# THE NEW STRONG'S® CONCISE CONCORDANCE

# VINE'S CONCISE DICTIONARY OF THE BIBLE

# STRONG'S CONCISE CONCORDANCE & VINE'S CONCISE DICTIONARY OF THE BIBLE

*Two Bible Reference Classics In One Handy Volume*

THOMAS NELSON PUBLISHERS
Nashville

Published in Nashville, Tennessee, by Thomas Nelson, Inc.



The publisher wishes to acknowledge the editorial and composition services of James A. Swa
son, John R. Kohlenberger III, and Multnomah Graphics.

**Library of Congress Cataloging-in-Publication Data**

Vine, W. E. (William Edwy), 1873–1949.
Vine's concise dictionary of the Bible. Strong's concise concordance omnibus.
p. cm.
ISBN 0-7852-4254-6
1. Bible Dictionaries. 2. Bible Concordances, English.
I. Strong, James, 1822–1894. Strong's concise concordance omnibus.
II. Title. III. Title: Concise expository dictionary. IV. Title:
Concise concordance omnibus. V. Title: Strong's concise concordance omnibus.
BS440.V755 1999
220.3—dc21 99–29685
CIP

Printed in the United States of America

15 - 07

# THE NEW STRONG'S® CONCISE CONCORDANCE

# STRONG'S
## CONCISE
# CONCORDANCE

# PREFACE

For over a century, Bible readers have relied on *Strong's Exhaustive Concordance of the Bible* to guide them to any passage in the King James Version. Recently this standard reference work has been completely re-typeset and corrected as *The New Strong's*™ *Exaustive Concordance of the Bible. The New Strong's*™ family of reference works continues the Strong's tradition of dependable information and clear presentation.

*The New Strong's*™ *Concise Concordance of the Bible* contains not only the clear typography of the Exhaustive edition but other special features as well. Proper names for people and places that share the same name have been separated and grouped under the appropriate entry. Variant spellings of proper names from other versions of the Bible have been listed and cross-referenced to the King James spelling, allowing this concordance to be used with modern translations.

This *Concise* edition is designed to serve better the needs of the average reader. It preserves the excellent scholarship of Dr. James Strong in a more convenient format, providing a complete concordance without the Hebrew and Greek detail. It is easily portable, with clear, legible type.

To accomplish this more manageable size, this edition eliminates 168 words that the reader is not likely to use in searching for particular passages in Scripture:

a
about
according
after
again
against
all
also
am
among
an
and
any
are
art
as
at
away
be
because
been
before
both
brought
but
by
came
cast
cause
children
city
come
days
did
do
done
down
even
every
fathers
for
forth
from
given
go
good
great
had
hand
hast
hath
have
he
her
high
him
himself
his
how
hundred
I
if
in
into
is
it
land
let
like
made
make
man
many
may
me
men
mine
more
my
neither

no
nor
not
now
O
of
off
on
one
ones
or
our
out
over
own
part
parts
pass
people
place
places
put

said
saith
same
saw
say
saying
see
sent
set
shall, shalt
she
should
so
sons
sought
spake
speak
take
than
that
the
thee

their
them
themselves
then
there
therefore
therein
thereof
thereon
thereto
these
they
thine
thing(s)
this
those
thou
thy
time
to
took
two

unto
up
upon
us
was
way
we
went
were
what
when
which
who
whom
will
with
ye
yea
yet
you
your

Entries for the following forty words have been condensed by retaining the m
important passages enabling the user to quickly find specific verses:

Aaron
another
behold
bring
called
Christ
David
day
earth
eat

Egypt
evil
father
give
God
hear
heard
heart
heaven
holy

house
Israel
Jerusalem
Jesus
Judah
king
know
lord
midst
might

Moses
name
servant
servants
son
together
voice
word
words
years

# CONCORDANCE

**A** See PREFACE.

**AARON** (*a'-ur-un*) See PREFACE. SEE ALSO AARON'S, AARONITES. *First high priest of Israel; brother of Moses.*
Is not *A* the Levite thy brother ... Ex 4:14
*A* went in, and told Pharaoh, Thus ... Ex 5:1
*A* cast down his rod before ... Ex 7:10
LORD spake unto Moses, Say unto *A* ... Ex 7:19
*A* did so, as the LORD commanded ... Ex 7:20
and *A* and Hur stayed up his hands, ... Ex 17:12
take thou unto thee *A* thy brother ... Ex 28:1
me in the priest's office, even *A* ... Ex 28:1
ears, and brought them unto *A* ... Ex 32:3
when *A* saw it, he built an altar ... Ex 32:5
they made the calf, which *A* made ... Ex 32:35
Take *A* and his sons with him, and ... Lev 8:2
And Moses brought *A* and his sons, ... Lev 8:6
And the LORD spake unto *A*, saying, ... Lev 10:8
*A* and his sons shall go in, and ... Num 4:19
against Moses and against *A* ... Num 16:3
the rod of *A* for the house of ... Num 17:8
LORD spake unto Moses and *A* ... Num 20:12
*A* died there in the top of the ... Num 20:28
But *A* and his sons offered upon ... 1Chr 6:49
and *A* whom he had chosen ... Ps 105:26
wife was of the daughters of *A* ... Lk 1:5
Saying unto *A*, Make us gods to go ... Acts 7:40
that is called of God, as was *A* ... Heb 5:4
be called after the order of *A* ... Heb 7:11

**AARONITES** (*a'-ur-un-ites*) *Priests; Aaron's descendants.*
Jehoiada was the leader of the *A* ... 1Chr 12:27
of the *A*, Zadok ... 1Chr 27:17

**AARON'S** (*a'-ur-uns*)
Eleazar *A* son took him one of the ... Ex 6:25
but *A* rod swallowed up their rods ... Ex 7:12
Abihu, Eleazar and Ithamar, *A* sons ... Ex 28:1
that they may make *A* garments to ... Ex 28:3
and they shall be upon *A* heart ... Ex 28:30
And it shall be upon *A* forehead ... Ex 28:38
for *A* sons thou shalt make coats, ... Ex 28:40
of the ram of *A* consecration ... Ex 29:26
And it shall be *A* and his sons' by ... Ex 29:28
*A* sons, shall bring the blood, and ... Lev 1:5
*A* sons, shall lay the parts, the ... Lev 1:8
*A* sons, shall sprinkle his blood ... Lev 1:11
bring it to *A* sons the priests ... Lev 2:2
of the meat offerings shall be *A* ... Lev 2:3
of the meat offering shall be *A* ... Lev 2:10
*A* sons the priests shall sprinkle ... Lev 3:2
*A* sons shall burn it on the altar ... Lev 3:5
*A* sons shall sprinkle the blood ... Lev 3:8
but the breast shall be *A* ... Lev 7:31
of the anointing oil upon *A* head ... Lev 8:12
And Moses brought *A* sons, and put ... Lev 8:13
it upon the tip of *A* right ear ... Lev 8:23
And he brought *A* sons, and Moses ... Lev 8:24
And he put all upon *A* hands ... Lev 8:27
*A* sons presented unto him the ... Lev 9:12
*A* sons presented unto him the ... Lev 9:18
And it shall be *A* and his sons' ... Lev 24:9
thou shalt write *A* name upon the ... Num 17:3
Bring *A* rod again before the ... Num 17:10
down upon the beard, even *A* beard ... Ps 133:2
*A* rod that budded, and the tables ... Heb 9:4

**ABADDON** (*ab-ad'-dun*) *Angel of the Abyss.*
name in the Hebrew tongue is *A* ... Rev 9:11

**ABAGTHA** (*ab-ag'-thah*) *Servant of King Ahaseurus.*
Biztha, Harbona, Bigtha, and *A* ... Est 1:10

**ABANA** (*ab-ay'-nah*) *A river in Syria.*
Are not *A* and Pharpar, rivers of ... 2Kin 5:12

**ABANAH** See ABANA.

**ABARIM** (*ab'-ar-im*) See IJE-ABARIM. *A mountain range in Moab.*
Get thee up into this mount *A* ... Num 27:12
and pitched in the mountains of *A* ... Num 33:47
departed from the mountains of *A* ... Num 33:48
Get thee up into this mountain *A* ... Deut 32:49

**ABASE**
every one that is proud, and *a* him ... Job 40:11
nor *a* himself for the noise of ... Is 31:4
is low, and *a* him that is high ... Eze 21:26
walk in pride he is able to *a* ... Dan 4:37

**ABASED**
shall exalt himself shall be *a* ... Mt 23:12
exalteth himself shall be *a* ... Lk 14:11
that exalteth himself shall be *a* ... Lk 18:14
I know both how to be *a*, and I ... Phil 4:12

**ABASING**
Have I committed an offence in *a* ... 2Cor 11:7

**ABATED**
and fifty days the waters were *a* ... Gen 8:3
to see if the waters were *a* from ... Gen 8:8
waters were *a* from off the earth ... Gen 8:11
it shall be *a* from thy estimation ... Lev 27:18
not dim, nor his natural force *a* ... Deut 34:7
Then their anger was *a* toward him ... Judg 8:3

**ABBA** (*ab'-bah*) *Aramaic for "Father."*
And he said, *A*, Father, all things ... Mk 14:36
of adoption, whereby we cry, *A* ... Rom 8:15
Son into your hearts, crying, *A* ... Gal 4:6

**ABDA** (*ab'-dah*)
*1. Father of Adoniram.*
Adoniram the son of *A* was over ... 1Kin 4:6
*2. A chief Levite after the exile.*
*A* the son of Shammua, the son of ... Neh 11:17

**ABDEEL** (*ab'-de-el*) *Father of Shelemiah.*
Azriel, and Shelemiah the son of *A* ... Jer 36:26

**ABDI** (*ab'-di*)
*1. Levite grandfather of Ethan.*
the son of Kishi, the son of *A* ... 1Chr 6:44
sons of Merari, Kish the son of *A* ... 2Chr 29:12
*2. Married a foreigner while in exile.*
Zechariah, and Jehiel, and *A* ... Ezr 10:26

**ABDIEL** (*ab'-de-el*) *Son of Guni.*
Ahi the son of *A*, the son of Guni ... 1Chr 5:15

**ABDON** (*ab'-dun*)
*1. Levitical city in Asher.*
her suburbs, *A* with her suburbs, ... Josh 21:30
suburbs, and *A* with her suburbs, ... 1Chr 6:74
*2. A judge of Israel.*
after him *A* the son of Hillel, a ... Judg 12:13
And *A* the son of Hillel the ... Judg 12:15
*3. A Benjamite in Jerusalem.*
And *A*, and Zichri, and Hanan, ... 1Chr 8:23
*4. Son of Jehiel.*
And his firstborn son *A*, and Zur, ... 1Chr 8:30
And his firstborn son *A*, then Zur, ... 1Chr 9:36
*5. Son of Micah.*
*A* the son of Micah, and Shaphan ... 2Chr 34:20

**ABED-NEGO** (*ab-ed'-ne-go*) *A companion of Daniel in captivity.*
and to Azariah, of *A* ... Dan 1:7
and he set Shadrach, Meshach, and *A* . Dan 2:49
Babylon, Shadrach, Meshach, and *A* ... Dan 3:12
to bring Shadrach, Meshach, and *A* ... Dan 3:13
true, O Shadrach, Meshach, and *A* ... Dan 3:14
Shadrach, Meshach, and *A*, answered .. Dan 3:16
against Shadrach, Meshach, and *A* ... Dan 3:19
to bind Shadrach, Meshach, and *A* ... Dan 3:20
took up Shadrach, Meshach, and *A* ... Dan 3:22
men, Shadrach, Meshach, and *A* ... Dan 3:23
and said, Shadrach, Meshach, and *A* ... Dan 3:26
Then Shadrach, Meshach, and *A* ... Dan 3:26
God of Shadrach, Meshach, and *A* ... Dan 3:28
God of Shadrach, Meshach, and *A* ... Dan 3:29
promoted Shadrach, Meshach, and *A* ... Dan 3:30

**ABEL** (*a'-bel*)
*1. Second son of Adam.*
And she again bare his brother *A* ... Gen 4:2
*A* was a keeper of sheep, but Cain ... Gen 4:2
And *A*, he also brought of the ... Gen 4:4
And the LORD had respect unto *A* ... Gen 4:4
And Cain talked with *A* his brother ... Gen 4:8
rose up against *A* his brother ... Gen 4:8
unto Cain, Where is *A* thy brother ... Gen 4:9
me another seed instead of *A* ... Gen 4:25
from the blood of righteous *A* ... Mt 23:35
From the blood of *A* unto the ... Lk 11:51
By faith *A* offered unto God a ... Heb 11:4
better things than that of *A* ... Heb 12:24
*2. Great stone near Beth-shemesh.*
even unto the great stone of *A* ... 1Sa 6:18
*3. A city in Naphtali.*
all the tribes of Israel unto *A* ... 2Sa 20:14
besieged him in *A* of Beth-maachah ... 2Sa 20:15
shall surely ask counsel at *A* ... 2Sa 20:18

**ABEL ACACIA GROVE** See ABEL-SHITTIM.

**ABEL BETH MAACAH** See BETH-MAACHAH.

**ABEL-BETH-MAACHAH** (*a'-bel-beth-ma'-a-kah*) *A city in northern Israel.*
and smote Ijon, and Dan, and *A* ... 1Kin 15:20
of Assyria, and took Ijon, and *A* ... 2Kin 15:29

**ABEL-MAIM** (*a'-bel-ma'-im*) *Another name for Abel-beth-maachah.*
and they smote Ijon, and Dan, and *A*. 2Chr 16:4

**ABEL-MEHOLAH** (*a'-bel-me-ho'-lah*) *A city in Issachar.*
Zererath, and to the border of *A* ... Judg 7:22
Jezreel, from Beth-shean to *A* ... 1Kin 4:12
Elisha the son of Shaphat of *A* ... 1Kin 19:16

**ABEL-MIZRAIM** (*a'-bel-miz'-ra-im*) *A place east of the Jordan River.*
the name of it was called *A* ... Gen 50:11

**ABEL-SHITTIM** (*a'-bel-shit'-tim*) *A place in Moab.*
even unto *A* in the plains of Moab ... Num 33:49

**ABEZ** (*a'-bez*) *A place in Issachar.*
And Rabbith, and Kishion, and *A* ... Josh 19:20

**ABHOR**
and my soul shall not *a* you ... Lev 26:11
or if your soul *a* my judgments ... Lev 26:15
idols, and my soul shall *a* you ... Lev 26:30
them away, neither will I *a* them ... Lev 26:44
it, and thou shalt utterly *a* it ... Deut 7:26
Thou shalt not *a* an Edomite ... Deut 23:7
thou shalt not *a* an Egyptian ... Deut 23:7
people Israel utterly to *a* him ... 1Sa 27:12
and mine own clothes shall *a* me ... Job 9:31
They *a* me, they flee far from me, ... Job 30:10
Wherefore I *a* myself, and repent ... Job 42:6
the LORD will *a* the bloody ... Ps 5:6
I hate and *a* lying ... Ps 119:163
people curse, nations shall *a* him ... Prov 24:24
Do not *a* us, for thy name's sake, ... Jer 14:21
gate, and they *a* him that speaketh ... Amos 5:10
I *a* the excellency of Jacob, and ... Amos 6:8
that *a* judgment, and pervert all ... Mic 3:9
*A* that which is evil ... Rom 12:9

**ABHORRED**
to be *a* in the eyes of Pharaoh ... Ex 5:21
things, and therefore I *a* them ... Lev 20:23
because their soul *a* my statutes ... Lev 26:43
he *a* them, because of the ... Deut 32:19
for men *a* the offering of the ... 1Sa 2:17
that thou art *a* of thy father ... 2Sa 16:21
he *a* Israel, and reigned over ... 1Kin 11:25
All my inward friends *a* me ... Job 19:19
For he hath not despised nor *a* ... Ps 22:24
he was wroth, and greatly *a* Israel ... Ps 78:59
But thou hast cast off and *a* ... Ps 89:38
insomuch that he *a* his own ... Ps 106:40
he that is *a* of the LORD shall ... Prov 22:14
he hath *a* his sanctuary, he hath ... Lam 2:7
and hast made thy beauty to be *a* ... Eze 16:25
them, and their soul also *a* me ... Zec 11:8

**ABHORREST**
the land that thou *a* shall be ... Is 7:16
thou that *a* idols, dost thou ... Rom 2:22

**ABHORRETH**
So that his life *a* bread, and his ... Job 33:20
the covetous, whom the LORD *a* ... Ps 10:3
he *a* not evil ... Ps 36:4
Their soul *a* all manner of meat ... Ps 107:18
to him whom the nation *a* ... Is 49:7

**ABHORRING**
they shall be an *a* unto all flesh ... Is 66:24

**ABI** (*a'-bi*) See ABI-ABLON, ABI-EZER. *Mother of King Hezekiah.*
His mother's name also was *A* ... 2Kin 18:2

**ABIA** (*ab-i'-ah*) See ABIAH, ABIJAH, ABIJAM.
*1. A son of Rehoboam.*
Rehoboam, *A* his son, Asa his son, ... 1Chr 3:10
and Roboam begat *A* ... Mt 1:7
and *A* begat Asa ... Mt 1:7
*2. A priest.*
Zacharias, of the course of *A* ... Lk 1:5

**ABIAH** (*ab-i'-ah*) See ABIA.
*1. A son of Samuel.*
and the name of his second, *A* ... 1Sa 8:2
the firstborn Vashni, and *A* ... 1Chr 6:28
*2. Mother of Ashur.*
then *A* Hezron's wife bare him ... 1Chr 2:24

*3. Son of Becher.*
and Omri, and Jerimoth, and *A* 1Chr 7:8

**ABI-ALBON** (*ab'-i-al'-bun*) *A "mighty man" of David.*
*A* the Arbathite, Azmaveth the 2Sa 23:31

**ABIASAPH** (*ab-i'-as-af*) See EBI-ASAPH. *A son of Korah.*
Assir, and Elkanah, and *A* Ex 6:24

**ABIATHAR** (*ab-i'-uth-ur*) See ABITHAR'S. *High Priest during David's reign.*
the son of Ahitub, named *A* 1Sa 22:20
*A* shewed David that Saul had 1Sa 22:21
And David said unto *A*, I knew it 1Sa 22:22
when *A* the son of Ahimelech fled 1Sa 23:6
and he said to *A* the priest 1Sa 23:9
And David said to *A* the priest 1Sa 30:7
*A* brought thither the ephod to 1Sa 30:7
Ahitub, and Ahimelech the son of *A* 2Sa 8:17
*A* went up, until all the people 2Sa 15:24
thy son, and Jonathan the son of *A* 2Sa 15:27
*A* carried the ark of God again to 2Sa 15:29
with thee Zadok and *A* the priests 2Sa 15:35
tell it to Zadok and *A* the priests 2Sa 15:35
to *A* the priests, Thus and thus 2Sa 17:15
to *A* the priests, saying, Speak 2Sa 19:11
and Zadok and *A* were the priests 2Sa 20:25
of Zeruiah, and with *A* the priest 1Kin 1:7
*A* the priest, and Joab the captain 1Kin 1:19
of the host, and *A* the priest 1Kin 1:25
the son of *A* the priest came 1Kin 1:42
for *A* the priest, and for Joab the 1Kin 2:22
unto *A* the priest said the king 1Kin 2:26
So Solomon thrust out *A* from 1Kin 2:27
did the king put in the room of *A* 1Kin 2:35
and Zadok and *A* were the priests 1Kin 4:4
*A* the priests, and for the Levites 1Chr 15:11
Ahitub, and Abimelech the son of *A* 1Chr 18:16
priest, and Ahimelech the son of *A* 1Chr 24:6
Jehoiada the son of Benaiah, and *A* 1Chr 27:34
in the days of *A* the high priest Mk 2:26

**ABIATHAR'S** (*ab-i'-uth-urs*)
Zadok's son, and Jonathan *A* son 2Sa 15:36

**ABIB** (*a'-bib*) See TEL-ABIB. *First month of the Hebrew year.*
day came ye out in the month *A* Ex 13:4
the time appointed of the month *A* Ex 23:15
thee, in the time of the month *A* Ex 34:18
for in the month *A* thou camest Ex 34:18
Observe the month of *A*, and keep Deut 16:1
for in the month of *A* the LORD Deut 16:1

**ABIDA** (*ab'-id-ah*) See ABIDAH. *A son of Midian.*
and Epher, and Henoch, and *A* 1Chr 1:33

**ABIDAH** (*ab'-id-ah*) See ABIDA. *Same as Abida.*
Ephah, and Epher, and Hanoch, and *A* Gen 25:4

**ABIDAN** (*ab'-id-an*) *Son of Gideoni.*
*A* the son of Gideoni Num 1:11
shall be *A* the son of Gideoni Num 2:22
On the ninth day *A* the son of Num 7:60
offering of *A* the son of Gideoni Num 7:65
Benjamin was *A* the son of Gideoni Num 10:24

**ABIDE**
but we will *a* in the street all Gen 19:2
young men, *A* ye here with the ass Gen 22:5
Let the damsel *a* with us a few Gen 24:55
*a* with me Gen 29:19
let thy servant *a* instead of the Gen 44:33
*a* ye every man in his place, let Ex 16:29
Therefore shall ye *a* at the door Lev 8:35
*a* with thee all night until the Lev 19:13
earth, and they *a* over against me Num 22:5
do ye *a* without the camp seven Num 31:19
Every thing that may *a* the fire Num 31:23
he shall *a* in it unto the death Num 35:25
shall *a* in your cities which I Deut 3:19
Judah shall *a* in their coast on Josh 18:5
the house of Joseph shall *a* in Josh 18:5
but *a* here fast by my maidens Ruth 2:8
the LORD, and there *a* for ever 1Sa 1:22
God of Israel shall not *a* with us 1Sa 5:7
*a* in a secret place, and hide 1Sa 19:2
unto David, *A* not in the hold 1Sa 22:5
*A* thou with me, fear not 1Sa 22:23
made also to *a* at the brook Besor 1Sa 30:21
and Israel, and Judah, *a* in tents 2Sa 11:11
to thy place, and *a* with the king 2Sa 15:19
will I be, and with him will I *a* 2Sa 16:18
place for thee to *a* in for ever 1Kin 8:13
*a* now at home 2Chr 25:19
that ye *a* in the siege in 2Chr 32:10
nor *a* in the paths thereof Job 24:13
*a* in the covert to lie in wait Job 38:40
to serve thee, or *a* by thy crib Job 39:9
who shall *a* in thy tabernacle Ps 15:1
I will *a* in thy tabernacle for Ps 61:4
He shall *a* before God for ever Ps 61:7
shall *a* under the shadow of the Ps 91:1
her feet *a* not in her house Prov 7:11
he that hath it shall *a* satisfied Prov 19:23
for that shall *a* with him of his Eccl 8:15
not be able to *a* his indignation Jer 10:10
If ye will still *a* in this land Jer 42:10
the LORD, no man shall *a* there Jer 49:18
there shall no man *a* there Jer 49:33
so shall no man *a* there, neither Jer 50:40
Thou shalt *a* for me many days Hos 3:3
shall *a* many days without a king Hos 3:4
the sword shall *a* on his cities Hos 11:6
and who can *a* it Joel 2:11
and they shall *a* Mic 5:4
who can *a* in the fierceness of Nah 1:6
But who may *a* the day of his Mal 3:2
there *a* till ye go thence Mt 10:11
there *a* till ye depart from that Mk 6:10
house ye enter into, there *a* Lk 9:4
for to day I must *a* at thy house Lk 19:5
him, saying, *A* with us Lk 24:29
on me should not *a* in darkness Jn 12:46
that he may *a* with you for ever Jn 14:16
*A* in me, and I in you Jn 15:4
itself, except it *a* in the vine Jn 15:4
no more can ye, except ye *a* in me Jn 15:4
If a man *a* not in me, he is cast Jn 15:6
If ye *a* in me, and my words *a* Jn 15:7
*a* in me, and my words *a* in you Jn 15:7
ye shall *a* in my love Jn 15:10
commandments, and *a* in his love Jn 15:10
it pleased Silas to *a* there still Acts 15:34
come into my house, and *a* there Acts 16:15
that bonds and afflictions *a* me Acts 20:23
Except these *a* in the ship Acts 27:31
if they *a* not still in unbelief Rom 11:23
If any man's work *a* which he hath 1Cor 3:14
good for them if they *a* even as I 1Cor 7:8
Let every man *a* in the same 1Cor 7:20
he is called, therein *a* with God 1Cor 7:24
But she is happier if she so *a* 1Cor 7:40
And it may be that I will *a* 1Cor 16:6
Nevertheless to *a* in the flesh is Phil 1:24
confidence, I know that I shall *a* Phil 1:25
thee to *a* still at Ephesus 1Ti 1:3
Let that therefore *a* in you 1Jn 2:24
taught you, ye shall *a* in him 1Jn 2:27
And now, little children, *a* in him 1Jn 2:28

**ABIDETH**
all that *a* not the fire ye shall Num 31:23
king, Behold, he *a* at Jerusalem 2Sa 16:3
*a* on the rock, upon the crag of Job 39:28
man being in honour *a* not Ps 49:12
them, even he that *a* of old Ps 55:19
established the earth, and it *a* Ps 119:90
cannot be removed, but *a* for ever Ps 125:1
reproof of life *a* among the wise Prov 15:31
but the earth *a* for ever Eccl 1:4
He that *a* in this city shall die Jer 21:9
but the wrath of God *a* on him Jn 3:36
the servant *a* not in the house Jn 8:35
but the Son *a* ever Jn 8:35
the ground and die, it *a* alone Jn 12:24
of the law that Christ *a* for ever Jn 12:34
He that *a* in me, and I in him, the Jn 15:5
now *a* faith, hope, charity, these 1Cor 13:13
we believe not, yet he *a* faithful 2Ti 2:13
*a* a priest continually Heb 7:3
God, which liveth and *a* for ever 1Pet 1:23
He that saith he *a* in him ought 1Jn 2:6
loveth his brother *a* in the light 1Jn 2:10
and the word of God *a* in you 1Jn 2:14
doeth the will of God *a* for ever 1Jn 2:17
ye have received of him *a* in you 1Jn 2:27
Whosoever *a* in him sinneth not 1Jn 3:6
loveth not his brother *a* in death 1Jn 3:14
And hereby we know that he *a* in us 1Jn 3:24
*a* not in the doctrine of Christ 2Jn 9
He that *a* in the doctrine of 2Jn 9

**ABIDING**
he saw Israel *a* in his tents Num 24:2
*a* with her in the chamber Judg 16:9
liers in wait *a* in the chamber Judg 16:12
driven me out this day from *a* in 1Sa 26:19
as a shadow, and there is none *a* 1Chr 29:15
country shepherds *a* in the field Lk 2:8
And ye have not his word *a* in you Jn 5:38
were in that city *a* certain days Acts 16:12
hath eternal life *a* in him 1Jn 3:15

**ABIEL** (*a'-be-el*)
*1. Grandfather of King Saul.*
whose name was Kish, the son of *A* 1Sa 9:1
father of Abner was the son of *A* 1Sa 14:51
*2. A "mighty man" of David.*
brooks of Gaash, *A* the Arbathite 1Chr 11:32

**ABI-EZER** (*ab-i-e'-zur*) See ABIEZRITE, JEEZER.
*1. A descendant of Manasseh.*
and *A* was gathered after him Judg 6:34
better than the vintage of *A* Judg 8:2

**ABIEZER**
for the children of *A*, and for the Josh 17:2
*A* the Anethothite, Mebunnai the 2Sa 23:27
Hammoleketh bare Ishod, and *A* 1Chr 7:18
the Tekoite, *A* the Antothite 1Chr 11:28
ninth month was *A* the Anetothite 1Chr 27:12

**ABI-EZRITE** (*ab-i-ez'-rite*) See ABI-EZRITES. *A descendant of Abiezer.*
that pertained unto Joash the *A* Judg 6:11

**ABI-EZRITES** (*ab-i-ez'-rites*)
day it is yet in Ophrah of the *A* Judg 6:24
his father, in Ophrah of the *A* Judg 8:32

**ABIGAIL** (*ab'-e-gul*)
*1. A wife of David.*
and the name of his wife *A* 1Sa 25:3
But one of the young men told *A* 1Sa 25:14
Then *A* made haste, and took two 1Sa 25:18
when *A* saw David, she hasted, and 1Sa 25:23
And David said to *A*, Blessed be 1Sa 25:32
And *A* came to Nabal 1Sa 25:36
sent and communed with *A* 1Sa 25:39
of David were come to *A* to Carmel 1Sa 25:40
*A* hasted, and arose, and rode upon 1Sa 25:42
*A* the Carmelitess, Nabal's wife 1Sa 27:3
*A* the wife of Nabal the Carmelite 1Sa 30:5
*A* Nabal's wife the Carmelite 2Sa 2:2
of *A* the wife of Nabal the 2Sa 3:3
Daniel, of *A* the Carmelitess 1Chr 3:1
*2. Mother of Amosa.*
that went in to *A* the daughter of 2Sa 17:25
Whose sisters were Zeruiah, and *A* 1Chr 2:16
And *A* bare Amasa 1Chr 2:17

**ABIHAIL** (*ab-e-ha'-il*)
*1. Head of Levital family of Merari.*
of Merari was Zuriel the son of *A* Num 3:35
*2. Wife of Abishur.*
name of the wife of Abishur was *A* 1Chr 2:29
*3. Chief of a family of Gad.*
the children of *A* the son of Huri 1Chr 5:14
*4. Descendant of Eliab.*
*A* the daughter of Eliab the son 2Chr 11:18
*5. Father of Esther.*
the daughter of *A* the uncle of Est 2:15
the queen, the daughter of *A* Est 9:29

**ABIHU** (*a-bi'-hew*) *A son of Aaron.*
and she bare him Nadab, and *A* Ex 6:23
LORD, thou, and Aaron, Nadab, and *A* Ex 24:1
up Moses, and Aaron, Nadab, and *A* Ex 24:9
office, even Aaron, Nadab and *A* Ex 28:1
And Nadab and *A*, the sons of Aaron Lev 10:1
Nadab the firstborn, and *A* Num 3:2
*A* died before the LORD, when they Num 3:4
unto Aaron was born Nadab, and *A* Num 26:60
*A* died, when they offered strange Num 26:61
Nadab, and *A*, Eleazar, and Ithamar 1Chr 6:3
Nadab, and *A*, Eleazar, and Ithamar 1Chr 24:1
*A* died before their father, and 1Chr 24:2

**ABIHUD** (*a-bi'-hud*) *A son of Bela.*
Bela were, Addar, and Gera, and *A* 1Chr 8:3

**ABIJAH** (*a-bi'-jah*) See ABIA, ABIJAM.
*1. A son of Jeroboam I.*
At that time *A* the son of 1Kin 14:1
*2. A priest during David's reign.*
to Hakkoz, the eighth to *A* 1Chr 24:10
*3. A son of Rehoboam.*
which bare him *A*, and Attai, and 2Chr 11:20
Rehoboam made *A* the son of 2Chr 11:22
*A* his son reigned in his stead 2Chr 12:16
began *A* to reign over Judah 2Chr 13:1
And there was war between *A* 2Chr 13:2
*A* set the battle in array with an 2Chr 13:3
*A* stood up upon mount Zemaraim 2Chr 13:4
Jeroboam and all Israel before *A* 2Chr 13:15
*A* and his people slew them 2Chr 13:17
*A* pursued after Jeroboam, and took 2Chr 13:19
strength again in the days of *A* 2Chr 13:20
But *A* waxed mighty, and married 2Chr 13:21
And the rest of the acts of *A* 2Chr 13:22
So *A* slept with his fathers, and 2Chr 14:1
*4. Mother of King Hezekiah.*
And his mother's name was *A* 2Chr 29:1
*5. A priest in Nehemiah's time.*
Meshullam, *A*, Mijamin Neh 10:7
*6. A priest who returned from Exile under Zerubbabel.*
Iddo, Ginnetho, *A* Neh 12:4
Of *A*, Zichri Neh 12:17

**ABIJAM** (*a-bi'-jum*) *Son and successor of King Rehoboam.*
*A* his son reigned in his stead 1Kin 14:31
son of Nebat reigned *A* over Judah 1Kin 15:1
Now the rest of the acts of *A* 1Kin 15:7
And there was war between *A* 1Kin 15:7
And *A* slept with his fathers 1Kin 15:8

**ABILENE** (*ab-i-le'-ne*) *A Roman tetrarchy in northern Palestine.*
and Lysanias the tetrarch of *A* Lk 3:1

**ABILITY**
according to his *a* that vowed Lev 27:8
They gave after their *a* unto the Ezr 2:69
We after our *a* have redeemed our Neh 5:8
such as had *a* in them to stand in Dan 1:4
man according to his several *a* Mt 25:15
every man according to his *a* Acts 11:29
it as of the *a* which God giveth 1Pet 4:11

**ABIMAEL** (*a-bim'-ah-el*) *A son of Joktan in Arabia.*
And Obal, and *A*, and Sheba Gen 10:28
And Ebal, and *A*, and Sheba 1Chr 1:22

**ABIMELECH** (*a-bim'-e-lek*) See ABIMELECH'S.
*1. Philistine king in Abraham's time.*
*A* king of Gerar sent, and took Gen 20:2
But God came to *A* in a dream by Gen 20:3
But *A* had not come near her Gen 20:4
Therefore *A* rose early in the Gen 20:8
Then *A* called Abraham, and said Gen 20:9
*A* said unto Abraham, What sawest Gen 20:10
*A* took sheep, and oxen, and Gen 20:14
*A* said, Behold, my land is before Gen 20:15
and God healed *A*, and his wife, and Gen 20:17
all the wombs of the house of *A* Gen 20:18

came to pass at that time, that *A* ........ Gen 21:22
Abraham reproved *A* because of a ...... Gen 21:25
*A* said, I wot not who hath done ........ Gen 21:26
and oxen, and gave them unto *A* ......... Gen 21:27
*A* said unto Abraham, What mean ..... Gen 21:29
then *A* rose up, and Phichol the ......... Gen 21:32
Isaac went unto *A* king of the .............. Gen 26:1
that *A* king of the Philistines ............... Gen 26:8
*A* called Isaac, and said, Behold, ........... Gen 26:9
*A* said, What is this thou hast ............. Gen 26:10
*A* charged all his people, saying, .......... Gen 26:11
*A* said unto Isaac, Go from us ............ Gen 26:16
Then *A* went to him from Gerar, and Gen 26:26
*2. Son of Gideon.*
him a son, whose name he called *A* .... Judg 8:31
*A* the son of Jerubbaal went to ............. Judg 9:1
their hearts inclined to follow *A* ........... Judg 9:3
wherewith *A* hired vain and light .......... Judg 9:4
of Millo, and went, and made *A* king .... Judg 9:6
in that ye have made *A* king ................. Judg 9:16
upon one stone, and have made *A* ....... Judg 9:18
this day, then rejoice ye in *A* ............... Judg 9:19
if not, let fire come out from *A* ............. Judg 9:20
the house of Millo, and devour *A* ......... Judg 9:20
there, for fear of *A* his brother ............ Judg 9:21
When *A* had reigned three years ........... Judg 9:22
God sent an evil spirit between *A* ........ Judg 9:23
dealt treacherously with *A* .................... Judg 9:23
be laid upon *A* their brother ................. Judg 9:24
and it was told *A* .................................... Judg 9:25
and did eat and drink, and cursed *A* ... Judg 9:27
the son of Ebed said, Who is *A* ............ Judg 9:28
then would I remove *A* .......................... Judg 9:29
And he said to *A*, Increase thine ......... Judg 9:29
he sent messengers unto *A* privily ........ Judg 9:31
*A* rose up, and all the people that ........ Judg 9:34
*A* rose up, and the people that ............. Judg 9:35
wherewith thou saidst, Who is *A* .......... Judg 9:38
men of Shechem, and fought with *A* .. Judg 9:39
*A* chased him, and he fled before ......... Judg 9:40
And *A* dwelt at Arumah ......................... Judg 9:41
and they told *A* ..................................... Judg 9:42
And *A*, and the company that was ...... Judg 9:44
*A* fought against the city all .............. Judg 9:45
And it was told *A*, that all the ............. Judg 9:47
*A* gat him up to mount Zalmon, he ..... Judg 9:48
*A* took an axe in his hand, and cut ..... Judg 9:48
man his bough, and followed *A* ............ Judg 9:49
Then went *A* to Thebez, and ................ Judg 9:50
*A* came unto the tower, and fought .... Judg 9:52
men of Israel saw that *A* was dead ...... Judg 9:55
God rendered the wickedness of *A* ...... Judg 9:56
after *A* there arose to defend .............. Judg 10:1
Who smote *A* the son of ...................... 2Sa 11:21
*3. Son of Abiathar the High Priest.*
*A* the son of Abiathar, were the ......... 1Chr 18:16
*4. Used in title of Psalm 34.*
he changed his behaviour before *A* .......... Ps 34:*t*

**ABIMELECH'S** (*a-bim'-e-leks*)
which *A* servants had violently ........... Gen 21:25
piece of a millstone upon *A* head ......... Judg 9:53

**ABINADAB** (*a-bin'-ah-dab*)
*1. A Levite of Kirjath-jearim.*
into the house of *A* in the hill .................. 1Sa 7:1
the house of *A* that was in Gibeah .......... 2Sa 6:3
and Uzzah and Ahio, the sons of *A* ......... 2Sa 6:3
house of *A* which was at Gibeah ............... 2Sa 6:4
a new cart out of the house of *A* ......... 1Chr 13:7
*2. A brother of David.*
Then Jesse called *A*, and made him ....... 1Sa 16:8
first born, and next unto him *A* ............ 1Sa 17:13
*A* the second, and Shimma the third ... 1Chr 2:13
*3. A son of King Saul.*
Philistines slew Jonathan, and *A* ............ 1Sa 31:2
Jonathan, and Malchi-shua, and *A* ...... 1Chr 8:33
Jonathan, and Malchi-shua, and *A* ...... 1Chr 9:39
Philistines slew Jonathan, and *A* ....... 1Chr 10:2
*4. Father of an officer of Solomon.*
The son of *A*, in all the region ............. 1Kin 4:11

**ABINOAM** (*a-bin'-o-am*) *Father of Barak.*
son of *A* out of Kedesh-naphtali ............. Judg 4:6
of *A* was gone up to mount Tabor ......... Judg 4:12
and Barak the son of *A* on that day ...... Judg 5:1
captivity captive, thou son of *A* ........... Judg 5:12

**ABIRAM** (*a-bi'-rum*)
*1. A conspirator against Moses.*
the son of Levi, and Dathan and *A* ..... Num 16:1
sent to call Dathan and *A* .................... Num 16:12
tabernacle of Korah, Dathan, and *A*. Num 16:24
went unto Dathan and *A* ..................... Num 16:25
tabernacle of Korah, Dathan, and *A*. Num 16:27
*A* came out, and stood in the door .... Num 16:27
Nemuel, and Dathan, and *A* ................. Num 26:9
This is that Dathan and *A*, which ......... Num 26:9
And what he did unto Dathan and *A*. Deut 11:6
and covered the company of *A* ........... Ps 106:17
*2. Son of Hiel the Bethelite.*
thereof in *A* his firstborn ..................... 1Kin 16:34

**ABISHAG** (*ab'-e-shag*) *An attendant of David.*
found *A* a Shunammite, and brought .... 1Kin 1:3
*A* the Shunammite ministered unto ..... 1Kin 1:15
that he give me *A* the Shunammite ..... 1Kin 2:17
Let *A* the Shunammite be given to ...... 1Kin 2:21
And why dost thou ask *A* the .............. 1Kin 2:22

**ABISHAI** (*ab'-e-shahee*) *David's nephew.*
to *A* the son of Zeruiah, brother ......... 1Sa 26:6
*A* said, I will go down with thee ............ 1Sa 26:6
*A* came to the people by night ............... 1Sa 26:7
Then said *A* to David, God hath ............ 1Sa 26:8
And David said to *A*, Destroy him ......... 1Sa 26:9
sons of Zeruiah there, Joab, and *A* ....... 2Sa 2:18
also and *A* pursued after Abner ............ 2Sa 2:24
*A* his brother slew Abner, because ......... 2Sa 3:30
into the hand of *A* his brother ............. 2Sa 10:10
then fled they also before *A* ................ 2Sa 10:14
Then said *A* the son of Zeruiah .............. 2Sa 16:9
And David said to *A*, and to all his ...... 2Sa 16:11
the hand of *A* the son of Zeruiah ........... 2Sa 18:2
And the king commanded Joab and *A* .. 2Sa 18:5
the king charged thee and *A* ................ 2Sa 18:12
But *A* the son of Zeruiah answered ..... 2Sa 19:21
And David said to *A*, Now shall ............. 2Sa 20:6
*A* his brother pursued after Sheba ....... 2Sa 20:10
But *A* the son of Zeruiah .................... 2Sa 21:17
And *A*, the brother of Joab, the ........... 2Sa 23:18
*A*, and Joab, and Asahel, three ............. 1Chr 2:16
*A* the brother of Joab, he was ............ 1Chr 11:20
*A* the son Zeruiah slew of the ........... 1Chr 18:12
unto the hand of *A* his brother ........... 1Chr 19:11
fled before *A* his brother ..................... 1Chr 19:15

**ABISHALOM** (*a-bish'-ah-lum*) See ABSALOM.
*Father of Maachah.*
was Maachah, the daughter of *A* ......... 1Kin 15:2
was Maachah, the daughter of *A* ....... 1Kin 15:10

**ABISHUA** (*a-bish'-u-ah*) *Son of Phinehas.*
begat Phinehas, Phinehas begat *A* ......... 1Chr 6:4
*A* begat Bukki, and Bukki begat ............ 1Chr 6:5
son, Phinehas his son, *A* his son, ......... 1Chr 6:50
And *A*, and Naaman, and Ahoah, .......... 1Chr 8:4
The son of *A*, the son of Phinehas ........... Ezr 7:5

**ABISHUR** (*ab'-e-shur*) *A son of Shammai.*
Nadab, and *A* ........................................ 1Chr 2:28
name of the wife of *A* was Abihail ...... 1Chr 2:29

**ABITAL** (*ab'-e-tal*) *A wife of David.*
fifth, Shephatiah the son of *A* .................. 2Sa 3:4
The fifth, Shephatiah of *A* ..................... 1Chr 3:3

**ABITUB** (*ab'-e-tub*) *Son of Shahareim.*
And of Hushim he begat *A*, and ............ 1Chr 8:11

**ABIUD** (*a-bi'-ud*) *A descendant of Zerubbabel; ancestor of Jesus.*
And Zorobabel begat *A* .............................. Mt 1:13
and *A* begat Eliakim ................................ Mt 1:13

**ABJECTS**
the *a* gathered themselves ....................... Ps 35:15

**ABLE**
the land was not *a* to bear them .......... Gen 13:6
if thou be *a* to number them ................. Gen 15:5
me and the children be *a* to endure .... Gen 33:14
one cannot be *a* to see the earth .............. Ex 10:5
thou art not *a* to perform it .................... Ex 18:18
out of all the people *a* men ..................... Ex 18:21
then thou shalt be *a* to endure ............... Ex 18:23
Moses chose *a* men out of all .................. Ex 18:25
Moses was not *a* to enter into the ......... Ex 40:35
if he be not *a* to bring a lamb, ................... Lev 5:7
But if he be not *a* to bring two ............... Lev 5:11
if she be not *a* to bring a lamb, ................ Lev 12:8
pigeons, such as he is *a* to get .............. Lev 14:22
Even such as he is *a* to get ................... Lev 14:31
whose hand is not *a* to get that ............. Lev 14:32
himself be *a* to redeem it ........................ Lev 25:26
But if he be not *a* to restore it ............. Lev 25:28
or if he be *a*, he may redeem ................. Lev 25:49
all that are *a* to go forth to war ............. Num 1:3
all that were *a* to go forth to .................. Num 1:20
all that were *a* to go forth to .................. Num 1:22
all that were *a* to go forth to .................. Num 1:24
all that were *a* to go forth to .................. Num 1:26
all that were *a* to go forth to .................. Num 1:28
all that were *a* to go forth to .................. Num 1:30
all that were *a* to go forth to .................. Num 1:32
all that were *a* to go forth to .................. Num 1:34
all that were *a* to go forth to .................. Num 1:36
all that were *a* to go forth to .................. Num 1:38
all that were *a* to go forth to .................. Num 1:40
all that were *a* to go forth to .................. Num 1:42
all that were *a* to go forth to .................. Num 1:45
I am not *a* to bear all this .................... Num 11:14
for we are well *a* to overcome it .......... Num 13:30
We be not *a* to go up against the ...... Num 13:31
Because the LORD was not *a* to ........... Num 14:16
I shall be *a* to overcome them ............. Num 22:11
am I not *a* indeed to promote thee .... Num 22:37
all that are *a* to go to war in ............... Num 26:2
I am not *a* to bear you myself ................. Deut 1:9
no man be *a* to stand before thee ....... Deut 7:24
Because the LORD was not *a* to ........... Deut 9:28
no man be *a* to stand before you ....... Deut 11:25
that thou art not *a* to carry it .............. Deut 14:24
Every man shall give as he is *a* ........... Deut 16:17
There shall not any man be *a* to ............ Josh 1:5
then I shall be *a* to drive them ............ Josh 14:12
no man hath been *a* to stand ............... Josh 23:9
what was I *a* to do in comparison ......... Judg 8:3
Who is *a* to stand before this ................ 1Sa 6:20
If he be *a* to fight with me, and ............ 1Sa 17:9
Thou art not *a* to go against this ......... 1Sa 17:33
for who is *a* to judge this thy so ........... 1Kin 3:9
were not *a* utterly to destroy ................ 1Kin 9:21
all that were *a* to put on armour .......... 2Kin 3:21
if thou be *a* on thy part to set ........... 2Kin 18:23
for he shall not be *a* to deliver ........... 2Kin 18:29
men *a* to bear buckler and sword, ....... 1Chr 5:18
very *a* men for the work of the ........... 1Chr 9:13
*a* men for strength for the .................. 1Chr 26:8
that we should be *a* to offer so .......... 1Chr 29:14
But who is *a* to build him an ................. 2Chr 2:6
*a* to receive the burnt offerings .............. 2Chr 7:7
so that none is *a* to withstand .............. 2Chr 20:6
they were not *a* to go to Tarshish ..... 2Chr 20:37
*a* to go forth to war, that could ........... 2Chr 25:5
The LORD is *a* to give thee much .......... 2Chr 25:9
*a* to deliver their lands out of .......... 2Chr 32:13
that your God should be *a* to ............. 2Chr 32:14
*a* to deliver his people out of ............. 2Chr 32:15
we are not *a* to stand without, ............. Ezr 10:13
we are not *a* to build the wall ............. Neh 4:10
who then is *a* to stand before me ......... Job 41:10
them that they were not *a* to rise ........... Ps 18:38
which they are not *a* to perform ............. Ps 21:11
down, and shall not be *a* to rise .............. Ps 36:12
me, so that I am not *a* to look up ........... Ps 40:12
but who is *a* to stand before envy .......... Prov 27:4
yet shall he not be *a* to find it .............. Eccl 8:17
if thou be *a* on thy part to set .................. Is 36:8
he shall not be *a* to deliver you .............. Is 36:14
thou shalt not be *a* to put if off ............... Is 47:11
so be thou shalt be *a* to profit .................. Is 47:12
not be *a* to abide his indignation ........... Jer 10:10
they shall not be *a* to escape ................... Jer 11:11
he shall not be *a* to hide himself ........... Jer 49:10
from whom I am not *a* to rise up ........ Lam 1:14
their gold shall not be *a* to .................... Eze 7:19
*a* to live for his righteousness ............... Eze 33:12
lambs as he shall be *a* to give ................ Eze 46:5
to the lambs as he is *a* to give ............ Eze 46:11
Art thou *a* to make known unto me .... Dan 2:26
our God whom we serve is *a* to .............. Dan 3:17
not *a* to make known unto me the ....... Dan 4:18
but thou art *a* ....................................... Dan 4:18
walk in pride he is *a* to abase .............. Dan 4:37
*a* to deliver thee from the lions ........... Dan 6:20
the land is not *a* to bear all his ........... Amos 7:10
*a* to deliver them in the day of ........... Zeph 1:18
that God is *a* of these stones to ................. Mt 3:9
Believe ye that I am *a* to do this ............ Mt 9:28
but are not *a* to kill the soul ................... Mt 10:28
which is *a* to destroy both soul .............. Mt 10:28
He that is *a* to receive it, let ................. Mt 19:12
Are ye *a* to drink of the cup that .......... Mt 20:22
They say unto him, We are *a* ................ Mt 20:22
no man was *a* to answer him a word ... Mt 22:46
I am *a* to destroy the temple of ............ Mt 26:61
them, as they were *a* to hear it .............. Mk 4:33
not *a* to speak, until the day ................... Lk 1:20
That God is *a* of these stones to ............... Lk 3:8
If ye then be not *a* to do that ............... Lk 12:26
to enter in, and shall not be *a* .............. Lk 13:24
is not *a* to finish it, all that ................... Lk 14:29
to build, and was not *a* to finish ........... Lk 14:30
consulteth whether he be *a* with ........... Lk 14:31
not be *a* to gainsay nor resist ................ Lk 21:15
no man is *a* to pluck them out of .......... Jn 10:29
now they were not *a* to draw it ................. Jn 21:6
they were not *a* to resist the ............... Acts 6:10
our fathers nor we were *a* to bear ..... Acts 15:10
which is *a* to build you up, and to ...... Acts 20:32
said he, which among you are *a* .......... Acts 25:5
he was *a* also to perform ..................... Rom 4:21
shall be *a* to separate us from ............. Rom 8:39
for God is *a* to graff them in .............. Rom 11:23
for God is *a* to make him stand .............. Rom 14:4
*a* also to admonish one another ........... Rom 15:14
hitherto ye were not *a* to bear it .......... 1Cor 3:2
neither yet now are ye *a* ...................... 1Cor 3:2
not one that shall be *a* to judge ............ 1Cor 6:5
to be tempted above that ye are *a* ..... 1Cor 10:13
that ye may be *a* to bear it .............. 1Cor 10:13
that we may be *a* to comfort them .......... 2Cor 1:4
Who also hath made us *a* ministers ........ 2Cor 3:6
God is *a* to make all grace abound ........ 2Cor 9:8
May be *a* to comprehend with all .......... Eph 3:18
Now unto him that is *a* to do ................ Eph 3:20
that ye may be *a* to stand against .......... Eph 6:11
that ye may be *a* to withstand in ........... Eph 6:13
wherewith ye shall be *a* to quench ......... Eph 6:16
to the working whereby he is *a* ............. Phil 3:21
am persuaded that he is *a* to keep ........... 2Ti 1:12
who shall be *a* to teach others ................. 2Ti 2:2
never *a* to come to the knowledge ........... 2Ti 3:7
which are *a* to make thee wise ................ 2Ti 3:15
that he may be *a* by sound ..................... Titus 1:9
he is *a* to succour them that are ............. Heb 2:18
that was *a* to save him from death ......... Heb 5:7
Wherefore he is *a* also to save ............... Heb 7:25
that God was *a* to raise him up ........... Heb 11:19
which is *a* to save your souls ................... Jas 1:21
*a* also to bridle the whole body .................. Jas 3:2
who is *a* to save and to destroy ................ Jas 4:12
*a* after my decease to have these ......... 2Pet 1:15
Now unto him that is *a* to keep ................ Jude 24
was *a* to open the book, neither .............. Rev 5:3
and who shall be *a* to stand ................. Rev 6:17
who is *a* to make war with him ............ Rev 13:4
no man was *a* to enter into the ............ Rev 15:8

**ABNER** (*ab'-nur*) See ABNER'S. *King Saul's military commander.*
of the captain of his host was *A* ........... 1Sa 14:50
Ner the father of *A* was the son .......... 1Sa 14:51
the Philistine, he said unto *A* ............. 1Sa 17:55
the captain of the host, *A* ..................... 1Sa 17:55
*A* said, As thy soul liveth, O ................ 1Sa 17:55

*A* took him, and brought him before... 1Sa 17:57
*A* sat by Saul's side, and David's 1Sa 20:25
*A* the son of Ner, the captain of 1Sa 26:5
but *A* and the people lay round 1Sa 26:7
to *A* the son of Ner, saying, 1Sa 26:14
Answerest thou not, *A* 1Sa 26:14
Then *A* answered and said, Who art ... 1Sa 26:14
And David said to *A*, Art not thou 1Sa 26:15
But *A* the son of Ner, captain of 2Sa 2:8
*A* the son of Ner, and the servants 2Sa 2:12
*A* said to Joab, Let the young men 2Sa 2:14
*A* was beaten, and the men of 2Sa 2:17
And Asahel pursued after *A* 2Sa 2:19
nor to the left from following *A* 2Sa 2:19
Then *A* looked behind him, and said 2Sa 2:20
*A* said to him, Turn thee aside to 2Sa 2:21
*A* said again to Asahel, Turn thee 2Sa 2:22
wherefore *A* with the hinder end 2Sa 2:23
also and Abishai pursued after *A* 2Sa 2:24
themselves together after *A* 2Sa 2:25
Then *A* called to Joab, and said, 2Sa 2:26
And *A* and his men walked all that 2Sa 2:29
And Joab returned from following *A* 2Sa 2:30
that *A* made himself strong for 2Sa 3:6
and Ish-bosheth said to *A*, 2Sa 3:7
Then was *A* very wroth for the 2Sa 3:8
So do God to *A*, and more also, 2Sa 3:9
could not answer *A* a word again 2Sa 3:11
*A* sent messengers to David on his 2Sa 3:12
Then said *A* unto him, Go, return 2Sa 3:16
*A* had communication with the 2Sa 3:17
*A* also spake in the ears of 2Sa 3:19
*A* went also to speak in the ears 2Sa 3:19
So *A* came to David to Hebron, and 2Sa 3:20
And David made *A* and the men that ... 2Sa 3:20
*A* said unto David, I will arise 2Sa 3:21
And David sent *A* away 2Sa 3:21
but *A* was not with David in 2Sa 3:22
*A* the son of Ner came to the king 2Sa 3:23
behold, *A* came unto thee 2Sa 3:24
Thou knowest *A* the son of Ner, 2Sa 3:25
David, he sent messengers after *A* 2Sa 3:26
when *A* was returned to Hebron, 2Sa 3:27
the blood of *A* the son of Ner 2Sa 3:28
and Abishai his brother slew *A* 2Sa 3:30
with sackcloth, and mourn before *A* 2Sa 3:31
And they buried *A* in Hebron 2Sa 3:32
voice, and wept at the grave of *A* 2Sa 3:32
And the king lamented over *A* 2Sa 3:33
and said, Died *A* as a fool dieth 2Sa 3:33
the king to slay *A* the son of Ner 2Sa 3:37
heard that *A* was dead in Hebron 2Sa 4:1
in the sepulchre of *A* in Hebron 2Sa 4:12
unto *A* the son of Ner, and unto 1Kin 2:5
*A* the son of Ner, captain of the 1Kin 2:32
*A* the son of Ner, and Joab the son... 1Chr 26:28
of Benjamin, Jaasiel the son of *A* 1Chr 27:21

**ABNER'S** (*ab'-nurs*)
of *A* men, so that three hundred 2Sa 2:31

**ABOARD**
over unto Phenicia, we went *a* Acts 21:2

**ABODE**
he *a* with him the space of a Gen 29:14
But his bow *a* in strength Gen 49:24
of the LORD *a* upon mount Sinai Ex 24:16
because the cloud *a* thereon Ex 40:35
and in the place where the cloud *a* Num 9:17
as long as the cloud *a* upon the Num 9:18
of the LORD they *a* in their tents Num 9:20
when the cloud *a* from even unto Num 9:21
of Israel *a* in their tents Num 9:22
and *a* at Hazeroth Num 11:35
and the people *a* in Kadesh Num 20:1
the princes of Moab *a* with Balaam Num 22:8
Israel *a* in Shittim, and the Num 25:1
So ye *a* in Kadesh many days, Deut 1:46
unto the days that ye *a* there Deut 1:46
So we *a* in the valley over Deut 3:29
then I *a* in the mount forty days Deut 9:9
*a* there three days, until the Josh 2:22
that they *a* in their places in Josh 5:8
*a* between Beth-el and Ai, on the Josh 8:9
Gilead *a* beyond Jordan Judg 5:17
sea shore, and *a* in his breaches Judg 5:17
and Israel *a* in Kadesh Judg 11:17
and he *a* with him three days Judg 19:4
*a* in the rock Rimmon four months... Judg 20:47
*a* there till even before God, and Judg 21:2
So the woman *a*, and gave her son 1Sa 1:23
while the ark *a* in Kirjath-jearim 1Sa 7:2
them, *a* in Gibeah of Benjamin 1Sa 13:16
(now Saul *a* in Gibeah under a 1Sa 22:6
David *a* in the wilderness in 1Sa 23:14
David *a* in the wood, and Jonathan 1Sa 23:18
*a* in the wilderness of Maon 1Sa 23:25
two hundred *a* by the stuff 1Sa 25:13
But David *a* in the wilderness, and 1Sa 26:3
for two hundred *a* behind, which 1Sa 30:10
David had *a* two days in Ziklag 2Sa 1:1
So Uriah *a* in Jerusalem that day, 2Sa 11:12
vow while I *a* at Geshur in Syria 2Sa 15:8
him up into a loft, where he *a* 1Kin 17:19
But I know thy *a*, and thy going 2Kin 19:27
there *a* we in tents three days Ezr 8:15
Jerusalem, and *a* there three days Ezr 8:32
But I know thy *a*, and thy going Is 37:28
So Jeremiah *a* in the court of the Jer 38:28
And while they *a* in Galilee Mt 17:22
Mary *a* with her about three Lk 1:56
neither *a* in any house, but in Lk 8:27
*a* in the mount that is called the Lk 21:37
like a dove, and it *a* upon him Jn 1:32
he dwelt, and *a* with him that day Jn 1:39
and he *a* there two days Jn 4:40
unto them, he *a* still in Galilee Jn 7:9
*a* not in the truth, because there Jn 8:44
and there he *a* Jn 10:40
he *a* two days still in the same Jn 11:6
unto him, and make our *a* with him Jn 14:23
where *a* both Peter, and James, and Acts 1:13
Judaea to Caesarea, and there *a* Acts 12:19
Long time therefore *a* they Acts 14:3
there they *a* long time with the Acts 14:28
Silas and Timotheus *a* there still Acts 17:14
he *a* with them, and wrought Acts 18:3
And there *a* three months Acts 20:3
where we *a* seven days Acts 20:6
brethren, and *a* with them one day Acts 21:7
of the seven; and *a* with him Acts 21:8
Peter, and *a* with him fifteen days Gal 1:18
Erastus *a* at Corinth 2Ti 4:20

**ABODEST**
Why *a* thou among the sheepfolds, Judg 5:16

**ABOLISH**
And the idols he shall utterly *a* Is 2:18

**ABOLISHED**
my righteousness shall not be *a* Is 51:6
cut down, and your works may be *a* Eze 6:6
to the end of that which is *a* 2Cor 3:13
Having *a* in his flesh the enmity, Eph 2:15
Jesus Christ, who hath *a* death 2Ti 1:10

**ABOMINABLE**
or any *a* unclean thing, and eat of Lev 7:21
*a* with any creeping thing that Lev 11:43
not any one of these *a* customs Lev 18:30
at all on the third day, it is *a* Lev 19:7
not make your souls *a* by beast Lev 20:25
Thou shalt not eat any *a* thing Deut 14:3
for the king's word was *a* to Joab 1Chr 21:6
put away the *a* idols out of all 2Chr 15:8
How much more *a* and filthy is man, Job 15:16
corrupt, they have done *a* works Ps 14:1
are they, and have done *a* iniquity Ps 53:1
out of thy grave like an *a* branch Is 14:19
broth of *a* things is in their Is 65:4
of their detestable and *a* things Jer 16:18
do not this *a* thing that I hate Jer 44:4
neither came there *a* flesh into Eze 4:14
*a* beasts, and all the idols of the Eze 8:10
hast committed more *a* than they Eze 16:52
and the scant measure that is *a* Mic 6:10
I will cast *a* filth upon thee, and Nah 3:6
in works they deny him, being *a* Titus 1:16
banquetings, and *a* idolatries 1Pet 4:3
fearful, and unbelieving, and the *a* Rev 21:8

**ABOMINABLY**
he did very *a* in following idols, 1Kin 21:26

**ABOMINATION**
for that is an *a* unto the Gen 43:32
is an *a* unto the Egyptians Gen 46:34
for we shall sacrifice the *a* of Ex 8:26
shall we sacrifice the *a* of the Ex 8:26
it shall be an *a*, and the soul Lev 7:18
they shall be an *a* unto you Lev 11:10
They shall be even an *a* unto you Lev 11:11
ye shall have their carcases in *a* Lev 11:11
that shall be an *a* unto you Lev 11:12
shall have in *a* among the fowls Lev 11:13
shall not be eaten, they are an *a* Lev 11:13
all four, shall be an *a* unto you Lev 11:20
four feet, shall be an *a* unto you Lev 11:23
upon the earth shall be an *a* Lev 11:41
for they are an *a* Lev 11:42
with womankind: it is *a* Lev 18:22
both of them have committed an *a* Lev 20:13
for it is an *a* to the LORD thy Deut 7:25
thou bring an *a* into thine house Deut 7:26
for every *a* to the LORD, which he Deut 12:31
that such *a* is wrought among you ... Deut 13:14
for that is an *a* unto the LORD Deut 17:1
that such *a* is wrought in Israel Deut 17:4
things are an *a* unto the LORD Deut 18:12
do so are *a* unto the LORD thy God Deut 22:5
these are *a* unto the LORD thy God... Deut 23:18
for that is *a* before the LORD Deut 24:4
are an *a* unto the LORD thy God Deut 25:16
an *a* unto the LORD, the work of Deut 27:15
was had in *a* with the Philistines 1Sa 13:4
Milcom the *a* of the Ammonites 1Kin 11:5
the *a* of Moab, in the hill that 1Kin 11:7
the *a* of the children of Ammon 1Kin 11:7
Ashtoreth the *a* of the Zidonians 2Kin 23:13
for Chemosh the *a* of the Moabites... 2Kin 23:13
for Milcom the *a* of the children 2Kin 23:13
thou hast made me an *a* unto them Ps 88:8
For the froward is *a* to the LORD Prov 3:32
yea, seven are an *a* unto him Prov 6:16
and wickedness is an *a* to my lips Prov 8:7
A false balance is *a* to the LORD Prov 11:1
a froward heart are *a* to the LORD Prov 11:20
Lying lips are *a* to the LORD Prov 12:22
but it is *a* to fools to depart Prov 13:19
of the wicked is an *a* to the LORD Prov 15:8
the wicked is an *a* unto the LORD Prov 15:9
the wicked are an *a* to the LORD Prov 15:26
in heart is an *a* to the LORD Prov 16:5
It is an *a* to kings to commit Prov 16:12
even they both are *a* to the LORD Prov 17:15
of them are alike *a* to the LORD Prov 20:10
weights are an *a* unto the LORD Prov 20:23
The sacrifice of the wicked is *a* Prov 21:27
and the scorner is an *a* to men Prov 24:9
law, even his prayer shall be *a* Prov 28:9
An unjust man is an *a* to the just Prov 29:27
in the way is *a* to the wicked Prov 29:27
incense is an *a* unto me Is 1:13
an *a* is he that chooseth you Is 41:24
I make the residue thereof an *a* Is 44:19
eating swine's flesh, and the *a* Is 66:17
land, and made mine heritage an *a* Jer 2:7
ashamed when they had committed *a* Jer 6:15
ashamed when they had committed *a* Jer 8:12
mind, that they should do this *a* Jer 32:35
haughty, and committed *a* before me. Eze 16:50
to the idols, hath committed *a* Eze 18:12
one hath committed *a* with his Eze 22:11
stand upon your sword, ye work *a* Eze 33:26
place the *a* that maketh desolate Dan 11:31
the *a* that maketh desolate set up Dan 12:11
an *a* is committed in Israel and in Mal 2:11
shall see the *a* of desolation Mt 24:15
ye shall see the *a* of desolation Mk 13:14
men is *a* in the sight of God Lk 16:15
neither whatsoever worketh *a* Rev 21:27

**ABOMINATIONS**
shall not commit any of these *a* Lev 18:26
(For all these *a* have the men of Lev 18:27
shall commit any of these *a* Lev 18:29
do after the *a* of those nations Deut 18:9
because of these *a* the LORD thy Deut 18:12
you not to do after all their *a* Deut 20:18
And ye have seen their *a*, and their.. Deut 29:17
with *a* provoked they him to anger Deut 32:16
*a* of the nations which the LORD 1Kin 14:24
according to the *a* of the heathen 2Kin 16:3
after the *a* of the heathen, whom 2Kin 21:2
king of Judah hath done these *a* 2Kin 21:11
all the *a* that were spied in the 2Kin 23:24
after the *a* of the heathen whom 2Chr 28:3
like unto the *a* of the heathen, 2Chr 33:2
Josiah took away all the *a* out of 2Chr 34:33
his *a* which he did, and that which 2Chr 36:8
after all the *a* of the heathen 2Chr 36:14
lands, doing according to their *a* Ezr 9:1
people of the lands, with their *a* Ezr 9:11
with the people of these *a* Ezr 9:14
there are seven *a* in his heart Prov 26:25
their soul delighteth in their *a* Is 66:3
put away thine *a* out of my sight Jer 4:1
are delivered to do all these *a* Jer 7:10
they have set their *a* in the Jer 7:30
thine *a* on the hills in the Jer 13:27
But they set their *a* in the house Jer 32:34
because of the *a* which ye have Jer 44:22
the like, because of all thine *a* Eze 5:9
things, and with all thine *a* Eze 5:11
have committed in all their *a* Eze 6:9
Alas for all the evil *a* of the Eze 6:11
recompense upon thee all thine *a* Eze 7:3
thine *a* shall be in the midst of Eze 7:4
recompense thee for all thine *a* Eze 7:8
thine *a* that are in the midst of Eze 7:9
they made the images of their *a* Eze 7:20
even the great *a* that the house Eze 8:6
and thou shalt see greater *a* Eze 8:6
the wicked *a* that they do here Eze 8:9
shalt see greater *a* that they do Eze 8:13
shalt see greater *a* than these Eze 8:15
the *a* which they commit here Eze 8:17
that cry for all the *a* that be Eze 9:4
all the *a* thereof from thence Eze 11:18
detestable things and their *a* Eze 11:21
*a* among the heathen whither they Eze 12:16
away your faces from all your *a* Eze 14:6
cause Jerusalem to know her *a* Eze 16:2
And in all thine *a* and thy Eze 16:22
and with all the idols of thy *a* Eze 16:36
this lewdness above all thine *a* Eze 16:43
ways, nor done after their *a* Eze 16:47
multiplied thine *a* more than they Eze 16:51
all thine *a* which thou hast done Eze 16:51
borne thy lewdness and thine *a* Eze 16:58
he hath done all these *a* Eze 18:13
the *a* that the wicked man doeth Eze 18:24
to know the *a* of their fathers Eze 20:4
away every man the *a* of his eyes Eze 20:7
man cast away the *a* of their eyes Eze 20:8
commit ye whoredom after their *a* Eze 20:30
thou shalt shew her all her *a* Eze 22:2
yea, declare unto them their *a* Eze 23:36
their *a* which they have committed Eze 33:29
for your iniquities and for your *a* Eze 36:31
their *a* that they have committed Eze 43:8
let it suffice you of all your *a* Eze 44:6
my covenant because of all your *a* Eze 44:7
their *a* which they have committed Eze 44:13
for the overspreading of *a* he Dan 9:27
their *a* were according as they Hos 9:10
his *a* from between his teeth Zec 9:7
golden cup in her hand full of *a* Rev 17:4
AND *A* OF THE EARTH Rev 17:5

**ABOUND**
man shall *a* with blessings Prov 28:20
And because iniquity shall *a* Mt 24:12
entered, that the offence might *a* Rom 5:20

abounded, grace did much more *a* ... Rom 5:20
continue in sin, that grace may *a* ... Rom 6:1
believing, that ye may *a* in hope ... Rom 15:13
the sufferings of Christ *a* in us ... 2Cor 1:5
as ye *a* in every thing, in faith, ... 2Cor 8:7
see that ye *a* in this grace also ... 2Cor 8:7
to make all grace *a* toward you ... 2Cor 9:8
things, may *a* to every good work ... 2Cor 9:8
that your love may *a* yet more ... Phil 1:9
to be abased, and I know how to *a* ... Phil 4:12
full and to be hungry, both to *a* ... Phil 4:12
fruit that may *a* to your account ... Phil 4:17
But I have all, and *a* ... Phil 4:18
*a* in love one toward another, and ... 1Th 3:12
to please God, so ye would *a* more ... 1Th 4:1
if these things be in you, and *a* ... 2Pet 1:8

**ABOUNDED**
*a* through my lie unto his glory ... Rom 3:7
Jesus Christ, hath *a* unto many ... Rom 5:15
But where sin *a*, grace did much ... Rom 5:20
their deep poverty *a* unto the ... 2Cor 8:2
Wherein he hath *a* toward us in ... Eph 1:8

**ABOUNDETH**
a furious man *a* in transgression ... Prov 29:22
our consolation also *a* by Christ ... 2Cor 1:5
of you all toward each other *a* ... 2Th 1:3

**ABOUNDING**
were no fountains *a* with water ... Prov 8:24
always *a* in the work of the Lord, ... 1Cor 15:58
*a* therein with thanksgiving ... Col 2:7

**ABOUT** See PREFACE.

**ABOVE**
waters which were *a* the firmament ... Gen 1:7
fowl that may fly *a* the earth in ... Gen 1:20
thou art cursed *a* all cattle ... Gen 3:14
*a* every beast of the field ... Gen 3:14
in a cubit shalt thou finish it *a* ... Gen 6:16
and it was lift up *a* the earth ... Gen 7:17
and of the dew of heaven from *a* ... Gen 27:39
And, behold, the LORD stood *a* it ... Gen 28:13
thee one portion *a* thy brethren ... Gen 48:22
thee with blessings of heaven *a* ... Gen 49:25
of thy father have prevailed *a* ... Gen 49:26
they dealt proudly he was *a* them ... Ex 18:11
treasure unto me *a* all people ... Ex 19:5
of any thing that is in heaven *a* ... Ex 20:4
put the mercy seat *a* upon the ark ... Ex 25:21
with thee from *a* the mercy seat ... Ex 25:22
a covering *a* of badgers' skins ... Ex 26:14
*a* the head of it unto one ring ... Ex 26:24
*a* the curious girdle of the ephod ... Ex 28:27
that it may be *a* the curious ... Ex 28:28
and the caul that is *a* the liver ... Ex 29:13
the caul *a* the liver, and the two ... Ex 29:22
from twenty years old and *a* ... Ex 30:14
covering of badgers' skins *a* that ... Ex 36:19
*a* the curious girdle of the ephod ... Ex 39:20
that it might be *a* the curious ... Ex 39:21
covering of the tent *a* upon it ... Ex 40:19
put the mercy seat *a* upon the ark ... Ex 40:20
the caul *a* the liver, with the ... Lev 3:4
the caul *a* the liver, with the ... Lev 3:10
the caul *a* the liver, with the ... Lev 3:15
the caul *a* the liver, with the ... Lev 4:9
and the caul that is *a* the liver ... Lev 7:4
the caul *a* the liver, and the two ... Lev 8:16
the caul *a* the liver, and the two ... Lev 8:25
the caul *a* the liver of the sin ... Lev 9:10
kidneys, and the caul *a* the liver ... Lev 9:19
which have legs *a* their feet ... Lev 11:21
it be from sixty years old and *a* ... Lev 27:7
*a* them that were redeemed by the ... Num 3:49
badgers' skins that is *a* upon it ... Num 4:25
*a* all the men which were upon the ... Num 12:3
then lift ye up yourselves *a* the ... Num 16:3
the LORD he is God in heaven *a* ... Deut 4:39
of any thing that is in heaven *a* ... Deut 5:8
*a* all people that are upon the ... Deut 7:6
shalt be blessed *a* all people ... Deut 7:14
even you *a* all people, as it is ... Deut 10:15
*a* all the nations that are upon ... Deut 14:2
be not lifted up *a* his brethren ... Deut 17:20
beat him *a* these with many ... Deut 25:3
to make thee high *a* all nations ... Deut 26:19
high *a* all nations of the earth ... Deut 28:1
and thou shalt be *a* only, and thou ... Deut 28:13
shall get up *a* thee very high ... Deut 28:43
and multiply thee *a* thy fathers ... Deut 30:5
your God, he is God in heaven *a* ... Josh 2:11
the waters that come down from *a* ... Josh 3:13
which came down from *a* stood ... Josh 3:16
Blessed *a* women shall Jael the ... Judg 5:24
shall she be *a* women in the tent ... Judg 5:24
and honourest thy sons *a* me ... 1Sa 2:29
He sent from *a*, he took me ... 2Sa 22:17
*a* them that rose up against me ... 2Sa 22:49
with cedar *a* upon the beams ... 1Kin 7:3
*a* were costly stones, after the ... 1Kin 7:11
pillars had pomegranates also *a* ... 1Kin 7:20
and the sea was set *a* upon them ... 1Kin 7:25
the ledges there was a base *a* ... 1Kin 7:29
the chapiter and *a* was a cubit ... 1Kin 7:31
the ark and the staves thereof *a* ... 1Kin 8:7
is no God like thee, in heaven *a* ... 1Kin 8:23
But hast done evil *a* all that ... 1Kin 14:9
*a* all that their fathers had done ... 1Kin 14:22
LORD *a* all that were before him ... 1Kin 16:30
hath done wickedly *a* all that the ... 2Kin 21:11
set his throne *a* the throne of ... 2Kin 25:28
Judah prevailed *a* his brethren ... 1Chr 5:2
also is to be feared *a* all gods ... 1Chr 16:25
from twenty years old and *a* ... 1Chr 23:27
among the thirty, and *a* the thirty ... 1Chr 27:6
*a* all that I have prepared for ... 1Chr 29:3
and thou art exalted as head *a* all ... 1Chr 29:11
for great is our God *a* all gods ... 2Chr 2:5
and the sea was set *a* upon them ... 2Chr 4:4
the ark and the staves thereof *a* ... 2Chr 5:8
of Absalom *a* all his wives ... 2Chr 11:21
priest, which stood *a* the people ... 2Chr 24:20
them from twenty years old and *a* ... 2Chr 25:5
images, that were on high *a* them ... 2Chr 34:4
From *a* the horse gate repaired ... Neh 3:28
man, and feared God *a* many ... Neh 7:2
(for he was *a* all the people ... Neh 8:5
which is exalted *a* all blessing ... Neh 9:5
*a* the house of David, even unto ... Neh 12:37
from *a* the gate of Ephraim, and ... Neh 12:39
*a* the old gate, and *a* the fish ... Neh 12:39
king loved Esther *a* all the women ... Est 2:17
set his seat *a* all the princes ... Est 3:1
he had advanced him *a* the princes ... Est 5:11
let not God regard it from *a* ... Job 3:4
*a* shall his branch be cut off ... Job 18:16
the price of wisdom is *a* rubies ... Job 28:18
portion of God is there from *a* ... Job 31:2
have denied the God that is *a* ... Job 31:28
hast set thy glory *a* the heavens ... Ps 8:1
are far *a* out of his sight ... Ps 10:5
He sent from *a*, he took me, he ... Ps 18:16
thou liftest me up *a* those that ... Ps 18:48
up *a* mine enemies round about me ... Ps 27:6
the oil of gladness *a* thy fellows ... Ps 45:7
shall call to the heavens from *a* ... Ps 50:4
exalted, O God, *a* the heavens ... Ps 57:5
let thy glory be *a* all the earth ... Ps 57:5
exalted, O God, *a* the heavens ... Ps 57:11
let thy glory be *a* all the earth ... Ps 57:11
had commanded the clouds from *a* ... Ps 78:23
God, and a great King *a* all gods ... Ps 95:3
he is to be feared *a* all gods ... Ps 96:4
LORD, art high *a* all the earth ... Ps 97:9
thou art exalted far *a* all gods ... Ps 97:9
he is high *a* all the people ... Ps 99:2
as the heaven is high *a* the earth ... Ps 103:11
the waters stood *a* the mountains ... Ps 104:6
thy mercy is great *a* the heavens ... Ps 108:4
exalted, O God, *a* the heavens ... Ps 108:5
thy glory *a* all the earth ... Ps 108:5
The LORD is high *a* all nations ... Ps 113:4
and his glory *a* the heavens ... Ps 113:4
I love thy commandments *a* gold ... Ps 119:127
yea, *a* fine gold ... Ps 119:127
and that our Lord is *a* all gods ... Ps 135:5
out the earth *a* the waters ... Ps 136:6
not Jerusalem *a* my chief joy ... Ps 137:6
magnified thy word *a* all thy name ... Ps 138:2
Send thine hand from *a* ... Ps 144:7
ye waters that be *a* the heavens ... Ps 148:4
his glory is *a* the earth and ... Ps 148:13
When he established the clouds *a* ... Prov 8:28
The way of life is *a* to the wise ... Prov 15:24
for her price is far *a* rubies ... Prov 31:10
small cattle *a* all that were in ... Eccl 2:7
man hath no preeminence *a* a beast ... Eccl 3:19
and shall be exalted *a* the hills ... Is 2:2
*A* it stood the seraphims ... Is 6:2
in the depth, or in the height *a* ... Is 7:11
my throne *a* the stars of God ... Is 14:13
I will ascend *a* the heights of ... Is 14:14
Drop down, ye heavens, from *a* ... Is 45:8
mourn, and the heavens *a* be black ... Jer 4:28
to me *a* the sand of the seas ... Jer 15:8
heart is deceitful *a* all things ... Jer 17:9
If heaven *a* can be measured, and ... Jer 31:37
which was *a* the chamber of ... Jer 35:4
set his throne *a* the throne of ... Jer 52:32
From *a* hath he sent fire into my ... Lam 1:13
forth over their heads *a* ... Eze 1:22
*a* the firmament that was over ... Eze 1:26
the appearance of a man *a* upon it ... Eze 1:26
in the firmament that was *a* the ... Eze 10:1
the God of Israel was over them *a* ... Eze 10:19
the God of Israel was over them *a* ... Eze 11:22
lewdness *a* all thine abominations ... Eze 16:43
itself any more *a* the nations ... Eze 29:15
his height was exalted *a* all the ... Eze 31:5
them, and the skin covered them *a* ... Eze 37:8
To that *a* the door, even unto the ... Eze 41:17
From the ground unto *a* the door ... Eze 41:20
was preferred *a* the presidents ... Dan 6:3
and he shall be strong *a* him ... Dan 11:5
and magnify himself *a* every god ... Dan 11:36
he shall magnify himself *a* all ... Dan 11:37
yet I destroyed his fruit from *a* ... Amos 2:9
it shall be exalted *a* the hills ... Mic 4:1
merchants *a* the stars of heaven ... Nah 3:16
The disciple is not *a* his master ... Mt 10:24
nor the servant *a* his lord ... Mt 10:24
Added yet this *a* all, that he ... Lk 3:20
The disciple is not *a* his master ... Lk 6:40
were sinners *a* all the Galilaeans ... Lk 13:2
*a* all men that dwelt in Jerusalem ... Lk 13:4
that cometh from *a* is *a* all ... Jn 3:31
that cometh from *a* is *a* all ... Jn 3:31
that cometh from heaven is *a* all ... Jn 3:31
*a* unto them that had eaten ... Jn 6:13
I am from *a* ... Jn 8:23
except it were given thee from *a* ... Jn 19:11
I will shew wonders in heaven *a* ... Acts 2:19
For the man was *a* forty years old ... Acts 4:22
*a* the brightness of the sun, ... Acts 26:13
is, to bring Christ down from *a* ... Rom 10:6
man esteemeth one day *a* another ... Rom 14:5
of men *a* that which is written ... 1Cor 4:6
to be tempted *a* that ye are able ... 1Cor 10:13
he was seen of *a* five hundred ... 1Cor 15:6
*a* strength, insomuch that we ... 2Cor 1:8
abundant, in stripes *a* measure ... 2Cor 11:23
in Christ *a* fourteen years ago ... 2Cor 12:2
me *a* that which he seeth me to be ... 2Cor 12:6
lest I should be exalted *a* ... 2Cor 12:7
I should be exalted *a* measure ... 2Cor 12:7
*a* many my equals in mine own ... Gal 1:14
But Jerusalem which is *a* is free ... Gal 4:26
Far *a* all principality, and power, ... Eph 1:21
*a* all that we ask or think ... Eph 3:20
and Father of all, who is *a* all ... Eph 4:6
ascended up far *a* all heavens ... Eph 4:10
*A* all, taking the shield of faith ... Eph 6:16
him a name which is *a* every name ... Phil 2:9
seek those things which are *a* ... Col 3:1
Set your affection on things *a* ... Col 3:2
*a* all these things put on charity ... Col 3:14
exalteth himself *a* all that is ... 2Th 2:4
but *a* a servant, a brother ... Philem 16
the oil of gladness *a* thy fellows ... Heb 1:9
*A* when he said, Sacrifice and ... Heb 10:8
and every perfect gift is from *a* ... Jas 1:17
This wisdom descendeth not from *a* ... Jas 3:15
that is from *a* is first pure ... Jas 3:17
But *a* all things, my brethren, ... Jas 5:12
*a* all things have fervent charity ... 1Pet 4:8
I wish *a* all things that thou ... 3Jn 2

**ABRAHAM** (*a'-bra-ham*) See ABRAHAM'S, ABRAM. *Father of the nation of Israel.*
Abram, but thy name shall be *A* ... Gen 17:5
And God said unto *A*, Thou shalt ... Gen 17:9
And God said unto *A*, As for Sarai ... Gen 17:15
Then *A* fell upon his face, and ... Gen 17:17
*A* said unto God, O that Ishmael ... Gen 17:18
with him, and God went up from *A* ... Gen 17:22
*A* took Ishmael his son, and all ... Gen 17:23
*A* was ninety years old and nine, ... Gen 17:24
selfsame day was *A* circumcised ... Gen 17:26
*A* hastened into the tent unto ... Gen 18:6
*A* ran unto the herd, and fetcht a ... Gen 18:7
Now *A* and Sarah were old and well .. Gen 18:11
And the LORD said unto *A*, ... Gen 18:13
*A* went with them to bring them on ... Gen 18:16
Shall I hide from *A* that thing ... Gen 18:17
Seeing that *A* shall surely become ... Gen 18:18
*A* that which he hath spoken of ... Gen 18:19
but *A* stood yet before the LORD ... Gen 18:22
*A* drew near, and said, Wilt thou ... Gen 18:23
*A* answered and said, Behold now, I ... Gen 18:27
as he had left communing with *A* ... Gen 18:33
*A* returned unto his place ... Gen 18:33
*A* gat up early in the morning to ... Gen 19:27
the plain, that God remembered *A* ... Gen 19:29
*A* journeyed from thence toward ... Gen 20:1
*A* said of Sarah his wife, She is ... Gen 20:2
Then Abimelech called *A*, and said ... Gen 20:9
And Abimelech said unto *A*, What ... Gen 20:10
*A* said, Because I thought, Surely ... Gen 20:11
and gave them unto *A*, and restored .. Gen 20:14
So *A* prayed unto God ... Gen 20:17
bare *A* a son in his old age, at ... Gen 21:2
*A* called the name of his son that ... Gen 21:3
*A* circumcised his son Isaac being ... Gen 21:4
*A* was an hundred years old, when ... Gen 21:5
said, Who would have said unto *A* ... Gen 21:7
*A* made a great feast the same day ... Gen 21:8
which she had born unto *A* ... Gen 21:9
Wherefore she said unto *A* ... Gen 21:10
And God said unto *A*, Let it not be ... Gen 21:12
*A* rose up early in the morning, ... Gen 21:14
captain of his host spake unto *A* ... Gen 21:22
And *A* said, I will swear ... Gen 21:24
*A* reproved Abimelech because of a ... Gen 21:25
*A* took sheep and oxen, and gave ... Gen 21:27
*A* set seven ewe lambs of the ... Gen 21:28
And Abimelech said unto *A*, What ... Gen 21:29
*A* planted a grove in Beer-sheba, ... Gen 21:33
*A* sojourned in the Philistines' ... Gen 21:34
things, that God did tempt *A* ... Gen 22:1
and said unto him, *A* ... Gen 22:1
*A* rose up early in the morning, ... Gen 22:3
third day *A* lifted up his eyes ... Gen 22:4
*A* said unto his young men, Abide ... Gen 22:5
*A* took the wood of the burnt ... Gen 22:6
And Isaac spake unto *A* his father ... Gen 22:7
*A* said, My son, God will provide ... Gen 22:8
*A* built an altar there, and laid ... Gen 22:9
*A* stretched forth his hand, and ... Gen 22:10
of heaven, and said, *A*, *A* ... Gen 22:11
*A* lifted up his eyes, and looked, ... Gen 22:13
*A* went and took the ram, and ... Gen 22:13
*A* called the name of that place ... Gen 22:14
*A* out of heaven the second time ... Gen 22:15
So *A* returned unto his young men, ... Gen 22:19
and *A* dwelt at Beer-sheba ... Gen 22:19
these things, that it was told *A* ... Gen 22:20
*A* came to mourn for Sarah, and to ... Gen 23:2
*A* stood up from before his dead, ... Gen 23:3
the children of Heth answered *A* ... Gen 23:5
*A* stood up, and bowed himself to ... Gen 23:7
Ephron the Hittite answered *A* in ... Gen 23:10

*A* bowed down himself before the ... Gen 23:12
And Ephron answered *A*, saying unto Gen 23:14
And *A* hearkened unto Ephron ... Gen 23:16
*A* weighed to Ephron the silver, ... Gen 23:16
Unto *A* for a possession in the ... Gen 23:18
*A* buried Sarah his wife in the ... Gen 23:19
were made sure unto *A* for a ... Gen 23:20
*A* was old, and well stricken in ... Gen 24:1
LORD had blessed *A* in all things ... Gen 24:1
*A* said unto his eldest servant of ... Gen 24:2
*A* said unto him, Beware thou that ... Gen 24:6
under the thigh of *A* his master ... Gen 24:9
said, O LORD God of my master *A* ... Gen 24:12
kindness unto my master *A* ... Gen 24:12
be the LORD God of my master *A* ... Gen 24:27
said, O LORD God of my master *A* ... Gen 24:42
the LORD God of my master *A* ... Gen 24:48
Then again *A* took a wife, and her ... Gen 25:1
*A* gave all that he had unto Isaac ... Gen 25:5
of the concubines, which *A* had ... Gen 25:6
*A* gave gifts, and sent them away ... Gen 25:6
Then *A* gave up the ghost, and died ... Gen 25:8
The field which *A* purchased of ... Gen 25:10
there was *A* buried, and Sarah his ... Gen 25:10
came to pass after the death of *A* ... Gen 25:11
Sarah's handmaid, bare unto *A* ... Gen 25:12
*A* begat Isaac ... Gen 25:19
famine that was in the days of *A* ... Gen 26:1
which I sware unto *A* thy father ... Gen 26:3
Because that *A* obeyed my voice, ... Gen 26:5
in the days of *A* his father ... Gen 26:15
in the days of *A* his father ... Gen 26:18
stopped them after the death of *A* ... Gen 26:18
I am the God of *A* thy father ... Gen 26:24
And give thee the blessing of *A* ... Gen 28:4
a stranger, which God gave unto *A* ... Gen 28:4
I am the LORD God of *A* thy father ... Gen 28:13
God of my father, the God of *A* ... Gen 31:42
The God of *A*, and the God of Nahor. Gen 31:53
Jacob said, O God of my father *A* ... Gen 32:9
And the land which I gave *A* ... Gen 35:12
Arbah, which is Hebron, where *A* ... Gen 35:27
God, before whom my fathers *A* ... Gen 48:15
them, and the name of my fathers *A* . Gen 48:16
which *A* bought with the field of ... Gen 49:30
There they buried *A* and Sarah his ... Gen 49:31
which *A* bought with the field for ... Gen 50:13
unto the land which he sware to *A* ... Gen 50:24
remembered his covenant with *A* ... Ex 2:24
God of thy father, the God of *A* ... Ex 3:6
God of your fathers, the God of *A* ... Ex 3:15
God of your fathers, the God of *A* ... Ex 3:16
of their fathers, the God of *A* ... Ex 4:5
And I appeared unto *A*, unto Isaac, ... Ex 6:3
which I did swear to give it to *A* ... Ex 6:8
Remember *A*, Isaac, and Israel, thy ... Ex 32:13
the land which I sware unto *A* ... Ex 33:1
covenant with *A* will I remember ... Lev 26:42
see the land which I sware unto *A* ... Num 32:11
LORD sware unto your fathers, *A* ... Deut 1:8
he sware unto thy fathers, to *A* ... Deut 6:10
LORD sware unto thy fathers, *A* ... Deut 9:5
Remember thy servants, *A*, Isaac, ... Deut 9:27
hath sworn unto thy fathers, to *A* ... Deut 29:13
LORD sware unto thy fathers, to *A* ... Deut 30:20
is the land which I sware unto *A* ... Deut 34:4
time, even Terah, the father of *A* ... Josh 24:2
I took your father *A* from the ... Josh 24:3
came near, and said, LORD God of *A* . 1Kin 18:36
because of his covenant with *A* ... 2Kin 13:23
Abram; the same is *A* ... 1Chr 1:27
The sons of *A*; Isaac, and ... 1Chr 1:28
And *A* begat Isaac ... 1Chr 1:34
the covenant which he made with *A* 1Chr 16:16
O LORD God of *A*, Isaac, and of ... 1Chr 29:18
the seed of *A* thy friend for ever ... 2Chr 20:7
turn again unto the LORD God of *A* ... 2Chr 30:6
and gavest him the name of *A* ... Neh 9:7
even the people of the God of *A* ... Ps 47:9
O ye seed of *A* his servant ... Ps 105:6
Which covenant he made with *A* ... Ps 105:9
holy promise, and *A* his servant ... Ps 105:42
saith the LORD, who redeemed *A* ... Is 29:22
chosen, the seed of *A* my friend ... Is 41:8
Look unto *A* your father, and unto ... Is 51:2
though *A* be ignorant of us, and ... Is 63:16
to be rulers over the seed of *A* ... Jer 33:26
*A* was one, and he inherited the ... Eze 33:24
truth to Jacob, and the mercy to *A* ... Mic 7:20
the son of David, the son of *A* ... Mt 1:1
*A* begat Isaac ... Mt 1:2
from *A* to David are fourteen ... Mt 1:17
We have *A* to our father ... Mt 3:9
to raise up children unto *A* ... Mt 3:9
and west, and shall sit down with *A* ... Mt 8:11
I am the God of *A*, and the God of ... Mt 22:32
him, saying, I am the God of *A* ... Mk 12:26
As he spake to our fathers, to *A* ... Lk 1:55
which he sware to our father *A* ... Lk 1:73
We have *A* to our father ... Lk 3:8
to raise up children unto *A* ... Lk 3:8
of Isaac, which was the son of *A* ... Lk 3:34
this woman, being a daughter of *A* ... Lk 13:16
of teeth, when ye shall see *A* ... Lk 13:28
seeth *A* afar off, and Lazarus in ... Lk 16:23
And he cried and said, Father *A* ... Lk 16:24
But *A* said, Son, remember that ... Lk 16:25
*A* saith unto him, They have Moses ... Lk 16:29
And he said, Nay, father *A* ... Lk 16:30
as he also is a son of *A* ... Lk 19:9
he calleth the Lord the God of *A* ... Lk 20:37
and said unto him, *A* is our father ... Jn 8:39
ye would do the works of *A* ... Jn 8:39
of God: this did not *A* ... Jn 8:40
*A* is dead, and the prophets ... Jn 8:52
thou greater than our father *A* ... Jn 8:53
Your father *A* rejoiced to see my ... Jn 8:56
years old, and hast thou seen *A* ... Jn 8:57
I say unto you, Before *A* was ... Jn 8:58
The God of *A*, and of Isaac, and of ... Acts 3:13
with our fathers, saying unto *A* ... Acts 3:25
glory appeared unto our father *A* ... Acts 7:2
so *A* begat Isaac, and circumcised ... Acts 7:8
laid in the sepulchre that *A* ... Acts 7:16
nigh, which God had sworn to *A* ... Acts 7:17
God of thy fathers, the God of *A* ... Acts 7:32
children of the stock of *A* ... Acts 13:26
we say then that *A* our father ... Rom 4:1
For if *A* were justified by works, ... Rom 4:2
*A* believed God, and it was counted ... Rom 4:3
reckoned to *A* for righteousness ... Rom 4:9
of that faith of our father *A* ... Rom 4:12
heir of the world, was not to *A* ... Rom 4:13
also which is of the faith of *A* ... Rom 4:16
because they are the seed of *A* ... Rom 9:7
am an Israelite, of the seed of *A* ... Rom 11:1
Are they the seed of *A* ... 2Cor 11:22
Even as *A* believed God, and it was ... Gal 3:6
the same are the children of *A* ... Gal 3:7
preached before the gospel unto *A* ... Gal 3:8
faith are blessed with faithful *A* ... Gal 3:9
That the blessing of *A* might come ... Gal 3:14
Now to *A* and his seed were the ... Gal 3:16
but God gave it to *A* by promise ... Gal 3:18
that *A* had two sons, the one by a ... Gal 4:22
but he took on him the seed of *A* ... Heb 2:16
For when God made promise to *A* ... Heb 6:13
who met *A* returning from the ... Heb 7:1
To whom also *A* gave a tenth part ... Heb 7:2
*A* gave the tenth of the spoils ... Heb 7:4
they come out of the loins of *A* ... Heb 7:5
from them received tithes of *A* ... Heb 7:6
tithes, payed tithes in *A* ... Heb 7:9
By faith *A*, when he was called to ... Heb 11:8
By faith *A*, when he was tried, ... Heb 11:17
Was not *A* our father justified by ... Jas 2:21
*A* believed God, and it was imputed ... Jas 2:23
Even as Sarah obeyed *A*, calling ... 1Pet 3:6

**ABRAHAM'S** (*a'-bra-hams*)
male among the men of *A* house ... Gen 17:23
because of Sarah *A* wife ... Gen 20:18
in *A* sight because of his son ... Gen 21:11
did bear to Nahor, *A* brother ... Gen 22:23
*A* brother, with her pitcher upon ... Gen 24:15
And he said, I am *A* servant ... Gen 24:34
when *A* servant heard their words, ... Gen 24:52
nurse, and *A* servant, and his men ... Gen 24:59
years of *A* life which he lived ... Gen 25:7
*A* son, whom Hagar the Egyptian, ... Gen 25:12
the generations of Isaac, *A* son ... Gen 25:19
thy seed for my servant *A* sake ... Gen 26:24
the daughter of Ishmael *A* son ... Gen 28:9
the sons of Keturah, *A* concubine ... 1Chr 1:32
by the angels into *A* bosom ... Lk 16:22
They answered him, We be *A* seed ... Jn 8:33
I know that ye are *A* seed ... Jn 8:37
unto them, If ye were *A* children ... Jn 8:39
be Christ's, then are ye *A* seed ... Gal 3:29

**ABRAM** (*a'-brum*) See ABRAHAM, ABRAM'S.
*Abraham's original name.*
lived seventy years, and begat *A* ... Gen 11:26
Terah begat *A*, Nahor, and Haran ... Gen 11:27
And *A* and Nahor took them wives ... Gen 11:29
And Terah took *A* his son, and Lot ... Gen 11:31
Now the LORD had said unto *A* ... Gen 12:1
So *A* departed, as the LORD had ... Gen 12:4
*A* was seventy and five years old ... Gen 12:4
*A* took Sarai his wife, and Lot his ... Gen 12:5
*A* passed through the land unto ... Gen 12:6
And the LORD appeared unto *A* ... Gen 12:7
*A* journeyed, going on still ... Gen 12:9
*A* went down into Egypt to sojourn ... Gen 12:10
when *A* was come into Egypt, the ... Gen 12:14
he entreated *A* well for her sake ... Gen 12:16
And Pharaoh called *A*, and said, ... Gen 12:18
*A* went up out of Egypt, he, and ... Gen 13:1
*A* was very rich in cattle, in ... Gen 13:2
there *A* called on the name of the ... Gen 13:4
And Lot also, which went with *A* ... Gen 13:5
*A* said unto Lot, Let there be no ... Gen 13:8
*A* dwelled in the land of Canaan, ... Gen 13:12
And the LORD said unto *A*, after ... Gen 13:14
Then *A* removed his tent, and came ... Gen 13:18
had escaped, and told *A* the Hebrew ... Gen 14:13
and these were confederate with *A* ... Gen 14:13
when *A* heard that his brother was ... Gen 14:14
Blessed be *A* of the most high God ... Gen 14:19
And the king of Sodom said unto *A* ... Gen 14:21
*A* said to the king of Sodom, I ... Gen 14:22
shouldest say, I have made *A* rich ... Gen 14:23
the LORD came unto *A* in a vision ... Gen 15:1
in a vision, saying, Fear not, *A* ... Gen 15:1
*A* said, Lord GOD, what wilt thou ... Gen 15:2
*A* said, Behold, to me thou hast ... Gen 15:3
the carcases, *A* drove them away ... Gen 15:11
down, a deep sleep fell upon *A* ... Gen 15:12
And he said unto *A*, Know of a ... Gen 15:13
the LORD made a covenant with *A* ... Gen 15:18
And Sarai said unto *A*, Behold now, ... Gen 16:2
*A* hearkened to the voice of Sarai ... Gen 16:2
after *A* had dwelt ten years in ... Gen 16:3
to her husband *A* to be his wife ... Gen 16:3
And Sarai said unto *A*, My wrong be ... Gen 16:5
But *A* said unto Sarai, Behold, ... Gen 16:6
And Hagar bare *A* a son ... Gen 16:15
*A* called his son's name, which ... Gen 16:15
*A* was fourscore and six years old, ... Gen 16:16
old, when Hagar bare Ishmael to *A* ... Gen 16:16
when *A* was ninety years old and ... Gen 17:1
and nine, the LORD appeared to *A* ... Gen 17:1
And *A* fell on his face ... Gen 17:3
thy name any more be called *A* ... Gen 17:5
*A*; the same is Abraham ... 1Chr 1:27
LORD the God, who didst choose *A* ... Neh 9:7

**ABRAM'S** (*a'-brums*)
the name of *A* wife was Sarai ... Gen 11:29
daughter in law, his son *A* wife ... Gen 11:31
plagues because of Sarai *A* wife ... Gen 12:17
between the herdmen of *A* cattle ... Gen 13:7
*A* brother's son, who dwelt in ... Gen 14:12
Now Sarai *A* wife bare him no ... Gen 16:1
Sarai *A* wife took Hagar her maid ... Gen 16:3

**ABROAD**
of the Canaanites spread *a* ... Gen 10:18
lest we be scattered *a* upon the ... Gen 11:4
So the LORD scattered them *a* from ... Gen 11:8
did the LORD scatter them *a* upon ... Gen 11:9
And he brought him forth *a* ... Gen 15:5
they had brought them forth *a* ... Gen 19:17
thou shalt spread *a* to the west ... Gen 28:14
*a* throughout all the land of ... Ex 5:12
I will spread *a* my hands unto the ... Ex 9:29
spread *a* his hands unto the LORD ... Ex 9:33
of the flesh *a* out of the house ... Ex 12:46
walk *a* upon his staff, then shall ... Ex 21:19
he spread *a* the tent over the ... Ex 40:19
scab spread much *a* in the skin ... Lev 13:7
a leprosy break out *a* in the skin ... Lev 13:12
if it spread much *a* in the skin ... Lev 13:22
it be spread much *a* in the skin ... Lev 13:27
shall tarry *a* out of his tent ... Lev 14:8
she be born at home, or born *a* ... Lev 18:9
they spread them all *a* for ... Num 11:32
shall he go *a* out of the camp ... Deut 23:10
whither thou shalt go forth *a* ... Deut 23:12
be, when thou wilt ease thyself *a* ... Deut 23:13
Thou shalt stand *a*, and the man to .. Deut 24:11
bring out the pledge *a* unto thee ... Deut 24:11
her young, spreadeth *a* her wings ... Deut 32:11
thirty daughters, whom he sent *a* ... Judg 12:9
daughters from *a* for his sons ... Judg 12:9
out both of them, he and Samuel, *a* ... 1Sa 9:26
they were spread *a* upon all the ... 1Sa 30:16
the street, and did spread them *a* ... 2Sa 22:43
walkest *a* any whither, that thou ... 1Kin 2:42
borrow thee vessels *a* of all thy ... 2Kin 4:3
let us send *a* unto our brethren ... 1Chr 13:2
spread themselves *a* in the valley ... 1Chr 14:13
his name spread *a* even to the ... 2Chr 26:8
And his name spread far *a* ... 2Chr 26:15
to carry it out *a* into the brook ... 2Chr 29:16
as soon as the commandment came *a* 2Chr 31:5
scatter you *a* among the nations ... Neh 1:8
queen shall come *a* unto all women ... Est 1:17
is a certain people scattered *a* ... Est 3:8
lion's whelps are scattered *a* ... Job 4:11
He wandereth *a* for bread, saying, ... Job 15:23
Cast *a* the rage of thy wrath ... Job 40:11
when he goeth *a*, he telleth it ... Ps 41:6
thine arrows also went *a* ... Ps 77:17
Let thy fountains be dispersed *a* ... Prov 5:16
scattereth *a* the inhabitants ... Is 24:1
doth he not cast *a* the fitches ... Is 28:25
that spreadeth *a* the earth by ... Is 44:24
pour it out upon the children *a* ... Jer 6:11
*a* the sword bereaveth, at home ... Lam 1:20
till ye have scattered them *a* ... Eze 34:21
prosperity shall yet be spread *a* ... Zec 1:17
for I have spread you *a* as the ... Zec 2:6
hereof went *a* into all that land ... Mt 9:26
spread *a* his fame in all that ... Mt 9:31
they fainted, and were scattered *a* ... Mt 9:36
not with me scattereth *a* ... Mt 12:30
of the flock shall be scattered *a* ... Mt 26:31
immediately his fame spread *a* ... Mk 1:28
to blaze *a* the matter, insomuch ... Mk 1:45
secret, but that it should come *a* ... Mk 4:22
(for his name was spread *a* ... Mk 6:14
all these sayings were noised *a* ... Lk 1:65
they made known *a* the saying ... Lk 2:17
more went there a fame *a* of him ... Lk 5:15
that shall not be known and come *a* ... Lk 8:17
of God that were scattered *a* ... Jn 11:52
this saying *a* among the brethren ... Jn 21:23
Now when this was noised *a* ... Acts 2:6
they were all scattered *a* ... Acts 8:1
they that were scattered *a* went ... Acts 8:4
Now they which were scattered *a* ... Acts 11:19
*a* in our hearts by the Holy Ghost ... Rom 5:5
obedience is come *a* unto all men ... Rom 16:19
is written, He hath dispersed *a* ... 2Cor 9:9
faith to God-ward is spread *a* ... 1Th 1:8
tribes which are scattered *a* ... Jas 1:1

**ABRONAH** See EBRONAH.

**ABSALOM** (*ab'-sal-um*) *A son of David.*
*A* the son of Maacah the daughter ... 2Sa 3:3
that *A* the son of David had a ... 2Sa 13:1

A her brother said unto her, Hath 2Sa 13:20
A spake unto his brother Amnon 2Sa 13:22
for A hated Amnon, because he had 2Sa 13:22
that A had sheepshearers in 2Sa 13:23
A invited all the king's sons 2Sa 13:23
A came to the king, and said, 2Sa 13:24
And the king said to A, Nay, my 2Sa 13:25
Then said A, If not, I pray thee, 2Sa 13:26
But A pressed him, that he let 2Sa 13:27
Now A had commanded his servants, 2Sa 13:28
the servants of A did unto Amnon 2Sa 13:29
as A had commanded 2Sa 13:29
A hath slain all the king's sons, 2Sa 13:30
for by the appointment of A this 2Sa 13:32
But A fled 2Sa 13:34
But A fled, and went to Talmai, 2Sa 13:37
So A fled, and went to Geshur, and 2Sa 13:38
David longed to go forth unto A 2Sa 13:39
the king's heart was toward A 2Sa 14:1
bring the young man A again 2Sa 14:21
Geshur, and brought A to Jerusalem 2Sa 14:23
So A returned to his own house, 2Sa 14:24
much praised as A for his beauty 2Sa 14:25
unto A there were born three sons 2Sa 14:27
So A dwelt two full years in 2Sa 14:28
Therefore A sent for Joab, to 2Sa 14:29
came to A unto his house, and said 2Sa 14:31
A answered Joab, Behold, I sent 2Sa 14:32
and when he had called for A 2Sa 14:33
and the king kissed A 2Sa 14:33
that A prepared him chariots and 2Sa 15:1
A rose up early, and stood beside 2Sa 15:2
then A called unto him, and said, 2Sa 15:2
A said unto him, See, thy matters 2Sa 15:3
A said moreover, Oh that I were 2Sa 15:4
on this manner did A to all 2Sa 15:6
so A stole the hearts of the men 2Sa 15:6
that A said unto the king, I pray 2Sa 15:7
But A sent spies throughout all 2Sa 15:10
shall say, A reigneth in Hebron 2Sa 15:10
with A went two hundred men out 2Sa 15:11
A sent for Ahithophel the 2Sa 15:12
increased continually with A 2Sa 15:12
of the men of Israel are after A 2Sa 15:13
we shall not else escape from A 2Sa 15:14
is among the conspirators with A 2Sa 15:31
return to the city, and say unto A 2Sa 15:34
city, and A came into Jerusalem 2Sa 15:37
into the hand of A thy son 2Sa 16:8
And A, and all the people the men 2Sa 16:15
David's friend, was come unto A 2Sa 16:16
A, that Hushai said unto A 2Sa 16:16
A said to Hushai, Is this thy 2Sa 16:17
And Hushai said unto A, Nay 2Sa 16:18
Then said A to Ahithophel, Give 2Sa 16:20
And Ahithophel said unto A 2Sa 16:21
So they spread A a tent upon the 2Sa 16:22
A went in unto his father's 2Sa 16:22
both with David and with A 2Sa 16:23
Moreover Ahithophel said unto A 2Sa 17:1
And the saying pleased A well 2Sa 17:4
Then said A, Call now Hushai the 2Sa 17:5
And when Hushai was come to A 2Sa 17:6
A spake unto him, saying, 2Sa 17:6
And Hushai said unto A, The 2Sa 17:7
among the people that follow A 2Sa 17:9
And A and all the men of Israel 2Sa 17:14
the LORD might bring evil upon A 2Sa 17:14
and thus did Ahithophel counsel A 2Sa 17:15
a lad saw them, and told A 2Sa 17:18
A passed over Jordan, he and all 2Sa 17:24
A made Amasa captain of the host 2Sa 17:25
A pitched in the land of Gilead 2Sa 17:26
with the young man, even with A 2Sa 18:5
the captains charge concerning A 2Sa 18:5
A met the servants of David 2Sa 18:9
A rode upon a mule, and the mule 2Sa 18:9
Behold, I saw A hanged in an oak 2Sa 18:10
that none touch the young man A 2Sa 18:12
them through the heart of A 2Sa 18:14
compassed about and smote A 2Sa 18:15
And they took A, and cast him into 2Sa 18:17
Now A in his lifetime had taken 2Sa 18:18
said, Is the young man A safe 2Sa 18:29
Cushi, Is the young man A safe 2Sa 18:32
my son A, my son, my son A 2Sa 18:33
God I had died for thee, O A 2Sa 18:33
king weepeth and mourneth for A 2Sa 19:1
loud voice, O my son A, O A 2Sa 19:4
that if A had lived, and all we 2Sa 19:6
he is fled out of the land for A 2Sa 19:9
And A, whom we anointed over us, 2Sa 19:10
Bichri do us more harm than did A 2Sa 20:6
and his mother bare him after A 1Kin 1:6
I fled because of A thy brother 1Kin 2:7
though he turned not after A 1Kin 2:28
A the son of Maachah the daughter 1Chr 3:2
he took Maachah the daughter of A. 2Chr 11:20
daughter of A above all his wives 2Chr 11:21
when he fled from A his son Ps 3:t

**ABSALOM'S** (*ab'-sal-ums*)
I love Tamar, my brother A sister 2Sa 13:4
desolate in her brother A house 2Sa 13:20
A servants set the field on fire 2Sa 14:30
when A servants came to the woman. 2Sa 17:20
is called unto this day, A place 2Sa 18:18

**ABSENCE**
them in the a of the multitude Lk 22:6
only, but now much more in my a Phil 2:12

**ABSENT**
when we are a one from another Gen 31:49
as a in body, but present in 1Cor 5:3
the body, we are a from the Lord 2Cor 5:6
rather to be a from the body 2Cor 5:8
that, whether present or a 2Cor 5:9
but being a am bold toward you 2Cor 10:1
in word by letters when we are a 2Cor 10:11
being a now I write to them which 2Cor 13:2
I write these things being a 2Cor 13:10
I come and see you, or else be a Phil 1:27
For though I be a in the flesh Col 2:5

**ABSTAIN**
that they a from pollutions of Acts 15:20
That ye a from meats offered to Acts 15:29
that ye should a from fornication 1Th 4:3
A from all appearance of evil 1Th 5:22
and commanding to a from meats 1Ti 4:3
a from fleshly lusts, which war 1Pet 2:11

**ABSTINENCE**
But after long a Paul stood forth Acts 27:21

**ABUNDANCE**
of heart, for the a of all things Deut 28:47
shall suck of the a of the seas Deut 33:19
for out of the a of my complaint 1Sa 1:16
the spoil of the city in great a 2Sa 12:30
oxen and fat cattle and sheep in a 1Kin 1:19
oxen and fat cattle and sheep in a 1Kin 1:25
there came no more such a of 1Kin 10:10
trees that are in the vale, for a 1Kin 10:27
for there is a sound of a of rain 1Kin 18:41
David prepared iron in a for the 1Chr 22:3
brass in a without weight 1Chr 22:3
Also cedar trees in a 1Chr 22:4
for it is in a 1Chr 22:14
there are workmen with thee in a 1Chr 22:15
stones, and marble stones in a 1Chr 29:2
sacrifices in a for all Israel 1Chr 29:21
trees that are in the vale for a 2Chr 1:15
Even to prepare me timber in a 2Chr 2:9
made all these vessels in great a 2Chr 4:18
that bare spices, and gold in a 2Chr 9:1
of gold, and of spices great a 2Chr 9:9
that are in the low plains in a 2Chr 9:27
and he gave them victual in a 2Chr 11:23
carried away sheep and camels in a 2Chr 14:15
fell to him out of Israel in a 2Chr 15:9
and he had riches and honour in a 2Chr 17:5
had riches and honour in a 2Chr 18:1
killed sheep and oxen for him in a 2Chr 18:2
they found among them in a both 2Chr 20:25
by day, and gathered money in a 2Chr 24:11
the burnt offerings were in a 2Chr 29:35
in a the firstfruits of corn 2Chr 31:5
and made darts and shields in a 2Chr 32:5
of flocks and herds in a 2Chr 32:29
oliveyards, and fruit trees in a Neh 9:25
from another,) and royal wine in a Est 1:7
and a of waters cover thee Job 22:11
he giveth meat in a Job 36:31
that a of waters may cover thee Job 38:34
themselves in the a of peace Ps 37:11
trusted in the a of his riches Ps 52:7
a of peace so long as the moon Ps 72:7
land brought forth frogs in a Ps 105:30
he that loveth a with increase Eccl 5:10
but the a of the rich will not Eccl 5:12
for the a of milk that they shall Is 7:22
Therefore the a they have gotten, Is 15:7
and for the great a of thine Is 47:9
because the a of the sea shall be Is 60:5
delighted with the a of her glory Is 66:11
reveal unto them the a of peace Jer 33:6
a of idleness was in her and in Eze 16:49
By reason of the a of his horses Eze 26:10
and silver, and apparel, in great a Zec 14:14
for out of the a of the heart the Mt 12:34
be given, and he shall have more a Mt 13:12
be given, and he shall have a Mt 25:29
all they did cast in of their a Mk 12:44
for of the a of the heart his Lk 6:45
in the a of the things which he Lk 12:15
For all these have of their a Lk 21:4
they which receive a of grace Rom 5:17
of affliction the a of their joy 2Cor 8:2
that now at this time your a may 2Cor 8:14
that their a also may be a supply 2Cor 8:14
a which is administered by us 2Cor 8:20
through the a of the revelations 2Cor 12:7
through the a of her delicacies Rev 18:3

**ABUNDANT**
and a in goodness and truth, Ex 34:6
be as this day, and much more a Is 56:12
a in treasures, thine end is come Jer 51:13
these we bestow more a honour 1Cor 12:23
parts have more a comeliness 1Cor 12:23
having given more a honour to 1Cor 12:24
that the a grace might through 2Cor 4:15
affection is more a toward you 2Cor 7:15
the saints, but is a also by many 2Cor 9:12
in labours more a, in stripes 2Cor 11:23
a in Jesus Christ for me by my Phil 1:26
Lord was exceeding a with faith 1Ti 1:14
which according to his a mercy 1Pet 1:3

**ABUNDANTLY**
Let the waters bring forth a the Gen 1:20
which the waters brought forth a Gen 1:21
they may breed a in the earth Gen 8:17
bring forth a in the earth, and Gen 9:7
were fruitful, and increased a Ex 1:7
river shall bring forth frogs a Ex 8:3
and the water came out a, and the Num 20:11
wine, and oil, and oxen, and sheep a 1Chr 12:40
David prepared a before his death 1Chr 22:5
saying, Thou hast shed blood a 1Chr 22:8
of all things brought they in a 2Chr 31:5
into whose hand God bringeth a Job 12:6
do drop and distil upon man a Job 36:28
They shall be a satisfied with Ps 36:8
waterest the ridges thereof a Ps 65:10
I will a bless her provision Ps 132:15
They shall a utter the memory of Ps 145:7
drink, yea, drink a, O beloved Song 5:1
every one shall howl, weeping a Is 15:3
It shall blossom a, and rejoice Is 35:2
to our God, for he will a pardon Is 55:7
and that they might have it more a Jn 10:10
I laboured more a than they all 1Cor 15:10
the world, and more a to you-ward 2Cor 1:12
love which I have more a unto you 2Cor 2:4
by you according to our rule a 2Cor 10:15
though the more a I love you 2Cor 12:15
that is able to do exceeding a Eph 3:20
endeavoured the more a to see 1Th 2:17
Which he shed on us a through Titus 3:6
willing more a to shew unto the Heb 6:17
shall be ministered unto you a 2Pet 1:11

**ABUSE**
and thrust me through, and a me 1Sa 31:4
these uncircumcised come and a me 1Chr 10:4
that I a not my power in the 1Cor 9:18

**ABUSED**
a her all the night until the Judg 19:25

**ABUSERS**
nor a of themselves with mankind, 1Cor 6:9

**ABUSING**
that use this world, as not a it 1Cor 7:31

**ACBOR** See ACHBOR.

**ACCAD** (*ak'-kad*) *A city of Shinar.*
was Babel, and Erech, and A Gen 10:10

**ACCEPT**
peradventure he will a of me Gen 32:20
the owner of it shall a thereof Ex 22:11
they then a of the punishment of Lev 26:41
they shall a of the punishment of Lev 26:43
and a the work of his hands Deut 33:11
against me, let him a an offering 1Sa 26:19
the king, The LORD thy God a thee 2Sa 24:23
Will ye a his person Job 13:8
you, if ye do secretly a persons Job 13:10
a any man's person, neither let Job 32:21
for him will I a Job 42:8
and a thy burnt sacrifice Ps 20:3
a the persons of the wicked Ps 82:2
A, I beseech thee, the freewill Ps 119:108
It is not good to a the person of Prov 18:5
the LORD doth not a them Jer 14:10
and an oblation, I will not a them Jer 14:12
there will I a them, and there Eze 20:40
I will a you with your sweet Eze 20:41
and I will a you, saith the Lord Eze 43:27
meat offerings, I will not a them Amos 5:22
with thee, or a thy person Mal 1:8
neither will I a an offering at Mal 1:10
should I a this of your hand Mal 1:13
We a it always, and in all places, Acts 24:3

**ACCEPTABLE**
for it shall not be a for you Lev 22:20
let him be a to his brethren, and Deut 33:24
be a in thy sight, O LORD, my Ps 19:14
unto thee, O LORD, in an a time Ps 69:13
of the righteous know what is a Prov 10:32
judgment is more a to the LORD Prov 21:3
sought to find out a words Eccl 12:10
In an a time have I heard thee, Is 49:8
a fast, and an a day to the LORD Is 58:5
To proclaim the a year of the Is 61:2
your burnt offerings are not a Jer 6:20
let my counsel be a unto thee Dan 4:27
To preach the a year of the Lord Lk 4:19
a unto God, which is your Rom 12:1
may prove what is that good, and a Rom 12:2
things serveth Christ is a to God Rom 14:18
up of the Gentiles might be a Rom 15:16
Proving what is a unto the Lord Eph 5:10
of a sweet smell, a sacrifice a Phil 4:18
a in the sight of God our Saviour 1Ti 2:3
for that is good and a before God 1Ti 5:4
a to God by Jesus Christ 1Pet 2:5
it patiently, this is a with God 1Pet 2:20

**ACCEPTABLY**
we may serve God a with reverence Heb 12:28

**ACCEPTANCE**
come up with a on mine altar Is 60:7

**ACCEPTATION**
saying, and worthy of all a 1Ti 1:15
saying and worthy of all a 1Ti 4:9

**ACCEPTED**
doest well, shalt thou not be a Gen 4:7
I have a thee concerning this Gen 19:21
they may be a before the LORD Ex 28:38
it shall be a for him to make Lev 1:4

the third day, it shall not be a ............... Lev 7:18
should it have been a in the................. Lev 10:19
it shall not be a........................................ Lev 19:7
it shall be perfect to be a ..................... Lev 22:21
but for a vow it shall not be a ............. Lev 22:23
they shall not be a for you ................... Lev 22:25
thenceforth it shall be a for an............ Lev 22:27
before the LORD, to be a for you ......... Lev 23:11
he was a in the sight of all the ............. 1Sa 18:5
thy voice, and have a thy person ......... 1Sa 25:35
a of the multitude of his.......................... Est 10:3
the LORD also a Job.................................. Job 42:9
shall be a upon mine altar.......................... Is 56:7
I pray thee, be a before thee ................ Jer 37:20
our supplication be a before thee ........... Jer 42:2
No prophet is a in his own ...................... Lk 4:24
righteousness, is a with him.................. Acts 10:35
Jerusalem may be a of the saints....... Rom 15:31
or absent, we may be a of him ............... 2Cor 5:9
I have heard thee in a time a................. 2Cor 6:2
behold, now is the a time........................ 2Cor 6:2
it is a according to that a man ............ 2Cor 8:12
For indeed he a the exhortation........... 2Cor 8:17
gospel, which ye have not a................... 2Cor 11:4
he hath made us a in the beloved ........... Eph 1:6

**ACCEPTEST**
neither a thou the person of any, .......... Lk 20:21

**ACCEPTETH**
How much less to him that a not......... Job 34:19
for God now a thy works........................ Eccl 9:7
but the LORD a them not ......................... Hos 8:13
God a no man's person .............................. Gal 2:6

**ACCEPTING**
were tortured, not a deliverance.......... Heb 11:35

**ACCESS**
By whom also we have a by faith .......... Rom 5:2
For through him we both have a by...... Eph 2:18
a with confidence by the faith of.......... Eph 3:12

**ACCHO** (ak'-ko) *A coastal city in Asher.*
drive out the inhabitants of A............... Judg 1:31

**ACCO** See ACCHO.

**ACCOMPANIED**
certain brethren from Joppa a him .... Acts 10:23
Moreover these six brethren a me...... Acts 11:12
there a him into Asia Sopater of............ Acts 20:4
And they a him unto the ship ............ Acts 20:38

**ACCOMPANY**
you, and things that a salvation ............. Heb 6:9

**ACCOMPANYING**
was at Gibeah, a the ark of God............. 2Sa 6:4

**ACCOMPLISH**
unto the LORD to a his vow.................. Lev 22:21
and thou shalt a my desire ..................... 1Kin 5:9
that he may rest, till he shall a ............... Job 14:6
they a a diligent search............................. Ps 64:6
but it shall a that which I ....................... Is 55:11
ye will surely a your vows ..................... Jer 44:25
thus will I a my fury upon them............. Eze 6:12
thee, and a mine anger upon thee ........... Eze 7:8
Thus will I a my wrath upon the......... Eze 13:15
to a my anger against them in the ........ Eze 20:8
to a my anger against them in the ...... Eze 20:21
that he would a seventy years in.............. Dan 9:2
which he should a at Jerusalem............... Lk 9:31

**ACCOMPLISHED**
the mouth of Jeremiah might be a.... 2Chr 36:22
the days of their purifications a .............. Est 2:12
It shall be a before his time, and.......... Job 15:32
The desire a is sweet to the soul ....... Prov 13:19
unto her, that her warfare is a.................. Is 40:2
to pass, when seventy years are a.......... Jer 25:12
and of your dispersions are a ............... Jer 25:34
be a at Babylon I will visit you............... Jer 29:10
they shall be a in that day ..................... Jer 39:16
The LORD hath a his fury...................... Lam 4:11
punishment of thine iniquity is a.......... Lam 4:22
And when thou hast a them, lie.............. Eze 4:6
Thus shall mine anger be a..................... Eze 5:13
when I have a my fury in them.............. Eze 5:13
prosper till the indignation be a........ Dan 11:36
when he shall have a to scatter............. Dan 12:7
days of his ministration were a ............... Lk 1:23
the days were a that she should................ Lk 2:6
when eight days were a for the................ Lk 2:21
to the law of Moses were a ...................... Lk 2:22
how am I straitened till it be a............... Lk 12:50
the Son of man shall be a........................ Lk 18:31
is written must yet be a in me................. Lk 22:37
that all things were now a ...................... Jn 19:28
And when we had a those days.............. Acts 21:5
a in your brethren that are in.................. 1Pet 5:9

**ACCOMPLISHING**
tabernacle, a the service of God .............. Heb 9:6

**ACCOMPLISHMENT**
to signify the a of the days of ............. Acts 21:26

**ACCORD**
a of thy harvest thou shalt not............... Lev 25:5
Joshua and with Israel, with one a ......... Josh 9:2
continued with one a in prayer............. Acts 1:14
were all with one a in one place............ Acts 2:1
daily with one a in the temple.............. Acts 2:46
up their voice to God with one a.......... Acts 4:24
all with one a in Solomon's porch........ Acts 5:12
ears, and ran upon him with one a...... Acts 7:57
the people with one a gave heed ............ Acts 8:6
which opened to them of his own a... Acts 12:10
but they came with one a to him ....... Acts 12:20
us, being assembled with one a.......... Acts 15:25
with one a against Paul, and ............. Acts 18:12
with one a into the theatre.................. Acts 19:29
of his own a he went unto you............ 2Cor 8:17
the same love, being of one a ................. Phil 2:2

**ACCORDING** See PREFACE.

**ACCORDINGLY**
a he will repay, fury to his ...................... Is 59:18

**ACCOUNT**
of every one that passeth the a ............ 2Kin 12:4
was the number put in the a of......... 1Chr 27:24
to the number of their a by the......... 2Chr 26:11
for he giveth not a of any of his.......... Job 33:13
of man, that thou makest a of him ........ Ps 144:3
one by one, to find out the a.................. Eccl 7:27
they shall give a thereof in the .............. Mt 12:36
would take a of his servants.................. Mt 18:23
give an a of thy stewardship..................... Lk 16:2
may give an a of this concourse ......... Acts 19:40
us shall give a of himself to God........ Rom 14:12
Let a man so a of us, as of the ............... 1Cor 4:1
fruit that may abound to your a.............. Phil 4:17
thee ought, put that on mine a.............. Philem 18
souls, as they that must give a............ Heb 13:17
Who shall give a to him that is.............. 1Pet 4:5
a that the longsuffering of our ............. 2Pet 3:15

**ACCOUNTED**
Which also were a giants, as the ......... Deut 2:11
(That also was a a land of giants......... Deut 2:20
it was nothing a of in the days.......... 1Kin 10:21
it was not any thing a of in the .......... 2Chr 9:20
it shall be a to the Lord for a ............... Ps 22:30
for wherein is he to be a of...................... Is 2:22
are a to rule over the Gentiles............ Mk 10:42
But they which shall be a worthy........... Lk 20:35
that ye may be a worthy to escape ....... Lk 21:36
of them should be a the greatest ........... Lk 22:24
we are a as sheep for the ..................... Rom 8:36
it was a to him for righteousness ............ Gal 3:6

**ACCOUNTING**
A that God was able to raise him........ Heb 11:19

**ACCOUNTS**
princes might give a unto them.............. Dan 6:2

**ACCURSED**
for he that is hanged is a of God ....... Deut 21:23
And the city shall be a, even it, ........... Josh 6:17
keep yourselves from the a thing ......... Josh 6:18
lest ye make yourselves a....................... Josh 6:18
when ye take of the a thing................... Josh 6:18
a trespass in the a thing.......................... Josh 7:1
of Judah, took of the a thing .................. Josh 7:1
have even taken of the a thing ............ Josh 7:11
enemies, because they were a .............. Josh 7:12
ye destroy the a from among you ......... Josh 7:12
There is an a thing in the midst............ Josh 7:13
away the a thing from among you......... Josh 7:13
a thing shall be burnt with fire ............ Josh 7:15
commit a trespass in the a thing ....... Josh 22:20
who transgressed in the thing a........... 1Chr 2:7
an hundred years old shall be a............. Is 65:20
a from Christ for my brethren ................ Rom 9:3
the Spirit of God calleth Jesus a ......... 1Cor 12:3
preached unto you, let him be a.............. Gal 1:8
ye have received, let him be a................ Gal 1:9

**ACCUSATION**
wrote they unto him an a against ............ Ezr 4:6
up over his head his a written.............. Mt 27:37
of his a was written over ..................... Mk 15:26
they might find an a against him............... Lk 6:7
any thing from any man by false a ......... Lk 19:8
What a bring ye against this man ......... Jn 18:29
they brought none a of such .............. Acts 25:18
Against an elder receive not an a ............ 1Ti 5:19
bring not railing a against them........... 2Pet 2:11
not bring against him a railing a .............. Jude 9

**ACCUSE**
A not a servant unto his master,........ Prov 30:10
that they might a him ........................... Mt 12:10
that they might a him ............................. Mk 3:2
to no man, neither a any falsely.............. Lk 3:14
his mouth, that they might a him.......... Lk 11:54
And they began to a him, saying,............ Lk 23:2
those things whereof ye a him .............. Lk 23:14
that I will a you to the Father ............... Jn 5:45
that they might have to a him.................. Jn 8:6
forth, Tertullus began to a him .......... Acts 24:2
these things, whereof we a him ........... Acts 24:8
the things whereof they now a me .... Acts 24:13
a this man, if there be any .................. Acts 25:5
these things whereof these a me ....... Acts 25:11
I had ought to a my nation of............ Acts 28:19
a your good conversation in ................ 1Pet 3:16

**ACCUSED**
came near, and a the Jews....................... Dan 3:8
those men which had a Daniel ............... Dan 6:24
when he was a of the chief................... Mt 27:12
the chief priests a him of many................ Mk 15:3
the same was a unto him that he.............. Lk 16:1
scribes stood and vehemently a him ..... Lk 23:10
wherefore he was a of the Jews.......... Acts 22:30
the cause wherefore they a him......... Acts 23:28
Whom I perceived to be a of.............. Acts 23:29
before that he which is a have.......... Acts 25:16
things whereof I am a of the Jews....... Acts 26:2
king Agrippa, I am a of the Jews ......... Acts 26:7
children not a of riot or unruly.............. Titus 1:6
which a them before our God day....... Rev 12:10

**ACCUSER**
for the a of our brethren is cast........... Rev 12:10

**ACCUSERS**
Woman, where are those thine a.............. Jn 8:10
gave commandment to his a also to .. Acts 23:30
when thine a are also come ............... Acts 23:35
Commanding his a to come unto.......... Acts 24:8
accused have the a face to face........... Acts 25:16
Against whom when the a stood up .. Acts 25:18
affection, trucebreakers, false a................. 2Ti 3:3
as becometh holiness, not false a .......... Titus 2:3

**ACCUSETH**
there is one that a you, even.................... Jn 5:45

**ACCUSING**
a or else excusing one another ............ Rom 2:15

**ACCUSTOMED**
do good, that are a to do evil ................ Jer 13:23

**ACELDAMA** (as-el'-dam-ah) *A burial ground bought with Judas' betrayal money.*
called in their proper tongue, A ............ Acts 1:19

**ACHAIA** (ak-ah'-yah) *Roman province in Greece.*
when Gallio was the deputy of A ....... Acts 18:12
he was disposed to pass into A............ Acts 18:27
through Macedonia and A.................... Acts 19:21
A to make a certain contribution.......... Rom 15:26
the firstfruits of A unto Christ............. Rom 16:5
that it is the firstfruits of A ................ 1Cor 16:15
all the saints which are in all A.............. 2Cor 1:1
that A was ready a year ago ................... 2Cor 9:2
this boasting in the regions of A ........ 2Cor 11:10
that believe in Macedonia and A ............ 1Th 1:7
Lord not only in Macedonia and A.......... 1Th 1:8

**ACHAICUS** (ak-ah'-yah-cus) *A Corinthian who visited Paul in Philippi.*
of Stephanas and Fortunatus and A.. 1Cor 16:17
by Stephanus, and Fortunatus, and A..... 1Cor s

**ACHAN** (a'-kan) See ACHAR. *Soldier under Joshua executed for disobedience.*
for A, the son of Carmi, the son ............ Josh 7:1
and A, the son of Carmi, the son.......... Josh 7:18
And Joshua said unto A, My son,......... Josh 7:19
A answered Joshua, and said,............... Josh 7:20
took A the son of Zerah, and the ......... Josh 7:24
Did not A the son of Zerah commit... Josh 22:20

**ACHAR** (a'-kar) See ACHAN. *A form of Achan.*
A, the troubler of Israel, who.................. 1Chr 2:7

**ACHAZ** (a'-kaz) See AHAZ. *The Greek form of Ahaz.*
and Joatham begat A.................................. Mt 1:9
and A begat Ezekias ................................... Mt 1:9

**ACHBOR** (ak'-bor)
*1. Father of an Edomite king.*
the son of A reigned in his stead......... Gen 36:38
And Baal-hanan the son of A died........ Gen 36:39
the son of A reigned in his stead ......... 1Chr 1:49
*2. A messenger of Josiah to Huldah.*
A the son of Michaiah, and Shaphan 2Kin 22:12
the priest, and Ahikam, and A ........... 2Kin 22:14
*3. Father of Elnathan.*
namely, Elnathan the son of A ............. Jer 26:22
and Elnathan the son of A .................... Jer 36:12

**ACHIM** (a'-kim) *Son of Sadoc;ancestor of Jesus.*
and Sadoc begat A ................................... Mt 1:14
and A begat Eliud..................................... Mt 1:14

**ACHISH** (a'-kish)
*1. A king of Gath who aided David.*
went to A the king of Gath .................. 1Sa 21:10
the servants of A said unto him ........... 1Sa 21:11
sore afraid of A the king of Gath ......... 1Sa 21:12
Then said A unto his servants, Lo........ 1Sa 21:14
men that were with him unto A............. 1Sa 27:2
And David dwelt with A at Gath ........... 1Sa 27:3
And David said unto A, If I have.......... 1Sa 27:5
Then A gave him Ziklag that day.......... 1Sa 27:6
and returned, and came to A................. 1Sa 27:9
A said, Whither have ye made a........... 1Sa 27:10
A believed David, saying, He hath ....... 1Sa 27:12
A said unto David, Know thou ............. 1Sa 28:1
And David said to A, Surely thou ......... 1Sa 28:2
A said to David, Therefore will I .......... 1Sa 28:2
passed on in the rereward with A .......... 1Sa 29:2
A said unto the princes of the............... 1Sa 29:3
Then A called David, and said unto....... 1Sa 29:6
And David said unto A, But what.......... 1Sa 29:8
A answered and said to David, I............. 1Sa 29:9
*2. A king of Gath during Solomon's reign.*
of Shimei ran away unto A son of....... 1Kin 2:39
went to Gath to A to seek his............... 1Kin 2:40

**ACHMETHA** (ak'-meth-ah) *A city in Media.*
And there was found at A, in the ............... Ezr 6:2

**ACHOR** (a'-kor) *A valley near Jericho.*
brought them unto the valley of A ...... Josh 7:24
place was called, The valley of A.......... Josh 7:26

toward Debir from the valley of *A* ....... Josh 15:7
the valley of *A* a place for the................. Is 65:10
the valley of *A* for a door of .................. Hos 2:15

**ACHSA** (*ak'-sah*) See ACHSAH. *Daughter of Caleb.*
and the daughter of Caleb was *A* ........ 1Chr 2:49

**ACHSAH** (*ak'-sah*) See ACHSA. *A form of Achsa.*
to him will I give *A* my daughter ....... Josh 15:16
he gave him *A* his daughter to............ Josh 15:17
to him will I give *A* my daughter......... Judg 1:12
he gave him *A* his daughter to ............ Judg 1:13

**ACHSHAPH** (*ak'-shaf*) *A Phoenician city in Asher.*
of Shimron, and to the king of *A*.......... Josh 11:1
the king of *A*, one................................ Josh 12:20
Helkath, and Hali, and Beten, and *A* . Josh 19:25

**ACHZIB** (*ak'-zib*) See CHEZIB.
*1. A town in western Judah.*
And Keilah, and *A*, and Mareshah...... Josh 15:44
the houses of *A* shall be a lie to ............ Mic 1:14
*2. A coastal city in Asher.*
at the sea from the coast to *A*............ Josh 19:29
of Zidon, nor of Ahlab, nor of *A*.......... Judg 1:31

**ACKNOWLEDGE**
But he shall *a* the son of the.............. Deut 21:17
neither did he *a* his brethren................ Deut 33:9
For I *a* my transgressions......................... Ps 51:3
In all thy ways *a* him, and he ................ Prov 3:6
and, ye that are near, *a* my might........... Is 33:13
all that see them shall *a* them.................... Is 61:9
of us, and Israel *a* us not......................... Is 63:16
Only *a* thine iniquity, that thou............... Jer 3:13
We *a*, O LORD, our wickedness, and ..... Jer 14:20
so will I *a* them that are carried.............. Jer 24:5
a strange god, whom he shall *a*........... Dan 11:39
till they *a* their offence, and.................. Hos 5:15
let him *a* that the things that I.......... 1Cor 14:37
therefore *a* ye them that are such ..... 1Cor 16:18
unto you, than what ye read or *a* ........ 2Cor 1:13
trust ye shall *a* even to the end........... 2Cor 1:13

**ACKNOWLEDGED**
And Judah *a* them, and said, She....... Gen 38:26
I *a* my sin unto thee, and mine.............. Ps 32:5
As also ye have *a* us in part .............. 2Cor 1:14

**ACKNOWLEDGEMENT**
to the *a* of the mystery of God,................. Col 2:2

**ACKNOWLEDGETH**
[ but ] he that *a* the Son hath ................. 1Jn 2:23

**ACKNOWLEDGING**
repentance to the *a* of the truth.............. 2Ti 2:25
the *a* of the truth which is after ............ Titus 1:1
may become effectual by the *a* of.......... Philem 6

**ACQUAINT**
*A* now thyself with him, and be at....... Job 22:21

**ACQUAINTANCE**
it to them, every man of his *a*.............. 2Kin 12:5
receive no more money of your *a* ........ 2Kin 12:7
mine *a* are verily estranged from........... Job 19:13
that had been of his *a* before................ Job 42:11
neighbours, and a fear to mine *a*............ Ps 31:11
mine equal, my guide, and mine *a*.......... Ps 55:13
hast put away mine *a* far from me............ Ps 88:8
from me, and mine *a* into darkness........ Ps 88:18
him among their kinsfolk and *a*.............. Lk 2:44
And all his *a*, and the women that ......... Lk 23:49
*a* to minister or come unto him .......... Acts 24:23

**ACQUAINTED**
down, and art *a* with all my ways.......... Ps 139:3
a man of sorrows, and *a* with grief........... Is 53:3

**ACQUAINTING**
yet *a* mine heart with wisdom ................ Eccl 2:3

**ACQUIT**
thou wilt not *a* me from mine.............. Job 10:14
and will not at all *a* the wicked.............. Nah 1:3

**ACRE**
as it were an half *a* of land.................. 1Sa 14:14

**ACRES**
ten *a* of vineyard shall yield one............... Is 5:10

**ACSAH** See ACHSA.

**ACSHAPH** See ACHSHAPH.

**ACT**
to pass his *a*, his strange *a*....................... Is 28:21
the *a* of violence is in their ...................... Is 59:6
taken in adultery, in the very *a*.................. Jn 8:4

**ACTIONS**
and by him *a* are weighed........................ 1Sa 2:3

**ACTIVITY**
knowest any men of *a* among them ..... Gen 47:6

**ACTS**
And his miracles, and his *a*................ Deut 11:3
great *a* of the LORD which he did ........ Deut 11:7
the righteous *a* of the LORD................ Judg 5:11
even the righteous *a* toward the ........... Judg 5:11
all the righteous *a* of the LORD ............ 1Sa 12:7
of Kabzeel, who had done many *a*......... 2Sa 23:20
I heard in mine own land of thy *a*........ 1Kin 10:6
And the rest of the *a* of Solomon....... 1Kin 11:41
in the book of the *a* of Solomon.......... 1Kin 11:41
And the rest of the *a* of Jeroboam ....... 1Kin 14:19
Now the rest of the *a* of Rehoboam .. 1Kin 14:29
Now the rest of the *a* of Abijam .......... 1Kin 15:7
The rest of all the *a* of Asa ................ 1Kin 15:23
Now the rest of the *a* of Nadab .......... 1Kin 15:31
Now the rest of the *a* of Baasha............. 1Kin 16:5
Now the rest of the *a* of Elah............... 1Kin 16:14
Now the rest of the *a* of Zimri............. 1Kin 16:20
Now the rest of the *a* of Omri.............. 1Kin 16:27
Now the rest of the *a* of Ahab.............. 1Kin 22:39
the rest of the *a* of Jehoshaphat.......... 1Kin 22:45
Now the rest of the *a* of Ahaziah......... 2Kin 1:18
And the rest of the *a* of Joram ............. 2Kin 8:23
Now the rest of the *a* of Jehu ............. 2Kin 10:34
And the rest of the *a* of Joash ............ 2Kin 12:19
Now the rest of the *a* of Jehoahaz........ 2Kin 13:8
And the rest of the *a* of Joash ............ 2Kin 13:12
Now the rest of the *a* of Jehoash ......... 2Kin 14:15
And the rest of the *a* of Amaziah....... 2Kin 14:18
Now the rest of the *a* of Jeroboam .... 2Kin 14:28
And the rest of the *a* of Azariah .......... 2Kin 15:6
And the rest of the *a* of Zachariah ..... 2Kin 15:11
And the rest of the *a* of Shallum ......... 2Kin 15:15
And the rest of the *a* of Menahem...... 2Kin 15:21
And the rest of the *a* of Pekahiah...... 2Kin 15:26
And the rest of the *a* of Pekah ........... 2Kin 15:31
Now the rest of the *a* of Jotham ......... 2Kin 15:36
Now the rest of the *a* of Ahaz ............ 2Kin 16:19
And the rest of the *a* of Hezekiah....... 2Kin 20:20
Now the rest of the *a* of Manasseh.... 2Kin 21:17
Now the rest of the *a* of Amon............. 2Kin 21:25
the *a* that he had done in Beth-el ....... 2Kin 23:19
Now the rest of the *a* of Josiah ........... 2Kin 23:28
the rest of the *a* of Jehoiakim............... 2Kin 24:5
of Kabzeel, who had done many *a* ..... 1Chr 11:22
Now the *a* of David the king,............... 1Chr 29:29
heard in mine own land of thine *a* ........ 2Chr 9:5
Now the rest of the *a* of Solomon ....... 2Chr 9:29
Now the *a* of Rehoboam, first and..... 2Chr 12:15
And the rest of the *a* of Abijah .......... 2Chr 13:22
the *a* of Asa, first and last, lo,............ 2Chr 16:11
the rest of the *a* of Jehoshaphat ......... 2Chr 20:34
Now the rest of the *a* of Amaziah ........ 2Chr 25:26
Now the rest of the *a* of Uzziah.......... 2Chr 26:22
Now the rest of the *a* of Jotham........... 2Chr 27:7
Now the rest of his *a* and of all.......... 2Chr 28:26
Now the rest of the *a* of Hezekiah ...... 2Chr 32:32
Now the rest of the *a* of Manasseh ... 2Chr 33:18
Now the rest of the *a* of Josiah .......... 2Chr 35:26
the rest of the *a* of Jehoiakim............... 2Chr 36:8
all the *a* of his power and of his............... Est 10:2
his *a* unto the children of Israel.............. Ps 103:7
utter the mighty *a* of the LORD ................ Ps 106:2
and shall declare thy mighty *a*................. Ps 145:4
of the might of thy terrible *a* ................. Ps 145:6
to the sons of men his mighty *a* .......... Ps 145:12
Praise him for his mighty *a*..................... Ps 150:2

**ACZIB** See ACHZIB.

**ADADAH** (*ad'-ad-ah*) *A city in southern Judah.*
And Kinah, and Dimonah, and *A* ....... Josh 15:22

**ADAH** (*a'-dah*)
*1. A wife of Lemech.*
the name of the one was *A*..................... Gen 4:19
And *A* bare Jabal.................................... Gen 4:20
And Lamech said unto his wives, *A*........ Gen 4:23
*2. A wife of Esau.*
*A* the daughter of Elon the ..................... Gen 36:2
And *A* bare to Esau Eliphaz..................... Gen 36:4
the son of *A* the wife of Esau................ Gen 36:10
were the sons of *A* Esau's wife ............ Gen 36:12
these were the sons of *A* ........................ Gen 36:16

**ADAIAH** (*ad-a-i'-yah*)
*1. Grandfather of King Josiah.*
the daughter of *A* of Boscath ................ 2Kin 22:1
*2. A Levite descendant of Gershon.*
the son of Zerah, the son of *A*............... 1Chr 6:41
*3. A son of Shimhi.*
And *A*, and Beraiah, and Shimrath,...... 1Chr 8:21
*4. A Levite of Jerusalem.*
*A* the son of Jeroham, the son of......... 1Chr 9:12
*5. Father of Maaseiah.*
of Obed, and Maaseiah the son of *A* ... 2Chr 23:1
*6. Married a foreign wife in Exile.*
Meshullam, Malluch, and *A*, Jashub, ... Ezr 10:29
*7. Married a foreign wife in Exile.*
And Shelemiah, and Nathan, and *A*..... Ezr 10:39
*8. A descendant of Pharez.*
the son of Hazaiah, the son of *A*........... Neh 11:5
*9. An Aaronite Levite.*
*A* the son of Jeroham, the son of ........ Neh 11:12

**ADALIA** (*ad-al-i'-yah*) *A son of Haman.*
And Poratha, and *A*, and Aridatha, .......... Est 9:8

**ADAM** (*ad'-um*) See ADAM'S.
*1. First man created by God.*
brought them unto *A* to see what.......... Gen 2:19
whatsoever *A* called every living........... Gen 2:19
*A* gave names to all cattle, and to.......... Gen 2:20
but for *A* there was not found an .......... Gen 2:20
a deep sleep to fall upon *A*.................... Gen 2:21
*A* said, This is now bone of my.............. Gen 2:23
and *A* and his wife hid themselves.......... Gen 3:8
And the LORD God called unto *A* ............ Gen 3:9
unto *A* he said, Because thou hast......... Gen 3:17
*A* called his wife's name Eve ................. Gen 3:20
Unto *A* also and to his wife did ............ Gen 3:21
And *A* knew Eve his wife........................ Gen 4:1
And *A* knew his wife again..................... Gen 4:25
the book of the generations of *A*............. Gen 5:1
them, and called their name *A*............... Gen 5:2
*A* lived an hundred and thirty................. Gen 5:3
the days of *A* after he had ..................... Gen 5:4
all the days that *A* lived were ................ Gen 5:5
when he separated the sons of *A*........ Deut 32:8
*A*, Sheth, Enosh,...................................... 1Chr 1:1
I covered my transgressions as *A*......... Job 31:33
of Seth, which was the son of *A* ............. Lk 3:38
death reigned from *A* to Moses ............ Rom 5:14
For as in *A* all die, even so in.............. 1Cor 15:22
The first man *A* was made a living..... 1Cor 15:45
the last *A* was made a quickening..... 1Cor 15:45
For *A* was first formed, then Eve............ 1Ti 2:13
*A* was not deceived, but the woman...... 1Ti 2:14
And Enoch also, the seventh from *A*...... Jude 14
*2. A town in Manasseh.*
an heap very far from the city *A*.......... Josh 3:16

**ADAMAH** (*ad'-am-ah*) *A walled city in Naphtali.*
And *A*, and Ramah, and Hazor, .......... Josh 19:36

**ADAMANT**
As an *a* harder than flint have I.............. Eze 3:9
made their hearts as an *a* stone ............ Zec 7:12

**ADAMI** (*ad'-am-i*) *A variant of Adamah.*
from Allon to Zaanannim, and *A*........ Josh 19:33

**ADAMI NEKEB** See NEKEB.

**ADAM'S** (*ad'-ums*)
the similitude of *A* transgression.......... Rom 5:14

**ADAR** (*a'-dar*) See ADDAR, ATAROTH-ADAR.
*1. A city in southern Judah.*
along to Hezron, and went up to *A*...... Josh 15:3
*2. Twelfth month of the Hebrew year.*
on the third day of the month *A* ........... Ezr 6:15
month, that is, the month *A*.................... Est 3:7
month, which is the month *A* ................ Est 3:13
month, which is the month *A* ................ Est 8:12
month, that is, the month *A*.................... Est 9:1
day also of the month *A*, and slew ......... Est 9:15
the thirteenth day of the month *A* ......... Est 9:17
of the month *A* a day of gladness........... Est 9:19
the fourteenth day of the month *A* ........ Est 9:21

**ADBEEL** (*ad'-be-el*) *Son of Ishmael.*
and Kedar, and *A*, and Mibsam,........... Gen 25:13
then Kedar, and *A*, and Mibsam,........... 1Chr 1:29

**ADD**
The LORD shall *a* to me another .......... Gen 30:24
shall *a* the fifth part thereto,.................. Lev 5:16
shall *a* the fifth part more........................ Lev 6:5
then he shall *a* a fifth part..................... Lev 27:13
then he shall *a* the fifth part of .............. Lev 27:15
then he shall *a* the fifth part of .............. Lev 27:19
shall *a* a fifth part of it.......................... Lev 27:27
he shall *a* thereto the fifth part ............. Lev 27:31
*a* unto it the fifth part thereof,................. Num 5:7
and to them ye shall *a* a forty.............. Num 35:6
Ye shall not *a* unto the word................... Deut 4:2
thou shalt not *a* thereto, nor.............. Deut 12:32
then shalt thou *a* three cities................ Deut 19:9
to *a* drunkenness to thirst ................... Deut 29:19
LORD thy God *a* unto the people ............. 2Sa 24:3
heavy yoke, I will *a* to your yoke ...... 1Kin 12:11
heavy, and I will *a* to your yoke ........ 1Kin 12:14
I will *a* unto thy days fifteen............... 2Kin 20:6
and thou mayest *a* thereto .................. 1Chr 22:14
yoke heavy, but I will *a* thereto........... 2Chr 10:14
ye intend to *a* more to our sins ........... 2Chr 28:13
*A* iniquity unto their iniquity.................... Ps 69:27
and peace, shall they *a* to thee ................ Prov 3:2
*A* thou not unto his words, lest............. Prov 30:6
*a* ye year to year....................................... Is 29:1
that they may *a* sin to sin........................... Is 30:1
I will *a* unto thy days fifteen ..................... Is 38:5
can *a* one cubit unto his stature ............. Mt 6:27
can *a* to his stature one cubit................. Lk 12:25
supposing to *a* affliction to my............... Phil 1:16
diligence, *a* to your faith virtue.............. 2Pet 1:5
If any man shall *a* unto these............... Rev 22:18
God shall *a* unto him the plagues.......... Rev 22:18

**ADDAN** (*ad'-dan*) *Home of some Exiles in Babylon.*
Tel-melah, Tel-harsa, Cherub, *A* ........... Ezr 2:59

**ADDAR** (*ad'-dar*) See ADAR, ATAROTH-ADDAR.
*Son of Bela.*
And the sons of Bela were, *A*................. 1Chr 8:3

**ADDED**
and he *a* no more.................................... Deut 5:22
for we have *a* unto all our sins ............. 1Sa 12:19
there were *a* besides unto them.............. Jer 36:32
for the LORD hath *a* grief to my................. Jer 45:3
excellent majesty was *a* unto me ........... Dan 4:36
these things shall be *a* unto you............... Mt 6:33
*A* yet this above all, that he...................... Lk 3:20
these things shall be *a* unto you ............. Lk 12:31
as they heard these things, he *a*.............. Lk 19:11
the same day there were *a* unto ............ Acts 2:41
the Lord *a* to the church daily ............. Acts 2:47
were the more *a* to the Lord................ Acts 5:14
much people was *a* unto the Lord..... Acts 11:24
in conference *a* nothing to me .................. Gal 2:6
It was *a* because of.................................. Gal 3:19

**ADDER**
an *a* in the path, that biteth the ......... Gen 49:17
the deaf *a* that stoppeth her ear ............... Ps 58:4
shalt tread upon the lion and *a* .............. Ps 91:13
a serpent, and stingeth like an *a* ........ Prov 23:32

**ADDERS'**
*a* poison is under their lips ...................... Ps 140:3

**ADDETH**
For he *a* rebellion unto his sin, ............ Job 34:37
rich, and he *a* no sorrow with it ........ Prov 10:22
mouth, and *a* learning to his lips ........ Prov 16:23
no man disannulleth, or *a* thereto .......... Gal 3:15

**ADDI** (*ad'-di*) *Son of Cozam; ancestor of Jesus.*
of Melchi, which was the son of *A* .......... Lk 3:28

**ADDICTED**
that they have *a* themselves to .......... 1Cor 16:15

**ADDITION**
molten, at the side of every *a* ............... 1Kin 7:30

**ADDITIONS**
were certain *a* made of thin work ........ 1Kin 7:29
of every one, and *a* round about .......... 1Kin 7:36

**ADDON** (*ad'-don*) *A form of Addan.*
Tel-melah, Tel-haresha, Cherub, *A* ........ Neh 7:61

**ADER** (*a'-dur*) *A son of Beriah.*
And Zebadiah, and Arad, and *A* .......... 1Chr 8:15

**ADIEL** (*a'-de-el*)
*1. A descendant of Simeon.*
and Jeshohaiah, and Asaiah, and *A* ..... 1Chr 4:36
*2. Father of Massiai.*
and Maasiai the son of *A*, the son ....... 1Chr 9:12
*3. Father of Azmaveth.*
was Azmaveth the son of *A* ............... 1Chr 27:25

**ADIN** (*a'-din*)
*1. Family who returned from exile.*
The children of *A*, four hundred ............ Ezr 2:15
The children of *A*, six hundred ............. Neh 7:20
*2. Family who sealed the covenant with Nehemiah.*
Adonijah, Bigvai, *A*, ............................... Neh 10:16
*3. An exilic family with Ezra.*
Of the sons also of *A* ................................ Ezr 8:6

**ADINA** (*ad'-in-ah*) *A "mighty man" of David.*
*A* the son of Shiza the Reubenite, ..... 1Chr 11:42

**ADINO** (*ad'-in-o*) *A "mighty man" of David.*
the same was *A* the Eznite ..................... 2Sa 23:8

**ADITHAIM** (*ad-ith-a'-im*) *A city in the plain of Judah.*
Sharaim, and *A*, and Gederah ............. Josh 15:36

**ADJURE**
How many times shall I *a* thee ........... 1Kin 22:16
How many times shall I *a* thee .......... 2Chr 18:15
I *a* thee by the living God, that ............ Mt 26:63
I *a* thee by God, that thou ..................... Mk 5:7
We *a* you by Jesus whom Paul .......... Acts 19:13

**ADJURED**
Joshua *a* them at that time, .................. Josh 6:26
for Saul had *a* the people .................... 1Sa 14:24

**ADLAI** (*ad'-la-i*) *Father of Shapat.*
valleys was Shaphat the son of *A* ...... 1Chr 27:29

**ADMAH** (*ad'-mah*) *A city destroyed with Sodom and Gomorrah.*
unto Sodom, and Gomorrah, and *A* .... Gen 10:19
of Gomorrah, Shinab king of *A* ............ Gen 14:2
of Gomorrah, and the king of *A* ........... Gen 14:8
of Sodom, and Gomorrah, *A*, and ...... Deut 29:23
how shall I make thee as *A* .................... Hos 11:8

**ADMATHA** (*ad'-math-ah*) *A prince of Persia.*
unto him was Carshena, Shethar, *A* ....... Est 1:14

**ADMINISTERED**
which is *a* by us to the glory of ........... 2Cor 8:19
this abundance which is *a* by us .......... 2Cor 8:20

**ADMINISTRATION**
For the *a* of this service not ............... 2Cor 9:12

**ADMINISTRATIONS**
And there are differences of *a* ............. 1Cor 12:5

**ADMIRATION**
persons in *a* because of advantage .......... Jude 16
saw her, I wondered with great *a* .......... Rev 17:6

**ADMIRED**
to be *a* in all them that believe ............. 2Th 1:10

**ADMONISH**
able also to *a* one another .................. Rom 15:14
over you in the Lord, and *a* you ........... 1Th 5:12
an enemy, but *a* him as a brother ........... 2Th 3:15

**ADMONISHED**
king, who will no more be *a* .................. Eccl 4:13
further, by these, my son, be *a* ........... Eccl 12:12
that I have *a* you this day ..................... Jer 42:19
was now already past, Paul *a* them ...... Acts 27:9
as Moses was *a* of God when he was ..... Heb 8:5

**ADMONISHING**
*a* one another in psalms and hymns ...... Col 3:16

**ADMONITION**
and they are written for our *a* ........... 1Cor 10:11
in the nurture and *a* of the Lord ............. Eph 6:4

the first and second *a* reject ................. Titus 3:10

**ADNA** (*ad'-nah*) See ADNAH.
*1. Married a foreigner while in exile.*
*A*, and Chelal, Benaiah, Maaseiah, ....... Ezr 10:30
*2. A priest during Joiakim's reign.*
Of Harim, *A* ........................................... Neh 12:15

**ADNAH** (*ad'-nah*) See ADNA.
*1. A captain in David's army.*
there fell to him of Manasseh, *A* ........ 1Chr 12:20
*2. A commander in Jehoshaphat's army.*
*A* the chief, and with him mighty ...... 2Chr 17:14

**ADO**
unto them, Why make ye this *a* ............ Mk 5:39

**ADONI-BEZEK** (*ad'-on-i-be'-zek*) *A lord of a Canaanite city.*
And they found *A* in Bezek ..................... Judg 1:5
But *A* fled ................................................ Judg 1:6
*A* said, Threescore and ten kings, .......... Judg 1:7

**ADONIJAH** (*ad-on-i'-jah*) See TOB-ADONIJAH.
*1. A son of David.*
the fourth, *A* the son of Haggith .............. 2Sa 3:4
Then *A* the son of Haggith exalted ........ 1Kin 1:5
and they following *A* helped him .......... 1Kin 1:7
to David, were not with *A* ...................... 1Kin 1:8
*A* slew sheep and oxen and fat ............... 1Kin 1:9
Hast thou not heard that *A* the ............ 1Kin 1:11
why then doth *A* reign .......................... 1Kin 1:13
And now, behold, *A* reigneth ................ 1Kin 1:18
*A* shall reign after me, and he ............. 1Kin 1:24
him, and say, God save king *A* ............. 1Kin 1:25
And *A* and all the guests that were ...... 1Kin 1:41
and *A* said unto him, Come in ............ 1Kin 1:42
answered and said to *A* ......................... 1Kin 1:43
that were with *A* were afraid ................ 1Kin 1:49
*A* feared because of Solomon, and ........ 1Kin 1:50
Behold, *A* feareth king Solomon ........... 1Kin 1:51
*A* the son of Haggith came to ................ 1Kin 2:13
Solomon, to speak unto him for *A* ....... 1Kin 2:19
be given to *A* thy brother to wife ......... 1Kin 2:21
ask Abishag the Shunammite for *A* ....... 1Kin 2:22
if *A* have not spoken this word ........... 1Kin 2:23
*A* shall be put to death this day ........... 1Kin 2:24
for Joab had turned after *A* ................... 1Kin 2:28
the fourth, *A* the son of Haggith ............ 1Chr 3:2
*2. A Levite under King Jehoshaphat.*
Shemiramoth, and Jehonathan, and *A* 2Chr 17:8
*3. A clan leader who sealed the covenant with Nehemiah.*
*A*, Bigvai, Adin, ..................................... Neh 10:16

**ADONIKAM** (*ad-on-i'-kam*) *A family in exile.*
The children of *A*, six hundred ............. Ezr 2:13
And of the last sons of *A*, whose ........... Ezr 8:13
The children of *A*, six hundred ............. Neh 7:18

**ADONIRAM** (*ad-on-i'-ram*) See ADORAM. *A tribute officer under Solomon.*
*A* the son of Abda was over the ............ 1Kin 4:6
and *A* was over the levy ....................... 1Kin 5:14

**ADONI-ZEDEK** (*ad'-on-i-ze'-dek*) *Canaanite king slain by Joshua.*
when *A* king of Jerusalem had ............... Josh 10:1
Wherefore *A* king of Jerusalem ............. Josh 10:3

**ADOPTION**
ye have received the Spirit of *a* ............ Rom 8:15
ourselves, waiting for the *a* .................. Rom 8:23
to whom pertaineth the *a*, and the ......... Rom 9:4
we might receive the *a* of sons ................ Gal 4:5
predestinated us unto the *a* of ................ Eph 1:5

**ADORAIM** (*ad-o-ra'-im*) *A city built by Rehoboam.*
And *A*, and Lachish, and Azekah, ......... 2Chr 11:9

**ADORAM** (*ad-o'-ram*) See ADONIRAM.
*1. A tribute officer under David.*
And *A* was over the tribute ................ 2Sa 20:24
*2. A tribute officer under Solomon.*
Then king Rehoboam sent *A* .............. 1Kin 12:18

**ADORN**
that women *a* themselves in modest ......... 1Ti 2:9
that they may *a* the doctrine of ........... Titus 2:10

**ADORNED**
shalt again be *a* with thy tabrets ............ Jer 31:4
how it was *a* with goodly stones ............. Lk 21:5
*a* themselves, being in subjection ........... 1Pet 3:5
as a bride *a* for her husband ................. Rev 21:2

**ADORNETH**
as a bride *a* herself with her ................... Is 61:10

**ADORNING**
Whose *a* let it not be that ..................... 1Pet 3:3
outward *a* of plaiting the hair ................. 1Pet 3:3

**ADRAMMELECH** (*a-dram'-mel-ek*)
*1. A god of the Avites.*
burnt their children in fire to *A* .......... 2Kin 17:31
*2. A son of Sennacherib.*
house of Nisroch his god, that *A* ......... 2Kin 19:37
house of Nisroch his god, that *A* ............ Is 37:38

**ADRAMYTTIAN** See ADRAMYTTIUM.

**ADRAMYTTIUM** (*a-dram-mit'-te-um*) *A seaport of Mysia in Asia Minor.*
And entering into a ship of *A* ................ Acts 27:2

**ADRIA** (*a'-dre-ah*) *The Adriatic Sea.*
as we were driven up and down in *A* Acts 27:27

**ADRIATIC** See ADRIA.

**ADRIEL** (*a'-dre-el*) *Husband of Merab, Saul's daughter.*
unto *A* the Meholathite to wife ............. 1Sa 18:19
whom she brought up for *A* the son ..... 2Sa 21:8

**ADULLAM** (*a-dul'-lam*) See ADULLAMITE.
*1. A city south of Jerusalem.*
the king of *A*, one ................................ Josh 12:15
Jarmuth, and *A*, Socoh, and Azekah,. Josh 15:35
And Beth-zur, and Shoco, and *A* ............ 2Chr 11:7
Zanoah, *A*, and in their villages, .......... Neh 11:30
he shall come unto *A* the glory of ........... Mic 1:15
*2. A large cave near the city of Adullam.*
thence, and escaped to the cave *A* ......... 1Sa 22:1
harvest time unto the cave of *A* ........... 2Sa 23:13
rock to David, into the cave of *A* ...... 1Chr 11:15

**ADULLAMITE** (*a-dul'-lam-ite*) *A native of Adullam.*
and turned in to a certain *A* .................. Gen 38:1
he and his friend Hirah the *A* .............. Gen 38:12
by the hand of his friend the *A* ............ Gen 38:20

**ADULTERER**
with his neighbour's wife, the *a* ........... Lev 20:10
The eye also of the *a* waiteth for .......... Job 24:15
the sorceress, the seed of the *a* ............... Is 57:3

**ADULTERERS**
him, and hast been partaker with *a* ....... Ps 50:18
for they be all *a*, an assembly of ............... Jer 9:2
For the land is full of *a* ......................... Jer 23:10
They are all *a*, as an oven heated .......... Hos 7:4
the sorcerers, and against the *a* ............. Mal 3:5
men are, extortioners, unjust, *a* ........... Lk 18:11
fornicators, nor idolaters, nor *a* ........... 1Cor 6:9
whoremongers and *a* God will judge .... Heb 13:4
Ye *a* and adulteresses, know ye not ........ Jas 4:4

**ADULTERESS**
the *a* shall surely be put to .................. Lev 20:10
the *a* will hunt for the precious ........... Prov 6:26
beloved of her friend, yet an *a* ................ Hos 3:1
man, she shall be called an *a* ................. Rom 7:3
so that she is no *a*, though she ............... Rom 7:3

**ADULTERESSES**
judge them after the manner of *a* ........ Eze 23:45
because they are *a*, and blood is .......... Eze 23:45
Ye adulterers and *a*, know ye not ............ Jas 4:4

**ADULTERIES**
I have seen thine *a*, and thy ................. Jer 13:27
said I unto her that was old in *a* .......... Eze 23:43
her *a* from between her breasts ............. Hos 2:2
proceed evil thoughts, murders, *a* ........ Mt 15:19
of men, proceed evil thoughts, *a* ............. Mk 7:21

**ADULTEROUS**
Such is the way of an *a* woman ......... Prov 30:20
*a* generation seeketh after a sign ........... Mt 12:39
*a* generation seeketh after a sign ............ Mt 16:4
of me and of my words in this *a* ............. Mk 8:38

**ADULTERY**
Thou shalt not commit *a* ........................ Ex 20:14
*a* with another man's wife ..................... Lev 20:10
even he that committeth *a* with ............. Lev 20:10
Neither shalt thou commit *a* ................. Deut 5:18
committeth *a* with a woman lacketh .. Prov 6:32
committed *a* I had put her away .............. Jer 3:8
committed *a* with stones and with ........... Jer 3:9
the full, they then committed *a* ................ Jer 5:7
ye steal, murder, and commit *a* ............... Jer 7:9
they commit *a*, and walk in lies ............. Jer 23:14
have committed *a* with their .................. Jer 29:23
But as a wife that committeth *a* ........... Eze 16:32
That they have committed *a* ................. Eze 23:37
their idols have they committed *a* ......... Eze 23:37
and stealing, and committing *a* ................ Hos 4:2
and your spouses shall commit *a* ........... Hos 4:13
your spouses when they commit *a* .......... Hos 4:14
old time, Thou shalt not commit *a* ............. Mt 5:27
*a* with her already in his heart ............... Mt 5:28
causeth her to commit *a* ......................... Mt 5:32
her that is divorced committeth *a* ........... Mt 5:32
shall marry another, committeth *a* ........... Mt 19:9
which is put away doth commit *a* ........... Mt 19:9
murder, Thou shalt not commit *a* ........... Mt 19:18
another, committeth *a* against her ...... Mk 10:11
to another, she committeth *a* .............. Mk 10:12
the commandments, Do not commit *a* Mk 10:19
and marrieth another, committeth *a* ...... Lk 16:18
from her husband committeth *a* ............. Lk 16:18
the commandments, Do not commit *a* . Lk 18:20
unto him a woman taken in *a* ................... Jn 8:3
Master, this woman was taken in *a* ........... Jn 8:4
sayest a man should not commit *a* ...... Rom 2:22
dost thou commit *a*? ............................... Rom 2:22
For this, Thou shalt not commit *a* ........ Rom 13:9
*A*, fornication, uncleanness, ................... Gal 5:19
For he that said, Do not commit *a* ......... Jas 2:11
Now if thou commit no *a*, yet if .............. Jas 2:11
Having eyes full of *a*, and that ............. 2Pet 2:14
them that commit *a* with her into ......... Rev 2:22

**ADUMMIM** (*a-dum'-mim*)
that is before the going up to *A* ........... Josh 15:7
is over against the going up of *A* ....... Josh 18:17

**ADVANCED**
It is the LORD that *a* Moses ... 1Sa 12:6
*a* him, and set his seat above all ... Est 3:1
how he had *a* him above the ... Est 5:11
whereunto the king *a* him ... Est 10:2

**ADVANTAGE**
What *a* will it be unto thee ... Job 35:3
What *a* then hath the Jew ... Rom 3:1
Lest Satan should get an *a* of us ... 2Cor 2:11
in admiration because of *a* ... Jude 16

**ADVANTAGED**
For what is a man *a*, if he gain ... Lk 9:25

**ADVANTAGETH**
what *a* it me, if the dead rise ... 1Cor 15:32

**ADVENTURE**
which would not *a* to set the sole ... Deut 28:56
not *a* himself into the theatre ... Acts 19:31

**ADVENTURED**
*a* his life far, and delivered you ... Judg 9:17

**ADVERSARIES**
and an adversary unto thine *a* ... Ex 23:22
lest their *a* should behave ... Deut 32:27
and will render vengeance to his *a* ... Deut 32:43
Art thou for us, or for our *a* ... Josh 5:13
The *a* of the LORD shall be broken ... 1Sa 2:10
ye should this day be *a* unto me ... 2Sa 19:22
Now when the *a* of Judah and ... Ezr 4:1
our *a* said, They shall not know, ... Neh 4:11
render evil for good are mine *a* ... Ps 38:20
mine *a* are all before thee ... Ps 69:19
and consumed that are *a* to my soul ... Ps 71:13
and turned my hand against their *a* ... Ps 81:14
set up the right hand of his *a* ... Ps 89:42
For my love they are my *a* ... Ps 109:4
reward of mine *a* from the LORD ... Ps 109:20
Let mine *a* be clothed with shame, ... Ps 109:29
Ah, I will ease me of mine *a* ... Is 1:24
set up the *a* of Rezin against him ... Is 9:11
the *a* of Judah shall be cut off ... Is 11:13
he will repay, fury to his *a* ... Is 59:18
our *a* have trodden down thy ... Is 63:18
to make thy name known to thine *a* ... Is 64:2
and all thine *a*, every one of them ... Jer 30:16
that he may avenge him of his *a* ... Jer 46:10
and their *a* said, We offend not, ... Jer 50:7
Her *a* are the chief, her enemies ... Lam 1:5
the *a* saw her, and did mock at her ... Lam 1:7
that his *a* should be round about ... Lam 1:17
hath set up the horn of thine *a* ... Lam 2:17
shall be lifted up upon thine *a* ... Mic 5:9
LORD will take vengeance on his *a* ... Nah 1:2
things, all his *a* were ashamed ... Lk 13:17
which all your *a* shall not be ... Lk 21:15
unto me, and there are many *a* ... 1Cor 16:9
And in nothing terrified by your *a* ... Phil 1:28
which shall devour the *a* ... Heb 10:27

**ADVERSARY**
an *a* unto thine adversaries ... Ex 23:22
in the way for an *a* against him ... Num 22:22
her *a* also provoked her sore, for ... 1Sa 1:6
in the battle he be an *a* to us ... 1Sa 29:4
is neither *a* nor evil occurrent ... 1Kin 5:4
LORD stirred up an *a* unto Solomon ... 1Kin 11:14
And God stirred him up another *a* ... 1Kin 11:23
he was an *a* to Israel all the ... 1Kin 11:25
And Esther said, The *a* and enemy is ... Est 7:6
that mine *a* had written a book ... Job 31:35
how long shall the *a* reproach ... Ps 74:10
who is mine *a*? ... Is 50:8
The *a* hath spread out his hand ... Lam 1:10
stood with his right hand as an *a* ... Lam 2:4
not have believed that the *a* ... Lam 4:12
An *a* there shall be even round ... Amos 3:11
Agree with thine *a* quickly ... Mt 5:25
lest at any time the *a* deliver ... Mt 5:25
with thine *a* to the magistrate ... Lk 12:58
him, saying, Avenge me of mine *a* ... Lk 18:3
to the *a* to speak reproachfully ... 1Ti 5:14
because your *a* the devil, as a ... 1Pet 5:8

**ADVERSITIES**
saved you out of all your *a* ... 1Sa 10:19
thou hast known my soul in *a* ... Ps 31:7

**ADVERSITY**
redeemed my soul out of all *a* ... 2Sa 4:9
for God did vex them with all *a* ... 2Chr 15:6
for I shall never be in *a* ... Ps 10:6
But in mine *a* they rejoiced, and ... Ps 35:15
give him rest from the days of *a* ... Ps 94:13
times, and a brother is born for *a* ... Prov 17:17
If thou faint in the day of *a* ... Prov 24:10
but in the day of *a* consider ... Eccl 7:14
the Lord give you the bread of *a* ... Is 30:20
and them which suffer *a*, as being ... Heb 13:3

**ADVERTISE**
I will *a* thee what this people ... Num 24:14
And I thought to *a* thee, saying, ... Ruth 4:4

**ADVICE**
consider of it, take *a*, and speak ... Judg 19:30
give here your *a* and counsel ... Judg 20:7
And blessed be thy *a*, and blessed ... 1Sa 25:33
that our *a* should not be first ... 2Sa 19:43
What *a* give ye that we may return ... 2Chr 10:9
them after the *a* of the young men ... 2Chr 10:14
Then Amaziah king of Judah took *a*. 2Chr 25:17
and with good *a* make war ... Prov 20:18
And herein I give my *a* ... 2Cor 8:10

**ADVISE**
now *a*, and see what answer I shall ... 2Sa 24:13
How do ye *a* that I may answer ... 1Kin 12:6
Now therefore *a* thyself what word .. 1Chr 21:12

**ADVISED**
but with the well *a* is wisdom ... Prov 13:10
the more part *a* to depart thence ... Acts 27:12

**ADVISEMENT**
Philistines upon *a* sent him away ... 1Chr 12:19

**ADVOCATE**
we have an *a* with the Father, ... 1Jn 2:1

**AENEAS** (*e'-ne-as*) *A paralytic healed by Peter.*
he found a certain man named *A* ... Acts 9:33
And Peter said unto him, *A* ... Acts 9:34

**AENON** (*e'-non*) *A place in the valley of Shechem.*
was baptizing in *A* near to Salim ... Jn 3:23

**AFAR**
his eyes, and saw the place *a* off ... Gen 22:4
And when they saw him *a* off ... Gen 37:18
And his sister stood *a* off ... Ex 2:4
it, they removed, and stood *a* off ... Ex 20:18
And the people stood *a* off ... Ex 20:21
and worship ye *a* off ... Ex 24:1
*a* off from the camp, and called it ... Ex 33:7
body, or be in a journey *a* off ... Num 9:10
stood on the top of an hill *a* off ... 1Sa 26:13
went, and stood to view *a* off ... 2Kin 2:7
when the man of God saw her *a* off ... 2Kin 4:25
and the noise was heard *a* off ... Ezr 3:13
of Jerusalem was heard even *a* off ... Neh 12:43
they lifted up their eyes *a* off ... Job 2:12
I will fetch my knowledge from *a* ... Job 36:3
man may behold it *a* off ... Job 36:25
and he smelleth the battle *a* off ... Job 39:25
prey, and her eyes behold *a* off ... Job 39:29
Why standest thou *a* off, O LORD ... Ps 10:1
and my kinsmen stand *a* off ... Ps 38:11
them that are *a* off upon the sea ... Ps 65:5
but the proud he knoweth *a* off ... Ps 138:6
understandest my thought *a* off ... Ps 139:2
she bringeth her food from *a* ... Prov 31:14
shall carry her *a* off to sojourn ... Is 23:7
and justice standeth *a* off ... Is 59:14
and Javan, to the isles *a* off ... Is 66:19
the LORD, and not a God *a* off ... Jer 23:23
for, lo, I will save thee from *a* ... Jer 30:10
and declare it in the isles *a* off ... Jer 31:10
I will save thee from *a* off ... Jer 46:27
remember the LORD *a* off, and let ... Jer 51:50
and rebuke strong nations *a* off ... Mic 4:3
But Peter followed him *a* off unto ... Mt 26:58
women were there beholding *a* off ... Mt 27:55
But when he saw Jesus *a* off ... Mk 5:6
a fig tree *a* off having leaves ... Mk 11:13
And Peter followed him *a* off ... Mk 14:54
were also women looking on *a* off ... Mk 15:40
torments, and seeth Abraham *a* off ... Lk 16:23
were lepers, which stood *a* off ... Lk 17:12
And the publican, standing *a* off ... Lk 18:13
And Peter followed *a* off ... Lk 22:54
him from Galilee, stood *a* off ... Lk 23:49
and to all that are *a* off ... Acts 2:39
peace to you which were *a* off ... Eph 2:17
but having seen them *a* off ... Heb 11:13
is blind, and cannot see *a* off ... 2Pet 1:9
Standing *a* off for the fear of ... Rev 18:10
shall stand *a* off for the fear of ... Rev 18:15
many as trade by sea, stood *a* off ... Rev 18:17

**AFFAIRS**
to God, and *a* of the king ... 1Chr 26:32
will guide his *a* with discretion ... Ps 112:5
over the *a* of the province of ... Dan 2:49
the *a* of the province of Babylon ... Dan 3:12
But that ye also may know my *a* ... Eph 6:21
purpose, that ye might know our *a* ... Eph 6:22
be absent, I may hear of your *a* ... Phil 1:27
himself with the *a* of this life ... 2Ti 2:4

**AFFECT**
They zealously *a* you, but not ... Gal 4:17
exclude you, that ye might *a* them ... Gal 4:17

**AFFECTED**
minds evil *a* against the brethren ... Acts 14:2
*a* always in a good thing, and not ... Gal 4:18

**AFFECTETH**
Mine eye *a* mine heart because of ... Lam 3:51

**AFFECTION**
because I have set my *a* to the ... 1Chr 29:3
without natural *a*, implacable, ... Rom 1:31
his inward *a* is more abundant ... 2Cor 7:15
Set your *a* on things above, not ... Col 3:2
uncleanness, inordinate *a* ... Col 3:5
Without natural *a*, trucebreakers, ... 2Ti 3:3

**AFFECTIONATELY**
So being *a* desirous of you, we ... 1Th 2:8

**AFFECTIONED**
Be kindly *a* one to another with ... Rom 12:10

**AFFECTIONS**
God gave them up unto vile *a* ... Rom 1:26
crucified the flesh with the *a* ... Gal 5:24

**AFFINITY**
Solomon made *a* with Pharaoh king ... 1Kin 3:1
abundance, and joined *a* with Ahab ... 2Chr 18:1
join in *a* with the people of ... Ezr 9:14

**AFFIRM**
as some *a* that we say,) Let us do ... Rom 3:8
what they say, nor whereof they *a* ... 1Ti 1:7
I will that thou *a* constantly ... Titus 3:8

**AFFIRMED**
hour after another confidently *a* ... Lk 22:59
But she constantly *a* that it was ... Acts 12:15
was dead, whom Paul *a* to be alive ... Acts 25:19

**AFFLICT**
they shall *a* them four hundred ... Gen 15:13
If thou shalt *a* my daughters ... Gen 31:50
to *a* them with their burdens ... Ex 1:11
Ye shall not *a* any widow, or ... Ex 22:22
If thou *a* them in any wise, and ... Ex 22:23
ye shall *a* your souls, and do no ... Lev 16:29
ye shall *a* your souls, by a ... Lev 16:31
ye shall *a* your souls, and offer ... Lev 23:27
of rest, and ye shall *a* your souls ... Lev 23:32
*a* Asshur, and shall *a* Eber ... Num 24:24
and ye shall *a* your souls ... Num 29:7
every binding oath to *a* the soul ... Num 30:13
that we may bind him to *a* him ... Judg 16:5
thou mightest be bound to *a* thee ... Judg 16:6
and she began to *a* him, and his ... Judg 16:19
of wickedness *a* them any more ... 2Sa 7:10
I will for this *a* the seed of ... 1Kin 11:39
their sin, when thou dost *a* them ... 2Chr 6:26
that we might *a* ourselves before ... Ezr 8:21
he will not *a* ... Job 37:23
how thou didst *a* the people ... Ps 44:2
*a* them, even he that abideth of ... Ps 55:19
nor the son of wickedness *a* him ... Ps 89:22
O LORD, and *a* thine heritage ... Ps 94:5
destroy all them that *a* my soul ... Ps 143:12
*a* her by the way of the sea ... Is 9:1
into the hand of them that *a* thee ... Is 51:23
a day for a man to *a* his soul ... Is 58:5
hold thy peace, and *a* us very sore ... Is 64:12
down, and to destroy, and to *a* ... Jer 31:28
For he doth not *a* willingly nor ... Lam 3:33
they *a* the just, they take a ... Amos 5:12
they shall *a* you from the ... Amos 6:14
thee, I will *a* thee no more ... Nah 1:12
time I will undo all that *a* thee ... Zeph 3:19

**AFFLICTED**
But the more they *a* them, the ... Ex 1:12
shall not be *a* in that same day ... Lev 23:29
Wherefore hast thou *a* thy servant ... Num 11:11
*a* us, and laid upon us hard ... Deut 26:6
me, and the Almighty hath *a* me ... Ruth 1:21
the *a* people thou wilt save ... 2Sa 22:28
because thou hast been *a* in all ... 1Kin 2:26
in all wherein my father was *a* ... 1Kin 2:26
*a* them, and delivered them into ... 2Kin 17:20
To him that is *a* pity should be ... Job 6:14
*a* me, they have also let loose ... Job 30:11
and he heareth the cry of the *a* ... Job 34:28
For thou wilt save the *a* people ... Ps 18:27
abhorred the affliction of the *a* ... Ps 22:24
for I am desolate and *a* ... Ps 25:16
do justice to the *a* and needy ... Ps 82:3
thou hast *a* me with all thy waves ... Ps 88:7
I am *a* and ready to die from my ... Ps 88:15
the days wherein thou hast *a* us ... Ps 90:15
A Prayer of the *a*, when he is ... Ps 102:t
of their iniquities, are *a* ... Ps 107:17
I was greatly *a* ... Ps 116:10
Before I was *a* I went astray ... Ps 119:67
is good for me that I have been *a* ... Ps 119:71
thou in faithfulness hast *a* me ... Ps 119:75
I am *a* very much ... Ps 119:107
time have they *a* me from my youth ... Ps 129:1
time have they *a* me from my youth ... Ps 129:2
will maintain the cause of the *a* ... Ps 140:12
All the days of the *a* are evil ... Prov 15:15
neither oppress the *a* in the gate ... Prov 22:22
hateth those that are *a* by it ... Prov 26:28
the judgment of any of the *a* ... Prov 31:5
he lightly *a* the land of Zebulun ... Is 9:1
and will have mercy upon his *a* ... Is 49:13
Therefore hear now this, thou *a* ... Is 51:21
stricken, smitten of God, and *a* ... Is 53:4
He was oppressed, and he was *a* ... Is 53:7
O thou *a*, tossed with tempest, and ... Is 54:11
wherefore have we *a* our soul ... Is 58:3
the hungry, and satisfy the *a* soul ... Is 58:10
The sons also of them that *a* thee ... Is 60:14
In all their affliction he was *a* ... Is 63:9
priests sigh, her virgins are *a* ... Lam 1:4
for the LORD hath *a* her for the ... Lam 1:5
wherewith the LORD hath *a* me in ... Lam 1:12
driven out, and her that I have *a* ... Mic 4:6
Though I have *a* thee, I will ... Nah 1:12
leave in the midst of thee an *a* ... Zeph 3:12
shall they deliver you up to be *a* ... Mt 24:9
And whether we be *a*, it is for ... 2Cor 1:6
feet, if she have relieved the *a* ... 1Ti 5:10
being destitute, *a*, tormented ... Heb 11:37
Be *a*, and mourn, and weep ... Jas 4:9
Is any among you *a* ... Jas 5:13

**AFFLICTEST**
from their sin, when thou *a* them ... 1Kin 8:35

**AFFLICTION**
because the LORD hath heard thy *a* ... Gen 16:11
the LORD hath looked upon my *a* ... Gen 29:32

God hath seen mine *a* and the ... Gen 31:42
be fruitful in the land of my *a* ... Gen 41:52
I have surely seen the *a* of my ... Ex 3:7
*a* of Egypt unto the land of the ... Ex 3:17
that he had looked upon their *a* ... Ex 4:31
therewith, even the bread of *a* ... Deut 16:3
our voice, and looked on our *a* ... Deut 26:7
look on the *a* of thine handmaid ... 1Sa 1:11
that the LORD will look on mine *a* ... 2Sa 16:12
bread of *a* and with water of *a* ... 1Kin 22:27
For the LORD saw the *a* of Israel ... 2Kin 14:26
bread of *a* and with water of *a* ... 2Chr 18:26
house,) and cry unto thee in our *a* ... 2Chr 20:9
And when he was in *a*, he besought ... 2Chr 33:12
in the province are in great *a* ... Neh 1:3
didst see the *a* of our fathers in ... Neh 9:9
Although *a* cometh not forth of ... Job 5:6
therefore see thou mine *a* ... Job 10:15
the days of *a* have taken hold ... Job 30:16
the days of *a* prevented me ... Job 30:27
and be holden in cords of *a* ... Job 36:8
He delivereth the poor in his *a* ... Job 36:15
hast thou chosen rather than *a* ... Job 36:21
abhorred the *a* of the afflicted ... Ps 22:24
Look upon mine *a* and my pain ... Ps 25:18
thy face, and forgettest our *a* ... Ps 44:24
thou laidst *a* upon our loins ... Ps 66:11
Mine eye mourneth by reason of *a* ... Ps 88:9
Nevertheless he regarded their *a* ... Ps 106:44
shadow of death, being bound in *a* ... Ps 107:10
brought low through oppression, *a* ... Ps 107:39
he the poor on high from *a* ... Ps 107:41
This is my comfort in my *a* ... Ps 119:50
then have perished in mine *a* ... Ps 119:92
Consider mine *a*, and deliver me ... Ps 119:153
of adversity, and the water of *a* ... Is 30:20
chosen thee in the furnace of *a* ... Is 48:10
In all their *a* he was afflicted, ... Is 63:9
publisheth *a* from mount Ephraim ... Jer 4:15
time of evil and in the time of *a* ... Jer 15:11
and my refuge in the day of *a* ... Jer 16:19
Why criest thou for thine *a* ... Jer 30:15
to come, and his *a* hasteth fast ... Jer 48:16
gone into captivity because of *a* ... Lam 1:3
remembered in the days of her *a* ... Lam 1:7
O LORD, behold my *a* ... Lam 1:9
seen *a* by the rod of his wrath ... Lam 3:1
Remembering mine *a* and my misery, ... Lam 3:19
in their *a* they will seek me ... Hos 5:15
not grieved for the *a* of Joseph ... Amos 6:6
not have looked on their *a* in the ... Obad 13
by reason of mine *a* unto the LORD ... Jonah 2:2
*a* shall not rise up the second ... Nah 1:9
I saw the tents of Cushan in *a* ... Hab 3:7
and they helped forward the *a* ... Zec 1:15
out or came in because of the *a* ... Zec 8:10
shall pass through the sea with *a* ... Zec 10:11
when *a* or persecution ariseth for ... Mk 4:17
For in those days shall be *a* ... Mk 13:19
of Egypt and Chanaan, and great *a* ... Acts 7:11
I have seen the *a* of my people ... Acts 7:34
For out of much *a* and anguish of ... 2Cor 2:4
For our light *a*, which is but for ... 2Cor 4:17
of *a* the abundance of their joy ... 2Cor 8:2
supposing to add *a* to my bonds ... Phil 1:16
that ye did communicate with my *a* ... Phil 4:14
received the word in much *a* ... 1Th 1:6
comforted over you in all our *a* ... 1Th 3:7
suffer *a* with the people of God ... Heb 11:25
fatherless and widows in their *a* ... Jas 1:27
for an example of suffering *a* ... Jas 5:10

**AFFLICTIONS**

Many are the *a* of the righteous ... Ps 34:19
remember David, and all his *a* ... Ps 132:1
And delivered him out of all his *a* ... Acts 7:10
saying that bonds and *a* abide me ... Acts 20:23
of God, in much patience, in *a* ... 2Cor 6:4
*a* of Christ in my flesh for his ... Col 1:24
no man should be moved by these *a* ... 1Th 3:3
but be thou partaker of the *a* of ... 2Ti 1:8
Persecutions, *a*, which came unto ... 2Ti 3:11
thou in all things, endure *a* ... 2Ti 4:5
ye endured a great fight of *a* ... Heb 10:32
both by reproaches and *a* ... Heb 10:33
knowing that the same *a* are ... 1Pet 5:9

**AFFORDING**

be full, *a* all manner of store ... Ps 144:13

**AFFRIGHT**

to *a* them, and to trouble them ... 2Chr 32:18

**AFFRIGHTED**

Thou shalt not be *a* at them ... Deut 7:21
as they that went before were *a* ... Job 18:20
He mocketh at fear, and is not *a* ... Job 39:22
My heart panted, fearfulness *a* me ... Is 21:4
fire, and the men of war are *a* ... Jer 51:32
and they were *a* ... Mk 16:5
And he saith unto them, Be not *a* ... Mk 16:6
But they were terrified and *a* ... Lk 24:37
and the remnant were *a*, and gave ... Rev 11:13

**AFOOT**

ran *a* thither out of all cities, ... Mk 6:33
minding himself to go *a* ... Acts 20:13

**AFORE**

*a* Isaiah was gone out into the ... 2Kin 20:4
which withereth *a* it groweth up ... Ps 129:6
For *a* the harvest, when the bud ... Is 18:5
*a* he that was escaped came ... Eze 33:22
(Which he had promised *a* by his ... Rom 1:2
which he had *a* prepared unto ... Rom 9:23
(as I wrote *a* in few words, ... Eph 3:3

**AFOREHAND**

she is come *a* to anoint my body ... Mk 14:8

**AFORETIME**

where *a* they laid the meat ... Neh 13:5
and *a* I was as a tabret ... Job 17:6
My people went down *a* into Egypt ... Is 52:4
Their children also shall be as *a* ... Jer 30:20
before his God, as he did *a* ... Dan 6:10
Pharisees him that *a* was blind ... Jn 9:13
*a* were written for our learning ... Rom 15:4

**AFRAID**

voice in the garden, and I was *a* ... Gen 3:10
for she was *a* ... Gen 18:15
and the men were sore *a* ... Gen 20:8
And he was *a*, and said, How ... Gen 28:17
and said to Laban, Because I was *a* ... Gen 31:31
Then Jacob was greatly *a* and ... Gen 32:7
heart failed them, and they were *a* ... Gen 42:28
the bundles of money, they were *a* ... Gen 42:35
And the men were *a*, because they ... Gen 43:18
for he was *a* to look upon God ... Ex 3:6
and they were sore *a* ... Ex 14:10
The people shall hear, and be *a* ... Ex 15:14
they were *a* to come nigh him ... Ex 34:30
down, and none shall make you *a* ... Lev 26:6
wherefore then were ye not *a* to ... Num 12:8
And Moab was sore *a* of the people ... Num 22:3
ye shall not be *a* of the face of ... Deut 1:17
Dread not, neither be *a* of them ... Deut 1:29
and they shall be *a* of you ... Deut 2:4
for ye were *a* by reason of the ... Deut 5:5
Thou shalt not be *a* of them ... Deut 7:18
all the people of whom thou art *a* ... Deut 7:19
For I was *a* of the anger and hot ... Deut 9:19
thou shalt not be *a* of him ... Deut 18:22
more than thou, be not *a* of them ... Deut 20:1
and they shall be *a* of thee ... Deut 28:10
of Egypt, which thou wast *a* of ... Deut 28:60
fear not, nor be *a* of them ... Deut 31:6
be not *a*, neither be thou ... Josh 1:9
therefore we were sore *a* of our ... Josh 9:24
Joshua, Be not *a* because of them ... Josh 11:6
saying, Whosoever is fearful and *a* ... Judg 7:3
at midnight, that the man was *a* ... Ruth 3:8
And the Philistines were *a* ... 1Sa 4:7
they were *a* of the Philistines ... 1Sa 7:7
they were dismayed, and greatly *a* ... 1Sa 17:11
fled from him, and were sore *a* ... 1Sa 17:24
And Saul was *a* of David, because ... 1Sa 18:12
very wisely, he was *a* of him ... 1Sa 18:15
Saul was yet the more *a* of David ... 1Sa 18:29
Ahimelech was *a* at the meeting of ... 1Sa 21:1
was sore *a* of Achish the king of ... 1Sa 21:12
Behold, we be *a* here in Judah ... 1Sa 23:3
host of the Philistines, he was *a* ... 1Sa 28:5
the king said unto her, Be not *a* ... 1Sa 28:13
along on the earth, and was sore *a* ... 1Sa 28:20
for he was sore *a* ... 1Sa 31:4
How wast thou not *a* to stretch ... 2Sa 1:14
David was *a* of the LORD that day, ... 2Sa 6:9
because the people have made me *a* ... 2Sa 14:15
weak handed, and will make him *a* ... 2Sa 17:2
floods of ungodly men made me *a* ... 2Sa 22:5
they shall be *a* out of their ... 2Sa 22:46
that were with Adonijah were *a* ... 1Kin 1:49
be not *a* of him ... 2Kin 1:15
But they were exceedingly *a* ... 2Kin 10:4
Be not *a* of the words which thou ... 2Kin 19:6
for they were *a* of the Chaldees ... 2Kin 25:26
for he was sore *a* ... 1Chr 10:4
David was *a* of God that day, ... 1Chr 13:12
for he was *a* because of the sword ... 1Chr 21:30
Be not *a* nor dismayed by reason ... 2Chr 20:15
be not *a* nor dismayed for the ... 2Chr 32:7
Then I was very sore *a*, ... Neh 2:2
the people, Be not ye *a* of them ... Neh 4:14
For they all made us *a*, saying, ... Neh 6:9
was he hired, that I should be *a* ... Neh 6:13
Then Haman was *a* before the king ... Est 7:6
that which I was *a* of is come ... Job 3:25
neither shalt thou be *a* of ... Job 5:21
neither shalt thou be *a* of the ... Job 5:22
ye see my casting down, and are *a* ... Job 6:21
I am *a* of all my sorrows, I know ... Job 9:28
down, and none shall make thee *a* ... Job 11:19
not his excellency make you *a* ... Job 13:11
and let not thy dread make me *a* ... Job 13:21
and anguish shall make him *a* ... Job 15:24
shall make him *a* on every side ... Job 18:11
Be ye *a* of the sword ... Job 19:29
Even when I remember I am *a* ... Job 21:6
when I consider, I am *a* of him ... Job 23:15
wherefore I was *a*, and durst not ... Job 32:6
my terror shall not make thee *a* ... Job 33:7
thou make him *a* as a grasshopper ... Job 39:20
up himself, the mighty are *a* ... Job 41:25
I will not be *a* of ten thousands ... Ps 3:6
floods of ungodly men made me *a* ... Ps 18:4
be *a* out of their close places ... Ps 18:45
of whom shall I be *a* ... Ps 27:1
Be not thou *a* when one is made ... Ps 49:16
What time I am *a*, I will trust in ... Ps 56:3
I will not be *a* what man can do ... Ps 56:11
parts are *a* at thy tokens ... Ps 65:8
they were *a* ... Ps 77:16
make them *a* with thy storm ... Ps 83:15
Thou shalt not be *a* for the ... Ps 91:5
He shall not be *a* of evil tidings ... Ps 112:7
is established, he shall not be *a* ... Ps 112:8
and I am *a* of thy judgments ... Ps 119:120
liest down, thou shalt not be *a* ... Prov 3:24
Be not *a* of sudden fear, neither ... Prov 3:25
She is not *a* of the snow for her ... Prov 31:21
shall be *a* of that which is high ... Eccl 12:5
fear ye their fear, nor be *a* ... Is 8:12
in Zion, be not *a* of the Assyrian ... Is 10:24
Ramah is *a* ... Is 10:29
I will trust, and not be *a* ... Is 12:2
And they shall be *a* ... Is 13:8
down, and none shall make them *a* ... Is 17:2
and it shall be *a* and fear because ... Is 19:16
thereof shall be *a* in himself ... Is 19:17
And they shall be *a* and ashamed of ... Is 20:5
he will not be *a* of their voice ... Is 31:4
princes shall be *a* of the ensign ... Is 31:9
The sinners in Zion are *a* ... Is 33:14
Be not *a* of the words that thou ... Is 37:6
lift it up, be not *a* ... Is 40:9
the ends of the earth were *a* ... Is 41:5
Fear ye not, neither be *a* ... Is 44:8
of men, neither be ye *a* of their ... Is 51:7
that thou shouldest be *a* of a man ... Is 51:12
whom hast thou been *a* or feared ... Is 57:11
Be not *a* of their faces ... Jer 1:8
at this, and be horribly *a* ... Jer 2:12
Be not *a* of them ... Jer 10:5
when Urijah heard it, he was *a* ... Jer 26:21
quiet, and none shall make him *a* ... Jer 30:10
the words, they were *a* both one ... Jer 36:16
Yet they were not *a*, nor rent ... Jer 36:24
I am *a* of the Jews that are ... Jer 38:19
of the men of whom thou art *a* ... Jer 39:17
for they were *a* of them, because ... Jer 41:18
Be not *a* of the king of Babylon, ... Jer 42:11
of whom ye are *a* ... Jer 42:11
be not *a* of him, saith the LORD ... Jer 42:11
and the famine, whereof ye were *a* ... Jer 42:16
at ease, and none shall make him *a* ... Jer 46:27
be not *a* of them ... Eze 2:6
neither be *a* of their words, ... Eze 2:6
be not *a* of their words, nor be ... Eze 2:6
and their kings shall be sore *a* ... Eze 27:35
to make the careless Ethiopians *a* ... Eze 30:9
shall be horribly *a* for thee ... Eze 32:10
safely, and none shall make them *a* ... Eze 34:28
their land, and none made them *a* ... Eze 39:26
I saw a dream which made me *a* ... Dan 4:5
and when he came, I was *a*, and fell ... Dan 8:17
Be not *a*, ye beasts of the field ... Joel 2:22
the city, and the people not be *a* ... Amos 3:6
Then the mariners were *a*, and ... Jonah 1:5
Then were the men exceedingly *a* ... Jonah 1:10
and none shall make them *a* ... Mic 4:4
they shall be *a* of the LORD our ... Mic 7:17
lion's whelp, and none made them *a* ... Nah 2:11
of beasts, which made them *a* ... Hab 2:17
I have heard thy speech, and was *a* ... Hab 3:2
down, and none shall make them *a* ... Zeph 3:13
me, and was *a* before my name ... Mal 2:5
Herod, he was *a* to go thither ... Mt 2:22
be not *a* ... Mt 14:27
saw the wind boisterous, he was *a* ... Mt 14:30
on their face, and were sore *a* ... Mt 17:6
them, and said, Arise, and be not *a* ... Mt 17:7
And I was *a*, and went and hid thy ... Mt 25:25
said Jesus unto them, Be not *a* ... Mt 28:10
and they were *a* ... Mk 5:15
ruler of the synagogue, Be not *a* ... Mk 5:36
be not *a* ... Mk 6:50
for they were sore *a* ... Mk 9:6
that saying, and were *a* to ask him ... Mk 9:32
and as they followed, they were *a* ... Mk 10:32
thing to any man for they were *a* ... Mk 16:8
and they were sore *a* ... Lk 2:9
And they being *a* wondered, saying ... Lk 8:25
and they were *a* ... Lk 8:35
Be not *a* of them that kill the ... Lk 12:4
And as they were *a*, and bowed down ... Lk 24:5
and they were *a* ... Jn 6:19
be not *a* ... Jn 6:20
be troubled, neither let it be *a* ... Jn 14:27
that saying, he was the more *a* ... Jn 19:8
but they were all *a* of him ... Acts 9:26
when he looked on him, he was *a* ... Acts 10:4
the night by a vision, Be not *a* ... Acts 18:9
saw indeed the light, and were *a* ... Acts 22:9
and the chief captain also was *a* ... Acts 22:29
thou then not be *a* of the power ... Rom 13:3
thou do that which is evil, be *a* ... Rom 13:4
I am *a* of you, lest I have ... Gal 4:11
they were not *a* of the king's ... Heb 11:23
are not *a* with any amazement ... 1Pet 3:6
be not *a* of their terror, neither ... 1Pet 3:14
they are not *a* to speak evil of ... 2Pet 2:10

**AFRESH**

to themselves the Son of God *a* ... Heb 6:6

**AFTER** See PREFACE.

**AFTERNOON**

And they tarried until *a*, and they ... Judg 19:8

**AFTERWARD**

*a* were the families of the ... Gen 10:18
*a* shall they come out with great ... Gen 15:14
me, and *a* I will see his face ... Gen 32:20
*a* came out his brother, that had ... Gen 38:30

*a* Moses and Aaron went in, and told...... Ex 5:1
*a* all the children of Israel came............ Ex 34:32
*a* he shall kill the burnt........................ Lev 14:19
*a* the priest shall go in to see............... Lev 14:36
in water, and *a* come into the camp.... Lev 16:26
*a* he shall come into the camp.............. Lev 16:28
shall *a* eat of the holy things.................. Lev 22:7
*a* shall cause the woman to drink.......... Num 5:26
*a* the people removed from................. Num 12:16
*a* he shall come into the camp, and..... Num 19:7
*a* shalt thou be gathered unto thy......... Num 31:2
*a* ye shall come into the camp............ Num 31:24
then *a* ye shall return, and be............ Num 32:22
*a* the hands of all the people.............. Deut 17:7
thou shalt not glean it *a*.................. Deut 24:21
and *a* may ye go your way.................... Josh 2:16
*a* he read all the words of the............... Josh 8:34
*a* Joshua smote them, and slew them Josh 10:26
and *a* I brought you out ....................... Josh 24:5
*a* the children of Judah went down....... Judg 1:9
and *a* shall thine hands be .................. Judg 7:11
And it came to pass *a*, that he............... Judg 16:4
morsel of bread, and *a* go your way.... Judg 19:5
And it came to pass *a*, that.................... 1Sa 24:5
David also arose *a*, and went out......... 1Sa 24:8
*a* when David heard it, he said, I .......... 2Sa 3:28
*a* Hezron went in to the daughter ....... 1Chr 2:21
*a* they made ready for themselves,.... 2Chr 35:14
*a* offered the continual burnt................ Ezr 3:5
*A* I came unto the house of................... Neh 6:10
counsel, and *a* receive me to glory......... Ps 73:24
*a* thou shalt be called, The city............... Is 1:26
*a* did more grievously afflict her.............. Is 9:1
And *a*, saith the LORD, I will.................. Jer 21:7
But *a* they turned, and caused the....... Jer 34:11
*a* it shall be inhabited, as in.................. Jer 46:26
And *a* I will bring again the ................... Jer 49:6
*A* he brought me to the temple, and ..... Eze 41:1
*A* he brought me to the gate, even....... Eze 43:1
*A* he brought me again unto the.......... Eze 47:1
*A* he measured a thousand .................... Eze 47:5
*a* I rose up, and did the king's ............... Dan 8:27
*A* shall the children of Israel................. Hos 3:5
And it shall come to pass *a*..................... Joel 2:28
forty nights, he was *a* an hungred ........... Mt 4:2
but *a* he repented, and went................... Mt 21:29
ye had seen it, repented not *a*............... Mt 21:32
*A* came also the other virgins,................ Mt 25:11
*a*, when affliction or persecution............. Mk 4:17
*A* he appeared unto the eleven as ........ Mk 16:14
they were ended, he *a* hungered ............... Lk 4:2
And it came to pass *a*, that he................... Lk 8:1
*a* thou shalt eat and drink ...................... Lk 17:8
but *a* he said within himself,................... Lk 18:4
*A* Jesus findeth him in the temple............ Jn 5:14
And *a* they desired a king .................... Acts 13:21
*a* they that are Christ's at his ............. 1Cor 15:23
*a* that which is spiritual....................... 1Cor 15:46
then would he not *a* have spoken ........... Heb 4:8
nevertheless *a* it yieldeth the................ Heb 12:11
For ye know how that *a*, when he...... Heb 12:17
*a* destroyed them that believed.................. Jude 5

**AFTERWARDS**
*a* she bare a daughter, and called....... Gen 30:21
*a* he will let you go hence......................... Ex 11:1
*a* the hand of all the people................... Deut 13:9
*a* they eat that be bidden ...................... 1Sa 9:13
mark, and *a* we will speak........................ Job 18:2
but *a* his mouth shall be filled............ Prov 20:17
and *a* build thine house ..................... Prov 24:27
He that rebuketh a man *a* shall........... Prov 28:23
a wise man keepeth it in till *a*........... Prov 29:11
*A* the spirit took me up, and................ Eze 11:24
but thou shalt follow me *a*..................... Jn 13:36
*A* I came into the regions of................... Gal 1:21
faith which should *a* be revealed............ Gal 3:23

**AGABUS** (*ag'-ab-us*) *A Christian prophet.*
stood up one of them named *A*........... Acts 11:28
Judaea a certain prophet, named *A*.... Acts 21:10

**AGAG** (*a'-gag*) See AGAGITE. *A king of Amalek during Exodus.*
his king shall be higher than *A* ............ Num 24:7
he took *A* the king of the......................... 1Sa 15:8
But Saul and the people spared *A*........... 1Sa 15:9
have brought *A* the king of Amalek.... 1Sa 15:20
Bring ye hither to me *A* the king......... 1Sa 15:32
*A* came unto him delicately .................. 1Sa 15:32
*A* said, Surely the bitterness of............ 1Sa 15:32
Samuel hewed *A* in pieces before........... 1Sa 15:33

**AGAGITE** (*ag'-ag-ite*) *A member of an Amalekite tribe.*
Haman the son of Hammedatha the *A*..... Est 3:1
Haman the son of Hammedatha the *A*.. Est 3:10
away the mischief of Haman the *A*.......... Est 8:3
Haman the son of Hammedatha the *A*..... Est 8:5
the son of Hammedatha, the *A*............... Est 9:24

**AGAIN** See PREFACE.

**AGAINST** See PREFACE.

**AGAR** (*a'-gar*) See HAGAR. *Greek form of Hagar.*
gendereth to bondage, which is *A*.......... Gal 4:24
For this *A* is mount Sinai in.................... Gal 4:25

**AGATE**
And the third row a ligure, an *a*............ Ex 28:19
And the third row, a ligure, an *a*........... Ex 39:12
and fine linen, and coral, and *a*........... Eze 27:16

**AGATES**
And I will make thy windows of *a*.......... Is 54:12

**AGE**
shalt be buried in a good old *a*............ Gen 15:15
were old and well stricken in *a*........... Gen 18:11
bare Abraham a son in his old *a*........... Gen 21:2
have born him a son in his old *a*........... Gen 21:7
was old, and well stricken in *a*.............. Gen 24:1
ghost, and died in a good old *a*.............. Gen 25:8
he was the son of his old *a*................... Gen 37:3
old man, and a child of his old *a* ......... Gen 44:20
so the whole *a* of Jacob was an............ Gen 47:28
the eyes of Israel were dim for *a*......... Gen 48:10
from the *a* of fifty years they.............. Num 8:25
Joshua waxed old and stricken in *a*..... Josh 23:1
them, I am old and stricken in *a* ........ Josh 23:2
son of Joash died in a good old *a*.......... Judg 8:32
and a nourisher of thine old *a*............ Ruth 4:15
die in the flower of their *a* ................... 1Sa 2:33
eyes were set by reason of his *a*.......... 1Kin 14:4
in the time of his old *a* he was........... 1Kin 15:23
from the *a* of thirty years ..................... 1Chr 23:3
from the *a* of twenty years and.......... 1Chr 23:24
And he died in a good old *a* ............... 1Chr 29:28
man, or him that stooped for *a*........... 2Chr 36:17
come to thy grave in a full *a* ................... Job 5:26
I pray thee, of the former *a*..................... Job 8:8
thine *a* shall be clearer than the........... Job 11:17
in whom old *a* was perished .................. Job 30:2
mine *a* is as nothing before thee............ Ps 39:5
me not off in the time of old *a*............... Ps 71:9
still bring forth fruit in old *a*................. Ps 92:14
Mine *a* is departed, and is removed ........ Is 38:12
And even to your old *a* I am he .............. Is 46:4
his staff in his hand for very *a*............... Zec 8:4
she was of the *a* of twelve years.............. Mk 5:42
also conceived a son in her old *a*.............. Lk 1:36
she was of a great *a*, and had.................. Lk 2:36
to be about thirty years of *a* .................. Lk 3:23
daughter, about twelve years of *a* ........... Lk 8:42
he is of *a*............................................ Jn 9:21
said his parents, He is of *a* ..................... Jn 9:23
if she pass the flower of her *a*.............. 1Cor 7:36
to them that are of full *a*...................... Heb 5:14
of a child when she was past *a* ............. Heb 11:11

**AGED**
Now Barzillai was a very *a* man........... 2Sa 19:32
away the understanding of the *a*.......... Job 12:20
both the grayheaded and very *a* men.. Job 15:10
and the *a* arose, and stood up .............. Job 29:8
neither do the *a* understand.................. Job 32:9
the *a* with him that is full of ................... Jer 6:11
That the *a* men be sober, grave,........... Titus 2:2
The *a* women likewise, that they.......... Titus 2:3
being such an one as Paul the *a*........... Philem 9

**AGEE** (*ag'-ee*) *Father of a "mighty man" of David.*
Shammah the son of *A* the Hararite.... 2Sa 23:11

**AGES**
That in the *a* to come he might.............. Eph 2:7
Which in other *a* was not made.............. Eph 3:5
by Christ Jesus throughout all *a*............ Eph 3:21
which hath been hid from *a*................... Col 1:26

**AGO**
asses that were lost three days *a*............ 1Sa 9:20
heard long *a* how I have done it ........ 2Kin 19:25
was builded these many years *a* .............. Ezr 5:11
unto him that fashioned it long *a*............ Is 22:11
Hast thou not heard long *a*..................... Is 37:26
have repented long *a* in sackcloth.......... Mt 11:21
How long is it *a* since this came .............. Mk 9:21
they had a great while *a* repented.......... Lk 10:13
Four days *a* I was fasting until ............. Acts 10:30
while *a* God made choice among us .... Acts 15:7
but also to be forward a year *a* ............ 2Cor 8:10
that Achaia was ready a year *a*............. 2Cor 9:2
in Christ above fourteen years *a* .......... 2Cor 12:2

**AGONE**
because three days *a* I fell sick............. 1Sa 30:13

**AGONY**
being in an *a* he prayed more ................ Lk 22:44

**AGREE**
*A* with thine adversary quickly,................ Mt 5:25
That if two of you shall *a* on................. Mt 18:19
didst not thou *a* with me for a.............. Mt 20:13
so did their witness *a* together.............. Mk 14:59
to this *a* the words of the.................... Acts 15:15
and these three *a* in one......................... 1Jn 5:8
to fulfil his will, and to *a*....................... Rev 17:17

**AGREED**
walk together, except they be *a* ........... Amos 3:3
when he had *a* with the labourers........... Mt 20:2
but their witness *a* not together ........... Mk 14:56
for the Jews had *a* already ....................... Jn 9:22
How is it that ye have *a* together........... Acts 5:9
And to him they *a* ............................... Acts 5:40
The Jews have *a* to desire thee........... Acts 23:20
when they *a* not among themselves,. Acts 28:25

**AGREEMENT**
Make an *a* with me by a present,....... 2Kin 18:31
death, and with hell are we at *a* ............ Is 28:15
your *a* with hell shall not stand.............. Is 28:18
Make an *a* with me by a present,............. Is 36:16
king of the north to make an *a* ............. Dan 11:6
what *a* hath the temple of God .............. 2Cor 6:16

**AGREETH**
and thy speech *a* thereto ........................ Mk 14:70
out of the new *a* not with the old............ Lk 5:36

**AGRIPPA** (*ag-rip'-pah*) *Great-grandson of Herod the Great.*
And after certain days king *A* ............. Acts 25:13
Then *A* said unto Festus, I would ....... Acts 25:22
when *A* was come, and Bernice, with Acts 25:23
And Festus said, King *A*, and all......... Acts 25:24
specially before thee, O king *A* ........... Acts 25:26
Then *A* said unto Paul, Thou art .......... Acts 26:1
I think myself happy, king *A*................. Acts 26:2
For which hope's sake, king *A* .............. Acts 26:7
Whereupon, O king *A*, I was not......... Acts 26:19
King *A*, believest thou the.................. Acts 26:27
Then *A* said unto Paul, Almost ........... Acts 26:28
Then said *A* unto Festus, This man ... Acts 26:32

**AGROUND**
two seas met, they ran the ship *a*....... Acts 27:41

**AGUE**
consumption, and the burning *a* .......... Lev 26:16

**AGUR** (*a'-gur*) *Son of Jakeh.*
The words of *A* the son of Jakeh,........ Prov 30:1

**AH**
them not say in their hearts, *A* .............. Ps 35:25
*A* sinful nation, a people laden...................... Is 1:4
the mighty One of Israel, *A* ........................ Is 1:24
Then said I, *A*, Lord GOD............................ Jer 1:6
Then said I, *A*, Lord GOD.......................... Jer 4:10
Then said I, *A*, Lord GOD.......................... Jer 14:13
for him, saying, *A* my brother.................... Jer 22:18
or, *A* sister................................................ Jer 22:18
lament for him, saying, *A* lord ................. Jer 22:18
or, *A* his glory ........................................... Jer 22:18
*A* Lord GOD................................................ Jer 32:17
will lament thee, saying, *A* lord............... Jer 34:5
Then said I, *A* Lord GOD ......................... Eze 4:14
and cried, and said, *A* Lord GOD............... Eze 9:8
a loud voice, and said, *A* Lord GOD ..... Eze 11:13
Then said I, *A* Lord GOD ....................... Eze 20:49
*a*.............................................................. Eze 21:15
wagging their heads, and saying, *A*...... Mk 15:29

**AHA**
wide against me, and said, *A*, *a*.............. Ps 35:21
shame that say unto me, *A*, *a*................. Ps 40:15
of their shame that say, *A*, *a* ....................... Ps 70:3
he warmeth himself, and saith, *A*........... Is 44:16
Because thou saidst, *A*, against............... Eze 25:3
hath said against Jerusalem, *A* ............... Eze 26:2
enemy hath said against you, *A* ............. Eze 36:2

**AHAB** (*a'-hab*) See AHAB'S.
*1. A king of Israel.*
*A* his son reigned in his stead ............ 1Kin 16:28
*A* the son of Omri to reign over ......... 1Kin 16:29
*A* the son of Omri reigned over.......... 1Kin 16:29
*A* the son of Omri did evil in the......... 1Kin 16:30
And *A* made a grove.............................. 1Kin 16:33
*A* did more to provoke the LORD........ 1Kin 16:33
of Gilead, said unto *A*, As the.............. 1Kin 17:1
saying, Go, shew thyself unto *A*........... 1Kin 18:1
went to shew himself unto *A* ............... 1Kin 18:2
*A* called Obadiah, which was the .......... 1Kin 18:3
*A* said unto Obadiah, Go into the ........ 1Kin 18:5
*A* went one way by himself, and......... 1Kin 18:6
thy servant into the hand of *A* ............ 1Kin 18:9
and so when I come and tell *A*........... 1Kin 18:12
So Obadiah went to meet *A* ............... 1Kin 18:16
and *A* went to meet Elijah.................. 1Kin 18:16
when *A* saw Elijah, that *A* said .......... 1Kin 18:17
So *A* sent unto all the children........... 1Kin 18:20
And Elijah said unto *A*, Get thee ....... 1Kin 18:41
So *A* went up to eat and to drink ....... 1Kin 18:42
And he said, Go up, say unto *A*.......... 1Kin 18:44
*A* rode, and went to Jezreel............... 1Kin 18:45
ran before *A* to the entrance of........... 1Kin 18:46
*A* told Jezebel all that Elijah ................ 1Kin 19:1
he sent messengers to *A* king of .......... 1Kin 20:2
a prophet unto *A* king of Israel .......... 1Kin 20:13
And *A* said, By whom .......................... 1Kin 20:14
Then said *A*, I will send thee.............. 1Kin 20:34
the palace of *A* king of Samaria .......... 1Kin 21:1
*A* spake unto Naboth, saying, Give ..... 1Kin 21:2
And Naboth said to *A*, The LORD......... 1Kin 21:3
*A* came into his house heavy and ........ 1Kin 21:4
was dead, that Jezebel said to *A*......... 1Kin 21:15
when *A* heard that Naboth was dead 1Kin 21:16
that *A* rose up to go down to the....... 1Kin 21:16
go down to meet *A* king of Israel ....... 1Kin 21:18
*A* said to Elijah, Hast thou found........ 1Kin 21:20
will cut off from *A* him that ................ 1Kin 21:21
Him that dieth of *A* in the city ............ 1Kin 21:24
But there was none like unto *A*........... 1Kin 21:25
when *A* heard those words, that he... 1Kin 21:27
Seest thou how *A* humbleth himself . 1Kin 21:29
LORD said, Who shall persuade *A*....... 1Kin 22:20
Now the rest of the acts of *A*............. 1Kin 22:39
So *A* slept with his fathers.................. 1Kin 22:40
fourth year of *A* king of Israel............ 1Kin 22:41
the son of *A* unto Jehoshaphat........... 1Kin 22:49
Ahaziah the son of *A* began to ........... 1Kin 22:51
Israel after the death of *A*...................... 2Kin 1:1
Now Jehoram the son of *A* began to..... 2Kin 3:1
when *A* was dead, that the king of........ 2Kin 3:5
Joram the son of *A* king of Israel ........ 2Kin 8:16
of Israel, as did the house of *A*........... 2Kin 8:18
the daughter of *A* was his wife............ 2Kin 8:18

year of Joram the son of *A* king 2Kin 8:25
in the way of the house of *A* 2Kin 8:27
the LORD, as did the house of *A* 2Kin 8:27
the son in law of the house of *A* 2Kin 8:27
he went with Joram the son of *A* 2Kin 8:28
see Joram the son of *A* in Jezreel 2Kin 8:29
smite the house of *A* thy master 2Kin 9:7
the whole house of *A* shall perish 2Kin 9:8
I will cut off from *A* him that 2Kin 9:8
I will make the house of *A* like 2Kin 9:9
rode together after *A* his father 2Kin 9:25
year of Joram the son of *A* began 2Kin 9:29
*A* had seventy sons in Samaria 2Kin 10:1
spake concerning the house of *A* 2Kin 10:10
of the house of *A* in Jezreel 2Kin 10:11
that remained unto *A* in Samaria 2Kin 10:17
unto them, *A* served Baal a little 2Kin 10:18
hast done unto the house of *A* 2Kin 10:30
a grove, as did *A* king of Israel 2Kin 21:3
and the plummet of the house of *A* 2Kin 21:13
and joined affinity with *A* 2Chr 18:1
he went down to *A* to Samaria 2Chr 18:2
*A* killed sheep and oxen for him in 2Chr 18:2
*A* king of Israel said unto 2Chr 18:3
Who shall entice *A* king of Israel 2Chr 18:19
like as did the house of *A* 2Chr 21:6
he had the daughter of *A* to wife 2Chr 21:6
the whoredoms of the house of *A* 2Chr 21:13
in the ways of the house of *A* 2Chr 22:3
of the LORD like the house of *A* 2Chr 22:4
went with Jehoram the son of *A* 2Chr 22:5
Jehoram the son of *A* at Jezreel 2Chr 22:6
to cut off the house of *A* 2Chr 22:7
judgment upon the house of *A* 2Chr 22:8
all the works of the house of *A* Mic 6:16

*2. A false prophet during the Exile.*
of *A* the son of Kolaiah, and of Jer 29:21
make thee like Zedekiah and like *A* Jer 29:22

**AHAB'S** (*a'-habs*)
So she wrote letters in *A* name 1Kin 21:8
them that brought up *A* children 2Kin 10:1

**AHARAH** (*a-har'-ah*) See AHER, AHIRAM, EHI. *Third son of Benjamin.*
the second, and *A* the third, 1Chr 8:1

**AHARHEL** (*a-har'-hel*) *A descendant of Judah.*
the families of *A* the son of 1Chr 4:8

**AHASAI** (*a-ha'-sa-i*) *Family of returned exiles.*
the son of Azareel, the son of *A* Neh 11:13

**AHASBAI** (*a-has'-ba-i*) *Father of a "mighty man" of David.*
Eliphelet the son of *A*, the son 2Sa 23:34

**AHASUERUS** (*a-has-u-e'-rus*) See AHASUERUS'.
*1. A Persian king, Cambyses.*
And in the reign of *A*, in the Ezr 4:6

**AHASUERUS'** (*a-has-u-e'-rus*) *Refers to Ahasuerus 3.*
And he wrote in the king *A* name Est 8:10

**AHASUERUS** (*a-has-u-e'-rus*)
*1. A Persian king, Cambyses*
And in the reign of *A* Ezr 4:6
*2. Father of Darius the Mede.*
first year of Darius the son of *A* Dan 9:1
*3. A king of Persia, Xerxes.*
it came to pass in the days of *A* Est 1:1
(this is *A* which reigned from Est 1:1
when the king *A* sat on the throne Est 1:2
house which belonged to king *A* Est 1:9
in the presence of *A* the king Est 1:10
of the king *A* by the chamberlains Est 1:15
all the provinces of the king *A* Est 1:16
The king *A* commanded Vashti the Est 1:17
Vashti come no more before king *A* Est 1:19
the wrath of king *A* was appeased Est 2:1
turn was come to go in to king *A* Est 2:12
*A* into his house royal in the Est 2:16
sought to lay hand on the king *A* Est 2:21
king *A* promote Haman the son of Est 3:1
throughout the whole kingdom of *A* Est 3:6
in the twelfth year of king *A* Est 3:7
And Haman said unto king *A* Est 3:8
the name of king *A* was it written Est 3:12
sought to lay hand on the king *A* Est 6:2
Then the king *A* answered and said Est 7:5
On that day did the king *A* give Est 8:1
Then the king *A* said unto Esther Est 8:7
in all the provinces of king *A* Est 8:12
all the provinces of the king *A* Est 9:2
all the provinces of the king *A* Est 9:20
provinces of the kingdom of *A* Est 9:30
the king *A* laid a tribute upon Est 10:1
the Jew was next unto king *A* Est 10:3

**AHAVA** (*a-ha'-vah*) See IVA. *A river of Babylon.*
to the river than runneth to *A* Ezr 8:15
a fast there, at the river of *A* Ezr 8:21
we departed from the river of *A* Ezr 8:31

**AHAZ** (*a'-haz*) See ACHAZ.
*1. A king of Judah.*
*A* his son reigned in his stead 2Kin 15:38
of Pekah the son of Remaliah *A* 2Kin 16:1
Twenty years old was *A* when he 2Kin 16:2
and they besieged *A*, but could not 2Kin 16:5
So *A* sent messengers to 2Kin 16:7
*A* took the silver and gold that 2Kin 16:8
king *A* went to Damascus to meet 2Kin 16:10
king *A* sent to Urijah the priest 2Kin 16:10
king *A* had sent from Damascus 2Kin 16:11
against king *A* came from Damascus 2Kin 16:11
king *A* commanded Urijah the 2Kin 16:15
to all that king *A* commanded 2Kin 16:16
king *A* cut off the borders of the 2Kin 16:17
of the acts of *A* which he did 2Kin 16:19
*A* slept with his fathers, and was 2Kin 16:20
In the twelfth year of *A* king of 2Kin 17:1
that Hezekiah the son of *A* king 2Kin 18:1
it had gone down in the dial of *A* 2Kin 20:11
the top of the upper chamber of *A* 2Kin 23:12
*A* his son, Hezekiah his son, 1Chr 3:13
*A* his son reigned in his stead 2Chr 27:9
*A* was twenty years old when he 2Chr 28:1
At that time did king *A* send unto 2Chr 28:16
low because of *A* king of Israel 2Chr 28:19
For *A* took away a portion out of 2Chr 28:21
this is that king *A* 2Chr 28:22
*A* gathered together the vessels 2Chr 28:24
*A* slept with his fathers, and they 2Chr 28:27
which king *A* in his reign did 2Chr 29:19
in the days of Uzziah, Jotham, *A* Is 1:1
the days of *A* the son of Jotham Is 7:1
Isaiah, Go forth now to meet *A* Is 7:3
the LORD spake again unto *A* Is 7:10
But *A* said, I will not ask, Is 7:12
that king *A* died was this burden Is 14:28
is gone down in the sun dial of *A* Is 38:8
in the days of Uzziah, Jotham, *A* Hos 1:1
in the days of Jotham, *A*, and Mic 1:1
*2. A Benjaminite and relative of Saul.*
Pithon, and Melech, and Tarea, and *A* 1Chr 8:35
And *A* begat Jehoadah 1Chr 8:36
and Melech, and Tahrea, and *A* 1Chr 9:41
And *A* begat Jarah 1Chr 9:42

**AHAZIAH** (*a-haz-i'-ah*) See AZARIAH, JEHOAHAZ.
*1. A king of Israel.*
*A* his son reigned in his stead 1Kin 22:40
Then said *A* the son of Ahab unto 1Kin 22:49
*A* the son of Ahab began to reign 1Kin 22:51
*A* fell down through a lattice in 2Kin 1:2
of the acts of *A* which he did 2Kin 1:18
*A* his son, Joash his son, 1Chr 3:11
himself with *A* king of Israel 2Chr 20:35
thou hast joined thyself with *A* 2Chr 20:37
*2. Son and successor of King Jehoram of Judah.*
*A* his son reigned in his stead 2Kin 8:24
did *A* the son of Jehoram king of 2Kin 8:25
twenty years old was *A* when he 2Kin 8:26
*A* the son of Jehoram king of 2Kin 8:29
*A* king of Judah was come down to 2Kin 9:16
*A* king of Judah went out, each in 2Kin 9:21
his hands, and fled, and said to *A* 2Kin 9:23
There is treachery, O *A* 2Kin 9:23
But when *A* the king of Judah saw 2Kin 9:27
Ahab began *A* to reign over Judah 2Kin 9:29
the brethren of *A* king of Judah 2Kin 10:13
We are the brethren of *A* 2Kin 10:13
of *A* saw that her son was dead 2Kin 11:1
of king Joram, sister of *A* 2Kin 11:2
took Joash the son of *A* 2Kin 11:2
Jehoshaphat, and Jehoram, and *A* 2Kin 12:18
year of Joash the son of *A* king 2Kin 13:1
the son of Jehoash the son of *A* 2Kin 14:13
*A* his youngest son king in his 2Chr 22:1
So *A* the son of Jehoram king of 2Chr 22:1
two years old was *A* when he began 2Chr 22:2
the destruction of *A* was of God 2Chr 22:7
and the sons of the brethren of *A* 2Chr 22:8
that ministered to *A* 2Chr 22:8
And he sought *A* 2Chr 22:9
So the house of *A* had no power to 2Chr 22:9
of *A* saw that her son was dead 2Chr 22:10
the king, took Joash the son of *A* 2Chr 22:11
(for she was the sister of *A* 2Chr 22:11

**AHBAN** (*ah'-ban*) *A descendant of Pharez.*
was Abihail, and she bare him *A* 1Chr 2:29

**AHER** (*a'-hur*) See AHARAH. *A descendant of Benjamin.*
of Ir, and Hushim, the sons of *A* 1Chr 7:12

**AHI** (*a'-hi*)
*1. A son of Abdiel.*
*A* the son of Abdiel, the son of 1Chr 5:15
*2. A chief of the Asherites.*
*A*, and Rohgah, Jehubbah, and Aram. 1Chr 7:34

**AHIAH** (*a-hi'-ah*) See AHIJAH.
*1. Grandson of Phinehas.*
And *A*, the son of Ahitub, 1Sa 14:3
And Saul said unto *A*, Bring hither 1Sa 14:18
*2. A scribe of Solomon.*
Elihoreph and *A*, the sons of 1Kin 4:3
*3. A descendant of Benjamin.*
And Naaman, and *A*, and Gera, he 1Chr 8:7

**AHIAM** (*a-hi'-ah*) *Son of Shemidah.*
*A* the son of Sharar the Hararite, 2Sa 23:33
*A* the son of Sacar the Hararite, 1Chr 11:35

**AHIAN** (*a-hi'-an*)
And the sons of Shemidah were, *A* 1Chr 7:19

**AHIEZER** (*a-hi-e'-zer*)
*1. One who numbered the people.*
*A* the son of Ammishaddai Num 1:12
shall be *A* the son of Ammishaddai Num 2:25
On the tenth day *A* the son of Num 7:66
of *A* the son of Ammishaddai Num 7:71
over his host was *A* the son of Num 10:25
*2. A chief of the Benjamites.*
The chief was *A*, then Joash, the 1Chr 12:3

**AHIHUD** (*a-hi'-hud*)
*1. A prince of Asher.*
of Asher, *A* the son of Shelomi Num 34:27
*2. A Benjamite of the Ehud family.*
removed them, and begat Uzza, and *A*. 1Chr 8:7

**AHIJAH** (*a-hi'-jah*) See AHIAH, AHIMELECH.
*1. A prophet during the reigns of Solomon and Rehoboam.*
that the prophet *A* the Shilonite 1Kin 11:29
*A* caught the new garment that was 1Kin 11:30
which the LORD spake by *A* the 1Kin 12:15
there is *A* the prophet, which 1Kin 14:2
Shiloh, and came to the house of *A* 1Kin 14:4
But *A* could not see 1Kin 14:4
And the LORD said unto *A*, Behold, 1Kin 14:5
when *A* heard the sound of her 1Kin 14:6
hand of his servant *A* the prophet 1Kin 14:18
by his servant *A* the Shilonite 1Kin 15:29
the prophecy of *A* the Shilonite 2Chr 9:29
*A* the Shilonite to Jeroboam the 2Chr 10:15
*2. Father of Baasha.*
And Baasha the son of *A*, of the 1Kin 15:27
of *A* to reign over all Israel in 1Kin 15:33
the house of Baasha the son of *A* 1Kin 21:22
the house of Baasha the son of *A* 2Kin 9:9
*3. Son of Jerahmeel.*
and Oren, and Ozem, and *A* 1Chr 2:25
*4. A "mighty man" of David.*
the Mecherathite, *A* the Pelonite, 1Chr 11:36
*5. A treasury official under David.*
*A* was over the treasures of the 1Chr 26:20
*6. A Levite who renewed the covenant.*
And *A*, Hanan, Anan, Neh 10:26

**AHIKAM** (*a-hi'-kam*) *An officer in Josiah's court.*
*A* the son of Shaphan, and Achbor 2Kin 22:12
So Hilkiah the priest, and *A* 2Kin 22:14
he made Gedaliah the son of *A* 2Kin 25:22
*A* the son of Shaphan, and Abdon 2Chr 34:20
Nevertheless the hand of *A* the Jer 26:24
the son of *A* the son of Shaphan Jer 39:14
the son of *A* the son of Shaphan Jer 40:5
Gedaliah the son of *A* to Mizpah Jer 40:6
the son of *A* governor in the land Jer 40:7
Gedaliah the son of *A* the son of Jer 40:9
the son of *A* the son of Shaphan Jer 40:11
the son of *A* believed them not Jer 40:14
But Gedaliah the son of *A* said Jer 40:16
Gedaliah the son of *A* to Mizpah Jer 41:1
smote Gedaliah the son of *A* the Jer 41:2
Come to Gedaliah the son of *A* Jer 41:6
to Gedaliah the son of *A* Jer 41:10
had slain Gedaliah the son of *A* Jer 41:16
had slain Gedaliah the son of *A* Jer 41:18
the son of *A* the son of Shaphan Jer 43:6

**AHILUD** (*a-hi'-lud*) *Father of a recorder under David and Solomon.*
the son of *A* was recorder 2Sa 8:16
the son of *A* was recorder 2Sa 20:24
Jehoshaphat the son of *A*, the 1Kin 4:3
Baana the son of *A* 1Kin 4:12
and Jehoshaphat the son of *A* 1Chr 18:15

**AHIMAAZ** (*a-him'-a-az*)
*1. Father of Ahinoam.*
was Ahinoam, the daughter of *A* 1Sa 14:50
*2. Son of Zadok.*
*A* thy son, and Jonathan the son of 2Sa 15:27
*A* Zadok's son, and Jonathan 2Sa 15:36
Jonathan and *A* stayed by En-rogel 2Sa 17:17
the house, they said, Where is *A* 2Sa 17:20
Then said *A* the son of Zadok, Let 2Sa 18:19
Then said *A* the son of Zadok yet 2Sa 18:22
Then *A* ran by the way of the 2Sa 18:23
the running of *A* the son of Zadok 2Sa 18:27
*A* called, and said unto the king, 2Sa 18:28
*A* answered, When Joab sent the 2Sa 18:29
begat Zadok, and Zadok begat *A* 1Chr 6:8
*A* begat Azariah, and Azariah begat 1Chr 6:9
Zadok his son, *A* his son 1Chr 6:53
*3. An officer of Solomon.*
*A* was in Naphtali 1Kin 4:15

**AHIMAN** (*a-hi'-man*)
*1. A giant of Anak.*
where *A*, Sheshai, and Talmai, the Num 13:22
three sons of Anak, Sheshai, and *A* Josh 15:14
and they slew Sheshai, and *A* Judg 1:10
*2. A Levite Temple servant.*
and Akkub, and Talmon, and *A* 1Chr 9:17

**AHIMELECH** (*a-him'-el-ek*)
*1. A priest.*
came David to Nob to *A* the priest 1Sa 21:1
*A* was afraid at the meeting of 1Sa 21:1
And David said unto *A* the priest 1Sa 21:2
And David said unto *A*, And is there 1Sa 21:8
to Nob, to *A* the son of Ahitub 1Sa 22:9
king sent to call *A* the priest 1Sa 22:11
Then *A* answered the king, and said 1Sa 22:14
said, Thou shalt surely die, *A* 1Sa 22:16
the sons of *A* the son of Ahitub 1Sa 22:20
son of *A* fled to David to Keilah 1Sa 23:6
*A* the son of Abiathar, were the 2Sa 8:17
*A* of the sons of Ithamar, 1Chr 24:3
*A* the son of Abiathar, and before 1Chr 24:6
of David the king, and Zadok, and *A* 1Chr 24:31

David is come to the house of *A* .............. Ps 52:*t*
*2. A Hittite officer.*
said to *A* the Hittite, and to .................... 1Sa 26:6

**AHIMELECH'S** (*a-him'-el-eks*) *Refers to Ahimelech 1.*
*A* son, I pray thee, bring me .................... 1Sa 30:7

**AHIMOTH**
Amasai, and *A* .......................................... 1Chr 6:25

**AHINADAB** (*a-hin'-ad-ab*) *A son of Iddo.*
*A* the son of Iddo had Mahanaim ........ 1Kin 4:14

**AHINOAM** (*a-hin'-o-am*)
*1. A wife of King Saul.*
And the name of Saul's wife was *A* ..... 1Sa 14:50
*2. A wife of David.*
David also took *A* of Jezreel .................. 1Sa 25:43
*A* the Jezreelitess, and Abigail ................ 1Sa 27:3
*A* the Jezreelitess, and Abigail ................ 1Sa 30:5
*A* the Jezreelitess, and Abigail ................ 2Sa 2:2
was Amnon, of *A* the Jezreelitess ............ 2Sa 3:2
Amnon, of *A* the Jezreelitess .................. 1Chr 3:1

**AHIO** (*a-hi'-o*)
*1. A son of Abinadab.*
and Uzzah and *A*, the sons of .................. 2Sa 6:3
and *A* went before the ark ........................ 2Sa 6:4
and Uzza and *A* drave the cart ................ 1Chr 13:7
*2. A son of Beriah the Benjamite.*
And *A*, Shashak, and Jeremoth, ........... 1Chr 8:14
*3. A son of Jehiel.*
And Gedor, and *A*, and Zacher ............. 1Chr 8:31
and *A*, and Zechariah .............................. 1Chr 9:37

**AHIRA** (*a-hi'-rah*) *A chief of Nephtali.*
*A* the son of Enan .................................. Num 1:15
shall be *A* the son of Enan .................... Num 2:29
the twelfth day *A* the son of Enan ....... Num 7:78
the offering of *A* the son of Enan ........ Num 7:83
of Naphtali was *A* the son of Enan ... Num 10:27

**AHIRAM** (*a-hi'-rum*) See AHARAH, AHIRAMITES.
*A descendant of Benjamin.*
of *A*, the family of the ........................... Num 26:38

**AHIRAMITES** (*a-hi'-rum-ites*) *Desendants of Ahiram.*
of Ahiram, the family of the *A* ........... Num 26:38

**AHISAMACH** (*a-his'-am-ak*) *Father of Aholiab.*
with him Aholiab, the son of *A* ............... Ex 31:6
both he, and Aholiab, the son of *A* ........ Ex 35:34
And with him was Aholiab, son of *A* .... Ex 38:23

**AHISHAHAR** (*a-hish'-a-har*) *A son of Bilhan.*
and Zethan, and Tharshish, and *A* ...... 1Chr 7:10

**AHISHAR** (*a-hi'-shar*) *Governor of the palace under Solomon.*
And *A* was over the household .............. 1Kin 4:6

**AHITHOPHEL** (*a-hith'-o-fel*) *A counsellor of David.*
Absalom sent for *A* the Gilonite ........... 2Sa 15:12
*A* is among the conspirators with ........ 2Sa 15:31
the counsel of *A* into foolishness .......... 2Sa 15:31
for me defeat the counsel of *A* .............. 2Sa 15:34
came to Jerusalem, and *A* with him .... 2Sa 16:15
Then said Absalom to *A*, Give ............... 2Sa 16:20
*A* said unto Absalom, Go in unto ......... 2Sa 16:21
And the counsel of *A*, which he ........... 2Sa 16:23
the counsel of *A* both with David ........ 2Sa 16:23
Moreover *A* said unto Absalom, Let ...... 2Sa 17:1
*A* hath spoken after this manner ........... 2Sa 17:6
The counsel that *A* hath given is ........... 2Sa 17:7
is better than the counsel of *A* ............. 2Sa 17:14
to defeat the good counsel of *A* ............ 2Sa 17:14
thus did *A* counsel Absalom and the ... 2Sa 17:15
for thus hath *A* counselled .................... 2Sa 17:21
when *A* saw that his counsel was ........ 2Sa 17:23
Eliam the son of *A* the Gilonite ............ 2Sa 23:34
*A* was the king's counsellor ................. 1Chr 27:33
after *A* was Jehoiada the son of ......... 1Chr 27:34

**AHITUB** (*a-hi'-tub*)
*1. The son of Phinehas.*
And Ahiah, the son of *A*, ......................... 1Sa 14:3
to Nob, to Ahimelech the son of *A* ......... 1Sa 22:9
the priest, the son of *A*, and all ............ 1Sa 22:11
said, Hear now, thou son of *A* ............... 1Sa 22:12
sons of Ahimelech the son of *A* ............. 1Sa 22:20
*2. Father of the high priest during David's reign.*
And Zadok the son of *A*, and .................. 2Sa 8:17
begat Amariah, and Amariah begat *A* .. 1Chr 6:7
*A* begat Zadok, and Zadok begat ........... 1Chr 6:8
son, Amariah his son, *A* his son, .......... 1Chr 6:52
And Zadok the son of *A*, and ............... 1Chr 18:16
the son of Zadok, the son of *A* ................ Ezr 7:2
*3. A priest seven generations later than Ahitub 2.*
begat Amariah, and Amariah begat *A* 1Chr 6:11
*A* begat Zadok, and Zadok begat .......... 1Chr 6:12
*4. A priest in Nehemiah's time.*
the son of Meraioth, the son of *A* ........ 1Chr 9:11
the son of Meraioth, the son of *A* ....... Neh 11:11

**AHLAB** (*ah'-lab*) *A city of Asher.*
inhabitants of Zidon, nor of *A* ............. Judg 1:31

**AHLAI** (*ah'-lahee*)
*1. A daughter of Sheshan.*
And the children of Sheshan; *A* ........... 1Chr 2:31
*2. Father of a "mighty man" of David.*
the Hittite, Zabad the son of *A* ........... 1Chr 11:41

**AHOAH** (*a-ho'-ah*) See AHOHITE. *The son of Bela.*
And Abishua, and Naaman, and *A* ........ 1Chr 8:4

**AHOHITE** (*a-ho'-hite*)
*1. A descendant of Ahoah.*
Zalmon the *A*, Maharai the .................... 2Sa 23:28
Eleazar the son of Dodo, the *A* .......... 1Chr 11:12
the Hushathite, Ilai the *A* .................... 1Chr 11:29
the second month was Dodai an *A* ...... 1Chr 27:4
*2. A rendering of "son of Ahohi."*
was Eleazar the son of Dodo the *A* ....... 2Sa 23:9

**AHOLAH** (*a-ho'-lah*) *A name for Samaria and the Ten Tribes.*
names of them were *A* the elder ............ Eze 23:4
Samaria is *A*, and Jerusalem ................... Eze 23:4
*A* played the harlot when she was ......... Eze 23:5
Son of man, wilt thou judge *A* ............. Eze 23:36
so went they in unto *A* and unto ......... Eze 23:44

**AHOLIAB** (*a-ho'-lee-ab*) *A Danite craftsman.*
behold, I have given with him *A* .............. Ex 31:6
that he may teach, both he, and *A* ........ Ex 35:34
Then wrought Bezaleel and *A* ................. Ex 36:1
And Moses called Bezaleel and *A* .......... Ex 36:2
And with him was *A*, son of ................... Ex 38:23

**AHOLIBAH** (*a-hol'-ib-ah*) *A name for Jerusalem and Judah.*
Aholah the elder, and *A* her sister ....... Eze 23:4
Samaria is Aholah, and Jerusalem *A* ..... Eze 23:4
And when her sister *A* saw this ............ Eze 23:11
Therefore, O *A*, thus saith the .............. Eze 23:22
man, wilt thou judge Aholah and *A* .... Eze 23:36
they in unto Aholah and unto *A* .......... Eze 23:44

**AHOLIBAMAH** (*a-hol'-ib-a'-mah*)
*1. A wife of Esau.*
*A* the daughter of Anah the .................. Gen 36:2
*A* bare Jeush, and Jaalam, and Korah .. Gen 36:5
And these were the sons of *A* ............. Gen 36:14
are the sons of *A* Esau's wife .............. Gen 36:18
came of *A* the daughter of Anah ......... Gen 36:18
Dishon, and *A* the daughter of Anah . Gen 36:25
*2. A chief from Esau.*
Duke *A*, duke Elah, duke Pinon, ......... Gen 36:41
Duke *A*, duke Elah, duke Pinon, .......... 1Chr 1:52

**AHUMAI** (*a-hoo'-mahee*) *Grandson of Shobal.*
and Jahath begat *A*, and Lahad .............. 1Chr 4:2

**AHUZAM** (*a-hoo'-zam*) *A son of Ashur.*
And Naarah bare him *A*, and Hepher, .. 1Chr 4:6

**AHUZZAM** See AHUZAM.

**AHUZZATH** (*a-huz'-zath*) *A friend of Ahimilech the Philistine king.*
*A* one of his friends, and Phichol .......... Gen 26:26

**AHZAI** See AHASAI.

**AI** (*a'-i*) See AIATH, AIJA, HAI. *A city near Bethel in Benjamin.*
Joshua sent men from Jericho to *A* ....... Josh 7:2
And the men went up and viewed *A* ..... Josh 7:2
thousand men go up and smite *A* ......... Josh 7:3
and they fled before the men of *A* ......... Josh 7:4
the men of *A* smote of them about ........ Josh 7:5
with thee, and arise, go up to *A* ............. Josh 8:1
given into thy hand the king of *A* .......... Josh 8:1
And thou shalt do to *A* and her king ..... Josh 8:2
people of war, to go up against *A* .......... Josh 8:3
and *A*, on the west side of *A* ................ Josh 8:9
of Israel, before the people to *A* ........... Josh 8:10
and pitched on the north side of *A* ....... Josh 8:11
was a valley between them and *A* ....... Josh 8:11
in ambush between Beth-el and *A* ......... Josh 8:12
pass, when the king of *A* saw it ............. Josh 8:14
all the people that were in *A* ............... Josh 8:16
not a man left in *A* or Beth-el .............. Josh 8:17
that is in thy hand toward *A* ................. Josh 8:18
when the men of *A* looked behind ........ Josh 8:20
again, and slew the men of *A* ............... Josh 8:21
the king of *A* they took alive, and ........ Josh 8:23
the inhabitants of *A* in the field ........... Josh 8:24
the Israelites returned unto *A* .............. Josh 8:24
thousand, even all the men of *A* ........... Josh 8:25
all the inhabitants of *A* ......................... Josh 8:26
And Joshua burnt *A*, and made it an ... Josh 8:28
the king of *A* he hanged on a tree ........ Josh 8:29
had done unto Jericho and to *A* ............. Josh 9:3
had heard how Joshua had taken *A* .... Josh 10:1
and her king, so he had done to *A* ....... Josh 10:1
and because it was greater than *A* ....... Josh 10:2
the king of *A*, which is beside ............... Josh 12:9
The men of Beth-el and *A*, two ............... Ezr 2:28
The men of Beth-el and *A*, an ................ Neh 7:32
Howl, O Heshbon, for *A* is spoiled ......... Jer 49:3

**AIAH** (*a-i'-ah*) See AJAH.
*1. A son of Zibeon the Horite.*
*A*, and Anah ........................................... 1Chr 1:40
*2. The father of Saul's concubine.*
was Rizpah, the daughter of *A* .............. 2Sa 3:7
sons of Rizpah the daughter of *A* .......... 2Sa 21:8
the daughter of *A* took sackcloth ........ 2Sa 21:10
what Rizpah the daughter of *A* ............ 2Sa 21:11

**AIATH** (*a-i'-ath*) See AI.. *A form of Ai.*
He is come to *A*, he is passed to .............. Is 10:28

**AIDED**
which *a* him in the killing of his ........... Judg 9:24

**AIJA** (*a-i'-jah*) See AI. *A form of Ai.*
dwelt at Michmash, and *A* ..................... Neh 11:31

**AIJALON** (*a-ij'-el-on*) See AJALON.
*1. A Levitical city in Dan.*
*A* with her suburbs, Gath-rimmon ..... Josh 21:24
would dwell in mount Heres in *A* ........ Judg 1:35
*2. A place in Zebulun.*
was buried in *A* in the country of ...... Judg 12:12
*3. A town between Benjamin and Judah.*
that day from Michmash to *A* ............... 1Sa 14:31
fathers of the inhabitants of *A* ............. 1Chr 8:13
Zorah, and *A*, and Hebron .................. 2Chr 11:10
*4. A Levitical city in Ephraim.*
And *A* with her suburbs, and ................ 1Chr 6:69

**AIJELETH** (*a-ij'-el-eth*) *A musical notation.*
the chief Musician upon *A* Shahar ........... Ps 22:*t*

**AILED**
What *a* thee, O thou sea, that ................. Ps 114:5

**AILETH**
and said unto her, What *a* thee .......... Gen 21:17
and said unto Micah, What *a* thee ..... Judg 18:23
that ye say unto me, What *a* thee ..... Judg 18:24
What *a* the people that they weep ......... 1Sa 11:5
king said unto her, What *a* thee ............ 2Sa 14:5
king said unto her, What *a* thee .......... 2Kin 6:28
What *a* thee now, that thou art ................. Is 22:1

**AIN** (*ah'-yin*) See EN.
*1. A place between Riblah and the Sea of Chinnereth.*
to Riblah, on the east side of *A* .......... Num 34:11
*2. A Levitical city in Simeon.*
And Lebaoth, and Shilhim, and *A* ...... Josh 15:32
*A*, Remmon, and Ether, and Ashan ...... Josh 19:7
*A* with her suburbs, and Juttah ........... Josh 21:16
their villages were, Etam, and *A* .......... 1Chr 4:32

**AIR**
sea, and over the fowl of the *a* ............. Gen 1:26
sea, and over the fowl of the *a* ............. Gen 1:28
earth, and to every fowl of the *a* .......... Gen 1:30
the field, and every fowl of the *a* .......... Gen 2:19
cattle, and to the fowl of the *a* ............. Gen 2:20
thing, and the fowls of the *a* .................... Gen 6:7
Of fowls also of the *a* by sevens ................ Gen 7:3
and upon every fowl of the *a* ..................... Gen 9:2
winged fowl that flieth in the *a* ........... Deut 4:17
be meat unto all fowls of the *a* ........... Deut 28:26
thy flesh unto the fowls of the *a* .......... 1Sa 17:44
this day unto the fowls of the *a* .......... 1Sa 17:46
of the *a* to rest on them by day ........... 2Sa 21:10
shall the fowls of the *a* eat ................. 1Kin 14:11
shall the fowls of the *a* eat ................... 1Kin 16:4
shall the fowls of the *a* eat ................. 1Kin 21:24
and the fowls of the *a*, and they .............. Job 12:7
close from the fowls of the *a* ................. Job 28:21
that no *a* can come between them ....... Job 41:16
The fowl of the *a*, and the fish of ............... Ps 8:8
The way of an eagle in the *a* ............... Prov 30:19
for a bird of the *a* shall carry ............... Eccl 10:20
Behold the fowls of the *a* ........................... Mt 6:26
and the birds of the *a* have nests ............. Mt 8:20
so that the birds of the *a* come ............. Mt 13:32
side, and the fowls of the *a* came ............... Mk 4:4
so that the fowls of the *a* may ................ Mk 4:32
and the fowls of the *a* devoured it ............. Lk 8:5
and birds of the *a* have nests ...................... Lk 9:58
the fowls of the *a* lodged in the ............ Lk 13:19
things, and fowls of the *a* .................. Acts 10:12
things, and fowls of the *a* ..................... Acts 11:6
clothes, and threw dust into the *a* ...... Acts 22:23
I, not as one that beateth the *a* ........... 1Cor 9:26
for ye shall speak into the *a* ................ 1Cor 14:9
the prince of the power of the *a* ............... Eph 2:2
clouds, to meet the Lord in the *a* ........... 1Th 4:17
the *a* were darkened by reason of .......... Rev 9:2
poured out his vial into the *a* ............... Rev 16:17

**AJAH** (*a'-jah*) See AIAH. *A son of Zibeon the Horite.*
both *A*, and Anah ................................. Gen 36:24

**AJALON** (*aj'-a-lon*) See AIJALON.
*1. A valley of Dan.*
and thou, Moon, in the valley of *A* .... Josh 10:12
*2. A Levitical city in Dan.*
And Shaalabbin, and *A*, and Jethlah,. Josh 19:42
*3. A town between Benjamin and Judah.*
and had taken Beth-shemesh, and *A*. 2Chr 28:18

**AKAN** (*a'-kan*) See JAAKAN, JAKAN. *A son of Ezer.*
Bilhan, and Zaavan, and *A* .................... Gen 36:27

**AKEL DAMA** See ACELDAMA.

**AKKAD** See ACCAD.

**AKKUB** (*ak'-kub*)
*1. A descendant of David.*
and Eliashib, and Pelaiah, and *A* .......... 1Chr 3:24
*2. A Levitical gatekeeper.*
the porters were, Shallum, and *A* ......... 1Chr 9:17
Moreover the porters, *A*, Talmon, ....... Neh 11:19
Obadiah, Meshullam, Talmon, *A* .......... Neh 12:25
*3. A family of Levitical porters.*
of Talmon, the children of *A* .................... Ezr 2:42
of Talmon, the children of *A* ................... Neh 7:45
*4. A family of returned exiles.*
of Hagabah, the children of *A* ................. Ezr 2:45
*5. A priest in Ezra's time.*
and Bani, and Sherebiah, Jamin, *A* ......... Neh 8:7

**AKRABBIM** (*ac-rab'-bim*) See MAALE-ACRABBIM. *An ascent south of the Dead Sea.*
from the south to the ascent of *A* ....... Num 34:4
was from the going up to *A* .................. Judg 1:36

**ALABASTER**
*a* box of very precious ointment .............. Mt 26:7
an *a* box of ointment of spikenard ......... Mk 14:3

brought an *a* box of ointment, Lk 7:37

**ALAMETH** (*al'-am-eth*) *A son of Becher.*
and Abiah, and Anathoth, and *A* 1Chr 7:8

**ALAMMELECH** (*a-lam'-mel-ek*) *A town in Asher.*
And *A*, and Amad, and Misheal Josh 19:26

**ALAMOTH** (*al'-am-oth*) *A musical notation.*
and Benaiah, with psalteries on *A* 1Chr 15:20
the sons of Korah, A Song upon *A* Ps 46:*t*

**ALARM**
When ye blow an *a*, then the camps... Num 10:5
When ye blow an *a* the second time... Num 10:6
blow an *a* for their journeys Num 10:6
blow, but ye shall not sound an *a* Num 10:7
shall blow an *a* with the trumpets Num 10:9
trumpets to cry *a* against you 2Chr 13:12
of the trumpet, the *a* of war Jer 4:19
that I will cause an *a* of war to Jer 49:2
sound an *a* in my holy mountain Joel 2:1
*a* against the fenced cities, and Zeph 1:16

**ALAS**
And Aaron said unto Moses, *A* Num 12:11
took up his parable, and said, *A* Num 24:23
And Joshua said, *A*, O Lord GOD, Josh 7:7
angel of the LORD, Gideon said, *A* Judg 6:22
he rent his clothes, and said, *A* Judg 11:35
they mourned over him, saying, *A* 1Kin 13:30
And the king of Israel said, *A* 2Kin 3:10
and he cried, and said, *A*, master 2Kin 6:5
And his servant said unto him, *A* 2Kin 6:15
*A*! for that day is great Jer 30:7
*A* for all the evil abominations Eze 6:11
*A* for the day Joel 1:15
say in all the highways, *A*! *a*! Amos 5:16
fear of her torment, saying, *A* Rev 18:10
*a* that great city Babylon, that Rev 18:10
And saying, *A*, *a* that great Rev 18:16
weeping and wailing, saying, *A* Rev 18:19
*a* that great city, wherein were Rev 18:19

**ALBEIT**
*a* I have not spoken Eze 13:7
*a* I do not say to thee how thou Philem 19

**ALEMETH** (*al-e'-meth*)
*1. A Levitical city in Benjamin.*
*A* with her suburbs, and Anathoth 1Chr 6:60
*2. A descendant of Jonathan.*
and Jehoadah begat *A* 1Chr 8:36
and Jarah begat *A* 1Chr 9:42

**ALEXANDER** (*al-ex-an'-dur*)
*1. Son of Simeon who bore Jesus'cross.*
of the country, the father of *A* Mk 15:21
*2. A Christian leader in Jerusalem.*
and Caiaphas, and John, and *A* Acts 4:6
*3. A participant in the Ephesian riot.*
they drew *A* out of the multitude, Acts 19:33
*A* beckoned with the hand, and Acts 19:33
*4. An opponent of Paul.*
Of whom is Hymenaeus and *A* 1Ti 1:20
*A* the coppersmith did me much 2Ti 4:14

**ALEXANDRIA** (*al-ex-an'-dree-ah*) See ALEXANDRIANS. *A city in Egypt.*
Jew named Apollos, born at *A* Acts 18:24
a ship of *A* sailing into Italy Acts 27:6
months we departed in a ship of *A* Acts 28:11

**ALEXANDRIAN** See ALEXANDRIA.

**ALEXANDRIANS** (*al-ex-an'-dree-uns*) *Residents of Alexandria.*
Libertines, and Cyrenians, and *A* Acts 6:9

**ALGUM**
trees, and *a* trees, out of Lebanon 2Chr 2:8
gold from Ophir, brought *a* trees 2Chr 9:10
the king made of the *a* trees 2Chr 9:11

**ALIAH** (*a-li'-ah*) See ALVAH. *A chief of Edom.*
duke Timnah, duke *A*, duke Jetheth... 1Chr 1:51

**ALIAN** (*a-li'-un*) See ALVAN. *A son of Shobal.*
*A*, and Manahath, and Ebal, Shephi, ... 1Chr 1:40

**ALIEN**
I have been an *a* in a strange Ex 18:3
or thou mayest sell it unto an *a* Deut 14:21
I am an *a* in their sight Job 19:15
an *a* unto my mother's children Ps 69:8
the sons of the *a* shall be your Is 61:5

**ALIENATE**
nor *a* the firstfruits of the land Eze 48:14

**ALIENATED**
them, and her mind was *a* from them. Eze 23:17
then my mind was *a* from her Eze 23:18
as my mind was *a* from her sister Eze 23:18
thee, from whom thy mind is *a* Eze 23:22
of them from whom thy mind is *a* Eze 23:28
being *a* from the life of God Eph 4:18
And you, that were sometime *a* Col 1:21

**ALIENS**
to strangers, our houses to *a* Lam 5:2
being *a* from the commonwealth of Eph 2:12
to flight the armies of the *a* Heb 11:34

**ALIKE**
and the clean shall eat of them *a* Deut 12:22
the clean person shall eat it *a* Deut 15:22
they shall part *a* 1Sa 30:24
They shall lie down *a* in the dust Job 21:26
He fashioneth their hearts *a* Ps 33:15
and the light are both *a* to thee Ps 139:12
both of them are *a* abomination to Prov 20:10
day and a contentious woman are *a* Prov 27:15
All things come *a* to all Eccl 9:2
whether they both shall be *a* good Eccl 11:6
another esteemeth every day *a* Rom 14:5

**ALIVE**
the ark, to keep them *a* with thee Gen 6:19
come unto thee, to keep them *a* Gen 6:20
to keep seed *a* upon the face of Gen 7:3
and Noah only remained *a*, and they... Gen 7:23
me, but they will save thee *a* Gen 12:12
saying, Is your father yet *a* Gen 43:7
Is he yet *a* Gen 43:27
is in good health, he is yet *a* Gen 43:28
told him, saying, Joseph is yet *a* Gen 45:26
Joseph my son is yet *a* Gen 45:28
thy face, because thou art yet *a* Gen 46:30
this day, to save much people *a* Gen 50:20
but saved the men children *a* Ex 1:17
and have saved the men children *a* Ex 1:18
and every daughter ye shall save *a* Ex 1:22
and see whether they be yet *a* Ex 4:18
be certainly found in his hand *a* Ex 22:4
sons of Aaron which were left *a* Lev 10:16
is to be cleansed two birds *a* Lev 14:4
be presented *a* before the LORD Lev 16:10
upon them that are left *a* of you Lev 26:36
went down *a* into the pit, and the Num 16:33
until there was none left him *a* Num 21:35
I had slain thee, and saved her *a* Num 22:33
Have ye saved all the women *a* Num 31:15
with him, keep *a* for yourselves Num 31:18
are *a* every one of you this day Deut 4:4
who are all of us here *a* this day Deut 5:3
that he might preserve us *a* Deut 6:24
thou shalt save *a* nothing that Deut 20:16
while I am yet *a* with you this Deut 31:27
I kill, and I make *a* Deut 32:39
And that ye will save *a* my father Josh 2:13
Joshua saved Rahab the harlot *a* Josh 6:25
And the king of Ai they took *a* Josh 8:23
behold, the LORD hath kept me *a* Josh 14:10
liveth, if ye had saved them *a* Judg 8:19
*a* of the women of Jabesh-gilead Judg 21:14
The LORD killeth, and maketh *a* 1Sa 2:6
Agag the king of the Amalekites *a* 1Sa 15:8
and left neither man nor woman *a* 1Sa 27:9
saved neither man nor woman *a* 1Sa 27:11
and with one full line to keep *a* 2Sa 8:2
Behold, while the child was yet *a* 2Sa 12:18
for the child, while it was *a* 2Sa 12:21
said, While the child was yet *a* 2Sa 12:22
while he was yet *a* in the midst 2Sa 18:14
to save the horses and mules *a* 1Kin 18:5
come out for peace, take them *a* 1Kin 20:18
be come out for war, take them *a* 1Kin 20:18
And he said, Is he yet *a* 1Kin 20:32
for Naboth is not *a*, but dead 1Kin 21:15
Am I God, to kill and to make *a* 2Kin 5:7
if they save us *a*, we shall live 2Kin 7:4
the city, we shall catch them *a* 2Kin 7:12
And he said, Take them *a* 2Kin 10:14
And they took them *a* 2Kin 10:14
other ten thousand left *a* did the 2Chr 25:12
and none can keep *a* his own soul Ps 22:29
thou hast kept me *a*, that I Ps 30:3
and to keep them *a* in famine Ps 33:19
will preserve him, and keep him *a* Ps 41:2
us swallow them up *a* as the grave Prov 1:12
than the living which are yet *a* Eccl 4:2
children, I will preserve them *a* Jer 49:11
is sold, although they were yet *a* Eze 7:13
the souls *a* that come unto you Eze 13:18
to save the souls *a* that should Eze 13:19
right, he shall save his soul *a* Eze 18:27
and whom he would he kept *a* Dan 5:19
deceiver said, while he was yet *a* Mt 27:63
when they had heard that he was *a* Mk 16:11
my son was dead, and is *a* again Lk 15:24
brother was dead, and is *a* again Lk 15:32
angels, which said that he was *a* Lk 24:23
*a* after his passion by many Acts 1:3
saints and widows, presented her *a* Acts 9:41
And they brought the young man *a* Acts 20:12
dead, whom Paul affirmed to be *a* Acts 25:19
but *a* unto God through Jesus Rom 6:11
as those that are *a* from the dead Rom 6:13
For I was *a* without the law once Rom 7:9
so in Christ shall all be made *a* 1Cor 15:22
of the Lord, that we which are *a* 1Th 4:15
Then we which are *a* and remain 1Th 4:17
I am *a* for evermore, Amen Rev 1:18
the last, which was dead, and is *a* Rev 2:8
These both were cast *a* into a Rev 19:20

**ALL** See PREFACE.

**ALLAMMELECH** See ALAMMELECH.

**ALLEGING**
Opening and *a*, that Christ must Acts 17:3

**ALLEGORY**
Which things are an *a* Gal 4:24

**ALLELUIA** (*al-le-loo'-yah*) *Greek form of Hallelujah.*
much people in heaven, saying, *A* Rev 19:1
And again they said, *A* Rev 19:3
saying, Amen; *A* Rev 19:4
of mighty thunderings, saying, *A* Rev 19:6

**ALLIED**
of our God, was *a* unto Tobiah Neh 13:4

**ALLON** (*al'-lon*) See ALLON-BACHUTH, ELON.
*1. A city in Naphtali.*
from *A* to Zaanannim, and Adami, Josh 19:33
*2. A chief of a Simeonite family.*
the son of Shiphi, the son of *A* 1Chr 4:37

**ALLON-BACHUTH** (*al'-lon-bak'-ooth*) *A place near Bethel.*
and the name of it was called *A* Gen 35:8

**ALLOW**
ye *a* the deeds of your fathers Lk 11:48
God, which they themselves also *a* Acts 24:15
For that which I do I *a* not Rom 7:15

**ALLOWANCE**
his *a* was a continual *a* 2Kin 25:30

**ALLOWED**
But as we were *a* of God to be put 1Th 2:4

**ALLOWETH**
himself in that thing which he *a* Rom 14:22

**ALLURE**
Therefore, behold, I will *a* her Hos 2:14
they *a* through the lusts of the 2Pet 2:18

**ALMIGHTY** *A term for God meaning sufficient or all-powerful.*
and said unto him, I am the *A* God Gen 17:1
God *A* bless thee, and make thee Gen 28:3
And God said unto him, I am God *A*.. Gen 35:11
God *A* give you mercy before the Gen 43:14
God *A* appeared unto me at Luz in Gen 48:3
and by the *A*, who shall bless thee Gen 49:25
unto Jacob, by the name of God *A* Ex 6:3
which saw the vision of the *A* Num 24:4
which saw the vision of the *A* Num 24:16
for the *A* hath dealt very Ruth 1:20
me, and the *A* hath afflicted me Ruth 1:21
not thou the chastening of the *A* Job 5:17
the arrows of the *A* are within me Job 6:4
he forsaketh the fear of the *A* Job 6:14
or doth the *A* pervert justice Job 8:3
and make thy supplication to the *A* Job 8:5
find out the *A* unto perfection Job 11:7
Surely I would speak to the *A* Job 13:3
himself against the *A* Job 15:25
What is the *A*, that we should Job 21:15
shall drink of the wrath of the *A* Job 21:20
Is it any pleasure to the *A* Job 22:3
and what can the *A* do for them Job 22:17
If thou return to the *A*, thou Job 22:23
the *A* shall be thy defence, and Job 22:25
thou have thy delight in the *A* Job 22:26
heart soft, and the *A* troubleth me Job 23:16
times are not hidden from the *A* Job 24:1
and the *A*, who hath vexed my soul Job 27:2
Will he delight himself in the *A* Job 27:10
is with the *A* will I not conceal Job 27:11
which they shall receive of the *A* Job 27:13
When the *A* was yet with me, when Job 29:5
inheritance of the *A* from on high Job 31:2
that the *A* would answer me, and Job 31:35
the inspiration of the *A* giveth Job 32:8
the breath of the *A* hath given me Job 33:4
and from the *A*, that he should Job 34:10
will the *A* pervert judgment Job 34:12
neither will the *A* regard it Job 35:13
Touching the *A*, we cannot find Job 37:23
with the *A* instruct him Job 40:2
When the *A* scattered kings in it, Ps 68:14
abide under the shadow of the *A* Ps 91:1
come as a destruction from the *A* Is 13:6
waters, as the voice of the *A* Eze 1:24
as the voice of the *A* God when he Eze 10:5
from the *A* shall it come Joel 1:15
and daughters, saith the Lord *A* 2Cor 6:18
was, and which is to come, the *A* Rev 1:8
Holy, holy, holy, Lord God *A* Rev 4:8
We give thee thanks, O Lord God *A* Rev 11:17
are thy works, Lord God *A* Rev 15:3
altar say, Even so, Lord God *A* Rev 16:7
battle of that great day of God *A* Rev 16:14
the fierceness and wrath of *A* God Rev 19:15
for the Lord God *A* and the Lamb Rev 21:22

**ALMODAD** (*al-mo'-dad*) *A descendant of Shem.*
And Joktan begat *A* Gen 10:26
And Joktan begat *A* 1Chr 1:20

**ALMON** (*al'-mon*) *A Levitical town in Benjamin.*
suburbs, and *A* with her suburbs Josh 21:18

**ALMOND**
the *a* tree shall flourish, and the Eccl 12:5
I said, I see a rod of an *a* tree Jer 1:11

**ALMON-DIBLATHAIM** (*al'-mon-dib-lath-a'-im*) *An encampment of Israel in the Wilderness.*
from Dibon-gad, and encamped in *A* Num 33:46
And they removed from *A*, and Num 33:47

**ALMONDS**
spices, and myrrh, nuts, and *a* Gen 43:11
Three bowls made like unto *a* Ex 25:33
made like *a* in the other branch Ex 25:33

be four bowls made like unto *a* ... Ex 25:34
the fashion of *a* in one branch ... Ex 37:19
made like *a* in another branch ... Ex 37:19
were four bowls made like *a* ... Ex 37:20
and bloomed blossoms, and yielded *a*. Num 17:8

**ALMOST**
they be *a* ready to stone me ... Ex 17:4
as for me, my feet were *a* gone ... Ps 73:2
my soul had *a* dwelt in silence ... Ps 94:17
They had *a* consumed me upon earth. Ps 119:87
I was *a* in all evil in the midst ... Prov 5:14
the next sabbath day came *a* the ... Acts 13:44
but *a* throughout all Asia, this ... Acts 19:26
when the seven days were *a* ended ... Acts 21:27
*A* thou persuadest me to be a ... Acts 26:28
hear me this day, were both *a* ... Acts 26:29
*a* all things are by the law ... Heb 9:22

**ALMS**
that ye do not your *a* before men ... Mt 6:1
Therefore when thou doest thine *a* ... Mt 6:2
But when thou doest *a*, let not ... Mt 6:3
That thine *a* may be in secret ... Mt 6:4
But rather give *a* of such things ... Lk 11:41
Sell that ye have, and give *a* ... Lk 12:33
to ask *a* of them that entered ... Acts 3:2
to go into the temple asked an *a* ... Acts 3:3
*a* at the Beautiful gate of the ... Acts 3:10
which gave much *a* to the people ... Acts 10:2
thine *a* are come up for a ... Acts 10:4
thine *a* are had in remembrance in ... Acts 10:31
I came to bring *a* to my nation ... Acts 24:17

**ALMSDEEDS**
of good works and *a* which she did ... Acts 9:36

**ALMUG**
Ophir great plenty of *a* trees ... 1Kin 10:11
the king made of the *a* trees ... 1Kin 10:12
there came no such *a* trees ... 1Kin 10:12

**ALOES**
as the trees of lign *a* which the ... Num 24:6
thy garments smell of myrrh, and *a* ... Ps 45:8
perfumed my bed with myrrh, *a* ... Prov 7:17
myrrh and *a*, with all the chief ... Song 4:14
brought a mixture of myrrh and *a* ... Jn 19:39

**ALONE**
not good that the man should be *a* ... Gen 2:18
And Jacob was left *a* ... Gen 32:24
brother is dead, and he is left *a* ... Gen 42:38
he *a* is left of his mother, and ... Gen 44:20
thee in Egypt, saying, Let us *a* ... Ex 14:12
why sittest thou thyself *a* ... Ex 18:14
not able to perform it thyself *a* ... Ex 18:18
Moses *a* shall come near the LORD ... Ex 24:2
Now therefore let me *a*, that my ... Ex 32:10
he shall dwell *a* ... Lev 13:46
able to bear all this people *a* ... Num 11:14
that thou bear it not thyself *a* ... Num 11:17
lo, the people shall dwell *a* ... Num 23:9
am not able to bear you myself *a* ... Deut 1:9
How can I myself *a* bear your ... Deut 1:12
Let me *a*, that I may destroy them ... Deut 9:14
So the LORD *a* did lead him, and ... Deut 32:12
then shall dwell in safety *a* ... Deut 33:28
perished not *a* in his iniquity ... Josh 22:20
which he had for himself *a* ... Judg 3:20
let me *a* two months, that I may ... Judg 11:37
and said unto him, Why art thou *a* ... 1Sa 21:1
let him *a*, and let him curse ... 2Sa 16:11
looked, and behold a man running *a* ... 2Sa 18:24
And the king said, If he be *a* ... 2Sa 18:25
Behold another man running *a* ... 2Sa 18:26
and they two were *a* in the field ... 1Kin 11:29
And the man of God said, Let her *a* ... 2Kin 4:27
thou art the God, even thou *a* ... 2Kin 19:15
And he said, Let him *a* ... 2Kin 23:18
So they let his bones *a*, with the ... 2Kin 23:18
whom *a* God hath chosen, is yet ... 1Chr 29:1
the work of this house of God *a* ... Ezr 6:7
Thou, even thou, art LORD *a* ... Neh 9:6
scorn to lay hands on Mordecai *a* ... Est 3:6
I only am escaped *a* to tell thee ... Job 1:15
I only am escaped *a* to tell thee ... Job 1:16
I only am escaped *a* to tell thee ... Job 1:17
I only am escaped *a* to tell thee ... Job 1:19
let me *a* ... Job 7:16
nor let me *a* till I swallow down ... Job 7:19
Which *a* spreadeth out the heavens ... Job 9:8
cease then, and let me *a*, that I ... Job 10:20
Hold your peace, let me *a* ... Job 13:13
Unto whom *a* the earth was given ... Job 15:19
Or have eaten my morsel myself *a* ... Job 31:17
thou, whose name *a* is JEHOVAH ... Ps 83:18
thou art God *a* ... Ps 86:10
am as a sparrow *a* upon the house ... Ps 102:7
To him who *a* doeth great wonders ... Ps 136:4
for his name *a* is excellent ... Ps 148:13
scornest, thou *a* shalt bear it ... Prov 9:12
There is one *a*, and there is not a ... Eccl 4:8
to him that is *a* when he falleth ... Eccl 4:10
but how can one be warm *a* ... Eccl 4:11
the LORD *a* shall be exalted in ... Is 2:11
the LORD *a* shall be exalted in ... Is 2:17
that they may be placed *a* in the ... Is 5:8
none shall be *a* in his appointed ... Is 14:31
thou art the God, even thou *a* ... Is 37:16
stretcheth forth the heavens *a* ... Is 44:24
Behold, I was left *a* ... Is 49:21
for I called him *a*, and blessed ... Is 51:2
I have trodden the winepress *a* ... Is 63:3
I sat *a* because of thy hand ... Jer 15:17
gates nor bars, which dwell *a* ... Jer 49:31
He sitteth *a* and keepeth silence ... Lam 3:28
I Daniel *a* saw the vision ... Dan 10:7
Therefore I was left *a*, and saw ... Dan 10:8
let him *a* ... Hos 4:17
Assyria, a wild ass *a* by himself ... Hos 8:9
Man shall not live by bread *a* ... Mt 4:4
evening was come, he was there *a* ... Mt 14:23
Let them *a* ... Mt 15:14
his fault between thee and him *a* ... Mt 18:15
Saying, Let us *a* ... Mk 1:24
And when he was *a*, they that were ... Mk 4:10
and when they were *a*, he expounded ... Mk 4:34
of the sea, and he *a* on the land ... Mk 6:47
And Jesus said, Let her *a* ... Mk 14:6
gave him to drink, saying, Let *a* ... Mk 15:36
man shall not live by bread *a* ... Lk 4:4
Saying, Let us *a* ... Lk 4:34
Who can forgive sins, but God *a* ... Lk 5:21
to eat but for the priests *a* ... Lk 6:4
came to pass, as he was *a* praying ... Lk 9:18
voice was past, Jesus was found *a* ... Lk 9:36
my sister hath left me to serve *a* ... Lk 10:40
let it *a* this year also, till I ... Lk 13:8
again into a mountain himself *a* ... Jn 6:15
his disciples were gone away *a* ... Jn 6:22
and Jesus was left *a*, and the woman ... Jn 8:9
for I am not *a*, but I and the ... Jn 8:16
the Father hath not left me *a* ... Jn 8:29
If we let him thus *a*, all men ... Jn 11:48
Then said Jesus, Let her *a* ... Jn 12:7
the ground and die, it abideth *a* ... Jn 12:24
to his own, and shall leave me *a* ... Jn 16:32
and yet I am not *a*, because the ... Jn 16:32
Neither pray I for these *a* ... Jn 17:20
from these men, and let them *a* ... Acts 5:38
that not *a* at Ephesus, but almost ... Acts 19:26
it was not written for his sake *a* ... Rom 4:23
and I am left *a*, and they seek my ... Rom 11:3
he have rejoicing in himself *a* ... Gal 6:4
it good to be left at Athens *a* ... 1Th 3:1
the high priest *a* once every year ... Heb 9:7
hath not works, is dead, being *a* ... Jas 2:17

**ALONG**
her maidens walked *a* by the ... Ex 2:5
the fire ran *a* upon the ground ... Ex 9:23
but we will go *a* by the king's ... Num 21:22
of Zin *a* by the coast of Edom ... Num 34:3
I will go *a* by the high way, I ... Deut 2:27
chased them *a* the way that goeth ... Josh 10:10
and passed *a* to Zin, and ascended ... Josh 15:3
passed *a* to Hezron, and went up to ... Josh 15:3
and passed *a* by the north of ... Josh 15:6
passed *a* unto the side of mount ... Josh 15:10
passed *a* to mount Baalah, and went. Josh 15:11
passeth *a* unto the borders of ... Josh 16:2
the border went *a* on the right ... Josh 17:7
passed *a* toward the side over ... Josh 18:18
the border passed *a* to the side ... Josh 18:19
from thence passeth on *a* on the ... Josh 19:13
the children of the east lay *a* in ... Judg 7:12
it, that the tent lay *a* ... Judg 7:13
all that came *a* that way by them ... Judg 9:25
another company come *a* by the ... Judg 9:37
Then they went *a* through the ... Judg 11:18
that be *a* by the coasts of Arnon ... Judg 11:26
liers in wait drew themselves *a* ... Judg 20:37
went *a* the highway, lowing as ... 1Sa 6:12
straightway all *a* on the earth ... 1Sa 28:20
her husband went with her *a* ... 2Sa 3:16
Shimei went *a* on the hill's side ... 2Sa 16:13
*a* by the altar and the temple ... 2Kin 11:11
*a* by the altar and the temple, by ... 2Chr 23:10
them, weeping all *a* as he went ... Jer 41:6

**ALOOF**
my friends stand *a* from my sore ... Ps 38:11

**ALOTH** (*a'-loth*) See BEALOTH. *A region near Asher.*
of Hushai was in Asher and in *A* ... 1Kin 4:16

**ALOUD**
And he wept *a* ... Gen 45:2
mocked them, and said, Cry *a* ... 1Kin 18:27
And they cried *a*, and cut ... 1Kin 18:28
and many shouted *a* for joy ... Ezr 3:12
I cry *a*, but there is no judgment ... Job 19:7
shall sing *a* of thy righteousness ... Ps 51:14
and at noon, will I pray, and cry *a* ... Ps 55:17
I will sing *a* of thy mercy in the ... Ps 59:16
Sing *a* unto God our strength ... Ps 81:1
her saints shall shout *a* for joy ... Ps 132:16
let them sing *a* upon their beds ... Ps 149:5
they shall cry *a* from the sea ... Is 24:14
forth into singing, and cry *a* ... Is 54:1
Cry *a*, spare not, lift up thy ... Is 58:1
Then an herald cried *a*, To you it ... Dan 3:4
He cried *a*, and said thus, Hew ... Dan 4:14
The king cried *a* to bring in the ... Dan 5:7
cry *a* at Beth-aven, after thee, O ... Hos 5:8
Now why dost thou cry out *a* ... Mic 4:9
the multitude crying *a* began to ... Mk 15:8

**ALPHA** (*al'-fah*) *First letter of Greek alphabet.*
I am *A* and Omega, the beginning and .. Rev 1:8
Saying, I am *A* and Omega, the ... Rev 1:11
I am *A* and Omega, the beginning and Rev 21:6
I am *A* and Omega ... Rev 22:13

**ALPHAEUS** (*al-fe'-us*) See CLEOPAS.
*1. Father of the apostle James.*
James the son of *A*, and Lebbaeus, ... Mt 10:3
and Thomas, and James the son of *A* ... Mk 3:18
and Thomas, James the son of *A* ... Lk 6:15
and Matthew, James the son of *A* ... Acts 1:13
*2. Father of the apostle Levi.*
he saw Levi the son of *A* sitting ... Mk 2:14

**ALREADY**
have offended against the LORD *a* ... 2Chr 28:13
are brought unto bondage *a* ... Neh 5:5
it hath been *a* of old time ... Eccl 1:10
even that which hath been *a* done ... Eccl 2:12
that which is to be hath *a* been ... Eccl 3:15
I praised the dead which are *a* ... Eccl 4:2
That which hath been is named *a* ... Eccl 6:10
yea, I have cursed them *a* ... Mal 2:2
adultery with her *a* in his heart ... Mt 5:28
unto you, That Elias is come *a* ... Mt 17:12
marvelled if he were *a* dead ... Mk 15:44
what will I, if it be *a* kindled ... Lk 12:49
that believeth not is condemned *a* ... Jn 3:18
for they are white *a* to harvest ... Jn 4:35
for the Jews had agreed *a* ... Jn 9:22
answered them, I have told you *a* ... Jn 9:27
had lain in the grave four days *a* ... Jn 11:17
Jesus, and saw that he was dead *a* ... Jn 19:33
there were three men *a* come unto ... Acts 11:11
because the fast was now *a* past ... Acts 27:9
present in spirit, have judged *a* ... 1Cor 5:3
bewail many which have sinned *a* ... 2Cor 12:21
Not as though I had *a* attained ... Phil 3:12
attained, either were *a* perfect ... Phil 3:12
whereto we have *a* attained ... Phil 3:16
mystery of iniquity doth *a* work ... 2Th 2:7
For some are *a* turned aside after ... 1Ti 5:15
that the resurrection is past *a* ... 2Ti 2:18
even now *a* is it in the world ... 1Jn 4:3
ye have *a* hold fast till I come ... Rev 2:25

**ALSO** See PREFACE.

**ALTAR**
Noah builded an *a* unto the LORD ... Gen 8:20
offered burnt offerings on the *a* ... Gen 8:20
builded he an *a* unto the LORD ... Gen 12:7
he builded an *a* unto the LORD ... Gen 12:8
Unto the place of the *a*, which he ... Gen 13:4
and built there an *a* unto the LORD ... Gen 13:18
and Abraham built an *a* there ... Gen 22:9
laid him on the *a* upon the wood ... Gen 22:9
And he builded an *a* there, and ... Gen 26:25
And he erected there an *a*, and ... Gen 33:20
and make there an *a* unto God ... Gen 35:1
I will make there an *a* unto God ... Gen 35:3
And he built there an *a*, and called ... Gen 35:7
And Moses built an *a*, and called ... Ex 17:15
An *a* of earth thou shalt make ... Ex 20:24
thou wilt make me an *a* of stone ... Ex 20:25
thou go up by steps unto mine *a* ... Ex 20:26
thou shalt take him from mine *a* ... Ex 21:14
builded an *a* under the hill, and ... Ex 24:4
the blood he sprinkled on the *a* ... Ex 24:6
shalt make an *a* of shittim wood ... Ex 27:1
the *a* shall be foursquare ... Ex 27:1
the compass of the *a* beneath ... Ex 27:5
may be even to the midst of the *a* ... Ex 27:5
thou shalt make staves for the *a* ... Ex 27:6
be upon the two sides of the *a* ... Ex 27:7
*a* to minister in the holy place ... Ex 28:43
horns of the *a* with thy finger ... Ex 29:12
blood beside the bottom of the *a* ... Ex 29:12
them, and burn them upon the *a* ... Ex 29:13
it round about upon the *a* ... Ex 29:16
burn the whole ram upon the *a* ... Ex 29:18
the blood upon the *a* round about ... Ex 29:20
of the blood that is upon the *a* ... Ex 29:21
burn them upon the *a* for a burnt ... Ex 29:25
and thou shalt cleanse the *a* ... Ex 29:36
shalt make an atonement for the *a* ... Ex 29:37
and it shall be an *a* most holy ... Ex 29:37
toucheth the *a* shall be holy ... Ex 29:37
which thou shalt offer upon the *a* ... Ex 29:38
of the congregation, and the *a* ... Ex 29:44
thou shalt make an *a* to burn ... Ex 30:1
of the congregation and the *a* ... Ex 30:18
come near to the *a* to minister ... Ex 30:20
his vessels, and the *a* of incense ... Ex 30:27
the *a* of burnt offering with all ... Ex 30:28
furniture, and the *a* of incense ... Ex 31:8
the *a* of burnt offering with all ... Ex 31:9
saw it, he built an *a* before it ... Ex 32:5
And the incense *a*, and his staves ... Ex 35:15
The *a* of burnt offering, with his ... Ex 35:16
the incense *a* of shittim wood ... Ex 37:25
he made the *a* of burnt offering ... Ex 38:1
he made all the vessels of the *a* ... Ex 38:3
he made for the *a* a brasen grate ... Ex 38:4
the rings on the sides of the *a* ... Ex 38:7
he made the *a* hollow with boards ... Ex 38:7
the congregation, and the brasen *a* ... Ex 38:30
it, and all the vessels of the *a* ... Ex 38:30
And the golden *a*, and the anointing ... Ex 39:38
The brasen *a*, and his grate of ... Ex 39:39
thou shalt set the *a* of gold for ... Ex 40:5
thou shalt set the *a* of the burnt ... Ex 40:6
tent of the congregation and the *a* ... Ex 40:7
the *a* of the burnt offering ... Ex 40:10
his vessels, and sanctify the *a* ... Ex 40:10
and it shall be an *a* most holy ... Ex 40:10
he put the golden *a* in the tent ... Ex 40:26

he put the *a* of burnt offering by ... Ex 40:29
tent of the congregation and the *a* ... Ex 40:30
and when they came near unto the *a* ... Ex 40:32
about the tabernacle and the *a* ... Ex 40:33
the *a* that is by the door of the ... Lev 1:5
priest shall put fire upon the *a* ... Lev 1:7
on the fire which is upon the *a* ... Lev 1:8
priest shall burn all on the *a* ... Lev 1:9
the *a* northward before the LORD ... Lev 1:11
his blood round about upon the *a* ... Lev 1:11
on the fire which is upon the *a* ... Lev 1:12
it all, and burn it upon the *a* ... Lev 1:13
priest shall bring it unto the *a* ... Lev 1:15
off his head, and burn it on the *a* ... Lev 1:15
be wrung out at the side of the *a* ... Lev 1:15
it beside the *a* on the east part ... Lev 1:16
priest shall burn it upon the *a* ... Lev 1:17
the memorial of it upon the *a* ... Lev 2:2
he shall bring it unto the *a* ... Lev 2:8
and shall burn it upon the *a* ... Lev 2:9
burnt on the *a* for a sweet savour ... Lev 2:12
the blood upon the *a* round about ... Lev 3:2
on the *a* upon the burnt sacrifice ... Lev 3:5
thereof round about upon the *a* ... Lev 3:8
priest shall burn it upon the *a* ... Lev 3:11
thereof upon the *a* round about ... Lev 3:13
priest shall burn them upon the *a* ... Lev 3:16
the *a* of sweet incense before the ... Lev 4:7
of the *a* of the burnt offering ... Lev 4:7
upon the *a* of the burnt offering ... Lev 4:10
of the *a* which is before the LORD ... Lev 4:18
of the *a* of the burnt offering ... Lev 4:18
from him, and burn it upon the *a* ... Lev 4:19
horns of the *a* of burnt offering ... Lev 4:25
bottom of the *a* of burnt offering ... Lev 4:25
shall burn all his fat upon the *a* ... Lev 4:26
horns of the *a* of burnt offering ... Lev 4:30
thereof at the bottom of the *a* ... Lev 4:30
the *a* for a sweet savour unto the ... Lev 4:31
horns of the *a* of burnt offering ... Lev 4:34
thereof at the bottom of the *a* ... Lev 4:34
priest shall burn them upon the *a* ... Lev 4:35
offering upon the side of the *a* ... Lev 5:9
wrung out at the bottom of the *a* ... Lev 5:9
thereof, and burn it on the *a* ... Lev 5:12
the *a* all night unto the morning ... Lev 6:9
the fire of the *a* shall be ... Lev 6:9
with the burnt offering on the *a* ... Lev 6:10
and he shall put them beside the *a* ... Lev 6:10
the fire upon the *a* shall be ... Lev 6:12
shall ever be burning upon the *a* ... Lev 6:13
it before the LORD, before the *a* ... Lev 6:14
it upon the *a* for a sweet savour ... Lev 6:15
sprinkle round about upon the *a* ... Lev 7:2
*a* for an offering made by fire ... Lev 7:5
shall burn the fat upon the *a* ... Lev 7:31
thereof upon the *a* seven times ... Lev 8:11
seven times, and anointed the *a* ... Lev 8:11
the *a* round about with his finger ... Lev 8:15
his finger, and purified the *a* ... Lev 8:15
the blood at the bottom of the *a* ... Lev 8:15
and Moses burned it upon the *a* ... Lev 8:16
the blood upon the *a* round about ... Lev 8:19
burnt the whole ram upon the *a* ... Lev 8:21
the blood upon the *a* round about ... Lev 8:24
burnt them on the *a* upon the ... Lev 8:28
of the blood which was upon the *a* ... Lev 8:30
said unto Aaron, Go unto the *a* ... Lev 9:7
Aaron therefore went unto the *a* ... Lev 9:8
and put it upon the horns of the *a* ... Lev 9:9
the blood at the bottom of the *a* ... Lev 9:9
sin offering, he burnt upon the *a* ... Lev 9:10
sprinkled round about upon the *a* ... Lev 9:12
and he burnt them upon the *a* ... Lev 9:13
upon the burnt offering on the *a* ... Lev 9:14
thereof, and burnt it upon the *a* ... Lev 9:17
sprinkled upon the *a* round about ... Lev 9:18
and he burnt the fat upon the *a* ... Lev 9:20
consumed upon the *a* the burnt ... Lev 9:24
it without leaven beside the *a* ... Lev 10:12
and the meat offering upon the *a* ... Lev 14:20
from off the *a* before the LORD ... Lev 16:12
the *a* that is before the LORD ... Lev 16:18
the horns of the *a* round about ... Lev 16:18
of the congregation, and the *a* ... Lev 16:20
offering shall he burn upon the *a* ... Lev 16:25
of the congregation, and for the *a* ... Lev 16:33
sprinkle the blood upon the *a* of ... Lev 17:6
*a* to make an atonement for your ... Lev 17:11
vail, nor come nigh unto the *a* ... Lev 21:23
of them upon the *a* unto the LORD ... Lev 22:22
by the *a* round about, and the ... Num 3:26
upon the golden *a* they shall ... Num 4:11
take away the ashes from the *a* ... Num 4:13
basons, all the vessels of the *a* ... Num 4:14
by the *a* round about, and their ... Num 4:26
the LORD, and offer it upon the *a* ... Num 5:25
thereof, and burn it upon the *a* ... Num 5:26
instruments thereof, both the *a* ... Num 7:1
offered for dedicating of the *a* ... Num 7:10
their offering before the *a* ... Num 7:10
day, for the dedicating of the *a* ... Num 7:11
This was the dedication of the *a* ... Num 7:84
This was the dedication of the *a* ... Num 7:88
plates for a covering of the *a* ... Num 16:38
plates for a covering of the *a* ... Num 16:39
put fire therein from off the *a* ... Num 16:46
vessels of the sanctuary and the *a* ... Num 18:3
sanctuary, and the charge of the *a* ... Num 18:5
office for every thing of the *a* ... Num 18:7
sprinkle their blood upon the *a* ... Num 18:17
offered on every *a* a bullock ... Num 23:2
offered upon every *a* a bullock ... Num 23:4
a bullock and a ram on every *a* ... Num 23:14
a bullock and a ram on every *a* ... Num 23:30
upon the *a* of the LORD thy God ... Deut 12:27
upon the *a* of the LORD thy God ... Deut 12:27
unto the *a* of the LORD thy God ... Deut 16:21
before the *a* of the LORD thy God ... Deut 26:4
there shalt thou build an *a* ... Deut 27:5
the LORD thy God, an *a* of stones ... Deut 27:5
Thou shalt build the *a* of the ... Deut 27:6
burnt sacrifice upon thine *a* ... Deut 33:10
Then Joshua built an *a* unto the ... Josh 8:30
an *a* of whole stones, over which ... Josh 8:31
for the *a* of the LORD, even unto ... Josh 9:27
*a* by Jordan, a great *a* ... Josh 22:10
*a* over against the land of Canaan ... Josh 22:11
in that ye have builded you an *a* ... Josh 22:16
an *a* beside the *a* of the LORD ... Josh 22:19
That we have built us an *a* to ... Josh 22:23
us now prepare to build us an *a* ... Josh 22:26
the pattern of the *a* of the LORD ... Josh 22:28
to build an *a* for burnt offerings ... Josh 22:29
beside the *a* of the LORD our God ... Josh 22:29
children of Gad called the *a* Ed ... Josh 22:34
built an *a* there unto the LORD ... Judg 6:24
throw down the *a* of Baal that thy ... Judg 6:25
build an *a* unto the LORD thy God ... Judg 6:26
the *a* of Baal was cast down, and ... Judg 6:28
offered upon the *a* that was built ... Judg 6:28
he hath cast down the *a* of Baal ... Judg 6:30
because one hath cast down his *a* ... Judg 6:31
because he hath thrown down his *a* ... Judg 6:32
up toward heaven from off the *a* ... Judg 13:20
ascended in the flame of the *a* ... Judg 13:20
rose early, and built there an *a* ... Judg 21:4
my priest, to offer upon mine *a* ... 1Sa 2:28
I shall not cut off from mine *a* ... 1Sa 2:33
there he built an *a* unto the LORD ... 1Sa 7:17
And Saul built an *a* unto the LORD ... 1Sa 14:35
the same was the first *a* that he ... 1Sa 14:35
rear an *a* unto the LORD in the ... 2Sa 24:18
to build an *a* unto the LORD, that ... 2Sa 24:21
built there an *a* unto the LORD ... 2Sa 24:25
caught hold on the horns of the *a* ... 1Kin 1:50
caught hold on the horns of the *a* ... 1Kin 1:51
they brought him down from the *a* ... 1Kin 1:53
caught hold on the horns of the *a* ... 1Kin 2:28
and, behold, he is by the *a* ... 1Kin 2:29
did Solomon offer upon that *a* ... 1Kin 3:4
so covered the *a* which was of ... 1Kin 6:20
also the whole *a* that was by the ... 1Kin 6:22
the *a* of gold, and the table of ... 1Kin 7:48
Solomon stood before the *a* of the ... 1Kin 8:22
come before thine *a* in this house ... 1Kin 8:31
from before the *a* of the LORD ... 1Kin 8:54
because the brasen *a* that was ... 1Kin 8:64
peace offerings upon the *a* which ... 1Kin 9:25
the *a* that was before the LORD ... 1Kin 9:25
Judah, and he offered upon the *a* ... 1Kin 12:32
So he offered upon the *a* which he ... 1Kin 12:33
and he offered upon the *a*, and ... 1Kin 12:33
stood by the *a* to burn incense ... 1Kin 13:1
he cried against the *a* in the ... 1Kin 13:2
of the LORD, and said, O *a*, *a* ... 1Kin 13:2
the *a* shall be rent, and the ashes ... 1Kin 13:3
cried against the *a* in Beth-el ... 1Kin 13:4
he put forth his hand from the *a* ... 1Kin 13:4
The *a* also was rent ... 1Kin 13:5
the ashes poured out from the *a* ... 1Kin 13:5
the LORD against the *a* in Beth-el ... 1Kin 13:32
he reared up an *a* for Baal in the ... 1Kin 16:32
leaped upon the *a* which was made ... 1Kin 18:26
he repaired the *a* of the LORD ... 1Kin 18:30
an *a* in the name of the LORD ... 1Kin 18:32
and he made a trench about the *a* ... 1Kin 18:32
the water ran round about the *a* ... 1Kin 18:35
of the temple, along by the *a* ... 2Kin 11:11
lid of it, and set it beside the *a* ... 2Kin 12:9
saw an *a* that was at Damascus ... 2Kin 16:10
the priest the fashion of the *a* ... 2Kin 16:10
Urijah the priest built an *a* ... 2Kin 16:11
from Damascus, the king saw the *a* .. 2Kin 16:12
and the king approached to the *a* ... 2Kin 16:12
his peace offerings, upon the *a* ... 2Kin 16:13
And he brought also the brasen *a* ... 2Kin 16:14
of the house, from between the *a* ... 2Kin 16:14
put it on the north side of the *a* ... 2Kin 16:14
Upon the great *a* burn the morning .. 2Kin 16:15
the brasen *a* shall be for me to ... 2Kin 16:15
before this *a* in Jerusalem ... 2Kin 18:22
to the *a* of the LORD in Jerusalem ... 2Kin 23:9
Moreover the *a* that was at ... 2Kin 23:15
to sin, had made, both that *a* ... 2Kin 23:15
and burned them upon the *a* ... 2Kin 23:16
done against the *a* of Beth-el ... 2Kin 23:17
upon the *a* of the burnt offering ... 1Chr 6:49
on the *a* of incense, and were ... 1Chr 6:49
upon the *a* of the burnt offering ... 1Chr 16:40
set up an *a* unto the LORD in the ... 1Chr 21:18
that I may build an *a* therein ... 1Chr 21:22
built there an *a* unto the LORD ... 1Chr 21:26
fire upon the *a* of burnt offering ... 1Chr 21:26
the *a* of the burnt offering, were ... 1Chr 21:29
this is the *a* of the burnt ... 1Chr 22:1
for the *a* of incense refined gold ... 1Chr 28:18
Moreover the brasen *a*, that ... 2Chr 1:5
to the brasen *a* before the LORD ... 2Chr 1:6
Moreover he made an *a* of brass ... 2Chr 4:1
house of God, the golden *a* also ... 2Chr 4:19
stood at the east end of the *a* ... 2Chr 5:12
he stood before the *a* of the LORD ... 2Chr 6:12
come before thine *a* in this house ... 2Chr 6:22
because the brasen *a* which ... 2Chr 7:7
dedication of the *a* seven days ... 2Chr 7:9
the LORD on the *a* of the LORD ... 2Chr 8:12
and renewed the *a* of the LORD ... 2Chr 15:8
of the temple, along by the *a* ... 2Chr 23:10
incense upon the *a* of incense ... 2Chr 26:16
LORD, from beside the incense *a* ... 2Chr 26:19
the *a* of burnt offering, with all ... 2Chr 29:18
they are before the *a* of the LORD ... 2Chr 29:19
offer them on the *a* of the LORD ... 2Chr 29:21
blood, and sprinkled it on the *a* ... 2Chr 29:22
sprinkled the blood upon the *a* ... 2Chr 29:22
sprinkled the blood upon the *a* ... 2Chr 29:22
with their blood upon the *a* ... 2Chr 29:24
the burnt offering upon the *a* ... 2Chr 29:27
Ye shall worship before one *a* ... 2Chr 32:12
And he repaired the *a* of the LORD ... 2Chr 33:16
offerings upon the *a* of the LORD ... 2Chr 35:16
builded the *a* of the God of ... Ezr 3:2
they set the *a* upon his bases ... Ezr 3:3
offer them upon the *a* of the ... Ezr 7:17
to burn upon the *a* of the LORD ... Neh 10:34
so will I compass thine *a* ... Ps 26:6
Then will I go unto the *a* of God ... Ps 43:4
they offer bullocks upon thine *a* ... Ps 51:19
even unto the horns of the *a* ... Ps 118:27
with the tongs from off the *a* ... Is 6:6
In that day shall there be an *a* ... Is 19:19
*a* as chalkstones that are beaten ... Is 27:9
Ye shall worship before this *a* ... Is 36:7
shall be accepted upon mine *a* ... Is 56:7
come up with acceptance on mine *a* ... Is 60:7
The Lord hath cast off his *a* ... Lam 2:7
northward at the gate of the *a* ... Eze 8:5
LORD, between the porch and the *a* ... Eze 8:16
in, and stood beside the brasen *a* ... Eze 9:2
keepers of the charge of the *a* ... Eze 40:46
the *a* that was before the house ... Eze 40:47
The *a* of wood was three cubits ... Eze 41:22
of the *a* after the cubits ... Eze 43:13
be the higher place of the *a* ... Eze 43:13
So the *a* shall be four cubits ... Eze 43:15
and from the *a* and upward shall be ... Eze 43:15
the *a* shall be twelve cubits long ... Eze 43:16
*a* in the day when they shall make ... Eze 43:18
and they shall cleanse the *a* ... Eze 43:22
Seven days shall they purge the *a* ... Eze 43:26
your burnt offerings upon the *a* ... Eze 43:27
corners of the settle of the *a* ... Eze 45:19
house, at the south side of the *a* ... Eze 47:1
howl, ye ministers of the *a* ... Joel 1:13
weep between the porch and the *a* ... Joel 2:17
clothes laid to pledge by every *a* ... Amos 2:8
horns of the *a* shall be cut off ... Amos 3:14
saw the Lord standing upon the *a* ... Amos 9:1
bowls, and as the corners of the *a* ... Zec 9:15
be like the bowls before the *a* ... Zec 14:20
offer polluted bread upon mine *a* ... Mal 1:7
kindle fire on mine *a* for nought ... Mal 1:10
covering the *a* of the LORD with ... Mal 2:13
if thou bring thy gift to the *a* ... Mt 5:23
Leave there thy gift before the *a* ... Mt 5:24
Whosoever shall swear by the *a* ... Mt 23:18
or the *a* that sanctifieth the ... Mt 23:19
therefore shall swear by the *a* ... Mt 23:20
slew between the temple and the *a* ... Mt 23:35
right side of the *a* of incense ... Lk 1:11
which perished between the *a* ... Lk 11:51
devotions, I found an *a* with this ... Acts 17:23
*a* are partakers with the *a* ... 1Cor 9:13
the sacrifices partakers of the *a* ... 1Cor 10:18
no man gave attendance at the *a* ... Heb 7:13
We have an *a*, whereof they have ... Heb 13:10
offered Isaac his son upon the *a* ... Jas 2:21
I saw under the *a* the souls of ... Rev 6:9
angel came and stood at the *a* ... Rev 8:3
*a* which was before the throne ... Rev 8:3
and filled it with fire of the *a* ... Rev 8:5
the golden *a* which is before God ... Rev 9:13
the temple of God, and the *a* ... Rev 11:1
another angel came out from the *a* ... Rev 14:18
I heard another out of the *a* say ... Rev 16:7

## ALTARS

But ye shall destroy their *a* ... Ex 34:13
and the candlestick, and the *a* ... Num 3:31
unto Balak, Build me here seven *a* ... Num 23:1
unto him, I have prepared seven *a* ... Num 23:4
top of Pisgah, and built seven *a* ... Num 23:14
unto Balak, Build me here seven *a* ... Num 23:29
ye shall destroy their *a*, and ... Deut 7:5
And ye shall overthrow their *a* ... Deut 12:3
ye shall throw down their *a* ... Judg 2:2
thy covenant, thrown down thine *a* .. 1Kin 19:10
thy covenant, thrown down thine *a* .. 1Kin 19:14
his *a* and his images brake they in ... 2Kin 11:18
the priest of Baal before the *a* ... 2Kin 11:18
whose *a* Hezekiah hath taken away,. 2Kin 18:22
and he reared up *a* for Baal ... 2Kin 21:3
he built *a* in the house of the ... 2Kin 21:4
he built *a* for all the host of ... 2Kin 21:5
the *a* that were on the top of the ... 2Kin 23:12
the *a* which Manasseh had made in .. 2Kin 23:12
places that were there upon the *a* ... 2Kin 23:20
away the *a* of the strange gods ... 2Chr 14:3
and brake it down, and brake his *a* ... 2Chr 23:17
the priest of Baal before the *a* ... 2Chr 23:17

he made him a in every corner of...... 2Chr 28:24
took away the a that were in.............. 2Chr 30:14
all the a for incense took they........... 2Chr 30:14
the a out of all Judah and.................. 2Chr 31:1
away his high places and his a........... 2Chr 32:12
and he reared up a for Baalim........... 2Chr 33:3
Also he built a in the house of............ 2Chr 33:4
he built a for all the host of................ 2Chr 33:5
all the a that he had built in.............. 2Chr 33:15
they brake down the a of Baalim......... 2Chr 34:4
bones of the priests upon their a.......... 2Chr 34:5
And when he had broken down the a 2Chr 34:7
may lay her young, even thine a............. Ps 84:3
And he shall not look to the a............... Is 17:8
whose a Hezekiah hath taken away,........ Is 36:7
burneth incense upon a of brick............... Is 65:3
set up a to that shameful thing............. Jer 11:13
even a to burn incense unto Baal.......... Jer 11:13
and upon the horns of your a................. Jer 17:1
their children remember their a.............. Jer 17:2
your a shall be desolate, and your.......... Eze 6:4
your bones round about your a............... Eze 6:5
that your a may be laid waste and.......... Eze 6:6
their idols round about their a.............. Eze 6:13
Ephraim hath made many a to sin........ Hos 8:11
a shall be unto him to sin..................... Hos 8:11
his fruit he hath increased the a........... Hos 10:1
he shall break down their a.................. Hos 10:2
thistle shall come up on their a............ Hos 10:8
their a are as heaps in the.................... Hos 12:11
will also visit the a of Beth-el............... Amos 3:14
prophets, and digged down thine a...... Rom 11:3

**ALTASCHITH**
To the chief Musician, A, Michtam.......... Ps 57:t
To the chief Musician, A, Michtam.......... Ps 58:t
To the chief Musician, A, Michtam.......... Ps 59:t
To the chief Musician, A, A Psalm........... Ps 75:t

**AL-TASHHETH** See AL-TASCHITH.

**ALTER**
He shall not a it, nor change it,............ Lev 27:10
that whosoever shall a this word........... Ezr 6:11
that shall put to their hand to a............. Ezr 6:12
nor a the thing that is gone out............. Ps 89:34

**ALTERED**
and the Medes, that it be not a.............. Est 1:19
fashion of his countenance was a........... Lk 9:29

**ALTERETH**
Medes and Persians, which a not.......... Dan 6:8
Medes and Persians, which a not.......... Dan 6:12

**ALTHOUGH**
the Philistines, a that was near............. Ex 13:17
a there was a plague in the................. Josh 22:17
A my house be not so with God............ 2Sa 23:5
desire, a he make it not to grow........... 2Sa 23:5
A I have sent unto thee, saying,........... 1Kin 20:5
a the enemy could not countervail.......... Est 7:4
a thou movedst me against him, to.......... Job 2:3
A affliction cometh not forth of.............. Job 5:6
A thou sayest thou shalt not see.......... Job 35:14
a I was an husband unto them,............. Jer 31:32
is sold, a they were yet alive................ Eze 7:13
A I have cast them far off among.......... Eze 11:16
a I have scattered them among the...... Eze 11:16
A the fig tree shall not blossom,........... Hab 3:17
A all shall be offended, yet will............ Mk 14:29
a the works were finished from........... Heb 4:3

**ALTOGETHER**
done a according to the cry of it.......... Gen 18:21
surely thrust you out hence a.................. Ex 11:1
And mount Sinai was a on a smoke...... Ex 19:18
make thyself a a prince over us......... Num 16:13
behold, thou hast blessed them a........ Num 23:11
thou hast a blessed them these.......... Num 24:10
But if her husband a hold his............. Num 30:14
That which is a just shalt thou.......... Deut 16:20
that he would not destroy him a......... 2Chr 12:12
For if thou a holdest thy peace........... Est 4:14
that ye would a hold your peace......... Job 13:5
why then are ye thus a vain................ Job 27:12
the LORD are true and righteous a......... Ps 19:9
man at his best state is a vanity............ Ps 39:5
I was a such an one as thyself.............. Ps 50:21
they are a become filthy........................ Ps 53:3
they are a lighter than vanity................ Ps 62:9
lo, O LORD, thou knowest it a................. Ps 139:4
yea, he is a lovely............................... Song 5:16
saith, Are not my princes a kings............. Is 10:8
but these have a broken the yoke,............ Jer 5:5
But they are a brutish and foolish.......... Jer 10:8
wilt thou be a unto me as a liar,............ Jer 15:18
will not leave thee a unpunished........... Jer 30:11
he that shall a go unpunished.............. Jer 49:12
Thou wast a born in sins, and dost......... Jn 9:34
a such as I am, except these............. Acts 26:29
Yet not a with the fornicators of......... 1Cor 5:10
Or saith he it a for our sakes............. 1Cor 9:10

**ALUSH** (*a'-lush*) *An Israelite encampment during the Exodus.*
from Dophkah, and encamped in A.. Num 33:13
And they removed from A, and.......... Num 33:14

**ALVAH** (*al'-vah*) See ALIAH. *An Edomite chief.*
duke Timnah, duke A, duke Jetheth.. Gen 36:40

**ALVAN** (*al'-van*) See ALIAN. *A son of Shobal the Horite.*
A, and Manahath, and Ebal, Shepho,. Gen 36:23

**ALWAY**
the table shewbread before me a.......... Ex 25:30
So it was a........................................ Num 9:16
and his commandments, a.................... Deut 11:1
be only oppressed and crushed a....... Deut 28:33
son shall eat bread a at my table.......... 2Sa 9:10
a light a before me in Jerusalem....... 1Kin 11:36
him to give him a a light.................... 2Kin 8:19
I would not live a................................ Job 7:16
needy shall not a be forgotten................. Ps 9:18
heart to perform thy statutes a.......... Ps 119:112
Happy is the man that feareth a....... Prov 28:14
and, lo, I am with you a, even............. Mt 28:20
but your time is a ready........................... Jn 7:6
to the people, and prayed to God a....... Acts 10:2
not see, and bow down their back a.. Rom 11:10
For we which live are a delivered....... 2Cor 4:11
As sorrowful, yet a rejoicing............... 2Cor 6:10
Rejoice in the Lord a............................. Phil 4:4
Let your speech be a with grace............ Col 4:6
be saved, to fill up their sins a.............. 1Th 2:16
to give thanks a to God for you............. 2Th 2:13
said, The Cretians are a liars............... Titus 1:12
They do a err in their heart................ Heb 3:10

**ALWAYS**
shall not a strive with man................... Gen 6:3
to cause the lamp to burn a.................. Ex 27:20
it shall be a upon his forehead,............ Ex 28:38
keep all my commandments a............. Deut 5:29
the LORD our God, for our good a......... Deut 6:24
of the LORD thy God are a upon it.... Deut 11:12
learn to fear the LORD thy God a....... Deut 14:23
Be ye mindful a of his covenant.......... 1Chr 16:15
good unto me, but a evil..................... 2Chr 18:7
will he a call upon God...................... Job 27:10
Great men are not a wise.................... Job 32:9
His ways are a grievous........................ Ps 10:5
I have set the LORD a before me.............. Ps 16:8
He will not a chide............................ Ps 103:9
be thou ravished a with her love.......... Prov 5:19
delight, rejoicing a before him............ Prov 8:30
Let thy garments be a white................. Eccl 9:8
ever, neither will I be a wroth............... Is 57:16
and her womb to be a great with me... Jer 20:17
Israel, which have been a waste........... Eze 38:8
do a behold the face of my Father.......... Mt 18:10
For ye have the poor a with you.......... Mt 26:11
but me ye have not a......................... Mt 26:11
And a, night and day, he was in the....... Mk 5:5
For ye have the poor with you a........... Mk 14:7
but me ye have not a........................... Mk 14:7
end, that men ought a to pray................ Lk 18:1
Watch ye therefore, and pray a............. Lk 21:36
for I do a those things that.................... Jn 8:29
And I knew that thou hearest me a....... Jn 11:42
For the poor a ye have with you............ Jn 12:8
but me ye have not a............................ Jn 12:8
temple, whither the Jews a resort.......... Jn 18:20
foresaw the Lord a before my face....... Acts 2:25
ye do a resist the Holy Ghost............... Acts 7:51
We accept it a, and in all places,......... Acts 24:3
to have a a conscience void of............ Acts 24:16
mention of you a in my prayers............ Rom 1:9
I thank my God a on your behalf.......... 1Cor 1:4
a abounding in the work of the.......... 1Cor 15:58
which a causeth us to triumph in........ 2Cor 2:14
A bearing about in the body the.......... 2Cor 4:10
Therefore we are a confident............... 2Cor 5:6
a having all sufficiency in all.............. 2Cor 9:8
affected a in a good thing..................... Gal 4:18
Giving thanks a for all things............... Eph 5:20
Praying a with all prayer and.............. Eph 6:18
A in every prayer of mine for you.......... Phil 1:4
but that with all boldness, as a........... Phil 1:20
my beloved, as ye have a obeyed........... Phil 2:12
Jesus Christ, praying a for you............... Col 1:3
a labouring fervently for you in............ Col 4:12
give thanks to God a for you all............. 1Th 1:2
ye have good remembrance of us a......... 1Th 3:6
are bound to thank God a for you........... 2Th 1:3
Wherefore also we pray a for you.......... 2Th 1:11
give you peace a by all means............. 2Th 3:16
mention of thee a in my prayers........... Philem 4
the priests went a into the first............. Heb 9:6
be ready a to give an answer to........... 1Pet 3:15
not be negligent to put you a in.......... 2Pet 1:12
these things a in remembrance........... 2Pet 1:15

**AM** See PREFACE.

**AMAD** (*a'-mad*) *A town on the border of Asher.*
And Alammelech, and A...................... Josh 19:26

**AMAL** (*a'-mal*) *A descendant of Asher.*
and Imna, and Shelesh, and A.............. 1Chr 7:35

**AMALEK** (*am'-al-ek*) See AMALEKITE.
*1. The son of Eliphaz.*
and she bare to Eliphaz A.................. Gen 36:12
duke Gatam, and duke A................... Gen 36:16
and Gatam, Kenaz, and Timna, and A 1Chr 1:36
*2. Descendants of Amalek.*
Then came A, and fought with................ Ex 17:8
out men, and go out, fight with A.......... Ex 17:9
had said to him, and fought with A....... Ex 17:10
he let down his hand, A prevailed.......... Ex 17:11
And Joshua discomfited A and his......... Ex 17:13
of A from under heaven..................... Ex 17:14
the LORD will have war with A.............. Ex 17:16
And when he looked on A, he took... Num 24:20
A was the first of the nations............ Num 24:20
Remember what A did unto thee by. Deut 25:17
of A from under heaven..................... Deut 25:19
him the children of Ammon and A...... Judg 3:13
there a root of them against A............. Judg 5:14
that which A did to Israel...................... 1Sa 15:2
Now go and smite A, and utterly........... 1Sa 15:3
And Saul came to a city of A................ 1Sa 15:5
have brought Agag the king of A........ 1Sa 15:20
his fierce wrath upon A,.................... 1Sa 28:18
and of the Philistines, and of A............ 2Sa 8:12
from the Philistinesand, from A......... 1Chr 18:11
Gebal, and Ammon, and A...................... Ps 83:7

**AMALEKITE** (*am'-al-ek-ite*) See AMALEKITES.
*A descendant of Amalek.*
man of Egypt, servant to an A............. 1Sa 30:13
And I answered him, I am an A.............. 2Sa 1:8
I am the son of a stranger, an A.......... 2Sa 1:13

**AMALEKITES** (*am'-al-ek-ites*)
and smote all the country of the A....... Gen 14:7
The A dwell in the land of the.......... Num 13:29
(Now the A and the Canaanites......... Num 14:25
For the A and the Canaanites are..... Num 14:43
Then the A came down, and the.......... Num 14:45
the Midianites came up, and the A......... Judg 6:3
Then all the Midianites and the A....... Judg 6:33
And the Midianites and the A............. Judg 7:12
The Zidonians also, and the A.......... Judg 10:12
of Ephraim, in the mount of the A.... Judg 12:15
gathered an host, and smote the A...... 1Sa 14:48
get you down from among the A............. 1Sa 15:6
Kenites departed from among the A...... 1Sa 15:6
Saul smote the A from Havilah............. 1Sa 15:7
took Agag the king of the A alive.......... 1Sa 15:8
They have brought them from the A.. 1Sa 15:15
utterly destroy the sinners the A.......... 1Sa 15:18
and have utterly destroyed the A......... 1Sa 15:20
to me Agag the king of the A.............. 1Sa 15:32
and the Gezrites, and the A................. 1Sa 27:8
that the A had invaded the south,......... 1Sa 30:1
all that the A had carried away.......... 1Sa 30:18
from the slaughter of the A................... 2Sa 1:1
rest of the A that were escaped........... 1Chr 4:43

**AMAM** (*a'-mam*) *A city near Shema and Moladah.*
A, and Shema, and Moladah,............... Josh 15:26

**AMANA** (*am-a'-nah*) *A city in southern Judah.*
look from the top of A, from the.......... Song 4:8

**AMARIAH** (*am-a-ri'-ah*)
*1. A descendant of Aaron.*
begat A, and A begat Ahitub,................ 1Chr 6:7
A his son, Ahitub his son,..................... 1Chr 6:52
The son of A, the son of Azariah,............ Ezr 7:3
*2. A High Priest during Solomon's reign.*
begat Amariah, and A begat Ahitub,... 1Chr 6:11
*3. A descendant of Kohath.*
A the second, Jahaziel the third,......... 1Chr 23:19
A the second, Jahaziel the third,......... 1Chr 24:23
*4. Chief priest during Jehoshaphat's reign.*
A the chief priest is over you in.......... 2Chr 19:11
*5. A Levite in Hezekiah's time.*
and Jeshua, and Shemaiah, A............ 2Chr 31:15
*6. Married a foreign wife in Exile.*
Shallum, A, and Joseph......................... Ezr 10:42
*7. A priest who sealed the covenant with Nehemiah.*
Pashur, A, Malchijah,.............................. Neh 10:3
A, Malluch, Hattush,............................... Neh 12:2
of A, Jehohanan..................................... Neh 12:13
*8. A descendant of Judah.*
son of Zechariah, the son of A............. Neh 11:4
*9. An ancestor of Zephaniah the prophet.*
the son of Gedaliah, the son of A.......... Zeph 1:1

**AMASA** (*am'-a-sah*)
*1. David's nephew.*
Absalom made A captain of the............ 2Sa 17:25
which A was a man's son, whose.......... 2Sa 17:25
And say ye to A, Art thou not of.......... 2Sa 19:13
Then said the king to A, Assemble........ 2Sa 20:4
So A went to assemble the men of......... 2Sa 20:5
is in Gibeon, A went before them........... 2Sa 20:8
And Joab said to A, Art thou in............ 2Sa 20:9
And Joab took A, by the beard with..... 2Sa 20:9
But A took no heed to the sword......... 2Sa 20:10
A wallowed in blood in the midst.......... 2Sa 20:12
he removed A out of the highway......... 2Sa 20:12
unto A the son of Jether, whom he....... 1Kin 2:5
A the son of Jether, captain of............ 1Kin 2:32
And Abigail bare A.............................. 1Chr 2:17
the father of A was Jether the............. 1Chr 2:17
*2. An Ephraimite who opposed the slavery of the Jews.*
A the son of Hadlai, stood up............ 2Chr 28:12

**AMASAI** (*am'-as-ahee*)
*1. A descendant of Kohath.*
A, and Ahimoth.................................... 1Chr 6:25
the son of Mahath, the son of A.......... 1Chr 6:35
arose, Mahath the son of A................ 2Chr 29:12
*2. A captain in David's army.*
Then the spirit came upon A................ 1Chr 12:18
*3. A Levite who helped relocate the Ark.*
Jehoshaphat, and Nethaneel, and A.. 1Chr 15:24

**AMASHAI** (*am'-ash-ahee*) *A priest of the Emmer family.*
A the son of Azareel, the son of.......... Neh 11:13

**AMASHSAI** See AMASHI.

**AMASIAH** (*am-a-si'-ah*) *Chief captain of Jehoshaphat's army.*
next him was *A* the son of Zichri, 2Chr 17:16

**AMAZED**
Then the dukes of Edom shall be *a* Ex 15:15
again, the men of Benjamin were *a* Judg 20:41
They were *a*, they answered no Job 32:15
they shall be *a* one at another Is 13:8
I will make many people *a* at thee Eze 32:10
And all the people were *a*, and said Mt 12:23
heard it, they were exceedingly *a* Mt 19:25
And they were all *a*, insomuch that Mk 1:27
insomuch that they were all *a* Mk 2:12
they were sore *a* in themselves Mk 6:51
they beheld him, were greatly *a* Mk 9:15
and they were *a* Mk 10:32
and John, and began to be sore *a* Mk 14:33
for they trembled and were *a* Mk 16:8
And when they saw him, they were *a* Lk 2:48
And they were all *a*, and spake Lk 4:36
And they were all *a*, and they Lk 5:26
they were all *a* at the mighty Lk 9:43
And they were all *a* and marvelled, Acts 2:7
And they were all *a*, and were in Acts 2:12
But all that heard him were *a* Acts 9:21

**AMAZEMENT**
*a* at that which had happened unto Acts 3:10
and are not afraid with any *a* 1Pet 3:6

**AMAZIAH** (*am-a-zi'-ah*)
*1. Son and successor of King Joash of Judah.*
*A* his son reigned in his stead 2Kin 12:21
he fought against *A* king of Judah 2Kin 13:12
*A* the son of Joash king of Judah 2Kin 14:1
Then *A* sent messengers to Jehoash 2Kin 14:8
of Israel sent to *A* king of Judah 2Kin 14:9
But *A* would not hear 2Kin 14:11
*A* king of Judah looked one 2Kin 14:11
of Israel took *A* king of Judah 2Kin 14:13
he fought with *A* king of Judah 2Kin 14:15
*A* the son of Joash king of Judah 2Kin 14:17
And the rest of the acts of *A* 2Kin 14:18
him king instead of his father *A* 2Kin 14:21
In the fifteenth year of *A* the 2Kin 14:23
son of *A* king of Judah to reign 2Kin 15:1
to all that his father *A* had done 2Kin 15:3
*A* his son, Azariah his son, 1Chr 3:12
*A* his son reigned in his stead 2Chr 24:27
*A* was twenty and five years old 2Chr 25:1
Moreover *A* gathered Judah 2Chr 25:5
*A* said to the man of God, But 2Chr 25:9
Then *A* separated them, to wit, 2Chr 25:10
*A* strengthened himself, and led 2Chr 25:11
of the army which *A* sent back 2Chr 25:13
after that *A* was come from the 2Chr 25:14
of the LORD was kindled against *A* 2Chr 25:15
Then *A* king of Judah took advice, 2Chr 25:17
of Israel sent to *A* king of Judah 2Chr 25:18
But *A* would not hear 2Chr 25:20
*A* king of Judah, at Beth-shemesh, 2Chr 25:21
of Israel took *A* king of Judah 2Chr 25:23
*A* the son of Joash king of Judah 2Chr 25:25
Now the rest of the acts of *A* 2Chr 25:26
Now after the time that *A* did 2Chr 25:27
king in the room of his father *A* 2Chr 26:1
to all that his father *A* did 2Chr 26:4
*2. A Simeonite.*
Jamlech, and Joshah the son of *A* 1Chr 4:34
*3. A Levite from the Merari family.*
son of Hashabiah, the son of *A* 1Chr 6:45
*4. Priest of the idols at Bethel.*
Then *A* the priest of Beth-el sent Amos 7:10
Also *A* said unto Amos, O thou Amos 7:12
Then answered Amos, and said to *A*. Amos 7:14

**AMBASSADOR**
but a faithful *a* is health Prov 13:17
an *a* is sent unto the heathen, Jer 49:14
an *a* is sent among the heathen, Obad 1
For which I am an *a* in bonds Eph 6:20

**AMBASSADORS**
and made as if they had been *a* Josh 9:4
the *a* of the princes of Babylon 2Chr 32:31
But he sent *a* to him, saying, 2Chr 35:21
That sendeth *a* by the sea Is 18:2
at Zoan, and his *a* came to Hanes Is 30:4
the *a* of peace shall weep Is 33:7
him in sending his *a* into Egypt Eze 17:15
Now then we are *a* for Christ 2Cor 5:20

**AMBASSAGE**
a great way off, he sendeth an *a* Lk 14:32

**AMBER**
midst thereof as the colour of *a* Eze 1:4
And I saw as the colour of *a* Eze 1:27
of brightness, as the colour of *a* Eze 8:2

**AMBUSH**
lay thee an *a* for the city behind Josh 8:2
Then ye shall rise up from the *a* Josh 8:7
and they went to lie in *a*, and Josh 8:9
them to lie in *a* between Beth-el Josh 8:12
in *a* against him behind the city Josh 8:14
the *a* arose quickly out of their Josh 8:19
saw that the *a* had taken the city Josh 8:21

**AMBUSHES**
up the watchmen, prepare the *a* Jer 51:12

**AMBUSHMENT**
But Jeroboam caused an *a* to come 2Chr 13:13
Judah, and the *a* was behind them 2Chr 13:13

**AMBUSHMENTS**
the LORD set *a* against the 2Chr 20:22

**AMEN**
*1. A term meaning "so be it."*
And the woman shall say, *A*, *a* Num 5:22
the people shall answer and say, *A* Deut 27:15
and all the people shall say, *A* Deut 27:16
And all the people shall say, *A* Deut 27:17
And all the people shall say, *A* Deut 27:18
And all the people shall say, *A* Deut 27:19
And all the people shall say, *A* Deut 27:20
And all the people shall say, *A* Deut 27:21
And all the people shall say, *A* Deut 27:22
And all the people shall say, *A* Deut 27:23
And all the people shall say, *A* Deut 27:24
And all the people shall say, *A* Deut 27:25
And all the people shall say, *A* Deut 27:26
answered the king, and said, *A* 1Kin 1:36
And all the people said, *A* 1Chr 16:36
And all the congregation said, *A* Neh 5:13
all the people answered, *A*, *A* Neh 8:6
*A*, and *A* Ps 41:13
*A*, and *A* Ps 72:19
*A*, and *A* Ps 89:52
and let all the people say, *A* Ps 106:48
Even the prophet Jeremiah said, *A* Jer 28:6
and the glory, for ever. *A*. Mt 6:13
the end of the world. *A*. Mt 28:20
with signs following. *A*. Mk 16:20
praising and blessing God. *A*. Lk 24:53
that should be written. *A*. Jn 21:25
who is blessed for ever. *A*. Rom 1:25
God blessed for ever. *A*. Rom 9:5
to whom be glory for ever. *A*. Rom 11:36
peace be with you all. *A*. Rom 15:33
Jesus Christ be with you. *A*. Rom 16:20
Jesus Christ be with you all. *A*. Rom 16:24
through Jesus Christ for ever. *A*. Rom 16:27
say *A* at thy giving of thanks 1Cor 14:16
with you all in Christ Jesus. *A*. 1Cor 16:24
God in him are yea, and in him *A* 2Cor 1:20
Holy Ghost, be with you all. *A*. 2Cor 13:14
be glory for ever and ever. *A*. Gal 1:5
Christ be with your spirit. *A*. Gal 6:18
all ages, world without end. *A*. Eph 3:21
Lord Jesus Christ in sincerity. *A*. Eph 6:24
be glory for ever and ever. *A*. Phil 4:20
Jesus Christ be with you all. *A*. Phil 4:23
Grace be with you. *A*. Col 4:18
Jesus Christ be with you. *A*. 1Th 5:28
Jesus Christ be with you all. *A*. 2Th 3:18
glory for ever and ever. *A*. 1Ti 1:17
honour and power everlasting. *A*. 1Ti 6:16
Grace be with thee. *A*. 1Ti 6:21
be glory for ever and ever. *A*. 2Ti 4:18
Grace be with you. *A*. 2Ti 4:22
Grace be with you all. *A*. Titus 3:15
Christ be with your spirit. *A*. Philem 25
be glory for ever and ever. *A*. Heb 13:21
Grace be with you all. *A*. Heb 13:25
dominion for ever and ever. *A*. 1Pet 4:11
dominion for ever and ever. *A*. 1Pet 5:11
all that are in Christ Jesus. *A*. 1Pet 5:14
glory both now and for ever. *A*. 2Pet 3:18
keep yourselves from idols. *A*. 1Jn 5:21
thy elect sister greet thee. *A*. 2Jn 13
power, both now and ever. *A*. Jude 25
dominion for ever and ever. *A*. Rev 1:6
Even so, *A*. Rev 1:7
I am alive for evermore, *A* Rev 1:18
And the four beasts said, *A* Rev 5:14
Saying, *A*: Blessing, and glory Rev 7:12
our God for ever and ever. *A*. Rev 7:12
sat on the throne, saying, *A*; Rev 19:4
Surely I come quickly. *A*. Rev 22:20
Jesus Christ be with you all. *A*. Rev 22:21
*2. A title of Christ.*
These things saith the *A*, the Rev 3:14

**AMEND**
LORD, to repair and *a* the house 2Chr 34:10
*A* your ways and your doings, and I Jer 7:3
For if ye throughly *a* your ways Jer 7:5
Therefore now *a* your ways Jer 26:13
*a* your doings, and go not after Jer 35:15
them the hour when he began to *a* Jn 4:52

**AMENDS**
he shall make *a* for the harm that Lev 5:16

**AMERCE**
they shall *a* him in an hundred Deut 22:19

**AMETHYST**
row a ligure, an agate, and an *a* Ex 28:19
row, a ligure, an agate, and an *a* Ex 39:12
the twelfth, an *a* Rev 21:20

**AMI** (*a'-mi*) *A family of returned exiles.*
of Zebaim, the children of *A* Ezr 2:57

**AMIABLE**
How *a* are thy tabernacles, O LORD Ps 84:1

**AMINADAB** (*a-min'-a-dab*) See AMMINADAB. *Son of Aram; ancestor of Jesus.*
And Aram begat *A* Mt 1:4
and *A* begat Naasson Mt 1:4
Which was the son of *A*, which was Lk 3:33

**AMISS**
We have sinned, we have done *a* 2Chr 6:37
which speak any thing *a* against Dan 3:29
but this man hath done nothing *a* Lk 23:41
and receive not, because ye ask *a* Jas 4:3

**AMITTAI** (*a-mit'-tahee*) *Father of Jonah.*
his servant Jonah, the son of *A* 2Kin 14:25
LORD came unto Jonah the son of *A* Jonah 1:1

**AMMAH** (*am'-mah*) See METHEG-AMMAH. *A hill near Gibeon.*
they were come to the hill of *A* 2Sa 2:24

**AMMI** (*am'-mi*) See AMMI-NADIB, BEN-AMMI, LO-AMMI. *A name given to Israel by Hosea meaning "my people."*
Say ye unto your brethren, *A* Hos 2:1

**AMMIEL** (*am'-me-el*) See ELIAM.
*1. A spy for Moses.*
of Dan, *A* the son of Gemalli Num 13:12
*2. A Manassehite of Lodebar.*
the house of Machir, the son of *A* 2Sa 9:4
the house of Machir, the son of *A* 2Sa 9:5
Machir the son of *A* of Lo-debar 2Sa 17:27
*3. Father of a wife of David.*
of Bath-shua the daughter of *A* 1Chr 3:5
*4. A Levite Tabernacle servant.*
*A* the sixth, Issachar the seventh 1Chr 26:5

**AMMIHUD** (*am-mi'-hud*)
*1. Father of Elishama.*
Elishama the son of *A* Num 1:10
shall be Elishama the son of *A* Num 2:18
seventh day Elishama the son of *A* Num 7:48
offering of Elishama the son of *A* Num 7:53
host was Elishama the son of *A* Num 10:22
*A* his son, Elishama his son, 1Chr 7:26
*2. A Simeonite.*
of Simeon, Shemuel the son of *A* Num 34:20
*3. A Naphtalite.*
of Naphtali, Pedahel the son of *A* Num 34:28
*4. Father of the king of Geshur.*
and went to Talmai, the son of *A* 2Sa 13:37
*5. A son of Omri.*
Uthai the son of *A*, the son of 1Chr 9:4

**AMMINADAB** (*am-min'-a-dab*) See AMINADAB, AMMI-NADIB.
*1. Aaron's father-in-law.*
took him Elisheba, daughter of *A* Ex 6:23
*2. A prince of Judah.*
Nahshon the son of *A* Num 1:7
Nahshon the son of *A* shall be Num 2:3
day was Nahshon the son of *A* Num 7:12
offering of Nahshon the son of *A* Num 7:17
his host was Nahshon the son of *A* Num 10:14
Hezron begat Ram, and Ram begat *A* Ruth 4:19
*A* begat Nahshon Ruth 4:20
And Ram begat *A* 1Chr 2:10
*A* begat Nahshon, prince of the 1Chr 2:10
*3. A son of Kohath.*
*A* his son, Korah his son, Assir 1Chr 6:22
*4. A Levite who relocated the Ark.*
*A* the chief, and his brethren an 1Chr 15:10
and Joel, Shemaiah, and Eliel, and *A* 1Chr 15:11

**AMMI-NADIB**
made me like the chariots of *A* Song 6:12

**AMMISHADDAI** (*am-mi-shad'-dahee*) *Father of the chief of the tribe of Dan.*
Ahiezer the son of *A* Num 1:12
Dan shall be Ahiezer the son of *A* Num 2:25
tenth day Ahiezer the son of *A* Num 7:66
offering of Ahiezer the son of *A* Num 7:71
his host was Ahiezer the son of *A* Num 10:25

**AMMIZABAD** (*am-miz'-a-bad*) *Son of a captain of David.*
and in his course was *A* his son 1Chr 27:6

**AMMON** (*am'-mon*)
*1. Territory in Jordan.*
the children of *A* unto this day Gen 19:38
even unto the children of *A* Num 21:24
of the children of *A* was strong Num 21:24
over against the children of *A* Deut 2:19
the children of *A* any possession Deut 2:19
the children of *A* thou camest not Deut 2:37
in Rabbath of the children of *A* Deut 3:11
the border of the children of *A* Deut 3:16
the border of the children of *A* Josh 12:2
the border of the children of *A* Josh 13:10
the land of the children of *A* Josh 13:25
unto him the children of *A* Judg 3:13
and the gods of the children of *A* Judg 10:6
the hands of the children of *A* Judg 10:7
Moreover the children of *A* passed Judg 10:9
Amorites, from the children of *A* Judg 10:11
Then the children of *A* were Judg 10:17
fight against the children of *A* Judg 10:18
that the children of *A* made war Judg 11:4
of *A* made war against Israel Judg 11:5
may fight with the children of *A* Judg 11:6
fight against the children of *A* Judg 11:8
fight against the children of *A* Judg 11:9
the king of the children of *A* Judg 11:12
the king of the children of *A* Judg 11:13
the king of the children of *A* Judg 11:14
nor the land of the children of *A* Judg 11:15

of Israel and the children of *A* ........... Judg 11:27
the king of the children of *A* ............... Judg 11:28
over unto the children of *A* .................. Judg 11:29
the children of *A* into mine hands ..... Judg 11:30
in peace from the children of *A* ......... Judg 11:31
of *A* to fight against them ..................... Judg 11:32
Thus the children of *A* were ................. Judg 11:33
even of the children of *A* ...................... Judg 11:36
fight against the children of *A* ............. Judg 12:1
strife with the children of *A* ................ Judg 12:2
over against the children of *A* ............. Judg 12:3
children of *A* came against you ........... 1Sa 12:12
and against the children of *A* ............... 1Sa 14:47
of Moab, and of the children of *A* .......... 2Sa 8:12
king of the children of *A* died .............. 2Sa 10:1
the land of the children of *A* ................ 2Sa 10:2
of *A* said unto Hanun their lord ............ 2Sa 10:3
when the children of *A* saw that ........... 2Sa 10:6
David, the children of *A* sent ............... 2Sa 10:6
And the children of *A* came out ............. 2Sa 10:8
array against the children of *A* ............ 2Sa 10:10
of *A* be too strong for thee ..................... 2Sa 10:11
when the children of *A* saw that ........... 2Sa 10:14
returned from the children of *A* ........... 2Sa 10:14
help the children of *A* any more ............ 2Sa 10:19
they destroyed the children of *A* ........... 2Sa 11:1
the sword of the children of *A* ................ 2Sa 12:9
Rabbah of the children of *A* ................... 2Sa 12:26
the cities of the children of *A* ............... 2Sa 12:31
of Rabbah of the children of *A* ............. 2Sa 17:27
abomination of the children of *A* .......... 1Kin 11:7
the god of the children of *A* .................. 1Kin 11:33
abomination of the children of *A* ........ 2Kin 23:13
and bands of the children of *A* ............. 2Kin 24:2
Moab, and from the children of *A* ...... 1Chr 18:11
king of the children of *A* died ............. 1Chr 19:1
of the children of *A* to Hanun ............... 1Chr 19:2
the children of *A* said to Hanun ........... 1Chr 19:3
when the children of *A* saw that ........... 1Chr 19:6
the children of *A* sent a thousand ........ 1Chr 19:6
the children of *A* gathered .................... 1Chr 19:7
And the children of *A* came out ............ 1Chr 19:9
array against the children of *A* ........... 1Chr 19:11
of *A* be too strong for thee .................... 1Chr 19:12
when the children of *A* saw that ........... 1Chr 19:15
help the children of *A* any more ........ 1Chr 19:19
the country of the children of *A* .......... 1Chr 20:1
the cities of the children of *A* ............. 1Chr 20:3
of Moab, and the children of *A* ............ 2Chr 20:1
And now, behold, the children of *A* ... 2Chr 20:10
against the children of *A* ...................... 2Chr 20:22
For the children of *A* and Moab ........... 2Chr 20:23
the children of *A* gave him the ............. 2Chr 27:5
the children of *A* pay unto him ............ 2Chr 27:5
had married wives of Ashdod, of *A* ...... Neh 13:23
Gebal, and *A*, and Amalek ........................... Ps 83:7
the children of *A* shall obey them .......... Is 11:14
and Edom, and the children of *A* ............. Jer 9:26
and Moab, and the children of *A* .......... Jer 25:21
captivity of the children of *A* .................... Jer 49:6
and the chief of the children of *A* ........ Dan 11:41
of the children of *A*, and for four ...... Amos 1:13
revilings of the children of *A* ................. Zeph 2:8
and the children of *A* as Gomorrah ...... Zeph 2:9

**AMMONITE** (*am'-mon-ite*) See AMMONITES, AMMONITESS. *A descendant of Ammon.*
An *A* or Moabite shall not enter ........... Deut 23:3
Then Nahash the *A* came up .................... 1Sa 11:1
Nahash the *A* answered them, On .......... 1Sa 11:2
Zelek the *A*, Nahari the ......................... 2Sa 23:37
Zelek the *A*, Naharai the ....................... 1Chr 11:39
and Tobiah the servant, the *A* .............. Neh 2:10
and Tobiah the servant, the *A* .............. Neh 2:19
Now Tobiah the *A* was by him ................ Neh 4:3
was found written, that the *A* ............... Neh 13:1

**AMMONITES** (*am'-mon-ites*)
the *A* call them Zamzummims .............. Deut 2:20
slew the *A* until the heat of the ............. 1Sa 11:11
Pharaoh, women of the Moabites, *A* ... 1Kin 11:1
Milcom the abomination of the *A* ......... 1Kin 11:5
and with them other beside the *A* ....... 2Chr 20:1
the *A* gave gifts to Uzziah .................... 2Chr 26:8
also with the king of the *A* .................... 2Chr 27:5
Perizzites, the Jebusites, the *A* .................. Ezr 9:1
Tobiah, and the Arabians, and the *A* ...... Neh 4:7
of Moab, and to the king of the *A* .......... Jer 27:3
that were in Moab, and among the *A* .. Jer 40:11
that Baalis the king of the *A* ................ Jer 40:14
and departed to go over to the *A* ........... Jer 41:10
with eight men, and went to the *A* ....... Jer 41:15
Concerning The *A*, thus saith the ........... Jer 49:1
to be heard in Rabbah of the *A* .............. Jer 49:2
may come to Rabbath of the *A* ............ Eze 21:20
the Lord GOD concerning the *A* ........... Eze 21:28
man, set thy face against the *A* ............ Eze 25:2
And say unto the *A*, Hear the word ...... Eze 25:3
the *A* a couchingplace for flocks ........... Eze 25:5
the men of the east with the *A* ............. Eze 25:10
that the *A* may not be remembered ..... Eze 25:10

**AMMONITESS** (*am'-mon-i-tess*)
name was Naamah an *A* ....................... 1Kin 14:21
name was Naamah an *A* ....................... 1Kin 14:31
name was Naamah an *A* ...................... 2Chr 12:13
Zabad the son of Shimeath an *A* ......... 2Chr 24:26

**AMNON** (*am'-non*) See AMNON'S.
*1. A son of David.*
and his firstborn was *A*, of ......................... 2Sa 3:2
*A* the son of David loved her .................. 2Sa 13:1
*A* was so vexed, that he fell sick ............ 2Sa 13:2
*A* thought it hard for him to do ............. 2Sa 13:2
But *A* had a friend, whose name ........... 2Sa 13:3
*A* said unto him, I love Tamar, my ......... 2Sa 13:4
So *A* lay down, and made himself .......... 2Sa 13:6
*A* said unto the king, I pray thee ........... 2Sa 13:6
*A* said, Have out all men from me ......... 2Sa 13:9
*A* said unto Tamar, Bring the meat ..... 2Sa 13:10
into the chamber to *A* her brother ....... 2Sa 13:10
Then *A* hated her exceedingly ............. 2Sa 13:15
*A* said unto her, Arise, be gone ............ 2Sa 13:15
Hath *A* thy brother been with thee ..... 2Sa 13:20
brother *A* neither good nor bad ............ 2Sa 13:22
for Absalom hated *A*, because he .......... 2Sa 13:22
thee, let my brother *A* go with us ......... 2Sa 13:26
pressed him, that he let *A* ................... 2Sa 13:27
and when I say unto you, Smite *A* ...... 2Sa 13:28
unto *A* as Absalom had commanded ... 2Sa 13:29
for *A* only is dead ................................... 2Sa 13:32
for *A* only is dead ................................... 2Sa 13:33
for he was comforted concerning *A* ...... 2Sa 13:39
the firstborn *A*, of Ahinoam the ............ 1Chr 3:1
*2. A son of Shimon.*
And the sons of Shimon were, *A* ......... 1Chr 4:20

**AMNON'S** (*am'-nons*) *Refers to Amnon 1.*
Go now to thy brother *A* house ............. 2Sa 13:7
Tamar went to her brother *A* house ....... 2Sa 13:8
Mark ye now when *A* heart is merry .. 2Sa 13:28

**AMOK** (*a'-mok*) *A priest who returned from Exile under Zerubbabel.*
Sallu, *A*, Hilkiah, Jedaiah ........................ Neh 12:7
of *A*, Eber ................................................. Neh 12:20

**AMON** (*a'-mon*)
*1. A governor of Samaria.*
carry him back unto *A* the .................. 1Kin 22:26
carry him back to *A* the governor ..... 2Chr 18:25
*2. Son and successor of King Manasseh of Judah.*
*A* his son reigned in his stead ............ 2Kin 21:18
*A* was twenty and two years old ........ 2Kin 21:19
the servants of *A* conspired ................ 2Kin 21:23
that had conspired against king *A* ..... 2Kin 21:24
of the acts of *A* which he did ............. 2Kin 21:25
*A* his son, Josiah his son ....................... 1Chr 3:14
*A* his son reigned in his stead ........... 2Chr 33:20
*A* was two and twenty years old ........ 2Chr 33:21
for *A* sacrificed unto all the ................ 2Chr 33:22
but *A* trespassed more and more ....... 2Chr 33:23
that had conspired against king *A* ..... 2Chr 33:25
Josiah the son of *A* king of Judah ............ Jer 1:2
Josiah the son of *A* king of Judah ......... Jer 25:3
the days of Josiah the son of *A* ............. Zeph 1:1
and Manasses begat *A* ............................. Mt 1:10
and *A* begat Josias ................................... Mt 1:10
*3. A descendant of Solomon who returned from the Exile under Zerubbabel.*
of Zebaim, the children of *A* .................. Neh 7:59

**AMONG** See PREFACE.

**AMONGST**
God *a* the trees of the garden .................. Gen 3:8
of a buryingplace *a* you .......................... Gen 23:9

**AMORITE** (*am'-o-rite*) *A descendant of Canaan, Ham's son.*
And the Jebusite, and the *A* ................. Gen 10:16
dwelt in the plain of Mamre the *A* ........ Gen 14:13
the hand of the *A* with my sword ....... Gen 48:22
drive out the Canaanite, the *A* ................ Ex 33:2
I drive out before thee the *A* .................. Ex 34:11
the *A* which was in it ........................... Num 32:39
given into thine hand Sihon the *A* ...... Deut 2:24
Lebanon, the Hittite, and the *A* ............. Josh 9:1
east and on the west, and to the *A* ...... Josh 11:3
The Jebusite also, and the *A* ................ 1Chr 1:14
thy father was an *A*, and thy ................. Eze 16:3
an Hittite, and your father an *A* .......... Eze 16:45
Yet destroyed I the *A* before them ...... Amos 2:9
to possess the land of the *A* ................ Amos 2:10

**AMORITES** (*am'-o-rites*)
of the Amalekites, and also the *A* ......... Gen 14:7
iniquity of the *A* is not yet full ............ Gen 15:16
And the *A*, and the Canaanites, and ... Gen 15:21
and the Hittites, and the *A* ........................ Ex 3:8
and the Hittites, and the *A* ...................... Ex 3:17
and the Hittites, and the *A* ...................... Ex 13:5
thee, and bring thee in unto the *A* ........ Ex 23:23
and the Jebusites, and the *A* ............... Num 13:29
cometh out of the coasts of the *A* ....... Num 21:13
of Moab, between Moab and the *A* ... Num 21:13
unto Sihon king of the *A*, saying, ...... Num 21:21
dwelt in all the cities of the *A* ........... Num 21:25
city of Sihon the king of the *A* .......... Num 21:26
unto Sihon king of the *A* ..................... Num 21:29
Israel dwelt in the land of the *A* ........ Num 21:31
drove out the *A* that were there .......... Num 21:32
didst unto Sihon king of the *A* ........... Num 21:34
all that Israel had done to the *A* ......... Num 22:2
kingdom of Sihon king of the *A* .......... Num 32:33
had slain Sihon the king of the *A* .......... Deut 1:4
and go to the mount of the *A* .................. Deut 1:7
the way of the mountain of the *A* ......... Deut 1:19
come unto the mountain of the *A* ......... Deut 1:20
deliver us into the hand of the *A* ......... Deut 1:27
And the *A*, which dwelt in that ............ Deut 1:44
didst unto Sihon king of the *A* .............. Deut 3:2
hand of the two kings of the *A* .............. Deut 3:8
and the *A* call it Shenir ........................ Deut 3:9
the land of Sihon king of the *A* ........... Deut 4:46
of Bashan, two kings of the *A* .............. Deut 4:47
and the Girgashites, and the *A* ............... Deut 7:1
namely, the Hittites, and the *A* .......... Deut 20:17
to Sihon and to Og, kings of the *A* ..... Deut 31:4
did unto the two kings of the *A* ............ Josh 2:10
and the Girgashites, and the *A* ............. Josh 3:10
pass, when all the kings of the *A* ........... Josh 5:1
deliver us into the hand of the *A* ........... Josh 7:7
he did to the two kings of the *A* ........... Josh 9:10
Therefore the five kings of the *A* ......... Josh 10:5
for all the kings of the *A* that ............... Josh 10:6
*A* before the children of Israel ............. Josh 10:12
Sihon king of the *A*, who dwelt in ....... Josh 12:2
the Hittites, the *A*, and the ..................... Josh 12:8
Aphek, to the borders of the *A* ............. Josh 13:4
the cities of Sihon king of the *A* ........ Josh 13:10
kingdom of Sihon king of the *A* .......... Josh 13:21
you into the land of the *A* ..................... Josh 24:8
Jericho fought against you, the *A* ...... Josh 24:11
you, even the two kings of the *A* ......... Josh 24:12
the flood, or the gods of the *A* ............ Josh 24:15
even the *A* which dwelt in the .............. Josh 24:18
the *A* forced the children of Dan ......... Judg 1:34
But the *A* would dwell in mount .......... Judg 1:35
the coast of the *A* was from the ........... Judg 1:36
the Canaanites, Hittites, and *A* ............. Judg 3:5
fear not the gods of the *A* ..................... Judg 6:10
side Jordan in the land of the *A* ........... Judg 10:8
from the Egyptians, and from the *A* .. Judg 10:11
unto Sihon king of the *A*, the ............. Judg 11:19
possessed all the land of the *A* ............ Judg 11:21
possessed all the coasts of the *A* ........ Judg 11:22
*A* from before his people Israel ........... Judg 11:23
was peace between Israel and the *A* ..... 1Sa 7:14
but of the remnant of the *A* .................... 2Sa 21:2
country of Sihon king of the *A* ............. 1Kin 4:19
people that were left of the *A* ............... 1Kin 9:20
to all things as did the *A* ..................... 1Kin 21:26
wickedly above all that the *A* did ...... 2Kin 21:11
left of the Hittites, and the *A* ................. 2Chr 8:7
Moabites, the Egyptians, and the *A* ......... Ezr 9:1
Canaanites, the Hittites, the *A* ................. Neh 9:8
Sihon king of the *A*, and Og king ......... Ps 135:11
Sihon king of the *A* ................................ Ps 136:19

**AMOS** (*a'-mos*)
*1. A prophet during the reign of Uzziah.*
The words of *A*, who was among the .. Amos 1:1
And the LORD said unto me, *A* ............. Amos 7:8
*A* hath conspired against thee in .......... Amos 7:10
For thus *A* saith, Jeroboam shall ......... Amos 7:11
Also Amaziah said unto *A*, O thou .... Amos 7:12
Then answered *A*, and said to .............. Amos 7:14
And he said, *A*, what seest thou ........... Amos 8:2
*2. Son of Naum; an ancestor of Jesus.*
which was the son of *A*, which ................ Lk 3:25

**AMOUNTING**
gold, *a* to six hundred talents ................ 2Chr 3:8

**AMOZ** (*a'-moz*) *Father of Isaiah.*
Isaiah the prophet the son of *A* ........... 2Kin 19:2
the son of *A* sent to Hezekiah ............ 2Kin 19:20
Isaiah the son of *A* came to him .......... 2Kin 20:1
Isaiah the prophet, the son of *A* ....... 2Chr 26:22
the prophet Isaiah the son of *A* ......... 2Chr 32:20
Isaiah the prophet, the son of *A* ....... 2Chr 32:32
The vision of Isaiah the son of *A* ................ Is 1:1
the son of *A* saw concerning Judah ............ Is 2:1
which Isaiah the son of *A* did see ............. Is 13:1
the LORD by Isaiah the son of *A* .............. Is 20:2
Isaiah the prophet the son of *A* ............... Is 37:2
the son of *A* sent unto Hezekiah ............ Is 37:21
the son of *A* came unto him ..................... Is 38:1

**AMPHIPOLIS** (*am-fip'-o-lis*) *A city in Macedonia.*
when they had passed through *A* ......... Acts 17:1

**AMPLIAS** (*am'-ple-as*) *A Christian acquaintance of Paul's.*
Greet *A* my beloved in the Lord ........... Rom 16:8

**AMRAM** (*am'-ram*) See AMRAMITES, AMRAM'S, HEMDAN.
*1. Father of Moses and Aaron.*
*A*, and Izhar, and Hebron, and Uzziel ..... Ex 6:18
*A* took him Jochebed his father's ............ Ex 6:20
of the life of *A* were an hundred ............. Ex 6:20
*A*, and Izehar, Hebron, and Uzziel ....... Num 3:19
And Kohath begat *A* ........................... Num 26:58
bare unto *A* Aaron and Moses ............ Num 26:59
*A*, Izhar, and Hebron, and Uzziel ........... 1Chr 6:2
And the children of *A* ............................. 1Chr 6:3
And the sons of Kohath were, *A* ......... 1Chr 6:18
*A*, Izhar, Hebron, and Uzziel, four ..... 1Chr 23:12
The sons of *A* ......................................... 1Chr 23:13
Of the sons of *A* ..................................... 1Chr 24:20
*2. Married a foreign wife in Exile.*
Maadai, *A*, and Uel, ................................... Ezr 10:34
*3. A son of Dishon.*
*A*, and Eshban, and Ithran, and ............ 1Chr 1:41

**AMRAMITES** (*am'-ram-ites*) *Descendants of Amram 1.*
of Kohath was the family of the *A* ...... Num 3:27
Of the *A*, and the Izharites, the .......... 1Chr 26:23

**AMRAM'S** (*am'-rams*)
the name of *A* wife was Jochebed, .... Num 26:59

**AMRAPHEL** (*am'-raf-el*) *King of Shinar in Abraham's time.*
in the days of *A* king of Shinar .............. Gen 14:1

A king of Shinar, and Arioch king........ Gen 14:9

**AMZI** (*am'-zi*)
*1. A son of Merari.*
The son of *A*, the son of Bani,.............. 1Chr 6:46
*2. Ancestor of Adaiah.*
the son of Pelaliah, the son of *A*......... Neh 11:12

**AN** See PREFACE.

**ANAB** (*a'-nab*) *A Canaanite city.*
from Hebron, from Debir, from *A*....... Josh 11:21
And *A*, and Eshtemoh, and Anim,....... Josh 15:50

**ANAH** (*a'-nah*)
*1. A daughter of Zibeon.*
of *A* the daughter of Zibeon the............ Gen 36:2
the daughter of *A* the daughter of...... Gen 36:14
of Aholibamah the daughter of *A*....... Gen 36:18
And the children of *A* were these....... Gen 36:25
and Aholibamah the daughter of *A*.... Gen 36:25
*2. A son of Seir.*
Shobal, and Zibeon, and *A*................. Gen 36:20
duke Shobal, duke Zibeon, duke *A*...... Gen 36:29
Shobal, and Zibeon, and *A*.................... 1Chr 1:38
*3. A son of Zibeon.*
both Ajah, and *A*................................ Gen 36:24
this was that *A* that found the............. Gen 36:24
Aiah, and *A*........................................ 1Chr 1:40
The sons of *A*...................................... 1Chr 1:41

**ANAHARATH** (*an-a-ha'-rath*) *A town in Issachar.*
And Haphraim, and Shihon, and *A*.... Josh 19:19

**ANAIAH** (*an-a-i'-ah*)
*1. A priest who assisted Ezra.*
stood Mattithiah, and Shema, and *A*...... Neh 8:4
*2. A Jew who sealed the covenant.*
Pelatiah, Hanan, *A*,............................... Neh 10:22

**ANAK** (*a'-nak*) See ANAKIMS. *The son of Arba.*
and Talmai, the children of *A*............ Num 13:22
we saw the children of *A* there.......... Num 13:28
we saw the giants, the sons of *A*....... Num 13:33
stand before the children of *A*................ Deut 9:2
the city of Arba the father of *A*.......... Josh 15:13
drove thence the three sons of *A*........ Josh 15:14
and Talmai, the children of *A*............. Josh 15:14
the city of Arba the father of *A*.......... Josh 21:11
thence the three sons of *A*.................... Judg 1:20

**ANAKIM** See ANAKIMS.

**ANAKIMS** (*an'-ak-ims*) *Descendants of Anak.*
have seen the sons of the *A* there....... Deut 1:28
great, and many, and tall, as the *A*..... Deut 2:10
were accounted giants, as the *A*.......... Deut 2:11
great, and many, and tall, as the *A*..... Deut 2:21
and tall, the children of the *A*................ Deut 9:2
cut off the *A* from the mountains,...... Josh 11:21
There was none of the *A* left in.......... Josh 11:22
in that day how the *A* were there....... Josh 14:12
Arba was a great man among the *A*.. Josh 14:15

**ANAKITES** See ANAKIMS.

**ANAMIM** (*an'-am-im*) *A people of northern Egypt.*
And Mizraim begat Ludim, and *A*....... Gen 10:13
And Mizraim begat Ludim, and *A*........ 1Chr 1:11

**ANAMITES** See ANAMIM.

**ANAMMELECH** (*a-nam'-mel-ek*) *A god of the Babylonians.*
in fire to Adrammelech and *A*............ 2Kin 17:31

**ANAN** (*a'-nan*) *An Israelite who sealed the covenant under Nehemiah.*
And Ahijah, Hanan, *A*,........................... Neh 10:26

**ANANI** (*an-a'-ni*) *A son of Elioneai.*
and Johanan, and Dalaiah, and *A*........ 1Chr 3:24

**ANANIAH** (*an-an-i'-ah*) See ANANIAS.
*1. Grandfather of Azariah.*
the son of *A* by his house....................... Neh 3:23
*2. A town in Benjamin.*
And at Anathoth, Nob, *A*,..................... Neh 11:32

**ANANIAS** (*an-an-i'-as*) See ANANIAH.
*1. A Christian who tried to deceive the apostles.*
But a certain man named *A*.................... Acts 5:1
But Peter said, *A*, why hath Satan......... Acts 5:3
*A* hearing these words fell down,........... Acts 5:5
*2. A Christian who aided Paul.*
disciple at Damascus, named *A*............. Acts 9:10
him said the Lord in a vision, *A*........... Acts 9:10
a vision a man named *A* coming in....... Acts 9:12
Then *A* answered, Lord, I have............. Acts 9:13
*A* went his way, and entered into......... Acts 9:17
And one *A*, a devout man according.. Acts 22:12
*3. The High Priest who interrogated Paul.*
the high priest *A* commanded them..... Acts 23:2
after five days *A* the high priest........... Acts 24:1

**ANATH** (*a'-nath*) See BETH-ANATH. *Father of Shamgar the judge.*
him was Shamgar the son of *A*............. Judg 3:31
the days of Shamgar the son of *A*......... Judg 5:6

**ANATHEMA** (*a-nath'-em-ah*) *Greek word for "accursed."*
Christ, let him be *A* Maranatha......... 1Cor 16:22

**ANATHOTH** (*an'-a-thoth*) See ANETOTHITE.
*1. A Levitical city in Benjamin.*
*A* with her suburbs, and Almon with Josh 21:18
said the king, Get thee to *A*.................. 1Kin 2:26
suburbs, and *A* with her suburbs......... 1Chr 6:60
The men of *A*, an hundred twenty......... Ezr 2:23
The men of *A*, an hundred twenty........ Neh 7:27
And at *A*, Nob, Ananiah,....................... Neh 11:32
to be heard unto Laish, O poor *A*........... Is 10:30
were in *A* in the land of Benjamin............ Jer 1:1
saith the LORD of the men of *A*............. Jer 11:21
will bring evil upon the men of *A*......... Jer 11:23
thou not reproved Jeremiah of *A*......... Jer 29:27
Buy thee my field that is in *A*................... Jer 32:7
field, I pray thee, that is in *A*.................. Jer 32:8
my uncle's son, that was in *A*................. Jer 32:9
*2. A son of Becher.*
Omri, and Jerimoth, and Abiah, and *A*. 1Chr 7:8
*3. An Israelite who sealed the covenant under Nehemiah.*
Hariph, *A*, Nebai,.................................... Neh 10:19

**ANATHOTHITE** See ANTOTHITE.

**ANCESTORS**
remember the covenant of their *a*....... Lev 26:45

**ANCHOR**
hope we have as an *a* of the soul.......... Heb 6:19

**ANCHORS**
they cast four *a* out of the stern.......... Acts 27:29
have cast *a* out of the foreship............ Acts 27:30
And when they had taken up the *a*... Acts 27:40

**ANCIENT**
chief things of the *a* mountains.......... Deut 33:15
that *a* river, the river Kishon................ Judg 5:21
of *a* times that I have formed it.......... 2Kin 19:25
And these are *a* things........................... 1Chr 4:22
of the fathers, who were *a* men.............. Ezr 3:12
With the *a* is wisdom.............................. Job 12:12
days of old, the years of *a* times............. Ps 77:5
Remove not the *a* landmark................ Prov 22:28
prophet, and the prudent, and the *a*........... Is 3:2
himself proudly against the *a*.................... Is 3:5
The *a* and honourable, he is the................ Is 9:15
of the wise, the son of *a* kings................ Is 19:11
whose antiquity is of *a* days..................... Is 23:7
of *a* times, that I have formed it............ Is 37:26
since I appointed the *a* people................ Is 44:7
hath declared this from *a* time............... Is 45:21
from *a* times the things that are............. Is 46:10
upon the *a* hast thou very heavily........... Is 47:6
awake, as in the *a* days, in the................ Is 51:9
mighty nation, it is an *a* nation............... Jer 5:15
in their ways from the *a* paths.............. Jer 18:15
Then they began at the *a* men................... Eze 9:6
even the *a* high places are ours............... Eze 36:2
the *A* of days did sit, whose...................... Dan 7:9
heaven, and came to the *A* of days....... Dan 7:13
Until the *A* of days came, and.............. Dan 7:22

**ANCIENTS**
As saith the proverb of the *a*............... 1Sa 24:13
I understand more than the *a*............ Ps 119:100
judgment with the *a* of his people............ Is 3:14
and before his *a* gloriously..................... Is 24:23
take of the *a* of the people........................ Jer 19:1
and of the *a* of the priests......................... Jer 19:1
the priest, and counsel from the *a*.......... Eze 7:26
of the *a* of the house of Israel................. Eze 8:11
hast thou seen what the *a* of the............. Eze 8:12
The *a* of Gebal and the wise men.......... Eze 27:9

**ANCLE**
*a* bones received strength......................... Acts 3:7

**ANCLES**
the waters were to the *a*.......................... Eze 47:3

**AND** See PREFACE.

**ANDREW** (*an'-drew*) *One of the twelve disciples.*
*A* his brother, casting a net into............... Mt 4:18
is called Peter, and *A* his brother............. Mt 10:2
*A* his brother casting a net into................ Mk 1:16
into the house of Simon and *A*................ Mk 1:29
And *A*, and Philip, and Bartholomew,.... Mk 3:18
and John and *A* asked him privately,.... Mk 13:3
*A* his brother, James and John,................. Lk 6:14
speak, and followed him, was *A*............... Jn 1:40
was of Bethsaida, the city of *A*................ Jn 1:44
One of his disciples, *A*, Simon.................. Jn 6:8
Philip cometh and telleth *A*.................... Jn 12:22
and again *A* and Philip tell Jesus........... Jn 12:22
Peter, and James, and John, and *A*...... Acts 1:13

**ANDRONICUS** (*an-dro-ni'-cus*) *A relative of Paul.*
Salute *A* and Junia, my kinsmen, and. Rom 16:7

**ANEM** (*a'-nem*) See EN-GANNIM. *A Levitical city in Issachar.*
suburbs, and *A* with her suburbs......... 1Chr 6:73

**ANER** (*a'-nur*)
*1. An ally of Abraham.*
of Eshcol, and brother of *A*.................. Gen 14:13
of the men which went with me, *A*.... Gen 14:24
*2. A Levitical city in Manasseh.*
*A* with her suburbs, and Bileam............ 1Chr 6:70

**ANETHOTHITE** (*an'-e-thoth-ite*) See ANETOTHITE. *A native of Anathoth.*
Abiezer the *A*, Mebunnai the................ 2Sa 23:27

**ANETOTHITE** (*an'-e-toth-ite*) See ANETHOTHITE, ANTOTHITE. *Same as Anethothite.*
the ninth month was Abiezer the *A*.. 1Chr 27:12

**ANGEL**
the *a* of the LORD found her by a.......... Gen 16:7
the *a* of the LORD said unto her,............ Gen 16:9
the *a* of the LORD said unto her,.......... Gen 16:10
the *a* of the LORD said unto her,.......... Gen 16:11
the *a* of God called to Hagar out......... Gen 21:17
the *a* of the LORD called unto him...... Gen 22:11
the *a* of the LORD called unto.............. Gen 22:15
he shall send his *a* before thee.............. Gen 24:7
I walk, will send his *a* with thee......... Gen 24:40
the *a* of God spake unto me in a.......... Gen 31:11
The *a* which redeemed me from all.... Gen 48:16
the *a* of the LORD appeared unto................ Ex 3:2
the *a* of God, which went before.......... Ex 14:19
I send an *A* before thee, to keep........... Ex 23:20
For mine *A* shall go before thee,........... Ex 23:23
mine *A* shall go before thee.................. Ex 32:34
And I will send an *a* before thee............. Ex 33:2
he heard our voice, and sent an *a*..... Num 20:16
the *a* of the LORD stood in the........... Num 22:22
the ass saw the *a* of the LORD............ Num 22:23
But the *a* of the LORD stood in a........ Num 22:24
the ass saw the *a* of the LORD............ Num 22:25
the *a* of the LORD went further,.......... Num 22:26
the ass saw the *a* of the LORD............ Num 22:27
he saw the *a* of the LORD standing.... Num 22:31
the *a* of the LORD said unto him,...... Num 22:32
said unto the *a* of the LORD,.............. Num 22:34
the *a* of the LORD said unto................ Num 22:35
an *a* of the LORD came up from............. Judg 2:1
when the *a* of the LORD spake................ Judg 2:4
said the *a* of the LORD, curse ye........... Judg 5:23
And there came an *a* of the LORD......... Judg 6:11
the *a* of the LORD appeared unto........... Judg 6:12
the *a* of God said unto him, Take........ Judg 6:20
Then the *a* of the LORD put forth......... Judg 6:21
Then the *a* of the LORD departed.......... Judg 6:21
that he was an *a* of the LORD.............. Judg 6:22
an *a* of the LORD face to face............... Judg 6:22
the *a* of the LORD appeared unto........... Judg 13:3
the countenance of an *a* of God........... Judg 13:6
the *a* of God came again unto the......... Judg 13:9
the *a* of the LORD said unto.................. Judg 13:13
said unto the *a* of the LORD................. Judg 13:15
the *a* of the LORD said unto.................. Judg 13:16
not that he was an *a* of the LORD...... Judg 13:16
said unto the *a* of the LORD................. Judg 13:17
the *a* of the LORD said unto him,........ Judg 13:18
and the *a* did wonderously.................... Judg 13:19
that the *a* of the LORD ascended......... Judg 13:20
But the *a* of the LORD did no more....... Judg 13:21
knew that he was an *a* of the LORD.. Judg 13:21
good in my sight, as an *a* of God........... 1Sa 29:9
for as an *a* of God, so is my lord........... 2Sa 14:17
to the wisdom of an *a* of God............... 2Sa 14:20
lord the king is as an *a* of God............. 2Sa 19:27
when the *a* stretched out his hand...... 2Sa 24:16
said to the *a* that destroyed the........... 2Sa 24:16
the *a* of the LORD was by the................ 2Sa 24:16
saw the *a* that smote the people........... 2Sa 24:17
an *a* spake unto me by the word of... 1Kin 13:18
then an *a* touched him, and said.......... 1Kin 19:5
the *a* of the LORD came again the......... 1Kin 19:7
But the *a* of the LORD said to................ 2Kin 1:3
the *a* of the LORD said unto................... 2Kin 1:15
that the *a* of the LORD went out,......... 2Kin 19:35
the *a* of the LORD destroying............... 1Chr 21:12
God sent an *a* unto Jerusalem to....... 1Chr 21:15
said to the *a* that destroyed, It........... 1Chr 21:15
the *a* of the LORD stood by the............ 1Chr 21:15
saw the *a* of the LORD stand.............. 1Chr 21:16
Then the *a* of the LORD commanded. 1Chr 21:18
Ornan turned back, and saw the *a*..... 1Chr 21:20
And the LORD commanded the *a*........ 1Chr 21:27
of the sword of the *a* of the LORD...... 1Chr 21:30
And the LORD sent an *a*, which cut... 2Chr 32:21
The *a* of the LORD encampeth round....... Ps 34:7
let the *a* of the LORD chase them............ Ps 35:5
let the *a* of the LORD persecute.............. Ps 35:6
neither say thou before the *a*.................. Eccl 5:6
Then the *a* of the LORD went forth......... Is 37:36
the *a* of his presence saved them............ Is 63:9
and Abed-nego, who hath sent his *a*.... Dan 3:28
My God hath sent his *a*, and hath......... Dan 6:22
Yea, he had power over the *a*................. Hos 12:4
the *a* that talked with me said................. Zec 1:9
they answered the *a* of the LORD.......... Zec 1:11
Then the *a* of the LORD answered.......... Zec 1:12
the LORD answered the *a* that................. Zec 1:13
So the *a* that communed with me......... Zec 1:14
I said unto the *a* that talked.................. Zec 1:19
the *a* that talked with me went............... Zec 2:3
another *a* went out to meet him,............. Zec 2:3
standing before the *a* of the LORD........... Zec 3:1
garments, and stood before the *a*............ Zec 3:3
the *a* of the LORD stood by..................... Zec 3:5
the *a* of the LORD protested unto............ Zec 3:6
the *a* that talked with me came.............. Zec 4:1
spake to the *a* that talked with.............. Zec 4:4
Then the *a* that talked with me.............. Zec 4:5
Then the *a* that talked with me.............. Zec 5:5
Then said I to the *a* that talked............ Zec 5:10
said unto the *a* that talked with.............. Zec 6:4
the *a* answered and said unto me,........... Zec 6:5
as the *a* of the LORD before them........... Zec 12:8
the *a* of the Lord appeared unto............... Mt 1:20

the *a* of the Lord had bidden him ... Mt 1:24
the *a* of the Lord appeareth to ... Mt 2:13
an *a* of the Lord appeareth in a ... Mt 2:19
for the *a* of the Lord descended ... Mt 28:2
the *a* answered and said unto the ... Mt 28:5
there appeared unto him an *a* of ... Lk 1:11
But the *a* said unto him, Fear not ... Lk 1:13
And Zacharias said unto the *a* ... Lk 1:18
the *a* answering said unto him, I ... Lk 1:19
in the sixth month the *a* Gabriel ... Lk 1:26
the *a* came in unto her, and said, ... Lk 1:28
the *a* said unto her, Fear not, ... Lk 1:30
Then said Mary unto the *a* ... Lk 1:34
the *a* answered and said unto her, ... Lk 1:35
And the *a* departed from her ... Lk 1:38
the *a* of the Lord came upon them, ... Lk 2:9
the *a* said unto them, Fear not ... Lk 2:10
the *a* a multitude of the heavenly ... Lk 2:13
which was so named of the *a* ... Lk 2:21
there appeared an *a* unto him from ... Lk 22:43
For an *a* went down at a certain ... Jn 5:4
others said, An *a* spake to him ... Jn 12:29
But the *a* of the Lord by night ... Acts 5:19
as it had been the face of an *a* ... Acts 6:15
*a* of the Lord in a flame of fire ... Acts 7:30
*a* which appeared to him in the ... Acts 7:35
in the wilderness with the *a* ... Acts 7:38
the *a* of the Lord spake unto ... Acts 8:26
day an *a* of God coming in to him ... Acts 10:3
when the *a* which spake unto ... Acts 10:7
was warned from God by an holy *a* ... Acts 10:22
how he had seen an *a* in his house ... Acts 11:13
the *a* of the Lord came upon him, ... Acts 12:7
the *a* said unto him, Gird thyself ... Acts 12:8
was true which was done by the *a* ... Acts 12:9
forthwith the *a* departed from him ... Acts 12:10
that the Lord hath sent his *a* ... Acts 12:11
Then said they, It is his *a* ... Acts 12:15
immediately the *a* of the Lord ... Acts 12:23
is no resurrection, neither *a* ... Acts 23:8
spirit or an *a* hath spoken to him ... Acts 23:9
by me this night the *a* of God ... Acts 27:23
is transformed into an *a* of light ... 2Cor 11:14
or an *a* from heaven, preach any ... Gal 1:8
but received me as an *a* of God ... Gal 4:14
signified it by his *a* unto his ... Rev 1:1
Unto the *a* of the church of ... Rev 2:1
unto the *a* of the church in ... Rev 2:8
to the *a* of the church in ... Rev 2:12
unto the *a* of the church in ... Rev 2:18
unto the *a* of the church in ... Rev 3:1
to the *a* of the church in ... Rev 3:7
unto the *a* of the church of the ... Rev 3:14
I saw a strong *a* proclaiming with ... Rev 5:2
I saw another *a* ascending from ... Rev 7:2
And another *a* came and stood at the ... Rev 8:3
the *a* took the censer, and filled ... Rev 8:5
The first *a* sounded, and there ... Rev 8:7
And the second *a* sounded, and as it ... Rev 8:8
And the third *a* sounded, and there ... Rev 8:10
And the fourth *a* sounded, and the ... Rev 8:12
heard an *a* flying through the ... Rev 8:13
And the fifth *a* sounded, and I saw ... Rev 9:1
which is the *a* of the bottomless ... Rev 9:11
And the sixth *a* sounded, and I ... Rev 9:13
Saying to the sixth *a* which had ... Rev 9:14
I saw another mighty *a* come down ... Rev 10:1
the *a* which I saw stand upon the ... Rev 10:5
of the voice of the seventh *a* ... Rev 10:7
is open in the hand of the *a* ... Rev 10:8
And I went unto the *a*, and said ... Rev 10:9
the *a* stood, saying, Rise, and ... Rev 11:1
And the seventh *a* sounded ... Rev 11:15
I saw another *a* fly in the midst ... Rev 14:6
And there followed another *a* ... Rev 14:8
the third *a* followed them, saying ... Rev 14:9
another *a* came out of the temple, ... Rev 14:15
another *a* came out from the temple ... Rev 14:17
another *a* came out from the altar ... Rev 14:18
the *a* thrust in his sickle into ... Rev 14:19
the second *a* poured out his vial ... Rev 16:3
the third *a* poured out his vial ... Rev 16:4
I heard the *a* of the waters say, ... Rev 16:5
the fourth *a* poured out his vial ... Rev 16:8
the fifth *a* poured out his vial ... Rev 16:10
the sixth *a* poured out his vial ... Rev 16:12
the seventh *a* poured out his vial ... Rev 16:17
the *a* said unto me, Wherefore ... Rev 17:7
another *a* come down from heaven ... Rev 18:1
a mighty *a* took up a stone like a ... Rev 18:21
I saw an *a* standing in the sun ... Rev 19:17
I saw an *a* come down from heaven, ... Rev 20:1
of a man, that is, of the *a* ... Rev 21:17
*a* to shew unto his servants the ... Rev 22:6
*a* which shewed me these things ... Rev 22:8
I Jesus have sent mine *a* to ... Rev 22:16

### ANGEL'S

up before God out of the *a* hand ... Rev 8:4
the little book out of the *a* hand ... Rev 10:10

### ANGELS

there came two *a* to Sodom at even ... Gen 19:1
then the *a* hastened Lot, saying, ... Gen 19:15
behold the *a* of God ascending and ... Gen 28:12
his way, and the *a* of God met him ... Gen 32:1
his *a* he charged with folly ... Job 4:18
him a little lower than the *a* ... Ps 8:5
thousand, even thousands of *a* ... Ps 68:17
by sending evil *a* among them ... Ps 78:49
shall give his *a* charge over thee ... Ps 91:11
Bless the LORD, ye his *a*, that ... Ps 103:20
Who maketh his *a* spirits ... Ps 104:4
Praise ye him, all his *a* ... Ps 148:2
He shall give his *a* charge ... Mt 4:6
*a* came and ministered unto him ... Mt 4:11
and the reapers are the *a* ... Mt 13:39
Son of man shall send forth his *a* ... Mt 13:41
the *a* shall come forth, and sever ... Mt 13:49
glory of his Father with his *a* ... Mt 16:27
That in heaven their *a* do always ... Mt 18:10
but are as the *a* of God in heaven ... Mt 22:30
he shall send his *a* with a great ... Mt 24:31
not the *a* of heaven, but my ... Mt 24:36
glory, and all the holy *a* with him ... Mt 25:31
prepared for the devil and his *a* ... Mt 25:41
me more than twelve legions of *a* ... Mt 26:53
the *a* ministered unto him ... Mk 1:13
of his Father with the holy *a* ... Mk 8:38
but are as the *a* which are in ... Mk 12:25
And then shall he send his *a* ... Mk 13:27
not the *a* which are in heaven, ... Mk 13:32
as the *a* were gone away from them ... Lk 2:15
shall give his *a* charge over thee ... Lk 4:10
in his Father's, and of the holy *a* ... Lk 9:26
also confess before the *a* of God ... Lk 12:8
be denied before the *a* of God ... Lk 12:9
the *a* of God over one sinner that ... Lk 15:10
was carried by the *a* into ... Lk 16:22
for they are equal unto the *a* ... Lk 20:36
they had also seen a vision of *a* ... Lk 24:23
the *a* of God ascending and ... Jn 1:51
seeth two *a* in white sitting, the ... Jn 20:12
the law by the disposition of *a* ... Acts 7:53
neither death, nor life, nor *a* ... Rom 8:38
spectacle unto the world, and to *a* ... 1Cor 4:9
Know ye not that we shall judge *a* ... 1Cor 6:3
on her head because of the *a* ... 1Cor 11:10
with the tongues of men and of *a* ... 1Cor 13:1
it was ordained by *a* in the hand ... Gal 3:19
humility and worshipping of *a* ... Col 2:18
from heaven with his mighty *a* ... 2Th 1:7
in the Spirit, seen of *a*, ... 1Ti 3:16
Lord Jesus Christ, and the elect *a* ... 1Ti 5:21
made so much better than the *a* ... Heb 1:4
of the *a* said he at any time ... Heb 1:5
let all the *a* of God worship him ... Heb 1:6
of the *a* he saith ... Heb 1:7
Who maketh his *a* spirits ... Heb 1:7
But to which of the *a* said he at ... Heb 1:13
the word spoken by *a* was stedfast ... Heb 2:2
For unto the *a* hath he not put in ... Heb 2:5
him a little lower than the *a* ... Heb 2:7
the *a* for the suffering of death ... Heb 2:9
took not on him the nature of *a* ... Heb 2:16
and to an innumerable company of *a*. Heb 12:22
some have entertained *a* unawares ... Heb 13:2
which things the *a* desire to look ... 1Pet 1:12
*a* and authorities and powers being ... 1Pet 3:22
God spared not the *a* that sinned ... 2Pet 2:4
Whereas *a*, which are greater in ... 2Pet 2:11
the *a* which kept not their first ... Jude 6
are the *a* of the seven churches ... Rev 1:20
before my Father, and before his *a* ... Rev 3:5
of many *a* round about the throne ... Rev 5:11
after these things I saw four *a* ... Rev 7:1
with a loud voice to the four *a* ... Rev 7:2
all the *a* stood round about the ... Rev 7:11
I saw the seven *a* which stood ... Rev 8:2
the seven *a* which had the seven ... Rev 8:6
of the trumpet of the three *a* ... Rev 8:13
Loose the four *a* which are bound ... Rev 9:14
the four *a* were loosed, which ... Rev 9:15
his *a* fought against the dragon ... Rev 12:7
and the dragon fought and his *a* ... Rev 12:7
his *a* were cast out with him ... Rev 12:9
in the presence of the holy *a* ... Rev 14:10
seven *a* having the seven last ... Rev 15:1
the seven *a* came out of the ... Rev 15:6
*a* seven golden vials full of the ... Rev 15:7
of the seven *a* were fulfilled ... Rev 15:8
the temple saying to the seven *a* ... Rev 16:1
seven *a* which had the seven vials ... Rev 17:1
came unto me one of the seven *a* ... Rev 21:9
gates, and at the gates twelve *a* ... Rev 21:12

### ANGELS'

Man did eat *a* food ... Ps 78:25

### ANGER

brother's *a* turn away from thee ... Gen 27:45
Jacob's *a* was kindled against ... Gen 30:2
let not thine *a* burn against thy ... Gen 44:18
for in their *a* they slew a man, ... Gen 49:6
Cursed be their *a*, for it was ... Gen 49:7
the *a* of the LORD was kindled ... Ex 4:14
out from Pharaoh in a great *a* ... Ex 11:8
Moses' *a* waxed hot, and he cast ... Ex 32:19
Let not the *a* of my lord wax hot ... Ex 32:22
and his *a* was kindled ... Num 11:1
the *a* of the LORD was kindled ... Num 11:10
the *a* of the LORD was kindled ... Num 12:9
God's *a* was kindled because he ... Num 22:22
Balaam's *a* was kindled, and he ... Num 22:27
Balak's *a* was kindled against ... Num 24:10
the *a* of the LORD was kindled ... Num 25:3
that the fierce *a* of the LORD may ... Num 25:4
the LORD's *a* was kindled the same ... Num 32:10
the LORD's *a* was kindled against ... Num 32:13
*a* of the LORD toward Israel ... Num 32:14
LORD thy God, to provoke him to *a* ... Deut 4:25
*a* of the LORD thy God be kindled ... Deut 6:15
so will the *a* of the LORD be ... Deut 7:4
of the LORD, to provoke him to *a* ... Deut 9:18
For I was afraid of the *a* ... Deut 9:19
turn from the fierceness of his *a* ... Deut 13:17
him, but then the *a* of the LORD ... Deut 29:20
which the LORD overthrew in his *a* ... Deut 29:23
meaneth the heat of this great *a* ... Deut 29:24
the *a* of the LORD was kindled ... Deut 29:27
them out of their land in *a* ... Deut 29:28
Then my *a* shall be kindled ... Deut 31:17
to provoke him to *a* through the ... Deut 31:29
provoked they him to *a* ... Deut 32:16
me to *a* with their vanities ... Deut 32:21
them to *a* with a foolish nation ... Deut 32:21
For a fire is kindled in mine *a* ... Deut 32:22
the *a* of the LORD was kindled ... Josh 7:1
from the fierceness of his *a* ... Josh 7:26
then shall the *a* of the LORD be ... Josh 23:16
them, and provoked the LORD to *a* ... Judg 2:12
the *a* of the LORD was hot against ... Judg 2:14
the *a* of the LORD was hot against ... Judg 2:20
Therefore the *a* of the LORD was ... Judg 3:8
Let not thine *a* be hot against me ... Judg 6:39
Then their *a* was abated toward ... Judg 8:3
son of Ebed, his *a* was kindled ... Judg 9:30
the *a* of the LORD was hot against ... Judg 10:7
his *a* was kindled, and he went up ... Judg 14:19
his *a* was kindled greatly ... 1Sa 11:6
Eliab's *a* was kindled against ... 1Sa 17:28
Then Saul's *a* was kindled against ... 1Sa 20:30
arose from the table in fierce *a* ... 1Sa 20:34
the *a* of the LORD was kindled ... 2Sa 6:7
David's *a* was greatly kindled ... 2Sa 12:5
again the *a* of the LORD was ... 2Sa 24:1
molten images, to provoke me to *a* ... 1Kin 14:9
groves, provoking the LORD to *a* ... 1Kin 14:15
the LORD God of Israel to *a* ... 1Kin 15:30
provoke me to *a* with their sins ... 1Kin 16:2
in provoking him to *a* with the ... 1Kin 16:7
Israel to *a* with their vanities ... 1Kin 16:13
Israel to *a* with their vanities ... 1Kin 16:26
the LORD God of Israel to *a* than ... 1Kin 16:33
thou hast provoked me to *a* ... 1Kin 21:22
provoked to *a* the LORD God of ... 1Kin 22:53
the *a* of the LORD was kindled ... 2Kin 13:3
things to provoke the LORD to *a* ... 2Kin 17:11
of the LORD, to provoke him to *a* ... 2Kin 17:17
of the LORD, to provoke him to *a* ... 2Kin 21:6
sight, and have provoked me to *a* ... 2Kin 21:15
to *a* with all the works of their ... 2Kin 22:17
had made to provoke the LORD to *a* .. 2Kin 23:19
wherewith his *a* was kindled ... 2Kin 23:26
For through the *a* of the LORD it ... 2Kin 24:20
the *a* of the LORD was kindled ... 1Chr 13:10
wherefore their *a* was greatly ... 2Chr 25:10
and they returned home in great *a* ... 2Chr 25:10
Wherefore the *a* of the LORD was ... 2Chr 25:15
provoked to *a* the LORD God of his ... 2Chr 28:25
of the LORD, to provoke him to *a* ... 2Chr 33:6
to *a* with all the works of their ... 2Chr 34:25
thee to *a* before the builders ... Neh 4:5
gracious and merciful, slow to *a* ... Neh 9:17
wroth, and his *a* burned in him ... Est 1:12
which overturneth them in his *a* ... Job 9:5
If God will not withdraw his *a* ... Job 9:13
He teareth himself in his *a* ... Job 18:4
God distributeth sorrows in his *a* ... Job 21:17
not so, he hath visited in his *a* ... Job 35:15
O lord, rebuke me not in thine *a* ... Ps 6:1
Arise, O LORD, in thine *a* ... Ps 7:6
fiery oven in the time of thine *a* ... Ps 21:9
put not thy servant away in *a* ... Ps 27:9
For his *a* endureth but a moment ... Ps 30:5
Cease from *a*, and forsake wrath ... Ps 37:8
in my flesh because of thine *a* ... Ps 38:3
in thine *a* cast down the people, ... Ps 56:7
let thy wrathful *a* take hold of ... Ps 69:24
why doth thine *a* smoke against ... Ps 74:1
hath he in *a* shut up his tender ... Ps 77:9
*a* also came up against Israel ... Ps 78:21
many a time turned he his *a* away ... Ps 78:38
upon them the fierceness of his *a* ... Ps 78:49
He made a way to his *a* ... Ps 78:50
him to *a* with their high places ... Ps 78:58
from the fierceness of thine *a* ... Ps 85:3
cause thine *a* toward us to cease ... Ps 85:4
out thine *a* to all generations ... Ps 85:5
For we are consumed by thine *a* ... Ps 90:7
Who knoweth the power of thine *a* ... Ps 90:11
merciful and gracious, slow to *a* ... Ps 103:8
will he keep his *a* for ever ... Ps 103:9
him to *a* with their inventions ... Ps 106:29
slow to *a*, and of great mercy ... Ps 145:8
but grievous words stir up *a* ... Prov 15:1
is slow to *a* appeaseth strife ... Prov 15:18
He that is slow to *a* is better ... Prov 16:32
of a man deferreth his *a* ... Prov 19:11
whoso provoketh him to *a* sinneth ... Prov 20:2
A gift in secret pacifieth *a* ... Prov 21:14
and the rod of his *a* shall fail ... Prov 22:8
is cruel, and *a* is outrageous ... Prov 27:4
for *a* resteth in the bosom of ... Eccl 7:9
the Holy One of Israel unto *a* ... Is 1:4
Therefore is the *a* of the LORD ... Is 5:25
For all this his *a* is not turned ... Is 5:25
for the fierce *a* of Rezin with ... Is 7:4
For all this his *a* is not turned ... Is 9:12
For all this his *a* is not turned ... Is 9:17
For all this his *a* is not turned ... Is 9:21
For all this his *a* is not turned ... Is 10:4

O Assyrian, the rod of mine *a* Is 10:5
mine *a* in their destruction Is 10:25
thine *a* is turned away, and thou Is 12:1
called my mighty ones for mine *a* Is 13:3
cruel both with wrath and fierce *a* Is 13:9
and in the day of his fierce *a* Is 13:13
he that ruled the nations in *a* Is 14:6
from far, burning with his *a* Is 30:27
with the indignation of his *a* Is 30:30
poured upon him the fury of his *a* Is 42:25
name's sake will I defer mine *a* Is 48:9
for I will tread them in mine *a* Is 63:3
tread down the people in mine *a* Is 63:6
me to *a* continually to my face Is 65:3
to render his *a* with fury Is 66:15
surely his *a* shall turn from me Jer 2:35
Will he reserve his *a* for ever Jer 3:5
not cause mine *a* to fall upon you Jer 3:12
and I will not keep *a* for ever Jer 3:12
for the fierce *a* of the LORD is Jer 4:8
of the LORD, and by his fierce *a* Jer 4:26
that they may provoke me to *a* Jer 7:18
Do they provoke me to *a* Jer 7:19
Behold, mine *a* and my fury shall Jer 7:20
me to *a* with their graven images Jer 8:19
not in thine *a*, lest thou bring Jer 10:24
themselves to provoke me to *a* in Jer 11:17
of the fierce *a* of the LORD Jer 12:13
for a fire is kindled in mine *a* Jer 15:14
ye have kindled a fire in mine *a* Jer 17:4
with them in the time of thine *a* Jer 18:23
and with a strong arm, even in *a* Jer 21:5
The *a* of the LORD shall not Jer 23:20
provoke me not to *a* with the Jer 25:6
that ye might provoke me to *a* Jer 25:7
of the fierce *a* of the LORD Jer 25:37
and because of his fierce *a* Jer 25:38
The fierce *a* of the LORD shall Jer 30:24
other gods, to provoke me to *a* Jer 32:29
to *a* with the work of their hands Jer 32:30
to me as a provocation of mine *a* Jer 32:31
they have done to provoke me to *a* Jer 32:32
I have driven them in mine *a* Jer 32:37
men, whom I have slain in mine *a* Jer 33:5
for great is the *a* and the fury Jer 36:7
As mine *a* and my fury hath been Jer 42:18
have committed to provoke me to *a* Jer 44:3
mine *a* was poured forth, and was Jer 44:6
evil upon them, even my fierce *a* Jer 49:37
from the fierce *a* of the LORD Jer 51:45
For through the *a* of the LORD it Jer 52:3
me in the day of his fierce *a* Lam 1:12
of Zion with a cloud in his *a* Lam 2:1
his footstool in the day of his *a* Lam 2:1
fierce *a* all the horn of Israel Lam 2:3
the indignation of his *a* the king Lam 2:6
slain them in the day of thine *a* Lam 2:21
*a* none escaped nor remained Lam 2:22
Thou hast covered with *a*, and Lam 3:43
destroy them in *a* from under the Lam 3:66
he hath poured out his fierce *a* Lam 4:11
The *a* of the LORD hath divided Lam 4:16
Thus shall mine *a* be accomplished Eze 5:13
execute judgments in thee in *a* Eze 5:15
and I will send mine *a* upon thee Eze 7:3
and accomplish mine *a* upon thee Eze 7:8
have returned to provoke me to *a* Eze 8:17
an overflowing shower in mine *a* Eze 13:13
thy whoredoms, to provoke me to *a* Eze 16:26
to accomplish my *a* against them Eze 20:8
to accomplish my *a* against them Eze 20:21
so will I gather you in mine *a* Eze 22:20
do in Edom according to mine *a* Eze 25:14
will even do according to thine *a* Eze 35:11
I have consumed them in mine *a* Eze 43:8
I beseech thee, let thine *a* Dan 9:16
shall be destroyed, neither in *a* Dan 11:20
mine *a* is kindled against them Hos 8:5
execute the fierceness of mine *a* Hos 11:9
provoked him to *a* most bitterly Hos 12:14
I gave thee a king in mine *a* Hos 13:11
for mine *a* is turned away from Hos 14:4
gracious and merciful, slow to *a* Joel 2:13
his *a* did tear perpetually, and he Amos 1:11
and turn away from his fierce *a* Jonah 3:9
God, and merciful, slow to *a* Jonah 4:2
And I will execute vengeance in *a* Mic 5:15
he retaineth not his *a* for ever Mic 7:18
The LORD is slow to *a*, and great Nah 1:3
abide in the fierceness of his *a* Nah 1:6
was thine *a* against the rivers Hab 3:8
didst thresh the heathen in *a* Hab 3:12
before the fierce *a* of the LORD Zeph 2:2
day of the LORD's *a* come upon you Zeph 2:2
be hid in the day of the LORD's *a* Zeph 2:3
indignation, even all my fierce *a* Zeph 3:8
Mine *a* was kindled against the Zec 10:3
looked round about on them with *a* Mk 3:5
by a foolish nation I will *a* you Rom 10:19
all bitterness, and wrath, and *a* Eph 4:31
*a*, wrath, malice, blasphemy, Col 3:8
provoke not your children to *a* Col 3:21

**ANGERED**
They *a* him also at the waters of Ps 106:32

**ANGLE**
all they that cast *a* into the Is 19:8
take up all of them with the *a* Hab 1:15

**ANGRY**
him, Oh let not the LORD be *a* Gen 18:30
he said, Oh let not the Lord be *a* Gen 18:32
nor *a* with yourselves, that ye Gen 45:5
he was *a* with Eleazar and Ithamar, Lev 10:16
Also the LORD was *a* with me for Deut 1:37
LORD was *a* with me for your sakes Deut 4:21
so that the LORD was *a* with you Deut 9:8
the LORD was very *a* with Aaron to Deut 9:20
lest *a* fellows run upon thee, and Judg 18:25
then be ye *a* for this matter 2Sa 19:42
thou be *a* with them, and deliver 1Kin 8:46
And the LORD was *a* with Solomon 1Kin 11:9
the LORD was very *a* with Israel 2Kin 17:18
thou be *a* with them, and deliver 2Chr 6:36
wouldest not thou be *a* with us Ezr 9:14
I was very *a* when I heard their Neh 5:6
Kiss the Son, lest he be *a* Ps 2:12
God is *a* with the wicked every Ps 7:11
in thy sight when once thou art *a* Ps 76:7
wilt thou be *a* for ever Ps 79:5
how long wilt thou be *a* against Ps 80:4
Wilt thou be *a* with us for ever Ps 85:5
He that is soon *a* dealeth Prov 14:17
with a contentious and an *a* woman Prov 21:19
Make no friendship with an *a* man Prov 22:24
so doth an *a* countenance a Prov 25:23
An *a* man stirreth up strife, and a Prov 29:22
should God be *a* at thy voice Eccl 5:6
not hasty in thy spirit to be *a* Eccl 7:9
mother's children were *a* with me Song 1:6
though thou wast *a* with me Is 12:1
be quiet, and will be no more *a* Eze 16:42
For this cause the king was *a* Dan 2:12
exceedingly, and he was very *a* Jonah 4:1
the LORD, Doest thou well to be *a* Jonah 4:4
thou well to be *a* for the gourd Jonah 4:9
And he said, I do well to be *a* Jonah 4:9
That whosoever is *a* with his Mt 5:22
house being *a* said to his servant Lk 14:21
And he was *a*, and would not go in Lk 15:28
are ye *a* at me, because I have Jn 7:23
Be ye *a*, and sin not Eph 4:26
not selfwilled, not soon *a* Titus 1:7
And the nations were *a*, and thy Rev 11:18

**ANGUISH**
in that we saw the *a* of his soul Gen 42:21
not unto Moses for *a* of spirit Ex 6:9
and be in *a* because of thee Deut 2:25
for *a* is come upon me, because my 2Sa 1:9
will speak in the *a* of my spirit Job 7:11
and *a* shall make him afraid Job 15:24
and *a* have taken hold on me Ps 119:143
distress and *a* cometh upon you Prov 1:27
trouble and darkness, dimness of *a* Is 8:22
into the land of trouble and *a* Is 30:6
the *a* as of her that bringeth Jer 4:31
*a* hath taken hold of us, and pain, Jer 6:24
*a* and sorrows have taken her, as a Jer 49:24
*a* took hold of him, and pangs as Jer 50:43
she remembereth no more the *a* Jn 16:21
Tribulation and *a*, upon every soul Rom 2:9
*a* of heart I wrote unto you with 2Cor 2:4

**ANIAM** (*a'-ne-am*) *A son of Shemida.*
Shechem, and Likhi, and *A* 1Chr 7:19

**ANIM** (*a'-nim*) *A city in Judah.*
And Anab, and Eshtemoh, and *A* Josh 15:50

**ANISE**
for ye pay tithe of mint and *a* Mt 23:23

**ANNA** (*an'-nah*) *A prophetess.*
And there was one *A*, a prophetess, Lk 2:36

**ANNAS** (*an'-nas*) *A High Priest during Jesus' ministry.*
*A* and Caiaphas being the high Lk 3:2
And led him away to *A* first Jn 18:13
Now *A* had sent him bound unto Jn 18:24
*A* the high priest, and Caiaphas, Acts 4:6

**ANOINT**
and shalt *a* them, and consecrate Ex 28:41
pour it upon his head, and *a* him Ex 29:7
for it, and thou shalt *a* it Ex 29:36
thou shalt *a* the tabernacle of Ex 30:26
And thou shalt *a* Aaron and his sons Ex 30:30
*a* the tabernacle, and all that is Ex 40:9
thou shalt *a* the altar of the Ex 40:10
And thou shalt *a* the laver Ex 40:11
and *a* him, and sanctify him Ex 40:13
And thou shalt *a* them Ex 40:15
as thou didst *a* their father Ex 40:15
And the priest, whom he shall *a* Lev 16:32
but thou shalt not *a* thyself with Deut 28:40
on a time to *a* a king over them Judg 9:8
If in truth ye *a* me king over you Judg 9:15
*a* thee, and put thy raiment upon Ruth 3:3
thou shalt *a* him to be captain 1Sa 9:16
The LORD sent me to *a* thee to be 1Sa 15:1
thou shalt *a* unto me him whom I 1Sa 16:3
And the LORD said, Arise, *a* him 1Sa 16:12
*a* not thyself with oil, but be as 2Sa 14:2
Nathan the prophet *a* him there 1Kin 1:34
*a* Hazael to be king over Syria 1Kin 19:15
thou *a* to be king over Israel 1Kin 19:16
thou *a* to be prophet in thy room 1Kin 19:16
ye princes, and *a* the shield Is 21:5
prophecy, and to *a* the most Holy Dan 9:24
neither did I *a* myself at all Dan 10:3
*a* themselves with the chief Amos 6:6
thou shalt not *a* thee with oil Mic 6:15
*a* thine head, and wash thy face Mt 6:17
to *a* my body to the burying Mk 14:8
that they might come and *a* him Mk 16:1
My head with oil thou didst not *a* Lk 7:46
*a* thine eyes with eyesalve, that Rev 3:18

**ANOINTED**
and wafers unleavened *a* with oil Ex 29:2
to be *a* therein, and to be Ex 29:29
or unleavened wafers *a* with oil Lev 2:4
If the priest that is *a* do sin Lev 4:3
the priest that is *a* shall take Lev 4:5
the priest that is *a* shall bring Lev 4:16
the LORD in the day when he is *a* Lev 6:20
is *a* in his stead shall offer it Lev 6:22
and unleavened wafers *a* with oil Lev 7:12
Israel, in the day that he *a* them Lev 7:36
*a* the tabernacle and all that was Lev 8:10
*a* the altar and all his vessels, Lev 8:11
head, and *a* him, to sanctify him Lev 8:12
Aaron, the priests which were *a* Num 3:3
of unleavened bread *a* with oil Num 6:15
up the tabernacle, and had *a* it Num 7:1
had *a* them, and sanctified them Num 7:1
altar in the day that it was *a* Num 7:10
altar, in the day when it was *a* Num 7:84
of the altar, after that it was *a* Num 7:88
which was *a* with the holy oil Num 35:25
king, and exalt the horn of his *a* 1Sa 2:10
shall walk before mine *a* for ever 1Sa 2:35
*a* thee to be captain over his 1Sa 10:1
before the LORD, and before his *a* 1Sa 12:3
his *a* is witness this day, that 1Sa 12:5
the LORD *a* thee king over Israel 1Sa 15:17
Surely the LORD's *a* is before him 1Sa 16:6
*a* him in the midst of his 1Sa 16:13
unto my master, the LORD's *a* 1Sa 24:6
seeing he is the *a* of the LORD 1Sa 24:6
for he is the LORD's *a* 1Sa 24:10
his hand against the LORD's *a* 1Sa 26:9
mine hand against the LORD's *a* 1Sa 26:11
kept your master, the LORD's *a* 1Sa 26:16
mine hand against the LORD's *a* 1Sa 26:23
hand to destroy the LORD's *a* 2Sa 1:14
saying, I have slain the LORD's *a* 2Sa 1:16
though he had not been *a* with oil 2Sa 1:21
there they *a* David king over the 2Sa 2:4
of Judah have *a* me king over them 2Sa 2:7
I am this day weak, though *a* king 2Sa 3:39
they *a* David king over Israel 2Sa 5:3
they had *a* David king over Israel 2Sa 5:17
I *a* thee king over Israel, and I 2Sa 12:7
*a* himself, and changed his apparel 2Sa 12:20
And Absalom, whom we *a* over us 2Sa 19:10
because he cursed the LORD's *a* 2Sa 19:21
and sheweth mercy to his *a* 2Sa 22:51
the *a* of the God of Jacob, and the 2Sa 23:1
of the tabernacle, and *a* Solomon 1Kin 1:39
prophet have *a* him king in Gihon 1Kin 1:45
had *a* him king in the room of his 1Kin 5:1
I have *a* thee king over Israel 2Kin 9:3
I have *a* thee king over the 2Kin 9:6
I have *a* thee king over Israel 2Kin 9:12
and they made him king, and *a* him 2Kin 11:12
*a* him, and made him king in his 2Kin 23:30
they *a* David king over Israel, 1Chr 11:3
David was *a* king over all Israel 1Chr 14:8
Saying, Touch not mine *a*, and do 1Chr 16:22
*a* him unto the LORD to be the 1Chr 29:22
turn not away the face of thine *a* 2Chr 6:42
whom the LORD had *a* to cut off 2Chr 22:7
And Jehoiada and his sons *a* him 2Chr 23:11
*a* them, and carried all the feeble 2Chr 28:15
the LORD, and against his *a* Ps 2:2
and sheweth mercy to his *a* Ps 18:50
know I that the LORD saveth his *a* Ps 20:6
is the saving strength of his *a* Ps 28:8
hath *a* thee with the oil of Ps 45:7
and look upon the face of thine *a* Ps 84:9
with my holy oil have I *a* him Ps 89:20
thou hast been wroth with thine *a* Ps 89:38
the footsteps of thine *a* Ps 89:51
I shall be *a* with fresh oil Ps 92:10
Saying, Touch not mine *a*, and do Ps 105:15
turn not away the face of thine *a* Ps 132:10
I have ordained a lamp for mine *a* Ps 132:17
Thus saith the LORD to his *a* Is 45:1
because the LORD hath *a* me to Is 61:1
the *a* of the LORD, was taken in Lam 4:20
from thee, and I *a* thee with oil Eze 16:9
Thou art the *a* cherub that Eze 28:14
even for salvation with thine *a* Hab 3:13
said he, These are the two *a* ones Zec 4:14
*a* with oil many that were sick, Mk 6:13
because he hath *a* me to preach Lk 4:18
feet, and *a* them with the ointment Lk 7:38
but this woman hath *a* my feet Lk 7:46
he *a* the eyes of the blind man Jn 9:6
*a* mine eyes, and said unto me, Go Jn 9:11
which *a* the Lord with ointment Jn 11:2
*a* the feet of Jesus, and wiped his Jn 12:3
child Jesus, whom thou hast *a* Acts 4:27
How God *a* Jesus of Nazareth with Acts 10:38
with you in Christ, and hath *a* us 2Cor 1:21
hath *a* thee with the oil of Heb 1:9

**ANOINTEDST**
Beth-el, where thou *a* the pillar Gen 31:13

**ANOINTEST**
thou *a* my head with oil Ps 23:5

**ANOINTING**
for the light, spices for *a* oil Ex 25:6
Then shalt thou take the *a* oil Ex 29:7

upon the altar, and of the *a* oil Ex 29:21
it shall be an holy *a* oil Ex 30:25
This shall be an holy *a* oil unto Ex 30:31
And the *a* oil, and sweet incense Ex 31:11
the light, and spices for *a* oil Ex 35:8
and his staves, and the *a* oil Ex 35:15
for the light, and for the *a* oil Ex 35:28
And he made the holy *a* oil Ex 37:29
And the golden altar, and the *a* oil Ex 39:38
And thou shalt take the *a* oil Ex 40:9
for their *a* shall surely be an Ex 40:15
is the portion of the *a* of Aaron Lev 7:35
of the *a* of his sons, out of the Lev 7:35
and the garments, and the *a* oil Lev 8:2
And Moses took the *a* oil, and Lev 8:10
he poured of the *a* oil upon Lev 8:12
And Moses took of the *a* oil Lev 8:30
for the *a* oil of the LORD is upon Lev 10:7
whose head the *a* oil was poured Lev 21:10
for the crown of the *a* oil of his Lev 21:12
daily meat offering, and the *a* oil Num 4:16
I given them by reason of the *a* Num 18:8
be destroyed because of the *a* Is 10:27
*a* him with oil in the name of the Jas 5:14
But the *a* which ye have received 1Jn 2:27
but as the same *a* teacheth you of 1Jn 2:27

**ANON**
word, and *a* with joy receiveth it Mt 13:20
fever, and *a* they tell him of her Mk 1:30

**ANOTHER** See PREFACE.
and shalt be turned into *a* man 1Sa 10:6
mine eyes shall behold, and not *a* Job 19:27
and let *a* take his office Ps 109:8
and discover not a secret to *a* Prov 25:9
Let *a* man praise thee, and not Prov 27:2
and my glory will I not give to *a* Is 42:8
and call his servants by *a* name Is 65:15
and thou shalt not be for *a* man Hos 3:3
let no man strive, nor reprove *a* Hos 4:4
should come, or do we look for *a* Mt 11:3
and *a* said, Is it I Mk 14:19
Then said he to *a*, And how much Lk 16:7
and he shall give you *a* Comforter Jn 14:16
he that cometh preacheth *a* Jesus 2Cor 11:4
Which is not *a* Gal 1:7
in himself alone, and not in *a* Gal 6:4
But exhort one *a* daily, while it Heb 3:13

**ANOTHER'S**
may not understand one *a* speech Gen 11:7
And if one man's ox hurt *a* Ex 21:35
ye also ought to wash one *a* feet Jn 13:14
his own, but every man *a* wealth 1Cor 10:24
Bear ye one *a* burdens, and so Gal 6:2

**ANSWER**
*a* for me in time to come, when it Gen 30:33
shall give Pharaoh an *a* of peace Gen 41:16
And his brethren could not *a* him Gen 45:3
be, if it make thee *a* of peace Deut 20:11
And they shall *a* and say, Our hands Deut 21:7
and spit in his face, and shall *a* Deut 25:9
And all the people shall *a* Deut 27:15
Then ye shall *a* them, That the Josh 4:7
yea, she returned *a* to herself Judg 5:29
then he would *a* him, Nay 1Sa 2:16
what if thy father *a* thee roughly 1Sa 20:10
he could not *a* Abner a word again 2Sa 3:11
see what *a* I shall return to him 2Sa 24:13
And they shall *a*, Because they 1Kin 9:9
advise that I may *a* this people 1Kin 12:6
*a* them, and speak good words to 1Kin 12:7
give ye that we may *a* this people 1Kin 12:9
was neither voice, nor any to *a* 1Kin 18:29
any salute thee, *a* him not again 2Kin 4:29
was, saying, *A* him not 2Kin 18:36
ye me to return *a* to this people 2Chr 10:6
we may return *a* to this people 2Chr 10:9
Thus shalt thou *a* the people that 2Chr 10:10
Then sent the king an *a* unto Ezr 4:17
then they returned *a* by letter Ezr 5:5
And thus they returned us *a* Ezr 5:11
peace, and found nothing to *a* Neh 5:8
Mordecai commanded to *a* Esther Est 4:13
bade them return Mordecai this *a* Est 4:15
if there be any that will *a* thee Job 5:1
he cannot *a* him one of a thousand Job 9:3
How much less shall I *a* him Job 9:14
were righteous, yet would I not *a* Job 9:15
man, as I am, that I should *a* him Job 9:32
Then call thou, and I will *a* Job 13:22
or let me speak, and *a* thou me Job 13:22
Thou shalt call, and I will *a* thee Job 14:15
my servant, and he gave me no *a* Job 19:16
do my thoughts cause me to *a* Job 20:2
my understanding causeth me to *a* Job 20:3
the words which he would *a* me Job 23:5
he visiteth, what shall I *a* him Job 31:14
is, that the Almighty would *a* me Job 31:35
these three men ceased to *a* Job Job 32:1
because they had found no *a* Job 32:3
Elihu saw that there was no *a* in Job 32:5
neither will I *a* him with your Job 32:14
I will *a* also my part, I also Job 32:17
I will open my lips and *a* Job 32:20
If thou canst *a* me, set thy words Job 33:5
I will *a* thee, that God is Job 33:12
thou hast any thing to say, *a* me Job 33:32
I will *a* thee, and thy companions Job 35:4
There they cry, but none giveth *a* Job 35:12
will demand of thee, and *a* thou me Job 38:3
that reproveth God, let him *a* it Job 40:2
what shall I *a* thee Job 40:4
but I will not *a* Job 40:5
have mercy also upon me, and *a* me Ps 27:7
in righteousness wilt thou *a* us Ps 65:5
for thou wilt *a* me Ps 86:7
call upon me, and I will *a* him Ps 91:15
the day when I call *a* me speedily Ps 102:2
save with thy right hand, and *a* me Ps 108:6
to *a* him that reproacheth me Ps 119:42
in thy faithfulness *a* me, and in Ps 143:1
call upon me, but I will not *a* Prov 1:28
A soft *a* turneth away wrath Prov 15:1
hath joy by the *a* of his mouth Prov 15:23
of the righteous studieth to *a* Prov 15:28
the *a* of the tongue, is from the Prov 16:1
that thou mightest *a* the words of Prov 22:21
his lips that giveth a right *a* Prov 24:26
*A* not a fool according to his Prov 26:4
*A* a fool according to his folly Prov 26:5
that I may *a* him that reproacheth Prov 27:11
he understand he will not *a* Prov 29:19
I called him, but he gave me no *a* Song 5:6
What shall one then *a* the Is 14:32
he shall hear it, he will *a* thee Is 30:19
was, saying, *A* him not Is 36:21
I asked of them, could *a* a word Is 41:28
cry unto him, yet can he not *a* Is 46:7
I called, was there none to *a* Is 50:2
thou call, and the LORD shall *a* Is 58:9
when I called, ye did not *a* Is 65:12
that before they call, I will *a* Is 65:24
because when I called, none did *a* Is 66:4
then shalt thou *a* them, Like as Jer 5:19
but they will not *a* thee Jer 7:27
Then they shall *a*, Because they Jer 22:9
Call unto me, and I will *a* thee Jer 33:3
thing the LORD shall *a* you Jer 42:4
people which had given him that *a* Jer 44:20
I the LORD will *a* him that cometh Eze 14:4
I the LORD will *a* him by myself Eze 14:7
that thou shalt *a*, For the Eze 21:7
careful to *a* thee in this matter Dan 3:16
Yea, the LORD will *a* and say unto Joel 2:19
for there is no *a* of God Mic 3:7
what I shall *a* when I am reproved Hab 2:1
beam out of the timber shall *a* it Hab 2:11
Then he shall *a*, Those with which Zec 13:6
no man was able to *a* him a word Mt 22:46
Then shall the righteous *a* him Mt 25:37
And the King shall *a* and say unto Mt 25:40
Then shall they also *a* him Mt 25:44
Then shall he *a* them, saying Mt 25:45
*a* me, and I will tell you by what Mk 11:29
*a* me Mk 11:30
neither wist they what to *a* him Mk 14:40
And he from within shall *a* Lk 11:7
how or what thing ye shall *a* Lk 12:11
and he shall *a* and say unto you, I Lk 13:25
they could not *a* him again to Lk 14:6
and *a* me Lk 20:3
and they marvelled at his *a* Lk 20:26
meditate before what ye shall *a* Lk 21:14
I also ask you, ye will not *a* me Lk 22:68
that we may give an *a* to them Jn 1:22
But Jesus gave him no *a* Jn 19:9
the more cheerfully *a* for myself Acts 24:10
have licence to *a* for himself Acts 25:16
because I shall *a* for myself this Acts 26:2
what saith the *a* of God unto him Rom 11:4
Mine *a* to them that do examine me 1Cor 9:3
that ye may have somewhat to *a* 2Cor 5:12
know how ye ought to *a* every man Col 4:6
At my first *a* no man stood with 2Ti 4:16
be ready always to give an *a* to 1Pet 3:15
but the *a* of a good conscience 1Pet 3:21

**ANSWERABLE**
*a* to the hangings of the court Ex 38:18

**ANSWERED**
And Abraham *a* and said Gen 18:27
And the children of Heth *a* Abraham Gen 23:5
Ephron the Hittite *a* Abraham in Gen 23:10
Ephron *a* Abraham, saying unto him Gen 23:14
Then Laban and Bethuel *a* and said Gen 24:50
And Isaac *a* and said unto Esau Gen 27:37
And Isaac his father *a* and said Gen 27:39
And Rachel and Leah *a* Gen 31:14
And Jacob *a* and said to Laban Gen 31:31
and Jacob *a* and said to Laban, What Gen 31:36
And Laban *a* and said unto Jacob Gen 31:43
And the sons of Jacob *a* Shechem Gen 34:13
who *a* me in the day of my Gen 35:3
And Joseph *a* and said, This is the Gen 40:18
Joseph *a* Pharaoh, saying, It is Gen 41:16
And Reuben *a* them, saying, Spake I Gen 42:22
And they *a*, Thy servant our father Gen 43:28
And Moses *a* and said, But, behold Ex 4:1
And Miriam *a* them, Sing ye to the Ex 15:21
And all the people *a* together Ex 19:8
spake, and God *a* him by a voice Ex 19:19
all the people *a* with one voice Ex 24:3
of Moses, one of his young men, *a* Num 11:28
And Balaam *a* and said unto the Num 22:18
And he *a* and said, Must I not take Num 23:12
But Balaam *a* and said unto Balak Num 23:26
Gad and the children of Reuben *a* Num 32:31
And ye *a* me, and said, The thing Deut 1:14
Then ye *a* and said unto me, We Deut 1:41
they *a* Joshua, saying, All that Josh 1:16
And the men *a* her, Our life for Josh 2:14
Achan *a* Joshua, and said, Indeed I Josh 7:20
they *a* Joshua, and said, Because Josh 9:24
Who *a*, Give me a blessing Josh 15:19
And Joshua *a* them, If thou be a Josh 17:15
and the half tribe of Manasseh *a* Josh 22:21
And the people *a* and said, God Josh 24:16
Her wise ladies *a* her, yea, she Judg 5:29
And his fellow *a* and said, This is Judg 7:14
the men of Penuel *a* him as the Judg 8:8
as the men of Succoth had *a* him Judg 8:8
And they *a*, As thou art, so were Judg 8:18
And they *a*, We will willingly give Judg 8:25
king of the children of Ammon *a* Judg 11:13
And they *a*, Samson, the son in law Judg 15:6
And they *a*, To bind Samson are we Judg 15:10
Then *a* the five men that went to Judg 18:14
But none *a* Judg 19:28
of the woman that was slain, *a* Judg 20:4
And they *a* him, The LORD bless Ruth 2:4
that was set over the reapers *a* Ruth 2:6
And Boaz *a* and said unto her, It Ruth 2:11
And she *a*, I am Ruth thine Ruth 3:9
And Hannah *a* and said, No, my lord 1Sa 1:15
Then Eli *a* and said, Go in peace 1Sa 1:17
and he *a*, Here am I 1Sa 3:4
And he *a*, I called not, my son 1Sa 3:6
Then Samuel *a*, Speak 1Sa 3:10
And he *a*, Here am I 1Sa 3:16
And the messenger *a* and said 1Sa 4:17
But she *a* not, neither did she 1Sa 4:20
And they *a*, Let the ark of the God 1Sa 5:8
They *a*, Five golden emerods, and 1Sa 6:4
And the servant *a* Saul again 1Sa 9:8
And they *a* them, and said, He is 1Sa 9:12
And Samuel *a* Saul, and said, I am 1Sa 9:19
And Saul *a* and said, Am not I a 1Sa 9:21
And one of the same place *a* 1Sa 10:12
And the LORD *a*, Behold, he hath 1Sa 10:22
And Nahash the Ammonite *a* them 1Sa 11:2
And they *a*, He is witness 1Sa 12:5
men of the garrison *a* Jonathan 1Sa 14:12
Then *a* one of the people, and said 1Sa 14:28
But he *a* him not that day 1Sa 14:37
among all the people that *a* him 1Sa 14:39
And Saul *a*, God do so and more also 1Sa 14:44
Then *a* one of the servants, and 1Sa 16:18
the people *a* him after this 1Sa 17:27
the people *a* him again after the 1Sa 17:30
And David *a*, I am the son of thy 1Sa 17:58
the women *a* one another as they 1Sa 18:7
And Michal *a* Saul, He said unto me 1Sa 19:17
And Jonathan *a* Saul, David 1Sa 20:28
Jonathan *a* Saul his father, and 1Sa 20:32
And the priest *a* David, and said 1Sa 21:4
David *a* the priest, and said unto 1Sa 21:5
Then *a* Doeg the Edomite, which 1Sa 22:9
And he *a*, Here I am, my lord 1Sa 22:12
Then Ahimelech *a* the king 1Sa 22:14
And the LORD *a* him and said, Arise 1Sa 23:4
Nabal *a* David's servants, and said 1Sa 25:10
Then *a* David and said to Ahimelech 1Sa 26:6
Then Abner *a* and said, Who art 1Sa 26:14
And David *a* and said, Behold the 1Sa 26:22
of the LORD, the LORD *a* him not 1Sa 28:6
And Saul *a*, I am sore distressed 1Sa 28:15
And Achish *a* and said to David, I 1Sa 29:9
And he *a* him, Pursue 1Sa 30:8
Then *a* all the wicked men and men 1Sa 30:22
And he *a*, That the people are fled 2Sa 1:4
And I *a*, Here am I 2Sa 1:7
I *a* him, I am an Amalekite 2Sa 1:8
And he *a*, I am the son of a 2Sa 1:13
And he *a*, I am 2Sa 2:20
David *a* Rechab and Baanah his 2Sa 4:9
And he *a*, Behold thy servant 2Sa 9:6
And she *a* him, Nay, my brother, do 2Sa 13:12
son of Shimeah David's brother, *a* 2Sa 13:32
And she *a*, I am indeed a widow 2Sa 14:5
Then the king *a* and said unto the 2Sa 14:18
And the woman *a* and said, As thy 2Sa 14:19
And Absalom *a* Joab, Behold, I sent 2Sa 14:32
Ittai *a* the king, and said, As the 2Sa 15:21
But the people *a*, Thou shalt not 2Sa 18:3
And Ahimaaz *a*, When Joab sent the 2Sa 18:29
And Cushi *a*, The enemies of my 2Sa 18:32
But Abishai the son of Zeruiah *a* 2Sa 19:21
And he *a*, My lord, O king, my 2Sa 19:26
And the king *a*, Chimham shall go 2Sa 19:38
men of Judah *a* the men of Israel 2Sa 19:42
men of Israel *a* the men of Judah 2Sa 19:43
And he *a*, I am he 2Sa 20:17
And he *a*, I do hear 2Sa 20:17
And Joab *a* and said, Far be it, far 2Sa 20:20
And the LORD *a*, It is for Saul, and 2Sa 21:1
they *a* the king, The man that 2Sa 21:5
unto the LORD, but he *a* them not 2Sa 22:42
Then king David *a* and said, Call 1Kin 1:28
the son of Jehoiada *a* the king 1Kin 1:36
And Jonathan *a* and said to Adonijah 1Kin 1:43
And king Solomon *a* and said unto 1Kin 2:22
Thus said Joab, and thus he *a* me 1Kin 2:30
Then the king *a* and said, Give her 1Kin 3:27
And he *a*, Nothing 1Kin 11:22
the king *a* the people roughly, and 1Kin 12:13
unto them, the people *a* the king 1Kin 12:16
And the king *a* and said unto the 1Kin 13:6
And he *a* him, I am 1Kin 18:8
And he *a*, I have not troubled 1Kin 18:18
the people *a* him not a word 1Kin 18:21
And all the people *a* and said, It 1Kin 18:24

was no voice, nor any that *a* 1Kin 18:26
And the king of Israel *a* and said, 1Kin 20:4
And the king of Israel *a* and said, 1Kin 20:11
And he *a*, Thou 1Kin 20:14
and he *a*, I will not give thee my 1Kin 21:6
And he *a*, I have found thee 1Kin 21:20
And he *a* him, Go, and prosper 1Kin 22:15
And they *a* him, He was an hairy 2Kin 1:8
And Elijah *a* and said to the 2Kin 1:10
And he *a* and said unto him, O man 2Kin 1:11
And Elijah *a* and said unto them, If 2Kin 1:12
And he *a*, Yea, I know it 2Kin 2:5
And he *a*, The way through the 2Kin 3:8
the king of Israel's servants *a* 2Kin 3:11
And she *a*, I dwell among mine own 2Kin 4:13
And Gehazi *a*, Verily she hath no 2Kin 4:14
And she *a*, It is well 2Kin 4:26
And he *a*, Go ye 2Kin 6:2
And he *a*, I will go 2Kin 6:3
And he *a*, Fear not 2Kin 6:16
And he *a*, Thou shalt not smite 2Kin 6:22
And she *a*, This woman said unto me 2Kin 6:28
the king leaned *a* the man of God 2Kin 7:2
And one of his servants *a* and said, 2Kin 7:13
that lord *a* the man of God, and 2Kin 7:19
And he *a*, Because I know the evil 2Kin 8:12
And Elisha *a*, The LORD hath shewed 2Kin 8:13
And he *a*, He told me that thou 2Kin 8:14
And Jehu *a*, What hast thou to do 2Kin 9:19
And he *a*, What peace, so long as 2Kin 9:22
And they *a*, We are the brethren of 2Kin 10:13
And Jehonadab *a*, It is 2Kin 10:15
their peace, and *a* him not a word 2Kin 18:36
And Hezekiah *a*, It is a light 2Kin 20:10
And Hezekiah *a*, All the things 2Kin 20:15
David went out to meet them, and *a* 1Chr 12:17
And Joab *a*, The LORD make his 1Chr 21:3
he *a* him from heaven by fire upon 1Chr 21:26
David saw that the LORD had *a* him 1Chr 21:28
the king of Tyre *a* in writing 2Chr 2:11
And it shall be *a*, Because they 2Chr 7:22
And the king *a* them roughly 2Chr 10:13
*a* them after the advice of the 2Chr 10:14
unto them, the people *a* the king 2Chr 10:16
he *a* him, I am as thou art, and my 2Chr 18:3
And the man of God *a*, The LORD is 2Chr 25:9
Then Hezekiah *a* and said, Now ye 2Chr 29:31
of the house of Zadok *a* him 2Chr 31:10
And Hilkiah *a* and said to Shaphan 2Chr 34:15
she *a* them, Thus saith the LORD 2Chr 34:23
one of the sons of Elam, *a* Ezr 10:2
Then all the congregation *a* Ezr 10:12
Then *a* I them, and said unto them, Neh 2:20
I *a* them after the same manner Neh 6:4
And all the people *a*, Amen, Amen, Neh 8:6
Memucan *a* before the king and the Est 1:16
And Esther *a*, If it seem good unto Est 5:4
Then *a* Esther, and said, My Est 5:7
Haman *a* the king, For the man Est 6:7
Then Esther the queen *a* and said, Est 7:3
Then the king Ahasuerus *a* Est 7:5
Then Satan *a* the LORD, and said, Job 1:7
Then Satan *a* the LORD, and said, Job 1:9
Satan *a* the LORD, and said, From Job 2:2
Satan *a* the LORD, and said, Skin Job 2:4
Then Eliphaz the Temanite *a* Job 4:1
But Job *a* and said, Job 6:1
Then *a* Bildad the Shuhite, and Job 8:1
Then Job *a* and said, Job 9:1
If I had called, and he had *a* me Job 9:16
Then *a* Zophar the Naamathite, and Job 11:1
not the multitude of words be *a* Job 11:2
And Job *a* and said, Job 12:1
Then *a* Eliphaz the Temanite, and Job 15:1
Then Job *a* and said, Job 16:1
Then *a* Bildad the Shuhite, and Job 18:1
Then Job *a* and said, Job 19:1
Then *a* Zophar the Naamathite, and Job 20:1
But Job *a* and said, Job 21:1
Then Eliphaz the Temanite *a* Job 22:1
Then Job *a* and said, Job 23:1
Then *a* Bildad the Shuhite, and Job 25:1
But Job *a* and said, Job 26:1
the son of Barachel the Buzite *a* Job 32:6
Job, or that *a* his words Job 32:12
They were amazed, they *a* no more Job 32:15
but stood still, and *a* no more Job 32:16
Furthermore Elihu *a* and said, Job 34:1
Then the LORD *a* Job out of the Job 38:1
Moreover the LORD *a* Job, and said, Job 40:1
Then Job *a* the LORD, and said, Job 40:3
Then *a* the LORD unto Job out of Job 40:6
Then Job *a* the LORD, and said, Job 42:1
unto the LORD, but he *a* them not Ps 18:41
I *a* thee in the secret place of Ps 81:7
upon the LORD, and he *a* them Ps 99:6
the LORD *a* me, and set me in a Ps 118:5
And he *a*, Until the cities be Is 6:11
And he *a* and said, Babylon is Is 21:9
their peace, and *a* him not a word Is 36:21
And Hezekiah *a*, All that is in Is 39:4
and I called you, but ye *a* not Jer 7:13
Then *a* I, and said, So be it, O Jer 11:5
his brother, What hath the LORD *a* Jer 23:35
What hath the LORD *a* thee Jer 23:37
unto them, but they have not *a* Jer 35:17
Then Baruch *a* them, He pronounced Jer 36:18
in Pathros, *a* Jeremiah, saying, Jer 44:15
Then I *a* them, The word of the Eze 24:20
And I *a*, O Lord GOD, thou knowest Eze 37:3
The king *a* and said to the Dan 2:5
They *a* again and said, Let the Dan 2:7
The king *a* and said, I know of Dan 2:8
The Chaldeans *a* before the king, Dan 2:10
Then Daniel *a* with counsel and Dan 2:14
He *a* and said to Arioch the king's Dan 2:15
Daniel *a* and said, Blessed be the Dan 2:20
The king *a* and said to Daniel, Dan 2:26
Daniel *a* in the presence of the Dan 2:27
The king *a* unto Daniel, and said, Dan 2:47
Meshach, and Abed-nego, *a* Dan 3:16
They *a* and said unto the king, Dan 3:24
He *a* and said, Lo, I see four men Dan 3:25
Belteshazzar *a* and said, My lord, Dan 4:19
Then Daniel *a* and said before the Dan 5:17
The king *a* and said, The thing is Dan 6:12
Then *a* they and said before the Dan 6:13
Then *a* Amos, and said to Amaziah, Amos 7:14
what Balaam the son of Beor *a* him Mic 6:5
And the LORD *a* me, and said, Write Hab 2:2
And the priests *a* and said, No Hag 2:12
And the priests *a* and said, It Hag 2:13
Then *a* Haggai, and said, So is Hag 2:14
stood among the myrtle trees *a* Zec 1:10
they *a* the angel of the LORD that Zec 1:11
Then the angel of the LORD *a* Zec 1:12
the LORD *a* the angel that talked Zec 1:13
And he *a* me, These are the horns Zec 1:19
And he *a* and spake unto those that Zec 3:4
So I *a* and spake to the angel that Zec 4:4
the angel that talked with me *a* Zec 4:5
Then he *a* and spake unto me, Zec 4:6
Then *a* I, and said unto him, What Zec 4:11
I *a* again, and said unto him, What Zec 4:12
And he *a* me and said, Knowest thou Zec 4:13
And I *a*, I see a flying roll Zec 5:2
Then I *a* and said unto the angel Zec 6:4
And the angel *a* and said unto me, Zec 6:5
But he *a* and said, It is written, Mt 4:4
The centurion *a* and said, Lord, I Mt 8:8
Jesus *a* and said unto them, Go and Mt 11:4
At that time Jesus *a* and said, I Mt 11:25
the scribes and of the Pharisees *a* Mt 12:38
But he *a* and said unto them, An Mt 12:39
But he *a* and said unto him that Mt 12:48
He *a* and said unto them, Because Mt 13:11
He *a* and said unto them, He that Mt 13:37
And Peter *a* him and said, Lord, if Mt 14:28
But he *a* and said unto them, Why Mt 15:3
But he *a* and said, Every plant, Mt 15:13
Then *a* Peter and said unto him, Mt 15:15
But he *a* her not a word Mt 15:23
But he *a* and said, I am not sent Mt 15:24
But he *a* and said, It is not meet Mt 15:26
Then Jesus *a* and said unto her, O Mt 15:28
He *a* and said unto them, When it Mt 16:2
And Simon Peter *a* and said, Thou Mt 16:16
And Jesus *a* and said unto him, Mt 16:17
Then *a* Peter, and said unto Jesus, Mt 17:4
And Jesus *a* and said unto them, Mt 17:11
Then Jesus *a* and said, O faithless Mt 17:17
And he *a* and said unto them, Have Mt 19:4
Then *a* Peter and said unto him, Mt 19:27
But he *a* one of them, and said, Mt 20:13
But Jesus *a* and said, Ye know not Mt 20:22
Jesus *a* and said unto them, Verily Mt 21:21
And Jesus *a* and said unto them, I Mt 21:24
they *a* Jesus, and said, We cannot Mt 21:27
He *a* and said, I will not Mt 21:29
And he *a* and said, I go sir Mt 21:30
And Jesus *a* and spake unto them Mt 22:1
Jesus *a* and said unto them, Ye do Mt 22:29
And Jesus *a* and said unto them, Mt 24:4
But the wise *a*, saying, Not so Mt 25:9
But he *a* and said, Verily I say Mt 25:12
His lord *a* and said unto him, Thou Mt 25:26
And he *a* and said, He that dippeth Mt 26:23
Then Judas, which betrayed him, *a* Mt 26:25
Peter *a* and said unto him, Though Mt 26:33
And the high priest *a* and said unto Mt 26:63
They *a* and said, He is guilty of Mt 26:66
priests and elders, he *a* nothing Mt 27:12
And he *a* him to never a word Mt 27:14
The governor *a* and said unto them, Mt 27:21
Then *a* all the people, and said, Mt 27:25
And the angel *a* and said unto the Mt 28:5
he *a* them, saying, Who is my Mk 3:33
And he *a*, saying, My name is Mk 5:9
He *a* and said unto them, Give ye Mk 6:37
He *a* and said unto them, Well hath Mk 7:6
And she *a* and said unto him, Yes, Mk 7:28
And his disciples *a* him, From Mk 8:4
And they *a*, John the Baptist Mk 8:28
And Peter *a* and said to Jesus, Mk 9:5
And he *a* and told them, Elias Mk 9:12
And one of the multitude *a* Mk 9:17
And John *a* him, saying, Master, we Mk 9:38
And he *a* and said unto them, What Mk 10:3
And Jesus *a* and said unto them, For Mk 10:5
And he *a* and said unto him, Master, Mk 10:20
And Jesus *a* and said, Verily I say Mk 10:29
And Jesus *a* and said unto him, What Mk 10:51
And Jesus *a* and said unto it, No Mk 11:14
And Jesus *a* and said unto them, I Mk 11:29
And they *a* and said unto Jesus, We Mk 11:33
that he had *a* them well, asked Mk 12:28
And Jesus *a* him, The first of all Mk 12:29
Jesus saw that he *a* discreetly Mk 12:34
And Jesus *a* and said, while he Mk 12:35
And he *a* and said unto them, It is Mk 14:20
And Jesus *a* and said unto them, Are Mk 14:48
he held his peace, and *a* nothing Mk 14:61
but he *a* nothing Mk 15:3
But Jesus yet *a* nothing Mk 15:5
But Pilate *a* them, saying, Will Mk 15:9
And Pilate *a* and said again unto Mk 15:12
And the angel *a* and said unto her, Lk 1:35
And his mother *a* and said, Not so Lk 1:60
John *a*, saying unto them all, I Lk 3:16
And Jesus *a* him, saying, It is Lk 4:4
And Jesus *a* and said unto him, Get Lk 4:8
Simon *a* and said, I suppose that Lk 7:43
And he *a* and said unto them, My Lk 8:21
he *a* him, saying, Fear not Lk 8:50
And John *a* and said, Master, we saw Lk 9:49
said unto him, Thou hast *a* right Lk 10:28
And Jesus *a* and said unto her, Lk 10:41
Then *a* one of the lawyers, and Lk 11:45
the synagogue *a* with indignation Lk 13:14
The Lord then *a* him, and said, Lk 13:15
*a* them, saying, Which of you Lk 14:5
he *a* them and said, The kingdom of Lk 17:20
And they *a* and said unto him, Where Lk 17:37
And he *a* and said unto them, I tell Lk 19:40
And he *a* and said unto them, I will Lk 20:3
And they *a*, that they could not Lk 20:7
They *a* and said, Caesar's Lk 20:24
And Jesus *a* and said, Suffer ye Lk 22:51
he *a* him and said, Thou sayest it Lk 23:3
but he *a* him nothing Lk 23:9
And he *a*, No Jn 1:21
John *a* them, saying, I baptize Jn 1:26
Jesus *a* and said unto him, Before Jn 1:48
Nathanael *a* and saith unto him, Jn 1:49
Jesus *a* and said unto him, Because Jn 1:50
Then *a* the Jews and said unto him, Jn 2:18
Jesus *a* and said unto them, Jn 2:19
Jesus *a* and said unto him, Verily, Jn 3:3
Jesus *a*, Verily, verily, I say Jn 3:5
Nicodemus *a* and said unto him, How Jn 3:9
Jesus *a* and said unto him, Art Jn 3:10
John *a* and said, A man can receive Jn 3:27
Jesus *a* and said unto her, If thou Jn 4:10
Jesus *a* and said unto her, Jn 4:13
The woman *a* and said, I have no Jn 4:17
The impotent man *a* him, Sir, I Jn 5:7
He *a* them, He that made me whole, Jn 5:11
But Jesus *a* them, My Father Jn 5:17
Then *a* Jesus and said unto them, Jn 5:19
Philip *a* him, Two hundred Jn 6:7
Jesus *a* them and said, Verily, Jn 6:26
Jesus *a* and said unto them, This Jn 6:29
Jesus therefore *a* and said unto Jn 6:43
Then Simon Peter *a* him, Lord, to Jn 6:68
Jesus *a* them, Have not I chosen Jn 6:70
Jesus *a* them, and said, My Jn 7:16
The people *a* and said, Thou hast a Jn 7:20
Jesus *a* and said unto them, I have Jn 7:21
The officers *a*, Never man spake Jn 7:46
Then *a* them the Pharisees, Are ye Jn 7:47
They *a* and said unto him, Art thou Jn 7:52
Jesus *a* and said unto them, Though Jn 8:14
Jesus *a*, Ye neither know me, nor Jn 8:19
They *a* him, We be Abraham's seed, Jn 8:33
Jesus *a* them, Verily, verily, I Jn 8:34
They *a* and said unto him, Abraham Jn 8:39
Then *a* the Jews, and said unto him Jn 8:48
Jesus *a*, I have not a devil Jn 8:49
Jesus *a*, If I honour myself, my Jn 8:54
Jesus *a*, Neither hath this man Jn 9:3
He *a* and said, A man that is Jn 9:11
His parents *a* them and said, We Jn 9:20
He *a* and said, Whether he be a Jn 9:25
He *a* them, I have told you Jn 9:27
The man *a* and said unto them, Why Jn 9:30
They *a* and said unto him, Thou Jn 9:34
He *a* and said, Who is he, Lord, Jn 9:36
Jesus *a* them, I told you, and ye Jn 10:25
Jesus *a* them, Many good works Jn 10:32
The Jews *a* him, saying, For a Jn 10:33
Jesus *a* them, Is it not written Jn 10:34
Jesus *a*, Are there not twelve Jn 11:9
And Jesus *a* them, saying, The hour Jn 12:23
Jesus *a* and said, This voice came Jn 12:30
The people *a* him, We have heard Jn 12:34
Jesus *a* and said unto him, What I Jn 13:7
Jesus *a* him, If I wash thee not, Jn 13:8
Jesus *a*, He it is, to whom I Jn 13:26
Jesus *a* him, Whither I go, thou Jn 13:36
Jesus *a* him, Wilt thou lay down Jn 13:38
Jesus *a* and said unto him, If a Jn 14:23
Jesus *a* them, Do ye now believe Jn 16:31
They *a* him, Jesus of Nazareth Jn 18:5
Jesus *a*, I have told you that I Jn 18:8
Jesus *a* him, I spake openly to Jn 18:20
Jesus *a* him, If I have spoken Jn 18:23
They *a* and said unto him, If he Jn 18:30
Jesus *a* him, Sayest thou this Jn 18:34
Pilate *a*, Am I a Jew Jn 18:35
Jesus *a*, My kingdom is not of Jn 18:36
Jesus *a*, Thou sayest that I am a Jn 18:37
The Jews *a* him, We have a law, and Jn 19:7
Jesus *a*, Thou couldest have no Jn 19:11
The chief priests *a*, We have no Jn 19:15
Pilate *a*, What I have written I Jn 19:22
And Thomas *a* and said unto him, My Jn 20:28
They *a* him, No Jn 21:5
he *a* unto the people, Ye men of Acts 3:12
But Peter and John *a* and said unto Acts 4:19
Peter *a* unto her, Tell me whether Acts 5:8

Peter and the other apostles *a*.............. Acts 5:29
Then *a* Simon, and said, Pray ye to..... Acts 8:24
And the eunuch *a* Philip, and said,....... Acts 8:34
And he *a* and said, I believe that......... Acts 8:37
Then Ananias *a*, Lord, I have............... Acts 9:13
Then *a* Peter,......................................... Acts 10:46
But the voice *a* me again from............. Acts 11:9
had held their peace, James *a*............ Acts 15:13
And the evil spirit *a* and said,............. Acts 19:15
Then Paul *a*, What mean ye to weep. Acts 21:13
And I *a*, Who art thou, Lord................. Acts 22:8
And the chief captain *a*, With a.......... Acts 22:28
had beckoned unto him to speak, *a*... Acts 24:10
to come, Felix trembled, and *a*........... Acts 24:25
But Festus *a*, that Paul should be......... Acts 25:4
While he *a* for himself, Neither............ Acts 25:8
*a* Paul, and said, Wilt thou go up.......... Acts 25:9
had conferred with the council, *a*....... Acts 25:12
To whom I *a*, It is not the manner.... Acts 25:16
forth the hand, and *a* for himself......... Acts 26:1
And one of the elders *a*, saying............ Rev 7:13

**ANSWEREDST**
Thou *a* them, O LORD our God................. Ps 99:8
In the day when I cried thou *a* me........ Ps 138:3

**ANSWEREST**
of Ner, saying, *A* thou not, Abner....... 1Sa 26:14
what emboldeneth thee that thou *a*...... Job 16:3
and said unto him, *A* thou nothing....... Mt 26:62
Jesus, saying, *A* thou nothing.............. Mk 14:60
him again, saying, *A* thou nothing......... Mk 15:4
*A* thou the high priest so....................... Jn 18:22

**ANSWERETH**
*a* me no more, neither by prophets...... 1Sa 28:15
and the God that *a* by fire.................. 1Kin 18:24
who calleth upon God, and he *a* him..... Job 12:4
He that *a* a matter before he.............. Prov 18:13
but the rich *a* roughly.......................... Prov 18:23
As in water face *a* to face.................... Prov 27:19
because God *a* him in the joy of.......... Eccl 5:20
but money *a* all things......................... Eccl 10:19
And Peter *a* and saith unto him,............ Mk 8:29
He *a* him, and saith, O faithless............. Mk 9:19
But Jesus *a* again, and saith unto......... Mk 10:24
He *a* and saith unto them, He that......... Lk 3:11
*a* to Jerusalem which now is, and.......... Gal 4:25

**ANSWERING**
Jesus *a* said unto him, Suffer it............... Mt 3:15
Jesus *a* saith unto them, Have ............. Mk 11:22
Jesus *a* saith unto them, Neither.......... Mk 11:33
Jesus *a* said unto them, Render to ....... Mk 12:17
Jesus *a* said unto them, Do ye not....... Mk 12:24
Jesus *a* said unto him, Seest thou.......... Mk 13:2
Jesus *a* them began to say, Take........... Mk 13:5
he *a* said unto him, Thou sayest............ Mk 15:2
the angel *a* said unto him, I am ............. Lk 1:19
Jesus *a* said unto him, It is said ............ Lk 4:12
Simon *a* said unto him, Master, we........... Lk 5:5
he *a* said unto them, What reason........... Lk 5:22
Jesus *a* said unto them, They that........... Lk 5:31
Jesus *a* them said, Have ye not................ Lk 6:3
Then Jesus *a* said unto them, Go............ Lk 7:22
Jesus *a* said unto him, Simon, I............... Lk 7:40
They *a* said, John the Baptist.................. Lk 9:19
Peter *a* said, The Christ of God............... Lk 9:20
And Jesus *a* said, O faithless and.......... Lk 9:41
he *a* said, Thou shalt love the............... Lk 10:27
And Jesus *a* said, A certain man............ Lk 10:30
Jesus *a* said unto them, Suppose............ Lk 13:2
he *a* said unto him, Lord, let it............... Lk 13:8
Jesus *a* spake unto the lawyers and........ Lk 14:3
he *a* said to his father, Lo,..................... Lk 15:29
And Jesus *a* said, Were there not ........... Lk 17:17
Jesus *a* said unto them, The.................. Lk 20:34
certain of the scribes *a* said.................. Lk 20:39
But the other *a* rebuked him.................. Lk 23:40
*a* said unto him, Art thou only a.............. Lk 24:18
not *a* again ........................................... Titus 2:9

**ANSWERS**
seeing in your *a* there remaineth.......... Job 21:34
because of his *a* for wicked men .......... Job 34:36
at his understanding and *a* ..................... Lk 2:47

**ANT**
Go to the *a*, thou sluggard..................... Prov 6:6

**ANTHOTHIJAH** See ANTOTHIJAH.

**ANTICHRIST**
ye have heard that *a* shall come............ 1Jn 2:18
He is *a*, that denieth the Father........... 1Jn 2:22
and this is that spirit of *a*..................... 1Jn 4:3
This is a deceiver and an *a*........................ 2Jn 7

**ANTICHRISTS**
come, even now are there many *a*......... 1Jn 2:18

**ANTIOCH** (*an'-te-ok*)
*1. A city in Syria.*
and Nicolas a proselyte of *A*.................. Acts 6:5
far as Phenice, and Cyprus, and *A*..... Acts 11:19
which, when they were come to *A*..... Acts 11:20
that he should go as far as *A*............. Acts 11:22
found him, he brought him unto *A*.... Acts 11:26
were called Christians first in *A*........ Acts 11:26
prophets from Jerusalem unto *A*........ Acts 11:27
that was at *A* certain prophets............. Acts 13:1
And thence sailed to *A*, from............. Acts 14:26
their own company to *A* with Paul.... Acts 15:22
which are of the Gentiles in *A*........... Acts 15:23
were dismissed, they came to *A*.......... Acts 15:30
also and Barnabas continued in *A*...... Acts 15:35
the church, he went down to *A*.......... Acts 18:22
But when Peter was come to *A*............. Gal 2:11
*2. A city in Pisidia.*
Perga, they came to *A* in Pisidia......... Acts 13:14
came thither certain Jews from *A*...... Acts 14:19
to Lystra, and to Iconium, and *A*........ Acts 14:21
which came unto me at *A*, at.................. 2Ti 3:11

**ANTIPAS** (*an'-tip-as*) *A Christian martyr.*
wherein *A* was my faithful martyr........ Rev 2:13

**ANTIPATRIS** (*an-tip'-at-ris*) *A city in northern Palestine.*
and brought him by night to *A*.......... Acts 23:31

**ANTIQUITY**
whose *a* is of ancient days..................... Is 23:7

**ANTOTHIJAH** (*an-to-thi'-jah*) *Son of Shashak.*
And Hananiah, and Elam, and *A*.......... 1Chr 8:24

**ANTOTHITE** (*an'-to-thite*) See ANETOTHITE. *A native of Anathoth.*
Ikkesh the Tekoite, Abiezer the *A*..... 1Chr 11:28
and Berachah, and Jehu the *A*............. 1Chr 12:3

**ANTS**
The *a* are a people not strong,............ Prov 30:25

**ANUB** (*a'-nub*) *A descendant of Judah.*
And Coz begat *A*, and Zobebah, and.... 1Chr 4:8

**ANVIL**
the hammer him that smote the *a*........... Is 41:7

**ANY** See PREFACE.

**APACE**
And he came *a*, and drew near............ 2Sa 18:25
Kings of armies did flee *a*..................... Ps 68:12
are beaten down, and are fled *a*............. Jer 46:5

**APART**
That thou shalt set *a* unto the................ Ex 13:12
she shall be put *a* seven days............... Lev 15:19
she is put *a* for her uncleanness........... Lev 18:19
*a* him that is godly for himself.................. Ps 4:3
her that was set *a* for pollution............ Eze 22:10
family of the house of David *a*............ Zec 12:12
of David *a*, and their wives *a*............... Zec 12:12
of Nathan *a*, and their wives *a*............ Zec 12:12
of Levi *a*, and their wives *a*................. Zec 12:13
of Shimei *a*, and their wives *a*............ Zec 12:13
family *a*, and their wives *a* ................. Zec 12:14
by ship into a desert place *a*................ Mt 14:13
went up into a mountain *a* to pray....... Mt 14:23
them up into an high mountain *a*.......... Mt 17:1
came the disciples to Jesus *a*............... Mt 17:19
the twelve disciples *a* in the way.......... Mt 20:17
Come ye yourselves *a* into a.................. Mk 6:31
an high mountain *a* by themselves.......... Mk 9:2
Wherefore lay *a* all filthiness and.......... Jas 1:21

**APELLES** (*a-pel'-leze*) *A Christian acquaintance of Paul.*
Salute *A* approved in Christ ............... Rom 16:10

**APES**
gold, and silver, ivory, and *a*.............. 1Kin 10:22
gold, and silver, ivory, and *a*............... 2Chr 9:21

**APHARSACHITES** (*a-far'-sak-ites*) See APHARSATHCHITES. *An Assyrian tribe.*
and his companions the *A*, which............ Ezr 5:6
and your companions the *A*..................... Ezr 6:6

**APHARSATHCHITES** (*a-far'-sath-kites*) See APHARSACHITES, APHARSITES. *Same as Apharsachites.*
the Dinaites, the *A*, the............................ Ezr 4:9

**APHARSITES** (*a-far'-sites*) See APHARSATHCHITES. *Same as Apharsachites*
the Tarpelites, the *A*, the.......................... Ezr 4:9

**APHEK** (*a'-fek*) See APHIK.
*1. A Canaanite city.*
The king of *A*, one ............................... Josh 12:18
and the Philistines pitched in *A*............... 1Sa 4:1
together all their armies to *A*................ 1Sa 29:1
*2. A city in Asher.*
is beside the Sidonians, unto *A*............ Josh 13:4
Ummah also, and *A*, and Rehob............ Josh 19:30
*3. Place where Ahab defeated Benhadad.*
the Syrians, and went up to *A*............ 1Kin 20:26
But the rest fled to *A*, into the............. 1Kin 20:30
thou shalt smite the Syrians in *A*....... 2Kin 13:17

**APHEKAH** (*af-e'-kah*) *A city in Judah.*
and Beth-tappuah, and *A*.................... Josh 15:53

**APHIAH** (*af-i'-ah*) *An ancestor of Saul.*
son of Bechorath, the son of *A*............... 1Sa 9:1

**APHIK** (*a'-fik*) See APHEK. *Same as Aphek 2.*
Achzib, nor of Helbah, nor of *A*........... Judg 1:31

**APHRAH** (*af'-rah*) See BETH-LEAPHRAH, OPHRAH. *A city in Benjamin.*
in the house of *A* roll thyself in.............. Mic 1:10

**APHSES** (*af'-seze*) *A Levite chief.*
to Hezir, the eighteenth to *A*............. 1Chr 24:15

**APIECE**
take five shekels *a* by the poll .............. Num 3:47
incense, weighing ten shekels *a*............ Num 7:86
of their princes gave him a rod *a*.......... Num 17:6
brass, of eighteen cubits high *a*............ 1Kin 7:15
Every one had four faces *a*.................... Eze 10:21
And the doors had two leaves *a*........... Eze 41:24
neither have two coats *a*............................ Lk 9:3
containing two or three firkins *a*............... Jn 2:6

**APOLLONIA** (*ap-ol-lo'-ne-ah*) *A city in Macedonia.*
passed through Amphipolis and *A*........ Acts 17:1

**APOLLOS** (*ap-ol'-los*) *A Christian Jew from Alexandria.*
And a certain Jew named *A*, born at. Acts 18:24
while *A* was at Corinth, Paul................ Acts 19:1
and I of *A*........................................... 1Cor 1:12
and another, I am of *A*............................. 1Cor 3:4
Who then is Paul, and who is *A*.............. 1Cor 3:5
I have planted, *A* watered....................... 1Cor 3:6
Whether Paul, or *A*, or Cephas, or....... 1Cor 3:22
to myself and to *A* for your sakes.......... 1Cor 4:6
As touching our brother *A*................... 1Cor 16:12
*A* on their journey diligently,.............. Titus 3:13

**APOLLYON** (*ap-ol'-le-on*) *The angel of the Abyss.*
the Greek tongue hath his name *A*....... Rev 9:11

**APOSTLE**
Jesus Christ, called to be an *a*................. Rom 1:1
as I am the *a* of the Gentiles.............. Rom 11:13
called to be an *a* of Jesus Christ............ 1Cor 1:1
Am I not an *a*............................................ 1Cor 9:1
If I be not an *a* unto others..................... 1Cor 9:2
am not meet to be called an *a*............... 1Cor 15:9
an *a* of Jesus Christ by the will............... 2Cor 1:1
Truly the signs of an *a* were ............... 2Cor 12:12
Paul, an *a*, (not of men, neither................. Gal 1:1
an *a* of Jesus Christ by the will.................. Eph 1:1
an *a* of Jesus Christ by the will.................. Col 1:1
an *a* of Jesus Christ by the........................ 1Ti 1:1
I am ordained a preacher, and an *a*.......... 1Ti 2:7
an *a* of Jesus Christ by the will................. 2Ti 1:1
am appointed a preacher, and an *a*......... 2Ti 1:11
an *a* of Jesus Christ, according .............. Titus 1:1
heavenly calling, consider the *A*............. Heb 3:1
an *a* of Jesus Christ, to the ...................... 1Pet 1:1
an *a* of Jesus Christ, to them.................. 2Pet 1:1

**APOSTLES**
names of the twelve *a* are these ............ Mt 10:2
the *a* gathered themselves....................... Mk 6:30
twelve, whom also he named *a* ................ Lk 6:13
And the *a*, when they were returned...... Lk 9:10
I will send them prophets and *a*............ Lk 11:49
the *a* said unto the Lord,.......................... Lk 17:5
down, and the twelve *a* with him .......... Lk 22:14
told these things unto the *a*.................. Lk 24:10
unto the *a* whom he had chosen ............ Acts 1:2
he was numbered with the eleven *a*.... Acts 1:26
Peter and to the rest of the *a*................ Acts 2:37
and signs were done by the *a*............... Acts 2:43
with great power gave the *a*................. Acts 4:33
who by the *a* was surnamed................. Acts 4:36
hands of the *a* were many signs........... Acts 5:12
And laid their hands on the *a*................ Acts 5:18
Peter and the other *a* answered............ Acts 5:29
to put the *a* forth a little space ............ Acts 5:34
and when they had called the *a*............. Acts 5:40
Whom they set before the *a* ................... Acts 6:6
Judaea and Samaria, except the *a*......... Acts 8:1
Now when the *a* which were at.............. Acts 8:14
took him, and brought him to the *a*..... Acts 9:27
And the *a* and brethren that were in... Acts 11:1
with the Jews, and part with the *a*...... Acts 14:4
Which when the *a*, Barnabas and....... Acts 14:14
go up to Jerusalem unto the *a* ............. Acts 15:2
of the church, and of the *a* .................. Acts 15:4
And the *a* and elders came together..... Acts 15:6
Then pleased it the *a* and elders, ........ Acts 15:22
The *a* and elders and brethren send... Acts 15:23
from the brethren unto the *a*............... Acts 15:33
keep, that were ordained of the *a*......... Acts 16:4
who are of note among the *a*................. Rom 16:7
God hath set forth us the *a* last ........... 1Cor 4:9
a wife, as well as other *a* ....................... 1Cor 9:5
set some in the church, first *a* ........... 1Cor 12:28
Are all *a*?............................................ 1Cor 12:29
then of all the *a*.................................... 1Cor 15:7
For I am the least of the *a*.................... 1Cor 15:9
a whit behind the very chiefest *a*.......... 2Cor 11:5
For such are false *a*, deceitful ............. 2Cor 11:13
themselves into the *a* of Christ............ 2Cor 11:13
am I behind the very chiefest *a*........... 2Cor 12:11
to them which were *a* before me............ Gal 1:17
But other of the *a* saw I none................ Gal 1:19
upon the foundation of the *a*.................. Eph 2:20
is now revealed unto his holy *a* ............... Eph 3:5
And he gave some, *a*............................... Eph 4:11
burdensome, as the *a* of Christ................ 1Th 2:6
of us the *a* of the Lord and ..................... 2Pet 3:2
of the *a* of our Lord Jesus Christ............. Jude 17
tried them which say they are *a* ............. Rev 2:2
her, thou heaven, and ye holy *a*............ Rev 18:20
names of the twelve *a* of the Lamb..... Rev 21:14

**APOSTLES'**
stedfastly in the *a* doctrine.................. Acts 2:42
And laid them down at the *a* feet......... Acts 4:35
money, and laid it at the *a* feet............ Acts 4:37
part, and laid it at the *a* feet................... Acts 5:2
that through laying on of the *a* ............ Acts 8:18

**APOSTLESHIP**
- take part of this ministry and *a* ... Acts 1:25
- whom we have received grace and *a* ... Rom 1:5
- seal of mine *a* are ye in the Lord ... 1Cor 9:2
- to the *a* of the circumcision ... Gal 2:8

**APOTHECARIES**
- Hananiah the son of one of the *a* ... Neh 3:8

**APOTHECARIES'**
- of spices prepared by the *a* art ... 2Chr 16:14

**APOTHECARY**
- compound after the art of the *a* ... Ex 30:25
- confection after the art of the *a* ... Ex 30:35
- according to the work of the *a* ... Ex 37:29
- *a* to send forth a stinking savour ... Eccl 10:1

**APPAIM** *(ap'-pa-im) A son of Nadab.*
- Seled, and *A* ... 1Chr 2:30
- And the sons of *A* ... 1Chr 2:31

**APPAREL**
- by the year, and a suit of *a* ... Judg 17:10
- asses, and the camels, and the *a* ... 1Sa 27:9
- on ornaments of gold upon your *a* ... 2Sa 1:24
- himself, and changed his *a* ... 2Sa 12:20
- mourner, and put on now mourning *a* .. 2Sa 14:2
- of his ministers, and their *a* ... 1Kin 10:5
- of his ministers, and their *a* ... 2Chr 9:4
- his cupbearers also, and their *a* ... 2Chr 9:4
- priests in their *a* with trumpets ... Ezr 3:10
- that Esther put on her royal *a* ... Est 5:1
- Let the royal *a* be brought which ... Est 6:8
- And let this *a* and horse be ... Est 6:9
- Haman, Make haste, and take the *a* ... Est 6:10
- Then took Haman the *a* and the ... Est 6:11
- of the king in royal *a* of blue ... Est 8:15
- The changeable suits of *a* ... Is 3:22
- our own bread, and wear our own *a* ... Is 4:1
- this that is glorious in his *a* ... Is 63:1
- Wherefore art thou red in thine *a* ... Is 63:2
- work, and in chests of rich *a* ... Eze 27:24
- as are clothed with strange *a* ... Zeph 1:8
- together, gold, and silver, and *a* ... Zec 14:14
- two men stood by them in white *a* ... Acts 1:10
- set day Herod, arrayed in royal *a* ... Acts 12:21
- no man's silver, or gold, or *a* ... Acts 20:33
- adorn themselves in modest *a* ... 1Ti 2:9
- man with a gold ring, in goodly *a* ... Jas 2:2
- of gold, or of putting on of *a* ... 1Pet 3:3

**APPARELLED**
- daughters that were virgins *a* ... 2Sa 13:18
- they which are gorgeously *a* ... Lk 7:25

**APPARENTLY**
- I speak mouth to mouth, even *a* ... Num 12:8

**APPEAL**
- I *a* unto Caesar ... Acts 25:11
- was constrained to *a* unto Caesar ... Acts 28:19

**APPEALED**
- answered, Hast thou *a* unto Caesar ... Acts 25:12
- But when Paul had *a* to be ... Acts 25:21
- he himself hath *a* to Augustus ... Acts 25:25
- if he had not *a* unto Caesar ... Acts 26:32

**APPEAR**
- one place, and let the dry land *a* ... Gen 1:9
- made the white *a* which was in the ... Gen 30:37
- none shall *a* before me empty ... Ex 23:15
- males shall *a* before the Lord GOD ... Ex 23:17
- none shall *a* before me empty ... Ex 34:20
- children *a* before the Lord GOD ... Ex 34:23
- when thou shalt go up to *a* before ... Ex 34:24
- to day the LORD will *a* unto you ... Lev 9:4
- of the LORD shall *a* unto you ... Lev 9:6
- if it *a* still in the garment, ... Lev 13:57
- for I will *a* in the cloud upon ... Lev 16:2
- in a year shall all thy males *a* ... Deut 16:16
- they shall not *a* before the LORD ... Deut 16:16
- When all Israel is come to *a* ... Deut 31:11
- the LORD did no more *a* to Manoah ... Judg 13:21
- that he may *a* before the LORD, and ... 1Sa 1:22
- Did I plainly *a* unto the house of ... 1Sa 2:27
- that night did God *a* unto Solomon ... 2Chr 1:7
- when shall I come and *a* before God ... Ps 42:2
- Let thy work *a* unto thy servants, ... Ps 90:16
- up Zion, he shall *a* in his glory ... Ps 102:16
- The flowers *a* on the earth ... Song 2:12
- goats, that *a* from mount Gilead ... Song 4:1
- flock of goats that *a* from Gilead ... Song 6:5
- whether the tender grape *a* ... Song 7:12
- When ye come to *a* before me ... Is 1:12
- but he shall *a* to your joy ... Is 66:5
- thy face, that thy shame may *a* ... Jer 13:26
- in all your doings your sins do *a* ... Eze 21:24
- that they may *a* unto men to fast ... Mt 6:16
- That thou *a* not unto men to fast, ... Mt 6:18
- which indeed *a* beautiful outward, ... Mt 23:27
- outwardly *a* righteous unto men ... Mt 23:28
- then shall *a* the sign of the Son ... Mt 24:30
- for ye are as graves which *a* not ... Lk 11:44
- of God should immediately *a* ... Lk 19:11
- priests and all their council to *a* ... Acts 22:30
- in the which I will *a* unto thee ... Acts 26:16
- But sin, that it might *a* sin ... Rom 7:13
- For we must all *a* before the ... 2Cor 5:10
- the sight of God might *a* unto you ... 2Cor 7:12
- not that we should *a* approved ... 2Cor 13:7
- Christ, who is our life, shall *a* ... Col 3:4
- shall ye also *a* with him in glory ... Col 3:4
- that thy profiting may *a* to all ... 1Ti 4:15
- now to *a* in the presence of God ... Heb 9:24
- he *a* the second time without sin ... Heb 9:28
- not made of things which do *a* ... Heb 11:3
- shall the ungodly and the sinner *a* ... 1Pet 4:18
- when the chief Shepherd shall *a* ... 1Pet 5:4
- that, when he shall *a*, we may ... 1Jn 2:28
- it doth not yet *a* what we shall ... 1Jn 3:2
- but we know that, when he shall *a* ... 1Jn 3:2
- shame of thy nakedness do not *a* ... Rev 3:18

**APPEARANCE**
- as it were the *a* of fire, until ... Num 9:15
- by day, and the *a* of fire by night ... Num 9:16
- for man looketh on the outward *a* ... 1Sa 16:7
- And this was their *a* ... Eze 1:5
- their *a* was like burning coals of ... Eze 1:13
- and like the *a* of lamps ... Eze 1:13
- returned as the *a* of a flash of ... Eze 1:14
- The *a* of the wheels and their work ... Eze 1:16
- and their *a* and their work was as ... Eze 1:16
- as the *a* of a sapphire stone ... Eze 1:26
- as the *a* of a man above upon it ... Eze 1:26
- as the *a* of fire round about ... Eze 1:27
- from the *a* of his loins even ... Eze 1:27
- from the *a* of his loins even ... Eze 1:27
- I saw as it were the *a* of fire ... Eze 1:27
- As the *a* of the bow that is in ... Eze 1:28
- so was the *a* of the brightness ... Eze 1:28
- This was the *a* of the likeness of ... Eze 1:28
- and lo a likeness as the *a* of fire ... Eze 8:2
- from the *a* of his loins even ... Eze 8:2
- as the *a* of brightness, as the ... Eze 8:2
- as the *a* of the likeness of a ... Eze 10:1
- the *a* of the wheels was as the ... Eze 10:9
- whose *a* was like the *a* ... Eze 40:3
- the *a* of the one as the *a* ... Eze 41:21
- the *a* of the chambers which were ... Eze 42:11
- it was according to the *a* of the ... Eze 43:3
- stood before me as the *a* of a man ... Dan 8:15
- and his face as the *a* of lightning ... Dan 10:6
- me one like the *a* of a man, ... Dan 10:18
- *a* of them is as the *a* of horses ... Joel 2:4
- Judge not according to the *a* ... Jn 7:24
- to answer them which glory in *a* ... 2Cor 5:12
- on things after the outward *a* ... 2Cor 10:7
- Abstain from all *a* of evil ... 1Th 5:22

**APPEARANCES**
- And as for their *a*, they four had ... Eze 10:10
- by the river of Chebar, their *a* ... Eze 10:22

**APPEARED**
- the LORD *a* unto Abram, and said, ... Gen 12:7
- unto the LORD, who *a* unto him ... Gen 12:7
- old and nine, the LORD *a* to Abram ... Gen 17:1
- the LORD *a* unto him in the plains ... Gen 18:1
- And the LORD *a* unto him, and said, ... Gen 26:2
- the LORD *a* unto him the same ... Gen 26:24
- that *a* unto thee when thou ... Gen 35:1
- because there God *a* unto him ... Gen 35:7
- God *a* unto Jacob again, when he ... Gen 35:9
- God Almighty *a* unto me at Luz in ... Gen 48:3
- the angel of the LORD *a* unto him ... Ex 3:2
- *a* unto me, saying, I have surely ... Ex 3:16
- The LORD hath not *a* unto thee ... Ex 4:1
- God of Jacob, hath *a* unto thee ... Ex 4:5
- I *a* unto Abraham, unto Isaac, and ... Ex 6:3
- his strength when the morning *a* ... Ex 14:27
- glory of the LORD *a* in the cloud ... Ex 16:10
- of the LORD *a* unto all the people ... Lev 9:23
- the glory of the LORD *a* in the ... Num 14:10
- the glory of the LORD *a* unto all ... Num 16:19
- it, and the glory of the LORD *a* ... Num 16:42
- the glory of the LORD *a* unto them ... Num 20:6
- the LORD *a* in the tabernacle in a ... Deut 31:15
- the angel of the LORD *a* unto him ... Judg 6:12
- of the LORD *a* unto the woman ... Judg 13:3
- Behold, the man hath *a* unto me ... Judg 13:10
- the LORD *a* again in Shiloh ... 1Sa 3:21
- And the channels of the sea *a* ... 2Sa 22:16
- In Gibeon the LORD *a* to Solomon ... 1Kin 3:5
- That the LORD *a* to Solomon the ... 1Kin 9:2
- as he had *a* unto him at Gibeon ... 1Kin 9:2
- which had *a* unto him twice ... 1Kin 11:9
- there *a* a chariot of fire, and ... 2Kin 2:11
- where the LORD *a* unto David his ... 2Chr 3:1
- the LORD *a* to Solomon by night, ... 2Chr 7:12
- of the morning till the stars *a* ... Neh 4:21
- The LORD hath *a* of old unto me, ... Jer 31:3
- *a* over them as it were a sapphire ... Eze 10:1
- there *a* in the cherubims the form ... Eze 10:8
- she *a* in her height with the ... Eze 19:11
- days their countenances *a* fairer ... Dan 1:15
- Belshazzar a vision *a* unto me ... Dan 8:1
- after that which *a* unto me at the ... Dan 8:1
- of the Lord *a* unto him in a dream ... Mt 1:20
- diligently what time the star *a* ... Mt 2:7
- fruit, then *a* the tares also ... Mt 13:26
- there *a* unto them Moses and Elias ... Mt 17:3
- the holy city, and *a* unto many ... Mt 27:53
- there *a* unto them Elias with ... Mk 9:4
- he *a* first to Mary Magdalene, out ... Mk 16:9
- After that he *a* in another form ... Mk 16:12
- Afterward he *a* unto the eleven as ... Mk 16:14
- there *a* unto him an angel of the ... Lk 1:11
- And of some, that Elias had *a* ... Lk 9:8
- Who *a* in glory, and spake of his ... Lk 9:31
- there *a* an angel unto him from ... Lk 22:43
- risen indeed, and hath *a* to Simon ... Lk 24:34
- there *a* unto them cloven tongues ... Acts 2:3
- The God of glory *a* unto our ... Acts 7:2
- there *a* to him in the wilderness ... Acts 7:30
- angel which *a* to him in the bush ... Acts 7:35
- that *a* unto thee in the way as ... Acts 9:17
- a vision *a* to Paul in the night ... Acts 16:9
- for I have *a* unto thee for this ... Acts 26:16
- sun nor stars in many days *a* ... Acts 27:20
- salvation hath *a* to all men ... Titus 2:11
- of God our Saviour toward man *a* ... Titus 3:4
- hath he *a* to put away sin by the ... Heb 9:26
- there *a* a great wonder in heaven ... Rev 12:1
- there *a* another wonder in heaven ... Rev 12:3

**APPEARETH**
- But when raw flesh *a* in him ... Lev 13:14
- as the leprosy *a* in the skin of ... Lev 13:43
- him into thy hand, as *a* this day ... Deut 2:30
- one of them in Zion *a* before God ... Ps 84:7
- The hay *a*, and the tender grass ... Prov 27:25
- for evil *a* out of the north, and ... Jer 6:1
- and who shall stand when he *a* ... Mal 3:2
- the Lord *a* to Joseph in a dream ... Mt 2:13
- an angel of the Lord *a* in a dream ... Mt 2:19
- that *a* for a little time, and then ... Jas 4:14

**APPEARING**
- until the *a* of our Lord Jesus ... 1Ti 6:14
- the *a* of our Saviour Jesus Christ ... 2Ti 1:10
- the quick and the dead at his *a* ... 2Ti 4:1
- all them also that love his *a* ... 2Ti 4:8
- the glorious *a* of the great God ... Titus 2:13
- glory at the *a* of Jesus Christ ... 1Pet 1:7

**APPEASE**
- I will *a* him with the present ... Gen 32:20

**APPEASED**
- the wrath of king Ahasuerus was *a* ... Est 2:1
- the townclerk had *a* the people ... Acts 19:35

**APPEASETH**
- he that is slow to anger *a* strife ... Prov 15:18

**APPERTAIN**
- up, with all that *a* unto them ... Num 16:30
- for to thee doth it *a* ... Jer 10:7

**APPERTAINED**
- and all the men that *a* unto Korah ... Num 16:32
- They, and all that *a* to them ... Num 16:33
- the palace which *a* to the house ... Neh 2:8

**APPERTAINETH**
- and give it unto him to whom it *a* ... Lev 6:5
- It *a* not unto thee, Uzziah, to ... 2Chr 26:18

**APPETITE**
- or fill the *a* of the young lions, ... Job 38:39
- if thou be a man given to *a* ... Prov 23:2
- mouth, and yet the *a* is not filled ... Eccl 6:7
- he is faint, and his soul hath *a* ... Is 29:8

**APPHIA** *(af'-fee-ah) A Christian acquaintance of Paul.*
- And to our beloved *A*, and Archippus .. Philem 2

**APPII** *(ap'-pe-i) A place south of Rome.*
- came to meet us as far as *A* forum ... Acts 28:15

**APPIUS** See APPII.

**APPLE**
- he kept him as the *a* of his eye ... Deut 32:10
- Keep me as the *a* of the eye ... Ps 17:8
- and my law as the *a* of thine eye ... Prov 7:2
- As the *a* tree among the trees of ... Song 2:3
- I raised thee up under the *a* tree ... Song 8:5
- let not the *a* of thine eye cease ... Lam 2:18
- the *a* tree, even all the trees of ... Joel 1:12
- you toucheth the *a* of his eye ... Zec 2:8

**APPLES**
- A word fitly spoken is like *a* of ... Prov 25:11
- with flagons, comfort me with *a* ... Song 2:5
- and the smell of thy nose like *a* ... Song 7:8

**APPLIED**
- I *a* mine heart to know, and to ... Eccl 7:25
- *a* my heart unto every work that ... Eccl 8:9
- When I *a* mine heart to know ... Eccl 8:16

**APPLY**
- that we may *a* our hearts unto ... Ps 90:12
- *a* thine heart to understanding ... Prov 2:2
- *a* thine heart unto my knowledge ... Prov 22:17
- *A* thine heart unto instruction, ... Prov 23:12

**APPOINT**
- *A* me thy wages, and I will give it ... Gen 30:28
- let him *a* officers over the land, ... Gen 41:34
- then I will *a* thee a place ... Ex 21:13
- shalt *a* it for the service of the ... Ex 30:16
- I will even *a* over you terror, ... Lev 26:16
- But thou shalt *a* the Levites over ... Num 1:50
- And thou shalt *a* Aaron and his sons.. Num 3:10
- *a* them every one to his service ... Num 4:19
- ye shall *a* unto them in charge ... Num 4:27
- refuge, which ye shall *a* for the ... Num 35:6
- Then ye shall *a* you cities to be ... Num 35:11
- *A* out for you cities of refuge, ... Josh 20:2
- *a* them for himself, for his ... 1Sa 8:11
- he will *a* him captains over ... 1Sa 8:12
- to *a* me ruler over the people of ... 2Sa 6:21
- Moreover I will *a* a place for my ... 2Sa 7:10
- my lord the king shall *a* ... 2Sa 15:15
- to all that thou shalt *a* ... 1Kin 5:6
- the place that thou shalt *a* me ... 1Kin 5:9
- to *a* their brethren to be the ... 1Chr 15:16
- *a* watches of the inhabitants of ... Neh 7:3
- let the king *a* officers in all ... Est 2:3

thou wouldest *a* me a set time ............. Job 14:13
salvation will God *a* for walls ..................... Is 26:1
To *a* unto them that mourn in Zion ......... Is 61:3
I will *a* over them four kinds, .................. Jer 15:3
chosen man, that I may *a* over her ....... Jer 49:19
and who will *a* me the time .................... Jer 49:19
chosen man, that I may *a* over her ....... Jer 50:44
and who will *a* me the time .................... Jer 50:44
*a* a captain against her ............................ Jer 51:27
*a* thee two ways, that the sword .............. Eze 21:19
*A* a way, that the sword may come ..... Eze 21:20
to *a* captains, to open the mouth ......... Eze 21:22
to *a* battering rams against the ............ Eze 21:22
ye shall *a* the possession of the ............ Eze 45:6
*a* themselves one head, and they .......... Hos 1:11
*a* him his portion with the ...................... Mt 24:51
will *a* him his portion with the ............... Lk 12:46
I *a* unto you a kingdom, as my .............. Lk 22:29
whom we may *a* over this business ....... Acts 6:3

**APPOINTED**
hath *a* me another seed instead of ......... Gen 4:25
At the time *a* I will return unto ........... Gen 18:14
thou hast *a* for thy servant Isaac ........ Gen 24:14
hath *a* out for my master's son ............ Gen 24:44
the LORD *a* a set time, saying, To ............ Ex 9:5
in the time *a* of the month Abib ............ Ex 23:15
keep the passover at his *a* season .......... Num 9:2
ye shall keep it in his *a* season ............. Num 9:3
*a* season among the children of .............. Num 9:7
of the LORD in his *a* season .................. Num 9:13
he and all his people, at a time *a* ............ Josh 8:14
they *a* Kedesh in Galilee in mount ........ Josh 20:7
These were the cities *a* for all .............. Josh 20:9
six hundred men *a* with weapons of.. Judg 18:11
the six hundred men *a* with their ....... Judg 18:16
that were *a* with weapons of war ...... Judg 18:17
Now there was an *a* sign between ..... Judg 20:38
to the set time that Samuel had *a* .......... 1Sa 13:8
thou camest not within the days *a* ...... 1Sa 13:11
and Samuel standing as *a* over them .. 1Sa 19:20
field at the time *a* with David ............. 1Sa 20:35
I have *a* my servants to such and .......... 1Sa 21:2
shall have *a* thee ruler over .................. 1Sa 25:30
his place which thou hast *a* him ............. 1Sa 29:4
For the LORD had *a* to defeat the ......... 2Sa 17:14
the set time which he had *a* him ............ 2Sa 20:5
the morning even to the time *a* ............ 2Sa 24:15
I have *a* him to be ruler over ............... 1Kin 1:35
*a* him victuals, and gave him land ..... 1Kin 11:18
the third day, as the king had *a* ......... 1Kin 12:12
man whom I *a* to utter destruction ... 1Kin 20:42
the king *a* the lord on whose hand ...... 2Kin 7:17
So the king *a* unto her a certain ............ 2Kin 8:6
Jehu *a* fourscore men without, and ... 2Kin 10:24
the priest *a* officers over the .............. 2Kin 11:18
the king of Assyria *a* unto ................... 2Kin 18:14
*a* unto all manner of service of ........... 1Chr 6:48
were *a* for all the work of the ............. 1Chr 6:49
were *a* to oversee the vessels .............. 1Chr 9:29
So the Levites *a* Heman the son of ... 1Chr 15:17
were *a* to sound with cymbals of ...... 1Chr 15:19
he *a* certain of the Levites to ............... 1Chr 16:4
And he *a*, according to the order ........... 2Chr 8:14
he *a* singers unto the LORD, and ........ 2Chr 20:21
Also Jehoiada *a* the offices of .............. 2Chr 23:18
Hezekiah *a* the courses of the .............. 2Chr 31:2
He *a* also the king's portion of .............. 2Chr 31:3
which I have *a* for your fathers ............ 2Chr 33:8
and they that the king had *a* ............. 2Chr 34:22
*a* the Levites, from twenty years ................ Ezr 3:8
the princes had *a* for the service ........... Ezr 8:20
in our cities come at *a* times ................ Ezr 10:14
from the time that I was *a* to be .......... Neh 5:14
thou hast also *a* prophets to .................... Neh 6:7
the singers and the Levites were *a* ......... Neh 7:1
in their rebellion *a* a captain to ............ Neh 9:17
at times *a* year by year, to burn .......... Neh 10:34
*a* two great companies of them ........... Neh 12:31
at that time were some *a* over the ...... Neh 12:44
*a* the wards of the priests and the ....... Neh 13:30
for the wood offering, at times *a* ........ Neh 13:31
for so the king had *a* to all the .................. Est 1:8
the keeper of the women, *a* ................... Est 2:15
whom he had *a* to attend upon her, ......... Est 4:5
to their *a* time every year ..................... Est 9:27
days of Purim in their times *a* .............. Est 9:31
Is there not an *a* time to man ................. Job 7:1
and wearisome nights are *a* to me ........... Job 7:3
thou hast *a* his bounds that he .............. Job 14:5
the days of my *a* time will I wait .......... Job 14:14
the heritage *a* unto him by God ........... Job 20:29
the thing that is *a* for me .................... Job 23:14
to the house *a* for all living ................. Job 30:23
given us like sheep *a* for meat ................ Ps 44:11
*a* a law in Israel, which he ...................... Ps 78:5
thou those that are *a* to die .................. Ps 79:11
in the new moon, in the time *a* .................. Ps 81:3
loose those that are *a* to death ............ Ps 102:20
He *a* the moon for seasons .................... Ps 104:19
and will come home at the day *a* ........... Prov 7:20
when he *a* the foundations of the ........ Prov 8:29
all such as are *a* to destruction ........... Prov 31:8
your *a* feasts my soul hateth ..................... Is 1:14
shall be alone in his *a* times .................. Is 14:31
the *a* barley and the rie in their .............. Is 28:25
since I *a* the ancient people ....................... Is 44:7
us the *a* weeks of the harvest ................... Jer 5:24
in the heaven knoweth her *a* times ............ Jer 8:7
if I have not *a* the ordinances of ........... Jer 33:25
he hath passed the time *a* ..................... Jer 46:17
there hath he *a* it ........................................ Jer 47:7
I have *a* thee each day for a year ............. Eze 4:6
which have *a* my land into their ............ Eze 36:5
it in the *a* place of the house ................. Eze 43:21
the king *a* them a daily provision ........... Dan 1:5
who hath *a* your meat and your .............. Dan 1:10
for at the time *a* the end shall ............. Dan 8:19
was true, but the time *a* was long ......... Dan 10:1
the end shall be at the time *a* .............. Dan 11:27
At the time *a* he shall return, and ........ Dan 11:29
because it is yet for a time *a* ................ Dan 11:35
hear ye the rod, and who hath *a* it ........... Mic 6:9
the vision is yet for an *a* time ................... Hab 2:3
disciples did as Jesus had *a* them ......... Mt 26:19
potter's field, as the Lord *a* me ............. Mt 27:10
a mountain where Jesus had *a* them ..... Mt 28:16
no more than that which is *a* you ........... Lk 3:13
the Lord *a* other seventy also ................... Lk 10:1
as my Father hath *a* unto me ................. Lk 22:29
And they *a* two, Joseph called .............. Acts 1:23
in the wilderness, as he had *a* ............... Acts 7:44
determined the times before *a* ............. Acts 17:26
Because he hath *a* a day, in the .......... Acts 17:31
for so had he *a*, minding himself ......... Acts 20:13
things which are *a* for thee to do ........ Acts 22:10
And when they had *a* him a day ......... Acts 28:23
last, as it were *a* to death ..................... 1Cor 4:9
until the time *a* of the father ................... Gal 4:2
know that we are *a* thereunto ................. 1Th 3:3
For God hath not *a* us to wrath .............. 1Th 5:9
Whereunto I am *a* a preacher ................. 2Ti 1:11
in every city, as I had *a* thee ................. Titus 1:5
whom he hath *a* heir of all things ........... Heb 1:2
was faithful to him that *a* him ................. Heb 3:2
as it is *a* unto men once to die, ............. Heb 9:27
whereunto also they were *a* ..................... 1Pet 2:8

**APPOINTETH**
that he *a* over it whomsoever he .......... Dan 5:21

**APPOINTMENT**
At the *a* of Aaron and his sons ............ Num 4:27
for by the *a* of Absalom this hath ........ 2Sa 13:32
according to the *a* of the priests ............... Ezr 6:9
for they had made an *a* together ............ Job 2:11

**APPREHEND**
with a garrison, desirous to *a* me ....... 2Cor 11:32
if that I may *a* that for which ............... Phil 3:12

**APPREHENDED**
And when he had *a* him, he put him ... Acts 12:4
which also I am *a* of Christ Jesus .......... Phil 3:12
I count not myself to have *a* .................. Phil 3:13

**APPROACH**
None of you shall *a* to any that .............. Lev 18:6
thou shalt not *a* to his wife .................... Lev 18:14
Also thou shalt not *a* unto a ................... Lev 18:19
if a woman *a* unto any beast, and ........ Lev 20:16
let him not *a* to offer the bread ............ Lev 21:17
hath a blemish, he shall not *a* ................ Lev 21:18
when they *a* unto the most holy ............. Num 4:19
battle, that the priest shall *a* .............. Deut 20:2
ye *a* this day unto battle against ........... Deut 20:3
thy days *a* that thou must die ............ Deut 31:14
are with me, will *a* unto the city ............ Josh 8:5
can make his sword to *a* unto him ....... Job 40:19
and causest to *a* unto thee ........................ Ps 65:4
draw near, and he shall *a* unto me ....... Jer 30:21
engaged his heart to *a* unto me ............. Jer 30:21
where the priests that *a* unto the ........ Eze 42:13
shall *a* to those things which are ........ Eze 42:14
which *a* unto me, to minister unto ...... Eze 43:19
the light which no man can *a* unto ........ 1Ti 6:16

**APPROACHED**
Wherefore *a* ye so nigh unto the ......... 2Sa 11:20
the king *a* to the altar, and ............... 2Kin 16:12

**APPROACHETH**
faileth not, where no thief *a* .................... Lk 12:33

**APPROACHING**
they take delight in *a* to God ................... Is 58:2
the more, as ye see the day *a* ............... Heb 10:25

**APPROVE**
their posterity *a* their sayings .................. Ps 49:13
ye shall *a* by your letters ...................... 1Cor 16:3
That ye may *a* things that are ................. Phil 1:10

**APPROVED**
a man *a* of God among you by .............. Acts 2:22
is acceptable to God, and *a* of men .... Rom 14:18
Salute Apelles *a* in Christ ...................... Rom 16:10
that they which are *a* may be made .. 1Cor 11:19
In all things ye have *a* ............................ 2Cor 7:11
he that commendeth himself is *a* ......... 2Cor 10:18
not that we should appear *a* .................. 2Cor 13:7
Study to shew thyself *a* unto God .......... 2Ti 2:15

**APPROVEST**
*a* the things that are more .................... Rom 2:18

**APPROVETH**
man in his cause, the Lord *a* not .......... Lam 3:36

**APPROVING**
But in all things *a* ourselves as ............... 2Cor 6:4

**APRONS**
together, and made themselves *a* ........... Gen 3:7
unto the sick handkerchiefs or *a* ........ Acts 19:12

**APT**
*a* for war, even them the king of ....... 2Kin 24:16
of them that were *a* to the war ........... 1Chr 7:40
given to hospitality, *a* to teach ................ 1Ti 3:2
all men, *a* to teach, patient, ..................... 2Ti 2:24

**AQUILA** (*ac'-quil-ah*) *A Christian acquaintance of Paul.*
And found a certain Jew named *A* ....... Acts 18:2
Syria, and with him Priscilla and *A* .... Acts 18:18
whom when *A* and Priscilla had .......... Acts 18:26
*A* my helpers in Christ Jesus ................... Rom 16:3
*A* and Priscilla salute you much in .... 1Cor 16:19
Salute Prisca and *A*, and the ................... 2Ti 4:19

**AR** (*ar*) *The capital of Moab.*
goeth down to the dwelling of *A* ....... Num 21:15
it hath consumed *A* of Moab ................ Num 21:28
because I have given *A* unto the ........... Deut 2:9
Thou art to pass over through *A* ......... Deut 2:18
and the Moabites which dwell in *A* ...... Deut 2:29
Because in the night *A* of Moab is ............ Is 15:1

**ARA** (*a'-rah*) *A son of Jether.*
Jephunneh, and Pispah, and *A* ............. 1Chr 7:38

**ARAB** (*a'-rab*) See ARBITE. *A city in Judah.*
*A*, and Dumah, and Eshean, ................. Josh 15:52

**ARABAH** (*ar'-ab-ah*) See BETH-ARABAH. *The Jordan Valley.*
the side over against *A* northward ..... Josh 18:18
and went down unto *A* ....................... Josh 18:18

**ARABIA** (*a-ra'-be-ah*) *The northern part of the Arabian peninsula.*
and of all the kings of *A* ...................... 1Kin 10:15
And all the kings of *A* and .................... 2Chr 9:14
The burden upon *A* ................................ Is 21:13
In the forest in *A* shall ye lodge .............. Is 21:13
And all the kings of *A*, and all the ........ Jer 25:24
*A*, and all the princes of Kedar, ............. Eze 27:21
but I went into *A*, and returned ............... Gal 1:17
For this Agar is mount Sinai in *A* .......... Gal 4:25

**ARABIAN** (*a-ra'-be-un*) See ARABIANS. *An inhabitant of Arabia.*
the Ammonite, and Geshem the *A* ......... Neh 2:19
and Tobiah, and Geshem the *A* ................ Neh 6:1
shall the *A* pitch tent there .................... Is 13:20
as the *A* in the wilderness ........................ Jer 3:2

**ARABIANS** (*a-ra'-be-uns*)
the *A* brought him flocks, seven ........ 2Chr 17:11
of the Philistines, and of the *A* .......... 2Chr 21:16
*A* to the camp had slain all the ........... 2Chr 22:1
against the *A* that dwelt in ................... 2Chr 26:7
Sanballat, and Tobiah, and the *A* ........... Neh 4:7
Cretes and *A*, we do hear them ............. Acts 2:11

**ARABS** See ARABIANS.

**ARAD** (*a'-rad*)
*1. A Canaanite king.*
when king *A* the Canaanite, which ..... Num 21:1
king *A* the Canaanite, which dwelt ... Num 33:40
*2. A district in Judah.*
the king of *A*, one ................................. Josh 12:14
which lieth in the south of *A* ................. Judg 1:16
*3. A son of Beriah.*
And Zebadiah, and *A*, and Ader, .......... 1Chr 8:15

**ARAH** (*a'-rah*)
*1. A son of Ulla.*
*A*, and Haniel, and Rezia ....................... 1Chr 7:39
*2. A family of exiles who returned under Zerubbabel.*
The children of *A*, seven hundred ............ Ezr 2:5
The children of *A*, six hundred .............. Neh 7:10
*3. Grandfather of Tobiah's wife.*
in law of Shechaniah the son of *A* ........ Neh 6:18

**ARAM** (*a'-ram*) See ARAMITESS, ARAM-NAHARAIM, ARAM-ZOBAH, BETH-ARAM, PADAN-ARAM, SYRIA.
*1. The son of Shem.*
Arphaxad, and Lud, and *A* .................... Gen 10:22
And the children of *A* ........................... Gen 10:23
Arphaxad, and Lud, and *A* ..................... 1Chr 1:17
*2. The son of Kemuel.*
and Kemuel the father of *A* ................... Gen 22:21
*3. Another name for Syria.*
of Moab hath brought me from *A* ....... Num 23:7
*4. A district of Canaan.*
And he took Geshur, and *A*, with the. 1Chr 2:23
*5. The son of Shamer.*
Ahi, and Rohgah, Jehubbah, and *A* ...... 1Chr 7:34
and Esrom begat *A* ................................... Mt 1:3
And *A* begat Aminadab ............................ Mt 1:4
Aminadab, which was the son of *A* ......... Lk 3:33

**ARAMEAN** See ARAMITESS.

**ARAMITESS** (*a'-ram-i-tes*) See SYRIAN. *Manasseh's concubine.*
(but his concubine the *A* bare .............. 1Chr 7:14

**ARAM-NAHARAIM** (*a'-ram-na-ha-ra'-im*) See MESOPOTAMIA. *The area between the Tigris and Euphrates rivers.*
when he strove with *A* and with ............... Ps 60:*t*

**ARAM-ZOBAH** (*a'-ram-zo'-bah*) *The area between the Orontes and Euphrates rivers.*
with Aram-naharaim and with *A* ............. Ps 60:*t*

**ARAN** (*a'-ran*) See BETH-ARAN. *The son of Seir the Horite.*
of Dishan are these; Uz, and A ... Gen 36:28
sons of Dishan; Uz, and A ... 1Chr 1:42

**ARARAT** (*ar'-ar-at*) See ARMENIA. *A district in Armenia.*
month, upon the mountains of A ... Gen 8:4
against her the kingdoms of A ... Jer 51:27

**ARAUNAH** (*a-raw'-nah*) See ORNAN. *A Jebusite.*
threshingplace of A the Jebusite ... 2Sa 24:16
threshingfloor of A the Jebusite ... 2Sa 24:18
A looked, and saw the king and his ... 2Sa 24:20
A went out, and bowed himself ... 2Sa 24:20
A said, Wherefore is my lord the ... 2Sa 24:21
A said unto David, Let my lord ... 2Sa 24:22
All these things did A, as a king ... 2Sa 24:23
A said unto the king, The LORD ... 2Sa 24:23
And the king said unto A, Nay ... 2Sa 24:24

**ARBA** (*ar'-bah*) See ARBAH, ARBATHITE, ARBITE, KIRJATH-ABBA. *Father of Anakim.*
even the city of A the father of ... Josh 15:13
the city of A the father of Anak ... Josh 21:11

**ARBAH** (*ar'-bah*) See ARBA. *Another name for Hebron.*
unto Mamre, unto the city of A ... Gen 35:27

**ARBATHITE** (*ar'-bath-ite*) *A native of Arbah.*
Abi-albon the A, Azmaveth the ... 2Sa 23:31
the brooks of Gaash, Abiel the A ... 1Chr 11:32

**ARBITE** (*ar'-bite*) *A native of Arab.*
the Carmelite, Paarai the A ... 2Sa 23:35

**ARCHANGEL**
a shout, with the voice of the a ... 1Th 4:16
Yet Michael the a, when ... Jude 9

**ARCHELAUS** (*ar-ke-la'-us*) *A son of Herod the Great.*
But when he heard that A did ... Mt 2:22

**ARCHER**
in the wilderness, and became an a ... Gen 21:20
bendeth let the a bend his bow ... Jer 51:3

**ARCHERS**
The a have sorely grieved him, and ... Gen 49:23
a in the places of drawing water ... Judg 5:11
against Saul, and the a hit him ... 1Sa 31:3
and he was sore wounded of the a ... 1Sa 31:3
Ulam were mighty men of valour, a ... 1Chr 8:40
the a hit him ... 1Chr 10:3
and he was wounded of the a ... 1Chr 10:3
the a shot at king Josiah ... 2Chr 35:23
His a compass me round about, he ... Job 16:13
And the residue of the number of a ... Is 21:17
together, they are bound by the a ... Is 22:3
together the a against Babylon ... Jer 50:29

**ARCHES**
round about, and likewise to the a ... Eze 40:16
the a thereof were after the ... Eze 40:21
And their windows, and their a ... Eze 40:22
the a thereof were before them ... Eze 40:22
the a thereof according to these ... Eze 40:24
in the a thereof round about ... Eze 40:25
the a thereof were before them ... Eze 40:26
the a thereof, according to these ... Eze 40:29
in the a thereof round about ... Eze 40:29
the a round about were five and ... Eze 40:30
the a thereof were toward the ... Eze 40:31
the a thereof, were according to ... Eze 40:33
in the a thereof round about ... Eze 40:33
the a thereof were toward the ... Eze 40:34
the a thereof, and the windows to ... Eze 40:36

**ARCHEVITES** (*ar'-ke-vites*) *Chaldean settlers in Samaria.*
Tarpelites, the Apharsites, the A ... Ezr 4:9

**ARCHI** (*ar'-kee*) See ARCHITE. *A border city of Ephraim.*
unto the borders of A to Ataroth ... Josh 16:2

**ARCHIPPUS** (*ar-kip'-pus*) *A Christian acquaintance of Paul.*
And say to A, Take heed to the ... Col 4:17
A our fellowsoldier, and to the ... Philem 2

**ARCHITE** (*ar'-kite*) See ARCHI. *A friend of David.*
Hushai the A came to meet him ... 2Sa 15:32
came to pass, when Hushai the A ... 2Sa 16:16
Call now Hushai the A also ... 2Sa 17:5
The counsel of Hushai the A is ... 2Sa 17:14
Hushai the A was the king's ... 1Chr 27:33

**ARCHITES** See ARCHI.

**ARCTURUS** (*ark-tu'-rus*) *Another name for "the Great Bear."*
Which maketh A, Orion, and ... Job 9:9
canst thou guide A with his sons ... Job 38:32

**ARD** (*ard*) See ARDITES.
*1. A son of Benjamin.*
Muppim, and Huppim, and A ... Gen 46:21
*2. A son of Bela.*
And the sons of Bela were A ... Num 26:40
of A, the family of the Ardites ... Num 26:40

**ARDITES** (*ar'-dites*) *Descendants of Bela.*
of Ard, the family of the A ... Num 26:40

**ARDON** (*ar'-don*) *A son of Caleb.*
Jesher, and Shobab, and A ... 1Chr 2:18

**ARE** See PREFACE.

**ARELI** (*a-re'-li*) See ARELITES. *A son of Gad.*
and Ezbon, Eri, and Arodi, and A ... Gen 46:16
of A, the family of the Arelites ... Num 26:17

**ARELITES** (*a-re'-lites*) See ARELI. *Descendants of Areli.*
of Areli, the family of the A ... Num 26:17

**AREOPAGITE** (*a-re-op'-a-jite*) *A title of Dionysius.*
the which was Dionysius the A ... Acts 17:34

**AREOPAGUS** (*a-re-op'-a-gus*) See AREOPAGITE, MARS'-HILL. *A plaza in Athens.*
took him, and brought him unto A ... Acts 17:19

**ARETAS** (*ar'-e-tas*) *A north Arabian ruler.*
A the king kept the city of the ... 2Cor 11:32

**ARGOB** (*ar'-gob*)
*1. A district of Og in Bashan.*
cities, all the region of A ... Deut 3:4
all the region of A, with all ... Deut 3:13
took all the country of A unto ... Deut 3:14
also pertained the region of A ... 1Kin 4:13
*2. An official of King Pekah of Israel.*
of the king's house, with A ... 2Kin 15:25

**ARGUING**
but what doth your a reprove ... Job 6:25

**ARGUMENTS**
him, and fill my mouth with a ... Job 23:4

**ARIDAI** (*a-rid'-a-i*) *A son of Haman.*
And Parmashta, and Arisai, and A ... Est 9:9

**ARIDATHA** (*a-rid'-a-thah*) *A son of Haman.*
And Poratha, and Adalia, and A ... Est 9:8

**ARIEH** (*a-ri'-eh*) *A companion of Argob.*
the king's house, with Argob and A .. 2Kin 15:25

**ARIEL** (*a'-re-el*) See JERUSALEM.
*1. An emissary of Ezra.*
Then sent I for Eliezer, for A ... Ezr 8:16
*2. A name for Jerusalem.*
Woe to Ariel, to A, the city ... Is 29:1
Yet I will distress A, and there ... Is 29:2
and it shall be unto me as A ... Is 29:2
the nations that fight against A ... Is 29:7

**ARIGHT**
a will I shew the salvation of ... Ps 50:23
that set not their heart a ... Ps 78:8
of the wise useth knowledge a ... Prov 15:2
the cup, when it moveth itself a ... Prov 23:31
and heard, but they spake not a ... Jer 8:6

**ARIMATHAEA** (*ar-im-ath-e'-ah*) *Another name for Ramah.*
come, there came a rich man of A ... Mt 27:57
Joseph of A, an honourable ... Mk 15:43
he was of A, a city of the Jews ... Lk 23:51
And after this Joseph of A ... Jn 19:38

**ARIMATHEA** See ARIMATHAEA.

**ARIOCH** (*a'-re-ok*)
*1. King of Ellasar in Assyria.*
A king of Ellasar, Chedorlaomer ... Gen 14:1
of Shinar, and A king of Ellasar ... Gen 14:9
*2. Captain of Nebuchadnezzar's guard.*
wisdom to A the captain of the ... Dan 2:14
said to A the king's captain, Why ... Dan 2:15
Then A made the thing known to ... Dan 2:15
Therefore Daniel went in unto A ... Dan 2:24
Then A brought in Daniel before ... Dan 2:25

**ARISAI** (*a-ris'-a-i*) *A son of Haman.*
And Parmashta, and A, and Aridai, and.. Est 9:9

**ARISE**
A, walk through the land in the ... Gen 13:17
angels hastened Lot, saying, A ... Gen 19:15
A, lift up the lad, and hold him ... Gen 21:18
a, I pray thee, sit and eat of my ... Gen 27:19
unto his father, Let my father a ... Gen 27:31
and a, flee thou to Laban my ... Gen 27:43
A, go to Padan-aram, to the house ... Gen 28:2
now a, get thee out from this ... Gen 31:13
And God said unto Jacob, A ... Gen 35:1
And let us a, and go up to Beth-el ... Gen 35:3
there shall a after them seven ... Gen 41:30
the lad with me, and we will a ... Gen 43:8
Take also your brother, and a ... Gen 43:13
And the LORD said unto me, A ... Deut 9:12
And the LORD said unto me, A ... Deut 10:11
If there a among you a prophet ... Deut 13:1
If there a a matter too hard for ... Deut 17:8
then shalt thou a, and get thee up ... Deut 17:8
now therefore a, go over this ... Josh 1:2
the people of war with thee, and a ... Josh 8:1
a, Barak, and lead thy captivity ... Judg 5:12
that the LORD said unto him, A ... Judg 7:9
the host of Israel, and said, A ... Judg 7:15
And they said, A, that we may go ... Judg 18:9
to a up out of the city with a ... Judg 20:40
of the servants with thee, and a ... 1Sa 9:3
And the LORD said, A, anoint him ... 1Sa 16:12
the LORD answered him and said, A ... 1Sa 23:4
to Joab, Let the young men now a ... 2Sa 2:14
And Joab said, Let them a ... 2Sa 2:14
Abner said unto David, I will a ... 2Sa 3:21
if so be that the king's wrath a ... 2Sa 11:20
And Amnon said unto her, A ... 2Sa 13:15
were with him at Jerusalem, A ... 2Sa 15:14
twelve thousand men, and I will a ... 2Sa 17:1
king David, and said unto David, A ... 2Sa 17:21
Now therefore a, go forth, and ... 2Sa 19:7
them, that they could not a ... 2Sa 22:39
thee shall any a like unto thee ... 1Kin 3:12
And Jeroboam said to his wife, A ... 1Kin 14:2
A thou therefore, get thee to ... 1Kin 14:12
A, get thee to Zarephath, which ... 1Kin 17:9
touched him, and said unto him, A ... 1Kin 19:5
time, and touched him, and said, A ... 1Kin 19:7
a, and eat bread, and let thine ... 1Kin 21:7
that Jezebel said to Ahab, A ... 1Kin 21:15
A, go down to meet Ahab king of ... 1Kin 21:18
said to Elijah the Tishbite, A ... 2Kin 1:3
had restored to life, saying, A ... 2Kin 8:1
make him a up from among his ... 2Kin 9:2
A therefore, and be doing, and the ... 1Chr 22:16
a therefore, and build ye the ... 1Chr 22:19
Now therefore a, O LORD God, into ... 2Chr 6:41
A ... Ezr 10:4
therefore we his servants will a ... Neh 2:20
Thus shall there a too much ... Est 1:18
deliverance a to the Jews from ... Est 4:14
I lie down, I say, When shall I a ... Job 7:4
and upon whom doth not his light a ... Job 25:3
A, O LORD ... Ps 3:7
A, O LORD, in thine anger, lift ... Ps 7:6
A, O LORD ... Ps 9:19
A, O LORD ... Ps 10:12
of the needy, now will I a ... Ps 12:5
A, O LORD, disappoint him, cast ... Ps 17:13
a, cast us not off for ever ... Ps 44:23
A for our help, and redeem us for ... Ps 44:26
Let God a, let his enemies be ... Ps 68:1
A, O God, plead thine own cause ... Ps 74:22
who should a and declare them to ... Ps 78:6
A, O God, judge the earth ... Ps 82:8
shall the dead a and praise thee ... Ps 88:10
when the waves thereof a, thou ... Ps 89:9
Thou shalt a, and have mercy upon ... Ps 102:13
when they a, let them be ashamed ... Ps 109:28
A, O LORD, into thy rest ... Ps 132:8
when wilt thou a out of thy sleep ... Prov 6:9
Her children a up, and call her ... Prov 31:28
A, my love, my fair one, and come ... Song 2:13
a, ye princes, and anoint the ... Is 21:5
a, pass over to Chittim ... Is 23:12
with my dead body shall they a ... Is 26:19
but will a against the house of ... Is 31:2
of rulers, Kings shall see and a ... Is 49:7
a, and sit down, O Jerusalem ... Is 52:2
A, shine; ... Is 60:1
but the LORD shall a upon thee ... Is 60:2
therefore gird up thy loins, and a ... Jer 1:17
of their trouble they will say, A ... Jer 2:27
let them a, if they can save thee ... Jer 2:28
a, and let us go up at noon ... Jer 6:4
a, and let us go by night, and let ... Jer 6:5
Shall they fall, and not a ... Jer 8:4
which is upon thy loins, and a ... Jer 13:4
that the LORD said unto me, A ... Jer 13:6
A, and go down to the potter's ... Jer 18:2
A ye, and let us go up to Zion ... Jer 31:6
and they said, A, and let us go ... Jer 46:16
A ye, go up to Kedar, and spoil ... Jer 49:28
A, get you up unto the wealthy ... Jer 49:31
A, cry out in the night ... Lam 2:19
and he said unto me, A, go forth ... Eze 3:22
after thee shall a another ... Dan 2:39
and they said thus unto it, A ... Dan 7:5
which shall a out of the earth ... Dan 7:17
are ten kings that shall a ... Dan 7:24
shall a tumult a among thy people ... Hos 10:14
by whom shall Jacob a ... Amos 7:2
by whom shall Jacob a ... Amos 7:5
A ye, and let us rise up against ... Obad 1
A, go to Nineveh, that great city ... Jonah 1:2
a, call upon thy God, if so be ... Jonah 1:6
A, go unto Nineveh, that great ... Jonah 3:2
came to pass, when the sun did a ... Jonah 4:8
A ye, and depart ... Mic 2:10
A and thresh, O daughter of Zion ... Mic 4:13
A, contend thou before the ... Mic 6:1
when I fall, I shall a ... Mic 7:8
to the dumb stone, A, it shall ... Hab 2:19
a with healing in his wings ... Mal 4:2
to Joseph in a dream, saying, A ... Mt 2:13
Saying, A, and take the young ... Mt 2:20
or to say, A, and walk ... Mt 9:5
he to the sick of the palsy,) A ... Mt 9:6
came and touched them, and said, A ... Mt 17:7
For there shall a false Christs ... Mt 24:24
or to say, A, and take up thy bed ... Mk 2:9
I say unto thee, A, and take up ... Mk 2:11
Damsel, I say unto thee, a ... Mk 5:41
of the palsy,) I say unto thee, A ... Lk 5:24
Young man, I say unto thee, A ... Lk 7:14
hand, and called, saying, Maid, a ... Lk 8:54
I will a and go to my father, and ... Lk 15:18
And he said unto him, A, go thy ... Lk 17:19
why do thoughts a in your hearts ... Lk 24:38
A, let us go hence ... Jn 14:31
Lord spake unto Philip, saying, A ... Acts 8:26
And the Lord said unto him, A ... Acts 9:6

And the Lord said unto him, *A* ............ Acts 9:11
*a*, and make thy bed ............ Acts 9:34
him to the body said, Tabitha, *a* ............ Acts 9:40
*A* therefore, and get thee down, and. Acts 10:20
I heard a voice saying unto me, *A* ....... Acts 11:7
him up, saying, *A* up quickly ............ Acts 12:7
of your own selves shall men *a* ............ Acts 20:30
And the Lord said unto me, *A* ............ Acts 22:10
*a*, and be baptized, and wash away.... Acts 22:16
*a* from the dead, and Christ shall .......... Eph 5:14
the day star *a* in your hearts ............ 2Pet 1:19

**ARISETH**
there *a* a little cloud out of the.......... 1Kin 18:44
The sun *a*, they gather themselves....... Ps 104:22
there *a* light in the darkness.............. Ps 112:4
The sun also *a*, and the sun goeth .......... Eccl 1:5
when he *a* to shake terribly the.............. Is 2:19
when he *a* to shake terribly the.............. Is 2:21
but when the sun *a* they flee away....... Nah 3:17
persecution *a* because of the word....... Mt 13:21
persecution *a* for the word's sake.......... Mk 4:17
for out of Galilee *a* no prophet.............. Jn 7:52
there *a* another priest,.............. Heb 7:15

**ARISING**
the king *a* from the banquet of.............. Est 7:7

**ARISTARCHUS** (*ar-is-tar'-cus*) *A companion of Paul.*
and having caught Gaius and *A*.......... Acts 19:29
and of the Thessalonians, *A*.............. Acts 20:4
one *A*, a Macedonian of.............. Acts 27:2
*A* my fellowprisoner saluteth you,.......... Col 4:10
Marcus, *A*, Demas, Lucas, my.............. Philem 24

**ARISTOBULUS** See ARISTOBULUS'.

**ARISTOBULUS'** (*a-rus-to-bu'-luz*) *A Christian acquaintance of Paul.*
them which are of *A* household.......... Rom 16:10

**ARK**
Make thee an *a* of gopher wood........... Gen 6:14
rooms shalt thou make in the *a*............ Gen 6:14
The length of the *a* shall be.............. Gen 6:15
A window shalt thou make to the *a*..... Gen 6:16
the door of the *a* shalt thou set............ Gen 6:16
and thou shalt come into the *a*............ Gen 6:18
sort shalt thou bring into the *a*............ Gen 6:19
thou and all thy house into the *a*........... Gen 7:1
sons' wives with him, into the *a*........... Gen 7:7
two and two unto Noah into the *a*........ Gen 7:9
of his sons with them, into the *a*........... Gen 7:13
they went in unto Noah into the *a*........ Gen 7:15
increased, and bare up the *a*.............. Gen 7:17
the *a* went upon the face of the........... Gen 7:18
they that were with him in the *a*........... Gen 7:23
cattle that was with him in the *a*........... Gen 8:1
the *a* rested in the seventh month.......... Gen 8:4
window of the *a* which he had made..... Gen 8:6
she returned unto him into the *a*........... Gen 8:9
pulled her in unto him into the *a*........... Gen 8:9
sent forth the dove out of the *a*........... Gen 8:10
removed the covering of the *a*.............. Gen 8:13
Go forth of the *a*, thou, and thy........... Gen 8:16
kinds, went forth out of the *a*.............. Gen 8:19
from all that go out of the *a*.............. Gen 9:10
of Noah, that went forth of the *a*.......... Gen 9:18
took for him an *a* of bulrushes.............. Ex 2:3
she saw the *a* among the flags.............. Ex 2:5
shall make an *a* of shittim wood........... Ex 25:10
the rings by the sides of the *a*.............. Ex 25:14
that the *a* may be borne with them...... Ex 25:14
shall be in the rings of the *a*.............. Ex 25:15
thou shalt put into the *a* the.............. Ex 25:16
the mercy seat above upon the *a*........... Ex 25:21
in the *a* thou shalt put the.............. Ex 25:21
are upon the *a* of the testimony........... Ex 25:22
the vail the *a* of the testimony.............. Ex 26:33
put the mercy seat upon the *a* of........... Ex 26:34
that is by the *a* of the testimony.......... Ex 30:6
and the *a* of the testimony,.............. Ex 30:26
the *a* of the testimony, and the.............. Ex 31:7
The *a*, and the staves thereof,.............. Ex 35:12
made the *a* of shittim wood.............. Ex 37:1
sides of the *a*, to bear the *a*.............. Ex 37:5
The *a* of the testimony, and the........... Ex 39:35
therein the *a* of the testimony.............. Ex 40:3
cover the *a* with the vail.............. Ex 40:3
before the *a* of the testimony.............. Ex 40:5
and put the testimony into the *a*........... Ex 40:20
and set the staves on the *a*.............. Ex 40:20
the mercy seat above upon the *a*........... Ex 40:20
he brought the *a* into the.............. Ex 40:21
covered the *a* of the testimony.............. Ex 40:21
mercy seat, which is upon the *a*........... Lev 16:2
And their charge shall be the *a*........... Num 3:31
cover the *a* of testimony with it.......... Num 4:5
that was upon the *a* of testimony......... Num 7:89
the *a* of the covenant of the LORD..... Num 10:33
when the *a* set forward, that.............. Num 10:35
nevertheless the *a* of the.............. Num 14:44
mount, and make thee an *a* of wood.. Deut 10:1
and thou shalt put them in the *a*........... Deut 10:2
I made an *a* of shittim wood, and........ Deut 10:3
tables in the *a* which I had made........ Deut 10:5
to bear the *a* of the covenant of........... Deut 10:8
which bare the *a* of the covenant........ Deut 31:9
which bare the *a* of the covenant....... Deut 31:25
put it in the side of the *a* of.............. Deut 31:26
When ye see the *a* of the covenant........ Josh 3:3
Take up the *a* of the covenant, and....... Josh 3:6
took up the *a* of the covenant.............. Josh 3:6
that bear the *a* of the covenant........... Josh 3:8
the *a* of the covenant of the Lord.......... Josh 3:11
that bear the *a* of the LORD.............. Josh 3:13
the priests bearing the *a* of the............ Josh 3:14
bare the *a* were come unto Jordan....... Josh 3:15
of the priests that bare the *a*.............. Josh 3:15
the priests that bare the *a* of.............. Josh 3:17
Pass over before the *a* of the.............. Josh 4:5
the *a* of the covenant of the LORD........... Josh 4:7
bare the *a* of the covenant stood.......... Josh 4:9
*a* stood in the midst of Jordan.............. Josh 4:10
that the *a* of the LORD passed.............. Josh 4:11
that bear the *a* of the testimony........... Josh 4:16
the *a* of the covenant of the LORD........ Josh 4:18
*a* seven trumpets of rams' horns............ Josh 6:4
Take up the *a* of the covenant, and........ Josh 6:6
horns before the *a* of the LORD.............. Josh 6:6
pass on before the *a* of the LORD.......... Josh 6:7
the *a* of the covenant of the LORD.......... Josh 6:8
and the rereward came after the *a*.......... Josh 6:9
So the *a* of the LORD compassed............ Josh 6:11
priests took up the *a* of the LORD......... Josh 6:12
of rams' horns before the *a* of.............. Josh 6:13
came after the *a* of the LORD.............. Josh 6:13
*a* of the LORD until the eventide............ Josh 7:6
judges, stood on this side the *a*........... Josh 8:33
which bare the *a* of the covenant......... Josh 8:33
(for the *a* of the covenant of God...... Judg 20:27
where the *a* of God was, and Samuel...... 1Sa 3:3
Let us fetch the *a* of the.............. 1Sa 4:3
might bring from thence the *a* of............ 1Sa 4:4
were there with the *a* of the.............. 1Sa 4:4
when the *a* of the covenant of the.......... 1Sa 4:5
they understood that the *a* of the........... 1Sa 4:6
And the *a* of God was taken.............. 1Sa 4:11
heart trembled for the *a* of God............ 1Sa 4:13
dead, and the *a* of God is taken........... 1Sa 4:17
he made mention of the *a* of God.......... 1Sa 4:18
that the *a* of God was taken.............. 1Sa 4:19
because the *a* of God was taken,........... 1Sa 4:21
for the *a* of God is taken.............. 1Sa 4:22
the Philistines took the *a* of God........... 1Sa 5:1
the Philistines took the *a* of God........... 1Sa 5:2
earth before the *a* of the LORD.............. 1Sa 5:3
ground before the *a* of the LORD............ 1Sa 5:4
The *a* of the God of Israel shall.............. 1Sa 5:7
with the *a* of the God of Israel.............. 1Sa 5:8
Let the *a* of the God of Israel be........... 1Sa 5:8
they carried the *a* of the God of............ 1Sa 5:8
they sent the *a* of God to Ekron............ 1Sa 5:10
as the *a* of God came to Ekron,............ 1Sa 5:10
the *a* of the God of Israel to us............ 1Sa 5:10
Send away the *a* of the God of............. 1Sa 5:11
the *a* of the LORD was in the.............. 1Sa 6:1
shall we do to the *a* of the LORD........... 1Sa 6:2
If ye send away the *a* of the God............ 1Sa 6:3
take the *a* of the LORD, and lay it.......... 1Sa 6:8
they laid the *a* of the LORD upon........... 1Sa 6:11
up their eyes, and saw the *a*.............. 1Sa 6:13
took down the *a* of the LORD.............. 1Sa 6:15
they set down the *a* of the LORD............ 1Sa 6:18
had looked into the *a* of the LORD.......... 1Sa 6:19
brought again the *a* of the LORD............ 1Sa 6:21
and brought up the *a* of the LORD........... 1Sa 7:1
his son to keep the *a* of the LORD........... 1Sa 7:1
to pass, while the *a* abode in.............. 1Sa 7:2
Ahiah, Bring hither the *a* of God......... 1Sa 14:18
For the *a* of God was at that time....... 1Sa 14:18
bring up from thence the *a* of God.......... 2Sa 6:2
they set the *a* of God upon a new........... 2Sa 6:3
Gibeah, accompanying the *a* of God....... 2Sa 6:4
and Ahio went before the *a*.............. 2Sa 6:4
forth his hand to the *a* of God.............. 2Sa 6:6
and there he died by the *a* of God.......... 2Sa 6:7
How shall the *a* of the LORD come........... 2Sa 6:9
*a* of the LORD unto him into the............ 2Sa 6:10
the *a* of the LORD continued in.............. 2Sa 6:11
unto him, because of the *a* of God......... 2Sa 6:12
brought up the *a* of God from the.......... 2Sa 6:12
that when they that bare the *a* of......... 2Sa 6:13
the *a* of the LORD with shouting............ 2Sa 6:15
as the *a* of the LORD came into.............. 2Sa 6:16
they brought in the *a* of the LORD.......... 2Sa 6:17
but the *a* of God dwelleth within............ 2Sa 7:2
And Uriah said unto David, The *a*....... 2Sa 11:11
bearing the *a* of the covenant of.......... 2Sa 15:24
and they set down the *a* of God........... 2Sa 15:24
Carry back the *a* of God into the........... 2Sa 15:25
Abiathar carried the *a* of God.............. 2Sa 15:29
because thou barest the *a* of the.......... 1Kin 2:26
stood before the *a* of the.............. 1Kin 3:15
to set there the *a* of the.............. 1Kin 6:19
that they might bring up the *a* of.......... 1Kin 8:1
and the priests took up the *a*.............. 1Kin 8:3
they brought up the *a* of the LORD......... 1Kin 8:4
him, were with him before the *a*........... 1Kin 8:5
the priests brought in the *a* of.............. 1Kin 8:6
two wings over the place of the *a*.......... 1Kin 8:7
and the cherubims covered the *a*........... 1Kin 8:7
There was nothing in the *a* save........... 1Kin 8:9
have set there a place for the *a*........... 1Kin 8:21
LORD, after that the *a* had rest........... 1Chr 6:31
again the *a* of our God to us.............. 1Chr 13:3
to bring the *a* of God from.............. 1Chr 13:5
up thence the *a* of God the LORD.......... 1Chr 13:6
they carried the *a* of God in a.............. 1Chr 13:7
put forth his hand to hold the *a*........... 1Chr 13:9
because he put his hand to the *a*....... 1Chr 13:10
I bring the *a* of God home to me....... 1Chr 13:12
So David brought not the *a* home..... 1Chr 13:13
the *a* of God remained with the......... 1Chr 13:14
prepared a place for the *a* of God......... 1Chr 15:1
the *a* of God but the Levites.............. 1Chr 15:2
LORD chosen to carry the *a* of God..... 1Chr 15:2
to bring up the *a* of the LORD.............. 1Chr 15:3
that ye may bring up the *a* of the..... 1Chr 15:12
the *a* of the LORD God of Israel.......... 1Chr 15:14
of the Levites bare the *a* of God......... 1Chr 15:15
were doorkeepers for the *a*.............. 1Chr 15:23
the trumpets before the *a* of God...... 1Chr 15:24
Jehiah were doorkeepers for the *a*....... 1Chr 15:24
went to bring up the *a* of the.............. 1Chr 15:25
the Levites that bare the *a* of.............. 1Chr 15:26
all the Levites that bare the *a*.............. 1Chr 15:27
the *a* of the covenant of the LORD....... 1Chr 15:28
as the *a* of the covenant of the.......... 1Chr 15:29
So they brought the *a* of God.............. 1Chr 16:1
minister before the *a* of the LORD........ 1Chr 16:4
the *a* of the covenant of God.............. 1Chr 16:6
the *a* of the covenant of the LORD....... 1Chr 16:37
minister before the *a* continually.......... 1Chr 16:37
but the *a* of the covenant of the.......... 1Chr 17:1
to bring the *a* of the covenant of....... 1Chr 22:19
the *a* of the covenant of the LORD......... 1Chr 28:2
covered the *a* of the covenant of....... 1Chr 28:18
But the *a* of God had David.............. 2Chr 1:4
to bring up the *a* of the covenant.......... 2Chr 5:2
and the Levites took up the *a*.............. 2Chr 5:4
And they brought up the *a*, and the...... 2Chr 5:5
assembled unto him before the *a*........... 2Chr 5:6
the priests brought in the *a* of............ 2Chr 5:7
wings over the place of the *a*.............. 2Chr 5:8
and the cherubims covered the *a*........... 2Chr 5:8
they drew out the staves of the *a*.......... 2Chr 5:9
seen from the *a* before the oracle.......... 2Chr 5:9
There was nothing in the *a* save.......... 2Chr 5:10
And in it have I put the *a*.............. 2Chr 6:11
thou, and the *a* of thy strength............ 2Chr 6:41
whereunto the *a* of the LORD hath........ 2Chr 8:11
Put the holy *a* in the house which...... 2Chr 35:3
thou, and the *a* of thy strength.............. Ps 132:8
The *a* of the covenant of the LORD......... Jer 3:16
day that Noe entered into the *a*............ Mt 24:38
day that Noe entered into the *a*............ Lk 17:27
the *a* of the covenant overlaid.............. Heb 9:4
prepared an *a* to the saving of.............. Heb 11:7
while the *a* was a preparing,.............. 1Pet 3:20
his temple the *a* of his testament......... Rev 11:19

**ARKITE** (*ar'-kite*) *A tribe descended from Canaan.*
And the Hivite, and the *A*, and the..... Gen 10:17
And the Hivite, and the *A*, and the..... 1Chr 1:15

**ARKITES** See ARCHI.

**ARM**
redeem you with a stretched out *a*........... Ex 6:6
by the greatness of thine *a* they.......... Ex 15:16
*A* some of yourselves unto the war..... Num 31:3
hand, and by a stretched out *a*............ Deut 4:34
hand and by a stretched out *a*............ Deut 5:15
hand, and the stretched out *a*............ Deut 7:19
power and by thy stretched out *a*........ Deut 9:29
hand, and his stretched out *a*............ Deut 11:2
hand, and with an outstretched *a*......... Deut 26:8
teareth the *a* with the crown of......... Deut 33:20
come, that I will cut off thine *a*............ 1Sa 2:31
the *a* of thy father's house, that............ 1Sa 2:31
and the bracelet that was on his *a*......... 2Sa 1:10
hand, and of thy stretched out *a*........... 1Kin 8:42
great power and a stretched out *a*...... 2Kin 17:36
hand, and thy stretched out *a*.............. 2Chr 6:32
With his is an *a* of flesh.............. 2Chr 32:8
how savest thou the *a* that hath............ Job 26:2
Then let mine *a* fall from my.............. Job 31:22
mine *a* be broken from the bone........... Job 31:22
by reason of the *a* of the mighty........... Job 35:9
the high *a* shall be broken.............. Job 38:15
Hast thou an *a* like God.............. Job 40:9
Break thou the *a* of the wicked.............. Ps 10:15
neither did their own *a* save them........... Ps 44:3
but thy right hand, and thine *a*.............. Ps 44:3
with thine *a* redeemed thy people........... Ps 77:15
thine enemies with thy strong *a*............ Ps 89:10
Thou hast a mighty *a*.............. Ps 89:13
mine *a* also shall strengthen him........... Ps 89:21
his right hand, and his holy *a*.............. Ps 98:1
hand, and with a stretched out *a*......... Ps 136:12
heart, as a seal upon thine *a*.............. Song 8:6
every man the flesh of his own *a*............ Is 9:20
and reapeth the ears with his *a*.............. Is 17:5
shew the lighting down of his *a*............ Is 30:30
be thou their *a* every morning.............. Is 33:2
hand, and his *a* shall rule for him.......... Is 40:10
shall gather the lambs with his *a*.......... Is 40:11
his *a* shall be on the Chaldeans.............. Is 48:14
on mine *a* shall they trust.............. Is 51:5
put on strength, O *a* of the LORD.......... Is 51:9
LORD hath made bare his holy *a* in........ Is 52:10
to whom is the *a* of the LORD.............. Is 53:1
therefore his *a* brought salvation.......... Is 59:16
by the *a* of his strength, Surely.............. Is 62:8
therefore mine own *a* brought.............. Is 63:5
hand of Moses with his glorious *a*........... Is 63:12
in man, and maketh flesh his *a*.............. Jer 17:5
hand and with a strong *a*, even in.......... Jer 21:5
power and by my outstretched *a*........... Jer 27:5
great power and stretched out *a*........... Jer 32:17
hand, and with a stretched out *a*........... Jer 32:21
his *a* is broken, saith the LORD.............. Jer 48:25

thine *a* shall be uncovered, and ... Eze 4:7
hand, and with a stretched out *a* ... Eze 20:33
hand, and with a stretched out *a* ... Eze 20:34
I have broken the *a* of Pharaoh ... Eze 30:21
and they that were his *a*, that ... Eze 31:17
not retain the power of the *a* ... Dan 11:6
neither shall he stand, nor his *a* ... Dan 11:6
the sword shall be upon his *a* ... Zec 11:17
his *a* shall be clean dried up, and ... Zec 11:17
hath shewed strength with his *a* ... Lk 1:51
to whom hath the *a* of the Lord ... Jn 12:38
with an high *a* brought he them ... Acts 13:17
*a* yourselves likewise with the ... 1Pet 4:1

**ARMAGEDDON** (*ar-mag-ed'-don*) *Scene of the last great battle of time.*
called in the Hebrew tongue *A* ... Rev 16:16

**ARMED**
he *a* his trained servants, born ... Gen 14:14
tribe, twelve thousand *a* for war ... Num 31:5
*a* before the children of Israel ... Num 32:17
if ye will go *a* before the LORD ... Num 32:20
will go all of you *a* over Jordan ... Num 32:21
pass over, every man *a* for war ... Num 32:27
Jordan, every man *a* to battle ... Num 32:29
will not pass over with you *a* ... Num 32:30
We will pass over *a* before the ... Num 32:32
ye shall pass over *a* before your ... Deut 3:18
shall pass before your brethren *a* ... Josh 1:14
passed over *a* before the children ... Josh 4:12
let him that is *a* pass on before ... Josh 6:7
the *a* men went before the priests ... Josh 6:9
the *a* men went before them ... Josh 6:13
the *a* men that were in the host ... Judg 7:11
he was *a* with a coat of mail ... 1Sa 17:5
Saul *a* David with his armour, and ... 1Sa 17:38
also he *a* him with a coat of mail ... 1Sa 17:38
They were *a* with bows, and could ... 1Chr 12:2
that were ready *a* to the war ... 1Chr 12:23
eight hundred, ready *a* to the war ... 1Chr 12:24
with him *a* men with bow and shield 2Chr 17:17
So the *a* men left the captives and ... 2Chr 28:14
he goeth on to meet the *a* men ... Job 39:21
The children of Ephraim, being *a* ... Ps 78:9
and thy want as an *a* man ... Prov 6:11
and thy want as an *a* man ... Prov 24:34
therefore the *a* soldiers of Moab ... Is 15:4
When a strong man *a* keepeth his ... Lk 11:21

**ARMENIA** (*ar-me'-ne-ah*) *A region between the lower ends of the Black and Caspian seas.*
they escaped into the land of *A* ... 2Kin 19:37
they escaped into the land of *A* ... Is 37:38

**ARMHOLES**
under thine *a* under the cords ... Jer 38:12
women that sew pillows to all *a* ... Eze 13:18

**ARMIES**
of Egypt according to their *a* ... Ex 6:26
upon Egypt, and bring forth mine *a* ... Ex 7:4
day have I brought your *a* out of ... Ex 12:17
of the land of Egypt by their *a* ... Ex 12:51
shall number them by their *a* ... Num 1:3
of Judah pitch throughout their *a* ... Num 2:3
four hundred, throughout their *a* ... Num 2:9
of Reuben according to their *a* ... Num 2:10
and fifty, throughout their *a* ... Num 2:16
of Ephraim according to their *a* ... Num 2:18
and an hundred, throughout their *a* ... Num 2:24
be on the north side by their *a* ... Num 2:25
of Judah according to their *a* ... Num 10:14
set forward according to their *a* ... Num 10:18
set forward according to their *a* ... Num 10:22
of Israel according to their *a* ... Num 10:28
their *a* under the hand of Moses ... Num 33:1
of the *a* to lead the people ... Deut 20:9
together their *a* to battle ... 1Sa 17:1
and cried unto the *a* of Israel ... 1Sa 17:8
I defy the *a* of Israel this day ... 1Sa 17:10
out of the *a* of the Philistines, ... 1Sa 17:23
defy the *a* of the living God ... 1Sa 17:26
defied the *a* of the living God ... 1Sa 17:36
hosts, the God of the *a* of Israel ... 1Sa 17:45
against the *a* of the Philistines ... 1Sa 23:3
their *a* together for warfare ... 1Sa 28:1
together all their *a* to Aphek ... 1Sa 29:1
And when all the captains of the *a* ... 2Kin 25:23
great, and the captains of the *a* ... 2Kin 25:26
the valiant men of the *a* were ... 1Chr 11:26
sent the captains of his *a* ... 2Chr 16:4
Is there any number of his *a* ... Job 25:3
and goest not forth with our *a* ... Ps 44:9
which didst not go out with our *a* ... Ps 60:10
Kings of *a* did flee apace ... Ps 68:12
As it were the company of two *a* ... Song 6:13
and his fury upon all their *a* ... Is 34:2
and he sent forth his *a*, and ... Mt 22:7
see Jerusalem compassed with *a* ... Lk 21:20
to flight the *a* of the aliens ... Heb 11:34
the *a* which were in heaven ... Rev 19:14
kings of the earth, and their *a* ... Rev 19:19

**ARMONI** (*ar-mo'-ni*) *A son of King Saul.*
Aiah, whom she bare unto Saul, *A* ... 2Sa 21:8

**ARMOUR**
the young man that bare his *a* ... 1Sa 14:1
to the young man that bare his *a* ... 1Sa 14:6
And Saul armed David with his *a* ... 1Sa 17:38
David girded his sword upon his *a* ... 1Sa 17:39
but he put his *a* in his tent ... 1Sa 17:54
his head, and stripped off his *a* ... 1Sa 31:9
they put his *a* in the house of ... 1Sa 31:10
the young men, and take thee his *a* ... 2Sa 2:21
bare Joab's *a* compassed about ... 2Sa 18:15
of gold, and garments, and *a* ... 1Kin 10:25
and they washed his *a* ... 1Kin 22:38
all that were able to put on *a* ... 2Kin 3:21
horses, a fenced city also, and *a* ... 2Kin 10:2
and all the house of his *a* ... 2Kin 20:13
him, they took his head, and his *a* ... 1Chr 10:9
they put his *a* in the house of ... 1Chr 10:10
the *a* of the house of the forest ... Is 22:8
and all the house of his *a* ... Is 39:2
them clothed with all sorts of *a* ... Eze 38:4
him all his *a* wherein he trusted ... Lk 11:22
and let us put on the *a* of light ... Rom 13:12
by the *a* of righteousness on the ... 2Cor 6:7
Put on the whole *a* of God ... Eph 6:11
take unto you the whole *a* of God ... Eph 6:13

**ARMOURBEARER**
hastily unto the young man his *a* ... Judg 9:54
his *a* said unto him, Do all that ... 1Sa 14:7
answered Jonathan and his *a* ... 1Sa 14:12
And Jonathan said unto his *a* ... 1Sa 14:12
upon his feet, and his *a* after him ... 1Sa 14:13
and his *a* slew after him ... 1Sa 14:13
his *a* made, was about twenty men, ... 1Sa 14:14
Jonathan and his *a* were not there ... 1Sa 14:17
and he became his *a* ... 1Sa 16:21
Then said Saul unto his *a* ... 1Sa 31:4
But his *a* would not ... 1Sa 31:4
when his *a* saw that Saul was dead ... 1Sa 31:5
died, and his three sons, and his *a* ... 1Sa 31:6
*a* to Joab the son of Zeruiah, ... 2Sa 23:37
Then said Saul to his *a*, Draw thy ... 1Chr 10:4
But his *a* would not ... 1Chr 10:4
when his *a* saw that Saul was dead ... 1Chr 10:5
the *a* of Joab the son of Zeruiah, ... 1Chr 11:39

**ARMOURY**
the *a* at the turning of the wall ... Neh 3:19
tower of David builded for an *a* ... Song 4:4
The LORD hath opened his *a* ... Jer 50:25

**ARMS**
the *a* of his hands were made ... Gen 49:24
underneath are the everlasting *a* ... Deut 33:27
the cords that were upon his *a* ... Judg 15:14
them from off his *a* like a thread ... Judg 16:12
bow of steel is broken by mine *a* ... 2Sa 22:35
and smote Jehoram between his *a* ... 2Kin 9:24
the *a* of the fatherless have been ... Job 22:9
bow of steel is broken by mine *a* ... Ps 18:34
For the *a* of the wicked shall be ... Ps 37:17
strength, and strengtheneth her *a* ... Prov 31:17
it with the strength of his *a* ... Is 44:12
shall bring thy sons in their *a* ... Is 49:22
mine *a* shall judge the people ... Is 51:5
and I will tear them from your *a* ... Eze 13:20
of Egypt, and will break his *a* ... Eze 30:22
I will strengthen the *a* of the ... Eze 30:24
but I will break Pharaoh's *a* ... Eze 30:24
the *a* of the king of Babylon ... Eze 30:25
the *a* of Pharaoh shall fall down ... Eze 30:25
his *a* of silver, his belly and his ... Dan 2:32
eyes as lamps of fire, and his *a* ... Dan 10:6
the *a* of the south shall not ... Dan 11:15
with the *a* of a flood shall they ... Dan 11:22
*a* shall stand on his part, and ... Dan 11:31
bound and strengthened their *a* ... Hos 7:15
to go, taking them by their *a* ... Hos 11:3
and when he had taken him in his *a* ... Mk 9:36
And he took them up in his *a* ... Mk 10:16
Then took he him up in his *a* ... Lk 2:28

**ARMY**
the chief captain of his *a* ... Gen 26:26
and his horsemen, and his *a* ... Ex 14:9
what he did unto the *a* of Egypt ... Deut 11:4
Sisera, the captain of Jabin's *a* ... Judg 4:7
we should give bread unto thine *a* ... Judg 8:6
to Abimelech, Increase thine *a* ... Judg 9:29
they slew of the *a* in the field ... 1Sa 4:2
a man of Benjamin out of the *a* ... 1Sa 4:12
I am he that came out of the *a* ... 1Sa 4:16
and I fled to day out of the *a* ... 1Sa 4:16
battle in array, *a* against *a* ... 1Sa 17:21
battle in array, *a* against *a* ... 1Sa 17:21
the carriage, and ran into the *a* ... 1Sa 17:22
ran toward the *a* to meet the ... 1Sa 17:48
the *a* which followed them ... 1Kin 20:19
And number thee an *a* ... 1Kin 20:25
like the *a* that thou hast lost, ... 1Kin 20:25
the *a* of the Chaldees pursued ... 2Kin 25:5
all his *a* were scattered from him ... 2Kin 25:5
all the *a* of the Chaldees, that ... 2Kin 25:10
Joab led forth the power of the *a* ... 1Chr 20:1
general of the king's *a* was Joab ... 1Chr 27:34
with an *a* of valiant men of war ... 2Chr 13:3
Asa had an *a* of men that bare ... 2Chr 14:8
as they went out before the *a* ... 2Chr 20:21
For the *a* of the Syrians came ... 2Chr 24:24
let not the *a* of Israel go with ... 2Chr 25:7
I have given to the *a* of Israel ... 2Chr 25:9
the *a* that was come to him out of ... 2Chr 25:10
of the *a* which Amaziah sent back ... 2Chr 25:13
And under their hand was an *a* ... 2Chr 26:13
king had sent captains of the *a* ... Neh 2:9
the *a* of Samaria, and said, What ... Neh 4:2
and dwelt as a king in the *a* ... Job 29:25
terrible as an *a* with banners ... Song 6:4
and terrible as an *a* with banners ... Song 6:10
unto king Hezekiah with a great *a* ... Is 36:2
forth the chariot and horse, the *a* ... Is 43:17
of Babylon's *a* besieged Jerusalem ... Jer 32:2
king of Babylon, and all his *a* ... Jer 34:1
*a* fought against Jerusalem ... Jer 34:7
hand of the king of Babylon's *a* ... Jer 34:21
fear of the *a* of the Chaldeans ... Jer 35:11
for fear of the *a* of the Syrians ... Jer 35:11
Then Pharaoh's *a* was come forth ... Jer 37:5
Behold, Pharaoh's *a*, which is ... Jer 37:7
*a* of the Chaldeans that fight ... Jer 37:10
that when the *a* of the Chaldeans ... Jer 37:11
Jerusalem for fear of Pharaoh's *a* ... Jer 37:11
hand of the king of Babylon's *a* ... Jer 38:3
all his *a* against Jerusalem, and ... Jer 39:1
Chaldeans' *a* pursued after them ... Jer 39:5
against the *a* of Pharaoh-necho ... Jer 46:2
for they shall march with an *a* ... Jer 46:22
of Babylon came, he and all his *a* ... Jer 52:4
But the *a* of the Chaldeans ... Jer 52:8
all his *a* was scattered from him ... Jer 52:8
all the *a* of the Chaldeans, that ... Jer 52:14
shall Pharaoh with his mighty *a* ... Eze 17:17
of Lud and of Phut were in thine *a* ... Eze 27:10
The men of Arvad with thine *a* ... Eze 27:11
his *a* to serve a great service ... Eze 29:18
yet had he no wages, nor his *a* ... Eze 29:18
it shall be the wages for his *a* ... Eze 29:19
all his *a* slain by the sword, ... Eze 32:31
their feet, an exceeding great *a* ... Eze 37:10
bring thee forth, and all thine *a* ... Eze 38:4
a great company, and a mighty *a* ... Eze 38:15
were in his *a* to bind Shadrach ... Dan 3:20
to his will in the *a* of heaven ... Dan 4:35
which shall come with an *a* ... Dan 11:7
certain years with a great *a* ... Dan 11:13
king of the south with a great *a* ... Dan 11:25
with a very great and mighty *a* ... Dan 11:25
him, and his *a* shall overflow ... Dan 11:26
utter his voice before his *a* ... Joel 2:11
far off from you the northern *a* ... Joel 2:20
my great *a* which I sent among you ... Joel 2:25
about mine house because of the *a* ... Zec 9:8
then came I with an *a*, and rescued ... Acts 23:27
the number of the *a* of the ... Rev 9:16
on the horse, and against his *a* ... Rev 19:19

**ARNAN** (*ar'-nan*) *Descendants of David.*
sons of Rephaiah, the sons of *A* ... 1Chr 3:21

**ARNON** (*ar'-non*) *A river in southern Canaan.*
and pitched on the other side of *A* ... Num 21:13
for *A* is the border of Moab, ... Num 21:13
Red sea, and in the brooks of *A* ... Num 21:14
his land from *A* unto Jabbok ... Num 21:24
land out of his hand, even unto *A* ... Num 21:26
the lords of the high places of *A* ... Num 21:28
Moab, which is in the border of *A* ... Num 22:36
journey, and pass over the river *A* ... Deut 2:24
is by the brink of the river of *A* ... Deut 2:36
the river of *A* unto mount Hermon ... Deut 3:8
Aroer, which is by the river *A* ... Deut 3:12
unto the river *A* half the valley ... Deut 3:16
is by the bank of the river *A* ... Deut 4:48
from the river *A* unto mount ... Josh 12:1
is upon the bank of the river *A* ... Josh 12:2
is upon the bank of the river *A* ... Josh 13:9
is on the bank of the river *A* ... Josh 13:16
from *A* even unto Jabbok, and unto ... Judg 11:13
and pitched on the other side of *A* ... Judg 11:18
for *A* was the border of Moab ... Judg 11:18
from *A* even unto Jabbok, and from ... Judg 11:22
that be along by the coasts of *A* ... Judg 11:26
Aroer, which is by the river *A* ... 2Kin 10:33
Moab shall be at the fords of *A* ... Is 16:2
tell ye it in *A*, that Moab is ... Jer 48:20

**AROD** (*a'-rod*) See ARODITES. *A son of Gad.*
Of *A*, the family of the Arodites ... Num 26:17

**ARODI** (*ar'-o-di*) See ARODITES. *Descendants of Arod.*
Haggi, Shuni, and Ezbon, Eri, and *A* ... Gen 46:16

**ARODITES** (*a'-ro-dites*) *Same as Arodi.*
Of Arod, the family of the *A* ... Num 26:17

**AROER** (*ar'-o-ur*)
*1. A city in the valley of Jabbok.*
Gad built Dibon, and Ataroth, and *A* Num 32:34
unto *A* that is before Rabbah ... Josh 13:25
over Jordan, and pitched in *A* ... 2Sa 24:5
The cities of *A* are forsaken ... Is 17:2
*2. An Amorite city.*
From *A*, which is by the brink of ... Deut 2:36
we possessed at that time, from *A* ... Deut 3:12
From *A*, which is by the bank of ... Deut 4:48
dwelt in Heshbon, and ruled from *A* ... Josh 12:2
From *A*, that is upon the bank of ... Josh 13:9
And their coast was from *A* ... Josh 13:16
in Heshbon and her towns, and in *A*. Judg 11:26
And he smote them from *A*, even ... Judg 11:33
and the Manassites, from *A* ... 2Kin 10:33
the son of Joel, who dwelt in *A* ... 1Chr 5:8
O inhabitant of *A*, stand by the ... Jer 48:19
*3. A city in southern Judah.*
And to them which were in *A* ... 1Sa 30:28

**AROERITE** (*ar'-o-ur-ite*) *A native of Aroer.*
Jehiel the sons of Hothan the *A* ... 1Chr 11:44

**AROSE**
And when the morning *a*, then the ... Gen 19:15
when she lay down, nor when she *a* .. Gen 19:33

and the younger *a*, and lay with him. Gen 19:35
when she lay down, nor when she *a*.. Gen 19:35
and he *a*, and went to Mesopotamia,.. Gen 24:10
Rebekah *a*, and her damsels Gen 24:61
in the field, and, lo, my sheaf *a* Gen 37:7
And she *a*, and went away, and laid... Gen 38:19
Now there *a* up a new king over Ex 1:8
there *a* not a prophet since in Deut 34:10
So Joshua *a*, and all the people of Josh 8:3
the ambush *a* quickly out of their Josh 8:19
And the men *a*, and went away Josh 18:8
son of Zippor, king of Moab, *a* Josh 24:9
there *a* another generation after Judg 2:10
And he *a* out of his seat Judg 3:20
And Deborah *a*, and went with Barak.. Judg 4:9
in Israel, until that I Deborah *a* Judg 5:7
that I *a* a mother in Israel Judg 5:7
the city *a* early in the morning Judg 6:28
And Gideon *a*, and slew Zebah and Judg 8:21
after Abimelech there *a* to defend Judg 10:1
And after him *a* Jair, a Gileadite, Judg 10:3
And Manoah *a*, and went after his Judg 13:11
*a* at midnight, and took the doors Judg 16:3
And her husband *a*, and went after Judg 19:3
when they *a* early in the morning, Judg 19:5
he *a* early in the morning on the Judg 19:8
And all the people *a* as one man Judg 20:8
And the children of Israel *a* Judg 20:18
Then she *a* with her daughters in Ruth 1:6
And Samuel *a* and went to Eli, and 1Sa 3:6
And he *a* and went to Eli, and said, 1Sa 3:8
of Ashdod *a* early on the morrow 1Sa 5:3
when they *a* early on the morrow 1Sa 5:4
And they *a* early 1Sa 9:26
And Saul *a*, and they went out both 1Sa 9:26
And Samuel *a*, and gat him up from ... 1Sa 13:15
when he *a* against me, I caught 1Sa 17:35
to pass, when the Philistine *a* 1Sa 17:48
the men of Israel and of Judah *a* 1Sa 17:52
Wherefore David *a* and went, he and.. 1Sa 18:27
and Jonathan *a*, and Abner sat by 1Sa 20:25
So Jonathan *a* from the table in 1Sa 20:34
David *a* out of a place toward the 1Sa 20:41
And he *a* and departed 1Sa 20:42
And David *a*, and fled that day for 1Sa 21:10
which were about six hundred, *a* 1Sa 23:13
And Jonathan Saul's son *a*, and went. 1Sa 23:16
And they *a*, and went to Ziph before.. 1Sa 23:24
Then David *a*, and cut off the 1Sa 24:4
David also *a* afterward, and went 1Sa 24:8
And David *a*, and went down to the 1Sa 25:1
And she *a*, and bowed herself on her... 1Sa 25:41
And Abigail hasted, and *a*, and rode... 1Sa 25:42
Then Saul *a*, and went down to the 1Sa 26:2
And David *a*, and came to the place 1Sa 26:5
And David *a*, and he passed over 1Sa 27:2
So he *a* from the earth, and sat 1Sa 28:23
All the valiant men *a*, and went 1Sa 31:12
Then there *a* and went over by 2Sa 2:15
And David *a*, and went with all the 2Sa 6:2
that David *a* from off his bed, and 2Sa 11:2
And the elders of his house *a* 2Sa 12:17
Then David *a* from the earth, and 2Sa 12:20
Then all the king's sons *a* 2Sa 13:29
Then the king *a*, and tare his 2Sa 13:31
So Joab *a* and went to Geshur, and 2Sa 14:23
Then Joab *a*, and came to Absalom 2Sa 14:31
So he *a*, and went to Hebron 2Sa 15:9
Then David *a*, and all the people 2Sa 17:22
he saddled his ass, and *a* 2Sa 17:23
Then the king *a*, and sat in the 2Sa 19:8
He *a*, and smote the Philistines 2Sa 23:10
feared because of Solomon, and *a* 1Kin 1:50
And Shimei *a*, and saddled his ass, 1Kin 2:40
she *a* at midnight, and took my son 1Kin 3:20
he *a* from before the altar of the 1Kin 8:54
they *a* out of Midian, and came to 1Kin 11:18
And Jeroboam *a*, and fled into Egypt 1Kin 11:40
And Jeroboam's wife did so, and *a* 1Kin 14:4
And Jeroboam's wife *a* 1Kin 14:17
So he *a* and went to Zarephath 1Kin 17:10
And when he saw that, he *a* 1Kin 19:3
And he *a*, and did eat and drink, and.. 1Kin 19:8
Then he *a*, and went after Elijah, 1Kin 19:21
And he *a*, and went down with him 2Kin 1:15
And he *a*, and followed her 2Kin 4:30
Wherefore they *a* and fled in the 2Kin 7:7
the king *a* in the night, and said 2Kin 7:12
And the woman *a*, and did after the 2Kin 8:2
And he *a*, and went into the house 2Kin 9:6
And he *a* and departed, and came to. 2Kin 10:12
saw that her son was dead, she *a* 2Kin 11:1
And his servants *a*, and made a 2Kin 12:20
when they *a* early in the morning, 2Kin 19:35
neither after him *a* there any 2Kin 23:25
and the captains of the armies, *a* 2Kin 25:26
They *a*, all the valiant men, and 1Chr 10:12
that there *a* war at Gezer with 1Chr 20:4
saw that her son was dead, she *a* 2Chr 22:10
Then the Levites *a*, Mahath the 2Chr 29:12
*a* and took away the altars 2Chr 30:14
Then the priests the Levites *a* 2Chr 30:27
of the LORD *a* against his people 2Chr 36:16
I *a* up from my heaviness Ezr 9:5
Then *a* Ezra, and made the chief Ezr 10:5
I *a* in the night, I and some few Neh 2:12
So Esther *a*, and stood before the Est 8:4
Then Job *a*, and rent his mantle, Job 1:20
I *a*, and they spake against me Job 19:18
and the aged *a*, and stood up Job 29:8
When God *a* to judgment, to save Ps 76:9
hasteth to his place where he *a* Eccl 1:5
when they *a* early in the morning, Is 37:36
Then *a* Ishmael the son of Jer 41:2
Then I *a*, and went forth into the Eze 3:23
Then the king *a* very early in the Dan 6:19
So Jonah *a*, and went unto Nineveh,.. Jonah 3:3
he *a* from his throne, and he laid Jonah 3:6
When he *a*, he took the young Mt 2:14
And he *a*, and took the young child Mt 2:21
and she *a*, and ministered unto them Mt 8:15
there *a* a great tempest in the Mt 8:24
Then he *a*, and rebuked the winds Mt 8:26
And he *a*, and departed to his house Mt 9:7
And he *a*, and followed him Mt 9:9
And Jesus *a*, and followed him, and Mt 9:19
her by the hand, and the maid *a* Mt 9:25
Then all those virgins *a*, and Mt 25:7
And the high priest *a*, and said Mt 26:62
of the saints which slept *a* Mt 27:52
And immediately he *a*, took up the Mk 2:12
And he *a* and followed him Mk 2:14
there *a* a great storm of wind, and Mk 4:37
And he *a*, and rebuked the wind, and.... Mk 4:39
And straightway the damsel *a* Mk 5:42
And from thence he *a*, and went into.... Mk 7:24
and he *a* Mk 9:27
he *a* from thence, and cometh into Mk 10:1
there *a* certain, and bare false Mk 14:57
Mary *a* in those days, and went Lk 1:39
he *a* out of the synagogue, and Lk 4:38
and immediately she *a* and Lk 4:39
And he *a* and stood forth Lk 6:8
and when the flood *a*, the stream Lk 6:48
Then he *a*, and rebuked the wind and.... Lk 8:24
came again, and she *a* straightway Lk 8:55
Then there *a* a reasoning among Lk 9:46
there *a* a mighty famine in that Lk 15:14
And he *a*, and came to his father Lk 15:20
And the whole multitude of them *a* Lk 23:1
Then *a* Peter, and ran unto the Lk 24:12
Then there *a* a question between Jn 3:25
the sea *a* by reason of a great Jn 6:18
she *a* quickly, and came unto him Jn 11:29
And the young men *a*, wound him up,.. Acts 5:6
there *a* a murmuring of the Acts 6:1
Then there *a* certain of the Acts 6:9
Till another king *a*, which knew Acts 7:18
And he *a* and went Acts 8:27
And Saul *a* from the earth Acts 9:8
he received sight forthwith, and *a* Acts 9:18
And he *a* immediately Acts 9:34
Then Peter *a* and went with them Acts 9:39
upon the persecution that *a* about Acts 11:19
the same time there *a* no small Acts 19:23
there *a* a dissension between the Acts 23:7
And there *a* a great cry Acts 23:9
were of the Pharisees' part *a* Acts 23:9
when there *a* a great dissension, Acts 23:10
But not long after there *a* Acts 27:14
there *a* a smoke out of the pit, Rev 9:2

**ARPAD** (*ar'pad*) *A city near Hamath.*
are the gods of Hamath, and of *A* 2Kin 18:34
king of Hamath, and the king of *A* 2Kin 19:13
is not Hamath as *A* Is 10:9
Hamath is confounded, and *A* Jer 49:23

**ARPHAD** (*ar'-fad*) See ARPAD. *Same as Arpad.*
Where are the gods of Hamath and *A* ... Is 36:19
king of Hamath, and the king of *A* Is 37:13

**ARPHAXAD**
Asshur, and *A*, and Lud Gen 10:22
And *A* begat Salah Gen 10:24
begat *A* two years after the flood Gen 11:10
he begat *A* five hundred years Gen 11:11
*A* lived five and thirty years, and Gen 11:12
*A* lived after he begat Salah four Gen 11:13
Asshur, and *A*, and Lud 1Chr 1:17
*A* begat Shelah, and Shelah begat 1Chr 1:18
Shem, *A*, Shelah, 1Chr 1:24
of Cainan, which was the son of *A* Lk 3:36

**ARRAY**
*a* to fight against them at Gibeah Judg 20:20
set their battle again in *a* in Judg 20:22
put themselves in *a* the first day Judg 20:22
themselves in *a* against Gibeah Judg 20:30
put themselves in *a* at Baal-tamar Judg 20:33
themselves in *a* against Israel 1Sa 4:2
set the battle in *a* against the 1Sa 17:2
come out to set your battle in *a* 1Sa 17:8
had put the battle in *a*, army 1Sa 17:21
put the battle in *a* at the 2Sa 10:8
put them in *a* against the Syrians 2Sa 10:9
that he might put them in *a* 2Sa 10:10
set themselves in *a* against David 2Sa 10:17
his servants, Set yourselves in *a* 1Kin 20:12
themselves in *a* against the city 1Kin 20:12
put the battle in *a* before the 1Chr 19:9
put them in *a* against the Syrians 1Chr 19:10
they set themselves in *a* against 1Chr 19:11
set the battle in *a* against them 1Chr 19:17
battle in *a* against the Syrians 1Chr 19:17
Abijah set the battle in *a* with 2Chr 13:3
*a* against him with eight hundred 2Chr 13:3
they set the battle in *a* in the 2Chr 14:10
that they may *a* the man withal Est 6:9
do set themselves in *a* against me Job 6:4
*a* thyself with glory and beauty Job 40:10
set themselves in *a* at the gate Is 22:7
set in *a* as men for war against Jer 6:23
he shall *a* himself with the land Jer 43:12
set themselves in *a* against her Jer 50:9
Put yourselves in *a* against Jer 50:14
upon horses, every one put in *a* Jer 50:42
a strong people set in battle *a* Joel 2:5
or gold, or pearls, or costly *a* 1Ti 2:9

**ARRAYED**
*a* him in vestures of fine linen, Gen 41:42
being *a* in white linen, having 2Chr 5:12
*a* them, and shod them, and gave 2Chr 28:15
*a* Mordecai, and brought him on Est 6:11
glory was not *a* like one of these Mt 6:29
glory was not *a* like one of these Lk 12:27
*a* him in a gorgeous robe, and sent Lk 23:11
*a* in royal apparel, sat upon his Acts 12:21
these which are *a* in white robes Rev 7:13
And the woman was *a* in purple Rev 17:4
she should be *a* in fine linen Rev 19:8

**ARRIVED**
they *a* at the country of the Lk 8:26
and the next day we *a* at Samos Acts 20:15

**ARROGANCY**
let not *a* come out of your mouth 1Sa 2:3
pride, and *a*, and the evil way, and Prov 8:13
I will cause the *a* of the proud Is 13:11
proud) his loftiness, and his *a* Jer 48:29

**ARROW**
lad ran, he shot an *a* beyond him 1Sa 20:36
of the *a* which Jonathan had shot 1Sa 20:37
and said, Is not the *a* beyond thee 1Sa 20:37
the *a* went out at his heart, and 2Kin 9:24
The *a* of the LORD's deliverance, 2Kin 13:17
the *a* of deliverance from Syria 2Kin 13:17
this city, nor shoot an *a* there 2Kin 19:32
The *a* cannot make him flee Job 41:28
ready their *a* upon the string Ps 11:2
God shall shoot at them with an *a* Ps 64:7
nor for the *a* that flieth by day Ps 91:5
a maul, and a sword, and a sharp *a*... Prov 25:18
this city, nor shoot an *a* there Is 37:33
Their tongue is as an *a* shot out Jer 9:8
and set me as a mark for the *a* Lam 3:12
his *a* shall go forth as the Zec 9:14

**ARROWS**
and pierce them through with his *a*.... Num 24:8
I will spend mine *a* upon them Deut 32:23
will make mine *a* drunk with blood.. Deut 32:42
I will shoot three *a* on the side 1Sa 20:20
a lad, saying, Go, find out the *a* 1Sa 20:21
the *a* are on this side of thee, 1Sa 20:21
Behold, the *a* are beyond thee 1Sa 20:22
find out now the *a* which I shoot 1Sa 20:36
Jonathan's lad gathered up the *a* 1Sa 20:38
And he sent out *a*, and scattered 2Sa 22:15
said unto him, Take bow and *a* 2Kin 13:15
And he took unto him bow and *a* 2Kin 13:15
And he said, Take the *a* 2Kin 13:18
shooting *a* out of a bow, even of 1Chr 12:2
and upon the bulwarks, to shoot *a*... 2Chr 26:15
For the *a* of the Almighty are Job 6:4
he ordaineth his *a* against the Ps 7:13
Yea, he sent out his *a*, and Ps 18:14
thou shalt make ready thine *a* Ps 21:12
For thine *a* stick fast in me, and Ps 38:2
Thine *a* are sharp in the heart of Ps 45:5
men, whose teeth are spears and *a* Ps 57:4
he bendeth his bow to shoot his *a* Ps 58:7
bend their bows to shoot their *a* Ps 64:3
There brake he the *a* of the bow Ps 76:3
thine *a* also went abroad Ps 77:17
Sharp *a* of the mighty, with coals Ps 120:4
As *a* are in the hand of a mighty Ps 127:4
shoot out thine *a*, and destroy Ps 144:6
mad man who casteth firebrands, *a*... Prov 26:18
Whose *a* are sharp, and all their Is 5:28
With *a* and with bows shall men Is 7:24
their *a* shall be as of a mighty Jer 50:9
the bow, shoot at her, spare no *a* Jer 50:14
Make bright the *a* Jer 51:11
He hath caused the *a* of his Lam 3:13
upon them the evil *a* of famine Eze 5:16
he made his *a* bright, he Eze 21:21
will cause thine *a* to fall out of Eze 39:3
the bucklers, the bows and the *a* Eze 39:9
at the light of thine *a* they went Hab 3:11

**ART** See PREFACE.

**ARTAXERXES** (*ar-tax-erx'-ees*) See ARTAXERXES'.
*1. A Persian king known as Longimanus.*
And in the days of *A* wrote Bishlam Ezr 4:7
companions, unto *A* king of Persia Ezr 4:7
to *A* the king in this sort Ezr 4:8
unto him, even unto *A* the king Ezr 4:11

**ARTAXERXES'** (*ar-tax-erx'-eez*) *Refers to Artaxerxes I.*
Now when the copy of king *A* Ezr 4:23

**ARTAXERXES** (*ar-tax-erx'-ees*)
*1. A Persian king known as Longimanus.*
And in the days of *A* Ezr 4:7
unto *A*, king of Persia Ezr 4:7
*A* the king of this sort Ezr 4:8
even unto *A* the king Ezr 4:11
*2. A Persian king known as Cambyses.*
and Darius, and *A* king of Persia Ezr 6:14
*3. A Persian king known as Darius.*
in the reign of *A* king of Persia Ezr 7:1
in the seventh year of *A* the king Ezr 7:7
king *A* gave unto Ezra the priest Ezr 7:11
*A*, king of kings, unto Ezra the Ezr 7:12

even I *A* the king, do make a ........ Ezr 7:21
in the reign of *A* the king ........ Ezr 8:1
the twentieth year of *A* the king ........ Neh 2:1
and thirtieth year of *A* the king ........ Neh 5:14
thirtieth year of *A* king of ........ Neh 13:6

**ARTEMAS** (*ar'-te-mas*) *A companion of Paul.*
When I shall send *A* unto thee ........ Titus 3:12

**ARTEMIS** See DIANA.

**ARTIFICER**
an instructer of every *a* in brass ........ Gen 4:22
the counsellor, and the cunning *a* ........ Is 3:3

**ARTIFICERS**
work to be made by the hands of *a* ..... 1Chr 29:5
Even to the *a* and builders gave ........ 2Chr 34:11

**ARTILLERY**
Jonathan gave his *a* unto his lad ........ 1Sa 20:40

**ARTS**
*a* brought their books together ........ Acts 19:19

**ARUBBOTH** See ARUBOTH.

**ARUBOTH** (*ar'-u-both*) *A district of Solomon's rule.*
The son of Hesed, in *A* ........ 1Kin 4:10

**ARUMAH** (*a-ru'-mah*) *A place in Ephraim.*
And Abimelech dwelt at *A* ........ Judg 9:41

**ARVAD** (*ar'-vad*) See ARVADITE. *An island near Zidon.*
of Zidon and *A* were thy mariners ........ Eze 27:8
The men of *A* with thine army were ... Eze 27:11

**ARVADITE** (*ar'-vad-ite*) *Descendants of Canaan.*
the *A*, and the Zemarite ........ Gen 10:18
And the *A*, and the Zemarite, and the 1Chr 1:16

**ARVADITES** See ARVADITE.

**ARZA** (*ar'-zah*) *A steward of King Elah of Israel.*
himself drunk in the house of *A* ........ 1Kin 16:9

**AS** See PREFACE.

**ASA** (*a'-sah*) See ASA'S.
*1. A king of Judah.*
*A* his son reigned in his stead ........ 1Kin 15:8
of Israel reigned *A* over Judah ........ 1Kin 15:9
*A* did that which was right in the ...... 1Kin 15:11
*A* destroyed her idol, and burnt it ...... 1Kin 15:13
And there was war between *A* ........ 1Kin 15:16
out or come in to *A* king of Judah .... 1Kin 15:17
Then *A* took all the silver and the ...... 1Kin 15:18
king *A* sent them to Ben-hadad, ........ 1Kin 15:18
Ben-hadad hearkened unto king *A* .... 1Kin 15:20
Then king *A* made a proclamation ........ 1Kin 15:22
king *A* built with them Geba of ........ 1Kin 15:22
The rest of all the acts of *A* ........ 1Kin 15:23
*A* slept with his fathers, and was ....... 1Kin 15:24
second year of *A* king of Judah ........ 1Kin 15:25
Even in the third year of *A* king ........ 1Kin 15:28
And there was war between *A* ........ 1Kin 15:32
In the third year of *A* king of ........ 1Kin 15:33
sixth year of *A* king of Judah ........ 1Kin 16:8
seventh year of *A* king of Judah ........ 1Kin 16:10
seventh year of *A* king of Judah ........ 1Kin 16:15
first year of *A* king of Judah ........ 1Kin 16:23
eighth year of *A* king of Judah ........ 1Kin 16:29
Jehoshaphat the son of *A* began to ... 1Kin 22:41
in all the ways of *A* his father ........ 1Kin 22:43
in the days of his father *A* ........ 1Kin 22:46
*A* his son, Jehoshaphat his son, ........ 1Chr 3:10
*A* his son reigned in his stead ........ 2Chr 14:1
*A* did that which was good and ........ 2Chr 14:2
*A* had an army of men that bare ........ 2Chr 14:8
Then *A* went out against him, and .... 2Chr 14:10
*A* cried unto the LORD his God, and .. 2Chr 14:11
smote the Ethiopians before *A* ........ 2Chr 14:12
*A* and the people that ........ 2Chr 14:13
And he went out to meet *A*, and said. 2Chr 15:2
and said unto him, Hear ye me, *A* ....... 2Chr 15:2
when *A* heard these words, and the .... 2Chr 15:8
fifteenth year of the reign of *A* ........ 2Chr 15:10
Maachah the mother of *A* the king ... 2Chr 15:16
*A* cut down her idol, and stamped ....... 2Chr 15:16
of *A* was perfect all his days ........ 2Chr 15:17
thirtieth year of the reign of *A* ........ 2Chr 15:19
*A* Baasha king of Israel came up ........ 2Chr 16:1
out or come in to *A* king of Judah ...... 2Chr 16:1
Then *A* brought out silver and gold .... 2Chr 16:2
Ben-hadad hearkened unto king *A* ...... 2Chr 16:4
Then *A* the king took all Judah ........ 2Chr 16:6
the seer came to *A* king of Judah ........ 2Chr 16:7
Then *A* was wroth with the seer, ........ 2Chr 16:10
*A* oppressed some of the people ........ 2Chr 16:10
And, behold, the acts of *A* ........ 2Chr 16:11
*A* in the thirty and ninth year of ....... 2Chr 16:12
*A* slept with his fathers, and died ...... 2Chr 16:13
which *A* his father had taken ........ 2Chr 17:2
walked in the way of *A* his father ...... 2Chr 20:32
in the ways of *A* king of Judah ........ 2Chr 21:12
was it which *A* the king had made ........ Jer 41:9
and Abia begat *A* ........ Mt 1:7
And *A* begat Josaphat ........ Mt 1:8
*2. Chief of a Levite family.*
and Berechiah the son of *A* ........ 1Chr 9:16

**ASAHEL** (*as'-a-hel*)
*1. The son of Zeruiah, David's sister.*
there, Joab, and Abishai, and *A* ........ 2Sa 2:18
*A* was as light of foot as a wild ........ 2Sa 2:18
And *A* pursued after Abner ........ 2Sa 2:19
behind him, and said, Art thou *A* ........ 2Sa 2:20
But *A* would not turn aside from ........ 2Sa 2:21
And Abner said again to *A*, Turn ........ 2Sa 2:22
to the place where *A* fell down ........ 2Sa 2:23
servants nineteen men and *A* ........ 2Sa 2:30
And they took up *A*, and buried him ..... 2Sa 2:32
for the blood of *A* his brother ........ 2Sa 3:27
brother *A* at Gibeon in the battle ........ 2Sa 3:30
*A* the brother of Joab was one of ........ 2Sa 23:24
Abishai, and Joab, and *A*, three ........ 1Chr 2:16
*A* the brother of Joab, Elhanan ........ 1Chr 11:26
month was *A* the brother of Joab ........ 1Chr 27:7
*2. A Levite teacher.*
and Nethaniah, and Zebadiah, and *A*.. 2Chr 17:8
*3. A Levite officer.*
and Azaziah, and Nahath, and *A* ....... 2Chr 31:13
*4. Father of Jonathan.*
Only Jonathan the son of *A* ........ Ezr 10:15

**ASAHIAH** (*as-a-hi'-ah*) See ASAIAH. *An officer of King Josiah.*
*A* a servant of the king's, saying ........ 2Kin 22:12
and Achbor, and Shaphan, and *A* ...... 2Kin 22:14

**ASAIAH** (*as-a'-yah*)
*1. A descendant of Simeon.*
and Jaakobah, and Jeshohaiah, and *A* 1Chr 4:36
*2. A descendant of Libni.*
son, Haggiah his son, *A* his son ........ 1Chr 6:30
*3. A Shilonite of Jerusalem.*
*A* the firstborn, and his sons ........ 1Chr 9:5
*4. A descendant of Merari.*
*A* the chief, and his brethren two ........ 1Chr 15:6
and for the Levites, for Uriel, *A* ........ 1Chr 15:11
*5. Same as Asahiah.*
*A* a servant of the king's, saying ........ 2Chr 34:20

**ASAPH** (*a'-saf*) See ASAPH'S.
*1. Father of Joah.*
and Joah the son of *A* the recorder ... 2Kin 18:18
and Joah the son of *A* the recorder ... 2Kin 18:37
the scribe, and Joah, the son of *A* ........ Is 36:22
*2. A musician of David and Solomon.*
And his brother *A*, who stood on ........ 1Chr 6:39
even *A* the son of Berachiah, the ........ 1Chr 6:39
brethren, *A* the son of Berechiah ....... 1Chr 15:17
So the singers, Heman, *A*, and ........ 1Chr 15:19
*A* the chief, and next to him ........ 1Chr 16:5
but *A* made a sound with cymbals ...... 1Chr 16:5
thank the LORD into the hand of *A* ..... 1Chr 16:7
ark of the covenant of the LORD *A* .... 1Chr 16:37
to the service of the sons of *A* ........ 1Chr 25:1
Of the sons of *A* ........ 1Chr 25:2
of Asaph under the hands of *A* ........ 1Chr 25:2
to the king's order to *A*, ........ 1Chr 25:6
lot came forth for *A* to Joseph ........ 1Chr 25:9
the singers, all of them of *A* ........ 2Chr 5:12
a Levite of the sons of *A* ........ 2Chr 20:14
and of the sons of *A* ........ 2Chr 29:13
words of David, and of *A* the seer ..... 2Chr 29:30
the sons of *A* were in their place ...... 2Chr 35:15
commandment of David, and *A* ........ 2Chr 35:15
the children of *A*, an hundred ........ Ezr 2:41
the sons of *A* with cymbals ........ Ezr 3:10
the children of *A*, an hundred ........ Neh 7:44
the son of Zabdi, the son of *A* ........ Neh 11:17
Of the sons of *A*, the singers ........ Neh 11:22
the son of Zaccur, the son of *A* ........ Neh 12:35
*A* of old there were chief of the ........ Neh 12:46
*A* Psalm of *A* ........ Ps 50:*t*
*A* Psalm of *A* ........ Ps 73:*t*
Maschil of *A* ........ Ps 74:*t*
Altaschith, *A* Psalm or Song of *A* ........ Ps 75:*t*
on Neginoth, *A* Psalm or Song of *A* ........ Ps 76:*t*
to Jeduthun, *A* Psalm of *A* ........ Ps 77:*t*
Maschil of *A* ........ Ps 78:*t*
*A* Psalm of *A* ........ Ps 79:*t*
Shoshannim-Eduth, *A* Psalm of *A* ........ Ps 80:*t*
upon Gittith, *A* Psalm of *A* ........ Ps 81:*t*
*A* Psalm of *A* ........ Ps 82:*t*
*A* Song or Psalm of *A* ........ Ps 83:*t*
*3. A Levite family in post-exilic Jerusalem.*
the son of Zichri, the son of *A* ........ 1Chr 9:15
*4. Descendants of Merari.*
the son of Kore, of the sons of *A* ........ 1Chr 26:1
*5. A Persian official.*
a letter unto *A* the keeper of the ........ Neh 2:8

**ASAPH'S** (*a'-safs*) *Refers to Asaph 1.*
and Joah, *A* son, the recorder ........ Is 36:3

**ASAREEL** (*a-sar'-e-el*) *A son of Jehaleleel.*
Ziph, and Ziphah, Tiria, and *A* ........ 1Chr 4:16

**ASARELAH** (*as-a-re'-lah*) See JESHARELAH. *A son of a musician of David.*
and Joseph, and Nethaniah, and *A* ...... 1Chr 25:2

**ASA'S** (*a'-sahz*) *Refers to Asa 1.*
nevertheless *A* heart was perfect ...... 1Kin 15:14

**ASCEND**
the people shall *a* up every man ........ Josh 6:5
Who shall *a* into the hill of the ........ Ps 24:3
He causeth the vapours to *a* from ........ Ps 135:7
If I *a* up into heaven, thou art ........ Ps 139:8
I will *a* into heaven, I will ........ Is 14:13
I will *a* above the heights of the ........ Is 14:14
he causeth the vapors to *a* from ........ Jer 10:13
he causeth the vapors to *a* from ........ Jer 51:16
Thou shalt *a* and come like a storm ...... Eze 38:9
of man *a* up where he was before ........ Jn 6:62
I *a* unto my Father, and your ........ Jn 20:17
heart, Who shall *a* into heaven ........ Rom 10:6
shall *a* out of the bottomless pit ........ Rev 17:8

**ASCENDED**
the smoke thereof *a* as the smoke ........ Ex 19:18
they *a* by the south, and came unto . Num 13:22
smoke of the city *a* up to heaven ........ Josh 8:20
and that the smoke of the city *a* ........ Josh 8:21
So Joshua *a* from Gilgal, he, and ........ Josh 10:7
*a* up on the south side unto ........ Josh 15:3
LORD *a* in the flame of the altar ........ Judg 13:20
flame of the city *a* up to heaven ........ Judg 20:40
Thou hast *a* on high, thou hast ........ Ps 68:18
Who hath *a* up into heaven, or ........ Prov 30:4
no man hath *a* up to heaven, but ........ Jn 3:13
for I am not yet *a* to my Father ........ Jn 20:17
David is not *a* into the heavens ........ Acts 2:34
after three days he *a* from ........ Acts 25:1
When he *a* up on high, he led ........ Eph 4:8
(Now that he *a*, what is it but ........ Eph 4:9
that *a* up far above all heavens ........ Eph 4:10
*a* up before God out of the ........ Rev 8:4
they *a* up to heaven in a cloud ........ Rev 11:12

**ASCENDETH**
the beast that *a* out of the ........ Rev 11:7
of their torment *a* up for ever ........ Rev 14:11

**ASCENDING**
and behold the angels of God *a* ........ Gen 28:12
I saw gods *a* out of the earth ........ 1Sa 28:13
he went before, *a* up to Jerusalem ........ Lk 19:28
open, and the angels of God *a* ........ Jn 1:51
saw another angel *a* from the east ........ Rev 7:2

**ASCENT**
the south to the *a* of Akrabbim ........ Num 34:4
went up by the *a* of mount Olivet ........ 2Sa 15:30
his *a* by which he went up unto ........ 1Kin 10:5
his *a* by which he went up into ........ 2Chr 9:4

**ASCRIBE**
*a* ye greatness unto our God ........ Deut 32:3
will *a* righteousness to my Maker ........ Job 36:3
*A* ye strength unto God ........ Ps 68:34

**ASCRIBED**
They have *a* unto David ten ........ 1Sa 18:8
to me they have *a* but thousands ........ 1Sa 18:8

**ASENATH** (*as'-e-nath*) *A great-grandson of Solomon.*
he gave him to wife *A* the ........ Gen 41:45
came, which *A* the daughter of ........ Gen 41:50
Ephraim, which *A* the daughter of ..... Gen 46:20

**ASER** (*a'-sur*) See ASHER. *Greek form of Asher.*
of Phanuel, of the tribe of *A* ........ Lk 2:36
Of the tribe of *A* were sealed ........ Rev 7:6

**ASH**
he planteth an *a*, and the rain ........ Is 44:14

**ASHAMED**
man and his wife, and were not *a* ........ Gen 2:25
should she not be *a* seven days ........ Num 12:14
And they tarried till they were *a* ........ Judg 3:25
because the men were greatly *a* ........ 2Sa 10:5
as people being *a* steal away when ........ 2Sa 19:3
when they urged him till he was *a* ........ 2Kin 2:17
stedfastly, until he was *a* ........ 2Kin 8:11
for the men were greatly *a* ........ 1Chr 19:5
the priests and the Levites were *a* ..... 2Chr 30:15
For I was *a* to require of the ........ Ezr 8:22
And said, O my God, I am *a* ........ Ezr 9:6
they came thither, and were *a* ........ Job 6:20
mockest, shall no man make thee *a* ........ Job 11:3
ye are not *a* that ye make ........ Job 19:3
Let all mine enemies be *a* ........ Ps 6:10
let them return and be *a* suddenly ........ Ps 6:10
let me not be *a*, let not mine ........ Ps 25:2
let none that wait on thee be *a* ........ Ps 25:3
let them be *a* which transgress ........ Ps 25:3
let me not be *a* ........ Ps 25:20
let me never be *a* ........ Ps 31:1
Let me not be *a*, O LORD ........ Ps 31:17
let the wicked be *a*, and let them ........ Ps 31:17
and their faces were not *a* ........ Ps 34:5
Let them be *a* and brought to ........ Ps 35:26
shall not be *a* in the evil time ........ Ps 37:19
Let them be *a* and confounded ........ Ps 40:14
GOD of hosts, be *a* for my sake ........ Ps 69:6
Let them be *a* and confounded that ........ Ps 70:2
O let not the oppressed return *a* ........ Ps 74:21
which hate me may see it, and be *a* ........ Ps 86:17
when they arise, let them be *a* ........ Ps 109:28
Then shall I not be *a*, when I ........ Ps 119:6
before kings, and will not be *a* ........ Ps 119:46
Let the proud be *a* ........ Ps 119:78
that I be not *a* ........ Ps 119:80
and let me not be *a* of my hope ........ Ps 119:116
they shall not be *a*, but they ........ Ps 127:5
but she that maketh *a* is as ........ Prov 12:4
For they shall be *a* of the oaks ........ Is 1:29
*a* of Ethiopia their expectation, ........ Is 20:5
Be thou *a*, O Zidon ........ Is 23:4
shall be confounded, and the sun *a* ........ Is 24:23
be *a* for their envy at the people ........ Is 26:11
Jacob, Jacob shall not now be *a* ........ Is 29:22
They were all *a* of a people that ........ Is 30:5
Lebanon is *a* and hewn down ........ Is 33:9

incensed against thee shall be *a*.............. Is 41:11
back, they shall be greatly *a*.................... Is 42:17
that they may be *a*........................................ Is 44:9
all his fellows shall be *a*........................... Is 44:11
fear, and they shall be *a* together............ Is 44:11
They shall be *a*, and also.......................... Is 45:16
ye shall not be *a* nor confounded............ Is 45:17
incensed against him shall be *a*.............. Is 45:24
shall not be *a* that wait for me .............. Is 49:23
and I know that I shall not be *a*.............. Is 50:7
for thou shalt not be *a* ............................. Is 54:4
shall rejoice, but ye shall be *a*................ Is 65:13
to your joy, and they shall be *a*.............. Is 66:5
As the thief is *a* when he is ..................... Jer 2:26
so is the house of Israel *a* ...................... Jer 2:26
thou also shalt be *a* of Egypt.................. Jer 2:36
as thou wast *a* of Assyria.......................... Jer 2:36
forehead, thou refusedst to be *a*.............. Jer 3:3
Were they *a* when they had..................... Jer 6:15
nay, they were not at all *a*...................... Jer 6:15
The wise men are *a*, they are................... Jer 8:9
Were they *a* when they had...................... Jer 8:12
nay, they were not at all *a*...................... Jer 8:12
they shall be *a* of your revenues ............ Jer 12:13
they were *a* and confounded, and ........... Jer 14:3
in the earth, the plowmen were *a* ............ Jer 14:4
she hath been *a* and confounded............. Jer 15:9
all that forsake thee shall be *a*............... Jer 17:13
they shall be greatly *a*.............................. Jer 20:11
surely then shalt thou be *a*...................... Jer 22:22
I was *a*, yea, even confounded,............... Jer 31:19
And Moab shall be *a* of Chemosh ............ Jer 48:13
as the house of Israel was *a* of .............. Jer 48:13
she that bare you shall be *a*.................... Jer 50:12
which are *a* of thy lewd way..................... Eze 16:27
shalt remember thy ways, and be *a*........ Eze 16:61
terror they are *a* of their might.............. Eze 32:30
be *a* and confounded for your own.......... Eze 36:32
that they may be *a* of their...................... Eze 43:10
if they be *a* of all that they..................... Eze 43:11
they shall be *a* because of their.............. Hos 4:19
Israel shall be *a* of his own.................... Hos 10:6
Be ye *a*, O ye husbandmen........................ Joel 1:11
and my people shall never be *a*.............. Joel 2:26
and my people shall never be *a*.............. Joel 2:27
Then shall the seers be *a*.......................... Mic 3:7
thou not be *a* for all thy doings.............. Zeph 3:11
for her expectation shall be *a*................. Zec 9:5
be *a* every one of his vision..................... Zec 13:4
therefore shall be *a* of me........................ Mk 8:38
also shall the Son of man be *a*................ Mk 8:38
For whosoever shall be *a* of me............... Lk 9:26
of him shall the Son of man be *a*............. Lk 9:26
all his adversaries were *a*....................... Lk 13:17
to beg I am *a* ............................................ Lk 16:3
For I am not *a* of the gospel of............... Rom 1:16
And hope maketh not *a*............................ Rom 5:5
those things whereof ye are now *a*......... Rom 6:21
believeth on him shall not be *a*............. Rom 9:33
believeth on him shall not be *a*............. Rom 10:11
thing to him of you, I am not *a*.............. 2Cor 7:14
ye) should be *a* in this same................... 2Cor 9:4
destruction, I should not be *a*................ 2Cor 10:8
that in nothing I shall be *a*..................... Phil 1:20
with him, that he may be *a*..................... 2Th 3:14
Be not thou therefore *a* of the................. 2Ti 1:8
nevertheless I am not *a*.......................... 2Ti 1:12
me, and was not *a* of my chain............... 2Ti 1:16
workman that needeth not to be *a*.......... 2Ti 2:15
is of the contrary part may be *a*.............. Titus 2:8
he is not *a* to call them brethren........... Heb 2:11
wherefore God is not *a* to be.................. Heb 11:16
they may be *a* that falsely accuse.......... 1Pet 3:16
as a Christian, let him not be *a*.............. 1Pet 4:16
not be *a* before him at his coming ......... 1Jn 2:28

**ASHAN** (*a'-shan*) See COR-ASHAN. *A Levitical city in Judah.*
Libnah, and Ether, and *A*,.................... Josh 15:42
Ain, Remmon, and Ether, and *A*............. Josh 19:7
and Ain, Rimmon, and Tochen, and *A* 1Chr 4:32
And *A* with her suburbs, and............... 1Chr 6:59

**ASHARELAH** See ASARELAH.

**ASHBEA** (*ash'-be-ah*) *Descendants of Shelah.*
fine linen, of the house of *A*................. 1Chr 4:21

**ASHBEL** (*ash'-bel*) See ASHBELITES. *A son of Benjamin.*
were Belah, and Becher, and *A*............ Gen 46:21
of *A*, the family of the.......................... Num 26:38
*A* the second, and Aharah the third...... 1Chr 8:1

**ASHBELITES** (*ash'-bel-ites*) *Descendants of Ashbel.*
of Ashbel, the family of the *A* ............ Num 26:38

**ASHCHENAZ** (*ash'-ke-naz*) See ASHKENAZ.
*1. A son of Gomer.*
*A*, and Riphath, and Togarmah ............ 1Chr 1:6
*2. A tribe near Armenia.*
kingdoms of Ararat, Minni, and *A* ........ Jer 51:27

**ASHDOD** (*ash'-dod*) See ASHDODITES, AZOTUS. *A Philistine city.*
only in Gaza, in Gath, and in *A*........... Josh 11:22
unto the sea, all that lay near *A* .......... Josh 15:46
*A* with her towns and her villages,...... Josh 15:47
brought it from Eben-ezer unto *A*......... 1Sa 5:1
when they of *A* arose early on the........... 1Sa 5:3
of Dagon in *A* unto this day..................... 1Sa 5:5
the LORD was heavy upon them of *A*...... 1Sa 5:6
smote them with emerods, even *A*........... 1Sa 5:6
when the men of *A* saw that it was......... 1Sa 5:7
for *A* one, for Gaza one, for................... 1Sa 6:17
wall of Jabneh, and the wall of *A* ........ 2Chr 26:6
and built cities about *A* ....................... 2Chr 26:6
Jews that had married wives of *A*....... Neh 13:23
spake half in the speech of *A* .............. Neh 13:24
the year that Tartan came unto *A* .......... Is 20:1
sent him,) and fought against *A* .......... Is 20:1
and Ekron, and the remnant of *A* ......... Jer 25:20
cut off the inhabitant from *A*................. Amos 1:8
Publish in the palaces at *A*.................... Amos 3:9
shall drive out *A* at the noonday........... Zeph 2:4
And a bastard shall dwell in *A*.............. Zec 9:6

**ASHDODITES** (*ash'-dod-ites*) See ASHDOTHITES. *Inhabitants of Ashdod.*
and the Ammonites, and the *A*.............. Neh 4:7

**ASHDOTHITES** (*ash'-doth-ites*) See ASHDODITES. *Same as Ashdodites.*
the Gazathites, and the *A*, the............... Josh 13:3

**ASHDOTH-PISGAH** (*ash''-doth-piz'gah*) *The eastern slope of Mt. Pisgah.*
the salt sea, under *A* eastward ............. Deut 3:17
and from the south, under *A* ................ Josh 12:3
And Beth-peor, and *A*, and.................. Josh 13:20

**ASHER** (*ash'-ur*) See ASER, ASHERITES.
*1. A son of Jacob by Zilpah.*
and she called his name *A*.................... Gen 30:13
Gad, and *A*: these are the sons ........... Gen 35:26
And the sons of *A* ................................ Gen 46:17
Out of *A* his bread shall be fat,............ Gen 49:20
Dan, and Naphtali, Gad, and *A*.............. Ex 1:4
of the daughter of *A* was Sarah .......... Num 26:46
and Benjamin, Naphtali, Gad, and *A*..... 1Chr 2:2
The sons of *A*; Imnah, and Isuah......... 1Chr 7:30
All these were the children of *A* ......... 1Chr 7:40
*2. A tribe descended from Asher 1.*
Of *A*........................................................ Num 1:13
Of the children of *A*, by their............... Num 1:40
of them, even of the tribe of *A*............. Num 1:41
by him shall be the tribe of *A*.............. Num 2:27
of *A* shall be Pagiel the son of.............. Num 2:27
prince of the children of *A* ................. Num 7:72
of *A* was Pagiel the son of Ocran ...... Num 10:26
Of the tribe of *A*, Sethur the son ....... Num 13:13
Of the children of *A* after their ........... Num 26:44
of *A* according to those that were..... Num 26:47
of the tribe of the children of *A* ......... Num 34:27
Reuben, Gad, and *A*, and Zebulun,.... Deut 27:13
of *A* he said, Let Asher be .................. Deut 33:24
of *A* according to their families.......... Josh 19:24
of *A* according to their families.......... Josh 19:31
reacheth to *A* on the west side, .......... Josh 19:34
and out of the tribe of *A*...................... Josh 21:6
And out of the tribe of *A*, Mishal ....... Josh 21:30
Neither did *A* drive out the.................. Judg 1:31
*A* continued on the sea shore, and ...... Judg 5:17
and he sent messengers unto *A* ........... Judg 6:35
out of Naphtali, and out of *A*.............. Judg 7:23
and out of the tribe of *A*..................... 1Chr 6:62
And out of the tribe of *A* .................... 1Chr 6:74
And of *A*, such as went forth to.......... 1Chr 12:36
Nevertheless divers of *A* and.............. 2Chr 30:11
the west side, a portion for *A*.............. Eze 48:2
And by the border of *A*, from the ......... Eze 48:3
one gate of Gad, one gate of *A* ........... Eze 48:34
*3. A town in Manasseh.*
Manasseh was from *A* to Michmethah Josh 17:7
met together in *A* on the north............ Josh 17:10
in *A* Beth-shean and her towns............ Josh 17:11
Baanah the son of Hushai was in *A* .... 1Kin 4:16

**ASHERITES** (*ash'-ur-ites*) *Same as Asher 2.*
But the *A* dwelt among the.................. Judg 1:32

**ASHES**
the Lord, which am but dust and *a* .... Gen 18:27
you handfuls of *a* of the furnace............... Ex 9:8
they took *a* of the furnace, and............... Ex 9:10
make his pans to receive his *a*................ Ex 27:3
east part, by the place of the *a*.............. Lev 1:16
where the *a* are poured out, and............. Lev 4:12
where the *a* are poured out shall ........... Lev 4:12
take up the *a* which the fire hath ........... Lev 6:10
carry forth the *a* without the................... Lev 6:11
take away the *a* from the altar............... Num 4:13
gather up the *a* of the heifer................. Num 19:9
he that gathereth the *a* of the.............. Num 19:10
of the *a* of the burnt heifer of............. Num 19:17
Tamar put *a* on her head, and rent...... 2Sa 13:19
the *a* that are upon it shall be.............. 1Kin 13:3
the *a* poured out from the altar,........... 1Kin 13:5
himself with *a* upon his face ............... 1Kin 20:38
took the *a* away from his face ............. 1Kin 20:41
carried the *a* of them unto.................... 2Kin 23:4
and put on sackcloth with *a*.................... Est 4:1
and many lay in sackcloth and *a* ............ Est 4:3
and he sat down among the *a*................. Job 2:8
Your remembrances are like unto *a* .... Job 13:12
and I am become like dust and *a* .......... Job 30:19
myself, and repent in dust and *a* ........... Job 42:6
For I have eaten *a* like bread .............. Ps 102:9
scattereth the hoar frost like *a*............ Ps 147:16
He feedeth on *a*...................................... Is 44:20
spread sackcloth and *a* under him ......... Is 58:5
to give unto them beauty for *a*............... Is 61:3
sackcloth, and wallow thyself in *a*......... Jer 6:26
and wallow yourselves in the *a*............. Jer 25:34
of the dead bodies, and of the *a*............. Jer 31:40
stones, he hath covered me with *a*....... Lam 3:16
shall wallow themselves in the *a*......... Eze 27:30
I will bring thee to *a* upon the............. Eze 28:18
with fasting, and sackcloth, and *a* ......... Dan 9:3
him with sackcloth, and sat in *a*......... Jonah 3:6
for they shall be *a* under the................. Mal 4:3
long ago in sackcloth and *a* .................. Mt 11:21
sitting in sackcloth and *a*...................... Lk 10:13
the *a* of an heifer sprinkling the............ Heb 9:13
Gomorrah into *a* condemned them ........ 2Pet 2:6

**ASHHUR** See ASHUR.

**ASHIMA** (*ash'-im-ah*) *An idol of Hamath.*
and the men of Hamath made *A* ........ 2Kin 17:30

**ASHKELON** (*ash'-ke-lon*) See ASKELON, ESHKALONITES. *A Philistine city.*
upon him, and he went down to *A* .... Judg 14:19
the land of the Philistines, and *A* ......... Jer 25:20
*A* is cut off with the remnant of............. Jer 47:5
hath given it a charge against *A* ........... Jer 47:7
that holdeth the sceptre from *A* .......... Amos 1:8
be forsaken, and *A* a desolation............ Zeph 2:4
in the houses of *A* shall they lie ........... Zeph 2:7
*A* shall see it, and fear ............................ Zec 9:5
Gaza, and *A* shall not be inhabited.......... Zec 9:5

**ASHKENAZ** (*ash'-ke-naz*) See ASHCHENAZ. *A son of Gomer.*
*A*, and Riphath, and Togarmah.............. Gen 10:3

**ASHNAH** (*ash'-nah*)
*1. A town in Judah near Dan.*
valley, Eshtaol, and Zoreah, and *A*..... Josh 15:33
*2. A town in Judah on the plains.*
And Jiphtah, and *A*, and Nezib,.......... Josh 15:43

**ASHPENAZ** (*ash'-pe-naz*) *A prince of the eunuchs under Nebuchadnezzar.*
the king spake unto *A* the master .......... Dan 1:3

**ASHRIEL** (*ash'-re-el*) See ASRIEL. *A grandson of Manasseh.*
*A*, whom she bare .................................. 1Chr 7:14

**ASHTAROTH** (*ash'-ta-roth*) See ASHTERATHITE, ASHTEROTH, ASTORETH, ASTAROTH, BEESHTERAH.
*1. A god of the Philistines, Phoenicians, and Zidonians.*
the LORD, and served Baal and *A* ......... Judg 2:13
the LORD, and served Baalim, and *A* ... Judg 10:6
*A* from among you, and prepare your...... 1Sa 7:3
Israel did put away Baalim and *A* .......... 1Sa 7:4
LORD, and have served Baalim and *A*.. 1Sa 12:10
put his armour in the house of *A* .......... 1Sa 31:10
*2. A city in Bashan.*
Og king of Bashan, which was at *A*..... Josh 9:10
of the giants, that dwelt at *A* ............... Josh 12:4
Og in Bashan, which reigned in *A*...... Josh 13:12
And half Gilead, and *A*, and Edrei,..... Josh 13:31
*3. A Levitical city in Manasseh.*
suburbs, and *A* with her suburbs ......... 1Chr 6:71

**ASHTERATHITE** (*ash'-ter-a-thite*) *Family name of Uzziah.*
Uzzia the *A*, Shama and Jehiel the.... 1Chr 11:44

**ASHTEROTH** (*ash'-te-roth*) *A city in Og.*
smote the Rephaims in *A* Karnaim....... Gen 14:5

**ASHTEROTH-KARNAIM** See ASHTEROTH.

**ASHTORETH** (*ash'-to-reth*) See ASHTAROTH. *Same as Ashtaroth 1.*
For Solomon went after *A* the............. 1Kin 11:5
have worshipped *A* the goddess of..... 1Kin 11:33
for *A* the abomination of the.............. 2Kin 23:13

**ASHUR** (*ash'-ur*) See ASHURITES, ASSHUR, ASSUR, ASSYRIA. *A son of Hezron.*
bare him *A* the father of Tekoa ............ 1Chr 2:24
*A* the father of Tekoa had two.............. 1Chr 4:5

**ASHURBANIPAL** See ASNAPPER.

**ASHURITES** (*ash'-ur-ites*) See ASSHURIM. *A tribe in the plain of Esdraelon.*
king over Gilead, and over the *A* ............ 2Sa 2:9
the company of the *A* have made........ Eze 27:6

**ASHVATH** (*ash'-vath*) *A descendant of Asher.*
Pasach, and Bimhal, and *A* .................... 1Chr 7:33

**ASIA** (*a'-she-ah*)
*1. A Roman province.*
and Cappadocia, in Pontus, and *A*.......... Acts 2:9
and of them of Cilicia and of *A*............... Acts 6:9
Ghost to preach the word in *A* ............. Acts 16:6
in *A* heard the word of the Lord........... Acts 19:10
himself stayed in *A* for a season.......... Acts 19:22
And certain of the chief of *A*................ Acts 19:31
him into *A* Sopater of Berea ............... Acts 20:4
and of *A*, Tychicus and Trophimus...... Acts 20:4
he would not spend the time in *A* ....... Acts 20:16
the first day that I came into *A* ........... Acts 20:18
The churches of *A* salute you ............ 1Cor 16:19
our trouble which came to us in *A*......... 2Cor 1:8
are in *A* be turned away from me.......... 2Ti 1:15
Pontus, Galatia, Cappadocia, *A* .............. 1Pet 1:1
the seven churches which are in *A* .......... Rev 1:4
the seven churches which are in *A* ....... Rev 1:11
*2. Another name for Asia Minor.*
but almost throughout all *A* ............... Acts 19:26
should be destroyed, whom all *A*......... Acts 19:27
ended, the Jews which were of *A*......... Acts 21:27
Whereupon certain Jews from *A* ........ Acts 24:18

to sail by the coasts of *A* ..... Acts 27:2

**ASIDE**
And Moses said, I will now turn *a* ..... Ex 3:3
LORD saw that he turned *a* to see ..... Ex 3:4
They have turned *a* quickly out of ..... Ex 32:8
unto them, If any man's wife go *a* ..... Num 5:12
if thou hast not gone *a* to ..... Num 5:19
But if thou hast gone *a* to ..... Num 5:20
when a wife goeth *a* to another ..... Num 5:29
the ass turned *a* out of the way ..... Num 22:23
ye shall not turn *a* to the right ..... Deut 5:32
turned *a* out of the way which I ..... Deut 9:12
ye had turned *a* quickly out of ..... Deut 9:16
be not deceived, and ye turn *a* ..... Deut 11:16
but turn *a* out of the way which I ..... Deut 11:28
that he turn not *a* from the ..... Deut 17:20
thou shalt not go *a* from any of ..... Deut 28:14
turn *a* from the way which I have ..... Deut 31:29
that ye turn not *a* therefrom to ..... Josh 23:6
he turned *a* to see the carcase of ..... Judg 14:8
We will not turn *a* hither into ..... Judg 19:12
And they turned *a* thither, to go ..... Judg 19:15
turn *a*, sit down here ..... Ruth 4:1
And he turned *a*, and sat down ..... Ruth 4:1
turned not *a* to the right hand or ..... 1Sa 6:12
but turned *a* after lucre, and took ..... 1Sa 8:3
yet turn not *a* from following the ..... 1Sa 12:20
And turn ye not *a* ..... 1Sa 12:21
Turn thee *a* to thy right hand or ..... 2Sa 2:21
not turn *a* from following of him ..... 2Sa 2:21
Turn thee *a* from following me ..... 2Sa 2:22
Howbeit he refused to turn *a* ..... 2Sa 2:23
Joab took him *a* in the gate to ..... 2Sa 3:27
but David carried it *a* into the ..... 2Sa 6:10
And the king said unto him, Turn *a* ..... 2Sa 18:30
And he turned *a*, and stood still ..... 2Sa 18:30
turned not *a* from any thing that ..... 1Kin 15:5
and, behold, a man turned *a* ..... 1Kin 20:39
they turned *a* to fight against ..... 1Kin 22:32
he turned not *a* from it, doing ..... 1Kin 22:43
thou shalt set *a* that which is ..... 2Kin 4:4
turned not *a* to the right hand or ..... 2Kin 22:2
but carried it *a* into the house ..... 1Chr 13:13
paths of their way are turned *a* ..... Job 6:18
They are all gone *a*, they are all ..... Ps 14:3
proud, nor such as turn *a* to lies ..... Ps 40:4
they were turned *a* like a ..... Ps 78:57
hate the work of them that turn *a* ..... Ps 101:3
As for such as turn *a* unto their ..... Ps 125:5
*a* by the flocks of thy companions ..... Song 1:7
whither is thy beloved turned *a* ..... Song 6:1
To turn *a* the needy from judgment ..... Is 10:2
turn *a* the just for a thing of ..... Is 29:21
turn *a* out of the path, cause the ..... Is 30:11
deceived heart hath turned him *a* ..... Is 44:20
turneth *a* to tarry for a night ..... Jer 14:8
or who shall go *a* to ask how thou ..... Jer 15:5
He hath turned *a* my ways, and ..... Lam 3:11
To turn *a* the right of a man ..... Lam 3:35
turn *a* the way of the meek ..... Amos 2:7
they turn *a* the poor in the gate ..... Amos 5:12
that turn *a* the stranger from his ..... Mal 3:5
he turned *a* into the parts of ..... Mt 2:22
For laying *a* the commandment of ..... Mk 7:8
he took him *a* from the multitude, ..... Mk 7:33
went *a* privately into a desert ..... Lk 9:10
supper, and laid *a* his garments ..... Jn 13:4
them to go *a* out of the council ..... Acts 4:15
and went with him *a* privately ..... Acts 23:19
And when they were gone *a*, they ..... Acts 26:31
have turned *a* unto vain jangling ..... 1Ti 1:6
are already turned *a* after Satan ..... 1Ti 5:15
let us lay *a* every weight, and the ..... Heb 12:1
Wherefore laying *a* all malice ..... 1Pet 2:1

**ASIEL** (*a'-se'-el*) *Grandfather of Jehu.*
the son of Seraiah, the son of *A* ..... 1Chr 4:35

**ASK**
it that thou dost *a* after my name ..... Gen 32:29
*A* me never so much dowry and gift, ..... Gen 34:12
who shall *a* counsel for him after ..... Num 27:21
For *a* now of the days that are ..... Deut 4:32
*a* from the one side of heaven ..... Deut 4:32
and make search, and *a* diligently ..... Deut 13:14
*a* thy father, and he will shew ..... Deut 32:7
that when your children *a* their ..... Josh 4:6
When your children shall *a* their ..... Josh 4:21
him to *a* of her father a field ..... Josh 15:18
him to *a* of her father a field ..... Judg 1:14
*A* counsel, we pray thee, of God, ..... Judg 18:5
sins this evil, to *a* us a king ..... 1Sa 12:19
*A* thy young men, and they will ..... 1Sa 25:8
Wherefore then dost thou *a* of me ..... 1Sa 28:16
the thing that I shall *a* thee ..... 2Sa 14:18
shall surely *a* counsel at Abel ..... 2Sa 20:18
now I *a* one petition of thee, ..... 1Kin 2:16
said unto her, *A* on, my mother ..... 1Kin 2:20
why dost thou *a* Abishag the ..... 1Kin 2:22
*a* for him the kingdom also ..... 1Kin 2:22
said, *A* what I shall give thee ..... 1Kin 3:5
to *a* a thing of thee for her son ..... 1Kin 14:5
*A* what I shall do for thee, ..... 2Kin 2:9
him, *A* what I shall give thee ..... 2Chr 1:7
together, to *a* help of the LORD ..... 2Chr 20:4
But *a* now the beasts, and they ..... Job 12:7
*A* of me, and I shall give thee the ..... Ps 2:8
*A* thee a sign of the LORD thy God ..... Is 7:11
*a* it either in the depth, or in ..... Is 7:11
But Ahaz said, I will not *a* ..... Is 7:12
*A* me of things to come concerning ..... Is 45:11
they *a* of me the ordinances of ..... Is 58:2
*a* for the old paths, where is the ..... Jer 6:16
go aside to *a* how thou doest ..... Jer 15:5
*A* ye now among the heathen, who ..... Jer 18:13
or a priest, shall *a* thee ..... Jer 23:33
*A* ye now, and see whether a man ..... Jer 30:6
Jeremiah, I will *a* thee a thing ..... Jer 38:14
*a* him that fleeth, and her that ..... Jer 48:19
They shall *a* the way to Zion with ..... Jer 50:5
the young children *a* bread ..... Lam 4:4
that whosoever shall *a* a petition ..... Dan 6:7
that every man that shall *a* a ..... Dan 6:12
My people *a* counsel at their ..... Hos 4:12
*A* now the priests concerning the ..... Hag 2:11
*A* ye of the LORD rain in the time ..... Zec 10:1
ye have need of, before ye *a* him ..... Mt 6:8
*A*, and it shall be given you ..... Mt 7:7
of you, whom if his son *a* bread ..... Mt 7:9
Or if he *a* a fish, will he give ..... Mt 7:10
good things to them that *a* him ..... Mt 7:11
give her whatsoever she would *a* ..... Mt 14:7
any thing that they shall *a* ..... Mt 18:19
and said, Ye know not what ye *a* ..... Mt 20:22
whatsoever ye shall *a* in prayer ..... Mt 21:22
I also will *a* you one thing, ..... Mt 21:24
forth *a* him any more questions ..... Mt 22:46
that they should *a* Barabbas ..... Mt 27:20
*A* of me whatsoever thou wilt, and ..... Mk 6:22
Whatsoever thou shalt *a* of me ..... Mk 6:23
unto her mother, What shall I *a* ..... Mk 6:24
saying, and were afraid to *a* him ..... Mk 9:32
unto them, Ye know not what ye *a* ..... Mk 10:38
I will also *a* of you one question ..... Mk 11:29
that durst *a* him any question ..... Mk 12:34
unto them, I will *a* you one thing ..... Lk 6:9
away thy goods *a* them not again ..... Lk 6:30
they feared to *a* him of that ..... Lk 9:45
And I say unto you, *A*, and it shall ..... Lk 11:9
If a son shall *a* bread of any of ..... Lk 11:11
or if he *a* a fish, will he for a ..... Lk 11:11
Or if he shall *a* an egg, will he ..... Lk 11:12
Holy Spirit to them that *a* him ..... Lk 11:13
much, of him they will *a* the more ..... Lk 12:48
And if any man *a* you, Why do ye ..... Lk 19:31
I will also *a* you one thing ..... Lk 20:3
not *a* him any question at all ..... Lk 20:40
And if I also *a* you, ye will not ..... Lk 22:68
Levites from Jerusalem to *a* him ..... Jn 1:19
*a* him: he shall speak ..... Jn 9:21
He is of age; *a* him ..... Jn 9:23
whatsoever thou wilt *a* of God ..... Jn 11:22
that he should *a* who it should be ..... Jn 13:24
whatsoever ye shall *a* in my name ..... Jn 14:13
If ye shall *a* any thing in my ..... Jn 14:14
ye shall *a* what ye will, and it ..... Jn 15:7
shall *a* of the Father in my name ..... Jn 15:16
that they were desirous to *a* him ..... Jn 16:19
in that day ye shall *a* me nothing ..... Jn 16:23
Whatsoever ye shall *a* the Father ..... Jn 16:23
*a*, and ye shall receive, that your ..... Jn 16:24
At that day ye shall *a* in my name ..... Jn 16:26
not that any man should *a* thee ..... Jn 16:30
*a* them which heard me, what I ..... Jn 18:21
none of the disciples durst *a* him ..... Jn 21:12
to *a* alms of them that entered ..... Acts 3:2
I *a* therefore for what intent ye ..... Acts 10:29
let them *a* their husbands at home ..... 1Cor 14:35
above all that we *a* or think ..... Eph 3:20
you lack wisdom, let him *a* of God ..... Jas 1:5
But let him *a* in faith, nothing ..... Jas 1:6
yet ye have not, because ye *a* not ..... Jas 4:2
Ye *a*, and receive not ..... Jas 4:3
because ye *a* amiss ..... Jas 4:3
And whatsoever we *a*, we receive of ..... 1Jn 3:22
if we *a* any thing according to ..... 1Jn 5:14
that he hear us, whatsoever we *a* ..... 1Jn 5:15
is not unto death, he shall *a* ..... 1Jn 5:16

**ASKED**
I *a* her, and said, Whose daughter ..... Gen 24:47
of the place *a* him of his wife ..... Gen 26:7
And Jacob *a* him, and said, Tell me, ..... Gen 32:29
and the man *a* him, saying, What ..... Gen 37:15
Then he *a* the men of that place, ..... Gen 38:21
he *a* Pharaoh's officers that were ..... Gen 40:7
The man *a* us straitly of our ..... Gen 43:7
he *a* them of their welfare, and ..... Gen 43:27
My lord *a* his servants, saying, ..... Gen 44:19
they *a* each other of their ..... Ex 18:7
*a* not counsel at the mouth of the ..... Josh 9:14
they gave him the city which he *a* ..... Josh 19:50
the children of Israel *a* the LORD ..... Judg 1:1
He *a* water, and she gave him milk ..... Judg 5:25
And when they enquired and *a* ..... Judg 6:29
but I *a* him not whence he was, ..... Judg 13:6
*a* counsel of God, and said, Which ..... Judg 20:18
*a* counsel of the LORD, saying, ..... Judg 20:23
petition that thou hast *a* of him ..... 1Sa 1:17
Because I have *a* him of the LORD ..... 1Sa 1:20
me my petition which I *a* of him ..... 1Sa 1:27
the people that *a* of him a king ..... 1Sa 8:10
Saul *a* counsel of God, Shall I go ..... 1Sa 14:37
and he *a* and said, Where are Samuel ..... 1Sa 19:22
David earnestly *a* leave of me ..... 1Sa 20:6
David earnestly *a* leave of me to ..... 1Sa 20:28
that Solomon had *a* this thing ..... 1Kin 3:10
Because thou hast *a* this thing ..... 1Kin 3:11
hast not *a* for thyself long life ..... 1Kin 3:11
neither hast *a* riches for thyself ..... 1Kin 3:11
nor hast *a* the life of thine ..... 1Kin 3:11
but hast *a* for thyself ..... 1Kin 3:11
thee that which thou hast not *a* ..... 1Kin 3:13
all her desire, whatsoever she *a* ..... 1Kin 10:13
he said, Thou hast *a* a hard thing ..... 2Kin 2:10
And when the king *a* the woman ..... 2Kin 8:6
heart, and thou hast not *a* riches ..... 2Chr 1:11
neither yet hast *a* long life ..... 2Chr 1:11
but hast *a* wisdom and knowledge ..... 2Chr 1:11
all her desire, whatsoever she *a* ..... 2Chr 9:12
Then *a* we those elders, and said ..... Ezr 5:9
We *a* their names also, to certify ..... Ezr 5:10
I *a* them concerning the Jews that ..... Neh 1:2
Have ye not *a* them that go by the ..... Job 21:29
He *a* life of thee, and thou gavest ..... Ps 21:4
The people *a*, and he brought ..... Ps 105:40
Egypt, and have not *a* at my mouth ..... Is 30:2
when I *a* of them, could answer a ..... Is 41:28
sought of them that *a* not for me ..... Is 65:1
they *a* Baruch, saying, Tell us ..... Jer 36:17
the king *a* him secretly in his ..... Jer 37:17
princes unto Jeremiah, and *a* him ..... Jer 38:27
that *a* such things at any ..... Dan 2:10
*a* him the truth of all this ..... Dan 7:16
And they *a* him, saying, Is it ..... Mt 12:10
he *a* his disciples, saying, Whom ..... Mt 16:13
And his disciples *a* him, saying, ..... Mt 17:10
is no resurrection, and *a* him, ..... Mt 22:23
*a* him a question, tempting him, ..... Mt 22:35
gathered together, Jesus *a* them ..... Mt 22:41
and the governor *a* him, saying, ..... Mt 27:11
the twelve *a* of him the parable ..... Mk 4:10
he *a* him, What is thy name ..... Mk 5:9
with haste unto the king, and *a* ..... Mk 6:25
the Pharisees and scribes *a* him ..... Mk 7:5
his disciples *a* him concerning ..... Mk 7:17
he *a* them, How many loaves have ..... Mk 8:5
him, he *a* him if he saw ought ..... Mk 8:23
and by the way he *a* his disciples ..... Mk 8:27
And they *a* him, saying, Why say ..... Mk 9:11
he *a* the scribes, What question ..... Mk 9:16
he *a* his father, How long is it ..... Mk 9:21
his disciples *a* him privately ..... Mk 9:28
and being in the house he *a* them ..... Mk 9:33
*a* him, Is it lawful for a man to ..... Mk 10:2
in the house his disciples *a* him ..... Mk 10:10
*a* him, Good Master, what shall I ..... Mk 10:17
and they *a* him, saying, ..... Mk 12:18
*a* him, Which is the first ..... Mk 12:28
John and Andrew *a* him privately, ..... Mk 13:3
*a* Jesus, saying, Answerest thou ..... Mk 14:60
Again the high priest *a* him ..... Mk 14:61
And Pilate *a* him, Art thou the ..... Mk 15:2
Pilate *a* him again, saying, ..... Mk 15:4
he *a* him whether he had been any ..... Mk 15:44
he *a* for a writing table, and ..... Lk 1:63
And the people *a* him, saying, What ..... Lk 3:10
And his disciples *a* him, saying, ..... Lk 8:9
And Jesus *a* him, saying, What is ..... Lk 8:30
he *a* them, saying, Whom say the ..... Lk 9:18
*a* what these things meant ..... Lk 15:26
And a certain ruler *a* him, saying, ..... Lk 18:18
pass by, he *a* what it meant ..... Lk 18:36
when he was come near, he *a* him, ..... Lk 18:40
And they *a* him, saying, Master, we ..... Lk 20:21
and they *a* him, ..... Lk 20:27
And they *a* him, saying, Master, ..... Lk 21:7
*a* him, saying, Prophesy, who is ..... Lk 22:64
And Pilate *a* him, saying, Art thou ..... Lk 23:3
he *a* whether the man were a ..... Lk 23:6
And they *a* him, What then ..... Jn 1:21
And they *a* him, and said unto him, ..... Jn 1:25
thou wouldest have *a* of him ..... Jn 4:10
Then *a* they him, What man is that ..... Jn 5:12
And his disciples *a* him, saying, ..... Jn 9:2
*a* him how he had received his ..... Jn 9:15
And they *a* them, saying, Is this ..... Jn 9:19
Hitherto have ye *a* nothing in my ..... Jn 16:24
Then *a* he them again, Whom seek ..... Jn 18:7
The high priest then *a* Jesus of ..... Jn 18:19
they *a* of him, saying, Lord, wilt ..... Acts 1:6
to go into the temple *a* an alms ..... Acts 3:3
had set them in the midst, they *a* ..... Acts 4:7
and the high priest *a* them ..... Acts 5:27
*a* whether Simon, which was ..... Acts 10:18
*a* him, What is that thou hast to ..... Acts 23:19
he *a* of what province he was ..... Acts 23:34
I *a* him whether he would go to ..... Acts 25:20
unto them that *a* not after me ..... Rom 10:20

**ASKELON** (*as'-ke-lon*) See ASHKELON. *A Philistine city.*
*A* with the coast thereof, and ..... Judg 1:18
one, for Gaza one, for *A* one ..... 1Sa 6:17
it not in the streets of *A* ..... 2Sa 1:20

**ASKEST**
Why *a* thou thus after my name, ..... Judg 13:18
*a* drink of me, which am a woman ..... Jn 4:9
Why *a* thou me? ..... Jn 18:21

**ASKETH**
*a* thee, saying, Whose art thou ..... Gen 32:17
thy son *a* thee in time to come ..... Ex 13:14
when thy son *a* thee in time to ..... Deut 6:20
hands earnestly, the prince *a* ..... Mic 7:3
and the judge *a* for a reward ..... Mic 7:3
Give to him that *a* thee, and from ..... Mt 5:42
For every one that *a* receiveth ..... Mt 7:8
Give to every man that *a* of thee ..... Lk 6:30
For every one that *a* receiveth ..... Lk 11:10
and none of you *a* me, Whither ..... Jn 16:5
an answer to every man that *a* you ..... 1Pet 3:15

**ASKING**
of the LORD, in *a* you a king 1Sa 12:17
also for *a* counsel of one that 1Chr 10:13
heart by *a* meat for their lust Ps 78:18
hearing them, and *a* them questions Lk 2:46
So when they continued *a* him Jn 8:7
*a* no question for conscience sake 1Cor 10:25
*a* no question for conscience sake 1Cor 10:27

**ASLEEP**
for he was fast *a* and weary Judg 4:21
for they were all *a* 1Sa 26:12
lips of those that are *a* to speak Song 7:9
and he lay, and was fast *a* Jonah 1:5
but he was *a* Mt 8:24
the disciples, and findeth them *a* Mt 26:40
And he came and found them *a* again Mt 26:43
part of the ship, *a* on a pillow Mk 4:38
returned, he found them *a* again Mk 14:40
But as they sailed he fell *a* Lk 8:23
when he had said this, he fell *a* Acts 7:60
present, but some are fallen *a* 1Cor 15:6
fallen *a* in Christ are perished 1Cor 15:18
concerning them which are *a* 1Th 4:13
not prevent them which are *a* 1Th 4:15
for since the fathers fell *a* 2Pet 3:4

**ASNAH** (*as'-nah*) *A family of exiles.*
The children of *A*, the children Ezr 2:50

**ASNAPPER** (*as-nap'-pur*) *An Assyrian king.*
noble *A* brought over, and set in Ezr 4:10

**ASP**
shall play on the hole of the *a* Is 11:8

**ASPATHA** (*as'-pa-thah*) *A son of Haman.*
And Parshandatha, and Dalphon, and *A*. Est 9:7

**ASPS**
dragons, and the cruel venom of *a* Deut 32:33
it is the gall of *a* within him Job 20:14
He shall suck the poison of *a* Job 20:16
the poison of *a* is under their Rom 3:13

**ASRIEL** (*as'-re-el*) See ASHRIEL, ASRIELITES. *A grandson of Manasseh.*
And of *A*, the family of the Num 26:31
Helek, and for the children of *A* Josh 17:2

**ASRIELITES** (*as'-re-el-ites*) *Descendants of Asriel.*
And of Asriel, the family of the *A* Num 26:31

**ASS**
in the morning, and saddled his *a* Gen 22:3
men, Abide ye here with the *a* Gen 22:5
give his *a* provender in the inn Gen 42:27
clothes, and laded every man his *a* Gen 44:13
Issachar is a strong *a* couching Gen 49:14
his sons, and set them upon an *a* Ex 4:20
every firstling of an *a* thou Ex 13:13
nor his ox, nor his *a*, nor any Ex 20:17
an ox or an *a* fall therein Ex 21:33
alive, whether it be ox, or *a* Ex 22:4
whether it be for ox, for *a* Ex 22:9
deliver unto his neighbour an *a* Ex 22:10
enemy's ox or his *a* going astray Ex 23:4
If thou see the *a* of him that Ex 23:5
thine *a* may rest, and the son of Ex 23:12
But the firstling of an *a* thou Ex 34:20
I have not taken one *a* from them Num 16:15
in the morning, and saddled his *a* Num 22:21
Now he was riding upon his *a* Num 22:22
the *a* saw the angel of the LORD Num 22:23
the *a* turned aside out of the way Num 22:23
and Balaam smote the *a*, to turn Num 22:23
when the *a* saw the angel of the Num 22:25
when the *a* saw the angel of the Num 22:27
and he smote the *a* with a staff Num 22:27
LORD opened the mouth of the *a* Num 22:28
And Balaam said unto the *a* Num 22:29
the *a* said unto Balaam Num 22:30
Am not I thine *a*, Num 22:30
smitten thine *a* these three times Num 22:32
the *a* saw me, and turned from me Num 22:33
nor thine ox, nor thine *a* Deut 5:14
his maidservant, his ox, or his *a* Deut 5:21
manner shalt thou do with his *a* Deut 22:3
shalt not see thy brother's *a* or Deut 22:4
plow with an ox and an *a* together Deut 22:10
thine *a* shall be violently taken Deut 28:31
and old, and ox, and sheep, and *a* Josh 6:21
and she lighted off her *a* Josh 15:18
and she lighted from off her *a* Judg 1:14
neither sheep, nor ox, nor *a* Judg 6:4
sons that rode on thirty *a* colts Judg 10:4
rode on threescore and ten *a* colts Judg 12:14
a new jawbone of an *a* Judg 15:15
said, With the jawbone of an *a* Judg 15:16
with the jaw of an *a* have I slain Judg 15:16
the man took her up upon an *a* Judg 19:28
or whose *a* have I taken 1Sa 12:3
suckling, ox and sheep, camel and *a* 1Sa 15:3
Jesse took an *a* laden with bread, 1Sa 16:20
it was so, as she rode on the *a* 1Sa 25:20
she hasted, and lighted off the *a* 1Sa 25:23
and arose, and rode upon an *a* 1Sa 25:42
not followed, he saddled his *a* 2Sa 17:23
said, I will saddle me an *a* 2Sa 19:26
And Shimei arose, and saddled his *a* 1Kin 2:40
unto his sons, Saddle me the *a* 1Kin 13:13
So they saddled him the *a* 1Kin 13:13
that he saddled for him the *a* 1Kin 13:23
the *a* stood by it, the lion also 1Kin 13:24
his sons, saying, Saddle me the *a* 1Kin 13:27
carcase cast in the way, and the *a* 1Kin 13:28
eaten the carcase, nor torn the *a* 1Kin 13:28
man of God, and laid it upon the *a* 1Kin 13:29
Then she saddled an *a*, and said to 2Kin 4:24
Doth the wild *a* bray when he hath Job 6:5
away the *a* of the fatherless Job 24:3
Who hath sent out the wild *a* free Job 39:5
loosed the bands of the wild *a* Job 39:5
for the horse, a bridle for the *a* Prov 26:3
owner, and the *a* his master's crib Is 1:3
the feet of the ox and the *a* Is 32:20
A wild *a* used to the wilderness, Jer 2:24
be buried with the burial of an *a* Jer 22:19
a wild *a* alone by himself Hos 8:9
lowly, and riding upon an *a* Zec 9:9
and upon a colt the foal of an *a* Zec 9:9
mule, of the camel, and of the *a* Zec 14:15
ye shall find an *a* tied, and a Mt 21:2
thee, meek, and sitting upon an *a* Mt 21:5
and a colt the foal of an *a* Mt 21:5
And brought the *a*, and the colt, and Mt 21:7
his ox or his *a* from the stall Lk 13:15
an *a* or an ox fallen into a pit Lk 14:5
when he had found a young *a* Jn 12:14
the dumb *a* speaking with man's 2Pet 2:16

**ASSAULT**
and province that would *a* them Est 8:11
when there was an *a* made both of Acts 14:5

**ASSAULTED**
*a* the house of Jason, and sought Acts 17:5

**ASSAY**
If we *a* to commune with thee, Job 4:2

**ASSAYED**
Or hath God *a* to go and take him a Deut 4:34
upon his armour, and he *a* to go 1Sa 17:39
he *a* to join himself to the Acts 9:26
they *a* to go into Bithynia Acts 16:7

**ASSAYING**
Egyptians *a* to do were drowned Heb 11:29

**ASSEMBLE**
them, all the assembly shall *a* Num 10:3
*A* me the men of Judah within 2Sa 20:4
Amasa went to *a* the men of Judah 2Sa 20:5
shall *a* the outcasts of Israel, Is 11:12
*A* yourselves and come Is 45:20
All ye, *a* yourselves, and hear Is 48:14
*A* yourselves, and let us go into Jer 4:5
*a* yourselves, and let us enter Jer 8:14
*a* all the beasts of the field, Jer 12:9
I will *a* them into the midst of Jer 21:4
*a* you out of the countries where Eze 11:17
the field, *A* yourselves, and come Eze 39:17
shall *a* a multitude of great Dan 11:10
they *a* themselves for corn and Hos 7:14
*a* the elders, gather the children Joel 2:16
*A* yourselves, and come, all ye Joel 3:11
*A* yourselves upon the mountains Amos 3:9
I will surely *a*, O Jacob, all of Mic 2:12
will I *a* her that halteth, and I Mic 4:6
that I may *a* the kingdoms, to Zeph 3:8

**ASSEMBED**
which *a* at the door of the Ex 38:8
they *a* all the congregation Num 1:18
of Israel *a* together at Shiloh Josh 18:1
of Israel *a* themselves together Judg 10:17
they lay with the women that *a* at 1Sa 2:22
that were with him *a* themselves 1Sa 14:20
Then Solomon *a* the elders of 1Kin 8:1
And all the men of Israel *a* 1Kin 8:2
of Israel, that were *a* unto him 1Kin 8:5
he *a* all the house of Judah, with 1Kin 12:21
David *a* the children of Aaron, and 1Chr 15:4
David *a* all the princes of Israel 1Chr 28:1
Then Solomon *a* the elders of 2Chr 5:2
*a* themselves unto the king in the 2Chr 5:3
of Israel that were *a* unto him 2Chr 5:6
And on the fourth day they *a* 2Chr 20:26
there *a* at Jerusalem much people 2Chr 30:13
Then were *a* unto me every one Ezr 9:4
there *a* unto him out of Israel a Ezr 10:1
of Israel were *a* with fasting Neh 9:1
the Jews that were at Shushan *a* Est 9:18
For, lo, the kings were *a* Ps 48:4
together, and let the people be *a* Is 43:9
*a* themselves by troops in the Jer 5:7
thy company that are *a* unto thee Eze 38:7
princes *a* together to the king, Dan 6:6
Then these men *a*, and found Daniel Dan 6:11
Then these men *a* unto the king Dan 6:15
Then *a* together the chief priests Mt 26:3
the scribes and the elders were *a* Mt 26:57
when they were *a* with the elders, Mt 28:12
with him were *a* all the chief Mk 14:53
were *a* for fear of the Jews Jn 20:19
being *a* together with them, Acts 1:4
shaken where they were *a* together Acts 4:31
to pass, that a whole year they *a* Acts 11:26
being *a* with one accord, to send Acts 15:25

**ASSEMBLIES**
the *a* of violent men have sought Ps 86:14
fastened by the masters of *a* Eccl 12:11
and sabbaths, the calling of *a* Is 1:13
of mount Zion, and upon her *a* Is 4:5
laws and my statutes in all mine *a* Eze 44:24
I will not smell in your solemn *a* Amos 5:21

**ASSEMBLING**
the lookingglasses of the women *a* Ex 38:8
Not forsaking the *a* of ourselves Heb 10:25

**ASSEMBLY**
unto their *a*, mine honour, be not Gen 49:6
the whole *a* of the congregation Ex 12:6
to kill this whole *a* with hunger Ex 16:3
be hid from the eyes of the *a* Lev 4:13
the *a* was gathered together unto Lev 8:4
it is a solemn *a* Lev 23:36
whole *a* of the children of Israel Num 8:9
use them for the calling of the *a* Num 10:2
them, all the *a* shall assemble Num 10:3
the *a* of the congregation of the Num 14:5
hundred and fifty princes of the *a* Num 16:2
went from the presence of the *a* Num 20:6
and gather thou the *a* together Num 20:8
day ye shall have a solemn *a* Num 29:35
the LORD spake unto all your *a* in Deut 5:22
of the fire in the day of the *a* Deut 9:10
of the fire in the day of the *a* Deut 10:4
be a solemn *a* to the LORD thy God Deut 16:8
God in Horeb in the day of the *a* Deut 18:16
in the *a* of the people of God Judg 20:2
camp from Jabesh-gilead to the *a* Judg 21:8
all this *a* shall know that the 1Sa 17:47
Proclaim a solemn *a* for Baal 2Kin 10:20
eighth day they made a solemn *a* 2Chr 7:9
the whole *a* took counsel to keep 2Chr 30:23
And I set a great *a* against them Neh 5:7
on the eighth day was a solemn *a* Neh 8:18
the *a* of the wicked have inclosed Ps 22:16
be feared in the *a* of the saints Ps 89:7
praise him in the *a* of the elders Ps 107:32
in the *a* of the upright, and in Ps 111:1
midst of the congregation and *a* Prov 5:14
upon the *a* of young men together Jer 6:11
an *a* of treacherous men Jer 9:2
I sat not in the *a* of the mockers Jer 15:17
spake to all the *a* of the people Jer 26:17
to come up against Babylon an *a* Jer 50:9
he hath called an *a* against me to Lam 1:15
destroyed his places of the *a* Lam 2:6
not be in the *a* of my people Eze 13:9
with an *a* of people, which shall Eze 23:24
ye a fast, call a solemn *a* Joel 1:14
sanctify a fast, call a solemn *a* Joel 2:15
are sorrowful for the solemn *a* Zeph 3:18
for the *a* was confused Acts 19:32
shall be determined in a lawful *a* Acts 19:39
thus spoken, he dismissed the *a* Acts 19:41
To the general *a* and church of the Heb 12:23
your *a* a man with a gold ring Jas 2:2

**ASSENT**
good to the king with one *a* 2Chr 18:12

**ASSENTED**
And the Jews also *a*, saying that Acts 24:9

**ASSES**
had sheep, and oxen, and he *a* Gen 12:16
and maidservants, and she *a* Gen 12:16
and maidservants, and camels, and *a*. Gen 24:35
and menservants, and camels, and *a* Gen 30:43
And I have oxen, and *a*, flocks, and Gen 32:5
kine, and ten bulls, twenty she *a* Gen 32:15
sheep, and their oxen, and their *a* Gen 34:28
as he fed the *a* of Zibeon his Gen 36:24
they laded their *a* with the corn Gen 42:26
and take us for bondmen, and our *a* Gen 43:18
and he gave their *a* provender Gen 43:24
were sent away, they and their *a* Gen 44:3
ten *a* laden with the good things Gen 45:23
ten she *a* laden with corn and Gen 45:23
cattle of the herds, and for the *a* Gen 47:17
upon the horses, upon the *a* Ex 9:3
and of the beeves, and of the *a* Num 31:28
persons, of the beeves, of the *a* Num 31:30
And threescore and one thousand *a* Num 31:34
the *a* were thirty thousand and Num 31:39
And thirty thousand *a* and five Num 31:45
daughters, and his oxen, and his *a* Josh 7:24
and took old sacks upon their *a* Josh 9:4
Speak, ye that ride on white *a* Judg 5:10
with him, and a couple of *a* Judg 19:3
there were with him two *a* saddled Judg 19:10
both straw and provender for our *a* Judg 19:19
and gave provender unto the *a* Judg 19:21
goodliest young men, and your *a* 1Sa 8:16
the *a* of Kish Saul's father were 1Sa 9:3
thee, and arise, go seek the *a* 1Sa 9:3
my father leave caring for the *a* 1Sa 9:5
as for thine *a* that were lost 1Sa 9:20
The *a* which thou wentest to seek 1Sa 10:2
hath left the care of the *a* 1Sa 10:2
And he said, To seek the *a* 1Sa 10:14
us plainly that the *a* were found 1Sa 10:16
and sucklings, and oxen, and *a* 1Sa 22:19
cakes of figs, and laid them on *a* 1Sa 25:18
the sheep, and the oxen, and the *a* 1Sa 27:9
him, with a couple of *a* saddled 2Sa 16:1
The *a* be for the king's household 2Sa 16:2
of the young men, and one of the *a* 2Kin 4:22
and their horses, and their *a* 2Kin 7:7
*a* tied, and the tents as they were 2Kin 7:10
of *a* two thousand, and of men an 1Chr 5:21
and Naphtali, brought bread on *a* 1Chr 12:40

over the *a* was Jehdeiah the ... 1Chr 27:30
all the feeble of them upon *a* ... 2Chr 28:15
their *a*, six thousand seven ... Ezr 2:67
seven hundred and twenty *a* ... Neh 7:69
bringing in sheaves, and lading *a* ... Neh 13:15
of oxen, and five hundred she *a* ... Job 1:3
the *a* feeding beside them ... Job 1:14
as wild *a* in the desert, go they ... Job 24:5
yoke of oxen, and a thousand she *a* ... Job 42:12
the wild *a* quench their thirst ... Ps 104:11
of horsemen, a chariot of *a* ... Is 21:7
upon the shoulders of young *a* ... Is 30:6
the young *a* that ear the ground ... Is 30:24
dens for ever, a joy of wild *a* ... Is 32:14
the wild *a* did stand in the high ... Jer 14:6
whose flesh is as the flesh of *a* ... Eze 23:20
his dwelling was with the wild *a* ... Dan 5:21

**ASSHUR** (*ash'-ur*) See ASHUR, ASSUR, ASSYRIA.
*1. The builder of Nineveh.*
Out of that land went forth *A* ... Gen 10:11
*2. A son of Shem.*
and *A*, and Arphaxad, and Lud ... Gen 10:22
Elam, and *A*, and Arphaxad, and Lud, 1Chr 1:17
*3. Another name for Assyria.*
until *A* shall carry thee away ... Num 24:22
of Chittim, and shall afflict *A* ... Num 24:24
Eden, the merchants of Sheba, *A* ... Eze 27:23
*A* is there and all her company ... Eze 32:22
*A* shall not save us ... Hos 14:3

**ASSHURIM** (*ash'-u-rim*) See ASHURITES.
*Descendants of Dedan.*
And the sons of Dedan were *A* ... Gen 25:3

**ASSHURITES** See ASSHURIM.

**ASSIGNED**
had a portion *a* them of Pharaoh ... Gen 47:22
they *a* Bezer in the wilderness ... Josh 20:8
that he *a* Uriah unto a place ... 2Sa 11:16

**ASSIR** (*as'-sur*)
*1. A son of Korah.*
*A*, and Elkanah, and Abiasaph ... Ex 6:24
son, Korah his son, *A* his son, ... 1Chr 6:22
*2. A son of Ebiasaph.*
Ebiasaph his son, and *A* his son, ... 1Chr 6:23
The son of Tahath, the son of *A* ... 1Chr 6:37
*3. A son of Jeconiah.*
*A*, Salathiel his son, ... 1Chr 3:17

**ASSIST**
that ye *a* her in whatsoever ... Rom 16:2

**ASSOCIATE**
*A* yourselves, O ye people, and ye ... Is 8:9

**ASSOS** (*as'-sos*) *A seaport of Mysia in Asia Minor.*
before to ship, and sailed unto *A* ... Acts 20:13
And when he met with us at *A* ... Acts 20:14

**ASS'S**
his *a* colt unto the choice vine ... Gen 49:11
until an *a* head was sold for ... 2Kin 6:25
man be born like a wild *a* colt ... Job 11:12
King cometh, sitting on an *a* colt ... Jn 12:15

**ASSUR** (*As'-sur*) See ASSHUR. *Same as Asshur 3.*
the days of Esar-haddon king of *A* ... Ezr 4:2
*A* also is joined with them ... Ps 83:8

**ASSURANCE**
and shalt have none *a* of thy life ... Deut 28:66
quietness and *a* for ever ... Is 32:17
he hath given *a* unto all men ... Acts 17:31
of the full *a* of understanding ... Col 2:2
in the Holy Ghost, and in much *a* ... 1Th 1:5
the full *a* of hope unto the end ... Heb 6:11
a true heart in full *a* of faith ... Heb 10:22

**ASSURE**
shall *a* our hearts before him ... 1Jn 3:19

**ASSURED**
unto it, and it shall be *a* to him ... Lev 27:19
give you *a* peace in this place ... Jer 14:13
hast learned and hast been *a* of ... 2Ti 3:14

**ASSUREDLY**
said unto David, Know thou *a* ... 1Sa 28:1
*A* Solomon thy son shall reign ... 1Kin 1:13
*A* Solomon thy son shall reign ... 1Kin 1:17
*A* Solomon thy son shall reign ... 1Kin 1:30
this land *a* with my whole heart ... Jer 32:41
If thou wilt *a* go forth unto the ... Jer 38:17
drink of the cup have *a* drunken ... Jer 49:12
all the house of Israel know *a* ... Acts 2:36
*a* gathering that the Lord had ... Acts 16:10

**ASSWAGE**
of my lips should *a* your grief ... Job 16:5

**ASSWAGED**
over the earth, and the waters *a* ... Gen 8:1
Though I speak, my grief is not *a* ... Job 16:6

**ASSYRIA** (*as-sir'-e-ah*) See ASSHUR, ASSYRIAN.
*A Mesopotamian empire.*
which goeth toward the east of *A* ... Gen 2:14
Egypt, as thou goest toward *A* ... Gen 25:18
Pul the king of *A* came against ... 2Kin 15:19
silver, to give to the king of *A* ... 2Kin 15:20
So the king of *A* turned back ... 2Kin 15:20
came Tiglath-pileser king of *A* ... 2Kin 15:29
and carried them captive to *A* ... 2Kin 15:29
to Tiglath-pileser king of *A* ... 2Kin 16:7
it for a present to the king of *A* ... 2Kin 16:8
the king of *A* hearkened unto him ... 2Kin 16:9
for the king of *A* went up against ... 2Kin 16:9
to meet Tiglath-pileser king of *A* ... 2Kin 16:10
of the LORD for the king of *A* ... 2Kin 16:18
him came up Shalmaneser king of *A* .. 2Kin 17:3
the king of *A* found conspiracy in ... 2Kin 17:4
no present to the king of *A* ... 2Kin 17:4
the king of *A* shut him up ... 2Kin 17:4
Then the king of *A* came up ... 2Kin 17:5
Hoshea the king of *A* took Samaria ... 2Kin 17:6
and carried Israel away into *A* ... 2Kin 17:6
their own land to *A* unto this day ... 2Kin 17:23
the king of *A* brought men from ... 2Kin 17:24
they spake to the king of *A* ... 2Kin 17:26
Then the king of *A* commanded ... 2Kin 17:27
he rebelled against the king of *A* ... 2Kin 18:7
king of *A* came up against Samaria ... 2Kin 18:9
the king of *A* did carry away ... 2Kin 18:11
did carry away Israel unto *A* ... 2Kin 18:11
did Sennacherib king of *A* come up ... 2Kin 18:13
sent to the king of *A* to Lachish ... 2Kin 18:14
the king of *A* appointed unto ... 2Kin 18:14
and gave it to the king of *A* ... 2Kin 18:16
And the king of *A* sent Tartan ... 2Kin 18:17
the great king, the king of *A* ... 2Kin 18:19
pledges to my lord the king of *A* ... 2Kin 18:23
of the great king, the king of *A* ... 2Kin 18:28
into the hand of the king of *A* ... 2Kin 18:30
for thus saith the king of *A* ... 2Kin 18:31
out of the hand of the king of *A* ... 2Kin 18:33
whom the king of *A* his master ... 2Kin 19:4
the king of *A* have blasphemed me ... 2Kin 19:6
found the king of *A* warring ... 2Kin 19:8
into the hand of the king of *A* ... 2Kin 19:10
kings of *A* have done to all lands ... 2Kin 19:11
the kings of *A* have destroyed the ... 2Kin 19:17
king of *A* I have heard ... 2Kin 19:20
the LORD concerning the king of *A* ... 2Kin 19:32
So Sennacherib king of *A* departed ... 2Kin 19:36
out of the hand of the king of *A* ... 2Kin 20:6
king of *A* to the river Euphrates ... 2Kin 23:29
king of *A* carried away captive ... 1Chr 5:6
up the spirit of Pul king of *A* ... 1Chr 5:26
of Tilgath-pilneser king of *A* ... 1Chr 5:26
unto the kings of *A* to help him ... 2Chr 28:16
king of *A* came unto him, and ... 2Chr 28:20
and gave it unto the king of *A* ... 2Chr 28:21
out of the hand of the kings of *A* ... 2Chr 30:6
Sennacherib king of *A* came ... 2Chr 32:1
Why should the kings of *A* come ... 2Chr 32:4
nor dismayed for the king of *A* ... 2Chr 32:7
this did Sennacherib king of *A* ... 2Chr 32:9
Thus saith Sennacherib king of *A* ... 2Chr 32:10
out of the hand of the king of *A* ... 2Chr 32:11
in the camp of the king of *A* ... 2Chr 32:21
hand of Sennacherib the king of *A* ... 2Chr 32:22
of the host of the king of *A* ... 2Chr 33:11
heart of the king of *A* unto them ... Ezr 6:22
of the kings of *A* unto this day ... Neh 9:32
even the king of *A* ... Is 7:17
the bee that is in the land of *A* ... Is 7:18
the river, by the king of *A* ... Is 7:20
taken away before the king of *A* ... Is 8:4
and many, even the king of *A* ... Is 8:7
the stout heart of the king of *A* ... Is 10:12
which shall be left, from *A* ... Is 11:11
which shall be left, from *A* ... Is 11:16
be a highway out of Egypt to *A* ... Is 19:23
Egypt, and the Egyptian into *A* ... Is 19:23
be the third with Egypt and with *A* ... Is 19:24
*A* the work of my hands, and Israel ... Is 19:25
Sargon the king of *A* sent him ... Is 20:1
So shall the king of *A* lead away ... Is 20:4
be delivered from the king of *A* ... Is 20:6
ready to perish in the land of *A* ... Is 27:13
king of *A* came up against all the ... Is 36:1
the king of *A* sent Rabshakeh from ... Is 36:2
the great king, the king of *A* ... Is 36:4
thee, to my master the king of *A* ... Is 36:8
of the great king, the king of *A* ... Is 36:13
into the hand of the king of *A* ... Is 36:15
for thus saith the king of *A* ... Is 36:16
out of the hand of the king of *A* ... Is 36:18
whom the king of *A* his master ... Is 37:4
the king of *A* have blasphemed me ... Is 37:6
found the king of *A* warring ... Is 37:8
into the hand of the king of *A* ... Is 37:10
of *A* have done to all lands by ... Is 37:11
the kings of *A* have laid waste ... Is 37:18
me against Sennacherib king of *A* ... Is 37:21
the LORD concerning the king of *A* ... Is 37:33
So Sennacherib king of *A* departed ... Is 37:37
out of the hand of the king of *A* ... Is 38:6
hast thou to do in the way of *A* ... Jer 2:18
Egypt, as thou wast ashamed of *A* ... Jer 2:36
the king of *A* hath devoured him ... Jer 50:17
as I have punished the king of *A* ... Jer 50:18
that were the chosen men of *A* ... Eze 23:7
they call to Egypt, they go to *A* ... Hos 7:11
For they are gone up to *A* ... Hos 8:9
shall eat unclean things in *A* ... Hos 9:3
*A* for a present to king Jareb ... Hos 10:6
and as a dove out of the land of *A* ... Hos 11:11
the land of *A* with the sword ... Mic 5:6
he shall come even to thee from *A* ... Mic 7:12
shepherds slumber, O king of *A* ... Nah 3:18
against the north, and destroy *A* ... Zeph 2:13
of Egypt, and gather them out of *A* ... Zec 10:10
the pride of *A* shall be brought ... Zec 10:11

**ASSYRIAN** (*as-sir'-e-un*) See ASSYRIANS. *An inhabitant of Assyria.*
O *A*, the rod of mine anger, and ... Is 10:5
in Zion, be not afraid of the *A* ... Is 10:24
I will break the *A* in my land ... Is 14:25
the *A* shall come into Egypt, and ... Is 19:23
til the *A* founded it for them ... Is 23:13
LORD shall the *A* be beaten down ... Is 30:31
Then shall the *A* fall with the ... Is 31:8
the *A* oppressed them without ... Is 52:4
the *A* was a cedar in Lebanon with ... Eze 31:3
wound, then went Ephraim to the *A* ... Hos 5:13
but the *A* shall be his king, ... Hos 11:5
when the *A* shall come into our ... Mic 5:5
shall he deliver us from the *A* ... Mic 5:6

**ASSYRIANS** (*as-sir'-e-uns*)
of the *A* an hundred fourscore ... 2Kin 19:35
Egyptians shall serve with the *A* ... Is 19:23
in the camp of the *A* an hundred ... Is 37:36
to the Egyptians, and to the *A* ... Lam 5:6
played the whore also with the *A* ... Eze 16:28
lovers, on the *A* her neighbours, ... Eze 23:5
lovers, into the hand of the *A* ... Eze 23:9
doted upon the *A* her neighbours ... Eze 23:12
and Koa, and all the *A* with them ... Eze 23:23
do make a covenant with the *A* ... Hos 12:1

**ASTAROTH** (*as'-ta-roth*) See ASHTAROTH. *A city in Bashan.*
Bashan, which dwelt at *A* in Edrei ... Deut 1:4

**ASTONIED**
and of my beard, and sat down *a* ... Ezr 9:3
I sat *a* until the evening ... Ezr 9:4
Upright men shall be *a* at this ... Job 17:8
after him shall be *a* at his day ... Job 18:20
As many were *a* at thee ... Is 52:14
Why shouldest thou be as a man *a* ... Jer 14:9
be *a* one with another, and consume ... Eze 4:17
Nebuchadnezzar the king was *a* ... Dan 3:24
was *a* for one hour, and his ... Dan 4:19
in him, and his lords were *a* ... Dan 5:9

**ASTONISHED**
dwell therein shall be *a* at it ... Lev 26:32
one that passeth by it shall be *a* ... 1Kin 9:8
Mark me, and be *a*, and lay your ... Job 21:5
tremble, and are *a* at his reproof ... Job 26:11
Be *a*, O ye heavens, at this, and ... Jer 2:12
and the priests shall be *a* ... Jer 4:9
that passeth thereby shall be *a* ... Jer 18:16
that passeth thereby shall be *a* ... Jer 19:8
one that goeth by it shall be *a* ... Jer 49:17
that goeth by Babylon shall be *a* ... Jer 50:13
remained there *a* among them seven ... Eze 3:15
at every moment, and be *a* at thee ... Eze 26:16
of the isles shall be *a* at thee ... Eze 27:35
the people shall be *a* at thee ... Eze 28:19
I was *a* at the vision, but none ... Dan 8:27
the people were *a* at his doctrine ... Mt 7:28
insomuch that they were *a* ... Mt 13:54
they were *a* at his doctrine ... Mt 22:33
they were *a* at his doctrine ... Mk 1:22
And they were *a* with a great ... Mk 5:42
and many hearing him were *a* ... Mk 6:2
And were beyond measure *a*, saying, ... Mk 7:37
the disciples were *a* at his words ... Mk 10:24
they were *a* out of measure, ... Mk 10:26
the people was *a* at his doctrine ... Mk 11:18
him were *a* at his understanding ... Lk 2:47
they were *a* at his doctrine ... Lk 4:32
For he was *a*, and all that were ... Lk 5:9
And her parents were *a* ... Lk 8:56
also of our company made us *a* ... Lk 24:22
*a* said, Lord, what wilt thou have ... Acts 9:6
which believed were *a*, as many as ... Acts 10:45
the door, and saw him, they were *a* ... Acts 12:16
being *a* at the doctrine of the ... Acts 13:12

**ASTONISHMENT**
and blindness, and *a* of heart ... Deut 28:28
And thou shalt become an *a* ... Deut 28:37
shall be an *a* to every one that ... 2Chr 7:21
delivered them to trouble, to *a* ... 2Chr 29:8
made us to drink the wine of *a* ... Ps 60:3
*a* hath taken hold on me ... Jer 8:21
destroy them, and make them an *a* ... Jer 25:9
shall be a desolation, and an *a* ... Jer 25:11
to make them a desolation, an *a* ... Jer 25:18
the earth, to be a curse, and an *a* ... Jer 29:18
shall be an execration, and an *a* ... Jer 42:18
shall be an execration, and an *a* ... Jer 44:12
your land a desolation, and an *a* ... Jer 44:22
dwelling place for dragons, an *a* ... Jer 51:37
become an *a* among the nations ... Jer 51:41
drink water by measure, and with *a* ... Eze 4:16
an *a* unto the nations that are ... Eze 5:15
and drink their water with *a* ... Eze 12:19
and sorrow, with the cup of *a* ... Eze 23:33
I will smite every horse with *a* ... Zec 12:4
were astonished with a great *a* ... Mk 5:42

**ASTRAY**
enemy's ox or his ass going *a* ... Ex 23:4
brother's ox or his sheep go *a* ... Deut 22:1
they go *a* as soon as they be born ... Ps 58:3
Before I was afflicted I went *a* ... Ps 119:67
I have gone *a* like a lost sheep ... Ps 119:176
of his folly he shall go *a* ... Prov 5:23
her ways, go not *a* in her paths ... Prov 7:25

righteous to go *a* in an evil way........ Prov 28:10
All we like sheep have gone *a*................... Is 53:6
have caused them to go *a*, they................ Jer 50:6
Israel may go no more *a* from me....... Eze 14:11
far from me, when Israel went *a*........ Eze 44:10
which went *a* away from me after........ Eze 44:10
children of Israel went *a* from me....... Eze 44:15
which went not *a* when the................ Eze 48:11
the children of Israel went *a*.............. Eze 48:11
as the Levites went *a*............................ Eze 48:11
sheep, and one of them be gone *a*........ Mt 18:12
and seeketh that which is gone *a*......... Mt 18:12
ninety and nine which went not *a*........ Mt 18:13
For ye were as sheep going *a*............... 1Pet 2:25
the right way, and are gone *a*.............. 2Pet 2:15

**ASTROLOGER**
such things at any magician, or *a*........ Dan 2:10

**ASTROLOGERS**
Let now the *a*, the stargazers,.................. Is 47:13
*a* that were in all his realm..................... Dan 1:20
to call the magicians, and the *a*............... Dan 2:2
cannot the wise men, the *a*...................... Dan 2:27
Then came in the magicians, the *a*......... Dan 4:7
cried aloud to bring in the *a*.................... Dan 5:7
made master of the magicians, *a*........... Dan 5:11
And now the wise men, the *a*................... Dan 5:15

**ASUNDER**
but shall not divide it *a*.......................... Lev 1:17
neck, but shall not divide it *a*.................. Lev 5:8
clave *a* that was under them.............. Num 16:31
of fire, and parted them both *a*............ 2Kin 2:11
at ease, but he hath broken me *a*......... Job 16:12
about, he cleaveth my reins *a*.............. Job 16:13
Let us break their bands *a*....................... Ps 2:3
he hath cut *a* the cords of the................ Ps 129:4
of the whole earth cut in *a*.................... Jer 50:23
great pain, and No shall be rent *a*........ Eze 30:16
he beheld, and drove *a* the nations........ Hab 3:6
staff, even Beauty, and cut it *a*............. Zec 11:10
Then I cut *a* mine other staff,............... Zec 11:14
together, let not man put *a*..................... Mt 19:6
And shall cut him *a*, and appoint.......... Mt 24:51
chains had been plucked *a* by him.......... Mk 5:4
together, let not man put *a*..................... Mk 10:9
he burst *a* in the midst, and all............. Acts 1:18
departed in *a* one from the other........ Acts 15:39
even to the dividing *a* of soul................. Heb 4:12
were stoned, they were sawn *a*............. Heb 11:37

**ASUPPIM** *Storage for temple gods.*
and to his sons the house of *A*.......... 1Chr 26:15
four a day, and toward *A* two............. 1Chr 26:17

**ASYNCRITUS** (*a-sin'-cri-tus*) *A Christian acquaintance of Paul.*
Salute *A*, Phlegon, Hermas,................. Rom 16:14

**AT** See PREFACE.

**ATAD** (*a'-tad*) See ABEL-MIZRAIM. *A place east of the Jordan.*
came to the threshingfloor of *A*.......... Gen 50:10
the mourning in the floor of *A*............ Gen 50:11

**ATARAH** (*at'-a-rah*) *A wife of Jerahmeel.*
another wife, whose name was *A*........ 1Chr 2:26

**ATAROTH** (*at'-a-roth*) See ATAROTH-ADAR, ATROTH.
*1. A city east of the Jordan.*
*A*, and Dibon, and Jazer, and Nimrah, Num 32:3
children of Gad built Dibon, and *A*... Num 32:34
*2. A city in Ephraim.*
unto the borders of Archi to *A*............ Josh 16:2
And it went down from Janohah to *A* Josh 16:7
*3. A city in Judah.*
and the Netophathites, *A*, the............. 1Chr 2:54

**ATAROTH-ADAR** (*at''-a-roth-a'-dar*) See ATAROTH-ADDAR. *A city on the border of Benjamin.*
and the border descended to *A*........... Josh 18:13

**ATAROTH-ADDAR** (*at''-a-roth-ad'-dar*) See ATAROTH-ADAR. *Same as Ataroth-adar.*
on the east side was *A*, unto................. Josh 16:5

**ATE**
*a* the sacrifices of the dead................... Ps 106:28
I *a* no pleasant bread, neither............... Dan 10:3
of the angel's hand, and *a* it up........... Rev 10:10

**ATER** (*a'-tur*)
*1. An ancestor of an exiled family.*
The children of *A* of Hezekiah............... Ezr 2:16
The children of *A* of Hezekiah.............. Neh 7:21
*2. An exiled family who returned under Zerubbabel.*
of Shallum, the children of *A*................. Ezr 2:42
of Shallum, the children of *A*................. Neh 7:45
*3. An Israelite who sealed the covenant with Nehemiah.*
*A*, Hizkijah, Azzur,................................. Neh 10:17

**ATHACH** (*a'-thak*) *A city in Judah.*
and to them which were in *A*................ 1Sa 30:30

**ATHAIAH** (*ath-a-i'-ah*) *A son of Uzziah*
*A* the son of Uzziah, the son of............ Neh 11:4

**ATHALIAH** (*ath-a-li'-ah*)
*1. Daughter of Jezebel.*
And his mother's name was *A*.............. 2Kin 8:26
when *A* the mother of Ahaziah saw.... 2Kin 11:1
nurse, in the bedchamber from *A*......... 2Kin 11:2
*A* did reign over the land...................... 2Kin 11:3
when *A* heard the noise of the............. 2Kin 11:13
*A* rent her clothes, and cried,.............. 2Kin 11:14
they slew *A* with the sword beside.... 2Kin 11:20
also was *A* the daughter of Omri........ 2Chr 22:2
But when *A* the mother of Ahaziah.. 2Chr 22:10
of Ahaziah,) hid him from *A*............... 2Chr 22:11
and *A* reigned over the land............... 2Chr 22:12
Now when *A* heard the noise of the . 2Chr 23:12
Then *A* rent her clothes, and said,..... 2Chr 23:13
they had slain *A* with the sword......... 2Chr 23:21
For the sons of *A*, that wicked............ 2Chr 24:7
*2. A son of Jeroham.*
and Shehariah, and *A*.......................... 1Chr 8:26
*3. Father of Jeshiah.*
Jeshaiah the son of *A*, and with.............. Ezr 8:7

**ATHENIANS** (*a-the'-ne-uns*) *Citizens of Athens*
(For all the *A* and strangers which.... Acts 17:21

**ATHENS** (*ath'-ens*) See ATHENIANS. *A city in Greece.*
conducted Paul brought him unto *A*. Acts 17:15
while Paul waited for them at *A*........ Acts 17:16
Mars' hill, and said, Ye men of *A*........ Acts 17:22
these things Paul departed from *A*....... Acts 18:1
it good to be left at *A* alone...................... 1Th 3:1
Thessalonians was written from *A*........... 1Th s
Thessalonians was written from *A*........... 2Th s

**ATHIRST**
And he was sore *a*, and called on....... Judg 15:18
and when thou art *a*, go unto the......... Ruth 2:9
when saw we thee an hungred, or *a*..... Mt 25:44
I will give unto him that is *a* of............ Rev 21:6
And let him that is *a* come.................. Rev 22:17

**ATHLAI** (*ath'-lahee*) *Married a foreign wife in exile.*
Jehohanan, Hananiah, Zabbai, and *A*.. Ezr 10:28

**ATONEMENT**
things wherewith the *a* was made........ Ex 29:33
bullock for a sin offering for *a*............. Ex 29:36
when thou hast made an *a* for it.......... Ex 29:36
shalt make an *a* for the altar................ Ex 29:37
Aaron shall make an *a* upon the.......... Ex 30:10
he make *a* upon it throughout your...... Ex 30:10
to make an *a* for your souls.................. Ex 30:15
thou shalt take the *a* money of............ Ex 30:16
to make an *a* for your souls.................. Ex 30:16
I shall make an *a* for your sin............ Ex 32:30
for him to make *a* for him...................... Lev 1:4
priest shall make an *a* for them........... Lev 4:20
the priest shall make an *a* for.............. Lev 4:26
priest shall make an *a* for him............. Lev 4:31
an *a* for his sin that he hath................ Lev 4:35
the priest shall make an *a* for.............. Lev 5:6
the priest shall make an *a* for.............. Lev 5:10
the priest shall make an *a* for.............. Lev 5:13
the priest shall make an *a* for.............. Lev 5:16
make an *a* for him concerning his......... Lev 5:18
make an *a* for him before the LORD........ Lev 6:7
the priest that maketh *a*........................ Lev 7:7
to do, to make an *a* for you................. Lev 8:34
make an *a* for thyself, and for the........ Lev 9:7
the people, and make an *a* for them...... Lev 9:7
to make *a* for them before the............ Lev 10:17
the LORD, and make an *a* for her......... Lev 12:7
priest shall make an *a* for her.............. Lev 12:8
make an *a* for him before the LORD..... Lev 14:18
make an *a* for him that is to be........... Lev 14:19
priest shall make an *a* for him............ Lev 14:20
to be waved, to make an *a* for him....... Lev 14:21
to make an *a* for him before the......... Lev 14:29
the priest shall make an *a* for............ Lev 14:31
and make an *a* for the house............... Lev 14:53
the priest shall make an *a* for............ Lev 15:15
the priest shall make an *a* for............ Lev 15:30
make an *a* for himself, and for his....... Lev 16:6
the LORD, to make an *a* with him.......... Lev 16:10
and shall make an *a* for himself.......... Lev 16:11
he shall make an *a* for the holy........... Lev 16:16
in to make an *a* in the holy place........ Lev 16:17
and have made an *a* for himself.......... Lev 16:17
the LORD, and make an *a* for it............ Lev 16:18
make an *a* for himself, and for the...... Lev 16:24
in to make *a* in the holy place............. Lev 16:27
the priest make an *a* for you............... Lev 16:30
father's stead, shall make the *a*......... Lev 16:32
he shall make an *a* for the holy........... Lev 16:33
he shall make an *a* for the.................. Lev 16:33
shall make an *a* for the priests........... Lev 16:33
to make an *a* for the children of......... Lev 16:34
altar to make an *a* for your souls......... Lev 17:11
that maketh an *a* for the soul............. Lev 17:11
the priest shall make an *a* for............ Lev 19:22
month there shall be a day of *a*.......... Lev 23:27
for it is a day of *a*............................... Lev 23:28
to make an *a* for you before the......... Lev 23:28
in the day of *a* shall ye make the......... Lev 25:9
beside the ram of the *a*......................... Num 5:8
whereby an *a* shall be made for............ Num 5:8
offering, and make an *a* for him.......... Num 6:11
to make an *a* for the Levites............... Num 8:12
to make an *a* for the children of......... Num 8:19
Aaron made an *a* for them to............... Num 8:21
the priest shall make an *a* for.......... Num 15:25
the priest shall make an *a* for.......... Num 15:28
the LORD, to make an *a* for him......... Num 15:28
and make an *a* for them..................... Num 16:46
and made an *a* for the people............ Num 16:47
made an *a* for the children of............. Num 25:13
offering, to make an *a* for you............ Num 28:22
the goats, to make an *a* for you.......... Num 28:30
offering, to make an *a* for you............. Num 29:5
beside the sin offering of *a*................. Num 29:11
to make an *a* for our souls before...... Num 31:50
and wherewith shall I make the *a*........ 2Sa 21:3
holy, and to make an *a* for Israel......... 1Chr 6:49
to make an *a* for all Israel.................. 2Chr 29:24
offerings to make an *a* for Israel......... Neh 10:33
whom we have now received the *a*..... Rom 5:11

**ATONEMENTS**
blood of the sin offering of *a*................ Ex 30:10

**ATROTH** (*a'-troth*) See ATAROTH. *A city in Gad.*
And *A*, Shophan, and Jaazer, and...... Num 32:35

**ATROTH BETH JOAB** See ATROTH.

**ATTAI** (*at'-tahee*)
*1. A grandson of Sheshan.*
and she bare him *A*.............................. 1Chr 2:35
*A* begat Nathan, and Nathan begat..... 1Chr 2:36
*2. A Gadite in David's army.*
*A* the sixth, Eliel the seventh,............. 1Chr 12:11
*3. A son of Rehoboam.*
which bare him Abijah, and *A*............ 2Chr 11:20

**ATTAIN**
it is high, I cannot *a* unto it.................... Ps 139:6
shall *a* unto wise counsels...................... Prov 1:5
as his hand shall *a* unto, and an........... Eze 46:7
it be ere they *a* to innocency................... Hos 8:5
any means they might *a* to Phenice... Acts 27:12
If by any means I might *a* unto............ Phil 3:11

**ATTAINED**
have not *a* unto the days of the.......... Gen 47:9
howbeit he *a* not unto the first............ 2Sa 23:19
but he *a* not to the first three............. 2Sa 23:23
howbeit he *a* not to the first.............. 1Chr 11:21
but *a* not to the first three.................. 1Chr 11:25
have *a* to righteousness, even the....... Rom 9:30
hath not *a* to the law of...................... Rom 9:31
Not as though I had already *a*............. Phil 3:12
whereto we have already *a*.................. Phil 3:16
doctrine, whereunto thou hast *a*............... 1Ti 4:6

**ATTALIA** (*at-ta-li'-ah*) *A seaport near Perga.*
in Perga, they went down into *A*........ Acts 14:25

**ATTEND**
he had appointed to *a* upon her................ Est 4:5
*a* unto my cry, give ear unto my............... Ps 17:1
*A* unto me, and hear me........................ Ps 55:2
*a* unto my prayer..................................... Ps 61:1
and *a* to the voice of my.......................... Ps 86:6
*A* unto my cry........................................ Ps 142:6
and *a* to know understanding................. Prov 4:1
My son, *a* to my words......................... Prov 4:20
*a* unto my wisdom, and bow thine.......... Prov 5:1
*a* to the words of my mouth.................. Prov 7:24
that ye may *a* upon the Lord................ 1Cor 7:35

**ATTENDANCE**
the *a* of his ministers, and their.......... 1Kin 10:5
the *a* of his ministers, and their............ 2Chr 9:4
give *a* to reading, to exhortation............ 1Ti 4:13
which no man gave *a* at the altar........... Heb 7:13

**ATTENDED**
I *a* unto you, and, behold, there.......... Job 32:12
he hath *a* to the voice of my................... Ps 66:19
that she *a* unto the things which....... Acts 16:14

**ATTENDING**
*a* continually upon this very................... Rom 13:6

**ATTENT**
let thine ears be *a* unto the................ 2Chr 6:40
mine ears *a* unto the prayer that.......... 2Chr 7:15

**ATTENTIVE**
Let thine ear now be *a*, and thine.......... Neh 1:6
let now thine ear be *a* to the................. Neh 1:11
were *a* unto the book of the law............. Neh 8:3
let thine ears be *a* to the voice.............. Ps 130:2
people were very *a* to hear him.............. Lk 19:48

**ATTENTIVELY**
Hear *a* the noise of his voice, and......... Job 37:2

**ATTIRE**
a woman with the *a* of an harlot.......... Prov 7:10
her ornaments, or a bride her *a*............. Jer 2:32
in dyed *a* upon their heads.................. Eze 23:15

**ATTIRED**
the linen mitre shall he be *a*................. Lev 16:4

**AUDIENCE**
in the *a* of the children of Heth........... Gen 23:10
the *a* of the people of the land............ Gen 23:13
in the *a* of the sons of Heth............... Gen 23:16
read in the *a* of the people.................... Ex 24:7
I pray thee, speak in thine *a*................ 1Sa 25:24
in the *a* of our God, keep and seek..... 1Chr 28:8
of Moses in the *a* of the people............. Neh 13:1
sayings in the *a* of the people.................. Lk 7:1
Then in the *a* of all the people............... Lk 20:45
and ye that fear God, give *a*............... Acts 13:16
gave *a* to Barnabas and Paul,............... Acts 15:12
they gave him *a* unto this word,......... Acts 22:22

**AUGMENT**
to *a* yet the fierce anger of the.......... Num 32:14

**AUGUSTAN** See AUGUSTUS.

**AUGUSTUS** (*aw-gus'-tus*) See AUGUSTUS', CAESAR. *An emperor of Rome.*
went out a decree from Caesar *A*.............. Lk 2:1
be reserved unto the hearing of *A*...... Acts 25:21
he himself hath appealed to *A*............ Acts 25:25

**AUGUSTUS'** (*aw-gus'-tus*)
Julius, a centurion of *A* band.................. Acts 27:1

**AUL**
bore his ear through with an *a*................ Ex 21:6
Then thou shalt take an *a*.................. Deut 15:17

**AUNT**
she is thine *a*............................................ Lev 18:14

**AUSTERE**
thee, because thou art an *a* man............ Lk 19:21
Thou knewest that I was an *a* man...... Lk 19:22

**AUTHOR**
For God is not the *a* of confusion...... 1Cor 14:33
he became the *a* of eternal...................... Heb 5:9
Looking unto Jesus the *a* and................ Heb 12:2

**AUTHORITIES**
angels and *a* and powers being made .. 1Pet 3:22

**AUTHORITY**
the Jew, wrote with all *a*.......................... Est 9:29
When the righteous are in *a*................. Prov 29:2
he taught them as one having *a*................. Mt 7:29
For I am a man under *a*, having................ Mt 8:9
are great exercise *a* upon them.............. Mt 20:25
By what *a* doest thou these things........ Mt 21:23
and who gave thee this *a*.......................... Mt 21:23
you by what *a* I do these things............ Mt 21:24
I you by what *a* I do these things........ Mt 21:27
he taught them as one that had *a*.......... Mk 1:22
for with *a* commandeth he even the...... Mk 1:27
great ones exercise *a* upon them.......... Mk 10:42
By what *a* doest thou these things...... Mk 11:28
thee this *a* to do these things.............. Mk 11:28
you by what *a* I do these things.............. Mk 11:29
you by what *a* I do these things.............. Mk 11:33
gave *a* to his servants, and to................ Mk 13:34
for with *a* and power he commandeth.... Lk 4:36
For I also am a man set under *a*................. Lk 7:8
*a* over all devils, and to cure.................... Lk 9:1
have thou *a* over ten cities.................... Lk 19:17
by what *a* doest thou these things.......... Lk 20:2
who is he that gave thee this *a*................ Lk 20:2
I you by what *a* I do these things............ Lk 20:8
the power and *a* of the governor............ Lk 20:20
they that exercise *a* upon them.............. Lk 22:25
hath given him *a* to execute.................... Jn 5:27
an eunuch of great *a* under................... Acts 8:27
here he hath *a* from the chief............... Acts 9:14
having received *a* from the chief.......... Acts 26:10
as I went to Damascus with *a*................ Acts 26:12
have put down all rule and all *a*............ 1Cor 15:24
boast somewhat more of our *a*............. 2Cor 10:8
kings, and for all that are in *a*................ 1Ti 2:2
nor to usurp *a* over the man................... 1Ti 2:12
and exhort, and rebuke with all *a*...... Titus 2:15
power, and his seat, and great *a*............ Rev 13:2

**AVA** (*a'-vah*) See IVAH. *An area near Babylon.*
and from Cuthah, and from *A*............ 2Kin 17:24

**AVAILETH**
Yet all this *a* me nothing.......................... Est 5:13
neither circumcision *a* any thing............... Gal 5:6
neither circumcision *a* any thing............. Gal 6:15
prayer of a righteous man *a* much......... Jas 5:16

**AVEN** See BETH-AVEN. *Another name for Heliopolis, in Egypt.*
The young men of *A* and of.................. Eze 30:17
The high places also of *A*........................ Hos 10:8
inhabitant from the plain of *A*............... Amos 1:5

**AVENGE**
Thou shalt not *a*, nor bear any............. Lev 19:18
that shall *a* the quarrel of my.............. Lev 26:25
*A* the children of Israel of the............... Num 31:2
and *a* the LORD of Midian..................... Num 31:3
for he will *a* the blood of his.............. Deut 32:43
and thee, and the LORD *a* me of thee.. 1Sa 24:12
that I may *a* the blood of my................. 2Kin 9:7
to *a* themselves on their enemies............ Est 8:13
and *a* me of mine enemies.......................... Is 1:24
that he may *a* him of his...................... Jer 46:10
I will *a* the blood of Jezreel...................... Hos 1:4
saying, *A* me of mine adversary................ Lk 18:3
widow troubleth me, I will *a* her.............. Lk 18:5
And shall not God *a* his own elect.......... Lk 18:7
you that he will *a* them speedily.............. Lk 18:8
*a* not yourselves, but rather give........ Rom 12:19
*a* our blood on them that dwell on........ Rev 6:10

**AVENGED**
If Cain shall be *a* sevenfold.................... Gen 4:24
until the people had *a* themselves...... Josh 10:13
done this, yet will I be *a* of you.............. Judg 15:7
that I may be at once *a* of the............. Judg 16:28
that I may be *a* on mine enemies.......... 1Sa 14:24
to be *a* of the king's enemies................ 1Sa 18:25
or that my lord hath *a* himself............... 1Sa 25:31
the LORD hath *a* my lord the king............ 2Sa 4:8
LORD hath *a* him of his enemies............ 2Sa 18:19
for the LORD hath *a* thee this day.......... 2Sa 18:31
shall not my soul be *a* on such a.............. Jer 5:9
shall not my soul be *a* on such a............ Jer 5:29
shall not my soul be *a* on such a.............. Jer 9:9
*a* him that was oppressed, and............. Acts 7:24
for God hath *a* you on her...................... Rev 18:20
hath *a* the blood of his servants............. Rev 19:2

**AVENGER**
you cities for refuge from the *a*.......... Num 35:12
Lest the *a* of the blood pursue.............. Deut 19:6
into the hand of the *a* of blood........... Deut 19:12
your refuge from the *a* of blood.......... Josh 20:3
if the *a* of blood pursue after............... Josh 20:5
die by the hand of the *a* of blood.......... Josh 20:9
mightest still the enemy and the *a*............ Ps 8:2
by reason of the enemy and *a*................ Ps 44:16
the Lord is the *a* of all such..................... 1Th 4:6

**AVENGETH**
It is God that *a* me, and that................ 2Sa 22:48
It is God that *a* me, and subdueth.......... Ps 18:47

**AVENGING**
ye the LORD for the *a* of Israel............... Judg 5:2
from *a* thyself with thine own.............. 1Sa 25:26
from *a* myself with mine own hand..... 1Sa 25:33

**AVERSE**
by securely as men *a* from war............... Mic 2:8

**AVIM** (*a'-vim*) See AVIMS, AVITES. *A city near Bethel.*
And *A*, and Parah, and Ophrah,.......... Josh 18:23

**AVIMS** (*a'-vims*) See AVIM. *A Canaanite tribe.*
the *A* which dwelt in Hazerim,............ Deut 2:23

**AVITES** (*a'-vites*) See AVIM.
*1. Same as Avims.*
and the Ekronites; also the *A*............... Josh 13:3
*2. A tribe moved to Samaria.*
the *A* made Nibhaz and Tartak, and. 2Kin 17:31

**AVITH** (*a'-vith*) *Capital of Edom.*
and the name of his city was *A*............ Gen 36:35
and the name of his city was *A*........... 1Chr 1:46

**AVOID**
*A* it, pass not by it, turn from.............. Prov 4:15
and *a* them............................................... Rom 16:17
to *a* fornication, let every man.............. 1Cor 7:2
foolish and unlearned questions *a*.......... 2Ti 2:23
But *a* foolish questions, and................... Titus 3:9

**AVOIDED**
David *a* out of his presence twice......... 1Sa 18:11

**AVOIDING**
*A* this, that no man should blame........ 2Cor 8:20
*a* profane and vain babblings, and.......... 1Ti 6:20

**AVOUCHED**
Thou hast *a* the LORD this day to...... Deut 26:17
the LORD hath *a* thee this day to....... Deut 26:18

**AVVA** See AVA.

**AVVIM** See AVITES.

**AWAIT**
But their laying *a* was known of.......... Acts 9:24

**AWAKE**
*A*, *a*, Deborah............................................ Judg 5:12
*a*, *a*, utter a song........................................ Judg 5:12
surely now he would *a* for thee.................. Job 8:6
be no more, they shall not *a*.................... Job 14:12
*a* for me to the judgment that...................... Ps 7:6
I shall be satisfied, when I *a*.................... Ps 17:15
*a* to my judgment, even unto my............ Ps 35:23
*A*, why sleepest thou, O Lord................. Ps 44:23
*A* up, my glory.............................................. Ps 57:8
*a*, psaltery and harp..................................... Ps 57:8
I myself will *a* early...................................... Ps 57:8
*a* to help me, and behold.............................. Ps 59:4
*A* to visit all the heathen............................. Ps 59:5
*A*, psaltery and harp.................................... Ps 108:2
I myself will *a* early.................................... Ps 108:2
when I *a*, I am still with thee................ Ps 139:18
when shall I *a*............................................ Prov 23:35
nor *a* my love, till he please..................... Song 2:7
nor *a* my love, till he please..................... Song 3:5
*A*, O north wind.......................................... Song 4:16
nor *a* my love, until he please................. Song 8:4
*A* and sing, ye that dwell in dust............. Is 26:19
*A*, *a*, put on strength, O arm........................ Is 51:9
*a*, as in the ancient days, in the.................. Is 51:9
*A*, *a*, stand up, O Jerusalem,..................... Is 51:17
*A*, *a*; put on thy strength............................. Is 52:1
in the dust of the earth shall *a*................. Dan 12:2
*A*, ye drunkards, and weep....................... Joel 1:5
*a* that shall vex thee, and thou.................. Hab 2:7
him that saith to the wood, *A*................... Hab 2:19
*A*, O sword, against my shepherd,.......... Zec 13:7
and they *a* him, and say unto him,.......... Mk 4:38
and when they were *a*, they saw his......... Lk 9:32
that I may *a* him out of sleep.................... Jn 11:11
it is high time to *a* out of sleep.............. Rom 13:11
*A* to righteousness, and sin not............ 1Cor 15:34
*A* thou that sleepest, and arise.................. Eph 5:14

**AWAKED**
Jacob *a* out of his sleep, and he........... Gen 28:16
he *a* out of his sleep, and went............ Judg 16:14
saw it, nor knew it, neither *a*............... 1Sa 26:12
he sleepeth, and must be *a*.................... 1Kin 18:27
him, saying, The child is not *a*.............. 2Kin 4:31
I *a*; for the LORD sustained me....................... Ps 3:5
Then the Lord *a* as one out of................ Ps 78:65
Upon this I *a*, and beheld........................ Jer 31:26

**AWAKEST**
so, O Lord, when thou *a*, thou................. Ps 73:20
and when thou *a*, it shall talk................. Prov 6:22

**AWAKETH**
As a dream when one *a*.............................. Ps 73:20
but he *a*, and his soul is empty................... Is 29:8
but he *a*, and, behold, he is faint............... Is 29:8

**AWAKING**
of the prison *a* out of his sleep........... Acts 16:27

**AWARE**
Or ever I was *a*, my soul made me...... Song 6:12
O Babylon, and thou wast not *a*............ Jer 50:24
and in an hour that he is not *a* of......... Mt 24:50
walk over them are not *a* of them.......... Lk 11:44
and at an hour when he is not *a*............ Lk 12:46

**AWAY** See PREFACE.

**AWE**
Stand in *a*, and sin not................................... Ps 4:4
of the world stand in *a* of him.................. Ps 33:8
heart standeth in *a* of thy word............ Ps 119:161

**AWOKE**
Noah *a* from his wine, and knew........... Gen 9:24
So Pharaoh *a*............................................... Gen 41:4
And Pharaoh *a*, and, behold, it was...... Gen 41:7
So I *a*........................................................ Gen 41:21
he *a* out of his sleep, and said, I........... Judg 16:20
And Solomon *a*............................................ 1Kin 3:15
*a* him, saying, Lord, save us....................... Mt 8:25
*a* him, saying, Master, master, we.......... Lk 8:24

**AX**
by forcing an *a* against them.............. Deut 20:19
share, and his coulter, and his *a*.......... 1Sa 13:20
the *a* head fell into the water.................. 2Kin 6:5
Shall the *a* boast itself against............... Is 10:15
hands of the workman, with the *a*........... Jer 10:3
Thou art my battle *a* and weapons....... Jer 51:20
now also the *a* is laid unto the................. Mt 3:10

**AXE**
with the *a* to cut down the tree.......... Deut 19:5
Abimelech took an *a* in his hand........... Judg 9:48
there was neither hammer nor *a*............. 1Kin 6:7
now also the *a* is laid unto the.................... Lk 3:9

**AXES**
and for the forks, and for the *a*............ 1Sa 13:21
under *a* of iron, and made them............ 2Sa 12:31
with harrows of iron, and with *a*......... 1Chr 20:3
lifted up *a* upon the thick trees................ Ps 74:5
work thereof at once with *a*...................... Ps 74:6
army, and come against her with *a*...... Jer 46:22
with his *a* he shall break down.............. Eze 26:9

**AXLETREES**
the *a* of the wheels were joined........... 1Kin 7:32
their *a*, and their naves, and their........ 1Kin 7:33

**AZAL** (*a'-zal*) *A place near Jerusalem.*
the mountains shall reach unto *A*......... Zec 14:5

**AZALIAH** (*az-a-li'-ah*) *Father of Shaphan.*
king sent Shaphan the son of *A*........... 2Kin 22:3
he sent Shaphan the son of *A*............... 2Chr 34:8

**AZANIAH** (*az-a-ni'-ah*) *Father of Jeshua.*
both Jeshua the son of *A*, Binnui.......... Neh 10:9

**AZARAEL** (*a-zar'-a-el*) See AZAREEL. *A priest from the Immer family.*
And his brethren, Shemaiah, and *A*.... Neh 12:36

**AZAREEL** (*a-zar'-e-el*) See AZARAEL.
*1. A Korahite in David's army.*
Elkanah, and Jesiah, and *A*, and.......... 1Chr 12:6
*2. A priest during David's time.*
The eleventh to *A*, he, his sons,......... 1Chr 25:18
*3. A Danite prince during David's time.*
Of Dan, *A* the son of Jeroham.............. 1Chr 27:22
*4. Married a foreign wife in exile.*
*A*, and Shelemiah, Shemariah,............... Ezr 10:41
*5. Same as Azarael.*
and Amashai the son of *A*, the son..... Neh 11:13

**AZAREL** See AZAREEL.

**AZARIAH** (*az-a-ri'-ah*) See AHAZIAH.
*1. A descendant of Zadok.*
*A* the son of Zadok the priest,............... 1Kin 4:2
*2. Captain of Solomon's guard.*
*A* the son of Nathan was over the........... 1Kin 4:5
*3. A king of Judah.*
And all the people of Judah took *A*... 2Kin 14:21
Jeroboam king of Israel began *A*........ 2Kin 15:1
And the rest of the acts of *A*............... 2Kin 15:6
So *A* slept with his fathers..................... 2Kin 15:7
eighth year of *A* king of Judah.............. 2Kin 15:8
thirtieth year of *A* king of Judah....... 2Kin 15:17
In the fiftieth year of *A* king of.......... 2Kin 15:23
fiftieth year of *A* king of Judah.......... 2Kin 15:27
*A* his son, Jotham his son,..................... 1Chr 3:12
*4. A descendant of Judah.*
*A*................................................................ 1Chr 2:8
*5. A descendant of Jerahmeel.*
Obed begat Jehu, and Jehu begat *A*.... 1Chr 2:38
*A* begat Helez, and Helez begat............ 1Chr 2:39
*6. A son of Ahimaaz.*
And Ahimaaz begat *A*, and Azariah...... 1Chr 6:9
*7. Grandson of Ahimaah.*

And Johanan begat *A*, (he it is............ 1Chr 6:10
*A* begat Amariah, and Amariah begat 1Chr 6:11
*8. A son of Hilkiah.*
begat Hilkiah, and Hilkiah begat *A*..... 1Chr 6:13
*A* begat Seraiah, and Seraiah begat..... 1Chr 6:14
*A* the son of Hilkiah, the son of.......... 1Chr 9:11
the son of Seraiah, the son of *A*.............. Ezr 7:1
*9. A descendant of Kohath.*
the son of Joel, the son of *A*................. 1Chr 6:36
*10. A prophet sent to King Asa.*
God came upon *A* the son of Oded..... 2Chr 15:1
*11. A son of King Jehoshaphat.*
the sons of Jehoshaphat, *A*.................. 2Chr 21:2
*12. A brother of King Jehoram.*
and Jehiel, and Zechariah, and *A*......... 2Chr 21:2
*13. A son of King Jehoram.*
*A* the son of Jehoram king of.............. 2Chr 22:6
*14. A conspirator with Joash.*
*A* the son of Jeroham, and Ishmael..... 2Chr 23:1
*15. Another conspirator with Joash.*
*A* the son of Obed, and Maaseiah........ 2Chr 23:1
*16. A High Priest.*
*A* the priest went in after him,.......... 2Chr 26:17
*A* the chief priest, and all the............. 2Chr 26:20
*17. A chief of Ephraim.*
*A* the son of Johanan, Berechiah....... 2Chr 28:12
*18. Father of Joel.*
of Amasai, and Joel the son of *A*....... 2Chr 29:12
*19. Helped cleanse the Temple.*
Abdi, and *A* the son of Jehalelel......... 2Chr 29:12
*20. A chief priest.*
*A* the chief priest of the house........... 2Chr 31:10
*A* the ruler of the house of God......... 2Chr 31:13
*21. Great-grandfather of Zadok.*
The son of Amariah, the son of *A*........ Ezr 7:3
*22. A repairer of the Jerusalem walls.*
After him repaired *A* the son of............ Neh 3:23
from the house of *A* unto the............... Neh 3:24
*23. An exile with Zerubbabel.*
Zerubbabel, Jeshua, Nehemiah, *A*.......... Neh 7:7
*24. A priest with Ezra.*
Hodijah, Maaseiah, Kelita, *A*.................. Neh 8:7
*25. A priest who renewed the covenant.*
Seraiah, *A*, Jeremiah,............................. Neh 10:2
*26. A prince of Judah.*
And *A*, Ezra, and Meshullam,............... Neh 12:33
*27. The son of Hoshaiah.*
Then spake *A* the son of Hoshaiah,........ Jer 43:2
*28. A companion of Daniel.*
Daniel, Hananiah, Mishael, and *A*.......... Dan 1:6
and to *A*, of Abed-nego......................... Dan 1:7
Daniel, Hananiah, Mishael, and *A*.......... Dan 1:11
Daniel, Hananiah, Mishael, and *A*.......... Dan 1:19
known to Hananiah, Mishael, and *A*.... Dan 2:17

**AZARYAHU** See AZARIAH.

**AZAZ** (*a'-zaz*) *Father of Bela.*
And Bela the son of *A*, the son of.......... 1Chr 5:8

**AZAZIAH** (*az-a-zi'-ah*)
*1. A Levite who relocated the Ark.*
and Obed-edom, and Jeiel, and *A*....... 1Chr 15:21
*2. Father of Hoshea.*
of Ephraim, Hoshea the son of *A*........ 1Chr 27:20
*3. A Levite during Hezekiah's reign.*
And Jehiel, and *A*, and Nahath, and.. 2Chr 31:13

**AZBUK** (*az'-buk*) *Father of Nehemiah.*
repaired Nehemiah the son of *A*........... Neh 3:16

**AZEKAH** (*a-ze'-kah*) *A town in Judah.*
to Beth-horon, and smote them to *A*. Josh 10:10
from heaven upon them unto *A*........... Josh 10:11
Jarmuth, and Adullam, Socoh, and *A* Josh 15:35
and pitched between Shochoh and *A*.... 1Sa 17:1
And Adoraim, and Lachish, and *A*....... 2Chr 11:9
and the fields thereof, at *A*................. Neh 11:30
against Lachish, and against *A*............ Jer 34:7

**AZEL** (*a'-zel*) See JAAZIEL. *A descendant of King Saul.*
son, Eleasah his son, *A* his son............ 1Chr 8:37
*A* had six sons, whose names are......... 1Chr 8:38
All these were the sons of *A*................ 1Chr 8:38
son, Eleasah his son, *A* his son............ 1Chr 9:43
*A* had six sons, whose names are.......... 1Chr 9:44
these were the sons of *A*...................... 1Chr 9:44

**AZEM** (*a'-zem*) See EZEM. *A city in Judah.*
Baalah, and Iim, and *A*,...................... Josh 15:29
And Hazar-shual, and Balah, and *A*..... Josh 19:3

**AZGAD** (*az'-gad*)
*1. A family of exiles.*
The children of *A*, a thousand two......... Ezr 2:12
The children of *A*, two thousand............ Neh 7:17
*2. An exile with Ezra.*
And of the sons of *A*............................. Ezr 8:12
*3. A family who sealed the covenant.*
Bunni, *A*, Bebai,.................................. Neh 10:15

**AZIEL** (*a'-ze-el*) *A Levite who relocated the Ark.*
And Zechariah, and *A*, and................. 1Chr 15:20

**AZIZA** (*a-zi'-zah*) *Married a foreigner in exile.*
and Jeremoth, and Zabad, and *A*.......... Ezr 10:27

**AZMAVETH** (*az-ma'-veth*) See BETH-AZMAVETH.
*1. A 'mighty man' of David.*
the Arbathite, *A* the Barhumite,........... 2Sa 23:31
*A* the Baharumite, Eliahba the........... 1Chr 11:33
*2. A descendant of Jonathan.*
and Jehoadah begat Alemeth, and *A*.. 1Chr 8:36
and Jarah begat Alemeth, and *A*........... 1Chr 9:42
*3. Father of Jeziel and Pelet.*
Jeziel, and Pelet, the sons of *A*............ 1Chr 12:3
*4. A village on the border of Judah.*
The children of *A*, forty and two.......... Ezr 2:24
and out of the fields of Geba and *A*.... Neh 12:29
*5. A treasurer of David.*
treasures was *A* the son of Adiel....... 1Chr 27:25

**AZMON** (*az'-mon*) See HESHMON. *A place in southern Canaan.*
to Hazar-addar, and pass on to *A*........ Num 34:4
from *A* unto the river of Egypt............ Num 34:5
From thence it passed toward *A*.......... Josh 15:4

**AZNOTH-TABOR** (*az''-noth-ta'-bor*) *Hills on the border of Naphtali.*
the coast turneth westward to *A*........ Josh 19:34

**AZOR** (*a'-zor*) *Great-grandson of Zorobabel.*
and Eliakim begat *A*.............................. Mt 1:13
And *A* begat Sadoc................................ Mt 1:14

**AZOTUS** (*a-zo'-tus*) See ASHDOD. *Greek form of Ashdod.*
But Philip was found at *A*..................... Acts 8:40

**AZRIEL** (*az'-re-el*)
*1. Chief of a family of Manasseh.*
Epher, and Ishi, and Eliel, and *A*.......... 1Chr 5:24
*2. Father of Jerimoth*
Naphtali, Jerimoth the son of *A*......... 1Chr 27:19
*3. Father of Seraiah.*
and Seraiah the son of *A*, and.............. Jer 36:26

**AZRIKAM** (*az'-ri-kam*)
*1. A son of Neariah.*
Elioenai, and Hezekiah, and *A*............. 1Chr 3:23
*2. A son of Azel.*
sons, whose names are these, *A*.......... 1Chr 8:38
sons, whose names are these, *A*.......... 1Chr 9:44
*3. A descendant of Merari.*
the son of Hasshub, the son of *A*.......... 1Chr 9:14
the son of Hashub, the son of *A*.......... Neh 11:15
*4. Governor of the house of King Ahaz.*
*A* the governor of the house, and........ 2Chr 28:7

**AZUBAH** (*a-zu'-bah*)
*1. Mother of King Jehoshaphat.*
his mother's name was *A* the............. 1Kin 22:42
his mother's name was *A* the............. 2Chr 20:31
*2. Wife of Caleb.*
begat children of *A* his wife................ 1Chr 2:18
when *A* was dead, Caleb took unto..... 1Chr 2:19

**AZUR** (*a'-zur*) See AZZUR.
*1. Father of Hananiah.*
Hananiah the son of *A* the prophet........ Jer 28:1
*2. Father of Jaazaniah.*
whom I saw Jaazaniah the son of *A*..... Eze 11:1

**AZZAH** (*az'-zah*) See GAZA. *A Philistine city.*
dwelt in Hazerim, even unto *A*............ Deut 2:23
the river, from Tiphsah even to *A*........ 1Kin 4:24
Philistines, and Ashkelon, and *A*.......... Jer 25:20

**AZZAN** (*az'-zan*) *A prince of Issachar.*
of Issachar, Paltiel the son of *A*.......... Num 34:26

**AZZUR** (*az'-zur*) *An Israelite who sealed the covenant under Nehemiah.*
Ater, Hizkijah, *A*,................................. Neh 10:17

# B

**BAAL** (*ba'-al*) See BAAL-BERITH, BAALE, BAAL-GAD, BAAL-HAMON, BAAL-HANAN, BAAL-HAZOR, BAAL-HERMON, BAALIM, BAAL-MEON, BAAL-PEOR, BAAL-PERAZIM, , BAAL-SHALISHA, BAAL-TAMAR.
*1. Chief god of the Canaanites.*
him up into the high places of *B*........ Num 22:41
forsook the LORD, and served *B*............ Judg 2:13
altar of *B* that thy father hath............ Judg 6:25
the altar of *B* was cast down, and........ Judg 6:28
he hath cast down the altar of *B*.......... Judg 6:30
against him, Will ye plead for *B*.......... Judg 6:31
Let *B* plead against him, because.......... Judg 6:32
Zidonians, and went and served *B*..... 1Kin 16:31
altar for *B* in the house of *B*.............. 1Kin 16:32
and the prophets of *B* four hundred.. 1Kin 18:19
but if *B*, then follow him.................... 1Kin 18:21
said unto the prophets of *B*................ 1Kin 18:25
called on the name of *B* from............. 1Kin 18:26
even until noon, saying, O *B*.............. 1Kin 18:26
unto them, Take the prophets of *B*...... 1Kin 18:40
knees which have not bowed unto *B* 1Kin 19:18
For he served *B*, and worshipped....... 1Kin 22:53
of *B* that his father had made.................. 2Kin 3:2
unto them, Ahab served *B* a little....... 2Kin 10:18
unto me all the prophets of *B*............ 2Kin 10:19
have a great sacrifice to do to *B*......... 2Kin 10:19
destroy the worshippers of *B*.............. 2Kin 10:19
Proclaim a solemn assembly for *B*...... 2Kin 10:20
and all the worshippers of *B* came...... 2Kin 10:21
And they came into the house of *B*.... 2Kin 10:21
the house of *B* was full from one....... 2Kin 10:21
for all the worshippers of *B*................ 2Kin 10:22
of Rechab, into the house of *B*........... 2Kin 10:23
and said unto the worshippers of *B*... 2Kin 10:23
but the worshippers of *B* only............. 2Kin 10:23
to the city of the house of *B*.............. 2Kin 10:25
the images out of the house of *B*....... 2Kin 10:26
brake down the image of *B*................. 2Kin 10:27
and brake down the house of *B*.......... 2Kin 10:27
Jehu destroyed *B* out of Israel............ 2Kin 10:28
the land went into the house of *B*...... 2Kin 11:18
the priest of *B* before the altars......... 2Kin 11:18
the host of heaven, and served *B*....... 2Kin 17:16
and he reared up altars for *B*.............. 2Kin 21:3
the vessels that were made for *B*......... 2Kin 23:4
also that burned incense unto *B*.......... 2Kin 23:5
the people went to the house of *B*..... 2Chr 23:17
the priest of *B* before the altars.......... 2Chr 23:17
and the prophets prophesied by *B*........ Jer 2:8
falsely, and burn incense unto *B*............. Jer 7:9
altars to burn incense unto *B*............... Jer 11:13
anger in offering incense unto *B*......... Jer 11:17
taught my people to swear by *B*........... Jer 12:16
built also the high places of *B*.............. Jer 19:5
fire for burnt offerings unto *B*.............. Jer 19:5
they prophesied in *B*, and caused.......... Jer 23:13
have forgotten my name for *B*.............. Jer 23:27
they have offered incense unto *B*......... Jer 32:29
they built the high places of *B*............ Jer 32:35
gold, which they prepared for *B*.............. Hos 2:8
but when he offended in *B*................... Hos 13:1
the remnant of *B* from this place........... Zeph 1:4
bowed the knee to the image of *B*...... Rom 11:4
*2. A city in Simeon.*
about the same cities, unto *B*.............. 1Chr 4:33
*3. A descendant of Reuben.*
son, Reaia his son, *B* his son,............... 1Chr 5:5
*4. A descendant of Benjamin.*
son Abdon, and Zur, and Kish, and *B*. 1Chr 8:30
Abdon, then Zur, and Kish, and *B*...... 1Chr 9:36

**BAALAH** (*ba'-al-ah*) See BAALE, BALEH, BILHAH, KIRJATH-BAAL.
*1. A city in Judah.*
and the border was drawn to *B*............ Josh 15:9
from *B* westward unto mount Seir..... Josh 15:10
*B*, and Iim, and Azem........................ Josh 15:29
went up, and all Israel, to *B*............... 1Chr 13:6
*2. A hill in Judah.*
and passed along to mount *B*.............. Josh 15:11

**BAALATH** (*ba'-al-ath*) See BAALATH-BEER. *A town in Dan.*
And Eltekeh, and Gibbethon, and *B*... Josh 19:44
And *B*, and Tadmor in the wilderness. 1Kin 9:18
And *B*, and all the store cities.............. 2Chr 8:6

**BAALATH-BEER** (*ba''-al-ath-be'-ur*) *A city in Simeon.*
round about these cities to *B*................ Josh 19:8

**BAAL-BERITH** (*ba''-al-be'-rith*) *An idol.*
after Baalim, and made *B* their god..... Judg 8:33
of silver out of the house of *B*............. Judg 9:4

**BAALE** (*ba'-al-eh*) *A form of Baalah.*
were with him from *B* of Judah............ 2Sa 6:2

**BAALE-JUDAH** See BAALE.

**BAAL-GAD** (*ba''-al-gad'*) *A Canaanite city.*
even unto *B* in the valley of................ Josh 11:17
from *B* in the valley of Lebanon........... Josh 12:7
from *B* under mount Hermon unto...... Josh 13:5

**BAAL-HAMON** (*ba''-al-ha'-mon*) *A place near Samaria.*
Solomon had a vineyard at *B*.............. Song 8:11

**BAAL-HANAN** (*ba'-al-ha'-nan*)
*1. A king of Edom.*
*B* the son of Achbor reigned in............ Gen 36:38
*B* the son of Achbor died, and............. Gen 36:39
*B* the son of Achbor reigned in............ 1Chr 1:49
when *B* was dead, Hadad reigned in... 1Chr 1:50
*2. A superintendent for David.*
the low plains was *B* the Gederite..... 1Chr 27:28

**BAAL-HAZOR** (*ba''-al-ha'-zor*) See HAZOR. *A place near Ephraim.*
Absalom had sheepshearers in *B*.......... 2Sa 13:23

**BAAL-HERMON** (*ba''-al-her'-mon*) *A city near Mt. Hermon.*
from mount *B* unto the entering in....... Judg 3:3
they increased from Bashan unto *B*.... 1Chr 5:23

**BAALI** (*ba'-al-i*) *A rejected title of God.*
and shalt call me no more *B*................... Hos 2:16

**BAALIM** (*ba'-al-im*) See BAAL. *Plural of Baal.*
sight of the LORD, and served *B*........... Judg 2:11
the LORD their God, and served *B*........ Judg 3:7
again, and went a whoring after *B*...... Judg 8:33
sight of the LORD, and served *B*........... Judg 10:6
our God, and also served *B*................... Judg 10:10
children of Israel did put away *B*............ 1Sa 7:4
the LORD, and have served *B*.............. 1Sa 12:10
the LORD, and thou hast followed *B*.. 1Kin 18:18
David, and sought not unto *B*............. 2Chr 17:3
the LORD did they bestow upon *B*........ 2Chr 24:7
and made also molten images for *B*..... 2Chr 28:2
and he reared up altars for *B*.............. 2Chr 33:3
the altars of *B* in his presence.............. 2Chr 34:4
polluted, I have not gone after *B*.......... Jer 2:23
of their own heart, and after *B*.............. Jer 9:14
will visit upon her the days of *B*............ Hos 2:13
the names of *B* out of her mouth.......... Hos 2:17
they sacrificed unto *B*, and burned........ Hos 11:2

**BAALIS** (*ba'-al-is*) *A king of the Ammonites.*
Dost thou certainly know that B.......... Jer 40:14

**BAAL-MEON** (*ba''-al-me'-on*) See BETH-BAAL-MEON. *A Reubenite town.*
Nebo, and B, (their names.................. Num 32:38
in Aroer, even unto Nebo and B............. 1Chr 5:8
of the country, Beth-jeshimoth, B.......... Eze 25:9

**BAAL-PEOR** (*ba''-al-pe'-or*) See PEOR. *A Moabite idol.*
And Israel joined himself unto B......... Num 25:3
his men that were joined unto B.......... Num 25:5
what the LORD did because of B............ Deut 4:3
for all the men that followed B.............. Deut 4:3
joined themselves also unto B............... Ps 106:28
but they went to B, and separated......... Hos 9:10

**BAAL-PERAZIM** (*ba''-al-per'-a-zim*) *A place near the valley of Rephaim.*
And David came to B, and David........... 2Sa 5:20
called the name of that place B............. 2Sa 5:20
So they came up to B.......................... 1Chr 14:11
called the name of that place B.......... 1Chr 14:11

**BAAL'S** (*ba'-als*)
but B prophets are four hundred........ 1Kin 18:22

**BAAL-SHALISHA** (*ba''-al-shal'-i-shah*) *A place in Ephraim*
And there came a man from B.............. 2Kin 4:42

**BAAL-TAMAR** (*ba''-al-ta'-mar*) *A place in Benjamin.*
and put themselves in array at B....... Judg 20:33

**BAAL-ZEBUB** (*ba''-al-ze'-bub*) See BEELZEBUB. *A Philistine idol.*
enquire of B the god of Ekron ............... 2Kin 1:2
to enquire of B the god of Ekron........... 2Kin 1:3
to enquire of B the god of Ekron........... 2Kin 1:6
to enquire of B the god of Ekron........ 2Kin 1:16

**BAAL-ZEPHON** (*ba''-al-ze'-fon*) *A place near the Rea Sea crossing.*
Migdol and the sea, over against B.......... Ex 14:2
sea, beside Pi-hahiroth, before B............. Ex 14:9
Pi-hahiroth, which is before B............. Num 33:7

**BAANA** (*ba'-an-ah*) See BAANAH.
*1. An officer in Solomon's army.*
B the son of Ahilud................................ 1Kin 4:12
*2. Father of Zadok.*
them repaired Zadok the son of B.......... Neh 3:4

**BAANAH** (*ba'-an-ah*) See BAANA.
*1. A captain in Ishbosheth's army.*
the name of the one was B........................ 2Sa 4:2
the Beerothite, Rechab and B.................. 2Sa 4:5
Rechab and B his brother escaped............ 2Sa 4:6
B his brother, the sons of Rimmon........... 2Sa 4:9
*2. Father of Heleb.*
Heleb the son of B, a................................ 2Sa 23:29
the son of B the Netophathite............ 1Chr 11:30
*3. An officer in Solomon's army.*
B the son of Hushai was in Asher......... 1Kin 4:16
*4. An exile who returned with Zerubbabel.*
Bilshan, Mizpar, Bigvai, Rehum, B........... Ezr 2:2
Mispereth, Bigvai, Nehum, B.................. Neh 7:7
Malluch, Harim, B................................. Neh 10:27

**BAARA** (*ba'-ar-ah*) *A wife of Shaharaim.*
Hushim and B were his wives.................. 1Chr 8:8

**BAASEIAH** (*ba-as-i'-ah*) *A Gersonite Levite.*
The son of Michael, the son of B.......... 1Chr 6:40

**BAASHA** (*ba'-ash-ah*) *A king of Israel.*
B king of Israel all their days............. 1Kin 15:16
B king of Israel went up against........ 1Kin 15:17
thy league with B king of Israel.......... 1Kin 15:19
when B heard thereof, that he............ 1Kin 15:21
thereof, wherewith B had builded...... 1Kin 15:22
B the son of Ahijah, of the house....... 1Kin 15:27
B smote him at Gibbethon, which...... 1Kin 15:27
Asa king of Judah did B slay him....... 1Kin 15:28
B king of Israel all their days............ 1Kin 15:32
B the son of Ahijah to reign over...... 1Kin 15:33
Jehu the son of Hanani against B........ 1Kin 16:1
will take away the posterity of B.......... 1Kin 16:3
Him that dieth of B in the city............. 1Kin 16:4
Now the rest of the acts of B................ 1Kin 16:5
So B slept with his fathers, and........... 1Kin 16:6
the word of the LORD against B........... 1Kin 16:7
B to reign over Israel in Tirzah............ 1Kin 16:8
that he slew all the house of B.......... 1Kin 16:11
Zimri destroy all the house of B........ 1Kin 16:12
against B by Jehu the prophet............ 1Kin 16:12
For all the sins of B, and the............. 1Kin 16:13
the house of B the son of Ahijah...... 1Kin 21:22
the house of B the son of Ahijah............ 2Kin 9:9
year of the reign of Asa B king........... 2Chr 16:1
thy league with B king of Israel........... 2Chr 16:3
when B heard it, that he left off.......... 2Chr 16:5
thereof, wherewith B was building...... 2Chr 16:6
made for fear of B king of Israel............ Jer 41:9

**BABBLER**
and a b is no better............................ Eccl 10:11
some said, What will this b say........... Acts 17:18

**BABBLING**
who hath b........................................... Prov 23:29

**BABBLINGS**
trust, avoiding profane and vain b.......... 1Ti 6:20
But shun profane and vain b................. 2Ti 2:16

**BABE**
and, behold, the b wept................................ Ex 2:6
of Mary, the b leaped in her womb.......... Lk 1:41
the b leaped in my womb for joy............. Lk 1:44
Ye shall find the b wrapped in................ Lk 2:12
and the b lying in a manger.................... Lk 2:16
for he is a b.......................................... Heb 5:13

**BABEL** (*ba'-bel*) See BABYLON. *A city in the plain of Shinar.*
beginning of his kingdom was B.......... Gen 10:10
is the name of it called B........................ Gen 11:9

**BABES**
Out of the mouth of b and........................... Ps 8:2
of their substance to their b................... Ps 17:14
and b shall rule over them............................ Is 3:4
and hast revealed them unto b.............. Mt 11:25
never read, Out of the mouth of b......... Mt 21:16
and hast revealed them unto b.............. Lk 10:21
of the foolish, a teacher of b............... Rom 2:20
carnal, even as unto b in Christ............ 1Cor 3:1
As newborn b, desire the sincere........... 1Pet 2:2

**BABYLON** (*bab'-il-un*) See BABEL, BABYLONIANS, BABYLONISH, BABYLON'S, CHALDEA, SHESHACH. *Capital of the Babylonian Empire; located on the Euphrates River.*
of Assyria brought men from B.......... 2Kin 17:24
the men of B made Succoth-benoth,. 2Kin 17:30
the son of Baladan, king of B.............. 2Kin 20:12
from a far country, even from B.......... 2Kin 20:14
this day, shall be carried into B.......... 2Kin 20:17
in the palace of the king of B.............. 2Kin 20:18
Nebuchadnezzar king of B came up.... 2Kin 24:1
for the king of B had taken from.......... 2Kin 24:7
of B came up against Jerusalem......... 2Kin 24:10
king of B came against the city.......... 2Kin 24:11
Judah went out to the king of B......... 2Kin 24:12
the king of B took him in the............. 2Kin 24:12
he carried away Jehoiachin to B......... 2Kin 24:15
captivity from Jerusalem to B............ 2Kin 24:15
of B brought captive to B.................. 2Kin 24:16
the king of B made Mattaniah his...... 2Kin 24:17
rebelled against the king of B............ 2Kin 24:20
Nebuchadnezzar king of B came........... 2Kin 25:1
him up to the king of B to Riblah........ 2Kin 25:6
of brass, and carried him to B............. 2Kin 25:7
of king Nebuchadnezzar king of B....... 2Kin 25:8
guard, a servant of the king of B........ 2Kin 25:8
that fell away to the king of B............ 2Kin 25:11
and carried the brass of them to B.... 2Kin 25:13
them to the king of B to Riblah.......... 2Kin 25:20
And the king of B smote them............ 2Kin 25:21
Nebuchadnezzar king of B had left.... 2Kin 25:22
heard that the king of B had made...... 2Kin 25:23
the land, and serve the king of B...... 2Kin 25:24
that Evil-merodach king of B in.......... 2Kin 25:27
the kings that were with him in B..... 2Kin 25:28
away to B for their transgression........... 1Chr 9:1
ambassadors of the princes of B......... 2Chr 32:31
with fetters, and carried him to B....... 2Chr 33:11
came up Nebuchadnezzar king of B.... 2Chr 36:6
him in fetters, to carry him to B.......... 2Chr 36:6
of the house of the LORD to B.............. 2Chr 36:7
and put them in his temple at B........... 2Chr 36:7
sent, and brought him to B................. 2Chr 36:10
all these he brought to B.................... 2Chr 36:18
the sword carried he away to B.......... 2Chr 36:20
brought up from B unto Jerusalem........ Ezr 1:11
B had carried away unto B....................... Ezr 2:1
of Nebuchadnezzar the king of B........... Ezr 5:12
and carried the people away into B........ Ezr 5:12
of B the same king Cyrus made a........... Ezr 5:13
brought them into the temple of B.......... Ezr 5:14
king take out of the temple of B............ Ezr 5:14
house, which is there at B..................... Ezr 5:17
the treasures were laid up in B............... Ezr 6:1
at Jerusalem, and brought unto B........... Ezr 6:5
This Ezra went up from B.......................... Ezr 7:6
month began he to go up from B............... Ezr 7:9
find in all the province of B................... Ezr 7:16
them that went up with me from B............ Ezr 8:1
the king of B had carried away............... Neh 7:6
king of B came I unto the king............. Neh 13:6
the king of B had carried away.............. Est 2:6
Rahab and B to them that know me....... Ps 87:4
By the rivers of B, there we sat............ Ps 137:1
O daughter of B, who art to be............. Ps 137:8
The burden of B, which Isaiah the............ Is 13:1
And B, the glory of kingdoms, the.......... Is 13:19
proverb against the king of B.................. Is 14:4
hosts, and cut off from B the name........ Is 14:22
and said, B is fallen, is fallen................... Is 21:9
the son of Baladan, king of B.................... Is 39:1
far country unto me, even from B............... Is 39:3
this day, shall be carried to B................... Is 39:6
in the palace of the king of B.................. Is 39:7
For your sake I have sent to B............... Is 43:14
the dust, O virgin daughter of B................ Is 47:1
he will do his pleasure on B................... Is 48:14
Go ye forth of B, flee ye from.............. Is 48:20
into the hand of the king of B................ Jer 20:4
shall carry them captive into B.............. Jer 20:4
and take them, and carry them to B........ Jer 20:5
and thou shalt come to B, and there...... Jer 20:6
king of B maketh war against us........... Jer 21:2
ye fight against the king of B................ Jer 21:4
hand of Nebuchadrezzar king of B.......... Jer 21:7
into the hand of the king of B............... Jer 21:10
hand of Nebuchadrezzar king of B....... Jer 22:25
of B had carried away captive................. Jer 24:1
and had brought them to B.................... Jer 24:1
year of Nebuchadrezzar king of B.......... Jer 25:1
and Nebuchadrezzar the king of B.......... Jer 25:9
serve the king of B seventy years......... Jer 25:11
that I will punish the king of B............ Jer 25:12
of Nebuchadnezzar the king of B............ Jer 27:6
same Nebuchadnezzar the king of B...... Jer 27:8
under the yoke of the king of B.............. Jer 27:8
Ye shall not serve the king of B............. Jer 27:9
under the yoke of the king of B............ Jer 27:11
under the yoke of the king of B............ Jer 27:12
that will not serve the king of B.......... Jer 27:13
Ye shall not serve the king of B........... Jer 27:14
shortly be brought again from B........... Jer 27:16
serve the king of B, and live................ Jer 27:17
and at Jerusalem, go not to B.............. Jer 27:18
Nebuchadnezzar king of B took not...... Jer 27:20
king of Judah from Jerusalem to B....... Jer 27:20
They shall be carried to B................... Jer 27:22
broken the yoke of the king of B............ Jer 28:2
of B took away from this place.............. Jer 28:3
this place, and carried them to B........... Jer 28:3
of Judah, that went into B..................... Jer 28:4
break the yoke of the king of B.............. Jer 28:4
captive, from B into this place............... Jer 28:6
of B from the neck of all nations.......... Jer 28:11
serve Nebuchadnezzar king of B.......... Jer 28:14
away captive from Jerusalem to B........... Jer 29:1
king of Judah sent unto B to................. Jer 29:3
Nebuchadnezzar king of B) saying.......... Jer 29:3
away from Jerusalem unto B.................... Jer 29:4
at B I will visit you, and perform.......... Jer 29:10
hath raised us up prophets in B............ Jer 29:15
I have sent from Jerusalem to B........... Jer 29:20
hand of Nebuchadrezzar king of B......... Jer 29:21
captivity of Judah which are in B......... Jer 29:22
whom the king of B roasted in the....... Jer 29:22
therefore he sent unto us in B.............. Jer 29:28
into the hand of the king of B................ Jer 32:3
into the hand of the king of B................ Jer 32:4
And he shall lead Zedekiah to B............ Jer 32:5
hand of Nebuchadrezzar king of B....... Jer 32:28
of the king of B by the sword.............. Jer 32:36
when Nebuchadnezzar king of B............. Jer 34:1
into the hand of the king of B................ Jer 34:2
behold the eyes of the king of B............ Jer 34:3
to mouth, and thou shalt go to B............ Jer 34:3
king of B came up into the land............ Jer 35:11
The king of B shall certainly................. Jer 36:29
whom Nebuchadrezzar king of B.............. Jer 37:1
into the hand of the king of B.............. Jer 37:17
The king of B shall not come................ Jer 37:19
by the hand of the king of B................ Jer 38:23
came Nebuchadrezzar king of B.............. Jer 39:1
princes of the king of B came in............. Jer 39:3
of the princes o the king of B............... Jer 39:3
up to Nebuchadnezzar king of B to........ Jer 39:5
Then the king of B slew the sons........... Jer 39:6
also the king of B slew all the.............. Jer 39:6
with chains, to carry him to B.............. Jer 39:7
B the remnant of the people that........... Jer 39:9
Now Nebuchadrezzar king of B gave.... Jer 39:11
were carried away captive unto B.......... Jer 40:1
unto thee to come with me into B.......... Jer 40:4
unto thee to come with me into B......... Jer 40:4
whom the king of B hath made.............. Jer 40:5
heard that the king of B had made......... Jer 40:7
not carried away captive to B................. Jer 40:7
the land, and serve the king of B........... Jer 40:9
heard that the king of B had left.......... Jer 40:11
whom the king of B had made................ Jer 41:2
whom the king of B made governor..... Jer 41:18
Be not afraid of the king of B............... Jer 42:11
and carry us away captives into B.......... Jer 43:3
take Nebuchadrezzar the king of B...... Jer 43:10
hand of Nebuchadrezzar king of B........ Jer 44:30
of B smote in the fourth year of............. Jer 46:2
king of B should come and smite.......... Jer 46:13
hand of Nebuchadrezzar king of B........ Jer 46:26
king of B shall smite, thus saith.......... Jer 49:28
for Nebuchadrezzar king of B hath...... Jer 49:30
that the LORD spake against B................ Jer 50:1
B is taken, Bel is confounded,.............. Jer 50:2
Remove out of the midst of B................ Jer 50:8
cause to come up against B an............... Jer 50:9
goeth by B shall be astonished............. Jer 50:13
in array against B round about............. Jer 50:14
Cut off the sower from B, and him....... Jer 50:16
king of B hath broken his bones............. Jer 50:17
I will punish the king of B.................... Jer 50:18
how is B become a desolation............... Jer 50:23
thee, and thou art also taken, O B.......... Jer 50:24
and escape out of the land of B............ Jer 50:28
together the archers against B.............. Jer 50:29
and disquiet the inhabitants of B.......... Jer 50:34
and upon the inhabitants of B............... Jer 50:35
against thee, O daughter of B.............. Jer 50:42
The king of B hath heard the................ Jer 50:43
that he hath taken against B................. Jer 50:45
taking of B the earth is moved............. Jer 50:46
Behold, I will raise up against B............. Jer 51:1
And will send unto B fanners.................. Jer 51:2
Flee out of the midst of B....................... Jer 51:6
B hath been a golden cup in the.............. Jer 51:7
B is suddenly fallen and destroyed......... Jer 51:8
We would have healed B, but she.......... Jer 51:9
for his device is against B.................... Jer 51:11
the standard upon the walls of B........... Jer 51:12
against the inhabitants of B................. Jer 51:12

And I will render unto *B* and to all ... Jer 51:24
LORD shall be performed against *B* ... Jer 51:29
to make the land of *B* a ... Jer 51:29
The mighty men of *B* have forborn ... Jer 51:30
to shew the king of *B* that his ... Jer 51:31
The daughter of *B* is like a ... Jer 51:33
the king of *B* hath devoured me ... Jer 51:34
to me and to my flesh be upon *B* ... Jer 51:35
*B* shall become heaps, a dwelling ... Jer 51:37
how is *B* become an astonishment ... Jer 51:41
The sea is come up upon *B* ... Jer 51:42
And I will punish Bel in *B* ... Jer 51:44
yea, the wall of *B* shall fall ... Jer 51:44
upon the graven images of *B* ... Jer 51:47
that is therein, shall sing for *B* ... Jer 51:48
As *B* hath caused the slain of ... Jer 51:49
so at *B* shall fall the slain of ... Jer 51:49
Though *B* should mount up to ... Jer 51:53
A sound of a cry cometh from *B* ... Jer 51:54
Because the LORD hath spoiled *B* ... Jer 51:55
is come upon her, even upon *B* ... Jer 51:56
The broad walls of *B* shall be ... Jer 51:58
*B* in the fourth year of his reign ... Jer 51:59
the evil that should come upon *B* ... Jer 51:60
words that are written against *B* ... Jer 51:60
to Seraiah, When thou comest to *B* ... Jer 51:61
thou shalt say, Thus shall *B* sink ... Jer 51:64
rebelled against the king of *B* ... Jer 52:3
Nebuchadrezzar king of *B* came ... Jer 52:4
*B* to Riblah in the land of Hamath ... Jer 52:9
the king of *B* slew the sons of ... Jer 52:10
the king of *B* bound him in chains ... Jer 52:11
and carried him to *B* ... Jer 52:11
year of Nebuchadrezzar king of *B* ... Jer 52:12
guard, which served the king of *B* ... Jer 52:12
away, that fell to the king of *B* ... Jer 52:15
all the brass of them to *B* ... Jer 52:17
them to the king of *B* to Riblah ... Jer 52:26
And the king of *B* smote them ... Jer 52:27
that Evil-merodach king of *B* in ... Jer 52:31
the kings that were with him in *B* ... Jer 52:32
diet given him of the king of *B* ... Jer 52:34
I will bring him to *B* to the land ... Eze 12:13
Behold, the king of *B* is come to ... Eze 17:12
and led them with him to *B* ... Eze 17:12
in the midst of *B* he shall die ... Eze 17:16
snare, and I will bring him to *B* ... Eze 17:20
and brought him to the king of *B* ... Eze 19:9
sword of the king of *B* may come ... Eze 21:19
For the king of *B* stood at the ... Eze 21:21
the king of *B* set himself against ... Eze 24:2
Tyrus Nebuchadrezzar king of *B* ... Eze 26:7
Nebuchadrezzar king of *B* caused ... Eze 29:18
unto Nebuchadrezzar king of *B* ... Eze 29:19
hand of Nebuchadrezzar king of *B* ... Eze 30:10
the arms of the king of *B* ... Eze 30:24
the arms of the king of *B* ... Eze 30:25
into the hand of the king of *B* ... Eze 30:25
king of *B* shall come upon thee ... Eze 32:11
king of *B* unto Jerusalem, and ... Dan 1:1
to destroy all the wise men of *B* ... Dan 2:12
forth to slay the wise men of *B* ... Dan 2:14
the rest of the wise men of *B* ... Dan 2:18
to destroy the wise men of *B* ... Dan 2:24
Destroy not the wise men of *B* ... Dan 2:24
over the whole province of *B* ... Dan 2:48
over all the wise men of *B* ... Dan 2:48
the affairs of the province of *B* ... Dan 2:49
of Dura, in the province of *B* ... Dan 3:1
the affairs of the province of *B* ... Dan 3:12
Abed-nego, in the province of *B* ... Dan 3:30
all the wise men of *B* before me ... Dan 4:6
in the palace of the kingdom of *B* ... Dan 4:29
and said, Is not this great *B* ... Dan 4:30
and said to the wise men of *B* ... Dan 5:7
king of *B* Daniel had a dream ... Dan 7:1
field, and thou shalt go even to *B* ... Mic 4:10
dwellest with the daughter of *B* ... Zec 2:7
of Jedaiah, which are come from *B* ... Zec 6:10
time they were carried away to *B* ... Mt 1:11
And after they were brought to *B* ... Mt 1:12
into *B* are fourteen generations ... Mt 1:17
into *B* unto Christ are fourteen ... Mt 1:17
and I will carry you away beyond *B* ... Acts 7:43
The church that is at *B*, elected ... 1Pet 5:13
*B* is fallen, is fallen, that ... Rev 14:8
great *B* came in remembrance ... Rev 16:19
*B* THE GREAT, THE MOTHER OF ... Rev 17:5
*B* the great is fallen, is fallen, ... Rev 18:2
Alas, alas that great city *B* ... Rev 18:10
that great city *B* be thrown down ... Rev 18:21

**BABYLONIA** See BABYLONISH.

**BABYLONIAN** See CHALDEANS'.

**BABYLONIANS** (*bab-il-o'-ne-ans*) See CHALDEANS. *Inhabitants of Babylonia.*
Apharsites, the Archevites, the *B* ... Ezr 4:9
the manner of the *B* of Chaldea ... Eze 23:15
the *B* came to her into the bed of ... Eze 23:17
The *B*, and all the Chaldeans, ... Eze 23:23

**BABYLONISH** (*bab-il-o'-nish*) See BABYLONIANS.
the spoils a goodly *B* garment ... Josh 7:21

**BABYLON'S** (*bab'-il-ons*)
For then the king of *B* army ... Jer 32:2
When the king of *B* army fought ... Jer 34:7
the hand of the king of *B* army ... Jer 34:21
the hand of the king of *B* army ... Jer 38:3
forth unto the king of *B* princes ... Jer 38:17
go forth to the king of *B* princes ... Jer 38:18
forth to the king of *B* princes ... Jer 38:22
and all the king of *B* princes ... Jer 39:13

**BACA** (*ba'-cah*) *A valley near Jerusalem.*
the valley of *B* make it a well ... Ps 84:6

**BACHRITES** (*bak'-rites*) *Descendants of Becher.*
of Becher, the family of the *B* ... Num 26:35

**BACK**
he brought *b* all the goods, and ... Gen 14:16
And they said, Stand *b* ... Gen 19:9
his wife looked *b* from behind him ... Gen 19:26
to pass, as he drew *b* his hand ... Gen 38:29
neither hath he kept *b* any thing ... Gen 39:9
the LORD caused the sea to go *b* ... Ex 14:21
wife, after he had sent her *b* ... Ex 18:2
surely bring it *b* to him again ... Ex 23:4
and thou shalt see my *b* parts ... Ex 33:23
wherefore are we kept *b*, that we ... Num 9:7
brought *b* word unto them ... Num 13:26
thee, I will get me *b* again ... Num 22:34
LORD hath kept thee *b* from honour ... Num 24:11
dig therewith, and shalt turn *b* ... Deut 23:13
turned *b* upon the pursuers ... Josh 8:20
For Joshua drew not his hand *b* ... Josh 8:26
And Joshua at that time turned *b* ... Josh 11:10
Else if ye do in any wise go *b* ... Josh 23:12
unto the LORD, and I cannot go *b* ... Judg 11:35
turned and went *b* unto his house ... Judg 18:26
in law is gone *b* unto her people ... Ruth 1:15
*b* with Naomi out of the country ... Ruth 2:6
turned his *b* to go from Samuel ... 1Sa 10:9
for he is turned *b* from following ... 1Sa 15:11
hath kept me *b* from hurting thee ... 1Sa 25:34
the bow of Jonathan turned not *b* ... 2Sa 1:22
can I bring him *b* again ... 2Sa 12:23
thou, and take *b* thy brethren ... 2Sa 15:20
Carry *b* the ark of God into the ... 2Sa 15:25
I will bring *b* all the people ... 2Sa 17:3
for Joab held *b* the people ... 2Sa 18:16
not a word of bringing the king *b* ... 2Sa 19:10
to bring the king *b* to his house ... 2Sa 19:11
ye the last to bring *b* the king ... 2Sa 19:12
turn *b* again, that I may die in ... 2Sa 19:37
first had in bringing *b* our king ... 2Sa 19:43
Bring him *b* with thee into thine ... 1Kin 13:18
So he went *b* with him, and did eat ... 1Kin 13:19
the prophet that brought him *b* ... 1Kin 13:20
But camest *b*, and hast eaten bread ... 1Kin 13:22
the prophet whom he had brought *b* ... 1Kin 13:23
him *b* from the way heard thereof ... 1Kin 13:26
it upon the ass, and brought it *b* ... 1Kin 13:29
and hast cast me behind thy *b* ... 1Kin 14:9
brought them *b* into the guard ... 1Kin 14:28
hast turned their heart *b* again ... 1Kin 18:37
And he said unto him, Go *b* again ... 1Kin 19:20
And he returned *b* from him ... 1Kin 19:21
carry him *b* unto Amon the ... 1Kin 22:26
that they turned *b* from pursuing ... 1Kin 22:33
the messengers turned *b* unto him ... 2Kin 1:5
them, Why are ye now turned *b* ... 2Kin 1:5
that fell from him, and went *b* ... 2Kin 2:13
And he turned *b*, and looked on them ... 2Kin 2:24
king Joram went *b* to be healed in ... 2Kin 8:29
So the king of Assyria turned *b* ... 2Kin 15:20
I will turn thee *b* by the way by ... 2Kin 19:28
ten degrees, or go *b* ten degrees ... 2Kin 20:9
And Ornan turned *b*, and saw the ... 1Chr 21:20
And when Judah looked *b*, behold, ... 2Chr 13:14
carry him *b* to Amon the governor ... 2Chr 18:25
they turned *b* again from pursuing ... 2Chr 18:32
brought them *b* unto the LORD God ... 2Chr 19:4
of the army which Amaziah sent *b* ... 2Chr 25:13
and brought the king word *b* again ... 2Chr 34:16
and viewed the wall, and turned *b* ... Neh 2:15
Neither have I gone *b* from the ... Job 23:12
He holdeth *b* the face of his ... Job 26:9
He keepeth *b* his soul from the ... Job 33:18
To bring *b* his soul from the pit, ... Job 33:30
Because they turned *b* from him ... Job 34:27
turneth he *b* from the sword ... Job 39:22
When mine enemies are turned *b* ... Ps 9:3
when the LORD bringeth *b* the ... Ps 14:7
Keep *b* thy servant also from ... Ps 19:13
shalt thou make them turn their *b* ... Ps 21:12
let them be turned *b* and brought ... Ps 35:4
us to turn *b* from the enemy ... Ps 44:10
Our heart is not turned *b* ... Ps 44:18
Every one of them is gone *b* ... Ps 53:3
When God bringeth *b* the captivity ... Ps 53:6
then shall mine enemies turn *b* ... Ps 56:9
Let them be turned *b* for a reward ... Ps 70:3
turned *b* in the day of battle ... Ps 78:9
Yea, they turned *b* and tempted God ... Ps 78:41
But turned *b*, and dealt ... Ps 78:57
So will not we go *b* from thee ... Ps 80:18
thou hast brought *b* the captivity ... Ps 85:1
Jordan was driven *b* ... Ps 114:3
Jordan, that thou wast driven *b* ... Ps 114:5
The plowers plowed upon my *b* ... Ps 129:3
and turned *b* that hate Zion ... Ps 129:5
but a rod is for the *b* of him ... Prov 10:13
and stripes for the *b* of fools ... Prov 19:29
ass, and a rod for the fool's *b* ... Prov 26:3
out, and who shall turn it *b* ... Is 14:27
and will not call *b* his words ... Is 31:2
I will turn thee *b* by the way by ... Is 37:29
cast all my sins behind thy *b* ... Is 38:17
They shall be turned *b*, they ... Is 42:17
and to the south, Keep not *b* ... Is 43:6
rebellious, neither turned away *b* ... Is 50:5
I gave my *b* to the smiters, and my ... Is 50:6
they have turned their *b* unto me ... Jer 2:27
the LORD is not turned *b* from us ... Jer 4:8
neither will I turn *b* from it ... Jer 4:28
turn *b* thine hand as a ... Jer 6:9
*b* by a perpetual backsliding ... Jer 8:5
They are turned *b* to the ... Jer 11:10
I will shew them the *b*, and not ... Jer 18:17
I will turn *b* the weapons of war ... Jer 21:4
And they have turned unto me the *b* ... Jer 32:33
mire, and they are turned away *b* ... Jer 38:22
Now while he was not yet gone *b* ... Jer 40:5
Go *b* also to Gedaliah the son of ... Jer 40:5
I will keep nothing *b* from you ... Jer 42:4
them dismayed and turned away *b* ... Jer 46:5
and are fled apace, and look not *b* ... Jer 46:5
for they also are turned *b* ... Jer 46:21
not look *b* to their children for ... Jer 47:3
keepeth *b* his sword from blood ... Jer 48:10
hath Moab turned the *b* with shame ... Jer 48:39
Flee ye, turn *b*, dwell deep, O ... Jer 49:8
for my feet, he hath turned me *b* ... Lam 1:13
he hath drawn *b* his right hand ... Lam 2:3
me, and cast me behind thy *b* ... Eze 23:35
I will not go *b*, neither will I ... Eze 24:14
And I will turn thee *b*, and put ... Eze 38:4
that is brought *b* from the sword ... Eze 38:8
And I will turn thee *b*, and leave ... Eze 39:2
Then he brought me *b* the way of ... Eze 44:1
which had upon the *b* of it four ... Dan 7:6
For Israel slideth *b* as a ... Hos 4:16
but none shall look *b* ... Nah 2:8
that are turned *b* from the LORD ... Zeph 1:6
when I turn *b* your captivity ... Zeph 3:20
return *b* to take his clothes ... Mt 24:18
rolled *b* the stone from the door, ... Mt 28:2
turn *b* again for to take up his ... Mk 13:16
they turned *b* again to Jerusalem, ... Lk 2:45
the ship, and returned *b* again ... Lk 8:37
hand to the plough, and looking *b* ... Lk 9:62
saw that he was healed, turned *b* ... Lk 17:15
let him likewise not return *b* ... Lk 17:31
time many of his disciples went *b* ... Jn 6:66
thus said, she turned herself *b* ... Jn 20:14
kept *b* part of the price, his ... Acts 5:2
to keep *b* part of the price of ... Acts 5:3
hearts turned *b* again into Egypt ... Acts 7:39
how I kept *b* nothing that was ... Acts 20:20
see, and bow down their *b* alway ... Rom 11:10
but if any man draw *b*, my soul ... Heb 10:38
of them who draw *b* unto perdition ... Heb 10:39
which is of you kept *b* by fraud ... Jas 5:4

**BACKBITERS**
*B*, haters of God, despiteful, ... Rom 1:30

**BACKBITETH**
He that *b* not with his tongue, ... Ps 15:3

**BACKBITING**
an angry countenance a *b* tongue ... Prov 25:23

**BACKBITINGS**
envyings, wraths, strifes, *b* ... 2Cor 12:20

**BACKBONE**
shall he take off hard by the *b* ... Lev 3:9

**BACKS**
enemies turn their *b* unto thee ... Ex 23:27
their *b* before their enemies ... Josh 7:8
but turned their *b* before their ... Josh 7:12
Therefore they turned their *b* ... Judg 20:42
of the LORD, and turned their *b* ... 2Chr 29:6
and cast thy law behind their *b* ... Neh 9:26
with their *b* toward the temple of ... Eze 8:16
And their whole body, and their *b* ... Eze 10:12

**BACKSIDE**
the flock to the *b* of the desert ... Ex 3:1
hang over the *b* of the tabernacle ... Ex 26:12
a book written within and on the *b* ... Rev 5:1

**BACKSLIDER**
The *b* in heart shall be filled ... Prov 14:14

**BACKSLIDING**
that which *b* Israel hath done ... Jer 3:6
*b* Israel committed adultery I had ... Jer 3:8
The *b* Israel hath justified ... Jer 3:11
thou *b* Israel, saith the LORD ... Jer 3:12
O *b* children, saith the LORD ... Jer 3:14
ye *b* children, and I will heal ... Jer 3:22
slidden back by a perpetual *b* ... Jer 8:5
thou go about, O thou *b* daughter ... Jer 31:22
thy flowing valley, O *b* daughter ... Jer 49:4
Israel slideth back as a *b* heifer ... Hos 4:16
my people are bent to *b* from me ... Hos 11:7
I will heal their *b*, I will love ... Hos 14:4

**BACKSLIDINGS**
thee, and thy *b* shall reprove thee ... Jer 2:19
children, and I will heal your *b* ... Jer 3:22
many, and their *b* are increased ... Jer 5:6
for our *b* are many ... Jer 14:7

**BACKWARD**
both their shoulders, and went *b* ... Gen 9:23
and their faces were *b*, and they ... Gen 9:23
so that his rider shall fall *b* ... Gen 49:17
seat *b* by the side of the gate ... 1Sa 4:18
the shadow return *b* ten degrees ... 2Kin 20:10
brought the shadow ten degrees *b* ... 2Kin 20:11

and *b*, but I cannot perceive him .......... Job 23:8
let them be driven *b* and put to .......... Ps 40:14
let them be turned *b*, and put to .......... Ps 70:2
unto anger, they are gone away *b*.......... Is 1:4
that they might go, and fall *b* .......... Is 28:13
sun dial of Ahaz, ten degrees *b*.......... Is 38:8
that turneth wise men *b*, and.......... Is 44:25
And judgment is turned away *b*.......... Is 59:14
of their evil heart, and went *b*.......... Jer 7:24
saith the LORD, thou art gone *b*.......... Jer 15:6
yea, she sigheth, and turneth *b*.......... Lam 1:8
unto them, I am he, they went *b*.......... Jn 18:6

**BAD**
cannot speak unto thee *b* or good ...... Gen 24:50
not to Jacob either good or *b*.......... Gen 31:24
not to Jacob either good or *b*.......... Gen 31:29
good for a *b*, or a *b* for a good.......... Lev 27:10
value it, whether it be good or *b*.......... Lev 27:12
it, whether it be good or *b*.......... Lev 27:14
search whether it be good or *b*.......... Lev 27:33
dwell in, whether it be good or *b*....... Num 13:19
either good or *b* of mine own mind... Num 24:13
brother Amnon neither good nor *b*.......... 2Sa 13:22
the king to discern good and *b*.......... 2Sa 14:17
I may discern between good and *b*........ 1Kin 3:9
the *b* city, and have set up the.......... Ezr 4:12
not be eaten, they were so *b*.......... Jer 24:2
into vessels, but cast the *b* away.......... Mt 13:48
all as many as they found, both *b*.......... Mt 22:10
done, whether it be good or *b*.......... 2Cor 5:10

**BADE**
And the man did as Joseph *b*.......... Gen 43:17
up till the morning, as Moses *b*.......... Ex 16:24
*b* stone them with stones.......... Num 14:10
did unto them as the LORD *b* him.......... Josh 11:9
all that her mother in law *b* her.......... Ruth 3:6
and some *b* me kill thee.......... 1Sa 24:10
(Also he *b* them teach the.......... 2Sa 1:18
for thy servant Joab, he *b* me.......... 2Sa 14:19
on the third day, as the king *b*.......... 2Chr 10:12
Then Esther *b* them return.......... Est 4:15
understood they how that he *b*.......... Mt 16:12
And he that *b* thee and him come and... Lk 14:9
that when he that *b* thee cometh.......... Lk 14:10
said he also to him that *b* him.......... Lk 14:12
made a great supper, and *b* many.......... Lk 14:16
the Spirit *b* me go with them,.......... Acts 11:12
But *b* them farewell, saying, I.......... Acts 18:21
*b* that he should be examined by.......... Acts 22:24

**BADEST**
have done according as thou *b* me..... Gen 27:19

**BADGERS'**
*b* skins, and shittim wood,.......... Ex 25:5
and a covering above of *b* skins.......... Ex 26:14
*b* skins, and shittim wood,.......... Ex 35:7
of rams, and *b* skins, brought them....... Ex 35:23
a covering of *b* skins above that.......... Ex 36:19
red, and the covering of *b* skins.......... Ex 39:34
thereon the covering of *b* skins.......... Num 4:6
same with a covering of *b* skins.......... Num 4:8
within a covering of *b* skins.......... Num 4:10
it with a covering of *b* skins.......... Num 4:11
them with a covering of *b* skins.......... Num 4:12
upon it a covering of *b* skins.......... Num 4:14
the covering of the *b* skins that.......... Num 4:25
work, and shod thee with *b* skin.......... Eze 16:10

**BADNESS**
in all the land of Egypt for *b*.......... Gen 41:19

**BAG**
not have in thy *b* divers weights........ Deut 25:13
in a shepherd's *b* which he had.......... 1Sa 17:40
And David put his hand in his *b*.......... 1Sa 17:49
transgression is sealed up in a *b*.......... Job 14:17
He hath taken a *b* of money with.......... Prov 7:20
the weights of the *b* are his work...... Prov 16:11
They lavish gold out of the *b*.......... Is 46:6
with the *b* of deceitful weights.......... Mic 6:11
to put it into a *b* with holes.......... Hag 1:6
he was a thief, and had the *b*.......... Jn 12:6
thought, because Judas had the *b*.......... Jn 13:29

**BAGS**
two talents of silver in two *b*.......... 2Kin 5:23
came up, and they put up in *b*.......... 2Kin 12:10
yourselves *b* which wax not old.......... Lk 12:33

**BAHARUMITE** (*ba-ha'-rum-ite*) See BARHUMITE. *Inhabitants of Bahurim.*
Azmaveth the *B*, Eliahba the.......... 1Chr 11:33

**BAHURIM** (*ba-hu'-rim*) See BAHARUMITE. *A village near Jerusalem.*
her along weeping behind her to *B*........ 2Sa 3:16
And when king David came to *B*.......... 2Sa 16:5
and came to a man's house in *B*.......... 2Sa 17:18
Gera, a Benjamite, which was of *B*...... 2Sa 19:16
the son of Gera, a Benjamite of *B*.......... 1Kin 2:8

**BAJITH** (*ba'-jith*) *A temple in Moab.*
He is gone up to *B*, and to Dibon,.......... Is 15:2

**BAKBAKKAR** (*bak-bak'-kar*) *A Levite who returned from exile.*
And *B*, Heresh, and Galal, and.......... 1Chr 9:15

**BAKBUK** (*bak'-buk*) *A family who returned from exile.*
The children of *B*, the children.......... Ezr 2:51
The children of *B*, the children.......... Neh 7:53

**BAKBUKIAH** (*bak-buk-i'-ah*) *A Levite exile who resettled in Jerusalem.*
*B* the second among his brethren,.......... Neh 11:17
Also *B* and Unni, their brethren,.......... Neh 12:9
Mattaniah, and *B*, Obadiah,.......... Neh 12:25

**BAKE**
did *b* unleavened bread, and they.......... Gen 19:3
*b* that which ye will *b* to day,.......... Ex 16:23
flour, and *b* twelve cakes thereof.......... Lev 24:5
ten women shall *b* your bread in.......... Lev 26:26
did *b* unleavened bread thereof.......... 1Sa 28:24
in his sight, and did *b* the cakes.......... 2Sa 13:8
thou shalt *b* it with dung that.......... Eze 4:12
where they shall *b* the meat.......... Eze 46:20

**BAKED**
they *b* unleavened cakes of the.......... Ex 12:39
*b* it in pans, and made cakes of it.......... Num 11:8
and for that which is *b* in the pan..... 1Chr 23:29
also I have *b* bread upon the.......... Is 44:19

**BAKEMEATS**
of all manner of *b* for Pharaoh .......... Gen 40:17

**BAKEN**
of a meat offering *b* in the oven.......... Lev 2:4
be a meat offering *b* in a pan.......... Lev 2:5
meat offering *b* in the frying pan.......... Lev 2:7
It shall not be *b* with leaven.......... Lev 6:17
and when it is *b*, thou shalt bring.......... Lev 6:21
the *b* pieces of the meat offering.......... Lev 6:21
offering that is *b* in the oven.......... Lev 7:9
they shall be *b* with leaven.......... Lev 23:17
there was a cake *b* on the coals.......... 1Kin 19:6

**BAKER**
his *b* had offended their lord the.......... Gen 40:1
the *b* of the king of Egypt, which.......... Gen 40:5
When the chief *b* saw that the.......... Gen 40:16
of the chief *b* among his servants.......... Gen 40:20
But he hanged the chief *b*.......... Gen 40:22
house, both me and the chief *b*.......... Gen 41:10
as an oven heated by the *b*.......... Hos 7:4
their *b* sleepeth all the night.......... Hos 7:6

**BAKERS**
and against the chief of the *b*.......... Gen 40:2
and to be cooks, and to be *b*.......... 1Sa 8:13

**BAKERS'**
of bread out of the *b* street.......... Jer 37:21

**BAKETH**
yea, he kindleth it, and *b* bread.......... Is 44:15

**BALAAM** (*ba'-la-am*) See BALAAM'S. *Son of Beor.*
unto *B* the son of Beor to Pethor.......... Num 22:5
and they came unto *B*, and spake.......... Num 22:7
the princes of Moab abode with *B*.......... Num 22:8
And God came unto *B*.......... Num 22:9
*B* said unto God, Balak the son of..... Num 22:10
And God said unto *B*, Thou shalt..... Num 22:12
*B* rose up in the morning, and said.... Num 22:13
*B* refuseth to come with us.......... Num 22:14
And they came to *B*.......... Num 22:16
*B* answered and said unto the.......... Num 22:18
And God came unto *B* at night.......... Num 22:20
*B* rose up in the morning, and.......... Num 22:21
*B* smote the ass, to turn her into.......... Num 22:23
the LORD, she fell down under *B*.......... Num 22:27
of the ass, and she said unto *B*.......... Num 22:28
*B* said unto the ass, Because thou..... Num 22:29
And the ass said unto *B*, Am not I..... Num 22:30
the LORD opened the eyes of *B*.......... Num 22:31
*B* said unto the angel of the LORD.......... Num 22:34
the angel of the LORD said unto *B*.......... Num 22:35
So *B* went with the princes of.......... Num 22:35
when Balak heard that *B* was come.. Num 22:36
And Balak said unto *B*, Did I not.......... Num 22:37
*B* said unto Balak, Lo, I am come.......... Num 22:38
*B* went with Balak, and they came.......... Num 22:39
oxen and sheep, and sent to *B*.......... Num 22:40
on the morrow, that Balak took *B*..... Num 22:41
*B* said unto Balak, Build me here.......... Num 23:1
And Balak did as *B* had spoken.......... Num 23:2
*B* offered on every altar a.......... Num 23:2
*B* said unto Balak, Stand by thy.......... Num 23:3
And God met *B*.......... Num 23:4
And Balak said unto *B*, What hast.... Num 23:11
And the LORD met *B*.......... Num 23:16
And Balak said unto *B*, Neither.......... Num 23:25
But *B* answered and said unto Balak Num 23:26
And Balak said unto *B*, Come, I.......... Num 23:27
Balak brought *B* unto the top of.......... Num 23:28
*B* said unto Balak, Build me here.......... Num 23:29
And Balak did as *B* had said.......... Num 23:30
when *B* saw that it pleased the.......... Num 24:1
*B* lifted up his eyes, and he saw.......... Num 24:2
*B* the son of Beor hath said, and.......... Num 24:3
anger was kindled against *B*.......... Num 24:10
and Balak said unto *B*, I called.......... Num 24:10
*B* said unto Balak, Spake I not.......... Num 24:12
*B* the son of Beor hath said, and.......... Num 24:15
*B* rose up, and went and returned to Num 24:25
*B* also the son of Beor they slew.......... Num 31:8
Israel, through the counsel of *B*.......... Num 31:16
*B* the son of Beor of Pethor of.......... Deut 23:4
thy God would not hearken unto *B*.... Deut 23:5
*B* also the son of Beor, the.......... Josh 13:22
called *B* the son of Beor to curse.......... Josh 24:9
But I would not hearken unto *B*.......... Josh 24:10
but hired *B* against them, that he.......... Neh 13:2
what *B* the son of Beor answered.......... Mic 6:5
the way of *B* the son of Bosor.......... 2Pet 2:15
after the error of *B* for reward.......... Jude 11
them that hold the doctrine of *B*.......... Rev 2:14

**BALAAM'S**
crushed *B* foot against the wall.......... Num 22:25
*B* anger was kindled, and he smote... Num 22:27
And the LORD put a word in *B* mouth Num 23:5

**BALAC** (*ba'-lak*) See BALAK. *Greek form of Balak.*
of Balaam, who taught *B* to cast a.......... Rev 2:14

**BALADAN** (*bal'-adan*) See BERODACH-BALADAN, MERODACH-BALADAN. *Father of a Babylonian king.*
Berodach-baladan, the son of *B*.......... 2Kin 20:12
Merodach-baladan, the son of *B*.......... Is 39:1

**BALAH** (*ba'-lah*) See BAALAH. *A city in Simeon.*
And Hazar-shual, and *B*, and Azem,.... Josh 19:3

**BALAK** (*ba'-lak*) See BALAC, BALAK'S. *A king of Moab.*
*B* the son of Zippor saw all that.......... Num 22:2
*B* the son of Zippor was king of.......... Num 22:4
and spake unto him the words of *B*.... Num 22:7
*B* the son of Zippor, king of Moab.... Num 22:10
and said unto the princes of *B*.......... Num 22:13
Moab rose up, and they went unto *B* Num 22:14
*B* sent yet again princes, more,.......... Num 22:15
Thus saith *B* the son of Zippor,.......... Num 22:16
and said unto the servants of *B*.......... Num 22:18
If *B* would give me his house full..... Num 22:18
Balaam went with the princes of *B*... Num 22:35
*B* heard that Balaam was come.......... Num 22:36
*B* said unto Balaam, Did I not.......... Num 22:37
And Balaam said unto *B*, Lo, I am.... Num 22:38
And Balaam went with *B*, and they.. Num 22:39
*B* offered oxen and sheep, and sent... Num 22:40
that *B* took Balaam, and brought...... Num 22:41
And Balaam said unto *B*, Build me...... Num 23:1
*B* did as Balaam had spoken.......... Num 23:2
and *B* and Balaam offered on every.... Num 23:2
And Balaam said unto *B*, Stand by..... Num 23:3
mouth, and said, Return unto *B*.......... Num 23:5
*B* the king of Moab hath brought.......... Num 23:7
*B* said unto Balaam, What hast.......... Num 23:11
*B* said unto him, Come, I pray.......... Num 23:13
And he said unto *B*, Stand here by.... Num 23:15
mouth, and said, Go again unto *B*.......... Num 23:16
*B* said unto him, What hath the.......... Num 23:17
his parable, and said, Rise up, *B*.......... Num 23:18
*B* said unto Balaam, Neither curse..... Num 23:25
Balaam answered and said unto *B*.... Num 23:26
*B* said unto Balaam, Come, I pray..... Num 23:27
*B* brought Balaam unto the top of...... Num 23:28
And Balaam said unto *B*, Build me..... Num 23:29
*B* did as Balaam had said, and.......... Num 23:30
*B* said unto Balaam, I called thee..... Num 24:10
And Balaam said unto *B*, Spake I...... Num 24:12
If *B* would give me his house full..... Num 24:13
and *B* also went his way.......... Num 24:25
Then *B* the son of Zippor, king of........ Josh 24:9
better than *B* the son of Zippor.......... Judg 11:25
remember now what *B* king of Moab..... Mic 6:5

**BALAK'S** (*ba'-laks*)
*B* anger was kindled against.......... Num 24:10

**BALANCE**
Let me be weighed in an even *b*.......... Job 31:6
to be laid in the *b*, they are.......... Ps 62:9
A false *b* is abomination to the.......... Prov 11:1
A just weight and *b* are the LORD's... Prov 16:11
and a false *b* is not good.......... Prov 20:23
in scales, and the hills in a *b*.......... Is 40:12
as the small dust of the *b*.......... Is 40:15
the bag, and weigh silver in the *b*.......... Is 46:6

**BALANCES**
Just *b*, just weights, a just.......... Lev 19:36
calamity laid in the *b* together.......... Job 6:2
and weighed him the money in the *b*... Jer 32:10
then take thee *b* to weigh.......... Eze 5:1
Ye shall have just *b*, and a just.......... Eze 45:10
Thou art weighed in the *b*.......... Dan 5:27
the *b* of deceit are in his hand.......... Hos 12:7
and falsifying the *b* by deceit.......... Amos 8:5
count them pure with the wicked *b*...... Mic 6:11
him had a pair of *b* in his hand.......... Rev 6:5

**BALANCINGS**
thou know the *b* of the clouds.......... Job 37:16

**BALD**
the *b* locust after his kind, and.......... Lev 11:22
is fallen off his head, he is *b*.......... Lev 13:40
toward his face, he is forehead *b*.......... Lev 13:41
And if there be in the *b* head.......... Lev 13:42
or *b* forehead, a white reddish.......... Lev 13:42
his *b* head, or his *b* forehead.......... Lev 13:42
*b* head, or in his *b* forehead.......... Lev 13:43
said unto him, Go up, thou *b* head.......... 2Kin 2:23
go up, thou *b* head.......... 2Kin 2:23
nor make themselves *b* for them.......... Jer 16:6
For every head shall be *b*.......... Jer 48:37
themselves utterly *b* for thee.......... Eze 27:31
every head was made *b*, and every..... Eze 29:18
Make thee *b*, and poll thee for thy........ Mic 1:16

**BALDNESS**
shall not make *b* upon their head .......... Lev 21:5
nor make any *b* between your eyes .... Deut 14:1
and instead of well set hair *b* ..................... Is 3:24
on all their heads shall be *b* ..................... Is 15:2
weeping, and to mourning, and to *b*....... Is 22:12
*B* is come upon Gaza ................................ Jer 47:5
faces, and *b* upon all their heads ............ Eze 7:18
all loins, and *b* upon every head ......... Amos 8:10
enlarge thy *b* as the eagle ....................... Mic 1:16

**BALL**
toss thee like a *b* into a large .................. Is 22:18

**BALM**
their camels bearing spicery and *b*...... Gen 37:25
the man a present, a little *b*.............. Gen 43:11
Is there no *b* in Gilead ............................ Jer 8:22
Go up into Gilead, and take *b*.............. Jer 46:11
take *b* for her pain, if so be she .............. Jer 51:8
and honey, and oil, and *b*.......................... Eze 27:17

**BAMAH** (*ba'-mah*) See BAMOTH. *Places where Israel sacrificed to idols.*
thereof is called *B* unto this day.......... Eze 20:29

**BAMOTH** (*ba'-moth*) See BAMOTH-BAAL. *A city on the Arnon River.*
and from Nahaliel to *B*......................... Num 21:19
from *B* in the valley, that is in........... Num 21:20

**BAMOTH-BAAL** (*ba'-moth-ba'-al*) *A Moabite town.*
Dibon, and *B*, and Beth-baal-meon,.... Josh 13:17

**BAND**
with a *b* round about the hole,.............. Ex 39:23
and there went with him a *b* of men... 1Sa 10:26
him, and became captain over a *b* ..... 1Kin 11:24
behold, they spied a *b* of men ............ 2Kin 13:21
and made them captains of the *b*....... 1Chr 12:18
David against the *b* of the rovers ...... 1Chr 12:21
for the *b* of men that came with .......... 2Chr 22:1
of the king a *b* of soldiers ....................... Ezr 8:22
unicorn with his *b* in the furrow .......... Job 39:10
the earth, even with a *b* of iron ............ Dan 4:15
the earth, even with a *b* of iron ............. Dan 4:23
unto him the whole *b* of soldiers .......... Mt 27:27
and they call together the whole *b*....... Mk 15:16
then, having received a *b* of men ............ Jn 18:3
Then the *b* and the captain and............ Jn 18:12
of the *b* called the Italian *b*.................... Acts 10:1
unto the chief captain of the *b*............ Acts 21:31
a centurion of Augustus' *b* ..................... Acts 27:1

**BANDED**
certain of the Jews *b* together............ Acts 23:12

**BANDS**
herds, and the camels, into two *b* ........ Gen 32:7
and now I am become two *b*.............. Gen 32:10
I have broken the *b* of your yoke .......... Lev 26:13
his *b* loosed from off his hands........... Judg 15:14
two men that were captains of *b*.............. 2Sa 4:2
So the *b* of Syria came no more........... 2Kin 6:23
the *b* of the Moabites invaded the ..... 2Kin 13:20
Pharaoh-nechoh put him in *b* at ....... 2Kin 23:33
against him *b* of the Chaldees ............. 2Kin 24:2
*b* of the Syrians, and *b* of the............... 2Kin 24:2
*b* of the children of Ammon, and ......... 2Kin 24:2
were *b* of soldiers for war, six ................ 1Chr 7:4
*b* that were ready armed to the.......... 1Chr 12:23
men, that went out to war by *b* ......... 2Chr 26:11
The Chaldeans made out three *b*............ Job 1:17
Pleiades, or loose the *b* of Orion ........... Job 38:31
hath loosed the *b* of the wild ass............ Job 39:5
Let us break their *b* asunder ........................ Ps 2:3
For there are no *b* in their death ........... Ps 73:4
death, and brake their *b* in sunder ....... Ps 107:14
The *b* of the wicked have robbed .......... Ps 119:61
go they forth all of them by *b*............... Prov 30:27
snares and nets, and her hands as *b*..... Eccl 7:26
lest your *b* be made strong..................... Is 28:22
thyself from the *b* of thy neck ................ Is 52:2
to loose the *b* of wickedness, to.............. Is 58:6
broken thy yoke, and burst thy *b*.............. Jer 2:20
they shall put *b* upon thee...................... Eze 3:25
behold, I will lay *b* upon thee..................... Eze 4:8
him to help him, and all his *b* .............. Eze 12:14
all his *b* shall fall by the sword ............ Eze 17:21
I have broken the *b* of their yoke ......... Eze 34:27
Gomer, and all his *b* ............................... Eze 38:6
the north quarters, and all his *b* ............ Eze 38:6
the land, thou, and all thy *b* .................... Eze 38:9
will rain upon him, and upon his *b*...... Eze 38:22
of Israel, thou, and all thy *b* ................... Eze 39:4
cords of a man, with *b* of love................ Hos 11:4
Beauty, and the other I called *B*.............. Zec 11:7
asunder mine other staff, even *B*........ Zec 11:14
and he brake the *b*, and was driven ........... Lk 8:29
and every one's *b* were loosed............. Acts 16:26
Jews, he loosed him from his *b* ........... Acts 22:30
the sea, and loosed the rudder *b* ......... Acts 27:40
*b* having nourishment ministered,.......... Col 2:19

**BANI** (*ba'-ni*)
*1. A "mighty man" of David.*
of Nathan of Zobah, *B* the Gadite,....... 2Sa 23:36
*2. A Levite descendant of Merari.*
The son of Amzi, the son of *B* .............. 1Chr 6:46
*3. A descendant of Pharez.*
the son of Imri, the son of *B*................... 1Chr 9:4
*4. A family of exiles.*
The children of *B*, six hundred ................ Ezr 2:10
And of the sons of *B* ............................... Ezr 10:29
*5. Father whose sons married foreign wives.*
Of the sons of *B* ........................................ Ezr 10:34
*6. A Jewish descendant of a foreign woman.*
And *B*, and Binnui, Shimei, .................... Ezr 10:38
*7. Father of Rehum.*
the Levites, Rehum the son of *B* ........... Neh 3:17
Also Jeshua, and *B*, and Sherebiah, ........ Neh 8:7
of the Levites, Jeshua, and *B*.................... Neh 9:4
Levites, Jeshua, and Kadmiel, *B* ............... Neh 9:5
*8. A priest who assisted Ezra.*
Shebaniah, Bunni, Sherebiah, *B*................ Neh 9:4
Hodijah, *B*, Beninu ................................ Neh 10:13
*9. An Israelite who renewed the covenant under Nehemiah.*
Pahath-moab, Elam, Zatthu, *B*............. Neh 10:14
*10. A family of exiles.*
Jerusalem was Uzzi the son of *B*......... Neh 11:22

**BANISHED**
doth not fetch home again his *b*........... 2Sa 14:13
that his *b* be not expelled from............ 2Sa 14:14

**BANISHMENT**
whether it be unto death, or to *b* ........... Ezr 7:26
thee false burdens and causes of *b*....... Lam 2:14

**BANK**
I stood upon the *b* of the river............ Gen 41:17
which is by the *b* of the river ............... Deut 4:48
which is upon the *b* of the river ............ Josh 12:2
that is upon the *b* of the river ............... Josh 13:9
that is on the *b* of the river................. Josh 13:16
they cast up a *b* against the city ........... 2Sa 20:15
back, and stood by the *b* of Jordan ...... 2Kin 2:13
shield, nor cast a *b* against it ............. 2Kin 19:32
shields, nor cast a *b* against it.................. Is 37:33
at the *b* of the river were very................. Eze 47:7
by the river upon the *b* thereof .......... Eze 47:12
this side of the *b* of the river................ Dan 12:5
that side of the *b* of the river ................ Dan 12:5
not thou my money into the *b* ............. Lk 19:23

**BANKS**
all his *b* all the time of harvest ............ Josh 3:15
place, and flowed over all his *b*............. Josh 4:18
when it had overflown all his *b* .......... 1Chr 12:15
channels, and go over all his *b*..................... Is 8:7
man's voice between the *b* of Ulai........... Dan 8:16

**BANNER**
Thou hast given a *b* to them that.............. Ps 60:4
house, and his *b* over me was love........ Song 2:4
Lift ye up a *b* upon the high..................... Is 13:2

**BANNERS**
of our God we will set up our *b*............... Ps 20:5
terrible as an army with *b*..................... Song 6:4
and terrible as an army with *b* ............. Song 6:10

**BANQUET**
*b* that I have prepared for him ................ Est 5:4
Haman came to the *b* that Esther .............. Est 5:5
said unto Esther at the *b* of wine.............. Est 5:6
Haman come to the *b* that I shall............... Est 5:8
the *b* that she had prepared but............. Est 5:12
merrily with the king unto the *b* ............ Est 5:14
the *b* that Esther had prepared............... Est 6:14
Haman came to *b* with Esther the.............. Est 7:1
the second day at the *b* of wine ............... Est 7:2
the king arising from the *b* of.................... Est 7:7
into the place of the *b* of wine.................. Est 7:8
the companions make a *b* of him .......... Job 41:6
his lords, came into the *b* house.......... Dan 5:10
the *b* of them that stretched.................. Amos 6:7

**BANQUETING**
He brought me to the *b* house .............. Song 2:4

**BANQUETINGS**
excess of wine, revellings, *b* ................... 1Pet 4:3

**BAPTISM**
and Sadducees come to his *b*................... Mt 3:7
the *b* that I am baptized with............... Mt 20:22
be baptized with the *b* that I am .......... Mt 20:23
The *b* of John, whence was it.............. Mt 21:25
preach the *b* of repentance for.................. Mk 1:4
be baptized with the *b* that I am .......... Mk 10:38
with the *b* that I am baptized .............. Mk 10:39
The *b* of John, was it from heaven......... Mk 11:30
preaching the *b* of repentance for............. Lk 3:3
being baptized with the *b* of John ........... Lk 7:29
But I have a *b* to be baptized................. Lk 12:50
The *b* of John, was it from heaven........... Lk 20:4
Beginning from the *b* of John............... Acts 1:22
after the *b* which John preached......... Acts 10:37
preached before his coming the *b*........ Acts 13:24
Lord, knowing only the *b* of John....... Acts 18:25
And they said, Unto John's *b* ............... Acts 19:3
baptized with the *b* of repentance........ Acts 19:4
buried with him by *b* into death ............. Rom 6:4
One Lord, one faith, one *b*....................... Eph 4:5
Buried with him in *b*, wherein................ Col 2:12
*b* doth also now save us (not the ........... 1Pet 3:21

**BAPTISMS**
Of the doctrine of *b*, and of ...................... Heb 6:2

**BAPTIST** (*bap'-tist*) See BAPTIST'S. *John, the forerunner of Jesus.*
In those days came John the *B*.................. Mt 3:1
risen a greater than John the *B* .............. Mt 11:11
from the days of John the *B* until .......... Mt 11:12
his servants, This is John the *B*............... Mt 14:2
Some say that thou art John the *B* ....... Mt 16:14
he spake unto them of John the *B* ....... Mt 17:13
That John the *B* was risen from.............. Mk 6:14
she said, The head of John the *B* ............ Mk 6:24
a charger the head of John the *B* ........... Mk 6:25
And they answered, John the *B* ............. Mk 8:28
John *B* hath sent us unto thee, ................ Lk 7:20
a greater prophet than John the *B* .......... Lk 7:28
For John the *B* came neither ................... Lk 7:33
They answering said, John the *B* ............. Lk 9:19

**BAPTIST'S** (*bap'-tists*)
me here John *B* head in a charger.......... Mt 14:8

**BAPTIZE**
I indeed *b* you with water unto ............... Mt 3:11
he shall *b* you with the Holy .................... Mt 3:11
John did *b* in the wilderness, and .............. Mk 1:4
but he shall *b* you with the Holy ................ Mk 1:8
I indeed *b* you with water ........................ Lk 3:16
he shall *b* you with the Holy..................... Lk 3:16
them, saying, I *b* with water...................... Jn 1:26
he that sent me to *b* with water................ Jn 1:33
For Christ sent me not to *b*................... 1Cor 1:17

**BAPTIZED**
And were *b* of him in Jordan,....................... Mt 3:6
Jordan unto John, to be *b* of him ............ Mt 3:13
I have need to be *b* of thee ..................... Mt 3:14
And Jesus, when he was *b*, went up ....... Mt 3:16
*b* with the baptism that I am *b*............... Mt 20:22
*b* with the baptism that I am *b* .............. Mt 20:23
were all *b* of him in the river of................ Mk 1:5
I indeed have *b* you with water ................ Mk 1:8
and was *b* of John in Jordan....................... Mk 1:9
*b* with the baptism that I am *b*............ Mk 10:38
am *b* withal shall ye be *b*...................... Mk 10:39
believeth and is *b* shall be saved.......... Mk 16:16
that came forth to be *b* of him .................. Lk 3:7
Then came also publicans to be *b* ............. Lk 3:12
Now when all the people were *b*............... Lk 3:21
to pass, that Jesus also being *b* ................ Lk 3:21
being *b* with the baptism of John ............ Lk 7:29
themselves, being not *b* of him................. Lk 7:30
But I have a baptism to be *b* with......... Lk 12:50
there he tarried with them, and *b* ........... Jn 3:22
and they came, and were *b* ....................... Jn 3:23
*b* more disciples than John,........................ Jn 4:1
(Though Jesus himself *b* not...................... Jn 4:2
the place where John at first *b*.............. Jn 10:40
For John truly *b* with water ................... Acts 1:5
but ye shall be *b* with the Holy................ Acts 1:5
be *b* every one of you in the name ...... Acts 2:38
gladly received his word were *b*............ Acts 2:41
name of Jesus Christ, they were *b* ........ Acts 8:12
and when he was *b*, he continued.......... Acts 8:13
only they were *b* in the name of........... Acts 8:16
what doth hinder me to be *b* ................ Acts 8:36
and he *b* him......................................... Acts 8:38
forthwith, and arose, and was *b*............ Acts 9:18
water, that these should not be *b*........ Acts 10:47
to be *b* in the name of the Lord.......... Acts 10:48
he said, John indeed *b* with water...... Acts 11:16
but ye shall be *b* with the Holy ........... Acts 11:16
And when she was *b*, and her .............. Acts 16:15
and was *b*, he and all his, ..................... Acts 16:33
hearing believed, and were *b* ............... Acts 18:8
them, Unto what then were ye *b*............ Acts 19:3
John verily *b* with the baptism of.......... Acts 19:4
they were *b* in the name of the............. Acts 19:5
arise, and be *b*, and wash away thy ... Acts 22:16
that so many of us as were *b* into.......... Rom 6:3
Christ were *b* into his death .................... Rom 6:3
or were ye *b* in the name of Paul......... 1Cor 1:13
I thank God that I *b* none of you......... 1Cor 1:14
say that I had *b* in mine own name ....... 1Cor 1:15
I *b* also the household of...................... 1Cor 1:16
I know not whether I *b* any other....... 1Cor 1:16
were all *b* unto Moses in the.............. 1Cor 10:2
Spirit are we all *b* into one body....... 1Cor 12:13
they do which are *b* for the dead....... 1Cor 15:29
why are they then *b* for the dead ...... 1Cor 15:29
*b* into Christ have put on Christ.............. Gal 3:27

**BAPTIZEST**
Why *b* thou then, if thou be not.............. Jn 1:25

**BAPTIZETH**
is he which *b* with the Holy Ghost .......... Jn 1:33
witness, behold, the same *b* .................... Jn 3:26

**BAPTIZING**
*b* them in the name of the Father,........ Mt 28:19
beyond Jordan, where John was *b* ............ Jn 1:28
therefore am I come *b* with water ........... Jn 1:31
John also was *b* in Aenon near to ............ Jn 3:23

**BAR**
the middle *b* in the midst of the............ Ex 26:28
he made the middle *b* to shoot .............. Ex 36:33
skins, and shall put it upon a *b*............. Num 4:10
skins, and shall put them on a *b* ........... Num 4:12
posts, and went away with them, *b*..... Judg 16:3
them shut the doors, and *b* them ............ Neh 7:3
will break also the *b* of Damascus ....... Amos 1:5

**BARABBAS** (*ba-rab'-bas*) *A criminal released instead of Jesus.*
then a notable prisoner, called *B* ........... Mt 27:16
*B*, or Jesus which is called..................... Mt 27:17
multitude that they should ask *B* .......... Mt 27:20
They said, *B* .......................................... Mt 27:21
Then released he *B* unto them ............... Mt 27:26
And there was one named *B*, which....... Mk 15:7
should rather release *B* unto them ....... Mk 15:11

people, released *B* unto them, and........ Mk 15:15
this man, and release unto us *B*............ Lk 23:18
saying, Not this man, but *B*.................... Jn 18:40
Now *B* was a robber................................ Jn 18:40

**BARACHEL** (*bar'-ak-el*) *Father of Elihu.*
of Elihu the son of *B* the Buzite.............. Job 32:2
Elihu the son of *B* the Buzite.................. Job 32:6

**BARACHIAH** See BARACHIAS.

**BARACHIAS** (*bar'-ak-i'-as*) *Father of Zachariah.*
the blood of Zacharias son of *B*............ Mt 23:35

**BARAK** (*ba'rak*) *A captain in Deborah's army.*
called *B* the son of Abinoam out........... Judg 4:6
*B* said unto her, If thou wilt go............ Judg 4:8
arose, and went with *B* to Kedesh......... Judg 4:9
*B* called Zebulun and Naphtali to........ Judg 4:10
they shewed Sisera that *B* the son........ Judg 4:12
And Deborah said unto *B*, Up............... Judg 4:14
So *B* went down from mount Tabor,... Judg 4:14
the edge of the sword before *B*............. Judg 4:15
But *B* pursued after the chariots,......... Judg 4:16
as *B* pursued Sisera, Jael came........... Judg 4:22
*B* the son of Abinoam on that day,........ Judg 5:1
arise, *B*, and lead thy captivity............. Judg 5:12
even Issachar, and also *B*..................... Judg 5:15
me to tell of Gedeon, and of *B*............ Heb 11:32

**BARAKEL** See BARACHEL.

**BARBARIAN**
be unto him that speaketh a *b*........... 1Cor 14:11
speaketh shall be a *b* unto me............ 1Cor 14:11
nor uncircumcision, *B*, Scythian,............ Col 3:11

**BARBARIANS**
when the *b* saw the venomous beast... Acts 28:4
both to the Greeks, and to the *B*.......... Rom 1:14

**BARBAROUS**
the *b* people shewed us no little........... Acts 28:2

**BARBED**
thou fill his skin with *b* irons.................. Job 41:7

**BARBER'S**
sharp knife, take thee a *b* razor............... Eze 5:1

**BARE**
*b* Cain, and said, I have gotten a............ Gen 4:1
she again *b* his brother Abel.................... Gen 4:2
and she conceived, and *b* Enoch.............. Gen 4:17
And Adah *b* Jabal.................................. Gen 4:20
she also *b* Tubal-cain, an........................ Gen 4:22
she *b* a son, and called his name............ Gen 4:25
they *b* children to them, the same.......... Gen 6:4
*b* up the ark, and it was lift up............. Gen 7:17
Abram's wife *b* him no children.............. Gen 16:1
And Hagar *b* Abram a son...................... Gen 16:15
his son's name, which Hagar *b*.............. Gen 16:15
when Hagar *b* Ishmael to Abram............ Gen 16:16
And the firstborn *b* a son, and............... Gen 19:37
And the younger, she also *b* a son...... Gen 19:38
and they *b* children.............................. Gen 20:17
*b* Abraham a son in his old age,........... Gen 21:2
unto him, whom Sarah *b* to him............ Gen 21:3
she *b* also Tebah, and Gaham, and..... Gen 22:24
of Milcah, which she *b* unto Nahor.... Gen 24:24
Sarah my master's wife *b* a son to...... Gen 24:36
son, whom Milcah *b* unto him............. Gen 24:47
she *b* him Zimran, and Jokshan, and... Gen 25:2
Sarah's handmaid, *b* unto Abraham... Gen 25:12
years old when she *b* them................... Gen 25:26
*b* a son, and she called his name.......... Gen 29:32
she conceived again, and *b* a son........ Gen 29:33
she conceived again, and *b* a son........ Gen 29:34
she conceived again, and *b* a son........ Gen 29:35
saw that she *b* Jacob no children.......... Gen 30:1
conceived, and *b* Jacob a son................ Gen 30:5
again, and *b* Jacob a second son.......... Gen 30:7
Zilpah Leah's maid *b* Jacob a son....... Gen 30:10
Leah's maid *b* Jacob a second son...... Gen 30:12
and *b* Jacob the fifth son..................... Gen 30:17
again, and *b* Jacob the sixth son......... Gen 30:19
And afterwards she *b* a daughter......... Gen 30:21
And she conceived, and *b* a son.......... Gen 30:23
then all the cattle *b* speckled............... Gen 31:8
then *b* all the cattle ringstraked............. Gen 31:8
I *b* the loss of it.................................. Gen 31:39
which she *b* unto Jacob, went out........ Gen 34:1
And Adah *b* to Esau Eliphaz................ Gen 36:4
and Bashemath *b* Reuel........................ Gen 36:4
And Aholibamah *b* Jeush, and Jaalam, Gen 36:5
and she *b* to Eliphaz Amalek.............. Gen 36:12
she *b* to Esau Jeush, and Jaalam,........ Gen 36:14
And she conceived, and *b* a son........... Gen 38:3
she conceived again, and *b* a son......... Gen 38:4
yet again conceived, and *b* a son.......... Gen 38:5
he was at Chezib, when she *b* him....... Gen 38:5
priest of On *b* unto him...................... Gen 41:50
know that my wife *b* me two sons...... Gen 44:27
which she *b* unto Jacob in.................. Gen 46:15
these she *b* unto Jacob, even............... Gen 46:18
priest of On *b* unto him...................... Gen 46:20
and she *b* these unto Jacob................ Gen 46:25
the woman conceived, and *b* a son............ Ex 2:2
she *b* him a son, and he called his........... Ex 2:22
and she *b* him Aaron and Moses............. Ex 6:20
she *b* him Nadab, and Abihu,................. Ex 6:23
and she *b* him Phinehas........................ Ex 6:25
how I *b* you on eagles' wings, and.......... Ex 19:4
shall be rent, and his head *b*................... Lev 13:45

whether it be *b* within or without........ Lev 13:55
they *b* it between two upon a............. Num 13:23
whom her mother *b* to Levi in............ Num 26:59
*b* unto Amram Aaron and.................... Num 26:59
how that the LORD thy God *b* thee..... Deut 1:31
which *b* the ark of the covenant.......... Deut 31:9
which *b* the ark of the covenant.......... Deut 31:25
as they that *b* the ark were come......... Josh 3:15
the feet of the priests that *b*.................. Josh 3:15
the priests that *b* the ark of the........... Josh 3:17
*b* the ark of the covenant stood............ Josh 4:9
For the priests which *b* the ark............ Josh 4:10
when the priests that *b* the ark............. Josh 4:18
which *b* the ark of the covenant........... Josh 8:33
the people that *b* the present............... Judg 3:18
she also *b* him a son, whose name......... Judg 8:31
And Gilead's wife *b* him sons............... Judg 11:2
and his wife was barren, and *b* not......... Judg 13:2
And the woman *b* a son, and called.. Judg 13:24
Pharez, whom Tamar *b* unto Judah.... Ruth 4:12
her conception, and she *b* a son......... Ruth 4:13
had conceived, that she *b* a son............ 1Sa 1:20
*b* three sons and two daughters............ 1Sa 2:21
the young man that *b* his armour........... 1Sa 14:1
the young man that *b* his armour........... 1Sa 14:6
the man that *b* the shield went............ 1Sa 17:41
that when they that *b* the ark of............ 2Sa 6:13
became his wife, and *b* him a son......... 2Sa 11:27
that Uriah's wife *b* unto David.............. 2Sa 12:15
she *b* a son, and he called his................ 2Sa 12:24
ten young men that *b* Joab's................... 2Sa 18:15
whom she *b* unto Saul, Armoni and...... 2Sa 21:8
his mother *b* him after Absalom............ 1Kin 1:6
and ten thousand that *b* burdens........... 1Kin 5:15
which *b* rule over the people that........ 1Kin 9:23
train, with camels that *b* spices............ 1Kin 10:2
Tahpenes *b* him Genubath his son..... 1Kin 11:20
the LORD, that the guard *b* them......... 1Kin 14:28
*b* a son at that season that.................. 2Kin 4:17
and they *b* them before him................. 2Kin 5:23
she *b* Zimran, and Jokshan, and.......... 1Chr 1:32
his daughter in law *b* him Pharez.......... 1Chr 2:4
And Abigail *b* Amasa............................ 1Chr 2:17
unto him Ephrath, which *b* him Hur... 1Chr 2:19
and she *b* him Segub............................ 1Chr 2:21
then Abiah Hezron's wife *b* him.......... 1Chr 2:24
she *b* him Ahban, and Molid................. 1Chr 2:29
and she *b* him Attai.............................. 1Chr 2:35
*b* Haran, and Moza, and Gazez.............. 1Chr 2:46
concubine, *b* Sheber, and Tirhanah..... 1Chr 2:48
She *b* also Shaaph the father of.......... 1Chr 2:49
Naarah *b* him Ahuzam, and Hepher,..... 1Chr 4:6
Because I *b* him with sorrow................ 1Chr 4:9
she *b* Miriam, and Shammai, and.......... 1Chr 4:17
his wife Jehudijah *b* Jered the............. 1Chr 4:18
Ashriel, whom she *b*............................. 1Chr 7:14
*b* Machir the father of Gilead.............. 1Chr 7:14
the wife of Machir *b* a son.................. 1Chr 7:16
And his sister Hammoleketh *b* Ishod.. 1Chr 7:18
*b* a son, and he called his name......... 1Chr 7:23
children of Judah that *b* shield............ 1Chr 12:24
*b* the ark of God upon their............... 1Chr 15:15
God helped the Levites that *b* the..... 1Chr 15:26
and all the Levites that *b* the ark...... 1Chr 15:27
that *b* rule over the people.................. 2Chr 8:10
company, and camels that *b* spices....... 2Chr 9:1
Which *b* him children.......................... 2Chr 11:19
which *b* him Abijah, and Attai, and.. 2Chr 11:20
had an army of men that *b* targets...... 2Chr 14:8
that *b* shields and drew bows, two...... 2Chr 14:8
the wall, and they that *b* burdens......... Neh 4:17
even their servants *b* rule over............. Neh 5:15
and bitterness to her that *b* him......... Prov 17:25
she that *b* thee shall rejoice............... Prov 23:25
the choice one of her that *b* her.......... Song 6:9
brought thee forth that *b* thee............ Song 8:5
and she conceived, and *b* a son................ Is 8:3
Elam *b* the quiver with chariots............ Is 22:6
strip you, and make you *b*, and gird....... Is 32:11
make *b* the leg, uncover the thigh.......... Is 47:2
father, and unto Sarah that *b* you........... Is 51:2
The LORD hath made *b* his holy arm...... Is 52:10
he *b* the sin of many, and made.............. Is 53:12
he *b* them, and carried them all............... Is 63:9
discovered, and thy heels made *b*.......... Jer 13:22
their mothers that *b* them..................... Jer 16:3
wherein my mother *b* me be blessed...... Jer 20:14
out, and thy mother that *b* thee........... Jer 22:26
But I have made Esau *b*, I have............ Jer 49:10
she that *b* you shall be ashamed........... Jer 50:12
I *b* it upon my shoulder in their.......... Eze 12:7
whereas thou wast naked and *b*............. Eze 16:7
youth, when thou wast naked and *b*... Eze 16:22
jewels, and leave thee naked and *b*....... Eze 16:39
the sceptres of them that *b* rule.......... Eze 19:11
and they were mine, and they *b* sons.... Eze 23:4
and shall leave thee naked and *b*......... Eze 23:29
their sons, whom they *b* unto me......... Eze 23:37
which conceived, and *b* him a son........... Hos 1:3
conceived again, and *b* a daughter.......... Hos 1:6
she conceived, and *b* a son.................... Hos 1:8
he hath made it clean *b*, and cast........... Joel 1:7
infirmities, and *b* our sicknesses........... Mt 8:17
For many *b* false witness against.......... Mk 14:56
*b* false witness against him,................... Mk 14:57
all *b* him witness, and wondered at......... Lk 4:22
they that *b* him stood still..................... Lk 7:14
up, and *b* fruit an hundredfold.................. Lk 8:8
Blessed is the womb that *b* thee............. Lk 11:27
barren, and the wombs that never *b*..... Lk 23:29

John *b* witness of him, and cried,............. Jn 1:15
John *b* record, saying, I saw the............... Jn 1:32
*b* record that this is the Son of.................. Jn 1:34
And they *b* it................................................ Jn 2:8
he *b* witness unto the truth....................... Jn 5:33
bag, and *b* what was put therein................ Jn 12:6
him from the dead, *b* record..................... Jn 12:17
And he that saw it *b* record..................... Jn 19:35
*b* them witness, giving them the............ Acts 15:8
but *b* grain, it may chance of.............. 1Cor 15:37
Who his own self *b* our sins in.............. 1Pet 2:24
Who *b* record of the word of God,.......... Rev 1:2
which *b* twelve manner of fruits,........... Rev 22:2

**BAREFOOT**
his head covered, and he went *b*........... 2Sa 15:30
And he did so, walking naked and *b*........ Is 20:2
*b* three years for a sign and...................... Is 20:3
young and old, naked and *b*...................... Is 20:4

**BAREST**
because thou *b* the ark of the............... 1Kin 2:26
thou never *b* rule over them.................... Is 63:19
Jordan, to whom thou *b* witness.............. Jn 3:26

**BARHUMITE** (*bar'hu-mite*) See BAHARUMITE. *A form of Baharumite.*
the Arbathite, Azmaveth the *B*............. 2Sa 23:31

**BARIAH** (*ba-ri'-ah*) *Grandson of Shechaniah.*
Hattush, and Igeal, and *B*, and............. 1Chr 3:22

**BAR-JESUS** (*bar-je'-sus*) See ELYMAS. *Another name of Elymas.*
prophet, a Jew, whose name was *B*...... Acts 13:6

**BAR-JONA** (*bar-jo'-nah*) See SIMON. *Another name of Simon Peter.*
him, Blessed art thou, Simon *B*............. Mt 16:17

**BAR-JONAH** See BAR-JONA.

**BARK**
are all dumb dogs, they cannot *b*........... Is 56:10

**BARKED**
my vine waste, and *b* my fig tree........... Joel 1:7

**BARKOS** (*bar'-cos*). *A family who returned from the exile.*
The children of *B*, the children................ Ezr 2:53
The children of *B*, the children............. Neh 7:55

**BARLEY**
And the flax and the *b* was smitten......... Ex 9:31
for the *b* was in the ear, and the............. Ex 9:31
a homer of *b* seed shall be valued........ Lev 27:16
tenth part of an ephah of *b* meal.......... Num 5:15
A land of wheat, and *b*, and vines,......... Deut 8:8
a cake of *b* bread tumbled into.............. Judg 7:13
in the beginning of *b* harvest................. Ruth 1:22
and it was about an ephah of *b*.............. Ruth 2:17
glean unto the end of *b* harvest............ Ruth 2:23
he winnoweth *b* to night in the............... Ruth 3:2
it, he measured six measures of *b*........ Ruth 3:15
six measures of *b* gave he me.............. Ruth 3:17
is near mine, and he hath *b* there........ 2Sa 14:30
earthen vessels, and wheat, and *b*........ 2Sa 17:28
in the beginning of *b* harvest.................. 2Sa 21:9
*B* also and straw for the horses and.... 1Kin 4:28
firstfruits, twenty loaves of *b*.............. 2Kin 4:42
and two measures of *b* for a shekel....... 2Kin 7:1
and two measures of *b* for a shekel....... 2Kin 7:16
Two measures of *b* for a shekel............ 2Kin 7:18
was a parcel of ground full of *b*......... 1Chr 11:13
and twenty thousand measures of *b*... 2Chr 2:10
Now therefore the wheat, and the *b*... 2Chr 2:15
of wheat, and ten thousand of *b*........... 2Chr 27:5
of wheat, and cockle instead of *b*......... Job 31:40
wheat and the appointed *b* and the........ Is 28:25
in the field, of wheat, and of *b*............... Jer 41:8
thou also unto thee wheat, and *b*........... Eze 4:9
And thou shalt eat it as *b* cakes............ Eze 4:12
among my people for handfuls of *b*..... Eze 13:19
part of an ephah of an homer of *b*....... Eze 45:13
of *b*, and an half homer of *b*.................. Hos 3:2
for the wheat and for the *b*..................... Joel 1:11
here, which hath five *b* loaves.................. Jn 6:9
fragments of the five *b* loaves................. Jn 6:13
three measures of *b* for a penny............ Rev 6:6

**BARN**
thy seed, and gather it into thy *b*......... Job 39:12
Is the seed yet in the *b*.......................... Hag 2:19
but gather the wheat into my *b*............ Mt 13:30
neither have storehouse nor *b*............... Lk 12:24

**BARNABAS** (*bar'-na-bas*) See JOSES. *A companion of Paul.*
by the apostles was surnamed *B*.......... Acts 4:36
But *B* took him, and brought him to... Acts 9:27
and they sent forth *B*, that he............ Acts 11:22
Then departed *B* to Tarsus................... Acts 11:25
to the elders by the hands of *B*........... Acts 11:30
And *B* and Saul returned from............ Acts 12:25
as *B*, and Simeon that was called......... Acts 13:1
Holy Ghost said, Separate me *B*........... Acts 13:2
who called for *B* and Saul, and.......... Acts 13:7
proselytes followed Paul and *B*........... Acts 13:43
*B* waxed bold, and said, It was........... Acts 13:46
persecution against Paul and *B*........... Acts 13:50
And they called *B*, Jupiter................... Acts 14:12
Which when the apostles, *B*................. Acts 14:14
day he departed with *B* to Derbe........ Acts 14:20
*B* had no small dissension and............. Acts 15:2
they determined that Paul and *B*......... Acts 15:2

silence, and gave audience to *B* ......... Acts 15:12
to Antioch with Paul and *B* ................ Acts 15:22
men unto you with our beloved *B*...... Acts 15:25
*B* continued in Antioch, teaching ........ Acts 15:35
some days after Paul said unto *B* ....... Acts 15:36
*B* determined to take with them......... Acts 15:37
so *B* took Mark, and sailed unto......... Acts 15:39
Or I only and *B*, have not we power..... 1Cor 9:6
went up again to Jerusalem with *B* ........ Gal 2:1
*B* the right hands of fellowship.............. Gal 2:9
insomuch that *B* also was carried........... Gal 2:13
you, and Marcus, sister's son to *B*.......... Col 4:10

**BARNFLOOR**
out of the *b*, or out of the...................... 2Kin 6:27

**BARNS**
So shall thy *b* be filled with.................. Prov 3:10
desolate, the *b* are broken down............ Joel 1:17
do they reap, nor gather into *b*............... Mt 6:26
I will pull down my *b*, and build ........... Lk 12:18

**BARREL**
but an handful of meal in a *b*............. 1Kin 17:12
The *b* of meal shall not waste,............ 1Kin 17:14
the *b* of meal wasted not, neither ...... 1Kin 17:16

**BARRELS**
Fill four *b* with water, and pour......... 1Kin 18:33

**BARREN**
But Sarai was *b*.................................... Gen 11:30
for his wife, because she was *b*........... Gen 25:21
but Rachel was *b*.................................. Gen 29:31
cast their young, nor be *b*...................... Ex 23:26
not be male or female *b* among you ... Deut 7:14
and his wife was *b*, and bare not......... Judg 13:2
unto her, Behold now, thou art *b*.......... Judg 13:3
so that the *b* hath born seven.................. 1Sa 2:5
water is naught, and the ground *b*....... 2Kin 2:19
thence any more death or *b* land......... 2Kin 2:21
entreateth the *b* that beareth not......... Job 24:21
and the *b* land his dwellings ................ Job 39:6
He maketh the *b* woman to keep .......... Ps 113:9
and the *b* womb.................................... Prov 30:16
twins, and none is *b* among them.......... Song 4:2
and there is not one *b* among them..... Song 6:6
Sing, O *b*, thou that didst not.................. Is 54:1
and will drive him into a land *b*............ Joel 2:20
because that Elisabeth was *b*.................... Lk 1:7
month with her, who was called *b*........ Lk 1:36
they shall say, Blessed are the *b*......... Lk 23:29
Rejoice, thou *b* that bearest not ............ Gal 4:27
you that ye shall neither be *b*................ 2Pet 1:8

**BARRENNESS**
A fruitful land into *b*, for the................. Ps 107:34

**BARS**
thou shalt make *b* of shittim wood........ Ex 26:26
five *b* for the boards of the................... Ex 26:27
five *b* for the boards of the side............ Ex 26:27
of gold for places for the *b* ................... Ex 26:29
shalt overlay the *b* with gold ................. Ex 26:29
his taches, and his boards, his *b*............ Ex 35:11
he made *b* of shittim wood..................... Ex 36:31
five *b* for the boards of the.................... Ex 36:32
five *b* for the boards of the.................... Ex 36:32
*b*, and overlaid the *b* with gold............. Ex 36:34
his taches, his boards, his *b* ................. Ex 39:33
thereof, and put in the *b* thereof............ Ex 40:18
the *b* thereof, and the pillars................ Num 3:36
the *b* thereof, and the pillars................. Num 4:31
with high walls, gates, and *b*................. Deut 3:5
into a town that hath gates and *b* .......... 1Sa 23:7
cities with walls and brasen *b*.............. 1Kin 4:13
cities, with walls, gates, and *b* ............. 2Chr 8:5
walls, and towers, gates, and *b* ........... 2Chr 14:7
locks thereof, and the *b* thereof.............. Neh 3:3
locks thereof, and the *b* thereof.............. Neh 3:6
the *b* thereof, and a thousand ................ Neh 3:13
locks thereof, and the *b* thereof............ Neh 3:14
the *b* thereof, and the wall of the........... Neh 3:15
shall go down to the *b* of the pit .......... Job 17:16
for it my decreed place, and set *b* ........ Job 38:10
his bones are like *b* of iron.................. Job 40:18
cut the *b* of iron in sunder ................... Ps 107:16
strengthened the *b* of thy gates ............ Ps 147:13
are like the *b* of a castle..................... Prov 18:19
and cut in sunder the *b* of iron ................. Is 45:2
which have neither gates nor *b* ............. Jer 49:31
her *b* are broken ................................... Jer 51:30
he hath destroyed and broken her *b*...... Lam 2:9
and having neither *b* nor gates............ Eze 38:11
the earth with her *b* was about me......... Jonah 2:6
the fire shall devour thy *b*..................... Nah 3:13

**BARSABAS** (*bar'-sab-as*) See JOSEPH, JUDAS, JUSTUS.
*1. A candidate for apostle.*
appointed two, Joseph called *B* ............. Acts 1:23
*2. A disciple sent to Antioch with Silas.*
namely, Judas surnamed *B*, and.......... Acts 15:22

**BARSABBAS** See BARSABAS.

**BARTHOLOMEW** (*bar-thol'-o-mew*) See NATHANAEL. *One of Jesus' twelve disciples.*
Philip, and *B*; Thomas, and........................ Mt 10:3
And Andrew, and Philip, and *B*............... Mk 3:18
James and John, Philip and *B* ................... Lk 6:14
and Andrew, Philip, and Thomas, *B*..... Acts 1:13

**BARTIMAEUS** (*bar-ti-me'-us*) *A blind beggar.*
a great number of people, blind *B*......... Mk 10:46

**BARUCH** (*ba'-rook*)
*1. A son of Zabbai.*
After him *B* the son of Zabbai .............. Neh 3:20
Daniel, Ginnethon, *B*,............................. Neh 10:6
*2. A descendant of Perez.*
And Maaseiah the son of *B*, the son..... Neh 11:5
*3. The scribe of Jeremiah.*
purchase unto *B* the son of Neriah ....... Jer 32:12
I charged *B* before them, saying,........... Jer 32:13
purchase unto *B* the son of Neriah ....... Jer 32:16
called *B* the son of Neriah...................... Jer 36:4
*B* wrote from the mouth of...................... Jer 36:4
And Jeremiah commanded *B*, saying,....... Jer 36:5
*B* the son of Neriah did according........... Jer 36:8
Then read *B* in the book the words ...... Jer 36:10
when *B* read the book in the ears ......... Jer 36:13
the son of Cushi, unto *B*....................... Jer 36:14
So *B* the son of Neriah took the........... Jer 36:14
So *B* read it in their ears...................... Jer 36:15
both one and other, and said unto *B*.... Jer 36:16
And they asked *B*, saying, Tell us ........ Jer 36:17
Then *B* answered them, He..................... Jer 36:18
Then said the princes unto *B*................. Jer 36:19
to take *B* the scribe and Jeremiah......... Jer 36:26
the words which *B* wrote at the ............ Jer 36:27
roll, and gave it to *B* the scribe............ Jer 36:32
But *B* the son of Neriah setteth.............. Jer 43:3
prophet, and *B* the son of Neriah ........... Jer 43:6
spake unto *B* the son of Neriah .............. Jer 45:1
the God of Israel, unto thee, O *B* ........... Jer 45:2

**BARZILLAI** (*bar-zil'-la-i*)
*1. A friend of David.*
*B* the Gileadite of Rogelim,................. 2Sa 17:27
*B* the Gileadite came down from ......... 2Sa 19:31
Now *B* was a very aged man, even ...... 2Sa 19:32
And the king said unto *B*, Come .......... 2Sa 19:33
*B* said unto the king, How long............ 2Sa 19:34
was come over, the king kissed *B* ....... 2Sa 19:39
unto the sons of *B* the Gileadite........... 1Kin 2:7
of Koz, the children of *B*...................... Ezr 2:61
the daughters of *B* the Gileadite.......... Ezr 2:61
of Koz, the children of *B* ..................... Neh 7:63
of *B* the Gileadite to wife .................... Neh 7:63
*2. Husband of Merab.*
the son of *B* the Meholathite.................... 2Sa 21:8

**BASE**
will be *b* in mine own sight..................... 2Sa 6:22
cubits was the length of one *b*............ 1Kin 7:27
the ledges there was a *b* above .......... 1Kin 7:29
every *b* had four brasen wheels,.......... 1Kin 7:30
was round after the work of the *b*....... 1Kin 7:31
the wheels were joined to the *b* .......... 1Kin 7:32
to the four corners of one *b* ................ 1Kin 7:34
were of the very *b* itself....................... 1Kin 7:34
in the top of the *b* was there a ........... 1Kin 7:35
on the top of the *b* the ledges ............. 1Kin 7:35
of fools, yea, children of *b* men........... Job 30:8
the *b* against the honourable .................... Is 3:5
That the kingdom might be *b* ............... Eze 17:14
they shall be there a *b* kingdom .......... Eze 29:14
and set there upon her own *b*............... Zec 5:11
and *b* before all the people, ..................... Mal 2:9
*b* things of the world, and things.......... 1Cor 1:28
who in presence am *b* among you ....... 2Cor 10:1

**BASEMATH** See BASMATH.

**BASER**
lewd fellows of the *b* sort ...................... Acts 17:5

**BASES**
And he made ten *b* of brass.................. 1Kin 7:27
the work of the *b* was on this............... 1Kin 7:28
this manner he made the ten *b*............. 1Kin 7:37
every one of the ten *b* one laver .......... 1Kin 7:38
he put five *b* on the right side.............. 1Kin 7:39
ten *b*, and ten lavers on the *b* ............. 1Kin 7:43
Ahaz cut off the borders of the *b*....... 2Kin 16:17
the house of the LORD, and the *b* ....... 2Kin 25:13
the *b* which Solomon had made for... 2Kin 25:16
*b*, and lavers made he upon the *b*........ 2Chr 4:14
And they set the altar upon his *b*.............. Ezr 3:3
the sea, and concerning the *b* ............... Jer 27:19
the house of the LORD, and the *b*........... Jer 52:17
bulls that were under the *b*................... Jer 52:20

**BASEST**
It shall be the *b* of the kingdoms ......... Eze 29:15
setteth up over it the *b* of men.............. Dan 4:17

**BASHAN** (*ba'-shan*) See BASHAN-HAVOTH-JAIR. *Kingdom of King Og.*
turned and went up by the way of *B* Num 21:33
Og the king of *B* went out against..... Num 21:33
and the kingdom of Og king of *B*...... Num 32:33
in Heshbon, and Og the king of *B*......... Deut 1:4
turned, and went up the way to *B*.......... Deut 3:1
Og the king of *B* came out against......... Deut 3:1
our hands Og also, the king of *B* ........... Deut 3:3
of Argob, the kingdom of Og in *B* ......... Deut 3:4
plain, and all Gilead, and all *B* ........... Deut 3:10
cities of the kingdom of Og in *B*.......... Deut 3:10
For only Og king of *B* remained of...... Deut 3:11
And the rest of Gilead, and all *B*......... Deut 3:13
the region of Argob, with all *B*............. Deut 3:13
and Golan in *B*, of the Manassites......... Deut 4:43
land, and the land of Og king of *B*....... Deut 4:47
of Heshbon, and Og the king of *B* ........ Deut 29:7
lambs, and rams of the breed of *B*..... Deut 32:14
he shall leap from *B* ............................. Deut 33:22
of Heshbon, and to Og king of *B* .......... Josh 9:10
And the coast of Og king of *B*............... Josh 12:4
Hermon, and in Salcah, and in all *B* .... Josh 12:5
Hermon, and all *B* unto Salcah ........... Josh 13:11
All the kingdom of Og in *B*................... Josh 13:12
coast was from Mahanaim, all *B*........... Josh 13:30
all the kingdom of Og king of *B* .......... Josh 13:30
the towns of Jair, which are in *B*......... Josh 13:30
cities of the kingdom of Og in *B*.......... Josh 13:31
war, therefore he had Gilead and *B* ..... Josh 17:1
beside the land of Gilead and *B*.............. Josh 17:5
Golan in *B* out of the tribe of.................. Josh 20:8
the half tribe of Manasseh in *B* ............ Josh 21:6
gave Golan in *B* with her suburbs...... Josh 21:27
Moses had given possession in *B* .......... Josh 22:7
region of Argob, which is in *B* ............. 1Kin 4:13
the Amorites, and of Og king of *B* ....... 1Kin 4:19
the river Arnon, even Gilead and *B*... 2Kin 10:33
in the land of *B* unto Salchah .............. 1Chr 5:11
next, and Jaanai, and Shaphat in *B*...... 1Chr 5:12
And they dwelt in Gilead in *B* ............ 1Chr 5:16
increased from *B* unto Baal-hermon..... 1Chr 5:23
out of the tribe of Manasseh in *B*......... 1Chr 6:62
Golan in *B* with her suburbs, and ........ 1Chr 6:71
and the land of Og king of *B*................. Neh 9:22
strong bulls of *B* have beset me............. Ps 22:12
hill of God is as the hill of *B*................. Ps 68:15
an high hill as the hill of *B*.................... Ps 68:15
said, I will bring again from *B*............... Ps 68:22
of the Amorites, and Og king of *B* ....... Ps 135:11
And Og the king of *B* ........................... Ps 136:20
up, and upon all the oaks of *B* .................. Is 2:13
and *B* and Carmel shake off their............ Is 33:9
and lift up thy voice in *B*....................... Jer 22:20
and he shall feed on Carmel and *B* ...... Jer 50:19
Of the oaks of *B* have they made........... Eze 27:6
all of them fatlings of *B*........................ Eze 39:18
Hear this word, ye kine of *B*.................. Amos 4:1
let them feed in *B* and Gilead, as ........... Mic 7:14
*B* languisheth, and Carmel, and the........ Nah 1:4
howl, O ye oaks of *B* ............................... Zec 11:2

**BASHAN-HAVOTH-JAIR** (*ba'''-shan-ha''-voth-ja'-ur*) *Same as Argob.*
called them after his own name, *B*...... Deut 3:14

**BASHEMATH** (*bash'-e-math*) See BASMATH.
*1. Daughter of Elon the Hittite.*
*B* the daughter of Elon the ................... Gen 26:34
*2. Daughter of Ishmael.*
*B* Ishmael's daughter, sister of................ Gen 36:3
and *B* bare Reuel ...................................... Gen 36:4
the son of *B* the wife of Esau............... Gen 36:10
were the sons of *B* Esau's wife............. Gen 36:13
are the sons of *B* Esau's wife................. Gen 36:17

**BASKET**
in the uppermost *b* there was of........... Gen 40:17
them out of the *b* upon my head........... Gen 40:17
*b*, and bring them in the *b*...................... Ex 29:3
one wafer out of the *b* of the................. Ex 29:23
and the bread that is in the *b* ............... Ex 29:32
rams, and a *b* of unleavened bread.......... Lev 8:2
out of the *b* of unleavened bread,.......... Lev 8:26
that is in the *b* of consecrations.............. Lev 8:31
a *b* of unleavened bread, cakes of.......... Num 6:15
with the *b* of unleavened bread............. Num 6:17
one unleavened cake out of the *b*......... Num 6:19
thee, and shalt put it in a *b*.................... Deut 26:2
take the *b* out of thine hand.................. Deut 26:4
Blessed shall be thy *b* and thy............... Deut 28:5
Cursed shall be thy *b* and thy............. Deut 28:17
the flesh he put in a *b*, and he............... Judg 6:19
One *b* had very good figs, even............... Jer 24:2
the other *b* had very naughty figs........... Jer 24:2
behold a *b* of summer fruit ................... Amos 8:1
And I said, A *b* of summer fruit............ Amos 8:2
let him down by the wall in a *b*............. Acts 9:25
through a window in a *b* was I let..... 2Cor 11:33

**BASKETS**
I had three white *b* on my head............ Gen 40:16
The three *b* are three days.................... Gen 40:18
persons, and put their heads in *b* ......... 2Kin 10:7
as a grapegatherer into the *b* .................... Jer 6:9
two *b* of figs were set before the............. Jer 24:1
that remained twelve *b* full................... Mt 14:20
meat that was left seven *b* full............... Mt 15:37
and how many *b* ye took up...................... Mt 16:9
and how many *b* ye took up.................... Mt 16:10
they took up twelve *b* full of the............ Mk 6:43
broken meat that was left seven *b* .......... Mk 8:8
how many *b* full of fragments took......... Mk 8:19
how many *b* full of fragments took......... Mk 8:20
that remained to them twelve *b*............... Lk 9:17
and filled twelve *b* with the .................... Jn 6:13

**BASMATH** (*bas'-math*) See BASHEMATH. *A daughter of Solomon.*
he also took *B* the daughter of ............ 1Kin 4:15

**BASON**
it in the blood that is in the *b*............... Ex 12:22
with the blood that is in the *b* ............... Ex 12:22
gave gold by weight for every *b*......... 1Chr 28:17
by weight for every *b* of silver........... 1Chr 28:17
that he poureth water into a *b*................. Jn 13:5

**BASONS**
half of the blood, and put it in *b* .............. Ex 24:6
ashes, and his shovels, and his *b*.............. Ex 27:3
pots, and the shovels, and the *b*............... Ex 38:3

and the shovels, and the *b* ... Num 4:14
Brought beds, and *b*, and earthen ... 2Sa 17:28
lavers, and the shovels, and the *b* ... 1Kin 7:40
pots, and the shovels, and the *b* ... 1Kin 7:45
bowls, and the snuffers, and the *b* ... 1Kin 7:50
LORD bowls of silver, snuffers, *b* ... 2Kin 12:13
for the golden *b* he gave gold by ... 1Chr 28:17
And he made an hundred *b* of gold ... 2Chr 4:8
pots, and the shovels, and the *b* ... 2Chr 4:11
And the snuffers, and the *b* ... 2Chr 4:22
Thirty *b* of gold, silver *b* ... Ezr 1:10
Also twenty *b* of gold, of a ... Ezr 8:27
a thousand drams of gold, fifty *b* ... Neh 7:70
And the *b*, and the firepans, and the ... Jer 52:19

**BASTARD**
A *b* shall not enter into the ... Deut 23:2
a *b* shall dwell in Ashdod, and I ... Zec 9:6

**BASTARDS**
all are partakers, then are ye *b* ... Heb 12:8

**BAT**
kind, and the lapwing, and the *b* ... Lev 11:19
kind, and the lapwing, and the *b* ... Deut 14:18

**BATH**
of vineyard shall yield one *b* ... Is 5:10
and a just ephah, and a just *b* ... Eze 45:10
the *b* shall be of one measure ... Eze 45:11
that the *b* may contain the tenth ... Eze 45:11
the *b* of oil, ye shall offer the ... Eze 45:14
tenth part of a *b* out of the cor ... Eze 45:14

**BATHE**
*b* himself in water, and be unclean ... Lev 15:5
*b* himself in water, and be unclean ... Lev 15:6
*b* himself in water, and be unclean ... Lev 15:7
*b* himself in water, and be unclean ... Lev 15:8
*b* himself in water, and be unclean ... Lev 15:10
*b* himself in water, and be unclean ... Lev 15:11
*b* his flesh in running water, and ... Lev 15:13
they shall both *b* themselves in ... Lev 15:18
*b* himself in water, and be unclean ... Lev 15:21
*b* himself in water, and be unclean ... Lev 15:22
*b* himself in water, and be unclean ... Lev 15:27
and *b* his flesh in water, and ... Lev 16:26
and *b* his flesh in water, and ... Lev 16:28
*b* himself in water, and be unclean ... Lev 17:15
he wash them not, nor *b* his flesh ... Lev 17:16
he shall *b* his flesh in water, and ... Num 19:7
*b* his flesh in water, and shall be ... Num 19:8
*b* himself in water, and shall be ... Num 19:19

**BATHED**
For my sword shall be *b* in heaven ... Is 34:5

**BATH-RABBIM** (*bath-rab'-bim*) *A gate at Heshbon.*
in Heshbon, by the gate of *B* ... Song 7:4

**BATHS**
it contained two thousand *b* ... 1Kin 7:26
one laver contained forty *b* ... 1Kin 7:38
and twenty thousand *b* of wine ... 2Chr 2:10
and twenty thousand *b* of oil ... 2Chr 2:10
received and held three thousand *b* ... 2Chr 4:5
wheat, and to an hundred *b* of wine ... Ezr 7:22
and to an hundred *b* of oil ... Ezr 7:22
cor, which is an homer of ten *b* ... Eze 45:14
for ten *b* are an homer ... Eze 45:14

**BATH-SHEBA** (*bath'-she-bah*) See BATH-SHUA. *A wife of David.*
And one said, Is not this *B* ... 2Sa 11:3
And David comforted *B* his wife ... 2Sa 12:24
unto *B* the mother of Solomon ... 1Kin 1:11
*B* went in unto the king into the ... 1Kin 1:15
*B* bowed, and did obeisance unto ... 1Kin 1:16
David answered and said, Call me *B* ... 1Kin 1:28
Then *B* bowed with her face to the ... 1Kin 1:31
came to *B* the mother of Solomon ... 1Kin 2:13
And *B* said, Well ... 1Kin 2:18
*B* therefore went unto king ... 1Kin 2:19
him, after he had gone in to *B* ... Ps 51:*t*

**BATH-SHUA** (*bath'-shu-ah*) See BATH-SHEBA. *A form of Bath-sheba.*
of *B* the daughter of Ammiel ... 1Chr 3:5

**BATS**
worship, to the moles and to the *b* ... Is 2:20

**BATTERED**
that were with Joab *b* the wall ... 2Sa 20:15

**BATTERING**
set *b* rams against it round about ... Eze 4:2
to appoint *b* rams against the ... Eze 21:22

**BATTLE**
they joined *b* with them in the ... Gen 14:8
all his people, to the *b* at Edrei ... Num 21:33
hundreds, which came from the *b* ... Num 31:14
men of war which went to the *b* ... Num 31:21
war upon them, who went out to *b* .. Num 31:27
men of war which went out to *b* ... Num 31:28
for war, before the LORD to *b* ... Num 32:27
over Jordan, every man armed to *b* .. Num 32:29
neither contend with them in *b* ... Deut 2:9
it, and contend with him in *b* ... Deut 2:24
and all his people, to *b* at Edrei ... Deut 3:1
out to *b* against thine enemies ... Deut 20:1
when ye are come nigh unto the *b* ... Deut 20:2
day unto *b* against your enemies ... Deut 20:3
his house, lest he die in the *b* ... Deut 20:5
his house, lest he die in the *b* ... Deut 20:6
his house, lest he die in the *b* ... Deut 20:7
came out against us unto *b* ... Deut 29:7
over before the LORD unto *b* ... Josh 4:13
city went out against Israel to *b* ... Josh 8:14
all other they took in *b* ... Josh 11:19
should come against Israel in *b* ... Josh 11:20
intend to go up against them in *b* ... Josh 22:33
from *b* before the sun was up ... Judg 8:13
to go out to *b* against the ... Judg 20:14
to the *b* against the children of ... Judg 20:18
went out to *b* against Benjamin ... Judg 20:20
set their *b* again in array in the ... Judg 20:22
Shall I go up again to *b* against ... Judg 20:23
out to *b* against the children of ... Judg 20:28
of all Israel, and the *b* was sore ... Judg 20:34
men of Israel retired in the *b* ... Judg 20:39
down before us, as in the first *b* ... Judg 20:39
but the *b* overtook them ... Judg 20:42
out against the Philistines to *b* ... 1Sa 4:1
and when they joined *b*, Israel was ... 1Sa 4:2
drew near to *b* against Israel ... 1Sa 7:10
it came to pass in the day of *b* ... 1Sa 13:22
themselves, and they came to the *b* ... 1Sa 14:20
followed hard after them in the *b* ... 1Sa 14:22
the *b* passed over unto Beth-aven ... 1Sa 14:23
together their armies to *b* ... 1Sa 17:1
set the *b* in array against the ... 1Sa 17:2
come out to set your *b* in array ... 1Sa 17:8
went and followed Saul to the *b* ... 1Sa 17:13
the *b* were Eliab the first born ... 1Sa 17:13
the fight, and shouted for the *b* ... 1Sa 17:20
had put the *b* in array, army ... 1Sa 17:21
down that thou mightest see the *b* ... 1Sa 17:28
for the *b* is the LORD'S, and he ... 1Sa 17:47
or he shall descend into *b* ... 1Sa 26:10
thou shalt go out with me to *b* ... 1Sa 28:1
let him not go down with us to *b* ... 1Sa 29:4
lest in the *b* he be an adversary ... 1Sa 29:4
shall not go up with us to the *b* ... 1Sa 29:9
part is that goeth down to the *b* ... 1Sa 30:24
the *b* went sore against Saul, and ... 1Sa 31:3
the people are fled from the *b* ... 2Sa 1:4
fallen in the midst of the *b* ... 2Sa 1:25
there was a very sore *b* that day ... 2Sa 2:17
brother Asahel at Gibeon in the *b* ... 2Sa 3:30
put the *b* in array at the ... 2Sa 10:8
of the *b* was against him before ... 2Sa 10:9
unto the *b* against the Syrians ... 2Sa 10:13
the time when kings go forth to *b* ... 2Sa 11:1
in the forefront of the hottest *b* ... 2Sa 11:15
make thy *b* more strong against ... 2Sa 11:25
that thou go to *b* in thine own ... 2Sa 17:11
the *b* was in the wood of Ephraim ... 2Sa 18:6
For the *b* was there scattered ... 2Sa 18:8
steal away when they flee in *b* ... 2Sa 19:3
we anointed over us, is dead in *b* ... 2Sa 19:10
shalt go no more out with us to *b* ... 2Sa 21:17
that there was again a *b* with the ... 2Sa 21:18
there was again a *b* in Gob with ... 2Sa 21:19
And there was yet a *b* in Gath ... 2Sa 21:20
hast girded me with strength to *b* ... 2Sa 22:40
were there gathered together to *b* ... 2Sa 23:9
go out to *b* against their enemy ... 1Kin 8:44
he said, Who shall order the *b* ... 1Kin 20:14
the seventh day the *b* was joined ... 1Kin 20:29
went out into the midst of the *b* ... 1Kin 20:39
go with me to *b* to Ramoth-gilead ... 1Kin 22:4
I go against Ramoth-gilead to *b* ... 1Kin 22:6
we go against Ramoth-gilead to *b* ... 1Kin 22:15
myself, and enter into the *b* ... 1Kin 22:30
himself, and went into the *b* ... 1Kin 22:30
And the *b* increased that day ... 1Kin 22:35
thou go with me against Moab to *b* ... 2Kin 3:7
that the *b* was too sore for him ... 2Kin 3:26
for they cried to God in the *b* ... 1Chr 5:20
fit to go out for war and *b* ... 1Chr 7:11
to *b* was twenty and six thousand ... 1Chr 7:40
the *b* went sore against Saul, and ... 1Chr 10:3
were gathered together to *b* ... 1Chr 11:13
and men of war fit for the *b* ... 1Chr 12:8
the Philistines against Saul to *b* ... 1Chr 12:19
Zebulun, such as went forth to *b* ... 1Chr 12:33
of Asher, such as went forth to *b* ... 1Chr 12:36
of instruments of war for the *b* ... 1Chr 12:37
that then thou shalt go out to *b* ... 1Chr 14:15
from their cities, and came to *b* ... 1Chr 19:7
put the *b* in array before the ... 1Chr 19:9
the *b* was set against him before ... 1Chr 19:10
before the Syrians unto the *b* ... 1Chr 19:14
set the *b* in array against them ... 1Chr 19:17
So when David had put the *b* in ... 1Chr 19:17
the time that kings go out to *b* ... 1Chr 20:1
Abijah set the *b* in array with an ... 2Chr 13:3
Jeroboam also set the *b* in array ... 2Chr 13:3
the *b* was before and behind ... 2Chr 13:14
they set the *b* in array in the ... 2Chr 14:10
Shall we go to Ramoth-gilead to *b* ... 2Chr 18:5
shall we go to Ramoth-gilead to *b* ... 2Chr 18:14
myself, and will go to the *b* ... 2Chr 18:29
and they went to the *b* ... 2Chr 18:29
And the *b* increased that day ... 2Chr 18:34
came against Jehoshaphat to *b* ... 2Chr 20:1
for the *b* is not yours, but God's ... 2Chr 20:15
shall not need to fight in this *b* ... 2Chr 20:17
go, do it, be strong for the *b* ... 2Chr 25:8
they should not go with him to *b* ... 2Chr 25:13
him, as a king ready to the *b* ... Job 15:24
of trouble, against the day of *b* ... Job 38:23
and he smelleth the *b* afar off ... Job 39:25
hand upon him, remember the *b* ... Job 41:8
me with strength unto the *b* ... Ps 18:39
and mighty, the LORD mighty in *b* ... Ps 24:8
from the *b* that was against me ... Ps 55:18
shield, and the sword, and the *b* ... Ps 76:3
bows, turned back in the day of *b* ... Ps 78:9
not made him to stand in the *b* ... Ps 89:43
covered my head in the day of *b* ... Ps 140:7
is prepared against the day of *b* ... Prov 21:31
nor the *b* to the strong, neither ... Eccl 9:11
For every *b* of the warrior is ... Is 9:5
hosts mustereth the host of the *b* ... Is 13:4
with the sword, nor dead in *b* ... Is 22:2
briers and thorns against me in *b* ... Is 27:4
them that turn the *b* to the gate ... Is 28:6
his anger, and the strength of *b* ... Is 42:25
as the horse rusheth into the *b* ... Jer 8:6
men be slain by the sword in *b* ... Jer 18:21
and shield, and draw near to *b* ... Jer 46:3
against her, and rise up to the *b* ... Jer 49:14
A sound of *b* is in the land, and ... Jer 50:22
put in array, like a man to the *b* ... Jer 50:42
Thou art my *b* ax and weapons of ... Jer 51:20
but none goeth to the *b* ... Eze 7:14
in the *b* in the day of the LORD ... Eze 13:5
neither in anger, nor in *b* ... Dan 11:20
stirred up to *b* with a very great ... Dan 11:25
by bow, nor by sword, nor by *b* ... Hos 1:7
the *b* out of the earth, and will ... Hos 2:18
the *b* in Gibeah against the ... Hos 10:9
Beth-arbel in the day of *b* ... Hos 10:14
as a strong people set in *b* array ... Joel 2:5
with shouting in the day of *b* ... Amos 1:14
let us rise up against her in *b* ... Obad 1
the *b* bow shall be cut off ... Zec 9:10
them as his goodly horse in the *b* ... Zec 10:3
the nail, out of him the *b* bow ... Zec 10:4
the mire of the streets in the *b* ... Zec 10:5
nations against Jerusalem to *b* ... Zec 14:2
as when he fought in the day of *b* ... Zec 14:3
shall prepare himself to the *b* ... 1Cor 14:8
like unto horses prepared unto *b* ... Rev 9:7
of many horses running to *b* ... Rev 9:9
to gather them to the *b* of that ... Rev 16:14
to gather them together to *b* ... Rev 20:8

**BATTLEMENT**
thou shalt make a *b* for thy roof ... Deut 22:8

**BATTLEMENTS**
take away her *b* ... Jer 5:10

**BATTLES**
go out before us, and fight our *b* ... 1Sa 8:20
for me, and fight the LORD'S *b* ... 1Sa 18:17
lord fighteth the *b* of the LORD ... 1Sa 25:28
Out of the spoils won in *b* did ... 1Chr 26:27
God to help us, and to fight our *b* ... 2Chr 32:8
in *b* of shaking will he fight ... Is 30:32

**BAVAI** (*bav'-a-i*) *A descendant of Henadad.*
*B* the son of Henadad, the ruler ... Neh 3:18

**BAVVAI** See BAVAI.

**BAY**
from the *b* that looketh southward ... Josh 15:2
the *b* of the sea at the uttermost ... Josh 15:5
*b* of the salt sea at the south ... Josh 18:19
himself like a green *b* tree ... Ps 37:35
chariot grisled and *b* horses ... Zec 6:3
the *b* went forth, and sought to go ... Zec 6:7

**BAZLITH** (*baz-'lith*) See BAZLUTH. *A family who returned from exile.*
The children of *B*, the children ... Neh 7:54

**BAZLUTH** (*baz'-luth*) See BAZLITH. *A form of Bazlith.*
The children of *B*, the children ... Ezr 2:52

**BDELLIUM**
there is *b* and the onyx stone ... Gen 2:12
colour thereof as the colour of *b* ... Num 11:7

**BE** See PREFACE.

**BEACON**
till ye be left as a *b* upon the ... Is 30:17

**BEALIAH** (*be-a-li'-ah*) *A warrior in David's army.*
Eluzai, and Jerimoth, and *B* ... 1Chr 12:5

**BEALOTH** (*be'-a-loth*) See ALOTH. *A city in Judah.*
Ziph, and Telem, and *B*, ... Josh 15:24

**BEAM**
went away with the pin of the *b* ... Judg 16:14
his spear was like a weaver's *b* ... 1Sa 17:7
whose spear was like a weaver's *b* ... 2Sa 21:19
the thick *b* were before them ... 1Kin 7:6
and take thence every man a *b* ... 2Kin 6:2
But as one was felling a *b* ... 2Kin 6:5
was a spear like a weaver's *b* ... 1Chr 11:23
spear staff was like a weaver's *b* ... 1Chr 20:5
the *b* out of the timber shall ... Hab 2:11
but considerest not the *b* that is ... Mt 7:3
behold, a *b* is in thine own eye ... Mt 7:4
first cast out the *b* out of thine ... Mt 7:5
but perceivest not the *b* that is ... Lk 6:41
the *b* that is in thine own eye ... Lk 6:42
cast out first the *b* out of thine ... Lk 6:42

**BEAMS**
that the *b* should not be fastened ... 1Kin 6:6
and covered the house with *b* ... 1Kin 6:9

hewed stone, and a row of cedar *b* 1Kin 6:36
with cedar *b* upon the pillars 1Kin 7:2
with cedar above upon the *b* 1Kin 7:3
hewed stones, and a row of cedar *b* 1Kin 7:12
He overlaid also the house, the *b* 2Chr 3:7
*b* for the gates of the palace Neh 2:8
who also laid the *b* thereof Neh 3:3
they laid the *b* thereof, and set Neh 3:6
Who layeth the *b* of his chambers Ps 104:3
The *b* of our house are cedar, and Song 1:17

**BEANS**

and flour, and parched corn, and *b* 2Sa 17:28
unto thee wheat, and barley, and *b* Eze 4:9

**BEAR**

is greater than I can *b* Gen 4:13
the land was not able to *b* them Gen 13:6
art with child, and shalt *b* a son Gen 16:11
that is ninety years old, *b* Gen 17:17
wife shall *b* thee a son indeed Gen 17:19
which Sarah shall *b* unto thee at Gen 17:21
Shall I of a surety *b* a child Gen 18:13
these eight Milcah did *b* to Nahor Gen 22:23
she shall *b* upon my knees, that I Gen 30:3
*b* them because of their cattle Gen 36:7
then let me *b* the blame for ever Gen 43:9
then I shall *b* the blame to my Gen 44:32
and bowed his shoulder to *b* Gen 49:15
they shall *b* the burden with thee Ex 18:22
Thou shalt not *b* false witness Ex 20:16
of the staves to *b* the table Ex 25:27
two sides of the altar, to *b* it Ex 27:7
Aaron shall *b* their names before Ex 28:12
Aaron shall *b* the names of the Ex 28:29
Aaron shall *b* the judgment of the Ex 28:30
that Aaron may *b* the iniquity of Ex 28:38
that they *b* not iniquity, and die Ex 28:43
for the staves to *b* it withal Ex 30:4
sides of the ark, to *b* the ark Ex 37:5
for the staves to *b* the table Ex 37:14
them with gold, to *b* the table Ex 37:15
for the staves to *b* it withal Ex 37:27
of the altar, to *b* it withal Ex 38:7
it, then he shall *b* his iniquity Lev 5:1
guilty, and shall *b* his iniquity Lev 5:17
eateth of it shall *b* his iniquity Lev 7:18
it you to *b* the iniquity of the Lev 10:17
But if she *b* a maid child, then Lev 12:5
the goat shall *b* upon him all Lev 16:22
then he shall *b* his iniquity Lev 17:16
eateth it shall *b* his iniquity Lev 19:8
nor *b* any grudge against the Lev 19:18
he shall *b* his iniquity Lev 20:17
they shall *b* their iniquity Lev 20:19
they shall *b* their sin Lev 20:20
lest they *b* sin for it, and die Lev 22:9
Or suffer them to *b* the iniquity Lev 22:16
curseth his God shall *b* his sin Lev 24:15
they shall *b* the tabernacle, and Num 1:50
sons of Kohath shall come to *b* it Num 4:15
they shall *b* the curtains of the Num 4:25
this woman shall *b* her iniquity Num 5:31
should *b* upon their shoulders Num 7:9
season, that man shall *b* his sin Num 9:13
I am not able to *b* all this Num 11:14
they shall *b* the burden of the Num 11:17
that thou *b* it not thyself alone Num 11:17
How long shall I *b* with this evil Num 14:27
*b* your whoredoms, until your Num 14:33
shall ye *b* your iniquities, even Num 14:34
*b* the iniquity of the sanctuary Num 18:1
thy sons with thee shall *b* the Num 18:1
the congregation, lest they *b* sin Num 18:22
they shall *b* their iniquity Num 18:23
ye shall *b* no sin by reason of it Num 18:32
then he shall *b* her iniquity Num 30:15
am not able to *b* you myself alone Deut 1:9
I myself alone *b* your cumbrance Deut 1:12
thee, as a man doth *b* his son Deut 1:31
Neither shalt thou *b* false Deut 5:20
to *b* the ark of the covenant of Deut 10:8
her children which she shall *b* Deut 28:57
that *b* the ark of the covenant Josh 3:8
that *b* the ark of the LORD Josh 3:13
that *b* the ark of the testimony Josh 4:16
seven priests shall *b* before the Josh 6:4
let seven priests *b* seven Josh 6:6
thou shalt conceive, and *b* a son Judg 13:3
thou shalt conceive, and *b* a son Judg 13:5
thou shalt conceive, and *b* a son Judg 13:7
to night, and should also *b* sons Ruth 1:12
and there came a lion, and a *b* 1Sa 17:34
slew both the lion and the *b* 1Sa 17:36
lion, and out of the paw of the *b* 1Sa 17:37
as a *b* robbed of her whelps in 2Sa 17:8
*b* the king tidings, how that the 2Sa 18:19
Thou shalt not *b* tidings this day 2Sa 18:20
but thou shalt *b* tidings another 2Sa 18:20
this day thou shalt *b* no tidings 2Sa 18:20
it was not my son, which I did *b* 1Kin 3:21
to *b* witness against him, saying 1Kin 21:10
which thou puttest on me will I *b* 2Kin 18:14
root downward, and *b* fruit upward 2Kin 19:30
men, men able to *b* buckler 1Chr 5:18
and ten thousand men to *b* burdens 2Chr 2:2
should *b* rule in his own house Est 1:22
I *b* up the pillars of it Ps 75:3
how I do *b* in my bosom the Ps 89:50
They shall *b* thee up in their Ps 91:12
scornest, thou alone shalt *b* it Prov 9:12
hand of the diligent shall *b* rule Prov 12:24
Let a *b* robbed of her whelps meet Prov 17:12
but a wounded spirit who can *b* Prov 18:14
As a roaring lion, and a ranging *b* Prov 28:15
and for four which it cannot *b* Prov 30:21
whereof every one *b* twins Song 4:2
I am weary to *b* them Is 1:14
*b* a son, and shall call his name Is 7:14
And the cow and the *b* shall feed Is 11:7
root downward, and *b* fruit upward Is 37:31
I have made, and I will *b* Is 46:4
They *b* him upon the shoulder Is 46:7
that *b* the vessels of the LORD Is 52:11
for he shall *b* their iniquities Is 53:11
O barren, thou that didst not *b* Is 54:1
the priests *b* rule by their means Jer 5:31
this is a grief, and I must *b* it Jer 10:19
*b* no burden on the sabbath day Jer 17:21
not to *b* a burden, even entering Jer 17:27
to husbands, that they may *b* sons Jer 29:6
because I did *b* the reproach of Jer 31:19
that the LORD could no longer *b* Jer 44:22
was unto me as a *b* lying in wait Lam 3:10
that he *b* the yoke in his youth Lam 3:27
it thou shalt *b* their iniquity Eze 4:4
so shalt thou *b* the iniquity of Eze 4:5
thou shalt *b* the iniquity of the Eze 4:6
thou *b* it upon thy shoulders Eze 12:6
shall *b* upon his shoulder in the Eze 12:12
they shall *b* the punishment of Eze 14:10
*b* thine own shame for thy sins Eze 16:52
*b* thy shame, in that thou hast Eze 16:52
thou mayest *b* thine own shame Eze 16:54
and that it might *b* fruit Eze 17:8
*b* fruit, and be a goodly cedar Eze 17:23
doth not the son *b* the iniquity Eze 18:19
The son shall not *b* the iniquity Eze 18:20
father *b* the iniquity of the son Eze 18:20
therefore *b* thou also thy Eze 23:35
ye shall *b* the sins of your idols Eze 23:49
*b* their shame with them that go Eze 32:30
neither *b* the shame of the Eze 34:29
you, they shall *b* their shame Eze 36:7
neither shalt thou *b* the reproach Eze 36:15
they shall even *b* their iniquity Eze 44:10
they shall *b* their iniquity Eze 44:12
but they shall *b* their shame Eze 44:13
that they *b* them not out into the Eze 46:20
which shall *b* rule over all the Dan 2:39
beast, a second, like to a *b* Dan 7:5
dried up, they shall *b* no fruit Hos 9:16
I will meet them as a *b* that is Hos 13:8
flee from a lion, and a *b* met him Amos 5:19
is not able to *b* all his words Amos 7:10
therefore ye shall *b* the reproach Mic 6:16
I will *b* the indignation of the Mic 7:9
all they that *b* silver are cut Zeph 1:11
If one *b* holy flesh in the skirt Hag 2:12
me, Whither do these *b* the ephah Zec 5:10
he shall *b* the glory, and shall Zec 6:13
whose shoes I am not worthy to *b* Mt 3:11
their hands they shall *b* thee up Mt 4:6
Thou shalt not *b* false witness Mt 19:18
him they compelled to *b* his cross Mt 27:32
Do not *b* false witness, Defraud Mk 10:19
and Rufus, to *b* his cross Mk 15:21
wife Elisabeth shall *b* thee a son Lk 1:13
their hands they shall *b* thee up Lk 4:11
Truly ye *b* witness that ye allow Lk 11:48
And if it *b* fruit, well Lk 13:9
And whosoever doth not *b* his cross Lk 14:27
though he *b* long with them Lk 18:7
Do not *b* false witness, Honour Lk 18:20
that he might *b* it after Jesus Lk 23:26
to *b* witness of the Light, that Jn 1:7
but was sent to *b* witness of that Jn 1:8
*b* unto the governor of the feast Jn 2:8
Ye yourselves *b* me witness Jn 3:28
If I *b* witness of myself, my Jn 5:31
*b* witness of me, that the Father Jn 5:36
Though I *b* record of myself, yet Jn 8:14
I am one that *b* witness of myself Jn 8:18
name, they *b* witness of me Jn 10:25
branch cannot *b* fruit of itself Jn 15:4
glorified, that ye *b* much fruit Jn 15:8
And ye also shall *b* witness Jn 15:27
you, but ye cannot *b* them now Jn 16:12
evil, *b* witness of the evil Jn 18:23
that I should *b* witness unto the Jn 18:37
to *b* my name before the Gentiles Acts 9:15
our fathers nor we were able to *b* Acts 15:10
would that I should *b* with you Acts 18:14
the high priest doth *b* me witness Acts 22:5
so must thou *b* witness also at Acts 23:11
could not *b* up into the wind, we Acts 27:15
For I *b* them record that they Rom 10:2
Thou shalt not *b* false witness Rom 13:9
to *b* the infirmities of the weak Rom 15:1
hitherto ye were not able to *b* it 1Cor 3:2
that ye may be able to *b* it 1Cor 10:13
we shall also *b* the image of the 1Cor 15:49
I *b* record, yea, and beyond their 2Cor 8:3
Would to God ye could *b* with me a 2Cor 11:1
and indeed *b* with me 2Cor 11:1
ye might well *b* with him 2Cor 11:4
for I *b* you record, that, if it Gal 4:15
you shall *b* his judgment Gal 5:10
*B* ye one another's burdens, and so Gal 6:2
every man shall *b* his own burden Gal 6:5
for I *b* in my body the marks of Gal 6:17
For I *b* him record, that he hath Col 4:13
*b* children, guide the house, give 1Ti 5:14
offered to *b* the sins of many Heb 9:28
my brethren, *b* olive berries Jas 3:12
*b* witness, and shew unto you that 1Jn 1:2
are three that *b* record in heaven 1Jn 5:7
are three that *b* witness in earth 1Jn 5:8
yea, and we also *b* record 3Jn 12
how thou canst not *b* them which Rev 2:2
his feet were as the feet of a *b* Rev 13:2

**BEARD**

a plague upon the head or the *b* Lev 13:29
even a leprosy upon the head or *b* Lev 13:30
his hair off his head and his *b* Lev 14:9
thou mar the corners of thy *b* Lev 19:27
shave off the corner of their *b* Lev 21:5
against me, I caught him by his *b* 1Sa 17:35
his spittle fall down upon his *b* 1Sa 21:13
his feet, nor trimmed his *b* 2Sa 19:24
by the *b* with the right hand to 2Sa 20:9
the hair of my head and of my *b* Ezr 9:3
upon the *b*, even Aaron's *b* Ps 133:2
and it shall also consume the *b* Is 7:20
be baldness, and every *b* cut off Is 15:2
shall be bald, and every *b* clipped Jer 48:37
upon thine head and upon thy *b* Eze 5:1

**BEARDS**

off the one half of their *b* 2Sa 10:4
at Jericho until your *b* be grown 2Sa 10:5
at Jericho until your *b* be grown 1Chr 19:5
men, having their *b* shaven Jer 41:5

**BEARERS**

of them to be *b* of burdens 2Chr 2:18
they were over the *b* of burdens 2Chr 34:13
The strength of the *b* of burdens Neh 4:10

**BEAREST**

now, thou art barren, and *b* not Judg 13:3
that thou *b* unto thy people Ps 106:4
him, Thou *b* record of thyself Jn 8:13
thou *b* not the root, but the root Rom 11:18
Rejoice, thou barren that *b* not Gal 4:27

**BEARETH**

whosoever *b* ought of the carcase Lev 11:25
he that *b* the carcase of them Lev 11:28
he also that *b* the carcase of it Lev 11:40
he that *b* any of those things Lev 15:10
father *b* the sucking child Num 11:12
*b* shall succeed in the name of Deut 25:6
be among you a root that *b* gall Deut 29:18
that it is not sown, nor *b* Deut 29:23
taketh them, *b* them on her wings Deut 32:11
up in me *b* witness to my face Job 16:8
entreateth the barren that *b* not Job 24:21
A man that *b* false witness Prov 25:18
but when the wicked *b* rule Prov 29:2
whereof every one *b* twins Song 6:6
spring, for the tree *b* her fruit Joel 2:22
which also *b* fruit, and bringeth Mt 13:23
is another that *b* witness of me Jn 5:32
that sent me *b* witness of me Jn 8:18
Every branch in me that *b* not Jn 15:2
and every branch that *b* fruit Jn 15:2
The Spirit itself *b* witness with Rom 8:16
for he *b* not the sword in vain Rom 13:4
*B* all things, believeth all 1Cor 13:7
But that which *b* thorns and briers Heb 6:8
it is the Spirit that *b* witness 1Jn 5:6

**BEARING**

have given you every herb *b* seed Gen 1:29
LORD hath restrained me from *b* Gen 16:2
his name Judah; and left *b* Gen 29:35
When Leah saw that she had left *b* Gen 30:9
with their camels *b* spicery Gen 37:25
set forward, *b* the tabernacle Num 10:17
set forward, *b* the sanctuary Num 10:21
and the priests the Levites *b* it Josh 3:3
the priests *b* the ark of the Josh 3:14
that the seven priests *b* the Josh 6:8
seven priests *b* seven trumpets of Josh 6:13
one *b* a shield went before him 1Sa 17:7
*b* the ark of the covenant of God 2Sa 15:24
*b* precious seed, shall doubtless Ps 126:6
you a man *b* a pitcher of water Mk 14:13
meet you, *b* a pitcher of water Lk 22:10
he *b* his cross went forth into a Jn 19:17
their conscience also *b* witness Rom 2:15
my conscience also *b* me witness Rom 9:1
Always *b* about in the body the 2Cor 4:10
God also *b* them witness, both Heb 2:4
without the camp, *b* his reproach Heb 13:13

**BEARS**

forth two she *b* out of the wood 2Kin 2:24
We roar all like *b*, and mourn sore Is 59:11

**BEAST**

*b* of the earth after his kind Gen 1:24
God made the *b* of the earth after Gen 1:25
to every *b* of the earth, and to Gen 1:30
God formed every *b* of the field Gen 2:19
air, and to every *b* of the field Gen 2:20
was more subtil than any *b* of the Gen 3:1
above every *b* of the field Gen 3:14
both man, and *b*, and the creeping Gen 6:7
Of every clean *b* thou shalt take Gen 7:2
every *b* after his kind, and all Gen 7:14
of fowl, and of cattle, and of *b* Gen 7:21
Every *b*, every creeping thing, and Gen 8:19

and took of every clean *b*, and of ... Gen 8:20
be upon every *b* of the earth ... Gen 9:2
hand of every *b* will I require it ... Gen 9:5
of every *b* of the earth with you ... Gen 9:10
the ark, to every *b* of the earth ... Gen 9:10
every *b* of theirs be ours ... Gen 34:23
Some evil *b* hath devoured him ... Gen 37:20
an evil *b* hath devoured him ... Gen 37:33
and it became lice in man, and in *b* ... Ex 8:17
were lice upon man, and upon *b* ... Ex 8:18
with blains upon man, and upon *b* ... Ex 9:9
with blains upon man, and upon *b* ... Ex 9:10
*b* which shall be found in the ... Ex 9:19
of Egypt, upon man, and upon *b* ... Ex 9:22
was in the field, both man and *b* ... Ex 9:25
move his tongue, against man or *b* ... Ex 11:7
the land of Egypt, both man and *b* ... Ex 12:12
of Israel, both of man and of *b* ... Ex 13:2
cometh of a *b* which thou hast ... Ex 13:12
of man, and the firstborn of *b* ... Ex 13:15
whether it be *b* or man, it shall ... Ex 19:13
and the dead *b* shall be his ... Ex 21:34
be eaten, and shall put in his *b* ... Ex 22:5
or an ox, or a sheep, or any *b* ... Ex 22:10
Whosoever lieth with a *b* shall ... Ex 22:19
the *b* of the field multiply ... Ex 23:29
it be a carcase of an unclean *b* ... Lev 5:2
of man, or any unclean *b*, or any ... Lev 7:21
the fat of the *b* that dieth of ... Lev 7:24
whosoever eateth the fat of the *b* ... Lev 7:25
whether it be of fowl or of *b* ... Lev 7:26
The carcases of every *b* which ... Lev 11:26
And if any *b*, of which ye may eat, ... Lev 11:39
between the *b* that may be eaten ... Lev 11:47
the *b* that may not be eaten ... Lev 11:47
catcheth any *b* or fowl that may ... Lev 17:13
any *b* to defile thyself therewith ... Lev 18:23
before a *b* to lie down thereto ... Lev 18:23
And if a man lie with a *b*, he ... Lev 20:15
and ye shall slay the *b* ... Lev 20:15
And if a woman approach unto any *b* ... Lev 20:16
shalt kill the woman, and the *b* ... Lev 20:16
make your souls abominable by *b* ... Lev 20:25
he that killeth a *b* shall make it ... Lev 24:18
shall make it good; *b* for *b* ... Lev 24:18
shall make it good; *b* for *b* ... Lev 24:18
And he that killeth a *b*, he shall ... Lev 24:21
for the *b* that are in thy land, ... Lev 25:7
And if it be a *b*, whereof men ... Lev 27:9
shall at all change *b* for *b* ... Lev 27:10
And if it be any unclean *b* ... Lev 27:11
present the *b* before the priest ... Lev 27:11
And if it be of an unclean *b* ... Lev 27:27
that he hath, both of man and *b* ... Lev 27:28
in Israel, both man and *b* ... Num 3:13
of Israel are mine, both man and *b* ... Num 8:17
was taken, both of man and of *b* ... Num 31:26
of fifty, both of man and of *b* ... Num 31:47
The likeness of any *b* that is on ... Deut 4:17
every *b* that parteth the hoof, and ... Deut 14:6
that lieth with any manner of *b* ... Deut 27:21
the men of every city, as the *b* ... Judg 20:48
by a wild *b* that was in Lebanon ... 2Kin 14:9
by a wild *b* that was in Lebanon ... 2Chr 25:18
neither was there any *b* with me ... Neh 2:12
save the *b* that I rode upon ... Neh 2:12
the *b* that was under me to pass ... Neh 2:14
or that the wild *b* may break them ... Job 39:15
O LORD, thou preservest man and *b* ... Ps 36:6
For every *b* of the forest is mine ... Ps 50:10
I was as a *b* before thee ... Ps 73:22
the wild *b* of the field doth ... Ps 80:13
drink to every *b* of the field ... Ps 104:11
of Egypt, both of man and *b* ... Ps 135:8
He giveth to the *b* his food ... Ps 147:9
man regardeth the life of his *b* ... Prov 12:10
man hath no preeminence above a *b* ... Eccl 3:19
the spirit of the *b* that goeth ... Eccl 3:21
nor any ravenous *b* shall go up ... Is 35:9
The *b* of the field shall honour ... Is 43:20
they are a burden to the weary *b* ... Is 46:1
As a *b* goeth down into the valley ... Is 63:14
this place, upon man, and upon *b* ... Jer 7:20
of the heavens and the *b* are fled ... Jer 9:10
of this city, both man and *b* ... Jer 21:6
the *b* that are upon the ground, ... Jer 27:5
of man, and with the seed of *b* ... Jer 31:27
It is desolate without man or *b* ... Jer 32:43
desolate without man and without *b* ... Jer 33:10
without inhabitant, and without *b* ... Jer 33:10
desolate without man and without *b* ... Jer 33:12
to cease from thence man and *b* ... Jer 36:29
they shall depart, both man and *b* ... Jer 50:3
remain in it, neither man nor *b* ... Jer 51:62
and will cut off man and *b* from it ... Eze 14:13
that I cut off man and *b* from it ... Eze 14:17
to cut off from it man and *b* ... Eze 14:19
and the famine, and the noisome *b* ... Eze 14:21
to cut off from it man and *b* ... Eze 14:21
and will cut off man and *b* from it ... Eze 25:13
and cut off man and *b* out of thee ... Eze 29:8
nor foot of *b* shall pass through ... Eze 29:11
meat to every *b* of the field ... Eze 34:8
neither shall the *b* of the land ... Eze 34:28
I will multiply upon you man and *b* ... Eze 36:11
to every *b* of the field, Assemble ... Eze 39:17
or torn, whether it be fowl or *b* ... Eze 44:31
And behold another *b*, a second, ... Dan 7:5
the *b* had also four heads ... Dan 7:6
visions, and behold a fourth *b* ... Dan 7:7
beheld even till the *b* was slain ... Dan 7:11
know the truth of the fourth *b* ... Dan 7:19
The fourth *b* shall be the fourth ... Dan 7:23
the wild *b* shall tear them ... Hos 13:8
saying, Let neither man nor *b* ... Jonah 3:7
*b* be covered with sackcloth, and ... Jonah 3:8
bind the chariot to the swift *b* ... Mic 1:13
I will consume man and *b* ... Zeph 1:3
hire for man, nor any hire for *b* ... Zec 8:10
and wine, and set him on his own *b* ... Lk 10:34
the venomous *b* hang on his hand ... Acts 28:4
he shook off the *b* into the fire ... Acts 28:5
if so much as a *b* touch the ... Heb 12:20
the first *b* was like a lion, and ... Rev 4:7
the second *b* like a calf ... Rev 4:7
the third *b* had a face as a man, ... Rev 4:7
the fourth *b* was like a flying ... Rev 4:7
seal, I heard the second *b* say ... Rev 6:3
seal, I heard the third *b* say ... Rev 6:5
the voice of the fourth *b* say ... Rev 6:7
the *b* that ascendeth out of the ... Rev 11:7
saw a *b* rise up out of the sea, ... Rev 13:1
the *b* which I saw was like unto a ... Rev 13:2
the world wondered after the *b* ... Rev 13:3
which gave power unto the *b* ... Rev 13:4
and they worshipped the *b* ... Rev 13:4
saying, Who is like unto the *b* ... Rev 13:4
I beheld another *b* coming up out ... Rev 13:11
power of the first *b* before him ... Rev 13:12
therein to worship the first *b* ... Rev 13:12
power to do in the sight of the *b* ... Rev 13:14
should make an image to the *b* ... Rev 13:14
give life unto the image of the *b* ... Rev 13:15
image of the *b* should both speak ... Rev 13:15
image of the *b* should be killed ... Rev 13:15
the mark, or the name of the *b* ... Rev 13:17
count the number of the *b* ... Rev 13:18
voice, If any man worship the *b* ... Rev 14:9
day nor night, who worship the *b* ... Rev 14:11
had gotten the victory over the *b* ... Rev 15:2
men which had the mark of the *b* ... Rev 16:2
his vial upon the seat of the *b* ... Rev 16:10
and out of the mouth of the *b* ... Rev 16:13
sit upon a scarlet coloured *b* ... Rev 17:3
of the *b* that carrieth her, which ... Rev 17:7
The *b* that thou sawest was, and is ... Rev 17:8
when they behold the *b* that was ... Rev 17:8
the *b* that was, and is not, even ... Rev 17:11
as kings one hour with the *b* ... Rev 17:12
power and strength unto the *b* ... Rev 17:13
which thou sawest upon the *b* ... Rev 17:16
and give their kingdom unto the *b* ... Rev 17:17
And I saw the *b*, and the kings of ... Rev 19:19
the *b* was taken, and with him the ... Rev 19:20
had received the mark of the *b* ... Rev 19:20
and which had not worshipped the *b* ... Rev 20:4
of fire and brimstone, where the *b* ... Rev 20:10

**BEAST'S**

let a *b* heart be given unto him ... Dan 4:16

**BEASTS**

of *b* that are not clean by two, ... Gen 7:2
Of clean *b*, and of *b* that are ... Gen 7:8
That which was torn of *b* I ... Gen 31:39
and his cattle, and all his *b* ... Gen 36:6
lade your *b*, and go, get you unto ... Gen 45:17
and all the firstborn of *b* ... Ex 11:5
that is torn of *b* in the field ... Ex 22:31
what they leave the *b* of the ... Ex 23:11
fat of that which is torn with *b* ... Lev 7:24
These are the *b* which ye shall ... Lev 11:2
all the *b* that are on the earth ... Lev 11:2
and cheweth the cud, among the *b* ... Lev 11:3
manner of *b* that go on all four ... Lev 11:27
This is the law of the *b*, and of ... Lev 11:46
or that which was torn with *b* ... Lev 17:15
put difference between clean *b* ... Lev 20:25
of itself, or is torn with *b* ... Lev 22:8
I will rid evil *b* out of the land ... Lev 26:6
I will also send wild *b* among you ... Lev 26:22
Only the firstling of the *b* ... Lev 27:26
LORD, whether it be of men or *b* ... Num 18:15
of unclean *b* shalt thou redeem ... Num 18:15
the congregation and their *b* drink ... Num 20:8
drank, and their *b* also ... Num 20:11
all the prey, both of men and of *b* ... Num 31:11
of the flocks, of all manner of *b* ... Num 31:30
their goods, and for all their *b* ... Num 35:3
lest the *b* of the field increase ... Deut 7:22
These are the *b* which ye shall ... Deut 14:4
and cheweth the cud among the *b* ... Deut 14:6
unto the *b* of the earth, and no ... Deut 28:26
send the teeth of *b* upon them ... Deut 32:24
the air, and to the *b* of the field ... 1Sa 17:44
to the wild *b* of the earth ... 1Sa 17:46
nor the *b* of the field by night ... 2Sa 21:10
he spake also of *b*, and of fowl, ... 1Kin 4:33
alive, that we lose not all the *b* ... 1Kin 18:5
ye, and your cattle, and your *b* ... 2Kin 3:17
and stalls for all manner of *b* ... 2Chr 32:28
gold, and with goods, and with *b* ... Ezr 1:4
with gold, with goods, and with *b* ... Ezr 1:6
be afraid of the *b* of the earth ... Job 5:22
the *b* of the field shall be at ... Job 5:23
But ask now the *b*, and they shall ... Job 12:7
Wherefore are we counted as *b* ... Job 18:3
us more than the *b* of the earth ... Job 35:11
Then the *b* go into dens, and ... Job 37:8
where all the *b* of the field play ... Job 40:20
oxen, yea, and the *b* of the field ... Ps 8:7
he is like the *b* that perish ... Ps 49:12
not, is like the *b* that perish ... Ps 49:20
the wild *b* of the field are mine ... Ps 50:11
saints unto the *b* of the earth ... Ps 79:2
wherein all the *b* of the forest ... Ps 104:20
both small and great *b* ... Ps 104:25
*B*, and all cattle ... Ps 148:10
She hath killed her *b* ... Prov 9:2
A lion which is strongest among *b* ... Prov 30:30
see that they themselves are *b* ... Eccl 3:18
the sons of men befalleth *b* ... Eccl 3:19
of rams, and the fat of fed *b* ... Is 1:11
But wild *b* of the desert shall ... Is 13:21
the wild *b* of the islands shall ... Is 13:22
and to the *b* of the earth ... Is 18:6
all the *b* of the earth shall ... Is 18:6
The burden of the *b* of the south ... Is 30:6
The wild *b* of the desert shall ... Is 34:14
with the wild *b* of the island ... Is 34:14
nor the *b* thereof sufficient for ... Is 40:16
their idols were upon the *b* ... Is 46:1
All ye *b* of the field, come to ... Is 56:9
yea, all ye *b* in the forest ... Is 56:9
and upon mules, and upon swift *b* ... Is 66:20
heaven, and for the *b* of the earth ... Jer 7:33
the *b* are consumed, and the birds ... Jer 12:4
assemble all the *b* of the field ... Jer 12:9
the *b* of the earth, to devour and ... Jer 15:3
heaven, and for the *b* of the earth ... Jer 16:4
heaven, and for the *b* of the earth ... Jer 19:7
the *b* of the field have I given ... Jer 27:6
given him the *b* of the field also ... Jer 28:14
heaven, and to the *b* of the earth ... Jer 34:20
Therefore the wild *b* of the ... Jer 50:39
wild *b* of the islands shall dwell ... Jer 50:39
I send upon you famine and evil *b* ... Eze 5:17
creeping things, and abominable *b* ... Eze 8:10
If I cause noisome *b* to pass ... Eze 14:15
may pass through because of the *b* ... Eze 14:15
for meat to the *b* of the field ... Eze 29:5
*b* of the field bring forth their ... Eze 31:6
all the *b* of the field shall be ... Eze 31:13
I will fill the *b* of the whole ... Eze 32:4
I will destroy also all the *b* ... Eze 32:13
nor the hoofs of *b* trouble them ... Eze 32:13
I give to the *b* to be devoured ... Eze 33:27
meat to all the *b* of the field ... Eze 34:5
will cause the evil *b* to cease ... Eze 34:25
the *b* of the field, and all ... Eze 38:20
to the *b* of the field to be ... Eze 39:4
the *b* of the field and the fowls ... Dan 2:38
the *b* of the field had shadow ... Dan 4:12
let the *b* get away from under it, ... Dan 4:14
the *b* in the grass of the earth ... Dan 4:15
under which the *b* of the field ... Dan 4:21
be with the *b* of the field ... Dan 4:23
shall be with the *b* of the field ... Dan 4:25
shall be with the *b* of the field ... Dan 4:32
and his heart was made like the *b* ... Dan 5:21
four great *b* came up from the sea ... Dan 7:3
all the *b* that were before it ... Dan 7:7
As concerning the rest of the *b* ... Dan 7:12
These great *b*, which are four, ... Dan 7:17
so that no *b* might stand before ... Dan 8:4
the *b* of the field shall eat them ... Hos 2:12
for them with the *b* of the field ... Hos 2:18
with the *b* of the field, and with ... Hos 4:3
How do the *b* groan ... Joel 1:18
The *b* of the field cry also unto ... Joel 1:20
Be not afraid, ye *b* of the field ... Joel 2:22
the peace offerings of your fat *b* ... Amos 5:22
a lion among the *b* of the forest ... Mic 5:8
cover thee, and the spoil of *b* ... Hab 2:17
of her, all the *b* of the nations ... Zeph 2:14
a place for *b* to lie down in ... Zeph 2:15
of all the *b* that shall be in ... Zec 14:15
and was with the wild *b* ... Mk 1:13
have ye offered to me slain *b* ... Acts 7:42
of fourfooted *b* of the earth ... Acts 10:12
*b* of the earth, and wild *b* ... Acts 10:12
*b* of the earth, and wild *b* ... Acts 11:6
And provide them *b*, that they may ... Acts 23:24
man, and to birds, and fourfooted *b* ... Rom 1:23
I have fought with *b* at Ephesus ... 1Cor 15:32
flesh of men, another flesh of *b* ... 1Cor 15:39
Cretians are alway liars, evil *b* ... Titus 1:12
For the bodies of those *b* ... Heb 13:11
For every kind of *b*, and of birds, ... Jas 3:7
But these, as natural brute *b* ... 2Pet 2:12
they know naturally, as brute *b* ... Jude 10
were four *b* full of eyes before ... Rev 4:6
the four *b* had each of them six ... Rev 4:8
And when those *b* give glory ... Rev 4:9
of the throne and of the four *b* ... Rev 5:6
he had taken the book, the four *b* ... Rev 5:8
round about the throne and the *b* ... Rev 5:11
And the four *b* said, Amen ... Rev 5:14
thunder, one of the four *b* saying ... Rev 6:1
in the midst of the four *b* say ... Rev 6:6
death, and with the *b* of the earth ... Rev 6:8
and about the elders and the four *b* ... Rev 7:11
the throne, and before the four *b* ... Rev 14:3
one of the four *b* gave unto the ... Rev 15:7
and fine flour, and wheat, and *b* ... Rev 18:13
elders and the four *b* fell down and ... Rev 19:4

**BEAT**

thou shalt *b* some of it very ... Ex 30:36
they did *b* the gold into thin ... Ex 39:3
or *b* it in a mortar, and baked it ... Num 11:8
*b* him above these with many ... Deut 25:3

he *b* down the tower of Penuel, and ... Judg 8:17
*b* down the city, and sowed it with ..... Judg 9:45
*b* at the door, and spake to the .......... Judg 19:22
*b* out that she had gleaned .......... Ruth 2:17
Then did I *b* them as small as the ......... 2Sa 22:43
they *b* down the cities, and on ......... 2Kin 3:25
Three times did Joash *b* him .......... 2Kin 13:25
of the LORD, did the king *b* down ....... 2Kin 23:12
Then did I *b* them small as the .......... Ps 18:42
I will *b* down his foes before his .......... Ps 89:23
Thou shalt *b* him with the rod, and... Prov 23:14
they shall *b* their swords into .......... Is 2:4
ye that ye *b* my people to pieces .......... Is 3:15
that the LORD shall *b* off from .......... Is 27:12
*b* them small, and shalt make the .......... Is 41:15
*B* your plowshares into swords, and ..... Joel 3:10
the sun *b* upon the head of Jonah, ...... Jonah 4:8
they shall *b* their swords into .......... Mic 4:3
thou shalt *b* in pieces many .......... Mic 4:13
winds blew, and *b* upon that house ........ Mt 7:25
winds blew, and *b* upon that house ........ Mt 7:27
*b* one, and killed another, and .......... Mt 21:35
the waves *b* into the ship, so .......... Mk 4:37
*b* him, and sent him away empty .......... Mk 12:3
the stream *b* vehemently upon that ....... Lk 6:48
which the stream did *b* vehemently ........ Lk 6:49
shall begin to *b* the menservants .......... Lk 12:45
but the husbandmen *b* him, and sent.... Lk 20:10
they *b* him also, and entreated him ....... Lk 20:11
clothes, and commanded to *b* them ... Acts 16:22
*b* him before the judgment seat .......... Acts 18:17
*b* in every synagogue them that ......... Acts 22:19

**BEATEN**
had set over them, were *b* .......... Ex 5:14
and, behold, thy servants are *b* .......... Ex 5:16
of *b* work shalt thou make them, .......... Ex 25:18
of *b* work shall the candlestick .......... Ex 25:31
shall be one *b* work of pure gold .......... Ex 25:36
pure oil olive *b* for the light .......... Ex 27:20
fourth part of an hin of *b* oil .......... Ex 29:40
*b* out of one piece made he them, .......... Ex 37:7
of *b* work made he the candlestick .......... Ex 37:17
of it was one *b* work of pure gold .......... Ex 37:22
even corn *b* out of full ears .......... Lev 2:14
part of the *b* corn thereof, and .......... Lev 2:16
full of sweet incense *b* small .......... Lev 16:12
pure oil olive *b* for the light .......... Lev 24:2
of the candlestick was of *b* gold .......... Num 8:4
the flowers thereof, was *b* work .......... Num 8:4
fourth part of an hin of *b* oil .......... Num 28:5
the wicked man be worthy to be *b* ....... Deut 25:2
down, and to be *b* before his face, ....... Deut 25:2
as if they were *b* before them .......... Josh 8:15
and Abner was *b*, and the men of .......... 2Sa 2:17
two hundred targets of *b* gold .......... 1Kin 10:16
three hundred shields of *b* gold .......... 1Kin 10:17
thousand measures of *b* wheat .......... 2Chr 2:10
two hundred targets of *b* gold .......... 2Chr 9:15
six hundred shekels of *b* gold .......... 2Chr 9:15
hundred shields made he of *b* gold ...... 2Chr 9:16
had *b* the graven images into .......... 2Chr 34:7
they have *b* me, and I felt it not ....... Prov 23:35
chalkstones that are *b* in sunder .......... Is 27:9
fitches are *b* out with a staff .......... Is 28:27
LORD shall the Assyrian be *b* down ....... Is 30:31
and their mighty ones are *b* down .......... Jer 46:5
thereof shall be *b* to pieces .......... Mic 1:7
in the synagogues ye shall be *b* .......... Mk 13:9
shall be *b* with many stripes .......... Lk 12:47
shall be *b* with few stripes .......... Lk 12:48
*b* them, they commanded that they ..... Acts 5:40
They have *b* us openly .......... Acts 16:37
Thrice was I *b* with rods, once .......... 2Cor 11:25

**BEATEST**
When thou *b* thine olive tree, .......... Deut 24:20
for if thou *b* him with the rod, .......... Prov 23:13

**BEATETH**
I, not as one that *b* the air .......... 1Cor 9:26

**BEATING**
they went on *b* down one another ....... 1Sa 14:16
*b* some, and killing some .......... Mk 12:5
the soldiers, they left *b* of Paul .......... Acts 21:32

**BEAUTIES**
in the *b* of holiness from the .......... Ps 110:3

**BEAUTIFUL**
but Rachel was *b* and well favoured... Gen 29:17
among the captives a *b* woman .......... Deut 21:11
and withal of a *b* countenance .......... 1Sa 16:12
and of a *b* countenance .......... 1Sa 25:3
the woman was very *b* to look upon ..... 2Sa 11:2
mother, and the maid was fair and *b* ....... Est 2:7
*B* for situation, the joy of the .......... Ps 48:2
made every thing *b* in his time .......... Eccl 3:11
Thou art *b*, O my love, as Tirzah, .......... Song 6:4
How *b* are thy feet with shoes, O .......... Song 7:1
shall the branch of the LORD be *b* .......... Is 4:2
put on thy *b* garments, O .......... Is 52:1
How *b* upon the mountains are the .......... Is 52:7
our *b* house, where our fathers .......... Is 64:11
that was given thee, thy *b* flock .......... Jer 13:20
strong staff broken, and the *b* rod ....... Jer 48:17
a *b* crown upon thine head .......... Eze 16:12
and thou wast exceeding *b*, and thou . Eze 16:13
*b* crowns upon their heads .......... Eze 23:42
which indeed appear *b* outward .......... Mt 23:27
of the temple which is called *B* .......... Acts 3:2
alms at the *B* gate of the temple .......... Acts 3:10

How *b* are the feet of them that .......... Rom 10:15

**BEAUTIFY**
to *b* the house of the LORD which .......... Ezr 7:27
he will *b* the meek with salvation .......... Ps 149:4
to *b* the place of my sanctuary .......... Is 60:13

**BEAUTY**
thy brother for glory and for *b* .......... Ex 28:2
make for them, for glory and for *b* ........ Ex 28:40
The *b* of Israel is slain upon thy .......... 2Sa 1:19
much praised as Absalom for his *b* ...... 2Sa 14:25
the LORD in the *b* of holiness .......... 1Chr 16:29
house with precious stones for *b* .......... 2Chr 3:6
should praise the *b* of holiness .......... 2Chr 20:21
the people and the princes her *b* .......... Est 1:11
and array thyself with glory and *b* ....... Job 40:10
life, to behold the *b* of the LORD .......... Ps 27:4
the LORD in the *b* of holiness .......... Ps 29:2
thou makest his *b* to consume away ..... Ps 39:11
the king greatly desire thy *b* .......... Ps 45:11
their *b* shall consume in the .......... Ps 49:14
Out of Zion, the perfection of *b* .......... Ps 50:2
let the *b* of the LORD our God be .......... Ps 90:17
and *b* are in his sanctuary .......... Ps 96:6
the LORD in the *b* of holiness .......... Ps 96:9
not after her *b* in thine heart .......... Prov 6:25
the *b* of old men is the grey head ....... Prov 20:29
Favour is deceitful, and *b* is vain ....... Prov 31:30
and burning instead of *b* .......... Is 3:24
the *b* of the Chaldees' excellency .......... Is 13:19
whose glorious *b* is a fading .......... Is 28:1
And the glorious *b*, which is on .......... Is 28:4
of glory, and for a diadem of *b* .......... Is 28:5
eyes shall see the king in his *b* .......... Is 33:17
man, according to the *b* of a man .......... Is 44:13
there is no *b* that we should .......... Is 53:2
to give unto them *b* for ashes .......... Is 61:3
of Zion all her *b* is departed .......... Lam 1:6
unto the earth the *b* of Israel .......... Lam 2:1
that men call The perfection of *b* .......... Lam 2:15
As for the *b* of his ornament, he .......... Eze 7:20
forth among the heathen for thy *b* ...... Eze 16:14
thou didst trust in thine own *b* .......... Eze 16:15
hast made thy *b* to be abhorred, .......... Eze 16:25
thou hast said, I am of perfect *b* .......... Eze 27:3
thy builders have perfected thy *b* .......... Eze 27:4
they have made thy *b* perfect .......... Eze 27:11
against the *b* of thy wisdom .......... Eze 28:7
full of wisdom, and perfect in *b* .......... Eze 28:12
was lifted up because of thy *b* .......... Eze 28:17
of God was like unto him in his *b* .......... Eze 31:8
Whom dost thou pass in *b* .......... Eze 32:19
his *b* shall be as the olive tree, .......... Hos 14:6
goodness, and how great is his *b* .......... Zec 9:17
the one I called *B*, and the other .......... Zec 11:7
And I took my staff, even *B* .......... Zec 11:10

**BEBAI** (*beb'-a-i*)
*1. Father of returned exiles.*
The children of *B*, six hundred .......... Ezr 2:11
The children of *B*, six hundred .......... Neh 7:16
*2. Father of returned exiles with Ezra.*
And of the sons of *B* .......... Ezr 8:11
Zechariah the son of *B*, and with .......... Ezr 8:11
Of the sons also of *B* .......... Ezr 10:28
*3. One who sealed the covenant.*
Bunni, Azgad, *B*, .......... Neh 10:15

**BECAME**
and man *b* a living soul .......... Gen 2:7
was parted, and *b* into four heads ........ Gen 2:10
the same *b* mighty men which were ........ Gen 6:4
him, and she *b* a pillar of salt .......... Gen 19:26
and she *b* my wife .......... Gen 20:12
in the wilderness, and *b* an archer .......... Gen 21:20
took Rebekah, and she *b* his wife ....... Gen 24:67
and grew until he *b* very great .......... Gen 26:13
For thy servant *b* surety for the .......... Gen 44:32
so the land *b* Pharaoh's .......... Gen 47:20
only, which *b* not Pharaoh's .......... Gen 47:26
bear, and *b* a servant unto tribute ...... Gen 49:15
daughter, and he *b* her son .......... Ex 2:10
on the ground, and it *b* a serpent .......... Ex 4:3
it, and it *b* a rod in his hand .......... Ex 4:4
his servants, and it *b* a serpent .......... Ex 7:10
man his rod, and they *b* serpents .......... Ex 7:12
it *b* lice in man, and in beast .......... Ex 8:17
all the dust of the land *b* lice .......... Ex 8:17
it *b* a boil breaking forth with .......... Ex 9:10
land of Egypt since it *b* a nation .......... Ex 9:24
so it *b* one tabernacle .......... Ex 36:13
Miriam *b* leprous, white as snow .......... Num 12:10
and they *b* a sign .......... Num 26:10
*b* there a nation, great, mighty, .......... Deut 26:5
the people melted, and *b* as water .......... Josh 7:5
Hebron therefore *b* the .......... Josh 14:14
it *b* the inheritance of the .......... Josh 24:32
among them, and *b* tributaries .......... Judg 1:30
of Beth-anath *b* tributaries unto .......... Judg 1:33
so that they *b* tributaries. .......... Judg 1:35
which thing *b* a snare unto Gideon ..... Judg 8:27
*b* as flax that was burnt with .......... Judg 15:14
one of his sons, who *b* his priest .......... Judg 17:5
and the young man *b* his priest .......... Judg 17:12
in her bosom, and *b* nurse unto it ....... Ruth 4:16
Therefore it *b* a proverb, Is Saul .......... 1Sa 10:12
and he *b* his armourbearer .......... 1Sa 16:21
Saul *b* David's enemy continually ....... 1Sa 18:29
and he *b* a captain over them .......... 1Sa 22:2
within him, and he *b* as a stone .......... 1Sa 25:37
of David, and *b* his wife .......... 1Sa 25:42

*b* one troop, and stood on the top .......... 2Sa 2:25
to flee, that he fell, and *b* lame .......... 2Sa 4:4
so the Moabites *b* David's .......... 2Sa 8:2
the Syrians *b* servants to David, .......... 2Sa 8:6
they of Edom *b* David's servants .......... 2Sa 8:14
she *b* his wife, and bare him a son ........ 2Sa 11:27
*b* captain over a band, when David ... 1Kin 11:24
And this thing *b* a sin .......... 1Kin 12:30
him again, and *b* as it was before ......... 1Kin 13:6
he *b* one of the priests of the .......... 1Kin 13:33
this thing *b* sin unto the house .......... 1Kin 13:34
Hoshea *b* his servant, and gave him ..... 2Kin 17:3
*b* vain, and went after the heathen .... 2Kin 17:15
Jehoiakim *b* his servant three .......... 2Kin 24:1
the Moabites *b* David's servants, .......... 1Chr 18:2
the Syrians *b* David's servants, .......... 1Chr 18:6
the Edomites *b* David's servants ........ 1Chr 18:13
with David, and *b* his servants .......... 1Chr 19:19
So Jotham *b* mighty, because he .......... 2Chr 27:6
*b* fat, and delighted themselves in .......... Neh 9:25
of the people of the land *b* Jews .......... Est 8:17
and I *b* a proverb to them .......... Ps 69:11
they *b* as dung for the earth .......... Ps 83:10
I *b* also a reproach unto them .......... Ps 109:25
they *b* as women .......... Jer 51:30
*b* a spreading vine of low stature .......... Eze 17:6
so it *b* a vine, and brought forth .......... Eze 17:6
it *b* a young lion, and it learned .......... Eze 19:3
he *b* a young lion, and learned to .......... Eze 19:6
and she *b* famous among women .......... Eze 23:10
his branches *b* long because of .......... Eze 31:5
they *b* meat to all the beasts of .......... Eze 34:5
surely because my flock *b* a prey .......... Eze 34:8
my flock *b* meat to every beast of .......... Eze 34:8
which *b* a prey and derision to the ....... Eze 36:4
*b* like the chaff of the summer .......... Dan 2:35
the image *b* a great mountain .......... Dan 2:35
according to his will, and *b* great .......... Dan 8:4
toward the ground, and I *b* dumb ....... Dan 10:15
in the day that he *b* a stranger .......... Obad 12
did shake, and *b* as dead men .......... Mt 28:4
And his raiment *b* shining, .......... Mk 9:3
he *b* very hungry, and would have ..... Acts 10:10
but *b* vain in their imaginations, .......... Rom 1:21
to be wise, they *b* fools, .......... Rom 1:22
from sin, ye *b* the servants of .......... Rom 6:18
And unto the Jews I *b* as a Jew .......... 1Cor 9:20
To the weak *b* I as weak, that I .......... 1Cor 9:22
but when I *b* a man, I put away ........ 1Cor 13:11
yet for your sakes he *b* poor .......... 2Cor 8:9
*b* obedient unto death, even the .......... Phil 2:8
ye *b* followers of us, and of the .......... 1Th 1:6
*b* followers of the churches of .......... 1Th 2:14
For it *b* him, for whom are all .......... Heb 2:10
he *b* the author of eternal .......... Heb 5:9
For such an high priest *b* us .......... Heb 7:26
whilst ye *b* companions of them .......... Heb 10:33
*b* heir of the righteousness which .......... Heb 11:7
the sun *b* black as sackcloth of .......... Rev 6:12
of hair, and the moon *b* as blood .......... Rev 6:12
the third part of the sea *b* blood .......... Rev 8:8
part of the waters *b* wormwood .......... Rev 8:11
it *b* as the blood of a dead man .......... Rev 16:3
and they *b* blood .......... Rev 16:4

**BECAMEST**
and thou, LORD, *b* their God .......... 1Chr 17:22
the Lord GOD, and thou *b* mine .......... Eze 16:8

**BECAUSE** See PREFACE.

**BECHER** (*be'-ker*) See BACHRITES.
*1. A son of Benjamin.*
sons of Benjamin were Belah, and *B* .. Gen 46:21
Bela, and *B*, and Jediael, three .......... 1Chr 7:6
And the sons of *B* .......... 1Chr 7:8
All these are the sons of *B* .......... 1Chr 7:8
*2. A son of Ephraim.*
of *B*, the family of the Bachrites ........ Num 26:35

**BECHERITES** See BACHRITES.

**BECHORATH** (*be-ko'-rath*) *An ancestor of King Saul.*
the son of Zeror, the son of *B* .......... 1Sa 9:1

**BECKONED**
for he *b* unto them, and remained .......... Lk 1:22
they *b* unto their partners, which .......... Lk 5:7
Simon Peter therefore *b* to him .......... Jn 13:24
Alexander *b* with the hand, and .......... Acts 19:33
*b* with the hand unto the people .......... Acts 21:40
governor had *b* unto him to speak ...... Acts 24:10

**BECKONING**
*b* unto them with the hand to hold .... Acts 12:17
*b* with his hand said, Men of .......... Acts 13:16

**BECOME**
the man is *b* as one of us, to .......... Gen 3:22
the waters shall no more *b* a .......... Gen 9:15
Abraham shall surely *b* a great .......... Gen 18:18
and he is *b* great .......... Gen 24:35
and now I am *b* two bands .......... Gen 32:10
with you, and we will *b* one people .... Gen 34:16
see what will *b* of his dreams .......... Gen 37:20
he also shall *b* a people, and he .......... Gen 48:19
his seed shall *b* a multitude of .......... Gen 48:19
shall *b* blood upon the dry land .......... Ex 4:9
Pharaoh, and it shall *b* a serpent .......... Ex 7:9
of water, that they may *b* blood .......... Ex 7:19
that it may *b* lice throughout all .......... Ex 8:16
it shall *b* small dust in all the .......... Ex 9:9
and song, and he is *b* my salvation ........ Ex 15:2

O LORD, is *b* glorious in power ... Ex 15:6
lest the land *b* desolate, and the ... Ex 23:29
we wot not what is *b* of him ... Ex 32:1
we wot not what is *b* of him ... Ex 32:23
the land *b* full of wickedness ... Lev 19:29
shall enter into her, and *b* bitter ... Num 5:24
*b* bitter, and her belly shall ... Num 5:27
this day thou art *b* the people of ... Deut 27:9
thou shalt *b* an astonishment, a ... Deut 28:37
our shoes are *b* old by reason of ... Josh 9:13
go from me, and I shall *b* weak ... Judg 16:17
from thee, and is *b* thine enemy ... 1Sa 28:16
and thou, LORD, art *b* their God ... 2Sa 7:24
about, and is *b* my brother's ... 1Kin 2:15
thee what shall *b* of the child ... 1Kin 14:3
and they shall *b* a prey and a spoil ... 2Kin 21:14
that they should *b* a desolation ... 2Kin 22:19
did, and what should *b* of her ... Est 2:11
my skin is broken, and *b* loathsome ... Job 7:5
which are ready to *b* heaps ... Job 15:28
*b* old, yea, are mighty in power ... Job 21:7
I am *b* like dust and ashes ... Job 30:19
Thou art *b* cruel to me ... Job 30:21
they are all together *b* filthy ... Ps 14:3
I *b* like them that go down into ... Ps 28:1
they are altogether *b* filthy ... Ps 53:3
and *b* not vain in robbery ... Ps 62:10
I am *b* a stranger unto my ... Ps 69:8
Let their table *b* a snare before ... Ps 69:22
their welfare, let it *b* a trap ... Ps 69:22
We are *b* a reproach to our ... Ps 79:4
and let his prayer *b* sin ... Ps 109:7
and song, and is *b* my salvation ... Ps 118:14
heard me, and art *b* my salvation ... Ps 118:21
is *b* the head stone of the corner ... Ps 118:22
For I am *b* like a bottle in the ... Ps 119:83
have him *b* his son at the length ... Prov 29:21
is the faithful city *b* an harlot ... Is 1:21
Thy silver is *b* dross, thy wine ... Is 1:22
all the land shall *b* briers ... Is 7:24
he also is *b* my salvation ... Is 12:2
thee, Art thou also *b* weak as we ... Is 14:10
art thou *b* like unto us ... Is 14:10
of Pharaoh is *b* brutish ... Is 19:11
The princes of Zoan are *b* fools ... Is 19:13
the vision of all is *b* unto you ... Is 29:11
thereof shall *b* burning pitch ... Is 34:9
the parched ground shall *b* a pool ... Is 35:7
Their webs shall not *b* garments ... Is 59:6
A little one shall *b* a thousand ... Is 60:22
after vanity, and are *b* vain ... Jer 2:5
*b* another man's, shall he return ... Jer 3:1
And the prophets shall *b* wind ... Jer 5:13
therefore they are *b* great ... Jer 5:27
*b* a den of robbers in your eyes ... Jer 7:11
For the pastors are *b* brutish ... Jer 10:21
this house shall *b* a desolation ... Jer 22:5
field, and Jerusalem shall *b* heaps ... Jer 26:18
that Bozrah shall *b* a desolation ... Jer 49:13
how is Babylon *b* a desolation ... Jer 50:23
and they shall *b* as women ... Jer 50:37
And Babylon shall *b* heaps, a ... Jer 51:37
how is Babylon *b* an astonishment ... Jer 51:41
how is she *b* as a widow ... Lam 1:1
provinces, how is she *b* tributary ... Lam 1:1
with her, they are *b* her enemies ... Lam 1:2
her princes are *b* like harts that ... Lam 1:6
for I am *b* vile ... Lam 1:11
How is the gold *b* dim ... Lam 4:1
daughter of my people is *b* cruel ... Lam 4:3
is withered, it is *b* like a stick ... Lam 4:8
Thou art *b* guilty in thy blood ... Eze 22:4
house of Israel is to me *b* dross ... Eze 22:18
Because ye are all *b* dross ... Eze 22:19
it shall *b* a spoil to the nations ... Eze 26:5
is *b* like the garden of Eden ... Eze 36:35
and ruined cities are *b* fenced ... Eze 36:35
they shall *b* one in thine hand ... Eze 37:17
king, that art grown and *b* strong ... Dan 4:22
thy people are *b* a reproach to ... Dan 9:16
shall *b* strong with a small ... Dan 11:23
And Ephraim said, Yet I am *b* rich ... Hos 12:8
and his spring shall *b* dry ... Hos 13:15
Samaria shall *b* desolate ... Hos 13:16
see what would *b* of the city ... Jonah 4:5
field, and Jerusalem shall *b* heaps ... Mic 3:12
their goods shall *b* a booty ... Zeph 1:13
how is she *b* a desolation, a ... Zeph 2:15
Zerubbabel thou shalt *b* a plain ... Zec 4:7
*b* as little children, ye shall ... Mt 18:3
the same is *b* the head of the ... Mt 21:42
will make you to *b* fishers of men ... Mk 1:17
is *b* the head of the corner ... Mk 12:10
the same is *b* the head of the ... Lk 20:17
he power to *b* the sons of God ... Jn 1:12
which is *b* the head of the corner ... Acts 4:11
we wot not what is *b* of him ... Acts 7:40
the soldiers, what was *b* of Peter ... Acts 12:18
they are together *b* unprofitable ... Rom 3:12
the world may *b* guilty before God ... Rom 3:19
that he might *b* the father of ... Rom 4:18
*b* servants to God, ye have your ... Rom 6:22
ye also are *b* dead to the law by ... Rom 7:4
might *b* exceeding sinful ... Rom 7:13
in this world, let him *b* a fool ... 1Cor 3:18
let him not *b* uncircumcised ... 1Cor 7:18
*b* a stumblingblock to them that ... 1Cor 8:9
I am *b* as sounding brass, or a ... 1Cor 13:1
*b* the firstfruits of them that ... 1Cor 15:20
behold, all things are *b* new ... 2Cor 5:17
I am *b* a fool in glorying ... 2Cor 12:11
Am I therefore *b* your enemy ... Gal 4:16
Christ is *b* of no effect unto you ... Gal 5:4
the things which *b* sound doctrine ... Titus 2:1
*b* effectual by the acknowledging ... Philem 6
are *b* such as have need of milk, ... Heb 5:12
are *b* judges of evil thoughts ... Jas 2:4
thou art *b* a transgressor of the ... Jas 2:11
are *b* the kingdoms of our Lord ... Rev 11:15
is *b* the habitation of devils, and ... Rev 18:2

**BECOMETH**
holiness *b* thine house, O LORD, ... Ps 93:5
He *b* poor that dealeth with a ... Prov 10:4
Excellent speech *b* not a fool ... Prov 17:7
*b* surety in the presence of his ... Prov 17:18
is born in his kingdom *b* poor ... Eccl 4:14
for thus it *b* us to fulfil all ... Mt 3:15
the word, and he *b* unfruitful ... Mt 13:22
*b* a tree, so that the birds of ... Mt 13:32
the word, and it *b* unfruitful ... Mk 4:19
*b* greater than all herbs, and ... Mk 4:32
as *b* saints, and that ye assist ... Rom 16:2
once named among you, as *b* saints ... Eph 5:3
be as it *b* the gospel of Christ ... Phil 1:27
But (which *b* women professing ... 1Ti 2:10
be in behaviour as *b* holiness ... Titus 2:3

**BECORATH** See BECHORATH.

**BED**
himself, and sat upon the *b* ... Gen 48:2
thou wentest up to thy father's *b* ... Gen 49:4
gathered up his feet into the *b* ... Gen 49:33
thy bedchamber, and upon thy *b* ... Ex 8:3
and he die not, but keepeth his *b* ... Ex 21:18
Every *b*, whereon he lieth that ... Lev 15:4
his *b* shall wash his clothes ... Lev 15:5
her *b* shall wash his clothes ... Lev 15:21
And if it be on her *b*, or on any ... Lev 15:23
all the *b* whereon he lieth shall ... Lev 15:24
Every *b* whereon she lieth all the ... Lev 15:26
her as the *b* of her separation ... Lev 15:26
an image, and laid it in the *b* ... 1Sa 19:13
Bring him up to me in the *b* ... 1Sa 19:15
there was an image in the *b* ... 1Sa 19:16
from the earth, and sat upon the *b* ... 1Sa 28:23
who lay on a *b* at noon ... 2Sa 4:5
he lay on his *b* in his bedchamber ... 2Sa 4:7
in his own house upon his *b* ... 2Sa 4:11
that David arose from off his *b* ... 2Sa 11:2
*b* with the servants of his lord ... 2Sa 11:13
unto him, Lay thee down on thy *b* ... 2Sa 13:5
the king bowed himself upon the *b* ... 1Kin 1:47
abode, and laid him upon his own *b* .. 1Kin 17:19
And he laid him down upon his *b* ... 1Kin 21:4
that *b* on which thou art gone up ... 2Kin 1:4
that *b* on which thou art gone up ... 2Kin 1:6
that *b* on which thou art gone up ... 2Kin 1:16
and let us set for him there a *b* ... 2Kin 4:10
laid him on the *b* of the man of ... 2Kin 4:21
was dead, and laid upon his *b* ... 2Kin 4:32
as he defiled his father's *b* ... 1Chr 5:1
laid him in the *b* which was ... 2Chr 16:14
the priest, and slew him on his *b* ... 2Chr 24:25
upon the *b* whereon Esther was ... Est 7:8
My *b* shall comfort me, my couch ... Job 7:13
I have made my *b* in the darkness ... Job 17:13
men, in slumberings upon the *b* ... Job 33:15
also with pain upon his *b* ... Job 33:19
with your own heart upon your *b* ... Ps 4:4
all the night make I my *b* to swim ... Ps 6:6
He deviseth mischief upon his *b* ... Ps 36:4
him upon the *b* of languishing ... Ps 41:3
make all his *b* in his sickness ... Ps 41:3
When I remember thee upon my *b* ... Ps 63:6
of my house, nor go up into my *b* ... Ps 132:3
if I make my *b* in hell, behold, ... Ps 139:8
I have decked my *b* with coverings ... Prov 7:16
I have perfumed my *b* with myrrh ... Prov 7:17
take away thy *b* from under thee ... Prov 22:27
so doth the slothful upon his *b* ... Prov 26:14
also our *b* is green ... Song 1:16
By night on my *b* I sought him ... Song 3:1
Behold his *b*, which is Solomon's ... Song 3:7
His cheeks are as a *b* of spices ... Song 5:13
For the *b* is shorter than that a ... Is 28:20
high mountain hast thou set thy *b* ... Is 57:7
thou hast enlarged thy *b*, and made ... Is 57:8
thou lovedst their *b* where thou ... Is 57:8
came to her into the *b* of love ... Eze 23:17
And satest upon a stately *b* ... Eze 23:41
They have set her a *b* in the ... Eze 32:25
visions of thy head upon thy *b* ... Dan 2:28
came into thy mind upon thy *b* ... Dan 2:29
afraid, and the thoughts upon my *b* ... Dan 4:5
the visions of mine head in my *b* ... Dan 4:10
the visions of my head upon my *b* ... Dan 4:13
and visions of his head upon his *b* ... Dan 7:1
in Samaria in the corner of a *b* ... Amos 3:12
sick of the palsy, lying on a *b* ... Mt 9:2
the palsy,) Arise, take up thy *b* ... Mt 9:6
they let down the *b* wherein the ... Mk 2:4
to say, Arise, and take up thy *b* ... Mk 2:9
thee, Arise, and take up thy *b* ... Mk 2:11
he arose, took up the *b*, and went ... Mk 2:12
put under a bushel, or under a *b* ... Mk 4:21
and her daughter laid upon the *b* ... Mk 7:30
men brought in a *b* a man which ... Lk 5:18
a vessel, or putteth it under a *b* ... Lk 8:16
and my children are with me in *b* ... Lk 11:7
there shall be two men in one *b* ... Lk 17:34
unto him, Rise, take up thy *b* ... Jn 5:8
was made whole, and took up his *b* ... Jn 5:9
lawful for thee to carry thy *b* ... Jn 5:10
same said unto me, Take up thy *b* ... Jn 5:11
said unto thee, Take up thy *b* ... Jn 5:12
which had kept his *b* eight years ... Acts 9:33
arise, and make thy *b* ... Acts 9:34
in all, and the *b* undefiled ... Heb 13:4
Behold, I will cast her into a *b* ... Rev 2:22

**BEDAD** (*be'-dad*) *Father of Hadad.*
died, and Hadad the son of *B* ... Gen 36:35
was dead, Hadad the son of *B* ... 1Chr 1:46

**BEDAN** (*be'-dan*)
*1. A judge of Israel.*
And the LORD sent Jerubbaal, and *B* ... 1Sa 12:11
*2. A descendant of Manasseh.*
And the sons of Ulam; *B* ... 1Chr 7:17

**BEDCHAMBER**
into thine house, and into thy *b* ... Ex 8:3
house, he lay on his bed in his *b* ... 2Sa 4:7
words that thou speakest in thy *b* ... 2Kin 6:12
in the *b* from Athaliah, so that ... 2Kin 11:2
and put him and his nurse in a *b* ... 2Chr 22:11
and curse not the rich in thy *b* ... Eccl 10:20

**BEDEIAH** (*be-de'-yah*) *Married a foreign wife in exile.*
Benaiah, *B*, Chelluh, ... Ezr 10:35

**BED'S**
bowed himself upon the *b* head ... Gen 47:31

**BEDS**
Brought *b*, and basons, and earthen ... 2Sa 17:28
the *b* were of gold and silver, ... Est 1:6
let them sing aloud upon their *b* ... Ps 149:5
to the *b* of spices, to feed in ... Song 6:2
they shall rest in their *b* ... Is 57:2
when they howled upon their *b* ... Hos 7:14
That lie upon *b* of ivory, and ... Amos 6:4
and work evil upon their *b* ... Mic 2:1
about in *b* those that were sick ... Mk 6:55
the streets, and laid them on *b* ... Acts 5:15

**BEDSTEAD**
his *b* was a *b* of iron ... Deut 3:11

**BEE**
for the *b* that is in the land of ... Is 7:18

**BEELIADA** (*be-e-li'-ad-ah*) *A son of David.*
And Elishama, and *B*, and Eliphalet ... 1Chr 14:7

**BEELZEBUB** (*be-el'-ze-bub*) See BAAL-ZEBUB. *Chief of evil spirits.*
called the master of the house *B* ... Mt 10:25
but by *B* the prince of the devils ... Mt 12:24
if I by *B* cast out devils, by ... Mt 12:27
from Jerusalem said, He hath *B* ... Mk 3:22
through *B* the chief of the devils ... Lk 11:15
that I cast out devils through *B* ... Lk 11:18
if I by *B* cast out devils, by ... Lk 11:19

**BEELZEBULL** See BEELZEBUB.

**BEEN** See PREFACE.

**BEER** (*be'-ur*) See BAALITH-BEER, BEER-ELIM, BEER-LAHAI-ROI, BEER-SHEBA.
*1. An Israelite post beyond the Arnon River.*
And from thence they went to *B* ... Num 21:16
*2. A town in Judah.*
ran away, and fled, and went to *B* ... Judg 9:21

**BEERA** (*be-e'-rah*) *Son of Zophah.*
and Shilshah, and Ithran, and *B* ... 1Chr 7:37

**BEERAH** (*be-e'-rah*) *A Reubenite prince.*
*B* his son, whom Tilgath-pilneser ... 1Chr 5:6

**BEER-ELIM** (*be'-ur-e'-lim*) *A well in Moab.*
and the howling thereof unto *B* ... Is 15:8

**BEERI** (*be-e'-ri*)
*1. Father of Judith.*
the daughter of *B* the Hittite ... Gen 26:34
*2. Father of Hosea.*
came unto Hosea, the son of *B* ... Hos 1:1

**BEER-LAHAI-ROI** (*be'''-ur-la''-hahe-ro'-e*) *A well.*
Wherefore the well was called *B* ... Gen 16:14

**BEEROTH** (*be-e'-roth*) See BEROTHITE.
*1. An Israelite encampment during the Exodus.*
*B* of the children of Jaakan to ... Deut 10:6
*2. A Hivvite city in Canaan.*
were Gibeon, and Chephirah, and *B* ... Josh 9:17
Gibeon, and Ramah, and *B*, ... Josh 18:25
(for *B* also was reckoned to ... 2Sa 4:2
of Kirjath-arim, Chephirah, and *B* ... Ezr 2:25
Kirjath-jearim, Chephirah, and *B* ... Neh 7:29

**BEEROTHITE** (*be-er'-o-thite*) See BEEROTHITES, BEROTHITE. *An inhabitant of Beeroth.*
Rechab, the sons of Rimmon a *B* ... 2Sa 4:2
And the sons of Rimmon the *B* ... 2Sa 4:5
brother, the sons of Rimmon the *B* ... 2Sa 4:9
Zelek the Ammonite, Nahari the *B* ... 2Sa 23:37

**BEEROTHITES** (*be-er'-o-thites*)
the *B* fled to Gittaim, and were 2Sa 4:3

**BEER-SHEBA** (*be-ur'-she-bah*) *A Canaanite city.*
wandered in the wilderness of *B* Gen 21:14
Wherefore he called that place *B* Gen 21:31
Thus they made a covenant at *B* Gen 21:32
And Abraham planted a grove in *B* Gen 21:33
rose up and went together to *B* Gen 22:19
and Abraham dwelt at *B* Gen 22:19
And he went up from thence to *B* Gen 26:23
of the city is *B* unto this day Gen 26:33
Jacob went out from *B* Gen 28:10
all that he had, and came to *B* Gen 46:1
And Jacob rose up from *B* Gen 46:5
And Hazar-shual, and *B*, and Josh 15:28
they had in their inheritance *B* Josh 19:2
as one man, from Dan even to *B* Judg 20:1
even to *B* knew that Samuel was 1Sa 3:20
they were judges in *B* 1Sa 8:2
and over Judah, from Dan even to *B* 2Sa 3:10
unto thee, from Dan even to *B* 2Sa 17:11
of Israel, from Dan even to *B* 2Sa 24:2
to the south of Judah, even to *B* 2Sa 24:7
even to *B* seventy thousand men 2Sa 24:15
his fig tree, from Dan even to *B* 1Kin 4:25
went for his life, and came to *B* 1Kin 19:3
his mother's name was Zibiah of *B* 2Kin 12:1
burned incense, from Geba to *B* 2Kin 23:8
And they dwelt at *B*, and Moladah, 1Chr 4:28
number Israel from *B* even to Dan 1Chr 21:2
people from *B* to mount Ephraim 2Chr 19:4
name also was Zibiah of *B* 2Chr 24:1
from *B* even to Dan, that they 2Chr 30:5
And at Hazar-shual, and at *B* Neh 11:27
they dwelt from *B* unto the valley Neh 11:30
into Gilgal, and pass not to *B* Amos 5:5
and, The manner of *B* liveth Amos 8:14

**BEES**
you, and chased you, as *b* do Deut 1:44
behold, there was a swarm of *b* Judg 14:8
They compassed me about like *b* Ps 118:12

**BE-ESHTARAH** See BEESH-TERAH.

**BEESH-TERAH** (*be-esh'te-rah*) See ASHTAROTH. *A Levitical city in Manasseh.*
and *B* with her suburbs Josh 21:27

**BEETLE**
the *b* after his kind, and the Lev 11:22

**BEEVES**
a male without blemish, of the *b* Lev 22:19
a freewill offering in *b* or sheep Lev 22:21
both of the persons, and of the *b* Num 31:28
fifty, of the persons, of the *b* Num 31:30
threescore and twelve thousand *b* Num 31:33
the *b* were thirty and six thousand Num 31:38
And thirty and six thousand *b* Num 31:44

**BEFALL**
Lest peradventure mischief *b* him Gen 42:4
if mischief *b* him by the way in Gen 42:38
also from me, and mischief *b* him Gen 44:29
shall *b* you in the last days Gen 49:1
evils and troubles shall *b* them Deut 31:17
evil will *b* you in the latter Deut 31:29
There shall no evil *b* thee Ps 91:10
*b* thy people in the latter days Dan 10:14
the things that shall *b* me there Acts 20:22

**BEFALLEN**
and such things have *b* me Lev 10:19
all the travel that hath *b* us Num 20:14
many evils and troubles are *b* them Deut 31:21
us, why then is all this *b* us Judg 6:13
he thought, Something hath *b* him 1Sa 20:26
every thing that had *b* him Est 6:13
what was *b* to the possessed of Mt 8:33

**BEFALLETH**
*b* the sons of men *b* beasts Eccl 3:19
even one thing *b* them Eccl 3:19

**BEFELL**
and told him all that *b* unto them Gen 42:29
told him all things that *b* them Josh 2:23
thee than all the evil that *b* 2Sa 19:7
that saw it told them how it *b* to Mk 5:16
which *b* me by the lying in wait Acts 20:19

**BEFORE** See PREFACE.

**BEFOREHAND**
take no thought *b* what ye shall Mk 13:11
make up *b* your bounty, whereof ye 2Cor 9:5
Some men's sins are open *b* 1Ti 5:24
good works of some are manifest *b* 1Ti 5:25
signify, when it testified *b* the 1Pet 1:11

**BEFORETIME**
The Horims also dwelt in Seir *b* Deut 2:12
for Hazor *b* was the head of all Josh 11:10
unwittingly, and hated him not *b* Josh 20:5
(*B* in Israel, when a man went to 1Sa 9:9
a Prophet was *b* called a Seer 1Sa 9:9
when all that knew him *b* saw that 1Sa 10:11
afflict them any more, as *b* 2Sa 7:10
Israel dwelt in their tents, as *b* 2Kin 13:5
Now I had not been *b* sad in his Neh 2:1
and *b*, that we may say, He is Is 41:26
which *b* in the same city used Acts 8:9

**BEG**
be continually vagabonds, and *b* Ps 109:10
therefore shall he *b* in harvest Prov 20:4
to *b* I am ashamed Lk 16:3

**BEGAN**
then *b* men to call upon the name Gen 4:26
when men *b* to multiply on the Gen 6:1
Noah *b* to be an husbandman, and he Gen 9:20
he *b* to be a mighty one in the Gen 10:8
seven years of dearth *b* to come Gen 41:54
*b* at the eldest, and left at the Gen 44:12
the people *b* to commit whoredom Num 25:1
*b* Moses to declare this law, Deut 1:5
the Spirit of the LORD *b* to move Judg 13:25
she *b* to afflict him, and his Judg 16:19
head *b* to grow again after he was Judg 16:22
and when the day *b* to spring Judg 19:25
they *b* to smite of the people, and Judg 20:31
the battle, Benjamin *b* to smite Judg 20:39
But when the flame *b* to arise up Judg 20:40
his eyes *b* to wax dim, that he 1Sa 3:2
when he *b* to reign over Israel 2Sa 2:10
years old when he *b* to reign 2Sa 5:4
that he *b* to build the house of 1Kin 6:1
one years old when he *b* to reign 1Kin 14:21
Nadab the son of Jeroboam *b* to 1Kin 15:25
*b* Baasha the son of Ahijah to 1Kin 15:33
*b* Elah the son of Baasha to reign 1Kin 16:8
when he *b* to reign, as soon as he 1Kin 16:11
Judah *b* Omri to reign over Israel 1Kin 16:23
year of Asa king of Judah *b* Ahab 1Kin 16:29
Asa *b* to reign over Judah in the 1Kin 22:41
five years old when he *b* to reign 1Kin 22:42
Ahaziah the son of Ahab *b* to 1Kin 22:51
Now Jehoram the son of Ahab *b* to 2Kin 3:1
king of Judah *b* to reign 2Kin 8:16
old was he when he *b* to reign 2Kin 8:17
was Ahaziah when he *b* to reign 2Kin 8:26
*b* Ahaziah to reign over Judah 2Kin 9:29
the LORD *b* to cut Israel short 2Kin 10:32
was Jehoash when he *b* to reign 2Kin 11:21
year of Jehu Jehoash *b* to reign 2Kin 12:1
Judah Jehoahaz the son of Jehu *b* 2Kin 13:1
year of Joash king of Judah *b* 2Kin 13:10
five years old when he *b* to reign 2Kin 14:2
of Israel *b* to reign in Samaria 2Kin 14:23
*b* Azariah son of Amaziah king of 2Kin 15:1
old was he when he *b* to reign 2Kin 15:2
of Jabesh *b* to reign in the nine 2Kin 15:13
*b* Menahem the son of Gadi to 2Kin 15:17
Pekahiah the son of Menahem *b* to 2Kin 15:23
*b* to reign over Israel in Samaria 2Kin 15:27
*b* Jotham the son of Uzziah king 2Kin 15:32
old was he when he *b* to reign 2Kin 15:33
In those days the LORD *b* to send 2Kin 15:37
Jotham king of Judah *b* to reign 2Kin 16:1
old was Ahaz when he *b* to reign 2Kin 16:2
year of Ahaz king of Judah *b* 2Kin 17:1
of Ahaz king of Judah *b* to reign 2Kin 18:1
old was he when he *b* to reign 2Kin 18:2
years old when he *b* to reign 2Kin 21:1
two years old when he *b* to reign 2Kin 21:19
years old when he *b* to reign 2Kin 22:1
years old when he *b* to reign 2Kin 23:31
five years old when he *b* to reign 2Kin 23:36
years old when he *b* to reign 2Kin 24:8
one years old when he *b* to reign 2Kin 24:18
*b* to reign did lift up the head 2Kin 25:27
he *b* to be mighty upon the earth 1Chr 1:10
the son of Zeruiah *b* to number 1Chr 27:24
Then Solomon *b* to build the house 2Chr 3:1
he *b* to build in the second day 2Chr 3:2
years old when he *b* to reign 2Chr 12:13
year of king Jeroboam *b* Abijah to 2Chr 13:1
And when they *b* to sing and to 2Chr 20:22
five years old when he *b* to reign 2Chr 20:31
two years old when he *b* to reign 2Chr 21:5
old was he when he *b* to reign 2Chr 21:20
was Ahaziah when he *b* to reign 2Chr 22:2
years old when he *b* to reign 2Chr 24:1
five years old when he *b* to reign 2Chr 25:1
old was Uzziah when he *b* to reign 2Chr 26:3
five years old when he *b* to reign 2Chr 27:1
years old when he *b* to reign 2Chr 27:8
years old when he *b* to reign 2Chr 28:1
Hezekiah *b* to reign when he was 2Chr 29:1
Now they *b* on the first day of 2Chr 29:17
And when the burnt offering *b* 2Chr 29:27
the song of the LORD *b* also with 2Chr 29:27
In the third month they *b* to lay 2Chr 31:7
Since the people *b* to bring the 2Chr 31:10
in every work that he *b* in the 2Chr 31:21
years old when he *b* to reign 2Chr 33:1
years old when he *b* to reign 2Chr 33:21
years old when he *b* to reign 2Chr 34:1
he *b* to seek after the God of 2Chr 34:3
twelfth year he *b* to purge Judah 2Chr 34:3
years old when he *b* to reign 2Chr 36:2
five years old when he *b* to reign 2Chr 36:5
years old when he *b* to reign 2Chr 36:9
years old when he *b* to reign 2Chr 36:11
*b* they to offer burnt offerings Ezr 3:6
*b* Zerubbabel the son of Shealtiel Ezr 3:8
*b* to build the house of God which Ezr 5:2
month *b* he to go up from Babylon Ezr 7:9
that the breaches *b* to be stopped Neh 4:7
when the gates of Jerusalem *b* to Neh 13:19
years old when he *b* to reign Jer 52:1
Then they *b* at the ancient men Eze 9:6
Jonah *b* to enter into the city a Jonah 3:4
From that time Jesus *b* to preach Mt 4:17
departed, Jesus *b* to say unto the Mt 11:7
Then *b* he to upbraid the cities Mt 11:20
*b* to pluck the ears of corn, and Mt 12:1
From that time forth *b* Jesus to Mt 16:21
*b* to rebuke him, saying, Be it Mt 16:22
*b* every one of them to say unto Mt 26:22
*b* to be sorrowful and very heavy Mt 26:37
Then *b* he to curse and to swear, Mt 26:74
as it *b* to dawn toward the first Mt 28:1
*b* to publish it much, and to blaze Mk 1:45
and his disciples *b*, as they went, Mk 2:23
he *b* again to teach by the sea Mk 4:1
they *b* to pray him to depart out Mk 5:17
*b* to publish in Decapolis how Mk 5:20
he *b* to teach in the synagogue Mk 6:2
*b* to send them forth by two and Mk 6:7
he *b* to teach them many things Mk 6:34
*b* to carry about in beds those Mk 6:55
*b* to question with him, seeking Mk 8:11
he *b* to teach them, that the Son Mk 8:31
took him, and *b* to rebuke him Mk 8:32
Then Peter *b* to say unto him, Lo, Mk 10:28
*b* to tell them what things should Mk 10:32
they *b* to be much displeased with Mk 10:41
he *b* to cry out, and say, Jesus, Mk 10:47
*b* to cast out them that sold and Mk 11:15
he *b* to speak unto them by Mk 12:1
And Jesus answering them *b* to say Mk 13:5
they *b* to be sorrowful, and to say Mk 14:19
*b* to be sore amazed, and to be Mk 14:33
some *b* to spit on him, and to Mk 14:65
*b* to say to them that stood by, Mk 14:69
But he *b* to curse and to swear, Mk 14:71
the multitude crying aloud *b* to Mk 15:8
*b* to salute him, Hail, King of Mk 15:18
which have been since the world *b* Lk 1:70
Jesus himself *b* to be about Lk 3:23
he *b* to say unto them, This day Lk 4:21
the ships, so that they *b* to sink Lk 5:7
and the Pharisees *b* to reason Lk 5:21
was dead sat up, and *b* to speak Lk 7:15
he *b* to speak unto the people Lk 7:24
*b* to wash his feet with tears, and Lk 7:38
him *b* to say within themselves Lk 7:49
And when the day *b* to wear away Lk 9:12
he *b* to say, This is an evil Lk 11:29
the Pharisees *b* to urge him Lk 11:53
he *b* to say unto his disciples Lk 12:1
with one consent *b* to make excuse Lk 14:18
Saying, This man *b* to build Lk 14:30
and he *b* to be in want Lk 15:14
And they *b* to be merry Lk 15:24
of the disciples *b* to rejoice Lk 19:37
*b* to cast out them that sold Lk 19:45
Then *b* he to speak to the people Lk 20:9
And they *b* to enquire among Lk 22:23
they *b* to accuse him, saying, We Lk 23:2
them the hour when he *b* to amend Jn 4:52
Since the world *b* was it not Jn 9:32
*b* to wash the disciples' feet, and Jn 13:5
of all that Jesus *b* both to do Acts 1:1
*b* to speak with other tongues, as Acts 2:4
holy prophets since the world *b* Acts 3:21
*b* at the same scripture, and Acts 8:35
*b* from Galilee, after the baptism Acts 10:37
as I *b* to speak, the Holy Ghost Acts 11:15
he *b* to speak boldly in the Acts 18:26
Tertullus *b* to accuse him, saying Acts 24:2
he had broken it, he *b* to eat Acts 27:35
was kept secret since the world *b* Rom 16:25
Christ Jesus before the world *b* 2Ti 1:9
lie, promised before the world *b* Titus 1:2
which at the first *b* to be spoken Heb 2:3

**BEGAT**
and Irad *b* Mehujael Gen 4:18
and Mehujael *b* Methusael Gen 4:18
and Methusael *b* Lamech Gen 4:18
*b* a son in his own likeness, Gen 5:3
and he *b* sons and daughters Gen 5:4
hundred and five years, and *b* Enos Gen 5:6
after he *b* Enos eight hundred Gen 5:7
years, and *b* sons and daughters Gen 5:7
lived ninety years, and *b* Cainan Gen 5:9
Enos lived after he *b* Cainan Gen 5:10
years, and *b* sons and daughters Gen 5:10
seventy years, and *b* Mahalaleel Gen 5:12
And Cainan lived after he *b* Gen 5:13
years, and *b* sons and daughters Gen 5:13
sixty and five years, and *b* Jared Gen 5:15
after he *b* Jared eight hundred Gen 5:16
years, and *b* sons and daughters Gen 5:16
sixty and two years, and he *b* Enoch Gen 5:18
Jared lived after he *b* Enoch Gen 5:19
years, and *b* sons and daughters Gen 5:19
and five years, and *b* Methuselah Gen 5:21
*b* Methuselah three hundred years Gen 5:22
and *b* sons and daughters Gen 5:22
and seven years, and *b* Lamech Gen 5:25
Methuselah lived after he *b* Gen 5:26
two years, and *b* sons and daughters Gen 5:26
eighty and two years, and *b* a son Gen 5:28
Lamech lived after he *b* Noah five Gen 5:30
years, and *b* sons and daughters Gen 5:30
and Noah *b* Shem, Ham, and Japheth Gen 5:32
Noah *b* three sons, Shem, Ham, and Gen 6:10
And Cush *b* Nimrod Gen 10:8
Mizraim *b* Ludim, and Gen 10:13
Canaan *b* Sidon his firstborn, and Gen 10:15
And Arphaxad *b* Salah Gen 10:24

B

and Salah *b* Eber ... Gen 10:24
Joktan *b* Almodad, and Sheleph, and. Gen 10:26
*b* Arphaxad two years after the ... Gen 11:10
Shem lived after he *b* Arphaxad ... Gen 11:11
years, and *b* sons and daughters ... Gen 11:11
five and thirty years, and *b* Salah ... Gen 11:12
after he *b* Salah four hundred ... Gen 11:13
years, and *b* sons and daughters ... Gen 11:13
lived thirty years, and *b* Eber ... Gen 11:14
after he *b* Eber four hundred ... Gen 11:15
years, and *b* sons and daughters ... Gen 11:15
four and thirty years, and *b* Peleg ... Gen 11:16
after he *b* Peleg four hundred ... Gen 11:17
years, and *b* sons and daughters ... Gen 11:17
lived thirty years, and *b* Reu ... Gen 11:18
lived after he *b* Reu two hundred ... Gen 11:19
years, and *b* sons and daughters ... Gen 11:19
two and thirty years, and *b* Serug ... Gen 11:20
after he *b* Serug two hundred ... Gen 11:21
years, and *b* sons and daughters ... Gen 11:21
lived thirty years, and *b* Nahor ... Gen 11:22
Serug lived after he *b* Nahor two ... Gen 11:23
years, and *b* sons and daughters ... Gen 11:23
nine and twenty years, and *b* Terah ... Gen 11:24
lived after he *b* Terah an hundred ... Gen 11:25
years, and *b* sons and daughters ... Gen 11:25
and *b* Abram, Nahor, and Haran ... Gen 11:26
Terah *b* Abram, Nahor, and Haran ... Gen 11:27
and Haran *b* Lot ... Gen 11:27
and Bethuel *b* Rebekah ... Gen 22:23
And Jokshan *b* Sheba, and Dedan ... Gen 25:3
Abraham *b* Isaac ... Gen 25:19
which they *b* in your land ... Lev 25:45
and Machir *b* Gilead ... Num 26:29
And Kohath *b* Amram ... Num 26:58
Of the Rock that *b* thee thou art ... Deut 32:18
and Gilead *b* Jephthah ... Judg 11:1
Pharez *b* Hezron, ... Ruth 4:18
And Hezron *b* Ram ... Ruth 4:19
and Ram *b* Amminadab ... Ruth 4:19
And Amminadab *b* Nahshon, and ... Ruth 4:20
Nahshon, and Nahshon *b* Salmon ... Ruth 4:20
Salmon *b* Boaz, and Boaz *b* Obed ... Ruth 4:21
Obed *b* Jesse ... Ruth 4:22
and Jesse *b* David ... Ruth 4:22
And Cush *b* Nimrod ... 1Chr 1:10
Mizraim *b* Ludim, and ... 1Chr 1:11
Canaan *b* Zidon his firstborn, and ... 1Chr 1:13
And Arphaxad *b* Shelah ... 1Chr 1:18
and Shelah *b* Eber ... 1Chr 1:18
Joktan *b* Almodad, and Sheleph, and.. 1Chr 1:20
And Abraham *b* Isaac ... 1Chr 1:34
And Ram *b* Amminadab ... 1Chr 2:10
and Amminadab *b* Nahshon ... 1Chr 2:10
And Nahshon *b* Salma ... 1Chr 2:11
and Salma *b* Boaz ... 1Chr 2:11
Boaz *b* Obed, and Obed *b* Jesse, ... 1Chr 2:12
Jesse *b* his firstborn Eliab, and ... 1Chr 2:13
Caleb the son of Hezron *b* ... 1Chr 2:18
Hur *b* Uri, and Uri *b* Bezaleel ... 1Chr 2:20
And Segub *b* Jair, who had three and. 1Chr 2:22
Attai *b* Nathan ... 1Chr 2:36
and Nathan *b* Zabad ... 1Chr 2:36
Zabad *b* Ephlal ... 1Chr 2:37
Ephlal *b* Obed ... 1Chr 2:37
And Obed *b* Jehu ... 1Chr 2:38
and Jehu *b* Azariah ... 1Chr 2:38
And Azariah *b* Helez ... 1Chr 2:39
and Helez *b* Eleasah ... 1Chr 2:39
And Eleasah *b* Sisamai ... 1Chr 2:40
and Sisamai *b* Shallum ... 1Chr 2:40
Shallum *b* Jekamiah ... 1Chr 2:41
and Jekamiah *b* Elishama ... 1Chr 2:41
And Shema *b* Raham, the father of ... 1Chr 2:44
and Rekem *b* Shammai ... 1Chr 2:44
and Haran *b* Gazez ... 1Chr 2:46
Reaiah the son of Shobal *b* Jahath ... 1Chr 4:2
and Jahath *b* Ahumai, and Lahad ... 1Chr 4:2
Coz *b* Anub, and Zobebah, and the ... 1Chr 4:8
the brother of Shuah *b* Mehir ... 1Chr 4:11
Eshton *b* Beth-rapha, and Paseah, ... 1Chr 4:12
And Meonothai *b* Ophrah ... 1Chr 4:14
and Seraiah *b* Joab, the father of ... 1Chr 4:14
Eleazar *b* Phinehas ... 1Chr 6:4
Phinehas *b* Abishua ... 1Chr 6:4
And Abishua *b* Bukki ... 1Chr 6:5
and Bukki *b* Uzzi ... 1Chr 6:5
And Uzzi *b* Zerahiah ... 1Chr 6:6
and Zerahiah *b* Meraioth ... 1Chr 6:6
Meraioth *b* Amariah ... 1Chr 6:7
and Amariah *b* Ahitub ... 1Chr 6:7
And Ahitub *b* Zadok ... 1Chr 6:8
and Zadok *b* Ahimaaz ... 1Chr 6:8
And Ahimaaz *b* Azariah ... 1Chr 6:9
and Azariah *b* Johanan ... 1Chr 6:9
And Johanan *b* Azariah, (he it is ... 1Chr 6:10
And Azariah *b* Amariah ... 1Chr 6:11
and Amariah *b* Ahitub ... 1Chr 6:11
And Ahitub *b* Zadok ... 1Chr 6:12
and Zadok *b* Shallum ... 1Chr 6:12
And Shallum *b* Hilkiah ... 1Chr 6:13
and Hilkiah *b* Azariah ... 1Chr 6:13
And Azariah *b* Seraiah ... 1Chr 6:14
and Seraiah *b* Jehozadak ... 1Chr 6:14
Heber *b* Japhlet, and Shomer, and ... 1Chr 7:32
Now Benjamin *b* Bela his firstborn ... 1Chr 8:1
them, and *b* Uzza, and Ahihud ... 1Chr 8:7
Shaharaim *b* children in the ... 1Chr 8:8
he *b* of Hodesh his wife, Jobab, ... 1Chr 8:9
And of Hushim he *b* Abitub, and ... 1Chr 8:11
And Mikloth *b* Shimeah ... 1Chr 8:32
And Ner *b* Kish, and Kish *b* Saul ... 1Chr 8:33
Saul *b* Jonathan, and Malchi-shua, ... 1Chr 8:33
and Merib-baal *b* Micah ... 1Chr 8:34
And Ahaz *b* Jehoadah ... 1Chr 8:36
and Jehoadah *b* Alemeth, and ... 1Chr 8:36
and Zimri *b* Moza, ... 1Chr 8:36
And Moza *b* Binea ... 1Chr 8:37
And Mikloth *b* Shimeam ... 1Chr 9:38
And Ner *b* Kish ... 1Chr 9:39
and Kish *b* Saul ... 1Chr 9:39
Saul *b* Jonathan, and Malchi-shua, ... 1Chr 9:39
and Merib-baal *b* Micah ... 1Chr 9:40
And Ahaz *b* Jarah ... 1Chr 9:42
Jarah *b* Alemeth, and Azmaveth, and. 1Chr 9:42
and Zimri *b* Moza ... 1Chr 9:42
And Moza *b* Binea ... 1Chr 9:43
David *b* more sons and daughters ... 1Chr 14:3
*b* twenty and eight sons, and ... 2Chr 11:21
*b* twenty and two sons, and sixteen.. 2Chr 13:21
and he *b* sons and daughters ... 2Chr 24:3
Jeshua *b* Joiakim ... Neh 12:10
Joiakim also *b* Eliashib ... Neh 12:10
and Eliashib *b* Joiada ... Neh 12:10
Joiada *b* Jonathan ... Neh 12:11
and Jonathan *b* Jaddua ... Neh 12:11
unto thy father that *b* thee ... Prov 23:22
fathers that *b* them in this land ... Jer 16:3
brought her, and he that *b* her ... Dan 11:6
his mother that *b* him shall say ... Zec 13:3
his mother that *b* him shall ... Zec 13:3
Abraham *b* Isaac ... Mt 1:2
and Isaac *b* Jacob ... Mt 1:2
and Jacob *b* Judas and his brethren ... Mt 1:2
Judas *b* Phares and Zara of Thamar ... Mt 1:3
and Phares *b* Esrom ... Mt 1:3
and Esrom *b* Aram ... Mt 1:3
And Aram *b* Aminadab ... Mt 1:4
and Aminadab *b* Naasson ... Mt 1:4
and Naasson *b* Salmon ... Mt 1:4
And Salmon *b* Booz of Rachab ... Mt 1:5
and Booz *b* Obed of Ruth ... Mt 1:5
and Obed *b* Jesse ... Mt 1:5
And Jesse *b* David the king ... Mt 1:6
David the king *b* Solomon of her ... Mt 1:6
And Solomon *b* Roboam ... Mt 1:7
and Roboam *b* Abia ... Mt 1:7
and Abia *b* Asa ... Mt 1:7
And Asa *b* Josaphat ... Mt 1:8
and Josaphat *b* Joram ... Mt 1:8
and Joram *b* Ozias ... Mt 1:8
And Ozias *b* Joatham ... Mt 1:9
and Joatham *b* Achaz ... Mt 1:9
and Achaz *b* Ezekias ... Mt 1:9
And Ezekias *b* Manasses ... Mt 1:10
and Manasses *b* Amon ... Mt 1:10
and Amon *b* Josias ... Mt 1:10
Josias *b* Jechonias and his ... Mt 1:11
to Babylon, Jechonias *b* Salathiel ... Mt 1:12
and Salathiel *b* Zorobabel ... Mt 1:12
And Zorobabel *b* Abiud ... Mt 1:13
and Abiud *b* Eliakim ... Mt 1:13
and Eliakim *b* Azor ... Mt 1:13
And Azor *b* Sadoc ... Mt 1:14
and Sadoc *b* Achim ... Mt 1:14
and Achim *b* Eliud ... Mt 1:14
And Eliud *b* Eleazar ... Mt 1:15
and Eleazar *b* Matthan ... Mt 1:15
and Matthan *b* Jacob ... Mt 1:15
Jacob *b* Joseph the husband of ... Mt 1:16
and so Abraham *b* Isaac, and ... Acts 7:8
and Isaac *b* Jacob ... Acts 7:8
Jacob *b* the twelve patriarchs ... Acts 7:8
of Madian, where he *b* two sons ... Acts 7:29
Of his own will *b* he us with the ... Jas 1:18
that *b* loveth him also that is ... 1Jn 5:1

## BEGET
twelve princes shall he *b* ... Gen 17:20
When thou shalt *b* children ... Deut 4:25
Thou shalt *b* sons and daughters, ... Deut 28:41
from thee, which thou shalt *b* ... 2Kin 20:18
If a man *b* an hundred children, ... Eccl 6:3
from thee, which thou shall *b* ... Is 39:7
ye wives, and *b* sons and daughters ... Jer 29:6
If he *b* a son that is a robber, a ... Eze 18:10
Now, lo, if he *b* a son, that ... Eze 18:14
which shall *b* children among you ... Eze 47:22

## BEGETTEST
issue, which thou *b* after them ... Gen 48:6
unto his father, What *b* thou ... Is 45:10

## BEGETTETH
He that *b* a fool doeth it to his ... Prov 17:21
he that *b* a wise child shall have ... Prov 23:24
he *b* a son, and there is nothing ... Eccl 5:14

## BEGGAR
lifteth up the *b* from the ... 1Sa 2:8
was a certain *b* named Lazarus ... Lk 16:20
it came to pass, that the *b* died ... Lk 16:22

## BEGGARLY
*b* elements, whereunto ye desire ... Gal 4:9

## BEGGED
to Pilate, and *b* the body of Jesus ... Mt 27:58
Pilate, and *b* the body of Jesus ... Lk 23:52
Is not this he that sat and *b* ... Jn 9:8

## BEGGING
forsaken, nor his seed *b* bread ... Ps 37:25
sat by the highway side *b* ... Mk 10:46
blind man sat by the way side *b* ... Lk 18:35

## BEGIN
and this they *b* to do ... Gen 11:6
*b* to possess it, and contend with ... Deut 2:24
This day will I *b* to put the ... Deut 2:25
*b* to possess, that thou mayest ... Deut 2:31
*b* to number the seven weeks from ... Deut 16:9
This day will I *b* to magnify thee ... Josh 3:7
What man is he that will *b* to ... Judg 10:18
he shall *b* to deliver Israel out ... Judg 13:5
when I *b*, I will also make an end ... 1Sa 3:12
Did I then *b* to enquire of God ... 1Sa 22:15
Jehoram king of Judah *b* to reign ... 2Kin 8:25
was the principal to *b* the ... Neh 11:17
I *b* to bring evil on the city ... Jer 25:29
and *b* at my sanctuary ... Eze 9:6
And shall *b* to smite his ... Mt 24:49
*b* not to say within yourselves, ... Lk 3:8
shall *b* to beat the menservants ... Lk 12:45
ye *b* to stand without, and to ... Lk 13:25
Then shall ye *b* to say, We have ... Lk 13:26
thou *b* with shame to take the ... Lk 14:9
all that behold it *b* to mock him ... Lk 14:29
these things *b* to come to pass ... Lk 21:28
Then shall they *b* to say to the ... Lk 23:30
Do we *b* again to commend ... 2Cor 3:1
must *b* at the house of God ... 1Pet 4:17
and if it first *b* at us, what ... 1Pet 4:17
angel, when he shall *b* to sound ... Rev 10:7

## BEGINNEST
weeks from such time as thou *b* to ... Deut 16:9

## BEGINNING
In the *b* God created the heaven ... Gen 1:1
the *b* of his kingdom was Babel, ... Gen 10:10
where his tent had been at the *b* ... Gen 13:3
still ill favoured, as at the *b* ... Gen 41:21
the *b* of my strength, the ... Gen 49:3
shall be unto you the *b* of months ... Ex 12:2
from the *b* of the year even unto ... Deut 11:12
for he is the *b* of his strength ... Deut 21:17
from the *b* of revenges upon the ... Deut 32:42
camp in the *b* of the middle watch ... Judg 7:19
in the *b* of barley harvest ... Ruth 1:22
in the latter end than at the *b* ... Ruth 3:10
in the *b* of barley harvest ... 2Sa 21:9
from the *b* of harvest until water ... 2Sa 21:10
so it was at the *b* of their ... 2Kin 17:25
waste them any more, as at the *b* ... 1Chr 17:9
in the *b* of his reign, wrote they ... Ezr 4:6
Though thy *b* was small, yet thy ... Job 8:7
latter end of Job more than his *b* ... Job 42:12
of the LORD is the *b* of wisdom ... Ps 111:10
Thy word is true from the *b* ... Ps 119:160
of the LORD is the *b* of knowledge ... Prov 1:7
possessed me in the *b* of his way ... Prov 8:22
up from everlasting, from the *b* ... Prov 8:23
of the LORD is the *b* of wisdom ... Prov 9:10
The *b* of strife is as when one ... Prov 17:14
may be gotten hastily at the *b* ... Prov 20:21
God maketh from the *b* to the end ... Eccl 3:11
end of a thing than the *b* thereof ... Eccl 7:8
The *b* of the words of his mouth ... Eccl 10:13
and thy counsellors as at the *b* ... Is 1:26
terrible from their *b* hitherto ... Is 18:2
terrible from their *b* hitherto ... Is 18:7
it not been told you from the *b* ... Is 40:21
the generations from the *b* ... Is 41:4
Who hath declared from the *b* ... Is 41:26
Declaring the end from the *b* ... Is 46:10
the former things from the *b* ... Is 48:3
from the *b* declared it to thee ... Is 48:5
created now, and not from the *b* ... Is 48:7
not spoken in secret from the *b* ... Is 48:16
For since the *b* of the world men ... Is 64:4
*b* is the place of our sanctuary ... Jer 17:12
In the *b* of the reign of ... Jer 26:1
In the *b* of the reign of ... Jer 27:1
in the *b* of the reign of Zedekiah ... Jer 28:1
*b* of the reign of Zedekiah king ... Jer 49:34
in the *b* of the watches pour out ... Lam 2:19
in the *b* of the year, in the ... Eze 40:1
I had seen in the vision at the *b* ... Dan 9:21
At the *b* of thy supplications the ... Dan 9:23
The *b* of the word of the LORD by ... Hos 1:2
the *b* of the shooting up of the ... Amos 7:1
she is the *b* of the sin to the ... Mic 1:13
*b* to sink, he cried, saying, Lord ... Mt 14:30
made them at the *b* made them male ... Mt 19:4
but from the *b* it was not so ... Mt 19:8
*b* from the last unto the first ... Mt 20:8
All these are the *b* of sorrows ... Mt 24:8
the *b* of the world to this time ... Mt 24:21
The *b* of the gospel of Jesus ... Mk 1:1
But from the *b* of the creation ... Mk 10:6
such as was not from the *b* of the ... Mk 13:19
unto us, which from the *b* were ... Lk 1:2
*b* from Galilee to this place ... Lk 23:5
*b* at Moses and all the prophets, ... Lk 24:27
among all nations, *b* at Jerusalem ... Lk 24:47
In the *b* was the Word, and the ... Jn 1:1
The same was in the *b* with God ... Jn 1:2
Every man at the *b* doth set forth ... Jn 2:10
This *b* of miracles did Jesus in ... Jn 2:11
For Jesus knew from the *b* who ... Jn 6:64
*b* at the eldest, even unto the ... Jn 8:9
that I said unto you from the *b* ... Jn 8:25

He was a murderer from the *b* ... Jn 8:44
ye have been with me from the *b* ... Jn 15:27
I said not unto you at the *b* ... Jn 16:4
*B* from the baptism of John, unto ... Acts 1:22
rehearsed the matter from the *b* ... Acts 11:4
fell on them, as on us at the *b* ... Acts 11:15
his works from the *b* of the world ... Acts 15:18
Which knew me from the *b*, if they ... Acts 26:5
which from the *b* of the world ... Eph 3:9
that in the *b* of the gospel, when ... Phil 4:15
who is the *b*, the firstborn from ... Col 1:18
because God hath from the *b* ... 2Th 2:13
in the *b* hast laid the foundation ... Heb 1:10
Christ, if we hold the *b* of our ... Heb 3:14
descent, having neither *b* of days ... Heb 7:3
end is worse with them than the *b* ... 2Pet 2:20
were from the *b* of the creation ... 2Pet 3:4
That which was from the *b* ... 1Jn 1:1
which ye had from the *b* ... 1Jn 2:7
which ye have heard from the *b* ... 1Jn 2:7
have known him that is from the *b* ... 1Jn 2:13
have known him that is from the *b* ... 1Jn 2:14
which ye have heard from the *b* ... 1Jn 2:24
from the *b* shall remain in you ... 1Jn 2:24
for the devil sinneth from the *b* ... 1Jn 3:8
message that ye heard from the *b* ... 1Jn 3:11
but that which we had from the *b* ... 2Jn 5
That, as ye have heard from the *b* ... 2Jn 6
I am Alpha and Omega, the *b* ... Rev 1:8
the *b* of the creation of God ... Rev 3:14
I am Alpha and Omega, the *b* ... Rev 21:6
I am Alpha and Omega, the *b* ... Rev 22:13

### BEGINNINGS
in the *b* of your months, ye shall ... Num 10:10
in the *b* of your months ye shall ... Num 28:11
do better unto you than at your *b* ... Eze 36:11
these are the *b* of sorrows ... Mk 13:8

### BEGOTTEN
*b* Seth were eight hundred years ... Gen 5:4
*b* of thy father, she is thy ... Lev 18:11
have I *b* them, that thou ... Num 11:12
The children that are *b* of them ... Deut 23:8
and ten sons of his body *b* ... Judg 8:30
or who hath *b* the drops of dew ... Job 38:28
this day have I *b* thee ... Ps 2:7
thine heart, Who hath *b* me these ... Is 49:21
for they have *b* strange children ... Hos 5:7
as of the only *b* of the Father ... Jn 1:14
the only *b* Son, which is in the ... Jn 1:18
that he gave his only *b* Son ... Jn 3:16
the name of the only *b* Son of God ... Jn 3:18
my Son, this day have I *b* thee ... Acts 13:33
I have *b* you through the gospel ... 1Cor 4:15
whom I have *b* in my bonds ... Philem 10
my Son, this day have I *b* thee ... Heb 1:5
art my Son, to day have I *b* thee ... Heb 5:5
offered up his only *b* son ... Heb 11:17
to his abundant mercy hath *b* us ... 1Pet 1:3
his only *b* Son into the world ... 1Jn 4:9
loveth him also that is *b* of him ... 1Jn 5:1
but he that is *b* of God keepeth ... 1Jn 5:18
the first *b* of the dead, and the ... Rev 1:5

### BEGUILE
lest any man should *b* you with ... Col 2:4
Let no man *b* you of your reward ... Col 2:18

### BEGUILED
the woman said, The serpent *b* me ... Gen 3:13
wherefore then hast thou *b* me ... Gen 29:25
wherewith they have *b* you in the ... Num 25:18
saying, Wherefore have ye *b* us ... Josh 9:22
as the serpent *b* Eve through his ... 2Cor 11:3

### BEGUILING
*b* unstable souls ... 2Pet 2:14

### BEGUN
the plague is *b* ... Num 16:46
the plague was *b* among the people ... Num 16:47
I have *b* to give Sihon and his ... Deut 2:31
thou hast *b* to shew thy servant ... Deut 3:24
before whom thou hast *b* to fall ... Est 6:13
undertook to do as they had *b* ... Est 9:23
And when he had *b* to reckon ... Mt 18:24
desired Titus, that as he had *b* ... 2Cor 8:6
for you, who have *b* before ... 2Cor 8:10
having *b* in the Spirit, are ye ... Gal 3:3
that he which hath *b* a good work ... Phil 1:6
for when they have *b* to wax ... 1Ti 5:11

### BEHALF
the *b* of the children of Israel ... Ex 27:21
sent messengers to David on his *b* ... 2Sa 3:12
to shew himself strong in the *b* ... 2Chr 16:9
I have yet to speak on God's *b* ... Job 36:2
own *b* shall cause the reproach ... Dan 11:18
I am glad therefore on your *b* ... Rom 16:19
I thank my God always on your *b* ... 1Cor 1:4
may be given by many on our *b* ... 2Cor 1:11
you occasion to glory on our *b* ... 2Cor 5:12
and of our boasting on your *b* ... 2Cor 8:24
you should be in vain in this *b* ... 2Cor 9:3
it is given in the *b* of Christ ... Phil 1:29
but let him glorify God on this *b* ... 1Pet 4:16

### BEHAVE
should *b* themselves strangely ... Deut 32:27
let us *b* ourselves valiantly for ... 1Chr 19:13
I will *b* myself wisely in a ... Ps 101:2
the child shall *b* himself proudly ... Is 3:5
Doth not *b* itself unseemly, ... 1Cor 13:5
know how thou oughtest to *b* ... 1Ti 3:15

### BEHAVED
sent him, and *b* himself wisely ... 1Sa 18:5
David *b* himself wisely in all his ... 1Sa 18:14
saw that he *b* himself very wisely ... 1Sa 18:15
that David *b* himself more wisely ... 1Sa 18:30
I *b* myself as though he had been ... Ps 35:14
Surely I have *b* and quieted myself ... Ps 131:2
as they have *b* themselves ill in ... Mic 3:4
unblameably we *b* ourselves among ... 1Th 2:10
for we *b* not ourselves disorderly ... 2Th 3:7

### BEHAVETH
he *b* himself uncomely toward his ... 1Cor 7:36

### BEHAVIOUR
And he changed his *b* before them ... 1Sa 21:13
he changed his *b* before Abimelech ... Ps 34:*t*
wife, vigilant, sober, of good *b* ... 1Ti 3:2
that they be in *b* as becometh ... Titus 2:3

### BEHEADED
heifer that is *b* in the valley ... Deut 21:6
*b* him, and took his head, and gat ... 2Sa 4:7
he sent, and *b* John in the prison ... Mt 14:10
he said, It is John, whom I *b* ... Mk 6:16
he went and *b* him in the prison, ... Mk 6:27
And Herod said, John have I *b* ... Lk 9:9
were *b* for the witness of Jesus ... Rev 20:4

### BEHELD
the Egyptians *b* the woman that ... Gen 12:14
*b* all the plain of Jordan, that ... Gen 13:10
all the land of the plain, and *b* ... Gen 19:28
Jacob *b* the countenance of Laban, ... Gen 31:2
Israel *b* Joseph's sons, and said, ... Gen 48:8
when he *b* the serpent of brass, ... Num 21:9
He hath not *b* iniquity in Jacob, ... Num 23:21
that *b* while Samson made sport ... Judg 16:27
David *b* the place where Saul lay, ... 1Sa 26:5
as he was destroying, the LORD *b* ... 1Chr 21:15
If I *b* the sun when it shined, or ... Job 31:26
I *b* the transgressors, and was ... Ps 119:158
I looked on my right hand, and *b* ... Ps 142:4
*b* among the simple ones, I ... Prov 7:7
Then I *b* all the work of God, ... Eccl 8:17
For I *b*, and there was no man ... Is 41:28
I *b* the earth, and, lo, it was ... Jer 4:23
I *b* the mountains, and, lo, they ... Jer 4:24
I *b*, and, lo, there was no man, and ... Jer 4:25
I *b*, and, lo, the fruitful place ... Jer 4:26
Upon this I awaked, and *b* ... Jer 31:26
Now as I *b* the living creatures, ... Eze 1:15
Then I *b*, and lo a likeness as the ... Eze 8:2
And when I *b*, lo, the sinews and ... Eze 37:8
I *b* till the wings thereof were ... Dan 7:4
After this I *b*, and lo another, ... Dan 7:6
I *b* till the thrones were cast ... Dan 7:9
I *b* then because of the voice of ... Dan 7:11
I *b* even till the beast was slain ... Dan 7:11
I *b*, and the same horn made war ... Dan 7:21
he *b*, and drove asunder the ... Hab 3:6
But Jesus *b* them, and said unto ... Mt 19:26
all the people, when they *b* him ... Mk 9:15
*b* how the people cast money into ... Mk 12:41
of Joses *b* where he was laid ... Mk 15:47
I *b* Satan as lightning fall from ... Lk 10:18
he *b* the city, and wept over it, ... Lk 19:41
he *b* them, and said, What is this ... Lk 20:17
But a certain maid *b* him as he ... Lk 22:56
*b* the sepulchre, and how his body ... Lk 23:55
he *b* the linen clothes laid by ... Lk 24:12
we *b* his glory, the glory as of ... Jn 1:14
And when Jesus *b* him, he said, ... Jn 1:42
spoken these things, while they *b* ... Acts 1:9
*b* your devotions, I found an ... Acts 17:23
And I *b*, and, lo, in the midst of ... Rev 5:6
And I *b*, and I heard the voice of ... Rev 5:11
And I *b*, and lo a black horse ... Rev 6:5
I *b* when he had opened the sixth ... Rev 6:12
After this I *b*, and, lo, a great ... Rev 7:9
And I *b*, and heard an angel flying ... Rev 8:13
and their enemies *b* them ... Rev 11:12
I *b* another beast coming up out ... Rev 13:11

### BEHEMOTH
Behold now *b*, which I made with ... Job 40:15

### BEHIND
in the tent door, which was *b* him ... Gen 18:10
look not *b* thee, neither stay ... Gen 19:17
his wife looked back from *b* him ... Gen 19:26
behold *b* him a ram caught in a ... Gen 22:13
and, behold, also he is *b* us ... Gen 32:18
Behold, thy servant Jacob is *b* us ... Gen 32:20
there shall not an hoof be left *b* ... Ex 10:26
maidservant that is *b* the mill ... Ex 11:5
of Israel, removed and went *b* them ... Ex 14:19
their face, and stood *b* them ... Ex 14:19
If there be yet many years *b* ... Lev 25:51
pitch *b* the tabernacle westward ... Num 3:23
even all that were feeble *b* thee ... Deut 25:18
thee an ambush for the city *b* it ... Josh 8:2
against the city, even *b* the city ... Josh 8:4
in ambush against him *b* the city ... Josh 8:14
when the men of Ai looked *b* them ... Josh 8:20
behold, it is *b* Kirjath-jearim ... Judg 18:12
the Benjamites looked *b* them ... Judg 20:40
wrapped in a cloth *b* the ephod ... 1Sa 21:9
And when Saul looked *b* him ... 1Sa 24:8
those that were left *b* stayed ... 1Sa 30:9
for two hundred abode *b*, which ... 1Sa 30:10
And when he looked *b* him, he saw ... 2Sa 1:7
Then Abner looked *b* him, and said, ... 2Sa 2:20
that the spear came out *b* him ... 2Sa 2:23
along weeping *b* her to Bahurim ... 2Sa 3:16
but fetch a compass *b* them ... 2Sa 5:23
was against him before and *b* ... 2Sa 10:9
by the way of the hill side *b* him ... 2Sa 13:34
the top of the throne was round *b* ... 1Kin 10:19
anger, and hast cast me *b* thy back ... 1Kin 14:9
sound of his master's feet *b* him ... 2Kin 6:32
turn thee *b* me ... 2Kin 9:18
turn thee *b* me ... 2Kin 9:19
part at the gate *b* the guard ... 2Kin 11:6
was set against him before and *b* ... 1Chr 19:10
ambushment to come about *b* them ... 2Chr 13:13
and the ambushment was *b* them ... 2Chr 13:13
the battle was before and *b* ... 2Chr 13:14
I in the lower places *b* the wall ... Neh 4:13
the rulers were *b* all the house ... Neh 4:16
and cast thy law *b* their backs ... Neh 9:26
and castest my words *b* thee ... Ps 50:17
Thou hast beset me *b* and before, ... Ps 139:5
behold, he standeth *b* our wall ... Song 2:9
before, and the Philistines *b* ... Is 9:12
ears shall hear a word *b* thee ... Is 30:21
hast cast all my sins *b* thy back ... Is 38:17
*B* the doors also and the posts ... Is 57:8
gardens *b* one tree in the midst ... Is 66:17
I heard *b* me a voice of a great ... Eze 3:12
cast me *b* thy back, therefore ... Eze 23:35
the separate place which was *b* it ... Eze 41:15
and *b* them a flame burneth ... Joel 2:3
*b* them a desolate wilderness ... Joel 2:3
repent, and leave a blessing *b* him ... Joel 2:14
*b* him were there red horses, ... Zec 1:8
of blood twelve years, came *b* him ... Mt 9:20
and said unto Peter, Get thee *b* me ... Mt 16:23
of Jesus, came in the press *b* ... Mk 5:27
Peter, saying, Get thee *b* me ... Mk 8:33
die, and leave his wife *b* him ... Mk 12:19
Jesus tarried *b* in Jerusalem ... Lk 2:43
and said unto him, Get thee *b* me ... Lk 4:8
stood at his feet *b* him weeping ... Lk 7:38
Came *b* him, and touched the border ... Lk 8:44
So that ye come *b* in no gift ... 1Cor 1:7
whit *b* the very chiefest apostles ... 2Cor 11:5
for in nothing am I *b* the very ... 2Cor 12:11
those things which are *b*, and ... Phil 3:13
fill up that which is *b* of the ... Col 1:24
heard *b* me a great voice, as of a ... Rev 1:10
beasts full of eyes before and *b* ... Rev 4:6

### BEHOLD See PREFACE.
thing that he had made, and, *b* ... Gen 1:31
And, *b*, I am with thee, and will ... Gen 28:15
And the LORD said unto Satan, *B* ... Job 1:12
And unto man he said, *B*, the fear ... Job 28:28
man may *b* it afar off ... Job 36:25
*B*, I am vile ... Job 40:4
if I make my bed in hell, *b* ... Ps 139:8
*B*, a virgin shall conceive, and ... Is 7:14
*B*, I and the children whom the ... Is 8:18
*B*, God is my salvation ... Is 12:2
the cities of Judah, *B* your God ... Is 40:9
shall say to Zion, *B*, *b* them ... Is 41:27
*b*, it is I ... Is 52:6
*B* me, *b* me, unto a nation ... Is 65:1
*B*, I am the LORD, the God of all ... Jer 32:27
*b*, and see if there be any sorrow ... Lam 1:12
*b*, thy King cometh unto thee ... Zec 9:9
*B*, a virgin shall be with child, ... Mt 1:23
Tell ye the daughter of Sion, *B* ... Mt 21:5
*b* the place where they laid him ... Mk 16:6
And, *b*, thou shalt conceive in thy ... Lk 1:31
for, *b*, I bring you good tidings ... Lk 2:10
*B* my hands and my feet, that it is ... Lk 24:39
And, *b*, I send the promise of my ... Lk 24:49
*B* the Lamb of God, which taketh ... Jn 1:29
he saith, *B* the Lamb of God ... Jn 1:36
*b*, thy King cometh, sitting on an ... Jn 12:15
Pilate saith unto them, *B* the man ... Jn 19:5
saith unto the Jews, *B* your King ... Jn 19:14
unto his mother, Woman, *b* thy son ... Jn 19:26
he to the disciple, *B* thy mother ... Jn 19:27
And said, *B*, I see the heavens ... Acts 7:56
for, *b*, he prayeth, ... Acts 9:11
*b*, all things are become new ... 2Cor 5:17
*b*, now is the accepted time ... 2Cor 6:2
*b*, now is the day of salvation ... 2Cor 6:2
*B*, what manner of love the Father ... 1Jn 3:1
*B*, I come quickly ... Rev 3:11
*B*, I stand at the door, and knock ... Rev 3:20
*B*, I come as a thief ... Rev 16:15
voice out of heaven saying, *B* ... Rev 21:3
that sat upon the throne said, *B* ... Rev 21:5
*B*, I come quickly ... Rev 22:7

### BEHOLDEST
for thou *b* mischief and spite, to ... Ps 10:14
why *b* thou the mote that is in ... Mt 7:3
why *b* thou the mote that is in ... Lk 6:41
when thou thyself *b* not the beam ... Lk 6:42

### BEHOLDETH
he *b* not the way of the vineyards ... Job 24:18
He *b* all high things ... Job 41:34
he *b* all the sons of men ... Ps 33:13
For he *b* himself, and goeth his ... Jas 1:24

### BEHOLDING
Turn away mine eyes from *b* vanity ... Ps 119:37
place, *b* the evil and the good ... Prov 15:3

saving the *b* of them with their Ecc1 5:11
many women were there *b* afar off Mt 27:55
Then Jesus *b* him loved him, and Mk 10:21
And the people stood *b* Lk 23:35
*b* the things which were done, Lk 23:48
stood afar off, *b* these things Lk 23:49
*b* the man which was healed Acts 4:14
*b* the miracles and signs which Acts 8:13
who stedfastly *b* him, and Acts 14:9
earnestly *b* the council, said, Acts 23:1
with open face *b* as in a glass 2Cor 3:18
*b* your order, and the stedfastness Col 2:5
he is like unto a man *b* his Jas 1:23

**BEHOVED**
thus it *b* Christ to suffer, and to Lk 24:46
Wherefore in all things it *b* him Heb 2:17

**BEING**
have pleasure, my lord *b* old also Gen 18:12
the LORD *b* merciful unto him Gen 19:16
his son Isaac *b* eight days old Gen 21:4
I *b* in the way, the LORD led me Gen 24:27
I *b* few in number, they shall Gen 34:30
his people, *b* old and full of days Gen 35:29
*b* seventeen years old, was Gen 37:2
*b* an hundred and ten years old Gen 50:26
their kneadingtroughs *b* bound up Ex 12:34
that openeth the matrix, *b* males Ex 13:15
the owner thereof *b* not with it Ex 22:14
Foursquare it shall be *b* doubled Ex 28:16
of them that cry for *b* overcome Ex 32:18
the breadth thereof, *b* doubled Ex 39:9
*b* a chief man among his people, Lev 21:4
*b* taken from the children of Lev 24:8
princes of Israel, *b* twelve men Num 1:44
a wall *b* on this side, and a wall Num 22:24
*b* in her father's house in her Num 30:3
*b* yet in her youth in her Num 30:16
*b* the rest of the prey which the Num 31:32
Baal-meon, (their names *b* changed Num 32:38
*b* the kingdom of Og, gave I unto Deut 3:13
*b* matters of controversy within Deut 17:8
she cried not, *b* in the city Deut 22:24
our enemies themselves *b* judges Deut 32:31
of you be freed from *b* bondmen Josh 9:23
Aaron, *b* of the families of the Josh 21:10
*b* an hundred and ten years old Josh 24:29
*b* an hundred and ten years old Judg 2:8
*b* threescore and ten persons, upon Judg 9:5
*b* a child, girded with a linen 1Sa 2:18
also rejected thee from *b* king 1Sa 15:23
thee from *b* king over Israel 1Sa 15:26
a great space *b* between them 1Sa 26:13
of salt, *b* eighteen thousand men 2Sa 8:13
*b* the king's son, lean from day 2Sa 13:4
*b* stronger than she, forced her, 2Sa 13:14
as people *b* ashamed steal away 2Sa 19:3
he *b* girded with a new sword, 2Sa 21:16
noise of the city *b* in an uproar 1Kin 1:41
from *b* priest unto the LORD 1Kin 2:27
Hadad *b* yet a little child 1Kin 11:17
even her he removed from *b* queen 1Kin 15:13
in *b* like the house of Jeroboam 1Kin 16:7
of Israel, *b* seven thousand 1Kin 20:15
Jehoshaphat *b* then king of Judah, 2Kin 8:16
*b* seventy persons, were with the 2Kin 10:6
*b* told, into the hands of them 2Kin 12:11
*b* over the host of the LORD, were 1Chr 9:19
household *b* taken for Eleazar 1Chr 24:6
*b* arrayed in white linen, having 2Chr 5:12
men, *b* mighty men of valour 2Chr 13:3
king, he removed her from *b* queen 2Chr 15:16
and departed without *b* desired 2Chr 21:20
in a several house, *b* a leper 2Chr 26:21
*b* set up, let him be hanged Ezr 6:11
*b* guilty, they offered a ram of Ezr 10:19
*b* as I am, would go into the Neh 6:11
of the provinces, *b* before him Est 1:3
(the vessels *b* diverse one from Est 1:7
out, *b* hastened by the king's Est 3:15
*b* hastened and pressed on by the Est 8:14
who ever perished, *b* innocent Job 4:7
*b* wholly at ease and quiet Job 21:23
Job died, *b* old and full of days Job 42:17
Nevertheless man *b* in honour Ps 49:12
*b* girded with power Ps 65:6
*b* mine enemies wrongfully, are Ps 69:4
*b* armed, and carrying bows, turned Ps 78:9
*b* full of compassion, forgave Ps 78:38
us cut them off from *b* a nation Ps 83:4
to my God while I have my *b* Ps 104:33
*b* bound in affliction and iron Ps 107:10
see my substance, yet *b* unperfect Ps 139:16
unto my God while I have any *b* Ps 146:2
shall keep thy foot from *b* taken Prov 3:26
that *b* often reproved hardeneth Prov 29:1
all hold swords, *b* expert in war Song 3:8
midst thereof *b* paved with love Song 3:10
she *b* desolate shall sit upon the Is 3:26
is taken away from *b* a city Is 17:1
or *b* his counsellor hath taught Is 40:13
but the sinner *b* an hundred years Is 65:20
Withhold thy foot from *b* unshod Jer 2:25
*b* desolate it mourneth unto me Jer 12:11
from *b* a pastor to follow thee Jer 17:16
*b* a nation before me for ever Jer 31:36
*b* an Hebrew or an Hebrewess, go Jer 34:9
when he had taken him *b* bound in Jer 40:1
let us cut it off from *b* a nation Jer 48:2
be destroyed from *b* a people Jer 48:42
*b* planted, shall it prosper Eze 17:10
multitude *b* at ease was with her Eze 23:42
which *b* brought forth into the Eze 47:8
*b* in the midst of that which is Eze 48:22
*b* gathered together, saw these Dan 3:27
*b* about threescore and two years Dan 5:31
his windows *b* open in his chamber Dan 6:10
Now that *b* broken, whereas four Dan 8:22
*b* caused to fly swiftly, touched Dan 9:21
*b* a just man, and not willing to Mt 1:19
which *b* interpreted is, God with Mt 1:23
Then Joseph *b* raised from sleep Mt 1:24
*b* warned of God in a dream that Mt 2:12
*b* warned of God in a dream, he Mt 2:22
*b* evil, know how to give good Mt 7:11
*b* evil, speak good things Mt 12:34
*b* before instructed of her mother Mt 14:8
*b* grieved for the hardness of Mk 3:5
*b* interpreted, Damsel, I say unto Mk 5:41
days the multitude *b* very great Mk 8:1
*b* in the house he asked them, Mk 9:33
*b* in Bethany in the house of Mk 14:3
*b* interpreted, The place of a Mk 15:22
*b* interpreted, My God, my God, Mk 15:34
*b* delivered out of the hand of Lk 1:74
espoused wife, *b* great with child Lk 2:5
Pontius Pilate *b* governor of Lk 3:1
Herod *b* tetrarch of Galilee, and Lk 3:1
Caiaphas *b* the high priests, the Lk 3:2
*b* reproved by him for Herodias Lk 3:19
pass, that Jesus also *b* baptized Lk 3:21
*b* (as was supposed) the son of Lk 3:23
Jesus *b* full of the Holy Ghost Lk 4:1
*B* forty days tempted of the devil Lk 4:2
synagogues, *b* glorified of all Lk 4:15
*b* baptized with the baptism of Lk 7:29
themselves, *b* not baptized of him Lk 7:30
they *b* afraid wondered, saying Lk 8:25
*b* evil, know how to give good Lk 11:13
*b* a daughter of Abraham, whom Lk 13:16
house *b* angry said to his servant Lk 14:21
*b* in torments, and seeth Abraham Lk 16:23
of God, *b* the children of the Lk 20:36
*b* brought before kings and rulers Lk 21:12
*b* of the number of the twelve Lk 22:3
*b* in an agony he prayed more Lk 22:44
*b* interpreted, Master,) where Jn 1:38
*b* interpreted, the Christ Jn 1:41
*b* wearied with his journey, sat Jn 4:6
*b* a Jew, askest drink of me, Jn 4:9
a multitude *b* in that place Jn 5:13
betray him, *b* one of the twelve Jn 6:71
Jesus by night, *b* one of them,) Jn 7:50
it, *b* convicted by their own Jn 8:9
*b* a man, makest thyself God Jn 10:33
*b* the high priest that same year, Jn 11:49
but *b* high priest that year, he Jn 11:51
And supper *b* ended, the devil Jn 13:2
unto you, *b* yet present with you Jn 14:25
*b* his kinsman whose ear Peter cut Jn 18:26
*b* a disciple of Jesus, but Jn 19:38
*b* the first day of the week, when Jn 20:19
then came Jesus, the doors *b* shut Jn 20:26
*b* seen of them forty days, and Acts 1:3
*b* assembled together with them, Acts 1:4
*b* delivered by the determinate Acts 2:23
Therefore *b* a prophet, and knowing Acts 2:30
Therefore *b* by the right hand of Acts 2:33
hour of prayer, *b* the ninth hour Acts 3:1
*B* grieved that they taught the Acts 4:2
*b* let go, they went to their own Acts 4:23
*b* interpreted, The son of Acts 4:36
his wife also *b* privy to it Acts 5:2
*b* full of the Holy Ghost, looked Acts 7:55
*b* sent forth by the Holy Ghost, Acts 13:4
*b* astonished at the doctrine of Acts 13:12
*b* a cripple from his mother's Acts 14:8
*b* brought on their way by the Acts 15:3
*b* read in the synagogues every Acts 15:21
*b* assembled with one accord, to Acts 15:25
*b* prophets also themselves, Acts 15:32
*b* recommended by the brethren Acts 15:40
*b* grieved, turned and said to the Acts 16:18
*b* Jews, do exceedingly trouble Acts 16:20
neither to observe, *b* Romans Acts 16:21
*b* Romans, and have cast us into Acts 16:37
we live, and move, and have our *b* Acts 17:28
*b* fervent in the spirit, he spake Acts 18:25
there *b* no cause whereby we may Acts 19:40
*b* fallen into a deep sleep Acts 20:9
*b* led by the hand of them that Acts 22:11
*b* exceedingly mad against them, I Acts 26:11
of Thessalonica, *b* with us Acts 27:2
we *b* exceedingly tossed with a Acts 27:18
*b* understood by the things that Rom 1:20
*B* filled with all unrighteousness Rom 1:29
*b* instructed out of the law Rom 2:18
*b* witnessed by the law and the Rom 3:21
*B* justified freely by his grace Rom 3:24
which he had yet *b* uncircumcised Rom 4:11
which he had *b* yet uncircumcised Rom 4:12
And *b* not weak in faith, he Rom 4:19
*b* fully persuaded that, what he Rom 4:21
Therefore *b* justified by faith, Rom 5:1
*b* now justified by his blood, we Rom 5:9
*b* reconciled, we shall be saved Rom 5:10
Knowing that Christ *b* raised from Rom 6:9
*B* then made free from sin, ye Rom 6:18
But now *b* made free from sin, and Rom 6:22
that *b* dead wherein we were held Rom 7:6
(For the children *b* not yet born Rom 9:11
For they *b* ignorant of God's Rom 10:3
*b* a wild olive tree, wert graffed Rom 11:17
*b* many, are one body in Christ, Rom 12:5
*b* sanctified by the Holy Ghost Rom 15:16
*b* reviled, we bless 1Cor 4:12
*b* persecuted, we suffer it 1Cor 4:12
*B* defamed, we intreat 1Cor 4:13
Is any man called *b* circumcised 1Cor 7:18
Art thou called *b* a servant 1Cor 7:21
*b* a servant, is the Lord's 1Cor 7:22
*b* free, is Christ's servant 1Cor 7:22
conscience *b* weak is defiled 1Cor 8:7
(*b* not without law to God, but 1Cor 9:21
For we *b* many are one bread, and 1Cor 10:17
one body, *b* many, are one body 1Cor 12:12
If so be that *b* clothed we shall 2Cor 5:3
tabernacle do groan, *b* burdened 2Cor 5:4
but *b* more forward, of his own 2Cor 8:17
*B* enriched in every thing to all 2Cor 9:11
but *b* absent am bold toward you 2Cor 10:1
myself from *b* burdensome unto you 2Cor 11:9
*b* crafty, I caught you with guile 2Cor 12:16
*b* absent now I write to them 2Cor 13:2
I write these things *b* absent 2Cor 13:10
lest *b* present I should use 2Cor 13:10
*b* more exceedingly zealous of the Gal 1:14
*b* a Greek, was compelled to be Gal 2:3
*b* a Jew, livest after the manner Gal 2:14
of the law, *b* made a curse for us Gal 3:13
*b* predestinated according to the Eph 1:11
your understanding *b* enlightened Eph 1:18
that ye *b* in time past Gentiles Eph 2:11
*b* aliens from the commonwealth of Eph 2:12
Jesus Christ himself *b* the chief Eph 2:20
*b* rooted and grounded in love, Eph 3:17
*b* alienated from the life of God Eph 4:18
Who *b* past feeling have given Eph 4:19
*B* confident of this very thing, Phil 1:6
*B* filled with the fruits of Phil 1:11
*b* of one accord, of one mind Phil 2:2
*b* in the form of God, thought it Phil 2:6
*b* found in fashion as a man, he Phil 2:8
*b* made conformable unto his death Phil 3:10
*b* fruitful in every good work, and Col 1:10
*b* knit together in love, and unto Col 2:2
*b* dead in your sins and the Col 2:13
So *b* affectionately desirous of 1Th 2:8
*b* taken from you for a short time 1Th 2:17
but the woman *b* deceived was in 1Ti 2:14
lest *b* lifted up with pride he 1Ti 3:6
of a deacon, *b* found blameless 1Ti 3:10
*b* mindful of thy tears, that I 2Ti 1:4
worse, deceiving, and *b* deceived 2Ti 3:13
*b* abominable, and disobedient, and Titus 1:16
That *b* justified by his grace, we Titus 3:7
sinneth, *b* condemned of himself Titus 3:11
*b* such an one as Paul the aged, Philem 9
Who *b* the brightness of his glory Heb 1:3
*B* made so much better than the Heb 1:4
himself hath suffered *b* tempted Heb 2:18
a promise *b* left us of entering Heb 4:1
not *b* mixed with faith in them Heb 4:2
*b* made perfect, he became the Heb 5:9
first *b* by interpretation King of Heb 7:2
For the priesthood *b* changed Heb 7:12
But Christ *b* come an high priest Heb 9:11
by it he *b* dead yet speaketh Heb 11:4
*b* warned of God of things not Heb 11:7
*b* destitute, afflicted, tormented Heb 11:37
as *b* yourselves also in the body Heb 13:3
he *b* not a forgetful hearer, but Jas 1:25
hath not works, is dead, *b* alone Jas 2:17
*b* much more precious than of gold 1Pet 1:7
*B* born again, not of corruptible 1Pet 1:23
at the word, *b* disobedient 1Pet 2:8
*b* dead to sins, should live unto 1Pet 2:24
*b* in subjection unto their own 1Pet 3:5
as *b* heirs together of the grace 1Pet 3:7
*b* put to death in the flesh, but 1Pet 3:18
powers *b* made subject unto him 1Pet 3:22
Neither as *b* lords over God's 1Pet 5:3
but *b* ensamples to the flock 1Pet 5:3
*b* overflowed with water, perished 2Pet 3:6
wherein the heavens *b* on fire 2Pet 3:12
*b* led away with the error of the 2Pet 3:17
*b* turned, I saw seven golden Rev 1:12
And she *b* with child cried, Rev 12:2
*b* the firstfruits unto God and to Rev 14:4

**BEKAH**
A *b* for every man, that is, half Ex 38:26

**BEKERITE** See BACHRITES.

**BEL** (*bel*) See BAAL. *A Babylonian god.*
*B* boweth down, Nebo stoopeth, Is 46:1
*B* is confounded, Merodach is Jer 50:2
And I will punish *B* in Babylon Jer 51:44

**BELA** (*be'-lah*) See BELAH, BELAITES.
*1. Another name for Zoar.*
king of Zeboiim, and the king of *B* Gen 14:2
the king of *B* (the same is Zoar Gen 14:8
*2. An Edomite king.*
*B* the son of Beor reigned in Edom Gen 36:32
*B* died, and Jobab the son of Zerah Gen 36:33
*B* the son of Beor 1Chr 1:43
when *B* was dead, Jobab the son of 1Chr 1:44
*3. A son of Benjamin.*
of *B*, the family of the Belaites Num 26:38
And the sons of *B* were Ard Num 26:40

*B*, and Becher, and Jediael, three .... 1Chr 7:6
And the sons of *B* .... 1Chr 7:7
Benjamin begat *B* his firstborn .... 1Chr 8:1
And the sons of *B* were, Addar, and.... 1Chr 8:3
*4. A son of Azaz the Reubenite.*
*B* the son of Azaz, the son of.... 1Chr 5:8

**BELAH** (*be'-lah*) See BELA. *A form of Bela.*
And the sons of Benjamin were *B*.... Gen 46:21

**BELAITES** (*be'-lah-ites*) *Descendants of Bela.*
of Bela, the family of the *B* .... Num 26:38

**BELCH**
they *b* out with their mouth .... Ps 59:7

**BELIAL** (*be'-le-al*) *A title for a "worthless person."*
Certain men, the children of *B* .... Deut 13:13
of the city, certain sons of *B* .... Judg 19:22
us the men, the children of *B* .... Judg 20:13
handmaid for a daughter of *B* .... 1Sa 1:16
the sons of Eli were sons of *B* .... 1Sa 2:12
But the children of *B* said .... 1Sa 10:27
for he is such a son of *B* .... 1Sa 25:17
I pray thee, regard this man of *B* .... 1Sa 25:25
all the wicked men and men of *B* .... 1Sa 30:22
thou bloody man, and thou man of *B* .... 2Sa 16:7
happened to be there a man of *B* .... 2Sa 20:1
But the sons of *B* shall be all of .... 2Sa 23:6
And set two men, sons of *B* .... 1Kin 21:10
came in two men, children of *B* .... 1Kin 21:13
the men of *B* witnessed against .... 1Kin 21:13
him vain men, the children of *B* .... 2Chr 13:7
what concord hath Christ with *B* .... 2Cor 6:15

**BELIED**
They have *b* the LORD, and said, It .... Jer 5:12

**BELIEF**
of the Spirit and *b* of the truth .... 2Th 2:13

**BELIEVE**
But, behold, they will not *b* me .... Ex 4:1
That they may *b* that the LORD God .... Ex 4:5
to pass, if they will not *b* thee .... Ex 4:8
that they will *b* the voice of the .... Ex 4:8
if they will not *b* also these two .... Ex 4:9
with thee, and *b* thee for ever .... Ex 19:9
how long will it be ere they *b* me .... Num 14:11
ye did not *b* the LORD your God .... Deut 1:32
that did not *b* in the LORD their .... 2Kin 17:14
*B* in the LORD your God, so shall .... 2Chr 20:20
*b* his prophets, so shall ye .... 2Chr 20:20
on this manner, neither yet *b* him .... 2Chr 32:15
yet would I not *b* that he had .... Job 9:16
Wilt thou *b* him, that he will .... Job 39:12
When he speaketh fair, *b* him not .... Prov 26:25
If ye will not *b*, surely ye shall .... Is 7:9
*b* me, and understand that I am he .... Is 43:10
*b* them not, though they speak .... Jer 12:6
in your days, which ye will not *b* .... Hab 1:5
*B* ye that I am able to do this .... Mt 9:28
these little ones which *b* in me .... Mt 18:6
us, Why did ye not then *b* him .... Mt 21:25
afterward, that ye might *b* him .... Mt 21:32
*b* it not .... Mt 24:23
*b* it not .... Mt 24:26
from the cross, and we will *b* him .... Mt 27:42
repent ye, and *b* the gospel .... Mk 1:15
synagogue, Be not afraid, only *b* .... Mk 5:36
said unto him, If thou canst *b* .... Mk 9:23
and said with tears, Lord, I *b* .... Mk 9:24
of these little ones that *b* in me .... Mk 9:42
but shall *b* that those things .... Mk 11:23
*b* that ye receive them, and ye .... Mk 11:24
say, Why then did ye not *b* him .... Mk 11:31
*b* him not .... Mk 13:21
the cross, that we may see and *b* .... Mk 15:32
signs shall follow them that *b* .... Mk 16:17
their hearts, lest they should *b* .... Lk 8:12
have no root, which for a while *b* .... Lk 8:13
*b* only, and she shall be made .... Lk 8:50
If I tell you, ye will not *b* .... Lk 22:67
slow of heart to *b* all that the .... Lk 24:25
that all men through him might *b* .... Jn 1:7
even to them that *b* on his name .... Jn 1:12
and ye *b* not, how shall ye *b* .... Jn 3:12
*b* me, the hour cometh, when ye .... Jn 4:21
And said unto the woman, Now we *b* .... Jn 4:42
signs and wonders, ye will not *b* .... Jn 4:48
whom he hath sent, him ye *b* not .... Jn 5:38
How can ye *b*, which receive .... Jn 5:44
But if ye *b* not his writings .... Jn 5:47
how shall ye *b* my words .... Jn 5:47
that ye *b* on him whom he hath .... Jn 6:29
then, that we may see, and *b* thee .... Jn 6:30
ye also have seen me, and *b* not .... Jn 6:36
there are some of you that *b* not .... Jn 6:64
And we *b* and are sure that thou art .... Jn 6:69
neither did his brethren *b* in him .... Jn 7:5
which they that *b* on him should .... Jn 7:39
for if ye *b* not that I am he, ye .... Jn 8:24
I tell you the truth, ye *b* me not .... Jn 8:45
say the truth, why do ye not *b* me .... Jn 8:46
the Jews did not *b* concerning him .... Jn 9:18
Dost thou *b* on the Son of God .... Jn 9:35
he, Lord, that I might *b* on him .... Jn 9:36
And he said, Lord, I *b* .... Jn 9:38
But ye *b* not, because ye are not .... Jn 10:26
the works of my Father, *b* me not .... Jn 10:37
ye *b* not me, *b* the works .... Jn 10:38
that ye may know, and *b*, that the .... Jn 10:38
not there, to the intent ye may *b* .... Jn 11:15
I *b* that thou art the Christ, the .... Jn 11:27
thee, that, if thou wouldest *b* .... Jn 11:40
that they may *b* that thou hast .... Jn 11:42
thus alone, all men will *b* on him .... Jn 11:48
*b* in the light, that ye may be .... Jn 12:36
Therefore they could not *b* .... Jn 12:39
words, and *b* not, I judge him not .... Jn 12:47
to pass, ye may *b* that I am he .... Jn 13:19
ye *b* in God, *b* also in me .... Jn 14:1
*B* me that I am in the Father, and .... Jn 14:11
or else *b* me for the very works' .... Jn 14:11
it is come to pass, ye might *b* .... Jn 14:29
Of sin, because they *b* not on me .... Jn 16:9
by this we *b* that thou camest .... Jn 16:30
Jesus answered them, Do ye now *b* .... Jn 16:31
shall *b* on me through their word .... Jn 17:20
that the world may *b* that thou .... Jn 17:21
he saith true, that ye might *b* .... Jn 19:35
hand into his side, I will not *b* .... Jn 20:25
that ye might *b* that Jesus is the .... Jn 20:31
I *b* that Jesus Christ is the Son .... Acts 8:37
by him all that *b* are justified .... Acts 13:39
work which ye shall in no wise *b* .... Acts 13:41
hear the word of the gospel, and *b* .... Acts 15:7
But we *b* that through the grace .... Acts 15:11
*B* on the Lord Jesus Christ, and .... Acts 16:31
that they should *b* on him which .... Acts 19:4
of Jews there are which *b* .... Acts 21:20
As touching the Gentiles which *b* .... Acts 21:25
for I *b* God, that it shall be .... Acts 27:25
For what if some did not *b* .... Rom 3:3
unto all and upon all them that *b* .... Rom 3:22
be the father of all them that *b* .... Rom 4:11
if we *b* on him that raised up .... Rom 4:24
we *b* that we shall also live with .... Rom 6:8
shalt *b* in thine heart that God .... Rom 10:9
how shall they *b* in him of whom .... Rom 10:14
from them that do not *b* in Judaea .... Rom 15:31
of preaching to save them that *b* .... 1Cor 1:21
If any of them that *b* not bid you .... 1Cor 10:27
and I partly *b* it .... 1Cor 11:18
for a sign, not to them that *b* .... 1Cor 14:22
but to them that *b* not .... 1Cor 14:22
serveth not for them that *b* .... 1Cor 14:22
but for them which *b* .... 1Cor 14:22
the minds of them which *b* not .... 2Cor 4:4
we also *b*, and therefore speak .... 2Cor 4:13
might be given to them that *b* .... Gal 3:22
of his power to us-ward who *b* .... Eph 1:19
of Christ, not only to *b* on him .... Phil 1:29
to all that *b* in Macedonia .... 1Th 1:7
ourselves among you that *b* .... 1Th 2:10
worketh also in you that *b* .... 1Th 2:13
For if we *b* that Jesus died and .... 1Th 4:14
*b* (because our testimony among .... 2Th 1:10
that they should *b* a lie .... 2Th 2:11
*b* on him to life everlasting .... 1Ti 1:16
with thanksgiving of them which *b* .... 1Ti 4:3
men, specially of those that *b* .... 1Ti 4:10
If we *b* not, yet he abideth .... 2Ti 2:13
but of them that *b* to the saving .... Heb 10:39
cometh to God must *b* that he is .... Heb 11:6
the devils also *b*, and tremble .... Jas 2:19
Who by him do *b* in God, that .... 1Pet 1:21
therefore which *b* he is precious .... 1Pet 2:7
That we should *b* on the name of .... 1Jn 3:23
*b* not every spirit, but try the .... 1Jn 4:1
have I written unto you that *b* on .... 1Jn 5:13
that ye may *b* on the name of the .... 1Jn 5:13

**BELIEVED**
And he *b* in the LORD .... Gen 15:6
heart fainted, for he *b* them not .... Gen 45:26
And the people *b* .... Ex 4:31
*b* the LORD, and his servant Moses .... Ex 14:31
and Aaron, Because ye *b* me not .... Num 20:12
ye *b* him not, nor hearkened to .... Deut 9:23
And Achish *b* David, saying, He .... 1Sa 27:12
Howbeit I *b* not the words, until .... 1Kin 10:7
Howbeit I *b* not their words, .... 2Chr 9:6
I laughed on them, they *b* it not .... Job 29:24
unless I had *b* to see the .... Ps 27:13
Because they *b* not in God .... Ps 78:22
*b* not for his wondrous works .... Ps 78:32
Then *b* they his words .... Ps 106:12
land, they *b* not his word .... Ps 106:24
I *b*, therefore have I spoken .... Ps 116:10
for I have *b* thy commandments .... Ps 119:66
Who hath *b* our report .... Is 53:1
the son of Ahikam *b* them not .... Jer 40:14
would not have *b* that the .... Lam 4:12
upon him, because he *b* in his God .... Dan 6:23
So the people of Nineveh *b* God .... Jonah 3:5
and as thou hast *b*, so be it done .... Mt 8:13
of righteousness, and ye *b* him not .... Mt 21:32
publicans and the harlots *b* him .... Mt 21:32
and had been seen of her, *b* not .... Mk 16:11
neither *b* they them .... Mk 16:13
because they *b* not them which had .... Mk 16:14
which are most surely *b* among us .... Lk 1:1
And blessed is she that *b* .... Lk 1:45
will say, Why then *b* ye him not .... Lk 20:5
as idle tales, and they *b* them not .... Lk 24:11
And while they yet *b* not for joy .... Lk 24:41
and his disciples *b* on him .... Jn 2:11
they *b* the scripture, and the word .... Jn 2:22
many *b* in his name, when they saw .... Jn 2:23
because he hath not *b* in the name .... Jn 3:18
*b* on him for the saying of the .... Jn 4:39
many more *b* because of his own .... Jn 4:41
the man *b* the word that Jesus had .... Jn 4:50
and himself *b*, and his whole house .... Jn 4:53
*b* Moses, ye would have *b* me .... Jn 5:46
who they were that *b* not, and who .... Jn 6:64
And many of the people *b* on him .... Jn 7:31
or of the Pharisees *b* on him .... Jn 7:48
spake these words, many *b* on him .... Jn 8:30
to those Jews which *b* on him .... Jn 8:31
them, I told you, and ye *b* not .... Jn 10:25
And many *b* on him there .... Jn 10:42
things which Jesus did, *b* on him .... Jn 11:45
the Jews went away, and *b* on Jesus .... Jn 12:11
them, yet they *b* not on him .... Jn 12:37
Lord, who hath *b* our report .... Jn 12:38
chief rulers also many *b* on him .... Jn 12:42
have *b* that I came out from God .... Jn 16:27
they have *b* that thou didst send .... Jn 17:8
to the sepulchre, and he saw, and *b* .... Jn 20:8
thou hast seen me, thou hast *b* .... Jn 20:29
that have not seen, and yet have *b* .... Jn 20:29
all that *b* were together, and had .... Acts 2:44
of them which heard the word *b* .... Acts 4:4
of them that *b* were of one heart .... Acts 4:32
But when they *b* Philip preaching .... Acts 8:12
Then Simon himself *b* also .... Acts 8:13
*b* not that he was a disciple .... Acts 9:26
and many *b* in the Lord .... Acts 9:42
which *b* were astonished, as many .... Acts 10:45
who *b* on the Lord Jesus Christ .... Acts 11:17
and a great number *b*, and turned .... Acts 11:21
when he saw what was done, *b* .... Acts 13:12
were ordained to eternal life *b* .... Acts 13:48
the Jews and also of the Greeks *b* .... Acts 14:1
them to the Lord, on whom they *b* .... Acts 14:23
the sect of the Pharisees which *b* .... Acts 15:5
woman, which was a Jewess, and *b* .... Acts 16:1
And some of them *b*, and consorted .... Acts 17:4
But the Jews which *b* not, moved .... Acts 17:5
Therefore many of them *b* .... Acts 17:12
certain men clave unto him, and *b* .... Acts 17:34
*b* on the Lord with all his house .... Acts 18:8
many of the Corinthians hearing *b* .... Acts 18:8
much which had *b* through grace .... Acts 18:27
the Holy Ghost since ye *b* .... Acts 19:2
*b* not, but spake evil of that way .... Acts 19:9
And many that *b* came .... Acts 19:18
synagogue them that *b* on thee .... Acts 22:19
the centurion *b* the master .... Acts 27:11
some *b* the things which were .... Acts 28:24
which were spoken, and some *b* not .... Acts 28:24
Abraham *b* God, and it was counted .... Rom 4:3
nations,) before him whom he *b* .... Rom 4:17
Who against hope *b* in hope .... Rom 4:18
on him in whom they have not *b* .... Rom 10:14
Lord, who hath *b* our report .... Rom 10:16
ye in times past have not *b* God .... Rom 11:30
Even so have these also now not *b* .... Rom 11:31
salvation nearer than when we *b* .... Rom 13:11
but ministers by whom ye *b* .... 1Cor 3:5
you, unless ye have *b* in vain .... 1Cor 15:2
or they, so we preach, and so ye *b* .... 1Cor 15:11
according as it is written, I *b* .... 2Cor 4:13
even we have *b* in Jesus Christ, .... Gal 2:16
Even as Abraham *b* God, and it was .... Gal 3:6
in whom also after that ye *b* .... Eph 1:13
among you was *b*) in that day .... 2Th 1:10
be damned who *b* not the truth .... 2Th 2:12
*b* on in the world, received up .... 1Ti 3:16
for I know whom I have *b*, and am .... 2Ti 1:12
that they which have *b* in God .... Titus 3:8
his rest, but to them that *b* not .... Heb 3:18
For we which have *b* do enter into .... Heb 4:3
perished not with them that *b* not .... Heb 11:31
which saith, Abraham *b* God .... Jas 2:23
*b* the love that God hath to us .... 1Jn 4:16
destroyed them that *b* not .... Jude 5

**BELIEVERS**
*b* were the more added to the Lord .... Acts 5:14
but be thou an example of the *b* .... 1Ti 4:12

**BELIEVEST**
because thou *b* not my words .... Lk 1:20
thee under the fig tree, *b* thou .... Jn 1:50
*B* thou this .... Jn 11:26
*B* thou not that I am in the .... Jn 14:10
If thou *b* with all thine heart, .... Acts 8:37
King Agrippa, *b* thou the prophets .... Acts 26:27
I know that thou *b* .... Acts 26:27
Thou *b* that there is one God .... Jas 2:19

**BELIEVETH**
He *b* not that he shall return out .... Job 15:22
neither *b* he that it is the sound .... Job 39:24
The simple *b* every word .... Prov 14:15
he that *b* shall not make haste .... Is 28:16
things are possible to him that *b* .... Mk 9:23
He that *b* and is baptized shall be .... Mk 16:16
but he that *b* not shall be damned .... Mk 16:16
That whosoever *b* in him should .... Jn 3:15
that whosoever *b* in him should .... Jn 3:16
He that *b* on him is not condemned .... Jn 3:18
but he that *b* not is condemned .... Jn 3:18
He that *b* on the Son hath .... Jn 3:36
he that *b* not the Son shall not .... Jn 3:36
*b* on him that sent me, hath .... Jn 5:24
he that *b* on me shall never .... Jn 6:35
*b* on him, may have everlasting .... Jn 6:40
He that *b* on me hath everlasting .... Jn 6:47
He that *b* on me, as the scripture .... Jn 7:38
he that *b* in me, though he were .... Jn 11:25
liveth and *b* in me shall never die .... Jn 11:26

cried and said, He that *b* on me ... Jn 12:44
*b* not on me, but on him that sent ... Jn 12:44
that whosoever *b* on me should not ... Jn 12:46
I say unto you, He that *b* on me ... Jn 14:12
*b* in him shall receive remission ... Acts 10:43
salvation to every one that *b* ... Rom 1:16
justifier of him which *b* in Jesus ... Rom 3:26
but *b* on him that justifieth the ... Rom 4:5
whosoever *b* on him shall not be ... Rom 9:33
righteousness to every one that *b* ... Rom 10:4
heart man *b* unto righteousness ... Rom 10:10
Whosoever *b* on him shall not be ... Rom 10:11
For one *b* that he may eat all ... Rom 14:2
brother hath a wife that *b* not ... 1Cor 7:12
which hath an husband that *b* not ... 1Cor 7:13
*b* all things, hopeth all things, ... 1Cor 13:7
and there come in one that *b* not ... 1Cor 14:24
hath he that *b* with an infidel ... 2Cor 6:15
man or woman that *b* have widows ... 1Ti 5:16
he that *b* on him shall not be ... 1Pet 2:6
Whosoever *b* that Jesus is the ... 1Jn 5:1
but he that *b* that Jesus is the ... 1Jn 5:5
He that *b* on the Son of God hath ... 1Jn 5:10
he that *b* not God hath made him a ... 1Jn 5:10
because he *b* not the record that ... 1Jn 5:10

## BELIEVING

ye shall ask in prayer, *b* ... Mt 21:22
and be not faithless, but *b* ... Jn 20:27
that *b* ye might have life through ... Jn 20:31
*b* in God with all his house ... Acts 16:34
*b* all things which are written in ... Acts 24:14
you with all joy and peace in *b* ... Rom 15:13
And they that have *b* masters ... 1Ti 6:2
though now ye see him not, yet *b* ... 1Pet 1:8

## BELL

A golden *b* and a pomegranate ... Ex 28:34
and a pomegranate, a golden *b* ... Ex 28:34
A *b* and a pomegranate, a *b* and a ... Ex 39:26

## BELLIES

alway liars, evil beasts, slow *b* ... Titus 1:12

## BELLOW

heifer at grass, and *b* as bulls ... Jer 50:11

## BELLOWS

The *b* are burned, the lead is ... Jer 6:29

## BELLS

*b* of gold between them round ... Ex 28:33
they made *b* of pure gold ... Ex 39:25
and put the *b* between the ... Ex 39:25
there be upon the *b* of the horses ... Zec 14:20

## BELLY

upon thy *b* shalt thou go, and dust ... Gen 3:14
Whatsoever goeth upon the *b* ... Lev 11:42
thigh to rot, and thy *b* to swell ... Num 5:21
bowels, to make thy *b* to swell ... Num 5:22
her *b* shall swell, and her thigh ... Num 5:27
and the woman through her *b* ... Num 25:8
thigh, and thrust it into his *b* ... Judg 3:21
not draw the dagger out of his *b* ... Judg 3:22
over against the *b* which was by ... 1Kin 7:20
ghost when I came out of the *b* ... Job 3:11
fill his *b* with the east wind ... Job 15:2
and their *b* prepareth deceit ... Job 15:35
God shall cast them out of his *b* ... Job 20:15
shall not feel quietness in his *b* ... Job 20:20
When he is about to fill his *b* ... Job 20:23
my *b* is as wine which hath no ... Job 32:19
force is in the navel of his *b* ... Job 40:16
whose *b* thou fillest with thy hid ... Ps 17:14
art my God from my mother's *b* ... Ps 22:10
with grief, yea, my soul and my *b* ... Ps 31:9
our *b* cleaveth unto the earth ... Ps 44:25
but the *b* of the wicked shall ... Prov 13:25
into the innermost parts of the *b* ... Prov 18:8
A man's *b* shall be satisfied with ... Prov 18:20
all the inward parts of the *b* ... Prov 20:27
stripes the inward parts of the *b* ... Prov 20:30
into the innermost parts of the *b* ... Prov 26:22
his *b* is as bright ivory overlaid ... Song 5:14
thy *b* is like an heap of wheat ... Song 7:2
which are borne by me from the *b* ... Is 46:3
formed thee in the *b* I knew thee ... Jer 1:5
filled his *b* with my delicates ... Jer 51:34
Son of man, cause thy *b* to eat ... Eze 3:3
and his arms of silver, his *b* ... Dan 2:32
Jonah was in the *b* of the fish ... Jonah 1:17
LORD his God out of the fish's *b* ... Jonah 2:1
out of the *b* of hell cried I, and ... Jonah 2:2
When I heard, my *b* trembled ... Hab 3:16
and three nights in the whale's *b* ... Mt 12:40
in at the mouth goeth into the *b* ... Mt 15:17
into his heart, but into the *b* ... Mk 7:19
*b* with the husks that the swine ... Lk 15:16
out of his *b* shall flow rivers of ... Jn 7:38
Jesus Christ, but their own *b* ... Rom 16:18
Meats for the *b*, and the *b* for ... 1Cor 6:13
destruction, whose God is their *b* ... Phil 3:19
and it shall make thy *b* bitter ... Rev 10:9
I had eaten it, my *b* was bitter ... Rev 10:10

## BELONG

Do not interpretations *b* to God ... Gen 40:8
the possession of the land did *b* ... Lev 27:24
and over all things that *b* to it ... Num 1:50
The secret things *b* unto the LORD ... Deut 29:29
which are revealed *b* unto us ... Deut 29:29
shields of the earth *b* unto God ... Ps 47:9
unto GOD the Lord *b* the issues ... Ps 68:20
These things also *b* to the wise ... Prov 24:23
To the Lord our God *b* mercies ... Dan 9:9
my name, because ye *b* to Christ ... Mk 9:41
the things which *b* unto thy peace ... Lk 19:42
for the things that *b* to the Lord ... 1Cor 7:32

## BELONGED

on the border of Manasseh *b* to ... Josh 17:8
of the herdmen that *b* to Saul ... 1Sa 21:7
the mighty men which *b* to David ... 1Kin 1:8
which *b* to the Philistines ... 1Kin 15:27
which *b* to the Philistines ... 1Kin 16:15
which *b* to Judah, for Israel, are ... 2Kin 14:28
All these *b* to the sons of Machir ... 1Chr 2:23
which *b* to Judah, to bring up ... 1Chr 13:6
the burial which *b* to the kings ... 2Chr 26:23
house which *b* to king Ahasuerus ... Est 1:9
with such things as *b* to her ... Est 2:9
he *b* unto Herod's jurisdiction ... Lk 23:7

## BELONGEST

said unto him, To whom *b* thou ... 1Sa 30:13

## BELONGETH

This is it that *b* unto the ... Num 8:24
To me *b* vengeance ... Deut 32:35
by Gibeah, which *b* to Benjamin ... Judg 19:14
into Gibeah that *b* to Benjamin ... Judg 20:4
which *b* to Judah, and pitched ... 1Sa 17:1
upon the coast which *b* to Judah ... 1Sa 30:14
which *b* to Zidon, and dwell there ... 1Kin 17:9
which *b* to Judah, and left his ... 1Kin 19:3
at Beth-shemesh, which *b* to Judah ... 2Kin 14:11
at Beth-shemesh, which *b* to Judah ... 2Chr 25:21
for this matter *b* unto thee ... Ezr 10:4
Salvation *b* unto the LORD ... Ps 3:8
that power *b* unto God ... Ps 62:11
Also unto thee, O Lord, *b* mercy ... Ps 62:12
O LORD God, to whom vengeance *b* ... Ps 94:1
O God, to whom vengeance *b* ... Ps 94:1
O Lord, righteousness *b* unto thee ... Dan 9:7
to us *b* confusion of face, to our ... Dan 9:8
But strong meat *b* to them that ... Heb 5:14
hath said, Vengeance *b* unto me ... Heb 10:30

## BELONGING

the service of the sanctuary *b* ... Num 7:9
a part of the field *b* unto Boaz ... Ruth 2:3
Philistines *b* to the five lords ... 1Sa 6:18
meddleth with strife *b* not to him ... Prov 26:17
*b* to the city called Bethsaida ... Lk 9:10

## BELOVED

If a man have two wives, one *b* ... Deut 21:15
born him children, both the *b* ... Deut 21:15
he may not make the son of the *b* ... Deut 21:16
The *b* of the LORD shall dwell in ... Deut 33:12
who was *b* of his God, and God made ... Neh 13:26
That thy *b* may be delivered ... Ps 60:5
That thy *b* may be delivered ... Ps 108:6
for so he giveth his *b* sleep ... Ps 127:2
only *b* in the sight of my mother ... Prov 4:3
My *b* is unto me as a cluster of ... Song 1:14
Behold, thou art fair, my *b* ... Song 1:16
so is my *b* among the sons ... Song 2:3
The voice of my *b* ... Song 2:8
My *b* is like a roe or a young ... Song 2:9
My *b* spake, and said unto me, Rise ... Song 2:10
My *b* is mine, and I am his ... Song 2:16
the shadows flee away, turn, my *b* ... Song 2:17
Let my *b* come into his garden, and ... Song 4:16
drink, yea, drink abundantly, O *b* ... Song 5:1
the voice of my *b* that knocketh ... Song 5:2
My *b* put in his hand by the hole ... Song 5:4
I rose up to open to my *b* ... Song 5:5
I opened to my *b* ... Song 5:6
but my *b* had withdrawn himself, ... Song 5:6
of Jerusalem, if ye find my *b* ... Song 5:8
thy *b* more than another *b* ... Song 5:9
thy *b* more than another *b* ... Song 5:9
My *b* is white and ruddy, the ... Song 5:10
This is my *b*, and this is my ... Song 5:16
Whither is thy *b* gone, O thou ... Song 6:1
whither is thy *b* turned aside ... Song 6:1
My *b* is gone down into his garden ... Song 6:2
am my beloved's, and my *b* is mine ... Song 6:3
mouth like the best wine for my *b* ... Song 7:9
Come, my *b*, let us go forth into ... Song 7:11
I have laid up for thee, O my *b* ... Song 7:13
wilderness, leaning upon her *b* ... Song 8:5
Make haste, my *b*, and be thou like ... Song 8:14
of my *b* touching his vineyard ... Is 5:1
What hath my *b* to do in mine ... Jer 11:15
I have given the dearly *b* of my ... Jer 12:7
for thou art greatly *b* ... Dan 9:23
me, O Daniel, a man greatly *b* ... Dan 10:11
And said, O man greatly *b*, fear ... Dan 10:19
love a woman *b* of her friend, yet ... Hos 3:1
even the *b* fruit of their womb ... Hos 9:16
heaven, saying, This is my *b* Son ... Mt 3:17
my *b*, in whom my soul is well ... Mt 12:18
which said, This is my *b* Son ... Mt 17:5
heaven, saying, Thou art my *b* Son ... Mk 1:11
cloud, saying, This is my *b* Son ... Mk 9:7
which said, Thou art my *b* Son ... Lk 3:22
cloud, saying, This is my *b* Son ... Lk 9:35
I will send my *b* son ... Lk 20:13
men unto you with our *b* Barnabas ... Acts 15:25
*b* of God, called to be saints ... Rom 1:7
and her *b*, which was not *b* ... Rom 9:25
they are *b* for the fathers' sakes ... Rom 11:28
Dearly *b*, avenge not yourselves ... Rom 12:19
Greet Amplias my *b* in the Lord ... Rom 16:8
helper in Christ, and Stachys my *b* ... Rom 16:9
Salute the *b* Persis, which ... Rom 16:12
but as my *b* sons I warn you ... 1Cor 4:14
you Timotheus, who is my *b* son ... 1Cor 4:17
Wherefore, my dearly *b*, flee from ... 1Cor 10:14
my *b* brethren, be ye stedfast, ... 1Cor 15:58
therefore these promises dearly *b* ... 2Cor 7:1
but we do all things, dearly *b* ... 2Cor 12:19
he hath made us accepted in the *b* ... Eph 1:6
a *b* brother and faithful minister ... Eph 6:21
Wherefore, my *b*, as ye have ... Phil 2:12
Therefore, my brethren dearly *b* ... Phil 4:1
fast in the Lord, my dearly *b* ... Phil 4:1
as the elect of God, holy and *b* ... Col 3:12
unto you, who is a *b* brother ... Col 4:7
*b* brother, who is one of you ... Col 4:9
the *b* physician, and Demas, greet ... Col 4:14
Knowing, brethren *b*, your ... 1Th 1:4
brethren *b* of the Lord, because ... 2Th 2:13
because they are faithful and *b* ... 1Ti 6:2
To Timothy, my dearly *b* son ... 2Ti 1:2
unto Philemon our dearly *b* ... Philem 1
And to our *b* Apphia, and Archippus ... Philem 2
but above a servant, a brother *b* ... Philem 16
But, *b*, we are persuaded better ... Heb 6:9
Do not err, my *b* brethren ... Jas 1:16
my *b* brethren, let every man be ... Jas 1:19
my *b* brethren, Hath not God ... Jas 2:5
Dearly *b*, I beseech you as ... 1Pet 2:11
*B*, think it not strange ... 1Pet 4:12
excellent glory, This is my *b* Son ... 2Pet 1:17
This second epistle, *b*, I now ... 2Pet 3:1
But, *b*, be not ignorant of this ... 2Pet 3:8
Wherefore, *b*, seeing that ye look ... 2Pet 3:14
even as our *b* brother Paul also ... 2Pet 3:15
Ye therefore, *b*, seeing ye know ... 2Pet 3:17
*B*, now are we the sons of God, and ... 1Jn 3:2
*B*, if our heart condemn us not, ... 1Jn 3:21
*B*, believe not every spirit, but ... 1Jn 4:1
*B*, let us love one another ... 1Jn 4:7
*B*, if God so loved us, we ought ... 1Jn 4:11
*B*, I wish above all things that ... 3Jn 2
*B*, thou doest faithfully ... 3Jn 5
*B*, follow not that which is evil, ... 3Jn 11
*B*, when I gave all diligence to ... Jude 3
But, *b*, remember ye the words ... Jude 17
But ye, *b*, building up yourselves ... Jude 20
the saints about, and the *b* city ... Rev 20:9

## BELOVED'S

I am my *b*, and my beloved is mine ... Song 6:3
I am my *b*, and his desire is ... Song 7:10

## BELSHAZZAR (*bel-shaz'-ar*) *A Babylonian king.*

*B* the king made a great feast to ... Dan 5:1
*B*, whiles he tasted the wine, ... Dan 5:2
Then was king *B* greatly troubled, ... Dan 5:9
And thou his son, O *B*, hast not ... Dan 5:22
Then commanded *B*, and they clothed ... Dan 5:29
In that night was *B* the king of ... Dan 5:30
In the first year of *B* king of ... Dan 7:1
king *B* a vision appeared unto me ... Dan 8:1

## BELTESHAZZAR (*bel-te-shaz'-ar*) See DANIEL. *The Babylonian name given to Daniel.*

he gave unto Daniel the name of *B* ... Dan 1:7
said to Daniel, whose name was *B* ... Dan 2:26
in before me, whose name was *B* ... Dan 4:8
O *B*, master of the magicians, ... Dan 4:9
Now thou, O *B*, declare the ... Dan 4:18
Then Daniel, whose name was *B* ... Dan 4:19
The king spake, and said, *B* ... Dan 4:19
*B* answered and said, My lord, the ... Dan 4:19
Daniel, whom the king named *B* ... Dan 5:12
Daniel, whose name was called *B* ... Dan 10:1

## BEMOAN

or who shall *b* thee ... Jer 15:5
neither go to lament nor *b* them ... Jer 16:5
not for the dead, neither *b* him ... Jer 22:10
All ye that are about him, *b* him ... Jer 48:17
who will *b* her ... Nah 3:7

## BEMOANED

and they *b* him, and comforted him ... Job 42:11

## BEMOANING

heard Ephraim *b* himself thus ... Jer 31:18

## BEN (*ben*) *A Levite.*

the second degree, Zechariah, *B* ... 1Chr 15:18

## BENAIAH (*ben-ay'-ah*)

*1. An officer of David.*

*B* the son of Jehoiada was over ... 2Sa 8:18
*B* the son of Jehoiada was over ... 2Sa 20:23
*B* the son of Jehoiada, the son of ... 2Sa 23:20
These things did *B* the son of ... 2Sa 23:22
*B* the son of Jehoiada, and Nathan ... 1Kin 1:8
But Nathan the prophet, and *B* ... 1Kin 1:10
*B* the son of Jehoiada, and thy ... 1Kin 1:26
prophet, and *B* the son of Jehoiada ... 1Kin 1:32
*B* the son of Jehoiada answered ... 1Kin 1:36
*B* the son of Jehoiada, and the ... 1Kin 1:38
*B* the son of Jehoiada, and the ... 1Kin 1:44
the hand of *B* the son of Jehoiada ... 1Kin 2:25
Then Solomon sent *B* the son of ... 1Kin 2:29
*B* came to the tabernacle of the ... 1Kin 2:30
*B* brought the king word again, ... 1Kin 2:30
So *B* the son of Jehoiada went up, ... 1Kin 2:34
the king put *B* the son of ... 1Kin 2:35
commanded *B* the son of Jehoiada ... 1Kin 2:46

B the son of Jehoiada was over... 1Kin 4:4
B the son of Jehoiada, the son of... 1Chr 11:22
These things did B the son of... 1Chr 11:24
B the son of Jehoiada was over... 1Chr 18:17
month was B the son of Jehoiada... 1Chr 27:5
This is that B, who was mighty... 1Chr 27:6

*2. A "mighty man" of David.*
B the Pirathonite, Hiddai of the... 2Sa 23:30
of Benjamin, B the Pirathonite,... 1Chr 11:31
month was B the Pirathonite... 1Chr 27:14

*3. A Simeonite family chief.*
and Adiel, and Jesimiel, and B... 1Chr 4:36

*4. A priest of David.*
and Jehiel, and Unni, Eliab, and B... 1Chr 15:18
Eliab, and Maaseiah, and B... 1Chr 15:20
and Amasai, and Zechariah, and B... 1Chr 15:24
and Mattithiah, and Eliab, and B... 1Chr 16:5
B also and Jahaziel the priests... 1Chr 16:6

*5. Father of Jehoida.*
was Jehoiada the son of B... 1Chr 27:34

*6. Grandfather of Jehaziel.*
son of Zechariah, the son of B... 2Chr 20:14

*7. A Levite during Hezekiah's reign.*
and Ismachiah, and Mahath, and B... 2Chr 31:13

*8. A descendant of Parosh.*
and Eleazar, and Malchijah, and B... Ezr 10:25

*9. A son of Pahath-moab.*
Adna, and Chelal, B, Maaseiah,... Ezr 10:30

*10. A son of Bani.*
B, Bedeiah, Chelluh,... Ezr 10:35

*11. A son of Nebo.*
Zabad, Zebina, Jadau, and Joel, B... Ezr 10:43

*12. Father of Pelatiah.*
of Azur, and Pelatiah the son of B... Eze 11:1
that Pelatiah the son of B died... Eze 11:13

**BEN-AMMI** (*ben-am'-mi*) *A son of Lot.*
bare a son, and called his name B... Gen 19:38

**BENCHES**
have made thy b of ivory, brought... Eze 27:6

**BEND**
For, lo, the wicked b their bow... Ps 11:2
b their bows to shoot their... Ps 64:3
they b their tongues like their... Jer 9:3
Lydians, that handle and b the bow... Jer 46:9
all ye that b the bow, shoot at... Jer 50:14
all ye that b the bow, camp... Jer 50:29
bendeth let the archer b his bow... Jer 51:3
this vine did b her roots toward... Eze 17:7

**BEN DEKER** See DEKAR.

**BENDETH**
when he b his bow to shoot his... Ps 58:7
Against him that b let the archer... Jer 51:3

**BENDING**
thee shall come b unto thee... Is 60:14

**BENEATH**
she was buried b Beth-el under an... Gen 35:8
above, or that is in the earth b... Ex 20:4
they shall be coupled together b... Ex 26:24
under the compass of the altar b... Ex 27:5
b upon the hem of it thou shalt... Ex 28:33
hands, and brake them b the mount... Ex 32:19
And they were coupled b, and... Ex 36:29
thereof b unto the midst of it... Ex 38:4
that is in the waters b the earth... Deut 4:18
heaven above, and upon the earth b... Deut 4:39
above, or that is in the earth b... Deut 5:8
that is in the waters b the earth... Deut 5:8
only, and thou shalt not be b... Deut 28:13
and for the deep that coucheth b... Deut 33:13
in heaven above, and in earth b... Josh 2:11
of Midian was b him in the valley... Judg 7:8
which is by Zartanah b Jezreel... 1Kin 4:12
b the lions and oxen were certain... 1Kin 7:29
in heaven above, or on earth b... 1Kin 8:23
His roots shall be dried up b... Job 18:16
that he may depart from hell b... Prov 15:24
Hell from b is moved for thee to... Is 14:9
heavens, and look upon the earth b... Is 51:6
of the earth searched out b... Jer 31:37
from above, and his roots from b... Amos 2:9
as Peter was b in the palace,... Mk 14:66
he said unto them, Ye are from b... Jn 8:23
above, and signs in the earth b... Acts 2:19

**BENE BARAK** See BENE-BERAK.

**BENE-BERAK** (*be'-ne-be'-rak*) *A city in Dan.*
and B, and Gath-rimmon,... Josh 19:45

**BENEFACTORS**
authority upon them are called b... Lk 22:25

**BENEFIT**
according to the b done unto him... 2Chr 32:25
wherewith I said I would b them... Jer 18:10
that ye might have a second b... 2Cor 1:15
and beloved, partakers of the b... 1Ti 6:2
that thy b should not be as it... Philem 14

**BENEFITS**
Lord, who daily loadeth us with b... Ps 68:19
my soul, and forget not all his b... Ps 103:2
the LORD for all his b toward me... Ps 116:12

**BENE JAAKAN** See BENE-JAAKAN.

**BENE-JAAKAN** (*be'-ne-ja'-a-kan*) *Namesake of several wells.*
from Moseroth, and pitched in B... Num 33:31
And they removed from B, and... Num 33:32

**BENEVOLENCE**
render unto the wife due b... 1Cor 7:3

**BEN-HADAD** (*ben'ha-dad*)

*1. A Syrian king, son of Tabrimon.*
and king Asa sent them to B... 1Kin 15:18
So B hearkened unto king Asa, and... 1Kin 15:20
sent to B king of Syria, that... 2Chr 16:2
B hearkened unto king Asa, and... 2Chr 16:4

*2. A Syrian king during Ahab's reign.*
B the king of Syria gathered all... 1Kin 20:1
and said unto him, Thus saith B... 1Kin 20:2
again, and said, Thus speaketh B... 1Kin 20:5
he said unto the messengers of B... 1Kin 20:9
B sent unto him, and said, The... 1Kin 20:10
when B heard this message, as he... 1Kin 20:12
But B was drinking himself drunk... 1Kin 20:16
B sent out, and they told him,... 1Kin 20:17
B the king of Syria escaped on an... 1Kin 20:20
that B numbered the Syrians, and... 1Kin 20:26
B fled, and came into the city,... 1Kin 20:30
and said, Thy servant B saith... 1Kin 20:32
and they said, Thy brother B... 1Kin 20:33
Then B came forth to him... 1Kin 20:33
B said unto him, The cities,... 1Kin 20:34
that B king of Syria gathered all... 2Kin 6:24
B the king of Syria was sick... 2Kin 8:7
Thy son B king of Syria hath sent... 2Kin 8:9

*3. A Syrian king, son of Hazael.*
into the hand of B the son of... 2Kin 13:3
B his son reigned in his stead... 2Kin 13:24
of B the son of Hazael the cities... 2Kin 13:25
shall devour the palaces of B... Amos 1:4

*4. A title for all the Syrian kings.*
it shall consume the palaces of B... Jer 49:27

**BEN-HAIL** (*ben-ha'-il*) *A prince of Judah.*
he sent to his princes, even to B... 2Chr 17:7

**BEN-HANAN** (*ben-ha'-nan*) *A son of Shimon.*
Shimon were, Amnon, and Rinnah, B. 1Chr 4:20

**BENINU** (*ben'-i-nu*) *A Levite who renewed the covenant.*
Hodijah, Bani, B... Neh 10:13

**BENJAMIN** (*ben'-ja-min*) See BENJAMIN'S, BENJAMITE.

*1. Youngest son of Jacob.*
but his father called him B... Gen 35:18
Joseph, and B... Gen 35:24
But B, Joseph's brother, Jacob... Gen 42:4
is not, and ye will take B away... Gen 42:36
away your other brother, and B... Gen 43:14
double money in their hand, and B... Gen 43:15
And when Joseph saw B with them... Gen 43:16
up his eyes, and saw his brother B... Gen 43:29
see, and the eyes of my brother B... Gen 45:12
and B wept upon his neck... Gen 45:14
but to B he gave three hundred... Gen 45:22
Joseph, and B... Gen 46:19
And the sons of B were Belah... Gen 46:21
Issachar, Zebulun, and B,... Ex 1:3
Dan, Joseph, and B, Naphtali, Gad,... 1Chr 2:2
The sons of B... 1Chr 7:6
Now B begat Bela his firstborn,... 1Chr 8:1

*2. One of the twelve tribes comprising Israel.*
B shall ravin as a wolf:... Gen 49:27
Of B... Num 1:11
Of the children of B, by their... Num 1:36
of them, even of the tribe of B... Num 1:37
Then the tribe of B... Num 2:22
of B shall be Abidan the son of... Num 2:22
prince of the children of B... Num 7:60
B was Abidan the son of Gideoni... Num 10:24
Of the tribe of B, Palti the son... Num 13:9
The sons of B after their... Num 26:38
sons of B after their families... Num 26:41
Of the tribe of B, Elidad the son... Num 34:21
and Issachar, and Joseph, and B... Deut 27:12
of B he said, The beloved of the... Deut 33:12
of B came up according to their... Josh 18:11
inheritance of the children of B... Josh 18:20
of B according to their families... Josh 18:21
of B according to their families... Josh 18:28
Simeon, and out of the tribe of B... Josh 21:4
And out of the tribe of B, Gibeon... Josh 21:17
the children of B did not drive... Judg 1:21
of B in Jerusalem unto this day... Judg 1:21
after thee, B, among thy people... Judg 5:14
also against Judah, and against B... Judg 10:9
by Gibeah, which belongeth to B... Judg 19:14
(Now the children of B heard that... Judg 20:3
into Gibeah that belongeth to B... Judg 20:4
do, when they come to Gibeah of B.. Judg 20:10
men through all the tribe of B... Judg 20:12
But the children of B would not... Judg 20:13
But the children of B gathered... Judg 20:14
the children of B were numbered... Judg 20:15
And the men of Israel, beside B... Judg 20:17
battle against the children of B... Judg 20:18
went out to battle against B... Judg 20:20
the children of B came forth out... Judg 20:21
the children of B my brother... Judg 20:23
the children of B the second day... Judg 20:24
B went forth against them out of... Judg 20:25
the children of B my brother... Judg 20:28
children of B on the third day... Judg 20:30
the children of B went out... Judg 20:31
And the children of B said... Judg 20:32
And the LORD smote B before Israel. Judg 20:35
So the children of B saw that... Judg 20:36
B began to smite and kill of the... Judg 20:39
again, the men of B were amazed... Judg 20:41
there fell of B eighteen thousand... Judg 20:44
fell that day of B were twenty... Judg 20:46
again upon the children of B... Judg 20:48
give his daughter unto B to wife... Judg 21:1
repented them for B their brother... Judg 21:6
to speak to the children of B... Judg 21:13
B came again at that time... Judg 21:14
And the people repented them for B. Judg 21:15
the women are destroyed out of B... Judg 21:16
for them that be escaped of B... Judg 21:17
be he that giveth a wife to B... Judg 21:18
they commanded the children of B... Judg 21:20
of Shiloh, and go to the land of B... Judg 21:21
And the children of B did so... Judg 21:23
ran a man of B out of the army... 1Sa 4:12
Now there was a man of B, whose... 1Sa 9:1
thee a man out of the land of B... 1Sa 9:16
the families of the tribe of B... 1Sa 9:21
in the border of B at Zelzah... 1Sa 10:2
near, the tribe of B was taken... 1Sa 10:20
B to come near by their families... 1Sa 10:21
were with Jonathan in Gibeah of B... 1Sa 13:2
up from Gilgal unto Gibeah of B... 1Sa 13:15
with them, abode in Gibeah of B... 1Sa 13:16
of Saul in Gibeah of B looked... 1Sa 14:16
and over Ephraim, and over B... 2Sa 2:9
went over by number twelve of B... 2Sa 2:15
the children of B gathered... 2Sa 2:25
of David had smitten of B... 2Sa 2:31
Abner also spake in the ears of B... 2Sa 3:19
good to the whole house of B... 2Sa 3:19
Beerothite, of the children of B... 2Sa 4:2
Beeroth also was reckoned to B... 2Sa 4:2
were a thousand men of B with him... 2Sa 19:17
they in the country of B in Zelah... 2Sa 21:14
of Gibeah of the children of B... 2Sa 23:29
Shimei the son of Elah, in B... 1Kin 4:18
of Judah, with the tribe of B... 1Kin 12:21
unto all the house of Judah and B... 1Kin 12:23
Asa built with them Geba of B... 1Kin 15:22
And out of the tribe of B... 1Chr 6:60
of the tribe of the children of B... 1Chr 6:65
All these are of the sons of B... 1Chr 8:40
of Judah, and of the children of B... 1Chr 9:3
And of the sons of B... 1Chr 9:7
pertained to the children of B... 1Chr 11:31
bow, even of Saul's brethren of B... 1Chr 12:2
there came of the children of B... 1Chr 12:16
And of the children of B, the... 1Chr 12:29
B counted he not among them... 1Chr 21:6
of B, Jaasiel the son of Abner... 1Chr 27:21
B an hundred and fourscore... 2Chr 11:1
and to all Israel in Judah and B... 2Chr 11:3
in Judah and in B fenced cities... 2Chr 11:10
having Judah and B on his side... 2Chr 11:12
all the countries of Judah and B... 2Chr 11:23
and out of B, that bare shields and... 2Chr 14:8
ye me, Asa, and all Judah and B... 2Chr 15:2
out of all the land of Judah and B... 2Chr 15:8
And he gathered all Judah and B... 2Chr 15:9
And of B... 2Chr 17:17
throughout all Judah and B... 2Chr 25:5
the altars out of all Judah and B... 2Chr 31:1
of Israel, and of all Judah and B... 2Chr 34:9
in Jerusalem and B to stand to it... 2Chr 34:32
of the fathers of Judah and B... Ezr 1:5
B heard that the children of the... Ezr 4:1
B gathered themselves together... Ezr 10:9
of Judah, and of the children of B... Neh 11:4
And these are the sons of B... Neh 11:7
The children also of B from Geba... Neh 11:31
were divisions in Judah, and in B... Neh 11:36
There is little B with their... Ps 68:27
Before Ephraim and B and Manasseh... Ps 80:2
were in Anathoth in the land of B... Jer 1:1
O ye children of B, gather... Jer 6:1
Jerusalem, and from the land of B... Jer 17:26
which is in the country of B... Jer 32:8
take witnesses in the land of B... Jer 32:44
of the south, and in the land of B... Jer 33:13
to go into the land of B, to... Jer 37:12
of Judah and the border of B... Eze 48:22
west side, B shall have a portion... Eze 48:23
And by the border of B, from the... Eze 48:24
one gate of Joseph, one gate of B... Eze 48:32
at Beth-aven, after thee, O B... Hos 5:8
and B shall possess Gilead... Obad 19
of Cis, a man of the tribe of B... Acts 13:21
of Abraham, of the tribe of B... Rom 11:1
of Israel, of the tribe of B... Phil 3:5
Of the tribe of B were sealed... Rev 7:8

*3. Great-grandson of Benjamin 1.*
Jeush, and B, and Ehud, and... 1Chr 7:10

*4. A descendant of Harim.*
B, Malluch, and Shemariah... Ezr 10:32

*5. A repairer of the Jerusalem wall.*
After him repaired B and Hashub... Neh 3:23

*6. Purified the Jerusalem wall.*
Judah, and B, and Shemaiah, and... Neh 12:34

*7. A gate of Jerusalem.*
that were in the high gate of B... Jer 20:2
And when he was in the gate of B... Jer 37:13
then sitting in the gate of B... Jer 38:7

**BENJAMIN'S** (*ben'-ja-mins*)

*1. Refers to Benjamin 1.*
but B mess was five times so much... Gen 43:34
and the cup was found in B sack... Gen 44:12
he fell upon his brother B neck... Gen 45:14

*2. Refers to Benjamin 7.*

from *B* gate unto the place of the........ Zec 14:10

**BENJAMITE** (*ben'-ja-mite*) See BENJAMITES. *A descendant of Benjamin.*
Ehud the son of Gera, a *B*.................... Judg 3:15
Bechorath, the son of Aphiah, a *B*........... 1Sa 9:1
answered and said, Am not I a *B*.......... 1Sa 9:21
much more now may this *B* do it.......... 2Sa 16:11
And Shimei the son of Gera, a *B*.......... 2Sa 19:16
was Sheba, the son of Bichri, a *B*.......... 2Sa 20:1
a *B* of Bahurim, which cursed me.......... 1Kin 2:8
of Shimei, the son of Kish, a *B*.................. Est 2:5
the words of Cush the *B*................................ Ps 7:t

**BENJAMITES** (*ben'-ja-mites*)
but the men of the place were *B*........ Judg 19:16
of the *B* that day twenty and five........ Judg 20:35
men of Israel gave place to the *B*...... Judg 20:36
the *B* looked behind them, and,.......... Judg 20:40
they inclosed the *B* round about.......... Judg 20:43
passed through the land of the *B*............. 1Sa 9:4
stood about him, Hear now, ye *B*.......... 1Sa 22:7
Abiezer the Anetothite, of the *B*........ 1Chr 27:12

**BENO** (*be'-no*) *A descendant of Merari.*
*B*.......................................................... 1Chr 24:26
*B*, and Shoham, and Zaccur................ 1Chr 24:27

**BEN-ONI** (*ben-o'-ni*) *Rachel's second son.*
died) that she called his name *B*.......... Gen 35:18

**BENT**
he hath *b* his bow, and made it................. Ps 7:12
have *b* their bow, to cast down.............. Ps 37:14
are sharp, and all their bows *b*.................. Is 5:28
drawn sword, and from the *b* bow.......... Is 21:15
He hath *b* his bow like an enemy.............. Lam 2:4
He hath *b* his bow, and set me as a..... Lam 3:12
my people are *b* to backsliding.............. Hos 11:7
When I have *b* Judah for me,.................. Zec 9:13

**BEN-ZOHETH** (*ben-zo'-heth*) *A descendant of Caleb.*
sons of Ishi were, Zoheth, and *B*.......... 1Chr 4:20

**BEON** (*be'-on*) *A place east of the Jordan River.*
and Shebam, and Nebo, and *B*............. Num 32:3

**BEOR** (*be'-or*)
*1. Father of Bela.*
Bela the son of *B* reigned in Edom...... Gen 36:32
Bela the son of *B*................................. 1Chr 1:43
*2. Father of Balaam.*
Balaam the son of *B* to Pethor............ Num 22:5
Balaam the son of *B* hath said............ Num 24:3
Balaam the son of *B* hath said............ Num 24:15
Balaam also the son of *B* they............ Num 31:8
son of *B* of Pethor of Mesopotamia...... Deut 23:4
Balaam also the son of *B*, the............ Josh 13:22
Balaam the son of *B* to curse you......... Josh 24:9
what Balaam the son of *B* answered....... Mic 6:5

**BERA** (*be'-rah*) *King of Sodom.*
made war with *B* king of Sodom........... Gen 14:2

**BERACAH** See BERACHAH.

**BERACHAH** (*ber'-a-kah*)
*1. A Benjamite warrior in David's army.*
and *B*, and Jehu the Antothite,............ 1Chr 12:3
*2. A valley in Judah.*
themselves in the valley of *B*........... 2Chr 20:26
place was called, The valley of *B*........ 2Chr 20:26

**BERACHIAH** (*ber-a-ki'-ah*) See BERECHIAH. *Father of Asaph.*
hand, even Asaph the son of *B*............ 1Chr 6:39

**BERAIAH** (*ber-a-i'-ah*) *A son of Shimhi.*
and *B*, and Shimrath............................ 1Chr 8:21

**BERAKIAH** See BERACHIAH.

**BEREA** (*be-re'-a*) *A city in Macedonia.*
Paul and Silas by night unto *B*.......... Acts 17:10
of God was preached of Paul at *B*...... Acts 17:13
him into Asia Sopater of *B*.................. Acts 20:4

**BEREAVE**
do I labour, and *b* my soul of good......... Eccl 4:8
I will *b* them of children, I will.............. Jer 15:7
evil beasts, and they shall *b* thee............ Eze 5:17
no more henceforth *b* them of men..... Eze 36:12
neither *b* thy nations any more,.......... Eze 36:14
their children, yet will I *b* them.............. Hos 9:12

**BEREAVED**
Me have ye *b* of my children............... Gen 42:36
*b* of my children, I am *b*.................... Gen 43:14
wives be *b* of their children................. Jer 18:21
up men, and hast *b* thy nations.......... Eze 36:13
as a bear that is *b* of her whelps............ Hos 13:8

**BEREAVETH**
abroad the sword *b*, at home there...... Lam 1:20

**BERECHIAH** (*ber-e-ki'-ah*) See BERACHIAH.
*1. A descendant of King Jehoiakim.*
And Hashubah, and Ohel, and *B*.......... 1Chr 3:20
*2. Same as Berachiah.*
his brethren, Asaph the son of *B*........ 1Chr 15:17
*3. A Levite near Jerusalem.*
*B* the son of Asa, the son of................. 1Chr 9:16
*4. A Levite doorkeeper.*
And *B* and Elkanah were...................... 1Chr 15:23
*5. An Ephraimite.*
*B* the son of Meshillemoth, and.......... 2Chr 28:12
*6. Father of Meshullam.*
repaired Meshullam the son of *B*............ Neh 3:4
son of *B* over against his chamber........ Neh 3:30
of Meshullam the son of *B*..................... Neh 6:18
*7. Father of Zechariah.*
LORD unto Zechariah, the son of *B*......... Zec 1:1
LORD unto Zechariah, the son of *B*......... Zec 1:7

**BERED** (*be'-red*)
*1. A place in southern Canaan.*
behold, it is between Kadesh and *B*.... Gen 16:14
*2. An Ephraimite.*
*B* his son, and Tahath his son, and...... 1Chr 7:20

**BEREKIAH** See BERECHIAH.

**BERI** (*be'-ri*) See BERITES. *Son of Zophah.*
and Harnepher, and Shual, and *B*........ 1Chr 7:36

**BERIAH** (*be-ri'-ah*) See BERIITES.
*1. A son of Asher.*
Jimnah, and Ishuah, and Isui, and *B*.. Gen 46:17
and the sons of *B*.................................. Gen 46:17
of *B*, the family of the Beriites............. Num 26:44
Of the sons of *B*.................................. Num 26:45
Imnah, and Isuah, and Ishuai, and *B*.. 1Chr 7:30
And the sons of *B*................................. 1Chr 7:31
*2. A son of Ephraim.*
a son, and he called his name *B*.......... 1Chr 7:23
*3. A son of Elpaal.*
*B* also, and Shema, who were heads... 1Chr 8:13
and Ispah, and Joha, the sons of *B*...... 1Chr 8:16
*4. A Levite.*
Jahath, Zina, and Jeush, and *B*........ 1Chr 23:10
but Jeush and *B* had not many sons. 1Chr 23:11

**BERIITES** (*be-ri'-ites*) *Descendants of Beriah 1.*
of Beriah, the family of the *B*............ Num 26:44

**BERITES** (*be'-rites*) *Descendants of Beri.*
and to Beth-maachah, and all the *B*.... 2Sa 20:14

**BERITH** (*be'-rith*) See BAAL-BERITH. *Idol at Shechem.*
an hold of the house of the god *B*......... Judg 9:46

**BERNICE** (*bur-ni'-see*) *Daughter of Herod Agrippa.*
*B* came unto Caesarea to salute.......... Acts 25:13
when Agrippa was come, and *B*.......... Acts 25:23
rose up, and the governor, and *B*......... Acts 26:30

**BERODACH-BALADAN** (*ber-o'-dak-bal'-a-dan*) See MERODACH-BALADAN. *A king of Babylon.*
At that time *B*, the son of.................... 2Kin 20:12

**BEROEA** See BEREA.

**BEROTHAH** (*ber-o'-thah*) See BEROTHAI, BEROTHITE. *A city near Hamath.*
Hamath, *B*, Sibraim, which is................ Eze 47:16

**BEROTHAI** (*ber'-o-thahee*) See BEROTHAH. *A city of Hadadezer.*
And from Betah, and from *B*, cities......... 2Sa 8:8

**BEROTHITE** (*be'-ro-thite*) See BEEROTHITE. *A native of Beeroth.*
Zelek the Ammonite, Naharai the *B*. 1Chr 11:39

**BERRIES**
two or three *b* in the top of the................. Is 17:6
tree, my brethren, bear olive *b*............... Jas 3:12

**BERYL**
And the fourth row a *b*, and an onyx... Ex 28:20
And the fourth row, a *b*, an onyx,....... Ex 39:13
are as gold rings set with the *b*.......... Song 5:14
was like unto the colour of a *b*............... Eze 1:16
was as the colour of a *b* stone............. Eze 10:9
topaz, and the diamond, the *b*............ Eze 28:13
His body also was like the *b*................ Dan 10:6
the eighth, *b*...................................... Rev 21:20

**BESAI** (*be'-sahee*) *A family of exiles.*
of Paseah, the children of *B*.................. Ezr 2:49
The children of *B*, the children.............. Neh 7:52

**BESEECH**
we *b* thee, three days' journey............ Ex 3:18
I *b* thee, shew me thy glory................. Ex 33:18
I *b* thee, lay not the sin upon us........ Num 12:11
Heal her now, O God, I *b* thee.......... Num 12:13
I *b* thee, let the power of my.............. Num 14:17
I *b* thee, the iniquity of this.............. Num 14:19
I *b* thee, tell thy servant.................... 1Sa 23:11
I *b* thee, and his servants go with........ 2Sa 13:24
I humbly *b* thee that I may find............. 2Sa 16:4
I *b* thee, O LORD, take away the.......... 2Sa 24:10
I *b* thee, save thou us out of his.......... 2Kin 19:19
I *b* thee, O LORD, remember now.......... 2Kin 20:3
I *b* thee, do away the iniquity of.......... 1Chr 21:8
I *b* thee, thine eyes be open, and......... 2Chr 6:40
I *b* thee, O LORD God of heaven,............. Neh 1:5
I *b* thee, the word that thou.................. Neh 1:8
I *b* thee, let now thine ear be.............. Neh 1:11
I *b* thee, that thou hast made me.......... Job 10:9
I *b* thee, and I will speak...................... Job 42:4
we *b* thee, O God of hosts...................... Ps 80:14
I *b* thee, deliver my soul...................... Ps 116:4
Save now, I *b* thee, O LORD.................. Ps 118:25
I *b* thee, send now prosperity.............. Ps 118:25
I *b* thee, the freewill offerings............ Ps 119:108
I *b* thee, how I have walked.................... Is 38:3
we *b* thee, we are all thy people............. Is 64:9
We *b* thee, let this man be put to.............. Jer 38:4
I *b* thee, the voice of the LORD,............. Jer 38:20
we *b* thee, our supplication be................ Jer 42:2
thy servants, I *b* thee, ten days.............. Dan 1:12
I *b* thee, let thine anger and thy.......... Dan 9:16
O Lord GOD, forgive, I *b* thee............... Amos 7:2
I, O Lord GOD, cease, I *b* thee............... Amos 7:5
We *b* thee, O LORD, we *b*.................... Jonah 1:14
I *b* thee, my life from me...................... Jonah 4:3
*b* God that he will be gracious................... Mal 1:9
they *b* him to put his hand upon............ Mk 7:32
I *b* thee, torment me not...................... Lk 8:28
I *b* thee, look upon my son.................... Lk 9:38
I *b* thee, suffer me to speak unto....... Acts 21:39
wherefore I *b* thee to hear me.............. Acts 26:3
I *b* you therefore, brethren, by............ Rom 12:1
Now I *b* you, brethren, for the.......... Rom 15:30
Now I *b* you, brethren, mark them.... Rom 16:17
Now I *b* you, brethren, by the............. 1Cor 1:10
Wherefore I *b* you, be ye..................... 1Cor 4:16
I *b* you, brethren, (ye know the......... 1Cor 16:15
Wherefore I *b* you that ye would........... 2Cor 2:8
as though God did *b* you by us............. 2Cor 5:20
*b* you also that ye receive not............... 2Cor 6:1
Now I Paul myself *b* you by the........... 2Cor 10:1
But I *b* you, that I may not be............. 2Cor 10:2
Brethren, I *b* you, be as I am................. Gal 4:12
*b* you that ye walk worthy of the........... Eph 4:1
I *b* Euodias, and *b* Syntyche,................ Phil 4:2
*b* Syntyche, that they be of the.............. Phil 4:2
Furthermore then we *b* you...................... 1Th 4:1
but we *b* you, brethren, that ye............ 1Th 4:10
we *b* you, brethren, to know them......... 1Th 5:12
Now we *b* you, brethren, by the............. 2Th 2:1
for love's sake I rather *b* thee................ Philem 9
I *b* thee for my son Onesimus,............. Philem 10
But I *b* you the rather to do this.......... Heb 13:19
I *b* you, brethren, suffer the.............. Heb 13:22
I *b* you as strangers and pilgrims,........ 1Pet 2:11
And now I *b* thee, lady, not as.................. 2Jn 5

**BESEECHING**
came unto him a centurion, *b* him,............ Mt 8:5
*b* him, and kneeling down to him,.......... Mk 1:40
*b* him that he would come and heal.......... Lk 7:3

**BESET**
*b* the house round about, and beat.... Judg 19:22
*b* the house round about upon me....... Judg 20:5
bulls of Bashan have *b* me round.......... Ps 22:12
Thou hast *b* me behind and before,....... Ps 139:5
own doings have *b* them about.............. Hos 7:2
the sin which doth so easily *b* us.......... Heb 12:1

**BESIDE**
*b* the first famine that was in................ Gen 26:1
take other wives *b* my daughters........ Gen 31:50
on foot that were men, *b* children......... Ex 12:37
*b* Pi-hahiroth, before Baal-zephon............ Ex 14:9
pour all the blood *b* the bottom............. Ex 29:12
cast it *b* the altar on the east................ Lev 1:16
and he shall put them *b* the altar........... Lev 6:10
*b* the burnt sacrifice of the..................... Lev 9:17
eat it without leaven *b* the altar.......... Lev 10:12
*b* the other in her life time.................. Lev 18:18
*B* the sabbaths of the LORD, and.......... Lev 23:38
*b* your gifts, and *b* all your.................. Lev 23:38
*b* all your freewill offerings,................ Lev 23:38
*b* the ram of the atonement,................. Num 5:8
lain with thee *b* thine husband.............. Num 5:20
*b* that that his hand shall get................ Num 6:21
*b* this manna, before our eyes.............. Num 11:6
*b* them that died about the matter..... Num 16:49
and as cedar trees *b* the waters............ Num 24:6
*b* the continual burnt offering,........... Num 28:10
*b* the continual burnt offering,........... Num 28:15
Ye shall offer these *b* the burnt.......... Num 28:23
it shall be offered *b* the.................... Num 28:24
Ye shall offer them *b* the.................... Num 28:31
*B* the burnt offering of the month....... Num 29:6
*b* the sin offering of atonement,.......... Num 29:11
*b* the continual burnt offering,........... Num 29:16
*b* the continual burnt offering,........... Num 29:19
*b* the continual burnt offering,........... Num 29:22
*b* the continual burnt offering,........... Num 29:25
*b* the continual burnt offering,........... Num 29:28
*b* the continual burnt offering,........... Num 29:31
*b* the continual burnt offering,........... Num 29:34
*b* the continual burnt offering,........... Num 29:38
*b* your vows, and your freewill............ Num 29:39
*b* the rest of them that were................. Num 31:8
*b* unwalled towns a great many............... Deut 3:5
there is none else *b* him...................... Deut 4:35
Gilgal, *b* the plains of Moreh............... Deut 11:30
*b* that which cometh of the sale........... Deut 18:8
more for thee, *b* these three................. Deut 19:9
*b* the covenant which he made with... Deut 29:1
the city Adam, that is *b* Zaretan.......... Josh 3:16
which is *b* Beth-aven, on the east.......... Josh 7:2
king of Ai, which is *b* Beth-el............... Josh 12:9
and Mearah that is *b* the Sidonians....... Josh 13:4
*b* the land of Gilead and Bashan,.......... Josh 17:5
in building you an altar *b* the.............. Josh 22:19
*b* the altar of the LORD our God.......... Josh 22:29
and it be dry upon all the earth *b*........ Judg 6:37
pitched *b* the well of Harod................... Judg 7:1
*b* ornaments, and collars, and............... Judg 8:26
*b* the chains that were about................ Judg 8:26
*b* her he had neither son nor............... Judg 11:34
*b* the inhabitants of Gibeah,................ Judg 20:15
*b* Benjamin, were numbered four........ Judg 20:17
wait which they had set *b* Gibeah...... Judg 20:36
And she sat *b* the reapers.................... Ruth 2:14
there is none to redeem it *b* thee.......... Ruth 4:4

for there is none *b* thee 1Sa 2:2
to battle, and pitched *b* Eben-ezer 1Sa 4:1
stand *b* my father in the field 1Sa 19:3
neither is there any God *b* thee 2Sa 7:22
in Baal-hazor, which is *b* Ephraim 2Sa 13:23
stood *b* the way of the gate 2Sa 15:2
all his servants passed on *b* him 2Sa 15:18
and took my son from *b* me 1Kin 3:20
sheep, *b* harts, and roebucks, and 1Kin 4:23
*B* the chief of Solomon's officers 1Kin 5:16
in Ezion-geber, which is *b* Eloth 1Kin 9:26
*b* that which Solomon gave her of 1Kin 10:13
*B* that he had of the merchantmen, 1Kin 10:15
and two lions stood *b* the stays 1Kin 10:19
*b* the mischief that Hadad did 1Kin 11:25
lay my bones *b* his bones 1Kin 13:31
with the sword *b* the king's house 2Kin 11:20
set it *b* the altar, on the right 2Kin 12:9
*b* his sin wherewith he made Judah 2Kin 21:16
*b* the sons of the concubines, and 1Chr 3:9
neither is there any God *b* thee 1Chr 17:20
*b* that which she had brought unto 2Chr 9:12
*B* that which chapmen 2Chr 9:14
*b* those whom the king put in the 2Chr 17:19
with them other *b* the Ammonites 2Chr 20:1
LORD, from *b* the incense altar 2Chr 26:19
*B* their genealogy of males, from 2Chr 31:16
*b* the freewill offering for the Ezr 1:4
*b* all that was willingly offered Ezr 1:6
*B* their servants and their maids, Ezr 2:65
*b* forty shekels of silver Neh 5:15
*b* those that came unto us from Neh 5:17
*B* their manservants and their Neh 7:67
*b* him stood Mattithiah, and Shema, Neh 8:4
and the asses feeding *b* them Job 1:14
he leadeth me *b* the still waters Ps 23:2
upon earth that I desire *b* thee Ps 73:25
feed thy kids *b* the shepherds' Song 1:8
are ye that sow *b* all waters Is 32:20
and *b* me there is no saviour Is 43:11
and *b* me there is no God Is 44:6
Is there a God *b* me Is 44:8
none else, there is no God *b* me Is 45:5
the west, that there is none *b* me Is 45:6
and there is no God else *b* me Is 45:21
there is none *b* me Is 45:21
heart, I am, and none else *b* me Is 47:8
heart, I am, and none else *b* me Is 47:10
*b* those that are gathered unto Is 56:8
*b* thee, what he hath prepared for Is 64:4
princes which stood *b* the king Jer 36:21
in, and stood *b* the brasen altar Eze 9:2
he went in, and stood *b* the wheels Eze 10:6
also turned not from *b* them Eze 10:16
out, the wheels also were *b* them Eze 10:19
their wings, and the wheels *b* them Eze 11:22
thereof from *b* the great waters Eze 32:13
up, even for others *b* those Dan 11:4
for there is no saviour *b* me Hos 13:4
I am, and there is none *b* me Zeph 2:15
thousand men, *b* women and children Mt 14:21
thousand men, *b* women and children Mt 15:38
I have gained *b* them five talents Mt 25:20
gained two other talents *b* them Mt 25:22
for they said, He is *b* himself Mk 3:21
*b* all this, between us and you Lk 16:26
*b* all this, to day is the third Lk 24:21
voice, Paul, thou art *b* thyself Acts 26:24
For whether we be *b* ourselves 2Cor 5:13
*B* those things that are without, 2Cor 11:28
*b* this, giving all diligence, add 2Pet 1:5

**BESIDES**
unto Lot, Hast thou here any *b* Gen 19:12
*b* Jacob's sons' wives, all the Gen 46:26
*B* the cakes, he shall offer for Lev 7:13
not here a prophet of the LORD *b* 1Kin 22:7
not here a prophet of the LORD *b* 2Chr 18:6
other lords *b* thee have had Is 26:13
there were added *b* unto them many Jer 36:32
*b*, I know not whether I baptized 1Cor 1:16
unto me even thine own self *b* Philem 19

**BESIEGE**
thee, then thou shalt *b* it Deut 20:12
When thou shalt *b* a city a long Deut 20:19
he shall *b* thee in all thy gates, Deut 28:52
he shall *b* thee in all thy gates Deut 28:52
to Keilah, to *b* David and his men 1Sa 23:8
if their enemy *b* them in the land 1Kin 8:37
city, and his servants did *b* it 2Kin 24:11
if their enemies *b* them in the 2Chr 6:28
*b*, O Media Is 21:2
which *b* you without the walls, and Jer 21:4
to the Chaldeans that *b* you Jer 21:9

**BESIEGED**
children of Ammon, and *b* Rabbah 2Sa 11:1
*b* him in Abel of Beth-maachah, and 2Sa 20:15
Israel with him, and they *b* Tirzah 1Kin 16:17
*b* Samaria, and warred against it 1Kin 20:1
host, and went up, and *b* Samaria 2Kin 6:24
and, behold, they *b* it, until an 2Kin 6:25
and they *b* Ahaz, but could not 2Kin 16:5
to Samaria, and *b* it three years 2Kin 17:5
came up against Samaria, and *b* it 2Kin 18:9
up all the rivers of *b* places 2Kin 19:24
Jerusalem, and the city was *b* 2Kin 24:10
the city was *b* unto the eleventh 2Kin 25:2
of Ammon, and came and *b* Rabbah 1Chr 20:1
*b* it, and built great bulwarks Eccl 9:14
garden of cucumbers, as a *b* city Is 1:8
up all the rivers of the *b* places Is 37:25
of Babylon's army *b* Jerusalem Jer 32:2
when the Chaldeans that *b* Jer 37:5
against Jerusalem, and they *b* it Jer 39:1
So the city was *b* unto the Jer 52:5
face against it, and it shall be *b* Eze 4:3
is *b* shall die by the famine Eze 6:12
Babylon unto Jerusalem, and *b* it Dan 1:1

**BESODEIAH** (*bes-o-di'-ah*) *A repairer of Jerusalem's walls.*
Paseah, and Meshullam the son of *B* Neh 3:6

**BESOM**
it with the *b* of destruction Is 14:23

**BESOR** (*be'-sor*) *A brook in southern Judah.*
with him, and came to the brook *B* 1Sa 30:9
could not go over the brook *B* 1Sa 30:10
made also to abide at the brook *B* 1Sa 30:21

**BESOUGHT**
anguish of his soul, when he *b* us Gen 42:21
Moses *b* the LORD his God, and said Ex 32:11
I *b* the LORD at that time, saying Deut 3:23
David therefore *b* God for the 2Sa 12:16
And the man of God *b* the LORD 1Kin 13:6
*b* him, and said unto him, O man of 2Kin 1:13
And Jehoahaz *b* the LORD, and the 2Kin 13:4
he *b* the LORD his God, and humbled 2Chr 33:12
we fasted and *b* our God for this Ezr 8:23
*b* him with tears to put away the Est 8:3
*b* the LORD, and the LORD repented Jer 26:19
So the devils *b* him, saying, If Mt 8:31
they *b* him that he would depart Mt 8:34
*b* him that they might only touch Mt 14:36
*b* him, saying, Send her away Mt 15:23
*b* him, saying, Have patience with Mt 18:29
he *b* him much that he would not Mk 5:10
And all the devils *b* him, saying, Mk 5:12
*b* him greatly, saying, My little Mk 5:23
*b* him that they might touch if it Mk 6:56
she *b* him that he would cast Mk 7:26
unto him, and *b* him to touch him Mk 8:22
and they *b* him for her Lk 4:38
*b* him, saying, Lord, if thou wilt Lk 5:12
they *b* him instantly, saying, Lk 7:4
they *b* him that he would not Lk 8:31
they *b* him that he would suffer Lk 8:32
about *b* him to depart from them Lk 8:37
*b* him that he might be with him Lk 8:38
*b* him that he would come into his Lk 8:41
I *b* thy disciples to cast him out Lk 9:40
a certain Pharisee *b* him to dine Lk 11:37
they *b* him that he would tarry Jn 4:40
*b* him that he would come down, and Jn 4:47
*b* Pilate that their legs might Jn 19:31
*b* Pilate that he might take away Jn 19:38
the Gentiles *b* that these words Acts 13:42
and her household, she *b* us Acts 16:15
*b* them, and brought them out, and Acts 16:39
*b* him not to go up to Jerusalem Acts 21:12
him against Paul, and *b* him, Acts 25:2
Paul *b* them all to take meat, Acts 27:33
this thing I *b* the Lord thrice 2Cor 12:8
As I *b* thee to abide still at 1Ti 1:3

**BEST**
take of the *b* fruits in the land Gen 43:11
in the *b* of the land make thy Gen 47:6
in the *b* of the land, in the land Gen 47:11
of the *b* of his own field Ex 22:5
of the *b* of his own vineyard, Ex 22:5
All the *b* of the oil Num 18:12
all the *b* of the wine, and of the Num 18:12
of the LORD, of all the *b* thereof Num 18:29
have heaved the *b* thereof from it Num 18:30
have heaved from it the *b* of it Num 18:32
them marry to whom they think *b* Num 36:6
thy gates, where it liketh him *b* Deut 23:16
oliveyards, even the *b* of them 1Sa 8:14
the *b* of the sheep, and of the 1Sa 15:9
people spared the *b* of the sheep 1Sa 15:15
What seemeth you *b* I will do 2Sa 18:4
and overlaid it with the *b* gold 1Kin 10:18
Look even out the *b* and meetest of 2Kin 10:3
her maids unto the *b* place of the Est 2:9
verily every man at his *b* state Ps 39:5
like the *b* wine for my beloved Song 7:9
*b* of Lebanon, all that drink Eze 31:16
The *b* of them is as a brier Mic 7:4
servants, Bring forth the *b* robe Lk 15:22
But covet earnestly the *b* gifts 1Cor 12:31

**BESTEAD**
shall pass through it, hardly *b* Is 8:21

**BESTIR**
that then thou shalt *b* thyself 2Sa 5:24

**BESTOW**
that he may *b* upon you a blessing Ex 32:29
thou shalt *b* that money for Deut 14:26
the LORD did they *b* upon Baalim 2Chr 24:7
thou shalt have occasion to *b* Ezr 7:20
*b* it out of the king's treasure Ezr 7:20
have no room where to *b* my fruits Lk 12:17
there will I *b* all my fruits and Lk 12:18
upon these we *b* more abundant 1Cor 12:23
though I *b* all my goods to feed 1Cor 13:3

**BESTOWED**
whom he *b* in the cities for 1Kin 10:26
hand, and *b* them in the house 2Kin 5:24
the money to be *b* on workmen 2Kin 12:15
*b* upon him such royal majesty as 1Chr 29:25
whom he *b* in the chariot cities, 2Chr 9:25
to all that the LORD hath *b* on us Is 63:7
which he hath *b* on them according Is 63:7
reap that whereon ye *b* no labour Jn 4:38
Mary, who *b* much labour on us Rom 16:6
his grace which was *b* upon me was 1Cor 15:10
that for the gift *b* upon us by 2Cor 1:11
*b* on the churches of Macedonia 2Cor 8:1
lest I have *b* upon you labour in Gal 4:11
of love the Father hath *b* upon us 1Jn 3:1

**BETAH** (*be'-tah*) *A city of Hadadezer.*
And from *B*, and from Berothai, 2Sa 8:8

**BETEN** (*be'-ten*) *A city in Asher.*
border was Helkath, and Hali, and *B*. Josh 19:25

**BETHABARA** (*beth-ab'-ar-ah*) See BETHBARAH. *A place east of the Jordan River.*
were done in *B* beyond Jordan Jn 1:28

**BETH ACACIA** See BETH-SHITTAH.

**BETH-ANATH** (*beth'-a-nath*) *A city in Naphtali.*
Iron, and Migdal-el, Horem, and *B* Josh 19:38
nor the inhabitants of *B* Judg 1:33
of *B* became tributaries unto them Judg 1:33

**BETH-ANOTH** (*beth'-a-noth*) *A city in Judah.*
And Maarath, and *B*, and Eltekon Josh 15:59

**BETHANY** (*beth'-a-ny*) *A village near Jerusalem.*
and went out of the city into *B* Mt 21:17
Now when Jesus was in *B*, in the Mt 26:6
to Jerusalem, unto Bethphage and *B* Mk 11:1
went out unto *B* with the twelve Mk 11:11
when they were come from *B* Mk 11:12
being in *B* in the house of Simon Mk 14:3
was come nigh to Bethphage and *B* Lk 19:29
And he led them out as far as to *B* Lk 24:50
man was sick, named Lazarus, of *B* Jn 11:1
Now *B* was nigh unto Jerusalem, Jn 11:18
before the passover came to *B* Jn 12:1

**BETH APHRAH** See APHRAH.

**BETH-ARABAH** (*beth-ar'-ab-ah*) *A city of the Arabah.*
and passed along by the north of *B* Josh 15:6
In the wilderness, *B*, Middin, and Josh 15:61
And *B*, and Zemaraim, and Beth-el, Josh 18:22

**BETH-ARAM** (*beth'-a-ram*) *A city in Gad.*
And in the valley, *B*, and Josh 13:27

**BETH-ARBEL** (*beth-ar'-bel*) *A city destroyed by the Assyrians.*
as Shalman spoiled *B* in the day Hos 10:14

**BETH ASHBEA** See ASHBEA.

**BETH-AVEN** (*beth-a'-ven*) *A town in Benjamin.*
Jericho to Ai, which is beside *B* Josh 7:2
were at the wilderness of *B* Josh 18:12
in Michmash, eastward from *B* 1Sa 13:5
and the battle passed over unto *B* 1Sa 14:23
Gilgal, neither go ye up to *B* Hos 4:15
cry aloud at *B*, after thee, O Hos 5:8
fear because of the calves of *B* Hos 10:5

**BETH-AZMAVETH** (*beth-az'-maveth*) See AZMAVETH. *A village in Judah.*
The men of *B*, forty and two Neh 7:28

**BETH-BAAL-MEON** (*beth-ba'-al-me'-on*) *A Moabite town.*
Dibon, and Bamoth-baal, and *B* Josh 13:17

**BETH-BARAH** (*beth-ba'-rah*) See BETHABARA. *A place in Gad.*
before them the waters unto *B* Judg 7:24
and took the waters unto *B* Judg 7:24

**BETH-BIREI** (*beth-bir-e-i*) See BETH-LEBAOTH. *A town in Simeon.*
and Hazar-susim, and at *B*, and at 1Chr 4:31

**BETH BIRI** See BETH-BIREI.

**BETH-CAR** (*beth'-car*) *A Philistine stronghold in Judah.*
them, until they came under *B* 1Sa 7:11

**BETH-DAGON** (*beth-da'-gon*)
*1. A town in Judah.*
And Gederoth, *B*, and Naamah, and Josh 15:41
*2. A town in Asher.*
turneth toward the sunrising to *B* Josh 19:27

**BETH-DIBLATHAIM** (*beth-dib-lath-a'-im*) *A Moabite town.*
Dibon, and upon Nebo, and upon *B* Jer 48:22

**BETH-EL**
unto a mountain on the east of *B* Gen 12:8
having *B* on the west, and Hai on Gen 12:8
journeys from the south even to *B* Gen 13:3
been at the beginning, between *B* Gen 13:3
called the name of that place *B* Gen 28:19
I am the God of *B*, where thou Gen 31:13
unto Jacob, Arise, go up to *B* Gen 35:1
And let us arise, and go up to *B* Gen 35:3
in the land of Canaan, that is, *B* Gen 35:6
was buried beneath *B* under an oak Gen 35:8
place where God spake with him, *B* Gen 35:15

And they journeyed from *B*................. Gen 35:16
Beth-aven, on the east side of *B*.............. Josh 7:2
lie in ambush, and abode between *B*...... Josh 8:9
them to lie in ambush between *B*......... Josh 8:12
was not a man left in Ai or *B*............... Josh 8:17
the king of Ai, which is beside *B*......... Josh 12:9
the king of *B*, one.................................. Josh 12:16
from Jericho throughout mount *B*....... Josh 16:1
And goeth out from *B* to Luz.............. Josh 16:2
to the side of Luz, which is *B*............. Josh 18:13
and Zemaraim, and *B*............................ Josh 18:22
they also went up against *B*................. Judg 1:22
house of Joseph sent to descry *B*........... Judg 1:23
Ramah and *B* in mount Ephraim............. Judg 4:5
which is on the north side of *B*.......... Judg 21:19
that goeth up from *B* to Shechem ...... Judg 21:19
from year to year in circuit to *B*............ 1Sa 7:16
three men going up to God to *B*............ 1Sa 10:3
Saul in Michmash and in mount *B*.......... 1Sa 13:2
To them which were in *B*, and to.......... 1Sa 30:27
And he set the one in *B*, and the........ 1Kin 12:29
So did he in *B*, sacrificing unto.......... 1Kin 12:32
he placed in *B* the priests of the.......... 1Kin 12:32
the altar which he had made in *B*....... 1Kin 12:33
by the word of the LORD unto *B*............. 1Kin 13:1
had cried against the altar in *B*............ 1Kin 13:4
not by the way that he came to *B*...... 1Kin 13:10
there dwelt an old prophet in *B*.......... 1Kin 13:11
man of God had done that day in *B*.. 1Kin 13:11
the LORD against the altar in *B*........... 1Kin 13:32
for the LORD hath sent me to *B*............. 2Kin 2:2
So they went down to *B*.......................... 2Kin 2:2
were at *B* came forth to Elisha............... 2Kin 2:3
And he went up from thence unto *B*... 2Kin 2:23
the golden calves that were in *B*......... 2Kin 10:29
from Samaria came and dwelt in *B*.... 2Kin 17:28
carried the ashes of them unto *B*.......... 2Kin 23:4
Moreover the altar that was at *B*....... 2Kin 23:15
hast done against the altar of *B*......... 2Kin 23:17
the acts that he had done in *B*............. 2Kin 23:19
and habitations were, *B* and the.......... 1Chr 7:28
*B* with the towns thereof, and........... 2Chr 13:19
The men of *B* and Ai, two hundred........ Ezr 2:28
The men of *B* and Ai, an hundred.......... Neh 7:32
dwelt at Michmash, and Aija, and *B*... Neh 11:31
was ashamed of *B* their confidence....... Jer 48:13
So shall *B* do unto you because of ...... Hos 10:15
he found him in *B*, and there he.......... Hos 12:4
I will also visit the altars of *B*............ Amos 3:14
Come to *B*, and transgress..................... Amos 4:4
But seek not *B*, nor enter into............... Amos 5:5
and *B* shall come to nought.................... Amos 5:5
there be none to quench it in *B*............ Amos 5:6
Then Amaziah the priest of *B* sent..... Amos 7:10
prophesy not again any more at *B*..... Amos 7:13

**BETH-ELITE** (*beth'-el-ite*) *A native of Bethel.*
days did Hiel the *B* build Jericho........ 1Kin 16:34

**BETH-EMEK** (*beth-e'-mek*) *A town in Asher.*
toward the north side of *B*.................. Josh 19:27

**BETHER** (*be'-thur*) *A district in the Jordan valley.*
hart upon the mountains of *B*............. Song 2:17

**BETHESDA** (*beth-ez'-dah*) *A pool in Jerusalem.*
is called in the Hebrew tongue *B*................ Jn 5:2

**BETH-EZEL** (*beth-e'-zel*) *A city in Judah.*
not forth in the mourning of *B*............... Mic 1:11

**BETH-GADER** (*beth-ga'-der*) See GEDER. *A descendant of Caleb.*
Hareph the father of *B*.......................... 1Chr 2:51

**BETH-GAMUL** (*beth-ga'-mul*) *A Moabite town.*
And upon Kiriathaim, and upon *B*........ Jer 48:23

**BETH-HACCEREM** (*beth-hak'-se-rem*) *A town in Judah.*
of Rechab, the ruler of part of *B*........... Neh 3:14
and set up a sign of fire in *B*...................... Jer 6:1

**BETH HAKKEREM** See BETH-HACCEREM.

**BETH-HARAN** (*beth-ha'-ran*) See ELON-BETH-HARAN. *A city in Gad.*
And Beth-nimrah, and *B*, fenced........ Num 32:36

**BETH-HOGLA** (*beth-hog'-lah*) See BETH-HOGLAH. *A city in Benjamin.*
And the border went up to *B*................. Josh 15:6

**BETH HOGLAH** See BETH-HOGLA.

**BETH-HOGLAH** (*beth-hog'-lah*) See BETH-HOGLAH. *Same as Beth-hogla.*
along to the side of *B* northward........ Josh 18:19
their families were Jericho, and *B*....... Josh 18:21

**BETH-HORON** (*beth-ho'-ron*) *Two cities in Ephraim, near Benjamin.*
along the way that goeth up to *B*....... Josh 10:10
and were in the going down to *B*....... Josh 10:11
unto the coast of *B* the nether............ Josh 16:3
Ataroth-addar, unto *B* the upper.......... Josh 16:5
on the south side of the nether *B*....... Josh 18:13
that lieth before *B* southward............. Josh 18:14
suburbs, and *B* with her suburbs........ Josh 21:22
company turned the way to *B*............... 1Sa 13:18
built Gezer, and *B* the nether,............. 1Kin 9:17
suburbs, and *B* with her suburbs,......... 1Chr 6:68
who built *B* the nether, and the........... 1Chr 7:24
Also he built *B* the upper......................... 2Chr 8:5
*B* the nether, fenced cities, with............ 2Chr 8:5
Judah, from Samaria even unto *B*..... 2Chr 25:13

**BETHINK**
Yet if they shall *b* themselves in.......... 1Kin 8:47
Yet if they *b* themselves in the............. 2Chr 6:37

**BETH JESHIMOTH** See JESIMOTH.

**BETH-JESHIMOTH** (*beth-jesh'-im-oth*) See BETH-JESIMOTH. *Same as Beth-jesimoth.*
sea on the east, the way to *B*................ Josh 12:3
and Ashdoth-pisgah, and *B*,................ Josh 13:20
the glory of the country, *B*.................... Eze 25:9

**BETH-JESIMOTH** (*beth-jes'-im-oth*) See BETH-JESHIMOTH. *A Moabite city.*
from *B* even unto Abel-shittim in...... Num 33:49

**BETH-LE-APHRAH** See APHRAH.

**BETH-LEBAOTH** (*beth-leb'-a-oth*) See BETH-BISEI. *A town in Simeon.*
And *B*, and Sharuhen.............................. Josh 19:6

**BETH-LEHEM** (*beth'-le-hem*) See BETH-LEHEMITE, BETH-LEHEM-JUDAH.
*1. A city in Judah.*
in the way to Ephrath, which is *B*...... Gen 35:19
the same is *B*............................................. Gen 48:7
two went until they came to *B*.............. Ruth 1:19
to pass, when they were come to *B*.... Ruth 1:19
they came to *B* in the beginning........... Ruth 1:22
And, behold, Boaz came from *B*............ Ruth 2:4
in Ephratah, and be famous in *B*......... Ruth 4:11
the LORD spake, and came to *B*............. 1Sa 16:4
to feed his father's sheep at *B*.............. 1Sa 17:15
that he might run to *B* his city............ 1Sa 20:6
asked leave of me to go to *B*................ 1Sa 20:28
of his father, which was in *B*................. 2Sa 2:32
of the Philistines was then in *B*........ 2Sa 23:14
of the water of the well of *B*............. 2Sa 23:15
drew water out of the well of *B*......... 2Sa 23:16
Elhanan the son of Dodo of *B*............ 2Sa 23:24
garrison was then at *B*......................... 1Chr 11:16
of the water of the well of *B*............ 1Chr 11:17
drew water out of the well of *B*........ 1Chr 11:18
Elhanan the son of Dodo of *B*........... 1Chr 11:26
He built even *B*, and Etam, and........... 2Chr 11:6
The children of *B*, an hundred.................. Ezr 2:21
The men of *B* and Netophah, an............ Neh 7:26
*B* Ephratah, though thou be little........... Mic 5:2
*2. A town in Zebulun.*
and Shimron, and Idalah, and *B*........ Josh 19:15
*3. A town in Ephraim.*
him Ibzan of *B* judged Israel.................. Judg 12:8
died Ibzan, and was buried at *B*.......... Judg 12:10
*4. A descendant of Caleb.*
Salma the father of *B*, Hareph the....... 1Chr 2:51
*B*, and the Netophathites, Ataroth,...... 1Chr 2:54
of Ephratah, the father of *B*.................... 1Chr 4:4

**BETHLEHEM** *A town in Judea.*
of Chimham, which is by *B*..................... Jer 41:17
Now when Jesus was born in *B* of............ Mt 2:1
said unto him, In *B* of Judaea.................. Mt 2:5
And thou *B*, in the land of Juda,............... Mt 2:6
And he sent them to *B*, and said, Go........ Mt 2:8
all the children that were in *B*................ Mt 2:16
city of David, which is called *B*................. Lk 2:4
Let us now go even unto *B*...................... Lk 2:15
of David, and out of the town of *B*.......... Jn 7:42

**BETH-LEHEMITE** (*beth'-le-hem-ite*) *A native of Bethlehem.*
I will send thee to Jesse the *B*............... 1Sa 16:1
I have seen a son of Jesse the *B*........... 1Sa 16:18
son of thy servant Jesse the *B*............. 1Sa 17:58
the son of Jaare-oregim, a *B*................ 2Sa 21:19

**BETH-LEHEM-JUDAH** (*beth'-le-hem-ju'-dah*) *Same as Beth-lehem 1.*
out of *B* of the family of Judah............. Judg 17:7
departed out of the city from *B*............ Judg 17:8
said unto him, I am a Levite of *B*......... Judg 17:9
took to him a concubine out of *B*........ Judg 19:1
him unto her father's house to *B*......... Judg 19:2
We are passing from *B* toward the.... Judg 19:18
and I went to *B*, but I am now............ Judg 19:18
a certain man of *B* went to...................... Ruth 1:1
and Chilion, Ephrathites of *B*.................. Ruth 1:2
the son of that Ephrathite of *B*............ 1Sa 17:12

**BETH MAACAH**

**BETH-MAACHAH** (*beth-ma'-a-kah*) See ABEL-BETH-MAACHAH. *A city in Manasseh.*
of Israel unto Abel, and to *B*............... 2Sa 20:14
came and besieged him in Abel of *B*.... 2Sa 20:15

**BETH-MARCABOTH** (*beth-mar'-cab-oth*) *A city in Judah.*
And Ziklag, and *B*, and Hazar-susah, .. Josh 19:5
And at *B*, and Hazar-susim, and at........ 1Chr 4:31

**BETH-MEON** (*beth-me'-on*) See BETH-BAAL-MEON. *A Moabite city.*
and upon Beth-gamul, and upon *B*....... Jer 48:23

**BETH-NIMRAH** (*beth-nim'-rah*) See NIMRAH. *A city in Gad.*
And *B*, and Beth-haran, fenced........... Num 32:36
And in the valley, Beth-aram, and *B*.. Josh 13:27

**BETH OPHRAH** See APHRAH.

**BETH-PALET** (*beth-pa'-let*) See BETH-PELET. *A town in Judah.*
and Heshmon, and *B*............................ Josh 15:27

**BETH-PAZZEZ** (*beth-paz'-zez*) *A town in Issachar.*
and En-haddah, and *B*......................... Josh 19:21

**BETH PELET** See BETH-PALET.

**BETH-PEOR** (*beth-pe'-or*) *A Moabite city.*
in the valley over against *B*.................. Deut 3:29
in the valley over against *B*.................. Deut 4:46
the land of Moab, over against *B*......... Deut 34:6
And *B*, and Ashdoth-pisgah, and.......... Josh 13:20

**BETHPHAGE** (*beth'-fa-je*) *A village near Jerusalem.*
unto Jerusalem, and were come to *B*...... Mt 21:1
came nigh to Jerusalem, unto *B*............ Mk 11:1
pass, when he was come nigh to *B*........ Lk 19:29

**BETH-PHELET** (*beth'-fe-let*) See BETH-PALET. *A town in Judah.*
at Jeshua, and at Moladah, and at *B*.. Neh 11:26

**BETH-RAPHA** (*beth'-ra-fah*) *Son of Eshton.*
And Eshton begat *B*, and Paseah, and 1Chr 4:12

**BETH-REHOB** (*beth'-re-hob*) *A place in northern Canaan.*
was in the valley that lieth by *B*........ Judg 18:28
sent and hired the Syrians of *B*............. 2Sa 10:6

**BETHSAIDA** (*beth-sa'-dah*)
*1. A city in Galilee.*
woe unto thee, *B*.......................................... Mt 11:21
to the other side before unto *B*............... Mk 6:45
woe unto thee, *B*......................................... Lk 10:13
Now Philip was of *B*, the city of.............. Jn 1:44
Philip, which was of *B* of Galilee........... Jn 12:21
*2. A place east of Lake Gennesareth.*
And he cometh to *B*................................. Mk 8:22
belonging to the city called *B*.................. Lk 9:10

**BETH SHAN** See BETH-SHEAN.

**BETH-SHAN** (*beth'-shan*) See BETH-SHEAN. *A city in Manasseh.*
his body to the wall of *B*....................... 1Sa 31:10
of his sons from the wall of *B*.............. 1Sa 31:12
stolen them from the street of *B*.......... 2Sa 21:12

**BETH-SHEAN** (*beth-she'-an*) See BETH-SHAN. *Same as Beth-shan.*
had in Issachar and in Asher *B*........... Josh 17:11
of iron, both they who are of *B*............ Josh 17:16
drive out the inhabitants of *B*.............. Judg 1:27
Taanach and Megiddo, and all *B*.......... 1Kin 4:12
from *B* to Abel-meholah, even unto.... 1Kin 4:12
of the children of Manasseh, *B*............ 1Chr 7:29

**BETH SHEMESH** See SHEMESH.

**BETH-SHEMESH** (*beth'-she-mesh*) See BETH-SHEMITE.
*1. A town in Judah.*
the north side, and went down to *B*... Josh 15:10
suburbs, and *B* with her suburbs........ Josh 21:16
by the way of his own coast to *B*............ 1Sa 6:9
the straight way to the way of *B*........... 1Sa 6:12
after them unto the border of *B*........... 1Sa 6:12
they of *B* were reaping their................... 1Sa 6:13
the men of *B* offered burnt..................... 1Sa 6:15
And he smote the men of *B*, because.... 1Sa 6:19
And the men of *B* said, Who is able...... 1Sa 6:20
in Makaz, and in Shaalbim, and *B*........ 1Kin 4:9
one another in the face at *B*............... 2Kin 14:11
Jehoash the son of Ahaziah, at *B*....... 2Kin 14:13
suburbs, and *B* with her suburbs.......... 1Chr 6:59
he and Amaziah king of Judah, at *B*. 2Chr 25:21
Joash, the son of Jehoahaz, at *B*........ 2Chr 25:23
south of Judah, and had taken *B*....... 2Chr 28:18
*2. A city in Issachar.*
to Tabor, and Shahazimah, and *B*...... Josh 19:22
*3. A city in Naphtali.*
Horem, and Beth-anath, and *B*............ Josh 19:38
drive out the inhabitants of *B*............... Judg 1:33
nevertheless the inhabitants of *B*......... Judg 1:33
*4. A temple in Egypt.*
shall break also the images of *B*........... Jer 43:13

**BETH-SHEMITE** (*beth'-shem-ite*) *An inhabitant of Beth-shemesh.*
into the field of Joshua, a *B*................... 1Sa 6:14
day in the field of Joshua, the *B*........... 1Sa 6:18

**BETH-SHITTAH** (*beth-shit'-tah*) *A place in the Jordan valley.*
and the host fled to *B* in Zererath....... Judg 7:22

**BETH-TAPPUAH** (*beth-tap'-pu-ah*) *A city in Judah.*
And Janum, and *B*, and Aphekah,...... Josh 15:53

**BETHUEL** (*beth-u'-el*) See BETHUL.
*1. Son of Nahor.*
and Pildash, and Jidlaph, and *B*........... Gen 22:22
And *B* begat Rebekah............................. Gen 22:23
came out, who was born to *B*............... Gen 24:15
daughter of *B* the son of Milcah........... Gen 24:24
And she said, The daughter of *B*......... Gen 24:47
*B* answered and said, The thing............ Gen 24:50
the daughter of *B* the Syrian of........... Gen 25:20
to the house of *B* thy mother's.............. Gen 28:2
son of *B* the Syrian, the brother........... Gen 28:5

*2. A town in Simeon.*
And at *B*, and at Hormah, and at......... 1Chr 4:30

**BETHUL** (*beth'-ul*) See BETHUEL. *A city in Simeon.*
And Eltolad, and *B*, and Hormah,......... Josh 19:4

**BETHZATHA** See BETHESDA.

**BETHZOR** See BETH-ZUR.

**BETH-ZUR** (*beth'-zur*)
*1. A town in Judah.*
Halhul, *B*, and Gedor,........................... Josh 15:58
And *B*, and Shoco, and Adullam, ......... 2Chr 11:7
the ruler of the half part of *B*............... Neh 3:16
*2. A descendant of Caleb.*
and Maon was the father of *B*............. 1Chr 2:45

**BETIMES**
they rose up *b* in the morning, and .... Gen 26:31
by his messengers, rising up *b*............ 2Chr 36:15
If thou wouldest seek unto God *b*........... Job 8:5
rising *b* for a prey..................................... Job 24:5
that loveth him chasteneth him *b*........ Prov 13:24

**BETONIM** (*bet'-o-nim*) *A town in Gad.*
unto Ramath-mizpeh, and *B*................. Josh 13:26

**BETRAY**
be come to *b* me to mine enemies..... 1Chr 12:17
shall *b* one another, and shall.................. Mt 24:10
he sought opportunity to *b* him.............. Mt 26:16
you, that one of you shall *b* me............. Mt 26:21
in the dish, the same shall *b* me............. Mt 26:23
he is at hand that doth *b* me................. Mt 26:46
shall *b* the brother to death................... Mk 13:12
chief priests, to *b* him unto them........... Mk 14:10
how he might conveniently *b* him........... Mk 14:11
which eateth with me shall *b* me........... Mk 14:18
how he might *b* him unto them................ Lk 22:4
sought opportunity to *b* him unto.......... Lk 22:6
believed not, and who should *b* him........ Jn 6:64
for he it was that should *b* him............... Jn 6:71
Simon's son, which should *b* him ............. Jn 12:4
Iscariot, Simon's son, to *b* him................ Jn 13:2
For he knew who should *b* him................ Jn 13:11
you, that one of you shall *b* me.............. Jn 13:21

**BETRAYED**
and Judas Iscariot, who also *b* him......... Mt 10:4
shall be *b* into the hands of men ............ Mt 17:22
shall be *b* unto the chief priests............. Mt 20:18
Son of man is *b* to be crucified ................ Mt 26:2
man by whom the Son of man is *b*........ Mt 26:24
Then Judas, which *b* him, answered...... Mt 26:25
the Son of man is *b* into the................... Mt 26:45
Now he that *b* him gave them a............... Mt 26:48
that I have *b* the innocent blood............. Mt 27:4
Judas Iscariot, which also *b* him............ Mk 3:19
man by whom the Son of man is *b*...... Mk 14:21
the Son of man is *b* into the.................... Mk 14:41
he that *b* him had given them a............ Mk 14:44
ye shall be *b* both by parents, and...... Lk 21:16
woe unto that man by whom he is *b*.... Lk 22:22
And Judas also, which *b* him.................... Jn 18:2
And Judas also, which *b* him.................... Jn 18:5
in which he was *b* took bread............ 1Cor 11:23

**BETRAYERS**
of whom ye have been now the *b*........ Acts 7:52

**BETRAYEST**
*b* thou the Son of man with a kiss........ Lk 22:48

**BETRAYETH**
Then Judas, which had *b* him.................. Mt 27:3
lo, he that *b* me is at hand.................... Mk 14:42
the hand of him that *b* me is with.......... Lk 22:21
Lord, which is he that *b* thee.................. Jn 21:20

**BETROTH**
Thou shalt *b* a wife, and another....... Deut 28:30
I will *b* thee unto me for ever................ Hos 2:19
yea, I will *b* thee unto me in................... Hos 2:19
I will even *b* thee unto me in ................. Hos 2:20

**BETROTHED**
who hath *b* her to himself, then............... Ex 21:8
if he have *b* her unto his son, he............. Ex 21:9
a man entice a maid that is not *b*.......... Ex 22:16
*b* to an husband, and not at all............... Lev 19:20
man is there that hath *b* a wife............. Deut 20:7
is a virgin be *b* unto an husband ....... Deut 22:23
man find a *b* damsel in the field.......... Deut 22:25
the *b* damsel cried, and there was....... Deut 22:27
that is a virgin, which is not *b*............ Deut 22:28

**BETTER**
It is *b* that I give her to thee,.............. Gen 29:19
For it had been *b* for us to serve........... Ex 14:12
were it not *b* for us to return............... Num 14:3
of the grapes of Ephraim *b* than ........... Judg 8:2
of Shechem, Whether is *b* for you .......... Judg 9:2
now art thou any thing *b* than............ Judg 11:25
is it *b* for thee to be a priest.............. Judg 18:19
which is *b* to thee than seven................. Ruth 4:15
am not I *b* to thee than ten sons.............. 1Sa 1:8
to obey is *b* than sacrifice, and............. 1Sa 15:22
of thine, that is *b* than thou ................. 1Sa 15:28
there is nothing *b* for me than................ 1Sa 27:1
of Hushai the Archite is *b* than.......... 2Sa 17:14
therefore now it is *b* that thou.................. 2Sa 18:3
name of Solomon *b* than thy name...... 1Kin 1:47
*b* than he, and slew them with the...... 1Kin 2:32
for I am not *b* than my fathers........... 1Kin 19:4
thee for it a *b* vineyard than it ........... 1Kin 21:2
*b* than all the waters of Israel............... 2Kin 5:12
which were *b* than thyself.................. 2Chr 21:13
unto another that is *b* than she................ Est 1:19
that a righteous man hath is *b*................. Ps 37:16
thy lovingkindness is *b* than life............... Ps 63:3
*b* than an ox or bullock that hath............ Ps 69:31
thy courts is *b* than a thousand............. Ps 84:10
It is *b* to trust in the LORD than .............. Ps 118:8
It is *b* to trust in the LORD than .............. Ps 118:9
The law of thy mouth is *b* unto me..... Ps 119:72
For the merchandise of it is *b*............... Prov 3:14
For wisdom is *b* than rubies.................. Prov 8:11
My fruit is *b* than gold, yea.................. Prov 8:19
is *b* than he that honoureth.................. Prov 12:9
*B* is little with the fear of the............. Prov 15:16
*B* is a dinner of herbs where love........ Prov 15:17
*B* is a little with righteousness.............. Prov 16:8
How much *b* is it to get wisdom .......... Prov 16:16
*B* it is to be of an humble spirit .......... Prov 16:19
to anger is *b* than the mighty ............. Prov 16:32
*B* is a dry morsel, and quietness.......... Prov 17:1
*B* is the poor that walketh in his............ Prov 19:1
and a poor man is *b* than a liar ........... Prov 19:22
It is *b* to dwell in a corner of.............. Prov 21:9
It is *b* to dwell in the......................... Prov 21:19
For *b* it is that it be said unto.............. Prov 25:7
It is *b* to dwell in the corner of............ Prov 25:24
Open rebuke is *b* than secret love........ Prov 27:5
for *b* is a neighbour that is near......... Prov 27:10
*B* is the poor that walketh in his.......... Prov 28:6
There is nothing *b* for a man ................ Eccl 2:24
perceive that there is nothing *b* ........... Eccl 3:22
*b* is he than both they, which ................. Eccl 4:3
*B* is an handful with quietness,............... Eccl 4:6
Two are *b* than one .................................. Eccl 4:9
*B* is a poor and a wise child than .......... Eccl 4:13
*B* is it that thou shouldest not .............. Eccl 5:5
an untimely birth is *b* than he .............. Eccl 6:3
*B* is the sight of the eyes than .............. Eccl 6:9
vanity, what is man the *b*...................... Eccl 6:11
A good name is *b* than precious.............. Eccl 7:1
It is *b* to go to the house of.................... Eccl 7:2
Sorrow is *b* than laughter ........................ Eccl 7:3
countenance the heart is made *b*............. Eccl 7:3
It is *b* to hear the rebuke of the............. Eccl 7:5
*B* is the end of a thing than the ............. Eccl 7:8
is *b* than the proud in spirit.................... Eccl 7:8
the former days were *b* than these ........ Eccl 7:10
man hath no *b* thing under the sun ...... Eccl 8:15
living dog is *b* than a dead lion .............. Eccl 9:4
Wisdom is *b* than strength...................... Eccl 9:16
Wisdom is *b* than weapons of war........ Eccl 9:18
and a babbler is no *b*........................... Eccl 10:11
for thy love is *b* than wine..................... Song 1:2
how much *b* is thy love than wine...... Song 4:10
a name *b* than of sons and of.................... Is 56:5
be slain with the sword are *b* ................... Lam 4:9
will do *b* unto you than at your ........... Eze 36:11
times *b* than all the magicians .............. Dan 1:20
for then was it *b* with me than .................. Hos 2:7
be they *b* than these kingdoms ............. Amos 6:2
for it is *b* for me to die than to............. Jonah 4:3
It is *b* for me to die than to.................. Jonah 4:8
Art thou *b* than populous No, that ........... Nah 3:8
Are ye not much *b* than they ................... Mt 6:26
much then is a man *b* than a sheep..... Mt 12:12
in me, it were *b* for him that a................ Mt 18:6
it is *b* for thee to enter into.................... Mt 18:8
it is *b* for thee to enter into.................... Mt 18:9
it is *b* for him that a millstone................ Mk 9:42
it is *b* for thee to enter into................... Mk 9:43
it is *b* for thee to enter halt................... Mk 9:45
it is *b* for thee to enter into................... Mk 9:47
for he saith, The old is *b* ...................... Lk 5:39
much more are ye *b* than the fowls ..... Lk 12:24
It were *b* for him that a.......................... Lk 17:2
are we *b* than they.................................. Rom 3:9
for it is *b* to marry than to burn........... 1Cor 7:9
her not in marriage doeth *b* .................. 1Cor 7:38
neither, if we eat, are we the *b*.............. 1Cor 8:8
for it were *b* for me to die, than........... 1Cor 9:15
ye come together not for the *b*............ 1Cor 11:17
which is far *b*........................................... Phil 1:23
esteem other *b* than themselves............... Phil 2:3
made so much *b* than the angels.............. Heb 1:4
we are persuaded *b* things of you........... Heb 6:9
the less is blessed of the *b*...................... Heb 7:7
the bringing in of a *b* hope did............. Heb 7:19
made a surety of a *b* testament ............ Heb 7:22
is the mediator of a *b* covenant .............. Heb 8:6
was established upon *b* promises.............. Heb 8:6
with *b* sacrifices than these.................... Heb 9:23
that ye have in heaven a *b*................... Heb 10:34
But now they desire a *b* country .......... Heb 11:16
might obtain a *b* resurrection ............. Heb 11:35
provided some *b* thing for us................ Heb 11:40
that speaketh *b* things than that......... Heb 12:24
For it is *b*, if the will of God................ 1Pet 3:17
For it had been *b* for them not to.......... 2Pet 2:21

**BETTERED**
that she had, and was nothing *b*............ Mk 5:26

**BETWEEN**
And I will put enmity *b* thee................ Gen 3:15
woman, and *b* thy seed and her seed ... Gen 3:15
of the covenant which I make *b* me..... Gen 9:12
be for a token of a covenant *b* me........ Gen 9:13
my covenant, which is *b* me................... Gen 9:15
the everlasting covenant *b* God.............. Gen 9:16
which I have established *b* me.............. Gen 9:17
And Resen *b* Nineveh and Calah......... Gen 10:12
the beginning, *b* Beth-el and Hai.......... Gen 13:3
there was a strife *b* the herdmen........... Gen 13:7
*b* my herdmen and thy herdmen ........... Gen 13:8
lamp that passed *b* those pieces........... Gen 15:17
the LORD judge *b* me and thee............... Gen 16:5
behold, it is *b* Kadesh and Bered ......... Gen 16:14
And I will make my covenant *b* me ..... Gen 17:2
I will establish my covenant *b* me ........ Gen 17:7
*b* me and you and thy seed after......... Gen 17:10
country, and dwelled *b* Kadesh.............. Gen 20:1
and let it be for a witness *b* me ........... Gen 31:44
said, This heap is a witness *b* me .......... Gen 31:48
for he said, The LORD watch *b* me...... Gen 31:49
brought them out from *b* his knees...... Gen 48:12
nor a lawgiver from *b* his feet.............. Gen 49:10
ass couching down *b* two burdens...... Gen 49:14
I will put a division *b* my people............... Ex 8:23
sever *b* the cattle of Israel ........................ Ex 9:4
put a difference *b* the Egyptians .............. Ex 11:7
and for a memorial *b* thine eyes.............. Ex 13:9
and for frontlets *b* thine eyes................ Ex 13:16
*b* Migdol and the sea, over against.......... Ex 14:2
it came *b* the camp of the...................... Ex 14:20
of Sin, which is *b* Elim and Sinai, ........... Ex 16:1
and I judge *b* one and another, and I... Ex 18:16
oath of the LORD be *b* them both.......... Ex 22:11
from *b* the two cherubims which........... Ex 25:22
divide unto you *b* the holy place........... Ex 26:33
bells of gold *b* them round about.......... Ex 28:33
and thou shalt put it *b* the.................... Ex 30:18
for it is a sign *b* me and you ................ Ex 31:13
It is a sign *b* me and the children ........ Ex 31:17
put the bells *b* the pomegranates.......... Ex 39:25
round about *b* the pomegranates............ Ex 39:25
thou shalt set the laver *b* the................... Ex 40:7
he set the laver *b* the tent of .................. Ex 40:30
that ye may put difference *b* holy....... Lev 10:10
and unholy, and *b* unclean and clean. Lev 10:10
make a difference *b* the unclean .......... Lev 11:47
*b* the beast that may be eaten and...... Lev 11:47
put difference *b* clean beasts............... Lev 20:25
and *b* unclean fowls and clean............. Lev 20:25
laws, which the LORD made *b* him....... Lev 26:46
from *b* the two cherubims .................... Num 7:89
the flesh was yet *b* their teeth............ Num 11:33
they bare it *b* two upon a staff........... Num 13:23
And he stood *b* the dead and the....... Num 16:48
of Moab, *b* Moab and the Amorites... Num 21:13
thereof be divided *b* many.................. Num 26:56
*b* a man and his wife, *b* the................ Num 30:16
*b* them that took the war upon.......... Num 31:27
battle, and *b* all the congregation...... Num 31:27
shall judge *b* the slayer and the ......... Num 35:24
*b* Paran, and Tophel, and Laban, and... Deut 1:1
Hear the causes *b* your brethren........... Deut 1:16
and judge righteously *b* every man..... Deut 1:16
that day had no knowledge *b* good..... Deut 1:39
(I stood *b* the LORD and you at ............ Deut 5:5
be as frontlets *b* thine eyes.................... Deut 6:8
may be as frontlets *b* your eyes ......... Deut 11:18
nor make any baldness *b* your eyes.... Deut 14:1
*b* blood and blood, *b* plea and............. Deut 17:8
*b* stroke and stroke, being matters...... Deut 17:8
*b* whom the controversy is, shall ....... Deut 19:17
If there be a controversy *b* men........... Deut 25:1
that cometh out from *b* her feet ....... Deut 28:57
and he shall dwell *b* his shoulders ..... Deut 33:12
Yet there shall be a space *b* you............ Josh 3:4
abode *b* Beth-el and Ai, on the.............. Josh 8:9
now there was a valley *b* them ............ Josh 8:11
them to lie in ambush *b* Beth-el............ Josh 8:12
forth *b* the children of Judah............ Josh 18:11
hath made Jordan a border *b* us........ Josh 22:25
But that it may be a witness *b* us....... Josh 22:27
but it is a witness *b* us and you .......... Josh 22:28
witness *b* us that the LORD is God ..... Josh 22:34
the LORD, he put darkness *b* you.......... Josh 24:7
the palm tree of Deborah *b* Ramah....... Judg 4:5
for there was peace *b* Jabin the............. Judg 4:17
sent an evil spirit *b* Abimelech............. Judg 9:23
The LORD be witness *b* us.................. Judg 11:10
this day *b* the children of Israel.......... Judg 11:27
times in the camp of Dan *b* Zorah..... Judg 13:25
in the midst *b* two tails....................... Judg 15:4
and they set him *b* the pillars ............ Judg 16:25
him up, and buried him *b* Zorah ......... Judg 16:31
sign *b* the men of Israel and the ......... Judg 20:38
which dwelleth *b* the cherubims................ 1Sa 4:4
took a stone, and set it *b* Mizpeh............ 1Sa 7:12
And there was peace *b* Israel................. 1Sa 7:14
*b* the passages, by which Jonathan......... 1Sa 14:4
And Saul said, Cast lots *b* me.............. 1Sa 14:42
to Judah, and pitched *b* Shochoh........... 1Sa 17:1
and there was a valley *b* them............... 1Sa 17:3
a target of brass *b* his shoulders........... 1Sa 17:6
liveth, there is but a step *b* me ............. 1Sa 20:3
of, behold, the LORD be *b* thee ............. 1Sa 20:23
LORD, saying, The LORD be *b* me ......... 1Sa 20:42
*b* my seed and thy seed for ever............. 1Sa 20:42
The LORD judge *b* me and thee, and.... 1Sa 24:12
therefore be judge, and judge *b* me..... 1Sa 24:15
a great space being *b* them................. 1Sa 26:13
was long war *b* the house of Saul............ 2Sa 3:1
there was war *b* the house of Saul........... 2Sa 3:6
that dwelleth *b* the cherubims ................. 2Sa 6:2
and he was taken up *b* the heaven ........... 2Sa 18:9
David sat *b* the two gates ................... 2Sa 18:24
and can I discern *b* good and evil ....... 2Sa 19:35
the LORD's oath that was *b* them........... 2Sa 21:7

*b* David and Jonathan the son of ... 2Sa 21:7
people, that I may discern *b* good ... 1Kin 3:9
and there was peace *b* Hiram ... 1Kin 5:12
and the borders were *b* the ledges ... 1Kin 7:28
that were *b* the ledges were lions ... 1Kin 7:29
in the clay ground *b* Succoth ... 1Kin 7:46
And there was war *b* Rehoboam ... 1Kin 14:30
And there was war *b* Rehoboam ... 1Kin 15:6
And there was war *b* Abijam ... 1Kin 15:7
was war *b* Asa and Baasha ... 1Kin 15:16
There is a league *b* me and thee, ... 1Kin 15:19
*b* my father and thy father ... 1Kin 15:19
was war *b* Asa and Baasha ... 1Kin 15:32
So they divided the land *b* them ... 1Kin 18:6
How long halt ye *b* two opinions ... 1Kin 18:21
and put his face *b* his knees ... 1Kin 18:42
three years without war *b* Syria ... 1Kin 22:1
smote the king of Israel *b* the ... 1Kin 22:34
and smote Jehoram *b* his arms ... 2Kin 9:24
made a covenant *b* the LORD ... 2Kin 11:17
*b* the king also and the people ... 2Kin 11:17
from *b* the altar and the house of ... 2Kin 16:14
which dwellest *b* the cherubims ... 2Kin 19:15
the way of the gate *b* two walls ... 2Kin 25:4
that dwelleth *b* the cherubims ... 1Chr 13:6
of the LORD stand *b* the earth ... 1Chr 21:16
in the clay ground *b* Succoth ... 2Chr 4:17
And there were wars *b* Rehoboam ... 2Chr 12:15
And there was war *b* Abijah ... 2Chr 13:2
There is a league *b* me and thee, ... 2Chr 16:3
as there was *b* my father ... 2Chr 16:3
smote the king of Israel *b* the ... 2Chr 18:33
*b* blood and blood, *b* law and ... 2Chr 19:10
made a covenant *b* him ... 2Chr 23:16
*b* all the people, and *b* the ... 2Chr 23:16
*b* the going up of the corner unto ... Neh 3:32
that no air can come *b* them ... Job 41:16
that dwellest *b* the cherubims ... Ps 80:1
he sitteth *b* the cherubims ... Ps 99:1
to cease, and parteth *b* the mighty ... Prov 18:18
Ye made also a ditch *b* the two ... Is 22:11
that dwellest *b* the cherubims ... Is 37:16
iniquities have separated *b* you ... Is 59:2
execute judgment *b* a man and his ... Jer 7:5
passed *b* the parts thereof, ... Jer 34:18
which passed *b* the parts of the ... Jer 34:19
a true and faithful witness *b* us ... Jer 42:5
way of the gate *b* the two walls ... Jer 52:7
overtook her *b* the straits ... Lam 1:3
set it for a wall of iron *b* thee ... Eze 4:3
spirit lifted me up *b* the earth ... Eze 8:3
*b* the porch and the altar, were ... Eze 8:16
Go in *b* the wheels, even under ... Eze 10:2
of fire from *b* the cherubims ... Eze 10:2
the wheels, from *b* the cherubims ... Eze 10:6
*b* the cherubims unto the fire ... Eze 10:7
the fire that was *b* the cherubims ... Eze 10:7
hath executed true judgment *b* man ... Eze 18:8
my sabbaths, to be a sign *b* me ... Eze 20:12
and they shall be a sign *b* me ... Eze 20:20
have put no difference *b* the holy ... Eze 22:26
shewed difference *b* the unclean ... Eze 22:26
Behold, I judge *b* cattle and ... Eze 34:17
*b* the rams and the he goats ... Eze 34:17
will judge *b* the fat cattle and ... Eze 34:20
fat cattle and *b* the lean cattle ... Eze 34:20
and I will judge *b* cattle and ... Eze 34:22
*b* the little chambers were five ... Eze 40:7
*b* the chambers was the wideness ... Eze 41:10
that a palm tree was *b* a cherub ... Eze 41:18
make a separation *b* the sanctuary ... Eze 42:20
by my posts, and the wall *b* me ... Eze 43:8
people the difference *b* the holy ... Eze 44:23
them to discern *b* the unclean ... Eze 44:23
which is *b* the border of Damascus ... Eze 47:16
*b* the border of Judah and the ... Eze 48:22
the mouth of it *b* the teeth of it ... Dan 7:5
had a notable horn *b* his eyes ... Dan 8:5
a man's voice *b* the banks of Ulai ... Dan 8:16
the great horn that is *b* his eyes ... Dan 8:21
*b* the seas in the glorious holy ... Dan 11:45
her adulteries from *b* her breasts ... Hos 2:2
weep *b* the porch and the altar, and ... Joel 2:17
cannot discern *b* their right hand ... Jonah 4:11
lifted up the ephah *b* the earth ... Zec 5:9
chariots out from *b* two mountains ... Zec 6:1
of peace shall be *b* them both ... Zec 6:13
his abominations from *b* his teeth ... Zec 9:7
break the brotherhood *b* Judah ... Zec 11:14
the LORD hath been witness *b* thee ... Mal 2:14
discern *b* the righteous and the ... Mal 3:18
*b* him that serveth God and him ... Mal 3:18
go and tell him his fault *b* thee ... Mt 18:15
whom ye slew *b* the temple ... Mt 23:35
which perished *b* the altar ... Lk 11:51
*b* us and you there is a great gulf ... Lk 16:26
they were at enmity *b* themselves ... Lk 23:12
*b* some of John's disciples ... Jn 3:25
Peter was sleeping *b* two soldiers ... Acts 12:6
And put no difference *b* us ... Acts 15:9
contention was so sharp *b* them ... Acts 15:39
a dissension *b* the Pharisees ... Acts 23:7
aside, they talked *b* themselves ... Acts 26:31
their own bodies *b* themselves ... Rom 1:24
there is no difference *b* the Jew ... Rom 10:12
be able to judge *b* his brethren ... 1Cor 6:5
There is difference also *b* a wife ... 1Cor 7:34
the middle wall of partition *b* us ... Eph 2:14
is one God, and one mediator *b* God ... 1Ti 2:5

### BETWIXT
be a token of the covenant *b* me ... Gen 17:11
what is that *b* me and thee ... Gen 23:15
now an oath *b* us, even *b* us ... Gen 26:28
set three days' journey *b* himself ... Gen 30:36
that they may judge *b* us both ... Gen 31:37
see, God is witness *b* me and thee ... Gen 31:50
pillar, which I have cast *b* me ... Gen 31:51
God of their father, judge *b* us ... Gen 31:53
before me, and put a space *b* drove ... Gen 32:16
Neither is there any daysman *b* us ... Job 9:33
shine by the cloud that cometh *b* ... Job 36:32
shall lie all night *b* my breasts ... Song 1:13
I pray you, *b* me and my vineyard ... Is 5:3
by the gate *b* the two walls ... Jer 39:4
For I am in a strait *b* two ... Phil 1:23

### BEULAH (*be-u'-lah*) *A name of restored Israel.*
called Hephzi-bah, and thy land *B* ... Is 62:4

### BEWAIL
*b* the burning which the LORD hath ... Lev 10:6
*b* her father and her mother a full ... Deut 21:13
*b* my virginity, I and my fellows ... Judg 11:37
Therefore I will *b* with the ... Is 16:9
that I shall *b* many which have ... 2Cor 12:21
deliciously with her, shall *b* her ... Rev 18:9

### BEWAILED
and *b* her virginity upon the ... Judg 11:38
And all wept, and *b* her ... Lk 8:52
people, and of women, which also *b* ... Lk 23:27

### BEWAILETH
that *b* herself, that spreadeth ... Jer 4:31

### BEWARE
*B* that thou bring not my son ... Gen 24:6
*B* of him, and obey his voice, ... Ex 23:21
Then *b* lest thou forget the LORD, ... Deut 6:12
*B* that thou forget not the LORD ... Deut 8:11
*B* that there be not a thought in ... Deut 15:9
Now therefore *b*, I pray thee, and ... Judg 13:4
I said unto the woman let her *b* ... Judg 13:13
*B* that none touch the young man ... 2Sa 18:12
*B* that thou pass not such a place ... 2Kin 6:9
*b* lest he take thee away with his ... Job 36:18
a scorner, and the simple will *b* ... Prov 19:25
*B* lest Hezekiah persuade you, ... Is 36:18
*B* of false prophets, which come ... Mt 7:15
But *b* of men ... Mt 10:17
*b* of the leaven of the Pharisees ... Mt 16:6
that ye should *b* of the leaven of ... Mt 16:11
them not *b* of the leaven of bread ... Mt 16:12
*b* of the leaven of the Pharisees, ... Mk 8:15
*B* of the scribes, which love to ... Mk 12:38
*B* ye of the leaven of the ... Lk 12:1
Take heed, and *b* of covetousness ... Lk 12:15
*B* of the scribes, which desire to ... Lk 20:46
*B* therefore, lest that come upon ... Acts 13:40
*B* of dogs, *b* of evil workers ... Phil 3:2
*b* of the concision ... Phil 3:2
*B* lest any man spoil you through ... Col 2:8
*b* lest ye also, being led away ... 2Pet 3:17

### BEWITCHED
*b* the people of Samaria, giving ... Acts 8:9
time he had *b* them with sorceries ... Acts 8:11
foolish Galatians, who hath *b* you ... Gal 3:1

### BEWRAY
*b* not him that wandereth ... Is 16:3

### BEWRAYETH
of his right hand, which *b* itself ... Prov 27:16
he heareth cursing, and *b* it not ... Prov 29:24
for thy speech *b* thee ... Mt 26:73

### BEYOND
spread his tent *b* the tower of ... Gen 35:21
of Atad, which is *b* Jordan ... Gen 50:10
Abel-mizraim, which is *b* Jordan ... Gen 50:11
or if it run *b* the time of her ... Lev 15:25
I cannot go *b* the word of the ... Num 22:18
I cannot go *b* the commandment of ... Num 24:13
your God hath given them *b* Jordan ... Deut 3:20
the good land that is *b* Jordan ... Deut 3:25
Neither is it *b* the sea, that ... Deut 30:13
the Amorites, that were *b* Jordan ... Josh 9:10
*b* Jordan eastward, even as Moses ... Josh 13:8
inheritance *b* Jordan on the east ... Josh 18:7
passed *b* the quarries, and escaped ... Judg 3:26
Gilead abode *b* Jordan ... Judg 5:17
Behold, the arrows are *b* thee ... 1Sa 20:22
lad ran, he shot an arrow *b* him ... 1Sa 20:36
and said, Is not the arrow *b* thee ... 1Sa 20:37
the Syrians that were *b* the river ... 2Sa 10:16
unto the place that is *b* Jokneam ... 1Kin 4:12
and shall scatter them *b* the river ... 1Kin 14:15
the Syrians that were *b* the river ... 1Chr 19:16
from *b* the sea on this side Syria ... 2Chr 20:2
and unto the rest *b* the river ... Ezr 4:17
over all countries *b* the river ... Ezr 4:20
Tatnai, governor *b* the river, ... Ezr 6:6
which are *b* the river, be ye far ... Ezr 6:6
even of the tribute *b* the river ... Ezr 6:8
treasurers which are *b* the river ... Ezr 7:21
the people that are *b* the river ... Ezr 7:25
me to the governors *b* the river ... Neh 2:7
came to the governors *b* the river ... Neh 2:9
from *b* the tower of the furnaces ... Neh 12:38
by them *b* the river, by the king ... Is 7:20
*b* Jordan, in Galilee of the ... Is 9:1
which is *b* the rivers of Ethiopia ... Is 18:1
cast forth *b* the gates of ... Jer 22:19
of the isles which are *b* the sea ... Jer 25:22
to go into captivity *b* Damascus ... Amos 5:27
From *b* the rivers of Ethiopia my ... Zeph 3:10
*b* Jordan, Galilee of the Gentiles ... Mt 4:15
and from Judaea, and from *b* Jordan ... Mt 4:25
the coasts of Judaea *b* Jordan ... Mt 19:1
and from Idumaea, and from *b* Jordan ... Mk 3:8
amazed in themselves *b* measure ... Mk 6:51
were *b* measure astonished, saying ... Mk 7:37
were done in Bethabara *b* Jordan ... Jn 1:28
he that was with thee *b* Jordan ... Jn 3:26
went away again *b* Jordan into the ... Jn 10:40
I will carry you away *b* Babylon ... Acts 7:43
*b* their power they were willing ... 2Cor 8:3
not ourselves *b* our measure ... 2Cor 10:14
the gospel in the regions *b* you ... 2Cor 10:16
how that *b* measure I persecuted ... Gal 1:13
That no man go *b* and defraud his ... 1Th 4:6

### BEZAI (*be'-zahee*)
*1. A family of exiles.*
The children of *B*, three hundred ... Ezr 2:17
The children of *B*, three hundred ... Neh 7:23
*2. A family who renewed the covenant.*
Hodijah, Hashum, *B*, ... Neh 10:18

### BEZALEEL (*be-zal'-e-el*)
*1. A craftsman.*
called by name *B* the son of Uri ... Ex 31:2
called by name *B* the son of Uri ... Ex 35:30
Then wrought *B* and Aholiab, and ... Ex 36:1
And Moses called *B* and Aholiab, and ... Ex 36:2
*B* made the ark of shittim wood ... Ex 37:1
*B* the son of Uri, the son of Hur, ... Ex 38:22
And Hur begat Uri, and Uri begat *B* ... 1Chr 2:20
that *B* the son of Uri, the son of ... 2Chr 1:5
*2. Married a foreign wife in exile.*
Benaiah, Maaseiah, Mattaniah, *B* ... Ezr 10:30

### BEZALEL See BEZALEEL.

### BEZEK (*be'-zek*) See ADONI-BEZEK. *A place in the Jordan valley.*
of them in *B* ten thousand men ... Judg 1:4
And they found Adoni-bezek in *B* ... Judg 1:5
And when he numbered them in *B* ... 1Sa 11:8

### BEZER (*be'-zer*)
*1. A city of refuge.*
*B* in the wilderness, in the plain ... Deut 4:43
they assigned *B* in the wilderness ... Josh 20:8
*B* with her suburbs, and Jahazah ... Josh 21:36
*B* in the wilderness with her ... 1Chr 6:78
*2. A son of Liph.*
*B*, and Hod, and Shamma ... 1Chr 7:37

### BICHRI (*bik'-ri*) *Father of Sheba.*
name was Sheba, the son of *B* ... 2Sa 20:1
and followed Sheba the son of *B* ... 2Sa 20:2
son of *B* do us more harm than did ... 2Sa 20:6
pursue after Sheba the son of *B* ... 2Sa 20:7
pursued after Sheba the son of *B* ... 2Sa 20:10
pursue after Sheba the son of *B* ... 2Sa 20:13
Sheba the son of *B* by name ... 2Sa 20:21
the head of Sheba the son of *B* ... 2Sa 20:22

### BICHRITES See BERITES.

### BICRI

### BID
*b* them that they make them ... Num 15:38
until the day I *b* you shout ... Josh 6:10
*B* the servant pass on before us, ... 1Sa 9:27
ere thou *b* the people return from ... 2Sa 2:26
riding for me, except I *b* thee ... 2Kin 4:24
if the prophet had *b* thee do some ... 2Kin 5:13
will do all that thou shalt *b* us ... 2Kin 10:5
it the preaching that I *b* thee ... Jonah 3:2
a sacrifice, he hath *b* his guests ... Zeph 1:7
*b* me come unto thee on the water ... Mt 14:28
ye shall find, *b* to the marriage ... Mt 22:9
whatsoever they *b* you observe ... Mt 23:3
let me first go *b* them farewell ... Lk 9:61
*b* her therefore that she help me ... Lk 10:40
lest they also *b* thee again ... Lk 14:12
that believe not *b* you to a feast ... 1Cor 10:27
house, neither *b* him God speed ... 2Jn 10

### BIDDEN
and afterwards they eat that be *b* ... 1Sa 9:13
place among them that were *b* ... 1Sa 9:22
for the LORD hath *b* him ... 2Sa 16:11
the angel of the Lord had *b* him ... Mt 1:24
them that were *b* to the wedding ... Mt 22:3
saying, Tell them which are *b* ... Mt 22:4
they which were *b* were not worthy ... Mt 22:8
Pharisee which had *b* him saw it ... Lk 7:39
a parable to those which were *b* ... Lk 14:7
When thou art *b* of any man to a ... Lk 14:8
man than thou be *b* of him ... Lk 14:8
But when thou art *b*, go and sit ... Lk 14:10
time to say to them that were *b* ... Lk 14:17
were *b* shall taste of my supper ... Lk 14:24

### BIDDETH
For he that *b* him God speed is ... 2Jn 11

### BIDDING
son in law, and goeth at thy *b* ... 1Sa 22:14

### BIDKAR (*bid'-kar*) *A captain of Jehu.*
Then said Jehu to *B* his captain ... 2Kin 9:25

### BIER
king David himself followed the *b* ... 2Sa 3:31
And he came and touched the *b* ... Lk 7:14

**BIGTHA** (*big'-thah*) *A servant of Ahasuerus.*
Mehuman, Biztha, Harbona, *B* ... Est 1:10

**BIGTHAN** (*big'-than*) See BIGTHANA. *A conspirator against Ahasuerus.*
two of the king's chamberlains, *B* ... Est 2:21

**BIGTHANA** (*big'-than-ah*) See BIGTHAN. *Same as Bigthan.*
that Mordecai had told of *B* ... Est 6:2

**BIGVAI** (*big'-vahee*)
*1. A family chief with Zerubbabel.*
Mordecai, Bilshan, Mizpar, *B* ... Ezr 2:2
Mordecai, Bilshan, Mispereth, *B* ... Neh 7:7
*2. A family of exiles with Zerubbabel.*
The children of *B*, two thousand ... Ezr 2:14
The children of *B*, two thousand ... Neh 7:19
*3. A family of exiles with Ezra.*
Of the sons also of *B* ... Ezr 8:14
*4. A family who renewed the covenant.*
Adonijah, *B*, Adin, ... Neh 10:16

**BILDAD** (*bil'-dad*) *A friend of Job.*
*B* the Shuhite, and Zophar the ... Job 2:11
Then answered *B* the Shuhite ... Job 8:1
Then answered *B* the Shuhite ... Job 18:1
Then answered *B* the Shuhite ... Job 25:1
*B* the Shuhite and Zophar the ... Job 42:9

**BILEAM** (*bil'-e-am*) See IBLEAM. *A Levitical city in Manasseh.*
*B* with her suburbs, for the ... 1Chr 6:70

**BILGAH** (*bil'-gah*)
*1. A priest during David's time.*
The fifteenth to *B*, the sixteenth ... 1Chr 24:14
*2. A priest with Zerubbabel.*
Miamin, Maadiah, *B*, ... Neh 12:5
Of *B*, Shammua ... Neh 12:18

**BILGAI** (*bil'-gahee*) *A priest with Zerubbabel.*
Maaziah, *B*, Shemaiah ... Neh 10:8

**BILHAH** (*bil'-hah*) See BALAH.
*1. Mother of Dan and Naphtali.*
*B* his handmaid to be her maid ... Gen 29:29
And she said, Behold my maid *B* ... Gen 30:3
she gave him *B* her handmaid to ... Gen 30:4
*B* conceived, and bare Jacob a son ... Gen 30:5
*B* Rachel's maid conceived again, ... Gen 30:7
lay with *B* his father's concubine ... Gen 35:22
And the sons of *B*, Rachel's ... Gen 35:25
and the lad was with the sons of *B* ... Gen 37:2
These are the sons of *B*, which ... Gen 46:25
Jezer, and Shallum, the sons of *B* ... 1Chr 7:13
*2. A town in Simeon.*
And at *B*, and at Ezem, and at Tolad, . 1Chr 4:29

**BILHAN** (*bil'-han*)
*1. Son of Ezer.*
*B*, and Zaavan, and Akan ... Gen 36:27
*B*, and Zavan, and Jakan ... 1Chr 1:42
*2. Son of Jediael.*
*B* ... 1Chr 7:10
and the sons of *B* ... 1Chr 7:10

**BILL**
him write her a *b* of divorcement ... Deut 24:1
write her a *b* of divorcement, and ... Deut 24:3
Where is the *b* of your mother's ... Is 50:1
away, and given her a *b* of divorce ... Jer 3:8
to write a *b* of divorcement ... Mk 10:4
And he said unto him, Take thy *b* ... Lk 16:6
And he said unto him, Take thy *b* ... Lk 16:7

**BILLOWS**
waves and thy *b* are gone over me ... Ps 42:7
all thy *b* and thy waves passed ... Jonah 2:3

**BILSHAN** (*bil'-shan*) *A Jewish prince with Zerubbabel.*
Seraiah, Reelaiah, Mordecai, *B* ... Ezr 2:2
Raamiah, Nahamani, Mordecai, *B* ... Neh 7:7

**BIMHAL** (*bim'-hal*) *A son of Japlet.*
Pasach, and *B*, and Ashvath ... 1Chr 7:33

**BIND**
they shall *b* the breastplate by ... Ex 28:28
they did *b* the breastplate by his ... Ex 39:21
or swear an oath to *b* his soul ... Num 30:2
*b* herself by a bond, being in her ... Num 30:3
thou shalt *b* them for a sign upon ... Deut 6:8
*b* them for a sign upon your hand, ... Deut 11:18
*b* up the money in thine hand, and ... Deut 14:25
thou shalt *b* this line of scarlet ... Josh 2:18
To *b* Samson are we come up, to do . Judg 15:10
him, We are come down to *b* thee ... Judg 15:12
but we will *b* thee fast, and ... Judg 15:13
that we may *b* him to afflict him ... Judg 16:5
If they *b* me with seven green ... Judg 16:7
If they *b* me fast with new ropes ... Judg 16:11
and *b* it as a crown to me ... Job 31:36
Canst thou *b* the sweet influences ... Job 38:31
Canst thou *b* the unicorn with his ... Job 39:10
and *b* their faces in secret ... Job 40:13
or wilt thou *b* him for thy ... Job 41:5
To *b* his princes at his pleasure ... Ps 105:22
*b* the sacrifice with cords, even ... Ps 118:27
To *b* their kings with chains, and ... Ps 149:8
*b* them about thy neck ... Prov 3:3
*B* them continually upon thine ... Prov 6:21
*B* them upon thy fingers, write ... Prov 7:3
*B* up the testimony, seal the law ... Is 8:16
*b* them on thee, as a bride doeth ... Is 49:18
he hath sent me to *b* up the ... Is 61:1
that thou shalt *b* a stone to it ... Jer 51:63
shall *b* thee with them, and thou ... Eze 3:25
number, and *b* them in thy skirts ... Eze 5:3
*b* the tire of thine head upon ... Eze 24:17
healed, to put a roller to *b* it ... Eze 30:21
will *b* up that which was broken, ... Eze 34:16
were in his army to *b* Shadrach ... Dan 3:20
hath smitten, and he will *b* us up ... Hos 6:1
when they shall *b* themselves in ... Hos 10:10
*b* the chariot to the swift beast ... Mic 1:13
except he first *b* the strong man ... Mt 12:29
*b* them in bundles to burn them ... Mt 13:30
whatsoever thou shalt *b* on earth ... Mt 16:19
Whatsoever ye shall *b* on earth ... Mt 18:18
*B* him hand and foot, and take him ... Mt 22:13
For they *b* heavy burdens and ... Mt 23:4
he will first *b* the strong man ... Mk 3:27
and no man could *b* him, no, not ... Mk 5:3
to *b* all that call on thy name ... Acts 9:14
Gird thyself, and *b* on thy sandals ... Acts 12:8
So shall the Jews at Jerusalem *b* ... Acts 21:11

**BINDETH**
For he maketh sore, and *b* up ... Job 5:18
He *b* up the waters in his thick ... Job 26:8
He *b* the floods from overflowing ... Job 28:11
it *b* me about as the collar of my ... Job 30:18
they cry not when he *b* them ... Job 36:13
nor he that *b* sheaves his bosom ... Ps 129:7
in heart, and *b* up their wounds ... Ps 147:3
As he that *b* a stone in a sling, ... Prov 26:8
in the day that the LORD *b* up the ... Is 30:26

**BINDING**
we were *b* sheaves in the field, ... Gen 37:7
*B* his foal unto the vine, and his ... Gen 49:11
it shall have a *b* of woven work ... Ex 28:32
every *b* oath to afflict the soul, ... Num 30:13
this way unto the death, *b* ... Acts 22:4

**BINEA** (*bin'-e-ah*) *A son of Moza.*
And Moza begat *B* ... 1Chr 8:37
And Moza begat *B* ... 1Chr 9:43

**BINNUI** (*bin'-nu-ee*)
*1. A Levite who returned from exile.*
Jeshua, and Noadiah the son of *B* ... Ezr 8:33
*2. A descendant of Pahath-moab.*
Mattaniah, Bezaleel, and *B* ... Ezr 10:30
*3. A descendant of Bani.*
And Bani, and *B*, Shimei, ... Ezr 10:38
*4. A descendant of Henadad.*
After him repaired *B* the son of ... Neh 3:24
*B* of the sons of Henadad, Kadmiel ... Neh 10:9
*5. A family who returned from exile.*
The children of *B*, six hundred ... Neh 7:15
*6. A Levite with Zerubbabel.*
Jeshua, *B*, Kadmiel, Sherebiah, ... Neh 12:8

**BIRD**
his kind, every *b* of every sort ... Gen 7:14
As for the living *b*, he shall ... Lev 14:6
the living *b* in the blood of the ... Lev 14:6
of the *b* that was killed over the ... Lev 14:6
shall let the living *b* loose into ... Lev 14:7
and the scarlet, and the living *b* ... Lev 14:51
them in the blood of the slain *b* ... Lev 14:51
the house with the blood of the *b* ... Lev 14:52
water, and with the living *b* ... Lev 14:52
*b* out of the city into the open ... Lev 14:53
thou play with him as with a *b* ... Job 41:5
Flee as a *b* to your mountain ... Ps 11:1
Our soul is escaped as a *b* out of ... Ps 124:7
is spread in the sight of any *b* ... Prov 1:17
as a *b* from the hand of the ... Prov 6:5
as a *b* hasteth to the snare, and ... Prov 7:23
As the *b* by wandering, as the ... Prov 26:2
As a *b* that wandereth from her ... Prov 27:8
for a *b* of the air shall carry ... Eccl 10:20
rise up at the voice of the *b* ... Eccl 12:4
as a wandering *b* cast out of the ... Is 16:2
a ravenous *b* from the east ... Is 46:11
is unto me as a speckled *b* ... Jer 12:9
enemies chased me sore, like a *b* ... Lam 3:52
glory shall fly away like a *b* ... Hos 9:11
shall tremble as a *b* out of Egypt ... Hos 11:11
Can a *b* fall in a snare upon the ... Amos 3:5
of every unclean and hateful *b* ... Rev 18:2

**BIRD'S**
If a *b* nest chance to be before ... Deut 22:6

**BIRDS**
but the *b* divided he not ... Gen 15:10
the *b* did eat them out of the ... Gen 40:17
the *b* shall eat thy flesh from ... Gen 40:19
is to be cleansed two *b* alive ... Lev 14:4
shall command that one of the *b* ... Lev 14:5
take to cleanse the house two *b* ... Lev 14:49
the *b* in an earthen vessel over ... Lev 14:50
Of all clean *b* ye shall eat ... Deut 14:11
suffered neither the *b* of the air ... 2Sa 21:10
Where the *b* make their nests ... Ps 104:17
as the *b* that are caught in the ... Eccl 9:12
time of the singing of *b* is come ... Song 2:12
As *b* flying, so will the LORD of ... Is 31:5
all the *b* of the heavens were ... Jer 4:25
As a cage is full of *b*, so are ... Jer 5:27
the beasts are consumed, and the *b* ... Jer 12:4
the *b* round about are against her ... Jer 12:9
unto the ravenous *b* of every sort ... Eze 39:4
the *b* of the air have nests ... Mt 8:20
so that the *b* of the air come and ... Mt 13:32
holes, and *b* of the air have nests ... Lk 9:58
like to corruptible man, and to *b* ... Rom 1:23
of fishes, and another of *b* ... 1Cor 15:39
For every kind of beasts, and of *b* ... Jas 3:7

**BIRDS'**
and his nails like *b* claws ... Dan 4:33

**BIRSHA** (*bur'-shah*) *A king of Gomorrah.*
with *B* king of Gomorrah, Shinab ... Gen 14:2

**BIRTH**
other stone, according to their *b* ... Ex 28:10
the children are come to the *b* ... 2Kin 19:3
hidden untimely *b* I had not been ... Job 3:16
like the untimely *b* of a woman ... Ps 58:8
that an untimely *b* is better than ... Eccl 6:3
of death than the day of one's *b* ... Eccl 7:1
the children are come to the *b* ... Is 37:3
Shall I bring to the *b*, and not ... Is 66:9
Thy *b* and thy nativity is of the ... Eze 16:3
fly away like a bird, from the *b* ... Hos 9:11
Now the *b* of Jesus Christ was on ... Mt 1:18
and many shall rejoice at his *b* ... Lk 1:14
a man which was blind from his *b* ... Jn 9:1
of whom I travail in *b* again ... Gal 4:19
with child cried, travailing in *b* ... Rev 12:2

**BIRTHDAY**
third day, which was Pharaoh's *b* ... Gen 40:20
But when Herod's *b* was kept ... Mt 14:6
that Herod on his *b* made a supper ... Mk 6:21

**BIRTHRIGHT**
said, Sell me this day thy *b* ... Gen 25:31
what profit shall this *b* do to me ... Gen 25:32
and he sold his *b* unto Jacob ... Gen 25:33
thus Esau despised his *b* ... Gen 25:34
he took away my *b* ... Gen 27:36
the firstborn according to his *b* ... Gen 43:33
his *b* was given unto the sons of ... 1Chr 5:1
is not to be reckoned after the *b* ... 1Chr 5:1
but the *b* was Joseph's ... 1Chr 5:2
for one morsel of meat sold his *b* ... Heb 12:16

**BIRZAITH** See BIRZAVITH.

**BIRZAVITH** (*bur'za-vith*) *A descendant of Asher.*
Malchiel, who is the father of *B* ... 1Chr 7:31

**BISHLAM** (*bish'-lam*) *A commissioner of Artaxerxes.*
in the days of Artaxerxes wrote *B* ... Ezr 4:7

**BISHOP**
If a man desire the office of a *b* ... 1Ti 3:1
A *b* then must be blameless, the ... 1Ti 3:2
ordained the first *b* of the ... 2Ti s
For a *b* must be blameless, as the ... Titus 1:7
ordained the first *b* of the ... Titus s
the Shepherd and *B* of your souls ... 1Pet 2:25

**BISHOPRICK**
and his *b* let another take ... Acts 1:20

**BISHOPS**
which are at Philippi, with the *b* ... Phil 1:1

**BIT**
the people, and they *b* the people ... Num 21:6
mouth must be held in with *b* ... Ps 32:9
on the wall, and a serpent *b* him ... Amos 5:19

**BITE**
an hedge, a serpent shall *b* him ... Eccl 10:8
will *b* without enchantment ... Eccl 10:11
be charmed, and they shall *b* you ... Jer 8:17
the serpent, and he shall *b* them ... Amos 9:3
that *b* with their teeth, and cry, ... Mic 3:5
up suddenly that shall *b* thee ... Hab 2:7
But if ye *b* and devour one another ... Gal 5:15

**BITETH**
that *b* the horse heels, so that ... Gen 49:17
At the last it *b* like a serpent ... Prov 23:32

**BITHIA** See BITHIAH.

**BITHIAH** (*bith-i'-ah*) *Daughter of Pharaoh.*
these are the sons of *B* the ... 1Chr 4:18

**BITHRON** (*bith'-ron*) *A district in Arabah.*
Jordan, and went through all *B* ... 2Sa 2:29

**BITHYNIA** (*bith-in'-e-ah*) *A Roman province in Asia Minor.*
Mysia, they assayed to go into *B* ... Acts 16:7
Galatia, Cappadocia, Asia, and *B* ... 1Pet 1:1

**BITS**
we put *b* in the horses' mouths, ... Jas 3:3

**BITTEN**
to pass, that every one that is *b* ... Num 21:8
that if a serpent had *b* any man ... Num 21:9

**BITTER**
with a great and exceeding *b* cry ... Gen 27:34
their lives *b* with hard bondage ... Ex 1:14
with *b* herbs they shall eat it ... Ex 12:8
waters of Marah, for they were *b* ... Ex 15:23
shall have in his hand the *b* ... Num 5:18
be thou free from this *b* water ... Num 5:19
blot them out with the *b* water ... Num 5:23
*b* water that causeth the curse ... Num 5:24
shall enter into her, and become *b* ... Num 5:24
shall enter into her, and become *b* ... Num 5:27
with unleavened bread and *b* herbs ... Num 9:11
heat, and with *b* destruction ... Deut 32:24
of gall, their clusters are *b* ... Deut 32:32
of Israel, that it was very *b* ... 2Kin 14:26
and cried with a loud and a *b* cry ... Est 4:1

and life unto the *b* in soul ... Job 3:20
For thou writest *b* things against ... Job 13:26
Even to day is my complaint *b* ... Job 23:2
shoot their arrows, even *b* words ... Ps 64:3
But her end is *b* as wormwood ... Prov 5:4
soul every *b* thing is sweet ... Prov 27:7
I find more *b* than death the ... Eccl 7:26
*b* for sweet, and sweet for *b* ... Is 5:20
shall be *b* to them that drink it ... Is 24:9
see that it is an evil thing and *b* ... Jer 2:19
thy wickedness, because it is *b* ... Jer 4:18
an only son, most *b* lamentation ... Jer 6:26
Ramah, lamentation, and *b* weeping ... Jer 31:15
bitterness of heart and *b* wailing ... Eze 27:31
and the end thereof as a *b* day ... Amos 8:10
I raise up the Chaldeans, that *b* ... Hab 1:6
wives, and be not *b* against them ... Col 3:19
the same place sweet water and *b* ... Jas 3:11
But if ye have *b* envying and ... Jas 3:14
waters, because they were made *b* ... Rev 8:11
and it shall make thy belly *b* ... Rev 10:9
as I had eaten it, my belly was *b* ... Rev 10:10

**BITTERLY**
curse ye *b* the inhabitants ... Judg 5:23
hath dealt very *b* with me ... Ruth 1:20
I will weep *b*, labour not to ... Is 22:4
ambassadors of peace shall weep *b* ... Is 33:7
against thee, and shall cry *b* ... Eze 27:30
provoked him to anger most *b* ... Hos 12:14
the mighty man shall cry there *b* ... Zeph 1:14
And he went out, and wept *b* ... Mt 26:75
And Peter went out, and wept *b* ... Lk 22:62

**BITTERN**
make it a possession for the *b* ... Is 14:23
and the *b* shall possess it ... Is 34:11
the *b* shall lodge in the upper ... Zeph 2:14

**BITTERNESS**
And she was in *b* of soul, and ... 1Sa 1:10
Surely the *b* of death is past ... 1Sa 15:32
it will be *b* in the latter end ... 2Sa 2:26
will complain in the *b* of my soul ... Job 7:11
my breath, but filleth me with *b* ... Job 9:18
I will speak in the *b* of my soul ... Job 10:1
dieth in the *b* of his soul ... Job 21:25
The heart knoweth his own *b* ... Prov 14:10
father, and *b* to her that bare him ... Prov 17:25
all my years in the *b* of my soul ... Is 38:15
Behold, for peace I had great *b* ... Is 38:17
are afflicted, and she is in *b* ... Lam 1:4
He hath filled me with *b*, he hath ... Lam 3:15
and took me away, and I went in *b* ... Eze 3:14
with *b* sigh before their eyes ... Eze 21:6
weep for thee with *b* of heart ... Eze 27:31
son, and shall be in *b* for him ... Zec 12:10
that is in *b* for his firstborn ... Zec 12:10
that thou art in the gall of *b* ... Acts 8:23
mouth is full of cursing and *b* ... Rom 3:14
Let all *b*, and wrath, and anger, and ... Eph 4:31
lest any root of *b* springing up ... Heb 12:15

**BIZIOTHIAH** See BIZJOTHJAH.

**BIZJOTHJAH** *(biz-joth'-jah) A town in Judah.*
Hazar-shual, and Beer-sheba, and *B* ... Josh 15:28

**BIZTHA** *(biz'-thah) An eunuch of Ahasuerus.*
wine, he commanded Mehuman, *B* ... Est 1:10

**BLACK**
and that there is no *b* hair in it ... Lev 13:31
that there is *b* hair grown up ... Lev 13:37
that the heaven was *b* with clouds ... 1Kin 18:45
of red, and blue, and white, and *b* ... Est 1:6
My skin is *b* upon me, and my bones ... Job 30:30
in the evening, in the *b* ... Prov 7:9
I am *b*, but comely, O ye ... Song 1:5
Look not upon me, because I am *b* ... Song 1:6
locks are bushy, and *b* as a raven ... Song 5:11
mourn, and the heavens above be *b* ... Jer 4:28
I am *b* ... Jer 8:21
they are *b* unto the ground ... Jer 14:2
Our skin was *b* like an oven ... Lam 5:10
and in the second chariot *b* horses ... Zec 6:2
The *b* horses which are therein go ... Zec 6:6
not make one hair white or *b* ... Mt 5:36
And I beheld, and lo a *b* horse ... Rev 6:5
the sun became *b* as sackcloth of ... Rev 6:12

**BLACKER**
Their visage is *b* than a coal ... Lam 4:8

**BLACKISH**
Which are *b* by reason of the ice, ... Job 6:16

**BLACKNESS**
let the *b* of the day terrify it ... Job 3:5
I clothe the heavens with *b* ... Is 50:3
all faces shall gather *b* ... Joel 2:6
and the faces of them all gather *b* ... Nah 2:10
that burned with fire, nor unto *b* ... Heb 12:18
the *b* of darkness for ever ... Jude 13

**BLADE**
the haft also went in after the *b* ... Judg 3:22
and the fat closed upon the *b* ... Judg 3:22
mine arm fall from my shoulder *b* ... Job 31:22
But when the *b* was sprung up, and ... Mt 13:26
first the *b*, then the ear, after ... Mk 4:28

**BLAINS**
breaking forth with *b* upon man ... Ex 9:9
breaking forth with *b* upon man ... Ex 9:10

**BLAME**
then let me bear the *b* for ever ... Gen 43:9
bear the *b* to my father for ever ... Gen 44:32
that no man should *b* us in this ... 2Cor 8:20
without *b* before him in love ... Eph 1:4

**BLAMED**
thing, that the ministry be not *b* ... 2Cor 6:3
the face, because he was to be *b* ... Gal 2:11

**BLAMELESS**
and ye shall be *b* ... Gen 44:10
We will be *b* of this thine oath ... Josh 2:17
Now shall I be more *b* than the ... Judg 15:3
profane the sabbath, and are *b* ... Mt 12:5
and ordinances of the Lord *b* ... Lk 1:6
that ye may be *b* in the day of ... 1Cor 1:8
That ye may be *b* and harmless, the ... Phil 2:15
which is in the law, *b* ... Phil 3:6
body be preserved *b* unto the ... 1Th 5:23
A bishop then must be *b*, the ... 1Ti 3:2
office of a deacon, being found *b* ... 1Ti 3:10
in charge, that they may be *b* ... 1Ti 5:7
If any be *b*, the husband of one ... Titus 1:6
For a bishop must be *b*, as the ... Titus 1:7
him in peace, without spot, and *b* ... 2Pet 3:14

**BLASPHEME**
to the enemies of the LORD to *b* ... 2Sa 12:14
him, saying, Thou didst *b* God ... 1Kin 21:10
people, saying, Naboth did *b* God ... 1Kin 21:13
shall the enemy *b* thy name for ... Ps 74:10
wherewith soever they shall *b* ... Mk 3:28
But he that shall *b* against the ... Mk 3:29
synagogue, and compelled them to *b* ... Acts 26:11
that they may learn not to *b* ... 1Ti 1:20
Do not they *b* that worthy name by ... Jas 2:7
to *b* his name, and his tabernacle, ... Rev 13:6

**BLASPHEMED**
son *b* the name of the LORD ... Lev 24:11
of the king of Assyria have *b* me ... 2Kin 19:6
Whom hast thou reproached and *b* ... 2Kin 19:22
foolish people have *b* thy name ... Ps 74:18
of the king of Assyria have *b* me ... Is 37:6
Whom hast thou reproached and *b* ... Is 37:23
name continually every day is *b* ... Is 52:5
mountains, and *b* me upon the hills ... Is 65:7
in this your fathers have *b* me ... Eze 20:27
they opposed themselves, and *b* ... Acts 18:6
For the name of God is *b* among ... Rom 2:24
of God and his doctrine be not *b* ... 1Ti 6:1
that the word of God be not *b* ... Titus 2:5
*b* the name of God, which hath ... Rev 16:9
*b* the God of heaven because of ... Rev 16:11
men *b* God because of the plague ... Rev 16:21

**BLASPHEMER**
Who was before a *b*, and a ... 1Ti 1:13

**BLASPHEMERS**
nor yet *b* of your goddess ... Acts 19:37
covetous, boasters, proud, *b* ... 2Ti 3:2

**BLASPHEMEST**
and sent into the world, Thou *b* ... Jn 10:36

**BLASPHEMETH**
he that *b* the name of the LORD, ... Lev 24:16
when he *b* the name of the LORD, ... Lev 24:16
of him that reproacheth and *b* ... Ps 44:16
within themselves, This man *b* ... Mt 9:3
but unto him that *b* against the ... Lk 12:10

**BLASPHEMIES**
that I have heard all thy *b* which ... Eze 35:12
thefts, false witness, *b* ... Mt 15:19
Why doth this man thus speak *b* ... Mk 2:7
*b* wherewith soever they shall ... Mk 3:28
Who is this which speaketh *b* ... Lk 5:21
mouth speaking great things and *b* ... Rev 13:5

**BLASPHEMING**
by Paul, contradicting and *b* ... Acts 13:45

**BLASPHEMOUS**
him speak *b* words against Moses ... Acts 6:11
*b* words against this holy place ... Acts 6:13

**BLASPHEMOUSLY**
many other things *b* spake they ... Lk 22:65

**BLASPHEMY**
of trouble, and of rebuke, and *b* ... 2Kin 19:3
of trouble, and of rebuke, and of *b* ... Is 37:3
*b* shall be forgiven unto men ... Mt 12:31
but the *b* against the Holy Ghost ... Mt 12:31
clothes, saying, He hath spoken *b* ... Mt 26:65
behold, now ye have heard his *b* ... Mt 26:65
lasciviousness, an evil eye, *b* ... Mk 7:22
Ye have heard the *b* ... Mk 14:64
stone thee not; but for *b* ... Jn 10:33
anger, wrath, malice, *b*, filthy ... Col 3:8
I know the *b* of them which say ... Rev 2:9
and upon his heads the name of *b* ... Rev 13:1
opened his mouth in *b* against God ... Rev 13:6
beast, full of names of *b* ... Rev 17:3

**BLAST**
with the *b* of thy nostrils the ... Ex 15:8
make a long *b* with the ram's horn ... Josh 6:5
at the *b* of the breath of his ... 2Sa 22:16
Behold, I will send a *b* upon him ... 2Kin 19:7
By the *b* of God they perish, and ... Job 4:9
at the *b* of the breath of thy ... Ps 18:15
when the *b* of the terrible ones ... Is 25:4
Behold, I will send a *b* upon him ... Is 37:7

**BLASTED**
*b* with the east wind sprung up ... Gen 41:6
*b* with the east wind, sprung up ... Gen 41:23
the seven empty ears *b* with the ... Gen 41:27
as corn *b* before it be grown up ... 2Kin 19:26
as corn *b* before it be grown up ... Is 37:27

**BLASTING**
and with the sword, and with *b* ... Deut 28:22
famine, if there be pestilence, *b* ... 1Kin 8:37
be pestilence, if there be *b* ... 2Chr 6:28
I have smitten you with *b* ... Amos 4:9
I smote you with *b* and with mildew ... Hag 2:17

**BLASTUS** *(blas'-tus) A servant of Herod Agrippa I.*
him, and, having made *B* the king's ... Acts 12:20

**BLAZE**
to *b* abroad the matter, insomuch ... Mk 1:45

**BLEATING**
What meaneth then this *b* of the ... 1Sa 15:14

**BLEATINGS**
to hear the *b* of the flocks ... Judg 5:16

**BLEMISH**
Your lamb shall be without *b* ... Ex 12:5
bullock, and two rams without *b* ... Ex 29:1
let him offer a male without *b* ... Lev 1:3
shall bring it a male without *b* ... Lev 1:10
it without *b* before the LORD ... Lev 3:1
he shall offer it without *b* ... Lev 3:6
without *b* unto the LORD for a sin ... Lev 4:3
of the goats, a male without *b* ... Lev 4:23
of the goats, a female without *b* ... Lev 4:28
shall bring it a female without *b* ... Lev 4:32
a ram without *b* out of the flocks ... Lev 5:15
a ram without *b* out of the flock ... Lev 5:18
a ram without *b* out of the flock, ... Lev 6:6
for a burnt offering, without *b* ... Lev 9:2
both of the first year, without *b* ... Lev 9:3
shall take two he lambs without *b* ... Lev 14:10
lamb of the first year without *b* ... Lev 14:10
their generations that hath any *b* ... Lev 21:17
man he be that hath a *b*, he shall ... Lev 21:18
or that hath a *b* in his eye ... Lev 21:20
No man that hath a *b* of the seed ... Lev 21:21
he hath a *b* ... Lev 21:21
the altar, because he hath a *b* ... Lev 21:23
at your own will a male without *b* ... Lev 22:19
But whatsoever hath a *b*, that ... Lev 22:20
there shall be no *b* therein ... Lev 22:21
the sheaf an he lamb without *b* of ... Lev 23:12
lambs without *b* of the first year ... Lev 23:18
a man cause a *b* in his neighbour ... Lev 24:19
as he hath caused a *b* in a man ... Lev 24:20
without *b* for a burnt offering ... Num 6:14
year without *b* for a sin offering ... Num 6:14
one ram without *b* for peace ... Num 6:14
without spot, wherein is no *b* ... Num 19:2
they shall be unto you without *b* ... Num 28:19
they shall be unto you without *b*) ... Num 28:31
lambs of the first year without *b* ... Num 29:2
they shall be unto you without *b* ... Num 29:8
they shall be without *b* ... Num 29:13
lambs of the first year without *b* ... Num 29:20
lambs of the first year without *b* ... Num 29:23
lambs of the first year without *b* ... Num 29:29
lambs of the first year without *b* ... Num 29:32
lambs of the first year without *b* ... Num 29:36
And if there be any *b* therein ... Deut 15:21
lame, or blind, or have any ill *b* ... Deut 15:21
bullock, or sheep, wherein is *b* ... Deut 17:1
of his head there was no *b* in him ... 2Sa 14:25
without *b* for a sin offering ... Eze 43:22
offer a young bullock without *b* ... Eze 43:23
a ram out of the flock without *b* ... Eze 43:23
a ram out of the flock, without *b* ... Eze 43:25
take a young bullock without *b* ... Eze 45:18
seven rams without *b* daily the ... Eze 45:23
day shall be six lambs without *b* ... Eze 46:4
*b*, and a ram without *b* ... Eze 46:4
be a young bullock without *b* ... Eze 46:6
they shall be without *b* ... Eze 46:6
lamb of the first year without *b* ... Eze 46:13
Children in whom was no *b* ... Dan 1:4
it should be holy and without *b* ... Eph 5:27
of Christ, as of a lamb without *b* ... 1Pet 1:19

**BLEMISHES**
is in them, and *b* be in them ... Lev 22:25
Spots they are and *b*, sporting ... 2Pet 2:13

**BLESS**
a great nation, and I will *b* thee ... Gen 12:2
And I will *b* them that *b* thee ... Gen 12:3
And I will *b* her, and give thee a ... Gen 17:16
yea, I will *b* her, and she shall ... Gen 17:16
That in blessing I will *b* thee ... Gen 22:17
will be with thee, and will *b* thee ... Gen 26:3
I am with thee, and will *b* thee ... Gen 26:24
that my soul may *b* thee before I ... Gen 27:4
*b* thee before the LORD before my ... Gen 27:7
that he may *b* thee before his ... Gen 27:10
venison, that thy soul may *b* me ... Gen 27:19
venison, that my soul may *b* thee ... Gen 27:25
venison, that thy soul may *b* me ... Gen 27:31
*B* me, even me also, O my father ... Gen 27:34
*b* me, even me also, O my father ... Gen 27:38
And God Almighty *b* thee, and make ... Gen 28:3
not let thee go, except thou *b* me ... Gen 32:26

thee, unto me, and I will *b* them ... Gen 48:9
me from all evil, *b* the lads ... Gen 48:16
saying, In thee shall Israel *b* ... Gen 48:20
who shall *b* thee with blessings ... Gen 49:25
and *b* me also ... Ex 12:32
come unto thee, and I will *b* thee ... Ex 20:24
he shall *b* thy bread, and thy ... Ex 23:25
On this wise ye shall *b* the ... Num 6:23
The LORD *b* thee, and keep thee ... Num 6:24
and I will *b* them ... Num 6:27
I have received commandment to *b* .. Num 23:20
them at all, nor *b* them at all ... Num 23:25
it pleased the LORD to *b* Israel ... Num 24:1
*b* you, as he hath promised you ... Deut 1:11
thee, and *b* thee, and multiply thee ... Deut 7:13
he will also *b* the fruit of thy ... Deut 7:13
then thou shalt *b* the LORD thy ... Deut 8:10
to *b* in his name, unto this day ... Deut 10:8
that the LORD thy God may *b* thee ... Deut 14:29
for the LORD shall greatly *b* thee ... Deut 15:4
God shall *b* thee in all thy works ... Deut 15:10
the LORD thy God shall *b* thee in ... Deut 15:18
*b* thee in all thine increase ... Deut 16:15
to *b* in the name of the LORD ... Deut 21:5
that the LORD thy God may *b* thee ... Deut 23:20
in his own raiment, and *b* thee ... Deut 24:13
that the LORD thy God may *b* thee ... Deut 24:19
*b* thy people Israel, and the land ... Deut 26:15
mount Gerizim to *b* the people ... Deut 27:12
he shall *b* thee in the land which ... Deut 28:8
to *b* all the work of thine hand ... Deut 28:12
that he *b* himself in his heart, ... Deut 29:19
the LORD thy God shall *b* thee in ... Deut 30:16
*B*, LORD, his substance, and accept ... Deut 33:11
that they should *b* the people of ... Josh 8:33
*B* ye the LORD ... Judg 5:9
answered him, The LORD *b* thee ... Ruth 2:4
because he doth *b* the sacrifice ... 1Sa 9:13
David returned to *b* his household ... 2Sa 6:20
to *b* the house of thy servant ... 2Sa 7:29
to *b* him, because he had fought ... 2Sa 8:10
that ye may *b* the inheritance of ... 2Sa 21:3
came to *b* our lord king David ... 1Kin 1:47
Oh that thou wouldest *b* me indeed ... 1Chr 4:10
and David returned to *b* his house ... 1Chr 16:43
to *b* the house of thy servant ... 1Chr 17:27
to *b* in his name for ever ... 1Chr 23:13
Now *b* the LORD your God ... 1Chr 29:20
*b* the LORD your God for ever and ... Neh 9:5
thou, LORD, wilt *b* the righteous ... Ps 5:12
I will *b* the LORD, who hath given ... Ps 16:7
congregations will I *b* the LORD ... Ps 26:12
people, and *b* thine inheritance ... Ps 28:9
the LORD will *b* his people with ... Ps 29:11
I will *b* the LORD at all times ... Ps 34:1
they *b* with their mouth, but they ... Ps 62:4
Thus will I *b* thee while I live ... Ps 63:4
O *b* our God, ye people, and make ... Ps 66:8
God be merciful unto us, and *b* us ... Ps 67:1
God, even our own God, shall *b* us ... Ps 67:6
God shall *b* us ... Ps 67:7
*B* ye God in the congregations, ... Ps 68:26
Sing unto the LORD, *b* his name ... Ps 96:2
thankful unto him, and *b* his name ... Ps 100:4
*B* the LORD, O my soul ... Ps 103:1
is within me, *b* his holy name ... Ps 103:1
*B* the LORD, O my soul, and forget ... Ps 103:2
*B* the LORD, ye his angels, that ... Ps 103:20
*B* ye the LORD, all ye his hosts ... Ps 103:21
*B* the LORD, all his works in all ... Ps 103:22
*b* the LORD, O my soul ... Ps 103:22
*B* the LORD, O my soul ... Ps 104:1
*B* thou the LORD, O my soul ... Ps 104:35
Let them curse, but *b* thou ... Ps 109:28
he will *b* us ... Ps 115:12
he will *b* the house of Israel ... Ps 115:12
he will *b* the house of Aaron ... Ps 115:12
He will *b* them that fear the LORD ... Ps 115:13
But we will *b* the LORD from this ... Ps 115:18
The LORD shall *b* thee out of Zion ... Ps 128:5
we *b* you in the name of the LORD ... Ps 129:8
I will abundantly *b* her provision ... Ps 132:15
*b* ye the LORD, all ye servants of ... Ps 134:1
in the sanctuary, and *b* the LORD ... Ps 134:2
and earth *b* thee out of Zion ... Ps 134:3
*B* the LORD, O house of Israel ... Ps 135:19
*b* the LORD, O house of Aaron ... Ps 135:19
*B* the LORD, O house of Levi ... Ps 135:20
ye that fear the LORD, *b* the LORD ... Ps 135:20
I will *b* thy name for ever and ... Ps 145:1
Every day will I *b* thee ... Ps 145:2
and thy saints shall *b* thee ... Ps 145:10
let all flesh *b* his holy name for ... Ps 145:21
and doth not *b* their mother ... Prov 30:11
Whom the LORD of hosts shall *b* ... Is 19:25
himself in the earth shall *b* ... Is 65:16
nations shall *b* themselves in him ... Jer 4:2
The LORD *b* thee, O habitation of ... Jer 31:23
from this day will I *b* you ... Hag 2:19
*b* them that curse you, do good to ... Mt 5:44
*B* them that curse you, and pray ... Lk 6:28
his Son Jesus, sent him to *b* you ... Acts 3:26
*B* them which persecute you ... Rom 12:14
*b*, and curse not ... Rom 12:14
being reviled, we *b* ... 1Cor 4:12
The cup of blessing which we *b* ... 1Cor 10:16
when thou shalt *b* with the spirit ... 1Cor 14:16
Surely blessing I will *b* thee ... Heb 6:14
Therewith *b* we God, even the ... Jas 3:9

**BLESSED**

God *b* them, saying, Be fruitful, ... Gen 1:22
God *b* them, and God said unto them .. Gen 1:28
God *b* the seventh day, and ... Gen 2:3
*b* them, and called their name Adam ... Gen 5:2
God *b* Noah and his sons, and said ... Gen 9:1
*B* be the LORD God of Shem ... Gen 9:26
all families of the earth be *b* ... Gen 12:3
he *b* him, and said ... Gen 14:19
*B* be Abram of the most high God, ... Gen 14:19
*b* be the most high God, which ... Gen 14:20
Behold, I have *b* him, and will ... Gen 17:20
of the earth shall be *b* in him ... Gen 18:18
all the nations of the earth be *b* ... Gen 22:18
the LORD had *b* Abraham in all ... Gen 24:1
*B* be the LORD God of my master ... Gen 24:27
said, Come in, thou *b* of the LORD ... Gen 24:31
the LORD hath *b* my master greatly ... Gen 24:35
*b* the LORD God of my master ... Gen 24:48
they *b* Rebekah, and said unto her, ... Gen 24:60
Abraham, that God *b* his son Isaac ... Gen 25:11
all the nations of the earth be *b* ... Gen 26:4
and the LORD *b* him ... Gen 26:12
thou art now the *b* of the LORD ... Gen 26:29
so he *b* him ... Gen 27:23
*b* him, and said, See, the smell of ... Gen 27:27
of a field which the LORD hath *b* ... Gen 27:27
*b* be he that blesseth thee ... Gen 27:29
before thou camest, and have *b* him .. Gen 27:33
yea, and he shall be *b* ... Gen 27:33
wherewith his father *b* him ... Gen 27:41
*b* him, and charged him, and said ... Gen 28:1
Esau saw that Isaac had *b* Jacob ... Gen 28:6
that as he *b* him he gave him a ... Gen 28:6
the families of the earth be *b* ... Gen 28:14
for the daughters will call me *b* ... Gen 30:13
the LORD hath *b* me for thy sake ... Gen 30:27
the LORD hath *b* thee since my ... Gen 30:30
sons and his daughters, and *b* them ... Gen 31:55
And he *b* him there ... Gen 32:29
came out of Padan-aram, and *b* him ... Gen 35:9
that the LORD *b* the Egyptian's ... Gen 39:5
and Jacob *b* Pharaoh ... Gen 47:7
Jacob *b* Pharaoh, and went out from . Gen 47:10
in the land of Canaan, and *b* me, ... Gen 48:3
he *b* Joseph, and said, God, before ... Gen 48:15
he *b* them that day, saying, In ... Gen 48:20
father spake unto them, and *b* them .. Gen 49:28
to his blessing he *b* them ... Gen 49:28
*B* be the LORD, who hath delivered ... Ex 18:10
the LORD *b* the sabbath day ... Ex 20:11
and Moses *b* them ... Ex 39:43
*b* them, and came down from ... Lev 9:22
and came out, and *b* the people ... Lev 9:23
that he whom thou blessest is *b* ... Num 22:6
for they are *b* ... Num 22:12
thou hast *b* them altogether ... Num 23:11
and he hath *b* ... Num 23:20
*B* is he that blesseth thee, and ... Num 24:9
thou hast altogether *b* them these ... Num 24:10
For the LORD thy God hath *b* thee ... Deut 2:7
Thou shalt be *b* above all people ... Deut 7:14
the LORD thy God hath *b* thee ... Deut 12:7
when the LORD thy God hath *b* thee Deut 14:24
*b* thee thou shalt give unto him ... Deut 15:14
as the LORD thy God hath *b* thee ... Deut 16:10
*B* shalt thou be in the city, and ... Deut 28:3
*b* shalt thou be in the field ... Deut 28:3
*B* shall be the fruit of thy body, ... Deut 28:4
*B* shall be thy basket and thy ... Deut 28:5
*B* shalt thou be when thou comest ... Deut 28:6
*b* shalt thou be when thou goest ... Deut 28:6
*b* the children of Israel before ... Deut 33:1
*B* of the LORD be his land, for ... Deut 33:13
*B* be he that enlargeth Gad ... Deut 33:20
Let Asher be *b* with children ... Deut 33:24
And Joshua *b* him, and gave unto ... Josh 14:13
as the LORD hath *b* me hitherto ... Josh 17:14
So Joshua *b* them, and sent them ... Josh 22:6
unto their tents, then he *b* them ... Josh 22:7
and the children of Israel *b* God ... Josh 22:33
therefore he *b* you still ... Josh 24:10
*B* above women shall Jael the wife ... Judg 5:24
*b* shall she be above women in the ... Judg 5:24
the child grew, and the LORD *b* him .. Judg 13:24
*B* be thou of the LORD, my son ... Judg 17:2
*b* be he that did take knowledge ... Ruth 2:19
*B* be he of the LORD, who hath not ... Ruth 2:20
*B* be thou of the LORD, my ... Ruth 3:10
*B* be the LORD, which hath not ... Ruth 4:14
Eli *b* Elkanah and his wife, and ... 1Sa 2:20
unto him, *B* be thou of the LORD ... 1Sa 15:13
And Saul said, *B* be ye of the LORD ... 1Sa 23:21
*B* be the LORD God of Israel, ... 1Sa 25:32
*b* be thy advice, and *b* be ... 1Sa 25:33
*B* be the LORD, that hath pleaded ... 1Sa 25:39
to David, *B* be thou, my son David ... 1Sa 26:25
*B* be ye of the LORD, that ye have ... 2Sa 2:5
the LORD *b* Obed-edom, and all his ... 2Sa 6:11
The LORD hath *b* the house of ... 2Sa 6:12
he *b* the people in the name of ... 2Sa 6:18
of thy servant be *b* for ever ... 2Sa 7:29
he would not go, but *b* him ... 2Sa 13:25
*B* be the LORD thy God, which hath ... 2Sa 18:28
king kissed Barzillai, and *b* him ... 2Sa 19:39
and *b* be my rock ... 2Sa 22:47
*B* be the LORD God of Israel, ... 1Kin 1:48
And king Solomon shall be *b* ... 1Kin 2:45
*B* be the LORD this day, which ... 1Kin 5:7
*b* all the congregation of Israel ... 1Kin 8:14

*B* be the LORD God of Israel, ... 1Kin 8:15
*b* all the congregation of Israel ... 1Kin 8:55
*B* be the LORD, that hath given ... 1Kin 8:56
they *b* the king, and went unto ... 1Kin 8:66
*B* be the LORD thy God, which ... 1Kin 10:9
the LORD *b* the house of Obed-edom. 1Chr 13:14
he *b* the people in the name of ... 1Chr 16:2
*B* be the LORD God of Israel for ... 1Chr 16:36
O LORD, and it shall be *b* for ever ... 1Chr 17:27
for God *b* him ... 1Chr 26:5
Wherefore David *b* the LORD before .. 1Chr 29:10
*B* be thou, LORD God of Israel our ... 1Chr 29:10
all the congregation *b* the LORD ... 1Chr 29:20
*B* be the LORD God of Israel, that ... 2Chr 2:12
*b* the whole congregation of ... 2Chr 6:3
*B* be the LORD God of Israel, who ... 2Chr 6:4
*B* be the LORD thy God, which ... 2Chr 9:8
for there they *b* the LORD ... 2Chr 20:26
the Levites arose and *b* the people ... 2Chr 30:27
they *b* the LORD, and his people ... 2Chr 31:8
for the LORD hath *b* his people ... 2Chr 31:10
*B* be the LORD God of our fathers, ... Ezr 7:27
Ezra *b* the LORD, the great God ... Neh 8:6
*b* be thy glorious name, which is ... Neh 9:5
the people *b* all the men, that ... Neh 11:2
thou hast *b* the work of his hands ... Job 1:10
*b* be the name of the LORD ... Job 1:21
the ear heard me, then it *b* me ... Job 29:11
If his loins have not *b* me ... Job 31:20
So the LORD *b* the latter end of ... Job 42:12
*B* is the man that walketh not in ... Ps 1:1
*B* are all they that put their ... Ps 2:12
and *b* be my rock ... Ps 18:46
hast made him most *b* for ever ... Ps 21:6
*B* be the LORD, because he hath ... Ps 28:6
*B* be the LORD ... Ps 31:21
*B* is he whose transgression is ... Ps 32:1
*B* is the man unto whom the LORD ... Ps 32:2
*B* is the nation whose God is the ... Ps 33:12
*b* is the man that trusteth in him ... Ps 34:8
For such as be *b* of him shall ... Ps 37:22
and his seed is *b* ... Ps 37:26
*B* is that man that maketh the ... Ps 40:4
*B* is he that considereth the poor ... Ps 41:1
he shall be *b* upon the earth ... Ps 41:2
*B* be the LORD God of Israel from ... Ps 41:13
God hath *b* thee for ever ... Ps 45:2
while he lived he *b* his soul ... Ps 49:18
*B* is the man whom thou choosest, ... Ps 65:4
*B* be God, which hath not turned ... Ps 66:20
*B* be the Lord, who daily loadeth ... Ps 68:19
*B* be God ... Ps 68:35
and men shall be *b* in him ... Ps 72:17
all nations shall call him *b* ... Ps 72:17
*B* be the LORD God, the God of ... Ps 72:18
*b* be his glorious name for ever ... Ps 72:19
*B* are they that dwell in thy ... Ps 84:4
*B* is the man whose strength is in ... Ps 84:5
*b* is the man that trusteth in ... Ps 84:12
*B* is the people that know the ... Ps 89:15
*B* be the LORD for evermore ... Ps 89:52
*B* is the man whom thou chastenest ... Ps 94:12
*B* are they that keep judgment, and ... Ps 106:3
*B* be the LORD God of Israel from ... Ps 106:48
*B* is the man that feareth the ... Ps 112:1
of the upright shall be *b* ... Ps 112:2
*B* be the name of the LORD from ... Ps 113:2
Ye are *b* of the LORD which made ... Ps 115:15
*B* be he that cometh in the name ... Ps 118:26
we have *b* you out of the house of ... Ps 118:26
*B* are the undefiled in the way, ... Ps 119:1
*B* are they that keep his ... Ps 119:2
*B* art thou, O LORD ... Ps 119:12
*B* be the LORD, who hath not given ... Ps 124:6
*B* is every one that feareth the ... Ps 128:1
man be *b* that feareth the LORD ... Ps 128:4
*B* be the LORD out of Zion, which ... Ps 135:21
*B* be the LORD my strength, which ... Ps 144:1
he hath *b* thy children within ... Ps 147:13
Let thy fountain be *b* ... Prov 5:18
for *b* are they that keep my ways ... Prov 8:32
*B* is the man that heareth me ... Prov 8:34
The memory of the just is *b* ... Prov 10:7
his children are *b* after him ... Prov 20:7
the end thereof shall not be *b* ... Prov 20:21
hath a bountiful eye shall be *b* ... Prov 22:9
children arise up, and call her *b* ... Prov 31:28
*B* art thou, O land, when thy king ... Eccl 10:17
The daughters saw her, and *b* her ... Song 6:9
*B* be Egypt my people, and Assyria ... Is 19:25
*b* are all they that wait for him ... Is 30:18
*B* are ye that sow beside all ... Is 32:20
alone, and *b* him, and increased him ... Is 51:2
*B* is the man that doeth this, and ... Is 56:2
the seed which the LORD hath *b* ... Is 61:9
are the seed of the *b* of the LORD ... Is 65:23
incense, as if he *b* an idol ... Is 66:3
*B* is the man that trusteth in the ... Jer 17:7
wherein my mother bare me be *b* ... Jer 20:14
*B* be the glory of the LORD from ... Eze 3:12
Then Daniel *b* the God of heaven ... Dan 2:19
*B* be the name of God for ever and ... Dan 2:20
*B* be the God of Shadrach, Meshach ... Dan 3:28
I *b* the most High, and I praised ... Dan 4:34
*B* is he that waiteth, and cometh ... Dan 12:12
that sell them say, *B* be the LORD ... Zec 11:5
And all nations shall call you *b* ... Mal 3:12
*B* are the poor in spirit ... Mt 5:3
*B* are they that mourn ... Mt 5:4
*B* are the meek ... Mt 5:5

*B* are they which do hunger and Mt 5:6
*B* are the merciful Mt 5:7
*B* are the pure in heart Mt 5:8
*B* are the peacemakers Mt 5:9
*B* are they which are persecuted Mt 5:10
*B* are ye, when men shall revile Mt 5:11
*b* is he, whosoever shall not be Mt 11:6
But *b* are your eyes, for they see Mt 13:16
and looking up to heaven, he *b* Mt 14:19
*B* art thou, Simon Bar-jona Mt 16:17
*B* is he that cometh in the name Mt 21:9
*B* is he that cometh in the name Mt 23:39
*B* is that servant, whom his lord Mt 24:46
ye *b* of my Father, inherit the Mt 25:34
*b* it, and brake it, and gave it to Mt 26:26
he looked up to heaven, and *b* Mk 6:41
and he *b*, and commanded to set them Mk 8:7
his hands upon them, and *b* them Mk 10:16
*B* is he that cometh in the name Mk 11:9
*B* be the kingdom of our father Mk 11:10
did eat, Jesus took bread, and *b* Mk 14:22
thou the Christ, the Son of the *B* Mk 14:61
*b* art thou among women Lk 1:28
*B* art thou among women, and Lk 1:42
*b* is the fruit of thy womb Lk 1:42
And *b* is she that believed Lk 1:45
all generations shall call me *b* Lk 1:48
*B* be the Lord God of Israel Lk 1:68
in his arms, and *b* God, and said, Lk 2:28
And Simeon *b* them, and said unto Lk 2:34
disciples, and said, *B* be ye poor Lk 6:20
*B* are ye that hunger now Lk 6:21
*B* are ye that weep now Lk 6:21
*B* are ye, when men shall hate you Lk 6:22
*b* is he, whosoever shall not be Lk 7:23
he *b* them, and brake, and gave to Lk 9:16
*B* are the eyes which see the Lk 10:23
*B* is the womb that bare thee, and Lk 11:27
*b* are they that hear the word of Lk 11:28
*B* are those servants, whom the Lk 12:37
them so, *b* are those servants Lk 12:38
*B* is that servant, whom his lord Lk 12:43
*B* is he that cometh in the name Lk 13:35
And thou shalt be *b* Lk 14:14
*B* is he that shall eat bread in Lk 14:15
*B* be the King that cometh in the Lk 19:38
*B* are the barren, and the wombs Lk 23:29
*b* it, and brake, and gave to them Lk 24:30
he lifted up his hands, and *b* them Lk 24:50
it came to pass, while he *b* them Lk 24:51
*B* is the King of Israel that Jn 12:13
*b* are they that have not seen, and Jn 20:29
the kindreds of the earth be *b* Acts 3:25
It is more *b* to give than to Acts 20:35
the Creator, who is *b* for ever Rom 1:25
*B* are they whose iniquities are Rom 4:7
*B* is the man to whom the Lord Rom 4:8
who is over all, God *b* for ever Rom 9:5
*B* be God, even the Father of our 2Cor 1:3
which is *b* for evermore, knoweth 2Cor 11:31
In thee shall all nations be *b* Gal 3:8
faith are *b* with faithful Abraham Gal 3:9
*B* be the God and Father of our Eph 1:3
who hath *b* us with all spiritual Eph 1:3
the glorious gospel of the *b* God 1Ti 1:11
times he shall shew, who is the *b* 1Ti 6:15
Looking for that *b* hope, and the Titus 2:13
slaughter of the kings, and *b* him Heb 7:1
*b* him that had the promises Heb 7:6
the less is *b* of the better Heb 7:7
By faith Isaac *b* Jacob and Esau Heb 11:20
*b* both the sons of Joseph Heb 11:21
*B* is the man that endureth Jas 1:12
this man shall be *b* in his deed Jas 1:25
*B* be the God and Father of our 1Pet 1:3
*B* is he that readeth, and they Rev 1:3
*B* are the dead which die in the Rev 14:13
*B* is he that watcheth, and keepeth Rev 16:15
*B* are they which are called unto Rev 19:9
*B* and holy is he that hath part in Rev 20:6
*b* is he that keepeth the sayings Rev 22:7
*B* are they that do his Rev 22:14

### BLESSEDNESS
also describeth the *b* of the man Rom 4:6
Cometh this *b* then upon the Rom 4:9
Where is then the *b* ye spake of Gal 4:15

### BLESSEST
that he whom thou *b* is blessed Num 22:6
for thou *b*, O LORD, and it shall 1Chr 17:27
thou *b* the springing thereof Ps 65:10

### BLESSETH
and blessed be he that *b* thee Gen 27:29
Blessed is he that *b* thee Num 24:9
For the LORD thy God *b* thee Deut 15:6
*b* the covetous, whom the LORD Ps 10:3
He *b* them also, so that they are Ps 107:38
but he *b* the habitation of the Prov 3:33
He that *b* his friend with a loud Prov 27:14
That he who *b* himself in the Is 65:16

### BLESSING
and thou shalt be a *b* Gen 12:2
That in *b* I will bless thee, and Gen 22:17
bring a curse upon me, and not a *b* Gen 27:12
Isaac had made an end of *b* Jacob Gen 27:30
and hath taken away thy *b* Gen 27:35
now he hath taken away my *b* Gen 27:36
Hast thou not reserved a *b* for me Gen 27:36
his father, Hast thou but one *b* Gen 27:38
*b* wherewith his father blessed Gen 27:41
And give thee the *b* of Abraham Gen 28:4
my *b* that is brought to thee Gen 33:11
the *b* of the LORD was upon all Gen 39:5
to his *b* he blessed them Gen 49:28
may bestow upon you a *b* this day Ex 32:29
Then I will command my *b* upon you. Lev 25:21
I set before you this day a *b* Deut 11:26
A *b*, if ye obey the commandments Deut 11:27
put the *b* upon mount Gerizim Deut 11:29
according to the *b* of the LORD Deut 12:15
according to the *b* of the LORD Deut 16:17
the curse into a *b* unto thee Deut 23:5
The LORD shall command the *b* upon. Deut 28:8
things are come upon thee, the *b* Deut 30:1
set before you life and death, *b* Deut 30:19
And this is the *b*, wherewith Moses Deut 33:1
And this is the *b* of Judah Deut 33:7
let the *b* come upon the head of Deut 33:16
and full with the *b* of the LORD Deut 33:23
Who answered, Give me a *b* Josh 15:19
And she said unto him, Give me a *b* Judg 1:15
now this *b* which thine handmaid 1Sa 25:27
with thy *b* let the house of thy 2Sa 7:29
thee, take a *b* of thy servant 2Kin 5:15
which is exalted above all *b* Neh 9:5
our God turned the curse into a *b* Neh 13:2
The *b* of him that was ready to Job 29:13
thy *b* is upon thy people Ps 3:8
shall receive the *b* from the LORD Ps 24:5
as he delighted not in *b*, so let Ps 109:17
The *b* of the LORD be upon you Ps 129:8
there the LORD commanded the *b* Ps 133:3
The *b* of the LORD, it maketh rich Prov 10:22
By the *b* of the upright the city Prov 11:11
but *b* shall be upon the head of Prov 11:26
a good *b* shall come upon them Prov 24:25
even a *b* in the midst of the land Is 19:24
my *b* upon thine offspring Is 44:3
for a *b* is in it Is 65:8
places round about my hill a *b* Eze 34:26
there shall be showers of *b* Eze 34:26
that he may cause the *b* to rest Eze 44:30
repent, and leave a *b* behind him Joel 2:14
I save you, and ye shall be a *b* Zec 8:13
of heaven, and pour you out a *b* Mal 3:10
in the temple, praising and *b* God Lk 24:53
of the *b* of the gospel of Christ Rom 15:29
The cup of *b* which we bless, is 1Cor 10:16
That the *b* of Abraham might come Gal 3:14
is dressed, receiveth *b* from God Heb 6:7
Surely *b* I will bless thee, and Heb 6:14
he would have inherited the *b* Heb 12:17
of the same mouth proceedeth *b* Jas 3:10
but contrariwise *b* 1Pet 3:9
that ye should inherit a *b* 1Pet 3:9
and honour, and glory, and *b* Rev 5:12
are in them, heard I saying, *B* Rev 5:13
*B*, and glory, and wisdom, and Rev 7:12

### BLESSINGS
bless thee with *b* of heaven above Gen 49:25
*b* of the deep that lieth under, Gen 49:25
*b* of the breasts, and of the womb Gen 49:25
The *b* of thy father have Gen 49:26
the *b* of my progenitors unto the Gen 49:26
all these *b* shall come on thee, Deut 28:2
all the words of the law, the *b* Josh 8:34
him with the *b* of goodness Ps 21:3
*B* are upon the head of the just Prov 10:6
faithful man shall abound with *b* Prov 28:20
upon you, and I will curse your *b* Mal 2:2
*b* in heavenly places in Christ Eph 1:3

### BLEW
the LORD, and *b* with the trumpets Josh 6:8
priests that *b* with the trumpets Josh 6:9
and *b* with the trumpets Josh 6:13
when the priests *b* with the Josh 6:16
the priests *b* with the trumpets Josh 6:20
that he *b* a trumpet in the Judg 3:27
upon Gideon, and he *b* a trumpet Judg 6:34
they *b* the trumpets, and brake the Judg 7:19
three companies *b* the trumpets Judg 7:20
the three hundred *b* the trumpets Judg 7:22
Saul *b* the trumpet throughout all 1Sa 13:3
So Joab *b* a trumpet, and all the 2Sa 2:28
Joab *b* the trumpet, and the people 2Sa 18:16
he *b* a trumpet, and said, We have 2Sa 20:1
he *b* a trumpet, and they retired 2Sa 20:22
And they *b* the trumpet 1Kin 1:39
*b* with trumpets, saying, Jehu is 2Kin 9:13
land rejoiced, and *b* with trumpets 2Kin 11:14
the floods came, and the winds *b* Mt 7:25
the floods came, and the winds *b* Mt 7:27
by reason of a great wind that *b* Jn 6:18
And when the south wind *b* softly Acts 27:13
and after one day the south wind *b* Acts 28:13

### BLIND
or deaf, or the seeing, or the *b* Ex 4:11
put a stumblingblock before the *b* Lev 19:14
a *b* man, or a lame, or he that Lev 21:18
*B*, or broken, or maimed, or Lev 22:22
therein, as if it be lame, or *b* Deut 15:21
for a gift doth *b* the eyes of the Deut 16:19
the *b* to wander out of the way Deut 27:18
as the *b* gropeth in darkness, and Deut 28:29
bribe to *b* mine eyes therewith 1Sa 12:3
Except thou take away the *b* 2Sa 5:6
Jebusites, and the lame and the *b* 2Sa 5:8
Wherefore they said, The *b* 2Sa 5:8
I was eyes to the *b*, and feet was Job 29:15
LORD openeth the eyes of the *b* Ps 146:8
the eyes of the *b* shall see out Is 29:18
the eyes of the *b* shall be opened Is 35:5
To open the *b* eyes, to bring out Is 42:7
I will bring the *b* by a way that Is 42:16
and look, ye *b*, that ye may see Is 42:18
Who is *b*, but my servant Is 42:19
who is *b* as he that is perfect, Is 42:19
and *b* as the LORD's servant Is 42:19
Bring forth the *b* people that Is 43:8
His watchmen are *b* Is 56:10
We grope for the wall like the *b* Is 59:10
of the earth, and with them the *b* Jer 31:8
wandered as *b* men in the streets Lam 4:14
that they shall walk like *b* men Zeph 1:17
if ye offer the *b* for sacrifice Mal 1:8
two *b* men followed him, crying, Mt 9:27
the house, the *b* men came to him Mt 9:28
The *b* receive their sight, and the Mt 11:5
him one possessed with a devil, *b* Mt 12:22
healed him, insomuch that the *b* Mt 12:22
they be *b* leaders of the *b* Mt 15:14
they be *b* leaders of the *b* Mt 15:14
if the *b* lead the *b*, both Mt 15:14
And if the *b* lead the *b* Mt 15:14
with them those that were lame, *b* Mt 15:30
the lame to walk, and the *b* to see Mt 15:31
two *b* men sitting by the way side Mt 20:30
And the *b* and the lame came to him Mt 21:14
ye *b* guides, which say, Whosoever Mt 23:16
Ye fools and *b*: Mt 23:17
Ye fools and *b*: Mt 23:19
Ye *b* guides, which strain at a Mt 23:24
Thou *b* Pharisee, cleanse first Mt 23:26
and they bring a *b* man unto him Mk 8:22
he took the *b* man by the hand, and Mk 8:23
*b* Bartimaeus, the son of Timaeus, Mk 10:46
And they call the *b* man, saying Mk 10:49
The *b* man said unto him, Lord, Mk 10:51
and recovering of sight to the *b* Lk 4:18
them, Can the *b* lead the *b* Lk 6:39
many that were *b* he gave sight Lk 7:21
how that the *b* see, the lame walk Lk 7:22
poor, the maimed, the lame, the *b* Lk 14:13
the maimed, and the halt, and the *b* Lk 14:21
a certain *b* man sat by the way Lk 18:35
multitude of impotent folk, of *b* Jn 5:3
a man which was *b* from his birth Jn 9:1
his parents, that he was born *b* Jn 9:2
eyes of the *b* man with the clay Jn 9:6
before had seen him that he was *b* Jn 9:8
him that aforetime was *b* Jn 9:13
They say unto the *b* man again Jn 9:17
him, that he had been *b*, and Jn 9:18
your son, who ye say was born *b* Jn 9:19
is our son, and that he was born *b* Jn 9:20
called they the man that was *b* Jn 9:24
I know, that, whereas I was *b* Jn 9:25
the eyes of one that was born *b* Jn 9:32
they which see might be made *b* Jn 9:39
and said unto him, Are we *b* also Jn 9:40
said unto them, If ye were *b* Jn 9:41
a devil open the eyes of the *b* Jn 10:21
which opened the eyes of the *b* Jn 11:37
is upon thee, and thou shalt be *b* Acts 13:11
thou thyself art a guide of the *b* Rom 2:19
he that lacketh these things is *b* 2Pet 1:9
and miserable, and poor, and *b* Rev 3:17

### BLINDED
He hath *b* their eyes, and hardened Jn 12:40
obtained it, and the rest were *b* Rom 11:7
But their minds were *b* 2Cor 3:14
*b* the minds of them which believe 2Cor 4:4
that darkness hath *b* his eyes 1Jn 2:11

### BLINDETH
for the gift *b* the wise, and Ex 23:8

### BLINDFOLDED
And when they had *b* him, they Lk 22:64

### BLINDNESS
at the door of the house with *b* Gen 19:11
smite thee with madness, and *b* Deut 28:28
this people, I pray thee, with *b* 2Kin 6:18
he smote them with *b* according to 2Kin 6:18
every horse of the people with *b* Zec 12:4
that *b* in part is happened to Rom 11:25
because of the *b* of their heart Eph 4:18

### BLOOD
the voice of thy brother's *b* Gen 4:10
thy brother's *b* from thy hand Gen 4:11
thereof, which is the *b* thereof Gen 9:4
surely your *b* of your lives will Gen 9:5
Whoso sheddeth man's *b*, Gen 9:6
by man shall his *b* be shed Gen 9:6
Reuben said unto them, Shed no *b* Gen 37:22
our brother, and conceal his *b* Gen 37:26
and dipped the coat in the *b* Gen 37:31
behold, also his *b* is required Gen 42:22
and his clothes in the *b* of grapes Gen 49:11
shall become *b* upon the dry land Ex 4:9
and they shall be turned to *b* Ex 7:17
of water, that they may become *b* Ex 7:19
that there may be *b* throughout Ex 7:19
in the river were turned to *b* Ex 7:20
there was *b* throughout all the Ex 7:21
And they shall take of the *b* Ex 12:7
the *b* shall be to you for a token Ex 12:13
and when I see the *b*, I will pass Ex 12:13

| | |
|---|---|
| dip it in the *b* that is in the | Ex 12:22 |
| with the *b* that is in the bason | Ex 12:22 |
| he seeth the *b* upon the lintel | Ex 12:23 |
| there shall no *b* be shed for him | Ex 22:2 |
| there shall be *b* shed for him | Ex 22:3 |
| Thou shalt not offer the *b* of my | Ex 23:18 |
| And Moses took half of the *b* | Ex 24:6 |
| half of the *b* he sprinkled on the | Ex 24:6 |
| And Moses took the *b*, and sprinkled | Ex 24:8 |
| Behold the *b* of the covenant, | Ex 24:8 |
| take of the *b* of the bullock | Ex 29:12 |
| pour all the *b* beside the bottom | Ex 29:12 |
| the ram, and thou shalt take his *b* | Ex 29:16 |
| kill the ram, and take of his *b* | Ex 29:20 |
| sprinkle the *b* upon the altar | Ex 29:20 |
| of the *b* that is upon the altar | Ex 29:21 |
| with the *b* of the sin offering of | Ex 30:10 |
| Thou shalt not offer the *b* of my | Ex 34:25 |
| Aaron's sons, shall bring the *b* | Lev 1:5 |
| sprinkle the *b* round about upon | Lev 1:5 |
| shall sprinkle his *b* round about | Lev 1:11 |
| the *b* thereof shall be wrung out | Lev 1:15 |
| the *b* upon the altar round about | Lev 3:2 |
| *b* thereof round about upon the | Lev 3:8 |
| of Aaron shall sprinkle the *b* | Lev 3:13 |
| that ye eat neither fat nor *b* | Lev 3:17 |
| shall take of the bullock's *b* | Lev 4:5 |
| shall dip his finger in the *b* | Lev 4:6 |
| sprinkle of the *b* seven times | Lev 4:6 |
| priest shall put some of the *b* | Lev 4:7 |
| shall pour all the *b* of the | Lev 4:7 |
| *b* to the tabernacle of the | Lev 4:16 |
| dip his finger in some of the *b* | Lev 4:17 |
| he shall put some of the *b* upon | Lev 4:18 |
| shall pour out all the *b* at the | Lev 4:18 |
| *b* of the sin offering with his | Lev 4:25 |
| shall pour out his *b* at the | Lev 4:25 |
| of the *b* thereof with his finger | Lev 4:30 |
| shall pour out all the *b* thereof | Lev 4:30 |
| *b* of the sin offering with his | Lev 4:34 |
| shall pour out all the *b* thereof | Lev 4:34 |
| he shall sprinkle of the *b* of the | Lev 5:9 |
| the rest of the *b* shall be wrung | Lev 5:9 |
| of the *b* thereof upon any garment | Lev 6:27 |
| whereof any of the *b* is brought | Lev 6:30 |
| the *b* thereof shall he sprinkle | Lev 7:2 |
| the *b* of the peace offerings | Lev 7:14 |
| ye shall eat no manner of *b* | Lev 7:26 |
| it be that eateth any manner of *b* | Lev 7:27 |
| that offereth the *b* of the peace | Lev 7:33 |
| and Moses took the *b*, and put it | Lev 8:15 |
| poured the *b* at the bottom of the | Lev 8:15 |
| Moses sprinkled the *b* upon the | Lev 8:19 |
| and Moses took of the *b* of it | Lev 8:23 |
| Moses put of the *b* upon the tip | Lev 8:24 |
| Moses sprinkled the *b* upon the | Lev 8:24 |
| of the *b* which was upon the altar | Lev 8:30 |
| of Aaron brought the *b* unto him | Lev 9:9 |
| and he dipped his finger in the *b* | Lev 9:9 |
| poured out the *b* at the bottom of | Lev 9:9 |
| sons presented unto him the *b* | Lev 9:12 |
| sons presented unto him the *b* | Lev 9:18 |
| the *b* of it was not brought in | Lev 10:18 |
| in the *b* of her purifying three | Lev 12:4 |
| she shall continue in the *b* of | Lev 12:5 |
| cleansed from the issue of her *b* | Lev 12:7 |
| the living bird in the *b* of the | Lev 14:6 |
| of the *b* of the trespass offering | Lev 14:14 |
| upon the *b* of the trespass | Lev 14:17 |
| of the *b* of the trespass offering | Lev 14:25 |
| upon the place of the *b* of the | Lev 14:28 |
| dip them in the *b* of the slain | Lev 14:51 |
| the house with the *b* of the bird | Lev 14:52 |
| and her issue in her flesh be *b* | Lev 15:19 |
| *b* many days out of the time of | Lev 15:25 |
| take of the *b* of the bullock | Lev 16:14 |
| the *b* with his finger seven times | Lev 16:14 |
| bring his *b* within the vail, and | Lev 16:15 |
| do with that *b* as he did with the | Lev 16:15 |
| he did with the *b* of the bullock | Lev 16:15 |
| take of the *b* of the bullock | Lev 16:18 |
| of the *b* of the goat, and put it | Lev 16:18 |
| he shall sprinkle of the *b* upon | Lev 16:19 |
| whose *b* was brought in to make | Lev 16:27 |
| *b* shall be imputed unto that man | Lev 17:4 |
| he hath shed *b* | Lev 17:4 |
| *b* upon the altar of the LORD at | Lev 17:6 |
| you, that eateth any manner of *b* | Lev 17:10 |
| against that soul that eateth *b* | Lev 17:10 |
| the life of the flesh is in the *b* | Lev 17:11 |
| for it is the *b* that maketh an | Lev 17:11 |
| No soul of you shall eat *b* | Lev 17:12 |
| that sojourneth among you eat *b* | Lev 17:12 |
| shall even pour out the *b* thereof | Lev 17:13 |
| the *b* of it is for the life | Lev 17:14 |
| Ye shall eat the *b* of no manner | Lev 17:14 |
| of all flesh is the *b* thereof | Lev 17:14 |
| against the *b* of thy neighbour | Lev 19:16 |
| not eat any thing with the *b* | Lev 19:26 |
| his *b* shall be upon him | Lev 20:9 |
| their *b* shall be upon them | Lev 20:11 |
| their *b* shall be upon them | Lev 20:12 |
| their *b* shall be upon them | Lev 20:13 |
| their *b* shall be upon them | Lev 20:16 |
| uncovered the fountain of her *b* | Lev 20:18 |
| their *b* shall be upon them | Lev 20:27 |
| sprinkle their *b* upon the altar | Num 18:17 |
| take of her *b* with his finger | Num 19:4 |
| sprinkle of her *b* directly before | Num 19:4 |
| her skin, and her flesh, and her *b* | Num 19:5 |
| prey, and drink the *b* of the slain | Num 23:24 |
| The revenger of *b* himself shall | Num 35:19 |
| the revenger of *b* shall slay the | Num 35:21 |
| the revenger of *b* according to | Num 35:24 |
| of the hand of the revenger of *b* | Num 35:25 |
| the revenger of *b* find him | Num 35:27 |
| the revenger of *b* kill the slayer | Num 35:27 |
| he shall not be guilty of *b* | Num 35:27 |
| for *b* it defileth the land | Num 35:33 |
| of the *b* that is shed therein | Num 35:33 |
| but by the *b* of him that shed it | Num 35:33 |
| Only ye shall not eat the *b* | Deut 12:16 |
| be sure that thou eat not the *b* | Deut 12:23 |
| for the *b* is the life | Deut 12:23 |
| offerings, the flesh and the *b* | Deut 12:27 |
| the *b* of thy sacrifices shall be | Deut 12:27 |
| thou shalt not eat the *b* thereof | Deut 15:23 |
| in judgment, between *b* and *b* | Deut 17:8 |
| of the *b* pursue the slayer | Deut 19:6 |
| That innocent *b* be not shed in | Deut 19:10 |
| inheritance, and so *b* be upon thee | Deut 19:10 |
| into the hand of the avenger of *b* | Deut 19:12 |
| guilt of innocent *b* from Israel | Deut 19:13 |
| Our hands have not shed this *b* | Deut 21:7 |
| lay not innocent *b* unto thy | Deut 21:8 |
| the *b* shall be forgiven them | Deut 21:8 |
| of innocent *b* from among you | Deut 21:9 |
| thou bring not *b* upon thine house | Deut 22:8 |
| drink the pure *b* of the grape | Deut 32:14 |
| make mine arrows drunk with *b* | Deut 32:42 |
| and that with the *b* of the slain | Deut 32:42 |
| will avenge the *b* of his servants | Deut 32:43 |
| his *b* shall be upon his head, and | Josh 2:19 |
| his *b* shall be on our head, if | Josh 2:19 |
| your refuge from the avenger of *b* | Josh 20:3 |
| the avenger of *b* pursue after him | Josh 20:5 |
| by the hand of the avenger of *b* | Josh 20:9 |
| their *b* be laid upon Abimelech | Judg 9:24 |
| people did eat them with the *b* | 1Sa 14:32 |
| LORD, in that they eat with the *b* | 1Sa 14:33 |
| the LORD in eating with the *b* | 1Sa 14:34 |
| wilt thou sin against innocent *b* | 1Sa 19:5 |
| thee from coming to shed *b* | 1Sa 25:26 |
| that thou hast shed *b* causeless | 1Sa 25:31 |
| me this day from coming to shed *b* | 1Sa 25:33 |
| let not my *b* fall to the earth | 1Sa 26:20 |
| unto him, Thy *b* be upon thy head | 2Sa 1:16 |
| From the *b* of the slain, from the | 2Sa 1:22 |
| for the *b* of Asahel his brother | 2Sa 3:27 |
| the *b* of Abner the son of Ner | 2Sa 3:28 |
| now require his *b* of your hand | 2Sa 4:11 |
| of *b* to destroy any more, lest | 2Sa 14:11 |
| all the *b* of the house of Saul | 2Sa 16:8 |
| Amasa wallowed in *b* in the midst | 2Sa 20:12 |
| is not this the *b* of the men that | 2Sa 23:17 |
| shed the *b* of war in peace, and | 1Kin 2:5 |
| put the *b* of war upon his girdle | 1Kin 2:5 |
| thou down to the grave with *b* | 1Kin 2:9 |
| mayest take away the innocent *b* | 1Kin 2:31 |
| return his *b* upon his own head | 1Kin 2:32 |
| Their *b* shall therefore return | 1Kin 2:33 |
| thy *b* shall be upon thine own | 1Kin 2:37 |
| till the *b* gushed out upon them | 1Kin 18:28 |
| *b* of Naboth shall dogs lick thy | 1Kin 21:19 |
| of Naboth shall dogs lick thy *b* | 1Kin 21:19 |
| the *b* ran out of the wound into | 1Kin 22:35 |
| and the dogs licked up his *b* | 1Kin 22:38 |
| on the other side as red as *b* | 2Kin 3:22 |
| And they said, This is *b* | 2Kin 3:23 |
| that I may avenge the *b* of my | 2Kin 9:7 |
| the *b* of all the servants of the | 2Kin 9:7 |
| seen yesterday the *b* of Naboth | 2Kin 9:26 |
| the *b* of his sons, saith the LORD | 2Kin 9:26 |
| some of her *b* was sprinkled on the | 2Kin 9:33 |
| sprinkled the *b* of his peace | 2Kin 16:13 |
| all the *b* of the burnt offering | 2Kin 16:15 |
| all the *b* of the sacrifice | 2Kin 16:15 |
| shed innocent *b* very much | 2Kin 21:16 |
| for the innocent *b* that he shed | 2Kin 24:4 |
| filled Jerusalem with innocent *b* | 2Kin 24:4 |
| shall I drink the *b* of these men | 1Chr 11:19 |
| Thou hast shed *b* abundantly | 1Chr 22:8 |
| much *b* upon the earth in my sight | 1Chr 22:8 |
| been a man of war, and hast shed *b* | 1Chr 28:3 |
| their cities, between *b* and *b* | 2Chr 19:10 |
| the *b* of the sons of Jehoiada the | 2Chr 24:25 |
| and the priests received the *b* | 2Chr 29:22 |
| sprinkled the *b* upon the altar | 2Chr 29:22 |
| sprinkled the *b* upon the altar | 2Chr 29:22 |
| with their *b* upon the altar | 2Chr 29:24 |
| the priests sprinkled the *b* | 2Chr 30:16 |
| sprinkled the *b* from their hands | 2Chr 35:11 |
| O earth, cover not thou my *b* | Job 16:18 |
| Her young ones also suck up *b* | Job 39:30 |
| When he maketh inquisition for *b* | Ps 9:12 |
| offerings of *b* will I not offer | Ps 16:4 |
| What profit is there in my *b* | Ps 30:9 |
| of bulls, or drink the *b* of goats | Ps 50:13 |
| his feet in the *b* of the wicked | Ps 58:10 |
| dipped in the *b* of thine enemies | Ps 68:23 |
| shall their *b* be in his sight | Ps 72:14 |
| And had turned their rivers into *b* | Ps 78:44 |
| Their *b* have they shed like water | Ps 79:3 |
| *b* of thy servants which is shed | Ps 79:10 |
| and condemn the innocent *b* | Ps 94:21 |
| He turned their waters into *b* | Ps 105:29 |
| And shed innocent *b* | Ps 106:38 |
| even the *b* of their sons and of | Ps 106:38 |
| and the land was polluted with *b* | Ps 106:38 |
| with us, let us lay wait for *b* | Prov 1:11 |
| to evil, and make haste to shed *b* | Prov 1:16 |
| And they lay wait for their own *b* | Prov 1:18 |
| and hands that shed innocent *b* | Prov 6:17 |
| wicked are to lie in wait for *b* | Prov 12:6 |
| man that doeth violence to the *b* | Prov 28:17 |
| of the nose bringeth forth *b* | Prov 30:33 |
| delight not in the *b* of bullocks | Is 1:11 |
| your hands are full of *b* | Is 1:15 |
| shall have purged the *b* of | Is 4:4 |
| noise, and garments rolled in *b* | Is 9:5 |
| of Dimon shall be full of *b* | Is 15:9 |
| earth also shall disclose her *b* | Is 26:21 |
| his ears from hearing of *b* | Is 33:15 |
| shall be melted with their *b* | Is 34:3 |
| of the LORD is filled with *b* | Is 34:6 |
| fatness, and with the *b* of lambs | Is 34:6 |
| their land shall be soaked with *b* | Is 34:7 |
| shall be drunken with their own *b* | Is 49:26 |
| For your hands are defiled with *b* | Is 59:3 |
| make haste to shed innocent *b* | Is 59:7 |
| their *b* shall be sprinkled upon | Is 63:3 |
| as if he offered swine's *b* | Is 66:3 |
| the *b* of the souls of the poor | Jer 2:34 |
| shed not innocent *b* in this place | Jer 7:6 |
| pour out their *b* by the force of | Jer 18:21 |
| place with the *b* of innocents | Jer 19:4 |
| shed innocent *b* in this place | Jer 22:3 |
| and for to shed innocent *b* | Jer 22:17 |
| bring innocent *b* upon yourselves | Jer 26:15 |
| and made drunk with their *b* | Jer 46:10 |
| keepeth back his sword from *b* | Jer 48:10 |
| my *b* upon the inhabitants of | Jer 51:35 |
| that have shed the *b* of the just | Lam 4:13 |
| have polluted themselves with *b* | Lam 4:14 |
| but his *b* will I require at thine | Eze 3:18 |
| but his *b* will I require at thine | Eze 3:20 |
| *b* shall pass through thee | Eze 5:17 |
| great, and the land is full of *b* | Eze 9:9 |
| and pour out my fury upon it in *b* | Eze 14:19 |
| saw thee polluted in thine own *b* | Eze 16:6 |
| unto thee when thou wast in thy *b* | Eze 16:6 |
| unto thee when thou wast in thy *b* | Eze 16:6 |
| washed away thy *b* from thee | Eze 16:9 |
| bare, and wast polluted in thy *b* | Eze 16:22 |
| by the *b* of thy children, which | Eze 16:36 |
| wedlock and shed *b* are judged | Eze 16:38 |
| and I will give thee *b* in fury | Eze 16:38 |
| that is a robber, a shedder of *b* | Eze 18:10 |
| his *b* shall be upon him | Eze 18:13 |
| mother is like a vine in thy *b* | Eze 19:10 |
| thy *b* shall be in the midst of | Eze 21:32 |
| The city sheddeth *b* in the midst | Eze 22:3 |
| in thy *b* that thou hast shed | Eze 22:4 |
| in thee to their power to shed *b* | Eze 22:6 |
| men that carry tales to shed *b* | Eze 22:9 |
| have they taken gifts to shed *b* | Eze 22:12 |
| at thy *b* which hath been in the | Eze 22:13 |
| ravening the prey, to shed *b* | Eze 22:27 |
| *b* is in their hands, and with | Eze 23:37 |
| the manner of women that shed *b* | Eze 23:45 |
| and *b* is in their hands | Eze 23:45 |
| For her *b* is in the midst of her | Eze 24:7 |
| I have set her *b* upon the top of | Eze 24:8 |
| pestilence, and *b* into her street | Eze 28:23 |
| I will also water with thy *b* the | Eze 32:6 |
| his *b* shall be upon his own head | Eze 33:4 |
| his *b* shall be upon him | Eze 33:5 |
| but his *b* will I require at the | Eze 33:6 |
| but his *b* will I require at thine | Eze 33:8 |
| Ye eat with the *b*, and lift up | Eze 33:25 |
| eyes toward your idols, and shed *b* | Eze 33:25 |
| hast shed the *b* of the children | Eze 35:5 |
| *b*, and *b* shall pursue thee | Eze 35:6 |
| *b*, even *b* shall pursue thee | Eze 35:6 |
| my fury upon them for the *b* that | Eze 36:18 |
| him with pestilence and with *b* | Eze 38:22 |
| that ye may eat flesh, and drink *b* | Eze 39:17 |
| drink the *b* of the princes of the | Eze 39:18 |
| drink *b* till ye be drunken, of my | Eze 39:19 |
| thereon, and to sprinkle *b* thereon | Eze 43:18 |
| thou shalt take of the *b* thereof | Eze 43:20 |
| offer my bread, the fat and the *b* | Eze 44:7 |
| to offer unto me the fat and the *b* | Eze 44:15 |
| take of the *b* of the sin offering | Eze 45:19 |
| I will avenge the *b* of Jezreel | Hos 1:4 |
| break out, and *b* toucheth *b* | Hos 4:2 |
| iniquity, and is polluted with *b* | Hos 6:8 |
| shall he leave his *b* upon him | Hos 12:14 |
| in the heavens and in the earth, *b* | Joel 2:30 |
| into darkness, and the moon into *b* | Joel 2:31 |
| shed innocent *b* in their land | Joel 3:19 |
| their *b* that I have not cleansed | Joel 3:21 |
| and lay not upon us innocent *b* | Jonah 1:14 |
| They build up Zion with *b* | Mic 3:10 |
| they all lie in wait for *b* | Mic 7:2 |
| because of men's *b*, and for the | Hab 2:8 |
| him that buildeth a town with *b* | Hab 2:12 |
| them afraid, because of men's *b* | Hab 2:17 |
| their *b* shall be poured out as | Zeph 1:17 |
| take away his *b* out of his mouth | Zec 9:7 |
| by the *b* of thy covenant I have | Zec 9:11 |
| with an issue of *b* twelve years | Mt 9:20 |
| *b* hath not revealed it unto thee, | Mt 16:17 |
| them in the *b* of the prophets | Mt 23:30 |
| righteous *b* shed upon the earth | Mt 23:35 |
| *b* of righteous Abel unto the *b* | Mt 23:35 |
| For this is my *b* of the new | Mt 26:28 |
| I have betrayed the innocent *b* | Mt 27:4 |
| because it is the price of *b* | Mt 27:6 |
| field was called, The field of *b* | Mt 27:8 |

of the *b* of this just person ... Mt 27:24
His *b* be on us, and on our ... Mt 27:25
had an issue of *b* twelve years ... Mk 5:25
fountain of her *b* was dried up ... Mk 5:29
This is my *b* of the new testament ... Mk 14:24
having an issue of *b* twelve years ... Lk 8:43
her issue of *b* stanched ... Lk 8:44
That the *b* of all the prophets, ... Lk 11:50
From the *b* of Abel unto the *b* ... Lk 11:51
whose *b* Pilate had mingled with ... Lk 13:1
cup is the new testament in my *b* ... Lk 22:20
of *b* falling down to the ground ... Lk 22:44
Which were born, not of *b* ... Jn 1:13
of the Son of man, and drink his *b* ... Jn 6:53
eateth my flesh, and drinketh my *b* ... Jn 6:54
indeed, and my *b* is drink indeed ... Jn 6:55
eateth my flesh, and drinketh my *b* ... Jn 6:56
and forthwith came there out *b* ... Jn 19:34
that is to say, The field of *b* ... Acts 1:19
*b*, and fire, and vapour of smoke ... Acts 2:19
into darkness, and the moon into *b* ... Acts 2:20
to bring this man's *b* upon us ... Acts 5:28
from things strangled, and from *b* ... Acts 15:20
meats offered to idols, and from *b* ... Acts 15:29
hath made of one *b* all nations of ... Acts 17:26
Your *b* be upon your own heads ... Acts 18:6
I am pure from the *b* of all men ... Acts 20:26
he hath purchased with his own *b* ... Acts 20:28
offered to idols, and from *b* ... Acts 21:25
when the *b* of thy martyr Stephen ... Acts 22:20
Their feet are swift to shed *b* ... Rom 3:15
through faith in his *b*, to ... Rom 3:25
being now justified by his *b* ... Rom 5:9
the communion of the *b* of Christ ... 1Cor 10:16
cup is the new testament in my *b* ... 1Cor 11:25
of the body and *b* of the Lord ... 1Cor 11:27
*b* cannot inherit the kingdom of ... 1Cor 15:50
I conferred not with flesh and *b* ... Gal 1:16
we have redemption through his *b* ... Eph 1:7
are made nigh by the *b* of Christ ... Eph 2:13
we wrestle not against flesh and *b* ... Eph 6:12
we have redemption through his *b* ... Col 1:14
peace through the *b* of his cross ... Col 1:20
are partakers of flesh and *b* ... Heb 2:14
once every year, not without *b* ... Heb 9:7
Neither by the *b* of goats ... Heb 9:12
but by his own *b* he entered in ... Heb 9:12
For if the *b* of bulls and of goats ... Heb 9:13
much more shall the *b* of Christ ... Heb 9:14
testament was dedicated without *b* ... Heb 9:18
the law, he took the *b* of calves ... Heb 9:19
This is the *b* of the testament ... Heb 9:20
with *b* both the tabernacle ... Heb 9:21
are by the law purged with *b* ... Heb 9:22
shedding of *b* is no remission ... Heb 9:22
place every year with *b* of others ... Heb 9:25
not possible that the *b* of bulls ... Heb 10:4
the holiest by the *b* of Jesus ... Heb 10:19
counted the *b* of the covenant ... Heb 10:29
passover, and the sprinkling of *b* ... Heb 11:28
Ye have not yet resisted unto *b* ... Heb 12:4
to the *b* of sprinkling, that ... Heb 12:24
whose *b* is brought into the ... Heb 13:11
the people with his own *b* ... Heb 13:12
through the *b* of the everlasting ... Heb 13:20
of the *b* of Jesus Christ ... 1Pet 1:2
But with the precious *b* of Christ ... 1Pet 1:19
the *b* of Jesus Christ his Son ... 1Jn 1:7
is he that came by water and *b* ... 1Jn 5:6
by water only, but by water and *b* ... 1Jn 5:6
spirit, and the water, and the *b* ... 1Jn 5:8
us from our sins in his own *b* ... Rev 1:5
God by thy *b* out of every kindred ... Rev 5:9
avenge our *b* on them that dwell ... Rev 6:10
of hair, and the moon became as *b* ... Rev 6:12
them white in the *b* of the Lamb ... Rev 7:14
hail and fire mingled with *b* ... Rev 8:7
third part of the sea became *b* ... Rev 8:8
over waters to turn them to *b* ... Rev 11:6
overcame him by the *b* of the Lamb ... Rev 12:11
*b* came out of the winepress, even ... Rev 14:20
it became as the *b* of a dead man ... Rev 16:3
and they became *b* ... Rev 16:4
they have shed the *b* of saints ... Rev 16:6
thou hast given them *b* to drink ... Rev 16:6
drunken with the *b* of the saints ... Rev 17:6
with the *b* of the martyrs of ... Rev 17:6
her was found the *b* of prophets ... Rev 18:24
hath avenged the *b* of his ... Rev 19:2
with a vesture dipped in *b* ... Rev 19:13

**BLOODGUILTINESS**

Deliver me from *b*, O God, thou ... Ps 51:14

**BLOODTHIRSTY**

The *b* hate the upright ... Prov 29:10

**BLOODY**

Surely a *b* husband art thou to me ... Ex 4:25
A *b* husband thou art, because of ... Ex 4:26
Come out, come out, thou *b* man ... 2Sa 16:7
because thou art a *b* man ... 2Sa 16:8
is for Saul, and for his *b* house ... 2Sa 21:1
the LORD will abhor the *b* ... Ps 5:6
sinners, nor my life with *b* men ... Ps 26:9
*b* and deceitful men shall not live ... Ps 55:23
iniquity, and save me from *b* men ... Ps 59:2
from me therefore, ye *b* men ... Ps 139:19
for the land is full of *b* crimes ... Eze 7:23
judge, wilt thou judge the *b* city ... Eze 22:2
Woe to the *b* city, to the pot ... Eze 24:6
Woe to the *b* city ... Eze 24:9
Woe to the *b* city ... Nah 3:1
sick of a fever and of a *b* flux ... Acts 28:8

**BLOOMED**

*b* blossoms, and yielded almonds ... Num 17:8

**BLOSSOM**

rod, whom I shall choose, shall *b* ... Num 17:5
their *b* shall go up as dust ... Is 5:24
Israel shall *b* and bud, and fill ... Is 27:6
shall rejoice, and *b* as the rose ... Is 35:1
It shall *b* abundantly, and rejoice ... Is 35:2
Although the fig tree shall not *b* ... Hab 3:17

**BLOSSOMED**

the rod hath *b*, pride hath budded ... Eze 7:10

**BLOSSOMS**

it budded, and her *b* shot forth ... Gen 40:10
brought forth buds, and bloomed *b* ... Num 17:8

**BLOT**

*b* me, I pray thee, out of thy ... Ex 32:32
him will I *b* out of my book ... Ex 32:33
he shall *b* them out with the ... Num 5:23
*b* out their name from under ... Deut 9:14
that thou shalt *b* out the ... Deut 25:19
the LORD shall *b* out his name ... Deut 29:20
*b* out the name of Israel from ... 2Kin 14:27
if any *b* hath cleaved to mine ... Job 31:7
mercies *b* out my transgressions ... Ps 51:1
*b* out all mine iniquities ... Ps 51:9
a wicked man getteth himself a *b* ... Prov 9:7
neither *b* out their sin from thy ... Jer 18:23
I will not *b* out his name out of ... Rev 3:5

**BLOTTED**

sin be *b* out from before thee ... Neh 4:5
Let them be *b* out of the book of ... Ps 69:28
following let their name be *b* out ... Ps 109:13
the sin of his mother be *b* out ... Ps 109:14
I have *b* out, as a thick cloud, ... Is 44:22
that your sins may be *b* out ... Acts 3:19

**BLOTTETH**

I, even I, am he that *b* out thy ... Is 43:25

**BLOTTING**

*B* out the handwriting of ... Col 2:14

**BLOW**

Thou didst *b* with thy wind, the ... Ex 15:10
And when they shall *b* with them ... Num 10:3
if they *b* but with one trumpet, ... Num 10:4
When ye *b* an alarm, then the ... Num 10:5
When ye *b* an alarm the second ... Num 10:6
they shall *b* an alarm for their ... Num 10:6
be gathered together, ye shall *b* ... Num 10:7
shall *b* with the trumpets ... Num 10:8
then ye shall *b* an alarm with the ... Num 10:9
ye shall *b* with the trumpets over ... Num 10:10
and the trumpets to *b* in his hand ... Num 31:6
priests shall *b* with the trumpets ... Josh 6:4
When I *b* with a trumpet, I and all ... Judg 7:18
then *b* ye the trumpets also on ... Judg 7:18
in their right hands to *b* withal ... Judg 7:20
*b* ye with the trumpet, and say, ... 1Kin 1:34
did *b* with the trumpets before ... 1Chr 15:24
consumed by the *b* of thine hand ... Ps 39:10
an east wind to *b* in the heaven ... Ps 78:26
*B* up the trumpet in the new moon, ... Ps 81:3
he causeth his wind to *b*, and the ... Ps 147:18
*b* upon my garden, that the spices ... Song 4:16
and he shall also *b* upon them ... Is 40:24
*B* ye the trumpet in the land ... Jer 4:5
*b* the trumpet in Tekoa, and set up ... Jer 6:1
breach, with a very grievous *b* ... Jer 14:17
*b* the trumpet among the nations, ... Jer 51:27
I will *b* against thee in the fire ... Eze 21:31
to *b* the fire upon it, to melt it ... Eze 22:20
*b* upon you in the fire of my ... Eze 22:21
he *b* the trumpet, and warn the ... Eze 33:3
*b* not the trumpet, and the people ... Eze 33:6
*B* ye the cornet in Gibeah, and the ... Hos 5:8
*B* ye the trumpet in Zion, and ... Joel 2:1
*B* the trumpet in Zion, sanctify a ... Joel 2:15
brought it home, I did *b* upon it ... Hag 1:9
the Lord GOD shall *b* the trumpet ... Zec 9:14
And when ye see the south wind *b* ... Lk 12:55
wind should not *b* on the earth ... Rev 7:1

**BLOWETH**

when he *b* a trumpet, hear ye ... Is 18:3
the spirit of the LORD *b* upon it ... Is 40:7
that *b* the coals in the fire ... Is 54:16
The wind *b* where it listeth, and ... Jn 3:8

**BLOWING**

a memorial of *b* of trumpets ... Lev 23:24
it is a day of *b* the trumpets ... Num 29:1
going on, and *b* with the trumpets ... Josh 6:9
going on, and *b* with the trumpets ... Josh 6:13

**BLOWN**

a fire not *b* shall consume him ... Job 20:26
that the great trumpet shall be *b* ... Is 27:13
They have *b* the trumpet, even to ... Eze 7:14
Shall a trumpet be *b* in the city ... Amos 3:6

**BLUE**

And *b*, and purple, and scarlet, and ... Ex 25:4
of fine twined linen, and *b* ... Ex 26:1
of *b* upon the edge of the one ... Ex 26:4
And thou shalt make a vail of *b* ... Ex 26:31
for the door of the tent, of *b* ... Ex 26:36
an hanging of twenty cubits, of *b* ... Ex 27:16
And they shall take gold, and *b* ... Ex 28:5
make the ephod of gold, of *b* ... Ex 28:6
even of gold, of *b*, and purple, and ... Ex 28:8
of gold, of *b*, and of purple, and ... Ex 28:15
of the ephod with a lace of *b* ... Ex 28:28
the robe of the ephod all of *b* ... Ex 28:31
thou shalt make pomegranates of *b* ... Ex 28:33
And thou shalt put it on a *b* lace ... Ex 28:37
And *b*, and purple, and scarlet, and ... Ex 35:6
every man, with whom was found *b* ... Ex 35:23
which they had spun, both of *b* ... Ex 35:25
and of the embroiderer, in *b* ... Ex 35:35
of fine twined linen, and *b* ... Ex 36:8
he made loops of *b* on the edge of ... Ex 36:11
And he made a vail of *b*, and purple ... Ex 36:35
for the tabernacle door of *b* ... Ex 36:37
of the court was needlework, of *b* ... Ex 38:18
workman, and an embroiderer in *b* ... Ex 38:23
And of the *b*, and purple, and ... Ex 39:1
And he made the ephod of gold, *b* ... Ex 39:2
into wires, to work it in the *b* ... Ex 39:3
of gold, *b*, and purple, and scarlet ... Ex 39:5
of gold, *b*, and purple, and scarlet ... Ex 39:8
of the ephod with a lace of *b* ... Ex 39:21
the ephod of woven work, all of *b* ... Ex 39:22
of the robe pomegranates of *b* ... Ex 39:24
girdle of fine twined linen, and *b* ... Ex 39:29
And they tied unto it a lace of *b* ... Ex 39:31
over it a cloth wholly of *b* ... Num 4:6
they shall spread a cloth of *b* ... Num 4:7
And they shall take a cloth of *b* ... Num 4:9
they shall spread a cloth of *b* ... Num 4:11
and put them in a cloth of *b* ... Num 4:12
of the borders a ribband of *b* ... Num 15:38
and in purple, and crimson, and *b* ... 2Chr 2:7
and in timber, in purple, in *b* ... 2Chr 2:14
And he made the vail of *b*, and ... 2Chr 3:14
Where were white, green, and *b* ... Est 1:6
upon a pavement of red, and *b* ... Est 1:6
of the king in royal apparel of *b* ... Est 8:15
*b* and purple is their clothing ... Jer 10:9
Which were clothed with *b* ... Eze 23:6
*b* and purple from the isles of ... Eze 27:7
in *b* clothes, and broidered work, ... Eze 27:24

**BLUENESS**

The *b* of a wound cleanseth away ... Prov 20:30

**BLUNT**

If the iron be *b*, and he do not ... Eccl 10:10

**BLUSH**

*b* to lift up my face to thee, my ... Ezr 9:6
all ashamed, neither could they *b* ... Jer 6:15
all ashamed, neither could they *b* ... Jer 8:12

**BOANERGES** (*bo-an-er'-jees*) *Surname of James and John, the sons of Zebedee.*

and he surnamed them *B*, which is, ... Mk 3:17

**BOAR**

The *b* out of the wood doth waste ... Ps 80:13

**BOARD**

cubits shall be the length of a *b* ... Ex 26:16
shall be the breadth of one *b* ... Ex 26:16
tenons shall there be in one *b* ... Ex 26:17
under one *b* for his two tenons ... Ex 26:19
another *b* for his two tenons ... Ex 26:19
two sockets under one *b* ... Ex 26:21
and two sockets under another *b* ... Ex 26:21
two sockets under one *b* ... Ex 26:25
and two sockets under another *b* ... Ex 26:25
The length of a *b* was ten cubits ... Ex 36:21
and the breadth of a *b* one cubit ... Ex 36:21
One *b* had two tenons, equally ... Ex 36:22
under one *b* for his two tenons ... Ex 36:24
another *b* for his two tenons ... Ex 36:24
two sockets under one *b* ... Ex 36:26
and two sockets under another *b* ... Ex 36:26
silver, under every *b* two sockets ... Ex 36:30

**BOARDS**

thou shalt make *b* for the ... Ex 26:15
for all the *b* of the tabernacle ... Ex 26:17
make the *b* for the tabernacle ... Ex 26:18
twenty *b* on the south side ... Ex 26:18
of silver under the twenty *b* ... Ex 26:19
side there shall be twenty *b* ... Ex 26:20
westward thou shalt make six *b* ... Ex 26:22
two *b* shalt thou make for the ... Ex 26:23
And they shall be eight *b*, and ... Ex 26:25
five for the *b* of the one side of ... Ex 26:26
five bars for the *b* of the other ... Ex 26:27
five bars for the *b* of the side ... Ex 26:27
the *b* shall reach from end to end ... Ex 26:28
shalt overlay the *b* with gold ... Ex 26:29
Hollow with *b* shalt thou make it ... Ex 27:8
covering, his taches, and his *b* ... Ex 35:11
he made *b* for the tabernacle of ... Ex 36:20
for all the *b* of the tabernacle ... Ex 36:22
he made *b* for the tabernacle ... Ex 36:23
twenty *b* for the south side ... Ex 36:23
silver he made under the twenty *b* ... Ex 36:24
north corner, he made twenty *b* ... Ex 36:25
tabernacle westward he made six *b* ... Ex 36:27
two *b* made he for the corners of ... Ex 36:28
And there were eight *b* ... Ex 36:30
five for the *b* of the one side of ... Ex 36:31
five bars for the *b* of the other ... Ex 36:32
five bars for the *b* of the ... Ex 36:32
*b* from the one end to the other ... Ex 36:33
And he overlaid the *b* with gold ... Ex 36:34

he made the altar hollow with *b* ... Ex 38:7
his furniture, his taches, his *b* ... Ex 39:33
sockets, and set up the *b* thereof ... Ex 40:18
shall be the *b* of the tabernacle ... Num 3:36
the *b* of the tabernacle, and the ... Num 4:31
house with beams and *b* of cedar ... 1Kin 6:9
the house within with *b* of cedar ... 1Kin 6:15
and the walls with *b* of cedar ... 1Kin 6:16
will inclose her with *b* of cedar ... Song 8:9
thy ship *b* of fir trees of Senir ... Eze 27:5
And the rest, some on *b*, and some ... Acts 27:44

## BOAST

*b* himself as he that putteth it ... 1Kin 20:11
thine heart lifteth thee up to *b* ... 2Chr 25:19
soul shall make her *b* in the LORD ... Ps 34:2
In God we *b* all the day long, and ... Ps 44:8
*b* themselves in the multitude of ... Ps 49:6
workers of iniquity *b* themselves ... Ps 94:4
that *b* themselves of idols ... Ps 97:7
*B* not thyself of to morrow ... Prov 27:1
Shall the ax *b* itself against him ... Is 10:15
their glory shall ye *b* yourselves ... Is 61:6
the law, and makest thy *b* of God ... Rom 2:17
Thou that makest thy *b* of the law ... Rom 2:23
*B* not against the branches ... Rom 11:18
But if thou *b*, thou bearest not ... Rom 11:18
for which I *b* of you to them of ... 2Cor 9:2
For though I should *b* somewhat ... 2Cor 10:8
But we will not *b* of things ... 2Cor 10:13
not to *b* in another man's line of ... 2Cor 10:16
that I may *b* myself a little ... 2Cor 11:16
of works, lest any man should *b* ... Eph 2:9

## BOASTED

your mouth ye have *b* against me ... Eze 35:13
For if I have *b* any thing to him ... 2Cor 7:14

## BOASTERS

of God, despiteful, proud, *b* ... Rom 1:30
of their own selves, covetous, *b* ... 2Ti 3:2

## BOASTEST

Why *b* thou thyself in mischief, O ... Ps 52:1

## BOASTETH

For the wicked *b* of his heart's ... Ps 10:3
he is gone his way, then he *b* ... Prov 20:14
Whoso *b* himself of a false gift ... Prov 25:14
little member, and *b* great things ... Jas 3:5

## BOASTING

Theudas, *b* himself to be somebody ... Acts 5:36
Where is *b* then ... Rom 3:27
to you in truth, even so our *b* ... 2Cor 7:14
love, and of our *b* on your behalf ... 2Cor 8:24
lest our *b* of you should be in ... 2Cor 9:3
ashamed in this same confident *b* ... 2Cor 9:4
Not *b* of things without our ... 2Cor 10:15
this *b* in the regions of Achaia ... 2Cor 11:10
in this confidence of *b* ... 2Cor 11:17

## BOASTINGS

But now ye rejoice in your *b* ... Jas 4:16

## BOAT

there went over a ferry *b* to ... 2Sa 19:18
that there was none other *b* there ... Jn 6:22
not with his disciples into the *b* ... Jn 6:22
we had much work to come by the *b* ... Acts 27:16
had let down the *b* into the sea ... Acts 27:30
cut off the ropes of the *b* ... Acts 27:32

## BOATS

(Howbeit there came other *b* from ... Jn 6:23

## BOAZ (*bo'-az*) See Booz.

*1. Husband of Ruth.*
and his name was *B* ... Ruth 2:1
of the field belonging unto *B* ... Ruth 2:3
*B* came from Beth-lehem, and said ... Ruth 2:4
Then said *B* unto his servant that ... Ruth 2:5
Then said *B* unto Ruth, Hearest ... Ruth 2:8
*B* answered and said unto her, It ... Ruth 2:11
*B* said unto her, At mealtime come ... Ruth 2:14
*B* commanded his young men, saying ... Ruth 2:15
with whom I wrought to day is *B* ... Ruth 2:19
*B* to glean unto the end of barley ... Ruth 2:23
now is not *B* of our kindred, with ... Ruth 3:2
when *B* had eaten and drunk, and his ... Ruth 3:7
Then went *B* up to the gate, and ... Ruth 4:1
kinsman of whom *B* spake came by ... Ruth 4:1
Then said *B*, What day thou buyest ... Ruth 4:5
Therefore the kinsman said unto *B* ... Ruth 4:8
*B* said unto the elders, and unto ... Ruth 4:9
So *B* took Ruth, and she was his ... Ruth 4:13
And Salmon begat *B* ... Ruth 4:21
and *B* begat Obed ... Ruth 4:21
begat Salma, and Salma begat *B* ... 1Chr 2:11
*B* begat Obed, and Obed begat Jesse ... 1Chr 2:12
*2. A pillar in Solomon's Temple.*
and called the name thereof *B* ... 1Kin 7:21
and the name of that on the left *B* ... 2Chr 3:17

## BOCHERU (*bok'-er-u*) *A relative of Saul.*

whose names are these, Azrikam, *B* ... 1Chr 8:38
whose names are these, Azrikam, *B* ... 1Chr 9:44

## BOCHIM (*bo'-kim*) *A place near Gilgal.*

the LORD came up from Gilgal to *B* ... Judg 2:1
called the name of that place *B* ... Judg 2:5

## BODIES

the sight of my lord, but our *b* ... Gen 47:18
the *b* of his sons from the wall ... 1Sa 31:12
the *b* of his sons, and brought ... 1Chr 10:12
they were dead *b* fallen to the ... 2Chr 20:24
both riches with the dead *b* ... 2Chr 20:25
they have dominion over our *b* ... Neh 9:37
ashes, your *b* to *b* of clay ... Job 13:12
ashes, your *b* to *b* of clay ... Job 13:12
The dead *b* of thy servants have ... Ps 79:2
fill the places with the dead *b* ... Ps 110:6
And the whole valley of the dead *b* ... Jer 31:40
fill them with the dead *b* of men ... Jer 33:5
their dead *b* shall be for meat ... Jer 34:20
cast all the dead *b* of the men ... Jer 41:9
another, and two covered their *b* ... Eze 1:11
covered on that side, their *b* ... Eze 1:23
upon whose *b* the fire had no ... Dan 3:27
king's word, and yielded their *b* ... Dan 3:28
be many dead *b* in every place ... Amos 8:3
many *b* of the saints which slept ... Mt 27:52
that the *b* should not remain upon ... Jn 19:31
their own *b* between themselves ... Rom 1:24
*b* by his Spirit that dwelleth in ... Rom 8:11
present your *b* a living sacrifice ... Rom 12:1
Know ye not that your *b* are the ... 1Cor 6:15
There are also celestial *b* ... 1Cor 15:40
and *b* terrestrial ... 1Cor 15:40
love their wives as their own *b* ... Eph 5:28
our *b* washed with pure water ... Heb 10:22
For the *b* of those beasts, whose ... Heb 13:11
their dead *b* shall lie in the ... Rev 11:8
shall see their dead *b* three days ... Rev 11:9
their dead *b* to be put in graves ... Rev 11:9

## BODILY

in a *b* shape like a dove upon him ... Lk 3:22
but his *b* presence is weak, and ... 2Cor 10:10
all the fulness of the Godhead *b* ... Col 2:9
For *b* exercise profiteth little ... 1Ti 4:8

## BODY

as it were the *b* of heaven in his ... Ex 24:10
shall he go in to any dead *b* ... Lev 21:11
LORD he shall come at no dead *b* ... Num 6:6
defiled by the dead *b* of a man ... Num 9:6
defiled by the dead *b* of a man ... Num 9:7
be unclean by reason of a dead *b* ... Num 9:10
He that toucheth the dead *b* of ... Num 19:11
dead *b* of any man that is dead ... Num 19:13
in the open fields, or a dead *b* ... Num 19:16
His *b* shall not remain all night ... Deut 21:23
shall be the fruit of thy *b* ... Deut 28:4
in goods, in the fruit of thy *b* ... Deut 28:11
shall be the fruit of thy *b* ... Deut 28:18
eat the fruit of thine own *b* ... Deut 28:53
thine hand, in the fruit of thy *b* ... Deut 30:9
and ten sons of his *b* begotten ... Judg 8:30
they fastened his *b* to the wall ... 1Sa 31:10
all night, and took the *b* of Saul ... 1Sa 31:12
he had restored a dead *b* to life ... 2Kin 8:5
men, and took away the *b* of Saul ... 1Chr 10:12
the children's sake of mine own *b* ... Job 19:17
my skin worms destroy this *b* ... Job 19:26
is drawn, and cometh out of the *b* ... Job 20:25
Of the fruit of thy *b* will I set ... Ps 132:11
thy flesh and thy *b* are consumed ... Prov 5:11
fruitful field, both soul and *b* ... Is 10:18
with my dead *b* shall they arise ... Is 26:19
hast laid thy *b* as the ground ... Is 51:23
cast his dead *b* into the graves ... Jer 26:23
his dead *b* shall be cast out in ... Jer 36:30
were more ruddy in *b* than rubies ... Lam 4:7
And their whole *b*, and their backs ... Eze 10:12
his *b* was wet with the dew of ... Dan 4:33
his *b* was wet with the dew of ... Dan 5:21
his *b* destroyed, and given to the ... Dan 7:11
in my spirit in the midst of my *b* ... Dan 7:15
His *b* also was like the beryl, and ... Dan 10:6
the fruit of my *b* for the sin of ... Mic 6:7
by a dead *b* touch any of these ... Hag 2:13
not that thy whole *b* should be ... Mt 5:29
not that thy whole *b* should be ... Mt 5:30
The light of the *b* is the eye ... Mt 6:22
thy whole *b* shall be full of ... Mt 6:22
thy whole *b* shall be full of ... Mt 6:23
nor yet for your *b*, what ye shall ... Mt 6:25
than meat, and the *b* than raiment ... Mt 6:25
And fear not them which kill the *b* ... Mt 10:28
to destroy both soul and *b* in hell ... Mt 10:28
disciples came, and took up the *b* ... Mt 14:12
hath poured this ointment on my *b* ... Mt 26:12
this is my *b* ... Mt 26:26
Pilate, and begged the *b* of Jesus ... Mt 27:58
commanded the *b* to be delivered ... Mt 27:58
And when Joseph had taken the *b* ... Mt 27:59
she felt in her *b* that she was ... Mk 5:29
to anoint my *b* to the burying ... Mk 14:8
this is my *b* ... Mk 14:22
cloth cast about his naked *b* ... Mk 14:51
Pilate, and craved the *b* of Jesus ... Mk 15:43
he gave the *b* to Joseph ... Mk 15:45
The light of the *b* is the eye ... Lk 11:34
thy whole *b* also is full of light ... Lk 11:34
thy *b* also is full of darkness ... Lk 11:34
If thy whole *b* therefore be full ... Lk 11:36
afraid of them that kill the *b* ... Lk 12:4
neither for the *b*, what ye shall ... Lk 12:22
the *b* is more than raiment ... Lk 12:23
unto them, Wheresoever the *b* is ... Lk 17:37
This is my *b* which is given for ... Lk 22:19
Pilate, and begged the *b* of Jesus ... Lk 23:52
sepulchre, and how his *b* was laid ... Lk 23:55
found not the *b* of the Lord Jesus ... Lk 24:3
And when they found not his *b* ... Lk 24:23
he spake of the temple of his *b* ... Jn 2:21
he might take away the *b* of Jesus ... Jn 19:38
therefore, and took the *b* of Jesus ... Jn 19:38
Then took they the *b* of Jesus ... Jn 19:40
where the *b* of Jesus had lain ... Jn 20:12
and turning him to the *b* said ... Acts 9:40
So that from his *b* were brought ... Acts 19:12
considered not his own *b* now dead ... Rom 4:19
that the *b* of sin might be ... Rom 6:6
therefore reign in your mortal *b* ... Rom 6:12
to the law by the *b* of Christ ... Rom 7:4
me from the *b* of this death ... Rom 7:24
the *b* is dead because of sin ... Rom 8:10
do mortify the deeds of the *b* ... Rom 8:13
to wit, the redemption of our *b* ... Rom 8:23
as we have many members in one *b* ... Rom 12:4
are one *b* in Christ, and every one ... Rom 12:5
For I verily, as absent in *b* ... 1Cor 5:3
Now the *b* is not for fornication ... 1Cor 6:13
and the Lord for the *b* ... 1Cor 6:13
is joined to an harlot is one *b* ... 1Cor 6:16
that a man doeth is without the *b* ... 1Cor 6:18
sinneth against his own *b* ... 1Cor 6:18
know ye not that your *b* is the ... 1Cor 6:19
therefore glorify God in your *b* ... 1Cor 6:20
wife hath not power of her own *b* ... 1Cor 7:4
hath not power of his own *b* ... 1Cor 7:4
that she may be holy both in *b* ... 1Cor 7:34
But I keep under my *b*, and bring ... 1Cor 9:27
the communion of the *b* of Christ ... 1Cor 10:16
many are one bread, and one *b* ... 1Cor 10:17
this is my *b*, which is broken for ... 1Cor 11:24
shall be guilty of the *b* ... 1Cor 11:27
not discerning the Lord's *b* ... 1Cor 11:29
For as the *b* is one, and hath many ... 1Cor 12:12
one *b*, being many, are one *b* ... 1Cor 12:12
are we all baptized into one *b* ... 1Cor 12:13
For the *b* is not one member, but ... 1Cor 12:14
not the hand, I am not of the *b* ... 1Cor 12:15
is it therefore not of the *b* ... 1Cor 12:15
am not the eye, I am not of the *b* ... 1Cor 12:16
is it therefore not of the *b* ... 1Cor 12:16
If the whole *b* were an eye ... 1Cor 12:17
every one of them in the *b* ... 1Cor 12:18
all one member, where were the *b* ... 1Cor 12:19
they many members, yet but one *b* ... 1Cor 12:20
much more those members of the *b* ... 1Cor 12:22
And those members of the *b* ... 1Cor 12:23
God hath tempered the *b* together ... 1Cor 12:24
should be no schism in the *b* ... 1Cor 12:25
Now ye are the *b* of Christ ... 1Cor 12:27
though I give my *b* to be burned ... 1Cor 13:3
and with what *b* do they come ... 1Cor 15:35
sowest not that *b* that shall be ... 1Cor 15:37
But God giveth it a *b* as it hath ... 1Cor 15:38
him, and to every seed his own *b* ... 1Cor 15:38
It is sown a natural *b* ... 1Cor 15:44
it is raised a spiritual *b* ... 1Cor 15:44
There is a natural *b* ... 1Cor 15:44
and there is a spiritual *b* ... 1Cor 15:44
the *b* the dying of the Lord Jesus ... 2Cor 4:10
might be made manifest in our *b* ... 2Cor 4:10
whilst we are at home in the *b* ... 2Cor 5:6
rather to be absent from the *b* ... 2Cor 5:8
receive the things done in his *b* ... 2Cor 5:10
years ago, (whether in the *b* ... 2Cor 12:2
or whether out of the *b*, I cannot ... 2Cor 12:2
in the *b*, or out of the *b* ... 2Cor 12:3
for I bear in my *b* the marks of ... Gal 6:17
Which is his *b*, the fulness of ... Eph 1:23
unto God in one *b* by the cross ... Eph 2:16
be fellowheirs, and of the same *b* ... Eph 3:6
There is one *b*, and one Spirit ... Eph 4:4
the edifying of the *b* of Christ ... Eph 4:12
From whom the whole *b* fitly ... Eph 4:16
maketh increase of the *b* unto the ... Eph 4:16
and he is the saviour of the *b* ... Eph 5:23
For we are members of his *b* ... Eph 5:30
Christ shall be magnified in my *b* ... Phil 1:20
Who shall change our vile *b* ... Phil 3:21
like unto his glorious *b* ... Phil 3:21
And he is the head of the *b* ... Col 1:18
In the *b* of his flesh through ... Col 1:22
in putting off the *b* of the sins ... Col 2:11
but the *b* is of Christ ... Col 2:17
from which all the *b* by joints ... Col 2:19
humility, and neglecting of the *b* ... Col 2:23
which also ye are called in one *b* ... Col 3:15
*b* be preserved blameless unto the ... 1Th 5:23
but a *b* hast thou prepared me ... Heb 10:5
through the offering of the *b* of ... Heb 10:10
as being yourselves also in the *b* ... Heb 13:3
things which are needful to the *b* ... Jas 2:16
For as the *b* without the spirit ... Jas 2:26
able also to bridle the whole *b* ... Jas 3:2
and we turn about their whole *b* ... Jas 3:3
that it defileth the whole *b* ... Jas 3:6
our sins in his own *b* on the tree ... 1Pet 2:24
he disputed about the *b* of Moses ... Jude 9

## BODY'S

Christ in my flesh for his *b* sake ... Col 1:24

## BOHAN (*bo'-han*) *A namesake of a border stone.*

the stone of *B* the son of Reuben ... Josh 15:6
the stone of *B* the son of Reuben ... Josh 18:17

## BOIL

shall be a *b* breaking forth with ... Ex 9:9
it became a *b* breaking forth with ... Ex 9:10
for the *b* was upon the magicians ... Ex 9:11

*B* the flesh at the door of the ... Lev 8:31
even in the skin thereof, was a *b* ... Lev 13:18
in the place of the *b* there be a ... Lev 13:19
of leprosy broken out of the *b* ... Lev 13:20
and spread not, it is a burning *b* ... Lev 13:23
And they took and laid it on the *b* ... 2Kin 20:7
maketh the deep to *b* like a pot ... Job 41:31
lay it for a plaister upon the *b* ... Is 38:21
the fire causeth the waters to *b* ... Is 64:2
bones under it, and make it *b* well ... Eze 24:5
shall *b* the trespass offering ... Eze 46:20
are the places of them that *b* ... Eze 46:24
*b* the sacrifice of the people ... Eze 46:24

**BOILED**
them, and *b* their flesh with the ... 1Kin 19:21
So we *b* my son, and did eat him ... 2Kin 6:29
My bowels *b*, and rested not ... Job 30:27

**BOILING**
it was made with *b* places under ... Eze 46:23

**BOILS**
before Moses because of the *b* ... Ex 9:11
smote Job with sore *b* from the ... Job 2:7

**BOISTEROUS**
But when he saw the wind *b* ... Mt 14:30

**BOKERU** See BOCHERU.

**BOKIM** See BOCHIM.

**BOLD**
but the righteous are *b* as a lion ... Prov 28:1
Then Paul and Barnabas waxed *b* ... Acts 13:46
But Esaias is very *b*, and saith, I ... Rom 10:20
but being absent am *b* toward you ... 2Cor 10:1
that I may not be *b* when I am ... 2Cor 10:2
I think to be *b* against some ... 2Cor 10:2
Howbeit whereinsoever any is *b* ... 2Cor 11:21
(I speak foolishly,) I am *b* also ... 2Cor 11:21
are much more *b* to speak the word ... Phil 1:14
we were *b* in our God to speak ... 1Th 2:2
though I might be much *b* in ... Philem 8

**BOLDLY**
sword, and came upon the city *b* ... Gen 34:25
went in *b* unto Pilate, and craved ... Mk 15:43
But, lo, he speaketh *b*, and they ... Jn 7:26
how he had preached *b* at Damascus ... Acts 9:27
he spake *b* in the name of the ... Acts 9:29
abode they speaking *b* in the Lord ... Acts 14:3
began to speak *b* in the synagogue ... Acts 18:26
spake *b* for the space of three ... Acts 19:8
the more *b* unto you in some sort ... Rom 15:15
me, that I may open my mouth *b* ... Eph 6:19
that therein I may speak *b* ... Eph 6:20
Let us therefore come *b* unto the ... Heb 4:16
So that we may *b* say, The Lord is ... Heb 13:6

**BOLDNESS**
the *b* of his face shall be ... Eccl 8:1
Now when they saw the *b* of Peter ... Acts 4:13
that with all *b* they may speak ... Acts 4:29
they spake the word of God with *b* ... Acts 4:31
Great is my *b* of speech toward ... 2Cor 7:4
In whom we have *b* and access with ... Eph 3:12
be ashamed, but that with all *b* ... Phil 1:20
great *b* in the faith which is in ... 1Ti 3:13
*b* to enter into the holiest by ... Heb 10:19
that we may have *b* in the day of ... 1Jn 4:17

**BOLLED**
was in the ear, and the flax was *b* ... Ex 9:31

**BOLSTER**
a pillow of goats' hair for his *b* ... 1Sa 19:13
a pillow of goats' hair for his *b* ... 1Sa 19:16
stuck in the ground at his *b* ... 1Sa 26:7
now the spear that is at his *b* ... 1Sa 26:11
the cruse of water from Saul's *b* ... 1Sa 26:12
cruse of water that was at his *b* ... 1Sa 26:16

**BOLT**
from me, and *b* the door after her ... 2Sa 13:17

**BOLTED**
her out, and *b* the door after her ... 2Sa 13:18

**BOND**
an oath to bind his soul with a *b* ... Num 30:2
the LORD, and bind herself by a *b* ... Num 30:3
her *b* wherewith she hath bound ... Num 30:4
every *b* wherewith she hath bound ... Num 30:4
her soul by a *b* with an oath ... Num 30:10
every *b* wherewith she bound her ... Num 30:11
or concerning the *b* of her soul ... Num 30:12
He looseth the *b* of kings ... Job 12:18
you into the *b* of the covenant ... Eze 20:37
from this *b* on the sabbath day ... Lk 13:16
and in the *b* of iniquity ... Acts 8:23
Gentiles, whether we be *b* or free ... 1Cor 12:13
there is neither *b* nor free ... Gal 3:28
of the Spirit in the *b* of peace ... Eph 4:3
the Lord, whether he be *b* or free ... Eph 6:8
Barbarian, Scythian, *b* nor free ... Col 3:11
which is the *b* of perfectness ... Col 3:14
and great, rich and poor, free and *b* ... Rev 13:16
flesh of all men, both free and *b* ... Rev 19:18

**BONDAGE**
their lives bitter with hard *b* ... Ex 1:14
Israel sighed by reason of the *b* ... Ex 2:23
up unto God by reason of the *b* ... Ex 2:23
whom the Egyptians keep in *b* ... Ex 6:5
and I will rid you out of their *b* ... Ex 6:6
anguish of spirit, and for cruel *b* ... Ex 6:9
from Egypt, out of the house of *b* ... Ex 13:3
from Egypt, from the house of *b* ... Ex 13:14
of Egypt, out of the house of *b* ... Ex 20:2
of Egypt, from the house of *b* ... Deut 5:6
of Egypt, from the house of *b* ... Deut 6:12
of Egypt, from the house of *b* ... Deut 8:14
you out of the house of *b* ... Deut 13:5
of Egypt, from the house of *b* ... Deut 13:10
us, and laid upon us hard *b* ... Deut 26:6
of Egypt, from the house of *b* ... Josh 24:17
you forth out of the house of *b* ... Judg 6:8
us a little reviving in our *b* ... Ezr 9:8
God hath not forsaken us in our *b* ... Ezr 9:9
and, lo, we bring into *b* our sons ... Neh 5:5
are brought unto *b* already ... Neh 5:5
because the *b* was heavy upon this ... Neh 5:18
a captain to return to their *b* ... Neh 9:17
from the hard *b* wherein thou wast ... Is 14:3
and were never in *b* to any man ... Jn 8:33
they should bring them into *b* ... Acts 7:6
they shall be in *b* will I judge ... Acts 7:7
the spirit of *b* again to fear ... Rom 8:15
shall be delivered from the *b* of ... Rom 8:21
is not under *b* in such cases ... 1Cor 7:15
suffer, if a man bring you into *b* ... 2Cor 11:20
that they might bring us into *b* ... Gal 2:4
were in *b* under the elements of ... Gal 4:3
ye desire again to be in *b* ... Gal 4:9
mount Sinai, which gendereth to *b* ... Gal 4:24
is in *b* with her children ... Gal 4:25
again with the yoke of *b* ... Gal 5:1
all their lifetime subject to *b* ... Heb 2:15
of the same is he brought in *b* ... 2Pet 2:19

**BONDMAID**
with a woman, that is a *b* ... Lev 19:20
had two sons, the one by a *b* ... Gal 4:22

**BONDMAIDS**
Both thy bondmen, and thy *b* ... Lev 25:44
of them shall ye buy bondmen and *b* .. Lev 25:44

**BONDMAN**
instead of the lad a *b* to my lord ... Gen 44:33
wast a *b* in the land of Egypt ... Deut 15:15
that thou wast a *b* in Egypt ... Deut 16:12
that thou wast a *b* in Egypt ... Deut 24:18
wast a *b* in the land of Egypt ... Deut 24:22
and the mighty men, and every *b* ... Rev 6:15

**BONDMEN**
and fall upon us, and take us for *b* ... Gen 43:18
and we also will be my lord's *b* ... Gen 44:9
they shall not be sold as *b* ... Lev 25:42
Both thy *b*, and thy bondmaids, ... Lev 25:44
of them shall ye buy *b* and ... Lev 25:44
they shall be your *b* for ever ... Lev 25:46
that ye should not be their *b* ... Lev 26:13
son, We were Pharaoh's *b* in Egypt ... Deut 6:21
you out of the house of *b* ... Deut 7:8
be sold unto your enemies for *b* ... Deut 28:68
none of you be freed from being *b* ... Josh 9:23
of Israel did Solomon make no *b* ... 1Kin 9:22
take unto him my two sons to be *b* ... 2Kin 4:1
of Judah and Jerusalem for *b* ... 2Chr 28:10
For we were *b* ... Ezr 9:9
But if we had been sold for *b* ... Est 7:4
of Egypt, out of the house of *b* ... Jer 34:13

**BONDS**
or of her *b* wherewith she hath ... Num 30:5
her *b* wherewith she bound her ... Num 30:7
all her vows, or all her *b* ... Num 30:14
thou hast loosed my *b* ... Ps 116:16
broken the yoke, and burst the *b* ... Jer 5:5
Make thee *b* and yokes, and put them ... Jer 27:2
off thy neck, and will burst thy *b* ... Jer 30:8
and will burst thy *b* in sunder ... Nah 1:13
in every city, saying that *b* ... Acts 20:23
charge worthy of death or of *b* ... Acts 23:29
a certain man left in *b* by Felix ... Acts 25:14
such as I am, except these *b* ... Acts 26:29
nothing worthy of death or of *b* ... Acts 26:31
For which I am an ambassador in *b* ... Eph 6:20
inasmuch as both in my *b*, and in ... Phil 1:7
So that my *b* in Christ are ... Phil 1:13
Lord, waxing confident by my *b* ... Phil 1:14
to add affliction to my *b* ... Phil 1:16
Christ, for which I am also in *b* ... Col 4:3
Remember my *b* ... Col 4:18
as an evil doer, even unto *b* ... 2Ti 2:9
whom I have begotten in my *b* ... Philem 10
unto me in the *b* of the gospel ... Philem 13
ye had compassion of me in my *b* ... Heb 10:34
and scourgings, yea, moreover of *b* ... Heb 11:36
Remember them that are in *b* ... Heb 13:3

**BONDSERVANT**
not compel him to serve as a *b* ... Lev 25:39

**BONDSERVICE**
levy a tribute of *b* unto this day ... 1Kin 9:21

**BONDWOMAN**
unto Abraham, Cast out this *b* ... Gen 21:10
for the son of this *b* shall not ... Gen 21:10
of the lad, and because of thy *b* ... Gen 21:12
son of the *b* will I make a nation ... Gen 21:13
But he who was of the *b* was born ... Gal 4:23
Cast out the *b* and her son ... Gal 4:30
for the son of the *b* shall not be ... Gal 4:30
we are not children of the *b* ... Gal 4:31

**BONDWOMEN**
your enemies for bondmen and *b* ... Deut 28:68
for bondmen and *b* unto you ... 2Chr 28:10
we had been sold for bondmen and *b* ... Est 7:4

**BONE**
said, This is now *b* of my bones ... Gen 2:23
said to him, Surely thou art my *b* ... Gen 29:14
shall ye break a *b* thereof ... Ex 12:46
morning, nor break any *b* of it ... Num 9:12
or a *b* of a man, or a grave, ... Num 19:16
and upon him that touched a *b* ... Num 19:18
remember also that I am your *b* ... Judg 9:2
saying, Behold, we are thy *b* ... 2Sa 5:1
ye to Amasa, Art thou not of my *b* ... 2Sa 19:13
saying, Behold, we are thy *b* ... 1Chr 11:1
thine hand now, and touch his *b* ... Job 2:5
My *b* cleaveth to my skin and to my ... Job 19:20
and mine arm be broken from the *b* ... Job 31:22
all mine enemies upon the cheek *b* ... Ps 3:7
and a soft tongue breaketh the *b* ... Prov 25:15
came together, *b* to his *b* ... Eze 37:7
land, when any seeth a man's *b* ... Eze 39:15
A *b* of him shall not be broken ... Jn 19:36

**BONES**
said, This is now bone of my *b* ... Gen 2:23
ye shall carry up my *b* from hence ... Gen 50:25
Moses took the *b* of Joseph with ... Ex 13:19
carry up my *b* away hence with you ... Ex 13:19
enemies, and shall break their *b* ... Num 24:8
the *b* of Joseph, which the ... Josh 24:32
divided her, together with her *b* ... Judg 19:29
And they took their *b*, and buried ... 1Sa 31:13
Ye are my brethren, ye are my *b* ... 2Sa 19:12
David went and took the *b* of Saul ... 2Sa 21:12
the *b* of Jonathan his son from ... 2Sa 21:12
up from thence the *b* of Saul ... 2Sa 21:13
the *b* of Jonathan his son ... 2Sa 21:13
they gathered the *b* of them that ... 2Sa 21:13
the *b* of Saul and Jonathan his son ... 2Sa 21:14
men's *b* shall be burnt upon thee ... 1Kin 13:2
lay my *b* beside his *b* ... 1Kin 13:31
down, and touched the *b* of Elisha ... 2Kin 13:21
their places with the *b* of men ... 2Kin 23:14
took the *b* out of the sepulchres, ... 2Kin 23:16
let no man move his *b* ... 2Kin 23:18
So they let his *b* alone ... 2Kin 23:18
with the *b* of the prophet that ... 2Kin 23:18
and burned men's *b* upon them ... 2Kin 23:20
buried their *b* under the oak in ... 1Chr 10:12
he burnt the *b* of the priests ... 2Chr 34:5
which made all my *b* to shake ... Job 4:14
flesh, and hast fenced me with *b* ... Job 10:11
His *b* are full of the sin of his ... Job 20:11
his *b* are moistened with marrow ... Job 21:24
My *b* are pierced in me in the ... Job 30:17
my *b* are burned with heat ... Job 30:30
of his *b* with strong pain ... Job 33:19
his *b* that were not seen stick ... Job 33:21
His *b* are as strong pieces of ... Job 40:18
his *b* are like bars of iron ... Job 40:18
for my *b* are vexed ... Ps 6:2
all my *b* are out of joint ... Ps 22:14
I may tell all my *b* ... Ps 22:17
iniquity, and my *b* are consumed ... Ps 31:10
my *b* waxed old through my roaring ... Ps 32:3
He keepeth all his *b* ... Ps 34:20
All my *b* shall say, LORD, who is ... Ps 35:10
rest in my *b* because of my sin ... Ps 38:3
As with a sword in my *b*, mine ... Ps 42:10
that the *b* which thou hast broken ... Ps 51:8
for God hath scattered the *b* of ... Ps 53:5
my *b* are burned as an hearth ... Ps 102:3
groaning my *b* cleave to my skin ... Ps 102:5
water, and like oil into his *b* ... Ps 109:18
Our *b* are scattered at the ... Ps 141:7
to thy navel, and marrow to thy *b* ... Prov 3:8
ashamed is as rottenness in his *b* ... Prov 12:4
but envy the rottenness of the *b* ... Prov 14:30
and a good report maketh the *b* fat ... Prov 15:30
to the soul, and health to the *b* ... Prov 16:24
but a broken spirit drieth the *b* ... Prov 17:22
nor how the *b* do grow in the womb ... Eccl 11:5
a lion, so will he break all my *b* ... Is 38:13
in drought, and make fat thy *b* ... Is 58:11
your *b* shall flourish like an ... Is 66:14
out the *b* of the kings of Judah ... Jer 8:1
the *b* of his princes, and the ... Jer 8:1
the *b* of the priests, and the ... Jer 8:1
the *b* of the prophets, and the ... Jer 8:1
the *b* of the inhabitants of ... Jer 8:1
as a burning fire shut up in my *b* ... Jer 20:9
all my *b* shake ... Jer 23:9
king of Babylon hath broken his *b* ... Jer 50:17
above hath he sent fire into my *b* ... Lam 1:13
he hath broken my *b* ... Lam 3:4
their skin cleaveth to their *b* ... Lam 4:8
I will scatter your *b* round about ... Eze 6:5
fill it with the choice *b* ... Eze 24:4
and burn also the *b* under it ... Eze 24:5
them seethe the *b* of it therein ... Eze 24:5
it well, and let the *b* be burned ... Eze 24:10
iniquities shall be upon their *b* ... Eze 32:27
of the valley which was full of *b* ... Eze 37:1
me, Son of man, can these *b* live ... Eze 37:3
unto me, Prophesy upon these *b* ... Eze 37:4
and say unto them, O ye dry *b* ... Eze 37:4
saith the Lord GOD unto these *b* ... Eze 37:5
the *b* came together, bone to his ... Eze 37:7
these *b* are the whole house of ... Eze 37:11

Our *b* are dried, and our hope is.......... Eze 37:11
brake all their *b* in pieces or................ Dan 6:24
because he burned the *b* of the............ Amos 2:1
bring out the *b* out of the house ........ Amos 6:10
and their flesh from off their *b*................ Mic 3:2
and they break their *b*, and chop............ Mic 3:3
rottenness entered into my *b*.................. Hab 3:16
gnaw not the *b* till the morrow............ Zeph 3:3
are within full of dead men's *b*............ Mt 23:27
for a spirit hath not flesh and *b*............ Lk 24:39
ancle *b* received strength...................... Acts 3:7
body, of his flesh, and of his *b*............. Eph 5:30
gave commandment concerning his *b* Heb 11:22

## BONNETS
*b* shalt thou make for them, for............ Ex 28:40
and his sons, and put the *b* on them....... Ex 29:9
goodly *b* of fine linen, and linen............ Ex 39:28
with girdles, and put *b* upon them........... Lev 8:13
The *b*, and the ornaments of the.............. Is 3:20
have linen *b* upon their heads.............. Eze 44:18

## BOOK
This is the *b* of the generations.............. Gen 5:1
Write this for a memorial in a *b*.............. Ex 17:14
he took the *b* of the covenant, and......... Ex 24:7
out of thy *b* which thou hast................. Ex 32:32
me, him will I blot out of my *b*.............. Ex 32:33
shall write these curses in a *b*.............. Num 5:23
in the *b* of the wars of the LORD........ Num 21:14
him a copy of this law in a *b* out........ Deut 17:18
law that are written in this *b*............... Deut 28:58
not written in the *b* of this law.......... Deut 28:61
in this *b* shall lie upon him................. Deut 29:20
are written in this *b* of the law............ Deut 29:21
curses that are written in this *b*......... Deut 29:27
are written in this *b* of the law............ Deut 30:10
the words of this law in a *b*............... Deut 31:24
Take this *b* of the law, and put it...... Deut 31:26
This *b* of the law shall not...................... Josh 1:8
in the *b* of the law of Moses.................. Josh 8:31
is written in the *b* of the law................ Josh 8:34
this written in the *b* of Jasher............ Josh 10:13
by cities into seven parts in a *b*........... Josh 18:9
in the *b* of the law of Moses............... Josh 23:6
words in the *b* of the law of God........ Josh 24:26
the kingdom, and wrote it in a *b*........... 1Sa 10:25
it is written in the *b* of Jasher............. 2Sa 1:18
in the *b* of the acts of Solomon .......... 1Kin 11:41
they are written in the *b* of the........... 1Kin 14:19
are they not written in the *b* of........... 1Kin 14:29
are they not written in the *b* of........... 1Kin 15:7
are they not written in the *b* of........... 1Kin 15:23
are they not written in the *b* of........... 1Kin 15:31
are they not written in the *b* of........... 1Kin 16:5
are they not written in the *b* of........... 1Kin 16:14
are they not written in the *b* of........... 1Kin 16:20
are they not written in the *b* of........... 1Kin 16:27
are they not written in the *b* of........... 1Kin 22:39
are they not written in the *b* of........... 1Kin 22:45
are they not written in the *b* of........... 2Kin 1:18
are they not written in the *b* of........... 2Kin 8:23
are they not written in the *b* of........... 2Kin 10:34
are they not written in the *b* of........... 2Kin 12:19
are they not written in the *b* of........... 2Kin 13:8
are they not written in the *b* of........... 2Kin 13:12
in the *b* of the law of Moses................ 2Kin 14:6
are they not written in the *b* of........... 2Kin 14:15
are they not written in the *b* of........... 2Kin 14:18
are they not written in the *b* of........... 2Kin 14:28
are they not written in the *b* of........... 2Kin 15:6
they are written in the *b* of the........... 2Kin 15:11
they are written in the *b* of the........... 2Kin 15:15
are they not written in the *b* of........... 2Kin 15:21
they are written in the *b* of the........... 2Kin 15:26
they are written in the *b* of the........... 2Kin 15:31
are they not written in the *b* of........... 2Kin 15:36
are they not written in the *b* of........... 2Kin 16:19
are they not written in the *b* of........... 2Kin 20:20
are they not written in the *b* of........... 2Kin 21:17
*b* of the chronicles of the kings............ 2Kin 21:25
I have found the *b* of the law in ......... 2Kin 22:8
And Hilkiah gave the *b* to Shaphan.... 2Kin 22:8
the priest hath delivered me a *b*.......... 2Kin 22:10
the words of the *b* of the law.............. 2Kin 22:11
the words of this *b* that is found........ 2Kin 22:13
unto the words of this *b*, to do........... 2Kin 22:13
even all the words of the *b* which...... 2Kin 22:16
*b* of the covenant which was found.... 2Kin 23:2
that were written in this *b*................. 2Kin 23:3
written in the *b* of this covenant......... 2Kin 23:21
*b* that Hilkiah the priest found......... 2Kin 23:24
are they not written in the *b* of........... 2Kin 23:28
are they not written in the *b* of........... 2Kin 24:5
in the *b* of the kings of Israel.............. 1Chr 9:1
in the *b* of Samuel the seer................. 1Chr 29:29
in the *b* of Nathan the prophet,............ 1Chr 29:29
in the *b* of Gad the seer,...................... 1Chr 29:29
in the *b* of Nathan the prophet............ 2Chr 9:29
in the *b* of Shemaiah the prophet...... 2Chr 12:15
in the *b* of the kings of Judah............ 2Chr 16:11
had the *b* of the law of the LORD......... 2Chr 17:9
they are written in the *b* of Jehu....... 2Chr 20:34
in the *b* of the kings of Israel............. 2Chr 20:34
the story of the *b* of the kings............ 2Chr 24:27
in the law in the *b* of Moses................ 2Chr 25:4
in the *b* of the kings of Judah............. 2Chr 25:26
in the *b* of the kings of Israel............. 2Chr 27:7
in the *b* of the kings of Judah............. 2Chr 28:26
in the *b* of the kings of Judah and .... 2Chr 32:32
in the *b* of the kings of Israel............. 2Chr 33:18
Hilkiah the priest found a *b* of........... 2Chr 34:14
I have found the *b* of the law in......... 2Chr 34:15
delivered the *b* to Shaphan.................. 2Chr 34:15
Shaphan carried the *b* to the king..... 2Chr 34:16
the priest hath given me a *b*............... 2Chr 34:18
the words of the *b* that is found......... 2Chr 34:21
all that is written in this *b*................ 2Chr 34:21
curses that are written in the *b*.......... 2Chr 34:24
*b* of the covenant that was found...... 2Chr 34:30
which are written in this *b*.................. 2Chr 34:31
it is written in the *b* of Moses............ 2Chr 35:12
in the *b* of the kings of Israel............. 2Chr 35:27
in the *b* of the kings of Israel............. 2Chr 36:8
*b* of the records of thy fathers................ Ezr 4:15
thou find in the *b* of the records............ Ezr 4:15
it is written in the *b* of Moses................ Ezr 6:18
bring the *b* of the law of Moses............... Neh 8:1
attentive unto the *b* of the law............... Neh 8:3
Ezra opened the *b* in the sight of............ Neh 8:5
So they read in the *b* in the law.............. Neh 8:8
he read in the *b* of the law of................. Neh 8:18
read in the *b* of the law of the................ Neh 9:3
in the *b* of the chronicles..................... Neh 12:23
On that day they read in the *b* of.......... Neh 13:1
it was written in the *b* of the.................. Est 2:23
he commanded to bring the *b* of............... Est 6:1
and it was written in the *b*..................... Est 9:32
are they not written in the *b* of................ Est 10:2
oh that they were printed in a *b*.............. Job 19:23
mine adversary had written a *b*.............. Job 31:35
of the *b* it is written of me......................... Ps 40:7
are they not in thy *b*................................ Ps 56:8
out of the *b* of the living........................ Ps 69:28
in thy *b* all my members were................. Ps 139:16
the words of a *b* that is sealed................ Is 29:11
the *b* is delivered to him that is............... Is 29:12
the deaf hear the words of the *b*.............. Is 29:18
in a table, and note it in a *b*..................... Is 30:8
Seek ye out of the *b* of the LORD............... Is 34:16
all that is written in this *b*.................... Jer 25:13
I have spoken unto thee in a *b*.................. Jer 30:2
subscribed the *b* of the purchase............ Jer 32:12
Take thee a roll of a *b*, and write.............. Jer 36:2
unto him, upon a roll of a *b*...................... Jer 36:4
reading in the *b* the words of the............ Jer 36:8
Then read Baruch in the *b* the............... Jer 36:10
had heard out of the *b* all the................ Jer 36:11
when Baruch read the *b* in the.............. Jer 36:13
and I wrote them with ink in the *b*....... Jer 36:18
*b* which Jehoiakim king of Judah.......... Jer 36:32
in a *b* at the mouth of Jeremiah............... Jer 45:1
So Jeremiah wrote in a *b* all the............ Jer 51:60
made an end of reading this *b*............... Jer 51:63
and, lo, a roll of a *b* was therein............. Eze 2:9
shall be found written in the *b*............... Dan 12:1
shut up the words, and seal the *b*........... Dan 12:4
The *b* of the vision of Nahum the.............. Nah 1:1
a *b* of remembrance was written............. Mal 3:16
The *b* of the generation of Jesus................. Mt 1:1
ye not read in the *b* of Moses................. Mk 12:26
As it is written in the *b* of the.................... Lk 3:4
him the *b* of the prophet Esaias................. Lk 4:17
And when he had opened the *b*.................. Lk 4:17
And he closed the *b*, and he gave it.......... Lk 4:20
himself saith in the *b* of Psalms............. Lk 20:42
which are not written in this *b*............... Jn 20:30
it is written in the *b* of Psalms............... Acts 1:20
written in the *b* of the prophets............. Acts 7:42
in the *b* of the law to do them................ Gal 3:10
whose names are in the *b* of life.............. Phil 4:3
hyssop, and sprinkled both the *b*............. Heb 9:19
of the *b* it is written of me..................... Heb 10:7
and, What thou seest, write in a *b*............ Rev 1:11
out his name out of the *b* of life............... Rev 3:5
on the throne a *b* written within.............. Rev 5:1
Who is worthy to open the *b*...................... Rev 5:2
the earth, was able to open the *b*.............. Rev 5:3
worthy to open and to read the *b*............... Rev 5:4
hath prevailed to open the *b*..................... Rev 5:5
took the *b* out of the right hand................ Rev 5:7
And when he had taken the *b*..................... Rev 5:8
Thou art worthy to take the *b*................... Rev 5:9
had in his hand a little *b* open.............. Rev 10:2
take the little *b* which is open.............. Rev 10:8
unto him, Give me the little *b*................ Rev 10:9
I took the little *b* out of the.................. Rev 10:10
names are not written in the *b* of........... Rev 13:8
names were not written in the *b*............ Rev 17:8
another *b* was opened............................ Rev 20:12
which is the *b* of life............................. Rev 20:12
was not found written in the *b* of.......... Rev 20:15
written in the Lamb's *b* of life............... Rev 21:27
sayings of the prophecy of this *b*........... Rev 22:7
which keep the sayings of this *b*............. Rev 22:9
sayings of the prophecy of this *b*........ Rev 22:10
words of the prophecy of this *b*............ Rev 22:18
that are written in this *b*...................... Rev 22:18
words of the *b* of this prophecy............ Rev 22:19
his part out of the *b* of life.................. Rev 22:19
which are written in this *b*.................... Rev 22:19

## BOOKS
of making many *b* there is no end...... Eccl 12:12
was set, and the *b* were opened............ Dan 7:10
by *b* the number of the years.................. Dan 9:2
the *b* that should be written................... Jn 21:25
arts brought their *b* together.............. Acts 19:19
comest, bring with thee, and the *b*........... 2Ti 4:13
and the *b* were opened........................ Rev 20:12
which were written in the *b*................. Rev 20:12

## BOOTH
as a *b* that the keeper maketh................ Job 27:18
the city, and there made him a *b*.......... Jonah 4:5

## BOOTHS
house, and made *b* for his cattle.......... Gen 33:17
Ye shall dwell in *b* seven days.............. Lev 23:42
Israelites born shall dwell in *b*.............. Lev 23:42
children of Israel to dwell in *b*............ Lev 23:43
of Israel should dwell in *b* in................. Neh 8:14
of thick trees, to make *b*........................ Neh 8:15
them, and made themselves *b*.................. Neh 8:16
made *b*, and sat under the *b*................... Neh 8:17

## BOOTIES
and thou shalt be for *b* unto them.......... Hab 2:7

## BOOTY
And the *b*, being the rest of the......... Num 31:32
And their camels shall be a *b*............... Jer 49:32
their goods shall become a *b*............... Zeph 1:13

**BOOZ** (*bo'-oz*) See BOAZ. *Greek form of Boaz.*
And Salmon begat *B* of Rachab................ Mt 1:5
and *B* begat Obed of Ruth........................ Mt 1:5
of Obed, which was the son of *B*............ Lk 3:32

**BOR ASHAN** See CHOR-ASHAN.

## BORDER
the *b* of the Canaanites was from....... Gen 10:19
his *b* shall be unto Zidon..................... Gen 49:13
the mount, or touch the *b* of it............ Ex 19:12
thou shalt make unto it a *b* of an......... Ex 25:25
to the *b* thereof round about................. Ex 25:25
Over against the *b* shall the.................. Ex 25:27
the breastplate in the *b* thereof............ Ex 28:26
Also he made thereunto a *b* of an......... Ex 37:12
for the *b* thereof round about............... Ex 37:12
Over against the *b* were the rings.......... Ex 37:14
the breastplate, upon the *b* of it............ Ex 39:19
a city in the uttermost of thy *b*.......... Num 20:16
give Israel passage through his *b*....... Num 20:21
for Arnon is the *b* of Moab.................. Num 21:13
Ar, and lieth upon the *b* of Moab....... Num 21:15
Israel to pass through his *b*............... Num 21:23
for the *b* of the children of.................. Num 21:24
Moab, which is in the *b* of Arnon......... Num 22:36
in Ije-abarim, in the *b* of Moab.......... Num 33:44
your south *b* shall be the outmost........ Num 34:3
your *b* shall turn from the south.......... Num 34:4
the *b* shall fetch a compass from.......... Num 34:5
And as for the western *b*, ye shall........ Num 34:6
even have the great sea for a *b*............ Num 34:6
this shall be your west *b*..................... Num 34:6
And this shall be your north *b*............. Num 34:7
*b* unto the entrance of Hamath.............. Num 34:8
forth of the *b* shall be to Zedad............ Num 34:8
the *b* shall go on to Ziphron, and......... Num 34:9
this shall be your north *b*.................... Num 34:9
east *b* from Hazar-enan to Shepham Num 34:10
the *b* shall descend, and shall............. Num 34:11
the *b* shall go down to Jordan, and... Num 34:12
the *b* of the city of his refuge............ Num 35:26
the *b* even unto the river Jabbok,........ Deut 3:16
which is the *b* of the children of......... Deut 3:16
LORD thy God shall enlarge thy *b*...... Deut 12:20
Gilgal, in the east *b* of Jericho............ Josh 4:19
which is the *b* of the children of.......... Josh 12:2
unto the *b* of the Geshurites and.......... Josh 12:5
the *b* of Sihon king of Heshbon............ Josh 12:5
unto the *b* of the children of.............. Josh 13:10
the *b* of the Geshurites and................. Josh 13:11
the *b* of the children of Reuben............ Josh 13:23
was Jordan, and the *b* thereof............... Josh 13:23
from Mahanaim unto the *b* of Debir.. Josh 13:26
king of Heshbon, Jordan and his *b*..... Josh 13:27
even to the *b* of Edom the..................... Josh 15:1
their south *b* was from the shore ......... Josh 15:2
the east *b* was the salt sea, even .......... Josh 15:5
their *b* in the north quarter was............ Josh 15:5
the *b* went up to Beth-hogla, and.......... Josh 15:6
the *b* went up to the stone of............... Josh 15:6
the *b* went up toward Debir from......... Josh 15:7
the *b* passed toward the waters of ....... Josh 15:7
the *b* went up by the valley of............. Josh 15:8
the *b* went up to the top of the............. Josh 15:8
the *b* was drawn from the top of.......... Josh 15:9
the *b* was drawn to Baalah, which....... Josh 15:9
the *b* compassed from Baalah.............. Josh 15:10
the *b* went out unto the side of........... Josh 15:11
the *b* was drawn to Shicron, and.......... Josh 15:11
out of the *b* were at the sea................ Josh 15:11
the west *b* was to the great sea,.......... Josh 15:12
the great sea, and the *b* thereof......... Josh 15:47
the *b* of the children of Ephraim.......... Josh 16:5
even the *b* of their inheritance.............. Josh 16:5
the *b* went out toward the sea to.......... Josh 16:6
the *b* went about eastward unto............ Josh 16:6
The *b* went out from Tappuah............... Josh 16:8
the *b* went along on the right.............. Josh 17:7
but Tappuah on the *b* of Manasseh..... Josh 17:8
Manasseh's, and the sea is his *b*......... Josh 17:10
their *b* on the north side was.............. Josh 18:12
the *b* went up to the side of............... Josh 18:12
the *b* went over from thence............... Josh 18:13
the *b* descended to Ataroth-adar,......... Josh 18:13
the *b* was drawn thence, and................ Josh 18:14
the *b* went out on the west, and.......... Josh 18:15
the *b* came down to the end of the..... Josh 18:16
the *b* passed along to the side of......... Josh 18:19
the outgoings of the *b* were at............ Josh 18:19
Jordan was the *b* of it on the............. Josh 18:20

the *b* of their inheritance was — Josh 19:10
their *b* went up toward the sea, — Josh 19:11
unto the *b* of Chisloth-tabor — Josh 19:12
the *b* compasseth it on the north — Josh 19:14
their *b* was toward Jezreel, and — Josh 19:18
of their *b* were at Jordan — Josh 19:22
their *b* was Helkath, and Hali, and — Josh 19:25
Rakkon, with the *b* before Japho — Josh 19:46
hath made Jordan a *b* between us — Josh 22:25
in the *b* of his inheritance in — Josh 24:30
in the *b* of his inheritance in — Judg 2:9
to the *b* of Abel-meholah, unto — Judg 7:22
but came not within the *b* of Moab — Judg 11:18
for Arnon was the *b* of Moab — Judg 11:18
them unto the *b* of Beth-shemesh — 1Sa 6:12
in the *b* of Benjamin at Zelzah — 1Sa 10:2
turned to the way of the *b* that — 1Sa 13:18
his *b* at the river Euphrates — 2Sa 8:3
and unto the *b* of Egypt — 1Kin 4:21
and upward, and stood in the *b* — 2Kin 3:21
Philistines, and to the *b* of Egypt — 2Chr 9:26
them to the *b* of his sanctuary — Ps 78:54
will establish the *b* of the widow — Prov 15:25
a pillar at the *b* thereof to the — Is 19:19
enter into the height of his *b* — Is 37:24
shall come again to their own *b* — Jer 31:17
against her from the utmost *b* — Jer 50:26
will judge you in the *b* of Israel — Eze 11:10
will judge you in the *b* of Israel — Eze 11:11
Syene even unto the *b* of Ethiopia — Eze 29:10
the *b* thereof by the edge thereof — Eze 43:13
the *b* about it shall be half a — Eze 43:17
settle, and upon the *b* round about — Eze 43:20
the west *b* unto the east *b* — Eze 45:7
This shall be the *b*, whereby ye — Eze 47:13
this shall be the *b* of the land — Eze 47:15
is between the *b* of Damascus — Eze 47:16
of Damascus and the *b* of Hamath — Eze 47:16
the *b* from the sea shall be — Eze 47:17
the *b* of Damascus, and the north — Eze 47:17
northward, and the *b* of Hamath — Eze 47:17
from the *b* unto the east sea — Eze 47:18
shall be the great sea from the *b* — Eze 47:20
the *b* of Damascus northward, to — Eze 48:1
And by the *b* of Dan, from the east — Eze 48:2
by the *b* of Asher, from the east — Eze 48:3
by the *b* of Naphtali, from the — Eze 48:4
by the *b* of Manasseh, from the — Eze 48:5
by the *b* of Ephraim, from the — Eze 48:6
by the *b* of Reuben, from the east — Eze 48:7
by the *b* of Judah, from the east — Eze 48:8
most holy by the *b* of the Levites — Eze 48:12
over against the *b* of the priests — Eze 48:13
of the oblation toward the east *b* — Eze 48:21
twenty thousand toward the west *b* — Eze 48:21
prince's, between the *b* of Judah — Eze 48:22
the *b* of Benjamin, shall be for — Eze 48:22
by the *b* of Benjamin, from the — Eze 48:24
by the *b* of Simeon, from the east — Eze 48:25
by the *b* of Issachar, from the — Eze 48:26
by the *b* of Zebulun, from the — Eze 48:27
And by the *b* of Gad, at the south — Eze 48:28
the *b* shall be even from Tamar — Eze 48:28
remove them far from their *b* — Joel 3:6
that they might enlarge their *b* — Amos 1:13
their *b* greater than your *b* — Amos 6:2
have brought thee even to the *b* — Obad 7
themselves against their *b* — Zeph 2:8
And Hamath also shall *b* thereby — Zec 9:2
The *b* of wickedness, and, The — Mal 1:4
be magnified from the *b* of Israel — Mal 1:5
it were but the *b* of his garment — Mk 6:56
touched the *b* of his garment — Lk 8:44

**BORDERS**
were in all the *b* round about — Gen 23:17
to cities from one end of the *b* — Gen 47:21
I will smite all thy *b* with frogs — Ex 8:2
unto the *b* of the land of Canaan — Ex 16:35
before thee, and enlarge thy *b* — Ex 34:24
*b* of their garments throughout — Num 15:38
fringe of the *b* a ribband of blue — Num 15:38
left, until we have passed thy *b* — Num 20:17
high way, until we be past thy *b* — Num 21:22
the *b* of the city of his refuge — Num 35:27
in the *b* of Dor on the west, — Josh 11:2
all the *b* of the Philistines, and — Josh 13:2
Egypt, even unto the *b* of Ekron — Josh 13:3
Aphek, to the *b* of the Amorites — Josh 13:4
unto the *b* of Archi to Ataroth — Josh 16:2
they came unto the *b* of Jordan — Josh 22:10
in the *b* of Jordan, at the — Josh 22:11
they had *b*, and the *b* were — 1Kin 7:28
on the *b* that were between the — 1Kin 7:29
of it were gravings with their *b* — 1Kin 7:31
under the *b* were four wheels — 1Kin 7:32
the *b* thereof were of the same — 1Kin 7:35
on the *b* thereof, he graved — 1Kin 7:36
Ahaz cut off the *b* of the bases — 2Kin 16:17
the *b* thereof, from the tower of — 2Kin 18:8
enter into the lodgings of his *b* — 2Kin 19:23
suburbs of Sharon, upon their *b* — 1Chr 5:16
by the *b* of the children of — 1Chr 7:29
hast set all the *b* of the earth — Ps 74:17
He maketh peace in thy *b*, and — Ps 147:14
We will make thee *b* of gold with — Song 1:11
is gone round about the *b* of Moab — Is 15:8
all thy *b* of pleasant stones — Is 54:12
nor destruction within thy *b* — Is 60:18
all thy sins, even in all thy *b* — Jer 15:13
for sin, throughout all thy *b* — Jer 17:3
Thy *b* are in the midst of the — Eze 27:4
in all the *b* thereof round about — Eze 45:1
and when he treadeth within our *b* — Mic 5:6
in the *b* of Zabulon and Nephthalim — Mt 4:13
enlarge the *b* of their garments, — Mt 23:5
arose, and went into the *b* of Tyre — Mk 7:24

**BORE**
his master shall *b* his ear — Ex 21:6
or *b* his jaw through with a thorn — Job 41:2

**BORED**
*b* a hole in the lid of it, and set — 2Kin 12:9

**BORN**
And unto Enoch was *b* Irad — Gen 4:18
to him also there was *b* a son — Gen 4:26
and daughters were *b* unto them — Gen 6:1
them were sons *b* after the flood — Gen 10:1
even to him were children *b* — Gen 10:21
And unto Eber were *b* two sons — Gen 10:25
*b* in his own house, three hundred — Gen 14:14
one *b* in my house is mine heir — Gen 15:3
he that is *b* in the house, or — Gen 17:12
He that is *b* in thy house, and he — Gen 17:13
Shall a child be *b* unto him that — Gen 17:17
and all that were *b* in his house — Gen 17:23
*b* in the house, and bought with — Gen 17:27
of his son that was *b* unto him — Gen 21:3
when his son Isaac was *b* unto him — Gen 21:5
for I have *b* him a son in his old — Gen 21:7
which she had *b* unto Abraham — Gen 21:9
she hath also *b* children unto thy — Gen 22:20
who was *b* to Bethuel, son of — Gen 24:15
because I have *b* him three sons — Gen 29:34
me, because I have *b* him six sons — Gen 30:20
to pass, when Rachel had *b* Joseph — Gen 30:25
their children which they have *b* — Gen 31:43
which were *b* to him in Padan-aram — Gen 35:26
which were *b* unto him in the land — Gen 36:5
unto Joseph were *b* two sons — Gen 41:50
the land of Egypt were *b* Manasseh — Gen 46:20
of Rachel, which were *b* to Jacob — Gen 46:22
which were *b* him in Egypt, were — Gen 46:27
which were *b* unto thee in the — Gen 48:5
Every son that is *b* ye shall cast — Ex 1:22
be a stranger, or *b* in the land — Ex 12:19
be as one that is *b* in the land — Ex 12:48
she have *b* him sons or daughters — Ex 21:4
conceived seed, and *b* a man child — Lev 12:2
that hath *b* a male or a female — Lev 12:7
mother, whether she be *b* at home — Lev 18:9
or *b* abroad, even their nakedness — Lev 18:9
be unto you as one *b* among you — Lev 19:34
he that is *b* in his house — Lev 22:11
*b* shall dwell in booths — Lev 23:42
as he that is *b* in the land — Lev 24:16
and for him that was *b* in the land — Num 9:14
All that are *b* of the country — Num 15:13
both for him that is *b* among the — Num 15:29
whether he be *b* in the land — Num 15:30
And unto Aaron was *b* Nadab — Num 26:60
they have *b* him children, both — Deut 21:15
but all the people that were *b* in — Josh 5:5
as he that was *b* among them — Josh 8:33
do unto the child that shall be *b* — Judg 13:8
father, who was *b* unto Israel — Judg 18:29
thee than seven sons, hath *b* him — Ruth 4:15
saying, There is a son *b* to Naomi — Ruth 4:17
so that the barren hath *b* seven — 1Sa 2:5
for thou hast *b* a son — 1Sa 4:20
the battle were Eliab the first *b* — 1Sa 17:13
unto David were sons *b* in Hebron — 2Sa 3:2
These were *b* to David in Hebron — 2Sa 3:5
yet sons and daughters *b* to David — 2Sa 5:13
that were *b* unto him in Jerusalem — 2Sa 5:14
the child also that is *b* unto — 2Sa 12:14
Absalom there were *b* three sons — 2Sa 14:27
he also was *b* to the giant — 2Sa 21:20
These four were *b* to the giant in — 2Sa 21:22
a child shall be *b* unto the house — 1Kin 13:2
And unto Eber were *b* two sons — 1Chr 1:19
which three were *b* unto him of — 1Chr 2:3
of Hezron, that were *b* unto him — 1Chr 2:9
which were *b* unto him in Hebron — 1Chr 3:1
These six were *b* unto him in — 1Chr 3:4
And these were *b* unto him in — 1Chr 3:5
that were *b* in that land slew — 1Chr 7:21
These were *b* unto the giant in — 1Chr 20:8
Behold, a son shall be *b* to thee — 1Chr 22:9
unto Shemaiah his son were sons *b* — 1Chr 26:6
wives, and such as are *b* of them — Ezr 10:3
there were *b* unto him seven sons — Job 1:2
the day perish wherein I was *b* — Job 3:3
Yet man is *b* unto trouble, as the — Job 5:7
though man be *b* like a wild ass's — Job 11:12
Man that is *b* of a woman is of — Job 14:1
Art thou the first man that was *b* — Job 15:7
and he which is *b* of a woman — Job 15:14
he be clean that is *b* of a woman — Job 25:4
thou it, because thou wast then *b* — Job 38:21
unto a people that shall be *b* — Ps 22:31
go astray as soon as they be *b* — Ps 58:3
the children which should be *b* — Ps 78:6
this man was *b* there — Ps 87:4
This and that man was *b* in her — Ps 87:5
people, that this man was *b* there — Ps 87:6
a brother is *b* for adversity — Prov 17:17
and had servants *b* in my house — Eccl 2:7
A time to be *b*, and a time to die — Eccl 3:2
whereas also he that is *b* in his — Eccl 4:14
For unto us a child is *b*, unto us — Is 9:6
or shall a nation be *b* at once — Is 66:8
that are *b* in this place, and — Jer 16:3
Cursed be the day wherein I was *b* — Jer 20:14
A man child is *b* unto thee — Jer 20:15
country, where ye were not *b* — Jer 22:26
in the day thou wast *b* thy navel — Eze 16:4
in the day that thou wast *b* — Eze 16:5
you as *b* in the country among the — Eze 47:22
her as in the day that she was *b* — Hos 2:3
of Mary, of whom was *b* Jesus — Mt 1:16
Now when Jesus was *b* in Bethlehem — Mt 2:1
is he that is *b* King of the Jews — Mt 2:2
of them where Christ should be *b* — Mt 2:4
Among them that are *b* of women — Mt 11:11
which were so *b* from their — Mt 19:12
for that man if he had not been *b* — Mt 26:24
that man if he had never been *b* — Mk 14:21
that holy thing which shall be *b* — Lk 1:35
For unto you is *b* this day in the — Lk 2:11
Among those that are *b* of women — Lk 7:28
Which were *b*, not of blood, nor — Jn 1:13
thee, Except a man be *b* again — Jn 3:3
How can a man be *b* when he is old — Jn 3:4
into his mother's womb, and be *b* — Jn 3:4
thee, Except a man be *b* of water — Jn 3:5
That which is *b* of the flesh is — Jn 3:6
that which is *b* of the Spirit is — Jn 3:6
unto thee, Ye must be *b* again — Jn 3:7
every one that is *b* of the Spirit — Jn 3:8
We be not *b* of fornication — Jn 8:41
his parents, that he was *b* blind — Jn 9:2
your son, who ye say was *b* blind — Jn 9:19
our son, and that he was *b* blind — Jn 9:20
the eyes of one that was *b* blind — Jn 9:32
Thou wast altogether *b* in sins — Jn 9:34
that a man is *b* into the world — Jn 16:21
To this end was I *b*, and for this — Jn 18:37
our own tongue, wherein we were *b* — Acts 2:8
In which time Moses was *b* — Acts 7:20
*b* in Pontus, lately come from — Acts 18:2
*b* at Alexandria, an eloquent man, — Acts 18:24
*b* in Tarsus, a city in Cilicia, — Acts 22:3
And Paul said, But I was free *b* — Acts 22:28
(For the children being not yet *b* — Rom 9:11
as of one *b* out of due time — 1Cor 15:8
bondwoman was *b* after the flesh — Gal 4:23
But as then he that was *b* after — Gal 4:29
him that was *b* after the Spirit — Gal 4:29
By faith Moses, when he was *b* — Heb 11:23
Being *b* again, not of corruptible — 1Pet 1:23
doeth righteousness is *b* of him — 1Jn 2:29
Whosoever is *b* of God doth not — 1Jn 3:9
sin, because he is *b* of God — 1Jn 3:9
every one that loveth is *b* of God — 1Jn 4:7
Jesus is the Christ is *b* of God — 1Jn 5:1
For whatsoever is *b* of God — 1Jn 5:4
whosoever is *b* of God sinneth not — 1Jn 5:18
her child as soon as it was *b* — Rev 12:4

**BORNE**
that the ark may be *b* with them — Ex 25:14
that the table may be *b* with them — Ex 25:28
stood, and on which it was *b* up — Judg 16:29
I have *b* chastisement, I will not — Job 34:31
then I could have *b* it — Ps 55:12
for thy sake I have *b* reproach — Ps 69:7
which are *b* by me from the belly, — Is 46:3
Surely he hath *b* our griefs — Is 53:4
ye shall be *b* upon her sides, and — Is 66:12
they must needs be *b*, because — Jer 10:5
She that hath *b* seven languisheth — Jer 15:9
that thou hast *b* me a man of — Jer 15:10
because he hath *b* it upon him — Lam 3:28
we have *b* their iniquities — Lam 5:7
whom thou hast *b* unto me — Eze 16:20
Thou hast *b* thy lewdness and thine — Eze 16:58
yet have they *b* their shame with — Eze 32:24
yet have they *b* their shame with — Eze 32:25
because ye have *b* the shame of — Eze 36:6
that they have *b* their shame — Eze 39:26
But ye have *b* the tabernacle of — Amos 5:26
unto us, which have *b* the burden — Mt 20:12
heavy burdens and grievous to be *b* — Mt 23:4
of the palsy, which was *b* of four — Mk 2:3
men with burdens grievous to be *b* — Lk 11:46
sent me, hath *b* witness of me — Jn 5:37
Sir, if thou have *b* him hence — Jn 20:15
that he was *b* of the soldiers for — Acts 21:35
as we have *b* the image of the — 1Cor 15:49
Which have *b* witness of thy — 3Jn 6
And hast *b*, and hast patience, and — Rev 2:3

**BORROW**
woman shall *b* of her neighbour — Ex 3:22
let every man *b* of his neighbour, — Ex 11:2
if a man *b* ought of his neighbour — Ex 22:14
nations, but thou shalt not *b* — Deut 15:6
many nations, and thou shalt not *b* — Deut 28:12
*b* thee vessels abroad of all thy — 2Kin 4:3
*b* not a few — 2Kin 4:3
from him that would *b* of thee — Mt 5:42

**BORROWED**
they *b* of the Egyptians jewels of — Ex 12:35
for it was *b* — 2Kin 6:5
We have *b* money for the king's — Neh 5:4

**BORROWER**
the *b* is servant to the lender — Prov 22:7
as with the lender, so with the *b* — Is 24:2

**BORROWETH**
The wicked *b*, and payeth not again...... Ps 37:21

**BORSHAN** See CHOR-ASHAN.

**BOSCATH** (*bos'-cath*) See BOSKETH. *A city in Judah.*
the daughter of Adaiah of *B*.................. 2Kin 22:1

**BOSOM**
I have given my maid into thy *b*........... Gen 16:5
Put now thine hand into thy *b*.................. Ex 4:6
And he put his hand into his *b*.................. Ex 4:6
Put thine hand into thy *b* again................. Ex 4:7
he put his hand into his *b* again................ Ex 4:7
and plucked it out of his *b*....................... Ex 4:7
say unto me, Carry them in thy *b*..... Num 11:12
daughter, or the wife of thy *b*............. Deut 13:6
and toward the wife of his *b*.............. Deut 28:54
evil toward the husband of her *b*....... Deut 28:56
the child, and laid it in her *b*................ Ruth 4:16
of his own cup, and lay in his *b*............. 2Sa 12:3
and thy master's wives into thy *b*.......... 2Sa 12:8
him, and let her lie in thy *b*................... 1Kin 1:2
slept, and laid it in her *b*........................ 1Kin 3:20
and laid her dead child in my *b*........... 1Kin 3:20
And he took him out of her *b*............. 1Kin 17:19
by hiding mine iniquity in my *b*........... Job 31:33
prayer returned into mine own *b*........... Ps 35:13
pluck it out of thy *b*.............................. Ps 74:11
into their *b* their reproach....................... Ps 79:12
how I do bear in my *b* the..................... Ps 89:50
nor he that bindeth sheaves his *b*.......... Ps 129:7
embrace the *b* of a stranger.................. Prov 5:20
Can a man take fire in his *b*................. Prov 6:27
man taketh a gift out of the *b* to....... Prov 17:23
man hideth his hand in his *b*.............. Prov 19:24
and a reward in the *b* strong wrath... Prov 21:14
slothful hideth his hand in his *b*......... Prov 26:15
anger resteth in the *b* of fools................ Eccl 7:9
his arm, and carry them in his *b*............. Is 40:11
even recompense into their *b*.................... Is 65:6
their former work into their *b*.................. Is 65:7
of the fathers into the *b* of..................... Jer 32:18
poured out into their mothers' *b*........... Lam 2:12
from her that lieth in thy *b*..................... Mic 7:5
over, shall men give into your *b*............. Lk 6:38
by the angels into Abraham's *b*............. Lk 16:22
afar off, and Lazarus in his *b*................ Lk 16:23
which is in the *b* of the Father................. Jn 1:18
on Jesus' *b* one of his disciples............. Jn 13:23

**BOSOR** (*bo'-sor*) *Greek form of Besor.*
the way of Balaam the son of *B*........... 2Pet 2:15

**BOSSES**
upon the thick *b* of his bucklers........... Job 15:26

**BOTCH**
smite thee with the *b* of Egypt........... Deut 28:27
with a sore *b* that cannot be............... Deut 28:35

**BOTH** See PREFACE.

**BOTTLE**
a *b* of water, and gave it unto............. Gen 21:14
And the water was spent in the *b*....... Gen 21:15
went, and filled the *b* with water........ Gen 21:19
And she opened a *b* of milk................. Judg 4:19
a *b* of wine, and brought him unto........ 1Sa 1:24
and another carrying a *b* of wine............ 1Sa 10:3
a *b* of wine, and a kid, and sent........... 1Sa 16:20
of summer fruits, and a *b* of wine.......... 2Sa 16:1
put thou my tears into thy *b*..................... Ps 56:8
I am become like a *b* in the smoke...... Ps 119:83
Every *b* shall be filled with wine.......... Jer 13:12
every *b* shall be filled with wine........... Jer 13:12
Go and get a potter's earthen *b*.............. Jer 19:1
Then shalt thou break the *b* in.............. Jer 19:10
drink, that puttest thy *b* to him............. Hab 2:15

**BOTTLES**
sacks upon their asses, and wine *b*........ Josh 9:4
these *b* of wine, which we filled,........... Josh 9:13
two *b* of wine, and five sheep,.............. 1Sa 25:18
it is ready to burst like new *b*............... Job 32:19
or who can stay the *b* of heaven.......... Job 38:37
his vessels, and break their *b*................. Jer 48:12
have made him sick with *b* of wine........ Hos 7:5
do men put new wine into old *b*............. Mt 9:17
else the *b* break, and the wine................. Mt 9:17
wine runneth out, and the *b* perish......... Mt 9:17
but they put new wine into new *b*........... Mt 9:17
man putteth new wine into old *b*.............. Mk 2:22
the new wine doth burst the *b*................. Mk 2:22
spilled, and the *b* will be marred............ Mk 2:22
new wine must be put into new *b*............ Mk 2:22
man putteth new wine into old *b*.............. Lk 5:37
the new wine will burst the *b*.................. Lk 5:37
be spilled, and the *b* shall perish............ Lk 5:37
new wine must be put into new *b*............ Lk 5:38

**BOTTOM**
they sank into the *b* as a stone................ Ex 15:5
blood beside the *b* of the altar............... Ex 29:12
the *b* of the altar of the burnt................... Lev 4:7
the *b* of the altar of the burnt................. Lev 4:18
*b* of the altar of burnt offering.............. Lev 4:25
thereof at the *b* of the altar.................... Lev 4:30
thereof at the *b* of the altar.................... Lev 4:34
wrung out at the *b* of the altar................. Lev 5:9
the blood at the *b* of the altar................. Lev 8:15
the blood at the *b* of the altar................... Lev 9:9
it, and covereth the *b* of the sea.......... Job 36:30
the *b* thereof of gold, the...................... Song 3:10
even the *b* shall be a cubit, and............ Eze 43:13
from the *b* upon the ground even........ Eze 43:14
the *b* thereof shall be a cubit............... Eze 43:17
they came at the *b* of the den............... Dan 6:24
from my sight in the *b* of the sea......... Amos 9:3
myrtle trees that were in the *b*................ Zec 1:8
in twain from the top to the *b*............... Mt 27:51
in twain from the top to the *b*.............. Mk 15:38

**BOTTOMLESS**
was given the key of the *b* pit................. Rev 9:1
And he opened the *b* pit........................ Rev 9:2
which is the angel of the *b* pit.............. Rev 9:11
*b* pit shall make war against them........ Rev 11:7
and shall ascend out of the *b* pit........... Rev 17:8
having the key of the *b* pit.................... Rev 20:1
And cast him into the *b* pit.................... Rev 20:3

**BOTTOMS**
down to the *b* of the mountains............. Jonah 2:6

**BOUGH**
Joseph is a fruitful *b*........................... Gen 49:22
even a fruitful *b* by a well.................... Gen 49:22
cut down a *b* from the trees, and......... Judg 9:48
likewise cut down every man his *b*...... Judg 9:49
shall lop the *b* with terror.......................... Is 10:33
in the top of the uppermost *b*..................... Is 17:6
strong cities be as a forsaken *b*................ Is 17:9

**BOUGHS**
first day the *b* of goodly trees.............. Lev 23:40
the *b* of thick trees, and willows........... Lev 23:40
shalt not go over the *b* again............. Deut 24:20
under the thick *b* of a great oak........... 2Sa 18:9
bring forth *b* like a plant.......................... Job 14:9
the *b* thereof were like the................... Ps 80:10
She sent out her *b* unto the sea............ Ps 80:11
I will take hold of the *b* thereof.......... Song 7:8
When the *b* thereof are withered,............ Is 27:11
and it shall bring forth *b*..................... Eze 17:23
and his top was among the thick *b*....... Eze 31:3
his *b* were multiplied, and his.............. Eze 31:5
heaven made their nests in his *b*.......... Eze 31:6
the fir trees were not like his *b*........... Eze 31:8
shot up his top among the thick *b*....... Eze 31:10
his *b* are broken by all the................ Eze 31:12
up their top among the thick *b*........... Eze 31:14
the heaven dwelt in the *b* thereof......... Dan 4:12

**BOUGHT**
or *b* with money of any stranger,......... Gen 17:12
he that is *b* with thy money, must....... Gen 17:13
all that were *b* with his money,............ Gen 17:23
*b* with money of the stranger,.............. Gen 17:27
he *b* a parcel of a field, where............. Gen 33:19
*b* him of the hands of the........................ Gen 39:1
Canaan, for the corn which they *b*..... Gen 47:14
Joseph *b* all the land of Egypt............. Gen 47:20
the land of the priests *b* he not............ Gen 47:22
I have *b* you this day and your............. Gen 47:23
which Abraham *b* with the field of..... Gen 49:30
which Abraham *b* with the field........... Gen 50:13
man's servant that is *b* for money......... Ex 12:44
*b* it until the year of jubile................... Lev 25:28
for ever to him that *b* it........................ Lev 25:30
*b* him from the year that he was......... Lev 25:50
of the money that he was *b* for............ Lev 25:51
the LORD a field which he hath *b*........ Lev 27:22
return unto him of whom it was *b*...... Lev 27:24
he thy father that hath *b* thee............ Deut 32:6
a parcel of ground which Jacob *b*...... Josh 24:32
that I have *b* all that was.................... Ruth 4:9
little ewe lamb, which he had *b*............ 2Sa 12:3
So David *b* the threshingfloor and........ 2Sa 24:24
he *b* the hill Samaria of Shemer....... 1Kin 16:24
this wall, neither *b* we any land............ Neh 5:16
Thou hast *b* me no sweet cane with...... Is 43:24
I *b* the field of Hanameel my.................. Jer 32:9
And fields shall be *b* in this land........... Jer 32:43
So I *b* her to me for fifteen...................... Hos 3:2
and sold all that he had, and *b* it........ Mt 13:46
*b* in the temple, and overthrew the....... Mt 21:12
*b* with them the potter's field,................. Mt 27:7
*b* in the temple, and overthrew the...... Mk 11:15
he *b* fine linen, and took him down..... Mk 15:46
had *b* sweet spices, that they................. Mk 16:1
I have *b* a piece of ground, and I.......... Lk 14:18
I have *b* five yoke of oxen, and I........... Lk 14:19
they did eat, they drank, they *b*............ Lk 17:28
that sold therein, and them that *b*......... Lk 19:45
in the sepulchre that Abraham *b*.......... Acts 7:16
For ye are *b* with a price...................... 1Cor 6:20
Ye are *b* with a price........................... 1Cor 7:23
even denying the Lord that *b* them......... 2Pet 2:1

**BOUND**
*b* Isaac his son, and laid him on........... Gen 22:9
*b* upon his hand a scarlet thread,......... Gen 38:28
where the king's prisoners were *b*....... Gen 39:20
the place where Joseph was *b*................. Gen 40:3
which were *b* in the prison..................... Gen 40:5
be *b* in the house of your prison........... Gen 42:19
and *b* him before their eyes.................. Gen 42:24
life is *b* up in the lad's life.................. Gen 44:30
utmost *b* of the everlasting hills............ Gen 49:26
their kneadingtroughs being *b* up.......... Ex 12:34
ephod, and *b* it unto him therewith.......... Lev 8:7
which hath no covering *b* upon it..... Num 19:15
wherewith she hath *b* her soul............... Num 30:4
she hath *b* her soul shall stand.............. Num 30:4
wherewith she hath *b* her soul.............. Num 30:5
lips, wherewith she *b* her soul.............. Num 30:6
she *b* her soul shall stand...................... Num 30:7
lips, wherewith she *b* her soul............... Num 30:8
wherewith they have *b* their souls...... Num 30:9
or *b* her soul by a bond with an......... Num 30:10
she *b* her soul shall stand.................... Num 30:11
she *b* the scarlet line in the.................... Josh 2:21
bottles, old, and rent, and *b* up.............. Josh 9:4
they *b* him with two new cords, and. Judg 15:13
mightest be *b* to afflict thee.................. Judg 16:6
dried, and she *b* him with them............ Judg 16:8
wherewith thou mightest be *b*.............. Judg 16:10
*b* him therewith, and said unto him.. Judg 16:12
me wherewith thou mightest be *b*..... Judg 16:13
*b* him with fetters of brass.................. Judg 16:21
the soul of my lord shall be *b* in........... 1Sa 25:29
Thy hands were not *b*, nor thy.............. 2Sa 3:34
*b* two talents of silver in two................ 2Kin 5:23
shut him up, and *b* him in prison......... 2Kin 17:4
*b* him with fetters of brass, and........... 2Kin 25:7
*b* him with fetters, and carried........... 2Chr 33:11
*b* him in fetters, to carry him to.......... 2Chr 36:6
And if they be *b* in fetters...................... Job 36:8
take it to the *b* thereof, and that.......... Job 38:20
out those which are *b* with chains.......... Ps 68:6
Thou hast set a *b* that they may............ Ps 104:9
being *b* in affliction and iron................. Ps 107:10
Foolishness is *b* in the heart of........... Prov 22:15
who hath *b* the waters in a................... Prov 30:4
not been closed, neither *b* up.................... Is 1:6
they are *b* by the archers.......................... Is 22:3
are found in thee are *b* together.............. Is 22:3
of the prison to them that are *b*.............. Is 61:1
the *b* of the sea by a perpetual................ Jer 5:22
cause, that thou mayest be *b* up............ Jer 30:13
*b* him with chains, to carry him............... Jer 39:7
when he had taken him being *b* in......... Jer 40:1
king of Babylon *b* him in chains............ Jer 52:11
transgressions is *b* by his hand.............. Lam 1:14
*b* with cords, and made of cedar,.......... Eze 27:24
it shall not be *b* up to be healed.......... Eze 30:21
neither have ye *b* up that which............. Eze 34:4
these men were *b* in their coats............. Dan 3:21
fell down *b* into the midst of the............ Dan 3:23
Did not we cast three men *b* into.......... Dan 3:24
The wind hath *b* her up in her.............. Hos 4:19
were like them that remove the *b*.......... Hos 5:10
Though I have *b* and strengthened....... Hos 7:15
The iniquity of Ephraim is *b* up........... Hos 13:12
her great men were *b* in chains.............. Nah 3:10
*b* him, and put him in prison for............. Mt 14:3
on earth shall be *b* in heaven................ Mt 16:19
on earth shall be *b* in heaven................ Mt 18:18
And when they had *b* him, they led........ Mt 27:2
he had been often *b* with fetters.............. Mk 5:4
*b* him in prison for Herodias'.................. Mk 6:17
*b* Jesus, and carried him away, and........ Mk 15:1
which lay *b* with them that had.............. Mk 15:7
and he was kept *b* with chains................. Lk 8:29
*b* up his wounds, pouring in oil............. Lk 10:34
of Abraham, whom Satan hath *b*............ Lk 13:16
*b* hand and foot with graveclothes.......... Jn 11:44
his face was *b* about with a..................... Jn 11:44
of the Jews took Jesus, and *b* him,........ Jn 18:12
Now Annas had sent him *b* unto............ Jn 18:24
might bring them *b* unto Jerusalem....... Acts 9:2
them *b* unto the chief priests................. Acts 9:21
two soldiers, *b* with two chains............. Acts 12:6
I go *b* in the spirit unto....................... Acts 20:22
*b* his own hands and feet, and said,... Acts 21:11
for I am ready not to be *b* only........... Acts 21:13
him to be *b* with two chains................. Acts 21:33
which were there *b* unto Jerusalem..... Acts 22:5
as they *b* him with thongs, Paul........... Acts 22:25
a Roman, and because he had *b* him. Acts 22:29
*b* themselves under a curse,................. Acts 23:12
We have *b* ourselves under a great..... Acts 23:14
which have *b* themselves with an ...... Acts 23:21
the Jews a pleasure, left Paul *b*........... Acts 24:27
of Israel I am *b* with this chain ......... Acts 28:20
is *b* by the law to her husband so.......... Rom 7:2
Art thou *b* unto a wife......................... 1Cor 7:27
The wife is *b* by the law as long........... 1Cor 7:39
We are *b* to thank God always for......... 2Th 1:3
But we are *b* to give thanks alway........ 2Th 2:13
but the word of God is not *b*...................... 2Ti 2:9
that are in bonds, as *b* with them.......... Heb 13:3
*b* in the great river Euphrates................ Rev 9:14
Satan, and *b* him a thousand years,...... Rev 20:2

**BOUNDS**
thou shalt set *b* unto the people............ Ex 19:12
Set *b* about the mount, and.................. Ex 19:23
I will set thy *b* from the Red sea.......... Ex 23:31
he set the *b* of the people................... Deut 32:8
his *b* that he cannot pass....................... Job 14:5
hath compassed the waters with *b*....... Job 26:10
have removed the *b* of the people.......... Is 10:13
the *b* of their habitation....................... Acts 17:26

**BOUNTIFUL**
He that hath a *b* eye shall be.............. Prov 22:9
nor the churl said to be *b*........................... Is 32:5

**BOUNTIFULLY**
because he hath dealt *b* with me............... Ps 13:6
the LORD hath dealt *b* with thee............ Ps 116:7
Deal *b* with thy servant, that I............ Ps 119:17
for thou shalt deal *b* with me................ Ps 142:7
soweth *b* shall reap also *b*................... 2Cor 9:6

**BOUNTIFULNESS**
enriched in every thing to all *b* 2Cor 9:11

**BOUNTY**
Solomon gave her of his royal *b* 1Kin 10:13
you, and make up beforehand your *b* 2Cor 9:5
might be ready, as a matter of *b* 2Cor 9:5

**BOW**
I do set my *b* in the cloud, and it Gen 9:13
that the *b* shall be seen in the Gen 9:14
the *b* shall be in the cloud Gen 9:16
thy weapons, thy quiver and thy *b* Gen 27:3
thee, and nations *b* down to thee Gen 27:29
thy mother's sons *b* down to thee Gen 27:29
thy brethren indeed come to *b* Gen 37:10
they cried before him, *B* the knee Gen 41:43
with my sword and with my *b* Gen 48:22
children shall *b* down before thee Gen 49:8
But his *b* abode in strength, and Gen 49:24
*b* down themselves unto me, saying Ex 11:8
Thou shalt not *b* down thyself to Ex 20:5
Thou shalt not *b* down to their Ex 23:24
in your land, to *b* down unto it Lev 26:1
Thou shalt not *b* down thyself Deut 5:9
nor *b* yourselves unto them Josh 23:7
with thy sword, nor with thy *b* Josh 24:12
them, and to *b* down unto them Judg 2:19
even to his sword, and to his *b* 1Sa 18:4
of Judah the use of the *b* 2Sa 1:18
the *b* of Jonathan turned not back 2Sa 1:22
so that a *b* of steel is broken by 2Sa 22:35
certain man drew a *b* at a venture 1Kin 22:34
I *b* myself in the house of Rimmon 2Kin 5:18
when I *b* down myself in the house 2Kin 5:18
with thy sword and with thy *b* 2Kin 6:22
Jehu drew a *b* with his full 2Kin 9:24
And Elisha said unto him, Take *b* 2Kin 13:15
And he took unto him *b* and arrows. 2Kin 13:15
Israel, Put thine hand upon the *b* 2Kin 13:16
nor *b* yourselves to them, nor 2Kin 17:35
*b* down thine ear, and hear 2Kin 19:16
and sword, and to shoot with *b* 1Chr 5:18
and shooting arrows out of a *b* 1Chr 12:2
and with him armed men with *b* 2Chr 17:17
certain man drew a *b* at a venture 2Chr 18:33
the *b* of steel shall strike him Job 20:24
my *b* was renewed in my hand Job 29:20
let others *b* down upon her Job 31:10
They *b* themselves, they bring Job 39:3
he hath bent his *b*, and made it Ps 7:12
For, lo, the wicked bend their *b* Ps 11:2
so that a *b* of steel is broken by Ps 18:34
to the dust shall *b* before him Ps 22:29
*B* down thine ear to me Ps 31:2
the sword, and have bent their *b* Ps 37:14
For I will not trust in my *b* Ps 44:6
he breaketh the *b*, and cutteth the Ps 46:9
bendeth his *b* to shoot his arrows Ps 58:7
the wilderness shall *b* before him Ps 72:9
brake he the arrows of the *b* Ps 76:3
turned aside like a deceitful *b* Ps 78:57
*B* down thine ear, O LORD, hear me Ps 86:1
O come, let us worship and *b* down Ps 95:6
*B* thy heavens, O LORD, and come Ps 144:5
*b* thine ear to my understanding Prov 5:1
The evil *b* before the good Prov 14:19
*B* down thine ear, and hear the Prov 22:17
the strong men shall *b* themselves Eccl 12:3
Without me they shall *b* down Is 10:4
drawn sword, and from the bent *b* Is 21:15
and as driven stubble to his *b* Is 41:2
That unto me every knee shall *b* Is 45:23
They stoop, they *b* down together Is 46:2
they shall *b* down to thee with Is 49:23
*B* down, that we may go over Is 51:23
is it to *b* down his head as a Is 58:5
they that despised thee shall *b* Is 60:14
ye shall all *b* down to the Is 65:12
Pul, and Lud, that draw the *b* Is 66:19
They shall lay hold on *b* and spear Jer 6:23
tongues like their *b* for lies Jer 9:3
that handle and bend the *b* Jer 46:9
I will break the *b* of Elam Jer 49:35
all ye that bend the *b*, shoot at Jer 50:14
all ye that bend the *b*, camp Jer 50:29
They shall hold the *b* and the Jer 50:42
bendeth let the archer bend his *b* Jer 51:3
He hath bent his *b* like an enemy Lam 2:4
He hath bent his *b*, and set me as Lam 3:12
As the appearance of the *b* that Eze 1:28
I will smite thy *b* out of thy Eze 39:3
that I will break the *b* of Israel Hos 1:5
God, and will not save them by *b* Hos 1:7
and I will break the *b* and the Hos 2:18
they are like a deceitful *b* Hos 7:16
he stand that handleth the *b* Amos 2:15
*b* myself before the high God Mic 6:6
the perpetual hills did *b* Hab 3:6
Thy *b* was made quite naked, Hab 3:9
the battle *b* shall be cut off Zec 9:10
filled the *b* with Ephraim, and Zec 9:13
the nail, out of him the battle *b* Zec 10:4
see, and *b* down their back alway Rom 11:10
Lord, every knee shall *b* to me Rom 14:11
For this cause I *b* my knees unto Eph 3:14
name of Jesus every knee should *b* Phil 2:10
and he that sat on him had a *b* Rev 6:2

**BOWED**
*b* himself toward the ground, Gen 18:2
he *b* himself with his face toward Gen 19:1
*b* himself to the people of the Gen 23:7
Abraham *b* down himself before the Gen 23:12
the man *b* down his head, and Gen 24:26
I *b* down my head, and worshipped Gen 24:48
*b* himself to the ground seven Gen 33:3
children, and they *b* themselves Gen 33:6
came near, and *b* themselves Gen 33:7
and Rachel, and they *b* themselves Gen 33:7
*b* down themselves before him with Gen 42:6
*b* themselves to him to the earth Gen 43:26
they *b* down their heads, and made Gen 43:28
Israel *b* himself upon the bed's Gen 47:31
he *b* himself with his face to the Gen 48:12
*b* his shoulder to bear, and became Gen 49:15
then they *b* their heads and Ex 4:31
And the people *b* the head and Ex 12:27
*b* his head toward the earth, and Ex 34:8
he *b* down his head, and fell flat Num 22:31
did eat, and *b* down to their gods Num 25:2
gods, and *b* yourselves to them Josh 23:16
*b* themselves unto them, and Judg 2:12
gods, and *b* themselves unto them Judg 2:17
At her feet he *b*, he fell, he lay Judg 5:27
at her feet he *b*, he fell Judg 5:27
where he *b*, there he fell down Judg 5:27
*b* down upon their knees to drink Judg 7:6
he *b* himself with all his might Judg 16:30
*b* herself to the ground, and said Ruth 2:10
she *b* herself and travailed 1Sa 4:19
ground, and *b* himself three times 1Sa 20:41
face to the earth, and *b* himself 1Sa 24:8
face, and *b* herself to the ground, 1Sa 25:23
*b* herself on her face to the 1Sa 25:41
face to the ground, and *b* himself 1Sa 28:14
he *b* himself, and said, What is 2Sa 9:8
*b* himself, and thanked the king 2Sa 14:22
*b* himself on his face to the 2Sa 14:33
Cushi *b* himself unto Joab, and ran 2Sa 18:21
he *b* the heart of all the men of 2Sa 19:14
He *b* the heavens also, and came 2Sa 22:10
*b* himself before the king on his 2Sa 24:20
And Bath-sheba *b*, and did obeisance 1Kin 1:16
he *b* himself before the king with 1Kin 1:23
Then Bath-sheba *b* with her face 1Kin 1:31
the king *b* himself upon the bed 1Kin 1:47
*b* himself to king Solomon 1Kin 1:53
*b* himself unto her, and sat down 1Kin 2:19
knees which have not *b* unto Baal 1Kin 19:18
*b* themselves to the ground before 2Kin 2:15
*b* herself to the ground, and took 2Kin 4:37
*b* himself to David with his face 1Chr 21:21
*b* down their heads, and worshipped. 1Chr 29:20
they *b* themselves with their 2Chr 7:3
Jehoshaphat *b* his head with his 2Chr 20:18
*b* down himself before them, and 2Chr 25:14
present with him *b* themselves 2Chr 29:29
they *b* their heads and worshipped 2Chr 29:30
they *b* their heads, and worshipped Neh 8:6
that were in the king's gate, *b* Est 3:2
But Mordecai *b* not, nor did him Est 3:2
Haman saw that Mordecai *b* not Est 3:5
He *b* the heavens also, and came Ps 18:9
I *b* down heavily, as one that Ps 35:14
I am *b* down greatly Ps 38:6
For our soul is *b* down to the Ps 44:25
my soul is *b* down Ps 57:6
up all those that be *b* down Ps 145:14
LORD raiseth them that are *b* down Ps 146:8
of men shall be *b* down, and the Is 2:11
loftiness of man shall be *b* down Is 2:17
I was *b* down at the hearing of it Is 21:3
they *b* the knee before him, and Mt 27:29
was *b* together, and could in no Lk 13:11
*b* down their faces to the earth, Lk 24:5
he *b* his head, and gave up the Jn 19:30
who have not *b* the knee to the Rom 11:4

**BOWELS**
thine own *b* shall be thine heir Gen 15:4
shall be separated from thy *b* Gen 25:23
for his *b* did yearn upon his Gen 43:30
the curse shall go into thy *b* Num 5:22
which shall proceed out of thy *b* 2Sa 7:12
my son, which came forth of my *b* 2Sa 16:11
shed out his *b* to the ground, and 2Sa 20:10
for her *b* yearned upon her son, 1Kin 3:26
sickness by disease of thy *b* 2Chr 21:15
until thy *b* fall out by reason of 2Chr 21:15
his *b* with an incurable disease 2Chr 21:18
his *b* fell out by reason of his 2Chr 21:19
*b* slew him there with the sword 2Chr 32:21
Yet his meat in his *b* is turned Job 20:14
My *b* boiled, and rested not Job 30:27
it is melted in the midst of my *b* Ps 22:14
that took me out of my mother's *b* Ps 71:6
let it come into his *b* like water Ps 109:18
door, and my *b* were moved for him Song 5:4
Wherefore my *b* shall sound like Is 16:11
the offspring of thy *b* like the Is 48:19
from the *b* of my mother hath he Is 49:1
strength, the sounding of thy *b* Is 63:15
My *b*, my *b* Jer 4:19
therefore my *b* are troubled for Jer 31:20
my *b* are troubled Lam 1:20
my *b* are troubled, my liver is Lam 2:11
fill thy *b* with this roll that I Eze 3:3
their souls, neither fill their *b* Eze 7:19
midst, and all his *b* gushed out Acts 1:18
ye are straitened in your own *b* 2Cor 6:12
you all in the *b* of Jesus Christ Phil 1:8
of the Spirit, if any *b* and Phil 2:1
beloved, *b* of mercies, kindness, Col 3:12
because the *b* of the saints are Philem 7
receive him, that is, mine own *b* Philem 12
refresh my *b* in the Lord Philem 20
shutteth up his *b* of compassion 1Jn 3:17

**BOWETH**
likewise every one that *b* down Judg 7:5
And the mean man *b* down, and the Is 2:9
Bel *b* down, Nebo stoopeth, their Is 46:1

**BOWING**
the LORD, *b* himself to the earth Gen 24:52
their eyes *b* down to the earth Ps 17:11
as a *b* wall shall ye be, and as a Ps 62:3
*b* their knees worshipped him Mk 15:19

**BOWL**
one silver *b* of seventy shekels, Num 7:13
one silver *b* of seventy shekels, Num 7:19
one silver *b* of seventy shekels, Num 7:25
one silver *b* of seventy shekels, Num 7:31
one silver *b* of seventy shekels, Num 7:37
a silver *b* of seventy shekels, Num 7:43
one silver *b* of seventy shekels, Num 7:49
one silver *b* of seventy shekels, Num 7:55
one silver *b* of seventy shekels, Num 7:61
one silver *b* of seventy shekels, Num 7:67
one silver *b* of seventy shekels, Num 7:73
one silver *b* of seventy shekels, Num 7:79
and thirty shekels, each *b* seventy Num 7:85
of the fleece, a *b* full of water Judg 6:38
loosed, or the golden *b* be broken Eccl 12:6
with a *b* upon the top of it, and Zec 4:2
one upon the right side of the *b* Zec 4:3

**BOWLS**
*b* thereof, to cover withal Ex 25:29
his shaft, and his branches, his *b* Ex 25:31
Three *b* made like unto almonds, Ex 25:33
three *b* made like almonds in the Ex 25:33
be four *b* made like unto almonds Ex 25:34
dishes, and his spoons, and his *b* Ex 37:16
his shaft, and his branch, his *b* Ex 37:17
Three *b* made after the fashion of Ex 37:19
three *b* made like almonds in Ex 37:19
were four *b* made like almonds Ex 37:20
dishes, and the spoons, and the *b* Num 4:7
of silver, twelve silver *b* Num 7:84
the two *b* of the chapiters that 1Kin 7:41
to cover the two *b* of the 1Kin 7:41
to cover the two *b* of the 1Kin 7:42
And the *b*, and the snuffers, and the 1Kin 7:50
the house of the LORD *b* of silver 2Kin 12:13
And the firepans, and the *b* 2Kin 25:15
gold for the fleshhooks, and the *b* 1Chr 28:17
and the snuffers, and the *b* Jer 52:18
basons, and the firepans, and the *b* Jer 52:19
That drink wine in *b*, and anoint Amos 6:6
and they shall be filled like *b* Zec 9:15
be like the *b* before the altar Zec 14:20

**BOWMEN**
the noise of the horsemen and *b* Jer 4:29

**BOWS**
The *b* of the mighty men are 1Sa 2:4
They were armed with *b*, and could 1Chr 12:2
that bare shields and drew *b* 2Chr 14:8
and helmets, and habergeons, and *b*. 2Chr 26:14
swords, their spears, and their *b* Neh 4:13
the spears, the shields, and the *b* Neh 4:16
heart, and their *b* shall be broken Ps 37:15
bend their *b* to shoot their Ps 64:3
being armed, and carrying *b* Ps 78:9
are sharp, and all their *b* bent Is 5:28
with *b* shall men come thither Is 7:24
Their *b* also shall dash the young Is 13:18
every one of their *b* is broken Jer 51:56
shields and the bucklers, the *b* Eze 39:9

**BOWSHOT**
a good way off, as it were a *b* Gen 21:16

**BOX**
take this *b* of oil in thine hand, 2Kin 9:1
Then take the *b* of oil, and pour 2Kin 9:3
the pine, and the *b* tree together Is 41:19
the *b* together, to beautify the Is 60:13
*b* of very precious ointment Mt 26:7
a woman having an alabaster *b* of Mk 14:3
and she brake the *b*, and poured it Mk 14:3
an alabaster *b* of ointment Lk 7:37

**BOY**
have given a *b* for an harlot, and Joel 3:3

**BOYS**
And the *b* grew Gen 25:27
of the city shall be full of *b* Zec 8:5

**BOZEZ** (*bo'-zez*) *A rock near Michmash.*
and the name of the one was *B* 1Sa 14:4

**BOZKATH** (*boz'-kath*) *A city in Judah.*
Lachish, and *B*, and Eglon, Josh 15:39

**BOZRAH** (*boz'-rah*)
*1. The capital city of Edom.*
Zerah of *B* reigned in his stead Gen 36:33
Zerah of *B* reigned in his stead 1Chr 1:44
the LORD hath a sacrifice in *B* Is 34:6
Edom, with dyed garments from *B* Is 63:1
that *B* shall become a desolation, Jer 49:13

eagle, and spread his wings over *B* ... Jer 49:22
shall devour the palaces of *B* ... Amos 1:12
them together as the sheep of *B* ... Mic 2:12
2. *A place in Moab.*
And upon Kerioth, and upon *B* ... Jer 48:24

## BRACELET
the *b* that was on his arm, and ... 2Sa 1:10

## BRACELETS
two *b* for her hands of ten ... Gen 24:22
*b* upon his sister's hands, and ... Gen 24:30
her face, and the *b* upon her hands ... Gen 24:47
And she said, Thy signet, and thy *b* ... Gen 38:18
whose are these, the signet, and *b* ... Gen 38:25
willing hearted, and brought *b* ... Ex 35:22
of jewels of gold, chains, and *b* ... Num 31:50
The chains, and the *b*, and the ... Is 3:19
I put *b* upon thy hands, and a ... Eze 16:11
which put *b* upon their hands, and ... Eze 23:42

## BRAKE
*b* every tree of the field ... Ex 9:25
all the people *b* off the golden ... Ex 32:3
and *b* them beneath the mount ... Ex 32:19
hands, and *b* them before your eyes ... Deut 9:17
*b* the pitchers that were in their ... Judg 7:19
*b* the pitchers, and held the lamps ... Judg 7:20
head, and all to *b* his skull ... Judg 9:53
he *b* the withs, as a thread of ... Judg 16:9
he *b* them from off his arms like ... Judg 16:12
side of the gate, and his neck *b* ... 1Sa 4:18
the three mighty men *b* through ... 2Sa 23:16
they *b* down the image of Baal, and ... 2Kin 10:27
*b* down the house of Baal, and made ... 2Kin 10:27
the house of Baal, and *b* it down ... 2Kin 11:18
his images *b* they in pieces ... 2Kin 11:18
*b* down the wall of Jerusalem from ... 2Kin 14:13
*b* the images, and cut down the ... 2Kin 18:4
*b* in pieces the brasen serpent ... 2Kin 18:4
he *b* down the houses of the ... 2Kin 23:7
*b* down the high places of the ... 2Kin 23:8
*b* them down from thence, and cast ... 2Kin 23:12
he *b* in pieces the images, and cut ... 2Kin 23:14
altar and the high place he *b* down ... 2Kin 23:15
*b* down the walls of Jerusalem ... 2Kin 25:10
the three *b* through the host of ... 1Chr 11:18
*b* down the images, and cut down ... 2Chr 14:3
*b* into it, and carried away all ... 2Chr 21:17
*b* it down, and *b* his altars and ... 2Chr 23:17
*b* down the wall of Jerusalem from ... 2Chr 25:23
*b* down the wall of Gath, and the ... 2Chr 26:6
*b* the images in pieces, and cut ... 2Chr 31:1
they *b* down the altars of Baalim ... 2Chr 34:4
he *b* in pieces, and made dust of ... 2Chr 34:4
*b* down the wall of Jerusalem, and ... 2Chr 36:19
I *b* the jaws of the wicked, and ... Job 29:17
sea with doors, when it *b* forth ... Job 38:8
*b* up for it my decreed place, and ... Job 38:10
There *b* he the arrows of the bow, ... Ps 76:3
he *b* the whole staff of bread ... Ps 105:16
*b* the trees of their coasts ... Ps 105:33
the plague *b* in upon them ... Ps 106:29
death, and *b* their bands in sunder ... Ps 107:14
which my covenant they *b*, ... Jer 31:32
*b* down the walls of Jerusalem ... Jer 39:8
*b* down all the walls of Jerusalem ... Jer 52:14
of the LORD, the Chaldeans *b* ... Jer 52:17
despised, and whose covenant he *b* ... Eze 17:16
troubled, and his sleep *b* from him ... Dan 2:1
iron and clay, and *b* them to pieces ... Dan 2:34
that it *b* in pieces the iron, the ... Dan 2:45
*b* all their bones in pieces or ... Dan 6:24
*b* in pieces, and stamped the ... Dan 7:7
*b* in pieces, and stamped the ... Dan 7:19
smote the ram, and *b* his two horns ... Dan 8:7
up to heaven, he blessed, and *b* ... Mt 14:19
*b* them, and gave to his disciples, ... Mt 15:36
*b* it, and gave it to the disciples ... Mt 26:26
loaves, and gave thanks, and *b* ... Mk 8:6
When I *b* the five loaves among ... Mk 8:19
she *b* the box, and poured it on ... Mk 14:3
*b* it and gave to them, and said, ... Mk 14:22
and their net *b* ... Lk 5:6
he *b* the bands, and was driven of ... Lk 8:29
to heaven, he blessed them, and *b* ... Lk 9:16
*b* it, and gave unto them, saying, ... Lk 22:19
took bread, and blessed it, and *b* ... Lk 24:30
*b* the legs of the first, and of ... Jn 19:32
dead already, they *b* not his legs ... Jn 19:33
when he had given thanks, he *b* it ... 1Cor 11:24

## BRAKEST
in the first tables, which thou *b* ... Ex 34:1
in the first tables which thou *b* ... Deut 10:2
thou *b* the heads of the dragons ... Ps 74:13
Thou *b* the heads of leviathan in ... Ps 74:14
they leaned upon thee, thou *b* ... Eze 29:7

## BRAMBLE
said all the trees unto the *b* ... Judg 9:14
the *b* said unto the trees, If in ... Judg 9:15
not, let fire come out of the *b* ... Judg 9:15
nor of a *b* bush gather they ... Lk 6:44

## BRAMBLES
*b* in the fortresses thereof ... Is 34:13

## BRANCH
with a knop and a flower in one *b* ... Ex 25:33
made like almonds in the other *b* ... Ex 25:33
his shaft, and his *b*, his bowls, ... Ex 37:17
the fashion of almonds in one *b* ... Ex 37:19
made like almonds in another *b* ... Ex 37:19
cut down from thence a *b* with one ... Num 13:23
his *b* shooteth forth in his ... Job 8:16
that the tender *b* thereof will ... Job 14:7
time, and his *b* shall not be green ... Job 15:32
and above shall his *b* be cut off ... Job 18:16
the dew lay all night upon my *b* ... Job 29:19
the *b* that thou madest strong for ... Ps 80:15
righteous shall flourish as a *b* ... Prov 11:28
In that day shall the *b* of the ... Is 4:2
off from Israel head and tail, *b* ... Is 9:14
a *B* shall grow out of his roots ... Is 11:1
of thy grave like an abominable *b* ... Is 14:19
forsaken bough, and an uppermost *b* ... Is 17:9
head or tail, *b* or rush, may do ... Is 19:15
the *b* of the terrible ones shall ... Is 25:5
the *b* of my planting, the work of ... Is 60:21
raise unto David a righteous *B* ... Jer 23:5
that time, will I cause the *B* of ... Jer 33:15
they put the *b* to their nose ... Eze 8:17
or than a *b* which is among the ... Eze 15:2
took the highest *b* of the cedar ... Eze 17:3
the highest *b* of the high cedar ... Eze 17:22
But out of a *b* of her roots shall ... Dan 11:7
will bring forth my servant the *B* ... Zec 3:8
the man whose name is The *B* ... Zec 6:12
leave them neither root nor *b* ... Mal 4:1
When his *b* is yet tender, and ... Mt 24:32
When her *b* is yet tender, and ... Mk 13:28
Every *b* in me that beareth not ... Jn 15:2
every *b* that beareth fruit, he ... Jn 15:2
As the *b* cannot bear fruit of ... Jn 15:4
in me, he is cast forth as a *b* ... Jn 15:6

## BRANCHES
And in the vine were three *b* ... Gen 40:10
The three *b* are three days ... Gen 40:12
whose *b* run over the wall ... Gen 49:22
his shaft, and his *b*, his bowls, ... Ex 25:31
six *b* shall come out of the sides ... Ex 25:32
three *b* of the candlestick out of ... Ex 25:32
three *b* of the candlestick out of ... Ex 25:32
so in the six *b* that come out of ... Ex 25:33
be a knop under two *b* of the same ... Ex 25:35
and a knop under two *b* of the same ... Ex 25:35
and a knop under two *b* of the same ... Ex 25:35
according to the six *b* that ... Ex 25:35
their *b* shall be of the same ... Ex 25:36
six *b* going out of the sides ... Ex 37:18
three *b* of the candlestick out of ... Ex 37:18
three *b* of the candlestick out of ... Ex 37:18
so throughout the six *b* going out ... Ex 37:19
And a knop under two *b* of the same ... Ex 37:21
and a knop under two *b* of the same ... Ex 37:21
and a knop under two *b* of the same ... Ex 37:21
to the six *b* going out of it ... Ex 37:21
knops and their *b* were of the same ... Ex 37:22
*b* of palm trees, and the boughs of ... Lev 23:40
fetch olive *b*, and pine *b* ... Neh 8:15
and myrtle *b*, and palm *b* ... Neh 8:15
*b* of thick trees, to make booths, ... Neh 8:15
the flame shall dry up his *b* ... Job 15:30
the sea, and her *b* unto the river ... Ps 80:11
which sing among the *b* ... Ps 104:12
her *b* are stretched out, they are ... Is 16:8
in the outmost fruitful *b* thereof ... Is 17:6
and take away and cut down the *b* ... Is 18:5
down, and consume the *b* thereof ... Is 27:10
it, and the *b* of it are broken ... Jer 11:16
whose *b* turned toward him, and the ... Eze 17:6
became a vine, and brought forth *b* ... Eze 17:6
and shot forth her *b* toward him ... Eze 17:7
that it might bring forth *b* ... Eze 17:8
in the shadow of the *b* thereof ... Eze 17:23
full of *b* by reason of many ... Eze 19:10
was exalted among the thick *b* ... Eze 19:11
with the multitude of her *b* ... Eze 19:11
is gone out of a rod of her *b* ... Eze 19:14
a cedar in Lebanon with fair *b* ... Eze 31:3
his *b* became long because of the ... Eze 31:5
under his *b* did all the beasts of ... Eze 31:6
greatness, in the length of his *b* ... Eze 31:7
chesnut trees were not like his *b* ... Eze 31:8
fair by the multitude of his *b* ... Eze 31:9
all the valleys his *b* are fallen ... Eze 31:12
of the field shall be upon his *b* ... Eze 31:13
ye shall shoot forth your *b* ... Eze 36:8
down the tree, and cut off his *b* ... Dan 4:14
under it, and the fowls from his *b* ... Dan 4:14
upon whose *b* the fowls of the ... Dan 4:21
cities, and shall consume his *b* ... Hos 11:6
His *b* shall spread, and his beauty ... Hos 14:6
the *b* thereof are made white ... Joel 1:7
them out, and marred their vine *b* ... Nah 2:2
What be these two olive *b* which ... Zec 4:12
come and lodge in the *b* thereof ... Mt 13:32
others cut down *b* from the trees ... Mt 21:8
herbs, and shooteth out great *b* ... Mk 4:32
others cut down *b* off the trees ... Mk 11:8
of the air lodged in the *b* of it ... Lk 13:19
Took *b* of palm trees, and went ... Jn 12:13
I am the vine, ye are the *b* ... Jn 15:5
if the root be holy, so are the *b* ... Rom 11:16
And if some of the *b* be broken off ... Rom 11:17
Boast not against the *b* ... Rom 11:18
The *b* were broken off, that I ... Rom 11:19
if God spared not the natural *b* ... Rom 11:21
these, which be the natural *b* ... Rom 11:24

## BRAND
is not this a *b* plucked out of ... Zec 3:2

## BRANDISH
when I shall *b* my sword before ... Eze 32:10

## BRANDS
And when he had set the *b* on fire ... Judg 15:5

## BRASEN
four *b* rings in the four corners ... Ex 27:4
burnt offering, with his *b* grate ... Ex 35:16
he made for the altar a *b* grate ... Ex 38:4
twenty, and their *b* sockets twenty ... Ex 38:10
the *b* altar, and the *b* grate ... Ex 38:30
The *b* altar, and his grate of ... Ex 39:39
and if it be sodden in a *b* pot ... Lev 6:28
the priest took the *b* censers ... Num 16:39
great cities with walls and *b* bars ... 1Kin 4:13
And every base had four *b* wheels ... 1Kin 7:30
because the *b* altar that was ... 1Kin 8:64
made in their stead *b* shields ... 1Kin 14:27
And he brought also the *b* altar ... 2Kin 16:14
the *b* altar shall be for me to ... 2Kin 16:15
off the *b* oxen that were under it ... 2Kin 16:17
brake in pieces the *b* serpent ... 2Kin 18:4
the *b* sea that was in the house ... 2Kin 25:13
wherewith Solomon made the *b* sea ... 1Chr 18:8
Moreover the *b* altar, that ... 2Chr 1:5
to the *b* altar before the LORD ... 2Chr 1:6
For Solomon had made a *b* scaffold ... 2Chr 6:13
because the *b* altar which Solomon ... 2Chr 7:7
*b* walls against the whole land, ... Jer 1:18
unto this people a fenced *b* wall ... Jer 15:20
the *b* sea that was in the house ... Jer 52:17
twelve *b* bulls that were under ... Jer 52:20
in, and stood beside the *b* altar ... Eze 9:2
and pots, *b* vessels, and of tables ... Mk 7:4

## BRASS
of every artificer in *b* and iron ... Gen 4:22
gold, and silver, and *b*, ... Ex 25:3
thou shalt make fifty taches of *b* ... Ex 26:11
cast five sockets of *b* for them ... Ex 26:37
and thou shalt overlay it with *b* ... Ex 27:2
thereof thou shalt make of *b* ... Ex 27:3
for it a grate of network of *b* ... Ex 27:4
wood, and overlay them with *b* ... Ex 27:6
twenty sockets shall be of *b* ... Ex 27:10
and their twenty sockets of *b* ... Ex 27:11
of silver, and their sockets of *b* ... Ex 27:17
linen, and their sockets of *b* ... Ex 27:18
pins of the court, shall be of *b* ... Ex 27:19
Thou shalt also make a laver of *b* ... Ex 30:18
and his foot also of *b* ... Ex 30:18
in gold, and in silver, and in *b* ... Ex 31:4
gold, and silver, and *b*, ... Ex 35:5
*b* brought the LORD's offering ... Ex 35:24
in gold, and in silver, and in *b* ... Ex 35:32
he made fifty taches of *b* to ... Ex 36:18
but their five sockets were of *b* ... Ex 36:38
and he overlaid it with *b* ... Ex 38:2
the vessels thereof made he of *b* ... Ex 38:3
the four ends of the grate of *b* ... Ex 38:5
wood, and overlaid them with *b* ... Ex 38:6
And he made the laver of *b* ... Ex 38:8
and the foot of it of *b* ... Ex 38:8
and their sockets of *b* twenty ... Ex 38:11
sockets for the pillars were of *b* ... Ex 38:17
four, and their sockets of *b* four ... Ex 38:19
the court round about, were of *b* ... Ex 38:20
the *b* of the offering was seventy ... Ex 38:29
brasen altar, and his grate of *b* ... Ex 39:39
as iron, and your earth as *b* ... Lev 26:19
And Moses made a serpent of *b* ... Num 21:9
when he beheld the serpent of *b* ... Num 21:9
the gold, and the silver, the *b* ... Num 31:22
of whose hills thou mayest dig *b* ... Deut 8:9
that is over thy head shall be *b* ... Deut 28:23
Thy shoes shall be iron and *b* ... Deut 33:25
silver, and gold, and vessels of *b* ... Josh 6:19
and the gold, and the vessels of *b* ... Josh 6:24
silver, and with gold, and with *b* ... Josh 22:8
and bound him with fetters of *b* ... Judg 16:21
had an helmet of *b* upon his head ... 1Sa 17:5
was five thousand shekels of *b* ... 1Sa 17:5
he had greaves of *b* upon his legs ... 1Sa 17:6
a target of *b* between his ... 1Sa 17:6
put an helmet of *b* upon his head ... 1Sa 17:38
king David took exceeding much *b* ... 2Sa 8:8
vessels of gold, and vessels of *b* ... 2Sa 8:10
hundred shekels of *b* in weight ... 2Sa 21:16
was a man of Tyre, a worker in *b* ... 1Kin 7:14
and cunning to work all works in *b* ... 1Kin 7:14
For he cast two pillars of *b* ... 1Kin 7:15
he made two chapiters of molten *b* ... 1Kin 7:16
And he made ten bases of *b* ... 1Kin 7:27
brasen wheels, and plates of *b* ... 1Kin 7:30
Then made he ten lavers of *b* ... 1Kin 7:38
of the LORD, were of bright *b* ... 1Kin 7:45
was the weight of the *b* found out ... 1Kin 7:47
and bound him with fetters of *b* ... 2Kin 25:7
the pillars of *b* that were in the ... 2Kin 25:13
carried the *b* of them to Babylon ... 2Kin 25:13
all the vessels of *b* wherewith ... 2Kin 25:14
the *b* of all these vessels was ... 2Kin 25:16
and the chapiter upon it was *b* ... 2Kin 25:17
chapiter round about, all of *b* ... 2Kin 25:17
to sound with cymbals of *b* ... 1Chr 15:19
brought David very much *b* ... 1Chr 18:8
the pillars, and the vessels of *b* ... 1Chr 18:8
of vessels of gold and silver and *b* ... 1Chr 18:10

*b* in abundance without weight 1Chr 22:3
and of *b* and iron without weight 1Chr 22:14
Of the gold, the silver, and the *b* 1Chr 22:16
and the *b* for things of *b* 1Chr 29:2
of *b* eighteen thousand talents, 1Chr 29:7
in gold, and in silver, and in *b* 2Chr 2:7
work in gold, and in silver, in *b* 2Chr 2:14
Moreover he made an altar of *b* 2Chr 4:1
overlaid the doors of them with *b* 2Chr 4:9
the house of the LORD of bright *b* 2Chr 4:16
for the weight of the *b* could not 2Chr 4:18
king Rehoboam made shields of *b* 2Chr 12:10
*b* to mend the house of the LORD 2Chr 24:12
or is my flesh of *b* Job 6:12
*b* is molten out of the stone Job 28:2
bones are as strong pieces of *b* Job 40:18
as straw, and *b* as rotten wood Job 41:27
For he hath broken the gates of *b* Ps 107:16
break in pieces the gates of *b* Is 45:2
is an iron sinew, and thy brow *b* Is 48:4
For *b* I will bring gold, and for Is 60:17
will bring silver, and for wood *b* Is 60:17
they are *b* and iron Jer 6:28
Also the pillars of *b* that were Jer 52:17
carried all the *b* of them to Jer 52:17
all the vessels of *b* wherewith Jer 52:18
the *b* of all these vessels was Jer 52:20
And a chapiter of *b* was upon it Jer 52:22
chapiters round about, all of *b* Jer 52:22
like the colour of burnished *b* Eze 1:7
all they are *b*, and tin, and iron, Eze 22:18
As they gather silver, and *b* Eze 22:20
that the *b* of it may be hot, and Eze 24:11
vessels of *b* in thy market Eze 27:13
was like the appearance of *b* Eze 40:3
his belly and his thighs of *b* Dan 2:32
was the iron, the clay, the *b* Dan 2:35
and another third kingdom of *b* Dan 2:39
brake in pieces the iron, the *b* Dan 2:45
even with a band of iron and *b* Dan 4:15
even with a band of iron and *b* Dan 4:23
gods of gold, and of silver, of *b* Dan 5:4
the gods of silver, and gold, of *b* Dan 5:23
were of iron, and his nails of *b* Dan 7:19
feet like in colour to polished *b* Dan 10:6
iron, and I will make thy hoofs *b* Mic 4:13
the mountains were mountains of *b* Zec 6:1
nor silver, nor *b* in your purses, Mt 10:9
I am become as sounding *b* 1Cor 13:1
And his feet like unto fine *b* Rev 1:15
fire, and his feet are like fine *b* Rev 2:18
and idols of gold, and silver, and *b* Rev 9:20
of most precious wood, and of *b* Rev 18:12

### BRAVERY
the *b* of their tinkling ornaments Is 3:18

### BRAWLER
but patient, not a *b*, not 1Ti 3:3

### BRAWLERS
speak evil of no man, to be no *b* Titus 3:2

### BRAWLING
the housetop, than with a *b* woman Prov 21:9
the housetop, than with a *b* woman Prov 25:24

### BRAY
Doth the wild ass *b* when he hath Job 6:5
Though thou shouldest *b* a fool in Prov 27:22

### BRAYED
Among the bushes they *b* Job 30:7

### BREACH
this *b* be upon thee Gen 38:29
*B* for *b*, eye for eye, tooth Lev 24:20
and ye shall know my *b* of promise Num 14:34
made a *b* in the tribes of Israel Judg 21:15
before me, as the *b* of waters 2Sa 5:20
the LORD had made a *b* upon Uzzah 2Sa 6:8
wheresoever any *b* shall be found 2Kin 12:5
the LORD had made a *b* upon Uzza 1Chr 13:11
the LORD our God made a *b* upon us 1Chr 15:13
that there was no *b* left therein Neh 6:1
He breaketh me with *b* upon *b* Job 16:14
chosen stood before him in the *b* Ps 106:23
therein is a *b* in the spirit Prov 15:4
let us make a *b* therein for us, Is 7:6
be to you as a *b* ready to fall Is 30:13
bindeth up the *b* of his people Is 30:26
be called, The repairer of the *b* Is 58:12
people is broken with a great *b* Jer 14:17
for thy *b* is great like the sea Lam 2:13
into a city wherein is made a *b* Eze 26:10

### BREACHES
the sea shore, and abode in his *b* Judg 5:17
repaired the *b* of the city of 1Kin 11:27
them repair the *b* of the house 2Kin 12:5
not repaired the *b* of the house 2Kin 12:6
repair ye not the *b* of the house 2Kin 12:7
deliver it for the *b* of the house 2Kin 12:7
to repair the *b* of the house 2Kin 12:8
the *b* of the house of the LORD 2Kin 12:12
to repair the *b* of the house 2Kin 22:5
that the *b* began to be stopped, Neh 4:7
heal the *b* thereof Ps 60:2
also the *b* of the city of David Is 22:9
And ye shall go out at the *b* Amos 4:3
will smite the great house with *b* Amos 6:11
fallen, and close up the *b* thereof Amos 9:11

### BREAD
of thy face shalt thou eat *b* Gen 3:19
king of Salem brought forth *b* Gen 14:18
And I will fetch a morsel of *b* Gen 18:5
a feast, and did bake unleavened *b* Gen 19:3
early in the morning, and took *b* Gen 21:14
Then Jacob gave Esau *b* and pottage. Gen 25:34
gave the savoury meat and the *b* Gen 27:17
I go, and will give me *b* to eat Gen 28:20
and called his brethren to eat *b* Gen 31:54
and they did eat *b*, and tarried all Gen 31:54
And they sat down to eat *b* Gen 37:25
save the *b* which he did eat Gen 39:6
all the land of Egypt there was *b* Gen 41:54
the people cried to Pharaoh for *b* Gen 41:55
that they should eat *b* there Gen 43:25
himself, and said, Set on *b* Gen 43:31
might not eat *b* with the Hebrews Gen 43:32
she asses laden with corn and *b* Gen 45:23
his father's household, with *b* Gen 47:12
there was no *b* in all the land Gen 47:13
unto Joseph, and said, Give us *b* Gen 47:15
Joseph gave them *b* in exchange Gen 47:17
he fed them with *b* for all their Gen 47:17
buy us and our land for *b*, and we Gen 47:19
Out of Asher his *b* shall be fat Gen 49:20
call him, that he may eat *b* Ex 2:20
roast with fire, and unleavened *b* Ex 12:8
days shall ye eat unleavened *b* Ex 12:15
*b* from the first day until the Ex 12:15
observe the feast of unleavened *b* Ex 12:17
even, ye shall eat unleavened *b* Ex 12:18
shall ye eat unleavened *b* Ex 12:20
shall no leavened *b* be eaten Ex 13:3
days thou shalt eat unleavened *b* Ex 13:6
Unleavened *b* shall be eaten seven Ex 13:7
no leavened *b* be seen with thee Ex 13:7
and when we did eat *b* to the full Ex 16:3
I will rain *b* from heaven for you Ex 16:4
and in the morning *b* to the full Ex 16:8
morning ye shall be filled with *b* Ex 16:12
This is the *b* which the LORD hath Ex 16:15
day they gathered twice as much *b* Ex 16:22
the sixth day the *b* of two days Ex 16:29
that they may see the *b* wherewith Ex 16:32
to eat *b* with Moses' father in Ex 18:12
keep the feast of unleavened *b* Ex 23:15
shalt eat unleavened *b* seven days Ex 23:15
of my sacrifice with leavened *b* Ex 23:18
your God, and he shall bless thy *b* Ex 23:25
And unleavened *b*, and cakes Ex 29:2
one loaf of *b*, and one cake of oiled Ex 29:23
*b* that is before the LORD Ex 29:23
the *b* that is in the basket, by Ex 29:32
of the consecrations, or of the *b* Ex 29:34
of unleavened *b* shalt thou keep Ex 34:18
days thou shalt eat unleavened *b* Ex 34:18
he did neither eat *b*, nor drink Ex 34:28
he set the *b* in order upon it Ex 40:23
with unleavened *b* shall it be Lev 6:16
leavened *b* with the sacrifice of Lev 7:13
rams, and a basket of unleavened *b* Lev 8:2
out of the basket of unleavened *b* Lev 8:26
cake, and a cake of oiled *b* Lev 8:26
there eat it with the *b* that is Lev 8:31
of the *b* shall ye burn with fire Lev 8:32
the *b* of their God, they do offer Lev 21:6
for he offereth the *b* of thy God Lev 21:8
to offer the *b* of his God Lev 21:17
nigh to offer the *b* of his God Lev 21:21
He shall eat the *b* of his God Lev 21:22
hand shall ye offer the *b* of your Lev 22:25
of unleavened *b* unto the LORD Lev 23:6
days ye must eat unleavened *b* Lev 23:6
And ye shall eat neither *b* Lev 23:14
ye shall offer with the *b* seven Lev 23:18
*b* of the first fruits for a wave Lev 23:20
it may be on the *b* for a memorial Lev 24:7
ye shall eat your *b* to the full Lev 26:5
I have broken the staff of your *b* Lev 26:26
shall bake your *b* in one oven Lev 26:26
you your *b* again by weight Lev 26:26
the continual *b* shall be thereon Num 4:7
And a basket of unleavened *b* Num 6:15
of unleavened *b* anointed with oil Num 6:15
with the basket of unleavened *b* Num 6:17
it, and eat it with unleavened *b* Num 9:11
for they are *b* for us Num 14:9
when ye eat of the *b* of the land Num 15:19
for there is no *b*, neither is Num 21:5
and our soul loatheth this light *b* Num 21:5
my *b* for my sacrifices made by Num 28:2
days shall unleavened *b* be eaten Num 28:17
that man doth not live by *b* only Deut 8:3
shalt eat *b* without scarceness Deut 8:9
neither did eat *b* nor drink water Deut 9:9
I did neither eat *b*, nor drink Deut 9:18
shalt eat no leavened *b* with it Deut 16:3
thou eat unleavened *b* therewith Deut 16:3
even the *b* of affliction Deut 16:3
there shall be no leavened *b* seen Deut 16:4
days thou shalt eat unleavened *b* Deut 16:8
in the feast of unleavened *b* Deut 16:16
Because they met you not with *b* Deut 23:4
Ye have not eaten *b*, neither have Deut 29:6
all the *b* of their provision was Josh 9:5
This our *b* we took hot for our Josh 9:12
a cake of barley *b* tumbled into Judg 7:13
loaves of *b* unto the people that Judg 8:5
we should give *b* unto thine army Judg 8:6
that we should give *b* unto thy Judg 8:15
me, I will not eat of thy *b* Judg 13:16
thine heart with a morsel of *b* Judg 19:5
and there is *b* and wine also for me Judg 19:19
his people in giving them *b* Ruth 1:6
come thou hither, and eat of the *b* Ruth 2:14
have hired out themselves for *b* 1Sa 2:5
piece of silver and a morsel of *b* 1Sa 2:36
that I may eat a piece of *b* 1Sa 2:36
for the *b* is spent in our vessels 1Sa 9:7
carrying three loaves of *b* 1Sa 10:3
and give thee two loaves of *b* 1Sa 10:4
And Jesse took an ass laden with *b* 1Sa 16:20
me five loaves of *b* in mine hand 1Sa 21:3
is no common *b* under mine hand 1Sa 21:4
but there is hallowed *b* 1Sa 21:4
the *b* is in a manner common, yea, 1Sa 21:5
So the priest gave him hallowed *b* 1Sa 21:6
for there was no *b* there but the 1Sa 21:6
to put hot *b* in the day when it 1Sa 21:6
in that thou hast given him *b* 1Sa 22:13
Shall I then take my *b*, and my 1Sa 25:11
for he had eaten no *b* all the day 1Sa 28:20
me set a morsel of *b* before thee 1Sa 28:22
and did bake unleavened *b* thereof 1Sa 28:24
him to David, and gave him *b* 1Sa 30:11
for he had eaten no *b*, nor drunk 1Sa 30:12
on the sword, or that lacketh *b* 2Sa 3:29
to me, and more also, if I taste *b* 2Sa 3:35
as men, to every one a cake of *b* 2Sa 6:19
thou shalt eat *b* at my table 2Sa 9:7
son shall eat *b* alway at my table 2Sa 9:10
neither did he eat *b* with them 2Sa 12:17
they set *b* before him, and he did 2Sa 12:20
dead, thou didst rise and eat *b* 2Sa 12:21
upon them two hundred loaves of *b* 2Sa 16:1
and the *b* and summer fruit for the 2Sa 16:2
neither will I eat *b* nor drink 1Kin 13:8
of the LORD, saying, Eat no *b* 1Kin 13:9
him, Come home with me, and eat *b* 1Kin 13:15
neither will I eat *b* nor drink 1Kin 13:16
Thou shalt eat no *b* nor drink 1Kin 13:17
thine house, that he may eat *b* 1Kin 13:18
did eat *b* in his house, and drank 1Kin 13:19
But camest back, and hast eaten *b* 1Kin 13:22
LORD did say to thee, Eat no *b* 1Kin 13:22
to pass, after he had eaten *b* 1Kin 13:23
And the ravens brought him *b* 1Kin 17:6
and flesh in the morning, and *b* 1Kin 17:6
a morsel of *b* in thine hand 1Kin 17:11
in a cave, and fed them with *b* 1Kin 18:4
in a cave, and fed them with *b* 1Kin 18:13
away his face, and would eat no *b* 1Kin 21:4
so sad, that thou eatest no *b* 1Kin 21:5
arise, and eat *b*, and let thine 1Kin 21:7
and feed him with *b* of affliction 1Kin 22:27
and she constrained him to eat *b* 2Kin 4:8
by, he turned in thither to eat *b* 2Kin 4:8
man of God *b* of the firstfruits 2Kin 4:42
set *b* and water before them, that 2Kin 6:22
land of corn and wine, a land of *b* 2Kin 18:32
unleavened *b* among their brethren 2Kin 23:9
there was no *b* for the people of 2Kin 25:3
he did eat *b* continually before 2Kin 25:29
brought *b* on asses, and on camels, 1Chr 12:40
woman, to every one a loaf of *b* 1Chr 16:3
even in the feast of unleavened *b* 2Chr 8:13
and feed him with *b* of affliction 2Chr 18:26
unleavened *b* in the second month 2Chr 30:13
kept the feast of unleavened *b* 2Chr 30:21
feast of unleavened *b* seven days 2Chr 35:17
unleavened *b* seven days with joy Ezr 6:22
he came thither, he did eat no *b* Ezr 10:6
not eaten the *b* of the governor Neh 5:14
people, and had taken of them *b* Neh 5:15
not I the *b* of the governor Neh 5:18
gavest them *b* from heaven for Neh 9:15
not the children of Israel with *b* Neh 13:2
He wandereth abroad for *b* Job 15:23
hast withholden *b* from the hungry Job 22:7
shall not be satisfied with *b* Job 27:14
for the earth, out of it cometh *b* Job 28:5
So that his life abhorreth *b* Job 33:20
did eat *b* with him in his house Job 42:11
eat up my people as they eat *b* Ps 14:4
forsaken, nor his seed begging *b* Ps 37:25
I trusted, which did eat of my *b* Ps 41:9
eat up my people as they eat *b* Ps 53:4
can he give *b* also Ps 78:20
feedest them with the *b* of tears Ps 80:5
so that I forget to eat my *b* Ps 102:4
For I have eaten ashes like *b* Ps 102:9
*b* which strengtheneth man's heart Ps 104:15
he brake the whole staff of *b* Ps 105:16
them with the *b* of heaven Ps 105:40
let them seek their *b* also out of Ps 109:10
up late, to eat the *b* of sorrows Ps 127:2
I will satisfy her poor with *b* Ps 132:15
For they eat the *b* of wickedness Prov 4:17
a man is brought to a piece of *b* Prov 6:26
Come, eat of my *b*, and drink of Prov 9:5
*b* eaten in secret is pleasant Prov 9:17
honoureth himself, and lacketh *b* Prov 12:9
land shall be satisfied with *b* Prov 12:11
and thou shalt be satisfied with *b* Prov 20:13
*B* of deceit is sweet to a man Prov 20:17
he giveth of his *b* to the poor Prov 22:9
Eat thou not the *b* of him that Prov 23:6
be hungry, give him *b* to eat Prov 25:21
his land shall have plenty of *b* Prov 28:19

for for a piece of *b* that man Prov 28:21
and eateth not the *b* of idleness Prov 31:27
eat thy *b* with joy, and drink thy Eccl 9:7
strong, neither yet *b* to the wise Eccl 9:11
Cast thy *b* upon the waters Eccl 11:1
and the staff, the whole stay of *b* Is 3:1
house is neither *b* nor clothing Is 3:7
saying, We will eat our own *b* Is 4:1
with their *b* him that fled Is 21:14
*B* corn is bruised Is 28:28
Lord give you the *b* of adversity Is 30:20
*b* of the increase of the earth, Is 30:23
*b* shall be given him Is 33:16
land of corn and wine, a land of *b* Is 36:17
yea, he kindleth it, and baketh *b* Is 44:15
also I have baked *b* upon the Is 44:19
pit, nor that his *b* should fail Is 51:14
money for that which is not *b* Is 55:2
to the sower, and *b* to the eater Is 55:10
not to deal thy *b* to the hungry Is 58:7
eat up thine harvest, and thy *b* Jer 5:17
of *b* out of the bakers' street Jer 37:21
until all the *b* in the city were Jer 37:21
there is no more *b* in the city Jer 38:9
they did eat *b* together in Mizpah Jer 41:1
the trumpet, nor have hunger of *b* Jer 42:14
so that there was no *b* for the Jer 52:6
he did continually eat *b* before Jer 52:33
All her people sigh, they seek *b* Lam 1:11
the young children ask *b*, and no Lam 4:4
Assyrians, to be satisfied with *b* Lam 5:6
We gat our *b* with the peril of Lam 5:9
vessel, and make thee *b* thereof Eze 4:9
defiled *b* among the Gentiles Eze 4:13
shalt prepare thy *b* therewith Eze 4:15
break the staff of *b* in Jerusalem Eze 4:16
and they shall eat *b* by weight Eze 4:16
That they may want *b* and water, and Eze 4:17
and will break your staff of *b* Eze 5:16
eat thy *b* with quaking, and drink Eze 12:18
eat their *b* with carefulness Eze 12:19
of barley and for pieces of *b* Eze 13:19
break the staff of the *b* thereof Eze 14:13
sister Sodom, pride, fulness of *b* Eze 16:49
hath given his *b* to the hungry Eze 18:7
hath given his *b* to the hungry Eze 18:16
thy lips, and eat not the *b* of men Eze 24:17
your lips, nor eat the *b* of men Eze 24:22
in it to eat *b* before the LORD Eze 44:3
even my house, when ye offer my *b* Eze 44:7
unleavened *b* shall be eaten Eze 45:21
I ate no pleasant *b*, neither came Dan 10:3
my lovers, that give me my *b* Hos 2:5
be unto them as the *b* of mourners Hos 9:4
for their *b* for their soul shall Hos 9:4
want of *b* in all your places Amos 4:6
the land of Judah, and there eat *b* Amos 7:12
in the land, not a famine of *b* Amos 8:11
they that eat thy *b* have laid a Obad 7
and with his skirt do touch *b* Hag 2:12
offer polluted *b* upon mine altar Mal 1:7
that these stones be made *b* Mt 4:3
Man shall not live by *b* alone Mt 4:4
Give us this day our daily *b* Mt 6:11
of you, whom if his son ask *b* Mt 7:9
not their hands when they eat *b* Mt 15:2
not meet to take the children's *b* Mt 15:26
have so much *b* in the wilderness Mt 15:33
they had forgotten to take *b* Mt 16:5
It is because we have taken no *b* Mt 16:7
because ye have brought no *b* Mt 16:8
spake it not to you concerning *b* Mt 16:11
not beware of the leaven of *b* Mt 16:12
*b* the disciples came to Jesus Mt 26:17
as they were eating, Jesus took *b* Mt 26:26
they could not so much as eat *b* Mk 3:20
no scrip, no *b*, no money in their Mk 6:8
the villages, and buy themselves *b* Mk 6:36
buy two hundred pennyworth of *b* Mk 6:37
his disciples eat *b* with defiled Mk 7:2
but eat *b* with unwashen hands Mk 7:5
not meet to take the children's *b* Mk 7:27
men with *b* here in the wilderness Mk 8:4
disciples had forgotten to take *b* Mk 8:14
It is because we have no *b* Mk 8:16
reason ye, because ye have no *b* Mk 8:17
the passover, and of unleavened *b* Mk 14:1
And the first day of unleavened *b* Mk 14:12
And as they did eat, Jesus took *b* Mk 14:22
this stone that it be made *b* Lk 4:3
man shall not live by *b* alone Lk 4:4
eating *b* nor drinking wine Lk 7:33
staves, nor scrip, neither *b* Lk 9:3
Give us day by day our daily *b* Lk 11:3
If a son shall ask *b* of any of Lk 11:11
to eat *b* on the sabbath day Lk 14:1
shall eat *b* in the kingdom of God Lk 14:15
of my father's have *b* enough Lk 15:17
feast of unleavened *b* drew nigh Lk 22:1
Then came the day of unleavened *b* Lk 22:7
And he took *b*, and gave thanks, and Lk 22:19
sat at meat with them, he took *b* Lk 24:30
known of them in breaking of *b* Lk 24:35
Philip, Whence shall we buy *b* Jn 6:5
Two hundred pennyworth of *b* is Jn 6:7
the place where they did eat *b* Jn 6:23
He gave them *b* from heaven to eat Jn 6:31
gave you not that *b* from heaven Jn 6:32
giveth you the true *b* from heaven Jn 6:32
For the *b* of God is he which Jn 6:33
Lord, evermore give us this *b* Jn 6:34
unto them, I am the *b* of life Jn 6:35
I am the *b* which came down from Jn 6:41
I am that *b* of life Jn 6:48
This is the *b* which cometh down Jn 6:50
I am the living *b* which came down Jn 6:51
if any man eat of this *b*, he Jn 6:51
the *b* that I will give is my Jn 6:51
This is that *b* which came down Jn 6:58
of this *b* shall live for ever Jn 6:58
He that eateth *b* with me hath Jn 13:18
there, and fish laid thereon, and *b* Jn 21:9
Jesus then cometh, and taketh *b* Jn 21:13
fellowship, and in breaking of *b* Acts 2:42
breaking *b* from house to house, Acts 2:46
were the days of unleavened *b* Acts 12:3
after the days of unleavened *b* Acts 20:6
came together to break *b*, Paul Acts 20:7
come up again, and had broken *b* Acts 20:11
he had thus spoken, he took *b* Acts 27:35
the unleavened *b* of sincerity 1Cor 5:8
The *b* which we break, is it not 1Cor 10:16
For we being many are one *b* 1Cor 10:17
are all partakers of that one *b* 1Cor 10:17
in which he was betrayed took *b* 1Cor 11:23
For as often as ye eat this *b* 1Cor 11:26
whosoever shall eat this *b* 1Cor 11:27
and so let him eat of that *b* 1Cor 11:28
both minister *b* for your food 2Cor 9:10
did we eat any man's *b* for nought 2Th 3:8
they work, and eat their own *b* 2Th 3:12

**BREADTH**

the *b* of it fifty cubits, and the Gen 6:15
length of it and in the *b* of it Gen 13:17
a cubit and a half the *b* thereof Ex 25:10
a cubit and a half the *b* thereof Ex 25:17
thereof, and a cubit the *b* thereof Ex 25:23
a border of an hand *b* round about Ex 25:25
the *b* of one curtain four cubits Ex 26:2
the *b* of one curtain four cubits Ex 26:8
half shall be the *b* of one board Ex 26:16
for the *b* of the court on the Ex 27:12
the *b* of the court on the east Ex 27:13
the *b* fifty every where, and the Ex 27:18
and a span shall be the *b* thereof Ex 28:16
thereof, and a cubit the *b* thereof Ex 30:2
the *b* of one curtain four cubits Ex 36:9
cubits was the *b* of one curtain Ex 36:15
the *b* of a board one cubit and a Ex 36:21
and a cubit and a half the *b* of it Ex 37:1
one cubit and a half the *b* thereof Ex 37:6
thereof, and a cubit the *b* thereof Ex 37:10
a cubit, and the *b* of it a cubit Ex 37:25
and five cubits the *b* thereof Ex 38:1
height in the *b* was five cubits Ex 38:18
thereof, and a span the *b* thereof Ex 39:9
and four cubits the *b* of it Deut 3:11
could sling stones at an hair *b* Judg 20:16
the *b* thereof twenty cubits, and 1Kin 6:2
according to the *b* of the house 1Kin 6:3
ten cubits was the *b* thereof 1Kin 6:3
in length, and twenty cubits in *b* 1Kin 6:20
the *b* thereof fifty cubits, and 1Kin 7:2
the *b* thereof thirty cubits 1Kin 7:6
And it was an hand *b* thick 1Kin 7:26
and four cubits the *b* thereof 1Kin 7:27
cubits, and the *b* twenty cubits 2Chr 3:3
according to the *b* of the house 2Chr 3:4
according to the *b* of the house 2Chr 3:8
the *b* thereof twenty cubits 2Chr 3:8
and twenty cubits the *b* thereof 2Chr 4:1
the *b* thereof threescore cubits Ezr 6:3
the *b* of the waters is straitened Job 37:10
thou perceived the *b* of the earth Job 38:18
shall fill the *b* of thy land Is 8:8
long by the cubit and an hand *b* Eze 40:5
he measured the *b* of the building Eze 40:5
he measured the *b* of the entry of Eze 40:11
the *b* was five and twenty cubits, Eze 40:13
Then he measured the *b* from the Eze 40:19
length thereof, and the *b* thereof Eze 40:20
the *b* five and twenty cubits Eze 40:21
the *b* five and twenty cubits Eze 40:25
the *b* five and twenty cubits Eze 40:36
the *b* of the gate was three Eze 40:48
cubits, and the *b* eleven cubits Eze 40:49
which was the *b* of the tabernacle Eze 41:1
the *b* of the door was ten cubits Eze 41:2
and the *b*, twenty cubits Eze 41:2
the *b* of the door, seven cubits Eze 41:3
and the *b*, twenty cubits, before Eze 41:4
the *b* of every side chamber, four Eze 41:5
therefore the *b* of the house was Eze 41:7
the *b* of the place that was left Eze 41:11
Also the *b* of the face of the Eze 41:14
door, and the *b* was fifty cubits Eze 42:2
was a walk of ten cubits *b* inward Eze 42:4
The cubit is a cubit and an hand *b* Eze 43:13
the *b* a cubit, and the border Eze 43:13
be two cubits, and the *b* one cubit Eze 43:14
four cubits, and the *b* one cubit Eze 43:14
the *b* shall be ten thousand Eze 45:1
in length, with five hundred in *b* Eze 45:2
and the *b* of ten thousand Eze 45:3
length, and the ten thousand of *b* Eze 45:5
and twenty thousand reeds in *b* Eze 48:8
length, and of ten thousand in *b* Eze 48:9
toward the west ten thousand in *b* Eze 48:10
toward the east ten thousand in *b* Eze 48:10
in length, and ten thousand in *b* Eze 48:13
thousand, and the *b* ten thousand Eze 48:13
that are left in the *b* over Eze 48:15
and the *b* thereof six cubits Dan 3:1
march through the *b* of the land Hab 1:6
to see what is the *b* thereof Zec 2:2
and the *b* thereof ten cubits Zec 5:2
with all saints what is the *b* Eph 3:18
went up on the *b* of the earth Rev 20:9
the length is as large as the *b* Rev 21:16
The length and the *b* and the height Rev 21:16

**BREAK**

Lot, and came near to *b* the door Gen 19:9
that thou shalt *b* his yoke from Gen 27:40
neither shall ye *b* a bone thereof Ex 12:46
it, then thou shalt *b* his neck Ex 13:13
lest they *b* through unto the LORD Ex 19:21
lest the LORD *b* forth upon them Ex 19:22
the people *b* through to come up Ex 19:24
lest he *b* forth upon them Ex 19:24
If fire *b* out, and catch in thorns Ex 22:6
quite *b* down their images Ex 23:24
*B* off the golden earrings, which Ex 32:2
hath any gold, let them *b* it off Ex 32:24
*b* their images, and cut down their Ex 34:13
not, then shalt thou *b* his neck Ex 34:20
and ye shall *b* it Lev 11:33
if a leprosy *b* out abroad in the Lev 13:12
*b* out in the house, after that he Lev 14:43
he shall *b* down the house, the Lev 14:45
but that ye *b* my covenant Lev 26:15
I will *b* the pride of your power Lev 26:19
to *b* my covenant with them Lev 26:44
the morning, nor *b* any bone of it Num 9:12
shall *b* their bones, and pierce Num 24:8
he shall not *b* his word, he shall Num 30:2
*b* down their images, and cut down Deut 7:5
*b* their pillars, and burn their Deut 12:3
*b* my covenant which I have made Deut 31:16
and provoke me, and *b* my covenant Deut 31:20
I will never *b* my covenant with Judg 2:1
peace, I will *b* down this tower Judg 8:9
many servants now a days that *b* 1Sa 25:10
they came to Hebron at *b* of day 2Sa 2:32
*b* thy league with Baasha king of 1Kin 15:19
to *b* through even unto the king 2Kin 3:26
did the Chaldees *b* in pieces 2Kin 25:13
*b* thy league with Baasha king of 2Chr 16:3
Should we again *b* thy Ezr 9:14
he shall even *b* down their stone Neh 4:3
Wilt thou *b* a leaf driven to and Job 13:25
*b* me in pieces with words Job 19:2
He shall *b* in pieces mighty men Job 34:24
or that the wild beast may *b* them Job 39:15
Let us *b* their bands asunder, and Ps 2:3
Thou shalt *b* them with a rod of Ps 2:9
*B* thou the arm of the wicked and Ps 10:15
*B* their teeth, O God, in their Ps 58:6
*b* out the great teeth of the Ps 58:6
shall *b* in pieces the oppressor Ps 72:4
But now they *b* down the carved Ps 74:6
If they *b* my statutes, and keep Ps 89:31
My covenant will I not *b*, nor Ps 89:34
They *b* in pieces thy people, O Ps 94:5
oil, which shall not *b* my head Ps 141:5
a time to *b* down, and a time to Eccl 3:3
Until the day *b*, and the shadows Song 2:17
Until the day *b*, and the shadows Song 4:6
*b* down the wall thereof, and it Is 5:5
they *b* forth into singing Is 14:7
That I will *b* the Assyrian in my Is 14:25
*b* the clods of his ground Is 28:24
nor *b* it with the wheel of his Is 28:28
he shall *b* it as the breaking of Is 30:14
the wilderness shall waters *b* out Is 35:6
so will he *b* all my bones Is 38:13
A bruised reed shall he not *b* Is 42:3
*b* forth into singing, ye Is 44:23
I will *b* in pieces the gates of Is 45:2
*b* forth into singing, O mountains Is 49:13
*B* forth into joy, sing together, Is 52:9
*b* forth into singing, and cry Is 54:1
For thou shalt *b* forth on the Is 54:3
the hills shall *b* forth before Is 55:12
go free, and that ye *b* every yoke Is 58:6
thy light *b* forth as the morning Is 58:8
*b* forth upon all the inhabitants Jer 1:14
*B* up your fallow ground, and sow Jer 4:3
*b* not thy covenant with us Jer 14:21
Shall iron *b* the northern iron and Jer 15:12
Then shalt thou *b* the bottle in Jer 19:10
Even so will I *b* this people Jer 19:11
for I will *b* the yoke of the king Jer 28:4
Even so will I *b* the yoke of Jer 28:11
that I will *b* his yoke from off Jer 30:8
to *b* down, and to throw down, and Jer 31:28
If ye can *b* my covenant of the Jer 33:20
He shall *b* also the images of Jer 43:13
which I have built will I *b* down Jer 45:4
his vessels, and *b* their bottles Jer 48:12
I will *b* the bow of Elam, the Jer 49:35
for with thee will I *b* in pieces Jer 51:20
with thee will I *b* in pieces the Jer 51:21
with thee will I *b* in pieces the Jer 51:21
thee also will I *b* in pieces man Jer 51:22
with thee will I *b* in pieces old Jer 51:22
with thee will I *b* in pieces the Jer 51:22
I will also *b* in pieces with thee Jer 51:23
with thee will I *b* in pieces the Jer 51:23
with thee will I *b* in pieces Jer 51:23
I will *b* the staff of bread in Eze 4:16

will *b* your staff of bread ... Eze 5:16
So will I *b* down the wall that ye ... Eze 13:14
will *b* the staff of the bread ... Eze 14:13
thee, as women that *b* wedlock ... Eze 16:38
shall *b* down thy high places ... Eze 16:39
or shall he *b* the covenant, and be ... Eze 17:15
thou shalt *b* the sherds thereof, ... Eze 23:34
of Tyrus, and *b* down her towers ... Eze 26:4
axes he shall *b* down thy towers ... Eze 26:9
they shall *b* down thy walls, and ... Eze 26:12
of thee by thy hand, thou didst *b* ... Eze 29:7
when I shall *b* there the yokes of ... Eze 30:18
will *b* his arms, the strong, and ... Eze 30:22
but I will *b* Pharaoh's arms, and ... Eze 30:24
shall it *b* in pieces and bruise ... Dan 2:40
people, but it shall *b* in pieces ... Dan 2:44
*b* off thy sins by righteousness, ... Dan 4:27
tread it down, and *b* it in pieces ... Dan 7:23
that I will *b* the bow of Israel ... Hos 1:5
I will *b* the bow and the sword and ... Hos 2:18
committing adultery, they *b* out ... Hos 4:2
he shall *b* down their altars, he ... Hos 10:2
plow, and Jacob shall *b* his clods ... Hos 10:11
*b* up your fallow ground ... Hos 10:12
and they shall not *b* their ranks ... Joel 2:7
I will *b* also the bar of Damascus ... Amos 1:5
lest he *b* out like fire in the ... Amos 5:6
they *b* their bones, and chop them ... Mic 3:3
For now will I *b* his yoke from ... Nah 1:13
that I might *b* my covenant which ... Zec 11:10
that I might *b* the brotherhood ... Zec 11:14
Whosoever therefore shall *b* one ... Mt 5:19
and where thieves *b* through ... Mt 6:19
do not *b* through nor steal ... Mt 6:20
else the bottles *b*, and the wine ... Mt 9:17
A bruised reed shall he not *b* ... Mt 12:20
came together to *b* bread, Paul ... Acts 20:7
a long while, even till *b* of day ... Acts 20:11
ye to weep and to *b* mine heart ... Acts 21:13
The bread which we *b*, is it not ... 1Cor 10:16
*b* forth and cry, thou that ... Gal 4:27

### BREAKER
The *b* is come up before them ... Mic 2:13
but if thou be a *b* of the law ... Rom 2:25

### BREAKEST
Thou *b* the ships of Tarshish with ... Ps 48:7

### BREAKETH
he said, Let me go, for the day *b* ... Gen 32:26
For he *b* me with a tempest, and ... Job 9:17
he *b* down, and it cannot be built ... Job 12:14
He *b* me with breach upon breach, ... Job 16:14
The flood *b* out from the ... Job 28:4
voice of the LORD *b* the cedars ... Ps 29:5
the LORD *b* the cedars of Lebanon ... Ps 29:5
he *b* the bow, and cutteth the ... Ps 46:9
My soul *b* for the longing that it ... Ps 119:20
and a soft tongue *b* the bone ... Prov 25:15
whoso *b* an hedge, a serpent shall ... Eccl 10:8
is crushed *b* out into a viper ... Is 59:5
as one *b* a potter's vessel, that ... Jer 19:11
hammer that *b* the rock in pieces ... Jer 23:29
bread, and no man *b* it unto them ... Lam 4:4
forasmuch as iron *b* in pieces ... Dan 2:40
and as iron that *b* all these ... Dan 2:40

### BREAKING
with him until the *b* of the day ... Gen 32:24
shall be a boil *b* forth with ... Ex 9:9
it became a boil *b* forth with ... Ex 9:10
If a thief be found *b* up, and be ... Ex 22:2
hand like the *b* forth of waters ... 1Chr 14:11
upon me as a wide *b* in of waters ... Job 30:14
that there be no *b* in, nor going ... Ps 144:14
*b* down the walls, and of crying to ... Is 22:5
whose *b* cometh suddenly at an ... Is 30:13
he shall break it as the *b* of the ... Is 30:14
the oath in *b* the covenant ... Eze 16:59
the oath by *b* the covenant ... Eze 17:18
of man, with the *b* of thy loins ... Eze 21:6
place of the *b* forth of children ... Hos 13:13
was known of them in *b* of bread ... Lk 24:35
in *b* of bread, and in prayers ... Acts 2:42
*b* bread from house to house, did ... Acts 2:46
through *b* the law dishonourest ... Rom 2:23

### BREAKINGS
by reason of *b* they purify ... Job 41:25

### BREAST
thou shalt take the *b* of the ram ... Ex 29:26
the *b* of the wave offering ... Ex 29:27
made by fire, the fat with the *b* ... Lev 7:30
that the *b* may be waved for a ... Lev 7:30
but the *b* shall be Aaron's and his ... Lev 7:31
For the wave *b* and the heave ... Lev 7:34
And Moses took the *b*, and waved it ... Lev 8:29
And the wave *b* and heave shoulder ... Lev 10:14
the wave *b* shall they bring with ... Lev 10:15
for the priest, with the wave *b* ... Num 6:20
shall be thine, as the wave *b* ... Num 18:18
pluck the fatherless from the *b* ... Job 24:9
and shalt suck the *b* of kings ... Is 60:16
the sea monsters draw out the *b* ... Lam 4:3
head was of fine gold, his *b* ... Dan 2:32
unto heaven, but smote upon his *b* ... Lk 18:13
lying on Jesus' *b* saith unto him ... Jn 13:25
also leaned on his *b* at supper ... Jn 21:20

### BREASTPLATE
be set in the ephod, and in the *b* ... Ex 25:7
a *b*, and an ephod, and a robe, and a ... Ex 28:4
thou shalt make the *b* of judgment ... Ex 28:15
thou shalt make upon the *b* chains ... Ex 28:22
make upon the *b* two rings of gold ... Ex 28:23
rings on the two ends of the *b* ... Ex 28:23
which are on the ends of the *b* ... Ex 28:24
of the *b* in the border thereof ... Ex 28:26
they shall bind the *b* by the ... Ex 28:28
that the *b* be not loosed from the ... Ex 28:28
the *b* of judgment upon his heart ... Ex 28:29
put in the *b* of judgment the Urim ... Ex 28:30
the ephod, and the ephod, and the *b* ... Ex 29:5
set for the ephod, and for the *b* ... Ex 35:9
set, for the ephod, and for the *b* ... Ex 35:27
he made the *b* of cunning work, ... Ex 39:8
they made the *b* double ... Ex 39:9
upon the *b* chains at the ends ... Ex 39:15
rings in the two ends of the *b* ... Ex 39:16
two rings on the ends of the *b* ... Ex 39:17
put them on the two ends of the *b* ... Ex 39:19
they did bind the *b* by his rings ... Ex 39:21
that the *b* might not be loosed ... Ex 39:21
And he put the *b* upon him ... Lev 8:8
also he put in the *b* the Urim ... Lev 8:8
he put on righteousness as a *b* ... Is 59:17
having on the *b* of righteousness ... Eph 6:14
sober, putting on the *b* of faith ... 1Th 5:8

### BREASTPLATES
And they had *b* ... Rev 9:9
as it were *b* of iron ... Rev 9:9
having *b* of fire, and of jacinth, ... Rev 9:17

### BREASTS
lieth under, blessings of the *b* ... Gen 49:25
And they put the fat upon the *b* ... Lev 9:20
And the *b* and the right shoulder ... Lev 9:21
or why the *b* that I should suck ... Job 3:12
His *b* are full of milk, and his ... Job 21:24
when I was upon my mother's *b* ... Ps 22:9
let her *b* satisfy thee at all ... Prov 5:19
shall lie all night betwixt my *b* ... Song 1:13
Thy two *b* are like two young roes ... Song 4:5
Thy two *b* are like two young roes ... Song 7:3
thy *b* to clusters of grapes ... Song 7:7
now also thy *b* shall be as ... Song 7:8
that sucked the *b* of my mother ... Song 8:1
a little sister, and she hath no *b* ... Song 8:8
I am a wall, and my *b* like towers ... Song 8:10
the milk, and drawn from the *b* ... Is 28:9
with the *b* of her consolations ... Is 66:11
thy *b* are fashioned, and thine ... Eze 16:7
there were their *b* pressed ... Eze 23:3
bruised the *b* of her virginity ... Eze 23:8
thereof, and pluck off thine own *b* ... Eze 23:34
her adulteries from between her *b* ... Hos 2:2
them a miscarrying womb and dry *b* ... Hos 9:14
and those that suck the *b* ... Joel 2:16
of doves, tabering upon their *b* ... Nah 2:7
which were done, smote their *b* ... Lk 23:48
having their *b* girded with golden ... Rev 15:6

### BREATH
into his nostrils the *b* of life ... Gen 2:7
flesh, wherein is the *b* of life ... Gen 6:17
flesh, wherein is the *b* of life ... Gen 7:15
whose nostrils was the *b* of life ... Gen 7:22
blast of the *b* of his nostrils ... 2Sa 22:16
that there was no *b* left in him ... 1Kin 17:17
by the *b* of his nostrils are they ... Job 4:9
will not suffer me to take my *b* ... Job 9:18
thing, and the *b* of all mankind ... Job 12:10
by the *b* of his mouth shall he go ... Job 15:30
My *b* is corrupt, my days are ... Job 17:1
My *b* is strange to my wife, ... Job 19:17
All the while my *b* is in me ... Job 27:3
the *b* of the Almighty hath given ... Job 33:4
unto himself his spirit and his *b* ... Job 34:14
By the *b* of God frost is given ... Job 37:10
His *b* kindleth coals, and a flame ... Job 41:21
blast of the *b* of thy nostrils ... Ps 18:15
of them by the *b* of his mouth ... Ps 33:6
thou takest away their *b*, they ... Ps 104:29
is there any *b* in their mouths ... Ps 135:17
His *b* goeth forth, he returneth ... Ps 146:4
thing that hath *b* praise the LORD ... Ps 150:6
yea, they have all one *b* ... Eccl 3:19
whose *b* is in his nostrils ... Is 2:22
with the *b* of his lips shall he ... Is 11:4
And his *b*, as an overflowing ... Is 30:28
the *b* of the LORD, like a stream ... Is 30:33
your *b*, as fire, shall devour you ... Is 33:11
he that giveth *b* unto the people ... Is 42:5
and there is no *b* in them ... Jer 10:14
and there is no *b* in them ... Jer 51:17
The *b* of our nostrils, the ... Lam 4:20
I will cause *b* to enter into you, ... Eze 37:5
put *b* in you, and ye shall live ... Eze 37:6
but there was no *b* in them ... Eze 37:8
Come from the four winds, O *b* ... Eze 37:9
the *b* came into them, and they ... Eze 37:10
and the God in whose hand thy *b* is ... Dan 5:23
me, neither is there *b* left in me ... Dan 10:17
there is no *b* at all in the midst ... Hab 2:19
he giveth to all life, and *b* ... Acts 17:25

### BREATHE
there was not any left to *b* ... Josh 11:11
them, neither left they any to *b* ... Josh 11:14
me, and such as *b* out cruelty ... Ps 27:12
*b* upon these slain, that they may ... Eze 37:9

### BREATHED
*b* into his nostrils the breath of ... Gen 2:7
but utterly destroyed all that *b* ... Josh 10:40
left not to Jeroboam any that *b* ... 1Kin 15:29
he *b* on them, and saith unto them, ... Jn 20:22

### BREATHETH
shalt save alive nothing that *b* ... Deut 20:16

### BREATHING
hide not thine ear at my *b* ... Lam 3:56
yet *b* out threatenings and ... Acts 9:1

### BRED
morning, and it *b* worms, and stank ... Ex 16:20

### BREECHES
linen *b* to cover their nakedness ... Ex 28:42
linen *b* of fine twined linen, ... Ex 39:28
his linen *b* shall he put upon his ... Lev 6:10
have the linen *b* upon his flesh ... Lev 16:4
have linen *b* upon their loins ... Eze 44:18

### BREED
that they may *b* abundantly in the ... Gen 8:17
lambs, and rams of the *b* of Bashan ... Deut 32:14

### BREEDING
even the *b* of nettles, and ... Zeph 2:9

### BRETHEN
There were therefore seven *b* ... Lk 20:29

### BRETHREN
father, and told his two *b* without ... Gen 9:22
servants shall he be unto his *b* ... Gen 9:25
for we be *b* ... Gen 13:8
in the presence of all his *b* ... Gen 16:12
And said, I pray you, *b*, do not so ... Gen 19:7
me to the house of my master's *b* ... Gen 24:27
died in the presence of all his *b* ... Gen 25:18
be lord over thy *b*, and let thy ... Gen 27:29
all his *b* have I given to him for ... Gen 27:37
And Jacob said unto them, My *b* ... Gen 29:4
And he took his *b* with him ... Gen 31:23
Laban with his *b* pitched in the ... Gen 31:25
before our *b* discern thou what is ... Gen 31:32
here before my *b* and thy *b* ... Gen 31:37
And Jacob said unto his *b*, Gather ... Gen 31:46
called his *b* to eat bread ... Gen 31:54
unto her father and unto her *b* ... Gen 34:11
Jacob, Simeon and Levi, Dinah's *b* ... Gen 34:25
was feeding the flock with his *b* ... Gen 37:2
when his *b* saw that their father ... Gen 37:4
loved him more than all his *b* ... Gen 37:4
a dream, and he told it his *b* ... Gen 37:5
his *b* said to him, Shalt thou ... Gen 37:8
another dream, and told it his *b* ... Gen 37:9
it to his father, and to his *b* ... Gen 37:10
thy *b* indeed come to bow down ... Gen 37:10
And his *b* envied him ... Gen 37:11
his *b* went to feed their father's ... Gen 37:12
Do not thy *b* feed the flock in ... Gen 37:13
see whether it be well with thy *b* ... Gen 37:14
And he said, I seek my *b* ... Gen 37:16
And Joseph went after his *b* ... Gen 37:17
when Joseph was come unto his *b* ... Gen 37:23
And Judah said unto his *b*, What ... Gen 37:26
And his *b* were content ... Gen 37:27
And he returned unto his *b* ... Gen 37:30
that Judah went down from his *b* ... Gen 38:1
he die also, as his *b* did ... Gen 38:11
Joseph's ten *b* went down to buy ... Gen 42:3
Jacob sent not with his *b* ... Gen 42:4
Joseph's *b* came, and bowed ... Gen 42:6
And Joseph saw his *b*, and he knew ... Gen 42:7
And Joseph knew his *b*, but they ... Gen 42:8
said, Thy servants are twelve *b* ... Gen 42:13
let one of your *b* be bound in the ... Gen 42:19
And he said unto his *b*, My money ... Gen 42:28
We be twelve *b*, sons of our ... Gen 42:32
leave one of your *b* here with me ... Gen 42:33
his *b* came to Joseph's house ... Gen 44:14
and let the lad go up with his *b* ... Gen 44:33
made himself known unto his *b* ... Gen 45:1
And Joseph said unto his *b* ... Gen 45:3
his *b* could not answer him ... Gen 45:3
And Joseph said unto his *b* ... Gen 45:4
Moreover he kissed all his *b* ... Gen 45:15
after that his *b* talked with him ... Gen 45:15
saying, Joseph's *b* are come ... Gen 45:16
said unto Joseph, Say unto thy *b* ... Gen 45:17
So he sent his *b* away, and they ... Gen 45:24
And Joseph said unto his *b* ... Gen 46:31
Pharaoh, and say unto him, My *b* ... Gen 46:31
and said, My father and my *b* ... Gen 47:1
And he took some of his *b*, even ... Gen 47:2
And Pharaoh said unto his *b* ... Gen 47:3
and thy *b* are come unto thee ... Gen 47:5
make thy father and *b* to dwell ... Gen 47:6
Joseph placed his father and his *b* ... Gen 47:11
nourished his father, and his *b* ... Gen 47:12
of their *b* in their inheritance ... Gen 48:6
to thee one portion above thy *b* ... Gen 48:22
Simeon and Levi are *b* ... Gen 49:5
art he whom thy *b* shall praise ... Gen 49:8
him that was separate from his *b* ... Gen 49:26
all the house of Joseph, and his *b* ... Gen 50:8
returned into Egypt, he, and his *b* ... Gen 50:14
when Joseph's *b* saw that their ... Gen 50:15
thee now, the trespass of thy *b* ... Gen 50:17
his *b* also went and fell down ... Gen 50:18

And Joseph said unto his *b*... Gen 50:24
And Joseph died, and all his *b*... Ex 1:6
that he went out unto his *b*... Ex 2:11
smiting an Hebrew, one of his *b*... Ex 2:11
return unto my *b* which are in... Ex 4:18
carry your *b* from before the... Lev 10:4
but let your *b*, the whole house... Lev 10:6
is the high priest among his *b*... Lev 21:10
but over your *b* the children of... Lev 25:46
one of his *b* may redeem him... Lev 25:48
their *b* in the tabernacle of the... Num 8:26
all thy *b* the sons of Levi with... Num 16:10
thy *b* also of the tribe of Levi,... Num 18:2
I have taken your *b* the Levites... Num 18:6
when our *b* died before the LORD... Num 20:3
brought unto his *b* a Midianitish... Num 25:6
among the *b* of our father... Num 27:4
among their father's *b*... Num 27:7
give his inheritance unto his *b*... Num 27:9
And if he have no *b*, then ye shall... Num 27:10
inheritance unto his father's *b*... Num 27:10
And if his father have no *b*... Num 27:11
of Reuben, Shall your *b* go to war... Num 32:6
Hear the causes between your *b*... Deut 1:16
our *b* have discouraged our heart,... Deut 1:28
of your *b* the children of Esau... Deut 2:4
from our *b* the children of Esau... Deut 2:8
your *b* the children of Israel... Deut 3:18
LORD have given rest unto your *b*... Deut 3:20
part nor inheritance with his *b*... Deut 10:9
you a poor man of one of thy *b*... Deut 15:7
one from among thy *b* shalt thou... Deut 17:15
be not lifted up above his *b*... Deut 17:20
have no inheritance among their *b*... Deut 18:2
as all his *b* the Levites do,... Deut 18:7
from the midst of thee, of thy *b*... Deut 18:15
up a Prophet from among their *b*... Deut 18:18
his *b* of the children of Israel... Deut 24:7
and needy, whether he be of thy *b*... Deut 24:14
If *b* dwell together, and one of... Deut 25:5
neither did he acknowledge his *b*... Deut 33:9
him that was separated from his *b*... Deut 33:16
let him be acceptable to his *b*... Deut 33:24
ye shall pass before your *b* armed... Josh 1:14
the LORD have given your *b* rest... Josh 1:15
my father, and my mother, and my *b*.. Josh 2:13
father, and thy mother, and thy *b*... Josh 2:18
father, and her mother, and her *b*... Josh 6:23
Nevertheless my *b* that went up... Josh 14:8
us an inheritance among our *b*... Josh 17:4
among the *b* of their father... Josh 17:4
Ye have not left your *b* these... Josh 22:3
God hath given rest unto your *b*... Josh 22:4
*b* on this side Jordan westward... Josh 22:7
spoil of your enemies with your *b*... Josh 22:8
And he said, They were my *b*... Judg 8:19
to Shechem unto his mother's *b*... Judg 9:1
his mother's *b* spake of him in... Judg 9:3
slew his *b* the sons of Jerubbaal,... Judg 9:5
aided him in the killing of his *b*... Judg 9:24
the son of Ebed came with his *b*... Judg 9:26
Ebed and his *b* be come to Shechem... Judg 9:31
and Zebul thrust out Gaal and his *b*... Judg 9:41
father, in slaying his seventy *b*... Judg 9:56
Then Jephthah fled from his *b*... Judg 11:3
among the daughters of thy *b*... Judg 14:3
Then his *b* and all the house of... Judg 16:31
they came unto their *b* to Zorah... Judg 18:8
their *b* said unto them, What say... Judg 18:8
of Laish, and said unto their *b*... Judg 18:14
and said unto them, Nay, my *b*... Judg 19:23
of their *b* the children of Israel... Judg 20:13
their *b* come unto us to complain... Judg 21:22
be not cut off from among his *b*... Ruth 4:10
him in the midst of his *b*... 1Sa 16:13
Take now for thy *b* an ephah of... 1Sa 17:17
and run to the camp to thy *b*... 1Sa 17:17
thousand, and look how thy *b* fare... 1Sa 17:18
army, and came and saluted his *b*... 1Sa 17:22
away, I pray thee, and see my *b*... 1Sa 20:29
and when his *b* and all his father's... 1Sa 22:1
David, Ye shall not do so, my *b*... 1Sa 30:23
return from following their *b*... 2Sa 2:26
of Saul thy father, to his *b*... 2Sa 3:8
return thou, and take back thy *b*... 2Sa 15:20
Ye are my *b*, ye are my bones and... 2Sa 19:12
Why have our *b* the men of Judah... 2Sa 19:41
called all his *b* the king's sons,... 1Kin 1:9
your *b* the children of Israel... 1Kin 12:24
him arise up from among his *b*... 2Kin 9:2
Jehu met with the *b* of Ahaziah... 2Kin 10:13
answered, We are the *b* of Ahaziah... 2Kin 10:13
unleavened bread among their *b*... 2Kin 23:9
was more honourable than his *b*... 1Chr 4:9
but his *b* had not many children,... 1Chr 4:27
For Judah prevailed above his *b*... 1Chr 5:2
his *b* by their families, when the... 1Chr 5:7
their *b* of the house of their... 1Chr 5:13
their *b* the sons of Merari stood... 1Chr 6:44
Their *b* also the Levites were... 1Chr 6:48
their *b* among all the families of... 1Chr 7:5
his *b* came to comfort him... 1Chr 7:22
dwelt with their *b* in Jerusalem... 1Chr 8:32
Jeuel, and their *b*, six hundred and... 1Chr 9:6
And their *b*, according to their... 1Chr 9:9
And their *b*, heads of the house of... 1Chr 9:13
and Talmon, and Ahiman, and their *b* 1Chr 9:17
the son of Korah, and his *b*... 1Chr 9:19
And their *b*, which were in their... 1Chr 9:25
And other of their *b*, of the sons... 1Chr 9:32
dwelt with their *b* at Jerusalem... 1Chr 9:38
over against their *b*... 1Chr 9:38
bow, even of Saul's *b* of Benjamin... 1Chr 12:2
all their *b* were at their... 1Chr 12:32
for their *b* had prepared for them... 1Chr 12:39
abroad unto our *b* every where... 1Chr 13:2
his *b* an hundred and twenty... 1Chr 15:5
his *b* two hundred and twenty... 1Chr 15:6
his *b* an hundred and thirty... 1Chr 15:7
the chief, and his *b* two hundred... 1Chr 15:8
the chief, and his *b* fourscore... 1Chr 15:9
his *b* an hundred and twelve... 1Chr 15:10
yourselves, both ye and your *b*... 1Chr 15:12
their *b* to be the singers with... 1Chr 15:16
and of his *b*, Asaph the son of... 1Chr 15:17
and of the sons of Merari their *b*... 1Chr 15:17
with them their *b* of the second... 1Chr 15:18
into the hand of Asaph and his *b*... 1Chr 16:7
of the LORD Asaph and his *b*... 1Chr 16:37
And Obed-edom with their *b*... 1Chr 16:38
his *b* the priests, before the... 1Chr 16:39
their *b* the sons of Kish took... 1Chr 23:22
of the sons of Aaron their *b*... 1Chr 23:32
their *b* the sons of Aaron in the... 1Chr 24:31
over against their younger *b*... 1Chr 24:31
with their *b* that were instructed... 1Chr 25:7
to Gedaliah, who with his *b*... 1Chr 25:9
to Zaccur, he, his sons, and his *b*... 1Chr 25:10
to Izri, he, his sons, and his *b*... 1Chr 25:11
Nethaniah, he, his sons, and his *b*... 1Chr 25:12
Bukkiah, he, his sons, and his *b*... 1Chr 25:13
he, his sons, and his *b*, were... 1Chr 25:14
Jeshaiah, he, his sons, and his *b*... 1Chr 25:15
Mattaniah, he, his sons, and his *b*... 1Chr 25:16
to Shimei, he, his sons, and his *b*... 1Chr 25:17
Azareel, he, his sons, and his *b*... 1Chr 25:18
Hashabiah, he, his sons, and his *b*... 1Chr 25:19
Shubael, he, his sons, and his *b*... 1Chr 25:20
he, his sons, and his *b*, were... 1Chr 25:21
Jeremoth, he, his sons, and his *b*... 1Chr 25:22
Hananiah, he, his sons, and his *b*... 1Chr 25:23
he, his sons, and his *b*, were... 1Chr 25:24
to Hanani, he, his sons, and his *b*... 1Chr 25:25
Mallothi, he, his sons, and his *b*... 1Chr 25:26
Eliathah, he, his sons, and his *b*... 1Chr 25:27
to Hothir, he, his sons, and his *b*... 1Chr 25:28
Giddalti, he, his sons, and his *b*... 1Chr 25:29
Mahazioth, he, his sons, and his *b*... 1Chr 25:30
he, his sons, and his *b*, were... 1Chr 25:31
whose *b* were strong men, Elihu,... 1Chr 26:7
they and their sons and their *b*... 1Chr 26:8
And Meshelemiah had sons and *b*... 1Chr 26:9
sons and *b* of Hosah were thirteen... 1Chr 26:11
And his *b* by Eliezer... 1Chr 26:25
his *b* were over all the treasures... 1Chr 26:26
hand of Shelomith, and of his *b*... 1Chr 26:28
Hebronites, Hashabiah and his *b*... 1Chr 26:30
And his *b*, men of valour, were two.. 1Chr 26:32
Elihu, one of the *b* of David... 1Chr 27:18
his feet, and said, Hear me, my *b*... 1Chr 28:2
with their sons and their *b*... 2Chr 5:12
go up, nor fight against your *b*... 2Chr 11:4
chief, to be ruler among his *b*... 2Chr 11:22
shall come to you of your *b* that... 2Chr 19:10
come upon you, and upon your *b*... 2Chr 19:10
he had *b* the sons of Jehoshaphat,... 2Chr 21:2
slew all his *b* with the sword, and... 2Chr 21:4
also hast slain thy *b* of thy... 2Chr 21:13
and the sons of the *b* of Ahaziah... 2Chr 22:8
of their *b* two hundred thousand... 2Chr 28:8
ye have taken captive of your *b*... 2Chr 28:11
city of palm trees, to their *b*... 2Chr 28:15
And they gathered their *b*, and... 2Chr 29:15
wherefore their *b* the Levites did... 2Chr 29:34
like your fathers, and like your *b*... 2Chr 30:7
turn again unto the LORD, your *b*... 2Chr 30:9
to give to their *b* by courses... 2Chr 31:15
the fathers of your *b* the people... 2Chr 35:5
yourselves, and prepare your *b*... 2Chr 35:6
and Shemaiah and Nethaneel, his *b*... 2Chr 35:9
for their *b* the Levites prepared... 2Chr 35:15
his *b* the priests, and Zerubbabel... Ezr 3:2
the son of Shealtiel, and his *b*... Ezr 3:2
remnant of their *b* the priests... Ezr 3:8
Jeshua with his sons and his *b*... Ezr 3:9
their sons and their *b* the Levites... Ezr 3:9
for their *b* the priests, and for... Ezr 6:20
seem good to thee, and to thy *b*... Ezr 7:18
to his *b* the Nethinims, at the... Ezr 8:17
Sherebiah, with his sons and his *b*... Ezr 8:18
of the sons of Merari, his *b*... Ezr 8:19
and ten of their *b* with them... Ezr 8:24
the son of Jozadak, and his *b*... Ezr 10:18
That Hanani, one of my *b*, came,... Neh 1:2
rose up with his *b* the priests... Neh 3:1
After him repaired their *b*... Neh 3:18
And he spake before his *b* and the... Neh 4:2
and terrible, and fight for your *b*... Neh 4:14
So neither I, nor my *b*, nor my... Neh 4:23
wives against their *b* the Jews... Neh 5:1
flesh is as the flesh of our *b*... Neh 5:5
have redeemed our *b* the Jews... Neh 5:8
and will ye even sell your *b*... Neh 5:8
I likewise, and my *b*, and my... Neh 5:10
my *b* have not eaten the bread of... Neh 5:14
And their *b*, Shebaniah, Hodijah,... Neh 10:10
They clave to their *b*, their... Neh 10:29
their *b* that did the work of the... Neh 11:12
And his *b*, chief of the fathers,... Neh 11:13
And their *b*, mighty men of valour,... Neh 11:14
Bakbukiah the second among his *b*... Neh 11:17
their *b* that kept the gates, were... Neh 11:19
of their *b* in the days of Jeshua... Neh 12:7
the thanksgiving, he and his *b*... Neh 12:8
Also Bakbukiah and Unni, their *b*... Neh 12:9
with their *b* over against them,... Neh 12:24
And his *b*, Shemaiah, and Azarael,... Neh 12:36
was to distribute unto their *b*... Neh 13:13
of the multitude of his *b*... Est 10:3
My *b* have dealt deceitfully as a... Job 6:15
He hath put my *b* far from me... Job 19:13
came there unto him all his *b*... Job 42:11
them inheritance among their *b*... Job 42:15
I will declare thy name unto my *b*... Ps 22:22
I am become a stranger unto my *b*... Ps 69:8
For my *b* and companions' sakes, I... Ps 122:8
how pleasant it is for *b* to dwell... Ps 133:1
and he that soweth discord among *b*.. Prov 6:19
of the inheritance among the *b*... Prov 17:2
All the *b* of the poor do hate him... Prov 19:7
Your *b* that hated you, that cast... Is 66:5
they shall bring all your *b* for... Is 66:20
as I have cast out all your *b*... Jer 7:15
For even thy *b*, and the house of... Jer 12:6
of your *b* that are not gone forth... Jer 29:16
the son of Habaziniah, and his *b*... Jer 35:3
and slew them not among their *b*... Jer 41:8
his seed is spoiled, and his *b*... Jer 49:10
of man, thy *b*, even thy *b*... Eze 11:15
Say ye unto your *b*, Ammi... Hos 2:1
Though he be fruitful among his *b*... Hos 13:15
then the remnant of his *b* shall... Mic 5:3
and Jacob begat Judas and his *b*... Mt 1:2
Josias begat Jechonias and his *b*... Mt 1:11
by the sea of Galilee, saw two *b*... Mt 4:18
from thence, he saw other two *b*... Mt 4:21
And if ye salute your *b* only... Mt 5:47
his *b* stood without, desiring to... Mt 12:46
thy *b* stand without, desiring to... Mt 12:47
and who are my *b*... Mt 12:48
and said, Behold my mother and my *b*. Mt 12:49
and his *b*, James, and Joses, and... Mt 13:55
that hath forsaken houses, or *b*... Mt 19:29
indignation against the two *b*... Mt 20:24
Now there were with us seven *b*... Mt 22:25
and all ye are *b*... Mt 23:8
one of the least of these my *b*... Mt 25:40
go tell my *b* that they go into... Mt 28:10
There came then his *b* and his... Mk 3:31
thy *b* without seek for thee... Mk 3:32
saying, Who is my mother, or my *b*... Mk 3:33
and said, Behold my mother and my *b*.. Mk 3:34
no man that hath left house, or *b*... Mk 10:29
now in this time, houses, and *b*... Mk 10:30
Now there were seven *b*... Mk 12:20
came to him his mother and his *b*... Lk 8:19
thy *b* stand without, desiring to... Lk 8:20
my *b* are these which hear the... Lk 8:21
call not thy friends, nor thy *b*... Lk 14:12
and wife, and children, and *b*... Lk 14:26
For I have five *b*... Lk 16:28
hath left house, or parents, or *b*... Lk 18:29
be betrayed both by parents, and *b*... Lk 21:16
art converted, strengthen thy *b*... Lk 22:32
he, and his mother, and his *b*... Jn 2:12
His *b* therefore said unto him,... Jn 7:3
neither did his *b* believe in him... Jn 7:5
But when his *b* were gone up... Jn 7:10
but go to my *b*, and say unto them,... Jn 20:17
this saying abroad among the *b*... Jn 21:23
mother of Jesus, and with his *b*... Acts 1:14
Men and *b*, this scripture must... Acts 1:16
Men and *b*, let me freely speak... Acts 2:29
rest of the apostles, Men and *b*... Acts 2:37
And now, *b*, I wot that through... Acts 3:17
God raise up unto you of your *b*... Acts 3:22
Wherefore, *b*, look ye out among... Acts 6:3
And he said, Men, *b*, and fathers,... Acts 7:2
Joseph was made known to his *b*... Acts 7:13
his *b* the children of Israel... Acts 7:23
For he supposed his *b* would have... Acts 7:25
one again, saying, Sirs, ye are *b*... Acts 7:26
God raise up unto you of your *b*... Acts 7:37
Which when the *b* knew, they... Acts 9:30
certain *b* from Joppa accompanied... Acts 10:23
*b* that were in Judaea heard that... Acts 11:1
these six *b* accompanied me... Acts 11:12
unto the *b* which dwelt in Judaea... Acts 11:29
things unto James, and to the *b*... Acts 12:17
unto them, saying, Ye men and *b*... Acts 13:15
Men and *b*, children of the stock... Acts 13:26
unto you therefore, men and *b*... Acts 13:38
minds evil affected against the *b*... Acts 14:2
down from Judaea taught the *b*... Acts 15:1
caused great joy unto all the *b*... Acts 15:3
up, and said unto them, Men and *b*... Acts 15:7
James answered, saying, Men and *b*.. Acts 15:13
and Silas, chief men among the *b*... Acts 15:22
*b* send greeting unto the *b*... Acts 15:23
exhorted the *b* with many words,... Acts 15:32
from the *b* unto the apostles... Acts 15:33
visit our *b* in every city where... Acts 15:36
by the *b* unto the grace of God... Acts 15:40
of by the *b* that were at Lystra... Acts 16:2
and when they had seen the *b*... Acts 16:40
certain *b* unto the rulers of the... Acts 17:6
the *b* immediately sent away Paul... Acts 17:10
then immediately the *b* sent away... Acts 17:14
and then took his leave of the *b*... Acts 18:18
the *b* wrote, exhorting the... Acts 18:27

And now, *b*, I commend you to God, Acts 20:32
to Ptolemais, and saluted the *b* ... Acts 21:7
the *b* received us gladly ... Acts 21:17
Men, *b*, and fathers, hear ye my ... Acts 22:1
I received letters unto the *b* ... Acts 22:5
the council, said, Men and *b* ... Acts 23:1
Then said Paul, I wist not, *b* ... Acts 23:5
out in the council, Men and *b* ... Acts 23:6
Where we found *b*, and were desired Acts 28:14
when the *b* heard of us, they came ... Acts 28:15
he said unto them, Men and *b* ... Acts 28:17
neither any of the *b* that came ... Acts 28:21
I would not have you ignorant, *b* ... Rom 1:13
Know ye not, *b*, (for I speak to ... Rom 7:1
Wherefore, my *b*, ye also are ... Rom 7:4
Therefore, *b*, we are debtors, not ... Rom 8:12
be the firstborn among many *b* ... Rom 8:29
accursed from Christ for my *b* ... Rom 9:3
*B*, my heart's desire and prayer to ... Rom 10:1
For I would not, *b*, that ye ... Rom 11:25
I beseech you therefore, *b* ... Rom 12:1
also am persuaded of you, my *b* ... Rom 15:14
Nevertheless, *b*, I have written ... Rom 15:15
Now I beseech you, *b*, for the ... Rom 15:30
the *b* which are with them ... Rom 16:14
Now I beseech you, *b*, mark them ... Rom 16:17
Now I beseech you, *b*, by the name ... 1Cor 1:10
declared unto me of you, my *b* ... 1Cor 1:11
For ye see your calling, *b* ... 1Cor 1:26
And I, *b*, when I came to you, came ... 1Cor 2:1
And I, *b*, could not speak unto you ... 1Cor 3:1
And these things, *b*, I have in a ... 1Cor 4:6
be able to judge between his *b* ... 1Cor 6:5
wrong, and defraud, and that your *b* ... 1Cor 6:8
*B*, let every man, wherein he is ... 1Cor 7:24
But this I say, *b*, the time is ... 1Cor 7:29
But when ye sin so against the *b* ... 1Cor 8:12
as the *b* of the Lord, and Cephas ... 1Cor 9:5
Moreover, *b*, I would not that ye ... 1Cor 10:1
Now I praise you, *b*, that ye ... 1Cor 11:2
Wherefore, my *b*, when ye come ... 1Cor 11:33
Now concerning spiritual gifts, *b* ... 1Cor 12:1
Now, *b*, if I come unto you ... 1Cor 14:6
*B*, be not children in ... 1Cor 14:20
How is it then, *b* ... 1Cor 14:26
Wherefore, *b*, covet to prophesy, ... 1Cor 14:39
Moreover, *b*, I declare unto you ... 1Cor 15:1
of above five hundred *b* at once ... 1Cor 15:6
Now this I say, *b*, that flesh and ... 1Cor 15:50
Therefore, my beloved *b*, be ye ... 1Cor 15:58
for I look for him with the *b* ... 1Cor 16:11
him to come unto you with the *b* ... 1Cor 16:12
I beseech you, *b*, (ye know the ... 1Cor 16:15
All the *b* greet you ... 1Cor 16:20
For we would not, *b*, have you ... 2Cor 1:8
Moreover, *b*, we do you to wit of ... 2Cor 8:1
or our *b* be enquired of, they are ... 2Cor 8:23
Yet have I sent the *b*, lest our ... 2Cor 9:3
it necessary to exhort the *b* ... 2Cor 9:5
the *b* which came from Macedonia ... 2Cor 11:9
the sea, in perils among false *b* ... 2Cor 11:26
Finally, *b*, farewell ... 2Cor 13:11
all the *b* which are with me, unto ... Gal 1:2
But I certify you, *b*, that the ... Gal 1:11
of false *b* unawares brought in ... Gal 2:4
*B*, I speak after the manner of ... Gal 3:15
*B*, I beseech you, be as I am ... Gal 4:12
Now we, *b*, as Isaac was, are the ... Gal 4:28
So then, *b*, we are not children ... Gal 4:31
And I, *b*, if I yet preach ... Gal 5:11
For, *b*, ye have been called unto ... Gal 5:13
*B*, if a man be overtaken in a ... Gal 6:1
*B*, the grace of our Lord Jesus ... Gal 6:18
Finally, my *b*, be strong in the ... Eph 6:10
Peace be to the *b*, and love with ... Eph 6:23
I would ye should understand, *b* ... Phil 1:12
And many of the *b* in the Lord ... Phil 1:14
Finally, my *b*, rejoice in the ... Phil 3:1
*B*, I count not myself to have ... Phil 3:13
*B*, be followers together of me, ... Phil 3:17
my *b* dearly beloved and longed for ... Phil 4:1
Finally, *b*, whatsoever things are ... Phil 4:8
The *b* which are with me greet you ... Phil 4:21
faithful *b* in Christ which are at ... Col 1:2
Salute the *b* which are in ... Col 4:15
*b* beloved, your election of God ... 1Th 1:4
For yourselves, *b*, know our ... 1Th 2:1
For ye remember, *b*, our labour and ... 1Th 2:9
For ye, *b*, became followers of ... 1Th 2:14
But we, *b*, being taken from you ... 1Th 2:17
Therefore, *b*, we were comforted ... 1Th 3:7
then we beseech you, *b*, and exhort ... 1Th 4:1
the *b* which are in all Macedonia ... 1Th 4:10
but we beseech you, *b*, that ye ... 1Th 4:10
not have you to be ignorant, *b* ... 1Th 4:13
of the times and the seasons, *b* ... 1Th 5:1
But ye, *b*, are not in darkness, ... 1Th 5:4
And we beseech you, *b*, to know ... 1Th 5:12
Now we exhort you, *b*, warn them ... 1Th 5:14
*B*, pray for us ... 1Th 5:25
Greet all the *b* with an holy kiss ... 1Th 5:26
be read unto all the holy *b* ... 1Th 5:27
to thank God always for you, *b* ... 2Th 1:3
Now we beseech you, *b*, by the ... 2Th 2:1
*b* beloved of the Lord, because ... 2Th 2:13
Therefore, *b*, stand fast, and hold ... 2Th 2:15
Finally, *b*, pray for us, that the ... 2Th 3:1
Now we command you, *b*, in the ... 2Th 3:6
But ye, *b*, be not weary in well ... 2Th 3:13
If thou put the *b* in remembrance ... 1Ti 4:6
and the younger men as *b* ... 1Ti 5:1
despise them, because they are *b* ... 1Ti 6:2
Linus, and Claudia, and all the *b* ... 2Ti 4:21
he is not ashamed to call them *b* ... Heb 2:11
I will declare thy name unto my *b* ... Heb 2:12
him to be made like unto his *b* ... Heb 2:17
Wherefore, holy *b*, partakers of ... Heb 3:1
Take heed, *b*, lest there be in ... Heb 3:12
to the law, that is, of their *b* ... Heb 7:5
Having therefore, *b*, boldness to ... Heb 10:19
And I beseech you, *b*, suffer the ... Heb 13:22
My *b*, count it all joy when ye ... Jas 1:2
Do not err, my beloved *b* ... Jas 1:16
Wherefore, my beloved *b*, let ... Jas 1:19
My *b*, have not the faith of our ... Jas 2:1
Hearken, my beloved *b*, Hath not ... Jas 2:5
What doth it profit, my *b* ... Jas 2:14
My *b*, be not many masters, ... Jas 3:1
My *b*, these things ought not so ... Jas 3:10
Can the fig tree, my *b*, bear ... Jas 3:12
Speak not evil one of another, *b* ... Jas 4:11
Be patient therefore, *b*, unto the ... Jas 5:7
Grudge not one against another, *b* ... Jas 5:9
Take, my *b*, the prophets, who ... Jas 5:10
But above all things, my *b* ... Jas 5:12
*B*, if any of you do err from the ... Jas 5:19
unto unfeigned love of the *b* ... 1Pet 1:22
one of another, love as *b* ... 1Pet 3:8
in your *b* that are in the world ... 1Pet 5:9
Wherefore the rather, *b*, give ... 2Pet 1:10
*B*, I write no new commandment ... 1Jn 2:7
Marvel not, my *b*, if the world ... 1Jn 3:13
unto life, because we love the *b* ... 1Jn 3:14
to lay down our lives for the *b* ... 1Jn 3:16
rejoiced greatly, when the *b* came ... 3Jn 3
whatsoever thou doest to the *b* ... 3Jn 5
doth he himself receive the *b* ... 3Jn 10
fellowservants also and their *b* ... Rev 6:11
the accuser of our *b* is cast down ... Rev 12:10
of thy *b* that have the testimony ... Rev 19:10
of thy *b* the prophets, and of them ... Rev 22:9

### BRETHREN'S
lest his *b* heart faint as well as ... Deut 20:8

### BRIBE
*b* to blind mine eyes therewith ... 1Sa 12:3
afflict the just, they take a *b* ... Amos 5:12

### BRIBERY
consume the tabernacles of *b* ... Job 15:34

### BRIBES
aside after lucre, and took *b* ... 1Sa 8:3
and their right hand is full of *b* ... Ps 26:10
his hands from holding of *b* ... Is 33:15

### BRICK
to another, Go to, let us make *b* ... Gen 11:3
they had *b* for stone, and slime ... Gen 11:3
hard bondage, in morter, and in *b* ... Ex 1:14
give the people straw to make *b* ... Ex 5:7
task in making *b* both yesterday ... Ex 5:14
and they say to us, Make *b* ... Ex 5:16
burneth incense upon altars of *b* ... Is 65:3

### BRICKKILN
and made them pass through the *b* ... 2Sa 12:31
and hide them in the clay in the *b* ... Jer 43:9
the morter, make strong the *b* ... Nah 3:14

### BRICKS
And the tale of the *b*, which they ... Ex 5:8
shall ye deliver the tale of *b* ... Ex 5:18
from your *b* of your daily task ... Ex 5:19
The *b* are fallen down, but we ... Is 9:10

### BRIDE
bind them on thee, as a *b* doeth ... Is 49:18
as a *b* adorneth herself with her ... Is 61:10
bridegroom rejoiceth over the *b* ... Is 62:5
her ornaments, or a *b* her attire ... Jer 2:32
bridegroom, and the voice of the *b* ... Jer 7:34
bridegroom, and the voice of the *b* ... Jer 16:9
bridegroom, and the voice of the *b* ... Jer 25:10
bridegroom, and the voice of the *b* ... Jer 33:11
and the *b* out of her closet ... Joel 2:16
He that hath the *b* is the ... Jn 3:29
of the *b* shall be heard no more ... Rev 18:23
prepared as a *b* adorned for her ... Rev 21:2
hither, I will shew thee the *b* ... Rev 21:9
And the Spirit and the *b* say ... Rev 22:17

### BRIDECHAMBER
Can the children of the *b* mourn ... Mt 9:15
Can the children of the *b* fast ... Mk 2:19
make the children of the *b* fast ... Lk 5:34

### BRIDEGROOM
Which is as a *b* coming out of his ... Ps 19:5
as a *b* decketh himself with ... Is 61:10
as the *b* rejoiceth over the bride ... Is 62:5
of gladness, the voice of the *b* ... Jer 7:34
of gladness, the voice of the *b* ... Jer 16:9
of gladness, the voice of the *b* ... Jer 25:10
of gladness, the voice of the *b* ... Jer 33:11
let the *b* go forth of his chamber ... Joel 2:16
as long as the *b* is with them ... Mt 9:15
when the *b* shall be taken from ... Mt 9:15
and went forth to meet the *b* ... Mt 25:1
While the *b* tarried, they all ... Mt 25:5
a cry made, Behold, the *b* cometh ... Mt 25:6
they went to buy, the *b* came ... Mt 25:10
fast, while the *b* is with them ... Mk 2:19
long as they have the *b* with them ... Mk 2:19
when the *b* shall be taken away ... Mk 2:20
fast, while the *b* is with them ... Lk 5:34
when the *b* shall be taken away ... Lk 5:35
of the feast called the *b* ... Jn 2:9
He that hath the bride is the *b* ... Jn 3:29
but the friend of the *b*, which ... Jn 3:29
and the voice of the *b* and of the ... Rev 18:23

### BRIDEGROOM'S
greatly because of the *b* voice ... Jn 3:29

### BRIDLE
my *b* in thy lips, and I will turn ... 2Kin 19:28
also let loose the *b* before me ... Job 30:11
can come to him with his double *b* ... Job 41:13
must be held in with bit and *b* ... Ps 32:9
I will keep my mouth with a *b* ... Ps 39:1
a *b* for the ass, and a rod for the ... Prov 26:3
there shall be a *b* in the jaws of ... Is 30:28
my *b* in thy lips, and I will turn ... Is 37:29
able also to *b* the whole body ... Jas 3:2

### BRIDLES
winepress, even unto the horse *b* ... Rev 14:20

### BRIDLETH
*b* not his tongue, but deceiveth ... Jas 1:26

### BRIEFLY
it is *b* comprehended in this ... Rom 13:9
as I suppose, I have written *b* ... 1Pet 5:12

### BRIER
instead of the *b* shall come up ... Is 55:13
*b* unto the house of Israel ... Eze 28:24
The best of them is as a *b* ... Mic 7:4

### BRIERS
of the wilderness and with *b* ... Judg 8:7
and thorns of the wilderness and *b* ... Judg 8:16
but there shall come up *b* ... Is 5:6
it shall even be for *b* and thorns ... Is 7:23
all the land shall become *b* ... Is 7:24
not come thither the fear of *b* ... Is 7:25
it shall devour the *b* and thorns, ... Is 9:18
his thorns and his *b* in one day ... Is 10:17
who would set the *b* and thorns ... Is 27:4
people shall come up thorns and *b* ... Is 32:13
afraid of their words, though *b* ... Eze 2:6
*b* is rejected, and is nigh unto ... Heb 6:8

### BRIGANDINE
that lifteth himself up in his *b* ... Jer 51:3

### BRIGANDINES
the spears, and put on the *b* ... Jer 46:4

### BRIGHT
or *b* spot, and it be in the skin ... Lev 13:2
If the *b* spot be white in the ... Lev 13:4
be a white rising, or a *b* spot ... Lev 13:19
But if the *b* spot stay in his ... Lev 13:23
that burneth have a white *b* spot ... Lev 13:24
if the hair in the *b* spot be ... Lev 13:25
be no white hair in the *b* spot ... Lev 13:26
if the *b* spot stay in his place, ... Lev 13:28
*b* spots, even white *b* spots ... Lev 13:38
if the *b* spots in the skin of ... Lev 13:39
and for a scab, and for a *b* spot ... Lev 14:56
of the LORD, were of *b* brass ... 1Kin 7:45
the house of the LORD of *b* brass ... 2Chr 4:16
he scattereth his *b* cloud ... Job 37:11
now men see not the *b* light which ... Job 37:21
his belly is as *b* ivory overlaid ... Song 5:14
Make *b* the arrows ... Jer 51:11
and the fire was *b*, and out of the ... Eze 1:13
it is made *b*, it is wrapped up ... Eze 21:15
he made his arrows *b*, he ... Eze 21:21
*b* iron, cassia, and calamus, were ... Eze 27:19
All the *b* lights of heaven will I ... Eze 32:8
lifteth up both the *b* sword ... Nah 3:3
so the LORD shall make *b* clouds ... Zec 10:1
a *b* cloud overshadowed them ... Mt 17:5
as when the *b* shining of a candle ... Lk 11:36
man stood before me in *b* clothing ... Acts 10:30
the offspring of David, and the *b* ... Rev 22:16

### BRIGHTNESS
Through the *b* before him were ... 2Sa 22:13
shined, or the moon walking in *b* ... Job 31:26
At the *b* that was before him his ... Ps 18:12
for *b*, but we walk in darkness ... Is 59:9
kings to the *b* of thy rising ... Is 60:3
neither for *b* shall the moon give ... Is 60:19
thereof go forth as *b*, and the ... Is 62:1
a *b* was about it, and out of the ... Eze 1:4
of fire, and it had *b* round about ... Eze 1:27
appearance of the *b* round about ... Eze 1:28
upward, as the appearance of *b* ... Eze 8:2
full of the *b* of the LORD's glory ... Eze 10:4
and they shall defile thy *b* ... Eze 28:7
thy wisdom by reason of thy *b* ... Eze 28:17
whose *b* was excellent, stood ... Dan 2:31
mine honour and *b* returned unto me ... Dan 4:36
shine as the *b* of the firmament ... Dan 12:3
even very dark, and no *b* in it ... Amos 5:20
And his *b* was as the light ... Hab 3:4
above the *b* of the sun, shining ... Acts 26:13
destroy with the *b* of his coming ... 2Th 2:8
Who being the *b* of his glory ... Heb 1:3

### BRIM
were dipped in the *b* of the water ... Josh 3:15
from the one *b* to the other ... 1Kin 7:23
under the *b* of it round about ... 1Kin 7:24
the *b* thereof was wrought like ... 1Kin 7:26

was wrought like the *b* of a cup ... 1Kin 7:26
sea of ten cubits from *b* to *b* ... 2Chr 4:2
the *b* of it like the work of the ... 2Chr 4:5
like the work of the *b* of a cup ... 2Chr 4:5
And they filled them up to the *b* ... Jn 2:7

**BRIMSTONE**
upon Sodom and upon Gomorrah *b* ... Gen 19:24
that the whole land thereof is *b* ... Deut 29:23
*b* shall be scattered upon his ... Job 18:15
he shall rain snares, fire and *b* ... Ps 11:6
of the LORD, like a stream of *b* ... Is 30:33
pitch, and the dust thereof into *b* ... Is 34:9
and great hailstones, fire, and *b* ... Eze 38:22
*b* from heaven, and destroyed them ... Lk 17:29
of fire, and of jacinth, and *b* ... Rev 9:17
mouths issued fire and smoke and *b* ... Rev 9:17
and by the smoke, and by the *b* ... Rev 9:18
*b* in the presence of the holy ... Rev 14:10
a lake of fire burning with *b* ... Rev 19:20
cast into the lake of fire and *b* ... Rev 20:10
lake which burneth with fire and *b* ... Rev 21:8

**BRING** See PREFACE.
sort shalt thou *b* into the ark ... Gen 6:19
when I *b* a cloud over the earth, ... Gen 9:14
with them to *b* them on the way ... Gen 18:16
*b* them out unto us, that we may ... Gen 19:5
I shall *b* a curse upon me, and not ... Gen 27:12
But *b* your youngest brother unto ... Gen 42:20
two sons, if I *b* him not to thee ... Gen 42:37
wives, and *b* your father, and come ... Gen 45:19
*B* them, I pray thee, unto me, and ... Gen 48:9
shall *b* thee into the land of the ... Ex 13:5
of thy land thou shalt *b* into the ... Ex 23:19
to *b* thee into the place which I ... Ex 23:20
of a willing heart, let him *b* it ... Ex 35:5
The people *b* much more than ... Ex 36:5
then he will *b* us into this land, ... Num 14:8
the LORD was not able to *b* this ... Num 14:16
him will I *b* into the land ... Num 14:24
therefore ye shall not *b* this ... Num 20:12
*b* it unto me, and I will hear it ... Deut 1:17
When the LORD thy God shall *b* ... Deut 7:1
Then thou shalt *b* her home to ... Deut 21:12
*b* it unto us, that we may hear it ... Deut 30:12
Judah, and *b* him unto his people ... Deut 33:7
be weaned, and then I will *b* him ... 1Sa 1:22
if we go, what shall we *b* the man ... 1Sa 9:7
*B* the portion which I gave thee, ... 1Sa 9:23
shouldest thou *b* me to thy father ... 1Sa 20:8
to *b* about all Israel unto thee ... 2Sa 3:12
except thou first *b* Michal Saul's ... 2Sa 3:13
*b* him to me, and he shall not ... 2Sa 14:10
Why are ye the last to *b* the king ... 2Sa 19:11
to *b* his way upon his head ... 1Kin 8:32
*B* me a new cruse, and put salt ... 2Kin 2:20
I will *b* you to the man whom ye ... 2Kin 6:19
*b* an offering, and come before him ... 1Chr 16:29
did not our God *b* all this evil ... Neh 13:18
Did I say, *B* unto me ... Job 6:22
wilt thou *b* me into dust again ... Job 10:9
Who can *b* a clean thing out of an ... Job 14:4
know that thou wilt *b* me to death ... Job 30:23
To *b* back his soul from the pit, ... Job 33:30
and he shall *b* it to pass ... Ps 37:5
let them *b* me unto thy holy hill, ... Ps 43:3
Who will *b* me into the strong ... Ps 60:9
shall *b* peace to the people ... Ps 72:3
he shall *b* upon them their own ... Ps 94:23
Scornful men *b* a city into a ... Prov 29:8
for who shall *b* him to see what ... Eccl 3:22
God will *b* thee into judgment ... Eccl 11:9
For God shall *b* every work into ... Eccl 12:14
*b* thee into my mother's house, ... Song 8:2
The LORD shall *b* upon thee ... Is 7:17
them, and *b* them to their place ... Is 14:2
fort of thy walls shall he *b* down ... Is 25:12
Tell ye, and *b* them near ... Is 45:21
I *b* near my righteousness ... Is 46:13
Even them will I *b* to my holy ... Is 56:7
that thou *b* the poor that are ... Is 58:7
and for iron I will *b* silver ... Is 60:17
I will *b* forth a seed out of ... Is 65:9
will *b* their fears upon them ... Is 66:4
a family, and I will *b* you to Zion ... Jer 3:14
lest thou *b* me to nothing ... Jer 10:24
therefore I will *b* upon them all ... Jer 11:8
*b* upon them the day of evil, and ... Jer 17:18
I will *b* them from the north ... Jer 31:8
so will I *b* upon them all the ... Jer 32:42
I will *b* it health and cure, and I ... Jer 33:6
and of them that shall *b* the ... Jer 33:11
I will *b* a fear upon thee, saith ... Jer 49:5
will *b* a sword upon you, and I ... Eze 6:3
I will *b* you out of the midst ... Eze 11:9
that I would not *b* them into the ... Eze 20:15
to *b* thee upon the necks of them ... Eze 21:29
I will *b* them against thee on ... Eze 23:22
I will *b* them out from the people ... Eze 34:13
that I would *b* thee against them ... Eze 38:17
*b* her into the wilderness, and ... Hos 2:14
which say to their masters, *B* ... Amos 4:1
Yet will I *b* an heir unto thee, O ... Mic 1:15
And I will *b* them, and they shall ... Zec 8:8
*B* ye all the tithes into the ... Mal 3:10
she shall *b* forth a son, and thou ... Mt 1:21
shall *b* forth a son, and they ... Mt 1:23
be thou there until I *b* thee word ... Mt 2:13
Therefore if thou *b* thy gift to ... Mt 5:23
*b* him hither to me ... Mt 17:17
loose them, and *b* them unto me ... Mt 21:2
they *b* unto him one that was deaf ... Mk 7:32
*b* him unto me ... Mk 9:19
loose him, and *b* him ... Mk 11:2
*b* forth a son, and shalt call his ... Lk 1:31
I *b* you good tidings of great joy ... Lk 2:10
life, and *b* no fruit to perfection ... Lk 8:14
And when they *b* you unto the ... Lk 12:11
*B* forth the best robe, and put it ... Lk 15:22
*b* hither the fatted calf, and kill ... Lk 15:23
loose him, and *b* him hither ... Lk 19:30
them also I must *b*, and they shall ... Jn 10:16
*b* all things to your remembrance, ... Jn 14:26
What accusation *b* ye against this ... Jn 18:29
intend to *b* this man's blood upon ... Acts 5:28
that they should *b* them into ... Acts 7:6
he might *b* them bound unto ... Acts 9:2
to *b* them which were there bound ... Acts 22:5
them, and to *b* him into the castle ... Acts 23:10
wise, and will *b* to nothing the ... 1Cor 1:19
who shall *b* you into remembrance ... 1Cor 4:17
my body, and *b* it into subjection ... 1Cor 9:27
that ye may *b* me on my journey ... 1Cor 16:6
if a man *b* you into bondage, if a ... 2Cor 11:20
schoolmaster to *b* us unto Christ ... Gal 3:24
but *b* them up in the nurture and ... Eph 6:4
in Jesus will God *b* with him ... 1Th 4:14
unjust, that he might *b* us to God ... 1Pet 3:18
*b* not this doctrine, receive him ... 2Jn 10
whom if thou *b* forward on their ... 3Jn 6
of the earth do *b* their glory ... Rev 21:24
And they shall *b* the glory ... Rev 21:26

**BRINGERS**
the *b* up of the children, sent to ... 2Kin 10:5

**BRINGEST**
a valiant man, and *b* good tidings ... 1Kin 1:42
*b* me into judgment with thee ... Job 14:3
that *b* good tidings, get thee up ... Is 40:9
that *b* good tidings, lift up thy ... Is 40:9
For thou *b* certain strange things ... Acts 17:20

**BRINGETH**
which *b* you out from under the ... Ex 6:7
For I am the LORD that *b* you up ... Lev 11:45
*b* it not unto the door of the ... Lev 17:4
*b* it not unto the door of the ... Lev 17:9
For the LORD thy God *b* thee into ... Deut 8:7
that the field *b* forth year by ... Deut 14:22
he *b* down to the grave, and ... 1Sa 2:6
down to the grave, and *b* up ... 1Sa 2:6
he *b* low, and lifteth up ... 1Sa 2:7
the king said, He also *b* tidings ... 2Sa 18:26
that *b* down the people under me, ... 2Sa 22:48
that *b* me forth from mine enemies ... 2Sa 22:49
into whose hand God *b* abundantly ... Job 12:6
*b* out to light the shadow of ... Job 12:22
for wrath *b* the punishments of ... Job 19:29
that is hid *b* he forth to light ... Job 28:11
that *b* forth his fruit in his ... Ps 1:3
when the LORD *b* back the ... Ps 14:7
The LORD *b* the counsel of the ... Ps 33:10
man who *b* wicked devices to pass ... Ps 37:7
When God *b* back the captivity of ... Ps 53:6
he *b* out those which are bound ... Ps 68:6
he *b* them out of their distresses ... Ps 107:28
so he *b* them unto their desired ... Ps 107:30
he *b* the wind out of his ... Ps 135:7
mouth of the just *b* forth wisdom ... Prov 10:31
moving his lips he *b* evil to pass ... Prov 16:30
him, and *b* him before great men ... Prov 18:16
that causeth shame, and *b* reproach ... Prov 19:26
wicked, and *b* the wheel over them ... Prov 20:26
when he *b* it with a wicked mind ... Prov 21:27
to himself *b* his mother to shame ... Prov 29:15
He that delicately *b* up his ... Prov 29:21
The fear of man *b* a snare ... Prov 29:25
churning of milk *b* forth butter ... Prov 30:33
of the nose *b* forth blood ... Prov 30:33
forcing of wrath *b* forth strife ... Prov 30:33
she *b* her food from afar ... Prov 31:14
the wood that *b* forth trees ... Eccl 2:6
the Lord *b* up upon them the ... Is 8:7
For he *b* down them that dwell on ... Is 26:5
he *b* it even to the dust ... Is 26:5
That *b* the princes to nothing ... Is 40:23
that *b* out their host by number ... Is 40:26
Jerusalem one that *b* good tidings ... Is 41:27
Which *b* forth the chariot and ... Is 43:17
feet of him that *b* good tidings ... Is 52:7
that *b* good tidings of good, that ... Is 52:7
that *b* forth an instrument for ... Is 54:16
For as the earth *b* forth her bud ... Is 61:11
her that *b* forth her first child ... Jer 4:31
*b* forth the wind out of his ... Jer 10:13
*b* forth the wind out of his ... Jer 51:16
which *b* their iniquity to ... Eze 29:16
he *b* forth fruit unto himself ... Hos 10:1
feet of him that *b* good tidings ... Nah 1:15
that which the ground *b* forth ... Hag 1:11
therefore every tree which *b* not ... Mt 3:10
good tree *b* forth good fruit ... Mt 7:17
a corrupt tree *b* forth evil fruit ... Mt 7:17
Every tree that *b* not forth good ... Mt 7:19
of the heart *b* forth good things ... Mt 12:35
evil treasure *b* forth evil things ... Mt 12:35
*b* forth, some an hundredfold, ... Mt 13:23
which *b* forth out of his treasure ... Mt 13:52
*b* them up into an high mountain ... Mt 17:1
For the earth *b* forth fruit of ... Mk 4:28
every tree therefore which *b* not ... Lk 3:9
For a good tree *b* not forth ... Lk 6:43
heart *b* forth that which is good ... Lk 6:45
heart *b* forth that which is evil ... Lk 6:45
if it die, it *b* forth much fruit ... Jn 12:24
the same *b* forth much fruit ... Jn 15:5
*b* forth fruit, as it doth also in ... Col 1:6
For the grace of God that *b* ... Titus 2:11
when he *b* in the firstbegotten ... Heb 1:6
*b* forth herbs meet for them by ... Heb 6:7
hath conceived, it *b* forth sin ... Jas 1:15
it is finished, *b* forth death ... Jas 1:15

**BRINGING**
*b* them out from the land of Egypt ... Ex 12:42
the people were restrained from *b* ... Ex 36:6
*b* iniquity to remembrance ... Num 5:15
by *b* up a slander upon the land, ... Num 14:36
ye not a word of *b* the king back ... 2Sa 19:10
be first had in *b* back our king ... 2Sa 19:43
*b* gold, and silver, ivory, and apes ... 1Kin 10:22
I am *b* such evil upon Jerusalem ... 2Kin 21:12
came the ships of Tarshish *b* gold ... 2Chr 9:21
*b* in sheaves, and lading asses ... Neh 13:15
rejoicing, *b* his sheaves with him ... Ps 126:6
*b* burnt offerings, and sacrifices, ... Jer 17:26
*b* sacrifices of praise, unto the ... Jer 17:26
in *b* them forth out of the land ... Eze 20:9
by *b* upon us a great evil ... Dan 9:12
given to a nation *b* forth the ... Mt 21:43
*b* one sick of the palsy, which ... Mk 2:3
*b* the spices which they had ... Lk 24:1
*b* sick folks, and them which were ... Acts 5:16
*b* me into captivity to the law of ... Rom 7:23
*b* into captivity every thought to ... 2Cor 10:5
in *b* many sons unto glory, to ... Heb 2:10
but the *b* in of a better hope did ... Heb 7:19
*b* in the flood upon the world of ... 2Pet 2:5

**BRINK**
kine upon the *b* of the river ... Gen 41:3
it in the flags by the river's *b* ... Ex 2:3
by the river's *b* against he come ... Ex 7:15
which is by the *b* of the river of ... Deut 2:36
to the *b* of the water of Jordan ... Josh 3:8
to return to the *b* of the river ... Eze 47:6

**BROAD**
cubits long, and five cubits *b* ... Ex 27:1
let them make them *b* plates for a ... Num 16:38
they were made *b* plates for a ... Num 16:39
chamber was five cubits *b* ... 1Kin 6:6
and the middle was six cubits *b* ... 1Kin 6:6
and the third was seven cubits *b* ... 1Kin 6:6
cubits long, and five cubits *b* ... 2Chr 6:13
Jerusalem unto the *b* wall ... Neh 3:8
the furnaces even unto the *b* wall ... Neh 12:38
out of the strait into a *b* place ... Job 36:16
thy commandment is exceeding *b* ... Ps 119:96
in the *b* ways I will seek him ... Song 3:2
be unto us a place of *b* rivers ... Is 33:21
seek in the *b* places thereof, if ... Jer 5:1
The *b* walls of Babylon shall be ... Jer 51:58
of the gate, which was one reed *b* ... Eze 40:6
of the gate, which was one reed *b* ... Eze 40:6
was one reed long, and one reed *b* ... Eze 40:7
long, and five and twenty cubits *b* ... Eze 40:29
cubits long, and five cubits *b* ... Eze 40:30
long, and five and twenty cubits *b* ... Eze 40:33
long, and a cubit and an half *b* ... Eze 40:42
And within were hooks, an hand *b* ... Eze 40:43
long, and an hundred cubits *b* ... Eze 40:47
six cubits *b* on the one side, and ... Eze 41:1
six cubits *b* on the other side, ... Eze 41:1
the west was seventy cubits *b* ... Eze 41:12
as long as they, and as *b* as they ... Eze 42:11
reeds long, and five hundred *b* ... Eze 42:20
be twelve cubits long, twelve *b* ... Eze 43:16
fourteen *b* in the four squares ... Eze 43:17
of the city five thousand *b* ... Eze 45:6
of forty cubits long and thirty *b* ... Eze 46:22
one against another in the *b* ways ... Nah 2:4
*b* is the way, that leadeth to ... Mt 7:13
they make *b* their phylacteries, ... Mt 23:5

**BROADER**
than the earth, and *b* than the sea ... Job 11:9

**BROIDED**
not with *b* hair, or gold, or ... 1Ti 2:9

**BROIDERED**
a *b* coat, a mitre, and a girdle ... Ex 28:4
I clothed thee also with *b* work ... Eze 16:10
of fine linen, and silk, and *b* work ... Eze 16:13
And tookest thy *b* garments ... Eze 16:18
and put off their *b* garments ... Eze 26:16
Fine linen with *b* work from Egypt ... Eze 27:7
*b* work, and fine linen, and coral, ... Eze 27:16
*b* work, and in chests of rich ... Eze 27:24

**BROILED**
they gave him a piece of a *b* fish ... Lk 24:42

**BROKEN**
fountains of the great deep *b* up ... Gen 7:11
he hath *b* my covenant ... Gen 17:14
she said, How hast thou *b* forth ... Gen 38:29
wherein it is sodden shall be *b* ... Lev 6:28
for pots, they shall be *b* down ... Lev 11:35
of leprosy *b* out of the boil ... Lev 13:20
it is a leprosy *b* out of the ... Lev 13:25
which hath the issue, shall be *b* ... Lev 15:12
or scabbed, or hath his stones *b* ... Lev 21:20
Blind, or *b*, or maimed, or having ... Lev 22:22

is bruised, or crushed, or *b* Lev 22:24
I have *b* the bands of your yoke, Lev 26:13
when I have *b* the staff of your Lev 26:26
hath *b* his commandment, that soul.. Num 15:31
Then were the horsehoofs *b* by the Judg 5:22
as a thread of tow is *b* when it Judg 16:9
The bows of the mighty men are *b* 1Sa 2:4
of the LORD shall be *b* to pieces 1Sa 2:10
The LORD hath *b* forth upon mine 2Sa 5:20
a bow of steel is *b* by mine arms 2Sa 22:35
altar of the LORD that was *b* down 1Kin 18:30
the ships were *b* at Ezion-geber 1Kin 22:48
the house, that it be not *b* down 2Kin 11:6
And the city was *b* up, and all the 2Kin 25:4
God hath *b* in upon mine enemies 1Chr 14:11
the LORD hath *b* thy works 2Chr 20:37
And the ships were *b*, that they 2Chr 20:37
had *b* up the house of God 2Chr 24:7
that they all were *b* in pieces 2Chr 25:12
built up all the wall that was *b* 2Chr 32:5
Hezekiah his father had *b* down 2Chr 33:3
when he had *b* down the altars and 2Chr 34:7
wall of Jerusalem also is *b* down Neh 1:3
of Jerusalem, which were *b* down Neh 2:13
teeth of the young lions, are *b* Job 4:10
my skin is *b*, and become loathsome Job 7:5
at ease, but he hath *b* me asunder Job 16:12
are past, my purposes are *b* off Job 17:11
of the fatherless have been *b* Job 22:9
wickedness shall be *b* as a tree Job 24:20
mine arm be *b* from the bone Job 31:22
and the high arm shall be *b* Job 38:15
thou hast *b* the teeth of the Ps 3:7
a bow of steel is *b* by mine arms Ps 18:34
I am like a *b* vessel Ps 31:12
unto them that are of a *b* heart Ps 34:18
not one of them is *b* Ps 34:20
heart, and their bows shall be *b* Ps 37:15
the arms of the wicked shall be *b* Ps 37:17
I am feeble and sore *b* Ps 38:8
Though thou hast sore *b* us in the Ps 44:19
which thou hast *b* may rejoice Ps 51:8
sacrifices of God are a *b* spirit Ps 51:17
a *b* and a contrite heart, O God, Ps 51:17
he hath *b* his covenant Ps 55:20
thou hast *b* it Ps 60:2
Reproach hath *b* my heart Ps 69:20
hast thou then *b* down her hedges Ps 80:12
Thou hast *b* Rahab in pieces, as Ps 89:10
Thou hast *b* down all his hedges Ps 89:40
For he hath *b* the gates of brass, Ps 107:16
he might even slay the *b* in heart Ps 109:16
the snare is *b*, and we are escaped Ps 124:7
He healeth the *b* in heart Ps 147:3
his knowledge the depths are *b* up Prov 3:20
shall he be *b* without remedy Prov 6:15
of the heart the spirit is *b* Prov 15:13
but a *b* spirit drieth the bones Prov 17:22
the stone wall thereof was *b* down Prov 24:31
time of trouble is like a *b* tooth Prov 25:19
is like a city that is *b* down Prov 25:28
a threefold cord is not quickly *b* Eccl 4:12
loosed, or the golden bowl be *b* Eccl 12:6
the pitcher be *b* at the fountain Eccl 12:6
or the wheel *b* at the cistern Eccl 12:6
the latchet of their shoes be *b* Is 5:27
and five years shall Ephraim be *b* Is 7:8
and ye shall be *b* in pieces Is 8:9
and ye shall be *b* in pieces Is 8:9
and ye shall be *b* in pieces Is 8:9
shall stumble, and fall, and be *b* Is 8:15
For thou hast *b* the yoke of his Is 9:4
The LORD hath *b* the staff of the Is 14:5
rod of him that smote thee is *b* Is 14:29
have *b* down the principal plants Is 16:8
they shall be *b* in the purposes Is 19:10
gods he hath *b* unto the ground Is 21:9
the houses have ye *b* down to Is 22:10
*b* the everlasting covenant Is 24:5
The city of confusion is *b* down Is 24:10
The earth is utterly *b* down Is 24:19
are withered, they shall be *b* off Is 27:11
go, and fall backward, and be *b* Is 28:13
vessel that is *b* in pieces Is 30:14
he hath *b* the covenant, he hath Is 33:8
any of the cords thereof be *b* Is 33:20
in the staff of this *b* reed Is 36:6
*b* cisterns, that can hold no Jer 2:13
Tahapanes have *b* the crown of thy Jer 2:16
For of old time I have *b* thy yoke Jer 2:20
*b* down at the presence of the Jer 4:26
these have altogether *b* the yoke Jer 5:5
is spoiled, and all my cords are *b* Jer 10:20
the house of Judah have *b* my Jer 11:10
it, and the branches of it are *b* Jer 11:16
people is *b* with a great breach Jer 14:17
this man Coniah a despised *b* idol Jer 22:28
me is *b* because of the prophets Jer 23:9
I have *b* the yoke of the king of Jer 28:2
*b* the yoke from off the neck of Jer 28:12
Thou hast *b* the yokes of wood Jer 28:13
be *b* with David my servant Jer 33:21
*b* up from Jerusalem for fear of Jer 37:11
of the month, the city was *b* up Jer 39:2
say, How is the strong staff *b* Jer 48:17
for it is *b* down Jer 48:20
Moab is cut off, and his arm is *b* Jer 48:25
for I have *b* Moab like a vessel Jer 48:38
howl, saying, How is it *b* down Jer 48:39
Merodach is *b* in pieces Jer 50:2
her images are *b* in pieces Jer 50:2
king of Babylon hath *b* his bones Jer 50:17
whole earth cut in asunder and *b* Jer 50:23
her bars are *b* Jer 51:30
every one of their bows is *b* Jer 51:56
of Babylon shall be utterly *b* Jer 51:58
Then the city was *b* up, and all Jer 52:7
he hath destroyed and *b* her bars Lam 2:9
he hath *b* my bones Lam 3:4
He hath also *b* my teeth with Lam 3:16
and your images shall be *b* Eze 6:4
desolate, and your idols may be *b* Eze 6:6
because I am *b* with their whorish Eze 6:9
and my covenant that he hath *b* Eze 17:19
her strong rods were *b* and Eze 19:12
she is *b* that was the gates of Eze 26:2
the east wind hath *b* thee in the Eze 27:26
be *b* by the seas in the depths of Eze 27:34
her foundations shall be *b* down Eze 30:4
I have *b* the arm of Pharaoh king Eze 30:21
the strong, and that which was *b* Eze 30:22
his boughs are *b* by all the Eze 31:12
thou shalt be *b* in the midst of Eze 32:28
have ye bound up that which was *b* Eze 34:4
and will bind up that which was *b* Eze 34:16
when I have *b* the bands of their Eze 34:27
they have *b* my covenant because Eze 44:7
*b* to pieces together, and became Dan 2:35
be partly strong, and partly *b* Dan 2:42
was strong, the great horn was *b* Dan 8:8
Now that being *b*, whereas four Dan 8:22
but he shall be *b* without hand Dan 8:25
stand up, his kingdom shall be *b* Dan 11:4
from before him, and shall be *b* Dan 11:22
*b* in judgment, because he Hos 5:11
of Samaria shall be *b* in pieces Hos 8:6
desolate, the barns are *b* down Joel 1:17
so that the ship was like to be *b* Jonah 1:4
they have *b* up, and have passed Mic 2:13
And it was *b* in that day Zec 11:11
one, nor heal that that is *b* Zec 11:16
they took up of the *b* meat that Mt 15:37
fall on this stone shall be *b* Mt 21:44
suffered his house to be *b* up Mt 24:43
and when they had *b* it up, they Mk 2:4
him, and the fetters *b* in pieces Mk 5:4
they took up of the *b* meat that Mk 8:8
his house to be *b* through Lk 12:39
fall upon that stone shall be *b* Lk 20:18
he not only had *b* the sabbath Jn 5:18
the law of Moses should not be *b* Jn 7:23
and the scripture cannot be *b* Jn 10:35
Pilate that their legs might be *b* Jn 19:31
A bone of him shall not be *b* Jn 19:36
so many, yet was not the net *b* Jn 21:11
when the congregation was *b* up Acts 13:43
had *b* bread, and eaten, and talked Acts 20:11
and when he had *b* it, he began to Acts 27:35
but the hinder part was *b* with Acts 27:41
some on *b* pieces of the ship Acts 27:44
if some of the branches be *b* off Rom 11:17
say then, The branches were *b* off Rom 11:19
of unbelief they were *b* off Rom 11:20
is my body, which is *b* for you 1Cor 11:24
hath *b* down the middle wall of Eph 2:14
potter shall they be *b* to shivers Rev 2:27

## BROKENFOOTED
Or a man that is *b*, or Lev 21:19

## BROKENHANDED
a man that is brokenfooted, or *b* Lev 21:19

## BROKENHEARTED
he hath sent me to bind up the *b* Is 61:1
he hath sent me to heal the *b* Lk 4:18

## BROOD
doth gather her *b* under her wings Lk 13:34

## BROOK
them, and sent them over the *b* Gen 32:23
thick trees, and willows of the *b* Lev 23:40
And they came unto the *b* of Eshcol Num 13:23
The place was called the *b* Eshcol Num 13:24
I, and get you over the *b* Zered Deut 2:13
And we went over the *b* Zered Deut 2:13
we were come over the *b* Zered Deut 2:14
cast the dust thereof into the *b* Deut 9:21
five smooth stones out of the *b* 1Sa 17:40
with him, and came to the *b* Besor 1Sa 30:9
could not go over the *b* Besor 1Sa 30:10
made also to abide at the *b* Besor 1Sa 30:21
himself passed over the *b* Kidron 2Sa 15:23
They be gone over the *b* of water 2Sa 17:20
out, and passest over the *b* Kidron 1Kin 2:37
idol, and burnt it by the *b* Kidron 1Kin 15:13
and hide thyself by the *b* Cherith 1Kin 17:3
that thou shalt drink of the *b* 1Kin 17:4
he went and dwelt by the *b* Cherith 1Kin 17:5
and he drank of the *b* 1Kin 17:6
a while, that the *b* dried up 1Kin 17:7
brought them down to the *b* Kishon. 1Kin 18:40
Jerusalem, unto the *b* Kidron 2Kin 23:6
and burned it at the *b* Kidron 2Kin 23:6
dust of them into the *b* Kidron 2Kin 23:12
it, and burnt it at the *b* Kidron 2Chr 15:16
find them at the end of the *b* 2Chr 20:16
it out abroad into the *b* Kidron 2Chr 29:16
and cast them into the *b* Kidron 2Chr 30:14
the *b* that ran through the midst 2Chr 32:4
went I up in the night by the *b* Neh 2:15
have dealt deceitfully as a *b* Job 6:15
of the *b* compass him about Job 40:22
as to Jabin, at the *b* of Kison Ps 83:9
shall drink of the *b* in the way Ps 110:7
of wisdom as a flowing *b* Prov 18:4
away to the *b* of the willows Is 15:7
the fields unto the *b* of Kidron Jer 31:40
his disciples over the *b* Cedron Jn 18:1

## BROOKS
Red sea, and in the *b* of Arnon, Num 21:14
at the stream of the *b* that goeth Num 21:15
a good land, a land of *b* of water Deut 8:7
Hiddai of the *b* of Gaash 2Sa 23:30
fountains of water, and unto all *b* 1Kin 18:5
Hurai of the *b* of Gaash, Abiel 1Chr 11:32
as the stream of *b* they pass away Job 6:15
floods, the *b* of honey and butter Job 20:17
of Ophir as the stones of the *b* Job 22:24
hart panteth after the water *b* Ps 42:1
the *b* of defence shall be emptied Is 19:6
the *b*, by the mouth of the *b* Is 19:7
and every thing sown by the *b* Is 19:7
angle into the *b* shall lament Is 19:8

## BROTH
basket, and he put the *b* in a pot Judg 6:19
upon this rock, and pour out the *b* Judg 6:20
*b* of abominable things is in Is 65:4

## BROTHER
And she again bare his *b* Abel Gen 4:2
And Cain talked with Abel his *b* Gen 4:8
Cain rose up against Abel his *b* Gen 4:8
unto Cain, Where is Abel thy *b* Gen 4:9
at the hand of every man's *b* will Gen 9:5
the *b* of Japheth the elder, even Gen 10:21
*b* of Eshcol, and *b* of Aner Gen 14:13
*b* of Eshcol, and *b* of Aner Gen 14:13
that his *b* was taken captive Gen 14:14
and also brought again his *b* Lot Gen 14:16
even she herself said, He is my *b* Gen 20:5
shall come, say of me, He is my *b* Gen 20:13
I have given thy *b* a thousand Gen 20:16
born children unto thy *b* Nahor Gen 22:20
Huz his firstborn, and Buz his *b* Gen 22:21
did bear to Nahor, Abraham's *b* Gen 22:23
the wife of Nahor, Abraham's *b* Gen 24:15
And Rebekah had a *b*, and his name Gen 24:29
he gave also to her *b* and to her Gen 24:53
And her *b* and her mother said, Let Gen 24:55
And after that came his *b* out Gen 25:26
thy father speak unto Esau thy *b* Gen 27:6
Esau my *b* is a hairy man, and I am Gen 27:11
were hairy, as his *b* Esau's hands Gen 27:23
that Esau his *b* came in from his Gen 27:30
Thy *b* came with subtilty, and hath Gen 27:35
thou live, and shalt serve thy *b* Gen 27:40
then will I slay my *b* Jacob Gen 27:41
thy *b* Esau, as touching thee, Gen 27:42
flee thou to Laban my *b* to Haran Gen 27:43
daughters of Laban thy mother's *b* Gen 28:2
the *b* of Rebekah, Jacob's and Gen 28:5
daughter of Laban his mother's *b* Gen 29:10
the sheep of Laban his mother's *b* Gen 29:10
the flock of Laban his mother's *b* Gen 29:10
Rachel that he was her father's *b* Gen 29:12
unto Jacob, Because thou art my *b* Gen 29:15
Esau his *b* unto the land of Seir Gen 32:3
saying, We came to thy *b* Esau Gen 32:6
pray thee, from the hand of my *b* Gen 32:11
his hand a present for Esau his *b* Gen 32:13
When Esau my *b* meeteth thee Gen 32:17
until he came near to his *b* Gen 33:3
And Esau said, I have enough, my *b* Gen 33:9
from the face of Esau thy *b* Gen 35:1
he fled from the face of his *b* Gen 35:7
from the face of his *b* Jacob Gen 36:6
profit is it if we slay our *b* Gen 37:26
for he is our *b* and our flesh Gen 37:27
her, and raise up seed to thy *b* Gen 38:8
that he should give seed to his *b* Gen 38:9
that, behold, his *b* came out Gen 38:29
And afterward came out his *b* Gen 38:30
But Benjamin, Joseph's *b*, Jacob Gen 42:4
your youngest *b* come hither Gen 42:15
of you, and let him fetch your *b* Gen 42:16
But bring your youngest *b* unto me Gen 42:20
verily guilty concerning our *b* Gen 42:21
And bring your youngest *b* unto me Gen 42:34
so will I deliver you your *b* Gen 42:34
for his *b* is dead, and he is left Gen 42:38
face, except your *b* be with you Gen 43:3
If thou wilt send our *b* with us Gen 43:4
face, except your *b* be with you Gen 43:5
the man whether ye had yet a *b* Gen 43:6
have ye another *b* Gen 43:7
he would say, Bring your *b* down Gen 43:7
Take also your *b*, and arise, go Gen 43:13
he may send away your other *b* Gen 43:14
saw his *b* Benjamin, his mother's Gen 43:29
and said, Is this your younger *b* Gen 43:29
his bowels did yearn upon his *b* Gen 43:30
saying, Have ye a father, or a *b* Gen 44:19
his *b* is dead, and he alone is Gen 44:20
youngest *b* come down with you Gen 44:23
if our youngest *b* be with us Gen 44:26
except our youngest *b* be with us Gen 44:26
And he said, I am Joseph your *b* Gen 45:4
see, and the eyes of my *b* Benjamin Gen 45:12
fell upon his *b* Benjamin's neck Gen 45:14
but truly his younger *b* shall be Gen 48:19
Is not Aaron the Levite thy *b* Ex 4:14

Aaron thy *b* shall be thy prophet ... Ex 7:1
Aaron thy *b* shall speak unto ... Ex 7:2
take thou unto thee Aaron thy *b* ... Ex 28:1
for Aaron thy *b* for glory ... Ex 28:2
holy garments for Aaron thy *b* ... Ex 28:4
shalt put them upon Aaron thy *b* ... Ex 28:41
the camp, and slay every man his *b* ... Ex 32:27
man upon his son, and upon his *b* ... Ex 32:29
Moses, Speak unto Aaron thy *b* ... Lev 16:2
the nakedness of thy father's *b* ... Lev 18:14
not hate thy *b* in thine heart ... Lev 19:17
and for his daughter, and for his *b* ... Lev 21:2
If thy *b* be waxen poor, and hath ... Lev 25:25
he redeem that which his *b* sold ... Lev 25:25
if thy *b* be waxen poor, and fallen ... Lev 25:35
that thy *b* may live with thee ... Lev 25:36
if thy *b* that dwelleth by thee be ... Lev 25:39
thy *b* that dwelleth by him wax ... Lev 25:47
or for his mother, for his *b* ... Num 6:7
together, thou, and Aaron thy *b* ... Num 20:8
of Edom, Thus saith thy *b* Israel ... Num 20:14
as Aaron thy *b* was gathered ... Num 27:13
our *b* unto his daughters ... Num 36:2
between every man and his *b* ... Deut 1:16
If thy *b*, the son of thy mother, ... Deut 13:6
it of his neighbour, or of his *b* ... Deut 15:2
thy *b* thine hand shall release ... Deut 15:3
shut thine hand from thy poor *b* ... Deut 15:7
eye be evil against thy poor *b* ... Deut 15:9
open thine hand wide unto thy *b* ... Deut 15:11
And if thy *b*, an Hebrew man, or an. Deut 15:12
over thee, which is not thy *b* ... Deut 17:15
testified falsely against his *b* ... Deut 19:18
thought to have done unto his *b* ... Deut 19:19
case bring them again unto thy *b* ... Deut 22:1
if thy *b* be not nigh unto thee, ... Deut 22:2
thee until thy *b* seek after it ... Deut 22:2
for he is thy *b* ... Deut 23:7
not lend upon usury to thy *b* ... Deut 23:19
but unto thy *b* thou shalt not ... Deut 23:20
thou dost lend thy *b* any thing ... Deut 24:10
then thy *b* should seem vile unto ... Deut 25:3
her husband's *b* shall go in unto ... Deut 25:5
duty of an husband's *b* unto her ... Deut 25:5
the name of his *b* which is dead ... Deut 25:6
My husband's *b* refuseth to raise ... Deut 25:7
up unto his *b* a name in Israel ... Deut 25:7
the duty of my husband's *b* ... Deut 25:7
eye shall be evil toward his *b* ... Deut 28:54
as Aaron thy *b* died in mount Hor, ... Deut 32:50
of Kenaz, the *b* of Caleb, took it ... Josh 15:17
And Judah said unto Simeon his *b* ... Judg 1:3
son of Kenaz, Caleb's younger *b* ... Judg 1:13
And Judah went with Simeon his *b* ... Judg 1:17
son of Kenaz, Caleb's younger *b* ... Judg 3:9
for they said, He is our *b* ... Judg 9:3
of Shechem, because he is your *b* ... Judg 9:18
for fear of Abimelech his *b* ... Judg 9:21
be laid upon Abimelech their *b* ... Judg 9:24
the children of Benjamin my *b* ... Judg 20:23
the children of Benjamin my *b* ... Judg 20:28
them for Benjamin their *b* ... Judg 21:6
land, which was our *b* Elimelech's ... Ruth 4:3
the son of Ahitub, I-chabod's *b* ... 1Sa 14:3
Eliab his eldest *b* heard when he ... 1Sa 17:28
and my *b*, he hath commanded me to. 1Sa 20:29
*b* to Joab, saying, Who will go ... 1Sa 26:6
for thee, my *b* Jonathan ... 2Sa 1:26
I hold up my face to Joab thy *b* ... 2Sa 2:22
up every one from following his *b* ... 2Sa 2:27
for the blood of Asahel his *b* ... 2Sa 3:27
Joab and Abishai his *b* slew Abner ... 2Sa 3:30
because he had slain their *b* ... 2Sa 3:30
and Rechab and Baanah his *b* escaped ... 2Sa 4:6
answered Rechab and Baanah his *b* ... 2Sa 4:9
into the hand of Abishai his *b* ... 2Sa 10:10
the son of Shimeah David's *b* ... 2Sa 13:3
love Tamar, my *b* Absalom's sister ... 2Sa 13:4
Go now to thy *b* Amnon's house ... 2Sa 13:7
Tamar went to her *b* Amnon's house ... 2Sa 13:8
into the chamber to Amnon her *b* ... 2Sa 13:10
And she answered him, Nay, my *b* ... 2Sa 13:12
Absalom her *b* said unto her ... 2Sa 13:20
Hath Amnon thy *b* been with thee ... 2Sa 13:20
he is thy *b* ... 2Sa 13:20
desolate in her *b* Absalom's house ... 2Sa 13:20
Absalom spake unto his *b* Amnon ... 2Sa 13:22
let my *b* Amnon go with us ... 2Sa 13:26
the son of Shimeah David's *b* ... 2Sa 13:32
Deliver him that smote his *b* ... 2Sa 14:7
the life of his *b* whom he slew ... 2Sa 14:7
the son of Zeruiah, Joab's *b* ... 2Sa 18:2
Amasa, Art thou in health, my *b* ... 2Sa 20:9
Abishai his *b* pursued after Sheba ... 2Sa 20:10
slew the *b* of Goliath the Gittite ... 2Sa 21:19
Shimeah the *b* of David slew him ... 2Sa 21:21
the *b* of Joab, the son of Zeruiah ... 2Sa 23:18
Asahel the *b* of Joab was one of ... 2Sa 23:24
the mighty men, and Solomon his *b* ... 1Kin 1:10
I fled because of Absalom thy *b* ... 1Kin 2:7
given to Adonijah thy *b* to wife ... 1Kin 2:21
for he is mine elder *b* ... 1Kin 2:22
which thou hast given me, my *b* ... 1Kin 9:13
over him, saying, Alas, my *b* ... 1Kin 13:30
he is my *b* ... 1Kin 20:32
and they said, Thy *b* Ben-hadad ... 1Kin 20:33
his father's *b* king in his stead ... 2Kin 24:17
the sons of Jada the *b* of Shammai ... 1Chr 2:32
of Caleb the *b* of Jerahmeel were ... 1Chr 2:42
Chelub the *b* of Shuah begat Mehir ... 1Chr 4:11
his *b* Asaph, who stood on his ... 1Chr 6:39
and the name of his *b* was Sheresh ... 1Chr 7:16
And the sons of his *b* Helem ... 1Chr 7:35
And the sons of Eshek his *b* were ... 1Chr 8:39
And Abishai the *b* of Joab, he was ... 1Chr 11:20
armies were, Asahel the *b* of Joab ... 1Chr 11:26
Joel the *b* of Nathan, Mibhar the ... 1Chr 11:38
the son of Shimri, and Joha his *b* ... 1Chr 11:45
unto the hand of Abishai his *b* ... 1Chr 19:11
fled before Abishai his *b* ... 1Chr 19:15
the *b* of Goliath the Gittite ... 1Chr 20:5
son of Shimea David's *b* slew him ... 1Chr 20:7
The *b* of Michah was Isshiah ... 1Chr 24:25
Zetham, and Joel his *b*, which were .. 1Chr 26:22
month was Asahel the *b* of Joab ... 1Chr 27:7
Shimei his *b* was the next ... 2Chr 31:12
hand of Cononiah and Shimei his *b* .. 2Chr 31:13
Eliakim his *b* king over Judah ... 2Chr 36:4
And Necho took Jehoahaz his *b* ... 2Chr 36:4
Zedekiah his *b* king over Judah ... 2Chr 36:10
exact usury, every one of his *b* ... Neh 5:7
That I gave my *b* Hanani, and ... Neh 7:2
a pledge from thy *b* for nought ... Job 22:6
I am a *b* to dragons, and a ... Job 30:29
though he had been my friend or *b* ... Ps 35:14
can by any means redeem his *b* ... Ps 49:7
sittest and speakest against thy *b* ... Ps 50:20
a *b* is born for adversity ... Prov 17:17
*b* to him that is a great waster ... Prov 18:9
A *b* offended is harder to be won ... Prov 18:19
that sticketh closer than a *b* ... Prov 18:24
that is near than a *b* far off ... Prov 27:10
yea, he hath neither child nor *b* ... Eccl 4:8
O that thou wert as my *b*, that ... Song 8:1
his *b* of the house of his father ... Is 3:6
no man shall spare his *b* ... Is 9:19
fight every one against his *b* ... Is 19:2
and every one said to his *b* ... Is 41:6
and trust ye not in any *b* ... Jer 9:4
for every *b* will utterly supplant ... Jer 9:4
lament for him, saying, Ah my *b* ... Jer 22:18
neighbour, and every one to his *b* ... Jer 23:35
his neighbour, and every man his *b* ... Jer 31:34
of them, to wit, of a Jew his *b* ... Jer 34:9
ye go every man his *b* an Hebrew ... Jer 34:14
liberty, every one to his *b* ... Jer 34:17
spoiled his *b* by violence ... Eze 18:18
to another, every one to his *b* ... Eze 33:30
sword shall be against his *b* ... Eze 38:21
for son, or for daughter, for *b* ... Eze 44:25
He took his *b* by the heel in the ... Hos 12:3
did pursue his *b* with the sword ... Amos 1:11
*b* Jacob shame shall cover thee ... Obad 10
thy *b* in the day that he became a ... Obad 12
hunt every man his *b* with a net ... Mic 7:2
every one by the sword of his *b* ... Hag 2:22
and compassions every man to his *b* ... Zec 7:9
evil against his *b* in your heart ... Zec 7:10
Was not Esau Jacob's *b* ... Mal 1:2
every man against his *b*, by ... Mal 2:10
called Peter, and Andrew his *b* ... Mt 4:18
the son of Zebedee, and John his *b* ... Mt 4:21
his *b* without a cause shall be in ... Mt 5:22
and whosoever shall say to his *b* ... Mt 5:22
thy *b* hath ought against thee ... Mt 5:23
first be reconciled to thy *b* ... Mt 5:24
Or how wilt thou say to thy *b* ... Mt 7:4
is called Peter, and Andrew his *b* ... Mt 10:2
the son of Zebedee, and John his *b* ... Mt 10:2
*b* shall deliver up the *b* to death ... Mt 10:21
is in heaven, the same is my *b* ... Mt 12:50
sake, his *b* Philip's wife ... Mt 14:3
Peter, James, and John his *b* ... Mt 17:1
Moreover if thy *b* shall trespass ... Mt 18:15
hear thee, thou hast gained thy *b* ... Mt 18:15
how oft shall my *b* sin against me ... Mt 18:21
every one his *b* their trespasses ... Mt 18:35
his *b* shall marry his wife ... Mt 22:24
and raise up seed unto his *b* ... Mt 22:24
issue, left his wife unto his *b* ... Mt 22:25
Andrew his *b* casting a net into ... Mk 1:16
the son of Zebedee, and John his *b* ... Mk 1:19
Zebedee, and John the *b* of James ... Mk 3:17
the will of God, the same is my *b* ... Mk 3:35
and James, and John the *b* of James ... Mk 5:37
the *b* of James, and Joses, and of ... Mk 6:3
sake, his *b* Philip's wife ... Mk 6:17
wrote unto us, If a man's *b* die ... Mk 12:19
that his *b* should take his wife, ... Mk 12:19
and raise up seed unto his *b* ... Mk 12:19
*b* shall betray the *b* to death ... Mk 13:12
his *b* Philip tetrarch of Ituraea ... Lk 3:1
for Herodias his *b* Philip's wife ... Lk 3:19
named Peter,) and Andrew his *b* ... Lk 6:14
And Judas the *b* of James, and Judas ... Lk 6:16
canst thou say to thy *b*, *B* ... Lk 6:42
unto him, Master, speak to my *b* ... Lk 12:13
he said unto him, Thy *b* is come ... Lk 15:27
for this thy *b* was dead, and is ... Lk 15:32
If thy *b* trespass against thee, ... Lk 17:3
wrote unto us, If any man's *b* die ... Lk 20:28
that his *b* should take his wife, ... Lk 20:28
wife, and raise up seed unto his *b* ... Lk 20:28
him, was Andrew, Simon Peter's *b* ... Jn 1:40
He first findeth his own *b* Simon ... Jn 1:41
Andrew, Simon Peter's *b*, saith ... Jn 6:8
hair, whose *b* Lazarus was sick ... Jn 11:2
comfort them concerning their *b* ... Jn 11:19
been here, my *b* had not died ... Jn 11:21
unto her, Thy *b* shall rise again ... Jn 11:23
been here, my *b* had not died ... Jn 11:32
Zelotes, and Judas the *b* of James ... Acts 1:13
*B* Saul, the Lord, even Jesus, ... Acts 9:17
he killed James the *b* of John ... Acts 12:2
and said unto him, Thou seest, *b* ... Acts 21:20
*B* Saul, receive thy sight ... Acts 22:13
But why dost thou judge thy *b* ... Rom 14:10
why dost thou set at nought thy *b* ... Rom 14:10
But if thy *b* be grieved with thy ... Rom 14:15
any thing whereby thy *b* stumbleth .. Rom 14:21
city saluteth you, and Quartus a *b* ... Rom 16:23
will of God, and Sosthenes our *b* ... 1Cor 1:1
is called a *b* be a fornicator ... 1Cor 5:11
But *b* goeth to law with *b*, ... 1Cor 6:6
If any *b* hath a wife that ... 1Cor 7:12
A *b* or a sister is not under ... 1Cor 7:15
knowledge shall the weak *b* perish ... 1Cor 8:11
if meat make my *b* to offend ... 1Cor 8:13
lest I make my *b* to offend ... 1Cor 8:13
As touching our *b* Apollos ... 1Cor 16:12
the will of God, and Timothy our *b* ... 2Cor 1:1
because I found not Titus my *b* ... 2Cor 2:13
And we have sent with him the *b* ... 2Cor 8:18
And we have sent with them our *b* ... 2Cor 8:22
Titus, and with him I sent a *b* ... 2Cor 12:18
I none, save James the Lord's *b* ... Gal 1:19
how I do, Tychicus, a beloved *b* ... Eph 6:21
to send to you Epaphroditus, my *b* ... Phil 2:25
will of God, and Timotheus our *b* ... Col 1:1
unto you, who is a beloved *b* ... Col 4:7
Onesimus, a faithful and beloved *b* ... Col 4:9
And sent Timotheus, our *b*, and ... 1Th 3:2
defraud his *b* in any matter ... 1Th 4:6
every *b* that walketh disorderly ... 2Th 3:6
an enemy, but admonish him as a *b* ... 2Th 3:15
of Jesus Christ, and Timothy our *b* ... Philem 1
saints are refreshed by thee, *b* ... Philem 7
a *b* beloved, specially to me, but ... Philem 16
Yea, *b*, let me have joy of thee ... Philem 20
his neighbour, and every man his *b* ... Heb 8:11
Know ye that our *b* Timothy is set ... Heb 13:23
Let the *b* of low degree rejoice ... Jas 1:9
If a *b* or sister be naked, and ... Jas 2:15
He that speaketh evil of his *b* ... Jas 4:11
of his *b*, and judgeth his *b* ... Jas 4:11
Silvanus, a faithful *b* unto you ... 1Pet 5:12
even as our beloved *b* Paul also ... 2Pet 3:15
is in the light, and hateth his *b* ... 1Jn 2:9
He that loveth his *b* abideth in ... 1Jn 2:10
that hateth his *b* is in darkness ... 1Jn 2:11
neither he that loveth not his *b* ... 1Jn 3:10
of that wicked one, and slew his *b* ... 1Jn 3:12
loveth not his *b* abideth in death ... 1Jn 3:14
hateth his *b* is a murderer ... 1Jn 3:15
good, and seeth his *b* have need ... 1Jn 3:17
say, I love God, and hateth his *b* ... 1Jn 4:20
not his *b* whom he hath seen ... 1Jn 4:20
he who loveth God love his *b* also ... 1Jn 4:21
If any man see his *b* sin a sin ... 1Jn 5:16
*b* of James, to them that are ... Jude 1
I John, who also am your *b* ... Rev 1:9

**BROTHERHOOD**
I might break the *b* between Judah ... Zec 11:14
Love the *b* ... 1Pet 2:17

**BROTHERLY**
and remembered not the *b* covenant ... Amos 1:9
one to another with *b* love ... Rom 12:10
But as touching *b* love ye need ... 1Th 4:9
Let *b* love continue ... Heb 13:1
And to godliness *b* kindness ... 2Pet 1:7
and to *b* kindness charity ... 2Pet 1:7

**BROTHER'S**
Am I my *b* keeper ... Gen 4:9
the voice of thy *b* blood crieth ... Gen 4:10
receive thy *b* blood from thy hand ... Gen 4:11
And his *b* name was Jubal ... Gen 4:21
and his *b* name was Joktan ... Gen 10:25
Sarai his wife, and Lot his *b* son ... Gen 12:5
And they took Lot, Abram's *b* son ... Gen 14:12
master's *b* daughter unto his son ... Gen 24:48
until thy *b* fury turn away ... Gen 27:44
Until thy *b* anger turn away from ... Gen 27:45
unto Onan, Go in unto thy *b* wife ... Gen 38:8
when he went in unto his *b* wife ... Gen 38:9
the nakedness of thy *b* wife ... Lev 18:16
it is thy *b* nakedness ... Lev 18:16
And if a man shall take his *b* wife ... Lev 20:21
he hath uncovered his *b* nakedness ... Lev 20:21
Thou shalt not see thy *b* ox or ... Deut 22:1
and with all lost things of thy *b* ... Deut 22:3
Thou shalt not see thy *b* ass or ... Deut 22:4
man like not to take his *b* wife ... Deut 25:7
then let his *b* wife go up to the ... Deut 25:7
Then shall his *b* wife come unto ... Deut 25:9
will not build up his *b* house ... Deut 25:9
turned about, and is become my *b* ... 1Kin 2:15
and his *b* name was Joktan ... 1Chr 1:19
wine in their eldest *b* house ... Job 1:13
wine in their eldest *b* house ... Job 1:18
neither go into thy *b* house in ... Prov 27:10
the mote that is in thy *b* eye ... Mt 7:3
out the mote out of thy *b* eye ... Mt 7:5
for thee to have thy *b* wife ... Mk 6:18
the mote that is in thy *b* eye ... Lk 6:41
out the mote that is in thy *b* eye ... Lk 6:42
an occasion to fall in his *b* way ... Rom 14:13
were evil, and his *b* righteous ... 1Jn 3:12

**BROTHERS'**
unto their father's *b* sons ........ Num 36:11

**BROUGHT** See PREFACE.

**BROUGHTEST**
which thou *b* out of the land of ........ Ex 32:7
(for thou *b* up this people in thy ........ Num 14:13
the land whence thou *b* us out say ........ Deut 9:28
which thou *b* out by thy mighty ........ Deut 9:29
that leddest out and *b* in Israel ........ 2Sa 5:2
which thou *b* forth out of Egypt, ........ 1Kin 8:51
when thou *b* our fathers out of ........ 1Kin 8:53
that leddest out and *b* in Israel ........ 1Chr 11:2
*b* him forth out of Ur of the ........ Neh 9:7
*b* forth water for them out of the ........ Neh 9:15
*b* them into the land, concerning ........ Neh 9:23
Thou *b* us into the net ........ Ps 66:11
but thou *b* us out into a wealthy ........ Ps 66:12

**BROW**
is an iron sinew, and thy *b* brass ........ Is 48:4
led him unto the *b* of the hill ........ Lk 4:29

**BROWN**
all the *b* cattle among the sheep, ........ Gen 30:32
*b* among the sheep, that shall be ........ Gen 30:33
all the *b* among the sheep, and ........ Gen 30:35
all the *b* in the flock of Laban ........ Gen 30:40

**BRUISE**
it shall *b* thy head, and thou ........ Gen 3:15
head, and thou shalt *b* his heel ........ Gen 3:15
nor *b* it with his horsemen ........ Is 28:28
Yet it pleased the LORD to *b* him ........ Is 53:10
Thy *b* is incurable, and thy wound ........ Jer 30:12
shall it break in pieces and *b* ........ Dan 2:40
There is no healing of thy *b* ........ Nah 3:19
the God of peace shall *b* Satan ........ Rom 16:20

**BRUISED**
unto the LORD that which is *b* ........ Lev 22:24
upon the staff of this *b* reed ........ 2Kin 18:21
Bread corn is *b* ........ Is 28:28
A *b* reed shall he not break, and ........ Is 42:3
he was *b* for our iniquities ........ Is 53:5
there they *b* the teats of their ........ Eze 23:3
they *b* the breasts of her ........ Eze 23:8
A *b* reed shall he not break, and ........ Mt 12:20
to set at liberty them that are *b* ........ Lk 4:18

**BRUISES**
but wounds, and *b*, and putrifying ........ Is 1:6

**BRUISING**
in *b* thy teats by the Egyptians ........ Eze 23:21
*b* him hardly departeth from him ........ Lk 9:39

**BRUIT**
the noise of the *b* is come ........ Jer 10:22
all that hear the *b* of thee shall ........ Nah 3:19

**BRUTE**
But these, as natural *b* beasts ........ 2Pet 2:12
as *b* beasts, in those things they ........ Jude 10

**BRUTISH**
the *b* person perish, and leave ........ Ps 49:10
A *b* man knoweth not ........ Ps 92:6
Understand, ye *b* among the people ........ Ps 94:8
but he that hateth reproof is *b* ........ Prov 12:1
Surely I am more *b* than any man ........ Prov 30:2
of Pharaoh is become *b* ........ Is 19:11
But they are altogether *b* ........ Jer 10:8
Every man is *b* in his knowledge ........ Jer 10:14
For the pastors are become *b* ........ Jer 10:21
Every man is *b* by his knowledge ........ Jer 51:17
thee into the hand of *b* men ........ Eze 21:31

**BUCKET**
the nations are as a drop of a *b* ........ Is 40:15

**BUCKETS**
shall pour the water out of his *b* ........ Num 24:7

**BUCKLER**
he is a *b* to all them that trust ........ 2Sa 22:31
valiant men, men able to bear *b* ........ 1Chr 5:18
that could handle shield and *b* ........ 1Chr 12:8
my *b*, and the horn of my salvation ........ Ps 18:2
he is a *b* to all those that trust ........ Ps 18:30
Take hold of shield and *b*, and ........ Ps 35:2
truth shall be thy shield and *b* ........ Ps 91:4
he is a *b* to them that walk ........ Prov 2:7
Order ye the *b* and shield, and draw ........ Jer 46:3
which shall set against thee *b* ........ Eze 23:24
lift up the *b* against thee ........ Eze 26:8

**BUCKLERS**
captains of hundreds spears, and *b* ........ 2Chr 23:9
upon the thick bosses of his *b* ........ Job 15:26
whereon there hang a thousand *b* ........ Song 4:4
even a great company with *b* ........ Eze 38:4
both the shields and the *b* ........ Eze 39:9

**BUD**
the scent of water it will *b* ........ Job 14:9
to cause the *b* of the tender herb ........ Job 38:27
I make the horn of David to *b* ........ Ps 132:17
and the pomegranates *b* forth ........ Song 7:12
when the *b* is perfect, and the ........ Is 18:5
Israel shall blossom and *b* ........ Is 27:6
and maketh it bring forth and *b* ........ Is 55:10
as the earth bringeth forth her *b* ........ Is 61:11
to multiply as the *b* of the field ........ Eze 16:7
of the house of Israel to *b* forth ........ Eze 29:21
the *b* shall yield no meal ........ Hos 8:7

**BUDDED**
and it was as though it *b*, and her ........ Gen 40:10
Aaron for the house of Levi was *b* ........ Num 17:8
flourished, and the pomegranates *b* ........ Song 6:11
rod hath blossomed, pride hath *b* ........ Eze 7:10
had manna, and Aaron's rod that *b* ........ Heb 9:4

**BUDS**
was budded, and brought forth *b* ........ Num 17:8

**BUFFET**
to *b* him, and to say unto him, ........ Mk 14:65
the messenger of Satan to *b* me ........ 2Cor 12:7

**BUFFETED**
they spit in his face, and *b* him ........ Mt 26:67
and thirst, and are naked, and are *b* ... 1Cor 4:11
when ye be *b* for your faults, ye ........ 1Pet 2:20

**BUILD**
let us *b* us a city and a tower, ........ Gen 11:4
and they left off to *b* the city ........ Gen 11:8
thou shalt not *b* it of hewn stone ........ Ex 20:25
*B* me here seven altars, and ........ Num 23:1
*B* me here seven altars, and ........ Num 23:29
We will *b* sheepfolds here for our ........ Num 32:16
*B* you cities for your little ones ........ Num 32:24
thou shalt *b* bulwarks against the ........ Deut 20:20
will not *b* up his brother's house ........ Deut 25:9
there shalt thou *b* an altar unto ........ Deut 27:5
Thou shalt *b* the altar of the ........ Deut 27:6
thou shalt *b* an house, and thou ........ Deut 28:30
us now prepare to *b* us an altar ........ Josh 22:26
to *b* an altar for burnt offerings ........ Josh 22:29
*b* an altar unto the LORD thy God ........ Judg 6:26
which two did *b* the house of ........ Ruth 4:11
I will *b* him a sure house ........ 1Sa 2:35
Shalt thou *b* me an house for me ........ 2Sa 7:5
Why *b* ye not me an house of cedar ........ 2Sa 7:7
He shall *b* an house for my name, ........ 2Sa 7:13
saying, I will *b* thee an house ........ 2Sa 7:27
to *b* an altar unto the LORD, that ........ 2Sa 24:21
*B* thee an house in Jerusalem, and ........ 1Kin 2:36
*b* an house unto the name of the ........ 1Kin 5:3
I purpose to *b* an house unto the ........ 1Kin 5:5
he shall *b* an house unto my name ........ 1Kin 5:5
timber and stones to *b* the house ........ 1Kin 5:18
that he began to *b* the house of ........ 1Kin 6:1
tribes of Israel to *b* an house ........ 1Kin 8:16
to *b* an house for the name of the ........ 1Kin 8:17
heart to *b* an house unto my name ........ 1Kin 8:18
thou shalt not *b* the house ........ 1Kin 8:19
he shall *b* the house unto my name ........ 1Kin 8:19
for to *b* the house of the LORD, ........ 1Kin 9:15
Solomon desired to *b* in Jerusalem ........ 1Kin 9:19
then did he *b* Millo ........ 1Kin 9:24
Then did Solomon *b* an high place ........ 1Kin 11:7
*b* thee a sure house, as I built ........ 1Kin 11:38
did Hiel the Beth-elite *b* Jericho ........ 1Kin 16:34
and carpenters, to *b* him an house ........ 1Chr 14:1
Thou shalt not *b* me an house to ........ 1Chr 17:4
the LORD will *b* thee an house ........ 1Chr 17:10
He shall *b* me an house, and I will ........ 1Chr 17:12
that thou wilt *b* him an house ........ 1Chr 17:25
that I may *b* an altar therein ........ 1Chr 21:22
stones to *b* the house of God ........ 1Chr 22:2
charged him to *b* an house for the ........ 1Chr 22:6
it was in my mind to *b* an house ........ 1Chr 22:7
thou shalt not *b* an house unto my ........ 1Chr 22:8
He shall *b* an house for my name ........ 1Chr 22:10
*b* the house of the LORD thy God, ........ 1Chr 22:11
*b* ye the sanctuary of the LORD ........ 1Chr 22:19
I had in mine heart to *b* an house ........ 1Chr 28:2
Thou shalt not *b* an house for my ........ 1Chr 28:3
thy son, he shall *b* my house ........ 1Chr 28:6
to *b* an house for the sanctuary ........ 1Chr 28:10
to *b* thee an house for thine holy ........ 1Chr 29:16
to *b* the palace, for the which I ........ 1Chr 29:19
Solomon determined to *b* an house ........ 2Chr 2:1
didst send him cedars to *b* him an ........ 2Chr 2:3
I *b* an house to the name of the ........ 2Chr 2:4
And the house which I *b* is great ........ 2Chr 2:5
But who is able to *b* him an house ........ 2Chr 2:6
that I should *b* him an house ........ 2Chr 2:6
to *b* shall be wonderful great ........ 2Chr 2:9
that might *b* an house for the ........ 2Chr 2:12
Then Solomon began to *b* the house ........ 2Chr 3:1
he began to *b* in the second day ........ 2Chr 3:2
tribes of Israel to *b* an house in ........ 2Chr 6:5
to *b* an house for the name of the ........ 2Chr 6:7
heart to *b* an house for my name ........ 2Chr 6:8
thou shalt not *b* the house ........ 2Chr 6:9
he shall *b* the house for my name ........ 2Chr 6:9
Solomon desired to *b* in Jerusalem ........ 2Chr 8:6
Let us *b* these cities, and make ........ 2Chr 14:7
son of David king of Israel did *b* ........ 2Chr 35:3
he hath charged me to *b* him an ........ 2Chr 36:23
he hath charged me to *b* him an ........ Ezr 1:2
*b* the house of the LORD God of ........ Ezr 1:3
to go up to *b* the house of the ........ Ezr 1:5
said unto them, Let us *b* with you ........ Ezr 4:2
us to *b* an house unto our God ........ Ezr 4:3
*b* unto the LORD God of Israel ........ Ezr 4:3
began to *b* the house of God which ........ Ezr 5:2
commanded you to *b* this house ........ Ezr 5:3
Who commanded you to *b* this house ........ Ezr 5:9
*b* the house that was builded ........ Ezr 5:11
a decree to *b* this house of God ........ Ezr 5:13
was made of Cyrus the king to *b* ........ Ezr 5:17
the elders of the Jews *b* this ........ Ezr 6:7
sepulchres, that I may *b* it ........ Neh 2:5
let us *b* up the wall of Jerusalem ........ Neh 2:17
And they said, Let us rise up and *b* ........ Neh 2:18
we his servants will arise and *b* ........ Neh 2:20
gate did the sons of Hassenaah *b* ........ Neh 3:3
he *b* it, and set up the doors ........ Neh 3:14
he said, Even that which they *b* ........ Neh 4:3
we are not able to *b* the wall ........ Neh 4:10
destroy them, and not *b* them up ........ Ps 28:5
*b* thou the walls of Jerusalem ........ Ps 51:18
will *b* the cities of Judah ........ Ps 69:35
ever, and *b* up thy throne to all ........ Ps 89:4
When the LORD shall *b* up Zion ........ Ps 102:16
Except the LORD *b* the house ........ Ps 127:1
they labour in vain that *b* it ........ Ps 127:1
The LORD doth *b* up Jerusalem ........ Ps 147:2
and afterwards *b* thine house ........ Prov 24:27
to break down, and a time to *b* up ........ Eccl 3:3
we will *b* upon her a palace of ........ Song 8:9
but we will *b* with hewn stones ........ Is 9:10
he shall *b* my city, and he shall ........ Is 45:13
thee shall *b* the old waste places ........ Is 58:12
of strangers shall *b* up thy walls ........ Is 60:10
they shall *b* the old wastes, they ........ Is 61:4
And they shall *b* houses, and ........ Is 65:21
They shall not *b*, and another ........ Is 65:22
is the house that ye *b* unto me ........ Is 66:1
destroy, and to throw down, to *b* ........ Jer 1:10
and concerning a kingdom, to *b* ........ Jer 18:9
I will *b* me a wide house and large ........ Jer 22:14
and I will *b* them, and not pull ........ Jer 24:6
*B* ye houses, and dwell in them ........ Jer 29:5
*b* ye houses, and dwell in them ........ Jer 29:28
Again I will *b* thee, and thou ........ Jer 31:4
so will I watch over them, to *b* ........ Jer 31:28
Israel to return, and will *b* them ........ Jer 33:7
Neither shall ye *b* house, nor sow ........ Jer 35:7
Nor to *b* houses for us to dwell ........ Jer 35:9
in this land, then will I *b* you ........ Jer 42:10
*b* a fort against it, and cast a ........ Eze 4:2
let us *b* houses ........ Eze 11:3
to cast a mount, and to *b* a fort ........ Eze 21:22
and shall *b* houses, and plant ........ Eze 28:26
I the LORD *b* the ruined places ........ Eze 36:36
to *b* Jerusalem unto the Messiah ........ Dan 9:25
I will *b* it as in the days of old ........ Amos 9:11
they shall *b* the waste cities, and ........ Amos 9:14
They *b* up Zion with blood, and ........ Mic 3:10
they shall also *b* houses, but not ........ Zeph 1:13
and bring wood, and *b* the house ........ Hag 1:8
To *b* it an house in the land of ........ Zec 5:11
he shall *b* the temple of the LORD ........ Zec 6:12
Even he shall *b* the temple of the ........ Zec 6:13
*b* in the temple of the LORD, and ........ Zec 6:15
Tyrus did *b* herself a strong hold ........ Zec 9:3
return and *b* the desolate places ........ Mal 1:4
the LORD of hosts, They shall *b* ........ Mal 1:4
upon this rock I will *b* my church ........ Mt 16:18
because ye *b* the tombs of the ........ Mt 23:29
of God, and to *b* it in three days ........ Mt 26:61
within three days I will *b* ........ Mk 14:58
Woe unto you for ye *b* the ........ Lk 11:47
them, and ye *b* their sepulchres ........ Lk 11:48
pull down my barns, and *b* greater ........ Lk 12:18
of you, intending to *b* a tower ........ Lk 14:28
Saying, This man began to *b* ........ Lk 14:30
what house will ye *b* me ........ Acts 7:49
will *b* again the tabernacle of ........ Acts 15:16
I will *b* again the ruins thereof, ........ Acts 15:16
grace, which is able to *b* you up ........ Acts 20:32
lest I should *b* upon another ........ Rom 15:20
Now if any man *b* upon this ........ 1Cor 3:12
For if I *b* again the things which ........ Gal 2:18

**BUILDED**
he *b* a city, and called the name ........ Gen 4:17
Noah *b* an altar unto the LORD ........ Gen 8:20
*b* Nineveh, and the city Rehoboth, ........ Gen 10:11
which the children of men *b* ........ Gen 11:5
there *b* he an altar unto the LORD ........ Gen 12:7
there he *b* an altar unto the LORD ........ Gen 12:8
he *b* an altar there, and called ........ Gen 26:25
*b* an altar under the hill, and ........ Ex 24:4
unto the cities which they *b* ........ Num 32:38
in that ye have *b* you an altar ........ Josh 22:16
less this house that I have *b* ........ 1Kin 8:27
that this house, which I have *b* ........ 1Kin 8:43
thereof, wherewith Baasha had *b* ........ 1Kin 15:22
*b* for Ashtoreth the abomination ........ 2Kin 23:13
the house that is to be *b* for the ........ 1Chr 22:5
*b* the altar of the God of Israel, ........ Ezr 3:2
the children of the captivity *b* ........ Ezr 4:1
the king, that, if this city be *b* ........ Ezr 4:13
that, if this city be *b* again ........ Ezr 4:16
cease, and that this city be not *b* ........ Ezr 4:21
which is *b* with great stones, and ........ Ezr 5:8
that was *b* these many years ago ........ Ezr 5:11
which a great king of Israel *b* ........ Ezr 5:11
house of God be *b* in his place ........ Ezr 5:15
at Jerusalem, Let the house be *b* ........ Ezr 6:3
And the elders of the Jews *b* ........ Ezr 6:14
And they *b*, and finished it, ........ Ezr 6:14
priests, and they *b* the sheep gate ........ Neh 3:1
next unto him *b* the men of ........ Neh 3:2
next to them *b* Zaccur the son of ........ Neh 3:2
heard that we *b* the wall, he was ........ Neh 4:1
They which *b* on the wall, and they ........ Neh 4:17
sword girded by his side, and so *b* ........ Neh 4:18
heard that I had *b* the wall ........ Neh 6:1
therein, and the houses were not *b* ........ Neh 7:4
for the singers had *b* them ........ Neh 12:29
away an house which he *b* not ........ Job 20:19
Jerusalem is *b* as a city that is ........ Ps 122:3

Wisdom hath *b* her house, she hath Prov 9:1
Through wisdom is an house *b* Prov 24:3
I *b* me houses Eccl 2:4
tower of David *b* for an armoury Song 4:4
city shall be *b* upon her own heap Jer 30:18
He hath *b* against me, and Lam 3:5
and the wastes shall be *b* Eze 36:10
cities, and the wastes shall be *b* Eze 36:33
they sold, they planted, they *b* Lk 17:28
In whom ye also are *b* together Eph 2:22
inasmuch as he who hath *b* the Heb 3:3
For every house is *b* by some man Heb 3:4

**BUILDEDST**
goodly cities, which thou *b* not Deut 6:10

**BUILDER**
which hath foundations, whose *b* Heb 11:10

**BUILDERS**
Solomon's *b* and Hiram's *b* 1Kin 5:18
it out to the carpenters and *b* 2Kin 12:11
Unto carpenters, and *b*, and masons, 2Kin 22:6
*b* gave they it, to buy hewn stone 2Chr 34:11
when the *b* laid the foundation of Ezr 3:10
thee to anger before the *b* Neh 4:5
For the *b*, every one had his Neh 4:18
The stone which the *b* refused is Ps 118:22
thy *b* have perfected thy beauty Eze 27:4
The stone which the *b* rejected Mt 21:42
The stone which the *b* rejected is Mk 12:10
The stone which the *b* rejected Lk 20:17
which was set at nought of you *b* Acts 4:11
the stone which the *b* disallowed 1Pet 2:7

**BUILDEST**
When thou *b* a new house, then Deut 22:8
for which cause thou *b* the wall Neh 6:6
In that thou *b* thine eminent Eze 16:31
*b* it in three days, save thyself Mt 27:40
temple, and *b* it in three days, Mk 15:29

**BUILDETH**
riseth up and *b* this city Jericho Josh 6:26
He *b* his house as a moth, and as a Job 27:18
Every wise woman *b* her house Prov 14:1
Woe unto him that *b* his house by Jer 22:13
forgotten his Maker, and *b* temples Hos 8:14
It is he that *b* his stories in Amos 9:6
Woe to him that *b* a town with Hab 2:12
foundation, and another *b* thereon 1Cor 3:10
man take heed how he *b* thereupon 1Cor 3:10

**BUILDING**
in *b* you an altar beside the Josh 22:19
made an end of *b* his own house 1Kin 3:1
And the house, when it was in *b* 1Kin 6:7
in the house, while it was in *b* 1Kin 6:7
this house which thou art in *b* 1Kin 6:12
So was he seven years in *b* it 1Kin 6:38
But Solomon was *b* his own house 1Kin 7:1
the *b* of the house of the LORD 1Kin 9:1
that he left off *b* of Ramah 1Kin 15:21
God, and had made ready for the *b* 1Chr 28:2
for the *b* of the house of God 2Chr 3:3
it, that he left off *b* of Ramah 2Chr 16:5
thereof, wherewith Baasha was *b* 2Chr 16:6
of Judah, and troubled them in *b* Ezr 4:4
*b* the rebellious and the bad city, Ezr 4:12
names of the men that make this *b* Ezr 5:4
even until now hath it been in *b* Ezr 5:16
for the *b* of this house of God Ezr 6:8
much slothfulness the *b* decayeth Eccl 10:18
*b* forts, to cut off many persons Eze 17:17
he measured the breadth of the *b* Eze 40:5
Now the *b* that was before the Eze 41:12
the wall of the *b* was five cubits Eze 41:12
and the separate place, and the *b* Eze 41:13
he measured the length of the *b* Eze 41:15
was before the *b* toward the north Eze 42:1
and than the middlemost of the *b* Eze 42:5
therefore the *b* was straitened Eze 42:6
place, and over against the *b* Eze 42:10
there was a row of *b* round about Eze 46:23
and six years was this temple in *b* Jn 2:20
God's husbandry, ye are God's *b* 1Cor 3:9
dissolved, we have a *b* of God 2Cor 5:1
In whom all the *b* fitly framed Eph 2:21
that is to say, not of this *b* Heb 9:11
*b* up yourselves on your most holy Jude 20
the *b* of the wall of it was of Rev 21:18

**BUILDINGS**
to shew him the *b* of the temple Mt 24:1
of stones and what *b* are here Mk 13:1
him, Seest thou these great *b* Mk 13:2

**BUILT**
*b* there an altar unto the LORD Gen 13:18
Abraham *b* an altar there, and laid Gen 22:9
*b* him an house, and made booths Gen 33:17
he *b* there an altar, and called Gen 35:7
they *b* for Pharaoh treasure Ex 1:11
Moses *b* an altar, and called the Ex 17:15
saw it, he *b* an altar before it Ex 32:5
(Now Hebron was *b* seven years Num 13:22
let the city of Sihon be *b* Num 21:27
*b* seven altars, and offered a Num 23:14
And the children of Gad *b* Dibon Num 32:34
the children of Reuben *b* Heshbon Num 32:37
hast *b* goodly houses, and dwelt Deut 8:12
it shall not be *b* again Deut 13:16
is there that hath *b* a new house Deut 20:5
Then Joshua *b* an altar unto the Josh 8:30
he *b* the city, and dwelt therein Josh 19:50
*b* there an altar by Jordan Josh 22:10
*b* an altar over against the land Josh 22:11
That we have *b* us an altar to Josh 22:23
labour, and cities which ye *b* not Josh 24:13
*b* a city, and called the name Judg 1:26
Then Gideon *b* an altar there unto Judg 6:24
offered upon the altar that was *b* Judg 6:28
they *b* a city, and dwelt therein Judg 18:28
*b* there an altar, and offered Judg 21:4
there he *b* an altar unto the LORD 1Sa 7:17
Saul *b* an altar unto the LORD 1Sa 14:35
altar that he *b* unto the LORD 1Sa 14:35
David *b* round about from Millo and 2Sa 5:9
and they *b* David an house 2Sa 5:11
David *b* there an altar unto the 2Sa 24:25
house *b* unto the name of the LORD 1Kin 3:2
which king Solomon *b* for the LORD 1Kin 6:2
house he *b* chambers round about 1Kin 6:5
was *b* of stone made ready before 1Kin 6:7
So he *b* the house, and finished it 1Kin 6:9
then he *b* chambers against all 1Kin 6:10
So Solomon *b* the house, and 1Kin 6:14
he *b* the walls of the house 1Kin 6:15
he *b* twenty cubits on the sides 1Kin 6:16
he even *b* them for it within, 1Kin 6:16
he *b* the inner court with three 1Kin 6:36
He *b* also the house of the forest 1Kin 7:2
I have surely *b* thee an house to 1Kin 8:13
have *b* an house for the name of 1Kin 8:20
house that I have *b* for thy name 1Kin 8:44
house which I have *b* for thy name 1Kin 8:48
this house, which thou hast *b* 1Kin 9:3
when Solomon had *b* the two houses 1Kin 9:10
And Solomon *b* Gezer 1Kin 9:17
house which Solomon had *b* for her 1Kin 9:24
altar which he *b* unto the LORD 1Kin 9:25
and the house that he had *b* 1Kin 10:4
Solomon *b* Millo, and repaired the 1Kin 11:27
as I *b* for David, and will give 1Kin 11:38
Jeroboam *b* Shechem in 1Kin 12:25
went out from thence, and *b* Penuel 1Kin 12:25
For they also *b* them high places, 1Kin 14:23
*b* Ramah, that he might not suffer 1Kin 15:17
king Asa *b* with them Geba of 1Kin 15:22
he did, and the cities which he *b* 1Kin 15:23
*b* on the hill, and called the name 1Kin 16:24
the name of the city which he *b* 1Kin 16:24
Baal, which he had *b* in Samaria 1Kin 16:32
with the stones he *b* an altar in 1Kin 18:32
made, and all the cities that he *b* 1Kin 22:39
He *b* Elath, and restored it to 2Kin 14:22
He *b* the higher gate of the house 2Kin 15:35
Urijah the priest *b* an altar 2Kin 16:11
that they had *b* in the house 2Kin 16:18
they *b* them high places in all 2Kin 17:9
For he *b* up again the high places 2Kin 21:3
he *b* altars in the house of the 2Kin 21:4
he *b* altars for all the host of 2Kin 21:5
they *b* forts against it round 2Kin 25:1
that Solomon *b* in Jerusalem 1Chr 6:10
until Solomon had *b* the house of 1Chr 6:32
who *b* Beth-horon the nether, and 1Chr 7:24
and Shamed, who *b* Ono 1Chr 8:12
he *b* the city round about, even 1Chr 11:8
Why have ye not *b* me an house of 1Chr 17:6
David *b* there an altar unto the 1Chr 21:26
to be *b* to the name of the LORD 1Chr 22:19
But I have *b* an house of 2Chr 6:2
have *b* the house for the name of 2Chr 6:10
less this house which I have *b* 2Chr 6:18
I have *b* is called by thy name 2Chr 6:33
house which I have *b* for thy name 2Chr 6:34
house which I have *b* for thy name 2Chr 6:38
wherein Solomon had *b* the house 2Chr 8:1
to Solomon, Solomon *b* them 2Chr 8:2
he *b* Tadmor in the wilderness, and 2Chr 8:4
cities, which he *b* in Hamath 2Chr 8:4
Also he *b* Beth-horon the upper, 2Chr 8:5
the house that he had *b* for her 2Chr 8:11
which he had *b* before the porch, 2Chr 8:12
and the house that he had *b* 2Chr 9:3
*b* cities for defence in Judah 2Chr 11:5
He *b* even Beth-lehem 2Chr 11:6
he *b* fenced cities in Judah 2Chr 14:6
So they *b* and prospered 2Chr 14:7
*b* Ramah, to the intent that he 2Chr 16:1
he *b* therewith Geba and Mizpah 2Chr 16:6
he *b* in Judah castles, and cities 2Chr 17:12
have *b* thee a sanctuary therein 2Chr 20:8
He *b* Eloth, and restored it to 2Chr 26:2
*b* cities about Ashdod, and among 2Chr 26:6
Moreover Uzziah *b* towers in 2Chr 26:9
Also he *b* towers in the desert, 2Chr 26:10
He *b* the high gate of the house 2Chr 27:3
and on the wall of Ophel he *b* much 2Chr 27:3
Moreover he *b* cities in the 2Chr 27:4
and in the forests he *b* castles 2Chr 27:4
*b* up all the wall that was broken 2Chr 32:5
For he *b* again the high places 2Chr 33:3
Also he *b* altars in the house of 2Chr 33:4
he *b* altars for all the host of 2Chr 33:5
Now after this he *b* a wall 2Chr 33:14
all the altars that he had *b* in 2Chr 33:15
places wherein he *b* high places 2Chr 33:19
they *b* it, and set up the doors Neh 3:13
he *b* it, and covered it, and set up Neh 3:15
So *b* we the wall Neh 4:6
came to pass, when the wall was *b* Neh 7:1
which *b* desolate places for Job 3:14
down, and it cannot be *b* again Job 12:14
the Almighty, thou shalt be *b* up Job 22:23
he *b* his sanctuary like high Ps 78:69
Mercy shall be *b* up for ever Ps 89:2
*b* great bulwarks against it Eccl 9:14
*b* a tower in the midst of it, and Is 5:2
it shall never be *b* Is 25:2
cities of Judah, Ye shall be *b* Is 44:26
to Jerusalem, Thou shalt be *b* Is 44:28
they have *b* the high places of Jer 7:31
then shall they be *b* in the midst Jer 12:16
They have *b* also the high places Jer 19:5
build thee, and thou shalt be *b* Jer 31:4
that the city shall be *b* to the Jer 31:38
that they *b* it even unto this day Jer 32:31
they *b* the high places of Baal, Jer 32:35
which I have *b* will I break down Jer 45:4
*b* forts against it round about Jer 52:4
one *b* up a wall, and, lo, others Eze 13:10
That thou hast also *b* unto thee Eze 16:24
Thou hast *b* thy high place at Eze 16:25
thou shalt be *b* no more Eze 26:14
that I have *b* for the house of Dan 4:30
the street shall be *b* again Dan 9:25
ye have *b* houses of hewn stone, Amos 5:11
day that thy walls are to be *b* Mic 7:11
that the LORD's house should be *b* Hag 1:2
my house shall be *b* in it Zec 1:16
laid, that the temple might be *b* Zec 8:9
which *b* his house upon a rock Mt 7:24
which *b* his house upon the sand Mt 7:26
*b* a tower, and let it out to Mt 21:33
*b* a tower, and let it out to Mk 12:1
the hill whereon their city was *b* Lk 4:29
He is like a man which *b* an house Lk 6:48
*b* an house upon the earth Lk 6:49
and he hath *b* us a synagogue Lk 7:5
But Solomon *b* him an house Acts 7:47
abide which he hath *b* thereupon 1Cor 3:14
are *b* upon the foundation of the Eph 2:20
*b* up in him, and stablished in the Col 2:7
but he that *b* all things is God Heb 3:4
are *b* up a spiritual house, an 1Pet 2:5

**BUKKI** (*buk'-ki*)
1. *A high priest.*
And Abishua begat *B* 1Chr 6:5
and *B* begat Uzzi 1Chr 6:5
*B* his son, Uzzi his son, Zerahiah 1Chr 6:51
the son of Uzzi, the son of *B* Ezr 7:4
2. *A Danite prince.*
of Dan, *B* the son of Jogli Num 34:22

**BUKKIAH** (*buk-ki'-ah*) *A Levite musician.*
*B*, Mattaniah, Uzziel, Shebuel, and 1Chr 25:4
The sixth to *B*, he, his sons, and 1Chr 25:13

**BUL** (*bul*) *Eighth month of the Hebrew year.*
the eleventh year, in the month *B* 1Kin 6:38

**BULL**
Their *b* gendereth, and faileth not Job 21:10
the streets, as a wild *b* in a net Is 51:20

**BULLOCK**
Take one young *b*, and two rams Ex 29:1
them in the basket, with the *b* Ex 29:3
thou shalt cause a *b* to be Ex 29:10
hands upon the head of the *b* Ex 29:10
shalt kill the *b* before the LORD Ex 29:11
shalt take of the blood of the *b* Ex 29:12
But the flesh of the *b*, and his Ex 29:14
day a *b* for a sin offering for Ex 29:36
shall kill the *b* before the LORD Lev 1:5
a young *b* without blemish unto Lev 4:3
he shall bring the *b* unto the Lev 4:4
kill the *b* before the LORD Lev 4:4
*b* at the bottom of the altar of Lev 4:7
fat of the *b* for the sin offering Lev 4:8
the *b* of the sacrifice of peace Lev 4:10
And the skin of the *b*, and all his Lev 4:11
Even the whole *b* shall he carry Lev 4:12
shall offer a young *b* for the sin Lev 4:14
the head of the *b* before the LORD Lev 4:15
the *b* shall be killed before the Lev 4:15
he shall do with the *b* as he did Lev 4:20
did with the *b* for a sin offering Lev 4:20
forth the *b* without the camp Lev 4:21
burn him as he burned the first *b* Lev 4:21
a *b* for the sin offering, and two Lev 8:2
he brought the *b* for the sin Lev 8:14
of the *b* of the sin offering Lev 8:14
But the *b*, and his hide, his flesh Lev 8:17
Also a *b* and a ram for peace Lev 9:4
He slew also the *b* and the ram for Lev 9:18
And the fat of the *b* and of the ram Lev 9:19
with a young *b* for a sin offering Lev 16:3
offer his *b* of the sin offering Lev 16:6
bring the *b* of the sin offering Lev 16:11
shall kill the *b* of the sin Lev 16:11
shall take of the blood of the *b* Lev 16:14
as he did with the blood of the *b* Lev 16:15
shall take of the blood of the *b* Lev 16:18
the *b* for the sin offering, and Lev 16:27
Either a *b* or a lamb that hath Lev 22:23
When a *b*, or a sheep, or a goat, Lev 22:27
of the first year, and one young *b* Lev 23:18
One young *b*, one ram, one lamb of Num 7:15
One young *b*, one ram, one lamb of Num 7:21
One young *b*, one ram, one lamb of Num 7:27
One young *b*, one ram, one lamb of Num 7:33
One young *b*, one ram, one lamb of Num 7:39
One young *b*, one ram, one lamb of Num 7:45

One young *b*, one ram, one lamb of.... Num 7:51
One young *b*, one ram, one lamb of.... Num 7:57
One young *b*, one ram, one lamb of.... Num 7:63
One young *b*, one ram, one lamb of.... Num 7:69
One young *b*, one ram, one lamb of.... Num 7:75
One young *b*, one ram, one lamb of.... Num 7:81
a young *b* with his meat offering.......... Num 8:8
another young *b* shalt thou take .......... Num 8:8
a *b* for a burnt offering, or for.............. Num 15:8
Then shall he bring with a *b* a.............. Num 15:9
Thus shall it be done for one *b*........... Num 15:11
one young *b* for a burnt offering ....... Num 15:24
Balaam offered on every altar a *b*........ Num 23:2
have offered upon every altar a *b*....... Num 23:4
seven altars, and offered a *b* .............. Num 23:14
Balaam had said, and offered a *b* ....... Num 23:30
mingled with oil, for one *b*.................. Num 28:12
be half an hin of wine unto a *b*.......... Num 28:14
deals shall ye offer for a *b* .................. Num 28:20
oil, three tenth deals unto one *b*......... Num 28:28
one young *b*, one ram, and seven........ Num 29:2
oil, three tenth deals for a *b*................ Num 29:3
one young *b*, one ram, and seven........ Num 29:8
oil, three tenth deals to a *b* ................. Num 29:9
every *b* of the thirteen bullocks.......... Num 29:14
one *b*, one ram, seven lambs of........... Num 29:36
their drink offerings for the *b*............... Num 29:37
work with the firstling of thy *b*............. Deut 15:19
unto the LORD thy God any *b*................ Deut 17:1
is like the firstling of his *b*................... Deut 33:17
him, Take thy father's young *b*............. Judg 6:25
even the second *b* of seven years......... Judg 6:25
place, and take the second *b*................ Judg 6:26
the second *b* was offered upon the...... Judg 6:28
And they slew a *b*, and brought the...... 1Sa 1:25
them choose one *b* for themselves..... 1Kin 18:23
and I will dress the other *b*................. 1Kin 18:23
Choose you one *b* for yourselves ....... 1Kin 18:25
they took the *b* which was given....... 1Kin 18:26
cut the *b* in pieces, and laid him......... 1Kin 18:33
consecrate himself with a young *b*...... 2Chr 13:9
I will take no *b* out of thy house.............. Ps 50:9
than an ox or *b* that hath horns............ Ps 69:31
lion shall eat straw like the *b*................. Is 65:25
as a *b* unaccustomed to the yoke.......... Jer 31:18
a young *b* for a sin offering.................. Eze 43:19
Thou shalt take the *b* also of the......... Eze 43:21
as they did cleanse it with the *b*........... Eze 43:22
offer a young *b* without blemish........... Eze 43:23
they shall also prepare a young *b*......... Eze 43:25
take a young *b* without blemish........... Eze 45:18
the land a *b* for a sin offering.............. Eze 45:22
meat offering of an ephah for a *b*......... Eze 45:24
be a young *b* without blemish................. Eze 46:6
a meat offering, an ephah for a *b*........... Eze 46:7
offering shall be an ephah to a *b*........... Eze 46:11

**BULLOCK'S**
lay his hand upon the *b* head..................... Lev 4:4
shall take of the *b* blood............................ Lev 4:5
*b* blood to the tabernacle of the............ Lev 4:16

**BULLOCKS**
the burnt offering were twelve *b* .......... Num 7:87
offerings were twenty and four *b*............ Num 7:88
hands upon the heads of the *b* ............... Num 8:12
and prepare me here seven *b*............... Num 23:29
two young *b*, and one ram, seven...... Num 28:11
two young *b*, and one ram ................... Num 28:19
two young *b*, one ram, seven lambs.. Num 28:27
thirteen young *b*, two rams, and........... Num 29:13
every bullock of the thirteen *b*............ Num 29:14
day ye shall offer twelve young *b*.......... Num 29:17
their drink offerings for the *b*............. Num 29:18
And on the third day eleven *b*............. Num 29:20
their drink offerings for the *b*............. Num 29:21
And on the fourth day ten *b*.............. Num 29:23
their drink offerings for the *b*............ Num 29:24
And on the fifth day nine *b*............... Num 29:26
their drink offerings for the *b*............. Num 29:27
And on the sixth day eight *b*............... Num 29:29
their drink offerings for the *b*............. Num 29:30
And on the seventh day seven *b*............. Num 29:32
their drink offerings for the *b*............. Num 29:33
him up with her, with three *b*................ 1Sa 1:24
Let them therefore give us two *b*....... 1Kin 18:23
LORD, that they offered seven *b*.......... 1Chr 15:26
after that day, even a thousand *b*...... 1Chr 29:21
they brought seven *b*......................... 2Chr 29:21
So they killed the *b*, and the.............. 2Chr 29:22
brought, was threescore and ten *b*.... 2Chr 29:32
to the congregation a thousand *b*..... 2Chr 30:24
to the congregation a thousand *b*...... 2Chr 30:24
thousand, and three thousand *b*........... 2Chr 35:7
they have need of, both young *b*............ Ezr 6:9
of this house of God an hundred *b*......... Ezr 6:17
buy speedily with this money *b*.............. Ezr 7:17
twelve *b* for all Israel, ninety................. Ezr 8:35
take unto you now seven *b*................... Job 42:8
they offer *b* upon thine altar................. Ps 51:19
I will offer *b* with goats........................ Ps 66:15
I delight not in the blood of *b*.................. Is 1:11
them, and the *b* with the bulls.................. Is 34:7
in the midst of her like fatted *b*............ Jer 46:21
Slay all her *b* ........................................ Jer 50:27
rams, of lambs, and of goats, of *b*........ Eze 39:18
offering to the LORD, seven *b*................. Eze 45:23
they sacrifice *b* in Gilgal ....................... Hos 12:11

**BULLS**
their colts, forty kine, and ten *b*.......... Gen 32:15
Many *b* have compassed me.................... Ps 22:12
strong *b* of Bashan have beset me........... Ps 22:12
Will I eat the flesh of *b*.......................... Ps 50:13
spearmen, the multitude of the *b*........... Ps 68:30
them, and the bullocks with the *b*............. Is 34:7
heifer at grass, and bellow as *b*.......... Jer 50:11
twelve brasen *b* that were under.......... Jer 52:20
For if the blood of *b* and of goats......... Heb 9:13
not possible that the blood of *b*............. Heb 10:4

**BULRUSH**
is it to bow down his head as a *b*............. Is 58:5

**BULRUSHES**
him, she took for him an ark of *b*.............. Ex 2:3
in vessels of *b* upon the waters.................. Is 18:2

**BULWARKS**
thou shalt build *b* against the............ Deut 20:20
to be on the towers and upon the *b*.. 2Chr 26:15
Mark ye well her *b*, consider her........... Ps 48:13
it, and built great *b* against it ............... Eccl 9:14
will God appoint for walls and *b*............... Is 26:1

**BUNAH** *(boo'-nah) Son of Jerahmeel.*
were, Ram the firstborn, and *B*............. 1Chr 2:25

**BUNCH**
And ye shall take a *b* of hyssop ............. Ex 12:22

**BUNCHES**
bread, and an hundred *b* of raisins......... 2Sa 16:1
*b* of raisins, and wine, and oil, and.... 1Chr 12:40
treasures upon the *b* of camels.................. Is 30:6

**BUNDLE**
every man's *b* of money was in his..... Gen 42:35
*b* of life with the LORD thy God............ 1Sa 25:29
A *b* of myrrh is my wellbeloved........... Song 1:13
Paul had gathered a *b* of sticks............ Acts 28:3

**BUNDLES**
their father saw the *b* of money.......... Gen 42:35
and bind them in *b* to burn them .......... Mt 13:30

**BUNNI** *(bun'-ni)*
*1. A Levite with Ezra.*
and Bani, Kadmiel, Shebaniah, *B*............ Neh 9:4
*2. Father of Hashabiah.*
son of Hashabiah, the son of *B*........... Neh 11:15
*3. A family who renewed the covenant.*
*B*, Azgad, Bebai,........................................ Neh 10:15

**BURDEN**
they shall bear the *b* with thee.............. Ex 18:22
hateth thee lying under his *b*.................... Ex 23:5
These things are the *b* of the.............. Num 4:15
one to his service and to his *b*............. Num 4:19
And this is the charge of their *b* ........... Num 4:31
of the charge of their *b*........................ Num 4:32
the service of the *b* in the..................... Num 4:47
service, and according to his *b* ............ Num 4:49
that thou layest the *b* of all................... Num 11:11
they shall bear the *b* of the................. Num 11:17
bear your cumbrance, and your *b*........ Deut 1:12
then thou shalt be a *b* unto me ............ 2Sa 15:33
be yet a *b* unto my lord the king .......... 2Sa 19:35
thy servant two mules' *b* of earth........ 2Kin 5:17
of Damascus, forty camels' *b* ................ 2Kin 8:9
the LORD laid this *b* upon him.............. 2Kin 9:25
it shall not be a *b* upon your.................. 2Chr 35:3
that there should no *b* be brought...... Neh 13:19
thee, so that I am a *b* to myself............. Job 7:20
as an heavy *b* they are too heavy............ Ps 38:4
Cast thy *b* upon the LORD, and he ......... Ps 55:22
I removed his shoulder from the *b*........... Ps 81:6
and the grasshopper shall be a *b*.......... Eccl 12:5
hast broken the yoke of his *b*...................... Is 9:4
that his *b* shall be taken away ................ Is 10:27
The *b* of Babylon, which Isaiah ................ Is 13:1
his *b* depart from off their....................... Is 14:25
that king Ahaz died was this *b* ............... Is 14:28
The *b* of Moab......................................... Is 15:1
The *b* of Damascus ................................... Is 17:1
The *b* of Egypt ........................................ Is 19:1
The *b* of the desert of the sea ................ Is 21:1
The *b* of Dumah....................................... Is 21:11
The *b* upon Arabia .................................. Is 21:13
The *b* of the valley of vision .................... Is 22:1
the *b* that was upon it shall be ............... Is 22:25
The *b* of Tyre.............................................. Is 23:1
The *b* of the beasts of the south.............. Is 30:6
anger, and the *b* thereof is heavy............ Is 30:27
they are a *b* to the weary beast .............. Is 46:1
they could not deliver the *b*...................... Is 46:2
bear no *b* on the sabbath day, nor......... Jer 17:21
Neither carry forth a *b* out of .............. Jer 17:22
to bring in no *b* through the................. Jer 17:24
sabbath day, and not to bear a *b*.......... Jer 17:27
saying, What is the *b* of the LORD......... Jer 23:33
shalt then say unto them, What *b* ........ Jer 23:33
The *b* of the LORD, I will even ............... Jer 23:34
the *b* of the LORD shall ye.................... Jer 23:36
every man's word shall be his *b*............ Jer 23:36
since ye say, The *b* of the LORD............. Jer 23:38
The *b* of the LORD, and I have sent ...... Jer 23:38
shall not say, The *b* of the LORD........... Jer 23:38
This *b* concerneth the prince in............. Eze 12:10
for the *b* of the king of princes ............. Hos 8:10
The *b* of Nineveh..................................... Nah 1:1
The *b* which Habakkuk the prophet........ Hab 1:1
whom the reproach of it was a *b*.......... Zeph 3:18
The *b* of the word of the LORD in .......... Zec 9:1
The *b* of the word of the LORD for......... Zec 12:1
all that *b* themselves with it.................. Zec 12:3
The *b* of the word of the LORD to........... Mal 1:1
my yoke is easy, and my *b* is light ......... Mt 11:30
unto us, which have borne the *b* ............ Mt 20:12
to lay upon you no greater *b* than ..... Acts 15:28
the ship was to unlade her *b*................ Acts 21:3
But be it so, I did not *b* you.............. 2Cor 12:16
every man shall bear his own *b* ................ Gal 6:5
I will put upon you none other *b*........... Rev 2:24

**BURDENED**
this tabernacle do groan, being *b*........... 2Cor 5:4
that other men be eased, and ye *b*....... 2Cor 8:13

**BURDENS**
ass couching down between two *b*..... Gen 49:14
to afflict them with their *b* ....................... Ex 1:11
brethren, and looked on their *b*............... Ex 2:11
get you unto your *b* .................................... Ex 5:4
and ye make them rest from their *b* ......... Ex 5:5
from under the *b* of the Egyptians ............ Ex 6:6
from under the *b* of the Egyptians ............ Ex 6:7
Gershonites, to serve, and for *b* ........... Num 4:24
the Gershonites, in all their *b* ............. Num 4:27
unto them in charge all their *b* ............ Num 4:27
and ten thousand that bare *b*............... 1Kin 5:15
and ten thousand men to bear *b*............ 2Chr 2:2
of them to be bearers of *b* .................... 2Chr 2:18
greatness of the *b* laid upon him.......... 2Chr 24:27
they were over the bearers of *b* ........ 2Chr 34:13
of the bearers of *b* is decayed................ Neh 4:10
on the wall, and they that bare *b*.......... Neh 4:17
and figs, and all manner of *b*............... Neh 13:15
wickedness, to undo the heavy *b* ............ Is 58:6
but have seen for thee false *b*................. Lam 2:14
and ye take from him *b* of wheat....... Amos 5:11
For they bind heavy *b* and grievous ....... Mt 23:4
men with *b* grievous to be borne.......... Lk 11:46
the *b* with one of your fingers............... Lk 11:46
Bear ye one another's *b*, and so................ Gal 6:2

**BURDENSOME**
a *b* stone for all people .......................... Zec 12:3
kept myself from being *b* unto you..... 2Cor 11:9
be that I myself was not *b* to you..... 2Cor 12:13
and I will not be *b* to you ................... 2Cor 12:14
others, when we might have been *b* ....... 1Th 2:6

**BURIAL**
the *b* which belonged to the kings .... 2Chr 26:23
good, and also that he have no *b*.............. Eccl 6:3
not be joined with them in *b*.................... Is 14:20
be buried with the *b* of an ass................. Jer 22:19
on my body, she did it for my *b*.............. Mt 26:12
men carried Stephen to his *b*.................. Acts 8:2

**BURIED**
thou shalt be *b* in a good old age ........ Gen 15:15
Abraham *b* Sarah his wife in the......... Gen 23:19
Ishmael *b* him in the cave of.................. Gen 25:9
there was Abraham *b*, and Sarah his.. Gen 25:10
she was *b* beneath Beth-el under........... Gen 35:8
was *b* in the way to Ephrath,............... Gen 35:19
and his sons Esau and Jacob *b* him .... Gen 35:29
I *b* her there in the way of..................... Gen 48:7
There they *b* Abraham and Sarah his Gen 49:31
there they *b* Isaac and Rebekah his ... Gen 49:31
and there I *b* Leah ............................... Gen 49:31
*b* him in the cave of the field of .......... Gen 50:13
father, after he had *b* his father.......... Gen 50:14
because there they *b* the people......... Num 11:34
Miriam died there, and was *b* there...... Num 20:1
For the Egyptians *b* all their .............. Num 33:4
Aaron died, and there he was *b*.............. Deut 10:6
he *b* him in a valley in the land ........... Deut 34:6
they *b* him in the border of his ........... Josh 24:30
*b* they in Shechem, in a parcel of....... Josh 24:32
they *b* him in a hill that....................... Josh 24:33
they *b* him in the border of his.............. Judg 2:9
was *b* in the sepulchre of Joash............ Judg 8:32
and died, and was *b* in Shamir............. Judg 10:2
And Jair died, and was *b* in Camon..... Judg 10:5
was *b* in one of the cities of.................. Judg 12:7
Ibzan, and was *b* at Beth-lehem ......... Judg 12:10
was *b* in Aijalon in the country.......... Judg 12:12
was *b* in Pirathon in the land of.......... Judg 12:15
*b* him between Zorah and Eshtaol in Judg 16:31
will I die, and there will I be *b*.............. Ruth 1:17
*b* him in his house at Ramah................ 1Sa 25:1
*b* him in Ramah, even in his own........... 1Sa 28:3
*b* them under a tree at Jabesh, and..... 1Sa 31:13
were they that *b* Saul ................................ 2Sa 2:4
even unto Saul, and have *b* him ............. 2Sa 2:5
*b* him in the sepulchre of his................ 2Sa 2:32
And they *b* Abner in Hebron ................. 2Sa 3:32
*b* it in the sepulchre of Abner in ............ 2Sa 4:12
was *b* in the sepulchre of his............... 2Sa 17:23
be *b* by the grave of my father and ...... 2Sa 19:37
Jonathan his son *b* they in the.............. 2Sa 21:14
was *b* in the city of David.................... 1Kin 2:10
he was *b* in his own house in the.......... 1Kin 2:34
was *b* in the city of David his............ 1Kin 11:43
came to pass, after he had *b* him ....... 1Kin 13:31
wherein the man of God is *b*............... 1Kin 13:31
And they *b* him...................................... 1Kin 14:18
was *b* with his fathers in the.............. 1Kin 14:31
they *b* him in the city of David ........... 1Kin 15:8
was *b* with his fathers in the.............. 1Kin 15:24
his fathers, and was *b* in Tirzah .......... 1Kin 16:6
his fathers, and was *b* in Samaria ........ 1Kin 16:28
they *b* the king in Samaria ................... 1Kin 22:37
was *b* with his fathers in the............... 1Kin 22:50
was *b* with his fathers in the................. 2Kin 8:24
*b* him in his sepulchre with his.............. 2Kin 9:28
and they *b* him in Samaria.................... 2Kin 10:35

they *b* him with his fathers in 2Kin 12:21
and they *b* him in Samaria 2Kin 13:9
Joash was *b* in Samaria with the 2Kin 13:13
And Elisha died, and they *b* him 2Kin 13:20
was *b* in Samaria with the kings 2Kin 14:16
he was *b* at Jerusalem with his 2Kin 14:20
they *b* him with his fathers in 2Kin 15:7
was *b* with his fathers in the 2Kin 15:38
was *b* with his fathers in the 2Kin 16:20
was *b* in the garden of his own 2Kin 21:18
he was *b* in his sepulchre in the 2Kin 21:26
*b* him in his own sepulchre 2Kin 23:30
*b* their bones under the oak in 1Chr 10:12
he was *b* in the city of David his 2Chr 9:31
was *b* in the city of David 2Chr 12:16
they *b* him in the city of David 2Chr 14:1
they *b* him in his own sepulchres, 2Chr 16:14
was *b* with his fathers in the 2Chr 21:1
Howbeit they *b* him in the city of 2Chr 21:20
they had slain him, they *b* him 2Chr 22:9
they *b* him in the city of David 2Chr 24:16
they *b* him in the city of David, 2Chr 24:25
but they *b* him not in the 2Chr 24:25
*b* him with his fathers in the 2Chr 25:28
they *b* him with his fathers in 2Chr 26:23
they *b* him in the city of David 2Chr 27:9
they *b* him in the city, even in 2Chr 28:27
they *b* him in the chiefest of the 2Chr 32:33
they *b* him in his own house 2Chr 33:20
was *b* in one of the sepulchres of 2Chr 35:24
remain of him shall be *b* in death Job 27:15
And so I saw the wicked *b*, who had Eccl 8:10
shall not be gathered, nor be *b* Jer 8:2
neither shall they be *b* Jer 16:4
they shall not be *b*, neither Jer 16:6
shalt die, and shalt be *b* there Jer 20:6
He shall be *b* with the burial of Jer 22:19
lamented, neither gathered, nor *b* Jer 25:33
till the buriers have *b* it in the Eze 39:15
*b* it, and went and told Jesus Mt 14:12
the rich man also died, and was *b* Lk 16:22
David, that he is both dead and *b* Acts 2:29
up, and carried him out, and *b* him Acts 5:6
*b* thy husband are at the door Acts 5:9
her forth, *b* her by her husband Acts 5:10
Therefore we are *b* with him by Rom 6:4
And that he was *b*, and that he rose 1Cor 15:4
*B* with him in baptism, wherein Col 2:12

### BURIERS

till the *b* have buried it in the Eze 39:15

### BURN

make brick, and *b* them throughly Gen 11:3
thine anger *b* against thy servant Gen 44:18
the morning ye shall *b* with fire Ex 12:10
to cause the lamp to *b* always Ex 27:20
them, and *b* them upon the altar Ex 29:13
shalt thou *b* with fire without Ex 29:14
thou shalt *b* the whole ram upon Ex 29:18
*b* them upon the altar for a burnt Ex 29:25
then thou shalt *b* the remainder Ex 29:34
make an altar to *b* incense upon Ex 30:1
Aaron shall *b* thereon sweet Ex 30:7
he shall *b* incense upon it Ex 30:7
he shall *b* incense upon it, a Ex 30:8
to *b* offering made by fire unto Ex 30:20
priest shall *b* all on the altar Lev 1:9
it all, and *b* it upon the altar Lev 1:13
his head, and *b* it on the altar Lev 1:15
the priest shall *b* it upon the Lev 1:17
the priest shall *b* the memorial Lev 2:2
shall *b* it upon the altar Lev 2:9
for ye shall *b* no leaven, nor any Lev 2:11
the priest shall *b* the memorial Lev 2:16
Aaron's sons shall *b* it on the Lev 3:5
the priest shall *b* it upon the Lev 3:11
the priest shall *b* them upon the Lev 3:16
the priest shall *b* them upon the Lev 4:10
*b* him on the wood with fire Lev 4:12
from him, and *b* it upon the altar Lev 4:19
*b* him as he burned the first Lev 4:21
he shall *b* all his fat upon the Lev 4:26
the priest shall *b* it upon the Lev 4:31
the priest shall *b* them upon the Lev 4:35
*b* it on the altar, according to Lev 5:12
the priest shall *b* wood on it Lev 6:12
he shall *b* thereon the fat of the Lev 6:12
shall *b* it upon the altar for a Lev 6:15
the priest shall *b* them upon the Lev 7:5
the priest shall *b* the fat upon Lev 7:31
of the bread shall ye *b* with fire Lev 8:32
He shall therefore *b* that garment Lev 13:52
thou shalt *b* it in the fire Lev 13:55
thou shalt *b* that wherein the Lev 13:57
shall he *b* upon the altar Lev 16:25
they shall *b* in the fire their Lev 16:27
*b* the fat for a sweet savour unto Lev 17:6
cause the lamps to *b* continually Lev 24:2
*b* it upon the altar, and afterward Num 5:26
shalt *b* their fat for an offering Num 18:17
one shall *b* the heifer in his Num 19:5
blood, with her dung, shall he *b* Num 19:5
(for the mountain did *b* with fire Deut 5:23
*b* their graven images with fire Deut 7:5
their gods shall ye *b* with fire Deut 7:25
and *b* their groves with fire Deut 12:3
shalt *b* with fire the city, and Deut 13:16
shall *b* unto the lowest hell, and Deut 32:22
*b* their chariots with fire Josh 11:6
that did Joshua *b* Josh 11:13
of the tower to *b* it with fire Judg 9:52
we will *b* thine house upon thee Judg 12:1
us the riddle, lest we *b* thee Judg 14:15
not fail to *b* the fat presently 1Sa 2:16
to *b* incense, to wear an ephod 1Sa 2:28
stood by the altar to *b* incense 1Kin 13:1
places that *b* incense upon thee 1Kin 13:2
Upon the great altar *b* the 2Kin 16:15
of Israel did *b* incense to it 2Kin 18:4
*b* incense in the high places in 2Kin 23:5
to *b* incense before the LORD, to 1Chr 23:13
to *b* before him sweet incense, and 2Chr 2:4
save only to *b* sacrifice before 2Chr 2:6
that they should *b* after the 2Chr 4:20
they *b* unto the LORD every 2Chr 13:11
lamps thereof, to *b* every evening 2Chr 13:11
to *b* incense upon the altar of 2Chr 26:16
to *b* incense unto the LORD, but 2Chr 26:18
that are consecrated to *b* incense 2Chr 26:18
a censer in his hand to *b* incense 2Chr 26:19
to *b* incense unto other gods 2Chr 28:25
minister unto him, and *b* incense 2Chr 29:11
one altar, and *b* incense upon it 2Chr 32:12
to *b* upon the altar of the LORD Neh 10:34
shall thy jealousy *b* like fire Ps 79:5
shall thy wrath *b* like fire Ps 89:46
and they shall both *b* together Is 1:31
and it shall *b* and devour his Is 10:17
them, I would *b* them together Is 27:4
And Lebanon is not sufficient to *b* Is 40:16
Then shall it be for a man to *b* Is 44:15
the fire shall *b* them Is 47:14
*b* that none can quench it because Jer 4:4
*b* incense unto Baal, and walk Jer 7:9
and it shall *b*, and shall not be Jer 7:20
Hinnom, to *b* their sons and their Jer 7:31
even altars to *b* incense unto Jer 11:13
anger, which shall *b* upon you Jer 15:14
anger, which shall *b* for ever Jer 17:4
to *b* their sons with fire for Jer 19:5
and he shall *b* it with fire Jer 21:10
*b* that none can quench it, Jer 21:12
*b* it with the houses, upon whose Jer 32:29
and he shall *b* it with fire Jer 34:2
so shall they *b* odours for thee Jer 34:5
and and take it, and *b* it with fire Jer 34:22
king that he would not *b* the roll Jer 36:25
and take it, and *b* it with fire Jer 37:8
tent, and *b* this city with fire Jer 37:10
they shall *b* it with fire, and Jer 38:18
and he shall *b* them, and carry them Jer 43:12
Egyptians shall he *b* with fire Jer 43:13
in that they went to *b* incense Jer 44:3
to *b* no incense unto other gods Jer 44:5
to *b* incense unto the queen of Jer 44:17
But since we left off to *b* Jer 44:18
to *b* incense to the queen of Jer 44:25
Thou shalt *b* with fire a third Eze 5:2
the fire, and *b* them in the fire Eze 5:4
they shall *b* thine houses with Eze 16:41
*b* up their houses with fire Eze 23:47
*b* also the bones under it, and Eze 24:5
brass of it may be hot, and may *b* Eze 24:11
*b* the weapons, both the shields Eze 39:9
they shall *b* them with fire seven Eze 39:9
for they shall *b* the weapons with Eze 39:10
he shall *b* it in the appointed Eze 43:21
*b* incense upon the hills, under Hos 4:13
I will *b* her chariots in the Nah 2:13
*b* incense unto their drag Hab 1:16
cometh, that shall *b* as an oven Mal 4:1
day that cometh shall *b* them up Mal 4:1
but he will *b* up the chaff with Mt 3:12
and bind them in bundles to *b* them Mt 13:30
his lot was to *b* incense when he Lk 1:9
but the chaff he will *b* with fire Lk 3:17
Did not our heart *b* within us Lk 24:32
it is better to marry than to *b* 1Cor 7:9
who is offended, and I *b* not 2Cor 11:29
eat her flesh, and *b* her with fire Rev 17:16

### BURNED

the bush *b* with fire, and the bush Ex 3:2
burn him as he *b* the first Lev 4:21
Moses *b* it upon the altar Lev 8:16
the mountain *b* with fire unto the Deut 4:11
mount, and the mount *b* with fire Deut 9:15
*b* them with fire, after they had Josh 7:25
Israel *b* none of them, save Hazor Josh 11:13
smitten Ziklag, and *b* it with fire 1Sa 30:1
and, behold, it was *b* with fire 1Sa 30:3
and we *b* Ziklag with fire 1Sa 30:14
and David and his men *b* them 2Sa 5:21
they shall be utterly *b* with fire 2Sa 23:7
of the house of Baal, and *b* them 2Kin 10:26
*b* incense still in the high 2Kin 15:35
have *b* incense unto other gods, 2Kin 22:17
he *b* them without Jerusalem in 2Kin 23:4
them also that *b* incense unto 2Kin 23:5
*b* it at the brook Kidron, and 2Kin 23:6
where the priests had *b* incense 2Kin 23:8
*b* the chariots of the sun with 2Kin 23:11
*b* the high place, and stamped it 2Kin 23:15
small to powder, and *b* the grove 2Kin 23:15
*b* them upon the altar, and 2Kin 23:16
*b* men's bones upon them, and 2Kin 23:20
and they were *b* with fire 1Chr 14:12
them, and *b* incense unto them 2Chr 25:14
have not *b* incense nor offered 2Chr 29:7
have *b* incense unto other gods, 2Chr 34:25
the gates thereof are *b* with fire Neh 1:3
the gates thereof are *b* with fire Neh 2:17
heaps of the rubbish which are *b* Neh 4:2
very wroth, and his anger *b* in him Est 1:12
hath *b* up the sheep, and the Job 1:16
me, and my bones are *b* with heat Job 30:30
while I was musing the fire *b* Ps 39:3
they have *b* up all the synagogues Ps 74:8
It is *b* with fire, it is cut down Ps 80:16
and my bones are *b* as an hearth Ps 102:3
the flame *b* up the wicked Ps 106:18
bosom, and his clothes not be *b* Prov 6:27
hot coals, and his feet not be *b* Prov 6:28
your cities are *b* with fire Is 1:7
inhabitants of the earth are *b* Is 24:6
up shall they be *b* in the fire Is 33:12
it *b* him, yet he laid it not to Is 42:25
the fire, thou shalt not be *b* Is 43:2
I have *b* part of it in the fire Is 44:19
praised thee, is *b* up with fire Is 64:11
which have *b* incense upon the Is 65:7
have *b* incense unto other gods, Jer 1:16
his cities are *b* without Jer 2:15
The bellows are *b*, the lead is Jer 6:29
because they are *b* up, so that Jer 9:10
is *b* up like a wilderness, that Jer 9:12
they have *b* incense to vanity, and Jer 18:15
have *b* incense in it unto other Jer 19:4
upon whose roofs they have *b* Jer 19:13
that the king had *b* the roll Jer 36:27
the king of Judah hath *b* Jer 36:28
Thou hast *b* this roll, saying, Jer 36:29
king of Judah had *b* in the fire Jer 36:32
city shall not be *b* with fire Jer 38:17
cause this city to be *b* with fire Jer 38:23
the Chaldeans *b* the king's house, Jer 39:8
had *b* incense unto other gods Jer 44:15
when we *b* incense to the queen of Jer 44:19
The incense that ye *b* in the Jer 44:21
Because ye have *b* incense Jer 44:23
daughters shall be *b* with fire Jer 49:2
they have *b* her dwellingplaces Jer 51:30
the reeds they have *b* with fire Jer 51:32
high gates shall be *b* with fire Jer 51:58
*b* the house of the LORD, and the Jer 52:13
of the great men, *b* he with fire Jer 52:13
he *b* against Jacob like a flaming Lam 2:3
of it, and the midst of it is *b* Eze 15:4
fire hath devoured it, and it is *b* Eze 15:5
to the north shall be *b* therein Eze 20:47
it well, and let the bones be *b* Eze 24:10
wherein she *b* incense to them, and Hos 2:13
*b* incense to graven images Hos 11:2
the flame hath *b* all the trees of Joel 1:19
because he *b* the bones of the Amos 2:1
thereof shall be *b* with the fire Mic 1:7
the earth is *b* at his presence, Nah 1:5
are gathered and *b* in the fire Mt 13:40
murderers, and *b* up their city Mt 22:7
them into the fire, and they are *b* Jn 15:6
and *b* them before all men Acts 19:19
*b* in their lust one toward Rom 1:27
If any man's work shall be *b* 1Cor 3:15
and though I give my body to be *b* 1Cor 13:3
whose end is to be *b* Heb 6:8
that *b* with fire, nor unto Heb 12:18
for sin, are *b* without the camp Heb 13:11
that are therein shall be *b* up 2Pet 3:10
as if they *b* in a furnace Rev 1:15
she shall be utterly *b* with fire Rev 18:8

### BURNETH

the quick flesh that *b* have a Lev 13:24
he that *b* them shall wash his Lev 16:28
he that *b* her shall wash his Num 19:8
he *b* the chariot in the fire Ps 46:9
As the fire *b* a wood, and as the Ps 83:14
*b* up his enemies round about Ps 97:3
For wickedness *b* as the fire Is 9:18
He *b* part thereof in the fire Is 44:16
thereof as a lamp that *b* Is 62:1
As when the melting fire *b* Is 64:2
*b* incense upon altars of brick Is 65:3
nose, a fire that *b* all the day Is 65:5
he that *b* incense, as if he Is 66:3
him that *b* incense to his gods Jer 48:35
morning it *b* as a flaming fire Hos 7:6
and behind them a flame *b* Joel 2:3
take him up, and he that *b* him Amos 6:10
in the lake which *b* with fire Rev 21:8

### BURNING

a *b* lamp that passed between Gen 15:17
*B* for *b*, wound for wound, Ex 21:25
*B* for *b*, wound for wound, Ex 21:25
because of the *b* upon the altar Lev 6:9
of the altar shall be *b* in it Lev 6:9
upon the altar shall be *b* in it Lev 6:12
shall ever be *b* upon the altar Lev 6:13
bewail the *b* which the LORD hath Lev 10:6
and spread not, it is a *b* boil Lev 13:23
the skin whereof there is a hot *b* Lev 13:24
is a leprosy broken out of the *b* Lev 13:25
it is a rising of the *b*, and the Lev 13:28
it is an inflammation of the *b* Lev 13:28
of *b* coals of fire from off the Lev 16:12
the *b* ague, that shall consume Lev 26:16
take up the censers out of the *b* Num 16:37
the midst of the *b* of the heifer Num 19:6
and with an extreme *b*, and with Deut 28:22
is brimstone, and salt, and *b* Deut 29:23
hunger, and devoured with *b* heat Deut 32:24

they made a very great *b* for him 2Chr 16:14
And his people made no *b* for him 2Chr 21:19
like the *b* of his fathers 2Chr 21:19
Out of his mouth go *b* lamps Job 41:19
Let *b* coals fall upon them Ps 140:10
in his lips there is as a *b* fire Prov 16:27
As coals are to *b* coals, and wood Prov 26:21
*B* lips and a wicked heart are like Prov 26:23
and *b* instead of beauty Is 3:24
judgment, and by the spirit of *b* Is 4:4
but this shall be with *b* and fuel Is 9:5
a *b* like the *b* of a fire Is 10:16
a *b* like the *b* of a fire Is 10:16
*b* with his anger, and the burden Is 30:27
land thereof shall become *b* pitch Is 34:9
as a *b* fire shut up in my bones Jer 20:9
a fire on the hearth *b* before him Jer 36:22
*b* incense unto other gods in the Jer 44:8
was like *b* coals of fire, and like Eze 1:13
the midst of a *b* fiery furnace Dan 3:6
the midst of a *b* fiery furnace Dan 3:11
the midst of a *b* fiery furnace Dan 3:15
us from the *b* fiery furnace Dan 3:17
them into the *b* fiery furnace Dan 3:20
the midst of the *b* fiery furnace Dan 3:21
the midst of the *b* fiery furnace Dan 3:23
the mouth of the *b* fiery furnace Dan 3:26
flame, and his wheels as *b* fire Dan 7:9
and given to the *b* flame Dan 7:11
a firebrand plucked out of the *b* Amos 4:11
*b* coals went forth at his feet Hab 3:5
be girded about, and your lights *b* Lk 12:35
He was a *b* and a shining light Jn 5:35
is no sooner risen with a *b* heat Jas 1:11
lamps of fire *b* before the throne Rev 4:5
as it were a great mountain *b* Rev 8:8
*b* as it were a lamp, and it fell Rev 8:10
they shall see the smoke of her *b* Rev 18:9
when they saw the smoke of her *b* Rev 18:18
a lake of fire *b* with brimstone Rev 19:20

**BURNINGS**

people shall be as the *b* of lime Is 33:12
us shall dwell with everlasting *b* Is 33:14
with the *b* of thy fathers, the Jer 34:5

**BURNISHED**

like the colour of *b* brass Eze 1:7

**BURNT**

offered *b* offerings on the altar Gen 8:20
offer him there for a *b* offering Gen 22:2
clave the wood for the *b* offering Gen 22:3
took the wood of the *b* offering Gen 22:6
is the lamb for a *b* offering Gen 22:7
himself a lamb for a *b* offering Gen 22:8
offered him up for a *b* offering Gen 22:13
Bring her forth, and let her be *b* Gen 38:24
sight, why the bush is not *b* Ex 3:3
and *b* offerings, that we may Ex 10:25
took a *b* offering and sacrifices Ex 18:12
sacrifice thereon thy *b* offerings Ex 20:24
Israel, which offered *b* offerings Ex 24:5
it is a *b* offering unto the LORD Ex 29:18
upon the altar for a *b* offering Ex 29:25
*b* offering throughout your Ex 29:42
nor *b* sacrifice, nor meat Ex 30:9
the altar of *b* offering with all Ex 30:28
the altar of *b* offering with all Ex 31:9
offered *b* offerings, and brought Ex 32:6
*b* it in the fire, and ground it to Ex 32:20
The altar of *b* offering, with his Ex 35:16
he made the altar of *b* offering Ex 38:1
*b* offering before the door of the Ex 40:6
the altar of the *b* offering Ex 40:10
he *b* sweet incense thereon Ex 40:27
he put the altar of *b* offering by Ex 40:29
and offered upon it the *b* offering Ex 40:29
If his offering be a *b* sacrifice Lev 1:3
upon the head of the *b* offering Lev 1:4
And he shall flay the *b* offering Lev 1:6
to be a *b* sacrifice, an offering Lev 1:9
of the goats, for a *b* sacrifice Lev 1:10
it is a *b* sacrifice, an offering Lev 1:13
if the *b* sacrifice for his Lev 1:14
it is a *b* sacrifice, an offering Lev 1:17
but they shall not be *b* on the Lev 2:12
on the altar upon the *b* sacrifice Lev 3:5
of the altar of the *b* offering Lev 4:7
upon the altar of the *b* offering Lev 4:10
are poured out shall he be *b* Lev 4:12
of the altar of the *b* offering Lev 4:18
the *b* offering before the LORD Lev 4:24
horns of the altar of *b* offering Lev 4:25
bottom of the altar of *b* offering Lev 4:25
in the place of the *b* offering Lev 4:29
horns of the altar of *b* offering Lev 4:30
where they kill the *b* offering Lev 4:33
horns of the altar of *b* offering Lev 4:34
and the other for a *b* offering Lev 5:7
offer the second for a *b* offering Lev 5:10
This is the law of the *b* offering Lev 6:9
It is the *b* offering, because of Lev 6:9
with the *b* offering on the altar Lev 6:10
lay the *b* offering in order upon Lev 6:12
it shall be wholly *b* Lev 6:22
for the priest shall be wholly *b* Lev 6:23
In the place where the *b* offering Lev 6:25
it shall be *b* in the fire Lev 6:30
*b* offering shall they kill the Lev 7:2
offereth any man's *b* offering Lev 7:8
*b* offering which he hath offered Lev 7:8
third day shall be *b* with fire Lev 7:17
it shall be *b* with fire Lev 7:19
This is the law of the *b* offering Lev 7:37
he *b* with fire without the camp Lev 8:17
the ram for the *b* offering Lev 8:18
Moses *b* the head, and the pieces, Lev 8:20
Moses *b* the whole ram upon the Lev 8:21
it was a *b* sacrifice for a sweet Lev 8:21
*b* them on the altar upon the Lev 8:28
on the altar upon the *b* offering Lev 8:28
and a ram for a *b* offering Lev 9:2
without blemish, for a *b* offering Lev 9:3
thy *b* offering, and make an Lev 9:7
sin offering, he *b* upon the altar Lev 9:10
the hide he *b* with fire without Lev 9:11
And he slew the *b* offering Lev 9:12
presented the *b* offering unto him Lev 9:13
and he *b* them upon the altar Lev 9:13
*b* them upon the *b* offering on Lev 9:14
*b* them upon the *b* offering on Lev 9:14
And he brought the *b* offering Lev 9:16
*b* it upon the altar Lev 9:17
beside the *b* sacrifice of the Lev 9:17
he *b* the fat upon the altar Lev 9:20
and the *b* offering, and peace Lev 9:22
upon the altar the *b* offering Lev 9:24
offering, and, behold, it was *b* Lev 10:16
their *b* offering before the LORD Lev 10:19
the first year for a *b* offering Lev 12:6
the one for the *b* offering Lev 12:8
it shall be *b* in the fire Lev 13:52
the *b* offering, in the holy place Lev 14:13
he shall kill the *b* offering Lev 14:19
priest shall offer the *b* offering Lev 14:20
and the other a *b* offering Lev 14:22
and the other for a *b* offering Lev 14:31
and the other for a *b* offering Lev 15:15
and the other for a *b* offering Lev 15:30
and a ram for a *b* offering Lev 16:3
and one ram for a *b* offering Lev 16:5
forth, and offer his *b* offering Lev 16:24
the *b* offering of the people, and Lev 16:24
that offereth a *b* offering or Lev 17:8
day, it shall be *b* in the fire Lev 19:6
they shall be *b* with fire Lev 20:14
she shall be *b* with fire Lev 21:9
unto the LORD for a *b* offering Lev 22:18
for a *b* offering unto the LORD Lev 23:12
they shall be for a *b* offering Lev 23:18
a *b* offering, and a meat offering, Lev 23:37
and the other for a *b* offering Num 6:11
without blemish for a *b* offering Num 6:14
sin offering, and his *b* offering Num 6:16
the first year, for a *b* offering Num 7:15
the first year, for a *b* offering Num 7:21
the first year, for a *b* offering Num 7:27
the first year, for a *b* offering Num 7:33
the first year, for a *b* offering Num 7:39
the first year, for a *b* offering Num 7:45
the first year, for a *b* offering Num 7:51
the first year, for a *b* offering Num 7:57
the first year, for a *b* offering Num 7:63
the first year, for a *b* offering Num 7:69
the first year, for a *b* offering Num 7:75
the first year, for a *b* offering Num 7:81
All the oxen for the *b* offering Num 7:87
and the other for a *b* offering Num 8:12
trumpets over your *b* offerings Num 10:10
the fire of the LORD *b* among them Num 11:1
the fire of the LORD *b* among them Num 11:3
a *b* offering, or a sacrifice in Num 15:3
with the *b* offering or sacrifice Num 15:5
a bullock for a *b* offering Num 15:8
young bullock for a *b* offering Num 15:24
they that were *b* had offered Num 16:39
*b* heifer of purification for sin Num 19:17
Balak, Stand by thy *b* offering Num 23:3
lo, he stood by his *b* sacrifice Num 23:6
Stand here by thy *b* offering Num 23:15
he stood by his *b* offering Num 23:17
day, for a continual *b* offering Num 28:3
It is a continual *b* offering Num 28:6
This is the *b* offering of every Num 28:10
beside the continual *b* offering Num 28:10
offer a *b* offering unto the LORD Num 28:11
for a *b* offering of a sweet Num 28:13
this is the *b* offering of every Num 28:14
beside the continual *b* offering Num 28:15
for a *b* offering unto the LORD Num 28:19
the *b* offering in the morning Num 28:23
is for a continual *b* offering Num 28:23
beside the continual *b* offering Num 28:24
But ye shall offer the *b* offering Num 28:27
beside the continual *b* offering Num 28:31
ye shall offer a *b* offering for a Num 29:2
Beside the *b* offering of the Num 29:6
offering, and the daily *b* offering Num 29:6
But ye shall offer a *b* offering Num 29:8
and the continual *b* offering Num 29:11
And ye shall offer a *b* offering Num 29:13
beside the continual *b* offering Num 29:16
beside the continual *b* offering Num 29:19
beside the continual *b* offering Num 29:22
beside the continual *b* offering Num 29:25
beside the continual *b* offering Num 29:28
beside the continual *b* offering Num 29:31
beside the continual *b* offering Num 29:34
But ye shall offer a *b* offering Num 29:36
beside the continual *b* offering Num 29:38
for your *b* offerings, and for your Num 29:39
they *b* all their cities wherein Num 31:10
*b* it with fire, and stamped it, and Deut 9:21
ye shall bring your *b* offerings Deut 12:6
your *b* offerings, and your Deut 12:11
*b* offerings in every place that Deut 12:13
thou shalt offer thy *b* offerings Deut 12:14
thou shalt offer thy *b* offerings Deut 12:27
have *b* in the fire to their gods Deut 12:31
thou shalt offer *b* offerings Deut 27:6
They shall be *b* with hunger Deut 32:24
whole *b* sacrifice upon thine Deut 33:10
they *b* the city with fire, and all Josh 6:24
thing shall be *b* with fire Josh 7:15
And Joshua *b* Ai, and made it an Josh 8:28
they offered thereon *b* offerings Josh 8:31
*b* their chariots with fire Josh 11:9
and he *b* Hazor with fire Josh 11:11
or if to offer thereon *b* offering Josh 22:23
not for *b* offering, nor for Josh 22:26
before him with our *b* offerings Josh 22:27
not for *b* offerings, nor for Josh 22:28
to build an altar for *b* offerings Josh 22:29
offer a *b* sacrifice with the wood Judg 6:26
will offer it up for a *b* offering Judg 11:31
if thou wilt offer a *b* offering Judg 13:16
not have received a *b* offering Judg 13:23
*b* up both the shocks, and also the Judg 15:5
*b* her and her father with fire Judg 15:6
as flax that was *b* with fire Judg 15:14
sword, and *b* the city with fire Judg 18:27
offered *b* offerings and peace Judg 20:26
offered *b* offerings and peace Judg 21:4
Also before they *b* the fat 1Sa 2:15
offered the kine a *b* offering 1Sa 6:14
Beth-shemesh offered *b* offerings 1Sa 6:15
offered it for a *b* offering 1Sa 7:9
was offering up the *b* offering 1Sa 7:10
to offer *b* offerings, and to 1Sa 10:8
Bring hither a *b* offering to me 1Sa 13:9
And he offered the *b* offering 1Sa 13:9
an end of offering the *b* offering 1Sa 13:10
and offered a *b* offering 1Sa 13:12
as great delight in *b* offerings 1Sa 15:22
came to Jabesh, and *b* them there 1Sa 31:12
and David offered *b* offerings 2Sa 6:17
an end of offering *b* offerings 2Sa 6:18
here be oxen for *b* sacrifice 2Sa 24:22
neither will I offer *b* offerings 2Sa 24:24
offered *b* offerings and peace 2Sa 24:25
and *b* incense in high places 1Kin 3:3
a thousand *b* offerings did 1Kin 3:4
LORD, and offered up *b* offerings 1Kin 3:15
for there he offered *b* offerings 1Kin 8:64
little to receive the *b* offerings 1Kin 8:64
*b* it with fire, and slain the 1Kin 9:16
did Solomon offer *b* offerings 1Kin 9:25
he *b* incense upon the altar that 1Kin 9:25
which *b* incense and sacrificed 1Kin 11:8
upon the altar, and *b* incense 1Kin 12:33
men's bones shall be *b* upon thee 1Kin 13:2
idol, and *b* it by the brook Kidron 1Kin 15:13
*b* the king's house over him with 1Kin 16:18
and pour it on the *b* sacrifice 1Kin 18:33
fell, and consumed the *b* sacrifice 1Kin 18:38
*b* incense yet in the high places 1Kin 22:43
*b* up the two captains of the 2Kin 1:14
offered him for a *b* offering upon 2Kin 3:27
*b* offering nor sacrifice unto 2Kin 5:17
*b* offerings, Jehu appointed 2Kin 10:24
an end of offering the *b* offering 2Kin 10:25
*b* incense in the high places 2Kin 12:3
*b* incense on the high places 2Kin 14:4
*b* incense still on the high 2Kin 15:4
*b* incense in the high places, and 2Kin 16:4
And he *b* his *b* offering 2Kin 16:13
altar burn the morning *b* offering 2Kin 16:15
and the king's *b* sacrifice 2Kin 16:15
with the *b* offering of all the 2Kin 16:15
all the blood of the *b* offering 2Kin 16:15
there they *b* incense in all the 2Kin 17:11
the Sepharvites *b* their children 2Kin 17:31
he *b* the house of the LORD, and 2Kin 25:9
great man's house *b* he with fire 2Kin 25:9
upon the altar of the *b* offering 1Chr 6:49
and they offered *b* sacrifices 1Chr 16:1
end of offering the *b* offerings 1Chr 16:2
To offer *b* offerings unto the 1Chr 16:40
*b* offering continually morning 1Chr 16:40
the oxen also for *b* offerings 1Chr 21:23
nor offer *b* offerings without 1Chr 21:24
offered *b* offerings and peace 1Chr 21:26
fire upon the altar of *b* offering 1Chr 21:26
and the altar of the *b* offering 1Chr 21:29
of the *b* offering for Israel 1Chr 22:1
to offer all *b* sacrifices unto 1Chr 23:31
offered *b* offerings unto the LORD 1Chr 29:21
a thousand *b* offerings upon it 2Chr 1:6
for the *b* offerings morning and 2Chr 2:4
*b* offering they washed in them 2Chr 4:6
and consumed the *b* offering 2Chr 7:1
for there he offered *b* offerings 2Chr 7:7
able to receive the *b* offerings 2Chr 7:7
Then Solomon offered *b* offerings 2Chr 8:12
and every evening *b* sacrifices 2Chr 13:11
it, and *b* it at the brook Kidron 2Chr 15:16
to offer the *b* offerings of the 2Chr 23:18
they offered *b* offerings in the 2Chr 24:14
Moreover he *b* incense in the 2Chr 28:3
*b* his children in the fire, after 2Chr 28:3
*b* incense in the high places, and 2Chr 28:4

*b* offerings in the holy place .... 2Chr 29:7
LORD, and the altar of *b* offering .... 2Chr 29:18
commanded that the *b* offering .... 2Chr 29:24
the *b* offering upon the altar .... 2Chr 29:27
when the *b* offering began, the .... 2Chr 29:27
until the *b* offering was finished .... 2Chr 29:28
were of a free heart *b* offerings .... 2Chr 29:31
And the number of the *b* offerings .... 2Chr 29:32
were for a *b* offering to the LORD .... 2Chr 29:32
not flay all the *b* offerings .... 2Chr 29:34
also the *b* offerings were in .... 2Chr 29:35
offerings for every *b* offering .... 2Chr 29:35
brought in the *b* offerings into .... 2Chr 30:15
and Levites for *b* offerings .... 2Chr 31:2
his substance for the *b* offerings .... 2Chr 31:3
evening *b* offerings, and the *b* .... 2Chr 31:3
he *b* the bones of the priests .... 2Chr 34:5
And they removed the *b* offerings .... 2Chr 35:12
busied in offering of *b* offerings .... 2Chr 35:14
to offer *b* offerings upon the .... 2Chr 35:16
they *b* the house of God, and brake .. 2Chr 36:19
*b* all the palaces thereof with .... 2Chr 36:19
to offer *b* offerings thereon, as .... Ezr 3:2
they offered *b* offerings thereon .... Ezr 3:3
even *b* offerings morning and .... Ezr 3:3
offered the daily *b* offerings by .... Ezr 3:4
offered the continual *b* offering .... Ezr 3:5
offer *b* offerings unto the LORD .... Ezr 3:6
for the *b* offerings of the God of .... Ezr 6:9
offered *b* offerings unto the God .... Ezr 8:35
all this was a *b* offering unto .... Ezr 8:35
and for the continual *b* offering .... Neh 10:33
offered *b* offerings according to .... Job 1:5
up for yourselves a *b* offering .... Job 42:8
and accept thy *b* sacrifice .... Ps 20:3
*b* offering and sin offering hast .... Ps 40:6
thy sacrifices or thy *b* offerings .... Ps 50:8
thou delightest not in *b* offering .... Ps 51:16
*b* offering and whole *b* offering .... Ps 51:19
into thy house with *b* offerings .... Ps 66:13
thee *b* sacrifices of fatlings .... Ps 66:15
I am full of the *b* offerings of .... Is 1:11
sufficient for a *b* offering .... Is 40:16
small cattle of thy *b* offerings .... Is 43:23
their *b* offerings and their .... Is 56:7
I hate robbery for *b* offering .... Is 61:8
your *b* offerings are not .... Jer 6:20
Put your *b* offerings unto your .... Jer 7:21
concerning *b* offerings or .... Jer 7:22
and when they offer *b* offering .... Jer 14:12
south, bringing *b* offerings, and .... Jer 17:26
fire for *b* offerings unto Baal .... Jer 19:5
before me to offer *b* offerings .... Jer 33:18
and will make thee a *b* mountain .... Jer 51:25
where they washed the *b* offering .... Eze 40:38
to slay thereon the *b* offering .... Eze 40:39
of hewn stone for the *b* offering .... Eze 40:42
they slew the *b* offering and the .... Eze 40:42
to offer *b* offerings thereon, and .... Eze 43:18
up for a *b* offering unto the LORD .... Eze 43:24
your *b* offerings upon the altar .... Eze 43:27
they shall slay the *b* offering .... Eze 44:11
for a *b* offering, and for peace .... Eze 45:15
prince's part to give *b* offerings .... Eze 45:17
the *b* offering, and the peace .... Eze 45:17
prepare a *b* offering to the LORD .... Eze 45:23
according to the *b* offering .... Eze 45:25
shall prepare his *b* offering .... Eze 46:2
the *b* offering that the prince .... Eze 46:4
shall prepare a voluntary *b* .... Eze 46:12
he shall prepare his *b* offering .... Eze 46:12
Thou shalt daily prepare a *b* .... Eze 46:13
for a continual *b* offering .... Eze 46:15
of God more than *b* offerings .... Hos 6:6
Though ye offer me *b* offerings .... Amos 5:22
come before him with *b* offerings .... Mic 6:6
more than all whole *b* offerings .... Mk 12:33
In *b* offerings and sacrifices for .... Heb 10:6
*b* offerings and offering for sin .... Heb 10:8
the third part of trees was *b* up .... Rev 8:7
and all green grass was *b* up .... Rev 8:7

**BURST**
it is ready to *b* like new bottles .... Job 32:19
presses shall *b* out with new wine .... Prov 3:10
broken thy yoke, and *b* thy bands .... Jer 2:20
broken the yoke, and *b* the bonds .... Jer 5:5
will *b* thy bonds, and strangers .... Jer 30:8
will *b* thy bonds in sunder .... Nah 1:13
the new wine doth *b* the bottles .... Mk 2:22
the new wine will *b* the bottles .... Lk 5:37
he *b* asunder in the midst, and all .... Acts 1:18

**BURSTING**
*b* of it a sherd to take fire from .... Is 30:14

**BURY**
that I may *b* my dead out of my .... Gen 23:4
of our sepulchres *b* thy dead .... Gen 23:6
but that thou mayest *b* thy dead .... Gen 23:6
should *b* my dead out of my sight .... Gen 23:8
*b* thy dead .... Gen 23:11
of me, and I will *b* my dead there .... Gen 23:13
*b* therefore thy dead .... Gen 23:15
*b* me not, I pray thee, in Egypt .... Gen 47:29
*b* me in their buryingplace .... Gen 47:30
*b* me with my fathers in the cave .... Gen 49:29
of Canaan, there shalt thou *b* me .... Gen 50:5
*b* my father, and I will come again .... Gen 50:5
*b* thy father, according as he .... Gen 50:6
And Joseph went up to *b* his father .... Gen 50:7
went up with him to *b* his father .... Gen 50:14
shalt in any wise *b* him that day .... Deut 21:23
said, and fall upon him, and *b* him .... 1Kin 2:31
host was gone up to *b* the slain .... 1Kin 11:15
to the city, to mourn and to *b* him .... 1Kin 13:29
then *b* me in the sepulchre .... 1Kin 13:31
shall mourn for him, and *b* him .... 1Kin 14:13
and there shall be none to *b* her .... 2Kin 9:10
now this cursed woman, and *b* her .... 2Kin 9:34
And they went to *b* her .... 2Kin 9:35
and there was none to *b* them .... Ps 79:3
for they shall *b* in Tophet .... Jer 7:32
and they shall have none to *b* them .... Jer 14:16
they shall *b* them in Tophet .... Jer 19:11
till there be no place to *b* .... Jer 19:11
and there shall they *b* Gog .... Eze 39:11
people of the land shall *b* them .... Eze 39:13
passing through the land to *b* .... Eze 39:14
them up, Memphis shall *b* them .... Hos 9:6
me first to go and *b* my father .... Mt 8:21
and let the dead *b* their dead .... Mt 8:22
potter's field, to *b* strangers in .... Mt 27:7
me first to go and *b* my father .... Lk 9:59
him, Let the dead *b* their dead .... Lk 9:60
as the manner of the Jews is to *b* .... Jn 19:40

**BURYING**
to pass, as they were *b* a man .... 2Kin 13:21
the house of Israel be *b* of them .... Eze 39:12
to anoint my body to the *b* .... Mk 14:8
day of my *b* hath she kept this .... Jn 12:7

**BURYINGPLACE**
me a possession of a *b* with you .... Gen 23:4
a possession of a *b* amongst you .... Gen 23:9
of a *b* by the sons of Heth .... Gen 23:20
of Egypt, and bury me in their *b* .... Gen 47:30
Hittite for a possession of a *b* .... Gen 49:30
of a *b* of Ephron the Hittite .... Gen 50:13
Eshtaol in the *b* of Manoah his .... Judg 16:31

**BUSH**
of fire out of the midst of a *b* .... Ex 3:2
the *b* burned with fire .... Ex 3:2
and the *b* was not consumed .... Ex 3:2
sight, why the *b* is not burnt .... Ex 3:3
him out of the midst of the *b* .... Ex 3:4
will of him that dwelt in the *b* .... Deut 33:16
how in the *b* God spake unto him, .... Mk 12:26
nor of a bramble *b* gather they .... Lk 6:44
even Moses shewed at the *b* .... Lk 20:37
Lord in a flame of fire in a *b* .... Acts 7:30
which appeared to him in the *b* .... Acts 7:35

**BUSHEL**
a candle, and put it under a *b* .... Mt 5:15
brought to be put under a *b* .... Mk 4:21
a secret place, neither under a *b* .... Lk 11:33

**BUSHES**
Who cut up mallows by the *b* .... Job 30:4
Among the *b* they brayed .... Job 30:7
and upon all thorns, and upon all *b* .... Is 7:19

**BUSHY**
most fine gold, his locks are *b* .... Song 5:11

**BUSIED**
*b* in offering of burnt offerings .... 2Chr 35:14

**BUSINESS**
went into the house to do his *b* .... Gen 39:11
shall he be charged with any *b* .... Deut 24:5
yours, if ye utter not this our *b* .... Josh 2:14
And if thou utter this our *b* .... Josh 2:20
and had no *b* with any man .... Judg 18:7
they had no *b* with any man .... Judg 18:28
thyself when the *b* was in hand .... 1Sa 20:19
The king hath commanded me a *b* .... 1Sa 21:2
of the *b* whereabout I send thee .... 1Sa 21:2
the king's *b* required haste .... 1Sa 21:8
for the outward *b* over Israel .... 1Chr 26:29
westward in all the *b* of the LORD .... 1Chr 26:30
and the Levites wait upon their *b* .... 2Chr 13:10
he had much *b* in the cities of .... 2Chr 17:13
Howbeit in the *b* of the .... 2Chr 32:31
the outward *b* of the house of God .... Neh 11:16
over the *b* of the house of God .... Neh 11:22
the Levites, every one in his *b* .... Neh 13:30
that have the charge of the *b* .... Est 3:9
that do *b* in great waters .... Ps 107:23
thou a man diligent in his *b* .... Prov 22:29
cometh through the multitude of *b* .... Eccl 5:3
to see the *b* that is done upon .... Eccl 8:16
I rose up, and did the king's *b* .... Dan 8:27
I must be about my Father's *b* .... Lk 2:49
whom we may appoint over this *b* .... Acts 6:3
Not slothful in *b* .... Rom 12:11
whatsoever *b* she hath need of you .... Rom 16:2
to be quiet, and to do your own *b* .... 1Th 4:11

**BUSY**
And as thy servant was *b* here .... 1Kin 20:40

**BUSYBODIES**
working not at all, but are *b* .... 2Th 3:11
only idle, but tattlers also and *b* .... 1Ti 5:13

**BUSYBODY**
or as a *b* in other men's matters .... 1Pet 4:15

**BUT** See PREFACE.

**BUTLER**
that the *b* of the king of Egypt .... Gen 40:1
of his dream, the *b* and the baker .... Gen 40:5
the chief *b* told his dream to .... Gen 40:9
manner when thou wast his *b* .... Gen 40:13
lifted up the head of the chief *b* .... Gen 40:20
he restored the chief *b* unto his .... Gen 40:21
not the chief *b* remember Joseph .... Gen 40:23
spake the chief *b* unto Pharaoh .... Gen 41:9

**BUTLERS**
against the chief of the *b* .... Gen 40:2

**BUTLERSHIP**
the chief butler unto his *b* again .... Gen 40:21

**BUTTER**
And he took *b*, and milk, and the .... Gen 18:8
*B* of kine, and milk of sheep, with .... Deut 32:14
brought forth *b* in a lordly dish .... Judg 5:25
And honey, and *b*, and sheep, and .... 2Sa 17:29
floods, the brooks of honey and *b* .... Job 20:17
When I washed my steps with *b* .... Job 29:6
of his mouth were smoother than *b* .... Ps 55:21
churning of milk bringeth forth *b* .... Prov 30:33
*B* and honey shall he eat, that he .... Is 7:15
they shall give, he shall eat *b* .... Is 7:22
for *b* and honey shall every one .... Is 7:22

**BUTTOCKS**
in the middle, even to their *b* .... 2Sa 10:4
in the midst hard by their *b* .... 1Chr 19:4
even with their *b* uncovered .... Is 20:4

**BUY**
Egypt to Joseph for to *b* corn .... Gen 41:57
thither, and *b* for us from thence .... Gen 42:2
went down to *b* corn in Egypt .... Gen 42:3
to *b* corn among those that came .... Gen 42:5
From the land of Canaan to *b* food .... Gen 42:7
but to *b* food are thy servants .... Gen 42:10
Go again, *b* us a little food .... Gen 43:2
we will go down and *b* thee food .... Gen 43:4
down at the first time to *b* food .... Gen 43:20
down in our hands to *b* food .... Gen 43:22
Go again, and *b* us a little food .... Gen 44:25
*b* us and our land for bread, and we .... Gen 47:19
If thou *b* an Hebrew servant, six .... Ex 21:2
But if the priest *b* any soul with .... Lev 22:11
thou shalt *b* of thy neighbour .... Lev 25:15
of them shall ye *b* bondmen .... Lev 25:44
among you, of them shall ye *b* .... Lev 25:45
Ye shall *b* meat of them for money .... Deut 2:6
ye shall also *b* water of them for .... Deut 2:6
and no man shall *b* you .... Deut 28:68
*B* it before the inhabitants, and .... Ruth 4:4
thou must *b* it also of Ruth the .... Ruth 4:5
said unto Boaz, *B* it for thee .... Ruth 4:8
To *b* the threshingfloor of thee, .... 2Sa 24:21
but I will surely *b* it of thee at .... 2Sa 24:24
to *b* timber and hewed stone to .... 2Kin 12:12
to *b* timber and hewn stone to .... 2Kin 22:6
but I will verily *b* it for the .... 1Chr 21:24
to *b* hewn stone, and timber for .... 2Chr 34:11
That thou mayest *b* speedily with .... Ezr 7:17
and houses, that we might *b* corn .... Neh 5:3
that we would not *b* it of them on .... Neh 10:31
*B* the truth, and sell it not .... Prov 23:23
come ye, *b*, and eat .... Is 55:1
*b* wine and milk without money and .... Is 55:1
*B* thee my field that is in .... Jer 32:7
of redemption is thine to *b* it .... Jer 32:7
*B* my field, I pray thee, that is .... Jer 32:8
*b* it for thyself .... Jer 32:8
*B* thee the field for money, and .... Jer 32:25
Men shall *b* fields for money, and .... Jer 32:44
That we may *b* the poor for silver .... Amos 8:6
and *b* themselves victuals .... Mt 14:15
that sell, and *b* for yourselves .... Mt 25:9
And while they went to *b*, the .... Mt 25:10
villages, and *b* themselves bread .... Mk 6:36
*b* two hundred pennyworth of bread .... Mk 6:37
*b* meat for all this people .... Lk 9:13
him sell his garment, and *b* one .... Lk 22:36
gone away unto the city to *b* meat .... Jn 4:8
Philip, Whence shall we *b* bread .... Jn 6:5
*B* those things that we have need .... Jn 13:29
and they that *b*, as though they .... 1Cor 7:30
and continue there a year, and *b* .... Jas 4:13
I counsel thee to *b* of me gold .... Rev 3:18
And that no man might *b* or sell .... Rev 13:17

**BUYER**
naught, it is naught, saith the *b* .... Prov 20:14
as with the *b*, so with the seller .... Is 24:2
let not the *b* rejoice, nor the .... Eze 7:12

**BUYEST**
or *b* ought of thy neighbour's .... Lev 25:14
What day thou *b* the field of the .... Ruth 4:5

**BUYETH**
She considereth a field, and *b* it .... Prov 31:16
all that he hath, and *b* that field .... Mt 13:44
for no man *b* their merchandise .... Rev 18:11

**BUZ** (*buz*)
*1. Son of Nahor.*
*B* his brother, and Kemuel the .... Gen 22:21
*2. A Gadite.*
the son of Jahdo, the son of *B* .... 1Chr 5:14
*3. A tribe in northern Arabia.*
Dedan, and Tema, and *B*, and all that .. Jer 25:23

**BUZI** (*boo'-zi*) See BUZITE. *Father of Ezekiel.*
Ezekiel the priest, the son of *B* .... Eze 1:3

**BUZITE** (*boo'-zite*) *A member of Buz 3.*
Elihu the son of Barachel the *B* .... Job 32:2
son of Barachel the *B* answered .... Job 32:6

**BY** See PREFACE.

**BYWAYS**
the travellers walked through *b* ............ Judg 5:6

**BYWORD**
astonishment, a proverb, and a *b* ....... Deut 28:37
a proverb and a *b* among all people ....... 1Kin 9:7
proverb and a *b* among all nations ...... 2Chr 7:20
made me also a *b* of the people ............... Job 17:6
I their song, yea, I am their *b* .................. Job 30:9
Thou makest us a *b* among the .............. Ps 44:14

# C

**CAB**
the fourth part of a *c* of dove's ............ 2Kin 6:25

**CABBON** (*cab'-bon*) *A town in Judah.*
And C, and Lahmam, and Kithlish, .... Josh 15:40

**CABINS**
into the dungeon, and into the *c* ........ Jer 37:16

**CABUL** (*ca'-bul*) *A town in Asher.*
goeth out to C on the left hand, ......... Josh 19:27
them the land of C unto this day ......... 1Kin 9:13

**CAESAR** (*se'-zur*) See CAESAR'S. *Title for the Roman Emperor.*
it lawful to give tribute unto C ............. Mt 22:17
Render therefore unto C the ................... Mt 22:21
Is it lawful to give tribute to C ............. Mk 12:14
Render to C the things that are .............. Mk 12:17
went out a decree from C Augustus .......... Lk 2:1
year of the reign of Tiberius C .................. Lk 3:1
for us to give tribute unto C ................... Lk 20:22
Render therefore unto C the ................... Lk 20:25
forbidding to give tribute to C ................. Lk 23:2
himself a king speaketh against C ............ Jn 19:12
answered, We have no king but C ............ Jn 19:15
to pass in the days of Claudius C ....... Acts 11:28
do contrary to the decrees of C ............. Acts 17:7
the temple, nor yet against C ................ Acts 25:8
I appeal unto C ........................................ Acts 25:11
Hast thou appealed unto C .................... Acts 25:12
unto C shalt thou go .............................. Acts 25:12
kept till I might send him to C .............. Acts 25:21
if he had not appealed unto C ............... Acts 26:32
thou must be brought before C ............. Acts 27:24
was constrained to appeal unto C ...... Acts 28:19

**CAESAREA** (*ses-a-re'-ah*)
*1. A town north of Galilee.*
into the coasts of C Philippi ..................... Mt 16:13
into the towns of C Philippi ...................... Mk 8:27
*2. A Judean Mediterranean port.*
all the cities, till he came to C ............... Acts 8:40
knew, they brought him down to C ......... Acts 9:30
certain man in C called Cornelius .......... Acts 10:1
morrow after they entered into C ........ Acts 10:24
where I was, sent from C unto me ....... Acts 11:11
And he went down from Judaea to C Acts 12:19
And when he had landed at C ............... Acts 18:22
company departed, and came unto C .. Acts 21:8
certain of the disciples of C ................. Acts 21:16
two hundred soldiers to go to C ............ Acts 23:23
Who, when they came to C, and ............ Acts 23:33
he ascended from C to Jerusalem ......... Acts 25:1
that Paul should be kept at C ............... Acts 25:4
ten days, he went down unto C .............. Acts 25:6
came unto C to salute Festus .............. Acts 25:13

**CAESAR'S** (*se'-zurs*)
They say unto him, C .................................. Mt 22:21
Caesar the things which are C ................ Mt 22:21
And they said unto him, C ....................... Mk 12:16
to Caesar the things that are C .............. Mk 12:17
They answered and said, C ....................... Lk 20:24
unto Caesar the things which be C ....... Lk 20:25
man go, thou art not C friend .................. Jn 19:12
I stand at C judgment seat, where ..... Acts 25:10
they that are of C household .................. Phil 4:22

**CAGE**
As a *c* is full of birds, so are ..................... Jer 5:27
a *c* of every unclean and hateful ........... Rev 18:2

**CAIAPHAS** (*cah'-ya-fus*) *A High Priest during Jesus' time.*
the high priest, who was called C ........... Mt 26:3
led him away to C the high priest ......... Mt 26:57
C being the high priests, the ........................ Lk 3:2
And one of them, named C, being .......... Jn 11:49
for he was father in law to C ................... Jn 18:13
Now C was he, which gave counsel ....... Jn 18:14
him bound unto C the high priest ......... Jn 18:24
Then led they Jesus from C unto ........... Jn 18:28
And Annas the high priest, and C ........... Acts 4:6

**CAIN** See TUBAL-CAIN.
*1. Eldest son of Adam and Eve.*
and she conceived, and bare C .................. Gen 4:1
but C was a tiller of the ground ............... Gen 4:2
that C brought of the fruit of ................... Gen 4:3
But unto C and to his offering he ............ Gen 4:5
And C was very wroth, and his ................ Gen 4:5
And the LORD said unto C, Why art ....... Gen 4:6
C talked with Abel his brother ................. Gen 4:8
that C rose up against Abel his ................ Gen 4:8
And the LORD said unto C, Where is ...... Gen 4:9
And C said unto the LORD, My ................ Gen 4:13
Therefore whosoever slayeth C ............... Gen 4:15
And the LORD set a mark upon C ............ Gen 4:15
C went out from the presence of ........... Gen 4:16
And C knew his wife ................................ Gen 4:17
If C shall be avenged sevenfold, ............ Gen 4:24
seed instead of Abel, whom C slew ....... Gen 4:25
a more excellent sacrifice than C ........... Heb 11:4
Not as C, who was of that wicked ......... 1Jn 3:12
they have gone in the way of C ............... Jude 11
*2. A town in Judah.*
C, Gibeah, and Timnah .......................... Josh 15:57

**CAINAN** (*ca'-nun*) See KENAN. *Son of Enos.*
lived ninety years, and begat C ................ Gen 5:9
after he begat C eight hundred ............. Gen 5:10
C lived seventy years, and begat ........... Gen 5:12
C lived after he begat Mahalaleel ......... Gen 5:13
all the days of C were nine ..................... Gen 5:14
Which was the son of C, which was ....... Lk 3:36
Maleleel, which was the son of C ........... Lk 3:37

**CAKE**
one *c* of oiled bread, and one ................. Ex 29:23
LORD, he took one unleavened *c* ............. Lev 8:26
a *c* of oiled bread, and one wafer, .......... Lev 8:26
two tenth deals shall be in one *c* ............ Lev 24:5
one unleavened *c* out of the .................... Num 6:19
Ye shall offer up a *c* of the .................... Num 15:20
a *c* of barley bread tumbled into ............ Judg 7:13
gave him a piece of a *c* of figs .............. 1Sa 30:12
as men, to every one a *c* of bread .......... 2Sa 6:19
thy God liveth, I have not a *c* ............. 1Kin 17:12
make me thereof a little *c* first ........... 1Kin 17:13
there was a *c* baken on the coals, ........ 1Kin 19:6
Ephraim is a *c* not turned .......................... Hos 7:8

**CAKES**
it, and make *c* upon the hearth .............. Gen 18:6
they baked unleavened *c* of the ............. Ex 12:39
*c* unleavened tempered with oil, .............. Ex 29:2
it shall be unleavened *c* of fine ................ Lev 2:4
unleavened *c* mingled with oil ................. Lev 7:12
*c* mingled with oil, of fine flour ............... Lev 7:12
Besides the *c*, he shall offer for ............... Lev 7:13
flour, and bake twelve *c* thereof ............. Lev 24:5
*c* of fine flour mingled with oil, ............. Num 6:15
baked it in pans, and made *c* of it ....... Num 11:8
after the passover, unleavened *c* ........... Josh 5:11
unleavened *c* of an ephah of flour ....... Judg 6:19
the flesh and the unleavened *c* ............. Judg 6:20
the flesh and the unleavened *c* ............. Judg 6:21
the flesh and the unleavened *c* ............. Judg 6:21
raisins, and two hundred *c* of figs ........ 1Sa 25:18
make me a couple of *c* in my sight ........ 2Sa 13:6
made *c* in his sight, and did bake ........... 2Sa 13:8
in his sight, and did bake the *c* ............... 2Sa 13:8
Tamar took the *c* which she had ........... 2Sa 13:10
*c* of figs, and bunches of raisins, ........ 1Chr 12:40
offering, and for the unleavened *c* ..... 1Chr 23:29
to make *c* to the queen of heaven, ......... Jer 7:18
did we make her *c* to worship her ......... Jer 44:19
And thou shalt eat it as barley *c* ........... Eze 4:12

**CALAH** (*ca'-lah*) *An Assyrian city.*
and the city Rehoboth, and C ............... Gen 10:11
And Resen between Nineveh and C .... Gen 10:12

**CALAMITIES**
refuge, until these *c* be overpast .............. Ps 57:1
prayer also shall be in their *c* ............... Ps 141:5
he that is glad at *c* shall not be ............ Prov 17:5

**CALAMITY**
for the day of their *c* is at hand ......... Deut 32:35
prevented me in the day of my *c* ........... 2Sa 22:19
my *c* laid in the balances .............................. Job 6:2
my path, they set forward my *c* ............ Job 30:13
prevented me in the day of my *c* .............. Ps 18:18
I also will laugh at your *c* ....................... Prov 1:26
shall his *c* come suddenly ....................... Prov 6:15
son is the *c* of his father ........................ Prov 19:13
For their *c* shall rise suddenly ............. Prov 24:22
house in the day of thy *c* ...................... Prov 27:10
the face, in the day of their *c* ................ Jer 18:17
day of their *c* was come upon them ...... Jer 46:21
The *c* of Moab is near to come, and ....... Jer 48:16
will bring the *c* of Esau upon him ........... Jer 49:8
I will bring their *c* from all .................... Jer 49:32
the sword in the time of their *c* ............. Eze 35:5
my people in the day of their *c* ........... Obad 13
affliction in the day of their *c* ............. Obad 13
substance in the day of their *c* ............ Obad 13

**CALAMUS**
of sweet *c* two hundred and fifty .......... Ex 30:23
*c* and cinnamon, with all trees of ........ Song 4:14
bright iron, cassia, and *c* ....................... Eze 27:19

**CALCOL** (*cal'-col*) See CHALCOL. *A son of Zerah.*
Zimri, and Ethan, and Heman, and C ... 1Chr 2:6

**CALDRON**
it into the pan, or kettle, or *c* ................. 1Sa 2:14
as out of a seething pot or *c* .................. Job 41:20
this city is the *c*, and we be the ............ Eze 11:3
the flesh, and this city is the *c* ............... Eze 11:7
This city shall not be your *c* .................. Eze 11:11
the pot, and as flesh within the *c* ............. Mic 3:3

**CALDRONS**
sod they in pots, and in *c* ..................... 2Chr 35:13
The *c* also, and the shovels, and ............ Jer 52:18
firepans, and the bowls, and the *c* ......... Jer 52:19

**CALEB** (*ca'-leb*) See CALEB'S, CALEB-EPHRATAH, CHELLUBAI.
*1. A son of Jephunneh.*
of Judah, C the son of Jephunneh ....... Num 13:6
C stilled the people before Moses ........ Num 13:30
C the son of Jephunneh, which ............ Num 14:6
But my servant C, because he had .... Num 14:24
save C the son of Jephunneh, and ....... Num 14:30
C the son of Jephunneh, which ........... Num 14:38
save C the son of Jephunneh, and ..... Num 26:65
Save C the son of Jephunneh the ...... Num 32:12
of Judah, C the son of Jephunneh ..... Num 34:19
Save C the son of Jephunneh .............. Deut 1:36
C the son of Jephunneh the ................. Josh 14:6
gave unto C the son of Jephunneh ..... Josh 14:13
of C the son of Jephunneh the ........... Josh 14:14
unto C the son of Jephunneh he ......... Josh 15:13
C drove thence the three sons of ......... Josh 15:14
And C said, He that smiteth ................. Josh 15:16
son of Kenaz, the brother of C ............. Josh 15:17
C said unto her, What wouldest ........... Josh 15:18
gave they to C the son of ..................... Josh 21:12
And C said, He that smiteth ................... Judg 1:12
C said unto her, What wilt thou ........... Judg 1:14
C gave her the upper springs and ......... Judg 1:15
And they gave Hebron unto C ............... Judg 1:20
and he was of the house of C .................. 1Sa 25:3
to Judah, and upon the south of C ...... 1Sa 30:14
and the daughter of C was Achsa ........ 1Chr 2:49
And the sons of C the son of ............... 1Chr 4:15
they gave to C the son of ..................... 1Chr 6:56
*2. A son of Hezron.*
C the son of Hezron begat ..................... 1Chr 2:18
C took unto him Ephrath, which ........... 1Chr 2:19
Now the sons of C the brother of ......... 1Chr 2:42
*3. A son of Hur.*
were the sons of C the son of Hur ....... 1Chr 2:50

**CALEB-EPHRATAH** (*ca'-leb-ef'-ra-tah*) *The place where Hezron died.*
after that Hezron was dead in C .......... 1Chr 2:24

**CALEB-EPHRATHAH** See CALEB-EPHRATAH.

**CALEB'S** (*ca'-lebs*) *Refers to Caleb 1.*
C younger brother, took it ..................... Judg 1:13
son of Kenaz, C younger brother ........... Judg 3:9
C concubine, bare Haran, and Moza, .. 1Chr 2:46
C concubine, bare Sheber, and ............ 1Chr 2:48

**CALF**
the herd, and fetcht a *c* tender ............. Gen 18:7
the *c* which he had dressed, and ............ Gen 18:8
after he had made it a molten *c* ............... Ex 32:4
they have made them a molten *c* ............ Ex 32:8
unto the camp, that he saw the *c* .......... Ex 32:19
he took the *c* which they had made ...... Ex 32:20
fire, and there came out this *c* ............... Ex 32:24
people, because they made the *c* ........... Ex 32:35
Take thee a young *c* for a sin .................... Lev 9:2
and a *c* and a lamb, both of the ............... Lev 9:3
slew the *c* of the sin offering, ................... Lev 9:8
God, and had made you a molten *c* ...... Deut 9:16
the *c* which ye had made, and burnt .. Deut 9:21
woman had a fat *c* in the house ........... 1Sa 28:24
they had made them a molten *c* ............ Neh 9:18
cow calveth, and casteth not her *c* ...... Job 21:10
maketh them also to skip like a *c* ........... Ps 29:6
They made a *c* in Horeb, and ................ Ps 106:19
and the *c* and the young lion and the ...... Is 11:6
there shall the *c* feed, and there ............. Is 27:10
me, when they cut the *c* in twain ......... Jer 34:18
passed between the parts of the *c* ......... Jer 34:19
Thy *c*, O Samaria, hath cast thee ............. Hos 8:5
but the *c* of Samaria shall be .................. Hos 8:6
And bring hither the fatted *c* ................ Lk 15:23
father hath killed the fatted *c* .............. Lk 15:27
hast killed for him the fatted *c* ............ Lk 15:30
they made a *c* in those days, and ......... Acts 7:41
and the second beast like a *c* ...................... Rev 4:7

**CALF'S**
was like the sole of a *c* foot ........................ Eze 1:7

**CALKERS**
men thereof were in thee thy *c* ............. Eze 27:9
mariners, and thy pilots, thy *c* ............. Eze 27:27

**CALL**
Adam to see what he would *c* them ..... Gen 2:19
then began men to *c* upon the name ..... Gen 4:26
son, and shalt *c* his name Ishmael ..... Gen 16:11
thou shalt not *c* her name Sarai ......... Gen 17:15
thou shalt *c* his name Isaac .................. Gen 17:19
We will *c* the damsel, and enquire ...... Gen 24:57
the daughters will *c* me blessed ........... Gen 30:13
to pass, when Pharaoh shall *c* you ....... Gen 46:33
*c* to thee a nurse of the Hebrew .................. Ex 2:7
*c* him, that he may eat bread ................... Ex 2:20
one *c* thee, and thou eat of his .............. Ex 34:15
And Moses sent to *c* Dathan ................ Num 16:12
to *c* him, saying, Behold, there ............. Num 22:5
him, If the men come to *c* thee .......... Num 22:20
send unto thee to *c* thee ..................... Num 22:37
but the Moabites *c* them Emims ........... Deut 2:11
the Ammonites *c* them Zamzummims Deut 2:20
Hermon the Sidonians *c* Sirion ................ Deut 3:9
and the Amorites *c* it Shenir .................. Deut 3:9
all things that we *c* upon him for ........... Deut 4:7
I *c* heaven and earth to witness ............ Deut 4:26
elders of his city shall *c* him ............... Deut 25:8
thou shalt *c* them to mind among ........ Deut 30:1

I c heaven and earth to record Deut 30:19
c Joshua, and present yourselves Deut 31:14
c heaven and earth to record Deut 31:28
They shall c the people unto the Deut 33:19
didst not c us to go with thee Judg 12:1
C for Samson, that he may make us. Judg 16:25
and to c peaceably unto them Judg 21:13
C me not Naomi, c me Mara Ruth 1:20
why then c ye me Naomi, seeing Ruth 1:21
for thou didst c me 1Sa 3:6
for thou didst c me 1Sa 3:8
and it shall be, if he c thee 1Sa 3:9
I will c unto the LORD, and he 1Sa 12:17
c Jesse to the sacrifice, and I 1Sa 16:3
sent to c Ahimelech the priest 1Sa 22:11
C now Hushai the Archite also, and 2Sa 17:5
I will c on the LORD, who is 2Sa 22:4
answered and said, C me Bath-sheba 1Kin 1:28
C me Zadok the priest, and Nathan 1Kin 1:32
in all that they c for unto thee 1Kin 8:52
me to c my sin to remembrance 1Kin 17:18
c ye on the name of your gods, and 1Kin 18:24
I will c on the name of the LORD 1Kin 18:24
c on the name of your gods, but 1Kin 18:25
gone to c Micaiah spake unto him 1Kin 22:13
his servant, C this Shunammite 2Kin 4:12
And he said, C her 2Kin 4:15
and said, C this Shunammite 2Kin 4:36
c on the name of the LORD his God 2Kin 5:11
Now therefore c unto me all the 2Kin 10:19
c upon his name, make known his 1Chr 16:8
went to c Micaiah spake to him 2Chr 18:12
C now, if there be any that will Job 5:1
Then c thou, and I will answer Job 13:22
Thou shalt c, and I will answer Job 14:15
will he always c upon God Job 27:10
Hear me when I c, O God of my Ps 4:1
LORD will hear when I c unto him Ps 4:3
eat bread, and c not upon the LORD Ps 14:4
I will c upon the LORD, who is Ps 18:3
let the king hear us when we c Ps 20:9
they c their lands after their Ps 49:11
He shall c to the heavens from Ps 50:4
c upon me in the day of trouble Ps 50:15
As for me, I will c upon God Ps 55:16
all nations shall c him blessed Ps 72:17
I c to remembrance my song in the Ps 77:6
us, and we will c upon thy name Ps 80:18
unto all them that c upon thee Ps 86:5
of my trouble I will c upon thee Ps 86:7
He shall c upon me, and I will Ps 91:15
among them that c upon his name Ps 99:6
in the day when I c answer me Ps 102:2
c upon his name Ps 105:1
therefore will I c upon him as Ps 116:2
c upon the name of the LORD Ps 116:13
will c upon the name of the LORD Ps 116:17
unto all them that c upon him Ps 145:18
to all that c upon him in truth Ps 145:18
Then shall they c upon me Prov 1:28
c understanding thy kinswoman Prov 7:4
Unto you, O men, I c Prov 8:4
To c passengers who go right on Prov 9:15
arise up, and c her blessed Prov 31:28
Woe unto them that c evil good Is 5:20
shall c his name Immanuel Is 7:14
C his name Maher-shalal-hash-baz Is 8:3
c upon his name, declare his Is 12:4
Lord GOD of hosts c to weeping Is 22:12
that I will c my servant Eliakim Is 22:20
will not c back his words Is 31:2
They shall c the nobles thereof Is 34:12
the sun shall he c upon my name Is 41:25
another shall c himself by the Is 44:5
And who, as I, shall c, and shall Is 44:7
which c thee by thy name, am the Is 45:3
For they c themselves of the holy Is 48:2
when I c unto them, they stand up Is 48:13
thou shalt c a nation that thou Is 55:5
c ye upon him while he is near Is 55:6
wilt thou c this a fast, and an Is 58:5
Then shalt thou c, and the LORD Is 58:9
c the sabbath a delight, the holy Is 58:13
and they shall c thee, The city of Is 60:14
but thou shalt c thy walls Is 60:18
shall c you the Ministers of our Is 61:6
And they shall c them, The holy Is 62:12
c his servants by another name Is 65:15
come to pass, that before they c Is 65:24
I will c all the families of the Jer 1:15
At that time they shall c Jer 3:17
and I said, Thou shalt c me Jer 3:19
Reprobate silver shall men c them Jer 6:30
thou shalt also c unto them Jer 7:27
c for the mourning women, that Jer 9:17
families that c not on thy name Jer 10:25
for I will c for a sword upon all Jer 25:29
Then shall ye c upon me, and ye Jer 29:12
C unto me, and I will answer thee, Jer 33:3
C together the archers against Jer 50:29
c together against her the Jer 51:27
men c The perfection of beauty Lam 2:15
but he will c to remembrance the Eze 21:23
I will c for the corn, and will Eze 36:29
I will c for a sword against him Eze 38:21
they shall c it The valley of Eze 39:11
king commanded to c the magicians Dan 2:2
said unto him, C his name Jezreel Hos 1:4
unto him, C her name Lo-ruhamah Hos 1:6
Then said God, C his name Lo-ammi Hos 1:9
LORD, that thou shalt c me Ishi Hos 2:16
and shalt c me no more Baali Hos 2:16
they c to Egypt, they go to Hos 7:11
c a solemn assembly, gather the Joel 1:14
a fast, c a solemn assembly Joel 2:15
that whosoever shall c on the Joel 2:32
the remnant whom the LORD shall c Joel 2:32
they shall c the husbandman to Amos 5:16
c upon thy God, if so be that God Jonah 1:6
that they may all c upon the name Zeph 3:9
hosts, shall ye c every man his Zec 3:10
they shall c on my name, and I Zec 13:9
and they shall c them, The border Mal 1:4
all nations shall c you blessed Mal 3:12
And now we c the proud happy Mal 3:15
thou shalt c his name JESUS Mt 1:21
they shall c his name Emmanuel, Mt 1:23
I am not come to c the righteous Mt 9:13
they c them of his household Mt 10:25
C the labourers, and give them Mt 20:8
sent forth his servants to c them Mt 22:3
doth David in spirit c him Lord Mt 22:43
If David then c him Lord Mt 22:45
c no man your father upon the Mt 23:9
I came not to c the righteous Mk 2:17
they c the blind man, saying unto Mk 10:49
whom ye c the King of the Jews Mk 15:12
they c together the whole band Mk 15:16
thou shalt c his name John Lk 1:13
a son, and shalt c his name JESUS Lk 1:31
generations shall c me blessed Lk 1:48
I came not to c the righteous Lk 5:32
why c ye me, Lord, Lord, and do Lk 6:46
c not thy friends, nor thy Lk 14:12
c the poor, the maimed, the lame, Lk 14:13
c thy husband, and come hither Jn 4:16
Ye c me Master and Lord Jn 13:13
Henceforth I c you not servants Jn 15:15
that whosoever shall c on the Acts 2:21
many as the Lord our God shall c Acts 2:39
to bind all that c on thy name Acts 9:14
c for one Simon, whose surname is Acts 10:5
cleansed, that c not thou common Acts 10:15
not c any man common or unclean Acts 10:28
c hither Simon, whose surname is Acts 10:32
cleansed, that c not thou common Acts 11:9
c for Simon, whose surname is Acts 11:13
took upon them to c over them Acts 19:13
after the way which they c heresy Acts 24:14
season, I will c for thee Acts 24:25
I will c them my people, which Rom 9:25
is rich unto all that c upon him Rom 10:12
For whosoever shall c upon the Rom 10:13
How then shall they c on him in Rom 10:14
with all that in every place c 1Cor 1:2
Moreover I c God for a record 2Cor 1:23
When I c to remembrance the 2Ti 1:5
with them that c on the Lord out 2Ti 2:22
is not ashamed to c them brethren Heb 2:11
But c to remembrance the former Heb 10:32
let him c for the elders of the Jas 5:14
if ye c on the Father, who 1Pet 1:17

**CALLED** See PREFACE.
God c the light Day, and the Gen 1:5
Day, and the darkness he c Night Gen 1:5
God c the firmament Heaven Gen 1:8
And God c the dry land Earth Gen 1:10
together of the waters c he Seas Gen 1:10
whatsoever Adam c every living Gen 2:19
she shall be c Woman, because she Gen 2:23
c their name Adam, in the day Gen 5:2
is the name of it c Babel Gen 11:9
thy name any more be c Abram Gen 17:5
the angel of the LORD c unto him Gen 22:11
shall not be c any more Jacob Gen 35:10
and he c his name Israel Gen 35:10
but his father c him Benjamin Gen 35:18
God c unto him out of the midst Ex 3:4
Then Pharaoh c for Moses and Aaron Ex 8:8
c for Moses and Aaron, and said Ex 9:27
the LORD c unto him out of the Ex 19:3
Moses c all Israel, and said unto Deut 5:1
because it is c the LORD's Deut 15:2
art c by the name of the LORD Deut 28:10
That the LORD c Samuel 1Sa 3:4
for he that is now c a Prophet 1Sa 9:9
whose name is c by the name of 2Sa 6:2
city, and it be c after my name 2Sa 12:28
c all his brethren the king's 1Kin 1:9
c on the name of Baal from 1Kin 18:26
Jabez c on the God of Israel, 1Chr 4:10
offerings, and c upon the LORD 1Chr 21:26
which are c by my name, shall 2Chr 7:14
her, and that she were c by name Est 2:14
the inner court, who is not c Est 4:11
I have c upon thee, for thou wilt Ps 17:6
they have not c upon God Ps 53:4
that have not c upon thy name Ps 79:6
I have c daily upon thee, I have Ps 88:9
Then c I upon the name of the Ps 116:4
and his name shall be c Wonderful Is 9:6
it shall be c The way of holiness Is 35:8
But thou hast not c upon me Is 43:22
which are c by the name of Israel Is 48:1
unto me, O Jacob and Israel, my c Is 48:12
for mine house shall be c an Is 56:7
that they might be c trees of Is 61:3
bring the day that thou hast c Lam 1:21
Thou hast c as in a solemn day my Lam 2:22
thereof is c Bamah unto this day Eze 20:29
now let Daniel be c, and he will Dan 5:12
was born Jesus, who is c Christ Mt 1:16
and he c his name JESUS Mt 1:25
for they shall be c the children Mt 5:9
he shall be c the least in the Mt 5:19
the same shall be c great in the Mt 5:19
is not his mother c Mary Mt 13:55
Jesus c a little child unto him, Mt 18:2
for many be c, but few chosen Mt 20:16
c them, and said, What will ye Mt 20:32
My house shall be c the house of Mt 21:13
But be not ye c Rabbi Mt 23:8
or Jesus which is c Christ Mt 27:17
still, and commanded him to be c Mk 10:49
Peter c to mind the word that Mk 14:72
shall be c the Son of the Highest Lk 1:32
of thee shall be c the Son of God Lk 1:35
kindred that is c by this name Lk 1:61
father, how he would have him c Lk 1:62
the child, his name was c JESUS Lk 2:21
am no more worthy to be c thy son Lk 15:19
these servants to be c unto him Lk 19:15
to the place, which is c Calvary Lk 23:33
him, Before that Philip c thee Jn 1:48
Messias cometh, which is c Christ Jn 4:25
A man that is c Jesus made clay, Jn 9:11
the street which is c Straight Acts 9:11
the disciples were c Christians Acts 11:26
who c for Barnabas and Saul, and Acts 13:7
Gentiles, upon whom my name is c Acts 15:17
be c in question for this day's Acts 19:40
of the dead I am c in question Acts 23:6
Paul the prisoner c me unto him Acts 23:18
c to be an apostle, separated Rom 1:1
are ye also the c of Jesus Christ Rom 1:6
Behold, thou art c a Jew, and Rom 2:17
to them who are the c according Rom 8:28
there shall they be c the Rom 9:26
by whom ye were c unto the 1Cor 1:9
But unto them which are c 1Cor 1:24
mighty, not many noble, are c 1Cor 1:26
if any man that is c a brother be 1Cor 5:11
Is any man c being circumcised 1Cor 7:18
the same calling wherein he was c 1Cor 7:20
Art thou c being a servant 1Cor 7:21
let every man, wherein he is c 1Cor 7:24
c you into the grace of Christ Gal 1:6
ye have been c unto liberty Gal 5:13
who are c Uncircumcision by that Eph 2:11
the vocation wherewith ye are c Eph 4:1
even as ye are c in one hope of Eph 4:4
which also ye are c in one body Col 3:15
himself above all that is c God 2Th 2:4
Whereunto he c you by our gospel, 2Th 2:14
life, whereunto thou art also c 1Ti 6:12
of science falsely so c 1Ti 6:20
daily, while it is c To day Heb 3:13
himself, but he that is c of God Heb 5:4
they which are c might receive Heb 9:15
is not ashamed to be c their God Heb 11:16
refused to be c the son of Heb 11:24
worthy name by the which ye are c Jas 2:7
he was c the Friend of God Jas 2:23
the praises of him who hath c you 1Pet 2:9
For even hereunto were ye c 1Pet 2:21
knowing that ye are thereunto c 1Pet 3:9
of him that hath c us to glory 2Pet 1:3
we should be c the sons of God 1Jn 3:1
preserved in Jesus Christ, and c Jude 1
name of the star is c Wormwood Rev 8:11
which spiritually is c Sodom Rev 11:8
and they that are with him are c Rev 17:14
Blessed are they which are c unto Rev 19:9

**CALLEDST**
us thus, that thou c us not Judg 8:1
for thou c me 1Sa 3:5
Thou c in trouble, and I delivered Ps 81:7
Thus thou c to remembrance the Eze 23:21

**CALLEST**
said unto him, Why c thou me good Mt 19:17
said unto him, Why c thou me good Mk 10:18
said unto him, Why c thou me good Lk 18:19

**CALLETH**
that the stranger c to thee for 1Kin 8:43
that the stranger c to thee for 2Chr 6:33
who c upon God, and he answereth Job 12:4
Deep c unto deep at the noise of Ps 42:7
he c them all by their names Ps 147:4
and his mouth c for strokes Prov 18:6
He c to me out of Seir, Watchman, Is 21:11
he c them all by names by the Is 40:26
None c for justice, nor any Is 59:4
is none that c upon thy name Is 64:7
is none among them that c unto me Hos 7:7
that c for the waters of the sea, Amos 5:8
he that c for the waters of the Amos 9:6
that, said, This man c for Elias Mt 27:47
and c unto him whom he would Mk 3:13
he c thee Mk 10:49
therefore himself c him Lord Mk 12:37
heard it said, Behold, he c Elias Mk 15:35
he c together his friends and Lk 15:6
it, she c her friends and her Lk 15:9
when he c the Lord the God of Lk 20:37
David therefore c him Lord Lk 20:44
he c his own sheep by name, and Jn 10:3
The Master is come, and c for thee Jn 11:28
c those things which be not as Rom 4:17
not of works, but of him that c Rom 9:11

Spirit of God *c* Jesus accursed 1Cor 12:3
cometh not of him that *c* you Gal 5:8
Faithful is he that *c* you 1Th 5:24
which *c* herself a prophetess, to Rev 2:20

**CALLING**
them for the *c* of the assembly Num 10:2
the *c* of assemblies, I cannot Is 1:13
*c* the generations from the Is 41:4
*C* a ravenous bird from the east, Is 46:11
in *c* to remembrance the days of Eze 23:19
markets, and *c* unto their fellows, Mt 11:16
without, sent unto him, *c* him Mk 3:31
Peter *c* to remembrance saith unto Mk 11:21
*c* unto him the centurion, he Mk 15:44
John *c* unto him two of his Lk 7:19
*c* one to another, and saying, We Lk 7:32
*c* upon God, and saying, Lord Jesus Acts 7:59
*c* on the name of the Lord Acts 22:16
*c* of God are without repentance Rom 11:29
For ye see your *c*, brethren, how 1Cor 1:26
the same *c* wherein he was called 1Cor 7:20
know what is the hope of his *c* Eph 1:18
are called in one hope of your *c* Eph 4:4
the high *c* of God in Christ Jesus Phil 3:14
would count you worthy of this *c* 2Th 1:11
us, and called us with an holy *c* 2Ti 1:9
partakers of the heavenly *c* Heb 3:1
Sarah obeyed Abraham, *c* him lord 1Pet 3:6
give diligence to make your *c* 2Pet 1:10

**CALM**
He maketh the storm a *c*, so that Ps 107:29
that the sea may be *c* unto us Jonah 1:11
so shall the sea be *c* unto you Jonah 1:12
and there was a great *c* Mt 8:26
ceased, and there was a great *c* Mk 4:39
and they ceased, and there was a *c* Lk 8:24

**CALNEH** (*cal'-neh*) See CALNO, CANNEH. *A center of Babylonian worship.*
Babel, and Erech, and Accad, and C Gen 10:10
Pass ye unto C, and see Amos 6:2

**CALNO** (*cal'-no*) See CALNEH. *Same as Calneh.*
Is not C as Carchemish Is 10:9

**CALVARY**
to the place, which is called C Lk 23:33

**CALVE**
thou mark when the hinds do *c* Job 39:1
of the LORD maketh the hinds to *c* Ps 29:9

**CALVED**
Yea, the hind also *c* in the field Jer 14:5

**CALVES**
bring their *c* home from them 1Sa 6:7
cart, and shut up their *c* at home 1Sa 6:10
and took sheep, and oxen, and *c* 1Sa 14:32
counsel, and made two *c* of gold 1Kin 12:28
unto the *c* that he had made 1Kin 12:32
the golden *c* that were in Beth-el 2Kin 10:29
them molten images, even two *c* 2Kin 17:16
for the *c* which he had made 2Chr 11:15
and there are with you golden *c* 2Chr 13:8
with the *c* of the people, till Ps 68:30
because of the *c* of Beth-aven Hos 10:5
the men that sacrifice kiss the *c* Hos 13:2
will we render the *c* of our lips Hos 14:2
the *c* out of the midst of the Amos 6:4
offerings, with *c* of a year old Mic 6:6
grow up as *c* of the stall Mal 4:2
by the blood of goats and *c* Heb 9:12
the law, he took the blood of *c* Heb 9:19

**CALVETH**
their cow *c*, and casteth not her Job 21:10

**CAME** See PREFACE.

**CAMEL**
saw Isaac, she lighted off the *c* Gen 24:64
as the *c*, because he cheweth the Lev 11:4
as the *c*, and the hare, and the Deut 14:7
and suckling, ox and sheep, *c* 1Sa 15:3
the horse, of the mule, of the *c* Zec 14:15
It is easier for a *c* to go Mt 19:24
strain at a gnat, and swallow a *c* Mt 23:24
It is easier for a *c* to go Mk 10:25
For it is easier for a *c* to go Lk 18:25

**CAMEL'S**
and put them in the *c* furniture Gen 31:34
John had his raiment of *c* hair Mt 3:4
And John was clothed with *c* hair Mk 1:6

**CAMELS**
maidservants, and she asses, and *c* Gen 12:16
ten *c* of the *c* of his master Gen 24:10
he made his *c* to kneel down Gen 24:11
and I will give thy *c* drink also Gen 24:14
I will draw water for thy *c* also Gen 24:19
draw water, and drew for all his *c* Gen 24:20
as the *c* had done drinking, that Gen 24:22
he stood by the *c* at the well Gen 24:30
the house, and room for the *c* Gen 24:31
and he ungirded his *c* Gen 24:32
gave straw and provender for the *c* Gen 24:32
and maidservants, and *c*, and asses Gen 24:35
and I will also draw for thy *c* Gen 24:44
and I will give thy *c* drink also Gen 24:46
and she made the *c* drink also Gen 24:46
damsels, and they rode upon the *c* Gen 24:61
and, behold, the *c* were coming Gen 24:63
and menservants, and *c*, and asses Gen 30:43
set his sons and his wives upon *c* Gen 31:17
and the flocks, and herds, and the *c* Gen 32:7
Thirty milch *c* with their colts, Gen 32:15
with their *c* bearing spicery Gen 37:25
upon the asses, upon the *c* Ex 9:3
their *c* were without number Judg 6:5
their *c* were without number, as Judg 7:12
the oxen, and the asses, and the *c* 1Sa 27:9
young men, which rode upon *c* 1Sa 30:17
with *c* that bare spices, and very 1Kin 10:2
of their *c* fifty thousand, and of 1Chr 5:21
brought bread on asses, and on *c* 1Chr 12:40
Over the *c* also was Obil the 1Chr 27:30
*c* that bare spices, and gold in 2Chr 9:1
*c* in abundance, and returned to 2Chr 14:15
Their *c*, four hundred thirty and Ezr 2:67
Their *c*, four hundred thirty and Neh 7:69
horseback, and riders on mules, *c* Est 8:10
*c* went out, being hastened and Est 8:14
sheep, and three thousand *c* Job 1:3
three bands, and fell upon the *c* Job 1:17
thousand sheep, and six thousand *c* Job 42:12
of asses, and a chariot of *c* Is 21:7
treasures upon the bunches of *c* Is 30:6
multitude of *c* shall cover thee Is 60:6
and all their vessels, and their *c* Jer 49:29
their *c* shall be a booty, and the Jer 49:32
I will make Rabbah a stable for *c* Eze 25:5

**CAMELS'**
that were on their *c* necks Judg 8:21
that were about their *c* necks Judg 8:26
forty *c* burden, and came and stood 2Kin 8:9

**CAMEST**
Sarai's maid, whence *c* thou Gen 16:8
unto the land from whence thou *c* Gen 24:5
I have eaten of all before thou *c* Gen 27:33
for in it thou *c* out from Egypt Ex 23:15
month Abib thou *c* out from Egypt Ex 34:18
wherefore *c* thou not unto me Num 22:37
the children of Ammon thou *c* not Deut 2:37
for thou *c* forth out of the land Deut 16:3
remember the day when thou *c* Deut 16:3
that thou *c* forth out of Egypt Deut 16:6
that thou *c* not within the days 1Sa 13:11
he said, Why *c* thou down hither 1Sa 17:28
*C* thou not from thy journey 2Sa 11:10
Whereas thou *c* but yesterday, 2Sa 15:20
again by the same way that thou *c* 1Kin 13:9
the man of God that *c* from Judah 1Kin 13:14
to go by the way that thou *c* 1Kin 13:17
But *c* back, and hast eaten bread 1Kin 13:22
back by the way by which thou *c* 2Kin 19:28
Thou *c* down also upon mount Sinai Neh 9:13
back by the way by which thou *c* Is 37:29
we looked not for, thou *c* down Is 64:3
before thou *c* forth out of the Jer 1:5
thou *c* forth with thy rivers, and Eze 32:2
how *c* thou in hither not having a Mt 22:12
him, Rabbi, when *c* thou hither Jn 6:25
that thou *c* forth from God Jn 16:30
unto thee in the way as thou *c* Acts 9:17

**CAMON** (*ca'-mon*) *A town in Gilead.*
And Jair died, and was buried in C Judg 10:5

**CAMP**
which went before the *c* of Israel Ex 14:19
between the *c* of the Egyptians Ex 14:20
the Egyptians and the *c* of Israel Ex 14:20
quails came up, and covered the *c* Ex 16:13
people that was in the *c* trembled Ex 19:16
out of the *c* to meet with God Ex 19:17
thou burn with fire without the *c* Ex 29:14
There is a noise of war in the *c* Ex 32:17
soon as he came nigh unto the *c* Ex 32:19
Moses stood in the gate of the *c* Ex 32:26
gate to gate throughout the *c* Ex 32:27
the *c*, afar off from the *c* Ex 33:7
which was without the *c* Ex 33:7
And he turned again into the *c* Ex 33:11
to be proclaimed throughout the *c* Ex 36:6
without the *c* unto a clean place Lev 4:12
forth the bullock without the *c* Lev 4:21
without the *c* unto a clean place Lev 6:11
he burnt with fire without the *c* Lev 8:17
he burnt with fire without the *c* Lev 9:11
before the sanctuary out of the *c* Lev 10:4
them in their coats out of the *c* Lev 10:5
without the *c* shall his Lev 13:46
shall go forth out of the *c* Lev 14:3
that he shall come into the *c* Lev 14:8
and afterward come into the *c* Lev 16:26
one carry forth without the *c* Lev 16:27
he shall come into the *c* Lev 16:28
an ox, or lamb, or goat, in the *c* Lev 17:3
or that killeth it out of the *c* Lev 17:3
Israel strove together in the *c* Lev 24:10
that hath cursed without the *c* Lev 24:14
him that had cursed out of the *c* Lev 24:23
tents, every man by his own *c* Num 1:52
they of the standard of the *c* of Num 2:3
in the *c* of Judah were an hundred Num 2:9
*c* of Reuben according to their Num 2:10
the *c* of Reuben were an hundred Num 2:16
shall set forward with the *c* of Num 2:17
the Levites in the midst of the *c* Num 2:17
shall be the standard of the *c* of Num 2:18
the *c* of Ephraim were an hundred Num 2:24
The standard of the *c* of Dan Num 2:25
they that were numbered in the *c* Num 2:31
when the *c* setteth forward, Aaron Num 4:5
as the *c* is to set forward Num 4:15
they put out of the *c* every leper Num 5:2
without the *c* shall ye put them Num 5:3
so, and put them out without the *c* Num 5:4
of the *c* of the children of Judah Num 10:14
the standard of the *c* of Reuben Num 10:18
the standard of the *c* of the Num 10:22
the standard of the *c* of the Num 10:25
day, when they went out of the *c* Num 10:34
in the uttermost parts of the *c* Num 11:1
dew fell upon the *c* in the night Num 11:9
remained two of the men in the *c* Num 11:26
and they prophesied in the *c* Num 11:26
and Medad do prophesy in the *c* Num 11:27
And Moses gat him into the *c* Num 11:30
sea, and let them fall by the *c* Num 11:31
the other side, round about the *c* Num 11:31
for themselves round about the *c* Num 11:32
be shut out from the *c* seven days Num 12:14
shut out from the *c* seven days Num 12:15
Moses, departed not out of the *c* Num 14:44
him with stones without the *c* Num 15:35
brought him without the *c* Num 15:36
may bring her forth without the *c* Num 19:3
he shall come into the *c*, and the Num 19:7
up without the *c* in a clean place Num 19:9
unto the *c* at the plains of Moab, Num 31:12
forth to meet them without the *c* Num 31:13
ye abide without the *c* seven days Num 31:19
ye shall come into the *c* Num 31:24
shall he go abroad out of the *c* Deut 23:10
he shall not come within the *c* Deut 23:10
he shall come into the *c* again Deut 23:11
have a place also without the *c* Deut 23:12
God walketh in the midst of thy *c* Deut 23:14
therefore shall thy *c* be holy Deut 23:14
and thy stranger that is in thy *c* Deut 29:11
abode in their places in the *c* Josh 5:8
into the *c*, and lodged in the *c* Josh 6:11
city once, and returned into the *c* Josh 6:14
make the *c* of Israel a curse, and Josh 6:18
left them without the *c* of Israel Josh 6:23
to Joshua unto the *c* at Gilgal Josh 9:6
unto Joshua to the *c* to Gilgal Josh 10:6
with him, unto the *c* to Gilgal Josh 10:15
*c* to Joshua at Makkedah in peace Josh 10:21
with him, unto the *c* to Gilgal Josh 10:43
I come to the outside of the *c* Judg 7:17
also on every side of all the *c* Judg 7:18
came unto the outside of the *c* in Judg 7:19
in his place round about the *c* Judg 7:21
in the *c* of Dan between Zorah Judg 13:25
there came none to the *c* from Judg 21:8
brought them unto the *c* to Shiloh Judg 21:12
the people were come into the *c* 1Sa 4:3
of the LORD came into the *c* 1Sa 4:5
shout in the *c* of the Hebrews 1Sa 4:6
of the LORD was come into the *c* 1Sa 4:6
they said, God is come into the *c* 1Sa 4:7
the *c* of the Philistines in three 1Sa 13:17
went up with them into the *c* from 1Sa 14:21
out of the *c* of the Philistines 1Sa 17:4
run to the *c* to thy brethren 1Sa 17:17
go down with me to Saul to the *c* 1Sa 26:6
a man came out of the *c* from Saul 2Sa 1:2
Out of the *c* of Israel am I 2Sa 1:3
over Israel that day in the *c* 1Kin 16:16
when they came to the *c* of Israel 2Kin 3:24
and such a place shall be my *c* 2Kin 6:8
to go unto the *c* of the Syrians 2Kin 7:5
uttermost part of the *c* of Syria 2Kin 7:5
even the *c* as it was, and fled for 2Kin 7:7
to the uttermost part of the *c* 2Kin 7:8
We came to the *c* of the Syrians 2Kin 7:10
are they gone out of the *c* to 2Kin 7:12
smote in the *c* of the Assyrians 2Kin 19:35
to the *c* had slain all the eldest 2Chr 22:1
captains in the *c* of the king of 2Chr 32:21
it fall in the midst of their *c* Ps 78:28
They envied Moses also in the *c* Ps 106:16
I will *c* against thee round about Is 29:3
smote in the *c* of the Assyrians Is 37:36
the bow, *c* against it round about Jer 50:29
set the *c* also against it, and set Eze 4:2
for his *c* is very great Joel 2:11
which *c* in the hedges in the cold Nah 3:17
for sin, are burned without the *c* Heb 13:11
therefore unto him without the *c* Heb 13:13
compassed the *c* of the saints Rev 20:9

**CAMPED**
there Israel *c* before the mount Ex 19:2

**CAMPHIRE**
is unto me as a cluster of *c* in Song 1:14
*c*, with spikenard, Song 4:13

**CAMPS**
*c* throughout their hosts were six Num 2:32
that they defile not their *c* Num 5:3
and for the journeying of the *c* Num 10:2
then the *c* that lie on the east Num 10:5
then the *c* that lie on the south Num 10:6
all the *c* throughout their hosts Num 10:25
*c* to come up unto your nostrils Amos 4:10

**CAN**
is greater than I *c* bear Gen 4:13
so that if a man *c* number the Gen 13:16
what *c* I do this day unto these Gen 31:43

how then c I do this great — Gen 39:9
there is none that c interpret it — Gen 41:15
C we find such a one as this is, — Gen 41:38
food, as much as they c carry — Gen 44:1
a man as I c certainly divine — Gen 44:15
I know that he c speak well — Ex 4:14
get you straw where ye c find it — Ex 5:11
young pigeons, such as he c get — Lev 14:30
Who c count the dust of Jacob, and — Num 23:10
How c I myself alone bear your — Deut 1:12
that c do according to thy works, — Deut 3:24
how c I dispossess them — Deut 7:17
Who c stand before the children — Deut 9:2
I c no more go out and come in — Deut 31:2
any that c deliver out of my hand — Deut 32:39
if ye c certainly declare it me — Judg 14:12
peradventure he c shew us our way — 1Sa 9:6
And Samuel said, How c I go — 1Sa 16:2
me now a man that c play well — 1Sa 16:17
what c he have more but the — 1Sa 18:8
for who c stretch forth his hand — 1Sa 26:9
shalt know what thy servant c do — 1Sa 28:2
what c David say more unto thee — 2Sa 7:20
Who c tell whether God will be — 2Sa 12:22
c I bring him back again — 2Sa 12:23
none c turn to the right hand or — 2Sa 14:19
me every thing that ye c hear — 2Sa 15:36
c I discern between good and evil — 2Sa 19:35
c thy servant taste what I eat or — 2Sa 19:35
c I hear any more the voice of — 2Sa 19:35
c skill to hew timber like unto — 1Kin 5:6
What c David speak more to thee — 1Chr 17:18
for who c judge this thy people, — 2Chr 1:10
that c skill to grave with the — 2Chr 2:7
for I know that thy servants c — 2Chr 2:8
For how c I endure to see the — Est 8:6
or how c I endure to see the — Est 8:6
when they c find the grave — Job 3:22
but who c withhold himself from — Job 4:2
C that which is unsavoury be — Job 6:6
C the rush grow up without mire — Job 8:11
c the flag grow without water — Job 8:11
he taketh away, who c hinder him — Job 9:12
there is none that c deliver out — Job 10:7
together, then who c hinder him — Job 11:10
a man, and there c be no opening — Job 12:14
Who c bring a clean thing out of — Job 14:4
wherewith he c do no good — Job 15:3
C a man be profitable unto God, — Job 22:2
c he judge through the dark cloud — Job 22:13
what c the Almighty do for them — Job 22:17
is in one mind, and who c turn him — Job 23:13
How then c man be justified with — Job 25:4
or how c he be clean that is born — Job 25:4
of his power who c understand — Job 26:14
who then c make trouble — Job 34:29
his face, who then c behold him — Job 34:29
or who c say, Thou hast wrought — Job 36:23
neither c the number of his years — Job 36:26
Also c any understand the — Job 36:29
Who c number the clouds in wisdom — Job 38:37
or who c stay the bottles of — Job 38:37
thine own right hand c save thee — Job 40:14
he that made him c make his sword — Job 40:19
he trusteth that he c draw up — Job 40:23
Who c discover the face of his — Job 41:13
or who c come to him with his — Job 41:13
Who c open the doors of his face — Job 41:14
that no air c come between them — Job 41:16
that no thought c be withholden — Job 42:2
what c the righteous do — Ps 11:3
Who c understand his errors — Ps 19:12
none c keep alive his own soul — Ps 22:29
they are more than c be numbered — Ps 40:5
None of them c by any means — Ps 49:7
not fear what flesh c do unto me — Ps 56:4
be afraid what man c do unto me — Ps 56:11
your pots c feel the thorns — Ps 58:9
C God furnish a table in the — Ps 78:19
c he give bread also — Ps 78:20
c he provide flesh for his people — Ps 78:20
For who in the heaven c be — Ps 89:6
mighty c be likened unto the Lord — Ps 89:6
Who c utter the mighty acts of — Ps 106:2
who c shew forth all his praise — Ps 106:2
what c man do unto me — Ps 118:6
who c stand before his cold — Ps 147:17
C a man take fire in his bosom, — Prov 6:27
C one go upon hot coals, and his — Prov 6:28
but a wounded spirit who c bear — Prov 18:14
but a faithful man who c find — Prov 20:6
Who c say, I have made my heart — Prov 20:9
how c a man then understand his — Prov 20:24
seven men that c render a reason — Prov 26:16
Who c find a virtuous woman — Prov 31:10
for what c the man do that cometh — Eccl 2:12
For who c eat, or who else c — Eccl 2:25
or who else c hasten hereunto, — Eccl 2:25
so that no man c find out the — Eccl 3:11
nothing c be put to it, nor any — Eccl 3:14
but how c one be warm alone — Eccl 4:11
for who c tell a man what shall — Eccl 6:12
for who c make that straight, — Eccl 7:13
exceeding deep, who c find it out — Eccl 7:24
for who c tell him when it shall — Eccl 8:7
be after him, who c tell him — Eccl 10:14
neither c the floods drown it — Song 8:7
a man c stretch himself on it — Is 28:20
than that he c wrap himself in it — Is 28:20
death c not celebrate thee — Is 38:18
who among them c declare this — Is 43:9
there is none that c deliver out — Is 43:13
yet c he not answer, nor save him — Is 46:7
C a woman forget her sucking — Is 49:15
dogs which c never have enough — Is 56:11
cisterns, that c hold no water — Jer 2:13
her occasion who c turn her away — Jer 2:24
if they c save thee in the time — Jer 2:28
C a maid forget her ornaments, or — Jer 2:32
burn that none c quench it — Jer 4:4
if ye c find a man, if there be — Jer 5:1
yet c they not prevail — Jer 5:22
yet c they not pass over it — Jer 5:22
so that none c pass through them — Jer 9:10
neither c men hear the voice of — Jer 9:10
C the Ethiopian change his skin, — Jer 13:23
of the Gentiles that c cause rain — Jer 14:22
or c the heavens give showers — Jer 14:22
who c know it? — Jer 17:9
and burn that none c quench it — Jer 21:12
C any hide himself in secret — Jer 23:24
If heaven above c be measured — Jer 31:37
If ye c break my covenant of the — Jer 33:20
that c do any thing against you — Jer 38:5
How c it be quiet, seeing the — Jer 47:7
who c heal thee? — Lam 2:13
C thine heart endure, or c — Eze 22:14
or c thine hands be strong, in — Eze 22:14
secret that they c hide from thee — Eze 28:3
c play well on an instrument — Eze 33:32
Son of man, c these bones live — Eze 37:3
I shall know that ye c shew me — Dan 2:9
that c shew the king's matter — Dan 2:10
that c shew it before the king — Dan 2:11
that c deliver after this sort — Dan 3:29
none c stay his hand, or say unto — Dan 4:35
For how c the servant of this my — Dan 10:17
and who c abide it? — Joel 2:11
C two walk together, except they — Amos 3:3
C a bird fall in a snare upon the — Amos 3:5
hath spoken, who c but prophesy — Amos 3:8
Who c tell if God will turn and — Jonah 3:9
none evil c come upon us — Mic 3:11
in pieces, and none c deliver — Mic 5:8
Who c stand before his — Nah 1:6
who c abide in the fierceness of — Nah 1:6
No man c serve two masters — Mt 6:24
c add one cubit unto his stature — Mt 6:27
neither c a corrupt tree bring — Mt 7:18
unto them, C the children of the — Mt 9:15
Or else how c one enter into a — Mt 12:29
O generation of vipers, how c ye — Mt 12:34
ye c discern the face of the sky — Mt 16:3
but c ye not discern the signs of — Mt 16:3
saying, Who then c be saved — Mt 19:25
how c ye escape the damnation of — Mt 23:33
your way, make it as sure as ye c — Mt 27:65
who c forgive sins but God only — Mk 2:7
unto them, C the children of the — Mk 2:19
How c Satan cast out Satan — Mk 3:23
No man c enter into a strong — Mk 3:27
entering into him c defile him — Mk 7:15
From whence c a man satisfy these — Mk 8:4
no fuller on earth c white them — Mk 9:3
This kind c come forth by nothing — Mk 9:29
that c lightly speak evil of me — Mk 9:39
themselves, Who then c be saved — Mk 10:26
c ye drink of the cup that I — Mk 10:38
And they said unto him, We c — Mk 10:39
Who c forgive sins, but God alone — Lk 5:21
C ye make the children of the — Lk 5:34
C the blind lead the blind — Lk 6:39
that have no more that they c do — Lk 12:4
of you with taking thought c add — Lk 12:25
ye c discern the face of the sky — Lk 12:56
No servant c serve two masters — Lk 16:13
neither c they pass to us, that — Lk 16:26
it said, Who then c be saved — Lk 18:26
Neither c they die any more — Lk 20:36
C there any good thing come out — Jn 1:46
for no man c do these miracles — Jn 3:2
How c a man be born when he is — Jn 3:4
c he enter the second time into — Jn 3:4
unto him, How c these things be — Jn 3:9
A man c receive nothing, except — Jn 3:27
The Son c do nothing of himself, — Jn 5:19
I c of mine own self do nothing — Jn 5:30
How c ye believe, which receive — Jn 5:44
No man c come to me, except the — Jn 6:44
How c this man give us his flesh — Jn 6:52
who c hear it? — Jn 6:60
that no man c come unto me, — Jn 6:65
night cometh, when no man c work — Jn 9:4
How c a man that is a sinner do — Jn 9:16
C a devil open the eyes of the — Jn 10:21
and how c we know the way — Jn 14:5
no more c ye, except ye abide in — Jn 15:4
for without me ye c do nothing — Jn 15:5
And he said, How c I, except some — Acts 8:31
C any man forbid water, that — Acts 10:47
Neither c they prove the things — Acts 24:13
law of God, neither indeed c be — Rom 8:7
be for us, who c be against us — Rom 8:31
neither c he know them, because — 1Cor 2:14
For other foundation c no man lay — 1Cor 3:11
that no man c say that Jesus is — 1Cor 12:3
For we c do nothing against the — 2Cor 13:8
I c do all things through Christ — Phil 4:13
For what thanks c we render to — 1Th 3:9
it is certain we c carry nothing — 1Ti 6:7
which no man c approach unto — 1Ti 6:16
whom no man hath seen, nor c see — 1Ti 6:16
Who c have compassion on the — Heb 5:2
c never with those sacrifices — Heb 10:1
which c never take away sins — Heb 10:11
c faith save him? — Jas 2:14
But the tongue c no man tame — Jas 3:8
C the fig tree, my brethren, bear — Jas 3:12
so c no fountain both yield salt — Jas 3:12
how c he love God whom he hath — 1Jn 4:20
an open door, and no man c shut it — Rev 3:8
which neither c see, nor hear, — Rev 9:20

**CANA** (*ca'-nah*) *A village in Galilee.*
was a marriage in C of Galilee — Jn 2:1
did Jesus in C of Galilee — Jn 2:11
came again into C of Galilee — Jn 4:46
and Nathanael of C in Galilee — Jn 21:2

**CANAAN** (*ca'-na-an*) See Canaanite.
*1. Son of Ham.*
and Ham is the father of C — Gen 9:18
And Ham, the father of C, saw the — Gen 9:22
And he said, Cursed be C — Gen 9:25
and C shall be his servant — Gen 9:26
and C shall be his servant — Gen 9:27
Cush, and Mizraim, and Phut, and C — Gen 10:6
C begat Sidon his firstborn, and — Gen 10:15
Cush, and Mizraim, Put, and C — 1Chr 1:8
C begat Zidon his firstborn, and — 1Chr 1:13
*2. Place where Canaanites dwell.*
to go into the land of C — Gen 11:31
forth to go into the land of C — Gen 12:5
and into the land of C they came — Gen 12:5
Abram dwelled in the land of C — Gen 13:12
dwelt ten years in the land of C — Gen 16:3
art a stranger, all the land of C — Gen 17:8
same is Hebron in the land of C — Gen 23:2
same is Hebron in the land of C — Gen 23:19
take a wife of the daughters of C — Gen 28:1
take a wife of the daughters of C — Gen 28:6
of C pleased not Isaac his father — Gen 28:8
Isaac his father in the land of C — Gen 31:18
which is in the land of C — Gen 33:18
to Luz, which is in the land of C — Gen 35:6
his wives of the daughters of C — Gen 36:2
born unto him in the land of C — Gen 36:5
which he had got in the land of C — Gen 36:6
was a stranger, in the land of C — Gen 37:1
the famine was in the land of C — Gen 42:5
From the land of C to buy food — Gen 42:7
sons of one man in the land of C — Gen 42:13
their father unto the land of C — Gen 42:29
with our father in the land of C — Gen 42:32
unto thee out of the land of C — Gen 44:8
and go, get you unto the land of C — Gen 45:17
came into the land of C unto — Gen 45:25
they had gotten in the land of C — Gen 46:6
Er and Onan died in the land of C — Gen 46:12
which were in the land of C — Gen 46:31
are come out of the land of C — Gen 47:1
famine is sore in the land of C — Gen 47:4
all the land of C fainted by — Gen 47:13
of Egypt, and in the land of C — Gen 47:14
of Egypt, and in the land of C — Gen 47:15
unto me at Luz in the land of C — Gen 48:3
by me in the land of C in the way — Gen 48:7
is before Mamre, in the land of C — Gen 49:30
digged for me in the land of C — Gen 50:5
carried him into the land of C — Gen 50:13
them, to give them the land of C — Ex 6:4
inhabitants of C shall melt away — Ex 15:15
unto the borders of the land of C — Ex 16:35
ye be come into the land of C — Lev 14:34
after the doings of the land of C — Lev 18:3
Egypt, to give you the land of C — Lev 25:38
they may search the land of C — Num 13:2
them to spy out the land of C — Num 13:17
Er and Onan died in the land of C — Num 26:19
among you in the land of C — Num 32:30
the Lord into the land of C — Num 32:32
in the south in the land of C — Num 33:40
over Jordan into the land of C — Num 33:51
When ye come into the land of C — Num 34:2
even the land of C with the — Num 34:2
of Israel in the land of C — Num 34:29
over Jordan into the land of C — Num 35:10
shall ye give in the land of C — Num 35:14
and behold the land of C, which I — Deut 32:49
fruit of the land of C that year — Josh 5:12
Israel inherited in the land of C — Josh 14:1
them at Shiloh in the land of C — Josh 21:2
Shiloh, which is in the land of C — Josh 22:9
Jordan, that are in the land of C — Josh 22:10
altar over against the land of C — Josh 22:11
of Gilead, unto the land of C — Josh 22:32
him throughout all the land of C — Josh 24:3
had not known all the wars of C — Judg 3:1
into the hand of Jabin king of C — Judg 4:2
C before the children of Israel — Judg 4:23
against Jabin the king of C — Judg 4:24
had destroyed Jabin king of C — Judg 4:24
then fought the kings of C in — Judg 5:19
Shiloh, which is in the land of C — Judg 21:12
thee will I give the land of C — 1Chr 16:18
thee will I give the land of C — Ps 105:11
sacrificed unto the idols of C — Ps 106:38
Bashan, and all the kingdoms of C — Ps 135:11
of Egypt speak the language of C — Is 19:18
thy nativity is of the land of C — Eze 16:3
in the land of C unto Chaldea — Eze 16:29

O *C*, the land of the Philistines, ... Zeph 2:5
a woman of *C* came out of the same ... Mt 15:22

**CANAANITE** (*ca'-na-an-ite*) See CANAANITES, CANAANITESS, CANAANITISH, ZELOTES.
*Descendants of Canaan.*
the *C* was then in the land ... Gen 12:6
and the *C* and the Perizzite dwelled ... Gen 13:7
there a daughter of a certain *C* ... Gen 38:2
shall drive out the Hivite, the *C* ... Ex 23:28
and I will drive out the *C* ... Ex 33:2
before thee the Amorite, and the *C* ... Ex 34:11
And when king Arad the *C*, which ... Num 21:1
And king Arad the *C*, which dwelt ... Num 33:40
Hittite, and the Amorite, the *C* ... Josh 9:1
to the *C* on the east and on the ... Josh 11:3
which is counted to the *C* ... Josh 13:3
the *C* in the house of the LORD of ... Zec 14:21
Simon the *C*, and Judas Iscariot, ... Mt 10:4
and Thaddaeus, and Simon the *C* ... Mk 3:18

**CANAANITES** (*ca'-na-an-ites*)
families of the *C* spread abroad ... Gen 10:18
border of the *C* was from Sidon ... Gen 10:19
And the Amorites, and the *C* ... Gen 15:21
my son of the daughters of the *C* ... Gen 24:3
my son of the daughters of the *C* ... Gen 24:37
of the land, among the *C* and the ... Gen 34:30
inhabitants of the land, the *C* ... Gen 50:11
unto the place of the *C*, and the ... Ex 3:8
of Egypt unto the land of the *C* ... Ex 3:17
bring thee into the land of the *C* ... Ex 13:5
bring thee into the land of the *C* ... Ex 13:11
and the Perizzites, and the *C* ... Ex 23:23
the *C* dwell by the sea, and by the ... Num 13:29
the *C* dwelt in the valley ... Num 14:25
the *C* are there before you, and ye ... Num 14:43
the *C* which dwelt in that hill, ... Num 14:45
of Israel, and delivered up the *C* ... Num 21:3
sea side, to the land of the *C* ... Deut 1:7
and the Amorites, and the *C* ... Deut 7:1
goeth down, in the land of the *C* ... Deut 11:30
Hittites, and the Amorites, the *C* ... Deut 20:17
drive out from before you the *C* ... Josh 3:10
and all the kings of the *C* ... Josh 5:1
For the *C* and all the inhabitants ... Josh 7:9
Hittites, the Amorites, and the *C* ... Josh 12:8
the south, all the land of the *C* ... Josh 13:4
not out the *C* that dwelt in Gezer ... Josh 16:10
but the *C* dwell among the ... Josh 16:10
but the *C* would dwell in that ... Josh 17:12
that they put the *C* to tribute ... Josh 17:13
all the *C* that dwell in the land ... Josh 17:16
for thou shalt drive out the *C* ... Josh 17:18
and the Perizzites, and the *C* ... Josh 24:11
go up for us against the *C* first ... Judg 1:1
that we may fight against the *C* ... Judg 1:3
and the LORD delivered the *C* ... Judg 1:4
against him, and they slew the *C* ... Judg 1:5
went down to fight against the *C* ... Judg 1:9
the *C* that dwelt in Hebron ... Judg 1:10
they slew the *C* that inhabited ... Judg 1:17
but the *C* would dwell in that ... Judg 1:27
that they put the *C* to tribute ... Judg 1:28
out the *C* that dwelt in Gezer ... Judg 1:29
but the *C* dwelt in Gezer among ... Judg 1:29
but the *C* dwelt among them, and ... Judg 1:30
the Asherites dwelt among the *C* ... Judg 1:32
but he dwelt among the *C*, the ... Judg 1:33
of the Philistines, and all the *C* ... Judg 3:3
of Israel dwelt among the *C* ... Judg 3:5
of the Hivites, and of the *C* ... 2Sa 24:7
slain the *C* that dwelt in the ... 1Kin 9:16
their abominations, even of the *C* ... Ezr 9:1
him to give the land of the *C* ... Neh 9:8
inhabitants of the land, the *C* ... Neh 9:24
shall possess that of the *C* ... Obad 20

**CANAANITESS** (*ca'-na-an-ite-ess*)
him of the daughter of Shua the *C* ... 1Chr 2:3

**CANAANITISH** (*ca'-na-an-i-tish*)
and Shaul the son of a *C* woman ... Gen 46:10
and Shaul the son of a *C* woman ... Ex 6:15

**CANDACE** (*can'-da-see*) *Name for a dynasty of Ethiopian queens.*
under *C* queen of the Ethiopians ... Acts 8:27

**CANDLE**
his *c* shall be put out with him ... Job 18:6
How oft is the *c* of the wicked ... Job 21:17
When his *c* shined upon my head, ... Job 29:3
For thou wilt light my *c* ... Ps 18:28
of man is the *c* of the LORD ... Prov 20:27
the *c* of the wicked shall be put ... Prov 24:20
her *c* goeth not out by night ... Prov 31:18
millstones, and the light of the *c* ... Jer 25:10
Neither do men light a *c*, and put ... Mt 5:15
Is a *c* brought to be put under a ... Mk 4:21
No man, when he hath lighted a *c* ... Lk 8:16
No man, when he hath lighted a *c* ... Lk 11:33
of a *c* doth give thee light ... Lk 11:36
one piece, doth not light a *c* ... Lk 15:8
the light of a *c* shall shine no ... Rev 18:23
and they need no *c*, neither light ... Rev 22:5

**CANDLES**
I will search Jerusalem with *c* ... Zeph 1:12

**CANDLESTICK**
thou shalt make a *c* of pure gold ... Ex 25:31
beaten work shall the *c* be made ... Ex 25:31
of the *c* out of the one side ... Ex 25:32
of the *c* out of the other side ... Ex 25:32
branches that come out of the *c* ... Ex 25:33
in the *c* shall be four bowls made ... Ex 25:34
that proceed out of the *c* ... Ex 25:35
the *c* over against the table on ... Ex 26:35
and all his vessels, and the *c* ... Ex 30:27
the pure *c* with all his furniture ... Ex 31:8
The *c* also for the light, and his ... Ex 35:14
he made the *c* of pure gold ... Ex 37:17
of beaten work made he the *c* ... Ex 37:17
three branches of the *c* out of ... Ex 37:18
three branches of the *c* out of ... Ex 37:18
six branches going out of the *c* ... Ex 37:19
in the *c* were four bowls made ... Ex 37:20
The pure *c*, with the lamps ... Ex 39:37
and thou shalt bring in the *c* ... Ex 40:4
he put the *c* in the tent of the ... Ex 40:24
*c* before the LORD continually ... Lev 24:4
the ark, and the table, and the *c* ... Num 3:31
cover the *c* of the light, and his ... Num 4:9
give light over against the *c* ... Num 8:2
lamps thereof over against the *c* ... Num 8:3
this work of the *c* was of beaten ... Num 8:4
shewed Moses, so he made the *c* ... Num 8:4
and a table, and a stool, and a *c* ... 2Kin 4:10
of gold, by weight for every *c* ... 1Chr 28:15
silver by weight, both for the *c* ... 1Chr 28:15
according to the use of every *c* ... 1Chr 28:15
the *c* of gold with the lamps ... 2Chr 13:11
wrote over against the *c* upon the ... Dan 5:5
behold a *c* all of gold, with a ... Zec 4:2
upon the right side of the *c* ... Zec 4:11
put it under a bushel, but on a *c* ... Mt 5:15
and not to be set on a *c* ... Mk 4:21
but setteth it on a *c*, that they ... Lk 8:16
under a bushel, but on a *c* ... Lk 11:33
the first, wherein was the *c* ... Heb 9:2
will remove thy *c* out of his ... Rev 2:5

**CANDLESTICKS**
the *c* of pure gold, five on the ... 1Kin 7:49
Even the weight for the *c* of gold ... 1Chr 28:15
for the *c* of silver by weight, ... 1Chr 28:15
he made ten *c* of gold according ... 2Chr 4:7
Moreover the *c* with their lamps, ... 2Chr 4:20
bowls, and the caldrons, and the *c* ... Jer 52:19
turned, I saw seven golden *c* ... Rev 1:12
in the midst of the seven *c* one ... Rev 1:13
right hand, and the seven golden *c* ... Rev 1:20
the seven *c* which thou sawest are ... Rev 1:20
the midst of the seven golden *c* ... Rev 2:1
the two *c* standing before the God ... Rev 11:4

**CANE**
bought me no sweet *c* with money ... Is 43:24
the sweet *c* from a far country ... Jer 6:20

**CANKER**
their word will eat as doth a *c* ... 2Ti 2:17

**CANKERED**
Your gold and silver is *c* ... Jas 5:3

**CANKERWORM**
locust hath left hath the *c* eaten ... Joel 1:4
that which the *c* hath left hath ... Joel 1:4
that the locust hath eaten, the *c* ... Joel 2:25
it shall eat thee up like the *c* ... Nah 3:15
make thyself many as the *c* ... Nah 3:15
the *c* spoileth, and fleeth away ... Nah 3:16

**CANNEH** (*can'-neh*) See CALNEH. *A place in southern Arabia.*
Haran, and *C*, and Eden, the ... Eze 27:23

**CANNOT**
I *c* escape to the mountain, lest ... Gen 19:19
for I *c* do any thing till thou be ... Gen 19:22
we *c* speak unto thee bad or good ... Gen 24:50
And they said, We *c*, until all the ... Gen 29:8
lord that I *c* rise up before thee ... Gen 31:35
which *c* be numbered for multitude ... Gen 32:12
We *c* do this thing, to give our ... Gen 34:14
to Judah, and said, I *c* find her ... Gen 38:22
we *c* tell who put our money in ... Gen 43:22
The lad *c* leave his father ... Gen 44:22
And we said, We *c* go down ... Gen 44:26
that one *c* be able to see the ... Ex 10:5
The people *c* come up to mount ... Ex 19:23
if he be poor, and *c* get so much ... Lev 14:21
I *c* go beyond the word of the ... Num 22:18
and I *c* reverse it ... Num 23:20
I *c* go beyond the commandment of ... Num 24:13
the land *c* be cleansed of the ... Num 35:33
a sore botch that *c* be healed ... Deut 28:35
the people, Ye *c* serve the LORD ... Josh 24:19
unto the LORD, and I *c* go back ... Judg 11:35
But if ye *c* declare it me, then ... Judg 14:13
I *c* redeem it for myself, lest I ... Ruth 4:6
for I *c* redeem it ... Ruth 4:6
which *c* profit nor deliver ... 1Sa 12:21
said unto Saul, I *c* go with these ... 1Sa 17:39
thy soul liveth, O king, I *c* tell ... 1Sa 17:55
that a man *c* speak to him ... 1Sa 25:17
thinking, David *c* come in ... 2Sa 5:6
which *c* be gathered up again ... 2Sa 14:14
because they *c* be taken with ... 2Sa 23:6
that *c* be numbered nor counted ... 1Kin 3:8
heaven of heavens *c* contain thee ... 1Kin 8:27
he *c* find thee, he shall slay me ... 1Kin 18:12
heaven of heavens *c* contain him ... 2Chr 2:6
heaven of heavens *c* contain thee ... 2Chr 6:18
of the LORD, that ye *c* prosper ... 2Chr 24:20
for we *c* stand before thee ... Ezr 9:15
great work, so that I *c* come down ... Neh 6:3
so that their hands *c* perform ... Job 5:12
*c* my taste discern perverse ... Job 6:30
he *c* answer him one of a thousand ... Job 9:3
down, and it *c* be built again ... Job 12:14
his bounds that he *c* pass ... Job 14:5
for I *c* find one wise man among ... Job 17:10
fenced up my way that I *c* pass ... Job 19:8
and backward, but I *c* perceive him ... Job 23:8
he doth work, but I *c* behold him ... Job 23:9
the right hand, that I *c* see him ... Job 23:9
It *c* be gotten for gold, neither ... Job 28:15
It *c* be valued with the gold of ... Job 28:16
gold and the crystal *c* equal it ... Job 28:17
we *c* be satisfied ... Job 31:31
consumed away, that it *c* be seen ... Job 33:21
a great ransom *c* deliver thee ... Job 36:18
doeth he, which we *c* comprehend ... Job 37:5
for we *c* order our speech by ... Job 37:19
the Almighty, we *c* find him out ... Job 37:23
together, that they *c* be sundered ... Job 41:17
they *c* be moved ... Job 41:23
of him that layeth at him *c* hold ... Job 41:26
The arrow *c* make him flee ... Job 41:28
they *c* be reckoned up in order ... Ps 40:5
I am so troubled that I *c* speak ... Ps 77:4
I am shut up, and I *c* come forth ... Ps 88:8
is stablished, that it *c* be moved ... Ps 93:1
which *c* be removed, but abideth ... Ps 125:1
it is high, I *c* attain unto it ... Ps 139:6
and for four which it *c* bear ... Prov 30:21
man *c* utter it ... Eccl 1:8
is crooked *c* be made straight ... Eccl 1:15
which is wanting *c* be numbered ... Eccl 1:15
that a man *c* find out the work ... Eccl 8:17
a man *c* tell what shall be ... Eccl 10:14
Many waters *c* quench love ... Song 8:7
of assemblies, I *c* away with ... Is 1:13
and he saith, I *c* ... Is 29:11
For the grave *c* praise thee ... Is 38:18
into the pit *c* hope for thy truth ... Is 38:18
shut their eyes, that they *c* see ... Is 44:18
hearts, that they *c* understand ... Is 44:18
that he *c* deliver his soul, nor ... Is 44:20
and pray unto a god that *c* save ... Is 45:20
at all, that it *c* redeem ... Is 50:2
are all dumb dogs, they *c* bark ... Is 56:10
are shepherds that *c* understand ... Is 56:11
the troubled sea, when it *c* rest ... Is 57:20
is not shortened, that it *c* save ... Is 59:1
his ear heavy, that it *c* hear ... Is 59:1
in the street, and equity *c* enter ... Is 59:14
behold, I *c* speak ... Jer 1:6
I *c* hold my peace, because thou ... Jer 4:19
decree, that it *c* pass it ... Jer 5:22
uncircumcised, and they *c* hearken ... Jer 6:10
in lying words, that *c* profit ... Jer 7:8
needs be borne, because they *c* go ... Jer 10:5
for they *c* do evil, neither also ... Jer 10:5
as a mighty man that *c* save ... Jer 14:9
*c* I do with you as this potter ... Jer 18:6
that *c* be made whole again ... Jer 19:11
that *c* be eaten, they are so evil ... Jer 24:3
which *c* be eaten, they are so ... Jer 24:8
that *c* be eaten, they are so evil ... Jer 29:17
the host of heaven *c* be numbered ... Jer 33:22
I *c* go into the house of the LORD ... Jer 36:5
the LORD, though it *c* be searched ... Jer 46:23
it *c* be quiet ... Jer 49:23
hedged me about, that I *c* get out ... Lam 3:7
that we *c* go in our streets ... Lam 4:18
king hath demanded *c* the wise men ... Dan 2:27
which *c* be measured nor numbered ... Hos 1:10
*c* discern between their right ... Jonah 4:11
*c* be satisfied, but gathereth ... Hab 2:5
that is set on an hill *c* be hid ... Mt 5:14
Ye *c* serve God and mammon ... Mt 6:24
A good tree *c* bring forth evil ... Mt 7:18
All men *c* receive this saying, ... Mt 19:11
Jesus, and said, We *c* tell ... Mt 21:27
Thinkest thou that I *c* now pray ... Mt 26:53
himself he *c* save ... Mt 27:42
bridegroom with them, they *c* fast ... Mk 2:19
itself, that kingdom *c* stand ... Mk 3:24
itself, that house *c* stand ... Mk 3:25
he *c* stand, but hath an end ... Mk 3:26
into the man, it *c* defile him ... Mk 7:18
and said unto Jesus, We *c* tell ... Mk 11:33
himself he *c* save ... Mk 15:31
I *c* rise and give thee ... Lk 11:7
for it *c* be that a prophet perish ... Lk 13:33
for they *c* recompense thee ... Lk 14:14
a wife, and therefore I *c* come ... Lk 14:20
life also, he *c* be my disciple ... Lk 14:26
come after me, *c* be my disciple ... Lk 14:27
that he hath, he *c* be my disciple ... Lk 14:33
I *c* dig ... Lk 16:3
Ye *c* serve God and mammon ... Lk 16:13
would pass from hence to you *c* ... Lk 16:26
he *c* see the kingdom of God ... Jn 3:3
he *c* enter into the kingdom of ... Jn 3:5
The world *c* hate you ... Jn 7:7
and where I am, thither ye *c* come ... Jn 7:34
and where I am, thither ye *c* come ... Jn 7:36
but ye *c* tell whence I come, and ... Jn 8:14
whither I go, ye *c* come ... Jn 8:21
he saith, Whither I go, ye *c* come ... Jn 8:22
even because ye *c* hear my word ... Jn 8:43
and the scripture *c* be broken ... Jn 10:35

the Jews, Whither I go, ye c come Jn 13:33
Lord, why c I follow thee now Jn 13:37
whom the world c receive, because Jn 14:17
As the branch c bear fruit of Jn 15:4
unto you, but ye c bear them now Jn 16:12
we c tell what he saith Jn 16:18
and we c deny it Acts 4:16
For we c but speak the things Acts 4:20
it be of God, ye c overthrow it Acts 5:39
manner of Moses, ye c be saved Acts 15:1
these things c be spoken against Acts 19:36
abide in the ship, ye c be saved Acts 27:31
are in the flesh c please God Rom 8:8
with groanings which c be uttered Rom 8:26
But if they c contain, let them 1Cor 7:9
Ye c drink the cup of the Lord, 1Cor 10:21
ye c be partakers of the Lord's 1Cor 10:21
the eye c say unto the hand, I 1Cor 12:21
blood c inherit the kingdom of 1Cor 15:50
(whether in the body, I c tell 2Cor 12:2
whether out of the body, I c tell 2Cor 12:2
or out of the body, I c tell 2Cor 12:3
c disannul, that it should make Gal 3:17
so that ye c do the things that Gal 5:17
they that are otherwise c be hid 1Ti 5:25
he c deny himself 2Ti 2:13
life, which God, that c lie Titus 1:2
Sound speech, that c be condemned Titus 2:8
have not an high priest which c Heb 4:15
of which we c now speak Heb 9:5
which c be shaken may remain Heb 12:27
a kingdom which c be moved Heb 12:28
for God c be tempted with evil, Jas 1:13
and desire to have, and c obtain Jas 4:2
c see afar off, and hath forgotten 2Pet 1:9
and that c cease from sin 2Pet 2:14
he c sin, because he is born of 1Jn 3:9

**CANST**
that thou c understand a dream to Gen 41:15
he said, Thou c not see my face Ex 33:20
whereof thou c not be healed Deut 28:27
thou c not stand before thine Josh 7:13
How c thou say, I love thee, when Judg 16:15
C thou bring me down to this 1Sa 30:15
wheresoever thou c sojourn 2Kin 8:1
gold that thou c find in all the Ezr 7:16
C thou by searching find out God Job 11:7
c thou find out the Almighty unto Job 11:7
what c thou do? Job 11:8
what c thou know? Job 11:8
Or darkness, that thou c not see Job 22:11
If thou c answer me, set thy Job 33:5
C thou bind the sweet influences Job 38:31
C thou bring forth Mazzaroth in Job 38:32
or c thou guide Arcturus with his Job 38:32
c thou set the dominion thereof Job 38:33
C thou lift up thy voice to the Job 38:34
C thou send lightnings, that they Job 38:35
or c thou mark when the hinds do Job 39:1
C thou number the months that Job 39:2
C thou bind the unicorn with his Job 39:10
C thou make him afraid as a Job 39:20
or c thou thunder with a voice Job 40:9
C thou draw out leviathan with an Job 41:1
C thou put an hook into his nose Job 41:2
C thou fill his skin with barbed Job 41:7
I know that thou c do every thing Job 42:2
all the things thou c desire are Prov 3:15
that thou c not know them Prov 5:6
is his son's name, if thou c tell Prov 30:4
speech than thou c perceive Is 33:19
that thou c not understand Is 33:19
How c thou say, I am not polluted Jer 2:23
then how c thou contend with Jer 12:5
whose words thou c not understand Eze 3:6
that thou c make interpretations, Dan 5:16
now if thou c read the writing, Dan 5:16
evil, and c not look on iniquity Hab 1:13
because thou c not make one hair Mt 5:36
thou wilt, thou c make me clean Mt 8:2
thou wilt, thou c make me clean Mk 1:40
but if thou c do any thing, have Mk 9:22
said unto him, If thou c believe Mk 9:23
thou wilt, thou c make me clean Lk 5:12
Either how c thou say to thy Lk 6:42
but c not tell whence it cometh, Jn 3:8
I go, thou c not follow me now Jn 13:36
Who said, C thou speak Greek Acts 21:37
how thou c not bear them which Rev 2:2

**CAPERNAUM** (*ca-pur'-na-um*) *A city in Galilee.*
Nazareth, he came and dwelt in C Mt 4:13
And when Jesus was entered into C Mt 8:5
And thou, C, which art exalted Mt 11:23
And when they were come to C Mt 17:24
And they went into C Mk 1:21
he entered into C after some days Mk 2:1
And he came to C Mk 9:33
we have heard done in C, do also Lk 4:23
And came down to C, a city of Lk 4:31
of the people, he entered into C Lk 7:1
And thou, C, which art exalted to Lk 10:15
After this he went down to C Jn 2:12
nobleman, whose son was sick at C Jn 4:46
and went over the sea toward C Jn 6:17
also took shipping, and came to C Jn 6:24
the synagogue, as he taught in C Jn 6:59

**CAPHTHORIM** (*caf'-tho-rim*) See CAPHTORIM. *People of Caphtor.*
whom came the Philistines,) and C 1Chr 1:12

**CAPHTOR** (*caf'-tor*) See CAPHTORIM. *Original land of the Philistines.*
which came forth out of C Deut 2:23
the remnant of the country of C Jer 47:4
and the Philistines from C Amos 9:7

**CAPHTORIM** (*caf'-to-rim*) See CAPHTHORIM, CAPHTORIMS. *Same as Caphthorim.*
out of whom came Philistim,) and C Gen 10:14

**CAPHTORIMS** (*caf'-to-rims*) See CAPHTORIM.
Hazerim, even unto Azzah, the C Deut 2:23

**CAPHTORITES** See CAPHTORIMS.

**CAPPADOCIA** (*cap-pa-do'-she-ah*) *A Roman province in Asia Minor.*
Mesopotamia, and in Judaea, and C Acts 2:9
throughout Pontus, Galatia, C 1Pet 1:1

**CAPTAIN**
Phichol the chief c of his host Gen 21:22
Phichol the chief c of his host Gen 21:32
Phichol the chief c of his army Gen 26:26
of Pharaoh's, and c of the guard Gen 37:36
c of the guard, an Egyptian, Gen 39:1
the house of the c of the guard Gen 40:3
the c of the guard charged Joseph Gen 40:4
in the c of the guard's house Gen 41:10
servant to the c of the guard Gen 41:12
be c of the children of Judah Num 2:3
the son of Zuar shall be c of the Num 2:5
be c of the children of Zebulun Num 2:7
the c of the children of Reuben Num 2:10
the c of the children of Simeon Num 2:12
the c of the sons of Gad shall be Num 2:14
the c of the sons of Ephraim Num 2:18
the c of the children of Manasseh Num 2:20
the c of the sons of Benjamin Num 2:22
the c of the children of Dan Num 2:25
the c of the children of Asher Num 2:27
the c of the children of Naphtali Num 2:29
one to another, Let us make a c Num 14:4
but as c of the host of the LORD Josh 5:14
the c of the LORD's host said Josh 5:15
the c of whose host was Sisera, Judg 4:2
the c of Jabin's army, with his Judg 4:7
unto Jephthah, Come, and be our c Judg 11:6
made him head and c over them Judg 11:11
him to be c over my people Israel 1Sa 9:16
thee to be c over his inheritance 1Sa 10:1
c of the host of Hazor, and into 1Sa 12:9
him to be c over his people 1Sa 13:14
the name of the c of his host was 1Sa 14:50
unto the c of their thousand 1Sa 17:18
the c of the host, Abner, whose 1Sa 17:55
made him his c over a thousand 1Sa 18:13
and he became a c over them 1Sa 22:2
the son of Ner, the c of his host 1Sa 26:5
of Ner, c of Saul's host, took 2Sa 2:8
and thou shalt be a c over Israel 2Sa 5:2
soul, he shall be chief and c 2Sa 5:8
Shobach the c of the host of 2Sa 10:16
smote Shobach the c of their host 2Sa 10:18
Absalom made Amasa c of the host 2Sa 17:25
if thou be not c of the host 2Sa 19:13
therefore he was their c 2Sa 23:19
said to Joab the c of the host 2Sa 24:2
priest, and Joab the c of the host 1Kin 1:19
c of the host of Israel, and Amasa 1Kin 2:32
of Jether, c of the host of Judah 1Kin 2:32
Joab the c of the host was gone 1Kin 11:15
that Joab the c of the host was 1Kin 11:21
became c over a band, when David 1Kin 11:24
c of half his chariots, conspired 1Kin 16:9
the c of the host, king over 1Kin 16:16
him a c of fifty with his fifty 2Kin 1:9
and said to the c of fifty 2Kin 1:10
another c of fifty with his fifty 2Kin 1:11
he sent again a c of the third 2Kin 1:13
the third c of fifty went up, and 2Kin 1:13
the king, or to the c of the host 2Kin 4:13
c of the host of the king of 2Kin 5:1
I have an errand to thee, O c 2Kin 9:5
And he said, To thee, O c 2Kin 9:5
Then said Jehu to Bidkar his c 2Kin 9:25
a c of his, conspired against him 2Kin 15:25
one c of the least of my master's 2Kin 18:24
tell Hezekiah the c of my people 2Kin 20:5
c of the guard, a servant of the 2Kin 25:8
that were with the c of the guard 2Kin 25:10
did Nebuzar-adan the c of the 2Kin 25:11
But the c of the guard left of 2Kin 25:12
the c of the guard took away 2Kin 25:15
the c of the guard took Seraiah 2Kin 25:18
Nebuzar-adan c of the guard took 2Kin 25:20
first shall be chief and c 1Chr 11:6
for he was their c 1Chr 11:21
a c of the Reubenites, and thirty 1Chr 11:42
Shophach the c of the host of 1Chr 19:16
killed Shophach the c of the host 1Chr 19:18
The third c of the host for the 1Chr 27:5
The fourth c for the fourth month 1Chr 27:7
The fifth c for the fifth month 1Chr 27:8
The sixth c for the sixth month 1Chr 27:9
The seventh c for the seventh 1Chr 27:10
The eighth c for the eighth month 1Chr 27:11
The ninth c for the ninth month 1Chr 27:12
The tenth c for the tenth month 1Chr 27:13
The eleventh c for the eleventh 1Chr 27:14
The twelfth c for the twelfth 1Chr 27:15
God himself is with us for our c 2Chr 13:12
next to him was Jehohanan the c 2Chr 17:15
a c to return to their bondage Neh 9:17
The c of fifty, and the honourable Is 3:3
one c of the least of my master's Is 36:9
a c of the ward was there, whose Jer 37:13
Then Nebuzar-adan the c of the Jer 39:9
But Nebuzar-adan the c of the Jer 39:10
Nebuzar-adan the c of the guard Jer 39:11
the c of the guard sent, and Jer 39:13
the c of the guard had let him go Jer 40:1
the c of the guard took Jeremiah, Jer 40:2
So the c of the guard gave him Jer 40:5
whom Nebuzar-adan the c of the Jer 41:10
the c of the guard had left with Jer 43:6
appoint a c against her Jer 51:27
c of the guard, which served the Jer 52:12
that were with the c of the guard Jer 52:14
Then Nebuzar-adan the c of the Jer 52:15
But Nebuzar-adan the c of the Jer 52:16
took the c of the guard away Jer 52:19
the c of the guard took Seraiah Jer 52:24
So Nebuzar-adan the c of the Jer 52:26
the c of the guard carried away Jer 52:30
Arioch the c of the king's guard Dan 2:14
and said to Arioch the king's c Dan 2:15
Then the band and the c and Jn 18:12
the c of the temple, and the Acts 4:1
the c of the temple and the chief Acts 5:24
Then went the c with the officers Acts 5:26
came unto the chief c of the band Acts 21:31
and when they saw the chief c Acts 21:32
Then the chief c came near Acts 21:33
castle, he said unto the chief c Acts 21:37
The chief c commanded him to be Acts 22:24
that, he went and told the chief c Acts 22:26
Then the chief c came, and said Acts 22:27
And the chief c answered, With a Acts 22:28
the chief c also was afraid, Acts 22:29
a great dissension, the chief c Acts 23:10
council signify to the chief c Acts 23:15
this young man unto the chief c Acts 23:17
and brought him to the chief c Acts 23:18
Then the chief c took him by the Acts 23:19
So the chief c then let the young Acts 23:22
But the chief c Lysias came upon Acts 24:7
the chief c shall come down Acts 24:22
prisoners to the c of the guard Acts 28:16
to make the c of their salvation Heb 2:10

**CAPTAINS**
and c over every one of them Ex 14:7
his chosen c also are drowned in Ex 15:4
with the c over thousands, and Num 31:14
c over hundreds, which came from Num 31:14
the c of thousands, and c Num 31:48
c of hundreds, came near unto Num 31:48
of the c of thousands, and of the Num 31:52
of the c of hundreds, was sixteen Num 31:52
the gold of the c of thousands Num 31:54
c over thousands, and c Deut 1:15
c over hundreds, and c over Deut 1:15
c over fifties, and c over Deut 1:15
c over tens, and officers among Deut 1:15
that they shall make c of the Deut 20:9
your c of your tribes, your Deut 29:10
said unto the c of the men of war Josh 10:24
will appoint him c over thousands 1Sa 8:12
over thousands, and c over fifties 1Sa 8:12
and make you all c of thousands 1Sa 22:7
of thousands, and c of hundreds 1Sa 22:7
had two men that were c of bands 2Sa 4:2
set c of thousands and c of 2Sa 18:1
and c of hundreds over them 2Sa 18:1
the c charge concerning Absalom 2Sa 18:5
in the seat, chief among the c 2Sa 23:8
and against the c of the host 2Sa 24:4
the c of the host went out from 2Sa 24:4
the c of the host, and Abiathar 1Kin 1:25
the two c of the hosts of Israel 1Kin 2:5
and his princes, and his c 1Kin 9:22
sent the c of the hosts which he 1Kin 15:20
place, and put c in their rooms 1Kin 20:24
two c that had rule over his 1Kin 22:31
when the c of the chariots saw 1Kin 22:32
when the c of the chariots 1Kin 22:33
burnt up the two c of the former 2Kin 1:14
about, and the c of the chariots 2Kin 8:21
the c of the host were sitting 2Kin 9:5
said to the guard and to the c 2Kin 10:25
the c cast them out, and went to 2Kin 10:25
rulers over hundreds, with the c 2Kin 11:4
the c over the hundreds did 2Kin 11:9
to the c over hundreds did the 2Kin 11:10
commanded the c of the hundreds 2Kin 11:15
rulers over hundreds, and the c 2Kin 11:19
when all the c of the armies, 2Kin 25:23
the c of the armies, arose, and 2Kin 25:26
Seir, having for their c Pelatiah 1Chr 4:42
a Hachmonite, the chief of the c 1Chr 11:11
Now three of the thirty c went 1Chr 11:15
of the sons of Gad, c of the host 1Chr 12:14
Amasai, who was chief of the c 1Chr 12:18
them, and made them c of the band 1Chr 12:18
c of the thousands that were of 1Chr 12:20
of valour, and were c in the host 1Chr 12:21
father's house twenty and two c 1Chr 12:28
And of Naphtali a thousand c 1Chr 12:34
consulted with the c of thousands 1Chr 13:1
the c over thousands, went 1Chr 15:25
the c of the host separated to 1Chr 25:1
the c over thousands and hundreds, 1Chr 26:26
the c of the host, had dedicated 1Chr 26:26
c of thousands and hundreds, and 1Chr 27:1

Perez was the chief of all the c ... 1Chr 27:3
the c of the companies that ... 1Chr 28:1
the c over the thousands, and ... 1Chr 28:1
c over the hundreds, and the ... 1Chr 28:1
the c of thousands and of hundreds ... 1Chr 29:6
to the c of thousands and of ... 2Chr 1:2
men of war, and chief of his c ... 2Chr 8:9
c of his chariots and horsemen ... 2Chr 8:9
put c in them, and store of ... 2Chr 11:11
sent the c of his armies against ... 2Chr 16:4
Of Judah, the c of thousands ... 2Chr 17:14
c of the chariots that were with ... 2Chr 18:30
when the c of the chariots saw ... 2Chr 18:31
when the c of the chariots ... 2Chr 18:32
him in, and the c of the chariots ... 2Chr 21:9
took the c of hundreds, Azariah ... 2Chr 23:1
to the c of hundreds spears ... 2Chr 23:9
the priest brought out the c of ... 2Chr 23:14
And he took the c of hundreds ... 2Chr 23:20
made them c over thousands, and ... 2Chr 25:5
c over hundreds, according to the ... 2Chr 25:5
of Hananiah, one of the king's c ... 2Chr 26:11
he set c of war over the people, ... 2Chr 32:6
c in the camp of the king of ... 2Chr 32:21
the c of the host of the king of ... 2Chr 33:11
put c of war in all the fenced ... 2Chr 33:14
the king had sent c of the army ... Neh 2:9
afar off, the thunder of the c ... Job 39:25
for thou hast taught them to be c ... Jer 13:21
Now when all the c of the forces ... Jer 40:7
all the c of the forces that were ... Jer 40:13
all the c of the forces that were ... Jer 41:11
all the c of the forces that were ... Jer 41:13
all the c of the forces that were ... Jer 41:16
Then all the c of the forces, and ... Jer 42:1
all the c of the forces which ... Jer 42:8
all the c of the forces, and all ... Jer 43:4
all the c of the forces, took all ... Jer 43:5
thee will I break in pieces c ... Jer 51:23
the c thereof, and all the rulers ... Jer 51:28
princes, and her wise men, her c ... Jer 51:57
for Jerusalem, to appoint c ... Eze 21:22
Which were clothed with blue, c ... Eze 23:6
the Assyrians her neighbours, c ... Eze 23:12
of them desirable young men, c ... Eze 23:23
princes, the governors, and the c ... Dan 3:2
the princes, the governors, and c ... Dan 3:3
And the princes, governors, and c ... Dan 3:27
the counsellors, and the c ... Dan 6:7
thy c as the great grasshoppers, ... Nah 3:17
a supper to his lords, high c ... Mk 6:21
with the chief priests and c ... Lk 22:4
c of the temple, and the elders, ... Lk 22:52
of hearing, with the chief c ... Acts 25:23
and the rich men, and the chief c ... Rev 6:15
flesh of kings, and the flesh of c ... Rev 19:18

## CAPTIVE

that his brother was taken c ... Gen 14:14
ones, and their wives took they c ... Gen 34:29
of the c that was in the dungeon ... Ex 12:29
Asshur shall carry thee away c ... Num 24:22
hands, and thou hast taken them c ... Deut 21:10
Barak, and lead thy captivity c ... Judg 5:12
enemies, which led them away c ... 1Kin 8:48
before them who carried them c ... 1Kin 8:50
had brought away c out of the ... 2Kin 5:2
thou hast taken c with thy sword ... 2Kin 6:22
and carried them c to Assyria ... 2Kin 15:29
carried the people of it c to Kir ... 2Kin 16:9
of Babylon brought c to Babylon ... 2Kin 24:16
king of Assyria carried away c ... 1Chr 5:6
land whither they are carried c ... 2Chr 6:37
children of Judah carry away c ... 2Chr 25:12
c of their brethren two hundred ... 2Chr 28:8
ye have taken c of your brethren ... 2Chr 28:11
before them that lead them c ... 2Chr 30:9
high, thou hast led captivity c ... Ps 68:18
us away c required of us a song ... Ps 137:3
my children, and am desolate, a c ... Is 49:21
mighty, or the lawful c delivered ... Is 49:24
The c exile hasteneth that he may ... Is 51:14
of thy neck, O c daughter of Zion ... Is 52:2
of Jerusalem c in the fifth month ... Jer 1:3
LORD's flock is carried away c ... Jer 13:17
shall be carried away c all of it ... Jer 13:19
it shall be wholly carried away c ... Jer 13:19
shall carry them c into Babylon ... Jer 20:4
place whither they have led him c ... Jer 22:12
of Babylon had carried away c ... Jer 24:1
that are carried away c of Judah ... Jer 24:5
when he carried away c Jeconiah ... Jer 27:20
and all that is carried away c ... Jer 28:6
away c from Jerusalem to Babylon ... Jer 29:1
I caused you to be carried away c ... Jer 29:14
of the guard carried away c into ... Jer 39:9
were carried away c of Jerusalem ... Jer 40:1
were carried away c unto Babylon ... Jer 40:1
not carried away c to Babylon ... Jer 40:7
Then Ishmael carried away c all ... Jer 41:10
of Nethaniah carried them away c ... Jer 41:10
away c from Mizpah cast about ... Jer 41:14
of the guard carried away c ... Jer 52:15
away c out of his own land ... Jer 52:27
Nebuchadrezzar carried away c ... Jer 52:28
c from Jerusalem eight hundred ... Jer 52:29
of the guard carried away c of ... Jer 52:30
away c the whole captivity ... Amos 1:6
Therefore now shall they go c ... Amos 6:7
c with the first that go c ... Amos 6:7
led away c out of their own land ... Amos 7:11
carried away c his forces ... Obad 11
And Huzzab shall be led away c ... Nah 2:7
be led away c into all nations ... Lk 21:24
up on high, he led captivity c ... Eph 4:8
who are taken c by him at his ... 2Ti 2:26
lead c silly women laden with ... 2Ti 3:6

## CAPTIVES

as c taken with the sword ... Gen 31:26
took all the women of Midian c ... Num 31:9
And they brought the c, and the ... Num 31:12
your c on the third day, and on ... Num 31:19
seest among the c a beautiful ... Deut 21:11
blood of the slain and of the c ... Deut 32:42
And had taken the women c, that ... 1Sa 30:2
and their daughters, were taken c ... 1Sa 30:3
And David's two wives were taken c ... 1Sa 30:5
away c unto the land of the enemy ... 1Kin 8:46
land whither they were carried c ... 1Kin 8:47
land of them that carried them c ... 1Kin 8:47
of valour, even ten thousand c ... 2Kin 24:14
they carry them away c unto a ... 2Chr 6:36
whither they have carried them c ... 2Chr 6:38
away a great multitude of them c ... 2Chr 28:5
therefore, and deliver the c again ... 2Chr 28:11
shall not bring in the c hither ... 2Chr 28:13
So the armed men left the c ... 2Chr 28:14
by name rose up, and took the c ... 2Chr 28:15
smitten Judah, and carried away c ... 2Chr 28:17
of all those that carried them c ... Ps 106:46
and they shall take them c ... Is 14:2
them c, whose c they were ... Is 14:2
prisoners, and the Ethiopians c ... Is 20:4
my city, and he shall let go my c ... Is 45:13
Even the c of the mighty shall be ... Is 49:25
to proclaim liberty to the c ... Is 61:1
of Judah, with all the c of Judah ... Jer 28:4
elders which were carried away c ... Jer 29:1
unto all that are carried away c ... Jer 29:4
caused you to be carried away c ... Jer 29:7
and carry us away c into Babylon ... Jer 43:3
burn them, and carry them away c ... Jer 43:12
for thy sons are taken c, and thy ... Jer 48:46
c, and thy daughters c ... Jer 48:46
that took them c held them fast ... Jer 50:33
as I was among the c by the river ... Eze 1:1
whither they shall be carried c ... Eze 6:9
of thy c in the midst of them ... Eze 16:53
found a man of the c of Judah ... Dan 2:25
shall also carry c into Egypt ... Dan 11:8
to preach deliverance to the c ... Lk 4:18

## CAPTIVITY

into c unto Sihon king of the ... Num 21:29
the raiment of her c from off her ... Deut 21:13
for they shall go into c ... Deut 28:41
the LORD thy God will turn thy c ... Deut 30:3
Barak, and lead thy c captive ... Judg 5:12
the day of the c of the land ... Judg 18:30
those carried he into c from ... 2Kin 24:15
thirtieth year of the c of ... 2Kin 25:27
dwelt in their steads until the c ... 1Chr 5:22
And Jehozadak went into c, when ... 1Chr 6:15
unto thee in the land of their c ... 2Chr 6:37
their soul in the land of their c ... 2Chr 6:38
and our wives are in c for this ... 2Chr 29:9
the c that were brought up from ... Ezr 1:11
that went up out of the c ... Ezr 2:1
come out of the c unto Jerusalem ... Ezr 3:8
the c builded the temple unto the ... Ezr 4:1
the rest of the children of the c ... Ezr 6:16
the children of the c kept the ... Ezr 6:19
for all the children of the c ... Ezr 6:20
which were come again out of c ... Ezr 6:21
which were come out of the c ... Ezr 8:35
of the lands, to the sword, to c ... Ezr 9:7
unto all the children of the c ... Ezr 10:7
And the children of the c did so ... Ezr 10:16
escaped, which were left of the c ... Neh 1:2
c there in the province are in ... Neh 1:3
them for a prey in the land of c ... Neh 4:4
that went up out of the c ... Neh 7:6
again out of the c made booths ... Neh 8:17
the c which had been carried away ... Est 2:6
And the LORD turned the c of Job ... Job 42:10
bringeth back the c of his people ... Ps 14:7
bringeth back the c of his people ... Ps 53:6
on high, thou hast led c captive ... Ps 68:18
And delivered his strength into c ... Ps 78:61
hast brought back the c of Jacob ... Ps 85:1
LORD turned again the c of Zion ... Ps 126:1
Turn again our c, O LORD, as the ... Ps 126:4
my people are gone into c ... Is 5:13
carry thee away with a mighty c ... Is 22:17
but themselves are gone into c ... Is 46:2
are for the c, to the c ... Jer 15:2
in thine house shall go into c ... Jer 20:6
and thy lovers shall go into c ... Jer 22:22
and I will turn away your c ... Jer 29:14
not gone forth with you into c ... Jer 29:16
word of the LORD, all ye of the c ... Jer 29:20
c of Judah which are in Babylon ... Jer 29:22
Babylon, saying, This c is long ... Jer 29:28
Send to all them of the c ... Jer 29:31
again the c of my people Israel ... Jer 30:3
thy seed from the land of their c ... Jer 30:10
one of them, shall go into c ... Jer 30:16
again the c of Jacob's tents ... Jer 30:18
when I shall bring again their c ... Jer 31:23
I will cause their c to return ... Jer 32:44
And I will cause the c of Judah ... Jer 33:7
the c of Israel to return, and ... Jer 33:7
cause to return the c of the land ... Jer 33:11
I will cause their c to return ... Jer 33:26
and such as are for c to c ... Jer 43:11
and such as are for c to c ... Jer 43:11
furnish thyself to go into c ... Jer 46:19
thy seed from the land of their c ... Jer 46:27
go forth into c with his priests ... Jer 48:7
neither hath he gone into c ... Jer 48:11
the c of Moab in the latter days ... Jer 48:47
for their king shall go into c ... Jer 49:3
I will bring again the c of the ... Jer 49:6
I will bring again the c of Elam ... Jer 49:39
thirtieth year of the c of ... Jer 52:31
Judah is gone into c because of ... Lam 1:3
are gone into c before the enemy ... Lam 1:5
and my young men are gone into c ... Lam 1:18
iniquity, to turn away thy c ... Lam 2:14
no more carry thee away into c ... Lam 4:22
fifth year of king Jehoiachin's c ... Eze 1:2
And go, get thee to them of the c ... Eze 3:11
came to them of the c at Tel-abib ... Eze 3:15
into Chaldea, to them of the c ... Eze 11:24
c all the things that the LORD ... Eze 11:25
as they that go forth into c ... Eze 12:4
my stuff by day, as stuff for c ... Eze 12:7
they shall remove and go into c ... Eze 12:11
When I shall bring again their c ... Eze 16:53
the c of Sodom and her daughters, ... Eze 16:53
the c of Samaria and her daughters ... Eze 16:53
then will I bring again the c of ... Eze 16:53
of Judah, when they went into c ... Eze 25:3
I will bring again the c of Egypt ... Eze 29:14
and these cities shall go into c ... Eze 30:17
and her daughters shall go into c ... Eze 30:18
pass in the twelfth year of our c ... Eze 33:21
went into c for their iniquity ... Eze 39:23
will I bring again the c of Jacob ... Eze 39:25
be led into c among the heathen ... Eze 39:28
five and twentieth year of our c ... Eze 40:1
of the children of the c of Judah ... Dan 5:13
of the children of the c of Judah ... Dan 6:13
by the sword, and by flame, by c ... Dan 11:33
I returned the c of my people ... Hos 6:11
shall bring again the c of Judah ... Joel 3:1
of Syria shall go into c unto Kir ... Amos 1:5
carried away captive the whole c ... Amos 1:6
delivered up the whole c to Edom ... Amos 1:9
And their king shall go into c ... Amos 1:15
for Gilgal shall surely go into c ... Amos 5:5
you to go into c beyond Damascus ... Amos 5:27
go into c forth of his land ... Amos 7:17
though they go into c before ... Amos 9:4
the c of my people of Israel ... Amos 9:14
the c of this host of the ... Obad 20
the c of Jerusalem, which is in ... Obad 20
they are gone into c from thee ... Mic 1:16
she carried away, she went into c ... Nah 3:10
shall gather the c as the sand ... Hab 1:9
visit them, and turn away their c ... Zeph 2:7
turn back your c before your eyes ... Zeph 3:20
Take of them of the c, even of ... Zec 6:10
of the city shall go forth into c ... Zec 14:2
bringing me into c to the law of ... Rom 7:23
bringing into c every thought to ... 2Cor 10:5
he led c captive, and gave gifts ... Eph 4:8
into c shall go into c ... Rev 13:10

## CARBUNCLE

be a sardius, a topaz, and a c ... Ex 28:17
was a sardius, a topaz, and a c ... Ex 39:10
sapphire, the emerald, and the c ... Eze 28:13

## CARBUNCLES

of agates, and thy gates of c ... Is 54:12

## CARCAS (*car'-cas*) *A servant of King Ahasuerus.*

Bigtha, and Abagtha, Zethar, and C ... Est 1:10

## CARCASE

whether it be a c of an unclean ... Lev 5:2
or a c of unclean cattle, or the ... Lev 5:2
or the c of unclean creeping ... Lev 5:2
their c shall ye not touch ... Lev 11:8
whosoever toucheth the c of them ... Lev 11:24
c of them shall wash his clothes ... Lev 11:25
whoso toucheth their c shall be ... Lev 11:27
he that beareth the c of them ... Lev 11:28
their c falleth shall be unclean ... Lev 11:35
toucheth their c shall be unclean ... Lev 11:36
if any part of their c fall upon ... Lev 11:37
any part of their c fall thereon ... Lev 11:38
he that toucheth the c thereof ... Lev 11:39
he that eateth of the c of it ... Lev 11:40
he also that beareth the c of it ... Lev 11:40
flesh, nor touch their dead c ... Deut 14:8
thy c shall be meat unto all ... Deut 28:26
take his c down from the tree ... Josh 8:29
aside to see the c of the lion ... Judg 14:8
and honey in the c of the lion ... Judg 14:8
honey out of the c of the lion ... Judg 14:9
thy c shall not come unto the ... 1Kin 13:22
his c was cast in the way, and the ... 1Kin 13:24
it, the lion also stood by the c ... 1Kin 13:24
saw the c cast in the way ... 1Kin 13:25
and the lion standing by the c ... 1Kin 13:25
found his c cast in the way, and ... 1Kin 13:28
ass and the lion standing by the c ... 1Kin 13:28
the lion had not eaten the c ... 1Kin 13:28
took up the c of the man of God ... 1Kin 13:29
he laid his c in his own grave ... 1Kin 13:30

the c of Jezebel shall be as dung .......... 2Kin 9:37
as a c trodden under feet .......... Is 14:19
For wheresoever the c is, there .......... Mt 24:28

**CARCASES**
the fowls came down upon the c .......... Gen 15:11
shall have their c in abomination .......... Lev 11:11
The c of every beast which .......... Lev 11:26
cast your c upon the c of .......... Lev 26:30
Your c shall fall in this .......... Num 14:29
But as for you, your c, they .......... Num 14:32
until your c be wasted in the .......... Num 14:33
I will give the c of the host of .......... 1Sa 17:46
their c were torn in the midst of .......... Is 5:25
shall come up out of their c .......... Is 34:3
look upon the c of the men that .......... Is 66:24
the c of this people shall be .......... Jer 7:33
Even the c of men shall fall as .......... Jer 9:22
their c shall be meat for the .......... Jer 16:4
with the c of their detestable .......... Jer 16:18
their c will I give to be meat .......... Jer 19:7
I will lay the dead c of the .......... Eze 6:5
nor by the c of their kings in .......... Eze 43:7
the c of their kings, far from me .......... Eze 43:9
of slain, and a great number of c .......... Nah 3:3
whose c fell in the wilderness .......... Heb 3:17

**CARCHEMISH** (*car'-ke-mish*) See CHARCHEMISH. *A city on the Euphrates River.*
Is not Calno as C .......... Is 10:9
was by the river Euphrates in C .......... Jer 46:2

**CARE**
hath left the c of the asses .......... 1Sa 10:2
flee away, they will not c for us .......... 2Sa 18:3
of us die, will they c for us .......... 2Sa 18:3
careful for us with all this c .......... 2Kin 4:13
nation, that dwelleth without c .......... Jer 49:31
eat bread by weight, and with c .......... Eze 4:16
the c of this world, and the .......... Mt 13:22
him to an inn, and took c of him .......... Lk 10:34
and said unto him, Take c of him .......... Lk 10:35
dost thou not c that my sister .......... Lk 10:40
c not for it .......... 1Cor 7:21
Doth God take c for oxen .......... 1Cor 9:9
have the same c one for another .......... 1Cor 12:25
but that our c for you in the .......... 2Cor 7:12
which put the same earnest c into .......... 2Cor 8:16
the c of all the churches .......... 2Cor 11:28
will naturally c for your state .......... Phil 2:20
that now at the last your c of me .......... Phil 4:10
how shall he take c of the church .......... 1Ti 3:5
Casting all your c upon him .......... 1Pet 5:7

**CAREAH** (*ca-re'-ah*) See KAREAH. *Father of Johanan.*
and Johanan the son of C, and .......... 2Kin 25:23

**CARED**
no man c for my soul .......... Ps 142:4
not that he c for the poor .......... Jn 12:6
Gallio c for none of those things .......... Acts 18:17

**CAREFUL**
thou hast been c for us with all .......... 2Kin 4:13
shall not be c in the year of .......... Jer 17:8
we are not c to answer thee in .......... Dan 3:16
her, Martha, Martha, thou art c .......... Lk 10:41
Be c for nothing .......... Phil 4:6
wherein ye were also c, but ye .......... Phil 4:10
might be c to maintain good works .......... Titus 3:8

**CAREFULLY**
Only if thou c hearken unto the .......... Deut 15:5
of Maroth waited c for good .......... Mic 1:12
I sent him therefore the more c .......... Phil 2:28
though he sought it c with tears .......... Heb 12:17

**CAREFULNESS**
water with trembling and with c .......... Eze 12:18
They shall eat their bread with c .......... Eze 12:19
But I would have you without c .......... 1Cor 7:32
what c it wrought in you, yea, .......... 2Cor 7:11

**CARELESS**
were therein, how they dwelt c .......... Judg 18:7
hear my voice, ye c daughters .......... Is 32:9
shall ye be troubled, ye c women .......... Is 32:10
be troubled, ye c ones .......... Is 32:11
to make the c Ethiopians afraid .......... Eze 30:9

**CARELESSLY**
to pleasures, that dwellest c .......... Is 47:8
them that dwell c in the isles .......... Eze 39:6
the rejoicing city that dwelt c .......... Zeph 2:15

**CARES**
the c of this world, and the .......... Mk 4:19
go forth, and are choked with c .......... Lk 8:14
c of this life, and so that day .......... Lk 21:34

**CAREST**
neither c thou for any man .......... Mt 22:16
c thou not that we perish .......... Mk 4:38
thou art true, and c for no man .......... Mk 12:14

**CARETH**
land which the LORD thy God c for .......... Deut 11:12
hireling, and c not for the sheep .......... Jn 10:13
He that is unmarried c for the .......... 1Cor 7:32
But he that is married c for the .......... 1Cor 7:33
The unmarried woman c for the .......... 1Cor 7:34
but she that is married c for the .......... 1Cor 7:34
for he c for you .......... 1Pet 5:7

**CARING**
my father leave c for the asses .......... 1Sa 9:5

**CARKAS** See CARCAS.

**CARMEL** (*car'-mel*) See CARMELITE.
*1. A mountain range in Canaan.*
the king of Jokneam of C, one .......... Josh 12:22
and reacheth to C westward .......... Josh 19:26
Samuel, saying, Saul came to C .......... 1Sa 15:12
to me all Israel unto mount C .......... 1Kin 18:19
prophets together unto mount C .......... 1Kin 18:20
And Elijah went up to the top of C .......... 1Kin 18:42
And he went from thence to mount C .......... 2Kin 2:25
unto the man of God to mount C .......... 2Kin 4:25
and into the forest of his C .......... 2Kin 19:23
in the mountains, and in C .......... 2Chr 26:10
Thine head upon thee is like C .......... Song 7:5
and C shake off their fruits .......... Is 33:9
unto it, the excellency of C .......... Is 35:2
border, and the forest of his C .......... Is 37:24
as C by the sea, so shall he come .......... Jer 46:18
habitation, and he shall feed on C .......... Jer 50:19
the top of C shall wither .......... Amos 1:2
hide themselves in the top of C .......... Amos 9:3
in the wood, in the midst of C .......... Mic 7:14
Bashan languisheth, and C, and the .......... Nah 1:4
*2. A town in Judah.*
Maon, C, and Ziph, and Juttah, .......... Josh 15:55
Maon, whose possessions were in C .......... 1Sa 25:2
and he was shearing his sheep in C .......... 1Sa 25:2
the young men, Get you up to C .......... 1Sa 25:5
all the while they were in C .......... 1Sa 25:7
David were come to Abigail to C .......... 1Sa 25:40

**CARMELITE** (*car'-mel-ite*) See CARMELITESS. *An inhabitant of Carmel 2.*
Abigail the wife of Nabal the C .......... 1Sa 30:5
and Abigail Nabal's wife the C .......... 2Sa 2:2
Abigail the wife of Nabal the C .......... 2Sa 3:3
Hezrai the C, Paarai the Arbite, .......... 2Sa 23:35
Hezro the C, Naarai the son of .......... 1Chr 11:37

**CARMELITESS** (*car'-mel-i-tess*)
Jezreelitess, and Abigail the C .......... 1Sa 27:3
second Daniel, of Abigail the C .......... 1Chr 3:1

**CARMI** (*car'-mi*) See CARMITES.
*1. Father of Achan.*
for Achan, the son of C, the son .......... Josh 7:1
and Achan, the son of C, the son .......... Josh 7:18
And the sons of C .......... 1Chr 2:7
Pharez, Hezron, and C, and Hur, and .......... 1Chr 4:1
*2. A son of Reuben.*
and Phallu, and Hezron, and C .......... Gen 46:9
Hanoch, and Pallu, Hezron, and C .......... Ex 6:14
of C, the family of the Carmites .......... Num 26:6
Hanoch, and Pallu, Hezron, and C .......... 1Chr 5:3

**CARMITES** (*car'-mites*) *Descendants of Carmi 2.*
of Carmi, the family of the C .......... Num 26:6

**CARNAL**
but I am c, sold under sin .......... Rom 7:14
Because the c mind is enmity .......... Rom 8:7
to minister unto them in c things .......... Rom 15:27
as unto spiritual, but as unto c .......... 1Cor 3:1
For ye are yet c .......... 1Cor 3:3
and divisions, are ye not c .......... 1Cor 3:3
are ye not c? .......... 1Cor 3:4
if we shall reap your c things .......... 1Cor 9:11
weapons of our warfare are not c .......... 2Cor 10:4
after the law of a c commandment .......... Heb 7:16
c ordinances, imposed on them .......... Heb 9:10

**CARNALLY**
lie c with thy neighbour's wife .......... Lev 18:20
And whosoever lieth c with a woman .......... Lev 19:20
And a man lie with her c, and it be .......... Num 5:13
For to be c minded is death .......... Rom 8:6

**CARPENTER**
So the c encouraged the goldsmith .......... Is 41:7
The c stretcheth out his rule .......... Is 44:13
Is not this the c, the son of .......... Mk 6:3

**CARPENTER'S**
Is not this the c son .......... Mt 13:55

**CARPENTERS**
to David, and cedar trees, and c .......... 2Sa 5:11
and they laid it out to the c .......... 2Kin 12:11
Unto c, and builders, and masons, .......... 2Kin 22:6
of cedars, with masons and c .......... 1Chr 14:1
c to repair the house of the LORD .......... 2Chr 24:12
also unto the masons, and to the c .......... Ezr 3:7
the princes of Judah, with the c .......... Jer 24:1
of Judah and Jerusalem, and the c .......... Jer 29:2
And the LORD shewed me four c .......... Zec 1:20

**CARPUS** (*car'-pus*) *A friend of Paul.*
cloke that I left at Troas with C .......... 2Ti 4:13

**CARRIAGE**
the cattle and the c before them .......... Judg 18:21
David left his c in the hand of .......... 1Sa 17:22
the hand of the keeper of the c .......... 1Sa 17:22

**CARRIAGES**
at Michmash he hath laid up his c .......... Is 10:28
your c were heavy loaden .......... Is 46:1
after those days we took up our c .......... Acts 21:15

**CARRIED**
he c away all his cattle, and all .......... Gen 31:18
c away my daughters, as captives .......... Gen 31:26
of Israel c Jacob their father .......... Gen 46:5
For his sons c him into the land .......... Gen 50:13
c them in their coats out of the .......... Lev 10:5
c them over with them unto the .......... Josh 4:8
c them up to the top of an hill .......... Judg 16:3
of Israel be c about unto Gath .......... 1Sa 5:8
they c the ark of the God of .......... 1Sa 5:8
that, after they had c it about .......... 1Sa 5:9
but c them away, and went on their .......... 1Sa 30:2
that the Amalekites had c away .......... 1Sa 30:18
but David c it aside into the .......... 2Sa 6:10
Abiathar c the ark of God again .......... 2Sa 15:29
land whither they were c captives .......... 1Kin 8:47
land of them that c them captives .......... 1Kin 8:47
before them who c them captive .......... 1Kin 8:50
c him up into a loft, where he .......... 1Kin 17:19
Then they c him forth out of the .......... 1Kin 21:13
c thence silver, and gold, and .......... 2Kin 7:8
c thence also, and went and hid it .......... 2Kin 7:8
his servants c him in a chariot .......... 2Kin 9:28
c them captive to Assyria .......... 2Kin 15:29
c the people of it captive to Kir .......... 2Kin 16:9
c Israel away into Assyria, and .......... 2Kin 17:6
whom the LORD c away before them .......... 2Kin 17:11
So was Israel c away out of their .......... 2Kin 17:23
they had c away from Samaria came .......... 2Kin 17:28
whom they c away from thence .......... 2Kin 17:33
this day, shall be c into Babylon .......... 2Kin 20:17
c the ashes of them unto Beth-el .......... 2Kin 23:4
his servants c him in a chariot .......... 2Kin 23:30
he c out thence all the treasures .......... 2Kin 24:13
he c away all Jerusalem, and all .......... 2Kin 24:14
he c away Jehoiachin to Babylon, .......... 2Kin 24:15
those c he into captivity from .......... 2Kin 24:15
of brass, and c him to Babylon .......... 2Kin 25:7
c the brass of them to Babylon .......... 2Kin 25:13
So Judah was c away out of their .......... 2Kin 25:21
king of Assyria c away captive .......... 1Chr 5:6
and he c them away, even the .......... 1Chr 5:26
when the LORD c away Judah .......... 1Chr 6:15
who were c away to Babylon for .......... 1Chr 9:1
they c the ark of God in a new .......... 1Chr 13:7
but c it aside into the house of .......... 1Chr 13:13
land whither they are c captive .......... 2Chr 6:37
whither they have c them captives .......... 2Chr 6:38
he c away also the shields of .......... 2Chr 12:9
they c away very much spoil .......... 2Chr 14:13
c away sheep and camels in .......... 2Chr 14:15
they c away the stones of Ramah, .......... 2Chr 16:6
c away all the substance that was .......... 2Chr 21:17
it, and c it to his place again .......... 2Chr 24:11
c away a great multitude of them .......... 2Chr 28:5
the children of Israel c away .......... 2Chr 28:8
c all the feeble of them upon .......... 2Chr 28:15
smitten Judah, and c away captives .......... 2Chr 28:17
with fetters, and c him to Babylon .......... 2Chr 33:11
Shaphan c the book to the king, .......... 2Chr 34:16
his brother, and c him to Egypt .......... 2Chr 36:4
Nebuchadnezzar also c of the .......... 2Chr 36:7
the sword c he away to Babylon .......... 2Chr 36:20
of those which had been c away .......... Ezr 2:1
Babylon had c away unto Babylon .......... Ezr 2:1
c the people away into Babylon .......... Ezr 5:12
of those that had been c away .......... Ezr 8:35
of those that had been c away .......... Ezr 9:4
of them that had been c away .......... Ezr 10:6
of those that had been c away .......... Ezr 10:8
of those that had been c away .......... Neh 7:6
the king of Babylon had c away .......... Neh 7:6
Who had been c away from .......... Est 2:6
been c away with Jeconiah king of .......... Est 2:6
the king of Babylon had c away .......... Est 2:6
have c them away, yea, and slain .......... Job 1:17
of the froward is c headlong .......... Job 5:13
I should have been c from the .......... Job 10:19
though the mountains be c into .......... Ps 46:2
of all those that c them captives .......... Ps 106:46
For there they that c us away .......... Ps 137:3
this day, shall be c to Babylon .......... Is 39:6
which are c from the womb .......... Is 46:3
shall be c upon their shoulders .......... Is 49:22
our griefs, and c our sorrows .......... Is 53:4
c them all the days of old .......... Is 63:9
LORD's flock is c away captive .......... Jer 13:17
Judah shall be c away captive all .......... Jer 13:19
it shall be wholly c away captive .......... Jer 13:19
king of Babylon had c away .......... Jer 24:1
that are c away captive of Judah .......... Jer 24:5
when he c away captive Jeconiah .......... Jer 27:20
They shall be c to Babylon .......... Jer 27:22
this place, and c them to Babylon .......... Jer 28:3
all that is c away captive, from .......... Jer 28:6
elders which were c away captives .......... Jer 29:1
c away captive from Jerusalem to .......... Jer 29:1
unto all that are c away captives .......... Jer 29:4
to be c away from Jerusalem unto .......... Jer 29:4
caused you to be c away captives .......... Jer 29:7
I caused you to be c away captive .......... Jer 29:14
the captain of the guard c away .......... Jer 39:9
were c away captive of Jerusalem .......... Jer 40:1
which were c away captive unto .......... Jer 40:1
of them that were not c away .......... Jer 40:7
Then Ishmael c away captive all .......... Jer 41:10
of Nethaniah c them away captive .......... Jer 41:10
c away captive from Mizpah cast .......... Jer 41:14
c him up unto the king of Babylon .......... Jer 52:9
c him to Babylon, and put him in .......... Jer 52:11
the captain of the guard c away .......... Jer 52:15
c all the brass of them to .......... Jer 52:17
Thus Judah was c away captive out .......... Jer 52:27

Nebuchadrezzar c away captive Jer 52:28
year of Nebuchadrezzar he c away Jer 52:29
the captain of the guard c away Jer 52:30
whither they shall be c captives Eze 6:9
c it into a land of traffick Eze 17:4
c me out in the spirit of the Eze 37:1
which he c into the land of Dan 1:2
the wind c them away, that no Dan 2:35
It shall be also c unto Assyria Hos 10:6
Assyrians, and oil is c into Egypt Hos 12:1
have c into your temples my Joel 3:5
because they c away captive the Amos 1:6
c away captive his forces Obad 11
Yet was she c away, she went into Nah 3:10
time they were c away to Babylon Mt 1:11
c him away, and delivered him to Mk 15:1
there was a dead man c out Lk 7:12
died, and was c by the angels into Lk 16:22
from them, and c up into heaven Lk 24:51
lame from his mother's womb was c Acts 3:2
up, and c him out, and buried him Acts 5:6
were c over into Sychem, and laid Acts 7:16
devout men c Stephen to his Acts 8:2
him to be c into the castle Acts 21:34
c away unto these dumb idols, 1Cor 12:2
c away with their dissimulation Gal 2:13
c about with every wind of Eph 4:14
Be not c about with divers and Heb 13:9
clouds that are c with a tempest 2Pet 2:17
without water, c about of winds Jude 12
her to be c away of the flood Rev 12:15
So he c me away in the spirit Rev 17:3
he c me away in the spirit to a Rev 21:10

### CARRIEST
Thou c them away as with a flood Ps 90:5

### CARRIETH
and as chaff that the storm c away Job 21:18
The east wind c him away, and he Job 27:21
woman, and of the beast that c her Rev 17:7

### CARRY
going to c it down to Egypt Gen 37:25
c corn for the famine of your Gen 42:19
c down the man a present, a Gen 43:11
sacks, c it again in your hand Gen 43:12
with food, as much as they can c Gen 44:1
which Joseph had sent to c him Gen 45:27
which Pharaoh had sent to c him Gen 46:5
thou shalt c me out of Egypt, and Gen 47:30
ye shall c up my bones from hence Gen 50:25
thou shalt not c forth ought of Ex 12:46
ye shall c up my bones away hence Ex 13:19
to c us forth out of Egypt Ex 14:11
go not with me, c us not up hence Ex 33:15
c forth without the camp unto a Lev 4:12
he shall c forth the bullock Lev 4:21
c forth the ashes without the Lev 6:11
c your brethren from before the Lev 10:4
he shall c them forth out of the Lev 14:45
shall one c forth without the Lev 16:27
C them in thy bosom, as a nursing Num 11:12
Asshur shall c thee away captive Num 24:22
so that thou art not able to c it Deut 14:24
Thou shalt c much seed out into Deut 28:38
ye shall c them over with you, and Josh 4:3
c these ten cheeses unto the 1Sa 17:18
unto him, Go, c them to the city 1Sa 20:40
C back the ark of God into the 2Sa 15:25
to c over the king's household 2Sa 19:18
so that they c them away captives 1Kin 8:46
shall c thee whither I know not 1Kin 18:12
then c him out, and stone him, 1Kin 21:10
c him back unto Amon the governor 1Kin 22:26
hand, and c me out of the host 1Kin 22:34
to a lad, C him to his mother 2Kin 4:19
c him to an inner chamber 2Kin 9:2
C thither one of the priests whom 2Kin 17:27
the king of Assyria did c away 2Kin 18:11
the captain of the guard c away 2Kin 25:11
to c tidings unto their idols, and 1Chr 10:9
None ought to c the ark of God 1Chr 15:2
LORD chosen to c the ark of God 1Chr 15:2
shall no more c the tabernacle 1Chr 23:26
thou shalt c it up to Jerusalem 2Chr 2:16
they c them away captives unto a 2Chr 6:36
c him back to Amon the governor 2Chr 18:25
that thou mayest c me out of the 2Chr 18:33
more than they could c away 2Chr 20:25
children of Judah c away captive 2Chr 25:12
c forth the filthiness out of the 2Chr 29:5
to c it out abroad into the brook 2Chr 29:16
in fetters, to c him to Babylon 2Chr 36:6
c them into the temple that is in Ezr 5:15
to c the silver and gold, which Ezr 7:15
Why doth thine heart c thee away Job 15:12
he dieth he shall c nothing away Ps 49:17
which he may c away in his hand Eccl 5:15
bird of the air shall c the voice Eccl 10:20
shall c it away safe, and none Is 5:29
shall they c away to the brook of Is 15:7
the LORD will c thee away with a Is 22:17
her own feet shall c her afar off Is 23:7
they will c their riches upon the Is 30:6
c them in his bosom, and shall Is 40:11
and the wind shall c them away Is 41:16
even to hoar hairs will I c you Is 46:4
even I will c, and will deliver Is 46:4
him upon the shoulder, they c him Is 46:7
the wind shall c them all away Is 57:13
Neither c forth a burden out of Jer 17:22
he shall c them captive into Jer 20:4
take them, and c them to Babylon Jer 20:5
with chains, to c him to Babylon Jer 39:7
that he should c him home Jer 39:14
c us away captives into Babylon Jer 43:3
them, and c them away captives Jer 43:12
he will no more c thee away into Lam 4:22
in their sight, and c out thereby Eze 12:5
c it forth in the twilight Eze 12:6
through the wall to c out thereby Eze 12:12
men that c tales to shed blood Eze 22:9
to c away silver and gold, to take Eze 38:13
shall also c captives into Egypt Dan 11:8
began to c about in beds those Mk 6:55
c any vessel through the temple Mk 11:16
C neither purse, nor scrip, nor Lk 10:4
not lawful for thee to c thy bed Jn 5:10
c thee whither thou wouldest not Jn 21:18
at the door, and shall c thee out Acts 5:9
I will c you away beyond Babylon Acts 7:43
is certain we can c nothing out 1Ti 6:7

### CARRYING
one c three kids, and another 1Sa 10:3
another c three loaves of bread, 1Sa 10:3
another c a bottle of wine 1Sa 10:3
c bows, turned back in the day of Ps 78:9
unto the c away of Jerusalem Jer 1:3
from David until the c away into Mt 1:17
from the c away into Babylon unto Mt 1:17
c her forth, buried her by her Acts 5:10

### CARSHENA (*car-she'-nah*) *A Persian prince.*
And the next unto him was C Est 1:14

### CART
Now therefore make a new c 1Sa 6:7
no yoke, and tie the kine to the c 1Sa 6:7
of the LORD, and lay it upon the c 1Sa 6:8
milch kine, and tied them to the c 1Sa 6:10
the ark of the LORD upon the c 1Sa 6:11
the c came into the field of 1Sa 6:14
and they clave the wood of the c 1Sa 6:14
set the ark of God upon a new c 2Sa 6:3
sons of Abinadab, drave the new c 2Sa 6:3
c out of the house of Abinadab 1Chr 13:7
and Uzza and Ahio drave the c 1Chr 13:7
and sin as it were with a c rope Is 5:18
neither is a c wheel turned about Is 28:27
break it with the wheel of his c Is 28:28
as a c is pressed that is full of Amos 2:13

### CARVED
house, and fetched the c image Judg 18:18
the house within was c with knops 1Kin 6:18
he c all the walls of the house 1Kin 6:29
about with c figures of cherubims 1Kin 6:29
he c upon them carvings of 1Kin 6:32
he c thereon cherubims and palm 1Kin 6:35
with gold fitted upon the c work 1Kin 6:35
And he set a c image, the idol 2Chr 33:7
the c images which Manasseh his 2Chr 33:22
the c images, and the molten 2Chr 34:3
the c images, and the molten 2Chr 34:4
But now they break down the c Ps 74:6
with c works, with fine linen of Prov 7:16

### CARVING
in c of timber, to work in all Ex 31:5
in c of wood, to make any manner Ex 35:33

### CARVINGS
carved upon them c of cherubims 1Kin 6:32

### CASE
did see that they were in evil c Ex 5:19
this is the c of the slayer, Deut 19:4
thou shalt in any c bring them Deut 22:1
In any c thou shalt deliver him Deut 24:13
that people, that is in such a c Ps 144:15
ye shall in no c enter into the Mt 5:20
If the c of the man be so with Mt 19:10
been now a long time in that c Jn 5:6

### CASEMENT
of my house I looked through my c Prov 7:6

### CASES
is not under bondage in such c 1Cor 7:15

### CASIPHIA (*cas-if'-e-ah*) *A place in Syria.*
Iddo the chief at the place C Ezr 8:17
the Nethinims, at the place C Ezr 8:17

### CASLUHIM (*cas'-loo-him*) *Descendants of Mizraim.*
And Pathrusim, and C, (out of whom Gen 10:14
and C, (of whom came 1Chr 1:12

### CASLUHITES See CASLUHIM.

### CASSIA
of c five hundred shekels, after Ex 30:24
smell of myrrh, and aloes, and c Ps 45:8
bright iron, c, and calamus, were Eze 27:19

### CAST See PREFACE.

### CASTAWAY
to others, I myself should be a c 1Cor 9:27

### CASTEDST
thou c them down into destruction Ps 73:18

### CASTEST
thou c off fear, and restrainest Job 15:4
and c my words behind thee Ps 50:17
LORD, why c thou off my soul Ps 88:14

### CASTETH
cow calveth, and c not her calf Job 21:10
he c the wicked down to the Ps 147:6
He c forth his ice like morsels Ps 147:17
but he c away the substance of Prov 10:3
Slothfulness c into a deep sleep Prov 19:15
c down the strength of the Prov 21:22
As a mad man who c firebrands Prov 26:18
with gold, and c silver chains Is 40:19
As a fountain c out her waters, Jer 6:7
so she c out her wickedness Jer 6:7
He c out devils through the Mt 9:34
of the devils c he out devils Mk 3:22
He c out devils through Beelzebub Lk 11:15
but perfect love c out fear 1Jn 4:18
and c them out of the church 3Jn 10
as a fig tree c her untimely figs Rev 6:13

### CASTING
c them down to the ground 2Sa 8:2
all of them had one c, one 1Kin 7:37
c himself down before the house Ezr 10:1
ye see my c down, and are afraid Job 6:21
they have defiled by c down the Ps 74:7
his crown by c it to the ground Ps 89:39
by c up mounts, and building forts Eze 17:17
thy c down shall be in the midst Mic 6:14
his brother, c a net into the sea Mt 4:18
and parted his garments, c lots Mt 27:35
his brother c a net into the sea Mk 1:16
we saw one c out devils in thy Mk 9:38
c away his garment, rose, and came Mk 10:50
c lots upon them, what every man Mk 15:24
we saw one c out devils in thy Lk 9:49
he was c out a devil, and it was Lk 11:14
saw the rich men c their gifts Lk 21:1
poor widow c in thither two mites Lk 21:2
For if the c away of them be the Rom 11:15
C down imaginations, and every 2Cor 10:5
C all your care upon him 1Pet 5:7

### CASTLE
David took the c of Zion, which 1Chr 11:5
And David dwelt in the c 1Chr 11:7
are like the bars of a c Prov 18:19
him to be carried into the c Acts 21:34
as Paul was to be led into the c Acts 21:37
him to be brought into the c Acts 22:24
them, and to bring him into the c Acts 23:10
he went and entered into the c Acts 23:16
go with him, and returned to the c Acts 23:32

### CASTLES
by their towns, and by their c Gen 25:16
they dwelt, and all their goodly c Num 31:10
their c in their coasts, of the 1Chr 6:54
and in the villages, and in the c 1Chr 27:25
and he built in Judah c, and cities 2Chr 17:12
and in the forests he built c 2Chr 27:4

### CASTOR (*cas'-tor*) *Patron god of sailors.*
in the isle, whose sign was C Acts 28:11

### CATCH
c in thorns, so that the stacks Ex 22:6
c you every man his wife of the Judg 21:21
from him, and did hastily c it 1Kin 20:33
we shall c them alive, and get 2Kin 7:12
he lieth in wait to c the poor Ps 10:9
he doth c the poor, when he Ps 10:9
net that he hath hid c himself Ps 35:8
extortioner c all that he hath Ps 109:11
they set a trap, they c men Jer 5:26
lion, and it learned to c the prey Eze 19:3
lion, and learned to c the prey Eze 19:6
they c them in their net, and Hab 1:15
Herodians, to c him in his words Mk 12:13
from henceforth thou shalt c men Lk 5:10
seeking to c something out of his Lk 11:54

### CATCHETH
c any beast or fowl that may be Lev 17:13
c away that which was sown in his Mt 13:19
and the wolf c them, and scattereth Jn 10:12

### CATERPILLER
mildew, locust, or if there be c 1Kin 8:37
also their increase unto the c Ps 78:46
like the gathering of the c Is 33:4
hath left hath the c eaten Joel 1:4
eaten, the cankerworm, and the c Joel 2:25

### CATERPILLERS
or mildew, locusts, or c 2Chr 6:28
spake, and the locusts came, and c Ps 105:34
fill thee with men, as with c Jer 51:14
horses to come up as the rough c Jer 51:27

### CATTLE
living creature after his kind, c Gen 1:24
c after their kind, and every Gen 1:25
fowl of the air, and over the c Gen 1:26
And Adam gave names to all c Gen 2:20
this, thou art cursed above all c Gen 3:14
in tents, and of such as have c Gen 4:20
of c after their kind, of every Gen 6:20
all the c after their kind, and Gen 7:14
the earth, both of fowl, and of c Gen 7:21
of the ground, both man, and c Gen 7:23
all the c that was with him in Gen 8:1
all flesh, both of fowl, and of c Gen 8:17
with you, of the fowl, of the c Gen 9:10
And Abram was very rich in c Gen 13:2
c and the herdmen of Lot's c Gen 13:7

the c should be gathered together Gen 29:7
thee, and how thy c was with me Gen 30:29
all the speckled and spotted c Gen 30:32
all the brown c among the sheep, Gen 30:32
and brought forth c ringstraked Gen 30:39
and put them not unto Laban's c Gen 30:40
the stronger c did conceive Gen 30:41
the eyes of the c in the gutters Gen 30:41
But when the c were feeble Gen 30:42
exceedingly, and had much c Gen 30:43
then all the c bare speckled Gen 31:8
then bare all the c ringstraked Gen 31:8
taken away the c of your father Gen 31:9
at the time that the c conceived Gen 31:10
upon the c were ringstraked Gen 31:10
leap upon the c are ringstraked Gen 31:12
And he carried away all his c Gen 31:18
the c of his getting, which he Gen 31:18
daughters, and six years for thy c Gen 31:41
these c are my c, and all Gen 31:43
according as the c that goeth Gen 33:14
house, and made booths for his c Gen 33:17
sons were with his c in the field Gen 34:5
Shall not their c and their Gen 34:23
persons of his house, and his c Gen 36:6
not bear them because of their c Gen 36:7
And they took their c, and their Gen 46:6
their trade hath been to feed c Gen 46:32
c from our youth even until now Gen 46:34
then make them rulers over my c Gen 47:6
And Joseph said, Give your c Gen 47:16
and I will give you for your c Gen 47:16
they brought their c unto Joseph Gen 47:17
for the c of the herds, and for Gen 47:17
for all their c for that year Gen 47:17
my lord also hath our herds of c Gen 47:18
upon thy c which is in the field Ex 9:3
sever between the c of Israel Ex 9:4
of Israel and the c of Egypt Ex 9:4
and all the c of Egypt died Ex 9:6
but of the c of the children of Ex 9:6
of the c of the Israelites dead Ex 9:7
therefore now, and gather thy c Ex 9:19
his c flee into the houses Ex 9:20
servants and his c in the field Ex 9:21
Our c also shall go with us Ex 10:26
and all the firstborn of c Ex 12:29
and herds, even very much c Ex 12:38
our children and our c with thirst Ex 17:3
nor thy maidservant, nor thy c Ex 20:10
and every firstling among thy c Ex 34:19
bring your offering of the c Lev 1:2
beast, or a carcase of unclean c Lev 5:2
Thou shalt not let thy c gender Lev 19:19
And for thy c, and for the beast Lev 25:7
your children, and destroy your c Lev 26:22
the c of the Levites instead of Num 3:41
the c of the children of Israel Num 3:41
the c of the Levites instead of Num 3:45
of the Levites instead of their c Num 3:45
that we and our c should die there Num 20:4
my c drink of thy water, then I Num 20:19
and took the spoil of all their c Num 31:9
had a very great multitude of c Num 32:1
the place was a place for c Num 32:1
c, and thy servants have c Num 32:4
build sheepfolds here for our c Num 32:16
wives, our flocks, and all our c Num 32:26
of them shall be for their c Num 35:3
Only the c we took for a prey Deut 2:35
But all the c, and the spoil of Deut 3:7
and your little ones, and your c Deut 3:19
(for I know that ye have much c Deut 3:19
nor thine ass, nor any of thy c Deut 5:14
barren among you, or among your c Deut 7:14
grass in thy fields for thy c Deut 11:15
the c thereof, with the edge of Deut 13:15
and the little ones, and the c Deut 20:14
thy ground, and the fruit of thy c Deut 28:4
body, and in the fruit of thy c Deut 28:11
he shall eat the fruit of thy c Deut 28:51
body, and in the fruit of thy c Deut 30:9
your little ones, and your c Josh 1:14
the c thereof, shall ye take for Josh 8:2
Only the c and the spoil of that Josh 8:27
spoil of these cities, and the c Josh 11:14
with their suburbs for their c Josh 14:4
the suburbs thereof for our c Josh 21:2
your tents, and with very much c Josh 22:8
For they came up with their c Judg 6:5
and put the little ones and the c Judg 18:21
and brought away their c, and 1Sa 23:5
they drave before those other c 1Sa 30:20
fat c by the stone of Zoheleth, 1Kin 1:9
And he hath slain oxen and fat c 1Kin 1:19
day, and hath slain oxen and fat c 1Kin 1:25
for the c that followed them 2Kin 3:9
ye may drink, both ye, and your c 2Kin 3:17
because their c were multiplied 1Chr 5:9
And they took away their c 1Chr 5:21
came down to take away their c 1Chr 7:21
They smote also the tents of c 2Chr 14:15
for he had much c, both in the 2Chr 26:10
thousand and six hundred small c 2Chr 35:8
offerings five thousand small c 2Chr 35:9
over our bodies, and over our c Neh 9:37
of our sons, and of our c, as it Neh 10:36
the c also concerning the vapour Job 36:33
the c upon a thousand hills Ps 50:10
gave up their c also to the hail Ps 78:48
the grass to grow for the c Ps 104:14
suffereth not their c to decrease Ps 107:38
Beasts, and all c Ps 148:10
small c above all that were in Eccl 2:7
and for the treading of lesser c Is 7:25
in that day shall thy c feed in Is 30:23
small c of thy burnt offerings Is 43:23
upon the beasts, and upon the c Is 46:1
can men hear the voice of the c Jer 9:10
the multitude of their c a spoil Jer 49:32
I judge between c and c Eze 34:17
fat c and between the lean c Eze 34:20
I will judge between c and c Eze 34:22
the nations, which have gotten c Eze 38:12
silver and gold, to take away c Eze 38:13
the herds of c are perplexed, Joel 1:18
and also much c Jonah 4:11
forth, and upon men, and upon c Hag 1:11
the multitude of men and c therein Zec 2:4
taught me to keep c from my youth Zec 13:5
a servant plowing or feeding c Lk 17:7
and his children, and his c Jn 4:12

**CAUDA** See CLAUDA.

**CAUGHT**
behold behind him a ram c in a Gen 22:13
she c him by his garment, saying, Gen 39:12
c it, and it became a rod in his Ex 4:4
prey which the men of war had c Num 31:32
c him, and cut off his thumbs and Judg 1:6
c a young man of the men of Judg 8:14
c three hundred foxes, and took Judg 15:4
of them that danced, whom they c Judg 21:23
I c him by his beard, and smote 1Sa 17:35
they c every one his fellow by 2Sa 2:16
his head c hold of the oak, and he 2Sa 18:9
c hold on the horns of the altar 1Kin 1:50
he hath c hold on the horns of 1Kin 1:51
c hold on the horns of the altar 1Kin 2:28
Ahijah c the new garment that was 1Kin 11:30
the hill, she c him by the feet 2Kin 4:27
and they c him, (for he was hid in 2Chr 22:9
So she c him, and kissed him, and Prov 7:13
the birds that are c in the snare Eccl 9:12
thou art found, and also c Jer 50:24
c him, and said unto him, O thou Mt 14:31
And they c him, and cast him out of Mt 21:39
And they c him, and beat him, and Mk 12:3
For oftentimes it had c him Lk 8:29
and that night they c nothing Jn 21:3
of the fish which ye have now c Jn 21:10
c him, and brought him to the Acts 6:12
Spirit of the Lord c away Philip Acts 8:39
their gains was gone, they c Paul Acts 16:19
and having c Gaius and Aristarchus, Acts 19:29
the Jews c me in the temple Acts 26:21
And when the ship was c, and could Acts 27:15
such an one c up to the third 2Cor 12:2
How that he was c up into 2Cor 12:4
being crafty, I c you with guile 2Cor 12:16
remain shall be c up together 1Th 4:17
and her child was c up unto God Rev 12:5

**CAUL**
the c that is above the liver, and Ex 29:13
the c above the liver, and the two Ex 29:22
the c above the liver, with the Lev 3:4
the c above the liver, with the Lev 3:10
the c above the liver, with the Lev 3:15
the c above the liver, with the Lev 4:9
the c that is above the liver, Lev 7:4
the c above the liver, and the two Lev 8:16
the c above the liver, and the two Lev 8:25
the c above the liver of the sin Lev 9:10
kidneys, and the c above the liver Lev 9:19
will rend the c of their heart, Hos 13:8

**CAULS**
about their feet, and their c Is 3:18

**CAUSE** See PREFACE.

**CAUSED**
for the LORD God had not c it to Gen 2:5
the LORD God c a deep sleep to Gen 2:21
when God c me to wander from my Gen 20:13
For God hath c me to be fruitful Gen 41:52
the LORD c the sea to go back by Ex 14:21
they c it to be proclaimed Ex 36:6
as he hath c a blemish in a man, Lev 24:20
these c the children of Israel, Num 31:16
I have c thee to see it with Deut 34:4
she c him to shave off the seven Judg 16:19
when Samuel had c all the tribes 1Sa 10:20
When he had c the tribe of 1Sa 10:21
Jonathan c David to swear again, 1Sa 20:17
have c thee to rest from all 2Sa 7:11
c Solomon to ride upon king 1Kin 1:38
they have c him to ride upon the 1Kin 1:44
c a seat to be set for the king's 1Kin 2:19
he c him to come up into the 1Kin 20:33
they c their sons and their 2Kin 17:17
c the children of Israel to dwell 2Chr 8:2
But Jeroboam c an ambushment to 2Chr 13:13
c the inhabitants of Jerusalem to 2Chr 21:11
he c his children to pass through 2Chr 33:6
he c all that were present in 2Chr 34:32
the God that hath c his name to Ezr 6:12
c the people to understand the Neh 8:7
c them to understand the reading Neh 8:8
he c the gallows to be made Est 5:14
I c the widow's heart to sing for Job 29:13
or have c the eyes of the widow Job 31:16
or have c the owners thereof to Job 31:39
c the light of his cloud to shine Job 37:15
c the dayspring to know his place Job 38:12
Thou hast c men to ride over our Ps 66:12
sea, and c them to pass through Ps 78:13
c waters to run down like rivers Ps 78:16
He c an east wind to blow in the Ps 78:26
upon which thou hast c me to hope Ps 119:49
fair speech she c him to yield Prov 7:21
they have c Egypt to err in every Is 19:14
I have not c thee to serve with Is 43:23
he c the waters to flow out of Is 48:21
Spirit of the LORD c him to rest Is 63:14
c my people Israel to inherit Jer 12:14
so have I c to cleave unto me the Jer 13:11
I have c him to fall upon it Jer 15:8
they have c them to stumble in Jer 18:15
c my people Israel to err Jer 23:13
had c my people to hear my words, Jer 23:22
whom I have c to be carried away Jer 29:4
of the city whither I have c you Jer 29:7
again into the place whence I c Jer 29:14
he c you to trust in a lie Jer 29:31
therefore thou hast c all this Jer 32:23
c the servants and the handmaids, Jer 34:11
c every man his servant, and every Jer 34:16
ones have c a cry to be heard Jer 48:4
I have c wine to fail from the Jer 48:33
have c them to go astray, they Jer 50:6
As Babylon hath c the slain of Jer 51:49
the LORD hath c the solemn feasts Lam 2:6
he hath c thine enemy to rejoice Lam 2:17
He hath c the arrows of his Lam 3:13
and he c me to eat that roll Eze 3:2
I have c thee to multiply as the Eze 16:7
Wherefore I c them to go forth Eze 20:10
in that they c to pass through Eze 20:26
thou hast c thy days to draw near Eze 22:4
have also c their sons, whom they Eze 23:37
till I have c my fury to rest Eze 24:13
c his army to serve a great Eze 29:18
down to the grave I c a mourning Eze 31:15
I c Lebanon to mourn for him, and Eze 31:15
which c terror in the land of the Eze 32:23
which c their terror in the land Eze 32:24
though their terror was c in the Eze 32:25
though they c their terror in the Eze 32:26
For I have c my terror in the Eze 32:32
c me to pass by them round about Eze 37:2
which c them to be led into Eze 39:28
c the house of Israel to fall Eze 44:12
c me to pass by the four corners Eze 46:21
c me to return to the brink of Eze 47:6
being c to fly swiftly, touched Dan 9:21
of whoredoms hath c them to err Hos 4:12
their lies c them to err, after Amos 2:4
I c it to rain upon one city, and Amos 4:7
c it not to rain upon another Amos 4:7
he c it to be proclaimed and Jonah 3:7
I have c thine iniquity to pass Zec 3:4
ye have c many to stumble at the Mal 2:8
have c that even this man should Jn 11:37
they c great joy unto all the Acts 15:3
But if any have c grief, he hath 2Cor 2:5

**CAUSELESS**
that thou hast shed blood c 1Sa 25:31
so the curse c shall not come Prov 26:2

**CAUSES**
thou mayest bring the c unto God Ex 18:19
the hard c they brought unto Ex 18:26
Hear the c between your brethren, Deut 1:16
when for all the c whereby Jer 3:8
false burdens and c of banishment Lam 2:14
hast pleaded the c of my soul Lam 3:58
For these c the Jews caught me in Acts 26:21

**CAUSEST**
thou c me to ride upon it, and Job 30:22
c to approach unto thee, that he Ps 65:4

**CAUSETH**
the bitter water that c the curse Num 5:18
bitter water that c the curse Num 5:19
this water that c the curse shall Num 5:22
the bitter water that c the curse Num 5:24
the water that c the curse shall Num 5:24
that the water that c the curse Num 5:27
c them to wander in a wilderness Job 12:24
my understanding c me to answer Job 20:3
He c it to come, whether for Job 37:13
He c the grass to grow for the Ps 104:14
and c them to wander in the Ps 107:40
He c the vapours to ascend from Ps 135:7
he c his wind to blow, and the Ps 147:18
in harvest is a son that c shame Prov 10:5
winketh with the eye c sorrow Prov 10:10
wrath is against him that c shame Prov 14:35
have rule over a son that c shame Prov 17:2
The lot c contentions to cease, Prov 18:18
his mother, is a son that c shame Prov 19:26
that c to err from the words of Prov 19:27
Whoso c the righteous to go Prov 28:10
as the garden c the things that Is 61:11
the fire c the waters to boil, to Is 64:2
he c the vapors to ascend from Jer 10:13
he c the vapors to ascend from Jer 51:16
as the sea c his waves to come up Eze 26:3
with any thing that c sweat Eze 44:18
c her to commit adultery Mt 5:32

which always c us to triumph in 2Cor 2:14
which c through us thanksgiving 2Cor 9:11
c the earth and them which dwell Rev 13:12
he c all, both small and great, Rev 13:16

**CAUSEWAY**
by the c of the going up, ward 1Chr 26:16
At Parbar westward, four at the c 1Chr 26:18

**CAUSING**
c the lips of those that are Song 7:9
jaws of the people, c them to err Is 30:28
in c you to return to this place Jer 29:10
c their flocks to lie down Jer 33:12

**CAVE**
and he dwelt in a c, he and his two Gen 19:30
he may give me the c of Machpelah Gen 23:9
the c that is therein, I give it Gen 23:11
the c which was therein, and all Gen 23:17
the c of the field of Machpelah Gen 23:19
the c that is therein, were made Gen 23:20
buried him in the c of Machpelah Gen 25:9
c that is in the field of Ephron Gen 49:29
In the c that is in the field of Gen 49:30
of the c that is therein was from Gen 49:32
buried him in the c of the field Gen 50:13
hid themselves in a c at Makkedah Josh 10:16
are found hid in a c at Makkedah Josh 10:17
stones upon the mouth of the c Josh 10:18
Joshua, Open the mouth of the c Josh 10:22
five kings unto me out of the c Josh 10:22
five kings unto him out of the c Josh 10:23
cast them into the c wherein they Josh 10:27
and escaped to the c Adullam 1Sa 22:1
by the way, where was a c 1Sa 24:3
remained in the sides of the c 1Sa 24:3
But Saul rose up out of the c 1Sa 24:7
afterward, and went out of the c 1Sa 24:8
to day into mine hand in the c 1Sa 24:10
time unto the c of Adullam 2Sa 23:13
and hid them by fifty in a c 1Kin 18:4
LORD's prophets by fifty in a c 1Kin 18:13
And he came thither unto a c 1Kin 19:9
stood in the entering in of the c 1Kin 19:13
to David, into the c of Adullam 1Chr 11:15
when he fled from Saul in the c Ps 57:*t*
A Prayer when he was in the c Ps 142:*t*
It was a c, and a stone lay upon Jn 11:38

**CAVE'S**
laid great stones in the c mouth Josh 10:27

**CAVES**
which are in the mountains, and c Judg 6:2
people did hide themselves in c 1Sa 13:6
in c of the earth, and in the Job 30:6
into the c of the earth, for fear Is 2:19
in the c shall die of the Eze 33:27
and in dens and c of the earth Heb 11:38

**CEASE**
and day and night shall not c Gen 8:22
and the thunder shall c, neither Ex 9:29
shall c waiting upon the service Num 8:25
they prophesied, and did not c Num 11:25
I will make to c from me the Num 17:5
shall never c out of the land Deut 15:11
of them to c from among men Deut 32:26
children c from fearing the LORD Josh 22:25
of you, and after that I will c Judg 15:7
Benjamin my brother, or shall I c Judg 20:28
C not to cry unto the LORD our 1Sa 7:8
of Ramah, and let his work c 2Chr 16:5
to cause these men to c, and that Ezr 4:21
Jews, and made them to c by force Ezr 4:23
they could not cause them to c Ezr 5:5
slay them, and cause the work to c Neh 4:11
why should the work c, whilst I Neh 6:3
There the wicked c from troubling Job 3:17
c then, and let me alone, that I Job 10:20
tender branch thereof will not c Job 14:7
C from anger, and forsake wrath Ps 37:8
He maketh wars to c unto the end Ps 46:9
cause thine anger toward us to c Ps 85:4
Thou hast made his glory to c Ps 89:44
The lot causeth contentions to c Prov 18:18
C, my son, to hear the Prov 19:27
honour for a man to c from strife Prov 20:3
yea, strife and reproach shall c Prov 22:10
c from thine own wisdom Prov 23:4
the grinders c because they are Eccl 12:3
c to do evil Is 1:16
C ye from man, whose breath is in Is 2:22
while, and the indignation shall c Is 10:25
the arrogancy of the proud to c Is 13:11
made their vintage shouting to c Is 16:10
also shall c from Ephraim Is 17:3
sighing thereof have I made to c Is 21:2
One of Israel to c from before us Is 30:11
when thou shalt c to spoil Is 33:1
Then will I cause to c from the Jer 7:34
night and day, and let them not c Jer 14:17
I will cause to c out of this Jer 16:9
neither shall c from yielding Jer 17:8
c from being a nation before me Jer 31:36
shall cause to c from thence man Jer 36:29
I will cause to c in Moab Jer 48:35
let not the apple of thine eye c Lam 2:18
and your idols may be broken and c Eze 6:6
make the pomp of the strong to c Eze 7:24
I will make this proverb to c Eze 12:23
I will cause thee to c from Eze 16:41
make thy lewdness to c from thee Eze 23:27
lewdness to c out of the land Eze 23:48
cause the noise of thy songs to c Eze 26:13
c by the hand of Nebuchadrezzar Eze 30:10
their images to c out of Noph Eze 30:13
of her strength shall c in her Eze 30:18
the pomp of her strength shall c Eze 33:28
cause them to c from feeding the Eze 34:10
evil beasts to c out of the land Eze 34:25
sacrifice and the oblation to c Dan 9:27
the reproach offered by him to c Dan 11:18
will cause to c the kingdom of Hos 1:4
also cause all her mirth to c Hos 2:11
Then said I, O Lord GOD, c Amos 7:5
wilt thou not c to pervert the Acts 13:10
there be tongues, they shall c 1Cor 13:8
C not to give thanks for you, Eph 1:16
do not c to pray for you, and to Col 1:9
and that cannot c from sin 2Pet 2:14

**CEASED**
it c to be with Sarah after the Gen 18:11
and the thunders and hail c Ex 9:33
the hail and the thunders were c Ex 9:34
the manna c on the morrow after Josh 5:12
they c not from their own doings, Judg 2:19
The inhabitants of the villages c Judg 5:7
they c in Israel, until that I Judg 5:7
and they that were hungry c 1Sa 2:5
words in the name of David, and c 1Sa 25:9
Then c the work of the house of Ezr 4:24
So it c unto the second year of Ezr 4:24
these three men c to answer Job Job 32:1
they did tear me, and c not Ps 35:15
sore ran in the night, and c not Ps 77:2
and say, How hath the oppressor c Is 14:4
the golden city c Is 14:4
The elders have c from the gate Lam 5:14
The joy of our heart is c Lam 5:15
the sea c from her raging Jonah 1:15
come into the ship, the wind c Mt 14:32
And the wind c, and there was a Mk 4:39
and the wind c Mk 6:51
in hath not c to kiss my feet Lk 7:45
and they c, and there was a calm Lk 8:24
in a certain place, when he c Lk 11:1
they c not to teach and preach Acts 5:42
And after the uproar was c Acts 20:1
I c not to warn every one night Acts 20:31
he would not be persuaded, we c Acts 21:14
is the offence of the cross c Gal 5:11
he also hath c from his own works Heb 4:10
they not have c to be offered Heb 10:2
in the flesh hath c from sin 1Pet 4:1

**CEASETH**
for the godly man c Ps 12:1
is precious, and it c for ever Ps 49:8
is no talebearer, the strife c Prov 26:20
is at an end, the spoiler c Is 16:4
The mirth of tabrets c, the noise Is 24:8
endeth, the joy of the harp c Is 24:8
lie waste, the wayfaring man c Is 33:8
c not, without any intermission, Lam 3:49
who c from raising after he hath Hos 7:4
said, This man c not to speak Acts 6:13

**CEASING**
the LORD in c to pray for you 1Sa 12:23
but prayer was made without c of Acts 12:5
that without c I make mention of Rom 1:9
without c your work of faith 1Th 1:3
cause also thank we God without c 1Th 2:13
Pray without c 1Th 5:17
that without c I have remembrance 2Ti 1:3

**CEDAR**
c wood, and scarlet, and hyssop Lev 14:4
the c wood, and the scarlet, and Lev 14:6
c wood, and scarlet, and hyssop Lev 14:49
And he shall take the c wood Lev 14:51
living bird, and with the c wood Lev 14:52
And the priest shall take c wood Num 19:6
as c trees beside the waters Num 24:6
c trees, and carpenters, and masons 2Sa 5:11
See now, I dwell in an house of c 2Sa 7:2
Why build ye not me an house of c 2Sa 7:7
from the c tree that is in 1Kin 4:33
hew me c trees out of Lebanon 1Kin 5:6
thy desire concerning timber of c 1Kin 5:8
So Hiram gave Solomon c trees 1Kin 5:10
house with beams and boards of c 1Kin 6:9
on the house with timber of c 1Kin 6:10
the house within with boards of c 1Kin 6:15
and the walls with boards of c 1Kin 6:16
the c of the house within was 1Kin 6:18
all was c 1Kin 6:18
covered the altar which was of c 1Kin 6:20
hewed stone, and a row of c beams 1Kin 6:36
upon four rows of c pillars 1Kin 7:2
with c beams upon the pillars 1Kin 7:2
it was covered with c above upon 1Kin 7:3
it was covered with c from one 1Kin 7:7
hewed stones, and a row of c beams 1Kin 7:12
furnished Solomon with c trees 1Kin 9:11
sent to the c that was in Lebanon 2Kin 14:9
cut down the tall c trees thereof 2Kin 19:23
Also c trees in abundance 1Chr 22:4
Tyre brought much c wood to David 1Chr 22:4
c trees made he as the sycomore 2Chr 1:15
Send me also c trees, fir trees, 2Chr 2:8
c trees made he as the sycomore 2Chr 9:27
sent to the c that was in Lebanon 2Chr 25:18
to bring c trees from Lebanon to Ezr 3:7
He moveth his tail like a c Job 40:17
he shall grow like a c in Lebanon Ps 92:12
The beams of our house are c Song 1:17
will inclose her with boards of c Song 8:9
plant in the wilderness the c Is 41:19
and it is cieled with c, and Jer 22:14
because thou closest thyself in c Jer 22:15
took the highest branch of the c Eze 17:3
the highest branch of the high c Eze 17:22
and bear fruit, and be a goodly c Eze 17:23
bound with cords, and made of c Eze 27:24
the Assyrian was a c in Lebanon Eze 31:3
for he shall uncover the c work Zeph 2:14
for the c is fallen Zec 11:2

**CEDARS**
and devour the c of Lebanon Judg 9:15
measures of hewed stones, and c 1Kin 7:11
c made he to be as the sycomore 1Kin 10:27
to David, and timber of c, with 1Chr 14:1
Lo, I dwell in an house of c 1Chr 17:1
ye not built me an house of c 1Chr 17:6
didst send him c to build him an 2Chr 2:3
voice of the LORD breaketh the c Ps 29:5
LORD breaketh the c of Lebanon Ps 29:5
thereof were like the goodly c Ps 80:10
the c of Lebanon, which he hath Ps 104:16
fruitful trees, and all c Ps 148:9
is as Lebanon, excellent as the c Song 5:15
And upon all the c of Lebanon Is 2:13
but we will change them into c Is 9:10
the c of Lebanon, saying, Since Is 14:8
will cut down the tall c thereof Is 37:24
He heweth him down c, and taketh Is 44:14
they shall cut down thy choice c Jer 22:7
that makest thy nest in the c Jer 22:23
they have taken c from Lebanon to Eze 27:5
The c in the garden of God could Eze 31:8
was like the height of the c Amos 2:9
that the fire may devour thy c Zec 11:1

**CEDRON** (*se'-drun*) See KIDRON. *Same as Kidron.*
his disciples over the brook C Jn 18:1

**CELEBRATE**
even, shall ye c your sabbath Lev 23:32
ye shall c it in the seventh Lev 23:41
praise thee, death can not c thee Is 38:18

**CELESTIAL**
There are also c bodies, and 1Cor 15:40
but the glory of the c is one 1Cor 15:40

**CELLARS**
wine c was Zabdi the Shiphmite 1Chr 27:27
over the c of oil was Joash 1Chr 27:28

**CENCHREA** (*sen'-kre-ah*) *Harbor city for Corinth.*
having shorn his head in C Acts 18:18
of the church which is at C Rom 16:1
Phebe servant of the church at C Rom *s*

**CENCHREAE** See CENCHREA.

**CENSER**
Aaron, took either of them his c Lev 10:1
he shall take a c full of burning Lev 16:12
And take every man his c, and put Num 16:17
before the LORD every man his c Num 16:17
also, and Aaron, each of you his c Num 16:17
And they took every man his c Num 16:18
Moses said unto Aaron, Take a c Num 16:46
had a c in his hand to burn 2Chr 26:19
with every man his c in his hand Eze 8:11
Which had the golden c, and the Heb 9:4
at the altar, having a golden c Rev 8:3
And the angel took the c, and Rev 8:5

**CENSERS**
minister about it, even the c Num 4:14
Take you c, Korah, and all his Num 16:6
censer, two hundred and fifty c Num 16:17
take up the c out of the burning Num 16:37
The c of these sinners against Num 16:38
the priest took the brasen c Num 16:39
the spoons, and the c of pure gold 1Kin 7:50
basons, and the spoons, and the c 2Chr 4:22

**CENTURION**
there came unto him a c, Mt 8:5
The c answered and said, Lord, I Mt 8:8
And Jesus said unto the c, Go thy Mt 8:13
Now when the c, and they that were Mt 27:54
And when the c, which stood over Mk 15:39
and calling unto him the c Mk 15:44
And when he knew it of the c Mk 15:45
the c sent friends to him, saying Lk 7:6
Now when the c saw what was done, Lk 23:47
a c of the band called the Acts 10:1
And they said, Cornelius the c Acts 10:22
said unto the c that stood by Acts 22:25
When the c heard that, he went and Acts 22:26
And he commanded a c to keep Paul Acts 24:23
Julius, a c of Augustus' band Acts 27:1
there the c found a ship of Acts 27:6
Nevertheless the c believed the Acts 27:11
Paul said to the c and to the Acts 27:31
But the c, willing to save Paul, Acts 27:43
the c delivered the prisoners to Acts 28:16

**CENTURION'S**
And a certain *c* servant, who was............. Lk 7:2

**CENTURIONS**
immediately took soldiers and *c*.......... Acts 21:32
Paul called one of the *c* unto him....... Acts 23:17
And he called unto him two *c*............ Acts 23:23

**CEPHAS** (*se'-fas*) See PETER. *Name given to Simon Peter.*
thou shalt be called C, which is ............... Jn 1:42
and I of C............................................. 1Cor 1:12
Whether Paul, or Apollos, or C............ 1Cor 3:22
as the brethren of the Lord, and C........... 1Cor 9:5
And that he was seen of C, then of..... 1Cor 15:5
And when James, C, and John, who........ Gal 2:9

**CEREMONIES**
and according to all the *c* thereof.......... Num 9:3

**CERTAIN**
And he lighted upon a *c* place............. Gen 28:11
a *c* man found him, and, behold, he..... Gen 37:15
and turned in to a *c* Adullamite............. Gen 38:1
there a daughter of a *c* Canaanite ........ Gen 38:2
gather a *c* rate every day, that I ............. Ex 16:4
And there were *c* men, who were............ Num 9:6
with *c* of the children of Israel,........... Num 16:2
C men, the children of Belial,............... Deut 13:13
if it be truth, and the thing *c*............. Deut 13:14
it be true, and the thing *c*.................... Deut 17:4
to his fault, by a *c* number ................ Deut 25:2
a *c* woman cast a piece of a ................. Judg 9:53
there was a *c* man of Zorah, of ............ Judg 13:2
that there was a *c* Levite ..................... Judg 19:1
*c* sons of Belial, beset the house........... Judg 19:22
a *c* man of Beth-lehem-judah went....... Ruth 1:1
Now there was a *c* man of........................ 1Sa 1:1
Now a *c* man of the servants of .............. 1Sa 21:7
a *c* man saw it, and told Joab, and ...... 2Sa 18:10
thou shalt know for *c* that thou........... 1Kin 2:37
unto thee, saying, Know for a *c*............ 1Kin 2:42
oxen were *c* additions made of ............ 1Kin 7:29
*c* Edomites of his father's.................. 1Kin 11:17
a *c* man of the sons of the.................. 1Kin 20:35
a *c* man drew a bow at a venture, ..... 1Kin 22:34
Now there cried a *c* woman of the ........ 2Kin 4:1
appointed unto her a *c* officer ............... 2Kin 8:6
*c* of them had the charge of the........... 1Chr 9:28
he appointed *c* of the Levites to........... 1Chr 16:4
Then there went *c*, and told David...... 1Chr 19:5
Even after a *c* rate every day,.............. 2Chr 8:13
after *c* years he went down to.............. 2Chr 18:2
a *c* man drew a bow at a venture,..... 2Chr 18:33
Then *c* of the heads of the................ 2Chr 28:12
with *c* chief of the fathers,.................... Ezr 10:16
came, he and *c* men of Judah.................. Neh 1:2
down and wept, and mourned *c* days..... Neh 1:4
at Jerusalem dwelt *c* of the.................... Neh 11:4
that a *c* portion should be for ............. Neh 11:23
*c* of the priests' sons with..................... Neh 12:35
after *c* days obtained I leave of ............ Neh 13:6
smote *c* of them, and plucked off......... Neh 13:25
the palace there was a *c* Jew ................ Est 2:5
There is a *c* people scattered................. Est 3:8
But know ye for *c*, that if ye put.......... Jer 26:15
Then rose up *c* of the elders of............. Jer 26:17
*c* men with him into Egypt .................... Jer 26:22
That there came *c* from Shechem ........... Jer 41:5
*c* of the poor of the people.................... Jer 52:15
*c* of the poor of the land for.................. Jer 52:16
Then came *c* of the elders of ................ Eze 14:1
that *c* of the elders of Israel .................. Eze 20:1
that he should bring *c* of the................. Dan 1:3
and the dream is *c*, and the.................... Dan 2:45
that time *c* Chaldeans came near............ Dan 3:8
There are *c* Jews whom thou hast.......... Dan 3:12
unto that *c* saint which spake................ Dan 8:13
fainted, and was sick *c* days ................ Dan 8:27
behold a *c* man clothed in linen,............ Dan 10:5
after *c* years with a great army ........... Dan 11:13
a *c* scribe came, and said unto him ........ Mt 8:19
*c* of the scribes said within........................ Mt 9:3
behold, there came a *c* ruler ..................... Mt 9:18
Then *c* of the scribes and of the ............ Mt 12:38
there came to him a *c* man ..................... Mt 17:14
of heaven likened unto a *c* king ............. Mt 18:23
desiring a *c* thing of him.......................... Mt 20:20
A *c* man had two sons............................... Mt 21:28
There was a *c* householder...................... Mt 21:33
of heaven is like unto a *c* king................. Mt 22:2
But there were *c* of the scribes................... Mk 2:6
a *c* woman, which had an issue of ......... Mk 5:25
synagogue's house *c* which said.............. Mk 5:35
*c* of the scribes, which came from ............. Mk 7:1
For a *c* woman, whose young.................... Mk 7:25
*c* of them that stood there said ................ Mk 11:5
A *c* man planted a vineyard, and .............. Mk 12:1
send unto him *c* of the Pharisees............. Mk 12:13
And there came a *c* poor widow ............... Mk 12:42
there followed him a *c* young man....... Mk 14:51
And there arose *c*, and bare false ......... Mk 14:57
a *c* priest named Zacharias, of.................. Lk 1:5
to pass, when he was in a *c* city ............. Lk 5:12
And it came to pass on a *c* day ................ Lk 5:17
*c* of the Pharisees said unto them.............. Lk 6:2
a *c* centurion's servant, who was.............. Lk 7:2
There was a *c* creditor which had............ Lk 7:41
*c* women, which had been healed of ......... Lk 8:2
it was told him by *c* which said.............. Lk 8:20
Now it came to pass on a *c* day ............... Lk 8:22
met him out of the city a *c* man .............. Lk 8:27
a *c* man said unto him, Lord, I ................ Lk 9:57
a *c* lawyer stood up, and tempted............ Lk 10:25
A *c* man went down from Jerusalem .... Lk 10:30
came down a *c* priest that way ............. Lk 10:31
But a *c* Samaritan, as he....................... Lk 10:33
that he entered into a *c* village............... Lk 10:38
a *c* woman named Martha received ...... Lk 10:38
as he was praying in a *c* place.................. Lk 11:1
a *c* woman of the company lifted .......... Lk 11:27
a *c* Pharisee besought him to dine.......... Lk 11:37
The ground of a *c* rich man.................... Lk 12:16
A *c* man had a fig tree planted in ............ Lk 13:6
day there came *c* of the Pharisees ......... Lk 13:31
there was a *c* man before him ................... Lk 14:2
A *c* man made a great supper, and........ Lk 14:16
And he said, A *c* man had two sons....... Lk 15:11
disciples, There was a *c* rich man ............ Lk 16:1
There was a *c* rich man, which was....... Lk 16:19
there was a *c* beggar named................... Lk 16:20
And as he entered into a *c* village .......... Lk 17:12
he spake this parable unto *c* ...................... Lk 18:9
a *c* ruler asked him, saying, Good.......... Lk 18:18
a *c* blind man sat by the way side .......... Lk 18:35
A *c* nobleman went into a far................ Lk 19:12
A *c* man planted a vineyard, and .............. Lk 20:9
came to him *c* of the Sadducees............. Lk 20:27
Then *c* of the scribes answering.............. Lk 20:39
he saw also a *c* poor widow ...................... Lk 21:2
But a *c* maid beheld him as he sat......... Lk 22:56
(Who for a *c* sedition made in the .......... Lk 23:19
prepared, and *c* others with them .............. Lk 24:1
*c* women also of our company made..... Lk 24:22
*c* of them which were with us went........ Lk 24:24
And there was a *c* nobleman ..................... Jn 4:46
down at a *c* season into the pool............... Jn 5:4
a *c* man was there, which had an................ Jn 5:5
Now a *c* man was sick, named.................... Jn 11:1
there were *c* Greeks among them ............ Jn 12:20
a *c* man lame from his mother's ............ Acts 3:2
But a *c* man named Ananias, with .......... Acts 5:1
privy to it, and brought a *c* part ........... Acts 5:2
there arose *c* of the synagogue .............. Acts 6:9
But there was a *c* man, called ............... Acts 8:9
way, they came unto a *c* water............. Acts 8:36
there was a *c* disciple at...................... Acts 9:10
Then was Saul *c* days with the .............. Acts 9:19
he found a *c* man named Aeneas............ Acts 9:33
Joppa a *c* disciple named Tabitha.......... Acts 9:36
There was a *c* man in Caesarea ............. Acts 10:1
a *c* vessel descending unto him,............ Acts 10:11
*c* brethren from Joppa accompanied.. Acts 10:23
prayed they him to tarry *c* days........... Acts 10:48
A *c* vessel descend, as it had................ Acts 11:5
his hands to vex *c* of the church ........... Acts 12:1
that was at Antioch *c* prophets ............. Acts 13:1
Paphos, they found a *c* sorcerer............ Acts 13:6
there sat a *c* man at Lystra,................... Acts 14:8
came thither *c* Jews from Antioch ..... Acts 14:19
*c* men which came down from Judaea Acts 15:1
*c* other of them, should go up to ........... Acts 15:2
But there rose up *c* of the sect............... Acts 15:5
that *c* which went out from us ........... Acts 15:24
a *c* disciple was there, named............... Acts 16:1
Timotheus, the son of a *c* woman ......... Acts 16:1
were in that city abiding *c* days......... Acts 16:12
a *c* woman named Lydia, a seller......... Acts 16:14
a *c* damsel possessed with a.................. Acts 16:16
took unto them *c* lewd fellows of............ Acts 17:5
*c* brethren unto the rulers of the........... Acts 17:6
Then *c* philosophers of the.................. Acts 17:18
For thou bringest *c* strange.................. Acts 17:20
as *c* also of your own poets have........ Acts 17:28
Howbeit *c* men clave unto him, and.. Acts 17:34
found a *c* Jew named Aquila, born.......... Acts 18:2
and entered into a *c* man's house.......... Acts 18:7
a *c* Jew named Apollos, born at........... Acts 18:24
and finding *c* disciples,........................ Acts 19:1
Then *c* of the vagabond Jews,............. Acts 19:13
For a *c* man named Demetrius, a ......... Acts 19:24
*c* of the chief of Asia, which ............... Acts 19:31
there sat in a window a *c* young .......... Acts 20:9
came down from Judaea a *c* prophet. Acts 21:10
There went with us also *c* of the ........ Acts 21:16
*c* of the Jews banded together, and ... Acts 23:12
for he hath a *c* thing to tell him ........ Acts 23:17
with a *c* orator named Tertullus, .......... Acts 24:1
Whereupon *c* Jews from Asia found.. Acts 24:18
And after *c* days, when Felix came..... Acts 24:24
after *c* days king Agrippa and ............ Acts 25:13
There is a *c* man left in bonds by ....... Acts 25:14
But had *c* questions against him......... Acts 25:19
Of whom I have no *c* thing to............. Acts 25:26
*c* other prisoners unto one named........ Acts 27:1
running under a *c* island which is ...... Acts 27:16
we must be cast upon a *c* island........... Acts 27:26
discovered a *c* creek with a shore ...... Acts 27:39
Achaia to make a *c* contribution......... Rom 15:26
have no *c* dwellingplace place............... 1Cor 4:11
For before that *c* came from James....... Gal 2:12
it is *c* we can carry nothing out .............. 1Ti 6:7
But one in a *c* place testified,.................. Heb 2:6
For he spake in a *c* place of the................ Heb 4:4
Again, he limiteth a *c* day ....................... Heb 4:7
But a *c* fearful looking for of............... Heb 10:27
For there are *c* men crept in...................... Jude 4

**CERTAINLY**
I will *c* return unto thee..................... Gen 18:10
We saw *c* that the LORD was with ...... Gen 26:28
could we *c* know that he would say..... Gen 43:7
that such a man as I can *c* divine......... Gen 44:15
will *c* requite us all the evil................. Gen 50:15
And he said, C I will be with thee ........... Ex 3:12
If the theft be *c* found in his..................... Ex 22:4
he hath *c* trespassed against the ............ Lev 5:19
congregation shall *c* stone him ............ Lev 24:16
Because it was *c* told thy........................ Josh 9:24
if ye can *c* declare it me within ........... Judg 14:12
Thy father *c* knoweth that I have.......... 1Sa 20:3
for if I knew *c* that evil were ................. 1Sa 20:9
thy servant hath *c* heard that ............... 1Sa 23:10
for the LORD will *c* make my lord .......... 1Sa 25:28
even so will I *c* do this day .................... 1Kin 1:30
unto him, Thou mayest *c* recover .......... 2Kin 8:10
If thou *c* return in peace, then ............ 2Chr 18:27
for riches *c* make themselves ................. Prov 23:5
Lo, *c* in vain made he it............................. Jer 8:8
Do we not *c* know that every ................ Jer 13:12
Ye shall *c* drink........................................ Jer 25:28
The king of Babylon shall *c* come.......... Jer 36:29
Dost thou *c* know that Baalis the .......... Jer 40:14
know *c* that I have admonished you.... Jer 42:19
Now therefore know *c* that ye............... Jer 42:22
But we will *c* do whatsoever thing......... Jer 44:17
*c* this is the day that we looked.............. Lam 2:16
and one shall *c* come, and overflow,... Dan 11:10
shall *c* come after certain years .......... Dan 11:13
C this was a righteous man ..................... Lk 23:47

**CERTAINTY**
Know for a *c* that the LORD your ....... Josh 23:13
and come ye again to me with the *c* ... 1Sa 23:23
know the *c* of the words of truth....... Prov 22:21
I know of *c* that ye would gain ............... Dan 2:8
know the *c* of those things.......................... Lk 1:4
not know the *c* for the tumult ........... Acts 21:34
*c* wherefore he was accused of the.... Acts 22:30

**CERTIFIED**
have we sent and *c* the king................... Ezr 4:14
Esther *c* the king thereof in ................... Est 2:22

**CERTIFY**
there come word from you to *c* me ..... 2Sa 15:28
We *c* the king that, if this city ............... Ezr 4:16
to *c* thee, that we might write................. Ezr 5:10
Also we *c* you, that touching any............ Ezr 7:24
But I *c* you, brethren, that the............... Gal 1:11

**CHAFED**
they be *c* in their minds, as a .................. 2Sa 17:8

**CHAFF**
as *c* that the storm carrieth away ........ Job 21:18
but are like the *c* which the wind.............. Ps 1:4
Let them be as *c* before the wind ............ Ps 35:5
and the flame consumeth the *c*................ Is 5:24
shall be chased as the *c* of the .............. Is 17:13
shall be as *c* that passeth away.............. Is 29:5
Ye shall conceive *c*, ye shall ................... Is 33:11
and shalt make the hills as *c* .................. Is 41:15
What is the *c* to the wheat .................... Jer 23:28
became like the *c* of the summer .......... Dan 2:35
as the *c* that is driven with the ............ Hos 13:3
before the day pass as the *c*.................... Zeph 2:2
up the *c* with unquenchable fire ............... Mt 3:12
but the *c* he will burn with fire ................ Lk 3:17

**CHAIN**
put a gold *c* about his neck ................. Gen 41:42
work, and wreaths of *c* work ................ 1Kin 7:17
compasseth them about as a *c* .................. Ps 73:6
eyes, with one *c* of thy neck.................. Song 4:9
he hath made my *c* heavy ....................... Lam 3:7
Make a *c*................................................. Eze 7:23
thy hands, and a *c* on thy neck ........... Eze 16:11
have a *c* of gold about his neck,.............. Dan 5:7
have a *c* of gold about thy neck,............ Dan 5:16
put a *c* of gold about his neck,.............. Dan 5:29
of Israel I am bound with this *c* .......... Acts 28:20
me, and was not ashamed of my *c*............ 2Ti 1:16
pit and a great *c* in his hand .................. Rev 20:1

**CHAINS**
two *c* of pure gold at the ends................ Ex 28:14
the wreathen *c* to the ouches .................. Ex 28:14
*c* at the ends of wreathen work of ......... Ex 28:22
*c* of gold in the two rings which ............ Ex 28:24
*c* thou shalt fasten in the two................. Ex 28:25
the breastplate *c* at the ends.................. Ex 39:15
they put the two wreathen *c* of............... Ex 39:17
two ends of the two wreathen *c*.............. Ex 39:18
hath gotten, of jewels of gold, *c*............ Num 31:50
beside the *c* that were about.................. Judg 8:26
the *c* of gold before the oracle ............... 1Kin 6:21
and set thereon palm trees and *c*............ 2Chr 3:5
And he made *c*, as in the oracle,............ 2Chr 3:16
and put them on the *c*............................. 2Chr 3:16
out those which are bound with *c*............. Ps 68:6
To bind their kings with *c*........................ Ps 149:8
thy head, and *c* about thy neck ................ Prov 1:9
jewels, thy neck with *c* of gold .............. Song 1:10
The *c*, and the bracelets, and the .............. Is 3:19
with gold, and casteth silver *c*................ Is 40:19
in *c* they shall come over, and ............... Is 45:14
eyes, and bound him with *c* ................... Jer 39:7
in *c* among all that were carried.............. Jer 40:1
the *c* which were upon thine hand ........... Jer 40:4
king of Babylon bound him in *c* ............. Jer 52:11
they brought him with *c* unto the .......... Eze 19:4
And they put him in ward in *c* ............... Eze 19:9
all her great men were bound in *c*.......... Nah 3:10
could bind him, no, not with *c* ................... Mk 5:3
often bound with fetters and *c*................... Mk 5:4

c his raiment, and came in unto Gen 41:14
be c unto white, he shall come Lev 13:16
the plague have not c his colour Lev 13:55
Baal-meon, (their names being c Num 32:38
he c his behaviour before them, 1Sa 21:13
c his apparel, and came into the 2Sa 12:20
stead, and c his name to Zedekiah 2Kin 24:17
And c his prison garments 2Kin 25:29
of my disease is my garment c Job 30:18
when he c his behaviour before Ps 34:*t*
change them, and they shall be c Ps 102:26
Thus they c their glory into the Ps 106:20
boldness of his face shall be c Eccl 8:1
c the ordinance, broken the Is 24:5
Hath a nation c their gods Jer 2:11
but my people have c their glory Jer 2:11
in him, and his scent is not c Jer 48:11
And c his prison garments Jer 52:33
how is the most fine gold c Lam 4:1
she hath c my judgments into Eze 5:6
before me, till the time be c Dan 2:9
his visage was c against Shadrach Dan 3:19
neither were their coats c Dan 3:27
have c the king's word, and Dan 3:28
Let his heart be c from man's Dan 4:16
Then the king's countenance was c Dan 5:6
and his countenance was c in him Dan 5:9
nor let thy countenance be c Dan 5:10
the writing, that it be not c Dan 6:8
the king establisheth may be c Dan 6:15
might not be c concerning Daniel Dan 6:17
me, and my countenance c in me Dan 7:28
he hath c the portion of my Mic 2:4
they c their minds, and said that Acts 28:6
c the glory of the uncorruptible Rom 1:23
Who c the truth of God into a lie Rom 1:25
all sleep, but we shall all be c 1Cor 15:51
incorruptible, and we shall be c 1Cor 15:52
are c into the same image from 2Cor 3:18
fold them up, and they shall be c Heb 1:12
For the priesthood being c Heb 7:12

**CHANGERS**
doves, and the c of money sitting Jn 2:14

**CHANGERS'**
and poured out the c money Jn 2:15

**CHANGES**
he gave each man c of raiment Gen 45:22
of silver, and five c of raiment Gen 45:22
of gold, and ten c of raiment 2Kin 5:5
of silver, and two c of garments 2Kin 5:22
with two c of garments, and laid 2Kin 5:23
c and war are against me Job 10:17
Because they have no c, therefore Ps 55:19

**CHANGEST**
thou c his countenance, and Job 14:20

**CHANGETH**
to his own hurt, and c not Ps 15:4
he c the times and the seasons Dan 2:21

**CHANGING**
redeeming and concerning c Ruth 4:7

**CHANNEL**
LORD shall beat off from the c of Is 27:12

**CHANNELS**
the c of the sea appeared, the 2Sa 22:16
Then the c of waters were seen, Ps 18:15
he shall come up over all his c Is 8:7

**CHANT**
That c to the sound of the viol, Amos 6:5

**CHAPEL**
for it is the king's c, and it is Amos 7:13

**CHAPITER**
of the one c was five cubits 1Kin 7:16
of the other c was five cubits 1Kin 7:16
seven for the one c 1Kin 7:17
and seven for the other c 1Kin 7:17
and so did he for the other c 1Kin 7:18
rows round about upon the other c 1Kin 7:20
And the mouth of it within the c 1Kin 7:31
and the c upon it was brass 2Kin 25:17
the height of the c three cubits 2Kin 25:17
upon the c round about, all of 2Kin 25:17
the c that was on the top of each 2Chr 3:15
And a c of brass was upon it Jer 52:22
height of one c was five cubits Jer 52:22

**CHAPITERS**
and he overlaid their c and their Ex 36:38
overlaying of their c of silver Ex 38:17
and the overlaying of their c Ex 38:19
the pillars, and overlaid their c Ex 38:28
he made two c of molten brass, to 1Kin 7:16
for the c which were upon the top 1Kin 7:17
to cover the c that were upon the 1Kin 7:18
the c that were upon the top of 1Kin 7:19
the c upon the two pillars had 1Kin 7:20
the two bowls of the c that were 1Kin 7:41
to cover the two bowls of the c 1Kin 7:41
the c that were upon the pillars 1Kin 7:42
the c which were on the top of 2Chr 4:12
c which were on the top of the 2Chr 4:12
the c which were upon the pillars 2Chr 4:13
upon the c round about, all of Jer 52:22

**CHAPMEN**
Beside that which c and merchants 2Chr 9:14

**CHAPT**
Because the ground is c, for Jer 14:4

**CHARASHIM** (*car'-a-shim*) *Place founded by Joab.*
the father of the valley of C 1Chr 4:14

**CHARCHEMISH** (*car'-ke-mish*) See CARCHEMISH. *Same as Carchemish.*
to fight against C by Euphrates 2Chr 35:20

**CHARGE**
obeyed my voice, and kept my c Gen 26:5
as he blessed him he gave him a c Gen 28:6
gave them a c unto the children Ex 6:13
c the people, lest they break Ex 19:21
keep the c of the LORD, that ye Lev 8:35
the Levites shall keep the c of Num 1:53
And they shall keep his c, and the Num 3:7
the c of the whole congregation Num 3:7
the c of the children of Israel, Num 3:8
the c of the sons of Gershon in Num 3:25
keeping the c of the sanctuary Num 3:28
their c shall be the ark, and the Num 3:31
that keep the c of the sanctuary Num 3:32
c of the sons of Merari shall be Num 3:36
keeping the c of the sanctuary Num 3:38
the c of the children of Israel Num 3:38
unto them in c all their burdens Num 4:27
their c shall be under the hand Num 4:28
this is the c of their burden, Num 4:31
of the c of their burden Num 4:32
the priest shall c her by an oath Num 5:19
Then the priest shall c the woman Num 5:21
the congregation, to keep the c Num 8:26
unto the Levites touching their c Num 8:26
of Israel kept the c of the LORD Num 9:19
they kept the c of the LORD Num 9:23
And they shall keep thy c, and the Num 18:3
the c of all the tabernacle Num 18:3
keep the c of the tabernacle of Num 18:4
shall keep the c of the sanctuary Num 18:5
sanctuary, and the c of the altar Num 18:5
I also have given thee the c of Num 18:8
give him a c in their sight Num 27:19
hands upon him, and gave him a c Num 27:23
Levites, which keep the c of the Num 31:30
Levites, which kept the c of the Num 31:47
men of war which are under our c Num 31:49
But c Joshua, and encourage him, Deut 3:28
the LORD thy God, and keep his c Deut 11:1
unto thy people of Israel's c Deut 21:8
that I may give him a c Deut 31:14
he gave Joshua the son of Nun a c Deut 31:23
but have kept the c of the Josh 22:3
I will give c concerning thee 2Sa 14:8
the captains c concerning Absalom 2Sa 18:5
keep the c of the LORD thy God, 1Kin 2:3
every man according to his c 1Kin 4:28
all the c of the house of Joseph 1Kin 11:28
leaned to have the c of the gate 2Kin 7:17
because the c was upon them, and 1Chr 9:27
certain of them had the c of the 1Chr 9:28
give thee c concerning Israel, 1Chr 22:12
the c of the tabernacle of the 1Chr 23:32
the c of the holy place, and the 1Chr 23:32
the c of the sons of Aaron their 1Chr 23:32
for we keep the c of the LORD our 2Chr 13:11
therefore the Levites had the c 2Chr 30:17
of the palace, c over Jerusalem Neh 7:2
to c ourselves yearly with the Neh 10:32
that have the c of the business Est 3:9
to c her that she should go in Est 4:8
hath given him a c over the earth Job 34:13
they laid to my c things that I Ps 35:11
shall give his angels c over thee Ps 91:11
I c you, O ye daughters of Song 2:7
I c you, O ye daughters of Song 3:5
I c you, O daughters of Jerusalem Song 5:8
beloved, that thou dost so c us Song 5:9
I c you, O daughters of Jerusalem Song 8:4
of my wrath will I give him a c Is 10:6
king of Babylon gave c concerning Jer 39:11
given it a c against Ashkelon Jer 47:7
which had the c of the men of war Jer 52:25
Cause them that have c over the Eze 9:1
the keepers of the c of the house Eze 40:45
the keepers of the c of the altar Eze 40:46
kept the c of mine holy things Eze 44:8
but ye have set keepers of my c Eze 44:8
having c at the gates of the Eze 44:11
keepers of the c of the house Eze 44:14
that kept the c of my sanctuary Eze 44:15
unto me, and they shall keep my c Eze 44:16
which have kept my c, which went Eze 48:11
ways, and if thou wilt keep my c Zec 3:7
give his angels c concerning thee Mt 4:6
I c thee, come out of him, and Mk 9:25
shall give his angels c over thee Lk 4:10
Lord, lay not this sin to their c Acts 7:60
who had the c of all her treasure Acts 8:27
Who, having received such a c Acts 16:24
his c worthy of death or of bonds Acts 23:29
any thing to the c of God's elect Rom 8:33
the gospel of Christ without c 1Cor 9:18
I c you by the Lord that this 1Th 5:27
that thou mightest c some that 1Ti 1:3
This c I commit unto thee, son 1Ti 1:18
And these things give in c 1Ti 5:7
I c thee before God, and the Lord 1Ti 5:21
I give thee c in the sight of God 1Ti 6:13
C them that are rich in this 1Ti 6:17
I c thee therefore before God, and 2Ti 4:1
it may not be laid to their c 2Ti 4:16

**CHARGEABLE**
now go, lest we be c unto thee 2Sa 13:25
before me were c unto the people Neh 5:15
you, and wanted, I was c to no man 2Cor 11:9
we would not be c unto any of you 1Th 2:9
we might not be c to any of you 2Th 3:8

**CHARGED**
Abimelech c all his people, Gen 26:11
c him, and said unto him, Thou Gen 28:1
of the guard c Joseph with them Gen 40:4
he c them, and said unto them, I Gen 49:29
Pharaoh c all his people, saying, Ex 1:22
I c your judges at that time, Deut 1:16
shall he be c with any business Deut 24:5
Moses c the people the same day, Deut 27:11
Joshua c them that went to Josh 18:8
the servant of the LORD c you Josh 22:5
have I not c the young men that Ruth 2:9
father c the people with the oath 1Sa 14:27
Thy father straitly c the people 1Sa 14:28
c the messenger, saying, When 2Sa 11:19
in our hearing the king c thee 2Sa 18:12
he c Solomon his son, saying, 1Kin 2:1
that I have c thee with 1Kin 2:43
For so was it c me by the word of 1Kin 13:9
whom the LORD had c them, that 2Kin 17:15
c them, saying, Ye shall not fear 2Kin 17:35
c him to build an house for the 1Chr 22:6
judgments which the LORD c Moses 1Chr 22:13
he c them, saying, Thus shall ye 2Chr 19:9
he hath c me to build him an 2Chr 36:23
he hath c me to build him an Ezr 1:2
c that they should not be opened Neh 13:19
for Mordecai had c her that she Est 2:10
as Mordecai had c her Est 2:20
sinned not, nor c God foolishly Job 1:22
and his angels he c with folly Job 4:18
I c Baruch before them, saying, Jer 32:13
father in all that he hath c us Jer 35:8
and Jesus straitly c them, saying, Mt 9:30
c them that they should not make Mt 12:16
Then c he his disciples that they Mt 16:20
from the mountain, Jesus c them Mt 17:9
And he straitly c him, and Mk 1:43
he straitly c them that they Mk 3:12
he c them straitly that no man Mk 5:43
he c them that they should tell Mk 7:36
but the more he c them, so much Mk 7:36
he c them, saying, Take heed, Mk 8:15
he c them that they should tell Mk 8:30
he c them that they should tell Mk 9:9
many c him that he should hold Mk 10:48
And he c him to tell no man Lk 5:14
but he c them that they should Lk 8:56
And he straitly c them, and Lk 9:21
c him, See thou tell no man that Acts 23:22
c every one of you, as a father 1Th 2:11
them, and let not the church be c 1Ti 5:16

**CHARGEDST**
for thou c us, saying, Set bounds Ex 19:23

**CHARGER**
And his offering was one silver c Num 7:13
for his offering one silver c Num 7:19
His offering was one silver c Num 7:25
c of the weight of an hundred Num 7:31
His offering was one silver c Num 7:37
c of the weight of an hundred Num 7:43
His offering was one silver c Num 7:49
c of the weight of an hundred Num 7:55
His offering was one silver c Num 7:61
His offering was one silver c Num 7:67
His offering was one silver c Num 7:73
His offering was one silver c Num 7:79
Each c of silver weighing an Num 7:85
here John Baptist's head in a c Mt 14:8
And his head was brought in a c Mt 14:11
by in a c the head of John the Mk 6:25
And brought his head in a c Mk 6:28

**CHARGERS**
twelve c of silver, twelve silver Num 7:84
thirty c of gold, a thousand Ezr 1:9
of gold, a thousand c of silver Ezr 1:9

**CHARGES**
and the Levites to their c 2Chr 8:14
c according to their courses 2Chr 31:16
in their c by their courses 2Chr 31:17
And he set the priests in their c 2Chr 35:2
be at c with them, that they may Acts 21:24
a warfare any time at his own c 1Cor 9:7

**CHARGEST**
that thou c me to day with a 2Sa 3:8

**CHARGING**
c the jailer to keep them safely Acts 16:23
c them before the Lord that they 2Ti 2:14

**CHARIOT**
ride in the second c which he had Gen 41:43
And Joseph made ready his c Gen 46:29
And he made ready his c, and took Ex 14:6
And took off their c wheels Ex 14:25
Sisera lighted down off his c Judg 4:15

Why is his *c* so long in coming ........ Judg 5:28
and David houghed all the *c* horses ........ 2Sa 8:4
was like the work of a *c* wheel ........ 1Kin 7:33
a *c* came up and went out of Egypt .. 1Kin 10:29
made speed to get him up to his *c* ..... 1Kin 12:18
up, say unto Ahab, Prepare thy *c* ........ 1Kin 18:44
horse for horse, and *c* for *c* ........ 1Kin 20:25
horse for horse, and *c* for *c* ........ 1Kin 20:25
caused him to come up into the *c* ........ 1Kin 20:33
he said unto the driver of his *c* ........ 1Kin 22:34
up in his *c* against the Syrians ........ 1Kin 22:35
the wound into the midst of the *c* ..... 1Kin 22:35
one washed the *c* in the pool of ........ 1Kin 22:38
there appeared a *c* of fire ........ 2Kin 2:11
the *c* of Israel, and the horsemen ........ 2Kin 2:12
with his horses and with his *c* ........ 2Kin 5:9
down from the *c* to meet him ........ 2Kin 5:21
again from his *c* to meet thee ........ 2Kin 5:26
They took therefore two *c* horses ........ 2Kin 7:14
So Jehu rode in a *c*, and went to ........ 2Kin 9:16
And his *c* was made ready ........ 2Kin 9:21
of Judah went out, each in his *c* ........ 2Kin 9:21
heart, and he sunk down in his *c* ........ 2Kin 9:24
and said, Smite him also in the *c* ........ 2Kin 9:27
carried him in a *c* to Jerusalem ........ 2Kin 9:28
he took him up to him into the *c* ........ 2Kin 10:15
So they made him ride in his *c* ........ 2Kin 10:16
the *c* of Israel, and the horsemen ........ 2Kin 13:14
him in a *c* dead from Megiddo ........ 2Kin 23:30
also houghed all the *c* horses ........ 1Chr 18:4
pattern of the *c* of the cherubims ........ 1Chr 28:18
which he placed in the *c* cities ........ 2Chr 1:14
a *c* for six hundred shekels of ........ 2Chr 1:17
Solomon had, and all the *c* cities ........ 2Chr 8:6
whom he bestowed in the *c* cities ........ 2Chr 9:25
made speed to get him up to his *c* ........ 2Chr 10:18
therefore he said to his *c* man ........ 2Chr 18:33
*c* against the Syrians until the ........ 2Chr 18:34
therefore took him out of that *c* ........ 2Chr 35:24
him in the second *c* that he had ........ 2Chr 35:24
he burneth the *c* in the fire ........ Ps 46:9
O God of Jacob, both the *c* ........ Ps 76:6
who maketh the clouds his *c* ........ Ps 104:3
a *c* of the wood of Lebanon ........ Song 3:9
he saw a *c* with a couple of ........ Is 21:7
a *c* of asses, and a *c* of ........ Is 21:7
behold, here cometh a *c* of men ........ Is 21:9
Which bringeth forth the *c* ........ Is 43:17
thee will I break in pieces the *c* ........ Jer 51:21
bind the *c* to the swift beast ........ Mic 1:13
In the first *c* were red horses ........ Zec 6:2
and in the second *c* black horses ........ Zec 6:2
And in the third *c* white horses ........ Zec 6:3
and in the fourth *c* grisled ........ Zec 6:3
I will cut off the *c* from Ephraim ........ Zec 9:10
sitting in his *c* read Esaias the ........ Acts 8:28
near, and join thyself to this *c* ........ Acts 8:29
he commanded the *c* to stand still ........ Acts 8:38

**CHARIOTS**
And there went up with him both *c* ..... Gen 50:9
And he took six hundred chosen *c* ........ Ex 14:7
all the *c* of Egypt, and captains ........ Ex 14:7
*c* of Pharaoh, and his horsemen, and ...... Ex 14:9
and upon all his host, upon his *c* ........ Ex 14:17
honour upon Pharaoh, upon his *c* ........ Ex 14:18
even all Pharaoh's horses, his *c* ........ Ex 14:23
upon the Egyptians, upon their *c* ........ Ex 14:26
waters returned, and covered the *c* ........ Ex 14:28
Pharaoh's *c* and his host hath he ........ Ex 15:4
of Pharaoh went in with his *c* ........ Ex 15:19
unto their horses, and to their *c* ........ Deut 11:4
enemies, and seest horses, and *c* ........ Deut 20:1
with horses and *c* very many ........ Josh 11:4
horses, and burn their *c* with fire ........ Josh 11:6
and burnt their *c* with fire ........ Josh 11:9
land of the valley have *c* of iron ........ Josh 17:16
though they have iron *c*, and ........ Josh 17:18
pursued after your fathers with *c* ........ Josh 24:6
because they had *c* of iron ........ Judg 1:19
for he had nine hundred *c* of iron ........ Judg 4:3
of Jabin's army, with his *c* ........ Judg 4:7
gathered together all his *c* ........ Judg 4:13
even nine hundred *c* of iron ........ Judg 4:13
discomfited Sisera, and all his *c* ........ Judg 4:15
But Barak pursued after the *c* ........ Judg 4:16
Why tarry the wheels of his *c* ........ Judg 5:28
them for himself, for his *c* ........ 1Sa 8:11
and some shall run before his *c* ........ 1Sa 8:11
of war, and instruments of his *c* ........ 1Sa 8:12
with Israel, thirty thousand *c* ........ 1Sa 13:5
and, lo, the *c* and horsemen ........ 2Sa 1:6
David took from him a thousand *c* ........ 2Sa 8:4
reserved of them for an hundred *c* ........ 2Sa 8:4
of seven hundred *c* of the Syrians ........ 2Sa 10:18
this, that Absalom prepared him *c* ........ 2Sa 15:1
and he prepared him *c* and horsemen, .. 1Kin 1:5
stalls of horses for his *c* ........ 1Kin 4:26
Solomon had, and cities for his *c* ........ 1Kin 9:19
his captains, and rulers of his *c* ........ 1Kin 9:22
And Solomon gathered together *c* ..... 1Kin 10:26
had a thousand and four hundred *c* .. 1Kin 10:26
he bestowed in the cities for *c* ........ 1Kin 10:26
Zimri, captain of half his *c* ........ 1Kin 16:9
kings with him, and horses, and *c* ........ 1Kin 20:1
out, and smote the horses and *c* ........ 1Kin 20:21
captains that had rule over his *c* ........ 1Kin 22:31
captains of the *c* saw Jehoshaphat .... 1Kin 22:32
when the captains of the *c* ........ 1Kin 22:33
sent he thither horses, and *c* ........ 2Kin 6:14
the city both with horses and *c* ........ 2Kin 6:15
*c* of fire round about Elisha ........ 2Kin 6:17
the Syrians to hear a noise of *c* ........ 2Kin 7:6
to Zair, and all the *c* with him ........ 2Kin 8:21
about, and the captains of the *c* ........ 2Kin 8:21
with you, and there are with you *c* ..... 2Kin 10:2
but fifty horsemen, and ten *c* ........ 2Kin 13:7
and put thy trust on Egypt for *c* ........ 2Kin 18:24
With the multitude of my *c* I am ........ 2Kin 19:23
burned the *c* of the sun with fire ........ 2Kin 23:11
David took from him a thousand *c* ........ 1Chr 18:4
but reserved of them an hundred *c* ..... 1Chr 18:4
talents of silver to hire them *c* ........ 1Chr 19:6
hired thirty and two thousand *c* ........ 1Chr 19:7
thousand men which fought in *c* ........ 1Chr 19:18
And Solomon gathered *c* ........ 2Chr 1:14
had a thousand and four hundred *c* ..... 2Chr 1:14
captains, and captains of his *c* ........ 2Chr 8:9
thousand stalls for horses and *c* ........ 2Chr 9:25
With twelve hundred *c*, and ........ 2Chr 12:3
thousand, and three hundred *c* ........ 2Chr 14:9
a huge host, with very many *c* ........ 2Chr 16:8
of the *c* that were with him ........ 2Chr 18:30
captains of the *c* saw Jehoshaphat .... 2Chr 18:31
when the captains of the *c* ........ 2Chr 18:32
princes, and all his *c* with him ........ 2Chr 21:9
him in, and the captains of the *c* ........ 2Chr 21:9
Some trust in *c*, and some in ........ Ps 20:7
The *c* of God are twenty thousand, ........ Ps 68:17
company of horses in Pharaoh's *c* ........ Song 1:9
made me like the *c* of Ammi-nadib ........ Song 6:12
is there any end of their *c* ........ Is 2:7
bare the quiver with *c* of men ........ Is 22:6
valleys shall be full of *c* ........ Is 22:7
there the *c* of thy glory shall be ........ Is 22:18
and stay on horses, and trust in *c* ........ Is 31:1
and put thy trust on Egypt for *c* ........ Is 36:9
By the multitude of my *c* am I ........ Is 37:24
with his *c* like a whirlwind, to ........ Is 66:15
all nations upon horses, and in *c* ........ Is 66:20
his *c* shall be as a whirlwind ........ Jer 4:13
the throne of David, riding in *c* ........ Jer 17:25
the throne of David, riding in *c* ........ Jer 22:4
and rage, ye *c* ........ Jer 46:9
horses, at the rushing of his *c* ........ Jer 47:3
their horses, and upon their *c* ........ Jer 50:37
shall come against thee with *c* ........ Eze 23:24
the north, with horses, and with *c* ........ Eze 26:7
and of the wheels, and of the *c* ........ Eze 26:10
in precious clothes for *c* ........ Eze 27:20
at my table with horses and *c* ........ Eze 39:20
him like a whirlwind, with *c* ........ Dan 11:40
Like the noise of *c* on the tops ........ Joel 2:5
of thee, and I will destroy thy *c* ........ Mic 5:10
the *c* shall be with flaming ........ Nah 2:3
The *c* shall rage in the streets, ........ Nah 2:4
and I will burn her *c* in the smoke ........ Nah 2:13
horses, and of the jumping *c* ........ Nah 3:2
horses and thy *c* of salvation ........ Hab 3:8
and I will overthrow the *c* ........ Hag 2:22
there came four *c* out from ........ Zec 6:1
of *c* of many horses running to ........ Rev 9:9
beasts, and sheep, and horses, and *c* ... Rev 18:13

**CHARITABLY**
thy meat, now walkest thou not *c* ..... Rom 14:15

**CHARITY**
puffeth up, but *c* edifieth ........ 1Cor 8:1
men and of angels, and have not *c* ..... 1Cor 13:1
remove mountains, and have not *c* ..... 1Cor 13:2
body to be burned, and have not *c* ..... 1Cor 13:3
*C* suffereth long, and is kind ........ 1Cor 13:4
*c* envieth not ........ 1Cor 13:4
*c* vaunteth not itself, is not ........ 1Cor 13:4
*C* never faileth ........ 1Cor 13:8
And now abideth faith, hope, *c* ........ 1Cor 13:13
but the greatest of these is *c* ........ 1Cor 13:13
Follow after *c*, and desire ........ 1Cor 14:1
all your things be done with *c* ........ 1Cor 16:14
above all these things put on *c* ........ Col 3:14
good tidings of your faith and *c* ........ 1Th 3:6
the *c* of every one of you all ........ 2Th 1:3
is *c* out of a pure heart, and of a ........ 1Ti 1:5
if they continue in faith and *c* ........ 1Ti 2:15
in word, in conversation, in *c* ........ 1Ti 4:12
follow righteousness, faith, *c* ........ 2Ti 2:22
purpose, faith, longsuffering, *c* ........ 2Ti 3:10
temperate, sound in faith, in *c* ........ Titus 2:2
have fervent *c* among yourselves ........ 1Pet 4:8
for *c* shall cover the multitude ........ 1Pet 4:8
ye one another with a kiss of *c* ........ 1Pet 5:14
and to brotherly kindness *c* ........ 2Pet 1:7
of thy *c* before the church ........ 3Jn 6
are spots in your feasts of *c* ........ Jude 12
I know thy works, and *c*, and ........ Rev 2:19

**CHARMED**
among you, which will not be *c* ........ Jer 8:17

**CHARMER**
Or a *c*, or a consulter with ........ Deut 18:11

**CHARMERS**
not hearken to the voice of *c* ........ Ps 58:5
seek to the idols, and to the *c* ........ Is 19:3

**CHARMING**
of charmers, *c* never so wisely ........ Ps 58:5

**CHARRAN** (*car'-ran*) See HARAN. *Greek form of Haran.*
Mesopotamia, before he dwelt in *C* ........ Acts 7:2
of the Chaldaeans, and dwelt in *C* ........ Acts 7:4

**CHASE**
ye shall *c* your enemies, and they ........ Lev 26:7
And five of you shall *c* an hundred ........ Lev 26:8
of a shaken leaf shall *c* them ........ Lev 26:36
How should one *c* a thousand ........ Deut 32:30
One man of you shall *c* a thousand ........ Josh 23:10
let the angel of the LORD *c* them ........ Ps 35:5

**CHASED**
*c* you, as bees do, and destroyed ........ Deut 1:44
for they *c* them from before the ........ Josh 7:5
wilderness wherein they *c* them ........ Josh 8:24
*c* them along the way that goeth ........ Josh 10:10
*c* them unto great Zidon, and unto ..... Josh 11:8
And Abimelech *c* him, and he fled ........ Judg 9:40
*c* them, and trode them down with ... Judg 20:43
therefore I *c* him from me ........ Neh 13:28
darkness, and *c* out of the world ........ Job 18:18
he shall be *c* away as a vision of ........ Job 20:8
And it shall be as the *c* roe ........ Is 13:14
shall be *c* as the chaff of the ........ Is 17:13
Mine enemies *c* me sore, like a ........ Lam 3:52

**CHASETH**
*c* away his mother, is a son that ........ Prov 19:26

**CHASING**
from *c* after the Philistines ........ 1Sa 17:53

**CHASTE**
you as a *c* virgin to Christ ........ 2Cor 11:2
To be discreet, *c*, keepers at ........ Titus 2:5
While they behold your *c* ........ 1Pet 3:2

**CHASTEN**
I will *c* him with the rod of men, ........ 2Sa 7:14
anger, neither *c* me in thy hot ........ Ps 6:1
neither *c* me in thy hot ........ Ps 38:1
*C* thy son while there is hope, and ..... Prov 19:18
to *c* thyself before thy God, thy ........ Dan 10:12
As many as I love, I rebuke and *c* ........ Rev 3:19

**CHASTENED**
and that, when they have *c* him ........ Deut 21:18
He is *c* also with pain upon his ........ Job 33:19
*c* my soul with fasting, that was ........ Ps 69:10
been plagued, and *c* every morning ........ Ps 73:14
The LORD hath *c* me sore ........ Ps 118:18
we are *c* of the Lord, that we ........ 1Cor 11:32
as *c*, and not killed ........ 2Cor 6:9
*c* us after their own pleasure ........ Heb 12:10

**CHASTENEST**
Blessed is the man whom thou *c* ........ Ps 94:12

**CHASTENETH**
heart, that, as a man *c* his son ........ Deut 8:5
son, so the LORD thy God *c* thee ........ Deut 8:5
he that loveth him *c* him betimes ..... Prov 13:24
For whom the Lord loveth he *c* ........ Heb 12:6
son is he whom the father *c* not ........ Heb 12:7

**CHASTENING**
not thou the *c* of the Almighty ........ Job 5:17
despise not the *c* of the LORD ........ Prov 3:11
a prayer when thy *c* was upon them ...... Is 26:16
not thou the *c* of the Lord ........ Heb 12:5
If ye endure *c*, God dealeth with ........ Heb 12:7
Now no *c* for the present seemeth ........ Heb 12:11

**CHASTISE**
will *c* you seven times for your ........ Lev 26:28
city shall take that man and *c* him .... Deut 22:18
but I will *c* you with scorpions ........ 1Kin 12:11
but I will *c* you with scorpions ........ 1Kin 12:14
but I will *c* you with scorpions ........ 2Chr 10:11
but I will *c* you with scorpions ........ 2Chr 10:14
I will *c* them, as their ........ Hos 7:12
in my desire that I should *c* them ........ Hos 10:10
I will therefore *c* him, and ........ Lk 23:16
I will therefore *c* him, and let ........ Lk 23:22

**CHASTISED**
my father hath *c* you with whips ........ 1Kin 12:11
my father also *c* you with whips ........ 1Kin 12:14
my father *c* you with whips, but I ........ 2Chr 10:11
my father *c* you with whips, but I ........ 2Chr 10:14
hast *c* me, and I was *c* ........ Jer 31:18

**CHASTISEMENT**
seen the *c* of the LORD your God ........ Deut 11:2
be said unto God, I have borne *c* ........ Job 34:31
the *c* of our peace was upon him ........ Is 53:5
with the *c* of a cruel one, for ........ Jer 30:14
But if ye be without *c*, whereof ........ Heb 12:8

**CHASTISETH**
He that *c* the heathen, shall not ........ Ps 94:10

**CHATTER**
a crane or a swallow, so did I *c* ........ Is 38:14

**CHEBAR** (*ke'-bar*) *A river in Mesopotamia.*
the captives by the river of *C* ........ Eze 1:1
of the Chaldeans by the river *C* ........ Eze 1:3
that dwelt by the river of *C* ........ Eze 3:15
which I saw by the river of *C* ........ Eze 3:23
that I saw by the river of *C* ........ Eze 10:15
God of Israel by the river of *C* ........ Eze 10:20
which I saw by the river of *C* ........ Eze 10:22
vision that I saw by the river *C* ........ Eze 43:3

**CHECK**
I have heard the *c* of my reproach ........ Job 20:3

**CHECKER**
And nets of *c* work, and wreaths of .... 1Kin 7:17

**CHEDORLAOMER** (*ke'-dor-la'-o-mer*) *An Elamite king.*
*C* king of Elam, and Tidal king of ........ Gen 14:1

Twelve years they served C .................. Gen 14:4
And in the fourteenth year came C ...... Gen 14:5
With C the king of Elam, and with....... Gen 14:9
return from the slaughter of C.............. Gen 14:17

**CHEEK**
near, and smote Micaiah on the c...... 1Kin 22:24
near, and smote Micaiah upon the c. 2Chr 18:23
me upon the c reproachfully.................. Job 16:10
all mine enemies upon the c bone............ Ps 3:7
He giveth his c to him that..................... Lam 3:30
he hath the c teeth of a great.................. Joel 1:6
of Israel with a rod upon the c................ Mic 5:1
shall smite thee on thy right c ................ Mt 5:39
on the one c offer also the other.............. Lk 6:29

**CHEEKS**
priest the shoulder, and the two c......... Deut 18:3
Thy c are comely with rows of............ Song 1:10
His c are as a bed of spices, as............ Song 5:13
my c to them that plucked off the ........... Is 50:6
night, and her tears are on her c ............ Lam 1:2

**CHEER**
shall c up his wife which he hath ........ Deut 24:5
let thy heart c thee in the days ............ Eccl 11:9
Son, be of good c...................................... Mt 9:2
unto them, saying, Be of good c ............ Mt 14:27
and saith unto them, Be of good c ......... Mk 6:50
but be of good c........................................ Jn 16:33
by him, and said, Be of good c ............ Acts 23:11
now I exhort you to be of good c....... Acts 27:22
Wherefore, sirs, be of good c.............. Acts 27:25
Then were they all of good c............... Acts 27:36

**CHEERETH**
I leave my wine, which c God ............. Judg 9:13

**CHEERFUL**
heart maketh a c countenance .......... Prov 15:13
joy and gladness, and c feasts............... Zec 8:19
corn shall make the young men c............ Zec 9:17
for God loveth a c giver .......................... 2Cor 9:7

**CHEERFULLY**
I do the more c answer for myself..... Acts 24:10

**CHEERFULNESS**
he that sheweth mercy, with c ............. Rom 12:8

**CHEESE**
c of kine, for David, and for the.......... 2Sa 17:29
out as milk, and curdled me like c....... Job 10:10

**CHEESES**
carry these ten c unto the....................... 1Sa 17:18

**CHELAL** (*ke'-lal*) *Married a foreign wife in exile.*
Adna, and C, Benaiah, Maaseiah,.......... Ezr 10:30

**CHELLUH** (*kel'-loo*) *Married a foreign wife in exile.*
Benaiah, Bedeiah, C,.............................. Ezr 10:35

**CHELUB** (*ke'-lub*)
*1. A descendant of Caleb.*
C the brother of Shuah begat ............... 1Chr 4:11
*2. Father of Ezri.*
the ground was Ezri the son of C...... 1Chr 27:26

**CHELUBAI** (*ke-loo'-bahee*) *Son of Hezron.*
Jerahmeel, and Ram, and C..................... 1Chr 2:9

**CHELUH** See CHELLUH.

**CHELUHI** See CHELLUH.

**CHEMARIMS** (*kem'-a-rims*) *Idolatrous priests of Judah.*
the name of the C with the....................... Zeph 1:4

**CHEMOSH** (*ke'-mosh*) *A Moabite god.*
thou art undone, O people of C.......... Num 21:29
not thou possess that which C thy.... Judg 11:24
Solomon build an high place for C....... 1Kin 11:7
C the god of the Moabites, and........... 1Kin 11:33
for C the abomination of the................. 2Kin 23:13
C shall go forth into captivity ................ Jer 48:7
And Moab shall be ashamed of C.......... Jer 48:13
the people of C perisheth...................... Jer 48:46

**CHENAANAH** (*ke-na'-a-nah*)
*1. Father of Zedekiah.*
Zedekiah the son of C made him ....... 1Kin 22:11
Zedekiah the son of C went near....... 1Kin 22:24
Zedekiah the son of C had made ...... 2Chr 18:10
Zedekiah the son of C came near ...... 2Chr 18:23
*2. Brother of Ehud.*
Benjamin, and Ehud, and C.................... 1Chr 7:10

**CHENANI** (*ken'-a-ni*) *A Levite helper of Ezra.*
Bunni, Sherebiah, Bani, and C.................. Neh 9:4

**CHENANIAH** (*ken-a-ni'-ah*) See CONONIAH.
*1. A chief Levite during David's reign.*
And C, chief of the Levites, was......... 1Chr 15:22
C the master of the song with the..... 1Chr 15:27
*2. An officer in David's army.*
Of the Izharites, C and his sons ......... 1Chr 26:29

**CHEPHAR-AMMONI** See CHEPHAR-HAAMMONAI.

**CHEPHAR-HAAMMONAI** (*ke'-far-ha-am'-mo-nahee*) *A town in Benjamin.*
And C, and Ophni, and Gaba ................... Josh 18:24

**CHEPHIRAH** (*ke-fi'-rah*) *A Hittite village in Benjamin.*
their cities were Gibeon, and C............. Josh 9:17

And Mizpeh, and C, and Mozah,......... Josh 18:26
The children of Kirjath-arim, C............... Ezr 2:25
The men of Kirjath-jearim, C................... Neh 7:29

**CHERAN** (*ke'-ran*) *Son of Dishon.*
and Eshban, and Ithran, and C ............ Gen 36:26
Eshban, and Ithran, and C..................... 1Chr 1:41

**CHERETHIMS** (*ker'-e-thims*) See CHERETHITES. *A Philistine tribe.*
and I will cut off the C, and .................. Eze 25:16

**CHERETHITES** (*ker'-e-thites*) See CHERETHIMS.
*1. Same as Cherethims.*
invasion upon the south of the C......... 1Sa 30:14
sea coast, the nation of the C............... Zeph 2:5
*2. Executioners and runners in David's army.*
of Jehoiada was over both the C............ 2Sa 8:18
and all the C, and all the ..................... 2Sa 15:18
after him Joab's men, and the C............ 2Sa 20:7
son of Jehoiada was over the C........... 2Sa 20:23
the son of Jehoiada, and the C............. 1Kin 1:38
the son of Jehoiada, and the C.............. 1Kin 1:44
son of Jehoiada was over the C.......... 1Chr 18:17

**CHERISH**
before the king, and let her c him.......... 1Kin 1:2

**CHERISHED**
c the king, and ministered to him .......... 1Kin 1:4

**CHERISHETH**
c it, even as the Lord the church........... Eph 5:29
even as a nurse c her children.................. 1Th 2:7

**CHERITH** (*ke'-rith*) *A brook in Gilead.*
and hide thyself by the brook C........... 1Kin 17:3
he went and dwelt by the brook C ...... 1Kin 17:5

**CHERUB** (*ke'-rub*)
*1. A winged celestial being.*
make one c on the one end, and the..... Ex 25:19
the other c on the other end .................. Ex 25:19
One c on the end on this side, and .......... Ex 37:8
another c on the other end on.................. Ex 37:8
And he rode upon a c, and did fly........ 2Sa 22:11
cubits was the one wing of the c ......... 1Kin 6:24
cubits the other wing of the c.............. 1Kin 6:24
the other c was ten cubits...................... 1Kin 6:25
of the one c was ten cubits..................... 1Kin 6:26
and so was it of the other c.................... 1Kin 6:26
the wing of the other c touched............ 1Kin 6:27
wing of the one c was five cubits ......... 2Chr 3:11
to the wing of the other c...................... 2Chr 3:11
of the other c was five cubits................. 2Chr 3:12
to the wing of the other c....................... 2Chr 3:12
And he rode upon a c, and did fly ........... Ps 18:10
of Israel was gone up from the c ............. Eze 9:3
the wheels, even under the c.................... Eze 10:2
of the LORD went up from the c .............. Eze 10:4
one c stretched forth his hand................. Eze 10:7
the cherubims, one wheel by one c.......... Eze 10:9
and another wheel by another c............... Eze 10:9
first face was the face of a c................... Eze 10:14
art the anointed c that covereth............. Eze 28:14
I will destroy thee, O covering c ............ Eze 28:16
tree was between a c and a c .................. Eze 41:18
and every c had two faces ...................... Eze 41:18
*2. An exile who returned with Zerubbabel.*
up from Tel-melah, Tel-harsa, C............... Ezr 2:59
from Tel-melah, Tel-haresha, C............... Neh 7:61

**CHERUBIM**
the east of the garden of Eden C........... Gen 3:24
the c shall stretch forth their .................. Ex 25:20

**CHERUBIMS**
And thou shalt make two c of gold....... Ex 25:18
the c on the two ends thereof................. Ex 25:19
seat shall the faces of the c be............... Ex 25:20
from between the two c which are.......... Ex 25:22
with c of cunning work shalt thou........... Ex 26:1
with c shall it be made............................ Ex 26:31
with c of cunning work made he.............. Ex 36:8
with c made he it of cunning work ....... Ex 36:35
And he made two c of gold, beaten........ Ex 37:7
he the c on the two ends thereof............. Ex 37:8
the c spread out their wings on............... Ex 37:9
seatward were the faces of the c.............. Ex 37:9
testimony, from between the two c..... Num 7:89
which dwelleth between the c................... 1Sa 4:4
hosts that dwelleth between the c ............ 2Sa 6:2
he made two c of olive tree .................. 1Kin 6:23
both the c were of one measure and... 1Kin 6:25
he set the c within the inner.................. 1Kin 6:27
forth the wings of the c, so that............ 1Kin 6:27
And he overlaid the c with gold........... 1Kin 6:28
about with carved figures of c .............. 1Kin 6:29
he carved upon them carvings of c........ 1Kin 6:32
gold, and spread gold upon the c .......... 1Kin 6:32
And he carved thereon c and palm....... 1Kin 6:35
the ledges were lions, oxen, and c........ 1Kin 7:29
the borders thereof, he graved c............ 1Kin 7:36
even under the wings of the c ................. 1Kin 8:6
For the c spread forth their two.............. 1Kin 8:7
the c covered the ark and the.................. 1Kin 8:7
which dwellest between the c............... 2Kin 19:15
LORD, that dwelleth between the c...... 1Chr 13:6
pattern of the chariot of the c ............. 1Chr 28:18
and graved c on the walls....................... 2Chr 3:7
house he made two c of image work .. 2Chr 3:10
the wings of the c were twenty............. 2Chr 3:11
The wings of these c spread.................. 2Chr 3:13
fine linen, and wrought c thereon......... 2Chr 3:14
even under the wings of the c ................ 2Chr 5:7

For the c spread forth their..................... 2Chr 5:8
the c covered the ark and the................. 2Chr 5:8
thou that dwellest between the c ............. Ps 80:1
he sitteth between the c .......................... Ps 99:1
that dwellest between the c...................... Is 37:16
c there appeared over them as it.......... Eze 10:1
coals of fire from between the c............ Eze 10:2
Now the c stood on the right side.......... Eze 10:3
the wheels, from between the c............. Eze 10:6
c unto the fire that was between ........... Eze 10:7
the fire that was between the c.............. Eze 10:7
there appeared in the c the form........... Eze 10:8
behold the four wheels by the c ............ Eze 10:9
And the c were lifted up........................ Eze 10:15
And when the c went, the wheels........ Eze 10:16
when the c lifted up their wings.......... Eze 10:16
of the house, and stood over the c....... Eze 10:18
the c lifted up their wings, and............ Eze 10:19
and I knew that they were the c........... Eze 10:20
Then did the c lift up their................... Eze 11:22
And it was made with c and palm ....... Eze 41:18
ground unto above the door were c .... Eze 41:20
on the doors of the temple, c ............... Eze 41:25
over it the c of glory shadowing.............. Heb 9:5

**CHERUBIMS'**
the sound of the c wings was.................. Eze 10:5

**CHESALON** (*kes'-a-lon*) *A landmark in Judah.*
side of mount Jearim, which is C........ Josh 15:10

**CHESED** (*ke'-sed*) *A son of Nahor.*
And C, and Hazo, and Pildash, and..... Gen 22:22

**CHESIL** (*ke'-sil*) *A Canaanite town.*
And Eltolad, and C, and Hormah,....... Josh 15:30

**CHESNUT**
poplar, and of the hazel and c tree ..... Gen 30:37
the c trees were not like his.................... Eze 31:8

**CHEST**
But Jehoiada the priest took a c........... 2Kin 12:9
there was much money in the c......... 2Kin 12:10
king's commandment they made a c... 2Chr 24:8
and brought in, and cast into the c... 2Chr 24:10
that at what time the c was................ 2Chr 24:11
officer came and emptied the c........... 2Chr 24:11

**CHESTS**
in c of rich apparel, bound with ........... Eze 27:24

**CHESULLOTH** (*ke-sul'-loth*) See CHISLOTH-TABOR. *A town in Issachar.*
border was toward Jezreel, and C....... Josh 19:18

**CHEW**
ye not eat of them that c the cud.......... Lev 11:4
not eat of them that c the cud ............. Deut 14:7
for they c the cud, but divide................ Deut 14:7

**CHEWED**
between their teeth, ere it was c........ Num 11:33

**CHEWETH**
c the cud, among the beasts, that.......... Lev 11:3
the camel, because he c the cud............ Lev 11:4
the coney, because he c the cud............ Lev 11:5
And the hare, because he c the cud ...... Lev 11:6
yet he c not the cud ................................ Lev 11:7
nor c the cud, are unclean unto ........... Lev 11:26
c the cud among the beasts, that.......... Deut 14:6
yet c not the cud, it is unclean............. Deut 14:8

**CHEZIB** (*ke'-zib*) See ACHZIB, CHOZEBA. *A Canaanite village.*
and he was at C, when she bare him.... Gen 38:5

**CHICKENS**
gathereth her c under her wings ........... Mt 23:37

**CHIDE**
the people did c with Moses.................... Ex 17:2
said unto them, Why c ye with me ......... Ex 17:2
they did c with him sharply..................... Judg 8:1
He will not always c................................ Ps 103:9

**CHIDING**
because of the c of the children .............. Ex 17:7

**CHIDON** (*ki'-don*) See NACHON. *Place where Uzzah died.*
came unto the threshingfloor of C....... 1Chr 13:9

**CHIEF**
Phichol the c captain of his host ......... Gen 21:22
Phichol the c captain of his host.......... Gen 21:32
Phichol the c captain of his army........ Gen 26:26
against the c of the butlers, and............ Gen 40:2
against the c of the bakers...................... Gen 40:2
the c butler told his dream to................. Gen 40:9
When the c baker saw that the ........... Gen 40:16
up the head of the c butler .................... Gen 40:20
of the c baker among his servants ....... Gen 40:20
he restored the c butler unto his.......... Gen 40:21
But he hanged the c baker..................... Gen 40:22
Yet did not the c butler remember....... Gen 40:23
Then spake the c butler unto ................. Gen 41:9
house, both me and the c baker ........... Gen 41:10
being a c man among his people,............ Lev 21:4
the c of the house of the father ............ Num 3:24
the c of the house of the father ............ Num 3:30
c over the c of the Levites..................... Num 3:32
the c of the house of the father ............ Num 3:35
the c of the congregation....................... Num 4:34
the c of Israel numbered, after.............. Num 4:46
a prince of a c house among the........ Num 25:14
people, and of a c house in Midian.... Num 25:15
the c fathers of the congregation....... Num 31:26

the *c* fathers of the tribes of ... Num 32:28
the *c* fathers of the families of ... Num 36:1
the *c* fathers of the children of ... Num 36:1
So I took the *c* of your tribes, ... Deut 1:15
for the *c* things of the ancient ... Deut 33:15
princes, of each *c* house a prince ... Josh 22:14
the *c* of all the people, even of ... Judg 20:2
hither, all the *c* of the people ... 1Sa 14:38
the *c* of the things which should ... 1Sa 15:21
of David's soul, he shall be *c* ... 2Sa 5:8
and David's sons were *c* rulers ... 2Sa 8:18
Jairite was a *c* ruler about David ... 2Sa 20:26
in the seat, *c* among the captains ... 2Sa 23:8
three of the thirty *c* went down ... 2Sa 23:13
son of Zeruiah, was *c* among three ... 2Sa 23:18
Beside the *c* of Solomon's ... 1Kin 5:16
the *c* of the fathers of the ... 1Kin 8:1
These were the *c* of the officers ... 1Kin 9:23
the hands of the *c* of the guard ... 1Kin 14:27
guard took Seraiah the *c* priest ... 2Kin 25:18
and of him came the *c* ruler ... 1Chr 5:2
was reckoned, were the *c*, Jeiel, ... 1Chr 5:7
Joel the *c*, and Shapham the next, ... 1Chr 5:12
*c* of the house of their fathers ... 1Chr 5:15
all of them *c* men ... 1Chr 7:3
men of valour, *c* of the princes ... 1Chr 7:40
by their generations, *c* men ... 1Chr 8:28
All these men were *c* of the ... 1Chr 9:9
Shallum was the *c* ... 1Chr 9:17
these Levites, the four *c* porters ... 1Chr 9:26
*c* of the fathers of the Levites, ... 1Chr 9:33
These *c* fathers of the Levites ... 1Chr 9:34
fathers of the Levites were *c* ... 1Chr 9:34
the Jebusites first shall be *c* ... 1Chr 11:6
Zeruiah went first up, and was *c* ... 1Chr 11:6
These also are the *c* of the ... 1Chr 11:10
Hachmonite, the *c* of the captains ... 1Chr 11:11
of Joab, he was *c* of the three ... 1Chr 11:20
The *c* was Ahiezer, then Joash, ... 1Chr 12:3
who was *c* of the captains, and he ... 1Chr 12:18
Uriel the *c*, and his brethren an ... 1Chr 15:5
Asaiah the *c*, and his brethren two ... 1Chr 15:6
Joel the *c*, and his brethren an ... 1Chr 15:7
Shemaiah the *c*, and his brethren ... 1Chr 15:8
Eliel the *c*, and his brethren ... 1Chr 15:9
Amminadab the *c*, and his brethren .. 1Chr 15:10
Ye are the *c* of the fathers of ... 1Chr 15:12
David spake to the *c* of the ... 1Chr 15:16
*c* of the Levites, was for song ... 1Chr 15:22
Asaph the *c*, and next to him ... 1Chr 16:5
of David were *c* about the king ... 1Chr 18:17
the *c* was Jehiel, and Zetham, and ... 1Chr 23:8
These were the *c* of the fathers ... 1Chr 23:9
And Jahath was the *c* ... 1Chr 23:11
of Gershom, Shebuel was the *c* ... 1Chr 23:16
of Eliezer were, Rehabiah the *c* ... 1Chr 23:17
Shelomith the *c* ... 1Chr 23:18
even the *c* of the fathers, as ... 1Chr 23:24
there were more *c* men found of ... 1Chr 24:4
*c* men of the house of their ... 1Chr 24:4
before the *c* of the fathers of ... 1Chr 24:6
the *c* of the fathers of the ... 1Chr 24:31
Simri the *c*, (for though he was ... 1Chr 26:10
yet his father made him the *c* ... 1Chr 26:10
the porters, even among the *c* men ... 1Chr 26:12
*c* fathers, even of Laadan the ... 1Chr 26:21
the *c* fathers, the captains over ... 1Chr 26:26
the Hebronites was Jerijah the *c* ... 1Chr 26:31
and seven hundred *c* fathers ... 1Chr 26:32
the *c* fathers and captains of ... 1Chr 27:1
the children of Perez was the *c* ... 1Chr 27:3
the son of Jehoiada, a *c* priest ... 1Chr 27:5
Then the *c* of the fathers and ... 1Chr 29:6
the LORD to be the *c* governor ... 1Chr 29:22
all Israel, the *c* of the fathers ... 2Chr 1:2
the *c* of the fathers of the ... 2Chr 5:2
*c* of his captains, and captains of ... 2Chr 8:9
And these were the *c* of king ... 2Chr 8:10
Abijah the son of Maachah the *c* ... 2Chr 11:22
the hands of the *c* of the guard ... 2Chr 12:10
Adnah the *c*, and with him mighty ... 2Chr 17:14
of the *c* of the fathers of Israel ... 2Chr 19:8
Amariah the *c* priest is over you ... 2Chr 19:11
the *c* of the fathers of Israel, ... 2Chr 23:2
king called for Jehoiada the *c* ... 2Chr 24:6
The whole number of the *c* of the ... 2Chr 26:12
And Azariah the *c* priest, and all ... 2Chr 26:20
Azariah the *c* priest of the house ... 2Chr 31:10
*c* of the Levites, gave unto the ... 2Chr 35:9
Moreover all the *c* of the priests ... 2Chr 36:14
Then rose up the *c* of the fathers ... Ezr 1:5
some of the *c* of the fathers, ... Ezr 2:68
*c* of the fathers, who were ... Ezr 3:12
to the *c* of the fathers, and said ... Ezr 4:2
the rest of the *c* of the fathers ... Ezr 4:3
the men that were the *c* of them ... Ezr 5:10
the son of Aaron the *c* priest ... Ezr 7:5
of Israel *c* men to go up with me ... Ezr 7:28
are now the *c* of their fathers ... Ezr 8:1
and for Meshullam, *c* men ... Ezr 8:16
Iddo the *c* at the place Casiphia ... Ezr 8:17
twelve of the *c* of the priests ... Ezr 8:24
them before the *c* of the priests ... Ezr 8:29
*c* of the fathers of Israel, at ... Ezr 8:29
hath been *c* in this trespass ... Ezr 9:2
arose Ezra, and made the *c* priests ... Ezr 10:5
with certain *c* of the fathers, ... Ezr 10:16
some of the *c* of the fathers gave ... Neh 7:70
some of the *c* of the fathers gave ... Neh 7:71
the *c* of the fathers of all the ... Neh 8:13
The *c* of the people ... Neh 10:14
Now these are the *c* of the ... Neh 11:3
*c* of the fathers, two hundred ... Neh 11:13
of the *c* of the Levites, had the ... Neh 11:16
These were the *c* of the priests ... Neh 12:7
priests, the *c* of the fathers ... Neh 12:12
were recorded *c* of the fathers ... Neh 12:22
the *c* of the fathers, were ... Neh 12:23
And the *c* of the Levites ... Neh 12:24
old there were *c* of the singers ... Neh 12:46
the *c* of the people of the earth ... Job 12:24
I chose out their way, and sat *c* ... Job 29:25
He is the *c* of the ways of God ... Job 40:19
To the *c* Musician on Neginoth, A ... Ps 4:*t*
To the *c* Musician upon Nehiloth, ... Ps 5:*t*
To the *c* Musician on Neginoth ... Ps 6:*t*
To the *c* Musician upon Gittith, A ... Ps 8:*t*
To the *c* Musician upon ... Ps 9:*t*
To the *c* Musician, A Psalm of ... Ps 11:*t*
To the *c* Musician upon Sheminith, ... Ps 12:*t*
To the *c* Musician, A Psalm of ... Ps 13:*t*
To the *c* Musician, A Psalm of ... Ps 14:*t*
To the *c* Musician, A Psalm of ... Ps 18:*t*
To the *c* Musician, A Psalm of ... Ps 19:*t*
To the *c* Musician, A Psalm of ... Ps 20:*t*
To the *c* Musician, A Psalm of ... Ps 21:*t*
To the *c* Musician upon Aijeleth ... Ps 22:*t*
To the *c* Musician, A Psalm of ... Ps 31:*t*
To the *c* Musician, A Psalm of ... Ps 36:*t*
To the *c* Musician, even to ... Ps 39:*t*
To the *c* Musician, A Psalm of ... Ps 40:*t*
To the *c* Musician, A Psalm of ... Ps 41:*t*
To the *c* Musician, Maschil, for ... Ps 42:*t*
To the *c* Musician for the sons of ... Ps 44:*t*
To the *c* Musician upon Shoshannim ... Ps 45:*t*
To the *c* Musician for the sons of ... Ps 46:*t*
To the *c* Musician, A Psalm for ... Ps 47:*t*
To the *c* Musician, A Psalm for ... Ps 49:*t*
To the *c* Musician, A Psalm of ... Ps 51:*t*
To the *c* Musician, Maschil, A ... Ps 52:*t*
To the *c* Musician upon Mahalath, ... Ps 53:*t*
To the *c* Musician on Neginoth, ... Ps 54:*t*
To the *c* Musician on Neginoth, ... Ps 55:*t*
To the *c* Musician upon ... Ps 56:*t*
To the *c* Musician, Altaschith, ... Ps 57:*t*
To the *c* Musician, Altaschith, ... Ps 58:*t*
To the *c* Musician, Altaschith, ... Ps 59:*t*
To the *c* Musician upon ... Ps 60:*t*
To the *c* Musician upon Neginah, A ... Ps 61:*t*
To the *c* Musician, to Jeduthun, A ... Ps 62:*t*
To the *c* Musician, A Psalm of ... Ps 64:*t*
To the *c* Musician, A Psalm and ... Ps 65:*t*
To the *c* Musician, A Song or ... Ps 66:*t*
To the *c* Musician on Neginoth, A ... Ps 67:*t*
To the *c* Musician, A Psalm or ... Ps 68:*t*
To the *c* Musician upon Shoshannim ... Ps 69:*t*
To the *c* Musician, A Psalm of ... Ps 70:*t*
To the *c* Musician, Altaschith, A ... Ps 75:*t*
To the *c* Musician on Neginoth, A ... Ps 76:*t*
To the *c* Musician, to Jeduthun, A ... Ps 77:*t*
the *c* of their strength in the ... Ps 78:51
To the *c* Musician upon ... Ps 80:*t*
To the *c* Musician upon Gittith, A ... Ps 81:*t*
To the *c* Musician upon Gittith, A ... Ps 84:*t*
To the *c* Musician, A Psalm for ... Ps 85:*t*
for the sons of Korah to the *c* ... Ps 88:*t*
the *c* of all their strength ... Ps 105:36
To the *c* Musician, A Psalm of ... Ps 109:*t*
not Jerusalem above my *c* joy ... Ps 137:6
To the *c* Musician, A Psalm of ... Ps 139:*t*
To the *c* Musician, A Psalm of ... Ps 140:*t*
She crieth in the *c* place of ... Prov 1:21
a whisperer separateth *c* friends ... Prov 16:28
and aloes, with all the *c* spices ... Song 4:14
even all the *c* ones of the earth ... Is 14:9
thee from the *c* men thereof ... Is 41:9
to be captains, and as *c* over thee ... Jer 13:21
who was also *c* governor in the ... Jer 20:1
shout among the *c* of the nations ... Jer 31:7
bow of Elam, the *c* of their might ... Jer 49:35
guard took Seraiah the *c* priest ... Jer 52:24
Her adversaries are the *c* ... Lam 1:5
in thy fairs with *c* of all spices ... Eze 27:22
the *c* prince of Meshech and Tubal ... Eze 38:2
the *c* prince of Meshech and Tubal ... Eze 38:3
the *c* prince of Meshech and Tubal ... Eze 39:1
*c* of the governors over all the ... Dan 2:48
lo, Michael, one of the *c* princes ... Dan 10:13
the *c* of the children of Ammon ... Dan 11:41
which are named *c* of the nations ... Amos 6:1
themselves with the *c* ointments ... Amos 6:6
To the *c* singer on my stringed ... Hab 3:19
he had gathered all the *c* priests ... Mt 2:4
*c* priests and scribes, and be ... Mt 16:21
be betrayed unto the *c* priests ... Mt 20:18
And whosoever will be *c* among you ... Mt 20:27
And when the *c* priests and scribes ... Mt 21:15
the *c* priests and the elders of ... Mt 21:23
And when the *c* priests and ... Mt 21:45
the *c* seats in the synagogues, ... Mt 23:6
assembled together the *c* priests ... Mt 26:3
Iscariot, went unto the *c* priests ... Mt 26:14
and staves, from the *c* priests ... Mt 26:47
Now the *c* priests, and elders, and ... Mt 26:59
was come, all the *c* priests ... Mt 27:1
pieces of silver to the *c* priests ... Mt 27:3
the *c* priests took the silver ... Mt 27:6
he was accused of the *c* priests ... Mt 27:12
But the *c* priests and elders ... Mt 27:20
Likewise also the *c* priests ... Mt 27:41
the *c* priests and Pharisees came ... Mt 27:62
shewed unto the *c* priests all the ... Mt 28:11
captains, and *c* estates of Galilee ... Mk 6:21
of the *c* priests, and scribes, and ... Mk 8:31
be delivered unto the *c* priests ... Mk 10:33
*c* priests heard it, and sought how ... Mk 11:18
there come to him the *c* priests ... Mk 11:27
the *c* seats in the synagogues, and ... Mk 12:39
the *c* priests and the scribes ... Mk 14:1
twelve, went unto the *c* priests ... Mk 14:10
and staves, from the *c* priest ... Mk 14:43
were assembled all the *c* priests ... Mk 14:53
the *c* priests and all the council ... Mk 14:55
the *c* priests held a consultation ... Mk 15:1
the *c* priests accused him of many ... Mk 15:3
For he knew that the *c* priests ... Mk 15:10
But the *c* priests moved the ... Mk 15:11
Likewise also the *c* priests ... Mk 15:31
*c* priests and scribes, and be slain ... Lk 9:22
Beelzebub the *c* of the devils ... Lk 11:15
into the house of one of the *c* ... Lk 14:1
how they chose out the *c* rooms ... Lk 14:7
which was the *c* among the ... Lk 19:2
But the *c* priests and the scribes ... Lk 19:47
the *c* of the people sought to ... Lk 19:47
the *c* priests and the scribes came ... Lk 20:1
the *c* priests and the scribes the ... Lk 20:19
and the *c* rooms at feasts ... Lk 20:46
the *c* priests and scribes sought ... Lk 22:2
and communed with the *c* priests ... Lk 22:4
and he that is *c*, as he that doth ... Lk 22:26
Jesus said unto the *c* priests ... Lk 22:52
the *c* priests and the scribes came ... Lk 22:66
Then said Pilate to the *c* priests ... Lk 23:4
the *c* priests and scribes stood and ... Lk 23:10
had called together the *c* priests ... Lk 23:13
of the *c* priests prevailed ... Lk 23:23
And how the *c* priests and our ... Lk 24:20
the *c* priests sent officers to ... Jn 7:32
the officers to the *c* priests ... Jn 7:45
Then gathered the *c* priests ... Jn 11:47
Now both the *c* priests and the ... Jn 11:57
But the *c* priests consulted that ... Jn 12:10
Nevertheless among the *c* rulers ... Jn 12:42
and officers from the *c* priests ... Jn 18:3
the *c* priests have delivered thee ... Jn 18:35
When the *c* priests therefore and ... Jn 19:6
The *c* priests answered, We have ... Jn 19:15
Then said the *c* priests of the ... Jn 19:21
reported all that the *c* priests ... Acts 4:23
the *c* priests heard these things, ... Acts 5:24
*c* priests to bind all that call ... Acts 9:14
them bound unto the *c* priests ... Acts 9:21
the *c* men of the city, and raised ... Acts 13:50
because he was the *c* speaker ... Acts 14:12
Silas, *c* men among the brethren ... Acts 15:22
which is the *c* city of that part ... Acts 16:12
and of the *c* women not a few ... Acts 17:4
the *c* ruler of the synagogue, ... Acts 18:8
the *c* ruler of the synagogue, and ... Acts 18:17
*c* of the priests, which did so ... Acts 19:14
And certain of the *c* of Asia ... Acts 19:31
unto the *c* captain of the band ... Acts 21:31
and when they saw the *c* captain ... Acts 21:32
Then the *c* captain came near, and ... Acts 21:33
he said unto the *c* captain ... Acts 21:37
The *c* captain commanded him to be. Acts 22:24
he went and told the *c* captain ... Acts 22:26
Then the *c* captain came, and said ... Acts 22:27
the *c* captain answered, With a ... Acts 22:28
the *c* captain also was afraid, ... Acts 22:29
bands, and commanded the *c* priests. Acts 22:30
the *c* captain, fearing lest Paul ... Acts 23:10
And they came to the *c* priests ... Acts 23:14
*c* captain that he bring him down ... Acts 23:15
this young man unto the *c* captain ... Acts 23:17
and brought him to the *c* captain ... Acts 23:18
Then the *c* captain took him by ... Acts 23:19
So the *c* captain then let the ... Acts 23:22
But the *c* captain Lysias came ... Acts 24:7
When Lysias the *c* captain shall ... Acts 24:22
the *c* of the Jews informed him ... Acts 25:2
the *c* priests and the elders of ... Acts 25:15
of hearing, with the *c* captains ... Acts 25:23
authority from the *c* priests ... Acts 26:10
and commission from the *c* priests ... Acts 26:12
of the *c* man of the island ... Acts 28:7
called the *c* of the Jews together ... Acts 28:17
himself being the *c* corner stone ... Eph 2:20
of whom I am *c* ... 1Ti 1:15
I lay in Sion a *c* corner stone ... 1Pet 2:6
when the *c* Shepherd shall appear, ... 1Pet 5:4
the *c* captains, and the mighty men ... Rev 6:15

**CHIEFEST**

*c* of all the offerings of Israel ... 1Sa 2:29
made them sit in the *c* place ... 1Sa 9:22
the *c* of the herdmen that ... 1Sa 21:7
they buried him in the *c* of the ... 2Chr 32:33
ruddy, the *c* among ten thousand ... Song 5:10
And whosoever of you will be the *c* ... Mk 10:44
a whit behind the very *c* apostles ... 2Cor 11:5
am I behind the very *c* apostles ... 2Cor 12:11
the *c* city of Phrygia Pacatiana ... 1Ti *s*

**CHIEFLY**

*c*, because that unto them were ... Rom 3:2
*c* they that are of Caesar's ... Phil 4:22
But *c* them that walk after the ... 2Pet 2:10

**CHILD**

she had no *c* ... Gen 11:30
unto her, Behold, thou art with *c* ... Gen 16:11

Every man c among you shall be ... Gen 17:10
every man c in your generations, ... Gen 17:12
the uncircumcised man c whose ... Gen 17:14
Shall a c be born unto him that ... Gen 17:17
Shall I of a surety bear a c ... Gen 18:13
of Lot with c by their father ... Gen 19:36
the c grew, and was weaned ... Gen 21:8
it on her shoulder, and the c ... Gen 21:14
she cast the c under one of the ... Gen 21:15
Let me not see the death of the c ... Gen 21:16
brethren, and said, The c is not ... Gen 37:30
behold, she is with c by whoredom ... Gen 38:24
man, whose these are, am I with c ... Gen 38:25
saying, Do not sin against the c ... Gen 42:22
a c of his old age, a little one ... Gen 44:20
saw him that he was a goodly c ... Ex 2:2
with pitch, and put the c therein ... Ex 2:3
she had opened it, she saw the c ... Ex 2:6
that she may nurse the c for thee ... Ex 2:7
said unto her, Take this c away ... Ex 2:9
And the woman took the c, and ... Ex 2:9
the c grew, and she brought him ... Ex 2:10
strive, and hurt a woman with c ... Ex 21:22
any widow, or fatherless c ... Ex 22:22
conceived seed, and born a man c ... Lev 12:2
But if she bear a maid c, then ... Lev 12:5
widow, or divorced, and have no c ... Lev 22:13
father beareth the sucking c ... Num 11:12
and one of them die, and have no c ... Deut 25:5
and she was his only c ... Judg 11:34
for the c shall be a Nazarite ... Judg 13:5
for the c shall be a Nazarite to ... Judg 13:7
do unto the c that shall be born ... Judg 13:8
How shall we order the c, and how ... Judg 13:12
the c grew, and the LORD blessed ... Judg 13:24
And Naomi took the c, and laid it ... Ruth 4:16
give unto thine handmaid a man c ... 1Sa 1:11
not go up until the c be weaned ... 1Sa 1:22
and the c was young ... 1Sa 1:24
bullock, and brought the c to Eli ... 1Sa 1:25
For this c I prayed ... 1Sa 1:27
the c did minister unto the LORD ... 1Sa 2:11
before the LORD, being a c ... 1Sa 2:18
the c Samuel grew before the LORD ... 1Sa 2:21
the c Samuel grew on, and was in ... 1Sa 2:26
the c Samuel ministered unto the ... 1Sa 3:1
that the LORD had called the c ... 1Sa 3:8
law, Phinehas' wife, was with c ... 1Sa 4:19
And she named the c I-chabod ... 1Sa 4:21
no c unto the day of her death ... 2Sa 6:23
told David, and said, I am with c ... 2Sa 11:5
the c also that is born unto thee ... 2Sa 12:14
the LORD struck the c that ... 2Sa 12:15
therefore besought God for the c ... 2Sa 12:16
the seventh day, that the c died ... 2Sa 12:18
to tell him that the c was dead ... 2Sa 12:18
while the c was yet alive, we ... 2Sa 12:18
if we tell him that the c is dead ... 2Sa 12:18
perceived that the c was dead ... 2Sa 12:19
unto his servants, Is the c dead ... 2Sa 12:19
thou didst fast and weep for the c ... 2Sa 12:21
but when the c was dead, thou ... 2Sa 12:21
While the c was yet alive, I ... 2Sa 12:22
to me, that the c may live ... 2Sa 12:22
and I am but a little c ... 1Kin 3:7
I was delivered of a c with her ... 1Kin 3:17
this woman's c died in the night ... 1Kin 3:19
and laid her dead c in my bosom ... 1Kin 3:20
in the morning to give my c suck ... 1Kin 3:21
said, Divide the living c in two ... 1Kin 3:25
the living c was unto the king ... 1Kin 3:26
O my lord, give her the living c ... 1Kin 3:26
and said, Give her the living c ... 1Kin 3:27
Hadad being yet a little c ... 1Kin 11:17
a c shall be born unto the house ... 1Kin 13:2
thee what shall become of the c ... 1Kin 14:3
into the city, the c shall die ... 1Kin 14:12
threshold of the door, the c died ... 1Kin 14:17
himself upon the c three times ... 1Kin 17:21
the soul of the c came into him ... 1Kin 17:22
And Elijah took the c, and brought ... 1Kin 17:23
answered, Verily she hath no c ... 2Kin 4:14
when the c was grown, it fell on ... 2Kin 4:18
is it well with the c ... 2Kin 4:26
my staff upon the face of the c ... 2Kin 4:29
And the mother of the c said ... 2Kin 4:30
the staff upon the face of the c ... 2Kin 4:31
him, saying, The c is not awaked ... 2Kin 4:31
the c was dead, and laid upon his ... 2Kin 4:32
And he went up, and lay upon the c ... 2Kin 4:34
he stretched himself upon the c ... 2Kin 4:34
and the flesh of the c waxed warm ... 2Kin 4:34
the c sneezed seven times ... 2Kin 4:35
and the c opened his eyes ... 2Kin 4:35
like unto the flesh of a little c ... 2Kin 5:14
and rip up their women with c ... 2Kin 8:12
that were with c he ripped up ... 2Kin 15:16
said, There is a man c conceived ... Job 3:3
as a c that is weaned of his ... Ps 131:2
my soul is even as a weaned c ... Ps 131:2
Even a c is known by his doings, ... Prov 20:11
Train up a c in the way he should ... Prov 22:6
is bound in the heart of a c ... Prov 22:15
not correction from the c ... Prov 23:13
a wise c shall have joy of him ... Prov 23:24
but a c left to himself bringeth ... Prov 29:15
a c shall have him become his son ... Prov 29:21
he hath neither c nor brother ... Eccl 4:8
a wise c than an old and foolish ... Eccl 4:13
with the second c that shall ... Eccl 4:15
O land, when thy king is a c ... Eccl 10:16
in the womb of her that is with c ... Eccl 11:5
the c shall behave himself ... Is 3:5
For before the c shall know to ... Is 7:16
For before the c shall have ... Is 8:4
For unto us a c is born, unto us ... Is 9:6
be few, that a c may write them ... Is 10:19
a little c shall lead them ... Is 11:6
the sucking c shall play on the ... Is 11:8
the weaned c shall put his hand ... Is 11:8
Like as a woman with c, that ... Is 26:17
We have been with c, we have been ... Is 26:18
Can a woman forget her sucking c ... Is 49:15
that didst not travail with c ... Is 54:1
for the c shall die an hundred ... Is 65:20
she was delivered of a man c ... Is 66:7
for I am a c ... Jer 1:6
said unto me, Say not, I am a c ... Jer 1:7
that bringeth forth her first c ... Jer 4:31
A man c is born unto thee ... Jer 20:15
whether a man doth travail with c ... Jer 30:6
and the lame, the woman with c ... Jer 31:8
that travaileth with c together ... Jer 31:8
is he a pleasant c ... Jer 31:20
cut off from you man and woman, c ... Jer 44:7
The tongue of the sucking c ... Lam 4:4
When Israel was a c, then I loved ... Hos 11:1
their women with c shall be ... Hos 13:16
up the women with c of Gilead ... Amos 1:13
found with c of the Holy Ghost ... Mt 1:18
Behold, a virgin shall be with c ... Mt 1:23
search diligently for the young c ... Mt 2:8
stood over where the young c was ... Mt 2:9
they saw the young c with Mary ... Mt 2:11
Arise, and take the young c ... Mt 2:13
seek the young c to destroy him ... Mt 2:13
he arose, he took the young c ... Mt 2:14
Arise, and take the young c ... Mt 2:20
And he arose, and took the young c ... Mt 2:21
to death, and the father the c ... Mt 10:21
the c was cured from that very ... Mt 17:18
Jesus called a little c unto him ... Mt 18:2
humble himself as this little c ... Mt 18:4
little c in my name receiveth me ... Mt 18:5
the c of hell than yourselves ... Mt 23:15
And woe unto them that are with c ... Mt 24:19
And he said, Of a c ... Mk 9:21
the father of the c cried out ... Mk 9:24
And he took a c, and set him in the ... Mk 9:36
the kingdom of God as a little c ... Mk 10:15
But woe to them that are with c ... Mk 13:17
And they had no c, because that ... Lk 1:7
day they came to circumcise the c ... Lk 1:59
What manner of c shall this be ... Lk 1:66
And thou, c, shalt be called the ... Lk 1:76
the c grew, and waxed strong in ... Lk 1:80
espoused wife, being great with c ... Lk 2:5
was told them concerning this c ... Lk 2:17
for the circumcising of the c ... Lk 2:21
parents brought in the c Jesus ... Lk 2:27
this c is set for the fall and ... Lk 2:34
the c grew, and waxed strong in ... Lk 2:40
the c Jesus tarried behind in ... Lk 2:43
for he is mine only c ... Lk 9:38
unclean spirit, and healed the c ... Lk 9:42
thought of their heart, took a c ... Lk 9:47
this c in my name receiveth me ... Lk 9:48
c shall in no wise enter therein ... Lk 18:17
But woe unto them that are with c ... Lk 21:23
him, Sir, come down ere my c die ... Jn 4:49
soon as she is delivered of the c ... Jn 16:21
a truth against thy holy c Jesus ... Acts 4:27
by the name of thy holy c Jesus ... Acts 4:30
him, when as yet he had no c ... Acts 7:5
thou c of the devil, thou enemy ... Acts 13:10
I was a c, I spake as a c ... 1Cor 13:11
I understood as a c ... 1Cor 13:11
I thought as a c ... 1Cor 13:11
the heir, as long as he is a c ... Gal 4:1
as travail upon a woman with c ... 1Th 5:3
that from a c thou hast known the ... 2Ti 3:15
was delivered of a c when she was ... Heb 11:11
they saw he was a proper c ... Heb 11:23
And she being with c cried ... Rev 12:2
for to devour her c as soon as it ... Rev 12:4
And she brought forth a man c ... Rev 12:5
her c was caught up unto God, and ... Rev 12:5
which brought forth the man c ... Rev 12:13

**CHILDBEARING**
she shall be saved in c, if they ... 1Ti 2:15

**CHILDHOOD**
you from my c unto this day ... 1Sa 12:2
for c and youth are vanity ... Eccl 11:10

**CHILDISH**
became a man, I put away c things ... 1Cor 13:11

**CHILDLESS**
wilt thou give me, seeing I go c ... Gen 15:2
they shall die c ... Lev 20:20
they shall be c ... Lev 20:21
As thy sword hath made women c ... 1Sa 15:33
shall thy mother be c among women ... 1Sa 15:33
the LORD, Write ye this man c ... Jer 22:30
took her to wife, and he died c ... Lk 20:30

**CHILDREN** See PREFACE.

**CHILDREN'S**
father, that is ours, and our c ... Gen 31:16
thy c children, and thy flocks, and ... Gen 45:10
of all that is the c of Israel ... Ex 9:4
children, and upon the c children ... Ex 34:7
c children, and ye shall have ... Deut 4:25
thy c for ever, because thou hast ... Josh 14:9
children, and their c children ... 2Kin 17:41
for the c sake of mine own body ... Job 19:17
his righteousness unto c children ... Ps 103:17
thou shalt see thy c children ... Ps 128:6
an inheritance to his c children ... Prov 13:22
C children are the crown of old ... Prov 17:6
with your c children will I plead ... Jer 2:9
the c teeth are set on edge ... Jer 31:29
the c teeth are set on edge ... Eze 18:2
their c children for ever ... Eze 37:25
is not meet to take the c bread ... Mt 15:26
is not meet to take the c bread ... Mk 7:27
the table eat of the c crumbs ... Mk 7:28

**CHILD'S**
maid went and called the c mother ... Ex 2:8
let this c soul come into him ... 1Kin 17:21
flesh shall be fresher than a c ... Job 33:25
which sought the young c life ... Mt 2:20

**CHILEAB** (*kil'-e-ab*) See DANIEL. *A son of David.*
And his second, C, of Abigail the ... 2Sa 3:3

**CHILION** (*kil'-e-on*) See CHILION'S. *A son of Elimelech.*
name of his two sons Mahlon and C ... Ruth 1:2
and C died also both of them ... Ruth 1:5

**CHILION'S** (*kil'-e-ons*)
Elimelech's, and all that was C ... Ruth 4:9

**CHILMAD** (*kil'-mad*) *An area between Assyria and Arabia.*
merchants of Sheba, Asshur, and C ... Eze 27:23

**CHIMHAM** (*kim'-ham*) *A servant of David.*
But behold thy servant C ... 2Sa 19:37
C shall go over with me, and I ... 2Sa 19:38
to Gilgal, and C went on with him ... 2Sa 19:40
and dwelt in the habitation of C ... Jer 41:17

**CHIMNEY**
and as the smoke out of the c ... Hos 13:3

**CHINNERETH** (*kin'-ne-reth*) See CHINNEROTH, CINNEROTH, GENNESARET. *A district around the Sea of Galilee.*
the side of the sea of C eastward ... Num 34:11
from C even unto the sea of the ... Deut 3:17
sea of C on the other side Jordan ... Josh 13:27
Zer, and Hammath, Rakkath, and C ... Josh 19:35

**CHINNEROTH** (*kin'-ne-roth*) See CHINNERETH. *Same as Chinnereth.*
and of the plains south of C ... Josh 11:2
plain to the sea of C on the east ... Josh 12:3

**CHIOS** (*ki'-os*) *An island near Greece.*
came the next day over against C ... Acts 20:15

**CHISLEU** (*kis'-lew*) *Ninth month of the Hebrew year.*
And it came to pass in the month C ... Neh 1:1
day of the ninth month, even in C ... Zec 7:1

**CHISLEV** See CHISLEU.

**CHISLON** (*kis'-lon*) *Father of Elidad.*
of Benjamin, Elidad the son of C ... Num 34:21

**CHISLOTH-TABOR** (*kis'-loth-ta'-bor*) See CHESULLOTH. *A city in Zebulon.*
sunrising unto the border of C ... Josh 19:12

**CHITTIM** (*kit'-tim*) See KITTIM. *Descendants of Javan.*
come come from the coast of C ... Num 24:24
from the land of C it is revealed ... Is 23:1
arise, pass over to C ... Is 23:12
For pass over the isles of C ... Jer 2:10
brought out of the isles of C ... Eze 27:6
For the ships of C shall come ... Dan 11:30

**CHIUN** (*ki'-un*) See REMPHAN. *Another name for the god Saturn.*
C your images, the star of your ... Amos 5:26

**CHLOE** (*clo'-e*) *A Christian acquaintance of Paul.*
them which are of the house of C ... 1Cor 1:11

**CHLOE'S** See CHLOE.

**CHODE**
Jacob was wroth, and c with Laban ... Gen 31:36
And the people c with Moses ... Num 20:3

**CHOICE**
in the c of our sepulchres bury ... Gen 23:6
and his ass's colt unto the c vine ... Gen 49:11
all your c vows which ye vow unto ... Deut 12:11
a c young man, and a goodly ... 1Sa 9:2
chose of all the c men of Israel ... 2Sa 10:9
fenced city, and every c city ... 2Kin 3:19
and the c fir trees thereof ... 2Kin 19:23
heads of their father's house, c ... 1Chr 7:40
chose out of all the c of Israel ... 1Chr 19:10
them three hundred thousand c men ... 2Chr 25:5
daily was one ox and six c sheep ... Neh 5:18
and knowledge rather than c gold ... Prov 8:10
and my revenue than c silver ... Prov 8:19
tongue of the just is as c silver ... Prov 10:20
she is the c one of her that bare ... Song 6:9
and the c fir trees thereof ... Is 37:24

they shall cut down thy c cedars.......... Jer 22:7
fill it with the c bones.......... Eze 24:4
Take the c of the flock, and burn.......... Eze 24:5
and all the trees of Eden, the c.......... Eze 31:16
while ago God made c among us.......... Acts 15:7

**CHOICEST**
and planted it with the c vine.......... Is 5:2
that thy c valleys shall be full.......... Is 22:7

**CHOKE**
c the word, and he becometh.......... Mt 13:22
c the word, and it becometh.......... Mk 4:19

**CHOKED**
the thorns sprung up, and c them.......... Mt 13:7
c it, and it yielded no fruit.......... Mk 4:7
and were c in the sea.......... Mk 5:13
thorns sprang up with it, and c it.......... Lk 8:7
are c with cares and riches and.......... Lk 8:14
place into the lake, and were c.......... Lk 8:33

**CHOLER**
he was moved with c against him.......... Dan 8:7
the south shall be moved with c.......... Dan 11:11

**CHOOSE**
C us out men, and go out, fight.......... Ex 17:9
that the man whom the LORD doth c.. Num 16:7
the man's rod, whom I shall c.......... Num 17:5
set his love upon you, nor c you.......... Deut 7:7
c out of all your tribes to put.......... Deut 12:5
c to cause his name to dwell.......... Deut 12:11
LORD shall c in one of thy tribes.......... Deut 12:14
which the LORD thy God shall c.......... Deut 12:18
the place which the LORD shall c.......... Deut 12:26
shall c to place his name there.......... Deut 14:23
God shall c to set his name there.......... Deut 14:24
which the LORD thy God shall c.......... Deut 14:25
the place which the LORD shall c.......... Deut 15:20
shall c to place his name there.......... Deut 16:2
God shall c to place his name in.......... Deut 16:6
which the LORD thy God shall c.......... Deut 16:7
the place which the LORD shall c.......... Deut 16:15
God in the place which he shall c.......... Deut 16:16
which the LORD thy God shall c.......... Deut 17:8
the LORD shall c shall shew thee.......... Deut 17:10
whom the LORD thy God shall c.......... Deut 17:15
the place which the LORD shall c.......... Deut 18:6
he shall c in one of thy gates.......... Deut 23:16
shall c to place his name there.......... Deut 26:2
therefore c life, that both thou.......... Deut 30:19
God in the place which he shall c.......... Deut 31:11
in the place which he should c.......... Josh 9:27
c you this day whom ye will serve.......... Josh 24:15
did I c him out of all the tribes.......... 1Sa 2:28
c you a man for you, and let him.......... 1Sa 17:8
and all the men of Israel, c.......... 2Sa 16:18
Let me now c out twelve thousand.......... 2Sa 17:1
of Saul, whom the LORD did c.......... 2Sa 21:6
c thee one of them, that I may do.......... 2Sa 24:12
the city which the LORD did c out.......... 1Kin 14:21
let them c one bullock for.......... 1Kin 18:23
C you one bullock for yourselves,.......... 1Kin 18:25
c thee one of them, that I may do.......... 1Chr 21:10
him, Thus saith the LORD, C thee.......... 1Chr 21:11
LORD the God, who didst c Abram.......... Neh 9:7
c out my words to reason with him.......... Job 9:14
Let us c to us judgment.......... Job 34:4
thou refuse, or whether thou c.......... Job 34:33
teach in the way that he shall c.......... Ps 25:12
He shall c our inheritance for us.......... Ps 47:4
did not c the fear of the LORD.......... Prov 1:29
oppressor, and c none of his ways.......... Prov 3:31
to refuse the evil, and c the good.......... Is 7:15
c the good, the land that thou.......... Is 7:16
on Jacob, and will yet c Israel.......... Is 14:1
One of Israel, and he shall c thee.......... Is 49:7
c the things that please me, and.......... Is 56:4
did c that wherein I delighted.......... Is 65:12
I also will c their delusions, and.......... Is 66:4
c thou a place, c it at the.......... Eze 21:19
c it at the head of the way to.......... Eze 21:19
Zion, and shall yet c Jerusalem.......... Zec 1:17
land, and shall c Jerusalem again.......... Zec 2:12
yet what I shall c I wot not.......... Phil 1:22

**CHOOSEST**
thou c the tongue of the crafty.......... Job 15:5
Blessed is the man whom thou c.......... Ps 65:4

**CHOOSETH**
So that my soul c strangling.......... Job 7:15
c a tree that will not rot.......... Is 40:20
an abomination is he that c you.......... Is 41:24

**CHOOSING**
C rather to suffer affliction.......... Heb 11:25

**CHOP**
c them in pieces, as for the pot,.......... Mic 3:3

**CHOR-ASHAN** (*cor-a'-shan*) *A town in Judah.*
and to them which were in C.......... 1Sa 30:30

**CHORAZIN** (*co-ra'-zin*) *A city near Capernaum.*
Woe unto thee, C.......... Mt 11:21
Woe unto thee, C.......... Lk 10:13

**CHOSE**
them wives of all which they c.......... Gen 6:2
Then Lot c him all the plain of.......... Gen 13:11
Moses c able men out of all.......... Ex 18:25
therefore he c their seed after.......... Deut 4:37
he c their seed after them, even.......... Deut 10:15
Joshua c out thirty thousand.......... Josh 8:3
They c new gods.......... Judg 5:8
Saul c him three thousand men of.......... 1Sa 13:2
c him five smooth stones out of.......... 1Sa 17:40
which c me before thy father, and.......... 2Sa 6:21
he c of all the choice men of.......... 2Sa 10:9
I c no city out of all the tribes.......... 1Kin 8:16
but I c David to be over my.......... 1Kin 8:16
David my servant's sake, whom I c... 1Kin 11:34
he c out of all the choice of.......... 1Chr 19:10
c me before all the house of my.......... 1Chr 28:4
out of the land of Egypt I c no.......... 2Chr 6:5
neither c I any man to be a ruler.......... 2Chr 6:5
I c out their way, and sat chief,.......... Job 29:25
c not the tribe of Ephraim.......... Ps 78:67
But c the tribe of Judah, the.......... Ps 78:68
He c David also his servant, and.......... Ps 78:70
c that in which I delighted not.......... Is 66:4
In the day when I c Israel.......... Eze 20:5
and of them he c twelve, whom also.......... Lk 6:13
how they c out the chief rooms.......... Lk 14:7
they c Stephen, a man full of.......... Acts 6:5
people of Israel c our fathers.......... Acts 13:17
Paul c Silas, and departed, being.......... Acts 15:40

**CHOSEN**
And he took six hundred c chariots.......... Ex 14:7
his c captains also are drowned.......... Ex 15:4
even him whom he hath c will he.......... Num 16:5
the LORD thy God hath c thee to.......... Deut 7:6
which the LORD thy God hath c to.... Deut 12:21
the LORD hath c thee to be a.......... Deut 14:2
hath c to place his name there.......... Deut 16:11
hath c him out of all thy tribes.......... Deut 18:5
God hath c to minister unto him.......... Deut 21:5
that ye have c you the LORD.......... Josh 24:22
cry unto the gods which ye have c.... Judg 10:14
numbered seven hundred c.......... Judg 20:15
seven hundred c men lefthanded.......... Judg 20:16
thousand c men out of all Israel.......... Judg 20:34
king which ye shall have c you.......... 1Sa 8:18
See ye him whom the LORD hath c.......... 1Sa 10:24
behold the king whom ye have c.......... 1Sa 12:13
Neither hath the LORD c this.......... 1Sa 16:8
Neither hath the LORD c this.......... 1Sa 16:9
Jesse, The LORD hath not c these.......... 1Sa 16:10
do not I know that thou hast c.......... 1Sa 20:30
thousand c men out of all Israel.......... 1Sa 24:2
having three thousand c men of.......... 1Sa 26:2
together all the c men of Israel.......... 2Sa 6:1
of thy people which thou hast c.......... 1Kin 3:8
toward the city which thou hast c.......... 1Kin 8:44
the city which thou hast c.......... 1Kin 8:48
Jerusalem's sake which I have c.......... 1Kin 11:13
the city which I have c out of.......... 1Kin 11:32
the city which I have c me to put.......... 1Kin 11:36
and fourscore thousand c men.......... 1Kin 12:21
which I have c out of all tribes.......... 2Kin 21:7
city Jerusalem which I have c.......... 2Kin 23:27
All these which were c to be.......... 1Chr 9:22
for them hath the LORD c to carry.......... 1Chr 15:2
ye children of Jacob, his c ones.......... 1Chr 16:13
Jeduthun, and the rest that were c.... 1Chr 16:41
for he hath c Judah to be the.......... 1Chr 28:4
he hath c Solomon my son to sit.......... 1Chr 28:5
for I have c him to be my son, and.......... 1Chr 28:6
for the LORD hath c thee to build.......... 1Chr 28:10
my son, whom alone God hath c.......... 1Chr 29:1
But I have c Jerusalem, that my.......... 2Chr 6:6
have c David to be over my people.......... 2Chr 6:6
this city which thou hast c.......... 2Chr 6:34
toward the city which thou hast c.......... 2Chr 6:38
have c this place to myself for.......... 2Chr 7:12
For now have I c and sanctified.......... 2Chr 7:16
and fourscore thousand c men.......... 2Chr 11:1
the city which the LORD had c out.......... 2Chr 12:13
even four hundred thousand c men.......... 2Chr 13:3
with eight hundred thousand c men... 2Chr 13:3
five hundred thousand c men.......... 2Chr 13:17
for the LORD hath c you to stand.......... 2Chr 29:11
which I have c before all the.......... 2Chr 33:7
I have c to set my name there.......... Neh 1:9
for this hast thou c rather than.......... Job 36:21
he hath c for his own inheritance.......... Ps 33:12
and smote down the c men of Israel.......... Ps 78:31
I have made a covenant with my c.......... Ps 89:3
exalted one c out of the people.......... Ps 89:19
ye children of Jacob his c.......... Ps 105:6
and Aaron whom he had c.......... Ps 105:26
with joy, and his c with gladness.......... Ps 105:43
That I may see the good of thy c.......... Ps 106:5
had not Moses his c stood before.......... Ps 106:23
I have c the way of truth.......... Ps 119:30
for I have c thy precepts.......... Ps 119:173
For the LORD hath c Zion.......... Ps 132:13
For the LORD hath c Jacob unto.......... Ps 135:4
rather to be c than silver.......... Prov 16:16
rather to be c than great riches.......... Prov 22:1
for the gardens that ye have c.......... Is 1:29
my servant, Jacob whom I have c.......... Is 41:8
I have c thee, and not cast thee.......... Is 41:9
LORD, and my servant whom I have c... Is 43:10
to give drink to my people, my c.......... Is 43:20
and Israel, whom I have c.......... Is 44:1
and thou, Jesurun, whom I have c.......... Is 44:2
I have c thee in the furnace of.......... Is 48:10
Is it such a fast that I have c.......... Is 58:5
not this the fast that I have c.......... Is 58:6
your name for a curse unto my c.......... Is 65:15
they have c their own ways, and.......... Is 66:3
death shall be c rather than life.......... Jer 8:3
families which the LORD hath c.......... Jer 33:24
his c young men are gone down to.......... Jer 48:15
and who is a c man, that I may.......... Jer 49:19
and who is a c man, that I may.......... Jer 50:44
that were the c men of Assyria.......... Eze 23:7
withstand, neither his c people.......... Dan 11:15
for I have c thee, saith the LORD.......... Hag 2:23
that hath c Jerusalem rebuke thee.......... Zec 3:2
Behold my servant, whom I have c.......... Mt 12:18
for many be called, but few c.......... Mt 20:16
many are called, but few are c.......... Mt 22:14
the elect's sake, whom he hath c.......... Mk 13:20
Mary hath c that good part, which.......... Lk 10:42
if he be Christ, the c of God.......... Lk 23:35
them, Have not I c you twelve.......... Jn 6:70
I know whom I have c.......... Jn 13:18
not c me, but I have c you.......... Jn 15:16
but I have c you out of the world.......... Jn 15:19
unto the apostles whom he had c.......... Acts 1:2
whether of these two thou hast c.......... Acts 1:24
for he is a c vessel unto me, to.......... Acts 9:15
unto witnesses c before of God.......... Acts 10:41
to send c men of their own.......... Acts 15:22
to send c men unto you with our.......... Acts 15:25
God of our fathers hath c thee.......... Acts 22:14
Salute Rufus c in the Lord.......... Rom 16:13
But God hath c the foolish things.......... 1Cor 1:27
God hath c the weak things of the.......... 1Cor 1:27
which are despised, hath God c.......... 1Cor 1:28
but who was also c of the.......... 2Cor 8:19
According as he hath c us in him.......... Eph 1:4
c you to salvation through.......... 2Th 2:13
who hath c him to be a soldier.......... 2Ti 2:4
Hath not God c the poor of this.......... Jas 2:5
but c of God, and precious,.......... 1Pet 2:4
But ye are a c generation.......... 1Pet 2:9
are with him are called, and c.......... Rev 17:14

**CHOZEBA** (*ko-ze'-bah*) See CHEZIB. *A city in Judah.*
And Jokim, and the men of C.......... 1Chr 4:22

**CHRIST** (*krist*) See PREFACE. SEE ALSO ANTICHRIST, CHRISTIAN, CHRIST'S, CHRIST, JESUS, MESSIAH. *A title of Jesus of Nazareth; Greek for Messiah.*
birth of Jesus C was on this wise.......... Mt 1:18
of them where C should be born.......... Mt 2:4
answered and said, Thou art the C.......... Mt 16:16
for one is your Master, even C.......... Mt 23:8
come in my name, saying, I am C.......... Mt 24:5
shall say unto you, Lo, here is C.......... Mt 24:23
Saying, Prophesy unto us, thou C.......... Mt 26:68
my name, because ye belong to C.......... Mk 9:41
Let C the King of Israel descend.......... Mk 15:32
before he had seen the Lord's C.......... Lk 2:26
Thou art C the Son of God.......... Lk 4:41
let him save himself, if he be C.......... Lk 23:35
on him, saying, If thou be C.......... Lk 23:39
Ought not C to have suffered.......... Lk 24:26
and thus it behoved C to suffer.......... Lk 24:46
Messias cometh, which is called C.......... Jn 4:25
but when C cometh, no man knoweth.... Jn 7:27
Shall C come out of Galilee.......... Jn 7:41
That C cometh of the seed of.......... Jn 7:42
any man did confess that he was C.......... Jn 9:22
I believe that thou art the C.......... Jn 11:27
the law that C abideth for ever.......... Jn 12:34
he would raise up C to sit on his.......... Acts 2:30
that C should suffer, he hath so.......... Acts 3:18
Samaria, and preached C unto them.......... Acts 8:5
he preached C in the synagogues.......... Acts 9:20
that C must needs have suffered,.......... Acts 17:3
That C should suffer, and that he.......... Acts 26:23
in due time C died for the.......... Rom 5:6
were yet sinners, C died for us.......... Rom 5:8
that like as C was raised up from.......... Rom 6:4
Knowing that C being raised from.......... Rom 6:9
dead to the law by the body of C.......... Rom 7:4
any man have not the Spirit of C.......... Rom 8:9
if C be in you, the body is dead.......... Rom 8:10
he that raised up C from the dead.......... Rom 8:11
accursed from C for my brethren.......... Rom 9:3
as concerning the flesh C came.......... Rom 9:5
For C is the end of the law for.......... Rom 10:4
to bring C down from above.......... Rom 10:6
to bring up C again from the dead.......... Rom 10:7
For to this end C both died.......... Rom 14:9
with thy meat, for whom C died.......... Rom 14:15
serveth C is acceptable to God.......... Rom 14:18
For even C pleased not himself.......... Rom 15:3
as C also received us to the.......... Rom 15:7
which C hath not wrought by me.......... Rom 15:18
the gospel, not where C was named.. Rom 15:20
the firstfruits of Achaia unto C.......... Rom 16:5
But we preach C crucified.......... 1Cor 1:23
C the power of God, and the wisdom.. 1Cor 1:24
and C is God's.......... 1Cor 3:23
For even C our passover is.......... 1Cor 5:7
and one Lord Jesus C, by whom are.......... 1Cor 8:6
brother perish, for whom C died.......... 1Cor 8:11
to God, but under the law to C.......... 1Cor 9:21
and that Rock was C.......... 1Cor 10:4
Neither let us tempt C, as some.......... 1Cor 10:9
how that C died for our sins.......... 1Cor 15:3
Now if C be preached that he rose.... 1Cor 15:12
rise not, then is not C raised.......... 1Cor 15:16
if C be not raised, your faith is.......... 1Cor 15:17
C the firstfruits.......... 1Cor 15:23
have we through C to God-ward.......... 2Cor 3:4
we have known C after the flesh.......... 2Cor 5:16

Therefore if any man be in C ... 2Cor 5:17
To wit, that God was in *C* ... 2Cor 5:19
what concord hath C with Belial ... 2Cor 6:15
you as a chaste virgin to C ... 2Cor 11:2
law, but by the faith of Jesus C ... Gal 2:16
even we have believed in Jesus C ... Gal 2:16
be justified by the faith of C ... Gal 2:16
we seek to be justified by C ... Gal 2:17
I am crucified with C ... Gal 2:20
yet not I, but C liveth in me ... Gal 2:20
the law, then C is dead in vain ... Gal 2:21
C hath redeemed us from the curse ... Gal 3:13
schoolmaster to bring us unto C ... Gal 3:24
then an heir of God through C ... Gal 4:7
again until C be formed in you ... Gal 4:19
wherewith C hath made us free ... Gal 5:1
C shall profit you nothing ... Gal 5:2
C is become of no effect unto you ... Gal 5:4
in the cross of our Lord Jesus C ... Gal 6:14
at that time ye were without C ... Eph 2:12
That C may dwell in your hearts ... Eph 3:17
things, which is the head, even C ... Eph 4:15
But ye have not so learned C ... Eph 4:20
dead, and C shall give thee light ... Eph 5:14
as the church is subject unto C ... Eph 5:24
even as C also loved the church, ... Eph 5:25
but I speak concerning C and the ... Eph 5:32
of your heart, as unto C ... Eph 6:5
Some indeed preach C even of envy ... Phil 1:15
The one preach C of contention ... Phil 1:16
or in truth, C is preached ... Phil 1:18
so now also C shall be magnified ... Phil 1:20
For to me to live is C, and to die ... Phil 1:21
the knowledge of C Jesus my Lord ... Phil 3:8
through C which strengtheneth me ... Phil 4:13
of the world, and not after C ... Col 2:8
When C, who is our life, shall ... Col 3:4
but C is all, and in all ... Col 3:11
even as C forgave you, so also do ... Col 3:13
for ye serve the Lord C ... Col 3:24
the dead in C shall rise first ... 1Th 4:16
in the name of our Lord Jesus C ... 2Th 3:6
before God, and the Lord Jesus C ... 1Ti 5:21
But C as a son over his own house ... Heb 3:6
So also C glorified not himself ... Heb 5:5
But C being come an high priest ... Heb 9:11
For C is not entered into the ... Heb 9:24
So C was once offered to bear the ... Heb 9:28
Jesus C the same yesterday, and to ... Heb 13:8
because C also suffered for us, ... 1Pet 2:21
Forasmuch then as C hath suffered ... 1Pet 4:1
that denieth that Jesus is the C ... 1Jn 2:22
kingdoms of our Lord, and of his C ... Rev 11:15
of our God, and the power of his C ... Rev 12:10

**CHRISTIAN** (*kris'-tyan*) See CHRISTIANS. *A follower of Jesus Christ.*
thou persuadest me to be a C ... Acts 26:28
Yet if any man suffer as a C ... 1Pet 4:16

**CHRISTIANS** (*kris'-tyans*)
were called C first in Antioch ... Acts 11:26

**CHRIST'S** (*krists*)
for the Lord Jesus C sake ... Rom 15:30
And ye are C ... 1Cor 3:23
We are fools for C sake, but ye ... 1Cor 4:10
called, being free, is C servant ... 1Cor 7:22
they that are C at his coming ... 1Cor 15:23
came to Troas to preach C gospel ... 2Cor 2:12
we pray you in C stead, be ye ... 2Cor 5:20
man trust to himself that he is C ... 2Cor 10:7
he is C, even so are we C ... 2Cor 10:7
in distresses for C sake ... 2Cor 12:10
And if ye be C, then are ye ... Gal 3:29
they that are C have crucified ... Gal 5:24
even as God for C sake hath ... Eph 4:32
not the things which are Jesus C ... Phil 2:21
ye are partakers of C sufferings ... 1Pet 4:13

**CHRISTS** (*krists*)
For there shall arise false C ... Mt 24:24
For false C and false prophets ... Mk 13:22

**CHRONICLES**
of the c of the kings of Israel ... 1Kin 14:19
of the c of the kings of Judah ... 1Kin 14:29
of the c of the kings of Judah ... 1Kin 15:7
of the c of the kings of Judah ... 1Kin 15:23
of the c of the kings of Israel ... 1Kin 15:31
of the c of the kings of Israel ... 1Kin 16:5
of the c of the kings of Israel ... 1Kin 16:14
of the c of the kings of Israel ... 1Kin 16:20
of the c of the kings of Israel ... 1Kin 16:27
of the c of the kings of Israel ... 1Kin 22:39
of the c of the kings of Judah ... 1Kin 22:45
of the c of the kings of Israel ... 2Kin 1:18
of the c of the kings of Judah ... 2Kin 8:23
of the c of the kings of Israel ... 2Kin 10:34
of the c of the kings of Judah ... 2Kin 12:19
of the c of the kings of Israel ... 2Kin 13:8
of the c of the kings of Israel ... 2Kin 13:12
of the c of the kings of Israel ... 2Kin 14:15
of the c of the kings of Judah ... 2Kin 14:18
of the c of the kings of Israel ... 2Kin 14:28
of the c of the kings of Judah ... 2Kin 15:6
of the c of the kings of Israel ... 2Kin 15:11
of the c of the kings of Israel ... 2Kin 15:15
of the c of the kings of Israel ... 2Kin 15:21
of the c of the kings of Israel ... 2Kin 15:26
of the c of the kings of Israel ... 2Kin 15:31
of the c of the kings of Judah ... 2Kin 15:36
of the c of the kings of Judah ... 2Kin 16:19
of the c of the kings of Judah ... 2Kin 20:20
of the c of the kings of Judah ... 2Kin 21:17
of the c of the kings of Judah ... 2Kin 21:25
of the c of the kings of Judah ... 2Kin 23:28
of the c of the kings of Judah ... 2Kin 24:5
account of the C of king David ... 1Chr 27:24
were written in the book of the c ... Neh 12:23
the book of the c before the king ... Est 2:23
the book of records of the c ... Est 6:1
of the c of the kings of Media ... Est 10:2

**CHRYSOLITE**
the seventh, c ... Rev 21:20

**CHRYSOPRASUS**
the tenth, a c ... Rev 21:20

**CHUB** (*cub*) *Allies of Egypt.*
and all the mingled people, and C ... Eze 30:5

**CHUN** (*kun*) *A city in Aran-zobah.*
Likewise from Tibhath, and from C ... 1Chr 18:8

**CHURCH**
upon this rock I will build my c ... Mt 16:18
to hear them, tell it unto the c ... Mt 18:17
but if he neglect to hear the c ... Mt 18:17
the Lord added to the c daily ... Acts 2:47
And great fear came upon all the c ... Acts 5:11
is he, that was in the c in the ... Acts 7:38
the c which was at Jerusalem ... Acts 8:1
for Saul, he made havock of the c ... Acts 8:3
of the c which was in Jerusalem ... Acts 11:22
assembled themselves with the c ... Acts 11:26
his hands to vex certain of the c ... Acts 12:1
ceasing of the c unto God for him ... Acts 12:5
Now there were in the c that was ... Acts 13:1
ordained them elders in every c ... Acts 14:23
and had gathered the c together ... Acts 14:27
brought on their way by the c ... Acts 15:3
they were received of the c ... Acts 15:4
and elders, with the whole c ... Acts 15:22
and gone up, and saluted the c ... Acts 18:22
and called the elders of the c ... Acts 20:17
overseers, to feed the c of God ... Acts 20:28
of the c which is at Cenchrea ... Rom 16:1
Likewise greet the c that is in ... Rom 16:5
mine host, and of the whole c ... Rom 16:23
servant of the c at Cenchrea ... Rom *s*
Unto the c of God which is at ... 1Cor 1:2
as I teach every where in every c ... 1Cor 4:17
who are least esteemed in the c ... 1Cor 6:4
the Gentiles, nor to the c of God ... 1Cor 10:32
when ye come together in the c ... 1Cor 11:18
or despise ye the c of God ... 1Cor 11:22
And God hath set some in the c ... 1Cor 12:28
that prophesieth edifieth the c ... 1Cor 14:4
that the c may receive edifying ... 1Cor 14:5
excel to the edifying of the c ... 1Cor 14:12
Yet in the c I had rather speak ... 1Cor 14:19
If therefore the whole c be come ... 1Cor 14:23
let him keep silence in the c ... 1Cor 14:28
shame for women to speak in the c ... 1Cor 14:35
because I persecuted the c of God ... 1Cor 15:9
with the c that is in their house ... 1Cor 16:19
unto the c of God which is at ... 2Cor 1:1
measure I persecuted the c of God ... Gal 1:13
the head over all things to the c ... Eph 1:22
the c the manifold wisdom of God ... Eph 3:10
Unto him be glory in the c by ... Eph 3:21
as Christ is the head of the c ... Eph 5:23
Therefore as the c is subject ... Eph 5:24
even as Christ also loved the c ... Eph 5:25
it to himself a glorious c ... Eph 5:27
it, even as the Lord the c ... Eph 5:29
speak concerning Christ and the c ... Eph 5:32
zeal, persecuting the c ... Phil 3:6
no c communicated with me as ... Phil 4:15
he is the head of the body, the c ... Col 1:18
his body's sake, which is the c ... Col 1:24
the c which is in his house ... Col 4:15
also in the c of the Laodiceans ... Col 4:16
unto the c of the Thessalonians ... 1Th 1:1
unto the c of the Thessalonians ... 2Th 1:1
he take care of the c of God ... 1Ti 3:5
which is the c of the living God, ... 1Ti 3:15
them, and let not the c be charged ... 1Ti 5:16
bishop of the c of the Ephesians ... 2Ti *s*
bishop of the c of the Cretians ... Titus *s*
and to the c in thy house ... Philem 2
in the midst of the c will I sing ... Heb 2:12
c of the firstborn, which are ... Heb 12:23
him call for the elders of the c ... Jas 5:14
The c that is at Babylon, elected ... 1Pet 5:13
of thy charity before the c ... 3Jn 6
I wrote unto the c ... 3Jn 9
and casteth them out of the c ... 3Jn 10
angel of the c of Ephesus write ... Rev 2:1
angel of the c in Smyrna write ... Rev 2:8
angel of the c in Pergamos write ... Rev 2:12
angel of the c in Thyatira write ... Rev 2:18
angel of the c in Sardis write ... Rev 3:1
And to the angel of the c in ... Rev 3:7
unto the angel of the c of the ... Rev 3:14

**CHURCHES**
Then had the c rest throughout ... Acts 9:31
and Cilicia, confirming the c ... Acts 15:41
so were the c established in the ... Acts 16:5
which are neither robbers of c ... Acts 19:37
also all the c of the Gentiles ... Rom 16:4
The c of Christ salute you ... Rom 16:16
And so ordain I in all c ... 1Cor 7:17
such custom, neither the c of God ... 1Cor 11:16
as in all c of the saints ... 1Cor 14:33
your women keep silence in the c ... 1Cor 14:34
given order to the c of Galatia ... 1Cor 16:1
The c of Asia salute you ... 1Cor 16:19
bestowed on the c of Macedonia ... 2Cor 8:1
the gospel throughout all the c ... 2Cor 8:18
the c to travel with us with this ... 2Cor 8:19
they are the messengers of the c ... 2Cor 8:23
shew ye to them, and before the c ... 2Cor 8:24
I robbed other c, taking wages of ... 2Cor 11:8
me daily, the care of all the c ... 2Cor 11:28
ye were inferior to other c ... 2Cor 12:13
with me, unto the c of Galatia ... Gal 1:2
was unknown by face unto the c of ... Gal 1:22
became followers of the c of God ... 1Th 2:14
in the c of God for your patience ... 2Th 1:4
to the seven c which are in Asia ... Rev 1:4
the seven c which are in Asia ... Rev 1:11
are the angels of the seven c ... Rev 1:20
which thou sawest are the seven c ... Rev 1:20
what the Spirit saith unto the c ... Rev 2:7
what the Spirit saith unto the c ... Rev 2:11
what the Spirit saith unto the c ... Rev 2:17
all the c shall know that I am he ... Rev 2:23
what the Spirit saith unto the c ... Rev 2:29
what the Spirit saith unto the c ... Rev 3:6
what the Spirit saith unto the c ... Rev 3:13
what the Spirit saith unto the c ... Rev 3:22
unto you these things in the c ... Rev 22:16

**CHURL**
nor the c said to be bountiful ... Is 32:5
also of the c are evil ... Is 32:7

**CHURLISH**
but the man was c and evil in his ... 1Sa 25:3

**CHURNING**
Surely the c of milk bringeth ... Prov 30:33

**CHUSHAN-RISHATHAIM** (*cu'-shan-rish-a-tha'-im*) *A king of Mesopotamia.*
the hand of C king of Mesopotamia ... Judg 3:8
of Israel served C eight years ... Judg 3:8
the LORD delivered C king of ... Judg 3:10
and his hand prevailed against C ... Judg 3:10

**CHUZA** (*cu'-zah*) *A steward of Herod Antipas.*
the wife of C Herod's steward ... Lk 8:3

**CIELED**
greater house he c with fir tree ... 2Chr 3:5
it is c with cedar, and painted ... Jer 22:14
c with wood round about, and from ... Eze 41:16
O ye, to dwell in your c houses ... Hag 1:4

**CIELING**
the house, and the walls of the c ... 1Kin 6:15

**CILICIA** (*sil-ish'-yah*) *A Roman province in Asia Minor.*
and Alexandrians, and of them of C ... Acts 6:9
Gentiles in Antioch and Syria and C ... Acts 15:23
And he went through Syria and C ... Acts 15:41
am a Jew of Tarsus, a city in C ... Acts 21:39
Jew, born in Tarsus, a city in C ... Acts 22:3
he understood that he was of C ... Acts 23:34
we had sailed over the sea of C ... Acts 27:5
into the regions of Syria and C ... Gal 1:21

**CINNAMON**
of sweet c half so much, even two ... Ex 30:23
my bed with myrrh, aloes, and c ... Prov 7:17
calamus and c, with all trees of ... Song 4:14
c, and odours, and ointments ... Rev 18:13

**CINNEROTH** (*sin'-ne-roth*) See CHINNEROTH. *Same as Chinneroth.*
and Abel-beth-maachah, and all C ... 1Kin 15:20

**CIRCLE**
sitteth upon the c of the earth ... Is 40:22

**CIRCUIT**
from year to year in c to Beth-el ... 1Sa 7:16
and he walketh in the c of heaven ... Job 22:14
his c unto the ends of it ... Ps 19:6

**CIRCUITS**
again according to his c ... Eccl 1:6

**CIRCUMCISE**
ye shall c the flesh of your ... Gen 17:11
C therefore the foreskin of your ... Deut 10:16
LORD thy God will c thine heart ... Deut 30:6
c again the children of Israel ... Josh 5:2
is the cause why Joshua did c ... Josh 5:4
C yourselves to the LORD, and take ... Jer 4:4
day they came to c the child ... Lk 1:59
and ye on the sabbath day c a man ... Jn 7:22
That it was needful to c them ... Acts 15:5
ought not to c their children ... Acts 21:21

**CIRCUMCISED**
man child among you shall be c ... Gen 17:10
days old shall be c among you ... Gen 17:12
with thy money, must needs be c ... Gen 17:13
flesh of his foreskin is not c ... Gen 17:14
c the flesh of their foreskin in ... Gen 17:23
when he was c in the flesh of his ... Gen 17:24
when he was c in the flesh of his ... Gen 17:25
In the selfsame day was Abraham c ... Gen 17:26
of the stranger, were c with him ... Gen 17:27
Abraham c his son Isaac being ... Gen 21:4
be, that every male of you be c ... Gen 34:15
will not hearken unto us, to be c ... Gen 34:17

us be c, as they are c ... Gen 34:22
and every male was c, all that ... Gen 34:24
for money, when thou hast c him ... Ex 12:44
the LORD, let all his males be c ... Ex 12:48
flesh of his foreskin shall be c ... Lev 12:3
c the children of Israel at the ... Josh 5:3
the people that came out were c ... Josh 5:5
out of Egypt, them they had not c ... Josh 5:5
up in their stead, them Joshua c ... Josh 5:7
they had not c them by the way ... Josh 5:7
are c with the uncircumcised ... Jer 9:25
Isaac, and c him the eighth day ... Acts 7:8
Except ye be c after the manner ... Acts 15:1
your souls, saying, Ye must be c ... Acts 15:24
c him because of the Jews which ... Acts 16:3
believe, though they be not c ... Rom 4:11
Is any man called being c ... 1Cor 7:18
let him not be c ... 1Cor 7:18
a Greek, was compelled to be c ... Gal 2:3
say unto you, that if ye be c ... Gal 5:2
again to every man that is c ... Gal 5:3
flesh, they constrain you to be c ... Gal 6:12
themselves who are c keep the law ... Gal 6:13
but desire to have you c, that ... Gal 6:13
C the eighth day, of the stock of ... Phil 3:5
In whom also ye are c with the ... Col 2:11

**CIRCUMCISING**

they had done c all the people ... Josh 5:8
for the c of the child, his name ... Lk 2:21

**CIRCUMCISION**

thou art, because of the c ... Ex 4:26
Moses therefore gave unto you c ... Jn 7:22
man on the sabbath day receive c ... Jn 7:23
And he gave him the covenant of c ... Acts 7:8
they of the c which believed were ... Acts 10:45
were of the c contended with him ... Acts 11:2
For c verily profiteth, if thou ... Rom 2:25
thy c is made uncircumcision ... Rom 2:25
uncircumcision be counted for c ... Rom 2:26
c dost transgress the law ... Rom 2:27
neither is that c, which is ... Rom 2:28
c is that of the heart, in the ... Rom 2:29
or what profit is there of c ... Rom 3:1
shall justify the c by faith ... Rom 3:30
blessedness then upon the c only ... Rom 4:9
when he was in c, or in ... Rom 4:10
Not in c, but in uncircumcision ... Rom 4:10
And he received the sign of c ... Rom 4:11
the father of c to them who are ... Rom 4:12
to them who are not of the c only ... Rom 4:12
of the c for the truth of God ... Rom 15:8
C is nothing, and uncircumcision ... 1Cor 7:19
gospel of the c was unto Peter ... Gal 2:7
Peter to the apostleship of the c ... Gal 2:8
the heathen, and they unto the c ... Gal 2:9
fearing them which were of the c ... Gal 2:12
neither c availeth any thing ... Gal 5:6
And I, brethren, if I yet preach c ... Gal 5:11
neither c availeth any thing ... Gal 6:15
the C in the flesh made by hands ... Eph 2:11
For we are the c, which worship ... Phil 3:3
with the c made without hands ... Col 2:11
of the flesh by the c of Christ ... Col 2:11
c nor uncircumcision, Barbarian, ... Col 3:11
called Justus, who are of the c ... Col 4:11
specially they of the c ... Titus 1:10

**CIRCUMSPECT**

that I have said unto you be c ... Ex 23:13

**CIRCUMSPECTLY**

See then that ye walk c, not as ... Eph 5:15

**CIS** (*sis*) See KISH. *Father of King Saul.*

gave unto them Saul the son of C ... Acts 13:21

**CISTERN**

ye every one the waters of his c ... 2Kin 18:31
Drink waters out of thine own c ... Prov 5:15
or the wheel broken at the c ... Eccl 12:6
every one the waters of his own c ... Is 36:16

**CISTERNS**

hewed them out c, broken c ... Jer 2:13

**CITIES**

Lot dwelled in the c of the plain ... Gen 13:12
And he overthrew those c, and all ... Gen 19:25
and all the inhabitants of the c ... Gen 19:25
God destroyed the c of the plain ... Gen 19:29
when he overthrew the c in the ... Gen 19:29
the c that were round about them ... Gen 35:5
and let them keep food in the c ... Gen 41:35
and laid up the food in the c ... Gen 41:48
he removed them to c from one end .. Gen 47:21
they built for Pharaoh treasure c ... Ex 1:11
the c of the Levites, and the ... Lev 25:32
the houses of the c of their ... Lev 25:32
for the houses of the c of the ... Lev 25:33
of their c may not be sold ... Lev 25:34
gathered together within your c ... Lev 26:25
And I will make your c waste ... Lev 26:31
be desolate, and your c waste ... Lev 26:33
what c they be that they dwell in ... Num 13:19
the c are walled, and very great ... Num 13:28
I will utterly destroy their c ... Num 21:2
utterly destroyed them and their c ... Num 21:3
And Israel took all these c ... Num 21:25
in all the c of the Amorites ... Num 21:25
all their c wherein they dwelt ... Num 31:10
cattle, and c for our little ones ... Num 32:16
c because of the inhabitants of ... Num 32:17
Build you c for your little ones, ... Num 32:24
shall be there in the c of Gilead ... Num 32:26
with the c thereof in the coasts, ... Num 32:33
even the c of the country round ... Num 32:33
and Beth-haran, fenced c ... Num 32:36
unto the c which they builded ... Num 32:38
of their possession c to dwell in ... Num 35:2
for the c round about them ... Num 35:2
the c shall they have to dwell in ... Num 35:3
And the suburbs of the c, which ye ... Num 35:4
be to them the suburbs of the c ... Num 35:5
among the c which ye shall give ... Num 35:6
there shall be six c for refuge ... Num 35:6
them ye shall add forty and two c ... Num 35:6
So all the c which ye shall give ... Num 35:7
Levites shall be forty and eight c ... Num 35:7
the c which ye shall give shall ... Num 35:8
every one shall give of his c ... Num 35:8
c to be c of refuge for you ... Num 35:11
they shall be unto you c for ... Num 35:12
of these c which ye shall give ... Num 35:13
six c shall ye have for refuge ... Num 35:13
give three c on this side Jordan ... Num 35:14
three c shall ye give in the land ... Num 35:14
which shall be c of refuge ... Num 35:14
These six c shall be a refuge, ... Num 35:15
into what c we shall come ... Deut 1:22
the c are great and walled up to ... Deut 1:28
And we took all his c at that time ... Deut 2:34
the spoil of the c which we took ... Deut 2:35
nor unto the c in the mountains, ... Deut 2:37
And we took all his c at that time ... Deut 3:4
took not from them, threescore c ... Deut 3:4
All these c were fenced with high ... Deut 3:5
the cattle, and the spoil of the c ... Deut 3:7
All the c of the plain, and all ... Deut 3:10
c of the kingdom of Og in Bashan ... Deut 3:10
the c thereof, gave I unto the ... Deut 3:12
shall abide in your c which I ... Deut 3:19
Then Moses severed three c on ... Deut 4:41
unto one of these c he might live ... Deut 4:42
to give thee great and goodly c ... Deut 6:10
c great and fenced up to heaven, ... Deut 9:1
shalt hear say in one of thy c ... Deut 13:12
them, and dwellest in their c ... Deut 19:1
Thou shalt separate three c for ... Deut 19:2
he shall flee unto one of those c ... Deut 19:5
shalt separate three c for thee ... Deut 19:7
thou add three c more for thee ... Deut 19:9
and fleeth into one of these c ... Deut 19:11
the c which are very far off from ... Deut 20:15
are not of the c of these nations ... Deut 20:15
But of the c of these people, ... Deut 20:16
they shall measure unto the c ... Deut 21:2
came unto their c on the third ... Josh 9:17
Now their c were Gibeon, and ... Josh 9:17
great city, as one of the royal c ... Josh 10:2
them not to enter into their c ... Josh 10:19
of them entered into fenced c ... Josh 10:20
thereof, and all the c thereof ... Josh 10:37
thereof, and all the c thereof ... Josh 10:39
all the c of those kings, and all ... Josh 11:12
But as for the c that stood still ... Josh 11:13
And all the spoil of these c ... Josh 11:14
them utterly with their c ... Josh 11:21
all the c of Sihon king of the ... Josh 13:10
all her c that are in the plain ... Josh 13:17
all the c of the plain, and all ... Josh 13:21
after their families, the c ... Josh 13:23
all the c of Gilead, and half the ... Josh 13:25
Gad after their families, the c ... Josh 13:28
which are in Bashan, threescore c ... Josh 13:30
c of the kingdom of Og in Bashan, ... Josh 13:31
save c to dwell in, with their ... Josh 14:4
that the c were great and fenced ... Josh 14:12
went out to the c of mount Ephron ... Josh 15:9
the uttermost c of the tribe of ... Josh 15:21
all the c are twenty and nine, ... Josh 15:32
fourteen c with their villages ... Josh 15:36
sixteen c with their villages ... Josh 15:41
nine c with their villages ... Josh 15:44
eleven c with their villages ... Josh 15:51
nine c with their villages ... Josh 15:54
ten c with their villages ... Josh 15:57
six c with their villages ... Josh 15:59
two c with their villages ... Josh 15:60
six c with their villages ... Josh 15:62
the separate c for the children ... Josh 16:9
all the c with their villages ... Josh 16:9
these c of Ephraim are among the ... Josh 17:9
are among the c of Manasseh ... Josh 17:9
out the inhabitants of those c ... Josh 17:12
described it by c into seven ... Josh 18:9
Now the c of the tribe of the ... Josh 18:21
twelve c with their villages ... Josh 18:24
fourteen c with their villages ... Josh 18:28
thirteen c and their villages ... Josh 19:6
four c and their villages ... Josh 19:7
about these c to Baalath-beer ... Josh 19:8
twelve c with their villages ... Josh 19:15
these c with their villages ... Josh 19:16
sixteen c with their villages ... Josh 19:22
to their families, the c and their ... Josh 19:23
two c with their villages ... Josh 19:30
these c with their villages ... Josh 19:31
And the fenced c are Ziddim ... Josh 19:35
nineteen c with their villages ... Josh 19:38
to their families, the c and their ... Josh 19:39
these c with their villages ... Josh 19:48
Appoint out for you c of refuge ... Josh 20:2
doth flee unto one of those c ... Josh 20:4
These were the c appointed for ... Josh 20:9
of Moses to give us c to dwell in ... Josh 21:2
commandment of the LORD, these c ... Josh 21:3
the tribe of Benjamin, thirteen c ... Josh 21:4
the half tribe of Manasseh, ten c ... Josh 21:5
of Manasseh in Bashan, thirteen c ... Josh 21:6
of the tribe of Zebulun, twelve c ... Josh 21:7
these c with their suburbs ... Josh 21:8
these c which are here mentioned ... Josh 21:9
nine c out of those two tribes ... Josh 21:16
four c ... Josh 21:18
All the c of the children of ... Josh 21:19
were thirteen c with their ... Josh 21:19
even they had the c of their lot ... Josh 21:20
Beth-horon with her suburbs; four c.. Josh 21:22
with her suburbs; four c ... Josh 21:24
with her suburbs; two c ... Josh 21:25
All the c were ten with their ... Josh 21:26
Beesh-terah with her suburbs; two c. Josh 21:27
En-gannim with her suburbs; four c.. Josh 21:29
Rehob with her suburbs; four c ... Josh 21:31
Kartan with her suburbs; three c ... Josh 21:32
All the c of the Gershonites ... Josh 21:33
thirteen c with their suburbs ... Josh 21:33
Nahalal with her suburbs; four c ... Josh 21:35
Mephaath with her suburbs; four c ... Josh 21:37
four c in all ... Josh 21:39
So all the c for the children of ... Josh 21:40
were by their lot twelve c ... Josh 21:40
All the c of the Levites within ... Josh 21:41
eight c with their suburbs ... Josh 21:41
These c were every one with their ... Josh 21:42
thus were all these c ... Josh 21:42
c which ye built not, and ye dwell ... Josh 24:13
ass colts, and they had thirty c ... Judg 10:4
in all the c that be along by the ... Judg 11:26
come to Minnith, even twenty c ... Judg 11:33
buried in one of the c of Gilead ... Judg 12:7
together out of the c unto Gibeah ... Judg 20:14
at that time out of the c twenty ... Judg 20:15
them which came out of the c they .. Judg 20:42
fire all the c that they came to ... Judg 20:48
inheritance, and repaired the c ... Judg 21:23
to the number of all the c of the ... 1Sa 6:18
the five lords, both of fenced c ... 1Sa 6:18
the c which the Philistines had ... 1Sa 7:14
women came out of all c of Israel ... 1Sa 18:6
in the c of the Jerahmeelites ... 1Sa 30:29
were in the c of the Kenites ... 1Sa 30:29
were dead, they forsook the c ... 1Sa 31:7
go up into any of the c of Judah ... 2Sa 2:1
and they dwelt in the c of Hebron ... 2Sa 2:3
c of Hadadezer, king David took ... 2Sa 8:8
people, and for the c of our God ... 2Sa 10:12
the c of the children of Ammon ... 2Sa 12:31
him, lest he get him fenced c ... 2Sa 20:6
to all the c of the Hivites, and ... 2Sa 24:7
threescore great c with walls ... 1Kin 4:13
them in the land of their c ... 1Kin 8:37
twenty c in the land of Galilee ... 1Kin 9:11
the c which Solomon had given him ... 1Kin 9:12
What c are these which thou hast ... 1Kin 9:13
all the c of store that Solomon ... 1Kin 9:19
c for his chariots ... 1Kin 9:19
c for his horsemen, and that which ... 1Kin 9:19
he bestowed in the c for chariots ... 1Kin 10:26
which dwelt in the c of Judah ... 1Kin 12:17
which are in the c of Samaria ... 1Kin 13:32
he had against the c of Israel ... 1Kin 15:20
the c which he built, are they ... 1Kin 15:23
And Ben-hadad said unto him, The c 1Kin 20:34
all the c that he built, are they ... 1Kin 22:39
And they beat down the c, and on ... 2Kin 3:25
Ben-hadad the son of Hazael the c ... 2Kin 13:25
him, and recovered the c of Israel ... 2Kin 13:25
Gozan, and in the c of the Medes ... 2Kin 17:6
them high places in all their c ... 2Kin 17:9
placed them in the c of Samaria ... 2Kin 17:24
and dwelt in the c thereof ... 2Kin 17:24
and placed in the c of Samaria ... 2Kin 17:26
in their c wherein they dwelt ... 2Kin 17:29
Gozan, and in the c of the Medes ... 2Kin 18:11
against all the fenced c of Judah ... 2Kin 18:13
waste fenced c into ruinous heaps ... 2Kin 19:25
the high places in the c of Judah ... 2Kin 23:5
the priests out of the c of Judah ... 2Kin 23:8
that were in the c of Samaria ... 2Kin 23:19
twenty c in the land of Gilead ... 1Chr 2:22
towns thereof, even threescore c ... 1Chr 2:23
These were their c unto the reign ... 1Chr 4:31
and Tochen, and Ashan, five c ... 1Chr 4:32
that were round about the same c ... 1Chr 4:33
of Aaron they gave the c of Judah ... 1Chr 6:57
All their c throughout their ... 1Chr 6:60
their families were thirteen c ... 1Chr 6:60
were c given out of the half ... 1Chr 6:61
tribe of Manasseh, by lot, ten c ... 1Chr 6:61
of Manasseh in Bashan, thirteen c ... 1Chr 6:62
of the tribe of Zebulun, twelve c ... 1Chr 6:63
these c with their suburbs ... 1Chr 6:64
the children of Benjamin, these c ... 1Chr 6:65
of the sons of Kohath had c of ... 1Chr 6:66
of the c of refuge, Shechem in ... 1Chr 6:67
their possessions in their c were ... 1Chr 9:2
dead, then they forsook their c ... 1Chr 10:7
and Levites which are in their c ... 1Chr 13:2
c of Hadarezer, brought David ... 1Chr 18:8
themselves together from their c ... 1Chr 19:7
people, and for the c of our God ... 1Chr 19:13

the c of the children of Ammon 1Chr 20:3
in the fields, in the c, and in 1Chr 27:25
which he placed in the chariot c 2Chr 1:14
them in the c of their land 2Chr 6:28
That the c which Huram had 2Chr 8:2
wilderness, and all the store c 2Chr 8:4
Beth-horon the nether, fenced c 2Chr 8:5
all the store c that Solomon had, 2Chr 8:6
and all the chariot c 2Chr 8:6
the c of the horsemen, and all 2Chr 8:6
whom he bestowed in the chariot c 2Chr 9:25
that dwelt in the c of Judah 2Chr 10:17
built c for defence in Judah 2Chr 11:5
in Judah and in Benjamin fenced c 2Chr 11:10
he took the fenced c which 2Chr 12:4
took c from him, Beth-el with the 2Chr 13:19
the c of Judah the high places 2Chr 14:5
And he built fenced c in Judah 2Chr 14:6
unto Judah, Let us build these c 2Chr 14:7
smote all the c round about Gerar 2Chr 14:14
and they spoiled all the c 2Chr 14:14
out of the c which he had taken 2Chr 15:8
armies against the c of Israel 2Chr 16:4
and all the store c of Naphtali 2Chr 16:4
in all the fenced c of Judah 2Chr 17:2
in the c of Ephraim, which Asa 2Chr 17:2
to teach in the c of Judah 2Chr 17:7
throughout all the c of Judah 2Chr 17:9
in Judah castles, and c of store 2Chr 17:12
much business in the c of Judah 2Chr 17:13
the fenced c throughout all Judah 2Chr 17:19
all the fenced c of Judah 2Chr 19:5
brethren that dwell in their c 2Chr 19:10
even out of all the c of Judah 2Chr 20:4
things, with fenced c in Judah 2Chr 21:3
Levites out of all the c of Judah 2Chr 23:2
them, Go out unto the c of Judah 2Chr 24:5
battle, fell upon the c of Judah 2Chr 25:13
built c about Ashdod, and among 2Chr 26:6
Moreover he built c in the 2Chr 27:4
invaded the c of the low country 2Chr 28:18
went out to the c of Judah 2Chr 31:1
his possession, into their own c 2Chr 31:1
that dwelt in the c of Judah 2Chr 31:6
in the c of the priests, in their 2Chr 31:15
fields of the suburbs of their c 2Chr 31:19
and encamped against the fenced c 2Chr 32:1
Moreover he provided him c 2Chr 32:29
war in all the fenced c of Judah 2Chr 33:14
And so did he in the c of Manasseh 2Chr 34:6
the Nethinims, dwelt in their c Ezr 2:70
and all Israel in their c Ezr 2:70
children of Israel were in the c Ezr 3:1
over, and set in the c of Samaria Ezr 4:10
in our c come at appointed times Ezr 10:14
and all Israel, dwelt in their c Neh 7:73
of Israel were in their c Neh 7:73
and proclaim in all their c Neh 8:15
And they took strong c, and a fat Neh 9:25
in all the c of our tillage Neh 10:37
and nine parts to dwell in other c Neh 11:1
but in the c of Judah dwelt every Neh 11:3
one in his possession in their c Neh 11:3
were in all the c of Judah Neh 11:20
them out of the fields of the c Neh 12:44
themselves together in their c Est 9:2
And he dwelleth in desolate c Job 15:28
and thou hast destroyed c Ps 9:6
and will build the c of Judah Ps 69:35
your c are burned with fire Is 1:7
Until the c be wasted without Is 6:11
and destroyed the c thereof Is 14:17
fill the face of the world with c Is 14:21
The c of Aroer are forsaken Is 17:2
strong c be as a forsaken bough Is 17:9
In that day shall five c in the Is 19:18
covenant, he hath despised the c Is 33:8
all the defenced c of Judah Is 36:1
defenced c into ruinous heaps Is 37:26
say unto the c of Judah, Behold Is 40:9
the c thereof lift up their voice Is 42:11
to the c of Judah, Ye shall be Is 44:26
the desolate c to be inhabited Is 54:3
and they shall repair the waste c Is 61:4
Thy holy c are a wilderness, Zion Is 64:10
and against all the c of Judah Jer 1:15
his c are burned without Jer 2:15
the number of thy c are thy gods Jer 2:28
and let us go into the defenced c Jer 4:5
thy c shall be laid waste, Jer 4:7
voice against the c of Judah Jer 4:16
all the c thereof were broken Jer 4:26
leopard shall watch over their c Jer 5:6
shall impoverish thy fenced c Jer 5:17
what they do in the c of Judah Jer 7:17
to cease from the c of Judah Jer 7:34
let us enter into the defenced c Jer 8:14
I will make the c of Judah Jer 9:11
to make the c of Judah desolate, Jer 10:22
all these words in the c of Judah Jer 11:6
Then shall the c of Judah Jer 11:12
the number of thy c were thy gods Jer 11:13
The c of the south shall be shut Jer 13:19
shall come from the c of Judah Jer 17:26
let that man be as the c which Jer 20:16
c which are not inhabited Jer 22:6
the c of Judah, and the kings Jer 25:18
and speak unto all the c of Judah Jer 26:2
Israel, turn again to these thy c Jer 31:21
in the c thereof, when I shall Jer 31:23
in all the c thereof together, Jer 31:24
in the c of Judah Jer 32:44
in the c of the mountains Jer 32:44
in the c of the valley Jer 32:44
and in the c of the south Jer 32:44
beast, even in the c of Judah Jer 33:10
beast, and in all the c thereof Jer 33:12
In the c of the mountains Jer 33:13
in the c of the vale Jer 33:13
in the c of the south Jer 33:13
in the c of Judah, shall the Jer 33:13
and against all the c thereof Jer 34:1
against all the c of Judah that Jer 34:7
c remained of the c of Judah Jer 34:7
I will make the c of Judah a Jer 34:22
Judah that come out of their c Jer 36:6
the c of Judah unto Jerusalem Jer 36:9
made governor over the c of Judah Jer 40:5
dwell in your c that ye have Jer 40:10
and upon all the c of Judah Jer 44:2
and was kindled in the c of Judah Jer 44:6
in the c of Judah, and in the Jer 44:17
that ye burned in the c of Judah Jer 44:21
for the c thereof shall be Jer 48:9
spoiled, and gone up out of her c Jer 48:15
upon all the c of the land of Jer 48:24
that dwell in Moab, leave the c Jer 48:28
Gad, and his people dwell in his c Jer 49:1
all the c thereof shall be Jer 49:13
and the neighbour c thereof Jer 49:18
and I will kindle a fire in his c Jer 50:32
and the neighbour c thereof Jer 50:40
Her c are a desolation, a dry Jer 51:43
and the maids in the c of Judah Lam 5:11
the c shall be laid waste Eze 6:6
the c that are inhabited shall be Eze 12:20
palaces, and he laid waste their c Eze 19:7
open the side of Moab from the c Eze 25:9
from his c which are on his Eze 25:9
like the c that are not inhabited Eze 26:19
her c among the c that are Eze 29:12
her c shall be in the midst of Eze 30:7
midst of the c that are wasted Eze 30:7
these c shall go into captivity Eze 30:17
I will lay thy c waste, and thou Eze 35:4
and thy c shall not return Eze 35:9
to the c that are forsaken, which Eze 36:4
the c shall be inhabited, and the Eze 36:10
also cause you to dwell in the c Eze 36:33
ruined c are become fenced, and Eze 36:35
so shall the waste c be filled Eze 36:38
they that dwell in the c of Eze 39:9
mount, and take the most fenced c Dan 11:15
and Judah hath multiplied fenced c Hos 8:14
but I will send a fire upon his c Hos 8:14
And the sword shall abide on his c Hos 11:6
that may save thee in all thy c Hos 13:10
cleanness of teeth in all your c Amos 4:6
So two or three c wandered unto Amos 4:8
and they shall build the waste c Amos 9:14
shall possess the c of the south Obad 20
I will cut off the c of thy land Mic 5:11
so will I destroy thy c Mic 5:14
Assyria, and from the fortified c Mic 7:12
and alarm against the fenced c Zeph 1:16
their c are destroyed, so that Zeph 3:6
on the c of Judah, against which Zec 1:12
My c through prosperity shall yet Zec 1:17
the c thereof round about her, Zec 7:7
and the inhabitants of many c Zec 8:20
And Jesus went about all the c Mt 9:35
have gone over the c of Israel Mt 10:23
to teach and to preach in their c Mt 11:1
the c wherein most of his mighty Mt 11:20
followed him on foot out of the c Mt 14:13
and ran afoot thither out of all c Mk 6:33
he entered, into villages, or c Mk 6:56
kingdom of God to other c also Lk 4:43
And he went through the c and Lk 13:22
have thou authority over ten c Lk 19:17
to him, Be thou also over five c Lk 19:19
the c round about unto Jerusalem Acts 5:16
through he preached in all the c Acts 8:40
c of Lycaonia, and unto the region Acts 14:6
And as they went through the c Acts 16:4
them even unto strange c Acts 26:11
And turning the c of Sodom 2Pet 2:6
the c about them in like manner, Jude 7
the c of the nations fell Rev 16:19

### CITIZEN
himself to a c of that country Lk 15:15
in Cilicia, a c of no mean city Acts 21:39

### CITIZENS
But his c hated him, and sent a Lk 19:14

**CITY** See PREFACE.

### CLAD
he had c himself with a new 1Kin 11:29
was c with zeal as a cloke Is 59:17

### CLAMOROUS
A foolish woman is c Prov 9:13

### CLAMOUR
and wrath, and anger, and c Eph 4:31

### CLAP
Men shall c their hands at him, Job 27:23
O c your hands, all ye people Ps 47:1
Let the floods c their hands Ps 98:8
of the field shall c their hands Is 55:12
All that pass by c their hands at Lam 2:15
thee shall c the hands over thee Nah 3:19

### CLAPPED
they c their hands, and said, God 2Kin 11:12
Because thou hast c thine hands Eze 25:6

C

### CLAPPETH
he c his hands among us, and Job 34:37

**CLAUDA** (*claw'-dah*) *An island near Crete.*
certain island which is called C Acts 27:16

**CLAUDIA** (*claw'-de-ah*) *A Roman Christian.*
thee, and Pudens, and Linus, and C 2Ti 4:21

**CLAUDIUS** (*claw'-de-us*)
*1. A Roman emperor.*
to pass in the days of C Caesar Acts 11:28
(because that C had commanded all Acts 18:2
*2. A Roman officer in Jerusalem.*
C Lysias unto the most excellent Acts 23:26

### CLAVE
c the wood for the burnt offering Gen 22:3
his soul c unto Dinah the Gen 34:3
that the ground c asunder that Num 16:31
But God c an hollow place that Judg 15:19
but Ruth c unto her Ruth 1:14
they c the wood of the cart, and 1Sa 6:14
men of Judah c unto their king 2Sa 20:2
his hand c unto the sword 2Sa 23:10
Solomon c unto these in love 1Kin 11:2
For he c to the LORD, and departed 2Kin 18:6
They c to their brethren, their Neh 10:29
He c the rocks in the wilderness, Ps 78:15
he c the rock also, and the waters Is 48:21
Howbeit certain men c unto him Acts 17:34

### CLAWS
and cleaveth the cleft into two c Deut 14:6
and his nails like birds' c Dan 4:33
fat, and tear their c in pieces Zec 11:16

### CLAY
in the c ground between Succoth 1Kin 7:46
in the c ground between Succoth 2Chr 4:17
in them that dwell in houses of c Job 4:19
that thou hast made me as the c Job 10:9
ashes, your bodies to bodies of c Job 13:12
dust, and prepare raiment as the c Job 27:16
I also am formed out of the c Job 33:6
It is turned as c to the seal Job 38:14
horrible pit, out of the miry c Ps 40:2
be esteemed as the potter's c Is 29:16
and as the potter treadeth c Is 41:25
Shall the c say to him that Is 45:9
we are the c, and thou our potter Is 64:8
the vessel that he made of c was Jer 18:4
as the c is in the potter's hand, Jer 18:6
them in the c in the brickkiln Jer 43:9
feet part of iron and part of c Dan 2:33
his feet that were of iron and c Dan 2:34
Then was the iron, the c, the Dan 2:35
feet and toes, part of potters' c Dan 2:41
sawest the iron mixed with miry c Dan 2:41
were part of iron, and part of c Dan 2:42
sawest iron mixed with miry c Dan 2:43
even as iron is not mixed with c Dan 2:43
pieces the iron, the brass, the c Dan 2:45
go into c, and tread the morter, Nah 3:14
that ladeth himself with thick c Hab 2:6
made c of the spittle, and he Jn 9:6
eyes of the blind man with the c Jn 9:6
A man that is called Jesus made c Jn 9:11
sabbath day when Jesus made the c Jn 9:14
He put c upon mine eyes, and I Jn 9:15
not the potter power over the c Rom 9:21

### CLEAN
Of every c beast thou shalt take Gen 7:2
of beasts that are not c by two Gen 7:2
Of c beasts, and of beasts that Gen 7:8
and of beasts that are not c Gen 7:8
c beast, and of every c fowl Gen 8:20
gods that are among you, and be c Gen 35:2
without the camp unto a c place Lev 4:12
without the camp unto a c place Lev 6:11
all that be c shall eat thereof Lev 7:19
unholy, and between unclean and c Lev 10:10
shall ye eat in a c place Lev 10:14
is plenty of water, shall be c Lev 11:36
is to be sown, it shall be c Lev 11:37
between the unclean and the c Lev 11:47
for her, and she shall be c Lev 12:8
the priest shall pronounce him c Lev 13:6
shall wash his clothes, and be c Lev 13:6
him c that hath the plague Lev 13:13
he is c Lev 13:13
him c that hath the plague Lev 13:17
he is c Lev 13:17
the priest shall pronounce him c Lev 13:23
the priest shall pronounce him c Lev 13:28
the priest shall pronounce him c Lev 13:34
shall wash his clothes, and be c Lev 13:34
the scall is healed, he is c Lev 13:37
the priest shall pronounce him c Lev 13:37
he is c Lev 13:39
yet is he c Lev 13:40
yet is he c Lev 13:41
the second time, and shall be c Lev 13:58
thing of skins, to pronounce it c Lev 13:59
be cleansed two birds alive and c Lev 14:4

times, and shall pronounce him c ... Lev 14:7
in water, that he may be c ... Lev 14:8
flesh in water, and he shall be c ... Lev 14:9
the priest that maketh him c ... Lev 14:11
the man that is to be made c ... Lev 14:11
for him, and he shall be c ... Lev 14:20
shall pronounce the house c ... Lev 14:48
and it shall be c ... Lev 14:53
it is unclean, and when it is c ... Lev 14:57
the issue spit upon him that is c ... Lev 15:8
in running water, and shall be c ... Lev 15:13
and after that she shall be c ... Lev 15:28
that ye may be c from all your ... Lev 16:30
then shall he be c ... Lev 17:15
put difference between c beasts ... Lev 20:25
and between unclean fowls and c ... Lev 20:25
of the holy things, until he be c ... Lev 22:4
the sun is down, he shall be c ... Lev 22:7
thou shalt not make c riddance of ... Lev 23:22
woman be not defiled, but be c ... Num 5:28
clothes, and so make themselves c ... Num 8:7
But the man that is c, and is not ... Num 9:13
every one that is c in thy house ... Num 18:11
every one that is c in thine ... Num 18:13
a man that is c shall gather up ... Num 19:9
up without the camp in a c place ... Num 19:9
on the seventh day he shall be c ... Num 19:12
the seventh day he shall not be c ... Num 19:12
a c person shall take hyssop, and ... Num 19:18
the c person shall sprinkle upon ... Num 19:19
in water, and shall be c at even ... Num 19:19
the fire, and it shall be c ... Num 31:23
the seventh day, and ye shall be c ... Num 31:24
the c may eat thereof, as of the ... Deut 12:15
the c shall eat of them alike ... Deut 12:22
Of all c birds ye shall eat ... Deut 14:11
But of all c fowls ye may eat ... Deut 14:20
the c person shall eat it alike, ... Deut 15:22
that is not c by reason of ... Deut 23:10
people were passed c over Jordan ... Josh 3:17
people were c passed over Jordan ... Josh 4:1
all the people were c passed over ... Josh 4:11
hath befallen him, he is not c ... 1Sa 20:26
surely he is not c ... 1Sa 20:26
again to thee, and thou shalt be c ... 2Kin 5:10
may I not wash in them, and be c ... 2Kin 5:12
he saith to thee, Wash, and be c ... 2Kin 5:13
of a little child, and he was c ... 2Kin 5:14
for every one that was not c ... 2Chr 30:17
and make my hands never so c ... Job 9:30
is pure, and I am c in thine eyes ... Job 11:4
Who can bring a c thing out of an ... Job 14:4
What is man, that he should be c ... Job 15:14
heavens are not c in his sight ... Job 15:15
he that hath c hands shall be ... Job 17:9
or how can he be c that is born ... Job 25:4
I am c without transgression, I ... Job 33:9
The fear of the LORD is c ... Ps 19:9
He that hath c hands, and a pure ... Ps 24:4
me with hyssop, and I shall be c ... Ps 51:7
Create in me a c heart, O God ... Ps 51:10
even to such as are of a c heart ... Ps 73:1
Is his mercy c gone for ever ... Ps 77:8
Where no oxen are, the crib is c ... Prov 14:4
of a man are c in his own eyes ... Prov 16:2
can say, I have made my heart c ... Prov 20:9
to the good and to the c, and to ... Eccl 9:2
Wash you, make you c ... Is 1:16
down, the earth is c dissolved ... Is 24:19
so that there is no place c ... Is 28:8
the ground shall eat c provender ... Is 30:24
be ye c, that bear the vessels of ... Is 52:11
a c vessel into the house of the ... Is 66:20
wilt thou not be made c ... Jer 13:27
between the unclean and the c ... Eze 22:26
will I sprinkle c water upon you ... Eze 36:25
and ye shall be c ... Eze 36:25
between the unclean and the c ... Eze 44:23
he hath made it c bare, and cast ... Joel 1:7
his arm shall be c dried up ... Zec 11:17
thou wilt, thou canst make me c ... Mt 8:2
be thou c ... Mt 8:3
for ye make c the outside of the ... Mt 23:25
the outside of them may be c also ... Mt 23:26
he wrapped it in a c linen cloth ... Mt 27:59
thou wilt, thou canst make me c ... Mk 1:40
be thou c ... Mk 1:41
thou wilt, thou canst make me c ... Lk 5:12
be thou c ... Lk 5:13
make c the outside of the cup ... Lk 11:39
behold, all things are c unto you ... Lk 11:41
his feet, but is c every whit ... Jn 13:10
and ye are c, but not all ... Jn 13:10
said he, Ye are not all c ... Jn 13:11
Now ye are c through the word ... Jn 15:3
I am c ... Acts 18:6
those that were c escaped from ... 2Pet 2:18
be arrayed in fine linen, c ... Rev 19:8
clothed in fine linen, white and c ... Rev 19:14

## CLEANNESS
according to the c of my hands ... 2Sa 22:21
according to my c in his eye ... 2Sa 22:25
according to the c of my hands ... Ps 18:20
according to the c of my hands in ... Ps 18:24
I also have given you c of teeth ... Amos 4:6

## CLEANSE
and thou shalt c the altar ... Ex 29:36
he shall take to c the house two ... Lev 14:49
he shall c the house with the ... Lev 14:52
c it, and hallow it from the ... Lev 16:19
to c you, that ye may be clean ... Lev 16:30
the children of Israel, and c them ... Num 8:6
thou do unto them, to c them ... Num 8:7
and thou shalt c them, and offer ... Num 8:15
an atonement for them to c them ... Num 8:21
to c the house of the LORD ... 2Chr 29:15
of the house of the LORD, to c it ... 2Chr 29:16
that they should c themselves ... Neh 13:22
c thou me from secret faults ... Ps 19:12
iniquity, and c me from my sin ... Ps 51:2
shall a young man c his way ... Ps 119:9
my people, not to fan, nor to c ... Jer 4:11
I will c them from all their ... Jer 33:8
from all your idols, will I c you ... Eze 36:25
they have sinned, and will c them ... Eze 37:23
of them, that they may c the land ... Eze 39:12
the face of the earth, to c it ... Eze 39:14
Thus shall they c the land ... Eze 39:16
thus shalt thou c and purge it ... Eze 43:20
and they shall c the altar ... Eze 43:22
as they did c it with the bullock ... Eze 43:22
blemish, and c the sanctuary ... Eze 45:18
For I will c their blood that I ... Joel 3:21
c the lepers, raise the dead, ... Mt 10:8
c first that which is within the ... Mt 23:26
let us c ourselves from all ... 2Cor 7:1
c it with the washing of water by ... Eph 5:26
C your hands, ye sinners ... Jas 4:8
to c us from all unrighteousness ... 1Jn 1:9

## CLEANSED
so it shall be c ... Lev 11:32
she shall be c from the issue of ... Lev 12:7
that is to be c two birds alive ... Lev 14:4
be c from the leprosy seven times ... Lev 14:7
he that is to be c shall wash his ... Lev 14:8
right ear of him that is to be c ... Lev 14:14
right ear of him that is to be c ... Lev 14:17
the head of him that is to be c ... Lev 14:18
is to be c from his uncleanness ... Lev 14:19
right ear of him that is to be c ... Lev 14:25
right ear of him that is to be c ... Lev 14:28
the head of him that is to be c ... Lev 14:29
that is to be c before the LORD ... Lev 14:31
hath an issue is c of his issue ... Lev 15:13
But if she be c of her issue ... Lev 15:28
the land cannot be c of the blood ... Num 35:33
which we are not c until this day ... Josh 22:17
We have c all the house of the ... 2Chr 29:18
had not c themselves, yet did ... 2Chr 30:18
though he be not c according to ... 2Chr 30:19
altars, and c Judah and Jerusalem ... 2Chr 34:5
commanded, and they c the chambers. Neh 13:9
Thus c I them from all strangers, ... Neh 13:30
I have, if I be c from my sin ... Job 35:3
Verily I have c my heart in vain, ... Ps 73:13
Thou art the land that is not c ... Eze 22:24
In the day that I shall have c ... Eze 36:33
And after he is c, they shall ... Eze 44:26
then shall the sanctuary be c ... Dan 8:14
their blood that I have not c ... Joel 3:21
And immediately his leprosy was c ... Mt 8:3
the lame walk, the lepers are c ... Mt 11:5
departed from him, and he was c ... Mk 1:42
and none of them was c, saving ... Lk 4:27
the lame walk, the lepers are c ... Lk 7:22
that, as they went, they were c ... Lk 17:14
said, Were there not ten c ... Lk 17:17
the second time, What God hath c ... Acts 10:15
from heaven, What God hath c ... Acts 11:9

## CLEANSETH
but the wind passeth, and c them ... Job 37:21
blueness of a wound c away evil ... Prov 20:30
Christ his Son c us from all sin ... 1Jn 1:7

## CLEANSING
been seen of the priest for his c ... Lev 13:7
much in the skin after his c ... Lev 13:35
of the leper in the day of his c ... Lev 14:2
day for his c unto the priest ... Lev 14:23
that which pertaineth to his c ... Lev 14:32
to himself seven days for his c ... Lev 15:13
his head in the day of his c ... Num 6:9
thou hast made an end of c it ... Eze 43:23
offer for thy c those things ... Mk 1:44
to the priest, and offer for thy c ... Lk 5:14

## CLEAR
thou shalt be c from this my oath ... Gen 24:8
shalt thou be c from this my oath ... Gen 24:41
one, thou shalt be c from my oath ... Gen 24:41
or how shall we c ourselves ... Gen 44:16
will by no means c the guilty ... Ex 34:7
the earth by c shining after rain ... 2Sa 23:4
and be c when thou judgest ... Ps 51:4
c as the sun, and terrible as an ... Song 6:10
place like a c heat upon herbs ... Is 18:4
darken the earth in the c day ... Amos 8:9
that the light shall not be c ... Zec 14:6
yourselves to be c in this matter ... 2Cor 7:11
like a jasper stone, c as crystal ... Rev 21:11
was pure gold, like unto c glass ... Rev 21:18
c as crystal, proceeding out of ... Rev 22:1

## CLEARER
age shall be c than the noonday ... Job 11:17

## CLEARING
and by no means c the guilty ... Num 14:18
what c of yourselves, yea, what ... 2Cor 7:11

## CLEARLY
my lips shall utter knowledge c ... Job 33:3
then shalt thou see c to cast out ... Mt 7:5
was restored, and saw every man c ... Mk 8:25
then shalt thou see c to pull out ... Lk 6:42
creation of the world are c seen ... Rom 1:20

## CLEARNESS
were the body of heaven in his c ... Ex 24:10

## CLEAVE
mother, and shall c unto his wife ... Gen 2:24
he shall c it with the wings ... Lev 1:17
But ye that did c unto the LORD ... Deut 4:4
serve, and to him shalt thou c ... Deut 10:20
in all his ways, and to c unto him ... Deut 11:22
ye shall serve him, and c unto him ... Deut 13:4
there shall c nought of the ... Deut 13:17
make the pestilence c unto thee ... Deut 28:21
and they shall c unto thee ... Deut 28:60
and that thou mayest c unto him ... Deut 30:20
to c unto him, and to serve him ... Josh 22:5
But c unto the LORD your God, as ... Josh 23:8
c unto the remnant of these ... Josh 23:12
of Naaman shall c unto thee ... 2Kin 5:27
the clods c fast together ... Job 38:38
Thou didst c the fountain and the ... Ps 74:15
it shall not c to me ... Ps 101:3
my groaning my bones c to my skin ... Ps 102:5
let my tongue c to the roof of my ... Ps 137:6
they shall c to the house of ... Is 14:1
so have I caused to c unto me the ... Jer 13:11
I will make thy tongue c to the ... Eze 3:26
they shall not c one to another ... Dan 2:43
but many shall c to them with ... Dan 11:34
Thou didst c the earth with ... Hab 3:9
the mount of Olives shall c in ... Zec 14:4
and mother, and shall c to his wife ... Mt 19:5
and mother, and c to his wife ... Mk 10:7
heart they would c unto the Lord ... Acts 11:23
c to that which is good ... Rom 12:9

## CLEAVED
Nevertheless he c unto the sins ... 2Kin 3:3
their tongue c to the roof of ... Job 29:10
if any blot hath c to mine hands ... Job 31:7

## CLEAVETH
c the cleft into two claws, and ... Deut 14:6
he c my reins asunder, and doth ... Job 16:13
My bone c to my skin and to my ... Job 19:20
and my tongue c to my jaws ... Ps 22:15
say they, c fast unto him ... Ps 41:8
our belly c unto the earth ... Ps 44:25
My soul c unto the dust ... Ps 119:25
cutteth and c wood upon the earth ... Ps 141:7
and he that c wood shall be ... Eccl 10:9
For as the girdle c to the loins ... Jer 13:11
c to the roof of his mouth for ... Lam 4:4
their skin c to their bones ... Lam 4:8
dust of your city, which c on us ... Lk 10:11

## CLEFT
cleaveth the c into two claws, and ... Deut 14:6
him, and the valleys shall be c ... Mic 1:4

## CLEFTS
that art in the c of the rock ... Song 2:14
To go into the c of the rocks ... Is 2:21
dwellest in the c of the rock ... Jer 49:16
and the little house with c ... Amos 6:11
dwellest in the c of the rock ... Obad 3

## CLEMENCY
hear us of thy c a few words ... Acts 24:4

## CLEMENT (*clem'-ent*) *A companion of Paul.*
me in the gospel, with C also ... Phil 4:3

## CLEOPAS (*cle'-o-pas*) See ALPHAEUS, CLEOPHAS. *A disciple on Emmaus Road.*
the one of them, whose name was C ... Lk 24:18

## CLEOPHAS (*cle'-o-fas*) See CLEOPAS. *Husband of Mary.*
sister, Mary the wife of C ... Jn 19:25

## CLIFF
they come up by the c of Ziz ... 2Chr 20:16

## CLIFFS
To dwell in the c of the valleys ... Job 30:6

## CLIFT
will put thee in a c of the rock ... Ex 33:22

## CLIFTS
valleys under the c of the rocks ... Is 57:5

## CLIMB
thickets, and c up upon the rocks ... Jer 4:29
they shall c the wall like men of ... Joel 2:7
they shall c up upon the houses ... Joel 2:9
though they c up to heaven, ... Amos 9:2

## CLIMBED
Jonathan c up upon his hands and ... 1Sa 14:13
c up into a sycomore tree to see ... Lk 19:4

## CLIMBETH
but c up some other way, the same ... Jn 10:1

## CLIPPED
shall be bald, and every beard c ... Jer 48:37

## CLODS
clothed with worms and c of dust ... Job 7:5
The c of the valley shall be ... Job 21:33
the c cleave fast together ... Job 38:38

break the c of his ground ... Is 28:24
plow, and Jacob shall break his c ... Hos 10:11
The seed is rotten under their c ... Joel 1:17

### CLOKE
and was clad with zeal as a c ... Is 59:17
thy coat, let him have thy c also ... Mt 5:40
him that taketh away thy c forbid ... Lk 6:29
now they have no c for their sin ... Jn 15:22
ye know, nor a c of covetousness ... 1Th 2:5
The c that I left at Troas with ... 2Ti 4:13
liberty for a c of maliciousness ... 1Pet 2:16

### CLOPAS See CLEOPHAS.

### CLOSE
eyes of her husband, and be kept c ... Num 5:13
be afraid out of their c places ... 2Sa 22:46
while he yet kept himself c ... 1Chr 12:1
kept c from the fowls of the air ... Job 28:21
shut up together as with a c seal ... Job 41:15
be afraid out of their c places ... Ps 18:45
shall follow c after you there in ... Jer 42:16
And I saw him come c unto the ram ... Dan 8:7
c up the breaches thereof ... Amos 9:11
And they kept it c, and told no man ... Lk 9:36
thence, they sailed c by Crete ... Acts 27:13

### CLOSED
c up the flesh instead thereof ... Gen 2:21
For the LORD had fast c up all ... Gen 20:18
the pit, and the earth c upon them ... Num 16:33
the fat c upon the blade, so that ... Judg 3:22
they have not been c, neither ... Is 1:6
deep sleep, and hath c your eyes ... Is 29:10
for the words are c up and sealed ... Dan 12:9
the depth c me round about, the ... Jonah 2:5
and their eyes they have c ... Mt 13:15
he c the book, and he gave it ... Lk 4:20
and their eyes have they c ... Acts 28:27

### CLOSER
that sticketh c than a brother ... Prov 18:24

### CLOSEST
because thou c thyself in cedar ... Jer 22:15

### CLOSET
and the bride out of her c ... Joel 2:16
thou prayest, enter into thy c ... Mt 6:6

### CLOSETS
in c shall be proclaimed upon the ... Lk 12:3

### CLOTH
spread over it a c wholly of blue ... Num 4:6
they shall spread a c of blue ... Num 4:7
spread upon them a c of scarlet ... Num 4:8
And they shall take a c of blue ... Num 4:9
they shall spread a c of blue ... Num 4:11
and put them in a c of blue ... Num 4:12
and spread a purple c thereon ... Num 4:13
they shall spread the c before ... Deut 22:17
bolster, and covered it with a c ... 1Sa 19:13
wrapped in a c behind the ephod ... 1Sa 21:9
cast a c upon him, when he saw ... 2Sa 20:12
morrow, that he took a thick c ... 2Kin 8:15
cast them away as a menstruous c ... Is 30:22
of new c unto an old garment ... Mt 9:16
he wrapped it in a clean linen c ... Mt 27:59
piece of new c on an old garment ... Mk 2:21
having a linen c cast about his ... Mk 14:51
And he left the linen c, and fled ... Mk 14:52

### CLOTHE
his sons, and c them with coats ... Ex 40:14
and she sent raiment to c Mordecai ... Est 4:4
I will also c her priests with ... Ps 132:16
His enemies will I c with shame ... Ps 132:18
shall c a man with rags ... Prov 23:21
I will c him with thy robe, and ... Is 22:21
thou shalt surely c thee with ... Is 49:18
I c the heavens with blackness, ... Is 50:3
they shall c themselves with ... Eze 26:16
ye c you with the wool, ye kill ... Eze 34:3
ye c you, but there is none warm ... Hag 1:6
I will c thee with change of ... Zec 3:4
if God so c the grass of the ... Mt 6:30
shall he not much more c you ... Mt 6:30
If then God so c the grass ... Lk 12:28
how much more will he c you ... Lk 12:28

### CLOTHED
make coats of skins, and c them ... Gen 3:21
c him with the robe, and put the ... Lev 8:7
who c you in scarlet, with other ... 2Sa 1:24
David was c with a robe of fine ... 1Chr 15:27
who were c in sackcloth, fell ... 1Chr 21:16
be c with salvation, and let thy ... 2Chr 6:41
c in their robes, and they sat in ... 2Chr 18:9
with the spoil c all that were ... 2Chr 28:15
the king's gate c with sackcloth ... Est 4:2
My flesh is c with worms and clods ... Job 7:5
hate thee shall be c with shame ... Job 8:22
Thou hast c me with skin and flesh ... Job 10:11
put on righteousness, and it c me ... Job 29:14
hast thou c his neck with thunder ... Job 39:19
let them be c with shame and ... Ps 35:26
The pastures are c with flocks ... Ps 65:13
reigneth, he is c with majesty ... Ps 93:1
the LORD is c with strength, ... Ps 93:1
thou art c with honour and majesty ... Ps 104:1
As he c himself with cursing like ... Ps 109:18
mine adversaries be c with shame ... Ps 109:29
priests be c with righteousness ... Ps 132:9
her household are c with scarlet ... Prov 31:21
for he hath c me with the ... Is 61:10
prince shall be c with desolation ... Eze 7:27
man among them was c with linen ... Eze 9:2
he called to the man c with linen ... Eze 9:3
the man c with linen, which had ... Eze 9:11
spake unto the man c with linen ... Eze 10:2
commanded the man c with linen ... Eze 10:6
of him that was c with linen ... Eze 10:7
I c thee also with broidered work ... Eze 16:10
Which were c with blue, captains ... Eze 23:6
rulers c most gorgeously, ... Eze 23:12
all of them c with all sorts of ... Eze 38:4
they shall be c with linen ... Eze 44:17
shall be c with scarlet, and have ... Dan 5:7
thou shalt be c with scarlet ... Dan 5:16
they c Daniel with scarlet, and ... Dan 5:29
behold a certain man c in linen ... Dan 10:5
And one said to the man c in linen ... Dan 12:6
And I heard the man c in linen ... Dan 12:7
all such as are c with strange ... Zeph 1:8
Now Joshua was c with filthy ... Zec 3:3
his head, and c him with garments ... Zec 3:5
or, Wherewithal shall we be c ... Mt 6:31
A man c in soft raiment ... Mt 11:8
Naked, and ye c me ... Mt 25:36
or naked, and c thee ... Mt 25:38
naked, and ye c me not ... Mt 25:43
John was c with camel's hair, and ... Mk 1:6
and had the legion, sitting, and c ... Mk 5:15
they c him with purple, and ... Mk 15:17
c in a long white garment ... Mk 16:5
A man c in soft raiment ... Lk 7:25
sitting at the feet of Jesus, c ... Lk 8:35
rich man, which was c in purple ... Lk 16:19
earnestly desiring to be c upon ... 2Cor 5:2
If so be that being c we shall ... 2Cor 5:3
but c upon, that mortality might ... 2Cor 5:4
to another, and be c with humility ... 1Pet 5:5
c with a garment down to the foot ... Rev 1:13
same shall be c in white raiment ... Rev 3:5
raiment, that thou mayest be c ... Rev 3:18
sitting, c in white raiment ... Rev 4:4
c with white robes, and palms in ... Rev 7:9
down from heaven, c with a cloud ... Rev 10:1
threescore days, c in sackcloth ... Rev 11:3
a woman c with the sun, and the ... Rev 12:1
c in pure and white linen, and ... Rev 15:6
that was c in fine linen, and ... Rev 18:16
he was c with a vesture dipped in ... Rev 19:13
c in fine linen, white and clean ... Rev 19:14

### CLOTHES
and he rent his c ... Gen 37:29
And Jacob rent his c, and put ... Gen 37:34
Then they rent their c, and laded ... Gen 44:13
his c in the blood of grapes ... Gen 49:11
in their c upon their shoulders ... Ex 12:34
morrow, and let them wash their c ... Ex 19:10
and they washed their c ... Ex 19:14
your heads, neither rend your c ... Lev 10:6
carcase of them shall wash his c ... Lev 11:25
carcase of them shall wash his c ... Lev 11:28
carcase of it shall wash his c ... Lev 11:40
carcase of it shall wash his c ... Lev 11:40
and he shall wash his c, and be ... Lev 13:6
and he shall wash his c, and be ... Lev 13:34
his c shall be rent, and his head ... Lev 13:45
to be cleansed shall wash his c ... Lev 14:8
and he shall wash his c, also he ... Lev 14:9
in the house shall wash his c ... Lev 14:47
in the house shall wash his c ... Lev 14:47
toucheth his bed shall wash his c ... Lev 15:5
hath the issue shall wash his c ... Lev 15:6
hath the issue shall wash his c ... Lev 15:7
then he shall wash his c, and ... Lev 15:8
of those things shall wash his c ... Lev 15:10
in water, he shall wash his c ... Lev 15:11
for his cleansing, and wash his c ... Lev 15:13
toucheth her bed shall wash his c ... Lev 15:21
she sat upon shall wash his c ... Lev 15:22
be unclean, and shall wash his c ... Lev 15:27
the scapegoat shall wash his c ... Lev 16:26
burneth them shall wash his c ... Lev 16:28
and shall put on the linen c ... Lev 16:32
he shall both wash his c ... Lev 17:15
uncover his head, nor rend his c ... Lev 21:10
flesh, and let them wash their c ... Num 8:7
purified, and they washed their c ... Num 8:21
searched the land, rent their c ... Num 14:6
Then the priest shall wash his c ... Num 19:7
her shall wash his c in water ... Num 19:8
of the heifer shall wash his c ... Num 19:10
purify himself, and wash his c ... Num 19:19
of separation shall wash his c ... Num 19:21
wash your c on the seventh day ... Num 31:24
your c are not waxen old upon you ... Deut 29:5
And Joshua rent his c, and fell to ... Josh 7:6
he saw her, that he rent his c ... Judg 11:35
the same day with his c rent ... 1Sa 4:12
And he stript off his c also ... 1Sa 19:24
camp from Saul with his c rent ... 2Sa 1:2
Then David took hold on his c ... 2Sa 1:11
that were with him, Rend your c ... 2Sa 3:31
stood by with their c rent ... 2Sa 13:31
his beard, nor washed his c ... 2Sa 19:24
and they covered him with c ... 1Kin 1:1
those words, that he rent his c ... 1Kin 21:27
and he took hold of his own c ... 2Kin 2:12
the letter, that he rent his c ... 2Kin 5:7
the king of Israel had rent his c ... 2Kin 5:8
Wherefore hast thou rent thy c ... 2Kin 5:8
of the woman, that he rent his c ... 2Kin 6:30
and Athaliah rent her c, and cried, ... 2Kin 11:14
to Hezekiah with their c rent ... 2Kin 18:37
heard it, that he rent his c ... 2Kin 19:1
of the law, that he rent his c ... 2Kin 22:11
and a curse, and hast rent thy c ... 2Kin 22:19
Then Athaliah rent her c, and said ... 2Chr 23:13
of the law, that he rent his c ... 2Chr 34:19
before me, and didst rend thy c ... 2Chr 34:27
me, none of us put off our c ... Neh 4:23
their c waxed not old, and their ... Neh 9:21
was done, Mordecai rent his c ... Est 4:1
mine own c shall abhor me ... Job 9:31
his bosom, and his c not be burned ... Prov 6:27
to Hezekiah with their c rent ... Is 36:22
heard it, that he rent his c ... Is 37:1
beards shaven, and their c rent ... Jer 41:5
shall strip thee also of thy c ... Eze 16:39
also strip thee out of thy c ... Eze 23:26
in precious c for chariots ... Eze 27:20
in all sorts of things, in blue c ... Eze 27:24
c laid to pledge by every altar ... Amos 2:8
the colt, and put on them their c ... Mt 21:7
field return back to take his c ... Mt 24:18
Then the high priest rent his c ... Mt 26:65
said, If I may touch but his c ... Mk 5:28
press, and said, Who touched my c ... Mk 5:30
Then the high priest rent his c ... Mk 14:63
from him, and put his own c on him ... Mk 15:20
and wrapped him in swaddling c ... Lk 2:7
the babe wrapped in swaddling c ... Lk 2:12
devils long time, and ware no c ... Lk 8:27
they spread their c in the way ... Lk 19:36
the linen c laid by themselves ... Lk 24:12
it in linen c with the spices ... Jn 19:40
looking in, saw the linen c lying ... Jn 20:5
and seeth the linen c lie ... Jn 20:6
head, not lying with the linen c ... Jn 20:7
their c at a young man's feet ... Acts 7:58
Paul, heard of, they rent their c ... Acts 14:14
the magistrates rent off their c ... Acts 16:22
cried out, and cast off their c ... Acts 22:23

### CLOTHEST
Though thou c thyself with ... Jer 4:30

### CLOTHING
and stripped the naked of their c ... Job 22:6
the naked to lodge without c ... Job 24:7
cause him to go naked without c ... Job 24:10
seen any perish for want of c ... Job 31:19
were sick, my c was sackcloth ... Ps 35:13
her c is of wrought gold ... Ps 45:13
The lambs are for thy c, and the ... Prov 27:26
her c is silk and purple ... Prov 31:22
Strength and honour are her c ... Prov 31:25
his father, saying, Thou hast c ... Is 3:6
my house is neither bread nor c ... Is 3:7
sufficiently, and for durable c ... Is 23:18
the garments of vengeance for c ... Is 59:17
blue and purple is their c ... Jer 10:9
which come to you in sheep's c ... Mt 7:15
they that wear soft c are in ... Mt 11:8
which love to go in long c ... Mk 12:38
a man stood before me in bright c ... Acts 10:30
to him that weareth the gay c ... Jas 2:3

### CLOTHS
the c of service, and the holy ... Ex 31:10
The c of service, to do service ... Ex 35:19
they made c of service, to do ... Ex 39:1
The c of service to do service in ... Ex 39:41

### CLOUD
I do set my bow in the c, and it ... Gen 9:13
when I bring a c over the earth ... Gen 9:14
the bow shall be seen in the c ... Gen 9:14
And the bow shall be in the c ... Gen 9:16
them by day in a pillar of a c ... Ex 13:21
away the pillar of the c by day ... Ex 13:22
the pillar of the c went from ... Ex 14:19
and it was a c and darkness to them ... Ex 14:20
the pillar of fire and of the c ... Ex 14:24
of the LORD appeared in the c ... Ex 16:10
Lo, I come unto thee in a thick c ... Ex 19:9
a thick c upon the mount, and the ... Ex 19:16
mount, and a c covered the mount ... Ex 24:15
the c covered it six days ... Ex 24:16
Moses out of the midst of the c ... Ex 24:16
went into the midst of the c ... Ex 24:18
And the LORD descended in the c ... Ex 34:5
Then a c covered the tent of the ... Ex 40:34
because the c abode thereon, and ... Ex 40:35
when the c was taken up from over ... Ex 40:36
But if the c were not taken up, ... Ex 40:37
For the c of the LORD was upon ... Ex 40:38
in the c upon the mercy seat ... Lev 16:2
that the c of the incense may ... Lev 16:13
up the c covered the tabernacle ... Num 9:15
the c covered it by day, and the ... Num 9:16
when the c was taken up from the ... Num 9:17
and in the place where the c abode ... Num 9:17
as long as the c abode upon the ... Num 9:18
when the c tarried long upon the ... Num 9:19
when the c was a few days upon ... Num 9:20
when the c abode from even unto ... Num 9:21
that the c was taken up in the ... Num 9:21
by night that the c was taken up ... Num 9:21
that the c tarried upon the ... Num 9:22
that the c was taken up from off ... Num 10:11
the c rested in the wilderness of ... Num 10:12

the c of the LORD was upon them ..... Num 10:34
And the LORD came down in a c ..... Num 11:25
came down in the pillar of the c ..... Num 12:5
the c departed from off the ..... Num 12:10
that thy c standeth over them, and ..... Num 14:14
by daytime in a pillar of a c ..... Num 14:14
the c covered it, and the glory of ..... Num 16:42
ye should go, and in a c by day ..... Deut 1:33
the midst of the fire, of the c ..... Deut 5:22
the tabernacle in a pillar of a c ..... Deut 31:15
the pillar of the c stood over ..... Deut 31:15
that the c filled the house of ..... 1Kin 8:10
to minister because of the c ..... 1Kin 8:11
ariseth a little c out of the sea ..... 1Kin 18:44
the house was filled with a c ..... 2Chr 5:13
to minister by reason of the c ..... 2Chr 5:14
the pillar of the c departed not ..... Neh 9:19
let a c dwell upon it ..... Job 3:5
As the c is consumed and vanisheth ..... Job 7:9
can he judge through the dark c ..... Job 22:13
the c is not rent under them ..... Job 26:8
and spreadeth his c upon it ..... Job 26:9
and my welfare passeth away as a c ..... Job 30:15
by the c that cometh betwixt ..... Job 36:32
watering he wearieth the thick c ..... Job 37:11
he scattereth his bright c ..... Job 37:11
the light of his c to shine ..... Job 37:15
When I made the c the garment ..... Job 38:9
daytime also he led them with a c ..... Ps 78:14
He spread a c for a covering ..... Ps 105:39
is as a c of the latter rain ..... Prov 16:15
Zion, and upon her assemblies, a c ..... Is 4:5
like a c of dew in the heat of ..... Is 18:4
the LORD rideth upon a swift c ..... Is 19:1
the heat with the shadow of a c ..... Is 25:5
I have blotted out, as a thick c ..... Is 44:22
thy transgressions, and, as a c ..... Is 44:22
Who are these that fly as a c ..... Is 60:8
of Zion with a c in his anger ..... Lam 2:1
hast covered thyself with a c ..... Lam 3:44
came out of the north, a great c ..... Eze 1:4
is in the c in the day of rain ..... Eze 1:28
a thick c of incense went up ..... Eze 8:11
the c filled the inner court ..... Eze 10:3
the house was filled with the c ..... Eze 10:4
a c shall cover her, and her ..... Eze 30:18
I will cover the sun with a c ..... Eze 32:7
be like a c to cover the land ..... Eze 38:9
Israel, as a c to cover the land ..... Eze 38:16
your goodness is as a morning c ..... Hos 6:4
they shall be as the morning c ..... Hos 13:3
a bright c overshadowed them ..... Mt 17:5
and behold a voice out of the c ..... Mt 17:5
there was a c that overshadowed ..... Mk 9:7
and a voice came out of the c ..... Mk 9:7
he thus spake, there came a c ..... Lk 9:34
feared as they entered into the c ..... Lk 9:34
there came a voice out of the c ..... Lk 9:35
When ye see a c rise out of the ..... Lk 12:54
of man coming in a c with power ..... Lk 21:27
a c received him out of their ..... Acts 1:9
all our fathers were under the c ..... 1Cor 10:1
all baptized unto Moses in the c ..... 1Cor 10:2
with so great a c of witnesses ..... Heb 12:1
from heaven, clothed with a c ..... Rev 10:1
they ascended up to heaven in a c ..... Rev 11:12
And I looked, and behold a white c ..... Rev 14:14
upon the c one sat like unto the ..... Rev 14:14
voice to him that sat on the c ..... Rev 14:15
he that sat on the c thrust in ..... Rev 14:16

### CLOUDS
midst of heaven, with darkness, c ..... Deut 4:11
dropped, the c also dropped water ..... Judg 5:4
waters, and thick c of the skies ..... 2Sa 22:12
riseth, even a morning without c ..... 2Sa 23:4
that the heaven was black with c ..... 1Kin 18:45
and his head reach unto the c ..... Job 20:6
Thick c are a covering to him ..... Job 22:14
up the waters in his thick c ..... Job 26:8
behold the c which are higher ..... Job 35:5
Which the c do drop and distil ..... Job 36:28
the spreadings of the c, or the ..... Job 36:29
With c he covereth the light ..... Job 36:32
thou know the balancings of the c ..... Job 37:16
bright light which is in the c ..... Job 37:21
thou lift up thy voice to the c ..... Job 38:34
Who can number the c in wisdom ..... Job 38:37
waters and thick c of the skies ..... Ps 18:11
was before him his thick c passed ..... Ps 18:12
faithfulness reacheth unto the c ..... Ps 36:5
heavens, and thy truth unto the c ..... Ps 57:10
and his strength is in the c ..... Ps 68:34
The c poured out water ..... Ps 77:17
he had commanded the c from above ..... Ps 78:23
C and darkness are round about him ..... Ps 97:2
who maketh the c his chariot ..... Ps 104:3
and thy truth reacheth unto the c ..... Ps 108:4
Who covereth the heaven with c ..... Ps 147:8
up, and the c drop down the dew ..... Prov 3:20
When he established the c above ..... Prov 8:28
himself of a false gift is like c ..... Prov 25:14
If the c be full of rain, they ..... Eccl 11:3
regardeth the c shall not reap ..... Eccl 11:4
nor the c return after the rain ..... Eccl 12:2
I will also command the c that ..... Is 5:6
ascend above the heights of the c ..... Is 14:14
Behold, he shall come up as c ..... Jer 4:13
of man came with the c of heaven ..... Dan 7:13
and of gloominess, a day of c ..... Joel 2:2
the c are the dust of his feet ..... Nah 1:3
and gloominess, a day of c ..... Zeph 1:15
so the LORD shall make bright c ..... Zec 10:1
in the c of heaven with power ..... Mt 24:30
and coming in the c of heaven ..... Mt 26:64
coming in the c with great power ..... Mk 13:26
and coming in the c of heaven ..... Mk 14:62
up together with them in the c ..... 1Th 4:17
c that are carried with a tempest ..... 2Pet 2:17
c they are without water, carried ..... Jude 12
Behold, he cometh with c ..... Rev 1:7

### CLOUDY
the c pillar descended, and stood ..... Ex 33:9
all the people saw the c pillar ..... Ex 33:10
them in the day by a c pillar ..... Neh 9:12
spake unto them in the c pillar ..... Ps 99:7
day of the LORD is near, a c day ..... Eze 30:3
they have been scattered in the c ..... Eze 34:12

### CLOUTED
c upon their feet, and old ..... Josh 9:5

### CLOUTS
and took thence old cast c ..... Jer 38:11
Put now these old cast c ..... Jer 38:12

### CLOVEN
or of them that divide the c hoof ..... Deut 14:7
them c tongues like as of fire ..... Acts 2:3

### CLOVENFOOTED
parteth the hoof, and is c ..... Lev 11:3
he divide the hoof, and be c ..... Lev 11:7
divideth the hoof, and is not c ..... Lev 11:26

### CLUSTER
a branch with one c of grapes ..... Num 13:23
because of the c of grapes which ..... Num 13:24
My beloved is unto me as a c of ..... Song 1:14
As the new wine is found in the c ..... Is 65:8
there is no c to eat ..... Mic 7:1

### CLUSTERS
the c thereof brought forth ripe ..... Gen 40:10
of gall, their c are bitter ..... Deut 32:32
corn, and an hundred c of raisins ..... 1Sa 25:18
cake of figs, and two c of raisins ..... 1Sa 30:12
and thy breasts to c of grapes ..... Song 7:7
breasts shall be as c of the vine ..... Song 7:8
gather the c of the vine of the ..... Rev 14:18

**CNIDUS** *(ni'-dus) A port town in southwestern Asia Minor.*
scarce were come over against C ..... Acts 27:7

### COAL
shall quench my c which is left ..... 2Sa 14:7
me, having a live c in his hand ..... Is 6:6
there shall not be a c to warm at ..... Is 47:14
Their visage is blacker than a c ..... Lam 4:8

### COALS
c of fire from off the altar ..... Lev 16:12
c were kindled by it ..... 2Sa 22:9
before him were c of fire kindled ..... 2Sa 22:13
there was a cake baken on the c ..... 1Kin 19:6
His breath kindleth c, and a flame ..... Job 41:21
c were kindled by it ..... Ps 18:8
passed, hail stones and c of fire ..... Ps 18:12
hail stones and c of fire ..... Ps 18:13
of the mighty, with c of juniper ..... Ps 120:4
Let burning c fall upon them ..... Ps 140:10
Can one go upon hot c, and his ..... Prov 6:28
For thou shalt heap c of fire ..... Prov 25:22
As c are to burning c, and ..... Prov 26:21
As c are to burning c ..... Prov 26:21
the c thereof are c of fire ..... Song 8:6
the tongs both worketh in the c ..... Is 44:12
baked bread upon the c thereof ..... Is 44:19
that bloweth the c in the fire ..... Is 54:16
was like burning c of fire ..... Eze 1:13
fill thine hand with c of fire ..... Eze 10:2
set it empty upon the c thereof ..... Eze 24:11
burning c went forth at his feet ..... Hab 3:5
there, who had made a fire of c ..... Jn 18:18
land, they saw a fire of c there ..... Jn 21:9
shalt heap c of fire on his head ..... Rom 12:20

### COAST
I bring the locusts into thy c ..... Ex 10:4
by the sea, and by the c of Jordan ..... Num 13:29
by the c of the land of Edom, ..... Num 20:23
Arnon, which is in the utmost c ..... Num 22:36
come come from the c of Chittim ..... Num 24:24
of Zin along by the c of Edom ..... Num 34:3
c of the salt sea eastward ..... Num 34:3
the c shall go down from Shepham ..... Num 34:11
Ye are to pass through the c of ..... Deut 2:4
Ar, the c of Moab, this day ..... Deut 2:18
the c thereof, from Chinnereth ..... Deut 3:17
the uttermost sea shall your c be ..... Deut 11:24
with thee in all thy c seven days ..... Deut 16:4
if the LORD thy God enlarge thy c ..... Deut 19:8
down of the sun, shall be your c ..... Josh 1:4
the c of Og king of Bashan, which ..... Josh 12:4
The king of Dor in the c of Dor ..... Josh 12:23
their c was from Aroer, that is ..... Josh 13:16
their c was Jazer, and all the ..... Josh 13:25
their c was from Mahanaim, all ..... Josh 13:30
the uttermost part of the south c ..... Josh 15:1
out of that c were at the sea ..... Josh 15:4
this shall be your south c ..... Josh 15:4
the great sea, and the c thereof ..... Josh 15:12
This is the c of the children of ..... Josh 15:12
children of Judah toward the c of ..... Josh 15:21
westward to the c of Japhleti ..... Josh 16:3
unto the c of Beth-horon the ..... Josh 16:3
the c of Manasseh was from Asher ..... Josh 17:7
the c descended unto the river ..... Josh 17:9
the c of Manasseh also was on the ..... Josh 17:9
abide in their c on the south ..... Josh 18:5
the c of their lot came forth ..... Josh 18:11
this was the south c ..... Josh 18:19
the c reacheth to Tabor, and ..... Josh 19:22
then the c turneth to Ramah, and ..... Josh 19:29
and the c turneth to Hosah ..... Josh 19:29
at the sea from the c to Achzib ..... Josh 19:29
their c was from Heleph, from ..... Josh 19:33
then the c turneth westward to ..... Josh 19:34
the c of their inheritance was ..... Josh 19:41
the c of the children of Dan went ..... Josh 19:47
took Gaza with the c thereof ..... Judg 1:18
and Askelon with the c thereof ..... Judg 1:18
and Ekron with the c thereof ..... Judg 1:18
the c of the Amorites was from ..... Judg 1:36
not Israel to pass through his c ..... Judg 11:20
way of his own c to Beth-shemesh ..... 1Sa 6:9
came no more into the c of Israel ..... 1Sa 7:13
me any more in any c of Israel ..... 1Sa 27:1
upon the c which belongeth to ..... 1Sa 30:14
He restored the c of Israel from ..... 2Kin 14:25
bless me indeed, and enlarge my c ..... 1Chr 4:10
destroy the remnant of the sea c ..... Eze 25:16
which is by the c of Hauran ..... Eze 47:16
to the c of the way of Hethlon ..... Eze 48:1
northward, to the c of Hamath ..... Eze 48:1
unto the inhabitants of the sea c ..... Zeph 2:5
the sea c shall be dwellings and ..... Zeph 2:6
the c shall be for the remnant of ..... Zeph 2:7
which is upon the sea c, in the ..... Mt 4:13
and from the sea c of Tyre ..... Lk 6:17

### COASTS
and rested in all the c of Egypt ..... Ex 10:14
one locust in all the c of Egypt ..... Ex 10:19
out of the c of the Amorites ..... Num 21:13
with the cities thereof in the c ..... Num 32:33
land of Canaan with the c thereof ..... Num 34:2
with the c thereof round about ..... Num 34:12
of Argob unto the c of Geshuri ..... Deut 3:14
divide the c of thy land, which ..... Deut 19:3
olive trees throughout all thy c ..... Deut 28:40
in all the c of the great sea ..... Josh 9:1
abide in their c on the north ..... Josh 18:5
by the c thereof round about, ..... Josh 18:20
land for inheritance by their c ..... Josh 19:49
all the c of the Amorites ..... Judg 11:22
that be along by the c of Arnon ..... Judg 11:26
family five men from their c ..... Judg 18:2
sent her into all the c of Israel ..... Judg 19:29
even Ashdod and the c thereof ..... 1Sa 5:6
the c thereof did Israel deliver ..... 1Sa 7:14
unto all the c of Israel ..... 1Sa 11:3
the c of Israel by the hands of ..... 1Sa 11:7
in any of the c of Israel ..... 2Sa 21:5
throughout all the c of Israel ..... 1Kin 1:3
smote them in all the c of Israel ..... 2Kin 10:32
the c thereof from Tirzah ..... 2Kin 15:16
their castles in their c, of the ..... 1Chr 6:54
c out of the tribe of Ephraim ..... 1Chr 6:66
throughout all the c of Israel ..... 1Chr 21:12
to him out of all their c ..... 2Chr 11:13
of flies, and lice in all their c ..... Ps 105:31
and brake the trees of their c ..... Ps 105:33
raised up from the c of the earth ..... Jer 25:32
them from the c of the earth ..... Jer 31:8
raised up from the c of the earth ..... Jer 50:41
of the land take a man of their c ..... Eze 33:2
Zidon, and all the c of Palestine ..... Joel 3:4
and in all the c thereof, from ..... Mt 2:16
he would depart out of their c ..... Mt 8:34
and departed into the c of Tyre ..... Mt 15:21
of Canaan came out of the same c ..... Mt 15:22
and came into the c of Magdala ..... Mt 15:39
into the c of Caesarea Philippi ..... Mt 16:13
came into the c of Judaea beyond ..... Mt 19:1
pray him to depart out of their c ..... Mk 5:17
departing from the c of Tyre ..... Mk 7:31
the midst of the c of Decapolis ..... Mk 7:31
cometh into the c of Judaea by ..... Mk 10:1
and expelled them out of their c ..... Acts 13:50
the upper c came to Ephesus ..... Acts 19:1
and throughout all the c of Judaea ..... Acts 26:20
meaning to sail by the c of Asia ..... Acts 27:2

### COAT
he made him a c of many colours ..... Gen 37:3
they stript Joseph out of his c ..... Gen 37:23
his c of many colours that was on ..... Gen 37:23
And they took Joseph's c, and ..... Gen 37:31
dipped the c in the blood ..... Gen 37:31
they sent the c of many colours, ..... Gen 37:32
whether it be thy son's c or no ..... Gen 37:32
it, and said, It is my son's c ..... Gen 37:33
and a robe, and a broidered c ..... Ex 28:4
embroider the c of fine linen ..... Ex 28:39
garments, and put upon Aaron the c ..... Ex 29:5
And he put upon him the c, and ..... Lev 8:7
He shall put on the holy linen c ..... Lev 16:4
his mother made him a little c ..... 1Sa 2:19
and he was armed with a c of mail ..... 1Sa 17:5
the weight of the c was five ..... 1Sa 17:5
he armed him with a c of mail ..... 1Sa 17:38
came to meet him with his c rent ..... 2Sa 15:32
me about as the collar of my c ..... Job 30:18
I have put off my c ..... Song 5:3

at the law, and take away thy c ... Mt 5:40
forbid not to take thy c also ... Lk 6:29
and also his c ... Jn 19:23
now the c was without seam, woven ... Jn 19:23
he girt his fisher's c unto him ... Jn 21:7

**COATS**
did the LORD God make c of skins ... Gen 3:21
Aaron's sons thou shalt make c ... Ex 28:40
his sons, and put c upon them ... Ex 29:8
they made c of fine linen of ... Ex 39:27
his sons, and clothe them with c ... Ex 40:14
put c upon them, and girded them ... Lev 8:13
them in their c out of the camp ... Lev 10:5
these men were bound in their c ... Dan 3:21
neither were their c changed ... Dan 3:27
for your journey, neither two c ... Mt 10:10
and not put on two c ... Mk 6:9
unto them, He that hath two c ... Lk 3:11
neither have two c apiece ... Lk 9:3
by him weeping, and shewing the c ... Acts 9:39

**COCK**
this night, before the c crow ... Mt 26:34
And immediately the c crew ... Mt 26:74
said unto him, Before the c crow ... Mt 26:75
night, before the c crow twice ... Mk 14:30
and the c crew ... Mk 14:68
And the second time the c crew ... Mk 14:72
unto him, Before the c crow twice ... Mk 14:72
the c shall not crow this day ... Lk 22:34
while he yet spake, the c crew ... Lk 22:60
said unto him, Before the c crow ... Lk 22:61
The c shall not crow, till thou ... Jn 13:38
and immediately the c crew ... Jn 18:27

**COCKATRICE**
root shall come forth a c ... Is 14:29

**COCKATRICE'**
shall put his hand on the c den ... Is 11:8
They hatch c eggs, and weave the ... Is 59:5

**COCKATRICES**
behold, I will send serpents, c ... Jer 8:17

**COCKCROWING**
even, or at midnight, or at the c ... Mk 13:35

**COCKLE**
of wheat, and c instead of barley ... Job 31:40

**COFFER**
in a c by the side thereof ... 1Sa 6:8
the c with the mice of gold and ... 1Sa 6:11
the c that was with it, wherein ... 1Sa 6:15

**COFFIN**
and he was put in a c in Egypt ... Gen 50:26

**COGITATIONS**
my c much troubled me, and my ... Dan 7:28

**COLD**
seedtime and harvest, and c ... Gen 8:22
they have no covering in the c ... Job 24:7
and c out of the north ... Job 37:9
who can stand before his c ... Ps 147:17
will not plow by reason of the c ... Prov 20:4
As the c of snow in the time of ... Prov 25:13
away a garment in c weather ... Prov 25:20
As c waters to a thirsty soul, so ... Prov 25:25
or shall the c flowing waters ... Jer 18:14
camp in the hedges in the c day ... Nah 3:17
of c water only in the name of a ... Mt 10:42
the love of many shall wax c ... Mt 24:12
for it was c ... Jn 18:18
present rain, and because of the c ... Acts 28:2
thirst, in fastings often, in c ... 2Cor 11:27
that thou art neither c nor hot ... Rev 3:15
I would thou wert c or hot ... Rev 3:15
lukewarm, and neither c nor hot ... Rev 3:16

**COLHOZEH**
repaired Shallun the son of C ... Neh 3:15
the son of Baruch, the son of C ... Neh 11:5

**COLLAR**
me about as the c of my coat ... Job 30:18

**COLLARS**
beside ornaments, and c, and purple ... Judg 8:26

**COLLECTION**
Judah and out of Jerusalem the c ... 2Chr 24:6
to bring in to the LORD the c ... 2Chr 24:9
concerning the c for the saints ... 1Cor 16:1

**COLLEGE**
she dwelt in Jerusalem in the c ... 2Kin 22:14
she dwelt in Jerusalem in the c ... 2Chr 34:22

**COLLOPS**
maketh c of fat on his flanks ... Job 15:27

**COLONY**
of that part of Macedonia, and a c ... Acts 16:12

**COLORS**
I will lay thy stones with fair c ... Is 54:11

**COLOSSE** (*co-los'-see*) See COLOSSIANS. *A city in Phrygia.*
brethren in Christ which are at C ... Col 1:2

**COLOSSIANS** (*co-los'-yans*) *Residents of Colosse.*
from Rome to the C by Tychicus ... Col *s*

**COLOUR**
the plague have not changed his c ... Lev 13:55
the c thereof as the c of ... Num 11:7
when it giveth his c in the cup ... Prov 23:31
midst thereof as the c of amber ... Eze 1:4
like the c of burnished brass ... Eze 1:7
was like unto the c of a beryl ... Eze 1:16
as the c of the terrible crystal ... Eze 1:22
And I saw as the c of amber ... Eze 1:27
of brightness, as the c of amber ... Eze 8:2
was as the c of a beryl stone ... Eze 10:9
his feet like in c to polished ... Dan 10:6
under c as though they would have ... Acts 27:30
arrayed in purple and scarlet c ... Rev 17:4

**COLOURED**
woman sit upon a scarlet c beast ... Rev 17:3

**COLOURS**
and he made him a coat of many c ... Gen 37:3
coat of many c that was on him ... Gen 37:23
And they sent the coat of many c ... Gen 37:32
to Sisera a prey of divers c ... Judg 5:30
a prey of divers c of needlework ... Judg 5:30
of divers c of needlework on both ... Judg 5:30
a garment of divers c upon her ... 2Sa 13:18
of divers c that was on her ... 2Sa 13:19
glistering stones, and of divers c ... 1Chr 29:2
thy high places with divers c ... Eze 16:16
of feathers, which had divers c ... Eze 17:3

**COLT**
his ass's c unto the choice vine ... Gen 49:11
man be born like a wild ass's c ... Job 11:12
upon a c the foal of an ass ... Zec 9:9
find an ass tied, and a c with her ... Mt 21:2
an ass, and a c the foal of an ass ... Mt 21:5
And brought the ass, and the c ... Mt 21:7
into it, ye shall find a c tied ... Mk 11:2
found the c tied by the door ... Mk 11:4
them, What do ye, loosing the c ... Mk 11:5
And they brought the c to Jesus ... Mk 11:7
entering ye shall find a c tied ... Lk 19:30
And as they were loosing the c ... Lk 19:33
unto them, Why loose ye the c ... Lk 19:33
cast their garments upon the c ... Lk 19:35
cometh, sitting on an ass's c ... Jn 12:15

**COLTS**
Thirty milch camels with their c ... Gen 32:15
sons that rode on thirty ass c ... Judg 10:4
rode on threescore and ten ass c ... Judg 12:14

**COME** See PREFACE.

**COMELINESS**
he hath no form nor c ... Is 53:2
for it was perfect through my c ... Eze 16:14
they set forth thy c ... Eze 27:10
for my c was turned in me into ... Dan 10:8
parts have more abundant c ... 1Cor 12:23

**COMELY**
a c person, and the LORD is with ... 1Sa 16:18
his power, nor his c proportion ... Job 41:12
for praise is c for the upright ... Ps 33:1
and praise is c ... Ps 147:1
go well, yea, four are c in going ... Prov 30:29
c for one to eat and to drink, and ... Eccl 5:18
I am black, but c, O ye daughters ... Song 1:5
Thy cheeks are c with rows of ... Song 1:10
voice, and thy countenance is c ... Song 2:14
of scarlet, and thy speech is c ... Song 4:3
c as Jerusalem, terrible as an ... Song 6:4
c for them that are escaped of ... Is 4:2
the daughter of Zion to a c ... Jer 6:2
upon you, but for that which is c ... 1Cor 7:35
is it c that a woman pray unto ... 1Cor 11:13
For our c parts have no need ... 1Cor 12:24

**COMERS**
make the c thereunto perfect ... Heb 10:1

**COMEST**
as thou c to Gerar, unto Gaza ... Gen 10:19
of Egypt, as thou c unto Zoar ... Gen 13:10
when thou c to my kindred ... Gen 24:41
when thou c nigh over against the ... Deut 2:19
When thou c nigh unto a city to ... Deut 20:10
When thou c into thy neighbour's ... Deut 23:24
When thou c into the standing ... Deut 23:25
shalt thou be when thou c in ... Deut 28:6
shalt thou be when thou c in ... Deut 28:19
said unto him, Whence c thou ... Judg 17:9
that thou c with such a company ... Judg 18:23
and whence c thou ... Judg 19:17
from Havilah until thou c to Shur ... 1Sa 15:7
coming, and said, C thou peaceably ... 1Sa 16:4
that thou c to me with staves ... 1Sa 17:43
Thou c to me with a sword, and ... 1Sa 17:45
said unto him, From whence c thou ... 2Sa 1:3
when thou c to see my face ... 2Sa 3:13
And she said, C thou peaceably ... 1Kin 2:13
and when thou c, anoint Hazael to ... 1Kin 19:15
said unto him, Whence c thou ... 2Kin 5:25
And when thou c thither, look out ... 2Kin 9:2
said unto Satan, Whence c thou ... Job 1:7
unto Satan, From whence c thou ... Job 2:2
When thou c to Babylon, and shalt ... Jer 51:61
and whence c thou ... Jonah 1:8
baptized of thee, and c thou to me ... Mt 3:14
me when thou c into thy kingdom ... Lk 23:42
at Troas with Carpus, when thou c ... 2Ti 4:13

**COMETH**
the virgin c forth to draw water ... Gen 24:43
his daughter c with the sheep ... Gen 29:6
And Leah said, A troop c ... Gen 30:11
also he c to meet thee, and four ... Gen 32:6
another, Behold, this dreamer c ... Gen 37:19
thy son Joseph c unto thee ... Gen 48:2
behold, he c forth to meet thee ... Ex 4:14
lo, he c forth to the water ... Ex 8:20
every firstling that c of a beast ... Ex 13:12
before the LORD, and when he c out ... Ex 28:35
when he c into the tabernacle of ... Ex 29:30
such water c shall be unclean ... Lev 11:34
the stranger that c nigh shall be ... Num 1:51
the stranger that c nigh shall be ... Num 3:10
the stranger that c nigh shall be ... Num 3:38
the spirit of jealousy c upon him ... Num 5:30
he c out of his mother's womb ... Num 12:12
Whosoever c any thing near unto ... Num 17:13
the stranger that c nigh shall be ... Num 18:7
that c out of the coasts of the ... Num 21:13
of whom c the family of the ... Num 26:5
beside that which c of the sale ... Deut 18:8
it shall be, when evening c on ... Deut 23:11
and cover that which c from thee ... Deut 23:13
that c out from between her feet ... Deut 28:57
that whatsoever c forth of the ... Judg 11:31
of any thing that c of the vine ... Judg 13:14
when it c among us, it may save ... 1Sa 4:3
that he saith c surely to pass ... 1Sa 9:6
Whosoever c not forth after Saul ... 1Sa 11:7
Wherefore c not the son of Jesse ... 1Sa 20:27
Therefore he c not unto the ... 1Sa 20:29
whatsoever c to thine hand unto ... 1Sa 25:8
And she said, An old man c up ... 1Sa 28:14
and when thy father c to see thee ... 2Sa 13:5
good man, and c with good tidings ... 2Sa 18:27
but c out of a far country for ... 1Kin 8:41
the wife of Jeroboam c to ask a ... 1Kin 14:5
for it shall be, when she c in ... 1Kin 14:5
and it shall be, when he c to us ... 2Kin 4:10
look, when the messenger c ... 2Kin 6:32
came to them, but he c not again ... 2Kin 9:18
even unto them, and c not again ... 2Kin 9:20
as soon as this letter c to you ... 2Kin 10:2
he that c within the ranges, let ... 2Kin 11:8
as he goeth out and as he c in ... 2Kin 11:8
all the money that c into any ... 2Kin 12:4
on the right side as one c into ... 2Kin 12:9
because he c to judge the earth ... 1Chr 16:33
thine holy name c of thine hand ... 1Chr 29:16
so that whosoever c to consecrate ... 2Chr 13:9
There c a great multitude against ... 2Chr 20:2
If, when evil c upon us, as the ... 2Chr 20:9
great company that c against us ... 2Chr 20:12
whosoever else c into the house ... 2Chr 23:7
be ye with the king when he c in ... 2Chr 23:7
long for death, but it c not ... Job 3:21
For my sighing c before I eat ... Job 3:24
Although affliction c not forth ... Job 5:6
afraid of destruction when it c ... Job 5:21
shock of corn c in in his season ... Job 5:26
He c forth like a flower, and is ... Job 14:2
the mountain falling c to nought ... Job 14:18
It is drawn, and c out of the body ... Job 20:25
sword c out of his gall ... Job 20:25
how oft c their destruction upon ... Job 21:17
his cry when trouble c upon him ... Job 27:9
for the earth, out of it c bread ... Job 28:5
Whence then c wisdom ... Job 28:20
shine by the cloud that c betwixt ... Job 36:32
Out of the south c the whirlwind ... Job 37:9
Fair weather c out of the north ... Job 37:22
a night, but joy c in the morning ... Ps 30:5
from him c my salvation ... Ps 62:1
For promotion c neither from the ... Ps 75:6
that passeth away, and c not again ... Ps 78:39
for he c, for he c to judge ... Ps 96:13
for he c to judge the earth ... Ps 98:9
Blessed be he that c in the name ... Ps 118:26
the hills, from whence c my help ... Ps 121:1
My help c from the LORD, which ... Ps 121:2
I will mock when your fear c ... Prov 1:26
When your fear c as desolation ... Prov 1:27
your destruction c as a whirlwind ... Prov 1:27
distress and anguish c upon you ... Prov 1:27
out of his mouth c knowledge ... Prov 2:6
of the wicked, when it c ... Prov 3:25
When pride c, then c shame ... Prov 11:2
the wicked c in his stead ... Prov 11:8
man is loathsome, and c to shame ... Prov 13:5
Only by pride c contention ... Prov 13:10
heart sick, but when the desire c ... Prov 13:12
When the wicked c, then c ... Prov 18:3
but his neighbour c and searcheth ... Prov 18:17
man's judgment c from the LORD ... Prov 29:26
away, and another generation c ... Eccl 1:4
the man do that c after the king ... Eccl 2:12
For out of prison he c to reign ... Eccl 4:14
For a dream c through the ... Eccl 5:3
For he c in with vanity, and ... Eccl 6:4
All that c is vanity ... Eccl 11:8
he c leaping upon the mountains ... Song 2:8
Who is this that c out of the ... Song 3:6
Who is this that c up from the ... Song 8:5
Behold, the day of the LORD c ... Is 13:9
so it c from the desert, from a ... Is 21:1
here c a chariot of men, with a ... Is 21:9
The watchman said, The morning c ... Is 21:12
he that c up out of the midst of ... Is 24:18

the LORD c out of his place to ... Is 26:21
This also c forth from the LORD ... Is 28:29
whose breaking c suddenly at an ... Is 30:13
the name of the LORD c from far ... Is 30:27
earth, and that which c out of it ... Is 42:5
For as the rain c down, and the ... Is 55:10
of Zion, Behold, thy salvation c ... Is 62:11
Who is this that c from Edom ... Is 63:1
To what purpose c there to me ... Jer 6:20
a people c from the north country ... Jer 6:22
and shall not see when good c ... Jer 17:6
and shall not see when heat c ... Jer 17:8
c from the rock of the field ... Jer 18:14
And when he c, he shall smite the ... Jer 43:11
Who is this that c up as a flood ... Jer 46:7
fair heifer, but destruction c ... Jer 46:20
it c out of the north ... Jer 46:20
Because of the day that c to ... Jer 47:4
there c up a nation against her ... Jer 50:3
A sound of a cry c from Babylon ... Jer 51:54
it c to pass, when the Lord ... Lam 3:37
it with dung that c out of man ... Eze 4:12
Destruction c; and they shall seek ... Eze 7:25
his face, and c to the prophet ... Eze 14:4
c according to the multitude of ... Eze 14:4
c to a prophet to enquire of him ... Eze 14:7
that which c into your mind shall ... Eze 20:32
because it c: and every heart ... Eze 21:7
behold, it c, and shall be brought ... Eze 21:7
and when this c, ye shall know ... Eze 24:24
for, lo, it c ... Eze 30:9
word that c forth from the LORD ... Eze 33:30
come unto thee as the people c ... Eze 33:31
And when this c to pass, (lo, it ... Eze 33:33
shall live whither the river c ... Eze 47:9
But he that c against him shall ... Dan 11:16
c to the thousand three hundred ... Dan 12:12
and the thief c in, and the troop ... Hos 7:1
for the day of the LORD c ... Joel 2:1
the LORD c forth out of his place ... Mic 1:3
when he c into our land, and when ... Mic 5:6
thy watchmen and thy visitation c ... Mic 7:4
when he c up unto the people, he ... Hab 3:16
behold, thy King c unto thee ... Zec 9:9
Behold, the day of the LORD c ... Zec 14:1
For, behold, the day c, that ... Mal 4:1
the day that c shall burn them up ... Mal 4:1
but he that c after me is ... Mt 3:11
Then c Jesus from Galilee to ... Mt 3:13
is more than these c of evil ... Mt 5:37
and to another, Come, and he c ... Mt 8:9
then c the wicked one, and ... Mt 13:19
but that which c out of the mouth ... Mt 15:11
take up the fish that first c up ... Mt 17:27
to that man by whom the offence c ... Mt 18:7
thy King c unto thee, meek, and ... Mt 21:5
Blessed is he that c in the name ... Mt 21:9
lord therefore of the vineyard c ... Mt 21:40
Blessed is he that c in the name ... Mt 23:39
the lightning c out of the east ... Mt 24:27
as ye think not the Son of man c ... Mt 24:44
when he c shall find so doing ... Mt 24:46
made, Behold, the bridegroom c ... Mt 25:6
the hour wherein the Son of man c ... Mt 25:13
time the lord of those servants c ... Mt 25:19
Then c Jesus with them unto a ... Mt 26:36
he c unto the disciples, and ... Mt 26:40
Then c he to his disciples, and ... Mt 26:45
There c one mightier than I after ... Mk 1:7
the multitude c together again, ... Mk 3:20
Satan c immediately, and taketh ... Mk 4:15
there c one of the rulers of the ... Mk 5:22
he c to the house of the ruler of ... Mk 5:38
watch of the night he c unto them ... Mk 6:48
That which c out of the man, that ... Mk 7:20
And he c to Bethsaida ... Mk 8:22
when he c in the glory of his ... Mk 8:38
told them, Elias verily c first ... Mk 9:12
c into the coasts of Judaea by ... Mk 10:1
Blessed is he that c in the name ... Mk 11:9
that c in the name of the Lord ... Mk 11:10
when the master of the house c ... Mk 13:35
the evening he c with the twelve ... Mk 14:17
And he c, and findeth them sleeping ... Mk 14:37
he c the third time, and saith ... Mk 14:41
c Judas, one of the twelve, and ... Mk 14:43
there c one of the maids of the ... Mk 14:66
but one mightier than I c ... Lk 3:16
Whosoever c to me, and heareth my ... Lk 6:47
and to another, Come, and he c ... Lk 7:8
then c the devil, and taketh away ... Lk 8:12
there c one from the ruler of the ... Lk 8:49
And when he c, he findeth it swept ... Lk 11:25
that when he c and knocketh, they ... Lk 12:36
when he c shall find watching ... Lk 12:37
for the Son of man c at an hour ... Lk 12:40
when he c shall find so doing ... Lk 12:43
ye say, There c a shower ... Lk 12:54
and it c to pass ... Lk 12:55
Blessed is he that c in the name ... Lk 13:35
that when he that bade thee c ... Lk 14:10
that c against him with twenty ... Lk 14:31
And when he c home, he calleth ... Lk 15:6
The kingdom of God c not with ... Lk 17:20
when the Son of man c, shall he ... Lk 18:8
that c in the name of the Lord ... Lk 19:38
every man that c into the world ... Jn 1:9
He that c after me is preferred ... Jn 1:15
After me c a man which is ... Jn 1:30
but canst not tell whence it c ... Jn 3:8
neither c to the light, lest his ... Jn 3:20
that doeth truth c to the light ... Jn 3:21
He that c from above is above all ... Jn 3:31
he that c from heaven is above ... Jn 3:31
Then c he to a city of Samaria, ... Jn 4:5
There c a woman of Samaria to ... Jn 4:7
Woman, believe me, the hour c ... Jn 4:21
But the hour c, and now is, when ... Jn 4:23
unto him, I know that Messias c ... Jn 4:25
four months, and then c harvest ... Jn 4:35
the honour that c from God only ... Jn 5:44
is he which c down from heaven ... Jn 6:33
he that c to me shall never ... Jn 6:35
him that c to me I will in no ... Jn 6:37
learned of the Father, c unto me ... Jn 6:45
bread which c down from heaven ... Jn 6:50
but when Christ c, no man knoweth ... Jn 7:27
on him, and said, When Christ c ... Jn 7:31
That Christ c of the seed of ... Jn 7:42
the night c, when no man can work ... Jn 9:4
The thief c not, but for to steal ... Jn 10:10
in himself c to the grave ... Jn 11:38
that c in the name of the Lord ... Jn 12:13
behold, thy King c, sitting on an ... Jn 12:15
Philip c and telleth Andrew ... Jn 12:22
Then c he to Simon Peter ... Jn 13:6
no man c unto the Father, but by ... Jn 14:6
for the prince of this world c ... Jn 14:30
But this c to pass, that the word ... Jn 15:25
yea, the time c, that whosoever ... Jn 16:2
but the time c, when I shall no ... Jn 16:25
Behold, the hour c, yea, is now ... Jn 16:32
c thither with lanterns and ... Jn 18:3
the week c Mary Magdalene early ... Jn 20:1
c to Simon Peter, and to the other ... Jn 20:2
Then c Simon Peter following him, ... Jn 20:6
Jesus then c, and taketh bread, and ... Jn 21:13
who, when he c, shall speak unto ... Acts 10:32
there c one after me, whose shoes ... Acts 13:25
this feast that c in Jerusalem ... Acts 18:21
C this blessedness then upon the ... Rom 4:9
So then faith c by hearing ... Rom 10:17
Then c the end, when he shall ... 1Cor 15:24
For if he that c preacheth ... 2Cor 11:4
that which c upon me daily, the ... 2Cor 11:28
This persuasion c not of him that ... Gal 5:8
c the wrath of God upon the ... Eph 5:6
things' sake the wrath of God c ... Col 3:6
Lord so c as a thief in the night ... 1Th 5:2
sudden destruction c upon them ... 1Th 5:3
strifes of words, whereof c envy ... 1Ti 6:4
in the rain that c oft upon it ... Heb 6:7
when he c into the world, he ... Heb 10:5
for he that c to God must believe ... Heb 11:6
c down from the Father of lights, ... Jas 1:17
the Lord c with ten thousands of ... Jude 14
Behold, he c with clouds ... Rev 1:7
which c down out of heaven from ... Rev 3:12
behold, the third woe c quickly ... Rev 11:14
and when he c, he must continue a ... Rev 17:10

### COMFIRMATION
c of the gospel, ye all are ... Phil 1:7

### COMFORT
This same shall c us concerning ... Gen 5:29
of bread, and c ye your hearts ... Gen 18:5
doth c himself, purposing to kill ... Gen 27:42
his daughters rose up to c him ... Gen 37:35
C thine heart with a morsel of ... Judg 19:5
C thine heart, I pray thee ... Judg 19:8
David sent to c him by the hand ... 2Sa 10:2
and his brethren came to c him ... 1Chr 7:22
David sent messengers to c him ... 1Chr 19:2
of Ammon to Hanun, to c him ... 1Chr 19:2
to mourn with him and to c him ... Job 2:11
Then should I yet have c ... Job 6:10
When I say, My bed shall c me ... Job 7:13
off my heaviness, and c myself ... Job 9:27
alone, that I may take c a little ... Job 10:20
How then c ye me in vain, seeing ... Job 21:34
thy rod and thy staff they c me ... Ps 23:4
greatness, and c me on every side ... Ps 71:21
This is my c in my affliction ... Ps 119:50
thy merciful kindness be for my c ... Ps 119:76
word, saying, When wilt thou c me ... Ps 119:82
me with flagons, c me with apples ... Song 2:5
weep bitterly, labour not to c me ... Is 22:4
C ye, c ye my people, saith ... Is 40:1
For the LORD shall c Zion ... Is 51:3
he will c all her waste places ... Is 51:3
by whom shall I c thee ... Is 51:19
Should I receive c in these ... Is 57:6
to c all that mourn ... Is 61:2
comforteth, so will I c you ... Is 66:13
When I would c myself against ... Jer 8:18
mourning, to c them for the dead ... Jer 16:7
mourning into joy, and will c them ... Jer 31:13
her lovers she hath none to c her ... Lam 1:2
hands, and there is none to c her ... Lam 1:17
there is none to c me ... Lam 1:21
equal to thee, that I may c thee ... Lam 2:13
And they shall c you, when ye see ... Eze 14:23
in that thou art a c unto them ... Eze 16:54
and the LORD shall yet c Zion ... Zec 1:17
they c in vain ... Zec 10:2
he said, Daughter, be of good c ... Mt 9:22
saying unto him, Be of good c ... Mk 10:49
unto her, Daughter, be of good c ... Lk 8:48
to c them concerning their ... Jn 11:19
in the c of the Holy Ghost, were ... Acts 9:31
c of the scriptures might have ... Rom 15:4
edification, and exhortation, and c ... 1Cor 14:3
of mercies, and the God of all c ... 2Cor 1:3
that we may be able to c them ... 2Cor 1:4
by the c wherewith we ourselves ... 2Cor 1:4
c him, lest perhaps such a one ... 2Cor 2:7
I am filled with c, I am ... 2Cor 7:4
we were comforted in your c ... 2Cor 7:13
Be perfect, be of good c, be of ... 2Cor 13:11
and that he might c your hearts ... Eph 6:22
Christ, if any c of love, if any ... Phil 2:1
you, that I also may be of good c ... Phil 2:19
your estate, and c your hearts ... Col 4:8
God, which have been a c unto me ... Col 4:11
to c you concerning your faith ... 1Th 3:2
Wherefore c one another with ... 1Th 4:18
Wherefore c yourselves together, ... 1Th 5:11
c the feebleminded, support the ... 1Th 5:14
C your hearts, and stablish you in ... 2Th 2:17

### COMFORTABLE
my lord the king shall now be c ... 2Sa 14:17
me with good words and c words ... Zec 1:13

### COMFORTABLY
speak c unto thy servants ... 2Sa 19:7
Hezekiah spake c unto all the ... 2Chr 30:22
city, and spake c to them, saying, ... 2Chr 32:6
Speak ye c to Jerusalem, and cry ... Is 40:2
wilderness, and speak c unto her ... Hos 2:14

### COMFORTED
Isaac was c after his mother's ... Gen 24:67
but he refused to be c ... Gen 37:35
and Judah was c, and went up unto ... Gen 38:12
he c them, and spake kindly unto ... Gen 50:21
for that thou hast c me, and for ... Ruth 2:13
David c Bath-sheba his wife, and ... 2Sa 12:24
for he was c concerning Amnon, ... 2Sa 13:39
c him over all the evil that the ... Job 42:11
my soul refused to be c ... Ps 77:2
LORD, hast holpen me, and c me ... Ps 86:17
and have c myself ... Ps 119:52
for the LORD hath c his people ... Is 49:13
for the LORD hath c his people ... Is 52:9
tossed with tempest, and not c ... Is 54:11
ye shall be c in Jerusalem ... Is 66:13
refused to be c for her children ... Jer 31:15
to rest upon them, and I will be c ... Eze 5:13
ye shall be c concerning the evil ... Eze 14:22
shall be c in the nether parts of ... Eze 31:16
shall be c over all his multitude ... Eze 32:31
her children, and would not be c ... Mt 2:18
for they shall be c ... Mt 5:4
but now he is c, and thou art ... Lk 16:25
c her, when they saw Mary, that ... Jn 11:31
seen the brethren, they c them ... Acts 16:40
man alive, and were not a little c ... Acts 20:12
that I may be c together with you ... Rom 1:12
all may learn, and all may be c ... 1Cor 14:31
we ourselves are c of God ... 2Cor 1:4
or whether we be c, it is for ... 2Cor 1:6
c us by the coming of Titus ... 2Cor 7:6
wherewith he was c in you ... 2Cor 7:7
we were c in your comfort ... 2Cor 7:13
That their hearts might be c ... Col 2:2
As ye know how we exhorted and c ... 1Th 2:11
we were c over you in all our ... 1Th 3:7

### COMFORTEDST
is turned away, and thou c me ... Is 12:1

### COMFORTER
were oppressed, and they had no c ... Eccl 4:1
but they had no c ... Eccl 4:1
she had no c ... Lam 1:9
because the c that should relieve ... Lam 1:16
and he shall give you another C ... Jn 14:16
But the C, which is the Holy ... Jn 14:26
But when the C is come, whom I ... Jn 15:26
the C will not come unto you ... Jn 16:7

### COMFORTERS
that he hath sent c unto thee ... 2Sa 10:3
that he hath sent c unto thee ... 1Chr 19:3
miserable c are ye all ... Job 16:2
and for c, but I found none ... Ps 69:20
whence shall I seek c for thee ... Nah 3:7

### COMFORTETH
as one that c the mourners ... Job 29:25
I, even I, am he that c you ... Is 51:12
As one whom his mother c, so will ... Is 66:13
Who c us in all our tribulation, ... 2Cor 1:4
that c those that are cast down, ... 2Cor 7:6

### COMFORTLESS
I will not leave you c ... Jn 14:18

### COMFORTS
within me thy c delight my soul ... Ps 94:19
restore c unto him and to his ... Is 57:18

### COMING
and, behold, the camels were c ... Gen 24:63
LORD hath blessed thee since my c ... Gen 30:30
thee, hinder thee from c unto me ... Num 22:16
heard of the c of the children of ... Num 33:40
Why is his chariot so long in c ... Judg 5:28
meet a company of prophets c down ... 1Sa 10:5
of the town trembled at his c ... 1Sa 16:4
I saw the son of Jesse c to Nob ... 1Sa 22:9
thee from c to shed blood ... 1Sa 25:26
me this day from c to shed blood ... 1Sa 25:33
thy c in with me in the host is ... 1Sa 29:6

of thy c unto me unto this day ... 1Sa 29:6
to know thy going out and thy c in ... 2Sa 3:25
his servants c on toward him ... 2Sa 24:20
the son of Rechab c to meet him ... 2Kin 10:15
the land at the c in of the year ... 2Kin 13:20
and thy going out, and thy c in ... 2Kin 19:27
Ahaziah was of God by c to Joram ... 2Chr 22:7
their c unto the house of God at ... Ezr 3:8
a bridegroom c out of his chamber ... Ps 19:5
for he seeth that his day is c ... Ps 37:13
thy c in from this time forth, and ... Ps 121:8
city, at the c in at the doors ... Prov 8:3
for thee to meet thee at thy c ... Is 14:9
shall hail, c down on the forest ... Is 32:19
and thy going out, and thy c in ... Is 37:28
and the things that are c, and ... Is 44:7
observe the time of their c ... Jer 8:7
an holy one c down from heaven, ... Dan 4:23
According to the days of thy c ... Mic 7:15
he had horns c out of his hand ... Hab 3:4
who may abide the day of his c ... Mal 3:2
prophet before the c of the great ... Mal 4:5
c out of the tombs, exceeding ... Mt 8:28
the Son of man c in his kingdom ... Mt 16:28
what shall be the sign of thy c ... Mt 24:3
so shall also the c of the Son of ... Mt 24:27
c in the clouds of heaven with ... Mt 24:30
so shall also the c of the Son of ... Mt 24:37
so shall also the c of the Son of ... Mt 24:39
his heart, My lord delayeth his c ... Mt 24:48
then at my c I should have ... Mt 25:27
c in the clouds of heaven ... Mt 26:64
straightway c up out of the water ... Mk 1:10
for there were many c and going, ... Mk 6:31
shall they see the Son of man c ... Mk 13:26
Lest c suddenly he find you ... Mk 13:36
c in the clouds of heaven ... Mk 14:62
c out of the country, the father ... Mk 15:21
she c in that instant gave thanks ... Lk 2:38
And as he was yet a c, the devil ... Lk 9:42
his heart, My lord delayeth his c ... Lk 12:45
by her continual c she weary me ... Lk 18:5
that at my c I might have ... Lk 19:23
things which are c on the earth ... Lk 21:26
of man c in a cloud with power ... Lk 21:27
c out of the country, and on him ... Lk 23:26
For, behold, the days are c ... Lk 23:29
c to him, and offering him vinegar ... Lk 23:36
who c after me is preferred ... Jn 1:27
day John seeth Jesus c unto him ... Jn 1:29
Jesus saw Nathanael c to him ... Jn 1:47
but while I am c, another ... Jn 5:7
I say unto you, The hour is c ... Jn 5:25
for the hour is c, in the which ... Jn 5:28
sheep are not, seeth the wolf c ... Jn 10:12
as she heard that Jesus was c ... Jn 11:20
that Jesus was c to Jerusalem ... Jn 12:12
before of the c of the Just One ... Acts 7:52
a vision a man named Ananias c in ... Acts 9:12
And he was with them c in and going ... Acts 9:28
day an angel of God c in to him ... Acts 10:3
And as Peter was c in, Cornelius ... Acts 10:25
c the baptism of repentance to ... Acts 13:24
who c thither went into the ... Acts 17:10
And while the day was c on ... Acts 27:33
been much hindered from c to you ... Rom 15:22
waiting for the c of our Lord ... 1Cor 1:7
they that are Christ's at his c ... 1Cor 15:23
I am glad of the c of Stephanas ... 1Cor 16:17
comforted us by the c of Titus ... 2Cor 7:6
And not by his c only, but by the ... 2Cor 7:7
is the third time I am c to you ... 2Cor 13:1
for me by my c to you again ... Phil 1:26
of our Lord Jesus Christ at his c ... 1Th 2:19
at the c of our Lord Jesus Christ ... 1Th 3:13
remain unto the c of the Lord ... 1Th 4:15
the c of our Lord Jesus Christ ... 1Th 5:23
by the c of our Lord Jesus Christ ... 2Th 2:1
with the brightness of his c ... 2Th 2:8
whose c is after the working of ... 2Th 2:9
brethren, unto the c of the Lord ... Jas 5:7
for the c of the Lord draweth ... Jas 5:8
To whom c, as unto a living stone ... 1Pet 2:4
c of our Lord Jesus Christ, but ... 2Pet 1:16
Where is the promise of his c ... 2Pet 3:4
hasting unto the c of the day of ... 2Pet 3:12
be ashamed before him at his c ... 1Jn 2:28
beast c up out of the earth ... Rev 13:11
c down from God out of heaven, ... Rev 21:2

## COMINGS

the c in thereof, and all the ... Eze 43:11

## COMMAND

him, that he will c his children ... Gen 18:19
according to that which I c thee ... Gen 27:8
Thy father did c before he died ... Gen 50:16
shalt speak all that I c thee ... Ex 7:2
LORD our God, as he shall c us ... Ex 8:27
God c thee so, then thou shalt be ... Ex 18:23
thou shalt c the children of ... Ex 27:20
thou that which I c thee this day ... Ex 34:11
C Aaron and his sons, saying, This ... Lev 6:9
Then the priest shall c that they ... Lev 13:54
Then shall the priest c to take ... Lev 14:4
the priest shall c that one of ... Lev 14:5
Then the priest shall c that they ... Lev 14:36
Then the priest shall c that they ... Lev 14:40
C the children of Israel, that ... Lev 24:2
Then I will c my blessing upon ... Lev 25:21
C the children of Israel, that ... Num 5:2
the LORD will c concerning you ... Num 9:8
C the children of Israel, and say ... Num 28:2
C the children of Israel, and say ... Num 34:2
C the children of Israel, that ... Num 35:2
c concerning the daughters of ... Num 36:6
c thou the people, saying, Ye are ... Deut 2:4
add unto the word which I c you ... Deut 4:2
the LORD your God which I c you ... Deut 4:2
which I c thee this day, that it ... Deut 4:40
his commandments, which I c thee ... Deut 6:2
which I c thee this day, shall be ... Deut 6:6
which I c thee this day, to do ... Deut 7:11
All the commandments which I c ... Deut 8:1
statutes, which I c thee this day ... Deut 8:11
which I c thee this day for thy ... Deut 10:13
which I c you this day, that ye ... Deut 11:8
which I c you this day, to love ... Deut 11:13
these commandments which I c you ... Deut 11:22
your God, which I c you this day ... Deut 11:27
of the way which I c you this day ... Deut 11:28
shall ye bring all that I c you ... Deut 12:11
thou shalt do all that I c thee ... Deut 12:14
all these words which I c thee ... Deut 12:28
What thing soever I c you ... Deut 12:32
which I c thee this day, to do ... Deut 13:18
which I c thee this day ... Deut 15:5
therefore I c thee, saying, Thou ... Deut 15:11
therefore I c thee this thing to ... Deut 15:15
unto them all that I shall c him ... Deut 18:18
Wherefore I c thee, saying, Thou ... Deut 19:7
which I c thee this day, to love ... Deut 19:9
therefore I c thee to do this ... Deut 24:18
therefore I c thee to do this ... Deut 24:22
which I c you this day ... Deut 27:1
which I c you this day, in mount ... Deut 27:4
statutes, which I c thee this day ... Deut 27:10
which I c thee this day, that the ... Deut 28:1
The LORD shall c the blessing ... Deut 28:8
which I c thee this day, to ... Deut 28:13
the words which I c thee this day ... Deut 28:14
statutes which I c thee this day ... Deut 28:15
to all that I c thee this day ... Deut 30:2
which I c thee this day ... Deut 30:8
which I c thee this day, it is ... Deut 30:11
In that I c thee this day to love ... Deut 30:16
which ye shall c your children to ... Deut 32:46
c the people, saying, Prepare you ... Josh 1:11
thou shalt c the priests that ... Josh 3:8
c ye them, saying, Take you hence ... Josh 4:3
C the priests that bear the ark ... Josh 4:16
servant, so did Moses c Joshua ... Josh 11:15
Let our lord now c thy servants ... 1Sa 16:16
Now therefore c thou that they ... 1Kin 5:6
hearken unto all that I c thee ... 1Kin 11:38
or if I c the locusts to devour ... 2Chr 7:13
Doth the eagle mount up at thy c ... Job 39:27
Yet the LORD will c his ... Ps 42:8
c deliverances for Jacob ... Ps 44:4
I will also c the clouds that ... Is 5:6
the work of my hands c ye me ... Is 45:11
whatsoever I c thee thou shalt ... Jer 1:7
speak unto them all that I c thee ... Jer 1:17
according to all which I c you ... Jer 11:4
all the words that I c thee to ... Jer 26:2
c them to say unto their masters, ... Jer 27:4
Behold, I will c, saith the LORD, ... Jer 34:22
whom thou didst c that they ... Lam 1:10
sea, thence will I c the serpent ... Amos 9:3
thence will I c the sword ... Amos 9:4
For, lo, I will c, and I will sift ... Amos 9:9
c that these stones be made bread ... Mt 4:3
Why did Moses then c to give a ... Mt 19:7
C therefore that the sepulchre be ... Mt 27:64
unto them, What did Moses c you ... Mk 10:3
c this stone that it be made ... Lk 4:3
c them to go out into the deep ... Lk 8:31
wilt thou that we c fire to come ... Lk 9:54
if ye do whatsoever I c you ... Jn 15:14
These things I c you, that ye ... Jn 15:17
Did not we straitly c you that ye ... Acts 5:28
to c them to keep the law of ... Acts 15:5
I c thee in the name of Jesus ... Acts 16:18
And unto the married I c, yet not ... 1Cor 7:10
will do the things which we c you ... 2Th 3:4
Now we c you, brethren, in the ... 2Th 3:6
Now them that are such we c ... 2Th 3:12
These things c and teach ... 1Ti 4:11

## COMMANDED

And the LORD God c the man ... Gen 2:16
whereof I c thee that thou ... Gen 3:11
of the tree, of which I c thee ... Gen 3:17
according to all that God c him ... Gen 6:22
unto all that the LORD c him ... Gen 7:5
and the female, as God had c Noah ... Gen 7:9
of all flesh, as God had c him ... Gen 7:16
Pharaoh c his men concerning him ... Gen 12:20
eight days old, as God had c him ... Gen 21:4
he c them, saying, Thus shall ye ... Gen 32:4
he c the foremost, saying, When ... Gen 32:17
so c he the second, and the third, ... Gen 32:19
Then Joseph c to fill their sacks ... Gen 42:25
he c the steward of his house, ... Gen 44:1
Now thou art c, this do ye ... Gen 45:19
land of Rameses, as Pharaoh had c ... Gen 47:11
Joseph c his servants the ... Gen 50:2
unto him according as he c them ... Gen 50:12
not as the king of Egypt c them ... Ex 1:17
all the signs which he had c him ... Ex 4:28
Pharaoh c the same day the ... Ex 5:6
and Aaron did as the LORD c them ... Ex 7:6
and they did so as the LORD had c ... Ex 7:10
and Aaron did so, as the LORD c ... Ex 7:20
and did as the LORD had c Moses ... Ex 12:28
as the LORD c Moses and Aaron, so ... Ex 12:50
the thing which the LORD hath c ... Ex 16:16
As the LORD c Moses, so Aaron ... Ex 16:34
these words which the LORD c him ... Ex 19:7
bread seven days, as I c thee ... Ex 23:15
to all things which I have c thee ... Ex 29:35
may make all that I have c thee ... Ex 31:6
that I have c thee shall they do ... Ex 31:11
out of the way which I c them ... Ex 32:8
Sinai, as the LORD had c him ... Ex 34:4
eat unleavened bread, as I c thee ... Ex 34:18
of Israel that which he was c ... Ex 34:34
the words which the LORD hath c ... Ex 35:1
is the thing which the LORD c ... Ex 35:4
and make all that the LORD hath c ... Ex 35:10
which the LORD had c to be made ... Ex 35:29
to all that the LORD had c ... Ex 36:1
work, which the LORD c to make ... Ex 36:5
made all that the LORD c Moses ... Ex 38:22
as the LORD c Moses ... Ex 39:1
as the LORD c Moses ... Ex 39:5
as the LORD c Moses ... Ex 39:7
as the LORD c Moses ... Ex 39:21
as the LORD c Moses ... Ex 39:26
as the LORD c Moses ... Ex 39:29
as the LORD c Moses ... Ex 39:31
to all that the LORD c Moses ... Ex 39:32
to all that the LORD c Moses ... Ex 39:42
had done it as the LORD had c ... Ex 39:43
to all that the LORD c him ... Ex 40:16
as the LORD c Moses ... Ex 40:19
as the LORD c Moses ... Ex 40:21
as the LORD had c Moses ... Ex 40:23
as the LORD c Moses ... Ex 40:25
as the LORD c Moses ... Ex 40:27
as the LORD c Moses ... Ex 40:29
as the LORD c Moses ... Ex 40:32
Which the LORD c to be given them ... Lev 7:36
Which the LORD c Moses in mount ... Lev 7:38
in the day that he c the children ... Lev 7:38
And Moses did as the LORD c him ... Lev 8:4
thing which the LORD c to be done ... Lev 8:5
as the LORD c Moses ... Lev 8:9
as the LORD c Moses ... Lev 8:13
as the LORD c Moses ... Lev 8:17
as the LORD c Moses ... Lev 8:21
as the LORD c Moses ... Lev 8:29
basket of consecrations, as I c ... Lev 8:31
day, so the LORD hath c to do ... Lev 8:34
for so I am c ... Lev 8:35
the LORD c by the hand of Moses ... Lev 8:36
c before the tabernacle of the ... Lev 9:5
the LORD c that ye should do ... Lev 9:6
as the LORD c ... Lev 9:7
as the LORD c Moses ... Lev 9:10
before the LORD; as Moses c ... Lev 9:21
the LORD, which he c them not ... Lev 10:1
for so I am c ... Lev 10:13
as the LORD hath c ... Lev 10:15
it in the holy place, as I c ... Lev 10:18
And he did as the LORD c Moses ... Lev 16:34
the thing which the LORD hath c ... Lev 17:2
of Israel did as the LORD c Moses ... Lev 24:23
which the LORD c Moses for the ... Lev 27:34
As the LORD c Moses, so he ... Num 1:19
to all that the LORD c Moses ... Num 1:54
as the LORD c Moses ... Num 2:33
to all that the LORD c Moses ... Num 2:34
the word of the LORD, as he was c ... Num 3:16
Moses numbered, as the LORD c him ... Num 3:42
of the LORD, as the LORD c Moses ... Num 3:51
of him, as the LORD c Moses ... Num 4:49
candlestick, as the LORD c Moses ... Num 8:3
unto all that the LORD c Moses ... Num 8:20
as the LORD had c Moses ... Num 8:22
to all that the LORD c Moses ... Num 9:5
hath c you by the hand of Moses ... Num 15:23
the day that the LORD c Moses ... Num 15:23
as the LORD c Moses ... Num 15:36
And Aaron took as Moses c, and ran ... Num 16:47
as the LORD c him, so did he ... Num 17:11
of the law which the LORD hath c ... Num 19:2
from before the LORD, as he c him ... Num 20:9
And Moses did as the LORD c ... Num 20:27
as the LORD c Moses and the ... Num 26:4
of judgment, as the LORD c Moses ... Num 27:11
And Moses did as the LORD c him ... Num 27:22
as the LORD c by the hand of ... Num 27:23
to all that the LORD c Moses ... Num 29:40
the thing which the LORD hath c ... Num 30:1
statutes, which the LORD c Moses ... Num 30:16
Midianites, as the LORD c Moses ... Num 31:7
of the law which the LORD c Moses ... Num 31:21
priest did as the LORD c Moses ... Num 31:31
the priest, as the LORD c Moses ... Num 31:41
as the LORD c Moses ... Num 31:47
them Moses c Eleazar the priest ... Num 32:28
Moses c the children of Israel, ... Num 34:13
which the LORD c to give unto the ... Num 34:13
These are they whom the LORD c to ... Num 34:29
The LORD c my lord to give the ... Num 36:2
my lord was c by the LORD to give ... Num 36:2
Moses c the children of Israel ... Num 36:5
Even as the LORD c Moses, so did ... Num 36:10
which the LORD c by the hand of ... Num 36:13
I c you at that time all the ... Deut 1:18
as the LORD our God c us ... Deut 1:19

to all that the LORD our God c us Deut 1:41
I c you at that time, saying, The Deut 3:18
I c Joshua at that time, saying, Deut 3:21
even as the LORD my God c me Deut 4:5
which he c you to perform, even Deut 4:13
the LORD c me at that time to Deut 4:14
as the LORD thy God hath c thee Deut 5:12
therefore the LORD thy God c thee Deut 5:15
as the LORD thy God hath c thee Deut 5:16
as the LORD your God hath c you Deut 5:32
the LORD your God hath c you Deut 5:33
the LORD your God c to teach you Deut 6:1
statutes, which he hath c thee Deut 6:17
which the LORD our God hath c you Deut 6:20
the LORD c us to do all these Deut 6:24
the LORD our God, as he hath c us Deut 6:25
out of the way which I c them Deut 9:12
the way which the LORD had c you Deut 9:16
there they be, as the LORD c me Deut 10:5
hath given thee, as I have c thee Deut 12:21
LORD thy God c thee to walk in Deut 13:5
of heaven, which I have not c Deut 17:3
which I have not c him to speak Deut 18:20
as the LORD thy God hath c thee Deut 20:17
as I c them, so ye shall observe Deut 24:8
which thou hast c me Deut 26:13
to all that thou hast c me Deut 26:14
hath c thee to do these statutes Deut 26:16
the elders of Israel c the people Deut 27:1
and his statutes which he c thee Deut 28:45
which the LORD c Moses to make Deut 29:1
commandments which I have c you Deut 31:5
And Moses c them, saying, At the Deut 31:10
That Moses c the Levites, which Deut 31:25
from the way which I have c you Deut 31:29
Moses c us a law, even the Deut 33:4
him, and did as the LORD c Moses Deut 34:9
which Moses my servant c thee Josh 1:7
Have not I c thee Josh 1:9
Then Joshua c the officers of the Josh 1:10
the servant of the LORD c you Josh 1:13
they c the people, saying, When Josh 3:3
of Israel did so as Joshua c Josh 4:8
was finished that the LORD c Josh 4:10
to all that Moses c Joshua Josh 4:10
Joshua therefore c the priests Josh 4:17
And Joshua had c the people Josh 6:10
my covenant which I c them Josh 7:11
he c them, saying, Behold, ye Josh 8:4
See, I have c you Josh 8:8
of the LORD which he c Joshua Josh 8:27
Joshua c that they should take Josh 8:29
the LORD c the children of Israel Josh 8:31
servant of the LORD had c before Josh 8:33
not a word of all that Moses c Josh 8:35
how that the LORD thy God c his Josh 9:24
down of the sun, that Joshua c Josh 10:27
as the LORD God of Israel c Josh 10:40
Moses the servant of the LORD c Josh 11:12
As the LORD c Moses his servant, Josh 11:15
of all that the LORD c Moses Josh 11:15
destroy them, as the LORD c Moses Josh 11:20
an inheritance, as I have c thee Josh 13:6
as the LORD c by the hand of Josh 14:2
As the LORD c Moses, so the Josh 14:5
The LORD c Moses to give us an Josh 17:4
The LORD c by the hand of Moses Josh 21:2
as the LORD c by the hand of Josh 21:8
the servant of the LORD c you Josh 22:2
my voice in all that I c you Josh 22:2
the LORD your God, which he c you Josh 23:16
covenant which I c their fathers Judg 2:20
which he c their fathers by the Judg 3:4
Hath not the LORD God of Israel c Judg 4:6
all that I c her let her observe Judg 13:14
c them, saying, Go and smite the Judg 21:10
Therefore they c the children of Judg 21:20
Boaz c his young men, saying, Let Ruth 2:15
which I have c in my habitation 1Sa 2:29
the LORD thy God, which he c thee 1Sa 13:13
the LORD hath c him to be captain 1Sa 13:14
kept that which the LORD c thee 1Sa 13:14
took, and went, as Jesse had c him 1Sa 17:20
Saul c his servants, saying, 1Sa 18:22
brother, he hath c me to be there 1Sa 20:29
The king hath c me a business 1Sa 21:2
send thee, and what I have c thee 1Sa 21:2
David c his young men, and they 2Sa 4:12
did so, as the LORD had c him 2Sa 5:25
whom I c to feed my people Israel 2Sa 7:7
as since the time that I c judges 2Sa 7:11
lord the king hath c his servant 2Sa 9:11
Now Absalom had c his servants 2Sa 13:28
have not I c you 2Sa 13:28
did unto Amnon as Absalom had c 2Sa 13:29
And the king c Joab and Abishai and 2Sa 18:5
performed all that the king c 2Sa 21:14
of Gad, went up as the LORD c 2Sa 24:19
So the king c Benaiah the son of 1Kin 2:46
And the king c, and they brought 1Kin 5:17
judgments, which he c our fathers 1Kin 8:58
to all that I have c thee 1Kin 9:4
had c him concerning this thing, 1Kin 11:10
he kept not that which the LORD c 1Kin 11:10
my statutes, which I have c thee 1Kin 11:11
which the LORD thy God c thee 1Kin 13:21
he c him all the days of his life 1Kin 15:5
I have c the ravens to feed thee 1Kin 17:4
I have c a widow woman there to 1Kin 17:9
the king of Syria c his thirty 1Kin 22:31
he c them, saying, This is the 2Kin 11:5
things that Jehoiada the priest c 2Kin 11:9
But Jehoiada the priest c the 2Kin 11:15
law of Moses, wherein the LORD c 2Kin 14:6
king Ahaz c Urijah the priest, 2Kin 16:15
according to all that king Ahaz c 2Kin 16:16
the law which I c your fathers 2Kin 17:13
Then the king of Assyria c 2Kin 17:27
the LORD c the children of Jacob 2Kin 17:34
which the LORD c Moses 2Kin 18:6
Moses the servant of the LORD c 2Kin 18:12
to all that I have c them 2Kin 21:8
law that my servant Moses c them 2Kin 21:8
the king c Hilkiah the priest, and 2Kin 22:12
the king c Hilkiah the high 2Kin 23:4
the king c all the people, saying 2Kin 23:21
Moses the servant of God had c 1Chr 6:49
David therefore did as God c him 1Chr 14:16
as Moses c according to the word 1Chr 15:15
the word which he c to a thousand 1Chr 16:15
of the LORD, which he c Israel 1Chr 16:40
whom I c to feed my people, 1Chr 17:6
since the time that I c judges to 1Chr 17:10
Is it not I that c the people to 1Chr 21:17
of the LORD c Gad to say to David 1Chr 21:18
And the LORD c the angel 1Chr 21:27
David c to gather together the 1Chr 22:2
David also c all the princes of 1Chr 22:17
to the order c unto them, 1Chr 23:31
the LORD God of Israel had c him 1Chr 24:19
to all that I have c thee 2Chr 7:17
for so had David the man of God c 2Chr 8:14
c Judah to seek the LORD God of 2Chr 14:4
Now the king of Syria had c the 2Chr 18:30
that Jehoiada the priest had c 2Chr 23:8
book of Moses, where the LORD c 2Chr 25:4
he c the priests the sons of 2Chr 29:21
for the king c that the burnt 2Chr 29:24
Hezekiah c to offer the burnt 2Chr 29:27
the princes c the Levites to sing 2Chr 29:30
Moreover he c the people that 2Chr 31:4
Then Hezekiah c to prepare 2Chr 31:11
c Judah and Jerusalem, saying, Ye 2Chr 32:12
heed to do all that I have c them 2Chr 33:8
c Judah to serve the LORD God of 2Chr 33:16
And the king c Hilkiah, and Ahikam 2Chr 34:20
for God c me to make haste 2Chr 35:21
the king of Persia hath c us Ezr 4:3
And I c, and search hath been made, Ezr 4:19
Who hath c you to build this Ezr 5:3
Who c you to build this house, and Ezr 5:9
Whatsoever is c by the God of Ezr 7:23
Which thou hast c by thy servants Ezr 9:11
which the LORD had c to Israel Neh 8:1
law which the LORD had c by Moses Neh 8:14
which was c to be given to the Neh 13:5
Then I c, and they cleansed the Neh 13:9
I c that the gates should be shut Neh 13:19
I c the Levites that they should Neh 13:22
he c Mehuman, Biztha, Harbona, Est 1:10
The king Ahasuerus c Vashti the Est 1:17
the king had so c concerning him Est 3:2
had c unto the king's lieutenants Est 3:12
Then Mordecai c to answer Esther, Est 4:13
to all that Esther had c him Est 4:17
he c to bring the book of records Est 6:1
all that Mordecai c unto the Jews Est 8:9
the king c it so to be done Est 9:14
he c by letters that his wicked Est 9:25
Hast thou c the morning since thy Job 38:12
did according as the LORD c them Job 42:9
to the judgment that thou hast c Ps 7:6
he c, and it stood fast Ps 33:9
Thy God hath c thy strength Ps 68:28
which he c our fathers, that they Ps 78:5
Though he had c the clouds from Ps 78:23
the word which he c to a thousand Ps 105:8
concerning whom the LORD c them Ps 106:34
he hath c his covenant for ever Ps 111:9
Thou hast c us to keep thy Ps 119:4
that thou hast c are righteous Ps 119:138
for there the LORD c the blessing Ps 133:3
for he c, and they were created Ps 148:5
I have c my sanctified ones, I Is 13:3
for my mouth it hath c, and his Is 34:16
and all their host have I c Is 45:12
and my molten image, hath c them Is 48:5
nor c them in the day that I Jer 7:22
But this thing c I them, saying, Jer 7:23
in all the ways that I have c you Jer 7:23
which I c them not, neither came Jer 7:31
Which I c your fathers in the day Jer 11:4
covenant, which I c them to do Jer 11:8
it by Euphrates, as the LORD c me Jer 13:5
which I c thee to hide there Jer 13:6
them not, neither have I c them Jer 14:14
sabbath day, as I c your fathers Jer 17:22
unto Baal, which I c not, nor Jer 19:5
yet I sent them not, nor c them Jer 23:32
had c him to speak unto all the Jer 26:8
my name, which I have not c them Jer 29:23
which I c them not, neither came Jer 32:35
the son of Rechab our father c us Jer 35:6
all that Jonadab our father c us Jer 35:10
that he c his sons not to drink Jer 35:14
of their father, which he c them Jer 35:16
unto all that he hath c you Jer 35:18
And Jeremiah c Baruch, saying, I Jer 36:5
that Jeremiah the prophet c him Jer 36:8
But the king c Jerahmeel the son Jer 36:26
Then Zedekiah the king c that Jer 37:21
Then the king c Ebed-melech the Jer 38:10
these words that the king had c Jer 38:27
to all that I have c thee Jer 50:21
c Seraiah the son of Neriah Jer 51:59
the LORD hath c concerning Jacob, Lam 1:17
that he had c in the days of old Lam 2:17
I have done as thou hast c me Eze 9:11
that when he had c the man Eze 10:6
And I did so as I was c Eze 12:7
I did in the morning as I was c Eze 24:18
So I prophesied as I was c Eze 37:7
So I prophesied as he c me Eze 37:10
Then the king c to call the Dan 2:2
c to destroy all the wise men of Dan 2:12
c that they should offer an Dan 2:46
cried aloud, To you it is c Dan 3:4
fury c to bring Shadrach, Meshach Dan 3:13
c that they should heat the Dan 3:19
he c the most mighty men that Dan 3:20
whereas they c to leave the stump Dan 4:26
c to bring the golden and silver Dan 5:2
Then c Belshazzar, and they Dan 5:29
Then the king c, and they brought Dan 6:16
c that they should take Daniel up Dan 6:23
And the king c, and they brought Dan 6:24
c the prophets, saying, Prophesy Amos 2:12
which I c my servants the Zec 1:6
which I c unto him in Horeb for Mal 4:4
and offer the gift that Moses c Mt 8:4
c them, saying, Go not into the Mt 10:5
at meat, he c it to be given her Mt 14:9
he c the multitude to sit down on Mt 14:19
For God c, saying, Honour thy Mt 15:4
he c the multitude to sit down on Mt 15:35
his lord c him to be sold, and his Mt 18:25
went, and did as Jesus c them Mt 21:6
Then Pilate c the body to be Mt 27:58
things whatsoever I have c you Mt 28:20
those things which Moses c Mk 1:44
c that something should be given Mk 5:43
c them that they should take Mk 6:8
and c his head to be brought Mk 6:27
he c them to make all sit down by Mk 6:39
he c the people to sit down on Mk 8:6
c to set them also before them Mk 8:7
still, and c him to be called Mk 10:49
unto them even as Jesus had c Mk 11:6
work, and c the porter to watch Mk 13:34
cleansing, according as Moses c Lk 5:14
(For he had c the unclean spirit Lk 8:29
and he c to give her meat Lk 8:55
c them to tell no man that thing Lk 9:21
Lord, it is done as thou hast c Lk 14:22
he did the things that were c him Lk 17:9
all those things which are c you Lk 17:10
c him to be brought unto him Lk 18:40
then he c these servants to be Lk 19:15
Now Moses in the law c us Jn 8:5
c them that they should not Acts 1:4
But when they had c them to go Acts 4:15
c them not to speak at all nor Acts 4:18
c to put the apostles forth a Acts 5:34
they c that they should not speak Acts 5:40
he c the chariot to stand still Acts 8:38
all things that are c thee of God Acts 10:33
he c us to preach unto the people Acts 10:42
he c them to be baptized in the Acts 10:48
c that they should be put to Acts 12:19
For so hath the Lord c us Acts 13:47
their clothes, and c to beat them Acts 16:22
(because that Claudius had c all Acts 18:2
c him to be bound with two chains Acts 21:33
he c him to be carried into the Acts 21:34
The chief captain c him to be Acts 22:24
c the chief priests and all their Acts 22:30
the high priest Ananias c them Acts 23:2
c the soldiers to go down, and to Acts 23:10
the soldiers, as it was c them Acts 23:31
he c him to be kept in Herod's Acts 23:35
he c a centurion to keep Paul, and Acts 24:23
seat c Paul to be brought Acts 25:6
c the man to be brought forth Acts 25:17
I c him to be kept till I might Acts 25:21
c that they which could swim Acts 27:43
but they are c to be under 1Cor 14:34
who c the light to shine out of 2Cor 4:6
with your own hands, as we c you 1Th 4:11
we were with you, this we c you 2Th 3:10
could not endure that which was c Heb 12:20
it was c them that they should Rev 9:4

**COMMANDEDST**

which thou c thy servant Moses Neh 1:7
that thou c thy servant Moses Neh 1:8
c them precepts, statutes, and Neh 9:14
of all that thou c them to do Jer 32:23

**COMMANDER**

a leader and c to the people Is 55:4

**COMMANDEST**

All that thou c us we will do Josh 1:16
thy words in all that thou c him Josh 1:18
c me to be smitten contrary to Acts 23:3

**COMMANDETH**

is the thing which the LORD c Ex 16:32
Thy servants will do as my lord c Num 32:25
Which c the sun, and it riseth not Job 9:7
c that they return from iniquity Job 36:10
c it not to shine by the cloud Job 36:32

that they may do whatsoever he c ... Job 37:12
For he c, and raiseth the stormy ... Ps 107:25
to pass, when the Lord c it not ... Lam 3:37
For, behold, the LORD c, and he ... Amos 6:11
for with authority c he even the ... Mk 1:27
power he c the unclean spirits, ... Lk 4:36
for he c even the winds and water, ... Lk 8:25
but now c all men every where to ... Acts 17:30

**COMMANDING**

had made an end of c his sons ... Gen 49:33
an end of c his twelve disciples ... Mt 11:1
C his accusers to come unto thee ... Acts 24:8
c to abstain from meats, which ... 1Ti 4:3

**COMMANDMENT**

according to the c of Pharaoh ... Gen 45:21
according to the c of the LORD ... Ex 17:1
which I will give thee in c unto ... Ex 25:22
he gave them in c all that the ... Ex 34:32
And Moses gave c, and they caused ... Ex 36:6
according to the c of Moses ... Ex 38:21
numbered at the c of the LORD ... Num 3:39
the c of the LORD by the hand of ... Num 4:37
according to the c of the LORD ... Num 4:41
According to the c of the LORD ... Num 4:49
At the c of the LORD the children ... Num 9:18
at the c of the LORD they pitched ... Num 9:18
according to the c of the LORD ... Num 9:20
according to the c of the LORD ... Num 9:20
At the c of the LORD they rested ... Num 9:23
at the c of the LORD they ... Num 9:23
at the c of the LORD by the hand ... Num 9:23
the c of the LORD by the hand of ... Num 10:13
Moses by the c of the LORD sent ... Num 13:3
ye transgress the c of the LORD ... Num 14:41
of the LORD, and hath broken his c ... Num 15:31
I have received c to bless ... Num 23:20
go beyond the c of the LORD ... Num 24:13
against my c in the desert of Zin ... Num 27:14
journeys by the c of the LORD ... Num 33:2
mount Hor at the c of the LORD ... Num 33:38
LORD had given him in c unto them ... Deut 1:3
the c of the LORD your God ... Deut 1:26
against the c of the LORD ... Deut 1:43
the c of the LORD your God ... Deut 9:23
that he turn not aside from the c ... Deut 17:20
For this c which I command thee ... Deut 30:11
be that doth rebel against thy c ... Josh 1:18
according to the c of the LORD ... Josh 8:8
according to the c of the LORD to ... Josh 15:13
Therefore according to the c of ... Josh 17:4
at the c of the LORD, these ... Josh 21:3
of the c of the LORD your God ... Josh 22:3
take diligent heed to do the c ... Josh 22:5
not rebel against the c of the ... 1Sa 12:14
rebel against the c of the LORD ... 1Sa 12:15
kept the c of the LORD thy God ... 1Sa 13:13
have performed the c of the LORD ... 1Sa 15:13
transgressed the c of the LORD ... 1Sa 15:24
thou despised the c of the LORD ... 2Sa 12:9
the c that I have charged thee ... 1Kin 2:43
hast not kept the c which the ... 1Kin 13:21
c which the LORD commanded the ... 2Kin 17:34
ordinances, and the law, and the c ... 2Kin 17:37
for the king's c was, saying, ... 2Kin 18:36
according to the c of Pharaoh ... 2Kin 23:35
Surely at the c of the LORD came ... 2Kin 24:3
their brethren were at their c ... 1Chr 12:32
their gods there, David gave a c ... 1Chr 14:12
people will be wholly at thy c ... 1Chr 28:21
according to the c of Moses ... 2Chr 8:13
they departed not from the c of ... 2Chr 8:15
and to do the law and the c ... 2Chr 14:4
blood and blood, between law and c. 2Chr 19:10
according to the c of Moses the ... 2Chr 24:6
at the king's c they made a chest ... 2Chr 24:8
stoned him with stones at the c ... 2Chr 24:21
according to the c of the king ... 2Chr 29:15
according to the c of David ... 2Chr 29:25
for so was the c of the LORD by ... 2Chr 29:25
and according to the c of the king ... 2Chr 30:6
one heart to do the c of the king ... 2Chr 30:12
And as soon as the c came abroad ... 2Chr 31:5
at the c of Hezekiah the king, and ... 2Chr 31:13
according to the king's c ... 2Chr 35:10
according to the c of David ... 2Chr 35:15
according to the c of king Josiah ... 2Chr 35:16
Give ye now c to cause these men ... Ezr 4:21
until another c shall be given ... Ezr 4:21
according to the c of the God of ... Ezr 6:14
and according to the c of Cyrus ... Ezr 6:14
I sent them with c unto Iddo the ... Ezr 8:17
that tremble at the c of our God ... Ezr 10:3
was the king's c concerning them ... Neh 11:23
according to the c of David the ... Neh 12:24
according to the c of David ... Neh 12:45
the king's c by his chamberlains ... Est 1:12
she hath not performed the c of ... Est 1:15
let there go a royal c from him ... Est 1:19
came to pass, when the king's c ... Est 2:8
for Esther did the c of Mordecai ... Est 2:20
transgressest thou the king's c ... Est 3:3
a c to be given in every province ... Est 3:14
being hastened by the king's c ... Est 3:15
whithersoever the king's c ... Est 4:3
gave him a c to Mordecai, to know ... Est 4:5
and gave him c unto Mordecai ... Est 4:10
a c to be given in every province ... Est 8:13
and pressed on by the king's c ... Est 8:14
city, whithersoever the king's c ... Est 8:17
of the same, when the king's c ... Est 9:1
gone back from the c of his lips ... Job 23:12
the c of the LORD is pure, ... Ps 19:8
thou hast given c to save me ... Ps 71:3
but thy c is exceeding broad ... Ps 119:96
He sendeth forth his c upon earth ... Ps 147:15
My son, keep thy father's c ... Prov 6:20
For the c is a lamp ... Prov 6:23
the waters should not pass his c ... Prov 8:29
feareth the c shall be rewarded ... Prov 13:13
He that keepeth the c keepeth his ... Prov 19:16
counsel thee to keep the king's c ... Eccl 8:2
Whoso keepeth the c shall feel no ... Eccl 8:5
the LORD hath given a c against ... Is 23:11
for the king's c was, saying, ... Is 36:21
none, but obey their father's c ... Jer 35:14
performed the c of their father ... Jer 35:16
the c of Jonadab your father ... Jer 35:18
for I have rebelled against his c ... Lam 1:18
because the king's c was urgent ... Dan 3:22
supplications the c came forth ... Dan 9:23
going forth of the c to restore ... Dan 9:25
he willingly walked after the c ... Hos 5:11
hath given a c concerning thee ... Nah 1:14
O ye priests, this c is for you ... Mal 2:1
that I have sent this c unto you ... Mal 2:4
he gave c to depart unto the ... Mt 8:18
the c of God by your tradition ... Mt 15:3
Thus have ye made the c of God of ... Mt 15:6
which is the great c in the law ... Mt 22:36
This is the first and great c ... Mt 22:38
For laying aside the c of God ... Mk 7:8
Full well ye reject the c of God ... Mk 7:9
him, Which is the first c of all ... Mk 12:28
this is the first c ... Mk 12:30
none other c greater than these ... Mk 12:31
transgressed I at any time thy c ... Lk 15:29
sabbath day according to the c ... Lk 23:56
This c have I received of my ... Jn 10:18
and the Pharisees had given a c ... Jn 11:57
which sent me, he gave me a c ... Jn 12:49
I know that his c is life ... Jn 12:50
A new c I give unto you, That ye ... Jn 13:34
and as the Father gave me c ... Jn 14:31
This is my c, That ye love one ... Jn 15:12
to whom we gave no such c ... Acts 15:24
and receiving a c unto Silas ... Acts 17:15
gave c to his accusers also to ... Acts 23:30
at Festus' c Paul was brought ... Acts 25:23
But sin, taking occasion by the c ... Rom 7:8
but when the c came, sin revived, ... Rom 7:9
And the c, which was ordained to ... Rom 7:10
For sin, taking occasion by the c ... Rom 7:11
the c holy, and just, and good ... Rom 7:12
that sin by the c might become ... Rom 7:13
and if there be any other c ... Rom 13:9
according to the c of the ... Rom 16:26
this by permission, and not of c ... 1Cor 7:6
virgins I have no c of the Lord ... 1Cor 7:25
I speak not by c, but by occasion ... 2Cor 8:8
which is the first c with promise ... Eph 6:2
by the c of God our Saviour ... 1Ti 1:1
Now the end of the c is charity ... 1Ti 1:5
thou keep this c without spot ... 1Ti 6:14
to the c of God our Saviour ... Titus 1:3
have a c to take tithes of the ... Heb 7:5
not after the law of a carnal c ... Heb 7:16
c going before for the weakness ... Heb 7:18
gave c concerning his bones ... Heb 11:22
were not afraid of the king's c ... Heb 11:23
the holy c delivered unto them ... 2Pet 2:21
of the c of us the apostles of ... 2Pet 3:2
I write no new c unto you ... 1Jn 2:7
but an old c which ye had from ... 1Jn 2:7
The old c is the word which ye ... 1Jn 2:7
a new c I write unto you, which ... 1Jn 2:8
And this is his c, That we should ... 1Jn 3:23
love one another, as he gave us c ... 1Jn 3:23
this c have we from him, That he ... 1Jn 4:21
have received a c from the Father ... 2Jn 4
though I wrote a new c unto thee ... 2Jn 5
This is the c, That, as ye have ... 2Jn 6

**COMMANDMENTS**

my voice, and kept my charge, my c ... Gen 26:5
sight, and wilt give ear to his c ... Ex 15:26
How long refuse ye to keep my c ... Ex 16:28
them that love me, and keep my c ... Ex 20:6
a law, and c which I have written ... Ex 24:12
words of the covenant, the ten c ... Ex 34:28
ignorance against any of the c of ... Lev 4:2
somewhat against any of the c of ... Lev 4:13
ignorance against any of the c of ... Lev 4:22
somewhat against any of the c of ... Lev 4:27
to be done by the c of the LORD ... Lev 5:17
Therefore shall ye keep my c ... Lev 22:31
walk in my statutes, and keep my c ... Lev 26:3
me, and will not do all these c ... Lev 26:14
so that ye will not do all my c ... Lev 26:15
These are the c, which the LORD ... Lev 27:34
and not observed all these c ... Num 15:22
and remember all the c of the LORD .. Num 15:39
ye may remember, and do all my c .. Num 15:40
These are the c and the judgments, .. Num 36:13
that ye may keep the c of the ... Deut 4:2
you to perform, even ten c ... Deut 4:13
therefore his statutes, and his c ... Deut 4:40
of them that love me and keep my c .. Deut 5:10
fear me, and keep all my c always ... Deut 5:29
I will speak unto thee all the c ... Deut 5:31
Now these are the c, the statutes ... Deut 6:1
to keep all his statutes and his c ... Deut 6:2
keep the c of the LORD your God ... Deut 6:17
these c before the LORD our God ... Deut 6:25
him and keep his c to a thousand ... Deut 7:9
Thou shalt therefore keep the c ... Deut 7:11
All the c which I command thee ... Deut 8:1
whether thou wouldest keep his c ... Deut 8:2
keep the c of the LORD thy God ... Deut 8:6
thy God, in not keeping his c ... Deut 8:11
to the first writing, the ten c ... Deut 10:4
To keep the c of the LORD ... Deut 10:13
and his judgments, and his c ... Deut 11:1
c which I command you this day ... Deut 11:8
hearken diligently unto my c ... Deut 11:13
all these c which I command you ... Deut 11:22
if ye obey the c of the LORD your ... Deut 11:27
obey the c of the LORD your God ... Deut 11:28
God, and fear him, and keep his c ... Deut 13:4
to keep all his c which I command ... Deut 13:18
to observe to do all these c ... Deut 15:5
shalt keep all these c to do them ... Deut 19:9
according to all thy c which thou ... Deut 26:13
I have not transgressed thy c ... Deut 26:13
and to keep his statutes, and his c ... Deut 26:17
thou shouldest keep all his c ... Deut 26:18
Keep all the c which I command ... Deut 27:1
of the LORD thy God, and do his c ... Deut 27:10
to do all his c which I command ... Deut 28:1
keep the c of the LORD thy God ... Deut 28:9
unto the c of the LORD thy God ... Deut 28:13
God, to observe to do all his c ... Deut 28:15
the LORD thy God, to keep his c ... Deut 28:45
do all his c which I command thee ... Deut 30:8
the LORD thy God, to keep his c ... Deut 30:10
in his ways, and to keep his c ... Deut 30:16
the c which I have commanded you ... Deut 31:5
in all his ways, and to keep his c ... Josh 22:5
in, obeying the c of the LORD ... Judg 2:17
hearken unto the c of the LORD ... Judg 3:4
me, and hath not performed my c ... 1Sa 15:11
to keep his statutes, and his c ... 1Kin 2:3
ways, to keep my statutes and my c ... 1Kin 3:14
keep all my c to walk in them ... 1Kin 6:12
in all his ways, and to keep his c ... 1Kin 8:58
in his statutes, and to keep his c ... 1Kin 8:61
children, and will not keep my c ... 1Kin 9:6
I chose, because he kept my c ... 1Kin 11:34
to keep my statutes and my c ... 1Kin 11:38
my servant David, who kept my c ... 1Kin 14:8
have forsaken the c of the LORD ... 1Kin 18:18
from your evil ways, and keep my c. 2Kin 17:13
they left all the c of the LORD ... 2Kin 17:16
not the c of the LORD their God ... 2Kin 17:19
following him, but kept his c ... 2Kin 18:6
after the LORD, and to keep his c ... 2Kin 23:3
if he be constant to do my c ... 1Chr 28:7
seek for all the c of the LORD ... 1Chr 28:8
a perfect heart, to keep thy c ... 1Chr 29:19
and forsake my statutes and my c ... 2Chr 7:19
of his father, and walked in his c ... 2Chr 17:4
transgress ye the c of the LORD ... 2Chr 24:20
God, and in the law, and in the c ... 2Chr 31:21
after the LORD, and to keep his c ... 2Chr 34:31
of the words of the c of the LORD ... Ezr 7:11
for we have forsaken thy c ... Ezr 9:10
Should we again break thy c ... Ezr 9:14
that love him and observe his c ... Neh 1:5
thee, and have not kept the c ... Neh 1:7
if ye turn unto me, and keep my c ... Neh 1:9
and true laws, good statutes and c ... Neh 9:13
necks, and hearkened not to thy c ... Neh 9:16
and hearkened not unto thy c ... Neh 9:29
thy law, nor hearkened unto thy c ... Neh 9:34
do all the c of the LORD our Lord ... Neh 10:29
the works of God, but keep his c ... Ps 78:7
my statutes, and keep not my c ... Ps 89:31
that remember his c to do them ... Ps 103:18
excel in strength, that do his c ... Ps 103:20
all his c are sure ... Ps 111:7
have all they that do his c ... Ps 111:10
that delighteth greatly in his c ... Ps 112:1
I have respect unto all thy c ... Ps 119:6
O let me not wander from thy c ... Ps 119:10
hide not thy c from me ... Ps 119:19
cursed, which do err from thy c ... Ps 119:21
I will run the way of thy c ... Ps 119:32
me to go in the path of thy c ... Ps 119:35
And I will delight myself in thy c ... Ps 119:47
also will I lift up unto thy c ... Ps 119:48
and delayed not to keep thy c ... Ps 119:60
for I have believed thy c ... Ps 119:66
that I may learn thy c ... Ps 119:73
All thy c are faithful ... Ps 119:86
Thou through thy c hast made me ... Ps 119:98
for I will keep the c of my God ... Ps 119:115
Therefore I love thy c above gold ... Ps 119:127
for I longed for thy c ... Ps 119:131
yet thy c are my delights ... Ps 119:143
and all thy c are truth ... Ps 119:151
for thy salvation, and done thy c ... Ps 119:166
for all thy c are righteousness ... Ps 119:172
for I do not forget thy c ... Ps 119:176
my words, and hide my c with thee ... Prov 2:1
but let thine heart keep my c ... Prov 3:1
keep my c, and live ... Prov 4:4
words, and lay up my c with thee ... Prov 7:1
Keep my c, and live ... Prov 7:2
The wise in heart will receive c ... Prov 10:8
Fear God, and keep his c ... Eccl 12:13
that thou hadst hearkened to my c ... Is 48:18

him, and to them that keep his c ........ Dan 9:4
the LORD, and have not kept his c ...... Amos 2:4
shall break one of these least c ........ Mt 5:19
for doctrines the c of men ........ Mt 15:9
wilt enter into life, keep the c ........ Mt 19:17
On these two c hang all the law ........ Mt 22:40
for doctrines the c of men ........ Mk 7:7
Thou knowest the c, Do not commit... Mk 10:19
him, The first of all the c is ........ Mk 12:29
before God, walking in all the c ........ Lk 1:6
Thou knowest the c, Do not commit .... Lk 18:20
If ye love me, keep my c ........ Jn 14:15
He that hath my c, and keepeth ........ Jn 14:21
If ye keep my c, ye shall abide ........ Jn 15:10
even as I have kept my Father's c ........ Jn 15:10
the Holy Ghost had given c unto ........ Acts 1:2
but the keeping of the c of God ........ 1Cor 7:19
unto you are the c of the Lord ........ 1Cor 14:37
even the law of c contained in ........ Eph 2:15
after the c and doctrines of men ........ Col 2:22
(touching whom ye received c ........ Col 4:10
For ye know what c we gave you by...... 1Th 4:2
c of men, that turn from the ........ Titus 1:14
we know him, if we keep his c ........ 1Jn 2:3
I know him, and keepeth not his c ........ 1Jn 2:4
of him, because we keep his c ........ 1Jn 3:22
keepeth his c dwelleth in him ........ 1Jn 3:24
when we love God, and keep his c ........ 1Jn 5:2
love of God, that we keep his c ........ 1Jn 5:3
and his c are not grievous ........ 1Jn 5:3
is love, that we walk after his c ........ 2Jn 6
her seed, which keep the c of God ...... Rev 12:17
are they that keep the c of God ........ Rev 14:12
Blessed are they that do his c ........ Rev 22:14

**COMMEND**
into thy hands I c my spirit ........ Lk 23:46
I c you to God, and to the word of .... Acts 20:32
c the righteousness of God ........ Rom 3:5
I c unto you Phebe our sister, ........ Rom 16:1
Do we begin again to c ourselves ........ 2Cor 3:1
For we c not ourselves again unto ...... 2Cor 5:12
with some that c themselves ........ 2Cor 10:12

**COMMENDATION**
some others, epistles of c to you ........ 2Cor 3:1
to you, or letters of c from you ........ 2Cor 3:1

**COMMENDED**
saw her, and c her before Pharaoh ..... Gen 12:15
A man shall be c according to his ...... Prov 12:8
Then I c mirth, because a man ........ Eccl 8:15
the lord c the unjust steward, ........ Lk 16:8
they c them to the Lord, on whom .... Acts 14:23
for I ought to have been c of you ...... 2Cor 12:11

**COMMENDETH**
But God c his love toward us, in ........ Rom 5:8
But meat c us not to God ........ 1Cor 8:8
For not he that c himself is ........ 2Cor 10:18
is approved, but whom the Lord c ..... 2Cor 10:18

**COMMENDING**
truth c ourselves to every man's ........ 2Cor 4:2

**COMMISSION**
c from the chief priests, ........ Acts 26:12

**COMMISSIONS**
they delivered the king's c unto ........ Ezr 8:36

**COMMIT**
Thou shalt not c adultery ........ Ex 20:14
If a soul c a trespass, and sin ........ Lev 5:15
c any of these things which are ........ Lev 5:17
c a trespass against the LORD, and ........ Lev 6:2
and shall not c any of these ........ Lev 18:26
For whosoever shall c any of ........ Lev 18:29
even the souls that c them shall ........ Lev 18:29
that ye c not any one of these ........ Lev 18:30
to c whoredom with Molech, from ........ Lev 20:5
When a man or woman shall c ........ Num 5:6
any sin that men c, to do ........ Num 5:6
c a trespass against him, ........ Num 5:12
the people began to c whoredom ........ Num 25:1
to c trespass against the LORD in ........ Num 31:16
Neither shalt thou c adultery ........ Deut 5:18
shall henceforth c no more any ........ Deut 19:20
c a trespass in the accursed ........ Josh 22:20
If he c iniquity, I will chasten ........ 2Sa 7:14
of Jerusalem to c fornication ........ 2Chr 21:11
and unto God would I c my cause ........ Job 5:8
that he should c iniquity ........ Job 34:10
Into thine hand I c my spirit ........ Ps 31:5
C thy way unto the LORD ........ Ps 37:5
C thy works unto the LORD, and thy... Prov 16:3
to kings to c wickedness ........ Prov 16:12
I will c thy government into his ........ Is 22:21
shall c fornication with all the ........ Is 23:17
c adultery, and swear falsely, and ........ Jer 7:9
and weary themselves to c iniquity ........ Jer 9:5
they c adultery, and walk in lies ........ Jer 23:14
c Jeremiah into the court of the ........ Jer 37:21
Wherefore c ye this great evil ........ Jer 44:7
and c iniquity, and I lay a ........ Eze 3:20
c the abominations which they c ........ Eze 8:17
didst c whoredom with them, ........ Eze 16:17
followeth thee to c whoredoms ........ Eze 16:34
thou shalt not c this lewdness ........ Eze 16:43
c ye whoredom after their ........ Eze 20:30
the midst of thee they c lewdness ........ Eze 22:9
Will they now c whoredoms with ........ Eze 23:43
and c iniquity, all his ........ Eze 33:13
they shall c whoredom, and shall ........ Hos 4:10
your daughters shall c whoredom ........ Hos 4:13
and your spouses shall c adultery ........ Hos 4:13
daughters when they c whoredom ........ Hos 4:14
your spouses when they c adultery ...... Hos 4:14
for they c lewdness ........ Hos 6:9
for they c falsehood ........ Hos 7:1
time, Thou shalt not c adultery ........ Mt 5:27
causeth her to c adultery ........ Mt 5:32
which is put away doth c adultery ........ Mt 19:9
murder, Thou shalt not c adultery ........ Mt 19:18
Do not c adultery, Do not kill, ........ Mk 10:19
did c things worthy of stripes, ........ Lk 12:48
who will c to your trust the true ........ Lk 16:11
Do not c adultery, Do not kill, ........ Lk 18:20
Jesus did not c himself unto them ........ Jn 2:24
that they which c such things are ....... Rom 1:32
against them which c such things ........ Rom 2:2
a man should not c adultery ........ Rom 2:22
dost thou c adultery ........ Rom 2:22
idols, dost thou c sacrilege ........ Rom 2:22
this, Thou shalt not c adultery ........ Rom 13:9
Neither let us c fornication ........ 1Cor 10:8
This charge I c unto thee ........ 1Ti 1:18
the same c thou to faithful men, ........ 2Ti 2:2
ye c sin, and are convinced of the ........ Jas 2:9
Do not c adultery, said also, Do ........ Jas 2:11
Now if thou c no adultery ........ Jas 2:11
according to the will of God c ........ 1Pet 4:19
is born of God doth not c sin ........ 1Jn 3:9
unto idols, and to c fornication ........ Rev 2:14
my servants to c fornication ........ Rev 2:20
them that c adultery with her ........ Rev 2:22

**COMMITTED**
he hath c all that he hath to my ........ Gen 39:8
prison c to Joseph's hand all the ........ Gen 39:22
for his sin that he hath c ........ Lev 4:35
for his trespass, which he hath c ........ Lev 5:7
customs, which were c before you ....... Lev 18:30
of them have c an abomination ........ Lev 20:13
for they c all these things, and ........ Lev 20:23
if ought be c by ignorance ........ Num 15:24
which have c that wicked thing, ........ Deut 17:5
if a man have c a sin worthy of ........ Deut 21:22
c a trespass in the accursed ........ Josh 7:1
have c against the God of Israel ........ Josh 22:16
because ye have not c this ........ Josh 22:31
for they have c lewdness and folly ...... Judg 20:6
perversely, we have c wickedness ....... 1Kin 8:47
with their sins which they had c ........ 1Kin 14:22
c them unto the hands of the ........ 1Kin 14:27
which he c against the LORD ........ 1Chr 10:13
c them to the hands of the chief ........ 2Chr 12:10
All that was c to thy servants, ........ 2Chr 34:16
we have c iniquity, we have done ........ Ps 106:6
For my people have c two evils ........ Jer 2:13
whereby backsliding Israel c ........ Jer 3:8
c adultery with stones and with ........ Jer 3:9
to the full, they then c adultery ........ Jer 5:7
horrible thing is c in the land ........ Jer 5:30
when they had c abomination ........ Jer 6:15
when they had c abomination ........ Jer 8:12
have c against the LORD our God ........ Jer 16:10
they have c villany in Israel ........ Jer 29:23
have c adultery with their ........ Jer 29:23
c him unto Gedaliah the son of ........ Jer 39:14
had c unto him men, and women, and... Jer 40:7
the captain of the guard had c to ........ Jer 41:10
have c to provoke me to anger ........ Jer 44:3
which they have c in the land of ........ Jer 44:9
the abominations which ye have c ........ Jer 44:22
have c in all their abominations ........ Eze 6:9
because they have c a trespass ........ Eze 15:8
Thou hast also c fornication with ........ Eze 16:26
and c abomination before me ........ Eze 16:50
hath Samaria c half of thy sins ........ Eze 16:51
hast c more abominable than they ...... Eze 16:52
to the idols, hath c abomination, ........ Eze 18:12
from all his sins that he hath c ........ Eze 18:21
his transgressions that he hath c ........ Eze 18:22
his wickedness that he hath c ........ Eze 18:27
his transgressions that he hath c ........ Eze 18:28
in that they have c a trespass ........ Eze 20:27
for all your evils that ye have c ........ Eze 20:43
one hath c abomination with his ........ Eze 22:11
they c whoredoms in Egypt ........ Eze 23:3
they c whoredoms in their youth ........ Eze 23:3
Thus she c her whoredoms with ........ Eze 23:7
That they have c adultery ........ Eze 23:37
their idols have they c adultery ........ Eze 23:37
for his iniquity that he hath c ........ Eze 33:13
c shall be mentioned unto him ........ Eze 33:16
abominations which they have c ........ Eze 33:29
abominations that they have c ........ Eze 43:8
abominations which they have c ........ Eze 44:13
have c iniquity, and have done ........ Dan 9:5
the land hath c great whoredom ........ Hos 1:2
they have c whoredom continually ....... Hos 4:18
and an abomination is c in Israel ........ Mal 2:11
c adultery with her already in ........ Mt 5:28
with him, who had c murder in the ...... Mk 15:7
and to whom men have c much ........ Lk 12:48
but hath c all judgment unto the ........ Jn 5:22
men and women c them to prison ........ Acts 8:3
or have c any thing worthy of ........ Acts 25:11
he had c nothing worthy of death ...... Acts 25:25
they c themselves unto the sea, ........ Acts 27:40
though I have c nothing against ........ Acts 28:17
them were c the oracles of God ........ Rom 3:2
of the gospel is c unto me ........ 1Cor 9:17
fornication, as some of them c ........ 1Cor 10:8
hath c unto us the word of ........ 2Cor 5:19
Have I c an offence in abasing ........ 2Cor 11:7
lasciviousness which they have c ........ 2Cor 12:21
the uncircumcision was c unto me ........ Gal 2:7
God, which was c to my trust ........ 1Ti 1:11
keep that which is c to thy trust ........ 1Ti 6:20
have c unto him against that day ........ 2Ti 1:12
That good thing which was c unto ........ 2Ti 1:14
which is c unto me according to ........ Titus 1:3
and if he have c sins, they shall ........ Jas 5:15
but c himself to him that judgeth ........ 1Pet 2:23
deeds which they have ungodly c ........ Jude 15
of the earth have c fornication ........ Rev 17:2
earth have c fornication with her ........ Rev 18:3
who have c fornication and lived ........ Rev 18:9

**COMMITTEST**
thou c whoredom, and Israel is ........ Hos 5:3

**COMMITTETH**
the man that c adultery with ........ Lev 20:10
even he that c adultery with his ........ Lev 20:10
the poor c himself unto thee ........ Ps 10:14
But whoso c adultery with a woman... Prov 6:32
that the house of Israel c here ........ Eze 8:6
But as a wife that c adultery ........ Eze 16:32
c iniquity, and doeth according to ....... Eze 18:24
c iniquity, and dieth in them ........ Eze 18:26
c iniquity, he shall even die ........ Eze 33:18
her that is divorced c adultery ........ Mt 5:32
shall marry another, c adultery ........ Mt 19:9
another, c adultery against her ........ Mk 10:11
to another, she c adultery ........ Mk 10:12
and marrieth another, c adultery ........ Lk 16:18
away from her husband c adultery ........ Lk 16:18
Whosoever c sin is the servant of ........ Jn 8:34
but he that c fornication sinneth ........ 1Cor 6:18
Whosoever c sin transgresseth ........ 1Jn 3:4
He that c sin is of the devil ........ 1Jn 3:8

**COMMITTING**
of life, without c iniquity ........ Eze 33:15
c adultery, they break out, and ........ Hos 4:2

**COMMODIOUS**
the haven was not c to winter in ........ Acts 27:12

**COMMON**
if any one of the c people sin ........ Lev 4:27
men die the c death of all men ........ Num 16:29
There is no c bread under mine ........ 1Sa 21:4
and the bread is in a manner c ........ 1Sa 21:5
the sun, and it is c among men ........ Eccl 6:1
into the graves of the c people ........ Jer 26:23
and shall eat them as c things ........ Jer 31:5
with the men of the c sort were ........ Eze 23:42
took Jesus into the c hall ........ Mt 27:27
the c people heard him gladly ........ Mk 12:37
together, and had all things c ........ Acts 2:44
but they had all things c ........ Acts 4:32
and put them in the c prison ........ Acts 5:18
any thing that is c or unclean ........ Acts 10:14
cleansed, that call not thou c ........ Acts 10:15
not call any man c or unclean ........ Acts 10:28
for nothing c or unclean hath at ........ Acts 11:8
cleansed, that call not thou c ........ Acts 11:9
taken you but such as is c to man ..... 1Cor 10:13
mine own son after the c faith ........ Titus 1:4
write unto you of the c salvation ........ Jude 3

**COMMONLY**
this saying is c reported among ........ Mt 28:15
It is reported c that there is ........ 1Cor 5:1

**COMMONWEALTH**
being aliens from the c of Israel ........ Eph 2:12

**COMMOTION**
a great c out of the north ........ Jer 10:22

**COMMOTIONS**
when ye shall hear of wars and c ........ Lk 21:9

**COMMUNE**
went out unto Jacob to c with him ...... Gen 34:6
I will c with thee from above the ........ Ex 25:22
C with David secretly, and say, ........ 1Sa 18:22
I will c with my father of thee ........ 1Sa 19:3
If we assay to c with thee ........ Job 4:2
c with your own heart upon your ........ Ps 4:4
they c of laying snares privily ........ Ps 64:5
I c with mine own heart ........ Ps 77:6

**COMMUNED**
he c with them, saying, If it be ........ Gen 23:8
Hamor c with them, saying, The ........ Gen 34:8
c with the men of their city, ........ Gen 34:20
c with them, and took from them ........ Gen 42:24
they c with him at the door of ........ Gen 43:19
c with them, and with all the ........ Judg 9:1
Samuel c with Saul upon the top ........ 1Sa 9:25
c with Abigail, to take her to ........ 1Sa 25:39
she c with him of all that was in ........ 1Kin 10:2
and they c with her ........ 2Kin 22:14
she c with him of all that was in ........ 2Chr 9:1
I c with mine own heart, saying, ........ Eccl 1:16
And the king c with them ........ Dan 1:19
So the angel that c with me said ........ Zec 1:14
c one with another what they ........ Lk 6:11
c with the chief priests and ........ Lk 22:4
pass, that, while they c together ........ Lk 24:15
him the oftener, and c with him ........ Acts 24:26

**COMMUNICATE**
c unto him that teacheth in all ........ Gal 6:6
that ye did c with my affliction ........ Phil 4:14

ready to distribute, willing to c ................ 1Ti 6:18
But to do good and to c forget not ..... Heb 13:16

**COMMUNICATED**
c unto them that gospel which I .............. Gal 2:2
no church c with me as concerning ...... Phil 4:15

**COMMUNICATION**
Abner had c with the elders of ................ 2Sa 3:17
them, Ye know the man, and his c ....... 2Kin 9:11
But let your c be, Yea, yea ........................ Mt 5:37
Let no corrupt c proceed out of ............. Eph 4:29
filthy c out of your mouth ......................... Col 3:8
That the c of thy faith may .................... Philem 6

**COMMUNICATIONS**
What manner of c are these that ........... Lk 24:17
evil c corrupt good manners ................. 1Cor 15:33

**COMMUNING**
as he had left c with Abraham ............. Gen 18:33
of c with him upon mount Sinai ............ Ex 31:18

**COMMUNION**
is it not the c of the blood of ............. 1Cor 10:16
is it not the c of the body of ................ 1Cor 10:16
what c hath light with darkness ........... 2Cor 6:14
the c of the Holy Ghost, be with ........ 2Cor 13:14

**COMPACT**
as a city that is c together ......................... Ps 122:3

**COMPACTED**
c by that which every joint ...................... Eph 4:16

**COMPANIED**
of these men which have c with us ...... Acts 1:21

**COMPANIES**
three hundred men into three c ............ Judg 7:16
the three c blew the trumpets, and ....... Judg 7:20
wait against Shechem in four c ........... Judg 9:34
and divided them into three c .............. Judg 9:43
the two other c ran upon all the .......... Judg 9:44
Saul put the people in three c .............. 1Sa 11:11
of the Philistines in three c .................. 1Sa 13:17
And the Syrians had gone out by c ........ 2Kin 5:2
in the c of the children of Levi ............. 1Chr 9:18
the captains of the c that ...................... 1Chr 28:1
appointed two great c of them ............. Neh 12:31
So stood the two c of them that ............ Neh 12:40
the c of Sheba waited for them ............. Job 6:19
O ye travelling c of Dedanim ................. Is 21:13
criest, let thy c deliver thee .................. Is 57:13
chariots, and with horsemen, and c ...... Eze 26:7
down by c upon the green grass ............ Mk 6:39

**COMPANION**
his brother, and every man his c ........... Ex 32:27
Samson's wife was given to his c ....... Judg 14:20
therefore I gave her to thy c ................. Judg 15:2
his wife, and given her to his c ............. Judg 15:6
the Archite was the king's c ............... 1Chr 27:33
to dragons, and a c to owls ................... Job 30:29
I am a c of all them that fear ............... Ps 119:63
but a c of fools shall be ....................... Prov 13:20
but he that is a c of riotous men ........... Prov 28:7
the same is the c of a destroyer .......... Prov 28:24
yet is she thy c, and the wife of ............... Mal 2:14
c in labour, and fellow soldier, .............. Phil 2:25
c in tribulation, and in the ........................ Rev 1:9

**COMPANIONS**
and she went with her c, and .............. Judg 11:38
brought thirty c to be with him .......... Judg 14:11
Tabeel, and the rest of their c ................ Ezr 4:7
scribe, and the rest of their c .................. Ezr 4:9
to the rest of their c that dwell ............. Ezr 4:17
Shimshai the scribe, and their c ............. Ezr 4:23
and Shethar-boznai, and their c ............... Ezr 5:3
his c the Apharsachites, which ................. Ezr 5:6
your c the Apharsachites, which ............... Ezr 6:6
river, Shethar-boznai, and their c ............ Ezr 6:13
answer thee, and thy c with thee ........... Job 35:4
Shall the c make a banquet of him ......... Job 41:6
the virgins her c that follow her ............ Ps 45:14
aside by the flocks of thy c .................... Song 1:7
the c hearken to thy voice ..................... Song 8:13
are rebellious, and c of thieves ................... Is 1:23
for the children of Israel his c .............. Eze 37:16
for all the house of Israel his c ............. Eze 37:16
Mishael, and Azariah, his c .................... Dan 2:17
Paul's c in travel, they rushed .............. Acts 19:29
whilst ye became c of them that .......... Heb 10:33

**COMPANIONS'**
c sakes, I will now say, Peace be ........... Ps 122:8

**COMPANY**
said, If Esau come to the one c ............... Gen 32:8
then the other c which is left ................. Gen 32:8
lodged that night in the c ...................... Gen 32:21
a c of nations shall be of thee, ............. Gen 35:11
a c of Ishmeelites came from ................. Gen 37:25
and it was a very great c ....................... Gen 50:9
they spake unto all the c of the ............. Num 14:7
unto Korah and unto all his c ................ Num 16:5
you censers, Korah, and all his c ........... Num 16:6
all thy c are gathered together ............ Num 16:11
all thy c before the LORD, thou, ........... Num 16:16
he be not as Korah, and as his c ......... Num 16:40
Now shall this c lick up all that ........... Num 22:4
against Aaron in the c of Korah ........... Num 26:9
with Korah, when that c died ............... Num 26:10
he was not in the c of them that .......... Num 27:3
the LORD in the c of Korah ................... Num 27:3
another c come along by the plain ...... Judg 9:37
the c that was with him, rushed ........... Judg 9:44
that thou comest with such a c ........... Judg 18:23
that thou shalt meet a c of ..................... 1Sa 10:5
behold, a c of prophets met him ........... 1Sa 10:10
one c turned unto the way that ............. 1Sa 13:17
another c turned the way to ................. 1Sa 13:18
another c turned to the way of ............ 1Sa 13:18
when they saw the c of the ................... 1Sa 19:20
thou bring me down to this c ............... 1Sa 30:15
I will bring thee down to this c ........... 1Sa 30:15
delivered the c that came against ........ 1Sa 30:23
the man of God, he and all his c ........... 2Kin 5:15
he spied the c of Jehu as he came ........ 2Kin 9:17
and said, I see a c ................................ 2Kin 9:17
at Jerusalem, with a very great c ............ 2Chr 9:1
great c that cometh against us ........... 2Chr 20:12
came with a small c of men ................ 2Chr 24:24
the other c of them that gave .............. Neh 12:38
thou hast made desolate all my c ........... Job 16:7
Which goeth in c with the workers ....... Job 34:8
walked unto the house of God in c ........ Ps 55:14
great was the c of those that ................ Ps 68:11
Rebuke the c of spearmen, the ............... Ps 68:30
and covered the c of Abiram ................ Ps 106:17
And a fire was kindled in their c .......... Ps 106:18
but he that keepeth c with ..................... Prov 29:3
to a c of horses in Pharaoh's ................. Song 1:9
As it were the c of two armies ............. Song 6:13
a great c shall return thither .................. Jer 31:8
also bring up a c against thee .............. Eze 16:40
great c make for him in the war, ......... Eze 17:17
I will bring up a c upon them .............. Eze 23:46
the c shall stone them with ................. Eze 23:47
the c of the Ashurites have made .......... Eze 27:6
in all thy c which is in the .................. Eze 27:27
all thy c in the midst of thee ............... Eze 27:34
over thee with a c of many people ......... Eze 32:3
Asshur is there and all her c ................ Eze 32:22
her c is round about her grave ............. Eze 32:23
even a great c with bucklers and .......... Eze 38:4
all thy c that are assembled unto ........... Eze 38:7
gathered thy c to take a prey ............... Eze 38:13
riding upon horses, a great c ............... Eze 38:15
so the c of priests murder in the ............. Hos 6:9
him to have been in the c ...................... Lk 2:44
there was a great c of publicans ............ Lk 5:29
the c of his disciples, and a .................... Lk 6:17
shall separate you from their c ............... Lk 6:22
them sit down by fifties in a c ................. Lk 9:14
behold, a man of the c cried out ............. Lk 9:38
of the c lifted up her voice .................. Lk 11:27
one of the c said unto him, .................... Lk 12:13
followed him a great c of people .......... Lk 23:27
also of our c made us astonished .......... Lk 24:22
saw a great c come unto him, he ............... Jn 6:5
let go, they went to their own c ............ Acts 4:23
a great c of the priests were .................. Acts 6:7
for a man that is a Jew to keep c ...... Acts 10:28
his c loosed from Paphos, they ............ Acts 13:13
their own c to Antioch with Paul ....... Acts 15:22
the baser sort, and gathered a c ......... Acts 17:5
we that were of Paul's c departed ....... Acts 21:8
I be somewhat filled with your c ........ Rom 15:24
epistle not to c with fornicators ............ 1Cor 5:9
written unto you not to keep c ............ 1Cor 5:11
have no c with him, that he may ........... 2Th 3:14
and to an innumerable c of angels ...... Heb 12:22
all the c in ships, and sailors, ........... Rev 18:17

**COMPARABLE**
c to fine gold, how are they .................... Lam 4:2

**COMPARE**
what likeness will ye c unto him ............ Is 40:18
c me, that we may be like ......................... Is 46:5
what comparison shall we c it ................. Mk 4:30
or c ourselves with some that .............. 2Cor 10:12

**COMPARED**
the heaven can be c unto the LORD .......... Ps 89:6
desire are not to be c unto her ............... Prov 3:15
be desired are not to be c to it ............... Prov 8:11
I have c thee, O my love, to a ................ Song 1:9
time are not worthy to be c with .......... Rom 8:18

**COMPARING**
c spiritual things with spiritual ............. 1Cor 2:13
c themselves among themselves, ........ 2Cor 10:12

**COMPARISON**
What have I done now in c of you ........ Judg 8:2
what was I able to do in c of you .......... Judg 8:3
your eyes in c of it as nothing .................. Hag 2:3
or with what c shall we compare ............ Mk 4:30

**COMPASS**
under the c of the altar beneath ............... Ex 27:5
grate of network under the c ................... Ex 38:4
Red sea, to c the land of Edom ............ Num 21:4
the border shall fetch a c from ............ Num 34:5
And ye shall c the city, all ye ................. Josh 6:3
ye shall c the city seven times ............... Josh 6:4
c the city, and let him that is ................. Josh 6:7
to Adar, and fetched a c to Karkaa ..... Josh 15:3
but fetch a c behind them ....................... 2Sa 5:23
cubits did c either of them about ......... 1Kin 7:15
cubits did c it round about ................... 1Kin 7:23
a round c of half a cubit high .............. 1Kin 7:35
they fetched a c of seven days' .............. 2Kin 3:9
ye shall c the king round about, .......... 2Kin 11:8
from brim to brim, round in c ................ 2Chr 4:2
cubits did c it round about .................... 2Chr 4:2
which did c it round about ..................... 2Chr 4:3
the Levites shall c the king ................. 2Chr 23:7
His archers c me round about, he ........... Job 16:13
willows of the brook c him about .......... Job 40:22
wilt thou c him as with a shield ............... Ps 5:12
of the people c thee about ......................... Ps 7:7
my deadly enemies, who c me about ....... Ps 17:9
so will I c thine altar, O LORD ................. Ps 26:6
thou shalt c me about with songs ............ Ps 32:7
the LORD, mercy shall c him about .......... Ps 32:10
of my heels shall c me about ................... Ps 49:5
the head of those that c me about ......... Ps 140:9
the righteous shall c me about .............. Ps 142:7
when he set a c upon the face of ........... Prov 8:27
and he marketh it out with the c .............. Is 44:13
that c yourselves about with ................... Is 50:11
the earth, A woman shall c a man ........ Jer 31:22
Gareb, and shall c about to Goath ......... Jer 31:39
fillet of twelve cubits did c it ................ Jer 52:21
wicked doth c about the righteous .......... Hab 1:4
for ye c sea and land to make one ....... Mt 23:15
c thee round, and keep thee in on ......... Lk 19:43
And from thence we fetched a c ......... Acts 28:13

**COMPASSED**
c the house round, both old and ............ Gen 19:4
we c mount Seir many days ..................... Deut 2:1
Ye have c this mountain long .................. Deut 2:3
So the ark of the LORD c the city ........ Josh 6:11
second day they c the city once ............ Josh 6:14
c the city after the same manner ......... Josh 6:15
day they c the city seven times ............. Josh 6:15
the border c from Baalah westward ... Josh 15:10
c the corner of the sea southward ....... Josh 18:14
c the land of Edom, and the land ....... Judg 11:18
they c him in, and laid wait for ............ Judg 16:2
for Saul and his men c David .............. 1Sa 23:26
that bare Joab's armour c about .......... 2Sa 18:15
When the waves of death c me .............. 2Sa 22:5
The sorrows of hell c me about ............ 2Sa 22:6
by night, and c the city about ............... 2Kin 6:14
an host c the city both with .................. 2Kin 6:15
the Edomites which c him about ........... 2Kin 8:21
Therefore they c about him to ............. 2Chr 18:31
smote the Edomites which c him in .... 2Chr 21:9
c about Ophel, and raised it up a ........ 2Chr 33:14
me, and hath c me with his net .............. Job 19:6
He hath c the waters with bounds, ....... Job 26:10
They have now c us in our steps ........... Ps 17:11
The sorrows of death c me ........................ Ps 18:4
The sorrows of hell c me about ................. Ps 18:5
Many bulls have c me ............................. Ps 22:12
For dogs have c me ................................ Ps 22:16
innumerable evils have c me about ........ Ps 40:12
they c me about together ........................ Ps 88:17
They c me about also with words ........... Ps 109:3
The sorrows of death c me ..................... Ps 116:3
All nations c me about .......................... Ps 118:10
They c me about ................................... Ps 118:11
yea, they c me about ............................. Ps 118:11
They c me about like bees ...................... Ps 118:12
me, and c me with gall and travel ........... Lam 3:5
and the floods c me about ...................... Jonah 2:3
The waters c me about, even to ............. Jonah 2:5
shall see Jerusalem c with armies .......... Lk 21:20
himself also is c with infirmity ................ Heb 5:2
after they were c about seven ............... Heb 11:30
Wherefore seeing we also are c ............. Heb 12:1
c the camp of the saints about, ............. Rev 20:9

**COMPASSEST**
Thou c my path and my lying down, ..... Ps 139:3

**COMPASSETH**
that is it which c the whole land ........... Gen 2:11
the same is it that c the whole .............. Gen 2:13
the border c it on the north side ......... Josh 19:14
Therefore pride c them about as a ........... Ps 73:6
Ephraim c me about with lies, and ...... Hos 11:12

**COMPASSING**
round about there were knops c it ....... 1Kin 7:24
in a cubit, c the sea round about .......... 1Kin 7:24
in a cubit, c the sea round about ........... 2Chr 4:3

**COMPASSION**
And she had c on him, and said, .............. Ex 2:6
have c upon thee, and multiply ......... Deut 13:17
have c upon thee, and will return ........ Deut 30:3
for ye have c on me .............................. 1Sa 23:21
give them c before them who ............... 1Kin 8:50
that they may have c on them ............... 1Kin 8:50
had c on them, and had respect ........... 2Kin 13:23
your children shall find c before ............ 2Chr 30:9
because he had c on his people .......... 2Chr 36:15
no c upon young man or maiden ........ 2Chr 36:17
But he, being full of c, forgave ............... Ps 78:38
thou, O Lord, art a God full of c ............ Ps 86:15
the LORD is gracious and full of c ........... Ps 111:4
he is gracious, and full of c ................... Ps 112:4
LORD is gracious, and full of c ............... Ps 145:8
not have c on the son of her womb ........ Is 49:15
have c on them, and will bring ............. Jer 12:15
yet will he have c according to ............... Lam 3:32
unto thee, to have c upon thee ............... Eze 16:5
again, he will have c upon us ................. Mic 7:19
he was moved with c on them .................. Mt 9:36
and was moved with c toward them ..... Mt 14:14
I have c on the multitude, ..................... Mt 15:32
of that servant was moved with c ......... Mt 18:27
have had c on thy fellowservant ............ Mt 18:33
So Jesus had c on them, and .................. Mt 20:34
And Jesus, moved with c, put forth ........ Mk 1:41

for thee, and hath had c on thee ........... Mk 5:19
and was moved with c toward them...... Mk 6:34
I have c on the multitude,................... Mk 8:2
thing, have c on us, and help us ........... Mk 9:22
the Lord saw her, he had c on her.......... Lk 7:13
when he saw him, he had c on him....... Lk 10:33
off, his father saw him, and had c.......... Lk 15:20
have c on whom I will have c............. Rom 9:15
Who can have c on the ignorant,........... Heb 5:2
For ye had c of me in my bonds,......... Heb 10:34
having c one of another, love as........... 1Pet 3:8
up his bowels of c from him ................ 1Jn 3:17
And of some have c, making a................. Jude 22

**COMPASSIONS**
consumed, because his c fail not.......... Lam 3:22
c every man to his brother ....................... Zec 7:9

**COMPEL**
thou shalt not c him to serve as.......... Lev 25:39
none did c ................................................ Est 1:8
whosoever shall c thee to go a................. Mt 5:41
they c one Simon a Cyrenian, who...... Mk 15:21
c them to come in, that my house......... Lk 14:23

**COMPELLED**
together with the woman, c him .......... 1Sa 28:23
fornication, and c Judah thereto ........ 2Chr 21:11
him they c to bear his cross................. Mt 27:32
synagogue, and c them to blaspheme Acts 26:11
ye have c me........................................ 2Cor 12:11
a Greek, was c to be circumcised............ Gal 2:3

**COMPELLEST**
why c thou the Gentiles to live.............. Gal 2:14

**COMPLAIN**
their brethren come unto us to c ...... Judg 21:22
I will c in the bitterness of my............... Job 7:11
the furrows likewise thereof c.............. Job 31:38
Wherefore doth a living man c.............. Lam 3:39

**COMPLAINED**
And when the people c, it..................... Num 11:1
I c, and my spirit was overwhelmed........ Ps 77:3

**COMPLAINERS**
These are murmurers, c, walking ............ Jude 16

**COMPLAINING**
that there be no c in our streets ........... Ps 144:14

**COMPLAINT**
for out of the abundance of my c.......... 1Sa 1:16
me, my couch shall ease my c................... Job 7:13
If I say, I will forget my c ..................... Job 9:27
I will leave my c upon myself................. Job 10:1
As for me, is my c to man ...................... Job 21:4
Even to day is my c bitter..................... Job 23:2
I mourn in my c, and make a noise ........ Ps 55:2
poureth out his c before the LORD .......... Ps 102:t
I poured out my c before him.................. Ps 142:2

**COMPLAINTS**
grievous c against Paul, which............. Acts 25:7

**COMPLETE**
seven sabbaths shall be c ..................... Lev 23:15
And ye are c in him, which is the.......... Col 2:10
and c in all the will of God.................... Col 4:12

**COMPOSITION**
other like it, after the c of it.................. Ex 30:32
according to the c thereof..................... Ex 30:37

**COMPOUND**
an ointment c after the art of................ Ex 30:25

**COMPOUNDETH**
Whosoever c any like it, or..................... Ex 30:33

**COMPREHEND**
doeth he, which we cannot c.................. Job 37:5
May be able to c with all saints ............ Eph 3:18

**COMPREHENDED**
c the dust of the earth in a ...................... Is 40:12
and the darkness c it not......................... Jn 1:5
it is briefly c in this saying,................... Rom 13:9

**CONANIAH** (*co-na-ni'-ah*) See CONONIAH. *A chief Levite during Josiah's time.*
C also, and Shemaiah and Nethaneel,. 2Chr 35:9

**CONCEAL**
slay our brother, and c his blood......... Gen 37:26
spare, neither shalt thou c him.............. Deut 13:8
is with the Almighty will I not c .......... Job 27:11
I will not c his parts, nor his................ Job 41:12
is the glory of God to c a thing ............ Prov 25:2
publish, and c not.................................. Jer 50:2

**CONCEALED**
for I have not c the words of the ........... Job 6:10
I have not c thy lovingkindness.............. Ps 40:10

**CONCEALETH**
of a faithful spirit c the matter........... Prov 11:13
A prudent man c knowledge ................ Prov 12:23

**CONCEIT**
and as an high wall in his own c......... Prov 18:11
lest he be wise in his own c................. Prov 26:5
thou a man wise in his own c ............... Prov 26:12
sluggard is wiser in his own c ............. Prov 26:16
The rich man is wise in his own c...... Prov 28:11

**CONCEITS**
ye should be wise in your own c ........ Rom 11:25
Be not wise in your own c ................... Rom 12:16

**CONCEIVE**
that they should c when they came ... Gen 30:38
the stronger cattle did c......................... Gen 30:41
that they might c among the rods ....... Gen 30:41
shall be free, and shall c seed................ Num 5:28
but thou shalt c, and bear a son............ Judg 13:3
For, lo, thou shalt c, and bear a............ Judg 13:5
unto me, Behold, thou shalt c................ Judg 13:7
They c mischief, and bring forth........... Job 15:35
and in sin did my mother c me ................ Ps 51:5
Behold, a virgin shall c, and bear............ Is 7:14
Ye shall c chaff, ye shall bring ................. Is 33:11
they c mischief, and bring forth............. Is 59:4
thou shalt c in thy womb, and................ Lk 1:31
received strength to c seed................... Heb 11:11

**CONCEIVED**
and she c, and bare Cain, and said,......... Gen 4:1
and she c, and bare Enoch...................... Gen 4:17
he went in unto Hagar, and she c ......... Gen 16:4
and when she saw that she had c ......... Gen 16:4
and when she saw that she had c ......... Gen 16:5
For Sarah c, and bare Abraham a .......... Gen 21:2
of him, and Rebekah his wife c............ Gen 25:21
And Leah c, and bare a son, and she.. Gen 29:32
she c again, and bare a son.................... Gen 29:33
she c again, and bare a son.................... Gen 29:34
she c again, and bare a son.................... Gen 29:35
And Bilhah c, and bare Jacob a son...... Gen 30:5
And Bilhah Rachel's maid c again......... Gen 30:7
God hearkened unto Leah, and she c. Gen 30:17
Leah c again, and bare Jacob the........ Gen 30:19
And she c, and bare a son .................... Gen 30:23
the flocks c before the rods, and ......... Gen 30:39
at the time that the cattle c................. Gen 31:10
And she c, and bare a son...................... Gen 38:3
she c again, and bare a son.................... Gen 38:4
And she yet again c, and bare a son..... Gen 38:5
came in unto her, and she c by him .... Gen 38:18
And the woman c, and bare a son ............ Ex 2:2
saying, If a woman have c seed.............. Lev 12:2
Have I c all this people......................... Num 11:12
was come about after Hannah had c..... 1Sa 1:20
visited Hannah, so that she c ................. 1Sa 2:21
And the woman c, and sent and told .... 2Sa 11:5
And the woman c, and bare a son at .. 2Kin 4:17
he went in to his wife, she c ................. 1Chr 7:23
was said, There is a man child c............. Job 3:3
hath c mischief, and brought forth ......... Ps 7:14
into the chamber of her that c me ....... Song 3:4
and she c, and bare a son ........................... Is 8:3
hath c a purpose against you ................ Jer 49:30
which c, and bare him a son .................... Hos 1:3
she c again, and bare a daughter............ Hos 1:6
she had weaned Lo-ruhamah, she c ........ Hos 1:8
she that c them hath done .................... Hos 2:5
for that which is c in her is of.................. Mt 1:20
those days his wife Elisabeth c................ Lk 1:24
she hath also c a son in her old............... Lk 1:36
angel before he was c in the womb......... Lk 2:21
why hast thou c this thing in ................. Acts 5:4
when Rebecca also had c by one.......... Rom 9:10
Then when lust hath c, it....................... Jas 1:15

**CONCEIVING**
speaking oppression and revolt, c.......... Is 59:13

**CONCEPTION**
multiply thy sorrow and thy c ............... Gen 3:16
in unto her, the LORD gave her c.......... Ruth 4:13
and from the womb, and from the c..... Hos 9:11

**CONCERN**
which c the Lord Jesus Christ............ Acts 28:31
things which c mine infirmities .......... 2Cor 11:30

**CONCERNETH**
LORD will perfect that which c me......... Ps 138:8
This burden c the prince in.................. Eze 12:10

**CONCERNING**
same shall comfort us c our work......... Gen 5:29
Pharaoh commanded his men c him... Gen 12:20
accepted thee c this thing also............. Gen 19:21
and sware to him c that matter ............. Gen 24:9
told him c the well which they ........... Gen 26:32
are verily guilty c our brother............. Gen 42:21
c the which I did swear to give............... Ex 6:8
made with you c all these words............ Ex 24:8
c things which ought not to be ................ Lev 4:2
c things which should not be done........ Lev 4:13
of the LORD his God c things................... Lev 4:22
an atonement for him as c his sin.......... Lev 4:26
c things which ought not to be .............. Lev 4:27
an atonement for him c his sin................ Lev 5:6
c his ignorance wherein he erred.......... Lev 5:18
which was lost, and lieth c it .................. Lev 6:3
for ever in your generations c............... Lev 6:18
C the feasts of the LORD, which ............ Lev 23:2
c the tithe of the herd, or of................ Lev 27:32
commanded Moses c the Levites........... Num 8:20
had commanded Moses c the Levites . Num 8:22
what the LORD will command c you ..... Num 9:8
LORD hath spoken good c Israel.......... Num 10:29
c which I sware to make you dwell .. Num 14:30
tribes c the children of Israel.............. Num 30:1
out of her lips c her vows .................... Num 30:12
or c the bond of her soul, shall.......... Num 30:12
c them Moses commanded .................. Num 32:28
c the daughters of Zelophehad.............. Num 36:6
unto Moses the man of God c me ........ Josh 14:6
the LORD your God spake c you ......... Josh 23:14
And Samson said c them, Now shall... Judg 15:3
c him that came not up to the............. Judg 21:5
former time in Israel c redeeming ......... Ruth 4:7
c changing, for to confirm all ................ Ruth 4:7
which I have spoken c his house ........... 1Sa 3:12
good that he hath spoken c thee.......... 1Sa 25:30
to day with a fault c this woman ............ 2Sa 3:8
thou hast spoken c thy servant ............. 2Sa 7:25
c his house, establish it for.................... 2Sa 7:25
David all the things c the war............... 2Sa 11:18
for he was comforted c Amnon ............ 2Sa 13:39
and I will give charge c thee .................. 2Sa 14:8
all the captains charge c Absalom.......... 2Sa 18:5
his word which he spake c me............... 1Kin 2:4
which he spake c the house of Eli ....... 1Kin 2:27
all thy desire c timber of cedar ............... 1Kin 5:8
and c timber of fir .................................. 1Kin 5:8
C this house which thou art in ............ 1Kin 6:12
Moreover c a stranger, that is.............. 1Kin 8:41
of Solomon c the name of the LORD.... 1Kin 10:1
Of the nations c which the LORD.......... 1Kin 11:2
had commanded him c this.................. 1Kin 11:10
he doth not prophesy good c me.......... 1Kin 22:8
he would prophesy no good c me......... 1Kin 22:18
the LORD hath spoken evil c thee........ 1Kin 22:23
LORD spake c the house of Ahab....... 2Kin 10:10
c whom the LORD had charged.......... 2Kin 17:15
that the LORD hath spoken c him....... 2Kin 19:21
the LORD c the king of Assyria .......... 2Kin 19:32
c the words of this book that is.......... 2Kin 22:13
all that which is written c us.............. 2Kin 22:13
to the word of the LORD c Israel ........ 1Chr 11:10
thou hast spoken c thy servant........... 1Chr 17:23
c his house be established for ............ 1Chr 17:23
to comfort him c his father .................. 1Chr 19:2
and give thee charge c Israel............... 1Chr 22:12
LORD charged Moses with c Israel..... 1Chr 22:13
Now c Moses the man of God, his..... 1Chr 23:14
C Rehabiah ........................................ 1Chr 24:21
C Kish .................................................. 1Chr 24:29
C the divisions of the porters ............... 1Chr 26:1
As c the sons of Laadan ..................... 1Chr 26:21
Moreover c the stranger, which is ....... 2Chr 6:32
c any matter, or c the treasures ........... 2Chr 8:15
and of Iddo the seer c genealogies .... 2Chr 12:15
also c Maachah the mother of Asa.... 2Chr 15:16
Now c his sons, and the greatness..... 2Chr 24:27
c the children of Israel and Judah ...... 2Chr 31:6
and the Levites c the heaps................... 2Chr 31:9
c the words of the book that is .......... 2Chr 34:21
saith the LORD God of Israel c............ 2Chr 34:26
answer by letter c this matter ................. Ezr 5:5
his pleasure to us c this matter ............. Ezr 5:17
Cyrus the king made a decree c.............. Ezr 6:3
counsellors, to enquire c Judah............... Ezr 7:14
is hope in Israel c this thing .................. Ezr 10:2
I asked them c the Jews that had........... Neh 1:2
of the captivity, and c Jerusalem............. Neh 1:2
c which thou hadst promised to ............ Neh 9:23
was the king's commandment c them Neh 11:23
hand in all matters c the people ........... Neh 11:24
c this, and wipe not out my good.......... Neh 13:14
my God, c this also, and spare me ...... Neh 13:22
the king had so commanded c him.......... Est 3:2
which they had seen c this matter.......... Est 9:26
The noise thereof sheweth c it.............. Job 36:33
it, the cattle also c the vapour .............. Job 36:33
c the words of Cush the Benjamite ............ Ps 7:t
C the words of men, by the word............ Ps 17:4
and speak wickedly c oppression.............. Ps 73:8
let it repent thee c thy servants.............. Ps 90:13
c whom the LORD commanded them ... Ps 106:34
precepts c all things to be right ........... Ps 119:128
C thy testimonies, I have known ........ Ps 119:152
repent himself c his servants ................ Ps 135:14
search out by wisdom c all things.......... Eccl 1:13
I said in mine heart c the estate............ Eccl 3:18
dost not enquire wisely c this ............... Eccl 7:10
son of Amoz, which he saw c Judah .......... Is 1:1
the son of Amoz saw c Judah ..................... Is 2:1
man's pen c Maher-shalal-hash-baz ............ Is 8:1
spoken c Moab since that time ................ Is 16:13
As at the report c Egypt, so...................... Is 23:5
c the house of Jacob, Jacob shall ............ Is 29:22
therefore have I cried c this..................... Is 30:7
he heard say c Tirhakah king of................. Is 37:9
which the LORD hath spoken c him .......... Is 37:22
the LORD c the king of Assyria ................ Is 37:33
me of things to come c my sons.............. Is 45:11
c the work of my hands command ye.... Is 45:11
c burnt offerings or sacrifices.................. Jer 7:22
came to Jeremiah c the dearth................ Jer 14:1
c the prophets that prophesy in ............. Jer 14:15
thus saith the LORD c the sons............... Jer 16:3
c the daughters that are born in............. Jer 16:3
c their mothers that bare them,.............. Jer 16:3
c their fathers that begat them................ Jer 16:3
instant I shall speak c a nation............... Jer 18:7
c a kingdom, to pluck up, and to ............ Jer 18:7
instant I shall speak c a nation............... Jer 18:9
c a kingdom, to build and to plant.......... Jer 18:9
c Jehoiakim the son of Josiah ............... Jer 22:18
the LORD of hosts c the prophets............ Jer 23:15
c all the people of Judah in the................ Jer 25:1
the LORD of hosts c the pillars .............. Jer 27:19
c the sea, and c the bases ....................... Jer 27:19
c the residue of the vessels that ............ Jer 27:19
c the vessels that remain in the............. Jer 27:21

Thus saith the LORD c Shemaiah ... Jer 29:31
c Israel and c Judah ... Jer 30:4
c this city, whereof ye say, It ... Jer 32:36
c the houses of this city, and ... Jer 33:4
c the houses of the kings of ... Jer 33:4
king of Babylon gave charge c ... Jer 39:11
The LORD hath said c you, O ye ... Jer 42:19
The word that came to Jeremiah c ... Jer 44:1
C The Ammonites, thus saith the ... Jer 49:1
C Edom, thus saith the LORD of ... Jer 49:7
C Damascus ... Jer 49:23
C Kedar, and c the kingdoms ... Jer 49:28
c the pillars, the height of one ... Jer 52:21
the LORD hath commanded c Jacob ... Lam 1:17
Israel which prophesy c Jerusalem ... Eze 13:16
a prophet to enquire of him c me ... Eze 14:7
ye shall be comforted c the evil ... Eze 14:22
even c all that I have brought ... Eze 14:22
this proverb c the land of Israel ... Eze 18:2
the Lord GOD c the Ammonites ... Eze 21:28
and c their reproach ... Eze 21:28
therefore c the land of Israel ... Eze 36:6
ears all that I say unto thee c ... Eze 44:5
C the ordinance of oil, the bath ... Eze 45:14
c the which I lifted up mine hand ... Eze 47:14
the God of heaven c this secret ... Dan 2:18
and made a proclamation c him ... Dan 5:29
against Daniel c the kingdom ... Dan 6:4
against him c the law of his God ... Dan 6:5
the king c the king's decree ... Dan 6:12
might not be changed c Daniel ... Dan 6:17
As c the rest of the beasts, they ... Dan 7:12
the vision c the daily sacrifice ... Dan 8:13
which he saw c Israel in the days ... Amos 1:1
Thus saith the Lord GOD c Edom ... Obad 1
of Judah, which he saw c Samaria ... Mic 1:1
Thus saith the LORD c the ... Mic 3:5
hath given a commandment c thee ... Nah 1:14
Ask now the priests c the law ... Hag 2:11
give his angels charge c thee ... Mt 4:6
to say unto the multitudes c John ... Mt 11:7
I spake it not to you c bread ... Mt 16:11
the devil, and also c the swine ... Mk 5:16
disciples asked him c the parable ... Mk 7:17
which was told them c this child ... Lk 2:17
to speak unto the people c John ... Lk 7:24
c the Son of man shall be ... Lk 18:31
for the things c me have an end ... Lk 22:37
C Jesus of Nazareth, which was a ... Lk 24:19
scriptures the things c himself ... Lk 24:27
prophets, and in the psalms, c me ... Lk 24:44
murmuring among the people c him ... Jn 7:12
people murmured such things c him ... Jn 7:32
the Jews did not believe c him ... Jn 9:18
to comfort them c their brother ... Jn 11:19
of David spake before c Judas ... Acts 1:16
For David speaketh c him, I ... Acts 2:25
the things c the kingdom of God ... Acts 8:12
as c that he raised him up from ... Acts 13:34
the things c the kingdom of God ... Acts 19:8
enquire any thing c other matters ... Acts 19:39
whereof they were informed c thee ... Acts 21:24
not receive thy testimony c me ... Acts 22:18
something more perfectly c him ... Acts 23:15
heard him c the faith in Christ ... Acts 24:24
c the crime laid against him ... Acts 25:16
letters out of Judaea c thee ... Acts 28:21
for as c this sect, we know that ... Acts 28:22
of God, persuading them c Jesus ... Acts 28:23
C his Son Jesus Christ our Lord, ... Rom 1:3
of whom as c the flesh Christ ... Rom 9:5
Esaias also crieth c Israel ... Rom 9:27
As c the gospel, they are enemies ... Rom 11:28
which is good, and simple c evil ... Rom 16:19
c him that hath so done this deed ... 1Cor 5:3
Now c the things whereof ye wrote ... 1Cor 7:1
Now c virgins I have no ... 1Cor 7:25
As c therefore the eating of ... 1Cor 8:4
Now c spiritual gifts, brethren, ... 1Cor 12:1
Now c the collection for the ... 1Cor 16:1
my partner and fellowhelper c you ... 2Cor 8:23
I speak as c reproach, as though ... 2Cor 11:21
That ye put off c the former ... Eph 4:22
but I speak c Christ and the ... Eph 5:32
C zeal, persecuting the church ... Phil 3:6
communicated with me as c giving ... Phil 4:15
and to comfort you c your faith ... 1Th 3:2
c them which are asleep, that ye ... 1Th 4:13
will of God in Christ Jesus c you ... 1Th 5:18
away c faith have made shipwreck ... 1Ti 1:19
professing have erred c the faith ... 1Ti 6:21
Who c the truth have erred, ... 2Ti 2:18
minds, reprobate c the faith ... 2Ti 3:8
Moses spake nothing c priesthood ... Heb 7:14
Jacob and Esau c things to come ... Heb 11:20
and gave commandment c his bones ... Heb 11:22
think it not strange c the fiery ... 1Pet 4:12
Lord is not slack c his promise ... 2Pet 3:9
unto you c them that seduce you ... 1Jn 2:26

### CONCISION
of evil workers, beware of the c ... Phil 3:2

### CONCLUDE
Therefore we c that a man is ... Rom 3:28

### CONCLUDED
c that they observe no such thing ... Acts 21:25
For God hath c them all in ... Rom 11:32
scripture hath c all under sin ... Gal 3:22

### CONCLUSION
Let us hear the c of the whole ... Eccl 12:13

### CONCORD
what c hath Christ with Belial ... 2Cor 6:15

### CONCOURSE
crieth in the chief place of c ... Prov 1:21
we may give an account of this c ... Acts 19:40

### CONCUBINE
And his c, whose name was Reumah, ... Gen 22:24
and lay with Bilhah his father's c ... Gen 35:22
Timna was c to Eliphaz Esau's son ... Gen 36:12
his c that was in Shechem, she ... Judg 8:31
who took to him a c out of ... Judg 19:1
his c played the whore against ... Judg 19:2
rose up to depart, he, and his c ... Judg 19:9
saddled, his c also was with him ... Judg 19:10
is my daughter a maiden, and his c ... Judg 19:24
so the man took his c, and brought ... Judg 19:25
the woman his c was fallen down ... Judg 19:27
a knife, and laid hold on his c ... Judg 19:29
belongeth to Benjamin, I and my c ... Judg 20:4
my c have they forced, that she ... Judg 20:5
And I took my c, and cut her in ... Judg 20:6
And Saul had a c, whose name was ... 2Sa 3:7
thou gone in unto my father's c ... 2Sa 3:7
of Aiah, the c of Saul, had done ... 2Sa 21:11
the sons of Keturah, Abraham's c ... 1Chr 1:32
And Ephah, Caleb's c, bare Haran, ... 1Chr 2:46
Maachah, Caleb's c, bare Sheber, ... 1Chr 2:48
(but his c the Aramitess bare ... 1Chr 7:14

### CONCUBINES
But unto the sons of the c ... Gen 25:6
And David took him more c and wives ... 2Sa 5:13
king left ten women, which were c ... 2Sa 15:16
Go in unto thy father's c ... 2Sa 16:21
went in unto his father's c in ... 2Sa 16:22
thy wives, and the lives of thy c ... 2Sa 19:5
the king took the ten women his c ... 2Sa 20:3
princesses, and three hundred c ... 1Kin 11:3
David, beside the sons of the c ... 1Chr 3:9
above all his wives and his c ... 2Chr 11:21
eighteen wives, and threescore c ... 2Chr 11:21
chamberlain, which kept the c ... Est 2:14
threescore queens, and fourscore c ... Song 6:8
yea, the queens and the c, and they ... Song 6:9
his princes, his wives, and his c ... Dan 5:2
his princes, his wives, and his c ... Dan 5:3
and thy lords, thy wives, and thy c ... Dan 5:23

### CONCUPISCENCE
wrought in me all manner of c ... Rom 7:8
inordinate affection, evil c ... Col 3:5
Not in the lust of c, even as the ... 1Th 4:5

### CONDEMN
and whom the judges shall c ... Ex 22:9
the righteous, and c the wicked ... Deut 25:1
myself, mine own mouth shall c me ... Job 9:20
I will say unto God, Do not c me ... Job 10:2
wilt thou c him that is most just ... Job 34:17
wilt thou c me, that thou mayest ... Job 40:8
nor c him when he is judged ... Ps 37:33
and c the innocent blood ... Ps 94:21
him from those that c his soul ... Ps 109:31
a man of wicked devices will he c ... Prov 12:2
who is he that shall c me ... Is 50:9
thee in judgment thou shalt c ... Is 54:17
this generation, and shall c it ... Mt 12:41
this generation, and shall c it ... Mt 12:42
they shall c him to death, ... Mt 20:18
they shall c him to death, and ... Mk 10:33
c not, and ye shall not be ... Lk 6:37
men of this generation, and c them ... Lk 11:31
this generation, and shall c it ... Lk 11:32
Son into the world to c the world ... Jn 3:17
unto her, Neither do I c thee ... Jn 8:11
I speak not this to c you ... 2Cor 7:3
For if our heart c us, God is ... 1Jn 3:20
Beloved, if our heart c us not ... 1Jn 3:21

### CONDEMNATION
seeing thou art in the same c ... Lk 23:40
And this is the c, that light is ... Jn 3:19
life, and shall not come into c ... Jn 5:24
for the judgment was by one to c ... Rom 5:16
judgment came upon all men to c ... Rom 5:18
There is therefore now no c to ... Rom 8:1
that ye come not together unto c ... 1Cor 11:34
if the ministration of c be glory ... 2Cor 3:9
he fall into the c of the devil ... 1Ti 3:6
we shall receive the greater c ... Jas 3:1
lest ye fall into c ... Jas 5:12
before of old ordained to this c ... Jude 4

### CONDEMNED
c the land in an hundred talents ... 2Chr 36:3
found no answer, and yet had c Job ... Job 32:3
he shall be judged, let him be c ... Ps 109:7
the c in the house of their god ... Amos 2:8
ye would not have c the guiltless ... Mt 12:7
and by thy words thou shalt be c ... Mt 12:37
him, when he saw that he was c ... Mt 27:3
they all c him to be guilty of ... Mk 14:64
condemn not, and ye shall not be c ... Lk 6:37
delivered him to be c to death ... Lk 24:20
He that believeth on him is not c ... Jn 3:18
that believeth not is c already ... Jn 3:18
hath no man c thee ... Jn 8:10
and for sin, c sin in the flesh ... Rom 8:3
we should not be c with the world ... 1Cor 11:32
Sound speech, that cannot be c ... Titus 2:8
and sinneth, being c of himself ... Titus 3:11
by the which he c the world ... Heb 11:7
Ye have c and killed the just ... Jas 5:6
another, brethren, lest ye be c ... Jas 5:9
Gomorrah into ashes c them with ... 2Pet 2:6

### CONDEMNEST
judgest another, thou c thyself ... Rom 2:1

### CONDEMNETH
Thine own mouth c thee, and not I ... Job 15:6
he that c the just, even they ... Prov 17:15
Who is he that c ... Rom 8:34
Happy is he that c not himself in ... Rom 14:22

### CONDEMNING
c the wicked, to bring his way ... 1Kin 8:32
they have fulfilled them in c him ... Acts 13:27

### CONDESCEND
but c to men of low estate ... Rom 12:16

### CONDITION
On this c will I make a covenant ... 1Sa 11:2

### CONDITIONS
ambassage, and desireth c of peace ... Lk 14:32

### CONDUCT
to c the king over Jordan ... 2Sa 19:15
the king, to c him over Jordan ... 2Sa 19:31
but c him forth in peace, that he ... 1Cor 16:11

### CONDUCTED
the people of Judah c the king ... 2Sa 19:40
they that c Paul brought him unto ... Acts 17:15

### CONDUIT
stood by the c of the upper pool, ... 2Kin 18:17
and how he made a pool, and a c ... 2Kin 20:20
at the end of the c of the upper ... Is 7:3
he stood by the c of the upper ... Is 36:2

### CONEY
And the c, because he cheweth the ... Lev 11:5
the camel, and the hare, and the c ... Deut 14:7

### CONFECTION
perfume, a c after the art of the ... Ex 30:35

### CONFECTIONARIES
will take your daughters to be c ... 1Sa 8:13

### CONFEDERACY
Say ye not, A c, to all them to ... Is 8:12
whom this people shall say, A c ... Is 8:12
All the men of thy c have brought ... Obad 7

### CONFEDERATE
and these were c with Abram ... Gen 14:13
they are c against thee ... Ps 83:5
saying, Syria is c with Ephraim ... Is 7:2

### CONFERENCE
somewhat in c added nothing to me ... Gal 2:6

### CONFERRED
he c with Joab the son of Zeruiah ... 1Kin 1:7
council, they c among themselves, ... Acts 4:15
when he had c with the council, ... Acts 25:12
immediately I c not with flesh and ... Gal 1:16

### CONFESS
that he shall c that he hath ... Lev 5:5
c over him all the iniquities of ... Lev 16:21
If they shall c their iniquity, ... Lev 26:40
Then they shall c their sin which ... Num 5:7
c thy name, and pray, and make ... 1Kin 8:33
c thy name, and turn from their ... 1Kin 8:35
c thy name, and pray and make ... 2Chr 6:24
c thy name, and turn from their ... 2Chr 6:26
c the sins of the children of ... Neh 1:6
Then will I also c unto thee that ... Job 40:14
I will c my transgressions unto ... Ps 32:5
therefore shall c me before men ... Mt 10:32
him will I c also before my ... Mt 10:32
Whosoever shall c me before men ... Lk 12:8
also c before the angels of God ... Lk 12:8
any man did c that he was Christ ... Jn 9:22
the Pharisees they did not c him ... Jn 12:42
but the Pharisees c both ... Acts 23:8
But this I c unto thee, that ... Acts 24:14
That if thou shalt c with thy ... Rom 10:9
and every tongue shall c to God ... Rom 14:11
For this cause I will c to thee ... Rom 15:9
that every tongue should c that ... Phil 2:11
C your faults one to another, and ... Jas 5:16
If we c our sins, he is faithful ... 1Jn 1:9
Whosoever shall c that Jesus is ... 1Jn 4:15
who c not that Jesus Christ is ... 2Jn 7
but I will c his name before my ... Rev 3:5

### CONFESSED
Ezra had prayed, and when he had c ... Ezr 10:1
c their sins, and the iniquities ... Neh 9:2
and another fourth part they c ... Neh 9:3
And he c, and denied not ... Jn 1:20
but c, I am not the Christ ... Jn 1:20
And many that believed came, and c. ... Acts 19:18
c that they were strangers and ... Heb 11:13

### CONFESSETH
but whoso c and forsaketh them ... Prov 28:13
Every spirit that c that Jesus ... 1Jn 4:2
every spirit that c not that ... 1Jn 4:3

**CONFESSING**
- c my sin and the sin of my people ... Dan 9:20
- of him in Jordan, c their sins ... Mt 3:6
- the river of Jordan, c their sins ... Mk 1:5

**CONFESSION**
- God of Israel, and make c unto him ... Josh 7:19
- making c to the LORD God of their ... 2Chr 30:22
- Now therefore make c unto the ... Ezr 10:11
- the LORD my God, and made my c ... Dan 9:4
- with the mouth c is made unto ... Rom 10:10
- Pontius Pilate witnessed a good c ... 1Ti 6:13

**CONFIDENCE**
- men of Shechem put their c in him ... Judg 9:26
- What c is this wherein thou ... 2Kin 18:19
- Is not this thy fear, thy c ... Job 4:6
- His c shall be rooted out of his ... Job 18:14
- to the fine gold, Thou art my c ... Job 31:24
- who art the c of all the ends of ... Ps 65:5
- in the LORD than to put c in man ... Ps 118:8
- the LORD than to put c in princes ... Ps 118:9
- For the LORD shall be thy c ... Prov 3:26
- the fear of the LORD is strong c ... Prov 14:26
- the strength of the c thereof ... Prov 21:22
- C in an unfaithful man in time of ... Prov 25:19
- in c shall be your strength ... Is 30:15
- What c is this wherein thou ... Is 36:4
- was ashamed of Beth-el their c ... Jer 48:13
- yea, they shall dwell with c ... Eze 28:26
- more the c of the house of Israel ... Eze 29:16
- a friend, put ye not c in a guide ... Mic 7:5
- the Lord Jesus Christ, with all c ... Acts 28:31
- in this c I was minded to come ... 2Cor 1:15
- having c in you all, that my joy ... 2Cor 2:3
- I have c in you in all things ... 2Cor 7:16
- upon the great c which I have in ... 2Cor 8:22
- when I am present with that c ... 2Cor 10:2
- foolishly, in this c of boasting ... 2Cor 11:17
- I have c in you through the Lord, ... Gal 5:10
- access with c by the faith of him ... Eph 3:12
- And having this c, I know that I ... Phil 1:25
- Jesus, and have no c in the flesh ... Phil 3:3
- I might also have c in the flesh ... Phil 3:4
- we have c in the Lord touching ... 2Th 3:4
- Having c in thy obedience I wrote ... Philem 21
- are we, if we hold fast the c ... Heb 3:6
- of our c stedfast unto the end ... Heb 3:14
- Cast not away therefore your c ... Heb 10:35
- he shall appear, we may have c ... 1Jn 2:28
- us not, then have we c toward God ... 1Jn 3:21
- this is the c that we have in him ... 1Jn 5:14

**CONFIDENCES**
- for the LORD hath rejected thy c ... Jer 2:37

**CONFIDENT**
- against me, in this will I be c ... Ps 27:3
- but the fool rageth, and is c ... Prov 14:16
- art c that thou thyself art a ... Rom 2:19
- Therefore we are always c ... 2Cor 5:6
- We are c, I say, and willing ... 2Cor 5:8
- ashamed in this same c boasting ... 2Cor 9:4
- Being c of this very thing, that ... Phil 1:6
- waxing c by my bonds, are much ... Phil 1:14

**CONFIDENTLY**
- one hour after another c affirmed ... Lk 22:59

**CONFIRM**
- changing, for to c all things ... Ruth 4:7
- in after thee, and c thy words ... 1Kin 1:14
- him to c the kingdom in his hand ... 2Kin 15:19
- to c this second letter of Purim ... Est 9:29
- To c these days of Purim in their ... Est 9:31
- thou didst c thine inheritance ... Ps 68:9
- weak hands, and c the feeble knees ... Is 35:3
- hope that they would c the word ... Eze 13:6
- he shall c the covenant with many ... Dan 9:27
- the Mede, even I, stood to c ... Dan 11:1
- to c the promises made unto the ... Rom 15:8
- Who shall also c you unto the end ... 1Cor 1:8
- ye would c your love toward him ... 2Cor 2:8

**CONFIRMATION**
- an oath for c is to them an end ... Heb 6:16

**CONFIRMED**
- For thou hast c to thyself thy ... 2Sa 7:24
- as the kingdom was c in his hand ... 2Kin 14:5
- LORD had c him king over Israel ... 1Chr 14:2
- hath c the same to Jacob for a ... 1Chr 16:17
- the decree of Esther c these ... Est 9:32
- c the same unto Jacob for a law, ... Ps 105:10
- he hath c his words, which he ... Dan 9:12
- with many words, and c them ... Acts 15:32
- testimony of Christ was c in you ... 1Cor 1:6
- a man's covenant, yet if it be c ... Gal 3:15
- that was c before of God in ... Gal 3:17
- was c unto us by them that heard ... Heb 2:3
- of his counsel, c it by an oath ... Heb 6:17

**CONFIRMETH**
- he c them, because he held his ... Num 30:14
- Cursed be he that c not all the ... Deut 27:26
- That c the word of his servant, ... Is 44:26

**CONFIRMING**
- c the word with signs following ... Mk 16:20
- C the souls of the disciples, and ... Acts 14:22
- Syria and Cilicia, c the churches ... Acts 15:41

**CONFISCATION**
- or to c of goods, or to ... Ezr 7:26

**CONFLICT**
- Having the same c which ye saw in ... Phil 1:30
- knew what great c I have for you ... Col 2:1

**CONFORMABLE**
- being made c unto his death ... Phil 3:10

**CONFORMED**
- to be c to the image of his Son ... Rom 8:29
- And be not c to this world ... Rom 12:2

**CONFOUND**
- there c their language, that they ... Gen 11:7
- because the LORD did there c the ... Gen 11:9
- lest I c thee before them ... Jer 1:17
- things of the world to c the wise ... 1Cor 1:27
- to c the things which are mighty ... 1Cor 1:27

**CONFOUNDED**
- power, they were dismayed and c ... 2Kin 19:26
- They were c because they had ... Job 6:20
- trusted in thee, and were not c ... Ps 22:5
- Let them be c and put to shame ... Ps 35:4
- c together that seek after my ... Ps 40:14
- that seek thee be c for my sake ... Ps 69:6
- c that seek after my soul ... Ps 70:2
- Let them be c and consumed that ... Ps 71:13
- for they are c, for they are ... Ps 71:24
- Let them be c and troubled for ... Ps 83:17
- C be all they that serve graven ... Ps 97:7
- Let them all be c and turned back ... Ps 129:5
- ye shall be c for the gardens ... Is 1:29
- that weave networks, shall be c ... Is 19:9
- Then the moon shall be c, and the ... Is 24:23
- power, they were dismayed and c ... Is 37:27
- thee shall be ashamed and c ... Is 41:11
- They shall be ashamed, and also c ... Is 45:16
- ashamed nor c world without end ... Is 45:17
- therefore shall I not be c ... Is 50:7
- neither be thou c ... Is 54:4
- we are greatly c, because we have ... Jer 9:19
- every founder is c by the graven ... Jer 10:14
- they were ashamed and c, and ... Jer 14:3
- she hath been ashamed and c ... Jer 15:9
- Let them be c that persecute me, ... Jer 17:18
- but let not me be c ... Jer 17:18
- and c for all thy wickedness ... Jer 22:22
- I was ashamed, yea, even c ... Jer 31:19
- The daughter of Egypt shall be c ... Jer 46:24
- Kiriathaim is c and taken ... Jer 48:1
- Misgab is c and dismayed ... Jer 48:1
- Moab is c ... Jer 48:20
- Hamath is c, and Arpad ... Jer 49:23
- say, Babylon is taken, Bel is c ... Jer 50:2
- her idols are c, her images are ... Jer 50:2
- Your mother shall be sore c ... Jer 50:12
- every founder is c by the graven ... Jer 51:17
- and her whole land shall be c ... Jer 51:47
- We are c, because we have heard ... Jer 51:51
- yea, be thou c also, and bear thy ... Eze 16:52
- mayest be c in all that thou hast ... Eze 16:54
- thou mayest remember, and be c ... Eze 16:63
- c for your own ways, O house of ... Eze 36:32
- be ashamed, and the diviners c ... Mic 3:7
- see and be c at all their might ... Mic 7:16
- the riders on horses shall be c ... Zec 10:5
- came together, and were c, because ... Acts 2:6
- c the Jews which dwelt at ... Acts 9:22
- believeth on him shall not be c ... 1Pet 2:6

**CONFUSED**
- of the warrior is with c noise ... Is 9:5
- for the assembly was c ... Acts 19:32

**CONFUSION**
- it is c ... Lev 18:23
- they have wrought c ... Lev 20:12
- the son of Jesse to thine own c ... 1Sa 20:30
- unto the c of thy mother's ... 1Sa 20:30
- to c of face, as it is this day ... Ezr 9:7
- I am full of c ... Job 10:15
- brought to c that devise my hurt ... Ps 35:4
- brought to c together that ... Ps 35:26
- My c is continually before me, and ... Ps 44:15
- be turned backward, and put to c ... Ps 70:2
- let me never be put to c ... Ps 71:1
- cover themselves with their own c ... Ps 109:29
- The city of c is broken down ... Is 24:10
- in the shadow of Egypt your c ... Is 30:3
- stretch out upon it the line of c ... Is 34:11
- their molten images are wind and c ... Is 41:29
- they shall go to c together that ... Is 45:16
- for c they shall rejoice in their ... Is 61:7
- our shame, and our c covereth us ... Jer 3:25
- to the c of their own faces ... Jer 7:19
- their everlasting c shall never ... Jer 20:11
- unto thee, but unto us c of faces ... Dan 9:7
- O Lord, to us belongeth c of face ... Dan 9:8
- the whole city was filled with c ... Acts 19:29
- For God is not the author of c ... 1Cor 14:33
- envying and strife is, there is c ... Jas 3:16

**CONGEALED**
- the depths were c in the heart of ... Ex 15:8

**CONGRATULATE**
- to c him, because he had fought ... 1Chr 18:10

**CONGREGATION**
- Speak ye unto all the c of Israel ... Ex 12:3
- the whole assembly of the c of ... Ex 12:6
- be cut off from the c of Israel ... Ex 12:19
- All the c of Israel shall keep it ... Ex 12:47
- all the c of the children of ... Ex 16:1
- the whole c of the children of ... Ex 16:2
- Say unto all the c of the ... Ex 16:9
- whole c of the children of Israel ... Ex 16:10
- and all the rulers of the c came ... Ex 16:22
- all the c of the children of ... Ex 17:1
- of the c without the vail ... Ex 27:21
- in unto the tabernacle of the c ... Ex 28:43
- door of the tabernacle of the c ... Ex 29:4
- before the tabernacle of the c ... Ex 29:10
- door of the tabernacle of the c ... Ex 29:11
- into the tabernacle of the c to ... Ex 29:30
- door of the tabernacle of the c ... Ex 29:32
- of the c before the LORD ... Ex 29:42
- sanctify the tabernacle of the c ... Ex 29:44
- of the tabernacle of the c ... Ex 30:16
- between the tabernacle of the c ... Ex 30:18
- go into the tabernacle of the c ... Ex 30:20
- the tabernacle of the c therewith ... Ex 30:26
- in the tabernacle of the c ... Ex 30:36
- The tabernacle of the c, and the ... Ex 31:7
- called it the Tabernacle of the c ... Ex 33:7
- out unto the tabernacle of the c ... Ex 33:7
- rulers of the c returned unto him ... Ex 34:31
- Moses gathered all the c of the ... Ex 35:1
- Moses spake unto all the c of the ... Ex 35:4
- all the c of the children of ... Ex 35:20
- work of the tabernacle of the c ... Ex 35:21
- door of the tabernacle of the c ... Ex 38:8
- of the c was an hundred talents ... Ex 38:25
- door of the tabernacle of the c ... Ex 38:30
- of the tent of the c finished ... Ex 39:32
- tabernacle, for the tent of the c ... Ex 39:40
- tabernacle of the tent of the c ... Ex 40:2
- tabernacle of the tent of the c ... Ex 40:6
- laver between the tent of the c ... Ex 40:7
- door of the tabernacle of the c ... Ex 40:12
- the table in the tent of the c ... Ex 40:22
- candlestick in the tent of the c ... Ex 40:24
- the tent of the c before the vail ... Ex 40:26
- tabernacle of the tent of the c ... Ex 40:29
- laver between the tent of the c ... Ex 40:30
- they went into the tent of the c ... Ex 40:32
- a cloud covered the tent of the c ... Ex 40:34
- to enter into the tent of the c ... Ex 40:35
- out of the tabernacle of the c ... Lev 1:1
- of the c before the LORD ... Lev 1:3
- door of the tabernacle of the c ... Lev 1:5
- door of the tabernacle of the c ... Lev 3:2
- it before the tabernacle of the c ... Lev 3:8
- it before the tabernacle of the c ... Lev 3:13
- of the c before the LORD ... Lev 4:4
- it to the tabernacle of the c ... Lev 4:5
- is in the tabernacle of the c ... Lev 4:7
- door of the tabernacle of the c ... Lev 4:7
- if the whole c of Israel sin ... Lev 4:13
- then the c shall offer a young ... Lev 4:14
- before the tabernacle of the c ... Lev 4:14
- the elders of the c shall lay ... Lev 4:15
- blood to the tabernacle of the c ... Lev 4:16
- is in the tabernacle of the c ... Lev 4:18
- door of the tabernacle of the c ... Lev 4:18
- it is a sin offering for the c ... Lev 4:21
- of the c they shall eat it ... Lev 6:16
- court of the tabernacle of the c ... Lev 6:26
- into the tabernacle of the c to ... Lev 6:30
- gather thou all the c together ... Lev 8:3
- door of the tabernacle of the c ... Lev 8:3
- door of the tabernacle of the c ... Lev 8:4
- And Moses said unto the c, This is ... Lev 8:5
- door of the tabernacle of the c ... Lev 8:31
- tabernacle of the c in seven days ... Lev 8:33
- of the tabernacle of the c day ... Lev 8:35
- before the tabernacle of the c ... Lev 9:5
- all the c drew near and stood ... Lev 9:5
- went into the tabernacle of the c ... Lev 9:23
- door of the tabernacle of the c ... Lev 10:7
- go into the tabernacle of the c ... Lev 10:9
- you to bear the iniquity of the c ... Lev 10:17
- door of the tabernacle of the c ... Lev 12:6
- door of the tabernacle of the c ... Lev 14:11
- door of the tabernacle of the c ... Lev 14:23
- door of the tabernacle of the c ... Lev 15:14
- door of the tabernacle of the c ... Lev 15:29
- he shall take of the c of the ... Lev 16:5
- door of the tabernacle of the c ... Lev 16:7
- he do for the tabernacle of the c ... Lev 16:16
- the c when he goeth in to make an ... Lev 16:17
- and for all the c of Israel ... Lev 16:17
- place, and the tabernacle of the c ... Lev 16:20
- come into the tabernacle of the c ... Lev 16:23
- for the tabernacle of the c ... Lev 16:33
- and for all the people of the c ... Lev 16:33
- door of the tabernacle of the c ... Lev 17:4
- door of the tabernacle of the c ... Lev 17:5
- door of the tabernacle of the c ... Lev 17:6
- door of the tabernacle of the c ... Lev 17:9
- Speak unto all the c of the ... Lev 19:2
- door of the tabernacle of the c ... Lev 19:21
- in the tabernacle of the c ... Lev 24:3
- head, and let all the c stone him ... Lev 24:14
- all the c shall certainly stone ... Lev 24:16
- Sinai, in the tabernacle of the c ... Num 1:1
- the c of the children of Israel ... Num 1:2
- These were the renowned of the c ... Num 1:16
- they assembled all the c together ... Num 1:18
- the c of the children of Israel ... Num 1:53
- of the c shall they pitch ... Num 2:2
- Then the tabernacle of the c ... Num 2:17

the charge of the whole c before Num 3:7
before the tabernacle of the c Num 3:7
of the tabernacle of the c Num 3:8
of the c shall be the tabernacle Num 3:25
door of the tabernacle of the c Num 3:25
the tabernacle of the c eastward Num 3:38
work in the tabernacle of the c Num 4:3
Kohath in the tabernacle of the c Num 4:4
Kohath in the tabernacle of the c Num 4:15
work in the tabernacle of the c Num 4:23
and the tabernacle of the c Num 4:25
door of the tabernacle of the c Num 4:25
in the tabernacle of the c Num 4:28
work of the tabernacle of the c Num 4:30
in the tabernacle of the c Num 4:31
in the tabernacle of the c Num 4:33
the chief of the c numbered the Num 4:34
work in the tabernacle of the c Num 4:35
in the tabernacle of the c Num 4:37
work in the tabernacle of the c Num 4:39
in the tabernacle of the c Num 4:41
work in the tabernacle of the c Num 4:43
burden in the tabernacle of the c Num 4:47
door of the tabernacle of the c Num 6:10
door of the tabernacle of the c Num 6:13
door of the tabernacle of the c Num 6:18
of the tabernacle of the c Num 7:5
of the c to speak with him Num 7:89
before the tabernacle of the c Num 8:9
of the tabernacle of the c Num 8:15
Israel in the tabernacle of the c Num 8:19
all the c of the children of Num 8:20
tabernacle of the c before Aaron Num 8:22
of the tabernacle of the c Num 8:24
in the tabernacle of the c Num 8:26
door of the tabernacle of the c Num 10:3
But when the c is to be gathered Num 10:7
them unto the tabernacle of the c Num 11:16
unto the tabernacle of the c Num 12:4
to all the c of the children of Num 13:26
word unto them, and unto all the c Num 13:26
all the c lifted up their voice, Num 14:1
the whole c said unto them, Would Num 14:2
the c of the children of Israel Num 14:5
But all the c bade stone them Num 14:10
in the tabernacle of the c before Num 14:10
shall I bear with this evil c Num 14:27
surely do it unto all this evil c Num 14:35
made all the c to murmur against Num 14:36
shall be both for you of the c Num 15:15
without the knowledge of the c Num 15:24
that all the c shall offer one Num 15:24
the c of the children of Israel Num 15:25
the c of the children of Israel Num 15:26
Moses and Aaron, and unto all the c Num 15:33
all the c shall stone him with Num 15:35
all the c brought him without the Num 15:36
of the assembly, famous in the c Num 16:2
you, seeing all the c are holy Num 16:3
above the c of the LORD Num 16:3
you from the c of Israel Num 16:9
to stand before the c to minister Num 16:9
tabernacle of the c with Moses Num 16:18
Korah gathered all the c against Num 16:19
door of the tabernacle of the c Num 16:19
the LORD appeared unto all the c Num 16:19
yourselves from among this c Num 16:21
wilt thou be wroth with all the c Num 16:22
Speak unto the c, saying, Get you Num 16:24
And he spake unto the c, saying, Num 16:26
and they perished from among the c Num 16:33
the c of the children of Israel Num 16:41
when the c was gathered against Num 16:42
toward the tabernacle of the c Num 16:42
before the tabernacle of the c Num 16:43
Get you up from among this c Num 16:45
incense, and go quickly unto the c Num 16:46
and ran into the midst of the c Num 16:47
door of the tabernacle of the c Num 16:50
of the c before the testimony Num 17:4
charge of the tabernacle of the c Num 18:4
of the tabernacle of the c Num 18:6
of the tabernacle of the c Num 18:21
come nigh the tabernacle of the c Num 18:22
of the tabernacle of the c Num 18:23
in the tabernacle of the c Num 18:31
tabernacle of the c seven times Num 19:4
it shall be kept for the c of the Num 19:9
shall be cut off from among the c Num 19:20
of Israel, even the whole c Num 20:1
And there was no water for the c Num 20:2
up the c of the LORD into this Num 20:4
door of the tabernacle of the c Num 20:6
so thou shalt give the c and their Num 20:8
Aaron gathered the c together Num 20:10
the c drank, and their beasts also Num 20:11
ye shall not bring this c into Num 20:12
of Israel, even the whole c Num 20:22
Hor in the sight of all the c Num 20:27
when all the c saw that Aaron was Num 20:29
in the sight of all the c of the Num 25:6
door of the tabernacle of the c Num 25:6
it, he rose up from among the c Num 25:7
Take the sum of all the c of the Num 26:2
which were famous in the c Num 26:9
before the princes and all the c Num 27:2
door of the tabernacle of the c Num 27:2
of Zin, in the strife of the c Num 27:14
all flesh, set a man over the c Num 27:16
that the c of the LORD be not as Num 27:17
the priest, and before all the c Num 27:19
that all the c of the children of Num 27:20
Israel with him, even all the c Num 27:21
the priest, and before all the c Num 27:22
unto the c of the children of Num 31:12
and all the princes of the c Num 31:13
a plague among the c of the LORD Num 31:16
and the chief fathers of the c Num 31:26
to battle, and between all the c Num 31:27
the c was three hundred thousand Num 31:43
it into the tabernacle of the c Num 31:54
and unto the princes of the c Num 32:2
LORD smote before the c of Israel Num 32:4
he stand before the c in judgment Num 35:12
Then the c shall judge between Num 35:24
the c shall deliver the slayer Num 35:25
the c shall restore him to the Num 35:25
not enter into the c of the LORD Deut 23:1
not enter into the c of the LORD Deut 23:2
not enter into the c of the LORD Deut 23:2
not enter into the c of the LORD Deut 23:3
into the c of the LORD for ever Deut 23:3
the c of the LORD in their third Deut 23:8
in the tabernacle of the c Deut 31:14
in the tabernacle of the c Deut 31:14
the c of Israel the words of this Deut 31:30
the inheritance of the c of Jacob Deut 33:4
not before all the c of Israel Josh 8:35
princes of the c sware unto them Josh 9:15
because the princes of the c had Josh 9:18
all the c murmured against the Josh 9:18
the princes said unto all the c Josh 9:19
drawers of water unto all the c Josh 9:21
and drawers of water for the c Josh 9:27
the whole c of the children of Josh 18:1
up the tabernacle of the c there Josh 18:1
door of the tabernacle of the c Josh 19:51
stand before the c for judgment Josh 20:6
until he stood before the c Josh 20:9
the whole c of the children of Josh 22:12
saith the whole c of the LORD Josh 22:16
was a plague in the c of the LORD Josh 22:17
wroth with the whole c of Israel Josh 22:18
wrath fell on all the c of Israel Josh 22:20
priest, and the princes of the c Josh 22:30
the c was gathered together as Judg 20:1
not up with the c unto the LORD Judg 21:5
the c sent thither twelve Judg 21:10
the whole c sent some to speak to Judg 21:13
Then the elders of the c said Judg 21:16
door of the tabernacle of the c 1Sa 2:22
LORD, and the tabernacle of the c 1Kin 8:4
all the c of Israel, that were 1Kin 8:5
and blessed all the c of Israel 1Kin 8:14
all the c of Israel stood 1Kin 8:14
presence of all the c of Israel 1Kin 8:22
blessed all the c of Israel with 1Kin 8:55
and all Israel with him, a great c 1Kin 8:65
all the c of Israel came, and 1Kin 12:3
sent and called him unto the c 1Kin 12:20
tabernacle of the c with singing 1Chr 6:32
door of the tabernacle of the c 1Chr 9:21
said unto all the c of Israel 1Chr 13:2
all the c said that they would do 1Chr 13:4
charge of the tabernacle of the c 1Chr 23:32
of all Israel the c of the LORD 1Chr 28:8
the king said unto all the c 1Chr 29:1
blessed the LORD before all the c 1Chr 29:10
And David said to all the c 1Chr 29:20
all the c blessed the LORD God of 1Chr 29:20
all the c with him, went to the 2Chr 1:3
the tabernacle of the c of God 2Chr 1:3
Solomon and the c sought unto it 2Chr 1:5
was at the tabernacle of the c 2Chr 1:6
before the tabernacle of the c 2Chr 1:13
ark, and the tabernacle of the c 2Chr 5:5
all the c of Israel that were 2Chr 5:6
and blessed the whole c of Israel 2Chr 6:3
all the c of Israel stood 2Chr 6:3
presence of all the c of Israel 2Chr 6:12
knees before all the c of Israel 2Chr 6:13
Israel with him, a very great c 2Chr 7:8
stood in the c of Judah and 2Chr 20:5
of the LORD in the midst of the c 2Chr 20:14
all the c made a covenant with 2Chr 23:3
of the c of Israel, for the 2Chr 24:6
before the princes and all the c 2Chr 28:14
offering before the king and the c 2Chr 29:23
all the c worshipped, and the 2Chr 29:28
the c brought in sacrifices and 2Chr 29:31
offerings, which the c brought 2Chr 29:32
all the c in Jerusalem, to keep 2Chr 30:2
pleased the king and all the c 2Chr 30:4
the second month, a very great c 2Chr 30:13
in the c that were not sanctified 2Chr 30:17
give to the c a thousand bullocks 2Chr 30:24
gave to the c a thousand bullocks 2Chr 30:24
all the c of Judah, with the 2Chr 30:25
all the c that came out of Israel 2Chr 30:25
daughters, through all the c 2Chr 31:18
The whole c together was forty and Ezr 2:64
of Israel a very great c of men Ezr 10:1
himself separated from the c of Ezr 10:8
Then all the c answered and said Ezr 10:12
now our rulers of all the c stand Ezr 10:14
And all the c said, Amen, and Neh 5:13
The whole c together was forty and Neh 7:66
the law before the c both of men Neh 8:2
all the c of them that were come Neh 8:17
come into the c of God for ever Neh 13:1
For the c of hypocrites shall be Job 15:34
I stood up, and I cried in the c Job 30:28
sinners in the c of the righteous Ps 1:5
So shall the c of the people Ps 7:7
midst of the c will I praise thee Ps 22:22
shall be of thee in the great c Ps 22:25
I have hated the c of evildoers Ps 26:5
give thee thanks in the great c Ps 35:18
righteousness in the great c Ps 40:9
and thy truth from the great c Ps 40:10
indeed speak righteousness, O c Ps 58:1
Thy c hath dwelt therein Ps 68:10
Remember thy c, which thou hast Ps 74:2
forget not the c of thy poor for Ps 74:19
the c I will judge uprightly Ps 75:2
standeth in the c of the mighty Ps 82:1
also in the c of the saints Ps 89:5
him also in the c of the people Ps 107:32
of the upright, and in the c Ps 111:1
and his praise in the c of saints Ps 149:1
in all evil in the midst of the c Prov 5:14
shall remain in the c of the dead Prov 21:16
be shewed before the whole c Prov 26:26
sit also upon the mount of the c Is 14:13
hear, ye nations, and know, O c Jer 6:18
their c shall be established Jer 30:20
they should not enter into thy c Lam 1:10
them, as their c hath heard Hos 7:12
Gather the people, sanctify the c Joel 2:16
cord by lot in the c of the LORD Mic 2:5
Now when the c was broken up, Acts 13:43

**CONGREGATIONS**
in the c will I bless the LORD Ps 26:12
Bless ye God in the c, even the Ps 68:26
roar in the midst of thy c Ps 74:4

**CONIAH** (*co-ni'-ah*) See JEHOIACHIN. *Another name for Jehoiachin.*
though C the son of Jehoiakim Jer 22:24
Is this man C a despised broken Jer 22:28
instead of C the son of Jehoiakim Jer 37:1

**CONIES**
and the rocks for the c Ps 104:18
The c are but a feeble folk, yet Prov 30:26

**CONONIAH** (*co-no-ni'-ah*) See CONANIAH. *A Levite during Hezekiah's time.*
over which C the Levite was ruler 2Chr 31:12
overseers under the hand of C 2Chr 31:13

**CONQUER**
he went forth conquering, and to c Rev 6:2

**CONQUERING**
and he went forth c, and to conquer Rev 6:2

**CONQUERORS**
than c through him that loved us Rom 8:37

**CONSCIENCE**
being convicted by their own c Jn 8:9
I have lived in all good c before Acts 23:1
to have always a c void of Acts 24:16
their c also bearing witness, and Rom 2:15
my c also bearing me witness in Rom 9:1
for wrath, but also for c sake Rom 13:5
for some with c of the idol unto 1Cor 8:7
their c being weak is defiled 1Cor 8:7
shall not the c of him which is 1Cor 8:10
brethren, and wound their weak c 1Cor 8:12
asking no question for c sake 1Cor 10:25
asking no question for c sake 1Cor 10:27
that shewed it, and for c sake 1Cor 10:28
C, I say, not thine own, but of 1Cor 10:29
liberty judged of another man's c 1Cor 10:29
is this, the testimony of our c 2Cor 1:12
every man's c in the sight of God 2Cor 4:2
of a pure heart, and of a good c 1Ti 1:5
Holding faith, and a good c 1Ti 1:19
mystery of the faith in a pure c 1Ti 3:9
having their c seared with a hot 1Ti 4:2
from my forefathers with pure c 2Ti 1:3
even their mind and c is defiled Titus 1:15
perfect, as pertaining to the c Heb 9:9
purge your c from dead works to Heb 9:14
should have had no more c of sins Heb 10:2
hearts sprinkled from an evil c Heb 10:22
for we trust we have a good c Heb 13:18
if a man for c toward God endure 1Pet 2:19
Having a good c 1Pet 3:16
the answer of a good c toward God 1Pet 3:21

**CONSCIENCES**
also are made manifest in your c 2Cor 5:11

**CONSECRATE**
make Aaron's garments to c him Ex 28:3
c them, and sanctify them, that Ex 28:41
and thou shalt c Aaron and his sons Ex 29:9
the atonement was made, to c Ex 29:33
seven days shalt thou c them Ex 29:35
c them, that they may minister Ex 30:30
C yourselves to day to the LORD, Ex 32:29
for seven days shall he c you Lev 8:33
whom he shall c to minister in Lev 16:32
he shall c unto the LORD the days Num 6:12
who then is willing to c his 1Chr 29:5
so that whosoever cometh to c 2Chr 13:9
and they shall c themselves Eze 43:26
I will c their gain unto the LORD Mic 4:13

### CONSECRATED
therein, and to be c in them — Ex 29:29
that is c to put on the garments, — Lev 21:10
whom he c to minister in the — Num 3:3
and iron, are c unto the LORD — Josh 6:19
c one of his sons, who became his — Judg 17:5
And Micah c the Levite — Judg 17:12
he c him, and he became one of the.. — 1Kin 13:33
that are c to burn incense — 2Chr 26:18
Now ye have c yourselves unto the .. — 2Chr 29:31
the c things were six hundred — 2Chr 29:33
were c unto the LORD their God — 2Chr 31:6
feasts of the LORD that were c — Ezr 3:5
the Son, who is c for evermore — Heb 7:28
way, which he hath c for us — Heb 10:20

### CONSECRATION
for it is a ram of c — Ex 29:22
breast of the ram of Aaron's c — Ex 29:26
is heaved up, of the ram of the c — Ex 29:27
thou shalt take the ram of the c — Ex 29:31
the other ram, the ram of c — Lev 8:22
for of the ram of c it was Moses' — Lev 8:29
the days of your c be at an end — Lev 8:33
because the c of his God is upon — Num 6:7
he hath defiled the head of his c — Num 6:9

### CONSECRATIONS
And if ought of the flesh of the c — Ex 29:34
trespass offering, and of the c — Lev 7:37
they were c for a sweet savour — Lev 8:28
bread that is in the basket of c — Lev 8:31

### CONSENT
But in this will we c unto you — Gen 34:15
Only herein will the men c unto — Gen 34:22
only let us c unto them, and they — Gen 34:23
Thou shalt not c unto him — Deut 13:8
but he would not c — Judg 11:17
and they came out with one c — 1Sa 11:7
him, Hearken not unto him, nor c — 1Kin 20:8
consulted together with one c — Ps 83:5
sinners entice thee, c thou not — Prov 1:10
of priests murder in the way by c — Hos 6:9
the LORD, to serve him with one c — Zeph 3:9
they all with one c began to make — Lk 14:18
I c unto the law that it is good — Rom 7:16
except it be with c for a time — 1Cor 7:5
c not to wholesome words, even — 1Ti 6:3

### CONSENTED
the priests c to receive no more — 2Kin 12:8
So he c to them in this matter, — Dan 1:14
The same had not c to the counsel — Lk 23:51
longer time with them, he c not — Acts 18:20

### CONSENTEDST
a thief, then thou c with him — Ps 50:18

### CONSENTING
Saul was c unto his death — Acts 8:1
c unto his death, and kept the — Acts 22:20

### CONSIDER
c that this nation is thy people — Ex 33:13
Then the priest shall c — Lev 13:13
c it in thine heart, that the — Deut 4:39
Thou shalt also c in thine heart — Deut 8:5
c the years of many generations — Deut 32:7
that they would c their latter — Deut 32:29
now therefore c what ye have to — Judg 18:14
c of it, take advice, and speak — Judg 19:30
for c how great things he hath — 1Sa 12:24
know and c what thou wilt do — 1Sa 25:17
wherefore c, I pray you, and see — 2Kin 5:7
will he not then c it — Job 11:11
when I c, I am afraid of him — Job 23:15
would not c any of his ways — Job 34:27
c the wondrous works of God — Job 37:14
c my meditation — Ps 5:1
When I c thy heavens, the work of — Ps 8:3
c my trouble which I suffer of — Ps 9:13
C and hear me, O LORD my God — Ps 13:3
C mine enemies — Ps 25:19
thou shalt diligently c his place — Ps 37:10
Hearken, O daughter, and c — Ps 45:10
well her bulwarks, c her palaces — Ps 48:13
Now c this, ye that forget God, — Ps 50:22
they shall wisely c of his doing — Ps 64:9
but I will c thy testimonies — Ps 119:95
C mine affliction, and deliver me — Ps 119:153
C how I love thy precepts — Ps 119:159
c her ways, and be wise — Prov 6:6
c diligently what is before thee — Prov 23:1
he that pondereth the heart c it — Prov 24:12
for they c not that they do evil — Eccl 5:1
C the work of God — Eccl 7:13
but in the day of adversity c — Eccl 7:14
not know, my people doth not c — Is 1:3
neither c the operation of his — Is 5:12
c thee, saying, Is this the man — Is 14:16
I will c in my dwelling place — Is 18:4
That they may see, and know, and c — Is 41:20
what they be, that we may c them — Is 41:22
neither c the things of old — Is 43:18
they had not heard shall they c — Is 52:15
c diligently, and see if there be — Jer 2:10
C ye, and call for the mourning — Jer 9:17
days ye shall c it perfectly — Jer 23:20
in the latter days ye shall c it — Jer 30:24
see, O LORD, and c — Lam 1:11
c to whom thou hast done this — Lam 2:20
c, and behold our reproach — Lam 5:1
it may be they will c, though — Eze 12:3
the matter, and c the vision — Dan 9:23
they c not in their hearts that I — Hos 7:2
C your ways — Hag 1:5
C your ways — Hag 1:7
c from this day and upward, from — Hag 2:15
C now from this day and upward, — Hag 2:18
the LORD's temple was laid, c it — Hag 2:18
C the lilies of the field, how — Mt 6:28
C the ravens — Lk 12:24
C the lilies how they grow — Lk 12:27
Nor c that it is expedient for us — Jn 11:50
together for to c of this matter — Acts 15:6
C what I say — 2Ti 2:7
c the Apostle and High Priest of — Heb 3:1
Now c how great this man was, — Heb 7:4
let us c one another to provoke — Heb 10:24
For c him that endured such — Heb 12:3

### CONSIDERED
but when I had c it in the — 1Kin 3:21
I have c the things which thou — 1Kin 5:8
Hast thou c my servant Job, that — Job 1:8
Hast thou c my servant Job, that — Job 2:3
for thou hast c my trouble — Ps 31:7
I have c the days of old, the — Ps 77:5
Then I saw, and c it well — Prov 24:32
c all the oppressions that are — Eccl 4:1
I c all travail, and every right — Eccl 4:4
I c all the living which walk — Eccl 4:15
For all this I c in my heart even — Eccl 9:1
I c the horns, and, behold, there — Dan 7:8
For they c not the miracle of the — Mk 6:52
I had fastened mine eyes, I c — Acts 11:6
And when he had c the thing — Acts 12:12
he c not his own body now dead, — Rom 4:19

### CONSIDEREST
C thou not what this people have — Jer 33:24
but c not the beam that is in — Mt 7:3

### CONSIDERETH
he c all their works — Ps 33:15
Blessed is he that c the poor — Ps 41:1
wisely c the house of the wicked — Prov 21:12
c not that poverty shall come — Prov 28:22
The righteous c the cause of the — Prov 29:7
She c a field, and buyeth it — Prov 31:16
none c in his heart, neither is — Is 44:19
sins which he hath done, and c — Eze 18:14
Because he c, and turneth away — Eze 18:28

### CONSIDERING
none c that the righteous is — Is 57:1
And as I was c, behold, an he goat — Dan 8:5
c thyself, lest thou also be — Gal 6:1
c the end of their conversation — Heb 13:7

### CONSIST
things, and by him all things c — Col 1:17

### CONSISTETH
for a man's life c not in the — Lk 12:15

### CONSOLATION
of c to drink for their father or — Jer 16:7
waiting for the c of Israel — Lk 2:25
for ye have received your c — Lk 6:24
being interpreted, The son of c — Acts 4:36
had read, they rejoiced for the c — Acts 15:31
c grant you to be likeminded one — Rom 15:5
so our c also aboundeth by Christ — 2Cor 1:5
we be afflicted, it is for your c — 2Cor 1:6
we be comforted, it is for your c — 2Cor 1:6
so shall ye be also of the c — 2Cor 1:7
but by the c wherewith he was — 2Cor 7:7
be therefore any c in Christ — Phil 2:1
and hath given us everlasting c — 2Th 2:16
c in thy love, because the bowels — Philem 7
to lie, we might have a strong c — Heb 6:18

### CONSOLATIONS
Are the c of God small with thee — Job 15:11
my speech, and let this be your c — Job 21:2
with the breasts of her c — Is 66:11

### CONSORTED
believed, and c with Paul and Silas — Acts 17:4

### CONSPIRACY
And the c was strong — 2Sa 15:12
his servants arose, and made a c — 2Kin 12:20
Now they made a c against him in — 2Kin 14:19
his c which he made, behold, they — 2Kin 15:15
made a c against Pekah the son of — 2Kin 15:30
king of Assyria found c in Hoshea — 2Kin 17:4
made a c against him in Jerusalem — 2Chr 25:27
A c is found among the men of — Jer 11:9
There is a c of her prophets in — Eze 22:25
than forty which had made this c — Acts 23:13

### CONSPIRATORS
is among the c with Absalom — 2Sa 15:31

### CONSPIRED
they c against him to slay him — Gen 37:18
That all of you have c against me — 1Sa 22:8
him, Why have ye c against me — 1Sa 22:13
house of Issachar, c against him — 1Kin 15:27
c against him, as he was in — 1Kin 16:9
encamped heard say, Zimri hath c — 1Kin 16:16
the son of Nimshi c against Joram — 2Kin 9:14
I c against my master, and slew — 2Kin 10:9
the son of Jabesh c against him — 2Kin 15:10
c against him, and smote him in — 2Kin 15:25
servants of Amon c against him — 2Kin 21:23
them that had c against king Amon.. — 2Kin 21:24
they c against him, and stoned him .. — 2Chr 24:21
his own servants c against him — 2Chr 24:25
these are they that c against him — 2Chr 24:26
And his servants c against him — 2Chr 33:24
them that had c against king Amon . — 2Chr 33:25
c all of them together to come and — Neh 4:8
Amos hath c against thee in the — Amos 7:10

### CONSTANT
if he be c to do my commandments — 1Chr 28:7

### CONSTANTLY
the man that heareth speaketh c — Prov 21:28
But she c affirmed that it was — Acts 12:15
things I will that thou affirm c — Titus 3:8

### CONSTELLATIONS
the c thereof shall not give — Is 13:10

### CONSTRAIN
they c you to be circumcised — Gal 6:12

### CONSTRAINED
and she c him to eat bread — 2Kin 4:8
straightway Jesus c his disciples — Mt 14:22
straightway he c his disciples to — Mk 6:45
But they c him, saying, Abide — Lk 24:29
And she c us — Acts 16:15
I was c to appeal unto Caesar — Acts 28:19

### CONSTRAINETH
the spirit within me c me — Job 32:18
For the love of Christ c us — 2Cor 5:14

### CONSTRAINT
the oversight thereof, not by c — 1Pet 5:2

### CONSULT
They only c to cast him down from — Ps 62:4

### CONSULTATION
priests held a c with the elders — Mk 15:1

### CONSULTED
king Rehoboam c with the old men, — 1Kin 12:6
c with the young men that were — 1Kin 12:8
David c with the captains of — 1Chr 13:1
when he had c with the people, he — 2Chr 20:21
Then I c with myself, and I — Neh 5:7
c against thy hidden ones — Ps 83:3
For they have c together with one — Ps 83:5
he c with images, he looked in — Eze 21:21
have c together to establish a — Dan 6:7
now what Balak king of Moab c — Mic 6:5
Thou hast c shame to thy house by — Hab 2:10
c that they might take Jesus by — Mt 26:4
But the chief priests c that they — Jn 12:10

### CONSULTER
or a c with familiar spirits, or — Deut 18:11

### CONSULTETH
c whether he be able with ten — Lk 14:31

### CONSUME
and the famine shall c the land — Gen 41:30
them, and that I may c them — Ex 32:10
to c them from the face of the — Ex 32:12
lest I c thee in the way — Ex 33:3
of thee in a moment, and c thee — Ex 33:5
ague, that shall c the eyes — Lev 26:16
that I may c them in a moment — Num 16:21
that I may c them as in a moment — Num 16:45
for this great fire will c us — Deut 5:25
thou shalt c all the people which — Deut 7:16
thou mayest not c them at once — Deut 7:22
for the locust shall c it — Deut 28:38
of thy land shall the locust c — Deut 28:42
shall c the earth with her — Deut 32:22
c you, after that he hath done — Josh 24:20
altar, shall be to c thine eyes — 1Sa 2:33
heaven, and c thee and thy fifty — 2Kin 1:10
heaven, and c thee and thy fifty — 2Kin 1:12
thou didst not utterly c them — Neh 9:31
to c them, and to destroy them — Est 9:24
fire shall c the tabernacles of — Job 15:34
a fire not blown shall c him — Job 20:26
Drought and heat c the snow waters .. — Job 24:19
they shall c — Ps 37:20
into smoke shall they c away — Ps 37:20
his beauty to c away like a moth — Ps 39:11
their beauty shall c in the grave — Ps 49:14
C them in wrath, c them, — Ps 59:13
their days did he c in vanity — Ps 78:33
and it shall also c the beard — Is 7:20
shall c the glory of his forest, — Is 10:18
down, and c the branches thereof — Is 27:10
I will surely c them, saith the — Jer 8:13
but I will c them by the sword, — Jer 14:12
it shall c the palaces of — Jer 49:27
c away for their iniquity — Eze 4:17
hailstones in my fury to c it — Eze 13:13
them in the wilderness, to c them — Eze 20:13
to c because of the glittering — Eze 21:28
will c thy filthiness out of thee — Eze 22:15
c the flesh, and spice it well, and — Eze 24:10
desolate, they are given us to c — Eze 35:12
c all these kingdoms, and it shall — Dan 2:44
take away his dominion, to c — Dan 7:26
shall c his branches, and devour — Hos 11:6
I will utterly c all things from — Zeph 1:2
I will c man and beast — Zeph 1:3
I will c the fowls of the heaven, — Zeph 1:3
shall c it with the timber — Zec 5:4
Their flesh shall c away while — Zec 14:12

their eyes shall c away in their Zec 14:12
their tongue shall c away in Zec 14:12
c them, even as Elias did Lk 9:54
whom the Lord shall c with the 2Th 2:8
that ye may c it upon your lusts Jas 4:3

**CONSUMED**
lest thou be c in the iniquity of Gen 19:15
to the mountain, lest thou be c Gen 19:17
in the day the drought c me Gen 31:40
with fire, and the bush was not c Ex 3:2
wrath, which c them as stubble Ex 15:7
or the field, be c therewith Ex 22:6
the ashes which the fire hath c Lev 6:10
c upon the altar the burnt Lev 9:24
c them that were in the uttermost Num 11:1
half c when he cometh out of his Num 12:12
this wilderness they shall be c Num 14:35
lest ye be c in all their sins Num 16:26
c the two hundred and fifty men Num 16:35
shall we be c with dying Num 17:13
it hath c Ar of Moab, and the Num 21:28
that I c not the children of Num 25:11
in the sight of the LORD, was c Num 32:13
among the host, until they were c Deut 2:15
when all the men of war were c Deut 2:16
until he have c thee from off the Deut 28:21
which came out of Egypt, were c Josh 5:6
of the sword, until they were c Josh 8:24
great slaughter, till they were c Josh 10:20
c the flesh and the unleavened Judg 6:21
still do wickedly, ye shall be c 1Sa 12:25
against them until they be c 1Sa 15:18
the king, The man that c us 2Sa 21:5
not again until I had c them 2Sa 22:38
I have c them, and wounded 2Sa 22:39
c the burnt sacrifice, and the 1Kin 18:38
Syrians, until thou have c them 1Kin 22:11
heaven, and c him and his fifty 2Kin 1:10
heaven, and c him and his fifty 2Kin 1:12
of the Israelites that are c 2Kin 7:13
in Aphek, till thou have c them 2Kin 13:17
Syria till thou hadst c it 2Kin 13:19
c the burnt offering and the 2Chr 7:1
whom the children of Israel c not 2Chr 8:8
shalt push Syria until they be c 2Chr 18:10
with us till thou hadst c us Ezr 9:14
the gates thereof are c with fire Neh 2:3
gates thereof were c with fire Neh 2:13
sheep, and the servants, and c them Job 1:16
breath of his nostrils are they c Job 4:9
they are c out of their place Job 6:17
As the cloud is c and vanisheth Job 7:9
though my reins be c within me Job 19:27
His flesh is c away, that it Job 33:21
Mine eye is c because of grief Ps 6:7
did I turn again till they were c Ps 18:37
mine eye is c with grief, yea, my Ps 31:9
mine iniquity, and my bones are c Ps 31:10
I am c by the blow of thine hand Ps 39:10
c that are adversaries to my soul Ps 71:13
they are utterly c with terrors Ps 73:19
The fire c their young men Ps 78:63
For we are c by thine anger, and Ps 90:7
For my days are c like smoke Ps 102:3
the sinners be c out of the earth Ps 104:35
They had almost c me upon earth Ps 119:87
My zeal hath c me, because mine Ps 119:139
when thy flesh and thy body are c Prov 5:11
that forsake the LORD shall be c Is 1:28
oppressors are c out of the land Is 16:4
to nought, and the scorner is c Is 29:20
thy face from us, and hast c us Is 64:7
and the mouse, shall be c together Is 66:17
thou hast c them, but they have Jer 5:3
burned, the lead is c of the fire Jer 6:29
after them, till I have c them Jer 9:16
him, and c him, and have made his Jer 10:25
the beasts are c, and the birds Jer 12:4
famine shall those prophets be c Jer 14:15
and they shall be c by the sword Jer 16:4
my days should be c with shame Jer 20:18
till they be c from off the land Jer 24:10
until I have c them by his hand Jer 27:8
until all the roll was c in the Jer 36:23
there, and they shall all be c Jer 44:12
they shall even be c by the sword Jer 44:12
have been c by the sword and by Jer 44:18
of Egypt shall be c by the sword Jer 44:27
after them, till I have c them Jer 49:37
and brought up hath mine enemy c Lam 2:22
LORD's mercies that we are not c Lam 3:22
they be c in the midst of thee Eze 5:12
ye shall be c in the midst Eze 13:14
the fire c them Eze 19:12
I have c them with the fire of my Eze 22:31
it, that the scum of it may be c Eze 24:11
they shall be no more c with Eze 34:29
wherefore I have c them in mine Eze 43:8
shall the fruit thereof be c Eze 47:12
which by his hand shall be c Dan 11:16
ye sons of Jacob are not c Mal 3:6
that ye be not c one of another Gal 5:15

**CONSUMETH**
And he, as a rotten thing, c Job 13:28
the remnant of them the fire c Job 22:20
is a fire that c to destruction Job 31:12
stubble, and the flame c the chaff Is 5:24

**CONSUMING**
For the LORD thy God is a c fire Deut 4:24
as a c fire he shall destroy them Deut 9:3
For our God is a c fire Heb 12:29

**CONSUMMATION**
it desolate, even until the c Dan 9:27

**CONSUMPTION**
even appoint over you terror, c Lev 26:16
LORD shall smite thee with a c Deut 28:22
the c decreed shall overflow with Is 10:22
Lord GOD of hosts shall make a c Is 10:23
from the Lord GOD of hosts a c Is 28:22

**CONTAIN**
heaven of heavens cannot c thee 1Kin 8:27
as great as would c two measures 1Kin 18:32
and heaven of heavens cannot c him 2Chr 2:6
heaven of heavens cannot c thee 2Chr 6:18
that the bath may c the tenth Eze 45:11
not c the books that should be Jn 21:25
But if they cannot c, let them 1Cor 7:9

**CONTAINED**
it c two thousand baths 1Kin 7:26
one laver c forty baths 1Kin 7:38
by nature the things c in the law Rom 2:14
of commandments c in ordinances Eph 2:15
also it is c in the scripture 1Pet 2:6

**CONTAINETH**
it c much Eze 23:32

**CONTAINING**
c two or three firkins apiece Jn 2:6

**CONTEMN**
Wherefore doth the wicked c God Ps 10:13
what if the sword c even the rod Eze 21:13

**CONTEMNED**
In whose eyes a vile person is c Ps 15:4
c the counsel of the most High Ps 107:11
for love, it would utterly be c Song 8:7
and the glory of Moab shall be c Is 16:14

**CONTEMNETH**
it c the rod of my son, as every Eze 21:10

**CONTEMPT**
Thus shall there arise too much c Est 1:18
He poureth c upon princes, and Job 12:21
or did the c of families terrify Job 31:34
He poureth c upon princes, and Ps 107:40
Remove from me reproach and c Ps 119:22
we are exceedingly filled with c Ps 123:3
ease, and with the c of the proud Ps 123:4
wicked cometh, then cometh also c Prov 18:3
glory, and to bring into c all the Is 23:9
and some to shame and everlasting c Dan 12:2

**CONTEMPTIBLE**
say, The table of the LORD is c Mal 1:7
thereof, even his meat, is c Mal 1:12
Therefore have I also made you c Mal 2:9
presence is weak, and his speech c 2Cor 10:10

**CONTEMPTUOUSLY**
and c against the righteous Ps 31:18

**CONTEND**
neither c with them in battle Deut 2:9
it, and c with him in battle Deut 2:24
If he will c with him, he cannot Job 9:3
will ye c for God Job 13:8
such as keep the law c with them Prov 28:4
neither may he c with him that is Eccl 6:10
for I will c with him that Is 49:25
who will c with me Is 50:8
For I will not c for ever Is 57:16
then how canst thou c with horses Jer 12:5
the voice of them that c with me Jer 18:19
the Lord GOD called to c by fire Amos 7:4
c thou before the mountains, and Mic 6:1
c for the faith which was once Jude 3

**CONTENDED**
Then c I with the rulers, and said Neh 13:11
Then I c with the nobles of Judah Neh 13:17
I c with them, and cursed them, and Neh 13:25
maidservant, when they c with me Job 31:13
them, even them that c with thee Is 41:12
of the circumcision c with him Acts 11:2

**CONTENDEST**
shew me wherefore thou c with me Job 10:2

**CONTENDETH**
Shall he that c with the Almighty Job 40:2
If a wise man c with a foolish Prov 29:9
contend with him that c with thee Is 49:25

**CONTENDING**
when c with the devil he disputed Jude 9

**CONTENT**
And his brethren were c Gen 37:27
Moses was c to dwell with the man Ex 2:21
when Moses heard that, he was c Lev 10:20
would to God we had been c Josh 7:7
the Levite was c to dwell with Judg 17:11
had said unto the man, Be c Judg 19:6
And Naaman said, Be c, take two 2Kin 5:23
And one said, Be c, I pray thee 2Kin 6:3
Now therefore be c, look upon me Job 6:28
neither will he rest c, though Prov 6:35
Pilate, willing to c the people Mk 15:15
and be c with your wages Lk 3:14
state I am, therewith to be c Phil 4:11
and raiment let us be therewith c 1Ti 6:8
be c with such things as ye have Heb 13:5
not c therewith, neither doth he 3Jn 10

**CONTENTION**
Only by pride cometh c Prov 13:10
therefore leave off c, before it Prov 17:14
A fool's lips enter into c Prov 18:6
the scorner, and c shall go out Prov 22:10
a man of c to the whole earth Jer 15:10
are that raise up strife and c Hab 1:3
the c was so sharp between them, Acts 15:39
The one preach Christ of c Phil 1:16
you the gospel of God with much c 1Th 2:2

**CONTENTIONS**
The lot causeth c to cease Prov 18:18
their c are like the bars of a Prov 18:19
the c of a wife are a continual Prov 19:13
who hath c Prov 23:29
Chloe, that there are c among you 1Cor 1:11
questions, and genealogies, and c Titus 3:9

**CONTENTIOUS**
in the wilderness, than with a c Prov 21:19
so is a c man to kindle strife Prov 26:21
rainy day and a c woman are alike Prov 27:15
But unto them that are c, and do Rom 2:8
But if any man seem to be c 1Cor 11:16

**CONTENTMENT**
godliness with c is great gain 1Ti 6:6

**CONTINUAL**
This shall be a c burnt offering Ex 29:42
the c bread shall be thereon Num 4:7
by day, for a c burnt offering Num 28:3
It is a c burnt offering, which Num 28:6
beside the c burnt offering, and Num 28:10
beside the c burnt offering, and Num 28:15
which is for a c burnt offering Num 28:23
beside the c burnt offering Num 28:24
them beside the c burnt offering Num 28:31
the c burnt offering, and the meat Num 29:11
beside the c burnt offering, his Num 29:16
beside the c burnt offering, and Num 29:19
beside the c burnt offering, and Num 29:22
beside the c burnt offering, his Num 29:25
beside the c burnt offering, and Num 29:28
beside the c burnt offering, his Num 29:31
beside the c burnt offering, his Num 29:34
beside the c burnt offering, and Num 29:38
his allowance was a c allowance 2Kin 25:30
for the c shewbread, and for the 2Chr 2:4
offered the c burnt offering Ezr 3:5
for the c meat offering, and for Neh 10:33
for the c burnt offering, of the Neh 10:33
of a merry heart hath a c feast Prov 15:15
of a wife are a c dropping Prov 19:13
A c dropping in a very rainy day Prov 27:15
people in wrath with a c stroke Is 14:6
of Luhith c weeping shall go up Jer 48:5
there was a c diet given him of Jer 52:34
sever out men of c employment Eze 39:14
morning for a c burnt offering Eze 46:15
lest by her c coming she weary me Lk 18:5
heaviness and c sorrow in my heart Rom 9:2

**CONTINUALLY**
of his heart was only evil c Gen 6:5
returned from off the earth c Gen 8:3
the waters decreased c until the Gen 8:5
for a memorial before the LORD c Ex 28:29
upon his heart before the LORD c Ex 28:30
of the first year day by day c Ex 29:38
to cause the lamps to burn c Lev 24:2
the morning before the LORD c Lev 24:3
candlestick before the LORD c Lev 24:4
set it in order before the LORD c Lev 24:8
the ark of the LORD went on c Josh 6:13
and Saul became David's enemy c 1Sa 18:29
shalt eat bread at my table c 2Sa 9:7
for he did eat c at the king's 2Sa 9:13
people increased c with Absalom 2Sa 15:12
before me c in the room of Joab 2Sa 19:13
which stand c before thee 1Kin 10:8
man of God, which passeth by us c 2Kin 4:9
he did eat bread c before him all 2Kin 25:29
the priests with trumpets c 1Chr 16:6
and his strength, seek his face c 1Chr 16:11
to minister before the ark c 1Chr 16:37
of the burnt offering c morning 1Chr 16:40
unto them, c before the LORD 1Chr 23:31
which stand c before thee 2Chr 9:7
between Rehoboam and Jeroboam c. 2Chr 12:15
LORD c all the days of Jehoiada 2Chr 24:14
Thus did Job c Job 1:5
his praise shall c be in my mouth Ps 34:1
yea, let them say c, Let the LORD Ps 35:27
halt, and my sorrow is c before me Ps 38:17
and thy truth c preserve me Ps 40:11
such as love thy salvation say c Ps 40:16
while they c say unto me, Where Ps 42:3
My confusion is c before me Ps 44:15
to have been c before me Ps 50:8
the goodness of God endureth c Ps 52:1
melt away as waters which run c Ps 58:7
and make their loins c to shake Ps 69:23
such as love thy salvation say c Ps 70:4
whereunto I may c resort Ps 71:3
my praise shall be c of thee Ps 71:6
But I will hope c, and will yet Ps 71:14
also shall be made for him c Ps 72:15
Nevertheless I am c with thee Ps 73:23
rise up against thee increaseth c Ps 74:23
Let his children be c vagabonds Ps 109:10

Let them be before the LORD c ... Ps 109:15
a girdle wherewith he is girded c ... Ps 109:19
shall I keep thy law c for ever ... Ps 119:44
My soul is c in my hand ... Ps 119:109
have respect unto thy statutes c ... Ps 119:117
c are they gathered together for ... Ps 140:2
his heart, he deviseth mischief c ... Prov 6:14
Bind them c upon thine heart, and ... Prov 6:21
it whirleth about c, and the wind ... Eccl 1:6
I stand c upon the watchtower in ... Is 21:8
thy walls are c before me ... Is 49:16
hast feared c every day because ... Is 51:13
my name c every day is blasphemed ... Is 52:5
And the LORD shall guide thee c ... Is 58:11
thy gates shall be open c ... Is 60:11
me to anger c to my face ... Is 65:3
before me c is grief and wounds ... Jer 6:7
offerings, and to do sacrifice c ... Jer 33:18
he did c eat bread before him all ... Jer 52:33
a meat offering c by a perpetual ... Eze 46:14
Thy God whom thou servest c ... Dan 6:16
is thy God, whom thou servest c ... Dan 6:20
they have committed whoredom c ... Hos 4:18
and judgment, and wait on thy God c .. Hos 12:6
so shall all the heathen drink c ... Obad 16
hath not thy wickedness passed c ... Nah 3:19
not spare c to slay the nations ... Hab 1:17
were c in the temple, praising and ... Lk 24:53
will give ourselves c to prayer ... Acts 6:4
of them that waited on him c ... Acts 10:7
attending c upon this very thing ... Rom 13:6
abideth a priest c ... Heb 7:3
year c make the comers thereunto ... Heb 10:1
the sacrifice of praise to God c ... Heb 13:15

**CONTINUANCE**
even great plagues, and of long c ... Deut 28:59
and sore sicknesses, and of long c ... Deut 28:59
which in c were fashioned, when ... Ps 139:16
in those is c, and we shall be ... Is 64:5
To them who by patient c in well ... Rom 2:7

**CONTINUE**
if he c a day or two, he shall ... Ex 21:21
she shall then c in the blood of ... Lev 12:4
she shall c in the blood of her ... Lev 12:5
you c following the LORD your God ... 1Sa 12:14
But now thy kingdom shall not c ... 1Sa 13:14
that it may c for ever before ... 2Sa 7:29
That the LORD may c his word ... 1Kin 2:4
neither shall his substance c ... Job 15:29
doth not mine eye c in their ... Job 17:2
O c thy lovingkindness unto them ... Ps 36:10
their houses shall c for ever ... Ps 49:11
children of thy servants shall c ... Ps 102:28
They c this day according to ... Ps 119:91
that c until night, till wine ... Is 5:11
vessel, that they may c many days ... Jer 32:14
he shall c more years than the ... Dan 11:8
because they c with me now three ... Mt 15:32
If ye c in my word, then are ye ... Jn 8:31
c ye in my love ... Jn 15:9
persuaded them to c in the grace ... Acts 13:43
exhorting them to c in the faith ... Acts 14:22
I c unto this day, witnessing ... Acts 26:22
Shall we c in sin, that grace may ... Rom 6:1
if thou c in his goodness ... Rom 11:22
of the gospel might c with you ... Gal 2:5
abide and c with you all for your ... Phil 1:25
If ye c in the faith grounded and ... Col 1:23
C in prayer, and watch in the same ... Col 4:2
if they c in faith and charity and ... 1Ti 2:15
c in them ... 1Ti 4:16
But c thou in the things which ... 2Ti 3:14
suffered to c by reason of death ... Heb 7:23
Let brotherly love c ... Heb 13:1
c there a year, and buy and sell, ... Jas 4:13
all things c as they were from ... 2Pet 3:4
you, ye also shall c in the Son ... 1Jn 2:24
was given unto him to c forty ... Rev 13:5
cometh, he must c a short space ... Rev 17:10

**CONTINUED**
and they c a season in ward ... Gen 40:4
Asher c on the sea shore, and ... Judg 5:17
the country of Moab, and c there ... Ruth 1:2
hath c even from the morning ... Ruth 2:7
as she c praying before the LORD, ... 1Sa 1:12
the ark of the LORD c in the ... 2Sa 6:11
they c three years without war ... 1Kin 22:1
all this c until the burnt ... 2Chr 29:28
also I c in the work of this wall ... Neh 5:16
Moreover Job c his parable ... Job 27:1
Moreover Job c his parable ... Job 29:1
his name shall be c as long as ... Ps 72:17
Daniel c even unto the first year ... Dan 1:21
c all night in prayer to God ... Lk 6:12
Ye are they which have c with me ... Lk 22:28
they c there not many days ... Jn 2:12
So when they c asking him ... Jn 8:7
there c with his disciples ... Jn 11:54
These all c with one accord in ... Acts 1:14
And they c stedfastly in the ... Acts 2:42
he c with Philip, and wondered, ... Acts 8:13
But Peter c knocking ... Acts 12:16
Barnabas c in Antioch, teaching ... Acts 15:35
he c there a year and six months, ... Acts 18:11
this c by the space of two years ... Acts 19:10
c his speech until midnight ... Acts 20:7
c fasting, having taken nothing ... Acts 27:33
because they c not in my covenant ... Heb 8:9
would no doubt have c with us ... 1Jn 2:19

**CONTINUETH**
fleeth also as a shadow, and c not ... Job 14:2
Cursed is every one that c not in ... Gal 3:10
c in supplications and prayers ... 1Ti 5:5
But this man, because he c ever ... Heb 7:24
c therein, he being not a ... Jas 1:25

**CONTINUING**
forth with fury, a c whirlwind ... Jer 30:23
c daily with one accord in the ... Acts 2:46
c instant in prayer ... Rom 12:12
For here have we no c city ... Heb 13:14

**CONTRADICTING**
which were spoken by Paul, c ... Acts 13:45

**CONTRADICTION**
without all c the less is blessed ... Heb 7:7
such c of sinners against himself ... Heb 12:3

**CONTRARIWISE**
So that c ye ought rather to ... 2Cor 2:7
But c, when they saw that the ... Gal 2:7
but c blessing ... 1Pet 3:9

**CONTRARY**
And if ye walk c unto me, and will ... Lev 26:21
things, but will walk c unto me ... Lev 26:23
Then will I also walk c unto you ... Lev 26:24
unto me, but walk c unto me ... Lev 26:27
Then I will walk c unto you also ... Lev 26:28
also they have walked c unto me ... Lev 26:40
I also have walked c unto them ... Lev 26:41
(though it was turned to the c ... Est 9:1
the c is in thee from other women ... Eze 16:34
unto thee, therefore thou art c ... Eze 16:34
for the wind was c ... Mt 14:24
for the wind was c unto them ... Mk 6:48
these all do c to the decrees of ... Acts 17:7
men to worship God c to the law ... Acts 18:13
me to be smitten c to the law ... Acts 23:3
things c to the name of Jesus of ... Acts 26:9
Cyprus, because the winds were c ... Acts 27:4
wert graffed c to nature into a ... Rom 11:24
offences c to the doctrine which ... Rom 16:17
these are c the one to the other ... Gal 5:17
was against us, which was c to us ... Col 2:14
not God, and are c to all men ... 1Th 2:15
thing that is c to sound doctrine ... 1Ti 1:10
is of the c part may be ashamed ... Titus 2:8

**CONTRIBUTION**
Achaia to make a certain c for ... Rom 15:26

**CONTRITE**
saveth such as be of a c spirit ... Ps 34:18
a c heart, O God, thou wilt not ... Ps 51:17
with him also that is of a c ... Is 57:15
to revive the heart of the c ones ... Is 57:15
of a c spirit, and trembleth at my ... Is 66:2

**CONTROVERSIES**
judgment of the LORD, and for c ... 2Chr 19:8

**CONTROVERSY**
matters of c within thy gates ... Deut 17:8
the men, between whom the c is ... Deut 19:17
and by their word shall every c ... Deut 21:5
If there be a c between men ... Deut 25:1
that when any man that had a c ... 2Sa 15:2
of recompences for the c of Zion ... Is 34:8
LORD hath a c with the nations ... Jer 25:31
in c they shall stand in judgment ... Eze 44:24
for the LORD hath a c with the ... Hos 4:1
The LORD hath also a c with Judah ... Hos 12:2
ye, O mountains, the LORD's c ... Mic 6:2
the LORD hath a c with his people ... Mic 6:2
without c great is the mystery of ... 1Ti 3:16

**CONVENIENT**
feed me with food c for me ... Prov 30:8
c for thee to go, thither go ... Jer 40:4
it seemeth c unto thee to go ... Jer 40:5
when a c day was come, that Herod ... Mk 6:21
when I have a c season, I will ... Acts 24:25
do those things which are not c ... Rom 1:28
come when he shall have c time ... 1Cor 16:12
nor jesting, which are not c ... Eph 5:4
to enjoin thee that which is c ... Philem 8

**CONVENIENTLY**
sought how he might c betray him ... Mk 14:11

**CONVERSANT**
strangers that were c among them ... Josh 8:35
as long as we were c with them ... 1Sa 25:15

**CONVERSATION**
to slay such as be of upright c ... Ps 37:14
his c aright will I shew the ... Ps 50:23
we have had our c in the world ... 2Cor 1:12
For ye have heard of my c in time ... Gal 1:13
c in times past in the lusts of ... Eph 2:3
the former c the old man, which ... Eph 4:22
Only let your c be as it becometh ... Phil 1:27
For our c is in heaven ... Phil 3:20
of the believers, in word, in c ... 1Ti 4:12
Let your c be without ... Heb 13:5
considering the end of their c ... Heb 13:7
good c his works with meekness of ... Jas 3:13
so be ye holy in all manner of c ... 1Pet 1:15
from your vain c received by ... 1Pet 1:18
Having your c honest among the ... 1Pet 2:12
word be won by the c of the wives ... 1Pet 3:1
your chaste c coupled with fear ... 1Pet 3:2
accuse your good c in Christ ... 1Pet 3:16
with the filthy c of the wicked ... 2Pet 2:7
ought ye to be in all holy c ... 2Pet 3:11

**CONVERSION**
declaring the c of the Gentiles ... Acts 15:3

**CONVERT**
understand with their heart, and c ... Is 6:10
err from the truth, and one c him ... Jas 5:19

**CONVERTED**
and sinners shall be c unto thee ... Ps 51:13
of the sea shall be c unto thee ... Is 60:5
with their heart, and should be c ... Mt 13:15
I say unto you, Except ye be c ... Mt 18:3
lest at any time they should be c ... Mk 4:12
and when thou art c, strengthen ... Lk 22:32
with their heart, and be c ... Jn 12:40
Repent ye therefore, and be c ... Acts 3:19
with their heart, and should be c ... Acts 28:27

**CONVERTETH**
that he which c the sinner from ... Jas 5:20

**CONVERTING**
the LORD is perfect, c the soul ... Ps 19:7

**CONVERTS**
and her c with righteousness ... Is 1:27

**CONVEY**
I will c them by sea in floats ... 1Kin 5:9
that they may c me over till I ... Neh 2:7

**CONVEYED**
for Jesus had c himself away ... Jn 5:13

**CONVICTED**
being c by their own conscience, ... Jn 8:9

**CONVINCE**
to exhort and to c the gainsayers ... Titus 1:9
to c all that are ungodly among ... Jude 15

**CONVINCED**
there was none of you that c Job ... Job 32:12
For he mightily c the Jews ... Acts 18:28
he is c of all, he is judged of ... 1Cor 14:24
are c of the law as transgressors ... Jas 2:9

**CONVINCETH**
Which of you c me of sin ... Jn 8:46

**CONVOCATION**
day there shall be an holy c ... Ex 12:16
there shall be an holy c to you ... Ex 12:16
is the sabbath of rest, an holy c ... Lev 23:3
first day ye shall have an holy c ... Lev 23:7
in the seventh day is an holy c ... Lev 23:8
that it may be an holy c unto you ... Lev 23:21
of blowing of trumpets, an holy c ... Lev 23:24
it shall be an holy c unto you ... Lev 23:27
the first day shall be an holy c ... Lev 23:35
day shall be an holy c unto you ... Lev 23:36
the first day shall be an holy c ... Num 28:18
day ye shall have an holy c ... Num 28:25
be out, ye shall have an holy c ... Num 28:26
month, ye shall have an holy c ... Num 29:1
of this seventh month an holy c ... Num 29:7

**CONVOCATIONS**
ye shall proclaim to be holy c ... Lev 23:2
feasts of the LORD, even holy c ... Lev 23:4
ye shall proclaim to be holy c ... Lev 23:37

**COOK**
And Samuel said unto the c ... 1Sa 9:23
the c took up the shoulder, and ... 1Sa 9:24

**COOKS**
to be confectionaries, and to be c ... 1Sa 8:13

**COOL**
in the garden in the c of the day ... Gen 3:8
finger in water, and c my tongue ... Lk 16:24

**COOS** (*co'-os*) *An island near Cnidus.*
with a straight course unto C ... Acts 21:1

**COPIED**
of Hezekiah king of Judah c out ... Prov 25:1

**COPING**
from the foundation unto the c ... 1Kin 7:9

**COPPER**
and two vessels of fine c, ... Ezr 8:27

**COPPERSMITH**
Alexander the c did me much evil ... 2Ti 4:14

**COPULATION**
man's seed of c go out from him ... Lev 15:16
skin, whereon is the seed of c ... Lev 15:17
whom man shall lie with seed of c ... Lev 15:18

**COPY**
that he shall write him a c of ... Deut 17:18
stones a c of the law of Moses ... Josh 8:32
This is the c of the letter that ... Ezr 4:11
Now when the c of king ... Ezr 4:23
The c of the letter that Tatnai, ... Ezr 5:6
Now this is the c of the letter ... Ezr 7:11
The c of the writing for a ... Est 3:14
Also he gave him the c of the ... Est 4:8
The c of the writing for a ... Est 8:13

**COR**
tenth part of a bath out of the c ......... Eze 45:14

**CORAL**
No mention shall be made of c ............ Job 28:18
work, and fine linen, and c .................... Eze 27:16

**CORBAN** (*cor'-ban*) *A sacred gift.*
to his father or mother, It is C ............... Mk 7:11

**CORD**
down by a c through the window......... Josh 2:15
Because he hath loosed my c................ Job 30:11
or his tongue with a c which thou......... Job 41:1
a threefold c is not quickly.................. Eccl 4:12
Or ever the silver c be loosed............... Eccl 12:6
have none that shall cast a c by............. Mic 2:5

**CORDS**
the pins of the court, and their c ........... Ex 35:18
hanging for the court gate, his c............ Ex 39:40
the c of it for all the service................. Num 3:26
and their pins, and their c...................... Num 3:37
the altar round about, and their c ....... Num 4:26
and their pins, and their c...................... Num 4:32
bound him with two new c.................. Judg 15:13
the c that were upon his arms............. Judg 15:14
fastened with c of fine linen..................... Est 1:6
be holden in c of affliction...................... Job 36:8
and cast away their c from us................... Ps 2:3
bind the sacrifice with c....................... Ps 118:27
cut asunder the c of the wicked ............ Ps 129:4
have hid a snare for me, and c .............. Ps 140:5
be holden with the c of his sins............ Prov 5:22
draw iniquity with c of vanity.................. Is 5:18
any of the c thereof be broken............... Is 33:20
spare not, lengthen thy c......................... Is 54:2
spoiled, and all my c are broken............ Jer 10:20
and they let down Jeremiah with c......... Jer 38:6
let them down by c into the.................. Jer 38:11
under thine armholes under the c .......... Jer 38:12
So they drew up Jeremiah with c........... Jer 38:13
of rich apparel, bound with c ............... Eze 27:24
I drew them with c of a man................... Hos 11:4
he had made a scourge of small c .......... Jn 2:15

**CORE** (*co'-ree*) See KORAH. *Greek form of Korah.*
perished in the gainsaying of C................ Jude 11

**CORIANDER**
and it was like c seed, white .................. Ex 16:31
And the manna was as c seed................ Num 11:7

**CORINTH** (*cor'-inth*) See CORINTHIANS, CORINTHUS. *Capital of Achaia.*
from Athens, and came to C.................. Acts 18:1
that, while Apollos was at C................. Acts 19:1
the church of God which is at C ............ 1Cor 1:2
the church of God which is at C ........... 2Cor 1:1
you I came not as yet unto C ............... 2Cor 1:23
Erastus abode at C................................ 2Ti 4:20

**CORINTHIANS** (*co-rin'-the-uns*) *Residents of Corinth.*
many of the C hearing believed, ........... Acts 18:8
The first epistle to the C was ................. 1Cor s
O ye C, our mouth is open unto............. 2Cor 6:11
the C was written from Philippi .............. 2Cor s

**CORINTHUS** (*co-rin'-thus*) See CORINTH. *Same as Corinth.*
Written to the Romans from C................. Rom s

**CORMORANT**
And the little owl, and the c.................. Lev 11:17
and the gier eagle, and the c.............. Deut 14:17
But the c and the bittern shall................. Is 34:11
both the c and the bittern shall ........... Zeph 2:14

**CORN**
of the earth, and plenty of c ................. Gen 27:28
and with c and wine have I................... Gen 27:37
seven ears of c came up upon one......... Gen 41:5
lay up c under the hand of.................... Gen 41:35
Joseph gathered c as the sand of.......... Gen 41:49
into Egypt to Joseph for to buy c.......... Gen 41:57
saw that there was c in Egypt............... Gen 42:1
heard that there is c in Egypt .............. Gen 42:2
went down to buy c in Egypt................. Gen 42:3
to buy c among those that came............ Gen 42:5
carry c for the famine of your............... Gen 42:19
to fill their sacks with c....................... Gen 42:25
they laded their asses with the c........... Gen 42:26
when they had eaten up the c................ Gen 43:2
of the youngest, and his c money ......... Gen 44:2
and ten she asses laden with c............. Gen 45:23
for the c which they bought.................. Gen 47:14
thorns, so that the stacks of c ................. Ex 22:6
or the standing c, or the field................. Ex 22:6
green ears of c dried by the fire............ Lev 2:14
even c beaten out of full ears................. Lev 2:14
it, part of the beaten c thereof.............. Lev 2:16
eat neither bread, nor parched c .......... Lev 23:14
were the c of the threshingfloor.......... Num 18:27
and the fruit of thy land, thy c.............. Deut 7:13
that thou mayest gather in thy c.......... Deut 11:14
thy gates the tithe of thy c.................. Deut 12:17
name there, the tithe of thy c.............. Deut 14:23
to put the sickle to the c....................... Deut 16:9
that thou hast gathered in thy c.......... Deut 16:13
The firstfruit also of thy c..................... Deut 18:4
the standing c of thy neighbour.......... Deut 23:25
unto thy neighbour's standing c .......... Deut 23:25
the ox when he treadeth out the c...... Deut 25:4
shall not leave thee either c ................ Deut 28:51
Jacob shall be upon a land of c.......... Deut 33:28
they did eat of the old c of the............... Josh 5:11
parched c in the selfsame day ............... Josh 5:11
eaten of the old c of the land ............... Josh 5:12
the standing c of the Philistines.......... Judg 15:5
shocks, and also the standing c............ Judg 15:5
glean ears of c after him in.................... Ruth 2:2
and he reached her parched c.............. Ruth 2:14
down at the end of the heap of c.......... Ruth 3:7
an ephah of this parched c.................. 1Sa 17:17
and five measures of parched c............ 1Sa 25:18
mouth, and spread ground c thereon .. 2Sa 17:19
and barley, and flour, and parched c... 2Sa 17:28
full ears of c in the husk .................... 2Kin 4:42
like your own land, a land of c .......... 2Kin 18:32
as c blasted before it be grown .......... 2Kin 19:26
in abundance the firstfruits of c.......... 2Chr 31:5
also for the increase of c..................... 2Chr 32:28
therefore we take up c for them............. Neh 5:2
and houses, that we might buy c ............ Neh 5:3
might exact of them money and c ........ Neh 5:10
part of the money, and of the c ............ Neh 5:11
shall bring the offering of the c ......... Neh 10:39
vessels, and the tithes of the c............. Neh 13:5
all Judah the tithe of the c.................. Neh 13:12
like as a shock of c cometh in in........... Job 5:26
reap every one his c in the field............ Job 24:6
off as the tops of the ears of c.............. Job 24:24
good liking, they grow up with c........... Job 39:4
than in the time that their c..................... Ps 4:7
thou preparest them c, when thou ........... Ps 65:9
also are covered over with c ................ Ps 65:13
of c in the earth upon the top of............ Ps 72:16
had given them of the c of heaven......... Ps 78:24
He that withholdeth c, the people...... Prov 11:26
the harvestman gathereth the c................ Is 17:5
threshing, and the c of my floor ........... Is 21:10
Bread c is bruised ................................. Is 28:28
like your own land, a land of c .............. Is 36:17
as c blasted before it be grown ............. Is 37:27
c to be meat for thine enemies................. Is 62:8
say to their mothers, Where is c........... Lam 2:12
and I will call for the c, and will ........ Eze 36:29
did not know that I gave her c .............. Hos 2:8
take away my c in the time ..................... Hos 2:9
And the earth shall hear the c .............. Hos 2:22
they assemble themselves for c ............ Hos 7:14
and loveth to tread out the c................ Hos 10:11
they shall revive as the c ...................... Hos 14:7
for the c is wasted................................... Joel 1:10
for the c is withered............................... Joel 1:17
people, Behold, I will send you c .......... Joel 2:19
moon be gone, that we may sell c ......... Amos 8:5
like as c is sifted in a sieve,................. Amos 9:9
upon the mountains, and upon the c..... Hag 1:11
c shall make the young men ................ Zec 9:17
on the sabbath day through the c ............ Mt 12:1
and began to pluck the ears of c ............ Mt 12:1
that he went through the c fields ......... Mk 2:23
they went, to pluck the ears of c........... Mk 2:23
after that the full c in the ear................ Mk 4:28
that he went through the c fields ............ Lk 6:1
disciples plucked the ears of c ................ Lk 6:1
Except a c of wheat fall into the ........... Jn 12:24
heard that there was c in Egypt ........... Acts 7:12
of the ox that treadeth out the c........... 1Cor 9:9
the ox that treadeth out the c ............... 1Ti 5:18

**CORNELIUS** (*cor-ne'-le-us*) *A Roman centurion converted by Peter.*
certain man in Caesarea called C ......... Acts 10:1
in to him, and saying unto him, C......... Acts 10:3
which spake unto C was departed......... Acts 10:7
C had made enquiry for Simon's......... Acts 10:17
which were sent unto him from C........ Acts 10:21
C the centurion, a just man, and........ Acts 10:22
C waited for them, and had called....... Acts 10:24
C met him, and fell down at his.......... Acts 10:25
C said, Four days ago I was................ Acts 10:30
And said, C, thy prayer is heard,......... Acts 10:31

**CORNER**
which is toward the north c.................... Ex 36:25
shave off the c of their beard ................. Lev 21:5
compassed the c of the sea................. Josh 18:14
from the right c of the temple to ....... 2Kin 11:11
to the left c of the temple .................... 2Kin 11:11
gate of Ephraim unto the c gate.......... 2Kin 14:13
the gate of Ephraim to the c gate ....... 2Chr 25:23
towers in Jerusalem at the c gate......... 2Chr 26:9
altars in every c of Jerusalem ............. 2Chr 28:24
of the wall, even unto the c.................... Neh 3:24
and to the going up of the c.................. Neh 3:31
between the going up of the c ............... Neh 3:32
or who laid the c stone thereof............... Job 38:6
is become the head stone of the c........ Ps 118:22
our daughters may be as c stones ........ Ps 144:12
through the street near her c.................. Prov 7:8
and lieth in wait at every c.................... Prov 7:12
to dwell in a c of the housetop ............ Prov 21:9
to dwell in the c of the housetop........ Prov 25:24
a tried stone, a precious c stone ............ Is 28:16
be removed into a c any more................ Is 30:20
Hananeel unto the gate of the c........... Jer 31:38
unto the c of the horse gate ................ Jer 31:40
and shall devour the c of Moab ............ Jer 48:45
not take of thee a stone for a c ........... Jer 51:26
in every c of the court there was......... Eze 46:21
in Samaria in the c of a bed................. Amos 3:12
Out of him came forth the c.................. Zec 10:4
the first gate, unto the c gate ............... Zec 14:10
same is become the head of the c.......... Mt 21:42
is become the head of the c ................... Mk 12:10
same is become the head of the c........... Lk 20:17
which is become the head of the c......... Acts 4:11
this thing was not done in a c............. Acts 26:26
himself being the chief c stone.............. Eph 2:20
I lay in Sion a chief c stone .................. 1Pet 2:6
same is made the head of the c .............. 1Pet 2:7

C

**CORNERS**
and put them in the four c thereof........ Ex 25:12
four c that are on the four feet ............. Ex 25:26
c of the tabernacle in the two................. Ex 26:23
they shall be for the two c...................... Ex 26:24
of it upon the four c thereof .................... Ex 27:2
rings in the four c thereof........................ Ex 27:4
crown of it, by the two c thereof.............. Ex 30:4
two boards made he for the c of............. Ex 36:28
did to both of them in both the c........... Ex 36:29
to be set by the four c of it....................... Ex 37:3
four c that were in the four feet ............ Ex 37:13
crown thereof, by the two c of it ........... Ex 37:27
horns thereof on the four c of it ............... Ex 38:2
wholly reap the c of thy field ................ Lev 19:9
not round the c of your heads .............. Lev 19:27
shalt thou mar the c of thy beard ......... Lev 19:27
c of thy field when thou reapest........... Lev 23:22
and shall smite the c of Moab............. Num 24:17
said, I would scatter them into c ....... Deut 32:26
and the four c thereof had.................... 1Kin 7:30
to the four c of one base ...................... 1Kin 7:34
and didst divide them into c ................. Neh 9:22
and smote the four c of the house ......... Job 1:19
from the four c of the earth.................... Is 11:12
and all that are in the utmost c ............... Jer 9:26
and all that are in the utmost c ............. Jer 25:23
them that are in the utmost c ............... Jer 49:32
come upon the four c of the land............. Eze 7:2
the c thereof, and the length ................ Eze 41:22
on the four c of the settle, and ............ Eze 43:20
upon the four c of the settle of............. Eze 45:19
pass by the four c of the court .............. Eze 46:21
In the four c of the court there .............. Eze 46:22
these four c were of one measure ......... Eze 46:22
bowls, and as the c of the altar ............ Zec 9:15
in the c of the streets, that........................... Mt 6:5
a great sheet knit at the four c .......... Acts 10:11
let down from heaven by four c............ Acts 11:5
on the four c of the earth ......................... Rev 7:1

**CORNET**
shouting, and with sound of the c ..... 1Chr 15:28
sound of c make a joyful noise ................ Ps 98:6
time ye hear the sound of the c............... Dan 3:5
people heard the sound of the c ............. Dan 3:7
shall hear the sound of the c ................ Dan 3:10
time ye hear the sound of the c............. Dan 3:15
Blow ye the c in Gibeah, and the............ Hos 5:8

**CORNETS**
and on timbrels, and on c, and on............ 2Sa 6:5
and with trumpets, and with c .......... 2Chr 15:14

**CORNFLOOR**
hast loved a reward upon every c........... Hos 9:1

**CORPSE**
of it, they came and took up his c.......... Mk 6:29

**CORPSES**
behold, they were all dead c.............. 2Kin 19:35
behold, they were all dead c ................... Is 37:36
and there is none end of their c.............. Nah 3:3
they stumble upon their c ...................... Nah 3:3

**CORRECT**
rebukes dost c man for iniquity ............. Ps 39:11
the heathen, shall not he c...................... Ps 94:10
C thy son, and he shall give thee ........ Prov 29:17
Thine own wickedness shall c thee.......... Jer 2:19
O LORD, c me, but with judgment.......... Jer 10:24
but I will c thee in measure, and............. Jer 30:11
of thee, but c thee in measure............... Jer 46:28

**CORRECTED**
A servant will not be c by words.......... Prov 29:19
fathers of our flesh which c us.............. Heb 12:9

**CORRECTETH**
happy is the man whom God c ................ Job 5:17
For whom the LORD loveth he c.............. Prov 3:12

**CORRECTION**
causeth it to come, whether for c......... Job 37:13
neither be weary of his c...................... Prov 3:11
as a fool to the c of the stocks............. Prov 7:22
C is grievous unto him that................. Prov 15:10
but the rod of c shall drive it.............. Prov 22:15
Withhold not c from the child............. Prov 23:13
they received no c.................................... Jer 2:30
they have refused to receive c ................. Jer 5:3
LORD their God, nor receiveth c ............. Jer 7:28
thou hast established them for c ............. Hab 1:12
she received not c.................................. Zeph 3:2
for doctrine, for reproof, for c .............. 2Ti 3:16

**CORRUPT**
The earth also was c before God........... Gen 6:11
the earth, and, behold, it was c............. Gen 6:12
Lest ye c yourselves, and make you..... Deut 4:16
shall c yourselves, and make a ............ Deut 4:25
ye will utterly c yourselves.................. Deut 31:29
My breath is c, my days are.................. Job 17:1
They are c, they have done..................... Ps 14:1

are c because of my foolishness Ps 38:5
C are they, and have done Ps 53:1
They are c, and speak wickedly Ps 73:8
troubled fountain, and a c spring Prov 25:26
nor according to your c doings Eze 20:44
she was more c in her inordinate Eze 23:11
c words to speak before me, till Dan 2:9
covenant shall he c by flatteries Dan 11:32
unto the Lord a c thing Mal 1:14
I will c your seed, and spread Mal 2:3
earth, where moth and rust doth c Mt 6:19
neither moth nor rust doth c Mt 6:20
but a c tree bringeth forth evil Mt 7:17
neither can a c tree bring forth Mt 7:18
the tree c, and his fruit c Mt 12:33
tree bringeth not forth c fruit Lk 6:43
neither doth a c tree bring forth Lk 6:43
communications c good manners 1Cor 15:33
as many, which c the word of God 2Cor 2:17
which is c according to the Eph 4:22
Let no c communication proceed Eph 4:29
disputings of men of c minds 1Ti 6:5
men of c minds, reprobate 2Ti 3:8
in those things they c themselves Jude 10
which did c the earth with her Rev 19:2

**CORRUPTED**
for all flesh had c his way upon Gen 6:12
the land was c by reason of the Ex 8:24
land of Egypt, have c themselves Ex 32:7
out of Egypt have c themselves Deut 9:12
They have c themselves, their Deut 32:5
c themselves more than their Judg 2:19
thou wast c more than they in all Eze 16:47
thou hast c thy wisdom by reason Eze 28:17
They have deeply c themselves Hos 9:9
rose early, and c all their doings Zeph 3:7
ye have c the covenant of Levi, Mal 2:8
wronged no man, we have c no man 2Cor 7:2
so your minds should be c from 2Cor 11:3
Your riches are c, and your Jas 5:2

**CORRUPTERS**
of evildoers, children that are c Is 1:4
they are all c Jer 6:28

**CORRUPTETH**
thief approacheth, neither moth c Lk 12:33

**CORRUPTIBLE**
into an image made like to c man Rom 1:23
they do it to obtain a c crown 1Cor 9:25
For this c must put on 1Cor 15:53
So when this c shall have put on 1Cor 15:54
were not redeemed with c things 1Pet 1:18
Being born again, not of c seed 1Pet 1:23
the heart, in that which is not c 1Pet 3:4

**CORRUPTING**
him the daughter of women, c her Dan 11:17

**CORRUPTION**
because their c is in them Lev 22:25
the right hand of the mount of c 2Kin 23:13
I have said to c, Thou art my Job 17:14
suffer thine Holy One to see c Ps 16:10
still live for ever, and not see c Ps 49:9
delivered it from the pit of c Is 38:17
was turned in me into c, and I Dan 10:8
thou brought up my life from c Jonah 2:6
suffer thine Holy One to see c Acts 2:27
hell, neither his flesh did see c Acts 2:31
dead, now no more to return to c Acts 13:34
suffer thine Holy One to see c Acts 13:35
laid unto his fathers, and saw c Acts 13:36
whom God raised again, saw no c Acts 13:37
of c into the glorious liberty of Rom 8:21
It is sown in c 1Cor 15:42
neither doth c inherit 1Cor 15:50
flesh shall of the flesh reap c Gal 6:8
having escaped the c that is in 2Pet 1:4
utterly perish in their own c 2Pet 2:12
themselves are the servants of c 2Pet 2:19

**CORRUPTLY**
And the people did yet c 2Chr 27:2
We have dealt very c against thee Neh 1:7

**COSAM** (*co'-sam*) *Son of Elmodam; ancestor of Jesus*
of Addi, which was the son of C Lk 3:28

**COST**
we eaten at all of the king's c 2Sa 19:42
of that which doth c me nothing 2Sa 24:24
offer burnt offerings without c 1Chr 21:24
not down first, and counteth the c Lk 14:28

**COSTLINESS**
in the sea by reason of her c Rev 18:19

**COSTLY**
c stones, and hewed stones, to lay 1Kin 5:17
All these were of c stones 1Kin 7:9
And the foundation was of c stones 1Kin 7:10
And above were c stones, after the 1Kin 7:11
of ointment of spikenard, very c Jn 12:3
or gold, or pearls, or c array 1Ti 2:9

**COTES**
manner of beasts, and c for flocks 2Chr 32:28

**COTTAGE**
Zion is left as a c in a vineyard Is 1:8
and shall be removed like a c Is 24:20

**COTTAGES**
c for shepherds, and folds for Zeph 2:6

**COUCH**
he went up to my c Gen 49:4
my c shall ease my complaint Job 7:13
When they c in their dens, and Job 38:40
I water my c with my tears Ps 6:6
of a bed, and in Damascus in a c Amos 3:12
his c into the midst before Jesus Lk 5:19
thee, Arise, and take up thy c Lk 5:24

**COUCHED**
he c as a lion, and as an old lion Gen 49:9
He c, he lay down as a lion, and Num 24:9

**COUCHES**
stretch themselves upon their c Amos 6:4
and laid them on beds and c Acts 5:15

**COUCHETH**
and for the deep that c beneath Deut 33:13

**COUCHING**
ass c down between two burdens Gen 49:14

**COUCHINGPLACE**
and the Ammonites a c for flocks Eze 25:5

**COULD**
so that they c not dwell together Gen 13:6
were dim, so that he c not see Gen 27:1
wherein they were strangers c not Gen 36:7
c not speak peaceably unto him Gen 37:4
but there was none that c Gen 41:8
it c not be known that they had Gen 41:21
was none that c declare it to me Gen 41:24
c we certainly know that he would Gen 43:7
Then Joseph c not refrain himself Gen 45:1
his brethren c not answer him Gen 45:3
dim for age, so that he c not see Gen 48:10
when she c not longer hide him, Ex 2:3
the Egyptians c not drink of the Ex 7:21
for they c not drink of the water Ex 7:24
bring forth lice, but they c not Ex 8:18
the magicians c not stand before Ex 9:11
c not tarry, neither had they Ex 12:39
they c not drink of the waters of Ex 15:23
that they c not keep the passover Num 9:6
the children of Israel c not Josh 7:12
of Judah c not drive them out Josh 15:63
Yet the children of Manasseh c Josh 17:12
but c not drive out the Judg 1:19
so that they c not any longer Judg 2:14
so that he c not draw the dagger Judg 3:22
that he c not do it by day, that Judg 6:27
for he c not frame to pronounce Judg 12:6
they c not in three days expound Judg 14:14
sojourn where he c find a place Judg 17:8
every one c sling stones at an Judg 20:16
rose up before one c know another Ruth 3:14
to wax dim, that he c not see 1Sa 3:2
eyes were dim, that he c not see 1Sa 4:15
sought him, he c not be found 1Sa 10:21
and went whithersoever they c go 1Sa 23:13
c not go over the brook Besor 1Sa 30:10
that they c not follow David 1Sa 30:21
he c not live after that he was 2Sa 1:10
he c not answer Abner a word 2Sa 3:11
c not find them, they returned to 2Sa 17:20
them, that they c not arise 2Sa 22:39
how that David my father c not 1Kin 5:3
that c not be told nor numbered 1Kin 8:5
So that the priests c not stand 1Kin 8:11
so that he c not pull it in again 1Kin 13:4
But Ahijah c not see 1Kin 14:4
king of Edom: but they c not 2Kin 3:26
And they c not eat thereof 2Kin 4:40
Ahaz, but c not overcome him 2Kin 16:5
c use both the right hand and the 1Chr 12:2
that c handle shield and buckler, 1Chr 12:8
fifty thousand, which c keep rank 1Chr 12:33
that c keep rank, came with a 1Chr 12:38
But David c not go before it to 1Chr 21:30
of the brass c not be found out 2Chr 4:18
which c not be told nor numbered 2Chr 5:6
So that the priests c not stand 2Chr 5:14
the priests c not enter into the 2Chr 7:2
and c not withstand them 2Chr 13:7
that they c not recover 2Chr 14:13
more than they c carry away 2Chr 20:25
that c handle spear and shield 2Chr 25:5
which c not deliver their own 2Chr 25:15
so that they c not flay all the 2Chr 29:34
For they c not keep it at that 2Chr 30:3
that c deliver his people out of 2Chr 32:14
all that c skill of instruments 2Chr 34:12
but they c not shew their Ezr 2:59
So that the people c not discern Ezr 3:13
that they c not cause them to Ezr 5:5
but they c not shew their Neh 7:61
and women, and all that c hear with Neh 8:2
women, and those that c understand Neh 8:3
c not speak in the Jews' language Neh 13:24
On that night c not the king Est 6:1
tongue, although the enemy c not Est 7:4
and no man c withstand them Est 9:2
but I c not discern the form Job 4:16
I also c speak as ye do Job 16:4
I c heap up words against you, and Job 16:4
of his highness I c not endure Job 31:23
sought him, but he c not be found Ps 37:36
then I c have borne it Ps 55:12
they have more than heart c wish Ps 73:7
floods, that they c not drink Ps 78:44
sought him, but I c not find him Song 5:6
What c have been done more to my Is 5:4
but c not prevail against it Is 7:1
a people that c not profit them Is 30:5
they c not well strengthen their Is 33:23
they c not spread the sail Is 33:23
I asked of them, c answer a word Is 41:28
they c not deliver the burden, Is 46:2
all ashamed, neither c they blush Jer 6:15
all ashamed, neither c they blush Jer 8:12
yet my mind c not be toward this Jer 15:1
with forbearing, and I c not stay Jer 20:9
which c not be eaten, they were Jer 24:2
So that the LORD c no longer bear Jer 44:22
so that men c not touch their Lam 4:14
for a nation that c not save us Lam 4:17
the garden of God c not hide him Eze 31:8
a river that I c not pass over Eze 47:5
a river that c not be passed over Eze 47:5
but they c not read the writing, Dan 5:8
but they c not shew the Dan 5:15
but they c find none occasion nor Dan 6:4
that c deliver out of his hand Dan 8:4
there was none that c deliver the Dan 8:7
yet c he not heal you, nor cure Hos 5:13
but they c not Jonah 1:13
disciples, and they c not cure him Mt 17:16
Why c not we cast him out Mt 17:19
c ye not watch with me one hour Mt 26:40
saw that he c prevail nothing Mt 27:24
insomuch that Jesus c no more Mk 1:45
when they c not come nigh unto Mk 2:4
so that they c not so much as eat Mk 3:20
no man c bind him, no, not with Mk 5:3
neither c any man tame him Mk 5:4
he c there do no mighty work, Mk 6:5
but she c not Mk 6:19
but he c not be hid Mk 7:24
and they c not Mk 9:18
Why c not we cast him out Mk 9:28
She hath done what she c Mk 14:8
out, he c not speak unto them Lk 1:22
when they c not find by what way Lk 5:19
that house, and c not shake it Lk 6:48
c not come at him for the press Lk 8:19
neither c be healed of any, Lk 8:43
and they c not Lk 9:40
c in no wise lift up herself Lk 13:11
they c not answer him again to Lk 14:6
c not for the press, because he Lk 19:3
c not find what they might do Lk 19:48
that they c not tell whence it Lk 20:7
they c not take hold of his words Lk 20:26
were not of God, he c do nothing Jn 9:33
C not this man, which opened the Jn 11:37
Therefore they c not believe Jn 12:39
c not contain the books that Jn 21:25
they c say nothing against it Acts 4:14
was I, that I c withstand God Acts 11:17
from which ye c not be justified Acts 13:39
when he c not know the certainty Acts 21:34
when I c not see for the glory of Acts 22:11
Paul, which they c not prove Acts 25:7
c not bear up into the wind, we Acts 27:15
commanded that they which c swim Acts 27:43
For what the law c not do Rom 8:3
For I c wish that myself were Rom 9:3
c not speak unto you as unto 1Cor 3:1
so that I c remove mountains, and 1Cor 13:2
c not stedfastly behold the face 2Cor 3:7
that the children of Israel c not 2Cor 3:13
Would to God ye c bear with me a 2Cor 11:1
law given which c have given life Gal 3:21
when we c no longer forbear 1Th 3:1
when I c no longer forbear, I 1Th 3:5
So we see that they c not enter Heb 3:19
because he c swear by no greater, Heb 6:13
that c not make him that did the Heb 9:9
(For they c not endure that which Heb 12:20
multitude, which no man c number Rev 7:9
no man c learn that song but the Rev 14:3

**COULDEST**
and done evil things as thou c Jer 3:5
them, and yet c not be satisfied Eze 16:28
c not thou watch one hour Mk 14:37
Thou c have no power at all Jn 19:11

**COULDST**
seeing thou c reveal this secret Dan 2:47

**COULTER**
every man his share, and his c 1Sa 13:20

**COULTERS**
for the mattocks, and for the c 1Sa 13:21

**COUNCIL**
the princes of Judah and their c Ps 68:27
Raca, shall be in danger of the c Mt 5:22
held a c against him, how they Mt 12:14
priests, and elders, and all the c Mt 26:59
all the c sought for witness Mk 14:55
elders and scribes and the whole c Mk 15:1
together, and led him into their c Lk 22:66
priests and the Pharisees a c Jn 11:47
them to go aside out of the c Acts 4:15
him, and called the c together Acts 5:21
them, they set them before the c Acts 5:27
Then stood there up one in the c Acts 5:34
from the presence of the c Acts 5:41

him, and brought him to the c Acts 6:12
And all that sat in the c, looking Acts 6:15
priests and all their c to appear Acts 22:30
Paul, earnestly beholding the c Acts 23:1
Pharisees, he cried out in the c Acts 23:6
Now therefore ye with the c Acts 23:15
down Paul to morrow into the c Acts 23:20
I brought him forth into their c Acts 23:28
in me, while I stood before the c Acts 24:20
when he had conferred with the c Acts 25:12

**COUNCILS**

they will deliver you up to the c Mt 10:17
they shall deliver you up to c Mk 13:9

**COUNSEL**

unto my voice, I will give thee c Ex 18:19
who shall ask c for him after the Num 27:21
Israel, through the c of Balaam Num 31:16
For they are a nation void of c Deut 32:28
asked not c at the mouth of the Josh 9:14
And they said unto him, Ask c Judg 18:5
give here your advice and c Judg 20:7
asked c of God, and said, Which of Judg 20:18
asked c of the LORD, saying, Judg 20:23
And Saul asked c of God, Shall I 1Sa 14:37
turn the c of Ahithophel into 2Sa 15:31
for me defeat the c of Ahithophel 2Sa 15:34
Give c among you what we shall do 2Sa 16:20
the c of Ahithophel, which he 2Sa 16:23
so was all the c of Ahithophel 2Sa 16:23
The c that Ahithophel hath given 2Sa 17:7
Therefore I c that all Israel be 2Sa 17:11
The c of Hushai the Archite is 2Sa 17:14
better than the c of Ahithophel 2Sa 17:14
defeat the good c of Ahithophel 2Sa 17:14
and thus did Ahithophel c Absalom 2Sa 17:15
saw that his c was not followed 2Sa 17:23
They shall surely ask c at Abel 2Sa 20:18
let me, I pray thee, give thee c 1Kin 1:12
he forsook the c of the old men 1Kin 12:8
What c give ye that we may answer 1Kin 12:9
old men's c that they gave him 1Kin 12:13
them after the c of the young men 1Kin 12:14
Whereupon the king took c 1Kin 12:28
took c with his servants, saying, 2Kin 6:8
are but vain words,) I have c 2Kin 18:20
also for asking c of one that had 1Chr 10:13
king Rehoboam took c with the old 2Chr 10:6
What c give ye me to return 2Chr 10:6
But he forsook the c which the 2Chr 10:8
took c with the young men that 2Chr 10:8
forsook the c of the old men 2Chr 10:13
He walked also after their c 2Chr 22:5
Art thou made of the king's c 2Chr 25:16
and hast not hearkened unto my c 2Chr 25:16
For the king had taken c, and his 2Chr 30:2
the whole assembly took c to keep 2Chr 30:23
He took c with his princes and his 2Chr 32:3
according to the c of my lord Ezr 10:3
according to the c of the princes Ezr 10:8
God had brought their c to nought Neh 4:15
and let us take c together Neh 6:7
the c of the froward is carried Job 5:13
and shine upon the c of the wicked Job 10:3
is wisdom and strength, he hath c Job 12:13
his own c shall cast him down Job 18:7
the c of the wicked is far from Job 21:16
but the c of the wicked is far Job 22:18
waited, and kept silence at my c Job 29:21
c by words without knowledge Job 38:2
that hideth c without knowledge Job 42:3
not in the c of the ungodly Ps 1:1
and the rulers take c together Ps 2:2
long shall I take c in my soul Ps 13:2
Ye have shamed the c of the poor Ps 14:6
the LORD, who hath given me c Ps 16:7
own heart, and fulfil all thy c Ps 20:4
while they took c together Ps 31:13
The LORD bringeth the c of the Ps 33:10
The c of the LORD standeth for Ps 33:11
We took sweet c together, and Ps 55:14
from the secret c of the wicked Ps 64:2
wait for my soul take c together Ps 71:10
Thou shalt guide me with thy c Ps 73:24
taken crafty c against thy people Ps 83:3
they waited not for his c Ps 106:13
they provoked him with their c Ps 106:43
contemned the c of the most High Ps 107:11
ye have set at nought all my c Prov 1:25
They would none of my c Prov 1:30
C is mine, and sound wisdom Prov 8:14
Where no c is, the people fall Prov 11:14
he that hearkeneth unto c is wise Prov 12:15
Without c purposes are Prov 15:22
Hear c, and receive instruction, Prov 19:20
nevertheless the c of the LORD Prov 19:21
C in the heart of man is like Prov 20:5
Every purpose is established by c Prov 20:18
nor c against the LORD Prov 21:30
For by wise c thou shalt make thy Prov 24:6
of a man's friend by hearty c Prov 27:9
I c thee to keep the king's Eccl 8:2
let the c of the Holy One of Is 5:19
have taken evil c against thee Is 7:5
Take c together, and it shall come Is 8:10
and understanding, the spirit of c Is 11:2
Take c, execute judgment Is 16:3
and I will destroy the c thereof Is 19:3
the c of the wise counsellors of Is 19:11
because of the c of the LORD of Is 19:17
hath taken this c against Tyre Is 23:8
of hosts, which is wonderful in c Is 28:29
to hide their c from the LORD Is 29:15
saith the LORD, that take c Is 30:1
they are but vain words) I have c Is 36:5
With whom took he c, and who Is 40:14
and performeth the c of his Is 44:26
yea, let them take c together Is 45:21
My c shall stand, and I will do Is 46:10
executeth my c from a far country Is 46:11
nor c from the wise, nor the word Jer 18:18
all their c against me to slay me Jer 18:23
I will make void the c of Judah Jer 19:7
hath stood in the c of the LORD Jer 23:18
But if they had stood in my c Jer 23:22
Great in c, and mighty in work Jer 32:19
and if I give thee c, wilt thou Jer 38:15
is c perished from the prudent Jer 49:7
Therefore hear the c of the LORD Jer 49:20
Babylon hath taken c against you Jer 49:30
hear ye the c of the LORD Jer 50:45
priest, and c from the ancients Eze 7:26
give wicked c in this city Eze 11:2
Then Daniel answered with c Dan 2:14
let my c be acceptable unto thee, Dan 4:27
My people ask c at their stocks, Hos 4:12
shall be ashamed of his own c Hos 10:6
neither understand they his c Mic 4:12
the c of peace shall be between Zec 6:13
took c how they might entangle Mt 22:15
elders of the people took c Mt 27:1
And they took c, and bought with Mt 27:7
with the elders, and had taken c Mt 28:12
straightway took c with the Mk 3:6
lawyers rejected the c of God Lk 7:30
same had not consented to the c Lk 23:51
took c together for to put him to Jn 11:53
which gave c to the Jews, that it Jn 18:14
delivered by the determinate c Acts 2:23
thy c determined before to be Acts 4:28
the heart, and took c to slay them Acts 5:33
for if this c or this work be of Acts 5:38
the Jews took c to kill him Acts 9:23
declare unto you all the c of God Acts 20:27
the soldiers' c was to kill the Acts 27:42
after the c of his own will Eph 1:11
promise the immutability of his c Heb 6:17
I c thee to buy of me gold tried Rev 3:18

**COUNSELED**

How hast thou c him that hath no Job 26:3

**COUNSELLED**

which he c in those days, was as 2Sa 16:23
and thus and thus have I c 2Sa 17:15
hath Ahithophel c against you 2Sa 17:21

**COUNSELLOR**

the Gilonite, David's c, from his 2Sa 15:12
for Zechariah his son, a wise c 1Chr 26:14
Jonathan David's uncle was a c 1Chr 27:32
And Ahithophel was the king's c 1Chr 27:33
mother was his c to do wickedly 2Chr 22:3
and the honourable man, and the c Is 3:3
name shall be called Wonderful, C Is 9:6
or being his c hath taught him Is 40:13
among them, and there was no c Is 41:28
is thy c perished? Mic 4:9
evil against the LORD, a wicked c Nah 1:11
of Arimathaea, an honourable c Mk 15:43
there was a man named Joseph, a c Lk 23:50
or who hath been his c Rom 11:34

**COUNSELLORS**

for they were his c after the 2Chr 22:4
And hired c against them, to Ezr 4:5
of the king, and of his seven c Ezr 7:14
his c have freely offered unto Ezr 7:15
unto me before the king, and his c Ezr 7:28
our God, which the king, and his c Ezr 8:25
c of the earth, which built Job 3:14
He leadeth c away spoiled, and Job 12:17
also are my delight, and my c Ps 119:24
multitude of c there is safety Prov 11:14
but to the c of peace is joy Prov 12:20
of c they are established Prov 15:22
in multitude of c there is safety Prov 24:6
thy c as at the beginning Is 1:26
the counsel of the wise c of Is 19:11
the judges, the treasurers, the c Dan 3:2
the judges, the treasurers, the c Dan 3:3
and spake, and said unto his c Dan 3:24
and captains, and the king's c Dan 3:27
and my c and my lords sought unto Dan 4:36
governors, and the princes, the c Dan 6:7

**COUNSELS**

it is turned round about by his c Job 37:12
let them fall by their own c Ps 5:10
and they walked in their own c Ps 81:12
shall attain unto wise c Prov 1:5
but the c of the wicked are Prov 12:5
to thee excellent things in c Prov 22:20
thy c of old are faithfulness and Is 25:1
wearied in the multitude of thy c Is 47:13
their ear, but walked in the c Jer 7:24
them, because of their own c Hos 11:6
of Ahab, and ye walk in their c Mic 6:16
make manifest the c of the hearts 1Cor 4:5

**COUNT**

shall make your c for the lamb Ex 12:4
then ye shall c the fruit thereof Lev 19:23
ye shall c unto you from the Lev 23:15
Then let him c the years of the Lev 25:27
jubile, then he shall c with him Lev 25:52
Who can c the dust of Jacob, and Num 23:10
C not thine handmaid for a 1Sa 1:16
and my maids, c me for a stranger Job 19:15
he see my ways, and c all my steps Job 31:4
The LORD shall c, when he writeth Ps 87:6
If I should c them, they are more Ps 139:18
I c them mine enemies Ps 139:22
Shall I c them pure with the Mic 6:11
neither c I my life dear unto Acts 20:24
I c all things but loss for the Phil 3:8
do c them but dung, that I may Phil 3:8
Brethren, I c not myself to have Phil 3:13
that our God would c you worthy 2Th 1:11
Yet c him not as an enemy, but 2Th 3:15
servants as are under the yoke c 1Ti 6:1
If thou c me therefore a partner, Philem 17
c it all joy when ye fall into Jas 1:2
we c them happy which endure Jas 5:11
as they that c it pleasure to 2Pet 2:13
promise, as some men c slackness 2Pet 3:9
c the number of the beast Rev 13:18

**COUNTED**

he c it to him for righteousness Gen 15:6
that shall be c stolen with me Gen 30:33
Are we not c of him strangers Gen 31:15
of testimony, as it was c Ex 38:21
be c as the fields of the country Lev 25:31
then it shall be c unto the Num 18:30
which is c to the Canaanite Josh 13:3
son Solomon shall be c offenders 1Kin 1:21
be numbered nor c for multitude 1Kin 3:8
Benjamin c he not among them 1Chr 21:6
as they were c by number of names 1Chr 23:24
for they were c faithful, and Neh 13:13
Wherefore are we c as beasts Job 18:3
Darts are c as stubble Job 41:29
we are c as sheep for the Ps 44:22
I am c with them that go down Ps 88:4
And that was c unto him for Ps 106:31
he holdeth his peace, is c wise Prov 17:28
it shall be c a curse to him Prov 27:14
hoofs shall be c like flint Is 5:28
fruitful field be c for a forest Is 32:15
where is he that c the towers Is 33:18
are c as the small dust of the Is 40:15
they are c to him less than Is 40:17
but they were c as a strange Hos 8:12
because they c him as a prophet Mt 14:5
for all men c John, that he was a Mk 11:32
rejoicing that they were c worthy Acts 5:41
they c the price of them, and Acts 19:19
be c for circumcision Rom 2:26
God, and it was c unto him for Rom 4:3
his faith is c for righteousness Rom 4:5
of the promise are c for the seed Rom 9:8
those I c loss for Christ Phil 3:7
that ye may be c worthy of the 2Th 1:5
me, for that he c me faithful 1Ti 1:12
well be c worthy of double honour 1Ti 5:17
For this man was c worthy of more Heb 3:3
But he whose descent is not c Heb 7:6
hath c the blood of the covenant, Heb 10:29

**COUNTENANCE**

was very wroth, and his c fell Gen 4:5
and why is thy c fallen Gen 4:6
And Jacob beheld the c of Laban Gen 31:2
unto them, I see your father's c Gen 31:5
Neither shalt thou c a poor man Ex 23:3
The LORD lift up his c upon thee Num 6:26
A nation of fierce c, which shall Deut 28:50
his c was like the c of Judg 13:6
did eat, and her c was no more sad 1Sa 1:18
unto Samuel, Look not on his c 1Sa 16:7
ruddy, and withal of a beautiful c 1Sa 16:12
a youth, and ruddy, and of a fair c 1Sa 17:42
and of a beautiful c 1Sa 25:3
she was a woman of a fair c 2Sa 14:27
And he settled his c stedfastly 2Kin 8:11
said unto me, Why is thy c sad Neh 2:2
why should not my c be sad Neh 2:3
thou changest his c, and sendest Job 14:20
the light of my c they cast not Job 29:24
up the light of thy c upon us Ps 4:6
through the pride of his c Ps 10:4
his c doth behold the upright Ps 11:7
him exceeding glad with thy c Ps 21:6
praise him for the help of his c Ps 42:5
him, who is the health of my c Ps 42:11
him, who is the health of my c Ps 43:5
thine arm, and the light of thy c Ps 44:3
perish at the rebuke of thy c Ps 80:16
O LORD, in the light of thy c Ps 89:15
secret sins in the light of thy c Ps 90:8
A merry heart maketh a cheerful c Prov 15:13
the light of the king's c is life Prov 16:15
so doth an angry c a backbiting Prov 25:23
sharpeneth the c of his friend Prov 27:17
of the c the heart is made better Eccl 7:3
of the stairs, let me see thy c Song 2:14
is thy voice, and thy c is comely Song 2:14
his c is as Lebanon, excellent as Song 5:15
The shew of their c doth witness Is 3:9
they shall be troubled in their c Eze 27:35
the c of the children that eat of Dan 1:13
Then the king's c was changed Dan 5:6
his c was changed in him, and his Dan 5:9

thee, nor let thy c be changed ... Dan 5:10
me, and my c changed in me ... Dan 7:28
to the full, a king of fierce c ... Dan 8:23
as the hypocrites, of a sad c ... Mt 6:16
His c was like lightning, and his ... Mt 28:3
the fashion of his c was altered ... Lk 9:29
make me full of joy with thy c ... Acts 2:28
of Moses for the glory of his c ... 2Cor 3:7
his c was as the sun shineth in ... Rev 1:16

**COUNTENANCES**
Then let our c be looked upon ... Dan 1:13
ten days their c appeared fairer ... Dan 1:15

**COUNTERVAIL**
could not c the king's damage ... Est 7:4

**COUNTETH**
he c me unto him as one of his ... Job 19:11
me, he c me for his enemy, ... Job 33:10
c the cost, whether he have ... Lk 14:28

**COUNTING**
c one by one, to find out the ... Eccl 7:27

**COUNTRIES**
after their tongues, in their c ... Gen 10:20
thy seed, I will give all these c ... Gen 26:3
give unto thy seed all these c ... Gen 26:4
all c came into Egypt to Joseph ... Gen 41:57
These are the c which Moses did ... Josh 13:32
these are the c which the ... Josh 14:1
and her towns, even three c ... Josh 17:11
they among all the gods of the c ... 2Kin 18:35
fame and of glory throughout all c ... 1Chr 22:5
and over all the kingdoms of the c ... 1Chr 29:30
throughout all the c of Judah ... 2Chr 11:23
service of the kingdoms of the c ... 2Chr 12:8
upon all the inhabitants of the c ... 2Chr 15:5
on all the kingdoms of those c ... 2Chr 20:29
c that pertained to the children ... 2Chr 34:33
because of the people of those c ... Ezr 3:3
ruled over all c beyond the river ... Ezr 4:20
shall wound the heads over many c ... Ps 110:6
and give ear, all ye of far c ... Is 8:9
waste all the nations, and their c ... Is 37:18
all c whither I have driven them ... Jer 23:3
from all c whither I had driven ... Jer 23:8
prophesied both against many c ... Jer 28:8
I will gather them out of all c ... Jer 32:37
Edom, and that were in all the c ... Jer 40:11
c that are round about her ... Eze 5:5
the c that are round about her ... Eze 5:6
shall be scattered through the c ... Eze 6:8
I have scattered them among the c ... Eze 11:16
in the c where they shall come ... Eze 11:16
assemble you out of the c where ... Eze 11:17
and disperse them in the c ... Eze 12:15
and disperse them through the c ... Eze 20:23
heathen, as the families of the c ... Eze 20:32
of the c wherein ye are scattered ... Eze 20:34
gather you out of the c wherein ... Eze 20:41
heathen, and a mocking to all c ... Eze 22:4
and disperse thee in the c ... Eze 22:15
cause thee to perish out of the c ... Eze 25:7
midst of the c that are desolate ... Eze 29:12
will disperse them through the c ... Eze 29:12
midst of the c that are desolate ... Eze 30:7
will disperse them through the c ... Eze 30:23
and disperse them among the c ... Eze 30:26
into the c which thou hast not ... Eze 32:9
people, and gather them from the c ... Eze 34:13
these two c shall be mine, and we ... Eze 35:10
they were dispersed through the c ... Eze 36:19
and gather you out of all c ... Eze 36:24
through all the c whither thou ... Dan 9:7
and he shall enter into the c ... Dan 11:40
many c shall be overthrown ... Dan 11:41
forth his hand also upon the c ... Dan 11:42
they shall remember me in far c ... Zec 10:9
that are in the c enter thereinto ... Lk 21:21

**COUNTRY**
unto Abram, Get thee out of thy c ... Gen 12:1
smote all the c of the Amalekites ... Gen 14:7
the smoke of the c went up as the ... Gen 19:28
from thence toward the south c ... Gen 20:1
But thou shalt go unto my c ... Gen 24:4
for he dwelt in the south c ... Gen 24:62
lived, eastward, unto the east c ... Gen 25:6
It must not be so done in our c ... Gen 29:26
unto mine own place, and to my c ... Gen 30:25
the land of Seir, the c of Edom ... Gen 32:3
saidst unto me, Return unto thy c ... Gen 32:9
Hamor the Hivite, prince of the c ... Gen 34:2
went into the c from the face of ... Gen 36:6
us, and took us for spies of the c ... Gen 42:30
And the man, the lord of the c ... Gen 42:33
land of Egypt, in the c of Goshen ... Gen 47:27
whether it be one of your own c ... Lev 16:29
whether it be one of your own c ... Lev 17:15
as for one of your own c ... Lev 24:22
be counted as the fields of the c ... Lev 25:31
All that are born of the c shall ... Num 15:13
pass, I pray thee, through thy c ... Num 20:17
valley, that is in the c of Moab ... Num 21:20
Even the c which the LORD smote ... Num 32:4
the cities of the c round about ... Num 32:33
the c of Argob unto the coasts of ... Deut 3:14
in the wilderness, in the plain c ... Deut 4:43
that I am come unto the c which ... Deut 26:3
of Israel to search out the c ... Josh 2:2
be come to search out all the c ... Josh 2:3
of the c do faint because of us ... Josh 2:24
two men that had spied out the c ... Josh 6:22
was noised throughout all the c ... Josh 6:27
them, saying, Go up and view the c ... Josh 7:2
Israel, We be come from a far c ... Josh 9:6
From a very far c thy servants ... Josh 9:9
inhabitants of our c spake to us ... Josh 9:11
smote all the c of the hills ... Josh 10:40
all the c of Goshen, even unto ... Josh 10:41
the hills, and all the south c ... Josh 11:16
the kings of the c which Joshua ... Josh 12:7
the wilderness, and in the south c ... Josh 12:8
of the hill c from Lebanon unto ... Josh 13:6
dukes of Sihon, dwelling in the c ... Josh 13:21
then get thee up to the wood c ... Josh 17:15
made an end of dividing the c ... Josh 19:51
is Hebron, in the hill c of Judah ... Josh 21:11
to go unto the c of Gilead ... Josh 22:9
the c was in quietness forty ... Judg 8:28
the inhabitants of that c ... Judg 11:21
in Aijalon in the c of Zebulun ... Judg 12:12
enemy, and the destroyer of our c ... Judg 16:24
went to spy out the c of Laish ... Judg 18:14
sent her throughout all the c of ... Judg 20:6
went to sojourn in the c of Moab ... Ruth 1:1
And they came into the c of Moab ... Ruth 1:2
might return from the c of Moab ... Ruth 1:6
for she had heard in the c of ... Ruth 1:6
returned out of the c of Moab ... Ruth 1:22
with Naomi out of the c of Moab ... Ruth 2:6
come again out of the c of Moab ... Ruth 4:3
the ark of the LORD was in the c ... 1Sa 6:1
of c villages, even unto the ... 1Sa 6:18
the camp from the c round about ... 1Sa 14:21
me a place in some town in the c ... 1Sa 27:5
time that David dwelt in the c of ... 1Sa 27:7
in the c of the Philistines ... 1Sa 27:11
all the c wept with a loud voice, ... 2Sa 15:23
over the face of all the c ... 2Sa 18:8
in the c of Benjamin in Zelah ... 2Sa 21:14
son of Uri was in the c of Gilead ... 1Kin 4:19
in the c of Sihon king of the ... 1Kin 4:19
of all the children of the east c ... 1Kin 4:30
of a far c for thy name's sake ... 1Kin 8:41
she turned and went to her own c ... 1Kin 10:13
and of the governors of the c ... 1Kin 10:15
that I may go to mine own c ... 1Kin 11:21
thou seekest to go to thine own c ... 1Kin 11:22
but the Syrians filled the c ... 1Kin 20:27
city, and every man to his own c ... 1Kin 22:36
the c was filled with water ... 2Kin 3:20
the Moabites, even in their c ... 2Kin 3:24
their c out of mine hand, that ... 2Kin 18:35
said, They are come from a far c ... 2Kin 20:14
begat children in the c of Moab ... 1Chr 8:8
wasted the c of the children of ... 1Chr 20:1
but is come from a far c for thy ... 2Chr 6:32
governors of the c brought gold ... 2Chr 9:14
much cattle, both in the low c ... 2Chr 26:10
invaded the cities of the low c ... 2Chr 28:18
to city through the c of Ephraim ... 2Chr 30:10
the plain c round about Jerusalem ... Neh 12:28
so is good news from a far c ... Prov 25:25
Your c is desolate, your cities ... Is 1:7
They come from a far c, from the ... Is 13:5
thee like a ball into a large c ... Is 22:18
are come from a far c unto me ... Is 39:3
executeth my counsel from a far c ... Is 46:11
I brought you into a plentiful c ... Jer 2:7
that watchers come from a far c ... Jer 4:16
and the sweet cane from a far c ... Jer 6:20
a people cometh from the north c ... Jer 6:22
of them that dwell in a far c ... Jer 8:19
commotion out of the north c ... Jer 10:22
no more, nor see his native c ... Jer 22:10
that bare thee, into another c ... Jer 22:26
of Israel out of the north c ... Jer 23:8
will bring them from the north c ... Jer 31:8
which is in the c of Benjamin ... Jer 32:8
in the c of Pathros, saying, ... Jer 44:1
north c by the river Euphrates ... Jer 46:10
the remnant of the c of Caphtor ... Jer 47:4
judgment is come upon the plain c ... Jer 48:21
of great nations from the north c ... Jer 50:9
us go every one into his own c ... Jer 51:9
out of the c where they sojourn ... Eze 20:38
into the c for the which I lifted ... Eze 20:42
his frontiers, the glory of the c ... Eze 25:9
the c shall be destitute of that ... Eze 32:15
all the inhabited places of the c ... Eze 34:13
issue out toward the east c ... Eze 47:8
be unto you as born in the c ... Eze 47:22
And Jacob fled into the c of Syria ... Hos 12:12
what is thy c? ... Jonah 1:8
my saying, when I was yet in my c ... Jonah 4:2
therein go forth into the north c ... Zec 6:6
go forth toward the south c ... Zec 6:6
c have quieted my spirit in the ... Zec 6:8
quieted my spirit in the north c ... Zec 6:8
east c, and from the west c ... Zec 8:7
into their own c another way ... Mt 2:12
side into the c of the Gergesenes ... Mt 8:28
abroad his fame in all that c ... Mt 9:31
when he was come into his own c ... Mt 13:54
without honour, save in his own c ... Mt 13:57
out into all that c round about ... Mt 14:35
husbandmen, and went into a far c ... Mt 21:33
as a man travelling into a far c ... Mt 25:14
into the c of the Gadarenes ... Mk 5:1
not send them away out of the c ... Mk 5:10
told it in the city, and in the c ... Mk 5:14
thence, and came into his own c ... Mk 6:1
without honour, but in his own c ... Mk 6:4
may go into the c round about ... Mk 6:36
into villages, or cities, or c ... Mk 6:56
husbandmen, and went into a far c ... Mk 12:1
passed by, coming out of the c ... Mk 15:21
they walked, and went into the c ... Mk 16:12
went into the hill c with haste ... Lk 1:39
all the hill c of Judaea ... Lk 1:65
And there were in the same c ... Lk 2:8
came into all the c about Jordan ... Lk 3:3
Capernaum, do also here in thy c ... Lk 4:23
prophet is accepted in his own c ... Lk 4:24
every place of the c round about ... Lk 4:37
arrived at the c of the Gadarenes ... Lk 8:26
told it in the city and in the c ... Lk 8:34
c of the Gadarenes round about ... Lk 8:37
c round about, and lodge, and get ... Lk 9:12
and took his journey into a far c ... Lk 15:13
himself to a citizen of that c ... Lk 15:15
a far c to receive for himself a ... Lk 19:12
went into a far c for a long time ... Lk 20:9
a Cyrenian, coming out of the c ... Lk 23:26
hath no honour in his own c ... Jn 4:44
unto a c near to the wilderness ... Jn 11:54
many went out of the c up to ... Jn 11:55
a Levite, and of the c of Cyprus ... Acts 4:36
unto him, Get thee out of thy c ... Acts 7:3
because their c was nourished by ... Acts 12:20
was nourished by the king's c ... Acts 12:20
was with the deputy of the c ... Acts 13:7
and went over all the c of Galatia ... Acts 18:23
that they drew near to some c ... Acts 27:27
of promise, as in a strange c ... Heb 11:9
plainly that they seek a c ... Heb 11:14
that c from whence they came out ... Heb 11:15
But now they desire a better c ... Heb 11:16

**COUNTRYMEN**
robbers, in perils by mine own c ... 2Cor 11:26
like things of your own c ... 1Th 2:14

**COUPLE**
c the curtains together with the ... Ex 26:6
thou shalt c five curtains by ... Ex 26:9
c the tent together, that it may ... Ex 26:11
of brass to c the tent together ... Ex 36:18
for it, to c it together ... Ex 39:4
servant with him, and a c of asses ... Judg 19:3
make me a c of cakes in my sight, ... 2Sa 13:6
with a c of asses saddled, and ... 2Sa 16:1
a chariot with a c of horsemen ... Is 21:7
of men, with a c of horsemen ... Is 21:9

**COUPLED**
be c together one to another ... Ex 26:3
shall be c one to another ... Ex 26:3
they shall be c together beneath, ... Ex 26:24
they shall be c together above ... Ex 26:24
he c the five curtains one unto ... Ex 36:10
curtains he c one unto another ... Ex 36:10
c the curtains one unto another ... Ex 36:13
he c five curtains by themselves, ... Ex 36:16
And they were c beneath, and ... Ex 36:29
c together at the head thereof, ... Ex 36:29
the two edges was it c together ... Ex 39:4
chaste conversation c with fear ... 1Pet 3:2

**COUPLETH**
of the curtain which c the second ... Ex 26:10
of the curtain which c the second ... Ex 36:17

**COUPLING**
from the selvedge in the c ... Ex 26:4
curtain, in the c of the second ... Ex 26:4
that is in the c of the second ... Ex 26:5
curtain that is outmost in the c ... Ex 26:10
over against the other c thereof ... Ex 28:27
from the selvedge in the c ... Ex 36:11
curtain, in the c of the second ... Ex 36:11
which was in the c of the second ... Ex 36:12
edge of the curtain in the c ... Ex 36:17
over against the other c thereof ... Ex 39:20

**COUPLINGS**
buy hewn stone, and timber for c ... 2Chr 34:11

**COURAGE**
And be ye of good c, and bring of ... Num 13:20
Be strong and of a good c, fear ... Deut 31:6
Israel, Be strong and of a good c ... Deut 31:7
and said, Be strong and of a good c ... Deut 31:23
Be strong and of a good c ... Josh 1:6
Be strong and of a good c ... Josh 1:9
only be strong and of a good c ... Josh 1:18
remain any more c in any man ... Josh 2:11
dismayed, be strong and of good c ... Josh 10:25
Be of good c, and let us play the ... 2Sa 10:12
Be of good c, and let us behave ... 1Chr 19:13
be strong, and of good c ... 1Chr 22:13
his son, Be strong and of good c ... 1Chr 28:20
of Oded the prophet, he took c ... 2Chr 15:8
be of good c, and do it ... Ezr 10:4
be of good c, and he shall ... Ps 27:14
Be of good c, and he shall ... Ps 31:24
said to his brother, Be of good c ... Is 41:6
his c against the king of the ... Dan 11:25
saw, he thanked God, and took c ... Acts 28:15

## COURAGEOUS

Only be thou strong and very c ... Josh 1:7
Be ye therefore very c to keep ... Josh 23:6
be c, and be valiant ... 2Sa 13:28
Be strong and c, be not afraid nor ... 2Chr 32:7
he that is c among the mighty ... Amos 2:16

## COURAGEOUSLY

Deal c, and the LORD shall be with ... 2Chr 19:11

## COURSE

of every c were twenty and four ... 1Chr 27:1
Over the first c for the first ... 1Chr 27:2
in his c were twenty and four ... 1Chr 27:2
over the c of the second month ... 1Chr 27:4
of his c was Mikloth also the ... 1Chr 27:4
in his c likewise were twenty and ... 1Chr 27:4
in his c were twenty and four ... 1Chr 27:5
in his c was Ammizabad his son ... 1Chr 27:6
in his c were twenty and four ... 1Chr 27:7
in his c were twenty and four ... 1Chr 27:8
in his c were twenty and four ... 1Chr 27:9
in his c were twenty and four ... 1Chr 27:10
in his c were twenty and four ... 1Chr 27:11
in his c were twenty and four ... 1Chr 27:12
in his c were twenty and four ... 1Chr 27:13
in his c were twenty and four ... 1Chr 27:14
in his c were twenty and four ... 1Chr 27:15
that ministered to the king by c ... 1Chr 28:1
and did not then wait by c ... 2Chr 5:11
sang together by c in praising ... Ezr 3:11
of the earth are out of c ... Ps 82:5
every one turned to his c ... Jer 8:6
their c is evil, and their force ... Jer 23:10
named Zacharias, of the c of Abia ... Lk 1:5
before God in the order of his c ... Lk 1:8
And as John fulfilled his c ... Acts 13:25
with a straight c to Samothracia ... Acts 16:11
that I might finish my c with joy ... Acts 20:24
came with a straight c unto Coos ... Acts 21:1
we had finished our c from Tyre ... Acts 21:7
the most by three, and that by c ... 1Cor 14:27
according to the c of this world ... Eph 2:2
word of the Lord may have free c ... 2Th 3:1
good fight, I have finished my c ... 2Ti 4:7
setteth on fire the c of nature ... Jas 3:6

## COURSES

the stars in their c fought ... Judg 5:20
ten thousand a month by c ... 1Kin 5:14
into c among the sons of Levi ... 1Chr 23:6
the king in any matter of the c ... 1Chr 27:1
Also for the c of the priests and ... 1Chr 28:13
the c of the priests and the ... 1Chr 28:21
the c of the priests to their ... 2Chr 8:14
also by their c at every gate ... 2Chr 8:14
the priest dismissed not the c ... 2Chr 23:8
appointed the c of the priests ... 2Chr 31:2
and the Levites after their c ... 2Chr 31:2
to give to their brethren by c ... 2Chr 31:15
charges according to their c ... 2Chr 31:16
in their charges by their c ... 2Chr 31:17
of your fathers, after your c ... 2Chr 35:4
place, and the Levites in their c ... 2Chr 35:10
and the Levites in their c ... Ezr 6:18
grass, as willows by the water c ... Is 44:4

## COURT

make the c of the tabernacle ... Ex 27:9
the c of fine twined linen of an ... Ex 27:9
for the breadth of the c on the ... Ex 27:12
the breadth of the c on the east ... Ex 27:13
for the gate of the c shall be an ... Ex 27:16
c shall be filleted with silver ... Ex 27:17
The length of the c shall be an ... Ex 27:18
thereof, and all the pins of the c ... Ex 27:19
The hangings of the c, his ... Ex 35:17
the hanging for the door of the c ... Ex 35:17
tabernacle, and the pins of the c ... Ex 35:18
And he made the c ... Ex 38:9
the c were of fine twined linen ... Ex 38:9
for the other side of the c gate ... Ex 38:15
All the hangings of the c round ... Ex 38:16
all the pillars of the c were ... Ex 38:17
the gate of the c was needlework ... Ex 38:18
to the hangings of the c ... Ex 38:18
of the c round about, were of ... Ex 38:20
the sockets of the c round about ... Ex 38:31
and the sockets of the c gate ... Ex 38:31
all the pins of the c round about ... Ex 38:31
The hangings of the c, his ... Ex 39:40
and the hanging for the c gate ... Ex 39:40
shalt set up the c round about ... Ex 40:8
hang up the hanging at the c gate ... Ex 40:8
he reared up the c round about ... Ex 40:33
set up the hanging of the c gate ... Ex 40:33
in the c of the tabernacle of the ... Lev 6:16
in the c of the tabernacle of the ... Lev 6:26
And the hangings of the c, and the ... Num 3:26
the curtain for the door of the c ... Num 3:26
the pillars of the c round about ... Num 3:37
And the hangings of the c, and the ... Num 4:26
for the door of the gate of the c ... Num 4:26
the pillars of the c round about ... Num 4:32
which had a well in his c ... 2Sa 17:18
he built the inner c with three ... 1Kin 6:36
had another c within the porch ... 1Kin 7:8
on the outside toward the great c ... 1Kin 7:9
the great c round about was with ... 1Kin 7:12
both for the inner c of the house ... 1Kin 7:12
c that was before the house of ... 1Kin 8:64
was gone out into the middle c ... 2Kin 20:4
he made the c of the priests ... 2Chr 4:9
great c, and doors for the c ... 2Chr 4:9
had set it in the midst of the c ... 2Chr 6:13
hallowed the middle of the c that ... 2Chr 7:7
of the LORD, before the new c ... 2Chr 20:5
in the c of the house of the LORD ... 2Chr 24:21
the c of the house of the LORD ... 2Chr 29:16
that was by the c of the prison ... Neh 3:25
in the c of the garden of the ... Est 1:5
before the c of the women's house ... Est 2:11
unto the king into the inner c ... Est 4:11
stood in the inner c of the ... Est 5:1
the queen standing in the c ... Est 5:2
And the king said, Who is in the c ... Est 6:4
the outward c of the king's house ... Est 6:4
Behold, Haman standeth in the c ... Est 6:5
of dragons, and a c for owls ... Is 34:13
he stood in the c of the LORD's ... Jer 19:14
Stand in the c of the LORD's ... Jer 26:2
shut up in the c of the prison ... Jer 32:2
uncle's son came to me in the c ... Jer 32:8
that sat in the c of the prison ... Jer 32:12
shut up in the c of the prison ... Jer 33:1
the scribe, in the higher c ... Jer 36:10
went in to the king into the c ... Jer 36:20
Jeremiah into the c of the prison ... Jer 37:21
remained in the c of the prison ... Jer 37:21
that was in the c of the prison ... Jer 38:6
remained in the c of the prison ... Jer 38:13
So Jeremiah abode in the c of the ... Jer 38:28
out of the c of the prison ... Jer 39:14
shut up in the c of the prison ... Jer 39:15
brought me to the door of the c ... Eze 8:7
the inner c of the LORD's house ... Eze 8:16
and the cloud filled the inner c ... Eze 10:3
the c was full of the brightness ... Eze 10:4
was heard even to the outer c ... Eze 10:5
of the c round about the gate ... Eze 40:14
brought he me into the outward c ... Eze 40:17
made for the c round about ... Eze 40:17
forefront of the inner c without ... Eze 40:19
the gate of the outward c that ... Eze 40:20
the gate of the inner c was over ... Eze 40:23
in the inner c toward the south ... Eze 40:27
to the inner c by the south gate ... Eze 40:28
thereof were toward the utter c ... Eze 40:31
into the inner c toward the east ... Eze 40:32
thereof were toward the outward c ... Eze 40:34
thereof were toward the utter c ... Eze 40:37
of the singers in the inner c ... Eze 40:44
So he measured the c, an hundred ... Eze 40:47
temple, and the porches of the c ... Eze 41:15
brought me forth into the utter c ... Eze 42:1
cubits which were for the inner c ... Eze 42:3
which was for the utter c ... Eze 42:3
toward the utter c on the ... Eze 42:7
in the utter c was fifty cubits ... Eze 42:8
goeth into them from the utter c ... Eze 42:9
the wall of the c toward the east ... Eze 42:10
the holy place into the utter c ... Eze 42:14
and brought me into the inner c ... Eze 43:5
in at the gates of the inner c ... Eze 44:17
in the gates of the inner c ... Eze 44:17
they go forth into the utter c ... Eze 44:19
into the utter c to the people ... Eze 44:19
when they enter into the inner c ... Eze 44:21
the sanctuary, unto the inner c ... Eze 44:27
posts of the gate of the inner c ... Eze 45:19
The gate of the inner c that ... Eze 46:1
them not out into the utter c ... Eze 46:20
brought me forth into the utter c ... Eze 46:21
pass by the four corners of the c ... Eze 46:21
corner of the c there was a c ... Eze 46:21
In the four corners of the c ... Eze 46:22
chapel, and it is the king's c ... Amos 7:13
But the c which is without the ... Rev 11:2

## COURTEOUS

as brethren, be pitiful, be c ... 1Pet 3:8

## COURTEOUSLY

Julius c entreated Paul, and gave ... Acts 27:3
us, and lodged us three days c ... Acts 28:7

## COURTS

two c of the house of the LORD ... 2Kin 21:5
two c of the house of the LORD ... 2Kin 23:12
the house of the LORD, in the c ... 1Chr 23:28
he shall build my house and my c ... 1Chr 28:6
of the c of the house of the LORD ... 1Chr 28:12
in the c of the house of the LORD ... 2Chr 23:5
two c of the house of the LORD ... 2Chr 33:5
roof of his house, and in their c ... Neh 8:16
in the c of the house of God, and ... Neh 8:16
in the c of the house of God ... Neh 13:7
thee, that he may dwell in thy c ... Ps 65:4
fainteth for the c of the LORD ... Ps 84:2
For a day in thy c is better than ... Ps 84:10
flourish in the c of our God ... Ps 92:13
an offering, and come into his c ... Ps 96:8
and into his c with praise ... Ps 100:4
In the c of the LORD's house, in ... Ps 116:19
in the c of the house of our God, ... Ps 135:2
this at your hand, to tread my c ... Is 1:12
drink it in the c of my holiness ... Is 62:9
fill the c with the slain ... Eze 9:7
pillars as the pillars of the c ... Eze 42:6
c joined of forty cubits long ... Eze 46:22
my house, and shalt also keep my c ... Zec 3:7
live delicately, are in kings' c ... Lk 7:25

## COUSIN

thy c Elisabeth, she hath also ... Lk 1:36

## COUSINS

her c heard how the Lord had ... Lk 1:58

## COVENANT

with thee will I establish my c ... Gen 6:18
behold, I establish my c with you ... Gen 9:9
And I will establish my c with you ... Gen 9:11
of the c which I make between me ... Gen 9:12
be for a token of a c between me ... Gen 9:13
And I will remember my c, which is ... Gen 9:15
the everlasting c between God ... Gen 9:16
Noah, This is the token of the c ... Gen 9:17
day the LORD made a c with Abram ... Gen 15:18
And I will make my c between me ... Gen 17:2
my c is with thee, and thou shalt ... Gen 17:4
I will establish my c between me ... Gen 17:7
generations for an everlasting c ... Gen 17:7
Thou shalt keep my c therefore ... Gen 17:9
This is my c, which ye shall keep ... Gen 17:10
be a token of the c betwixt me ... Gen 17:11
my c shall be in your flesh for ... Gen 17:13
your flesh for an everlasting c ... Gen 17:13
he hath broken my c ... Gen 17:14
I will establish my c with him ... Gen 17:19
with him for an everlasting c ... Gen 17:19
But my c will I establish with ... Gen 17:21
and both of them made a c ... Gen 21:27
Thus they made a c at Beer-sheba ... Gen 21:32
and let us make a c with thee ... Gen 26:28
come thou, let us make a c ... Gen 31:44
God remembered his c with Abraham ... Ex 2:24
also established my c with them ... Ex 6:4
and I have remembered my c ... Ex 6:5
my voice indeed, and keep my c ... Ex 19:5
Thou shalt make no c with them ... Ex 23:32
And he took the book of the c ... Ex 24:7
said, Behold the blood of the c ... Ex 24:8
generations, for a perpetual c ... Ex 31:16
And he said, Behold, I make a c ... Ex 34:10
lest thou make a c with the ... Ex 34:12
Lest thou make a c with the ... Ex 34:15
words I have made a c with thee ... Ex 34:27
the tables the words of the c ... Ex 34:28
thou suffer the salt of the c of ... Lev 2:13
of Israel by an everlasting c ... Lev 24:8
you, and establish my c with you ... Lev 26:9
but that ye break my c ... Lev 26:15
shall avenge the quarrel of my c ... Lev 26:25
will I remember my c with Jacob ... Lev 26:42
also my c with Isaac ... Lev 26:42
also my c with Abraham will I ... Lev 26:42
and to break my c with them ... Lev 26:44
remember the c of their ancestors ... Lev 26:45
the ark of the c of the LORD went ... Num 10:33
the ark of the c of the LORD ... Num 14:44
it is a c of salt for ever before ... Num 18:19
I give unto him my c of peace ... Num 25:12
even the c of an everlasting ... Num 25:13
And he declared unto you his c ... Deut 4:13
lest ye forget the c of the LORD ... Deut 4:23
nor forget the c of thy fathers ... Deut 4:31
our God made a c with us in Horeb ... Deut 5:2
made not this c with our fathers ... Deut 5:3
thou shalt make no c with them ... Deut 7:2
the faithful God, which keepeth c ... Deut 7:9
God shall keep unto thee the c ... Deut 7:12
that he may establish his c which ... Deut 8:18
even the tables of the c which ... Deut 9:9
stone, even the tables of the c ... Deut 9:11
of the c were in my two hands ... Deut 9:15
bear the ark of the c of the LORD ... Deut 10:8
thy God, in transgressing his c ... Deut 17:2
These are the words of the c ... Deut 29:1
beside the c which he made with ... Deut 29:1
therefore the words of this c ... Deut 29:9
into c with the LORD thy God ... Deut 29:12
with you only do I make this c ... Deut 29:14
to all the curses of the c that ... Deut 29:21
the c of the LORD God of their ... Deut 29:25
bare the ark of the c of the LORD ... Deut 31:9
break my c which I have made with ... Deut 31:16
and provoke me, and break my c ... Deut 31:20
bare the ark of the c of the LORD ... Deut 31:25
ark of the c of the LORD your God ... Deut 31:26
observed thy word, and kept thy c ... Deut 33:9
ark of the c of the LORD your God ... Josh 3:3
saying, Take up the ark of the c ... Josh 3:6
And they took up the ark of the c ... Josh 3:6
that bear the ark of the c ... Josh 3:8
the ark of the c of the Lord of ... Josh 3:11
ark of the c before the people ... Josh 3:14
that bare the ark of the c of the ... Josh 3:17
the ark of the c of the LORD ... Josh 4:7
which bare the ark of the c stood ... Josh 4:9
that bare the ark of the c of the ... Josh 4:18
them, Take up the ark of the c ... Josh 6:6
the ark of the c of the LORD ... Josh 6:8
my c which I commanded them ... Josh 7:11
transgressed the c of the LORD ... Josh 7:15
bare the ark of the c of the LORD ... Josh 8:33
the c of the LORD your God ... Josh 23:16
So Joshua made a c with the ... Josh 24:25
I will never break my c with you ... Judg 2:1
people hath transgressed my c ... Judg 2:20
(for the ark of the c of God was ... Judg 20:27
Let us fetch the ark of the c of ... 1Sa 4:3
ark of the c of the LORD of hosts ... 1Sa 4:4
with the ark of the c of God ... 1Sa 4:4

when the ark of the c of the LORD 1Sa 4:5
Make a c with us, and we will 1Sa 11:1
will I make a c with you, that I 1Sa 11:2
Then Jonathan and David made a c 1Sa 18:3
into a c of the LORD with thee 1Sa 20:8
So Jonathan made a c with the 1Sa 20:16
they two made a c before the LORD 1Sa 23:18
bearing the ark of the c of God 2Sa 15:24
made with me an everlasting c 2Sa 23:5
the ark of the c of the LORD 1Kin 3:15
the ark of the c of the LORD 1Kin 6:19
might bring up the ark of the c 1Kin 8:1
brought in the ark of the c of 1Kin 8:6
when the LORD made a c with the 1Kin 8:9
ark, wherein is the c of the LORD 1Kin 8:21
on earth beneath, who keepest c 1Kin 8:23
thee, and thou hast not kept my c 1Kin 11:11
of Israel have forsaken thy c 1Kin 19:10
of Israel have forsaken thy c 1Kin 19:14
I will send thee away with this c 1Kin 20:34
So he made a c with him, and sent 1Kin 20:34
made a c with them, and took an 2Kin 11:4
Jehoiada made a c between the 2Kin 11:17
because of his c with Abraham 2Kin 13:23
his c that he made with their 2Kin 17:15
With whom the LORD had made a c 2Kin 17:35
the c that I have made with you 2Kin 17:38
their God, but transgressed his c 2Kin 18:12
the words of the book of the c 2Kin 23:2
made a c before the LORD, to walk 2Kin 23:3
to perform the words of this c 2Kin 23:3
And all the people stood to the c 2Kin 23:3
is written in the book of this c 2Kin 23:21
David made a c with them in 1Chr 11:3
c of the LORD out of the house of 1Chr 15:25
bare the ark of the c of the LORD 1Chr 15:26
the c of the LORD with shouting 1Chr 15:28
as the ark of the c of the LORD 1Chr 15:29
before the ark of the c of God 1Chr 16:6
Be ye mindful always of his c 1Chr 16:15
Even of the c which he made with 1Chr 16:16
and to Israel for an everlasting c 1Chr 16:17
ark of the c of the LORD Asaph 1Chr 16:37
but the ark of the c of the LORD 1Chr 17:1
the ark of the c of the LORD 1Chr 22:19
for the ark of the c of the LORD 1Chr 28:2
the ark of the c of the LORD 1Chr 28:18
to bring up the ark of the c of 2Chr 5:2
brought in the ark of the c of 2Chr 5:7
when the LORD made a c with the 2Chr 5:10
ark, wherein is the c of the LORD 2Chr 6:11
which keepest c, and shewest mercy 2Chr 6:14
him and to his sons by a c of salt 2Chr 13:5
they entered into a c to seek the 2Chr 15:12
because of the c that he had made 2Chr 21:7
son of Zichri, into c with him 2Chr 23:1
all the congregation made a c 2Chr 23:3
And Jehoiada made a c between him 2Chr 23:16
a c with the LORD God of Israel 2Chr 29:10
the words of the book of the c 2Chr 34:30
made a c before the LORD, to walk 2Chr 34:31
to perform the words of the c 2Chr 34:31
did according to the c of God 2Chr 34:32
Now therefore let us make a c Ezr 10:3
and terrible God, that keepeth c Neh 1:5
madest a c with him to give the Neh 9:8
the terrible God, who keepest c Neh 9:32
of all this we make a sure c Neh 9:38
the c of the priesthood, and of Neh 13:29
I made a c with mine eyes Job 31:1
Will he make a c with thee Job 41:4
and truth unto such as keep his c Ps 25:10
and he will shew them his c Ps 25:14
have we dealt falsely in thy c Ps 44:17
made a c with me by sacrifice Ps 50:5
shouldest take my c in thy mouth Ps 50:16
he hath broken his c Ps 55:20
Have respect unto the c Ps 74:20
They kept not the c of God Ps 78:10
were they stedfast in his c Ps 78:37
I have made a c with my chosen, I Ps 89:3
my c shall stand fast with him Ps 89:28
My c will I not break, nor alter Ps 89:34
made void the c of thy servant Ps 89:39
To such as keep his c, and to Ps 103:18
He hath remembered his c for ever Ps 105:8
Which c he made with Abraham, and Ps 105:9
and to Israel for an everlasting c Ps 105:10
And he remembered for them his c Ps 106:45
he will ever be mindful of his c Ps 111:5
he hath commanded his c for ever Ps 111:9
If thy children will keep my c Ps 132:12
and forgetteth the c of her God Prov 2:17
broken the everlasting c Is 24:5
said, We have made a c with death Is 28:15
your c with death shall be Is 28:18
he hath broken the c, he hath Is 33:8
give thee for a c of the people Is 42:6
give thee for a c of the people Is 49:8
neither shall the c of my peace Is 54:10
make an everlasting c with you Is 55:3
please me, and take hold of my c Is 56:4
it, and taketh hold of my c Is 56:6
bed, and made thee a c with them Is 57:8
As for me, this is my c with them Is 59:21
make an everlasting c with them Is 61:8
The ark of the c of the LORD Jer 3:16
Hear ye the words of this c Jer 11:2
obeyeth not the words of this c Jer 11:3
Hear ye the words of this c Jer 11:6
upon them all the words of this c Jer 11:8
house of Judah have broken my c Jer 11:10
remember, break not thy c with us Jer 14:21
the c of the LORD their God Jer 22:9
that I will make a new c with the Jer 31:31
Not according to the c that I Jer 31:32
which my c they brake, although I Jer 31:32
But this shall be the c that I Jer 31:33
make an everlasting c with them Jer 32:40
If ye can break my c of the day Jer 33:20
my c of the night, and that there Jer 33:20
Then may also my c be broken with Jer 33:21
If my c be not with day and night, Jer 33:25
the king Zedekiah had made a c Jer 34:8
which had entered into the c Jer 34:10
I made a c with your fathers in Jer 34:13
ye had made a c before me in the Jer 34:15
men that have transgressed my c Jer 34:18
c which they had made before me Jer 34:18
to the LORD in a perpetual c that Jer 50:5
and entered into a c with thee Eze 16:8
the oath in breaking the c Eze 16:59
my c with thee in the days of thy Eze 16:60
unto thee an everlasting c Eze 16:60
for daughters, but not by thy c Eze 16:61
I will establish my c with thee Eze 16:62
made a c with him, and hath taken Eze 17:13
keeping of his c it might stand Eze 17:14
or shall he break the c, and be Eze 17:15
whose c he brake, even with him Eze 17:16
the oath by breaking the c Eze 17:18
my c that he hath broken, even it Eze 17:19
bring you into the bond of the c Eze 20:37
will make with them a c of peace Eze 34:25
will make a c of peace with them Eze 37:26
be an everlasting c with them Eze 37:26
broken my c because of all your Eze 44:7
and dreadful God, keeping the c Dan 9:4
he shall confirm the c with many Dan 9:27
yea, also the prince of the c Dan 11:22
heart shall be against the holy c Dan 11:28
indignation against the holy c Dan 11:30
with them that forsake the holy c Dan 11:30
c shall he corrupt by flatteries Dan 11:32
in that day will I make a c for Hos 2:18
like men have transgressed the c Hos 6:7
they have transgressed my c Hos 8:1
swearing falsely in making a c Hos 10:4
they do make a c with the Hos 12:1
and remembered not the brotherly c Amos 1:9
by the blood of thy c I have sent Zec 9:11
that I might break my c which I Zec 11:10
that my c might be with Levi, Mal 2:4
My c was with him of life and Mal 2:5
ye have corrupted the c of Levi Mal 2:8
by profaning the c of our fathers Mal 2:10
companion, and the wife of thy c Mal 2:14
even the messenger of the c Mal 3:1
and to remember his holy c Lk 1:72
of the c which God made with our Acts 3:25
he gave him the c of circumcision Acts 7:8
For this is my c unto them Rom 11:27
Though it be but a man's c Gal 3:15
And this I say, that the c Gal 3:17
he is the mediator of a better c Heb 8:6
For if that first c had been Heb 8:7
when I will make a new c with the Heb 8:8
Not according to the c that I Heb 8:9
they continued not in my c Heb 8:9
For this is the c that I will Heb 8:10
In that he saith, A new c Heb 8:13
Then verily the first c had also Heb 9:1
the ark of the c overlaid round Heb 9:4
budded, and the tables of the c Heb 9:4
This is the c that I will make Heb 10:16
hath counted the blood of the c Heb 10:29
Jesus the mediator of the new c Heb 12:24
the blood of the everlasting c Heb 13:20

## COVENANTBREAKERS

Without understanding, c, without Rom 1:31

## COVENANTED

according as I have c with David 2Chr 7:18
I c with you when ye came out of Hag 2:5
they c with him for thirty pieces Mt 26:15
were glad, and c to give him money Lk 22:5

## COVENANTS

adoption, and the glory, and the c Rom 9:4
for these are the two c Gal 4:24
strangers from the c of promise Eph 2:12

## COVER

they shall c the face of the Ex 10:5
man shall dig a pit, and not c it Ex 21:33
and bowls thereof, to c withal Ex 25:29
side and on that side, to c it Ex 26:13
breeches to c their nakedness Ex 28:42
will c thee with my hand while I Ex 33:22
bowls, and his covers to c withal Ex 37:16
and c the ark with the vail Ex 40:3
the leprosy c all the skin of him Lev 13:12
the cloud of the incense may c Lev 16:13
blood thereof, and c it with dust Lev 17:13
c the ark of testimony with it Num 4:5
the bowls, and covers to c withal Num 4:7
c the same with a covering of Num 4:8
c the candlestick of the light, Num 4:9
c it with a covering of badgers' Num 4:11
c them with a covering of Num 4:12
they c the face of the earth, and Num 22:5
c that which cometh from thee Deut 23:13
the LORD shall c him all the day Deut 33:12
and Saul went in to c his feet 1Sa 24:3
to c the chapiters that were upon 1Kin 7:18
to c the two bowls of the 1Kin 7:41
to c the two bowls of the 1Kin 7:42
the two wreaths to c the two 2Chr 4:12
to c the two pommels of the 2Chr 4:13
c not their iniquity, and let not Neh 4:5
c not thou my blood, and let my Job 16:18
dust, and the worms shall c them Job 21:26
and abundance of waters c thee Job 22:11
abundance of waters may c thee Job 38:34
The shady trees c him with their Job 40:22
He shall c thee with his feathers Ps 91:4
turn not again to c the earth Ps 104:9
let them c themselves with their Ps 109:29
Surely the darkness shall c me Ps 139:11
mischief of their own lips c them Ps 140:9
the LORD, as the waters c the sea Is 11:9
under thee, and the worms c thee Is 14:11
captivity, and will surely c thee Is 22:17
and shall no more c her slain Is 26:21
that c with a covering, but not Is 30:1
seest the naked, that thou c him Is 58:7
neither shall they c themselves Is 59:6
the darkness shall c the earth Is 60:2
multitude of camels shall c thee Is 60:6
I will go up, and will c the earth Jer 46:8
sackcloth, and horror shall c them Eze 7:18
thou shalt c thy face, that thou Eze 12:6
he shall c his face, that he see Eze 12:12
the ground, to c it with dust Eze 24:7
c not thy lips, and eat not the Eze 24:17
ye shall not c your lips, nor eat Eze 24:22
horses their dust shall c thee Eze 26:10
and great waters shall c thee Eze 26:19
as for her, a cloud shall c her Eze 30:18
I will c the heaven, and make the Eze 32:7
I will c the sun with a cloud, and Eze 32:7
c you with skin, and put breath in Eze 37:6
be like a cloud to c the land Eze 38:9
Israel, as a cloud to c the land Eze 38:16
my flax given to c her nakedness Hos 2:9
shall say to the mountains, C us Hos 10:8
brother Jacob shame shall c thee Obad 10
yea, they shall all c their lips Mic 3:7
shame shall c her which said unto Mic 7:10
the LORD, as the waters c the sea Hab 2:14
violence of Lebanon shall c thee Hab 2:17
to c his face, and to buffet him, Mk 14:65
and to the hills, C us Lk 23:30
indeed ought not to c his head 1Cor 11:7
for charity shall c the multitude 1Pet 4:8

## COVERED

under the whole heaven, were c Gen 7:19
and the mountains were c Gen 7:20
c the nakedness of their father Gen 9:23
she took a vail, and c herself Gen 24:65
c her with a vail, and wrapped Gen 38:14
because she had c her face Gen 38:15
came up, and c the land of Egypt Ex 8:6
For they c the face of the whole Ex 10:15
c the chariots, and the horsemen, Ex 14:28
The depths have c them Ex 15:5
with thy wind, the sea c them Ex 15:10
the quails came up, and c the camp Ex 16:13
the mount, and a cloud c the mount Ex 24:15
Sinai, and the cloud c it six days Ex 24:16
c with their wings over the mercy Ex 37:9
c the ark of the testimony Ex 40:21
Then a cloud c the tent of the Ex 40:34
the leprosy have c all his flesh Lev 13:13
to see when the holy things are c Num 4:20
six c wagons, and twelve oxen Num 7:3
up the cloud c the tabernacle Num 9:15
the cloud c it by day, and the Num 9:16
and, behold, the cloud c it Num 16:42
thick, thou art c with fatness Deut 32:15
the sea upon them, and c them Josh 24:7
the tent, she c him with a mantle Judg 4:18
milk, and gave him drink, and c him Judg 4:19
his bolster, and c it with a cloth 1Sa 19:13
and he is c with a mantle 1Sa 28:14
as he went up, and had his head c 2Sa 15:30
was with him c every man his head 2Sa 15:30
But the king c his face, and the 2Sa 19:4
they c him with clothes, but he 1Kin 1:1
c the house with beams and boards 1Kin 6:9
he c them on the inside with wood 1Kin 6:15
c the floor of the house with 1Kin 6:15
so c the altar which was of cedar 1Kin 6:20
c them with gold fitted upon the 1Kin 6:35
it was c with cedar above upon 1Kin 7:3
it was c with cedar from one side 1Kin 7:7
ark, and the cherubims c the ark 1Kin 8:7
c himself with sackcloth, and went 2Kin 19:1
c with sackcloth, to Isaiah the 2Kin 19:2
c the ark of the covenant of the 1Chr 28:18
ark, and the cherubims c the ark 2Chr 5:8
c it, and set up the doors thereof Neh 3:15
mourning, and having his head c Est 6:12
king's mouth, they c Haman's face Est 7:8
neither hath he c the darkness Job 23:17
If I c my transgressions as Adam, Job 31:33
is forgiven, whose sin is c Ps 32:1
and the shame of my face hath c me Ps 44:15
c us with the shadow of death Ps 44:19
valleys also are c over with corn Ps 65:13
the wings of a dove c with silver Ps 68:13

shame hath c my face ... Ps 69:7
let them be c with reproach and ... Ps 71:13
The hills were c with the shadow ... Ps 80:10
thou hast c all their sin ... Ps 85:2
thou hast c him with shame ... Ps 89:45
the waters c their enemies ... Ps 106:11
and c the company of Abiram ... Ps 106:17
thou hast c me in my mother's ... Ps 139:13
thou hast c my head in the day of ... Ps 140:7
nettles had c the face thereof, ... Prov 24:31
a potsherd c with silver dross ... Prov 26:23
Whose hatred is c by deceit ... Prov 26:26
his name shall be c with darkness ... Eccl 6:4
with twain he c his face ... Is 6:2
and with twain he c his feet ... Is 6:2
your rulers, the seers hath he c ... Is 29:10
c himself with sackcloth, and went ... Is 37:1
of the priests c with sackcloth ... Is 37:2
I have c thee in the shadow of ... Is 51:16
he hath c me with the robe of ... Is 61:10
and confounded, and c their heads ... Jer 14:3
were ashamed, they c their heads ... Jer 14:4
she is c with the multitude of ... Jer 51:42
shame hath c our faces ... Jer 51:51
How hath the Lord c the daughter ... Lam 2:1
stones, he hath c me with ashes ... Lam 3:16
Thou hast c with anger, and ... Lam 3:43
Thou hast c thyself with a cloud, ... Lam 3:44
to another, and two c their bodies ... Eze 1:11
which c on this side, and every ... Eze 1:23
which c on that side, their ... Eze 1:23
over thee, and c thy nakedness ... Eze 16:8
fine linen, and I c thee with silk ... Eze 16:10
hath c the naked with a garment ... Eze 18:7
hath c the naked with a garment, ... Eze 18:16
a rock, that it should not be c ... Eze 24:8
of Elishah was that which c thee ... Eze 27:7
I c the deep for him, and I ... Eze 31:15
them, and the skin c them above ... Eze 37:8
windows, and the windows were c ... Eze 41:16
c him with sackcloth, and sat in ... Jonah 3:6
beast be c with sackcloth, and cry ... Jonah 3:8
His glory c the heavens, and the ... Hab 3:3
the ship was c with the waves ... Mt 8:24
for there is nothing c, that ... Mt 10:26
For there is nothing c, that ... Lk 12:2
are forgiven, and whose sins are c ... Rom 4:7
or prophesying, having his head c ... 1Cor 11:4
For if the woman be not c ... 1Cor 11:6
be shorn or shaven, let her be c ... 1Cor 11:6

**COVEREDST**
Thou c it with the deep as with a ... Ps 104:6
thy broidered garments, and c them ... Eze 16:18

**COVEREST**
vesture, wherewith thou c thyself ... Deut 22:12
Who c thyself with light as with ... Ps 104:2

**COVERETH**
all the fat that c the inwards ... Ex 29:13
and the fat that c the inwards ... Ex 29:22
the fat that c the inwards ... Lev 3:3
and the fat that c the inwards ... Lev 3:9
the fat that c the inwards ... Lev 3:14
the fat that c the inwards ... Lev 4:8
and the fat that c the inwards ... Lev 7:3
that which c the inwards, and the ... Lev 9:19
which c the face of the earth ... Num 22:11
Surely he c his feet in his ... Judg 3:24
he c the faces of the judges ... Job 9:24
Because he c his face with his ... Job 15:27
it, and c the bottom of the sea ... Job 36:30
With clouds he c the light ... Job 36:32
violence c them as a garment ... Ps 73:6
him as the garment which c him ... Ps 109:19
Who c the heaven with clouds, who ... Ps 147:8
but violence c the mouth of the ... Prov 10:6
but violence c the mouth of the ... Prov 10:11
but love c all sins ... Prov 10:12
but a prudent man c shame ... Prov 12:16
He that c a transgression seeketh ... Prov 17:9
He that c his sins shall not ... Prov 28:13
our shame, and our confusion c us ... Jer 3:25
art the anointed cherub that c ... Eze 28:14
for one c violence with his ... Mal 2:16
c it with a vessel, or putteth it ... Lk 8:16

**COVERING**
and Noah removed the c of the ark ... Gen 8:13
he is to thee a c of the eyes ... Gen 20:16
For that is his c only, it is his ... Ex 22:27
c the mercy seat with their wings ... Ex 25:20
to be a c upon the tabernacle ... Ex 26:7
thou shalt make a c for the tent ... Ex 26:14
a c above of badgers' skins ... Ex 26:14
tabernacle, his tent, and his c ... Ex 35:11
mercy seat, and the vail of the c ... Ex 35:12
he made a c for the tent of rams' ... Ex 36:19
a c of badgers' skins above that ... Ex 36:19
the c of rams' skins dyed red, and ... Ex 39:34
the c of badgers' skins ... Ex 39:34
and the vail of the c ... Ex 39:34
put the c of the tent above upon ... Ex 40:19
and set up the vail of the c ... Ex 40:21
he shall put a c upon his upper ... Lev 13:45
the c thereof, and the hanging for ... Num 3:25
they shall take down the c vail ... Num 4:5
thereon the c of badgers' skins ... Num 4:6
same with a c of badgers' skins ... Num 4:8
within a c of badgers' skins ... Num 4:10
cover it with a c of badgers' ... Num 4:11
them with a c of badgers' skins ... Num 4:12
upon it a c of badgers' skins ... Num 4:14
made an end of c the sanctuary ... Num 4:15
of the congregation, his c ... Num 4:25
the c of the badgers' skins that ... Num 4:25
broad plates for a c of the altar ... Num 16:38
broad plates for a c of the altar ... Num 16:39
which hath no c bound upon it ... Num 19:15
spread a c over the well's mouth, ... 2Sa 17:19
Thick clouds are a c to him ... Job 22:14
that they have no c in the cold ... Job 24:7
him, and destruction hath no c ... Job 26:6
clothing, or any poor without c ... Job 31:19
He spread a cloud for a c ... Ps 105:39
the c of it of purple, the midst ... Song 3:10
And he discovered the c of Judah ... Is 22:8
of the c cast over all people ... Is 25:7
the c narrower than that he can ... Is 28:20
and that cover with a c, but not ... Is 30:1
Ye shall defile also the c of thy ... Is 30:22
and I make sackcloth their c ... Is 50:3
every precious stone was thy c ... Eze 28:13
O c cherub, from the midst of the ... Eze 28:16
c the altar of the LORD with ... Mal 2:13
for her hair is given her for a c ... 1Cor 11:15

**COVERINGS**
decked my bed with c of tapestry ... Prov 7:16
She maketh herself c of tapestry ... Prov 31:22

**COVERS**
c thereof, and bowls thereof, to ... Ex 25:29
his c to cover withal, of pure ... Ex 37:16
the bowls, and c to cover withal ... Num 4:7

**COVERT**
came down by the c of the hill ... 1Sa 25:20
the c for the sabbath that they ... 2Kin 16:18
abide in the c to lie in wait ... Job 38:40
in the c of the reed, and fens ... Job 40:21
will trust in the c of thy wings ... Ps 61:4
for a c from storm and from rain ... Is 4:6
be thou a c to them from the face ... Is 16:4
the wind, and a c from the tempest ... Is 32:2
He hath forsaken his c, as the ... Jer 25:38

**COVET**
Thou shalt not c thy neighbour's ... Ex 20:17
thou shalt not c thy neighbour's ... Ex 20:17
wife, neither shalt thou c thy ... Deut 5:21
they c fields, and take them by ... Mic 2:2
law had said, Thou shalt not c ... Rom 7:7
false witness, Thou shalt not c ... Rom 13:9
But c earnestly the best gifts ... 1Cor 12:31
c to prophesy, and forbid not to ... 1Cor 14:39

**COVETED**
shekels weight, then I c them ... Josh 7:21
I have c no man's silver, or gold ... Acts 20:33
which while some c after, they ... 1Ti 6:10

**COVETETH**
He c greedily all the day long ... Prov 21:26
Woe to him that c an evil ... Hab 2:9

**COVETOUS**
heart's desire, and blesseth the c ... Ps 10:3
And the Pharisees also, who were c ... Lk 16:14
of this world, or with the c ... 1Cor 5:10
a brother be a fornicator, or c ... 1Cor 5:11
Nor thieves, nor c, nor drunkards ... 1Cor 6:10
nor unclean person, nor c man ... Eph 5:5
but patient, not a brawler, not c ... 1Ti 3:3
be lovers of their own selves, c ... 2Ti 3:2
have exercised with c practices ... 2Pet 2:14

**COVETOUSNESS**
fear God, men of truth, hating c ... Ex 18:21
unto thy testimonies, and not to c ... Ps 119:36
but he that hateth c shall ... Prov 28:16
the iniquity of his c was I wroth ... Is 57:17
of them every one is given to c ... Jer 6:13
unto the greatest is given to c ... Jer 8:10
thine heart are not but for thy c ... Jer 22:17
is come, and the measure of thy c ... Jer 51:13
their heart goeth after their c ... Eze 33:31
coveteth an evil c to his house ... Hab 2:9
Thefts, c, wickedness, deceit, ... Mk 7:22
them, Take heed, and beware of c ... Lk 12:15
fornication, wickedness, c ... Rom 1:29
matter of bounty, and not as of c ... 2Cor 9:5
and all uncleanness, or c ... Eph 5:3
evil concupiscence, and c ... Col 3:5
as ye know, nor a cloke of c ... 1Th 2:5
your conversation be without c ... Heb 13:5
through c shall they with feigned ... 2Pet 2:3

**COVOCATION**
month ye shall have an holy c ... Num 29:12

**COW**
And whether it be c or ewe ... Lev 22:28
But the firstling of a c, or the ... Num 18:17
their c calveth, and casteth not ... Job 21:10
a man shall nourish a young c ... Is 7:21
And the c and the bear shall feed ... Is 11:7
every c at that which is before ... Amos 4:3

**COW'S**
I have given thee c dung for ... Eze 4:15

**COZ** (coz) *A descendant of Caleb.*
C begat Anub, and Zobebah, and the ... 1Chr 4:8

**COZBI** (coz'-bi) *A Midianite woman.*
woman that was slain was C ... Num 25:15
of Peor, and in the matter of C ... Num 25:18

**COZEBA** See CHOZEBA.

**CRACKLING**
For as the c of thorns under a ... Eccl 7:6

**CRACKNELS**
take with thee ten loaves, and c ... 1Kin 14:3

**CRAFT**
cause c to prosper in his hand ... Dan 8:25
how they might take him by c ... Mk 14:1
And because he was of the same c ... Acts 18:3
that by this c we have our wealth ... Acts 19:25
our c is in danger to be set at ... Acts 19:27
craftsman, of whatsoever c he be ... Rev 18:22

**CRAFTINESS**
He taketh the wise in their own c ... Job 5:13
But he perceived their c, and said ... Lk 20:23
He taketh the wise in their own c ... 1Cor 3:19
of dishonesty, not walking in c ... 2Cor 4:2
the sleight of men, and cunning c ... Eph 4:14

**CRAFTSMAN**
the work of the hands of the c ... Deut 27:15
and no c, of whatsoever craft he ... Rev 18:22

**CRAFTSMEN**
thousand captives, and all the c ... 2Kin 24:14
might, even seven thousand, and c ... 2Kin 24:16
for they were c ... 1Chr 4:14
Lod, and Ono, the valley of c ... Neh 11:35
all of it the work of the c ... Hos 13:2
brought no small gain unto the c ... Acts 19:24
the c which are with him, have a ... Acts 19:38

**CRAFTY**
the devices of the c, so that ... Job 5:12
thou choosest the tongue of the c ... Job 15:5
They have taken c counsel against ... Ps 83:3
nevertheless, being c, I caught ... 2Cor 12:16

**CRAG**
upon the c of the rock, and the ... Job 39:28

**CRANE**
Like a c or a swallow, so did I ... Is 38:14
and the turtle and the c and the ... Jer 8:7

**CRASHING**
and a great c from the hills ... Zeph 1:10

**CRAVED**
Pilate, and c the body of Jesus ... Mk 15:43

**CRAVETH**
for his mouth c it of him ... Prov 16:26

**CREATE**
C in me a clean heart, O God ... Ps 51:10
the LORD will c upon every ... Is 4:5
I form the light, and c darkness ... Is 45:7
I make peace, and c evil ... Is 45:7
I c the fruit of the lips ... Is 57:19
I c new heavens and a new earth ... Is 65:17
for ever in that which I c ... Is 65:18
I c Jerusalem a rejoicing, and her ... Is 65:18

**CREATED**
In the beginning God c the heaven ... Gen 1:1
God c great whales, and every ... Gen 1:21
So God c man in his own image ... Gen 1:27
in the image of God c he him ... Gen 1:27
male and female c he them ... Gen 1:27
from all his work which God c ... Gen 2:3
and of the earth when they were c ... Gen 2:4
In the day that God c man ... Gen 5:1
Male and female c he them ... Gen 5:2
Adam, in the day when they were c ... Gen 5:2
have c from the face of the earth ... Gen 6:7
day that God c man upon the earth ... Deut 4:32
and the south thou hast c them ... Ps 89:12
shall be c shall praise the LORD ... Ps 102:18
forth thy spirit, they are c ... Ps 104:30
for he commanded, and they were c ... Ps 148:5
and behold who hath c these things ... Is 40:26
the Holy One of Israel hath c it ... Is 41:20
he that c the heavens, and ... Is 42:5
thus saith the LORD that c thee ... Is 43:1
for I have c him for my glory, I ... Is 43:7
I the LORD have c it ... Is 45:8
made the earth, and c man upon it ... Is 45:12
saith the LORD that c the heavens ... Is 45:18
he c it not in vain, he formed it ... Is 45:18
They are c now, and not from the ... Is 48:7
I have c the smith that bloweth ... Is 54:16
I have c the waster to destroy ... Is 54:16
for the LORD hath c a new thing ... Jer 31:22
in the place where thou wast c ... Eze 21:30
thee in the day that thou wast c ... Eze 28:13
from the day that thou wast c ... Eze 28:15
hath not one God c us ... Mal 2:10
which God c unto this time ... Mk 13:19
was the man c for the woman ... 1Cor 11:9
c in Christ Jesus unto good works ... Eph 2:10
who c all things by Jesus Christ ... Eph 3:9
after God is c in righteousness ... Eph 4:24
For by him were all things c ... Col 1:16
all things were c by him, and for ... Col 1:16
after the image of him that c him ... Col 3:10
which God hath c to be received ... 1Ti 4:3
for thou hast c all things ... Rev 4:11
thy pleasure they are and were c ... Rev 4:11
who c heaven, and the things that ... Rev 10:6

**CREATETH**
c the wind, and declareth unto man ... Amos 4:13

**CREATION**
of the c God made them male ... Mk 10:6
the c which God created unto this ... Mk 13:19

C

things of him from the c of the Rom 1:20
we know that the whole c groaneth Rom 8:22
were from the beginning of the c 2Pet 3:4
the beginning of the c of God Rev 3:14

**CREATOR**

Remember now thy C in the days of Eccl 12:1
the C of the ends of the earth, Is 40:28
the c of Israel, your King Is 43:15
the creature more than the C Rom 1:25
well doing, as unto a faithful C 1Pet 4:19

**CREATURE**

the moving c that hath life Gen 1:20
and every living c that moveth Gen 1:21
forth the living c after his kind Gen 1:24
Adam called every living c Gen 2:19
every living c that is with you Gen 9:10
every living c that is with you, Gen 9:12
and every living c of all flesh Gen 9:15
every living c of all flesh that Gen 9:16
of every living c that moveth in Lev 11:46
of every c that creepeth upon the Lev 11:46
of the living c was in the wheels Eze 1:20
of the living c was in the wheels Eze 1:21
living c was as the colour of the Eze 1:22
This is the living c that I saw Eze 10:15
of the living c was in them Eze 10:17
This is the living c that I saw Eze 10:20
and preach the gospel to every c Mk 16:15
served the c more than the Rom 1:25
c waiteth for the manifestation Rom 8:19
For the c was made subject to Rom 8:20
Because the c itself also shall Rom 8:21
nor depth, nor any other c Rom 8:39
man be in Christ, he is a new c 2Cor 5:17
nor uncircumcision, but a new c Gal 6:15
God, the firstborn of every c Col 1:15
to every c which is under heaven Col 1:23
For every c of God is good, and 1Ti 4:4
Neither is there any c that is Heb 4:13
every c which is in heaven, and on Rev 5:13

**CREATURES**

houses shall be full of doleful c Is 13:21
the likeness of four living c Eze 1:5
for the likeness of the living c Eze 1:13
up and down among the living c Eze 1:13
And the living c ran and returned Eze 1:14
Now as I beheld the living c Eze 1:15
upon the earth by the living c Eze 1:15
And when the living c went Eze 1:19
when the living c were lifted up Eze 1:19
living c that touched one another Eze 3:13
be a kind of firstfruits of his c Jas 1:18
of the c which were in the sea Rev 8:9

**CREDITOR**

Every c that lendeth ought unto Deut 15:2
the c is come to take unto him my 2Kin 4:1
There was a certain c which had Lk 7:41

**CREDITORS**

or which of my c is it to whom I Is 50:1

**CREEK**

a certain c with a shore, into Acts 27:39

**CREEP**

All fowls that c, going upon all Lev 11:20
things that c upon the earth Lev 11:29
unclean to you among all that c Lev 11:31
things that c upon the earth Lev 11:42
beasts of the forest do c forth Ps 104:20
things that c upon the earth Eze 38:20
sort are they which c into houses 2Ti 3:6

**CREEPETH**

every thing that c upon the earth Gen 1:25
thing that c upon the earth Gen 1:26
every thing that c upon the earth Gen 1:30
every thing that c upon the earth Gen 7:8
every creeping thing that c upon Gen 7:14
thing that c upon the earth Gen 7:21
thing that c upon the earth Gen 8:17
whatsoever c upon the earth, Gen 8:19
every creeping thing that c upon Lev 11:41
with any creeping thing that c Lev 11:43
thing that c upon the earth Lev 11:44
creature that c upon the earth Lev 11:46
living thing that c on the ground Lev 20:25
of any thing that c on the ground Deut 4:18

**CREEPING**

c thing, and beast of the earth Gen 1:24
over every c thing that creepeth Gen 1:26
the c thing, and the fowls of the Gen 6:7
of every c thing of the earth Gen 6:20
every c thing that creepeth upon Gen 7:14
of every c thing that creepeth Gen 7:21
the c things, and the fowl of the Gen 7:23
of every c thing that creepeth Gen 8:17
Every beast, every c thing Gen 8:19
the carcase of unclean c things Lev 5:2
may ye eat of every flying c Lev 11:21
But all other flying c things Lev 11:23
the c things that creep upon the Lev 11:29
every c thing that creepeth upon Lev 11:41
hath more feet among all c things Lev 11:42
with any c thing that creepeth Lev 11:43
of c thing that creepeth upon the Lev 11:44
Or whosoever toucheth any c thing Lev 22:5
every c thing that flieth is Deut 14:19
of c things, and of fishes 1Kin 4:33
wherein are things c innumerable Ps 104:25
c things, and flying fowl Ps 148:10
and behold every form of c things Eze 8:10
all c things that creep upon the Eze 38:20
with the c things of the ground Hos 2:18
of the sea, as the c things Hab 1:14
c things, and fowls of the air Acts 10:12
c things, and fowls of the air Acts 11:6
and fourfooted beasts, and c things Rom 1:23

**CREPT**

are certain men c in unawares Jude 4

**CRESCENS** (*cres'-sens*) *A companion of Paul.*

C to Galatia, Titus unto Dalmatia 2Ti 4:10

**CRETE** (*creet*) See CRETES. *An island south of Greece.*

suffering us, we sailed under C Acts 27:7
which is an haven of C, and lieth Acts 27:12
thence, they sailed close by C Acts 27:13
me, and not have loosed from C Acts 27:21
For this cause left I thee in C Titus 1:5

**CRETES** (*creets*) See CRETIANS. *Inhabitants of Crete.*

C and Arabians, we do hear them Acts 2:11

**CRETIANS** (*cre'-shuns*) See CRETES. *Same as Cretes.*

The C are alway liars, evil Titus 1:12
bishop of the church of the C Titus *s*

**CREW**

And immediately the cock c Mt 26:74
and the cock c Mk 14:68
And the second time the cock c Mk 14:72
while he yet spake, the cock c Lk 22:60
and immediately the cock c Jn 18:27

**CRIB**

to serve thee, or abide by thy c Job 39:9
Where no oxen are, the c is clean Prov 14:4
owner, and the ass his master's c Is 1:3

**CRIED**

he c with a great and exceeding Gen 27:34
with me, and I c with a loud voice Gen 39:14
that I lifted up my voice and c Gen 39:15
as I lifted up my voice and c Gen 39:18
they c before him, Bow the knee Gen 41:43
the people c to Pharaoh for bread Gen 41:55
and he c, Cause every man to go Gen 45:1
reason of the bondage, and they c Ex 2:23
c unto Pharaoh, saying, Wherefore Ex 5:15
Moses c unto the LORD because of Ex 8:12
of Israel c out unto the LORD Ex 14:10
And he c unto the LORD Ex 15:25
Moses c unto the LORD, saying, Ex 17:4
And the people c unto Moses Num 11:2
Moses c unto the LORD, saying, Num 12:13
lifted up their voice, and c Num 14:1
when we c unto the LORD, he heard Num 20:16
the damsel, because she c not Deut 22:24
field, and the betrothed damsel c Deut 22:27
when we c unto the LORD God of Deut 26:7
when they c unto the LORD, he put Josh 24:7
of Israel c unto the LORD Judg 3:9
of Israel c unto the LORD Judg 3:15
of Israel c unto the LORD Judg 4:3
c through the lattice, Why is his Judg 5:28
of Israel c unto the LORD Judg 6:6
when the children of Israel c Judg 6:7
and they c, The sword of the LORD, Judg 7:20
and all the host ran, and c Judg 7:21
and lifted up his voice, and c Judg 9:7
of Israel c unto the LORD Judg 10:10
ye c to me, and I delivered you Judg 10:12
they c unto the children of Dan Judg 18:23
and told it, all the city c out 1Sa 4:13
Ekron, that the Ekronites c out 1Sa 5:10
Samuel c unto the LORD for Israel 1Sa 7:9
your fathers c unto the LORD, 1Sa 12:8
they c unto the LORD, and said, We 1Sa 12:10
he c unto the LORD all night 1Sa 15:11
c unto the armies of Israel, and 1Sa 17:8
Jonathan c after the lad, and said 1Sa 20:37
Jonathan c after the lad, Make 1Sa 20:38
c after Saul, saying, My lord the 1Sa 24:8
David c to the people, and to 1Sa 26:14
Samuel, she c with a loud voice 1Sa 28:12
And the watchman c, and told the 2Sa 18:25
the king c with a loud voice, O 2Sa 19:4
Then c a wise woman out of the 2Sa 20:16
upon the LORD, and c to my God 2Sa 22:7
he c against the altar in the 1Kin 13:2
which had c against the altar in 1Kin 13:4
he c unto the man of God that 1Kin 13:21
For the saying which he c by the 1Kin 13:32
he c unto the LORD, and said, O 1Kin 17:20
c unto the LORD, and said, O LORD 1Kin 17:21
they c aloud, and cut themselves 1Kin 18:28
passed by, he c unto the king 1Kin 20:39
and Jehoshaphat c out 1Kin 22:32
And Elisha saw it, and he c 2Kin 2:12
Now there c a certain woman of 2Kin 4:1
of the pottage, that they c out 2Kin 4:40
and he c, and said, Alas, master 2Kin 6:5
there c a woman unto him, saying, 2Kin 6:26
c to the king for her house and 2Kin 8:5
Athaliah rent her clothes, and c 2Kin 11:14
c with a loud voice in the Jews' 2Kin 18:28
the prophet c unto the LORD 2Kin 20:11
for they c to God in the battle, 1Chr 5:20
they c unto the LORD, and the 2Chr 13:14
Asa c unto the LORD his God, and 2Chr 14:11
but Jehoshaphat c out, and the 2Chr 18:31
Then they c with a loud voice in 2Chr 32:18
of Amoz, prayed and c to heaven 2Chr 32:20
c with a loud voice unto the LORD Neh 9:4
trouble, when they c unto thee Neh 9:27
c unto thee, thou heardest them Neh 9:28
c with a loud and a bitter cry Est 4:1
I delivered the poor that c Job 29:12
(they c after them as after a Job 30:5
up, and I c in the congregation Job 30:28
I c unto the LORD with my voice, Ps 3:4
upon the LORD, and c unto my God Ps 18:6
They c, but there was none to Ps 18:41
They c unto thee, and were Ps 22:5
but when he c unto him, he heard Ps 22:24
I c unto thee, and thou hast Ps 30:2
I c to thee, O LORD Ps 30:8
supplications when I c unto thee Ps 31:22
This poor man c, and the LORD Ps 34:6
I c unto him with my mouth, and he Ps 66:17
I c unto God with my voice, even Ps 77:1
God of my salvation, I have c day Ps 88:1
But unto thee have I c, O LORD Ps 88:13
Then they c unto the LORD in Ps 107:6
Then they c unto the LORD in Ps 107:13
I c with my whole heart Ps 119:145
I c unto thee Ps 119:146
the dawning of the morning, and c Ps 119:147
In my distress I c unto the LORD Ps 120:1
of the depths have I c unto thee Ps 130:1
In the day when I c thou Ps 138:3
I c unto the LORD with my voice Ps 142:1
I c unto thee, O LORD Ps 142:5
one c unto another, and said, Holy Is 6:3
moved at the voice of him that c Is 6:4
And he c, A lion Is 21:8
have I c concerning this, Their Is 30:7
c with a loud voice in the Jews' Is 36:13
Destruction upon destruction is c Jer 4:20
I c out, I c violence and Jer 20:8
c out, I c violence and spoil Jer 20:8
Their heart c unto the Lord, O Lam 2:18
They c unto them, Depart ye Lam 4:15
He c also in mine ears with a Eze 9:1
that I fell upon my face, and c Eze 9:8
it was c unto them in my hearing, Eze 10:13
c with a loud voice, and said, Ah Eze 11:13
Then an herald c aloud, To you it Dan 3:4
He c aloud, and said thus, Hew Dan 4:14
The king c aloud to bring in the Dan 5:7
he c with a lamentable voice unto Dan 6:20
they have not c unto me with Hos 7:14
c every man unto his god, and cast Jonah 1:5
Wherefore they c unto the LORD Jonah 1:14
I c by reason of mine affliction Jonah 2:2
out of the belly of hell c I Jonah 2:2
the city a day's journey, and he c Jonah 3:4
whom the former prophets have c Zec 1:4
Then c he upon me, and spake unto Zec 6:8
hath c by the former prophets Zec 7:7
it is come to pass, that as he c Zec 7:13
so they c, and I would not hear, Zec 7:13
And, behold, they c out, saying, Mt 8:29
and they c out for fear Mt 14:26
and beginning to sink, he c Mt 14:30
c unto him, saying, Have mercy on Mt 15:22
c out, saying, Have mercy on us, Mt 20:30
but they c the more, saying, Have Mt 20:31
went before, and that followed, c Mt 21:9
But they c out the more, saying, Mt 27:23
hour Jesus c with a loud voice Mt 27:46
when he had c again with a loud Mt 27:50
an unclean spirit; and he c out Mk 1:23
c with a loud voice, he came out Mk 1:26
him, fell down before him, and c Mk 3:11
c with a loud voice, and said, Mk 5:7
it had been a spirit, and c out Mk 6:49
the father of the child c out Mk 9:24
And the spirit c, and rent him sore Mk 9:26
but he c the more a great deal, Mk 10:48
before, and they that followed, c Mk 11:9
they c out again, Crucify him Mk 15:13
they c out the more exceedingly, Mk 15:14
hour Jesus c with a loud voice Mk 15:34
Jesus c with a loud voice, and Mk 15:37
against him, saw that he so c out Mk 15:39
and c out with a loud voice, Lk 4:33
he had said these things, he c Lk 8:8
he c out, and fell down before him Lk 8:28
a man of the company c out Lk 9:38
And he c and said, Father Abraham, Lk 16:24
And he c, saying, Jesus, thou son Lk 18:38
but he c so much the more, Thou Lk 18:39
they c out all at once, saying, Lk 23:18
But they c, saying, Crucify him, Lk 23:21
when Jesus had c with a loud Lk 23:46
John bare witness of him, and c Jn 1:15
Then c Jesus in the temple as he Jn 7:28
of the feast, Jesus stood and c Jn 7:37
he c with a loud voice, Lazarus, Jn 11:43
and went forth to meet him, and c Jn 12:13
Jesus c and said, He that Jn 12:44
Then c they all again, saying, Jn 18:40
and officers saw him, they c out Jn 19:6
but the Jews c out, saying, If Jn 19:12
But they c out, Away with him, Jn 19:15
Then they c out with a loud voice Acts 7:57
c with a loud voice, Lord, lay Acts 7:60

same followed Paul and us, and c....... Acts 16:17
But Paul c with a loud voice,............ Acts 16:28
c out, saying, Great is Diana of........... Acts 19:28
Some therefore c one thing................. Acts 19:32
the space of two hours c out............... Acts 19:34
some c one thing, some another,........ Acts 21:34
And as they c out, and cast off.......... Acts 22:23
wherefore they c so against him......... Acts 22:24
he c out in the council, Men and......... Acts 23:6
that I c standing among them,............ Acts 24:21
they c with a loud voice, saying,............ Rev 6:10
he c with a loud voice to the.................... Rev 7:2
c with a loud voice, saying,................... Rev 7:10
c with a loud voice, as when a.............. Rev 10:3
and when he had c, seven thunders...... Rev 10:3
And she being with child c.................... Rev 12:2
c with a loud cry to him that had........ Rev 14:18
he c mightily with a strong voice.......... Rev 18:2
c when they saw the smoke of her ...... Rev 18:18
cast dust on their heads, and c........... Rev 18:19
he c with a loud voice, saying to........ Rev 19:17

**CRIES**
the c of them which have reaped............ Jas 5:4

**CRIEST**
Moses, Wherefore c thou unto me......... Ex 14:15
Who art thou that c to the king.......... 1Sa 26:14
if thou c after knowledge, and................ Prov 2:3
When thou c, let thy companies............. Is 57:13
Why c thou for thine affliction............. Jer 30:15

**CRIETH**
blood c unto me from the ground......... Gen 4:10
come to pass, when he c unto me.......... Ex 22:27
and the soul of the wounded c out...... Job 24:12
shall deliver the needy when he c......... Ps 72:12
my flesh c out for the living God............ Ps 84:2
Wisdom c without................................. Prov 1:20
She c in the chief place of.................... Prov 1:21
She c at the gates, at the entry............. Prov 8:3
she c upon the highest places of............. Prov 9:3
is in pain, and c out in her pangs......... Is 26:17
of him that c in the wilderness................. Is 40:3
it c out against me.................................... Jer 12:8
The LORD's voice c unto the city.............. Mic 6:9
for she c after us.................................... Mt 15:23
taketh him, and he suddenly c out......... Lk 9:39
Esaias also c concerning Israel,............. Rom 9:27
is of you kept back by fraud, c................. Jas 5:4

**CRIME**
For this is an heinous c......................... Job 31:11
concerning the c laid against him....... Acts 25:16

**CRIMES**
for the land is full of bloody c................ Eze 7:23
to signify the c laid against him.......... Acts 25:27

**CRIMSON**
and in iron, and in purple, and c............ 2Chr 2:7
blue, and in fine linen, and in c........... 2Chr 2:14
the vail of blue, and purple, and c........ 2Chr 3:14
though they be red like c........................... Is 1:18
thou clothest thyself with c........................ Jer 4:30

**CRIPPLE**
being a c from his mother's womb,...... Acts 14:8

**CRISPING**
and the wimples, and the c pins,.............. Is 3:22

**CRISPUS** (*cris'-pus*) *A convert of Paul.*
And C, the chief ruler of the.................. Acts 18:8
I baptized none of you, but C.............. 1Cor 1:14

**CROOKBACKT**
Or c, or a dwarf, or that hath a........... Lev 21:20

**CROOKED**
are a perverse and c generation........... Deut 32:5
hand hath formed the c serpent........... Job 26:13
as turn aside unto their c ways.............. Ps 125:5
Whose ways are c, and they froward.. Prov 2:15
That which is c cannot be made........... Eccl 1:15
straight, which he hath made c............ Eccl 7:13
even leviathan that c serpent.................. Is 27:1
the c shall be made straight, and............ Is 40:4
before them, and c things straight.......... Is 42:16
make the c places straight......................... Is 45:2
they have made them c paths.................. Is 59:8
stone, he hath made my paths c............. Lam 3:9
the c shall be made straight, and............... Lk 3:5
rebuke, in the midst of a c...................... Phil 2:15

**CROP**
away his c with his feathers.................... Lev 1:16
I will c off from the top of his.............. Eze 17:22

**CROPPED**
He c off the top of his young.................. Eze 17:4

**CROSS**
And he that taketh not his c................ Mt 10:38
deny himself, and take up his c............ Mt 16:24
him they compelled to bear his c........... Mt 27:32
Son of God, come down from the c...... Mt 27:40
let him now come down from the c...... Mt 27:42
deny himself, and take up his c.............. Mk 8:34
and come, take up the c, and follow.... Mk 10:21
Alexander and Rufus, to bear his c...... Mk 15:21
thyself, and come down from the c....... Mk 15:30
of Israel descend now from the c......... Mk 15:32
himself, and take up his c daily.............. Lk 9:23
And whosoever doth not bear his c....... Lk 14:27
and on him they laid the c...................... Lk 23:26
he bearing his c went forth into............. Jn 19:17
wrote a title, and put it on the c............. Jn 19:19
by the c of Jesus his mother.................... Jn 19:25
upon the c on the sabbath day............... Jn 19:31
lest the c of Christ should be................ 1Cor 1:17
of the c is to them that perish............. 1Cor 1:18
is the offence of the c ceased.................. Gal 5:11
persecution for the c of Christ............... Gal 6:12
save in the c of our Lord Jesus............... Gal 6:14
unto God in one body by the c............. Eph 2:16
death, even the death of the c................... Phil 2:8
the enemies of the c of Christ............... Phil 3:18
peace through the blood of his c............ Col 1:20
of the way, nailing it to his c................. Col 2:14
was set before him endured the c......... Heb 12:2

**CROSSWAY**
thou have stood in the c, to cut............. Obad 14

**CROUCH**
c to him for a piece of silver and.......... 1Sa 2:36

**CROUCHETH**
He c, and humbleth himself, that........... Ps 10:10

**CROW**
this night, before the cock c.................. Mt 26:34
said unto him, Before the cock c............ Mt 26:75
night, before the cock c twice.................. Mk 14:30
unto him, Before the cock c twice......... Mk 14:72
the cock shall not c this day................... Lk 22:34
said unto him, Before the cock c............. Lk 22:61
unto thee, The cock shall not c............... Jn 13:38

**CROWN**
on the c of the head of him that......... Gen 49:26
upon it a c of gold round about............. Ex 25:11
make thereto a c of gold round.............. Ex 25:24
thou shalt make a golden c to the......... Ex 25:25
put the holy c upon the mitre.................. Ex 29:6
unto it a c of gold round about............... Ex 30:3
thou make to it under the c of it.............. Ex 30:4
made a c of gold to it round.................... Ex 37:2
made thereunto a c of gold round.......... Ex 37:11
made a c of gold for the border.............. Ex 37:12
unto it a c of gold round about.............. Ex 37:26
gold for it under the c thereof................ Ex 37:27
plate of the holy c of pure gold............... Ex 39:30
put the golden plate, the holy c................. Lev 8:9
for the c of the anointing oil of.............. Lev 21:12
the arm with the c of the head........... Deut 33:20
I took the c that was upon his................. 2Sa 1:10
their king's c from off his head........... 2Sa 12:30
to the c of his head there was no......... 2Sa 14:25
put the c upon him, and gave him..... 2Kin 11:12
David took the c of their king.............. 1Chr 20:2
king's son, and put upon him the c... 2Chr 23:11
before the king with the c royal............. Est 1:11
he set the royal c upon her head........... Est 2:17
the c royal which is set upon his.............. Est 6:8
white, and with a great c of gold........... Est 8:15
the sole of his foot unto his c................... Job 2:7
and taken the c from my head................. Job 19:9
shoulder, and bind it as a c to me........ Job 31:36
thou settest a c of pure gold on.................. Ps 21:3
thou hast profaned his c by..................... Ps 89:39
upon himself shall his c flourish........... Ps 132:18
a c of glory shall she deliver to.............. Prov 4:9
woman is a c to her husband................ Prov 12:4
The c of the wise is their riches.......... Prov 14:24
The hoary head is a c of glory............ Prov 16:31
children are the c of old men............... Prov 17:6
doth the c endure to every.................. Prov 27:24
c wherewith his mother crowned........ Song 3:11
c of the head of the daughters of............... Is 3:17
Woe to the c of pride, to the.................... Is 28:1
The c of pride, the drunkards of................. Is 28:3
LORD of hosts be for a c of glory............. Is 28:5
Thou shalt also be a c of glory.................. Is 62:3
have broken the c of thy head................. Jer 2:16
down, even the c of your glory.............. Jer 13:18
Moab, and the c of the head of the........ Jer 48:45
The c is fallen from our head................. Lam 5:16
a beautiful c upon thine head................ Eze 16:12
the diadem, and take off the c............... Eze 21:26
shall be as the stones of a c.................... Zec 9:16
they had platted a c of thorns.............. Mt 27:29
purple, and platted a c of thorns......... Mk 15:17
soldiers platted a c of thorns................... Jn 19:2
forth, wearing the c of thorns.................. Jn 19:5
do it to obtain a corruptible c............... 1Cor 9:25
and longed for, my joy and c...................... Phil 4:1
hope, or joy, or c of rejoicing.................. 1Th 2:19
up for me a c of righteousness................. 2Ti 4:8
he shall receive the c of life..................... Jas 1:12
ye shall receive a c of glory................... 1Pet 5:4
and I will give thee a c of life................. Rev 2:10
thou hast, that no man take thy c......... Rev 3:11
and a c was given unto him...................... Rev 6:2
upon her head a c of twelve stars.......... Rev 12:1
having on his head a golden c............. Rev 14:14

**CROWNED**
hast c him with glory and honour.............. Ps 8:5
the prudent are c with knowledge..... Prov 14:18
the crown wherewith his mother c..... Song 3:11
Thy c are as the locusts, and thy.......... Nah 3:17
for masteries, yet is he not c..................... 2Ti 2:5
of death, c with glory and honour.......... Heb 2:9

**CROWNEDST**
thou c him with glory and honour,......... Heb 2:7

**CROWNEST**
Thou c the year with thy goodness........ Ps 65:11

**CROWNETH**
who c thee with lovingkindness and...... Ps 103:4

**CROWNING**
the c city, whose merchants are................ Is 23:8

**CROWNS**
beautiful c upon their heads.................. Eze 23:42
take silver and gold, and make c............ Zec 6:11
the c shall be to Helem, and to.............. Zec 6:14
they had on their heads c of gold............. Rev 4:4
cast their c before the throne,................ Rev 4:10
heads were as it were c like gold.............. Rev 9:7
horns, and seven c upon his heads......... Rev 12:3
horns, and upon his horns ten c........... Rev 13:1
fire, and on his head were many c....... Rev 19:12

**CRUCIFIED**
Son of man is betrayed to be c................. Mt 26:2
all say unto him, Let him be c................. Mt 27:22
the more, saying, Let him be c............... Mt 27:23
Jesus, he delivered him to be c............... Mt 27:26
And they c him, and parted his.............. Mt 27:35
were there two thieves c with him......... Mt 27:38
also, which were c with him................... Mt 27:44
that ye seek Jesus, which was c............... Mt 28:5
when he had scourged him, to be c....... Mk 15:15
And when they had c him, they.......... Mk 15:24
was the third hour, and they c him....... Mk 15:25
they that were c with him reviled........ Mk 15:32
Jesus of Nazareth, which was c............ Mk 16:6
requiring that he might be c.................. Lk 23:23
called Calvary, there they c him............ Lk 23:33
the hands of sinful men, and be c............ Lk 24:7
condemned to death, and have c him... Lk 24:20
him therefore unto them to be c............. Jn 19:16
Where they c him, and two others........... Jn 19:18
Jesus was c was nigh to the city............ Jn 19:20
soldiers, when they had c Jesus............. Jn 19:23
of the other which was c with him......... Jn 19:32
where he was c there was a garden....... Jn 19:41
taken, and by wicked hands have c...... Acts 2:23
that same Jesus, whom ye have c........ Acts 2:36
Christ of Nazareth, whom ye c............ Acts 4:10
that our old man is c with him............... Rom 6:6
was Paul c for you?............................... 1Cor 1:13
But we preach Christ c, unto the......... 1Cor 1:23
you, save Jesus Christ, and him c.......... 1Cor 2:2
not have c the Lord of glory.................... 1Cor 2:8
though he was c through weakness.... 2Cor 13:4
I am c with Christ..................................... Gal 2:20
evidently set forth, c among you.............. Gal 3:1
they that are Christ's have c the............. Gal 5:24
by whom the world is c unto me............ Gal 6:14
Egypt, where also our Lord was c.......... Rev 11:8

**CRUCIFY**
mock, and to scourge, and to c him...... Mt 20:19
some of them ye shall kill and c........... Mt 23:34
on him, and led him away to c him...... Mt 27:31
And they cried out again, C him........... Mk 15:13
out the more exceedingly, C him.......... Mk 15:14
on him, and led him out to c him......... Mk 15:20
And with him they c two thieves.......... Mk 15:27
cried, saying, C him, c him.................... Lk 23:21
out, saying, C him, c him......................... Jn 19:6
unto them, Take ye him, and c him.......... Jn 19:6
not that I have power to c thee............. Jn 19:10
with him, away with him, c him............ Jn 19:15
unto them, Shall I c your King............. Jn 19:15
seeing they c to themselves the................ Heb 6:6

**CRUEL**
and their wrath, for it was c................... Gen 49:7
of spirit, and for c bondage........................ Ex 6:9
dragons, and the c venom of asps...... Deut 32:33
Thou art become c to me....................... Job 30:21
and they hate me with c hatred............... Ps 25:19
hand of the unrighteous and c man......... Ps 71:4
others, and thy years unto the c............... Prov 5:9
but he that is c troubleth his.................. Prov 11:17
mercies of the wicked are c.................. Prov 12:10
therefore a c messenger shall be........ Prov 17:11
Wrath is c, and anger is........................ Prov 27:4
jealousy is c as the grave...................... Song 8:6
c both with wrath and fierce anger........... Is 13:9
over into the hand of a c lord.................... Is 19:4
they are c, and have no mercy................. Jer 6:23
with the chastisement of a c one........... Jer 30:14
they are c, and will not shew................ Jer 50:42
daughter of my people is become c........ Lam 4:3
And others had trial of c mockings..... Heb 11:36

**CRUELLY**
father, because he c oppressed............. Eze 18:18

**CRUELTY**
instruments of c are in their................... Gen 49:5
That the c done to the threescore........ Judg 9:24
me, and such as breathe out c................ Ps 27:12
are full of the habitations of c.............. Ps 74:20
with c have ye ruled them..................... Eze 34:4

**CRUMBS**
yet the dogs eat of the c which............. Mt 15:27
the table eat of the children's c.............. Mk 7:28
desiring to be fed with the c.................. Lk 16:21

C

### CRUSE
the c of water, and let us go — 1Sa 26:11
the c of water from Saul's — 1Sa 26:12
the c of water that was at his — 1Sa 26:16
a c of honey, and go to him — 1Kin 14:3
a barrel, and a little oil in a c — 1Kin 17:12
neither shall the c of oil fail — 1Kin 17:14
neither did the c of oil fail — 1Kin 17:16
and a c of water at his head — 1Kin 19:6
And he said, Bring me a new c — 2Kin 2:20

### CRUSH
that the foot may c them, or that — Job 39:15
against me to c my young men — Lam 1:15
To c under his feet all the — Lam 3:34
which c the needy, which say to — Amos 4:1

### CRUSHED
LORD that which is bruised, or c — Lev 22:24
c Balaam's foot against the wall — Num 22:25
be only oppressed and c alway — Deut 28:33
which are c before the moth — Job 4:19
they are c in the gate, neither — Job 5:4
that which is c breaketh out into — Is 59:5
hath devoured me, he hath c me — Jer 51:34

### CRY
LORD said, Because the c of Sodom — Gen 18:20
according to the c of it, which — Gen 18:21
because the c of them is waxen — Gen 19:13
a great and exceeding bitter c — Gen 27:34
their c came up unto God by — Ex 2:23
have heard their c by reason of — Ex 3:7
the c of the children of Israel — Ex 3:9
therefore they c, saying, Let us — Ex 5:8
And there shall be a great c — Ex 11:6
and there was a great c in Egypt — Ex 12:30
they c at all unto me — Ex 22:23
I will surely hear their c — Ex 22:23
of them that c for being overcome — Ex 32:18
upon his upper lip, and shall c — Lev 13:45
about them fled at the c of them — Num 16:34
he c unto the LORD against thee, — Deut 15:9
lest he c against thee unto the — Deut 24:15
c unto the gods which ye have — Judg 10:14
the c of the city went up to — 1Sa 5:12
Cease not to c unto the LORD our — 1Sa 7:8
ye shall c out in that day — 1Sa 8:18
because their c is come unto me — 1Sa 9:16
I yet to c any more unto the king — 2Sa 19:28
my c did enter into his ears — 2Sa 22:7
my God, to hearken unto the c — 1Kin 8:28
mocked them, and said, C aloud — 1Kin 18:27
she went forth to c unto the king — 2Kin 8:3
my God, to hearken unto the c — 2Chr 6:19
trumpets to c alarm against you — 2Chr 13:12
c unto thee in our affliction, — 2Chr 20:9
there was a great c of the people — Neh 5:1
very angry when I heard their c — Neh 5:6
heardest their c by the Red sea — Neh 9:9
cried with a loud and a bitter c — Est 4:1
of the fastings and their c — Est 9:31
blood, and let my c have no place — Job 16:18
I c out of wrong, but I am not — Job 19:7
I c aloud, but there is no — Job 19:7
Will God hear his c when trouble — Job 27:9
I c unto thee, and thou dost not — Job 30:20
though they c in his destruction — Job 30:24
If my land c against me, or that — Job 31:38
So that they cause the c of the — Job 34:28
he heareth the c of the afflicted — Job 34:28
they make the oppressed to c — Job 35:9
they c out by reason of the arm — Job 35:9
There they c, but none giveth — Job 35:12
they c not when he bindeth them — Job 36:13
when his young ones c unto God — Job 38:41
Hearken unto the voice of my c — Ps 5:2
not the c of the humble — Ps 9:12
right, O LORD, attend unto my c — Ps 17:1
my c came before him, even into — Ps 18:6
I c in the daytime, but thou — Ps 22:2
O LORD, when I c with my voice — Ps 27:7
Unto thee will I c, O LORD my — Ps 28:1
when I c unto thee, when I lift — Ps 28:2
and his ears are open unto their c — Ps 34:15
The righteous c, and the LORD — Ps 34:17
O LORD, and give ear unto my c — Ps 39:12
inclined unto me, and heard my c — Ps 40:1
at noon, will I pray, and c aloud — Ps 55:17
When I c unto thee, then shall — Ps 56:9
I will c unto God most high — Ps 57:2
Hear my c, O God — Ps 61:1
of the earth will I c unto thee — Ps 61:2
for I c unto thee daily — Ps 86:3
incline thine ear unto my c — Ps 88:2
He shall c unto me, Thou art my — Ps 89:26
LORD, and let my c come unto thee — Ps 102:1
affliction, when he heard their c — Ps 106:44
Then they c unto the LORD in — Ps 107:19
Then they c unto the LORD in — Ps 107:28
Let my c come near before thee, O — Ps 119:169
Lord, I c unto thee — Ps 141:1
unto my voice, when I c unto thee — Ps 141:1
Attend unto my c — Ps 142:6
he also will hear their c — Ps 145:19
and to the young ravens which c — Ps 147:9
Doth not wisdom c — Prov 8:1
his ears at the c of the poor — Prov 21:13
he also shall c himself — Prov 21:13
heard in quiet more than the c of — Eccl 9:17
for righteousness, but behold a c — Is 5:7
child shall have knowledge to c — Is 8:4
C out and shout, thou inhabitant — Is 12:6
shall c in their desolate houses — Is 13:22
c, O city — Is 14:31
And Heshbon shall c, and Elealeh — Is 15:4
soldiers of Moab shall c out — Is 15:4
My heart shall c out for Moab — Is 15:5
shall raise up a c of destruction — Is 15:5
For the c is gone round about the — Is 15:8
for they shall c unto the LORD — Is 19:20
they shall c aloud from the sea — Is 24:14
c ye out, and c — Is 29:9
unto thee at the voice of thy c — Is 30:19
valiant ones shall c without — Is 33:7
the satyr shall c to his fellow — Is 34:14
c unto her, that her warfare is — Is 40:2
The voice said, C — Is 40:6
And he said, What shall I c — Is 40:6
He shall not c, nor lift up, nor — Is 42:2
he shall c, yea, roar — Is 42:13
now will I c like a travailing — Is 42:14
whose c is in the ships — Is 43:14
yea, one shall c unto him — Is 46:7
c aloud, thou that didst not — Is 54:1
C aloud, spare not, lift up thy — Is 58:1
thou shalt c, and he shall say, — Is 58:9
but ye shall c for sorrow of — Is 65:14
c in the ears of Jerusalem, — Jer 2:2
thou not from this time c unto me — Jer 3:4
c, gather together, and say, — Jer 4:5
neither lift up c nor prayer for — Jer 7:16
Behold the voice of the c of the — Jer 8:19
and though they shall c unto me — Jer 11:11
c unto the gods unto whom they — Jer 11:12
neither lift up a c or prayer for — Jer 11:14
they c unto me for their trouble — Jer 11:14
the c of Jerusalem is gone up — Jer 14:2
fast, I will not hear their c — Jer 14:12
Let a c be heard from their — Jer 18:22
let him hear the c in the morning — Jer 20:16
Go up to Lebanon, and c — Jer 22:20
in Bashan, and c from the passages — Jer 22:20
Howl, ye shepherds, and c — Jer 25:34
A voice of the c of the shepherds — Jer 25:36
upon the mount Ephraim shall c — Jer 31:6
thy c hath filled the land — Jer 46:12
They did c there, Pharaoh king of — Jer 46:17
then the men shall c, and all the — Jer 47:2
ones have caused a c to be heard — Jer 48:4
have heard a c of destruction — Jer 48:5
howl and c; tell ye it in Arnon — Jer 48:20
I will c out for all Moab — Jer 48:31
From the c of Heshbon even unto — Jer 48:34
c, ye daughters of Rabbah, gird — Jer 49:3
at the c the noise thereof was — Jer 49:21
and they shall c unto them — Jer 49:29
the c is heard among the nations — Jer 50:46
A sound of a c cometh from — Jer 51:54
Arise, c out in the night — Lam 2:19
Also when I c and shout, he — Lam 3:8
ear at my breathing, at my c — Lam 3:56
though they c in mine ears with a — Eze 8:18
that c for all the abominations — Eze 9:4
C and howl, son of man — Eze 21:12
Forbear to c, make no mourning — Eze 24:17
of thy fall, when the wounded c — Eze 26:15
the sound of the c of thy pilots — Eze 27:28
shall c bitterly, and shall cast — Eze 27:30
c aloud at Beth-aven, after thee, — Hos 5:8
Israel shall c unto me, My God, — Hos 8:2
your God, and c unto the LORD, — Joel 1:14
O LORD, to thee will I c — Joel 1:19
of the field c also unto thee — Joel 1:20
a young lion c out of his den — Amos 3:4
that great city, and c against it — Jonah 1:2
sackcloth, and c mightily unto God — Jonah 3:8
Then shall they c unto the LORD — Mic 3:4
that bite with their teeth, and c — Mic 3:5
Now why dost thou c out aloud — Mic 4:9
Stand, stand, shall they c — Nah 2:8
O LORD, how long shall I c — Hab 1:2
even c out unto thee of violence, — Hab 1:2
the stone shall c out of the wall — Hab 2:11
noise of a c from the fish gate — Zeph 1:10
mighty man shall c there bitterly — Zeph 1:14
C thou, saying, Thus saith the — Zec 1:14
C yet, saying, Thus saith the — Zec 1:17
He shall not strive, nor c — Mt 12:19
And at midnight there was a c made — Mt 25:6
of Nazareth, he began to c out — Mk 10:47
avenge his own elect, which c day — Lk 18:7
stones would immediately c out — Lk 19:40
And there arose a great c — Acts 23:9
Spirit of adoption, whereby we c — Rom 8:15
break forth and c, thou that — Gal 4:27
cried with a loud c to him that — Rev 14:18

### CRYING
when Eli heard the noise of the c — 1Sa 4:14
hand on her head, and went on c — 2Sa 13:19
regardeth he the c of the driver — Job 39:7
I am weary of my c — Ps 69:3
let not thy soul spare for his c — Prov 19:18
horseleach hath two daughters, c — Prov 30:15
walls, and of c to the mountains — Is 22:5
There is a c for wine in the — Is 24:11
heard in her, nor the voice of c — Is 65:19
A voice of c shall be from — Jer 48:3
thereof with shoutings, c, — Zec 4:7
with weeping, and with c out — Mal 2:13
The voice of one c in the — Mt 3:3
two blind men followed him, c — Mt 9:27
the children c in the temple, and — Mt 21:15
The voice of one c in the — Mk 1:3
the mountains, and in the tombs, c — Mk 5:5
the multitude c aloud began to — Mk 15:8
The voice of one c in the — Lk 3:4
c out, and saying, Thou art Christ — Lk 4:41
voice of one c in the wilderness — Jn 1:23
c with loud voice, came out of — Acts 8:7
ran in among the people, c out, — Acts 14:14
unto the rulers of the city, c — Acts 17:6
C out, Men of Israel, help — Acts 21:28
of the people followed after, c — Acts 21:36
c that he ought not to live any — Acts 25:24
of his Son into your hearts, c — Gal 4:6
and supplications with strong c — Heb 5:7
c with a loud voice to him that — Rev 14:15
more death, neither sorrow, nor c — Rev 21:4

### CRYSTAL
The gold and the c cannot equal it — Job 28:17
as the colour of the terrible c — Eze 1:22
was a sea of glass like unto c — Rev 4:6
like a jasper stone, clear as c — Rev 21:11
of water of life, clear as c — Rev 22:1

### CUBIT
in a c shalt thou finish it above — Gen 6:16
be the length thereof, and a c — Ex 25:10
half the breadth thereof, and a c — Ex 25:10
be the length thereof, and a c — Ex 25:17
c the breadth thereof, and a c — Ex 25:23
a c on the one side, and a c — Ex 26:13
be the length of a board, and a c — Ex 26:16
A c shall be the length thereof, — Ex 30:2
and a c the breadth thereof — Ex 30:2
and the breadth of a board one c — Ex 36:21
half was the length of it, and a c — Ex 37:1
a half the breadth of it, and a c — Ex 37:1
was the length thereof, and one c — Ex 37:6
c the breadth thereof, and a c — Ex 37:10
a c, and the breadth of it a c — Ex 37:25
of it, after the c of a man — Deut 3:11
had two edges, of a c length — Judg 3:16
knops compassing it, ten in a c — 1Kin 7:24
the chapiter and above was a c — 1Kin 7:31
after the work of the base, a c — 1Kin 7:31
a wheel was a c and half a c — 1Kin 7:32
a round compass of half a c high — 1Kin 7:35
ten in a c, compassing the sea — 2Chr 4:3
reed of six cubits long by the c — Eze 40:5
chambers was one c on this side — Eze 40:12
the space was one c on that side — Eze 40:12
a c and an half long, and a c — Eze 40:42
and an half broad, and one c high — Eze 40:42
breadth inward, a way of one c — Eze 42:4
The c is a c and an hand — Eze 43:13
The c is a c and an hand — Eze 43:13
be a c, and the breadth a c — Eze 43:13
two cubits, and the breadth one c — Eze 43:14
four cubits, and the breadth one c — Eze 43:14
border about it shall be half a c — Eze 43:17
bottom thereof shall be a c about — Eze 43:17
can add one c unto his stature — Mt 6:27
can add to his stature one c — Lk 12:25

### CUBITS
the ark shall be three hundred c — Gen 6:15
c, the breadth of it fifty c — Gen 6:15
and the height of it thirty c — Gen 6:15
Fifteen c upward did the waters — Gen 7:20
two c and a half shall be the — Ex 25:10
two c and a half shall be the — Ex 25:17
two c shall be the length thereof — Ex 25:23
shall be eight and twenty c — Ex 26:2
the breadth of one curtain four c — Ex 26:2
of one curtain shall be thirty c — Ex 26:8
the breadth of one curtain four c — Ex 26:8
Ten c shall be the length of a — Ex 26:16
five c long, and five c broad — Ex 27:1
height thereof shall be three c — Ex 27:1
of an hundred c long for one side — Ex 27:9
be hangings of an hundred c long — Ex 27:11
side shall be hangings of fifty c — Ex 27:12
side eastward shall be fifty c — Ex 27:13
of the gate shall be fifteen c — Ex 27:14
side shall be hangings fifteen c — Ex 27:15
shall be an hanging of twenty c — Ex 27:16
the court shall be an hundred c — Ex 27:18
the height five c of fine twined — Ex 27:18
two c shall be the height thereof — Ex 30:2
one curtain was twenty and eight c — Ex 36:9
the breadth of one curtain four c — Ex 36:9
of one curtain was thirty c — Ex 36:15
four c was the breadth of one — Ex 36:15
The length of a board was ten c — Ex 36:21
two c and a half was the length of — Ex 37:1
two c and a half was the length — Ex 37:6
two c was the length thereof, and — Ex 37:10
two c was the height of it — Ex 37:25
five c was the length thereof, and — Ex 38:1
five c the breadth thereof — Ex 38:1
three c the height thereof — Ex 38:1
fine twined linen, an hundred c — Ex 38:9
the hangings were an hundred c — Ex 38:11
side were hangings of fifty c — Ex 38:12
the east side eastward fifty c — Ex 38:13
side of the gate were fifteen c — Ex 38:14
hand, were hangings of fifteen c — Ex 38:15
twenty c was the length, and the — Ex 38:18
height in the breadth was five c — Ex 38:18
as it were two c high upon the — Num 11:31
outward a thousand c round about — Num 35:4

on the east side two thousand c Num 35:5
on the south side two thousand c Num 35:5
on the west side two thousand c Num 35:5
on the north side two thousand c Num 35:5
nine c was the length thereof, and Deut 3:11
four c the breadth of it, after Deut 3:11
about two thousand c by measure Josh 3:4
of Gath, whose height was six c 1Sa 17:4
length thereof was threescore c 1Kin 6:2
and the breadth thereof twenty c 1Kin 6:2
and the height thereof thirty c 1Kin 6:2
twenty c was the length thereof, 1Kin 6:3
ten c was the breadth thereof 1Kin 6:3
chamber was five c broad 1Kin 6:6
and the middle was six c broad 1Kin 6:6
and the third was seven c broad 1Kin 6:6
all the house, five c high 1Kin 6:10
he built twenty c on the sides of 1Kin 6:16
before it, was forty c long 1Kin 6:17
forepart was twenty c in length 1Kin 6:20
twenty c in breadth 1Kin 6:20
twenty c in the height thereof 1Kin 6:20
of olive tree, each ten c high 1Kin 6:23
five c was the one wing of the 1Kin 6:24
five c the other wing of the 1Kin 6:24
part of the other were ten c 1Kin 6:24
And the other cherub was ten c 1Kin 6:25
of the one cherub was ten c 1Kin 6:26
length thereof was an hundred c 1Kin 7:2
and the breadth thereof fifty c 1Kin 7:2
and the height thereof thirty c 1Kin 7:2
the length thereof was fifty c 1Kin 7:6
and the breadth thereof thirty c 1Kin 7:6
ten c, and stones of eight c 1Kin 7:10
brass, of eighteen c high apiece 1Kin 7:15
a line of twelve c did compass 1Kin 7:15
of the one chapiter was five c 1Kin 7:16
of the other chapiter was five c 1Kin 7:16
of lily work in the porch, four c 1Kin 7:19
ten c from the one brim to the 1Kin 7:23
about, and his height was five c 1Kin 7:23
a line of thirty c did compass it 1Kin 7:23
four c was the length of one base 1Kin 7:27
four c the breadth thereof, and 1Kin 7:27
and three c the height of it 1Kin 7:27
and every laver was four c 1Kin 7:38
the corner gate, four hundred c 2Kin 14:13
of the one pillar was eighteen c 2Kin 25:17
height of the chapiter three c 2Kin 25:17
man of great stature, five c high 1Chr 11:23
The length by c after the first 2Chr 3:3
first measure was threescore c 2Chr 3:3
c, and the breadth twenty c 2Chr 3:3
breadth of the house, twenty c 2Chr 3:4
breadth of the house, twenty c 2Chr 3:8
and the breadth thereof twenty c 2Chr 3:8
the cherubims were twenty c long 2Chr 3:11
wing of the one cherub was five c 2Chr 3:11
other wing was likewise five c 2Chr 3:11
of the other cherub was five c 2Chr 3:12
and the other wing was five c also 2Chr 3:12
spread themselves forth twenty c 2Chr 3:13
pillars of thirty and five c high 2Chr 3:15
top of each of them was five c 2Chr 3:15
twenty c the length thereof, and 2Chr 4:1
twenty c the breadth thereof, and 2Chr 4:1
and ten c the height thereof 2Chr 4:1
sea of ten c from brim to brim 2Chr 4:2
five c the height thereof 2Chr 4:2
a line of thirty c did compass it 2Chr 4:2
a brasen scaffold, of five c long 2Chr 6:13
five c broad, and three c 2Chr 6:13
the corner gate, four hundred c 2Chr 25:23
the height thereof threescore c Ezr 6:3
the breadth thereof threescore c Ezr 6:3
a thousand c on the wall unto the Neh 3:13
a gallows be made of fifty c high Est 5:14
also, the gallows fifty c high Est 7:9
of one pillar was eighteen c Jer 52:21
fillet of twelve c did compass it Jer 52:21
height of one chapiter was five c Jer 52:22
reed of six c long by the cubit Eze 40:5
the little chambers were five c Eze 40:7
he the porch of the gate, eight c Eze 40:9
and the posts thereof, two c Eze 40:9
of the entry of the gate, ten c Eze 40:11
length of the gate, thirteen c Eze 40:11
chambers were six c on this side Eze 40:12
and six c on that side Eze 40:12
the breadth was five and twenty c Eze 40:13
made also posts of threescore c Eze 40:14
of the inner gate were fifty c Eze 40:15
without, an hundred c eastward Eze 40:19
the length thereof was fifty c Eze 40:21
and the breadth five and twenty c Eze 40:21
from gate to gate an hundred c Eze 40:23
the length was fifty c Eze 40:25
and the breadth five and twenty c Eze 40:25
toward the south an hundred c Eze 40:27
it was fifty c long Eze 40:29
and five and twenty c broad Eze 40:29
about were five and twenty c long Eze 40:30
and five c broad Eze 40:30
it was fifty c long Eze 40:33
and five and twenty c broad Eze 40:33
the length was fifty c, and the Eze 40:36
and the breadth five and twenty c Eze 40:36
the court, an hundred c long Eze 40:47
and an hundred c broad Eze 40:47
five c on this side Eze 40:48
and five c on that side Eze 40:48
the gate was three c on this side Eze 40:48
and three c on that side Eze 40:48
length of the porch was twenty c Eze 40:49
and the breadth eleven c Eze 40:49
six c broad on the one side, and Eze 41:1
six c broad on the other side, Eze 41:1
the breadth of the door was ten c Eze 41:2
door were five c on the one side Eze 41:2
and five c on the other side Eze 41:2
the length thereof, forty c Eze 41:2
and the breadth, twenty c Eze 41:2
the post of the door, two c Eze 41:3
and the door, six c Eze 41:3
the breadth of the door, seven c Eze 41:3
the length thereof, twenty c Eze 41:4
and the breadth, twenty c, before Eze 41:4
the wall of the house, six c Eze 41:5
of every side chamber, four c Eze 41:5
were a full reed of six great c Eze 41:8
side chamber without, was five c Eze 41:9
was the wideness of twenty c Eze 41:10
was left was five c round about Eze 41:11
the west was seventy c broad Eze 41:12
was five c thick round about Eze 41:12
and the length thereof ninety c Eze 41:12
the house, an hundred c long Eze 41:13
walls thereof, an hundred c long Eze 41:13
toward the east, an hundred c Eze 41:14
on the other side, an hundred c Eze 41:15
altar of wood was three c high Eze 41:22
and the length thereof two c Eze 41:22
an hundred c was the north door Eze 42:2
and the breadth was fifty c Eze 42:2
Over against the twenty c which Eze 42:3
a walk of ten c breadth inward Eze 42:4
the length thereof was fifty c Eze 42:7
in the utter court was fifty c Eze 42:8
the temple were an hundred c Eze 42:8
measures of the altar after the c Eze 43:13
the lower settle shall be two c Eze 43:14
greater settle shall be four c Eze 43:14
So the altar shall be four c Eze 43:15
the altar shall be twelve c long Eze 43:16
settle shall be fourteen c long Eze 43:17
fifty c round about for the Eze 45:2
courts joined of forty c long Eze 46:22
he measured a thousand c Eze 47:3
whose height was threescore c Dan 3:1
and the breadth thereof six c Dan 3:1
the length thereof is twenty c Zec 5:2
and the breadth thereof ten c Zec 5:2
but as it were two hundred c Jn 21:8
an hundred and forty and four c Rev 21:17

**CUCKOW**

owl, and the night hawk, and the c Lev 11:16
owl, and the night hawk, and the c Deut 14:15

**CUCUMBERS**

the c, and the melons, and the Num 11:5
as a lodge in a garden of c Is 1:8

**CUD**

is clovenfooted, and cheweth the c Lev 11:3
not eat of them that chew the c Lev 11:4
camel, because he cheweth the c Lev 11:4
coney, because he cheweth the c Lev 11:5
hare, because he cheweth the c Lev 11:6
yet he cheweth not the c Lev 11:7
clovenfooted, nor cheweth the c Lev 11:26
cheweth the c among the beasts, Deut 14:6
not eat of them that chew the c Deut 14:7
for they chew the c, but divide Deut 14:7
the hoof, yet cheweth not the c Deut 14:8

**CUMBERED**

But Martha was c about much Lk 10:40

**CUMBERETH**

why c it the ground Lk 13:7

**CUMBRANCE**

can I myself alone bear your c Deut 1:12

**CUMI**

hand, and said unto her, Talitha c Mk 5:41

**CUMMIN**

the fitches, and scatter the c Is 28:25
wheel turned about upon the c Is 28:27
with a staff, and the c with a rod Is 28:27
pay tithe of mint and anise and c Mt 23:23

**CUN** See CHUN.

**CUNNING**

and Esau was a c hunter, a man of Gen 25:27
with cherubims of c work shalt Ex 26:1
and fine twined linen of c work Ex 26:31
and fine twined linen, with c work Ex 28:6
of judgment with c work Ex 28:15
To devise c works, to work in Ex 31:4
to make any manner of c work Ex 35:33
of the c workman, and of the Ex 35:35
and of those that devise c work Ex 35:35
cherubims of c work made he them Ex 36:8
cherubims made he it of c work Ex 36:35
a c workman, and an embroiderer in Ex 38:23
and in the fine linen, with c work Ex 39:3
he made the breastplate of c work Ex 39:8
who is a c player on an harp 1Sa 16:16
that is c in playing, and a mighty 1Sa 16:18
c to work all works in brass 1Kin 7:14
all manner of c men for every 1Chr 22:15
of the LORD, even all that were c 1Chr 25:7
therefore a man c to work in gold 2Chr 2:7
can skill to grave with the c men 2Chr 2:7
And now I have sent a c man 2Chr 2:13
be put to him, with thy c men 2Chr 2:14
with the c men of my lord David 2Chr 2:14
engines, invented by c men 2Chr 26:15
let my right hand forget her c Ps 137:5
work of the hands of a c workman Song 7:1
the c artificer, and the eloquent Is 3:3
he seeketh unto him a c workman Is 40:20
and send for c women, that they Jer 9:17
they are all the work of c men Jer 10:9
c in knowledge, and understanding Dan 1:4
c craftiness, whereby they lie in Eph 4:14

**CUNNINGLY**

not followed c devised fables 2Pet 1:16

**CUP**

Pharaoh's c was in my hand Gen 40:11
and pressed them into Pharaoh's c Gen 40:11
I gave the c into Pharaoh's hand Gen 40:11
deliver Pharaoh's c into his hand Gen 40:13
he gave the c into Pharaoh's hand Gen 40:21
And put my c, the silver c Gen 44:2
the c was found in Benjamin's Gen 44:12
he also with whom the c is found Gen 44:16
man in whose hand the c is found Gen 44:17
own meat, and drank of his own c 2Sa 12:3
was wrought like the brim of a c 1Kin 7:26
like the work of the brim of a c 2Chr 4:5
shall be the portion of their c Ps 11:6
of mine inheritance and of my c Ps 16:5
my c runneth over Ps 23:5
waters of a full c are wrung out Ps 73:10
the hand of the LORD there is a c Ps 75:8
I will take the c of salvation Ps 116:13
it giveth his colour in the c Prov 23:31
of the LORD the c of his fury Is 51:17
the dregs of the c of trembling Is 51:17
of thine hand the c of trembling Is 51:22
the dregs of the c of my fury Is 51:22
the c of consolation to drink for Jer 16:7
Take the wine c of this fury at Jer 25:15
Then took I the c at the LORD's Jer 25:17
take the c at thine hand to drink Jer 25:28
of the c have assuredly drunken Jer 49:12
a golden c in the LORD's hand Jer 51:7
the c also shall pass through Lam 4:21
will I give her c into thine hand Eze 23:31
drink of thy sister's c deep Eze 23:32
with the c of astonishment and Eze 23:33
with the c of thy sister Samaria Eze 23:33
the c of the LORD's right hand Hab 2:16
I will make Jerusalem a c of Zec 12:2
c of cold water only in the name Mt 10:42
of the c that I shall drink of Mt 20:22
Ye shall drink indeed of my c Mt 20:23
make clean the outside of the c Mt 23:25
first that which is within the c Mt 23:26
And he took the c, and gave thanks, Mt 26:27
possible, let this c pass from me Mt 26:39
if this c may not pass away from Mt 26:42
a c of water to drink in my name Mk 9:41
ye drink of the c that I drink of Mk 10:38
drink of the c that I drink of Mk 10:39
And he took the c, and when he had Mk 14:23
take away this c from me Mk 14:36
make clean the outside of the c Lk 11:39
And he took the c, and gave thanks, Lk 22:17
Likewise also the c after supper Lk 22:20
This c is the new testament in my Lk 22:20
be willing, remove this c from me Lk 22:42
the c which my Father hath given Jn 18:11
The c of blessing which we bless, 1Cor 10:16
Ye cannot drink the c of the Lord 1Cor 10:21
and the c of devils 1Cor 10:21
same manner also he took the c 1Cor 11:25
This c is the new testament in my 1Cor 11:25
eat this bread, and drink this c 1Cor 11:26
drink this c of the Lord, 1Cor 11:27
of that bread, and drink of that c 1Cor 11:28
into the c of his indignation Rev 14:10
to give unto her the c of the Rev 16:19
having a golden c in her hand Rev 17:4
in the c which she hath filled Rev 18:6

**CUPBEARER**

For I was the king's c Neh 1:11

**CUPBEARERS**

and their apparel, and his c 1Kin 10:5
his c also, and their apparel 2Chr 9:4

**CUPS**

and the bowls, and the c 1Chr 28:17
quantity, from the vessels of c Is 22:24
pots full of wine, and c, and I Jer 35:5
and the spoons, and the c Jer 52:19
to hold, as the washing of c Mk 7:4
men, as the washing of pots and c Mk 7:8

**CURDLED**

out as milk, and c me like cheese Job 10:10

**CURE**

health and c, and I will c them Jer 33:6
heal you, nor c you of your wound Hos 5:13
and they could not c him Mt 17:16
over all devils, and to c diseases Lk 9:1

**CURED**
for thou shalt not be c ... Jer 46:11
the child was c from that very ... Mt 17:18
in that same hour he c many of ... Lk 7:21
said unto him that was c, It is ... Jn 5:10

**CURES**
I do c to day and to morrow, and ... Lk 13:32

**CURIOUS**
the c girdle of the ephod, which ... Ex 28:8
above the c girdle of the ephod ... Ex 28:27
above the c girdle of the ephod ... Ex 28:28
gird him with the c girdle of the ... Ex 29:5
And to devise c works, to work in ... Ex 35:32
the c girdle of his ephod, that ... Ex 39:5
above the c girdle of the ephod ... Ex 39:20
above the c girdle of the ephod ... Ex 39:21
with the c girdle of the ephod ... Lev 8:7
used c arts brought their books ... Acts 19:19

**CURIOUSLY**
c wrought in the lowest parts of ... Ps 139:15

**CURRENT**
c money with the merchant ... Gen 23:16

**CURSE**
I will not again c the ground any ... Gen 8:21
thee, and c him that curseth thee ... Gen 12:3
and I shall bring a c upon me ... Gen 27:12
said unto him, Upon me be thy c ... Gen 27:13
nor c the ruler of thy people ... Ex 22:28
Thou shalt not c the deaf ... Lev 19:14
bitter water that causeth the c ... Num 5:18
bitter water that causeth the c ... Num 5:19
the woman, The LORD make thee a c. Num 5:21
the c shall go into thy bowels ... Num 5:22
bitter water that causeth the c ... Num 5:24
the c shall enter into her ... Num 5:24
the c shall enter into her ... Num 5:27
shall be a c among her people ... Num 5:27
I pray thee, c me this people ... Num 22:6
come now, c me them ... Num 22:11
thou shalt not c the people ... Num 22:12
I pray thee, c me this people ... Num 22:17
c me Jacob, and come, defy Israel ... Num 23:7
How shall I c, whom God hath not ... Num 23:8
I took thee to c mine enemies ... Num 23:11
and c me them from thence ... Num 23:13
Neither c them at all, nor bless ... Num 23:25
thou mayest c me them from thence Num 23:27
I called thee to c mine enemies ... Num 24:10
you this day a blessing and a c ... Deut 11:26
And a c, if ye will not obey the ... Deut 11:28
Gerizim, and the c upon mount Ebal Deut 11:29
Pethor of Mesopotamia, to c thee ... Deut 23:4
the c into a blessing unto thee ... Deut 23:5
shall stand upon mount Ebal to c ... Deut 27:13
he heareth the words of this c ... Deut 29:19
upon thee, the blessing and the c ... Deut 30:1
and make the camp of Israel a c ... Josh 6:18
Balaam the son of Beor to c you ... Josh 24:9
C ye Meroz, said the angel of the ... Judg 5:23
c ye bitterly the inhabitants ... Judg 5:23
upon them came the c of Jotham ... Judg 9:57
this dead dog c my lord the king ... 2Sa 16:9
so let him c, because the LORD ... 2Sa 16:10
LORD hath said unto him, C David ... 2Sa 16:10
let him alone, and let him c ... 2Sa 16:11
c in the day when I went to ... 1Kin 2:8
should become a desolation and a c .. 2Kin 22:19
their nobles, and entered into a c ... Neh 10:29
them, that he should c them ... Neh 13:2
God turned the c into a blessing ... Neh 13:2
he will c thee to thy face ... Job 1:11
he will c thee to thy face ... Job 2:5
c God, and die ... Job 2:9
Let them c it ... Job 3:8
that c the day, who are ready ... Job 3:8
to sin by wishing a c to his soul ... Job 31:30
their mouth, but they c inwardly ... Ps 62:4
Let them c, but bless thou ... Ps 109:28
The c of the LORD is in the house ... Prov 3:33
corn, the people shall c him ... Prov 11:26
him shall the people c, nations ... Prov 24:24
so the c causeless shall not come ... Prov 26:2
it shall be counted a c to him ... Prov 27:14
his eyes shall have many a c ... Prov 28:27
unto his master, lest he c thee ... Prov 30:10
lest thou hear thy servant c thee ... Eccl 7:21
C not the king, no not in thy ... Eccl 10:20
c not the rich in thy bedchamber ... Eccl 10:20
c their king and their God, and ... Is 8:21
hath the c devoured the earth ... Is 24:6
and upon the people of my c ... Is 34:5
and have given Jacob to the c ... Is 43:28
your name for a c unto my chosen ... Is 65:15
yet every one of them doth c me ... Jer 15:10
and a proverb, a taunt and a c ... Jer 24:9
astonishment, an hissing, and a c ... Jer 25:18
will make this city a c to all the ... Jer 26:6
kingdoms of the earth, to be a c ... Jer 29:18
of them shall be taken up a c by ... Jer 29:22
and an astonishment, and a c ... Jer 42:18
off, and that ye might be a c ... Jer 44:8
and an astonishment, and a c ... Jer 44:12
and an astonishment, and a c ... Jer 44:22
a reproach, a waste, and a c ... Jer 49:13
sorrow of heart, thy c unto them ... Lam 3:65
therefore the c is poured upon us ... Dan 9:11
This is the c that goeth forth ... Zec 5:3
as ye were a c among the heathen ... Zec 8:13
I will even send a c upon you ... Mal 2:2
and I will c your blessings ... Mal 2:2
Ye are cursed with a c ... Mal 3:9
come and smite the earth with a c ... Mal 4:6
enemies, bless them that c you ... Mt 5:44
Then began he to c and to swear, ... Mt 26:74
But he began to c and to swear, ... Mk 14:71
Bless them that c you, and pray ... Lk 6:28
and bound themselves under a c ... Acts 23:12
bound ourselves under a great c ... Acts 23:14
bless, and c not ... Rom 12:14
works of the law are under the c ... Gal 3:10
redeemed us from the c of the law ... Gal 3:13
being made a c for us ... Gal 3:13
and therewith c we men, which are ... Jas 3:9
And there shall be no more c ... Rev 22:3

**CURSED**
thou art c above all cattle, and ... Gen 3:14
c is the ground for thy sake ... Gen 3:17
now art thou c from the earth, ... Gen 4:11
the ground which the LORD hath c ... Gen 5:29
And he said, C be Canaan ... Gen 9:25
c be every one that curseth thee, ... Gen 27:29
C be their anger, for it was ... Gen 49:7
he hath c his father or his ... Lev 20:9
the name of the LORD, and c ... Lev 24:11
him that hath c without the camp ... Lev 24:14
him that had c out of the camp ... Lev 24:23
and he whom thou cursest is c ... Num 22:6
I curse, whom God hath not c ... Num 23:8
c is he that curseth thee ... Num 24:9
lest thou be a c thing like it ... Deut 7:26
for it is a c thing ... Deut 7:26
of the c thing to thine hand ... Deut 13:17
C be the man that maketh any ... Deut 27:15
C be he that setteth light by his ... Deut 27:16
C be he that removeth his ... Deut 27:17
C be he that maketh the blind to ... Deut 27:18
C be he that perverteth the ... Deut 27:19
C be he that lieth with his ... Deut 27:20
C be he that lieth with any ... Deut 27:21
C be he that lieth with his ... Deut 27:22
C be he that lieth with his ... Deut 27:23
C be he that smiteth his ... Deut 27:24
C be he that taketh reward to ... Deut 27:25
C be he that confirmeth not all ... Deut 27:26
C shalt thou be in the city, and ... Deut 28:16
c shalt thou be in the field ... Deut 28:16
C shall be thy basket and thy ... Deut 28:17
C shall be the fruit of thy body, ... Deut 28:18
C shalt thou be when thou comest ... Deut 28:19
c shalt thou be when thou goest ... Deut 28:19
C be the man before the LORD, ... Josh 6:26
Now therefore ye are c, and there ... Josh 9:23
did eat and drink, and c Abimelech ... Judg 9:27
C be he that giveth a wife to ... Judg 21:18
C be the man that eateth any food ... 1Sa 14:24
C be the man that eateth any food ... 1Sa 14:28
the Philistine c David by his ... 1Sa 17:43
c be they before the LORD ... 1Sa 26:19
came forth, and c still as he came ... 2Sa 16:5
And thus said Shimei when he c ... 2Sa 16:7
c as he went, and threw stones at ... 2Sa 16:13
because he c the LORD's anointed ... 2Sa 19:21
which c me with a grievous curse ... 1Kin 2:8
c them in the name of the LORD ... 2Kin 2:24
and said, Go, see now this c woman ... 2Kin 9:34
c them, and smote certain of them, ... Neh 13:25
sinned, and c God in their hearts ... Job 1:5
Job his mouth, and c his day ... Job 3:1
but suddenly I c his habitation ... Job 5:3
their portion is c in the earth ... Job 24:18
they that be c of him shall be ... Ps 37:22
hast rebuked the proud that are c ... Ps 119:21
thyself likewise hast c others ... Eccl 7:22
C be the man that obeyeth not the ... Jer 11:3
C be the man that trusteth in man ... Jer 17:5
C be the day wherein I was born ... Jer 20:14
C be the man who brought tidings ... Jer 20:15
C be he that doeth the work of ... Jer 48:10
c be he that keepeth back his ... Jer 48:10
But c be the deceiver, which hath ... Mal 1:14
I have c them already, because ye ... Mal 2:2
Ye are c with a curse ... Mal 3:9
left hand, Depart from me, ye c ... Mt 25:41
who knoweth not the law are c ... Jn 7:49
C is every one that continueth ... Gal 3:10
C is every one that hangeth on a ... Gal 3:13
with covetous practices; c children ... 2Pet 2:14

**CURSEDST**
from thee, about which thou c ... Judg 17:2
which thou c is withered away ... Mk 11:21

**CURSES**
shall write these c in a book ... Num 5:23
that all these c shall come upon ... Deut 28:15
Moreover all these c shall come ... Deut 28:45
all the c that are written in ... Deut 29:20
according to all the c of the ... Deut 29:21
to bring upon it all the c that ... Deut 29:27
all these c upon thine enemies ... Deut 30:7
even all the c that are written ... 2Chr 34:24

**CURSEST**
and he whom thou c is cursed ... Num 22:6

**CURSETH**
thee, and curse him that c thee ... Gen 12:3
cursed be every one that c thee ... Gen 27:29
he that c his father, or his ... Ex 21:17
For every one that c his father ... Lev 20:9
Whosoever c his God shall bear ... Lev 24:15
thee, and cursed is he that c thee ... Num 24:9
Whoso c his father or his mother, ... Prov 20:20
a generation that c their father ... Prov 30:11
He that c father or mother, let ... Mt 15:4
Whoso c father or mother, let him ... Mk 7:10

**CURSING**
the woman with an oath of c ... Num 5:21
The LORD shall send upon thee c ... Deut 28:20
you life and death, blessing and c ... Deut 30:19
me good for his c this day ... 2Sa 16:12
His mouth is full of c and deceit ... Ps 10:7
and for c and lying which they ... Ps 59:12
As he loved c, so let it come ... Ps 109:17
with c like as with his garment ... Ps 109:18
he heareth c, and bewrayeth it not ... Prov 29:24
Whose mouth is full of c and ... Rom 3:14
is rejected, and is nigh unto c ... Heb 6:8
mouth proceedeth blessing and c ... Jas 3:10

**CURSINGS**
of the law, the blessings and c ... Josh 8:34

**CURTAIN**
length of one c shall be eight ... Ex 26:2
the breadth of one c four cubits ... Ex 26:2
one c from the selvedge in the ... Ex 26:4
the uttermost edge of another c ... Ex 26:4
shalt thou make in the one c ... Ex 26:5
thou make in the edge of the c ... Ex 26:5
The length of one c shall be ... Ex 26:8
the breadth of one c four cubits ... Ex 26:8
shalt double the sixth c in the ... Ex 26:9
loops on the edge of the one c ... Ex 26:10
the c which coupleth the second ... Ex 26:10
the half c that remaineth, shall ... Ex 26:12
The length of one c was twenty ... Ex 36:9
the breadth of one c four cubits ... Ex 36:9
of one c from the selvedge in the ... Ex 36:11
the uttermost side of another c ... Ex 36:11
Fifty loops made he in one c ... Ex 36:12
made he in the edge of the c ... Ex 36:12
the loops held one c to another ... Ex 36:12
length of one c was thirty cubits ... Ex 36:15
cubits was the breadth of one c ... Ex 36:15
edge of the c in the coupling ... Ex 36:17
the c which coupleth the second ... Ex 36:17
the c for the door of the court, ... Num 3:26
out the heavens like a c ... Ps 104:2
stretcheth out the heavens as a c ... Is 40:22

**CURTAINS**
with ten c of fine twined linen ... Ex 26:1
every one of the c shall have one ... Ex 26:2
The five c shall be coupled ... Ex 26:3
other five c shall be coupled one ... Ex 26:3
couple the c together with the ... Ex 26:6
thou shalt make c of goats' hair ... Ex 26:7
eleven c shalt thou make ... Ex 26:7
the eleven c shall be all of one ... Ex 26:8
shalt couple five c by themselves ... Ex 26:9
six c by themselves, and shalt ... Ex 26:9
remaineth of the c of the tent ... Ex 26:12
the length of the c of the tent ... Ex 26:13
made ten c of fine twined linen ... Ex 36:8
the c were all of one size ... Ex 36:9
the five c one unto another ... Ex 36:10
the other five c he coupled one ... Ex 36:10
coupled the c one unto another ... Ex 36:13
he made c of goats' hair for the ... Ex 36:14
eleven c he made them ... Ex 36:14
the eleven c were of one size ... Ex 36:15
he coupled five c by themselves ... Ex 36:16
and six c by themselves ... Ex 36:16
bear the c of the tabernacle ... Num 4:25
the ark of God dwelleth within c ... 2Sa 7:2
of the LORD remaineth under c ... 1Chr 17:1
of Kedar, as the c of Solomon ... Song 1:5
forth the c of thine habitations ... Is 54:2
spoiled, and my c in a moment ... Jer 4:20
tent any more, and to set up my c ... Jer 10:20
shall take to themselves their c ... Jer 49:29
the c of the land of Midian did ... Hab 3:7

**CUSH** (*cush*) See ETHIOPIA.
*1. A son of Ham.*
C, and Mizraim, and Phut ... Gen 10:6
the sons of C; Seba, and Havilah ... Gen 10:7
And C begat Nimrod ... Gen 10:8
C, and Mizraim, Put, and Canaan ... 1Chr 1:8
the sons of C; Seba, and Havilah ... 1Chr 1:9
And C begat Nimrod ... 1Chr 1:10
*2. A Benjamite.*
the words of C the Benjamite ... Ps 7:t
*3. Land of descendants of Cush.*
Egypt, and from Pathros, and from C ... Is 11:11

**CUSHAN** (*cu'-shan*) See CHUSHAN-RISHATHAIM.
*Same as Chushan-rishathaim.*
saw the tents of C in affliction ... Hab 3:7

**CUSHAN-RISHATHIAM**

**CUSHI** (*cu'-shi*)
*1. Messenger of David.*
Then said Joab to C, Go tell the ... 2Sa 18:21
C bowed himself unto Joab, and ran ... 2Sa 18:21
me, I pray thee, also run after C ... 2Sa 18:22
way of the plain, and overran C ... 2Sa 18:23
And, behold, C came ... 2Sa 18:31
C said, Tidings, my lord the king ... 2Sa 18:31
And the king said unto C, Is the ... 2Sa 18:32
C answered, The enemies of my ... 2Sa 18:32

2. *Ancestor of Jehudi.*
son of Shelemiah, the son of C ... Jer 36:14
3. *Father of Zephaniah.*
came unto Zephaniah the son of C ... Zeph 1:1

## CUSTODY
And under the c and charge of the ... Num 3:36
unto the c of Hege the king's ... Est 2:3
to the c of Hegai, that Esther ... Est 2:8
to the c of Hegai, keeper of the ... Est 2:8
to the c of Shaashgaz, the king's ... Est 2:14

## CUSTOM
for the c of women is upon me ... Gen 31:35
And it was a c in Israel, ... Judg 11:39
the priest's c with the people ... 1Sa 2:13
by number, according to the c ... Ezr 3:4
they not pay toll, tribute, and c ... Ezr 4:13
and toll, tribute, and c, was paid ... Ezr 4:20
to impose toll, tribute, or c ... Ezr 7:24
sealed according to the law and c ... Jer 32:11
sitting at the receipt of c ... Mt 9:9
of the earth take c or tribute ... Mt 17:25
sitting at the receipt of c ... Mk 2:14
According to the c of the ... Lk 1:9
do for him after the c of the law ... Lk 2:27
after the c of the feast ... Lk 2:42
and, as his c was, he went into ... Lk 4:16
Levi, sitting at the receipt of c ... Lk 5:27
But ye have a c, that I should ... Jn 18:39
c to whom c; fear to whom fear ... Rom 13:7
be contentious, we have no such c ... 1Cor 11:16

## CUSTOMS
not any one of these abominable c ... Lev 18:30
For the c of the people are vain ... Jer 10:3
shall change the c which Moses ... Acts 6:14
And teach c, which are not lawful ... Acts 16:21
neither to walk after the c ... Acts 21:21
I know thee to be expert in all c ... Acts 26:3
or c of our fathers, yet was I ... Acts 28:17

## CUT
neither shall all flesh be c off ... Gen 9:11
that soul shall be c off from his ... Gen 17:14
c off the foreskin of her son, and ... Ex 4:25
thou shalt be c off from the ... Ex 9:15
soul shall be c off from Israel ... Ex 12:15
even that soul shall be c off ... Ex 12:19
and I will c them off ... Ex 23:23
thou shalt c the ram in pieces, ... Ex 29:17
shall even be c off from his ... Ex 30:33
shall even be c off from his ... Ex 30:38
that soul shall be c off from ... Ex 31:14
images, and c down their groves ... Ex 34:13
c it into wires, to work it in ... Ex 39:3
offering, and c it into his pieces ... Lev 1:6
he shall c it into his pieces, ... Lev 1:12
shall be c off from his people ... Lev 7:20
shall be c off from his people ... Lev 7:21
it shall be c off from his people ... Lev 7:25
shall be c off from his people ... Lev 7:27
And he c the ram into pieces ... Lev 8:20
that man shall be c off from ... Lev 17:4
even that man shall be c off from ... Lev 17:9
will c him off from among his ... Lev 17:10
eateth it shall be c off ... Lev 17:14
be c off from among their people ... Lev 18:29
that soul shall be c off from ... Lev 19:8
will c him off from among his ... Lev 20:3
will c him off, and all that go a ... Lev 20:5
will c him off from among his ... Lev 20:6
they shall be c off in the sight ... Lev 20:17
both of them shall be c off from ... Lev 20:18
that soul shall be c off from my ... Lev 22:3
or crushed, or broken, or c ... Lev 22:24
he shall be c off from among his ... Lev 23:29
c down your images, and cast your ... Lev 26:30
C ye not off the tribe of the ... Num 4:18
be c off from among his people ... Num 9:13
c down from thence a branch with ... Num 13:23
of Israel c down from thence ... Num 13:24
that soul shall be c off from ... Num 15:30
that soul shall utterly be c off ... Num 15:31
soul shall be c off from Israel ... Num 19:13
that soul shall be c off from ... Num 19:20
c down their groves, and burn ... Deut 7:5
c off the nations from before ... Deut 12:29
ye shall not c yourselves ... Deut 14:1
thy God hath c off the nations ... Deut 19:1
with the axe to c down the tree ... Deut 19:5
thou shalt not c them down (for ... Deut 20:19
thou shalt destroy and c them down ... Deut 20:20
or hath his privy member c off ... Deut 23:1
Then thou shalt c off her hand ... Deut 25:12
c off from the waters that come ... Josh 3:13
salt sea, failed, and were c off ... Josh 3:16
were c off before the ark of the ... Josh 4:7
the waters of Jordan were c off ... Josh 4:7
c off our name from the earth ... Josh 7:9
c off the Anakims from the ... Josh 11:21
c down for thyself there in the ... Josh 17:15
a wood, and thou shalt c it down ... Josh 17:18
all the nations that I have c off ... Josh 23:4
c off his thumbs and his great ... Judg 1:6
thumbs and their great toes c off ... Judg 1:7
c down the grove that is by it ... Judg 6:25
the grove which thou shalt c down ... Judg 6:26
the grove was c down that was by ... Judg 6:28
because he hath c down the grove ... Judg 6:30
c down a bough from the trees, and ... Judg 9:48
all the people likewise c down ... Judg 9:49
c her in pieces, and sent her ... Judg 20:6
There is one tribe c off from ... Judg 21:6
not c off from among his brethren ... Ruth 4:10
that I will c off thine arm, and ... 1Sa 2:31
whom I shall not c off from mine ... 1Sa 2:33
were c off upon the threshold ... 1Sa 5:4
him, and c off his head therewith ... 1Sa 17:51
But also thou shalt not c off thy ... 1Sa 20:15
not when the LORD hath c off the ... 1Sa 20:15
c off the skirt of Saul's robe ... 1Sa 24:4
because he had c off Saul's skirt ... 1Sa 24:5
for in that I c off the skirt of ... 1Sa 24:11
that thou wilt not c off my seed ... 1Sa 24:21
how he hath c off those that have ... 1Sa 28:9
they c off his head, and stripped ... 1Sa 31:9
c off their hands and their feet, ... 2Sa 4:12
have c off all thine enemies out ... 2Sa 7:9
c off their garments in the ... 2Sa 10:4
they c off the head of Sheba the ... 2Sa 20:22
Then will I c off Israel out of ... 1Kin 9:7
until he had c off every male in ... 1Kin 11:16
of Jeroboam, even to c it off ... 1Kin 13:34
will c off from Jeroboam him that ... 1Kin 14:10
who shall c off the house of ... 1Kin 14:14
when Jezebel c off the prophets ... 1Kin 18:4
c it in pieces, and lay it on wood ... 1Kin 18:23
c themselves after their manner ... 1Kin 18:28
c the bullock in pieces, and laid ... 1Kin 18:33
will c off from Ahab him that ... 1Kin 21:21
came to Jordan, they c down wood ... 2Kin 6:4
he c down a stick, and cast it in ... 2Kin 6:6
I will c off from Ahab him that ... 2Kin 9:8
the LORD began to c Israel short ... 2Kin 10:32
king Ahaz c off the borders of ... 2Kin 16:17
c down the groves, and brake in ... 2Kin 18:4
At that time did Hezekiah c off ... 2Kin 18:16
will c down the tall cedar trees ... 2Kin 19:23
c down the groves, and filled ... 2Kin 23:14
c in pieces all the vessels of ... 2Kin 24:13
have c off all thine enemies from ... 1Chr 17:8
c off their garments in the midst ... 1Chr 19:4
c them with saws, and with harrows ... 1Chr 20:3
can skill to c timber in Lebanon ... 2Chr 2:8
the hewers that c timber ... 2Chr 2:10
we will c wood out of Lebanon, as ... 2Chr 2:16
the images, and c down the groves ... 2Chr 14:3
Asa c down her idol, and stamped ... 2Chr 15:16
to c off the house of Ahab ... 2Chr 22:7
for he was c off from the house ... 2Chr 26:21
c in pieces the vessels of the ... 2Chr 28:24
c down the groves, and threw down ... 2Chr 31:1
which c off all the mighty men of ... 2Chr 32:21
on high above them, he c down ... 2Chr 34:4
c down all the idols throughout ... 2Chr 34:7
or where were the righteous c off ... Job 4:7
let loose his hand, and c me off ... Job 6:9
not c down, it withereth before ... Job 8:12
Whose hope shall be c off ... Job 8:14
If he c off, and shut up, or ... Job 11:10
forth like a flower, and is c down ... Job 14:2
hope of a tree, if it be c down ... Job 14:7
above shall his branch be c off ... Job 18:16
his months is c off in the midst ... Job 21:21
Which were c down out of time, ... Job 22:16
our substance is not c down ... Job 22:20
Because I was not c off before ... Job 23:17
c off as the tops of the ears of ... Job 24:24
Who c up mallows by the bushes, ... Job 30:4
when people are c off in their ... Job 36:20
The LORD shall c off all ... Ps 12:3
I am c off from before thine eyes ... Ps 31:22
to c off the remembrance of them ... Ps 34:16
soon be c down like the grass ... Ps 37:2
For evildoers shall be c off ... Ps 37:9
be cursed of him shall be c off ... Ps 37:22
seed of the wicked shall be c off ... Ps 37:28
when the wicked are c off ... Ps 37:34
end of the wicked shall be c off ... Ps 37:38
c them off in thy truth ... Ps 54:5
let them be as c in pieces ... Ps 58:7
of the wicked also will I c off ... Ps 75:10
He shall c off the spirit of ... Ps 76:12
is burned with fire, it is c down ... Ps 80:16
let us c them off from being a ... Ps 83:4
they are c off from thy hand ... Ps 88:5
thy terrors have c me off ... Ps 88:16
in the evening it is c down ... Ps 90:6
for it is soon c off, and we fly ... Ps 90:10
shall c them off in their own ... Ps 94:23
the LORD our God shall c them off ... Ps 94:23
his neighbour, him will I c off ... Ps 101:5
that I may c off all wicked doers ... Ps 101:8
c the bars of iron in sunder ... Ps 107:16
Let his posterity be c off ... Ps 109:13
that he may c off the memory of ... Ps 109:15
he hath c asunder the cords of ... Ps 129:4
of thy mercy c off mine enemies, ... Ps 143:12
shall be c off from the earth ... Prov 2:22
the froward tongue shall be c out ... Prov 10:31
expectation shall not be c off ... Prov 23:18
expectation shall not be c off ... Prov 24:14
the sycomores are c down, but we ... Is 9:10
LORD will c off from Israel head ... Is 9:14
and c off nations not a few ... Is 10:7
he shall c down the thickets of ... Is 10:34
of Judah shall be c off ... Is 11:13
how art thou c down to the ground ... Is 14:12
c off from Babylon the name, and ... Is 14:22
be baldness, and every beard c off ... Is 15:2
he shall both c off the sprigs ... Is 18:5
take away and c down the branches ... Is 18:5
be removed, and be c down, and fall ... Is 22:25
that was upon it shall be c off ... Is 22:25
that watch for iniquity are c off ... Is 29:20
as thorns c up shall they be ... Is 33:12
I will c down the tall cedars ... Is 37:24
I have c off like a weaver my ... Is 38:12
he will c me off with pining ... Is 38:12
c in sunder the bars of iron ... Is 45:2
for thee, that I c thee not off ... Is 48:9
c off nor destroyed from before ... Is 48:19
Art thou not it that hath c Rahab ... Is 51:9
for he was c off out of the land ... Is 53:8
sign that shall not be c off ... Is 55:13
name, that shall not be c off ... Is 56:5
as if he c off a dog's neck ... Is 66:3
is c off from their mouth ... Jer 7:28
C off thine hair, O Jerusalem, and ... Jer 7:29
to c off the children from ... Jer 9:21
let us c him off from the land of ... Jer 11:19
nor c themselves, nor make ... Jer 16:6
they shall c down thy choice ... Jer 22:7
are c down because of the fierce ... Jer 25:37
when they c the calf in twain, and ... Jer 34:18
he c it with the penknife, and ... Jer 36:23
having c themselves, with ... Jer 41:5
to c off from you man and woman, ... Jer 44:7
that ye might c yourselves off, ... Jer 44:8
for evil, and to c off all Judah ... Jer 44:11
They shall c down her forest, ... Jer 46:23
to c off from Tyrus and Zidon ... Jer 47:4
Ashkelon is c off with the ... Jer 47:5
how long wilt thou c thyself ... Jer 47:5
let us c it off from being a ... Jer 48:2
Also thou shalt be c down ... Jer 48:2
The horn of Moab is c off ... Jer 48:25
of war shall be c off in that day ... Jer 49:26
C off the sower from Babylon, and ... Jer 50:16
of the whole earth c in asunder ... Jer 50:23
of war shall be c off in that day ... Jer 50:30
be not c off in her iniquity ... Jer 51:6
to c it off, that none shall ... Jer 51:62
He hath c off in his fierce anger ... Lam 2:3
They have c off my life in the ... Lam 3:53
then I said, I am c off ... Lam 3:54
and your images may be c down ... Eze 6:6
I will c him off from the midst ... Eze 14:8
will c off man and beast from it ... Eze 14:13
so that I c off man and beast from ... Eze 14:17
to c off from it man and beast ... Eze 14:19
to c off from it man and beast ... Eze 14:21
wast born thy navel was not c ... Eze 16:4
c off the fruit thereof, that it ... Eze 17:9
forts, to c off many persons ... Eze 17:17
and will c off from thee the ... Eze 21:3
Seeing then that I will c off ... Eze 21:4
I will c thee off from the people ... Eze 25:7
will c off man and beast from it ... Eze 25:13
I will c off the Cherethims, and ... Eze 25:16
c off man and beast out of thee ... Eze 29:8
I will c off the multitude of No ... Eze 30:15
have c him off, and have left him ... Eze 31:12
c off from it him that passeth ... Eze 35:7
we are c off for our parts ... Eze 37:11
neither c down any out of the ... Eze 39:10
thereof, ye shall be c in pieces ... Dan 2:5
a stone was c out without hands ... Dan 2:34
was c out of the mountain without ... Dan 2:45
shall be c in pieces, and their ... Dan 3:29
c off his branches, shake off his ... Dan 4:14
two weeks shall Messiah be c off ... Dan 9:26
idols, that they may be c off ... Hos 8:4
her king is c off as the foam ... Hos 10:7
king of Israel utterly be c off ... Hos 10:15
for it is c off from your mouth ... Joel 1:5
the drink offering is c off from ... Joel 1:9
Is not the meat c off before our ... Joel 1:16
c off the inhabitant from the ... Amos 1:5
I will c off the inhabitant from ... Amos 1:8
I will c off the judge from the ... Amos 2:3
horns of the altar shall be c off ... Amos 3:14
c them in the head, all of them ... Amos 9:1
by night, (how art thou c off ... Obad 5
of Esau may be c off by slaughter ... Obad 9
and thou shalt be c off for ever ... Obad 10
to c off those of his that did ... Obad 14
all thine enemies shall be c off ... Mic 5:9
that I will c off thy horses out ... Mic 5:10
I will c off the cities of thy ... Mic 5:11
I will c off witchcrafts out of ... Mic 5:12
graven images also will I c off ... Mic 5:13
yet thus shall they be c down ... Nah 1:12
will I c off the graven image ... Nah 1:14
he is utterly c off ... Nah 1:15
I will c off thy prey from the ... Nah 2:13
the sword shall c thee off ... Nah 3:15
shall be c off from the fold ... Hab 3:17
I will c off man from off the ... Zeph 1:3
I will c off the remnant of Baal ... Zeph 1:4
the merchant people are c down ... Zeph 1:11
they that bear silver are c off ... Zeph 1:11
I have c off the nations ... Zeph 3:6
dwelling should not be c off ... Zeph 3:7
one that stealeth shall be c off ... Zec 5:3
one that sweareth shall be c off ... Zec 5:3
I will c off the pride of the ... Zec 9:6
I will c off the chariot from ... Zec 9:10
and the battle bow shall be c off ... Zec 9:10
also I c off in one month ... Zec 11:8
is to be c off, let it be c off ... Zec 11:9

c it asunder, that I might break Zec 11:10
Then I c asunder mine other staff Zec 11:14
not visit those that be c off Zec 11:16
with it shall be c in pieces Zec 12:3
that I will c off the names of Zec 13:2
two parts therein shall be c off Zec 13:8
shall not be c off from the city Zec 14:2
The LORD will c off the man that Mal 2:12
c it off, and cast it from thee Mt 5:30
c them off, and cast them from Mt 18:8
others c down branches from the Mt 21:8
shall c him asunder, and appoint Mt 24:51
if thy hand offend thee, c it off Mk 9:43
if thy foot offend thee, c it off Mk 9:45
others c down branches off the Mk 11:8
the high priest, and c off his ear Mk 14:47
will c him in sunder, and will Lk 12:46
c it down Lk 13:7
after that thou shalt c it down Lk 13:9
priest, and c off his right ear Lk 22:50
servant, and c off his right ear Jn 18:10
his kinsman whose ear Peter c off Jn 18:26
they were c to the heart, and took Acts 5:33
they were c to the heart, and they Acts 7:54
Then the soldiers c off the ropes Acts 27:32
c it short in righteousness Rom 9:28
thou also shalt be c off Rom 11:22
For if thou wert c out of the Rom 11:24
that I may c off occasion from 2Cor 11:12
were even c off which trouble you Gal 5:12

**CUTH** (*cuth*) See CUTHAH. *A Babylonian city.*
the men of C made Nergal, and the 2Kin 17:30

**CUTHAH** (*cu'-thah*) See CUTH. *Same as Cuth.*
men from Babylon, and from C 2Kin 17:24

**CUTTEST**
When thou c down thine harvest in Deut 24:19

**CUTTETH**
He c out rivers among the rocks Job 28:10
the bow, and c the spear in sunder Ps 46:9
the grave's mouth, as when one c Ps 141:7
the hand of a fool c off the feet Prov 26:6
for one c a tree out of the Jer 10:3
chambers, and c him out windows Jer 22:14

**CUTTING**
in c of stones, to set them, and Ex 31:5
in the c of stones, to set them, Ex 35:33
I said in the c off of my days, I Is 38:10
to thy house by c off many people Hab 2:10
crying, and c himself with stones Mk 5:5

**CUTTINGS**
Ye shall not make any c in your Lev 19:28
nor make any c in their flesh Lev 21:5
upon all the hands shall be c Jer 48:37

**CUZA** See CHUZA.

**CYMBAL**
sounding brass, or a tinkling c 1Cor 13:1

**CYMBALS**
timbrels, and on cornets, and on c 2Sa 6:5
and with timbrels, and with c 1Chr 13:8
musick, psalteries and harps and c 1Chr 15:16
to sound with c of brass 1Chr 15:19
and with trumpets, and with c 1Chr 15:28
but Asaph made a sound with c 1Chr 16:5
c for those that should make a 1Chr 16:42
harps, with psalteries, and with c 1Chr 25:1
in the house of the LORD, with c 1Chr 25:6
arrayed in white linen, having c 2Chr 5:12
voice with the trumpets and c 2Chr 5:13
in the house of the LORD with c 2Chr 29:25
Levites the sons of Asaph with c Ezr 3:10
and with singing, with c, Neh 12:27
Praise him upon the loud c Ps 150:5
him upon the high sounding c Ps 150:5

**CYPRESS**
him down cedars, and taketh the c Is 44:14

**CYPRUS** (*si'-prus*) *An island off the Syrian coast.*
a Levite, and of the country of C Acts 4:36
travelled as far as Phenice, and C Acts 11:19
And some of them were men of C Acts 11:20
and from thence they sailed to C Acts 13:4
took Mark, and sailed unto C Acts 15:39
Now when we had discovered C Acts 21:3
brought with them one Mnason of C Acts 21:16
from thence, we sailed under C Acts 27:4

**CYRENE** (*si-re'-ne*) See CYRENIAN. *A Libyan city.*
came out, they found a man of C Mt 27:32
and in the parts of Libya about C Acts 2:10
of them were men of Cyprus and C Acts 11:20
was called Niger, and Lucius of C Acts 13:1

**CYRENIAN** (*si-re'-he-an*) See CYRENIANS. *A native of Cyrene.*
And they compel one Simon a C Mk 15:21
laid hold upon one Simon, a C Lk 23:26

**CYRENIANS** (*si-re'-ne-ans*)
synagogue of the Libertines, and C Acts 6:9

**CYRENIUS** (*si-re'-ne-us*) *A Roman governor of Syria.*
made when C was governor of Syria Lk 2:2

**CYRUS** (*si'-rus*) *Founder of the Persian Empire.*
first year of C king of Persia 2Chr 36:22
up the spirit of C king of Persia 2Chr 36:22
Thus saith C king of Persia, All 2Chr 36:23
first year of C king of Persia Ezr 1:1
up the spirit of C king of Persia Ezr 1:1
Thus saith C king of Persia, The Ezr 1:2
Also C the king brought forth the Ezr 1:7
Even those did C king of Persia Ezr 1:8
that they had of C king of Persia Ezr 3:7
as king C the king of Persia hath Ezr 4:3
all the days of C king of Persia Ezr 4:5
But in the first year of C the Ezr 5:13
C made a decree to build this Ezr 5:13
those did C the king take out of Ezr 5:14
that a decree was made of C the Ezr 5:17
In the first year of C the king Ezr 6:3
the same C the king made a decree Ezr 6:3
according to the commandment of C Ezr 6:14
That saith of C, He is my Is 44:28
the LORD to his anointed, to C Is 45:1
unto the first year of king C Dan 1:21
and in the reign of C the Persian Dan 6:28
In the third year of C king of Dan 10:1

# D

**DABAREH** (*dab'-a-reh*) See DABARETH. *A Levitical city in Issachar.*
her suburbs, D with her suburbs, Josh 21:28

**DABBASHETH** (*dab'-ba-sheth*) *A border city of Issachar.*
sea, and Maralah, and reached to D Josh 19:11

**DABBESHETH** See DABBASHETH.

**DABERATH** (*dab'-e-rath*) See DABAREH. *Same as Dabareh.*
and then goeth out to D, and goeth Josh 19:12
her suburbs, D with her suburbs, 1Chr 6:72

**DAGGER**
made him a d which had two edges Judg 3:16
took the d from his right thigh, Judg 3:21
not draw the d out of his belly Judg 3:22

**DAGON** See BETH-DAGON, DAGON'S. *A Philistine god.*
great sacrifice unto D their god Judg 16:23
house of D, and set it by D 1Sa 5:2
D was fallen upon his face to the 1Sa 5:3
And they took D, and set him in his 1Sa 5:3
D was fallen upon his face to the 1Sa 5:4
and the head of D and both the 1Sa 5:4
the stump of D was left to him 1Sa 5:4
neither the priests of D, nor any 1Sa 5:5
of D in Ashdod unto this day 1Sa 5:5
sore upon us, and upon D our god 1Sa 5:7
his head in the temple of D 1Chr 10:10

**DAGON'S**
nor any that come into D house 1Sa 5:5

**DAILY**
your d tasks, as when there was Ex 5:13
from your bricks of your d task Ex 5:19
be twice as much as they gather d Ex 16:5
the d meat offering, and the Num 4:16
this manner ye shall offer d Num 28:24
the d burnt offering, and his meat Num 29:6
she pressed him d with her words Judg 16:16
a d rate for every day, all the 2Kin 25:30
his d portion for their service 2Chr 31:16
offered the d burnt offerings by Ezr 3:4
was prepared for me d was one ox Neh 5:18
pass, when they spake d unto him Est 3:4
soul, having sorrow in my heart d Ps 13:2
while they say d unto me, Where Ps 42:10
he fighting d oppresseth me Ps 56:1
enemies would d swallow me up Ps 56:2
that I may d perform my vows Ps 61:8
who d loadeth us with benefits, Ps 68:19
and d shall he be praised Ps 72:15
foolish man reproacheth thee d Ps 74:22
for I cry unto thee d Ps 86:3
LORD, I have called d upon thee Ps 88:9
came round about me d like water Ps 88:17
I was d his delight, rejoicing Prov 8:30
watching d at my gates, waiting Prov 8:34
Yet they seek me d, and delight to Is 58:2
d rising up early and sending them Jer 7:25
I am in derision d, every one Jer 20:7
unto me, and a derision, d Jer 20:8
that they should give him d a Jer 37:21
and Noph shall have distresses d Eze 30:16
without blemish d the seven days Eze 45:23
of the goats d for a sin offering Eze 45:23
Thou shalt d prepare a burnt Eze 46:13
the king appointed them a d Dan 1:5
by him the d sacrifice was taken Dan 8:11
the d sacrifice by reason of Dan 8:12
vision concerning the d sacrifice Dan 8:13
shall take away the d sacrifice Dan 11:31
And from the time that the d Dan 12:11
he d increaseth lies and Hos 12:1
Give us this day our d bread Mt 6:11
I sat d with you teaching in the Mt 26:55
I was d with you in the temple Mk 14:49
himself, and take up his cross d Lk 9:23
Give us day by day our d bread Lk 11:3
he taught d in the temple Lk 19:47
When I was d with you in the Lk 22:53
continuing d with one accord in Acts 2:46
church d such as should be saved Acts 2:47
whom they laid d at the gate of Acts 3:2
d in the temple, and in every Acts 5:42
neglected in the d ministration Acts 6:1
faith, and increased in number d Acts 16:5
and searched the scriptures d Acts 17:11
in the market d with them that Acts 17:17
disputing d in the school of one Acts 19:9
in Christ Jesus our Lord, I die d 1Cor 15:31
that which cometh upon me d 2Cor 11:28
But exhort one another d, while Heb 3:13
Who needeth not d, as those high Heb 7:27
priest standeth d ministering Heb 10:11
be naked, and destitute of d food Jas 2:15

**DAINTIES**
be fat, and he shall yield royal d Gen 49:20
and let me not eat of their d Ps 141:4
Be not desirous of his d Prov 23:3

**DAINTY**
bread, and his soul d meat Job 33:20
neither desire thou his d meats Prov 23:6
thee, and all things which were d Rev 18:14

**DALAIAH** (*dal-a-i'-ah*) See DELAIAH. *A descendant of Judah.*
and Akkub, and Johanan, and D 1Chr 3:24

**DALE**
of Shaveh, which is the king's d Gen 14:17
pillar, which is in the king's d 2Sa 18:18

**DALMANUTHA** (*dal-ma-nu'-thah*) *A village in Galilee.*
and came into the parts of D Mk 8:10

**DALMATIA** (*dal-ma'-she-ah*) *A Roman province west of Macedonia.*
Crescens to Galatia, Titus unto D 2Ti 4:10

**DALPHON** (*dal'-fon*) *A son of Haman.*
And Parshandatha, and D, and Aspatha Est 9:7

**DAM**
seven days it shall be with his d Ex 22:30
shall be seven days under the d Lev 22:27
the d sitting upon the young, or Deut 22:6
not take the d with the young Deut 22:6
shalt in any wise let the d go Deut 22:7

**DAMAGE**
why should d grow to the hurt of Ezr 4:22
not countervail the king's d Est 7:4
off the feet, and drinketh d Prov 26:6
and the king should have no d Dan 6:2
will be with hurt and much d Acts 27:10
might receive d by us in nothing 2Cor 7:9

**DAMARIS** (*dam'-a-ris*) *An Athenian convert of Paul.*
Areopagite, and a woman named D Acts 17:34

**DAMASCENES** (*dam-as-senes'*) *Inhabitants of Damascus.*
the city of the D with a garrison 2Cor 11:32

**DAMASCUS** (*da-mas'-cus*) See DAMASCENES, SYRIA-DAMASCUS. *A city in Syria.*
which is on the left hand of D Gen 14:15
of my house is this Eliezer of D Gen 15:2
when the Syrians of D came to 2Sa 8:5
David put garrisons in Syria of D 2Sa 8:6
and they went to D, and dwelt 1Kin 11:24
and dwelt therein, and reigned in D 1Kin 11:24
king of Syria, that dwelt at D 1Kin 15:18
on thy way to the wilderness of D 1Kin 19:15
shalt make streets for thee in D 1Kin 20:34
not Abana and Pharpar, rivers of D 2Kin 5:12
And Elisha came to D 2Kin 8:7
even of every good thing of D 2Kin 8:9
he warred, and how he recovered D 2Kin 14:28
king of Assyria went up against D 2Kin 16:9
king Ahaz went to D to meet 2Kin 16:10
and saw an altar that was at D 2Kin 16:10
that king Ahaz had sent from D 2Kin 16:11
it against king Ahaz came from D 2Kin 16:11
the king was come from D 2Kin 16:12
when the Syrians of D came to 1Chr 18:5
king of Syria, that dwelt at D 2Chr 16:2
spoil of them unto the king of D 2Chr 24:23
captives, and brought them to D 2Chr 28:5
he sacrificed unto the gods of D 2Chr 28:23
of Lebanon which looketh toward D Song 7:4
For the head of Syria is D Is 7:8
and the head of D is Rezin Is 7:8
and my mother, the riches of D Is 8:4
is not Samaria as D Is 10:9
The burden of D Is 17:1
D is taken away from being a city Is 17:1
Ephraim, and the kingdom from D Is 17:3
Concerning D. Hamath is confounded Jer 49:23
D is waxed feeble, and turneth Jer 49:24
kindle a fire in the wall of D Jer 49:27
D was thy merchant in the Eze 27:18
which is between the border of D Eze 47:16
be Hazar-enan, the border of D Eze 47:17
measure from Hauran, and from D Eze 47:18
the border of D northward Eze 48:1
For three transgressions of D Amos 1:3

I will break also the bar of *D* ... Amos 1:5
of a bed, and in *D* in a couch ... Amos 3:12
you to go into captivity beyond *D* ... Amos 5:27
*D* shall be the rest thereof ... Zec 9:1
letters to *D* to the synagogues ... Acts 9:2
as he journeyed, he came near *D* ... Acts 9:3
the hand, and brought him into *D* ... Acts 9:8
there was a certain disciple at *D* ... Acts 9:10
the disciples which were at *D* ... Acts 9:19
the Jews which dwelt at *D* ... Acts 9:22
boldly at *D* in the name of Jesus ... Acts 9:27
unto the brethren, and went to *D* ... Acts 22:5
was come nigh unto *D* about noon ... Acts 22:6
said unto me, Arise, and go into *D* ... Acts 22:10
that were with me, I came into *D* ... Acts 22:11
as I went to *D* with authority ... Acts 26:12
But shewed first unto them of *D* ... Acts 26:20
In *D* the governor under Aretas ... 2Cor 11:32
Arabia, and returned again unto *D* ... Gal 1:17

**DAMNABLE**
privily shall bring in *d* heresies ... 2Pet 2:1

**DAMNATION**
ye shall receive the greater *d* ... Mt 23:14
how can ye escape the *d* of hell ... Mt 23:33
but is in danger of eternal *d* ... Mk 3:29
these shall receive greater *d* ... Mk 12:40
the same shall receive greater *d* ... Lk 20:47
evil, unto the resurrection of *d* ... Jn 5:29
whose *d* is just ... Rom 3:8
shall receive to themselves *d* ... Rom 13:2
drinketh *d* to himself, not ... 1Cor 11:29
Having *d*, because they have cast ... 1Ti 5:12
not, and their *d* slumbereth not ... 2Pet 2:3

**DAMNED**
he that believeth not shall be *d* ... Mk 16:16
he that doubteth is *d* if he eat ... Rom 14:23
That they all might be *d* who ... 2Th 2:12

**DAMSEL**
that the *d* to whom I shall say, ... Gen 24:14
the *d* was very fair to look upon, ... Gen 24:16
And the *d* ran, and told them of her ... Gen 24:28
Let the *d* abide with us a few ... Gen 24:55
And they said, We will call the *d* ... Gen 24:57
of Jacob, and he loved the *d* ... Gen 34:3
and spake kindly unto the *d* ... Gen 34:3
saying, Get me this *d* to wife ... Gen 34:4
but give me the *d* to wife ... Gen 34:12
Then shall the father of the *d* ... Deut 22:15
them unto the father of the *d* ... Deut 22:19
virginity be not found for the *d* ... Deut 22:20
the *d* to the door of her father's ... Deut 22:21
If a *d* that is a virgin be ... Deut 22:23
the *d*, because she cried not, ... Deut 22:24
find a betrothed *d* in the field ... Deut 22:25
But unto the *d* thou shalt do ... Deut 22:26
there is in the *d* no sin worthy ... Deut 22:26
field, and the betrothed *d* cried ... Deut 22:27
If a man find a *d* that is a ... Deut 22:28
to every man a *d* or two ... Judg 5:30
when the father of the *d* saw him ... Judg 19:3
over the reapers, Whose *d* is this ... Ruth 2:5
It is the Moabitish *d* that came ... Ruth 2:6
So they sought for a fair *d* ... 1Kin 1:3
the *d* was very fair, and cherished ... 1Kin 1:4
in a charger, and given to the *d* ... Mt 14:11
a *d* came unto him, saying, Thou ... Mt 26:69
the *d* is not dead, but sleepeth ... Mk 5:39
the father and the mother of the *d* ... Mk 5:40
entereth in where the *d* was lying ... Mk 5:40
And he took the *d* by the hand ... Mk 5:41
which is, being interpreted, *D* ... Mk 5:41
And straightway the *d* arose ... Mk 5:42
him, the king said unto the *d* ... Mk 6:22
in a charger, and gave it to the *d* ... Mk 6:28
the *d* gave it to her mother ... Mk 6:28
Then saith the *d* that kept the ... Jn 18:17
a *d* came to hearken, named Rhoda ... Acts 12:13
a certain *d* possessed with a ... Acts 16:16

**DAMSEL'S**
*d* virginity unto the elders of ... Deut 22:15
the *d* father shall say unto the ... Deut 22:16
with her shall give unto the *d* ... Deut 22:29
the *d* father, retained him ... Judg 19:4
the *d* father said unto his son in ... Judg 19:5
for the *d* father had said unto ... Judg 19:6
the *d* father said, Comfort thine ... Judg 19:8
the *d* father, said unto him, ... Judg 19:9

**DAMSELS**
And Rebekah arose, and her *d* ... Gen 24:61
with five *d* of hers that went ... 1Sa 25:42
among them were the *d* playing ... Ps 68:25

**DAN** (*dan*) See DANITES, DAN-JAAN, LAISH, MAHANEH-DAN.
*1. A son of Jacob.*
therefore called she his name *D* ... Gen 30:6
*D*, and Naphtali ... Gen 35:25
And the sons of *D* ... Gen 46:23
*D* shall judge his people, as one ... Gen 49:16
*D* shall be a serpent by the way, ... Gen 49:17
*D*, and Naphtali, Gad, and Asher ... Ex 1:4
therein, and called Leshem, *D* ... Josh 19:47
after the name of *D* their father ... Josh 19:47
after the name of *D* their father ... Judg 18:29
*D*, Joseph, and Benjamin, Naphtali, ... 1Chr 2:2
*D* also and Javan going to and fro ... Eze 27:19
*2. A city and tribal territory in northern Canaan.*
eighteen, and pursued them unto *D* ... Gen 14:14
all the land of Gilead, unto *D* ... Deut 34:1
called the name of the city *D* ... Judg 18:29
from *D* even to Beer-sheba, with ... Judg 20:1
all Israel from *D* even to ... 1Sa 3:20
from *D* even to Beer-sheba ... 2Sa 3:10
from *D* even to Beer-sheba, as the ... 2Sa 17:11
from *D* even to Beer-sheba, and ... 2Sa 24:2
from *D* even to Beer-sheba seventy ... 2Sa 24:15
from *D* even to Beer-sheba, all ... 1Kin 4:25
Beth-el, and the other put he in *D* ... 1Kin 12:29
before the one, even unto *D* ... 1Kin 12:30
of Israel, and smote Ijon, and *D* ... 1Kin 15:20
in Beth-el, and that were in *D* ... 2Kin 10:29
Israel from Beer-sheba even to *D* ... 1Chr 21:2
and they smote Ijon, and *D*, and ... 2Chr 16:4
Israel, from Beer-sheba even to *D* ... 2Chr 30:5
For a voice declareth from *D* ... Jer 4:15
of his horses was heard from *D* ... Jer 8:16
a portion for *D* ... Eze 48:1
And by the border of *D*, from the ... Eze 48:2
gate of Benjamin, one gate of *D* ... Eze 48:32
of Samaria, and say, Thy god, O *D* ... Amos 8:14
*3. Tribe descended from Dan 1.*
of Ahisamach, of the tribe of *D* ... Ex 31:6
of Ahisamach, of the tribe of *D* ... Ex 35:34
of Ahisamach, of the tribe of *D* ... Ex 38:23
of Dibri, of the tribe of *D* ... Lev 24:11
Of *D*; Ahiezer the son ... Num 1:12
Of the children of *D*, by their ... Num 1:38
of them, even of the tribe of *D* ... Num 1:39
The standard of the camp of *D* ... Num 2:25
of *D* shall be Ahiezer the son of ... Num 2:25
of *D* were an hundred thousand ... Num 2:31
prince of the children of *D* ... Num 7:66
of the children of *D* set forward ... Num 10:25
Of the tribe of *D*, Ammiel the son ... Num 13:12
sons of *D* after their families ... Num 26:42
of *D* after their families ... Num 26:42
of the tribe of the children of *D* ... Num 34:22
Gad, and Asher, and Zebulun, *D* ... Deut 27:13
Dan he said, *D* is a lion's whelp ... Deut 33:22
of *D* according to their families ... Josh 19:40
of *D* went out too little for them ... Josh 19:47
therefore the children of *D* went ... Josh 19:47
of *D* according to their families ... Josh 19:48
Ephraim, and out of the tribe of *D* ... Josh 21:5
And out of the tribe of *D*, Eltekeh ... Josh 21:23
children of *D* into the mountain ... Judg 1:34
why did *D* remain in ships ... Judg 5:17
in the camp of *D* between Zorah ... Judg 13:25
the children of *D* sent of their ... Judg 18:2
which were of the children of *D* ... Judg 18:16
and overtook the children of *D* ... Judg 18:22
they cried unto the children of *D* ... Judg 18:23
the children of *D* said unto him ... Judg 18:25
the children of *D* went their way ... Judg 18:26
the children of *D* set up the ... Judg 18:30
were priests to the tribe of *D* ... Judg 18:30
Of *D*, Azareel the son of Jeroham ... 1Chr 27:22
of a woman of the daughters of *D* ... 2Chr 2:14

**DANCE**
of Shiloh come out to *d* in dances ... Judg 21:21
like a flock, and their children *d* ... Job 21:11
Let them praise his name in the *d* ... Ps 149:3
Praise him with the timbrel and *d* ... Ps 150:4
a time to mourn, and a time to *d* ... Eccl 3:4
there, and satyrs shall *d* there ... Is 13:21
shall the virgin rejoice in the *d* ... Jer 31:13
our *d* is turned into mourning ... Lam 5:15

**DANCED**
to their number, of them that *d* ... Judg 21:23
David *d* before the LORD with all ... 2Sa 6:14
piped unto you, and ye have not *d* ... Mt 11:17
of Herodias *d* before them ... Mt 14:6
the said Herodias came in, and *d* ... Mk 6:22
piped unto you, and ye have not *d* ... Lk 7:32

**DANCES**
after her with timbrels and with *d* ... Ex 15:20
meet him with timbrels and with *d* ... Judg 11:34
of Shiloh come out to dance in *d* ... Judg 21:21
sing one to another of him in *d* ... 1Sa 21:11
they sang one to another in *d* ... 1Sa 29:5
shalt go forth in the *d* of them ... Jer 31:4

**DANCING**
that he saw the calf, and the *d* ... Ex 32:19
cities of Israel, singing and *d* ... 1Sa 18:6
earth, eating and drinking, and *d* ... 1Sa 30:16
leaping and *d* before the LORD ... 2Sa 6:16
out at a window saw king David *d* ... 1Chr 15:29
turned for me my mourning into *d* ... Ps 30:11
the house, he heard musick and *d* ... Lk 15:25

**DANDLED**
her sides, and be *d* upon her knees ... Is 66:12

**DANGER**
shall be in *d* of the judgment ... Mt 5:21
shall be in *d* of the judgment ... Mt 5:22
shall be in *d* of the council ... Mt 5:22
shall be in *d* of hell fire ... Mt 5:22
but is in *d* of eternal damnation ... Mk 3:29
craft is in *d* to be set at nought ... Acts 19:27
For we are in *d* to be called in ... Acts 19:40

**DANGEROUS**
spent, and when sailing was now *d* ... Acts 27:9

**DANIEL** See BELTESHAZZAR.
*1. A son of David.*
the second *D*, of Abigail the ... 1Chr 3:1
*2. An Israelite who renewed the covenant.*
of the sons of Ithamar; *D* ... Ezr 8:2
*D*, Ginnethon, Baruch, ... Neh 10:6
*3. A major prophet.*
Though these three men, Noah, *D* ... Eze 14:14
Though Noah, *D*, and Job, were in ... Eze 14:20
Behold, thou art wiser than *D* ... Eze 28:3
were of the children of Judah, *D* ... Dan 1:6
for he gave unto *D* the name of ... Dan 1:7
But *D* purposed in his heart that ... Dan 1:8
Now God had brought *D* into favour ... Dan 1:9
prince of the eunuchs said unto *D* ... Dan 1:10
Then said *D* to Melzar, whom the ... Dan 1:11
of the eunuchs had set over *D* ... Dan 1:11
*D* had understanding in all ... Dan 1:17
them all was found none like *D* ... Dan 1:19
*D* continued even unto the first ... Dan 1:21
and they sought *D* and his fellows ... Dan 2:13
Then *D* answered with counsel and ... Dan 2:14
Arioch made the thing known to *D* ... Dan 2:15
Then *D* went in, and desired of the ... Dan 2:16
Then *D* went to his house, and made ... Dan 2:17
that *D* and his fellows should not ... Dan 2:18
revealed unto *D* in a night vision ... Dan 2:19
Then *D* blessed the God of heaven ... Dan 2:19
*D* answered and said, Blessed be ... Dan 2:20
Therefore *D* went in unto Arioch, ... Dan 2:24
Then Arioch brought in *D* before ... Dan 2:25
The king answered and said to *D* ... Dan 2:26
*D* answered in the presence of the ... Dan 2:27
upon his face, and worshipped *D* ... Dan 2:46
The king answered unto *D*, and said ... Dan 2:47
Then the king made *D* a great man ... Dan 2:48
Then *D* requested of the king, and ... Dan 2:49
but *D* sat in the gate of the king ... Dan 2:49
But at the last *D* came in before ... Dan 4:8
Then *D*, whose name was ... Dan 4:19
doubts, were found in the same *D* ... Dan 5:12
now let *D* be called, and he will ... Dan 5:12
Then was *D* brought in before the ... Dan 5:13
said unto Daniel, Art thou that *D* ... Dan 5:13
Then *D* answered and said before ... Dan 5:17
and they clothed *D* with scarlet ... Dan 5:29
of whom *D* was first ... Dan 6:2
Then this *D* was preferred above ... Dan 6:3
against *D* concerning the kingdom ... Dan 6:4
find any occasion against this *D* ... Dan 6:5
Now when *D* knew that the writing ... Dan 6:10
found *D* praying and making ... Dan 6:11
and said before the king, That *D* ... Dan 6:13
set his heart on *D* to deliver him ... Dan 6:14
king commanded, and they brought *D* ... Dan 6:16
Now the king spake and said unto *D* ... Dan 6:16
might not be changed concerning *D* ... Dan 6:17
with a lamentable voice unto *D* ... Dan 6:20
king spake and said to Daniel, O *D* ... Dan 6:20
Then said *D* unto the king, O king ... Dan 6:21
should take *D* up out of the den ... Dan 6:23
So *D* was taken up out of the den, ... Dan 6:23
those men which had accused *D* ... Dan 6:24
and fear before the God of *D* ... Dan 6:26
who hath delivered *D* from the ... Dan 6:27
So this *D* prospered in the reign ... Dan 6:28
king of Babylon *D* had a dream ... Dan 7:1
*D* spake and said, I saw in my ... Dan 7:2
I *D* was grieved in my spirit in ... Dan 7:15
As for me *D*, my cogitations much ... Dan 7:28
appeared unto me, even unto me *D* ... Dan 8:1
it came to pass, when I, even I *D* ... Dan 8:15
I *D* fainted, and was sick certain ... Dan 8:27
the first year of his reign I *D* ... Dan 9:2
and talked with me, and said, O *D* ... Dan 9:22
a thing was revealed unto *D* ... Dan 10:1
In those days I *D* was mourning ... Dan 10:2
And I *D* alone saw the vision ... Dan 10:7
And he said unto me, O *D*, a man ... Dan 10:11
Then said he unto me, Fear not, *D* ... Dan 10:12
But thou, O *D*, shut up the words, ... Dan 12:4
Then I *D* looked, and, behold, ... Dan 12:5
And he said, Go thy way, *D* ... Dan 12:9
spoken of by *D* the prophet ... Mt 24:15
spoken of by *D* the prophet ... Mk 13:14

**DANITES** (*dan'-ites*) *Descendants of Dan 1.*
of Zorah, of the family of the *D* ... Judg 13:2
*D* sought them an inheritance to ... Judg 18:1
thence of the family of the *D* ... Judg 18:11
of the *D* expert in war twenty and ... 1Chr 12:35

**DAN-JAAN** (*dan-ja'-an*) *A place between Gilead and Zidon.*
and they came to *D*, and about to ... 2Sa 24:6

**DANNAH** (*dan'-nah*) *A city in Judah.*
And *D*, and Kirjath-sannah, which is ... Josh 15:49

**DARA** (*da'-rah*) See DARDA. *A son of Zerah.*
Ethan, and Heman, and Calcol, and *D* ... 1Chr 2:6

**DARDA** (*dar'-dah*) See DARA. *A wise man.*
and Heman, and Chalcol, and *D* ... 1Kin 4:31

**DARE**
is so fierce that *d* stir him up ... Job 41:10
good man some would even *d* to die ... Rom 5:7
For I will not *d* to speak of any ... Rom 15:18
*D* any of you, having a matter ... 1Cor 6:1

For we *d* not make ourselves of … 2Cor 10:12

**DARIUS** (*da-ri'-us*)

*1. Darius Hystaspes, king of Persia.*
the reign of *D* king of Persia … Ezr 4:5
of the reign of *D* king of Persia … Ezr 4:24
cease, till the matter came to *D* … Ezr 5:5
the river, sent unto *D* the king … Ezr 5:6
Unto *D* the king, all peace … Ezr 5:7
Then *D* the king made a decree, and … Ezr 6:1
I *D* have made a decree … Ezr 6:12
to that which *D* the king had sent … Ezr 6:13
to the commandment of Cyrus, and *D*.. Ezr 6:14
year of the reign of *D* the king … Ezr 6:15
In the second year of *D* the king … Hag 1:1
in the second year of *D* the king … Hag 1:15
month, in the second year of *D* … Hag 2:10
month, in the second year of *D* … Zec 1:1
Sebat, in the second year of *D* … Zec 1:7
pass in the fourth year of king *D* … Zec 7:1

*2. Darius Nothus, king of Persia.*
to the reign of *D* the Persian … Neh 12:22

*3. Cyaxares, king of Media.*
*D* the Median took the kingdom, … Dan 5:31
It pleased *D* to set over the … Dan 6:1
and said thus unto him, King *D* … Dan 6:6
Wherefore king *D* signed the … Dan 6:9
Then king *D* wrote unto all people … Dan 6:25
prospered in the reign of *D* … Dan 6:28
year of *D* the son of Ahasuerus … Dan 9:1
I in the first year of *D* the Mede … Dan 11:1

**DARK**

the sun went down, and it was *d* … Gen 15:17
if the plague be somewhat *d* … Lev 13:6
than the skin, but be somewhat *d* … Lev 13:21
the other skin, but be somewhat *d* … Lev 13:26
in the skin, but it be somewhat *d* … Lev 13:28
the plague be somewhat *d* after … Lev 13:56
apparently, and not in *d* speeches … Num 12:8
of the gate, when it was *d* … Josh 2:5
*d* waters, and thick clouds of the … 2Sa 22:12
began to be *d* before the sabbath … Neh 13:19
of the twilight thereof be *d* … Job 3:9
They grope in the *d* without light … Job 12:25
shall be *d* in his tabernacle … Job 18:6
can he judge through the *d* cloud … Job 22:13
In the *d* they dig through houses, … Job 24:16
round about him were *d* waters … Ps 18:11
Let their way be *d* and slippery … Ps 35:6
I will open my *d* saying upon the … Ps 49:4
for the *d* places of the earth are … Ps 74:20
I will utter *d* sayings of old … Ps 78:2
thy wonders be known in the *d* … Ps 88:12
He sent darkness, and made it *d* … Ps 105:28
of the wise, and their *d* sayings … Prov 1:6
evening, in the black and *d* night … Prov 7:9
LORD, and their works are in the *d* … Is 29:15
in a *d* place of the earth … Is 45:19
feet stumble upon the *d* mountains … Jer 13:16
He hath set me in *d* places … Lam 3:6
the house of Israel do in the *d* … Eze 8:12
and make the stars thereof *d* … Eze 32:7
of heaven will I make *d* over thee … Eze 32:8
scattered in the cloudy and *d* day … Eze 34:12
and understanding *d* sentences … Dan 8:23
the sun and the moon shall be *d* … Joel 2:10
and maketh the day *d* with night … Amos 5:8
even very *d*, and no brightness in … Amos 5:20
and it shall be *d* unto you … Mic 3:6
and the day shall be *d* over them … Mic 3:6
light shall not be clear, nor *d* … Zec 14:6
full of light, having no part *d* … Lk 11:36
And it was now *d*, and Jesus was not … Jn 6:17
early, when it was yet *d*, unto … Jn 20:1
a light that shineth in a *d* place … 2Pet 1:19

**DARKEN**

I will *d* the earth in the clear … Amos 8:9

**DARKENED**

earth, so that the land was *d* … Ex 10:15
Let their eyes be *d*, that they … Ps 69:23
the moon, or the stars, be not *d* … Eccl 12:2
that look out of the windows be *d* … Eccl 12:3
the light is *d* in the heavens … Is 5:30
the LORD of hosts is the land *d* … Is 9:19
the sun shall be *d* in his going … Is 13:10
all joy is *d*, the mirth of the … Is 24:11
also the day shall be *d*, when I … Eze 30:18
The sun and the moon shall be *d* … Joel 3:15
his right eye shall be utterly *d* … Zec 11:17
of those days shall the sun be *d* … Mt 24:29
tribulation, the sun shall be *d* … Mk 13:24
And the sun was *d*, and the veil of … Lk 23:45
and their foolish heart was *d* … Rom 1:21
Let their eyes be *d*, that they … Rom 11:10
Having the understanding *d* … Eph 4:18
as the third part of them was *d* … Rev 8:12
the air were *d* by reason of the … Rev 9:2

**DARKENETH**

Who is this that *d* counsel by … Job 38:2

**DARKISH**

skin of their flesh be *d* white … Lev 13:39

**DARKLY**

For now we see through a glass, *d* … 1Cor 13:12

**DARKNESS**

*d* was upon the face of the deep … Gen 1:2
God divided the light from the *d* … Gen 1:4
Day, and the *d* he called Night … Gen 1:5
and to divide the light from the *d* … Gen 1:18
horror of great *d* fell upon him … Gen 15:12
that there may be *d* over the land … Ex 10:21
Egypt, even *d* which may be felt … Ex 10:21
there was a thick *d* in all the … Ex 10:22
*d* to them, but it gave light by … Ex 14:20
unto the thick *d* where God was … Ex 20:21
with *d*, clouds, and thick *d* … Deut 4:11
of the cloud, and of the thick *d* … Deut 5:22
voice out of the midst of the *d* … Deut 5:23
as the blind gropeth in *d* … Deut 28:29
he put *d* between you and the … Josh 24:7
the wicked shall be silent in *d* … 1Sa 2:9
and *d* was under his feet … 2Sa 22:10
he made *d* pavilions round about … 2Sa 22:12
and the LORD will lighten my *d* … 2Sa 22:29
he would dwell in the thick *d* … 1Kin 8:12
he would dwell in the thick *d* … 2Chr 6:1
Let that day be *d* … Job 3:4
Let *d* and the shadow of death … Job 3:5
that night, let *d* seize upon it … Job 3:6
They meet with *d* in the daytime … Job 5:14
not return, even to the land of *d* … Job 10:21
A land of *d*, as *d* itself … Job 10:22
order, and where the light is as *d* … Job 10:22
discovereth deep things out of *d* … Job 12:22
not that he shall return out of *d* … Job 15:22
the day of *d* is ready at his hand … Job 15:23
He shall not depart out of *d* … Job 15:30
the light is short because of *d* … Job 17:12
I have made my bed in the *d* … Job 17:13
shall be driven from light into *d* … Job 18:18
and he hath set *d* in my paths … Job 19:8
All *d* shall be hid in his secret … Job 20:26
Or *d*, that thou canst not see … Job 22:11
I was not cut off before the *d* … Job 23:17
he covered the *d* from my face … Job 23:17
He setteth an end to *d*, and … Job 28:3
the stones of *d*, and the shadow of … Job 28:3
by his light I walked through *d* … Job 29:3
I waited for light, there came *d* … Job 30:26
There is no *d*, nor shadow of … Job 34:22
order our speech by reason of *d* … Job 37:19
thick *d* a swaddlingband for it, … Job 38:9
and as for *d*, where is the place … Job 38:19
and *d* was under his feet … Ps 18:9
He made *d* his secret place … Ps 18:11
LORD my God will enlighten my *d* … Ps 18:28
they walk on in *d* … Ps 82:5
laid me in the lowest pit, in *d* … Ps 88:6
me, and mine acquaintance into *d* … Ps 88:18
the pestilence that walketh in *d* … Ps 91:6
Clouds and *d* are round about him … Ps 97:2
Thou makest *d*, and it is night … Ps 104:20
He sent *d*, and made it dark … Ps 105:28
Such as sit in *d* and in the shadow … Ps 107:10
He brought them out of *d* and the … Ps 107:14
there ariseth light in the *d* … Ps 112:4
Surely the *d* shall cover me … Ps 139:11
the *d* hideth not from thee … Ps 139:12
the *d* and the light are both alike … Ps 139:12
he hath made me to dwell in *d* … Ps 143:3
to walk in the ways of *d* … Prov 2:13
The way of the wicked is as *d* … Prov 4:19
shall be put out in obscure *d* … Prov 20:20
as far as light excelleth *d* … Eccl 2:13
but the fool walketh in *d* … Eccl 2:14
All his days also he eateth in *d* … Eccl 5:17
in with vanity, and departeth in *d* … Eccl 6:4
his name shall be covered with *d* … Eccl 6:4
let him remember the days of *d* … Eccl 11:8
that put *d* for light, and light … Is 5:20
for light, and light for *d* … Is 5:20
one look unto the land, behold *d* … Is 5:30
and behold trouble and *d*, dimness … Is 8:22
and they shall be driven to *d* … Is 8:22
in *d* have seen a great light … Is 9:2
see out of obscurity, and out of *d* … Is 29:18
them that sit in *d* out of the … Is 42:7
I will make *d* light before them, … Is 42:16
will give thee the treasures of *d* … Is 45:3
I form the light, and create *d* … Is 45:7
thou silent, and get thee into *d* … Is 47:5
to them that are in *d*, Shew … Is 49:9
of his servant, that walketh in *d* … Is 50:10
and thy *d* be as the noonday … Is 58:10
for brightness, but we walk in *d* … Is 59:9
the *d* shall cover the earth, and … Is 60:2
the earth, and gross *d* the people … Is 60:2
a land of *d* … Jer 2:31
LORD your God, before he cause *d* … Jer 13:16
of death, and make it gross *d* … Jer 13:16
them as slippery ways in the *d* … Jer 23:12
hath led me, and brought me into *d* … Lam 3:2
set *d* upon thy land, saith the … Eze 32:8
he knoweth what is in the *d* … Dan 2:22
A day of *d* and of gloominess, a … Joel 2:2
a day of clouds and of thick *d* … Joel 2:2
The sun shall be turned into *d* … Joel 2:31
that maketh the morning *d* … Amos 4:13
the day of the LORD is *d*, and not … Amos 5:18
not the day of the LORD be *d*? … Amos 5:20
when I sit in *d*, the LORD shall … Mic 7:8
*d* shall pursue his enemies … Nah 1:8
and desolation, a day of *d* … Zeph 1:15
a day of clouds and thick *d* … Zeph 1:15
which sat in *d* saw great light … Mt 4:16
thy whole body shall be full of *d* … Mt 6:23
be *d*, how great is that *d* … Mt 6:23
shall be cast out into outer *d* … Mt 8:12
What I tell you in *d*, that speak … Mt 10:27
away, and cast him into outer *d* … Mt 22:13
unprofitable servant into outer *d* … Mt 25:30
was *d* over all the land unto the … Mt 27:45
there was *d* over the whole land … Mk 15:33
give light to them that sit in *d* … Lk 1:79
evil, thy body also is full of *d* … Lk 11:34
light which is in thee be not *d* … Lk 11:35
in *d* shall be heard in the light … Lk 12:3
is your hour, and the power of *d* … Lk 22:53
there was a *d* over all the earth … Lk 23:44
And the light shineth in *d* … Jn 1:5
the *d* comprehended it not … Jn 1:5
men loved *d* rather than light, … Jn 3:19
followeth me shall not walk in *d* … Jn 8:12
the light, lest *d* come upon you … Jn 12:35
for he that walketh in *d* knoweth … Jn 12:35
on me should not abide in *d* … Jn 12:46
The sun shall be turned into *d* … Acts 2:20
there fell on him a mist and a *d* … Acts 13:11
and to turn them from *d* to light … Acts 26:18
a light of them which are in *d* … Rom 2:19
therefore cast off the works of *d* … Rom 13:12
to light the hidden things of *d* … 1Cor 4:5
the light to shine out of *d* … 2Cor 4:6
what communion hath light with *d* … 2Cor 6:14
For ye were sometimes *d*, but now … Eph 5:8
with the unfruitful works of *d* … Eph 5:11
the rulers of the *d* of this world … Eph 6:12
delivered us from the power of *d* … Col 1:13
But ye, brethren, are not in *d* … 1Th 5:4
we are not of the night, nor of *d* … 1Th 5:5
fire, nor unto blackness, and *d* … Heb 12:18
of *d* into his marvellous light … 1Pet 2:9
delivered them into chains of *d* … 2Pet 2:4
to whom the mist of *d* is reserved … 2Pet 2:17
light, and in him is no *d* at all … 1Jn 1:5
fellowship with him, and walk in *d* … 1Jn 1:6
because the *d* is past, and the … 1Jn 2:8
brother, is in *d* even until now … 1Jn 2:9
is in *d*, and walketh in *d* … 1Jn 2:11
because that *d* hath blinded his … 1Jn 2:11
in everlasting chains under *d* … Jude 6
the blackness of *d* for ever … Jude 13
and his kingdom was full of *d* … Rev 16:10

**DARKON** (*dar'-kon*) *A family of exiles.*

of Jaalah, the children of *D* … Ezr 2:56
of Jaala, the children of *D* … Neh 7:58

**DARLING**

my *d* from the power of the dog … Ps 22:20
destructions, my *d* from the lions … Ps 35:17

**DART**

the spear, the *d*, nor the … Job 41:26
Till a *d* strike through his liver … Prov 7:23
or thrust through with a *d* … Heb 12:20

**DARTS**

And he took three *d* in his hand … 2Sa 18:14
in the city of David, and made *d* … 2Chr 32:5
*D* are counted as stubble … Job 41:29
all the fiery *d* of the wicked … Eph 6:16

**DASH**

wilt *d* their children, and rip up … 2Kin 8:12
thou shalt *d* them in pieces like … Ps 2:9
lest thou *d* thy foot against a … Ps 91:12
Their bows also shall *d* the young … Is 13:18
I will *d* them one against another … Jer 13:14
lest at any time thou *d* thy foot … Mt 4:6
lest at any time thou *d* thy foot … Lk 4:11

**DASHED**

hath *d* in pieces the enemy … Ex 15:6
be *d* to pieces before their eyes … Is 13:16
the mother was *d* in pieces upon … Hos 10:14
infants shall be *d* in pieces … Hos 13:16
her young children also were *d* in … Nah 3:10

**DASHETH**

*d* thy little ones against the … Ps 137:9
He that *d* in pieces is come up … Nah 2:1

**DATHAN** (*da'-than*) *A conspirator against Moses.*

of Kohath, the son of Levi, and *D* … Num 16:1
And Moses sent to call *D* … Num 16:12
about the tabernacle of Korah, *D* … Num 16:24
rose up and went unto *D* … Num 16:25
from the tabernacle of Korah, *D* … Num 16:27
and *D* and Abiram came out … Num 16:27
Nemuel, and *D*, and Abiram … Num 26:9
This is that *D* and Abiram, which … Num 26:9
And what he did unto *D* and Abiram, … Deut 11:6
earth opened and swallowed up *D* … Ps 106:17

**DAUB**

Say unto them which *d* it with … Eze 13:11

**DAUBED**

*d* it with slime and with pitch, and … Ex 2:3
others *d* it with untempered … Eze 13:10
daubing wherewith ye have *d* it … Eze 13:12
ye have *d* with untempered morter … Eze 13:14
upon them that have *d* it with … Eze 13:15
no more, neither they that *d* it … Eze 13:15
her prophets have *d* them with … Eze 22:28

**DAUBING**

Where is the *d* wherewith ye have … Eze 13:12

**DAUGHTER**

the *d* of Haran, the father of … Gen 11:29
son's son, and Sarai his *d* in law … Gen 11:31

she is the *d* of my father, but ... Gen 20:12
but not the *d* of my mother ... Gen 20:12
And said, Whose *d* art thou ... Gen 24:23
I am the *d* of Bethuel the son of ... Gen 24:24
her, and said, Whose *d* art thou ... Gen 24:47
The *d* of Bethuel, Nahor's son, ... Gen 24:47
master's brother's *d* unto his son ... Gen 24:48
the *d* of Bethuel the Syrian of ... Gen 25:20
Judith the *d* of Beeri the Hittite ... Gen 26:34
Bashemath the *d* of Elon the ... Gen 26:34
the *d* of Ishmael Abraham's son ... Gen 28:9
Rachel his *d* cometh with the ... Gen 29:6
when Jacob saw Rachel the *d* of ... Gen 29:10
years for Rachel thy younger *d* ... Gen 29:18
evening, that he took Leah his *d* ... Gen 29:23
Laban gave unto his *d* Leah Zilpah ... Gen 29:24
him Rachel his *d* to wife also ... Gen 29:28
Laban gave to Rachel his *d* Bilhah ... Gen 29:29
And afterwards she bare a *d* ... Gen 30:21
And Dinah the *d* of Leah, which she ... Gen 34:1
clave unto Dinah the *d* of Jacob ... Gen 34:3
that he had defiled Dinah his *d* ... Gen 34:5
in Israel in lying with Jacob's *d* ... Gen 34:7
my son Shechem longeth for your *d* ... Gen 34:8
then will we take our *d*, and we ... Gen 34:17
he had delight in Jacob's *d* ... Gen 34:19
Adah the *d* of Elon the Hittite, ... Gen 36:2
Aholibamah the *d* of Anah the ... Gen 36:2
Anah the *d* of Zibeon the Hivite ... Gen 36:2
And Bashemath Ishmael's *d*, sister ... Gen 36:3
*d* of Anah the *d* of Zibeon ... Gen 36:14
came of Aholibamah the *d* of Anah ... Gen 36:18
and Aholibamah the *d* of Anah ... Gen 36:25
the *d* of Matred, the *d* of ... Gen 36:39
Judah saw there a *d* of a certain ... Gen 38:2
said Judah to Tamar his *d* in law ... Gen 38:11
in process of time the *d* of Shuah ... Gen 38:12
not that she was his *d* in law ... Gen 38:16
Tamar thy *d* in law hath played ... Gen 38:24
the *d* of Poti-pherah priest of On ... Gen 41:45
came, which Asenath the *d* of ... Gen 41:50
in Padan-aram, with his *d* Dinah ... Gen 46:15
whom Laban gave to Leah his *d* ... Gen 46:18
Ephraim, which Asenath the *d* of ... Gen 46:20
Laban gave unto Rachel his *d* ... Gen 46:25
but if it be a *d*, then she shall ... Ex 1:16
every *d* ye shall save alive ... Ex 1:22
Levi, and took to wife a *d* of Levi ... Ex 2:1
the *d* of Pharaoh came down to ... Ex 2:5
said his sister to Pharaoh's *d* ... Ex 2:7
Pharaoh's *d* said to her, Go ... Ex 2:8
Pharaoh's *d* said unto her, Take ... Ex 2:9
she brought him unto Pharaoh's *d* ... Ex 2:10
and he gave Moses Zipporah his *d* ... Ex 2:21
*d* of Amminadab, sister of Naashon ... Ex 6:23
thou, nor thy son, nor thy *d* ... Ex 20:10
if a man sell his *d* to be a ... Ex 21:7
gored a son, or have gored a *d* ... Ex 21:31
fulfilled, for a son, or for a *d* ... Lev 12:6
the *d* of thy father, or *d* ... Lev 18:9
*d*, or of thy daughter's *d* ... Lev 18:10
of thy father's wife's *d*, ... Lev 18:11
the nakedness of thy *d* in law ... Lev 18:15
the nakedness of a woman and her *d*. Lev 18:17
son's *d*, or her daughter's *d* ... Lev 18:17
Do not prostitute thy *d*, to cause ... Lev 19:29
And if a man lie with his *d* in law ... Lev 20:12
father's *d*, or his mother's *d* ... Lev 20:17
and for his son, and for his *d* ... Lev 21:2
the *d* of any priest, if she ... Lev 21:9
If the priest's *d* also be married ... Lev 22:12
But if the priest's *d* be a widow ... Lev 22:13
the *d* of Dibri, of the tribe of ... Lev 24:11
was slain was Cozbi, the *d* of Zur ... Num 25:15
the *d* of a prince of Midian, ... Num 25:18
the name of the *d* of Asher was ... Num 26:46
the *d* of Levi, whom her mother ... Num 26:59
inheritance to pass unto his *d* ... Num 27:8
And if he have no *d*, then ye shall ... Num 27:9
wife, between the father and his *d* ... Num 30:16
And every *d*, that possesseth an ... Num 36:8
thou, nor thy son, nor thy *d* ... Deut 5:14
thy *d* thou shalt not give unto ... Deut 7:3
nor his *d* shalt thou take unto ... Deut 7:3
thou, and thy son, and thy *d* ... Deut 12:18
thy mother, or thy son, or thy *d* ... Deut 13:6
God, thou, and thy son, and thy *d* ... Deut 16:11
feast, thou, and thy son, and thy *d* ... Deut 16:14
or his *d* to pass through the fire ... Deut 18:10
I gave my *d* unto this man to wife ... Deut 22:16
saying, I found not thy *d* a maid ... Deut 22:17
the *d* of his father, or the ... Deut 27:22
father, or the *d* of his mother ... Deut 27:22
toward her son, and toward her *d* ... Deut 28:56
will I give Achsah my *d* to wife ... Josh 15:16
he gave him Achsah his *d* to wife ... Josh 15:17
will I give Achsah my *d* to wife ... Judg 1:12
he gave him Achsah his *d* to wife ... Judg 1:13
his *d* came out to meet him with ... Judg 11:34
her he had neither son nor *d* ... Judg 11:34
his clothes, and said, Alas, my *d* ... Judg 11:35
went yearly to lament the *d* of ... Judg 11:40
Behold, here is my *d* a maiden ... Judg 19:24
give his *d* unto Benjamin to wife ... Judg 21:1
her *d* in law, with her, which ... Ruth 1:22
And she said unto her, Go, my *d* ... Ruth 2:2
unto Ruth, Hearest thou not, my *d* ... Ruth 2:8
And Naomi said unto her *d* in law ... Ruth 2:20
*d* in law, It is good, my *d* ... Ruth 2:22
mother in law said unto her, My *d* ... Ruth 3:1
Blessed be thou of the LORD, my *d* ... Ruth 3:10
And now, my *d*, fear not ... Ruth 3:11
law, she said, Who art thou, my *d* ... Ruth 3:16
Then said she, Sit still, my *d* ... Ruth 3:18
for thy *d* in law, which loveth ... Ruth 4:15
thine handmaid for a *d* of Belial ... 1Sa 1:16
his *d* in law, Phinehas' wife, was ... 1Sa 4:19
was Ahinoam, the *d* of Ahimaaz ... 1Sa 14:50
riches, and will give him his *d* ... 1Sa 17:25
to David, Behold my elder *d* Merab ... 1Sa 18:17
at the time when Merab Saul's *d* ... 1Sa 18:19
And Michal Saul's *d* loved David ... 1Sa 18:20
gave him Michal his *d* to wife ... 1Sa 18:27
and that Michal Saul's *d* loved him ... 1Sa 18:28
But Saul had given Michal his *d* ... 1Sa 25:44
the *d* of Talmai king of Geshur ... 2Sa 3:3
name was Rizpah, the *d* of Aiah ... 2Sa 3:7
thou first bring Michal Saul's *d* ... 2Sa 3:13
Michal Saul's *d* looked through a ... 2Sa 6:16
Michal the *d* of Saul came out to ... 2Sa 6:20
Therefore Michal the *d* of Saul ... 2Sa 6:23
the *d* of Eliam, the wife of Uriah ... 2Sa 11:3
his bosom, and was unto him as a *d* ... 2Sa 12:3
were born three sons, and one *d* ... 2Sa 14:27
in to Abigail the *d* of Nahash ... 2Sa 17:25
two sons of Rizpah the *d* of Aiah ... 2Sa 21:8
five sons of Michal the *d* of Saul ... 2Sa 21:8
Rizpah the *d* of Aiah took ... 2Sa 21:10
David what Rizpah the *d* of Aiah ... 2Sa 21:11
of Egypt, and took Pharaoh's *d* ... 1Kin 3:1
Taphath the *d* of Solomon to wife ... 1Kin 4:11
Basmath the *d* of Solomon to wife ... 1Kin 4:15
also an house for Pharaoh's *d* ... 1Kin 7:8
given it for a present unto his *d* ... 1Kin 9:16
But Pharaoh's *d* came up out of ... 1Kin 9:24
together with the *d* of Pharaoh ... 1Kin 11:1
was Maachah, the *d* of Abishalom ... 1Kin 15:2
was Maachah, the *d* of Abishalom ... 1Kin 15:10
the *d* of Ethbaal king of the ... 1Kin 16:31
name was Azubah the *d* of Shilhi ... 1Kin 22:42
for the *d* of Ahab was his wife ... 2Kin 8:18
the *d* of Omri king of Israel ... 2Kin 8:26
for she is a king's *d* ... 2Kin 9:34
the *d* of king Joram, sister of ... 2Kin 11:2
Give thy *d* to my son to wife ... 2Kin 14:9
name was Jerusha, the *d* of Zadok ... 2Kin 15:33
also was Abi, the *d* of Zachariah ... 2Kin 18:2
The virgin the *d* of Zion hath ... 2Kin 19:21
the *d* of Jerusalem hath shaken ... 2Kin 19:21
the *d* of Haruz of Jotbah ... 2Kin 21:19
the *d* of Adaiah of Boscath ... 2Kin 22:1
his *d* to pass through the fire to ... 2Kin 23:10
the *d* of Jeremiah of Libnah ... 2Kin 23:31
the *d* of Pedaiah of Rumah ... 2Kin 23:36
the *d* of Elnathan of Jerusalem ... 2Kin 24:8
the *d* of Jeremiah of Libnah ... 2Kin 24:18
the *d* of Matred, the *d* of ... 1Chr 1:50
of the *d* of Shua the Canaanitess ... 1Chr 2:3
Tamar his *d* in law bare him ... 1Chr 2:4
*d* of Machir the father of Gilead ... 1Chr 2:21
Sheshan gave his *d* to Jarha his ... 1Chr 2:35
and the *d* of Caleb was Achsa ... 1Chr 2:49
the *d* of Talmai king of Geshur ... 1Chr 3:2
of Bath-shua the *d* of Ammiel ... 1Chr 3:5
sons of Bithiah the *d* of Pharaoh ... 1Chr 4:18
his *d* was Sherah, who built ... 1Chr 7:24
that Michal the *d* of Saul looking ... 1Chr 15:29
Solomon brought up the *d* of ... 2Chr 8:11
Rehoboam took him Mahalath the *d* 2Chr 11:18
Abihail the *d* of Eliab the son of ... 2Chr 11:18
he took Maachah the *d* of Absalom .. 2Chr 11:20
Rehoboam loved Maachah the *d* of ... 2Chr 11:21
Michaiah the *d* of Uriel of Gibeah ... 2Chr 13:2
name was Azubah the *d* of Shilhi ... 2Chr 20:31
for he had the *d* of Ahab to wife ... 2Chr 21:6
also was Athaliah the *d* of Omri ... 2Chr 22:2
the *d* of the king, took Joash the ... 2Chr 22:11
the *d* of king Jehoram, the wife ... 2Chr 22:11
Give thy *d* to my son to wife ... 2Chr 25:18
also was Jerushah, the *d* of Zadok ... 2Chr 27:1
was Abijah, the *d* of Zechariah ... 2Chr 29:1
the *d* of Meshullam the son of ... Neh 6:18
that is, Esther, his uncle's *d* ... Est 2:7
were dead, took for his own *d* ... Est 2:7
the *d* of Abihail the uncle of ... Est 2:15
who had taken her for his *d* ... Est 2:15
the *d* of Abihail, and Mordecai the ... Est 9:29
in the gates of the *d* of Zion ... Ps 9:14
Hearken, O *d*, and consider, and ... Ps 45:10
the *d* of Tyre shall be there with ... Ps 45:12
The king's *d* is all glorious ... Ps 45:13
O *d* of Babylon, who art to be ... Ps 137:8
thy feet with shoes, O prince's *d* ... Song 7:1
the *d* of Zion is left as a ... Is 1:8
Lift up thy voice, O *d* of Gallim ... Is 10:30
the mount of the *d* of Zion ... Is 10:32
unto the mount of the *d* of Zion ... Is 16:1
spoiling of the *d* of my people ... Is 22:4
land as a river, O *d* of Tarshish ... Is 23:10
thou oppressed virgin, *d* of Zidon ... Is 23:12
the *d* of Zion, hath despised thee ... Is 37:22
the *d* of Jerusalem hath shaken ... Is 37:22
O virgin *d* of Babylon, sit on the ... Is 47:1
no throne, O *d* of the Chaldeans ... Is 47:1
darkness, O *d* of the Chaldeans ... Is 47:5
of thy neck, O captive *d* of Zion ... Is 52:2
world, Say ye to the *d* of Zion ... Is 62:11
toward the *d* of my people ... Jer 4:11
child, the voice of the *d* of Zion ... Jer 4:31
I have likened the *d* of Zion to a ... Jer 6:2
of the *d* of my people slightly ... Jer 6:14
for war against thee, O *d* of Zion ... Jer 6:23
O *d* of my people, gird thee with ... Jer 6:26
of the *d* of my people slightly ... Jer 8:11
the voice of the cry of the *d* of ... Jer 8:19
For the hurt of the *d* of my ... Jer 8:21
of the *d* of my people recovered ... Jer 8:22
the slain of the *d* of my people ... Jer 9:1
shall I do for the *d* of my people ... Jer 9:7
for the virgin *d* of my people is ... Jer 14:17
go about, O thou backsliding *d* ... Jer 31:22
balm, O virgin, the *d* of Egypt ... Jer 46:11
O thou *d* dwelling in Egypt, ... Jer 46:19
The *d* of Egypt shall be ... Jer 46:24
Thou *d* that dost inhabit Dibon, ... Jer 48:18
flowing valley, O backsliding *d* ... Jer 49:4
against thee, O *d* of Babylon ... Jer 50:42
The *d* of Babylon is like a ... Jer 51:33
the *d* of Jeremiah of Libnah ... Jer 52:1
from the *d* of Zion all her beauty ... Lam 1:6
the *d* of Judah, as in a winepress ... Lam 1:15
the *d* of Zion with a cloud in his ... Lam 2:1
strong holds of the *d* of Judah ... Lam 2:2
the tabernacle of the *d* of Zion ... Lam 2:4
in the *d* of Judah mourning ... Lam 2:5
destroy the wall of the *d* of Zion ... Lam 2:8
The elders of the *d* of Zion sit ... Lam 2:10
destruction of the *d* of my people ... Lam 2:11
I liken to thee, O *d* of Jerusalem ... Lam 2:13
comfort thee, O virgin *d* of Zion ... Lam 2:13
their head at the *d* of Jerusalem ... Lam 2:15
the Lord, O wall of the *d* of Zion ... Lam 2:18
destruction of the *d* of my people ... Lam 3:48
the *d* of my people is become ... Lam 4:3
of the iniquity of the *d* of my ... Lam 4:6
destruction of the *d* of my people ... Lam 4:10
O *d* of Edom, that dwellest in the ... Lam 4:21
is accomplished, O *d* of Zion ... Lam 4:22
visit thine iniquity, O *d* of Edom ... Lam 4:22
shall deliver neither son nor *d* ... Eze 14:20
As is the mother, so is her *d* ... Eze 16:44
Thou art thy mother's *d*, that ... Eze 16:45
hath lewdly defiled his *d* in law ... Eze 22:11
his sister, his father's *d* ... Eze 22:11
for mother, or for son, or for *d* ... Eze 44:25
for the king's *d* of the south ... Dan 11:6
he shall give him the *d* of women ... Dan 11:17
and took Gomer the *d* of Diblaim ... Hos 1:3
she conceived again, and bare a *d* ... Hos 1:6
of the sin to the *d* of Zion ... Mic 1:13
the strong hold of the *d* of Zion ... Mic 4:8
shall come to the *d* of Jerusalem ... Mic 4:8
O *d* of Zion, like a woman in ... Mic 4:10
Arise and thresh, O *d* of Zion ... Mic 4:13
thyself in troops, O *d* of troops ... Mic 5:1
the *d* riseth up against her ... Mic 7:6
the *d* in law against her mother ... Mic 7:6
even the *d* of my dispersed, shall ... Zeph 3:10
Sing, O *d* of Zion ... Zeph 3:14
all the heart, O *d* of Jerusalem ... Zeph 3:14
dwellest with the *d* of Babylon ... Zec 2:7
Sing and rejoice, O *d* of Zion ... Zec 2:10
Rejoice greatly, O *d* of Zion ... Zec 9:9
shout, O *d* of Jerusalem ... Zec 9:9
married the *d* of a strange god ... Mal 2:11
saying, My *d* is even now dead ... Mt 9:18
and when he saw her, he said, *D* ... Mt 9:22
the *d* against her mother, and the ... Mt 10:35
the *d* in law against her mother ... Mt 10:35
he that loveth son or *d* more than ... Mt 10:37
the *d* of Herodias danced before ... Mt 14:6
my *d* is grievously vexed with a ... Mt 15:22
her *d* was made whole from that ... Mt 15:28
Tell ye the *d* of Sion, Behold, ... Mt 21:5
My little *d* lieth at the point of ... Mk 5:23
And he said unto her, *D*, thy faith ... Mk 5:34
certain which said, Thy *d* is dead ... Mk 5:35
when the *d* of the said Herodias ... Mk 6:22
whose young *d* had an unclean ... Mk 7:25
cast forth the devil out of her *d* ... Mk 7:26
the devil is gone out of thy *d* ... Mk 7:29
out, and her *d* laid upon the bed ... Mk 7:30
the *d* of Phanuel, of the tribe of ... Lk 2:36
For he had one only *d*, about ... Lk 8:42
And he said unto her, *D*, be of ... Lk 8:48
saying to him, Thy *d* is dead ... Lk 8:49
the mother against the *d* ... Lk 12:53
and the *d* against the mother ... Lk 12:53
in law against her *d* in law ... Lk 12:53
the *d* in law against her mother ... Lk 12:53
being a *d* of Abraham, whom Satan ... Lk 13:16
Fear not, *d* of Sion ... Jn 12:15
Pharaoh's *d* took him up, and ... Acts 7:21
be called the son of Pharaoh's *d* ... Heb 11:24

**DAUGHTER'S**

daughter, or of thy *d* daughter ... Lev 18:10
or her *d* daughter, to uncover her ... Lev 18:17
are the tokens of my *d* virginity ... Deut 22:17

**DAUGHTERS**

and he begat sons and *d* ... Gen 5:4
seven years, and begat sons and *d* ... Gen 5:7
fifteen years, and begat sons and *d* ... Gen 5:10
forty years, and begat sons and *d* ... Gen 5:13
thirty years, and begat sons and *d* ... Gen 5:16
hundred years, and begat sons and *d* ... Gen 5:19
hundred years, and begat sons and *d* ... Gen 5:22
and two years, and begat sons and *d* ... Gen 5:26
and five years, and begat sons and *d* ... Gen 5:30
earth, and *d* were born unto them, ... Gen 6:1

the *d* of men that they were fair ..... Gen 6:2
of God came in unto the *d* of men ..... Gen 6:4
hundred years, and begat sons and *d*. Gen 11:11
three years, and begat sons and *d* ..... Gen 11:13
three years, and begat sons and *d* ..... Gen 11:15
thirty years, and begat sons and *d* ..... Gen 11:17
and nine years, and begat sons and *d* Gen 11:19
seven years, and begat sons and *d* ..... Gen 11:21
hundred years, and begat sons and *d*. Gen 11:23
years, and begat sons and *d* ..... Gen 11:25
I have two *d* which have not known ... Gen 19:8
son in law, and thy sons, and thy *d* .... Gen 19:12
sons in law, which married his *d* ..... Gen 19:14
take thy wife, and thy two *d* ..... Gen 19:15
and upon the hand of his two *d* ..... Gen 19:16
mountain, and his two *d* with him ..... Gen 19:30
dwelt in a cave, he and his two *d* ..... Gen 19:30
Thus were both the *d* of Lot with ..... Gen 19:36
my son of the *d* of the Canaanites ..... Gen 24:3
the *d* of the men of the city come ..... Gen 24:13
my son of the *d* of the Canaanites ..... Gen 24:37
my life because of the *d* of Heth ..... Gen 27:46
take a wife of the *d* of Heth ..... Gen 27:46
which are of the *d* of the land ..... Gen 27:46
take a wife of the *d* of Canaan ..... Gen 28:1
*d* of Laban thy mother's brother ..... Gen 28:2
take a wife of the *d* of Canaan ..... Gen 28:6
Esau seeing that the *d* of Canaan ..... Gen 28:8
And Laban had two *d* ..... Gen 29:16
for the *d* will call me blessed ..... Gen 30:13
to me, and carried away my *d* ..... Gen 31:26
me to kiss my sons and my *d* ..... Gen 31:28
take by force thy *d* from me ..... Gen 31:31
thee fourteen years for thy two *d* ..... Gen 31:41
These *d* are my *d*, and ..... Gen 31:43
Jacob, These *d* are my *d* ..... Gen 31:43
can I do this day unto these my *d* ..... Gen 31:43
If thou shalt afflict my *d* ..... Gen 31:50
take other wives beside my *d* ..... Gen 31:50
up, and kissed his sons and his *d* ..... Gen 31:55
went out to see the *d* of the land ..... Gen 34:1
with us, and give your *d* unto us ..... Gen 34:9
unto us, and take our *d* unto you ..... Gen 34:9
Then will we give our *d* unto you ..... Gen 34:16
and we will take your *d* to us ..... Gen 34:16
us take their *d* to us for wives ..... Gen 34:21
and let us give them our *d* ..... Gen 34:21
took his wives of the *d* of Canaan ..... Gen 36:2
his wives, and his sons, and his *d* ..... Gen 36:6
all his *d* rose up to comfort him ..... Gen 37:35
his *d*, and his sons' *d* ..... Gen 46:7
his *d* were thirty and three ..... Gen 46:15
the priest of Midian had seven *d* ..... Ex 2:16
And he said unto his *d*, And where ..... Ex 2:20
upon your sons, and upon your *d* ..... Ex 3:22
one of the *d* of Putiel to wife ..... Ex 6:25
old, with our sons and with our *d* ..... Ex 10:9
and she have born him sons or *d* ..... Ex 21:4
with her after the manner of *d* ..... Ex 21:9
wives, of your sons, and of your *d* ..... Ex 32:2
take of their *d* unto thy sons ..... Ex 34:16
their *d* go a whoring after their ..... Ex 34:16
and thy sons, and thy *d* with thee ..... Lev 10:14
the flesh of your *d* shall ye eat ..... Lev 26:29
to thy *d* with thee, by a statute ..... Num 18:11
thy *d* with thee, by a statute for ..... Num 18:19
his sons that escaped, and his *d* ..... Num 21:29
whoredom with the *d* of Moab ..... Num 25:1
son of Hepher had no sons, but *d* ..... Num 26:33
the names of the *d* of Zelophehad ..... Num 26:33
Then came the *d* of Zelophehad ..... Num 27:1
and these are the names of his *d* ..... Num 27:1
The *d* of Zelophehad speak right ..... Num 27:7
Zelophehad our brother unto his *d* ..... Num 36:2
concerning the *d* of Zelophehad ..... Num 36:6
so did the *d* of Zelophehad ..... Num 36:10
the *d* of Zelophehad, were married .... Num 36:11
God, ye, and your sons, and your *d* ... Deut 12:12
their *d* they have burnt in the ..... Deut 12:31
be no whore of the *d* of Israel ..... Deut 23:17
thy *d* shall be given unto another ..... Deut 28:32
Thou shalt beget sons and *d* ..... Deut 28:41
the flesh of thy sons and of thy *d* ..... Deut 28:53
of his sons, and of his *d* ..... Deut 32:19
of gold, and his sons, and his *d* ..... Josh 7:24
of Manasseh, had no sons, but *d* ..... Josh 17:3
and these are the names of his *d* ..... Josh 17:3
Because the *d* of Manasseh had an ..... Josh 17:6
they took their *d* to be their ..... Judg 3:6
gave their *d* to their sons, and ..... Judg 3:6
That the *d* of Israel went yearly ..... Judg 11:40
he had thirty sons, and thirty *d* ..... Judg 12:9
took in thirty *d* from abroad for ..... Judg 12:9
of the *d* of the Philistines ..... Judg 14:1
of the *d* of the Philistines ..... Judg 14:2
woman among the *d* of thy brethren .. Judg 14:3
not give them of our *d* to wives ..... Judg 21:7
may not give them wives of our *d* ..... Judg 21:18
if the *d* of Shiloh come out to ..... Judg 21:21
man his wife of the *d* of Shiloh ..... Judg 21:21
Then she arose with her *d* in law ..... Ruth 1:6
her two *d* in law with her ..... Ruth 1:7
Naomi said unto her two *d* in law ..... Ruth 1:8
And Naomi said, Turn again, my *d* ..... Ruth 1:11
Turn again, my *d*, go your way ..... Ruth 1:12
nay, my *d* ..... Ruth 1:13
wife, and to all her sons and her *d* ..... 1Sa 1:4
and bare three sons and two *d* ..... 1Sa 2:21
he will take your *d* to be ..... 1Sa 8:13
the names of his two *d* were these ..... 1Sa 14:49
wives, and their sons, and their *d* ..... 1Sa 30:3
man for his sons and for his *d* ..... 1Sa 30:6
nor great, neither sons nor *d* ..... 1Sa 30:19
lest the *d* of the Philistines ..... 2Sa 1:20
lest the *d* of the uncircumcised ..... 2Sa 1:20
Ye *d* of Israel, weep over Saul, ..... 2Sa 1:24
were yet sons and *d* born to David ..... 2Sa 5:13
*d* that were virgins apparelled ..... 2Sa 13:18
the lives of thy sons and of thy *d* ..... 2Sa 19:5
their *d* to pass through the fire, ..... 2Kin 17:17
Now Sheshan had no sons, but *d* ..... 1Chr 2:34
Shimei had sixteen sons and six *d* ..... 1Chr 4:27
and Zelophehad had *d* ..... 1Chr 7:15
and David begat more sons and *d* ..... 1Chr 14:3
died, and had no sons, but *d* ..... 1Chr 23:22
to Heman fourteen sons and three *d* ... 1Chr 25:5
son of a woman of the *d* of Dan ..... 2Chr 2:14
and eight sons, and threescore *d* ..... 2Chr 11:21
twenty and two sons, and sixteen *d* .. 2Chr 13:21
and he begat sons and *d* ..... 2Chr 24:3
thousand, women, sons, and *d* ..... 2Chr 28:8
the sword, and our sons and our *d* ..... 2Chr 29:9
wives, and their sons, and their *d* ..... 2Chr 31:18
which took a wife of the *d* of ..... Ezr 2:61
taken of their *d* for themselves ..... Ezr 9:2
give not your *d* unto their sons ..... Ezr 9:12
take their *d* unto your sons ..... Ezr 9:12
part of Jerusalem, he and his *d* ..... Neh 3:12
brethren, your sons, and your *d* ..... Neh 4:14
that said, We, our sons, and our *d* ..... Neh 5:2
our *d* to be servants ..... Neh 5:5
some of our *d* are brought unto ..... Neh 5:5
which took one of the *d* of ..... Neh 7:63
wives, their sons, and their *d* ..... Neh 10:28
that we would not give our *d* unto ..... Neh 10:30
nor take their *d* for our sons ..... Neh 10:30
not give your *d* unto their sons ..... Neh 13:25
nor take their *d* unto your sons ..... Neh 13:25
unto him seven sons and three *d* ..... Job 1:2
his *d* were eating and drinking ..... Job 1:13
thy *d* were eating and drinking ..... Job 1:18
He had also seven sons and three *d* ..... Job 42:13
found so fair as the *d* of Job ..... Job 42:15
Kings' *d* were among thy ..... Ps 45:9
let the *d* of Judah be glad, ..... Ps 48:11
the *d* of Judah rejoiced because ..... Ps 97:8
sons and their *d* unto devils, ..... Ps 106:37
blood of their sons and of their *d* ..... Ps 106:38
that our *d* may be as corner ..... Ps 144:12
The horseleach hath two *d* ..... Prov 30:15
Many *d* have done virtuously, but ..... Prov 31:29
all the *d* of musick shall be ..... Eccl 12:4
O ye *d* of Jerusalem, as the tents ..... Song 1:5
thorns, so is my love among the *d* ..... Song 2:2
O ye *d* of Jerusalem, by the roes, ..... Song 2:7
O ye *d* of Jerusalem, by the roes, ..... Song 3:5
with love, for the *d* of Jerusalem ..... Song 3:10
O ye *d* of Zion, and behold king ..... Song 3:11
O *d* of Jerusalem, if ye find my ..... Song 5:8
is my friend, O *d* of Jerusalem ..... Song 5:16
The *d* saw her, and blessed her ..... Song 6:9
O *d* of Jerusalem, that ye stir ..... Song 8:4
Because the *d* of Zion are haughty ..... Is 3:16
of the head of the *d* of Zion ..... Is 3:17
away the filth of the *d* of Zion ..... Is 4:4
so the *d* of Moab shall be at the ..... Is 16:2
hear my voice, ye careless *d* ..... Is 32:9
my *d* from the ends of the earth ..... Is 43:6
thy *d* shall be carried upon their ..... Is 49:22
name better than of sons and of *d* ..... Is 56:5
thy *d* shall be nursed at thy side ..... Is 60:4
herds, their sons and their *d* ..... Jer 3:24
thy sons and thy *d* should eat ..... Jer 5:17
their sons and their *d* in the fire ..... Jer 7:31
mouth, and teach your *d* wailing ..... Jer 9:20
their *d* shall die by famine ..... Jer 11:22
nor their sons, nor their *d* ..... Jer 14:16
thou have sons or *d* in this place ..... Jer 16:2
concerning the *d* that are born in ..... Jer 16:3
sons and the flesh of their *d* ..... Jer 19:9
Take ye wives, and beget sons and *d* ..... Jer 29:6
give your *d* to husbands ..... Jer 29:6
that they may bear sons and *d* ..... Jer 29:6
their *d* to pass through the fire ..... Jer 32:35
our wives, our sons, nor our *d* ..... Jer 35:8
were in Mizpah, even the king's *d* ..... Jer 41:10
and children, and the king's *d* ..... Jer 43:6
taken captives, and thy *d* captives ..... Jer 48:46
her *d* shall be burned with fire ..... Jer 49:2
ye *d* of Rabbah, gird you with ..... Jer 49:3
because of all the *d* of my city ..... Lam 3:51
face against the *d* of thy people ..... Eze 13:17
shall deliver neither sons nor *d* ..... Eze 14:16
shall deliver neither sons nor *d* ..... Eze 14:18
be brought forth, both sons and *d* ..... Eze 14:22
thou hast taken thy sons and thy *d* ..... Eze 16:20
the *d* of the Philistines, which ..... Eze 16:27
her *d* that dwell at thy left hand ..... Eze 16:46
thy right hand, is Sodom and her *d* ..... Eze 16:46
hath not done, she nor her *d* ..... Eze 16:48
as thou hast done, thou and thy *d* ..... Eze 16:48
idleness was in her and in her *d* ..... Eze 16:49
the captivity of Sodom and her *d* ..... Eze 16:53
the captivity of Samaria and her *d* ..... Eze 16:53
When thy sisters, Sodom and her *d* ..... Eze 16:55
her *d* shall return to their ..... Eze 16:55
thy *d* shall return to your former ..... Eze 16:55
of thy reproach of the *d* of Syria ..... Eze 16:57
the *d* of the Philistines, which ..... Eze 16:57
I will give them unto thee for *d* ..... Eze 16:61
two women, the *d* of one mother ..... Eze 23:2
were mine, and they bare sons and *d* .... Eze 23:4
they took her sons and her *d* ..... Eze 23:10
they shall take thy sons and thy *d* ..... Eze 23:25
shall slay their sons and their *d* ..... Eze 23:47
your *d* whom ye have left shall ..... Eze 24:21
minds, their sons and their *d* ..... Eze 24:25
her *d* which are in the field ..... Eze 26:6
with the sword thy *d* in the field ..... Eze 26:8
her *d* shall go into captivity ..... Eze 30:18
the *d* of the nations shall lament ..... Eze 32:16
the *d* of the famous nations, unto ..... Eze 32:18
therefore your *d* shall commit ..... Hos 4:13
I will not punish your *d* when ..... Hos 4:14
your *d* shall prophesy, your old ..... Joel 2:28
your *d* into the hand of the ..... Joel 3:8
thy *d* shall fall by the sword, and ..... Amos 7:17
and his wife was of the *d* of Aaron ..... Lk 1:5
*D* of Jerusalem, weep not for me, ..... Lk 23:28
your *d* shall prophesy, and your ..... Acts 2:17
And the same man had four *d* ..... Acts 21:9
you, and ye shall be my sons and *d* ..... 2Cor 6:18
whose *d* ye are, as long as ye do ..... 1Pet 3:6

**DAVID** See PREFACE. SEE ALSO DAVID'S.
*Second king of Israel.*
begat Jesse, and Jesse begat *D* ..... Ruth 4:22
came upon *D* from that day forward... 1Sa 16:13
that *D* took an harp, and played ..... 1Sa 16:23
a covenant with the house of *D* ..... 1Sa 20:16
So *D* reigned over all Israel, and ..... 1Chr 18:14
be broken with *D* my servant ..... Jer 33:21
multiply the seed of *D* my servant ..... Jer 33:22
*D* my servant, so that I will not ..... Jer 33:26
crying, and saying, Thou son of *D* ..... Mt 9:27
and said, Is not this the son of *D* ..... Mt 12:23
saying, Hosanna to the son of *D* ..... Mt 21:9
more a great deal, Thou son of *D* ..... Mk 10:48
was of the house and lineage of *D* ..... Lk 2:4
Christ cometh of the seed of *D* ..... Jn 7:42
For *D* speaketh concerning him, I ..... Acts 2:25
of *D* was raised from the dead ..... 2Ti 2:8
am the root and the offspring of *D* ..... Rev 22:16

**DAVID'S**
Saul became *D* enemy continually ..... 1Sa 18:29
also sent messengers unto *D* house ..... 1Sa 19:11
Michal *D* wife told him, saying, ..... 1Sa 19:11
it at the hand of *D* enemies ..... 1Sa 20:16
Saul's side, and *D* place was empty ..... 1Sa 20:25
the month, that *D* place was empty ..... 1Sa 20:27
*D* men said unto him, Behold, we ..... 1Sa 23:3
that *D* heart smote him, because ..... 1Sa 24:5
when *D* young men came, they spake .. 1Sa 25:9
And Nabal answered *D* servants ..... 1Sa 25:10
So *D* young men turned their way, ..... 1Sa 25:12
*D* wife, to Phalti the son of ..... 1Sa 25:44
And Saul knew *D* voice, and said, Is ... 1Sa 26:17
*D* two wives were taken captives, ..... 1Sa 30:5
cattle, and said, This is *D* spoil ..... 1Sa 30:20
there lacked of *D* servants ..... 2Sa 2:30
sixth, Ithream, by Eglah *D* wife ..... 2Sa 3:5
blind, that are hated of *D* soul ..... 2Sa 5:8
so the Moabites became *D* servants ..... 2Sa 8:2
they of Edom became *D* servants ..... 2Sa 8:14
and *D* sons were chief rulers ..... 2Sa 8:18
*D* servants came into the land of ..... 2Sa 10:2
Wherefore Hanun took *D* servants ..... 2Sa 10:4
*D* anger was greatly kindled ..... 2Sa 12:5
and it was set on *D* head ..... 2Sa 12:30
the son of Shimeah *D* brother ..... 2Sa 13:3
the son of Shimeah *D* brother ..... 2Sa 13:32
*D* counsellor, from his city, even ..... 2Sa 15:12
So Hushai *D* friend came into the ..... 2Sa 15:37
*D* friend, was come unto Absalom, ..... 2Sa 16:16
all *D* men with him, over Jordan ..... 2Sa 19:41
*D* heart smote him after that he ..... 2Sa 24:10
the prophet Gad, *D* seer, saying, ..... 2Sa 24:11
Solomon to ride upon king *D* mule ..... 1Kin 1:38
one tribe for my servant *D* sake ..... 1Kin 11:32
Nevertheless for *D* sake did the ..... 1Kin 15:4
did the priest give king *D* spears ..... 2Kin 11:10
sake, and for my servant *D* sake ..... 2Kin 19:34
sake, and for my servant *D* sake ..... 2Kin 20:6
and the Moabites became *D* servants . 1Chr 18:2
and the Syrians became *D* servants .... 1Chr 18:6
the Edomites became *D* servants ..... 1Chr 18:13
Wherefore Hanun took *D* servants ..... 1Chr 19:4
and it was set upon *D* head ..... 1Chr 20:2
son of Shimea *D* brother slew him ..... 1Chr 20:7
spake unto Gad, *D* seer, saying, ..... 1Chr 21:9
of the substance which was king *D* ... 1Chr 27:31
Also Jonathan *D* uncle was a ..... 1Chr 27:32
and shields, that had been king *D* ..... 2Chr 23:9
For thy servant *D* sake turn not ..... Ps 132:10
*D* Psalm of praise ..... Ps 145:*t*
sake, and for my servant *D* sake ..... Is 37:35
the kings that sit upon *D* throne ..... Jer 13:13
How say they that Christ is *D* son ..... Lk 20:41

**DAWN**
as it began to *d* toward the first ..... Mt 28:1
in a dark place, until the day *d* ..... 2Pet 1:19

**DAWNING**
rose early about the *d* of the day ..... Josh 6:15
the woman in the *d* of the day ..... Judg 19:26
let it see the *d* of the day ..... Job 3:9
to and fro unto the *d* of the day ..... Job 7:4
I prevented the *d* of the morning ..... Ps 119:147

**DAY** See PREFACE.
And God called the light *D* ... Gen 1:5
and the morning were the first *d* ... Gen 1:5
and the morning were the second *d* ... Gen 1:8
and the morning were the third *d* ... Gen 1:13
to divide the *d* from the night ... Gen 1:14
the greater light to rule the *d* ... Gen 1:16
And to rule over the *d* and over the ... Gen 1:18
and the morning were the fourth *d* ... Gen 1:19
and the morning were the fifth *d* ... Gen 1:23
and the morning were the sixth *d* ... Gen 1:31
on the seventh *d* God ended his ... Gen 2:2
he rested on the seventh *d* from ... Gen 2:2
And God blessed the seventh *d* ... Gen 2:3
in the *d* that the LORD God made ... Gen 2:4
Remember the sabbath *d*, to keep ... Ex 20:8
Keep the sabbath *d* to sanctify it ... Deut 5:12
For a *d* in thy courts is better ... Ps 84:10
not what a *d* may bring forth ... Prov 27:1
Behold the *d*, behold, it is come ... Eze 7:10
in that *d* when I make up my ... Mal 3:17
Give us this *d* our daily bread ... Mt 6:11
and be raised again the third *d* ... Mt 16:21
the third *d* he shall be raised ... Mt 17:23
the third *d* he shall rise again ... Mt 20:19
But of that *d* and hour knoweth no ... Mt 24:36
for ye know neither the *d* nor the ... Mt 25:13
killed, he shall rise the third *d* ... Mk 9:31
the third *d* he shall rise again ... Mk 10:34
But of that *d* and that hour ... Mk 13:32
For unto you is born this *d* in ... Lk 2:11
the third *d* he shall rise again ... Lk 18:33
This *d* is salvation come to this ... Lk 19:9
so that *d* come upon you unawares ... Lk 21:34
and the third *d* rise again ... Lk 24:7
to rise from the dead the third *d* ... Lk 24:46
raise it up again at the last *d* ... Jn 6:39
I will raise him up at the last *d* ... Jn 6:40
At that *d* ye shall know that I am ... Jn 14:20
Him God raised up the third *d* ... Acts 10:40
In the *d* when God shall judge the ... Rom 2:16
sake we are killed all the *d* long ... Rom 8:36
*d* according to the scriptures ... 1Cor 15:4
now is the *d* of salvation ... 2Cor 6:2
know perfectly that the *d* of the ... 1Th 5:2
To *d* if ye will hear his voice, ... Heb 3:7
that one *d* is with the Lord as a ... 2Pet 3:8
and a thousand years as one *d* ... 2Pet 3:8
But the *d* of the Lord will come ... 2Pet 3:10

**DAY'S**
as it were a *d* journey on this ... Num 11:31
as it were a *d* journey on the ... Num 11:31
But he himself went a *d* journey ... 1Kin 19:4
as every *d* work required ... 1Chr 16:37
also according unto this *d* decree ... Est 9:13
enter into the city a *d* journey ... Jonah 3:4
in the company, went a *d* journey ... Lk 2:44
Jerusalem a sabbath *d* journey ... Acts 1:12
in question for this *d* uproar ... Acts 19:40

**DAYS** See PREFACE.

**DAYS'**
he set three *d* journey betwixt ... Gen 30:36
pursued after him seven *d* journey ... Gen 31:23
thee, three *d* journey into the ... Ex 3:18
three *d* journey into the desert, ... Ex 5:3
We will go three *d* journey into ... Ex 8:27
mount of the LORD three *d* journey .. Num 10:33
them in the three *d* journey ... Num 10:33
went three *d* journey in the ... Num 33:8
(There are eleven *d* journey from ... Deut 1:2
unto him, Give us seven *d* respite ... 1Sa 11:3
be three *d* pestilence in thy land ... 2Sa 24:13
a compass of seven *d* journey ... 2Kin 3:9
great city of three *d* journey ... Jonah 3:3

**DAYSMAN**
Neither is there any *d* betwixt us ... Job 9:33

**DAYSPRING**
caused the *d* to know his place ... Job 38:12
whereby the *d* from on high hath ... Lk 1:78

**DAYTIME**
by *d* in a pillar of a cloud, and ... Num 14:14
They meet with darkness in the *d* ... Job 5:14
marked for themselves in the *d* ... Job 24:16
O my God, I cry in the *d*, but ... Ps 22:2
his lovingkindness in the *d* ... Ps 42:8
In the *d* also he led them with a ... Ps 78:14
a shadow in the *d* from the heat ... Is 4:6
upon the watchtower in the *d* ... Is 21:8
it pleasure to riot in the *d* ... 2Pet 2:13

**DEACON**
let them use the office of a *d* ... 1Ti 3:10
a *d* well purchase to themselves a ... 1Ti 3:13

**DEACONS**
Philippi, with the bishops and *d* ... Phil 1:1
Likewise must the *d* be grave ... 1Ti 3:8
Let the *d* be the husbands of one ... 1Ti 3:12

**DEAD**
him, Behold, thou art but a *d* man ... Gen 20:3
stood up from before his *d* ... Gen 23:3
I may bury my *d* out of my sight ... Gen 23:4
of our sepulchres bury thy *d* ... Gen 23:6
but that thou mayest bury thy *d* ... Gen 23:6
should bury my *d* out of my sight ... Gen 23:8
bury thy *d* ... Gen 23:11
of me, and I will bury my *d* there ... Gen 23:13
bury therefore thy *d* ... Gen 23:15
for his brother is *d*, and he is ... Gen 42:38
and his brother is *d*, and he alone ... Gen 44:20
saw that their father was *d* ... Gen 50:15
for all the men are *d* which ... Ex 4:19
of the cattle of the Israelites *d* ... Ex 9:7
a house where there was not one *d* ... Ex 12:30
for they said, We be all *d* men ... Ex 12:33
Egyptians *d* upon the sea shore ... Ex 14:30
and the *d* beast shall be his ... Ex 21:34
the *d* ox also they shall divide ... Ex 21:35
and the *d* shall be his own ... Ex 21:36
doth touch them, when they be *d* ... Lev 11:31
any of them, when they are *d* ... Lev 11:32
cuttings in your flesh for the *d* ... Lev 19:28
for the *d* among his people ... Lev 21:1
shall he go in to any *d* body ... Lev 21:11
thing that is unclean by the *d* ... Lev 22:4
and whosoever is defiled by the *d* ... Num 5:2
LORD he shall come at no *d* body ... Num 6:6
him, for that he sinned by the *d* ... Num 6:11
defiled by the *d* body of a man ... Num 9:6
defiled by the *d* body of a man ... Num 9:7
be unclean by reason of a *d* body ... Num 9:10
Let her not be as one *d*, of whom ... Num 12:12
And he stood between the *d* ... Num 16:48
He that toucheth the *d* body of ... Num 19:11
Whosoever toucheth the *d* body of ... Num 19:13
*d* body of any man that is *d* ... Num 19:13
in the open fields, or a *d* body ... Num 19:16
a bone, or one slain, or one *d* ... Num 19:18
congregation saw that Aaron was *d* .. Num 20:29
and *d* from among the people, ... Deut 2:16
between your eyes for the *d* ... Deut 14:1
flesh, nor touch their *d* carcase ... Deut 14:8
the wife of the *d* shall not marry ... Deut 25:5
name of his brother which is *d* ... Deut 25:6
nor given ought thereof for the *d* ... Deut 26:14
Moses my servant is *d* ... Josh 1:2
to pass, when the judge was *d* ... Judg 2:19
was fallen down *d* on the earth ... Judg 3:25
of the LORD, when Ehud was *d* ... Judg 4:1
her tent, behold, Sisera lay *d* ... Judg 4:22
he bowed, there he fell down *d* ... Judg 5:27
to pass, as soon as Gideon was *d* ... Judg 8:33
Israel saw that Abimelech was *d* ... Judg 9:55
So the *d* which he slew at his ... Judg 16:30
have they forced, that she is *d* ... Judg 20:5
you, as ye have dealt with the *d* ... Ruth 1:8
to the living and to the *d* ... Ruth 2:20
the Moabitess, the wife of the *d* ... Ruth 4:5
of the *d* upon his inheritance ... Ruth 4:5
of the *d* upon his inheritance ... Ruth 4:10
that the name of the *d* be not cut ... Ruth 4:10
also, Hophni and Phinehas, are *d* ... 1Sa 4:17
in law and her husband were *d* ... 1Sa 4:19
saw their champion was *d*, they ... 1Sa 17:51
after a *d* dog, after a flea ... 1Sa 24:14
when David heard that Nabal was *d* ... 1Sa 25:39
Now Samuel was *d*, and all Israel ... 1Sa 28:3
armourbearer saw that Saul was *d* ... 1Sa 31:5
and that Saul and his sons were *d* ... 1Sa 31:7
the people also are fallen and *d* ... 2Sa 1:4
and Jonathan his son are *d* also ... 2Sa 1:4
Saul and Jonathan his son be *d* ... 2Sa 1:5
for your master Saul is *d* ... 2Sa 2:7
heard that Abner was *d* in Hebron ... 2Sa 4:1
me, saying, Behold, Saul is *d* ... 2Sa 4:10
look upon such a *d* dog as I am ... 2Sa 9:8
Uriah the Hittite is *d* also ... 2Sa 11:21
some of the king's servants be *d* ... 2Sa 11:24
Uriah the Hittite is *d* also ... 2Sa 11:24
that Uriah her husband was *d* ... 2Sa 11:26
to tell him that the child was *d* ... 2Sa 12:18
we tell him that the child is *d* ... 2Sa 12:18
perceived that the child was *d* ... 2Sa 12:19
unto his servants, Is the child *d* ... 2Sa 12:19
And they said, He is *d* ... 2Sa 12:19
but when the child was *d*, thou ... 2Sa 12:21
But now he is *d*, wherefore should ... 2Sa 12:23
for Amnon only is *d* ... 2Sa 13:32
that all the king's sons are *d* ... 2Sa 13:33
for Amnon only is *d* ... 2Sa 13:33
concerning Amnon, seeing he was *d* ... 2Sa 13:39
had a long time mourned for the *d* ... 2Sa 14:2
widow woman, and mine husband is *d*. 2Sa 14:5
Why should this *d* dog curse my ... 2Sa 16:9
because the king's son is *d* ... 2Sa 18:20
anointed over us, is *d* in battle ... 2Sa 19:10
but *d* men before my lord the king ... 2Sa 19:28
laid her *d* child in my bosom ... 1Kin 3:20
my child suck, behold, it was *d* ... 1Kin 3:21
is my son, and the *d* is thy son ... 1Kin 3:22
but the *d* is thy son, and the ... 1Kin 3:22
that liveth, and thy son is the *d* ... 1Kin 3:23
but thy son is the *d*, and my son ... 1Kin 3:23
the captain of the host was *d* ... 1Kin 11:21
to his sons, saying, When I am *d* ... 1Kin 13:31
saying, Naboth is stoned, and is *d* ... 1Kin 21:14
that Naboth was stoned, and was *d* ... 1Kin 21:15
for Naboth is not alive, but *d* ... 1Kin 21:15
heard that Naboth was *d* ... 1Kin 21:16
it came to pass, when Ahab was *d* ... 2Kin 3:5
Thy servant my husband is *d* ... 2Kin 4:1
house, behold, the child was *d* ... 2Kin 4:32
he had restored a *d* body to life ... 2Kin 8:5
of Ahaziah saw that her son was *d* ... 2Kin 11:1
behold, they were all *d* corpses ... 2Kin 19:35
him in a chariot *d* from Megiddo ... 2Kin 23:30
And when Bela was *d*, Jobab the son .. 1Chr 1:44
And when Jobab was *d*, Husham of ... 1Chr 1:45
And when Husham was *d*, Hadad the. 1Chr 1:46
And when Hadad was *d*, Samlah of ... 1Chr 1:47
And when Samlah was *d*, Shaul of ... 1Chr 1:48
And when Shaul was *d*, Baal-hanan ... 1Chr 1:49
And when Baal-hanan was *d*, Hadad .. 1Chr 1:50
And when Azubah was *d*, Caleb took. 1Chr 2:19
Hezron was *d* in Caleb-ephratah ... 1Chr 2:24
armourbearer saw that Saul was *d* ... 1Chr 10:5
and that Saul and his sons were *d* ... 1Chr 10:7
they were *d* bodies fallen to the ... 2Chr 20:24
both riches with the *d* bodies ... 2Chr 20:25
of Ahaziah saw that her son was *d* ... 2Chr 22:10
when her father and mother were *d* ... Est 2:7
upon the young men, and they are *d* ... Job 1:19
*D* things are formed from under ... Job 26:5
forgotten as a *d* man out of mind ... Ps 31:12
and horse are cast into a *d* sleep ... Ps 76:6
The *d* bodies of thy servants have ... Ps 79:2
Free among the *d*, like the slain ... Ps 88:5
Wilt thou shew wonders to the *d* ... Ps 88:10
shall the *d* arise and praise thee ... Ps 88:10
and ate the sacrifices of the *d* ... Ps 106:28
fill the places with the *d* bodies ... Ps 110:6
The *d* praise not the LORD, ... Ps 115:17
as those that have been long *d* ... Ps 143:3
death, and her paths unto the *d* ... Prov 2:18
knoweth not that the *d* are there ... Prov 9:18
in the congregation of the *d* ... Prov 21:16
Wherefore I praised the *d* which ... Eccl 4:2
the *d* which are already *d* more ... Eccl 4:2
and after that they go to the *d* ... Eccl 9:3
dog is better than a *d* lion ... Eccl 9:4
but the *d* know not any thing, ... Eccl 9:5
*D* flies cause the ointment of the ... Eccl 10:1
for the living to the *d* ... Is 8:19
it stirreth up the *d* for thee ... Is 14:9
with the sword, nor *d* in battle ... Is 22:2
They are *d*, they shall not live ... Is 26:14
Thy *d* men shall live, together ... Is 26:19
together with my *d* body shall ... Is 26:19
and the earth shall cast out the *d* ... Is 26:19
behold, they were all *d* corpses ... Is 37:36
are in desolate places as *d* men ... Is 59:10
to comfort them for the *d* ... Jer 16:7
Weep ye not for the *d*, neither ... Jer 22:10
cast his *d* body into the graves ... Jer 26:23
the whole valley of the *d* bodies ... Jer 31:40
them with the *d* bodies of men ... Jer 33:5
their *d* bodies shall be for meat ... Jer 34:20
his *d* body shall be cast out in ... Jer 36:30
cast all the *d* bodies of the men ... Jer 41:9
places, as they that be *d* of old ... Lam 3:6
I will lay the *d* carcases of the ... Eze 6:5
cry, make no mourning for the *d* ... Eze 24:17
they shall come at no *d* person to ... Eze 44:25
of any thing that is *d* of itself ... Eze 44:31
there shall be many *d* bodies in ... Amos 8:3
by a *d* body touch any of these ... Hag 2:13
But when Herod was *d*, behold, an ... Mt 2:19
for they are *d* which sought the ... Mt 2:20
and let the *d* bury their *d* ... Mt 8:22
saying, My daughter is even now *d* ... Mt 9:18
for the maid is not *d*, but ... Mt 9:24
cleanse the lepers, raise the *d* ... Mt 10:8
the *d* are raised up, and the poor ... Mt 11:5
he is risen from the *d* ... Mt 14:2
of man be risen again from the *d* ... Mt 17:9
the resurrection of the *d* ... Mt 22:31
God is not the God of the *d* ... Mt 22:32
are within full of *d* men's bones ... Mt 23:27
people, He is risen from the *d* ... Mt 27:64
did shake, and became as *d* men ... Mt 28:4
that he is risen from the *d* ... Mt 28:7
which said, Thy daughter is *d* ... Mk 5:35
the damsel is not *d*, but sleepeth ... Mk 5:39
the Baptist was risen from the *d* ... Mk 6:14
he is risen from the *d* ... Mk 6:16
Son of man were risen from the *d* ... Mk 9:9
the rising from the *d* should mean ... Mk 9:10
and he was as one *d* ... Mk 9:26
insomuch that many said, He is *d* ... Mk 9:26
when they shall rise from the *d* ... Mk 12:25
And as touching the *d*, that they ... Mk 12:26
He is not the God of the *d* ... Mk 12:27
marvelled if he were already *d* ... Mk 15:44
whether he had been any while *d* ... Mk 15:44
there was a *d* man carried out, ... Lk 7:12
And he that was *d* sat up, and began ... Lk 7:15
the *d* are raised, to the poor the ... Lk 7:22
saying to him, Thy daughter is *d* ... Lk 8:49
she is not *d*, but sleepeth ... Lk 8:52
to scorn, knowing that she was *d* ... Lk 8:53
that John was risen from the *d* ... Lk 9:7
Let the *d* bury their *d* ... Lk 9:60
and departed, leaving him half *d* ... Lk 10:30
For this my son was *d*, and is ... Lk 15:24
for this thy brother was *d* ... Lk 15:32
if one went unto them from the *d* ... Lk 16:30
though one rose from the *d* ... Lk 16:31
and the resurrection from the *d* ... Lk 20:35
Now that the *d* are raised ... Lk 20:37
For he is not a God of the *d* ... Lk 20:38
seek ye the living among the *d* ... Lk 24:5
to rise from the *d* the third day ... Lk 24:46
therefore he was risen from the *d* ... Jn 2:22
as the Father raiseth up the *d* ... Jn 5:21
when the *d* shall hear the voice ... Jn 5:25
manna in the wilderness, and are *d* ... Jn 6:49
fathers did eat manna, and are *d* ... Jn 6:58

Abraham is *d*, and the prophets Jn 8:52
our father Abraham, which is *d* Jn 8:53
and the prophets are *d* Jn 8:53
unto them plainly, Lazarus is *d* Jn 11:14
believeth in me, though he were *d* Jn 11:25
the sister of him that was *d* Jn 11:39
for he hath been *d* four days Jn 11:39
the place where the *d* was laid Jn 11:41
And he that was *d* came forth Jn 11:44
Lazarus was which had been *d* Jn 12:1
*d*, whom he raised from the *d* Jn 12:1
whom he had raised from the *d* Jn 12:9
grave, and raised him from the *d* Jn 12:17
and saw that he was *d* already Jn 19:33
he must rise again from the *d* Jn 20:9
that he was risen from the *d* Jn 21:14
David, that he is both *d* and Acts 2:29
whom God hath raised from the *d* Acts 3:15
Jesus the resurrection from the *d* Acts 4:2
whom God raised from the *d* Acts 4:10
young men came in, and found her *d* Acts 5:10
thence, when his father was *d* Acts 7:4
with him after he rose from the *d* Acts 10:41
God to be the Judge of quick and *d* Acts 10:42
But God raised him from the *d* Acts 13:30
that he raised him up from the *d* Acts 13:34
the city, supposing he had been *d* Acts 14:19
and risen again from the *d* Acts 17:3
he hath raised him from the *d* Acts 17:31
of the resurrection of the *d* Acts 17:32
the third loft, and was taken up *d* Acts 20:9
resurrection of the *d* I am called Acts 23:6
shall be a resurrection of the *d* Acts 24:15
the resurrection of the *d* I am Acts 24:21
and of one Jesus, which was *d* Acts 25:19
you, that God should raise the *d* Acts 26:8
first that should rise from the *d* Acts 26:23
or fallen down *d* suddenly Acts 28:6
by the resurrection from the *d* Rom 1:4
even God, who quickeneth the *d* Rom 4:17
considered not his own body now *d* Rom 4:19
up Jesus our Lord from the *d* Rom 4:24
the offence of one many be *d* Rom 5:15
How shall we, that are *d* to sin Rom 6:2
the *d* by the glory of the Father Rom 6:4
For he that is *d* is freed from Rom 6:7
Now if we be *d* with Christ Rom 6:8
raised from the *d* dieth no more Rom 6:9
to be *d* indeed unto sin, but Rom 6:11
those that are alive from the *d* Rom 6:13
but if the husband be *d*, she is Rom 7:2
but if her husband be *d*, she is Rom 7:3
ye also are become *d* to the law Rom 7:4
to him who is raised from the *d* Rom 7:4
that being *d* wherein we were held Rom 7:6
For without the law sin was *d* Rom 7:8
the body is *d* because of sin Rom 8:10
up Jesus from the *d* dwell in you Rom 8:11
*d* shall also quicken your mortal Rom 8:11
bring up Christ again from the *d* Rom 10:7
God hath raised him from the *d* Rom 10:9
of them be, but life from the *d* Rom 11:15
he might be Lord both of the *d* Rom 14:9
but if her husband be *d*, she is 1Cor 7:39
preached that he rose from the *d* 1Cor 15:12
there is no resurrection of the *d* 1Cor 15:12
there be no resurrection of the *d* 1Cor 15:13
up, if so be that the *d* rise not 1Cor 15:15
For if the *d* rise not, then is 1Cor 15:16
now is Christ risen from the *d* 1Cor 15:20
also the resurrection of the *d* 1Cor 15:21
do which are baptized for the *d* 1Cor 15:29
if the *d* rise not at all 1Cor 15:29
are they then baptized for the *d* 1Cor 15:29
it me, if the *d* rise not 1Cor 15:32
will say, How are the *d* raised up 1Cor 15:35
also is the resurrection of the *d* 1Cor 15:42
sound, and the *d* shall be raised 1Cor 15:52
but in God which raiseth the *d* 2Cor 1:9
one died for all, then were all *d* 2Cor 5:14
Father, who raised him from the *d* Gal 1:1
I through the law am *d* to the law Gal 2:19
the law, then Christ is *d* in vain Gal 2:21
when he raised him from the *d* Eph 1:20
who were *d* in trespasses and sins Eph 2:1
Even when we were *d* in sins Eph 2:5
sleepest, and arise from the *d* Eph 5:14
unto the resurrection of the *d* Phil 3:11
the firstborn from the *d* Col 1:18
who hath raised him from the *d* Col 2:12
being *d* in your sins and the Col 2:13
Wherefore if ye be *d* with Christ Col 2:20
For ye are *d*, and your life is hid Col 3:3
heaven, whom he raised from the *d* 1Th 1:10
the *d* in Christ shall rise first 1Th 4:16
in pleasure is *d* while she liveth 1Ti 5:6
from the *d* according to my gospel 2Ti 2:8
For if we be *d* with him, we shall 2Ti 2:11
the *d* at his appearing and his 2Ti 4:1
of repentance from *d* works Heb 6:1
and of resurrection of the *d* Heb 6:2
purge your conscience from *d* Heb 9:14
is of force after men are *d* Heb 9:17
and by it he being *d* yet speaketh Heb 11:4
even of one, and him as good as *d* Heb 11:12
to raise him up, even from the *d* Heb 11:19
their *d* raised to life again Heb 11:35
again from the *d* our Lord Jesus Heb 13:20
faith, if it hath not works, is *d* Jas 2:17
that faith without works is *d* Jas 2:20
the body without the spirit is *d* Jas 2:26
so faith without works is *d* also Jas 2:26
of Jesus Christ from the *d* 1Pet 1:3
that raised him up from the *d* 1Pet 1:21
being *d* to sins, should live unto 1Pet 2:24
ready to judge the quick and the *d* 1Pet 4:5
preached also to them that are *d* 1Pet 4:6
withereth, without fruit, twice *d* Jude 12
and the first begotten of the *d* Rev 1:5
saw him, I fell at his feet as *d* Rev 1:17
I am he that liveth, and was *d* Rev 1:18
first and the last, which was *d* Rev 2:8
a name that thou livest, and art *d* Rev 3:1
their *d* bodies shall lie in the Rev 11:8
see their *d* bodies three days Rev 11:9
shall not suffer their *d* bodies Rev 11:9
is come, and the time of the *d* Rev 11:18
Blessed are the *d* which die in Rev 14:13
it became as the blood of a *d* man Rev 16:3
But the rest of the *d* lived not Rev 20:5
And I saw the *d*, small and great, Rev 20:12
the *d* were judged out of those Rev 20:12
gave up the *d* which were in it Rev 20:13
up the *d* which were in them Rev 20:13

### DEADLY

for there was a *d* destruction 1Sa 5:11
oppress me, from my *d* enemies Ps 17:9
the groanings of a *d* wounded man Eze 30:24
and if they drink any *d* thing Mk 16:18
an unruly evil, full of *d* poison Jas 3:8
and his *d* wound was healed Rev 13:3
beast, whose *d* wound was healed Rev 13:12

### DEADNESS

neither yet the *d* of Sarah's womb Rom 4:19

### DEAF

or who maketh the dumb, or *d* Ex 4:11
Thou shalt not curse the *d* Lev 19:14
But I, as a *d* man, heard not Ps 38:13
they are like the *d* adder that Ps 58:4
in that day shall the *d* hear the Is 29:18
the ears of the *d* shall be Is 35:5
Hear, ye *d* Is 42:18
or *d*, as my messenger that I sent Is 42:19
eyes, and the *d* that have ears Is 43:8
mouth, their ears shall be *d* Mic 7:16
the *d* hear, the dead are raised Mt 11:5
bring unto him one that was *d* Mk 7:32
he maketh both the *d* to hear Mk 7:37
*d* spirit, I charge thee, come out Mk 9:25
the *d* hear, the dead are raised, Lk 7:22

### DEAL

now will we *d* worse with thee, Gen 19:9
thou wilt not *d* falsely with me Gen 21:23
And now if ye will *d* kindly Gen 24:49
and I will *d* well with thee Gen 32:9
Should he *d* with our sister as Gen 34:31
*d* kindly and truly with me Gen 47:29
let us *d* wisely with them Ex 1:10
but let not Pharaoh *d* deceitfully Ex 8:29
he shall *d* with her after the Ex 21:9
thou shalt *d* with thy vineyard Ex 23:11
tenth *d* of flour mingled with the Ex 29:40
one tenth *d* of fine flour mingled Lev 14:21
not steal, neither *d* falsely Lev 19:11
if thou *d* thus with me, kill me, Num 11:15
tenth *d* of flour mingled with the Num 15:4
a several tenth *d* of flour Num 28:13
A several tenth *d* shalt thou Num 28:21
A several tenth *d* unto one lamb Num 28:29
one tenth *d* for one lamb, Num 29:4
A several tenth *d* for one lamb Num 29:10
a several tenth *d* to each lamb of Num 29:15
But thus shall ye *d* with them Deut 7:5
the land, that we will *d* kindly Josh 2:14
the LORD *d* kindly with you, as ye Ruth 1:8
Therefore thou shalt *d* kindly 1Sa 20:8
*D* gently for my sake with the 2Sa 18:5
As thou didst *d* with David my 2Chr 2:3
dwell therein, even so *d* with me 2Chr 2:3
*D* courageously, and the LORD shall 2Chr 19:11
lest I *d* with you after your Job 42:8
unto the fools, *D* not foolishly Ps 75:4
to *d* subtilly with his servants Ps 105:25
*D* bountifully with thy servant, Ps 119:17
*D* with thy servant according unto Ps 119:124
for thou shalt *d* bountifully with Ps 142:7
but they that *d* truly are his Prov 12:22
of uprightness will he *d* unjustly Is 26:10
make an end to *d* treacherously Is 33:1
they shall *d* treacherously with Is 33:1
wouldest *d* very treacherously Is 48:8
my servant shall *d* prudently Is 52:13
Is it not to *d* thy bread to the Is 58:7
happy that *d* very treacherously Jer 12:1
*d* thus with them in the time of Jer 18:23
if so be that the LORD will *d* Jer 21:2
Therefore will I also *d* in fury Eze 8:18
I will even *d* with thee as thou Eze 16:59
kept my judgments, to *d* truly Eze 18:9
the days that I shall *d* with thee Eze 22:14
they shall *d* furiously with thee Eze 23:25
they shall *d* with thee hatefully, Eze 23:29
he shall surely *d* with him Eze 31:11
thou seest, *d* with thy servants Dan 1:13
shall *d* against them, and shall Dan 11:7
upon them that *d* treacherously Hab 1:13
why do we *d* treacherously every Mal 2:10
let none *d* treacherously against Mal 2:15
that ye *d* not treacherously Mal 2:16
more a great *d* they published it Mk 7:36
but he cried the more a great *d* Mk 10:48

### DEALER

the treacherous *d* dealeth Is 21:2

### DEALERS

the treacherous *d* have dealt Is 24:16
the treacherous *d* have dealt very Is 24:16

### DEALEST

Wherefore *d* thou thus with thy Ex 5:15
*d* treacherously, and they dealt Is 33:1

### DEALETH

thus *d* Micah with me, and hath Judg 18:4
told me that he *d* very subtilly 1Sa 23:22
poor that *d* with a slack hand Prov 10:4
prudent man *d* with knowledge Prov 13:16
He that is soon angry *d* foolishly Prov 14:17
is his name, who *d* in proud wrath Prov 21:24
dealer *d* treacherously, and the Is 21:2
the priest every one *d* falsely Jer 6:13
the priest every one *d* falsely Jer 8:10
God *d* with you as with sons Heb 12:7

### DEALING

his violent *d* shall come down Ps 7:16

### DEALINGS

of your evil *d* by all this people 1Sa 2:23
have no *d* with the Samaritans Jn 4:9

### DEALS

three tenth *d* of fine flour for a Lev 14:10
thereof shall be two tenth *d* of Lev 23:13
two wave loaves of two tenth *d* Lev 23:17
two tenth *d* shall be in one cake Lev 24:5
for a meat offering two tenth *d* Num 15:6
*d* of flour mingled with half an Num 15:9
two tenth *d* of flour for a meat Num 28:9
three tenth *d* of flour for a meat Num 28:12
two tenth *d* of flour for a meat Num 28:12
three tenth *d* shall ye offer for Num 28:20
bullock, and two tenth *d* for a ram Num 28:20
three tenth *d* unto one bullock, Num 28:28
two tenth *d* unto one ram, Num 28:28
three tenth *d* for a bullock Num 29:3
and two tenth *d* for a ram Num 29:3
three tenth *d* to a bullock Num 29:9
and two tenth *d* to one ram, Num 29:9
three tenth *d* unto every bullock Num 29:14
two tenth *d* to each ram of the Num 29:14

### DEALT

when Sarai *d* hardly with her, she Gen 16:6
because God hath *d* graciously Gen 33:11
Wherefore *d* ye so ill with me, as Gen 43:6
Therefore God *d* well with the Ex 1:20
hast thou *d* thus with us, to Ex 14:11
they *d* proudly he was above them Ex 18:11
seeing he hath *d* deceitfully with Ex 21:8
if ye have *d* well with Jerubbaal Judg 9:16
If ye then have *d* truly and Judg 9:19
and the men of Shechem *d* Judg 9:23
as ye have *d* with the dead, and Ruth 1:8
hath *d* very bitterly with me Ruth 1:20
how that thou hast *d* well with me 1Sa 24:18
shall have *d* well with my lord 1Sa 25:31
he *d* among all the people, even 2Sa 6:19
for they *d* faithfully 2Kin 12:15
*d* with familiar spirits and 2Kin 21:6
hand, because they *d* faithfully 2Kin 22:7
he *d* to every one of Israel, both 1Chr 16:3
Even so *d* David with all the 1Chr 20:3
done amiss, and have *d* wickedly 2Chr 6:37
he *d* wisely, and dispersed of all 2Chr 11:23
*d* with a familiar spirit, and with 2Chr 33:6
We have *d* very corruptly against Neh 1:7
that they *d* proudly against them Neh 9:10
But they and our fathers *d* proudly Neh 9:16
yet they *d* proudly, and hearkened Neh 9:29
My brethren have *d* deceitfully as Job 6:15
because he hath *d* bountifully Ps 13:6
neither have we *d* falsely in thy Ps 44:17
*d* unfaithfully like their fathers Ps 78:57
He hath not *d* with us after our Ps 103:10
for the LORD hath *d* bountifully Ps 116:7
Thou hast *d* well with thy servant Ps 119:65
for they *d* perversely with me Ps 119:78
He hath not *d* so with any nation Ps 147:20
dealers have *d* treacherously Is 24:16
dealers have *d* very treacherously Is 24:16
they *d* not treacherously with Is 33:1
so have ye *d* treacherously with Jer 3:20
the house of Judah have *d* very Jer 5:11
even they have *d* treacherously Jer 12:6
all her friends have *d* Lam 1:2
in the midst of thee have they *d* Eze 22:7
Because that Edom hath *d* against Eze 25:12
the Philistines have *d* by revenge Eze 25:15
They have *d* treacherously against Hos 5:7
there have they *d* treacherously Hos 6:7
that hath *d* wondrously with you Joel 2:26
our doings, so hath he *d* with us Zec 1:6
Judah hath *d* treacherously, and an Mal 2:11
whom thou hast *d* treacherously Mal 2:14
Thus hath the Lord *d* with me in Lk 1:25
Son, why hast thou thus *d* with us Lk 2:48
The same *d* subtilly with our Acts 7:19
of the Jews have *d* with me Acts 25:24
according as God hath *d* to every Rom 12:3

**DEAR**

Is Ephraim my *d* son ... Jer 31:20
who was *d* unto him, was sick, and ... Lk 7:2
count I my life *d* unto myself ... Acts 20:24
followers of God, as *d* children ... Eph 5:1
of Epaphras our *d* fellowservant ... Col 1:7
us into the kingdom of his *d* Son ... Col 1:13
souls, because ye were *d* unto us ... 1Th 2:8

**DEARLY**

I have given the *d* beloved of my ... Jer 12:7
*D* beloved, avenge not yourselves, ... Rom 12:19
my *d* beloved, flee from idolatry ... 1Cor 10:14
these promises *d* beloved, let us ... 2Cor 7:1
*d* beloved, for your edifying ... 2Cor 12:19
Therefore, my brethren *d* beloved ... Phil 4:1
fast in the Lord, my *d* beloved ... Phil 4:1
To Timothy, my *d* beloved son ... 2Ti 1:2
unto Philemon our *d* beloved ... Philem 1
*D* beloved, I beseech you as ... 1Pet 2:11

**DEARTH**

seven years of *d* began to come ... Gen 41:54
and the *d* was in all lands ... Gen 41:54
and there was a *d* in the land ... 2Kin 4:38
If there be *d* in the land ... 2Chr 6:28
might buy corn, because of the *d* ... Neh 5:3
came to Jeremiah concerning the *d* ... Jer 14:1
Now there came a *d* over all the ... Acts 7:11
great *d* throughout all the world ... Acts 11:28

**DEATH**

Let me not see the *d* of the child ... Gen 21:16
comforted after his mother's *d* ... Gen 24:67
to pass after the *d* of Abraham ... Gen 25:11
his wife shall surely be put to *d* ... Gen 26:11
them after the *d* of Abraham ... Gen 26:18
old, I know not the day of my *d* ... Gen 27:2
thee before the LORD before my *d* ... Gen 27:7
he may bless thee before his *d* ... Gen 27:10
may take away from me this *d* only ... Ex 10:17
mount shall be surely put to *d* ... Ex 19:12
he die, shall be surely put to *d* ... Ex 21:12
mother, shall be surely put to *d* ... Ex 21:15
hand, he shall surely be put to *d* ... Ex 21:16
mother, shall surely be put to *d* ... Ex 21:17
his owner also shall be put to *d* ... Ex 21:29
a beast shall surely be put to *d* ... Ex 22:19
it shall surely be put to *d* ... Ex 31:14
day, he shall surely be put to *d* ... Ex 31:15
work therein shall be put to *d* ... Ex 35:2
the *d* of the two sons of Aaron ... Lev 16:1
they shall not be put to *d* ... Lev 19:20
he shall surely be put to *d* ... Lev 20:2
mother shall be surely put to *d* ... Lev 20:9
shall surely be put to *d* ... Lev 20:10
of them shall surely be put to *d* ... Lev 20:11
of them shall surely be put to *d* ... Lev 20:12
they shall surely be put to *d* ... Lev 20:13
he shall surely be put to *d* ... Lev 20:15
they shall surely be put to *d* ... Lev 20:16
wizard, shall surely be put to *d* ... Lev 20:27
LORD, he shall surely be put to *d* ... Lev 24:16
of the LORD, shall be put to *d* ... Lev 24:16
any man shall surely be put to *d* ... Lev 24:17
a man, he shall be put to *d* ... Lev 24:21
but shall surely be put to *d* ... Lev 27:29
cometh nigh shall be put to *d* ... Num 1:51
cometh nigh shall be put to *d* ... Num 3:10
cometh nigh shall be put to *d* ... Num 3:38
The man shall be surely put to *d* ... Num 15:35
men die the common *d* of all men ... Num 16:29
cometh nigh shall be put to *d* ... Num 18:7
Let me die the *d* of the righteous ... Num 23:10
murderer shall surely be put to *d* ... Num 35:16
murderer shall surely be put to *d* ... Num 35:17
murderer shall surely be put to *d* ... Num 35:18
him shall surely be put to *d* ... Num 35:21
it unto the *d* of the high priest ... Num 35:25
until the *d* of the high priest ... Num 35:28
but after the *d* of the high ... Num 35:28
to *d* by the mouth of witnesses ... Num 35:30
a murderer, which is guilty of *d* ... Num 35:31
but he shall be surely put to *d* ... Num 35:31
until the *d* of the priest ... Num 35:32
of dreams, shall be put to *d* ... Deut 13:5
be first upon him to put him to *d* ... Deut 13:9
is worthy of *d* be put to *d* ... Deut 17:6
witness he shall not be put to *d* ... Deut 17:6
be first upon him to put him to *d* ... Deut 17:7
whereas he was not worthy of *d* ... Deut 19:6
have committed a sin worthy of *d* ... Deut 21:22
and he be to be put to *d* ... Deut 21:22
in the damsel no sin worthy of *d* ... Deut 22:26
not be put to *d* for the children ... Deut 24:16
be put to *d* for the fathers ... Deut 24:16
shall be put to *d* for his own sin ... Deut 24:16
thee this day life and good, and *d* ... Deut 30:15
I have set before you life and *d* ... Deut 30:19
and how much more after my *d* ... Deut 31:27
my *d* ye will utterly corrupt ... Deut 31:29
children of Israel before his *d* ... Deut 33:1
Now after the *d* of Moses the ... Josh 1:1
him, he shall be put to *d* ... Josh 1:18
have, and deliver our lives from *d* ... Josh 2:13
until the *d* of the high priest ... Josh 20:6
Now after the *d* of Joshua it came ... Judg 1:1
jeoparded their lives unto the *d* ... Judg 5:18
let him be put to *d* whilst it is ... Judg 6:31
from the womb to the day of his *d* ... Judg 13:7
so that his soul was vexed unto *d* ... Judg 16:16
*d* were more than they which he ... Judg 16:30
Gibeah, that we may put them to *d* ... Judg 20:13
He shall surely be put to *d* ... Judg 21:5
also, if ought but *d* part thee ... Ruth 1:17
law since the *d* of thine husband ... Ruth 2:11
about the time of her *d* the women ... 1Sa 4:20
men, that we may put them to *d* ... 1Sa 11:12
not a man be put to *d* this day ... 1Sa 11:13
the bitterness of *d* is past ... 1Sa 15:32
see Saul until the day of his *d* ... 1Sa 15:35
is but a step between me and *d* ... 1Sa 20:3
I have occasioned the *d* of all ... 1Sa 22:22
came to pass after the *d* of Saul ... 2Sa 1:1
in their *d* they were not divided ... 2Sa 1:23
no child unto the day of her *d* ... 2Sa 6:23
two lines measured he to put to *d* ... 2Sa 8:2
shall be, whether in *d* or life ... 2Sa 15:21
not Shimei be put to *d* for this ... 2Sa 19:21
be put to *d* this day in Israel ... 2Sa 19:22
shut up unto the day of their *d* ... 2Sa 20:3
were put to *d* in the days of ... 2Sa 21:9
When the waves of *d* compassed me ... 2Sa 22:5
the snares of *d* prevented me ... 2Sa 22:6
not put thee to *d* with the sword ... 1Kin 2:8
shall be put to *d* this day ... 1Kin 2:24
for thou art worthy of *d* ... 1Kin 2:26
not at this time put thee to *d* ... 1Kin 2:26
in Egypt until the *d* of Solomon ... 1Kin 11:40
Israel after the *d* of Ahab ... 2Kin 1:1
thence any more *d* or barren land ... 2Kin 2:21
man of God, there is *d* in the pot ... 2Kin 4:40
not be put to *d* for the children ... 2Kin 14:6
be put to *d* for the fathers ... 2Kin 14:6
shall be put to *d* for his own sin ... 2Kin 14:6
king of Judah lived after the *d* ... 2Kin 14:17
was a leper unto the day of his *d* ... 2Kin 15:5
days was Hezekiah sick unto *d* ... 2Kin 20:1
prepared abundantly before his *d* ... 1Chr 22:5
God of Israel should be put to *d* ... 2Chr 15:13
after the *d* of his father to his ... 2Chr 22:4
the house, he shall be put to *d* ... 2Chr 23:7
Now after the *d* of Jehoiada came ... 2Chr 24:17
*d* of Joash son of Jehoahaz king ... 2Chr 25:25
was a leper unto the day of his *d* ... 2Chr 26:21
days Hezekiah was sick to the *d* ... 2Chr 32:24
Jerusalem did him honour at his *d* ... 2Chr 32:33
upon him, whether it be unto *d* ... Ezr 7:26
is one law of his to put him to *d* ... Est 4:11
and the shadow of *d* stain it ... Job 3:5
Which long for *d*, but it cometh ... Job 3:21
he shall redeem thee from *d* ... Job 5:20
and *d* rather than my life ... Job 7:15
of darkness and the shadow of *d* ... Job 10:21
and of the shadow of *d*, without ... Job 10:22
out to light the shadow of *d* ... Job 12:22
on my eyelids is the shadow of *d* ... Job 16:16
even the firstborn of *d* shall ... Job 18:13
to them even as the shadow of *d* ... Job 24:17
in the terrors of the shadow of *d* ... Job 24:17
of him shall be buried in *d* ... Job 27:15
of darkness, and the shadow of *d* ... Job 28:3
*d* say, We have heard the fame ... Job 28:22
know that thou wilt bring me to *d* ... Job 30:23
is no darkness, nor shadow of *d* ... Job 34:22
Have the gates of *d* been opened ... Job 38:17
seen the doors of the shadow of *d* ... Job 38:17
For in *d* there is no remembrance ... Ps 6:5
for him the instruments of *d* ... Ps 7:13
liftest me up from the gates of *d* ... Ps 9:13
eyes, lest I sleep the sleep of *d* ... Ps 13:3
The sorrows of *d* compassed me ... Ps 18:4
the snares of *d* prevented me ... Ps 18:5
brought me into the dust of *d* ... Ps 22:15
the valley of the shadow of *d* ... Ps 23:4
To deliver their soul from *d* ... Ps 33:19
covered us with the shadow of *d* ... Ps 44:19
he will be our guide even unto *d* ... Ps 48:14
*d* shall feed on them ... Ps 49:14
the terrors of *d* are fallen upon ... Ps 55:4
Let *d* seize upon them, and let ... Ps 55:15
hast delivered my soul from *d* ... Ps 56:13
the Lord belong the issues from *d* ... Ps 68:20
For there are no bands in their *d* ... Ps 73:4
he spared not their soul from *d* ... Ps 78:50
that liveth, and shall not see *d* ... Ps 89:48
those that are appointed to *d* ... Ps 102:20
in darkness and in the shadow of *d* ... Ps 107:10
of darkness and the shadow of *d* ... Ps 107:14
draw near unto the gates of *d* ... Ps 107:18
The sorrows of *d* compassed me ... Ps 116:3
hast delivered my soul from *d* ... Ps 116:8
the LORD is the *d* of his saints ... Ps 116:15
he hath not given me over unto *d* ... Ps 118:18
For her house inclineth unto *d* ... Prov 2:18
Her feet go down to *d* ... Prov 5:5
going down to the chambers of *d* ... Prov 7:27
all they that hate me love *d* ... Prov 8:36
righteousness delivereth from *d* ... Prov 10:2
righteousness delivereth from *d* ... Prov 11:4
evil pursueth it to his own *d* ... Prov 11:19
the pathway thereof there is no *d* ... Prov 12:28
to depart from the snares of *d* ... Prov 13:14
the end thereof are the ways of *d* ... Prov 14:12
to depart from the snares of *d* ... Prov 14:27
the righteous hath hope in his *d* ... Prov 14:32
of a king is as messengers of *d* ... Prov 16:14
the end thereof are the ways of *d* ... Prov 16:25
*D* and life are in the power of the ... Prov 18:21
to and fro of them that seek *d* ... Prov 21:6
them that are drawn unto *d* ... Prov 24:11
casteth firebrands, arrows, and *d* ... Prov 26:18
the day of *d* than the day of ... Eccl 7:1
find more bitter than *d* the woman ... Eccl 7:26
hath he power in the day of *d* ... Eccl 8:8
for love is strong as *d* ... Song 8:6
in the land of the shadow of *d* ... Is 9:2
He will swallow up *d* in victory ... Is 25:8
We have made a covenant with *d* ... Is 28:15
your covenant with *d* shall be ... Is 28:18
days was Hezekiah sick unto *d* ... Is 38:1
thee, *d* can not celebrate thee ... Is 38:18
wicked, and with the rich in his *d* ... Is 53:9
hath poured out his soul unto *d* ... Is 53:12
of drought, and of the shadow of *d* ... Jer 2:6
*d* shall be chosen rather than ... Jer 8:3
For *d* is come up into our windows ... Jer 9:21
he turn it into the shadow of *d* ... Jer 13:16
Such as are for *d*, to *d* ... Jer 15:2
Such as are for *d*, to *d* ... Jer 15:2
and let their men be put to *d* ... Jer 18:21
the way of life, and the way of *d* ... Jer 21:8
certain, that if ye put me to *d* ... Jer 26:15
and all Judah put him at all to *d* ... Jer 26:19
the king sought to put him to *d* ... Jer 26:21
of the people to put him to *d* ... Jer 26:24
thee, let this man be put to *d* ... Jer 38:4
wilt thou not surely put me to *d* ... Jer 38:15
soul, I will not put thee to *d* ... Jer 38:16
us, and we will not put thee to *d* ... Jer 38:25
that they might put us to *d* ... Jer 43:3
such as are for *d* to *d* ... Jer 43:11
in prison till the day of his *d* ... Jer 52:11
put them to *d* in Riblah in the ... Jer 52:27
a portion until the day of his *d* ... Jer 52:34
bereaveth, at home there is as *d* ... Lam 1:20
in the *d* of him that dieth ... Eze 18:32
for they are all delivered unto *d* ... Eze 31:14
pleasure in the *d* of the wicked ... Eze 33:11
I will redeem them from *d* ... Hos 13:14
O *d*, I will be thy plagues ... Hos 13:14
the shadow of *d* into the morning ... Amos 5:8
do well to be angry, even unto *d* ... Jonah 4:9
his desire as hell, and is as *d* ... Hab 2:5
And was there until the *d* of Herod ... Mt 2:15
shadow of *d* light is sprung up ... Mt 4:16
shall deliver up the brother to *d* ... Mt 10:21
and cause them to be put to *d* ... Mt 10:21
when he would have put him to *d* ... Mt 14:5
or mother, let him die the *d* ... Mt 15:4
here, which shall not taste of *d* ... Mt 16:28
and they shall condemn him to *d* ... Mt 20:18
exceeding sorrowful, even unto *d* ... Mt 26:38
against Jesus, to put him to *d* ... Mt 26:59
and said, He is guilty of *d* ... Mt 26:66
against Jesus to put him to *d* ... Mt 27:1
daughter lieth at the point of *d* ... Mk 5:23
or mother, let him die the *d* ... Mk 7:10
here, which shall not taste of *d* ... Mk 9:1
and they shall condemn him to *d* ... Mk 10:33
shall betray the brother to *d* ... Mk 13:12
shall cause them to be put to *d* ... Mk 13:12
him by craft, and put him to *d* ... Mk 14:1
is exceeding sorrowful unto *d* ... Mk 14:34
against Jesus to put him to *d* ... Mk 14:55
condemned him to be guilty of *d* ... Mk 14:64
in darkness and in the shadow of *d* ... Lk 1:79
Ghost, that he should not see *d* ... Lk 2:26
here, which shall not taste of *d* ... Lk 9:27
scourge him, and put him to *d* ... Lk 18:33
shall they cause to be put to *d* ... Lk 21:16
thee, both into prison, and to *d* ... Lk 22:33
worthy of *d* is done unto him ... Lk 23:15
I have found no cause of *d* in him ... Lk 23:22
led with him to be put to *d* ... Lk 23:32
him to be condemned to *d*, and have ... Lk 24:20
for he was at the point of *d* ... Jn 4:47
but is passed from *d* unto life ... Jn 5:24
my saying, he shall never see *d* ... Jn 8:51
saying, he shall never taste of *d* ... Jn 8:52
said, This sickness is not unto *d* ... Jn 11:4
Howbeit Jesus spake of his *d* ... Jn 11:13
together for to put him to *d* ... Jn 11:53
they might put Lazarus also to *d* ... Jn 12:10
signifying what *d* he should die ... Jn 12:33
lawful for us to put any man to *d* ... Jn 18:31
signifying what *d* he should die ... Jn 18:32
signifying by what *d* he should ... Jn 21:19
up, having loosed the pains of *d* ... Acts 2:24
And Saul was consenting unto his *d* ... Acts 8:1
that they should be put to *d* ... Acts 12:19
they found no cause of *d* in him ... Acts 13:28
I persecuted this way unto the *d* ... Acts 22:4
by, and consenting unto his *d* ... Acts 22:20
charge worthy of *d* or of bonds ... Acts 23:29
committed any thing worthy of *d* ... Acts 25:11
had committed nothing worthy of *d* ... Acts 25:25
and when they were put to *d* ... Acts 26:10
nothing worthy of *d* or of bonds ... Acts 26:31
there was no cause of *d* in me ... Acts 28:18
such things are worthy of *d* ... Rom 1:32
to God by the *d* of his Son ... Rom 5:10
into the world, and *d* by sin ... Rom 5:12
so *d* passed upon all men, for ... Rom 5:12
Nevertheless *d* reigned from Adam ... Rom 5:14
man's offence *d* reigned by one ... Rom 5:17
That as sin hath reigned unto *d* ... Rom 5:21
Christ were baptized into his *d* ... Rom 6:3
buried with him by baptism into *d* ... Rom 6:4
together in the likeness of his *d* ... Rom 6:5
*d* hath no more dominion over him ... Rom 6:9
whether of sin unto *d*, or of ... Rom 6:16

for the end of those things is *d* Rom 6:21
For the wages of sin is *d* Rom 6:23
to bring forth fruit unto *d* Rom 7:5
to life, I found to be unto *d* Rom 7:10
that which is good made *d* unto me Rom 7:13
working *d* in me by that which is Rom 7:13
me from the body of this *d* Rom 7:24
me free from the law of sin and *d* Rom 8:2
For to be carnally minded is *d* Rom 8:6
I am persuaded, that neither *d* Rom 8:38
or the world, or life, or *d* 1Cor 3:22
last, as it were appointed to *d* 1Cor 4:9
do shew the Lord's *d* till he come 1Cor 11:26
For since by man came *d*, by man 1Cor 15:21
that shall be destroyed is *d* 1Cor 15:26
*D* is swallowed up in victory 1Cor 15:54
O *d*, where is thy sting 1Cor 15:55
The sting of *d* is sin 1Cor 15:56
the sentence of *d* in ourselves 2Cor 1:9
delivered us from so great a *d* 2Cor 1:10
we are the savour of *d* unto *d* 2Cor 2:16
we are the savour of *d* unto *d* 2Cor 2:16
But if the ministration of *d* 2Cor 3:7
delivered unto *d* for Jesus' sake 2Cor 4:11
So then *d* worketh in us, but life 2Cor 4:12
the sorrow of the world worketh *d* 2Cor 7:10
whether it be by life, or by *d* Phil 1:20
and became obedient unto *d* Phil 2:8
even the *d* of the cross Phil 2:8
indeed he was sick nigh unto *d* Phil 2:27
work of Christ he was nigh unto *d* Phil 2:30
being made conformable unto his *d* Phil 3:10
the body of his flesh through *d* Col 1:22
Christ, who hath abolished *d* 2Ti 1:10
the angels for the suffering of *d* Heb 2:9
God should taste *d* for every man Heb 2:9
that through *d* he might destroy Heb 2:14
him that had the power of *d* Heb 2:14
them who through fear of *d* were Heb 2:15
that was able to save him from *d* Heb 5:7
to continue by reason of *d* Heb 7:23
new testament, that by means of *d* Heb 9:15
be the *d* of the testator Heb 9:16
that he should not see *d* Heb 11:5
it is finished, bringeth forth *d* Jas 1:15
his way shall save a soul from *d* Jas 5:20
God, being put to *d* in the flesh 1Pet 3:18
we have passed from *d* unto life 1Jn 3:14
not his brother abideth in *d* 1Jn 3:14
sin a sin which is not unto *d* 1Jn 5:16
life for them that sin not unto *d* 1Jn 5:16
There is a sin unto *d* 1Jn 5:16
and there is a sin not unto *d* 1Jn 5:17
and have the keys of hell and of *d* Rev 1:18
be thou faithful unto *d*, and I Rev 2:10
shall not be hurt of the second *d* Rev 2:11
I will kill her children with *d* Rev 2:23
and his name that sat on him was *D* Rev 6:8
sword, and with hunger, and with *d* Rev 6:8
And in those days shall men seek *d* Rev 9:6
to die, and *d* shall flee from them Rev 9:6
loved not their lives unto the *d* Rev 12:11
his heads as it were wounded to *d* Rev 13:3
her plagues come in one day, *d* Rev 18:8
such the second *d* hath no power Rev 20:6
and *d* and hell delivered up the Rev 20:13
And *d* and hell were cast into the Rev 20:14
This is the second *d* Rev 20:14
and there shall be no more *d* Rev 21:4
which is the second *d* Rev 21:8

**DEATHS**
They shall die of grievous *d* Jer 16:4
thou shalt die the *d* of them that Eze 28:8
Thou shalt die the *d* of the Eze 28:10
prisons more frequent, in *d* oft 2Cor 11:23

**DEBASE**
didst *d* thyself even unto hell Is 57:9

**DEBATE**
*D* thy cause with thy neighbour Prov 25:9
forth, thou wilt *d* with it Is 27:8
Behold, ye fast for strife and *d* Is 58:4
full of envy, murder, *d*, deceit, Rom 1:29

**DEBATES**
lest there be *d*, envyings, wraths 2Cor 12:20

**DEBIR** (*de'-bur*) See KIRJATH-SANNAH, KIRJATH-SEPHER.
*1. An Amorite king.*
unto *D* king of Eglon, saying, Josh 10:3
*2. A city in Judah.*
and all Israel with him, to *D* Josh 10:38
done to Hebron, so he did to *D* Josh 10:39
mountains, from Hebron, from *D* Josh 11:21
The king of *D*, one Josh 12:13
toward *D* from the valley of Achor Josh 15:7
up thence to the inhabitants of *D* Josh 15:15
and the name of *D* before was Josh 15:15
and Kirjath-sannah, which is *D* Josh 15:49
suburbs, and *D* with her suburbs, Josh 21:15
went against the inhabitants of *D* Judg 1:11
and the name of *D* before was Judg 1:11
her suburbs, *D* with her suburbs, 1Chr 6:58
*3. The boundary of Gad.*
Mahanaim unto the border of *D* Josh 13:26

**DEBORAH** (*deb'-o-rah*)
*1. Rebekah's nurse.*
But *D* Rebekah's nurse died, and Gen 35:8
*2. A judge of Israel.*
And *D*, a prophetess, the wife of Judg 4:4
the palm tree of *D* between Ramah Judg 4:5
*D* arose, and went with Barak to Judg 4:9
and *D* went up with him Judg 4:10
And *D* said unto Barak, Up Judg 4:14
Then sang *D* and Barak the son of Judg 5:1
in Israel, until that I *D* arose Judg 5:7
Awake, awake, *D* Judg 5:12
princes of Issachar were with *D* Judg 5:15

**DEBT**
and every one that was in *d* 1Sa 22:2
Go, sell the oil, and pay thy *d* 2Kin 4:7
year, and the exaction of every *d* Neh 10:31
loosed him, and forgave him the *d* Mt 18:27
prison, till he should pay the *d* Mt 18:30
I forgave thee all that *d* Mt 18:32
not reckoned of grace, but of *d* Rom 4:4

**DEBTOR**
hath restored to the *d* his pledge Eze 18:7
the gold of the temple, he is a *d* Mt 23:16
I am *d* both to the Greeks, and to Rom 1:14
that he is a *d* to do the whole Gal 5:3

**DEBTORS**
us our debts, as we forgive our *d* Mt 6:12
certain creditor which had two *d* Lk 7:41
one of his lord's *d* unto him Lk 16:5
Therefore, brethren, we are *d* Rom 8:12
and their *d* they are Rom 15:27

**DEBTS**
of them that are sureties for *d* Prov 22:26
And forgive us our *d*, as we Mt 6:12

**DECAPOLIS** (*de-cap'-o-lis*) *A district east of the Jordan River.*
of people from Galilee, and from *D* Mt 4:25
began to publish in *D* how great Mk 5:20
the midst of the coasts of *D* Mk 7:31

**DECAY**
poor, and fallen in *d* with thee Lev 25:35

**DECAYED**
of the bearers of burdens is *d* Neh 4:10
raise up the *d* places thereof Is 44:26

**DECAYETH**
fail from the sea, and the flood *d* Job 14:11
much slothfulness the building *d* Eccl 10:18
Now that which *d* and waxeth old is Heb 8:13

**DECEASE**
spake of his *d* which he should Lk 9:31
that ye may be able after my *d* to 2Pet 1:15

**DECEASED**
they are *d*, they shall not rise Is 26:14
when he had married a wife, *d* Mt 22:25

**DECEIT**
and their belly prepareth *d* Job 15:35
wickedness, nor my tongue utter *d* Job 27:4
or if my foot hath hasted to *d* Job 31:5
His mouth is full of cursing and *d* Ps 10:7
of his mouth are iniquity and *d* Ps 36:3
to evil, and thy tongue frameth *d* Ps 50:19
*d* and guile depart not from her Ps 55:11
He shall redeem their soul from *d* Ps 72:14
He that worketh *d* shall not dwell Ps 101:7
for their *d* is falsehood Ps 119:118
the counsels of the wicked are *d* Prov 12:5
but a false witness *d* Prov 12:17
*D* is in the heart of them that Prov 12:20
but the folly of fools is *d* Prov 14:8
Bread of *d* is sweet to a man Prov 20:17
lips, and layeth up *d* within him Prov 26:24
Whose hatred is covered by *d* Prov 26:26
neither was any *d* in his mouth Is 53:9
so are their houses full of *d* Jer 5:27
they hold fast *d*, they refuse to Jer 8:5
habitation is in the midst of *d* Jer 9:6
through *d* they refuse to know me, Jer 9:6
it speaketh *d* Jer 9:8
nought, and the *d* of their heart Jer 14:14
of the *d* of their own heart Jer 23:26
and the house of Israel with *d* Hos 11:12
the balances of *d* are in his hand Hos 12:7
and falsifying the balances by *d* Amos 8:5
houses with violence and *d* Zeph 1:9
covetousness, wickedness, *d* Mk 7:22
full of envy, murder, debate, *d* Rom 1:29
their tongues they have used *d* Rom 3:13
you through philosophy and vain *d* Col 2:8
For our exhortation was not of *d* 1Th 2:3

**DECEITFUL**
will abhor the bloody and *d* man Ps 5:6
but they devise *d* matters against Ps 35:20
O deliver me from the *d* and unjust Ps 43:1
devouring words, O thou *d* tongue Ps 52:4
*d* men shall not live out half Ps 55:23
were turned aside like a *d* bow Ps 78:57
the mouth of the *d* are opened Ps 109:2
lying lips, and from a *d* tongue Ps 120:2
The wicked worketh a *d* work Prov 11:18
but a *d* witness speaketh lies Prov 14:25
for they are *d* meat Prov 23:3
but the kisses of an enemy are *d* Prov 27:6
poor and the *d* man meet together Prov 29:13
Favour is *d*, and beauty is vain Prov 31:30
The heart is *d* above all things, Jer 17:9
they are like a *d* bow Hos 7:16
and with the bag of *d* weights Mic 6:11
their tongue is *d* in their mouth Mic 6:12
neither shall a *d* tongue be found Zeph 3:13
apostles, *d* workers, transforming 2Cor 11:13
corrupt according to the *d* lusts Eph 4:22

**DECEITFULLY**
Shechem and Hamor his father *d* Gen 34:13
but let not Pharaoh deal *d* any Ex 8:29
seeing he hath dealt *d* with her Ex 21:8
the thing which he hath *d* gotten Lev 6:4
brethren have dealt *d* as a brook Job 6:15
and talk *d* for him Job 13:7
his soul unto vanity, nor sworn *d* Ps 24:4
like a sharp rasor, working *d* Ps 52:2
that doeth the work of the LORD *d* Jer 48:10
made with him he shall work *d* Dan 11:23
nor handling the word of God *d* 2Cor 4:2

**DECEITFULNESS**
the *d* of riches, choke the word, Mt 13:22
the *d* of riches, and the lusts of Mk 4:19
be hardened through the *d* of sin Heb 3:13

**DECEITS**
imagine *d* all the day long Ps 38:12
unto us smooth things, prophesy *d* Is 30:10

**DECEIVABLENESS**
with all *d* of unrighteousness in 2Th 2:10

**DECEIVE**
of Ner, that he came to *d* thee 2Sa 3:25
did I not say, Do not *d* me 2Kin 4:28
the king, Let not Hezekiah *d* you 2Kin 18:29
God in whom thou trustest *d* thee 2Kin 19:10
therefore let not Hezekiah *d* you 2Chr 32:15
and *d* not with thy lips Prov 24:28
the king, Let not Hezekiah *d* you Is 36:14
*d* thee, saying, Jerusalem shall Is 37:10
they will *d* every one his Jer 9:5
*d* you, neither hearken to your Jer 29:8
*D* not yourselves, saying, The Jer 37:9
they wear a rough garment to *d* Zec 13:4
them, Take heed that no man *d* you Mt 24:4
and shall *d* many Mt 24:5
shall rise, and shall *d* many Mt 24:11
they shall *d* the very elect Mt 24:24
say, Take heed lest any man *d* you Mk 13:5
and shall *d* many Mk 13:6
fair speeches *d* the hearts of the Rom 16:18
Let no man *d* himself 1Cor 3:18
whereby they lie in wait to *d* Eph 4:14
Let no man *d* you with vain words Eph 5:6
Let no man *d* you by any means 2Th 2:3
we *d* ourselves, and the truth is 1Jn 1:8
Little children, let no man *d* you 1Jn 3:7
that he should *d* the nations no Rev 20:3
shall go out to *d* the nations Rev 20:8

**DECEIVED**
And your father hath *d* me, and Gen 31:7
violence, or hath *d* his neighbour Lev 6:2
that your heart be not *d* Deut 11:16
Michal, Why hast thou *d* me so 1Sa 19:17
Saul, saying, Why hast thou *d* me 1Sa 28:12
My lord, O king, my servant *d* me 2Sa 19:26
the *d* and the deceiver are his Job 12:16
not him that is *d* trust in vanity Job 15:31
mine heart have been *d* by a woman Job 31:9
whosoever is *d* thereby is not Prov 20:1
fools, the princes of Noph are *d* Is 19:13
a *d* heart hath turned him aside, Is 44:20
thou hast greatly *d* this people Jer 4:10
O LORD, thou hast *d* me, and I was Jer 20:7
thou hast *d* me, and I was *d* Jer 20:7
Thy terribleness hath *d* thee Jer 49:16
for my lovers, but they *d* me Lam 1:19
if the prophet be *d* when he hath Eze 14:9
I the LORD have *d* that prophet Eze 14:9
pride of thine heart hath *d* thee Obad 3
at peace with thee have *d* thee Obad 7
said, Take heed that ye be not *d* Lk 21:8
them the Pharisees, Are ye also *d* Jn 7:47
*d* me, and by it slew me Rom 7:11
Be not *d*: neither fornicators 1Cor 6:9
Be not *d*: evil communications 1Cor 15:33
Be not *d*; God is not Gal 6:7
And Adam was not *d*, but the woman 1Ti 2:14
but the woman being *d* was in the 1Ti 2:14
and worse, deceiving, and being *d* 2Ti 3:13
sometimes foolish, disobedient, *d* Titus 3:3
thy sorceries were all nations *d* Rev 18:23
with which he *d* them that had Rev 19:20
the devil that *d* them was cast Rev 20:10

**DECEIVER**
me, and I shall seem to him as a *d* Gen 27:12
the deceived and the *d* are his Job 12:16
But cursed be the *d*, which hath Mal 1:14
Sir, we remember that that *d* said Mt 27:63
This is a *d* and an antichrist 2Jn 7

**DECEIVERS**
as *d*, and yet true 2Cor 6:8
many unruly and vain talkers and *d* Titus 1:10
For many *d* are entered into the 2Jn 7

**DECEIVETH**
is the man that *d* his neighbour Prov 26:19
but he *d* the people Jn 7:12
when he is nothing, he *d* himself Gal 6:3
but *d* his own heart, this man's Jas 1:26
and Satan, which *d* the whole world Rev 12:9
*d* them that dwell on the earth by Rev 13:14

**DECEIVING**
shall wax worse and worse, *d* 2Ti 3:13
hearers only, *d* your own selves Jas 1:22

**DECEIVINGS**
own *d* while they feast with you 2Pet 2:13

**DECENTLY**
Let all things be done *d* and in 1Cor 14:40

**DECIDED**
thyself hast *d* it 1Kin 20:40

**DECISION**
multitudes in the valley of *d* Joel 3:14
LORD is near in the valley of *d* Joel 3:14

**DECK**
*D* thyself now with majesty and Job 40:10
They *d* it with silver and with Jer 10:4

**DECKED**
I have *d* my bed with coverings of Prov 7:16
I *d* thee also with ornaments, and Eze 16:11
Thus wast thou *d* with gold Eze 16:13
she *d* herself with her earrings Hos 2:13
*d* with gold and precious stones and Rev 17:4
*d* with gold, and precious stones, Rev 18:16

**DECKEDST**
*d* thy high places with divers Eze 16:16
*d* thyself with ornaments, Eze 23:40

**DECKEST**
though thou *d* thee with ornaments Jer 4:30

**DECKETH**
as a bridegroom *d* himself with Is 61:10

**DECLARATION**
the *d* of the greatness of Est 10:2
my speech, and my *d* with your ears Job 13:17
*d* of those things which are most Lk 1:1
Lord, and *d* of your ready mind 2Cor 8:19

**DECLARE**
was none that could *d* it to me Gen 41:24
Moab, began Moses to *d* this law Deut 1:5
shall *d* his cause in the ears of Josh 20:4
if ye can certainly *d* it me Judg 14:12
But if ye cannot *d* it me, then Judg 14:13
that he may *d* unto us the riddle, Judg 14:15
the words of the prophets *d* good 1Kin 22:13
*D* his glory among the heathen 1Chr 16:24
*d* good to the king with one 2Chr 18:12
to *d* it unto her, and to charge Est 4:8
of the sea shall *d* unto thee Job 12:8
that which I have seen I will *d* Job 15:17
Who shall *d* his way to his face Job 21:31
Then did he see it, and *d* it Job 28:27
I would *d* unto him the number of Job 31:37
*d*, if thou hast understanding Job 38:4
*d* if thou knowest it all Job 38:18
demand of thee, and *d* thou unto me Job 40:7
demand of thee, and *d* thou unto me Job 42:4
I will *d* the decree Ps 2:7
*d* among the people his doings Ps 9:11
The heavens *d* the glory of God Ps 19:1
I will *d* thy name unto my Ps 22:22
shall *d* his righteousness unto a Ps 22:31
shall it *d* thy truth Ps 30:9
For I will *d* mine iniquity Ps 38:18
if I would *d* and speak of them, Ps 40:5
heavens shall *d* his righteousness Ps 50:6
hast thou to do to *d* my statutes Ps 50:16
fear, and shall *d* the work of God Ps 64:9
I will *d* what he hath done for my Ps 66:16
that I may *d* all thy works Ps 73:28
name is near thy wondrous works *d* Ps 75:1
But I will *d* for ever Ps 75:9
arise and *d* them to their children Ps 78:6
*D* his glory among the heathen, Ps 96:3
The heavens *d* his righteousness, Ps 97:6
To *d* the name of the LORD in Zion Ps 102:21
*d* his works with rejoicing Ps 107:22
live, and *d* the works of the LORD Ps 118:17
and shall *d* thy mighty acts Ps 145:4
and I will *d* thy greatness Ps 145:6
in my heart even to *d* all this Eccl 9:1
they *d* their sin as Sodom, they Is 3:9
*d* his doings among the people, Is 12:4
watchman, let him *d* what he seeth Is 21:6
or *d* us things for to come Is 41:22
to pass, and new things do I *d* Is 42:9
*d* his praise in the islands Is 42:12
who among them can *d* this Is 43:9
*d* thou, that thou mayest be Is 43:26
as I, shall call, and shall *d* it Is 44:7
I *d* things that are right Is 45:19
and will not ye *d* it Is 48:6
with a voice of singing *d* ye Is 48:20
who shall *d* his generation Is 53:8
I will *d* thy righteousness, and Is 57:12
they shall *d* my glory among the Is 66:19
*D* ye in Judah, and publish in Jer 4:5
*D* this in the house of Jacob, and Jer 5:20
hath spoken, that he may *d* it Jer 9:12
*d* it in the isles afar off, and Jer 31:10
If I *d* it unto thee, wilt thou Jer 38:15
*D* unto us now what thou hast said Jer 38:25
answer you, I will *d* it unto you Jer 42:4
so *d* unto us, and we will do it Jer 42:20
*D* ye in Egypt, and publish in Jer 46:14
*D* ye among the nations, and Jer 50:2
to *d* in Zion the vengeance of the Jer 50:28
let us *d* in Zion the work of the Jer 51:10
that they may *d* all their Eze 12:16
*d* unto them their abominations Eze 23:36
*d* all that thou seest to the Eze 40:4
*d* the interpretation thereof, Dan 4:18
*D* ye it not at Gath, weep ye not Mic 1:10
to *d* unto Jacob his transgression Mic 3:8
even to day do I *d* that I will Zec 9:12
*D* unto us the parable of the Mt 13:36
unto him, *D* unto us this parable Mt 15:15
unto them thy name, and will *d* it Jn 17:26
who shall *d* his generation Acts 8:33
we *d* unto you glad tidings, how Acts 13:32
though a man *d* it unto you Acts 13:41
worship, him *d* I unto you Acts 17:23
For I have not shunned to *d* unto Acts 20:27
to *d* his righteousness for the Rom 3:25
To *d*, I say, at this time his Rom 3:26
for the day shall *d* it, because 1Cor 3:13
Now in this that I *d* unto you I 1Cor 11:17
I *d* unto you the gospel which I 1Cor 15:1
state shall Tychicus *d* unto you Col 4:7
I will *d* thy name unto my Heb 2:12
things *d* plainly that they seek a Heb 11:14
heard *d* we unto you, that ye also 1Jn 1:3
*d* unto you, that God is light, and 1Jn 1:5

**DECLARED**
that my name may be *d* throughout Ex 9:16
Moses *d* unto the children of Lev 23:44
they *d* their pedigrees after Num 1:18
because it was not *d* what should Num 15:34
he *d* unto you his covenant, which Deut 4:13
For thou hast *d* this day, that 2Sa 19:6
the words that were *d* unto them Neh 8:12
plentifully *d* the thing as it is Job 26:3
I have *d* thy faithfulness and thy Ps 40:10
hitherto have I *d* thy wondrous Ps 71:17
thou hast *d* thy strength among Ps 77:14
lovingkindness be *d* in the grave Ps 88:11
With my lips have I *d* all the Ps 119:13
I have *d* my ways, and thou Ps 119:26
A grievous vision is *d* unto me Is 21:2
God of Israel, have I *d* unto you Is 21:10
Who hath *d* from the beginning, Is 41:26
I have *d*, and have saved, and I Is 43:12
thee from that time, and have *d* it Is 44:8
who hath *d* this from ancient time Is 45:21
I have *d* the former things from Is 48:3
from the beginning *d* it to thee Is 48:5
among them hath *d* these things Is 48:14
Then Michaiah *d* unto them all the Jer 36:13
now I have this day *d* it to you Jer 42:21
she *d* unto him before all the Lk 8:47
of the Father, he hath *d* him Jn 1:18
I have *d* unto them thy name, and Jn 17:26
*d* unto them how he had seen the Acts 9:27
when he had *d* all these things Acts 10:8
*d* unto them how the Lord had Acts 12:17
they *d* all things that God had Acts 15:4
Simeon hath *d* how God at the Acts 15:14
he *d* particularly what things God Acts 21:19
Festus *d* Paul's cause unto the Acts 25:14
*d* to be the Son of God with power Rom 1:4
thee, and that my name might be *d* Rom 9:17
For it hath been *d* unto me of you 1Cor 1:11
*d* to be the epistle of Christ 2Cor 3:3
Who also *d* unto us your love in Col 1:8
as he hath *d* to his servants the Rev 10:7

**DECLARETH**
yea, there is none that *d* Is 41:26
For a voice *d* from Dan, and Jer 4:15
and their staff *d* unto them Hos 4:12
*d* unto man what is his thought, Amos 4:13

**DECLARING**
*D* the end from the beginning, and Is 46:10
*d* the conversion of the Gentiles Acts 15:3
*d* what miracles and wonders God Acts 15:12
*d* unto you the testimony of God 1Cor 2:1

**DECLINE**
to *d* after many to wrest judgment Ex 23:2
thou shalt not *d* from the Deut 17:11
yet do I not *d* from thy Ps 119:157
neither *d* from the words of my Prov 4:5
Let not thine heart *d* to her ways Prov 7:25

**DECLINED**
*d* neither to the right hand, nor 2Chr 34:2
his way have I kept, and not *d* Job 23:11
have our steps *d* from thy way Ps 44:18
yet have I not *d* from thy law Ps 119:51

**DECLINETH**
My days are like a shadow that *d* Ps 102:11
am gone like the shadow when it *d* Ps 109:23

**DECREASE**
suffereth not their cattle to *d* Ps 107:38
He must increase, but I must *d* Jn 3:30

**DECREASED**
the waters *d* continually until Gen 8:5

**DECREE**
So they established a *d* to make 2Chr 30:5
a *d* to build this house of God Ezr 5:13
that a *d* was made of Cyrus the Ezr 5:17
Then Darius the king made a *d* Ezr 6:1
*d* concerning the house of God at Ezr 6:3
Moreover I make a *d* what ye shall Ezr 6:8
Also I have made a *d*, that Ezr 6:11
I Darius have made a *d* Ezr 6:12
I make a *d*, that all they of the Ezr 7:13
do make a *d* to all the treasurers Ezr 7:21
when the king's *d* which he shall Est 1:20
his *d* was heard, and when many Est 2:8
the *d* was given in Shushan the Est 3:15
his *d* came, there was great Est 4:3
*d* that was given at Shushan to Est 4:8
the *d* was given at Shushan the Est 8:14
his *d* came, the Jews had joy and Est 8:17
his *d* drew near to be put in Est 9:1
also according unto this day's *d* Est 9:13
the *d* was given at Shushan Est 9:14
the *d* of Esther confirmed these Est 9:32
Thou shalt also *d* a thing Job 22:28
When he made a *d* for the rain Job 28:26
I will declare the *d* Ps 2:7
he hath made a *d* which shall not Ps 148:6
kings reign, and princes *d* justice Prov 8:15
When he gave to the sea his *d* Prov 8:29
Woe unto them that *d* unrighteous Is 10:1
bound of the sea by a perpetual *d* Jer 5:22
dream, there is but one *d* for you Dan 2:9
the *d* went forth that the wise Dan 2:13
Why is the *d* so hasty from the Dan 2:15
Thou, O king, hast made a *d* Dan 3:10
Therefore I make a *d*, That every Dan 3:29
Therefore made I a *d* to bring in Dan 4:6
is by the *d* of the watchers Dan 4:17
this is the *d* of the most High, Dan 4:24
statute, and to make a firm *d* Dan 6:7
Now, O king, establish the *d* Dan 6:8
signed the writing and the *d* Dan 6:9
the king concerning the king's *d* Dan 6:12
Hast thou not signed a *d*, that Dan 6:12
nor the *d* that thou hast signed, Dan 6:13
That no *d* nor statute which the Dan 6:15
I make a *d*, That in every Dan 6:26
Nineveh by the *d* of the king Jonah 3:7
day shall the *d* be far removed Mic 7:11
Before the *d* bring forth, before Zeph 2:2
went out a *d* from Caesar Augustus Lk 2:1

**DECREED**
done, and what was *d* against her Est 2:1
as they had *d* for themselves and Est 9:31
And brake up for it my *d* place Job 38:10
the consumption *d* shall overflow Is 10:22
hath so *d* in his heart that he 1Cor 7:37

**DECREES**
them that decree unrighteous *d* Is 10:1
delivered them the *d* for to keep Acts 16:4
do contrary to the *d* of Caesar Acts 17:7

**DEDAN** (*de'-dan*) See DEDANIM.
*1. A grandson of Cush.*
sons of Raamah; Sheba, and *D* Gen 10:7
sons of Raamah; Sheba, and *D* 1Chr 1:9
*2. A son of Jokshan.*
And Jokshan begat Sheba, and *D* Gen 25:3
the sons of *D* were Asshurim, and Gen 25:3
sons of Jokshan; Sheba, and *D* 1Chr 1:32
*3. A district between Sela and the Salt Sea.*
*D*, and Tema, and Buz, and all that Jer 25:23
dwell deep, O inhabitants of *D* Jer 49:8
they of *D* shall fall by the sword Eze 25:13
The men of *D* were thy merchants Eze 27:15
*D* was thy merchant in precious Eze 27:20
Sheba, and *D*, and the merchants of Eze 38:13

**DEDANIM** (*ded'-a-nim*) See DODANIM.
*Descendants of Raamah.*
O ye travelling companies of *D* Is 21:13

**DEDANITES** See DEDANIM.

**DEDICATE**
the battle, and another man *d* it Deut 20:5
king David did *d* unto the LORD 2Sa 8:11
*d* to maintain the house of the 1Chr 26:27
to *d* it to him, and to burn before 2Chr 2:4

**DEDICATED**
a new house, and hath not *d* it Deut 20:5
I had wholly *d* the silver unto Judg 17:3
gold that he had *d* of all nations 2Sa 8:11
which David his father had *d* 1Kin 7:51
of Israel *d* the house of the LORD 1Kin 8:63
the things which his father had *d* 1Kin 15:15
and the things which himself had *d* 1Kin 15:15
All the money of the *d* things 2Kin 12:4
fathers, kings of Judah, had *d* 2Kin 12:18
also king David *d* unto the LORD 1Chr 18:11
the treasures of the *d* things 1Chr 26:20
all the treasures of the *d* things 1Chr 26:26
the captains of the host, had *d* 1Chr 26:26
and Joab the son of Zeruiah, had *d* 1Chr 26:28
and whosoever had *d* any thing 1Chr 26:28
of the treasuries of the *d* things 1Chr 28:12
that David his father had *d* 2Chr 5:1
all the people *d* the house of God 2Chr 7:5
the things that his father had *d* 2Chr 15:18
and that he himself had *d* 2Chr 15:18
also all the *d* things of the 2Chr 24:7
tithes and the *d* things faithfully 2Chr 31:12
every *d* thing in Israel shall be Eze 44:29
testament was *d* without blood Heb 9:18

**DEDICATING**
the princes offered for *d* of the Num 7:10
his day, for the *d* of the altar Num 7:11

### DEDICATION
This was the *d* of the altar Num 7:84
This was the *d* of the altar Num 7:88
for they kept the *d* of the altar 2Chr 7:9
kept the *d* of this house of God Ezr 6:16
offered at the *d* of this house of Ezr 6:17
at the *d* of the wall of Jerusalem Neh 12:27
to keep the *d* with gladness, both Neh 12:27
Song at the *d* of the house of Ps 30:*t*
to come to the *d* of the image Dan 3:2
unto the *d* of the image that Dan 3:3
at Jerusalem the feast of the *d* Jn 10:22

### DEED
What *d* is this that ye have done Gen 44:15
in very *d* for this cause have I Ex 9:16
There was no such *d* done nor seen Judg 19:30
For in very *d*, as the LORD God of 1Sa 25:34
that Saul was come in very *d* 1Sa 26:4
because by this *d* thou hast given 2Sa 12:14
But will God in very *d* dwell with 2Chr 6:18
For this *d* of the queen shall Est 1:17
have heard of the *d* of the queen Est 1:18
to the counsel and *d* of them Lk 23:51
which was a prophet mighty in *d* Lk 24:19
good *d* done to the impotent man Acts 4:9
Gentiles obedient, by word and *d* Rom 15:18
that he that hath done this *d* 1Cor 5:2
him that hath so done this *d* 1Cor 5:3
be also in *d* when we are present 2Cor 10:11
And whatsoever ye do in word or *d* Col 3:17
man shall be blessed in his *d* Jas 1:25
but in *d* and in truth 1Jn 3:18

### DEEDS
thou hast done *d* unto me that Gen 20:9
make known his *d* among the people 1Chr 16:8
And his *d*, first and last, behold, 2Chr 35:27
is come upon us for our evil *d* Ezr 9:13
reported his good *d* before me Neh 6:19
wipe not out my good *d* that I Neh 13:14
Give them according to their *d* Ps 28:4
make known his *d* among the people Ps 105:1
According to their *d*, accordingly Is 59:18
they overpass the *d* of the wicked Jer 5:28
them according to their *d* Jer 25:14
ye allow the *d* of your fathers Lk 11:48
receive the due reward of our *d* Lk 23:41
light, because their *d* were evil Jn 3:19
lest his *d* should be reproved Jn 3:20
that his *d* may be made manifest, Jn 3:21
Ye do the *d* of your father Jn 8:41
and was mighty in words and in *d* Acts 7:22
and confessed, and shewed their *d* Acts 19:18
that very worthy *d* are done unto Acts 24:2
to every man according to his *d* Rom 2:6
Therefore by the *d* of the law Rom 3:20
by faith without the *d* of the law Rom 3:28
do mortify the *d* of the body Rom 8:13
in signs, and wonders, and mighty *d*. 2Cor 12:12
put off the old man with his *d* Col 3:9
day to day with their unlawful *d* 2Pet 2:8
speed is partaker of his evil *d* 2Jn 11
remember his *d* which he doeth 3Jn 10
ungodly *d* which they have ungodly Jude 15
hatest the *d* of the Nicolaitanes Rev 2:6
except they repent of their *d* Rev 2:22
sores, and repented not of their *d* Rev 16:11

### DEEMED
about midnight the shipmen *d* that Acts 27:27

### DEEP
was upon the face of the *d* Gen 1:2
the LORD God caused a *d* sleep to Gen 2:21
of the great *d* broken up, and the Gen 7:11
The fountains also of the *d* Gen 8:2
a *d* sleep fell upon Abram Gen 15:12
of the *d* that lieth under Gen 49:25
for the *d* that coucheth beneath, Deut 33:13
because a *d* sleep from the LORD 1Sa 26:12
when *d* sleep falleth on men, Job 4:13
He discovereth *d* things out of Job 12:22
when *d* sleep falleth upon men, in Job 33:15
and the face of the *d* is frozen Job 38:30
He maketh the *d* to boil like a Job 41:31
one would think the *d* to be hoary Job 41:32
thy judgments are a great *d* Ps 36:6
*D* calleth unto *d* at the noise Ps 42:7
*D* calleth unto *d* at the noise Ps 42:7
one of them, and the heart, is *d* Ps 64:6
I sink in *d* mire, where there is Ps 69:2
I am come into *d* waters, where Ps 69:2
hate me, and out of the *d* waters Ps 69:14
neither let the *d* swallow me up Ps 69:15
and didst cause it to take *d* root Ps 80:9
and thy thoughts are very *d* Ps 92:5
are the *d* places of the earth Ps 95:4
it with the *d* as with a garment Ps 104:6
the LORD, and his wonders in the *d* Ps 107:24
in the seas, and all *d* places Ps 135:6
into *d* pits, that they rise not Ps 140:10
the fountains of the *d* Prov 8:28
of a man's mouth are as *d* waters Prov 18:4
casteth into a *d* sleep Prov 19:15
the heart of man is like *d* water Prov 20:5
mouth of strange women is a *d* pit Prov 22:14
For a whore is a *d* ditch Prov 23:27
which is far off, and exceeding *d* Eccl 7:24
upon you the spirit of *d* sleep Is 29:10
Woe unto them that seek *d* to hide Is 29:15
he hath made it *d* and large Is 30:33
That saith to the *d*, Be dry, and I Is 44:27
sea, the waters of the great *d* Is 51:10
That led them through the *d* Is 63:13
Flee ye, turn back, dwell *d* Jer 49:8
Flee, get you far off, dwell *d* Jer 49:30
shalt drink of thy sister's cup *d* Eze 23:32
I shall bring up the *d* upon thee Eze 26:19
the *d* set him up on high with her Eze 31:4
I covered the *d* for him, and I Eze 31:15
Then will I make their waters *d* Eze 32:14
and to have drunk of the *d* waters Eze 34:18
He revealeth the *d* and secret Dan 2:22
I was in a *d* sleep on my face Dan 8:18
then was I in a *d* sleep on my Dan 10:9
fire, and it devoured the great *d* Amos 7:4
For thou hadst cast me into the *d* Jonah 2:3
the *d* uttered his voice, and Hab 3:10
unto Simon, Launch out into the *d* Lk 5:4
which built an house, and digged *d* Lk 6:48
command them to go out into the *d* Lk 8:31
to draw with, and the well is *d* Jn 4:11
being fallen into a *d* sleep Acts 20:9
Or, Who shall descend into the *d* Rom 10:7
things, yea, the *d* things of God 1Cor 2:10
their *d* poverty abounded unto the 2Cor 8:2
and a day I have been in the *d* 2Cor 11:25

### DEEPER
the plague in sight be *d* than the Lev 13:3
in sight be not *d* than the skin Lev 13:4
and it be in sight *d* than the skin Lev 13:25
if it be in sight *d* than the skin Lev 13:30
be not in sight *d* than the skin Lev 13:31
be not in sight *d* than the skin Lev 13:32
nor be in sight *d* than the skin Lev 13:34
*d* than hell; what canst thou know? Job 11:8
a people of a *d* speech than thou Is 33:19

### DEEPLY
of Israel have *d* revolted Is 31:6
They have *d* corrupted themselves, Hos 9:9
he sighed *d* in his spirit, and Mk 8:12

### DEEPNESS
because they had no *d* of earth Mt 13:5

### DEEPS
thou threwest into the *d*, as a Neh 9:11
lowest pit, in darkness, in the *d* Ps 88:6
the earth, ye dragons, and all *d* Ps 148:7
all the *d* of the river shall dry Zec 10:11

### DEER
and the roebuck, and the fallow *d* Deut 14:5

### DEFAMED
Being *d*, we intreat 1Cor 4:13

### DEFAMING
For I heard the *d* of many Jer 20:10

### DEFEAT
then mayest thou for me *d* the 2Sa 15:34
For the LORD had appointed to *d* 2Sa 17:14

### DEFENCE
their *d* is departed from them, and Num 14:9
and built cities for *d* in Judah 2Chr 11:5
Yea, the Almighty shall be thy *d* Job 22:25
My *d* is of God, which saveth the Ps 7:10
for an house of *d* to save me Ps 31:2
for God is my *d* Ps 59:9
for thou hast been my *d* and refuge Ps 59:16
for God is my *d*, and the God of my Ps 59:17
he is my *d* Ps 62:2
he is my *d* Ps 62:6
For the LORD is our *d* Ps 89:18
But the LORD is my *d* Ps 94:22
For wisdom is a *d* Eccl 7:12
and money is a *d* Eccl 7:12
upon all the glory shall be a *d* Is 4:5
the brooks of *d* shall be emptied Is 19:6
his place of *d* shall be the Is 33:16
and the *d* shall be prepared Nah 2:5
have made his *d* unto the people Acts 19:33
hear ye my *d* which I make now Acts 22:1
as both in my bonds, and in the *d* Phil 1:7
I am set for the *d* of the gospel Phil 1:17

### DEFENCED
of a *d* city a ruin Is 25:2
Yet the *d* city shall be desolate, Is 27:10
against all the *d* cities of Judah Is 36:1
waste *d* cities into ruinous heaps Is 37:26
have made thee this day a *d* city Jer 1:18
and let us go into the *d* cities Jer 4:5
and let us enter into the *d* cities Jer 8:14
for these *d* cities remained of Jer 34:7
and to Judah in Jerusalem the *d* Eze 21:20

### DEFEND
to *d* Israel Tola the son of Puah Judg 10:1
For I will *d* this city, to save 2Kin 19:34
I will *d* this city for mine own 2Kin 20:6
name of the God of Jacob *d* thee Ps 20:1
*d* me from them that rise up Ps 59:1
*D* the poor and fatherless Ps 82:3
the LORD of hosts *d* Jerusalem Is 31:5
For I will *d* this city to save it Is 37:35
and I will *d* this city Is 38:6
The LORD of hosts shall *d* them Zec 9:15
In that day shall the LORD *d* the Zec 12:8

### DEFENDED
*d* it, and slew the Philistines 2Sa 23:12
he *d* him, and avenged him that was Acts 7:24

### DEFENDEST
for joy, because thou *d* them Ps 5:11

### DEFENDING
*d* also he will deliver it Is 31:5

### DEFER
a vow unto God, *d* not to pay it Eccl 5:4
name's sake will I *d* mine anger Is 48:9
*d* not, for thine own sake, O my Dan 9:19

### DEFERRED
the young man *d* not to do the Gen 34:19
Hope *d* maketh the heart sick, but Prov 13:12
he *d* them, and said, When Lysias Acts 24:22

### DEFERRETH
discretion of a man *d* his anger Prov 19:11

### DEFIED
I defy, whom the LORD hath not *d* Num 23:8
seeing he hath *d* the armies of 1Sa 17:36
of Israel, whom thou hast *d* 1Sa 17:45
And when he *d* Israel, Jonathan the 2Sa 21:21
when they *d* the Philistines that 2Sa 23:9
But when he *d* Israel, Jonathan 1Chr 20:7

### DEFILE
neither shall ye *d* yourselves Lev 11:44
when they *d* my tabernacle that is Lev 15:31
wife, to *d* thyself with her Lev 18:20
any beast to *d* thyself therewith Lev 18:23
*D* not ye yourselves in any of Lev 18:24
not you out also, when ye *d* it Lev 18:28
that ye *d* not yourselves therein Lev 18:30
to *d* my sanctuary, and to profane Lev 20:3
But he shall not *d* himself Lev 21:4
nor *d* himself for his father, or Lev 21:11
not eat to *d* himself therewith Lev 22:8
that they *d* not their camps, in Num 5:3
*D* not therefore the land which ye Num 35:34
children of Ammon, did the king *d* 2Kin 23:13
how shall I *d* them? Song 5:3
Ye shall *d* also the covering of Is 30:22
is called by my name, to *d* it Jer 32:34
shall enter into it, and *d* it Eze 7:22
*D* the house, and fill the courts Eze 9:7
*d* not yourselves with the idols Eze 20:7
nor *d* yourselves with their idols Eze 20:18
against herself to *d* herself Eze 22:3
they shall *d* thy brightness Eze 28:7
ye *d* every one his neighbour's Eze 33:26
Neither shall they *d* themselves Eze 37:23
the house of Israel no more *d* Eze 43:7
at no dead person to *d* themselves Eze 44:25
no husband, they may *d* themselves Eze 44:25
in his heart that he would not *d* Dan 1:8
that he might not *d* himself Dan 1:8
and they *d* the man Mt 15:18
are the things which *d* a man Mt 15:20
that entering into him can *d* him Mk 7:15
those are they that *d* the man Mk 7:15
into the man, it cannot *d* him Mk 7:18
come from within, and *d* the man Mk 7:23
If any man *d* the temple of God, 1Cor 3:17
for them that *d* themselves with 1Ti 1:10
these filthy dreamers *d* the flesh Jude 8

### DEFILED
her, and lay with her, and *d* her Gen 34:2
that he had *d* Dinah his daughter Gen 34:5
because he had *d* Dinah their Gen 34:13
because they had *d* their sister Gen 34:27
be that a man shall be *d* withal Lev 5:3
them, that ye should be *d* thereby Lev 11:43
shall be in him he shall be *d* Lev 13:46
goeth from him, and is *d* therewith Lev 15:32
are *d* which I cast out before you Lev 18:24
And the land is *d* Lev 18:25
were before you, and the land is *d* Lev 18:27
after wizards, to be *d* by them Lev 19:31
There shall none be *d* for the Lev 21:1
for her may he be *d* Lev 21:3
and whosoever is *d* by the dead Num 5:2
and be kept close, and she be *d* Num 5:13
jealous of his wife, and she be *d* Num 5:14
of his wife, and she be not *d* Num 5:14
of thy husband, and if thou be *d* Num 5:20
come to pass, that, if she be *d* Num 5:27
And if the woman be not *d*, but be Num 5:28
instead of her husband, and is *d* Num 5:29
he hath *d* the head of his Num 6:9
because his separation was *d* Num 6:12
who were *d* by the dead body of a Num 9:6
We are *d* by the dead body of a Num 9:7
because he hath *d* the sanctuary Num 19:20
that thy land be not *d*, which Deut 21:23
the fruit of thy vineyard, be *d* Deut 22:9
be his wife, after that she is *d* Deut 24:4
*d* the high places where the 2Kin 23:8
he *d* Topheth, which is in the 2Kin 23:10
forasmuch as he *d* his father's 1Chr 5:1
they have *d* the priesthood Neh 13:29
my skin, and *d* my horn in the dust Job 16:15
they have *d* by casting down the Ps 74:7
thy holy temple have they *d* Ps 79:1
Thus were they *d* with their own Ps 106:39
The earth also is *d* under the Is 24:5
For your hands are *d* with blood Is 59:3
ye *d* my land, and made mine Jer 2:7
her whoredom, that she *d* the land Jer 3:9
because they have *d* my land Jer 16:18
shall be *d* as the place of Tophet Jer 19:13

their *d* bread among the Gentiles Eze 4:13
because thou hast *d* my sanctuary Eze 5:11
and their holy places shall be *d* Eze 7:24
neither hath *d* his neighbour's Eze 18:6
and *d* his neighbour's wife, Eze 18:11
hath not *d* his neighbour's wife, Eze 18:15
doings, wherein ye have been *d* Eze 20:43
hast *d* thyself in thine idols Eze 22:4
hath lewdly *d* his daughter in law Eze 22:11
all their idols she *d* herself Eze 23:7
Then I saw that she was *d* Eze 23:13
they *d* her with their whoredom, Eze 23:17
they have *d* my sanctuary in the Eze 23:38
Thou hast *d* thy sanctuaries by Eze 28:18
they *d* it by their own way and by Eze 36:17
they have even *d* my holy name by Eze 43:8
whoredom, and Israel is *d* Hos 5:3
whoredom of Ephraim, Israel is *d* Hos 6:10
thee, that say, Let her be *d* Mic 4:11
of his disciples eat bread with *d* Mk 7:2
hall, lest they should be *d* Jn 18:28
their conscience being weak is *d* 1Cor 8:7
but unto them that are *d* and Titus 1:15
their mind and conscience is *d* Titus 1:15
trouble you, and thereby many be *d*... Heb 12:15
which have not *d* their garments Rev 3:4
they which were not *d* with women Rev 14:4

**DEFILEDST**
then *d* thou it Gen 49:4

**DEFILETH**
every one that *d* it shall surely Ex 31:14
*d* the tabernacle of the LORD Num 19:13
for blood it *d* the land Num 35:33
goeth into the mouth *d* a man Mt 15:11
out of the mouth, this *d* a man Mt 15:11
with unwashen hands *d* not a man Mt 15:20
out of the man, that *d* the man Mk 7:20
that it *d* the whole body, and Jas 3:6
enter into it any thing that *d* Rev 21:27

**DEFRAUD**
Thou shalt not *d* thy neighbour Lev 19:13
*D* not, Honour thy father and Mk 10:19
Nay, ye do wrong, and *d*, and that 1Cor 6:8
*D* ye not one the other, except it 1Cor 7:5
*d* his brother in any matter 1Th 4:6

**DEFRAUDED**
or whom have I *d*? 1Sa 12:3
And they said, Thou hast not *d* us 1Sa 12:4
rather suffer yourselves to be *d* 1Cor 6:7
no man, we have *d* no man 2Cor 7:2

**DEFY**
curse me Jacob, and come, *d* Israel Num 23:7
or how shall I *d*, whom the LORD Num 23:8
I *d* the armies of Israel this day 1Sa 17:10
surely to *d* Israel is he come up 1Sa 17:25
that he should *d* the armies of 1Sa 17:26

**DEGENERATE**
then art thou turned into the *d* Jer 2:21

**DEGREE**
their brethren of the second *d* 1Chr 15:18
to the estate of a man of high *d* 1Chr 17:17
Surely men of low *d* are vanity Ps 62:9
and men of high *d* are a lie Ps 62:9
seats, and exalted them of low *d* Lk 1:52
purchase to themselves a good *d* 1Ti 3:13
Let the brother of low *d* rejoice Jas 1:9

**DEGREES**
shall the shadow go forward ten *d* 2Kin 20:9
or go back ten *d* 2Kin 20:9
for the shadow to go down ten *d* 2Kin 20:10
the shadow return backward ten *d* 2Kin 20:10
brought the shadow ten *d* backward. 2Kin 20:11
A Song of *d* Ps 120:*t*
A Song of *d* Ps 121:*t*
A Song of *d* of David Ps 122:*t*
A Song of *d* Ps 123:*t*
A Song of *d* of David Ps 124:*t*
A Song of *d* Ps 125:*t*
A Song of *d* Ps 126:*t*
A Song of *d* for Solomon Ps 127:*t*
A Song of *d* Ps 128:*t*
A Song of *d* Ps 129:*t*
A Song of *d* Ps 130:*t*
A Song of *d* of David Ps 131:*t*
A Song of *d* Ps 132:*t*
A Song of *d* of David Ps 133:*t*
A Song of *d* Ps 134:*t*
bring again the shadow of the *d* Is 38:8
sun dial of Ahaz, ten *d* backward Is 38:8
So the sun returned ten *d* Is 38:8
by which *d* it was gone down Is 38:8

**DEHAVITES** (*de-ha'-vites*) *Foreign settlers in Samaria.*
the Susanchites, the *D*, and the Ezr 4:9

**DEKAR** (*de'-kar*) *Father of an officer of Solomon.*
The son of *D*, in Makaz, and in 1Kin 4:9

**DELAIAH** (*del-a-i'-ah*) See DALAIAH.
*1. A priest of David.*
The three and twentieth to *D* 1Chr 24:18
*2. A family with a lost genealogy.*
The children of *D*, the children Ezr 2:60
The children of *D*, the children Neh 7:62
*3. An opponent of Nehemiah.*
son of *D* the son of Mehetabeel Neh 6:10
*4. A prince of Judah.*
*D* the son of Shemaiah, and Jer 36:12
Nevertheless Elnathan and *D* Jer 36:25

**DELAY**
Thou shalt not *d* to offer the Ex 22:29
he would not *d* to come to them Acts 9:38
without any *d* on the morrow I sat.... Acts 25:17

**DELAYED**
*d* to come down out of the mount Ex 32:1
*d* not to keep thy commandments Ps 119:60

**DELAYETH**
his heart, My lord *d* his coming Mt 24:48
his heart, My lord *d* his coming Lk 12:45

**DELECTABLE**
their *d* things shall not profit Is 44:9

**DELICACIES**
through the abundance of her *d* Rev 18:3

**DELICATE**
is tender among you, and very *d* Deut 28:54
*d* woman among you, which would .. Deut 28:56
no more be called tender and *d* Is 47:1
of Zion to a comely and *d* woman Jer 6:2
and poll thee for thy *d* children Mic 1:16

**DELICATELY**
And Agag came unto him *d* 1Sa 15:32
He that *d* bringeth up his servant Prov 29:21
They that did feed *d* are desolate Lam 4:5
gorgeously apparelled, and live *d* Lk 7:25

**DELICATENESS**
of her foot upon the ground for *d* Deut 28:56

**DELICATES**
hath filled his belly with my *d* Jer 51:34

**DELICIOUSLY**
glorified herself, and lived *d* Rev 18:7
lived *d* with her, shall bewail Rev 18:9

**DELIGHT**
because he had *d* in Jacob's Gen 34:19
If the LORD *d* in us, then he will Num 14:8
Only the LORD had a *d* in thy Deut 10:15
be, if thou have no *d* in her Deut 21:14
as great *d* in burnt offerings 1Sa 15:22
Behold, the king hath *d* in thee 1Sa 18:22
he thus say, I have no *d* in thee 2Sa 15:26
my lord the king *d* in this thing 2Sa 24:3
To whom would the king *d* to do Est 6:6
thou have thy *d* in the Almighty Job 22:26
Will he *d* himself in the Almighty Job 27:10
that he should *d* himself with God Job 34:9
But his *d* is in the law of the Ps 1:2
excellent, in whom is all my *d* Ps 16:3
*D* thyself also in the LORD Ps 37:4
shall *d* themselves in the Ps 37:11
I *d* to do thy will, O my God Ps 40:8
they *d* in lies Ps 62:4
thou the people that *d* in war Ps 68:30
within me thy comforts *d* my soul Ps 94:19
I will *d* myself in thy statutes Ps 119:16
Thy testimonies also are my *d* Ps 119:24
for therein do I *d* Ps 119:35
And I will *d* myself in thy Ps 119:47
but I *d* in thy law Ps 119:70
for thy law is my *d* Ps 119:77
and thy law is my *d* Ps 119:174
the scorners *d* in their scorning, Prov 1:22
*d* in the frowardness of the Prov 2:14
and I was daily his *d*, rejoicing Prov 8:30
but a just weight is his *d* Prov 11:1
upright in their way are his *d* Prov 11:20
they that deal truly are his *d* Prov 12:22
prayer of the upright is his *d* Prov 15:8
Righteous lips are the *d* of kings Prov 16:13
A fool hath no *d* in understanding Prov 18:2
*D* is not seemly for a fool Prov 19:10
them that rebuke him shall be *d* Prov 24:25
he shall give *d* unto thy soul Prov 29:17
under his shadow with great *d* Song 2:3
I *d* not in the blood of bullocks, Is 1:11
for gold, they shall not *d* in it Is 13:17
let your soul *d* itself in fatness Is 55:2
*d* to know my ways, as a nation Is 58:2
they take *d* in approaching to God Is 58:2
and call the sabbath a *d*, the holy Is 58:13
Then shalt thou *d* thyself in the Is 58:14
they have no *d* in it Jer 6:10
for in these things I *d*, saith Jer 9:24
of the covenant, whom ye *d* in Mal 3:1
For I *d* in the law of God after Rom 7:22

**DELIGHTED**
Saul's son *d* much in David 1Sa 19:2
delivered me, because he *d* in me 2Sa 22:20
which *d* in thee, to set thee on 1Kin 10:9
which *d* in thee to set thee on 2Chr 9:8
*d* themselves in thy great Neh 9:25
no more, except the king *d* in her Est 2:14
delivered me, because he *d* in me Ps 18:19
deliver him, seeing he *d* in him Ps 22:8
as he *d* not in blessing, so let Ps 109:17
did choose that wherein I *d* not Is 65:12
and chose that in which I *d* not Is 66:4
be *d* with the abundance of her Is 66:11

**DELIGHTEST**
thou *d* not in burnt offering Ps 51:16

**DELIGHTETH**
the man whom the king *d* to honour Est 6:6
the man whom the king *d* to honour Est 6:7
withal whom the king *d* to honour Est 6:9
the man whom the king *d* to honour Est 6:9
the man whom the king *d* to honour Est 6:11
and he *d* in his way Ps 37:23
the LORD, that *d* greatly in his Ps 112:1
He *d* not in the strength of the Ps 147:10
as a father the son in whom he *d* Prov 3:12
mine elect, in whom my soul *d* Is 42:1
for the LORD *d* in thee, and thy Is 62:4
ways, and their soul *d* in their Is 66:3
for ever, because he *d* in mercy Mic 7:18
of the LORD, and he *d* in them Mal 2:17

**DELIGHTS**
you in scarlet, with other *d* 2Sa 1:24
Unless thy law had been my *d* Ps 119:92
yet thy commandments are my *d* Ps 119:143
my *d* were with the sons of men Prov 8:31
the *d* of the sons of men, as Eccl 2:8
pleasant art thou, O love, for *d* Song 7:6

**DELIGHTSOME**
for ye shall be a *d* land, saith Mal 3:12

**DELILAH** (*de-li'-lah*) *Woman who betrayed Samson.*
valley of Sorek, whose name was *D*.... Judg 16:4
*D* said to Samson, Tell me, I pray Judg 16:6
*D* said unto Samson, Behold, thou Judg 16:10
*D* therefore took new ropes, and Judg 16:12
*D* said unto Samson, Hitherto thou... Judg 16:13
when *D* saw that he had told her Judg 16:18

**DELIVER**
*D* me, I pray thee, from the hand Gen 32:11
to *d* him to his father again Gen 37:22
thou shalt *d* Pharaoh's cup into Gen 40:13
so will I *d* you your brother, and Gen 42:34
*d* him into my hand, and I will Gen 42:37
I am come down to *d* them out of Ex 3:8
yet shall ye *d* the tale of bricks Ex 5:18
but God *d* him into his hand Ex 21:13
If a man shall *d* unto his Ex 22:7
If a man *d* unto his neighbour an Ex 22:10
thou shalt *d* it unto him by that Ex 22:26
for I will *d* the inhabitants of Ex 23:31
they shall *d* you your bread again Lev 26:26
If thou wilt indeed *d* this people Num 21:2
the congregation shall *d* the Num 35:25
to *d* us into the hand of the Deut 1:27
that he might *d* him into thy hand Deut 2:30
for I will *d* him, and all his Deut 3:2
thy God shall *d* them before thee Deut 7:2
the LORD thy God shall *d* thee Deut 7:16
thy God shall *d* them unto thee Deut 7:23
he shall *d* their kings into thine Deut 7:24
*d* him into the hand of the Deut 19:12
to *d* thee, and to give up thine Deut 23:14
Thou shalt not *d* unto his master Deut 23:15
In any case thou shalt *d* him the Deut 24:13
*d* her husband out of the hand of Deut 25:11
any that can *d* out of my hand Deut 32:39
have, and *d* our lives from death Josh 2:13
to *d* us into the hand of the Josh 7:7
your God will *d* it into your hand Josh 8:7
morrow about this time will I *d* Josh 11:6
then they shall not *d* the slayer Josh 20:5
I will *d* him into thine hand Judg 4:7
*d* the Midianites into thine hand Judg 7:7
Israel, Did not I *d* you from the Judg 10:11
wherefore I will *d* you no more Judg 10:13
let them *d* you in the time of Judg 10:14
*d* us only, we pray thee, this day Judg 10:15
the LORD *d* them before me, shall Judg 11:9
If thou shalt without fail *d* the Judg 11:30
he shall begin to *d* Israel out of Judg 13:5
that we may *d* thee into the hand Judg 15:12
fast, and *d* thee into their hand Judg 15:13
Now therefore *d* us the men Judg 20:13
I will *d* them into thine hand Judg 20:28
who shall *d* us out of the hand of 1Sa 4:8
he will *d* you out of the hand of 1Sa 7:3
Israel *d* out of the hands of the 1Sa 7:14
but now *d* us out of the hand of 1Sa 12:10
things, which cannot profit nor *d* 1Sa 12:21
wilt thou *d* them into the hand of 1Sa 14:37
he will *d* me out of the hand of 1Sa 17:37
the LORD *d* thee into mine hand 1Sa 17:46
for I will *d* the Philistines into 1Sa 23:4
of Keilah *d* me up into his hand 1Sa 23:11
Will the men of Keilah *d* me 1Sa 23:12
LORD said, They will *d* thee up 1Sa 23:12
our part shall be to *d* him into 1Sa 23:20
I will *d* thine enemy into thine 1Sa 24:4
cause, and *d* me out of thine hand 1Sa 24:15
LORD, and let him *d* me out of all 1Sa 26:24
Moreover the LORD will also *d* 1Sa 28:19
the LORD also shall *d* the host of 1Sa 28:19
nor *d* me into the hands of my 1Sa 30:15
*D* me my wife Michal, which I 2Sa 3:14
wilt thou *d* them into mine hand 2Sa 5:19
for I will doubtless *d* the 2Sa 5:19
*D* him that smote his brother, 2Sa 14:7
to *d* his handmaid out of the hand 2Sa 14:16
*d* him only, and I will depart from 2Sa 20:21
*d* them to the enemy, so that they 1Kin 8:46
that thou wouldest *d* thy servant 1Kin 18:9

Thou shalt *d* me thy silver, and ... 1Kin 20:5
I will *d* it into thine hand this ... 1Kin 20:13
therefore will I *d* all this great ... 1Kin 20:28
for the Lord shall *d* it into the ... 1Kin 22:6
for the LORD shall *d* it into the ... 1Kin 22:12
for the LORD shall *d* it into the ... 1Kin 22:15
to *d* them into the hand of Moab ... 2Kin 3:10
to *d* them into the hand of Moab ... 2Kin 3:13
he will *d* the Moabites also into ... 2Kin 3:18
but *d* it for the breaches of the ... 2Kin 12:7
he shall *d* you out of the hand of ... 2Kin 17:39
I will *d* thee two thousand horses ... 2Kin 18:23
be able to *d* you out of his hand ... 2Kin 18:29
saying, The LORD will surely *d* us ... 2Kin 18:30
you, saying, The LORD will *d* us ... 2Kin 18:32
that the LORD should *d* Jerusalem ... 2Kin 18:35
and I will *d* thee and this city out ... 2Kin 20:6
*d* them into the hand of their ... 2Kin 21:14
let them *d* it into the hand of ... 2Kin 22:5
wilt thou *d* them into mine hand ... 1Chr 14:10
for I will *d* them into thine hand ... 1Chr 14:10
*d* us from the heathen, that we ... 1Chr 16:35
*d* them over before their enemies, ... 2Chr 6:36
for God will *d* it into the king's ... 2Chr 18:5
for the LORD shall *d* it into the ... 2Chr 18:11
which could not *d* their own ... 2Chr 25:15
that he might *d* them into the ... 2Chr 25:20
*d* the captives again, which ye ... 2Chr 28:11
The LORD our God shall *d* us out ... 2Chr 32:11
to *d* their lands out of mine hand ... 2Chr 32:13
that could *d* his people out of ... 2Chr 32:14
be able to *d* you out of mine hand ... 2Chr 32:14
to *d* his people out of mine hand ... 2Chr 32:15
your God *d* you out of mine hand ... 2Chr 32:15
*d* his people out of mine hand ... 2Chr 32:17
those *d* thou before the God of ... Ezr 7:19
many times didst thou *d* them ... Neh 9:28
neither is there any to *d* them ... Job 5:4
He shall *d* thee in six troubles ... Job 5:19
*D* me from the enemy's hand ... Job 6:23
none that can *d* out of thine hand ... Job 10:7
He shall *d* the island of the ... Job 22:30
*D* him from going down to the pit ... Job 33:24
He will *d* his soul from going ... Job 33:28
then a great ransom cannot *d* thee ... Job 36:18
Return, O LORD, *d* my soul ... Ps 6:4
them that persecute me, and *d* me ... Ps 7:1
pieces, while there is none to *d* ... Ps 7:2
*d* my soul from the wicked, which ... Ps 17:13
trusted, and thou didst *d* them ... Ps 22:4
on the LORD that he would *d* him ... Ps 22:8
let him *d* him, seeing he ... Ps 22:8
*D* my soul from the sword ... Ps 22:20
O keep my soul, and *d* me ... Ps 25:20
*D* me not over unto the will of ... Ps 27:12
*d* me in thy righteousness ... Ps 31:1
*d* me speedily ... Ps 31:2
*d* me from the hand of mine ... Ps 31:15
neither shall he *d* any by his ... Ps 33:17
To *d* their soul from death, and to ... Ps 33:19
LORD shall help them, and *d* them ... Ps 37:40
he shall *d* them from the wicked, ... Ps 37:40
*D* me from all my transgressions ... Ps 39:8
Be pleased, O LORD, to *d* me ... Ps 40:13
the LORD will *d* him in time of ... Ps 41:1
thou wilt not *d* him unto the will ... Ps 41:2
O *d* me from the deceitful and ... Ps 43:1
I will *d* thee, and thou shalt ... Ps 50:15
in pieces, and there be none to *d* ... Ps 50:22
*D* me from bloodguiltiness, O God, ... Ps 51:14
wilt not thou *d* my feet from ... Ps 56:13
*D* me from mine enemies, O my God ... Ps 59:1
*D* me from the workers of iniquity ... Ps 59:2
*D* me out of the mire, and let me ... Ps 69:14
*d* me because of mine enemies ... Ps 69:18
Make haste, O God, to *d* me ... Ps 70:1
*D* me in thy righteousness, and ... Ps 71:2
*D* me, O my God, out of the hand ... Ps 71:4
for there is none to *d* him ... Ps 71:11
For he shall *d* the needy when he ... Ps 72:12
O *d* not the soul of thy ... Ps 74:19
*d* us, and purge away our sins, for ... Ps 79:9
*D* the poor and needy ... Ps 82:4
shall he *d* his soul from the hand ... Ps 89:48
Surely he shall *d* thee from the ... Ps 91:3
upon me, therefore will I *d* him ... Ps 91:14
I will *d* him, and honour him ... Ps 91:15
Many times did he *d* them ... Ps 106:43
thy mercy is good, *d* thou me ... Ps 109:21
O LORD, I beseech thee, *d* my soul ... Ps 116:4
*D* me from the oppression of man ... Ps 119:134
Consider mine affliction, and *d* me ... Ps 119:153
Plead my cause, and *d* me ... Ps 119:154
*d* me according to thy word ... Ps 119:170
*D* my soul, O LORD, from lying ... Ps 120:2
*D* me, O LORD, from the evil man ... Ps 140:1
*d* me from my persecutors ... Ps 142:6
*D* me, O LORD, from mine enemies ... Ps 143:9
*d* me out of great waters, from ... Ps 144:7
*d* me from the hand of strange ... Ps 144:11
To *d* thee from the way of the ... Prov 2:12
To *d* thee from the strange woman, ... Prov 2:16
of glory shall she *d* to thee ... Prov 4:9
*d* thyself, when thou art come ... Prov 6:3
*D* thyself as a roe from the hand ... Prov 6:5
of the upright shall *d* them ... Prov 11:6
mouth of the upright shall *d* them ... Prov 12:6
for if thou *d* him, yet thou must ... Prov 19:19
shalt *d* his soul from hell ... Prov 23:14
If thou forbear to *d* them that ... Prov 24:11
neither shall wickedness *d* those ... Eccl 8:8
it away safe, and none shall *d* it ... Is 5:29
a great one, and he shall *d* them ... Is 19:20
which men *d* to one that is ... Is 29:11
defending also he will *d* it ... Is 31:5
for he shall not be able to *d* you ... Is 36:14
saying, The LORD will surely *d* us ... Is 36:15
you, saying, The LORD will *d* us ... Is 36:18
that the LORD should *d* Jerusalem ... Is 36:20
And I will *d* thee and this city out ... Is 38:6
is none that can *d* out of my hand ... Is 43:13
prayeth unto it, and saith, *D* me ... Is 44:17
aside, that he cannot *d* his soul ... Is 44:20
they could not *d* the burden ... Is 46:2
even I will carry, and will *d* you ... Is 46:4
they shall not *d* themselves from ... Is 47:14
or have I no power to *d* ... Is 50:2
criest, let thy companies *d* thee ... Is 57:13
for I am with thee to *d* thee ... Jer 1:8
thee, saith the LORD, to *d* thee ... Jer 1:19
I *d* to the sword before their ... Jer 15:9
to *d* thee, saith the LORD ... Jer 15:20
I will *d* thee out of the hand of ... Jer 15:21
Therefore *d* up their children to ... Jer 18:21
Moreover I will *d* all the ... Jer 20:5
I will *d* Zedekiah king of Judah, ... Jer 21:7
*d* him that is spoiled out of the ... Jer 21:12
*d* the spoiled out of the hand of ... Jer 22:3
I will *d* them to be removed into ... Jer 24:9
will *d* them to be removed to all ... Jer 29:18
I will *d* them into the hand of ... Jer 29:21
lest they *d* me into their hand, ... Jer 38:19
said, They shall not *d* thee ... Jer 38:20
But I will *d* thee in that day, ... Jer 39:17
For I will surely *d* thee, and thou ... Jer 39:18
you, and to *d* you from his hand ... Jer 42:11
for to *d* us into the hand of the ... Jer 43:3
*d* such as are for death to death ... Jer 43:11
I will *d* them into the hand of ... Jer 46:26
Babylon, and *d* every man his soul ... Jer 51:6
*d* ye every man his soul from the ... Jer 51:45
that doth *d* us out of their hand ... Lam 5:8
*d* them in the day of the wrath of ... Eze 7:19
*d* you into the hands of strangers ... Eze 11:9
*d* my people out of your hand, and ... Eze 13:21
for I will *d* my people out of ... Eze 13:23
they should *d* but their own souls ... Eze 14:14
they shall *d* neither sons nor ... Eze 14:16
they shall *d* neither sons nor ... Eze 14:18
they shall *d* neither son nor ... Eze 14:20
they shall but *d* their own souls ... Eze 14:20
*d* thee into the hand of brutish ... Eze 21:31
I will *d* thee into the hand of ... Eze 23:28
therefore I will *d* thee to the ... Eze 25:4
will *d* thee for a spoil to the ... Eze 25:7
taketh warning shall *d* his soul ... Eze 33:5
shall not *d* him in the day of his ... Eze 33:12
for I will *d* my flock from their ... Eze 34:10
will *d* them out of all places ... Eze 34:12
that shall *d* you out of my hands ... Dan 3:15
to *d* us from the burning fiery ... Dan 3:17
he will *d* us out of thine hand, O ... Dan 3:17
God that can *d* after this sort ... Dan 3:29
set his heart on Daniel to *d* him ... Dan 6:14
going down of the sun to *d* him ... Dan 6:14
continually, he will *d* thee ... Dan 6:16
able to *d* thee from the lions ... Dan 6:20
any that could *d* out of his hand ... Dan 8:4
could *d* the ram out of his hand ... Dan 8:7
none shall *d* her out of mine hand ... Hos 2:10
how shall I *d* thee, Israel ... Hos 11:8
captivity, to *d* them up to Edom ... Amos 1:6
shall the mighty *d* himself ... Amos 2:14
swift of foot shall not *d* himself ... Amos 2:15
that rideth the horse *d* himself ... Amos 2:15
therefore will I *d* up the city ... Amos 6:8
his head, to *d* him from his grief ... Jonah 4:6
thus shall he *d* us from the ... Mic 5:6
teareth in pieces, and none can *d* ... Mic 5:8
shalt take hold, but shalt not *d* ... Mic 6:14
*d* them in the day of the LORD's ... Zeph 1:18
*D* thyself, O Zion, that dwellest ... Zec 2:7
I will *d* the men every one into ... Zec 11:6
of their hand I will not *d* them ... Zec 11:6
the adversary *d* thee to the judge ... Mt 5:25
the judge *d* thee to the officer, ... Mt 5:25
temptation, but *d* us from evil ... Mt 6:13
for they will *d* you up to the ... Mt 10:17
But when they *d* you up, take no ... Mt 10:19
the brother shall *d* up the ... Mt 10:21
shall *d* him to the Gentiles to ... Mt 20:19
Then shall they *d* you up to be ... Mt 24:9
give me, and I will *d* him unto you ... Mt 26:15
let him *d* him now, if he will ... Mt 27:43
shall *d* him to the Gentiles ... Mk 10:33
for they shall *d* you up to ... Mk 13:9
*d* you up, take no thought ... Mk 13:11
but *d* us from evil ... Lk 11:4
the judge *d* thee to the officer, ... Lk 12:58
they might *d* him unto the power ... Lk 20:20
that God by his hand would *d* them ... Acts 7:25
and am come down to *d* them ... Acts 7:34
shall *d* him into the hands of the ... Acts 21:11
no man may *d* me unto them ... Acts 25:11
of the Romans to *d* any man to die ... Acts 25:16
who shall *d* me from the body of ... Rom 7:24
To *d* such a one unto Satan for ... 1Cor 5:5
from so great a death, and doth *d* ... 2Cor 1:10
we trust that he will yet *d* us ... 2Cor 1:10
that he might *d* us from this ... Gal 1:4
the Lord shall *d* me from every ... 2Ti 4:18
*d* them who through fear of death ... Heb 2:15
The Lord knoweth how to *d* the ... 2Pet 2:9

## DELIVERANCE

to save your lives by a great *d* ... Gen 45:7
Thou hast given this great *d* into ... Judg 15:18
the LORD had given *d* unto Syria ... 2Kin 5:1
said, The arrow of the LORD's *d* ... 2Kin 13:17
and the arrow of *d* from Syria ... 2Kin 13:17
the LORD saved them by a great *d* ... 1Chr 11:14
but I will grant them some *d* ... 2Chr 12:7
and hast given us such *d* as this ... Ezr 9:13
*d* arise to the Jews from another ... Est 4:14
Great *d* giveth he to his king ... Ps 18:50
compass me about with songs of *d* ... Ps 32:7
not wrought any *d* in the earth ... Is 26:18
Zion and in Jerusalem shall be *d* ... Joel 2:32
But upon mount Zion shall be *d* ... Obad 17
to preach *d* to the captives, and ... Lk 4:18
were tortured, not accepting *d* ... Heb 11:35

## DELIVERANCES

command *d* for Jacob ... Ps 44:4

## DELIVERED

into your hand are they *d* ... Gen 9:2
which hath *d* thine enemies into ... Gen 14:20
her days to be *d* were fulfilled ... Gen 25:24
he *d* them into the hand of his ... Gen 32:16
he *d* him out of their hands ... Gen 37:21
are *d* ere the midwives come in ... Ex 1:19
An Egyptian *d* us out of the hand ... Ex 2:19
hast thou *d* thy people at all ... Ex 5:23
the Egyptians, and *d* our houses ... Ex 12:27
*d* me from the sword of Pharaoh ... Ex 18:4
the way, and how the LORD *d* them ... Ex 18:8
whom he had *d* out of the hand of ... Ex 18:9
who hath *d* you out of the hand of ... Ex 18:10
who hath *d* the people from under ... Ex 18:10
in that which was *d* him to keep ... Lev 6:2
or that which was *d* him to keep ... Lev 6:4
ye shall be *d* into the hand of ... Lev 26:25
of Israel, and *d* up the Canaanites ... Num 21:3
for I have *d* him into thy hand, ... Num 21:34
So there were *d* out of the ... Num 31:5
the LORD our God *d* him before us ... Deut 2:33
the LORD our God *d* all unto us ... Deut 2:36
So the LORD our God *d* into our ... Deut 3:3
of stone, and *d* them unto me ... Deut 5:22
the LORD *d* unto me two tables of ... Deut 9:10
God hath *d* it into thine hands ... Deut 20:13
God hath *d* them into thine hands ... Deut 21:10
*d* it unto the priests the sons of ... Deut 31:9
Truly the LORD hath *d* into our ... Josh 2:24
*d* them out of the hand of the ... Josh 9:26
for I have *d* them into thine hand ... Josh 10:8
LORD *d* up the Amorites before the ... Josh 10:12
God hath *d* them into your hand ... Josh 10:19
And the LORD *d* it also, and the ... Josh 10:30
the LORD *d* Lachish into the hand ... Josh 10:32
the LORD *d* them into the hand of ... Josh 11:8
the LORD *d* all their enemies into ... Josh 21:44
now ye have *d* the children of ... Josh 22:31
so I *d* you out of his hand ... Josh 24:10
and I *d* them into your hand ... Josh 24:11
I have *d* the land into his hand ... Judg 1:2
the LORD *d* the Canaanites and the ... Judg 1:4
he *d* them into the hands of ... Judg 2:14
which *d* them out of the hand of ... Judg 2:16
*d* them out of the hand of their ... Judg 2:18
neither *d* he them into the hand ... Judg 2:23
who *d* them, even Othniel the son ... Judg 3:9
the LORD *d* Chushan-rishathaim ... Judg 3:10
for the LORD hath *d* your enemies ... Judg 3:28
and he also *d* Israel ... Judg 3:31
hath *d* Sisera into thine hand ... Judg 4:14
They that are *d* from the noise of ... Judg 5:11
the LORD *d* them into the hand of ... Judg 6:1
I *d* you out of the hand of the ... Judg 6:9
*d* us into the hands of the ... Judg 6:13
for I have *d* it into thine hand ... Judg 7:9
into his hand hath God *d* Midian ... Judg 7:14
for the LORD hath *d* into your ... Judg 7:15
God hath *d* into your hands the ... Judg 8:3
when the LORD hath *d* Zebah ... Judg 8:7
for thou hast *d* us from the hand ... Judg 8:22
who had *d* them out of the hands ... Judg 8:34
*d* you out of the hand of Midian ... Judg 9:17
I *d* you out of their hand ... Judg 10:12
And the LORD God of Israel *d* Sihon ... Judg 11:21
the LORD *d* them into his hands ... Judg 11:32
ye *d* me not out of their hands ... Judg 12:2
And when I saw that ye *d* me not ... Judg 12:3
the LORD *d* them into my hand ... Judg 12:3
the LORD *d* them into the hand of ... Judg 13:1
Our god hath *d* Samson our enemy ... Judg 16:23
Our god hath *d* into our hands our ... Judg 16:24
was with child, near to be *d* ... 1Sa 4:19
*d* you out of the hand of the ... 1Sa 10:18
*d* you out of the hand of your ... 1Sa 12:11
for the LORD hath *d* them into our ... 1Sa 14:10
for the LORD hath *d* them into the ... 1Sa 14:12
*d* Israel out of the hands of them ... 1Sa 14:48
him, and *d* it out of his mouth ... 1Sa 17:35
The LORD that *d* me out of the paw ... 1Sa 17:37
God hath *d* him into mine hand ... 1Sa 23:7
but God *d* him not into his hand ... 1Sa 23:14
*d* thee to day into mine hand in ... 1Sa 24:10
the LORD had *d* me into thine hand ... 1Sa 24:18
God hath *d* thine enemy into thine ... 1Sa 26:8
for the LORD *d* thee into my hand ... 1Sa 26:23

*d* the company that came against ... 1Sa 30:23
have not *d* thee into the hand of ... 2Sa 3:8
the rest of the people he *d* into ... 2Sa 10:10
I *d* thee out of the hand of Saul ... 2Sa 12:7
the LORD hath *d* the kingdom into ... 2Sa 16:8
which hath *d* up the men that ... 2Sa 18:28
he *d* us out of the hand of the ... 2Sa 19:9
men of his sons be *d* unto us ... 2Sa 21:6
he *d* them into the hands of the ... 2Sa 21:9
in the day that the LORD had *d* ... 2Sa 22:1
He *d* me from my strong enemy, and .. 2Sa 22:18
he *d* me, because he delighted in ... 2Sa 22:20
Thou also hast *d* me from the ... 2Sa 22:44
thou hast *d* me from the violent ... 2Sa 22:49
I was *d* of a child with her in ... 1Kin 3:17
the third day after that I was *d* ... 1Kin 3:18
that this woman was *d* also ... 1Kin 3:18
the LORD hath *d* him unto the lion ... 1Kin 13:26
*d* them into the hand of his ... 1Kin 15:18
house, and *d* him unto his mother ... 1Kin 17:23
into whose hand they *d* the money ... 2Kin 12:15
he *d* them into the hand of Hazael ... 2Kin 13:3
*d* them into the hand of spoilers, ... 2Kin 17:20
this city shall not be *d* into the ... 2Kin 18:30
any of the gods of the nations *d* ... 2Kin 18:33
have they *d* Samaria out of mine ... 2Kin 18:34
that have *d* their country out of ... 2Kin 18:35
Jerusalem shall not be *d* into the ... 2Kin 19:10
and shalt thou be *d* ... 2Kin 19:11
*d* them which my fathers have ... 2Kin 19:12
money that was *d* into their hand ... 2Kin 22:7
have *d* it into the hand of them ... 2Kin 22:9
the priest hath *d* me a book ... 2Kin 22:10
Hagarites were *d* into their hand ... 1Chr 5:20
*d* it, and slew the Philistines ... 1Chr 11:14
Then on that day David *d* first ... 1Chr 16:7
the rest of the people he *d* unto ... 1Chr 19:11
God *d* them into their hand ... 2Chr 13:16
he *d* them into thine hand ... 2Chr 16:8
they shall be *d* into your hand ... 2Chr 18:14
*d* to the captains of hundreds ... 2Chr 23:9
the LORD *d* a very great host into ... 2Chr 24:24
Wherefore the LORD his God *d* him ... 2Chr 28:5
he was also *d* into the hand of ... 2Chr 28:5
he hath *d* them into your hand, and ... 2Chr 28:9
he hath *d* them to trouble, to ... 2Chr 29:8
*d* their people out of mine hand ... 2Chr 32:17
they *d* the money that was brought ... 2Chr 34:9
Hilkiah *d* the book to Shaphan ... 2Chr 34:15
have *d* it into the hand of the ... 2Chr 34:17
Babylon, and they were *d* unto one ... Ezr 5:14
he *d* us from the hand of the ... Ezr 8:31
they *d* the king's commissions ... Ezr 8:36
been *d* into the hand of the kings ... Ezr 9:7
horse be *d* to the hand of one of ... Est 6:9
God hath *d* me to the ungodly, and ... Job 16:11
it is *d* by the pureness of thine ... Job 22:30
so should I be *d* for ever from my ... Job 23:7
Because I *d* the poor that cried, ... Job 29:12
I have *d* him that without cause ... Ps 7:4
*d* him from the hand of all his ... Ps 18:t
He *d* me from my strong enemy, and ... Ps 18:17
he *d* me, because he delighted in ... Ps 18:19
Thou hast *d* me from the strivings ... Ps 18:43
thou hast *d* me from the violent ... Ps 18:48
They cried unto thee, and were *d* ... Ps 22:5
man is not *d* by much strength ... Ps 33:16
me, and *d* me from all my fears ... Ps 34:4
For he hath *d* me out of all ... Ps 54:7
He hath *d* my soul in peace from ... Ps 55:18
For thou hast *d* my soul from ... Ps 56:13
That thy beloved may be *d* ... Ps 60:5
let me be *d* from them that hate ... Ps 69:14
day when he *d* them from the enemy ... Ps 78:42
*d* his strength into captivity, and ... Ps 78:61
his hands were *d* from the pots ... Ps 81:6
calledst in trouble, and I *d* thee ... Ps 81:7
thou hast *d* my soul from the ... Ps 86:13
he *d* them out of their distresses ... Ps 107:6
*d* them from their destructions ... Ps 107:20
That thy beloved may be *d* ... Ps 108:6
For thou hast *d* my soul from ... Ps 116:8
The righteous is *d* out of trouble ... Prov 11:8
knowledge shall the just be *d* ... Prov 11:9
seed of the righteous shall be *d* ... Prov 11:21
walketh wisely, he shall be *d* ... Prov 28:26
and he by his wisdom *d* the city ... Eccl 9:15
to be *d* from the king of Assyria ... Is 20:6
the book is *d* to him that is not ... Is 29:12
he hath *d* them to the slaughter ... Is 34:2
this city shall not be *d* into the ... Is 36:15
any of the gods of the nations *d* ... Is 36:18
have they *d* Samaria out of my ... Is 36:19
that have *d* their land out of my ... Is 36:20
and shalt thou be *d* ... Is 37:11
*d* them which my fathers have ... Is 37:12
thou hast in love to my soul *d* it ... Is 38:17
mighty, or the lawful captive *d* ... Is 49:24
prey of the terrible shall be *d* ... Is 49:25
came, she was *d* of a man child ... Is 66:7
and say, We are *d* to do all these ... Jer 7:10
for he hath *d* the soul of the ... Jer 20:13
but shall surely be *d* into the ... Jer 32:4
Now when I had *d* the evidence of ... Jer 32:16
It shall be *d* into the hand of ... Jer 32:36
be taken, and *d* into his hand ... Jer 34:3
thou shalt be *d* into the hand of ... Jer 37:17
she shall be *d* into the hand of ... Jer 46:24
the Lord hath *d* me into their ... Lam 1:14
but thou hast *d* thy soul ... Eze 3:19
also thou hast *d* thy soul ... Eze 3:21
they only shall be *d*, but the ... Eze 14:16
they only shall be *d* themselves ... Eze 14:18
*d* them to cause them to pass ... Eze 16:21
*d* thee unto the will of them that ... Eze 16:27
he break the covenant, and be *d* ... Eze 17:15
Wherefore I have *d* her into the ... Eze 23:9
I have therefore *d* him into the ... Eze 31:11
for they are all *d* unto death ... Eze 31:14
she is *d* to the sword ... Eze 32:20
but thou hast *d* thy soul ... Eze 33:9
*d* them out of the hand of those ... Eze 34:27
*d* his servants that trusted in ... Dan 3:28
who hath *d* Daniel from the power ... Dan 6:27
that time thy people shall be *d* ... Dan 12:1
the name of the LORD shall be *d* ... Joel 2:32
because they *d* up the whole ... Amos 1:9
escapeth of them shall not be *d* ... Amos 9:1
neither shouldest thou have *d* up ... Obad 14
there shalt thou be *d* ... Mic 4:10
that he may be *d* from the power ... Hab 2:9
they that tempt God are even *d* ... Mal 3:15
All things are *d* unto me of my ... Mt 11:27
*d* him to the tormentors, till he ... Mt 18:34
and *d* unto them his goods ... Mt 25:14
*d* him to Pontius Pilate the ... Mt 27:2
knew that for envy they had *d* him ... Mt 27:18
Jesus, he *d* him to be crucified ... Mt 27:26
Pilate commanded the body to be *d* ... Mt 27:58
your tradition, which ye have *d* ... Mk 7:13
The Son of man is *d* into the ... Mk 9:31
shall be *d* unto the chief priests ... Mk 10:33
him away, and *d* him to Pilate ... Mk 15:1
chief priests had *d* him for envy ... Mk 15:10
*d* Jesus, when he had scourged him ... Mk 15:15
Even as they *d* them unto us ... Lk 1:2
time came that she should be *d* ... Lk 1:57
being *d* out of the hand of our ... Lk 1:74
accomplished that she should be *d* ... Lk 2:6
for that is *d* unto me ... Lk 4:6
there was *d* unto him the book of ... Lk 4:17
And he *d* him to his mother ... Lk 7:15
*d* him again to his father ... Lk 9:42
shall be *d* into the hands of men ... Lk 9:44
All things are *d* to me of my ... Lk 10:22
that thou mayest be *d* from him ... Lk 12:58
For he shall be *d* unto the ... Lk 18:32
*d* them ten pounds, and said unto ... Lk 19:13
but he *d* Jesus to their will ... Lk 23:25
The Son of man must be *d* into the ... Lk 24:7
our rulers *d* him to be condemned ... Lk 24:20
as soon as she is *d* of the child ... Jn 16:21
would not have *d* him up unto thee ... Jn 18:30
chief priests have *d* thee unto me ... Jn 18:35
I should not be *d* to the Jews ... Jn 18:36
therefore he that *d* me unto thee ... Jn 19:11
Then *d* he him therefore unto them ... Jn 19:16
being *d* by the determinate ... Acts 2:23
whom ye *d* up, and denied him in ... Acts 3:13
the customs which Moses *d* us ... Acts 6:14
*d* him out of all his afflictions, ... Acts 7:10
*d* him to four quaternions of ... Acts 12:4
hath *d* me out of the hand of ... Acts 12:11
together, they *d* the epistle ... Acts 15:30
they *d* them the decrees for to ... Acts 16:4
*d* the epistle to the governor, ... Acts 23:33
sail into Italy, they *d* Paul ... Acts 27:1
the centurion *d* the prisoners to ... Acts 28:16
yet was I *d* prisoner from ... Acts 28:17
Who was *d* for our offences, and ... Rom 4:25
form of doctrine which was *d* you ... Rom 6:17
But now we are *d* from the law ... Rom 7:6
creature itself also shall be *d* ... Rom 8:21
but *d* him up for us all, how ... Rom 8:32
That I may be *d* from them that do .. Rom 15:31
ordinances, as I *d* them to you ... 1Cor 11:2
Lord that which also I *d* unto you ... 1Cor 11:23
For I *d* unto you first of all ... 1Cor 15:3
when he shall have *d* up the ... 1Cor 15:24
Who *d* us from so great a death, ... 2Cor 1:10
*d* unto death for Jesus' sake ... 2Cor 4:11
Who hath *d* us from the power of ... Col 1:13
which *d* us from the wrath to come ... 1Th 1:10
And that we may be *d* from ... 2Th 3:2
whom I have *d* unto Satan, that ... 1Ti 1:20
but out of them all the Lord *d* me ... 2Ti 3:11
I was *d* out of the mouth of the ... 2Ti 4:17
was *d* of a child when she was ... Heb 11:11
*d* them into chains of darkness, ... 2Pet 2:4
*d* just Lot, vexed with the filthy ... 2Pet 2:7
the holy commandment *d* unto them .. 2Pet 2:21
which was once *d* unto the saints ... Jude 3
in birth, and pained to be *d* ... Rev 12:2
the woman which was ready to be *d* ... Rev 12:4
hell *d* up the dead which were in ... Rev 20:13

## DELIVEREDST

Therefore thou *d* them into the ... Neh 9:27
thou *d* unto me five talents ... Mt 25:20
thou *d* unto me two talents ... Mt 25:22

## DELIVERER

the LORD raised up a *d* to the ... Judg 3:9
LORD, the LORD raised them up a *d* ... Judg 3:15
And there was no *d*, because it was .. Judg 18:28
my rock, and my fortress, and my *d* ... 2Sa 22:2
my rock, and my fortress, and my *d* ... Ps 18:2
thou art my help and my *d* ... Ps 40:17
thou art my help and my *d* ... Ps 70:5
my high tower, and my *d* ... Ps 144:2
a *d* by the hand of the angel ... Acts 7:35
shall come out of Sion the *D* ... Rom 11:26

## DELIVEREST

which *d* the poor from him that is ... Ps 35:10
that which thou *d* will I give up ... Mic 6:14

## DELIVERETH

He *d* the poor in his affliction, ... Job 36:15
He *d* me from mine enemies ... Ps 18:48
them that fear him, and *d* them ... Ps 34:7
*d* them out of all their troubles ... Ps 34:17
but the LORD *d* him out of them ... Ps 34:19
he *d* them out of the hand of the ... Ps 97:10
who *d* David his servant from the ... Ps 144:10
but righteousness *d* from death ... Prov 10:2
but righteousness *d* from death ... Prov 11:4
A true witness *d* souls ... Prov 14:25
*d* girdles unto the merchant ... Prov 31:24
they are for a prey, and none *d* ... Is 42:22
He *d* and rescueth, and he worketh ... Dan 6:27

## DELIVERING

*d* you up to the synagogues, and ... Lk 21:12
*d* into prisons both men and women ... Acts 22:4
*D* thee from the people, and from ... Acts 26:17

## DELIVERY

draweth near the time of her *d* ... Is 26:17

## DELUSION

God shall send them strong *d* ... 2Th 2:11

## DELUSIONS

I also will choose their *d* ... Is 66:4

## DEMAND

for I will *d* of thee, and answer ... Job 38:3
I will *d* of thee, and declare thou ... Job 40:7
I will *d* of thee, and declare thou ... Job 42:4
the *d* by the word of the holy ... Dan 4:17

## DEMANDED

set over them, were beaten, and *d* ... Ex 5:14
David *d* of him how Joab did, and ... 2Sa 11:7
king hath *d* cannot the wise men ... Dan 2:27
he *d* of them where Christ should ... Mt 2:4
And the soldiers likewise *d* of him ... Lk 3:14
when he was *d* of the Pharisees, ... Lk 17:20
*d* who he was, and what he ... Acts 21:33

## DEMAS (*de'-mas*) *A companion of Paul.*

Luke, the beloved physician, and *D* ... Col 4:14
For *D* hath forsaken me, having ... 2Ti 4:10
Marcus, Aristarchus, *D*, Lucas, my ... Philem 24

## DEMETRIUS (*de-me'-tre-us*)

*1. An opponent of Paul.*
For a certain man named *D* ... Acts 19:24
Wherefore if *D*, and the craftsmen ... Acts 19:38
*2. Disciple commended by John.*
*D* hath good report of all men, and ... 3Jn 12

## DEMONSTRATION

but in *d* of the Spirit and of ... 1Cor 2:4

## DEN

wait secretly as a lion in his *d* ... Ps 10:9
put his hand on the cockatrice' *d* ... Is 11:8
become a *d* of robbers in your ... Jer 7:11
heaps, and a *d* of dragons ... Jer 9:11
Judah desolate, and a *d* of dragons ... Jer 10:22
shall be cast into the *d* of lions ... Dan 6:7
shall be cast into the *d* of lions ... Dan 6:12
and cast him into the *d* of lions ... Dan 6:16
and laid upon the mouth of the *d* ... Dan 6:17
went in haste unto the *d* of lions ... Dan 6:19
And when he came to the *d*, he ... Dan 6:20
take Daniel up out of the *d* ... Dan 6:23
Daniel was taken up out of the *d* ... Dan 6:23
cast them into the *d* of lions ... Dan 6:24
they came at the bottom of the *d* ... Dan 6:24
a young lion cry out of his *d* ... Amos 3:4
ye have made it a *d* of thieves ... Mt 21:13
ye have made it a *d* of thieves ... Mk 11:17
ye have made it a *d* of thieves ... Lk 19:46

## DENIED

Then Sarah *d*, saying, I laughed ... Gen 18:15
and I *d* him not ... 1Kin 20:7
for I should have *d* the God that ... Job 31:28
But he *d* before them all, saying, ... Mt 26:70
again he *d* with an oath, I do not ... Mt 26:72
But he *d*, saying, I know not, ... Mk 14:68
And he *d* it again ... Mk 14:70
When all *d*, Peter and they that ... Lk 8:45
be *d* before the angels of God ... Lk 12:9
he *d* him, saying, Woman, I know ... Lk 22:57
And he confessed, and *d* not ... Jn 1:20
crow, till thou hast *d* me thrice ... Jn 13:38
He *d* it, and said, I am not ... Jn 18:25
Peter then *d* again ... Jn 18:27
*d* him in the presence of Pilate, ... Acts 3:13
But ye *d* the Holy One and the Just ... Acts 3:14
he hath *d* the faith, and is worse ... 1Ti 5:8
my name, and hast not *d* my faith ... Rev 2:13
my word, and hast not *d* my name ... Rev 3:8

## DENIETH

But he that *d* me before men shall ... Lk 12:9
that *d* that Jesus is the Christ ... 1Jn 2:22
that *d* the Father and the Son ... 1Jn 2:22
Whosoever *d* the Son, the same ... 1Jn 2:23

**DENOUNCE**
I *d* unto you this day, that ye ... Deut 30:18

**DENS**
of Israel made them the *d* which ... Judg 6:2
Then the beasts go into *d* ... Job 37:8
When they couch in their *d* ... Job 38:40
and lay them down in their *d* ... Ps 104:22
and Hermon, from the lions' *d* ... Song 4:8
and towers shall be for *d* for ever ... Is 32:14
with prey, and his *d* with ravin ... Nah 2:12
deserts, and in mountains, and in *d* ... Heb 11:38
free man, hid themselves in the *d* ... Rev 6:15

**DENY**
unto you, lest ye *d* your God ... Josh 24:27
one petition of thee, *d* me not ... 1Kin 2:16
his place, then it shall *d* him ... Job 8:18
*d* me them not before I die ... Prov 30:7
*d* thee, and say, Who is the LORD ... Prov 30:9
whosoever shall *d* me before men ... Mt 10:33
him will I also *d* before my ... Mt 10:33
come after me, let him *d* himself ... Mt 16:24
cock crow, thou shalt *d* me thrice ... Mt 26:34
with thee, yet will I not *d* thee ... Mt 26:35
cock crow, thou shalt *d* me thrice ... Mt 26:75
come after me, let him *d* himself ... Mk 8:34
twice, thou shalt *d* me thrice ... Mk 14:30
I will not *d* thee in any wise ... Mk 14:31
twice, thou shalt *d* me thrice ... Mk 14:72
come after me, let him *d* himself ... Lk 9:23
which *d* that there is any ... Lk 20:27
thrice *d* that thou knowest me ... Lk 22:34
cock crow, thou shalt *d* me thrice ... Lk 22:61
and we cannot *d* it ... Acts 4:16
if we *d* him, he also will *d* us ... 2Ti 2:12
if we *d* him, he also will *d* us ... 2Ti 2:12
he cannot *d* himself ... 2Ti 2:13
but in works they *d* him, being ... Titus 1:16

**DENYING**
but *d* the power thereof ... 2Ti 3:5
*d* ungodliness and worldly lusts, ... Titus 2:12
even *d* the Lord that bought them, ... 2Pet 2:1
*d* the only Lord God, and our Lord ... Jude 4

**DEPART**
or if thou *d* to the right hand, ... Gen 13:9
sceptre shall not *d* from Judah ... Gen 49:10
And the frogs shall *d* from thee ... Ex 8:11
of flies may *d* from Pharaoh ... Ex 8:29
And Moses let his father in law *d* ... Ex 18:27
so that her fruit *d* from her ... Ex 21:22
And the LORD said unto Moses, *D* ... Ex 33:1
And then shall he *d* from thee ... Lev 25:41
but I will *d* to mine own land, and ... Num 10:30
unto the congregation, saying, *D* ... Num 16:26
lest they *d* from thy heart all ... Deut 4:9
didst *d* out of the land of Egypt ... Deut 9:7
law shall not *d* out of thy mouth ... Josh 1:8
So Joshua let the people *d* ... Josh 24:28
*D* not hence, I pray thee, until I ... Judg 6:18
*d* early from mount Gilead ... Judg 7:3
the morning, that he rose up to *d* ... Judg 19:5
And when the man rose up to *d* ... Judg 19:7
the morning on the fifth day to *d* ... Judg 19:8
And when the man rose up to *d* ... Judg 19:9
Saul said unto the Kenites, Go, *d* ... 1Sa 15:6
*d*, and get thee into the land of ... 1Sa 22:5
in the morning, and have light, *d* ... 1Sa 29:10
rose up early to *d* in the morning ... 1Sa 29:11
they may lead them away, and *d* ... 1Sa 30:22
mercy shall not *d* away from him ... 2Sa 7:15
and to morrow I will let thee *d* ... 2Sa 11:12
shall never *d* from thine house ... 2Sa 12:10
make speed to *d*, lest he overtake ... 2Sa 15:14
only, and I will *d* from the city ... 2Sa 20:21
statutes, I did not *d* from them ... 2Sa 22:23
Hadad said to Pharaoh, Let me *d* ... 1Kin 11:21
*D* yet for three days, then come ... 1Kin 12:5
of the LORD, and returned to *d* ... 1Kin 12:24
of Israel, that he may *d* from me ... 1Kin 15:19
of Israel, that he may *d* from me ... 2Chr 16:3
and God moved them to *d* from him. 2Chr 18:31
they might not *d* from their ... 2Chr 35:15
How long wilt thou not *d* from me ... Job 7:19
He shall not *d* out of darkness ... Job 15:30
The increase of his house shall *d* ... Job 20:28
they say unto God, *D* from us ... Job 21:14
Which said unto God, *D* from us ... Job 22:17
to *d* from evil is understanding ... Job 28:28
*D* from me, all ye workers of ... Ps 6:8
*D* from evil, and do good ... Ps 34:14
*D* from evil, and do good ... Ps 37:27
guile *d* not from her streets ... Ps 55:11
A froward heart shall *d* from me ... Ps 101:4
*D* from me, ye evildoers ... Ps 119:115
*d* from me therefore, ye bloody ... Ps 139:19
fear the LORD, and *d* from evil ... Prov 3:7
let not them *d* from thine eyes ... Prov 3:21
Let them not *d* from thine eyes ... Prov 4:21
*d* not from the words of my mouth ... Prov 5:7
to *d* from the snares of death ... Prov 13:14
to fools to *d* from evil ... Prov 13:19
to *d* from the snares of death ... Prov 14:27
that he may *d* from hell beneath ... Prov 15:24
fear of the LORD men *d* from evil ... Prov 16:6
of the upright is to *d* from evil ... Prov 16:17
evil shall not *d* from his house ... Prov 17:13
he is old, he will not *d* from it ... Prov 22:6
not his foolishness *d* from him ... Prov 27:22
The envy also of Ephraim shall *d* ... Is 11:13
shall his yoke *d* from off them ... Is 14:25
his burden *d* from off their ... Is 14:25
*D* ye, *d* ye, go ye out from ... Is 52:11
*d* ye, go ye out from thence, ... Is 52:11
For the mountains shall *d* ... Is 54:10
my kindness shall not *d* from thee ... Is 54:10
shall not *d* out of thy mouth, nor ... Is 59:21
lest my soul *d* from thee ... Jer 6:8
they that *d* from me shall be ... Jer 17:13
those ordinances *d* from before me ... Jer 31:36
that they shall not *d* from me ... Jer 32:40
Chaldeans shall surely *d* from us ... Jer 37:9
for they shall not *d* ... Jer 37:9
they shall remove, they shall *d* ... Jer 50:3
They cried unto them, *D* ye ... Lam 4:15
*d*, *d*, touch not ... Lam 4:15
*d*, *d*, touch not ... Lam 4:15
and my jealousy shall *d* from thee ... Eze 16:42
also to them when I *d* from them ... Hos 9:12
Arise ye, and *d* ... Mic 2:10
the sceptre of Egypt shall *d* away ... Zec 10:11
*d* from me, ye that work iniquity ... Mt 7:23
to *d* unto the other side ... Mt 8:18
he would *d* out of their coasts ... Mt 8:34
when ye *d* out of that house or ... Mt 10:14
said unto them, They need not *d* ... Mt 14:16
*D* from me, ye cursed, into ... Mt 25:41
pray him to *d* out of their coasts ... Mk 5:17
abide till ye *d* from that place ... Mk 6:10
nor hear you, when ye *d* thence ... Mk 6:11
thou thy servant *d* in peace ... Lk 2:29
that he should not *d* from them ... Lk 4:42
Jesus' knees, saying, *D* from me ... Lk 5:8
about besought him to *d* from them ... Lk 8:37
into, there abide, and thence *d* ... Lk 9:4
thee, thou shalt not *d* thence ... Lk 12:59
*d* from me, all ye workers of ... Lk 13:27
him, Get thee out, and *d* hence ... Lk 13:31
are in the midst of it *d* out ... Lk 21:21
*D* hence, and go into Judaea, that ... Jn 7:3
*d* out of this world unto the ... Jn 13:1
but if I *d*, I will send him unto ... Jn 16:7
they should not *d* from Jerusalem ... Acts 1:4
now therefore *d*, and go in peace ... Acts 16:36
desired them to *d* out of the city ... Acts 16:39
commanded all Jews to *d* from Rome .. Acts 18:2
them, ready to *d* on the morrow ... Acts 20:7
And he said unto me, *D* ... Acts 22:21
captain then let the young man *d* ... Acts 23:22
himself would *d* shortly thither ... Acts 25:4
part advised to *d* thence also ... Acts 27:12
not the wife *d* from her husband ... 1Cor 7:10
But and if she *d*, let her remain ... 1Cor 7:11
But if the unbelieving *d*, let him ... 1Cor 7:15
the unbelieving *d*, let him *d* ... 1Cor 7:15
thrice, that it might *d* from me ... 2Cor 12:8
betwixt two, having a desire to *d* ... Phil 1:23
times some shall *d* from the faith ... 1Ti 4:1
name of Christ *d* from iniquity ... 2Ti 2:19
*D* in peace, be ye warmed and ... Jas 2:16

**DEPARTED**
So Abram *d*, as the LORD had ... Gen 12:4
years old when he *d* out of Haran ... Gen 12:4
in Sodom, and his goods, and *d* ... Gen 14:12
and she *d*, and wandered in the ... Gen 21:14
of the camels of his master, and *d* ... Gen 24:10
Isaac *d* thence, and pitched his ... Gen 26:17
away, and they *d* from him in peace .. Gen 26:31
my sleep *d* from mine eyes ... Gen 31:40
and Laban *d*, and returned unto his ... Gen 31:55
And the man said, They are *d* hence .. Gen 37:17
asses with the corn, and *d* thence ... Gen 42:26
sent his brethren away, and they *d* ... Gen 45:24
For they were *d* from Rephidim ... Ex 19:2
*d* not out of the tabernacle ... Ex 33:11
of the children of Israel *d* from ... Ex 35:20
if the plague be *d* from them ... Lev 13:58
they *d* from the mount of the LORD .. Num 10:33
kindled against them; and he *d* ... Num 12:9
And the cloud *d* from off the ... Num 12:10
their defence is *d* from them ... Num 14:9
and Moses, *d* not out of the camp ... Num 14:44
the elders of Midian *d* with the ... Num 22:7
they *d* from Rameses in the first ... Num 33:3
they *d* from Succoth, and pitched ... Num 33:6
they *d* from before Pi-hahiroth, ... Num 33:8
they *d* from Dophkah ... Num 33:13
they *d* from Rephidim, and pitched ... Num 33:15
they *d* from Kibroth-hattaavah, and . Num 33:17
they *d* from Hazeroth, and pitched ... Num 33:18
they *d* from Rithmah, and pitched ... Num 33:19
they *d* from Rimmon-parez, and ... Num 33:20
they *d* from Tahath, and pitched at .. Num 33:27
they *d* from Hashmonah, and ... Num 33:30
they *d* from Moseroth, and pitched ... Num 33:31
they *d* from Ebronah, and encamped ... Num 33:35
they *d* from mount Hor, and pitched ... Num 33:41
they *d* from Zalmonah, and pitched ... Num 33:42
they *d* from Punon, and pitched in ... Num 33:43
they *d* from Oboth, and pitched in ... Num 33:44
they *d* from Iim, and pitched in ... Num 33:45
they *d* from the mountains of ... Num 33:48
when we *d* from Horeb, we went ... Deut 1:19
when she is *d* out of his house, ... Deut 24:2
And she sent them away, and they *d* .. Josh 2:21
*d* from the children of Israel out ... Josh 22:9
of the LORD *d* out of his sight ... Judg 6:21
they *d* every man unto his place ... Judg 9:55
not that the LORD was *d* from him ... Judg 16:20
the man *d* out of the city from ... Judg 17:8
Then the five men *d*, and came to ... Judg 18:7
So they turned and *d*, and put the ... Judg 18:21
that night, but he rose up and *d* ... Judg 19:10
of Israel *d* thence at that time ... Judg 21:24
The glory is *d* from Israel ... 1Sa 4:21
said, The glory is *d* from Israel ... 1Sa 4:22
not let the people go, and they *d* ... 1Sa 6:6
When thou art *d* from me to day, ... 1Sa 10:2
So the Kenites *d* from among the ... 1Sa 15:6
Spirit of the LORD *d* from Saul ... 1Sa 16:14
and the evil spirit *d* from him ... 1Sa 16:23
was with him, and was *d* from Saul ... 1Sa 18:12
And he arose and *d* ... 1Sa 20:42
David therefore *d* thence, and ... 1Sa 22:1
Then David *d*, and came into the ... 1Sa 22:5
arose and *d* out of Keilah, and went ... 1Sa 23:13
God is *d* from me, and answereth me .. 1Sa 28:15
seeing the LORD is *d* from thee ... 1Sa 28:16
So all the people *d* every one to ... 2Sa 6:19
Uriah *d* out of the king's house, ... 2Sa 11:8
And Nathan *d* unto his house ... 2Sa 12:15
came to pass, after they were *d* ... 2Sa 17:21
from the day the king *d* until the ... 2Sa 19:24
have not wickedly *d* from my God ... 2Sa 22:22
And the people *d* ... 1Kin 12:5
So Israel *d* unto their tents ... 1Kin 12:16
And Jeroboam's wife arose, and *d* ... 1Kin 14:17
So he *d* thence, and found Elisha ... 1Kin 19:19
And the messengers *d*, and brought ... 1Kin 20:9
as soon as thou art *d* from me ... 1Kin 20:36
And as soon as he was *d* from him ... 1Kin 20:36
So the prophet *d*, and waited for ... 1Kin 20:38
And Elijah *d* ... 2Kin 1:4
he *d* not therefrom ... 2Kin 3:3
they *d* from him, and returned to ... 2Kin 3:27
And he *d*, and took with him ten ... 2Kin 5:5
So he *d* from him a little way ... 2Kin 5:19
and he let the men go, and they *d* ... 2Kin 5:24
So he *d* from Elisha, and came to ... 2Kin 8:14
And he arose and *d*, and came to ... 2Kin 10:12
And when he was *d* thence, he ... 2Kin 10:15
Jehu *d* not from after them, to ... 2Kin 10:29
for he *d* not from the sins of ... 2Kin 10:31
he *d* not therefrom ... 2Kin 13:2
Nevertheless they *d* not from the ... 2Kin 13:6
he *d* not from all the sins of ... 2Kin 13:11
he *d* not from all the sins of ... 2Kin 14:24
he *d* not from the sins of ... 2Kin 15:9
he *d* not all his days from the ... 2Kin 15:18
he *d* not from the sins of ... 2Kin 15:24
he *d* not from the sins of ... 2Kin 15:28
they *d* not from them ... 2Kin 17:22
*d* not from following him, but ... 2Kin 18:6
heard that he was *d* from Lachish ... 2Kin 19:8
So Sennacherib king of Assyria *d* ... 2Kin 19:36
all the people *d* every man to his ... 1Chr 16:43
Wherefore Joab *d*, and went ... 1Chr 21:4
they *d* not from the commandment ... 2Chr 8:15
And the people *d* ... 2Chr 10:5
*d* not from it, doing that which ... 2Chr 20:32
years, and *d* without being desired ... 2Chr 21:20
And when they were *d* from him ... 2Chr 24:25
all his days they *d* not from ... 2Chr 34:33
Then we *d* from the river of Ahava ... Ezr 8:31
the cloud *d* not from them by day ... Neh 9:19
have not wickedly *d* from my God ... Ps 18:21
who drove him away, and he *d* ... Ps 34:t
Egypt was glad when they *d* ... Ps 105:38
I have not *d* from thy judgments ... Ps 119:102
the day that Ephraim *d* from Judah ... Is 7:17
heard that he was *d* from Lachish ... Is 37:8
So Sennacherib king of Assyria *d* ... Is 37:37
Mine age is *d*, and is removed from ... Is 38:12
the smiths, were *d* from Jerusalem ... Jer 29:2
of them, they *d* from Jerusalem ... Jer 37:5
*d* to go over to the Ammonites ... Jer 41:10
And they *d*, and dwelt in the ... Jer 41:17
of Zion all her beauty is *d* ... Lam 1:6
heart, which hath *d* from me ... Eze 6:9
Then the glory of the LORD *d* from ... Eze 10:18
The kingdom is *d* from thee ... Dan 4:31
thereof, because it is *d* from it ... Hos 10:5
But ye are *d* out of the way ... Mal 2:8
they had heard the king, they *d* ... Mt 2:9
they *d* into their own country ... Mt 2:12
And when they were *d*, behold, the ... Mt 2:13
mother by night, and *d* into Egypt ... Mt 2:14
into prison, he *d* into Galilee ... Mt 4:12
And he arose, and *d* to his house ... Mt 9:7
And when Jesus *d* thence, two blind ... Mt 9:27
But they, when they were *d* ... Mt 9:31
he *d* thence to teach and to preach ... Mt 11:1
And as they *d*, Jesus began to say ... Mt 11:7
And when he was *d* thence, he went ... Mt 12:9
these parables, he *d* thence ... Mt 13:53
he *d* thence by ship into a desert ... Mt 14:13
*d* into the coasts of Tyre and ... Mt 15:21
Jesus *d* from thence, and came nigh ... Mt 15:29
And he left them, and *d* ... Mt 16:4
and he *d* out of him ... Mt 17:18
he *d* from Galilee, and came into ... Mt 19:1
his hands on them, and *d* thence ... Mt 19:15
as they *d* from Jericho, a great ... Mt 20:29
went out, and *d* from the temple ... Mt 24:1
of silver in the temple, and *d* ... Mt 27:5
the door of the sepulchre, and *d* ... Mt 27:60
they *d* quickly from the sepulchre ... Mt 28:8
*d* into a solitary place, and there ... Mk 1:35
the leprosy *d* from him, and he was ... Mk 1:42
And he *d*, and began to publish in ... Mk 5:20

they *d* into a desert place by … Mk 6:32
he *d* into a mountain to pray … Mk 6:46
ship again *d* to the other side … Mk 8:13
they *d* thence, and passed through … Mk 9:30
he *d* to his own house … Lk 1:23
And the angel *d* from her … Lk 1:38
which *d* not from the temple, but … Lk 2:37
he *d* from him for a season … Lk 4:13
And when it was day, he *d* and went … Lk 4:42
the leprosy *d* from him … Lk 5:13
*d* to his own house, glorifying … Lk 5:25
the messengers of John were *d* … Lk 7:24
out of whom the devils were *d* … Lk 8:35
*d* besought him that he might be … Lk 8:38
And they *d*, and went through the … Lk 9:6
as they *d* from him, Peter said … Lk 9:33
his raiment, and wounded him, and *d* … Lk 10:30
And on the morrow when he *d* … Lk 10:35
clothes laid by themselves, and *d* … Lk 24:12
Judaea, and *d* again into Galilee … Jn 4:3
Now after two days he *d* thence … Jn 4:43
The man *d*, and told the Jews that … Jn 5:15
he *d* again into a mountain … Jn 6:15
These things spake Jesus, and *d* … Jn 12:36
they *d* from the presence of the … Acts 5:41
which spake unto Cornelius was *d* … Acts 10:7
Then *d* Barnabas to Tarsus, for to … Acts 11:25
and forthwith the angel *d* from him … Acts 12:10
And he *d*, and went into another … Acts 12:17
the Holy Ghost, *d* unto Seleucia … Acts 13:4
But when they *d* from Perga … Acts 13:14
the next day he *d* with Barnabas … Acts 14:20
who *d* from them from Pamphylia, … Acts 15:38
that they *d* in asunder one from … Acts 15:39
And Paul chose Silas, and *d* … Acts 15:40
they comforted them, and *d* … Acts 16:40
to him with all speed, they *d* … Acts 17:15
So Paul *d* from among them … Acts 17:33
these things Paul *d* from Athens … Acts 18:1
he *d* thence, and entered into a … Acts 18:7
had spent some time there, he *d* … Acts 18:23
he *d* from them, and separated the … Acts 19:9
and the diseases *d* from them … Acts 19:12
*d* for to go into Macedonia … Acts 20:1
even till break of day, so he *d* … Acts 20:11
had accomplished those days, we *d* … Acts 21:5
we that were of Paul's company *d* … Acts 21:8
Then straightway they *d* from him … Acts 22:29
and when we *d*, they laded us with … Acts 28:10
after three months we *d* in a ship … Acts 28:11
not among themselves, they *d* … Acts 28:25
had said these words, the Jews *d* … Acts 28:29
when I *d* from Macedonia, no … Phil 4:15
world, and is *d* unto Thessalonica … 2Ti 4:10
he therefore *d* for a season … Philem 15
the heaven *d* as a scroll when it … Rev 6:14
soul lusted after are *d* from thee … Rev 18:14
dainty and goodly are *d* from thee … Rev 18:14

**DEPARTETH**
wind carrieth him away, and he *d* … Job 27:21
wise man feareth, and *d* from evil … Prov 14:16
*d* in darkness, and his name shall … Eccl 6:4
he that *d* from evil maketh … Is 59:15
treacherously *d* from her husband … Jer 3:20
whose heart *d* from the LORD … Jer 17:5
the prey *d* not … Nah 3:1
and bruising him hardly *d* from him … Lk 9:39

**DEPARTING**
to pass, as her soul was in *d* … Gen 35:18
their *d* out of the land of Egypt … Ex 16:1
*d* away from our God, speaking … Is 59:13
even by *d* from thy precepts and … Dan 9:5
transgressed thy law, even by *d* … Dan 9:11
great whoredom, *d* from the LORD … Hos 1:2
And the people saw them *d*, and many … Mk 6:33
*d* from the coasts of Tyre and … Mk 7:31
John *d* from them returned to … Acts 13:13
that after my *d* shall grievous … Acts 20:29
in *d* from the living God … Heb 3:12
made mention of the *d* of the … Heb 11:22

**DEPARTURE**
sea shall be troubled at thy *d* … Eze 26:18
and the time of my *d* is at hand … 2Ti 4:6

**DEPOSED**
he was *d* from his kingly throne, … Dan 5:20

**DEPRIVED**
why should I be *d* also of you … Gen 27:45
Because God hath *d* her of wisdom … Job 39:17
I am *d* of the residue of my years … Is 38:10

**DEPTH**
The *d* saith, It is not in me … Job 28:14
walked in the search of the *d* … Job 38:16
he layeth up the *d* in storehouses … Ps 33:7
a compass upon the face of the *d* … Prov 8:27
for height, and the earth for *d* … Prov 25:3
ask it either in the *d*, or in the … Is 7:11
the *d* closed me round about, the … Jonah 2:5
were drowned in the *d* of the sea … Mt 18:6
up, because it had no *d* of earth … Mk 4:5
Nor height, nor *d*, nor any other … Rom 8:39
O the *d* of the riches both of the … Rom 11:33
is the breadth, and length, and *d* … Eph 3:18

**DEPTHS**
The *d* have covered them … Ex 15:5
the *d* were congealed in the heart … Ex 15:8
*d* that spring out of valleys and … Deut 8:7
again from the *d* of the sea … Ps 68:22
up again from the *d* of the earth … Ps 71:20
the *d* also were troubled … Ps 77:16
them drink as out of the great *d* … Ps 78:15
so he led them through the *d* … Ps 106:9
they go down again to the *d* … Ps 107:26
Out of the *d* have I cried unto … Ps 130:1
his knowledge the *d* are broken up … Prov 3:20
When there were no *d*, I was … Prov 8:24
her guests are in the *d* of hell … Prov 9:18
that hath made the *d* of the sea a … Is 51:10
be broken by the seas in the *d* of … Eze 27:34
their sins into the *d* of the sea … Mic 7:19
have not known the *d* of Satan … Rev 2:24

**DEPUTED**
but there is no man *d* of the king … 2Sa 15:3

**DEPUTIES**
and to the lieutenants, and the *d* … Est 8:9
and the lieutenants, and the *d* … Est 9:3
the law is open, and there are *d* … Acts 19:38

**DEPUTY**
a *d* was king … 1Kin 22:47
was with the *d* of the country … Acts 13:7
to turn away the *d* from the faith … Acts 13:8
Then the *d*, when he saw what was … Acts 13:12
when Gallio was the *d* of Achaia … Acts 18:12

**DERBE** (der'-by) *A south Galatian town.*
of it, and fled unto Lystra and *D* … Acts 14:6
he departed with Barnabas to *D* … Acts 14:20
Then came he to *D* and Lystra … Acts 16:1
and Gaius of *D*, and Timotheus … Acts 20:4

**DERIDE**
they shall *d* every strong hold … Hab 1:10

**DERIDED**
and they *d* him … Lk 16:14
the rulers also with them *d* him … Lk 23:35

**DERISION**
are younger than I have me in *d* … Job 30:1
the Lord shall have them in *d* … Ps 2:4
a *d* to them that are round about … Ps 44:13
shalt have all the heathen in *d* … Ps 59:8
*d* to them that are round about us … Ps 79:4
proud have had me greatly in *d* … Ps 119:51
I am in *d* daily, every one … Jer 20:7
made a reproach unto me, and a *d* … Jer 20:8
vomit, and he also shall be in *d* … Jer 48:26
For was not Israel a *d* unto thee … Jer 48:27
so shall Moab be a *d* and a … Jer 48:39
I was a *d* to all my people … Lam 3:14
be laughed to scorn and had in *d* … Eze 23:32
*d* to the residue of the heathen … Eze 36:4
this shall be their *d* in the land … Hos 7:16

**DESCEND**
and the border shall *d*, and shall … Num 34:11
or he shall *d* into battle … 1Sa 26:10
his glory shall not *d* after him … Ps 49:17
that rejoiceth, shall *d* into it … Is 5:14
with them that *d* into the pit … Eze 26:20
with them that *d* into the pit … Eze 31:16
of Israel *d* now from the cross … Mk 15:32
saw a vision, A certain vessel *d* … Acts 11:5
Who shall *d* into the deep … Rom 10:7
shall *d* from heaven with a shout … 1Th 4:16

**DESCENDED**
the LORD *d* upon it in fire … Ex 19:18
tabernacle, the cloudy pillar *d* … Ex 33:9
the LORD *d* in the cloud, and stood … Ex 34:5
the brook that *d* out of the mount … Deut 9:21
*d* from the mountain, and passed … Josh 2:23
the coast *d* unto the river Kanah, … Josh 17:9
the border *d* to Ataroth-adar, … Josh 18:13
*d* to the valley of Hinnom, to the … Josh 18:16
on the south, and *d* to En-rogel, … Josh 18:16
*d* to the stone of Bohan the son … Josh 18:17
as the dew that *d* upon the … Ps 133:3
ascended up into heaven, or *d* … Prov 30:4
And the rain *d*, and the floods came … Mt 7:25
And the rain *d*, and the floods came … Mt 7:27
angel of the Lord *d* from heaven … Mt 28:2
the Holy Ghost *d* in a bodily … Lk 3:22
the high priest *d* with the elders … Acts 24:1
what is it but that he also *d* … Eph 4:9
He that *d* is the same also that … Eph 4:10

**DESCENDETH**
This wisdom *d* not from above, but … Jas 3:15

**DESCENDING**
of God ascending and *d* on it … Gen 28:12
the Spirit of God *d* like a dove … Mt 3:16
the Spirit like a dove *d* upon him … Mk 1:10
I saw the Spirit *d* from heaven … Jn 1:32
whom thou shalt see the Spirit *d* … Jn 1:33
and *d* upon the Son of man … Jn 1:51
and a certain vessel *d* unto him … Acts 10:11
*d* out of heaven from God, … Rev 21:10

**DESCENT**
even now at the *d* of the mount of … Lk 19:37
father, without mother, without *d* … Heb 7:3
But he whose *d* is not counted … Heb 7:6

**DESCRIBE**
*d* it according to the inheritance … Josh 18:4
Ye shall therefore *d* the land … Josh 18:6
them that went to *d* the land … Josh 18:8
*d* it, and come again to me, that I … Josh 18:8

**DESCRIBED**
*d* it by cities into seven parts … Josh 18:9
he *d* unto him the princes of … Judg 8:14

**DESCRIBETH**
Even as David also *d* the … Rom 4:6
For Moses *d* the righteousness … Rom 10:5

**DESCRIPTION**
bring the *d* hither to me, that I … Josh 18:6

**DESCRY**
house of Joseph sent to *d* Beth-el … Judg 1:23

**DESERT**
flock to the backside of the *d* … Ex 3:1
three days' journey into the *d* … Ex 5:3
and were come to the *d* of Sinai … Ex 19:2
from the *d* unto the river … Ex 23:31
into the *d* of Zin in the first … Num 20:1
my commandment in the *d* of Zin … Num 27:14
they removed from the *d* of Sinai … Num 33:16
He found him in a *d* land, and in … Deut 32:10
Also he built towers in the *d* … 2Chr 26:10
Behold, as wild asses in the *d* … Job 24:5
render to them their *d* … Ps 28:4
and grieve him in the *d* … Ps 78:40
I am like an owl of the *d* … Ps 102:6
and tempted God in the *d* … Ps 106:14
beasts of the *d* shall lie there … Is 13:21
The burden of the *d* of the sea … Is 21:1
so it cometh from the *d*, from a … Is 21:1
The wild beasts of the *d* shall … Is 34:14
the *d* shall rejoice, and blossom … Is 35:1
break out, and streams in the *d* … Is 35:6
make straight in the *d* a highway … Is 40:3
I will set in the *d* the fir tree … Is 41:19
wilderness, and rivers in the *d* … Is 43:19
wilderness, and rivers in the *d* … Is 43:20
her *d* like the garden of the LORD … Is 51:3
shall be like the heath in the *d* … Jer 17:6
people that dwell in the *d* … Jer 25:24
a wilderness, a dry land, and a *d* … Jer 50:12
the wild beasts of the *d* with the … Jer 50:39
country, and go down into the *d* … Eze 47:8
by ship into a *d* place apart … Mt 14:13
to him, saying, This is a *d* place … Mt 14:15
unto you, Behold, he is in the *d* … Mt 24:26
city, but was without in *d* places … Mk 1:45
yourselves apart into a *d* place … Mk 6:31
they departed into a *d* place by … Mk 6:32
him, and said, This is a *d* place … Mk 6:35
departed and went into a *d* place … Lk 4:42
a *d* place belonging to the city … Lk 9:10
for we are here in a *d* place … Lk 9:12
fathers did eat manna in the *d* … Jn 6:31
Jerusalem unto Gaza, which is *d* … Acts 8:26

**DESERTS**
when he led them through the *d* … Is 48:21
wilderness, through a land of *d* … Jer 2:6
to their *d* will I judge them … Eze 7:27
are like the foxes in the *d* … Eze 13:4
was in the *d* till the day of his … Lk 1:80
they wandered in *d*, and in … Heb 11:38

**DESERVE**
us less than our iniquities *d* … Ezr 9:13

**DESERVETH**
thee less than thine iniquity *d* … Job 11:6

**DESERVING**
according to the *d* of his hands … Judg 9:16

**DESIRABLE**
rulers, all of them *d* young men … Eze 23:6
horses, all of them *d* young men … Eze 23:12
all of them *d* young men, captains … Eze 23:23

**DESIRE**
thy *d* shall be to thy husband, and … Gen 3:16
And unto thee shall be his *d* … Gen 4:7
for that ye did *d* … Ex 10:11
neither shall any man *d* thy land … Ex 34:24
Neither shalt thou *d* thy … Deut 5:21
thou shalt not *d* the silver or … Deut 7:25
come with all the *d* of his mind … Deut 18:6
hast a *d* unto her, that thou … Deut 21:11
I would *d* a request of you, that … Judg 8:24
And on whom is all the *d* of Israel … 1Sa 9:20
the *d* of thy soul to come down … 1Sa 23:20
is all my salvation, and all my *d* … 2Sa 23:5
I *d* one small petition of thee … 1Kin 2:20
I will do all thy *d* concerning … 1Kin 5:8
and thou shalt accomplish my *d* … 1Kin 5:9
fir trees according to all his *d* … 1Kin 5:10
all Solomon's *d* which he was … 1Kin 9:1
with gold, according to all his *d* … 1Kin 9:11
unto the queen of Sheba all her *d* … 1Kin 10:13
said, Did I *d* a son of my lord … 2Kin 4:28
to the queen of Sheba all her *d* … 2Chr 9:12
and sought him with their whole *d* … 2Chr 15:15
servants, who *d* to fear thy name … Neh 1:11
and I *d* to reason with God … Job 13:3
thou wilt have a *d* to the work of … Job 14:15
for we *d* not the knowledge of thy … Job 21:14
withheld the poor from their *d* … Job 31:16
behold, my *d* is, that the … Job 31:35
speak, for I *d* to justify thee … Job 33:32
My *d* is that Job may be tried … Job 34:36
*D* not the night, when people are … Job 36:20
wicked boasteth of his heart's *d* … Ps 10:3
hast heard the *d* of the humble … Ps 10:17
Thou hast given him his heart's *d* … Ps 21:2

D

Lord, all my *d* is before thee ..... Ps 38:9
and offering thou didst not *d* ..... Ps 40:6
the king greatly *d* thy beauty ..... Ps 45:11
hath seen his *d* upon mine enemies ..... Ps 54:7
let me see my *d* upon mine enemies ..... Ps 59:10
put to confusion, that *d* my hurt ..... Ps 70:2
upon earth that I *d* beside thee ..... Ps 73:25
for he gave them their own *d* ..... Ps 78:29
shall see my *d* on mine enemies ..... Ps 92:11
mine ears shall hear my *d* of the ..... Ps 92:11
he see his *d* upon his enemies ..... Ps 112:8
the *d* of the wicked shall perish ..... Ps 112:10
I see my *d* upon them that hate me ..... Ps 118:7
satisfiest the *d* of every living ..... Ps 145:16
He will fulfil the *d* of them that ..... Ps 145:19
all the things thou canst *d* are ..... Prov 3:15
but the *d* of the righteous shall ..... Prov 10:24
The *d* of the righteous is only ..... Prov 11:23
heart sick, but when the *d* cometh ..... Prov 13:12
The *d* accomplished is sweet to ..... Prov 13:19
Through *d* a man, having separated ..... Prov 18:1
The *d* of a man is his kindness ..... Prov 19:22
The *d* of the slothful killeth him ..... Prov 21:25
neither *d* thou his dainty meats ..... Prov 23:6
neither *d* to be with them ..... Prov 24:1
eyes than the wandering of the *d* ..... Eccl 6:9
be a burden, and *d* shall fail ..... Eccl 12:5
beloved's, and his *d* is toward me ..... Song 7:10
the *d* of our soul is to thy name, ..... Is 26:8
is no beauty that we should *d* him ..... Is 53:2
land whereunto they *d* to return ..... Jer 22:27
in the place whither ye *d* to go ..... Jer 42:22
have a *d* to return to dwell there ..... Jer 44:14
I take away from thee the *d* of ..... Eze 24:16
the *d* of your eyes, and that which ..... Eze 24:21
the *d* of their eyes, and that ..... Eze 24:25
That they would *d* mercies of the ..... Dan 2:18
nor the *d* of women, nor regard ..... Dan 11:37
It is in my *d* that I should ..... Hos 10:10
Woe unto you that *d* the day of ..... Amos 5:18
he uttereth his mischievous *d* ..... Mic 7:3
home, who enlargeth his *d* as hell ..... Hab 2:5
the *d* of all nations shall come ..... Hag 2:7
If any man *d* to be first, the ..... Mk 9:35
do for us whatsoever we shall *d* ..... Mk 10:35
unto you, What things soever ye *d* ..... Mk 11:24
*d* him to do as he had ever done ..... Mk 15:8
when ye shall *d* to see one of the ..... Lk 17:22
which *d* to walk in long robes, and ..... Lk 20:46
With *d* I have desired to eat this ..... Lk 22:15
The Jews have agreed to *d* thee ..... Acts 23:20
But we *d* to hear of thee what ..... Acts 28:22
Brethren, my heart's *d* and prayer ..... Rom 10:1
having a great *d* these many years ..... Rom 15:23
*d* spiritual gifts, but rather ..... 1Cor 14:1
when he told us your earnest *d* ..... 2Cor 7:7
what fear, yea, what vehement *d* ..... 2Cor 7:11
from them which *d* occasion ..... 2Cor 11:12
For though I would *d* to glory ..... 2Cor 12:6
whereunto ye *d* again to be in ..... Gal 4:9
I *d* to be present with you now, ..... Gal 4:20
ye that *d* to be under the law, do ..... Gal 4:21
As many as *d* to make a fair shew ..... Gal 6:12
but *d* to have you circumcised, ..... Gal 6:13
Wherefore I *d* that ye faint not ..... Eph 3:13
having a *d* to depart, and to be ..... Phil 1:23
Not because I *d* a gift ..... Phil 4:17
but I *d* fruit that may abound to ..... Phil 4:17
to *d* that ye might be filled with ..... Col 1:9
to see your face with great *d* ..... 1Th 2:17
If a man *d* the office of a bishop ..... 1Ti 3:1
we *d* that every one of you do ..... Heb 6:11
But now they *d* a better country, ..... Heb 11:16
*d* to have, and cannot obtain ..... Jas 4:2
things the angels *d* to look into ..... 1Pet 1:12
*d* the sincere milk of the word, ..... 1Pet 2:2
shall *d* to die, and death shall ..... Rev 9:6

## DESIRED

a tree to be *d* to make one wise, ..... Gen 3:6
ye have chosen, and whom ye have *d*. 1Sa 12:13
that which Solomon *d* to build in ..... 1Kin 9:19
all that Solomon *d* to build in ..... 2Chr 8:6
And he *d* many wives ..... 2Chr 11:23
and departed without being *d* ..... 2Chr 21:20
whatsoever she *d* was given her to ..... Est 2:13
shall not save of that which he *d* ..... Job 20:20
More to be *d* are they than gold, ..... Ps 19:10
One thing have I *d* of the LORD ..... Ps 27:4
bringeth them unto their *d* haven ..... Ps 107:30
he hath *d* it for his habitation ..... Ps 132:13
for I have *d* it ..... Ps 132:14
all the things that may be *d* are ..... Prov 8:11
There is treasure to be *d* ..... Prov 21:20
mine eyes *d* I kept not from them ..... Eccl 2:10
of the oaks which ye have *d* ..... Is 1:29
soul have I *d* thee in the night ..... Is 26:9
neither have I *d* the woeful day ..... Jer 17:16
*d* of the king that he would give ..... Dan 2:16
unto me now what we *d* of thee ..... Dan 2:23
For I *d* mercy, and not sacrifice ..... Hos 6:6
my soul *d* the firstripe fruit ..... Mic 7:1
gather together, O nation not *d* ..... Zeph 2:1
righteous men have *d* to see those ..... Mt 13:17
tempting *d* him that he would shew ..... Mt 16:1
one prisoner, whomsoever they *d* ..... Mk 15:6
one of the Pharisees *d* him that ..... Lk 7:36
And he *d* to see him ..... Lk 9:9
kings have *d* to see those things ..... Lk 10:24
With desire I have *d* to eat this ..... Lk 22:15
Satan hath *d* to have you, that he ..... Lk 22:31
cast into prison, whom they had *d* ..... Lk 23:25
*d* him, saying, Sir, we would see ..... Jn 12:21
*d* a murderer to be granted unto ..... Acts 3:14
*d* to find a tabernacle for the ..... Acts 7:46
he *d* Philip that he would come up ..... Acts 8:31
*d* of him letters to Damascus to ..... Acts 9:2
chamberlain their friend, *d* peace ..... Acts 12:20
*d* to hear the word of God ..... Acts 13:7
And afterward they *d* a king ..... Acts 13:21
yet *d* they Pilate that he should ..... Acts 13:28
*d* them to depart out of the city ..... Acts 16:39
When they *d* him to tarry longer ..... Acts 18:20
*d* favour against him, that he ..... Acts 25:3
were *d* to tarry with them seven ..... Acts 28:14
I greatly *d* him to come unto you ..... 1Cor 16:12
Insomuch that we *d* Titus, that as ..... 2Cor 8:6
I *d* Titus, and with him I sent a ..... 2Cor 12:18
the petitions that we *d* of him ..... 1Jn 5:15

## DESIREDST

According to all that thou *d* of ..... Deut 18:16
all that debt, because thou *d* me ..... Mt 18:32

## DESIRES

give thee the *d* of thine heart ..... Ps 37:4
not, O LORD, the *d* of the wicked ..... Ps 140:8
fulfilling the *d* of the flesh ..... Eph 2:3

## DESIREST

thou *d* truth in the inward parts ..... Ps 51:6
For thou *d* not sacrifice ..... Ps 51:16

## DESIRETH

or for whatsoever thy soul *d* ..... Deut 14:26
then take as much as thy soul *d* ..... 1Sa 2:16
The king *d* not any dowry, but an ..... 1Sa 18:25
unto David, Whatsoever thy soul *d* ..... 1Sa 20:4
reign over all that thine heart *d* ..... 2Sa 3:21
according to all that thy soul *d* ..... 1Kin 11:37
a servant earnestly *d* the shadow ..... Job 7:2
And what his soul *d*, even that he ..... Job 23:13
What man is he that *d* life ..... Ps 34:12
the hill which God *d* to dwell in ..... Ps 68:16
The wicked *d* the net of evil men ..... Prov 12:12
The soul of the sluggard *d* ..... Prov 13:4
The soul of the wicked *d* evil ..... Prov 21:10
for his soul of all that he *d* ..... Eccl 6:2
drunk old wine straightway *d* new ..... Lk 5:39
and *d* conditions of peace ..... Lk 14:32
of a bishop, he *d* a good work ..... 1Ti 3:1

## DESIRING

without, *d* to speak with him ..... Mt 12:46
without, *d* to speak with thee ..... Mt 12:47
him, and *d* a certain thing of him ..... Mt 20:20
stand without, *d* to see thee ..... Lk 8:20
*d* to be fed with the crumbs which ..... Lk 16:21
*d* him that he would not delay to ..... Acts 9:38
*d* him that he would not adventure ..... Acts 19:31
*d* to have judgment against him ..... Acts 25:15
earnestly *d* to be clothed upon ..... 2Cor 5:2
*d* greatly to see us, as we also ..... 1Th 3:6
*D* to be teachers of the law ..... 1Ti 1:7
Greatly *d* to see thee, being ..... 2Ti 1:4

## DESIROUS

Be not *d* of his dainties ..... Prov 23:3
for he was *d* to see him of a long ..... Lk 23:8
knew that they were *d* to ask him ..... Jn 16:19
a garrison, *d* to apprehend me ..... 2Cor 11:32
Let us not be *d* of vain glory ..... Gal 5:26
So being affectionately *d* of you ..... 1Th 2:8

## DESOLATE

not die, that the land be not *d* ..... Gen 47:19
lest the land become *d*, and the ..... Ex 23:29
and your high ways shall be *d* ..... Lev 26:22
and your land shall be *d*, and your ..... Lev 26:33
sabbaths, as long as it lieth *d* ..... Lev 26:34
long as it lieth *d* it shall rest ..... Lev 26:35
while she lieth *d* without them ..... Lev 26:43
So Tamar remained *d* in her ..... 2Sa 13:20
as she lay *d* she kept sabbath ..... 2Chr 36:21
earth, which built *d* places for ..... Job 3:14
And he dwelleth in *d* cities ..... Job 15:28
of hypocrites shall be *d*, and fire ..... Job 15:34
thou hast made *d* all my company ..... Job 16:7
the wilderness in former time *d* ..... Job 30:3
To satisfy the *d* and waste ground ..... Job 38:27
for I am *d* and afflicted ..... Ps 25:16
hate the righteous shall be *d* ..... Ps 34:21
them that trust in him shall be *d* ..... Ps 34:22
Let them be *d* for a reward of ..... Ps 40:15
Let their habitation be *d* ..... Ps 69:25
bread also out of their *d* places ..... Ps 109:10
my heart within me is *d* ..... Ps 143:4
Your country is *d*, your cities ..... Is 1:7
it in your presence, and it is *d* ..... Is 1:7
she being *d* shall sit upon the ..... Is 3:26
Of a truth many houses shall be *d* ..... Is 5:9
man, and the land be utterly *d* ..... Is 6:11
rest all of them in the *d* valleys ..... Is 7:19
fierce anger, to lay the land *d* ..... Is 13:9
shall cry in their *d* houses ..... Is 13:22
the waters of Nimrim shall be *d* ..... Is 15:6
and they that dwell therein are *d* ..... Is 24:6
Yet the defenced city shall be *d* ..... Is 27:10
cause to inherit the *d* heritages ..... Is 49:8
thy *d* places, and the land of thy ..... Is 49:19
I have lost my children, and am *d* ..... Is 49:21
of the *d* than the children of the ..... Is 54:1
make the *d* cities to be inhabited ..... Is 54:3
we are in *d* places as dead men ..... Is 59:10
thy land any more be termed *D* ..... Is 62:4
be horribly afraid, be ye very *d* ..... Jer 2:12
from his place to make thy land *d* ..... Jer 4:7
said, The whole land shall be *d* ..... Jer 4:27
lest I make thee *d*, a land not ..... Jer 6:8
for the land shall be *d* ..... Jer 7:34
I will make the cities of Judah *d* ..... Jer 9:11
to make the cities of Judah *d* ..... Jer 10:22
and have made his habitation *d* ..... Jer 10:25
pleasant portion a *d* wilderness ..... Jer 12:10
They have made it *d* ..... Jer 12:11
being *d* it mourneth unto me ..... Jer 12:11
the whole land is made *d*, because ..... Jer 12:11
To make their land *d*, and a ..... Jer 18:16
And I will make this city *d* ..... Jer 19:8
for their land is *d* because of ..... Jer 25:38
this city shall be *d* without an ..... Jer 26:9
It is *d* without man or beast ..... Jer 32:43
ye say shall be *d* without man ..... Jer 33:10
streets of Jerusalem, that are *d* ..... Jer 33:10
which is *d* without man and without ..... Jer 33:12
and they are wasted and *d*, as at ..... Jer 44:6
waste and *d* without an inhabitant ..... Jer 46:19
for the cities thereof shall be *d* ..... Jer 48:9
waters also of Nimrim shall be *d* ..... Jer 48:34
and it shall be a *d* heap, and her ..... Jer 49:2
their habitations *d* with them ..... Jer 49:20
her, which shall make her land *d* ..... Jer 50:3
but it shall be wholly *d* ..... Jer 50:13
make their habitation *d* with them ..... Jer 50:45
but thou shalt be *d* for ever ..... Jer 51:26
but that it shall be *d* for ever ..... Jer 51:62
all her gates are *d* ..... Lam 1:4
he hath made me *d* and faint all ..... Lam 1:13
my children are *d*, because the ..... Lam 1:16
he hath made me *d* ..... Lam 3:11
delicately are *d* in the streets ..... Lam 4:5
the mountain of Zion, which is *d* ..... Lam 5:18
And your altars shall be *d* ..... Eze 6:4
and the high places shall be *d* ..... Eze 6:6
may be laid waste and made *d* ..... Eze 6:6
upon them, and make the land *d* ..... Eze 6:14
more *d* than the wilderness toward ..... Eze 6:14
that her land may be *d* from all ..... Eze 12:19
waste, and the land shall be *d* ..... Eze 12:20
and they spoil it, so that it be *d* ..... Eze 14:15
but the land shall be *d* ..... Eze 14:16
And I will make the land *d* ..... Eze 15:8
And he knew their *d* palaces ..... Eze 19:7
and the land was *d*, and the fulness ..... Eze 19:7
womb, that I might make them *d* ..... Eze 20:26
the land of Israel, when it was *d* ..... Eze 25:3
and I will make it *d* from Teman ..... Eze 25:13
When I shall make thee a *d* city ..... Eze 26:19
of the earth, in places *d* of old ..... Eze 26:20
And the land of Egypt shall be *d* ..... Eze 29:9
land of Egypt utterly waste and *d* ..... Eze 29:10
*d* in the midst of the countries ..... Eze 29:12
midst of the countries that are *d* ..... Eze 29:12
laid waste shall be *d* forty years ..... Eze 29:12
they shall be *d* in the midst of ..... Eze 30:7
midst of the countries that are *d* ..... Eze 30:7
And I will make Pathros *d*, and will ..... Eze 30:14
I shall make the land of Egypt *d* ..... Eze 32:15
For I will lay the land most *d* ..... Eze 33:28
mountains of Israel shall be *d* ..... Eze 33:28
land most *d* because of all their ..... Eze 33:29
thee, and I will make thee most *d* ..... Eze 35:3
cities waste, and thou shalt be *d* ..... Eze 35:4
will I make mount Seir most *d* ..... Eze 35:7
Israel, saying, They are laid *d* ..... Eze 35:12
rejoiceth, I will make thee *d* ..... Eze 35:14
house of Israel, because it was *d* ..... Eze 35:15
thou shalt be *d*, O mount Seir, and ..... Eze 35:15
Because they have made you *d* ..... Eze 36:3
to the valleys, to the *d* wastes ..... Eze 36:4
the *d* land shall be tilled, ..... Eze 36:34
whereas it lay *d* in the sight of ..... Eze 36:34
This land that was *d* is become ..... Eze 36:35
and the waste and *d* and ruined ..... Eze 36:35
places, and plant that that was *d* ..... Eze 36:36
to turn thine hand upon the *d* ..... Eze 38:12
upon thy sanctuary that is *d* ..... Dan 9:17
abominations he shall make it *d* ..... Dan 9:27
shall be poured upon the *d* ..... Dan 9:27
the abomination that maketh *d* ..... Dan 11:31
abomination that maketh *d* set up ..... Dan 12:11
Ephraim shall be *d* in the day of ..... Hos 5:9
Samaria shall become *d* ..... Hos 13:16
clods, the garners are laid *d* ..... Joel 1:17
the flocks of sheep are made *d* ..... Joel 1:18
and behind them a *d* wilderness ..... Joel 2:3
drive him into a land barren and *d* ..... Joel 2:20
and Edom shall be a *d* wilderness ..... Joel 3:19
high places of Isaac shall be *d* ..... Amos 7:9
the idols thereof will I lay *d* ..... Mic 1:7
in making thee *d* because of thy ..... Mic 6:13
the land shall be *d* because of ..... Mic 7:13
their towers are *d* ..... Zeph 3:6
Thus the land was *d* after them ..... Zec 7:14
for they laid the pleasant land *d* ..... Zec 7:14
will return and build the *d* places ..... Mal 1:4
your house is left unto you *d* ..... Mt 23:38
your house is left unto you *d* ..... Lk 13:35
Psalms, Let his habitation be *d* ..... Acts 1:20
for the *d* hath many more children ..... Gal 4:27
she that is a widow indeed, and *d* ..... 1Ti 5:5
the whore, and shall make her *d* ..... Rev 17:16
for in one hour is she made *d* ..... Rev 18:19

**DESOLATION**
and bring your sanctuaries unto *d* Lev 26:31
And I will bring the land into *d* Lev 26:32
for ever, even a *d* unto this day Josh 8:28
that they should become a *d* 2Kin 22:19
who therefore gave them up to *d* 2Chr 30:7
in the *d* they rolled themselves Job 30:14
How are they brought into *d* Ps 73:19
When your fear cometh as *d* Prov 1:27
neither of the *d* of the wicked Prov 3:25
in the *d* which shall come from Is 10:3
and there shall be *d* Is 17:9
In the city is left *d*, and the Is 24:12
*d* shall come upon thee suddenly, Is 47:11
*d*, and destruction, and the famine, Is 51:19
is a wilderness, Jerusalem a *d* Is 64:10
that this house shall become a *d* Jer 22:5
And this whole land shall be a *d* Jer 25:11
princes thereof, to make them a *d* Jer 25:18
Judah a *d* without an inhabitant Jer 34:22
and, behold, this day they are a *d* Jer 44:2
therefore is your land a *d* Jer 44:22
that Bozrah shall become a *d* Jer 49:13
Also Edom shall be a *d* Jer 49:17
for dragons, and a *d* for ever Jer 49:33
become a *d* among the nations Jer 50:23
Babylon a *d* without an inhabitant Jer 51:29
Her cities are a *d*, a dry land, Jer 51:43
and a snare is come upon us, *d* Lam 3:47
prince shall be clothed with *d* Eze 7:27
with the cup of astonishment and *d* Eze 23:33
and the transgression of *d* Dan 8:13
he daily increaseth lies and *d* Hos 12:1
Egypt shall be a *d*, and Edom shall Joel 3:19
that I should make thee a *d* Mic 6:16
a booty, and their houses a *d* Zeph 1:13
distress, a day of wasteness and *d* Zeph 1:15
be forsaken, and Ashkelon a *d* Zeph 2:4
and saltpits, and a perpetual *d* Zeph 2:9
and will make Nineveh a *d*, and dry Zeph 2:13
*d* shall be in the thresholds Zeph 2:14
how is she become a *d*, a place Zeph 2:15
against itself is brought to *d* Mt 12:25
shall see the abomination of *d* Mt 24:15
ye shall see the abomination of *d* Mk 13:14
against itself is brought to *d* Lk 11:17
know that the *d* thereof is nigh Lk 21:20

**DESOLATIONS**
God, and to repair the *d* thereof Ezr 9:9
what *d* he hath made in the earth Ps 46:8
up thy feet unto the perpetual *d* Ps 74:3
they shall raise up the former *d* Is 61:4
the *d* of many generations Is 61:4
and an hissing, and perpetual *d* Jer 25:9
and will make it perpetual *d* Jer 25:12
I will make thee perpetual *d* Eze 35:9
years in the *d* of Jerusalem Dan 9:2
open thine eyes, and behold our *d* Dan 9:18
end of the war *d* are determined Dan 9:26

**DESPAIR**
and Saul shall *d* of me, to seek me 1Sa 27:1
*d* of all the labour which I took Eccl 2:20
we are perplexed, but not in *d* 2Cor 4:8

**DESPAIRED**
insomuch that we *d* even of life 2Cor 1:8

**DESPERATE**
and the speeches of one that is *d* Job 6:26
the day of grief and of *d* sorrow Is 17:11

**DESPERATELY**
above all things, and *d* wicked Jer 17:9

**DESPISE**
And if ye shall *d* my statutes Lev 26:15
they that *d* me shall be lightly 1Sa 2:30
why then did ye *d* us, that our 2Sa 19:43
so that they shall *d* their Est 1:17
therefore *d* not thou the Job 5:17
I would *d* my life Job 9:21
that thou shouldest *d* the work of Job 10:3
If I did *d* the cause of my Job 31:13
heart, O God, thou wilt not *d* Ps 51:17
awakest, thou shalt *d* their image Ps 73:20
destitute, and not *d* their prayer Ps 102:17
but fools *d* wisdom and instruction Prov 1:7
*d* not the chastening of the LORD Prov 3:11
Men do not *d* a thief, if he steal Prov 6:30
for he will *d* the wisdom of thy Prov 23:9
*d* not thy mother when she is old Prov 23:22
of Israel, Because ye *d* this word Is 30:12
thy lovers will *d* thee, they will Jer 4:30
say still unto them that *d* me Jer 23:17
all that honoured her *d* her Lam 1:8
which *d* thee round about Eze 16:57
that *d* them round about them Eze 28:26
I *d* your feast days, and I will Amos 5:21
you, O priests, that *d* my name Mal 1:6
hold to the one, and *d* the other Mt 6:24
Take heed that ye *d* not one of Mt 18:10
hold to the one, and *d* the other Lk 16:13
that eateth *d* him that eateth not Rom 14:3
or *d* ye the church of God, and 1Cor 11:22
Let no man therefore *d* him 1Cor 16:11
*D* not prophesyings 1Th 5:20
Let no man *d* thy youth 1Ti 4:12
masters, let them not *d* them 1Ti 6:2
Let no man *d* thee Titus 2:15
*d* not thou the chastening of the Heb 12:5
of uncleanness, and *d* government 2Pet 2:10
*d* dominion, and speak evil of Jude 8

**DESPISED**
her mistress was *d* in her eyes Gen 16:4
conceived, I was *d* in her eyes Gen 16:5
thus Esau *d* his birthright Gen 25:34
even because they *d* my judgments Lev 26:43
because that ye have *d* the LORD Num 11:20
know the land which ye have *d* Num 14:31
Because he hath *d* the word of the Num 15:31
this the people that thou hast *d* Judg 9:38
And they *d* him, and brought him no 1Sa 10:27
and she *d* him in her heart 2Sa 6:16
Wherefore hast thou *d* the 2Sa 12:9
because thou hast *d* me, and hast 2Sa 12:10
the daughter of Zion hath *d* thee 2Kin 19:21
and she *d* him in her heart 1Chr 15:29
*d* his words, and misused his 2Chr 36:16
*d* us, and said, What is this thing Neh 2:19
for we are *d* Neh 4:4
*d* in the thought of him that is Job 12:5
Yea, young children *d* me Job 19:18
of men, and *d* of the people Ps 22:6
For he hath not *d* nor abhorred Ps 22:24
to shame, because God hath *d* them Ps 53:5
they *d* the pleasant land, they Ps 106:24
I am small and *d* Ps 119:141
they *d* all my reproof Prov 1:30
and my heart *d* reproof Prov 5:12
is of a perverse heart shall be *d* Prov 12:8
He that is *d*, and hath a servant, Prov 12:9
the poor man's wisdom is *d* Eccl 9:16
yea, I should not be *d* Song 8:1
*d* the word of the Holy One of Is 5:24
he hath *d* the cities, he Is 33:8
the daughter of Zion, hath *d* thee Is 37:22
He is *d* and rejected of men Is 53:3
he was *d*, and we esteemed him not Is 53:3
all they that *d* thee shall bow Is 60:14
this man Coniah a *d* broken idol Jer 22:28
thus they have *d* my people Jer 33:24
and *d* among men Jer 49:15
hath *d* in the indignation of his Lam 2:6
which hast *d* the oath in breaking Eze 16:59
made him king, whose oath he *d* Eze 17:16
Seeing he *d* the oath by breaking Eze 17:18
surely mine oath that he hath *d* Eze 17:19
they *d* my judgments, which if a Eze 20:13
Because they *d* my judgments Eze 20:16
but had *d* my statutes, and had Eze 20:24
Thou hast *d* mine holy things, and Eze 22:8
are round about them, that *d* them Eze 28:24
because they have *d* the law of Amos 2:4
thou art greatly *d* Obad 2
For who hath *d* the day of small Zec 4:10
say, Wherein have we *d* thy name Mal 1:6
they were righteous, and *d* others Lk 18:9
great goddess Diana should be *d* Acts 19:27
the world, and things which are *d* 1Cor 1:28
ye are honourable, but we are *d* 1Cor 4:10
which was in my flesh ye *d* not Gal 4:14
He that *d* Moses' law died without Heb 10:28
But ye have *d* the poor Jas 2:6

**DESPISERS**
Behold, ye *d*, and wonder, and Acts 13:41
*d* of those that are good, 2Ti 3:3

**DESPISEST**
Or *d* thou the riches of his Rom 2:4

**DESPISETH**
God is mighty, and *d* not any Job 36:5
the poor, and *d* not his prisoners Ps 69:33
is void of wisdom *d* his neighbour Prov 11:12
Whoso *d* the word shall be Prov 13:13
is perverse in his ways *d* him Prov 14:2
He that *d* his neighbour sinneth Prov 14:21
A fool *d* his father's instruction Prov 15:5
but a foolish man *d* his mother Prov 15:20
instruction *d* his own soul Prov 15:32
but he that *d* his ways shall die Prov 19:16
*d* to obey his mother, the ravens Prov 30:17
he that *d* the gain of oppressions Is 33:15
his Holy One, to him whom man *d* Is 49:7
he that *d* you *d* me Lk 10:16
*d* me *d* him that sent me Lk 10:16
He therefore that *d*, *d* not man 1Th 4:8

**DESPISING**
*d* the shame, and is set down at Heb 12:2

**DESPITE**
thy *d* against the land of Israel Eze 25:6
hath done *d* unto the Spirit of Heb 10:29

**DESPITEFUL**
taken vengeance with a *d* heart Eze 25:15
with *d* minds, to cast it out for Eze 36:5
Backbiters, haters of God, *d* Rom 1:30

**DESPITEFULLY**
and pray for them which *d* use you Mt 5:44
and pray for them which *d* use you Lk 6:28
with their rulers, to use them *d* Acts 14:5

**DESTITUTE**
who hath not left *d* my master of Gen 24:27
will regard the prayer of the *d* Ps 102:17
leave not my soul *d* Ps 141:8
is joy to him that is *d* of wisdom Prov 15:21
the country shall be *d* of that Eze 32:15
*d* of the truth, supposing that 1Ti 6:5
being *d*, afflicted, tormented Heb 11:37
be naked, and *d* of daily food, Jas 2:15

**DESTROY**
I will *d* man whom I have created Gen 6:7
I will *d* them with the earth Gen 6:13
to *d* all flesh, wherein is the Gen 6:17
that I have made will I *d* from Gen 7:4
more be a flood to *d* the earth Gen 9:11
become a flood to *d* all flesh Gen 9:15
Wilt thou also *d* the righteous Gen 18:23
wilt thou also *d* and not spare the Gen 18:24
wilt thou *d* all the city for lack Gen 18:28
forty and five, I will not *d* it Gen 18:28
I will not *d* it for twenty's sake Gen 18:31
I will not *d* it for ten's sake Gen 18:32
For we will *d* this place, because Gen 19:13
and the LORD hath sent us to *d* it Gen 19:13
for the LORD will *d* this city Gen 19:14
to *d* the frogs from thee and thy Ex 8:9
shall not be upon you to *d* you Ex 12:13
my sword, my hand shall *d* them Ex 15:9
will *d* all the people to whom Ex 23:27
But ye shall *d* their altars Ex 34:13
the same soul will I *d* from among Lev 23:30
*d* your cattle, and make you few in Lev 26:22
I will *d* your high places, and cut Lev 26:30
to *d* them utterly, and to break my Lev 26:44
I will utterly *d* their cities Num 21:2
*d* all the children of Sheth Num 24:17
shall *d* him that remaineth of the Num 24:19
ye shall *d* all this people Num 32:15
*d* all their pictures, and *d* Num 33:52
the hand of the Amorites, to *d* us Deut 1:27
to *d* them from among the host, Deut 2:15
not forsake thee, neither *d* thee Deut 4:31
*d* thee from off the face of the Deut 6:15
smite them, and utterly *d* them Deut 7:2
against you, and *d* thee suddenly Deut 7:4
ye shall *d* their altars, and break Deut 7:5
hate him to their face, to *d* them Deut 7:10
shall *d* them with a mighty Deut 7:23
thou shalt *d* their name from Deut 7:24
a consuming fire he shall *d* them Deut 9:3
*d* them quickly, as the LORD hath Deut 9:3
Let me alone, that I may *d* them Deut 9:14
was wroth against you to *d* you Deut 9:19
the LORD had said he would *d* you Deut 9:25
*d* not thy people and thine Deut 9:26
and the LORD would not *d* thee Deut 10:10
Ye shall utterly *d* all the places Deut 12:2
*d* the names of them out of that Deut 12:3
But thou shalt utterly *d* them Deut 20:17
thou shalt not *d* the trees Deut 20:19
not trees for meat, thou shalt *d* Deut 20:20
will rejoice over you to *d* you Deut 28:63
he will *d* these nations from Deut 31:3
shall *d* both the young man and the Deut 32:25
and shall say, *D* them Deut 33:27
the hand of the Amorites, to *d* us Josh 7:7
except ye *d* the accursed from Josh 7:12
to *d* all the inhabitants of the Josh 9:24
that he might *d* them utterly Josh 11:20
favour, but that he might *d* them Josh 11:20
to *d* the land wherein the Josh 22:33
entered into the land to *d* it Judg 6:5
do, Ye shall utterly *d* every male Judg 21:11
utterly *d* all that they have, and 1Sa 15:3
lest I *d* you with them 1Sa 15:6
good, and would not utterly *d* them 1Sa 15:9
utterly *d* the sinners the 1Sa 15:18
to *d* the city for my sake 1Sa 23:10
that thou wilt not *d* my name out 1Sa 24:21
David said to Abishai, *D* him not 1Sa 26:9
people in to *d* the king thy lord 1Sa 26:15
hand to *d* the LORD's anointed 2Sa 1:14
and we will *d* the heir also 2Sa 14:7
revengers of blood to *d* any more 2Sa 14:11
lest they *d* my son 2Sa 14:11
hand of the man that would *d* me 2Sa 14:16
thou seekest to *d* a city and a 2Sa 20:19
me, that I should swallow up or *d* 2Sa 20:20
that I might *d* them that hate me 2Sa 22:41
his hand upon Jerusalem to *d* it 2Sa 24:16
also were not able utterly to *d* 1Kin 9:21
to *d* it from off the face of the 1Kin 13:34
Thus did Zimri *d* all the house of 1Kin 16:12
Yet the LORD would not *d* Judah 2Kin 8:19
might *d* the worshippers of Baal 2Kin 10:19
and Jacob, and would not *d* them 2Kin 13:23
LORD against this place to *d* it 2Kin 18:25
Go up against this land, and *d* it 2Kin 18:25
sent them against Judah to *d* it 2Kin 24:2
an angel unto Jerusalem to *d* it 1Chr 21:15
therefore I will not *d* them 2Chr 12:7
he would not *d* him altogether 2Chr 12:12
Seir, utterly to slay and *d* them 2Chr 20:23
every one helped to *d* another 2Chr 20:23
would not *d* the house of David 2Chr 21:7
God hath determined to *d* thee 2Chr 25:16
is with me, that he *d* thee not 2Chr 35:21
name to dwell there *d* all kings Ezr 6:12
to *d* this house of God which is Ezr 6:12
to *d* all the Jews that were Est 3:6
all the king's provinces, to *d* Est 3:13
for the Jews, to *d* them Est 4:7
was given at Shushan to *d* them Est 4:8
which he wrote to *d* the Jews Est 8:5
and to stand for their life, to *d* Est 8:11
against the Jews to *d* them Est 9:24
to consume them, and to *d* them Est 9:24
him, to *d* him without cause Job 2:3

that it would please God to *d* me Job 6:9
If he *d* him from his place, then Job 8:18
yet thou dost *d* me Job 10:8
after my skin worms *d* this body Job 19:26
Thou shalt *d* them that speak Ps 5:6
*D* thou them, O God Ps 5:10
that I might *d* them that hate me Ps 18:40
fruit shalt thou *d* from the earth Ps 21:10
of his hands, he shall *d* them Ps 28:5
that seek after my soul to *d* it Ps 40:14
shall likewise *d* thee for ever Ps 52:5
*D*, O Lord, and divide their Ps 55:9
those that seek my soul, to *d* it Ps 63:9
they that would *d* me, being mine Ps 69:4
hearts, Let us *d* them together Ps 74:8
I will early *d* all the wicked of Ps 101:8
he said that he would *d* them Ps 106:23
his wrath, lest he should *d* them Ps 106:23
They did not *d* the nations Ps 106:34
name of the LORD will I *d* them Ps 118:10
name of the LORD I will *d* them Ps 118:11
name of the LORD I will *d* them Ps 118:12
wicked have waited for me to *d* me Ps 119:95
*d* all them that afflict my soul Ps 143:12
shoot out thine arrows, and *d* them Ps 144:6
but all the wicked will he *d* Ps 145:20
prosperity of fools shall *d* them Prov 1:32
of transgressors shall *d* them Prov 11:3
The LORD will *d* the house of the Prov 15:25
of the wicked shall *d* them Prov 21:7
*d* the work of thine hands Eccl 5:6
why shouldest thou *d* thyself Eccl 7:16
to err, and *d* the way of thy paths Is 3:12
but it is in his heart to *d* Is 10:7
nor *d* in all my holy mountain Is 11:9
the LORD shall utterly *d* the Is 11:15
indignation, to *d* the whole land Is 13:5
he shall *d* the sinners thereof Is 13:9
I will *d* the counsel thereof Is 19:3
to *d* the strong holds thereof Is 23:11
he will *d* in this mountain the Is 25:7
to *d* the poor with lying words Is 32:7
LORD against this land to *d* it Is 36:10
Go up against this land, and *d* it Is 36:10
I will *d* and devour at once Is 42:14
as if he were ready to *d* Is 51:13
and I have created the waster to *d* Is 54:16
cluster, and one saith, *D* it not Is 65:8
sakes, that I may not *d* them all Is 65:8
nor *d* in all my holy mountain Is 65:25
out, and to pull down, and to *d* Jer 1:10
Go ye up upon her walls, and *d* Jer 5:10
by night, and let us *d* her palaces Jer 6:5
Let us *d* the tree with the fruit Jer 11:19
*d* that nation, saith the LORD Jer 12:17
spare, nor have mercy, but *d* them Jer 13:14
of the earth, to devour and *d* Jer 15:3
my hand against thee, and *d* thee Jer 15:6
I will *d* my people, since they Jer 15:7
*d* them with double destruction Jer 17:18
up, and to pull down, and to *d* it Jer 18:7
Woe be unto the pastors that *d* Jer 23:1
about, and will utterly *d* them Jer 25:9
down, and to throw down, and to *d* Jer 31:28
*d* this land, and shall cause to Jer 36:29
I will *d* the city and the Jer 46:8
he shall *d* thy strong holds Jer 48:18
they will *d* till they have enough Jer 49:9
will *d* from thence the king and Jer 49:38
utterly *d* after them, saith the Jer 50:21
her up as heaps, and *d* her utterly Jer 50:26
*d* ye utterly all her host Jer 51:3
is against Babylon, to *d* it Jer 51:11
and with thee will I *d* kingdoms Jer 51:20
The LORD hath purposed to *d* the Lam 2:8
*d* them in anger from under the Lam 3:66
and which I will send to *d* you Eze 5:16
I will *d* your high places Eze 6:3
wilt thou *d* all the residue of Eze 9:8
will *d* him from the midst of my Eze 14:9
of brutish men, and skilful to *d* Eze 21:31
to *d* souls, to get dishonest gain Eze 22:27
the land, that I should not *d* it Eze 22:30
I will *d* thee Eze 25:7
to *d* it for the old hatred Eze 25:15
*d* the remnant of the sea coast Eze 25:16
they shall *d* the walls of Tyrus, Eze 26:4
walls, and *d* thy pleasant houses Eze 26:12
and I will *d* thee, O covering Eze 28:16
shall be brought to *d* the land Eze 30:11
I will also *d* the idols, and I Eze 30:13
I will *d* also all the beasts Eze 32:13
but I will *d* the fat and the Eze 34:16
I saw when I came to *d* the city Eze 43:3
commanded to *d* all the wise men Dan 2:12
to *d* the wise men of Babylon Dan 2:24
*D* not the wise men of Babylon Dan 2:24
Hew the tree down, and *d* it Dan 4:23
consume and to *d* it unto the end Dan 7:26
he shall *d* wonderfully, and shall Dan 8:24
shall *d* the mighty and the holy Dan 8:24
heart, and by peace shall *d* many Dan 8:25
that shall come shall *d* the city Dan 9:26
portion of his meat shall *d* him Dan 11:26
go forth with great fury to *d* Dan 11:44
I will *d* her vines and her fig Hos 2:12
the night, and I will *d* thy mother Hos 4:5
I will not return to *d* Ephraim Hos 11:9
I will *d* it from off the face of Amos 9:8
not utterly *d* the house of Jacob Amos 9:8
even *d* the wise men out of Edom, Obad 8
it is polluted, it shall *d* you Mic 2:10
of thee, and I will *d* thy chariots Mic 5:10
so will I *d* thy cities Mic 5:14
Philistines, I will even *d* thee Zeph 2:5
against the north, and *d* Assyria Zeph 2:13
I will *d* the strength of the Hag 2:22
that I will seek to *d* all the Zec 12:9
he shall not *d* the fruits of your Mal 3:11
seek the young child to *d* him Mt 2:13
not that I am come to *d* the law Mt 5:17
I am not come to *d*, but to fulfil Mt 5:17
him which is able to *d* both soul Mt 10:28
against him, how they might *d* him Mt 12:14
will miserably *d* those wicked men Mt 21:41
I am able to *d* the temple of God, Mt 26:61
should ask Barabbas, and *d* Jesus Mt 27:20
art thou come to *d* us Mk 1:24
against him, how they might *d* him Mk 3:6
and into the waters, to *d* him Mk 9:22
and sought how they might *d* him Mk 11:18
*d* the husbandmen, and will give Mk 12:9
I will *d* this temple that is made Mk 14:58
art thou come to *d* us Lk 4:34
to save life, or to *d* it Lk 6:9
man is not come to *d* men's lives Lk 9:56
of the people sought to *d* him Lk 19:47
*d* these husbandmen, and shall give Lk 20:16
*D* this temple, and in three days I Jn 2:19
for to steal, and to kill, and to *d* Jn 10:10
of Nazareth shall *d* this place Acts 6:14
*D* not him with thy meat, for whom Rom 14:15
For meat *d* not the work of God Rom 14:20
I will *d* the wisdom of the wise, 1Cor 1:19
temple of God, him shall God *d* 1Cor 3:17
but God shall *d* both it and them 1Cor 6:13
shall *d* with the brightness of 2Th 2:8
that through death he might *d* him Heb 2:14
who is able to save and to *d* Jas 4:12
that he might *d* the works of the 1Jn 3:8
*d* them which *d* the earth Rev 11:18

## DESTROYED

every living substance was *d* Gen 7:23
they were *d* from the earth Gen 7:23
where, before the LORD *d* Sodom Gen 13:10
when God *d* the cities of the Gen 19:29
and I shall be *d*, I and my house Gen 34:30
thou not yet that Egypt is *d* Ex 10:7
LORD only, he shall be utterly *d* Ex 22:20
and they utterly *d* them and their Num 21:3
*d* you in Seir, even unto Hormah Deut 1:44
when they had *d* them from before Deut 2:12
but the LORD *d* them before them Deut 2:21
when he *d* the Horims from before Deut 2:22
*d* them, and dwelt in their stead Deut 2:23
that time, and utterly *d* the men Deut 2:34
And we utterly *d* them, as we did Deut 3:6
God hath *d* them from among you Deut 4:3
upon it, but shall utterly be *d* Deut 4:26
hide themselves from thee, be *d* Deut 7:20
destruction, until they be *d* Deut 7:23
thee, until thou have *d* them Deut 7:24
was angry with you to have *d* you Deut 9:8
angry with Aaron to have *d* him Deut 9:20
how the LORD hath *d* them unto Deut 11:4
that they be *d* from before thee Deut 12:30
unto for to do, until thou be *d* Deut 28:20
down upon thee, until thou be *d* Deut 28:24
and overtake thee, till thou be *d* Deut 28:45
thy neck, until he have *d* thee Deut 28:48
of thy land, until thou be *d* Deut 28:51
thy sheep, until he have *d* thee Deut 28:51
bring upon thee, until thou be *d* Deut 28:61
unto the land of them, whom he *d* Deut 31:4
Sihon and Og, whom ye utterly *d* Josh 2:10
they utterly *d* all that was in Josh 6:21
until he had utterly *d* all the Josh 8:26
had taken Ai, and had utterly *d* it Josh 10:1
and the king thereof he utterly *d* Josh 10:28
therein he utterly *d* that day Josh 10:35
but *d* it utterly, and all the Josh 10:37
utterly *d* all the souls that were Josh 10:39
but utterly *d* all that breathed, Josh 10:40
the sword, and he utterly *d* them Josh 11:12
the sword, until they had *d* them Josh 11:14
Joshua *d* them utterly with their Josh 11:21
until he have *d* you from off this Josh 23:15
and I *d* them from before you Josh 24:8
Zephath, and utterly *d* it Judg 1:17
until they had *d* Jabin king of Judg 4:24
*d* the increase of the earth, till Judg 6:4
*d* down to the ground of the Judg 20:21
*d* down to the ground of the Judg 20:25
the children of Israel *d* of the Judg 20:35
they *d* in the midst of them Judg 20:42
the women are *d* out of Benjamin Judg 21:16
a tribe be not *d* out of Israel Judg 21:17
he *d* them, and smote them with 1Sa 5:6
utterly *d* all the people with the 1Sa 15:8
and refuse, that they *d* utterly 1Sa 15:9
and the rest we have utterly *d* 1Sa 15:15
have utterly *d* the Amalekites 1Sa 15:20
which should have been utterly *d* 1Sa 15:21
they *d* the children of Ammon, and 2Sa 11:1
be *d* from remaining in any of the 2Sa 21:5
pursued mine enemies, and *d* them 2Sa 22:38
to the angel that *d* the people 2Sa 24:16
Asa *d* her idol, and burnt it by 1Kin 15:13
that breathed, until he had *d* him 1Kin 15:29
in Samaria, till he had *d* him 2Kin 10:17
Thus Jehu *d* Baal out of Israel 2Kin 10:28
she arose and *d* all the seed royal 2Kin 11:1
for the king of Syria had *d* them 2Kin 13:7
them which my fathers have *d* 2Kin 19:12
of Assyria have *d* the nations 2Kin 19:17
therefore they have *d* them 2Kin 19:18
which Hezekiah his father had *d* 2Kin 21:3
*d* before the children of Israel 2Kin 21:9
*d* them utterly unto this day, and 1Chr 4:41
the land, whom God *d* before them 1Chr 5:25
And Joab smote Rabbah, and *d* it 1Chr 20:1
months to be *d* before thy foes 1Chr 21:12
evil, and said to the angel that *d* 1Chr 21:15
for they were *d* before the LORD, 2Chr 14:13
And nation was *d* of nation 2Chr 15:6
turned from them, and *d* them not 2Chr 20:10
*d* all the seed royal of the house 2Chr 22:10
*d* all the princes of the people 2Chr 24:23
until they had utterly *d* them all 2Chr 31:1
nations that my fathers utterly *d* 2Chr 32:14
whom the LORD had *d* before the 2Chr 33:9
which the kings of Judah had *d* 2Chr 34:11
*d* all the goodly vessels thereof 2Chr 36:19
for which cause was this city *d* Ezr 4:15
who *d* this house, and carried the Ezr 5:12
it be written that they may be *d* Est 3:9
and thy father's house shall be *d* Est 4:14
are sold, I and my people, to be *d* Est 7:4
Jews slew and *d* five hundred men Est 9:6
*d* five hundred men in Shushan the Est 9:12
They are *d* from morning to Job 4:20
He hath *d* me on every side, and I Job 19:10
in the night, so that they are *d* Job 34:25
thou hast *d* the wicked, thou hast Ps 9:5
and thou hast *d* cities Ps 9:6
If the foundations be *d*, what can Ps 11:3
transgressors shall be *d* together Ps 37:38
thou hast *d* all them that go a Ps 73:27
their iniquity, and *d* them not Ps 78:38
and frogs, which *d* them Ps 78:45
He *d* their vines with hail, and Ps 78:47
is that they shall be *d* for ever Ps 92:7
of Babylon, who art to be *d* Ps 137:8
despiseth the word shall be *d* Prov 13:13
a companion of fools shall be *d* Prov 13:20
is that is *d* for want of judgment Prov 13:23
his neck, shall suddenly be *d* Prov 29:1
they that are led of them are *d* Is 9:16
the yoke shall be *d* because of Is 10:27
and *d* the cities thereof Is 14:17
because thou hast *d* thy land Is 14:20
*d* them, and made all their memory Is 26:14
he hath utterly *d* them, he hath Is 34:2
them which my fathers have *d* Is 37:12
therefore they have *d* them Is 37:19
been cut off nor *d* from before me Is 48:19
Many pastors have *d* my vineyard Jer 12:10
for all thy lovers are *d* Jer 22:20
Moab is *d* Jer 48:4
perish, and the plain shall be *d* Jer 48:8
Moab shall be *d* from being a Jer 48:42
Babylon is suddenly fallen and *d* Jer 51:8
*d* out of her the great voice Jer 51:55
he hath *d* his strong holds, and Lam 2:5
he hath *d* his places of the Lam 2:6
he hath *d* and broken her bars Lam 2:9
and say to thee, How art thou *d* Eze 26:17
like the *d* in the midst of the Eze 27:32
when all her helpers shall be *d* Eze 30:8
the multitude thereof shall be *d* Eze 32:12
a kingdom, which shall never be *d* Dan 2:44
kingdom that which shall not be *d* Dan 6:26
beast was slain, and his body *d* Dan 7:11
kingdom that which shall not be *d* Dan 7:14
but within few days he shall be *d* Dan 11:20
My people are *d* for lack of Hos 4:6
the sin of Israel, shall be *d* Hos 10:8
O Israel, thou hast *d* thyself Hos 13:9
Yet *d* I the Amorite before them, Amos 2:9
yet I *d* his fruit from above, and Amos 2:9
their cities are *d*, so that there Zeph 3:6
*d* those murderers, and burned up Mt 22:7
and the flood came, and *d* them all Lk 17:27
from heaven, and *d* them all Lk 17:29
shall be *d* from among the people Acts 3:23
Is not this he that *d* them which Acts 9:21
when he had *d* seven nations in Acts 13:19
and her magnificence should be *d* Acts 19:27
that the body of sin might be *d* Rom 6:6
tempted, and were *d* of serpents 1Cor 10:9
and were *d* of the destroyer 1Cor 10:10
enemy that shall be *d* is death 1Cor 15:26
cast down, but not *d* 2Cor 4:9
the faith which once he *d* Gal 1:23
build again the things which I *d* Gal 2:18
lest he that *d* the firstborn Heb 11:28
beasts, made to be taken and *d* 2Pet 2:12
afterward *d* them that believed Jude 5
third part of the ships were *d* Rev 8:9

## DESTROYER

will not suffer the *d* to come in Ex 12:23
the *d* of our country, which slew Judg 16:24
in prosperity the *d* shall come Job 15:21
kept me from the paths of the *d* Ps 17:4
the same is the companion of a *d* Prov 28:24
the *d* of the Gentiles is on his Jer 4:7
and were destroyed of the *d* 1Cor 10:10

## DESTROYERS

the grave, and his life to the *d* Job 33:22
thy *d* and they that made thee Is 49:17

And I will prepare *d* against thee ... Jer 22:7
O ye *d* of mine heritage, because ... Jer 50:11

**DESTROYEST**
and thou *d* the hope of man ... Job 14:19
the LORD, which *d* all the earth ... Jer 51:25
Thou that *d* the temple, and ... Mt 27:40
thou that *d* the temple, and ... Mk 15:29

**DESTROYETH**
which the LORD *d* before your face ... Deut 8:20
He *d* the perfect and the wicked ... Job 9:22
increaseth the nations, and *d* them ... Job 12:23
he that doeth it *d* his own soul ... Prov 6:32
with his mouth *d* his neighbour ... Prov 11:9
thy ways to that which *d* kings ... Prov 31:3
and a gift *d* the heart ... Eccl 7:7
but one sinner *d* much good ... Eccl 9:18

**DESTROYING**
of Heshbon, utterly *d* the men ... Deut 3:6
*d* it utterly, and all that is ... Deut 13:15
edge of the sword, utterly *d* them ... Josh 11:11
to all lands, by *d* them utterly ... 2Kin 19:11
land, and the angel of the LORD *d* ... 1Chr 21:12
and as he was *d*, the LORD beheld, ... 1Chr 21:15
a *d* storm, as a flood of mighty ... Is 28:2
to all lands by *d* them utterly ... Is 37:11
your prophets, like a *d* lion ... Jer 2:30
that rise up against me, a *d* wind ... Jer 51:1
O *d* mountain, saith the LORD, ... Jer 51:25
not withdrawn his hand from *d* ... Lam 2:8
man with his *d* weapon in his hand ... Eze 9:1
mine eye spared them from *d* them ... Eze 20:17

**DESTRUCTION**
destroy them with a mighty *d* ... Deut 7:23
burning heat, and with bitter *d* ... Deut 32:24
the city with a very great *d* ... 1Sa 5:9
for there was a deadly *d* ... 1Sa 5:11
a man whom I appointed to utter *d* .. 1Kin 20:42
the death of his father to his *d* ... 2Chr 22:4
the *d* of Ahaziah was of God by ... 2Chr 22:7
his heart was lifted up to his *d* ... 2Chr 26:16
endure to see the *d* of my kindred ... Est 8:6
of the sword, and slaughter, and *d* ... Est 9:5
be afraid of *d* when it cometh ... Job 5:21
At *d* and famine thou shalt laugh ... Job 5:22
*d* shall be ready at his side ... Job 18:12
how oft cometh their *d* upon them ... Job 21:17
His eyes shall see his *d*, and he ... Job 21:20
is reserved to the day of *d* ... Job 21:30
before him, and *d* hath no covering ... Job 26:6
*D* and death say, We have heard the... Job 28:22
up against me the ways of their *d* ... Job 30:12
grave, though they cry in his *d* ... Job 30:24
Is not *d* to the wicked ... Job 31:3
it is a fire that consumeth to *d* ... Job 31:12
For *d* from God was a terror to me ... Job 31:23
at the *d* of him that hated me ... Job 31:29
Let *d* come upon him at unawares ... Ps 35:8
into that very *d* let him fall ... Ps 35:8
bring them down into the pit of *d* ... Ps 55:23
thou castedst them down into *d* ... Ps 73:18
or thy faithfulness in *d* ... Ps 88:11
Thou turnest man to *d* ... Ps 90:3
nor for the *d* that wasteth at ... Ps 91:6
Who redeemeth thy life from *d* ... Ps 103:4
your *d* cometh as a whirlwind ... Prov 1:27
mouth of the foolish is near *d* ... Prov 10:14
the *d* of the poor is their ... Prov 10:15
but *d* shall be to the workers of ... Prov 10:29
wide his lips shall have *d* ... Prov 13:3
of people is the *d* of the prince ... Prov 14:28
Hell and *d* are before the LORD ... Prov 15:11
Pride goeth before *d*, and an ... Prov 16:18
that exalteth his gate seeketh *d* ... Prov 17:19
A fool's mouth is his *d*, and his ... Prov 18:7
Before *d* the heart of man is ... Prov 18:12
but *d* shall be to the workers of ... Prov 21:15
For their heart studieth *d* ... Prov 24:2
Hell and *d* are never full ... Prov 27:20
of all such as are appointed to *d* ... Prov 31:8
the *d* of the transgressors and of ... Is 1:28
cease, and mine anger in their *d* ... Is 10:25
come as a *d* from the Almighty ... Is 13:6
will sweep it with the besom of *d* ... Is 14:23
they shall raise up a cry of *d* ... Is 15:5
shall be called, The city of *d* ... Is 19:18
and the gate is smitten with *d* ... Is 24:12
places, and the land of thy *d* ... Is 49:19
desolation, and *d*, and the famine, ... Is 51:19
wasting and *d* are in their paths ... Is 59:7
wasting nor *d* within thy borders ... Is 60:18
evil from the north, and a great *d* ... Jer 4:6
*D* upon *d* is cried ... Jer 4:20
out of the north, and great *d* ... Jer 6:1
and destroy them with double *d* ... Jer 17:18
a very fair heifer, but *d* cometh ... Jer 46:20
Horonaim, spoiling and great *d* ... Jer 48:3
the enemies have heard a cry of *d* ... Jer 48:5
is in the land, and of great *d* ... Jer 50:22
great *d* from the land of the ... Jer 51:54
for the *d* of the daughter of my ... Lam 2:11
is come upon us, desolation and *d* ... Lam 3:47
*d* of the daughter of my people ... Lam 3:48
they were their meat in the *d* of ... Lam 4:10
which shall be for their *d* ... Eze 5:16
*D* cometh; and they shall seek ... Eze 7:25
bring thy *d* among the nations ... Eze 32:9
fled from me: *d* unto them ... Hos 7:13
lo, they are gone because of *d* ... Hos 9:6
O grave, I will be thy *d* ... Hos 13:14
as a *d* from the Almighty shall it ... Joel 1:15
of Judah in the day of their *d* ... Obad 12
destroy you, even with a sore *d* ... Mic 2:10
and there shall be no more utter *d* ... Zec 14:11
is the way, that leadeth to *d* ... Mt 7:13
*D* and misery are in their ways ... Rom 3:16
the vessels of wrath fitted to *d* ... Rom 9:22
unto Satan for the *d* of the flesh ... 1Cor 5:5
edification, and not for your *d* ... 2Cor 10:8
me to edification, and not to *d* ... 2Cor 13:10
Whose end is *d*, whose God is ... Phil 3:19
then sudden *d* cometh upon them, ... 1Th 5:3
be punished with everlasting *d* ... 2Th 1:9
lusts, which drown men in *d* ... 1Ti 6:9
and bring upon themselves swift *d* ... 2Pet 2:1
scriptures, unto their own *d* ... 2Pet 3:16

**DESTRUCTIONS**
*d* are come to a perpetual end ... Ps 9:6
rescue my soul from their *d* ... Ps 35:17
and delivered them from their *d* ... Ps 107:20

**DETAIN**
LORD, I pray thee, let us *d* thee ... Judg 13:15
unto Manoah, Though thou *d* me ... Judg 13:16

**DETAINED**
there that day, *d* before the LORD ... 1Sa 21:7

**DETERMINATE**
being delivered by the *d* counsel ... Acts 2:23

**DETERMINATION**
for my *d* is to gather the nations ... Zeph 3:8

**DETERMINE**
and he shall pay as the judges *d* ... Ex 21:22

**DETERMINED**
be sure that evil is *d* by him ... 1Sa 20:7
*d* by my father to come upon thee ... 1Sa 20:9
Jonathan knew that it was *d* of ... 1Sa 20:33
for evil is *d* against our master, ... 1Sa 25:17
of Absalom this hath been *d* from ... 2Sa 13:32
Solomon *d* to build an house for ... 2Chr 2:1
that God hath *d* to destroy thee ... 2Chr 25:16
evil *d* against him by the king ... Est 7:7
Seeing his days are *d*, the number ... Job 14:5
shall make a consumption, even *d* ... Is 10:23
hosts, which he hath *d* against it ... Is 19:17
even *d* upon the whole earth ... Is 28:22
weeks are *d* upon thy people ... Dan 9:24
end of the war desolations are *d* ... Dan 9:26
that *d* shall be poured upon the ... Dan 9:27
for that that is *d* shall be done ... Dan 11:36
the Son of man goeth, as it was *d* ... Lk 22:22
when he was *d* to let him go ... Acts 3:13
thy counsel *d* before to be done ... Acts 4:28
*d* to send relief unto the ... Acts 11:29
they *d* that Paul and Barnabas, and ... Acts 15:2
Barnabas *d* to take with them John ... Acts 15:37
hath *d* the times before appointed ... Acts 17:26
it shall be *d* in a lawful ... Acts 19:39
For Paul had *d* to sail by Ephesus ... Acts 20:16
to Augustus, I have *d* to send him ... Acts 25:25
when it was *d* that we should sail ... Acts 27:1
For I *d* not to know any thing ... 1Cor 2:2
But I *d* this with myself, that I ... 2Cor 2:1
for I have *d* there to winter ... Titus 3:12

**DETEST**
but thou shalt utterly *d* it ... Deut 7:26

**DETESTABLE**
with the carcases of their *d* ... Jer 16:18
sanctuary with all thy *d* things ... Eze 5:11
of their *d* things therein ... Eze 7:20
away all the *d* things thereof ... Eze 11:18
after the heart of their *d* things ... Eze 11:21
idols, nor with their *d* things ... Eze 37:23

**DEUEL** (*de-oo'-el*) See REUEL. *Father of Eliasaph.*
Eliasaph the son of *D* ... Num 1:14
sixth day Eliasaph the son of *D* ... Num 7:42
offering of Eliasaph the son of *D* ... Num 7:47
of Gad was Eliasaph the son of *D* ... Num 10:20

**DEVICE**
to find out every *d* which shall ... 2Chr 2:14
his *d* that he had devised against ... Est 8:3
by letters that his wicked *d* ... Est 9:25
they imagined a mischievous *d* ... Ps 21:11
further not his wicked *d* ... Ps 140:8
for there is no work, nor *d* ... Eccl 9:10
you, and devise a *d* against you ... Jer 18:11
for his *d* is against Babylon, to ... Jer 51:11
their *d* against me all the day ... Lam 3:62
stone, graven by art and man's *d* ... Acts 17:29

**DEVICES**
disappointeth the *d* of the crafty ... Job 5:12
the *d* which ye wrongfully imagine ... Job 21:27
in the *d* that they have imagined ... Ps 10:2
he maketh the *d* of the people of ... Ps 33:10
man who bringeth wicked *d* to pass ... Ps 37:7
and be filled with their own *d* ... Prov 1:31
a man of wicked *d* will he condemn ... Prov 12:2
and a man of wicked *d* is hated ... Prov 14:17
There are many *d* in a man's heart ... Prov 19:21
he deviseth wicked *d* to destroy ... Is 32:7
they had devised *d* against me ... Jer 11:19
but we will walk after our own *d* ... Jer 18:12
let us devise *d* against Jeremiah ... Jer 18:18
he shall forecast his *d* against ... Dan 11:24
they shall forecast *d* against him ... Dan 11:25
for we are not ignorant of his *d* ... 2Cor 2:11

**DEVIL**
wilderness to be tempted of the *d* ... Mt 4:1
Then the *d* taketh him up into the ... Mt 4:5
the *d* taketh him up into an ... Mt 4:8
Then the *d* leaveth him, and, ... Mt 4:11
him a dumb man possessed with a *d* ... Mt 9:32
when the *d* was cast out, the dumb ... Mt 9:33
and they say, He hath a *d* ... Mt 11:18
unto him one possessed with a *d* ... Mt 12:22
enemy that sowed them is the *d* ... Mt 13:39
is grievously vexed with a *d* ... Mt 15:22
And Jesus rebuked the *d* ... Mt 17:18
fire, prepared for the *d* and his ... Mt 25:41
him that was possessed with the *d* ... Mk 5:15
him that was possessed with the *d* ... Mk 5:16
the *d* prayed him that he might be ... Mk 5:18
forth the *d* out of her daughter ... Mk 7:26
the *d* is gone out of thy daughter ... Mk 7:29
house, she found the *d* gone out ... Mk 7:30
Being forty days tempted of the *d* ... Lk 4:2
the *d* said unto him, If thou be ... Lk 4:3
And the *d*, taking him up into an ... Lk 4:5
the *d* said unto him, All this ... Lk 4:6
when the *d* had ended all the ... Lk 4:13
had a spirit of an unclean *d* ... Lk 4:33
when the *d* had thrown him in the ... Lk 4:35
and ye say, He hath a *d* ... Lk 7:33
then cometh the *d*, and taketh away ... Lk 8:12
was driven of the *d* into the ... Lk 8:29
the *d* threw him down, and tare him ... Lk 9:42
And he was casting out a *d* ... Lk 11:14
when the *d* was gone out, the dumb ... Lk 11:14
you twelve, and one of you is a *d* ... Jn 6:70
answered and said, Thou hast a *d* ... Jn 7:20
Ye are of your father the *d* ... Jn 8:44
thou art a Samaritan, and hast a *d* ... Jn 8:48
Jesus answered, I have not a *d* ... Jn 8:49
Now we know that thou hast a *d* ... Jn 8:52
And many of them said, He hath a *d* ... Jn 10:20
the words of him that hath a *d* ... Jn 10:21
Can a *d* open the eyes of the ... Jn 10:21
the *d* having now put into the ... Jn 13:2
all that were oppressed of the *d* ... Acts 10:38
all mischief, thou child of the *d* ... Acts 13:10
Neither give place to the *d* ... Eph 4:27
stand against the wiles of the *d* ... Eph 6:11
into the condemnation of the *d* ... 1Ti 3:6
reproach and the snare of the *d* ... 1Ti 3:7
out of the snare of the *d* ... 2Ti 2:26
power of death, that is, the *d* ... Heb 2:14
Resist the *d*, and he will flee ... Jas 4:7
because your adversary the *d* ... 1Pet 5:8
that committeth sin is of the *d* ... 1Jn 3:8
for the *d* sinneth from the ... 1Jn 3:8
might destroy the works of the *d* ... 1Jn 3:8
and the children of the *d* ... 1Jn 3:10
when contending with the *d* he ... Jude 9
the *d* shall cast some of you into ... Rev 2:10
that old serpent, called the *D* ... Rev 12:9
for the *d* is come down unto you, ... Rev 12:12
that old serpent, which is the *D* ... Rev 20:2
the *d* that deceived them was cast ... Rev 20:10

**DEVILISH**
above, but is earthly, sensual, *d* ... Jas 3:15

**DEVILS**
offer their sacrifices unto *d* ... Lev 17:7
They sacrificed unto *d*, not to ... Deut 32:17
for the high places, and for the *d* ... 2Chr 11:15
sons and their daughters unto *d* ... Ps 106:37
those which were possessed with *d* ... Mt 4:24
and in thy name have cast out *d* ... Mt 7:22
many that were possessed with *d* ... Mt 8:16
met him two possessed with *d* ... Mt 8:28
So the *d* besought him, saying, If ... Mt 8:31
to the possessed of the *d* ... Mt 8:33
He casteth out *d* through the ... Mt 9:34
through the prince of the *d* ... Mt 9:34
raise the dead, cast out *d* ... Mt 10:8
This fellow doth not cast out *d* ... Mt 12:24
by Beelzebub the prince of the *d* ... Mt 12:24
And if I by Beelzebub cast out *d* ... Mt 12:27
But if I cast out *d* by the Spirit ... Mt 12:28
them that were possessed with *d* ... Mk 1:32
diseases, and cast out many *d* ... Mk 1:34
and suffered not the *d* to speak ... Mk 1:34
all Galilee, and cast out *d* ... Mk 1:39
heal sicknesses, and to cast out *d* ... Mk 3:15
of the *d* casteth he out *d* ... Mk 3:22
all the *d* besought him, saying, ... Mk 5:12
And they cast out many *d*, and ... Mk 6:13
saw one casting out *d* in thy name ... Mk 9:38
out of whom he had cast seven *d* ... Mk 16:9
In my name shall they cast out *d* ... Mk 16:17
*d* also came out of many, crying ... Lk 4:41
out of whom went seven *d* ... Lk 8:2
man, which had *d* long time ... Lk 8:27
because many *d* were entered into ... Lk 8:30
Then went the *d* out of the man, ... Lk 8:33
out of whom the *d* were departed ... Lk 8:35
was possessed of the *d* was healed ... Lk 8:36
Now the man out of whom the *d* ... Lk 8:38
power and authority over all *d* ... Lk 9:1
saw one casting out *d* in thy name ... Lk 9:49
even the *d* are subject unto us ... Lk 10:17
said, He casteth out *d* through ... Lk 11:15
Beelzebub the chief of the *d* ... Lk 11:15
I cast out *d* through Beelzebub ... Lk 11:18
And if I by Beelzebub cast out *d* ... Lk 11:19
with the finger of God cast out *d* ... Lk 11:20
that fox, Behold, I cast out *d* ... Lk 13:32

sacrifice, they sacrifice to *d* ... 1Cor 10:20
ye should have fellowship with *d* ... 1Cor 10:20
cup of the Lord, and the cup of *d* ... 1Cor 10:21
table, and of the table of *d* ... 1Cor 10:21
spirits, and doctrines of *d* ... 1Ti 4:1
the *d* also believe, and tremble ... Jas 2:19
that they should not worship *d* ... Rev 9:20
For they are the spirits of *d* ... Rev 16:14
and is become the habitation of *d* ... Rev 18:2

**DEVISE**
To *d* cunning works, to work in ... Ex 31:4
to *d* curious works, to work in ... Ex 35:32
and of those that *d* cunning work ... Ex 35:35
yet doth he *d* means, that his ... 2Sa 14:14
to confusion that *d* my hurt ... Ps 35:4
but they *d* deceitful matters ... Ps 35:20
against me do they *d* my hurt ... Ps 41:7
*D* not evil against thy neighbour, ... Prov 3:29
Do they not err that *d* evil ... Prov 14:22
shall be to them that *d* good ... Prov 14:22
his eyes to *d* froward things ... Prov 16:30
you, and *d* a device against you ... Jer 18:11
let us *d* devices against Jeremiah ... Jer 18:18
these are the men that *d* mischief ... Eze 11:2
Woe to them that *d* iniquity ... Mic 2:1
this family do I *d* an evil ... Mic 2:3

**DEVISED**
that *d* against us that we should ... 2Sa 21:5
which he had *d* of his own heart ... 1Kin 12:33
that he had *d* against the Jews ... Est 8:3
*d* by Haman the son of Hammedatha ... Est 8:5
had *d* against the Jews to destroy ... Est 9:24
which he *d* against the Jews, ... Est 9:25
they *d* to take away my life ... Ps 31:13
they had *d* devices against me ... Jer 11:19
they have *d* evil against it ... Jer 48:2
for the LORD hath both *d* and done ... Jer 51:12
hath done that which he had *d* ... Lam 2:17
not followed cunningly *d* fables ... 2Pet 1:16

**DEVISETH**
He *d* mischief upon his bed ... Ps 36:4
Thy tongue *d* mischiefs ... Ps 52:2
he *d* mischief continually ... Prov 6:14
An heart that *d* wicked ... Prov 6:18
A man's heart *d* his way ... Prov 16:9
He that *d* to do evil shall be ... Prov 24:8
he *d* wicked devices to destroy ... Is 32:7
But the liberal *d* liberal things ... Is 32:8

**DEVOTE**
that a man shall *d* unto the LORD ... Lev 27:28

**DEVOTED**
holy unto the LORD, as a field *d* ... Lev 27:21
Notwithstanding no *d* thing ... Lev 27:28
every *d* thing is most holy unto ... Lev 27:28
None *d*, which shall be ... Lev 27:29
which shall be *d* of men ... Lev 27:29
Every thing *d* in Israel shall be ... Num 18:14
thy servant, who is *d* to thy fear ... Ps 119:38

**DEVOTIONS**
as I passed by, and beheld your *d* ... Acts 17:23

**DEVOUR**
the morning he shall *d* the prey ... Gen 49:27
blood, and my sword shall *d* flesh ... Deut 32:42
and *d* the cedars of Lebanon ... Judg 9:15
*d* the men of Shechem, and the ... Judg 9:20
house of Millo, and *d* Abimelech ... Judg 9:20
said, Shall the sword *d* for ever ... 2Sa 2:26
command the locusts to *d* the land ... 2Chr 7:13
It shall *d* the strength of his ... Job 18:13
of death shall *d* his strength ... Job 18:13
wrath, and the fire shall *d* them ... Ps 21:9
a fire shall *d* before him ... Ps 50:3
wild beast of the field doth *d* it ... Ps 80:13
to *d* the poor from off the earth, ... Prov 30:14
strangers *d* it in your presence, ... Is 1:7
they shall *d* Israel with open ... Is 9:12
it shall *d* the briers and thorns, ... Is 9:18
*d* his thorns and his briers in one ... Is 10:17
of thine enemies shall *d* them ... Is 26:11
not of a mean man, shall *d* him ... Is 31:8
your breath, as fire, shall *d* you ... Is 33:11
I will destroy and *d* at once ... Is 42:14
ye beasts of the field, come to *d* ... Is 56:9
all that *d* him shall offend ... Jer 2:3
people wood, and it shall *d* them ... Jer 5:14
beasts of the field, come to *d* ... Jer 12:9
*d* from the one end of the land ... Jer 12:12
and the beasts of the earth, to *d* ... Jer 15:3
it shall *d* the palaces of ... Jer 17:27
it shall *d* all things round about ... Jer 21:14
that *d* thee shall be devoured ... Jer 30:16
and the sword shall *d*, and it shall ... Jer 46:10
sword shall *d* round about thee ... Jer 46:14
shall *d* the corner of Moab, and ... Jer 48:45
it shall *d* all round about him ... Jer 50:32
famine and pestilence shall *d* him ... Eze 7:15
and another fire shall *d* them ... Eze 15:7
it shall *d* every green tree in ... Eze 20:47
them through the fire, to *d* them ... Eze 23:37
midst of thee, it shall *d* thee ... Eze 28:18
the beast of the land *d* them ... Eze 34:28
thou shalt *d* men no more, neither ... Eze 36:14
thus unto it, Arise, *d* much flesh ... Dan 7:5
shall *d* the whole earth, and shall ... Dan 7:23
now shall a month *d* them with ... Hos 5:7
it shall *d* the palaces thereof ... Hos 8:14
*d* them, because of their own ... Hos 11:6
there will I *d* them like a lion ... Hos 13:8
which shall *d* the palaces of ... Amos 1:4
which shall *d* the palaces thereof ... Amos 1:7
which shall *d* the palaces thereof ... Amos 1:10
which shall *d* the palaces of ... Amos 1:12
it shall *d* the palaces thereof, ... Amos 1:14
it shall *d* the palaces of Kirioth ... Amos 2:2
it shall *d* the palaces of ... Amos 2:5
*d* it, and there be none to quench ... Amos 5:6
shall kindle in them, and *d* them ... Obad 18
the sword shall *d* thy young lions ... Nah 2:13
the fire shall *d* thy bars ... Nah 3:13
There shall the fire *d* thee ... Nah 3:15
was as to *d* the poor secretly ... Hab 3:14
and they shall *d*, and subdue with ... Zec 9:15
that the fire may *d* thy cedars ... Zec 11:1
they shall *d* all the people round ... Zec 12:6
for ye *d* widows' houses, and for a ... Mt 23:14
Which *d* widows' houses, and for a ... Mk 12:40
Which *d* widows' houses, and for a ... Lk 20:47
you into bondage, if a man *d* you ... 2Cor 11:20
*d* one another, take heed that ye ... Gal 5:15
which shall *d* the adversaries ... Heb 10:27
about, seeking whom he may *d* ... 1Pet 5:8
for to *d* her child as soon as it ... Rev 12:4

**DEVOURED**
hath quite *d* also our money ... Gen 31:15
say, Some evil beast hath *d* him ... Gen 37:20
an evil beast hath *d* him ... Gen 37:33
seven thin ears *d* the seven rank ... Gen 41:7
the thin ears *d* the seven good ... Gen 41:24
*d* them, and they died before the ... Lev 10:2
what time the fire *d* two hundred ... Num 26:10
from them, and they shall be *d* ... Deut 31:17
*d* with burning heat, and with ... Deut 32:24
the wood *d* more people that day ... 2Sa 18:8
people that day than the sword *d* ... 2Sa 18:8
and fire out of his mouth *d* ... 2Sa 22:9
and fire out of his mouth *d* ... Ps 18:8
of flies among them, which *d* them ... Ps 78:45
For they have *d* Jacob, and laid ... Ps 79:7
*d* the fruit of their ground ... Ps 105:35
ye shall be *d* with the sword ... Is 1:20
hath the curse *d* the earth ... Is 24:6
own sword hath *d* your prophets ... Jer 2:30
For shame hath *d* the labour of ... Jer 3:24
have *d* the land, and all that is ... Jer 8:16
*d* him, and consumed him, and have ... Jer 10:25
they that devour thee shall be *d* ... Jer 30:16
All that found them have *d* them ... Jer 50:7
the king of Assyria hath *d* him ... Jer 50:17
the king of Babylon hath *d* me ... Jer 51:34
it hath *d* the foundations thereof ... Lam 4:11
any work, when the fire hath *d* it ... Eze 15:5
thou sacrificed unto them to be *d* ... Eze 16:20
to catch the prey; it *d* men ... Eze 19:3
to catch the prey, and *d* men ... Eze 19:6
branches, which hath *d* her fruit ... Eze 19:14
they have *d* souls ... Eze 22:25
residue shall be *d* by the fire ... Eze 23:25
will I give to the beasts to be *d* ... Eze 33:27
the beasts of the field to be *d* ... Eze 39:4
it *d* and brake in pieces, and ... Dan 7:7
which *d*, brake in pieces, and ... Dan 7:19
an oven, and have *d* their judges ... Hos 7:7
Strangers have *d* his strength ... Hos 7:9
for the fire hath *d* the pastures ... Joel 1:19
the fire hath *d* the pastures of ... Joel 1:20
increased, the palmerworm *d* them ... Amos 4:9
it *d* the great deep, and did eat ... Amos 7:4
they shall be *d* as stubble fully ... Nah 1:10
be *d* by the fire of his jealousy ... Zeph 1:18
for all the earth shall be *d* with ... Zeph 3:8
and she shall be *d* with fire ... Zec 9:4
and the fowls came and *d* them up ... Mt 13:4
fowls of the air came and *d* it up ... Mk 4:4
and the fowls of the air *d* it ... Lk 8:5
which hath *d* thy living with ... Lk 15:30
from God out of heaven, and *d* them ... Rev 20:9

**DEVOURER**
will rebuke the *d* for your sakes ... Mal 3:11

**DEVOUREST**
say unto you, Thou land *d* up men ... Eze 36:13

**DEVOURETH**
for the sword *d* one as well as ... 2Sa 11:25
mouth of the wicked *d* iniquity ... Prov 19:28
the man who *d* that which is holy ... Prov 20:25
as the fire *d* the stubble ... Is 5:24
flaming fire, which *d* round about ... Lam 2:3
the fire *d* both the ends of it, ... Eze 15:4
A fire *d* before them ... Joel 2:3
flame of fire that *d* the stubble ... Joel 2:5
thy tongue when the wicked *d* the ... Hab 1:13
their mouth, and *d* their enemies ... Rev 11:5

**DEVOURING**
the glory of the LORD was like *d* ... Ex 24:17
Thou lovest all *d* words, O thou ... Ps 52:4
tempest, and the flame of *d* fire ... Is 29:6
and his tongue as a *d* fire ... Is 30:27
and with the flame of a *d* fire ... Is 30:30
us shall dwell with the *d* fire ... Is 33:14

**DEVOUT**
and the same man was just and *d* ... Lk 2:25
*d* men, out of every nation under ... Acts 2:5
*d* men carried Stephen to his ... Acts 8:2
A *d* man, and one that feared God ... Acts 10:2
a *d* soldier of them that waited ... Acts 10:7
But the Jews stirred up the *d* ... Acts 13:50
of the *d* Greeks a great multitude ... Acts 17:4
the Jews, and with the *d* persons ... Acts 17:17
a *d* man according to the law, ... Acts 22:12

**DEW**
God give thee of the *d* of heaven ... Gen 27:28
of the *d* of heaven from above ... Gen 27:39
in the morning the *d* lay round ... Ex 16:13
when the *d* that lay was gone up, ... Ex 16:14
when the *d* fell upon the camp in ... Num 11:9
my speech shall distil as the *d* ... Deut 32:2
things of heaven, for the *d* ... Deut 33:13
his heavens shall drop down *d* ... Deut 33:28
if the *d* be on the fleece only, ... Judg 6:37
wringed the *d* out of the fleece, ... Judg 6:38
all the ground let there be *d* ... Judg 6:39
there was *d* on all the ground ... Judg 6:40
of Gilboa, let there be no *d* ... 2Sa 1:21
as the *d* falleth on the ground ... 2Sa 17:12
there shall not be *d* nor rain ... 1Kin 17:1
the *d* lay all night upon my ... Job 29:19
who hath begotten the drops of *d* ... Job 38:28
thou hast the *d* of thy youth ... Ps 110:3
As the *d* of Hermon, and as the *d* ... Ps 133:3
up, and the clouds drop down the *d* ... Prov 3:20
his favour is as *d* upon the grass ... Prov 19:12
for my head is filled with *d* ... Song 5:2
like a cloud of *d* in the heat of ... Is 18:4
for thy *d* is as the *d* of herbs, ... Is 26:19
it be wet with the *d* of heaven ... Dan 4:15
it be wet with the *d* of heaven ... Dan 4:23
wet thee with the *d* of heaven ... Dan 4:25
body was wet with the *d* of heaven ... Dan 4:33
body was wet with the *d* of heaven ... Dan 5:21
as the early *d* it goeth away ... Hos 6:4
as the early *d* that passeth away, ... Hos 13:3
I will be as the *d* unto Israel ... Hos 14:5
many people as a *d* from the LORD ... Mic 5:7
heaven over you is stayed from *d* ... Hag 1:10
and the heavens shall give their *d* ... Zec 8:12

**DIADEM**
my judgment was as a robe and a *d* ... Job 29:14
for a *d* of beauty, unto the ... Is 28:5
a royal *d* in the hand of thy God ... Is 62:3
Remove the *d*, and take off the ... Eze 21:26

**DIAL**
it had gone down in the *d* of Ahaz ... 2Kin 20:11
is gone down in the sun *d* of Ahaz ... Is 38:8

**DIAMOND**
be an emerald, a sapphire, and a *d* ... Ex 28:18
an emerald, a sapphire, and a *d* ... Ex 39:11
of iron, and with the point of a *d* ... Jer 17:1
the sardius, topaz, and the *d* ... Eze 28:13

**DIANA** (*di-an'-ah*) *A Greek goddess.*
which made silver shrines for *D* ... Acts 19:24
goddess *D* should be despised ... Acts 19:27
Great is *D* of the Ephesians ... Acts 19:28
Great is *D* of the Ephesians ... Acts 19:34
worshipper of the great goddess *D* ... Acts 19:35

**DIBLAH** See DIBLATH.

**DIBLAIM** (*dib'-la-im*) *Father of Gomer.*
and took Gomer the daughter of *D* ... Hos 1:3

**DIBLATH** (*dib'-lath*) *A place in northern Canaan.*
than the wilderness toward *D* ... Eze 6:14

**DIBON** (*di'-bon*) See DIBON-GAD, DIMON.
*1. A Moabite city.*
Heshbon is perished even unto *D* ... Num 21:30
Ataroth, and *D*, and Jazer, and ... Num 32:3
And the children of Gad built *D* ... Num 32:34
He is gone up to Bajith, and to *D* ... Is 15:2
*2. An undefined city.*
and all the plain of Medeba unto *D* ... Josh 13:9
*D*, and Bamoth-baal, and ... Josh 13:17
Thou daughter that dost inhabit *D* ... Jer 48:18
And upon *D*, and upon Nebo ... Jer 48:22
*3. A town in Judah.*
in the villages thereof, and at *D* ... Neh 11:25

**DIBON-GAD** (*di'-bon-gad'*) *An encampment during the Exodus.*
from Iim, and pitched in *D* ... Num 33:45
And they removed from *D*, and ... Num 33:46

**DIBRI** (*dib'-ri*) *Father of Shelomith.*
was Shelomith, the daughter of *D* ... Lev 24:11

**DID** See PREFACE.

**DIDDEST**
as thou *d* the Egyptian yesterday ... Acts 7:28

**DIDST**
why *d* thou not tell me that she ... Gen 12:18
but thou *d* laugh ... Gen 18:15
I know that thou *d* this in the ... Gen 20:6
neither *d* thou tell me, neither ... Gen 21:26
Wherefore *d* thou flee away ... Gen 31:27
*d* not tell me, that I might have ... Gen 31:27
of my hand *d* thou require it, ... Gen 31:39
Thou *d* blow with thy wind, the ... Ex 15:10
as thou *d* anoint their father, ... Ex 40:15
thou shalt do to him as thou *d* ... Num 21:34
thou shalt do unto him as thou *d* ... Deut 3:2
from the day that thou *d* depart ... Deut 9:7
thou *d* drink the pure blood of ... Deut 32:14
whom thou *d* prove at Massah, and ... Deut 33:8

with whom thou *d* strive at the ... Deut 33:8
which thou *d* let us down by ... Josh 2:18
her king as thou *d* unto Jericho ... Josh 8:2
*d* not call us to go with thee ... Judg 12:1
thou *d* send come again unto us ... Judg 13:8
for thou *d* call me ... 1Sa 3:6
for thou *d* call me ... 1Sa 3:8
Wherefore then *d* thou not obey ... 1Sa 15:19
but *d* fly upon the spoil, and ... 1Sa 15:19
*d* evil in the sight of the LORD ... 1Sa 15:19
thou sawest it, and *d* rejoice ... 1Sa 19:5
come to the place where thou *d* ... 1Sa 20:19
men of my lord, whom thou *d* send ... 1Sa 25:25
why then *d* thou not go down unto ... 2Sa 11:10
For thou *d* it secretly ... 2Sa 12:12
thou *d* fast and weep for the child ... 2Sa 12:21
the child was dead, thou *d* rise ... 2Sa 12:21
the other that thou *d* unto me ... 2Sa 13:16
why *d* thou not smite him there to ... 2Sa 18:11
yet *d* thou set thy servant among ... 2Sa 19:28
*D* not thou, my lord, O king, ... 1Kin 1:13
that thou *d* to David my father ... 1Kin 2:44
thou *d* well that it was in thine ... 1Kin 8:18
For thou *d* separate them from ... 1Kin 8:53
All that thou *d* send for to thy ... 1Kin 20:9
Thou *d* blaspheme God and the king 1Kin 21:10
For thy people Israel *d* thou make ... 1Chr 17:22
As thou *d* deal with David my ... 2Chr 2:3
*d* send him cedars to build him an ... 2Chr 2:3
thou *d* well in that it was in ... 2Chr 6:8
because thou *d* rely on the LORD, ... 2Chr 16:8
who *d* drive out the inhabitants ... 2Chr 20:7
thou *d* humble thyself before God, ... 2Chr 34:27
*d* rend thy clothes, and weep ... 2Chr 34:27
who *d* choose Abram, and broughtest ... Neh 9:7
*d* see the affliction of our ... Neh 9:9
So *d* thou get thee a name, as it ... Neh 9:10
thou *d* divide the sea before them ... Neh 9:11
wonders that thou *d* among them ... Neh 9:17
forty years *d* thou sustain them ... Neh 9:21
*d* divide them into corners ... Neh 9:22
many times *d* thou deliver them ... Neh 9:28
Yet many years *d* thou forbear ... Neh 9:30
thou *d* not utterly consume them ... Neh 9:31
wherewith thou *d* testify against ... Neh 9:34
trusted, and thou *d* deliver them ... Ps 22:4
thou *d* make me hope when I was ... Ps 22:9
thou *d* hide thy face, and I was ... Ps 30:7
because thou *d* it ... Ps 39:9
and offering thou *d* not desire ... Ps 40:6
what work thou *d* in their days ... Ps 44:1
How thou *d* drive out the heathen ... Ps 44:2
how thou *d* afflict the people, and ... Ps 44:2
which *d* not go out with our ... Ps 60:10
when thou *d* march through the ... Ps 68:7
*d* send a plentiful rain ... Ps 68:9
whereby thou *d* confirm thine ... Ps 68:9
Surely thou *d* set them in ... Ps 73:18
Thou *d* divide the sea by thy ... Ps 74:13
Thou *d* cleave the fountain and the ... Ps 74:15
Thou *d* cause judgment to be heard ... Ps 76:8
*d* cause it to take deep root, and ... Ps 80:9
which *d* weaken the nations ... Is 14:12
thou *d* look in that day to the ... Is 22:8
thou *d* shew them no mercy ... Is 47:6
so that thou *d* not lay these ... Is 47:7
neither *d* remember the latter end ... Is 47:7
things, and thou *d* not know them ... Is 48:6
O barren, thou that *d* not bear ... Is 54:1
thou that *d* not travail with ... Is 54:1
*d* increase thy perfumes, and *d* ... Is 57:9
*d* debase thyself even unto hell ... Is 57:9
so *d* thou lead thy people, to ... Is 63:14
When thou *d* terrible things which ... Is 64:3
which thou *d* swear to their ... Jer 32:22
How *d* thou write all these words ... Jer 36:17
Thou *d* say, Woe is me now ... Jer 45:3
whom thou *d* command that they ... Lam 1:10
thou *d* eat fine flour, and honey, ... Eze 16:13
thou *d* prosper into a kingdom ... Eze 16:13
But thou *d* trust in thine own ... Eze 16:15
And of thy garments thou *d* take ... Eze 16:16
*d* commit whoredom with them, ... Eze 16:17
which thou *d* give unto them ... Eze 16:36
for whom thou *d* wash thyself ... Eze 23:40
thou *d* enrich the kings of the ... Eze 27:33
thou *d* break, and rend all their ... Eze 29:7
As thou *d* rejoice at the ... Eze 35:15
from the first day that thou *d* ... Dan 10:12
because thou *d* trust in thy way, ... Hos 10:13
that thou *d* ride upon thine ... Hab 3:8
Thou *d* cleave the earth with ... Hab 3:9
Thou *d* march through the land in ... Hab 3:12
thou *d* thresh the heathen in ... Hab 3:12
Thou *d* strike through with his ... Hab 3:14
Thou *d* walk through the sea with ... Hab 3:15
*d* not thou sow good seed in thy ... Mt 13:27
faith, wherefore *d* thou doubt ... Mt 14:31
*d* not thou agree with me for a ... Mt 20:13
head with oil thou *d* not anoint ... Lk 7:46
and reapest that thou *d* not sow ... Lk 19:21
have believed that thou *d* send me ... Jn 17:8
uncircumcised, and *d* eat with them ... Acts 11:3
hast thou that thou *d* not receive ... 1Cor 4:7
now if thou *d* receive it, why ... 1Cor 4:7
*d* set him over the works of thy ... Heb 2:7
unto me, Wherefore *d* thou marvel ... Rev 17:7

**DIDYMUS** (*did'-i-mus*) See THOMAS. *Another name for Thomas the apostle.*
said Thomas, which is called *D* ... Jn 11:16
one of the twelve, called *D* ... Jn 20:24
Simon Peter, and Thomas called *D* ... Jn 21:2

**DIE**
thereof thou shalt surely *d* ... Gen 2:17
shall ye touch it, lest ye *d* ... Gen 3:3
the woman, Ye shall not surely *d* ... Gen 3:4
that is in the earth shall *d* ... Gen 6:17
lest some evil take me, and I *d* ... Gen 19:19
thou that thou shalt surely *d* ... Gen 20:7
Behold, I am at the point to *d* ... Gen 25:32
Because I said, Lest I *d* for her ... Gen 26:9
my soul may bless thee before I *d* ... Gen 27:4
Give me children, or else I *d* ... Gen 30:1
one day, all the flock will *d* ... Gen 33:13
said, Lest peradventure he *d* also ... Gen 38:11
that we may live, and not *d* ... Gen 42:2
be verified, and ye shall not *d* ... Gen 42:20
that we may live, and not *d* ... Gen 43:8
it be found, both let him *d* ... Gen 44:9
his father, his father would *d* ... Gen 44:22
is not with us, that he will *d* ... Gen 44:31
I will go and see him before I *d* ... Gen 45:28
said unto Joseph, Now let me *d* ... Gen 46:30
why should we *d* in thy presence ... Gen 47:15
shall we *d* before thine eyes ... Gen 47:19
seed, that we may live, and not *d* ... Gen 47:19
time drew nigh that Israel must *d* ... Gen 47:29
said unto Joseph, Behold, I *d* ... Gen 48:21
made me swear, saying, Lo, I *d* ... Gen 50:5
said unto his brethren, I *d* ... Gen 50:24
fish that is in the river shall *d* ... Ex 7:18
there shall nothing *d* of all that ... Ex 9:4
down upon them, and they shall *d* ... Ex 9:19
thou seest my face thou shalt *d* ... Ex 10:28
in the land of Egypt shall *d* ... Ex 11:5
us away to *d* in the wilderness ... Ex 14:11
we should *d* in the wilderness ... Ex 14:12
not God speak with us, lest we *d* ... Ex 20:19
that smiteth a man, so that he *d* ... Ex 21:12
from mine altar, that he may *d* ... Ex 21:14
he *d* not, but keepeth his bed ... Ex 21:18
a rod, and he *d* under his hand ... Ex 21:20
a man or a woman, that they *d* ... Ex 21:28
ox hurt another's, that he *d* ... Ex 21:35
up, and be smitten that he *d* ... Ex 22:2
and it *d*, or be hurt, or driven ... Ex 22:10
neighbour, and it be hurt, or *d* ... Ex 22:14
when he cometh out, that he *d* not ... Ex 28:35
that they bear not iniquity, and *d* ... Ex 28:43
wash with water, that they *d* not ... Ex 30:20
and their feet, that they *d* not ... Ex 30:21
charge of the LORD, that ye *d* not ... Lev 8:35
lest ye *d*, and lest wrath come ... Lev 10:6
of the congregation, lest ye *d* ... Lev 10:7
of the congregation, lest ye *d* ... Lev 10:9
any beast, of which ye may eat, *d* ... Lev 11:39
that they *d* not in their ... Lev 15:31
that he *d* not ... Lev 16:2
upon the testimony, that he *d* not ... Lev 16:13
they shall *d* childless ... Lev 20:20
*d* therefore, if they profane it ... Lev 22:9
touch any holy thing, lest they *d* ... Num 4:15
that they may live, and not *d* ... Num 4:19
things are covered, lest they *d* ... Num 4:20
or for his sister, when they *d* ... Num 6:7
if any man *d* very suddenly by him ... Num 6:9
consumed, and there they shall *d* ... Num 14:35
If these men *d* the common death ... Num 16:29
from me, that they *d* not ... Num 17:10
unto Moses, saying, Behold, we *d* ... Num 17:12
tabernacle of the LORD shall *d* ... Num 17:13
that neither they, nor ye also, *d* ... Num 18:3
lest they bear sin, and *d* ... Num 18:22
the children of Israel, lest ye *d* ... Num 18:32
we and our cattle should *d* there ... Num 20:4
unto his people, and shall *d* there ... Num 20:26
of Egypt to *d* in the wilderness ... Num 21:5
Let me *d* the death of the ... Num 23:10
shall surely *d* in the wilderness ... Num 26:65
of Israel, saying, If a man *d* ... Num 27:8
that the manslayer *d* not, until ... Num 35:12
instrument of iron, so that he *d* ... Num 35:16
wherewith he may *d*, and he *d* ... Num 35:17
wherewith he may *d*, and he *d* ... Num 35:18
him by laying of wait, that he *d* ... Num 35:20
him with his hand, that he *d* ... Num 35:21
any stone, wherewith a man may *d* ... Num 35:23
and cast it upon him, that he *d* ... Num 35:23
any person to cause him to *d* ... Num 35:30
But I must *d* in this land, I must ... Deut 4:22
Now therefore why should we *d* ... Deut 5:25
our God any more, then we shall *d* ... Deut 5:25
stone him with stones, that he *d* ... Deut 13:10
them with stones, till they *d* ... Deut 17:5
the judge, even that man shall *d* ... Deut 17:12
great fire any more, that I *d* not ... Deut 18:16
gods, even that prophet shall *d* ... Deut 18:20
upon his neighbour, that he *d* ... Deut 19:5
and smite him mortally that he *d* ... Deut 19:11
avenger of blood, that he may *d* ... Deut 19:12
lest he *d* in the battle, and ... Deut 20:5
lest he *d* in the battle, and ... Deut 20:6
lest he *d* in the battle, and ... Deut 20:7
stone him with stones, that he *d* ... Deut 21:21
stone her with stones that she *d* ... Deut 22:21
then they shall both of them *d* ... Deut 22:22
them with stones that they *d* ... Deut 22:24
only that lay with her shall *d* ... Deut 22:25
or if the latter husband *d* ... Deut 24:3
then that thief shall *d* ... Deut 24:7
dwell together, and one of them *d* ... Deut 25:5
days approach that thou must *d* ... Deut 31:14
*d* in the mount whither thou goest ... Deut 32:50
Let Reuben live, and not *d* ... Deut 33:6
not *d* by the hand of the avenger ... Josh 20:9
thou shalt not *d* ... Judg 6:23
Bring out thy son, that he may *d* ... Judg 6:30
unto his wife, We shall surely *d* ... Judg 13:22
and now shall I *d* for thirst ... Judg 15:18
Let me *d* with the Philistines ... Judg 16:30
Where thou diest, will I *d* ... Ruth 1:17
*d* in the flower of their age ... 1Sa 2:33
one day they shall *d* both of them ... 1Sa 2:34
the LORD thy God, that we *d* not ... 1Sa 12:19
my son, he shall surely *d* ... 1Sa 14:39
in mine hand, and, lo, I must *d* ... 1Sa 14:43
for thou shalt surely *d*, Jonathan ... 1Sa 14:44
said unto Saul, Shall Jonathan *d* ... 1Sa 14:45
thou shalt not *d* ... 1Sa 20:2
of the LORD, that I *d* not ... 1Sa 20:14
unto me, for he shall surely *d* ... 1Sa 20:31
king said, Thou shalt surely *d* ... 1Sa 22:16
or his day shall come to *d* ... 1Sa 26:10
LORD liveth, ye are worthy to *d* ... 1Sa 26:16
for my life, to cause me to *d* ... 1Sa 28:9
him, that he may be smitten, and *d* ... 2Sa 11:15
done this thing shall surely *d* ... 2Sa 12:5
thou shalt not *d* ... 2Sa 12:13
is born unto thee shall surely *d* ... 2Sa 12:14
For we must needs *d*, and are as ... 2Sa 14:14
neither if half of us *d*, will ... 2Sa 18:3
unto Shimei, Thou shalt not *d* ... 2Sa 19:23
that I may *d* in mine own city, and ... 2Sa 19:37
shall be found in him, he shall *d* ... 1Kin 1:52
David drew nigh that he should *d* ... 1Kin 2:1
but I will *d* here ... 1Kin 2:30
certain that thou shalt surely *d* ... 1Kin 2:37
whither, that thou shalt surely *d* ... 1Kin 2:42
into the city, the child shall *d* ... 1Kin 14:12
my son, that we may eat it, and *d* ... 1Kin 17:12
for himself that he might *d* ... 1Kin 19:4
out, and stone him, that he may *d* ... 1Kin 21:10
art gone up, but shalt surely *d* ... 2Kin 1:4
art gone up, but shalt surely *d* ... 2Kin 1:6
art gone up, but shalt surely *d* ... 2Kin 1:16
Why sit we here until we *d* ... 2Kin 7:3
in the city, and we shall *d* there ... 2Kin 7:4
if we sit still here, we *d* also ... 2Kin 7:4
if they kill us, we shall but *d* ... 2Kin 7:4
shewed me that he shall surely *d* ... 2Kin 8:10
honey, that ye may live, and not *d* ... 2Kin 18:32
for thou shalt *d*, and not live ... 2Kin 20:1
shall not *d* for the children ... 2Chr 25:4
the children *d* for the fathers ... 2Chr 25:4
every man shall *d* for his own sin ... 2Chr 25:4
over yourselves to *d* by famine ... 2Chr 32:11
curse God, and *d* ... Job 2:9
they *d*, even without wisdom ... Job 4:21
and wisdom shall *d* with you ... Job 12:2
the stock thereof *d* in the ground ... Job 14:8
If a man *d*, shall he live again ... Job 14:14
till I *d* I will not remove mine ... Job 27:5
I shall *d* in my nest, and I shall ... Job 29:18
In a moment shall they *d*, and the ... Job 34:20
they shall *d* without knowledge ... Job 36:12
They *d* in youth, and their life is ... Job 36:14
speak evil of me, When shall he *d* ... Ps 41:5
For he seeth that wise men *d* ... Ps 49:10
those that are appointed to *d* ... Ps 79:11
But ye shall *d* like men, and fall ... Ps 82:7
ready to *d* from my youth up ... Ps 88:15
takest away their breath, they *d* ... Ps 104:29
I shall not *d*, but live, and ... Ps 118:17
He shall *d* without instruction ... Prov 5:23
but fools *d* for want of wisdom ... Prov 10:21
and he that hateth reproof shall *d* ... Prov 15:10
that despiseth his ways shall *d* ... Prov 19:16
him with the rod, he shall not *d* ... Prov 23:13
deny me them not before I *d* ... Prov 30:7
A time to be born, and a time to *d* ... Eccl 3:2
shouldest thou *d* before thy time ... Eccl 7:17
the living know that they shall *d* ... Eccl 9:5
for to morrow we shall *d* ... Is 22:13
not be purged from you till ye *d* ... Is 22:14
there shalt thou *d*, and there the ... Is 22:18
for thou shalt *d*, and not live ... Is 38:1
therein shall *d* in like manner ... Is 51:6
be afraid of a man that shall *d* ... Is 51:12
that he should not *d* in the pit ... Is 51:14
for the child shall *d* an hundred ... Is 65:20
for their worm shall not *d* ... Is 66:24
that thou *d* not by our hand ... Jer 11:21
young men shall *d* by the sword ... Jer 11:22
their daughters shall *d* by famine ... Jer 11:22
They shall *d* of grievous deaths ... Jer 16:4
and the small shall *d* in this land ... Jer 16:6
to Babylon, and there thou shalt *d* ... Jer 20:6
they shall *d* of a great ... Jer 21:6
in this city shall *d* by the sword ... Jer 21:9
But he shall *d* in the place ... Jer 22:12
and there shall ye *d* ... Jer 22:26
him, saying, Thou shalt surely *d* ... Jer 26:8
saying, This man is worthy to *d* ... Jer 26:11
This man is not worthy to *d* ... Jer 26:16
Why will ye *d*, thou and thy people ... Jer 27:13
this year thou shalt *d*, because ... Jer 28:16
But every one shall *d* for his own ... Jer 31:30
Thou shalt not *d* by the sword ... Jer 34:4
But thou shalt *d* in peace ... Jer 34:5
the scribe, lest I *d* there ... Jer 37:20

D

in this city shall *d* by the sword ............ Jer 38:2
he is like to *d* for hunger in the............. Jer 38:9
out of the dungeon, before he *d*............. Jer 38:10
these words, and thou shalt not *d*........ Jer 38:24
to Jonathan's house, to *d* there............ Jer 38:26
and there ye shall *d*.............................. Jer 42:16
they shall *d* by the sword, by the......... Jer 42:17
that ye shall *d* by the sword ................. Jer 42:22
they shall *d*, from the least even ......... Jer 44:12
the wicked, Thou shalt surely *d*............ Eze 3:18
man shall *d* in his iniquity................... Eze 3:18
he shall *d* in his iniquity ..................... Eze 3:19
before him, he shall *d*.......................... Eze 3:20
he shall *d* in his sin, and his .............. Eze 3:20
thee shall *d* with the pestilence ........... Eze 5:12
far off shall *d* of the pestilence............ Eze 6:12
is besieged shall *d* by the famine.......... Eze 6:12
the field shall *d* with the sword ............ Eze 7:15
see it, though he shall *d* there.............. Eze 12:13
slay the souls that should not *d*........... Eze 13:19
the midst of Babylon he shall *d*............ Eze 17:16
the soul that sinneth, it shall *d*.............. Eze 18:4
he shall surely *d*.................................... Eze 18:13
he shall not *d* for the iniquity ............... Eze 18:17
even he shall *d* in his iniquity ............... Eze 18:18
The soul that sinneth, it shall *d*............ Eze 18:20
shall surely live, he shall not *d*............ Eze 18:21
at all that the wicked should *d*............. Eze 18:23
hath sinned, in them shall he *d*............ Eze 18:24
that he hath done shall he *d*................. Eze 18:26
shall surely live, he shall not *d*............ Eze 18:28
for why will ye *d*, O house of................ Eze 18:31
thou shalt *d* the deaths of them ............ Eze 28:8
Thou shalt *d* the deaths of the............. Eze 28:10
O wicked man, thou shalt surely *d*........ Eze 33:8
man shall *d* in his iniquity................... Eze 33:8
he shall *d* in his iniquity ..................... Eze 33:9
for why will ye *d*, O house of............... Eze 33:11
hath committed, he shall *d* for it.......... Eze 33:13
the wicked, Thou shalt surely *d*............ Eze 33:14
shall surely live, he shall not *d*............ Eze 33:15
iniquity, he shall even *d* thereby ......... Eze 33:18
caves shall *d* of the pestilence.............. Eze 33:27
Moab shall *d* with tumult, with ............ Amos 2:2
in one house, that they shall *d*............. Amos 6:9
Jeroboam shall *d* by the sword .............. Amos 7:11
thou shalt *d* in a polluted land............. Amos 7:17
of my people shall *d* by the sword ........ Amos 9:10
better for me to *d* than to live.............. Jonah 4:3
and wished in himself to *d*.................... Jonah 4:8
better for me to *d* than to live.............. Jonah 4:8
we shall not *d*......................................... Hab 1:12
that that dieth, let it *d*.......................... Zec 11:9
therein shall be cut off and *d*................ Zec 13:8
or mother, let him *d* the death.............. Mt 15:4
Master, Moses said, If a man *d*............. Mt 22:24
him, Though I should *d* with thee.......... Mt 26:35
or mother, let him *d* the death ............. Mk 7:10
unto us, If a man's brother *d*................ Mk 12:19
If I should *d* with thee, I will................ Mk 14:31
unto him, was sick, and ready to *d*........... Lk 7:2
unto us, If any man's brother *d*............. Lk 20:28
he *d* without children, that his.............. Lk 20:28
Neither can they *d* any more ................. Lk 20:36
Sir, come down ere my child *d*.............. Jn 4:49
a man may eat thereof, and not *d*.......... Jn 6:50
seek me, and shall *d* in your sins............ Jn 8:21
you, that ye shall *d* in your sins............. Jn 8:24
I am he, ye shall *d* in your sins.............. Jn 8:24
also go, that we may *d* with him ........... Jn 11:16
and believeth in me shall never *d*......... Jn 11:26
one man should *d* for the people........... Jn 11:50
Jesus should *d* for that nation.............. Jn 11:51
wheat fall into the ground and *d*........... Jn 12:24
but if it *d*, it bringeth forth ................. Jn 12:24
signifying what death he should *d*.......... Jn 12:33
one man should *d* for the people ........... Jn 18:14
signifying what death he should *d*......... Jn 18:32
law, and by our law he ought to *d*............ Jn 19:7
that that disciple should not *d*.............. Jn 21:23
said not unto him, He shall not *d*.......... Jn 21:23
but also to *d* at Jerusalem for............. Acts 21:13
of death, I refuse not to *d*................... Acts 25:11
Romans to deliver any man to *d*............. Acts 25:16
for a righteous man will one *d*............... Rom 5:7
man some would even dare to *d*.............. Rom 5:7
live after the flesh, ye shall *d*.............. Rom 8:13
we *d*, we *d* unto the Lord....................... Rom 14:8
whether we live therefore, or *d*............. Rom 14:8
for it were better for me to *d*.............. 1Cor 9:15
For as in Adam all *d*, even so in........ 1Cor 15:22
Christ Jesus our Lord, I *d* daily .......... 1Cor 15:31
for to morrow we *d*............................. 1Cor 15:32
is not quickened, except it *d*.............. 1Cor 15:36
that ye are in our hearts to *d*.............. 2Cor 7:3
live is Christ, and to *d* is gain.............. Phil 1:21
here men that *d* receive tithes................ Heb 7:8
is appointed unto men once to *d*............ Heb 9:27
which remain, that are ready to *d*............ Rev 3:2
and shall desire to *d*, and death.............. Rev 9:6
Blessed are the dead which *d* in........... Rev 14:13

**DIED**
and thirty years: and he *d*...................... Gen 5:5
and twelve years: and he *d*...................... Gen 5:8
and five years: and he *d*......................... Gen 5:11
and ten years: and he *d*........................... Gen 5:14
and five years: and he *d*......................... Gen 5:17
*d*.............................................................. Gen 5:20
and nine years: and he *d*........................ Gen 5:27
and seven years: and he *d*...................... Gen 5:31
all flesh *d* that moved upon the............ Gen 7:21
all that was in the dry land, *d*.............. Gen 7:22
and fifty years: and he *d*....................... Gen 9:29
Haran *d* before his father Terah .......... Gen 11:28
and Terah *d* in Haran ........................... Gen 11:32
And Sarah *d* in Kirjath-arba.................. Gen 23:2
*d* in a good old age, an old man,............ Gen 25:8
and he gave up the ghost and *d*........... Gen 25:17
he *d* in the presence of all his .............. Gen 25:18
But Deborah Rebekah's nurse *d* ............ Gen 35:8
(for she *d*) that she called his.............. Gen 35:18
And Rachel *d*, and was buried in the . Gen 35:19
And Isaac gave up the ghost, and *d*... Gen 35:29
And Bela *d*, and Jobab the son of........ Gen 36:33
And Jobab *d*, and Husham .................. Gen 36:34
And Husham *d*, and Hadad................... Gen 36:35
And Hadad *d*, and Samlah................... Gen 36:36
And Samlah *d*, and Saul of Rehoboth Gen 36:37
And Saul *d*, and Baal-hanan the son .. Gen 36:38
And Baal-hanan the son of Achbor *d*. Gen 36:39
daughter of Shuah Judah's wife *d*...... Gen 38:12
Onan *d* in the land of Canaan.............. Gen 46:12
Rachel *d* by me in the land of.............. Gen 48:7
father did command before he *d*.......... Gen 50:16
So Joseph *d*, being an hundred and.... Gen 50:26
And Joseph *d*, and all his brethren, ........... Ex 1:6
of time, that the king of Egypt *d* ............ Ex 2:23
the fish that was in the river *d*................ Ex 7:21
the frogs *d* out of the houses,................ Ex 8:13
and all the cattle of Egypt *d*.................... Ex 9:6
the children of Israel *d* not one................ Ex 9:6
Would to God we had *d* by the hand ....... Ex 16:3
them, and they *d* before the LORD ......... Lev 10:2
offered before the LORD, and *d*............... Lev 16:1
eateth that which *d* of itself.................. Lev 17:15
Abihu *d* before the LORD, when............. Num 3:4
we had *d* in the land of Egypt .............. Num 14:2
God we had *d* in this wilderness .......... Num 14:2
*d* by the plague before the LORD.......... Num 14:37
stoned him with stones, and he *d*...... Num 15:36
Now they that *d* in the plague.............. Num 16:49
beside them that *d* about the............... Num 16:49
and Miriam *d* there, and was buried ... Num 20:1
Would God that we had *d* when our... Num 20:3
our brethren *d* before the LORD............ Num 20:3
Aaron *d* there in the top of the........... Num 20:28
and much people of Israel *d*................. Num 21:6
those that *d* in the plague were............ Num 25:9
with Korah, when that company *d*.... Num 26:10
the children of Korah *d* not.................. Num 26:11
Onan *d* in the land of Canaan .............. Num 26:19
And Nadab and Abihu *d*, when they. Num 26:61
Our father *d* in the wilderness,............ Num 27:3
but *d* in his own sin, and had no.......... Num 27:3
*d* there, in the fortieth year................ Num 33:38
years old when he *d* in mount Hor.... Num 33:39
there Aaron *d*, and there he was.......... Deut 10:6
Aaron thy brother *d* in mount Hor.... Deut 32:50
LORD *d* there in the land of Moab ......... Deut 34:5
and twenty years old when he *d*......... Deut 34:7
*d* in the wilderness by the way,............ Josh 5:4
upon them unto Azekah, and they *d*. Josh 10:11
they were more which *d* with............... Josh 10:11
Nun, the servant of the LORD, *d*.......... Josh 24:29
And Eleazar the son of Aaron *d*......... Josh 24:33
him to Jerusalem, and there he *d*.......... Judg 1:7
Nun, the servant of the LORD, *d* ........... Judg 2:8
which Joshua left when he *d*................ Judg 2:21
And Othniel the son of Kenaz *d*.......... Judg 3:11
asleep and weary. So he *d*.................... Judg 4:21
son of Joash *d* in a good old age ......... Judg 8:32
of the tower of Shechem *d* also........... Judg 9:49
man thrust him through, and he *d* ...... Judg 9:54
twenty and three years, and *d* ............. Judg 10:2
And Jair *d*, and was buried in Camon. Judg 10:5
Then *d* Jephthah the Gileadite, and..... Judg 12:7
Then *d* Ibzan, and was buried at........ Judg 12:10
And Elon the Zebulonite *d*, and was . Judg 12:12
son of Hillel the Pirathonite *d*.......... Judg 12:15
And Elimelech Naomi's husband *d*........ Ruth 1:3
Chilion *d* also both of them................... Ruth 1:5
gate, and his neck brake, and he *d*....... 1Sa 4:18
the men that *d* not were smitten............ 1Sa 5:12
rescued Jonathan, that he *d* not.......... 1Sa 14:45
And Samuel *d*; and all the Israelites...... 1Sa 25:1
that his heart *d* within him................. 1Sa 25:37
the LORD smote Nabal, that he *d*.......... 1Sa 25:38
upon his sword, and *d* with him ............ 1Sa 31:5
So Saul *d*, and his three sons, and ........ 1Sa 31:6
And he smote him that he *d*.................. 2Sa 1:15
there, and *d* in the same place.............. 2Sa 2:23
Asahel fell down and *d* stood still .......... 2Sa 2:23
three hundred and threescore men *d*...... 2Sa 2:31
under the fifth rib, that he *d*.................. 2Sa 3:27
and said, *D* Abner as a fool dieth .......... 2Sa 3:33
there he *d* by the ark of God.................. 2Sa 6:7
king of the children of Ammon *d* ........... 2Sa 10:1
of their host, who *d* there...................... 2Sa 10:18
and Uriah the Hittite *d* also................. 2Sa 11:17
the wall, that he *d* in Thebez................ 2Sa 11:21
the seventh day, that the child *d*.......... 2Sa 12:18
in order, and hanged himself, and *d*.... 2Sa 17:23
would God I had *d* for thee ................. 2Sa 18:33
lived, and all we had *d* this day ............. 2Sa 19:6
him not again; and he *d*....................... 2Sa 20:10
there *d* of the people from Dan.............. 2Sa 24:15
and he fell upon him that he *d*............. 1Kin 2:25
out, and fell upon him, that he *d*......... 1Kin 2:46
this woman's child *d* in the night.......... 1Kin 3:19
stoned him with stones, that he *d*...... 1Kin 12:18
of the door, the child *d*....................... 1Kin 14:17
house over him with fire, and *d*........... 1Kin 16:18
so Tibni *d*, and Omri reigned............... 1Kin 16:22
stoned him with stones, that he *d*...... 1Kin 21:13
against the Syrians, and *d* at even...... 1Kin 22:35
So the king *d*, and was brought to..... 1Kin 22:37
So he *d* according to the word of.......... 2Kin 1:17
on her knees till noon, and then *d*....... 2Kin 4:20
upon him in the gate, and he *d*.......... 2Kin 7:17
upon him in the gate, and he *d*............ 2Kin 7:20
it on his face, so that he *d*................... 2Kin 8:15
And he fled to Megiddo, and *d* there... 2Kin 9:27
his servants, smote him, and he *d*...... 2Kin 12:21
sick of his sickness whereof he *d*......... 2Kin 13:14
And Elisha *d*, and they buried him .... 2Kin 13:20
So Hazael king of Syria *d*.................... 2Kin 13:24
and he came to Egypt, and *d* there.... 2Kin 23:34
him, and smote Gedaliah, that he *d*... 2Kin 25:25
Hadad *d* also. And the dukes ................ 1Chr 1:51
but Seled *d* without children ............... 1Chr 2:30
Jether *d* without children.................... 1Chr 2:32
fell likewise on the sword, and *d*.......... 1Chr 10:5
So Saul *d*, and his three sons .............. 1Chr 10:6
and all his house *d* together................ 1Chr 10:6
So Saul *d* for his transgression ......... 1Chr 10:13
and there he *d* before God .................. 1Chr 13:10
king of the children of Ammon *d*.......... 1Chr 19:1
And Eleazar *d*, and had no sons, but. 1Chr 23:22
Abihu *d* before their father, and.......... 1Chr 24:2
he *d* in a good old age, full of............ 1Chr 29:28
stoned him with stones, that he *d*...... 2Chr 10:18
and the LORD struck him, and he *d*... 2Chr 13:20
*d* in the one and fortieth year of......... 2Chr 16:13
time of the sun going down he *d*.......... 2Chr 18:34
so he *d* of sore diseases ..................... 2Chr 21:19
and was full of days when he *d*.......... 2Chr 24:15
thirty years old was he when he *d*..... 2Chr 24:15
And when he *d*, he said, The LORD..... 2Chr 24:22
and slew him on his bed, and he *d* .... 2Chr 24:25
brought him to Jerusalem, and he *d*.. 2Chr 35:24
Why *d* I not from the womb..................... Job 3:11
So Job *d*, being old and full of............. Job 42:17
*d* I saw also the Lord sitting...................... Is 6:1
that king Ahaz *d* was this burden........... Is 14:28
So Hananiah the prophet *d* the............. Jer 28:17
Pelatiah the son of Benaiah *d* ............. Eze 11:13
and at even my wife *d* ........................... Eze 24:18
when he offended in Baal, he *d* ............... Hos 13:1
And last of all the woman *d* also.......... Mt 22:27
And the second took her, and *d*........... Mk 12:21
last of all the woman *d* also ................ Mk 12:22
came to pass, that the beggar *d* ............ Lk 16:22
the rich man also *d*, and was................ Lk 16:22
a wife, and *d* without children............... Lk 20:29
her to wife, and he *d* childless .............. Lk 20:30
and they left no children, and *d*............ Lk 20:31
Last of all the woman *d* also................ Lk 20:32
been here, my brother had not *d*........... Jn 11:21
been here, my brother had not *d*........... Jn 11:32
even this man should not have *d*........... Jn 11:37
Jacob went down into Egypt, and *d*..... Acts 7:15
days, that she was sick, and *d*............ Acts 9:37
due time Christ *d* for the ungodly.......... Rom 5:6
were yet sinners, Christ *d* for us ............ Rom 5:8
that he *d*, he *d* unto sin once ............. Rom 6:10
came, sin revived, and I *d* ...................... Rom 7:9
It is Christ that *d*, yea rather,............... Rom 8:34
For to this end Christ both *d*............... Rom 14:9
with thy meat, for whom Christ *d* ....... Rom 14:15
brother perish, for whom Christ *d*........ 1Cor 8:11
how that Christ *d* for our sins ............. 1Cor 15:3
thus judge, that if one *d* for all............. 2Cor 5:14
And that he *d* for all, that they ........... 2Cor 5:15
but unto him which *d* for them ............ 2Cor 5:15
For if we believe that Jesus *d*................ 1Th 4:14
Who *d* for us, that, whether we............. 1Th 5:10
law *d* without mercy under two or..... Heb 10:28
These all *d* in faith, not having ........... Heb 11:13
By faith Joseph, when he *d*................. Heb 11:22
were in the sea, and had life, *d*.............. Rev 8:9
many men *d* of the waters, because...... Rev 8:11
and every living soul *d* in the sea.......... Rev 16:3

**DIEST**
Where thou *d*, will I die, and................ Ruth 1:17

**DIET**
And for his *d*, there was a..................... Jer 52:34
there was a continual *d* given him......... Jer 52:34

**DIETH**
fat of the beast that *d* of itself............... Lev 7:24
That which *d* of itself, or is.................... Lev 22:8
the law, when a man *d* in a tent........ Num 19:14
eat of any thing that *d* of itself ........... Deut 14:21
and said, Died Abner as a fool *d*............ 2Sa 3:33
Him that *d* of Jeroboam in the........... 1Kin 14:11
him that *d* in the field shall the .......... 1Kin 14:11
Him that *d* of Baasha in the city .......... 1Kin 16:4
him that *d* of his in the fields ............... 1Kin 16:4
Him that *d* of Ahab in the city ........... 1Kin 21:24
him that *d* in the field shall the ......... 1Kin 21:24
But man *d*, and wasteth away.............. Job 14:10
One *d* in his full strength, being .......... Job 21:23
another *d* in the bitterness of............... Job 21:25
For when he *d* he shall carry................. Ps 49:17
When a wicked man *d*, his..................... Prov 11:7
And how *d* the wise man ....................... Eccl 2:16
as the one *d*, so *d* the other................... Eccl 3:19
is no water, and *d* for thirst.................... Is 50:2
he that eateth of their eggs *d*.................... Is 59:5
eaten of that which *d* of itself.............. Eze 4:14

committeth iniquity, and *d* in them ..... Eze 18:26
in the death of him that *d* ..... Eze 18:32
that that *d*, let it die ..... Zec 11:9
Where their worm *d* not, and the ..... Mk 9:44
Where their worm *d* not, and the ..... Mk 9:46
Where their worm *d* not, and the ..... Mk 9:48
raised from the dead *d* no more ..... Rom 6:9
himself, and no man *d* to himself ..... Rom 14:7

**DIFFER**
who maketh thee to *d* from another ..... 1Cor 4:7

**DIFFERENCE**
put a *d* between the Egyptians ..... Ex 11:7
And that ye may put *d* between holy.. Lev 10:10
To make a *d* between the unclean ..... Lev 11:47
put *d* between clean beasts ..... Lev 20:25
have put no *d* between the holy ..... Eze 22:26
they shewed *d* between the unclean.... Eze 22:26
my people the *d* between the holy ..... Eze 44:23
put no *d* between us and them, ..... Acts 15:9
for there is no *d* ..... Rom 3:22
For there is no *d* between the Jew ..... Rom 10:12
There is *d* also between a wife and ..... 1Cor 7:34
some have compassion, making a *d* ..... Jude 22

**DIFFERENCES**
there are *d* of administrations, ..... 1Cor 12:5

**DIFFERETH**
for one star *d* from another star ..... 1Cor 15:41
*d* nothing from a servant, though ..... Gal 4:1

**DIFFERING**
Having then gifts *d* according to ..... Rom 12:6

**DIG**
a pit, or if a man shall *d* a pit ..... Ex 21:33
whose hills thou mayest *d* brass ..... Deut 8:9
abroad, thou shalt *d* therewith ..... Deut 23:13
*d* for it more than for hid ..... Job 3:21
ye *d* a pit for your friend ..... Job 6:27
yea, thou shalt *d* about thee ..... Job 11:18
In the dark they *d* through houses ..... Job 24:16
me, Son of man, *d* now in the wall ..... Eze 8:8
*D* thou through the wall in their ..... Eze 12:5
they shall *d* through the wall to ..... Eze 12:12
Though they *d* into hell, thence ..... Amos 9:2
also, till I shall *d* about it ..... Lk 13:8
I cannot *d* ..... Lk 16:3

**DIGGED**
unto me, that I have *d* this well ..... Gen 21:30
had *d* in the days of Abraham his ..... Gen 26:15
Isaac *d* again the wells of water, ..... Gen 26:18
which they had *d* in the days of ..... Gen 26:18
Isaac's servants *d* in the valley ..... Gen 26:19
they *d* another well, and strove ..... Gen 26:21
from thence, and *d* another well ..... Gen 26:22
there Isaac's servants *d* a well ..... Gen 26:25
the well which they had *d* ..... Gen 26:32
their selfwill they *d* down a wall ..... Gen 49:6
in my grave which I have *d* for me ..... Gen 50:5
all the Egyptians *d* round about ..... Ex 7:24
The princes *d* the well ..... Num 21:18
the nobles of the people *d* it ..... Num 21:18
thou filledst not, and wells *d* ..... Deut 6:11
I have *d* and drunk strange waters, ..... 2Kin 19:24
in the desert, and *d* many wells ..... 2Chr 26:10
houses full of all goods, wells *d* ..... Neh 9:25
*d* it, and is fallen into the ditch ..... Ps 7:15
cause they have *d* for my soul ..... Ps 35:7
they have *d* a pit before me, into ..... Ps 57:6
until the pit be *d* for the wicked ..... Ps 94:13
The proud have *d* pits for me ..... Ps 119:85
it shall not be pruned, nor *d* ..... Is 5:6
that shall be *d* with the mattock ..... Is 7:25
I have *d*, and drunk water ..... Is 37:25
hole of the pit whence ye are *d* ..... Is 51:1
Then I went to Euphrates, and *d* ..... Jer 13:7
for they have *d* a pit for my soul ..... Jer 18:20
for they have *d* a pit to take me, ..... Jer 18:22
when I had *d* in the wall, behold ..... Eze 8:8
in the even I *d* through the wall ..... Eze 12:7
*d* a winepress in it, and built a ..... Mt 21:33
*d* in the earth, and hid his lord's ..... Mt 25:18
*d* a place for the winefat, and ..... Mk 12:1
*d* deep, and laid the foundation on ..... Lk 6:48
prophets, and *d* down thine altars ..... Rom 11:3

**DIGGEDST**
and wells digged, which thou *d* not ..... Deut 6:11

**DIGGETH**
An ungodly man *d* up evil ..... Prov 16:27
Whoso *d* a pit shall fall therein ..... Prov 26:27
He that *d* a pit shall fall into ..... Eccl 10:8

**DIGNITIES**
are not afraid to speak evil of *d* ..... 2Pet 2:10
dominion, and speak evil of *d* ..... Jude 8

**DIGNITY**
my strength, the excellency of *d* ..... Gen 49:3
*d* hath been done to Mordecai for ..... Est 6:3
Folly is set in great *d*, and the ..... Eccl 10:6
and their *d* shall proceed of ..... Hab 1:7

**DIKLAH** (*dik'-lah*) *A son of Joktan.*
And Hadoram, and Uzal, and *D* ..... Gen 10:27
Hadoram also, and Uzal, and *D* ..... 1Chr 1:21

**DILEAN** (*dil'-e-an*) *A city in Judah.*
And *D*, and Mizpeh, and Joktheel, ..... Josh 15:38

**DILIGENCE**
Keep thy heart with all *d* ..... Prov 4:23
give *d* that thou mayest be ..... Lk 12:58
he that ruleth, with *d* ..... Rom 12:8
and knowledge, and in all *d* ..... 2Cor 8:7
Do thy *d* to come shortly unto me ..... 2Ti 4:9
Do thy *d* to come before winter ..... 2Ti 4:21
one of you do shew the same *d* to ..... Heb 6:11
And beside this, giving all *d* ..... 2Pet 1:5
give *d* to make your calling and ..... 2Pet 1:10
when I gave all *d* to write unto ..... Jude 3

**DILIGENT**
judges shall make *d* inquisition ..... Deut 19:18
But take *d* heed to do the ..... Josh 22:5
they accomplish a *d* search ..... Ps 64:6
and my spirit made *d* search ..... Ps 77:6
but the hand of the *d* maketh rich ..... Prov 10:4
The hand of the *d* shall bear rule ..... Prov 12:24
substance of a *d* man is precious ..... Prov 12:27
soul of the *d* shall be made fat ..... Prov 13:4
The thoughts of the *d* tend only ..... Prov 21:5
thou a man *d* in his business ..... Prov 22:29
Be thou *d* to know the state of ..... Prov 27:23
proved *d* in many things ..... 2Cor 8:22
but now much more *d* ..... 2Cor 8:22
be *d* to come unto me to Nicopolis ..... Titus 3:12
be *d* that ye may be found of him ..... 2Pet 3:14

**DILIGENTLY**
If thou wilt *d* hearken to the ..... Ex 15:26
Moses *d* sought the goat of the ..... Lev 10:16
to thyself, and keep thy soul *d* ..... Deut 4:9
teach them *d* unto thy children ..... Deut 6:7
Ye shall *d* keep the commandments ... Deut 6:17
if ye shall hearken *d* unto my ..... Deut 11:13
For if ye shall *d* keep all these ..... Deut 11:22
enquire, and make search, and ask *d* Deut 13:14
hast heard of it, and enquired *d* ..... Deut 17:4
of leprosy, that thou observe *d* ..... Deut 24:8
if thou shalt hearken *d* unto the ..... Deut 28:1
Now the men did *d* observe whether. 1Kin 20:33
let it be *d* done for the house of ..... Ezr 7:23
Hear *d* my speech, and my ..... Job 13:17
Hear *d* my speech, and let this be ..... Job 21:2
thou shalt *d* consider his place, ..... Ps 37:10
us to keep thy precepts *d* ..... Ps 119:4
*d* to seek thy face, and I have ..... Prov 7:15
He that *d* seeketh good procureth ..... Prov 11:27
consider *d* what is before thee ..... Prov 23:1
he hearkened *d* with much heed ..... Is 21:7
hearken *d* unto me, and eat ye that ..... Is 55:2
and send unto Kedar, and consider *d* ..... Jer 2:10
if they will *d* learn the ways of ..... Jer 12:16
if ye *d* hearken unto me, saith ..... Jer 17:24
if ye will *d* obey the voice of ..... Zec 6:15
enquired of them *d* what time the ..... Mt 2:7
search *d* for the young child ..... Mt 2:8
he had *d* enquired of the wise men ..... Mt 2:16
house, and seek *d* till she find it ..... Lk 15:8
taught *d* the things of the Lord, ..... Acts 18:25
if she have *d* followed every good ..... 1Ti 5:10
in Rome, he sought me out very *d* ..... 2Ti 1:17
and Apollos on their journey *d* ..... Titus 3:13
rewarder of them that *d* seek him ..... Heb 11:6
Looking *d* lest any man fail of ..... Heb 12:15
have enquired and searched *d* ..... 1Pet 1:10

**DIM**
Isaac was old, and his eyes were *d* ..... Gen 27:1
the eyes of Israel were *d* for age ..... Gen 48:10
his eye was not *d*, nor his ..... Deut 34:7
place, and his eyes began to wax *d* ..... 1Sa 3:2
and his eyes were *d*, that he could ..... 1Sa 4:15
Mine eye also is *d* by reason of ..... Job 17:7
of them that see shall not be *d* ..... Is 32:3
How is the gold become *d* ..... Lam 4:1
for these things our eyes are *d* ..... Lam 5:17

**DIMINISH**
ye shall not *d* ought thereof ..... Ex 5:8
duty of marriage, shall he not *d* ..... Ex 21:10
thou shalt *d* the price of it ..... Lev 25:16
neither shall ye *d* ought from it ..... Deut 4:2
not add thereto, nor *d* from it ..... Deut 12:32
*d* not a word ..... Jer 26:2
therefore will I also *d* thee ..... Eze 5:11
for I will *d* them, that they ..... Eze 29:15

**DIMINISHED**
not ought of your work shall be *d* ..... Ex 5:11
gotten by vanity shall be *d* ..... Prov 13:11
the children of Kedar, shall be *d* ..... Is 21:17
may be increased there, and not *d* ..... Jer 29:6
have *d* thine ordinary food, and ..... Eze 16:27

**DIMINISHING**
the *d* of them the riches of the ..... Rom 11:12

**DIMNAH** (*dim'-nah*) *A Levitical city in Zebulun.*
*D* with her suburbs, Nahalal with ..... Josh 21:35

**DIMNESS**
trouble and darkness, *d* of anguish ..... Is 8:22
Nevertheless the *d* shall not be ..... Is 9:1

**DIMON** (*di'-mon*) See DIBON, DIMONAH. *A Moabite city.*
For the waters of *D* shall be full ..... Is 15:9
for I will bring more upon *D* ..... Is 15:9

**DIMONAH** (*di-mo'-nah*) See DIMON. *A city in Judah.*
And Kinah, and *D*, and Adadah, ..... Josh 15:22

**DINAH** See DINAH'S. *A daughter of Jacob.*
a daughter, and called her name *D* ..... Gen 30:21
*D* the daughter of Leah, which she ..... Gen 34:1
his soul clave unto *D* the ..... Gen 34:3
he had defiled *D* his daughter ..... Gen 34:5
he had defiled *D* their sister ..... Gen 34:13
took *D* out of Shechem's house, and.. Gen 34:26
Padan-aram, with his daughter *D* ..... Gen 46:15

D

**DINAH'S**
*D* brethren, took each man his ..... Gen 34:25

**DINAITES** (*di'-na-ites*) *Foreign settlers in Samaria.*
the *D*, the Apharsathchites, the ..... Ezr 4:9

**DINE**
these men shall *d* with me at noon ..... Gen 43:16
besought him to *d* with him ..... Lk 11:37
Jesus saith unto them, Come and *d* ..... Jn 21:12

**DINED**
So when they had *d*, Jesus saith ..... Jn 21:15

**DINHABAH** (*din'-ha-bah*) *Capital of Edom.*
and the name of his city was *D* ..... Gen 36:32
and the name of his city was *D* ..... 1Chr 1:43

**DINNER**
Better is a *d* of herbs where love ..... Prov 15:17
Behold, I have prepared my *d* ..... Mt 22:4
he had not first washed before *d* ..... Lk 11:38
When thou makest a *d* or a supper ..... Lk 14:12

**DIONYSIUS** (*di-on-ish'-yus*) *An Athenian convert of Paul.*
the which was *D* the Areopagite ..... Acts 17:34

**DIOTREPHES** (*di-ot'-re-feez*) *A believer condemned by John.*
but *D*, who loveth to have the ..... 3Jn 9

**DIP**
*d* it in the blood that is in the ..... Ex 12:22
the priest shall *d* his finger in ..... Lev 4:6
the priest shall *d* his finger in ..... Lev 4:17
and the hyssop, and shall *d* them ..... Lev 14:6
the priest shall *d* his right ..... Lev 14:16
*d* them in the blood of the slain ..... Lev 14:51
*d* it in the water, and sprinkle it ..... Num 19:18
let him *d* his foot in oil ..... Deut 33:24
*d* thy morsel in the vinegar ..... Ruth 2:14
that he may *d* the tip of his ..... Lk 16:24

**DIPPED**
goats, and *d* the coat in the blood ..... Gen 37:31
he *d* his finger in the blood, and ..... Lev 9:9
were *d* in the brim of the water ..... Josh 3:15
*d* it in an honeycomb, and put his ..... 1Sa 14:27
*d* himself seven times in Jordan, ..... 2Kin 5:14
*d* it in water, and spread it on ..... 2Kin 8:15
That thy foot may be *d* in the ..... Ps 68:23
give a sop, when I have *d* it ..... Jn 13:26
And when he had *d* the sop, he gave ..... Jn 13:26
clothed with a vesture *d* in blood ..... Rev 19:13

**DIPPETH**
He that *d* his hand with me in the ..... Mt 26:23
that *d* with me in the dish ..... Mk 14:20

**DIRECT**
to *d* his face unto Goshen ..... Gen 46:28
will I *d* my prayer unto thee ..... Ps 5:3
him, and he shall *d* thy paths ..... Prov 3:6
of the perfect shall *d* his way ..... Prov 11:5
but wisdom is profitable to *d* ..... Eccl 10:10
and I will *d* all his ways ..... Is 45:13
I will *d* their work in truth, and ..... Is 61:8
man that walketh to *d* his steps ..... Jer 10:23
Jesus Christ, *d* our way unto you ..... 1Th 3:11
the Lord *d* your hearts into the ..... 2Th 3:5

**DIRECTED**
Now he hath not *d* his words ..... Job 32:14
O that my ways were *d* to keep thy ..... Ps 119:5
Who hath *d* the Spirit of the LORD ..... Is 40:13

**DIRECTETH**
He *d* it under the whole heaven, ..... Job 37:3
but the LORD *d* his steps ..... Prov 16:9
as for the upright, he *d* his way ..... Prov 21:29

**DIRECTION**
by the *d* of the lawgiver, with ..... Num 21:18

**DIRECTLY**
sprinkle of her blood *d* before ..... Num 19:4
even the way *d* before the wall ..... Eze 42:12

**DIRT**
and the *d* came out ..... Judg 3:22
them out as the *d* in the streets ..... Ps 18:42
whose waters cast up mire and *d* ..... Is 57:20

**DISALLOW**
But if her father *d* her in the ..... Num 30:5

**DISALLOWED**
her, because her father *d* her ..... Num 30:5
But if her husband *d* her on the ..... Num 30:8
his peace at her, and *d* her not ..... Num 30:11
*d* indeed of men, but chosen of ..... 1Pet 2:4
the stone which the builders *d* ..... 1Pet 2:7

**DISANNUL**
Wilt thou also *d* my judgment ... Job 40:8
hath purposed, and who shall *d* it ... Is 14:27
and thirty years after, cannot *d* ... Gal 3:17

**DISANNULLED**
covenant with death shall be *d* ... Is 28:18

**DISANNULLETH**
yet if it be confirmed, no man *d* ... Gal 3:15

**DISANNULLING**
For there is verily a *d* of the ... Heb 7:18

**DISAPPOINT**
O LORD, *d* him, cast him down ... Ps 17:13

**DISAPPOINTED**
Without counsel purposes are *d* ... Prov 15:22

**DISAPPOINTETH**
He *d* the devices of the crafty, ... Job 5:12

**DISCERN**
before our brethren *d* thou what ... Gen 31:32
and she said, *D*, I pray thee, ... Gen 38:25
so is my lord the king to *d* good ... 2Sa 14:17
can I *d* between good and evil ... 2Sa 19:35
that I may *d* between good and bad ... 1Kin 3:9
understanding to *d* judgment ... 1Kin 3:11
So that the people could not *d* ... Ezr 3:13
but I could not *d* the form ... Job 4:16
cannot my taste *d* perverse things ... Job 6:30
cause them to *d* between the ... Eze 44:23
cannot *d* between their right hand ... Jonah 4:11
*d* between the righteous and the ... Mal 3:18
ye can *d* the face of the sky ... Mt 16:3
but can ye not *d* the signs of the ... Mt 16:3
ye can *d* the face of the sky and ... Lk 12:56
is it that ye do not *d* this time ... Lk 12:56
senses exercised to *d* both good ... Heb 5:14

**DISCERNED**
he *d* him not, because his hands ... Gen 27:23
the king of Israel *d* him that he ... 1Kin 20:41
I *d* among the youths, a young man ... Prov 7:7
because they are spiritually *d* ... 1Cor 2:14

**DISCERNER**
is a *d* of the thoughts and intents ... Heb 4:12

**DISCERNETH**
and a wise man's heart *d* both time ... Eccl 8:5

**DISCERNING**
to himself, not *d* the Lord's body ... 1Cor 11:29
to another *d* of spirits ... 1Cor 12:10

**DISCHARGE**
and there is no *d* in that war ... Eccl 8:8

**DISCHARGED**
and will cause them to be *d* there ... 1Kin 5:9

**DISCIPLE**
The *d* is not above his master, ... Mt 10:24
It is enough for the *d* that he be ... Mt 10:25
water only in the name of a *d* ... Mt 10:42
who also himself was Jesus' *d* ... Mt 27:57
The *d* is not above his master ... Lk 6:40
own life also, he cannot be my *d* ... Lk 14:26
and come after me, cannot be my *d* ... Lk 14:27
that he hath, he cannot be my *d* ... Lk 14:33
him, and said, Thou art his *d* ... Jn 9:28
Jesus, and so did another *d* ... Jn 18:15
that *d* was known unto the high ... Jn 18:15
Then went out that other *d* ... Jn 18:16
the *d* standing by, whom he loved, ... Jn 19:26
Then saith he to the *d*, Behold ... Jn 19:27
from that hour that *d* took her ... Jn 19:27
being a *d* of Jesus, but secretly ... Jn 19:38
to Simon Peter, and to the other *d* ... Jn 20:2
went forth, and that other *d* ... Jn 20:3
the other *d* did outrun Peter, and ... Jn 20:4
Then went in also that other *d* ... Jn 20:8
Therefore that *d* whom Jesus loved ... Jn 21:7
seeth the *d* whom Jesus loved ... Jn 21:20
that that *d* should not die ... Jn 21:23
This is the *d* which testifieth of ... Jn 21:24
there was a certain *d* at Damascus ... Acts 9:10
and believed not that he was a *d* ... Acts 9:26
Joppa a certain *d* named Tabitha ... Acts 9:36
and, behold, a certain *d* was there ... Acts 16:1
one Mnason of Cyprus, an old *d* ... Acts 21:16

**DISCIPLES**
seal the law among my *d* ... Is 8:16
he was set, his *d* came unto him ... Mt 5:1
And another of his *d* said unto him ... Mt 8:21
into a ship, his *d* followed him ... Mt 8:23
his *d* came to him, and awoke him, ... Mt 8:25
and sat down with him and his *d* ... Mt 9:10
saw it, they said unto his *d* ... Mt 9:11
Then came to him the *d* of John ... Mt 9:14
fast oft, but thy *d* fast not ... Mt 9:14
and followed him, and so did his *d* ... Mt 9:19
Then saith he unto his *d*, The ... Mt 9:37
had called unto him his twelve *d* ... Mt 10:1
an end of commanding his twelve *d* ... Mt 11:1
of Christ, he sent two of his *d* ... Mt 11:2
his *d* were an hungred, and began ... Mt 12:1
thy *d* do that which is not lawful ... Mt 12:2
forth his hand toward his *d* ... Mt 12:49
the *d* came, and said unto him, Why ... Mt 13:10
his *d* came unto him, saying, ... Mt 13:36
his *d* came, and took up the body, ... Mt 14:12
his *d* came to him, saying, This ... Mt 14:15
and gave the loaves to his *d* ... Mt 14:19
and the *d* to the multitude ... Mt 14:19
his *d* to get into a ship, and to ... Mt 14:22
when the *d* saw him walking on the ... Mt 14:26
Why do thy *d* transgress the ... Mt 15:2
Then came his *d*, and said unto him ... Mt 15:12
his *d* came and besought him, ... Mt 15:23
Then Jesus called his *d* unto him ... Mt 15:32
his *d* say unto him, Whence should ... Mt 15:33
and brake them, and gave to his *d* ... Mt 15:36
and the *d* to the multitude ... Mt 15:36
when his *d* were come to the other ... Mt 16:5
Caesarea Philippi, he asked his *d* ... Mt 16:13
Then charged he his *d* that they ... Mt 16:20
began Jesus to shew unto his *d* ... Mt 16:21
Then said Jesus unto his *d* ... Mt 16:24
And when the *d* heard it, they fell ... Mt 17:6
his *d* asked him, saying, Why then ... Mt 17:10
Then the *d* understood that he ... Mt 17:13
And I brought him to thy *d* ... Mt 17:16
Then came the *d* to Jesus apart, ... Mt 17:19
same time came the *d* unto Jesus ... Mt 18:1
His *d* say unto him, If the case ... Mt 19:10
and the *d* rebuked them ... Mt 19:13
Then said Jesus unto his *d* ... Mt 19:23
When his *d* heard it, they were ... Mt 19:25
the twelve *d* apart in the way ... Mt 20:17
of Olives, then sent Jesus two *d* ... Mt 21:1
the *d* went, and did as Jesus ... Mt 21:6
And when the *d* saw it, they ... Mt 21:20
him their *d* with the Herodians ... Mt 22:16
to the multitude, and to his *d* ... Mt 23:1
his *d* came to him for to shew him ... Mt 24:1
the *d* came unto him privately, ... Mt 24:3
these sayings, he said unto his *d* ... Mt 26:1
But when his *d* saw it, they had ... Mt 26:8
bread the *d* came to Jesus ... Mt 26:17
passover at thy house with my *d* ... Mt 26:18
the *d* did as Jesus had appointed ... Mt 26:19
and brake it, and gave it to the *d* ... Mt 26:26
Likewise also said all the *d* ... Mt 26:35
Gethsemane, and saith unto the *d* ... Mt 26:36
And he cometh unto the *d*, and ... Mt 26:40
Then cometh he to his *d*, and saith ... Mt 26:45
Then all the *d* forsook him ... Mt 26:56
lest his *d* come by night, and ... Mt 27:64
tell his *d* that he is risen from ... Mt 28:7
and did run to bring his *d* word ... Mt 28:8
And as they went to tell his *d* ... Mt 28:9
His *d* came by night, and stole him ... Mt 28:13
Then the eleven *d* went away into ... Mt 28:16
also together with Jesus and his *d* ... Mk 2:15
and sinners, they said unto his *d* ... Mk 2:16
the *d* of John and of the Pharisees ... Mk 2:18
unto him, Why do the *d* of John ... Mk 2:18
fast, but thy *d* fast not ... Mk 2:18
his *d* began, as they went, to ... Mk 2:23
himself with his *d* to the sea ... Mk 3:7
And he spake to his *d*, that a ... Mk 3:9
he expounded all things to his *d* ... Mk 4:34
his *d* said unto him, Thou seest ... Mk 5:31
and his *d* follow him ... Mk 6:1
when his *d* heard of it, they came ... Mk 6:29
his *d* came unto him, and said, ... Mk 6:35
gave them to his *d* to set before ... Mk 6:41
his *d* to get into the ship ... Mk 6:45
of his *d* eat bread with defiled ... Mk 7:2
Why walk not thy *d* according to ... Mk 7:5
his *d* asked him concerning the ... Mk 7:17
eat, Jesus called his *d* unto him ... Mk 8:1
his *d* answered him, From whence ... Mk 8:4
gave to his *d* to set before them ... Mk 8:6
he entered into a ship with his *d* ... Mk 8:10
Now the *d* had forgotten to take ... Mk 8:14
And Jesus went out, and his *d* ... Mk 8:27
and by the way he asked his *d* ... Mk 8:27
turned about and looked on his *d* ... Mk 8:33
people unto him with his *d* also ... Mk 8:34
And when he came to his *d*, he saw ... Mk 9:14
I spake to thy *d* that they should ... Mk 9:18
his *d* asked him privately, Why ... Mk 9:28
For he taught his *d*, and said unto ... Mk 9:31
in the house his *d* asked him ... Mk 10:10
his *d* rebuked those that brought ... Mk 10:13
round about, and saith unto his *d* ... Mk 10:23
the *d* were astonished at his ... Mk 10:24
he went out of Jericho with his *d* ... Mk 10:46
he sendeth forth two of his *d* ... Mk 11:1
And his *d* heard it ... Mk 11:14
And he called unto him his *d* ... Mk 12:43
one of his *d* saith unto him, ... Mk 13:1
his *d* said unto him, Where wilt ... Mk 14:12
And he sendeth forth two of his *d* ... Mk 14:13
shall eat the passover with my *d* ... Mk 14:14
his *d* went forth, and came into ... Mk 14:16
and he saith to his *d*, Sit ye here ... Mk 14:32
But go your way, tell his *d* ... Mk 16:7
Pharisees murmured against his *d* ... Lk 5:30
Why do the *d* of John fast often, ... Lk 5:33
likewise the *d* of the Pharisees ... Lk 5:33
his *d* plucked the ears of corn, ... Lk 6:1
was day, he called unto him his *d* ... Lk 6:13
plain, and the company of his *d* ... Lk 6:17
And he lifted up his eyes on his *d* ... Lk 6:20
many of his *d* went with him, and ... Lk 7:11
the *d* of John shewed him of all ... Lk 7:18
two of his *d* sent them to Jesus ... Lk 7:19
his *d* asked him, saying, What ... Lk 8:9
he went into a ship with his *d* ... Lk 8:22
he called his twelve *d* together ... Lk 9:1
And he said to his *d*, Make them ... Lk 9:14
gave to the *d* to set before the ... Lk 9:16
praying, his *d* were with him ... Lk 9:18
I besought thy *d* to cast him out ... Lk 9:40
Jesus did, he said unto his *d* ... Lk 9:43
And when his *d* James and John saw ... Lk 9:54
And he turned him unto his *d* ... Lk 10:23
one of his *d* said unto him, Lord, ... Lk 11:1
pray, as John also taught his *d* ... Lk 11:1
to say unto his *d* first of all ... Lk 12:1
And he said unto his *d*, Therefore ... Lk 12:22
And he said also unto his *d* ... Lk 16:1
Then said he unto the *d*, It is ... Lk 17:1
And he said unto the *d*, The days ... Lk 17:22
but when his *d* saw it, they ... Lk 18:15
of Olives, he sent two of his *d* ... Lk 19:29
of the *d* began to rejoice ... Lk 19:37
unto him, Master, rebuke thy *d* ... Lk 19:39
all the people he said unto his *d* ... Lk 20:45
shall eat the passover with my *d* ... Lk 22:11
and his *d* also followed him ... Lk 22:39
from prayer, and was come to his *d* ... Lk 22:45
after John stood, and two of his *d* ... Jn 1:35
the two *d* heard him speak, and ... Jn 1:37
both Jesus was called, and his *d* ... Jn 2:2
and his *d* believed on him ... Jn 2:11
mother, and his brethren, and his *d* ... Jn 2:12
his *d* remembered that it was ... Jn 2:17
his *d* remembered that he had said ... Jn 2:22
his *d* into the land of Judaea ... Jn 3:22
question between some of John's *d* ... Jn 3:25
made and baptized more *d* than John ... Jn 4:1
himself baptized not, but his *d* ... Jn 4:2
(For his *d* were gone away unto ... Jn 4:8
And upon this came his *d*, and ... Jn 4:27
the mean while his *d* prayed him ... Jn 4:31
said the *d* one to another ... Jn 4:33
and there he sat with his *d* ... Jn 6:3
One of his *d*, Andrew, Simon ... Jn 6:8
thanks, he distributed to the *d* ... Jn 6:11
the *d* to them that were set down ... Jn 6:11
were filled, he said unto his *d* ... Jn 6:12
his *d* went down unto the sea, ... Jn 6:16
one whereinto his *d* were entered ... Jn 6:22
went not with his *d* into the boat ... Jn 6:22
but that his *d* were gone away ... Jn 6:22
was not there, neither his *d* ... Jn 6:24
Many therefore of his *d*, when ... Jn 6:60
himself that his *d* murmured at it ... Jn 6:61
that time many of his *d* went back ... Jn 6:66
that thy *d* also may see the works ... Jn 7:3
my word, then are ye my *d* indeed ... Jn 8:31
his *d* asked him, saying, Master, ... Jn 9:2
will ye also be his *d* ... Jn 9:27
but we are Moses' *d* ... Jn 9:28
Then after that saith he to his *d* ... Jn 11:7
His *d* say unto him, Master, the ... Jn 11:8
Then said his *d*, Lord, if he ... Jn 11:12
and there continued with his *d* ... Jn 11:54
Then saith one of his *d*, Judas ... Jn 12:4
understood not his *d* at the first ... Jn 12:16
Then the *d* looked one on another, ... Jn 13:22
on Jesus' bosom one of his *d* ... Jn 13:23
all men know that ye are my *d* ... Jn 13:35
so shall ye be my *d* ... Jn 15:8
some of his *d* among themselves ... Jn 16:17
His *d* said unto him, Lo, now ... Jn 16:29
with his *d* over the brook Cedron ... Jn 18:1
the which he entered, and his *d* ... Jn 18:1
resorted thither with his *d* ... Jn 18:2
not thou also one of this man's *d* ... Jn 18:17
priest then asked Jesus of his *d* ... Jn 18:19
Art not thou also one of his *d* ... Jn 18:25
Then the *d* went away again unto ... Jn 20:10
told the *d* that she had seen the ... Jn 20:18
the doors were shut where the *d* ... Jn 20:19
Then were the *d* glad, when they ... Jn 20:20
The other *d* therefore said unto ... Jn 20:25
days again his *d* were within ... Jn 20:26
Jesus in the presence of his *d* ... Jn 20:30
to the *d* at the sea of Tiberias ... Jn 21:1
of Zebedee, and two other of his *d* ... Jn 21:2
but the *d* knew not that it was ... Jn 21:4
the other *d* came in a little ship ... Jn 21:8
none of the *d* durst ask him, Who ... Jn 21:12
Jesus shewed himself to his *d* ... Jn 21:14
stood up in the midst of the *d* ... Acts 1:15
number of the *d* was multiplied ... Acts 6:1
the multitude of the *d* unto them ... Acts 6:2
the number of the *d* multiplied in ... Acts 6:7
against the *d* of the Lord ... Acts 9:1
with the *d* which were at Damascus ... Acts 9:19
Then the *d* took him by night, and ... Acts 9:25
assayed to join himself to the *d* ... Acts 9:26
the *d* had heard that Peter was ... Acts 9:38
the *d* were called Christians ... Acts 11:26
Then the *d*, every man according ... Acts 11:29
the *d* were filled with joy, and ... Acts 13:52
as the *d* stood round about him, ... Acts 14:20
Confirming the souls of the *d* ... Acts 14:22
they abode long time with the *d* ... Acts 14:28
put a yoke upon the neck of the *d* ... Acts 15:10
in order, strengthening all the *d* ... Acts 18:23
exhorting the *d* to receive him ... Acts 18:27
and finding certain *d*, ... Acts 19:1
from them, and separated the *d* ... Acts 19:9
people, the *d* suffered him not ... Acts 19:30
Paul called unto him the *d* ... Acts 20:1
when the *d* came together to break ... Acts 20:7
things, to draw away *d* after them ... Acts 20:30

And finding *d*, we tarried there ... Acts 21:4
also certain of the *d* of Caesarea ... Acts 21:16

**DISCIPLES'**
and began to wash the *d* feet ... Jn 13:5

**DISCIPLINE**
He openeth also their ear to *d* ... Job 36:10

**DISCLOSE**
the earth also shall *d* her blood ... Is 26:21

**DISCOMFITED**
And Joshua *d* Amalek and his people ... Ex 17:13
*d* them, even unto Hormah ... Num 14:45
the LORD *d* them before Israel, and ... Josh 10:10
And the LORD *d* Sisera, and all his ... Judg 4:15
and Zalmunna, and *d* all the host ... Judg 8:12
upon the Philistines, and *d* them ... 1Sa 7:10
lightning, and *d* them ... 2Sa 22:15
he shot out lightnings, and *d* them ... Ps 18:14
and his young men shall be *d* ... Is 31:8

**DISCOMFITURE**
and there was a very great *d* ... 1Sa 14:20

**DISCONTENTED**
in debt, and every one that was *d* ... 1Sa 22:2

**DISCONTINUE**
shalt *d* from thine heritage that ... Jer 17:4

**DISCORD**
he soweth *d* ... Prov 6:14
he that soweth *d* among brethren ... Prov 6:19

**DISCOURAGE**
wherefore *d* ye the heart of the ... Num 32:7

**DISCOURAGED**
was much *d* because of the way ... Num 21:4
they *d* the heart of the children ... Num 32:9
fear not, neither be *d* ... Deut 1:21
our brethren have *d* our heart ... Deut 1:28
He shall not fail nor be *d* ... Is 42:4
children to anger, lest they be *d* ... Col 3:21

**DISCOVER**
wife, nor *d* his father's skirt ... Deut 22:30
we will *d* ourselves unto them ... 1Sa 14:8
Who can *d* the face of his garment ... Job 41:13
but that his heart may *d* itself ... Prov 18:2
*d* not a secret to another ... Prov 25:9
the LORD will *d* their secret ... Is 3:17
Therefore will I *d* thy skirts ... Jer 13:26
he will *d* thy sins ... Lam 4:22
will *d* thy nakedness unto them, ... Eze 16:37
now will I *d* her lewdness in the ... Hos 2:10
I will *d* the foundations thereof ... Mic 1:6
I will *d* thy skirts upon thy face ... Nah 3:5

**DISCOVERED**
thy nakedness be not *d* thereon ... Ex 20:26
he hath *d* her fountain, and she ... Lev 20:18
both of them *d* themselves unto ... 1Sa 14:11
When Saul heard that David was *d* ... 1Sa 22:6
foundations of the world were *d* ... 2Sa 22:16
of the world were *d* at thy rebuke ... Ps 18:15
he *d* the covering of Judah, and ... Is 22:8
for thou hast *d* thyself to ... Is 57:8
thine iniquity are thy skirts *d* ... Jer 13:22
they have not *d* thine iniquity, ... Lam 2:14
the foundation thereof shall be *d* ... Eze 13:14
thy nakedness *d* through thy ... Eze 16:36
Before thy wickedness was *d* ... Eze 16:57
in that your transgressions are *d* ... Eze 21:24
In thee have they *d* their ... Eze 22:10
These *d* her nakedness ... Eze 23:10
So she *d* her whoredoms, and ... Eze 23:18
her whoredoms, and *d* her nakedness. Eze 23:18
of thy whoredoms shall be *d* ... Eze 23:29
the iniquity of Ephraim was *d* ... Hos 7:1
Now when we had *d* Cyprus, we left ... Acts 21:3
but they *d* a certain creek with a ... Acts 27:39

**DISCOVERETH**
He *d* deep things out of darkness, ... Job 12:22
hinds to calve, and *d* the forests ... Ps 29:9

**DISCOVERING**
by *d* the foundation unto the neck ... Hab 3:13

**DISCREET**
let Pharaoh look out a man *d* ... Gen 41:33
thee all this, there is none so *d* ... Gen 41:39
To be *d*, chaste, keepers at home, ... Titus 2:5

**DISCREETLY**
when Jesus saw that he answered *d* ... Mk 12:34

**DISCRETION**
he will guide his affairs with *d* ... Ps 112:5
to the young man knowledge and *d* ... Prov 1:4
*D* shall preserve thee, ... Prov 2:11
keep sound wisdom and *d* ... Prov 3:21
That thou mayest regard *d* ... Prov 5:2
a fair woman which is without *d* ... Prov 11:22
The *d* of a man deferreth his ... Prov 19:11
his God doth instruct him to *d* ... Is 28:26
out the heavens by his *d* ... Jer 10:12

**DISDAINED**
about, and saw David, he *d* him ... 1Sa 17:42
whose fathers I would have *d* to ... Job 30:1

**DISEASE**
whether I shall recover of this *d* ... 2Kin 1:2
saying, Shall I recover of this *d* ... 2Kin 8:8
saying, Shall I recover of this *d* ... 2Kin 8:9
until his *d* was exceeding great ... 2Chr 16:12
yet in his *d* he sought not to the ... 2Chr 16:12
great sickness by *d* of thy bowels ... 2Chr 21:15
in his bowels with an incurable *d* ... 2Chr 21:18
of my *d* is my garment changed ... Job 30:18
are filled with a loathsome *d* ... Ps 38:7
An evil *d*, say they, cleaveth ... Ps 41:8
is vanity, and it is an evil *d* ... Eccl 6:2
all manner of *d* among the people ... Mt 4:23
and every *d* among the people ... Mt 9:35
of sickness and all manner of *d* ... Mt 10:1
made whole of whatsoever *d* he had ... Jn 5:4

**DISEASED**
his old age he was *d* in his feet ... 1Kin 15:23
of his reign was *d* in his feet ... 2Chr 16:12
The *d* have ye not strengthened, ... Eze 34:4
pushed all the *d* with your horns, ... Eze 34:21
which was *d* with an issue of ... Mt 9:20
brought unto him all that were *d* ... Mt 14:35
brought unto him all that were *d* ... Mk 1:32
which he did on them that were *d* ... Jn 6:2

**DISEASES**
put none of these *d* upon thee ... Ex 15:26
put none of the evil *d* of Egypt ... Deut 7:15
upon thee all the *d* of Egypt ... Deut 28:60
so he died of sore *d* ... 2Chr 21:19
(for they left him in great *d* ... 2Chr 24:25
who healeth all thy *d* ... Ps 103:3
that were taken with divers *d* ... Mt 4:24
many that were sick of divers *d* ... Mk 1:34
divers *d* brought them unto him ... Lk 4:40
him, and to be healed of their *d* ... Lk 6:17
over all devils, and to cure *d* ... Lk 9:1
the *d* departed from them, and the ... Acts 19:12
which had *d* in the island, came, ... Acts 28:9

**DISFIGURE**
for they *d* their faces, that they ... Mt 6:16

**DISGRACE**
do not *d* the throne of thy glory ... Jer 14:21

**DISGUISE**
*d* thyself, that thou be not known ... 1Kin 14:2
unto Jehoshaphat, I will *d* myself ... 1Kin 22:30
unto Jehoshaphat, I will *d* myself ... 2Chr 18:29

**DISGUISED**
Saul *d* himself, and put on other ... 1Sa 28:8
*d* himself with ashes upon his ... 1Kin 20:38
And the king of Israel *d* himself ... 1Kin 22:30
So the king of Israel *d* himself ... 2Chr 18:29
but *d* himself, that he might ... 2Chr 35:22

**DISGUISETH**
and *d* his face ... Job 24:15

**DISH**
forth butter in a lordly *d* ... Judg 5:25
Jerusalem as a man wipeth a *d* ... 2Kin 21:13
dippeth his hand with me in the *d* ... Mt 26:23
that dippeth with me in the *d* ... Mk 14:20

**DISHAN** (*di'-shan*) See DISHON. *A son of Seir.*
And Dishon, and Ezer, and *D* ... Gen 36:21
The children of *D* are these ... Gen 36:28
Duke Dishon, duke Ezer, duke *D* ... Gen 36:30
and Dishon, and Ezar, and *D* ... 1Chr 1:38
The sons of *D* ... 1Chr 1:42

**DISHES**
And thou shalt make the *d* thereof ... Ex 25:29
which were upon the table, his *d* ... Ex 37:16
of blue, and put thereon the *d* ... Num 4:7

**DISHON** (*di'-shon*) See DISHAN.
*1. A son of Seir.*
And *D*, and Ezer, and Dishan ... Gen 36:21
And these are the children of *D* ... Gen 36:26
Duke *D*, duke Ezer, duke Dishan ... Gen 36:30
Shobal, and Zibeon, and Anah, and *D* 1Chr 1:38
*2. A son of Anah.*
*D*, and Aholibamah the daughter of ... Gen 36:25
The sons of Anah; *D* ... 1Chr 1:41
And the sons of *D* ... 1Chr 1:41

**DISHONEST**
thy *d* gain which thou hast made ... Eze 22:13
to destroy souls, to get *d* gain ... Eze 22:27

**DISHONESTY**
renounced the hidden things of *d* ... 2Cor 4:2

**DISHONOUR**
meet for us to see the king's *d* ... Ezr 4:14
*d* that magnify themselves against ... Ps 35:26
my reproach, and my shame, and my *d* Ps 69:19
reproach and *d* that seek my hurt ... Ps 71:13
A wound and *d* shall he get ... Prov 6:33
I honour my Father, and ye do *d* me ... Jn 8:49
to *d* their own bodies between ... Rom 1:24
unto honour, and another unto *d* ... Rom 9:21
It is sown in *d* ... 1Cor 15:43
By honour and *d*, by evil report and ... 2Cor 6:8
and some to honour, and some to *d* ... 2Ti 2:20

**DISHONOUREST**
breaking the law *d* thou God ... Rom 2:23

**DISHONOURETH**
For the son *d* the father, the ... Mic 7:6
his head covered, *d* his head ... 1Cor 11:4
her head uncovered *d* her head ... 1Cor 11:5

**DISINHERIT**
*d* them, and will make of thee a ... Num 14:12

**DISMAYED**
fear not, neither be *d* ... Deut 31:8
be not afraid, neither be thou *d* ... Josh 1:9
Fear not, neither be thou *d* ... Josh 8:1
unto them, Fear not, nor be *d* ... Josh 10:25
of the Philistine, they were *d* ... 1Sa 17:11
were of small power, they were *d* ... 2Kin 19:26
dread not, nor be *d* ... 1Chr 22:13
fear not, nor be *d* ... 1Chr 28:20
Be not afraid nor *d* by reason of ... 2Chr 20:15
fear not, nor be *d* ... 2Chr 20:17
be not afraid nor *d* for the king ... 2Chr 32:7
I was *d* at the seeing of it ... Is 21:3
were of small power, they were *d* ... Is 37:27
be not *d* ... Is 41:10
or do evil, that we may be *d* ... Is 41:23
be not *d* at their faces, lest I ... Jer 1:17
wise men are ashamed, they are *d* ... Jer 8:9
be not *d* at the signs of heaven ... Jer 10:2
for the heathen are *d* at them ... Jer 10:2
be *d*, but let not me be *d* ... Jer 17:18
they shall fear no more, nor be *d* ... Jer 23:4
neither be *d*, O Israel ... Jer 30:10
Wherefore have I seen them *d* ... Jer 46:5
O my servant Jacob, and be not *d* ... Jer 46:27
Misgab is confounded and *d* ... Jer 48:1
Elam to be *d* before their enemies ... Jer 49:37
and they shall be *d* ... Jer 50:36
nor be *d* at their looks, though ... Eze 2:6
neither be *d* at their looks, ... Eze 3:9
mighty men, O Teman, shall be *d* ... Obad 9

**DISMAYING**
a *d* to all them about him ... Jer 48:39

**DISMISSED**
the priest *d* not the courses ... 2Chr 23:8
So when they were *d*, they came to ... Acts 15:30
thus spoken, he *d* the assembly ... Acts 19:41

**DISOBEDIENCE**
For as by one man's *d* many were ... Rom 5:19
in a readiness to revenge all *d* ... 2Cor 10:6
now worketh in the children of *d* ... Eph 2:2
of God upon the children of *d* ... Eph 5:6
God cometh on the children of *d* ... Col 3:6
*d* received a just recompence of ... Heb 2:2

**DISOBEDIENT**
who was *d* unto the word of the ... 1Kin 13:26
Nevertheless they were *d*, and ... Neh 9:26
the *d* to the wisdom of the just ... Lk 1:17
I was not *d* unto the heavenly ... Acts 26:19
of evil things, *d* to parents, ... Rom 1:30
stretched forth my hands unto a *d* ... Rom 10:21
man, but for the lawless and *d* ... 1Ti 1:9
*d* to parents, unthankful, unholy, ... 2Ti 3:2
deny him, being abominable, and *d* ... Titus 1:16
also were sometimes foolish, *d* ... Titus 3:3
but unto them which be *d*, the ... 1Pet 2:7
stumble at the word, being *d* ... 1Pet 2:8
Which sometime were *d*, when once ... 1Pet 3:20

**DISOBEYED**
thou hast *d* the mouth of the LORD ... 1Kin 13:21

**DISORDERLY**
from every brother that walketh *d* ... 2Th 3:6
behaved not ourselves *d* among you ... 2Th 3:7
are some which walk among you *d* ... 2Th 3:11

**DISPATCH**
and *d* them with their swords ... Eze 23:47

**DISPENSATION**
a *d* of the gospel is committed ... 1Cor 9:17
That in the *d* of the fulness of ... Eph 1:10
If ye have heard of the *d* of the ... Eph 3:2
according to the *d* of God which ... Col 1:25

**DISPERSE**
*D* yourselves among the people, and ... 1Sa 14:34
The lips of the wise *d* knowledge ... Prov 15:7
and *d* them in the countries ... Eze 12:15
*d* them through the countries ... Eze 20:23
*d* thee in the countries, and will ... Eze 22:15
will *d* them through the countries ... Eze 29:12
will *d* them through the countries ... Eze 30:23
*d* them among the countries ... Eze 30:26

**DISPERSED**
*d* of all his children throughout ... 2Chr 11:23
*d* among the people in all the ... Est 3:8
He hath *d*, he hath given to the ... Ps 112:9
Let thy fountains be *d* abroad ... Prov 5:16
gather together the *d* of Judah ... Is 11:12
they were *d* through the countries ... Eze 36:19
even the daughter of my *d* ... Zeph 3:10
go unto the *d* among the Gentiles ... Jn 7:35
as many as obeyed him, were *d* ... Acts 5:37
it is written, He hath *d* abroad ... 2Cor 9:9

**DISPERSIONS**
of your *d* are accomplished ... Jer 25:34

**DISPLAYED**
that it may be *d* because of the ... Ps 60:4

**DISPLEASE**
Let it not *d* my lord that I ... Gen 31:35
now therefore, if it *d* thee ... Num 22:34
that thou *d* not the lords of the ... 1Sa 29:7
Joab, Let not this thing *d* thee ... 2Sa 11:25
it *d* him, and he turn away his ... Prov 24:18

D

**DISPLEASED**
the thing which he did *d* the LORD Gen 38:10
the head of Ephraim, it *d* him Gen 48:17
people complained, it *d* the LORD Num 11:1
Moses also was *d* Num 11:10
But the thing *d* Samuel, when they 1Sa 8:6
very wroth, and the saying *d* him 1Sa 18:8
And David was *d*, because the LORD 2Sa 6:8
that David had done *d* the LORD 2Sa 11:27
his father had not *d* him at any 1Kin 1:6
went to his house heavy and *d* 1Kin 20:43
*d* because of the word which 1Kin 21:4
And David was *d*, because the LORD 1Chr 13:11
God was *d* with this thing 1Chr 21:7
scattered us, thou hast been *d* Ps 60:1
it *d* him that there was no Is 59:15
was sore *d* with himself, and set Dan 6:14
But it *d* Jonah exceedingly, and he Jonah 4:1
Was the LORD *d* against the rivers Hab 3:8
been sore *d* with your fathers Zec 1:2
I am very sore *d* with the heathen Zec 1:15
for I was but a little *d*, and they Zec 1:15
they were sore *d*, Mt 21:15
when Jesus saw it, he was much *d* Mk 10:14
began to be much *d* with James Mk 10:41
Herod was highly *d* with them of Acts 12:20

**DISPLEASURE**
was afraid of the anger and hot *d* Deut 9:19
Philistines, though I do them a *d* Judg 15:3
wrath, and vex them in his sore *d* Ps 2:5
neither chasten me in thy hot *d* Ps 6:1
neither chasten me in thy hot *d* Ps 38:1

**DISPOSED**
Or who hath *d* the whole world Job 34:13
Dost thou know when God *d* them Job 37:15
when he was *d* to pass into Achaia Acts 18:27
you to a feast, and ye be *d* to go 1Cor 10:27

**DISPOSING**
but the whole *d* thereof is of the Prov 16:33

**DISPOSITION**
the law by the *d* of angels Acts 7:53

**DISPOSSESS**
ye shall *d* the inhabitants of the Num 33:53
how can I *d* them Deut 7:17

**DISPOSSESSED**
*d* the Amorite which was in it Num 32:39
*d* the Amorites from before his Judg 11:23

**DISPUTATION**
*d* with them, they determined that Acts 15:2

**DISPUTATIONS**
receive ye, but not to doubtful *d* Rom 14:1

**DISPUTE**
the righteous might *d* with him Job 23:7

**DISPUTED**
What was it that ye *d* among Mk 9:33
way they had *d* among themselves Mk 9:34
Jesus, and *d* against the Grecians Acts 9:29
Therefore *d* he in the synagogue Acts 17:17
he *d* about the body of Moses Jude 9

**DISPUTER**
where is the *d* of this world 1Cor 1:20

**DISPUTING**
and of Asia, *d* with Stephen Acts 6:9
And when there had been much *d* Acts 15:7
for the space of three months, *d* Acts 19:8
*d* daily in the school of one Acts 19:9
me in the temple *d* with any man Acts 24:12

**DISPUTINGS**
things without murmurings and *d* Phil 2:14
Perverse *d* of men of corrupt 1Ti 6:5

**DISQUIET**
*d* the inhabitants of Babylon Jer 50:34

**DISQUIETED**
said to Saul, Why hast thou *d* me 1Sa 28:15
surely they are *d* in vain Ps 39:6
and why art thou *d* in me Ps 42:5
and why art thou *d* within me Ps 42:11
and why art thou *d* within me Ps 43:5
For three things the earth is *d* Prov 30:21

**DISQUIETNESS**
by reason of the *d* of my heart Ps 38:8

**DISSEMBLED**
*d* also, and they have put it even Josh 7:11
For ye *d* in your hearts, when ye Jer 42:20
the other Jews *d* likewise with Gal 2:13

**DISSEMBLERS**
neither will I go in with *d* Ps 26:4

**DISSEMBLETH**
He that hateth *d* with his lips Prov 26:24

**DISSENSION**
Paul and Barnabas had no small *d* Acts 15:2
there arose a *d* between the Acts 23:7
And when there arose a great *d* Acts 23:10

**DISSIMULATION**
Let love be without *d* Rom 12:9
was carried away with their *d* Gal 2:13

**DISSOLVE**
make interpretations, and *d* doubts Dan 5:16

**DISSOLVED**
all the inhabitants thereof are *d* Ps 75:3
thou, whole Palestina, art *d* Is 14:31
broken down, the earth is clean *d* Is 24:19
all the host of heaven shall be *d* Is 34:4
opened, and the palace shall be *d* Nah 2:6
house of this tabernacle were *d* 2Cor 5:1
that all these things shall be *d* 2Pet 3:11
heavens being on fire shall be *d* 2Pet 3:12

**DISSOLVEST**
ride upon it, and *d* my substance Job 30:22

**DISSOLVING**
*d* of doubts, were found in the Dan 5:12

**DISTAFF**
spindle, and her hands hold the *d* Prov 31:19

**DISTANT**
equally *d* one from another Ex 36:22

**DISTIL**
my speech shall *d* as the dew Deut 32:2
do drop and *d* upon man abundantly Job 36:28

**DISTINCTION**
they give a *d* in the sounds 1Cor 14:7

**DISTINCTLY**
in the book in the law of God *d* Neh 8:8

**DISTRACTED**
while I suffer thy terrors I am *d* Ps 88:15

**DISTRACTION**
attend upon the Lord without *d* 1Cor 7:35

**DISTRESS**
answered me in the day of my *d* Gen 35:3
therefore is this *d* come upon us Gen 42:21
*D* not the Moabites, neither Deut 2:9
*d* them not, nor meddle with them Deut 2:19
thine enemies shall *d* thee Deut 28:53
shall *d* thee in all thy gates Deut 28:55
enemy shall *d* thee in thy gates Deut 28:57
come unto me now when ye are in *d* Judg 11:7
And every one that was in *d* 1Sa 22:2
In my *d* I called upon the LORD, 2Sa 22:7
redeemed my soul out of all *d* 1Kin 1:29
in the time of his *d* did he 2Chr 28:22
Ye see the *d* that we are in, how Neh 2:17
pleasure, and we are in great *d* Neh 9:37
hast enlarged me when I was in *d* Ps 4:1
In my *d* I called upon the LORD, Ps 18:6
I called upon the LORD in *d* Ps 118:5
In my *d* I cried unto the LORD, and Ps 120:1
when *d* and anguish cometh Prov 1:27
a strength to the needy in his *d* Is 25:4
Yet I will *d* Ariel, and there Is 29:2
and her munition, and that *d* her Is 29:7
land at this once, and will *d* them Jer 10:18
for I am in *d* Lam 1:20
spoken proudly in the day of *d* Obad 12
that did remain in the day of *d* Obad 14
of wrath, a day of trouble and *d* Zeph 1:15
And I will bring *d* upon men Zeph 1:17
shall be great *d* in the land Lk 21:23
and upon the earth *d* of nations Lk 21:25
shall tribulation, or *d*, or Rom 8:35
this is good for the present *d* 1Cor 7:26
our affliction and *d* by your faith 1Th 3:7

**DISTRESSED**
Jacob was greatly afraid and *d* Gen 32:7
Moab was *d* because of the Num 22:3
and they were greatly *d* Judg 2:15
so that Israel was sore *d* Judg 10:9
a strait, (for the people were *d* 1Sa 13:6
the men of Israel were *d* that day 1Sa 14:24
And Saul answered, I am sore *d* 1Sa 28:15
And David was greatly *d* 1Sa 30:6
I am *d* for thee, my brother 2Sa 1:26
*d* him, but strengthened him not 2Chr 28:20
troubled on every side, yet not *d* 2Cor 4:8

**DISTRESSES**
O bring thou me out of my *d* Ps 25:17
he delivered them out of their *d* Ps 107:6
and he saved them out of their *d* Ps 107:13
and he saveth them out of their *d* Ps 107:19
he bringeth them out of their *d* Ps 107:28
and Noph shall have *d* daily Eze 30:16
afflictions, in necessities, in *d* 2Cor 6:4
in *d* for Christ's sake 2Cor 12:10

**DISTRIBUTE**
*d* for inheritance in the plains Josh 13:32
to *d* the oblations of the LORD, 2Chr 31:14
was to *d* unto their brethren Neh 13:13
*d* unto the poor, and thou shalt Lk 18:22
be rich in good works, ready to *d* 1Ti 6:18

**DISTRIBUTED**
*d* for inheritance to them Josh 14:1
And David *d* them, both Zadok of 1Chr 24:3
whom David had *d* in the house of 2Chr 23:18
he *d* to the disciples, and the Jn 6:11
But as God hath *d* to every man 1Cor 7:17
the rule which God hath *d* to us 2Cor 10:13

**DISTRIBUTETH**
God *d* sorrows in his anger Job 21:17

**DISTRIBUTING**
*D* to the necessity of saints Rom 12:13

**DISTRIBUTION**
*d* was made unto every man Acts 4:35
and for your liberal *d* unto them 2Cor 9:13

**DITCH**
Yet shalt thou plunge me in the *d* Job 9:31
fallen into the *d* which he made Ps 7:15
For a whore is a deep *d* Prov 23:27
Ye made also a *d* between the two Is 22:11
blind, both shall fall into the *d* Mt 15:14
they not both fall into the *d* Lk 6:39

**DITCHES**
LORD, Make this valley full of *d* 2Kin 3:16

**DIVERS**
not sow thy vineyard with *d* seeds Deut 22:9
not wear a garment of *d* sorts Deut 22:11
not have in thy bag *d* weights Deut 25:13
have in thine house *d* measures Deut 25:14
to Sisera a prey of *d* colours Judg 5:30
a prey of *d* colours of needlework Judg 5:30
of *d* colours of needlework on Judg 5:30
a garment of *d* colours upon her 2Sa 13:18
rent her garment of *d* colours 2Sa 13:19
of *d* colours, and all manner of 1Chr 29:2
*d* kinds of spices prepared by the 2Chr 16:14
*d* also of the princes of Israel 2Chr 21:4
Nevertheless *d* of Asher and 2Chr 30:11
He sent *d* sorts of flies among Ps 78:45
there came *d* sorts of flies, and Ps 105:31
*D* weights, and *d* measures, Prov 20:10
*D* weights are an abomination unto Prov 20:23
words there are also *d* vanities Eccl 5:7
thy high places with *d* colours Eze 16:16
of feathers, which had *d* colours Eze 17:3
that were taken with *d* diseases Mt 4:24
and earthquakes, in *d* places Mt 24:7
many that were sick of *d* diseases Mk 1:34
for *d* of them came from far Mk 8:3
shall be earthquakes in *d* places Mk 13:8
*d* diseases brought them unto him Lk 4:40
earthquakes shall be in *d* places Lk 21:11
But when *d* were hardened, and Acts 19:9
to another *d* kinds of tongues 1Cor 12:10
with sins, led away with *d* lusts 2Ti 3:6
deceived, serving *d* lusts Titus 3:3
in *d* manners spake in time past Heb 1:1
with *d* miracles, and gifts of the Heb 2:4
*d* washings, and carnal ordinances, Heb 9:10
Be not carried about with *d* Heb 13:9
when ye fall into *d* temptations Jas 1:2

**DIVERSE**
thy cattle gender with a *d* kind Lev 19:19
vessels being *d* one from another Est 1:7
their laws are *d* from all people Est 3:8
from the sea, *d* one from another Dan 7:3
it was *d* from all the beasts that Dan 7:7
which was *d* from all the others, Dan 7:19
which shall be *d* from all Dan 7:23
he shall be *d* from the first, and Dan 7:24

**DIVERSITIES**
Now there are *d* of gifts, but the 1Cor 12:4
there are *d* of operations, but it 1Cor 12:6
helps, governments, *d* of tongues 1Cor 12:28

**DIVIDE**
let it *d* the waters from the Gen 1:6
to *d* the day from the night Gen 1:14
to *d* the light from the darkness Gen 1:18
I will *d* them in Jacob, and Gen 49:7
and at night he shall *d* the spoil Gen 49:27
thine hand over the sea, and *d* it Ex 14:16
will overtake, I will *d* the spoil Ex 15:9
the live ox, and *d* the money of it Ex 21:35
and the dead ox also they shall *d* Ex 21:35
the vail shall *d* unto you between Ex 26:33
but shall not *d* it asunder Lev 1:17
neck, but shall not *d* it asunder Lev 5:8
cud, or of them that *d* the hoof Lev 11:4
the swine, though he *d* the hoof Lev 11:7
*d* the prey into two parts Num 31:27
ye shall *d* the land by lot for an Num 33:54
which shall *d* the land unto you Num 34:17
to *d* the land by inheritance Num 34:18
to *d* the inheritance unto the Num 34:29
or of them that *d* the cloven hoof Deut 14:7
chew the cud, but *d* not the hoof Deut 14:7
*d* the coasts of thy land, which Deut 19:3
*d* for an inheritance the land Josh 1:6
only *d* thou it by lot unto the Josh 13:6
Now therefore *d* this land for an Josh 13:7
they shall *d* it into seven parts Josh 18:5
*d* the spoil of your enemies with Josh 22:8
said, Thou and Ziba *d* the land 2Sa 19:29
*D* the living child in two, and 1Kin 3:25
neither mine nor thine, but *d* it 1Kin 3:26
thou didst *d* the sea before them, Neh 9:11
didst *d* them into corners Neh 9:22
the innocent shall *d* the silver Job 27:17
O Lord, and *d* their tongues Ps 55:9
I will *d* Shechem, and mete out the Ps 60:6
Thou didst *d* the sea by thy Ps 74:13
I will *d* Shechem, and mete out the Ps 108:7
than to *d* the spoil with the Prov 16:19
men rejoice when they *d* the spoil Is 9:3

Therefore will I *d* him a portion ... Is 53:12
he shall *d* the spoil with the ... Is 53:12
balances to weigh, and *d* the hair ... Eze 5:1
when ye shall *d* by lot the land ... Eze 45:1
So shall ye *d* this land unto you ... Eze 47:21
that ye shall *d* it by lot for an ... Eze 47:22
shall *d* by lot unto the tribes of ... Eze 48:29
shall *d* the land for gain ... Dan 11:39
that he *d* the inheritance with me ... Lk 12:13
this, and *d* it among yourselves ... Lk 22:17

**DIVIDED**
God *d* the light from the darkness ... Gen 1:4
*d* the waters which were under the ... Gen 1:7
of the Gentiles *d* in their lands ... Gen 10:5
for in his days was the earth *d* ... Gen 10:25
by these were the nations *d* in ... Gen 10:32
he *d* himself against them, he and ... Gen 14:15
*d* them in the midst, and laid each ... Gen 15:10
but the birds *d* he not ... Gen 15:10
he *d* the people that was with him ... Gen 32:7
he *d* the children unto Leah, and ... Gen 33:1
dry land, and the waters were *d* ... Ex 14:21
Unto these the land shall be *d* ... Num 26:53
the land shall be *d* by lot ... Num 26:55
thereof be *d* between many ... Num 26:56
which Moses *d* from the men that ... Num 31:42
hath *d* unto all nations under the ... Deut 4:19
When the Most High *d* to the ... Deut 32:8
of Israel did, and they *d* the land ... Josh 14:5
there Joshua *d* the land unto the ... Josh 18:10
*d* for an inheritance by lot in ... Josh 19:51
I have *d* unto you by lot these ... Josh 23:4
have they not *d* the prey ... Judg 5:30
he *d* the three hundred men into ... Judg 7:16
*d* them into three companies, and ... Judg 9:43
*d* her, together with her bones, ... Judg 19:29
and in their death they were not *d* ... 2Sa 1:23
people of Israel *d* into two parts ... 1Kin 16:21
So they *d* the land between them ... 1Kin 18:6
the waters, and they were *d* hither ... 2Kin 2:8
in his days the earth was *d* ... 1Chr 1:19
David *d* them into courses among ... 1Chr 23:6
and thus were they *d* ... 1Chr 24:4
Thus were they *d* by lot, one sort ... 1Chr 24:5
*d* them speedily among all the ... 2Chr 35:13
Who hath *d* a watercourse for the ... Job 38:25
that tarried at home *d* the spoil ... Ps 68:12
He *d* the sea, and caused them to ... Ps 78:13
*d* them an inheritance by line, and ... Ps 78:55
To him which *d* the Red sea into ... Ps 136:13
is the prey of a great spoil *d* ... Is 33:23
his hand hath *d* it unto them by ... Is 34:17
that *d* the sea, whose waves ... Is 51:15
The anger of the LORD hath *d* them ... Lam 4:16
neither shall they be *d* into two ... Eze 37:22
of iron, the kingdom shall be *d* ... Dan 2:41
Thy kingdom is *d*, and given to the ... Dan 5:28
shall be *d* toward the four winds ... Dan 11:4
Their heart is *d* ... Hos 10:2
and thy land shall be *d* by line ... Amos 7:17
turning away he hath *d* our fields ... Mic 2:4
thy spoil shall be *d* in the midst ... Zec 14:1
Every kingdom *d* against itself is ... Mt 12:25
every city or house *d* against ... Mt 12:25
Satan, he is *d* against himself ... Mt 12:26
if a kingdom be *d* against itself ... Mk 3:24
if a house be *d* against itself, ... Mk 3:25
rise up against himself, and be *d* ... Mk 3:26
the two fishes *d* he among them ... Mk 6:41
Every kingdom *d* against itself is ... Lk 11:17
a house *d* against a house falleth ... Lk 11:17
Satan also be *d* against himself ... Lk 11:18
shall be five in one house *d* ... Lk 12:52
father shall be *d* against the son ... Lk 12:53
he *d* unto them his living ... Lk 15:12
he *d* their land to them by lot ... Acts 13:19
the multitude of the city was *d* ... Acts 14:4
and the multitude was *d* ... Acts 23:7
Is Christ *d*? ... 1Cor 1:13
great city was *d* into three parts ... Rev 16:19

**DIVIDER**
made me a judge or a *d* over you ... Lk 12:14

**DIVIDETH**
the cud, but *d* not the hoof ... Lev 11:4
the cud, but *d* not the hoof ... Lev 11:5
the cud, but *d* not the hoof ... Lev 11:6
of every beast which *d* the hoof ... Lev 11:26
the swine, because it *d* the hoof ... Deut 14:8
He *d* the sea with his power, and ... Job 26:12
of the LORD *d* the flames of fire ... Ps 29:7
which *d* the sea when the waves ... Jer 31:35
as a shepherd *d* his sheep from ... Mt 25:32
he trusted, and *d* his spoils ... Lk 11:22

**DIVIDING**
of *d* the land for inheritance by ... Josh 19:49
they made an end of *d* the country ... Josh 19:51
*d* the water before them, to make ... Is 63:12
a time and times and the *d* of time ... Dan 7:25
*d* to every man severally as he ... 1Cor 12:11
rightly *d* the word of truth ... 2Ti 2:15
even to the *d* asunder of soul ... Heb 4:12

**DIVINATION**
the rewards of *d* in their hand ... Num 22:7
is there any *d* against Israel ... Num 23:23
through the fire, or that useth *d* ... Deut 18:10
pass through the fire, and used *d* ... 2Kin 17:17
unto you a false vision and *d* ... Jer 14:14
*d* within the house of Israel ... Eze 12:24
They have seen vanity and lying *d* ... Eze 13:6
and have ye not spoken a lying *d* ... Eze 13:7
head of the two ways, to use *d* ... Eze 21:21
hand was the *d* for Jerusalem ... Eze 21:22
them as a false *d* in their sight ... Eze 21:23
with a spirit of *d* met us ... Acts 16:16

**DIVINATIONS**
see no more vanity, nor divine *d* ... Eze 13:23

**DIVINE**
such a man as I can certainly *d* ... Gen 44:15
*d* unto me by the familiar spirit, ... 1Sa 28:8
A *d* sentence is in the lips of ... Prov 16:10
that see vanity, and that *d* lies ... Eze 13:9
no more vanity, nor *d* divinations ... Eze 13:23
whiles they *d* a lie unto thee, to ... Eze 21:29
unto you, that ye shall not *d* ... Mic 3:6
the prophets thereof *d* for money ... Mic 3:11
had also ordinances of *d* service ... Heb 9:1
According as his *d* power hath ... 2Pet 1:3
be partakers of the *d* nature ... 2Pet 1:4

**DIVINERS**
observers of times, and unto *d* ... Deut 18:14
called for the priests and the *d* ... 1Sa 6:2
of the liars, and maketh *d* mad ... Is 44:25
to your prophets, nor to your *d* ... Jer 27:9
Let not your prophets and your *d* ... Jer 29:8
be ashamed, and the *d* confounded ... Mic 3:7
the *d* have seen a lie, and have ... Zec 10:2

**DIVINETH**
drinketh, and whereby indeed he *d* ... Gen 44:5

**DIVINING**
*d* lies unto them, saying, Thus ... Eze 22:28

**DIVISION**
I will put a *d* between my people ... Ex 8:23
after the *d* of the families of ... 2Chr 35:5
you, Nay; but rather *d* ... Lk 12:51
So there was a *d* among the people ... Jn 7:43
And there was a *d* among them ... Jn 9:16
There was a *d* therefore again ... Jn 10:19

**DIVISIONS**
to their *d* by their tribes ... Josh 11:23
a possession according to their *d* ... Josh 12:7
of Israel according to their *d* ... Josh 18:10
For the *d* of Reuben there were ... Judg 5:15
For the *d* of Reuben there were ... Judg 5:16
Now these are the *d* of the sons ... 1Chr 24:1
Concerning the *d* of the porters ... 1Chr 26:1
these were the *d* of the porters ... 1Chr 26:12
These are the *d* of the porters ... 1Chr 26:19
*d* of the families of the fathers ... 2Chr 35:5
might give according to the *d* of ... 2Chr 35:12
they set the priests in their *d* ... Ezr 6:18
And of the Levites were *d* in Judah ... Neh 11:36
brethren, mark them which cause *d* ... Rom 16:17
and that there be no *d* among you ... 1Cor 1:10
you envying, and strife, and *d* ... 1Cor 3:3
I hear that there be *d* among you ... 1Cor 11:18

**DIVORCE**
away, and given her a bill of *d* ... Jer 3:8

**DIVORCED**
or a *d* woman, or profane, or an ... Lev 21:14
daughter be a widow, or *d* ... Lev 22:13
of a widow, and of her that is *d* ... Num 30:9
her that is *d* committeth adultery ... Mt 5:32

**DIVORCEMENT**
let him write her a bill of *d* ... Deut 24:1
her, and write her a bill of *d* ... Deut 24:3
is the bill of your mother's *d* ... Is 50:1
let him give her a writing of *d* ... Mt 5:31
command to give a writing of *d* ... Mt 19:7
suffered to write a bill of *d* ... Mk 10:4

**DIZAHAB** (*diz'-a-hab*) *A place in the Sinai wilderness.*
and Laban, and Hazeroth, and *D* ... Deut 1:1

**DO** See PREFACE.

**DOCTOR**
a *d* of the law, had in reputation ... Acts 5:34

**DOCTORS**
sitting in the midst of the *d* ... Lk 2:46
*d* of the law sitting by, which ... Lk 5:17

**DOCTRINE**
My *d* shall drop as the rain, my ... Deut 32:2
My *d* is pure, and I am clean in ... Job 11:4
For I give you good *d*, forsake ye ... Prov 4:2
shall he make to understand *d* ... Is 28:9
they that murmured shall learn *d* ... Is 29:24
the stock is a *d* of vanities ... Jer 10:8
people were astonished at his *d* ... Mt 7:28
but of the *d* of the Pharisees and ... Mt 16:12
they were astonished at his *d* ... Mt 22:33
And they were astonished at his *d* ... Mk 1:22
what new *d* is this ... Mk 1:27
and said unto them in his *d* ... Mk 4:2
people was astonished at his *d* ... Mk 11:18
And he said unto them in his *d* ... Mk 12:38
And they were astonished at his *d* ... Lk 4:32
My *d* is not mine, but his that ... Jn 7:16
his will, he shall know of the *d* ... Jn 7:17
of his disciples, and of his *d* ... Jn 18:19
stedfastly in the apostles' *d* ... Acts 2:42
have filled Jerusalem with your *d* ... Acts 5:28
astonished at the *d* of the Lord ... Acts 13:12
May we know what this new *d* ... Acts 17:19
form of *d* which was delivered you ... Rom 6:17
to the *d* which ye have learned ... Rom 16:17
or by prophesying, or by *d* ... 1Cor 14:6
one of you hath a psalm, hath a *d* ... 1Cor 14:26
about with every wind of *d* ... Eph 4:14
some that they teach no other *d* ... 1Ti 1:3
thing that is contrary to sound *d* ... 1Ti 1:10
the words of faith and of good *d* ... 1Ti 4:6
to reading, to exhortation, to *d* ... 1Ti 4:13
heed unto thyself, and unto the *d* ... 1Ti 4:16
they who labour in the word and *d* ... 1Ti 5:17
of God and his *d* be not blasphemed ... 1Ti 6:1
to the *d* which is according to ... 1Ti 6:3
But thou hast fully known my *d* ... 2Ti 3:10
of God, and is profitable for *d* ... 2Ti 3:16
with all longsuffering and *d* ... 2Ti 4:2
when they will not endure sound *d* ... 2Ti 4:3
be able by sound *d* both to exhort ... Titus 1:9
the things which become sound *d* ... Titus 2:1
in *d* shewing uncorruptness, ... Titus 2:7
that they may adorn the *d* of God ... Titus 2:10
the principles of the *d* of Christ ... Heb 6:1
Of the *d* of baptisms, and of ... Heb 6:2
and abideth not in the *d* of Christ ... 2Jn 9
that abideth in the *d* of Christ ... 2Jn 9
any unto you, and bring not this *d* ... 2Jn 10
them that hold the *d* of Balaam ... Rev 2:14
hold the *d* of the Nicolaitanes ... Rev 2:15
as many as have not this *d* ... Rev 2:24

**DOCTRINES**
teaching for *d* the commandments ... Mt 15:9
teaching for *d* the commandments ... Mk 7:7
the commandments and *d* of men ... Col 2:22
seducing spirits, and *d* of devils ... 1Ti 4:1
about with divers and strange *d* ... Heb 13:9

**DODAI** (*do'-dahee*) See DODO. *A captain in David's army.*
the second month was *D* an Ahohite.. 1Chr 27:4

**DODANIM** (*do'-da-nim*) See RODANIM. *Descendants of Javan.*
and Tarshish, Kittim, and *D* ... Gen 10:4
and Tarshish, Kittim, and *D* ... 1Chr 1:7

**DODAVAH** (*do'-da-vah*) *Father of Eliezer.*
Then Eliezer the son of *D* of ... 2Chr 20:37

**DODAVAHU** See DODAVAH.

**DODO** (*do'-do*) See DODAI.
*1. Grandfather of Tola.*
the son of Puah, the son of *D* ... Judg 10:1
*2. Father of Eleazar.*
Eleazar the son of *D* the Ahohite ... 2Sa 23:9
him was Eleazar the son of *D* ... 1Chr 11:12
*3. Father of Elhanan.*
the son of *D* of Beth-lehem ... 2Sa 23:24
the son of *D* of Beth-lehem ... 1Chr 11:26

**DOEG** (*do'-eg*) *Chief herdsman of King Saul.*
and his name was *D*, an Edomite, ... 1Sa 21:7
Then answered *D* the Edomite ... 1Sa 22:9
And the king said to *D*, Turn thou, ... 1Sa 22:18
*D* the Edomite turned, and he fell ... 1Sa 22:18
when *D* the Edomite was there, ... 1Sa 22:22
when *D* the Edomite came and told ... Ps 52:t

**DOER**
did there, he was the *d* of it ... Gen 39:22
the *d* of evil according to his ... 2Sa 3:39
plentifully rewardeth the proud *d* ... Ps 31:23
A wicked *d* giveth heed to false ... Prov 17:4
I suffer trouble, as an evil *d* ... 2Ti 2:9
a hearer of the word, and not a *d* ... Jas 1:23
but a *d* of the work, this man ... Jas 1:25
law, thou art not a *d* of the law ... Jas 4:11

**DOERS**
the hand of the *d* of the work ... 2Kin 22:5
let them give it to the *d* of the ... 2Kin 22:5
neither will he help the evil *d* ... Job 8:20
*d* from the city of the LORD ... Ps 101:8
but the *d* of the law shall be ... Rom 2:13
But be ye *d* of the word, and not ... Jas 1:22

**DOEST**
If thou *d* well, shalt thou not be ... Gen 4:7
if thou *d* not well, sin lieth at ... Gen 4:7
is with thee in all that thou *d* ... Gen 21:22
thing that thou *d* to the people ... Ex 18:14
The thing that thou *d* is not good ... Ex 18:17
when thou *d* that which is good and ... Deut 12:28
work of thine hand which thou *d* ... Deut 14:29
bless thee in all that thou *d* ... Deut 15:18
but thou *d* me wrong to war ... Judg 11:27
in, and to know all that thou *d* ... 2Sa 3:25
mayest prosper in all that thou *d* ... 1Kin 2:3
him, What *d* thou here, Elijah ... 1Kin 19:9
and said, What *d* thou here, Elijah ... 1Kin 19:13
and mark, and see what thou *d* ... 1Kin 20:22
will say unto him, What *d* thou ... Job 9:12
sinnest, what *d* thou against him ... Job 35:6
multiplied, what *d* thou unto him ... Job 35:6
when thou *d* well to thyself ... Ps 49:18
Thou art the God that *d* wonders ... Ps 77:14
art great, and *d* wondrous things ... Ps 86:10
Thou art good, and *d* good ... Ps 119:68
who may say unto him, What *d* thou ... Eccl 8:4
when thou *d* evil, then thou ... Jer 11:15
shall go aside to ask how thou *d* ... Jer 15:5
said unto thee, What *d* thou ... Eze 12:9
seeing thou *d* all these things, ... Eze 16:30

things are to us, that thou *d* so ... Eze 24:19
or say unto him, What *d* thou... Dan 4:35
the LORD, *D* thou well to be angry ... Jonah 4:4
*D* thou well to be angry for the ... Jonah 4:9
Therefore when thou *d* thine alms ... Mt 6:2
But when thou *d* alms, let not thy ... Mt 6:3
authority *d* thou these things ... Mt 21:23
authority *d* thou these things ... Mk 11:28
authority *d* thou these things ... Lk 20:2
seeing that thou *d* these things ... Jn 2:18
can do these miracles that thou *d* ... Jn 3:2
may see the works that thou *d* ... Jn 7:3
said Jesus unto him, That thou *d* ... Jn 13:27
saying, Take heed what thou *d* ... Acts 22:26
that judgest *d* the same things ... Rom 2:1
*d* the same, that thou shalt ... Rom 2:3
there is one God; thou *d* well ... Jas 2:19
thou *d* faithfully whatsoever thou ... 3Jn 5
whatsoever thou *d* to the brethren ... 3Jn 5

**DOETH**
seen all that Laban *d* unto thee ... Gen 31:12
for whosoever *d* any work therein, ... Ex 31:14
whosoever *d* any work in the ... Ex 31:15
whosoever *d* work therein shall be ... Ex 35:2
while he *d* somewhat against any ... Lev 4:27
in any of all these that a man *d* ... Lev 6:3
that *d* any work in that same day ... Lev 23:30
But the soul that *d* ought ... Num 15:30
who shall live when God *d* this ... Num 24:23
Which *d* great things and ... Job 5:9
Which *d* great things past finding ... Job 9:10
his soul desireth, even that he *d* ... Job 23:13
and *d* not good to the widow ... Job 24:21
great things *d* he, which we ... Job 37:5
and whatsoever he *d* shall prosper ... Ps 1:3
works, there is none that *d* good ... Ps 14:1
there is none that *d* good ... Ps 14:3
nor *d* evil to his neighbour, nor ... Ps 15:3
He that *d* these things shall ... Ps 15:5
there is none that *d* good ... Ps 53:1
there is none that *d* good ... Ps 53:3
who only *d* wondrous things ... Ps 72:18
he that *d* righteousness at all ... Ps 106:3
hand of the LORD *d* valiantly ... Ps 118:15
hand of the LORD *d* valiantly ... Ps 118:16
To him who alone *d* great wonders ... Ps 136:4
he that *d* it destroyeth his own ... Prov 6:32
The merciful man *d* good to his ... Prov 11:17
the heart of the foolish *d* not so ... Prov 15:7
a fool *d* it to his sorrow ... Prov 17:21
A merry heart *d* good like a ... Prov 17:22
A man that *d* violence to the ... Prov 28:17
and of mirth, What *d* it ... Eccl 2:2
I know that, whatsoever God *d* ... Eccl 3:14
and God *d* it, that men should fear ... Eccl 3:14
just man upon earth, that *d* good ... Eccl 7:20
for he *d* whatsoever pleaseth him ... Eccl 8:3
bind them on thee, as a bride *d* ... Is 49:18
Blessed is the man that *d* this ... Is 56:2
Wherefore *d* the LORD our God all ... Jer 5:19
Cursed be he that *d* the work of ... Jer 48:10
he escape that *d* such things ... Eze 17:15
that *d* the like to any one of ... Eze 18:10
that *d* not any of those duties, ... Eze 18:11
considereth, and *d* not such like, ... Eze 18:14
and *d* according to all the ... Eze 18:24
that the wicked man *d*, shall he ... Eze 18:24
*d* that which is lawful and right, ... Eze 18:27
he *d* according to his will in the ... Dan 4:35
in all his works which he *d* ... Dan 9:14
name, saith the LORD that *d* this ... Amos 9:12
will cut off the man that *d* this ... Mal 2:12
Every one that *d* evil is good in ... Mal 2:17
hand know what thy right hand *d* ... Mt 6:3
but he that *d* the will of my ... Mt 7:21
*d* them, I will liken him unto a ... Mt 7:24
*d* them not, shall be likened unto ... Mt 7:26
my servant, Do this, and he *d* it ... Mt 8:9
*d* them, I will shew you to whom ... Lk 6:47
*d* not, is like a man that without ... Lk 6:49
my servant, Do this, and he *d* it ... Lk 7:8
For every one that *d* evil hateth ... Jn 3:20
But he that *d* truth cometh to the ... Jn 3:21
for what things soever he *d* ... Jn 5:19
these also *d* the Son likewise ... Jn 5:19
him all things that himself *d* ... Jn 5:20
no man that *d* any thing in secret ... Jn 7:4
it hear him, and know what he *d* ... Jn 7:51
*d* his will, him he heareth ... Jn 9:31
for this man *d* many miracles ... Jn 11:47
dwelleth in me, he *d* the works ... Jn 14:10
knoweth not what his lord *d* ... Jn 15:15
will think that he *d* God service ... Jn 16:2
the Lord, who *d* all these things ... Acts 15:17
This man *d* nothing worthy of ... Acts 26:31
every soul of man that *d* evil ... Rom 2:9
there is none that *d* good ... Rom 3:12
That the man which *d* those things ... Rom 10:5
wrath upon him that *d* evil ... Rom 13:4
that a man *d* is without the body ... 1Cor 6:18
he will keep his virgin, *d* well ... 1Cor 7:37
giveth her in marriage *d* well ... 1Cor 7:38
her not in marriage *d* better ... 1Cor 7:38
*d* he it by the works of the law, ... Gal 3:5
The man that *d* them shall live in ... Gal 3:12
whatsoever good thing any man *d* ... Eph 6:8
But he that *d* wrong shall receive ... Col 3:25
*d* it not, to him it is sin ... Jas 4:17
but he that *d* the will of God ... 1Jn 2:17
ye know that every one that *d* ... 1Jn 2:29
he that *d* righteousness is ... 1Jn 3:7
whosoever *d* not righteousness is ... 1Jn 3:10
remember his deeds which he *d* ... 3Jn 10
He that *d* good is of God ... 3Jn 11
but he that *d* evil hath not seen ... 3Jn 11
he *d* great wonders, so that he ... Rev 13:13

**DOG**
shall not a *d* move his tongue ... Ex 11:7
of a whore, or the price of a *d* ... Deut 23:18
as a *d* lappeth, him shalt thou ... Judg 7:5
said unto David, Am I a *d* ... 1Sa 17:43
after a dead *d*, after a flea ... 1Sa 24:14
look upon such a dead *d* as I am ... 2Sa 9:8
Why should this dead *d* curse my ... 2Sa 16:9
But what, is thy servant a *d* ... 2Kin 8:13
darling from the power of the *d* ... Ps 22:20
they make a noise like a *d* ... Ps 59:6
and let them make a noise like a *d* ... Ps 59:14
As a *d* returneth to his vomit, so ... Prov 26:11
one that taketh a *d* by the ears ... Prov 26:17
for a living *d* is better than a ... Eccl 9:4
The *d* is turned to his own vomit ... 2Pet 2:22

**DOG'S**
and said, Am I a *d* head, which ... 2Sa 3:8
a lamb, as if he cut off a *d* neck ... Is 66:3

**DOGS**
ye shall cast it to the *d* ... Ex 22:31
in the city shall the *d* eat ... 1Kin 14:11
in the city shall the *d* eat ... 1Kin 16:4
In the place where *d* licked the ... 1Kin 21:19
of Naboth shall *d* lick thy blood ... 1Kin 21:19
The *d* shall eat Jezebel by the ... 1Kin 21:23
Ahab in the city the *d* shall eat ... 1Kin 21:24
the *d* licked up his blood ... 1Kin 22:38
the *d* shall eat Jezebel in the ... 2Kin 9:10
shall *d* eat the flesh of Jezebel ... 2Kin 9:36
have set with the *d* of my flock ... Job 30:1
For *d* have compassed me ... Ps 22:16
the tongue of thy *d* in the same ... Ps 68:23
all ignorant, they are all dumb *d* ... Is 56:10
they are greedy *d* which can never ... Is 56:11
the *d* to tear, and the fowls of ... Jer 15:3
not that which is holy unto the *d* ... Mt 7:6
bread, and to cast it to *d* ... Mt 15:26
yet the *d* eat of the crumbs which ... Mt 15:27
bread, and to cast it unto the *d* ... Mk 7:27
yet the *d* under the table eat of ... Mk 7:28
moreover the *d* came and licked his ... Lk 16:21
Beware of *d*, beware of evil ... Phil 3:2
For without are *d*, and sorcerers, ... Rev 22:15

**DOING**
hast now done foolishly in so *d* ... Gen 31:28
ye have done evil in so *d* ... Gen 44:5
fearful in praises, *d* wonders ... Ex 15:11
without *d* any thing else, go ... Num 20:19
in *d* wickedly in the sight of the ... Deut 9:18
So Hiram made an end of *d* all the ... 1Kin 7:40
*d* evil in the sight of the LORD ... 1Kin 16:19
*d* that which was right in the ... 1Kin 22:43
in *d* that which was evil in the ... 2Kin 21:16
Arise therefore, and be *d*, and the ... 1Chr 22:16
*d* that which was right in the ... 2Chr 20:32
*d* according to their abominations ... Ezr 9:1
I am *d* a great work, so that I ... Neh 6:3
in so *d* my maker would soon take ... Job 32:22
shall wisely consider of his *d* ... Ps 64:9
he is terrible in his *d* toward ... Ps 66:5
This is the LORD's *d* ... Ps 118:23
keepeth his hand from *d* any evil ... Is 56:2
from *d* thy pleasure on my holy ... Is 58:13
not *d* thine own ways, nor finding ... Is 58:13
this is the Lord's *d*, and it is ... Mt 21:42
when he cometh shall find so *d* ... Mt 24:46
This was the Lord's *d*, and it is ... Mk 12:11
when he cometh shall find so *d* ... Lk 12:43
who went about *d* good, and healing. Acts 10:38
they have found any evil *d* in me ... Acts 24:20
in well *d* seek for glory and ... Rom 2:7
for in so *d* thou shalt heap coals ... Rom 12:20
Now therefore perform the *d* of it ... 2Cor 8:11
And let us not be weary in well *d* ... Gal 6:9
*d* the will of God from the heart ... Eph 6:6
With good will *d* service, as to ... Eph 6:7
brethren, be not weary in well *d* ... 2Th 3:13
for in *d* this thou shalt both ... 1Ti 4:16
another, *d* nothing by partiality ... 1Ti 5:21
that with well *d* ye may put to ... 1Pet 2:15
be so, that ye suffer for well *d* ... 1Pet 3:17
for well *d*, than for evil *d* ... 1Pet 3:17
of their souls to him in well *d* ... 1Pet 4:19

**DOINGS**
After the *d* of the land of Egypt, ... Lev 18:3
after the *d* of the land of Canaan ... Lev 18:3
of the wickedness of thy *d* ... Deut 28:20
they ceased not from their own *d* ... Judg 2:19
man was churlish and evil in his *d* ... 1Sa 25:3
and not after the *d* of Israel ... 2Chr 17:4
declare among the people his *d* ... Ps 9:11
of all thy work, and talk of thy *d* ... Ps 77:12
Even a child is known by his *d* ... Prov 20:11
of your *d* from before mine eyes ... Is 1:16
their *d* are against the LORD, to ... Is 3:8
shall eat the fruit of their *d* ... Is 3:10
declare his *d* among the people, ... Is 12:4
it because of the evil of your *d* ... Jer 4:4
thy *d* have procured these things ... Jer 4:18
Israel, Amend your ways and your *d* ... Jer 7:3
amend your ways and your *d* ... Jer 7:5
then thou shewedst me their *d* ... Jer 11:18
according to the fruit of his *d* ... Jer 17:10
and make your ways and your *d* good. Jer 18:11
it, because of the evil of your *d* ... Jer 21:12
according to the fruit of your *d* ... Jer 21:14
visit upon you the evil of your *d* ... Jer 23:2
way, and from the evil of their *d* ... Jer 23:22
way, and from the evil of your *d* ... Jer 25:5
because of the evil of their *d* ... Jer 26:3
now amend your ways and your *d* ... Jer 26:13
according to the fruit of his *d* ... Jer 32:19
his evil way, and amend your *d* ... Jer 35:15
because of the evil of your *d* ... Jer 44:22
ye shall see their way and their *d* ... Eze 14:22
when ye see their ways and their *d* ... Eze 14:23
remember your ways, and all your *d* ... Eze 20:43
nor according to your corrupt *d* ... Eze 20:44
in all your *d* your sins do appear ... Eze 21:24
thy ways, and according to thy *d* ... Eze 24:14
it by their own way and by their *d* ... Eze 36:17
to their *d* I judged them ... Eze 36:19
your *d* that were not good, and ... Eze 36:31
ways, and reward them their *d* ... Hos 4:9
their *d* to turn unto their God ... Hos 5:4
now their own *d* have beset them ... Hos 7:2
for the wickedness of their *d* I ... Hos 9:15
according to his *d* will he ... Hos 12:2
are these his *d* ... Mic 2:7
behaved themselves ill in their *d* ... Mic 3:4
therein, for the fruit of their *d* ... Mic 7:13
early, and corrupted all their *d* ... Zeph 3:7
thou not be ashamed for all thy *d* ... Zeph 3:11
evil ways, and from your evil *d* ... Zec 1:4
our ways, and according to our *d* ... Zec 1:6

**DOLEFUL**
shall be full of *d* creatures ... Is 13:21
and lament with a *d* lamentation ... Mic 2:4

**DOMINION**
let them have *d* over the fish of ... Gen 1:26
have *d* over the fish of the sea, ... Gen 1:28
pass when thou shalt have the *d* ... Gen 27:40
shalt thou indeed have *d* over us ... Gen 37:8
shall come he that shall have *d* ... Num 24:19
have *d* over the nobles among the ... Judg 5:13
made me have *d* over the mighty ... Judg 5:13
the Philistines had *d* over Israel ... Judg 14:4
For he had *d* over all the region ... 1Kin 4:24
and in all the land of his *d* ... 1Kin 9:19
in his house, nor in all his *d* ... 2Kin 20:13
and Saraph, who had the *d* in Moab ... 1Chr 4:22
his *d* by the river Euphrates ... 1Chr 18:3
throughout all the land of his *d* ... 2Chr 8:6
from under the *d* of Judah ... 2Chr 21:8
so that they had the *d* over them ... Neh 9:28
also they have *d* over our bodies, ... Neh 9:37
*D* and fear are with him ... Job 25:2
canst thou set the *d* thereof in ... Job 38:33
Thou madest him to have *d* over ... Ps 8:6
let them not have *d* over me ... Ps 19:13
the upright shall have *d* over ... Ps 49:14
He shall have *d* also from sea to ... Ps 72:8
his works in all places of his *d* ... Ps 103:22
his sanctuary, and Israel his *d* ... Ps 114:2
not any iniquity have *d* over me ... Ps 119:133
thy *d* endureth throughout all ... Ps 145:13
besides thee have had *d* over us ... Is 26:13
in his house, nor in all his *d* ... Is 39:2
kingdoms of the earth of his *d* ... Jer 34:1
thereof, and all the land of his *d* ... Jer 51:28
his *d* is from generation to ... Dan 4:3
thy *d* to the end of the earth ... Dan 4:22
whose *d* is an everlasting *d* ... Dan 4:34
That in every *d* of my kingdom men ... Dan 6:26
his *d* shall be even unto the end ... Dan 6:26
and *d* was given to it ... Dan 7:6
they had their *d* taken away ... Dan 7:12
And there was given him *d*, and ... Dan 7:14
his *d* is an everlasting *d*, ... Dan 7:14
and they shall take away his *d* ... Dan 7:26
And the kingdom and *d*, and the ... Dan 7:27
up, that shall rule with great *d* ... Dan 11:3
according to his *d* which he ruled ... Dan 11:4
be strong above him, and have *d* ... Dan 11:5
his *d* shall be a great *d* ... Dan 11:5
shall it come, even the first *d* ... Mic 4:8
his *d* shall be from sea even to ... Zec 9:10
the Gentiles exercise *d* over them ... Mt 20:25
death hath no more *d* over him ... Rom 6:9
For sin shall not have *d* over you ... Rom 6:14
how that the law hath *d* over a ... Rom 7:1
that we have *d* over your faith ... 2Cor 1:24
and power, and might, and *d* ... Eph 1:21
be praise and *d* for ever and ever ... 1Pet 4:11
be glory and *d* for ever and ever ... 1Pet 5:11
defile the flesh, despise *d* ... Jude 8
Saviour, be glory and majesty, *d* ... Jude 25
be glory and *d* for ever and ever ... Rev 1:6

**DOMINIONS**
all *d* shall serve and obey him ... Dan 7:27
whether they be thrones, or *d* ... Col 1:16

**DONE** See PREFACE.

**DOOR**
not well, sin lieth at the *d* ... Gen 4:7
the *d* of the ark shalt thou set ... Gen 6:16
he sat in the tent *d* in the heat ... Gen 18:1
ran to meet them from the tent *d* ... Gen 18:2
And Sarah heard it in the tent *d* ... Gen 18:10
Lot went out at the *d* unto them ... Gen 19:6

and shut the *d* after him Gen 19:6
Lot, and came near to break the *d* Gen 19:9
house to them, and shut to the *d* Gen 19:10
the *d* of the house with blindness Gen 19:11
wearied themselves to find the *d* Gen 19:11
with him at the *d* of the house Gen 43:19
on the upper *d* post of the houses Ex 12:7
*d* of his house until the morning Ex 12:22
the LORD will pass over the *d* Ex 12:23
he shall also bring him to the *d* Ex 21:6
or unto the *d* post Ex 21:6
an hanging for the *d* of the tent Ex 26:36
the *d* of the tabernacle of the Ex 29:4
by the *d* of the tabernacle of the Ex 29:11
by the *d* of the tabernacle of the Ex 29:32
your generations at the *d* of the Ex 29:42
and stood every man at his tent *d* Ex 33:8
stood at the *d* of the tabernacle, Ex 33:9
pillar stand at the tabernacle *d* Ex 33:10
every man in his tent *d* Ex 33:10
the hanging for the *d* at the Ex 35:15
hanging for the *d* of the court Ex 35:17
for the tabernacle *d* of blue Ex 36:37
which assembled at the *d* of the Ex 38:8
to the *d* of the tabernacle of the Ex 38:30
the hanging for the tabernacle *d* Ex 39:38
of the *d* to the tabernacle Ex 40:5
*d* of the tabernacle of the tent Ex 40:6
his sons unto the *d* of the Ex 40:12
at the *d* of the tabernacle Ex 40:28
*d* of the tabernacle of the tent Ex 40:29
at the *d* of the tabernacle of the Lev 1:3
by the *d* of the tabernacle of the Lev 1:5
and kill it at the *d* of the Lev 3:2
the *d* of the tabernacle of the Lev 4:4
which is at the *d* of the Lev 4:7
which is at the *d* of the Lev 4:18
the *d* of the tabernacle of the Lev 8:3
the *d* of the tabernacle of the Lev 8:4
Boil the flesh at the *d* of the Lev 8:31
of the *d* of the tabernacle of the Lev 8:33
at the *d* of the tabernacle of the Lev 8:35
the *d* of the tabernacle of the Lev 10:7
unto the *d* of the tabernacle of Lev 12:6
at the *d* of the tabernacle of the Lev 14:11
unto the *d* of the tabernacle of Lev 14:23
the house to the *d* of the house Lev 14:38
the *d* of the tabernacle of the Lev 15:14
to the *d* of the tabernacle of the Lev 15:29
at the *d* of the tabernacle of the Lev 16:7
the *d* of the tabernacle of the Lev 17:4
unto the *d* of the tabernacle of Lev 17:5
at the *d* of the tabernacle of the Lev 17:6
the *d* of the tabernacle of the Lev 17:9
unto the *d* of the tabernacle of Lev 19:21
the hanging for the *d* of the Num 3:25
curtain for the *d* of the court Num 3:26
the hanging for the *d* of the Num 4:25
the hanging for the *d* of the gate Num 4:26
to the *d* of the tabernacle of the Num 6:10
the *d* of the tabernacle of the Num 6:13
at the *d* of the tabernacle of the Num 6:18
at the *d* of the tabernacle of the Num 10:3
every man in the *d* of his tent Num 11:10
stood in the *d* of the tabernacle, Num 12:5
stood in the *d* of the tabernacle Num 16:18
against them unto the *d* of the Num 16:19
stood in the *d* of their tents, and Num 16:27
the *d* of the tabernacle of the Num 16:50
the *d* of the tabernacle of the Num 20:6
the *d* of the tabernacle of the Num 25:6
by the *d* of the tabernacle of the Num 27:2
upon the *d* posts of thine house Deut 11:20
it through his ear unto the *d* Deut 15:17
to the *d* of her father's house Deut 22:21
over the *d* of the tabernacle Deut 31:15
at the *d* of the tabernacle of the Josh 19:51
her, Stand in the *d* of the tent Judg 4:20
went hard unto the *d* of the tower Judg 9:52
round about, and beat at the *d* Judg 19:22
fell down at the *d* of the man's Judg 19:26
fallen down at the *d* of the house Judg 19:27
at the *d* of the tabernacle of the 1Sa 2:22
But Uriah slept at the *d* of the 2Sa 11:9
from me, and bolt the *d* after her 2Sa 13:17
out, and bolted the *d* after her 2Sa 13:18
The *d* for the middle chamber was 1Kin 6:8
So also made he for the *d* of the 1Kin 6:33
leaves of the one *d* were folding 1Kin 6:34
of the other *d* were folding 1Kin 6:34
her feet, as she came in at the *d* 1Kin 14:6
came to the threshold of the *d* 1Kin 14:17
which kept the *d* of the king's 1Kin 14:27
thou shalt shut the *d* upon thee 2Kin 4:4
from him, and shut the *d* upon her 2Kin 4:5
called her, she stood in the *d* 2Kin 4:15
of God, and shut the *d* upon him 2Kin 4:21
shut the *d* upon them twain, and 2Kin 4:33
stood at the *d* of the house of 2Kin 5:9
*d*, and hold him fast at the *d* 2Kin 6:32
Then open the *d*, and flee, and 2Kin 9:3
And he opened the *d*, and fled 2Kin 9:10
the priests that kept the *d* put 2Kin 12:9
which the keepers of the *d* have 2Kin 22:4
order, and the keepers of the *d* 2Kin 23:4
and the three keepers of the *d* 2Kin 25:18
of the *d* of the tabernacle of the 1Chr 9:21
*d* of the house of Eliashib the Neh 3:20
from the *d* of the house of Neh 3:21
Teresh, of those which kept the *d* Est 2:21
the keepers of the *d*, who sought Est 6:2
laid wait at my neighbour's *d* Job 31:9
silence, and went not out of the *d* Job 31:34
Keep the *d* of my lips Ps 141:3
come not nigh the *d* of her house Prov 5:8
she sitteth at the *d* of her house Prov 9:14
As the *d* turneth upon his hinges, Prov 26:14
in his hand by the hole of the *d* Song 5:4
and if she be a *d*, we will inclose Song 8:9
the posts of the *d* moved at the Is 6:4
of Shallum, the keeper of the *d* Jer 35:4
and the three keepers of the *d* Jer 52:24
to the *d* of the inner gate, that Eze 8:3
brought me to the *d* of the court Eze 8:7
digged in the wall, behold a *d* Eze 8:8
Then he brought me to the *d* of Eze 8:14
at the *d* of the temple of the Eze 8:16
every one stood at the *d* of the Eze 10:19
behold at the *d* of the gate five Eze 11:1
and twenty cubits, *d* against *d* Eze 40:13
breadth of the *d* was ten cubits Eze 41:2
the sides of the *d* were five Eze 41:2
and measured the post of the *d* Eze 41:3
and the *d*, six cubits Eze 41:3
and the breadth of the *d*, seven Eze 41:3
one *d* toward the north, and Eze 41:11
another *d* toward the south Eze 41:11
The *d* posts, and the narrow Eze 41:16
three stories, over against the *d* Eze 41:16
To that above the *d*, even unto Eze 41:17
unto above the *d* were cherubims Eze 41:20
two leaves for the one *d* Eze 41:24
and two leaves for the other *d* Eze 41:24
an hundred cubits was the north *d* Eze 42:2
was a *d* in the head of the way Eze 42:12
the land shall worship at the *d* Eze 46:3
me again unto the *d* of the house Eze 47:1
valley of Achor for a *d* of hope Hos 2:15
said, Smite the lintel of the *d* Amos 9:1
and when thou hast shut thy *d* Mt 6:6
and the *d* was shut Mt 25:10
stone to the *d* of the sepulchre Mt 27:60
rolled back the stone from the *d* Mt 28:2
was gathered together at the *d* Mk 1:33
no, not so much as about the *d* Mk 2:2
found the colt tied by the *d* Mk 11:4
stone unto the *d* of the sepulchre Mk 15:46
stone from the *d* of the sepulchre Mk 16:3
the *d* is now shut, and my children Lk 11:7
risen up, and hath shut to the *d* Lk 13:25
without, and to knock at the *d* Lk 13:25
not by the *d* into the sheepfold Jn 10:1
*d* is the shepherd of the sheep Jn 10:2
unto you, I am the *d* of the sheep Jn 10:7
I am the *d* Jn 10:9
But Peter stood at the *d* without Jn 18:16
and spake unto her that kept the *d* Jn 18:16
damsel that kept the *d* unto Peter Jn 18:17
buried thy husband are at the *d* Acts 5:9
before the *d* kept the prison Acts 12:6
knocked at the *d* of the gate Acts 12:13
and when they had opened the *d* Acts 12:16
how he had opened the *d* of faith Acts 14:27
For a great *d* and effectual is 1Cor 16:9
a *d* was opened unto me of the 2Cor 2:12
open unto us a *d* of utterance Col 4:3
the judge standeth before the *d* Jas 5:9
I have set before thee an open *d* Rev 3:8
Behold, I stand at the *d*, and Rev 3:20
man hear my voice, and open the *d* Rev 3:20
behold, a *d* was opened in heaven Rev 4:1

**DOORKEEPER**
I had rather be a *d* in the house Ps 84:10

**DOORKEEPERS**
and Elkanah were *d* for the ark 1Chr 15:23
and Jehiah were *d* for the ark 1Chr 15:24

**DOORS**
*d* of thy house into the street Josh 2:19
shut the *d* of the parlour upon Judg 3:23
the *d* of the parlour were locked, Judg 3:24
opened not the *d* of the parlour Judg 3:25
of the *d* of my house to meet me Judg 11:31
took the *d* of the gate of the Judg 16:3
opened the *d* of the house, and Judg 19:27
opened the *d* of the house of the 1Sa 3:15
and scrabbled on the *d* of the gate 1Sa 21:13
oracle he made *d* of olive tree 1Kin 6:31
The two *d* also were of olive tree 1Kin 6:32
the two *d* were of fir tree 1Kin 6:34
And all the *d* and posts were square 1Kin 7:5
both for the *d* of the inner house 1Kin 7:50
for the *d* of the house, to wit, 1Kin 7:50
the *d* of the temple of the LORD 2Kin 18:16
the nails for the *d* of the gates 1Chr 22:3
and the *d* thereof, with gold 2Chr 3:7
great court, and *d* for the court 2Chr 4:9
overlaid the *d* of them with brass 2Chr 4:9
the inner *d* thereof for the most 2Chr 4:22
the *d* of the house of the temple, 2Chr 4:22
shall be porters of the *d* 2Chr 23:4
shut up the *d* of the house of the 2Chr 28:24
opened the *d* of the house of the 2Chr 29:3
have shut up the *d* of the porch 2Chr 29:7
the *d* had gathered of the hand of 2Chr 34:9
it, and set up the *d* of it Neh 3:1
thereof, and set up the *d* thereof Neh 3:3
thereof, and set up the *d* thereof Neh 3:6
built it, and set up the *d* thereof Neh 3:13
build it, and set up the *d* thereof Neh 3:14
it, and set up the *d* thereof Neh 3:15
not set up the *d* upon the gates Neh 6:1
let us shut the *d* of the temple Neh 6:10
was built, and I had set up the *d* Neh 7:1
stand by, let them shut the *d* Neh 7:3
not up the *d* of my mother's womb Job 3:10
but I opened my *d* to the Job 31:32
Or who shut up the sea with *d* Job 38:8
decreed place, and set bars and *d* Job 38:10
or hast thou seen the *d* of the Job 38:17
Who can open the *d* of his face Job 41:14
be ye lifted up, ye everlasting *d* Ps 24:7
lift them up, ye everlasting *d* Ps 24:9
above, and opened the *d* of heaven Ps 78:23
city, at the coming in at the *d* Prov 8:3
waiting at the posts of my *d* Prov 8:34
the *d* shall be shut in the Eccl 12:4
and shut thy *d* about thee Is 26:20
Behind the *d* also and the posts Is 57:8
in the *d* of the houses, and speak Eze 33:30
the *d* of the side chambers were Eze 41:11
temple and the sanctuary had two *d* Eze 41:23
the *d* had two leaves apiece, two Eze 41:24
on the *d* of the temple, cherubims Eze 41:25
and their *d* toward the north Eze 42:4
fashions, and according to their *d* Eze 42:11
according to the *d* of the Eze 42:12
keep the *d* of thy mouth from her Mic 7:5
Open thy *d*, O Lebanon, that the Zec 11:1
that would shut the *d* for nought Mal 1:10
that it is near, even at the *d* Mt 24:33
that it is nigh, even at the *d* Mk 13:29
when the *d* were shut where the Jn 20:19
the *d* being shut, and stood in the Jn 20:26
Lord by night opened the prison *d* Acts 5:19
standing without before the *d* Acts 5:23
immediately all the *d* were opened Acts 16:26
and seeing the prison *d* open Acts 16:27
and forthwith the *d* were shut Acts 21:30

**DOPHKAH** (*dof'-kah*) *An encampment during the Exodus.*
of Sin, and encamped in *D* Num 33:12
And they departed from *D*, and Num 33:13

**DOR** (*dor*) See EN-DOR. *A Canaanite city.*
in the borders of *D* on the west Josh 11:2
The king of *D* in the coast of *D* Josh 12:23
towns, and the inhabitants of *D* Josh 17:11
towns, nor the inhabitants of *D* Judg 1:27
Abinadab, in all the region of *D* 1Kin 4:11
towns, Megiddo and her towns, *D* 1Chr 7:29

**DORCAS** (*dor'-cas*) See TABITHA. *Disciple raised from the dead by Peter.*
by interpretation is called *D* Acts 9:36
coats and garments which *D* made Acts 9:39

**DOST**
it that thou *d* ask after my name Gen 32:29
when thou *d* overtake them, say Gen 44:4
*d* thou go to possess their land Deut 9:5
When thou *d* lend thy brother any Deut 24:10
the man to whom thou *d* lend shall Deut 24:11
Thou *d* but hate me, and lovest me Judg 14:16
after whom *d* thou pursue 1Sa 24:14
Wherefore then *d* thou ask of me 1Sa 28:16
why *d* thou ask Abishag the 1Kin 2:22
*D* thou now govern the kingdom of 1Kin 21:7
Now on whom *d* thou trust, that 2Kin 18:20
sin, when thou *d* afflict them 2Chr 6:26
For what *d* thou make request Neh 2:4
*D* thou still retain thine Job 2:9
And why *d* thou not pardon my Job 7:21
yet thou *d* destroy me Job 10:8
*d* thou open thine eyes upon such Job 14:3
*d* thou not watch over my sin Job 14:16
*d* thou restrain wisdom to thyself Job 15:8
unto thee, and thou *d* not hear me Job 30:20
Why *d* thou strive against him Job 33:13
*D* thou know when God disposed Job 37:15
*D* thou know the balancings of the Job 37:16
When thou with rebukes *d* correct Ps 39:11
why *d* thou cast me off Ps 43:2
*d* not increase thy wealth by Ps 44:12
thou *d* establish equity, thou Ps 99:4
honour, when thou *d* embrace her Prov 4:8
for thou *d* not enquire wisely Eccl 7:10
beloved, that thou *d* so charge us Song 5:9
*d* weigh the path of the just Is 26:7
now on whom *d* thou trust, that Is 36:5
Wherefore *d* thou prophesy, and say Jer 32:3
*D* thou certainly know that Baalis Jer 40:14
daughter that *d* inhabit Dibon Jer 48:18
Wherefore *d* thou forget us for Lam 5:20
thou *d* dwell among scorpions Eze 2:6
Whom *d* thou pass in beauty Eze 32:19
if thou *d* not speak to warn the Eze 33:8
Now why *d* thou cry out aloud Mic 4:9
Why *d* thou shew me iniquity, and Hab 1:3
*d* thou not care that my sister Lk 10:40
*D* not thou fear God, seeing thou Lk 23:40
what *d* thou work? Jn 6:30
born in sins, and *d* thou teach us Jn 9:34
*D* thou believe on the Son of God Jn 9:35
How long *d* thou make us to doubt Jn 10:24
him, Lord, *d* thou wash my feet Jn 13:6
should not steal, *d* thou steal Rom 2:21
adultery, *d* thou commit adultery Rom 2:22
idols, *d* thou commit sacrilege Rom 2:22
circumcision *d* transgress the law Rom 2:27
But why *d* thou judge thy brother Rom 14:10

or why *d* thou set at nought thy....... Rom 14:10
why *d* thou glory, as if thou.................... 1Cor 4:7
*d* thou not judge and avenge our......... Rev 6:10

### DOTE

and they shall *d*: a sword is................... Jer 50:36

### DOTED

she *d* on her lovers, on the.................... Eze 23:5
and with all on whom she *d*..................... Eze 23:7
of the Assyrians, upon whom she *d*...... Eze 23:9
She *d* upon the Assyrians her................ Eze 23:12
eyes, she *d* upon them, and sent.......... Eze 23:16
For she *d* upon their paramours,.......... Eze 23:20

### DOTH

For God *d* know that in the day ye........ Gen 3:5
*d* comfort himself, purposing to........... Gen 27:42
*d* my father yet live................................ Gen 45:3
*d* put a difference between the.............. Ex 11:7
I am the LORD that *d* sanctify you......... Ex 31:13
why *d* thy wrath wax hot against............ Ex 32:11
whosoever *d* touch them, when they.. Lev 11:31
*d* fall, it shall be unclean...................... Lev 11:32
of the fruits *d* he sell unto thee............ Lev 25:16
when the LORD *d* make thy thigh to... Num 5:21
the man whom the LORD *d* choose...... Num 16:7
the LORD *d* command concerning the. Num 36:6
the LORD our God *d* give unto us......... Deut 1:20
which the LORD our God *d* give us...... Deut 1:25
as a man *d* bear his son, in all............ Deut 1:31
this day that God *d* talk with man........ Deut 5:24
that man *d* not live by bread only......... Deut 8:3
the mouth of the LORD *d* man live........ Deut 8:3
of these nations the LORD *d* drive......... Deut 9:4
these nations the LORD thy God *d*......... Deut 9:5
what *d* the LORD thy God require...... Deut 10:12
He *d* execute the judgment of the..... Deut 10:18
for a gift *d* blind the eyes of............... Deut 16:19
abominations the LORD thy God *d*..... Deut 18:12
which the LORD thy God *d* give.......... Deut 20:16
God, he it is that *d* go with thee.......... Deut 31:6
he it is that *d* go before thee............... Deut 31:8
Whosoever he be that *d* rebel................ Josh 1:18
when he that *d* flee unto one of............ Josh 20:4
it shall be, when any man *d* come....... Judg 4:20
*d* know that thou art a virtuous.......... Ruth 3:11
because he *d* bless the sacrifice............. 1Sa 9:13
*D* not David hide himself with us.......... 1Sa 23:19
*D* not David hide himself in the............. 1Sa 26:1
Wherefore *d* my lord thus pursue........ 1Sa 26:18
as when one *d* hunt a partridge in....... 1Sa 26:20
that David *d* honour thy father............. 2Sa 10:3
for the king *d* speak this thing............. 2Sa 14:13
in that the king *d* not fetch home........ 2Sa 14:13
neither *d* God respect any person........ 2Sa 14:14
yet *d* he devise means, that his............ 2Sa 14:14
the king *d* sit in the gate....................... 2Sa 19:8
For thy servant *d* know that I............... 2Sa 19:20
but why *d* my lord the king.................... 2Sa 24:3
of that which *d* cost me nothing.......... 2Sa 24:24
the son of Haggith *d* reign..................... 1Kin 1:11
why then *d* Adonijah reign..................... 1Kin 1:13
for he *d* not prophesy good.................... 1Kin 22:8
spirit of Elijah *d* rest on Elisha........... 2Kin 2:15
that this man *d* send unto me to.......... 2Kin 5:7
that David *d* honour thy father............ 1Chr 19:3
why then *d* my lord require this........... 1Chr 21:3
as *d* thy people Israel, and may............ 2Chr 6:33
*D* not Hezekiah persuade you to........ 2Chr 32:11
*D* Job fear God for nought....................... Job 1:9
*D* not their excellency which is.............. Job 4:21
neither *d* trouble spring out of.............. Job 5:6
*D* the wild ass bray when he hath.......... Job 6:5
but what *d* your arguing reprove.......... Job 6:25
*D* God pervert judgment.......................... Job 8:3
or *d* the Almighty pervert justice.......... Job 8:3
*D* not the ear try words......................... Job 12:11
Why *d* thine heart carry thee away..... Job 15:12
my reins asunder, and *d* not spare....... Job 16:13
*d* not mine eye continue in their......... Job 17:2
And thou sayest, How *d* God know..... Job 22:13
On the left hand, where he *d* work....... Job 23:9
so *d* the grave those which have.......... Job 24:19
upon whom *d* not his light arise.......... Job 25:3
*D* not he see my ways, and count......... Job 31:4
Therefore *d* Job open his mouth in...... Job 35:16
he *d* establish them for ever, and........ Job 36:7
*D* the hawk fly by thy wisdom, and..... Job 39:26
*D* the eagle mount up at thy................ Job 39:27
By his neesings a light *d* shine............ Job 41:18
in his law *d* he meditate day and............... Ps 1:2
in his pride *d* persecute the poor............ Ps 10:2
in the secret places *d* he murder............ Ps 10:8
he *d* catch the poor, when he................... Ps 10:9
Wherefore *d* the wicked contemn........ Ps 10:13
his countenance *d* behold the.................. Ps 11:7
in his temple *d* every one speak............. Ps 29:9
because mine enemy *d* not triumph...... Ps 41:11
*D* not David hide himself with us........... Ps 54:*t*
for who, say they, *d* hear......................... Ps 59:7
he *d* send out his voice, and that........... Ps 68:33
And they say, How *d* God know.............. Ps 73:11
why *d* thine anger smoke against............ Ps 74:1
*d* his promise fail for evermore................ Ps 77:8
boar out of the wood *d* waste it.............. Ps 80:13
beast of the field *d* devour it.................. Ps 80:13
neither *d* a fool understand this............. Ps 92:6
therefore *d* my soul keep them.......... Ps 119:129
wait for the LORD, my soul *d* wait........... Ps 130:5
The LORD *d* build up Jerusalem............... Ps 147:2
These six things *d* the LORD hate........ Prov 6:16
*D* not wisdom cry?.................................... Prov 8:1
a stranger *d* not intermeddle with...... Prov 14:10
he that *d* keep his soul shall be............ Prov 22:5
*d* not he that pondereth the heart...... Prov 24:12
thy soul, *d* not he know it..................... Prov 24:12
so *d* an angry countenance a................. Prov 25:23
so *d* the slothful upon his bed............... Prov 26:14
so *d* the sweetness of a man's................ Prov 27:9
*d* the crown endure to every................ Prov 27:24
but the righteous *d* sing and................. Prov 29:6
and *d* not bless their mother................ Prov 30:11
her husband *d* safely trust in her....... Prov 31:11
so *d* a little folly him that is................. Eccl 10:1
and his right hand *d* embrace me......... Song 2:6
but Israel *d* not know.................................. Is 1:3
my people *d* not consider............................. Is 1:3
neither *d* the cause of the widow.............. Is 1:23
*d* take away from Jerusalem and................ Is 3:1
*d* witness against them................................. Is 3:9
neither *d* his heart think so...................... Is 10:7
*D* the plowman plow all day to sow....... Is 28:24
*d* he open and break the clods of........... Is 28:24
*d* he not cast abroad the fitches,.............. Is 28:25
For his God *d* instruct him to.................. Is 28:26
him to discretion, and *d* teach him......... Is 28:26
stream of brimstone, *d* kindle it.............. Is 30:33
the villages that Kedar *d* inhabit............ Is 42:11
an ash, and the rain *d* nourish it........... Is 44:14
day that I am he that *d* speak.................. Is 52:6
neither *d* justice overtake us...................... Is 59:9
glory for that which *d* not profit............ Jer 2:11
for to thee *d* it appertain........................ Jer 10:7
Wherefore *d* the way of the wicked....... Jer 12:1
the LORD *d* not accept them.................... Jer 14:10
yet every one of them *d* curse me.......... Jer 15:10
that none *d* return from his.................... Jer 23:14
see whether a man *d* travail with.......... Jer 30:6
him, as a shepherd *d* his flock................ Jer 31:10
why then *d* their king inherit Gad........ Jer 49:1
neither *d* any son of man pass.............. Jer 51:43
How *d* the city sit solitary, that............. Lam 1:1
For he *d* not afflict willingly.................. Lam 3:33
Wherefore *d* a living man complain..... Lam 3:39
there is none that *d* deliver us................ Lam 5:8
When a righteous man *d* turn from...... Eze 3:20
he *d* not sin, he shall surely................... Eze 3:21
*d* not the son bear the iniquity............ Eze 18:19
of me, *D* he not speak parables........... Eze 20:49
that *d* not understand shall fall........... Hos 4:14
of Israel *d* testify to his face.................. Hos 5:5
what *d* the LORD require of thee,........... Mic 6:8
judgment *d* never go forth...................... Hab 1:4
for the wicked *d* compass about............ Hab 1:4
every morning *d* he bring his................ Zeph 3:5
rust *d* corrupt, and where thieves........... Mt 6:19
neither moth nor rust *d* corrupt............. Mt 6:20
This fellow *d* not cast out devils........... Mt 12:24
*D* not your master pay tribute............... Mt 17:24
*d* he not leave the ninety and nine........ Mt 18:12
is put away *d* commit adultery............... Mt 19:9
How then *d* David in spirit call............. Mt 22:43
not what hour your Lord *d* come............ Mt 24:42
he is at hand that *d* betray me.............. Mt 26:46
Why *d* this man thus speak...................... Mk 2:7
the new wine *d* burst the bottles............ Mk 2:22
Why *d* this generation seek after............ Mk 8:12
My soul *d* magnify the Lord,..................... Lk 1:46
neither *d* a corrupt tree bring................. Lk 6:43
of a candle *d* give thee light.................. Lk 11:36
*d* not each one of you on the.................. Lk 13:15
as a hen *d* gather her brood under......... Lk 13:34
whosoever *d* not bear his cross,.............. Lk 14:27
*d* not leave the ninety and nine in.......... Lk 15:4
*d* not light a candle, and sweep.............. Lk 15:8
*D* he thank that servant because............ Lk 17:9
that is chief, as he that *d* serve............ Lk 22:26
beginning *d* set forth good wine.............. Jn 2:10
said unto them, *D* this offend you............ Jn 6:61
*D* our law judge any man, before............ Jn 7:51
how then *d* he now see.............................. Jn 9:19
Therefore *d* my Father love me,.............. Jn 10:17
even by him *d* this man stand here........ Acts 4:10
what *d* hinder me to be baptized........ Acts 8:36
the high priest *d* bear me witness........ Acts 22:5
much learning *d* make thee mad........ Acts 26:24
man seeth, why *d* he yet hope for........ Rom 8:24
unto me, Why *d* he yet find fault........ Rom 9:19
to the Lord he *d* not regard it.............. Rom 14:6
*D* God take care for oxen........................ 1Cor 9:9
*D* not even nature itself teach............ 1Cor 11:14
*D* not behave itself unseemly,.............. 1Cor 13:5
neither *d* corruption inherit............... 1Cor 15:50
so great a death, and *d* deliver............. 2Cor 1:10
much more *d* the ministration of........... 2Cor 3:9
for whatsoever *d* make manifest is........ Eph 5:13
as it *d* also in you, since the..................... Col 1:6
as a father *d* his children,...................... 1Th 2:11
of iniquity *d* already work...................... 2Th 2:7
their word will eat as *d* a canker.......... 2Ti 2:17
all shall wax old as *d* a garment.......... Heb 1:11
the sin which *d* so easily beset............. Heb 12:1
What *d* it profit, my brethren,............... Jas 2:14
to the body; what *d* it profit?................ Jas 2:16
*D* a fountain send forth at the............... Jas 3:11
and he *d* not resist you............................ Jas 5:6
*d* also now save us (not the................. 1Pet 3:21
and so *d* Marcus my son....................... 1Pet 5:13
it *d* not yet appear what we shall........... 1Jn 3:2
is born of God *d* not commit sin............. 1Jn 3:9
neither *d* he himself receive the............... 3Jn 10
and in righteousness he *d* judge.......... Rev 19:11

### DOTHAN

(*do'-than*) *A city in Manasseh.*
I heard them say, Let us go to *D*........ Gen 37:17
his brethren, and found them in *D*...... Gen 37:17
him, saying, Behold, he is in *D*............ 2Kin 6:13

### DOTING

but *d* about questions and strifes............ 1Ti 6:4

### DOUBLE

take *d* money in your hand................... Gen 43:12
they took *d* money in their hand,......... Gen 43:15
he shall restore *d*....................................... Ex 22:4
the thief be found, let him pay *d*............. Ex 22:7
he shall pay *d* unto his neighbour............ Ex 22:9
shalt *d* the sixth curtain in the................ Ex 26:9
they made the breastplate *d*.................... Ex 39:9
worth a *d* hired servant to thee.......... Deut 15:18
by giving him a *d* portion of all........... Deut 21:17
let a *d* portion of thy spirit be............... 2Kin 2:9
they were not of *d* heart....................... 1Chr 12:33
that they are *d* to that which is............. Job 11:6
can come to him with his *d* bridle....... Job 41:13
with a *d* heart do they speak..................... Ps 12:2
LORD's hand *d* for all her sins.................. Is 40:2
For your shame ye shall have *d*................ Is 61:7
land they shall possess the *d*..................... Is 61:7
their iniquity and their sin *d*................. Jer 16:18
destroy them with *d* destruction........... Jer 17:18
that I will render *d* unto thee................. Zec 9:12
be counted worthy of *d* honour............... 1Ti 5:17
A *d* minded man is unstable in all............ Jas 1:8
purify your hearts, ye *d* minded............. Jas 4:8
*d* unto her *d* according to...................... Rev 18:6
she hath filled fill to her *d*.................... Rev 18:6

### DOUBLED

dream was *d* unto Pharaoh twice........ Gen 41:32
Foursquare it shall be being *d*............... Ex 28:16
span the breadth thereof, being *d*........... Ex 39:9
let the sword be *d* the third time......... Eze 21:14

### DOUBLETONGUED

must the deacons be grave, not *d*............ 1Ti 3:8

### DOUBT

is without *d* rent in pieces.................... Gen 37:33
life shall hang in *d* before thee.......... Deut 28:66
No *d* but ye are the people, and............. Job 12:2
faith, wherefore didst thou *d*.................. Mt 14:31
*d* not, ye shall not only do this.............. Mt 21:21
shall not *d* in his heart, but.................... Mk 11:23
no *d* the kingdom of God is come.......... Lk 11:20
How long dost thou make us to *d*........... Jn 10:24
were all amazed, and were in *d*.......... Acts 2:12
No *d* this man is a murderer, whom.... Acts 28:4
For our sakes, no *d*, this is.................... 1Cor 9:10
for I stand in *d* of you............................. Gal 4:20
they would no *d* have continued........... 1Jn 2:19

### DOUBTED

but some *d*................................................ Mt 28:17
they *d* of them whereunto this............. Acts 5:24
Now while Peter *d* in himself what.... Acts 10:17
because I *d* of such manner of........... Acts 25:20

### DOUBTETH

he that *d* is damned if he eat,............. Rom 14:23

### DOUBTFUL

drink, neither be ye of *d* mind.............. Lk 12:29
but not to *d* disputations........................ Rom 14:1

### DOUBTING

on another, *d* of whom he spake............ Jn 13:22
down, and go with them, *d* nothing... Acts 10:20
bade me go with them, nothing *d*......... Acts 11:12
up holy hands, without wrath and *d*....... 1Ti 2:8

### DOUBTLESS

*D* ye shall not come into the land..... Num 14:30
for I will *d* deliver the.............................. 2Sa 5:19
shall *d* come again with rejoicing........... Ps 126:6
*D* thou art our father, though................ Is 63:16
unto others, yet *d* I am to you................ 1Cor 9:2
not expedient for me *d* to glory.......... 2Cor 12:1
Yea *d*, and I count all things but............ Phil 3:8

### DOUBTS

sentences, and dissolving of *d*.............. Dan 5:12
interpretations, and dissolve *d*............. Dan 5:16

### DOUGH

the people took their *d* before it........... Ex 12:34
baked unleavened cakes of the *d*.......... Ex 12:39
of your *d* for an heave offering.......... Num 15:20
Of the first of your *d* ye shall............... Num 15:21
bring the firstfruits of our *d*................. Neh 10:37
fire, and the women knead their *d*.......... Jer 7:18
the priest the first of your *d*................. Eze 44:30
after he hath kneaded the *d*.................... Hos 7:4

### DOVE

Also he sent forth a *d* from him............. Gen 8:8
But the *d* found no rest for the................ Gen 8:9
sent forth the *d* out of the ark............... Gen 8:10
the *d* came in to him in the.................... Gen 8:11
and sent forth the *d*.................................. Gen 8:12
Oh that I had wings like a *d*.................... Ps 55:6
wings of a *d* covered with silver........... Ps 68:13
O my *d*, that art in the clefts of............ Song 2:14
to me, my sister, my love, my *d*............. Song 5:2
My *d*, my undefiled is but one................ Song 6:9
I did mourn as a *d*.................................... Is 38:14
be like the *d* that maketh her nest......... Jer 48:28
is like a silly *d* without heart................ Hos 7:11

as a *d* out of the land of Assyria ... Hos 11:11
Spirit of God descending like a *d* ... Mt 3:16
the Spirit like a *d* descending ... Mk 1:10
a bodily shape like a *d* upon him ... Lk 3:22
descending from heaven like a *d* ... Jn 1:32

**DOVE'S**
the fourth part of a cab of *d* ... 2Kin 6:25

**DOVES**
eyes of *d* by the rivers of waters ... Song 5:12
like bears, and mourn sore like *d* ... Is 59:11
as the *d* to their windows ... Is 60:8
mountains like *d* of the valleys ... Eze 7:16
lead her as with the voice of *d* ... Nah 2:7
as serpents, and harmless as *d* ... Mt 10:16
and the seats of them that sold *d* ... Mt 21:12
and the seats of them that sold *d* ... Mk 11:15
that sold oxen and sheep and *d* ... Jn 2:14
And said unto them that sold *d* ... Jn 2:16

**DOVES'**
thou art fair; thou hast *d* eyes ... Song 1:15
thou hast *d* eyes within thy locks ... Song 4:1

**DOWN** See PREFACE.

**DOWNSITTING**
Thou knowest my *d* and mine ... Ps 139:2

**DOWNWARD**
Judah shall yet again take root *d* ... 2Kin 19:30
beast that goeth *d* to the earth ... Eccl 3:21
of Judah shall again take root *d* ... Is 37:31
appearance of his loins even *d* ... Eze 1:27
appearance of his loins even *d* ... Eze 8:2

**DOWRY**
God hath endued me with a good *d* ... Gen 30:20
Ask me never so much *d* and gift, ... Gen 34:12
according to the *d* of virgins ... Ex 22:17
The king desireth not any *d* ... 1Sa 18:25

**DRAG**
net, and gather them in their *d* ... Hab 1:15
net, and burn incense unto their *d* ... Hab 1:16

**DRAGGING**
cubits,) *d* the net with fishes ... Jn 21:8

**DRAGON**
valley, even before the *d* well ... Neh 2:13
the *d* shalt thou trample under ... Ps 91:13
he shall slay the *d* that is in ... Is 27:1
hath cut Rahab, and wounded the *d* ... Is 51:9
he hath swallowed me up like a *d* ... Jer 51:34
the great *d* that lieth in the ... Eze 29:3
and behold a great red *d*, having ... Rev 12:3
the *d* stood before the woman ... Rev 12:4
his angels fought against the *d* ... Rev 12:7
the *d* fought and his angels, ... Rev 12:7
the great *d* was cast out, that ... Rev 12:9
when the *d* saw that he was cast ... Rev 12:13
which the *d* cast out of his mouth ... Rev 12:16
the *d* was wroth with the woman, ... Rev 12:17
the *d* gave him his power, and his ... Rev 13:2
they worshipped the *d* which gave ... Rev 13:4
like a lamb, and he spake as a *d* ... Rev 13:11
come out of the mouth of the *d* ... Rev 16:13
And he laid hold on the *d*, that ... Rev 20:2

**DRAGONS**
Their wine is the poison of *d* ... Deut 32:33
I am a brother to *d*, and a ... Job 30:29
sore broken us in the place of *d* ... Ps 44:19
the heads of the *d* in the waters ... Ps 74:13
the LORD from the earth, ye *d* ... Ps 148:7
*d* in their pleasant palaces ... Is 13:22
and it shall be an habitation of *d* ... Is 34:13
in the habitation of *d*, where ... Is 35:7
the field shall honour me, the *d* ... Is 43:20
Jerusalem heaps, and a den of *d* ... Jer 9:11
of Judah desolate, and a den of *d* ... Jer 10:22
they snuffed up the wind like *d* ... Jer 14:6
Hazor shall be a dwelling for *d* ... Jer 49:33
heaps, a dwelling place for *d* ... Jer 51:37
I will make a wailing like the *d* ... Mic 1:8
waste for the *d* of the wilderness ... Mal 1:3

**DRAMS**
talents and ten thousand *d* ... 1Chr 29:7
and one thousand *d* of gold ... Ezr 2:69
basons of gold, of a thousand *d* ... Ezr 8:27
the treasure a thousand *d* of gold ... Neh 7:70
work twenty thousand *d* of gold ... Neh 7:71
was twenty thousand *d* of gold ... Neh 7:72

**DRANK**
he *d* of the wine, and was drunken ... Gen 9:21
so I *d*, and she made the camels ... Gen 24:46
and he brought him wine, and he *d* ... Gen 27:25
they *d*, and were merry ... Gen 43:34
abundantly, and the congregation *d* .. Num 20:11
*d* the wine of their drink ... Deut 32:38
*d* of his own cup, and lay in his ... 2Sa 12:3
bread in his house, and *d* water ... 1Kin 13:19
and he *d* of the brook ... 1Kin 17:6
meat, and of the wine which he *d* ... Dan 1:5
nor with the wine which he *d* ... Dan 1:8
*d* wine before the thousand ... Dan 5:1
and his concubines, *d* in them ... Dan 5:3
They *d* wine, and praised the gods ... Dan 5:4
and they all *d* of it ... Mk 14:23
They did eat, they *d*, they ... Lk 17:27
they did eat, they *d*, they bought ... Lk 17:28
*d* thereof himself, and his ... Jn 4:12

for they *d* of that spiritual Rock ... 1Cor 10:4

**DRAUGHT**
made it a *d* house unto this day ... 2Kin 10:27
belly, and is cast out into the *d* ... Mt 15:17
belly, and goeth out into the *d* ... Mk 7:19
and let down your nets for a *d* ... Lk 5:4
at the *d* of the fishes which they ... Lk 5:9

**DRAVE**
wheels, that they *d* them heavily ... Ex 14:25
they *d* not out the Canaanites ... Josh 16:10
which *d* them out from before you, ... Josh 24:12
the LORD *d* out from before us all ... Josh 24:18
he *d* out the inhabitants of the ... Judg 1:19
*d* them out from before you, and ... Judg 6:9
which they *d* before those other ... 1Sa 30:20
sons of Abinadab, *d* the new cart ... 2Sa 6:3
Syria, and *d* the Jews from Elath ... 2Kin 16:6
Jeroboam *d* Israel from following ... 2Kin 17:21
and Uzza and Ahio *d* the cart ... 1Chr 13:7
whom God *d* out before the face of ... Acts 7:45
he *d* them from the judgment seat ... Acts 18:16

**DRAW**
time that women go out to *d* water ... Gen 24:11
of the city come out to *d* water ... Gen 24:13
I will *d* water for thy camels ... Gen 24:19
again unto the well to *d* water ... Gen 24:20
virgin cometh forth to *d* water ... Gen 24:43
I will also *d* for thy camels ... Gen 24:44
And he said, *D* not nigh hither ... Ex 3:5
them, *D* out and take you a lamb ... Ex 12:21
I will *d* my sword, my hand shall ... Ex 15:9
will *d* out a sword after you ... Lev 26:33
so that he could not *d* the dagger ... Judg 3:22
*d* toward mount Tabor, and take ... Judg 4:6
I will *d* unto thee to the river ... Judg 4:7
*D* thy sword, and slay me, that men ... Judg 9:54
let us *d* near to one of these ... Judg 19:13
*d* them from the city unto the ... Judg 20:32
maidens going out to *d* water ... 1Sa 9:11
Let us *d* near hither unto God ... 1Sa 14:36
*D* ye near hither, all the chief ... 1Sa 14:38
*D* thy sword, and thrust me through ... 1Sa 31:4
we will *d* it into the river, ... 2Sa 17:13
*D* thy sword, and thrust me through .. 1Chr 10:4
and every man shall *d* after him ... Job 21:33
he trusteth that he can *d* up ... Job 40:23
Canst thou *d* out leviathan with ... Job 41:1
*D* me not away with the wicked, and ... Ps 28:3
*D* out also the spear, and stop the ... Ps 35:3
*D* nigh unto my soul, and redeem it ... Ps 69:18
is good for me to *d* near to God ... Ps 73:28
wilt thou *d* out thine anger to ... Ps 85:5
they *d* near unto the gates of ... Ps 107:18
They *d* nigh that follow after ... Ps 119:150
of understanding will *d* it out ... Prov 20:5
come not, nor the years *d* nigh ... Eccl 12:1
*D* me, we will run after thee ... Song 1:4
Woe unto them that *d* iniquity ... Is 5:18
of the Holy One of Israel *d* nigh ... Is 5:19
ye *d* water out of the wells of ... Is 12:3
people *d* near me with their mouth ... Is 29:13
*d* near together, ye that are ... Is 45:20
But *d* near hither, ye sons of the ... Is 57:3
a wide mouth, and *d* out the tongue ... Is 57:4
if thou *d* out thy soul to the ... Is 58:10
that *d* the bow, to Tubal, and ... Is 66:19
and I will cause him to *d* near ... Jer 30:21
and shield, and *d* near to battle ... Jer 46:3
of the flock shall *d* them out ... Jer 49:20
of the flock shall *d* them out ... Jer 50:45
the sea monsters *d* out the breast ... Lam 4:3
I will *d* out a sword after them ... Eze 5:2
I will *d* out a sword after them ... Eze 5:12
charge over the city to *d* near ... Eze 9:1
I will *d* out the sword after them ... Eze 12:14
will *d* forth my sword out of his ... Eze 21:3
hast caused thy days to *d* near ... Eze 22:4
they shall *d* their swords against ... Eze 28:7
they shall *d* their swords against ... Eze 30:11
*d* her and all her multitudes ... Eze 32:20
let all the men of war *d* near ... Joel 3:9
*D* thee waters for the siege, ... Nah 3:14
to *d* out fifty vessels out of the ... Hag 2:16
*D* out now, and bear unto the ... Jn 2:8
a woman of Samaria to *d* water ... Jn 4:7
Sir, thou hast nothing to *d* with ... Jn 4:11
not, neither come hither to *d* ... Jn 4:15
Father which hath sent me *d* him ... Jn 6:44
the earth, will *d* all men unto me ... Jn 12:32
now they were not able to *d* it ... Jn 21:6
to *d* away disciples after them ... Acts 20:30
by the which we *d* nigh unto God ... Heb 7:19
Let us *d* near with a true heart ... Heb 10:22
but if any man *d* back, my soul ... Heb 10:38
of them who *d* back unto perdition ... Heb 10:39
*d* you before the judgment seats ... Jas 2:6
*D* nigh to God, and he will *d* ... Jas 4:8

**DRAWER**
thy wood unto the *d* of thy water ... Deut 29:11

**DRAWERS**
wood and *d* of water unto all the ... Josh 9:21
*d* of water for the house of my ... Josh 9:23
*d* of water for the congregation, ... Josh 9:27

**DRAWETH**
the wife of the one *d* near for to ... Deut 25:11
now the day *d* toward evening, I ... Judg 19:9
He *d* also the mighty with his ... Job 24:22

his soul *d* near unto the grave, ... Job 33:22
when he *d* him into his net ... Ps 10:9
my life *d* nigh unto the grave ... Ps 88:3
that *d* near the time of her ... Is 26:17
The time is come, the day *d* near ... Eze 7:12
This people *d* nigh unto me with ... Mt 15:8
and the time *d* near ... Lk 21:8
for your redemption *d* nigh ... Lk 21:28
for the coming of the Lord *d* nigh ... Jas 5:8

D

**DRAWING**
archers in the places of *d* water ... Judg 5:11
the sea, and *d* nigh unto the ship ... Jn 6:19

**DRAWN**
way, and his sword *d* in his hand ... Num 22:23
way, and his sword *d* in his hand ... Num 22:31
and which hath not *d* in the yoke ... Deut 21:3
not hear, but shalt be *d* away ... Deut 30:17
him with his sword *d* in his hand ... Josh 5:13
till we have *d* them from the city ... Josh 8:6
were *d* away from the city ... Josh 8:16
the border was *d* from the top of ... Josh 15:9
and the border was *d* to Baalah ... Josh 15:9
and the border was *d* to Shicron ... Josh 15:11
And the border was *d* thence ... Josh 18:14
was *d* from the north, and went ... Josh 18:17
were *d* away from the city ... Judg 20:31
that which the young men have *d* ... Ruth 2:9
having a *d* sword in his hand ... 1Chr 21:16
It is *d*, and cometh out of the ... Job 20:25
The wicked have *d* out the sword ... Ps 37:14
than oil, yet were they *d* swords ... Ps 55:21
them that are *d* unto death ... Prov 24:11
from the swords, from the *d* sword ... Is 21:15
the milk, and *d* from the breasts ... Is 28:9
with the burial of an ass, *d* ... Jer 22:19
with lovingkindness have I *d* thee ... Jer 31:3
he hath *d* back his right hand ... Lam 2:3
have *d* forth my sword out of his ... Eze 21:5
thou, The sword, the sword is *d* ... Eze 21:28
all were *d* up again into heaven ... Acts 11:10
when he is *d* away of his own lust ... Jas 1:14

**DREAD**
the *d* of you shall be upon every ... Gen 9:2
Fear and *d* shall fall upon them ... Ex 15:16
*D* not, neither be afraid of them ... Deut 1:29
will I begin to put the *d* of thee ... Deut 2:25
the *d* of you upon all the land ... Deut 11:25
*d* not, nor be dismayed ... 1Chr 22:13
and his *d* fall upon you ... Job 13:11
let not thy *d* make me afraid ... Job 13:21
your fear, and let him be your *d* ... Is 8:13

**DREADFUL**
and said, How *d* is this place ... Gen 28:17
A *d* sound is in his ears ... Job 15:21
were so high that they were *d* ... Eze 1:18
and behold a fourth beast, *d* ... Dan 7:7
from all the others, exceeding *d* ... Dan 7:19
*d* God, keeping the covenant and ... Dan 9:4
They are terrible and *d* ... Hab 1:7
my name is *d* among the heathen ... Mal 1:14
of the great and *d* day of the LORD ... Mal 4:5

**DREAM**
came to Abimelech in a *d* by night ... Gen 20:3
And God said unto him in a *d* ... Gen 20:6
up mine eyes, and saw in a *d* ... Gen 31:10
angel of God spake unto me in a *d* ... Gen 31:11
Laban the Syrian in a *d* by night ... Gen 31:24
And Joseph dreamed a *d*, and he told .. Gen 37:5
this *d* which I have dreamed ... Gen 37:6
And he dreamed yet another *d* ... Gen 37:9
Behold, I have dreamed a *d* more ... Gen 37:9
What is this *d* that thou hast ... Gen 37:10
And they dreamed a *d* both of them ... Gen 40:5
each man his *d* in one night ... Gen 40:5
to the interpretation of his *d* ... Gen 40:5
unto him, We have dreamed a *d* ... Gen 40:8
chief butler told his *d* to Joseph ... Gen 40:9
and said to him, In my *d* ... Gen 40:9
unto Joseph, I also was in my *d* ... Gen 40:16
awoke, and, behold, it was a *d* ... Gen 41:7
and Pharaoh told them his *d* ... Gen 41:8
And we dreamed a *d* in one night ... Gen 41:11
to the interpretation of his *d* ... Gen 41:11
to his *d* he did interpret ... Gen 41:12
unto Joseph, I have dreamed a *d* ... Gen 41:15
understand a *d* to interpret it ... Gen 41:15
Pharaoh said unto Joseph, In my *d* ... Gen 41:17
And I saw in my *d*, and, behold, ... Gen 41:22
Pharaoh, The *d* of Pharaoh is one ... Gen 41:25
are seven years: the *d* is one ... Gen 41:26
for that the *d* was doubled unto ... Gen 41:32
and will speak unto him in a *d* ... Num 12:6
man that told a *d* unto his fellow ... Judg 7:13
and said, Behold, I dreamed a *d* ... Judg 7:13
Gideon heard the telling of the *d* ... Judg 7:15
to Solomon in a *d* by night ... 1Kin 3:5
and, behold, it was a *d* ... 1Kin 3:15
He shall fly away as a *d*, and ... Job 20:8
In a *d*, in a vision of the night, ... Job 33:15
As a *d* when one awaketh ... Ps 73:20
of Zion, we were like them that *d* ... Ps 126:1
For a *d* cometh through the ... Eccl 5:3
shall be as a *d* of a night vision ... Is 29:7
hath a *d*, let him tell a *d* ... Jer 23:28
unto them, I have dreamed a *d* ... Dan 2:3
spirit was troubled to know the *d* ... Dan 2:3
tell thy servants the *d*, and we ... Dan 2:4
will not make known unto me the *d* ... Dan 2:5

But if ye shew the *d*, and the ... Dan 2:6
therefore shew me the *d*, and the ... Dan 2:6
the king tell his servants the *d* ... Dan 2:7
will not make known unto me the *d* ... Dan 2:9
therefore tell me the *d*, and I ... Dan 2:9
unto me the *d* which I have seen ... Dan 2:26
Thy *d*, and the visions of thy head ... Dan 2:28
This is the *d*; and we will ... Dan 2:36
and the *d* is certain, and the ... Dan 2:45
I saw a *d* which made me afraid, ... Dan 4:5
me the interpretation of the *d* ... Dan 4:6
and I told the *d* before them ... Dan 4:7
and before him I told the *d* ... Dan 4:8
visions of my *d* that I have seen ... Dan 4:9
This *d* I king Nebuchadnezzar have ... Dan 4:18
said, Belteshazzar, let not the *d* ... Dan 4:19
the *d* be to them that hate thee, ... Dan 4:19
king of Babylon Daniel had a *d* ... Dan 7:1
then he wrote the *d*, and told the ... Dan 7:1
your old men shall *d* dreams ... Joel 2:28
the Lord appeared unto him in a *d* ... Mt 1:20
being warned of God in a *d* that ... Mt 2:12
Lord appeareth to Joseph in a *d* ... Mt 2:13
in a *d* to Joseph in Egypt ... Mt 2:19
being warned of God in a *d* ... Mt 2:22
this day in a *d* because of him ... Mt 27:19
and your old men shall *d* dreams ... Acts 2:17

**DREAMED**
And he *d*, and behold a ladder set ... Gen 28:12
Joseph *d* a dream, and he told it ... Gen 37:5
you, this dream which I have *d* ... Gen 37:6
he *d* yet another dream, and told ... Gen 37:9
Behold, I have *d* a dream more ... Gen 37:9
is this dream that thou hast *d* ... Gen 37:10
they *d* a dream both of them, each ... Gen 40:5
said unto him, We have *d* a dream ... Gen 40:8
of two full years, that Pharaoh *d* ... Gen 41:1
And he slept and *d* the second time ... Gen 41:5
we *d* a dream in one night, I and ... Gen 41:11
we *d* each man according to the ... Gen 41:11
I have *d* a dream, and there is ... Gen 41:15
the dreams which he *d* of them ... Gen 42:9
I *d* a dream, and, lo, a cake of ... Judg 7:13
saying, I have *d*, I have *d* ... Jer 23:25
dreams which ye cause to be *d* ... Jer 29:8
Nebuchadnezzar *d* dreams, ... Dan 2:1
I have *d* a dream, and my spirit ... Dan 2:3

**DREAMER**
to another, Behold, this *d* cometh ... Gen 37:19
or a *d* of dreams, and giveth thee ... Deut 13:1
that prophet, or that *d* of dreams ... Deut 13:3
or that *d* of dreams, shall be put ... Deut 13:5

**DREAMERS**
to your diviners, nor to your *d* ... Jer 27:9
these filthy *d* defile the flesh ... Jude 8

**DREAMETH**
even be as when an hungry man *d* ... Is 29:8
or as when a thirsty man *d* ... Is 29:8

**DREAMS**
hated him yet the more for his *d* ... Gen 37:8
see what will become of his *d* ... Gen 37:20
and he interpreted to us our *d* ... Gen 41:12
Joseph remembered the *d* which he ... Gen 42:9
you a prophet, or a dreamer of *d* ... Deut 13:1
prophet, or that dreamer of *d* ... Deut 13:3
prophet, or that dreamer of *d* ... Deut 13:5
answered him not, neither by *d* ... 1Sa 28:6
neither by prophets, nor by *d* ... 1Sa 28:15
Then thou scarest me with *d* ... Job 7:14
For in the multitude of *d* ... Eccl 5:7
to forget my name by their *d* ... Jer 23:27
them that prophesy false *d* ... Jer 23:32
neither hearken to your *d* which ... Jer 29:8
understanding in all visions and *d* ... Dan 1:17
Nebuchadnezzar dreamed *d* ... Dan 2:1
for to shew the king his *d* ... Dan 2:2
understanding, interpreting of *d* ... Dan 5:12
your old men shall dream *d* ... Joel 2:28
seen a lie, and have told false *d* ... Zec 10:2
and your old men shall dream *d* ... Acts 2:17

**DREGS**
but the *d* thereof, all the wicked ... Ps 75:8
thou hast drunken the *d* of the ... Is 51:17
even the *d* of the cup of my fury ... Is 51:22

**DRESS**
into the garden of Eden to *d* it ... Gen 2:15
and he hasted to *d* it ... Gen 18:7
*d* them, but shalt neither drink ... Deut 28:39
to *d* for the wayfaring man that ... 2Sa 12:4
*d* the meat in my sight, that I ... 2Sa 13:5
Amnon's house, and *d* him meat ... 2Sa 13:7
*d* it for me and my son, that we ... 1Kin 17:12
I will *d* the other bullock, and ... 1Kin 18:23
for yourselves, and *d* it first ... 1Kin 18:25

**DRESSED**
milk, and the calf which he had *d* ... Gen 18:8
all that is *d* in the fryingpan, ... Lev 7:9
of wine, and five sheep ready *d* ... 1Sa 25:18
*d* it for the man that was come to ... 2Sa 12:4
king, and had neither *d* his feet ... 2Sa 19:24
was given them, and they *d* it ... 1Kin 18:26
meet for them by whom it is *d* ... Heb 6:7

**DRESSER**
he unto the *d* of his vineyard ... Lk 13:7

**DRESSERS**
vine *d* in the mountains, and in ... 2Chr 26:10

**DRESSETH**
when he *d* the lamps, he shall ... Ex 30:7

**DREW**
And Abraham *d* near, and said, Wilt ... Gen 18:23
water, and *d* for all his camels ... Gen 24:20
down unto the well, and *d* water ... Gen 24:45
and they *d* and lifted up Joseph out ... Gen 37:28
as he *d* back his hand, that, ... Gen 38:29
the time *d* nigh that Israel must ... Gen 47:29
Because I *d* him out of the water ... Ex 2:10
*d* water, and filled the troughs to ... Ex 2:16
also *d* water enough for us, and ... Ex 2:19
And when Pharaoh *d* nigh, the ... Ex 14:10
Moses *d* near unto the thick ... Ex 20:21
and all the congregation *d* near ... Lev 9:5
*d* nigh, and came before the city, ... Josh 8:11
For Joshua *d* not his hand back, ... Josh 8:26
twenty thousand men that *d* sword ... Judg 8:10
But the youth *d* not his sword ... Judg 8:20
thousand footmen that *d* sword ... Judg 20:2
and six thousand men that *d* sword ... Judg 20:15
hundred thousand men that *d* sword ... Judg 20:17
all these *d* the sword ... Judg 20:25
all these *d* the sword ... Judg 20:35
liers in wait *d* themselves along ... Judg 20:37
thousand men that *d* the sword ... Judg 20:46
So he *d* off his shoe ... Ruth 4:8
*d* water, and poured it out before ... 1Sa 7:6
the Philistines *d* near to battle ... 1Sa 7:10
Then Saul *d* near to Samuel in the ... 1Sa 9:18
And the Philistine *d* near morning ... 1Sa 17:16
he *d* near to the Philistine ... 1Sa 17:40
came on and *d* near unto David ... 1Sa 17:41
*d* nigh to meet David, that David ... 1Sa 17:48
*d* it out of the sheath thereof, ... 1Sa 17:51
And Joab *d* nigh, and the people ... 2Sa 10:13
And he came apace, and *d* near ... 2Sa 18:25
he *d* me out of many waters ... 2Sa 22:17
*d* water out of the well of ... 2Sa 23:16
valiant men that *d* the sword ... 2Sa 24:9
Now the days of David *d* nigh that ... 1Kin 2:1
they *d* out the staves, that the ... 1Kin 8:8
a certain man *d* a bow at a ... 1Kin 22:34
seven hundred men that *d* swords ... 2Kin 3:26
Jehu *d* a bow with his full ... 2Kin 9:24
*d* water out of the well of ... 1Chr 11:18
*d* nigh before the Syrians unto ... 1Chr 19:14
*d* forth the Syrians that were ... 1Chr 19:16
hundred thousand men that *d* sword ... 1Chr 21:5
and ten thousand men that *d* sword ... 1Chr 21:5
they *d* out the staves of the ark, ... 2Chr 5:9
*d* bows, two hundred and fourscore ... 2Chr 14:8
a certain man *d* a bow at a ... 2Chr 18:33
So Esther *d* near, and touched the ... Est 5:2
his decree *d* near to be put in ... Est 9:1
he *d* me out of many waters ... Ps 18:16
were afraid, *d* near, and came ... Is 41:5
So they *d* up Jeremiah with cords, ... Jer 38:13
I *d* them with cords of a man, ... Hos 11:4
she *d* not near to her God ... Zeph 3:2
they *d* to shore, and sat down, and ... Mt 13:48
when they *d* nigh unto Jerusalem, ... Mt 21:1
when the time of the fruit *d* near ... Mt 21:34
*d* his sword, and struck a servant ... Mt 26:51
of Gennesaret, and *d* to the shore ... Mk 6:53
of them that stood by *d* a sword ... Mk 14:47
Then *d* near unto him all the ... Lk 15:1
*d* nigh to the house, he heard ... Lk 15:25
feast of unleavened bread *d* nigh ... Lk 22:1
*d* near unto Jesus to kiss him ... Lk 22:47
preparation, and the sabbath *d* on ... Lk 23:54
and reasoned, Jesus himself *d* near ... Lk 24:15
they *d* nigh unto the village, ... Lk 24:28
servants which *d* the water knew ... Jn 2:9
Simon Peter having a sword *d* it ... Jn 18:10
*d* the net to land full of great ... Jn 21:11
*d* away much people after him ... Acts 5:37
the time of the promise *d* nigh ... Acts 7:17
as he *d* near to behold it, the ... Acts 7:31
*d* nigh unto the city, Peter went ... Acts 10:9
*d* him out of the city, supposing ... Acts 14:19
*d* them into the marketplace unto ... Acts 16:19
he *d* out his sword, and would have ... Acts 16:27
they *d* Jason and certain brethren ... Acts 17:6
they *d* Alexander out of the ... Acts 19:33
Paul, and *d* him out of the temple ... Acts 21:30
that they *d* near to some country ... Acts 27:27
his tail *d* the third part of the ... Rev 12:4

**DREWEST**
Thou *d* near in the day that I ... Lam 3:57

**DRIED**
were *d* up from off the earth ... Gen 8:7
the waters were *d* up from off the ... Gen 8:13
day of the month, was the earth *d* ... Gen 8:14
green ears of corn *d* by the fire ... Lev 2:14
nor eat moist grapes, or *d* ... Num 6:3
But now our soul is *d* away ... Num 11:6
For we have heard how the LORD *d* ... Josh 2:10
For the LORD your God *d* up the ... Josh 4:23
which he *d* up from before us, ... Josh 4:23
heard that the LORD had *d* up the ... Josh 5:1
green withs that were never *d* ... Judg 16:7
green withs which had not been *d* ... Judg 16:8
*d* up, so that he could not pull ... 1Kin 13:4
a while, that the brook *d* up ... 1Kin 17:7
I *d* up all the rivers of besieged ... 2Kin 19:24
His roots shall be *d* up beneath ... Job 18:16
they are *d* up, they are gone away ... Job 28:4
My strength is *d* up like a ... Ps 22:15
my throat is *d* ... Ps 69:3
the Red sea also, and it was *d* up ... Ps 106:9
their multitude *d* up with thirst ... Is 5:13
the river shall be wasted and *d* up ... Is 19:5
defence shall be emptied and *d* up ... Is 19:6
have I *d* up all the rivers of the ... Is 37:25
thou not it which hath *d* the sea ... Is 51:10
places of the wilderness are *d* up ... Jer 23:10
and they shall be *d* up ... Jer 50:38
have *d* up the green tree, and have ... Eze 17:24
and the east wind *d* up her fruit ... Eze 19:12
behold, they say, Our bones are *d* ... Eze 37:11
is smitten, their root is *d* up ... Hos 9:16
and his fountain shall be *d* up ... Hos 13:15
the new wine is *d* up, the oil ... Joel 1:10
The vine is *d* up, and the fig tree ... Joel 1:12
for the rivers of waters are *d* up ... Joel 1:20
his arm shall be clean *d* up ... Zec 11:17
fountain of her blood was *d* up ... Mk 5:29
the fig tree *d* up from the roots ... Mk 11:20
and the water thereof was *d* up ... Rev 16:12

**DRIEDST**
thou *d* up mighty rivers ... Ps 74:15

**DRIETH**
and the flood decayeth and *d* up ... Job 14:11
but a broken spirit *d* the bones ... Prov 17:22
it dry, and *d* up all the rivers ... Nah 1:4

**DRINK**
let us make our father *d* wine ... Gen 19:32
their father *d* wine that night ... Gen 19:33
let us make him *d* wine this night ... Gen 19:34
father *d* wine that night also ... Gen 19:35
with water, and gave the lad *d* ... Gen 21:19
I pray thee, that I may *d* ... Gen 24:14
and she shall say, *D* ... Gen 24:14
and I will give thy camels *d* also ... Gen 24:14
*d* a little water of thy pitcher ... Gen 24:17
And she said, *D*, my lord ... Gen 24:18
upon her hand, and gave him *d* ... Gen 24:18
And when she had done giving him *d* ... Gen 24:19
little water of thy pitcher to *d* ... Gen 24:43
And she say to me, Both *d* thou ... Gen 24:44
and I said unto her, Let me *d* ... Gen 24:45
from her shoulder, and said, *D* ... Gen 24:46
and I will give thy camels *d* also ... Gen 24:46
and she made the camels *d* also ... Gen 24:46
And they did eat and *d*, he and the ... Gen 24:54
and he did eat and *d*, and rose up, ... Gen 25:34
a feast, and they did eat and *d* ... Gen 26:30
troughs when the flocks came to *d* ... Gen 30:38
conceive when they came to *d* ... Gen 30:38
he poured a *d* offering thereon, ... Gen 35:14
to *d* of the water of the river ... Ex 7:18
the Egyptians could not *d* of the ... Ex 7:21
about the river for water to *d* ... Ex 7:24
for they could not *d* of the water ... Ex 7:24
they could not *d* of the waters of ... Ex 15:23
Moses, saying, What shall we *d* ... Ex 15:24
was no water for the people to *d* ... Ex 17:1
said, Give us water that we may *d* ... Ex 17:2
out of it, that the people may *d* ... Ex 17:6
they saw God, and did eat and *d* ... Ex 24:11
an hin of wine for a *d* offering ... Ex 29:40
to the *d* offering thereof ... Ex 29:41
shall ye pour *d* offering thereon ... Ex 30:9
people sat down to eat and to *d* ... Ex 32:6
the children of Israel *d* of it ... Ex 32:20
neither eat bread, nor *d* water ... Ex 34:28
Do not *d* wine nor strong *d*, ... Lev 10:9
Do not *d* wine nor strong *d* ... Lev 10:9
all *d* that may be drunk in every ... Lev 11:34
the *d* offering thereof shall be ... Lev 23:13
their *d* offerings, even an ... Lev 23:18
*d* offerings, every thing upon his ... Lev 23:37
he shall cause the woman to *d* the ... Num 5:24
cause the woman to *d* the water ... Num 5:26
he hath made her to *d* the water ... Num 5:27
himself from wine and strong *d* ... Num 6:3
shall *d* no vinegar of wine, or ... Num 6:3
of wine, or vinegar of strong *d* ... Num 6:3
neither shall he *d* any liquor of ... Num 6:3
offering, and their *d* offerings ... Num 6:15
meat offering, and his *d* offering ... Num 6:17
that the Nazarite may *d* wine ... Num 6:20
a *d* offering shalt thou prepare ... Num 15:5
for a *d* offering thou shalt offer ... Num 15:7
thou shalt bring for a *d* offering ... Num 15:10
his *d* offering, according to the ... Num 15:24
neither is there any water to *d* ... Num 20:5
congregation and their beasts *d* ... Num 20:8
neither will we *d* of the water of ... Num 20:17
my cattle *d* of thy water, then I ... Num 20:19
we will not *d* of the waters of ... Num 21:22
prey, and *d* the blood of the slain ... Num 23:24
the *d* offering thereof shall be ... Num 28:7
unto the LORD for a *d* offering ... Num 28:7
as the *d* offering thereof, thou ... Num 28:8
oil, and the *d* offering thereof ... Num 28:9
burnt offering, and his *d* offering ... Num 28:10
their *d* offerings shall be half ... Num 28:14
burnt offering, and his *d* offering ... Num 28:15
burnt offering, and his *d* offering ... Num 28:24
blemish) and their *d* offerings ... Num 28:31
their *d* offerings, according unto ... Num 29:6

of it, and their *d* offerings ... Num 29:11
meat offering, and his *d* offering ... Num 29:16
their *d* offerings for the ... Num 29:18
thereof, and their *d* offerings ... Num 29:19
their *d* offerings for the ... Num 29:21
meat offering, and his *d* offering ... Num 29:22
their *d* offerings for the ... Num 29:24
meat offering, and his *d* offering ... Num 29:25
their *d* offerings for the ... Num 29:27
meat offering, and his *d* offering ... Num 29:28
their *d* offerings for the ... Num 29:30
meat offering, and his *d* offering ... Num 29:31
their *d* offerings for the ... Num 29:33
meat offering, and his *d* offering ... Num 29:34
their *d* offerings for the bullock ... Num 29:37
meat offering, and his *d* offering ... Num 29:38
for your *d* offerings, and for your ... Num 29:39
was no water for the people to *d* ... Num 33:14
of them for money, that ye may *d* ... Deut 2:6
me water for money, that I may *d* ... Deut 2:28
neither did eat bread nor *d* water ... Deut 9:9
nor *d* water, because of all your ... Deut 9:18
or for wine, or for strong *d* ... Deut 14:26
but shalt neither *d* of the wine ... Deut 28:39
have ye drunk wine or strong *d* ... Deut 29:6
thou didst *d* the pure blood of ... Deut 32:14
the wine of their *d* offerings ... Deut 32:38
I pray thee, a little water to *d* ... Judg 4:19
a bottle of milk, and gave him *d* ... Judg 4:19
boweth down upon his knees to *d* ... Judg 7:5
down upon their knees to *d* water ... Judg 7:6
of their god, and did eat and *d* ... Judg 9:27
*d* not wine nor strong *d* ... Judg 13:4
and *d* not wine nor strong *d* ... Judg 13:4
now *d* no wine nor strong ... Judg 13:7
no wine nor strong *d* ... Judg 13:7
neither let her *d* wine or strong ... Judg 13:14
let her *d* wine or strong *d* ... Judg 13:14
so they did eat and *d*, and lodged ... Judg 19:4
eat and *d* both of them together ... Judg 19:6
their feet, and did eat and *d* ... Judg 19:21
*d* of that which the young men ... Ruth 2:9
drunken neither wine nor strong *d* ... 1Sa 1:15
and they made him *d* water ... 1Sa 30:11
into mine house, to eat and to *d* ... 2Sa 11:11
him, he did eat and *d* before him ... 2Sa 11:13
be faint in the wilderness may *d* ... 2Sa 16:2
taste what I eat or what I *d* ... 2Sa 19:35
Oh that one would give me *d* of ... 2Sa 23:15
he would not *d* thereof, but ... 2Sa 23:16
therefore he would not *d* it ... 2Sa 23:17
*d* before him, and say, God save ... 1Kin 1:25
bread nor *d* water in this place ... 1Kin 13:8
nor *d* water, nor turn again by ... 1Kin 13:9
neither will I eat bread nor *d* ... 1Kin 13:16
eat no bread nor *d* water there ... 1Kin 13:17
that he may eat bread and *d* water ... 1Kin 13:18
thee, Eat no bread, and *d* no water ... 1Kin 13:22
that thou shalt *d* of the brook ... 1Kin 17:4
water in a vessel, that I may *d* ... 1Kin 17:10
unto Ahab, Get thee up, eat and *d* ... 1Kin 18:41
So Ahab went up to eat and to *d* ... 1Kin 18:42
And he did eat and *d*, and laid him ... 1Kin 19:6
And he arose, and did eat and *d* ... 1Kin 19:8
filled with water, that ye may *d* ... 2Kin 3:17
them, that they may eat and *d* ... 2Kin 6:22
into one tent, and did eat and *d* ... 2Kin 7:8
he was come in, he did eat and *d* ... 2Kin 9:34
and poured his *d* offering ... 2Kin 16:13
offering, and their *d* offerings ... 2Kin 16:15
*d* their own piss with you ... 2Kin 18:27
*d* ye every one the waters of his ... 2Kin 18:31
Oh that one would give me *d* of ... 1Chr 11:17
but David would not *d* of it ... 1Chr 11:18
shall I *d* the blood of these men ... 1Chr 11:19
Therefore he would not *d* it ... 1Chr 11:19
lambs, with their *d* offerings ... 1Chr 29:21
*d* before the LORD on that day ... 1Chr 29:22
them, and gave them to eat and to *d* 2Chr 28:15
the *d* offerings for every burnt ... 2Chr 29:35
and meat, and *d*, and oil, unto them ... Ezr 3:7
their *d* offerings, and offer them ... Ezr 7:17
he did eat no bread, nor *d* water ... Ezr 10:6
*d* the sweet, and send portions ... Neh 8:10
went their way to eat, and to *d* ... Neh 8:12
they gave them *d* in vessels of ... Est 1:7
the king and Haman sat down to *d* ... Est 3:15
and neither eat nor *d* three days ... Est 4:16
sisters to eat and to *d* with them ... Job 1:4
he shall *d* of the wrath of the ... Job 21:20
not given water to the weary to *d* ... Job 22:7
their *d* offerings of blood will I ... Ps 16:4
thou shalt make them *d* of the ... Ps 36:8
of bulls, or *d* the blood of goats ... Ps 50:13
thou hast made us to *d* the wine ... Ps 60:3
thirst they gave me vinegar to *d* ... Ps 69:21
shall wring them out, and *d* them ... Ps 75:8
gave them *d* as out of the great ... Ps 78:15
floods, that they could not *d* ... Ps 78:44
them tears to *d* in great measure ... Ps 80:5
mingled my *d* with weeping, ... Ps 102:9
They give *d* to every beast of the ... Ps 104:11
He shall *d* of the brook in the ... Ps 110:7
and *d* the wine of violence ... Prov 4:17
*D* waters out of thine own cistern ... Prov 5:15
*d* of the wine which I have ... Prov 9:5
is a mocker, strong *d* is raging ... Prov 20:1
Eat and *d*, saith he to thee ... Prov 23:7
be thirsty, give him water to *d* ... Prov 25:21
it is not for kings to *d* wine ... Prov 31:4
nor for princes strong *d* ... Prov 31:4
Lest they *d*, and forget the law, ... Prov 31:5
Give strong *d* unto him that is ... Prov 31:6
Let him *d*, and forget his poverty, ... Prov 31:7
man, than that he should eat and *d* ... Eccl 2:24
that every man should eat and *d* ... Eccl 3:13
and comely for one to eat and to *d* ... Eccl 5:18
the sun, than to eat, and to *d* ... Eccl 8:15
*d* thy wine with a merry heart ... Eccl 9:7
*d*, yea, *d* abundantly, O ... Song 5:1
yea, *d* abundantly, O beloved ... Song 5:1
I would cause thee to *d* of spiced ... Song 8:2
that they may follow strong *d* ... Is 5:11
them that are mighty to *d* wine ... Is 5:22
of strength to mingle strong *d* ... Is 5:22
watch in the watchtower, eat, *d* ... Is 21:5
let us eat and *d* ... Is 22:13
They shall not *d* wine with a song ... Is 24:9
strong *d* shall be bitter to them ... Is 24:9
shall be bitter to them that *d* it ... Is 24:9
through strong *d* are out of the ... Is 28:7
have erred through strong *d* ... Is 28:7
out of the way through strong *d* ... Is 28:7
stagger, but not with strong *d* ... Is 29:9
he will cause the *d* of the ... Is 32:6
*d* their own piss with you ... Is 36:12
*d* ye every one the waters of his ... Is 36:16
to give *d* to my people, my chosen ... Is 43:20
thou shalt no more *d* it again ... Is 51:22
will fill ourselves with strong *d* ... Is 56:12
hast thou poured a *d* offering ... Is 57:6
the stranger shall not *d* thy wine ... Is 62:8
have brought it together shall *d* ... Is 62:9
that furnish the *d* offering unto ... Is 65:11
behold, my servants shall *d* ... Is 65:13
Egypt, to *d* the waters of Sihor ... Jer 2:18
to *d* the waters of the river ... Jer 2:18
to pour out *d* offerings unto ... Jer 7:18
and given us water of gall to *d* ... Jer 8:14
and give them water of gall to *d* ... Jer 9:15
*d* for their father or for their ... Jer 16:7
to sit with them to eat and to *d* ... Jer 16:8
have poured out *d* offerings unto ... Jer 19:13
did not thy father eat and *d* ... Jer 22:15
make them *d* the water of gall ... Jer 23:15
to whom I send thee, to *d* it ... Jer 25:15
And they shall *d*, and be moved, and ... Jer 25:16
and made all the nations to *d* ... Jer 25:17
of Sheshach shall *d* after them ... Jer 25:26
*D* ye, and be drunken, and spue, and ... Jer 25:27
take the cup at thine hand to *d* ... Jer 25:28
Ye shall certainly *d* ... Jer 25:28
poured out *d* offerings unto other ... Jer 32:29
chambers, and give them wine to *d* ... Jer 35:2
and I said unto them, *D* ye wine ... Jer 35:5
But they said, We will *d* no wine ... Jer 35:6
us, saying, Ye shall *d* no wine ... Jer 35:6
to *d* no wine all our days, we, ... Jer 35:8
commanded his sons not to *d* wine ... Jer 35:14
for unto this day they *d* none ... Jer 35:14
to pour out *d* offerings unto her, ... Jer 44:17
to pour out *d* offerings unto her, ... Jer 44:18
poured out *d* offerings unto her, ... Jer 44:19
pour out *d* offerings unto her, ... Jer 44:19
to pour out *d* offerings unto her ... Jer 44:25
to *d* of the cup have assuredly ... Jer 49:12
but thou shalt surely *d* of it ... Jer 49:12
Thou shalt *d* also water by ... Eze 4:11
from time to time shalt thou *d* ... Eze 4:11
they shall *d* water by measure, and ... Eze 4:16
*d* thy water with trembling and ... Eze 12:18
*d* their water with astonishment, ... Eze 12:19
out there their *d* offerings ... Eze 20:28
Thou shalt *d* of thy sister's cup ... Eze 23:32
Thou shalt even *d* it and suck it ... Eze 23:34
fruit, and they shall *d* thy milk ... Eze 25:4
in their height, all that *d* water ... Eze 31:14
best of Lebanon, all that *d* water ... Eze 31:16
they *d* that which ye have fouled ... Eze 34:19
that ye may eat flesh, and *d* blood ... Eze 39:17
*d* the blood of the princes of the ... Eze 39:18
*d* blood till ye be drunken, of my ... Eze 39:19
Neither shall any priest *d* wine ... Eze 44:21
*d* offerings, in the feasts, and in ... Eze 45:17
appointed your meat and your *d* ... Dan 1:10
us pulse to eat, and water to *d* ... Dan 1:12
and the wine that they should *d* ... Dan 1:16
his concubines, might *d* therein ... Dan 5:2
wool and my flax, mine oil and my *d* ... Hos 2:5
Their *d* is sour ... Hos 4:18
the *d* offering is cut off from ... Joel 1:9
the *d* offering is withholden from ... Joel 1:13
a *d* offering unto the LORD your ... Joel 2:14
girl for wine, that they might *d* ... Joel 3:3
they *d* the wine of the condemned ... Amos 2:8
ye gave the Nazarites wine to *d* ... Amos 2:12
their masters, Bring, and let us *d* ... Amos 4:1
unto one city, to *d* water ... Amos 4:8
but ye shall not *d* wine of them ... Amos 5:11
That *d* wine in bowls, and anoint ... Amos 6:6
vineyards, and *d* the wine thereof ... Amos 9:14
*d* continually, yea, they shall *d* ... Obad 16
let them not feed, nor *d* water ... Jonah 3:7
unto thee of wine and of strong *d* ... Mic 2:11
sweet wine, but shalt not *d* wine ... Mic 6:15
him that giveth his neighbour *d* ... Hab 2:15
*d* thou also, and let thy foreskin ... Hab 2:16
but not *d* the wine thereof ... Zeph 1:13
ye *d*, but ye are not filled with ... Hag 1:6
but ye are not filled with *d* ... Hag 1:6
when ye did eat, and when ye did *d* ... Zec 7:6
yourselves, and *d* for yourselves ... Zec 7:6
and they shall *d*, and make a noise ... Zec 9:15
ye shall eat, or what ye shall *d* ... Mt 6:25
or, What shall we *d* ... Mt 6:31
whosoever shall give to *d* unto ... Mt 10:42
*d* of the cup that I shall *d* ... Mt 20:22
Ye shall *d* indeed of my cup, and ... Mt 20:23
and to eat and *d* with the drunken ... Mt 24:49
I was thirsty, and ye gave me *d* ... Mt 25:35
or thirsty, and gave thee *d* ... Mt 25:37
I was thirsty, and ye gave me no *d* ... Mt 25:42
to them, saying, *D* ye all of it ... Mt 26:27
I will not *d* henceforth of this ... Mt 26:29
until that day when I *d* it new ... Mt 26:29
pass away from me, except I *d* it ... Mt 26:42
vinegar to *d* mingled with gall ... Mt 27:34
tasted thereof, he would not *d* ... Mt 27:34
it on a reed, and gave him to *d* ... Mt 27:48
a cup of water to *d* in my name ... Mk 9:41
can ye *d* of the cup that I *d* ... Mk 10:38
*d* of the cup that I *d* of ... Mk 10:39
I will *d* no more of the fruit of ... Mk 14:25
until that day that I *d* it new in ... Mk 14:25
they gave him to *d* wine mingled ... Mk 15:23
it on a reed, and gave him to *d* ... Mk 15:36
if they *d* any deadly thing, it ... Mk 16:18
shall *d* neither wine nor strong ... Lk 1:15
neither wine nor strong *d* ... Lk 1:15
*d* with publicans and sinners ... Lk 5:30
but thine eat and *d* ... Lk 5:33
take thine ease, eat, *d*, and be ... Lk 12:19
ye shall eat, or what ye shall *d* ... Lk 12:29
and maidens, and to eat and *d* ... Lk 12:45
and afterward thou shalt eat and *d* ... Lk 17:8
I will not *d* of the fruit of the ... Lk 22:18
*d* at my table in my kingdom, and ... Lk 22:30
saith unto her, Give me to *d* ... Jn 4:7
thou, being a Jew, askest *d* of me ... Jn 4:9
that saith to thee, Give me to *d* ... Jn 4:10
*d* his blood, ye have no life in ... Jn 6:53
indeed, and my blood is *d* indeed ... Jn 6:55
let him come unto me, and *d* ... Jn 7:37
hath given me, shall I not *d* it ... Jn 18:11
sight, and neither did eat nor *d* ... Acts 9:9
*d* with him after he rose from the ... Acts 10:41
nor *d* till they had killed Paul ... Acts 23:12
nor *d* till they have killed him ... Acts 23:21
if he thirst, give him *d* ... Rom 12:20
kingdom of God is not meat and *d* ... Rom 14:17
to eat flesh, nor to *d* wine ... Rom 14:21
Have we not power to eat and to *d* ... 1Cor 9:4
all *d* the same spiritual *d* ... 1Cor 10:4
all *d* the same spiritual *d* ... 1Cor 10:4
The people sat down to eat and *d* ... 1Cor 10:7
Ye cannot *d* the cup of the Lord, ... 1Cor 10:21
Whether therefore ye eat, or *d* ... 1Cor 10:31
ye not houses to eat and to *d* in ... 1Cor 11:22
this do ye, as oft as ye *d* it ... 1Cor 11:25
*d* this cup, ye do shew the Lord's ... 1Cor 11:26
bread, and *d* this cup of the Lord, ... 1Cor 11:27
of that bread, and *d* of that cup ... 1Cor 11:28
all made to *d* into one Spirit ... 1Cor 12:13
let us eat and *d* ... 1Cor 15:32
judge you in meat, or in *d* ... Col 2:16
*D* no longer water, but use a ... 1Ti 5:23
because she made all nations *d* of ... Rev 14:8
The same shall *d* of the wine of ... Rev 14:10
thou hast given them blood to *d* ... Rev 16:6

## DRINKERS

all ye *d* of wine, because of the ... Joel 1:5

## DRINKETH

Is not this it in which my lord *d* ... Gen 44:5
*d* water of the rain of heaven ... Deut 11:11
the poison whereof *d* up my spirit ... Job 6:4
which *d* iniquity like water ... Job 15:16
who *d* up scorning like water ... Job 34:7
he *d* up a river, and hasteth not ... Job 40:23
cutteth off the feet, and *d* damage ... Prov 26:6
man dreameth, and, behold, he *d* ... Is 29:8
he *d* no water, and is faint ... Is 44:12
*d* with publicans and sinners ... Mk 2:16
Whosoever *d* of this water shall ... Jn 4:13
But whosoever *d* of the water that ... Jn 4:14
*d* my blood, hath eternal life ... Jn 6:54
*d* my blood, dwelleth in me, and I ... Jn 6:56
*d* unworthily, eateth and *d* ... 1Cor 11:29
For the earth which *d* in the rain ... Heb 6:7

## DRINKING

also, until they have done *d* ... Gen 24:19
to pass, as the camels had done *d* ... Gen 24:22
he shall have done eating and *d* ... Ruth 3:3
upon all the earth, eating and *d* ... 1Sa 30:16
the sea in multitude, eating and *d* ... 1Kin 4:20
all king Solomon's *d* vessels were ... 1Kin 10:21
*d* himself drunk in the house of ... 1Kin 16:9
heard this message, as he was *d* ... 1Kin 20:12
But Ben-hadad was *d* himself drunk ... 1Kin 20:16
David three days, eating and *d* ... 1Chr 12:39
all the *d* vessels of king Solomon ... 2Chr 9:20
the *d* was according to the law ... Est 1:8
*d* wine in their eldest brother's ... Job 1:13
*d* wine in their eldest brother's ... Job 1:18
sheep, eating flesh, and *d* wine ... Is 22:13
John came neither eating nor *d* ... Mt 11:18
The Son of man came eating and *d* ... Mt 11:19
the flood they were eating and *d* ... Mt 24:38
neither eating bread nor *d* wine ... Lk 7:33
Son of man is come eating and *d* ... Lk 7:34

*d* such things as they give Lk 10:7

**DRINKS**
Which stood only in meats and *d* Heb 9:10

**DRIVE**
shall he *d* them out of his land Ex 6:1
which shall *d* out the Hivite, the Ex 23:28
I will not *d* them out from before Ex 23:29
little I will *d* them out from Ex 23:30
thou shalt *d* them out before thee Ex 23:31
I will *d* out the Canaanite, the Ex 33:2
I *d* out before thee the Amorite, Ex 34:11
that I may *d* them out of the land Num 22:6
to overcome them, and *d* them out Num 22:11
Then ye shall *d* out all the Num 33:52
But if ye will not *d* out the Num 33:55
To *d* out nations from before thee Deut 4:38
so shalt thou *d* them out, and Deut 9:3
doth *d* them out from before thee Deut 9:4
doth *d* them out from before thee Deut 9:5
Then will the LORD *d* out all Deut 11:23
the LORD thy God doth *d* them out Deut 18:12
fail *d* out from before you the Josh 3:10
them will I *d* out from before the Josh 13:6
I shall be able to *d* them out Josh 14:12
of Judah could not *d* them out Josh 15:63
*d* out the inhabitants of those Josh 17:12
but did not utterly *d* them out Josh 17:13
for thou shalt *d* out the Josh 17:18
*d* them from out of your sight Josh 23:5
*d* out any of these nations from Josh 23:13
but could not *d* out the Judg 1:19
did not *d* out the Jebusites that Judg 1:21
Neither did Manasseh *d* out the Judg 1:27
and did not utterly *d* them out Judg 1:28
Neither did Ephraim *d* out the Judg 1:29
Neither did Zebulun *d* out the Judg 1:30
Neither did Asher *d* out the Judg 1:31
for they did not *d* them out Judg 1:32
Neither did Naphtali *d* out the Judg 1:33
I will not *d* them out from before Judg 2:3
I also will not henceforth *d* out Judg 2:21
God shall *d* out from before us Judg 11:24
an ass, and said to her servant, *D* 2Kin 4:24
who didst *d* out the inhabitants 2Chr 20:7
side, and shall *d* him to his feet Job 18:11
They *d* away the ass of the Job 24:3
How thou didst *d* out the heathen Ps 44:2
is driven away, so *d* them away Ps 68:2
shall *d* it far from him Prov 22:15
I will *d* thee from thy station, Is 22:19
all places whither I shall *d* them Jer 24:9
and that I should *d* you out Jer 27:10
that I might *d* you out, and that Jer 27:15
not, because the LORD did *d* them Jer 46:15
Gentiles, whither I will *d* them Eze 4:13
That they shall *d* thee from men Dan 4:25
they shall *d* thee from men, and Dan 4:32
I will *d* them out of mine house Hos 9:15
will *d* him into a land barren and Joel 2:20
they shall *d* out Ashdod at the Zeph 2:4
up into the wind, we let her *d* Acts 27:15

**DRIVEN**
thou hast *d* me out this day from Gen 4:14
they were *d* out from Pharaoh's Ex 10:11
or *d* away, no man seeing it Ex 22:10
until he hath *d* out his enemies Num 32:21
shouldest be *d* to worship them, Deut 4:19
the LORD thy God hath *d* thee Deut 30:1
If any of thine be *d* out unto the Deut 30:4
For the LORD hath *d* out from Josh 23:9
for they have *d* me out this day 1Sa 26:19
is wisdom *d* quite from me Job 6:13
Wilt thou break a leaf *d* to Job 13:25
He shall be *d* from light into Job 18:18
They were *d* forth from among men, Job 30:5
let them be *d* backward and put to Ps 40:14
As smoke is *d* away, so drive them Ps 68:2
Jordan was *d* back Ps 114:3
Jordan, that thou wast *d* back Ps 114:5
The wicked is *d* away in his Prov 14:32
and they shall be *d* to darkness Is 8:22
wither, be *d* away, and be no more Is 19:7
sword, and as *d* stubble to his bow Is 41:2
the places whither I have *d* them Jer 8:3
the lands whither he had *d* them Jer 16:15
*d* them away, and have not visited Jer 23:2
countries whither I have *d* them Jer 23:3
countries whither I had *d* them Jer 23:8
they shall be *d* on, and fall Jer 23:12
the places whither I have *d* you Jer 29:14
the nations whither I have *d* them Jer 29:18
whither I have *d* them in mine Jer 32:37
of all places whither they were *d* Jer 40:12
nations, whither they had been *d* Jer 43:5
the nations whither I have *d* thee Jer 46:28
ye shall be *d* out every man right Jer 49:5
the lions have *d* him away Jer 50:17
I have *d* him out for his Eze 31:11
again that which was *d* away Eze 34:4
bring again that which was *d* away Eze 34:16
he was *d* from men, and did eat Dan 4:33
he was *d* from the sons of men Dan 5:21
whither thou hast *d* them, because Dan 9:7
as the chaff that is *d* with the Hos 13:3
I will gather her that is *d* out Mic 4:6
and gather her that was *d* out Zeph 3:19
was *d* of the devil into the Lk 8:29
strake sail, and so were *d* Acts 27:17
night was come, as we were *d* up Acts 27:27

a wave of the sea *d* with the wind Jas 1:6
are *d* of fierce winds, yet are Jas 3:4

**DRIVER**
he said unto the *d* of his chariot 1Kin 22:34
regardeth he the crying of the *d* Job 39:7

**DRIVETH**
for he *d* furiously 2Kin 9:20
the chaff which the wind *d* away Ps 1:4
The north wind *d* away rain Prov 25:23
immediately the spirit *d* him into Mk 1:12

**DRIVING**
without *d* them out hastily Judg 2:23
the *d* is like the *d* of Jehu 2Kin 9:20
the *d* is like the *d* of Jehu 2Kin 9:20
by *d* out nations from before thy 1Chr 17:21

**DROMEDARIES**
*d* brought they unto the place 1Kin 4:28
on mules, camels, and young *d* Est 8:10
thee, the *d* of Midian and Ephah Is 60:6

**DROMEDARY**
thou art a swift *d* traversing her Jer 2:23

**DROP**
My doctrine shall *d* as the rain Deut 32:2
also his heavens shall *d* down dew Deut 33:28
Which the clouds do *d* and distil Job 36:28
and thy paths *d* fatness Ps 65:11
They *d* upon the pastures of the Ps 65:12
the clouds *d* down the dew Prov 3:20
a strange woman *d* as an honeycomb Prov 5:3
O my spouse, *d* as the honeycomb Song 4:11
nations are as a *d* of a bucket Is 40:15
*D* down, ye heavens, from above, Is 45:8
*d* thy word toward the south, and Eze 20:46
*d* thy word toward the holy places Eze 21:2
mountains shall *d* down new wine Joel 3:18
*d* not thy word against the house Amos 7:16
the mountains shall *d* sweet wine Amos 9:13

**DROPPED**
earth trembled, and the heavens *d* Judg 5:4
the clouds also *d* water Judg 5:4
the wood, behold, the honey *d* 1Sa 14:26
of harvest until water *d* upon 2Sa 21:10
and my speech *d* upon them Job 29:22
the heavens also *d* at the Ps 68:8
my hands *d* with myrrh, and my Song 5:5

**DROPPETH**
of the hands the house *d* through Eccl 10:18

**DROPPING**
of a wife are a continual *d* Prov 19:13
A continual *d* in a very rainy day Prov 27:15
lilies, *d* sweet smelling myrrh Song 5:13

**DROPS**
he maketh small the *d* of water Job 36:27
or who hath begotten the *d* of dew Job 38:28
my locks with the *d* of the night Song 5:2
*d* of blood falling down to the Lk 22:44

**DROPSY**
man before him which had the *d* Lk 14:2

**DROSS**
the wicked of the earth like *d* Ps 119:119
Take away the *d* from the silver, Prov 25:4
a potsherd covered with silver *d* Prov 26:23
Thy silver is become *d*, thy wine Is 1:22
thee, and purely purge away thy *d* Is 1:25
house of Israel is to me become *d* Eze 22:18
they are even the *d* of silver Eze 22:18
Because ye are all become *d* Eze 22:19

**DROUGHT**
in the day the *d* consumed me Gen 31:40
serpents, and scorpions, and *d* Deut 8:15
*D* and heat consume the snow waters Job 24:19
is turned into the *d* of summer Ps 32:4
and satisfy thy soul in *d* Is 58:11
and of pits, through a land of *d* Jer 2:6
not be careful in the year of *d* Jer 17:8
A *d* is upon her waters Jer 50:38
in the land of great *d* Hos 13:5
And I called for a *d* upon the land Hag 1:11

**DROVE**
So he *d* out the man Gen 3:24
the carcases, Abram *d* them away Gen 15:11
servants, every *d* by themselves Gen 32:16
me, and put a space betwixt *d* Gen 32:16
and put a space betwixt *d* and *d* Gen 32:16
thou by all this *d* which I met Gen 33:8
the shepherds came and *d* them away Ex 2:17
*d* out the Amorites that were Num 21:32
Caleb *d* thence the three sons of Josh 15:14
who *d* away the inhabitants of 1Chr 8:13
who *d* him away, and he departed Ps 34:*t*
beheld, and *d* asunder the nations Hab 3:6
he *d* them all out of the temple, Jn 2:15

**DROVES**
third, and all that followed the *d* Gen 32:19

**DROWN**
love, neither can the floods *d* it Song 8:7
which *d* men in destruction and 1Ti 6:9

**DROWNED**
also are *d* in the Red sea Ex 15:4
and it shall be cast out and *d* Amos 8:8
and shall be *d*, as by the flood of Amos 9:5

that he were *d* in the depth of Mt 18:6
Egyptians assaying to do were *d* Heb 11:29

**DROWSINESS**
*d* shall clothe a man with rags Prov 23:21

**DRUNK**
all drink that may be *d* in every Lev 11:34
neither have ye *d* wine or strong Deut 29:6
make mine arrows *d* with blood Deut 32:42
and when he had *d*, his spirit came Judg 15:19
And when Boaz had eaten and *d* Ruth 3:7
in Shiloh, and after they had *d* 1Sa 1:9
nor *d* any water, three days and 1Sa 30:12
and he made him *d* 2Sa 11:13
*d* water in the place, of the 1Kin 13:22
eaten bread, and after he had *d* 1Kin 13:23
drinking himself *d* in the house 1Kin 16:9
himself *d* in the pavilions 1Kin 20:16
and when they had eaten and *d* 2Kin 6:23
*d* strange waters, and with the 2Kin 19:24
I have *d* my wine with my milk Song 5:1
I have digged, and *d* water Is 37:25
which hast *d* at the hand of the Is 51:17
make them *d* in my fury, and I will Is 63:6
and made *d* with their blood Jer 46:10
And I will make *d* her princes Jer 51:57
to have *d* of the deep waters, but Eze 34:18
concubines, have *d* wine in them Dan 5:23
For as ye have *d* upon my holy Obad 16
No man also having *d* old wine Lk 5:39
*d* in thy presence, and thou hast Lk 13:26
and when men have well *d*, then Jn 2:10
be not *d* with wine, wherein is Eph 5:18
been made *d* with the wine of her Rev 17:2
For all nations have *d* of the Rev 18:3

**DRUNKARD**
he is a glutton, and a *d* Deut 21:20
For the *d* and the glutton shall Prov 23:21
goeth up into the hand of a *d* Prov 26:9
shall reel to and fro like a *d* Is 24:20
an idolater, or a railer, or a *d* 1Cor 5:11

**DRUNKARDS**
and I was the song of the *d* Ps 69:12
to the *d* of Ephraim, whose Is 28:1
the *d* of Ephraim, shall be Is 28:3
Awake, ye *d*, and weep Joel 1:5
and while they are drunken as *d* Nah 1:10
Nor thieves, nor covetous, nor *d* 1Cor 6:10

**DRUNKEN**
And he drank of the wine, and was *d* Gen 9:21
Eli thought she had been *d* 1Sa 1:13
unto her, How long wilt thou be *d* 1Sa 1:14
I have *d* neither wine nor strong 1Sa 1:15
within him for he was very *d* 1Sa 25:36
them to stagger like a *d* man Job 12:25
and fro, and stagger like a *d* man Ps 107:27
as a *d* man staggereth in his Is 19:14
they are *d*, but not with wine Is 29:9
they shall be *d* with their own Is 49:26
thou hast *d* the dregs of the cup Is 51:17
now this, thou afflicted, and *d* Is 51:21
I am like a *d* man, and like a man Jer 23:9
Drink ye, and be *d*, and spue, and Jer 25:27
Make ye him *d*: for he magnified Jer 48:26
drink of the cup have assuredly *d* Jer 49:12
hand, that made all the earth *d* Jer 51:7
the nations have *d* of her wine Jer 51:7
feasts, and I will make them *d* Jer 51:39
he hath made me *d* with wormwood Lam 3:15
thou shalt be *d*, and shalt make Lam 4:21
We have *d* our water for money Lam 5:4
full, and drink blood till ye be *d* Eze 39:19
and while they are *d* as drunkards Nah 1:10
Thou also shalt be *d* Nah 3:11
to him, and makest him *d* also Hab 2:15
and to eat and drink with the *d* Mt 24:49
and to eat and drink, and to be *d* Lk 12:45
serve me, till I have eaten and *d* Lk 17:8
For these are not *d*, as ye Acts 2:15
and one is hungry, and another is *d* 1Cor 11:21
be *d* are *d* in the night 1Th 5:7
I saw the woman *d* with the blood Rev 17:6

**DRUNKENNESS**
of mine heart, to add *d* to thirst Deut 29:19
for strength, and not for *d* Eccl 10:17
inhabitants of Jerusalem, with *d* Jer 13:13
Thou shalt be filled with *d* Eze 23:33
overcharged with surfeiting, and *d* Lk 21:34
not in rioting and *d*, not in Rom 13:13
Envyings, murders, *d*, revellings, Gal 5:21

**DRUSILLA** (*dru-sil'-lah*) *Wife of Felix.*
when Felix came with his wife *D* Acts 24:24

**DRY**
place, and let the *d* land appear Gen 1:9
And God called the *d* land Earth Gen 1:10
of all that was in the *d* land Gen 7:22
the face of the ground was *d* Gen 8:13
river, and pour it upon the *d* land Ex 4:9
become blood upon the *d* land Ex 4:9
children of Israel shall go on *d* Ex 14:16
night, and made the sea *d* land Ex 14:21
of the sea upon the *d* ground Ex 14:22
*d* land in the midst of the sea Ex 14:29
on *d* land in the midst of the sea Ex 15:19
offering, mingled with oil, and *d* Lev 7:10
it is a *d* scall, even a leprosy Lev 13:30
of the LORD stood firm on *d* Josh 3:17

passed over on *d* ground, until ... Josh 3:17
were lifted up unto the *d* land ... Josh 4:18
came over this Jordan on *d* land ... Josh 4:22
bread of their provision was *d* ... Josh 9:5
but now, behold, it is *d*, and it ... Josh 9:12
it be *d* upon all the earth beside ... Judg 6:37
let it now be *d* only upon the ... Judg 6:39
for it was *d* upon the fleece only ... Judg 6:40
they two went over on *d* ground ... 2Kin 2:8
midst of the sea on the *d* land ... Neh 9:11
the waters, and they *d* up ... Job 12:15
and wilt thou pursue the *d* stubble ... Job 13:25
the flame shall *d* up his branches ... Job 15:30
my flesh longeth for thee in a *d* ... Ps 63:1
He turned the sea into *d* land ... Ps 66:6
the rebellious dwell in a *d* land ... Ps 68:6
and his hands formed the *d* land ... Ps 95:5
they ran in the *d* places like a ... Ps 105:41
and the watersprings into *d* ground ... Ps 107:33
*d* ground into watersprings ... Ps 107:35
Better is a *d* morsel, and ... Prov 17:1
as the heat in a *d* place ... Is 25:5
as rivers of water in a *d* place ... Is 32:2
the *d* land springs of water ... Is 41:18
and hills, and *d* up all their herbs ... Is 42:15
islands, and I will *d* up the pools ... Is 42:15
and floods upon the *d* ground ... Is 44:3
That saith to the deep, Be *d* ... Is 44:27
and I will *d* up thy rivers ... Is 44:27
at my rebuke I *d* up the sea ... Is 50:2
and as a root out of a *d* ground ... Is 53:2
eunuch say, Behold, I am a *d* tree ... Is 56:3
A *d* wind of the high places in ... Jer 4:11
wilderness, a *d* land, and a desert ... Jer 50:12
I will *d* up her sea ... Jer 51:36
and make her springs *d* ... Jer 51:36
a *d* land, and a wilderness, a land ... Jer 51:43
have made the *d* tree to flourish ... Eze 17:24
planted in the wilderness, in a *d* ... Eze 19:13
tree in thee, and every *d* tree ... Eze 20:47
And I will make the rivers *d* ... Eze 30:12
and, lo, they were very *d* ... Eze 37:2
O ye *d* bones, hear the word of ... Eze 37:4
and set her like a *d* land ... Hos 2:3
a miscarrying womb and *d* breasts ... Hos 9:14
and his spring shall become *d* ... Hos 13:15
hath made the sea and the *d* land ... Jonah 1:9
vomited out Jonah upon the *d* land ... Jonah 2:10
rebuketh the sea, and maketh it *d* ... Nah 1:4
be devoured as stubble fully *d* ... Nah 1:10
and *d* like a wilderness ... Zeph 2:13
earth, and the sea, and the *d* land ... Hag 2:6
the deeps of the river shall *d* up ... Zec 10:11
man, he walketh through *d* places ... Mt 12:43
man, he walketh through *d* places ... Lk 11:24
tree, what shall be done in the *d* ... Lk 23:31
through the Red sea as by *d* land ... Heb 11:29

**DRYSHOD**
streams, and make men go over *d* ... Is 11:15

**DUE**
it is thy *d*, and thy sons' *d* ... Lev 10:13
they be thy *d*, and thy sons' *d* ... Lev 10:14
I will give you rain in *d* season ... Lev 26:4
offer unto me in their *d* season ... Num 28:2
rain of your land in his *d* season ... Deut 11:14
be the priest's *d* from the people ... Deut 18:3
their foot shall slide in *d* time ... Deut 32:35
sought him not after the *d* order ... 1Chr 15:13
LORD the glory *d* unto his name ... 1Chr 16:29
for the singers, *d* for every day ... Neh 11:23
LORD the glory *d* unto his name ... Ps 29:2
LORD the glory *d* unto his name ... Ps 96:8
give them their meat in *d* season ... Ps 104:27
them their meat in *d* season ... Ps 145:15
good from them to whom it is *d* ... Prov 3:27
and a word spoken in *d* season ... Prov 15:23
and thy princes eat in *d* season ... Eccl 10:17
pay all that was *d* unto him ... Mt 18:34
to give them meat in *d* season ... Mt 24:45
their portion of meat in *d* season ... Lk 12:42
for we receive the *d* reward of ... Lk 23:41
in *d* time Christ died for the ... Rom 5:6
tribute to whom tribute is *d* ... Rom 13:7
unto the wife *d* benevolence ... 1Cor 7:3
as of one born out of *d* time ... 1Cor 15:8
for in *d* season we shall reap, if ... Gal 6:9
all, to be testified in *d* time ... 1Ti 2:6
But hath in *d* times manifested ... Titus 1:3
that he may exalt you in *d* time ... 1Pet 5:6

**DUES**
Render therefore to all their *d* ... Rom 13:7

**DUKE**
firstborn son of Esau; *d* Teman ... Gen 36:15
*d* Omar, *d* Zepho, *d* Kenaz, ... Gen 36:15
*D* Korah, *d* Gatam, and *d* ... Gen 36:16
*D* Korah, *d* Gatam, and *d* Amalek ... Gen 36:16
*d* Nahath, *d* Zerah ... Gen 36:17
*d* Shammah, *d* ... Gen 36:17
*d* Jeush, *d* Jaalam, *d* Korah ... Gen 36:18
came of the Horites; *d* Lotan ... Gen 36:29
*d* Shobal, *d* Zibeon, *d* Anah, ... Gen 36:29
*D* Dishon, *d* Ezer, *d* Dishan ... Gen 36:30
by their names; *d* Timnah ... Gen 36:40
*d* Alvah, *d* Jetheth ... Gen 36:40
*D* Aholibamah, *d* Elah, *d* Pinon ... Gen 36:41
*D* Kenaz, *d* Teman, *d* Mibzar, ... Gen 36:42
*D* Magdiel, *d* Iram ... Gen 36:43
of Edom were; *d* Timnah ... 1Chr 1:51
*d* Aliah, *d* Jetheth ... 1Chr 1:51
*D* Aholibamah, *d* Elah, *d* Pinon ... 1Chr 1:52
*D* Kenaz, *d* Teman, *d* Mibzar, ... 1Chr 1:53
*D* Magdiel, *d* Iram ... 1Chr 1:54

**DUKES**
These were *d* of the sons of Esau ... Gen 36:15
these are the *d* that came of ... Gen 36:16
these are the *d* that came of ... Gen 36:17
these were the *d* that came of ... Gen 36:18
who is Edom, and these are their *d* ... Gen 36:19
these are the *d* of the Horites, ... Gen 36:21
These are the *d* that came of the ... Gen 36:29
these are the *d* that came of Hori ... Gen 36:30
among their *d* in the land of Seir ... Gen 36:30
names of the *d* that came of Esau ... Gen 36:40
these be the *d* of Edom, according ... Gen 36:43
Then the *d* of Edom shall be ... Ex 15:15
and Reba, which were *d* of Sihon ... Josh 13:21
And the *d* of Edom were ... 1Chr 1:51
These are the *d* of Edom ... 1Chr 1:54

**DULCIMER**
flute, harp, sackbut, psaltery, *d* ... Dan 3:5
harp, sackbut, psaltery, and *d* ... Dan 3:10
harp, sackbut, psaltery, and *d* ... Dan 3:15

**DULL**
and their ears are *d* of hearing ... Mt 13:15
and their ears are *d* of hearing ... Acts 28:27
seeing ye are *d* of hearing ... Heb 5:11

**DUMAH** (*doo'-mah*)
*1. Son of Ishmael.*
And Mishma, and *D*, and Massa, ... Gen 25:14
Mishma, and *D*, Massa, Hadad, and ... 1Chr 1:30
*2. A city in Judah.*
Arab, and *D*, and Eshean, ... Josh 15:52
*3. An undetermined city.*
The burden of *D*. He calleth to ... Is 21:11

**DUMB**
or who maketh the *d*, or deaf, or ... Ex 4:11
I was as a *d* man that openeth not ... Ps 38:13
I was *d* with silence, I held my ... Ps 39:2
I was *d*, I opened not my mouth ... Ps 39:9
Open thy mouth for the *d* in the ... Prov 31:8
hart, and the tongue of the *d* sing ... Is 35:6
a sheep before her shearers is *d* ... Is 53:7
all ignorant, they are all *d* dogs ... Is 56:10
thy mouth, that thou shalt be *d* ... Eze 3:26
thou shalt speak, and be no more *d* ... Eze 24:27
was opened, and I was no more *d* ... Eze 33:22
toward the ground, and I became *d* ... Dan 10:15
trusteth therein, to make *d* idols ... Hab 2:18
to the *d* stone, Arise, it shall ... Hab 2:19
they brought to him a *d* man ... Mt 9:32
devil was cast out, the *d* spake ... Mt 9:33
with a devil, blind, and *d* ... Mt 12:22
the blind and *d* both spake and saw ... Mt 12:22
those that were lame, blind, *d* ... Mt 15:30
when they saw the *d* to speak ... Mt 15:31
deaf to hear, and the *d* to speak ... Mk 7:37
my son, which hath a *d* spirit ... Mk 9:17
spirit, saying unto him, Thou *d* ... Mk 9:25
And, behold, thou shalt be *d* ... Lk 1:20
casting out a devil, and it was *d* ... Lk 11:14
devil was gone out, the *d* spake ... Lk 11:14
like a lamb *d* before his shearer, ... Acts 8:32
carried away unto these *d* idols ... 1Cor 12:2
the *d* ass speaking with man's ... 2Pet 2:16

**DUNG**
bullock, and his skin, and his *d* ... Ex 29:14
legs, and his inwards, and his *d* ... Lev 4:11
and his hide, his flesh, and his *d* ... Lev 8:17
skins, and their flesh, and their *d* ... Lev 16:27
flesh, and her blood, with her *d* ... Num 19:5
Jeroboam, as a man taketh away *d* ... 1Kin 14:10
*d* for five pieces of silver ... 2Kin 6:25
*d* upon the face of the field in ... 2Kin 9:37
that they may eat their own *d* ... 2Kin 18:27
the dragon well, and to the *d* port ... Neh 2:13
on the wall unto the *d* gate ... Neh 3:13
But the *d* gate repaired Malchiah ... Neh 3:14
upon the wall toward the *d* gate ... Neh 12:31
perish for ever like his own *d* ... Job 20:7
they became as *d* for the earth ... Ps 83:10
that they may eat their own *d* ... Is 36:12
they shall be for *d* upon the face ... Jer 8:2
fall as *d* upon the open field ... Jer 9:22
but they shall be as *d* upon the ... Jer 16:4
they shall be *d* upon the ground ... Jer 25:33
it with *d* that cometh out of man ... Eze 4:12
given thee cow's *d* for man's *d* ... Eze 4:15
given thee cow's *d* for man's *d* ... Eze 4:15
as dust, and their flesh as the *d* ... Zeph 1:17
spread *d* upon your faces ... Mal 2:3
even the *d* of your solemn feasts ... Mal 2:3
I shall dig about it, and *d* it ... Lk 13:8
things, and do count them but *d* ... Phil 3:8

**DUNGEON**
they should put me into the *d* ... Gen 40:15
brought him hastily out of the *d* ... Gen 41:14
of the captive that was in the *d* ... Ex 12:29
Jeremiah was entered into the *d* ... Jer 37:16
cast him into the *d* of Malchiah ... Jer 38:6
in the *d* there was no water, but ... Jer 38:6
they had put Jeremiah in the *d* ... Jer 38:7
whom they have cast into the *d* ... Jer 38:9
Jeremiah the prophet out of the *d* ... Jer 38:10
by cords into the *d* to Jeremiah ... Jer 38:11
and took him up out of the *d* ... Jer 38:13
have cut off my life in the *d* ... Lam 3:53
name, O LORD, out of the low *d* ... Lam 3:55

**DUNGHILL**
lifteth up the beggar from the *d* ... 1Sa 2:8
his house be made a *d* for this ... Ezr 6:11
and lifteth the needy out of the *d* ... Ps 113:7
straw is trodden down for the *d* ... Is 25:10
and your houses shall be made a *d* ... Dan 2:5
and their houses shall be made a *d* ... Dan 3:29
for the land, nor yet for the *d* ... Lk 14:35

**DUNGHILLS**
brought up in scarlet embrace *d* ... Lam 4:5

**DURA** (*doo'-rah*) *A plain in Babylonia.*
he set it up in the plain of *D* ... Dan 3:1

**DURABLE**
*d* riches and righteousness ... Prov 8:18
sufficiently, and for *d* clothing ... Is 23:18

**DURETH**
in himself, but *d* for a while ... Mt 13:21

**DURST**
that *d* presume in his heart to do ... Est 7:5
*d* not shew you mine opinion ... Job 32:6
neither *d* any man from that day ... Mt 22:46
no man after that *d* ask him any ... Mk 12:34
after that they *d* not ask him any ... Lk 20:40
none of the disciples *d* ask him ... Jn 21:12
of the rest *d* no man join himself ... Acts 5:13
Moses trembled, and *d* not behold ... Acts 7:32
*d* not bring against him a railing ... Jude 9

**DUST**
formed man of the *d* of the ground ... Gen 2:7
*d* shalt thou eat all the days of ... Gen 3:14
for *d* thou art, and unto *d* ... Gen 3:19
thy seed as the *d* of the earth ... Gen 13:16
man can number the *d* of the earth ... Gen 13:16
unto the Lord, which am but *d* ... Gen 18:27
shall be as the *d* of the earth ... Gen 28:14
smite the *d* of the land, that it ... Ex 8:16
smote the *d* of the earth, and it ... Ex 8:17
all the *d* of the land became lice ... Ex 8:17
it shall become small *d* in all ... Ex 9:9
they shall pour out the *d* that ... Lev 14:41
blood thereof, and cover it with *d* ... Lev 17:13
of the *d* that is in the floor of ... Num 5:17
Who can count the *d* of Jacob ... Num 23:10
even until it was as small as *d* ... Deut 9:21
I cast the *d* thereof into the ... Deut 9:21
the rain of thy land powder and *d* ... Deut 28:24
the poison of serpents of the *d* ... Deut 32:24
Israel, and put *d* upon their heads ... Josh 7:6
raiseth up the poor out of the *d* ... 1Sa 2:8
and threw stones at him, and cast *d* ... 2Sa 16:13
as small as the *d* of the earth ... 2Sa 22:43
as I exalted thee out of the *d* ... 1Kin 16:2
the wood, and the stones, and the *d* ... 1Kin 18:38
if the *d* of Samaria shall suffice ... 1Kin 20:10
made them like the *d* by threshing ... 2Kin 13:7
cast the *d* of them into the brook ... 2Kin 23:12
the *d* of the earth in multitude ... 2Chr 1:9
made *d* of them, and strowed it ... 2Chr 34:4
sprinkled *d* upon their heads ... Job 2:12
whose foundation is in the *d* ... Job 4:19
cometh not forth of the *d* ... Job 5:6
clothed with worms and clods of *d* ... Job 7:5
for now shall I sleep in the *d* ... Job 7:21
wilt thou bring me into *d* again ... Job 10:9
grow out of the *d* of the earth ... Job 14:19
skin, and defiled my horn in the *d* ... Job 16:15
our rest together is in the *d* ... Job 17:16
shall lie down with him in the *d* ... Job 20:11
shall lie down alike in the *d* ... Job 21:26
Then shalt thou lay up gold as *d* ... Job 22:24
Though he heap up silver as the *d* ... Job 27:16
and it hath *d* of gold ... Job 28:6
the mire, and I am become like *d* ... Job 30:19
and man shall turn again unto *d* ... Job 34:15
When the *d* groweth into hardness, ... Job 38:38
earth, and warmeth them in the *d* ... Job 39:14
Hide them in the *d* together ... Job 40:13
I abhor myself, and repent in *d* ... Job 42:6
and lay mine honour in the *d* ... Ps 7:5
small as the *d* before the wind ... Ps 18:42
brought me into the *d* of death ... Ps 22:15
to the *d* shall bow before him ... Ps 22:29
shall the *d* praise thee ... Ps 30:9
our soul is bowed down to the *d* ... Ps 44:25
and his enemies shall lick the *d* ... Ps 72:9
rained flesh also upon them as *d* ... Ps 78:27
stones, and favour the *d* thereof ... Ps 102:14
he remembereth that we are *d* ... Ps 103:14
they die, and return to their *d* ... Ps 104:29
raiseth up the poor out of the *d* ... Ps 113:7
My soul cleaveth unto the *d* ... Ps 119:25
part of the *d* of the world ... Prov 8:26
the *d*, and all turn to *d* again ... Eccl 3:20
Then shall the *d* return to the ... Eccl 12:7
the rock, and hide thee in the *d* ... Is 2:10
and their blossom shall go up as *d* ... Is 5:24
to the ground, even to the *d* ... Is 25:12
he bringeth it even to the *d* ... Is 26:5
Awake and sing, ye that dwell in *d* ... Is 26:19
speech shall be low out of the *d* ... Is 29:4
speech shall whisper out of the *d* ... Is 29:4
strangers shall be like small *d* ... Is 29:5
their *d* made fat with fatness ... Is 34:7

the *d* thereof into brimstone, and Is 34:9
comprehended the *d* of the earth Is 40:12
as the small *d* of the balance Is 40:15
gave them as the *d* to his sword Is 41:2
Come down, and sit in the *d* Is 47:1
and lick up the *d* of thy feet Is 49:23
Shake thyself from the *d* Is 52:2
*d* shall be the serpent's meat Is 65:25
have cast up *d* upon their heads Lam 2:10
He putteth his mouth in the *d* Lam 3:29
the ground, to cover it with *d* Eze 24:7
I will also scrape her *d* from her Eze 26:4
horses their *d* shall cover thee Eze 26:10
thy *d* in the midst of the water Eze 26:12
shall cast up *d* upon their heads, Eze 27:30
in the *d* of the earth shall awake Dan 12:2
That pant after the *d* of the Amos 2:7
of Aphrah roll thyself in the *d* Mic 1:10
shall lick the *d* like a serpent Mic 7:17
the clouds are the *d* of his feet Nah 1:3
thy nobles shall dwell in the *d* Nah 3:18
for they shall heap *d*, and take it Hab 1:10
blood shall be poured out as *d* Zeph 1:17
and heaped up silver as the *d* Zec 9:3
shake off the *d* of your feet Mt 10:14
shake off the *d* under your feet Mk 6:11
shake off the very *d* from your Lk 9:5
Even the very *d* of your city Lk 10:11
But they shook off the *d* of their Acts 13:51
clothes, and threw *d* into the air, Acts 22:23
they cast *d* on their heads, and Rev 18:19

## DUTIES

And that doeth not any of those *d* Eze 18:11

## DUTY

her *d* of marriage, shall he not Ex 21:10
perform the *d* of an husband's Deut 25:5
the *d* of my husband's brother Deut 25:7
as the *d* of every day required 2Chr 8:14
as the *d* of every day required Ezr 3:4
for this is the whole *d* of man Eccl 12:13
done that which was our *d* to do Lk 17:10
their *d* is also to minister unto Rom 15:27

## DWARF

Or crookbackt, or a *d*, or that Lev 21:20

## DWELL

the father of such as *d* in tents Gen 4:20
he shall *d* in the tents of Shem Gen 9:27
them, that they might *d* together Gen 13:6
so that they could not *d* together Gen 13:6
he shall *d* in the presence of all Gen 16:12
for he feared to *d* in Zoar Gen 19:30
*d* where it pleaseth thee Gen 20:15
of the Canaanites, among whom I *d* Gen 24:3
the Canaanites, in whose land I *d* Gen 24:37
*d* in the land which I shall tell Gen 26:2
now will my husband *d* with me Gen 30:20
And ye shall *d* with us Gen 34:10
*d* and trade ye therein, and get you Gen 34:10
we will *d* with you, and we will Gen 34:16
therefore let them *d* in the land Gen 34:21
consent unto us for to *d* with us Gen 34:22
unto them, and they will *d* with us Gen 34:23
go up to Beth-el, and *d* there Gen 35:1
than that they might *d* together Gen 36:7
thou shalt *d* in the land of Gen 45:10
that ye may *d* in the land of Gen 46:34
let thy servants *d* in the land of Gen 47:4
make thy father and brethren to *d* Gen 47:6
in the land of Goshen let them *d* Gen 47:6
Zebulun shall *d* at the haven of Gen 49:13
was content to *d* with the man Ex 2:21
of Goshen, in which my people *d* Ex 8:22
thou hast made for thee to *d* in Ex 15:17
They shall not *d* in thy land Ex 23:33
that I may *d* among them Ex 25:8
I will *d* among the children of Ex 29:45
of Egypt, that I may *d* among them Ex 29:46
he shall *d* alone Lev 13:46
whither I bring you to *d* therein Lev 20:22
Ye shall *d* in booths seven days Lev 23:42
Israelites born shall *d* in booths Lev 23:42
children of Israel to *d* in booths Lev 23:43
ye shall *d* in the land in safety Lev 25:18
your fill, and *d* therein in safety Lev 25:19
full, and *d* in your land safely Lev 26:5
your enemies which *d* therein Lev 26:32
camps, in the midst whereof I *d* Num 5:3
what the land is that they *d* in Num 13:19
cities they be that they *d* in Num 13:19
be strong that *d* in the land Num 13:28
The Amalekites *d* in the land of Num 13:29
the Amorites, *d* in the mountains Num 13:29
and the Canaanites *d* by the sea Num 13:29
I sware to make you *d* therein Num 14:30
lo, the people shall *d* alone Num 23:9
our little ones shall *d* in the Num 32:17
of the land, and *d* therein Num 33:53
vex you in the land wherein ye *d* Num 33:55
their possession cities to *d* in Num 35:2
cities shall they have to *d* in Num 35:3
come again to *d* in the land Num 35:32
ye shall inhabit, wherein I *d* Num 35:34
for I the LORD *d* among the Num 35:34
children of Esau, which *d* in Seir Deut 2:4
children of Esau which *d* in Seir Deut 2:29
and the Moabites which *d* in Ar Deut 2:29
which *d* in the champaign over Deut 11:30
ye shall possess it, and *d* therein Deut 11:31
*d* in the land which the LORD your Deut 12:10
about, so that ye *d* in safety Deut 12:10
to cause his name to *d* there Deut 12:11
God hath given thee to *d* there Deut 13:12
shalt *d* therein, and shalt say, I Deut 17:14
He shall *d* with thee, even among Deut 23:16
If brethren *d* together, and one of Deut 25:5
and thou shalt not *d* therein Deut 28:30
that thou mayest *d* in the land Deut 30:20
the LORD shall *d* in safety by him Deut 33:12
he shall *d* between his shoulders Deut 33:12
then shall *d* in safety alone Deut 33:28
Peradventure ye *d* among us Josh 9:7
when ye *d* among us Josh 9:22
*d* in the mountains are gathered Josh 10:6
the Maachathites *d* among the Josh 13:13
in the land, save cities to *d* in Josh 14:4
but the Jebusites *d* with the Josh 15:63
but the Canaanites *d* among the Josh 16:10
Canaanites would *d* in that land Josh 17:12
all the Canaanites that *d* in the Josh 17:16
a place, that he may *d* among them Josh 20:4
he shall *d* in that city, until he Josh 20:6
Moses to give us cities to *d* in Josh 21:2
ye built not, and ye *d* in them Josh 24:13
the Amorites, in whose land ye *d* Josh 24:15
but the Jebusites *d* with the Judg 1:21
Canaanites would *d* in that land Judg 1:27
But the Amorites would *d* in mount Judg 1:35
the Amorites, in whose land ye *d* Judg 6:10
that they should not *d* in Shechem Judg 9:41
*D* with me, and be unto me a father Judg 17:10
was content to *d* with the man Judg 17:11
them an inheritance to *d* in Judg 18:1
made them *d* in this place 1Sa 12:8
the country, that I may *d* there 1Sa 27:5
for why should thy servant *d* in 1Sa 27:5
I *d* in an house of cedar, but the 2Sa 7:2
build me an house for me to *d* in 2Sa 7:5
that they may *d* in a place of 2Sa 7:10
*d* there, and go not forth thence 1Kin 2:36
this woman *d* in one house 1Kin 3:17
I will *d* among the children of 1Kin 6:13
he would *d* in the thick darkness 1Kin 8:12
built thee an house to *d* in 1Kin 8:13
will God indeed *d* on the earth 1Kin 8:27
belongeth to Zidon, and *d* there 1Kin 17:9
I *d* among mine own people 2Kin 4:13
the place where we *d* with thee is 2Kin 6:1
us a place there, where we may *d* 2Kin 6:2
*d* there, and let him teach them 2Kin 17:27
*d* in the land, and serve the king 2Kin 25:24
I *d* in an house of cedars, but 1Chr 17:1
not build me an house to *d* in 1Chr 17:4
they shall *d* in their place, and 1Chr 17:9
that they may *d* in Jerusalem for 1Chr 23:25
build him an house to *d* therein 2Chr 2:3
he would *d* in the thick darkness 2Chr 6:1
very deed *d* with men on the earth 2Chr 6:18
the children of Israel to *d* there 2Chr 8:2
My wife shall not *d* in the house 2Chr 8:11
brethren that *d* in their cities 2Chr 19:10
companions that *d* in Samaria Ezr 4:17
name to *d* there destroy all kings Ezr 6:12
*d* in booths in the feast of the Neh 8:14
to bring one of ten to *d* in Neh 11:1
nine parts to *d* in other cities Neh 11:1
themselves to *d* at Jerusalem Neh 11:2
let a cloud *d* upon it Job 3:5
in them that *d* in houses of clay Job 4:19
wickedness *d* in thy tabernacles Job 11:14
It shall *d* in his tabernacle, Job 18:15
They that *d* in mine house, and my Job 19:15
To *d* in the cliffs of the valleys Job 30:6
LORD, only makest me *d* in safety Ps 4:8
neither shall evil *d* with thee Ps 5:4
who shall *d* in thy holy hill Ps 15:1
I will *d* in the house of the LORD Ps 23:6
the world, and they that *d* therein Ps 24:1
His soul shall *d* at ease Ps 25:13
that I may *d* in the house of the Ps 27:4
so shalt thou *d* in the land Ps 37:3
and *d* for evermore Ps 37:27
the land, and *d* therein for ever Ps 37:29
that he may *d* in thy courts Ps 65:4
They also that *d* in the uttermost Ps 65:8
the rebellious *d* in a dry land Ps 68:6
hill which God desireth to *d* in Ps 68:16
the LORD will *d* in it for ever Ps 68:16
the LORD God might *d* among them Ps 68:18
let none *d* in their tents Ps 69:25
that they may *d* there, and have it Ps 69:35
love his name shall *d* therein Ps 69:36
They that *d* in the wilderness Ps 72:9
of Israel to *d* in their tents Ps 78:55
are they that *d* in thy house Ps 84:4
than to *d* in the tents of Ps 84:10
that glory may *d* in our land Ps 85:9
the world, and they that *d* therein Ps 98:7
the land, that they may *d* with me Ps 101:6
shall not *d* within my house Ps 101:7
they found no city to *d* in Ps 107:4
wickedness of them that *d* therein Ps 107:34
there he maketh the hungry to *d* Ps 107:36
that I *d* in the tents of Kedar Ps 120:5
here will I *d*; for I have Ps 132:14
brethren to *d* together in unity Ps 133:1
*d* in the uttermost parts of the Ps 139:9
upright shall *d* in thy presence Ps 140:13
he hath made me to *d* in darkness Ps 143:3
hearkeneth unto me shall *d* safely Prov 1:33
the upright shall *d* in the land Prov 2:21
I wisdom *d* with prudence, and find Prov 8:12
It is better to *d* in a corner of Prov 21:9
It is better to *d* in the Prov 21:19
It is better to *d* in the corner Prov 25:24
I *d* in the midst of a people of Is 6:5
they that *d* in the land of the Is 9:2
wolf also shall *d* with the lamb Is 11:6
and owls shall *d* there, and satyrs Is 13:21
Let mine outcasts *d* with thee Is 16:4
for them that *d* in the wilderness Is 23:13
for them that *d* before the LORD Is 23:18
they that *d* therein are desolate Is 24:6
bringeth down them that *d* on high Is 26:5
Awake and sing, ye that *d* in dust Is 26:19
shall *d* in Zion at Jerusalem Is 30:19
shall *d* in the wilderness Is 32:16
my people shall *d* in a peaceable Is 32:18
Who among us shall *d* with the Is 33:14
who among us shall *d* with Is 33:14
He shall *d* on high Is 33:16
the people that *d* therein shall Is 33:24
also and the raven shall *d* in it Is 34:11
generation shall they *d* therein Is 34:17
them out as a tent to *d* in Is 40:22
give place to me that I may *d* Is 49:20
they that *d* therein shall die in Is 51:6
I *d* in the high and holy place, Is 57:15
The restorer of paths to *d* in Is 58:12
it, and my servants shall *d* there Is 65:9
forsaken, and not a man *d* therein Jer 4:29
will cause you to *d* in this place Jer 7:3
I cause you to *d* in this place Jer 7:7
the city, and those that *d* therein Jer 8:16
of them that *d* in a far country Jer 8:19
corners, that *d* in the wilderness Jer 9:26
wickedness of them that *d* therein Jer 12:4
all that *d* in thine house shall Jer 20:6
saved, and Israel shall *d* safely Jer 23:6
they shall *d* in their own land Jer 23:8
them that *d* in the land of Egypt Jer 24:8
*d* in the land that the LORD hath Jer 25:5
people that *d* in the desert Jer 25:24
they shall till it, and *d* therein Jer 27:11
Build ye houses, and *d* in them Jer 29:5
build ye houses, and *d* in them Jer 29:28
have a man to *d* among this people Jer 29:32
there shall *d* in Judah itself, and Jer 31:24
and I will cause them to *d* safely Jer 32:37
and Jerusalem shall *d* safely Jer 33:16
all your days ye shall *d* in tents Jer 35:7
to build houses for us to *d* in Jer 35:9
so we *d* at Jerusalem Jer 35:11
ye shall *d* in the land which I Jer 35:15
*d* with him among the people Jer 40:5
*d* in the land, and serve the king Jer 40:9
I will *d* at Mizpah to serve the Jer 40:10
*d* in your cities that ye have Jer 40:10
We will not *d* in this land, Jer 42:13
and there will we *d* Jer 42:14
to *d* in the land of Judah Jer 43:4
to *d* in the land of Judah Jer 43:5
Jews which *d* in the land of Egypt Jer 44:1
which *d* at Migdol, and at Jer 44:1
of Egypt, whither ye be gone to *d* Jer 44:8
them that *d* in the land of Egypt Jer 44:13
a desire to return to *d* there Jer 44:14
all Judah that *d* in the land of Jer 44:26
the city, and them that *d* therein Jer 47:2
without any to *d* therein Jer 48:9
O ye that *d* in Moab, leave the Jer 48:28
*d* in the rock, and be like the Jer 48:28
his people *d* in his cities Jer 49:1
*d* deep, O inhabitants of Dedan Jer 49:8
shall a son of man *d* in it Jer 49:18
*d* deep, O ye inhabitants of Hazor Jer 49:30
gates nor bars, which *d* alone Jer 49:31
there, nor any son of man *d* in it Jer 49:33
desolate, and none shall *d* therein Jer 50:3
of the islands shall *d* there Jer 50:39
and the owls shall *d* therein Jer 50:39
shall any son of man *d* therein Jer 50:40
against them that *d* in the midst Jer 51:1
thou dost *d* among scorpions Eze 2:6
of all them that *d* therein Eze 12:19
daughters that *d* at thy left hand Eze 16:46
under it shall *d* all fowl of Eze 17:23
the branches thereof shall they *d* Eze 17:23
then shall they *d* in their land Eze 28:25
they shall *d* safely therein, and Eze 28:26
they shall *d* with confidence, Eze 28:26
smite all them that *d* therein Eze 32:15
they shall *d* safely in the Eze 34:25
but they shall *d* safely, and none Eze 34:28
ye shall *d* in the land that I Eze 36:28
also cause you to *d* in the cities Eze 36:33
they shall *d* in the land that I Eze 37:25
and they shall *d* therein, even Eze 37:25
they shall *d* safely all of them Eze 38:8
that *d* safely, all of them Eze 38:11
that *d* in the midst of the land Eze 38:12
among them that *d* carelessly in Eze 39:6
they that *d* in the cities of Eze 39:9
where I will *d* in the midst of Eze 43:7
I will *d* in the midst of them for Eze 43:9
wheresoever the children of men *d* Dan 2:38
that *d* in all the earth Dan 4:1
that *d* in all the earth Dan 6:25
They shall not *d* in the LORD's Hos 9:3

yet make thee to *d* in tabernacles ......... Hos 12:9
They that *d* under his shadow ......... Hos 14:7
But Judah shall *d* for ever ......... Joel 3:20
of Israel be taken out that *d* in ......... Amos 3:12
stone, but ye shall not *d* in them ......... Amos 5:11
all that *d* therein shall mourn ......... Amos 9:5
thou shalt *d* in the field, and ......... Mic 4:10
because of them that *d* therein ......... Mic 7:13
which *d* solitarily in the wood, ......... Mic 7:14
the world, and all that *d* therein ......... Nah 1:5
thy nobles shall *d* in the dust ......... Nah 3:18
city, and of all that *d* therein ......... Hab 2:8
city, and of all that *d* therein ......... Hab 2:17
of all them that *d* in the land ......... Zeph 1:18
to *d* in your cieled houses, and ......... Hag 1:4
I will *d* in the midst of thee, ......... Zec 2:10
I will *d* in the midst of thee, and ......... Zec 2:11
will *d* in the midst of Jerusalem ......... Zec 8:3
old women *d* in the streets of ......... Zec 8:4
they shall *d* in the midst of ......... Zec 8:8
And a bastard shall *d* in Ashdod ......... Zec 9:6
And men shall *d* in it, and there ......... Zec 14:11
and they enter in and *d* there ......... Mt 12:45
and they enter in, and *d* there ......... Lk 11:26
*d* on the face of the whole earth ......... Lk 21:35
desolate, and let no man *d* therein ......... Acts 1:20
all ye that *d* at Jerusalem, be ......... Acts 2:14
to all them that *d* in Jerusalem ......... Acts 4:16
into this land, wherein ye now *d* ......... Acts 7:4
For they that *d* at Jerusalem ......... Acts 13:27
to *d* on all the face of the earth ......... Acts 17:26
but Paul was suffered to *d* by ......... Acts 28:16
that the Spirit of God *d* in you ......... Rom 8:9
up Jesus from the dead *d* in you ......... Rom 8:11
and she be pleased to *d* with him ......... 1Cor 7:12
and if he be pleased to *d* with her ......... 1Cor 7:13
I will *d* in them, and walk in them ......... 2Cor 6:16
That Christ may *d* in your hearts ......... Eph 3:17
that in him should all fulness *d* ......... Col 1:19
Let the word of Christ *d* in you ......... Col 3:16
*d* with them according to ......... 1Pet 3:7
Hereby know we that we *d* in him ......... 1Jn 4:13
to try them that *d* upon the earth ......... Rev 3:10
blood on them that *d* on the earth ......... Rev 6:10
on the throne shall *d* among them ......... Rev 7:15
they that *d* upon the earth shall ......... Rev 11:10
ye heavens, and ye that *d* in them ......... Rev 12:12
and them that *d* in heaven ......... Rev 13:6
all that *d* upon the earth shall ......... Rev 13:8
them which *d* therein to worship ......... Rev 13:12
deceiveth them that *d* on the ......... Rev 13:14
to them that *d* on the earth ......... Rev 13:14
unto them that *d* on the earth ......... Rev 14:6
they that *d* on the earth shall ......... Rev 17:8
he will *d* with them, and they ......... Rev 21:3

## DWELLED

the Perizzite *d* then in the land ......... Gen 13:7
Abram *d* in the land of Canaan, and ......... Gen 13:12
Lot *d* in the cities of the plain, ......... Gen 13:12
*d* between Kadesh and Shur, and ......... Gen 20:1
they *d* there about ten years ......... Ruth 1:4
on every side, and ye *d* safe ......... 1Sa 12:11

## DWELLERS

*d* on the earth, see ye, when he ......... Is 18:3
known unto all the *d* at Jerusalem ......... Acts 1:19
the *d* in Mesopotamia, and in ......... Acts 2:9

## DWELLEST

them, and *d* in their land ......... Deut 12:29
*d* in their cities, and in their ......... Deut 19:1
and possessest it, and *d* therein ......... Deut 26:1
which *d* between the cherubims, ......... 2Kin 19:15
thou that *d* between the cherubims ......... Ps 80:1
O thou that *d* in the heavens ......... Ps 123:1
Thou that *d* in the gardens, the ......... Song 8:13
hosts, O my people that *d* in Zion ......... Is 10:24
that *d* between the cherubims, ......... Is 37:16
that *d* carelessly, that sayest in ......... Is 47:8
O thou that *d* in the clefts of ......... Jer 49:16
O thou that *d* upon many waters, ......... Jer 51:13
of Edom, that *d* in the land of Uz ......... Lam 4:21
thee, O thou that *d* in the land ......... Eze 7:7
of man, thou *d* in the midst of a ......... Eze 12:2
thou that *d* in the clefts of the ......... Obad 3
that *d* with the daughter of ......... Zec 2:7
Master,) where *d* thou ......... Jn 1:38
I know thy works, and where thou *d* ... Rev 2:13

## DWELLETH

But the stranger that *d* with you ......... Lev 19:34
if thy brother that *d* by thee be ......... Lev 25:39
brother that *d* by him wax poor ......... Lev 25:47
and the people that *d* therein ......... Num 13:18
he *d* as a lion, and teareth the ......... Deut 33:20
she *d* in Israel even unto this ......... Josh 6:25
wherein the LORD's tabernacle *d* ......... Josh 22:19
which *d* between the cherubims ......... 1Sa 4:4
while he *d* in the country of the ......... 1Sa 27:11
that *d* between the cherubims ......... 2Sa 6:2
the ark of God *d* within curtains ......... 2Sa 7:2
that *d* between the cherubims, ......... 1Chr 13:6
he *d* in desolate cities, and in ......... Job 15:28
Where is the way where light *d* ......... Job 38:19
She *d* and abideth on the rock, ......... Job 39:28
to the LORD, which *d* in Zion ......... Ps 9:11
and the place where thine honour *d* ......... Ps 26:8
He that *d* in the secret place of ......... Ps 91:1
the LORD our God, who *d* on high, ......... Ps 113:5
out of Zion, which *d* at Jerusalem ......... Ps 135:21
seeing he *d* securely by thee ......... Prov 3:29
of hosts, which *d* in mount Zion ......... Is 8:18
for he *d* on high ......... Is 33:5
the people that *d* in this city ......... Jer 29:16
desolation, and no man *d* therein, ......... Jer 44:2
that *d* without care, saith the ......... Jer 49:31
a land wherein no man *d*, neither ......... Jer 51:43
she *d* among the heathen, she ......... Lam 1:3
that *d* at thy right hand, is ......... Eze 16:46
the king *d* that made him king ......... Eze 17:16
when my people of Israel *d* safely ......... Eze 38:14
darkness, and the light *d* with him ......... Dan 2:22
every one that *d* therein shall ......... Hos 4:3
for the LORD *d* in Zion ......... Joel 3:21
and every one mourn that *d* therein ......... Amos 8:8
by it, and by him that *d* therein ......... Mt 23:21
my blood, *d* in me, and I in him ......... Jn 6:56
but the Father that *d* in me ......... Jn 14:10
for he *d* with you, and shall be in ......... Jn 14:17
Howbeit the most High *d* not in ......... Acts 7:48
*d* not in temples made with hands ......... Acts 17:24
that do it, but sin that *d* in me ......... Rom 7:17
is, in my flesh,) *d* no good thing ......... Rom 7:18
that do it, but sin that *d* in me ......... Rom 7:20
by his Spirit that *d* in you ......... Rom 8:11
that the Spirit of God *d* in you ......... 1Cor 3:16
For in him *d* all the fulness of ......... Col 2:9
by the Holy Ghost which *d* in us ......... 2Ti 1:14
The spirit that *d* in us lusteth ......... Jas 4:5
earth, wherein *d* righteousness ......... 2Pet 3:13
how *d* the love of God in him ......... 1Jn 3:17
keepeth his commandments *d* in him ......... 1Jn 3:24
God *d* in us, and his love is ......... 1Jn 4:12
God *d* in him, and he in God ......... 1Jn 4:15
he that *d* in love *d* in God ......... 1Jn 4:16
the truth's sake, which *d* in us ......... 2Jn 2
slain among you, where Satan *d* ......... Rev 2:13

## DWELLING

their *d* was from Mesha, as thou ......... Gen 10:30
Jacob was a plain man, *d* in tents ......... Gen 25:27
thy *d* shall be the fatness of the ......... Gen 27:39
if a man sell a *d* house in a ......... Lev 25:29
that goeth down to the *d* of Ar ......... Num 21:15
dukes of Sihon, *d* in the country ......... Josh 13:21
hear thou in heaven thy *d* place ......... 1Kin 8:30
hear thou in heaven thy *d* place ......... 1Kin 8:39
Hear thou in heaven thy *d* place ......... 1Kin 8:43
in heaven thy *d* place, and ......... 1Kin 8:49
were in his city, *d* with Naboth ......... 1Kin 21:8
at the beginning of their *d* there ......... 2Kin 17:25
they ministered before the *d* ......... 1Chr 6:32
Now these are their *d* places ......... 1Chr 6:54
and a place for thy *d* for ever ......... 2Chr 6:2
hear thou from thy *d* place ......... 2Chr 6:21
hear thou from heaven thy *d* place ......... 2Chr 6:30
heavens, even from thy *d* place ......... 2Chr 6:33
heavens, even from thy *d* place ......... 2Chr 6:39
came up to his holy *d* place ......... 2Chr 30:27
on his people, and on his *d* place ......... 2Chr 36:15
the *d* place of the wicked shall ......... Job 8:22
where are the *d* places of the ......... Job 21:28
their *d* places to all generations ......... Ps 49:11
consume in the grave from their *d* ......... Ps 49:14
and pluck thee out of thy *d* place ......... Ps 52:5
defiled by casting down the *d* ......... Ps 74:7
and his *d* place in Zion ......... Ps 76:2
Jacob, and laid waste his *d* place ......... Ps 79:7
thou hast been our *d* place in all ......... Ps 90:1
shall any plague come nigh thy *d* ......... Ps 91:10
and oil in the *d* of the wise ......... Prov 21:20
against the *d* of the righteous ......... Prov 24:15
upon every *d* place of mount Zion ......... Is 4:5
I will consider in my *d* place ......... Is 18:4
O thou daughter *d* in Egypt ......... Jer 46:19
And Hazor shall be a *d* for dragons ......... Jer 49:33
a *d* place for dragons, an ......... Jer 51:37
all of them *d* without walls, and ......... Eze 38:11
profane place for the city, for *d* ......... Eze 48:15
whose *d* is not with flesh ......... Dan 2:11
thy *d* shall be with the beasts of ......... Dan 4:25
thy *d* shall be with the beasts of ......... Dan 4:32
his *d* was with the wild asses ......... Dan 5:21
I am the LORD your God *d* in Zion ......... Joel 3:17
Where is the *d* of the lions ......... Nah 2:11
so their *d* should not be cut off, ......... Zeph 3:7
Who had his *d* among the tombs ......... Mk 5:3
there were *d* at Jerusalem Jews, ......... Acts 2:5
Jews and Greeks also *d* at Ephesus ......... Acts 19:17
*d* in the light which no man can ......... 1Ti 6:16
*d* in tabernacles with Isaac and ......... Heb 11:9
that righteous man *d* among them ......... 2Pet 2:8

## DWELLINGPLACE

parable, and said, Strong is thy *d* ......... Num 24:21
and have no certain *d* place ......... 1Cor 4:11

## DWELLINGPLACES

tents, and have mercy on his *d* ......... Jer 30:18
they have burned her *d* ......... Jer 51:30
In all your *d* the cities shall be ......... Eze 6:6
will save them out of all their *d* ......... Eze 37:23
to possess the *d* that are not ......... Hab 1:6

## DWELLINGS

of Israel had light in their *d* ......... Ex 10:23
generations throughout all your *d* ......... Lev 3:17
or of beast, in any of your *d* ......... Lev 7:26
sabbath of the LORD in all your *d* ......... Lev 23:3
your generations in all your *d* ......... Lev 23:14
*d* throughout your generations ......... Lev 23:21
your generations in all your *d* ......... Lev 23:31
your generations in all your *d* ......... Num 35:29
nor any remaining in his *d* ......... Job 18:19
such are the *d* of the wicked ......... Job 18:21
and the barren land his *d* ......... Job 39:6
for wickedness is in their *d* ......... Ps 55:15
Zion more than all the *d* of Jacob ......... Ps 87:2
habitation, and in sure *d*, and in ......... Is 32:18
because our *d* have cast us out ......... Jer 9:19
in thee, and make their *d* in thee ......... Eze 25:4
And the sea coast shall be *d* ......... Zeph 2:6

## DWELT

*d* in the land of Nod, on the east ......... Gen 4:16
and they *d* there ......... Gen 11:2
they came unto Haran, and *d* there ......... Gen 11:31
*d* in the plain of Mamre, which is ......... Gen 13:18
Amorites, that *d* in Hazezon-tamar ......... Gen 14:7
who *d* in Sodom, and his goods, and ......... Gen 14:12
for he *d* in the plain of Mamre ......... Gen 14:13
after Abram had *d* ten years in ......... Gen 16:3
the cities in the which Lot *d* ......... Gen 19:29
*d* in the mountain, and his two ......... Gen 19:30
he *d* in a cave, he and his two ......... Gen 19:30
*d* in the wilderness, and became an ......... Gen 21:20
he *d* in the wilderness of Paran ......... Gen 21:21
and Abraham *d* at Beer-sheba ......... Gen 22:19
Ephron *d* among the children of ......... Gen 23:10
for he *d* in the south country ......... Gen 24:62
Isaac *d* by the well Lahai-roi ......... Gen 25:11
they *d* from Havilah unto Shur, ......... Gen 25:18
And Isaac *d* in Gerar ......... Gen 26:6
the valley of Gerar, and *d* there ......... Gen 26:17
when Israel *d* in that land, that ......... Gen 35:22
Thus *d* Esau in mount Seir ......... Gen 36:8
Jacob *d* in the land wherein his ......... Gen 37:1
went and *d* in her father's house ......... Gen 38:11
Israel *d* in the land of Egypt, in ......... Gen 47:27
Joseph *d* in Egypt, he, and his ......... Gen 50:22
and *d* in the land of Midian ......... Ex 2:15
who *d* in Egypt, was four hundred ......... Ex 12:40
the land of Egypt, wherein ye *d* ......... Lev 18:3
your sabbaths, when ye *d* upon it ......... Lev 26:35
and the Canaanites *d* in the valley ......... Num 14:25
Canaanites which *d* in that hill ......... Num 14:45
we have *d* in Egypt a long time ......... Num 20:15
which *d* in the south, heard tell ......... Num 21:1
Israel *d* in all the cities of the ......... Num 21:25
Thus Israel *d* in the land of the ......... Num 21:31
the Amorites, which *d* at Heshbon ......... Num 21:34
all their cities wherein they *d* ......... Num 31:10
and he *d* therein ......... Num 32:40
which *d* in the south in the land ......... Num 33:40
which *d* in Heshbon, and Og the ......... Deut 1:4
which *d* at Astaroth in Edrei ......... Deut 1:4
Ye have *d* long enough in this ......... Deut 1:6
which *d* in that mountain, came ......... Deut 1:44
which *d* in Seir, through the way ......... Deut 2:8
The Emims *d* therein in times past ......... Deut 2:10
The Horims also *d* in Seir ......... Deut 2:12
before them, and *d* in their stead ......... Deut 2:12
giants *d* therein in old time ......... Deut 2:20
them, and *d* in their stead ......... Deut 2:21
of Esau, which *d* in Seir, when he ......... Deut 2:22
*d* in their stead even unto this ......... Deut 2:22
And the Avims which *d* in Hazerim ......... Deut 2:23
them, and *d* in their stead ......... Deut 2:23
the Amorites, which *d* at Heshbon ......... Deut 3:2
who *d* at Heshbon, whom Moses and ......... Deut 4:46
built goodly houses, and *d* therein ......... Deut 8:12
we have *d* in the land of Egypt ......... Deut 29:16
will of him that *d* in the bush ......... Deut 33:16
town wall, and she *d* upon the wall ......... Josh 2:15
*d* on the other side Jordan ......... Josh 7:7
and that they *d* among them ......... Josh 9:16
who *d* in Heshbon, and ruled from ......... Josh 12:2
that *d* at Ashtaroth and at Edrei, ......... Josh 12:4
the Canaanites that *d* in Gezer ......... Josh 16:10
*d* therein, and called Leshem, Dan, ......... Josh 19:47
he built the city, and *d* therein ......... Josh 19:50
they possessed it, and *d* therein ......... Josh 21:43
the children of Reuben and Gad *d* ......... Josh 22:33
Your fathers *d* on the other side ......... Josh 24:2
ye *d* in the wilderness a long ......... Josh 24:7
which *d* on the other side Jordan ......... Josh 24:8
the Amorites which *d* in the land ......... Josh 24:18
that *d* in the mountain, and in the ......... Judg 1:9
the Canaanites that *d* in Hebron ......... Judg 1:10
they went and *d* among the people ......... Judg 1:16
the Canaanites that *d* in Gezer ......... Judg 1:29
but the Canaanites *d* in Gezer ......... Judg 1:29
but the Canaanites *d* among them ......... Judg 1:30
But the Asherites *d* among the ......... Judg 1:32
but he *d* among the Canaanites, ......... Judg 1:33
Hivites that *d* in mount Lebanon ......... Judg 3:3
of Israel *d* among the Canaanites ......... Judg 3:5
which *d* in Harosheth of the ......... Judg 4:2
she *d* under the palm tree of ......... Judg 4:5
*d* in tents on the east of Nobah ......... Judg 8:11
Joash went and *d* in his own house ......... Judg 8:29
*d* there, for fear of Abimelech ......... Judg 9:21
And Abimelech *d* at Arumah ......... Judg 9:41
he *d* in Shamir in mount Ephraim ......... Judg 10:1
brethren, and *d* in the land of Tob ......... Judg 11:3
While Israel *d* in Heshbon ......... Judg 11:26
*d* in the top of the rock Etam ......... Judg 15:8
were therein, how they *d* careless ......... Judg 18:7
they built a city, and *d* therein ......... Judg 18:28
repaired the cities, and *d* in them ......... Judg 21:23
and *d* with her mother in law ......... Ruth 2:23
he and Samuel went and *d* in Naioth ......... 1Sa 19:18
they *d* with him all the while ......... 1Sa 22:4
*d* in strong holds at En-gedi ......... 1Sa 23:29

David *d* with Achish at Gath, he 1Sa 27:3
the time that David *d* in the 1Sa 27:7
the Philistines came and *d* in them 1Sa 31:7
they *d* in the cities of Hebron 2Sa 2:3
So David *d* in the fort, and called 2Sa 5:9
Whereas I have not *d* in any house 2Sa 7:6
all that *d* in the house of Ziba 2Sa 9:12
So Mephibosheth *d* in Jerusalem 2Sa 9:13
So Absalom *d* two full years in 2Sa 14:28
Shimei *d* in Jerusalem many days 1Kin 2:38
And Judah and Israel *d* safely 1Kin 4:25
his house where he *d* had another 1Kin 7:8
the Canaanites that *d* in the city 1Kin 9:16
*d* therein, and reigned in Damascus 1Kin 11:24
Solomon, and Jeroboam *d* in Egypt 1Kin 12:2
which *d* in the cities of Judah 1Kin 12:17
in mount Ephraim, and *d* therein 1Kin 12:25
Now there *d* an old prophet in 1Kin 13:11
the city where the old prophet *d* 1Kin 13:25
that *d* at Damascus, saying, 1Kin 15:18
building of Ramah, and *d* in Tirzah 1Kin 15:21
*d* by the brook Cherith, that is 1Kin 17:5
of Israel *d* in their tents 2Kin 13:5
death, and *d* in a several house 2Kin 15:5
Elath, and *d* there unto this day 2Kin 16:6
and *d* in the cities thereof 2Kin 17:24
*d* in Beth-el, and taught them how 2Kin 17:28
in their cities wherein they *d* 2Kin 17:29
returned, and *d* at Nineveh 2Kin 19:36
(now she *d* in Jerusalem in the 2Kin 22:14
of the scribes which *d* at Jabez 1Chr 2:55
those that *d* among plants and 1Chr 4:23
there they *d* with the king for 1Chr 4:23
they *d* at Beer-sheba, and Moladah, 1Chr 4:28
they of Ham had *d* there of old 1Chr 4:40
this day, and *d* in their rooms 1Chr 4:41
escaped, and *d* there unto this day 1Chr 4:43
who *d* in Aroer, even unto Nebo and 1Chr 5:8
they *d* in their tents throughout 1Chr 5:10
of Gad *d* over against them 1Chr 5:11
they *d* in Gilead in Bashan, and in 1Chr 5:16
they *d* in their steads until the 1Chr 5:22
tribe of Manasseh *d* in the land 1Chr 5:23
In these *d* the children of Joseph 1Chr 7:29
These *d* in Jerusalem 1Chr 8:28
at Gibeon *d* the father of Gibeon 1Chr 8:29
these also *d* with their brethren 1Chr 8:32
*d* in their possessions in their 1Chr 9:2
in Jerusalem *d* of the children of 1Chr 9:3
that *d* in the villages of the 1Chr 9:16
these *d* at Jerusalem 1Chr 9:34
in Gibeon *d* the father of Gibeon, 1Chr 9:35
they also *d* with their brethren 1Chr 9:38
the Philistines came and *d* in them 1Chr 10:7
And David *d* in the castle 1Chr 11:7
For I have not *d* in an house 1Chr 17:5
that *d* in the cities of Judah 2Chr 10:17
Rehoboam *d* in Jerusalem, and built 2Chr 11:5
that *d* at Damascus, saying, 2Chr 16:2
Jehoshaphat *d* at Jerusalem 2Chr 19:4
they *d* therein, and have built 2Chr 20:8
the Arabians that *d* in Gur-baal 2Chr 26:7
*d* in a several house, being a 2Chr 26:21
and they *d* there 2Chr 28:18
that *d* in Judah, rejoiced 2Chr 30:25
that *d* in Judah, rejoiced 2Chr 30:25
that *d* in Jerusalem to give the 2Chr 31:4
that *d* in the cities of Judah, 2Chr 31:6
(now she *d* in Jerusalem in the 2Chr 34:22
*d* in their cities, and all Israel Ezr 2:70
Moreover the Nethinims *d* in Ophel Neh 3:26
the Jews which *d* by them came Neh 4:12
and all Israel, *d* in their cities Neh 7:73
of the people *d* at Jerusalem Neh 11:1
the province that *d* in Jerusalem Neh 11:3
but in the cities of Judah *d* Neh 11:3
at Jerusalem *d* certain of the Neh 11:4
All the sons of Perez that *d* at Neh 11:6
But the Nethinims *d* in Ophel Neh 11:21
of Judah *d* at Kirjath-arba Neh 11:25
they *d* from Beer-sheba unto the Neh 11:30
Benjamin from Geba *d* at Michmash Neh 11:31
There *d* men of Tyre also therein, Neh 13:16
that *d* in the unwalled towns, Est 9:19
and the honourable man *d* in it Job 22:8
*d* as a king in the army, as one Job 29:25
Thy congregation hath *d* therein Ps 68:10
mount Zion, wherein thou hast *d* Ps 74:2
my soul had almost *d* in silence Ps 94:17
My soul hath long *d* with him that Ps 120:6
neither shall it be *d* in from Is 13:20
to Ariel, the city where David *d* Is 29:1
went and returned, and *d* at Nineveh Is 37:37
passed through, and where no man *d* Jer 2:6
But we have *d* in tents, and have Jer 35:10
so he *d* among the people Jer 39:14
*d* with him among the people that Jer 40:6
*d* in the habitation of Chimham, Jer 41:17
that *d* in the land of Egypt Jer 44:15
neither shall it be *d* in from Jer 50:39
that *d* by the river of Chebar, and Eze 3:15
under his shadow *d* all great Eze 31:6
that *d* under his shadow in the Eze 31:17
of Israel *d* in their own land Eze 36:17
wherein your fathers have *d* Eze 37:25
when they *d* safely in their land, Eze 39:26
heaven *d* in the boughs thereof Dan 4:12
which the beasts of the field *d* Dan 4:21
rejoicing city that *d* carelessly Zeph 2:15
*d* in a city called Nazareth Mt 2:23
*d* in Capernaum, which is upon the Mt 4:13
on all that *d* round about them Lk 1:65
above all men that *d* in Jerusalem Lk 13:4
*d* among us, (and we beheld his Jn 1:14
They came and saw where he *d* Jn 1:39
before he *d* in Charran, Acts 7:2
the Chaldaeans, and *d* in Charran Acts 7:4
the Jews which *d* at Damascus Acts 9:22
to the saints which *d* at Lydda Acts 9:32
And all that *d* at Lydda and Saron Acts 9:35
the brethren which *d* in Judaea Acts 11:29
*d* as strangers in the land of Acts 13:17
so that all they which *d* in Asia Acts 19:10
of all the Jews which *d* there Acts 22:12
Paul *d* two whole years in his own Acts 28:30
which *d* first in thy grandmother 2Ti 1:5
them that *d* on the earth Rev 11:10

**DYED**
And rams' skins *d* red, and badgers' Ex 25:5
for the tent of rams' skins *d* red Ex 26:14
And rams' skins *d* red, and badgers' Ex 35:7
for the tent of rams' skins *d* red Ex 36:19
the covering of rams' skins *d* red Ex 39:34
with *d* garments from Bozrah Is 63:1
exceeding in *d* attire upon their Eze 23:15

**DYING**
shall we be consumed with *d* Num 17:13
took a wife, and *d* left no seed Mk 12:20
years of age, and she lay a *d* Lk 8:42
the body the *d* of the Lord Jesus 2Cor 4:10
as *d*, and, behold, we live 2Cor 6:9
By faith Jacob, when he was a *d* Heb 11:21

# E

**EACH**
laid *e* piece one against another Gen 15:10
took *e* man his sword, and came Gen 34:25
*e* man his dream in one night, Gen 40:5
*e* man according to the interpretation Gen 40:5
we dreamed *e* man according to the Gen 41:11
to *e* man according to his dream Gen 41:12
he gave *e* man changes of raiment Gen 45:22
they asked *e* other of their Ex 18:7
of *e* shall there be a like weight Ex 30:34
put pure frankincense upon *e* row Lev 24:7
*e* one was for the house of his Num 1:44
the princes, and for *e* one an ox Num 7:3
*e* prince on his day, for the Num 7:11
*E* charger of silver weighing an Num 7:85
and thirty shekels, *e* bowl seventy Num 7:85
*e* day for a year, shall ye bear Num 14:34
and Aaron, *e* of you his censer Num 16:17
for *e* prince one, according to Num 17:6
two tenth deals to *e* ram of the Num 29:14
a several tenth deal to *e* lamb of Num 29:15
among you three men for *e* tribe Josh 18:4
of *e* chief house a prince Josh 22:14
*e* one was an head of the house of Josh 22:14
*e* one resembled the children of a Judg 8:18
not to *e* man his wife in the war Judg 21:22
return *e* to her mother's house Ruth 1:8
*e* of you in the house of her Ruth 1:9
*e* man his month in a year made 1Kin 4:7
of olive tree, *e* ten cubits high 1Kin 6:23
king of Judah sat *e* on his throne 1Kin 22:10
*e* in his chariot, and they went 2Kin 9:21
of *e* man fifty shekels of silver, 2Kin 15:20
on *e* hand, and six on *e* foot 1Chr 20:6
top of *e* of them was five cubits 2Chr 3:15
rows of pomegranates on *e* wreath 2Chr 4:13
stays on *e* side of the sitting 2Chr 9:18
to the language of *e* people Neh 13:24
and peace have kissed *e* other Ps 85:10
which they made *e* one for himself Is 2:20
*e* one had six wings Is 6:2
of dragons, where *e* lay, shall be Is 35:7
*e* one walking in his uprightness Is 57:2
appointed thee *e* day for a year Eze 4:6
upon *e* post were palm trees Eze 40:16
measured *e* post of the porch, Eze 40:48
doth not *e* one of you on the Lk 13:15
of fire, and it sat upon *e* of them Acts 2:3
let *e* esteem other better than Phil 2:3
you all toward *e* other aboundeth 2Th 1:3
the four beasts had *e* of them six Rev 4:8

**EAGLE**
the *e*, and the ossifrage, and the Lev 11:13
and the pelican, and the gier *e* Lev 11:18
the *e*, and the ossifrage, and the Deut 14:12
And the pelican, and the gier *e* Deut 14:17
earth, as swift as the *e* flieth Deut 28:49
As an *e* stirreth up her nest, Deut 32:11
as the *e* that hasteth to the prey Job 9:26
Doth the *e* mount up at thy Job 39:27
fly away as an *e* toward heaven Prov 23:5
The way of an *e* in the air Prov 30:19
Behold, he shall fly as an *e* Jer 48:40
make thy nest as high as the *e* Jer 49:16
he shall come up and fly as the *e* Jer 49:22
four also had the face of an *e* Eze 1:10
and the fourth the face of an *e* Eze 10:14
A great *e* with great wings, Eze 17:3
another great *e* with great wings Eze 17:7
He shall come as an *e* against the Hos 8:1
thou exalt thyself as the *e* Obad 4
enlarge thy baldness as the *e* Mic 1:16
fly as the *e* that hasteth to eat Hab 1:8
fourth beast was like a flying *e* Rev 4:7
were given two wings of a great *e* Rev 12:14

**EAGLE'S**
thy youth is renewed like the *e* Ps 103:5
was like a lion, and had *e* wings Dan 7:4

**EAGLES**
they were swifter than *e*, they 2Sa 1:23
out, and the young *e* shall eat it Prov 30:17
shall mount up with wings as *e* Is 40:31
his horses are swifter than *e* Jer 4:13
swifter than the *e* of the heaven Lam 4:19
there will the *e* be gathered Mt 24:28
thither will the *e* be gathered Lk 17:37

**EAGLES'**
and how I bare you on *e* wings Ex 19:4
hairs were grown like *e* feathers Dan 4:33

**EAR**
for the barley was in the *e* Ex 9:31
wilt give *e* to his commandments, Ex 15:26
bore his *e* through with an aul Ex 21:6
the tip of the right *e* of Aaron Ex 29:20
tip of the right *e* of his sons Ex 29:20
upon the tip of Aaron's right *e* Lev 8:23
upon the tip of their right *e* Lev 8:24
it upon the tip of the right *e* of Lev 14:14
*e* of him that is to be cleansed Lev 14:17
it upon the tip of the right *e* of Lev 14:25
*e* of him that is to be cleansed Lev 14:28
your voice, nor give *e* unto you Deut 1:45
it through his *e* unto the door Deut 15:17
Give *e*, O ye heavens, and I will Deut 32:1
give *e*, O ye princes Judg 5:3
and will set them to *e* his ground 1Sa 8:12
in his *e* a day before Saul came 1Sa 9:15
LORD, bow down thine *e*, and hear 2Kin 19:16
but they would not give *e* 2Chr 24:19
Let thine *e* now be attentive, and Neh 1:6
let now thine *e* be attentive to Neh 1:11
yet would they not give *e* Neh 9:30
mine *e* received a little thereof Job 4:12
Doth not the *e* try words Job 12:11
mine *e* hath heard and understood Job 13:1
When the *e* heard me, then it Job 29:11
Unto me men gave *e*, and waited, and Job 29:21
I gave *e* to your reasons, whilst Job 32:11
give *e* unto me, ye that have Job 34:2
For the *e* trieth words, as the Job 34:3
also their *e* to discipline Job 36:10
of thee by the hearing of the *e* Job 42:5
Give *e* to my words, O LORD Ps 5:1
thou wilt cause thine *e* to hear Ps 10:17
give *e* unto my prayer, that goeth Ps 17:1
incline thine *e* unto me, and hear Ps 17:6
Bow down thine *e* to me Ps 31:2
O LORD, and give *e* unto my cry Ps 39:12
and consider, and incline thine *e* Ps 45:10
give *e*, all ye inhabitants of the Ps 49:1
will incline mine *e* to a parable Ps 49:4
give *e* to the words of my mouth Ps 54:2
Give *e* to my prayer, O God Ps 55:1
deaf adder that stoppeth her *e* Ps 58:4
incline thine *e* unto me, and save Ps 71:2
and he gave *e* unto me Ps 77:1
Give *e*, O my people, to my law Ps 78:1
Give *e*, O Shepherd of Israel, Ps 80:1
give *e*, O God of Jacob Ps 84:8
Bow down thine *e*, O LORD, hear me Ps 86:1
Give *e*, O LORD, unto my prayer Ps 86:6
incline thine *e* unto my cry Ps 88:2
He that planted the *e*, shall he Ps 94:9
incline thine *e* unto me Ps 102:2
he hath inclined his *e* unto me Ps 116:2
give *e* unto my voice, when I cry Ps 141:1
give *e* to my supplications Ps 143:1
thou incline thine *e* unto wisdom Prov 2:2
incline thine *e* unto my sayings Prov 4:20
bow thine *e* to my understanding Prov 5:1
nor inclined mine *e* to them that Prov 5:13
The *e* that heareth the reproof of Prov 15:31
a liar giveth *e* to a naughty Prov 17:4
the *e* of the wise seeketh Prov 18:15
The hearing *e*, and the seeing eye, Prov 20:12
Bow down thine *e*, and hear the Prov 22:17
wise reprover upon an obedient *e* Prov 25:12
away his *e* from hearing the law Prov 28:9
nor the *e* filled with hearing Eccl 1:8
Hear, O heavens, and give *e* Is 1:2
give *e* unto the law of our God, Is 1:10
and give *e*, all ye of far Is 8:9
Give ye *e*, and hear my voice Is 28:23
the young asses that *e* the ground Is 30:24
give *e* unto my speech Is 32:9
Incline thine *e*, O LORD, and hear Is 37:17
Who among you will give *e* to this Is 42:23
time that thine *e* was not opened Is 48:8
he wakeneth mine *e* to hear as the Is 50:4
The Lord GOD hath opened mine *e* Is 50:5
give *e* unto me, O my nation Is 51:4
Incline your *e*, and come unto me Is 55:3
neither his *e* heavy, that it Is 59:1
not heard, nor perceived by the *e* Is 64:4
their *e* is uncircumcised, and they Jer 6:10
not, nor inclined their *e* Jer 7:24
not unto me, nor inclined their *e* Jer 7:26
let your *e* receive the word of Jer 9:20

obeyed not, nor inclined their *e* ... Jer 11:8
Hear ye, and give *e* ... Jer 13:15
not, neither inclined their *e* ... Jer 17:23
nor inclined your *e* to hear ... Jer 25:4
unto me, neither inclined their *e* ... Jer 34:14
but ye have not inclined your *e* ... Jer 35:15
nor inclined their *e* to turn from ... Jer 44:5
hide not thine *e* at my breathing, ... Lam 3:56
O my God, incline thine *e* ... Dan 9:18
and give ye *e*, O house of the king ... Hos 5:1
Hear this, ye old men, and give *e* ... Joel 1:2
lion two legs, or a piece of an *e* ... Amos 3:12
and what ye hear in the *e*, that ... Mt 10:27
high priest's, and smote off his *e* ... Mt 26:51
first the blade, then the *e* ... Mk 4:28
after that the full corn in the *e* ... Mk 4:28
the high priest, and cut off his *e* ... Mk 14:47
which ye have spoken in the *e* in ... Lk 12:3
priest, and cut off his right *e* ... Lk 22:50
And he touched his *e*, and healed ... Lk 22:51
servant, and cut off his right *e* ... Jn 18:10
his kinsman whose *e* Peter cut off ... Jn 18:26
nor *e* heard, neither have entered ... 1Cor 2:9
if the *e* shall say, Because I am ... 1Cor 12:16
He that hath an *e*, let him hear ... Rev 2:7
He that hath an *e*, let him hear ... Rev 2:11
He that hath an *e*, let him hear ... Rev 2:17
He that hath an *e*, let him hear ... Rev 2:29
He that hath an *e*, let him hear ... Rev 3:6
He that hath an *e*, let him hear ... Rev 3:13
He that hath an *e*, let him hear ... Rev 3:22
If any man have an *e*, let him ... Rev 13:9

**EARED**
which is neither *e* nor sown ... Deut 21:4

**EARING**
shall neither be *e* nor harvest ... Gen 45:6
in *e* time and in harvest thou ... Ex 34:21

**EARLY**
your feet, and ye shall rise up *e* ... Gen 19:2
Abraham gat up *e* in the morning ... Gen 19:27
Abimelech rose *e* in the morning ... Gen 20:8
Abraham rose up *e* in the morning ... Gen 21:14
Abraham rose up *e* in the morning ... Gen 22:3
Jacob rose up *e* in the morning, ... Gen 28:18
*e* in the morning Laban rose up, ... Gen 31:55
Rise up *e* in the morning, and ... Ex 8:20
Rise up *e* in the morning, and ... Ex 9:13
rose up *e* in the morning, and ... Ex 24:4
they rose up *e* on the morrow, and ... Ex 32:6
Moses rose up *e* in the morning, ... Ex 34:4
they rose up *e* in the morning, and ... Num 14:40
Joshua rose *e* in the morning ... Josh 3:1
Joshua rose *e* in the morning, and ... Josh 6:12
that they rose *e* about the ... Josh 6:15
Joshua rose up *e* in the morning ... Josh 7:16
Joshua rose up *e* in the morning ... Josh 8:10
it, that they hasted and rose up *e* ... Josh 8:14
the city arose *e* in the morning ... Judg 6:28
for he rose up *e* on the morrow ... Judg 6:38
that were with him, rose up *e* ... Judg 7:1
depart *e* from mount Gilead ... Judg 7:3
the sun is up, thou shalt rise *e* ... Judg 9:33
when they arose *e* in the morning ... Judg 19:5
he arose *e* in the morning on the ... Judg 19:8
to morrow get you *e* on your way ... Judg 19:9
morrow, that the people rose *e* ... Judg 21:4
And they rose up in the morning *e* ... 1Sa 1:19
of Ashdod arose *e* on the morrow ... 1Sa 5:3
when they arose *e* on the morrow ... 1Sa 5:4
And they arose *e* ... 1Sa 9:26
when Samuel rose *e* to meet Saul ... 1Sa 15:12
David rose up *e* in the morning, ... 1Sa 17:20
Wherefore now rise up *e* in the ... 1Sa 29:10
soon as ye be up *e* in the morning ... 1Sa 29:10
his men rose up *e* to depart in ... 1Sa 29:11
And Absalom rose up *e*, and stood ... 2Sa 15:2
they rose up *e* in the morning, and ... 2Kin 3:22
of the man of God was risen *e* ... 2Kin 6:15
when they arose *e* in the morning ... 2Kin 19:35
they rose *e* in the morning, and ... 2Chr 20:20
Then Hezekiah the king rose *e* ... 2Chr 29:20
rose up *e* in the morning, and ... Job 1:5
shall help her, and that right *e* ... Ps 46:5
I myself will awake *e* ... Ps 57:8
*e* will I seek thee ... Ps 63:1
returned and enquired *e* after God ... Ps 78:34
O satisfy us *e* with thy mercy ... Ps 90:14
I will *e* destroy all the wicked ... Ps 101:8
I myself will awake *e* ... Ps 108:2
It is vain for you to rise up *e* ... Ps 127:2
they shall seek me *e*, but they ... Prov 1:28
that seek me *e* shall find me ... Prov 8:17
rising *e* in the morning, it shall ... Prov 27:14
Let us get up *e* to the vineyards ... Song 7:12
that rise up *e* in the morning ... Is 5:11
within me will I seek thee *e* ... Is 26:9
when they arose *e* in the morning ... Is 37:36
and I spake unto you, rising up *e* ... Jer 7:13
the prophets, daily rising up *e* ... Jer 7:25
even unto this day, rising *e* ... Jer 11:7
I have spoken unto you, rising *e* ... Jer 25:3
servants the prophets, rising *e* ... Jer 25:4
I sent unto you, both rising up *e* ... Jer 26:5
the prophets, rising up *e* ... Jer 29:19
though I taught them, rising up *e* ... Jer 32:33
I have spoken unto you, rising *e* ... Jer 35:14
the prophets, rising up *e* ... Jer 35:15
servants the prophets, rising *e* ... Jer 44:4
king arose very *e* in the morning ... Dan 6:19
affliction they will seek me *e* ... Hos 5:15
as the *e* dew it goeth away ... Hos 6:4
as the *e* dew that passeth away, ... Hos 13:3
but they rose *e*, and corrupted all ... Zeph 3:7
which went out *e* in the morning ... Mt 20:1
very *e* in the morning the first ... Mk 16:2
Now when Jesus was risen *e* the ... Mk 16:9
all the people came *e* in the ... Lk 21:38
very *e* in the morning, they came ... Lk 24:1
which were *e* at the sepulchre ... Lk 24:22
And And *e* in the morning he came ... Jn 8:1
*e* in the morning he came again ... Jn 8:2
of judgment: and it was *e* ... Jn 18:28
the week cometh Mary Magdalene *e* ... Jn 20:1
into the temple *e* in the morning ... Acts 5:21
for it, until he receive the *e* ... Jas 5:7

**EARNEST**
For the *e* expectation of the ... Rom 8:19
given the *e* of the Spirit in our ... 2Cor 1:22
given unto us the *e* of the Spirit ... 2Cor 5:5
when he told us your *e* desire ... 2Cor 7:7
which put the same *e* care into ... 2Cor 8:16
Which is the *e* of our inheritance ... Eph 1:14
According to my *e* expectation ... Phil 1:20
we ought to give the more *e* heed ... Heb 2:1

**EARNESTLY**
Did I not *e* send unto thee to ... Num 22:37
David *e* asked leave of me that he ... 1Sa 20:6
David *e* asked leave of me to go ... 1Sa 20:28
Zabbai *e* repaired the other piece ... Neh 3:20
As a servant *e* desireth the ... Job 7:2
For I *e* protested unto your ... Jer 11:7
I do *e* remember him still ... Jer 31:20
may do evil with both hands *e* ... Mic 7:3
in an agony he prayed more *e* ... Lk 22:44
*e* looked upon him, and said, This ... Lk 22:56
or why look ye so *e* on us ... Acts 3:12
*e* beholding the council, said, ... Acts 23:1
But covet *e* the best gifts ... 1Cor 12:31
*e* desiring to be clothed upon ... 2Cor 5:2
he prayed *e* that it might not ... Jas 5:17
exhort you that ye should *e* ... Jude 3

**EARNETH**
he that *e* wages *e* wages to ... Hag 1:6

**EARRING**
golden *e* of half a shekel weight ... Gen 24:22
came to pass, when he saw the *e* ... Gen 24:30
I put the *e* upon her face, and the ... Gen 24:47
money, and every one an *e* of gold ... Job 42:11
As an *e* of gold, and an ornament ... Prov 25:12

**EARRINGS**
all their *e* which were in their ... Gen 35:4
unto them, Break off the golden *e* ... Ex 32:2
golden *e* which were in their ears ... Ex 32:3
and brought bracelets, and *e* ... Ex 35:22
chains, and bracelets, rings, *e* ... Num 31:50
me every man the *e* of his prey ... Judg 8:24
(For they had golden *e*, because ... Judg 8:24
every man the *e* of his prey ... Judg 8:25
golden *e* that he requested was a ... Judg 8:26
and the tablets, and the *e* ... Is 3:20
*e* in thine ears, and a beautiful ... Eze 16:12
and she decked herself with her *e* ... Hos 2:13

**EARS**
told all these things in their *e* ... Gen 20:8
earrings which were in their *e* ... Gen 35:4
seven *e* of corn came up upon one ... Gen 41:5
And, behold, seven thin *e* and ... Gen 41:6
the seven thin *e* devoured the ... Gen 41:7
devoured the seven rank and full *e* ... Gen 41:7
seven *e* came up in one stalk, ... Gen 41:22
And, behold, seven *e*, withered, ... Gen 41:23
*e* devoured the seven good *e* ... Gen 41:24
the seven good *e* are seven years ... Gen 41:26
the seven empty *e* blasted with ... Gen 41:27
thee, speak a word in my lord's *e* ... Gen 44:18
in the *e* of Pharaoh, saying, ... Gen 50:4
mayest tell in the *e* of thy son ... Ex 10:2
Speak now in the *e* of the people ... Ex 11:2
and rehearse it in the *e* of Joshua ... Ex 17:14
which are in the *e* of your wives ... Ex 32:2
earrings which were in their *e* ... Ex 32:3
of thy firstfruits green *e* of ... Lev 2:14
even corn beaten out of full *e* ... Lev 2:14
nor parched corn, nor green *e* ... Lev 23:14
ye have wept in the *e* of the LORD ... Num 11:18
LORD, as ye have spoken in mine *e* ... Num 14:28
which I speak in your *e* this day ... Deut 5:1
pluck the *e* with thine hand ... Deut 23:25
see, and *e* to hear, unto this day ... Deut 29:4
may speak these words in their *e* ... Deut 31:28
Moses spake in the *e* of all the ... Deut 31:30
this song in the *e* of the people ... Deut 32:44
the *e* of the elders of that city ... Josh 20:4
proclaim in the *e* of the people ... Judg 7:3
in the *e* of all the men of ... Judg 9:2
brethren spake of him in the *e* of ... Judg 9:3
and spakest of also in mine *e* ... Judg 17:2
glean *e* of corn after him in ... Ruth 2:2
at which both the *e* of every one ... 1Sa 3:11
them in the *e* of the LORD ... 1Sa 8:21
tidings in the *e* of the people ... 1Sa 11:4
bleating of the sheep in mine *e* ... 1Sa 15:14
those words in the *e* of David ... 1Sa 18:23
also spake in the *e* of Benjamin ... 2Sa 3:19
the *e* of David in Hebron all that ... 2Sa 3:19
all that we have heard with our *e* ... 2Sa 7:22
and my cry did enter into his *e* ... 2Sa 22:7
full *e* of corn in the husk ... 2Kin 4:42
*e* of the people that are on the ... 2Kin 18:26
thy tumult is come up into mine *e* ... 2Kin 19:28
of it, both his *e* shall tingle ... 2Kin 21:12
he read in their *e* all the words ... 2Kin 23:2
all that we have heard with our *e* ... 1Chr 17:20
let thine *e* be attent unto the ... 2Chr 6:40
mine *e* attent unto the prayer ... 2Chr 7:15
he read in their *e* all the words ... 2Chr 34:30
the *e* of all the people were ... Neh 8:3
and my declaration with your *e* ... Job 13:17
A dreadful sound is in his *e* ... Job 15:21
off as the tops of the *e* of corn ... Job 24:24
heard the fame thereof with our *e* ... Job 28:22
Then he openeth the *e* of men ... Job 33:16
and openeth their *e* in oppression ... Job 36:15
came before him, even into his *e* ... Ps 18:6
his *e* are open unto their cry ... Ps 34:15
mine *e* hast thou opened ... Ps 40:6
We have heard with our *e*, O God, ... Ps 44:1
incline your *e* to the words of my ... Ps 78:1
mine *e* shall hear my desire of ... Ps 92:11
They have *e*, but they hear not ... Ps 115:6
let thine *e* be attentive to the ... Ps 130:2
They have *e*, but they hear not ... Ps 135:17
Whoso stoppeth his *e* at the cry ... Prov 21:13
Speak not in the *e* of a fool ... Prov 23:9
thine *e* to the words of knowledge ... Prov 23:12
one that taketh a dog by the *e* ... Prov 26:17
In mine *e* said the LORD of hosts, ... Is 5:9
people fat, and make their *e* heavy ... Is 6:10
their eyes, and hear with their *e* ... Is 6:10
after the hearing of his *e* ... Is 11:3
reapeth the *e* with his arm ... Is 17:5
*e* in the valley of Rephaim ... Is 17:5
in mine *e* by the LORD of hosts ... Is 22:14
thine *e* shall hear a word behind ... Is 30:21
the *e* of them that hear shall ... Is 32:3
that stoppeth his *e* from hearing ... Is 33:15
the *e* of the deaf shall be ... Is 35:5
in the *e* of the people that are ... Is 36:11
tumult, is come up into mine *e* ... Is 37:29
opening the *e*, but he heareth not ... Is 42:20
eyes, and the deaf that have *e* ... Is 43:8
other, shall say again in thine *e* ... Is 49:20
cry in the *e* of Jerusalem, saying ... Jer 2:2
which have *e*, and hear not ... Jer 5:21
heareth, his *e* shall tingle ... Jer 19:3
as ye have heard with your *e* ... Jer 26:11
speak all these words in your *e* ... Jer 26:15
this word that I speak in thine *e* ... Jer 28:7
in the *e* of all the people ... Jer 28:7
in the *e* of Jeremiah the prophet ... Jer 29:29
the *e* of the people in the LORD's ... Jer 36:6
thou shalt read them in the *e* of ... Jer 36:6
in the *e* of all the people ... Jer 36:10
the book in the *e* of the people ... Jer 36:13
hast read in the *e* of the people ... Jer 36:14
Sit down now, and read it in our *e* ... Jer 36:15
So Baruch read it in their *e* ... Jer 36:15
the words in the *e* of the king ... Jer 36:20
read it in the *e* of the king ... Jer 36:21
in the *e* of all the princes which ... Jer 36:21
thine heart, and hear with thine *e* ... Eze 3:10
cry in mine *e* with a loud voice ... Eze 8:18
also in mine *e* with a loud voice ... Eze 9:1
they have *e* to hear, and hear not ... Eze 12:2
forehead, and earrings in thine *e* ... Eze 16:12
take away thy nose and thine *e* ... Eze 23:25
thee to hear it with thine *e* ... Eze 24:26
thine eyes, and hear with thine *e* ... Eze 40:4
hear with thine *e* all that I say ... Eze 44:5
mouth, their *e* shall be deaf ... Mic 7:16
the shoulder, and stopped their *e* ... Zec 7:11
He that hath *e* to hear, let him ... Mt 11:15
and began to pluck the *e* of corn ... Mt 12:1
Who hath *e* to hear, let him hear ... Mt 13:9
their *e* are dull of hearing, and ... Mt 13:15
their eyes, and hear with their *e* ... Mt 13:15
and your *e*, for they hear ... Mt 13:16
Who hath *e* to hear, let him hear ... Mt 13:43
if this come to the governor's *e* ... Mt 28:14
they went, to pluck the *e* of corn ... Mk 2:23
unto them, He that hath *e* to hear ... Mk 4:9
If any man have *e* to hear ... Mk 4:23
If any man have *e* to hear ... Mk 7:16
and put his fingers into his *e* ... Mk 7:33
And straightway his *e* were opened ... Mk 7:35
and having *e*, hear ye not ... Mk 8:18
thy salutation sounded in mine *e* ... Lk 1:44
scripture fulfilled in your *e* ... Lk 4:21
disciples plucked the *e* of corn ... Lk 6:1
he cried, He that hath *e* to hear ... Lk 8:8
sayings sink down into your *e* ... Lk 9:44
He that hath *e* to hear, let him ... Lk 14:35
and uncircumcised in heart and *e* ... Acts 7:51
a loud voice, and stopped their *e* ... Acts 7:57
the *e* of the church which was in ... Acts 11:22
certain strange things to our *e* ... Acts 17:20
their *e* are dull of hearing, and ... Acts 28:27
their eyes, and hear with their *e* ... Acts 28:27
*e* that they should not hear ... Rom 11:8
teachers, having itching *e* ... 2Ti 4:3
turn away their *e* from the truth ... 2Ti 4:4
into the *e* of the Lord of Sabaoth ... Jas 5:4
his *e* are open unto their prayers ... 1Pet 3:12

**EARTH** See PREFACE.
God created the heaven and the *e* ... Gen 1:1
the *e* were finished, and all the ... Gen 2:1

And God looked upon the *e*, and, ... Gen 6:12
for the *e* is filled with violence ... Gen 6:13
I will destroy them with the *e* ... Gen 6:13
of a covenant between me and the *e* ... Gen 9:13
the nations of the *e* be blessed ... Gen 22:18
the nations of the *e* be blessed ... Gen 26:4
Then the *e* shook and trembled ... 2Sa 22:8
From going to and fro in the *e* ... Job 1:7
an appointed time to man upon *e* ... Job 7:1
is thy name in all the *e* ... Ps 8:1
The *e* is the LORD's, and the ... Ps 24:1
But the meek shall inherit the *e* ... Ps 37:11
All the *e* shall worship thee, and ... Ps 66:4
fear before him, all the *e* ... Ps 96:9
but the *e* abideth for ever ... Eccl 1:4
The *e* is utterly broken down ... Is 24:19
the *e* is clean dissolved, the ... Is 24:19
ye saved, all the ends of the *e* ... Is 45:22
for they shall inherit the *e* ... Mt 5:5
Ye are the salt of the *e* ... Mt 5:13
Thy will be done in *e*, as it is ... Mt 6:10
*e* shall pass away, but my words ... Mt 24:35
Heaven and *e* shall pass away ... Mk 13:31
on *e* peace, good will toward men ... Lk 2:14
The first man is of the *e* ... 1Cor 15:47
into the lower parts of the *e* ... Eph 4:9
things in heaven, and things in *e* ... Phil 2:10
strangers and pilgrims on the *e* ... Heb 11:13
he was cast out into the *e* ... Rev 12:9
And I saw a new heaven and a new *e* .. Rev 21:1

**EARTHEN**
But the *e* vessel wherein it is ... Lev 6:28
every *e* vessel, whereinto any of ... Lev 11:33
in an *e* vessel over running water ... Lev 14:5
in an *e* vessel over running water ... Lev 14:50
take holy water in an *e* vessel ... Num 5:17
*e* vessels, and wheat, and barley, ... 2Sa 17:28
Go and get a potter's *e* bottle ... Jer 19:1
and put them in an *e* vessel ... Jer 32:14
are they esteemed as *e* pitchers ... Lam 4:2
have this treasure in *e* vessels ... 2Cor 4:7

**EARTHLY**
If I have told you *e* things ... Jn 3:12
he that is of the earth is *e* ... Jn 3:31
For we know that if our *e* house ... 2Cor 5:1
in their shame, who mind *e* things ... Phil 3:19
not from above, but is *e*, sensual ... Jas 3:15

**EARTHQUAKE**
and after the wind an *e* ... 1Kin 19:11
but the LORD was not in the *e* ... 1Kin 19:11
And after the *e* a fire ... 1Kin 19:12
of hosts with thunder, and with *e* ... Is 29:6
of Israel, two years before the *e* ... Amos 1:1
*e* in the days of Uzziah king of ... Zec 14:5
him, watching Jesus, saw the *e* ... Mt 27:54
And, behold, there was a great *e* ... Mt 28:2
And suddenly there was a great *e* ... Acts 16:26
seal, and, lo, there was a great *e* ... Rev 6:12
and lightnings, and an *e* ... Rev 8:5
the same hour was there a great *e* ... Rev 11:13
in the *e* were slain of men seven ... Rev 11:13
voices, and thunderings, and an *e* ... Rev 11:19
and there was a great *e*, such as ... Rev 16:18
upon the earth, so mighty an *e* ... Rev 16:18

**EARTHQUAKES**
be famines, and pestilences, and *e* ... Mt 24:7
there shall be *e* in divers places ... Mk 13:8
great *e* shall be in divers places ... Lk 21:11

**EARTHY**
The first man is of the earth, *e* ... 1Cor 15:47
As is the *e*, such are they also ... 1Cor 15:48
such are they also that are *e* ... 1Cor 15:48
we have borne the image of the *e* ... 1Cor 15:49

**EASE**
when thou wilt *e* thyself abroad ... Deut 23:13
nations shalt thou find no *e* ... Deut 28:65
trode them down with *e* over ... Judg 20:43
now therefore *e* thou somewhat the ... 2Chr 10:4
*E* somewhat the yoke that thy ... 2Chr 10:9
me, my couch shall *e* my complaint ... Job 7:13
the thought of him that is at *e* ... Job 12:5
I was at *e*, but he hath broken me ... Job 16:12
full strength, being wholly at *e* ... Job 21:23
His soul shall dwell at *e* ... Ps 25:13
scorning of those that are at *e* ... Ps 123:4
I will *e* me of mine adversaries, ... Is 1:24
Rise up, ye women that are at *e* ... Is 32:9
Tremble, ye women that are at *e* ... Is 32:11
return, and be in rest and at *e* ... Jer 46:27
hath been at *e* from his youth ... Jer 48:11
multitude being at *e* was with her ... Eze 23:42
Woe to them that are at *e* in Zion ... Amos 6:1
with the heathen that are at *e* ... Zec 1:15
take thine *e*, eat, drink, and be ... Lk 12:19

**EASED**
and though I forbear, what am I *e* ... Job 16:6
I mean not that other men be *e* ... 2Cor 8:13

**EASIER**
so shall it be *e* for thyself ... Ex 18:22
For whether is *e*, to say, Thy ... Mt 9:5
It is *e* for a camel to go through ... Mt 19:24
Whether is it *e* to say to the ... Mk 2:9
It is *e* for a camel to go through ... Mk 10:25
Whether is *e*, to say, Thy sins be ... Lk 5:23
it is *e* for heaven and earth to ... Lk 16:17
For it is *e* for a camel to go ... Lk 18:25

**EASILY**
is not *e* provoked, thinketh no ... 1Cor 13:5
the sin which doth so *e* beset us ... Heb 12:1

**EAST**
goeth toward the *e* of Assyria ... Gen 2:14
he placed at the *e* of the garden ... Gen 3:24
the land of Nod, on the *e* of Eden ... Gen 4:16
unto Sephar a mount of the *e* ... Gen 10:30
as they journeyed from the *e* ... Gen 11:2
a mountain on the *e* of Beth-el ... Gen 12:8
on the west, and Hai on the *e* ... Gen 12:8
and Lot journeyed *e* ... Gen 13:11
eastward, unto the *e* country ... Gen 25:6
abroad to the west, and to the *e* ... Gen 28:14
the land of the people of the *e* ... Gen 29:1
blasted with the *e* wind sprung up ... Gen 41:6
thin, and blasted with the *e* wind ... Gen 41:23
empty ears blasted with the *e* ... Gen 41:27
the LORD brought an *e* wind upon ... Ex 10:13
the *e* wind brought the locusts ... Ex 10:13
by a strong *e* wind all that night ... Ex 14:21
*e* side eastward shall be fifty ... Ex 27:13
for the *e* side eastward fifty ... Ex 38:13
it beside the altar on the *e* part ... Lev 1:16
on the *e* side toward the rising ... Num 2:3
the tabernacle toward the *e* ... Num 3:38
on the *e* parts shall go forward ... Num 10:5
out of the mountains of the *e* ... Num 23:7
ye shall point out your *e* border ... Num 34:10
to Riblah, on the *e* side of Ain ... Num 34:11
on the *e* side two thousand cubits ... Num 35:5
in the *e* border of Jericho ... Josh 4:19
on the *e* side of Beth-el, and ... Josh 7:2
And to the Canaanite on the *e* ... Josh 11:3
Hermon, and all the plain on the *e* ... Josh 12:1
to the sea of Chinneroth on the *e* ... Josh 12:3
plain, even the salt sea on the *e* ... Josh 12:3
the *e* border was the salt sea, ... Josh 15:5
the water of Jericho on the *e* ... Josh 16:1
on the *e* side was Ataroth-addar ... Josh 16:5
passed by it on the *e* to Janohah ... Josh 16:6
north, and in Issachar on the *e* ... Josh 17:10
beyond Jordan on the *e*, which ... Josh 18:7
the border of it on the *e* side ... Josh 18:20
along on the *e* to Gittah-hepher ... Josh 19:13
and the children of the *e* ... Judg 6:3
the children of the *e* were ... Judg 6:33
all the children of the *e* lay ... Judg 7:12
hosts of the children of the *e* ... Judg 8:10
dwelt in tents on the *e* of Nobah ... Judg 8:11
came by the *e* side of the land of ... Judg 11:18
on the *e* side of the highway that ... Judg 21:19
all the children of the *e* country ... 1Kin 4:30
and three looking toward the *e* ... 1Kin 7:25
even unto the *e* side of the ... 1Chr 4:39
all the *e* land of Gilead ... 1Chr 5:10
on the *e* side of Jordan, were ... 1Chr 6:78
were the porters, toward the *e* ... 1Chr 9:24
of the valleys, both toward the *e* ... 1Chr 12:15
and three looking toward the *e* ... 2Chr 4:4
on the right side of the *e* end ... 2Chr 4:10
stood at the *e* end of the altar, ... 2Chr 5:12
them together into the *e* street ... 2Chr 29:4
Levite, the porter toward the *e* ... 2Chr 31:14
the water gate toward the *e* ... Neh 3:26
the keeper of the *e* gate ... Neh 3:29
greatest of all the men of the *e* ... Job 1:3
and fill his belly with the *e* wind ... Job 15:2
The *e* wind carrieth him away, and ... Job 27:21
the *e* wind upon the earth ... Job 38:24
ships of Tarshish with an *e* wind ... Ps 48:7
cometh neither from the *e* ... Ps 75:6
He caused an *e* wind to blow in ... Ps 78:26
As far as the *e* is from the west, ... Ps 103:12
them out of the lands, from the *e* ... Ps 107:3
they be replenished from the *e* ... Is 2:6
spoil them of the *e* together ... Is 11:14
wind in the day of the *e* wind ... Is 27:8
up the righteous man from the *e* ... Is 41:2
I will bring thy seed from the *e* ... Is 43:5
a ravenous bird from the *e* ... Is 46:11
with an *e* wind before the enemy ... Jer 18:17
is by the entry of the *e* gate ... Jer 19:2
of the horse gate toward the *e* ... Jer 31:40
Kedar, and spoil the men of the *e* ... Jer 49:28
LORD, and their faces toward the *e* ... Eze 8:16
worshipped the sun toward the *e* ... Eze 8:16
of the *e* gate of the LORD's house ... Eze 10:19
brought me unto the *e* gate of the ... Eze 11:1
is on the *e* side of the city ... Eze 11:23
when the *e* wind toucheth it ... Eze 17:10
the *e* wind dried up her fruit ... Eze 19:12
the men of the *e* for a possession ... Eze 25:4
men of the *e* with the Ammonites ... Eze 25:10
the *e* wind hath broken thee in ... Eze 27:26
passengers on the *e* of the sea ... Eze 39:11
gate which looketh toward the *e* ... Eze 40:6
gate that looketh toward the *e* ... Eze 40:22
toward the north, and toward the *e* ... Eze 40:23
into the inner court toward the *e* ... Eze 40:32
one at the side of the *e* gate ... Eze 40:44
the separate place toward the *e* ... Eze 41:14
was the entry on the *e* side ... Eze 42:9
wall of the court toward the *e* ... Eze 42:10
before the wall toward the *e* ... Eze 42:12
whose prospect is toward the *e* ... Eze 42:15
He measured the *e* side with the ... Eze 42:16
gate that looketh toward the *e* ... Eze 43:1
Israel came from the way of the *e* ... Eze 43:2
whose prospect is toward the *e* ... Eze 43:4
stairs shall look toward the *e* ... Eze 43:17
which looketh toward the *e* ... Eze 44:1
and from the *e* side eastward ... Eze 45:7
the west border unto the *e* border ... Eze 45:7
*e* shall be shut the six working ... Eze 46:1
gate that looketh toward the *e* ... Eze 46:12
of the house stood toward the *e* ... Eze 47:1
issue out toward the *e* country ... Eze 47:8
the *e* side ye shall measure from ... Eze 47:18
from the border unto the *e* sea ... Eze 47:18
And this is the *e* side ... Eze 47:18
for these are his sides *e* ... Eze 48:1
from the *e* side unto the west ... Eze 48:2
from the *e* side even unto the ... Eze 48:3
from the *e* side unto the west ... Eze 48:4
from the *e* side unto the west ... Eze 48:5
from the *e* side even unto the ... Eze 48:6
from the *e* side unto the west ... Eze 48:7
from the *e* side unto the west ... Eze 48:8
from the *e* side unto the west ... Eze 48:8
toward the *e* ten thousand in ... Eze 48:10
on the *e* side four thousand and ... Eze 48:16
toward the *e* two hundred and fifty ... Eze 48:17
the oblation toward the *e* border ... Eze 48:21
from the *e* side unto the west ... Eze 48:23
from the *e* side unto the west ... Eze 48:24
from the *e* side unto the west ... Eze 48:25
from the *e* side unto the west ... Eze 48:26
from the *e* side unto the west ... Eze 48:27
at the *e* side four thousand and ... Eze 48:32
toward the south, and toward the *e* ... Dan 8:9
But tidings out of the *e* and out ... Dan 11:44
and followeth after the *e* wind ... Hos 12:1
an *e* wind shall come, the wind of ... Hos 13:15
with his face toward the *e* sea ... Joel 2:20
and from the north even to the *e* ... Amos 8:12
sat on the *e* side of the city, and ... Jonah 4:5
God prepared a vehement *e* wind ... Jonah 4:8
faces shall sup up as the *e* wind ... Hab 1:9
save my people from the *e* country ... Zec 8:7
is before Jerusalem on the *e* ... Zec 14:4
in the midst thereof toward the *e* ... Zec 14:4
wise men from the *e* to Jerusalem ... Mt 2:1
we have seen his star in the *e* ... Mt 2:2
the star, which they saw in the *e* ... Mt 2:9
That many shall come from the *e* ... Mt 8:11
the lightning cometh out of the *e* ... Mt 24:27
And they shall come from the *e* ... Lk 13:29
angel ascending from the *e* ... Rev 7:2
kings of the *e* might be prepared ... Rev 16:12
On the *e* three gates ... Rev 21:13

**EASTER** *Passover.*
intending after *E* to bring him ... Acts 12:4

**EASTWARD**
God planted a garden *e* in Eden ... Gen 2:8
art northward, and southward, and *e*. Gen 13:14
his son, while he yet lived, *e* ... Gen 25:6
east side *e* shall be fifty cubits ... Ex 27:13
for the east side *e* fifty cubits ... Ex 38:13
his finger upon the mercy seat *e* ... Lev 16:14
tabernacle of the congregation *e* ... Num 3:38
to us on this side Jordan *e* ... Num 32:19
outmost coast of the salt sea *e* ... Num 34:3
side of the sea of Chinnereth *e* ... Num 34:11
this side Jordan near Jericho *e* ... Num 34:15
salt sea, under Ashdoth-pisgah *e* ... Deut 3:17
and northward, and southward, and *e* Deut 3:27
the plain on this side Jordan *e* ... Deut 4:49
and unto the valley of Mizpeh *e* ... Josh 11:8
Moses gave them, beyond Jordan *e* ... Josh 13:8
on the other side Jordan *e* ... Josh 13:27
other side Jordan, by Jericho, *e* ... Josh 13:32
went about *e* unto Taanath-shiloh ... Josh 16:6
turned from Sarid *e* toward the ... Josh 19:12
other side Jordan by Jericho *e* ... Josh 20:8
in Michmash, *e* from Beth-aven ... 1Sa 13:5
house *e* over against the south ... 1Kin 7:39
Get thee hence, and turn thee *e* ... 1Kin 17:3
From Jordan *e*, all the land of ... 2Kin 10:33
And he said, Open the window *e* ... 2Kin 13:17
*e* he inhabited unto the entering ... 1Chr 5:9
*e* Naaran, and westward Gezer, with .. 1Chr 7:28
waited in the king's gate *e* ... 1Chr 9:18
the lot *e* fell to Shelemiah ... 1Chr 26:14
*E* were six Levites, northward ... 1Chr 26:17
David, even unto the water gate *e* ... Neh 12:37
the LORD's house, which looketh *e* ... Eze 11:1
gate *e* were three on this side ... Eze 40:10
without, an hundred cubits *e* ... Eze 40:19
westward, and from the east side *e* ... Eze 45:7
the threshold of the house *e* ... Eze 47:1
gate by the way that looketh *e* ... Eze 47:2
the line in his hand went forth *e* ... Eze 47:3
portion shall be ten thousand *e* ... Eze 48:18

**EASY**
but knowledge is *e* unto him that ... Prov 14:6
For my yoke is *e*, and my burden is ... Mt 11:30
tongue words *e* to be understood ... 1Cor 14:9
*e* to be intreated, full of mercy ... Jas 3:17

**EAT** See PREFACE.
the garden thou mayest freely *e* ... Gen 2:16
and evil, thou shalt not *e* of it ... Gen 2:17
Ye shall not *e* of every tree of ... Gen 3:1
of the fruit thereof, and did *e* ... Gen 3:6
and he did *e* ... Gen 3:6
Ye shall not *e* any thing with the ... Lev 19:26
Only ye shall not *e* the blood ... Deut 12:16
him, and said unto him, Arise and *e* ... 1Kin 19:5

thy son, that we may *e* him to day 2Kin 6:28
Give thy son, that we may *e* him 2Kin 6:29
up corn for them, that we may *e* Neh 5:2
The meek shall *e* and be satisfied Ps 22:26
Man did *e* angels' food Ps 78:25
ye shall *e* the good of the land Is 1:19
come ye, buy, and *e* Is 55:1
For they shall *e*, and not have Hos 4:10
Thou shalt *e*, but not be Mic 6:14
ye *e*, but ye have not enough Hag 1:6
for your life, what ye shall *e* Mt 6:25
not their hands when they *e* bread Mt 15:2
but to *e* with unwashen hands Mt 15:20
the disciples, and said, Take, *e* Mt 26:26
And as they did *e*, Jesus took Mk 14:22
and gave to them, and said, Take, *e* Mk 14:22
*e* such things as are set before Lk 10:8
take thine ease, *e*, drink, and be Lk 12:19
Except ye *e* the flesh of the Son Jn 6:53
Rise, Peter; kill, and *e* Acts 10:13
Arise, Peter; slay and *e* Acts 11:7
that he may *e* all things Rom 14:2
Whether therefore ye *e*, or drink, 1Cor 10:31
he brake it, and said, Take, *e* 1Cor 11:24
I give to *e* of the tree of life Rev 2:7

**EATEN**
Hast thou *e* of the tree, whereof Gen 3:11
hast *e* of the tree, of which I Gen 3:17
unto thee of all food that is *e* Gen 6:21
that which the young men have *e* Gen 14:24
I have *e* of all before thou Gen 27:33
rams of thy flock have I not *e* Gen 31:38
And when they had *e* them up Gen 41:21
not be known that they had *e* them Gen 41:21
when they had *e* up the corn which Gen 43:2
In one house shall it be *e* Ex 12:46
shall no leavened bread be *e* Ex 13:3
bread shall be *e* seven days Ex 13:7
and his flesh shall not be *e* Ex 21:28
cause a field or vineyard to be *e* Ex 22:5
it shall not be *e*, because it is Ex 29:34
shall it be *e* in the holy place Lev 6:16
it shall not be *e* Lev 6:23
in the holy place shall it be *e* Lev 6:26
in the holy place, shall be *e* Lev 6:30
it shall be *e* in the holy place Lev 7:6
for thanksgiving shall be *e* the Lev 7:15
it shall be *e* the same day that Lev 7:16
the remainder of it shall be *e* Lev 7:16
be *e* at all on the third day Lev 7:18
any unclean thing shall not be *e* Lev 7:19
Wherefore have ye not *e* the sin Lev 10:17
have *e* it in the holy place Lev 10:18
if I had *e* the sin offering to Lev 10:19
they shall not be *e*, they are an Lev 11:13
Of all meat which may be *e* Lev 11:34
it shall not be *e* Lev 11:41
between the beast that may be *e* Lev 11:47
and the beast that may not be *e* Lev 11:47
any beast or fowl that may be *e* Lev 17:13
It shall be *e* the same day ye Lev 19:6
if it be *e* at all on the third Lev 19:7
it shall not be *e* of Lev 19:23
On the same day it shall be *e* up Lev 22:30
days shall unleavened bread be *e* Num 28:17
when thou shalt have *e* and be full Deut 6:11
When thou hast *e* and art full, Deut 8:10
Lest when thou hast *e* and art full Deut 8:12
as the roebuck and the hart is *e* Deut 12:22
they shall not be *e* Deut 14:19
vineyard, and hath not yet *e* of it Deut 20:6
I have not *e* thereof in my Deut 26:14
Ye have not *e* bread, neither have Deut 29:6
and they shall have *e* and filled Deut 31:20
had *e* of the old corn of the land Josh 5:12
And when Boaz had *e* and drunk, and Ruth 3:7
up after they had *e* in Shiloh 1Sa 1:9
if haply the people had *e* freely 1Sa 14:30
for he had *e* no bread all the day 1Sa 28:20
and when he had *e*, his spirit came 1Sa 30:12
for he had *e* no bread, nor drunk 1Sa 30:12
have we *e* at all of the king's 2Sa 19:42
hast *e* bread and drunk water in 1Kin 13:22
to pass, after he had *e* bread 1Kin 13:23
the lion had not *e* the carcase 1Kin 13:28
and when they had *e* and drunk, he 2Kin 6:23
my brethren have not *e* the bread Neh 5:14
is unsavoury be *e* without salt Job 6:6
as a garment that is moth *e* Job 13:28
Or have *e* my morsel myself alone, Job 31:17
the fatherless hath not *e* thereof Job 31:17
If I have *e* the fruits thereof Job 31:39
zeal of thine house hath *e* me up Ps 69:9
For I have *e* ashes like bread, and Ps 102:9
bread *e* in secret is pleasant Prov 9:17
thou hast *e* shalt thou vomit up Prov 23:8
I have *e* my honeycomb with my Song 5:1
for ye have *e* up the vineyard Is 3:14
thereof, and it shall be *e* up Is 5:5
and it shall return, and shall be *e* Is 6:13
I have roasted flesh, and *e* it Is 44:19
for they have *e* up Jacob, and Jer 10:25
figs, which could not be *e* Jer 24:2
evil, very evil, that cannot be *e* Jer 24:3
the evil figs, which cannot be *e* Jer 24:8
like vile figs, that cannot be *e* Jer 29:17
The fathers have *e* a sour grape Jer 31:29
up even till now have I not *e* of Eze 4:14
The fathers have *e* sour grapes Eze 18:2
hath not *e* upon the mountains, Eze 18:6
duties, but even hath *e* upon the Eze 18:11
That hath not *e* upon the Eze 18:15
you to have *e* up the good pasture Eze 34:18
unleavened bread shall be *e* Eze 45:21
ye have *e* the fruit of lies Hos 10:13
hath left hath the locust *e* Joel 1:4
hath left hath the cankerworm *e* Joel 1:4
hath left hath the caterpiller *e* Joel 1:4
the years that the locust hath *e* Joel 2:25
they that had *e* were about five Mt 14:21
they that had *e* were about four Mk 8:9
shall ye begin to say, We have *e* Lk 13:26
and serve me, till I have *e* Lk 17:8
zeal of thine house hath *e* me up Jn 2:17
and above unto them that had *e* Jn 6:13
very hungry, and would have *e* Acts 10:10
for I have never *e* any thing that Acts 10:14
he was *e* of worms, and gave up the Acts 12:23
again, and had broken bread, and *e* Acts 20:11
And when they had *e* enough Acts 27:38
and as soon as I had *e* it, my Rev 10:10

**EATER**
Out of the *e* came forth meat, and Judg 14:14
to the sower, and bread to the *e* Is 55:10
even fall into the mouth of the *e* Nah 3:12

**EATERS**
among riotous *e* of flesh Prov 23:20

**EATEST**
for in the day that thou *e* Gen 2:17
and why *e* thou not 1Sa 1:8
so sad, that thou *e* no bread 1Kin 21:5

**EATETH**
for whosoever *e* leavened bread Ex 12:15
for whosoever *e* that which is Ex 12:19
the soul that *e* of it shall bear Lev 7:18
But the soul that *e* of the flesh Lev 7:20
For whosoever *e* the fat of the Lev 7:25
even the soul that *e* it shall be Lev 7:25
it be that *e* any manner of blood Lev 7:27
he that *e* of the carcase of it Lev 11:40
he that *e* in the house shall wash Lev 14:47
that *e* any manner of blood Lev 17:10
against that soul that *e* blood Lev 17:10
whosoever *e* it shall be cut off Lev 17:14
every soul that *e* that which died Lev 17:15
Therefore every one that *e* it Lev 19:8
it, is a land that *e* up the Num 13:32
man that *e* any food until evening 1Sa 14:24
the man that *e* any food this day 1Sa 14:28
Whose harvest the hungry *e* up Job 5:5
soul, and never *e* with pleasure Job 21:25
he *e* grass as an ox Job 40:15
similitude of an ox that *e* grass Ps 106:20
The righteous *e* to the satisfying Prov 13:25
she *e*, and wipeth her mouth, and Prov 30:20
*e* not the bread of idleness Prov 31:27
together, and *e* his own flesh Eccl 4:5
his days also he *e* in darkness Eccl 5:17
eat thereof, but a stranger *e* it Eccl 6:2
it is yet in his hand he *e* it up Is 28:4
man dreameth, and, behold, he *e* Is 29:8
with part thereof he *e* flesh Is 44:16
he that *e* of their eggs dieth, and Is 59:5
every man that *e* the sour grape Jer 31:30
Why *e* your Master with publicans Mt 9:11
disciples, How is it that he *e* Mk 2:16
One of you which *e* with me shall Mk 14:18
receiveth sinners, and *e* with them Lk 15:2
Whoso *e* my flesh, and drinketh my Jn 6:54
He that *e* my flesh, and drinketh Jn 6:56
so he that *e* me, even he shall Jn 6:57
he that *e* of this bread shall Jn 6:58
He that *e* bread with me hath Jn 13:18
another, who is weak, *e* herbs Rom 14:2
*e* despise him that *e* not Rom 14:3
which *e* not judge him that *e* Rom 14:3
He that *e*, *e* to the Lord, Rom 14:6
*e* not, to the Lord he *e* not Rom 14:6
for that man who *e* with offence Rom 14:20
because he *e* not of faith Rom 14:23
*e* not of the fruit thereof 1Cor 9:7
*e* not of the milk of the flock 1Cor 9:7
*e* and drinketh unworthily, *e* 1Cor 11:29

**EATING**
every man according to his *e* Ex 12:4
it every man according to his *e* Ex 16:16
every man according to his *e* Ex 16:18
every man according to his *e* Ex 16:21
in his hands, and went on *e* Judg 14:9
man, until he shall have done *e* Ruth 3:3
the LORD in *e* with the blood 1Sa 14:34
abroad upon all the earth, *e* 1Sa 30:16
it as they had made an end of *e* 1Kin 1:41
is by the sea in multitude, *e* 1Kin 4:20
as they were *e* of the pottage, 2Kin 4:40
were with David three days, *e* 1Chr 12:39
his sons and his daughters were *e* Job 1:13
Thy sons and thy daughters were *e* Job 1:18
rain it upon him while he is *e* Job 20:23
*e* flesh, and drinking wine Is 22:13
midst, *e* swine's flesh, and the Is 66:17
an end of *e* the grass of the land Amos 7:2
John came neither *e* nor drinking Mt 11:18
The Son of man came *e* and drinking Mt 11:19
were before the flood they were *e* Mt 24:38
And as they were *e*, Jesus took Mt 26:26
neither *e* bread nor drinking wine Lk 7:33
The Son of man is come *e* and Lk 7:34
And in the same house remain, *e* Lk 10:7
the *e* of those things that are 1Cor 8:4
For in *e* every one taketh before 1Cor 11:21

**EBAL** (*e'-bal*) *Son of Shobal.*
Manahath, and *E*, Shepho, Gen 36:23
and the curse upon mount *E* Deut 11:29
command you this day, in mount *E* Deut 27:4
shall stand upon mount *E* to curse Deut 27:13
the LORD God of Israel in mount *E* Josh 8:30
half of them over against mount *E* Josh 8:33
And *E*, and Abimael, and Sheba, 1Chr 1:22
Alian, and Manahath, and *E*, Shephi, 1Chr 1:40

**EBED** (*e'-bed*) See EBED-MELECH.
*1. Father of Gaal.*
Gaal the son of *E* came with his Judg 9:26
And Gaal the son of *E* said Judg 9:28
the words of Gaal the son of *E* Judg 9:30
saying, Behold, Gaal the son of *E* Judg 9:31
And Gaal the son of *E* went out Judg 9:35
*2. A family of exiles.*
*E* the son of Jonathan, and with Ezr 8:6

**EBED-MELECH** (*e'-bed-me'-lek*) *An Ethiopian eunuch.*
Now when *E* the Ethiopian, one of Jer 38:7
*E* went forth out of the king's Jer 38:8
king commanded *E* the Ethiopian Jer 38:10
So *E* took the men with him, and Jer 38:11
*E* the Ethiopian said unto Jer 38:12
speak to *E* the Ethiopian, saying, Jer 39:16

**EBEN-EZER**
to battle, and pitched beside *E* 1Sa 4:1
and brought it from *E* unto Ashdod 1Sa 5:1
Shen, and called the name of it *E* 1Sa 7:12

**EBER** (*e'-bur*) See HEBER.
*1. A great-grandson of Shem.*
father of all the children of *E* Gen 10:21
and Salah begat *E* Gen 10:24
unto *E* were born two sons Gen 10:25
lived thirty years, and begat *E* Gen 11:14
after he begat *E* four hundred Gen 11:15
*E* lived four and thirty years, and Gen 11:16
*E* lived after he begat Peleg four Gen 11:17
begat Shelah, and Shelah begat *E* 1Chr 1:18
unto *E* were born two sons 1Chr 1:19
*E*, Peleg, Reu, 1Chr 1:25
*2. Descendants of Eber 1.*
Asshur, and shall afflict *E* Num 24:24
*3. Son of Elpaal.*
*E*, and Misham, and Shamed, who 1Chr 8:12
*4. A priest of the Amok family.*
Kallai; of Amok, *E* Neh 12:20

**EBEZ** See ABEZ.

**EBIASAPH** (*e-bi'-a-saf*) See ABIASAPH. *A great-grandson of Korah.*
*E* his son, and Assir his son, 1Chr 6:23
the son of Assir, the son of *E* 1Chr 6:37
the son of Kore, the son of *E* 1Chr 9:19

**EBONY**
for a present horns of ivory and *e* Eze 27:15

**EBRONAH** (*eb-ro'-nah*) *An encampment during the Exodus.*
from Jotbathah, and encamped at *E* Num 33:34
And they departed from *E*, and Num 33:35

**ECBATANA** See ACHMETHA.

**ED** (*ed*) *Name of an altar.*
of Gad called the altar *E* Josh 22:34

**EDAR** (*e'-dar*) See EDER. *A name of a watchtower.*
his tent beyond the tower of *E* Gen 35:21

**EDEN** (*e'-dun*)
*1. Original land of Adam and Eve.*
planted a garden eastward in *E* Gen 2:8
went out of *E* to water the garden Gen 2:10
into the garden of *E* to dress it Gen 2:15
him forth from the garden of *E* Gen 3:23
east of the garden of *E* Cherubim Gen 3:24
the land of Nod, on the east of *E* Gen 4:16
will make her wilderness like *E* Is 51:3
hast been in *E* the garden of God Eze 28:13
so that all the trees of *E* Eze 31:9
and all the trees of *E*, the choice Eze 31:16
in greatness among the trees of *E* Eze 31:18
of *E* unto the nether parts of the Eze 31:18
is become like the garden of *E* Eze 36:35
is as the garden of *E* before them Joel 2:3
*2. An undetermined place.*
the children of *E* which were in 2Kin 19:12
the children of *E* which were in Is 37:12
Haran, and Canneh, and *E*, the Eze 27:23
the sceptre from the house of *E* Amos 1:5
*3. Son of Joah.*
of Zimmah, and *E* the son of Joah 2Chr 29:12
*4. A Levite during Hezekiah's time.*
were *E*, and Miniamin, 2Chr 31:15

**EDER** (*e'-dur*) See EDAR. *A city in southern Judah.*
were Kabzeel, and *E* Josh 15:21
*2. A grandson of Merari.*
Mahli, and *E*, and Jeremoth, three 1Chr 23:23
Mahli, and *E*, and Jerimoth 1Chr 24:30

**EDGE**
his son with the *e* of the sword ... Gen 34:26
in the *e* of the wilderness ... Ex 13:20
people with the *e* of the sword ... Ex 17:13
the *e* of the one curtain from the ... Ex 26:4
uttermost *e* of another curtain ... Ex 26:4
loops shalt thou make in the *e* of ... Ex 26:5
the *e* of the one curtain that is ... Ex 26:10
fifty loops in the *e* of the ... Ex 26:10
on the *e* of one curtain from the ... Ex 36:11
fifty loops made he in the *e* of ... Ex 36:12
*e* of the curtain in the coupling ... Ex 36:17
fifty loops made he upon the *e* of ... Ex 36:17
smote him with the *e* of the sword ... Num 21:24
Etham, which is in the *e* of the ... Num 33:6
in the *e* of the land of Edom ... Num 33:37
that city with the *e* of the sword ... Deut 13:15
thereof, with the *e* of the sword ... Deut 13:15
thereof with the *e* of the sword ... Deut 20:13
and ass, with the *e* of the sword ... Josh 6:21
all fallen on the *e* of the sword ... Josh 8:24
smote it with the *e* of the sword ... Josh 8:24
smote it with the *e* of the sword ... Josh 10:28
smote it with the *e* of the sword ... Josh 10:30
smote it with the *e* of the sword ... Josh 10:32
smote it with the *e* of the sword ... Josh 10:35
smote it with the *e* of the sword ... Josh 10:37
them with the *e* of the sword ... Josh 10:39
therein with the *e* of the sword ... Josh 11:11
them with the *e* of the sword ... Josh 11:12
smote with the *e* of the sword ... Josh 11:14
even unto the *e* of the sea of ... Josh 13:27
smote it with the *e* of the sword ... Josh 19:47
it with the *e* of the sword ... Judg 1:8
the city with the *e* of the sword ... Judg 1:25
with the *e* of the sword before ... Judg 4:15
fell upon the *e* of the sword ... Judg 4:16
them with the *e* of the sword ... Judg 18:27
the city with the *e* of the sword ... Judg 20:37
them with the *e* of the sword ... Judg 20:48
with the *e* of the sword, with the ... Judg 21:10
people with the *e* of the sword ... 1Sa 15:8
smote he with the *e* of the sword ... 1Sa 22:19
and sheep, with the *e* of the sword ... 1Sa 22:19
the city with the *e* of the sword ... 2Sa 15:14
them with the *e* of the sword ... 2Kin 10:25
servants with the *e* of the sword ... Job 1:15
servants with the *e* of the sword ... Job 1:17
also turned the *e* of his sword ... Ps 89:43
be blunt, and he do not whet the *e* ... Eccl 10:10
them with the *e* of the sword ... Jer 21:7
the children's teeth are set on *e* ... Jer 31:29
his teeth shall be set on *e* ... Jer 31:30
the children's teeth are set on *e* ... Eze 18:2
the border thereof by the *e* ... Eze 43:13
shall fall by the *e* of the sword ... Lk 21:24
escaped the *e* of the sword, out ... Heb 11:34

**EDGES**
joined at the two *e* thereof ... Ex 28:7
by the two *e* was it coupled ... Ex 39:4
made him a dagger which had two *e* .. Judg 3:16
hath the sharp sword with two *e* ... Rev 2:12

**EDIFICATION**
his neighbour for his good to *e* ... Rom 15:2
speaketh unto men to *e*, and ... 1Cor 14:3
the Lord hath given us for *e* ... 2Cor 10:8
which the Lord hath given me to *e* ... 2Cor 13:10

**EDIFIED**
and Galilee and Samaria, and were *e* ... Acts 9:31
well, but the other is not *e* ... 1Cor 14:17

**EDIFIETH**
puffeth up, but charity *e* ... 1Cor 8:1
in an unknown tongue *e* himself ... 1Cor 14:4
he that prophesieth *e* the church ... 1Cor 14:4

**EDIFY**
wherewith one may *e* another ... Rom 14:19
for me, but all things *e* not ... 1Cor 10:23
*e* one another, even as also ye do ... 1Th 5:11

**EDIFYING**
that the church may receive *e* ... 1Cor 14:5
may excel to the *e* of the church ... 1Cor 14:12
Let all things be done unto *e* ... 1Cor 14:26
dearly beloved, for your *e* ... 2Cor 12:19
for the *e* of the body of Christ ... Eph 4:12
body unto the *e* of itself in love ... Eph 4:16
which is good to the use of *e* ... Eph 4:29
than godly *e* which is in faith ... 1Ti 1:4

**EDOM** (*e'-dum*) See EDOMITES, ESAU, IDUMEA, OBED-EDOM.
*1. Another name for Esau.*
children of Seir in the land of *E* ... Gen 36:21
that reigned in the land of *E* ... Gen 36:31
Bela the son of Beor reigned in *E* ... Gen 36:32
these be the dukes of *E*, ... Gen 36:43
the dukes of *E* shall be amazed ... Ex 15:15
from Kadesh unto the king of *E* ... Num 20:14
*E* said unto him, Thou shalt not ... Num 20:18
*E* came out against him with much .. Num 20:20
Thus *E* refused to give Israel ... Num 20:21
by the coast of the land of *E* ... Num 20:23
Red sea, to compass the land of *E* ... Num 21:4
*E* shall be a possession, Seir ... Num 24:18
Hor, in the edge of the land of *E* ... Num 33:37
of Zin along by the coast of *E* ... Num 34:3
even to the border of *E* the ... Josh 15:1
coast of *E* southward were Kabzeel ... Josh 15:21
marchedst out of the field of *E* ... Judg 5:4
messengers unto the king of *E* ... Judg 11:17
but the king of *E* would not ... Judg 11:17
and compassed the land of *E* ... Judg 11:18
children of Ammon, and against *E* ... 1Sa 14:47
And he put garrisons in *E* ... 2Sa 8:14
throughout all *E* put he garrisons ... 2Sa 8:14
all they of *E* became David's ... 2Sa 8:14
of the Red sea, in the land of *E* ... 1Kin 9:26
he was of the king's seed in *E* ... 1Kin 11:14
came to pass, when David was in *E* .. 1Kin 11:15
he had smitten every male in *E* ... 1Kin 11:15
he had cut off every male in *E* ... 1Kin 11:16
There was then no king in *E* ... 1Kin 22:47
way through the wilderness of *E* ... 2Kin 3:8
king of Judah, and the king of *E* ... 2Kin 3:9
the king of *E* went down to him ... 2Kin 3:12
there came water by the way of *E* ... 2Kin 3:20
through even unto the king of *E* ... 2Kin 3:26
In his days *E* revolted from under ... 2Kin 8:20
Yet *E* revolted from under the ... 2Kin 8:22
He slew of *E* in the valley of ... 2Kin 14:7
Thou hast indeed smitten *E* ... 2Kin 14:10
that reigned in the land of *E* ... 1Chr 1:43
And the dukes of *E* were ... 1Chr 1:51
These are the dukes of *E* ... 1Chr 1:54
from *E*, and from Moab ... 1Chr 18:11
And he put garrisons in *E* ... 1Chr 18:13
at the sea side in the land of *E* ... 2Chr 8:17
they sought after the gods of *E* ... 2Chr 25:20
smote of *E* in the valley of salt ... Ps 60:*t*
over *E* will I cast out my shoe ... Ps 60:8
who will lead me into *E* ... Ps 60:9
The tabernacles of *E*, and the ... Ps 83:6
over *E* will I cast out my shoe ... Ps 108:9
who will lead me into *E* ... Ps 108:10
the children of *E* in the day of ... Ps 137:7
they shall lay their hand upon *E* ... Is 11:14
Who is this that cometh from *E* ... Is 63:1
Egypt, and Judah, and *E*, and the ... Jer 9:26
*E*, and Moab, and the children of ... Jer 25:21
And send them to the king of *E* ... Jer 27:3
and among the Ammonites, and in *E* ... Jer 40:11
Concerning *E*, thus saith the LORD ... Jer 49:7
Also *E* shall be a desolation ... Jer 49:17
that he hath taken against *E* ... Jer 49:20
*E* be as the heart of a woman in ... Jer 49:22
and be glad, O daughter of *E* ... Lam 4:21
thine iniquity, O daughter of *E* ... Lam 4:22
Because that *E* hath dealt against ... Eze 25:12
also stretch out mine hand upon *E* ... Eze 25:13
I will lay my vengeance upon *E* by ... Eze 25:14
they shall do in *E* according to ... Eze 25:14
There is *E*, her kings, and all her ... Eze 32:29
escape out of his hand, even *E* ... Dan 11:41
*E* shall be a desolate wilderness, ... Joel 3:19
to deliver them up to *E* ... Amos 1:6
up the whole captivity to *E* ... Amos 1:9
For three transgressions of *E* ... Amos 1:11
bones of the king of *E* into lime ... Amos 2:1
they may possess the remnant of *E* ... Amos 9:12
saith the Lord GOD concerning *E* ... Obad 1
destroy the wise men out of *E* ... Obad 8
Whereas *E* saith, We are ... Mal 1:4
*2. Descendants of Esau.*
therefore was his name called *E* ... Gen 25:30
land of Seir, the country of *E* ... Gen 32:3
the generations of Esau, who is *E* ... Gen 36:1
Esau is *E* ... Gen 36:8
came of Eliphaz in the land of *E* ... Gen 36:16
came of Reuel in the land of *E* ... Gen 36:17
are the sons of Esau, who is *E* ... Gen 36:19

**EDOMITE** (*e'-dum-ite*) See EDOMITES. *A descendant of Esau.*
Thou shalt not abhor an *E* ... Deut 23:7
and his name was Doeg, an *E* ... 1Sa 21:7
Then answered Doeg the *E*, which ... 1Sa 22:9
And Doeg the *E* turned, and he fell ... 1Sa 22:18
day, when Doeg the *E* was there ... 1Sa 22:22
unto Solomon, Hadad the *E* ... 1Kin 11:14
of David, when Doeg the *E* came ... Ps 52:*t*

**EDOMITES** (*e'-dum-ites*)
the father of the *E* in mount Seir ... Gen 36:9
he is Esau the father of the *E* ... Gen 36:43
of the Moabites, Ammonites, *E* ... 1Kin 11:1
certain *E* of his father's ... 1Kin 11:17
smote the *E* which compassed him ... 2Kin 8:21
the son Zeruiah slew of the *E* in ... 1Chr 18:12
all the *E* became David's servants ... 1Chr 18:13
In his days the *E* revolted from ... 2Chr 21:8
smote the *E* which compassed him ... 2Chr 21:9
So the *E* revolted from under the ... 2Chr 21:10
come from the slaughter of the *E* ... 2Chr 25:14
Lo, thou hast smitten the *E* ... 2Chr 25:19
For again the *E* had come and ... 2Chr 28:17

**EDREI** (*ed'-re-i*)
*1. A city in Bashan.*
his people, to the battle at *E* ... Num 21:33
which dwelt at Astaroth in *E* ... Deut 1:4
and all his people, to battle at *E* ... Deut 3:1
and all Bashan, unto Salchah and *E* ... Deut 3:10
that dwelt at Ashtaroth and at *E* ... Josh 12:4
reigned in Ashtaroth and in *E* ... Josh 13:12
half Gilead, and Ashtaroth, and *E* ... Josh 13:31
*2. A city in Naphtali*
And Kedesh, and *E*, and En-hazor, ... Josh 19:37

**EFFECT**
she bound her soul, of none *e* ... Num 30:8
and they spake to her to that *e* ... 2Chr 34:22
devices of the people of none *e* ... Ps 33:10
the *e* of righteousness quietness ... Is 32:17
his lies shall not so *e* it ... Jer 48:30
at hand, and the *e* of every vision ... Eze 12:23
God of none *e* by your tradition ... Mt 15:6
of none *e* through your tradition ... Mk 7:13
make the faith of God without *e* ... Rom 3:3
and the promise made of none *e* ... Rom 4:14
the word of God hath taken none *e* ... Rom 9:6
Christ should be made of none *e* ... 1Cor 1:17
should make the promise of none *e* ... Gal 3:17
Christ is become of no *e* unto you ... Gal 5:4

**EFFECTED**
his own house, he prosperously *e* ... 2Chr 7:11

**EFFECTUAL**
*e* is opened unto me, and there are ... 1Cor 16:9
which is *e* in the enduring of the ... 2Cor 1:6
me by the *e* working of his power ... Eph 3:7
according to the *e* working in the ... Eph 4:16
of thy faith may become *e* by the ... Philem 6
The *e* fervent prayer of a ... Jas 5:16

**EFFECTUALLY**
(For he that wrought *e* in Peter ... Gal 2:8
which *e* worketh also in you that ... 1Th 2:13

**EFFEMINATE**
idolaters, nor adulterers, nor *e* ... 1Cor 6:9

**EGG**
any taste in the white of an *e* ... Job 6:6
Or if he shall ask an *e*, will he ... Lk 11:12

**EGGS**
whether they be young ones, or *e* ... Deut 22:6
upon the young, or upon the *e* ... Deut 22:6
Which leaveth her *e* in the earth ... Job 39:14
as one gathereth *e* that are left ... Is 10:14
They hatch cockatrice' *e*, and ... Is 59:5
he that eateth of their *e* dieth ... Is 59:5
As the partridge sitteth on *e* ... Jer 17:11

**EGLAH** (*eg'-lah*) See MICHAL. *A wife of David.*
sixth, Ithream, by *E* David's wife ... 2Sa 3:5
the sixth, Ithream by *E* his wife ... 1Chr 3:3

**EGLAIM** (*eg'-la-im*) See EN-EGLAIM. *A Moabite city.*
the howling thereof unto *E* ... Is 15:8

**EGLON** (*eg'-lon*)
*1. An Amorite city.*
Lachish, and unto Debir king of *E* ... Josh 10:3
king of Lachish, the king of *E* ... Josh 10:5
king of Lachish, and the king of *E* ... Josh 10:23
from Lachish Joshua passed unto *E* ... Josh 10:34
And Joshua went up from *E*, and all . Josh 10:36
to all that he had done to *E* ... Josh 10:37
The king of *E*, one ... Josh 12:12
Lachish, and Bozkath, and *E* ... Josh 15:39
*2. A Moabite king.*
the LORD strengthened *E* the king ... Judg 3:12
the children of Israel served *E* ... Judg 3:14
a present unto *E* the king of Moab ... Judg 3:15
the present unto *E* king of Moab ... Judg 3:17
and *E* was a very fat man ... Judg 3:17

**EGYPT** (*e'-jipt*) See PREFACE. SEE ALSO EGYPTIAN, MIZRAIM. *Kingdom in northeast Africa.*
went down into *E* to sojourn there ... Gen 12:10
sold him into *E* unto Potiphar ... Gen 37:36
your brother, whom ye sold into *E* ... Gen 45:4
land of Canaan, and came into *E* ... Gen 46:6
the children of Israel out of *E* ... Ex 3:10
of the land of *E* by their armies ... Ex 12:51
day, in which ye came out from *E* ... Ex 13:3
there is a people come out from *E* ... Num 22:5
Thou hast brought a vine out of *E* ... Ps 80:8
The burden of *E* ... Is 19:1
be a highway out of *E* to Assyria ... Is 19:23
*E* is like a very fair heifer, but ... Jer 46:20
And they committed whoredoms in *E* ... Eze 23:3
and they shall spoil the pomp of *E* ... Eze 32:12
and his mother, and flee into *E* ... Mt 2:13
By faith he forsook *E*, not ... Heb 11:27

**EGYPTIAN** (*e-jip'-shun*) See EGYPTIAN'S, EGYPTIANS.
*1. An inhabitant of Egypt.*
and she had an handmaid, an *E* ... Gen 16:1
wife took Hagar her maid the *E* ... Gen 16:3
Sarah saw the son of Hagar the *E* ... Gen 21:9
Abraham's son, whom Hagar the *E* ... Gen 25:12
captain of the guard, an *E* ... Gen 39:1
in the house of his master the *E* ... Gen 39:2
women are not as the *E* women ... Ex 1:19
he spied an *E* smiting an Hebrew, ... Ex 2:11
there was no man, he slew the *E* ... Ex 2:12
kill me, as thou killedst the *E* ... Ex 2:14
An *E* delivered us out of the hand ... Ex 2:19
woman, whose father was an *E* ... Lev 24:10
thou shalt not abhor an *E* ... Deut 23:7
And they found an *E* in the field ... 1Sa 30:11
And he slew an *E*, a goodly man ... 2Sa 23:21
the *E* had a spear in his hand ... 2Sa 23:21
And Sheshan had a servant, an *E* ... 1Chr 2:34
And he slew an *E*, a man of great ... 1Chr 11:23
the *E* into Assyria, and the ... Is 19:23
was oppressed, and smote the *E* ... Acts 7:24
as thou diddest the *E* yesterday ... Acts 7:28
Art not thou that *E*, which before ... Acts 21:38
*2. The Red Sea.*
destroy the tongue of the *E* sea ... Is 11:15

**EGYPTIAN'S** (*e-jip'-shuns*)
the E house for Joseph's sake ... Gen 39:5
the spear out of the E hand ... 2Sa 23:21
in the E hand was a spear like a ... 1Chr 11:23
the spear out of the E hand ... 1Chr 11:23

**EGYPTIANS** (*e-jip'-shuns*)
when the E shall see thee, that ... Gen 12:12
the E beheld the woman that she ... Gen 12:14
and Pharaoh said unto all the E ... Gen 41:55
storehouses, and sold unto the E ... Gen 41:56
them by themselves, and for the E ... Gen 43:32
because the E might not eat bread ... Gen 43:32
that is an abomination unto the E ... Gen 43:32
and the E and the house of Pharaoh ... Gen 45:2
is an abomination unto the E ... Gen 46:34
all the E came unto Joseph, and ... Gen 47:15
for the E sold every man his ... Gen 47:20
the E mourned for him threescore ... Gen 50:3
is a grievous mourning to the E ... Gen 50:11
the E made the children of Israel ... Ex 1:13
them out of the hand of the E ... Ex 3:8
wherewith the E oppress them ... Ex 3:9
favour in the sight of the E ... Ex 3:21
and ye shall spoil the E ... Ex 3:22
whom the E keep in bondage ... Ex 6:5
from under the burdens of the E ... Ex 6:6
from under the burdens of the E ... Ex 6:7
the E shall know that I am the ... Ex 7:5
the E shall lothe to drink of the ... Ex 7:18
the E could not drink of the ... Ex 7:21
all the E digged round about the ... Ex 7:24
the houses of the E shall be full ... Ex 8:21
of the E to the LORD our God ... Ex 8:26
of the E before their eyes ... Ex 8:26
the magicians, and upon all the E ... Ex 9:11
and the houses of all the E ... Ex 10:6
favour in the sight of the E ... Ex 11:3
put a difference between the E ... Ex 11:7
will pass through to smite the E ... Ex 12:23
in Egypt, when he smote the E ... Ex 12:27
and all his servants, and all the E ... Ex 12:30
the E were urgent upon the people ... Ex 12:33
of the E jewels of silver ... Ex 12:35
favour in the sight of the E ... Ex 12:36
And they spoiled the E ... Ex 12:36
that the E may know that I am the ... Ex 14:4
But the E pursued after them, all ... Ex 14:9
behold, the E marched after them ... Ex 14:10
us alone, that we may serve the E ... Ex 14:12
been better for us to serve the E ... Ex 14:12
for the E whom ye have seen to ... Ex 14:13
I will harden the hearts of the E ... Ex 14:17
the E shall know that I am the ... Ex 14:18
it came between the camp of the E ... Ex 14:20
the E pursued, and went in after ... Ex 14:23
the E through the pillar of fire ... Ex 14:24
and troubled the host of the E ... Ex 14:24
so that the E said, Let us flee ... Ex 14:25
fighteth for them against the E ... Ex 14:25
waters may come again upon the E ... Ex 14:26
and the E fled against it ... Ex 14:27
the LORD overthrew the E in the ... Ex 14:27
that day out of the hand of the E ... Ex 14:30
Israel saw the E dead upon the ... Ex 14:30
which the LORD did upon the E ... Ex 14:31
which I have brought upon the E ... Ex 15:26
to the E for Israel's sake, and ... Ex 18:8
out of the hand of the E ... Ex 18:9
you out of the hand of the E ... Ex 18:10
from under the hand of the E ... Ex 18:10
have seen what I did unto the E ... Ex 19:4
Wherefore should the E speak ... Ex 32:12
Then the E shall hear it, (for ... Num 14:13
the E vexed us, and our fathers ... Num 20:15
hand in the sight of all the E ... Num 33:3
For the E buried all their ... Num 33:4
the E evil entreated us, and ... Deut 26:6
the E pursued after your fathers ... Josh 24:6
put darkness between you and the E .. Josh 24:7
you out of the hand of the E ... Judg 6:9
Did not I deliver you from the E ... Judg 10:11
the E with all the plagues in the ... 1Sa 4:8
ye harden your hearts, as the E ... 1Sa 6:6
you out of the hand of the E ... 1Sa 10:18
Hittites, and the kings of the E ... 2Kin 7:6
Ammonites, the Moabites, the E ... Ezr 9:1
set the E against the E ... Is 19:2
the E will I give over into the ... Is 19:4
the E shall know the LORD in that ... Is 19:21
the E shall serve with the ... Is 19:23
Assyria lead away the E prisoners ... Is 20:4
For the E shall help in vain, and ... Is 30:7
Now the E are men, and not God ... Is 31:3
of the E shall he burn with fire ... Jer 43:13
We have given the hand to the E ... Lam 5:6
with the E thy neighbours ... Eze 16:26
the E for the paps of thy youth ... Eze 23:21
scatter the E among the nations ... Eze 29:12
E from the people whither they ... Eze 29:13
scatter the E among the nations ... Eze 30:23
scatter the E among the nations ... Eze 30:26
in all the wisdom of the E ... Acts 7:22
which the E assaying to do were ... Heb 11:29

**EHI** (*e'-hi*) See AHARAH. *A son of Benjamin.*
and Ashbel, Gera, and Naaman, E ... Gen 46:21

**EHUD** (*e'-hud*)
*1. A son of Gera.*
E the son of Gera, a Benjamite, a ... Judg 3:15
But E made him a dagger which had .. Judg 3:16
And E came unto him ... Judg 3:20
E said, I have a message from God ... Judg 3:20
E put forth his left hand, and ... Judg 3:21
Then E went forth through the ... Judg 3:23
E escaped while they tarried, and ... Judg 3:26
of the LORD, when E was dead ... Judg 4:1
*2. A great-grandson of Benjamin.*
Jeush, and Benjamin, and E, and ... 1Chr 7:10
And these are the sons of E ... 1Chr 8:6

**EIGHT**
Seth were e hundred years ... Gen 5:4
after he begat Enos e hundred ... Gen 5:7
after he begat Cainan e hundred ... Gen 5:10
he begat Mahalaleel e hundred ... Gen 5:13
after he begat Jared e hundred ... Gen 5:16
Mahalaleel were e hundred ninety ... Gen 5:17
he begat Enoch e hundred years ... Gen 5:19
he that is e days old shall be ... Gen 17:12
his son Isaac being e days old ... Gen 21:4
these e Milcah did bear to Nahor, ... Gen 22:23
length of one curtain shall be e ... Ex 26:2
And they shall be e boards ... Ex 26:25
e cubits, and the breadth of one ... Ex 36:9
And there were e boards ... Ex 36:30
e thousand and an hundred, ... Num 2:24
were e thousand and six hundred, ... Num 3:28
were e thousand and five hundred ... Num 4:48
e oxen he gave unto the sons of ... Num 7:8
And on the sixth day e bullocks ... Num 29:29
shall be forty and e cities ... Num 35:7
Zered, was thirty and e years ... Deut 2:14
e cities with their suburbs ... Josh 21:41
served Chushan-rishathaim e years ... Judg 3:8
and he judged Israel e years ... Judg 12:14
Now Eli was ninety and e years old ... 1Sa 4:15
and he had e sons ... 1Sa 17:12
up his spear against e hundred ... 2Sa 23:8
there were in Israel e hundred ... 2Sa 24:9
ten cubits, and stones of e cubits ... 1Kin 7:10
he reigned e years in Jerusalem ... 2Kin 8:17
in Samaria was twenty and e years ... 2Kin 10:36
Josiah was e years old when he ... 2Kin 22:1
e hundred, ready armed to the war ... 1Chr 12:24
e hundred, mighty men of valour, ... 1Chr 12:30
e thousand and six hundred ... 1Chr 12:35
their brethren, threescore and e ... 1Chr 16:38
by man, was thirty and e thousand ... 1Chr 23:3
e among the sons of Ithamar ... 1Chr 24:4
was two hundred fourscore and e ... 1Chr 25:7
e sons, and threescore daughters ... 2Chr 11:21
in array against him with e ... 2Chr 13:3
he reigned e years in Jerusalem ... 2Chr 21:5
he reigned in Jerusalem e years ... 2Chr 21:20
the house of the LORD in e days ... 2Chr 29:17
Josiah was e years old when he ... 2Chr 34:1
Jehoiachin was e years old when ... 2Chr 36:9
and Joab, two thousand e hundred ... Ezr 2:6
of Ater of Hezekiah, ninety and e ... Ezr 2:16
Anathoth, an hundred twenty and e ... Ezr 2:23
of Asaph, an hundred twenty and e ... Ezr 2:41
and with him twenty and e males ... Ezr 8:11
thousand and e hundred and eighteen. Neh 7:11
of Zattu, e hundred forty and five ... Neh 7:13
of Binnui, six hundred forty and e ... Neh 7:15
of Bebai, six hundred twenty and e ... Neh 7:16
of Ater of Hezekiah, ninety and e ... Neh 7:21
Hashum, three hundred twenty and e.. Neh 7:22
an hundred fourscore and e ... Neh 7:26
Anathoth, an hundred twenty and e ... Neh 7:27
of Asaph, an hundred forty and e ... Neh 7:44
of Shobai, an hundred thirty and e ... Neh 7:45
threescore and e valiant men ... Neh 11:6
Sallai, nine hundred twenty and e ... Neh 11:8
the house were e hundred twenty ... Neh 11:12
of valour, an hundred twenty and e ... Neh 11:14
a portion to seven, and also to e ... Eccl 11:2
escaped from Johanan with e men ... Jer 41:15
from Jerusalem e hundred thirty ... Jer 52:29
the porch of the gate, e cubits ... Eze 40:9
and the going up to it had e steps ... Eze 40:31
and the going up to it had e steps ... Eze 40:34
and the going up to it had e steps ... Eze 40:37
e tables, whereupon they slew ... Eze 40:41
shepherds, and e principal men ... Mic 5:5
when e days were accomplished for ... Lk 2:21
an e days after these sayings ... Lk 9:28
an infirmity thirty and e years ... Jn 5:5
after e days again his disciples ... Jn 20:26
which had kept his bed e years ... Acts 9:33
e souls were saved by water ... 1Pet 3:20

**EIGHTEEN**
his own house, three hundred and e ... Gen 14:14
Eglon the king of Moab e years ... Judg 3:14
e years, all the children of ... Judg 10:8
of Israel again e thousand men ... Judg 20:25
fell of Benjamin e thousand men ... Judg 20:44
of salt, being e thousand men ... 2Sa 8:13
of brass, of e cubits high apiece ... 1Kin 7:15
Jehoiachin was e years old when ... 2Kin 24:8
of the one pillar was e cubits ... 2Kin 25:17
half tribe of Manasseh e thousand ... 1Chr 12:31
in the valley of salt e thousand ... 1Chr 18:12
sons and brethren, strong men, e ... 1Chr 26:9
of brass e thousand talents, and ... 1Chr 29:7
(for he took e wives, and ... 2Chr 11:21
with him two hundred and e males ... Ezr 8:9
with his sons and his brethren, e ... Ezr 8:18
thousand and eight hundred and e ... Neh 7:11
height of one pillar was e cubits ... Jer 52:21
round about e thousand measures ... Eze 48:35
Or those e, upon whom the tower ... Lk 13:4
had a spirit of infirmity e years ... Lk 13:11
hath bound, lo, these e years ... Lk 13:16

**EIGHTEENTH**
Now in the e year of king ... 1Kin 15:1
over Israel in Samaria the e year ... 2Kin 3:1
pass in the e year of king Josiah ... 2Kin 22:3
But in the e year of king Josiah, ... 2Kin 23:23
to Hezir, the e to Aphses, ... 1Chr 24:15
The e to Hanani, he, his sons, and ... 1Chr 25:25
Now in the e year of king ... 2Chr 13:1
Now in the e year of his reign, ... 2Chr 34:8
In the e year of the reign of ... 2Chr 35:19
of Judah, which was the e year of ... Jer 32:1
In the e year of Nebuchadrezzar ... Jer 52:29

**EIGHTH**
on the e day thou shalt give it ... Ex 22:30
And it came to pass on the e day ... Lev 9:1
in the e day the flesh of his ... Lev 12:3
on the e day he shall take two he ... Lev 14:10
he shall bring them on the e day ... Lev 14:23
on the e day he shall take to him ... Lev 15:14
on the e day she shall take unto ... Lev 15:29
and from the e day and thenceforth ... Lev 22:27
on the e day shall be an holy ... Lev 23:36
on the e day shall be a sabbath ... Lev 23:39
And ye shall sow the e year ... Lev 25:22
on the e day he shall bring two ... Num 6:10
On the e day offered Gamaliel the ... Num 7:54
On the e day ye shall have a ... Num 29:35
month Bul, which is the e month ... 1Kin 6:38
On the e day he sent the people ... 1Kin 8:66
ordained a feast in the e month ... 1Kin 12:32
the fifteenth day of the e month ... 1Kin 12:33
e year of Asa king of Judah began ... 1Kin 16:29
e year of Azariah king of Judah ... 2Kin 15:8
him in the e year of his reign ... 2Kin 24:12
Johanan the e, Elzabad the ninth, ... 1Chr 12:12
to Hakkoz, the e to Abijah, ... 1Chr 24:10
The e to Jeshaiah, he, his sons, ... 1Chr 25:15
the seventh, Peulthai the e ... 1Chr 26:5
e captain for the e month ... 1Chr 27:11
in the e day they made a solemn ... 2Chr 7:9
on the e day of the month came ... 2Chr 29:17
For in the e year of his reign, ... 2Chr 34:3
on the e day was a solemn ... Neh 8:18
it shall be, that upon the e day ... Eze 43:27
In the e month, in the second ... Zec 1:1
that on the e day they came to ... Lk 1:59
and circumcised him the e day ... Acts 7:8
Circumcised the e day, of the ... Phil 3:5
but saved Noah the e person ... 2Pet 2:5
was, and is not, even he is the e ... Rev 17:11
the e, beryl ... Rev 21:20

**EIGHTIETH**
e year after the children of ... 1Kin 6:1

**EIGHTY**
And Methuselah lived an hundred e ... Gen 5:25
he begat Lamech seven hundred e ... Gen 5:26
And Lamech lived an hundred e ... Gen 5:28

**EITHER**
speak not to Jacob e good or bad ... Gen 31:24
speak not to Jacob e good or bad ... Gen 31:29
took e of them his censer, and put ... Lev 10:1
e in the warp, or in the woof, or ... Lev 13:49
e in the warp, or in the woof, or ... Lev 13:51
e in the warp, or in the woof, or ... Lev 13:53
e in the warp, or in the woof, or ... Lev 13:57
e warp, or woof, or whatsoever ... Lev 13:58
e in the warp, or woof, or any ... Lev 13:59
E a bullock or a lamb that hath ... Lev 22:23
E his uncle, or his uncle's son, ... Lev 25:49
When e man or woman shall ... Num 6:2
where was no way to turn e to the ... Num 22:26
to do e good or bad of mine own ... Num 24:13
e the sun, or moon, or any of the ... Deut 17:3
also shall not leave thee e corn ... Deut 28:51
e that all the sons of Jerubbaal, ... Judg 9:2
will do nothing e great or small ... 1Sa 20:2
e that thou hast shed blood ... 1Sa 25:31
e great or small, but carried ... 1Sa 30:2
did compass e of them about ... 1Kin 7:15
there were stays on e side on the ... 1Kin 10:19
e he is talking, or he is ... 1Kin 18:27
E three years' famine ... 1Chr 21:12
Judah sat e of them on his throne ... 2Chr 18:9
no man knoweth e love or hatred ... Eccl 9:1
e this or that, or whether they ... Eccl 11:6
ask it e in the depth, or in the ... Is 7:11
e the groves, or the images ... Is 17:8
e on the right hand, or on the ... Eze 21:16
for e he will hate the one, and ... Mt 6:24
E make the tree good, and his ... Mt 12:33
E how canst thou say to thy ... Lk 6:42
E what woman having ten pieces of ... Lk 15:8
for e he will hate the one, and ... Lk 16:13
on e side one, and Jesus in the ... Jn 19:18
but e to tell, or to hear some ... Acts 17:21
speak to you e by revelation ... 1Cor 14:6
attained, e were already perfect ... Phil 3:12
e a vine, figs ... Jas 3:12
on e side of the river, was there ... Rev 22:2

**EKER** (*e'-ker*) *Descendant of Judah.*
were, Maaz, and Jamin, and E ... 1Chr 2:27

**EKRON** (*ec'-ron*) See EKRONITES. *A Philistine city.*
unto the borders of E northward ... Josh 13:3
out unto the side of E northward ... Josh 15:11

*E*, with her towns and her villages ... Josh 15:45
From *E* even unto the sea, all ... Josh 15:46
And Elon, and Thimnathah, and *E* ... Josh 19:43
and *E* with the coast thereof ... Judg 1:18
they sent the ark of God to *E* ... 1Sa 5:10
pass, as the ark of God came to *E* ... 1Sa 5:10
they returned to *E* the same day ... 1Sa 6:16
one, for Gath one, for *E* one ... 1Sa 6:17
to Israel, from *E* even unto Gath ... 1Sa 7:14
the valley, and to the gates of *E* ... 1Sa 17:52
even unto Gath, and unto *E* ... 1Sa 17:52
of Baal-zebub the god of *E* ... 2Kin 1:2
of Baal-zebub the god of *E* ... 2Kin 1:3
of Baal-zebub the god of *E* ... 2Kin 1:6
of Baal-zebub the god of *E* ... 2Kin 1:16
and Ashkelon, and Azzah, and *E* ... Jer 25:20
I will turn mine hand against *E* ... Amos 1:8
noonday, and *E* shall be rooted up ... Zeph 2:4
it, and be very sorrowful, and *E* ... Zec 9:5
in Judah, and *E* as a Jebusite ... Zec 9:7

**EKRONITES** (*ek'-ron-ites*) *Inhabitants of Ekron.*
the Gittites, and the *E* ... Josh 13:3
that the *E* cried out, saying, ... 1Sa 5:10

**ELADAH** (*el'-a-dah*) *A descendant of Ephraim.*
*E* his son, and Tahath his son, ... 1Chr 7:20

**ELAH** (*e'-lah*)
*1. An Edomite prince.*
Duke Aholibamah, duke *E*, duke ... Gen 36:41
Duke Aholibamah, duke *E*, duke ... 1Chr 1:52
*2. A valley in Judah.*
and pitched by the valley of *E* ... 1Sa 17:2
Israel, were in the valley of *E* ... 1Sa 17:19
thou slewest in the valley of *E* ... 1Sa 21:9
*3. Father of Shimei.*
Shimei the son of *E*, in Benjamin ... 1Kin 4:18
*4. Son of King Baasha of Israel.*
*E* his son reigned in his stead ... 1Kin 16:6
*E* the son of Baasha to reign over ... 1Kin 16:8
Baasha, and the sins of *E* his son ... 1Kin 16:13
Now the rest of the acts of *E* ... 1Kin 16:14
*5. Father of King Hoshea of Israel.*
Hoshea the son of *E* made a ... 2Kin 15:30
Judah began Hoshea the son of *E* ... 2Kin 17:1
of Hoshea son of *E* king of Israel ... 2Kin 18:1
of Hoshea son of *E* king of Israel ... 2Kin 18:9
*6. A son of Caleb.*
of Jephunneh; Iru, *E* ... 1Chr 4:15
and the sons of *E*, even Kenaz ... 1Chr 4:15
*7. A Benjamite.*
*E* the son of Uzzi, the son of ... 1Chr 9:8

**ELAM** (*e'-lam*) See ELAMITES, PERSIA.
*1. A son of Shem.*
*E*, and Asshur, and Arphaxad ... Gen 10:22
*E*, and Asshur, and Arphaxad ... 1Chr 1:17
*2. Land of the Elamites.*
Ellasar, Chedorlaomer king of *E* ... Gen 14:1
With Chedorlaomer the king of *E* ... Gen 14:9
Pathros, and from Cush, and from *E* ... Is 11:11
Go up, O *E*: ... Is 21:2
*E* bare the quiver with chariots ... Is 22:6
of Zimri, and all the kings of *E* ... Jer 25:25
*E* in the beginning of the reign ... Jer 49:34
Behold, I will break the bow of *E* ... Jer 49:35
upon *E* will I bring the four ... Jer 49:36
the outcasts of *E* shall not come ... Jer 49:36
For I will cause *E* to be dismayed ... Jer 49:37
And I will set my throne in *E* ... Jer 49:38
bring again the captivity of *E* ... Jer 49:39
There is *E* and all her multitude ... Eze 32:24
which is in the province of *E* ... Dan 8:2
*3. Son of Shashak.*
And Hananiah, and *E* ... 1Chr 8:24
*4. A son of Meshelemiah.*
*E* the fifth, Jehohanan the sixth, ... 1Chr 26:3
*5. A family of exiles with Zerubbabel.*
The children of *E*, a thousand two ... Ezr 2:7
The children of *E*, a thousand two ... Neh 7:12
*6. A family of exiles with Zerubbabel.*
The children of the other *E* ... Ezr 2:31
The children of the other *E* ... Neh 7:34
*7. A family of exiles with Ezra.*
And of the sons of *E* ... Ezr 8:7
*8. An ancestor of Shechaniah.*
of Jehiel, one of the sons of *E* ... Ezr 10:2
And of the sons of *E* ... Ezr 10:26
*9. A chief who renewed the covenant.*
Parosh, Pahath-moab, *E*, Zatthu, ... Neh 10:14
*10. A priest who purified the wall.*
and Malchijah, and *E* ... Neh 12:42

**ELAMITES** (*e'-lam-ites*) See PERSIANS. *Foreign settlers in Samaria.*
the Dehavites, and the *E*, ... Ezr 4:9
Parthians, and Medes, and *E* ... Acts 2:9

**ELASAH** (*el'-a-sah*) See ELEASA.
*1. Married a foreign wife.*
Ishmael, Nethaneel, Jozabad, and *E* ... Ezr 10:22
*2. An ambassador of Hezekiah.*
By the hand of *E* the son of ... Jer 29:3

**ELATH** (*e'-lath*) See ELOTH. *An Elamite port.*
the way of the plain from *E* ... Deut 2:8
He built *E*, and restored it to ... 2Kin 14:22
of Syria recovered *E* to Syria ... 2Kin 16:6
and drave the Jews from *E* ... 2Kin 16:6
and the Syrians came to *E*, and ... 2Kin 16:6

**EL-BERITH** See BERITH.

**EL-BETH-EL**
an altar, and called the place *E* ... Gen 35:7

**ELDAAH** (*el'-da-ah*) *A son of Midian.*
Hanoch, and Abidah, and *E* ... Gen 25:4
Epher, and Henoch, and Abida, and *E* ... 1Chr 1:33

**ELDAD** (*el'-dad*) *An elder and prophet with Moses.*
camp, the name of the one was *E* ... Num 11:26
man, and told Moses, and said, *E* ... Num 11:27

**ELDER**
the brother of Japheth the *e* ... Gen 10:21
the *e* shall serve the younger ... Gen 25:23
these words of Esau her *e* son ... Gen 27:42
the name of the *e* was Leah ... Gen 29:16
Behold my *e* daughter Merab, her ... 1Sa 18:17
for he is mine *e* brother ... 1Kin 2:22
aged men, much *e* than thy father ... Job 15:10
because they were *e* than he ... Job 32:4
thine *e* sister is Samaria, she and ... Eze 16:46
receive thy sisters, thine *e* ... Eze 16:61
names of them were Aholah the *e* ... Eze 23:4
Now his *e* son was in the field ... Lk 15:25
The *e* shall serve the younger ... Rom 9:12
Rebuke not an *e*, but intreat him ... 1Ti 5:1
The *e* women as mothers ... 1Ti 5:2
Against an *e* receive not an ... 1Ti 5:19
you I exhort, who am also an *e* ... 1Pet 5:1
submit yourselves unto the *e* ... 1Pet 5:5
The *e* unto the elect lady and her ... 2Jn 1
The *e* unto the wellbeloved Gaius, ... 3Jn 1

**ELDERS**
of Pharaoh, the *e* of his house ... Gen 50:7
all the *e* of the land of Egypt, ... Gen 50:7
gather the *e* of Israel together, ... Ex 3:16
the *e* of Israel, unto the king of ... Ex 3:18
the *e* of the children of Israel ... Ex 4:29
called for all the *e* of Israel ... Ex 12:21
take with thee of the *e* of Israel ... Ex 17:5
in the sight of the *e* of Israel ... Ex 17:6
all the *e* of Israel, to eat bread ... Ex 18:12
and called for the *e* of the people ... Ex 19:7
and seventy of the *e* of Israel ... Ex 24:1
and seventy of the *e* of Israel ... Ex 24:9
And he said unto the *e*, Tarry ye ... Ex 24:14
the *e* of the congregation shall ... Lev 4:15
and his sons, and the *e* of Israel ... Lev 9:1
me seventy men of the *e* of Israel ... Num 11:16
knowest to be the *e* of the people ... Num 11:16
men of the *e* of the people ... Num 11:24
and gave it unto the seventy *e* ... Num 11:25
the camp, he and the *e* of Israel ... Num 11:30
the *e* of Israel followed him ... Num 16:25
And Moab said unto the *e* of Midian ... Num 22:4
*e* of Moab and the *e* of Midian ... Num 22:7
heads of your tribes, and your *e* ... Deut 5:23
Then the *e* of his city shall send ... Deut 19:12
Then thy *e* and thy judges shall ... Deut 21:2
even the *e* of that city shall ... Deut 21:3
the *e* of that city shall bring ... Deut 21:4
all the *e* of that city, that are ... Deut 21:6
him out unto the *e* of his city ... Deut 21:19
shall say unto the *e* of his city ... Deut 21:20
the *e* of the city in the gate ... Deut 22:15
father shall say unto the *e* ... Deut 22:16
cloth before the *e* of the city ... Deut 22:17
the *e* of that city shall take ... Deut 22:18
wife go up to the gate unto the *e* ... Deut 25:7
Then the *e* of his city shall call ... Deut 25:8
unto him in the presence of the *e* ... Deut 25:9
Moses with the *e* of Israel ... Deut 27:1
captains of your tribes, your *e* ... Deut 29:10
LORD, and unto all the *e* of Israel ... Deut 31:9
unto me all the *e* of your tribes ... Deut 31:28
thy *e*, and they will tell thee ... Deut 32:7
the *e* of Israel, and put dust upon ... Josh 7:6
the *e* of Israel, before the ... Josh 8:10
And all Israel, and their *e* ... Josh 8:33
Wherefore our *e* and all the ... Josh 9:11
in the ears of the *e* of that city ... Josh 20:4
for all Israel, and for their *e* ... Josh 23:2
and called for the *e* of Israel ... Josh 24:1
all the days of the *e* that ... Josh 24:31
all the days of the *e* that ... Judg 2:7
the *e* thereof, even threescore and ... Judg 8:14
And he took the *e* of the city ... Judg 8:16
the *e* of Gilead went to fetch ... Judg 11:5
said unto the *e* of Gilead ... Judg 11:7
the *e* of Gilead said unto ... Judg 11:8
said unto the *e* of Gilead ... Judg 11:9
the *e* of Gilead said unto ... Judg 11:10
went with the *e* of Gilead ... Judg 11:11
Then the *e* of the congregation ... Judg 21:16
took ten men of the *e* of the city ... Ruth 4:2
before the *e* of my people ... Ruth 4:4
And Boaz said unto the *e*, and unto ... Ruth 4:9
that were in the gate, and the *e* ... Ruth 4:11
the *e* of Israel said, Wherefore ... 1Sa 4:3
Then all the *e* of Israel gathered ... 1Sa 8:4
the *e* of Jabesh said unto him, ... 1Sa 11:3
before the *e* of my people, and ... 1Sa 15:30
the *e* of the town trembled at his ... 1Sa 16:4
of the spoil unto the *e* of Judah ... 1Sa 30:26
with the *e* of Israel, saying, Ye ... 2Sa 3:17
So all the *e* of Israel came to ... 2Sa 5:3
the *e* of his house arose, and went ... 2Sa 12:17
well, and all the *e* of Israel ... 2Sa 17:4
Absalom and the *e* of Israel ... 2Sa 17:15
saying, Speak unto the *e* of Judah ... 2Sa 19:11
Solomon assembled the *e* of Israel ... 1Kin 8:1
all the *e* of Israel came, and the ... 1Kin 8:3
called all the *e* of the land ... 1Kin 20:7
And all the *e* and all the people ... 1Kin 20:8
and sent the letters unto the *e* ... 1Kin 21:8
the men of his city, even the *e* ... 1Kin 21:11
his house, and the *e* sat with him ... 2Kin 6:32
came to him, he said to the *e* ... 2Kin 6:32
the rulers of Jezreel, to the *e* ... 2Kin 10:1
the *e* also, and the bringers up of ... 2Kin 10:5
the *e* of the priests, covered ... 2Kin 19:2
unto him all the *e* of Judah ... 2Kin 23:1
Therefore came all the *e* of ... 1Chr 11:3
the *e* of Israel, and the captains ... 1Chr 15:25
the *e* of Israel, who were clothed ... 1Chr 21:16
Solomon assembled the *e* of Israel ... 2Chr 5:2
And all the *e* of Israel came ... 2Chr 5:4
together all the *e* of Judah ... 2Chr 34:29
God was upon the *e* of the Jews ... Ezr 5:5
Then asked we those *e*, and said ... Ezr 5:9
the *e* of the Jews build this ... Ezr 6:7
*e* of these Jews for the building ... Ezr 6:8
the *e* of the Jews builded, and ... Ezr 6:14
counsel of the princes and the *e* ... Ezr 10:8
and with them the *e* of every city ... Ezr 10:14
him in the assembly of the *e* ... Ps 107:32
sitteth among the *e* of the land ... Prov 31:23
the *e* of the priests covered with ... Is 37:2
up certain of the *e* of the land ... Jer 26:17
of the *e* which were carried away ... Jer 29:1
mine *e* gave up the ghost in the ... Lam 1:19
The *e* of the daughter of Zion sit ... Lam 2:10
priests, they favoured not the *e* ... Lam 4:16
the faces of *e* were not honoured ... Lam 5:12
The *e* have ceased from the gate, ... Lam 5:14
the *e* of Judah sat before me, ... Eze 8:1
of the *e* of Israel unto me ... Eze 14:1
that certain of the *e* of Israel ... Eze 20:1
man, speak unto the *e* of Israel ... Eze 20:3
a solemn assembly, gather the *e* ... Joel 1:14
the congregation, assemble the *e* ... Joel 2:16
transgress the tradition of the *e* ... Mt 15:2
and suffer many things of the *e* ... Mt 16:21
the *e* of the people came unto him ... Mt 21:23
the *e* of the people, unto the ... Mt 26:3
chief priests and *e* of the people ... Mt 26:47
scribes and the *e* were assembled ... Mt 26:57
Now the chief priests, and *e* ... Mt 26:59
*e* of the people took counsel ... Mt 27:1
silver to the chief priests and *e* ... Mt 27:3
accused of the chief priests and *e* ... Mt 27:12
*e* persuaded the multitude that ... Mt 27:20
him, with the scribes and *e* ... Mt 27:41
they were assembled with the *e* ... Mt 28:12
holding the tradition of the *e* ... Mk 7:3
to the tradition of the *e* ... Mk 7:5
things, and be rejected of the *e* ... Mk 8:31
priests, and the scribes, and the *e* ... Mk 11:27
priest and the scribes and the *e* ... Mk 14:43
all the chief priests and the *e* ... Mk 14:53
held a consultation with the *e* ... Mk 15:1
sent unto him the *e* of the Jews ... Lk 7:3
things, and be rejected of the *e* ... Lk 9:22
scribes came upon him with the *e* ... Lk 20:1
captains of the temple, and the *e* ... Lk 22:52
the *e* of the people and the chief ... Lk 22:66
morrow, that their rulers, and *e* ... Acts 4:5
of the people, and *e* of Israel, ... Acts 4:8
priests and *e* had said unto them ... Acts 4:23
stirred up the people, and the *e* ... Acts 6:12
sent it to the *e* by the hands of ... Acts 11:30
ordained them *e* in every church ... Acts 14:23
apostles and *e* about this question ... Acts 15:2
church, and of the apostles and *e* ... Acts 15:4
*e* came together for to consider ... Acts 15:6
Then pleased it the apostles and *e* ... Acts 15:22
The apostles and *e* and brethren ... Acts 15:23
*e* which were at Jerusalem ... Acts 16:4
called the *e* of the church ... Acts 20:17
and all the *e* were present ... Acts 21:18
and all the estate of the *e* ... Acts 22:5
came to the chief priests and *e* ... Acts 23:14
high priest descended with the *e* ... Acts 24:1
the *e* of the Jews informed me, ... Acts 25:15
Let the *e* that rule well be ... 1Ti 5:17
ordain *e* in every city, as I had ... Titus 1:5
For by it the *e* obtained a good ... Heb 11:2
him call for the *e* of the church ... Jas 5:14
The *e* which are among you I ... 1Pet 5:1
twenty *e* sitting, clothed in ... Rev 4:4
twenty *e* fall down before him ... Rev 4:10
one of the *e* saith unto me, Weep ... Rev 5:5
beasts, and in the midst of the *e* ... Rev 5:6
twenty *e* fell down before the ... Rev 5:8
the throne and the beasts and the *e* ... Rev 5:11
twenty *e* fell down and worshipped ... Rev 5:14
about the throne, and about the *e* ... Rev 7:11
And one of the *e* answered, saying ... Rev 7:13
And the four and twenty *e*, which ... Rev 11:16
before the four beasts, and the *e* ... Rev 14:3
And the four and twenty *e* and the ... Rev 19:4

**ELDEST**
unto his *e* servant of his house ... Gen 24:2
not see, he called Esau his *e* son ... Gen 27:1
goodly raiment of her *e* son Esau ... Gen 27:15
And he searched, and began at the *e* ... Gen 44:12
of Reuben, Israel's *e* son ... Num 1:20
Reuben, the *e* son of Israel ... Num 26:5
the three *e* sons of Jesse went and ... 1Sa 17:13

the three *e* followed Saul 1Sa 17:14
Eliab his *e* brother heard when he 1Sa 17:28
Then he took his *e* son that 2Kin 3:27
to the camp had slain all the *e* 2Chr 22:1
wine in their *e* brother's house Job 1:13
wine in their *e* brother's house Job 1:18
one by one, beginning at the *e* Jn 8:9

**ELEAD** (*e'-le-ad*) *A descendant of Ephraim.*
Shuthelah his son, and Ezer, and *E* 1Chr 7:21

**ELEADAH** See ELADAH.

**ELEALEH** (*el-e-a'-leh*) *An Amorite village.*
and Nimrah, and Heshbon, and *E* Num 32:3
of Reuben built Heshbon, and *E* Num 32:37
And Heshbon shall cry, and *E* Is 15:4
with my tears, O Heshbon, and *E* Is 16:9
the cry of Heshbon even unto *E* Jer 48:34

**ELEASAH** (*el-e'-a-sah*) See ELASAH.
*1. A son of Helez.*
begat Helez, and Helez begat *E* 1Chr 2:39
*E* begat Sisamai, and Sisamai begat 1Chr 2:40
*2. A descendant of King Saul.*
his son, *E* his son, Azel his son 1Chr 8:37
his son, *E* his son, Azel his son 1Chr 9:43

**ELEAZAR** (*el-e-a'-zar*)
*1. A son of Aaron.*
she bare him Nadab, and Abihu, *E* Ex 6:23
*E* Aaron's son took him one of the Ex 6:25
even Aaron, Nadab and Abihu, *E* Ex 28:1
Moses said unto Aaron, and unto *E* Lev 10:6
Moses spake unto Aaron, and unto *E*. Lev 10:12
and he was angry with *E* Lev 10:16
Nadab the firstborn, and Abihu, *E* Num 3:2
and *E* and Ithamar ministered in the Num 3:4
*E* the son of Aaron the priest Num 3:32
to the office of *E* the son of Num 4:16
Speak unto *E* the son of Aaron the Num 16:37
*E* the priest took the brasen Num 16:39
shall give her unto *E* the priest Num 19:3
*E* the priest shall take of her Num 19:4
*E* his son, and bring them up unto Num 20:25
and put them upon *E* his son Num 20:26
and put them upon *E* his son Num 20:28
*E* came down from the mount Num 20:28
And when Phinehas, the son of *E* Num 25:7
Phinehas, the son of *E*, the son Num 25:11
unto *E* the son of Aaron the Num 26:1
*E* the priest spake with them in Num 26:3
was born Nadab, and Abihu, *E* Num 26:60
*E* the priest, who numbered the Num 26:63
before *E* the priest, and before Num 27:2
And set him before *E* the priest Num 27:19
shall stand before *E* the priest Num 27:21
and set him before *E* the priest Num 27:22
Phinehas the son of *E* the priest Num 31:6
*E* the priest, and unto the Num 31:12
*E* the priest, and all the princes Num 31:13
*E* the priest said unto the men of Num 31:21
*E* the priest, and the chief Num 31:26
and give it unto *E* the priest Num 31:29
*E* the priest did as the LORD Num 31:31
unto *E* the priest, as the LORD Num 31:41
*E* the priest took the gold of Num 31:51
*E* the priest took the gold of the Num 31:54
to *E* the priest, and unto the Num 32:2
Moses commanded *E* the Num 32:28
*E* the priest, and Joshua the son Num 34:17
*E* his son ministered in the Deut 10:6
which *E* the priest, and Joshua the Josh 14:1
came near before *E* the priest Josh 17:4
which *E* the priest, and Joshua the Josh 19:51
of the Levites unto *E* the priest Josh 21:1
Phinehas the son of *E* the priest Josh 22:13
Phinehas the son of *E* the priest Josh 22:31
Phinehas the son of *E* the priest Josh 22:32
And *E* the son of Aaron died Josh 24:33
And Phinehas, the son of *E* Judg 20:28
Nadab, and Abihu, *E*, and Ithamar 1Chr 6:3
*E* begat Phinehas, Phinehas begat 1Chr 6:4
*E* his son, Phinehas his son 1Chr 6:50
Phinehas the son of *E* was the 1Chr 9:20
Nadab, and Abihu, *E*, and Ithamar 1Chr 24:1
therefore *E* and Ithamar executed 1Chr 24:2
them, both Zadok of the sons of *E* 1Chr 24:3
of *E* than of the sons of Ithamar 1Chr 24:4
Among the sons of *E* there were 1Chr 24:4
of God, were of the sons of *E* 1Chr 24:5
household being taken for *E* 1Chr 24:6
the son of Phinehas, the son of *E* Ezr 7:5
*2. Son of Abinadab.*
sanctified *E* his son to keep the 1Sa 7:1
*3. A son of Dodo.*
after him was *E* the son of Dodo 2Sa 23:9
after him was *E* the son of Dodo, 1Chr 11:12
*4. Son of Mahli.*
The sons of Mahli; *E*, and Kish 1Chr 23:21
*E* died, and had no sons, but 1Chr 23:22
Of Mahli came *E*, who had no sons 1Chr 24:28
*5. Son of Phinehas.*
with him was *E* the son of Ezr 8:33
*6. Married a foreign wife.*
and Malchiah, and Miamin, and *E* Ezr 10:25
*7. A priest in Nehemiah's time.*
And Maaseiah, and Shemaiah, and *E*. Neh 12:42
*8. Son of Eliud; ancestor of Jesus.*
And Eliud begat *E* Mt 1:15
and *E* begat Matthan Mt 1:15

**ELECT**
mine *e*, in whom my soul Is 42:1
servant's sake, and Israel mine *e* Is 45:4
mine *e* shall inherit it, and my Is 65:9
mine *e* shall long enjoy the work Is 65:22
they shall deceive the very *e* Mt 24:24
his *e* from the four winds Mt 24:31
if it were possible, even the *e* Mk 13:22
his *e* from the four winds Mk 13:27
And shall not God avenge his own *e* Lk 18:7
thing to the charge of God's *e* Rom 8:33
Put on therefore, as the *e* of God Col 3:12
the *e* angels, that thou observe 1Ti 5:21
according to the faith of God's *e* Titus 1:1
*E* according to the foreknowledge 1Pet 1:2
in Sion a chief corner stone, *e* 1Pet 2:6
The elder unto the *e* lady 2Jn 1
of thy *e* sister greet thee 2Jn 13

**ELECTED**
*e* together with you, saluteth you 1Pet 5:13

**ELECTION**
of God according to *e* might stand Rom 9:11
according to the *e* of grace Rom 11:5
but the *e* hath obtained it, and Rom 11:7
but as touching the *e*, they are Rom 11:28
brethren beloved, your *e* of God 1Th 1:4
to make your calling and *e* sure 2Pet 1:10

**ELECT'S**
but for the *e* sake those days Mt 24:22
but for the *e* sake, whom he hath Mk 13:20
endure all things for the *e* sakes 2Ti 2:10

**EL-ELOHE-ISRAEL** (*el-el-o'-he-iz'-rah-el*) *An altar of Jacob near Shechem.*
there an altar, and called it *E* Gen 33:20

**ELEMENTS**
bondage under the *e* of the world Gal 4:3
again to the weak and beggarly *e* Gal 4:9
the *e* shall melt with fervent 2Pet 3:10
the *e* shall melt with fervent 2Pet 3:12

**ELEPH** (*e'-lef*) *A town in Benjamin.*
And Zelah, *E*, and Jebusi, which is Josh 18:28

**ELEVEN**
his *e* sons, and passed over the Gen 32:22
the *e* stars made obeisance to me Gen 37:9
*e* curtains shalt thou make Ex 26:7
the *e* curtains shall be all of Ex 26:8
*e* curtains he made them Ex 36:14
the *e* curtains were of one size Ex 36:15
And on the third day *e* bullocks Num 29:20
(There are *e* days' journey from Deut 1:2
*e* cities with their villages Josh 15:51
of us *e* hundred pieces of silver Judg 16:5
The *e* hundred shekels of silver Judg 17:2
when he had restored the *e* Judg 17:3
he reigned *e* years in Jerusalem 2Kin 23:36
he reigned *e* years in Jerusalem 2Kin 24:18
he reigned *e* years in Jerusalem 2Chr 36:5
reigned *e* years in Jerusalem 2Chr 36:11
he reigned *e* years in Jerusalem Jer 52:1
cubits, and the breadth *e* cubits Eze 40:49
Then the *e* disciples went away Mt 28:16
unto the *e* as they sat at meat Mk 16:14
told all these things unto the *e* Lk 24:9
found the *e* gathered together, and Lk 24:33
was numbered with the *e* apostles Acts 1:26
But Peter, standing up with the *e* Acts 2:14

**ELEVENTH**
On the *e* day Pagiel the son of Num 7:72
the fortieth year, in the *e* month Deut 1:3
And in the *e* year, in the month 1Kin 6:38
in the *e* year of Joram the son of 2Kin 9:29
unto the *e* year of king Zedekiah 2Kin 25:2
the tenth, Machbanai the *e* 1Chr 12:13
The *e* to Eliashib, the twelfth to 1Chr 24:12
The *e* to Azareel, he, his sons, 1Chr 25:18
The *e* captain for the *e* 1Chr 27:14
unto the end of the *e* year of Jer 1:3
in the *e* year of Zedekiah, in the Jer 39:2
unto the *e* year of king Zedekiah Jer 52:5
And it came to pass in the *e* year Eze 26:1
And it came to pass in the *e* year Eze 30:20
And it came to pass in the *e* year Eze 31:1
and twentieth day of the *e* month Zec 1:7
about the *e* hour he went out, and Mt 20:6
that were hired about the *e* hour Mt 20:9
the *e*, a jacinth Rev 21:20

**ELHANAN** (*el-ha'-nan*)
*1. Son of Jair.*
where *E* the son of Jaare-oregim, 2Sa 21:19
*E* the son of Jair slew Lahmi the 1Chr 20:5
*2. Son of Dodo.*
*E* the son of Dodo of Beth-lehem, 2Sa 23:24
*E* the son of Dodo of Beth-lehem, 1Chr 11:26

**ELI** (*e'-li*) See ELI'S, ELOI.
*1. A High Priest of Israel.*
And the two sons of *E*, Hophni and 1Sa 1:3
Now *E* the priest sat upon a seat 1Sa 1:9
the LORD, that *E* marked her mouth 1Sa 1:12
therefore *E* thought she had been 1Sa 1:13
*E* said unto her, How long wilt 1Sa 1:14
Then *E* answered and said, Go in 1Sa 1:17
and brought the child to *E* 1Sa 1:25
unto the LORD before *E* the priest 1Sa 2:11
Now the sons of *E* were sons of 1Sa 2:12
*E* blessed Elkanah and his wife, and 1Sa 2:20
Now *E* was very old, and heard all 1Sa 2:22
And there came a man of God unto *E* 1Sa 2:27
ministered unto the LORD before *E* 1Sa 3:1
when *E* was laid down in his place 1Sa 3:2
And he ran unto *E*, and said, Here 1Sa 3:5
And Samuel arose and went to *E* 1Sa 3:6
And he arose and went to *E*, and said 1Sa 3:8
*E* perceived that the LORD had 1Sa 3:8
Therefore *E* said unto Samuel, Go, 1Sa 3:9
*E* all things which I have spoken 1Sa 3:12
I have sworn unto the house of *E* 1Sa 3:14
feared to shew *E* the vision 1Sa 3:15
Then *E* called Samuel, and said, 1Sa 3:16
and the two sons of *E*, Hophni and 1Sa 4:4
and the two sons of *E*, Hophni and 1Sa 4:11
*E* sat upon a seat by the wayside 1Sa 4:13
when *E* heard the noise of the 1Sa 4:14
man came in hastily, and told *E* 1Sa 4:14
Now *E* was ninety and eight years 1Sa 4:15
And the man said unto *E*, I am he 1Sa 4:16
the son of Phinehas, the son of *E* 1Sa 14:3
the house of *E* in Shiloh 1Kin 2:27
*2. An Aramaic term for God.*
with a loud voice, saying, Eli, *E* Mt 27:46

**ELIAB** (*e'-le-ab*) See ELIAB'S, ELIEL.
*1. Son of Helon.*
*E* the son of Helon Num 1:9
*E* the son of Helon shall be Num 2:7
the third day *E* the son of Helon Num 7:24
offering of *E* the son of Helon Num 7:29
of Zebulun was *E* the son of Helon Num 10:16
*2. Father of Dathan.*
Dathan and Abiram, the sons of *E* Num 16:1
Dathan and Abiram, the sons of *E* Num 16:12
the sons of Pallu; *E* Num 26:8
And the sons of *E* Num 26:9
Dathan and Abiram, the sons of *E* Deut 11:6
*3. A son of Jesse.*
were come, that he looked on *E* 1Sa 16:6
the battle were *E* the first born 1Sa 17:13
*E* his eldest brother heard when 1Sa 17:28
And Jesse begat his firstborn *E* 1Chr 2:13
daughter of *E* the son of Jesse 2Chr 11:18
*4. A Levite ancestor of Samuel.*
*E* his son, Jeroham his son, 1Chr 6:27
*5. A leader in David's army.*
Obadiah the second, *E* the third, 1Chr 12:9
*6. A Levite in David's time.*
and Jehiel, and Unni, *E*, and 1Chr 15:18
and Jehiel, and Unni, and *E* 1Chr 15:20
and Jehiel, and Mattithiah, and *E* 1Chr 16:5

**ELIAB'S** (*e'-le-abs*)
*E* anger was kindled against David 1Sa 17:28

**ELIADA** (*e'-li'-a-dah*) See ELIADAH.
*1. A son of David.*
And Elishama, and *E*, and Eliphalet 2Sa 5:16
And Elishama, and *E*, and Eliphelet, 1Chr 3:8
*E* a mighty man of valour, and with 2Chr 17:17

**ELIADAH** (*e-li'-a-dah*) See ELIADA. *An opponent of King Saul.*
adversary, Rezon the son of *E* 1Kin 11:23

**ELIAH** (*e-li'-ah*) See ELIJAH. *A son of Jeroham.*
And Jaresiah, and *E*, and Zichri, the 1Chr 8:27
and Abdi, and Jeremoth, and *E* Ezr 10:26

**ELIAHBA** (*e-li'-ah-bah*) *A 'mighty man' of David.*
*E* the Shaalbonite, of the sons of 2Sa 23:32
Baharumite, *E* the Shaalbonite, 1Chr 11:33

**ELIAKIM** (*e-li'-a-kim*) See JEHOIAKIM.
*1. A son of Hilkiah.*
out to them *E* the son of Hilkiah 2Kin 18:18
Then said *E* the son of Hilkiah, 2Kin 18:26
Then came *E* the son of Hilkiah, 2Kin 18:37
And he sent *E*, which was over the 2Kin 19:2
my servant *E* the son of Hilkiah Is 22:20
Then came forth unto him *E* Is 36:3
Then said *E* and Shebna and Joah Is 36:11
Then came *E*, the son of Hilkiah, Is 36:22
And he sent *E*, who was over the Is 37:2
*2. Original name of Jehoiakim.*
Pharaoh-nechoh made *E* the son of 2Kin 23:34
the king of Egypt made *E* his 2Chr 36:4
*3. A priest who dedicated the wall.*
*E*, Maaseiah, Miniamin, Michaiah, Neh 12:41
*4. Son of Abiud; ancestor of Jesus.*
and Abiud begat *E* Mt 1:13
and *E* begat Azor Mt 1:13
of Jonan, which was the son of *E* Lk 3:30

**ELIAM** (*e'-le-am*)
*1. Father of Bathsheba.*
Bath-sheba, the daughter of *E* 2Sa 11:3
*2. A 'mighty man' of David.*
*E* the son of Ahithophel the 2Sa 23:34

**ELIAS** (*e-li'-as*) See ELIJAH. *Greek form of Elijah.*
if ye will receive it, this is *E* Mt 11:14
some, *E*; and others, Jeremias Mt 16:14
them Moses and *E* talking with him Mt 17:3
and one for Moses, and one for *E* Mt 17:4
scribes that *E* must first come Mt 17:10
*E* truly shall first come, and Mt 17:11
That *E* is come already, and they Mt 17:12
said, This man calleth for *E* Mt 27:47
let us see whether *E* will come to Mt 27:49

Others said, That it is *E* ... Mk 6:15
but some say, *E* ... Mk 8:28
appeared unto them *E* with Moses ... Mk 9:4
and one for Moses, and one for *E* ... Mk 9:5
scribes that *E* must first come ... Mk 9:11
*E* verily cometh first, and ... Mk 9:12
That *E* is indeed come, and they ... Mk 9:13
it said, Behold, he calleth *E* ... Mk 15:35
let us see whether *E* will come to ... Mk 15:36
him in the spirit and power of *E* ... Lk 1:17
were in Israel in the days of *E* ... Lk 4:25
But unto none of them was *E* sent ... Lk 4:26
And of some, that *E* had appeared ... Lk 9:8
but some say *E* ... Lk 9:19
two men, which were Moses and *E* ... Lk 9:30
and one for Moses, and one for *E* ... Lk 9:33
and consume them, even as *E* did ... Lk 9:54
Art thou *E*? ... Jn 1:21
if thou be not that Christ, nor *E* ... Jn 1:25
not what the scripture saith of *E* ... Rom 11:2
*E* was a man subject to like ... Jas 5:17

**ELIASAPH** (*e-li'-a-saf*)
*1. A chief of Gad.*
*E* the son of Deuel ... Num 1:14
Gad shall be *E* the son of Reuel ... Num 2:14
the sixth day *E* the son of Deuel ... Num 7:42
offering of *E* the son of Deuel ... Num 7:47
of Gad was *E* the son of Deuel ... Num 10:20
*2. A Gershonite leader.*
shall be *E* the son of Lael ... Num 3:24

**ELIASHIB** (*e-li'-a-shib*)
*1. A descendant of Judah.*
of Elioenai were, Hodaiah, and *E* ... 1Chr 3:24
*2. A priest in David's time.*
The eleventh to *E*, the twelfth to ... 1Chr 24:12
*3. Son of Joiakim.*
chamber of Johanan the son of *E* ... Ezr 10:6
Joiakim, Joiakim also begat *E* ... Neh 12:10
and *E* begat Joiada ... Neh 12:10
The Levites in the days of *E* ... Neh 12:22
the days of Johanan the son of *E* ... Neh 12:23
*4. Married a foreign wife.*
*E* ... Ezr 10:24
*5. Son of Zotta.*
Elioenai, *E*, Mattaniah, and ... Ezr 10:27
*6. Son of Bani.*
Vaniah, Meremoth, *E*, ... Ezr 10:36
*7. High Priest during Nehemiah's time.*
Then *E* the high priest rose up ... Neh 3:1
of the house of *E* the high priest ... Neh 3:20
from the door of the house of *E* ... Neh 3:21
even to the end of the house of *E* ... Neh 3:21
this, *E* the priest, having the ... Neh 13:4
of the evil that *E* did for Tobiah ... Neh 13:7
the son of *E* the high priest, was ... Neh 13:28

**ELIATHAH** (*e-li'-a-thah*) *A son of Heman.*
and Jerimoth, Hananiah, Hanani, *E* ... 1Chr 25:4
The twentieth to *E*, he, his sons, ... 1Chr 25:27

**ELIDAD** (*e-li'-dad*) *Son of Chislon.*
of Benjamin, *E* the son of Chislon ... Num 34:21

**ELIEHOENAI** See ELIHOENAI.

**ELIEL** (*e'-le-el*) See ELIAH.
*1. Head of the house of Manasseh.*
even Epher, and Ishi, and *E* ... 1Chr 5:24
*2. Son of Jeroham.*
the son of Jeroham, the son of *E* ... 1Chr 6:34
*3. A son of Shimhi.*
And Elienai, and Zilthai, and *E* ... 1Chr 8:20
*4. A son of Shashak.*
And Ishpan, and Heber, and *E* ... 1Chr 8:22
*5. A captain in David's army.*
*E* the Mahavite, and Jeribai, and ... 1Chr 11:46
*6. A 'mighty man' of David.*
*E*, and Obed, and Jasiel the ... 1Chr 11:47
*7. A Gadite ally of David.*
Attai the sixth, *E* the seventh, ... 1Chr 12:11
*8. A chief of Judah.*
*E* the chief, and his brethren ... 1Chr 15:9
*9. A chief Levite.*
Asaiah, and Joel, Shemaiah, and *E* ... 1Chr 15:11
*10. A Levite in Hezekiah's time.*
and Jerimoth, and Jozabad, and *E* ... 2Chr 31:13

**ELIENAI** (*e-li-e'-nahee*) *A son of Shimhi.*
And *E*, and Zilthai, and Eliel, ... 1Chr 8:20

**ELIEZER**
of my house is this *E* of Damascus ... Gen 15:2
And the name of the other was *E* ... Ex 18:4
Zemira, and Joash, and *E*, and ... 1Chr 7:8
and Zechariah, and Benaiah, and *E* ... 1Chr 15:24
sons of Moses were, Gershom, and *E* 1Chr 23:15
And the sons of *E* were, Rehabiah ... 1Chr 23:17
And *E* had none other sons ... 1Chr 23:17
And his brethren by *E* ... 1Chr 26:25
was *E* the son of Zichri ... 1Chr 27:16
Then *E* the son of Dodavah of ... 2Chr 20:37
Then sent I for *E*, for Ariel, for ... Ezr 8:16
Maaseiah, and *E*, and Jarib, and ... Ezr 10:18
Kelita,) Pethahiah, Judah, and *E* ... Ezr 10:23
*E*, Ishijah, Malchiah, Shemaiah, ... Ezr 10:31
of Jose, which was the son of *E* ... Lk 3:29

**ELIHOENAI** (*e-li-ho-e'-nahee*) See ELIOENAI. *A family of exiles.*
*E* the son of Zerahiah, and with ... Ezr 8:4

**ELIHOREPH** (*e-li-ho'-ref*) *A scribe of Solomon.*
*E* and Ahiah, the sons of Shisha, ... 1Kin 4:3

**ELIHU** (*e-li'-hew*)
*1. Great-grandfather of Samuel.*
the son of Jeroham, the son of *E* ... 1Sa 1:1
*2. A soldier of David.*
and Michael, and Jozabad, and *E* ... 1Chr 12:20
*3. A Tabernacle servant.*
whose brethren were strong men, *E* ... 1Chr 26:7
*4. Brother of David.*
Of Judah, *E*, one of the brethren ... 1Chr 27:18
*5. A friend of Job.*
Then was kindled the wrath of *E* ... Job 32:2
Now *E* had waited till Job had ... Job 32:4
When *E* saw that there was no ... Job 32:5
*E* the son of Barachel the Buzite ... Job 32:6
Furthermore *E* answered and said, ... Job 34:1
*E* spake moreover, and said, ... Job 35:1
*E* also proceeded, and said, ... Job 36:1

**ELIJAH** (*e-li'-jah*) See ELIAH, ELIAS.
*1. The prophet.*
*E* the Tishbite, who was of the ... 1Kin 17:1
*E* said unto her, Fear not ... 1Kin 17:13
did according to the saying of *E* ... 1Kin 17:15
of the LORD, which he spake by *E* ... 1Kin 17:16
And she said unto *E*, What have I ... 1Kin 17:18
And the LORD heard the voice of *E* ... 1Kin 17:22
*E* took the child, and brought him ... 1Kin 17:23
*E* said, See, thy son liveth ... 1Kin 17:23
And the woman said to *E*, Now by ... 1Kin 17:24
LORD came to *E* in the third year ... 1Kin 18:1
*E* went to shew himself unto Ahab ... 1Kin 18:2
was in the way, behold, *E* met him ... 1Kin 18:7
and said, Art thou that my lord *E* ... 1Kin 18:7
tell thy lord, Behold, *E* is here ... 1Kin 18:8
tell thy lord, Behold, *E* is here ... 1Kin 18:11
tell thy lord, Behold, *E* is here ... 1Kin 18:14
*E* said, As the LORD of hosts ... 1Kin 18:15
and Ahab went to meet *E* ... 1Kin 18:16
it came to pass, when Ahab saw *E* ... 1Kin 18:17
*E* came unto all the people, and ... 1Kin 18:21
Then said *E* unto the people, I, ... 1Kin 18:22
*E* said unto the prophets of Baal, ... 1Kin 18:25
that *E* mocked them, and said, Cry ... 1Kin 18:27
*E* said unto all the people, Come ... 1Kin 18:30
*E* took twelve stones, according ... 1Kin 18:31
that *E* the prophet came near, and ... 1Kin 18:36
*E* said unto them, Take the ... 1Kin 18:40
*E* brought them down to the brook ... 1Kin 18:40
*E* said unto Ahab, Get thee up, ... 1Kin 18:41
*E* went up to the top of Carmel ... 1Kin 18:42
And the hand of the LORD was on *E*. 1Kin 18:46
told Jezebel all that *E* had done ... 1Kin 19:1
Jezebel sent a messenger unto *E* ... 1Kin 19:2
unto him, What doest thou here, *E* ... 1Kin 19:9
when *E* heard it, that he wrapped ... 1Kin 19:13
and said, What doest thou here, *E* ... 1Kin 19:13
*E* passed by him, and cast his ... 1Kin 19:19
he left the oxen, and ran after *E* ... 1Kin 19:20
Then he arose, and went after *E* ... 1Kin 19:21
the LORD came to *E* the Tishbite ... 1Kin 21:17
And Ahab said to *E*, Hast thou ... 1Kin 21:20
the LORD came to *E* the Tishbite ... 1Kin 21:28
the LORD said to *E* the Tishbite ... 2Kin 1:3
And *E* departed ... 2Kin 1:4
And he said, It is *E* the Tishbite ... 2Kin 1:8
*E* answered and said to the captain ... 2Kin 1:10
*E* answered and said unto them, If ... 2Kin 1:12
and fell on his knees before *E* ... 2Kin 1:13
the angel of the LORD said unto *E* ... 2Kin 1:15
of the LORD which *E* had spoken ... 2Kin 1:17
up *E* into heaven by a whirlwind ... 2Kin 2:1
that *E* went with Elisha from ... 2Kin 2:1
*E* said unto Elisha, Tarry here, I ... 2Kin 2:2
*E* said unto him, Elisha, tarry ... 2Kin 2:4
*E* said unto him, Tarry, I pray ... 2Kin 2:6
*E* took his mantle, and wrapped it ... 2Kin 2:8
that *E* said unto Elisha, Ask what ... 2Kin 2:9
*E* went up by a whirlwind into ... 2Kin 2:11
mantle of *E* that fell from him ... 2Kin 2:13
mantle of *E* that fell from him ... 2Kin 2:14
said, Where is the LORD God of *E* ... 2Kin 2:14
The spirit of *E* doth rest on ... 2Kin 2:15
poured water on the hands of *E* ... 2Kin 3:11
by his servant *E* the Tishbite ... 2Kin 9:36
which he spake by his servant *E* ... 2Kin 10:10
of the LORD, which he spake to *E* ... 2Kin 10:17
writing to him from *E* the prophet ... 2Chr 21:12
I will send you *E* the prophet ... Mal 4:5
*2. Married a foreign wife.*
Maaseiah, and *E*, and Shemaiah, and .. Ezr 10:21

**ELIKA** (*e-li'-kah*) *A guard of David.*
the Harodite, *E* the Harodite, ... 2Sa 23:25

**ELIM** (*e'-lim*) See BEER-ELIM. *An encampment during the Exodus.*
And they came to *E*, where were ... Ex 15:27
And they took their journey from *E* ... Ex 16:1
of Sin, which is between *E* ... Ex 16:1
from Marah, and came unto *E* ... Num 33:9
in *E* were twelve fountains of ... Num 33:9
And they removed from *E*, and ... Num 33:10

**ELIMELECH** (*e-lim'-e-lek*) See ELIMELECH'S.
*Husband of Naomi.*
And the name of the man was *E* ... Ruth 1:2
And *E* Naomi's husband died ... Ruth 1:3
man of wealth, of the family of *E* ... Ruth 2:1
Boaz, who was of the kindred of *E* ... Ruth 2:3

**ELIMELECH'S**
of land, which was our brother *E* ... Ruth 4:3
that I have bought all that was *E* ... Ruth 4:9

**ELIOENAI** (*e-li-o-e'-nahee*) See ELIHOENAI.
*1. A son of Neariah.*
*E*, and Hezekiah, and Azrikam, three . 1Chr 3:23
And the sons of *E* were, Hodaiah, ... 1Chr 3:24
*2. A Simeonite prince.*
And *E*, and Jaakobah ... 1Chr 4:36
*3. A son of Becher.*
and Joash, and Eliezer, and *E* ... 1Chr 7:8
*4. A Temple servant.*
the sixth, *E* the seventh ... 1Chr 26:3
*5. Married a foreign wife.*
*E*, Maaseiah, Ishmael, Nethaneel, ... Ezr 10:22
*6. A son of Zattu.*
*E*, Eliashib, Mattaniah, and ... Ezr 10:27
*7. A priest during Nehemiah's time.*
Maaseiah, Miniamin, Michaiah, *E* ... Neh 12:41

**ELIPHAL** (*el'-i-fal*) *A captain in David's army.*
the Hararite, *E* the son of Ur, ... 1Chr 11:35

**ELIPHALET** (*e-lif'-a-let*) See ELIPHELET, ELPALET. *A son of David.*
And Elishama, and Eliada, and *E* ... 2Sa 5:16
And Elishama, and Beeliada, and *E* ... 1Chr 14:7

**ELIPHAZ** (*el'-if-az*)
*1. A son of Esau.*
And Adah bare to Esau *E* ... Gen 36:4
*E* the son of Adah the wife of ... Gen 36:10
And the sons of *E* were Teman ... Gen 36:11
was concubine to *E* Esau's son ... Gen 36:12
and she bare to *E* Amalek ... Gen 36:12
the sons of *E* the firstborn son ... Gen 36:15
came of *E* in the land of Edom ... Gen 36:16
*E*, Reuel, and Jeush, and Jaalam, and. 1Chr 1:35
The sons of *E*; Teman, and ... 1Chr 1:36
*2. A friend of Job.*
*E* the Temanite, and Bildad the ... Job 2:11
Then *E* the Temanite answered and ... Job 4:1
Then answered *E* the Temanite ... Job 15:1
Then *E* the Temanite answered and ... Job 22:1
the LORD said to *E* the Temanite ... Job 42:7
So *E* the Temanite and Bildad the ... Job 42:9

**ELIPHELEH** (*e-lif'-e-leh*) *A Levite singer.*
and Mattithiah, and *E* ... 1Chr 15:18
and *E*, and Mikneiah, ... 1Chr 15:21

**ELIPHELEHU** See ELIPHELEH.

**ELIPHELET** (*e-lif'-e-let*) See ELIPHALET.
*1. A 'mighty man' of David.*
*E* the son of Ahasbai, the son of ... 2Sa 23:34
*2. A son of David.*
Ibhar also, and Elishama, and *E* ... 1Chr 3:6
*3. Same as Eliphat.*
And Elishama, and Eliada, and *E* ... 1Chr 3:8
*4. A descendant of King Saul.*
Jehush the second, and *E* the third ... 1Chr 8:39
*5. A family of exiles.*
whose names are these, *E* ... Ezr 8:13
*6. A son of Hashum.*
Mattenai, Mattathah, Zabad, *E* ... Ezr 10:33

**ELI'S** (*e'-lize*) *Refers to Eli 1.*
that the iniquity of *E* house ... 1Sa 3:14

**ELISABETH** (*e-liz'-a-beth*) See ELISABETH'S.
*Mother of John the Baptist.*
of Aaron, and her name was *E* ... Lk 1:5
child, because that *E* was barren ... Lk 1:7
thy wife *E* shall bear thee a son, ... Lk 1:13
those days his wife *E* conceived ... Lk 1:24
And, behold, thy cousin *E*, she ... Lk 1:36
house of Zacharias, and saluted *E* ... Lk 1:40
when *E* heard the salutation of ... Lk 1:41
*E* was filled with the Holy Ghost ... Lk 1:41

**ELISABETH'S** (*e-liz'-a-beths*)
Now *E* full time came that she ... Lk 1:57

**ELISEUS** (*el-i-se'-us*) See ELISHA. *Greek form of Elisha.*
in the time of *E* the prophet ... Lk 4:27

**ELISHA** (*e-li'-shah*) See ELISEUS. *A prophet.*
and *E* the son of Shaphat of ... 1Kin 19:16
the sword of Jehu shall *E* slay ... 1Kin 19:17
found *E* the son of Shaphat, who ... 1Kin 19:19
Elijah went with *E* from Gilgal ... 2Kin 2:1
And Elijah said unto *E*, Tarry here ... 2Kin 2:2
*E* said unto him, As the LORD ... 2Kin 2:2
were at Beth-el came forth to *E* ... 2Kin 2:3
And Elijah said unto him, *E* ... 2Kin 2:4
that were at Jericho came to *E* ... 2Kin 2:5
over, that Elijah said unto *E* ... 2Kin 2:9
*E* said, I pray thee, let a double ... 2Kin 2:9
*E* saw it, and he cried, My father, ... 2Kin 2:12
and thither: and *E* went over ... 2Kin 2:14
spirit of Elijah doth rest on *E* ... 2Kin 2:15
the men of the city said unto *E* ... 2Kin 2:19
to the saying of *E* which he spake ... 2Kin 2:22
Here is *E* the son of Shaphat, ... 2Kin 3:11
*E* said unto the king of Israel, ... 2Kin 3:13
*E* said, As the LORD of hosts ... 2Kin 3:14
the sons of the prophets unto *E* ... 2Kin 4:1
*E* said unto her, What shall I do ... 2Kin 4:2
that *E* passed to Shunem, where ... 2Kin 4:8
season that *E* had said unto her ... 2Kin 4:17
when *E* was come into the house, ... 2Kin 4:32
And *E* came again to Gilgal ... 2Kin 4:38
when *E* the man of God had heard ... 2Kin 5:8

at the door of the house of *E* ... 2Kin 5:9
*E* sent a messenger unto him, ... 2Kin 5:10
the servant of *E* the man of God ... 2Kin 5:20
*E* said unto him, Whence comest ... 2Kin 5:25
sons of the prophets said unto *E* ... 2Kin 6:1
but *E*, the prophet that is in ... 2Kin 6:12
*E* prayed, and said, LORD, I pray ... 2Kin 6:17
and chariots of fire round about *E* ... 2Kin 6:17
*E* prayed unto the LORD, and said, ... 2Kin 6:18
according to the word of *E* ... 2Kin 6:18
*E* said unto them, This is not the ... 2Kin 6:19
come into Samaria, that *E* said ... 2Kin 6:20
And the king of Israel said unto *E* ... 2Kin 6:21
if the head of *E* the son of ... 2Kin 6:31
But *E* sat in his house, and the ... 2Kin 6:32
Then *E* said, Hear ye the word of ... 2Kin 7:1
Then spake *E* unto the woman, ... 2Kin 8:1
the great things that *E* hath done ... 2Kin 8:4
her son, whom *E* restored to life ... 2Kin 8:5
And *E* came to Damascus ... 2Kin 8:7
*E* said unto him, Go, say unto him ... 2Kin 8:10
*E* answered, The LORD hath shewed ... 2Kin 8:13
So he departed from *E*, and came to ... 2Kin 8:14
said to him, What said *E* to thee ... 2Kin 8:14
*E* the prophet called one of the ... 2Kin 9:1
Now *E* was fallen sick of his ... 2Kin 13:14
*E* said unto him, Take bow and ... 2Kin 13:15
*E* put his hands upon the king's ... 2Kin 13:16
Then *E* said, Shoot ... 2Kin 13:17
*E* died, and they buried him ... 2Kin 13:20
the man into the sepulchre of *E* ... 2Kin 13:21
down, and touched the bones of *E* ... 2Kin 13:21

**ELISHAH** (*e-li'-shah*) *A son of Javan.*
*E*, and Tarshish, Kittim, and ... Gen 10:4
*E*, and Tarshish, Kittim, and ... 1Chr 1:7
purple from the isles of *E* was ... Eze 27:7

**ELISHAMA** (*e-lish'-a-mah*) See ELISHUA.
*1. Grandfather of Joshua.*
*E* the son of Ammihud ... Num 1:10
shall be *E* the son of Ammihud ... Num 2:18
seventh day *E* the son of Ammihud ... Num 7:48
offering of *E* the son of Ammihud ... Num 7:53
over his host was *E* the son of ... Num 10:22
son, Ammihud his son, *E* his son, ... 1Chr 7:26
*2. A son of David.*
And *E*, and Eliada, and Eliphalet ... 2Sa 5:16
Ibhar also, and *E*, and Eliphelet, ... 1Chr 3:6
And *E*, and Eliada, and Eliphelet, ... 1Chr 3:8
And *E*, and Beeliada, and Eliphalet ... 1Chr 14:7
*3. A descendant of Judah.*
the son of Nethaniah the son of *E* ... Jer 41:1
*4. Son of Jekamiah.*
Jekamiah, and Jekamiah begat *E* ... 1Chr 2:41
*5. Same as Elishua.*
son of Nethaniah, the son of *E* ... 2Kin 25:25
*6. A priest who taught the law.*
and with them *E* and Jehoram, ... 2Chr 17:8
*7. A scribe of Jehoiakim.*
even *E* the scribe, and Delaiah the ... Jer 36:12
in the chamber of *E* the scribe ... Jer 36:20
he took it out of *E* the scribe's ... Jer 36:21

**ELISHAPHAT** (*e-lish'-a-fat*) *Assisted in making Joash king.*
*E* the son of Zichri, into ... 2Chr 23:1

**ELISHEBA** (*e-lish'-e-bah*) *Daughter of Amminadab.*
And Aaron took him *E*, daughter of ... Ex 6:23

**ELISHUA** (*e-lish'-oo-ah*) See ELISHAMA. *A son of David.*
Ibhar also, and *E*, and Nepheg, and ... 2Sa 5:15
And Ibhar, and *E*, and Elpalet, ... 1Chr 14:5

**ELIUD** (*e-li'-ud*) *Son of Achis;ancestor of Jesus.*
and Achim begat *E* ... Mt 1:14
And *E* begat Eleazar ... Mt 1:15

**ELIZABETH** See ELISABETH.

**ELIZAPHAN** (*e-liz'-a-fan*) See ELZAPHAN.
*1. Son of Uzziel.*
shall be *E* the son of Uzziel ... Num 3:30
Of the sons of *E* ... 1Chr 15:8
*2. Son of Parnach.*
of Zebulun, *E* the son of Parnach ... Num 34:25
*3. A family of Levites.*
And of the sons of *E* ... 2Chr 29:13

**ELIZUR** (*e-li'-zur*) *Son of Shedeur.*
*E* the son of Shedeur ... Num 1:5
shall be *E* the son of Shedeur ... Num 2:10
On the fourth day *E* the son of ... Num 7:30
offering of *E* the son of Shedeur ... Num 7:35
over his host was *E* the son of ... Num 10:18

**ELKANAH** (*el-ka'-nah*)
*1. A grandson of Korah.*
Assir, and *E*, and Abiasaph ... Ex 6:24
*E* his son, and Ebiasaph his son, ... 1Chr 6:23
*2. Father of Samuel.*
mount Ephraim, and his name was *E* ... 1Sa 1:1
when the time was that *E* offered ... 1Sa 1:4
Then said *E* her husband to her, ... 1Sa 1:8
and *E* knew Hannah his wife ... 1Sa 1:19
And the man *E*, and all his house, ... 1Sa 1:21
*E* her husband said unto her, Do ... 1Sa 1:23
*E* went to Ramah to his house ... 1Sa 2:11
And Eli blessed *E* and his wife, and ... 1Sa 2:20
son, Jeroham his son, *E* his son ... 1Chr 6:27
The son of *E*, the son of Jeroham, ... 1Chr 6:34
*3. A Levite.*
the sons of *E*; Amasai, and ... 1Chr 6:25
The son of *E*, the son of Joel, ... 1Chr 6:36
*4. A descendant of Kohath.*
the sons of *E* ... 1Chr 6:26
The son of Zuph, the son of *E* ... 1Chr 6:35
*5. Father of Asa.*
the son of Asa, the son of *E* ... 1Chr 9:16
*6. A soldier in David's army.*
*E*, and Jesiah, and Azareel, and ... 1Chr 12:6
*7. A Levite doorkeeper.*
*E* were doorkeepers for the ark ... 1Chr 15:23
*8. An officer of King Ahaz.*
*E* that was next to the king ... 2Chr 28:7

**ELKOSH** See ELKOHSHITE.

**ELKOSHITE**
book of the vision of Nahum the *E* ... Nah 1:1

**ELLASAR** (*el'-la-sar*) *A Babylonian city.*
king of Shinar, Arioch king of *E* ... Gen 14:1
of Shinar, and Arioch king of *E* ... Gen 14:9

**ELMODAM** (*el-mo'-dam*) *Son of Er.*
of Cosam, which was the son of *E* ... Lk 3:28

**ELMS**
hills, under oaks and poplars and *e* ... Hos 4:13

**ELNAAM** (*el-na'-am*) *Father of two of David's 'mighty men.'*
and Joshaviah, the sons of *E* ... 1Chr 11:46

**ELNATHAN** (*el-na'-than*)
*1. Father of Nehushta.*
the daughter of *E* of Jerusalem ... 2Kin 24:8
*E* the son of Achbor, and certain ... Jer 26:22
*E* the son of Achbor, and Gemariah ... Jer 36:12
Nevertheless *E* and Delaiah and ... Jer 36:25
*2. Name of three Levites during Ezra's time.*
for Ariel, for Shemaiah, and for *E* ... Ezr 8:16
and for Jarib, and for *E* ... Ezr 8:16
also for Joiarib, and for *E* ... Ezr 8:16

**ELOI** (*e-lo'-ee*) See ELI. *Same as Eli 2.*
a loud voice, saying, *E*, *E* ... Mk 15:34

**ELON** (*e'-lon*) See ELONITES.
*1. Esau's father-in-law.*
the daughter of *E* the Hittite ... Gen 26:34
the daughter of *E* the Hittite ... Gen 36:2
*2. A son of Zebulun.*
Sered, and *E*, and Jahleel ... Gen 46:14
of *E*, the family of the Elonites ... Num 26:26
*3. A Danite town.*
And *E*, and Thimnathah, and Ekron, ... Josh 19:43
*4. A judge of Israel.*
And after him *E*, a Zebulonite, ... Judg 12:11
*E* the Zebulonite died, and was ... Judg 12:12

**ELON-BETH-HANAN** (*e'-lon-beth-ha'-nan*) *A Danite town.*
Shaalbim, and Beth-shemesh, and *E* ... 1Kin 4:9

**ELONITES** (*e'-lon-ites*) *Descendants of Elon 2.*
of Elon, the family of the *E* ... Num 26:26

**ELOQUENT**
the LORD, O my Lord, I am not *e* ... Ex 4:10
artificer, and the *e* orator ... Is 3:3
an *e* man, and mighty in the ... Acts 18:24

**ELOTH** (*e'-loth*) See ELATH. *Same as Elath.*
in Ezion-geber, which is beside *E* ... 1Kin 9:26
Solomon to Ezion-geber, and to *E* ... 2Chr 8:17
He built *E*, and restored it to ... 2Chr 26:2

**ELPAAL** (*el-pa'-al*) *A son of Shaharaim.*
of Hushim he begat Abitub, and *E* ... 1Chr 8:11
The sons of *E*; Eber, and Misham ... 1Chr 8:12
Jezliah, and Jobab, the sons of *E* ... 1Chr 8:18

**ELPALET** (*el-pa'-let*) See ELIPHALET. *A son of David.*
And Ibhar, and Elishua, and *E* ... 1Chr 14:5

**EL-PARAN** (*el-pa'-ran*) *A place in southern Canaan.*
in their mount Seir, unto *E* ... Gen 14:6

**ELPELET** See ELPALET.

**ELSE**
Give me children, or *e* I die ... Gen 30:1
or *e* by the life of Pharaoh ... Gen 42:16
*E*, if thou wilt not let my people ... Ex 8:21
*E*, if thou refuse to let my ... Ex 10:4
only, without doing any thing *e* ... Num 20:19
there is none *e* beside him ... Deut 4:35
the earth beneath: there is none *e* ... Deut 4:39
*E* if ye do in any wise go back, ... Josh 23:12
This is nothing *e* save the sword ... Judg 7:14
if I taste bread, or ought *e* ... 2Sa 3:35
for we shall not *e* escape from ... 2Sa 15:14
is God, and that there is none *e* ... 1Kin 8:60
or *e* thou shalt pay a talent of ... 1Kin 20:39
or *e*, if it please thee, I will ... 1Kin 21:6
or *e* three days the sword of the ... 1Chr 21:12
whosoever *e* cometh into the house ... 2Chr 23:7
this is nothing *e* but sorrow of ... Neh 2:2
*e* would I give it ... Ps 51:16
or who *e* can hasten hereunto, ... Eccl 2:25
I am the LORD, and there is none *e* ... Is 45:5
I am the LORD, and there is none *e* ... Is 45:6
and there is none *e*, there is no ... Is 45:14
and there is none *e* ... Is 45:18
and there is no God *e* beside me ... Is 45:21
for I am God, and there is none *e* ... Is 45:22
for I am God, and there is none *e* ... Is 46:9
heart, I am, and none *e* beside me ... Is 47:8
heart, I am, and none *e* beside me ... Is 47:10
I am the LORD your God, and none *e* ... Joel 2:27
or *e* he will hold to the one, and ... Mt 6:24
*e* the bottles break, and the wine ... Mt 9:17
Or *e* how can one enter into a ... Mt 12:29
or *e* make the tree corrupt, and ... Mt 12:33
*e* the new piece that filled it up ... Mk 2:21
*e* the new wine doth burst the ... Mk 2:22
*e* the new wine will burst the ... Lk 5:37
Or *e*, while the other is yet a ... Lk 14:32
or *e* he will hold to the one, and ... Lk 16:13
or *e* believe me for the very ... Jn 14:11
spent their time in nothing *e* ... Acts 17:21
Or *e* let these same here say, if ... Acts 24:20
or *e* excusing one another ... Rom 2:15
*e* were your children unclean ... 1Cor 7:14
*E* when thou shalt bless with the ... 1Cor 14:16
*E* what shall they do which are ... 1Cor 15:29
or *e* be absent, I may hear of ... Phil 1:27
or *e* I will come unto thee ... Rev 2:5
or *e* I will come unto thee ... Rev 2:16

**ELTEKE** See ELTEKEH.

**ELTEKEH** (*el'-te-keh*) *A Danite city.*
And *E*, and Gibbethon, and Baalath, ... Josh 19:44
*E* with her suburbs, Gibbethon ... Josh 21:23

**ELTEKON** (*el'-te-kon*) *A city in Judah.*
And Maarath, and Beth-anoth, and *E* Josh 15:59

**ELTOLAD** (*el-to'-lad*) *A city in Judah.*
And *E*, and Chesil, and Hormah, ... Josh 15:30
And *E*, and Bethul, and Hormah, ... Josh 19:4

**ELUL** (*e'-lul*) *Sixth month of the Hebrew year.*
and fifth day of the month *E* ... Neh 6:15

**ELUZAI** (*e-loo'-zahee*) *A soldier in David's army.*
*E*, and Jerimoth, and Bealiah, and ... 1Chr 12:5

**ELYMAS** (*el'-i-mas*) See BAR-JESUS. *A sorcerer.*
But *E* the sorcerer (for so is his ... Acts 13:8

**ELZABAD** (*el'-za-bad*)
*1. A soldier in David's army.*
Johanan the eighth, *E* the ninth, ... 1Chr 12:12
*2. Son of Shemaiah.*
Othni, and Rephael, and Obed, *E* ... 1Chr 26:7

**ELZAPHAN** (*el'-za-fan*) See ELIZAPHAN. *A son of Uzziel.*
Mishael, and *E*, and Zithri ... Ex 6:22
And Moses called Mishael and *E* ... Lev 10:4

**EMBALM**
the physicians to *e* his father ... Gen 50:2

**EMBALMED**
and the physicians *e* Israel ... Gen 50:2
the days of those which are *e* ... Gen 50:3
and they *e* him, and he was put in a ... Gen 50:26

**EMBOLDENED**
of him which is weak be *e* to eat ... 1Cor 8:10

**EMBOLDENETH**
or what *e* thee that thou ... Job 16:3

**EMBRACE**
time of life, thou shalt *e* a son ... 2Kin 4:16
*e* the rock for want of a shelter ... Job 24:8
to honour, when thou dost *e* her ... Prov 4:8
*e* the bosom of a stranger ... Prov 5:20
a time to *e*, and a time to refrain ... Eccl 3:5
head, and his right hand doth *e* me ... Song 2:6
and his right hand should *e* me ... Song 8:3
brought up in scarlet *e* dunghills ... Lam 4:5

**EMBRACED**
*e* him, and kissed him, and brought ... Gen 29:13
*e* him, and fell on his neck, and ... Gen 33:4
and he kissed them, and *e* them ... Gen 48:10
*e* them, and departed for to go ... Acts 20:1
*e* them, and confessed that they ... Heb 11:13

**EMBRACING**
and a time to refrain from *e* ... Eccl 3:5
him, and *e* him said, Trouble not ... Acts 20:10

**EMBROIDER**
thou shalt *e* the coat of fine ... Ex 28:39

**EMBROIDERER**
the cunning workman, and of the *e* ... Ex 35:35
an *e* in blue, and in purple, and in ... Ex 38:23

**EMEK KEZIZ** See KEZIZ.

**EMERALD**
And the second row shall be an *e* ... Ex 28:18
And the second row, an *e*, a ... Ex 39:11
the jasper, the sapphire, the *e* ... Eze 28:13
throne, in sight like unto an *e* ... Rev 4:3
a chalcedony; the fourth, an *e* ... Rev 21:19

**EMERALDS**
they occupied in thy fairs with *e* ... Eze 27:16

**EMERODS**
the botch of Egypt, and with the *e* ... Deut 28:27
them, and smote them with *e* ... 1Sa 5:6
they had *e* in their secret parts ... 1Sa 5:9
died not were smitten with the *e* ... 1Sa 5:12
They answered, Five golden *e* ... 1Sa 6:4
ye shall make images of your *e* ... 1Sa 6:5
of gold and the images of their *e* ... 1Sa 6:11

these are the golden *e* which the .......... 1Sa 6:17

**EMIM** See EMIMS.

**EMIMS** (*e'-mims*) *A race of giants.*
the *E* in Shaveh Kiriathaim,................... Gen 14:5
The *E* dwelt therein in times past........ Deut 2:10
but the Moabites call them *E*................. Deut 2:11

**EMINENT**
also built unto thee an *e* place............. Eze 16:24
In that thou buildest thine *e*................ Eze 16:31
shall throw down thine *e* place.............. Eze 16:39
it upon an high mountain and *e*.......... Eze 17:22

**EMITES** See EMIMS.

**EMMANUEL** (*em-man'-uel*) See IMMANUEL. *A Messianic name.*
and they shall call his name *E*................. Mt 1:23

**EMMAUS** (*em'-ma-us*) *A village near Jerusalem.*
same day to a village called *E*................ Lk 24:13

**EMMOR** (*em'-mor*) See HAMOR. *Father of Sychem.*
sons of *E* the father of Sychem............ Acts 7:16

**EMPIRE**
be published throughout all his *e*........... Est 1:20

**EMPLOY**
life) to *e* them in the siege.................. Deut 20:19

**EMPLOYED**
for they were *e* in that work day.......... 1Chr 9:33
Tikvah were *e* about this matter.......... Ezr 10:15

**EMPLOYMENT**
sever out men of continual *e*................ Eze 39:14

**EMPTIED**
*e* her pitcher into the trough, and....... Gen 24:20
to pass as they *e* their sacks................. Gen 42:35
*e* the chest, and took it, and................ 2Chr 24:11
even thus be he shaken out, and *e* ....... Neh 5:13
the brooks of defence shall be *e*............. Is 19:6
The land shall be utterly *e* ...................... Is 24:3
hath not been *e* from vessel to............... Jer 48:11
for the emptiers have *e* them out........... Nah 2:2

**EMPTIERS**
for the *e* have emptied them out,........... Nah 2:2

**EMPTINESS**
of confusion, and the stones of *e*............ Is 34:11

**EMPTY**
thou hadst sent me away now *e*.......... Gen 31:42
and the pit was *e*, there was no........... Gen 37:24
the seven *e* ears blasted with the ........ Gen 41:27
when ye go, ye shall not go *e*.................. Ex 3:21
and none shall appear before me *e*....... Ex 23:15
And none shall appear before me *e*....... Ex 34:20
command that they *e* the house........... Lev 14:36
thou shalt not let him go away *e*......... Deut 15:13
not appear before the LORD *e*............... Deut 16:16
with *e* pitchers, and lamps within......... Judg 7:16
LORD hath brought me home again *e*. Ruth 1:21
Go not *e* unto thy mother in law.......... Ruth 3:17
the God of Israel, send it not *e*.............. 1Sa 6:3
because thy seat will be *e*..................... 1Sa 20:18
side, and David's place was *e*............... 1Sa 20:25
month, that David's place was *e*........... 1Sa 20:27
the sword of Saul returned not *e*........... 2Sa 1:22
thy neighbours, even *e* vessels.............. 2Kin 4:3
Thou hast sent widows away *e*............... Job 22:9
out the north over the *e* place............... Job 26:7
they *e* themselves upon the earth.......... Eccl 11:3
the LORD maketh the earth *e*................... Is 24:1
but he awaketh, and his soul is *e*............ Is 29:8
to make *e* the soul of the hungry,............ Is 32:6
returned with their vessels *e*................. Jer 14:3
shall *e* his vessels, and break................ Jer 48:12
fan her, and shall *e* her land.................. Jer 51:2
me, he hath made me an *e* vessel.......... Jer 51:34
Then set it *e* upon the coals................. Eze 24:11
Israel is an *e* vine, he bringeth............. Hos 10:1
She is *e*, and void, and waste................ Nah 2:10
Shall they therefore *e* their net............. Hab 1:17
pipes *e* the golden oil out of................... Zec 4:12
when he is come, he findeth it *e*............. Mt 12:44
and beat him, and sent him away *e*......... Mk 12:3
and the rich he hath sent *e* away ........... Lk 1:53
beat him, and sent him away *e*............... Lk 20:10
shamefully, and sent him away *e*........... Lk 20:11

**EMULATION**
to *e* them which are my flesh.............. Rom 11:14

**EMULATIONS**
witchcraft, hatred, variance, *e*............... Gal 5:20

**EN-MISHPAT**
And they returned, and came to *E*........ Gen 14:7

**ENABLED**
Jesus our Lord, who hath *e* me .............. 1Ti 1:12

**ENAIM**

**ENAM** (*e'-nam*) *A city in Judah.*
and En-gannim, Tappuah, and *E*......... Josh 15:34

**ENAN** (*e'-nan*) See HAZAR-ENAN. *Father of Ahira.*
Ahira the son of *E* ................................ Num 1:15
shall be Ahira the son of *E*................... Num 2:29
twelfth day Ahira the son of *E*.............. Num 7:78
offering of Ahira the son of *E*.............. Num 7:83
Naphtali was Ahira the son of *E*........ Num 10:27

**ENCAMP**
*e* before Pi-hahiroth, between ................. Ex 14:2
before it shall ye *e* by the sea ................. Ex 14:2
it, and shall *e* round about the ............ Num 1:50
as they *e*, so shall they set.................... Num 2:17
those that *e* by him shall be the........... Num 2:27
But those that *e* before the.................. Num 3:38
how we are to *e* in the wilderness..... Num 10:31
*e* against the city, and take it............... 2Sa 12:28
*e* round about my tabernacle................ Job 19:12
an host should *e* against me .................. Ps 27:3
I will *e* about mine house because.......... Zec 9:8

**ENCAMPED**
*e* in Etham, in the edge of the ............... Ex 13:20
they *e* there by the waters..................... Ex 15:27
where he *e* at the mount of God............... Ex 18:5
from Elim, and *e* by the Red sea....... Num 33:10
*e* in the wilderness of Sin.................... Num 33:11
of Sin, and *e* in Dophkah..................... Num 33:12
from Dophkah, and *e* in Alush ............. Num 33:13
*e* at Rephidim, where was no water.. Num 33:14
and *e* at Hazeroth.............................. Num 33:17
mount Shapher, and *e* in Haradah..... Num 33:24
from Makheloth, and *e* at Tahath...... Num 33:26
and *e* at Moseroth............................... Num 33:30
Bene-jaakan, and *e* at Hor-hagidgad. Num 33:32
from Jotbathah, and *e* at Ebronah...... Num 33:34
from Ebronah, and *e* at Ezion-gaber. Num 33:35
and *e* in Almon-diblathaim .................. Num 33:46
*e* in Gilgal, in the east border ............... Josh 4:19
children of Israel *e* in Gilgal................ Josh 5:10
*e* before Gibeon, and made war ............. Josh 10:5
*e* against it, and fought against............ Josh 10:31
they *e* against it, and fought................ Josh 10:34
they *e* against them, and destroyed....... Judg 6:4
*e* against Thebez, and took it............... Judg 9:50
gathered together, and *e* in Gilead........ Judg 10:17
together, and *e* in Mizpeh .................... Judg 10:17
the morning, and *e* against Gibeah.... Judg 20:19
up, and *e* against Jabesh-gilead.............. 1Sa 11:1
but the Philistines *e* in Michmash ........ 1Sa 13:16
my lord, are *e* in the open fields ........... 2Sa 11:11
the people were *e* against.................... 1Kin 16:15
the people that were *e* heard say ....... 1Kin 16:16
*e* in the valley of Rephaim.................. 1Chr 11:15
*e* against the fenced cities, and............ 2Chr 32:1

**ENCAMPETH**
The angel of the LORD *e* round ............... Ps 34:7
bones of him that *e* against thee .............. Ps 53:5

**ENCAMPING**
and overtook them *e* by the sea............... Ex 14:9

**ENCHANTER**
or an observer of times, or an *e* ........ Deut 18:10

**ENCHANTERS**
to your dreamers, nor to your *e*.............. Jer 27:9

**ENCHANTMENT**
neither shall ye use *e*, nor.................... Lev 19:26
there is no *e* against Jacob ................. Num 23:23
the serpent will bite without *e*............... Eccl 10:11

**ENCHANTMENTS**
did in like manner with their *e*................. Ex 7:11
of Egypt did so with their *e*...................... Ex 7:22
the magicians did so with their *e*............... Ex 8:7
with their *e* to bring forth lice.................. Ex 8:18
as at other times, to seek for *e*............. Num 24:1
the fire, and used divination and *e*..... 2Kin 17:17
and observed times, and used *e*.......... 2Kin 21:6
also he observed times, and used *e*...... 2Chr 33:6
the great abundance of thine *e*................. Is 47:9
Stand now with thine *e*, and with.......... Is 47:12

**ENCOUNTERED**
and of the Stoicks, *e* him.................... Acts 17:18

**ENCOURAGE**
*e* him: for he shall cause ........................ Deut 1:38
and *e* him, and strengthen him............. Deut 3:28
overthrow it: and *e* thou him ............... 2Sa 11:25
They *e* themselves in an evil................... Ps 64:5

**ENCOURAGED**
the men of Israel *e* themselves ............ Judg 20:22
but David *e* himself in the LORD............. 1Sa 30:6
that they might be *e* in the law............ 2Chr 31:4
*e* them to the service of the................ 2Chr 35:2
So the carpenter *e* the goldsmith .............. Is 41:7

**END**
The *e* of all flesh is come before............ Gen 6:13
after the *e* of the hundred and................ Gen 8:3
to pass at the *e* of forty days.................. Gen 8:6
which is in the *e* of his field................. Gen 23:9
had made an *e* of blessing Jacob ......... Gen 27:30
pass at the *e* of two full years.............. Gen 41:1
*e* of the borders of Egypt even to........ Gen 47:21
Egypt even to the other *e* thereof........ Gen 47:21
made an *e* of commanding his sons...... Gen 49:33
to the *e* thou mayest know that I............. Ex 8:22
pass at the *e* of the four hundred.......... Ex 12:41
which is in the *e* of the year ................. Ex 23:16
And make one cherub on the one *e* ......... Ex 25:19
the other cherub on the other *e* .............. Ex 25:19
boards shall reach from *e* to *e* ............... Ex 26:28
Moses, when he had made an *e* of........... Ex 31:18
of ingathering at the year's *e*................ Ex 34:22
from the one *e* to the other.................... Ex 36:33
One cherub on the *e* on this side ............ Ex 37:8
on the other *e* on that side...................... Ex 37:8
of your consecration be at an *e*............ Lev 8:33
when he hath made an *e* of................. Lev 16:20
To the *e* that the children of.................. Lev 17:5
his sons have made an *e* of..................... Num 4:15
as he had made an *e* of speaking...... Num 16:31
and let my last *e* be like his ............... Num 23:10
but his latter *e* shall be that he ......... Num 24:20
to do thee good at thy latter *e*............... Deut 8:16
to pass at the *e* of forty days ................ Deut 9:11
year even unto the *e* of the year........ Deut 11:12
from the one *e* of the earth even .......... Deut 13:7
unto the other *e* of the earth................ Deut 13:7
At the *e* of three years thou.................. Deut 14:28
At the *e* of every seven years ................ Deut 15:1
to the *e* that he should multiply............ Deut 17:16
to the *e* that he may prolong his ....... Deut 17:20
an *e* of speaking unto the people.......... Deut 20:9
When thou hast made an *e* of................ Deut 26:12
from the *e* of the earth, as swift........... Deut 28:49
from the one *e* of the earth even.......... Deut 28:64
At the *e* of every seven years, in ....... Deut 31:10
when Moses had made an *e* of............. Deut 31:24
I will see what their *e* shall be........... Deut 32:20
would consider their latter *e* ............... Deut 32:29
Moses made an *e* of speaking all........ Deut 32:45
when Israel had made an *e* of.............. Josh 8:24
it came to pass at the *e* of three .......... Josh 9:16
an *e* of slaying them with a very ........ Josh 10:20
sea, even unto the *e* of Jordan ............. Josh 15:5
which is at the *e* of the valley ............... Josh 15:8
was from the *e* of Kirjath-jearim........ Josh 18:15
the *e* of the mountain that lieth............ Josh 18:16
salt sea at the south *e* of Jordan.......... Josh 18:19
When they had made an *e* of ............... Josh 19:49
So they made an *e* of dividing the...... Josh 19:51
when he had made an *e* to offer.............. Judg 3:18
*e* of the staff that was in his.................. Judg 6:21
to pass at the *e* of two months ............. Judg 11:39
when he had made an *e* of speaking. Judg 15:17
behold, the day groweth to an *e*........... Judg 19:9
unto the *e* of barley harvest................... Ruth 2:23
down at the *e* of the heap of corn ......... Ruth 3:7
latter *e* than at the beginning.............. Ruth 3:10
I begin, I will also make an *e*.................. 1Sa 3:12
going down to the *e* of the city ............. 1Sa 9:27
he had made an *e* of prophesying ......... 1Sa 10:13
*e* of offering the burnt offering ............ 1Sa 13:10
wherefore he put forth the *e* of ............. 1Sa 14:27
the *e* of the rod that was in mine........... 1Sa 14:43
when he had made an *e* of speaking ..... 1Sa 18:1
when David had made an *e* of............... 1Sa 24:16
*e* of the spear smote him under............. 2Sa 2:23
be bitterness in the latter *e*..................... 2Sa 2:26
an *e* of offering burnt offerings.............. 2Sa 6:18
When thou hast made an *e* of................ 2Sa 11:19
as he had made an *e* of speaking .......... 2Sa 13:36
every year's *e* that he polled it.............. 2Sa 14:26
Jerusalem at the *e* of nine months.......... 2Sa 24:8
as they had made an *e* of eating ........... 1Kin 1:41
to pass at the *e* of three years.............. 1Kin 2:39
until he had made an *e* of ...................... 1Kin 3:1
So Hiram made an *e* of doing all........... 1Kin 7:40
an *e* of praying all this prayer............... 1Kin 8:54
to pass at the *e* of twenty years ........... 1Kin 9:10
to pass at the seven years' *e*................... 2Kin 8:3
was full from one *e* to another .............. 2Kin 10:21
as soon as he had made an *e* of.......... 2Kin 10:25
at the *e* of three years they took........ 2Kin 18:10
Jerusalem from one *e* to another ....... 2Kin 21:16
when David had made an *e* of............. 1Chr 16:2
on the right side of the east *e*............... 2Chr 4:10
stood at the east *e* of the altar .............. 2Chr 5:12
Solomon had made an *e* of praying....... 2Chr 7:1
to pass at the *e* of twenty years ............ 2Chr 8:1
find them at the *e* of the brook.......... 2Chr 20:16
when they had made an *e* of the ....... 2Chr 20:23
after the *e* of two years, his............... 2Chr 21:19
chest, until they had made an *e* .......... 2Chr 24:10
came to pass at the *e* of the year....... 2Chr 24:23
of the first month they made an *e*...... 2Chr 29:17
they had made an *e* of offering.......... 2Chr 29:29
from one *e* to another with their ............ Ezr 9:11
they made an *e* with all the men ......... Ezr 10:17
to the *e* of the house of Eliashib........... Neh 3:21
will they make an *e* in a day .................... Neh 4:2
and what is mine *e*, that I should............. Job 6:11
yet thy latter *e* should greatly................ Job 8:7
Shall vain words have an *e* ................... Job 16:3
it be ere ye make an *e* of words............. Job 18:2
the day and night come to an *e*........... Job 26:10
He setteth an *e* to darkness .................. Job 28:3
that Job may be tried unto the *e*......... Job 34:36
*e* of Job more than his beginning......... Job 42:12
of the wicked come to an *e*..................... Ps 7:9
are come to a perpetual *e*....................... Ps 9:6
their words to the *e* of the world........... Ps 19:4
forth is from the *e* of the heaven........... Ps 19:6
To the *e* that my glory may sing ........... Ps 30:12
for the *e* of that man is peace ............... Ps 37:37
the *e* of the wicked shall be cut............ Ps 37:38
LORD, make me to know mine *e* ............. Ps 39:4
to cease unto the *e* of the earth.............. Ps 46:9
From the *e* of the earth will I.................. Ps 61:2
then understood I their *e*....................... Ps 73:17
and thy years shall have no *e*............. Ps 102:27
man, and are at their wit's *e*.............. Ps 107:27
and I shall keep it unto the *e* .............. Ps 119:33
I have seen an *e* of all ........................... Ps 119:96

statutes alway, even unto the *e* ........ Ps 119:112
But her *e* is bitter as wormwood, ........ Prov 5:4
but the *e* thereof are the ways of ........ Prov 14:12
the *e* of that mirth is heaviness ........ Prov 14:13
but the *e* thereof are the ways of ........ Prov 16:25
mayest be wise in thy latter *e* ........ Prov 19:20
but the *e* thereof shall not be ........ Prov 20:21
For surely there is an *e* ........ Prov 23:18
not what to do in the *e* thereof ........ Prov 25:8
from the beginning to the *e* ........ Eccl 3:11
yet is there no *e* of all his ........ Eccl 4:8
There is no *e* of all the people, ........ Eccl 4:16
for that is the *e* of all men ........ Eccl 7:2
Better is the *e* of a thing than ........ Eccl 7:8
to the *e* that man should find ........ Eccl 7:14
the *e* of his talk is mischievous ........ Eccl 10:13
making many books there is no *e* ........ Eccl 12:12
is there any *e* of their treasures ........ Is 2:7
is there any *e* of their chariots ........ Is 2:7
unto them from the *e* of the earth ........ Is 5:26
at the *e* of the conduit of the ........ Is 7:3
and peace there shall be no *e* ........ Is 9:7
from the *e* of heaven, even the ........ Is 13:5
for the extortioner is at an *e* ........ Is 16:4
after the *e* of seventy years ........ Is 23:15
pass after the *e* of seventy years ........ Is 23:17
make an *e* to deal treacherously ........ Is 33:1
night wilt thou make an *e* of me ........ Is 38:12
night wilt thou make an *e* of me ........ Is 38:13
and know the latter *e* of them ........ Is 41:22
praise from the *e* of the earth ........ Is 42:10
nor confounded world without *e* ........ Is 45:17
Declaring the *e* from the ........ Is 46:10
didst remember the latter *e* of it ........ Is 47:7
it even to the *e* of the earth ........ Is 48:20
salvation unto the *e* of the earth ........ Is 49:6
unto the *e* of the world, Say ye ........ Is 62:11
unto the *e* of the eleventh year ........ Jer 1:3
will he keep it to the *e* ........ Jer 3:5
yet will I not make a full *e* ........ Jer 4:27
but make not a full *e* ........ Jer 5:10
I will not make a full *e* with you ........ Jer 5:18
will ye do in the *e* thereof V ........ Jer 5:31
said, He shall not see our last *e* ........ Jer 12:4
*e* of the land even to the other ........ Jer 12:12
even to the other *e* of the land ........ Jer 12:12
days, and at his *e* shall be a fool ........ Jer 17:11
one *e* of the earth even unto the ........ Jer 25:33
unto the other *e* of the earth ........ Jer 25:33
when Jeremiah had made an *e* of ........ Jer 26:8
evil, to give you an expected *e* ........ Jer 29:11
though I make a full *e* of all ........ Jer 30:11
will I not make a full *e* of thee ........ Jer 30:11
And there is hope in thine *e* ........ Jer 31:17
At the *e* of seven years let ye go ........ Jer 34:14
that when Jeremiah had made an *e* ........ Jer 43:1
until there be an *e* of them ........ Jer 44:27
for I will make a full *e* of all ........ Jer 46:28
I will not make a full *e* of thee ........ Jer 46:28
thine *e* is come, and the measure ........ Jer 51:13
that his city is taken at one *e* ........ Jer 51:31
made an *e* of reading this book ........ Jer 51:63
she remembereth not her last *e* ........ Lam 1:9
our *e* is near, our days are ........ Lam 4:18
for our *e* is come ........ Lam 4:18
to pass at the *e* of seven days ........ Eze 3:16
An *e*, the *e* is come upon the ........ Eze 7:2
Now is the *e* come upon thee, and I ........ Eze 7:3
An *e* is come, the *e* is come ........ Eze 7:6
wilt thou make a full *e* of the ........ Eze 11:13
neither did I make an *e* of them ........ Eze 20:17
to the *e* that they might know ........ Eze 20:26
when iniquity shall have an *e* ........ Eze 21:25
their iniquity shall have an *e* ........ Eze 21:29
At the *e* of forty years will I ........ Eze 29:13
To the *e* that none of all the ........ Eze 31:14
time that their iniquity had an *e* ........ Eze 35:5
after the *e* of seven months shall ........ Eze 39:14
the separate place at the *e* ........ Eze 41:12
Now when he had made an *e* of ........ Eze 42:15
hast made an *e* of cleansing it ........ Eze 43:23
From the north *e* to the coast of ........ Eze 48:1
that at the *e* thereof they might ........ Dan 1:5
at the *e* of ten days their ........ Dan 1:15
Now at the *e* of the days that the ........ Dan 1:18
thereof to the *e* of all the earth ........ Dan 4:11
dominion to the *e* of the earth ........ Dan 4:22
At the *e* of twelve months he ........ Dan 4:29
And at the *e* of the days I ........ Dan 4:34
dominion shall be even unto the *e* ........ Dan 6:26
and to destroy it unto the *e* ........ Dan 7:26
Hitherto is the *e* of the matter ........ Dan 7:28
time of the *e* shall be the vision ........ Dan 8:17
in the last *e* of the indignation ........ Dan 8:19
the time appointed the *e* shall be ........ Dan 8:19
and to make an *e* of sins, and to ........ Dan 9:24
the *e* thereof shall be with a ........ Dan 9:26
unto the *e* of the war desolations ........ Dan 9:26
in the *e* of years they shall join ........ Dan 11:6
for yet the *e* shall be at the ........ Dan 11:27
white, even to the time of the *e* ........ Dan 11:35
at the time of the *e* shall the ........ Dan 11:40
yet he shall come to his *e* ........ Dan 11:45
book, even to the time of the *e* ........ Dan 12:4
it be to the *e* of these wonders ........ Dan 12:6
shall be the *e* of these things ........ Dan 12:8
and sealed till the time of the *e* ........ Dan 12:9
But go thou thy way till the *e* be ........ Dan 12:13
in thy lot at the *e* of the days ........ Dan 12:13
the great houses shall have an *e* ........ Amos 3:15
to what *e* is it for you ........ Amos 5:18
that when they had made an *e* of ........ Amos 7:2
The *e* is come upon my people of ........ Amos 8:2
the *e* thereof as a bitter day ........ Amos 8:10
to the *e* that every one of the ........ Obad 9
an utter *e* of the place thereof ........ Nah 1:8
he will make an utter *e* ........ Nah 1:9
for there is none *e* of the store ........ Nah 2:9
there is none *e* of their corpses ........ Nah 3:3
but at the *e* it shall speak, and ........ Hab 2:3
endureth to the *e* shall be saved ........ Mt 10:22
when Jesus had made an *e* of ........ Mt 11:1
the harvest is the *e* of the world ........ Mt 13:39
it be in the *e* of this world ........ Mt 13:40
shall it be at the *e* of the world ........ Mt 13:49
coming, and of the *e* of the world ........ Mt 24:3
to pass, but the *e* is not yet ........ Mt 24:6
he that shall endure unto the *e* ........ Mt 24:13
and then shall the *e* come ........ Mt 24:14
from one *e* of heaven to the other ........ Mt 24:31
with the servants, to see the *e* ........ Mt 26:58
In the *e* of the sabbath, as it ........ Mt 28:1
even unto the *e* of the world ........ Mt 28:20
he cannot stand, but hath an *e* ........ Mk 3:26
but the *e* shall not be yet ........ Mk 13:7
he that shall endure unto the *e* ........ Mk 13:13
his kingdom there shall be no *e* ........ Lk 1:33
a parable unto them to this *e* ........ Lk 18:1
but the *e* is not by and by ........ Lk 21:9
things concerning me have an *e* ........ Lk 22:37
world, he loved them unto the *e* ........ Jn 13:1
To this *e* was I born, and for this ........ Jn 18:37
to the *e* they might not live ........ Acts 7:19
to the *e* ye may be established ........ Rom 1:11
to the *e* the promise might be ........ Rom 4:16
for the *e* of those things is ........ Rom 6:21
and the *e* everlasting life ........ Rom 6:22
For Christ is the *e* of the law ........ Rom 10:4
For to this *e* Christ both died, ........ Rom 14:9
shall also confirm you unto the *e* ........ 1Cor 1:8
Then cometh the *e*, when he shall ........ 1Cor 15:24
shall acknowledge even to the *e* ........ 2Cor 1:13
For to this *e* also did I write, ........ 2Cor 2:9
the *e* of that which is abolished ........ 2Cor 3:13
whose *e* shall be according to ........ 2Cor 11:15
all ages, world without *e* ........ Eph 3:21
Whose *e* is destruction, whose God ........ Phil 3:19
To the *e* he may stablish your ........ 1Th 3:13
Now the *e* of the commandment is ........ 1Ti 1:5
of the hope firm unto the *e* ........ Heb 3:6
confidence stedfast unto the *e* ........ Heb 3:14
whose *e* is to be burned ........ Heb 6:8
full assurance of hope unto the *e* ........ Heb 6:11
is to them an *e* of all strife ........ Heb 6:16
beginning of days, nor *e* of life ........ Heb 7:3
but now once in the *e* of the ........ Heb 9:26
considering the *e* of their ........ Heb 13:7
and have seen the *e* of the Lord ........ Jas 5:11
Receiving the *e* of your faith ........ 1Pet 1:9
hope to the *e* for the grace that ........ 1Pet 1:13
But the *e* of all things is at ........ 1Pet 4:7
what shall the *e* be of them that ........ 1Pet 4:17
the latter *e* is worse with them ........ 2Pet 2:20
and keepeth my works unto the *e* ........ Rev 2:26
and Omega, the beginning and the *e* ........ Rev 21:6
and Omega, the beginning and the *e* .. Rev 22:13

**ENDAMAGE**
so thou shalt *e* the revenue of ........ Ezr 4:13

**ENDANGER**
ye make me *e* my head to the king ........ Dan 1:10

**ENDANGERED**
cleaveth wood shall be *e* thereby ........ Eccl 10:9

**ENDEAVOUR**
Moreover I will *e* that ye may be ........ 2Pet 1:15

**ENDEAVOURED**
immediately we *e* to go into ........ Acts 16:10
*e* the more abundantly to see your ........ 1Th 2:17

**ENDEAVOURING**
*E* to keep the unity of the Spirit ........ Eph 4:3

**ENDEAVOURS**
to the wickedness of their *e* ........ Ps 28:4

**ENDED**
on the seventh day God *e* his work ........ Gen 2:2
was in the land of Egypt, were *e* ........ Gen 41:53
When that year was *e*, they came ........ Gen 47:18
of this song, until they were *e* ........ Deut 31:30
and mourning for Moses were *e* ........ Deut 34:8
until they have *e* all my harvest ........ Ruth 2:21
and so they *e* the matter ........ 2Sa 20:18
So was *e* all the work that king ........ 1Kin 7:51
help them, till the work was *e* ........ 2Chr 29:34
The words of Job are *e* ........ Job 31:40
of David the son of Jesse are *e* ........ Ps 72:20
days of thy mourning shall be *e* ........ Is 60:20
harvest is past, the summer is *e* ........ Jer 8:20
till thou hast *e* the days of thy ........ Eze 4:8
when Jesus had *e* these sayings ........ Mt 7:28
and when they were *e*, he afterward ........ Lk 4:2
devil had *e* all the temptation ........ Lk 4:13
Now when he had *e* all his sayings ........ Lk 7:1
And supper being *e*, the devil ........ Jn 13:2
After these things were *e* ........ Acts 19:21
when the seven days were almost *e* ... Acts 21:27

**ENDETH**
the noise of them that rejoice *e* ........ Is 24:8

**ENDING**
and Omega, the beginning and the *e* ........ Rev 1:8

**ENDLESS**
*e* genealogies, which minister ........ 1Ti 1:4
but after the power of an *e* life ........ Heb 7:16

**EN-DOR** *(en'-dor) A village near Mt. Tabor.*
towns, and the inhabitants of *E* ........ Josh 17:11
that hath a familiar spirit at *E* ........ 1Sa 28:7
Which perished at *E*: they became ........ Ps 83:10

**ENDOW**
he shall surely *e* her to be his ........ Ex 22:16

**E**

**ENDS**
in the two *e* of the mercy seat ........ Ex 25:18
cherubims on the two *e* thereof ........ Ex 25:19
two chains of pure gold at the *e* ........ Ex 28:14
*e* of wreathen work of pure gold ........ Ex 28:22
on the two *e* of the breastplate ........ Ex 28:23
are on the *e* of the breastplate ........ Ex 28:24
the other two *e* of the two ........ Ex 28:25
two *e* of the breastplate in the ........ Ex 28:26
on the two *e* of the mercy seat ........ Ex 37:7
cherubims on the two *e* thereof ........ Ex 37:8
the four *e* of the grate of brass ........ Ex 38:5
the breastplate chains at the *e* ........ Ex 39:15
in the two *e* of the breastplate ........ Ex 39:16
rings on the *e* of the breastplate ........ Ex 39:17
the two *e* of the two wreathen ........ Ex 39:18
on the two *e* of the breastplate ........ Ex 39:19
together to the *e* of the earth ........ Deut 33:17
shall judge the *e* of the earth ........ 1Sa 2:10
that the *e* of the staves were ........ 1Kin 8:8
that the *e* of the staves were ........ 2Chr 5:9
he looketh to the *e* of the earth ........ Job 28:24
lightning unto the *e* of the earth ........ Job 37:3
take hold of the *e* of the earth ........ Job 38:13
and his circuit unto the *e* of it ........ Ps 19:6
All the *e* of the world shall ........ Ps 22:27
praise unto the *e* of the earth ........ Ps 48:10
in Jacob unto the *e* of the earth ........ Ps 59:13
of all the *e* of the earth ........ Ps 65:5
all the *e* of the earth shall fear ........ Ps 67:7
the river unto the *e* of the earth ........ Ps 72:8
all the *e* of the earth have seen ........ Ps 98:3
to ascend from the *e* of the earth ........ Ps 135:7
a fool are in the *e* of the earth ........ Prov 17:24
all the *e* of the earth ........ Prov 30:4
far unto all the *e* of the earth ........ Is 26:15
the Creator of the *e* of the earth ........ Is 40:28
the *e* of the earth were afraid, ........ Is 41:5
taken from the *e* of the earth ........ Is 41:9
daughters from the *e* of the earth ........ Is 43:6
ye saved, all the *e* of the earth ........ Is 45:22
all the *e* of the earth shall see ........ Is 52:10
to ascend from the *e* of the earth ........ Jer 10:13
unto thee from the *e* of the earth ........ Jer 16:19
come even to the *e* of the earth ........ Jer 25:31
to ascend from the *e* of the earth ........ Jer 51:16
fire devoureth both the *e* of it ........ Eze 15:4
be great unto the *e* of the earth ........ Mic 5:4
river even to the *e* of the earth ........ Zec 9:10
salvation unto the *e* of the earth ........ Acts 13:47
words unto the *e* of the world ........ Rom 10:18
upon whom the *e* of the world are ... 1Cor 10:11

**ENDUED**
God hath *e* me with a good dowry ..... Gen 30:20
*e* with prudence and understanding, ... 2Chr 2:12
*e* with understanding, of Huram my ... 2Chr 2:13
until ye be *e* with power from on ........ Lk 24:49
*e* with knowledge among you ........ Jas 3:13

**ENDURE**
me and the children be able to *e* ........ Gen 33:14
so, then thou shalt be able to *e* ........ Ex 18:23
For how can I *e* to see the evil ........ Est 8:6
or how can I *e* to see the ........ Est 8:6
hold it fast, but it shall not *e* ........ Job 8:15
of his highness I could not *e* ........ Job 31:23
But the LORD shall *e* for ever ........ Ps 9:7
weeping may *e* for a night ........ Ps 30:5
thee as long as the sun and moon *e* ........ Ps 72:5
His name shall *e* for ever ........ Ps 72:17
also will I make to *e* for ever ........ Ps 89:29
His seed shall *e* for ever ........ Ps 89:36
thou, O LORD, shalt *e* for ever ........ Ps 102:12
shall perish, but thou shalt *e* ........ Ps 102:26
of the LORD shall *e* for ever ........ Ps 104:31
doth the crown *e* to every ........ Prov 27:24
Can thine heart *e*, or can thine ........ Eze 22:14
But he that shall *e* unto the end ........ Mt 24:13
and so *e* but for a time ........ Mk 4:17
but he that shall *e* unto the end ........ Mk 13:13
and tribulations that ye *e* ........ 2Th 1:4
Thou therefore *e* hardness ........ 2Ti 2:3
Therefore I *e* all things for the ........ 2Ti 2:10
they will not *e* sound doctrine ........ 2Ti 4:3
*e* afflictions, do the work of an ........ 2Ti 4:5
If ye *e* chastening, God dealeth ........ Heb 12:7
(For they could not *e* that which ........ Heb 12:20
we count them happy which *e* ........ Jas 5:11
for conscience toward God *e* grief ........ 1Pet 2:19

**ENDURED**
their time should have *e* for ever ........ Ps 81:15
*e* with much longsuffering the ........ Rom 9:22
what persecutions I *e* ........ 2Ti 3:11
And so, after he had patiently *e* ........ Heb 6:15

ye *e* a great fight of afflictions Heb 10:32
for he *e*, as seeing him who is Heb 11:27
was set before him *e* the cross Heb 12:2
For consider him that *e* such Heb 12:3

## ENDURETH

for his mercy *e* for ever 1Chr 16:34
because his mercy *e* for ever 1Chr 16:41
for his mercy *e* for ever 2Chr 5:13
for his mercy *e* for ever 2Chr 7:3
because his mercy *e* for ever 2Chr 7:6
for his mercy *e* for ever 2Chr 20:21
for his mercy *e* for ever toward Ezr 3:11
For his anger *e* but a moment Ps 30:5
the goodness of God *e* continually Ps 52:1
of peace so long as the moon *e* Ps 72:7
his truth *e* to all generations Ps 100:5
for his mercy *e* for ever Ps 106:1
for his mercy *e* for ever Ps 107:1
and his righteousness *e* for ever Ps 111:3
his praise *e* for ever Ps 111:10
and his righteousness *e* for ever Ps 112:3
his righteousness *e* for ever Ps 112:9
the truth of the LORD *e* for ever Ps 117:2
because his mercy *e* for ever Ps 118:1
say, that his mercy *e* for ever Ps 118:2
say, that his mercy *e* for ever Ps 118:3
say, that his mercy *e* for ever Ps 118:4
for his mercy *e* for ever Ps 118:29
righteous judgments *e* for ever Ps 119:160
Thy name, O LORD, *e* for ever Ps 135:13
for his mercy *e* for ever Ps 136:1
for his mercy *e* for ever Ps 136:2
for his mercy *e* for ever Ps 136:3
for his mercy *e* for ever Ps 136:4
for his mercy *e* for ever Ps 136:5
for his mercy *e* for ever Ps 136:6
for his mercy *e* for ever Ps 136:7
for his mercy *e* for ever Ps 136:8
for his mercy *e* for ever Ps 136:9
for his mercy *e* for ever Ps 136:10
for his mercy *e* for ever Ps 136:11
for his mercy *e* for ever Ps 136:12
for his mercy *e* for ever Ps 136:13
for his mercy *e* for ever Ps 136:14
for his mercy *e* for ever Ps 136:15
for his mercy *e* for ever Ps 136:16
for his mercy *e* for ever Ps 136:17
for his mercy *e* for ever Ps 136:18
for his mercy *e* for ever Ps 136:19
for his mercy *e* for ever Ps 136:20
for his mercy *e* for ever Ps 136:21
for his mercy *e* for ever Ps 136:22
for his mercy *e* for ever Ps 136:23
for his mercy *e* for ever Ps 136:24
for his mercy *e* for ever Ps 136:25
for his mercy *e* for ever Ps 136:26
thy mercy, O LORD, *e* for ever Ps 138:8
thy dominion *e* throughout all Ps 145:13
for his mercy *e* for ever Jer 33:11
but he that *e* to the end shall be Mt 10:22
which *e* unto everlasting life Jn 6:27
hopeth all things, *e* all things 1Cor 13:7
is the man that *e* temptation Jas 1:12
the word of the Lord *e* for ever 1Pet 1:25

## ENDURING

of the LORD is clean, *e* for ever Ps 19:9
which is effectual in the *e* of 2Cor 1:6
heaven a better and an *e* substance Heb 10:34

## EN-EGLAIM *(en-eg'-la-im) A place near the Salt Sea.*

upon it from En-gedi even unto *E* Eze 47:10

## ENEMIES

delivered thine *e* into thy hand Gen 14:20
shall possess the gate of his *e* Gen 22:17
shall be in the neck of thine *e* Gen 49:8
war, they join also unto our *e* Ex 1:10
I will be an enemy unto thine *e* Ex 23:22
I will make all thine *e* turn Ex 23:27
unto their shame among their *e* Ex 32:25
And ye shall chase your *e*, and they Lev 26:7
your *e* shall fall before you by Lev 26:8
in vain, for your *e* shall eat it Lev 26:16
ye shall be slain before your *e* Lev 26:17
your *e* which dwell therein shall Lev 26:32
hearts in the lands of their *e* Lev 26:36
no power to stand before your *e* Lev 26:37
land of your *e* shall eat you up Lev 26:38
them into the land of their *e* Lev 26:41
they be in the land of their *e* Lev 26:44
and ye shall be saved from your *e* Num 10:9
LORD, and let thine *e* be scattered Num 10:35
ye be not smitten before your *e* Num 14:42
I took thee to curse mine *e* Num 23:11
he shall eat up the nations his *e* Num 24:8
I called thee to curse mine *e* Num 24:10
shall be a possession for his *e* Num 24:18
driven out his *e* from before him Num 32:21
lest ye be smitten before your *e* Deut 1:42
out all thine *e* from before thee Deut 6:19
rest from all your *e* round about Deut 12:10
out to battle against thine *e* Deut 20:1
day unto battle against your *e* Deut 20:3
to fight for you against your *e* Deut 20:4
shalt eat the spoil of thine *e* Deut 20:14
forth to war against thine *e* Deut 21:10
host goeth forth against thine *e* Deut 23:9
and to give up thine *e* before thee Deut 23:14
rest from all thine *e* round about Deut 25:19
The LORD shall cause thine *e* that Deut 28:7
thee to be smitten before thine *e* Deut 28:25
sheep shall be given unto thine *e* Deut 28:31
shalt thou serve thine *e* which Deut 28:48
wherewith thine *e* shall distress Deut 28:53
wherewith thine *e* shall distress Deut 28:55
be sold unto your *e* for bondmen Deut 28:68
put all these curses upon thine *e* Deut 30:7
even our *e* themselves being Deut 32:31
I will render vengeance to mine *e* Deut 32:41
be thou an help to him from his *e* Deut 33:7
thine *e* shall be found liars unto Deut 33:29
their backs before their *e* Josh 7:8
could not stand before their *e* Josh 7:12
turned their backs before their *e* Josh 7:12
canst not stand before thine *e* Josh 7:13
avenged themselves upon their *e* Josh 10:13
ye not, but pursue after your *e* Josh 10:19
all your *e* against whom ye fight Josh 10:25
a man of all their *e* before them Josh 21:44
all their *e* into their hand Josh 21:44
of your *e* with your brethren Josh 22:8
from all their *e* round about Josh 23:1
the hands of their *e* round about Judg 2:14
any longer stand before their *e* Judg 2:14
their *e* all the days of the judge Judg 2:18
*e* the Moabites into your hand Judg 3:28
So let all thine *e* perish Judg 5:31
of all their *e* on every side Judg 8:34
vengeance for thee of thine *e* Judg 11:36
my mouth is enlarged over mine *e* 1Sa 2:1
save us out of the hand of our *e* 1Sa 4:3
us out of the hand of our *e* 1Sa 12:10
the hand of your *e* on every side 1Sa 12:11
that I may be avenged on mine *e* 1Sa 14:24
spoil of their *e* which they found 1Sa 14:30
against all his *e* on every side 1Sa 14:47
to be avenged of the king's *e* 1Sa 18:25
the *e* of David every one from the 1Sa 20:15
it at the hand of David's *e* 1Sa 20:16
also do God unto the *e* of David 1Sa 25:22
thine own hand, now let thine *e* 1Sa 25:26
and the souls of thine *e*, them 1Sa 25:29
against the *e* of my lord the king 1Sa 29:8
of the spoil of the *e* of the LORD 1Sa 30:26
and out of the hand of all their *e* 2Sa 3:18
forth upon mine *e* before me 2Sa 5:20
rest round about from all his *e* 2Sa 7:1
off all thine *e* out of thy sight 2Sa 7:9
thee to rest from all thine *e* 2Sa 7:11
to the *e* of the LORD to blaspheme 2Sa 12:14
LORD hath avenged him of his *e* 2Sa 18:19
The *e* of my lord the king, and all 2Sa 18:32
In that thou lovest thine *e* 2Sa 19:6
saved us out of the hand of our *e* 2Sa 19:9
him out of the hand of all his *e* 2Sa 22:1
so shall I be saved from mine *e* 2Sa 22:4
I have pursued mine *e*, and 2Sa 22:38
also given me the necks of mine *e* 2Sa 22:41
bringeth me forth from mine *e* 2Sa 22:49
flee three months before thine *e* 2Sa 24:13
hast asked the life of thine *e* 1Kin 3:11
soul, in the land of their *e* 1Kin 8:48
you out of the hand of all your *e* 2Kin 17:39
them into the hand of their *e* 2Kin 21:14
a prey and a spoil to all their *e* 2Kin 21:14
ye be come to betray me to mine *e* 1Chr 12:17
God hath broken in upon mine *e* by 1Chr 14:11
off all thine *e* from before thee 1Chr 17:8
I will subdue all thine *e* 1Chr 17:10
sword of thine *e* overtaketh thee 1Chr 21:12
rest from all his *e* round about 1Chr 22:9
honour, nor the life of thine *e* 2Chr 1:11
if their *e* besiege them in the 2Chr 6:28
go out to war against their *e* by 2Chr 6:34
deliver them over before their *e* 2Chr 6:36
made them to rejoice over their *e* 2Chr 20:27
fought against the *e* of Israel 2Chr 20:29
them into the hand of their *e* 2Chr 25:20
when our *e* heard that it was Neh 4:15
the reproach of the heathen our *e* Neh 5:9
the Arabian, and the rest of our *e* Neh 6:1
that when all our *e* heard thereof Neh 6:16
them into the hand of their *e* Neh 9:27
them out of the hand of their *e* Neh 9:27
thou them in the hand of their *e* Neh 9:28
to avenge themselves on their *e* Est 8:13
in the day that the *e* of the Jews Est 9:1
*e* with the stroke of the sword Est 9:5
lives, and had rest from their *e* Est 9:16
the Jews rested from their *e* Est 9:22
me unto him as one of his *e* Job 19:11
all mine *e* upon the cheek bone Ps 3:7
righteousness because of mine *e* Ps 5:8
waxeth old because of all mine *e* Ps 6:7
Let all mine *e* be ashamed Ps 6:10
because of the rage of mine *e* Ps 7:6
strength because of thine *e* Ps 8:2
When mine *e* are turned back, they Ps 9:3
as for all his *e*, he puffeth at Ps 10:5
that oppress me, from my deadly *e* Ps 17:9
him from the hand of all his *e* Ps 18:*t*
so shall I be saved from mine *e* Ps 18:3
I have pursued mine *e*, and Ps 18:37
also given me the necks of mine *e* Ps 18:40
He delivereth me from mine *e* Ps 18:48
hand shall find out all thine *e* Ps 21:8
me in the presence of mine *e* Ps 23:5
let not mine *e* triumph over me Ps 25:2
Consider mine *e*; for they are Ps 25:19
When the wicked, even mine *e* Ps 27:2
up above mine *e* round about me Ps 27:6
a plain path, because of mine *e* Ps 27:11
not over unto the will of mine *e* Ps 27:12
I was a reproach among all mine *e* Ps 31:11
me from the hand of mine *e* Ps 31:15
mine *e* wrongfully rejoice over me Ps 35:19
the *e* of the LORD shall be as the Ps 37:20
But mine *e* are lively, and they Ps 38:19
him unto the will of his *e* Ps 41:2
Mine *e* speak evil of me, When Ps 41:5
in my bones, mine *e* reproach me Ps 42:10
thee will we push down our *e* Ps 44:5
But thou hast saved us from our *e* Ps 44:7
in the heart of the king's *e* Ps 45:5
He shall reward evil unto mine *e* Ps 54:5
hath seen his desire upon mine *e* Ps 54:7
Mine *e* would daily swallow me up Ps 56:2
thee, then shall mine *e* turn back Ps 56:9
Deliver me from mine *e*, O my God Ps 59:1
let me see my desire upon mine *e* Ps 59:10
it is that shall tread down our *e* Ps 60:12
of thy power shall thine *e* submit Ps 66:3
God arise, let his *e* be scattered Ps 68:1
God shall wound the head of his *e* Ps 68:21
be dipped in the blood of thine *e* Ps 68:23
me, being mine *e* wrongfully Ps 69:4
deliver me because of mine *e* Ps 69:18
For mine *e* speak against me Ps 71:10
his *e* shall lick the dust Ps 72:9
Thine *e* roar in the midst of thy Ps 74:4
Forget not the voice of thine *e* Ps 74:23
but the sea overwhelmed their *e* Ps 78:53
he smote his *e* in the hinder Ps 78:66
our *e* laugh among themselves Ps 80:6
should soon have subdued their *e* Ps 81:14
For, lo, thine *e* make a tumult Ps 83:2
thine *e* with thy strong arm Ps 89:10
hast made all his *e* to rejoice Ps 89:42
Wherewith thine *e* have reproached Ps 89:51
For, lo, thine *e*, O LORD, for, lo Ps 92:9
for, lo, thine *e* shall perish Ps 92:9
shall see my desire on mine *e* Ps 92:11
and burneth up his *e* round about Ps 97:3
Mine *e* reproach me all the day Ps 102:8
made them stronger than their *e* Ps 105:24
And the waters covered their *e* Ps 106:11
Their *e* also oppressed them, and Ps 106:42
it is that shall tread down our *e* Ps 108:13
I make thine *e* thy footstool Ps 110:1
rule thou in the midst of thine *e* Ps 110:2
he see his desire upon his *e* Ps 112:8
hast made me wiser than mine *e* Ps 119:98
because mine *e* have forgotten thy Ps 119:139
Many are my persecutors and mine *e* Ps 119:157
speak with the *e* in the gate Ps 127:5
His *e* will I clothe with shame Ps 132:18
And hath redeemed us from our *e* Ps 136:24
hand against the wrath of mine *e* Ps 138:7
thine *e* take thy name in vain Ps 139:20
I count them mine *e* Ps 139:22
Deliver me, O LORD, from mine *e* Ps 143:9
And of thy mercy cut off mine *e* Ps 143:12
he maketh even his *e* to be at Prov 16:7
and avenge me of mine *e* Is 1:24
him, and join his *e* together Is 9:11
fire of thine *e* shall devour them Is 26:11
he shall prevail against his *e* Is 42:13
adversaries, recompence to his *e* Is 59:18
thy corn to be meat for thine *e* Is 62:8
rendereth recompence to his *e* Is 66:6
and his indignation toward his *e* Is 66:14
of my soul into the hand of her *e* Jer 12:7
to the sword before their *e* Jer 15:9
make thee to pass with thine *e* Jer 15:14
*e* in the land which thou knowest Jer 17:4
fall by the sword before their *e* Jer 19:7
and straitness, wherewith their *e* Jer 19:9
fall by the sword of their *e* Jer 20:4
I give into the hand of their *e* Jer 20:5
and into the hand of their *e* Jer 21:7
them into the hand of their *e* Jer 34:20
I give into the hand of their *e* Jer 34:21
of Egypt into the hand of his *e* Jer 44:30
the going down of Horonaim the *e* Jer 48:5
to be dismayed before their *e* Jer 49:37
with her, they are become her *e* Lam 1:2
are the chief, her *e* prosper Lam 1:5
all mine *e* have heard of my Lam 1:21
All thine *e* have opened their Lam 2:16
All our *e* have opened their Lam 3:46
Mine *e* chased me sore, like a Lam 3:52
them into the hand of their *e* Eze 39:23
interpretation thereof to thine *e* Dan 4:19
go into captivity before their *e* Amos 9:4
thee from the hand of thine *e* Mic 4:10
all thine *e* shall be cut off Mic 5:9
a man's *e* are the men of his own Mic 7:6
and he reserveth wrath for his *e* Nah 1:2
and darkness shall pursue his *e* Nah 1:8
be set wide open unto thine *e* Nah 3:13
which tread down their *e* in the Zec 10:5
But I say unto you, Love your *e* Mt 5:44
till I make thine *e* thy footstool Mt 22:44
till I make thine *e* thy footstool Mk 12:36
we should be saved from our *e* Lk 1:71
out of the hand of our *e* might Lk 1:74
unto you which hear, Love your *e* Lk 6:27
But love ye your *e*, and do good, Lk 6:35
But those mine *e*, which would not Lk 19:27

that thine e shall cast a trench ... Lk 19:43
Till I make thine e thy footstool ... Lk 20:43
For if, when we were e, we were ... Rom 5:10
they are e for your sakes ... Rom 11:28
he hath put all e under his feet ... 1Cor 15:25
that they are the e of the cross ... Phil 3:18
e in your mind by wicked works, ... Col 1:21
I make thine e thy footstool ... Heb 1:13
till his e be made his footstool ... Heb 10:13
their mouth, and devoureth their e ... Rev 11:5
and their e beheld them ... Rev 11:12

**ENEMIES'**
desolate, and ye be in your e land ... Lev 26:34
in their iniquity in your e lands ... Lev 26:39
them out of their e lands ... Eze 39:27

**ENEMY**
LORD, hath dashed in pieces the e ... Ex 15:6
The e said, I will pursue, I will ... Ex 15:9
then I will be an e unto thine ... Ex 23:22
delivered into the hand of the e ... Lev 26:25
against the e that oppresseth you ... Num 10:9
that he die, and was not his e ... Num 35:23
wherewith thine e shall distress ... Deut 28:57
that I feared the wrath of the e ... Deut 32:27
beginning of revenges upon the e ... Deut 32:42
thrust out the e from before thee ... Deut 33:27
Samson our e into our hand ... Judg 16:23
delivered into our hands our e ... Judg 16:24
shalt see an e in my habitation ... 1Sa 2:32
Saul became David's e continually ... 1Sa 18:29
me so, and sent away mine e ... 1Sa 19:17
deliver thine e into thine hand ... 1Sa 24:4
For if a man find his e, will he ... 1Sa 24:19
thine e into thine hand this day ... 1Sa 26:8
from thee, and is become thine e ... 1Sa 28:16
the son of Saul thine e, which ... 2Sa 4:8
He delivered me from my strong e ... 2Sa 22:18
be smitten down before the e ... 1Kin 8:33
if their e besiege them in the ... 1Kin 8:37
go out to battle against their e ... 1Kin 8:44
them, and deliver them to the e ... 1Kin 8:46
captives unto the land of the e ... 1Kin 8:46
Hast thou found me, O mine e ... 1Kin 21:20
be put to the worse before the e ... 2Chr 6:24
shall make thee fall before the e ... 2Chr 25:8
to help the king against the e ... 2Chr 26:13
help us against the e in the way ... Ezr 8:22
us from the hand of the e ... Ezr 8:31
the Agagite, the Jews' e ... Est 3:10
tongue, although the e could not ... Est 7:4
and e is this wicked Haman ... Est 7:6
the Jews' e unto Esther the queen ... Est 8:1
the e of the Jews, slew they ... Est 9:10
the e of all the Jews, had ... Est 9:24
face, and holdest me for thine e ... Job 13:24
mine e sharpeneth his eyes upon ... Job 16:9
Let mine e be as the wicked, and ... Job 27:7
me, he counteth me for his e ... Job 33:10
him that without cause is mine e ... Ps 7:4
Let the e persecute my soul, and ... Ps 7:5
that thou mightest still the e ... Ps 8:2
O thou e, destructions are come ... Ps 9:6
shall mine e be exalted over me ... Ps 13:2
Lest mine e say, I have prevailed ... Ps 13:4
He delivered me from my strong e ... Ps 18:17
shut me up into the hand of the e ... Ps 31:8
because mine e doth not triumph ... Ps 41:11
of the oppression of the e ... Ps 42:9
of the oppression of the e ... Ps 43:2
makest us to turn back from the e ... Ps 44:10
by reason of the e and avenger ... Ps 44:16
Because of the voice of the e ... Ps 55:3
For it was not an e that ... Ps 55:12
me, and a strong tower from the e ... Ps 61:3
my life from fear of the e ... Ps 64:1
even all that the e hath done ... Ps 74:3
shall the e blaspheme thy name ... Ps 74:10
that the e hath reproached, O ... Ps 74:18
when he delivered them from the e ... Ps 78:42
The e shall not exact upon him ... Ps 89:22
them from the hand of the e ... Ps 106:10
redeemed from the hand of the e ... Ps 107:2
For the e hath persecuted my soul ... Ps 143:3
Rejoice not when thine e falleth ... Prov 24:17
If thine e be hungry, give him ... Prov 25:21
the kisses of an e are deceitful ... Prov 27:6
When the e shall come in like a ... Is 59:19
he was turned to be their e ... Is 63:10
for the sword of the e and fear is ... Jer 6:25
verily I will cause the e to ... Jer 15:11
as with an east wind before the e ... Jer 18:17
thee with the wound of an e ... Jer 30:14
come again from the land of the e ... Jer 31:16
king of Babylon, his e, and that ... Jer 44:30
gone into captivity before the e ... Lam 1:5
fell into the hand of the e ... Lam 1:7
for the e hath magnified himself ... Lam 1:9
desolate, because the e prevailed ... Lam 1:16
his right hand from before the e ... Lam 2:3
He hath bent his bow like an e ... Lam 2:4
The Lord was as an e ... Lam 2:5
of the e the walls of her palaces ... Lam 2:7
thine e to rejoice over thee ... Lam 2:17
brought up hath mine e consumed ... Lam 2:22
the e should have entered into ... Lam 4:12
Because the e hath said against ... Eze 36:2
the e shall pursue him ... Hos 8:3
my people is risen up as an e ... Mic 2:8
Rejoice not against me, O mine e ... Mic 7:8
she that is mine e shall see it ... Mic 7:10
seek strength because of the e ... Nah 3:11
he hath cast out thine e ... Zeph 3:15
thy neighbour, and hate thine e ... Mt 5:43
his e came and sowed tares among ... Mt 13:25
unto them, An e hath done this ... Mt 13:28
The e that sowed them is the ... Mt 13:39
and over all the power of the e ... Lk 10:19
thou e of all righteousness, wilt ... Acts 13:10
Therefore if thine e hunger ... Rom 12:20
The last e that shall be ... 1Cor 15:26
Am I therefore become your e ... Gal 4:16
Yet count him not as an e ... 2Th 3:15
of the world is the e of God ... Jas 4:4

**ENEMY'S**
If thou meet thine e ox or his ... Ex 23:4
Or, Deliver me from the e hand ... Job 6:23
and his glory into the e hand ... Ps 78:61

**ENFLAMING**
E yourselves with idols under ... Is 57:5

**ENGAGED**
for who is this that e his heart ... Jer 30:21

**EN-GANNIM** (*en-gan'-nim*)
*1. A city in Judah.*
and E, Tappuah, and Enam ... Josh 15:34
*2. A city in Issachar.*
and E, and En-haddah, and ... Josh 19:21
her suburbs, E with her suburbs ... Josh 21:29

**EN-GEDI** (*en-ghe'-di*) See HAZAZON-TAMAR. *A town on the Salt Sea.*
and the city of Salt, and E ... Josh 15:62
and dwelt in strong holds at E ... 1Sa 23:29
David is in the wilderness of E ... 1Sa 24:1
be in Hazazon-tamar, which is E ... 2Chr 20:2
of camphire in the vineyards of E ... Song 1:14
it from E even unto En-eglaim ... Eze 47:10

**ENGINES**
And he made in Jerusalem e ... 2Chr 26:15
he shall set e of war against thy ... Eze 26:9

**ENGRAFTED**
receive with meekness the e word ... Jas 1:21

**ENGRAVE**
shalt thou e the two stones with ... Ex 28:11
I will e the graving thereof, ... Zec 3:9

**ENGRAVEN**
e in stones, was glorious, so ... 2Cor 3:7

**ENGRAVER**
With the work of an e in stone ... Ex 28:11
work all manner of work, of the e ... Ex 35:35
of the tribe of Dan, an e ... Ex 38:23

**ENGRAVINGS**
like the e of a signet, shalt ... Ex 28:11
names, like the e of a signet ... Ex 28:21
like the e of a signet, HOLINESS ... Ex 28:36
like the e of a signet, every one ... Ex 39:14
like to the e of a signet ... Ex 39:30

**EN-HADDAH** (*en-had'-dah*) *A city in Issachar.*
And Remeth, and En-gannim, and E ... Josh 19:21

**EN-HAKKORE** (*en-hak'-ko-re*) *A spring.*
he called the name thereof E ... Judg 15:19

**EN-HAZOR** (*en-ha'-zor*) *A city in Naphtali.*
And Kedesh, and Edrei, and E ... Josh 19:37

**ENJOIN**
e thee that which is convenient ... Philem 8

**ENJOINED**
and Esther the queen had e them ... Est 9:31
Who hath e him his way ... Job 36:23
which God hath e unto you ... Heb 9:20

**ENJOY**
shall the land e her sabbaths ... Lev 26:34
the land rest, and e her sabbaths ... Lev 26:34
shall e her sabbaths, while she ... Lev 26:43
e every man the inheritance of ... Num 36:8
but thou shalt not e them ... Deut 28:41
e it, which Moses the LORD's ... Josh 1:15
with mirth, therefore e pleasure ... Eccl 2:1
his soul e good in his labour ... Eccl 2:24
e the good of all his labour, it ... Eccl 3:13
to e the good of all his labour ... Eccl 5:18
mine elect shall long e the work ... Is 65:22
that by thee we e great quietness ... Acts 24:2
giveth us richly all things to e ... 1Ti 6:17
than to e the pleasures of sin ... Heb 11:25

**ENJOYED**
until the land had e her sabbaths ... 2Chr 36:21

**ENLARGE**
God shall e Japheth, and he shall ... Gen 9:27
before thee, and e thy borders ... Ex 34:24
LORD thy God shall e thy border ... Deut 12:20
if the LORD thy God e thy coast ... Deut 19:8
e my coast, and that thine hand ... 1Chr 4:10
when thou shalt e my heart ... Ps 119:32
E the place of thy tent, and let ... Is 54:2
that they might e their border ... Amos 1:13
e thy baldness as the eagle ... Mic 1:16
e the borders of their garments, ... Mt 23:5

**ENLARGED**
my mouth is e over mine enemies ... 1Sa 2:1
Thou hast e my steps under me ... 2Sa 22:37
thou hast e me when I was in ... Ps 4:1
Thou hast e my steps under me, ... Ps 18:36
The troubles of my heart are e ... Ps 25:17
Therefore hell hath e herself ... Is 5:14
thou hast e thy bed, and made thee ... Is 57:8
thine heart shall fear, and be e ... Is 60:5
is open unto you, our heart is e ... 2Cor 6:11
unto my children,) be ye also e ... 2Cor 6:13
that we shall be e by you ... 2Cor 10:15

**ENLARGEMENT**
at this time, then shall there e ... Est 4:14

**ENLARGETH**
he said, Blessed be he that e Gad ... Deut 33:20
he e the nations, and straiteneth ... Job 12:23
who e his desire as hell, and is ... Hab 2:5

**ENLARGING**
And there was an e, and a winding ... Eze 41:7

**ENLIGHTEN**
LORD my God will e my darkness ... Ps 18:28

**ENLIGHTENED**
and his eyes were e ... 1Sa 14:27
you, how mine eyes have been e ... 1Sa 14:29
to be e with the light of the ... Job 33:30
His lightnings e the world ... Ps 97:4
of your understanding being e ... Eph 1:18
for those who were once e ... Heb 6:4

**ENLIGHTENING**
of the LORD is pure, e the eyes ... Ps 19:8

**ENMITY**
I will put e between thee and the ... Gen 3:15
Or in e smite him with his hand, ... Num 35:21
he thrust him suddenly without e ... Num 35:22
they were at e between themselves ... Lk 23:12
the carnal mind is e against God ... Rom 8:7
abolished in his flesh the e ... Eph 2:15
cross, having slain the e thereby ... Eph 2:16
of the world is e with God ... Jas 4:4

**ENOCH** (*e'-nok*) See HENOCH.
*1. A son of Cain.*
and she conceived, and bare E ... Gen 4:17
And unto E was born Irad ... Gen 4:18
*2. A city built by Cain.*
after the name of his son, E ... Gen 4:17
*3. A son of Jared.*
sixty and two years, and he begat E ... Gen 5:18
he begat E eight hundred years ... Gen 5:19
E lived sixty and five years, and ... Gen 5:21
E walked with God after he begat ... Gen 5:22
all the days of E were three ... Gen 5:23
And E walked with God ... Gen 5:24
Mathusala, which was the son of E ... Lk 3:37
By faith E was translated that he ... Heb 11:5
E also, the seventh from Adam, ... Jude 14

**ENOS** (*e'-nos*) See ENOSH. *Son of Seth.*
and he called his name E ... Gen 4:26
hundred and five years, and begat E ... Gen 5:6
after he begat E eight hundred ... Gen 5:7
E lived ninety years, and begat ... Gen 5:9
E lived after he begat Cainan ... Gen 5:10
all the days of E were nine ... Gen 5:11
Which was the son of E, which was ... Lk 3:38

**ENOSH** (*e'-nosh*) See ENOS. *Same as Enos.*
Adam, Sheth, E, ... 1Chr 1:1

**ENOUGH**
We have both straw and provender e ... Gen 24:25
And Esau said, I have e, my ... Gen 33:9
with me, and because I have e ... Gen 33:11
behold, it is large e for them ... Gen 34:21
And Israel said, It is e ... Gen 45:28
and also drew water e for us ... Ex 2:19
Intreat the LORD (for it is e) ... Ex 9:28
e for the service of the work ... Ex 36:5
have dwelt long e in this mount ... Deut 1:6
compassed this mountain long e ... Deut 2:3
said, The hill is not e for us ... Josh 17:16
destroyed the people, It is e ... 2Sa 24:16
and said, It is e ... 1Kin 19:4
the angel that destroyed, It is e ... 1Chr 21:15
of the LORD, we have had e to eat ... 2Chr 31:10
have goats' milk e for thy food ... Prov 27:27
vain persons shall have poverty e ... Prov 28:19
yea, four things say not, It is e ... Prov 30:15
the fire that saith not, It is e ... Prov 30:16
dogs which can never have e ... Is 56:11
will destroy till they have e ... Jer 49:9
For they shall eat, and not have e ... Hos 4:10
not have stolen till they had e ... Obad 5
tear in pieces e for his whelps ... Nah 2:12
ye eat, but ye have not e ... Hag 1:6
shall not be room e to receive it ... Mal 3:10
It is e for the disciple that he ... Mt 10:25
lest there be not e for us ... Mt 25:9
it is e, the hour is come ... Mk 14:41
of my father's have bread e ... Lk 15:17
And he said unto them, It is e ... Lk 22:38
And when they had eaten e, they ... Acts 27:38

**ENQUIRE**
the damsel, and e at her mouth ... Gen 24:57
And she went to e of the LORD ... Gen 25:22
people come unto me to e of God ... Ex 18:15
that thou e not after their gods, ... Deut 12:30
Then shalt thou e, and make search ... Deut 13:14
that shall be in those days, and e ... Deut 17:9
e of thee, and say, Is there any ... Judg 4:20

when a man went to e of God 1Sa 9:9
E thou whose son the stripling is 1Sa 17:56
I then begin to e of God for him 1Sa 22:15
that I may go to her, and e of her 1Sa 28:7
said unto the king of Israel, E 1Kin 22:5
besides, that we might e of him 1Kin 22:7
by whom we may e of the LORD 1Kin 22:8
e of Baal-zebub the god of Ekron 2Kin 1:2
that ye go to e of Baal-zebub the 2Kin 1:3
that thou sendest to e of 2Kin 1:6
e of Baal-zebub the god of Ekron 2Kin 1:16
no God in Israel to e of his word 2Kin 1:16
that we may e of the LORD by him 2Kin 3:11
e of the LORD by him, saying, 2Kin 8:8
altar shall be for me to e by 2Kin 16:15
e of the LORD for me, and for the 2Kin 22:13
which sent you to e of the LORD 2Kin 22:18
had a familiar spirit, to e of it 1Chr 10:13
to e of his welfare, and to 1Chr 18:10
not go before it to e of God 1Chr 21:30
said unto the king of Israel, E 2Chr 18:4
besides, that we might e of him 2Chr 18:6
man, by whom we may e of the LORD 2Chr 18:7
who sent unto him to e of the 2Chr 32:31
e of the LORD for me, and for them 2Chr 34:21
who sent you to e of the LORD 2Chr 34:26
to e concerning Judah and Ezr 7:14
For e, I pray thee, of the former Job 8:8
the LORD, and to e in his temple Ps 27:4
for thou dost not e wisely Eccl 7:10
also the night: if ye will e Is 21:12
e ye: return, come Is 21:12
E, I pray thee, of the LORD for Jer 21:2
that sent you unto me to e of me Jer 37:7
prophet to e of him concerning me Eze 14:7
of Israel came to e of the LORD Eze 20:1
Are ye come to e of me Eze 20:3
enter, e who in it is worthy Mt 10:11
they began to e among themselves, Lk 22:23
Do ye e among yourselves of that Jn 16:19
e in the house of Judas for one Acts 9:11
But if ye e any thing concerning Acts 19:39
as though ye would e something Acts 23:15
as though they would e somewhat Acts 23:20
Whether any do e of Titus 2Cor 8:23

**ENQUIRED**
e diligently, and, behold, it be Deut 17:4
And when they e and asked, they Judg 6:29
the men of Succoth, and e of him Judg 8:14
children of Israel e of the LORD Judg 20:27
Therefore they e of the LORD 1Sa 10:22
he e of the LORD for him, and gave 1Sa 22:10
hast e of God for him, that he 1Sa 22:13
Therefore David e of the LORD 1Sa 23:2
Then David e of the LORD yet 1Sa 23:4
when Saul e of the LORD, the LORD 1Sa 28:6
David e at the LORD, saying, 1Sa 30:8
that David e of the LORD, saying, 2Sa 2:1
David e of the LORD, saying, 2Sa 5:19
when David e of the LORD, he said 2Sa 5:23
David sent and e after the woman 2Sa 11:3
was as if a man had e at the 2Sa 16:23
and David e of the LORD 2Sa 21:1
And e not of the LORD 1Chr 10:14
for we e not at it in the days of 1Chr 13:3
David e of God, saying, Shall I 1Chr 14:10
Therefore David e again of God 1Chr 14:14
returned and e early after God Ps 78:34
should I be e of at all by them Eze 14:3
GOD, I will not be e of by you Eze 20:3
and shall I be e of by you Eze 20:31
GOD, I will not be e of by you Eze 20:31
I will yet for this be e of by Eze 36:37
that the king e of them, he Dan 1:20
sought the LORD, nor e for him Zeph 1:6
e of them diligently what time Mt 2:7
had diligently e of the wise men Mt 2:16
Then e he of them the hour when Jn 4:52
or our brethren be e of, they are 2Cor 8:23
salvation the prophets have e 1Pet 1:10

**ENQUIREST**
That thou e after mine iniquity, Job 10:6

**ENQUIRY**
is holy, and after vows to make e Prov 20:25
had made e for Simon's house Acts 10:17

**ENRICH**
the king will e him with great 1Sa 17:25
thou didst e the kings of the Eze 27:33

**ENRICHED**
in every thing ye are e by him 1Cor 1:5
Being e in every thing to all 2Cor 9:11

**ENRICHEST**
thou greatly e it with the river Ps 65:9

**EN-RIMMON** (*en-rim'-mon*) See AIN, RIMMON. *A city in Judah.*
And at E, and at Zareah, and at Neh 11:29

**EN-ROGEL** (*en-ro'-ghel*) *A fountain near Jerusalem.*
the goings out thereof were at E Josh 15:7
on the south, and descended to E Josh 18:16
Jonathan and Ahimaaz stayed by E 2Sa 17:17
stone of Zoheleth, which is by E 1Kin 1:9

**ENSAMPLE**
walk so as ye have us for an e Phil 3:17
an e unto you to follow us 2Th 3:9
making them an e unto those that 2Pet 2:6

**ENSAMPLES**
things happened unto them for e 1Cor 10:11
So that we were e to all that 1Th 1:7
but being e to the flock 1Pet 5:3

**EN-SHEMESH** (*en-she'-mesh*) *A spring.*
passed toward the waters of E Josh 15:7
the north, and went forth to E Josh 18:17

**ENSIGN**
with the e of their father's Num 2:2
he will lift up an e to the Is 5:26
stand for an e of the people Is 11:10
shall set up an e for the nations Is 11:12
lifteth up an e on the mountains Is 18:3
a mountain, and as an e on an hill Is 30:17
princes shall be afraid of the e Is 31:9
lifted up as an e upon his land Zec 9:16

**ENSIGNS**
they set up their e for signs Ps 74:4

**ENSNARED**
reign not, lest the people be e Job 34:30

**ENSUE**
let him seek peace, and e it 1Pet 3:11

**ENTANGLE**
how they might e him in his talk Mt 22:15

**ENTANGLED**
They are e in the land, the Ex 14:3
be not e again with the yoke of Gal 5:1
Christ, they are again e therein 2Pet 2:20

**ENTANGLETH**
No man that warreth e himself 2Ti 2:4

**EN-TAPPUAH** (*en-tap'-poo-ah*) *A town in Manasseh.*
hand unto the inhabitants of E Josh 17:7

**ENTER**
he was come near to e into Egypt Gen 12:11
able to e into the tent of the Ex 40:35
all that e into the host, to do Num 4:3
all that e in to perform the Num 4:23
the curse shall e into her Num 5:24
the curse shall e into her Num 5:27
for he shall not e into the land Num 20:24
shall not e into the congregation Deut 23:1
A bastard shall not e into the Deut 23:2
e into the congregation of the Deut 23:2
e into the congregation of the Deut 23:3
e into the congregation of the Deut 23:3
e into the congregation of the Deut 23:8
That thou shouldest e into Deut 29:12
them not to e into their cities Josh 10:19
go, and to e to possess the land Judg 18:9
my cry did e into his ears 2Sa 22:7
and when thy feet e into the city 1Kin 14:12
myself, and e into the battle 1Kin 22:30
We will e into the city, then the 2Kin 7:4
A third part of you that e in on 2Kin 11:5
I will e into the lodgings of his 2Kin 19:23
the priests could not e into the 2Chr 7:2
unclean in any thing should e in 2Chr 23:19
e into his sanctuary, which he 2Chr 30:8
for the house that I shall e into Neh 2:8
for none might e into the king's Est 4:2
will he e with thee into judgment Job 22:4
that he should e into judgment Job 34:23
Their sword shall e into their Ps 37:15
they shall e into the king's Ps 45:15
they should not e into my rest Ps 95:11
E into his gates with Ps 100:4
into which the righteous shall e Ps 118:20
e not into judgment with thy Ps 143:2
E not into the path of the wicked Prov 4:14
A fool's lips e into contention, Prov 18:6
e not into the fields of the Prov 23:10
E into the rock, and hide thee in Is 2:10
The LORD will e into judgment Is 3:14
which keepeth the truth may e in Is 26:2
e thou into thy chambers, and shut Is 26:20
I will e into the height of his Is 37:24
He shall e into peace Is 57:2
in the street, and equity cannot e Is 59:14
that e in at these gates to Jer 7:2
let us e into the defenced cities Jer 8:14
if I e into the city, then behold Jer 14:18
E not into the house of mourning, Jer 16:5
that e in by these gates Jer 17:20
Then shall there e into the gates Jer 17:25
or who shall e into our Jer 21:13
thy people that e in by these Jer 22:2
then shall there e in by the Jer 22:4
Bethlehem, to go to e into Egypt, Jer 41:17
set your faces to e into Egypt Jer 42:15
you, when ye shall e into Egypt Jer 42:18
not e into thy congregation Lam 1:10
of his quiver to e into my reins Lam 3:13
for the robbers shall e into it Eze 7:22
neither shall they e into the Eze 13:9
they shall not e into the land of Eze 20:38
when he shall e into thy gates, Eze 26:10
as men e into a city wherein is Eze 26:10
I will cause breath to e into you Eze 37:5
When the priests e therein Eze 42:14
and no man shall e in by it Eze 44:2
he shall e by the way of the Eze 44:3
shall e into my sanctuary, of any Eze 44:9
They shall e into my sanctuary, Eze 44:16
that when they e in at the gates Eze 44:17
when they e into the inner court Eze 44:21
the prince shall e by the way of Eze 46:2
And when the prince shall e Eze 46:8
shall e into the fortress of the Dan 11:7
He shall also set his face to e Dan 11:17
He shall e peaceably even upon Dan 11:24
he shall e into the countries, and Dan 11:40
He shall e also into the glorious Dan 11:41
I will not e into the city Hos 11:9
they shall e in at the windows Joel 2:9
nor e into Gilgal, and pass not to Amos 5:5
Jonah began to e into the city a Jonah 3:4
it shall e into the house of the Zec 5:4
ye shall in no case e into the Mt 5:20
e into thy closet, and when thou Mt 6:6
E ye in at the strait gate Mt 7:13
shall e into the kingdom of Mt 7:21
city of the Samaritans e ye not Mt 10:5
city or town ye shall e, enquire Mt 10:11
Or else how can one e into a Mt 12:29
wicked than himself, and they e in Mt 12:45
ye shall not e into the kingdom Mt 18:3
to e into life halt or maimed Mt 18:8
thee to e into life with one eye Mt 18:9
but if thou wilt e into life Mt 19:17
e into the kingdom of heaven Mt 19:23
than for a rich man to e into the Mt 19:24
e thou into the joy of thy lord Mt 25:21
e thou into the joy of thy lord Mt 25:23
that ye e not into temptation Mt 26:41
no more openly e into the city Mk 1:45
No man can e into a strong man's Mk 3:27
swine, that we may e into them Mk 5:12
place soever ye e into a house Mk 6:10
out of him, and e no more into him Mk 9:25
for thee to e into life maimed Mk 9:43
for thee to e halt into life Mk 9:45
it is better for thee to e into Mk 9:47
child, he shall not e therein Mk 10:15
riches e into the kingdom of God Mk 10:23
to e into the kingdom of God Mk 10:24
than for a rich man to e into the Mk 10:25
into the house, neither e therein Mk 13:15
lest ye e into temptation Mk 14:38
thou shouldest e under my roof Lk 7:6
that they which e in may see the Lk 8:16
would suffer them to e into them Lk 8:32
And whatsoever house ye e into Lk 9:4
And into whatsoever house ye e Lk 10:5
And into whatsoever city ye e Lk 10:8
But into whatsoever city ye e Lk 10:10
and they e in, and dwell there Lk 11:26
Strive to e in at the strait gate Lk 13:24
I say unto you, will seek to e in Lk 13:24
child shall in no wise e therein Lk 18:17
riches e into the kingdom of God Lk 18:24
than for a rich man to e into the Lk 18:25
are in the countries e thereinto Lk 21:21
them, Pray that ye e not into Lk 22:40
lest ye e into temptation Lk 22:46
things, and to e into his glory Lk 24:26
can he e the second time into his Jn 3:4
he cannot e into the kingdom of Jn 3:5
by me if any man e in, he shall Jn 10:9
e into the kingdom of God Acts 14:22
grievous wolves e in among you Acts 20:29
They shall not e into my rest Heb 3:11
they should not e into his rest Heb 3:18
not e in because of unbelief Heb 3:19
have believed do e into rest Heb 4:3
if they shall e into my rest Heb 4:3
If they shall e into my rest Heb 4:5
that some must e therein, and they Heb 4:6
therefore to e into that rest Heb 4:11
boldness to e into the holiest by Heb 10:19
man was able to e into the temple Rev 15:8
there shall in no wise e into it Rev 21:27
may e in through the gates into Rev 22:14

**ENTERED**
In the selfsame day e Noah Gen 7:13
in unto him, and e into his house Gen 19:3
the earth when Lot e into Zoar Gen 19:23
tent, and e into Rachel's tent Gen 31:33
he e into his chamber, and wept Gen 43:30
as Moses e into the tabernacle, Ex 33:9
which are e into thine house Josh 2:3
they e into the city, and took it, Josh 8:19
of them e into fenced cities Josh 10:20
they e into the land to destroy Judg 6:5
they e into an hold of the house Judg 9:46
Abishai, and e into the city 2Sa 10:14
e into another tent, and carried 2Kin 7:8
as Jehu e in at the gate, she 2Kin 9:31
his brother, and e into the city 1Chr 19:15
when the king e into the house of 2Chr 12:11
they e into a covenant to seek 2Chr 15:12
howbeit he e not into the temple 2Chr 27:2
e into Judah, and encamped against 2Chr 32:1
e by the gate of the valley, and Neh 2:15
e into a curse, and into an oath, Neh 10:29
Hast thou e into the springs of Job 38:16
Hast thou e into the treasures of Job 38:22
but when ye e, ye defiled my land Jer 2:7
is e into our palaces, to cut off Jer 9:21
which had e into the covenant, Jer 34:10
Jeremiah was e into the dungeon Jer 37:16
the heathen e into her sanctuary Lam 1:10
the enemy should have e into the Lam 4:12

the spirit *e* into me when he ........ Eze 2:2
Then the spirit *e* into me........ Eze 3:24
*e* into a covenant with thee,........ Eze 16:8
when they *e* unto the heathen,........ Eze 36:20
they *e* into the wall which was of........ Eze 41:6
hath *e* in by it, therefore it ........ Eze 44:2
foreigners *e* into his gates, and ........ Obad 11
Thou shouldest not have *e* into ........ Obad 13
rottenness *e* into my bones, and I........ Hab 3:16
when Jesus was *e* into Capernaum ........ Mt 8:5
And when he was *e* into a ship ........ Mt 8:23
he *e* into a ship, and passed over,........ Mt 9:1
How he *e* into the house of God,........ Mt 12:4
the day that Noe *e* into the ark........ Mt 24:38
day he *e* into the synagogue........ Mk 1:21
they *e* into the house of Simon and........ Mk 1:29
again he *e* into Capernaum after........ Mk 2:1
he *e* again into the synagogue........ Mk 3:1
so that he *e* into a ship, and sat........ Mk 4:1
went out, and *e* into the swine........ Mk 5:13
And whithersoever he *e*, into........ Mk 6:56
when he was *e* into the house from........ Mk 7:17
*e* into an house, and would have no........ Mk 7:24
straightway he *e* into a ship with........ Mk 8:10
and as soon as ye be *e* into it........ Mk 11:2
Jesus *e* into Jerusalem, and into........ Mk 11:11
*e* into the house of Zacharias, and........ Lk 1:40
and *e* into Simon's house........ Lk 4:38
he *e* into one of the ships, which........ Lk 5:3
that he *e* into the synagogue and........ Lk 6:6
the people, he *e* into Capernaum........ Lk 7:1
I *e* into thine house, thou gavest........ Lk 7:44
many devils were *e* into him........ Lk 8:30
of the man, and *e* into the swine........ Lk 8:33
feared as they *e* into the cloud........ Lk 9:34
went, and *e* into a village of the........ Lk 9:52
that he *e* into a certain village........ Lk 10:38
ye *e* not in yourselves, and them........ Lk 11:52
as he *e* into a certain village,........ Lk 17:12
the day that Noe *e* into the ark........ Lk 17:27
And Jesus *e* and passed through........ Lk 19:1
Then *e* Satan into Judas surnamed........ Lk 22:3
when ye are *e* into the city,........ Lk 22:10
And they *e* in, and found not the........ Lk 24:3
ye are *e* into their labours........ Jn 4:38
*e* into a ship, and went over the........ Jn 6:17
whereinto his disciples were *e*........ Jn 6:22
And after the sop Satan *e* into him........ Jn 13:27
was a garden, into the which he *e*........ Jn 18:1
Then Pilate *e* into the judgment........ Jn 18:33
*e* into a ship immediately........ Jn 21:3
of them that *e* into the temple........ Acts 3:2
*e* with them into the temple,........ Acts 3:8
they *e* into the temple early in........ Acts 5:21
went his way, and *e* into the house........ Acts 9:17
morrow after they *e* into Caesarea........ Acts 10:24
hath at any time *e* into my mouth........ Acts 11:8
we *e* into the man's house........ Acts 11:12
*e* into the house of Lydia........ Acts 16:40
*e* into a certain man's house,........ Acts 18:7
but he himself *e* into the........ Acts 18:19
would have *e* in unto the people........ Acts 19:30
we *e* into the house of Philip the........ Acts 21:8
with them *e* into the temple........ Acts 21:26
*e* into the castle, and told Paul........ Acts 23:16
was *e* into the place of hearing,........ Acts 25:23
to whom Paul *e* in, and prayed, and........ Acts 28:8
by one man sin *e* into the world........ Rom 5:12
Moreover the law *e*, that the........ Rom 5:20
neither have *e* into the heart of........ 1Cor 2:9
*e* not in because of unbelief........ Heb 4:6
For he that is *e* into his rest........ Heb 4:10
the forerunner is for us *e*........ Heb 6:20
but by his own blood he *e* in once........ Heb 9:12
For Christ is not *e* into the holy........ Heb 9:24
*e* into the ears of the Lord of........ Jas 5:4
deceivers are *e* into the world........ 2Jn 7
of life from God *e* into them........ Rev 11:11

**ENTERETH**
every one that *e* into the service........ Num 4:30
every one that *e* into the service........ Num 4:35
every one that *e* into the service........ Num 4:39
every one that *e* into the service........ Num 4:43
even unto every one that *e* into........ 2Chr 31:16
When wisdom *e* into thine heart,........ Prov 2:10
A reproof *e* more into a wise man........ Prov 17:10
which *e* into their privy chambers........ Eze 21:14
the east, as one *e* into them........ Eze 42:12
he that *e* in by the way of the........ Eze 46:9
he that *e* by the way of the south........ Eze 46:9
that whatsoever *e* in at the mouth........ Mt 15:17
*e* in where the damsel was lying........ Mk 5:40
thing from without *e* into the man........ Mk 7:18
Because it *e* not into his heart,........ Mk 7:19
him into the house where he *e* in........ Lk 22:10
He that *e* not by the door into........ Jn 10:1
But he that *e* in by the door is........ Jn 10:2
which *e* into that within the veil........ Heb 6:19
as the high priest *e* into the........ Heb 9:25

**ENTERING**
at the *e* in of the tabernacle........ Ex 35:15
cast it at the *e* of the gate of........ Josh 8:29
Hermon unto the *e* into Hamath........ Josh 13:5
at the *e* of the gate of the city........ Josh 20:4
unto the *e* in of Hamath........ Judg 3:3
stood in the *e* of the gate of the........ Judg 9:35
even unto the *e* of the gate........ Judg 9:40
stood in the *e* of the gate of the........ Judg 9:44
Dan, stood by the *e* of the gate........ Judg 18:16
the priest stood in the *e* of the........ Judg 18:17
by *e* into a town that hath gates........ 1Sa 23:7
in array at the *e* in of the gate........ 2Sa 10:8
them even unto the *e* of the gate........ 2Sa 11:23
for the *e* of the oracle he made........ 1Kin 6:31
from the *e* in of Hamath unto the........ 1Kin 8:65
stood in the *e* in of the cave........ 1Kin 19:13
men at the *e* in of the gate........ 2Kin 7:3
at the *e* in of the gate until the........ 2Kin 10:8
the coast of Israel from the *e* of........ 2Kin 14:25
*e* in of the gate of Joshua the........ 2Kin 23:8
at the *e* in of the house of the........ 2Kin 23:11
*e* in of the wilderness from the........ 1Chr 5:9
Egypt even unto the *e* of Hemath........ 1Chr 13:5
from the *e* in of Hamath unto the........ 2Chr 7:8
the *e* in of the gate of Samaria........ 2Chr 18:9
part of you *e* on the sabbath........ 2Chr 23:4
stood at his pillar at the *e* in........ 2Chr 23:13
when she was come to the *e* of the... 2Chr 23:15
abroad even to the *e* in of Egypt........ 2Chr 26:8
even to the *e* in at the fish gate........ 2Chr 33:14
that there is no house, no *e* in........ Is 23:1
the *e* of the gates of Jerusalem........ Jer 1:15
even *e* in at the gates of........ Jer 17:27
mark well the *e* in of the house,........ Eze 44:5
*e* in of Hemath unto the river of........ Amos 6:14
ye them that are *e* to go in........ Mt 23:13
and the lusts of other things *e* in........ Mk 4:19
that *e* into him can defile him........ Mk 7:15
*e* into the ship again departed to........ Mk 8:13
*e* into the sepulchre, they saw a........ Mk 16:5
them that were *e* in ye hindered........ Lk 11:52
in the which at your *e* ye shall........ Lk 19:30
*e* into every house, and haling men........ Acts 8:3
*e* into a ship of Adramyttium, we........ Acts 27:2
manner of *e* in we had unto you........ 1Th 1:9
being left us of *e* into his rest........ Heb 4:1

**ENTERPRISE**
hands cannot perform their *e*........ Job 5:12

**ENTERTAIN**
Be not forgetful to *e* strangers........ Heb 13:2

**ENTERTAINED**
some have *e* angels unawares........ Heb 13:2

**ENTICE**
if a man *e* a maid that is not........ Ex 22:16
*e* thee secretly, saying, Let us........ Deut 13:6
*E* thy husband, that he may........ Judg 14:15
*E* him, and see wherein his great........ Judg 16:5
Who shall *e* Ahab king of Israel,........ 2Chr 18:19
the LORD, and said, I will *e* him........ 2Chr 18:20
the LORD said, Thou shalt *e* him........ 2Chr 18:21
My son, if sinners *e* thee........ Prov 1:10

**ENTICED**
And my heart hath been secretly *e*........ Job 31:27
saying, Peradventure he will be *e*........ Jer 20:10
drawn away of his own lust, and *e*........ Jas 1:14

**ENTICETH**
A violent man *e* his neighbour........ Prov 16:29

**ENTICING**
not with *e* words of man's wisdom........ 1Cor 2:4
should beguile you with *e* words........ Col 2:4

**ENTIRE**
work, that ye may be perfect and *e*........ Jas 1:4

**ENTRANCE**
your border unto the *e* of Hamath........ Num 34:8
the *e* into the city, and we will........ Judg 1:24
shewed them the *e* into the city........ Judg 1:25
before Ahab to the *e* of Jezreel........ 1Kin 18:46
in the *e* of the gate of Samaria........ 1Kin 22:10
And they went to the *e* of Gedor........ 1Chr 4:39
that kept the *e* of the king's........ 2Chr 12:10
The *e* of thy words giveth light........ Ps 119:130
the face of the gate of the *e*........ Eze 40:15
know our *e* in unto you, that it........ 1Th 2:1
For so an *e* shall be ministered........ 2Pet 1:11

**ENTRANCES**
land of Nimrod in the *e* thereof........ Mic 5:6

**ENTREAT**
I will cause the enemy to *e* thee........ Jer 15:11
*e* them evil four hundred years........ Acts 7:6

**ENTREATED**
he *e* Abram well for her sake........ Gen 12:16
hast thou so evil *e* this people........ Ex 5:22
And the Egyptians evil *e* us........ Deut 26:6
*e* them spitefully, and slew them........ Mt 22:6
shall be mocked, and spitefully *e*........ Lk 18:32
*e* him shamefully, and sent him........ Lk 20:11
evil *e* our fathers, so that they........ Acts 7:19
And Julius courteously *e* Paul........ Acts 27:3
before, and were shamefully *e*........ 1Th 2:2

**ENTREATETH**
He evil *e* the barren that beareth........ Job 24:21

**ENTRIES**
the *e* thereof were by the posts........ Eze 40:38

**ENTRY**
house, and the king's *e* without........ 2Kin 16:18
the LORD, were keepers of the *e*........ 1Chr 9:19
the *e* of the house, the inner........ 2Chr 4:22
at the *e* of the city, at the........ Prov 8:3
which is by the *e* of the east........ Jer 19:2
sat down in the *e* of the new gate........ Jer 26:10
at the *e* of the new gate of the........ Jer 36:10
*e* that is in the house of the........ Jer 38:14
which is at the *e* of Pharaoh's........ Jer 43:9
this image of jealousy in the *e*........ Eze 8:5
art situate at the *e* of the sea........ Eze 27:3
the breadth of the *e* of the gate........ Eze 40:11
up to the *e* of the north gate........ Eze 40:40
was the *e* on the east side........ Eze 42:9
After he brought me through the *e*........ Eze 46:19

**ENVIED**
and the Philistines *e* him........ Gen 26:14
no children, Rachel *e* her sister........ Gen 30:1
And his brethren *e* him........ Gen 37:11
They *e* Moses also in the camp, and........ Ps 106:16
this a man is *e* of his neighbour........ Eccl 4:4
were in the garden of God, *e* him........ Eze 31:9

**ENVIES**
all guile, and hypocrisies, and *e*........ 1Pet 2:1

**ENVIEST**
said unto him, *E* thou for my sake........ Num 11:29

**ENVIETH**
charity *e* not........ 1Cor 13:4

**ENVIOUS**
neither be thou *e* against the........ Ps 37:1
For I was *e* at the foolish, when........ Ps 73:3
Be not thou *e* against evil men,........ Prov 24:1
neither be thou *e* at the wicked........ Prov 24:19

**ENVIRON**
shall *e* us round, and cut off our........ Josh 7:9

**ENVY**
man, and *e* slayeth the silly one........ Job 5:2
*E* thou not the oppressor, and........ Prov 3:31
but *e* the rottenness of the bones........ Prov 14:30
Let not thine heart *e* sinners........ Prov 23:17
but who is able to stand before *e*........ Prov 27:4
love, and their hatred, and their *e*........ Eccl 9:6
The *e* also of Ephraim shall........ Is 11:13
Ephraim shall not *e* Judah........ Is 11:13
ashamed for their *e* at the people........ Is 26:11
according to thine *e* which thou........ Eze 35:11
For he knew that for *e* they had........ Mt 27:18
priests had delivered him for *e*........ Mk 15:10
And the patriarchs, moved with *e*........ Acts 7:9
they were filled with *e*, and........ Acts 13:45
which believed not, moved with *e*........ Acts 17:5
full of *e*, murder, debate, deceit........ Rom 1:29
indeed preach Christ even of *e*........ Phil 1:15
of words, whereof cometh *e*........ 1Ti 6:4
pleasures, living in malice and *e*........ Titus 3:3
that dwelleth in us lusteth to *e*........ Jas 4:5

**ENVYING**
and wantonness, not in strife and *e*... Rom 13:13
for whereas there is among you *e*........ 1Cor 3:3
one another, *e* one another........ Gal 5:26
But if ye have bitter *e* and strife........ Jas 3:14
For where *e* and strife is, there........ Jas 3:16

**ENVYINGS**
lest there be debates, *e*, wraths,........ 2Cor 12:20
*E*, murders, drunkenness,........ Gal 5:21

**EPAENETUS** (*ep-en'-e-tus*) *A Christian acquaintance of Paul.*
Salute my wellbeloved *E*, who is........ Rom 16:5

**EPAPHRAS** (*ep'-a-fras*) *A Christian acquaintance of Paul.*
As ye also learned of *E* our dear........ Col 1:7
*E*, who is one of you, a servant........ Col 4:12
There salute thee *E*, my........ Philem 23

**EPAPHRODITUS** (*e-paf-ro-di'-tus*) *A fellow-worker with Paul.*
it necessary to send to you *E*........ Phil 2:25
having received of *E* the things........ Phil 4:18
to the Philippians from Rome by *E*........ Phil s

**EPENETUS** See EPAENETUS.

**EPHAH** (*e'-fah*)
*1. A son of Midian; grandson of Abraham.*
*E*, and Epher, and Hanoch........ Gen 25:4
*E*, and Epher, and Henoch........ 1Chr 1:33
the dromedaries of Midian and *E*........ Is 60:6
*2. A concubine of Caleb.*
And *E*, Caleb's concubine, bare........ 1Chr 2:46
*3. A son of Jahdai.*
Gesham, and Pelet, and *E*........ 1Chr 2:47
*4. A grain measure.*
an omer is the tenth part of an *e*........ Ex 16:36
of an *e* of fine flour for a sin........ Lev 5:11
the tenth part of an *e* of fine........ Lev 6:20
balances, just weights, a just *e*........ Lev 19:36
tenth part of an *e* of barley meal........ Num 5:15
a tenth part of an *e* of flour for........ Num 28:5
unleavened cakes of an *e* of flour........ Judg 6:19
and it was about an *e* of barley........ Ruth 2:17
one *e* of flour, and a bottle of........ 1Sa 1:24
an *e* of this parched corn........ 1Sa 17:17
seed of an homer shall yield an *e*........ Is 5:10
have just balances, and a just *e*........ Eze 45:10
The *e* and the bath shall be of one........ Eze 45:11
the *e* the tenth part of an homer........ Eze 45:11
part of an *e* of an homer of wheat........ Eze 45:13
of an *e* of an homer of barley........ Eze 45:13
offering of an *e* for a bullock........ Eze 45:24
an *e* for a ram, and an hin of oil........ Eze 45:24
a ram, and an hin of oil for an *e*........ Eze 45:24
offering shall be an *e* for a ram........ Eze 46:5
to give, and an hin of oil to an *e*........ Eze 46:5

an *e* for a bullock, and ... Eze 46:7
an *e* for a ram, and for the lambs ... Eze 46:7
unto, and an hin of oil to an *e* ... Eze 46:7
shall be an *e* to a bullock ... Eze 46:11
an *e* to a ram, and to the lambs as ... Eze 46:11
to give, and an hin of oil to an *e* ... Eze 46:11
morning, the sixth part of an *e* ... Eze 46:14
forth wheat, making the *e* small ... Amos 8:5
This is an *e* that goeth forth ... Zec 5:6
sitteth in the midst of the *e* ... Zec 5:7
cast it into the midst of the *e* ... Zec 5:8
lifted up the *e* between the earth ... Zec 5:9
me, Whither do these bear the *e* ... Zec 5:10

**EPHAI** (*e'-fahee*) *Family who remained in Jerusalem during captivity.*
the sons of *E* the Netophathite, ... Jer 40:8

**EPHER** (*e'-fur*)
*1. A son of Midian; grandson of Abraham.*
*E*, and Hanoch, and Abidah ... Gen 25:4
*E*, and Henoch, and Abida, ... 1Chr 1:33
*2. A descendant of Judah.*
Ezra were, Jether, and Mered, and *E* .. 1Chr 4:17
*3. A chief of Manasseh.*
house of their fathers, even *E* ... 1Chr 5:24

**EPHES-DAMMIM**
between Shochoh and Azekah, in *E* ... 1Sa 17:1

**EPHESIAN** (*e-fe'-zheun*) See EPHESIANS. *A resident of Ephesus.*
him in the city Trophimus an *E* ... Acts 21:29

**EPHESIANS** (*e-fe'-zheuns*)
saying, Great is Diana of the *E* ... Acts 19:28
out, Great is Diana of the *E* ... Acts 19:34
*E* is a worshipper of the great ... Acts 19:35
from Rome unto the *E* by Tychicus ... Eph s
bishop of the church of the *E* ... 2Ti s

**EPHESUS** (*ef'-e-sus*) See EPHESIAN. *Capital of Roman province of Asia.*
And he came to *E*, and left them ... Acts 18:19
And he sailed from *E* ... Acts 18:21
in the scriptures, came to *E* ... Acts 18:24
the upper coasts came to *E* ... Acts 19:1
Jews and Greeks also dwelling at *E* .. Acts 19:17
see and hear, that not alone at *E* ... Acts 19:26
the people, he said, Ye men of *E* ... Acts 19:35
Paul had determined to sail by *E* ... Acts 20:16
And from Miletus he sent to *E* ... Acts 20:17
I have fought with beasts at *E* ... 1Cor 15:32
I will tarry at *E* until Pentecost ... 1Cor 16:8
God, to the saints which are at *E* ... Eph 1:1
besought thee to abide still at *E* ... 1Ti 1:3
things he ministered unto me at *E* ... 2Ti 1:18
And Tychicus have I sent to *E* ... 2Ti 4:12
unto *E*, and unto Smyrna, and unto ... Rev 1:11
angel of the church of *E* write ... Rev 2:1

**EPHLAL** (*ef'-lal*) *A descendant of Pharez.*
And Zabad begat *E*, and *E* begat ... 1Chr 2:37
begat *E*, and *E* begat Obed, ... 1Chr 2:37

**EPHOD** (*e'-fod*)
*1. Father of Hanniel.*
of Manasseh, Hanniel the son of *E* ... Num 34:23
*2. A priestly garment.*
and stones to be set in the *e* ... Ex 25:7
a breastplate, and an *e*, and a robe ... Ex 28:4
And they shall make the *e* of gold ... Ex 28:6
And the curious girdle of the *e* ... Ex 28:8
upon the shoulders of the *e* for ... Ex 28:12
work of the *e* thou shalt make it ... Ex 28:15
shoulderpieces of the *e* before it ... Ex 28:25
is in the side of the *e* inward ... Ex 28:26
the two sides of the *e* underneath ... Ex 28:27
above the curious girdle of the *e* ... Ex 28:27
of the *e* with a lace of blue ... Ex 28:28
above the curious girdle of the *e* ... Ex 28:28
be not loosed from the *e* ... Ex 28:28
the robe of the *e* all of blue ... Ex 28:31
the coat, and the robe of the *e* ... Ex 29:5
and the *e*, and the breastplate ... Ex 29:5
with the curious girdle of the *e* ... Ex 29:5
and stones to be set for the *e* ... Ex 35:9
and stones to be set, for the *e* ... Ex 35:27
And he made the *e* of gold, blue, ... Ex 39:2
And the curious girdle of his *e* ... Ex 39:5
them on the shoulders of the *e* ... Ex 39:7
work, like the work of the *e* ... Ex 39:8
on the shoulderpieces of the *e* ... Ex 39:18
was on the side of the *e* inward ... Ex 39:19
the two sides of the *e* underneath ... Ex 39:20
above the curious girdle of the *e* ... Ex 39:20
of the *e* with a lace of blue ... Ex 39:21
above the curious girdle of the *e* ... Ex 39:21
might not be loosed from the *e* ... Ex 39:21
the robe of the *e* of woven work ... Ex 39:22
put the *e* upon him, and he girded ... Lev 8:7
with the curious girdle of the *e* ... Lev 8:7
And Gideon made an *e* thereof ... Judg 8:27
an house of gods, and made an *e* ... Judg 17:5
there is in these houses an *e* ... Judg 18:14
took the graven image, and the *e* ... Judg 18:17
fetched the carved image, the *e* ... Judg 18:18
heart was glad, and he took the *e* ... Judg 18:20
a child, girded with a linen *e* ... 1Sa 2:18
incense, to wear an *e* before me ... 1Sa 2:28
priest in Shiloh, wearing an *e* ... 1Sa 14:3
wrapped in a cloth behind the *e* ... 1Sa 21:9
persons that did wear a linen *e* ... 1Sa 22:18
came down with an *e* in his hand ... 1Sa 23:6
the priest, Bring hither the *e* ... 1Sa 23:9
pray thee, bring me hither the *e* ... 1Sa 30:7
brought thither the *e* to David ... 1Sa 30:7
David was girded with a linen *e* ... 2Sa 6:14
also had upon him an *e* of linen ... 1Chr 15:27
without an image, and without an *e* ... Hos 3:4

**EPHPHATHA**
he sighed, and saith unto him, *E* ... Mk 7:34

**EPHRAIM** (*e'-fra-im*) See EPHRAIMITE, EPHRAIM'S, EPHRAIN.
*1. A son of Joseph.*
name of the second called he *E* ... Gen 41:52
of Egypt were born Manasseh and *E* .. Gen 46:20
him his two sons, Manasseh and *E* ... Gen 48:1
And now thy two sons, *E* and ... Gen 48:5
*E* in his right hand toward ... Gen 48:13
his right hand upon the head of *E* ... Gen 48:17
bless, saying, God make thee as *E* ... Gen 48:20
and he set *E* before Manasseh ... Gen 48:20
their families were Manasseh and *E* .. Num 26:28
And the sons of *E* ... 1Chr 7:20
*E* their father mourned many days, ... 1Chr 7:22
*2. One of the twelve tribes comprising Israel.*
children of Joseph: of *E* ... Num 1:10
namely, of the children of *E* ... Num 1:32
of them, even of the tribe of *E* ... Num 1:33
of *E* according to their armies ... Num 2:18
the captain of the sons of *E* ... Num 2:18
of *E* were an hundred thousand ... Num 2:24
prince of the children of *E* ... Num 7:48
*E* set forward according to their ... Num 10:22
Of the tribe of *E*, Oshea the son ... Num 13:8
sons of *E* after their families ... Num 26:35
of *E* according to those that were ... Num 26:37
of the tribe of the children of *E* ... Num 34:24
they are the ten thousands of *E* ... Deut 33:17
And all Naphtali, and the land of *E* ... Deut 34:2
were two tribes, Manasseh and *E* ... Josh 14:4
children of Joseph, Manasseh and *E* ... Josh 16:4
the border of the children of *E* ... Josh 16:5
children of *E* by their families ... Josh 16:8
cities for the children of *E* were ... Josh 16:9
belonged to the children of *E* ... Josh 17:8
these cities of *E* are among the ... Josh 17:9
the house of Joseph, even to *E* ... Josh 17:17
of the families of the tribe of *E* ... Josh 21:5
their lot out of the tribe of *E* ... Josh 21:20
Neither did *E* drive out the ... Judg 1:29
Out of *E* was there a root of them ... Judg 5:14
Then all the men of *E* gathered ... Judg 7:24
the men of *E* said unto him, Why ... Judg 8:1
of *E* better than the vintage of ... Judg 8:2
and against the house of *E* ... Judg 10:9
the men of *E* gathered themselves ... Judg 12:1
men of Gilead, and fought with *E* ... Judg 12:4
and the men of Gilead smote *E* ... Judg 12:4
of *E* among the Ephraimites ... Judg 12:4
in Pirathon in the land of *E* ... Judg 12:15
and over Jezreel, and over *E* ... 2Sa 2:9
coasts out of the tribe of *E* ... 1Chr 6:66
Benjamin, and of the children of *E* ... 1Chr 9:3
the children of *E* twenty thousand ... 1Chr 12:30
Pelonite, of the children of *E* ... 1Chr 27:10
Pirathonite, of the children of *E* ... 1Chr 27:14
Of the children of *E*, Hoshea the ... 1Chr 27:20
the strangers with them out of *E* ... 2Chr 15:9
of Judah, and in the cities of *E* ... 2Chr 17:2
wit, with all the children of *E* ... 2Chr 25:7
that was come to him out of *E* ... 2Chr 25:10
And Zichri, a mighty man of *E* ... 2Chr 28:7
of the heads of the children of *E* ... 2Chr 28:12
Judah, and wrote letters also to *E* ... 2Chr 30:1
to city through the country of *E* ... 2Chr 30:10
of the people, even many of *E* ... 2Chr 30:18
in *E* also and Manasseh, until they ... 2Chr 31:1
in the cities of Manasseh, and *E* ... 2Chr 34:6
of the hand of Manasseh and *E* ... 2Chr 34:9
*E* also is the strength of mine ... Ps 60:7
The children of *E*, being armed, ... Ps 78:9
and chose not the tribe of *E* ... Ps 78:67
Before *E* and Benjamin and Manasseh ... Ps 80:2
*E* also is the strength of mine ... Ps 108:8
Syria is confederate with *E* ... Is 7:2
Because Syria, *E*, and the son of ... Is 7:5
and five years shall *E* be broken ... Is 7:8
And the head of *E* is Samaria ... Is 7:9
from the day that *E* departed from ... Is 7:17
all the people shall know, even *E* ... Is 9:9
Manasseh, *E* ... Is 9:21
and *E*, Manasseh ... Is 9:21
The envy also of *E* shall depart ... Is 11:13
*E* shall not envy Judah ... Is 11:13
and Judah shall not vex *E* ... Is 11:13
fortress also shall cease from *E* ... Is 17:3
of pride, to the drunkards of *E* ... Is 28:1
of pride, the drunkards of *E* ... Is 28:3
even the whole seed of *E* ... Jer 7:15
to Israel, and *E* is my firstborn ... Jer 31:9
I have surely heard *E* bemoaning ... Jer 31:18
Is *E* my dear son ... Jer 31:20
it, For Joseph, the stick of *E* ... Eze 37:16
Joseph, which is in the hand of *E* ... Eze 37:19
the west side, a portion for *E* ... Eze 48:5
And by the border of *E*, from the ... Eze 48:6
*E* is joined to idols ... Hos 4:17
I know *E*, and Israel is not hid ... Hos 5:3
for now, O *E*, thou committest ... Hos 5:3
and *E* fall in their iniquity ... Hos 5:5
*E* shall be desolate in the day of ... Hos 5:9
*E* is oppressed and broken in ... Hos 5:11
will I be unto *E* as a moth ... Hos 5:12
When *E* saw his sickness, and Judah ... Hos 5:13
then went *E* to the Assyrian, and ... Hos 5:13
For I will be unto *E* as a lion ... Hos 5:14
O *E*, what shall I do unto thee ... Hos 6:4
there is the whoredom of *E* ... Hos 6:10
the iniquity of *E* was discovered ... Hos 7:1
*E*, he hath mixed himself among ... Hos 7:8
*E* is a cake not turned ... Hos 7:8
*E* also is like a silly dove ... Hos 7:11
*E* hath hired lovers ... Hos 8:9
Because *E* hath made many altars ... Hos 8:11
but *E* shall return to Egypt, and ... Hos 9:3
The watchman of *E* was with my God ... Hos 9:8
As for *E*, their glory shall fly ... Hos 9:11
*E*, as I saw Tyrus, is planted in ... Hos 9:13
but *E* shall bring forth his ... Hos 9:13
*E* is smitten, their root is dried ... Hos 9:16
*E* shall receive shame, and Israel ... Hos 10:6
*E* is as an heifer that is taught, ... Hos 10:11
I will make *E* to ride ... Hos 10:11
I taught *E* also to go, taking ... Hos 11:3
How shall I give thee up, *E* ... Hos 11:8
I will not return to destroy *E* ... Hos 11:9
*E* compasseth me about with lies, ... Hos 11:12
*E* feedeth on wind, and followeth ... Hos 12:1
*E* said, Yet I am become rich, I ... Hos 12:8
*E* provoked him to anger most ... Hos 12:14
When *E* spake trembling, he ... Hos 13:1
The iniquity of *E* is bound up ... Hos 13:12
*E* shall say, What have I to do ... Hos 14:8
shall possess the fields of *E* ... Obad 19
I will cut off the chariot from *E* ... Zec 9:10
for me, filled the bow with *E* ... Zec 9:13
they of *E* shall be like a mighty ... Zec 10:7
*3. Mountains in Samaria.*
if mount *E* be too narrow for thee ... Josh 17:15
even Timnath-serah in mount *E* ... Josh 19:50
Naphtali, and Shechem in mount *E* ... Josh 20:7
with her suburbs in mount *E* ... Josh 21:21
which is in mount *E*, on the ... Josh 24:30
which was given him in mount *E* ... Josh 24:33
Timnath-heres, in the mount of *E* ... Judg 2:9
a trumpet in the mountain of *E* ... Judg 3:27
Ramah and Beth-el in mount *E* ... Judg 4:5
messengers throughout all mount *E* ... Judg 7:24
and he dwelt in Shamir in mount *E* ... Judg 10:1
And there was a man of mount *E* ... Judg 17:1
he came to mount *E* to the house ... Judg 17:8
who when they came to mount *E* ... Judg 18:2
they passed thence unto mount *E* ... Judg 18:13
sojourning on the side of mount *E* ... Judg 19:1
even, which was also of mount *E* ... Judg 19:16
toward the side of mount *E* ... Judg 19:18
of Ramathaim-zophim, of mount *E* ... 1Sa 1:1
And he passed through mount *E* ... 1Sa 9:4
had hid themselves in mount *E* ... 1Sa 14:22
but a man of mount *E*, Sheba the ... 2Sa 20:21
The son of Hur, in mount *E* ... 1Kin 4:8
Jeroboam built Shechem in mount *E* 1Kin 12:25
*E* two young men of the sons of ... 2Kin 5:22
in mount *E* with her suburbs ... 1Chr 6:67
Zemaraim, which is in mount *E* ... 2Chr 13:4
which he had taken from mount *E* ... 2Chr 15:8
people from Beer-sheba to mount *E* ... 2Chr 19:4
affliction from mount *E* ... Jer 4:15
upon the mount *E* shall cry ... Jer 31:6
shall be satisfied upon mount *E* ... Jer 50:19
*4. A town near Absalom's farm.*
in Baal-hazor, which is beside *E* ... 2Sa 13:23
*5. Battle site between David's and Absalom's armies.*
the battle was in the wood of *E* ... 2Sa 18:6
*6. A northern gate at Jerusalem.*
gate of *E* unto the corner gate ... 2Kin 14:13
the gate of *E* to the corner gate ... 2Chr 25:23
and in the street of the gate of *E* ... Neh 8:16
And from above the gate of *E* ... Neh 12:39
*7. A city near Jerusalem.*
wilderness, into a city called *E* ... Jn 11:54

**EPHRAIMITE** (*e'-fra-im-ite*) See EPHRAIMITES. *A descendant of Ephraim.*
said unto him, Art thou an *E* ... Judg 12:5

**EPHRAIMITES** (*e'-fra-im-ites*)
dwell among the *E* unto this day ... Josh 16:10
fugitives of Ephraim among the *E* ... Judg 12:4
passages of Jordan before the *E* ... Judg 12:5
that when those *E* which were ... Judg 12:5
fell at that time of the *E* forty ... Judg 12:6

**EPHRAIM'S** (*e'-fra-ims*)
*1. Refers to Ephraim 1.*
hand, and laid it upon *E* head ... Gen 48:14
to remove it from *E* head unto ... Gen 48:17
Joseph saw *E* children of the ... Gen 50:23
*2. Refers to Ephraim 2.*
Southward it was *E*, and northward .. Josh 17:10

**EPHRAIN** (*e'-fra-in*) See EPHRAIM, EPHRON. *A city in Benjamin.*
and *E* with the towns thereof ... 2Chr 13:19

**EPHRATAH** (*ef'-rat-ah*) See BETHLEHEM, CALEB-EPHRATAH, EPHRATH, EPHRATHITE.
*1. Another name for Bethlehem-judah.*
and do thou worthily in *E*, and be ... Ruth 4:11
Lo, we heard of it at *E* ... Ps 132:6
But thou, Beth-lehem *E*, though ... Mic 5:2
*2. A wife of Caleb.*
son of Hur, the firstborn of *E* ... 1Chr 2:50

sons of Hur, the firstborn of *E*................ 1Chr 4:4

**EPHRATH** (*e'-frath*) See EPHRATAH.
*1. A city in Judah.*
was but a little way to come to *E*....... Gen 35:16
and was buried in the way to *E*.......... Gen 35:19
but a little way to come unto *E*............ Gen 48:7
buried her there in the way of *E*.......... Gen 48:7
*2. Same as Ephratah 2.*
was dead, Caleb took unto him *E*........ 1Chr 2:19

**EPHRATHAH** See EPHRATAH.

**EPHRATHITE** (*ef'-rath-ite*) See EPHRATHITES.
*An inhabitant of Bethlehem Judah.*
of Tohu, the son of Zuph, an *E*.............. 1Sa 1:1
son of that *E* of Beth-lehem-judah....... 1Sa 17:12
an *E* of Zereda, Solomon's servant .... 1Kin 11:26

**EPHRATHITES** (*ef'-rath-ites*)
and Chilion, *E* of Beth-lehem-judah...... Ruth 1:2

**EPHRON** (*e'-fron*) See EPHRAIM, EPHRAIN.
*1. Son of Zohar.*
for me to *E* the son of Zohar................ Gen 23:8
*E* dwelt among the children of............ Gen 23:10
*E* the Hittite answered Abraham in.... Gen 23:10
he spake unto *E* in the audience ......... Gen 23:13
*E* answered Abraham, saying unto ..... Gen 23:14
And Abraham hearkened unto *E*.......... Gen 23:16
Abraham weighed to *E* the silver......... Gen 23:16
And the field of *E*, which was in ......... Gen 23:17
in the field of *E* the son of.................... Gen 25:9
is in the field of *E* the Hittite.............. Gen 49:29
bought with the field of *E* the............. Gen 49:30
a buryingplace of *E* the Hittite............ Gen 50:13
*2. A mountain between Judah and Benjamin.*
went out to the cities of mount *E*........ Josh 15:9

**EPICUREANS** (*ep-i-cu-re'-ans*) *Followers of the philosopher Epicurus.*
certain philosophers of the *E*.............. Acts 17:18

**EPISTLE**
together, they delivered the *e*.............. Acts 15:30
delivered the *e* to the governor,.......... Acts 23:33
I Tertius, who wrote this *e*................ Rom 16:22
I wrote unto you in an *e* not to............... 1Cor 5:9
The first *e* to the Corinthians................ 1Cor s
Ye are our *e* written in our...................... 2Cor 3:2
the *e* of Christ ministered by us.............. 2Cor 3:3
the same *e* hath made you sorry............. 2Cor 7:8
The second *e* to the Corinthians ............ 2Cor s
when this *e* is read among you,............... Col 4:16
likewise read the *e* from Laodicea.......... Col 4:16
this *e* be read unto all the holy ............. 1Th 5:27
The first *e* unto the.................................... 1Th s
taught, whether by word, or our *e* ........ 2Th 2:15
man obey not our word by this *e*........ 2Th 3:14
which is the token in every *e*................. 2Th 3:17
The second *e* to the Thessalonians........... 2Th s
The second *e* unto Timotheus,................... 2Ti s
This second *e*, beloved, I now.................. 2Pet 3:1

**EPISTLES**
*e* of commendation to you, or.................. 2Cor 3:1
As also in all his *e*, speaking in ............ 2Pet 3:16

**EQUAL**
gold and the crystal cannot *e* it.............. Job 28:17
topaz of Ethiopia shall not *e* it.............. Job 28:19
eyes behold the things that are *e*............. Ps 17:2
But it was thou, a man mine *e*................ Ps 55:13
The legs of the lame are not *e* ............. Prov 26:7
will ye liken me, or shall I be *e*............... Is 40:25
will ye liken me, and make me *e*.............. Is 46:5
what shall I *e* to thee, that I................. Lam 2:13
say, The way of the Lord is not *e* ......... Eze 18:25
Is not my way *e*.................................. Eze 18:25
The way of the Lord is not *e*............... Eze 18:29
of Israel, are not my ways *e*................. Eze 18:29
say, The way of the Lord is not *e*......... Eze 33:17
as for them, their way is not *e*............. Eze 33:17
say, The way of the Lord is not *e* ......... Eze 33:20
and thou hast made them *e* unto us..... Mt 20:12
for they are *e* unto the angels .............. Lk 20:36
Father, making himself *e* with God.......... Jn 5:18
it not robbery to be *e* with God ............. Phil 2:6
servants that which is just and *e*............ Col 4:1
breadth and the height of it are *e*........ Rev 21:16

**EQUALITY**
But by an *e*, that now at this................ 2Cor 8:14
that there may be *e*.............................. 2Cor 8:14

**EQUALLY**
*e* distant one from another...................... Ex 36:22

**EQUALS**
many my *e* in mine own nation............. Gal 1:14

**EQUITY**
the world, and the people with *e*............. Ps 98:9
thou dost establish *e*, thou .................... Ps 99:4
justice, and judgment, and *e* .............. Prov 1:3
righteousness, and judgment, and *e* ...... Prov 2:9
good, nor to strike princes for *e* ......... Prov 17:26
wisdom, and in knowledge, and in *e* .... Eccl 2:21
reprove with *e* for the meek of................ Is 11:4
in the street, and *e* cannot enter ........... Is 59:14
abhor judgment, and pervert all *e* ........... Mic 3:9
he walked with me in peace and *e* .......... Mal 2:6

**ER** (*ur*)
*1. A son of Judah.*
and he called his name *E*................... Gen 38:3
took a wife for *E* his firstborn............... Gen 38:6
And *E*, Judah's firstborn, was................ Gen 38:7
*E*, and Onan, and Shelah ..................... Gen 46:12
but *E* and Onan died in the land of .... Gen 46:12
The sons of Judah were *E* and Onan Num 26:19
and *E* and Onan died in the land of.. Num 26:19
*E*, and Onan, and Shelah........................ 1Chr 2:3
And *E*, the firstborn of Judah, was........ 1Chr 2:3
*2. A son of Shelah.*
*E* the father of Lecah, and Laadah ...... 1Chr 4:21
*3. Father of Elmodan;ancestor of Jesus.*
Elmodam, which was the son of *E*......... Lk 3:28

**ERAN** (*e'-ran*) See ERANITES. *A son of Shathelah.*
of *E*, the family of the Eranites ......... Num 26:36

**ERANITES** (*e'-ran-ites*) *Descendants of Eran.*
of Eran, the family of the *E*................ Num 26:36

**ERASTUS** (*e-ras'-tus*)
*1. A fellow-worker with Paul.*
unto him, Timotheus and *E*................. Acts 19:22
*E* abode at Corinth................................... 2Ti 4:20
*2. A Corinthian city official.*
*E* the chamberlain of the city............. Rom 16:23

**ERE**
are delivered *e* the midwives come.......... Ex 1:19
*e* it was chewed, the wrath of the....... Num 11:33
long will it be *e* they believe me ........ Num 14:11
*e* the lamp of God went out in the.......... 1Sa 3:3
*e* thou bid the people return from......... 2Sa 2:26
but *e* the messenger came to him, ....... 2Kin 6:32
How long will it be *e* ye make an.......... Job 18:2
long will it be *e* thou be quiet .............. Jer 47:6
how long will it be *e* they attain.............. Hos 8:5
Sir, come down *e* my child die ............... Jn 4:49

**ERECH** (*e'-rek*) See ARCHEVITES. *A city in Shinar.*
of his kingdom was Babel, and *E*........ Gen 10:10

**ERECTED**
he *e* there an altar, and called it........... Gen 33:20

**ERI** (*e'-ri*) See ERITES. *A son of Gad.*
and Haggi, Shuni, and Ezbon, *E*......... Gen 46:16
of *E*, the family of the Erites............. Num 26:16

**ERITES** (*e'-rites*) *Descendants of Eri.*
of Eri, the family of the *E*.................... Num 26:16

**ERR**
the inhabitants of Jerusalem to *e*......... 2Chr 33:9
a people that do *e* in their heart ........... Ps 95:10
which do *e* from thy commandments.. Ps 119:21
all them that *e* from thy statutes........ Ps 119:118
Do they not *e* that devise evil............. Prov 14:22
to *e* from the words of knowledge....... Prov 19:27
which lead thee cause thee to *e*.................. Is 3:12
of this people cause them to *e*.................. Is 9:16
Egypt to *e* in every work thereof.............. Is 19:14
they *e* in vision, they stumble in................ Is 28:7
of the people, causing them to *e*............... Is 30:28
though fools, shall not *e* therein ............... Is 35:8
thou made us to *e* from thy ways ............ Is 63:17
and caused my people Israel to *e* ........... Jer 23:13
my people to *e* by their lies................... Jer 23:32
whoredoms hath caused them to *e*.......... Hos 4:12
and their lies caused them to *e*............ Amos 2:4
prophets that make my people *e*............... Mic 3:5
and said unto them, Ye do *e*.................... Mt 22:29
unto them, Do ye not therefore *e* ......... Mk 12:24
ye therefore do greatly *e*........................ Mk 12:27
They do alway *e* in their heart............... Heb 3:10
Do not *e*, my beloved brethren ................ Jas 1:16
if any of you do *e* from the truth............. Jas 5:19

**ERRAND**
not eat, until I have told mine *e*........... Gen 24:33
said, I have a secret *e* unto thee ........... Judg 3:19
and he said, I have an *e* to thee ............ 2Kin 9:5

**ERRED**
his ignorance wherein he *e*........................ Lev 5:18
And if ye have *e*, and not observed...... Num 15:22
the fool, and have *e* exceedingly ......... 1Sa 26:21
me to understand wherein I have *e*....... Job 6:24
And be it indeed that I have *e* ................ Job 19:4
yet I *e* not from thy precepts............... Ps 119:110
But they also have *e* through wine........... Is 28:7
the prophet have *e* through strong ............ Is 28:7
They also that *e* in spirit shall............... Is 29:24
they have *e* from the faith, and............... 1Ti 6:10
have *e* concerning the faith...................... 1Ti 6:21
Who concerning the truth have *e*.............. 2Ti 2:18

**ERRETH**
but he that refuseth reproof *e*............. Prov 10:17
of the month for every one that *e*.......... Eze 45:20

**ERROR**
and God smote him there for his *e* .......... 2Sa 6:7
mine *e* remaineth with myself................. Job 19:4
the angel, that it was an *e*...................... Eccl 5:6
as an *e* which proceedeth from the ...... Eccl 10:5
to utter *e* against the LORD, to................. Is 32:6
there any *e* or fault found in him............ Dan 6:4
so the last *e* shall be worse than............ Mt 27:64
of their *e* which was meet....................... Rom 1:27
*e* of his way shall save a soul.................... Jas 5:20
escaped from them who live in *e* ........... 2Pet 2:18
led away with the *e* of the wicked ........ 2Pet 3:17
of truth, and the spirit of *e* ..................... 1Jn 4:6
after the *e* of Balaam for reward ............. Jude 11

**ERRORS**
Who can understand his *e*........................ Ps 19:12
They are vanity, and the work of *e* ...... Jer 10:15
They are vanity, the work of *e* .............. Jer 51:18
and for the *e* of the people..................... Heb 9:7

**ESAIAS** (*e-sah'-yas*) See ISAIAH. *Greek form of Isaiah.*
was spoken of by the prophet *E* ............... Mt 3:3
which was spoken by *E* the prophet....... Mt 4:14
which was spoken by *E* the prophet....... Mt 8:17
which was spoken by *E* the prophet..... Mt 12:17
is fulfilled the prophecy of *E*.................. Mt 13:14
well did *E* prophesy of you,..................... Mt 15:7
Well hath *E* prophesied of you ................ Mk 7:6
of the words of *E* the prophet................. Lk 3:4
him the book of the prophet *E* .............. Lk 4:17
the Lord, as said the prophet *E*.............. Jn 1:23
That the saying of *E* the prophet........... Jn 12:38
because that *E* said again ....................... Jn 12:39
These things said *E*, when he saw.......... Jn 12:41
in his chariot read *E* the prophet.......... Acts 8:28
and heard him read the prophet *E* ........ Acts 8:30
by *E* the prophet unto our fathers...... Acts 28:25
*E* also crieth concerning Israel, ............ Rom 9:27
as *E* said before, Except the Lord........... Rom 9:29
For *E* saith, Lord, who hath.................. Rom 10:16
But *E* is very bold, and saith, I ........... Rom 10:20
*E* saith, There shall be a root of ......... Rom 15:12

**ESAR-HADDON** (*e'-zar-had'-dun*) *An Assyrian king.*
*E* his son reigned in his stead............... 2Kin 19:37
since the days of *E* king of Assur............ Ezr 4:2
*E* his son reigned in his stead.................. Is 37:38

**ESAU** (*e'-saw*)
*1. A son of Isaac.*
and they called his name *E*.................. Gen 25:25
*E* was a cunning hunter, a man of...... Gen 25:27
And Isaac loved *E*, because he did...... Gen 25:28
*E* came from the field, and he was...... Gen 25:29
*E* said to Jacob, Feed me, I pray.......... Gen 25:30
*E* said, Behold, I am at the point.......... Gen 25:32
Then Jacob gave *E* bread and ............. Gen 25:34
thus *E* despised his birthright............... Gen 25:34
*E* was forty years old when he............. Gen 26:34
he called *E* his eldest son, and ................ Gen 27:1
when Isaac spake to *E* his son................ Gen 27:5
*E* went to the field to hunt for.............. Gen 27:5
father speak unto *E* thy brother............. Gen 27:6
*E* my brother is a hairy man, and I..... Gen 27:11
raiment of her eldest son *E*.................. Gen 27:15
his father, I am *E* thy firstborn............ Gen 27:19
thou be my very son *E* or not................ Gen 27:21
but the hands are the hands of *E*......... Gen 27:22
he said, Art thou my very son *E*........... Gen 27:24
that *E* his brother came in from............ Gen 27:30
I am thy son, thy firstborn *E*............... Gen 27:32
when *E* heard the words of his............ Gen 27:34
And Isaac answered and said unto *E*. Gen 27:37
*E* said unto his father, Hast thou ......... Gen 27:38
*E* lifted up his voice, and wept............. Gen 27:38
*E* hated Jacob because of the............... Gen 27:41
*E* said in his heart, The days of............ Gen 27:41
these words of *E* her elder son............ Gen 27:42
unto him, Behold, thy brother *E*.......... Gen 27:42
When *E* saw that Isaac had blessed ..... Gen 28:6
*E* seeing that the daughters of............... Gen 28:8
Then went *E* unto Ishmael, and took... Gen 28:9
to *E* his brother unto the land of.......... Gen 32:3
shall ye speak unto my lord *E*................ Gen 32:4
saying, We came to thy brother *E*......... Gen 32:6
If *E* come to the one company, and....... Gen 32:8
of my brother, from the hand of *E*....... Gen 32:11
hand a present for *E* his brother.......... Gen 32:13
When *E* my brother meeteth thee,....... Gen 32:17
is a present sent unto my lord *E*......... Gen 32:18
this manner shall ye speak unto *E*...... Gen 32:19
*E* came, and with him four hundred..... Gen 33:1
*E* ran to meet him, and embraced........ Gen 33:4
*E* said, I have enough, my brother......... Gen 33:9
*E* said, Let me now leave with............ Gen 33:15
So *E* returned that day on his way...... Gen 33:16
from the face of *E* thy brother............... Gen 35:1
and his sons *E* and Jacob buried him. Gen 35:29
these are the generations of *E* .............. Gen 36:1
*E* took his wives of the daughters........ Gen 36:2
And Adah bare to *E* Eliphaz ................ Gen 36:4
these are the sons of *E*, which .............. Gen 36:5
*E* took his wives, and his sons, and ...... Gen 36:6
*E* in mount Seir: *E* is Edom................. Gen 36:8
these are the generations of *E* .............. Gen 36:9
the son of Adah the wife of *E*............. Gen 36:10
son of Bashemath the wife of *E*........... Gen 36:10
and she bare to *E* Jeush, and Jaalam . Gen 36:14
These were dukes of the sons of *E* .... Gen 36:15
of Eliphaz the firstborn son of *E*......... Gen 36:15
These are the sons of *E*, who is ........... Gen 36:19
names of the dukes that came of *E* .... Gen 36:40
he is *E* the father of the....................... Gen 36:43
And I gave unto Isaac Jacob and *E*...... Josh 24:4
and I gave unto *E* mount Seir ............. Josh 24:4
sons of Isaac; *E* and Israel................... 1Chr 1:34
Was not *E* Jacob's brother........................ Mal 1:2
And I hated *E*, and laid his.................... Mal 1:3
or profane person, as *E*, who for.......... Heb 12:16
*2. Descendants of Esau.*
your brethren the children of *E*............... Deut 2:4
Seir unto *E* for a possession.................... Deut 2:5
our brethren the children of *E*............... Deut 2:8
the children of *E* succeeded them........ Deut 2:12

As he did to the children of *E* Deut 2:22
children of *E* which dwell in Seir Deut 2:29
The sons of *E* 1Chr 1:35
bring the calamity of *E* upon him Jer 49:8
But I have made *E* bare, I have Jer 49:10
are the things of *E* searched out Obad 6
and the house of *E* for stubble Obad 18
any remaining of the house of *E* Obad 18
have I loved, but *E* have I hated Rom 9:13
*E* concerning things to come Heb 11:20
*3. A mountain.*
out of the mount of *E* Obad 8
of *E* may be cut off by slaughter Obad 9
shall possess the mount of *E* Obad 19
Zion to judge the mount of *E* Obad 21

**ESAU'S** (*e'-saws*) *Refers to Esau 1.*
and his hand took hold on *E* heel Gen 25:26
hairy, as his brother *E* hands Gen 27:23
of Rebekah, Jacob's and *E* mother Gen 28:5
These are the names of *E* sons Gen 36:10
was concubine to Eliphaz *E* son Gen 36:12
were the sons of Adah *E* wife Gen 36:12
were the sons of Bashemath *E* wife Gen 36:13
the daughter of Zibeon, *E* wife Gen 36:14
these are the sons of Reuel *E* son Gen 36:17
are the sons of Bashemath *E* wife Gen 36:17
are the sons of Aholibamah *E* wife Gen 36:18
the daughter of Anah, *E* wife Gen 36:18

**ESCAPE**
that he said, *E* for thy life Gen 19:17
*e* to the mountain, lest thou be Gen 19:17
I cannot *e* to the mountain, lest Gen 19:19
let me *e* thither, (is it not a Gen 19:20
Haste thee, *e* thither Gen 19:22
company which is left shall *e* Gen 32:8
they let none of them remain or *e* Josh 8:22
speedily *e* into the land of the 1Sa 27:1
so shall I *e* out of his hand 1Sa 27:1
we shall not else *e* from Absalom 2Sa 15:14
he get him fenced cities, and *e* us 2Sa 20:6
let not one of them *e* 1Kin 18:40
then let none go forth nor *e* out 2Kin 9:15
I have brought into your hands *e* 2Kin 10:24
they that *e* out of mount Zion 2Kin 19:31
God, to leave us a remnant to *e* Ezr 9:8
thou shalt *e* in the king's house Est 4:13
shall fail, and they shall not *e* Job 11:20
I would hasten my *e* from the Ps 55:8
Shall they *e* by iniquity Ps 56:7
righteousness, and cause me to *e* Ps 71:2
own nets, whilst that I withal *e* Ps 141:10
he that speaketh lies shall not *e* Prov 19:5
pleaseth God shall *e* from her Eccl 7:26
and how shall we *e* Is 20:6
they that *e* out of mount Zion Is 37:32
I will send those that *e* of them Is 66:19
which they shall not be able to *e* Jer 11:11
the principal of the flock to *e* Jer 25:35
not *e* out of the hand of the Jer 32:4
thou shalt not *e* out of his hand, Jer 34:3
thou shalt not *e* out of their Jer 38:18
thou shalt not *e* out of their Jer 38:23
none of them shall remain or *e* Jer 42:17
shall *e* or remain, that they Jer 44:14
shall return but such as shall *e* Jer 44:14
Yet a small number that *e* the Jer 44:28
flee away, nor the mighty man *e* Jer 46:6
every city, and no city shall *e* Jer 48:8
*e* out of the land of Babylon, to Jer 50:28
let none thereof *e* Jer 50:29
*e* the sword among the nations Eze 6:8
they that *e* of you shall remember Eze 6:9
But they that *e* of them shall Eze 7:16
shall *e*, and shall be on the Eze 7:16
shall he *e* that doeth such things Eze 17:15
all these things, he shall not *e* Eze 17:18
but these shall *e* out of his hand Dan 11:41
and the land of Egypt shall not *e* Dan 11:42
yea, and nothing shall *e* them Joel 2:3
cut off those of his that did *e* Obad 14
how can ye *e* the damnation of Mt 23:33
to *e* all these things that shall Lk 21:36
any of them should swim out, and *e* Acts 27:42
that thou shalt *e* the judgment of Rom 2:3
temptation also make a way to *e* 1Cor 10:13
and they shall not *e* 1Th 5:3
How shall we *e*, if we neglect so Heb 2:3
earth, much more shall not we *e* Heb 12:25

**ESCAPED**
And there came one that had *e* Gen 14:13
the residue of that which is *e* Ex 10:5
he hath given his sons that *e* Num 21:29
is *e* from his master unto thee Deut 23:15
Ehud *e* while they tarried, and Judg 3:26
the quarries, and *e* unto Seirath Judg 3:26
and there *e* not a man Judg 3:29
Ephraimites which were *e* said Judg 12:5
for them that be *e* of Benjamin Judg 21:17
but the people *e* 1Sa 14:41
and David fled, and *e* that night 1Sa 19:10
and he went, and fled, and *e* 1Sa 19:12
away mine enemy, that he is *e* 1Sa 19:17
So David fled, and *e*, and came to 1Sa 19:18
thence, and *e* to the cave Adullam 1Sa 22:1
son of Ahitub, named Abiathar, *e* 1Sa 22:20
Saul that David was *e* from Keilah 1Sa 23:13
there *e* not a man of them, save 1Sa 30:17
Out of the camp of Israel am I *e* 2Sa 1:3
and Rechab and Baanah his brother *e* 2Sa 4:6
Ben-hadad the king of Syria *e* on 1Kin 20:20
the remnant that is *e* of the 2Kin 19:30
they *e* into the land of Armenia 2Kin 19:37
of the Amalekites that were *e* 1Chr 4:43
king of Syria *e* out of thine hand 2Chr 16:7
fallen to the earth, and none *e* 2Chr 20:24
that are *e* out of the hand of the 2Chr 30:6
them that had *e* from the sword 2Chr 36:20
for we remain yet *e*, as it is Ezr 9:15
concerning the Jews that had *e* Neh 1:2
I only am *e* alone to tell thee Job 1:15
I only am *e* alone to tell thee Job 1:16
I only am *e* alone to tell thee Job 1:17
I only am *e* alone to tell thee Job 1:19
I am *e* with the skin of my teeth Job 19:20
Our soul is *e* as a bird out of Ps 124:7
the snare is broken, and we are *e* Ps 124:7
for them that are *e* of Israel Is 4:2
such as are *e* of the house of Is 10:20
the remnant that is *e* of the Is 37:31
they *e* into the land of Armenia Is 37:38
ye that are *e* of the nations Is 45:20
*e* from Johanan with eight men Jer 41:15
Ye that have *e* the sword, go away Jer 51:50
LORD's anger none *e* nor remained Lam 2:22
mouth be opened to him which is *e* Eze 24:27
that one that had *e* out of Eze 33:21
evening, afore he that was *e* came Eze 33:22
but he *e* out of their hand, Jn 10:39
that they *e* all safe to land Acts 27:44
And when they were *e*, then they Acts 28:1
whom, though he hath *e* the sea Acts 28:4
down by the wall, and *e* his hands 2Cor 11:33
*e* the edge of the sword, out of Heb 11:34
For if they *e* not who refused him Heb 12:25
having *e* the corruption that is 2Pet 1:4
those that were clean *e* from them 2Pet 2:18
For if after they have *e* the 2Pet 2:20

**ESCAPETH**
that him that *e* the sword of 1Kin 19:17
him that *e* from the sword of Jehu 1Kin 19:17
lions upon him that *e* of Moab Is 15:9
him that fleeth, and her that *e* Jer 48:19
That he that *e* in that day shall Eze 24:26
he that *e* of them shall not be Amos 9:1

**ESCAPING**
there should be no remnant nor *e* Ezr 9:14

**ESCHEW**
Let him *e* evil, and do good 1Pet 3:11

**ESCHEWED**
and one that feared God, and *e* evil Job 1:1

**ESCHEWETH**
one that feareth God, and *e* evil Job 1:8
one that feareth God, and *e* evil Job 2:3

**ESEK** (*e'-sek*) *A well in the valley of Geran.*
he called the name of the well *E* Gen 26:20

**ESHAN** See ESHEAN.

**ESH-BAAL** (*esh'-ba-al*) See ISH-BOSHETH. *A son of King Saul.*
and Abinadab, and *E* 1Chr 8:33
and Abinadab, and *E* 1Chr 9:39

**ESHBAN**
Hemdan, and *E*, and Ithran, and Gen 36:26
*E*, and Ithran, and Cheran 1Chr 1:41

**ESHCOL** (*esh'-col*)
*1. Brother of Mamre and Aner.*
Mamre the Amorite, brother of *E* Gen 14:13
men which went with me, Aner, *E* Gen 14:24
*2. A valley or brook in Hebron.*
And they came unto the brook of *E* Num 13:23
The place was called the brook *E* Num 13:24
they went up unto the valley of *E* Num 32:9
and came unto the valley of *E* Deut 1:24

**ESHEAN** (*esh'-e-an*) *A city in Judea.*
Arab, and Dumah, and *E*, Josh 15:52

**ESHEK** (*e'-shek*) *A descendant of King Saul.*
the sons of *E* his brother were, 1Chr 8:39

**ESHKALONITES** (*esh'-ka-lon-ites*) *Inhabitants of Ashkelon.*
and the Ashdothites, the *E* Josh 13:3

**ESHTAOL** (*esh'-ta-ol*) See ESHTAULITES. *A town in Judah.*
And in the valley, *E*, and Zoreah, Josh 15:33
their inheritance was Zorah, and *E* Josh 19:41
camp of Dan between Zorah and *E* Judg 13:25
*E* in the buryingplace of Manoah Judg 16:31
of valour, from Zorah, and from *E* Judg 18:2
unto their brethren to Zorah and *E* Judg 18:8
Danites, out of Zorah and out of *E* Judg 18:11

**ESHTAOLITES** See ESHTAULITES.

**ESHTAULITES** (*esh'-ta-u-lites*) *Inhabitants of Eshtaol.*
came the Zareathites, and the *E* 1Chr 2:53

**ESHTEMOA** (*esh-te-mo'-ah*) See ESHTEMOH.
*1. A Levitical town in Judah.*
suburbs, and *E* with her suburbs, Josh 21:14
and to them which were in *E* 1Sa 30:28
with her suburbs, and Jattir, and *E* 1Chr 6:57
*2. A descendant of Ezra.*
and Ishbah the father of *E* 1Chr 4:17
the Garmite, and *E* the Maachathite 1Chr 4:19

**ESHTEMOH** (*esh'-te-moh*) See ESHTEMOA. *Same as Eshtemoa 1.*
And Anab, and *E*, and Anim, Josh 15:50

**ESHTON** (*esh'-ton*) *Grandson of Chelub.*
Mehir, which was the father of *E* 1Chr 4:11
*E* begat Beth-rapha, and Paseah, and 1Chr 4:12

**ESLI** (*es'-li*) *Father of Naum; ancestor of Jesus.*
of Naum, which was the son of *E* Lk 3:25

**ESPECIALLY**
but *e* among my neighbours, and a Ps 31:11
*E* because I know thee to be Acts 26:3
*e* unto them who are of the Gal 6:10
*e* they who labour in the word and 1Ti 5:17
the books, but *e* the parchments 2Ti 4:13

**ESPIED**
in the inn, he *e* his money Gen 42:27
into a land that I had *e* for them Eze 20:6

**ESPOUSALS**
crowned him in the day of his *e* Song 3:11
of thy youth, the love of thine *e* Jer 2:2

**ESPOUSED**
which I *e* to me for an hundred 2Sa 3:14
his mother Mary was *e* to Joseph Mt 1:18
To a virgin *e* to a man whose name Lk 1:27
To be taxed with Mary his *e* wife Lk 2:5
for I have *e* you to one husband, 2Cor 11:2

**ESPY**
Kadesh-barnea to *e* out the land Josh 14:7
of Aroer, stand by the way, and *e* Jer 48:19

**ESROM** (*es'-rom*) See HEZRON. *Son of Phares; ancestor of Jesus.*
and Phares begat *E* Mt 1:3
and *E* begat Aram Mt 1:3
of Aram, which was the son of *E* Lk 3:33

**ESTABLISH**
with thee will I *e* my covenant Gen 6:18
I *e* my covenant with you, and with Gen 9:9
I will *e* my covenant with you Gen 9:11
I will *e* my covenant between me Gen 17:7
I will *e* my covenant with him for Gen 17:19
my covenant will I *e* with Isaac Gen 17:21
you, and *e* my covenant with you Lev 26:9
the soul, her husband may *e* it Num 30:13
that he may *e* his covenant which Deut 8:18
The LORD shall *e* thee an holy Deut 28:9
That he may *e* thee to day for a Deut 29:13
only the LORD *e* his word 1Sa 1:23
bowels, and I will *e* his kingdom 2Sa 7:12
*e* it for ever, and do as thou hast 2Sa 7:25
Then I will *e* the throne of thy 1Kin 9:5
son after him, and to *e* Jerusalem 1Kin 15:4
and I will *e* his kingdom 1Chr 17:11
I will *e* the throne of his 1Chr 22:10
Moreover I will *e* his kingdom for 1Chr 28:7
to *e* them for ever, therefore 2Chr 9:8
he doth *e* them for ever, and they Job 36:7
but *e* the just: for the righteous Ps 7:9
God will *e* it for ever Ps 48:8
the highest himself shall *e* her Ps 87:5
shalt thou *e* in the very heavens Ps 89:2
Thy seed will I *e* for ever Ps 89:4
*e* thou the work of our hands upon Ps 90:17
the work of our hands *e* thou it Ps 90:17
thou dost *e* equity, thou Ps 99:4
but he will *e* the border of the Prov 15:25
to *e* it with judgment and with Is 9:7
to *e* the earth, to cause to Is 49:8
And give him no rest, till he *e* Is 62:7
the LORD that formed it, to *e* it Jer 33:2
I will *e* unto thee an everlasting Eze 16:60
I will *e* my covenant with thee Eze 16:62
together to *e* a royal statute Dan 6:7
*e* the decree, and sign the writing Dan 6:8
exalt themselves to *e* the vision Dan 11:14
good, and *e* judgment in the gate Amos 5:15
yea, we *e* the law Rom 3:31
going about to *e* their own Rom 10:3
to *e* you, and to comfort you 1Th 3:2
first, that he may *e* the second Heb 10:9

**ESTABLISHED**
which I have *e* between me Gen 9:17
is because the thing is *e* by God Gen 41:32
I have also *e* my covenant with Ex 6:4
O Lord, which thy hands have *e* Ex 15:17
*e* for ever to him that bought it Lev 25:30
witnesses, shall the matter be *e* Deut 19:15
Hath he not made thee, and *e* thee Deut 32:6
was *e* to be a prophet of the LORD 1Sa 3:20
*e* thy kingdom upon Israel for 1Sa 13:13
the ground, thou shalt not be *e* 1Sa 20:31
Israel shall be *e* in thine hand 1Sa 24:20
LORD had *e* him king over Israel 2Sa 5:12
shall be *e* for ever before thee 2Sa 7:16
thy throne shall be *e* for ever 2Sa 7:16
servant David be *e* before thee 2Sa 7:26
and his kingdom was *e* greatly 1Kin 2:12
the LORD liveth, which hath *e* me 1Kin 2:24
be *e* before the LORD for ever 1Kin 2:45
the kingdom was *e* in the hand of 1Kin 2:46
throne shall be *e* for evermore 1Chr 17:14
his house be *e* for ever, and do as 1Chr 17:23
Let it even be *e*, that thy name 1Chr 17:24
thy servant be *e* before thee 1Chr 17:24
promise unto David my father be *e* 2Chr 1:9
when Rehoboam had *e* the kingdom 2Chr 12:1

LORD your God, so shall ye be *e* ......... 2Chr 20:20
when the kingdom was *e* to him ......... 2Chr 25:3
So they *e* a decree to make ......... 2Chr 30:5
Their seed is *e* in their sight ......... Job 21:8
thing, and it shall be *e* unto thee ......... Job 22:28
the seas, and *e* it upon the floods ......... Ps 24:2
feet upon a rock, and *e* my goings ......... Ps 40:2
For he *e* a testimony in Jacob, and ......... Ps 78:5
earth which he hath *e* for ever ......... Ps 78:69
With whom my hand shall be *e* ......... Ps 89:21
It shall be *e* for ever as the ......... Ps 89:37
Thy throne is *e* of old ......... Ps 93:2
the world also shall be *e* that it ......... Ps 96:10
their seed shall be *e* before thee ......... Ps 102:28
His heart is *e*, he shall not be ......... Ps 112:8
thou hast *e* the earth, and it ......... Ps 119:90
an evil speaker be *e* in the earth ......... Ps 140:11
hath he *e* the heavens ......... Prov 3:19
feet, and let all thy ways be *e* ......... Prov 4:26
When he *e* the clouds above ......... Prov 8:28
man shall not be *e* by wickedness ......... Prov 12:3
lip of truth shall be *e* for ever ......... Prov 12:19
of counsellors they are *e* ......... Prov 15:22
LORD, and thy thoughts shall be *e* ......... Prov 16:3
the throne is *e* by righteousness ......... Prov 16:12
Every purpose is *e* by counsel ......... Prov 20:18
and by understanding it is *e* ......... Prov 24:3
shall be *e* in righteousness ......... Prov 25:5
his throne shall be *e* for ever ......... Prov 29:14
who hath *e* all the ends of the ......... Prov 30:4
be *e* in the top of the mountains ......... Is 2:2
believe, surely ye shall not be *e* ......... Is 7:9
And in mercy shall the throne be *e* ......... Is 16:5
he hath *e* it, he created it not ......... Is 45:18
In righteousness shalt thou be *e* ......... Is 54:14
he hath *e* the world by his wisdom ......... Jer 10:12
congregation shall be *e* before me ......... Jer 30:20
he hath *e* the world by his wisdom ......... Jer 51:15
I was *e* in my kingdom, and ......... Dan 4:36
be *e* in the top of the mountains ......... Mic 4:1
thou hast *e* them for correction ......... Hab 1:12
and it shall be *e*, and set there ......... Zec 5:11
witnesses every word may be *e* ......... Mt 18:16
were the churches *e* in the faith ......... Acts 16:5
gift, to the end ye may be *e* ......... Rom 1:11
witnesses shall every word be *e* ......... 2Cor 13:1
which was *e* upon better promises ......... Heb 8:6
that the heart be *e* with grace ......... Heb 13:9
be *e* in the present truth ......... 2Pet 1:12

**ESTABLISHETH**
then he *e* all her vows, or all ......... Num 30:14
The king by judgment *e* the land ......... Prov 29:4
which the king *e* may be changed ......... Dan 6:15

**ESTABLISHMENT**
the *e* thereof, Sennacherib king ......... 2Chr 32:1

**ESTATE**
to the *e* of a man of high degree ......... 1Chr 17:17
*e* unto another that is better ......... Est 1:19
Who remembered us in our low *e* ......... Ps 136:23
saying, Lo, I am come to great *e* ......... Eccl 1:16
the *e* of the sons of men, that ......... Eccl 3:18
shall return to their former *e* ......... Eze 16:55
shall return to their former *e* ......... Eze 16:55
shall return to your former *e* ......... Eze 16:55
roots shall one stand up in his *e* ......... Dan 11:7
Then shall stand up in his *e* a ......... Dan 11:20
in his *e* shall stand up a vile ......... Dan 11:21
But in his *e* shall he honour the ......... Dan 11:38
the low *e* of his handmaiden ......... Lk 1:48
and all the *e* of the elders ......... Acts 22:5
but condescend to men of low *e* ......... Rom 12:16
that he might know your *e* ......... Col 4:8
which kept not their first *e* ......... Jude 6

**ESTATES**
will settle you after your old *e* ......... Eze 36:11
captains, and chief *e* of Galilee ......... Mk 6:21

**ESTEEM**
Will he *e* thy riches ......... Job 36:19
Therefore I *e* all thy precepts ......... Ps 119:128
yet we did *e* him stricken ......... Is 53:4
*e* other better than themselves ......... Phil 2:3
to *e* them very highly in love for ......... 1Th 5:13

**ESTEEMED**
lightly *e* the Rock of his ......... Deut 32:15
despise me shall be lightly *e* ......... 1Sa 2:30
I am a poor man, and lightly *e* ......... 1Sa 18:23
I have *e* the words of his mouth ......... Job 23:12
lips is *e* a man of understanding ......... Prov 17:28
shall be *e* as the potter's clay ......... Is 29:16
field shall be *e* as a forest ......... Is 29:17
he was despised, and we *e* him not ......... Is 53:3
how are they *e* as earthen ......... Lam 4:2
for that which is highly *e* among ......... Lk 16:15
who are least *e* in the church ......... 1Cor 6:4

**ESTEEMETH**
He *e* iron as straw, and brass as ......... Job 41:27
One man *e* one day above another ......... Rom 14:5
another *e* every day alike ......... Rom 14:5
but to him that *e* any thing to be ......... Rom 14:14

**ESTEEMING**
*E* the reproach of Christ greater ......... Heb 11:26

**ESTHER** (*est'-thur*) See ESTHER'S, HADASSAH.
*A Jewish queen.*
brought up Hadassah, that is, *E* ......... Est 2:7
that *E* was brought also unto the ......... Est 2:8
*E* had not shewed her people nor ......... Est 2:10
women's house, to know how *E* did ......... Est 2:11
Now when the turn of *E*, the ......... Est 2:15
*E* obtained favour in the sight of ......... Est 2:15
So *E* was taken unto king ......... Est 2:16
the king loved *E* above all the ......... Est 2:17
*E* had not yet shewed her kindred ......... Est 2:20
for *E* did the commandment of ......... Est 2:20
who told it unto *E* the queen ......... Est 2:22
*E* certified the king thereof in ......... Est 2:22
Then called *E* for Hatach, one of ......... Est 4:5
destroy them, to shew it unto *E* ......... Est 4:8
told *E* the words of Mordecai ......... Est 4:9
Again *E* spake unto Hatach, and ......... Est 4:10
Mordecai commanded to answer *E* ......... Est 4:13
Then *E* bade them return Mordecai ......... Est 4:15
to all that *E* had commanded him ......... Est 4:17
that *E* put on her royal apparel ......... Est 5:1
when the king saw *E* the queen ......... Est 5:2
the king held out to *E* the golden ......... Est 5:2
So *E* drew near, and touched the ......... Est 5:2
unto her, What wilt thou, queen *E* ......... Est 5:3
*E* answered, If it seem good unto ......... Est 5:4
that he may do as *E* hath said ......... Est 5:5
the banquet that *E* had prepared ......... Est 5:5
the king said unto *E* at the ......... Est 5:6
Then answered *E*, and said, My ......... Est 5:7
*E* the queen did let no man come ......... Est 5:12
the banquet that *E* had prepared ......... Est 6:14
came to banquet with *E* the queen ......... Est 7:1
unto *E* on the second day at the ......... Est 7:2
What is thy petition, queen *E* ......... Est 7:2
Then *E* the queen answered and said ......... Est 7:3
answered and said unto *E* the queen ......... Est 7:5
*E* said, The adversary and enemy is ......... Est 7:6
for his life to *E* the queen ......... Est 7:7
fallen upon the bed whereon *E* was ......... Est 7:8
the Jews' enemy unto *E* the queen ......... Est 8:1
for *E* had told what he was unto ......... Est 8:1
*E* set Mordecai over the house of ......... Est 8:2
*E* spake yet again before the king ......... Est 8:3
out the golden sceptre toward *E* ......... Est 8:4
So *E* arose, and stood before the ......... Est 8:4
Ahasuerus said unto *E* the queen ......... Est 8:7
I have given *E* the house of Haman ......... Est 8:7
And the king said unto *E* the queen ......... Est 9:12
Then said *E*, If it please the ......... Est 9:13
But when *E* came before the king ......... Est 9:25
Then *E* the queen, the daughter of ......... Est 9:29
*E* the queen had enjoined them, and ......... Est 9:31
the decree of *E* confirmed these ......... Est 9:32

**ESTHER'S** (*es'-thurs*)
and his servants, even *E* feast ......... Est 2:18
So *E* maids and her chamberlains ......... Est 4:4
And they told to Mordecai *E* words ......... Est 4:12

**ESTIMATE**
LORD, then the priest shall *e* it ......... Lev 27:14
as the priest shall *e* it, so ......... Lev 27:14

**ESTIMATION**
with thy *e* by shekels of silver ......... Lev 5:15
out of the flock, with thy *e* ......... Lev 5:18
out of the flock, with thy *e* ......... Lev 6:6
shall be for the LORD by thy *e* ......... Lev 27:2
thy *e* shall be of the male from ......... Lev 27:3
even thy *e* shall be fifty shekels ......... Lev 27:3
then thy *e* shall be thirty ......... Lev 27:4
then thy *e* shall be of the male ......... Lev 27:5
then thy *e* shall be of the male ......... Lev 27:6
for the female thy *e* shall be ......... Lev 27:6
then thy *e* shall be fifteen ......... Lev 27:7
But if he be poorer than thy *e* ......... Lev 27:8
a fifth part thereof unto thy *e* ......... Lev 27:13
of the money of thy *e* unto it ......... Lev 27:15
then thy *e* shall be according to ......... Lev 27:16
according to thy *e* it shall stand ......... Lev 27:17
and it shall be abated from thy *e* ......... Lev 27:18
of the money of thy *e* unto it ......... Lev 27:19
unto him the worth of thy *e* ......... Lev 27:23
he shall give thine *e* in that day ......... Lev 27:23
redeem it according to thine *e* ......... Lev 27:27
shall be sold according to thy *e* ......... Lev 27:27
thou redeem, according to thine *e* ......... Num 18:16

**ESTIMATIONS**
all thy *e* shall be according to ......... Lev 27:25

**ESTRANGED**
acquaintance are verily *e* from me ......... Job 19:13
The wicked are *e* from the womb ......... Ps 58:3
They were not *e* from their lust ......... Ps 78:30
have *e* this place, and have burned ......... Jer 19:4
because they are all *e* from me ......... Eze 14:5

**ETAM** (*e'-tam*)
*1. An area in western Judah.*
and dwelt in the top of the rock *E* ......... Judg 15:8
went to the top of the rock *E* ......... Judg 15:11
*2. A descendant of Judah.*
And these were of the father of *E* ......... 1Chr 4:3
*3. A village in Simeon.*
And their villages were, *E* ......... 1Chr 4:32
*4. A town in Judah.*
He built even Beth-lehem, and *E* ......... 2Chr 11:6

**ETERNAL**
The *e* God is thy refuge, and ......... Deut 33:27
I will make thee an *e* excellency ......... Is 60:15
I do, that I may have *e* life ......... Mt 19:16
but the righteous into life *e* ......... Mt 25:46
but is in danger of *e* damnation ......... Mk 3:29
I do that I may inherit *e* life ......... Mk 10:17
and in the world to come *e* life ......... Mk 10:30
what shall I do to inherit *e* life ......... Lk 10:25
what shall I do to inherit *e* life ......... Lk 18:18
not perish, but have *e* life ......... Jn 3:15
and gathereth fruit unto life *e* ......... Jn 4:36
in them ye think ye have *e* life ......... Jn 5:39
and drinketh my blood, hath *e* life ......... Jn 6:54
thou hast the words of *e* life ......... Jn 6:68
And I give unto them *e* life ......... Jn 10:28
world shall keep it unto life *e* ......... Jn 12:25
that he should give *e* life to as ......... Jn 17:2
And this is life *e*, that they ......... Jn 17:3
were ordained to *e* life believed ......... Acts 13:48
that are made, even his *e* power ......... Rom 1:20
and honour and immortality, *e* life ......... Rom 2:7
through righteousness unto *e* life ......... Rom 5:21
but the gift of God is *e* life ......... Rom 6:23
exceeding and *e* weight of glory ......... 2Cor 4:17
things which are not seen are *e* ......... 2Cor 4:18
made with hands, *e* in the heavens ......... 2Cor 5:1
According to the *e* purpose which ......... Eph 3:11
Now unto the King *e*, immortal ......... 1Ti 1:17
of faith, lay hold on *e* life ......... 1Ti 6:12
that they may lay hold on *e* life ......... 1Ti 6:19
is in Christ Jesus with *e* glory ......... 2Ti 2:10
In hope of *e* life, which God ......... Titus 1:2
according to the hope of *e* life ......... Titus 3:7
he became the author of *e* ......... Heb 5:9
of the dead, and of *e* judgment ......... Heb 6:2
having obtained *e* redemption for ......... Heb 9:12
who through the *e* Spirit offered ......... Heb 9:14
the promise of *e* inheritance ......... Heb 9:15
unto his *e* glory by Christ Jesus ......... 1Pet 5:10
and shew unto you that *e* life ......... 1Jn 1:2
he hath promised us, even *e* life ......... 1Jn 2:25
hath *e* life abiding in him ......... 1Jn 3:15
that God hath given to us *e* life ......... 1Jn 5:11
ye may know that ye have *e* life ......... 1Jn 5:13
This is the true God, and *e* life ......... 1Jn 5:20
suffering the vengeance of *e* fire ......... Jude 7
our Lord Jesus Christ unto *e* life ......... Jude 21

**ETERNITY**
and lofty One that inhabiteth *e* ......... Is 57:15

**ETHAM** (*e'-tham*) *An encampment during the Exodus.*
from Succoth, and encamped in *E* ......... Ex 13:20
from Succoth, and pitched in *E* ......... Num 33:6
And they removed from *E* ......... Num 33:7
journey in the wilderness of *E* ......... Num 33:8

**ETHAN** (*e'-than*)
*1. A wise man in Solomon's time.*
than *E* the Ezrahite, and Heman, and ......... 1Kin 4:31
Maschil of *E* the Ezrahite ......... Ps 89:*t*
*2. A son of Zerah.*
Zimri, and *E*, and Heman, and Calcol ......... 1Chr 2:6
And the sons of *E* ......... 1Chr 2:8
*3. A descendant of Gershon.*
The son of *E*, the son of Zimmah ......... 1Chr 6:42
*4. A descendant of Merari.*
*E* the son of Kishi, the son of ......... 1Chr 6:44
brethren, *E* the son of Kushaiah ......... 1Chr 15:17
the singers, Heman, Asaph, and *E* ......... 1Chr 15:19

**ETHANIM** (*eth'-a-nim*) *Seventh month of the Hebrew year.*
at the feast in the month *E* ......... 1Kin 8:2

**ETHBAAL** (*eth'-ba-al*) *Father of Jezebel.*
of *E* king of the Zidonians ......... 1Kin 16:31

**ETHER** (*e'-ther*) *A city in Judah.*
Libnah, and *E*, and Ashan ......... Josh 15:42
Ain, Remmon, and *E*, and Ashan ......... Josh 19:7

**ETHIOPIA** (*e-the-o'-pe-ah*) See CUSH, ETHIOPIAN.
*1. The land south of Egypt.*
compasseth the whole land of *E* ......... Gen 2:13
reigned from India even unto *E* ......... Est 1:1
which are from India unto *E* ......... Est 8:9
The topaz of *E* shall not equal it ......... Job 28:19
behold Philistia, and Tyre, with *E* ......... Ps 87:4
which is beyond the rivers of *E* ......... Is 18:1
Syene even unto the border of *E* ......... Eze 29:10
the rivers of *E* my suppliants ......... Zeph 3:10
and, behold, a man of *E*, an eunuch ......... Acts 8:27
*2. Inhabitants of Ethiopia.*
heard say of Tirhakah king of *E* ......... 2Kin 19:9
*E* shall soon stretch out her ......... Ps 68:31
and wonder upon Egypt and upon *E* ......... Is 20:3
ashamed of *E* their expectation ......... Is 20:5
say concerning Tirhakah king of *E* ......... Is 37:9
I gave Egypt for thy ransom, *E* ......... Is 43:3
of Egypt, and merchandise of *E* ......... Is 45:14
and great pain shall be in *E* ......... Eze 30:4
*E*, and Libya, and Lydia, and all the ......... Eze 30:5
Persia, *E*, and Libya with them ......... Eze 38:5
*E* and Egypt were her strength, and ......... Nah 3:9

**ETHIOPIAN**
the *E* woman whom he had married ......... Num 12:1
for he had married an *E* woman ......... Num 12:1
the *E* with an host of a thousand ......... 2Chr 14:9
Can the *E* change his skin, or the ......... Jer 13:23
Now when Ebed-melech the *E* ......... Jer 38:7
king commanded Ebed-melech the *E* ......... Jer 38:10
Ebed-melech the *E* said unto ......... Jer 38:12
Go and speak to Ebed-melech the *E* ......... Jer 39:16

**ETHIOPIANS** *Inhabitants of Ethiopia.*
the Lubim, the Sukkiims, and the *E*.... 2Chr 12:3
the LORD smote the *E* before Asa...... 2Chr 14:12
before Judah; and the *E* fled.............. 2Chr 14:12
the *E* were overthrown, that they..... 2Chr 14:13
Were not the *E* and the Lubims a........ 2Chr 16:8
Arabians, that were near the *E*........... 2Chr 21:16
the *E* captives, young and old,................... Is 20:4
the *E* and the Libyans, that handle......... Jer 46:9
to make the careless *E* afraid................. Eze 30:9
the *E* shall be at his steps...................... Dan 11:43
not as children of the *E* unto me.......... Amos 9:7
Ye *E* also, ye shall be slain by.............. Zeph 2:12
under Candace queen of the *E*.............. Acts 8:27

**ETH-KAZIN**

**ETHNAN** *(eth'-nan) Grandson of Ashur.*
were, Zereth, and Jezoar, and *E*............ 1Chr 4:7

**ETHNI** *(eth'-ni)* See JEATERAI. *Ancestor of Asaph.*
The son of *E*, the son of Zerah,............ 1Chr 6:41

**EUBULUS** *(yu-bu'-lus) A Christian acquaintance of Paul.*
*E* greeteth thee, and Pudens, and............ 2Ti 4:21

**EUNICE** *(yu-ni'-see) Mother of Timothy.*
grandmother Lois, and thy mother *E*....... 2Ti 1:5

**EUNUCH**
neither let the *e* say, Behold, I.................. Is 56:3
He took also out of the city an *e*............ Jer 52:25
an *e* of great authority under................ Acts 8:27
the *e* answered Philip, and said, I......... Acts 8:34
the *e* said, See, here is water.............. Acts 8:36
the water, both Philip and the *e*........... Acts 8:38
that the *e* saw him no more.................. Acts 8:39

**EUNUCHS**
looked out to him two or three *e*......... 2Kin 9:32
they shall be *e* in the palace of.......... 2Kin 20:18
they shalt be *e* in the palace of................ Is 39:7
unto the *e* that keep my sabbaths............ Is 56:4
the king, and the queen, and the *e*......... Jer 29:2
the princes of Jerusalem, the *e*............. Jer 34:19
one of the *e* which was in the................... Jer 38:7
women, and the children, and the *e*...... Jer 41:16
unto Ashpenaz the master of his *e*......... Dan 1:3
the prince of the *e* gave names............... Dan 1:7
of the *e* that he might not defile............ Dan 1:8
love with the prince of the *e*................. Dan 1:9
prince of the *e* said unto Daniel........... Dan 1:10
of the *e* had set over Daniel.................. Dan 1:11
of the *e* brought them in before............ Dan 1:18
For there are some *e*, which were......... Mt 19:12
and there are some *e*, which were.......... Mt 19:12
*e*, which were made *e* of men................. Mt 19:12
and there be *e*, which have made.......... Mt 19:12
which have made themselves *e* for....... Mt 19:12

**EUODIAS** *(yu-o'-de-as) A Christian at Philippi.*
I beseech *E*, and beseech Syntyche,........ Phil 4:2

**EUPHRATES** *(yu-fra'-teze) A river in Mesopotamia.*
And the fourth river is *E*........................ Gen 2:14
unto the great river, the river *E*.......... Gen 15:18
unto the great river, the river *E*............. Deut 1:7
from the river, the river *E*................... Deut 11:24
unto the great river, the river *E*............. Josh 1:4
recover his border at the river *E*............. 2Sa 8:3
king of Assyria to the river *E*.............. 2Kin 23:29
river of Egypt unto the river *E*............. 2Kin 24:7
the wilderness from the river *E*............... 1Chr 5:9
his dominion by the river *E*.................. 1Chr 18:3
to fight against Charchemish by *E*.... 2Chr 35:20
upon thy loins, and arise, go to *E*............ Jer 13:4
So I went, and hid it by *E*...................... Jer 13:5
LORD said unto me, Arise, go to *E*............ Jer 13:6
Then I went to *E*, and digged, and............ Jer 13:7
was by the river *E* in Carchemish.............. Jer 46:2
toward the north by the river *E*.............. Jer 46:6
the north country by the river *E*............ Jer 46:10
and cast it into the midst of *E*.............. Jer 51:63
are bound in the great river *E*............... Rev 9:14
his vial upon the great river *E*............. Rev 16:12

**EURAQUILO** See EUROCLYDON.

**EUROCLYDON** *(yu-roc'-lid-on) A Mediterranean wind.*
it a tempestuous wind, called *E*.......... Acts 27:14

**EUTYCHUS** *(yu'-tik-us) Youth restored to life.*
a certain young man named *E*.............. Acts 20:9

**EVANGELIST**
into the house of Philip the *e*............... Acts 21:8
afflictions, do the work of an *e*............... 2Ti 4:5

**EVANGELISTS**
and some, *e*; and some, pastors............. Eph 4:11

**EVE** *(eev) Wife of Adam.*
And Adam called his wife's name *E*...... Gen 3:20
And Adam knew *E* his wife...................... Gen 4:1
beguiled *E* through his subtilty............ 2Cor 11:3
For Adam was first formed, then *E*........ 1Ti 2:13

**EVEN** See PREFACE.

**EVENING**
And the *e* and the morning were the..... Gen 1:5
And the *e* and the morning were the..... Gen 1:8
And the *e* and the morning were the... Gen 1:13
And the *e* and the morning were the... Gen 1:19
And the *e* and the morning were the... Gen 1:23
And the *e* and the morning were the... Gen 1:31
the dove came in to him in the *e*.......... Gen 8:11
of water at the time of the *e*............... Gen 24:11
And it came to pass in the *e*................. Gen 29:23
came out of the field in the *e*............... Gen 30:16
of Israel shall kill it in the *e*................... Ex 12:6
give you in the *e* flesh to eat..................... Ex 16:8
Moses from the morning unto the *e*...... Ex 18:13
from *e* to morning before the LORD....... Ex 27:21
the *e* unto the morning before the......... Lev 24:3
when *e* cometh on, he shall wash...... Deut 23:11
upon the trees until the *e*.................... Josh 10:26
now the day draweth toward *e*............ Judg 19:9
man that eateth any food until *e*........... 1Sa 14:24
Philistine drew near morning and *e*...... 1Sa 17:16
even unto the *e* of the next day........... 1Sa 30:17
and bread and flesh in the *e*................. 1Kin 17:6
the offering of the *e* sacrifice.............. 1Kin 18:29
the offering of the *e* sacrifice.............. 1Kin 18:36
the *e* meat offering, and the............... 2Kin 16:15
offering continually morning and *e*... 1Chr 16:40
the burnt offerings morning and *e*......... 2Chr 2:4
every *e* burnt sacrifices and sweet..... 2Chr 13:11
lamps thereof, to burn every *e*............ 2Chr 13:11
*e* burnt offerings, and the burnt........... 2Chr 31:3
even burnt offerings morning and *e*........ Ezr 3:3
astonied until the *e* sacrifice.................... Ezr 9:4
at the *e* sacrifice I arose up..................... Ezr 9:5
In the *e* she went, and on the.................. Est 2:14
are destroyed from morning to *e*............. Job 4:20
*E*, and morning, and at noon, will I........ Ps 55:17
They return at *e*: they make a................... Ps 59:6
And at *e* let them return........................ Ps 59:14
of the morning and *e* to rejoice............... Ps 65:8
in the *e* it is cut down, and..................... Ps 90:6
work and to his labour until the *e*........ Ps 104:23
up of my hands as the *e* sacrifice.......... Ps 141:2
In the twilight, in the *e*........................ Prov 7:9
in the *e* withhold not thine hand.......... Eccl 11:6
of the *e* are stretched out........................ Jer 6:4
of the LORD was upon me in the *e*....... Eze 33:22
shall not be shut until the *e*.................. Eze 46:2
And the vision of the *e* and the............. Dan 8:26
about the time of the *e* oblation........... Dan 9:21
are more fierce than the *e* wolves............ Hab 1:8
shall they lie down in the *e*................... Zeph 2:7
her judges are *e* wolves......................... Zeph 3:3
that at *e* time it shall be light................ Zec 14:7
And when it was *e*, his disciples........... Mt 14:15
and when the *e* was come, he was.......... Mt 14:23
and said unto them, When it is *e*.............. Mt 16:2
in the *e* he cometh with the................... Mk 14:17
for it is toward *e*, and the day is........... Lk 24:29
Then the same day at *e*, being the.......... Jn 20:19
the prophets, from morning till *e*........ Acts 28:23

**EVENINGS**
a wolf of the *e* shall spoil them,................. Jer 5:6

**EVENINGTIDE**
And it came to pass in an *e*..................... 2Sa 11:2
And behold at *e* trouble.......................... Is 17:14

**EVENT**
that one *e* happeneth to them all.......... Eccl 2:14
there is one *e* to the righteous,............... Eccl 9:2
sun, that there is one *e* unto all.............. Eccl 9:3

**EVENTIDE**
to meditate in the field at the *e*........... Gen 24:63
the ark of the LORD until the *e*................ Josh 7:6
of Ai he hanged on a tree until *e*.......... Josh 8:29
now the *e* was come, he went out......... Mk 11:11
for it was now *e*...................................... Acts 4:3

**EVER**
of life, and eat, and live for *e*................. Gen 3:22
I give it, and to thy seed for *e*............. Gen 13:15
then let me bear the blame for *e*........... Gen 43:9
bear the blame to my father for *e*........ Gen 44:32
this is my name for *e*, and this is.............. Ex 3:15
it a feast by an ordinance for *e*............. Ex 12:14
generations by an ordinance for *e*.......... Ex 12:17
to thee and to thy sons for *e*.................. Ex 12:24
see them again no more for *e*................ Ex 14:13
The LORD shall reign for *e*..................... Ex 15:18
LORD shall reign for *e* and *e*................... Ex 15:18
with thee, and believe thee for *e*............... Ex 19:9
and he shall serve him for *e*.................... Ex 21:6
it shall be a statute for *e* unto............... Ex 27:21
shall be a statute for *e* unto him........... Ex 28:43
his sons' by a statute for *e* from............ Ex 29:28
shall be a statute for *e* to them............. Ex 30:21
and the children of Israel for *e*............... Ex 31:17
and they shall inherit it for *e*................. Ex 32:13
The fire shall *e* be burning upon............. Lev 6:13
It shall be a statute for *e* in.................... Lev 6:18
is a statute for *e* unto the LORD............... Lev 6:22
for *e* from among the children of.............. Lev 7:34
by a statute for *e* throughout.................. Lev 7:36
it shall be a statute for *e*........................ Lev 10:9
with thee, by a statute for *e*.................. Lev 10:15
shall be a statute for *e* unto you........... Lev 16:29
your souls, by a statute for *e*................ Lev 16:31
for *e* unto them throughout their............. Lev 17:7
it shall be a statute for *e*...................... Lev 23:14
for *e* in all your dwellings...................... Lev 23:21
it shall be a statute for *e*...................... Lev 23:31
statute for *e* in your generations.......... Lev 23:41
statute for *e* in your generations............. Lev 24:3
The land shall not be sold for *e*............. Lev 25:23
for *e* to him that bought it.................... Lev 25:30
they shall be your bondmen for *e*........ Lev 25:46
for *e* throughout your generations...... Num 10:8
an ordinance for *e* in your................... Num 15:15
thy sons, by an ordinance for *e*.............. Num 18:8
with thee, by a statute for *e*................ Num 18:11
with thee, by a statute for *e*................ Num 18:19
for *e* before the LORD unto thee......... Num 18:19
it shall be a statute for *e*..................... Num 18:23
among them, for a statute for *e*........... Num 19:10
upon which thou hast ridden *e*............ Num 22:30
was I *e* wont to do so unto thee......... Num 22:30
end shall be that he perish for *e*......... Num 24:20
and he also shall perish for *e*............ Num 24:24
Did *e* people hear the voice of................ Deut 4:33
LORD thy God giveth thee, for *e*............ Deut 4:40
and with their children for *e*................ Deut 5:29
thy children after thee for *e*................ Deut 12:28
and it shall be an heap for *e*.............. Deut 13:16
and he shall be thy servant for *e*....... Deut 15:17
the LORD, him and his sons for *e*.......... Deut 18:5
thy God, and to walk *e* in his ways..... Deut 19:9
congregation of the LORD for *e*............ Deut 23:3
prosperity all thy days for *e*................. Deut 23:6
a wonder, and upon thy seed for *e*.... Deut 28:46
unto us and to our children for *e*....... Deut 29:29
to heaven, and say, I live for *e*........... Deut 32:40
unto the children of Israel for *e*............ Josh 4:7
fear the LORD your God for *e*................. Josh 4:24
Ai, and made it an heap for *e*................. Josh 8:28
and thy children's for *e*, because .......... Josh 14:9
did he *e* strive against Israel,.............. Judg 11:25
or did he *e* fight against them,............ Judg 11:25
the LORD, and there abide for *e*.............. 1Sa 1:22
should walk before me for *e*.................... 1Sa 2:30
an old man in thine house for *e*............. 1Sa 2:32
walk before mine anointed for *e*............. 1Sa 2:35
for *e* for the iniquity which he................ 1Sa 3:13
with sacrifice nor offering for *e*............. 1Sa 3:14
thy kingdom upon Israel for *e*.............. 1Sa 13:13
thy kindness from my house for *e*......... 1Sa 20:15
LORD be between thee and me for *e*.... 1Sa 20:23
between my seed and thy seed for *e*.... 1Sa 20:42
he shall be my servant for *e*................. 1Sa 27:12
thee keeper of mine head for *e*................ 1Sa 28:2
Shall the sword devour for *e*.................. 2Sa 2:26
guiltless before the LORD for *e*.............. 2Sa 3:28
the throne of his kingdom for *e*.............. 2Sa 7:13
be established for *e* before thee............ 2Sa 7:16
throne shall be established for *e*........... 2Sa 7:16
to be a people unto thee for *e*................ 2Sa 7:24
his house, establish it for *e*................... 2Sa 7:25
let thy name be magnified for *e*.............. 2Sa 7:26
it may continue for *e* before thee........... 2Sa 7:29
of thy servant be blessed for *e*............... 2Sa 7:29
Let my lord king David live for *e*......... 1Kin 1:31
upon the head of his seed for *e*............. 1Kin 2:33
be peace for *e* from the LORD................ 1Kin 2:33
established before the LORD for *e*......... 1Kin 2:45
for Hiram was *e* a lover of David........... 1Kin 5:1
place for thee to abide in for *e*............... 1Kin 8:13
built, to put my name there for *e*........... 1Kin 9:3
of thy kingdom upon Israel for *e*........... 1Kin 9:5
the LORD loved Israel for *e*.................... 1Kin 10:9
the seed of David, but not for *e*.......... 1Kin 11:39
they will be thy servants for *e*.............. 1Kin 12:7
unto thee, and unto thy seed for *e*....... 2Kin 5:27
Israel, will I put my name for *e*............ 2Kin 21:7
and to minister unto him for *e*............... 1Chr 15:2
for his mercy endureth for *e*.............. 1Chr 16:34
be the LORD God of Israel for *e*.......... 1Chr 16:36
LORD God of Israel for *e* and *e*............ 1Chr 16:36
because his mercy endureth for *e*....... 1Chr 16:41
I will stablish his throne for *e*............ 1Chr 17:12
and in my kingdom for *e*..................... 1Chr 17:14
thou make thine own people for *e*........ 1Chr 17:22
his house be established for *e*............. 1Chr 17:23
thy name may be magnified for *e*......... 1Chr 17:24
that it may be before thee for *e*.......... 1Chr 17:27
and it shall be blessed for *e*............... 1Chr 17:27
of his kingdom over Israel for *e*.......... 1Chr 22:10
holy things, he and his sons for *e*...... 1Chr 23:13
and to bless in his name for *e*............ 1Chr 23:13
they may dwell in Jerusalem for *e*...... 1Chr 23:25
to be king over Israel for *e*.................... 1Chr 28:4
will establish his kingdom for *e*............ 1Chr 28:7
for your children after you for *e*........... 1Chr 28:8
him, he will cast thee off for *e*.............. 1Chr 28:9
Israel our father, for *e* and *e*............. 1Chr 29:10
fathers, keep this for *e* in the............. 1Chr 29:18
is an ordinance for *e* to Israel................. 2Chr 2:4
for his mercy endureth for *e*.................. 2Chr 5:13
and a place for thy dwelling for *e*.......... 2Chr 6:2
for his mercy endureth for *e*.................... 2Chr 7:3
because his mercy endureth for *e*........... 2Chr 7:6
that my name may be there for *e*.......... 2Chr 7:16
Israel, to establish them for *e*................ 2Chr 9:8
they will be thy servants for *e*............... 2Chr 10:7
over Israel to David for *e*...................... 2Chr 13:5
seed of Abraham thy friend for *e*........... 2Chr 20:7
for his mercy endureth for *e*................ 2Chr 20:21
light to him and to his sons for *e*.......... 2Chr 21:7
which he hath sanctified for *e*............... 2Chr 30:8
Jerusalem shall my name be for *e*.......... 2Chr 33:4
Israel, will I put my name for *e*............ 2Chr 33:7
endureth for *e* toward Israel..................... Ezr 3:11
their peace or their wealth for *e*.............. Ezr 9:12
to your children for *e*............................... Ezr 9:12
the king, Let the king live for *e*.................. Neh 2:3
the LORD your God for *e* and *e*.................. Neh 9:5
the congregation of God for *e*................... Neh 13:1

who e perished, being innocent ... Job 4:7
they perish for e without any ... Job 4:20
Thou prevailest for e against him ... Job 14:20
pen and lead in the rock for e ... Job 19:24
perish for e like his own dung ... Job 20:7
be delivered for e from my judge ... Job 23:7
yea, he doth establish them for e ... Job 36:7
thou take him for a servant for e ... Job 41:4
let them e shout for joy, because ... Ps 5:11
hast put out their name for e ... Ps 9:5
put out their name for e and e ... Ps 9:5
But the LORD shall endure for e ... Ps 9:7
the poor shall not perish for e ... Ps 9:18
The LORD is King for e and e ... Ps 10:16
The LORD is King for e and e ... Ps 10:16
them from this generation for e ... Ps 12:7
forget me, O LORD¿ for e? ... Ps 13:1
the LORD is clean, enduring for e ... Ps 19:9
it him, even length of days for e ... Ps 21:4
even length of days for e and e ... Ps 21:4
hast made him most blessed for e ... Ps 21:6
your heart shall live for e ... Ps 22:26
in the house of the LORD for e ... Ps 23:6
for they have been e of old ... Ps 25:6
Mine eyes are e toward the LORD ... Ps 25:15
them also, and lift them up for e ... Ps 28:9
yea, the LORD sitteth King for e ... Ps 29:10
will give thanks unto thee for e ... Ps 30:12
of the LORD standeth for e ... Ps 33:11
their inheritance shall be for e ... Ps 37:18
He is e merciful, and lendeth ... Ps 37:26
they are preserved for e ... Ps 37:28
the land, and dwell therein for e ... Ps 37:29
settest me before thy face for e ... Ps 41:12
long, and praise thy name for e ... Ps 44:8
arise, cast us not off for e ... Ps 44:23
God hath blessed thee for e ... Ps 45:2
Thy throne, O God, is for e ... Ps 45:6
throne, O God, is for e and e ... Ps 45:6
the people praise thee for e ... Ps 45:17
people praise thee for e and e ... Ps 45:17
God will establish it for e ... Ps 48:8
For this God is our God for e ... Ps 48:14
this God is our God for e and e ... Ps 48:14
is precious, and it ceaseth for e ... Ps 49:8
That he should still live for e ... Ps 49:9
their houses shall continue for e ... Ps 49:11
and my sin is e before me ... Ps 51:3
shall likewise destroy thee for e ... Ps 52:5
I trust in the mercy of God for e ... Ps 52:8
in the mercy of God for e and e ... Ps 52:8
I will praise thee for e, because ... Ps 52:9
abide in thy tabernacle for e ... Ps 61:4
He shall abide before God for e ... Ps 61:7
I sing praise unto thy name for e ... Ps 61:8
He ruleth by his power for e ... Ps 66:7
the LORD will dwell in it for e ... Ps 68:16
His name shall endure for e ... Ps 72:17
be his glorious name for e ... Ps 72:19
of my heart, and my portion for e ... Ps 73:26
why hast thou cast us off for e ... Ps 74:1
enemy blaspheme thy name for e ... Ps 74:10
congregation of thy poor for e ... Ps 74:19
But I will declare for e ... Ps 75:9
Will the Lord cast off for e ... Ps 77:7
Is his mercy clean gone for e ... Ps 77:8
which he hath established for e ... Ps 78:69
wilt thou be angry for e ... Ps 79:5
will give thee thanks for e ... Ps 79:13
time should have endured for e ... Ps 81:15
be confounded and troubled for e ... Ps 83:17
Wilt thou be angry with us for e ... Ps 85:5
of the mercies of the LORD for e ... Ps 89:1
Mercy shall be built up for e ... Ps 89:2
Thy seed will I establish for e ... Ps 89:4
also will I make to endure for e ... Ps 89:29
His seed shall endure for e ... Ps 89:36
be established for e as the moon ... Ps 89:37
wilt thou hide thyself for e ... Ps 89:46
or e thou hadst formed the earth ... Ps 90:2
they shall be destroyed for e ... Ps 92:7
thine house, O LORD, for e ... Ps 93:5
thou, O LORD, shalt endure for e ... Ps 102:12
will he keep his anger for e ... Ps 103:9
it should not be removed for e ... Ps 104:5
of the LORD shall endure for e ... Ps 104:31
remembered his covenant for e ... Ps 105:8
for his mercy endureth for e ... Ps 106:1
for his mercy endureth for e ... Ps 107:1
Thou art a priest for e after the ... Ps 110:4
his righteousness endureth for e ... Ps 111:3
he will e be mindful of his ... Ps 111:5
They stand fast for e and e, and ... Ps 111:8
They stand fast for e and e ... Ps 111:8
hath commanded his covenant for e ... Ps 111:9
his praise endureth for e ... Ps 111:10
his righteousness endureth for e ... Ps 112:3
he shall not be moved for e ... Ps 112:6
his righteousness endureth for e ... Ps 112:9
truth of the LORD endureth for e ... Ps 117:2
because his mercy endureth for e ... Ps 118:1
that his mercy endureth for e ... Ps 118:2
that his mercy endureth for e ... Ps 118:3
that his mercy endureth for e ... Ps 118:4
for his mercy endureth for e ... Ps 118:29
I keep thy law continually for e ... Ps 119:44
thy law continually for e and e ... Ps 119:44
For e, O LORD, thy word is ... Ps 119:89
for they are e with me ... Ps 119:98
have I taken as an heritage for e ... Ps 119:111
that thou hast founded them for e ... Ps 119:152
judgments endureth for e ... Ps 119:160
be removed, but abideth for e ... Ps 125:1
people from henceforth even for e ... Ps 125:2
the LORD from henceforth and for e ... Ps 131:3
This is my rest for e ... Ps 132:14
Thy name, O LORD, endureth for e ... Ps 135:13
for his mercy endureth for e ... Ps 136:1
for his mercy endureth for e ... Ps 136:2
for his mercy endureth for e ... Ps 136:3
for his mercy endureth for e ... Ps 136:4
for his mercy endureth for e ... Ps 136:5
for his mercy endureth for e ... Ps 136:6
for his mercy endureth for e ... Ps 136:7
for his mercy endureth for e ... Ps 136:8
for his mercy endureth for e ... Ps 136:9
for his mercy endureth for e ... Ps 136:10
for his mercy endureth for e ... Ps 136:11
for his mercy endureth for e ... Ps 136:12
for his mercy endureth for e ... Ps 136:13
for his mercy endureth for e ... Ps 136:14
for his mercy endureth for e ... Ps 136:15
for his mercy endureth for e ... Ps 136:16
for his mercy endureth for e ... Ps 136:17
for his mercy endureth for e ... Ps 136:18
for his mercy endureth for e ... Ps 136:19
for his mercy endureth for e ... Ps 136:20
for his mercy endureth for e ... Ps 136:21
for his mercy endureth for e ... Ps 136:22
for his mercy endureth for e ... Ps 136:23
for his mercy endureth for e ... Ps 136:24
for his mercy endureth for e ... Ps 136:25
for his mercy endureth for e ... Ps 136:26
thy mercy, O LORD, endureth for e ... Ps 138:8
and I will bless thy name for e ... Ps 145:1
will bless thy name for e and e ... Ps 145:1
and I will praise thy name for e ... Ps 145:2
praise thy name for e and e ... Ps 145:2
flesh bless his holy name for e ... Ps 145:21
bless his holy name for e and e ... Ps 145:21
which keepeth truth for e ... Ps 146:6
The LORD shall reign for e ... Ps 146:10
hath also stablished them for e ... Ps 148:6
stablished them for e and e ... Ps 148:6
the beginning, or e the earth was ... Prov 8:23
truth shall be established for e ... Prov 12:19
For riches are not for e ... Prov 27:24
throne shall be established for e ... Prov 29:14
but the earth abideth for e ... Eccl 1:4
wise more than of the fool for e ... Eccl 2:16
God doeth, it shall be for e ... Eccl 3:14
they any more a portion for e in ... Eccl 9:6
Or e the silver cord be loosed, ... Eccl 12:6
Or e I was aware, my soul made me... Song 6:12
from henceforth even for e ... Is 9:7
Trust ye in the LORD for e ... Is 26:4
he will not e be threshing it ... Is 28:28
may be for the time to come for e ... Is 30:8
the time to come for e and e ... Is 30:8
and towers shall be for dens for e ... Is 32:14
quietness and assurance for e ... Is 32:17
stakes thereof shall e be removed ... Is 33:20
smoke thereof shall go up for e ... Is 34:10
none shall pass through it for e ... Is 34:10
pass through it for e and e ... Is 34:10
they shall possess it for e ... Is 34:17
word of our God shall stand for e ... Is 40:8
saidst, I shall be a lady for e ... Is 47:7
but my salvation shall be for e ... Is 51:6
my righteousness shall be for e ... Is 51:8
For I will not contend for e ... Is 57:16
LORD, from henceforth and for e ... Is 59:21
they shall inherit the land for e ... Is 60:21
neither remember iniquity for e ... Is 64:9
rejoice for e in that which I ... Is 65:18
Will he reserve his anger for e ... Jer 3:5
and I will not keep anger for e ... Jer 3:12
to your fathers, for e and e ... Jer 7:7
anger, which shall burn for e ... Jer 17:4
and this city shall remain for e ... Jer 17:25
and to your fathers for e and e ... Jer 25:5
being a nation before me for e ... Jer 31:36
nor thrown down any more for e ... Jer 31:40
way, that they may fear me for e ... Jer 32:39
for his mercy endureth for e ... Jer 33:11
neither ye, nor your sons for e ... Jer 35:6
a man to stand before me for e ... Jer 35:19
dragons, and a desolation for e ... Jer 49:33
shall be no more inhabited for e ... Jer 50:39
but thou shalt be desolate for e ... Jer 51:26
that it shall be desolate for e ... Jer 51:62
the Lord will not cast off for e ... Lam 3:31
Thou, O LORD, remainest for e ... Lam 5:19
dost thou forget us for e ... Lam 5:20
their children's children for e ... Eze 37:25
David shall be their prince for e ... Eze 37:25
of the children of Israel for e ... Eze 43:7
dwell in the midst of them for e ... Eze 43:9
in Syriack, O king, live for e ... Dan 2:4
Blessed be the name of God for e ... Dan 2:20
be the name of God for e and e ... Dan 2:20
kingdoms, and it shall stand for e ... Dan 2:44
O king, live for e ... Dan 3:9
and honoured him that liveth for e ... Dan 4:34
spake and said, O king, live for e ... Dan 5:10
unto him, King Darius, live for e ... Dan 6:6
unto the king, O king, live for e ... Dan 6:21
all their bones in pieces or e ... Dan 6:24
the living God, and stedfast for e ... Dan 6:26
the kingdom for e, even for e ... Dan 7:18
for e, even for e and e ... Dan 7:18
righteousness as the stars for e ... Dan 12:3
as the stars for e and e ... Dan 12:3
for e that it shall be for a time ... Dan 12:7
I will betroth thee unto me for e ... Hos 2:19
there hath not been e the like ... Joel 2:2
But Judah shall dwell for e ... Joel 3:20
and he kept his wrath for e ... Amos 1:11
and thou shalt be cut off for e ... Obad 10
with her bars was about me for e ... Jonah 2:6
have ye taken away my glory for e ... Mic 2:9
name of the LORD our God for e ... Mic 4:5
of the LORD our God for e and e ... Mic 4:5
Zion from henceforth, even for e ... Mic 4:7
he retaineth not his anger for e ... Mic 7:18
the prophets, do they live for e ... Zec 1:5
the LORD hath indignation for e ... Mal 1:4
and the power, and the glory, for e ... Mt 6:13
grow on thee henceforward for e ... Mt 21:19
to this time, no, nor e shall be ... Mt 24:21
eat fruit of thee hereafter for e ... Mk 11:14
to do as he had e done unto them ... Mk 15:8
over the house of Jacob for e ... Lk 1:33
to Abraham, and to his seed for e ... Lk 1:55
unto him, Son, thou art e with me ... Lk 15:31
told me all things that e I did ... Jn 4:29
He told me all that e I did ... Jn 4:39
this bread, he shall live for e ... Jn 6:51
of this bread shall live for e ... Jn 6:58
abideth not in the house for e ... Jn 8:35
but the Son abideth e ... Jn 8:35
All that e came before me are ... Jn 10:8
the law that Christ abideth for e ... Jn 12:34
that he may abide with you for e ... Jn 14:16
I e taught in the synagogue, and ... Jn 18:20
or e he come near, are ready to ... Acts 23:15
the Creator, who is blessed for e ... Rom 1:25
is over all, God blessed for e ... Rom 9:5
to whom be glory for e ... Rom 11:36
glory through Jesus Christ for e ... Rom 16:27
his righteousness remaineth for e ... 2Cor 9:9
To whom be glory for e and e ... Gal 1:5
For no man e yet hated his own ... Eph 5:29
our Father be glory for e and e ... Phil 4:20
so shall we e be with the Lord ... 1Th 4:17
but e follow that which is good, ... 1Th 5:15
be honour and glory for e and e ... 1Ti 1:17
E learning, and never able to come ... 2Ti 3:7
to whom be glory for e and e ... 2Ti 4:18
thou shouldest receive him for e ... Philem 15
throne, O God, is for e and e ... Heb 1:8
Thou art a priest for e after the ... Heb 5:6
made an high priest for e after ... Heb 6:20
Thou art a priest for e after the ... Heb 7:17
Thou art a priest for e after the ... Heb 7:21
this man, because he continueth e ... Heb 7:24
seeing he e liveth to make ... Heb 7:25
one sacrifice for sins for e ... Heb 10:12
for e them that are sanctified ... Heb 10:14
yesterday, and to day, and for e ... Heb 13:8
to whom be glory for e and e ... Heb 13:21
which liveth and abideth for e ... 1Pet 1:23
word of the Lord endureth for e ... 1Pet 1:25
praise and dominion for e and e ... 1Pet 4:11
glory and dominion for e and e ... 1Pet 5:11
of darkness is reserved for e ... 2Pet 2:17
To him be glory both now and for e ... 2Pet 3:18
the will of God abideth for e ... 1Jn 2:17
in us, and shall be with us for e ... 2Jn 2
the blackness of darkness for e ... Jude 13
dominion and power, both now and e ... Jude 25
glory and dominion for e and e ... Rev 1:6
throne, who liveth for e and e ... Rev 4:9
him that liveth for e and e ... Rev 4:10
and unto the Lamb for e and e ... Rev 5:13
him that liveth for e and e ... Rev 5:14
be unto our God for e and e ... Rev 7:12
by him that liveth for e and e ... Rev 10:6
and he shall reign for e and e ... Rev 11:15
ascendeth up for e and e ... Rev 14:11
of God, who liveth for e and e ... Rev 15:7
her smoke rose up for e and e ... Rev 19:3
day and night for e and e ... Rev 20:10
and they shall reign for e and e ... Rev 22:5

**EVERLASTING**

the e covenant between God ... Gen 9:16
generations for an e covenant ... Gen 17:7
of Canaan, for an e possession ... Gen 17:8
in your flesh for an e covenant ... Gen 17:13
with him for an e covenant ... Gen 17:19
the name of the LORD, the e God ... Gen 21:33
after thee for an e possession ... Gen 48:4
the utmost bound of the e hills ... Gen 49:26
an e priesthood throughout their ... Ex 40:15
shall be an e statute unto you ... Lev 16:34
of Israel by an e covenant ... Lev 24:8
the covenant of an e priesthood ... Num 25:13
and underneath are the e arms ... Deut 33:27
hath made with me an e covenant ... 2Sa 23:5
and to Israel for an e covenant ... 1Chr 16:17
and be ye lifted up, ye e doors ... Ps 24:7
even lift them up, ye e doors ... Ps 24:9
Israel from e, and to e ... Ps 41:13
world, even from e to e ... Ps 90:2
thou art from e ... Ps 93:2
his mercy is e ... Ps 100:5
e to e upon them that ... Ps 103:17
and to Israel for an e covenant ... Ps 105:10
of Israel from e to e ... Ps 106:48
shall be in e remembrance ... Ps 112:6

is an *e* righteousness, and thy law...... Ps 119:142
of thy testimonies is *e*...... Ps 119:144
in me, and lead me in the way *e*...... Ps 139:24
Thy kingdom is an *e* kingdom...... Ps 145:13
I was set up from *e*, from the...... Prov 8:23
the righteous is an *e* foundation...... Prov 10:25
The *e* Father, The Prince of Peace...... Is 9:6
ordinance, broken the *e* covenant...... Is 24:5
in the LORD JEHOVAH is *e* strength...... Is 26:4
us shall dwell with *e* burnings...... Is 33:14
songs and *e* joy upon their heads...... Is 35:10
thou not heard, that the *e* God...... Is 40:28
in the LORD with an *e* salvation...... Is 45:17
*e* joy shall be upon their head...... Is 51:11
but with *e* kindness will I have...... Is 54:8
I will make an *e* covenant with...... Is 55:3
for an *e* sign that shall not be...... Is 55:13
I will give them an *e* name...... Is 56:5
shall be unto thee an *e* light...... Is 60:19
the LORD shall be thine *e* light...... Is 60:20
*e* joy shall be unto them...... Is 61:7
I will make an *e* covenant with...... Is 61:8
them, to make himself an *e* name...... Is 63:12
thy name is from *e*...... Is 63:16
is the living God, and an *e* king...... Jer 10:10
their *e* confusion shall never be...... Jer 20:11
I will bring an *e* reproach upon...... Jer 23:40
I have loved thee with an *e* love...... Jer 31:3
I will make an *e* covenant with...... Jer 32:40
establish unto thee an *e* covenant...... Eze 16:60
it shall be an *e* covenant with...... Eze 37:26
his kingdom is an *e* kingdom...... Dan 4:3
whose dominion is an *e* dominion...... Dan 4:34
his dominion is an *e* dominion...... Dan 7:14
whose kingdom is an *e* kingdom...... Dan 7:27
to bring in *e* righteousness, and...... Dan 9:24
earth shall awake, some to *e* life...... Dan 12:2
and some to shame and *e* contempt...... Dan 12:2
have been from of old, from *e*...... Mic 5:2
Art thou not from *e*, O LORD my...... Hab 1:12
the *e* mountains were scattered,...... Hab 3:6
his ways are *e*...... Hab 3:6
two feet to be cast into *e* fire...... Mt 18:8
and shall inherit *e* life...... Mt 19:29
from me, ye cursed, into *e* fire...... Mt 25:41
shall go away into *e* punishment...... Mt 25:46
receive you into *e* habitations...... Lk 16:9
and in the world to come life *e*...... Lk 18:30
not perish, but have *e* life...... Jn 3:16
believeth on the Son hath *e* life...... Jn 3:36
of water springing up into *e* life...... Jn 4:14
on him that sent me, hath *e* life...... Jn 5:24
meat which endureth unto *e* life...... Jn 6:27
believeth on him, may have *e* life...... Jn 6:40
that believeth on me hath *e* life...... Jn 6:47
that his commandment is life *e*...... Jn 12:50
yourselves unworthy of *e* life...... Acts 13:46
unto holiness, and the end *e* life...... Rom 6:22
to the commandment of the *e* God...... Rom 16:26
shall of the Spirit reap life *e*...... Gal 6:8
Who shall be punished with *e*...... 2Th 1:9
and hath given us *e* consolation...... 2Th 2:16
believe on him to life *e*...... 1Ti 1:16
to whom be honour and power *e*...... 1Ti 6:16
the blood of the *e* covenant...... Heb 13:20
into the *e* kingdom of our Lord...... 2Pet 1:11
he hath reserved in *e* chains...... Jude 6
having the *e* gospel to preach...... Rev 14:6

**EVERMORE**
be only oppressed and spoiled *e*...... Deut 28:29
unto David, and to his seed for *e*...... 2Sa 22:51
you, ye shall observe to do for *e*...... 2Kin 17:37
throne shall be established for *e*...... 1Chr 17:14
hand there are pleasures for *e*...... Ps 16:11
to David, and to his seed for *e*...... Ps 18:50
and dwell for *e*...... Ps 37:27
doth his promise fail for *e*...... Ps 77:8
and I will glorify thy name for *e*...... Ps 86:12
mercy will I keep for him for *e*...... Ps 89:28
Blessed be the LORD for *e*...... Ps 89:52
thou, LORD, art most high for *e*...... Ps 92:8
seek his face *e*...... Ps 105:4
unto all generations for *e*...... Ps 106:31
from this time forth and for *e*...... Ps 113:2
from this time forth and for *e*...... Ps 115:18
this time forth, and even for *e*...... Ps 121:8
also sit upon thy throne for *e*...... Ps 132:12
the blessing, even life for *e*...... Ps 133:3
in the midst of them for *e*...... Eze 37:26
be in the midst of them for *e*...... Eze 37:28
him, Lord, *e* give us this bread...... Jn 6:34
Christ, which is blessed for *e*...... 2Cor 11:31
Rejoice *e*...... 1Th 5:16
the Son, who is consecrated for *e*...... Heb 7:28
and, behold, I am alive for *e*...... Rev 1:18

**EVERY** See PREFACE.

**EVI** (*e'-vi*) *A Midian prince.*
namely, *E*, and Rekem, and Zur, and...... Num 31:8
with the princes of Midian, *E*...... Josh 13:21

**EVIDENCE**
And I subscribed the *e*, and sealed...... Jer 32:10
So I took the *e* of the purchase,...... Jer 32:11
I gave the *e* of the purchase unto...... Jer 32:12
this *e* of the purchase, both...... Jer 32:14
sealed, and this *e* which is open...... Jer 32:14
Now when I had delivered the *e* of...... Jer 32:16
for, the *e* of things not seen...... Heb 11:1

**EVIDENCES**
Take these *e*, this evidence of...... Jer 32:14
fields for money, and subscribe *e*...... Jer 32:44

**EVIDENT**
for it is *e* unto you if I lie...... Job 6:28
law in the sight of God, it is *e*...... Gal 3:11
to them an *e* token of perdition...... Phil 1:28
For it is *e* that our Lord sprang...... Heb 7:14
And it is yet far more *e*...... Heb 7:15

**EVIDENTLY**
He saw in a vision *e* about the...... Acts 10:3
Christ hath been *e* set forth...... Gal 3:1

**EVIL** See PREFACE.
be as gods, knowing good and *e*...... Gen 3:5
his heart was only *e* continually...... Gen 6:5
they brought up an *e* report of...... Num 13:32
LORD shall separate him unto *e*...... Deut 29:21
day life and good, and death and *e*...... Deut 30:15
*e* will befall you in the latter...... Deut 31:29
because ye will do *e* in the sight...... Deut 31:29
if it seem *e* unto you to serve...... Josh 24:15
an *e* spirit from God troubleth...... 1Sa 16:15
when the *e* spirit from God was...... 1Sa 16:23
the *e* spirit departed from him...... 1Sa 16:23
that the *e* spirit from God came...... 1Sa 18:10
the *e* spirit from the LORD was...... 1Sa 19:9
that feareth God, and escheweth *e*...... Job 1:8
shadow of death, I will fear no *e*...... Ps 23:4
Keep thy tongue from *e*, and thy...... Ps 34:13
There shall no *e* befall thee...... Ps 91:10
Ye that love the LORD, hate *e*...... Ps 97:10
For their feet run to *e*, and make...... Prov 1:16
and go not in the way of *e* men...... Prov 4:14
in every place, beholding the *e*...... Prov 15:3
while the *e* days come not, nor...... Eccl 12:1
that call *e* good, and good *e*...... Is 5:20
that he may know to refuse the *e*...... Is 7:15
and turn every man from his *e* way...... Jer 26:3
set my face against you for *e*...... Jer 44:11
An *e*, an only *e*, behold, is...... Eze 7:5
turn ye, turn ye from your *e* ways...... Eze 33:11
Seek good, and not *e*, that ye may...... Amos 5:14
Hate the *e*, and love the good, and...... Amos 5:15
that they turned from their *e* way...... Jonah 3:10
Who hate the good, and love the *e*...... Mic 3:2
maketh his sun to rise on the *e*...... Mt 5:45
temptation, but deliver us from *e*...... Mt 6:13
unto the day is the *e* thereof...... Mt 6:34
think ye *e* in your hearts...... Mt 9:4
said, Why, what *e* hath he done...... Mt 27:23
that can lightly speak *e* of me...... Mk 9:39
an *e* man out of the *e* treasure...... Lk 6:45
but deliver us from *e*...... Lk 11:4
light, because their deeds were *e*...... Jn 3:19
one that doeth *e* hateth the light...... Jn 3:20
the *e* spirit answered and said,...... Acts 19:15
but the *e* which I would not, that...... Rom 7:19
do good, *e* is present with me...... Rom 7:21
Abhor that which is *e*...... Rom 12:9
Recompense to no man *e* for *e*...... Rom 12:17
Be not overcome of *e*...... Rom 12:21
but overcome *e* with good...... Rom 12:21
not then your good be *e* spoken of...... Rom 14:16
easily provoked, thinketh no *e*...... 1Cor 13:5
the time, because the days are *e*...... Eph 5:16
See that none render *e* for *e*...... 1Th 5:15
Abstain from all appearance of *e*...... 1Th 5:22
of money is the root of all *e*...... 1Ti 6:10
To speak *e* of no man, to be no...... Titus 3:2
follow not that which is *e*...... 3Jn 11
he that doeth *e* hath not seen God...... 3Jn 11

**EVILDOER**
every one is an hypocrite and an *e*...... Is 9:17
or as a thief, or as an *e*...... 1Pet 4:15

**EVILDOERS**
have hated the congregation of *e*...... Ps 26:5
Fret not thyself because of *e*...... Ps 37:1
For *e* shall be cut off...... Ps 37:9
will rise up for me against the *e*...... Ps 94:16
Depart from me, ye *e*...... Ps 119:115
laden with iniquity, a seed of *e*...... Is 1:4
the seed of *e* shall never be...... Is 14:20
arise against the house of the *e*...... Is 31:2
of the poor from the hand of *e*...... Jer 20:13
strengthen also the hands of *e*...... Jer 23:14
they speak against you as *e*...... 1Pet 2:12
by him for the punishment of *e*...... 1Pet 2:14
they speak evil of you, as of *e*...... 1Pet 3:16

**EVILFAVOUREDNESS**
wherein is blemish, or any *e*...... Deut 17:1

**EVIL-MERODACH** (*e'-vil-mer'-o-dak*) *Son of Nebuchadnezzar.*
that *E* king of Babylon in the...... 2Kin 25:27
that *E* king of Babylon in the...... Jer 52:31

**EVILS**
they shall be devoured, and many *e*...... Deut 31:17
day, Are not these *e* come upon us...... Deut 31:17
*e* which they shall have wrought...... Deut 31:18
shall come to pass, when many *e*...... Deut 31:21
For innumerable *e* have compassed...... Ps 40:12
my people have committed two *e*...... Jer 2:13
*e* which they have committed in...... Eze 6:9
all your *e* that ye have committed...... Eze 20:43
for all the *e* which Herod had...... Lk 3:19

**EWE**
Abraham set seven *e* lambs of the...... Gen 21:28
What mean these seven *e* lambs...... Gen 21:29
For these seven *e* lambs shalt...... Gen 21:30
one *e* lamb of the first year...... Lev 14:10
And whether it be cow or *e*...... Lev 22:28
one *e* lamb of the first year...... Num 6:14
nothing, save one little *e* lamb...... 2Sa 12:3

**EWES**
thy *e* and thy she goats have not...... Gen 31:38
and twenty he goats, two hundred *e*...... Gen 32:14
From following the *e* great with...... Ps 78:71

**EXACT**
he shall not *e* it of his...... Deut 15:2
foreigner thou mayest *e* it again...... Deut 15:3
Ye *e* usury, every one of his...... Neh 5:7
might *e* of them money and corn...... Neh 5:10
and the oil, that ye *e* of them...... Neh 5:11
The enemy shall not *e* upon him...... Ps 89:22
pleasure, and *e* all your labours...... Is 58:3
*E* no more than that which is...... Lk 3:13

**EXACTED**
Menahem *e* the money of Israel,...... 2Kin 15:20
he *e* the silver and the gold of...... 2Kin 23:35

**EXACTETH**
God *e* of thee less than thine...... Job 11:6

**EXACTION**
year, and the *e* of every debt...... Neh 10:31

**EXACTIONS**
take away your *e* from my people...... Eze 45:9

**EXACTORS**
peace, and thine *e* righteousness...... Is 60:17

**EXALT**
my father's God, and I will *e* him...... Ex 15:2
*e* the horn of his anointed...... 1Sa 2:10
therefore shalt thou not *e* them...... Job 17:4
let us *e* his name together...... Ps 34:3
he shall *e* thee to inherit the...... Ps 37:34
not the rebellious *e* themselves...... Ps 66:7
But my horn shalt thou *e* like the...... Ps 92:10
*E* ye the LORD our God, and worship...... Ps 99:5
*E* the LORD our God, and worship at...... Ps 99:9
Let them *e* him also in the...... Ps 107:32
thou art my God, I will *e* thee...... Ps 118:28
lest they *e* themselves...... Ps 140:8
*E* her, and she shall promote thee...... Prov 4:8
*e* the voice unto them, shake the...... Is 13:2
I will *e* my throne above the...... Is 14:13
I will *e* thee, I will praise thy...... Is 25:1
*e* him that is low, and abase him...... Eze 21:26
neither shall it *e* itself any...... Eze 29:15
*e* themselves for their height...... Eze 31:14
*e* themselves to establish the...... Dan 11:14
and he shall *e* himself, and magnify...... Dan 11:36
High, none at all would *e* him...... Hos 11:7
Though thou *e* thyself as the...... Obad 4
whosoever shall *e* himself shall...... Mt 23:12
take of you, if a man *e* himself...... 2Cor 11:20
that he may *e* you in due time...... 1Pet 5:6

**EXALTED**
Agag, and his kingdom shall be *e*...... Num 24:7
LORD, mine horn is *e* in the LORD...... 1Sa 2:1
that he had *e* his kingdom for his...... 2Sa 5:12
*e* be the God of the rock of my...... 2Sa 22:47
the son of Haggith *e* himself...... 1Kin 1:5
Forasmuch as I *e* thee from among...... 1Kin 14:7
Forasmuch as I *e* thee out of the...... 1Kin 16:2
whom hast thou *e* thy voice...... 2Kin 19:22
thou art *e* as head above all...... 1Chr 29:11
which is *e* above all blessing and...... Neh 9:5
which mourn may be *e* to safety...... Job 5:11
They are *e* for a little while,...... Job 24:24
them for ever, and they are *e*...... Job 36:7
side, when the vilest men are *e*...... Ps 12:8
shall mine enemy be *e* over me...... Ps 13:2
let the God of my salvation be *e*...... Ps 18:46
Be thou *e*, LORD, in thine own...... Ps 21:13
I will be *e* among the heathen...... Ps 46:10
I will be *e* in the earth...... Ps 46:10
he is greatly *e*...... Ps 47:9
Be thou *e*, O God, above the...... Ps 57:5
Be thou *e*, O God, above the...... Ps 57:11
horns of the righteous shall be *e*...... Ps 75:10
thy righteousness shall they be *e*...... Ps 89:16
in thy favour our horn shall be *e*...... Ps 89:17
I have *e* one chosen out of the...... Ps 89:19
and in my name shall his horn be *e*...... Ps 89:24
thou art *e* far above all gods...... Ps 97:9
Be thou *e*, O God, above the...... Ps 108:5
his horn shall be *e* with honour...... Ps 112:9
The right hand of the LORD is *e*...... Ps 118:16
of the upright the city is *e*...... Prov 11:11
shall be *e* above the hills...... Is 2:2
LORD alone shall be *e* in that day...... Is 2:11
LORD alone shall be *e* in that day...... Is 2:17
of hosts shall be *e* in judgment...... Is 5:16
make mention that his name is *e*...... Is 12:4
you, and therefore will he be *e*...... Is 30:18
The LORD is *e*...... Is 33:5
now will I be *e*...... Is 33:10
whom hast thou *e* thy voice...... Is 37:23
Every valley shall be *e*, and every...... Is 40:4
a way, and my highways shall be *e*...... Is 49:11
deal prudently, he shall be *e*...... Is 52:13
have *e* the low tree, have dried...... Eze 17:24

her stature was *e* among the thick ...... Eze 19:11
Therefore his height was *e* above ........... Eze 31:5
trembling, he *e* himself in Israel ........... Hos 13:1
were filled, and their heart was *e* ........... Hos 13:6
it shall be *e* above the hills ........... Mic 4:1
which art *e* unto heaven, shalt be ........... Mt 11:23
shall humble himself shall be *e* ........... Mt 23:12
seats, and *e* them of low degree ........... Lk 1:52
Capernaum, which art *e* to heaven ........... Lk 10:15
that humbleth himself shall be *e* ........... Lk 14:11
that humbleth himself shall be *e* ........... Lk 18:14
being by the right hand of God *e* ........... Acts 2:33
Him hath God *e* with his right ........... Acts 5:31
*e* the people when they dwelt as ........... Acts 13:17
abasing myself that ye might be *e* ........... 2Cor 11:7
lest I should be *e* above measure ........... 2Cor 12:7
lest I should be *e* above measure ........... 2Cor 12:7
God also hath highly *e* him ........... Phil 2:9
degree rejoice in that he is *e* ........... Jas 1:9

**EXALTEST**
As yet *e* thou thyself against my ........... Ex 9:17

**EXALTETH**
Behold, God *e* by his power ........... Job 36:22
He also *e* the horn of his people, ........... Ps 148:14
that is hasty of spirit *e* folly ........... Prov 14:29
Righteousness *e* a nation ........... Prov 14:34
he that *e* his gate seeketh ........... Prov 17:19
For whosoever *e* himself shall be ........... Lk 14:11
for every one that *e* himself ........... Lk 18:14
every high thing that *e* itself ........... 2Cor 10:5
*e* himself above all that is ........... 2Th 2:4

**EXAMINATION**
O king Agrippa, that, after *e* had ........... Acts 25:26

**EXAMINE**
the tenth month to *e* the matter ........... Ezr 10:16
*E* me, O LORD, and prove me ........... Ps 26:2
to them that do *e* me is this ........... 1Cor 9:3
But let a man *e* himself, and so ........... 1Cor 11:28
*E* yourselves, whether ye be in ........... 2Cor 13:5

**EXAMINED**
having *e* him before you, have ........... Lk 23:14
If we this day be *e* of the good ........... Acts 4:9
he *e* the keepers, and commanded ........... Acts 12:19
that he should be *e* by scourging ........... Acts 22:24
from him which should have *e* him ........... Acts 22:29
Who, when they had *e* me, would ........... Acts 28:18

**EXAMINING**
by *e* of whom thyself mayest take ........... Acts 24:8

**EXAMPLE**
willing to make her a publick *e* ........... Mt 1:19
For I have given you an *e* ........... Jn 13:15
but be thou an *e* of the believers ........... 1Ti 4:12
fall after the same *e* of unbelief ........... Heb 4:11
Who serve unto the *e* and shadow of ........... Heb 8:5
for an *e* of suffering affliction, ........... Jas 5:10
suffered for us, leaving us an *e* ........... 1Pet 2:21
flesh, are set forth for an *e* ........... Jude 7

**EXAMPLES**
Now these things were our *e* ........... 1Cor 10:6

**EXCEED**
stripes he may give him, and not *e* ........... Deut 25:3
lest, if he should *e*, and beat him ........... Deut 25:3
shall *e* the righteousness of the ........... Mt 5:20
of righteousness *e* in glory ........... 2Cor 3:9

**EXCEEDED**
one with another, until David *e* ........... 1Sa 20:41
So king Solomon *e* all the kings ........... 1Kin 10:23
transgressions that they have *e* ........... Job 36:9

**EXCEEDEST**
for thou *e* the fame that I heard ........... 2Chr 9:6

**EXCEEDETH**
prosperity *e* the fame which I ........... 1Kin 10:7

**EXCEEDING**
thy shield, and thy *e* great reward ........... Gen 15:1
And I will make thee *e* fruitful ........... Gen 17:6
*e* bitter cry, and said unto his ........... Gen 27:34
and multiplied, and waxed *e* mighty ........... Ex 1:7
the voice of the trumpet *e* loud ........... Ex 19:16
to search it, is an *e* good land ........... Num 14:7
Talk no more so *e* proudly ........... 1Sa 2:3
king David took *e* much brass ........... 2Sa 8:8
The rich man had *e* many flocks ........... 2Sa 12:2
wisdom and understanding *e* much ........... 1Kin 4:29
because they were *e* many ........... 1Kin 7:47
he brought also *e* much spoil out ........... 1Chr 20:2
for the LORD must be *e* magnifical ........... 1Chr 22:5
and spears, and made them *e* strong. 2Chr 11:12
for there was *e* much spoil in ........... 2Chr 14:14
until his disease was *e* great ........... 2Chr 16:12
And Hezekiah had *e* much riches ........... 2Chr 32:27
thou hast made him *e* glad with ........... Ps 21:6
altar of God, unto God my *e* joy ........... Ps 43:4
but thy commandment is *e* broad ........... Ps 119:96
the earth, but they are *e* wise ........... Prov 30:24
*e* deep, who can find it out ........... Eccl 7:24
(he is *e* proud) his loftiness, and ........... Jer 48:29
of Israel and Judah is *e* great ........... Eze 9:9
and thou wast *e* beautiful, and thou ........... Eze 16:13
*e* in dyed attire upon their heads ........... Eze 23:15
upon their feet, an *e* great army ........... Eze 37:10
the fish of the great sea, *e* many ........... Eze 47:10
was urgent, and the furnace *e* hot ........... Dan 3:22
Then was the king *e* glad for him ........... Dan 6:23
*e* dreadful, whose teeth were of ........... Dan 7:19
little horn, which waxed *e* great ........... Dan 8:9
Now Nineveh was an *e* great city ........... Jonah 3:3
So Jonah was *e* glad of the gourd ........... Jonah 4:6
they rejoiced with *e* great joy ........... Mt 2:10
was *e* wroth, and sent forth, and ........... Mt 2:16
him up into an *e* high mountain ........... Mt 4:8
Rejoice, and be *e* glad ........... Mt 5:12
*e* fierce, so that no man might ........... Mt 8:28
And they were *e* sorry ........... Mt 17:23
And they were *e* sorrowful, and ........... Mt 26:22
unto them, My soul is *e* sorrowful ........... Mt 26:38
And the king was *e* sorry ........... Mk 6:26
became shining, *e* white as snow ........... Mk 9:3
My soul is *e* sorrowful unto death ........... Mk 14:34
Herod saw Jesus, he was *e* glad ........... Lk 23:8
was *e* fair, and nourished up in ........... Acts 7:20
commandment might become *e* sinful Rom 7:13
worketh for us a far more *e* ........... 2Cor 4:17
comfort, I am *e* joyful in all our ........... 2Cor 7:4
you for the *e* grace of God in you ........... 2Cor 9:14
what is the *e* greatness of his ........... Eph 1:19
the *e* riches of his grace in his ........... Eph 2:7
do *e* abundantly above all that we ........... Eph 3:20
Lord was *e* abundant with faith ........... 1Ti 1:14
ye may be glad also with *e* joy ........... 1Pet 4:13
Whereby are given unto us *e* great ........... 2Pet 1:4
presence of his glory with *e* joy ........... Jude 24
the plague thereof was *e* great ........... Rev 16:21

**EXCEEDINGLY**
waters prevailed *e* upon the earth ........... Gen 7:19
and sinners before the LORD *e* ........... Gen 13:13
her, I will multiply thy seed *e* ........... Gen 16:10
and thee, and will multiply thee *e* ........... Gen 17:2
fruitful, and will multiply him *e* ........... Gen 17:20
And Isaac trembled very *e*, and said... Gen 27:33
And the man increased *e*, and had ........... Gen 30:43
therein, and grew, and multiplied *e* ........... Gen 47:27
played the fool, and have erred *e* ........... 1Sa 26:21
Then Amnon hated her *e* ........... 2Sa 13:15
But they were *e* afraid, and said, ........... 2Kin 10:4
*e* in the sight of all Israel ........... 1Chr 29:25
was with him, and magnified him *e* ........... 2Chr 1:1
And Jehoshaphat waxed great *e* ........... 2Chr 17:12
for he strengthened himself *e* ........... 2Chr 26:8
it grieved them *e* that there was ........... Neh 2:10
Then was the queen *e* grieved ........... Est 4:4
Which rejoice *e*, and are glad, ........... Job 3:22
yea, let them *e* rejoice ........... Ps 68:3
But lusted *e* in the wilderness, ........... Ps 106:14
and I love them *e* ........... Ps 119:167
for we are *e* filled with contempt ........... Ps 123:3
Our soul is *e* filled with the ........... Ps 123:4
dissolved, the earth is moved *e* ........... Is 24:19
dreadful and terrible, and strong *e* ........... Dan 7:7
Then were the men *e* afraid ........... Jonah 1:10
Then the men feared the LORD *e* ........... Jonah 1:16
But it displeased Jonah *e* ........... Jonah 4:1
heard it, they were *e* amazed ........... Mt 19:25
And they feared *e*, and said one to ........... Mk 4:41
And they cried out the more *e* ........... Mk 15:14
Jews, do *e* trouble our city, ........... Acts 16:20
being *e* mad against them, I ........... Acts 26:11
we being *e* tossed with a tempest, ........... Acts 27:18
*e* the more joyed we for the joy ........... 2Cor 7:13
being more *e* zealous of the ........... Gal 1:14
day praying *e* that we might see ........... 1Th 3:10
because that your faith groweth *e* ........... 2Th 1:3
Moses said, I *e* fear and quake ........... Heb 12:21

**EXCEL**
as water, thou shalt not *e* ........... Gen 49:4
with harps on the Sheminith to *e* ........... 1Chr 15:21
that *e* in strength, that do his ........... Ps 103:20
images did *e* them of Jerusalem ........... Is 10:10
seek that ye may *e* to the ........... 1Cor 14:12

**EXCELLED**
Solomon's wisdom *e* the wisdom of ........... 1Kin 4:30

**EXCELLENCY**
*e* of dignity, and the *e* of power ........... Gen 49:3
in the greatness of thine *e* thou ........... Ex 15:7
thy help, and in his *e* on the sky ........... Deut 33:26
and who is the sword of thy *e* ........... Deut 33:29
Doth not their *e* which is in them ........... Job 4:21
Shall not his *e* make you afraid ........... Job 13:11
Though his *e* mount up to the ........... Job 20:6
with the voice of his *e* ........... Job 37:4
thyself now with majesty and *e* ........... Job 40:10
the *e* of Jacob whom he loved ........... Ps 47:4
to cast him down from his *e* ........... Ps 62:4
his *e* is over Israel, and his ........... Ps 68:34
but the *e* of knowledge is, that ........... Eccl 7:12
the beauty of the Chaldees' *e* ........... Is 13:19
the *e* of Carmel and Sharon, they ........... Is 35:2
of the LORD, and the *e* of our God ........... Is 35:2
I will make thee an eternal *e* ........... Is 60:15
the *e* of your strength, the ........... Eze 24:21
of hosts, I abhor the *e* of Jacob ........... Amos 6:8
LORD hath sworn by the *e* of Jacob ........... Amos 8:7
hath turned away the *e* of Jacob ........... Nah 2:2
of Jacob, as the *e* of Israel ........... Nah 2:2
came not with *e* of speech or of ........... 1Cor 2:1
that the *e* of the power may be of ........... 2Cor 4:7
the *e* of the knowledge of Christ ........... Phil 3:8

**EXCELLENT**
honour of his *e* majesty many days ........... Est 1:4
he is *e* in power, and in judgment, ........... Job 37:23
how *e* is thy name in all the ........... Ps 8:1
how *e* is thy name in all the ........... Ps 8:9
are in the earth, and to the *e* ........... Ps 16:3
How *e* is thy lovingkindness, O ........... Ps 36:7
*e* than the mountains of prey ........... Ps 76:4
it shall be an *e* oil, which shall ........... Ps 141:5
for his name alone is *e* ........... Ps 148:13
him according to his *e* greatness ........... Ps 150:2
for I will speak of *e* things ........... Prov 8:6
is more *e* than his neighbour ........... Prov 12:26
*E* speech becometh not a fool ........... Prov 17:7
understanding is of an *e* spirit ........... Prov 17:27
to thee *e* things in counsels ........... Prov 22:20
is as Lebanon, *e* as the cedars ........... Song 5:15
the fruit of the earth shall be *e* ........... Is 4:2
for he hath done *e* things ........... Is 12:5
in counsel, and *e* in working ........... Is 28:29
and thou art come to *e* ornaments ........... Eze 16:7
image, whose brightness was *e* ........... Dan 2:31
*e* majesty was added unto me ........... Dan 4:36
Forasmuch as an *e* spirit, and ........... Dan 5:12
*e* wisdom is found in thee ........... Dan 5:14
because an *e* spirit was in him ........... Dan 6:3
thee in order, most *e* Theophilus, ........... Lk 1:3
Claudius Lysias unto the most *e* ........... Acts 23:26
the things that are more *e* ........... Rom 2:18
yet shew I unto you a more *e* way.... 1Cor 12:31
ye may approve things that are *e* ........... Phil 1:10
obtained a more *e* name than they ........... Heb 1:4
he obtained a more *e* ministry ........... Heb 8:6
God a more *e* sacrifice than Cain ........... Heb 11:4
a voice to him from the *e* glory ........... 2Pet 1:17

**EXCELLEST**
virtuously, but thou *e* them all ........... Prov 31:29

**EXCELLETH**
Then I saw that wisdom *e* folly ........... Eccl 2:13
as far as light *e* darkness ........... Eccl 2:13
by reason of the glory that *e* ........... 2Cor 3:10

**EXCEPT**
*E* the God of my father, the God ........... Gen 31:42
not let thee go, *e* thou bless me ........... Gen 32:26
*e* your youngest brother come ........... Gen 42:15
*e* your brother be with you ........... Gen 43:3
*e* your brother be with you ........... Gen 43:5
For *e* we had lingered, surely now ........... Gen 43:10
*E* your youngest brother come down. Gen 44:23
*e* our youngest brother be with us ........... Gen 44:26
*e* the land of the priests only, ........... Gen 47:26
*e* thou make thyself altogether a ........... Num 16:13
*e* their Rock had sold them, and ........... Deut 32:30
*e* ye destroy the accursed from ........... Josh 7:12
*e* thou hadst hasted and come to ........... 1Sa 25:34
do God to Abner, and more also, *e* ........... 2Sa 3:9
*e* thou first bring Michal Saul's ........... 2Sa 3:13
*E* thou take away the blind and the ........... 2Sa 5:6
thy riding for me, *e* I bid thee ........... 2Kin 4:24
*e* the king delighted in her, and ........... Est 2:14
*e* such to whom the king shall ........... Est 4:11
*E* the LORD build the house, they ........... Ps 127:1
*e* the LORD keep the city, the ........... Ps 127:1
*e* they have done mischief ........... Prov 4:16
*E* the LORD of hosts had left unto ........... Is 1:9
*e* the gods, whose dwelling is not ........... Dan 2:11
worship any god, *e* their own God ........... Dan 3:28
Daniel, *e* we find it against him ........... Dan 6:5
walk together, *e* they be agreed ........... Amos 3:3
That *e* your righteousness shall ........... Mt 5:20
*e* he first bind the strong man ........... Mt 12:29
*E* ye be converted, and become as ........... Mt 18:3
*e* it be for fornication, and shall ........... Mt 19:9
*e* those days should be shortened, ........... Mt 24:22
*e* I drink it, thy will be done ........... Mt 26:42
*e* he will first bind the strong ........... Mk 3:27
*e* they wash their hands oft, eat ........... Mk 7:3
*e* they wash, they eat not ........... Mk 7:4
*e* that the Lord had shortened ........... Mk 13:20
*e* we should go and buy meat for ........... Lk 9:13
*e* ye repent, ye shall all ........... Lk 13:3
*e* ye repent, ye shall all ........... Lk 13:5
thou doest, *e* God be with him ........... Jn 3:2
*E* a man be born again, he cannot ........... Jn 3:3
*E* a man be born of water and of ........... Jn 3:5
*e* it be given him from heaven ........... Jn 3:27
*E* ye see signs and wonders, ye ........... Jn 4:48
*e* the Father which hath sent me ........... Jn 6:44
*E* ye eat the flesh of the Son of ........... Jn 6:53
*e* it were given unto him of my ........... Jn 6:65
*E* a corn of wheat fall into the ........... Jn 12:24
of itself, *e* it abide in the vine ........... Jn 15:4
no more can ye, *e* ye abide in me ........... Jn 15:4
*e* it were given thee from above ........... Jn 19:11
*E* I shall see in his hands the ........... Jn 20:25
Judaea and Samaria, *e* the apostles ........... Acts 8:1
*e* some man should guide me ........... Acts 8:31
*E* ye be circumcised after the ........... Acts 15:1
*E* it be for this one voice, that ........... Acts 24:21
such as I am, *e* these bonds ........... Acts 26:29
*E* these abide in the ship, ye ........... Acts 27:31
*e* the law had said, Thou shalt ........... Rom 7:7
*E* the Lord of Sabaoth had left us ........... Rom 9:29
shall they preach, *e* they be sent ........... Rom 10:15
*e* it be with consent for a time, ........... 1Cor 7:5
*e* he interpret, that the church ........... 1Cor 14:5
*e* I shall speak to you either by ........... 1Cor 14:6
*e* they give a distinction in the ........... 1Cor 14:7
*e* ye utter by the tongue words ........... 1Cor 14:9
sowest is not quickened, *e* it die ........... 1Cor 15:36
*e* it be that I myself was not ........... 2Cor 12:13
is in you, *e* ye be reprobates ........... 2Cor 13:5
*e* there come a falling away first ........... 2Th 2:3
not crowned, *e* he strive lawfully ........... 2Ti 2:5

out of his place, *e* thou repent Rev 2:5
*e* they repent of their deeds Rev 2:22

**EXCEPTED**
him, it is manifest that he is *e* 1Cor 15:27

**EXCESS**
they are full of extortion and *e* Mt 23:25
not drunk with wine, wherein is *e* Eph 5:18
lusts, *e* of wine, revellings, 1Pet 4:3
with them to the same *e* of riot 1Pet 4:4

**EXCHANGE**
gave them bread in *e* for horses Gen 47:17
the *e* thereof shall be holy Lev 27:10
the *e* of it shall not be for Job 28:17
shall not sell of it, neither *e* Eze 48:14
a man give in *e* for his soul Mt 16:26
a man give in *e* for his soul Mk 8:37

**EXCHANGERS**
to have put my money to the *e* Mt 25:27

**EXCLUDE**
yea, they would *e* you, that ye Gal 4:17

**EXCLUDED**
is boasting then? It is *e* Rom 3:27

**EXCUSE**
with one consent began to make *e* Lk 14:18
so that they are without *e* Rom 1:20
think ye that we *e* ourselves unto 2Cor 12:19

**EXCUSED**
I pray thee have me *e* Lk 14:18
I pray thee have me *e* Lk 14:19

**EXCUSING**
accusing or else *e* one another Rom 2:15

**EXECRATION**
and ye shall be an *e*, and an Jer 42:18
and they shall be an *e*, and an Jer 44:12

**EXECUTE**
gods of Egypt I will *e* judgment Ex 12:12
the priest shall *e* upon her all Num 5:30
that they may *e* the service of Num 8:11
He doth *e* the judgment of the Deut 10:18
*e* my judgments, and keep all my 1Kin 6:12
when wilt thou *e* judgment on them Ps 119:84
To *e* vengeance upon the heathen, Ps 149:7
To *e* upon them the judgment Ps 149:9
Take counsel, *e* judgment Is 16:3
if ye throughly *e* judgment Jer 7:5
*E* judgment in the morning, and Jer 21:12
*E* ye judgment and righteousness, Jer 22:3
shall *e* judgment and justice in Jer 23:5
and he shall *e* judgment and Jer 33:15
will *e* judgments in the midst of Eze 5:8
I will *e* judgments in thee, and Eze 5:10
when I shall *e* judgments in thee Eze 5:15
will *e* judgments among you Eze 11:9
*e* judgments upon thee in the Eze 16:41
I will *e* judgments upon Moab Eze 25:11
I will *e* great vengeance upon Eze 25:17
Zoan, and will *e* judgments in No Eze 30:14
Thus will I *e* judgments in Egypt Eze 30:19
*e* judgment and justice, take away Eze 45:9
I will not *e* the fierceness of Hos 11:9
I will *e* vengeance in anger and Mic 5:15
my cause, and *e* judgment for me Mic 7:9
*E* true judgment, and shew mercy and Zec 7:9
*e* the judgment of truth and peace Zec 8:16
him authority to *e* judgment also Jn 5:27
a revenger to *e* wrath upon him Rom 13:4
To *e* judgment upon all, and to Jude 15

**EXECUTED**
gods also the LORD *e* judgments Num 33:4
he *e* the justice of the LORD, and Deut 33:21
David *e* judgment and justice unto 2Sa 8:15
(he it is that *e* the priest's 1Chr 6:10
*e* judgment and justice among all 1Chr 18:14
Ithamar *e* the priest's office 1Chr 24:2
So they *e* judgment against Joash 2Chr 24:24
let judgment be *e* speedily upon Ezr 7:26
stood up Phinehas, and *e* judgment Ps 106:30
an evil work is not *e* speedily Eccl 8:11
shall not return, until he have *e* Jer 23:20
neither *e* my judgments, but have Eze 11:12
hath *e* true judgment between man Eze 18:8
hath *e* my judgments, hath walked Eze 18:17
they had not *e* my judgments Eze 20:24
for they had *e* judgment upon her Eze 23:10
I shall have *e* judgments in her Eze 28:22
when I have *e* judgments upon all Eze 28:26
see my judgment that I have *e* Eze 39:21
that while he *e* the priest's Lk 1:8

**EXECUTEDST**
nor *e* his fierce wrath upon 1Sa 28:18

**EXECUTEST**
thou *e* judgment and righteousness Ps 99:4

**EXECUTETH**
known by the judgment which he *e* Ps 9:16
The LORD *e* righteousness and Ps 103:6
Which *e* judgment for the Ps 146:7
the man that *e* my counsel from a Is 46:11
if there be any that *e* judgment Jer 5:1
for he is strong that *e* his word Joel 2:11

**EXECUTING**
in *e* that which is right in mine 2Kin 10:30
*e* the priest's office unto the 2Chr 11:14
when Jehu was *e* judgment upon the 2Chr 22:8

**EXECUTION**
decree drew near to be put in *e* Est 9:1

**EXECUTIONER**
And immediately the king sent an *e* Mk 6:27

**EXEMPTED**
throughout all Judah; none was *e* 1Kin 15:22

**EXERCISE**
neither do I *e* myself in great Ps 131:1
the LORD which *e* lovingkindness Jer 9:24
the Gentiles *e* dominion over them Mt 20:25
are great *e* authority upon them Mt 20:25
the Gentiles *e* lordship over them Mk 10:42
their great ones *e* authority upon Mk 10:42
the Gentiles *e* lordship over them Lk 22:25
they that *e* authority upon them Lk 22:25
And herein do I *e* myself, to have Acts 24:16
*e* thyself rather unto godliness 1Ti 4:7
For bodily *e* profiteth little 1Ti 4:8

**EXERCISED**
the sons of man to be *e* therewith Eccl 1:13
to the sons of men to be *e* in it Eccl 3:10
*e* robbery, and have vexed the poor Eze 22:29
senses *e* to discern both good Heb 5:14
unto them which are *e* thereby Heb 12:11
an heart they have *e* with 2Pet 2:14

**EXERCISETH**
he *e* all the power of the first Rev 13:12

**EXHORT**
other words did he testify and *e* Acts 2:40
now I *e* you to be of good cheer Acts 27:22
it necessary to *e* the brethren 2Cor 9:5
*e* you by the Lord Jesus, that as 1Th 4:1
Now we *e* you, brethren, warn them 1Th 5:14
*e* by our Lord Jesus Christ, that 2Th 3:12
I *e* therefore, that, first of all 1Ti 2:1
These things teach and *e* 1Ti 6:2
*e* with all longsuffering and 2Ti 4:2
able by sound doctrine both to *e* Titus 1:9
men likewise *e* to be sober minded Titus 2:6
*E* servants to be obedient unto Titus 2:9
These things speak, and *e*, and Titus 2:15
But *e* one another daily, while it Heb 3:13
elders which are among you I *e* 1Pet 5:1
*e* you that ye should earnestly Jude 3

**EXHORTATION**
many other things in his *e* Lk 3:18
have any word of *e* for the people Acts 13:15
parts, and had given them much *e* Acts 20:2
Or he that exhorteth, on *e* Rom 12:8
unto men to edification, and *e* 1Cor 14:3
For indeed he accepted the *e* 2Cor 8:17
For our *e* was not of deceit, nor 1Th 2:3
give attendance to reading, to *e* 1Ti 4:13
ye have forgotten the *e* which Heb 12:5
brethren, suffer the word of *e* Heb 13:22

**EXHORTED**
*e* them all, that with purpose of Acts 11:23
*e* the brethren with many words, Acts 15:32
As ye know how we *e* and comforted 1Th 2:11

**EXHORTETH**
Or he that *e*, on exhortation Rom 12:8

**EXHORTING**
*e* them to continue in the faith, Acts 14:22
*e* the disciples to receive him Acts 18:27
but *e* one another Heb 10:25
I have written briefly, *e* 1Pet 5:12

**EXILE**
thou art a stranger, and also an *e* 2Sa 15:19
The captive *e* hasteneth that he Is 51:14

**EXORCISTS**
certain of the vagabond Jews, *e* Acts 19:13

**EXPECTATION**
the *e* of the poor shall not Ps 9:18
for my *e* is from him Ps 62:5
but the *e* of the wicked shall Prov 10:28
man dieth, his *e* shall perish Prov 11:7
but the *e* of the wicked is wrath Prov 11:23
thine *e* shall not be cut off Prov 23:18
thy *e* shall not be cut off Prov 24:14
and ashamed of Ethiopia their *e* Is 20:5
that day, Behold, such is our *e* Is 20:6
for her *e* shall be ashamed Zec 9:5
And as the people were in *e* Lk 3:15
from all the *e* of the people of Acts 12:11
For the earnest *e* of the creature Rom 8:19
According to my earnest *e* Phil 1:20

**EXPECTED**
not of evil, to give you an *e* end Jer 29:11

**EXPECTING**
*e* to receive something of them Acts 3:5
From henceforth *e* till his Heb 10:13

**EXPEDIENT**
Nor consider that it is *e* for us Jn 11:50
It is *e* for you that I go away Jn 16:7
that it was *e* that one man should Jn 18:14
unto me, but all things are not *e* 1Cor 6:12
for me, but all things are not *e* 1Cor 10:23
for this is *e* for you, who have 2Cor 8:10
It is not *e* for me doubtless to 2Cor 12:1

**EXPEL**
he shall *e* them from before you, Josh 23:5
*e* me out of my father's house Judg 11:7

**EXPELLED**
of Israel *e* not the Geshurites Josh 13:13
he *e* thence the three sons of Judg 1:20
his banished be not *e* from him 2Sa 14:14
*e* them out of their coasts Acts 13:50

**EXPENCES**
let the *e* be given out of the Ezr 6:4
forthwith *e* be given unto these Ezr 6:8

**EXPERIENCE**
for I have learned by *e* that the Gen 30:27
my heart had great *e* of wisdom Eccl 1:16
And patience, *e* Rom 5:4
and *e*, hope Rom 5:4

**EXPERIMENT**
Whiles by the *e* of this 2Cor 9:13

**EXPERT**
*e* in war, with all instruments of 1Chr 12:33
And of the Danites *e* in war twenty 1Chr 12:35
battle, *e* in war, forty thousand 1Chr 12:36
all hold swords, being *e* in war Song 3:8
shall be as of a mighty *e* man Jer 50:9
know thee to be *e* in all customs Acts 26:3

**EXPIRED**
and the days were not *e* 1Sa 18:26
to pass, after the year was *e* 2Sa 11:1
when thy days be *e* that thou must 1Chr 17:11
pass, that after the year was *e* 1Chr 20:1
And when the year was *e*, king 2Chr 36:10
And when these days were *e* Est 1:5
And when these days are *e*, it Eze 43:27
And when forty years were *e* Acts 7:30
And when the thousand years are *e* Rev 20:7

**EXPLOITS**
and he shall do *e*, and return to Dan 11:28
God shall be strong, and do *e* Dan 11:32

**EXPOUND**
not in three days *e* the riddle Judg 14:14

**EXPOUNDED**
unto them which *e* the riddle Judg 14:19
he *e* all things to his disciples Mk 4:34
he *e* unto them in all the Lk 24:27
*e* it by order unto them, saying, Acts 11:4
*e* unto him the way of God more Acts 18:26
to whom he *e* and testified the Acts 28:23

**EXPRESS**
the *e* image of his person, and Heb 1:3

**EXPRESSED**
men which are *e* by their names Num 1:17
thousand, which were *e* by name 1Chr 12:31
were chosen, who were *e* by name 1Chr 16:41
men which were *e* by name rose up 2Chr 28:15
city, the men that were *e* by name 2Chr 31:19
all of them were *e* by name Ezr 8:20

**EXPRESSLY**
If I *e* say unto the lad, Behold, 1Sa 20:21
came *e* unto Ezekiel the priest Eze 1:3
Now the Spirit speaketh *e* 1Ti 4:1

**EXTEND**
there be none to *e* mercy unto him Ps 109:12
I will *e* peace to her like a Is 66:12

**EXTENDED**
hath *e* mercy unto me before the Ezr 7:28
but hath *e* mercy unto us in the Ezr 9:9

**EXTENDETH**
my goodness *e* not to thee Ps 16:2

**EXTINCT**
breath is corrupt, my days are *e* Job 17:1
they are *e*, they are quenched as Is 43:17

**EXTOL**
I will *e* thee, O LORD Ps 30:1
*e* him that rideth upon the Ps 68:4
I will *e* thee, my God, O king Ps 145:1
Now I Nebuchadnezzar praise and *e* Dan 4:37

**EXTOLLED**
mouth, and he was *e* with my tongue Ps 66:17
he shall be exalted and *e* Is 52:13

**EXTORTION**
gained of thy neighbours by *e* Eze 22:12
but within they are full of *e* Mt 23:25

**EXTORTIONER**
Let the *e* catch all that he hath Ps 109:11
for the *e* is at an end, the Is 16:4
a railer, or a drunkard, or an *e* 1Cor 5:11

**EXTORTIONERS**
that I am not as other men are, *e* Lk 18:11
world, or with the covetous, or *e* 1Cor 5:10
drunkards, nor revilers, nor *e* 1Cor 6:10

**EXTREME**
and with an *e* burning, and with ... Deut 28:22

**EXTREMITY**
yet he knoweth it not in great *e* ... Job 35:15

**EYE**
*E* for *e*, tooth for tooth, hand ... Ex 21:24
a man smite the *e* of his servant ... Ex 21:26
or the *e* of his maid, that it ... Ex 21:26
or that hath a blemish in his *e* ... Lev 21:20
*e* for *e*, tooth for tooth ... Lev 24:20
thine *e* shall have no pity upon ... Deut 7:16
neither shall thine *e* pity him ... Deut 13:8
thine *e* be evil against thy poor ... Deut 15:9
Thine *e* shall not pity him, but ... Deut 19:13
And thine *e* shall not pity ... Deut 19:21
*e* for *e*, tooth for tooth, hand ... Deut 19:21
thine *e* shall not pity her ... Deut 25:12
his *e* shall be evil toward his ... Deut 28:54
her *e* shall be evil toward the ... Deut 28:56
he kept him as the apple of his *e* ... Deut 32:10
his *e* was not dim, nor his ... Deut 34:7
but mine *e* spared thee ... 1Sa 24:10
to my cleanness in his *e* sight ... 2Sa 22:25
But the *e* of their God was upon ... Ezr 5:5
mine *e* shall no more see good ... Job 7:7
The *e* of him that hath seen me ... Job 7:8
up the ghost, and no *e* had seen me ... Job 10:18
mine *e* hath seen all this, mine ... Job 13:1
but mine *e* poureth out tears unto ... Job 16:20
doth not mine *e* continue in their ... Job 17:2
Mine *e* also is dim by reason of ... Job 17:7
The *e* also which saw him shall ... Job 20:9
The *e* also of the adulterer ... Job 24:15
saying, No *e* shall see me ... Job 24:15
the vulture's *e* hath not seen ... Job 28:7
his *e* seeth every precious thing ... Job 28:10
and when the *e* saw me, it gave ... Job 29:11
but now mine *e* seeth thee ... Job 42:5
Mine *e* is consumed because of ... Ps 6:7
Keep me as the apple of the *e* ... Ps 17:8
mine *e* is consumed with grief, ... Ps 31:9
I will guide thee with mine *e* ... Ps 32:8
the *e* of the LORD is upon them ... Ps 33:18
*e* that hate me without a cause ... Ps 35:19
Aha, aha, our *e* hath seen it ... Ps 35:21
mine *e* hath seen his desire upon ... Ps 54:7
Mine *e* mourneth by reason of ... Ps 88:9
Mine *e* also shall see my desire ... Ps 92:11
he that formed the *e*, shall he ... Ps 94:9
and my law as the apple of thine *e* ... Prov 7:2
winketh with the *e* causeth sorrow ... Prov 10:10
The hearing ear, and the seeing *e* ... Prov 20:12
a bountiful *e* shall be blessed ... Prov 22:9
bread of him that hath an evil *e* ... Prov 23:6
hasteth to be rich hath an evil *e* ... Prov 28:22
The *e* that mocketh at his father, ... Prov 30:17
the *e* is not satisfied with ... Eccl 1:8
neither is his *e* satisfied with ... Eccl 4:8
their *e* shall not spare children ... Is 13:18
for they shall see *e* to *e* ... Is 52:8
the ear, neither hath the *e* seen ... Is 64:4
mine *e* shall weep sore, and run ... Jer 13:17
mine *e*, mine *e* runneth down ... Lam 1:16
to the *e* in the tabernacle of the ... Lam 2:4
not the apple of thine *e* cease ... Lam 2:18
Mine *e* runneth down with rivers ... Lam 3:48
Mine *e* trickleth down, and ceaseth ... Lam 3:49
Mine *e* affecteth mine heart ... Lam 3:51
neither shall mine *e* spare ... Eze 5:11
mine *e* shall not spare thee, ... Eze 7:4
mine *e* shall not spare, neither ... Eze 7:9
mine *e* shall not spare, neither ... Eze 8:18
let not your *e* spare, neither ... Eze 9:5
mine *e* shall not spare, neither ... Eze 9:10
None *e* pitied thee, to do any of ... Eze 16:5
Nevertheless mine *e* spared them ... Eze 20:17
and let our *e* look upon Zion ... Mic 4:11
you toucheth the apple of his *e* ... Zec 2:8
upon his arm, and upon his right *e* ... Zec 11:17
his right *e* shall be utterly ... Zec 11:17
And if thy right *e* offend thee ... Mt 5:29
hath been said, An *e* for an *e* ... Mt 5:38
The light of the body is the *e* ... Mt 6:22
if therefore thine *e* be single ... Mt 6:22
But if thine *e* be evil, thy whole ... Mt 6:23
mote that is in thy brother's *e* ... Mt 7:3
the beam that is in thine own *e* ... Mt 7:3
pull out the mote out of thine *e* ... Mt 7:4
behold, a beam is in thine own *e* ... Mt 7:4
out the beam out of thine own *e* ... Mt 7:5
the mote out of thy brother's *e* ... Mt 7:5
if thine *e* offend thee, pluck it ... Mt 18:9
to enter into life with one *e* ... Mt 18:9
to go through the *e* of a needle ... Mt 19:24
Is thine *e* evil, because I am ... Mt 20:15
deceit, lasciviousness, an evil *e* ... Mk 7:22
if thine *e* offend thee, pluck it ... Mk 9:47
the kingdom of God with one *e* ... Mk 9:47
to go through the *e* of a needle ... Mk 10:25
mote that is in thy brother's *e* ... Lk 6:41
the beam that is in thine own *e* ... Lk 6:41
out the mote that is in thine *e* ... Lk 6:42
the beam that is in thine own *e* ... Lk 6:42
first the beam out of thine own *e* ... Lk 6:42
mote that is in thy brother's *e* ... Lk 6:42
The light of the body is the *e* ... Lk 11:34
therefore when thine *e* is single ... Lk 11:34
but when thine *e* is evil, thy ... Lk 11:34
camel to go through a needle's *e* ... Lk 18:25
*E* hath not seen, nor ear heard, ... 1Cor 2:9
shall say, Because I am not the *e* ... 1Cor 12:16
If the whole body were an *e* ... 1Cor 12:17
the *e* cannot say unto the hand, I ... 1Cor 12:21
moment, in the twinkling of an *e* ... 1Cor 15:52
every *e* shall see him, and they ... Rev 1:7

**EYEBROWS**
his head and his beard and his *e* ... Lev 14:9

**EYED**
Leah was tender *e* ... Gen 29:17
Saul *e* David from that day and ... 1Sa 18:9

**EYELIDS**
on my *e* is the shadow of death ... Job 16:16
are like the *e* of the morning ... Job 41:18
his eyes behold, his *e* try ... Ps 11:4
mine eyes, or slumber to mine *e* ... Ps 132:4
let thine *e* look straight before ... Prov 4:25
eyes, nor slumber to thine *e* ... Prov 6:4
let her take thee with her *e* ... Prov 6:25
and their *e* are lifted up ... Prov 30:13
our *e* gush out with waters ... Jer 9:18

**EYE'S**
let him go free for his *e* sake ... Ex 21:26

**EYES**
then your *e* shall be opened, and ... Gen 3:5
and that it was pleasant to the *e* ... Gen 3:6
the *e* of them both were opened, ... Gen 3:7
found grace in the *e* of the LORD ... Gen 6:8
And Lot lifted up his *e*, and beheld ... Gen 13:10
from him, Lift up now thine *e* ... Gen 13:14
mistress was despised in her *e* ... Gen 16:4
I was despised in her *e* ... Gen 16:5
And he lift up his *e* and looked, and ... Gen 18:2
ye to them as is good in your *e* ... Gen 19:8
he is to thee a covering of the *e* ... Gen 20:16
And God opened her *e* ... Gen 21:19
third day Abraham lifted up his *e* ... Gen 22:4
And Abraham lifted up his *e* ... Gen 22:13
and he lifted up his *e*, and saw, and ... Gen 24:63
And Rebekah lifted up her *e* ... Gen 24:64
his *e* were dim, so that he could ... Gen 27:1
if I have found favour in thine *e* ... Gen 30:27
*e* of the cattle in the gutters ... Gen 30:41
that I lifted up mine *e*, and saw ... Gen 31:10
And he said, Lift up now thine *e* ... Gen 31:12
and my sleep departed from mine *e* ... Gen 31:40
And Jacob lifted up his *e*, and ... Gen 33:1
And he lifted up his *e*, and saw the ... Gen 33:5
Let me find grace in your *e* ... Gen 34:11
and they lifted up their *e* ... Gen 37:25
wife cast her *e* upon Joseph ... Gen 39:7
was good in the *e* of Pharaoh ... Gen 41:37
in the *e* of all his servants ... Gen 41:37
and bound him before their *e* ... Gen 42:24
And he lifted up his *e*, and saw his ... Gen 43:29
that I may set mine *e* upon him ... Gen 44:21
And, behold, your *e* see, and the ... Gen 45:12
the *e* of my brother Benjamin, ... Gen 45:12
shall put his hand upon thine *e* ... Gen 46:4
shall we die before thine *e* ... Gen 47:19
Now the *e* of Israel were dim for ... Gen 48:10
His *e* shall be red with wine, and ... Gen 49:12
now I have found grace in your *e* ... Gen 50:4
be abhorred in the *e* of Pharaoh ... Ex 5:21
in the *e* of his servants, to put ... Ex 5:21
of the Egyptians before their *e* ... Ex 8:26
and for a memorial between thine *e* ... Ex 13:9
and for frontlets between thine *e* ... Ex 13:16
of Israel lifted up their *e* ... Ex 14:10
the *e* of the children of Israel ... Ex 24:17
be hid from the *e* of the assembly ... Lev 4:13
ways hide their *e* from the man ... Lev 20:4
ague, that shall consume the *e* ... Lev 26:16
be hid from the *e* of her husband ... Num 5:13
thou mayest be to us instead of *e* ... Num 10:31
beside this manna, before our *e* ... Num 11:6
your own heart and your own *e* ... Num 15:39
thou put out the *e* of these men ... Num 16:14
ye unto the rock before their *e* ... Num 20:8
to sanctify me in the *e* of the ... Num 20:12
the LORD opened the *e* of Balaam ... Num 22:31
And Balaam lifted up his *e* ... Num 24:2
the man whose *e* are open hath ... Num 24:3
a trance, but having his *e* open ... Num 24:4
the man whose *e* are open hath ... Num 24:15
a trance, but having his *e* open ... Num 24:16
me at the water before their *e* ... Num 27:14
of them shall be pricks in your *e* ... Num 33:55
for you in Egypt before your *e* ... Deut 1:30
Thine *e* have seen all that the ... Deut 3:21
and lift up thine *e* westward ... Deut 3:27
and behold it with thine *e* ... Deut 3:27
Your *e* have seen what the LORD ... Deut 4:3
things which thine *e* have seen ... Deut 4:9
thou lift up thine *e* unto heaven ... Deut 4:19
for you in Egypt before your *e* ... Deut 4:34
be as frontlets between thine *e* ... Deut 6:8
all his household, before our *e* ... Deut 6:22
temptations which thine *e* saw ... Deut 7:19
and brake them before your *e* ... Deut 9:17
things, which thine *e* have seen ... Deut 10:21
But your *e* have seen all the ... Deut 11:7
the *e* of the LORD thy God are ... Deut 11:12
be as frontlets between your *e* ... Deut 11:18
whatsoever is right in his own *e* ... Deut 12:8
in the *e* of the LORD thy God ... Deut 13:18
between your *e* for the dead ... Deut 14:1
gift doth blind the *e* of the wise ... Deut 16:19
blood, neither have our *e* seen it ... Deut 21:7
that she find no favour in his *e* ... Deut 24:1
ox shall be slain before thine *e* ... Deut 28:31
thine *e* shall look, and fail with ... Deut 28:32
of thine *e* which thou shalt see ... Deut 28:34
trembling heart, and failing of *e* ... Deut 28:65
of thine *e* which thou shalt see ... Deut 28:67
your *e* in the land of Egypt unto ... Deut 29:2
which thine *e* have seen, the ... Deut 29:3
*e* to see, and ears to hear, unto ... Deut 29:4
thee to see it with thine *e* ... Deut 34:4
Jericho, that he lifted up his *e* ... Josh 5:13
your sides, and thorns in your *e* ... Josh 23:13
your *e* have seen what I have done ... Josh 24:7
took him, and put out his *e* ... Judg 16:21
of the Philistines for my two *e* ... Judg 16:28
that which was right in his own *e* ... Judg 17:6
And when he had lifted up his *e* ... Judg 19:17
that which was right in his own *e* ... Judg 21:25
Let thine *e* be on the field that ... Ruth 2:9
Why have I found grace in thine *e* ... Ruth 2:10
shall be to consume thine *e* ... 1Sa 2:33
his *e* began to wax dim, that he ... 1Sa 3:2
his *e* were dim, that he could not ... 1Sa 4:15
and they lifted up their *e* ... 1Sa 6:13
I may thrust out all your right *e* ... 1Sa 11:2
bribe to blind mine *e* therewith ... 1Sa 12:3
the LORD will do before your *e* ... 1Sa 12:16
and his *e* were enlightened ... 1Sa 14:27
how mine *e* have been enlightened, ... 1Sa 14:29
I have found grace in thine *e* ... 1Sa 20:3
if I have found favour in thine *e* ... 1Sa 20:29
this day thine *e* have seen how ... 1Sa 24:10
young men find favour in thine *e* ... 1Sa 25:8
was precious in thine *e* this day ... 1Sa 26:21
much set by this day in mine *e* ... 1Sa 26:24
much set by in the *e* of the LORD ... 1Sa 26:24
I have now found grace in thine *e* ... 1Sa 27:5
to day in the *e* of the handmaids ... 2Sa 6:20
take thy wives before thine *e* ... 2Sa 12:11
kept the watch lifted up his *e* ... 2Sa 13:34
find favour in the *e* of the LORD ... 2Sa 15:25
unto the wall, and lifted up his *e* ... 2Sa 18:24
therefore what is good in thine *e* ... 2Sa 19:27
but thine *e* are upon the haughty, ... 2Sa 22:28
that the *e* of my lord the king ... 2Sa 24:3
the *e* of all Israel are upon thee ... 1Kin 1:20
this day, mine *e* even seeing it ... 1Kin 1:48
That thine *e* may be open toward ... 1Kin 8:29
That thine *e* may be open unto the ... 1Kin 8:52
and mine *e* and mine heart shall be ... 1Kin 9:3
I came, and mine *e* had seen it ... 1Kin 10:7
do that which is right in mine *e* ... 1Kin 11:33
for his *e* were set by reason of ... 1Kin 14:4
only which was right in mine *e* ... 1Kin 14:8
was right in the *e* of the LORD ... 1Kin 15:5
was right in the *e* of the LORD ... 1Kin 15:11
wrought evil in the *e* of the LORD ... 1Kin 16:25
whatsoever is pleasant in thine *e* ... 1Kin 20:6
was right in the *e* of the LORD ... 1Kin 22:43
his *e* upon his *e*, and his hands ... 2Kin 4:34
times, and the child opened his *e* ... 2Kin 4:35
LORD, I pray thee, open his *e* ... 2Kin 6:17
opened the *e* of the young man ... 2Kin 6:17
open the *e* of these men, that ... 2Kin 6:20
And the LORD opened their *e* ... 2Kin 6:20
thou shalt see it with thine *e* ... 2Kin 7:2
thou shalt see it with thine *e* ... 2Kin 7:19
that which is good in thine *e* ... 2Kin 10:5
that which is right in mine *e* ... 2Kin 10:30
open, LORD, thine *e*, and see ... 2Kin 19:16
and lifted up thine *e* on high ... 2Kin 19:22
thine *e* shall not see all the ... 2Kin 22:20
the sons of Zedekiah before his *e* ... 2Kin 25:7
and put out the *e* of Zedekiah ... 2Kin 25:7
right in the *e* of all the people ... 1Chr 13:4
this was a small thing in thine *e* ... 1Chr 17:17
And David lifted up his *e*, and saw ... 1Chr 21:16
do that which is good in his *e* ... 1Chr 21:23
That thine *e* may be open upon ... 2Chr 6:20
thine *e* be open, and let thine ... 2Chr 6:40
Now mine *e* shall be open, and mine ... 2Chr 7:15
and mine *e* and mine heart shall be ... 2Chr 7:16
I came, and mine *e* had seen it ... 2Chr 9:6
right in the *e* of the LORD his ... 2Chr 14:2
For the *e* of the LORD run to and ... 2Chr 16:9
but our *e* are upon thee ... 2Chr 20:12
was evil in the *e* of the LORD ... 2Chr 21:6
evil in the *e* of the LORD our God ... 2Chr 29:6
to hissing, as ye see with your *e* ... 2Chr 29:8
neither shall thine *e* see all the ... 2Chr 34:28
house was laid before their *e* ... Ezr 3:12
that our God may lighten our *e* ... Ezr 9:8
now be attentive, and thine *e* open ... Neh 1:6
much cast down in their own *e* ... Neh 6:16
despise their husbands in their *e* ... Est 1:17
king, and I be pleasing in his *e* ... Est 8:5
they lifted up their *e* afar off ... Job 2:12
womb, nor hid sorrow from mine *e* ... Job 3:10
an image was before mine *e* ... Job 4:16
thine *e* are upon me, and I am not ... Job 7:8
Hast thou *e* of flesh ... Job 10:4
is pure, and I am clean in thine *e* ... Job 11:4
But the *e* of the wicked shall ... Job 11:20
open thine *e* upon such an one ... Job 14:3
and what do thy *e* wink at, ... Job 15:12
enemy sharpeneth his *e* upon me ... Job 16:9
even the *e* of his children shall ... Job 17:5
mine *e* shall behold, and not ... Job 19:27
and their offspring before their *e* ... Job 21:8

His *e* shall see his destruction, ... Job 21:20
yet his *e* are upon their ways ... Job 24:23
he openeth his *e*, and he is not ... Job 27:19
is hid from the *e* of all living ... Job 28:21
I was *e* to the blind, and feet was ... Job 29:15
I made a covenant with mine *e* ... Job 31:1
and mine heart walked after mine *e* ... Job 31:7
or have caused the *e* of the widow ... Job 31:16
he was righteous in his own *e* ... Job 32:1
For his *e* are upon the ways of ... Job 34:21
not his *e* from the righteous ... Job 36:7
prey, and her *e* behold afar off ... Job 39:29
He taketh it with his *e* ... Job 40:24
his *e* are like the eyelids of the ... Job 41:18
his *e* are privily set against the ... Ps 10:8
his *e* behold, his eyelids try, ... Ps 11:4
lighten mine *e*, lest I sleep the ... Ps 13:3
In whose *e* a vile person is ... Ps 15:4
let thine *e* behold the things ... Ps 17:2
they have set their *e* bowing down ... Ps 17:11
LORD is pure, enlightening the *e* ... Ps 19:8
Mine *e* are ever toward the LORD ... Ps 25:15
lovingkindness is before mine *e* ... Ps 26:3
I am cut off from before thine *e* ... Ps 31:22
The *e* of the LORD are upon the ... Ps 34:15
is no fear of God before his *e* ... Ps 36:1
flattereth himself in his own *e* ... Ps 36:2
as for the light of mine *e* ... Ps 38:10
set them in order before thine *e* ... Ps 50:21
his *e* behold the nations ... Ps 66:7
mine *e* fail while I wait for my ... Ps 69:3
Let their *e* be darkened, that ... Ps 69:23
Their *e* stand out with fatness ... Ps 73:7
Thou holdest mine *e* waking ... Ps 77:4
Only with thine *e* shalt thou ... Ps 91:8
set no wicked thing before mine *e* ... Ps 101:3
Mine *e* shall be upon the faithful ... Ps 101:6
*e* have they, but they see not ... Ps 115:5
mine *e* from tears, and my feet ... Ps 116:8
it is marvellous in our *e* ... Ps 118:23
Open thou mine *e*, that I may ... Ps 119:18
Turn away mine *e* from beholding ... Ps 119:37
Mine *e* fail for thy word, saying, ... Ps 119:82
Mine *e* fail for thy salvation, and ... Ps 119:123
Rivers of waters run down mine *e* ... Ps 119:136
Mine *e* prevent the night watches, ... Ps 119:148
lift up mine *e* unto the hills ... Ps 121:1
Unto thee lift I up mine *e* ... Ps 123:1
as the *e* of servants look unto ... Ps 123:2
as the *e* of a maiden unto the ... Ps 123:2
so our *e* wait upon the LORD our ... Ps 123:2
is not haughty, nor mine *e* lofty ... Ps 131:1
I will not give sleep to mine *e* ... Ps 132:4
*e* have they, but they see not ... Ps 135:16
Thine *e* did see my substance, yet ... Ps 139:16
But mine *e* are unto thee, O GOD ... Ps 141:8
The *e* of all wait upon thee ... Ps 145:15
LORD openeth the *e* of the blind ... Ps 146:8
Be not wise in thine own *e* ... Prov 3:7
let not them depart from thine *e* ... Prov 3:21
Let them not depart from thine *e* ... Prov 4:21
Let thine *e* look right on, and let ... Prov 4:25
man are before the *e* of the LORD ... Prov 5:21
Give not sleep to thine *e* ... Prov 6:4
He winketh with his *e*, he ... Prov 6:13
the teeth, and as smoke to the *e* ... Prov 10:26
of a fool is right in his own *e* ... Prov 12:15
The *e* of the LORD are in every ... Prov 15:3
The light of the *e* rejoiceth the ... Prov 15:30
of a man are clean in his own *e* ... Prov 16:2
He shutteth his *e* to devise ... Prov 16:30
in the *e* of him that hath it ... Prov 17:8
but the *e* of a fool are in the ... Prov 17:24
away all evil with his *e* ... Prov 20:8
open thine *e*, and thou shalt be ... Prov 20:13
of a man is right in his own *e* ... Prov 21:2
findeth no favour in his *e* ... Prov 21:10
The *e* of the LORD preserve ... Prov 22:12
Wilt thou set thine *e* upon that ... Prov 23:5
let thine *e* observe my ways ... Prov 23:26
who hath redness of *e* ... Prov 23:29
Thine *e* shall behold strange ... Prov 23:33
the prince whom thine *e* have seen ... Prov 25:7
so the *e* of man are never ... Prov 27:20
but he that hideth his *e* shall ... Prov 28:27
the LORD lighteneth both their *e* ... Prov 29:13
that are pure in their own *e* ... Prov 30:12
O how lofty are their *e* ... Prov 30:13
whatsoever mine *e* desired I kept ... Eccl 2:10
The wise man's *e* are in his head ... Eccl 2:14
beholding of them with their *e* ... Eccl 5:11
the *e* than the wandering of the ... Eccl 6:9
nor night seeth sleep with his *e* ... Eccl 8:16
it is for the *e* to behold the sun ... Eccl 11:7
heart, and in the sight of thine *e* ... Eccl 11:9
thou hast doves' *e* ... Song 1:15
hast doves' *e* within thy locks ... Song 4:1
my heart with one of thine *e* ... Song 4:9
His *e* are as the *e* of doves by ... Song 5:12
Turn away thine *e* from me ... Song 6:5
thine *e* like the fishpools in ... Song 7:4
then was I in his *e* as one that ... Song 8:10
I will hide mine *e* from you ... Is 1:15
of your doings from before mine *e* ... Is 1:16
to provoke the *e* of his glory ... Is 3:8
stretched forth necks and wanton *e* ... Is 3:16
the *e* of the lofty shall be ... Is 5:15
them that are wise in their own *e* ... Is 5:21
for mine *e* have seen the King, ... Is 6:5
their ears heavy, and shut their *e* ... Is 6:10
lest they see with their *e* ... Is 6:10
judge after the sight of his *e* ... Is 11:3
dashed to pieces before their *e* ... Is 13:16
his *e* shall have respect to the ... Is 17:7
deep sleep, and hath closed your *e* ... Is 29:10
the *e* of the blind shall see out ... Is 29:18
but thine *e* shall see thy ... Is 30:20
the *e* of them that see shall not ... Is 32:3
shutteth his *e* from seeing evil ... Is 33:15
Thine *e* shall see the king in his ... Is 33:17
thine *e* shall see Jerusalem a ... Is 33:20
Then the *e* of the blind shall be ... Is 35:5
open thine *e*, O LORD, and see ... Is 37:17
and lifted up thine *e* on high ... Is 37:23
mine *e* fail with looking upward ... Is 38:14
Lift up your *e* on high, and behold ... Is 40:26
To open the blind *e*, to bring out ... Is 42:7
the blind people that have *e* ... Is 43:8
for he hath shut their *e*, that ... Is 44:18
be glorious in the *e* of the LORD ... Is 49:5
Lift up thine *e* round about ... Is 49:18
Lift up your *e* to the heavens, and ... Is 51:6
arm in the *e* of all the nations ... Is 52:10
and we grope as if we had no *e* ... Is 59:10
Lift up thine *e* round about ... Is 60:4
but did evil before mine *e* ... Is 65:12
because they are hid from mine *e* ... Is 65:16
but they did evil before mine *e* ... Is 66:4
Lift up thine *e* unto the high ... Jer 3:2
are not thine *e* upon the truth ... Jer 5:3
which have *e*, and see not ... Jer 5:21
become a den of robbers in your *e* ... Jer 7:11
mine *e* a fountain of tears, that ... Jer 9:1
that our *e* may run down with ... Jer 9:18
Lift up your *e*, and behold them ... Jer 13:20
their *e* did fail, because there ... Jer 14:6
Let mine *e* run down with tears ... Jer 14:17
cease out of this place in your *e* ... Jer 16:9
For mine *e* are upon all their ... Jer 16:17
is their iniquity hid from mine *e* ... Jer 16:17
and thine *e* shall behold it ... Jer 20:4
But thine *e* and thine heart are ... Jer 22:17
set mine *e* upon them for good ... Jer 24:6
he shall slay them before your *e* ... Jer 29:21
weeping, and thine *e* from tears ... Jer 31:16
his *e* shall behold his *e* ... Jer 32:4
for thine *e* are open upon all the ... Jer 32:19
thine *e* shall behold the *e* of ... Jer 34:3
the *e* of the king of Babylon ... Jer 34:3
Zedekiah in Riblah before his *e* ... Jer 39:6
Moreover he put out Zedekiah's *e* ... Jer 39:7
of many, as thine *e* do behold us ... Jer 42:2
was evil in the *e* of the LORD ... Jer 52:2
the sons of Zedekiah before his *e* ... Jer 52:10
Then he put out the *e* of Zedekiah ... Jer 52:11
Mine *e* do fail with tears, my ... Lam 2:11
our *e* as yet failed for our vain ... Lam 4:17
for these things our *e* are dim ... Lam 5:17
full of *e* round about them four ... Eze 1:18
departed from me, and with their *e* ... Eze 6:9
lift up thine *e* now the way ... Eze 8:5
So I lifted up mine *e* the way ... Eze 8:5
were full of *e* round about ... Eze 10:12
house, which have *e* to see ... Eze 12:2
he see not the ground with his *e* ... Eze 12:12
neither hath lifted up his *e* to ... Eze 18:6
hath lifted up his *e* to the idols ... Eze 18:12
neither hath lifted up his *e* to ... Eze 18:15
man the abominations of his *e* ... Eze 20:7
away the abominations of their *e* ... Eze 20:8
their *e* were after their fathers' ... Eze 20:24
bitterness sigh before their *e* ... Eze 21:6
have hid their *e* from my sabbaths ... Eze 22:26
soon as she saw them with her *e* ... Eze 23:16
not lift up thine *e* unto them ... Eze 23:27
wash thyself, paintedst thy *e* ... Eze 23:40
desire of thine *e* with a stroke ... Eze 24:16
strength, the desire of your *e* ... Eze 24:21
glory, the desire of their *e* ... Eze 24:25
lift up your *e* toward your idols, ... Eze 33:25
sanctified in you before their *e* ... Eze 36:23
be in thine hand before their *e* ... Eze 37:20
in thee, O Gog, before their *e* ... Eze 38:16
be known in the *e* of many nations ... Eze 38:23
Son of man, behold with thine *e* ... Eze 40:4
mark well, and behold with thine *e* ... Eze 44:5
lifted up mine *e* unto heaven ... Dan 4:34
in this horn were *e* like the *e* ... Dan 7:8
horn were *e* like the *e* of man ... Dan 7:8
even of that horn that had *e* ... Dan 7:20
Then I lifted up mine *e*, and saw, ... Dan 8:3
had a notable horn between his *e* ... Dan 8:5
between his *e* is the first king ... Dan 8:21
open thine *e*, and behold our ... Dan 9:18
Then I lifted up mine *e*, and ... Dan 10:5
his *e* as lamps of fire, and his ... Dan 10:6
shall be hid from mine *e* ... Hos 13:14
not the meat cut off before our *e* ... Joel 1:16
I will set mine *e* upon them for ... Amos 9:4
the *e* of the Lord GOD are upon ... Amos 9:8
mine *e* shall behold her ... Mic 7:10
Thou art of purer *e* than to ... Hab 1:13
back your captivity before your *e* ... Zeph 3:20
is it not in your *e* in comparison ... Hag 2:3
Then lifted I up mine *e*, and saw, ... Zec 1:18
I lifted up mine *e* again, and ... Zec 2:1
upon one stone shall be seven *e* ... Zec 3:9
they are the *e* of the LORD ... Zec 4:10
I turned, and lifted up mine *e* ... Zec 5:1
said unto me, Lift up now thine *e* ... Zec 5:5
Then lifted I up mine *e*, and ... Zec 5:9
And I turned, and lifted up mine *e* ... Zec 6:1
If it be marvellous in the *e* of ... Zec 8:6
it also be marvellous in mine *e* ... Zec 8:6
when the *e* of man, as of all the ... Zec 9:1
for now have I seen with mine *e* ... Zec 9:8
I will open mine *e* upon the house ... Zec 12:4
their *e* shall consume away in ... Zec 14:12
your *e* shall see, and ye shall say ... Mal 1:5
Then touched he their *e*, saying, ... Mt 9:29
And their *e* were opened ... Mt 9:30
and their *e* they have closed ... Mt 13:15
time they should see with their *e* ... Mt 13:15
But blessed are your *e*, for they ... Mt 13:16
when they had lifted up their *e* ... Mt 17:8
rather than having two *e* to be ... Mt 18:9
Lord, that our *e* may be opened ... Mt 20:33
on them, and touched their *e* ... Mt 20:34
their *e* received sight, and they ... Mt 20:34
and it is marvellous in our *e* ... Mt 21:42
for their *e* were heavy ... Mt 26:43
Having *e*, see ye not ... Mk 8:18
and when he had spit on his *e* ... Mk 8:23
he put his hands again upon his *e* ... Mk 8:25
than having two *e* to be cast into ... Mk 9:47
and it is marvellous in our *e* ... Mk 12:11
again, (for their *e* were heavy ... Mk 14:40
For mine *e* have seen thy ... Lk 2:30
the *e* of all them that were in ... Lk 4:20
lifted up his *e* on his disciples ... Lk 6:20
Blessed are the *e* which see the ... Lk 10:23
And in hell he lift up his *e* ... Lk 16:23
up so much as his *e* unto heaven ... Lk 18:13
but now they are hid from thine *e* ... Lk 19:42
But their *e* were holden that they ... Lk 24:16
their *e* were opened, and they knew ... Lk 24:31
I say unto you, Lift up your *e* ... Jn 4:35
When Jesus then lifted up his *e* ... Jn 6:5
he anointed the *e* of the blind ... Jn 9:6
unto him, How were thine *e* opened ... Jn 9:10
made clay, and anointed mine *e* ... Jn 9:11
made the clay, and opened his *e* ... Jn 9:14
them, He put clay upon mine *e* ... Jn 9:15
him, that he hath opened thine *e* ... Jn 9:17
or who hath opened his *e*, we know ... Jn 9:21
how opened he thine *e* ... Jn 9:26
is, and yet he hath opened mine *e* ... Jn 9:30
the *e* of one that was born blind ... Jn 9:32
a devil open the *e* of the blind ... Jn 10:21
which opened the *e* of the blind ... Jn 11:37
And Jesus lifted up his *e*, and said ... Jn 11:41
He hath blinded their *e*, and ... Jn 12:40
they should not see with their *e* ... Jn 12:40
and lifted up his *e* to heaven ... Jn 17:1
fastening his *e* upon him with ... Acts 3:4
when his *e* were opened, he saw no ... Acts 9:8
from his *e* as it had been scales ... Acts 9:18
And she opened her *e* ... Acts 9:40
which when I had fastened mine *e* ... Acts 11:6
the Holy Ghost, set his *e* on him ... Acts 13:9
To open their *e*, and to turn them ... Acts 26:18
and their *e* have they closed ... Acts 28:27
lest they should see with their *e* ... Acts 28:27
is no fear of God before their *e* ... Rom 3:18
*e* that they should not see, and ... Rom 11:8
Let their *e* be darkened, that ... Rom 11:10
before whose *e* Jesus Christ hath ... Gal 3:1
would have plucked out your own *e* ... Gal 4:15
The *e* of your understanding being ... Eph 1:18
opened unto the *e* of him with ... Heb 4:13
For the *e* of the Lord are over ... 1Pet 3:12
Having *e* full of adultery, and ... 2Pet 2:14
which we have seen with our *e* ... 1Jn 1:1
that darkness hath blinded his *e* ... 1Jn 2:11
the flesh, and the lust of the *e* ... 1Jn 2:16
his *e* were as a flame of fire ... Rev 1:14
who hath his *e* like unto a flame ... Rev 2:18
anoint thine *e* with eyesalve, ... Rev 3:18
were four beasts full of *e* before ... Rev 4:6
and they were full of *e* within ... Rev 4:8
having seven horns and seven *e* ... Rev 5:6
wipe away all tears from their *e* ... Rev 7:17
His *e* were as a flame of fire, and ... Rev 19:12
wipe away all tears from their *e* ... Rev 21:4

**EYESALVE**
and anoint thine eyes with *e* ... Rev 3:18

**EYESERVICE**
Not with *e*, as menpleasers ... Eph 6:6
not with *e*, as menpleasers ... Col 3:22

**EYESIGHT**
cleanness of my hands in his *e* ... Ps 18:24

**EYEWITNESSES**
which from the beginning were *e* ... Lk 1:2
but were *e* of his majesty ... 2Pet 1:16

**EZAR** (*e'-zar*) See EZER. *A son of Seir.*
Zibeon, and Anah, and Dishon, and *E* ... 1Chr 1:38

**EZBAI** (*ez'-bahee*) *Father of Naarai.*
Carmelite, Naarai the son of *E* ... 1Chr 11:37

**EZBON** (*ez'-bon*)
*1. Son of Gad.*
Ziphion, and Haggi, Shuni, and *E* ... Gen 46:16
*2. Son of Bela.*
*E*, and Uzzi, and Uzziel, and ... 1Chr 7:7

**EZEKIAS** (*ez-e-ki'-as*) See HEZEKIAH. *Greek form of Hezekiah.*
and Achaz begat *E* ... Mt 1:9

And *E* begat Manasses Mt 1:10

**EZEKIEL**
came expressly unto *E* the priest Eze 1:3
Thus *E* is unto you a sign Eze 24:24

**EZEL**
and shalt remain by the stone *E* 1Sa 20:19

**EZEM**
And at Bilhah, and at *E*, and at 1Chr 4:29

**EZER**
*1. Son of Seir the Horite.*
And Dishon, and *E*, and Dishan Gen 36:21
The children of *E* are these Gen 36:27
Duke Dishon, duke *E*, duke Dishan Gen 36:30
The sons of *E*; Bilhan 1Chr 1:42
*2. A descendant of Judah.*
Gedor, and *E* the father of Hushah 1Chr 4:4
*3. A son of Ephraim.*
son, and Shuthelah his son, and *E* 1Chr 7:21
*4. A Gadite who fought for David.*
*E* the first, Obadiah the second, 1Chr 12:9
*5. A Levite who repaired the Jerusalem wall.*
him repaired *E* the son of Jeshua Neh 3:19
*6. A priest in the time of Nehemiah.*
and Malchijah, and Elam, and *E* Neh 12:42

**EZION-GABER**
from Ebronah, and encamped at *E* Num 33:35
And they removed from *E*, and Num 33:36
the plain from Elath, and from *E* Deut 2:8
and they made the ships in *E* 2Chr 20:36

**EZION-GEBER** (*e'-ze-on-ghe'-bur*) See EZION-GABER. *An Israelite seaport.*
Solomon made a navy of ships in *E* 1Kin 9:26
for the ships were broken at *E* 1Kin 22:48
Then went Solomon to *E*, and to 2Chr 8:17

**EZNITE** (*ez'-nite*) *Descendant of Adino.*
the same was Adino the *E* 2Sa 23:8

**EZRA** (*ez'-rah*) See AZARIAH, EZRAHITE.
*1. A descendant of Judah.*
And the sons of *E* were, Jether, and 1Chr 4:17
*2. Priest who led exiles back to Jerusalem.*
*E* the son of Seraiah, the son of Ezr 7:1
This *E* went up from Babylon Ezr 7:6
For *E* had prepared his heart to Ezr 7:10
Artaxerxes gave unto *E* the priest Ezr 7:11
unto *E* the priest, a scribe of Ezr 7:12
that whatsoever *E* the priest Ezr 7:21
And thou, *E*, after the wisdom of Ezr 7:25
Now when *E* had prayed, and when he Ezr 10:1
of Elam, answered and said unto *E* Ezr 10:2
Then arose *E*, and made the chief Ezr 10:5
Then *E* rose up from before the Ezr 10:6
*E* the priest stood up, and said Ezr 10:10
*E* the priest, with certain chief Ezr 10:16
they spake unto *E* the scribe to Neh 8:1
*E* the priest brought the law Neh 8:2
*E* the scribe stood upon a pulpit Neh 8:4
*E* opened the book in the sight of Neh 8:5
*E* blessed the LORD, the great God Neh 8:6
*E* the priest the scribe, and the Neh 8:9
unto *E* the scribe, even to Neh 8:13
Of *E*, Meshullam Neh 12:13
of *E* the priest, the scribe Neh 12:26
And Azariah, *E*, and Meshullam, Neh 12:33
God, and *E* the scribe before them Neh 12:36
*3. A priest who returned from exile.*
Seraiah, Jeremiah, *E*, Neh 12:1

**EZRAH**

**EZRAHITE** (*ez'-rah-hite*)
than Ethan the *E*, and Heman, and 1Kin 4:31
Leannoth, Maschil of Heman the *E* Ps 88:*t*
Maschil of Ethan the *E* Ps 89:*t*

**EZRI** (*ez'-ri*) *A superindendent of David.*
ground was *E* the son of Chelub 1Chr 27:26

# F

**FABLES**
Neither give heed to *f* and endless 1Ti 1:4
refuse profane and old wives' *f* 1Ti 4:7
truth, and shall be turned unto *f* 2Ti 4:4
Not giving heed to Jewish *f* Titus 1:14
not followed cunningly devised *f* 2Pet 1:16

**FACE**
was upon the *f* of the deep Gen 1:2
moved upon the *f* of the waters Gen 1:2
is upon the *f* of all the earth Gen 1:29
watered the whole *f* of the ground Gen 2:6
In the sweat of thy *f* shalt thou Gen 3:19
this day from the *f* of the earth Gen 4:14
from thy *f* shall I be hid Gen 4:14
to multiply on the *f* of the earth Gen 6:1
created from the *f* of the earth Gen 6:7
alive upon the *f* of all the earth Gen 7:3
from off the *f* of the earth Gen 7:4
ark went upon the *f* of the waters Gen 7:18
was upon the *f* of the ground Gen 7:23
from off the *f* of the ground Gen 8:8
were on the *f* of the whole earth Gen 8:9
the *f* of the ground was dry Gen 8:13
upon the *f* of the whole earth Gen 11:4
upon the *f* of all the earth Gen 11:8
upon the *f* of all the earth Gen 11:9
with her, she fled from her *f* Gen 16:6
I flee from the *f* of my mistress Gen 16:8
And Abram fell on his *f* Gen 17:3
Then Abraham fell upon his *f* Gen 17:17
with his *f* toward the ground Gen 19:1
great before the *f* of the LORD Gen 19:13
and I put the earring upon her *f* Gen 24:47
come for my hire before thy *f* Gen 30:33
set his *f* toward the mount Gilead Gen 31:21
me, and afterward I will see his *f* Gen 32:20
for I have seen God *f* to *f* Gen 32:30
for therefore I have seen thy *f* Gen 33:10
as though I had seen the *f* of God Gen 33:10
from the *f* of Esau thy brother Gen 35:1
he fled from the *f* of his brother Gen 35:7
from the *f* of his brother Jacob Gen 36:6
because she had covered her *f* Gen 38:15
was over all the *f* of the earth Gen 41:56
us, saying, Ye shall not see my *f* Gen 43:3
unto us, Ye shall not see my *f* Gen 43:5
And he washed his *f*, and went out, Gen 43:31
you, ye shall see my *f* no more Gen 44:23
for we may not see the man's *f* Gen 44:26
to direct his *f* unto Goshen Gen 46:28
me die, since I have seen thy *f* Gen 46:30
I had not thought to see thy *f* Gen 48:11
himself with his *f* to the earth Gen 48:12
Joseph fell upon his father's *f* Gen 50:1
went and fell down before his *f* Gen 50:18
Moses fled from the *f* of Pharaoh Ex 2:15
And Moses hid his *f* Ex 3:6
shall cover the *f* of the earth Ex 10:5
covered the *f* of the whole earth Ex 10:15
heed to thyself, see my *f* no more Ex 10:28
thou seest my *f* thou shalt die Ex 10:28
I will see thy *f* again no more Ex 10:29
cloud went from before their *f* Ex 14:19
Let us flee from the *f* of Israel Ex 14:25
upon the *f* of the wilderness Ex 16:14
them from the *f* of the earth Ex 32:12
LORD spake unto Moses *f* to *f* Ex 33:11
that are upon the *f* of the earth Ex 33:16
he said, Thou canst not see my *f* Ex 33:20
but my *f* shall not be seen Ex 33:23
wist not that the skin of his *f* Ex 34:29
behold, the skin of his *f* shone Ex 34:30
with them, he put a vail on his *f* Ex 34:33
of Israel saw the *f* of Moses Ex 34:35
that the skin of Moses' *f* shone Ex 34:35
put the vail upon his *f* again Ex 34:35
the part of his head toward his *f* Lev 13:41
I will even set my *f* against that Lev 17:10
honour the *f* of the old man, and Lev 19:32
I will set my *f* against that man, Lev 20:3
I will set my *f* against that man Lev 20:5
even set my *f* against that soul Lev 20:6
And I will set my *f* against you Lev 26:17
LORD make his *f* shine upon thee Num 6:25
high upon the *f* of the earth Num 11:31
were upon the *f* of the earth Num 12:3
her father had but spit in her *f* Num 12:14
that thou LORD art seen *f* to *f* Num 14:14
heard it, he fell upon his *f* Num 16:4
one shall slay her before his *f* Num 19:3
they cover the *f* of the earth Num 22:5
which covereth the *f* of the earth Num 22:11
his head, and fell flat on his *f* Num 22:31
but he set his *f* toward the Num 24:1
not be afraid of the *f* of man Deut 1:17
LORD talked with you *f* to *f* in Deut 5:4
thee from off the *f* of the earth Deut 6:15
that are upon the *f* of the earth Deut 7:6
them that hate him to their *f* Deut 7:10
him, he will repay him to his *f* Deut 7:10
the LORD destroyeth before your *f* Deut 8:20
bring them down before thy *f* Deut 9:3
and to be beaten before his *f* Deut 25:2
off his foot, and spit in his *f* Deut 25:9
thee to be smitten before thy *f* Deut 28:7
taken away from before thy *f* Deut 28:31
shall give them up before your *f* Deut 31:5
and I will hide my *f* from them Deut 31:17
I will surely hide my *f* in that Deut 31:18
said, I will hide my *f* from them Deut 32:20
whom the LORD knew *f* to *f* Deut 34:10
Joshua fell on his *f* to the earth Josh 5:14
his *f* before the ark of the LORD Josh 7:6
liest thou thus upon thy *f* Josh 7:10
an angel of the LORD *f* to *f* Judg 6:22
Then she fell on her *f*, and bowed Ruth 2:10
Dagon was fallen upon his *f* to 1Sa 5:3
Dagon was fallen upon his *f* to 1Sa 5:4
he fell upon his *f* to the earth 1Sa 17:49
every one from the *f* of the earth 1Sa 20:15
fell on his *f* to the ground, and 1Sa 20:41
stooped with his *f* to the earth 1Sa 24:8
and fell before David on her *f* 1Sa 25:23
herself on her *f* to the earth 1Sa 25:41
earth before the *f* of the LORD 1Sa 26:20
stooped with his *f* to the ground 1Sa 28:14
hold up my *f* to Joab thy brother 2Sa 2:22
that is, Thou shalt not see my *f* 2Sa 3:13
when thou comest to see my *f* 2Sa 3:13
come unto David, he fell on his *f* 2Sa 9:6
she fell on her *f* to the ground 2Sa 14:4
Joab fell to the ground on his *f* 2Sa 14:22
house, and let him not see my *f* 2Sa 14:24
house, and saw not the king's *f* 2Sa 14:24
and saw not the king's *f* 2Sa 14:28
therefore let me see the king's *f* 2Sa 14:32
bowed himself on his *f* to the 2Sa 14:33
over the *f* of all the country 2Sa 18:8
earth upon his *f* before the king 2Sa 18:28
But the king covered his *f* 2Sa 19:4
the king on his *f* upon the ground 2Sa 24:20
the king with his *f* to the ground 1Kin 1:23
bowed with her *f* to the earth 1Kin 1:31
And the king turned his *f* about 1Kin 8:14
Intreat now the *f* of the LORD thy 1Kin 13:6
it from off the *f* of the earth 1Kin 13:34
and he knew him, and fell on his *f* 1Kin 18:7
put his *f* between his knees, 1Kin 18:42
he wrapped his *f* in his mantle 1Kin 19:13
himself with ashes upon his *f* 1Kin 20:38
and took the ashes away from his *f* 1Kin 20:41
his bed, and turned away his *f* 1Kin 21:4
my staff upon the *f* of the child 2Kin 4:29
the staff upon the *f* of the child 2Kin 4:31
in water, and spread it on his *f* 2Kin 8:15
and she painted her *f*, and tired 2Kin 9:30
he lifted up his *f* to the window 2Kin 9:32
shall be as dung upon the *f* of 2Kin 9:37
Hazael set his *f* to go up to 2Kin 12:17
down unto him, and wept over his *f*. 2Kin 13:14
let us look one another in the *f* 2Kin 14:8
another in the *f* at Beth-shemesh 2Kin 14:11
then wilt thou turn away the *f* of 2Kin 18:24
Then he turned his *f* to the wall 2Kin 20:2
strength, seek his *f* continually 1Chr 16:11
to David with his *f* to the ground 1Chr 21:21
And the king turned his *f*, and 2Chr 6:3
not away the *f* of thine anointed 2Chr 6:42
themselves, and pray, and seek my *f* 2Chr 7:14
his head with his *f* to the ground 2Chr 20:18
let us see one another in the *f* 2Chr 25:17
and they saw one another in the *f* 2Chr 25:21
will not turn away his *f* from you 2Chr 30:9
with shame of *f* to his own land 2Chr 32:21
would not turn his *f* from him 2Chr 35:22
and blush to lift up my *f* to thee Ezr 9:6
to a spoil, and to confusion of *f* Ezr 9:7
and Media, which saw the king's *f* Est 1:14
mouth, they covered Haman's *f* Est 7:8
and he will curse thee to thy *f* Job 1:11
and he will curse thee to thy *f* Job 2:5
Then a spirit passed before my *f* Job 4:15
thou lift up thy *f* without spot Job 11:15
Wherefore hidest thou thy *f* Job 13:24
covereth his *f* with his fatness Job 15:27
up in me beareth witness to my *f* Job 16:8
My *f* is foul with weeping, and on Job 16:16
shall declare his way to his *f* Job 21:31
and shalt lift up thy *f* unto God Job 22:26
he covered the darkness from my *f* Job 23:17
and disguiseth his *f* Job 24:15
holdeth back the *f* of his throne Job 26:9
me, and spare not to spit in my *f* Job 30:10
and he shall see his *f* with joy Job 33:26
and when he hideth his *f*, who then Job 34:29
the *f* of the world in the earth Job 37:12
the *f* of the deep is frozen Job 38:30
can discover the *f* of his garment Job 41:13
Who can open the doors of his *f* Job 41:14
make thy way straight before my *f* Ps 5:8
he hideth his *f* Ps 10:11
long wilt thou hide thy *f* from me Ps 13:1
behold thy *f* in righteousness Ps 17:15
thy strings against the *f* of them Ps 21:12
hath he hid his *f* from him Ps 22:24
that seek him, that seek thy *f* Ps 24:6
When thou saidst, Seek ye my *f* Ps 27:8
my heart said unto thee, Thy *f* Ps 27:8
Hide not thy *f* far from me Ps 27:9
thou didst hide thy *f*, and I was Ps 30:7
Make thy *f* to shine upon thy Ps 31:16
The *f* of the LORD is against them Ps 34:16
settest me before thy *f* for ever Ps 41:12
the shame of my *f* hath covered me Ps 44:15
Wherefore hidest thou thy *f* Ps 44:24
Hide thy *f* from my sins, and blot Ps 51:9
cause his *f* to shine upon us Ps 67:1
shame hath covered my *f* Ps 69:7
hide not thy *f* from thy servant Ps 69:17
O God, and cause thy *f* to shine Ps 80:3
of hosts, and cause thy *f* to shine Ps 80:7
of hosts, cause thy *f* to shine Ps 80:19
look upon the *f* of thine anointed Ps 84:9
why hidest thou thy *f* from me Ps 88:14
and truth shall go before thy *f* Ps 89:14
beat down his foes before his *f* Ps 89:23
Hide not thy *f* from me in the day Ps 102:2
and oil to make his *f* to shine Ps 104:15
Thou hidest thy *f*, they are Ps 104:29
thou renewest the *f* of the earth Ps 104:30
seek his *f* evermore Ps 105:4
Make thy *f* to shine upon thy Ps 119:135
not away the *f* of thine anointed Ps 132:10
hide not thy *f* from me, lest I be Ps 143:7
with an impudent *f* said unto him Prov 7:13
thee, diligently to seek thy *f* Prov 7:15
a compass upon the *f* of the depth Prov 8:27
A wicked man hardeneth his *f* Prov 21:29
nettles had covered the *f* thereof Prov 24:31
As in water *f* answereth to *f*, Prov 27:19
wisdom maketh his *f* to shine Eccl 8:1
of his *f* shall be changed Eccl 8:1
with twain he covered his *f* Is 6:2

that hideth his *f* from the house Is 8:17
nor fill the *f* of the world with Is 14:21
to them from the *f* of the spoiler Is 16:4
the world upon the *f* of the earth Is 23:17
destroy in this mountain the *f* of Is 25:7
fill the *f* of the world with Is 27:6
he hath made plain the *f* thereof Is 28:25
neither shall his *f* now wax pale Is 29:22
then wilt thou turn away the *f* of Is 36:9
turned his *f* toward the wall Is 38:2
with their *f* toward the earth Is 49:23
I hid not my *f* from shame Is 50:6
have I set my *f* like a flint Is 50:7
I hid my *f* from thee for a moment Is 54:8
your sins have hid his *f* from you Is 59:2
for thou hast hid thy *f* from us Is 64:7
me to anger continually to my *f* Is 65:3
the *f* thereof is toward the north Jer 1:13
back unto me, and not their *f* Jer 2:27
thou rentest thy *f* with painting Jer 4:30
for dung upon the *f* of the earth Jer 8:2
I discover thy skirts upon thy *f* Jer 13:26
as dung upon the *f* of the earth Jer 16:4
they are not hid from my *f* Jer 16:17
shew them the back, and not the *f* Jer 18:17
For I have set my *f* against this Jer 21:10
hand of them whose *f* thou fearest Jer 22:25
which are upon the *f* of the earth Jer 25:26
thee from off the *f* of the earth Jer 28:16
should remove it from before my *f* Jer 32:31
unto me the back, and not the *f* Jer 32:33
I have hid my *f* from this city Jer 33:5
I will set my *f* against you for Jer 44:11
water before the *f* of the Lord Lam 2:19
man before the *f* of the most High Lam 3:35
they four had the *f* of a man Eze 1:10
the *f* of a lion, on the right Eze 1:10
they four had the *f* of an ox on Eze 1:10
four also had the *f* of an eagle Eze 1:10
when I saw it, I fell upon my *f* Eze 1:28
I have made thy *f* strong against Eze 3:8
and I fell on my *f* Eze 3:23
set thy *f* against it, and it shall Eze 4:3
Therefore thou shalt set thy *f* Eze 4:7
set thy *f* toward the mountains of Eze 6:2
My *f* will I turn also from them Eze 7:22
I was left, that I fell upon my *f* Eze 9:8
first *f* was the *f* of a cherub Eze 10:14
second *f* was the *f* of a man Eze 10:14
and the third the *f* of a lion Eze 10:14
and the fourth the *f* of an eagle Eze 10:14
Then fell I down upon my *f* Eze 11:13
thou shalt cover thy *f*, that thou Eze 12:6
he shall cover his *f*, that he see Eze 12:12
set thy *f* against the daughters Eze 13:17
of their iniquity before their *f* Eze 14:3
of his iniquity before his *f* Eze 14:4
of his iniquity before his *f* Eze 14:7
I will set my *f* against that man, Eze 14:8
And I will set my *f* against them Eze 15:7
when I set my *f* against them Eze 15:7
will I plead with you *f* to *f* Eze 20:35
will I plead with you *f* to *f* Eze 20:35
set thy *f* toward the south, and Eze 20:46
set thy *f* toward Jerusalem, and Eze 21:2
left, whithersoever thy *f* is set Eze 21:16
set thy *f* against the Ammonites, Eze 25:2
set thy *f* against Zidon, and Eze 28:21
set thy *f* against Pharaoh king of Eze 29:2
upon all the *f* of the earth Eze 34:6
set thy *f* against mount Seir, and Eze 35:2
set thy *f* against Gog, the land Eze 38:2
my fury shall come up in my *f* Eze 38:18
that are upon the *f* of the earth Eze 38:20
remain upon the *f* of the earth Eze 39:14
therefore hid I my *f* from them Eze 39:23
unto them, and hid my *f* from them Eze 39:24
I hide my *f* any more from them Eze 39:29
from the *f* of the gate of the Eze 40:15
gate of the entrance unto the *f* Eze 40:15
the breadth of the *f* of the house Eze 41:14
So that the *f* of a man was toward Eze 41:19
the *f* of a young lion toward the Eze 41:19
and the *f* of the sanctuary Eze 41:21
upon the *f* of the porch without Eze 41:25
and I fell upon my *f* Eze 43:3
and I fell upon my *f* Eze 44:4
Nebuchadnezzar fell upon his *f* Dan 2:46
west on the *f* of the whole earth Dan 8:5
I was afraid, and fell upon my *f* Dan 8:17
sleep on my *f* toward the ground Dan 8:18
I set my *f* unto the Lord God, to Dan 9:3
to us belongeth confusion of *f* Dan 9:8
cause thy *f* to shine upon thy Dan 9:17
his *f* as the appearance of Dan 10:6
was I in a deep sleep on my *f* Dan 10:9
and my *f* toward the ground Dan 10:9
I set my *f* toward the ground, and Dan 10:15
He shall also set his *f* to enter Dan 11:17
he turn his *f* unto the isles Dan 11:18
Then he shall turn his *f* toward Dan 11:19
of Israel doth testify to his *f* Hos 5:5
their offence, and seek my *f* Hos 5:15
they are before my *f* Hos 7:2
of Israel testifieth to his *f* Hos 7:10
Before their *f* the people shall Joel 2:6
with his *f* toward the east sea, Joel 2:20
them out upon the *f* of the earth Amos 5:8
them out upon the *f* of the earth Amos 9:6
it from off the *f* of the earth Amos 9:8
he will even hide his *f* from them Mic 3:4
in pieces is come up before thy *f* Nah 2:1
discover thy skirts upon thy *f* Nah 3:5
over the *f* of the whole earth Zec 5:3
anoint thine head, and wash thy *f* Mt 6:17
I send my messenger before thy *f* Mt 11:10
ye can discern the *f* of the sky Mt 16:3
his *f* did shine as the sun, and Mt 17:2
heard it, they fell on their *f* Mt 17:6
angels do always behold the *f* of Mt 18:10
little farther, and fell on his *f* Mt 26:39
Then did they spit in his *f* Mt 26:67
I send my messenger before thy *f* Mk 1:2
to spit on him, and to cover his *f* Mk 14:65
for thou shalt go before the *f* of Lk 1:76
before the *f* of all people Lk 2:31
who seeing Jesus fell on his *f* Lk 5:12
I send my messenger before thy *f* Lk 7:27
set his *f* to go to Jerusalem Lk 9:51
And sent messengers before his *f* Lk 9:52
because his *f* was as though he Lk 9:53
two before his *f* into every city Lk 10:1
ye can discern the *f* of the sky Lk 12:56
And fell down on his *f* at his feet Lk 17:16
dwell on the *f* of the whole earth Lk 21:35
him, they struck him on the *f* Lk 22:64
his *f* was bound about with a Jn 11:44
the Lord always before my *f* Acts 2:25
saw his *f* as it had been the *f* Acts 6:15
out before the *f* of our fathers Acts 7:45
dwell on all the *f* of the earth Acts 17:26
of God, shall see my *f* no more Acts 20:25
they should see his *f* no more Acts 20:38
have the accusers *f* to *f* Acts 25:16
but then *f* to *f* 1Cor 13:12
down on his *f* he will worship God 1Cor 14:25
*f* of Moses for the glory of his 2Cor 3:7
which put a vail over his *f* 2Cor 3:13
with open *f* beholding as in a 2Cor 3:18
of God in the *f* of Jesus Christ 2Cor 4:6
if a man smite you on the *f* 2Cor 11:20
was unknown by *f* unto the Gal 1:22
Antioch, I withstood him to the *f* Gal 2:11
have not seen my *f* in the flesh Col 2:1
to see your *f* with great desire 1Th 2:17
that we might see your *f*, and 1Th 3:10
his natural *f* in a glass Jas 1:23
but the *f* of the Lord is against 1Pet 3:12
speak *f* to *f*, that our joy may 2Jn 12
come unto you, and speak *f* to *f* 2Jn 12
thee, and we shall speak *f* to *f* 3Jn 14
thee, and we shall speak *f* to *f* 3Jn 14
the third beast had a *f* as a man Rev 4:7
hide us from the *f* of him that Rev 6:16
his *f* was as it were the sun, and Rev 10:1
from the *f* of the serpent Rev 12:14
sat on it, from whose *f* the earth Rev 20:11
And they shall see his *f* Rev 22:4

**FACES**

their *f* were backward, and they Gen 9:23
men turned their *f* from thence Gen 18:22
set the *f* of the flocks toward Gen 30:40
him with their *f* to the earth Gen 42:6
laid before their *f* all these Ex 19:7
his fear may be before your *f* Ex 20:20
their *f* shall look one to another Ex 25:20
shall the *f* of the cherubims be Ex 25:20
with their *f* one to another Ex 37:9
were the *f* of the cherubims Ex 37:9
they shouted, and fell on their *f* Lev 9:24
Aaron fell on their *f* before all Num 14:5
And they fell upon their *f* Num 16:22
And they fell upon their *f* Num 16:45
and they fell upon their *f* Num 20:6
and fell on their *f* to the ground Judg 13:20
And they turned their *f*, and said Judg 18:23
day the *f* of all thy servants 2Sa 19:5
that all Israel set their *f* on me 1Kin 2:15
saw it, they fell on their *f* 1Kin 18:39
*f* were like the *f* of lions 1Chr 12:8
in sackcloth, fell upon their *f* 1Chr 21:16
feet, and their *f* were inward 2Chr 3:13
bowed themselves with their *f* to 2Chr 7:3
have turned away their *f* from the 2Chr 29:6
LORD with their *f* to the ground Neh 8:6
he covereth the *f* of the judges Job 9:24
and bind their *f* in secret Job 40:13
and their *f* were not ashamed Ps 34:5
Fill their *f* with shame Ps 83:16
and grind the *f* of the poor Is 3:15
their *f* shall be as flames Is 13:8
wipe away tears from off all *f* Is 25:8
we hid as it were our *f* from him Is 53:3
Be not afraid of their *f* Jer 1:8
be not dismayed at their *f* Jer 1:17
made their *f* harder than a rock Jer 5:3
to the confusion of their own *f* Jer 7:19
all *f* are turned into paleness Jer 30:6
set your *f* to enter into Egypt Jer 42:15
*f* to go into Egypt to sojourn Jer 42:17
that have set their *f* to go into Jer 44:12
to Zion with their *f* thitherward Jer 50:5
shame hath covered our *f* Jer 51:51
the *f* of elders were not honoured Lam 5:12
And every one had four *f*, and every Eze 1:6
and they four had their *f* and their Eze 1:8
As for the likeness of their *f* Eze 1:10
Thus were their *f* Eze 1:11
living creatures, with his four *f* Eze 1:15
thy face strong against their *f* Eze 3:8
and shame shall be upon all *f* Eze 7:18
LORD, and their *f* toward the east Eze 8:16
And every one had four *f* Eze 10:14
Every one had four *f* apiece Eze 10:21
the likeness of their *f* was the Eze 10:22
*f* which I saw by the river of Eze 10:22
turn away your *f* from all your Eze 14:6
all *f* from the south to the north Eze 20:47
and every cherub had two *f* Eze 41:18
for why should he see your *f* Dan 1:10
thee, but unto us confusion of *f* Dan 9:7
all *f* shall gather blackness Joel 2:6
and the *f* of them all gather Nah 2:10
their *f* shall sup up as the east Hab 1:9
seed, and spread dung upon your *f* Mal 2:3
for they disfigure their *f* Mt 6:16
bowed down their *f* to the earth Lk 24:5
fell before the throne on their *f* Rev 7:11
their *f* were as the *f* of men Rev 9:7
on their seats, fell upon their *f* Rev 11:16

**FADE**

Strangers shall *f* away, and they 2Sa 22:46
The strangers shall *f* away Ps 18:45
and we all do *f* as a leaf Is 64:6
the fig tree, and the leaf shall *f* Jer 8:13
for meat, whose leaf shall not *f* Eze 47:12
the rich man *f* away in his ways Jas 1:11

**FADETH**

shall be as an oak whose leaf *f* Is 1:30
*f* away, the world languisheth and Is 24:4
*f* away, the haughty people of the Is 24:4
The grass withereth, the flower *f* Is 40:7
The grass withereth, the flower *f* Is 40:8
that *f* not away, reserved in 1Pet 1:4
a crown of glory that *f* not away 1Pet 5:4

**FADING**

glorious beauty is a *f* flower Is 28:1
fat valley, shall be a *f* flower Is 28:4

**FAIL**

you for your cattle, if money *f* Gen 47:16
*f* with longing for them all the Deut 28:32
he will not *f* thee, nor forsake Deut 31:6
be with thee, he will not *f* thee Deut 31:8
I will not *f* thee, nor forsake Josh 1:5
that he will without *f* drive out Josh 3:10
If thou shalt without *f* deliver Judg 11:30
Let them not *f* to burn the fat 1Sa 2:16
no man's heart *f* because of him 1Sa 17:32
I should not *f* to sit with the 1Sa 20:5
them, and without *f* recover all 1Sa 30:8
let there not *f* from the house of 2Sa 3:29
there shall not *f* thee (said he) 1Kin 2:4
There shall not *f* thee a man in 1Kin 8:25
There shall not *f* thee a man upon 1Kin 9:5
neither shall the cruse of oil *f* 1Kin 17:14
neither did the cruse of oil *f* 1Kin 17:16
he will not *f* thee, nor forsake 1Chr 28:20
There shall not *f* thee a man in 2Chr 6:16
There shall not *f* thee a man to 2Chr 7:18
heed now that ye *f* not to do this Ezr 4:22
given them day by day without *f* Ezr 6:9
let nothing *f* of all that thou Est 6:10
unto them, so as it should not *f* Est 9:27
should not *f* from among the Jews Est 9:28
the eyes of the wicked shall *f* Job 11:20
As the waters *f* from the sea Job 14:11
the eyes of his children shall *f* Job 17:5
caused the eyes of the widow to *f* Job 31:16
for the faithful *f* from among the Ps 12:1
mine eyes *f* while I wait for my Ps 69:3
doth his promise *f* for evermore Ps 77:8
nor suffer my faithfulness to *f* Ps 89:33
Mine eyes *f* for thy word, saying, Ps 119:82
Mine eyes *f* for thy salvation, and Ps 119:123
and the rod of his anger shall *f* Prov 22:8
be a burden, and desire shall *f* Eccl 12:5
shall *f* in the midst thereof Is 19:3
the waters shall *f* from the sea Is 19:5
and all the glory of Kedar shall *f* Is 21:16
and they all shall *f* together Is 31:3
the drink of the thirsty to *f* Is 32:6
for the vintage shall *f*, the Is 32:10
no one of these shall *f*, none Is 34:16
mine eyes *f* with looking upward Is 38:14
He shall not *f* nor be discouraged Is 42:4
pit, nor that his bread should *f* Is 51:14
for the spirit should *f* before me Is 57:16
of water, whose waters *f* not Is 58:11
their eyes did *f*, because there Jer 14:6
me as a liar, and as waters that *f* Jer 15:18
wine to *f* from the winepresses Jer 48:33
Mine eyes do *f* with tears Lam 2:11
because his compassions *f* not Lam 3:22
and the new wine shall *f* in her Hos 9:2
to make the poor of the land to *f* Amos 8:4
the labour of the olive shall *f* Hab 3:17
that, when ye *f*, they may receive Lk 16:9
than one tittle of the law to *f* Lk 16:17
for thee, that thy faith *f* not Lk 22:32
there be prophecies, they shall *f* 1Cor 13:8
same, and thy years shall not *f* Heb 1:12
for the time would *f* me to tell Heb 11:32
any man *f* of the grace of God Heb 12:15

**FAILED**

and their heart *f* them, and they Gen 42:28
when money *f* in the land of Egypt Gen 47:15
the plain, even the salt sea, *f* Josh 3:16
There *f* not ought of any good Josh 21:45

that not one thing hath *f* of all Josh 23:14
and not one thing hath *f* thereof Josh 23:14
there hath not *f* one word of all 1Kin 8:56
My kinsfolk have *f*, and my Job 19:14
refuge *f* me; no man cared Ps 142:4
my soul *f* when he spake Song 5:6
their might hath *f* Jer 51:30
our eyes as yet *f* for our vain Lam 4:17

**FAILETH**

for the money *f* Gen 47:15
Their bull gendereth, and *f* not Job 21:10
my strength *f* because of mine Ps 31:10
heart panteth, my strength *f* me Ps 38:10
therefore my heart *f* me Ps 40:12
forsake me not when my strength *f* Ps 71:9
My flesh and my heart *f* Ps 73:26
and my flesh *f* of fatness Ps 109:24
my spirit *f* Ps 143:7
by the way, his wisdom *f* him Eccl 10:3
hay is withered away, the grass *f* Is 15:6
strong in power; not one *f* Is 40:26
and their tongue *f* for thirst Is 41:17
he is hungry, and his strength *f* Is 44:12
Yea, truth *f* Is 59:15
are prolonged, and every vision *f* Eze 12:22
his judgment to light, he *f* not Zeph 3:5
in the heavens that *f* not Lk 12:33
Charity never *f* 1Cor 13:8

**FAILING**

*f* of eyes, and sorrow of mind Deut 28:65
Men's hearts *f* them for fear, and Lk 21:26

**FAIN**

he would *f* flee out of his hand Job 27:22
he would *f* have filled his belly Lk 15:16

**FAINT**

came from the field, and he was *f* Gen 25:29
red pottage; for I am *f* Gen 25:30
let not your hearts *f*, fear not, Deut 20:3
heart *f* as well as his heart Deut 20:8
behind thee, when thou wast *f* Deut 25:18
of the land *f* because of you Josh 2:9
of the country do *f* because of us Josh 2:24
hundred men that were with him, *f* Judg 8:4
for they be *f*, and I am pursuing Judg 8:5
And the people were *f* 1Sa 14:28
and the people were very *f* 1Sa 14:31
which were so *f* that they could 1Sa 30:10
which were so *f* that they could 1Sa 30:21
wine, that such as be *f* in the 2Sa 16:2
and David waxed *f* 2Sa 21:15
If thou *f* in the day of adversity Prov 24:10
is sick, and the whole heart *f* Is 1:5
Therefore shall all hands be *f* Is 13:7
he awaketh, and, behold, he is *f* Is 29:8
He giveth power to the *f* Is 40:29
Even the youths shall *f* and be Is 40:30
and they shall walk, and not *f* Is 40:31
he drinketh no water, and is *f* Is 44:12
sorrow, my heart is *f* in me Jer 8:18
And lest your heart *f*, and ye fear Jer 51:46
made me desolate and *f* all the day Lam 1:13
sighs are many, and my heart is *f* Lam 1:22
that *f* for hunger in the top of Lam 2:19
For this our heart is *f* Lam 5:17
feeble, and every spirit shall *f* Eze 21:7
gates, that their heart may *f* Eze 21:15
virgins and young men *f* for thirst Amos 8:13
fasting, lest they *f* in the way Mt 15:32
houses, they will *f* by the way Mk 8:3
ought always to pray, and not to *f* Lk 18:1
we have received mercy, we *f* not 2Cor 4:1
For which cause we *f* not 2Cor 4:16
season we shall reap, if we *f* not Gal 6:9
Wherefore I desire that ye *f* not Eph 3:13
ye be wearied and *f* in your minds Heb 12:3
nor *f* when thou art rebuked of Heb 12:5

**FAINTED**

And Jacob's heart *f*, for he Gen 45:26
all the land of Canaan *f* by Gen 47:13
I had *f*, unless I had believed to Ps 27:13
and thirsty, their soul *f* in them Ps 107:5
Thy sons have *f*, they lie at the Is 51:20
I *f* in my sighing, and I find no Jer 45:3
the trees of the field *f* for him Eze 31:15
And I Daniel *f*, and was sick Dan 8:27
When my soul *f* within me I Jonah 2:7
upon the head of Jonah, that he *f* Jonah 4:8
on them, because they *f*, and were Mt 9:36
sake hast laboured, and hast not *f* Rev 2:3

**FAINTEST**

it is come upon thee, and thou *f* Job 4:5

**FAINTETH**

even *f* for the courts of the LORD Ps 84:2
My soul *f* for thy salvation Ps 119:81
be as when a standard-bearer *f* Is 10:18
earth, *f* not, neither is weary Is 40:28

**FAINTHEARTED**

man is there that is fearful and *f* Deut 20:8
neither be *f* for the two tails of Is 7:4
they are *f* Jer 49:23

**FAINTNESS**

*f* into their hearts in the lands Lev 26:36

**FAIR**

daughters of men that they were *f* Gen 6:2
thou art a *f* woman to look upon Gen 12:11
the woman that she was very *f* Gen 12:14
damsel was very *f* to look upon Gen 24:16
because she was *f* to look upon Gen 26:7
and ruddy, and of a *f* countenance 1Sa 17:42
the son of David had a *f* sister 2Sa 13:1
was a woman of a *f* countenance 2Sa 14:27
So they sought for a *f* damsel 1Kin 1:3
And the damsel was very *f*, and 1Kin 1:4
for she was *f* to look on Est 1:11
Let there be *f* young virgins Est 2:2
may gather together all the *f* Est 2:3
nor mother, and the maid was *f* Est 2:7
*F* weather cometh out of the north Job 37:22
so *f* as the daughters of Job Job 42:15
With her much *f* speech she caused Prov 7:21
so is a *f* woman which is without Prov 11:22
When he speaketh *f*, believe him Prov 26:25
Behold, thou art *f*, my love Song 1:15
behold, thou art *f* Song 1:15
Behold, thou art *f*, my beloved, Song 1:16
my love, my *f* one, and come away Song 2:10
my love, my *f* one, and come away Song 2:13
Behold, thou art *f*, my love Song 4:1
behold, thou art *f* Song 4:1
Thou art all *f*, my love Song 4:7
How *f* is thy love, my sister, my Song 4:10
*f* as the moon, clear as the sun, Song 6:10
How *f* and how pleasant art thou, O Song 7:6
be desolate, even great and *f* Is 5:9
will lay thy stones with *f* colors Is 54:11
in vain shalt thou make thyself *f* Jer 4:30
thy name, A green olive tree, *f* Jer 11:16
they speak *f* words unto thee Jer 12:6
Egypt is like a very *f* heifer Jer 46:20
taken thy *f* jewels of my gold Eze 16:17
and shall take thy *f* jewels Eze 16:39
and take away thy *f* jewels Eze 23:26
cedar in Lebanon with *f* branches Eze 31:3
Thus was he *f* in his greatness, Eze 31:7
I have made him *f* by the Eze 31:9
The leaves thereof were *f* Dan 4:12
Whose leaves were *f*, and the fruit Dan 4:21
but I passed over upon her *f* neck Hos 10:11
In that day shall the *f* virgins Amos 8:13
Let them set a *f* mitre upon his Zec 3:5
So they set a *f* mitre upon his Zec 3:5
ye say, It will be *f* weather Mt 16:2
was born, and was exceeding *f* Acts 7:20
which is called The *f* havens Acts 27:8
*f* speeches deceive the hearts of Rom 16:18
to make a *f* shew in the flesh Gal 6:12

**FAIRER**

not her younger sister *f* than she Judg 15:2
Thou art *f* than the children of Ps 45:2
their countenances appeared *f* Dan 1:15

**FAIREST**

O thou *f* among women, go thy way Song 1:8
beloved, O thou *f* among women Song 5:9
gone, O thou *f* among women Song 6:1

**FAIRS**

and lead, they traded in thy *f* Eze 27:12
traded in thy *f* with horses Eze 27:14
occupied in thy *f* with emeralds Eze 27:16
going to and fro occupied in thy *f* Eze 27:19
they occupied in thy *f* with chief Eze 27:22
Thy riches, and thy *f*, thy Eze 27:27

**FAITH**

children in whom is no *f* Deut 32:20
but the just shall live by his *f* Hab 2:4
more clothe you, O ye of little *f* Mt 6:30
you, I have not found so great *f* Mt 8:10
are ye fearful, O ye of little *f* Mt 8:26
Jesus seeing their *f* said unto Mt 9:2
thy *f* hath made thee whole Mt 9:22
to your *f* be it unto you Mt 9:29
said unto him, O thou of little *f* Mt 14:31
unto her, O woman, great is thy *f* Mt 15:28
said unto them, O ye of little *f* Mt 16:8
If ye have *f* as a grain of Mt 17:20
I say unto you, If ye have *f* Mt 21:21
of the law, judgment, mercy, and *f* Mt 23:23
When Jesus saw their *f*, he said Mk 2:5
how is it that ye have no *f* Mk 4:40
thy *f* hath made thee whole Mk 5:34
thy *f* hath made thee whole Mk 10:52
saith unto them, Have *f* in God Mk 11:22
And when he saw their *f*, he said Lk 5:20
you, I have not found so great *f* Lk 7:9
the woman, Thy *f* hath saved thee Lk 7:50
said unto them, Where is your *f* Lk 8:25
thy *f* hath made thee whole Lk 8:48
he clothe you, O ye of little *f* Lk 12:28
unto the Lord, Increase our *f* Lk 17:5
If ye had *f* as a grain of mustard Lk 17:6
thy *f* hath made thee whole Lk 17:19
shall he find *f* on the earth Lk 18:8
thy *f* hath saved thee Lk 18:42
for thee, that thy *f* fail not Lk 22:32
his name through *f* in his name Acts 3:16
the *f* which is by him hath given Acts 3:16
chose Stephen, a man full of *f* Acts 6:5
priests were obedient to the *f* Acts 6:7
And Stephen, full of *f* and power, Acts 6:8
and full of the Holy Ghost and of *f* Acts 11:24
turn away the deputy from the *f* Acts 13:8
that he had *f* to be healed Acts 14:9
them to continue in the *f* Acts 14:22
the door of *f* unto the Gentiles Acts 14:27
them, purifying their hearts by *f* Acts 15:9
the churches established in the *f* Acts 16:5
*f* toward our Lord Jesus Christ Acts 20:21
him concerning the *f* in Christ Acts 24:24
are sanctified by *f* that is in me Acts 26:18
to the *f* among all nations Rom 1:5
you all, that your *f* is spoken of Rom 1:8
you by the mutual *f* both of you Rom 1:12
of God revealed from *f* to *f* Rom 1:17
written, The just shall live by *f* Rom 1:17
make the *f* of God without effect Rom 3:3
of God which is by *f* of Jesus Rom 3:22
through *f* in his blood, to Rom 3:25
but by the law of *f* Rom 3:27
that a man is justified by *f* Rom 3:28
justify the circumcision by *f* Rom 3:30
and uncircumcision through *f* Rom 3:30
then make void the law through *f* Rom 3:31
the ungodly, his *f* is counted for Rom 4:5
for we say that *f* was reckoned to Rom 4:9
of the *f* which he had yet being Rom 4:11
of that *f* of our father Abraham Rom 4:12
through the righteousness of *f* Rom 4:13
*f* is made void, and the promise Rom 4:14
Therefore it is of *f*, that it Rom 4:16
also which is of the *f* of Abraham Rom 4:16
And being not weak in *f*, he Rom 4:19
but was strong in *f*, giving glory Rom 4:20
Therefore being justified by *f* Rom 5:1
by *f* into this grace wherein we Rom 5:2
the righteousness which is of *f* Rom 9:30
Because they sought it not by *f* Rom 9:32
is of *f* speaketh on this wise Rom 10:6
that is, the word of *f*, which we Rom 10:8
So then *f* cometh by hearing, and Rom 10:17
broken off, and thou standest by *f* Rom 11:20
to every man the measure of *f* Rom 12:3
according to the proportion of *f* Rom 12:6
that is weak in the *f* receive ye Rom 14:1
Hast thou *f*? Rom 14:22
eat, because he eateth not of *f* Rom 14:23
for whatsoever is not of *f* is sin Rom 14:23
nations for the obedience of *f* Rom 16:26
That your *f* should not stand in 1Cor 2:5
To another *f* by the same Spirit 1Cor 12:9
and though I have all *f*, so that I 1Cor 13:2
And now abideth *f*, hope, charity, 1Cor 13:13
vain, and your *f* is also vain 1Cor 15:14
be not raised, your *f* is vain 1Cor 15:17
Watch ye, stand fast in the *f* 1Cor 16:13
that we have dominion over your *f* 2Cor 1:24
for by *f* ye stand 2Cor 1:24
We having the same spirit of *f* 2Cor 4:13
(For we walk by *f*, not by sight 2Cor 5:7
as ye abound in every thing, in *f* 2Cor 8:7
when your *f* is increased, that we 2Cor 10:15
whether ye be in the *f* 2Cor 13:5
the *f* which once he destroyed Gal 1:23
but by the *f* of Jesus Christ, Gal 2:16
be justified by the *f* of Christ Gal 2:16
I live by the *f* of the Son of God Gal 2:20
the law, or by the hearing of *f* Gal 3:2
the law, or by the hearing of *f* Gal 3:5
that they which are of *f*, the Gal 3:7
justify the heathen through *f* Gal 3:8
So then they which be of *f* are Gal 3:9
for, The just shall live by *f* Gal 3:11
And the law is not of *f* Gal 3:12
promise of the Spirit through *f* Gal 3:14
that the promise by *f* of Jesus Gal 3:22
But before *f* came, we were kept Gal 3:23
shut up unto the *f* which should Gal 3:23
that we might be justified by *f* Gal 3:24
But after that *f* is come, we are Gal 3:25
of God by *f* in Christ Jesus Gal 3:26
the hope of righteousness by *f* Gal 5:5
but *f* which worketh by love Gal 5:6
gentleness, goodness, *f*, Gal 5:22
who are of the household of *f* Gal 6:10
heard of your *f* in the Lord Jesus Eph 1:15
by grace are ye saved through *f* Eph 2:8
with confidence by the *f* of him Eph 3:12
may dwell in your hearts by *f* Eph 3:17
One Lord, one *f*, one baptism, Eph 4:5
we all come in the unity of the *f* Eph 4:13
Above all, taking the shield of *f* Eph 6:16
to the brethren, and love with *f* Eph 6:23
for your furtherance and joy of *f* Phil 1:25
together for the *f* of the gospel Phil 1:27
sacrifice and service of your *f* Phil 2:17
which is through the *f* of Christ Phil 3:9
which is of God by *f* Phil 3:9
heard of your *f* in Christ Jesus Col 1:4
If ye continue in the *f* grounded Col 1:23
stedfastness of your *f* in Christ Col 2:5
up in him, and stablished in the *f* Col 2:7
the *f* of the operation of God Col 2:12
without ceasing your work of *f* 1Th 1:3
*f* to God-ward is spread abroad 1Th 1:8
to comfort you concerning your *f* 1Th 3:2
forbear, I sent to know your *f* 1Th 3:5
brought us good tidings of your *f* 1Th 3:6
affliction and distress by your *f* 1Th 3:7
that which is lacking in your *f* 1Th 3:10
putting on the breastplate of *f* 1Th 5:8
because that your *f* groweth 2Th 1:3
*f* in all your persecutions and 2Th 1:4
and the work of *f* with power 2Th 1:11
for all men have not *f* 2Th 3:2
Unto Timothy, my own son in the *f* 1Ti 1:2

than godly edifying which is in *f* 1Ti 1:4
conscience, and of *f* unfeigned 1Ti 1:5
was exceeding abundant with *f* 1Ti 1:14
Holding *f*, and a good conscience 1Ti 1:19
concerning *f* have made shipwreck 1Ti 1:19
a teacher of the Gentiles in *f* 1Ti 2:7
if they continue in *f* and charity 1Ti 2:15
of the *f* in a pure conscience 1Ti 3:9
great boldness in the *f* which is 1Ti 3:13
some shall depart from the *f* 1Ti 4:1
nourished up in the words of *f* 1Ti 4:6
in charity, in spirit, in *f* 1Ti 4:12
own house, he hath denied the *f* 1Ti 5:8
they have cast off their first *f* 1Ti 5:12
after, they have erred from the *f* 1Ti 6:10
after righteousness, godliness, *f* 1Ti 6:11
Fight the good fight of *f* 1Ti 6:12
have erred concerning the *f* 1Ti 6:21
the unfeigned *f* that is in thee 2Ti 1:5
which thou hast heard of me, in *f* 2Ti 1:13
and overthrow the *f* of some 2Ti 2:18
but follow righteousness, *f* 2Ti 2:22
minds, reprobate concerning the *f* 2Ti 3:8
manner of life, purpose, *f* 2Ti 3:10
*f* which is in Christ Jesus 2Ti 3:15
my course, I have kept the *f* 2Ti 4:7
according to the *f* of God's elect Titus 1:1
mine own son after the common *f* Titus 1:4
that they may be sound in the *f* Titus 1:13
grave, temperate, sound in *f* Titus 2:2
Greet them that love us in the *f* Titus 3:15
Hearing of thy love and *f*, which Philem 5
thy *f* may become effectual by the Philem 6
not being mixed with *f* in them Heb 4:2
dead works, and of *f* toward God, Heb 6:1
followers of them who through *f* Heb 6:12
true heart in full assurance of *f* Heb 10:22
of our *f* without wavering Heb 10:23
Now the just shall live by *f* Heb 10:38
Now *f* is the substance of things Heb 11:1
Through *f* we understand that the Heb 11:3
By *f* Abel offered unto God a more Heb 11:4
By *f* Enoch was translated that he Heb 11:5
But without *f* it is impossible to Heb 11:6
By *f* Noah, being warned of God of Heb 11:7
the righteousness which is by *f* Heb 11:7
By *f* Abraham, when he was called Heb 11:8
By *f* he sojourned in the land of Heb 11:9
Through *f* also Sara herself Heb 11:11
These all died in *f*, not having Heb 11:13
By *f* Abraham, when he was tried, Heb 11:17
By *f* Isaac blessed Jacob and Esau Heb 11:20
By *f* Jacob, when he was a dying, Heb 11:21
By *f* Joseph, when he died, made Heb 11:22
By *f* Moses, when he was born, was Heb 11:23
By *f* Moses, when he was come to Heb 11:24
By *f* he forsook Egypt, not Heb 11:27
Through *f* he kept the passover, Heb 11:28
By *f* they passed through the Red Heb 11:29
By *f* the walls of Jericho fell Heb 11:30
By *f* the harlot Rahab perished Heb 11:31
Who through *f* subdued kingdoms, Heb 11:33
obtained a good report through *f* Heb 11:39
the author and finisher of our *f* Heb 12:2
whose *f* follow, considering the Heb 13:7
trying of your *f* worketh patience Jas 1:3
But let him ask in *f*, nothing Jas 1:6
have not the *f* of our Lord Jesus Jas 2:1
the poor of this world rich in *f* Jas 2:5
though a man say he hath *f* Jas 2:14
can *f* save him? Jas 2:14
Even so *f*, if it hath not works, Jas 2:17
Yea, a man may say, Thou hast *f* Jas 2:18
shew me thy *f* without thy works, Jas 2:18
I will shew thee my *f* by my works Jas 2:18
that *f* without works is dead Jas 2:20
Seest thou how *f* wrought with his Jas 2:22
and by works was *f* made perfect Jas 2:22
is justified, and not by *f* only Jas 2:24
so *f* without works is dead also Jas 2:26
the prayer of *f* shall save the Jas 5:15
*f* unto salvation ready to be 1Pet 1:5
That the trial of your *f*, being 1Pet 1:7
Receiving the end of your *f* 1Pet 1:9
that your *f* and hope might be in 1Pet 1:21
Whom resist stedfast in the *f* 1Pet 5:9
precious *f* with us through the 2Pet 1:1
diligence, add to your *f* virtue 2Pet 1:5
overcometh the world, even our *f* 1Jn 5:4
earnestly contend for the *f* which Jude 3
up yourselves on your most holy *f* Jude 20
my name, and hast not denied my *f* Rev 2:13
and charity, and service, and *f* Rev 2:19
patience and the *f* of the saints Rev 13:10
of God, and the *f* of Jesus Rev 14:12

## FAITHFUL

who is *f* in all mine house Num 12:7
thy God, he is God, the *f* God Deut 7:9
And I will raise me up a *f* priest 1Sa 2:35
who is so *f* among all thy 1Sa 22:14
that are peaceable and *f* in Israel 2Sa 20:19
for he was a *f* man, and feared God Neh 7:2
foundest his heart *f* before thee Neh 9:8
for they were counted *f*, and their Neh 13:13
for the *f* fail from among the Ps 12:1
for the LORD preserveth the *f* Ps 31:23
moon, and as a *f* witness in heaven Ps 89:37
shall be upon the *f* of the land Ps 101:6
All thy commandments are *f* Ps 119:86
commanded are righteous and very *f* Ps 119:138
but he that is of a *f* spirit Prov 11:13
but a *f* ambassador is health Prov 13:17
A *f* witness will not lie Prov 14:5
but a *f* man who can find Prov 20:6
so is a *f* messenger to them that Prov 25:13
*F* are the wounds of a friend Prov 27:6
A *f* man shall abound with Prov 28:20
How is the *f* city become an Is 1:21
city of righteousness, the *f* city Is 1:26
I took unto me *f* witnesses to Is 8:2
because of the LORD that is *f* Is 49:7
*f* witness between us, if we do Jer 42:5
forasmuch as he was *f*, neither Dan 6:4
with God, and is *f* with the saints Hos 11:12
Who then is a *f* and wise servant, Mt 24:45
Well done, thou good and *f* servant Mt 25:21
thou hast been *f* over a few Mt 25:21
him, Well done, good and *f* servant Mt 25:23
thou hast been *f* over a few Mt 25:23
the Lord said, Who then is that *f* Lk 12:42
He that is *f* in that which is Lk 16:10
which is least is *f* also in much Lk 16:10
been *f* in the unrighteous mammon Lk 16:11
if ye have not been *f* in that Lk 16:12
thou hast been *f* in a very little Lk 19:17
judged me to be *f* to the Lord Acts 16:15
God is *f*, by whom ye were called 1Cor 1:9
stewards, that a man be found *f* 1Cor 4:2
*f* in the Lord, who shall bring 1Cor 4:17
mercy of the Lord to be *f* 1Cor 7:25
but God is *f*, who will not suffer 1Cor 10:13
faith are blessed with *f* Abraham Gal 3:9
and to the *f* in Christ Jesus Eph 1:1
*f* minister in the Lord, shall Eph 6:21
*f* brethren in Christ which are at Col 1:2
who is for you a *f* minister of Col 1:7
a *f* minister and fellowservant in Col 4:7
With Onesimus, a *f* and beloved Col 4:9
*F* is he that calleth you, who 1Th 5:24
But the Lord is *f*, who shall 2Th 3:3
me, for that he counted me *f* 1Ti 1:12
This is a *f* saying, and worthy of 1Ti 1:15
sober, *f* in all things 1Ti 3:11
This is a *f* saying and worthy of 1Ti 4:9
them service, because they are *f* 1Ti 6:2
the same commit thou to *f* men 2Ti 2:2
It is a *f* saying 2Ti 2:11
we believe not, yet he abideth *f* 2Ti 2:13
having *f* children not accused of Titus 1:6
Holding fast the *f* word as he Titus 1:9
This is a *f* saying, and these Titus 3:8
and *f* high priest in things Heb 2:17
Who was *f* to him that appointed Heb 3:2
also Moses was *f* in all his house Heb 3:2
verily was *f* in all his house Heb 3:5
(for he is *f* that promised Heb 10:23
she judged him *f* who had promised Heb 11:11
well doing, as unto a *f* Creator 1Pet 4:19
a *f* brother unto you, as I 1Pet 5:12
If we confess our sins, he is *f* 1Jn 1:9
Christ, who is the *f* witness Rev 1:5
be thou *f* unto death, and I will Rev 2:10
wherein Antipas was my *f* martyr Rev 2:13
things saith the Amen, the *f* Rev 3:14
him are called, and chosen, and *f* Rev 17:14
he that sat upon him was called *F* Rev 19:11
for these words are true and *f* Rev 21:5
said unto me, These sayings are *f* Rev 22:6

## FAITHFULLY

for they dealt *f* 2Kin 12:15
their hand, because they dealt *f* 2Kin 22:7
ye do in the fear of the LORD, *f* 2Chr 19:9
tithes and the dedicated things *f* 2Chr 31:12
And the men did the work *f* 2Chr 34:12
The king that *f* judgeth the poor, Prov 29:14
my word, let him speak my word *f* Jer 23:28
thou doest *f* whatsoever thou 3Jn 5

## FAITHFULNESS

man his righteousness and his *f* 1Sa 26:23
For there is no *f* in their mouth Ps 5:9
thy *f* reacheth unto the clouds Ps 36:5
I have declared thy *f* and thy Ps 40:10
or thy *f* in destruction Ps 88:11
known thy *f* to all generations Ps 89:1
thy *f* shalt thou establish in the Ps 89:2
thy *f* also in the congregation of Ps 89:5
or to thy *f* round about thee Ps 89:8
But my *f* and my mercy shall be Ps 89:24
from him, nor suffer my *f* to fail Ps 89:33
morning, and thy *f* every night, Ps 92:2
that thou in *f* hast afflicted me Ps 119:75
Thy *f* is unto all generations Ps 119:90
in thy *f* answer me, and in thy Ps 143:1
*f* the girdle of his reins Is 11:5
thy counsels of old are *f* Is 25:1
great is thy *f* Lam 3:23
even betroth thee unto me in *f* Hos 2:20

## FAITHLESS

Then Jesus answered and said, O *f* Mt 17:17
O *f* generation, how long shall I Mk 9:19
And Jesus answering said, O *f* Lk 9:41
and be not *f*, but believing Jn 20:27

## FALL

a deep sleep to *f* upon Adam Gen 2:21
*f* upon us, and take us for bondmen Gen 43:18
See that ye *f* not out by the way Gen 45:24
that his rider shall *f* backward Gen 49:17
lest he *f* upon us with pestilence Ex 5:3
Fear and dread shall *f* upon them Ex 15:16
it, and an ox or an ass *f* therein Ex 21:33
them, when they are dead, doth *f* Lev 11:32
if any part of their carcase *f* Lev 11:37
part of their carcase *f* thereon Lev 11:38
lest the land *f* to whoredom Lev 19:29
they shall *f* before you by the Lev 26:7
your enemies shall *f* before you Lev 26:8
they shall *f* when none pursueth Lev 26:36
they shall *f* one upon another, as Lev 26:37
let them *f* by the camp, as it Num 11:31
to *f* by the sword, that our wives Num 14:3
shall *f* in this wilderness Num 14:29
they shall *f* in this wilderness Num 14:32
you, and ye shall *f* by the sword Num 14:43
*f* unto you for an inheritance Num 34:2
ass or his ox *f* down by the way Deut 22:4
house, if any man *f* from thence Deut 22:8
of the city shall *f* down flat Josh 6:5
said, Rise thou, and *f* upon us Judg 8:21
that ye will not *f* upon me Judg 15:12
thirst, and *f* into the hand of the Judg 15:18
let *f* also some of the handfuls Ruth 2:16
thou know how the matter will *f* Ruth 3:18
none of his words *f* to the ground 1Sa 3:19
hair of his head *f* to the ground 1Sa 14:45
*f* by the hand of the Philistines 1Sa 18:25
let his spittle *f* down upon his 1Sa 21:13
not put forth their hand to *f* 1Sa 22:17
Turn thou, and *f* upon the priests 1Sa 22:18
let not my blood *f* to the earth 1Sa 26:20
and said, Go near, and *f* upon him 2Sa 1:15
hair of thy son *f* to the earth 2Sa 14:11
let us *f* now into the hand of the 2Sa 24:14
let me not *f* into the hand of man 2Sa 24:14
not an hair of him *f* to the earth 1Kin 1:52
Jehoiada, saying, Go, *f* upon him 1Kin 2:29
said, and *f* upon him, and bury him 1Kin 2:31
may go up and *f* at Ramoth-gilead 1Kin 22:20
let us *f* unto the host of the 2Kin 7:4
Know now that there shall *f* unto 2Kin 10:10
thy hurt, that thou shouldest *f* 2Kin 14:10
I will cause him to *f* by the 2Kin 19:7
He will *f* to his master Saul to 1Chr 12:19
let me *f* now into the hand of the 1Chr 21:13
but let me not *f* into the hand of 1Chr 21:13
may go up and *f* at Ramoth-gilead 2Chr 18:19
until thy bowels *f* out by reason 2Chr 21:15
make thee *f* before the enemy 2Chr 25:8
thine hurt, that thou shouldest *f* 2Chr 25:19
before whom thou hast begun to *f* Est 6:13
but shalt surely *f* before him Est 6:13
and his dread *f* upon you Job 13:11
Then let mine arm *f* from my Job 31:22
let them *f* by their own counsels Ps 5:10
are turned back, they shall *f* Ps 9:3
that the poor may *f* by his strong Ps 10:10
that very destruction let him *f* Ps 35:8
Though he *f*, he shall not be Ps 37:24
whereby the people *f* under thee Ps 45:5
They shall *f* by the sword Ps 63:10
own tongue to *f* upon themselves Ps 64:8
all kings shall *f* down before him Ps 72:11
he let it *f* in the midst of their Ps 78:28
*f* like one of the princes Ps 82:7
A thousand shall *f* at thy side Ps 91:7
thrust sore at me that I might *f* Ps 118:13
Let burning coals *f* upon them Ps 140:10
Let the wicked *f* into their own Ps 141:10
The LORD upholdeth all that *f* Ps 145:14
away, unless they cause some to *f* Prov 4:16
but a prating fool shall *f* Prov 10:8
but a prating fool shall *f* Prov 10:10
but the wicked shall *f* by his own Prov 11:5
Where no counsel is, the people *f* Prov 11:14
trusteth in his riches shall *f* Prov 11:28
and an haughty spirit before a *f* Prov 16:18
of the LORD shall *f* therein Prov 22:14
the wicked shall *f* into mischief Prov 24:16
diggeth a pit shall *f* therein Prov 26:27
he shall *f* himself into his own Prov 28:10
his heart shall *f* into mischief Prov 28:14
in his ways shall *f* at once Prov 28:18
the righteous shall see their *f* Prov 29:16
For if they *f*, the one will lift Eccl 4:10
diggeth a pit shall *f* into it Eccl 10:8
if the tree *f* toward the south, Eccl 11:3
Thy men shall *f* by the sword Is 3:25
among them shall stumble, and *f* Is 8:15
they shall *f* under the slain Is 10:4
Lebanon shall *f* by a mighty one Is 10:34
unto them shall *f* by the sword Is 13:15
be removed, and be cut down, and *f* Is 22:25
of the fear shall *f* into the pit Is 24:18
and it shall *f*, and not rise again Is 24:20
*f* backward, and be broken, and Is 28:13
be to you as a breach ready to *f* Is 30:13
slaughter, when the towers *f* Is 30:25
both he that helpeth shall *f* Is 31:3
and he that is holpen shall *f* down Is 31:3
the Assyrian *f* with the sword Is 31:8
and all their host shall *f* down Is 34:4
I will cause him to *f* by the Is 37:7
and the young men shall utterly *f* Is 40:30
shall I *f* down to the stock of a Is 44:19
they shall *f* down unto thee, they Is 45:14
they *f* down, yea, they worship Is 46:6
and mischief shall *f* upon thee Is 47:11
against thee shall *f* for thy sake Is 54:15
cause mine anger to *f* upon you Jer 3:12

they shall *f* among them that *f* Jer 6:15
sons together shall *f* upon them Jer 6:21
Shall they *f*, and not arise Jer 8:4
shall they *f* among them that *f* Jer 8:12
*f* as dung upon the open field Jer 9:22
caused him to *f* upon it suddenly Jer 15:8
I will cause them to *f* by the Jer 19:7
they shall *f* by the sword of Jer 20:4
shall be driven on, and *f* therein Jer 23:12
it shall *f* grievously upon the Jer 23:19
ye, and be drunken, and spue, and *f* Jer 25:27
ye shall *f* like a pleasant vessel Jer 25:34
it shall *f* with pain upon the Jer 30:23
I *f* not away to the Chaldeans Jer 37:14
and thou shalt not *f* by the sword Jer 39:18
and *f* in the land of Egypt Jer 44:12
*f* toward the north by the river Jer 46:6
He made many to *f*, yea, one fell Jer 46:16
the fear shall *f* into the pit Jer 48:44
is moved at the noise of their *f* Jer 49:21
young men shall *f* in her streets Jer 49:26
her young men *f* in the streets Jer 50:30
the most proud shall stumble and *f* Jer 50:32
Thus the slain shall *f* in the Jer 51:4
yea, the wall of Babylon shall *f* Jer 51:44
slain shall *f* in the midst of her Jer 51:47
caused the slain of Israel to *f* Jer 51:49
so at Babylon shall *f* the slain Jer 51:49
he hath made my strength to *f* Lam 1:14
a third part shall *f* by the sword Eze 5:12
the slain shall *f* in the midst of Eze 6:7
for they shall *f* by the sword Eze 6:11
that is near shall *f* by the sword Eze 6:12
Ye shall *f* by the sword Eze 11:10
morter, that it shall *f* Eze 13:11
ye, O great hailstones, shall *f* Eze 13:11
be discovered, and it shall *f* Eze 13:14
his bands shall *f* by the sword Eze 17:21
thy remnant shall *f* by the sword Eze 23:25
let no lot *f* upon it Eze 24:6
ye have left shall *f* by the sword Eze 24:21
of Dedan shall *f* by the sword Eze 25:13
isles shake at the sound of thy *f* Eze 26:15
isles tremble in the day of thy *f* Eze 26:18
shall *f* into the midst of the Eze 27:27
in the midst of thee shall *f* Eze 27:34
thou shalt *f* upon the open fields Eze 29:5
when the slain shall *f* in Egypt Eze 30:4
shall *f* with them by the sword Eze 30:5
also that uphold Egypt shall *f* Eze 30:6
shall they *f* in it by the sword Eze 30:6
of Pi-beseth shall *f* by the sword Eze 30:17
the sword to *f* out of his hand Eze 30:22
the arms of Pharaoh shall *f* down Eze 30:25
to shake at the sound of his *f* Eze 31:16
his own life, in the day of thy *f* Eze 32:10
will I cause thy multitude to *f* Eze 32:12
They shall *f* in the midst of them Eze 32:20
he shall not *f* thereby in the day Eze 33:12
the wastes shall *f* by the sword Eze 33:27
shall they *f* that are slain with Eze 35:8
cause thy nations to *f* any more Eze 36:15
down, and the steep places shall *f* Eze 38:20
every wall shall *f* to the ground Eze 38:20
arrows to *f* out of thy right hand Eze 39:3
Thou shalt *f* upon the mountains Eze 39:4
Thou shalt *f* upon the open field Eze 39:5
of Israel to *f* into iniquity Eze 44:12
this land shall *f* unto you for Eze 47:14
ye *f* down and worship the golden Dan 3:5
all kinds of musick, shall *f* down Dan 3:10
ye *f* down and worship the image Dan 3:15
but they shall *f* Dan 11:14
but he shall stumble and *f* Dan 11:19
and many shall *f* down slain Dan 11:26
yet they shall *f* by the sword Dan 11:33
Now when they shall *f*, they shall Dan 11:34
of them of understanding shall *f* Dan 11:35
Therefore shalt thou *f* in the day Hos 4:5
shall *f* with thee in the night Hos 4:5
that doth not understand shall *f* Hos 4:14
Ephraim *f* in their iniquity Hos 5:5
Judah also shall *f* with them Hos 5:5
their princes shall *f* by the Hos 7:16
and to the hills, F on us Hos 10:8
they shall *f* by the sword Hos 13:16
the transgressors shall *f* therein Hos 14:9
when they *f* upon the sword, they Joel 2:8
Can a bird *f* in a snare upon the Amos 3:5
be cut off, and *f* to the ground Amos 3:14
daughters shall *f* by the sword Amos 7:17
even they shall *f*, and never rise Amos 8:14
the least grain *f* upon the earth Amos 9:9
when I *f*, I shall arise Mic 7:8
they shall even *f* into the mouth Nah 3:12
I give thee, if thou wilt *f* down Mt 4:9
and great was the *f* of it Mt 7:27
one of them shall not *f* on the Mt 10:29
if it *f* into a pit on the sabbath Mt 12:11
both shall *f* into the ditch Mt 15:14
which *f* from their masters' table Mt 15:27
whosoever shall *f* on this stone Mt 21:44
but on whomsoever it shall *f* Mt 21:44
and the stars shall *f* from heaven Mt 24:29
And the stars of heaven shall *f* Mk 13:25
this child is set for the *f* Lk 2:34
they not both *f* into the ditch Lk 6:39
and in time of temptation *f* away Lk 8:13
Satan as lightning *f* from heaven Lk 10:18
Whosoever shall *f* upon that stone Lk 20:18
but on whomsoever it shall *f* Lk 20:18
they shall *f* by the edge of the Lk 21:24
to say to the mountains, F on us Lk 23:30
a corn of wheat *f* into the ground Jn 12:24
they should *f* into the quicksands Acts 27:17
of the boat, and let her *f* off Acts 27:32
*f* from the head of any of you Acts 27:34
they stumbled that they should *f* Rom 11:11
but rather through their *f* Rom 11:11
Now if the *f* of them be the Rom 11:12
or an occasion to *f* in his Rom 14:13
he standeth take heed lest he *f* 1Cor 10:12
he *f* into the condemnation of the 1Ti 3:6
lest he *f* into reproach and the 1Ti 3:7
will be rich *f* into temptation 1Ti 6:9
lest any man *f* after the same Heb 4:11
If they shall *f* away, to renew Heb 6:6
It is a fearful thing to *f* into Heb 10:31
when ye *f* into divers temptations Jas 1:2
lest ye *f* into condemnation Jas 5:12
do these things, ye shall never *f* 2Pet 1:10
*f* from your own stedfastness 2Pet 3:17
twenty elders *f* down before him Rev 4:10
F on us, and hide us from the face Rev 6:16
I saw a star *f* from heaven unto Rev 9:1

**FALLEN**

and why is thy countenance *f* Gen 4:6
man whose hair is *f* off his head Lev 13:40
he that hath his hair *f* off from Lev 13:41
poor, and *f* in decay with thee Lev 25:35
is *f* to us on this side Jordan Num 32:19
and that your terror is *f* upon us Josh 2:9
when they were all *f* on the edge Josh 8:24
their lord was *f* down dead on the Judg 3:25
*f* unto them among the tribes of Judg 18:1
the woman his concubine was *f* Judg 19:27
Dagon was *f* upon his face to the 1Sa 5:3
Dagon was *f* upon his face to the 1Sa 5:4
from the LORD was *f* upon them 1Sa 26:12
his three sons *f* in mount Gilboa 1Sa 31:8
and many of the people also are *f* 2Sa 1:4
not live after that he was *f* 2Sa 1:10
because they were *f* by the sword 2Sa 1:12
how are the mighty *f* 2Sa 1:19
How are the mighty *f* in the midst 2Sa 1:25
How are the mighty *f*, and the 2Sa 1:27
a great man *f* this day in Israel 2Sa 3:38
yea, they are *f* under my feet 2Sa 22:39
Now Elisha was *f* sick of his 2Kin 13:14
his sons *f* in mount Gilboa 1Chr 10:8
were dead bodies *f* to the earth 2Chr 20:24
our fathers have *f* by the sword 2Chr 29:9
Haman was *f* upon the bed whereon Est 7:8
The fire of God is *f* from heaven Job 1:16
is *f* into the ditch which he made Ps 7:15
The lines are *f* unto me in Ps 16:6
they are *f* under my feet Ps 18:38
They are brought down and *f* Ps 20:8
are the workers of iniquity *f* Ps 36:12
terrors of death are *f* upon me Ps 55:4
whereof they are *f* themselves Ps 57:6
reproached thee are *f* upon me Ps 69:9
is ruined, and Judah is *f* Is 3:8
The bricks are *f* down, but we Is 9:10
How art thou *f* from heaven Is 14:12
fruits and for thy harvest is *f* Is 16:9
he answered and said, Babylon is *f* Is 21:9
and said, Babylon is *f*, is *f* Is 21:9
the inhabitants of the world *f* Is 26:18
for truth is *f* in the street, and Is 59:14
Jews that are *f* to the Chaldeans Jer 38:19
and they are *f* both together Jer 46:12
the spoiler is *f* upon thy summer Jer 48:32
her foundations are *f*, her walls Jer 50:15
Babylon is suddenly *f* and Jer 51:8
my young men are *f* by the sword Lam 2:21
The crown is *f* from our head Lam 5:16
Lo, when the wall is *f*, shall it Eze 13:12
the valleys his branches are *f* Eze 31:12
all of them slain, *f* by the sword Eze 32:22
*f* by the sword, which caused Eze 32:23
*f* by the sword, which are gone Eze 32:24
that are *f* of the uncircumcised Eze 32:27
all their kings are *f* Hos 7:7
for thou hast *f* by thine iniquity Hos 14:1
The virgin of Israel is *f* Amos 5:2
the tabernacle of David that is *f* Amos 9:11
for the cedar is *f* Zec 11:2
have an ass or an ox *f* into a pit Lk 14:5
as yet he was *f* upon none of them Acts 8:16
of David, which is *f* down Acts 15:16
being *f* into a deep sleep Acts 20:9
when we were all *f* to the earth Acts 26:14
lest we should have *f* upon rocks Acts 27:29
swollen, or *f* down dead suddenly Acts 28:6
present, but some are *f* asleep 1Cor 15:6
Then they also which are *f* asleep 1Cor 15:18
ye are *f* from grace Gal 5:4
which happened unto me have *f* out Phil 1:12
therefore from whence thou art *f* Rev 2:5
saying, Babylon is *f*, is *f* Rev 14:8
five are *f*, and one is, and the Rev 17:10
Babylon the great is *f*, is *f* Rev 18:2

**FALLEST**

Thou *f* away to the Chaldeans Jer 37:13

**FALLETH**

when there *f* out any war, they Ex 1:10
vessel, whereinto any of them *f* Lev 11:33
their carcase *f* shall be unclean Lev 11:35
be in the place where his lot *f* Num 33:54
or that *f* on the sword, or that 2Sa 3:29
as a man *f* before wicked men, so 2Sa 3:34
him as the dew *f* on the ground 2Sa 17:12
night, when deep sleep *f* on men Job 4:13
night, when deep sleep *f* upon men Job 33:15
wicked messenger *f* into mischief Prov 13:17
a perverse tongue *f* into mischief Prov 17:20
For a just man *f* seven times Prov 24:16
Rejoice not when thine enemy *f* Prov 24:17
to him that is alone when he *f* Eccl 4:10
when it *f* suddenly upon them Eccl 9:12
in the place where the tree *f* Eccl 11:3
as the leaf *f* off from the vine Is 34:4
a graven image, and *f* down thereto Is 44:15
he *f* down unto it, and worshippeth Is 44:17
*f* to the Chaldeans that besiege Jer 21:9
whoso *f* not down and worshippeth Dan 3:6
whoso *f* not down and worshippeth, Dan 3:11
for ofttimes he *f* into the fire Mt 17:15
a house divided against a house *f* Lk 11:17
the portion of goods that *f* to me Lk 15:12
his own master he standeth or *f* Rom 14:4
grass, and the flower thereof *f* Jas 1:11
and the flower thereof *f* away 1Pet 1:24

**FALLING**

*f* into a trance, but having his Num 24:4
*f* into a trance, but having his Num 24:16
have upholden him that was *f* Job 4:4
the mountain *f* cometh to nought Job 14:18
not thou deliver my feet from *f* Ps 56:13
from tears, and my feet from *f* Ps 116:8
A righteous man *f* down before the Prov 25:26
as a *f* fig from the fig tree Is 34:4
*f* down before him, she declared Lk 8:47
of blood *f* down to the ground Lk 22:44
*f* headlong, he burst asunder in Acts 1:18
*f* into a place where two seas met Acts 27:41
so *f* down on his face he will 1Cor 14:25
except there come a *f* away first 2Th 2:3
that is able to keep you from *f* Jude 24

**FALLOW**

the *f* deer, and the wild goat, and Deut 14:5
Jerusalem, Break up your *f* ground Jer 4:3
break up your *f* ground Hos 10:12

**FALLOWDEER**

beside harts, and roebucks, and *f* 1Kin 4:23

**FALSE**

Thou shalt not bear *f* witness Ex 20:16
Thou shalt not raise a *f* report Ex 23:1
Keep thee far from a *f* matter Ex 23:7
Neither shalt thou bear *f* witness Deut 5:20
If a *f* witness rise up against Deut 19:16
if the witness be a *f* witness Deut 19:18
And they said, It is *f* 2Kin 9:12
For truly my words shall not be *f* Job 36:4
for *f* witnesses are risen up Ps 27:12
F witnesses did rise up Ps 35:11
therefore I hate every *f* way Ps 119:104
and I hate every *f* way Ps 119:128
be done unto thee, thou *f* tongue Ps 120:3
A *f* witness that speaketh lies, Prov 6:19
A *f* balance is abomination to the Prov 11:1
but a *f* witness deceit Prov 12:17
but a *f* witness will utter lies Prov 14:5
wicked doer giveth heed to *f* lips Prov 17:4
A *f* witness shall not be Prov 19:5
A *f* witness shall not be Prov 19:9
and a *f* balance is not good Prov 20:23
A *f* witness shall perish Prov 21:28
of a *f* gift is like clouds Prov 25:14
A man that beareth *f* witness Prov 25:18
they prophesy unto you a *f* vision Jer 14:14
them that prophesy *f* dreams Jer 23:32
Then said Jeremiah, It is *f* Jer 37:14
but have seen for thee *f* burdens Lam 2:14
as a *f* divination in their sight Eze 21:23
and love no *f* oath Zec 8:17
seen a lie, and have told *f* dreams Zec 10:2
against *f* swearers, and against Mal 3:5
Beware of *f* prophets, which come Mt 7:15
thefts, *f* witness, blasphemies Mt 15:19
Thou shalt not bear *f* witness Mt 19:18
many *f* prophets shall rise, and Mt 24:11
For there shall arise *f* Christs Mt 24:24
*f* prophets, and shall shew great Mt 24:24
sought *f* witness against Jesus, Mt 26:59
though many *f* witnesses came, yet Mt 26:60
At the last came two *f* witnesses Mt 26:60
not steal, Do not bear *f* witness Mk 10:19
For *f* Christs and *f* prophets Mk 13:22
For many bare *f* witness against Mk 14:56
bare *f* witness against him, Mk 14:57
their fathers to the *f* prophets Lk 6:26
not steal, Do not bear *f* witness Lk 18:20
from any man by *f* accusation Lk 19:8
set up *f* witnesses, which said, Acts 6:13
a *f* prophet, a Jew, whose name Acts 13:6
Thou shalt not bear *f* witness Rom 13:9
we are found *f* witnesses of God 1Cor 15:15
For such are *f* apostles, 2Cor 11:13
sea, in perils among *f* brethren 2Cor 11:26
that because of *f* brethren Gal 2:4
*f* accusers, incontinent, fierce, 2Ti 3:3
not *f* accusers, not given to much Titus 2:3
But there were *f* prophets also 2Pet 2:1
shall be *f* teachers among you 2Pet 2:1
because many *f* prophets are gone 1Jn 4:1

out of the mouth of the *f* prophet ....... Rev 16:13
with him the *f* prophet that ....... Rev 19:20
the *f* prophet are, and shall be....... Rev 20:10

## FALSEHOOD
wrought *f* against mine own life....... 2Sa 18:13
in your answers there remaineth *f*....... Job 21:34
mischief, and brought forth *f*....... Ps 7:14
for their deceit is *f*....... Ps 119:118
right hand is a right hand of *f*....... Ps 144:8
right hand is a right hand of *f*....... Ps 144:11
under *f* have we hid ourselves....... Is 28:15
of transgression, a seed of *f*....... Is 57:4
from the heart words of *f*....... Is 59:13
for his molten image is *f*....... Jer 10:14
forgotten me, and trusted in *f*....... Jer 13:25
for his molten image is *f*....... Jer 51:17
for they commit *f*; and the thief....... Hos 7:1
*f* do lie, saying, I will prophesy....... Mic 2:11

## FALSELY
that thou wilt not deal *f* with me....... Gen 21:23
concerning it, and sweareth *f*....... Lev 6:3
that about which he hath sworn *f*....... Lev 6:5
shall not steal, neither deal *f*....... Lev 19:11
ye shall not swear by my name *f*....... Lev 19:12
hath testified *f* against his....... Deut 19:18
have we dealt *f* in thy covenant....... Ps 44:17
surely they swear *f*....... Jer 5:2
The prophets prophesy *f*, and the....... Jer 5:31
the priest every one dealeth *f*....... Jer 6:13
and commit adultery, and swear *f*....... Jer 7:9
the priest every one dealeth *f*....... Jer 8:10
For they prophesy *f* unto you in....... Jer 29:9
for thou speakest *f* of Ishmael....... Jer 40:16
unto Jeremiah, Thou speakest *f*....... Jer 43:2
swearing *f* in making a covenant....... Hos 10:4
of him that sweareth *f* by my name....... Zec 5:4
all manner of evil against you *f*....... Mt 5:11
to no man, neither accuse any *f*....... Lk 3:14
of science *f* so called....... 1Ti 6:20
they may be ashamed that *f* accuse....... 1Pet 3:16

## FALSIFYING
and *f* the balances by deceit....... Amos 8:5

## FAME
the *f* thereof was heard in....... Gen 45:16
heard the *f* of thee will speak....... Num 14:15
his *f* was noised throughout all....... Josh 6:27
for we have heard the *f* of him....... Josh 9:9
his *f* was in all nations round....... 1Kin 4:31
*f* of Solomon concerning the name....... 1Kin 10:1
exceedeth the *f* which I heard....... 1Kin 10:7
the *f* of David went out into all....... 1Chr 14:17
be of exceeding magnifical, of *f*....... 1Chr 22:5
Sheba heard of the *f* of Solomon....... 2Chr 9:1
thou exceedest the *f* that I heard....... 2Chr 9:6
his *f* went out throughout all the....... Est 9:4
We have heard the *f* thereof with....... Job 28:22
off, that have not heard my *f*....... Is 66:19
We have heard the *f* thereof....... Jer 6:24
*f* in every land where they have....... Zeph 3:19
his *f* went throughout all Syria....... Mt 4:24
the *f* hereof went abroad into all....... Mt 9:26
spread abroad his *f* in all that....... Mt 9:31
tetrarch heard of the *f* of Jesus....... Mt 14:1
immediately his *f* spread abroad....... Mk 1:28
there went out a *f* of him through....... Lk 4:14
the *f* of him went out into every....... Lk 4:37
more went there a *f* abroad of him....... Lk 5:15

## FAMILIAR
not them that have *f* spirits....... Lev 19:31
after such as have *f* spirits....... Lev 20:6
or woman that hath a *f* spirit....... Lev 20:27
or a consulter with *f* spirits....... Deut 18:11
put away those that had *f* spirits....... 1Sa 28:3
me a woman that hath a *f* spirit....... 1Sa 28:7
that hath a *f* spirit at En-dor....... 1Sa 28:7
divine unto me by the *f* spirit....... 1Sa 28:8
cut off those that have *f* spirits....... 1Sa 28:9
and dealt with *f* spirits and....... 2Kin 21:6
the workers with *f* spirits....... 2Kin 23:24
of one that had a *f* spirit....... 1Chr 10:13
and dealt with a *f* spirit....... 2Chr 33:6
my *f* friends have forgotten me....... Job 19:14
Yea, mine own *f* friend, in whom I....... Ps 41:9
unto them that have *f* spirits....... Is 8:19
and to them that have *f* spirits....... Is 19:3
as of one that hath a *f* spirit....... Is 29:4

## FAMILIARS
All my *f* watched for my halting,....... Jer 20:10

## FAMILIES
after his tongue, after their *f*....... Gen 10:5
afterward were the *f* of the....... Gen 10:18
the sons of Ham, after their *f*....... Gen 10:20
the sons of Shem, after their *f*....... Gen 10:31
These are the *f* of the sons of....... Gen 10:32
in thee shall all *f* of the earth....... Gen 12:3
all the *f* of the earth be blessed....... Gen 28:14
of Esau, according to their *f*....... Gen 36:40
with bread, according to their *f*....... Gen 47:12
these be the *f* of Reuben....... Ex 6:14
these are the *f* of Simeon....... Ex 6:15
and Shimi, according to their *f*....... Ex 6:17
these are the *f* of Levi according....... Ex 6:19
these are the *f* of the Korhites....... Ex 6:24
the Levites according to their *f*....... Ex 6:25
you a lamb according to your *f*....... Ex 12:21
of their *f* that are with you,....... Lev 25:45
children of Israel, after their *f*....... Num 1:2
their pedigrees after their *f*....... Num 1:18
their generations, after their *f*....... Num 1:20
their generations, after their *f*....... Num 1:22
their generations, after their *f*....... Num 1:24
their generations, after their *f*....... Num 1:26
their generations, after their *f*....... Num 1:28
their generations, after their *f*....... Num 1:30
their generations, after their *f*....... Num 1:32
their generations, after their *f*....... Num 1:34
their generations, after their *f*....... Num 1:36
their generations, after their *f*....... Num 1:38
their generations, after their *f*....... Num 1:40
their generations, after their *f*....... Num 1:42
forward, every one after their *f*....... Num 2:34
of their fathers, by their *f*....... Num 3:15
of the sons of Gershon by their *f*....... Num 3:18
And the sons of Kohath by their *f*....... Num 3:19
And the sons of Merari by their *f*....... Num 3:20
These are the *f* of the Levites....... Num 3:20
these are the *f* of the....... Num 3:21
The *f* of the Gershonites shall....... Num 3:23
these are the *f* of the Kohathites....... Num 3:27
The *f* of the sons of Kohath shall....... Num 3:29
the *f* of the Kohathites shall be....... Num 3:30
these are the *f* of Merari....... Num 3:33
the house of the father of the *f*....... Num 3:35
of the LORD, throughout their *f*....... Num 3:39
the sons of Levi, after their *f*....... Num 4:2
*f* of the Kohathites from among....... Num 4:18
of their fathers, by their *f*....... Num 4:22
of the *f* of the Gershonites....... Num 4:24
This is the service of the *f* of....... Num 4:28
shalt number them after their *f*....... Num 4:29
of the *f* of the sons of Merari....... Num 4:33
of the Kohathites after their *f*....... Num 4:34
were numbered of them by their *f*....... Num 4:36
of the *f* of the Kohathites....... Num 4:37
of Gershon, throughout their *f*....... Num 4:38
of them, throughout their *f*....... Num 4:40
of the *f* of the sons of Gershon....... Num 4:41
of the *f* of the sons of Merari....... Num 4:42
throughout their *f*, by the house....... Num 4:42
numbered of them after their *f*....... Num 4:44
of the *f* of the sons of Merari....... Num 4:45
of Israel numbered, after their *f*....... Num 4:46
people weep throughout their *f*....... Num 11:10
These are the *f* of the Reubenites....... Num 26:7
The sons of Simeon after their *f*....... Num 26:12
These are the *f* of the Simeonites....... Num 26:14
The children of Gad after their *f*....... Num 26:15
These are the *f* of the children....... Num 26:18
sons of Judah after their *f* were....... Num 26:20
These are the *f* of Judah....... Num 26:22
sons of Issachar after their *f*....... Num 26:23
These are the *f* of Issachar....... Num 26:25
the sons of Zebulun after their *f*....... Num 26:26
These are the *f* of the....... Num 26:27
after their *f* were Manasseh....... Num 26:28
These are the *f* of Manasseh....... Num 26:34
the sons of Ephraim after their *f*....... Num 26:35
These are the *f* of the sons of....... Num 26:37
the sons of Joseph after their *f*....... Num 26:37
sons of Benjamin after their *f*....... Num 26:38
sons of Benjamin after their *f*....... Num 26:41
are the sons of Dan after their *f*....... Num 26:42
These are the *f* of Dan after....... Num 26:42
the *f* of Dan after their *f*....... Num 26:42
All the *f* of the Shuhamites,....... Num 26:43
children of Asher after their *f*....... Num 26:44
These are the *f* of the sons of....... Num 26:47
sons of Naphtali after their *f*....... Num 26:48
These are the *f* of Naphtali....... Num 26:50
of Naphtali according to their *f*....... Num 26:50
of the Levites after their *f*....... Num 26:57
These are the *f* of the Levites....... Num 26:58
of the *f* of Manasseh the son of....... Num 27:1
for an inheritance among your *f*....... Num 33:54
the chief fathers of the *f* of the....... Num 36:1
of the *f* of the sons of Joseph,....... Num 36:1
they were married into the *f* of....... Num 36:12
come according to the *f* thereof....... Josh 7:14
inheritance according to their *f*....... Josh 13:15
children of Reuben after their *f*....... Josh 13:23
children of Gad according their *f*....... Josh 13:24
the children of Gad after their *f*....... Josh 13:28
children of Manasseh by their *f*....... Josh 13:29
the children of Machir by their *f*....... Josh 13:31
the children of Judah by their *f*....... Josh 15:1
round about according to their *f*....... Josh 15:12
of Judah according to their *f*....... Josh 15:20
according to their *f* was thus....... Josh 16:5
children of Ephraim by their *f*....... Josh 16:8
children of Manasseh by their *f*....... Josh 17:2
the son of Joseph by their *f*....... Josh 17:2
came up according to their *f*....... Josh 18:11
round about, according to their *f*....... Josh 18:20
according to their *f* were Jericho....... Josh 18:21
of Benjamin according to their *f*....... Josh 18:28
of Simeon according to their *f*....... Josh 19:1
of Simeon according to their *f*....... Josh 19:8
of Zebulun according to their *f*....... Josh 19:10
of Zebulun according to their *f*....... Josh 19:16
of Issachar according to their *f*....... Josh 19:17
of Issachar according to their *f*....... Josh 19:23
of Asher according to their *f*....... Josh 19:24
of Asher according to their *f*....... Josh 19:31
of Naphtali according to their *f*....... Josh 19:32
of Naphtali according to their *f*....... Josh 19:39
of Dan according to their *f*....... Josh 19:40
of Dan according to their *f*....... Josh 19:48
out for the *f* of the Kohathites....... Josh 21:4
of the *f* of the tribe of Ephraim....... Josh 21:5
of the *f* of the tribe of Issachar....... Josh 21:6
*f* had out of the tribe of Reuben....... Josh 21:7
being of the *f* of the Kohathites,....... Josh 21:10
the *f* of the children of Kohath,....... Josh 21:20
*f* of the children of Kohath that....... Josh 21:26
of the *f* of the Levites, out of....... Josh 21:27
Gershonites according to their *f*....... Josh 21:33
unto the *f* of the children of....... Josh 21:34
the children of Merari by their *f*....... Josh 21:40
remaining of the *f* of the Levites....... Josh 21:40
the *f* of the tribe of Benjamin....... 1Sa 9:21
Benjamin to come near by their *f*....... 1Sa 10:21
And the *f* of Kirjath-jearim....... 1Chr 2:53
the *f* of the scribes which dwelt....... 1Chr 2:55
These are the *f* of the Zorathites....... 1Chr 4:2
the *f* of Aharhel the son of Harum....... 1Chr 4:8
the *f* of the house of them that....... 1Chr 4:21
names were princes in their *f*....... 1Chr 4:38
And his brethren by their *f*....... 1Chr 5:7
these are the *f* of the Levites....... 1Chr 6:19
of the *f* of the Kohathites....... 1Chr 6:54
their *f* were thirteen cities....... 1Chr 6:60
of Gershom throughout their *f* out....... 1Chr 6:62
given by lot, throughout their *f*....... 1Chr 6:63
the residue of the *f* of the sons....... 1Chr 6:66
their brethren among all the *f* of....... 1Chr 7:5
to the divisions of the *f* of the....... 2Chr 35:5
division of the *f* of the Levites....... 2Chr 35:5
divisions of the *f* of the people....... 2Chr 35:12
after their *f* with their swords....... Neh 4:13
did the contempt of *f* terrify me....... Job 31:34
God setteth the solitary in *f*....... Ps 68:6
maketh him *f* like a flock....... Ps 107:41
I will call all the *f* of the....... Jer 1:15
all the *f* of the house of Israel....... Jer 2:4
upon the *f* that call not on thy....... Jer 10:25
and take all the *f* of the north....... Jer 25:9
be the God of all the *f* of Israel....... Jer 31:1
The two *f* which the LORD hath....... Jer 33:24
as the *f* of the countries, to....... Eze 20:32
I known of all the *f* of the earth....... Amos 3:2
*f* through her witchcrafts....... Nah 3:4
All the *f* that remain, every....... Zec 12:14
will not come up of all the *f* of....... Zec 14:17

## FAMILY
that man, and against his *f*....... Lev 20:5
shall return every man unto his *f*....... Lev 25:10
and shall return unto his own *f*....... Lev 25:41
to the stock of the stranger's *f*....... Lev 25:47
unto him of his *f* may redeem him....... Lev 25:49
Gershon was the *f* of the Libnites....... Num 3:21
and the *f* of the Shimites....... Num 3:21
Kohath was the *f* of the Amramites....... Num 3:27
the *f* of the Izeharites, and the....... Num 3:27
the *f* of the Hebronites, and the....... Num 3:27
and the *f* of the Uzzielites....... Num 3:27
Merari was the *f* of the Mahlites....... Num 3:33
and the *f* of the Mushites....... Num 3:33
cometh the *f* of the Hanochites....... Num 26:5
of Pallu, the *f* of the Palluites....... Num 26:5
Hezron, the *f* of the Hezronites....... Num 26:6
of Carmi, the *f* of the Carmites....... Num 26:6
Nemuel, the *f* of the Nemuelites....... Num 26:12
of Jamin, the *f* of the Jaminites....... Num 26:12
Jachin, the *f* of the Jachinites....... Num 26:12
Of Zerah, the *f* of the Zarhites....... Num 26:13
of Shaul, the *f* of the Shaulites....... Num 26:13
Zephon, the *f* of the Zephonites....... Num 26:15
of Haggi, the *f* of the Haggites....... Num 26:15
of Shuni, the *f* of the Shunites....... Num 26:15
Of Ozni, the *f* of the Oznites....... Num 26:16
of Eri, the *f* of the Erites....... Num 26:16
Of Arod, the *f* of the Arodites....... Num 26:17
of Areli, the *f* of the Arelites....... Num 26:17
Shelah, the *f* of the Shelanites....... Num 26:20
of Pharez, the *f* of the Pharzites....... Num 26:20
of Zerah, the *f* of the Zarhites....... Num 26:20
Hezron, the *f* of the Hezronites....... Num 26:21
of Hamul, the *f* of the Hamulites....... Num 26:21
of Tola, the *f* of the Tolaites....... Num 26:23
of Pua, the *f* of the Punites....... Num 26:23
Jashub, the *f* of the Jashubites....... Num 26:24
Shimron, the *f* of the Shimronites....... Num 26:24
of Sered, the *f* of the Sardites....... Num 26:26
of Elon, the *f* of the Elonites....... Num 26:26
Jahleel, the *f* of the Jahleelites....... Num 26:26
Machir, the *f* of the Machirites....... Num 26:29
come the *f* of the Gileadites....... Num 26:29
Jeezer, the *f* of the Jeezerites....... Num 26:30
of Helek, the *f* of the Helekites....... Num 26:30
Asriel, the *f* of the Asrielites....... Num 26:31
Shechem, the *f* of the Shechemites....... Num 26:31
Shemida, the *f* of the Shemidaites....... Num 26:32
Hepher, the *f* of the Hepherites....... Num 26:32
the *f* of the Shuthalhites....... Num 26:35
of Becher, the *f* of the Bachrites....... Num 26:35
of Tahan, the *f* of the Tahanites....... Num 26:35
of Eran, the *f* of the Eranites....... Num 26:36
of Bela, the *f* of the Belaites....... Num 26:38
Ashbel, the *f* of the Ashbelites....... Num 26:38
Ahiram, the *f* of the Ahiramites....... Num 26:38
Shupham, the *f* of the Shuphamites....... Num 26:39
Hupham, the *f* of the Huphamites....... Num 26:39
of Ard, the *f* of the Ardites....... Num 26:40
of Naaman, the *f* of the Naamites....... Num 26:40
Shuham, the *f* of the Shuhamites....... Num 26:42
of Jimna, the *f* of the Jimnites....... Num 26:44

of Jesui, the *f* of the Jesuites ... Num 26:44
of Beriah, the *f* of the Beriites ... Num 26:44
of Heber, the *f* of the Heberites ... Num 26:45
the *f* of the Malchielites ... Num 26:45
Jahzeel, the *f* of the Jahzeelites ... Num 26:48
of Guni, the *f* of the Gunites ... Num 26:48
Of Jezer, the *f* of the Jezerites ... Num 26:49
Shillem, the *f* of the Shillemites ... Num 26:49
Gershon, the *f* of the Gershonites ... Num 26:57
Kohath, the *f* of the Kohathites ... Num 26:57
of Merari, the *f* of the Merarites ... Num 26:57
the *f* of the Libnites ... Num 26:58
the *f* of the Hebronites ... Num 26:58
the *f* of the Mahlites ... Num 26:58
the *f* of the Mushites ... Num 26:58
Mushites, the *f* of the Korathites ... Num 26:58
be done away from among his *f* ... Num 27:4
that is next to him of his *f* ... Num 27:11
only to the *f* of the tribe of ... Num 36:6
the *f* of the tribe of her father ... Num 36:8
tribe of the *f* of their father ... Num 36:12
be among you man, or woman, or *f* .. Deut 29:18
the *f* which the LORD shall take ... Josh 7:14
And he brought the *f* of Judah ... Josh 7:17
he took the *f* of the Zarhites ... Josh 7:17
he brought the *f* of the Zarhites ... Josh 7:17
they let go the man and all his *f* ... Judg 1:25
my *f* is poor in Manasseh, and I am ... Judg 6:15
with all the *f* of the house of ... Judg 9:1
of the *f* of the Danites, whose ... Judg 13:2
of the *f* of Judah, who was a ... Judg 17:7
*f* five men from their coasts ... Judg 18:2
thence of the *f* of the Danites ... Judg 18:11
unto a tribe and a *f* in Israel ... Judg 18:19
man to his tribe and to his *f* ... Judg 21:24
of wealth, of the *f* of Elimelech ... Ruth 2:1
my *f* the least of all the ... 1Sa 9:21
the *f* of Matri was taken, and Saul ... 1Sa 10:21
life, or my father's *f* in Israel ... 1Sa 18:18
sacrifice there for all the *f* ... 1Sa 20:6
for our *f* hath a sacrifice in the ... 1Sa 20:29
the whole *f* is risen against ... 2Sa 14:7
man of the *f* of the house of Saul ... 2Sa 16:5
neither did all their *f* multiply ... 1Chr 4:27
were left of the *f* of that tribe ... 1Chr 6:61
for the *f* of the remnant of the ... 1Chr 6:70
*f* of the half tribe of Manasseh ... 1Chr 6:71
ark of God remained with the *f* of ... 1Chr 13:14
every generation, every *f* ... Est 9:28
you one of a city, and two of a *f* ... Jer 3:14
them that remain of this evil *f* ... Jer 8:3
against the whole *f* which I ... Amos 3:1
against this *f* do I devise an ... Mic 2:3
land shall mourn, every *f* apart ... Zec 12:12
the *f* of the house of David apart ... Zec 12:12
the *f* of the house of Nathan ... Zec 12:12
The *f* of the house of Levi apart ... Zec 12:13
the *f* of Shimei apart, and their ... Zec 12:13
that remain, every *f* apart ... Zec 12:14
if the *f* of Egypt go not up, and ... Zec 14:18
Of whom the whole *f* in heaven ... Eph 3:15

**FAMINE**

And there was a *f* in the land ... Gen 12:10
for the *f* was grievous in the ... Gen 12:10
And there was a *f* in the land ... Gen 26:1
beside the first *f* that was in ... Gen 26:1
wind shall be seven years of *f* ... Gen 41:27
arise after them seven years of *f* ... Gen 41:30
the *f* shall consume the land ... Gen 41:30
by reason of that *f* following ... Gen 41:31
land against the seven years of *f* ... Gen 41:36
the land perish not through the *f* ... Gen 41:36
sons before the years of *f* came ... Gen 41:50
the *f* was over all the face of ... Gen 41:56
the *f* waxed sore in the land of ... Gen 41:56
because that the *f* was so sore in ... Gen 41:57
for the *f* was in the land of ... Gen 42:5
corn for the *f* of your houses ... Gen 42:19
take food for the *f* of your ... Gen 42:33
the *f* was sore in the land ... Gen 43:1
years hath the *f* been in the land ... Gen 45:6
for yet there are five years of *f* ... Gen 45:11
for the *f* is sore in the land of ... Gen 47:4
for the *f* was very sore, so that ... Gen 47:13
Canaan fainted by reason of the *f* ... Gen 47:13
because the *f* prevailed over them ... Gen 47:20
that there was a *f* in the land ... Ruth 1:1
Then there was a *f* in the days of ... 2Sa 21:1
Shall seven years of *f* come unto ... 2Sa 24:13
If there be in the land *f* ... 1Kin 8:37
And there was a sore *f* in Samaria ... 1Kin 18:2
And there was a great *f* in Samaria ... 2Kin 6:25
then the *f* is in the city, and we ... 2Kin 7:4
for the LORD hath called for a *f* ... 2Kin 8:1
month the *f* prevailed in the city ... 2Kin 25:3
Either three years' *f* ... 1Chr 21:12
judgment, or pestilence, or *f* ... 2Chr 20:9
give over yourselves to die by *f* ... 2Chr 32:11
In *f* he shall redeem thee from ... Job 5:20
destruction and *f* thou shalt laugh ... Job 5:22
For want and *f* they were solitary ... Job 30:3
death, and to keep them alive in *f* ... Ps 33:19
in the days of *f* they shall be ... Ps 37:19
he called for a *f* upon the land ... Ps 105:16
and I will kill thy root with *f* ... Is 14:30
and destruction, and the *f* ... Is 51:19
neither shall we see sword nor *f* ... Jer 5:12
and their daughters shall die by *f* ... Jer 11:22
them by the sword, and by the *f* ... Jer 14:12
sword, neither shall ye have *f* ... Jer 14:13
*f* shall not be in this land ... Jer 14:15
*f* shall those prophets be ... Jer 14:15
of Jerusalem because of the *f* ... Jer 14:16
behold them that are sick with *f* ... Jer 14:18
as are for the *f*, to the *f* ... Jer 15:2
be consumed by the sword, and by *f* ... Jer 16:4
up their children to the *f* ... Jer 18:21
from the sword, and from the *f* ... Jer 21:7
die by the sword, and by the *f* ... Jer 21:9
And I will send the sword, the *f* ... Jer 24:10
with the sword, and with the *f* ... Jer 27:8
people, by the sword, by the *f* ... Jer 27:13
send upon them the sword, the *f* ... Jer 29:17
them with the sword, with the *f* ... Jer 29:18
because of the sword, and of the *f* ... Jer 32:24
Babylon by the sword, and by the *f* ... Jer 32:36
to the pestilence, and to the *f* ... Jer 34:17
shall die by the sword, by the *f* ... Jer 38:2
in the land of Egypt, and the *f* ... Jer 42:16
shall die by the sword, by the *f* ... Jer 42:17
shall die by the sword, by the *f* ... Jer 42:22
consumed by the sword and by the *f* ... Jer 44:12
by the sword and by the *f* ... Jer 44:12
Jerusalem, by the sword, by the *f* ... Jer 44:13
consumed by the sword and by the *f* ... Jer 44:18
consumed by the sword and by the *f* ... Jer 44:27
the *f* was sore in the city, so ... Jer 52:6
an oven because of the terrible *f* ... Lam 5:10
with *f* shall they be consumed in ... Eze 5:12
upon them the evil arrows of *f* ... Eze 5:16
and I will increase the *f* upon you ... Eze 5:16
So will I send upon you *f* ... Eze 5:17
shall fall by the sword, by the *f* ... Eze 6:11
and is besieged shall die by the *f* ... Eze 6:12
and the pestilence and the *f* within ... Eze 7:15
and he that is in the city, *f* ... Eze 7:15
them from the sword, from the *f* ... Eze 12:16
thereof, and will send *f* upon it ... Eze 14:13
Jerusalem, the sword, and the *f* ... Eze 14:21
increase it, and lay no *f* upon you ... Eze 36:29
reproach of *f* among the heathen ... Eze 36:30
that I will send a *f* in the land ... Amos 8:11
not a *f* of bread, nor a thirst ... Amos 8:11
when great *f* was throughout all ... Lk 4:25
arose a mighty *f* in that land ... Lk 15:14
or distress, or persecution, or *f* ... Rom 8:35
one day, death, and mourning, and *f* ... Rev 18:8

**FAMINES**

and there shall be *f*, and ... Mt 24:7
places, and there shall be *f* ... Mk 13:8
shall be in divers places, and *f* ... Lk 21:11

**FAMISH**

the soul of the righteous to *f* ... Prov 10:3
for he will *f* all the gods of the ... Zeph 2:11

**FAMISHED**

when all the land of Egypt was *f* ... Gen 41:55
and their honourable men are *f* ... Is 5:13

**FAMOUS**

*f* in the congregation, men of ... Num 16:2
which were *f* in the congregation, ... Num 26:9
Ephratah, and be *f* in Beth-lehem ... Ruth 4:11
that his name may be *f* in Israel ... Ruth 4:14
*f* men, and heads of the house of ... 1Chr 5:24
*f* throughout the house of their ... 1Chr 12:30
A man was *f* according as he had ... Ps 74:5
And slew *f* kings ... Ps 136:18
and she became *f* among women ... Eze 23:10
and the daughters of the *f* nations ... Eze 32:18

**FAN**

with the shovel and with the *f* ... Is 30:24
Thou shalt *f* them, and the wind ... Is 41:16
daughter of my people, not to *f* ... Jer 4:11
I will *f* them with a *f* in the ... Jer 15:7
Babylon fanners, that shall *f* her ... Jer 51:2
Whose *f* is in his hand, and he ... Mt 3:12
Whose *f* is in his hand, and he ... Lk 3:17

**FANNERS**

And will send unto Babylon *f* ... Jer 51:2

**FAR**

That be *f* from thee to do after ... Gen 18:25
the wicked, that be *f* from thee ... Gen 18:25
out of the city, and not yet *f* off ... Gen 44:4
only ye shall not go very *f* away ... Ex 8:28
Keep thee *f* from a false matter ... Ex 23:7
*f* off about the tabernacle of the ... Num 2:2
his name there be too *f* from thee ... Deut 12:21
or *f* off from thee, from the one ... Deut 13:7
if the place be too *f* from thee ... Deut 14:24
which are very *f* off from thee ... Deut 20:15
a nation against thee from *f* ... Deut 28:49
that shall come from a *f* land ... Deut 29:22
from thee, neither is it *f* off ... Deut 30:11
an heap very *f* from the city Adam ... Josh 3:16
go not very *f* from the city, but ... Josh 8:4
We be come from a *f* country ... Josh 9:6
From a very *f* country thy ... Josh 9:9
saying, We are very *f* from you ... Josh 9:22
for you, and adventured his life *f* ... Judg 9:17
they were *f* from the Zidonians ... Judg 18:7
because it was *f* from Zidon ... Judg 18:28
by Jebus, the day was *f* spent ... Judg 19:11
the LORD saith, Be it *f* from me ... 1Sa 2:30
Jonathan said, *F* be it from thee ... 1Sa 20:9
be it *f* from me ... 1Sa 22:15
tarried in a place that was *f* off ... 2Sa 15:17
*F* be it, *f* be it from me, that ... 2Sa 20:20
*f* be it from me, that I should ... 2Sa 20:20
Be it *f* from me, O LORD, that I ... 2Sa 23:17
but cometh out of a *f* country for ... 1Kin 8:41
the land of the enemy, *f* or near ... 1Kin 8:46
They are come from a *f* country ... 2Kin 20:14
but is come from a *f* country for ... 2Chr 6:32
unto a land *f* off or near ... 2Chr 6:36
And his name spread *f* abroad ... 2Chr 26:15
the river, be ye *f* from thence ... Ezr 6:6
upon the wall, one *f* from another ... Neh 4:19
king Ahasuerus, both nigh and *f* ... Est 9:20
His children are *f* from safety ... Job 5:4
be in thine hand, put it *f* away ... Job 11:14
Withdraw thine hand *f* from me ... Job 13:21
He hath put my brethren *f* from me ... Job 19:13
of the wicked is *f* from me ... Job 21:16
of the wicked is *f* from me ... Job 22:18
iniquity *f* from thy tabernacles ... Job 22:23
abhor me, they flee *f* from me ... Job 30:10
*f* be it from God, that he should ... Job 34:10
thy judgments are *f* above out of ... Ps 10:5
why art thou so *f* from helping me ... Ps 22:1
Be not *f* from me ... Ps 22:11
But be not thou *f* from me ... Ps 22:19
Hide not thy face *f* from me ... Ps 27:9
O Lord, be not *f* from me ... Ps 35:22
O my God, be not *f* from me ... Ps 38:21
Lo, then would I wander *f* off ... Ps 55:7
O God, be not *f* from me ... Ps 71:12
they that are *f* from thee shall ... Ps 73:27
away mine acquaintance *f* from me ... Ps 88:8
and friend hast thou put *f* from me ... Ps 88:18
thou art exalted *f* above all gods ... Ps 97:9
As *f* as the east is from the west ... Ps 103:12
so *f* hath he removed our ... Ps 103:12
blessing, so let it be *f* from him ... Ps 109:17
they are *f* from thy law ... Ps 119:150
Salvation is *f* from the wicked ... Ps 119:155
and perverse lips put *f* from thee ... Prov 4:24
Remove thy way *f* from her ... Prov 5:8
The LORD is *f* from the wicked ... Prov 15:29
more do his friends go *f* from him ... Prov 19:7
his soul shall be *f* from them ... Prov 22:5
shall drive it *f* from him ... Prov 22:15
so is good news from a *f* country ... Prov 25:25
that is near than a brother *f* off ... Prov 27:10
Remove *f* from me vanity and lies ... Prov 30:8
for her price is *f* above rubies ... Prov 31:10
as *f* as light excelleth darkness ... Eccl 2:13
but it was *f* from me ... Eccl 7:23
That which is *f* off, and exceeding ... Eccl 7:24
an ensign to the nations from *f* ... Is 5:26
the LORD have removed men *f* away ... Is 6:12
give ear, all ye of *f* countries ... Is 8:9
which shall come from *f* ... Is 10:3
They come from a *f* country ... Is 13:5
them, and they shall flee *f* off ... Is 17:13
they shall turn the rivers *f* away ... Is 19:6
together, which have fled from *f* ... Is 22:3
thou hadst removed it *f* unto all ... Is 26:15
removed their heart *f* from me ... Is 29:13
name of the LORD cometh from *f* ... Is 30:27
Hear, ye that are *f* off, what I ... Is 33:13
the land that is very *f* off ... Is 33:17
are come from a *f* country unto me ... Is 39:3
bring my sons from *f*, and my ... Is 43:6
my counsel from a *f* country ... Is 46:11
that are *f* from righteousness ... Is 46:12
it shall not be *f* off, and my ... Is 46:13
and hearken, ye people, from *f* ... Is 49:1
Behold, these shall come from *f* ... Is 49:12
swallowed thee up shall be *f* away ... Is 49:19
thou shalt be *f* from oppression ... Is 54:14
didst send thy messengers *f* off ... Is 57:9
Peace, peace to him that is *f* off ... Is 57:19
Therefore is judgment *f* from us ... Is 59:9
but it is *f* off from us ... Is 59:11
thy sons shall come from *f* ... Is 60:4
first, to bring thy sons from *f* ... Is 60:9
me, that they are gone *f* from me ... Jer 2:5
watchers come from a *f* country ... Jer 4:16
bring a nation upon you from *f* ... Jer 5:15
the sweet cane from a *f* country ... Jer 6:20
of them that dwell in a *f* country ... Jer 8:19
mouth, and *f* from their reins ... Jer 12:2
And all the kings of the north, *f* ... Jer 25:26
to remove you *f* from your land ... Jer 27:10
of the land of Moab, *f* or near ... Jer 48:24
Thus *f* is the judgment of Moab ... Jer 48:47
Flee, get you *f* off, dwell deep ... Jer 49:30
Thus *f* are the words of Jeremiah ... Jer 51:64
relieve my soul is *f* from me ... Lam 1:16
removed my soul *f* off from peace ... Lam 3:17
He that is *f* off shall die of the ... Eze 6:12
have I set it *f* from them ... Eze 7:20
that I should go *f* off from my ... Eze 8:6
said, Get you *f* from the LORD ... Eze 11:15
cast them *f* off among the heathen ... Eze 11:16
of the times that are *f* off ... Eze 12:27
and those that be *f* from thee ... Eze 22:5
have sent for men to come from *f* ... Eze 23:40
*f* from me, and I will dwell in the ... Eze 43:9
that are gone away *f* from me ... Eze 44:10
that are near, and that are *f* off ... Dan 9:7
the fourth shall be *f* richer than ... Dan 11:2
But I will remove *f* off from you ... Joel 2:20
remove them *f* from their border ... Joel 3:6
to the Sabeans, to a people *f* off ... Joel 3:8
Ye that put *f* away the evil day ... Amos 6:3
her that was cast *f* off a strong ... Mic 4:7

F

day shall the decree be *f* removed Mic 7:11
their horsemen shall come from *f* Hab 1:8
they that are *f* off shall come and Zec 6:15
shall remember me in *f* countries Zec 10:9
but their heart is *f* from me Mt 15:8
saying, Be it *f* from thee, Lord Mt 16:22
and went into a *f* country Mt 21:33
a man travelling into a *f* country Mt 25:14
And when the day was now *f* spent Mk 6:35
and now the time is *f* passed Mk 6:35
but their heart is *f* from me Mk 7:6
for divers of them came from *f* Mk 8:3
and went into a *f* country Mk 12:1
Thou art not *f* from the kingdom Mk 12:34
is as a man taking a *f* journey Mk 13:34
he was now not *f* from the house Lk 7:6
took his journey into a *f* country Lk 15:13
*f* country to receive for himself Lk 19:12
went into a *f* country for a long Lk 20:9
and said, Suffer ye thus *f* Lk 22:51
evening, and the day is *f* spent Lk 24:29
led them out as *f* as to Bethany Lk 24:50
(for they were not *f* from land Jn 21:8
Stephen travelled as *f* as Phenice Acts 11:19
that he should go as *f* as Antioch Acts 11:22
though he be not *f* from every one Acts 17:27
for I will send thee *f* hence unto Acts 22:21
to meet us as *f* as Appii forum Acts 28:15
The night is *f* spent, the day is Rom 13:12
worketh for us a *f* more exceeding 2Cor 4:17
for we are come as *f* as to you 2Cor 10:14
*F* above all principality, and Eph 1:21
Jesus ye who sometimes were *f* off Eph 2:13
ascended up *f* above all heavens Eph 4:10
be with Christ; which is *f* better Phil 1:23
And it is yet *f* more evident Heb 7:15

**FARE**

and look how thy brethren *f* 1Sa 17:18
so he paid the *f* thereof, and went Jonah 1:3
shall do well. *F* ye well Acts 15:29

**FARED**

linen, and *f* sumptuously every day Lk 16:19

**FAREWELL**

but let me first go bid them *f* Lk 9:61
But bade them *f*, saying, I must Acts 18:21
what they had against him. *F.* Acts 23:30
Finally, brethren, *f* 2Cor 13:11

**FARM**

and went their ways, one to his *f* Mt 22:5

**FARTHER**

And he went a little *f*, and fell on Mt 26:39
he had gone a little *f* thence Mk 1:19
of Judaea by the *f* side of Jordan Mk 10:1

**FARTHING**

thou hast paid the uttermost *f* Mt 5:26
Are not two sparrows sold for a *f* Mt 10:29
in two mites, which make a *f* Mk 12:42

**FARTHINGS**

not five sparrows sold for two *f* Lk 12:6

**FASHION**

this is the *f* which thou shalt Gen 6:15
*f* thereof which was shewed thee Ex 26:30
the *f* of almonds in one branch Ex 37:19
and according to all the *f* of it 1Kin 6:38
the priest the *f* of the altar 2Kin 16:10
did not one *f* us in the womb Job 31:15
the *f* thereof, and the goings out Eze 43:11
saying, We never saw it on this *f* Mk 2:12
the *f* of his countenance was Lk 9:29
to the *f* that he had seen Acts 7:44
for the *f* of this world passeth 1Cor 7:31
And being found in *f* as a man Phil 2:8
grace of the *f* of it perisheth Jas 1:11

**FASHIONED**

*f* it with a graving tool, after Ex 32:4
*f* me together round about Job 10:8
Thy hands have made me and *f* me Ps 119:73
which in continuance were *f* Ps 139:16
unto him that *f* it long ago Is 22:11
thy breasts are *f*, and thine hair Eze 16:7
that it may be *f* like unto his Phil 3:21

**FASHIONETH**

He *f* their hearts alike Ps 33:15
*f* it with hammers, and worketh it Is 44:12
the clay say to him that *f* it Is 45:9

**FASHIONING**

not *f* yourselves according to the 1Pet 1:14

**FASHIONS**

were both according to their *f* Eze 42:11

**FAST**

For the LORD had *f* closed up all Gen 20:18
for he was *f* asleep and weary Judg 4:21
but we will bind thee *f*, and Judg 15:13
If they bind me *f* with new ropes Judg 16:11
but abide here *f* by my maidens Ruth 2:8
Thou shalt keep *f* by my young men Ruth 2:21
So she kept *f* by the maidens of Ruth 2:23
thou didst *f* and weep for the 2Sa 12:21
he is dead, wherefore should I *f* 2Sa 12:23
the letters, saying, Proclaim a *f* 1Kin 21:9
They proclaimed a *f*, and set 1Kin 21:12
door, and hold him *f* at the door 2Kin 6:32
proclaimed a *f* throughout all 2Chr 20:3
walls, and this work goeth *f* on Ezr 5:8
Then I proclaimed a *f* there Ezr 8:21
*f* ye for me, and neither eat nor Est 4:16
and my maidens will *f* likewise Est 4:16
still he holdeth *f* his integrity Job 2:3
he shall hold it *f*, but it shall Job 8:15
My righteousness I hold *f* Job 27:6
and the clods cleave *f* together Job 38:38
he commanded, and it stood *f* Ps 33:9
For thine arrows stick *f* in me Ps 38:2
say they, cleaveth *f* unto him Ps 41:8
strength setteth *f* the mountains Ps 65:6
covenant shall stand *f* with him Ps 89:28
They stand *f* for ever and ever, and Ps 111:8
Take *f* hold of instruction Prov 4:13
day of your *f* ye find pleasure Is 58:3
ye *f* for strife and debate, and to Is 58:4
ye shall not *f* as ye do this day, Is 58:4
Is it such a *f* that I have chosen Is 58:5
wilt thou call this a *f*, and an Is 58:5
Is not this the *f* that I have Is 58:6
they hold *f* deceit, they refuse Jer 8:5
When they *f*, I will not hear Jer 14:12
that they proclaimed a *f* before Jer 36:9
say ye, Stand *f*, and prepare thee Jer 46:14
come, and his affliction hasteth *f* Jer 48:16
took them captives held them *f* Jer 50:33
Sanctify ye a *f*, call a solemn Joel 1:14
the trumpet in Zion, sanctify a *f* Joel 2:15
and he lay, and was *f* asleep Jonah 1:5
believed God, and proclaimed a *f* Jonah 3:5
years, did ye at all *f* unto me Zec 7:5
The *f* of the fourth month, and the Zec 8:19
the *f* of the fifth Zec 8:19
the *f* of the seventh Zec 8:19
and the *f* of Zec 8:19
Moreover when ye *f*, be not, as Mt 6:16
they may appear unto men to *f* Mt 6:16
thou appear not unto men to *f* Mt 6:18
Why do we and the Pharisees *f* oft Mt 9:14
*f* oft, but thy disciples *f* not Mt 9:14
from them, and then shall they *f* Mt 9:15
hold him *f* Mt 26:48
and of the Pharisees used to *f* Mk 2:18
of John and of the Pharisees *f* Mk 2:18
but thy disciples *f* not Mk 2:18
children of the bridechamber *f* Mk 2:19
with them, they cannot *f* Mk 2:19
then shall they *f* in those days Mk 2:20
do the disciples of John *f* often Lk 5:33
children of the bridechamber *f* Lk 5:34
then shall they *f* in those days Lk 5:35
I *f* twice in the week, I give Lk 18:12
made their feet *f* in the stocks Acts 16:24
because the *f* was now already Acts 27:9
and the forepart stuck *f*, and Acts 27:41
stand *f* in the faith, quit you 1Cor 16:13
Stand *f* therefore in the liberty Gal 5:1
that ye stand *f* in one spirit Phil 1:27
so stand *f* in the Lord, my dearly Phil 4:1
live, if ye stand *f* in the Lord 1Th 3:8
hold *f* that which is good 1Th 5:21
Therefore, brethren, stand *f* 2Th 2:15
Hold *f* the form of sound words, 2Ti 1:13
Holding *f* the faithful word as he Titus 1:9
if we hold *f* the confidence and Heb 3:6
let us hold *f* our profession Heb 4:14
Let us hold *f* the profession of Heb 10:23
and thou holdest *f* my name Rev 2:13
have already hold *f* till I come Rev 2:25
hast received and heard, and hold *f* Rev 3:3
hold that *f* which thou hast, that Rev 3:11

**FASTED**

*f* that day until even, and offered Judg 20:26
*f* on that day, and said there, We 1Sa 7:6
a tree at Jabesh, and *f* seven days 1Sa 31:13
*f* until even, for Saul, and for 2Sa 1:12
and David *f*, and went in, and lay 2Sa 12:16
the child was yet alive, I *f* 2Sa 12:22
sackcloth upon his flesh, and *f* 1Kin 21:27
oak in Jabesh, and *f* seven days 1Chr 10:12
So we *f* and besought our God for Ezr 8:23
and mourned certain days, and *f* Neh 1:4
Wherefore have we *f*, say they, and Is 58:3
to the priests, saying, When ye *f* Zec 7:5
And when he had *f* forty days Mt 4:2
they ministered to the Lord, and *f* Acts 13:2
And when they had *f* and prayed, and Acts 13:3

**FASTEN**

*f* the wreathen chains to the Ex 28:14
thou shalt *f* in the two ouches Ex 28:25
to *f* it on high upon the mitre Ex 39:31
I will *f* him as a nail in a sure Is 22:23
they *f* it with nails and with Jer 10:4

**FASTENED**

chains they *f* in the two ouches Ex 39:18
*f* his sockets, and set up the Ex 40:18
temples, and *f* it into the ground Judg 4:21
she *f* it with the pin, and said Judg 16:14
they *f* his body to the wall of 1Sa 31:10
*f* upon his loins in the sheath 2Sa 20:8
be *f* in the walls of the house 1Kin 6:6
*f* his head in the temple of Dagon 1Chr 10:10
which were *f* to the throne, and 2Chr 9:18
*f* with cords of fine linen and Est 1:6
are the foundations thereof *f* Job 38:6
as nails *f* by the masters of Eccl 12:11
shall the nail that is *f* in the Is 22:25
he *f* it with nails, that it Is 41:7
an hand broad, *f* round about Eze 40:43
in the synagogue were *f* on him Lk 4:20
the which when I had *f* mine eyes Acts 11:6
out of the heat, and *f* on his hand Acts 28:3

**FASTENING**

*f* his eyes upon him with John, Acts 3:4

**FASTEST**

But thou, when thou *f*, anoint Mt 6:17

**FASTING**

of Israel were assembled with *f* Neh 9:1
mourning among the Jews, and *f* Est 4:3
I humbled my soul with *f* Ps 35:13
wept, and chastened my soul with *f* Ps 69:10
My knees are weak through *f* Ps 109:24
the LORD's house upon the *f* day Jer 36:6
his palace, and passed the night *f* Dan 6:18
prayer and supplications, with *f* Dan 9:3
me with all your heart, and with *f* Joel 2:12
and I will not send them away *f* Mt 15:32
goeth not out but by prayer and *f* Mt 17:21
them away *f* to their own houses Mk 8:3
by nothing, but by prayer and *f* Mk 9:29
days ago I was *f* until this hour Acts 10:30
church, and had prayed with *f* Acts 14:23
ye have tarried and continued *f* Acts 27:33
that ye may give yourselves to *f* 1Cor 7:5

**FASTINGS**

their seed, the matters of the *f* Est 9:31
the temple, but served God with *f* Lk 2:37
in labours, in watchings, in *f* 2Cor 6:5
in *f* often, in cold and nakedness 2Cor 11:27

**FAT**

of his flock and of the *f* thereof Gen 4:4
the seven well favoured and *f* kine Gen 41:4
did eat up the first seven *f* kine Gen 41:20
and ye shall eat the *f* of the land Gen 45:18
Out of Asher his bread shall be *f* Gen 49:20
neither shall the *f* of my Ex 23:18
thou shalt take all the *f* that Ex 29:13
the *f* that is upon them, and burn Ex 29:13
thou shalt take of the ram the *f* Ex 29:22
the *f* that covereth the inwards, Ex 29:22
the *f* that is upon them, and the Ex 29:22
lay the parts, the head, and the *f* Lev 1:8
pieces, with his head and his *f* Lev 1:12
the *f* that covereth the inwards, Lev 3:3
all the *f* that is upon the Lev 3:3
the *f* that is on them, which is Lev 3:4
the *f* thereof, and the whole rump, Lev 3:9
the *f* that covereth the inwards, Lev 3:9
all the *f* that is upon the Lev 3:9
the *f* that is upon them, which is Lev 3:10
the *f* that covereth the inwards, Lev 3:14
all the *f* that is upon the Lev 3:14
the *f* that is upon them, which is Lev 3:15
all the *f* is the LORD's Lev 3:16
that ye eat neither *f* nor blood Lev 3:17
the *f* of the bullock for the sin Lev 4:8
the *f* that covereth the inwards, Lev 4:8
all the *f* that is upon the Lev 4:8
the *f* that is upon them, which is Lev 4:9
he shall take all his *f* from him Lev 4:19
burn all his *f* upon the altar Lev 4:26
as the *f* of the sacrifice of Lev 4:26
shall take away all the *f* thereof Lev 4:31
as the *f* is taken away from off Lev 4:31
shall take away all the *f* thereof Lev 4:35
as the *f* of the lamb is taken Lev 4:35
the *f* of the peace offerings Lev 6:12
offer of it all the *f* thereof Lev 7:3
the *f* that covereth the inwards, Lev 7:3
the *f* that is on them, which is Lev 7:4
Ye shall eat no manner of *f* Lev 7:23
the *f* of the beast that dieth of Lev 7:24
the *f* of that which is torn with Lev 7:24
eateth the *f* of the beast Lev 7:25
the *f* with the breast, it shall Lev 7:30
shall burn the *f* upon the altar Lev 7:31
of the peace offerings, and the *f* Lev 7:33
he took all the *f* that was upon Lev 8:16
and the two kidneys, and their *f* Lev 8:16
the head, and the pieces, and the *f* Lev 8:20
And he took the *f*, and the rump, and Lev 8:25
all the *f* that was upon the Lev 8:25
and the two kidneys, and their *f* Lev 8:25
one wafer, and put them on the *f* Lev 8:26
But the *f*, and the kidneys, and the Lev 9:10
the *f* of the bullock and of the Lev 9:19
they put the *f* upon the breasts, Lev 9:20
he burnt the *f* upon the altar Lev 9:20
altar the burnt offering and the *f* Lev 9:24
offerings made by fire of the *f* Lev 10:15
the *f* of the sin offering shall Lev 16:25
burn the *f* for a sweet savour Lev 17:6
land is, whether it be *f* or lean Num 13:20
shalt burn their *f* for an Num 18:17
and filled themselves, and waxen *f* Deut 31:20
with *f* of lambs, and rams of the Deut 32:14
with the *f* of kidneys of wheat Deut 32:14
But Jeshurun waxed *f*, and kicked Deut 32:15
thou art waxen *f*, thou art grown Deut 32:15
Which did eat the *f* of their Deut 32:38
and Eglon was a very *f* man Judg 3:17
the *f* closed upon the blade, so Judg 3:22
Also before they burnt the *f* 1Sa 2:15
not fail to burn the *f* presently 1Sa 2:16
to make yourselves *f* with the 1Sa 2:29
and to hearken than the *f* of rams 1Sa 15:22

the woman had a *f* calf in the .... 1Sa 28:24
from the *f* of the mighty, the bow .... 2Sa 1:22
*f* cattle by the stone of Zoheleth .... 1Kin 1:9
*f* cattle and sheep in abundance, .... 1Kin 1:19
*f* cattle and sheep in abundance, .... 1Kin 1:25
Ten *f* oxen, and twenty oxen out of .... 1Kin 4:23
the *f* of the peace offerings .... 1Kin 8:64
the *f* of the peace offerings .... 1Kin 8:64
And they found *f* pasture and good, ... 1Chr 4:40
the *f* of the peace offerings, .... 2Chr 7:7
and the meat offerings, and the *f* .... 2Chr 7:7
with the *f* of the peace offerings .... 2Chr 29:35
offerings and the *f* until night .... 2Chr 35:14
unto them, Go your way, eat the *f* .... Neh 8:10
a *f* land, and possessed houses .... Neh 9:25
eat, and were filled, and became *f* .... Neh 9:25
*f* land which thou gavest before .... Neh 9:35
maketh collops of *f* on his flanks .... Job 15:27
They are inclosed in their own *f* .... Ps 17:10
All they that be *f* upon earth .... Ps 22:29
LORD shall be as the *f* of lambs .... Ps 37:20
they shall be *f* and flourishing .... Ps 92:14
Their heart is as *f* as grease .... Ps 119:70
The liberal soul shall be made *f* .... Prov 11:25
of the diligent shall be made *f* .... Prov 13:4
a good report maketh the bones *f* .... Prov 15:30
trust in the LORD shall be made *f* .... Prov 28:25
of rams, and the *f* of fed beasts .... Is 1:11
the waste places of the *f* ones .... Is 5:17
Make the heart of this people *f* .... Is 6:10
send among his *f* ones leanness .... Is 10:16
all people a feast of *f* things .... Is 25:6
of *f* things full of marrow, of .... Is 25:6
of the *f* valleys of them that are .... Is 28:1
is on the head of the *f* valley .... Is 28:4
of the earth, and it shall be *f* .... Is 30:23
it is made *f* with fatness, and .... Is 34:6
with the *f* of the kidneys of rams .... Is 34:6
and their dust made *f* with fatness .... Is 34:7
me with the *f* of thy sacrifices .... Is 43:24
in drought, and make *f* thy bones .... Is 58:11
They are waxen *f*, they shine .... Jer 5:28
because ye are grown *f* as the .... Jer 50:11
Ye eat the *f*, and ye clothe you .... Eze 34:3
in a *f* pasture shall they feed .... Eze 34:14
but I will destroy the *f* and the .... Eze 34:16
will judge between the *f* cattle .... Eze 34:20
ye shall eat *f* till ye be full .... Eze 39:19
when ye offer my bread, the *f* .... Eze 44:7
before me to offer unto me the *f* .... Eze 44:15
out of the *f* pastures of Israel .... Eze 45:15
peace offerings of your *f* beasts .... Amos 5:22
by them their portion is *f* .... Hab 1:16
he shall eat the flesh of the *f* .... Zec 11:16

**FATFLESHED**
seven well favoured kine and *f* .... Gen 41:2
up out of the river seven kine, *f* .... Gen 41:18

**FATHER** See PREFACE.
Therefore shall a man leave his *f* .... Gen 2:24
thou shalt be a *f* of many nations .... Gen 17:4
said, I am God, the God of thy *f* .... Gen 46:3
Honour thy *f* and thy mother .... Ex 20:12
Honour thy *f* and thy mother, as .... Deut 5:16
be my son, and I will be his *f* .... 1Chr 22:10
I was a *f* to the poor .... Job 29:16
A *f* of the fatherless, and a judge .... Ps 68:5
Like as a *f* pitieth his children, .... Ps 103:13
A wise son maketh a glad *f* .... Prov 10:1
A foolish son is a grief to his *f* .... Prov 17:25
son is the calamity of his *f* .... Prov 19:13
The mighty God, The everlasting *F* .... Is 9:6
Have we not all one *f* .... Mal 2:10
glorify your *F* which is in heaven .... Mt 5:16
thy *F* which seeth in secret .... Mt 6:4
for your *F* knoweth what things ye .... Mt 6:8
Our *F* which art in heaven, .... Mt 6:9
will of my *F* which is in heaven .... Mt 7:21
before my *F* which is in heaven .... Mt 10:32
before my *F* which is in heaven .... Mt 10:33
He that loveth *f* or mother more .... Mt 10:37
will of my *F* which is in heaven .... Mt 12:50
commanded, saying, Honour thy *f* .... Mt 15:4
this cause shall a man leave *f* .... Mt 19:5
Honour thy *f* and thy mother .... Mt 19:19
or brethren, or sisters, or *f* .... Mt 19:29
call no man your *f* upon the earth .... Mt 23:9
hand, Come, ye blessed of my *F* .... Mt 25:34
face, and prayed, saying, O my *F* .... Mt 26:39
them in the name of the *F* .... Mt 28:19
For Moses said, Honour thy *f* .... Mk 7:10
cause shall a man leave his *f* .... Mk 10:7
me first to go and bury my *f* .... Lk 9:59
knoweth who the Son is, but the *F* .... Lk 10:22
Our *F* which art in heaven, .... Lk 11:2
I will arise and go to my *f* .... Lk 15:18
bear false witness, Honour thy *f* .... Lk 18:20
Then said Jesus, *F*, forgive them .... Lk 23:34
My *F* worketh hitherto, and I work .... Jn 5:17
Not that any man hath seen the *F* .... Jn 6:46
it were given unto him of my *F* .... Jn 6:65
they unto him, Where is thy *F* .... Jn 8:19
Ye neither know me, nor my *F* .... Jn 8:19
ye should have known my *F* also .... Jn 8:19
that he spake to them of the *F* .... Jn 8:27
but as my *F* hath taught me, I .... Jn 8:28
the *F* hath not left me alone .... Jn 8:29
we have one *F*, even God .... Jn 8:41
As the *F* knoweth me, even so know .... Jn 10:15
I and my *F* are one .... Jn 10:30
and believe, that the *F* is in me .... Jn 10:38
no man cometh unto the *F*, but by .... Jn 14:6
ye should have known my *F* also .... Jn 14:7
unto him, Lord, shew us the *F* .... Jn 14:8
am in the *F*, and the *F* in me .... Jn 14:10
ye shall know that I am in my *F* .... Jn 14:20
vine, and my *F* is the husbandman .... Jn 15:1
up his eyes to heaven, and said, *F* .... Jn 17:1
Holy *F*, keep through thine own .... Jn 17:11
as my *F* hath sent me, even so .... Jn 20:21
made thee a *f* of many nations .... Rom 4:17
adoption, whereby we cry, Abba, *F* .... Rom 8:15
to us there is but one God, the *F* .... 1Cor 8:6
*F* of our Lord Jesus Christ, which .... 2Cor 11:31
*F* of all, who is above all, and .... Eph 4:6
Lord, to the glory of God the *F* .... Phil 2:11
And again, I will be to him a *F* .... Heb 1:5
cometh down from the *F* of lights .... Jas 1:17
love the *F* hath bestowed upon us .... 1Jn 3:1
that bear record in heaven, the *F* .... 1Jn 5:7
set down with my *F* in his throne .... Rev 3:21

**FATHERLESS**
not afflict any widow, or *f* child .... Ex 22:22
be widows, and your children *f* .... Ex 22:24
execute the judgment of the *f* .... Deut 10:18
thee,) and the stranger, and the *f* .... Deut 14:29
gates, and the stranger, and the *f* .... Deut 16:11
Levite, the stranger, and the *f* .... Deut 16:14
of the stranger, nor of the *f* .... Deut 24:17
be for the stranger, for the *f* .... Deut 24:19
be for the stranger, for the *f* .... Deut 24:20
be for the stranger, for the *f* .... Deut 24:21
the Levite, the stranger, the *f* .... Deut 26:12
and unto the stranger, to the *f* .... Deut 26:13
the judgment of the stranger, *f* .... Deut 27:19
Yea, ye overwhelm the *f*, and ye .... Job 6:27
the arms of the *f* have been .... Job 22:9
They drive away the ass of the *f* .... Job 24:3
They pluck the *f* from the breast, .... Job 24:9
the poor that cried, and the *f* .... Job 29:12
the *f* hath not eaten thereof .... Job 31:17
lifted up my hand against the *f* .... Job 31:21
thou art the helper of the *f* .... Ps 10:14
To judge the *f* and the oppressed, .... Ps 10:18
A father of the *f*, and a judge of .... Ps 68:5
Defend the poor and *f* .... Ps 82:3
and the stranger, and murder the *f* .... Ps 94:6
Let his children be *f*, and his .... Ps 109:9
be any to favour his *f* children .... Ps 109:12
he relieveth the *f* and widow .... Ps 146:9
not into the fields of the *f* .... Prov 23:10
the oppressed, judge the *f* .... Is 1:17
they judge not the *f*, neither .... Is 1:23
shall have mercy on their *f* .... Is 9:17
prey, and that they may rob the *f* .... Is 10:2
not the cause, the cause of the *f* .... Jer 5:28
oppress not the stranger, the *f* .... Jer 7:6
violence to the stranger, the *f* .... Jer 22:3
Leave thy *f* children, I will .... Jer 49:11
We are orphans and *f*, our mothers .... Lam 5:3
in thee have they vexed the *f* .... Eze 22:7
for in thee the *f* findeth mercy .... Hos 14:3
oppress not the widow, nor the *f* .... Zec 7:10
in his wages, the widow, and the *f* .... Mal 3:5
Father is this, To visit the *f* .... Jas 1:27

**FATHER'S**
and they saw not their *f* nakedness .... Gen 9:23
thy kindred, and from thy *f* house .... Gen 12:1
me to wander from my *f* house .... Gen 20:13
which took me from my *f* house .... Gen 24:7
is there room in thy *f* house for .... Gen 24:23
But thou shalt go unto my *f* house .... Gen 24:38
of my kindred, and of my *f* house .... Gen 24:40
For all the wells which his *f* .... Gen 26:15
come again to my *f* house in peace .... Gen 28:21
Rachel came with her *f* sheep .... Gen 29:9
Rachel that he was her *f* brother .... Gen 29:12
taken away all that was our *f* .... Gen 31:1
of that which was our *f* hath he .... Gen 31:1
I see your *f* countenance, that it .... Gen 31:5
inheritance for us in our *f* house .... Gen 31:14
stolen the images that were her *f* .... Gen 31:19
sore longedst after thy *f* house .... Gen 31:30
lay with Bilhah his *f* concubine .... Gen 35:22
the sons of Zilpah, his *f* wives .... Gen 37:2
to feed their *f* flock in Shechem .... Gen 37:12
Remain a widow at thy *f* house .... Gen 38:11
went and dwelt in her *f* house .... Gen 38:11
all my toil, and all my *f* house .... Gen 41:51
his brethren, and unto his *f* house .... Gen 46:31
my *f* house, which were in the .... Gen 46:31
all his *f* household, with bread, .... Gen 47:12
and he held up his *f* hand, to .... Gen 48:17
thou wentest up to thy *f* bed .... Gen 49:4
thy *f* children shall bow down .... Gen 49:8
And Joseph fell upon his *f* face .... Gen 50:1
and his brethren, and his *f* house .... Gen 50:8
in Egypt, he, and his *f* house .... Gen 50:22
troughs to water their *f* flock .... Ex 2:16
him Jochebed his *f* sister to wife .... Ex 6:20
my *f* God, and I will exalt him .... Ex 15:2
priest's office in his *f* stead .... Lev 16:32
The nakedness of thy *f* wife shalt .... Lev 18:8
it is thy *f* nakedness .... Lev 18:8
of thy *f* wife's daughter, .... Lev 18:11
the nakedness of thy *f* sister .... Lev 18:12
she is thy *f* near kinswoman .... Lev 18:12
the nakedness of thy *f* brother .... Lev 18:14
his *f* wife hath uncovered his .... Lev 20:11
hath uncovered his *f* nakedness .... Lev 20:11
his *f* daughter, or his mother's .... Lev 20:17
sister, nor of thy *f* sister .... Lev 20:19
and is returned unto her *f* house .... Lev 22:13
she shall eat of her *f* meat .... Lev 22:13
with the ensign of their *f* house .... Num 2:2
thy *f* house with thee shall bear .... Num 18:1
among their *f* brethren .... Num 27:7
inheritance unto his *f* brethren .... Num 27:10
being in her *f* house in her youth .... Num 30:3
yet in her youth in her *f* house .... Num 30:16
unto their *f* brothers' sons .... Num 36:11
damsel to the door of her *f* house .... Deut 22:21
to play the whore in her *f* house .... Deut 22:21
A man shall not take his *f* wife .... Deut 22:30
nor discover his *f* skirt .... Deut 22:30
be he that lieth with his *f* wife .... Deut 27:20
because he uncovereth his *f* skirt .... Deut 27:20
shew kindness unto my *f* house .... Josh 2:12
all thy *f* household, home unto .... Josh 2:18
her *f* household, and all that she .... Josh 6:25
and I am the least in my *f* house .... Judg 6:15
Take thy *f* young bullock, even .... Judg 6:25
because he feared his *f* household .... Judg 6:27
went unto his *f* house at Ophrah .... Judg 9:5
up against my *f* house this day .... Judg 9:18
shalt not inherit in our *f* house .... Judg 11:2
me, and expel me out of my *f* house .... Judg 11:7
thee and thy *f* house with fire .... Judg 14:15
and he went up to his *f* house .... Judg 14:19
her *f* house to Beth-lehem-judah .... Judg 19:2
she brought him into her *f* house .... Judg 19:3
arm, and the arm of thy *f* house .... 1Sa 2:31
on thee, and on all thy *f* house .... 1Sa 9:20
to feed his *f* sheep at Beth-lehem .... 1Sa 17:15
make his *f* house free in Israel .... 1Sa 17:25
Thy servant kept his *f* sheep .... 1Sa 17:34
go no more home to his *f* house .... 1Sa 18:2
or my *f* family in Israel, that I .... 1Sa 18:18
all his *f* house heard it, they .... 1Sa 22:1
son of Ahitub, and all his *f* house .... 1Sa 22:11
thou, and all thy *f* house .... 1Sa 22:16
of all the persons of thy *f* house .... 1Sa 22:22
destroy my name out of my *f* house .... 1Sa 24:21
thou gone in unto my *f* concubine .... 2Sa 3:7
of Joab, and on all his *f* house .... 2Sa 3:29
kindness for Jonathan thy *f* sake .... 2Sa 9:7
be on me, and on my *f* house .... 2Sa 14:9
have been thy *f* servant hitherto .... 2Sa 15:34
I have served in thy *f* presence .... 2Sa 16:19
Go in unto thy *f* concubines .... 2Sa 16:21
Absalom went in unto his *f* .... 2Sa 16:22
For all of my *f* house were but .... 2Sa 19:28
against me, and against my *f* house .... 2Sa 24:17
not do it for David thy *f* sake .... 1Kin 11:12
of his *f* servants with him .... 1Kin 11:17
shall be thicker than my *f* loins .... 1Kin 12:10
thy *f* house, in that ye have .... 1Kin 18:18
sons, and set him on his *f* throne .... 2Kin 10:3
and made him king in his *f* stead .... 2Kin 23:30
his *f* brother king in his stead .... 2Kin 24:17
forasmuch as he defiled his *f* bed .... 1Chr 5:1
Shemuel, heads of their *f* house .... 1Chr 7:2
of Asher, heads of their *f* house .... 1Chr 7:40
of his *f* house twenty and two .... 1Chr 12:28
God, be on me, and on my *f* house .... 1Chr 21:17
according to their *f* house .... 1Chr 23:11
with understanding, of Huram my *f* .... 2Chr 2:13
shall be thicker than my *f* loins .... 2Chr 10:10
slain thy brethren of thy *f* house .... 2Chr 21:13
king in his *f* stead in Jerusalem .... 2Chr 36:1
they could not shew their *f* house .... Ezr 2:59
both I and my *f* house have sinned .... Neh 1:6
they could not shew their *f* house .... Neh 7:61
thy *f* house shall be destroyed .... Est 4:14
thine own people, and thy *f* house .... Ps 45:10
For I was my *f* son, tender and .... Prov 4:3
keep thy *f* commandment, and .... Prov 6:20
son heareth his *f* instruction .... Prov 13:1
fool despiseth his *f* instruction .... Prov 15:5
thy *f* friend, forsake not .... Prov 27:10
thy people, and upon thy *f* house .... Is 7:17
a glorious throne to his *f* house .... Is 22:23
him all the glory of his *f* house .... Is 22:24
but obey their *f* commandment .... Jer 35:14
that seeth all his *f* sins which .... Eze 18:14
his sister, his *f* daughter .... Eze 22:11
it new with you in my *F* kingdom .... Mt 26:29
I must be about my *F* business .... Lk 2:49
in his own glory, and in his *F* .... Lk 9:26
for it is your *F* good pleasure to .... Lk 12:32
of my *f* have bread enough .... Lk 15:17
wouldest send him to my *f* house .... Lk 16:27
make not my *F* house an house of .... Jn 2:16
I am come in my *F* name, and ye .... Jn 5:43
this is the *F* will which hath .... Jn 6:39
the works that I do in my *F* name .... Jn 10:25
to pluck them out of my *F* hand .... Jn 10:29
In my *F* house are many mansions .... Jn 14:2
not mine, but the *F* which sent me .... Jn 14:24
as I have kept my *F* commandments .... Jn 15:10
up in his *f* house three months .... Acts 7:20
that one should have his *f* wife .... 1Cor 5:1
having his *F* name written in .... Rev 14:1

**FATHERS** See PREFACE.

**FATHERS'**
be the heads of their *f* houses .... Ex 6:14
nor thy *f* fathers have seen, .... Ex 10:6
one, according to their *f* houses .... Num 17:6

upward, throughout their *f* house .... Num 26:2
ye are risen up in your *f* stead .... Num 32:14
the place of my *f* sepulchres .... Neh 2:3
unto the city of my *f* sepulchres .... Neh 2:5
eyes were after their *f* idols .... Eze 20:24
they discovered their *f* nakedness .... Eze 22:10
have not done, nor his *f* fathers .... Dan 11:24
they are beloved for the *f* sakes .... Rom 11:28

**FATHOMS**
And sounded, and found it twenty *f* .. Acts 27:28
again, and found it fifteen *f* .... Acts 27:28

**FATLING**
the young lion and the *f* together .... Is 11:6

**FATLINGS**
and of the oxen, and of the *f* .... 1Sa 15:9
paces, he sacrificed oxen and *f* .... 2Sa 6:13
unto thee burnt sacrifices of *f* .... Ps 66:15
bullocks, all of them *f* of Bashan .... Eze 39:18
my *f* are killed, and all things .... Mt 22:4

**FATNESS**
the *f* of the earth, and plenty of .... Gen 27:28
shall be the *f* of the earth .... Gen 27:39
thick, thou art covered with *f* .... Deut 32:15
unto them, Should I leave my *f* .... Judg 9:9
he covereth his face with his *f* .... Job 15:27
on thy table should be full of *f* .... Job 36:16
satisfied with the *f* of thy house .... Ps 36:8
be satisfied as with marrow and *f* .... Ps 63:5
and thy paths drop *f* .... Ps 65:11
Their eyes stand out with *f* .... Ps 73:7
and my flesh faileth of *f* .... Ps 109:24
the *f* of his flesh shall wax lean .... Is 17:4
with blood, it is made fat with *f* .... Is 34:6
and their dust made fat with *f* .... Is 34:7
let your soul delight itself in *f* .... Is 55:2
the soul of the priests with *f* .... Jer 31:14
the root and *f* of the olive tree .... Rom 11:17

**FATS**
the *f* shall overflow with wine and .... Joel 2:24
the press is full, the *f* overflow .... Joel 3:13

**FATTED**
and fallowdeer, and *f* fowl .... 1Kin 4:23
the midst of her like *f* bullocks .... Jer 46:21
And bring hither the *f* calf .... Lk 15:23
thy father hath killed the *f* calf .... Lk 15:27
hast killed for him the *f* calf .... Lk 15:30

**FATTER**
*f* in flesh than all the children .... Dan 1:15

**FATTEST**
upon them, and slew the *f* of them .... Ps 78:31
upon the *f* places of the province .... Dan 11:24

**FAULT**
but the *f* is in thine own people .... Ex 5:16
his face, according to his *f* .... Deut 25:2
I have found no *f* in him since he .... 1Sa 29:3
with a *f* concerning this woman .... 2Sa 3:8
prepare themselves without my *f* .... Ps 59:4
could find none occasion nor *f* .... Dan 6:4
there any error or *f* found in him .... Dan 6:4
go and tell him his *f* between thee .... Mt 18:15
unwashen, hands, they found *f* .... Mk 7:2
people, I find no *f* in this man .... Lk 23:4
have found no *f* in this man .... Lk 23:14
them, I find in him no *f* at all .... Jn 18:38
may know that I find no *f* in him .... Jn 19:4
for I find no *f* in him .... Jn 19:6
unto me, Why doth he yet find *f* .... Rom 9:19
there is utterly a *f* among you .... 1Cor 6:7
if a man be overtaken in a *f* .... Gal 6:1
For finding *f* with them, he saith .... Heb 8:8
for they are without *f* before the .... Rev 14:5

**FAULTLESS**
if that first covenant had been *f* .... Heb 8:7
to present you *f* before the .... Jude 24

**FAULTS**
I do remember my *f* this day .... Gen 41:9
cleanse thou me from secret *f* .... Ps 19:12
Confess your *f* one to another, and .... Jas 5:16
when ye be buffeted for your *f* .... 1Pet 2:20

**FAULTY**
this thing as one which is *f* .... 2Sa 14:13
now shall they be found *f* .... Hos 10:2

**FAVOUR**
now I have found *f* in thy sight .... Gen 18:3
if I have found *f* in thine eyes .... Gen 30:27
gave him *f* in the sight of the .... Gen 39:21
I will give this people *f* in the .... Ex 3:21
the LORD gave the people *f* in the .... Ex 11:3
the LORD gave the people *f* in the .... Ex 12:36
have I not found *f* in thy sight .... Num 11:11
if I have found *f* in thy sight .... Num 11:15
that she find no *f* in his eyes .... Deut 24:1
the old, nor shew *f* to the young .... Deut 28:50
O Naphtali, satisfied with *f* .... Deut 33:23
and that they might have no *f* .... Josh 11:20
Let me find *f* in thy sight, my .... Ruth 2:13
was in *f* both with the LORD, and .... 1Sa 2:26
for he hath found *f* in my sight .... 1Sa 16:22
if I have found *f* in thine eyes .... 1Sa 20:29
young men find *f* in thine eyes .... 1Sa 25:8
nevertheless the lords *f* thee not .... 1Sa 29:6
if I shall find *f* in the eyes of .... 2Sa 15:25
Hadad found great *f* in the sight .... 1Kin 11:19
servant have found *f* in thy sight .... Neh 2:5
Esther obtained *f* in the sight of .... Est 2:15
*f* in his sight more than all the .... Est 2:17
that she obtained *f* in his sight .... Est 5:2
If I have found *f* in the sight of .... Est 5:8
If I have found *f* in thy sight .... Est 7:3
and if I have found *f* in his sight .... Est 8:5
Thou hast granted me life and *f* .... Job 10:12
with *f* wilt thou compass him as .... Ps 5:12
in his *f* is life .... Ps 30:5
by thy *f* thou hast made my .... Ps 30:7
that *f* my righteous cause .... Ps 35:27
because thou hadst a *f* unto them .... Ps 44:3
the people shall intreat thy *f* .... Ps 45:12
in thy *f* our horn shall be .... Ps 89:17
for the time to *f* her, yea, the .... Ps 102:13
her stones, and *f* the dust thereof .... Ps 102:14
with the *f* that thou bearest unto .... Ps 106:4
any to *f* his fatherless children .... Ps 109:12
A good man sheweth *f*, and lendeth .... Ps 112:5
I intreated thy *f* with my whole .... Ps 119:58
So shalt thou find *f* and good .... Prov 3:4
and shall obtain *f* of the LORD .... Prov 8:35
seeketh good procureth *f* .... Prov 11:27
good man obtaineth *f* of the LORD .... Prov 12:2
Good understanding giveth *f* .... Prov 13:15
among the righteous there is *f* .... Prov 14:9
The king's *f* is toward a wise .... Prov 14:35
his *f* is as a cloud of the latter .... Prov 16:15
thing, and obtaineth *f* of the LORD .... Prov 18:22
will intreat the *f* of the prince .... Prov 19:6
but his *f* is as dew upon the .... Prov 19:12
findeth no *f* in his eyes .... Prov 21:10
loving *f* rather than silver and .... Prov 22:1
*f* than he that flattereth with .... Prov 28:23
Many seek the ruler's *f* .... Prov 29:26
*F* is deceitful, and beauty is vain .... Prov 31:30
nor yet *f* to men of skill .... Eccl 9:11
I in his eyes as one that found *f* .... Song 8:10
Let *f* be shewed to the wicked .... Is 26:10
formed them will shew them no *f* .... Is 27:11
but in my *f* have I had mercy on .... Is 60:10
where I will not shew you *f* .... Jer 16:13
Now God had brought Daniel into *f* .... Dan 1:9
for thou hast found *f* with God .... Lk 1:30
stature, and in *f* with God and man .... Lk 2:52
having *f* with all the people .... Acts 2:47
his afflictions, and gave him *f* .... Acts 7:10
Who found *f* before God, and .... Acts 7:46
desired *f* against him, that he .... Acts 25:3

**FAVOURABLE**
Be *f* unto them for our sakes .... Judg 21:22
God, and he will be *f* unto him .... Job 33:26
and will he be *f* no more .... Ps 77:7
thou hast been *f* unto thy land .... Ps 85:1

**FAVOURED**
Rachel was beautiful and well *f* .... Gen 29:17
was a goodly person, and well *f* .... Gen 39:6
of the river seven well *f* kine .... Gen 41:2
them out of the river, ill *f* .... Gen 41:3
And the ill *f* and leanfleshed kine .... Gen 41:4
kine did eat up the seven well *f* .... Gen 41:4
seven kine, fatfleshed and well *f* .... Gen 41:18
up after them, poor and very ill *f* .... Gen 41:19
the ill *f* kine did eat up the .... Gen 41:20
but they were still ill *f* .... Gen 41:21
ill *f* kine that came up after .... Gen 41:27
priests, they *f* not the elders .... Lam 4:16
whom was no blemish, but well *f* .... Dan 1:4
Hail, thou that art highly *f* .... Lk 1:28

**FAVOUREST**
By this I know that thou *f* me .... Ps 41:11

**FAVOURETH**
by him, and said, He that *f* Joab .... 2Sa 20:11

**FEAR**
the *f* of you and the dread of you .... Gen 9:2
in a vision, saying, *F* not, Abram .... Gen 15:1
Surely the *f* of God is not in .... Gen 20:11
*f* not; for God hath heard .... Gen 21:17
*f* not, for I am with thee, and .... Gen 26:24
the *f* of Isaac, had been with me .... Gen 31:42
Jacob sware by the *f* of his .... Gen 31:53
for I *f* him, lest he will come and .... Gen 32:11
the midwife said unto her, *F* not .... Gen 35:17
for I *f* God .... Gen 42:18
he said, Peace be to you, *f* not .... Gen 43:23
*f* not to go down into Egypt .... Gen 46:3
And Joseph said unto them, *F* not .... Gen 50:19
Now therefore *f* ye not .... Gen 50:21
ye will not yet *f* the LORD God .... Ex 9:30
*F* ye not, stand still, and see the .... Ex 14:13
*F* and dread shall fall upon them .... Ex 15:16
people able men, such as *f* God .... Ex 18:21
Moses said unto the people, *F* not .... Ex 20:20
that his *f* may be before your .... Ex 20:20
I will send my *f* before thee .... Ex 23:27
Ye shall *f* every man his mother .... Lev 19:3
the blind, but shalt *f* thy God .... Lev 19:14
face of the old man, and *f* thy God .... Lev 19:32
but thou shalt *f* thy God .... Lev 25:17
but *f* thy God .... Lev 25:36
but shalt *f* thy God .... Lev 25:43
neither *f* ye the people of the .... Num 14:9
LORD is with us: *f* them not .... Num 14:9
LORD said unto Moses, *F* him not .... Num 21:34
*f* not, neither be discouraged .... Deut 1:21
the *f* of thee upon the nations .... Deut 2:25
the LORD said unto me, *F* him not .... Deut 3:2
Ye shall not *f* them .... Deut 3:22
that they may learn to *f* me all .... Deut 4:10
in them, that they would *f* me .... Deut 5:29
thou mightest *f* the LORD thy God .... Deut 6:2
Thou shalt *f* the LORD thy God, and .... Deut 6:13
to *f* the LORD our God, for our .... Deut 6:24
to walk in his ways, and to *f* him .... Deut 8:6
but to *f* the LORD thy God, to .... Deut 10:12
Thou shalt *f* the LORD thy God .... Deut 10:20
your God shall lay the *f* of you .... Deut 11:25
*f* him, and keep his commandments .... Deut 13:4
And all Israel shall hear, and *f* .... Deut 13:11
to *f* the LORD thy God always .... Deut 14:23
all the people shall hear, and *f* .... Deut 17:13
may learn to *f* the LORD his God .... Deut 17:19
which remain shall hear, and *f* .... Deut 19:20
*f* not, and do not tremble, neither .... Deut 20:3
and all Israel shall hear, and *f* .... Deut 21:21
that thou mayest *f* this glorious .... Deut 28:58
and thou shalt *f* day and night, and .. Deut 28:66
for the *f* of thine heart .... Deut 28:67
heart wherewith thou shalt *f* .... Deut 28:67
*f* not, nor be afraid of them .... Deut 31:6
*f* not, neither be dismayed .... Deut 31:8
*f* the LORD your God, and observe .... Deut 31:12
learn to *f* the LORD your God, as .... Deut 31:13
that ye might *f* the LORD your God .... Josh 4:24
*F* not, neither be thou dismayed .... Josh 8:1
LORD said unto Joshua, *F* them not .... Josh 10:8
*F* not, nor be dismayed, be strong .... Josh 10:25
done it for *f* of this thing .... Josh 22:24
Now therefore *f* the LORD, and .... Josh 24:14
turn in to me; *f* not .... Judg 4:18
*f* not the gods of the Amorites .... Judg 6:10
*f* not: thou shalt not die .... Judg 6:23
But if thou *f* to go down, go thou .... Judg 7:10
for *f* of Abimelech his brother .... Judg 9:21
And now, my daughter, *f* not .... Ruth 3:11
stood by her said unto her, *F* not .... 1Sa 4:20
the *f* of the LORD fell on the .... 1Sa 11:7
If ye will *f* the LORD, and serve .... 1Sa 12:14
said unto the people, *F* not .... 1Sa 12:20
Only *f* the LORD, and serve him in .... 1Sa 12:24
and fled that day for *f* of Saul .... 1Sa 21:10
Abide thou with me, *f* not .... 1Sa 22:23
And he said unto him, *F* not .... 1Sa 23:17
haste to get away for *f* of Saul .... 1Sa 23:26
And David said unto him, *F* not .... 2Sa 9:7
then kill him, *f* not .... 2Sa 13:28
be just, ruling in the *f* of God .... 2Sa 23:3
That they may *f* thee all the days .... 1Kin 8:40
to *f* thee, as do thy people .... 1Kin 8:43
And Elijah said unto her, *F* not .... 1Kin 17:13
but I thy servant *f* the LORD from .... 1Kin 18:12
that thy servant did *f* the LORD .... 2Kin 4:1
And he answered, *F* not .... 2Kin 6:16
them how they should *f* the LORD .... 2Kin 17:28
they *f* not the LORD, neither do .... 2Kin 17:34
saying, Ye shall not *f* other gods .... 2Kin 17:35
stretched out arm, him shall ye *f* .... 2Kin 17:36
and ye shall not *f* other gods .... 2Kin 17:37
neither shall ye *f* other gods .... 2Kin 17:38
But the LORD your God ye shall *f* .... 2Kin 17:39
*F* not to be the servants of the .... 2Kin 25:24
the LORD brought the *f* of him .... 1Chr 14:17
*F* before him, all the earth .... 1Chr 16:30
*f* not, nor be dismayed .... 1Chr 28:20
That they may *f* thee, to walk in .... 2Chr 6:31
*f* thee, as doth thy people Israel .... 2Chr 6:33
for the *f* of the LORD came upon .... 2Chr 14:14
the *f* of the LORD fell upon all .... 2Chr 17:10
Wherefore now let the *f* of the .... 2Chr 19:7
shall ye do in the *f* of the LORD .... 2Chr 19:9
*f* not, nor be dismayed .... 2Chr 20:17
the *f* of God was on all the .... 2Chr 20:29
for *f* was upon them because of .... Ezr 3:3
who desire to *f* thy name .... Neh 1:11
the *f* of our God because of the .... Neh 5:9
not I, because of the *f* of God .... Neh 5:15
that would have put me in *f* .... Neh 6:14
sent letters to put me in *f* .... Neh 6:19
for the *f* of the Jews fell upon .... Est 8:17
for the *f* of them fell upon all .... Est 9:2
because the *f* of Mordecai fell .... Est 9:3
Doth Job *f* God for nought .... Job 1:9
Is not this thy *f*, thy confidence .... Job 4:6
*F* came upon me, and trembling .... Job 4:14
forsaketh the *f* of the Almighty .... Job 6:14
me, and let not his *f* terrify me .... Job 9:34
Then would I speak, and not *f* him .... Job 9:35
shalt be stedfast, and shalt not *f* .... Job 11:15
Yea, thou castest off *f*, and .... Job 15:4
Their houses are safe from *f* .... Job 21:9
he reprove thee for *f* of thee .... Job 22:4
thee, and sudden *f* troubleth thee .... Job 22:10
Dominion and *f* are with him .... Job 25:2
the *f* of the LORD, that is wisdom .... Job 28:28
Did I *f* a great multitude, or did .... Job 31:34
Men do therefore *f* him .... Job 37:24
her labour is in vain without *f* .... Job 39:16
He mocketh at *f*, and is not .... Job 39:22
his like, who is made without *f* .... Job 41:33
Serve the LORD with *f*, and rejoice .... Ps 2:11
in thy *f* will I worship toward .... Ps 5:7
Put them in *f*, O LORD .... Ps 9:20
There were they in great *f* .... Ps 14:5
he honoureth them that *f* the LORD .... Ps 15:4
The *f* of the LORD is clean .... Ps 19:9
Ye that *f* the LORD, praise him .... Ps 22:23
*f* him, all ye the seed of Israel .... Ps 22:23

my vows before them that *f* him ... Ps 22:25
shadow of death, I will *f* no evil ... Ps 23:4
the LORD is with them that *f* him ... Ps 25:14
whom shall I *f*? ... Ps 27:1
against me, my heart shall not *f* ... Ps 27:3
and a *f* to mine acquaintance ... Ps 31:11
*f* was on every side ... Ps 31:13
hast laid up for them that *f* thee ... Ps 31:19
Let all the earth *f* the LORD ... Ps 33:8
the LORD is upon them that *f* him ... Ps 33:18
round about them that *f* him ... Ps 34:7
O *f* the LORD, ye his saints ... Ps 34:9
is no want to them that *f* him ... Ps 34:9
will teach you the *f* of the LORD ... Ps 34:11
that there is no *f* of God before ... Ps 36:1
many shall see it, and *f*, and shall ... Ps 40:3
Therefore will not we *f*, though ... Ps 46:2
*F* took hold upon them there, and ... Ps 48:6
Wherefore should I *f* in the days ... Ps 49:5
righteous also shall see, and *f* ... Ps 52:6
There were they in great *f* ... Ps 53:5
in great *f*, where no *f* was ... Ps 53:5
changes, therefore they *f* not God ... Ps 55:19
I will not *f* what flesh can do ... Ps 56:4
a banner to them that *f* thee ... Ps 60:4
heritage of those that *f* thy name ... Ps 61:5
my life from *f* of the enemy ... Ps 64:1
do they shoot at him, and *f* not ... Ps 64:4
And all men shall *f*, and shall ... Ps 64:9
Come and hear, all ye that *f* God ... Ps 66:16
the ends of the earth shall *f* him ... Ps 67:7
They shall *f* thee as long as the ... Ps 72:5
salvation is nigh them that *f* him ... Ps 85:9
unite my heart to *f* thy name ... Ps 86:11
even according to thy *f*, so is ... Ps 90:11
*f* before him, all the earth ... Ps 96:9
shall *f* the name of the LORD ... Ps 102:15
his mercy toward them that *f* him ... Ps 103:11
the LORD pitieth them that *f* him ... Ps 103:13
everlasting upon them that *f* him ... Ps 103:17
for the *f* of them fell upon them ... Ps 105:38
given meat unto them that *f* him ... Ps 111:5
The *f* of the LORD is the ... Ps 111:10
Ye that *f* the LORD, trust in the ... Ps 115:11
will bless them that *f* the LORD ... Ps 115:13
Let them now that *f* the LORD say ... Ps 118:4
I will not *f* ... Ps 118:6
servant, who is devoted to thy *f* ... Ps 119:38
Turn away my reproach which I *f* ... Ps 119:39
companion of all them that *f* thee ... Ps 119:63
They that *f* thee will be glad ... Ps 119:74
Let those that *f* thee turn unto ... Ps 119:79
My flesh trembleth for *f* of thee ... Ps 119:120
ye that *f* the LORD, bless the ... Ps 135:20
the desire of them that *f* him ... Ps 145:19
pleasure in them that *f* him ... Ps 147:11
The *f* of the LORD is the ... Prov 1:7
I will mock when your *f* cometh ... Prov 1:26
When your *f* cometh as desolation, ... Prov 1:27
did not choose the *f* of the LORD ... Prov 1:29
and shall be quiet from *f* of evil ... Prov 1:33
thou understand the *f* of the LORD ... Prov 2:5
*f* the LORD, and depart from evil ... Prov 3:7
Be not afraid of sudden *f* ... Prov 3:25
The *f* of the LORD is to hate evil ... Prov 8:13
The *f* of the LORD is the ... Prov 9:10
The *f* of the wicked, it shall ... Prov 10:24
The *f* of the LORD prolongeth days ... Prov 10:27
In the *f* of the LORD is strong ... Prov 14:26
The *f* of the LORD is a fountain ... Prov 14:27
Better is little with the *f* of ... Prov 15:16
The *f* of the LORD is the ... Prov 15:33
by the *f* of the LORD men depart ... Prov 16:6
The *f* of the LORD tendeth to life ... Prov 19:23
The *f* of a king is as the roaring ... Prov 20:2
the *f* of the LORD are riches, and ... Prov 22:4
but be thou in the *f* of the LORD ... Prov 23:17
*f* thou the LORD and the king ... Prov 24:21
The *f* of man bringeth a snare ... Prov 29:25
it, that men should *f* before him ... Eccl 3:14
but *f* thou God ... Eccl 5:7
be well with them that *f* God ... Eccl 8:12
that *f* God, which *f* before him ... Eccl 8:12
*F* God, and keep his commandments ... Eccl 12:13
thigh because of *f* in the night ... Song 3:8
for *f* of the LORD, and for the ... Is 2:10
for *f* of the LORD, and for the ... Is 2:19
for *f* of the LORD, and for the ... Is 2:21
*f* not, neither be fainthearted ... Is 7:4
not come thither the *f* of briers ... Is 7:25
neither *f* ye their *f*, nor be ... Is 8:12
neither *f* ye their *f*, nor be ... Is 8:12
and let him be your *f*, and let him ... Is 8:13
knowledge and of the *f* of the LORD ... Is 11:2
in the *f* of the LORD ... Is 11:3
from thy sorrow, and from thy *f* ... Is 14:3
*f* because of the shaking of the ... Is 19:16
hath he turned into *f* unto me ... Is 21:4
*F*, and the pit, and the snare, are ... Is 24:17
of the *f* shall fall into the pit ... Is 24:18
the terrible nations shall *f* thee ... Is 25:3
their *f* toward me is taught by ... Is 29:13
shall *f* the God of Israel ... Is 29:23
over to his strong hold for *f* ... Is 31:9
the *f* of the LORD is his treasure ... Is 33:6
a fearful heart, Be strong, *f* not ... Is 35:4
*F* thou not; for I am ... Is 41:10
hand, saying unto thee, *F* not ... Is 41:13
*F* not, thou worm Jacob, and ye men ... Is 41:14
that formed thee, O Israel, *F* not ... Is 43:1
*F* not: for I am with thee ... Is 43:5
*F* not, O Jacob, my servant ... Is 44:2
*F* ye not, neither be afraid ... Is 44:8
yet they shall *f*, and they shall ... Is 44:11
*f* ye not the reproach of men, ... Is 51:7
*F* not; for thou shalt not be ashamed ... Is 54:4
for thou shalt not *f* ... Is 54:14
So shall they *f* the name of the ... Is 59:19
together, and thine heart shall *f* ... Is 60:5
and hardened our heart from thy *f* ... Is 63:17
that my *f* is not in thee, saith ... Jer 2:19
*F* ye not me? saith the LORD ... Jer 5:22
Let us now *f* the LORD our God, ... Jer 5:24
the enemy and *f* is on every side ... Jer 6:25
Who would not *f* thee, O King of ... Jer 10:7
defaming of many, *f* on every side ... Jer 20:10
and they shall *f* no more, nor be ... Jer 23:4
did he not *f* the LORD, and ... Jer 26:19
heard a voice of trembling, of *f* ... Jer 30:5
Therefore *f* thou not, O my ... Jer 30:10
way, that they may *f* me for ever ... Jer 32:39
I will put my *f* in their hearts ... Jer 32:40
and they shall *f* and tremble for ... Jer 33:9
let us go to Jerusalem for *f* of ... Jer 35:11
for *f* of the army of the Syrians ... Jer 35:11
Jerusalem for *f* of Pharaoh's army ... Jer 37:11
*F* not to serve the Chaldeans ... Jer 40:9
for *f* of Baasha king of Israel ... Jer 41:9
for *f* was round about, saith the ... Jer 46:5
But *f* not thou, O my servant ... Jer 46:27
*F* thou not, O Jacob my servant, ... Jer 46:28
*F*, and the pit, and the snare, ... Jer 48:43
the *f* shall fall into the pit ... Jer 48:44
I will bring a *f* upon thee ... Jer 49:5
to flee, and *f* hath seized on her ... Jer 49:24
cry unto them, *F* is on every side ... Jer 49:29
for *f* of the oppressing sword ... Jer 50:16
ye *f* for the rumour that shall be ... Jer 51:46
*F* and a snare is come upon us, ... Lam 3:47
thou saidst, *F* not ... Lam 3:57
*f* them not, neither be dismayed ... Eze 3:9
I will put a *f* in the land of ... Eze 30:13
I *f* my lord the king, who hath ... Dan 1:10
*f* before the God of Daniel ... Dan 6:26
said he unto me, *F* not, Daniel ... Dan 10:12
O man greatly beloved, *f* not ... Dan 10:19
shall *f* the LORD and his goodness ... Hos 3:5
shall *f* because of the calves of ... Hos 10:5
*F* not, O land ... Joel 2:21
lion hath roared, who will not *f* ... Amos 3:8
I *f* the LORD, the God of heaven, ... Jonah 1:9
God, and shall *f* because of thee ... Mic 7:17
I said, Surely thou wilt *f* me ... Zeph 3:7
be said to Jerusalem, *F* thou not ... Zeph 3:16
the people did *f* before the LORD ... Hag 1:12
remaineth among you: *f* ye not ... Hag 2:5
*f* not, but let your hands be ... Zec 8:13
to the house of Judah: *f* ye not ... Zec 8:15
Ashkelon shall see it, and *f* ... Zec 9:5
if I be a master, where is my *f* ... Mal 1:6
for the *f* wherewith he feared me ... Mal 2:5
*f* not me, saith the LORD of hosts ... Mal 3:5
But unto you that *f* my name shall ... Mal 4:2
*f* not to take unto thee Mary thy ... Mt 1:20
*F* them not therefore ... Mt 10:26
*f* not them which kill the body, ... Mt 10:28
but rather *f* him which is able to ... Mt 10:28
*F* ye not therefore, ye are of ... Mt 10:31
and they cried out for *f* ... Mt 14:26
we *f* the people ... Mt 21:26
for *f* of him the keepers did ... Mt 28:4
and said unto the women, *F* not ye ... Mt 28:5
quickly from the sepulchre with *f* ... Mt 28:8
was troubled, and *f* fell upon him ... Lk 1:12
said unto him, *F* not, Zacharias ... Lk 1:13
angel said unto her, *F* not, Mary ... Lk 1:30
that *f* him from generation to ... Lk 1:50
*f* came on all that dwelt round ... Lk 1:65
enemies might serve him without *f* ... Lk 1:74
the angel said unto them, *F* not ... Lk 2:10
And Jesus said unto Simon, *F* not ... Lk 5:10
God, and were filled with *f* ... Lk 5:26
And there came a *f* on all ... Lk 7:16
for they were taken with great *f* ... Lk 8:37
he answered him, saying, *F* not ... Lk 8:50
will forewarn you whom ye shall *f* ... Lk 12:5
*F* him, which after he hath killed ... Lk 12:5
yea, I say unto you, *F* him ... Lk 12:5
*F* not therefore ... Lk 12:7
*F* not, little flock ... Lk 12:32
himself, Though I *f* not God ... Lk 18:4
Men's hearts failing them for *f* ... Lk 21:26
him, saying, Dost not thou *f* God ... Lk 23:40
openly of him for *f* of the Jews ... Jn 7:13
*F* not, daughter of Sion ... Jn 12:15
but secretly for *f* of the Jews ... Jn 19:38
were assembled for *f* of the Jews ... Jn 20:19
And *f* came upon every soul ... Acts 2:43
great *f* came on all them that ... Acts 5:5
great *f* came upon all the church, ... Acts 5:11
and walking in the *f* of the Lord ... Acts 9:31
Men of Israel, and ye that *f* God ... Acts 13:16
*f* fell on them all, and the name ... Acts 19:17
Saying, *F* not, Paul ... Acts 27:24
There is no *f* of God before their ... Rom 3:18
the spirit of bondage again to *f* ... Rom 8:15
Be not highminded, but *f* ... Rom 11:20
to whom custom; *f* to whom ... Rom 13:7
to whom *f*; honour to whom ... Rom 13:7
was with you in weakness, and in *f* ... 1Cor 2:3
that he may be with you without *f* ... 1Cor 16:10
holiness in the *f* of God ... 2Cor 7:1
what indignation, yea, what *f* ... 2Cor 7:11
obedience of you all, how with *f* ... 2Cor 7:15
But I *f*, lest by any means, as ... 2Cor 11:3
For I *f*, lest, when I come, I ... 2Cor 12:20
one to another in the *f* of God ... Eph 5:21
according to the flesh, with *f* ... Eph 6:5
bold to speak the word without *f* ... Phil 1:14
out your own salvation with *f* ... Phil 2:12
all, that others also may *f* ... 1Ti 5:20
hath not given us the spirit of *f* ... 2Ti 1:7
through *f* of death were all their ... Heb 2:15
Let us therefore *f*, lest, a ... Heb 4:1
not seen as yet, moved with *f* ... Heb 11:7
that Moses said, I exceedingly *f* ... Heb 12:21
with reverence and godly *f* ... Heb 12:28
I will not *f* what man shall do ... Heb 13:6
time of your sojourning here in *f* ... 1Pet 1:17
*F* God. Honour the king ... 1Pet 2:17
to your masters with all *f* ... 1Pet 2:18
conversation coupled with *f* ... 1Pet 3:2
that is in you with meekness and *f* ... 1Pet 3:15
There is no *f* in love ... 1Jn 4:18
but perfect love casteth out *f* ... 1Jn 4:18
because *f* hath torment ... 1Jn 4:18
you, feeding themselves without *f* ... Jude 12
And others save with *f*, pulling ... Jude 23
upon me, saying unto me, *F* not ... Rev 1:17
*F* none of those things which thou ... Rev 2:10
great *f* fell upon them which saw ... Rev 11:11
saints, and them that *f* thy name ... Rev 11:18
*F* God, and give glory to him ... Rev 14:7
Who shall not *f* thee, O Lord, and ... Rev 15:4
afar off for the *f* of her torment ... Rev 18:10
afar off for the *f* of her torment ... Rev 18:15
ye his servants, and ye that *f* him ... Rev 19:5

**FEARED**

for he *f* to dwell in Zoar ... Gen 19:30
for he *f* to say, She is my wife ... Gen 26:7
But the midwives *f* God, and did ... Ex 1:17
pass, because the midwives *f* God ... Ex 1:21
And Moses *f*, and said, Surely this ... Ex 2:14
He that *f* the word of the LORD ... Ex 9:20
and the people *f* the LORD, and ... Ex 14:31
and he *f* not God ... Deut 25:18
newly up, whom your fathers *f* not ... Deut 32:17
Were it not that I *f* the wrath of ... Deut 32:27
and they *f* him, as they *f* ... Josh 4:14
That they *f* greatly, because ... Josh 10:2
because he *f* his father's ... Judg 6:27
for he *f*, because he was yet a ... Judg 8:20
Samuel *f* to shew Eli the vision ... 1Sa 3:15
all the people greatly *f* the LORD ... 1Sa 12:18
for the people *f* the oath ... 1Sa 14:26
because I *f* the people, and obeyed ... 1Sa 15:24
a word again, because he *f* him ... 2Sa 3:11
So the Syrians *f* to help the ... 2Sa 10:19
the servants of David *f* to tell ... 2Sa 12:18
Adonijah *f* because of Solomon, and ... 1Kin 1:50
and they *f* the king ... 1Kin 3:28
(Now Obadiah *f* the LORD greatly ... 1Kin 18:3
of Egypt, and had *f* other gods, ... 2Kin 17:7
there, that they *f* not the LORD ... 2Kin 17:25
So they *f* the LORD, and made unto ... 2Kin 17:32
They *f* the LORD, and served their ... 2Kin 17:33
So these nations *f* the LORD ... 2Kin 17:41
he also is to be *f* above all gods ... 1Chr 16:25
And Jehoshaphat *f*, and set himself ... 2Chr 20:3
faithful man, and *f* God above many ... Neh 7:2
and upright, and one that *f* God ... Job 1:1
which I greatly *f* is come upon me ... Job 3:25
Thou, even thou, art to be *f* ... Ps 76:7
the earth *f*, and was still, ... Ps 76:8
unto him that ought to be *f* ... Ps 76:11
on safely, so that they *f* not ... Ps 78:53
God is greatly to be *f* in the ... Ps 89:7
he is to be *f* above all gods ... Ps 96:4
with thee, that thou mayest be *f* ... Ps 130:4
The isles saw it, and *f* ... Is 41:5
hast *f* continually every day ... Is 51:13
whom hast thou been afraid or *f* ... Is 57:11
treacherous sister Judah *f* not ... Jer 3:8
pass, that the sword, which ye *f* ... Jer 42:16
this day, neither have they *f* ... Jer 44:10
Ye have *f* the sword ... Eze 11:8
trembled and *f* before him ... Dan 5:19
because we *f* not the LORD ... Hos 10:3
Then the men *f* the LORD ... Jonah 1:16
for the fear wherewith he *f* me ... Mal 2:5
Then they that *f* the LORD spake ... Mal 3:16
him for them that *f* the LORD ... Mal 3:16
he *f* the multitude, because they ... Mt 14:5
they *f* the multitude, because ... Mt 21:46
they *f* greatly, saying, Truly ... Mt 27:54
they *f* exceedingly, and said one ... Mk 4:41
For Herod *f* John, knowing that he ... Mk 6:20
for they *f* him, because all the ... Mk 11:18
they *f* the people ... Mk 11:32
lay hold on him, but *f* the people ... Mk 12:12
they *f* as they entered into the ... Lk 9:34
they *f* to ask him of that saying ... Lk 9:45
which *f* not God, neither regarded ... Lk 18:2
For I *f* thee, because thou art an ... Lk 19:21
and they *f* the people ... Lk 20:19
for they *f* the people ... Lk 22:2
parents, because they *f* the Jews ... Jn 9:22
for they *f* the people, lest they ... Acts 5:26
one that *f* God with all his house ... Acts 10:2
and they *f*, when they heard that ... Acts 16:38

death, and was heard in that he *f* ......... Heb 5:7

### FEAREST
for now I know that thou *f* God.......... Gen 22:12
even of old, and thou *f* me not................ Is 57:11
hand of them whose face thou *f*........... Jer 22:25

### FEARETH
Behold, Adonijah *f* king Solomon ........ 1Kin 1:51
and an upright man, one that *f* God........ Job 1:8
and an upright man, one that *f* God........ Job 2:3
What man is he that *f* the LORD............ Ps 25:12
is the man that *f* the LORD..................... Ps 112:1
is every one that *f* the Lord.................. Ps 128:1
man be blessed that *f* the LORD............. Ps 128:4
but he that *f* the commandment ........ Prov 13:13
in his uprightness *f* the LORD ............... Prov 14:2
A wise man *f*, and departeth from ..... Prov 14:16
Happy is the man that *f* alway .......... Prov 28:14
but a woman that *f* the LORD............. Prov 31:30
for he that *f* God shall come ................ Eccl 7:18
because he *f* not before God............... Eccl 8:13
sweareth, as he that *f* an oath ................ Eccl 9:2
Who is among you that *f* the LORD ........ Is 50:10
a just man, and one that *f* God......... Acts 10:22
But in every nation he that *f* him....... Acts 10:35
and whosoever among you *f* God....... Acts 13:26
He that *f* is not made perfect in............. 1Jn 4:18

### FEARFUL
*f* in praises, doing wonders ..................... Ex 15:11
say, What man is there that is *f*........... Deut 20:8
and *f* name, THE LORD THY GOD .. Deut 28:58
people, saying, Whosoever is *f*................ Judg 7:3
Say to them that are of a *f* heart ............. Is 35:4
he saith unto them, Why are ye *f*.............. Mt 8:26
said unto them, Why are ye so *f*............. Mk 4:40
*f* sights and great signs shall.................. Lk 21:11
But a certain *f* looking for of............... Heb 10:27
It is a *f* thing to fall into the................ Heb 10:31
But the *f*, and unbelieving, and the...... Rev 21:8

### FEARFULLY
for I am *f* and wonderfully made.......... Ps 139:14

### FEARFULNESS
*F* and trembling are come upon me,........ Ps 55:5
My heart panted, *f* affrighted me............. Is 21:4
*f* hath surprised the hypocrites ................. Is 33:14

### FEARING
children cease from *f* the LORD ............ Josh 22:25
But the woman *f* and trembling,............. Mk 5:33
*f* lest Paul should have been ............... Acts 23:10
*f* lest they should fall into the.............. Acts 27:17
Then *f* lest we should have fallen....... Acts 27:29
himself, *f* them which were of the ......... Gal 2:12
but in singleness of heart, *f* God............. Col 3:22
not *f* the wrath of the king................... Heb 11:27

### FEARS
me, and delivered me from all my *f*......... Ps 34:4
*f* shall be in the way, and the................ Eccl 12:5
and will bring their *f* upon them .............. Is 66:4
were fightings, within were *f* .................. 2Cor 7:5

### FEAST
and he made them a *f*, and did bake .... Gen 19:3
Abraham made a great *f* the same.......... Gen 21:8
And he made them a *f*, and they did.. Gen 26:30
the men of the place, and made a *f*... Gen 29:22
that he made a *f* unto all his.................. Gen 40:20
that they may hold a *f* unto me in ............ Ex 5:1
we must hold a *f* unto the LORD .............. Ex 10:9
ye shall keep it a *f* to the LORD.............. Ex 12:14
ye shall keep it a *f* by an....................... Ex 12:14
observe the *f* of unleavened bread......... Ex 12:17
day shall be a *f* to the LORD ................... Ex 13:6
keep a *f* unto me in the year................... Ex 23:14
keep the *f* of unleavened bread ............. Ex 23:15
the *f* of harvest, the firstfruits ............... Ex 23:16
the *f* of ingathering, which is in.............. Ex 23:16
To morrow is a *f* to the LORD .................. Ex 32:5
The *f* of unleavened bread shalt............ Ex 34:18
thou shalt observe the *f* of weeks........... Ex 34:22
the *f* of ingathering at the .................... Ex 34:22
shall the sacrifice of the *f* of.................. Ex 34:25
*f* of unleavened bread unto the ............... Lev 23:6
*f* of tabernacles for seven days ............. Lev 23:34
ye shall keep a *f* unto the LORD............. Lev 23:39
ye shall keep it a *f* unto the .................. Lev 23:41
day of this month is the *f*...................... Num 28:17
ye shall keep a *f* unto the LORD ........... Num 29:12
thou shalt keep the *f* of weeks ............ Deut 16:10
Thou shalt observe the *f* of ................. Deut 16:13
And thou shalt rejoice in thy *f*............ Deut 16:14
*f* unto the LORD thy God in the.......... Deut 16:15
in the *f* of unleavened bread, and........ Deut 16:16
bread, and in the *f* of weeks................ Deut 16:16
and in the *f* of tabernacles.................... Deut 16:16
release, in the *f* of tabernacles,............ Deut 31:10
and Samson made there a *f*.................. Judg 14:10
me within the seven days of the *f*...... Judg 14:12
seven days, while their *f* lasted.......... Judg 14:17
there is a *f* of the LORD in................. Judg 21:19
he held a *f* in his house, like............... 1Sa 25:36
his house, like the *f* of a king.............. 1Sa 25:36
and the men that were with him a *f*...... 2Sa 3:20
made a *f* to all his servants.................. 1Kin 3:15
at the *f* in the month Ethanim............... 1Kin 8:2
And at that time Solomon held a *f*....... 1Kin 8:65
ordained a *f* in the eighth month ......... 1Kin 12:32
like unto the *f* that is in Judah,......... 1Kin 12:32
ordained a *f* unto the children of ....... 1Kin 12:33
*f* which was in the seventh month ........ 2Chr 5:3
Solomon kept the *f* seven days.............. 2Chr 7:8
seven days, and the *f* seven days........... 2Chr 7:9
even in the *f* of unleavened bread ....... 2Chr 8:13
bread, and in the *f* of weeks................. 2Chr 8:13
and in the *f* of tabernacles.................... 2Chr 8:13
much people to keep the *f* of............. 2Chr 30:13
present at Jerusalem kept the *f*.......... 2Chr 30:21
eat throughout the *f* seven days ......... 2Chr 30:22
the *f* of unleavened bread seven ......... 2Chr 35:17
kept also the *f* of tabernacles ................... Ezr 3:4
kept the *f* of unleavened bread ............... Ezr 6:22
in the *f* of the seventh month ................ Neh 8:14
And they kept the *f* seven days............. Neh 8:18
he made a *f* unto all his princes ................ Est 1:3
the king made a *f* unto all the.................. Est 1:5
a *f* for the women in the royal ................... Est 1:9
a great *f* unto all his princes ................... Est 2:18
and his servants, even Esther's *f*........... Est 2:18
the Jews had joy and gladness, a *f*......... Est 8:17
appointed, on our solemn *f* day................. Ps 81:3
a merry heart hath a continual *f*....... Prov 15:15
A *f* is made for laughter, and wine...... Eccl 10:19
unto all people a *f* of fat things ................ Is 25:6
a *f* of wines on the lees, of fat................. Is 25:6
LORD, as in the day of a solemn *f*......... Lam 2:7
the passover, a *f* of seven days ............ Eze 45:21
seven days of the *f* he shall ................ Eze 45:23
like in the *f* of the seven days............... Eze 45:25
the king made a great *f* to a................... Dan 5:1
her *f* days, her new moons, and her...... Hos 2:11
in the day of the *f* of the LORD................ Hos 9:5
as in the days of the solemn *f*................ Hos 12:9
I hate, I despise your *f* days ............... Amos 5:21
to keep the *f* of tabernacles.................. Zec 14:16
up to keep the *f* of tabernacles............. Zec 14:18
up to keep the *f* of tabernacles............. Zec 14:19
two days is the *f* of the passover ............ Mt 26:2
But they said, Not on the *f* day.............. Mt 26:5
of the *f* of unleavened bread the........... Mt 26:17
Now at that *f* the governor was............. Mt 27:15
days was the *f* of the passover ............... Mk 14:1
But they said, Not on the *f* day.............. Mk 14:2
Now at that *f* he released unto .............. Mk 15:6
year at the *f* of the passover .................. Lk 2:41
after the custom of the *f*......................... Lk 2:42
him a great *f* in his own house................ Lk 5:29
But when thou makest a *f*, call ............. Lk 14:13
Now the *f* of unleavened bread .............. Lk 22:1
release one unto them at the *f* .............. Lk 23:17
bear unto the governor of the *f* ................ Jn 2:8
When the ruler of the *f* had..................... Jn 2:9
the governor of the *f* called the ............... Jn 2:9
at the passover, in the *f* day .................... Jn 2:23
that he did at Jerusalem at the *f* ............. Jn 4:45
for they also went unto the *f*..................... Jn 4:45
this there was a *f* of the Jews.................... Jn 5:1
a *f* of the Jews, was nigh ........................... Jn 6:4
Now the Jews' *f* of tabernacles ................. Jn 7:2
Go ye up unto this *f*................................... Jn 7:8
I go not up yet unto this *f* ......................... Jn 7:8
then went he also up unto the *f* ............... Jn 7:10
Then the Jews sought him at the *f* ........... Jn 7:11
Now about the midst of the *f*................... Jn 7:14
last day, that great day of the *f* .............. Jn 7:37
Jerusalem the *f* of the dedication ............ Jn 10:22
that he will not come to the *f*.................. Jn 11:56
people that were come to the *f*............... Jn 12:12
that came up to worship at the *f*............. Jn 12:20
Now before the *f* of the passover, ........... Jn 13:1
we have need of against the *f* .................. Jn 13:29
this *f* that cometh in Jerusalem .......... Acts 18:21
Therefore let us keep the *f*..................... 1Cor 5:8
that believe not bid you to a *f* .............. 1Cor 10:27
deceivings while they *f* with you ......... 2Pet 2:13
of charity, when they *f* with you............ Jude 12

### FEASTED
*f* in their houses, every one his................. Job 1:4

### FEASTING
they, and made it a day of *f*..................... Est 9:17
rested, and made it a day of *f*................... Est 9:18
month Adar a day of gladness and *f*...... Est 9:19
they should make them days of *f*.............. Est 9:22
days of their *f* were gone about................ Job 1:5
than to go to the house of *f* ....................... Eccl 7:2
not also go into the house of *f*.................. Jer 16:8

### FEASTS
Concerning the *f* of the LORD ................ Lev 23:2
convocations, even these are my *f*.......... Lev 23:2
These are the *f* of the LORD ................... Lev 23:4
These are the *f* of the LORD.................. Lev 23:37
of Israel the *f* of the LORD ................... Lev 23:44
offering, or in your solemn *f* ................ Num 15:3
do unto the LORD in your set *f*........... Num 29:39
in the new moons, and on the set *f*... 1Chr 23:31
on the solemn *f* of the LORD our.............. 2Chr 2:4
the new moons, and on the solemn *f*.. 2Chr 8:13
the new moons, and for the set *f*.......... 2Chr 31:3
of all the set *f* of the LORD that ............... Ezr 3:5
of the new moons, for the set *f*............... Neh 10:33
With hypocritical mockers in *f*................ Ps 35:16
your appointed *f* my soul hateth .............. Is 1:14
and pipe, and wine, are in their *f*.............. Is 5:12
In their heat I will make their *f*........... Jer 51:39
because none come to the solemn *f*...... Lam 1:4
the LORD hath caused the solemn *f*........ Lam 2:6
of Jerusalem in her solemn *f* ............... Eze 36:38
and drink offerings, in the *f*................ Eze 45:17
before the LORD in the solemn *f* ............ Eze 46:9
And in the *f* and in the solemnities ..... Eze 46:11
her sabbaths, and all her solemn *f*......... Hos 2:11
I will turn your *f* into mourning.......... Amos 8:10
O Judah, keep thy solemn *f*..................... Nah 1:15
joy and gladness, and cheerful *f*............. Zec 8:19
even the dung of your solemn *f* ............... Mal 2:3
And love the uppermost rooms at *f*........ Mt 23:6
and the uppermost rooms at *f* ............... Mk 12:39
and the chief rooms at *f*......................... Lk 20:46
are spots in your *f* of charity.................... Jude 12

### FEATHERED
*f* fowls like as the sand of the ................ Ps 78:27
Speak unto every *f* fowl, and to .......... Eze 39:17

### FEATHERS
pluck away his crop with his *f*.............. Lev 1:16
or wings and *f* unto the ostrich ............ Job 39:13
silver, and her *f* with yellow gold .......... Ps 68:13
He shall cover thee with his *f*.................. Ps 91:4
wings, longwinged, full of *f*..................... Eze 17:3
eagle with great wings and many *f*........ Eze 17:7
hairs were grown like eagles' *f* ............. Dan 4:33

### FED
Jacob *f* the rest of Laban's.................... Gen 30:36
as he *f* the asses of Zibeon his ............ Gen 36:24
and they *f* in a meadow ............................ Gen 41:2
and they *f* in a meadow .......................... Gen 41:18
he *f* them with bread for all.................. Gen 47:17
the God which *f* me all my life .............. Gen 48:15
I have *f* you in the wilderness ............... Ex 16:32
*f* thee with manna, which thou ............. Deut 8:3
Who *f* thee in the wilderness with....... Deut 8:16
*f* them, but went not in unto them........ 2Sa 20:3
*f* them with bread and water................. 1Kin 18:4
*f* them with bread and water............... 1Kin 18:13
over the herds that *f* in Sharon ......... 1Chr 27:29
land, and verily thou shalt be *f*................ Ps 37:3
So he *f* them according to the................ Ps 78:72
He should have *f* them also with ............ Ps 81:16
of rams, and the fat of *f* beasts .................. Is 1:11
when I had *f* them to the full,................. Jer 5:7
They were as *f* horses in the ..................... Jer 5:8
oil, and honey, wherewith I *f* thee....... Eze 16:19
the wool, ye kill them that are *f*............ Eze 34:3
*f* themselves, and *f* not my flock ......... Eze 34:8
thereof, and all flesh was *f* of it............ Dan 4:12
they *f* him with grass like oxen,............ Dan 5:21
and I *f* the flock...................................... Zec 11:7
saw we thee an hungred, and *f* thee..... Mt 25:37
they that *f* the swine fled, and .............. Mk 5:14
When they that *f* them saw what.............. Lk 8:34
desiring to be *f* with the crumbs............ Lk 16:21
I have *f* you with milk, and not ............ 1Cor 3:2

### FEEBLE
But when the cattle were *f*................. Gen 30:42
even all that were *f* behind thee ........ Deut 25:18
hath many children is waxed *f*............... 1Sa 2:5
dead in Hebron, his hands were *f*............ 2Sa 4:1
carried all the *f* of them upon........... 2Chr 28:15
and said, What do these *f* Jews ............. Neh 4:2
hast strengthened the *f* knees ................ Job 4:3
I am *f* and sore broken.............................. Ps 38:8
there was not one *f* person among...... Ps 105:37
The conies are but a *f* folk.................. Prov 30:26
remnant shall be very small and *f*.......... Is 16:14
hands, and confirm the *f* knees .............. Is 35:3
our hands wax *f*........................................ Jer 6:24
Damascus is waxed *f*, and turneth......... Jer 49:24
of them, and his hands waxed *f*.............. Jer 50:43
All hands shall be *f*, and all ................ Eze 7:17
melt, and all hands shall be *f*............... Eze 21:7
he that is *f* among them at that............ Zec 12:8
the body, which seem to be more *f*... 1Cor 12:22
which hang down, and the *f* knees.... Heb 12:12

### FEEBLEMINDED
that are unruly, comfort the *f*................. 1Th 5:14

### FEEBLENESS
to their children for *f* of hands................. Jer 47:3

### FEEBLER
so the *f* were Laban's, and the............ Gen 30:42

### FEED
*F* me, I pray thee, with that same....... Gen 25:30
ye the sheep, and go and *f* them .......... Gen 29:7
this thing for me, I will again *f*............ Gen 30:31
his brethren went to *f* their ................. Gen 37:12
Do not thy brethren *f* the flock ........... Gen 37:13
where they *f* their flocks ..................... Gen 37:16
their trade hath been to *f* cattle .......... Gen 46:32
shall *f* in another man's field................. Ex 22:5
nor herds *f* before that mount ................ Ex 34:3
Saul to *f* his father's sheep at.............. 1Sa 17:15
Thou shalt *f* my people Israel, and ....... 2Sa 5:2
I commanded to *f* my people Israel......... 2Sa 7:7
me, and I will *f* thee with me in ........... 2Sa 19:33
the ravens to *f* thee there..................... 1Kin 17:4
*f* him with bread of affliction and....... 1Kin 22:27
Thou shalt *f* my people Israel, and...... 1Chr 11:2
whom I commanded to *f* my people.... 1Chr 17:6
*f* him with bread of affliction and ...... 2Chr 18:26
take away flocks, and *f* thereof............ Job 24:2
the worm shall *f* sweetly on him .......... Job 24:20
*f* them also, and lift them up for............ Ps 28:9
death shall *f* on them............................ Ps 49:14
brought him to *f* Jacob his people......... Ps 78:71
The lips of the righteous *f* many ....... Prov 10:21
*f* me with food convenient for me......... Prov 30:8
*f* thy kids beside the shepherds'............ Song 1:8

twins, which *f* among the lilies ... Song 4:5
to *f* in the gardens, and to gather ... Song 6:2
the lambs *f* after their manner ... Is 5:17
And the cow and the bear shall *f* ... Is 11:7
the firstborn of the poor shall *f* ... Is 14:30
there shall the calf *f*, and there ... Is 27:10
thy cattle *f* in large pastures ... Is 30:23
He shall *f* his flock like a ... Is 40:11
They shall *f* in the ways, and ... Is 49:9
I will *f* them that oppress thee ... Is 49:26
*f* thee with the heritage of Jacob ... Is 58:14
*f* your flocks, and the sons of the ... Is 61:5
wolf and the lamb shall *f* together ... Is 65:25
which shall *f* you with knowledge ... Jer 3:15
they shall *f* every one in his ... Jer 6:3
Behold, I will *f* them, even this ... Jer 9:15
the pastors that *f* my people ... Jer 23:2
over them which shall *f* them ... Jer 23:4
I will *f* them with wormwood, and ... Jer 23:15
he shall *f* on Carmel and Bashan, ... Jer 50:19
They that did *f* delicately are ... Lam 4:5
of Israel that do *f* themselves ... Eze 34:2
not the shepherds *f* the flocks ... Eze 34:2
but ye *f* not the flock ... Eze 34:3
shepherds *f* themselves any more ... Eze 34:10
*f* them upon the mountains of ... Eze 34:13
I will *f* them in a good pasture, ... Eze 34:14
in a fat pasture shall they *f* ... Eze 34:14
I will *f* my flock, and I will ... Eze 34:15
I will *f* them with judgment ... Eze 34:16
over them, and he shall *f* them ... Eze 34:23
he shall *f* them, and he shall be ... Eze 34:23
they that *f* of the portion of his ... Dan 11:26
now the LORD will *f* them as a ... Hos 4:16
and the winepress shall not *f* them ... Hos 9:2
let them not *f*, nor drink water ... Jonah 3:7
*f* in the strength of the LORD, in ... Mic 5:4
*F* thy people with thy rod, the ... Mic 7:14
let them *f* in Bashan and Gilead, ... Mic 7:14
they shall *f* thereupon ... Zeph 2:7
for they shall *f* and lie down, and ... Zeph 3:13
*F* the flock of the slaughter ... Zec 11:4
I will *f* the flock of slaughter, ... Zec 11:7
Then said I, I will not *f* you ... Zec 11:9
nor *f* that that standeth still ... Zec 11:16
him into his fields to *f* swine ... Lk 15:15
He saith unto him, *F* my lambs ... Jn 21:15
He saith unto him, *F* my sheep ... Jn 21:16
Jesus saith unto him, *F* my sheep ... Jn 21:17
to *f* the church of God, which he ... Acts 20:28
if thine enemy hunger, *f* him ... Rom 12:20
bestow all my goods to *f* the poor ... 1Cor 13:3
*F* the flock of God which is among ... 1Pet 5:2
midst of the throne shall *f* them ... Rev 7:17
that they should *f* her there a ... Rev 12:6

### FEEDEST
Thou *f* them with the bread of ... Ps 80:5
whom my soul loveth, where thou *f* ... Song 1:7

### FEEDETH
mouth of fools *f* on foolishness ... Prov 15:14
he *f* among the lilies ... Song 2:16
he *f* among the lilies ... Song 6:3
He *f* on ashes ... Is 44:20
Ephraim *f* on wind, and followeth ... Hos 12:1
yet your heavenly Father *f* them ... Mt 6:26
and God *f* them ... Lk 12:24
or who *f* a flock, and eateth not ... 1Cor 9:7

### FEEDING
was *f* the flock with his brethren ... Gen 37:2
and the asses *f* beside them ... Job 1:14
them to cease from *f* the flock ... Eze 34:10
the *f* place of the young lions, ... Nah 2:11
from them an herd of many swine *f* ... Mt 8:30
mountains a great herd of swine *f* ... Mk 5:11
of many swine *f* on the mountain ... Lk 8:32
a servant plowing or *f* cattle ... Lk 17:7
*f* themselves without fear ... Jude 12

### FEEL
My father peradventure will *f* me ... Gen 27:12
I pray thee, that I may *f* thee ... Gen 27:21
Suffer me that I may *f* the ... Judg 16:26
Surely he shall not *f* quietness ... Job 20:20
Before your pots can *f* the thorns ... Ps 58:9
commandment shall *f* no evil thing ... Eccl 8:5
if haply they might *f* after him ... Acts 17:27

### FEELING
Who being past *f* have given ... Eph 4:19
with the *f* of our infirmities ... Heb 4:15

### FEET
you, be fetched, and wash your *f* ... Gen 18:4
tarry all night, and wash your *f* ... Gen 19:2
camels, and water to wash his *f* ... Gen 24:32
the men's *f* that were with him ... Gen 24:32
water, and they washed their *f* ... Gen 43:24
nor a lawgiver from between his *f* ... Gen 49:10
he gathered up his *f* into the bed ... Gen 49:33
put off thy shoes from off thy *f* ... Ex 3:5
of her son, and cast it at his *f* ... Ex 4:25
girded, your shoes on your *f* ... Ex 12:11
there was under his *f* as it were ... Ex 24:10
that are on the four *f* thereof ... Ex 25:26
their hands and their *f* thereat ... Ex 30:19
shall wash their hands and their *f* ... Ex 30:21
that were in the four *f* thereof ... Ex 37:13
their hands and their *f* thereat ... Ex 40:31
the great toes of their right *f* ... Lev 8:24
which have legs above their *f* ... Lev 11:21
things, which have four *f* ... Lev 11:23
or whatsoever hath more *f* among ... Lev 11:42
thing else, go through on my *f* ... Num 20:19
only I will pass through on my *f* ... Deut 2:28
your *f* shall tread shall be yours ... Deut 11:24
cometh out from between her *f* ... Deut 28:57
and they sat down at thy *f* ... Deut 33:3
as soon as the soles of the *f* of ... Josh 3:13
the *f* of the priests that bare ... Josh 3:15
where the priests' *f* stood firm ... Josh 4:3
in the place where the *f* of the ... Josh 4:9
the soles of the priests' *f* were ... Josh 4:18
old shoes and clouted upon their *f* ... Josh 9:5
put your *f* upon the necks of ... Josh 10:24
put their *f* upon the necks of ... Josh 10:24
thy *f* have trodden shall be thine ... Josh 14:9
his *f* in his summer chamber ... Judg 3:24
up with ten thousand men at his *f* ... Judg 4:10
chariot, and fled away on his *f* ... Judg 4:15
*f* to the tent of Jael the wife of ... Judg 4:17
At her *f* he bowed, he fell, he ... Judg 5:27
at her *f* he bowed, he fell ... Judg 5:27
and they washed their *f*, and did ... Judg 19:21
shalt go in, and uncover his *f* ... Ruth 3:4
came softly, and uncovered his *f* ... Ruth 3:7
and, behold, a woman lay at his *f* ... Ruth 3:8
she lay at his *f* until the ... Ruth 3:14
He will keep the *f* of his saints ... 1Sa 2:9
up upon his hands and upon his *f* ... 1Sa 14:13
and Saul went in to cover his *f* ... 1Sa 24:3
And fell at his *f*, and said, Upon ... 1Sa 25:24
be a servant to wash the *f* of the ... 1Sa 25:41
nor thy *f* put into fetters ... 2Sa 3:34
had a son that was lame of his *f* ... 2Sa 4:4
and cut off their hands and their *f* ... 2Sa 4:12
yet a son, which is lame on his *f* ... 2Sa 9:3
and was lame on both his *f* ... 2Sa 9:13
down to thy house, and wash thy *f* ... 2Sa 11:8
and had neither dressed his *f* ... 2Sa 19:24
and darkness was under his *f* ... 2Sa 22:10
He maketh my *f* like hinds' *f* ... 2Sa 22:34
so that my *f* did not slip ... 2Sa 22:37
yea, they are fallen under my *f* ... 2Sa 22:39
in his shoes that were on his *f* ... 1Kin 2:5
put them under the soles of his *f* ... 1Kin 5:3
Ahijah heard the sound of her *f* ... 1Kin 14:6
when thy *f* enter into the city, ... 1Kin 14:12
old age he was diseased in his *f* ... 1Kin 15:23
the hill, she caught him by the *f* ... 2Kin 4:27
she went in, and fell at his *f* ... 2Kin 4:37
of his master's *f* behind him ... 2Kin 6:32
of her than the skull, and the *f* ... 2Kin 9:35
he revived, and stood up on his *f* ... 2Kin 13:21
with the sole of my *f* have I ... 2Kin 19:24
Neither will I make the *f* of ... 2Kin 21:8
the king stood up upon his *f* ... 1Chr 28:2
and they stood on their *f*, and ... 2Chr 3:13
his reign was diseased in his *f* ... 2Chr 16:12
not old, and their *f* swelled not ... Neh 9:21
the king, and fell down at his *f* ... Est 8:3
*f* is as a lamp despised in the ... Job 12:5
Thou puttest my *f* also in the ... Job 13:27
a print upon the heels of my *f* ... Job 13:27
is cast into a net by his own *f* ... Job 18:8
side, and shall drive him to his *f* ... Job 18:11
the blind, and *f* was I to the lame ... Job 29:15
they push away my *f*, and they ... Job 30:12
He putteth my *f* in the stocks ... Job 33:11
hast put all things under his *f* ... Ps 8:6
and darkness was under his *f* ... Ps 18:9
He maketh my *f* like hinds' *f*, ... Ps 18:33
under me, that my *f* did not slip ... Ps 18:36
they are fallen under my *f* ... Ps 18:38
they pierced my hands and my *f* ... Ps 22:16
shall pluck my *f* out of the net ... Ps 25:15
hast set my *f* in a large room ... Ps 31:8
clay, and set my *f* upon a rock, and ... Ps 40:2
us, and the nations under our *f* ... Ps 47:3
thou deliver my *f* from falling ... Ps 56:13
he shall wash his *f* in the blood ... Ps 58:10
suffereth not our *f* to be moved ... Ps 66:9
as for me, my *f* were almost gone ... Ps 73:2
Lift up thy *f* unto the perpetual ... Ps 74:3
dragon shalt thou trample under *f* ... Ps 91:13
Whose *f* they hurt with fetters ... Ps 105:18
*f* have they, but they walk not ... Ps 115:7
from tears, and my *f* from falling ... Ps 116:8
turned my *f* unto thy testimonies ... Ps 119:59
my *f* from every evil way, that I ... Ps 119:101
Thy word is a lamp unto my *f* ... Ps 119:105
Our *f* shall stand within thy ... Ps 122:2
For their *f* run to evil, and make ... Prov 1:16
Ponder the path of thy *f*, and let ... Prov 4:26
Her *f* go down to death ... Prov 5:5
his eyes, he speaketh with his *f* ... Prov 6:13
*f* that be swift in running to ... Prov 6:18
hot coals, and his *f* not be burned ... Prov 6:28
her *f* abide not in her house ... Prov 7:11
that hasteth with his *f* sinneth ... Prov 19:2
hand of a fool cutteth off the *f* ... Prov 26:6
spreadeth a net for his *f* ... Prov 29:5
I have washed my *f* ... Song 5:3
beautiful are thy *f* with shoes ... Song 7:1
and making a tinkling with their *f* ... Is 3:16
tinkling ornaments about their *f* ... Is 3:18
and with twain he covered his *f* ... Is 6:2
the head, and the hair of the *f* ... Is 7:20
as a carcase trodden under *f* ... Is 14:19
her own *f* shall carry her afar ... Is 23:7
even the *f* of the poor, and the ... Is 26:6
Ephraim, shall be trodden under *f* ... Is 28:3
forth thither the *f* of the ox ... Is 32:20
with the sole of my *f* have I ... Is 37:25
that he had not gone with his *f* ... Is 41:3
and lick up the dust of thy *f* ... Is 49:23
the *f* of him that bringeth good ... Is 52:7
Their *f* run to evil, and they make ... Is 59:7
make the place of my *f* glorious ... Is 60:13
down at the soles of thy *f* ... Is 60:14
before your *f* stumble upon the ... Jer 13:16
they have not refrained their *f* ... Jer 14:10
take me, and hid snares for my *f* ... Jer 18:22
thy *f* are sunk in the mire, and ... Jer 38:22
he hath spread a net for my *f* ... Lam 1:13
To crush under his *f* all the ... Lam 3:34
And their *f* were straight *f* ... Eze 1:7
the sole of their *f* was like the ... Eze 1:7
me, Son of man, stand upon thy *f* ... Eze 2:1
unto me, and set me upon my *f* ... Eze 2:2
into me, and set me upon my *f* ... Eze 3:24
hast opened thy *f* to every one ... Eze 16:25
and put on thy shoes upon thy *f* ... Eze 24:17
heads, and your shoes upon your *f* ... Eze 24:23
hands, and stamped with the *f* ... Eze 25:6
troubledst the waters with thy *f* ... Eze 32:2
*f* the residue of your pastures ... Eze 34:18
must foul the residue with your *f* ... Eze 34:18
which ye have trodden with your *f* ... Eze 34:19
which ye have fouled with your *f* ... Eze 34:19
lived, and stood up upon their *f* ... Eze 37:10
and the place of the soles of my *f* ... Eze 43:7
his *f* part of iron and part of ... Dan 2:33
upon his *f* that were of iron ... Dan 2:34
And whereas thou sawest the *f* ... Dan 2:41
toes of the *f* were part of iron ... Dan 2:42
and made stand upon the *f* as a man ... Dan 7:4
the residue with the *f* of it ... Dan 7:7
and stamped the residue with his *f* ... Dan 7:19
his *f* like in colour to polished ... Dan 10:6
the clouds are the dust of his *f* ... Nah 1:3
the *f* of him that bringeth good ... Nah 1:15
burning coals went forth at his *f* ... Hab 3:5
will make my *f* like hinds' *f* ... Hab 3:19
his *f* shall stand in that day ... Zec 14:4
while they stand upon their *f* ... Zec 14:12
ashes under the soles of your *f* ... Mal 4:3
they trample them under their *f* ... Mt 7:6
shake off the dust of your *f* ... Mt 10:14
and cast them down at Jesus' *f* ... Mt 15:30
two *f* to be cast into everlasting ... Mt 18:8
fellowservant fell down at his *f* ... Mt 18:29
And they came and held him by the *f* ... Mt 28:9
when he saw him, he fell at his *f* ... Mk 5:22
*f* for a testimony against them ... Mk 6:11
of him, and came and fell at his *f* ... Mk 7:25
than having two *f* to be cast into ... Mk 9:45
to guide our *f* into the way of ... Lk 1:79
stood at his *f* behind him weeping ... Lk 7:38
and began to wash his *f* with tears ... Lk 7:38
of her head, and kissed his *f* ... Lk 7:38
thou gavest me no water for my *f* ... Lk 7:44
she hath washed my *f* with tears ... Lk 7:44
in hath not ceased to kiss my *f* ... Lk 7:45
hath anointed my *f* with ointment ... Lk 7:46
sitting at the *f* of Jesus ... Lk 8:35
and he fell down at Jesus' *f* ... Lk 8:41
off the very dust from your *f* for ... Lk 9:5
Mary, which also sat at Jesus' *f* ... Lk 10:39
on his hand, and shoes on his *f* ... Lk 15:22
And fell down on his face at his *f* ... Lk 17:16
Behold my hands and my *f*, that it ... Lk 24:39
he shewed them his hands and his *f* ... Lk 24:40
wiped his *f* with her hair, whose ... Jn 11:2
saw him, she fell down at his *f* ... Jn 11:32
and anointed the *f* of Jesus ... Jn 12:3
wiped his *f* with her hair ... Jn 12:3
and began to wash the disciples' *f* ... Jn 13:5
him, Lord, dost thou wash my *f* ... Jn 13:6
him, Thou shalt never wash my *f* ... Jn 13:8
unto him, Lord, not my *f* only ... Jn 13:9
needeth not save to wash his *f* ... Jn 13:10
So after he had washed their *f* ... Jn 13:12
and Master, have washed your *f* ... Jn 13:14
ought to wash one another's *f* ... Jn 13:14
the head, and the other at the *f* ... Jn 20:12
and immediately his *f* and ancle ... Acts 3:7
laid them down at the apostles' *f* ... Acts 4:35
and laid it at the apostles' *f* ... Acts 4:37
and laid it at the apostles' *f* ... Acts 5:2
the *f* of them which have buried ... Acts 5:9
she down straightway at his *f* ... Acts 5:10
him, Put off thy shoes from thy *f* ... Acts 7:33
their clothes at a young man's *f* ... Acts 7:58
met him, and fell down at his *f* ... Acts 10:25
whose shoes of his *f* I am not ... Acts 13:25
the dust of their *f* against them ... Acts 13:51
man at Lystra, impotent in his *f* ... Acts 14:8
voice, Stand upright on thy *f* ... Acts 14:10
made their *f* fast in the stocks ... Acts 16:24
and bound his own hands and *f* ... Acts 21:11
in this city at the *f* of Gamaliel ... Acts 22:3
But rise, and stand upon thy *f* ... Acts 26:16
Their *f* are swift to shed blood ... Rom 3:15
How beautiful are the *f* of them ... Rom 10:15
bruise Satan under your *f* shortly ... Rom 16:20
nor again the head to the *f* ... 1Cor 12:21
hath put all enemies under his *f* ... 1Cor 15:25
hath put all things under his *f* ... 1Cor 15:27
hath put all things under his *f* ... Eph 1:22
your *f* shod with the preparation ... Eph 6:15

if she have washed the saints' *f* .............. 1Ti 5:10
things in subjection under his *f* .............. Heb 2:8
And make straight paths for your *f* .... Heb 12:13
his *f* like unto fine brass, as if................. Rev 1:15
saw him, I fell at his *f* as dead................ Rev 1:17
his *f* are like fine brass ........................... Rev 2:18
to come and worship before thy *f*........... Rev 3:9
sun, and his *f* as pillars of fire.............. Rev 10:1
them, and they stood upon their *f*....... Rev 11:11
the sun, and the moon under her *f* ...... Rev 12:1
his *f* were as the *f* of a bear................ Rev 13:2
I fell at his *f* to worship him................ Rev 19:10
*f* of the angel which shewed me........... Rev 22:8

**FEIGN**
*f* thyself to be a mourner, and put......... 2Sa 14:2
that she shall *f* herself to be................. 1Kin 14:5
which should *f* themselves just ............. Lk 20:20

**FEIGNED**
*f* himself mad in their hands, and......... 1Sa 21:13
that goeth not out of *f* lips......................... Ps 17:1
covetousness shall they with *f*................. 2Pet 2:3

**FEIGNEDLY**
me with her whole heart, but *f*............... Jer 3:10

**FEIGNEST**
why *f* thou thyself to be another ......... 1Kin 14:6
but thou *f* them out of thine own.......... Neh 6:8

**FELIX** (*fe'-lix*) See FELIX'. *A Roman procurator of Judea.*
him safe unto F the governor............. Acts 23:24
governor F sendeth greeting.............. Acts 23:26
and in all places, most noble F.......... Acts 24:3
when F heard these things, having .... Acts 24:22
when F came with his wife ................. Acts 24:24
F trembled, and answered, Go thy ..... Acts 24:25
and F, willing to shew the Jews a ...... Acts 24:27
a certain man left in bonds by F....... Acts 25:14

**FELIX'** (*fe'-lix*)
Porcius Festus came into F room ....... Acts 24:27

**FELL**
very wroth, and his countenance *f* ......... Gen 4:5
and Gomorrah fled, and *f* there ........... Gen 14:10
down, a deep sleep *f* upon Abram ....... Gen 15:12
of great darkness *f* upon him .............. Gen 15:12
And Abram *f* on his face ...................... Gen 17:3
Then Abraham *f* upon his face, and ... Gen 17:17
*f* on his neck, and kissed him................. Gen 33:4
they *f* before him on the ground......... Gen 44:14
he *f* upon his brother Benjamin's....... Gen 45:14
he *f* on his neck, and wept on his ....... Gen 46:29
Joseph *f* upon his father's face,............ Gen 50:1
went and *f* down before his face ......... Gen 50:18
there *f* of the people that day ................ Ex 32:28
they shouted, and *f* on their faces ......... Lev 9:24
goat upon which the LORD's lot *f*.......... Lev 16:9
on which the lot *f* to be the.................. Lev 16:10
that was among them *f* a lusting......... Num 11:4
when the dew *f* upon the camp in....... Num 11:9
in the night, the manna *f* upon it ........ Num 11:9
Aaron *f* on their faces before all ......... Num 14:5
heard it, he *f* upon his face.................. Num 16:4
they *f* upon their faces, and said,....... Num 16:22
And they *f* upon their faces .............. Num 16:45
and they *f* upon their faces ................. Num 20:6
the LORD, she *f* down under Balaam . Num 22:27
his head, and *f* flat on his face.......... Num 22:31
I *f* down before the LORD, as at........... Deut 9:18
Thus I *f* down before the LORD ............ Deut 9:25
nights, as I *f* down at the first.......... Deut 9:25
Joshua *f* on his face to the earth ........ Josh 5:14
shout, that the wall *f* down flat ........... Josh 6:20
*f* to the earth upon his face ................... Josh 7:6
it was, that all that *f* that day .............. Josh 8:25
and they *f* upon them.............................. Josh 11:7
Joseph *f* from Jordan by Jericho........... Josh 16:1
there *f* ten portions to Manasseh,.......... Josh 17:5
wrath *f* on all the congregation .......... Josh 22:20
all the host of Sisera *f* upon the.......... Judg 4:16
At her feet he bowed, he *f* ..................... Judg 5:27
at her feet he bowed, he *f*...................... Judg 5:27
he bowed, there he *f* down dead, .......... Judg 5:27
a tent, and smote it that it *f*................. Judg 7:13
for there *f* an hundred and twenty ........ Judg 8:10
there *f* at that time of the...................... Judg 12:6
*f* on their faces to the ground............. Judg 13:20
the house *f* upon the lords, and............ Judg 16:30
*f* down at the door of the man's............ Judg 19:26
there *f* of Benjamin eighteen................ Judg 20:44
So that all which *f* that day of............. Judg 20:46
Then she *f* on her face, and bowed..... Ruth 2:10
for there *f* of Israel thirty........................ 1Sa 4:10
that he *f* from off the seat......................... 1Sa 4:18
fear of the LORD *f* on the people.............. 1Sa 11:7
and they *f* before Jonathan................... 1Sa 14:13
he *f* upon his face to the earth ............. 1Sa 17:49
*f* down by the way to Shaaraim ............ 1Sa 17:52
*f* on his face to the ground, and ........... 1Sa 20:41
he *f* upon the priests, and slew on ........ 1Sa 22:18
*f* before David on her face, and ............ 1Sa 25:23
*f* at his feet, and said, Upon me,............ 1Sa 25:24
Then Saul *f* straightway all along ......... 1Sa 28:20
since he *f* unto me unto this day............. 1Sa 29:3
because three days agone I *f* sick ........ 1Sa 30:13
*f* down slain in mount Gilboa ................. 1Sa 31:1
Saul took a sword, and *f* upon it ........... 1Sa 31:4
he *f* likewise upon his sword, and .......... 1Sa 31:5
that he *f* to the earth, and did................... 2Sa 1:2
so they *f* down together .......................... 2Sa 2:16
he *f* down there, and died in the ............ 2Sa 2:23
to the place where Asahel *f* down........... 2Sa 2:23
she made haste to flee, that he *f* ............. 2Sa 4:4
David, he *f* on his face, and did ............... 2Sa 9:6
there *f* some of the people of the ......... 2Sa 11:17
that he *f* sick for his sister ................... 2Sa 13:2
she *f* on her face to the ground, ............ 2Sa 14:4
Joab *f* to the ground on his face,.......... 2Sa 14:22
he *f* down to the earth upon his........... 2Sa 18:28
of Gera *f* down before the king ........... 2Sa 19:18
and as he went forth it *f* out .................. 2Sa 20:8
they *f* all seven together, and................. 2Sa 21:9
*f* by the hand of David, and by the...... 2Sa 21:22
he *f* upon him that he died ................... 1Kin 2:25
who *f* upon two men more righteous.. 1Kin 2:32
up, and *f* upon him, and slew him......... 1Kin 2:34
out, and *f* upon him, that he died ........ 1Kin 2:46
Abijah the son of Jeroboam *f* sick ...... 1Kin 14:1
the mistress of the house, *f* sick ....... 1Kin 17:17
*f* on his face, and said, Art thou .......... 1Kin 18:7
Then the fire of the LORD *f*................. 1Kin 18:38
saw it, they *f* on their faces.............. 1Kin 18:39
and there a wall *f* upon twenty .......... 1Kin 20:30
Ahaziah *f* down through a lattice .......... 2Kin 1:2
*f* on his knees before Elijah, and.......... 2Kin 1:13
mantle of Elijah that *f* from him.......... 2Kin 2:13
mantle of Elijah that *f* from him.......... 2Kin 2:14
shall *f* every good tree, and stop ......... 2Kin 3:19
it *f* on a day, that Elisha passed ............ 2Kin 4:8
it *f* on a day, that he came..................... 2Kin 4:11
it *f* on a day, that he went out.............. 2Kin 4:18
*f* at his feet, and bowed herself............ 2Kin 4:37
the ax head *f* into the water.................... 2Kin 6:5
the man of God said, Where *f* it ............. 2Kin 6:6
And so it *f* out unto him ......................... 2Kin 7:20
the fugitives that *f* away to the.......... 2Kin 25:11
Hagarites, who *f* by their hand............ 1Chr 5:10
For there *f* down many slain,............... 1Chr 5:22
*f* down slain in mount Gilboa .............. 1Chr 10:1
Saul took a sword, and *f* upon it.......... 1Chr 10:4
he *f* likewise on the sword, and ........... 1Chr 10:5
there *f* some of Manasseh to David... 1Chr 12:19
there *f* to him of Manasseh, Adnah... 1Chr 12:20
they *f* by the hand of David, and......... 1Chr 20:8
there *f* of Israel seventy ...................... 1Chr 21:14
in sackcloth, *f* upon their faces ......... 1Chr 21:16
the lot eastward *f* to Shelemiah ......... 1Chr 26:14
because there *f* wrath for it............... 1Chr 27:24
so there *f* down slain of Israel ........... 2Chr 13:17
for they *f* to him out of Israel.............. 2Chr 15:9
the fear of the LORD *f* upon all........... 2Chr 17:10
of Jerusalem *f* before the LORD.......... 2Chr 20:18
his bowels *f* out by reason of his ....... 2Chr 21:19
*f* upon the cities of Judah, from ......... 2Chr 25:13
I *f* upon my knees, and spread out .......... Ezr 9:5
*f* down at his feet, and besought ............... Est 8:3
the fear of the Jews *f* upon them............ Est 8:17
fear of them *f* upon all people................. Est 9:2
the fear of Mordecai *f* upon them.......... Est 9:3
And the Sabeans *f* upon them................ Job 1:15
*f* upon the camels, and have................... Job 1:17
it *f* upon the young men, and they ........ Job 1:19
*f* down upon the ground, and............... Job 1:20
up my flesh, they stumbled and *f* ............ Ps 27:2
Their priests *f* by the sword.................. Ps 78:64
for the fear of them *f* upon them ......... Ps 105:38
they *f* down, and there was none to .... Ps 107:12
in the city, and those that *f* away........... Jer 39:9
that *f* to him, with the rest of ................ Jer 39:9
to fall, yea, one *f* upon another.............. Jer 46:16
in the city, and those that *f* away.......... Jer 52:15
that *f* to the king of Babylon, and........... Jer 52:15
when her people *f* into the hand............ Lam 1:7
the children *f* under the wood.............. Lam 5:13
I *f* upon my face, and I heard a.............. Eze 1:28
and I *f* on my face ................................. Eze 3:23
of the Lord GOD *f* there upon me............ Eze 8:1
that I *f* upon my face, and cried,.............. Eze 9:8
the Spirit of the LORD *f* upon me ........... Eze 11:5
Then *f* I down upon my face, and........ Eze 11:13
so *f* they all by the sword...................... Eze 39:23
and I *f* upon my face............................ Eze 43:3
and I *f* upon my face............................ Eze 44:4
Nebuchadnezzar *f* upon his face ........... Dan 2:46
*f* down and worshipped the golden........... Dan 3:7
*f* down bound into the midst of............. Dan 3:23
there *f* a voice from heaven,................... Dan 4:31
came up, and before whom three *f*.......... Dan 7:20
I was afraid, and *f* upon my face ............ Dan 8:17
but a great quaking *f* upon them ......... Dan 10:7
lots, and the lot *f* upon Jonah ............... Jonah 1:7
*f* down, and worshipped him.................... Mt 2:11
and it *f* not: for it was founded ................ Mt 7:25
and it *f*: and great was the fall ................. Mt 7:27
some seeds *f* by the way side, and.......... Mt 13:4
Some *f* upon stony places, where ........... Mt 13:5
And some *f* among thorns ....................... Mt 13:7
But other *f* into good ground, and............ Mt 13:8
they *f* on their face, and were ................ Mt 17:6
The servant therefore *f* down ................ Mt 18:26
fellowservant *f* down at his feet............ Mt 18:29
*f* on his face, and prayed, saying, ......... Mt 26:39
*f* down before him, and cried, ................. Mk 3:11
some *f* by the way side, and the .............. Mk 4:4
some *f* on stony ground, where it............ Mk 4:5
some *f* among thorns, and the................. Mk 4:7
other *f* on good ground, and did ............. Mk 4:8
he saw him, he *f* at his feet,.................. Mk 5:22
*f* down before him, and told him .......... Mk 5:33
of him, and came and *f* at his feet.......... Mk 7:25
he *f* on the ground, and wallowed .......... Mk 9:20
*f* on the ground, and prayed that,.......... Mk 14:35
was troubled, and fear *f* upon him.......... Lk 1:12
he *f* down at Jesus' knees, saying............ Lk 5:8
who seeing Jesus *f* on his face................ Lk 5:12
vehemently, and immediately it *f*............. Lk 6:49
he sowed, some *f* by the way side ............ Lk 8:5
And some *f* upon a rock.............................. Lk 8:6
And some *f* among thorns .......................... Lk 8:7
other *f* on good ground, and sprang.......... Lk 8:8
that which *f* among thorns are................. Lk 8:14
But as they sailed he *f* asleep ................. Lk 8:23
*f* down before him, and with a loud ........ Lk 8:28
he *f* down at Jesus' feet, and .................. Lk 8:41
*f* among thieves, which stripped............. Lk 10:30
unto him that *f* among the thieves......... Lk 10:36
upon whom the tower in Siloam *f* ............ Lk 13:4
*f* on his neck, and kissed him ................. Lk 15:20
which *f* from the rich man's table ......... Lk 16:21
*f* down on his face at his feet,................ Lk 17:16
she *f* down at his feet, saying.................. Jn 11:32
went backward, and *f* to the ground ....... Jn 18:6
which Judas by transgression *f*............ Acts 1:25
and the lot *f* upon Matthias.................. Acts 1:26
hearing these words *f* down................... Acts 5:5
Then *f* she down straightway at ........... Acts 5:10
he had said this, he *f* asleep ................. Acts 7:60
he *f* to the earth, and heard a................. Acts 9:4
immediately there *f* from his eyes ........ Acts 9:18
made ready, he *f* into a trance,............ Acts 10:10
*f* down at his feet, and worshipped .... Acts 10:25
the Holy Ghost *f* on all them.............. Acts 10:44
speak, the Holy Ghost *f* on them....... Acts 11:15
his chains *f* off from his hands............ Acts 12:7
immediately there *f* on him a mist ..... Acts 13:11
*f* on sleep, and was laid unto his......... Acts 13:36
*f* down before Paul and Silas, ............. Acts 16:29
fear *f* on them all, and the name ........ Acts 19:17
image which *f* down from Jupiter ...... Acts 19:35
*f* down from the third loft, and ............ Acts 20:9
*f* on him, and embracing him said,..... Acts 20:10
*f* on Paul's neck, and kissed him,........ Acts 20:37
I *f* unto the ground, and heard a ......... Acts 22:7
on them which *f*, severity .................... Rom 11:22
them that reproached thee *f* on me..... Rom 15:3
*f* in one day three and twenty ............ 1Cor 10:8
sinned, whose carcases *f* in the............. Heb 3:17
faith the walls of Jericho *f* down......... Heb 11:30
for since the fathers *f* asleep ................ 2Pet 3:4
saw him, I *f* at his feet as dead ............. Rev 1:17
twenty elders *f* down before the ............. Rev 5:8
the four and twenty elders *f* down.......... Rev 5:14
stars of heaven *f* unto the earth ............ Rev 6:13
*f* before the throne on their .................. Rev 7:11
there *f* a great star from heaven,.......... Rev 8:10
it *f* upon the third part of the................. Rev 8:10
great fear *f* upon them which saw ...... Rev 11:11
and the tenth part of the city *f* ............ Rev 11:13
*f* upon their faces, and worshipped ..... Rev 11:16
there *f* a noisome and grievous............. Rev 16:2
and the cities of the nations *f*.............. Rev 16:19
there *f* upon men a great hail out ....... Rev 16:21
elders and the four beasts *f* down........ Rev 19:4
I *f* at his feet to worship him.............. Rev 19:10
I *f* down to worship before the ............. Rev 22:8

**FELLED**
of water, and *f* all the good trees ......... 2Kin 3:25

**FELLER**
no *f* is come up against us ........................ Is 14:8

**FELLEST**
before wicked men, so *f* thou.................. 2Sa 3:34

**FELLING**
But as one was *f* a beam, the ax ........... 2Kin 6:5

**FELLOES**
and their naves, and their *f* .................. 1Kin 7:33

**FELLOW**
This one *f* came in to sojourn, and....... Gen 19:9
Wherefore smitest thou thy *f*.................... Ex 2:13
man that told a dream unto his *f*.......... Judg 7:13
his *f* answered and said, This is........... Judg 7:14
every man's sword against his *f* ........... Judg 7:22
man's sword was against his *f*............... 1Sa 14:20
this *f* to play the mad man in my.......... 1Sa 21:15
shall this *f* come into my house............ 1Sa 21:15
this *f* hath in the wilderness................. 1Sa 25:21
said unto him, Make this *f* return .......... 1Sa 29:4
every one his *f* by the head ................... 2Sa 2:16
Put this *f* in the prison, and feed....... 1Kin 22:27
wherefore came this mad *f* to thee....... 2Kin 9:11
Put this *f* in the prison, and feed....... 2Chr 18:26
fall, the one will lift up his *f*................ Eccl 4:10
and the satyr shall cry to his *f*............... Is 34:14
And they said every one to his *f*.......... Jonah 1:7
and against the man that is my *f*............ Zec 13:7
This *f* doth not cast out devils,.............. Mt 12:24
And said, This *f* said, I am able............. Mt 26:61
This *f* was also with Jesus of................. Mt 26:71
Of a truth this *f* also was with............... Lk 22:59
We found this *f* perverting the............... Lk 23:2
as for this *f*, we know not from .............. Jn 9:29
This *f* persuadeth men to worship...... Acts 18:13
Away with such a *f* from the earth.... Acts 22:22
have found this man a pestilent *f*.......... Acts 24:5
*f* soldier, but your messenger, and......... Phil 2:25
These only are my *f* workers unto ......... Col 4:11

**FELLOWCITIZENS**
but *f* with the saints, and of the ........ Eph 2:19

**FELLOWDISCIPLES**
is called Didymus, unto his *f*........ Jn 11:16

**FELLOWHEIRS**
That the Gentiles should be *f*........ Eph 3:6

**FELLOWHELPER**
is my partner and *f* concerning you .... 2Cor 8:23

**FELLOWHELPERS**
that we might be *f* to the truth........ 3Jn 8

**FELLOWLABOURER**
our *f* in the gospel of Christ, to........ 1Th 3:2
Philemon our dearly beloved, and *f*...... Philem 1

**FELLOWLABOURERS**
Clement also, and with other my *f*........ Phil 4:3
Aristarchus, Demas, Lucas, my *f*........ Philem 24

**FELLOWPRISONER**
Aristarchus my *f* saluteth you........ Col 4:10
Epaphras, my *f* in Christ Jesus........ Philem 23

**FELLOWPRISONERS**
and Junia, my kinsmen, and my *f*........ Rom 16:7

**FELLOW'S**
and thrust his sword in his *f* side........ 2Sa 2:16

**FELLOWS**
and bewail my virginity, I and my *f*.. Judg 11:37
lest angry *f* run upon thee, and........ Judg 18:25
as one of the vain *f* shamelessly........ 2Sa 6:20
the oil of gladness above thy *f*........ Ps 45:7
all his *f* shall be ashamed........ Is 44:11
and the tribes of Israel his *f*........ Eze 37:19
Daniel and his *f* to be slain........ Dan 2:13
his *f* should not perish with the........ Dan 2:18
look was more stout than his *f*........ Dan 7:20
thy *f* that sit before thee........ Zec 3:8
markets, and calling unto their *f*........ Mt 11:16
certain lewd *f* of the baser sort........ Acts 17:5
the oil of gladness above thy *f*........ Heb 1:9

**FELLOWSERVANT**
his *f* fell down at his feet, and........ Mt 18:29
also have had compassion on thy *f*........ Mt 18:33
learned of Epaphras our dear *f*........ Col 1:7
minister and *f* in the Lord........ Col 4:7
I am thy *f*, and of thy brethren........ Rev 19:10
for I am thy *f*, and of thy........ Rev 22:9

**FELLOWSERVANTS**
went out, and found one of his *f*........ Mt 18:28
So when his *f* saw what was done,........ Mt 18:31
And shall begin to smite his *f*........ Mt 24:49
little season, until their *f* also........ Rev 6:11

**FELLOWSHIP**
delivered him to keep, or in *f*........ Lev 6:2
of iniquity have *f* with thee........ Ps 94:20
in the apostles' doctrine and *f*........ Acts 2:42
the *f* of his Son Jesus Christ our........ 1Cor 1:9
that ye should have *f* with devils........ 1Cor 10:20
for what *f* hath righteousness........ 2Cor 6:14
take upon us the *f* of the........ 2Cor 8:4
and Barnabas the right hands of *f*........ Gal 2:9
see what is the *f* of the mystery........ Eph 3:9
have no *f* with the unfruitful........ Eph 5:11
For your *f* in the gospel from the........ Phil 1:5
if any *f* of the Spirit, if any........ Phil 2:1
the *f* of his sufferings, being........ Phil 3:10
that ye also may have *f* with us........ 1Jn 1:3
truly our *f* is with the Father,........ 1Jn 1:3
If we say that we have *f* with him........ 1Jn 1:6
we have *f* one with another, and........ 1Jn 1:7

**FELLOWSOLDIER**
Apphia, and Archippus our *f*........ Philem 2

**FELT**
he *f* him, and said, The voice is........ Gen 27:22
even darkness which may be *f*........ Ex 10:21
have beaten me, and I *f* it not........ Prov 23:35
she *f* in her body that she was........ Mk 5:29
beast into the fire, and *f* no harm........ Acts 28:5

**FEMALE**
male and *f* created he them........ Gen 1:27
Male and *f* created he them........ Gen 5:2
they shall be male and *f*........ Gen 6:19
thee by sevens, the male and his *f*........ Gen 7:2
clean by two, the male and his *f*........ Gen 7:2
air by sevens, the male and the *f*........ Gen 7:3
into the ark, the male and the *f*........ Gen 7:9
*f* of all flesh, as God had........ Gen 7:16
whether it be a male or *f*........ Lev 3:1
male or *f*, he shall offer it........ Lev 3:6
a *f* without blemish, for his sin........ Lev 4:28
bring it a *f* without blemish........ Lev 4:32
a *f* from the flock, a lamb or a........ Lev 5:6
her that hath born a male or a *f*........ Lev 12:7
And if it be a *f*, then thy........ Lev 27:4
shekels, and for the *f* ten shekels........ Lev 27:5
for the *f* thy estimation shall be........ Lev 27:6
shekels, and for the *f* ten shekels........ Lev 27:7
*f* shall ye put out, without the........ Num 5:3
figure, the likeness of male or *f*........ Deut 4:16
not be male or *f* barren among you .... Deut 7:14
the beginning made them male and *f*..... Mt 19:4
creation God made them male and *f*..... Mk 10:6
free, there is neither male nor *f*........ Gal 3:28

**FENCE**
shall ye be, and as a tottering *f*........ Ps 62:3

**FENCED**
in the *f* cities because of the........ Num 32:17
and Beth-haran, *f* cities........ Num 32:36
cities were *f* with high walls........ Deut 3:5
cities great and *f* up to heaven,........ Deut 9:1
*f* walls come down, wherein thou...... Deut 28:52
of them entered into *f* cities........ Josh 10:20
that the cities were great and *f*........ Josh 14:12
the *f* cities are Ziddim, Zer, and........ Josh 19:35
the five lords, both of *f* cities........ 1Sa 6:18
him, lest he get him *f* cities........ 2Sa 20:6
touch them must be *f* with iron........ 2Sa 23:7
And ye shall smite every *f* city........ 2Kin 3:19
horses, a *f* city also, and armour........ 2Kin 10:2
of the watchmen to the *f* city........ 2Kin 17:9
of the watchmen to the *f* city........ 2Kin 18:8
against all the *f* cities of Judah........ 2Kin 18:13
waste *f* cities into ruinous heaps........ 2Kin 19:25
*f* cities, with walls, gates, and........ 2Chr 8:5
in Judah and in Benjamin *f* cities...... 2Chr 11:10
and Benjamin, unto every *f* city........ 2Chr 11:23
he took the *f* cities which........ 2Chr 12:4
he built *f* cities in Judah........ 2Chr 14:6
in all the *f* cities of Judah........ 2Chr 17:2
the *f* cities throughout all Judah........ 2Chr 17:19
all the *f* cities of Judah........ 2Chr 19:5
things, with *f* cities in Judah........ 2Chr 21:3
and encamped against the *f* cities........ 2Chr 32:1
war in all the *f* cities of Judah........ 2Chr 33:14
hast *f* me with bones and sinews........ Job 10:11
He hath *f* up my way that I cannot...... Job 19:8
high tower, and upon every *f* wall........ Is 2:15
And he *f* it, and gathered out the........ Is 5:2
shall impoverish thy *f* cities........ Jer 5:17
unto this people a *f* brasen wall........ Jer 15:20
and ruined cities are become *f*........ Eze 36:35
mount, and take the most *f* cities........ Dan 11:15
and Judah hath multiplied *f* cities........ Hos 8:14
and alarm against the *f* cities........ Zeph 1:16

**FENS**
in the covert of the reed, and *f*........ Job 40:21

**FERRET**
And the *f*, and the chameleon, and...... Lev 11:30

**FERRY**
there went over a *f* boat to carry........ 2Sa 19:18

**FERVENT**
being *f* in the spirit, he spake........ Acts 18:25
*f* in spirit; serving the Lord........ Rom 12:11
mourning, your *f* mind toward me........ 2Cor 7:7
The effectual *f* prayer of a........ Jas 5:16
above all things have *f* charity........ 1Pet 4:8
elements shall melt with *f* heat........ 2Pet 3:10
elements shall melt with *f* heat........ 2Pet 3:12

**FERVENTLY**
always labouring *f* for you in........ Col 4:12
one another with a pure heart *f*........ 1Pet 1:22

**FESTUS** (*fes'-tus*) See YESTUS'. *A Roman procurator of Judea.*
Porcius *F* came into Felix' room........ Acts 24:27
Now when *F* was come into the........ Acts 25:1
But *F* answered, that Paul should........ Acts 25:4
But *F*, willing to do the Jews a........ Acts 25:9
Then *F*, when he had conferred........ Acts 25:12
came unto Caesarea to salute *F*........ Acts 25:13
*F* declared Paul's cause unto the........ Acts 25:14
Then Agrippa said unto *F*, I would........ Acts 25:22
*F* said, King Agrippa, and all men........ Acts 25:24
*F* said with a loud voice, Paul,........ Acts 26:24
said, I am not mad, most noble *F*........ Acts 26:25
Then said Agrippa unto *F*, This........ Acts 26:32

**FESTUS'** (*fes'-tus*)
at *F* commandment Paul was........ Acts 25:23

**FETCH**
I will *f* a morsel of bread, and........ Gen 18:5
*f* me from thence two good kids of........ Gen 27:9
obey my voice, and go *f* me them........ Gen 27:13
will send, and *f* thee from thence........ Gen 27:45
let him *f* your brother, and ye........ Gen 42:16
flags, she sent her maid to *f* it........ Ex 2:5
must we *f* you water out of this........ Num 20:10
the border shall *f* a compass from........ Num 34:5
*f* him thence, and deliver him into........ Deut 19:12
go into his house to *f* his pledge........ Deut 24:10
thou shalt not go again to *f* it........ Deut 24:19
and from thence will he *f* thee........ Deut 30:4
the elders of Gilead went to *f*........ Judg 11:5
to *f* victual for the people, that........ Judg 20:10
Let us *f* the ark of the covenant........ 1Sa 4:3
come ye down, and *f* it up to you........ 1Sa 6:21
said unto Jesse, Send and *f* him........ 1Sa 16:11
*f* him unto me, for he shall........ 1Sa 20:31
the young men come over and *f* it........ 1Sa 26:22
but *f* a compass behind them, and........ 2Sa 5:23
not *f* home again his banished........ 2Sa 14:13
To *f* about this form of speech........ 2Sa 14:20
*F* me, I pray thee, a little water........ 1Kin 17:10
And as she was going to *f* it........ 1Kin 17:11
he is, that I may send and *f* him........ 2Kin 6:13
*F* quickly Micaiah the son of Imla........ 2Chr 18:8
*f* olive branches, and pine........ Neh 8:15
I will *f* my knowledge from afar,........ Job 36:3
Come ye, say they, I will *f* wine........ Is 56:12
king sent Jehudi to *f* the roll........ Jer 36:21
them come themselves and *f* us out .. Acts 16:37

**FETCHED**
a little water, I pray you, be *f*........ Gen 18:4
he went, and *f*, and brought........ Gen 27:14
to Adar, and *f* a compass to Karkaa........ Josh 15:3
*f* the carved image, the ephod, and ... Judg 18:18
And they ran and *f* him thence........ 1Sa 10:23
as though they would have *f* wheat........ 2Sa 4:6
*f* him out of the house of Machir,........ 2Sa 9:5
*f* her to his house, and she became........ 2Sa 11:27
*f* thence a wise woman, and said........ 2Sa 14:2
sent and *f* Hiram out of Tyre........ 1Kin 7:13
*f* from thence gold, four hundred........ 1Kin 9:28
they *f* a compass of seven days'........ 2Kin 3:9
*f* the rulers over hundreds, with........ 2Kin 11:4
And they *f* up, and brought forth........ 2Chr 1:17
*f* them, and brought them again........ 2Chr 12:11
they *f* forth Urijah out of Egypt,........ Jer 26:23
And from thence we *f* a compass........ Acts 28:13

**FETCHETH**
his hand *f* a stroke with the axe........ Deut 19:5

**FETCHT**
*f* a calf tender and good, and gave........ Gen 18:7

**FETTERS**
and bound him with *f* of brass........ Judg 16:21
bound, nor thy feet put into *f*........ 2Sa 3:34
and bound him with *f* of brass........ 2Kin 25:7
the thorns, and bound him with *f*...... 2Chr 33:11
of Babylon, and bound him in *f*........ 2Chr 36:6
And if they be bound in *f*, and be........ Job 36:8
Whose feet they hurt with *f*........ Ps 105:18
and their nobles with *f* of iron........ Ps 149:8
he had been often bound with *f*........ Mk 5:4
by him, and the *f* broken in pieces........ Mk 5:4
kept bound with chains and in *f*........ Lk 8:29

**FEVER**
with a consumption, and with a *f*...... Deut 28:22
mother laid, and sick of a *f*........ Mt 8:14
her hand, and the *f* left her........ Mt 8:15
wife's mother lay sick of a *f*........ Mk 1:30
and immediately the *f* left her........ Mk 1:31
mother was taken with a great *f*........ Lk 4:38
stood over her, and rebuked the *f*........ Lk 4:39
the seventh hour the *f* left him........ Jn 4:52
father of Publius lay sick of a *f*........ Acts 28:8

**FEW**
the damsel abide with us a *f* days........ Gen 24:55
And tarry with him a *f* days........ Gen 27:44
they seemed unto him but a *f* days .... Gen 29:20
I being *f* in number, they shall........ Gen 34:30
*f* and evil have the days of the........ Gen 47:9
if there remain but *f* years unto........ Lev 25:52
cattle, and make you *f* in number........ Lev 26:22
when the cloud was a *f* days upon........ Num 9:20
they be strong or weak, *f* or many.... Num 13:18
to *f* thou shalt give the less........ Num 26:54
be divided between many and *f*........ Num 26:56
that have *f* ye shall give *f*........ Num 35:8
that have *f* ye shall give *f*........ Num 35:8
ye shall be left *f* in number........ Deut 4:27
and sojourned there with a *f*........ Deut 26:5
And ye shall be left *f* in number........ Deut 28:62
and let not his men be *f*........ Deut 33:6
for they are but *f*........ Josh 7:3
the LORD to save by many or by *f*........ 1Sa 14:6
those *f* sheep in the wilderness........ 1Sa 17:28
empty vessels; borrow not a *f*........ 2Kin 4:3
When ye were but *f*, even a *f*,........ 1Chr 16:19
When ye were but *f*, even a *f*........ 1Chr 16:19
But the priests were too *f*........ 2Chr 29:34
night, I and some *f* men with me........ Neh 2:12
but the people were *f* therein........ Neh 7:4
Are not my days *f*........ Job 10:20
is born of a woman is of *f* days........ Job 14:1
When a *f* years are come, then I........ Job 16:22
they were but a *f* men in number........ Ps 105:12
yea, very *f*, and strangers in it........ Ps 105:12
Let his days be *f*........ Ps 109:8
therefore let thy words be *f*........ Eccl 5:2
a little city, and *f* men within it........ Eccl 9:14
grinders cease because they are *f*........ Eccl 12:3
and cut off nations not a *f*........ Is 10:7
trees of his forest shall be *f*........ Is 10:19
earth are burned, and *f* men left........ Is 24:6
them, and they shall not be *f*........ Jer 30:19
(for we are left but a *f* of many........ Jer 42:2
also take thereof a *f* in number........ Eze 5:3
But I will leave a *f* men of them........ Eze 12:16
but within *f* days he shall be........ Dan 11:20
life, and *f* there be that find it........ Mt 7:14
but the labourers are *f*........ Mt 9:37
said, Seven, and a *f* little fishes........ Mt 15:34
for many be called, but *f* chosen........ Mt 20:16
many are called, but *f* are chosen........ Mt 22:14
been faithful over a *f* things........ Mt 25:21
been faithful over a *f* things........ Mt 25:23
laid his hands upon a *f* sick folk........ Mk 6:5
they had a *f* small fishes........ Mk 8:7
is great, but the labourers are *f*........ Lk 10:2
shall be beaten with *f* stripes........ Lk 12:48
are there *f* that be saved........ Lk 13:23
and of the chief women not a *f*........ Acts 17:4
were Greeks, and of men, not a *f*........ Acts 17:12
hear us of thy clemency a *f* words........ Acts 24:4
(as I wrote afore in *f* words........ Eph 3:3
For they verily for a *f* days........ Heb 12:10
a letter unto you in *f* words........ Heb 13:22

ark was a preparing, wherein *f* 1Pet 3:20
But I have a *f* things against Rev 2:14
I have a *f* things against thee Rev 2:20
Thou hast a *f* names even in Rev 3:4

### FEWER
to the *f* ye shall give the less Num 33:54

### FEWEST
for ye were the *f* of all people Deut 7:7

### FEWNESS
according to the *f* of years thou Lev 25:16

### FIDELITY
but shewing all good *f* Titus 2:10

### FIELD
every plant of the *f* before it Gen 2:5
herb of the *f* before it grew Gen 2:5
God formed every beast of the *f* Gen 2:19
air, and to every beast of the *f* Gen 2:20
the *f* which the LORD God had made Gen 3:1
and above every beast of the *f* Gen 3:14
thou shalt eat the herb of the *f* Gen 3:18
to pass, when they were in the *f* Gen 4:8
which is in the end of his *f* Gen 23:9
the *f* give I thee, and the cave Gen 23:11
I will give thee money for the *f* Gen 23:13
the *f* of Ephron, which was in Gen 23:17
which was before Mamre, the *f* Gen 23:17
all the trees that were in the *f* Gen 23:17
the *f* of Machpelah before Mamre Gen 23:19
And the *f*, and the cave that is Gen 23:20
meditate in the *f* at the eventide Gen 24:63
that walketh in the *f* to meet us Gen 24:65
in the *f* of Ephron the son of Gen 25:9
The *f* which Abraham purchased of Gen 25:10
a cunning hunter, a man of the *f* Gen 25:27
and Esau came from the *f*, and he Gen 25:29
and thy bow, and go out to the *f* Gen 27:3
Esau went to the *f* to hunt for Gen 27:5
a *f* which the LORD hath blessed Gen 27:27
looked, and behold a well in the *f* Gen 29:2
and found mandrakes in the *f* Gen 30:14
came out of the *f* in the evening Gen 30:16
Leah to the *f* unto his flock, Gen 31:4
And he bought a parcel of a *f* Gen 33:19
were with his cattle in the *f* Gen 34:5
out of the *f* when they heard it Gen 34:7
city, and that which was in the *f* Gen 34:28
who smote Midian in the *f* of Moab Gen 36:35
we were binding sheaves in the *f* Gen 37:7
behold, he was wandering in the *f* Gen 37:15
he had in the house, and in the *f* Gen 39:5
the food of the *f*, which was Gen 41:48
Egyptians sold every man his *f* Gen 47:20
be your own, for seed of the *f* Gen 47:24
is in the *f* of Ephron the Hittite Gen 49:29
that is in the *f* of Machpelah Gen 49:30
the *f* of Ephron the Hittite for a Gen 49:30
The purchase of the *f* and of the Gen 49:32
in the cave of the *f* of Machpelah Gen 50:13
with the *f* for a possession of a Gen 50:13
in all manner of service in the *f* Ex 1:14
upon thy cattle which is in the *f* Ex 9:3
and all that thou hast in the *f* Ex 9:19
which shall be found in the *f* Ex 9:19
servants and his cattle in the *f* Ex 9:21
and upon every herb of the *f* Ex 9:22
of Egypt all that was in the *f* Ex 9:25
hail smote every herb of the *f* Ex 9:25
and brake every tree of the *f* Ex 9:25
groweth for you out of the *f* Ex 10:5
trees, or in the herbs of the *f* Ex 10:15
day ye shall not find it in the *f* Ex 16:25
If a man shall cause a *f* or Ex 22:5
and shall feed in another man's *f* Ex 22:5
of the best of his own *f*, and of Ex 22:5
or the standing corn, or the *f* Ex 22:6
that is torn of beasts in the *f* Ex 22:31
the beasts of the *f* shall eat Ex 23:11
which thou hast sown in the *f* Ex 23:16
in thy labours out of the *f* Ex 23:16
the beast of the *f* multiply Ex 23:29
living bird loose into the open *f* Lev 14:7
which they offer in the open *f* Lev 17:5
wholly reap the corners of thy *f* Lev 19:9
not sow thy *f* with mingled seed Lev 19:19
of thy *f* when thou reapest Lev 23:22
Six years thou shalt sow thy *f* Lev 25:3
thou shalt neither sow thy *f* Lev 25:4
the increase thereof out of the *f* Lev 25:12
But the *f* of the suburbs of their Lev 25:34
the trees of the *f* shall yield Lev 26:4
part of a *f* of his possession Lev 27:16
If he sanctify his *f* from the Lev 27:17
sanctify his *f* after the jubile Lev 27:18
if he that sanctified the *f* will Lev 27:19
And if he will not redeem the *f* Lev 27:20
he have sold the *f* to another man Lev 27:20
But the *f*, when it goeth out in Lev 27:21
unto the LORD, as a *f* devoted Lev 27:21
the LORD a *f* which he hath bought Lev 27:22
*f* shall return unto him of whom Lev 27:24
of the *f* of his possession, shall Lev 27:28
ox licketh up the grass of the *f* Num 22:4
of the way, and went into the *f* Num 22:23
brought him into the *f* of Zophim Num 23:14
thy neighbour's house, his *f* Deut 5:21
of the *f* increase upon thee Deut 7:22
that the *f* bringeth forth year by Deut 14:22
*f* is man's life) to employ them Deut 20:19
to possess it, lying in the *f* Deut 21:1
find a betrothed damsel in the *f* Deut 22:25
For he found her in the *f* Deut 22:27
down thine harvest in thy *f* Deut 24:19
and hast forgot a sheaf in the *f* Deut 24:19
and blessed shalt thou be in the *f* Deut 28:3
and cursed shalt thou be in the *f* Deut 28:16
carry much seed out into the *f* Deut 28:38
the inhabitants of Ai in the *f* Josh 8:24
him to ask of her father a *f* Josh 15:18
him to ask of her father a *f* Judg 1:14
marchedst out of the *f* of Edom Judg 5:4
death in the high places of the *f* Judg 5:18
thee, and lie in wait in the *f* Judg 9:32
the people went out into the *f* Judg 9:42
companies, and laid wait in the *f* Judg 9:43
the woman as she sat in the *f* Judg 13:9
his work out of the *f* at even Judg 19:16
and the other to Gibeah in the *f* Judg 20:31
Naomi, Let me now go to the *f* Ruth 2:2
gleaned in the *f* after the Ruth 2:3
part of the *f* belonging unto Boaz Ruth 2:3
Go not to glean in another *f* Ruth 2:8
be on the *f* that they do reap Ruth 2:9
she gleaned in the *f* until even Ruth 2:17
they meet thee not in any other *f* Ruth 2:22
buyest the *f* of the hand of Naomi Ruth 4:5
in the *f* about four thousand men 1Sa 4:2
cart came into the *f* of Joshua 1Sa 6:14
unto this day in the *f* of Joshua 1Sa 6:18
came after the herd out of the *f* 1Sa 11:5
trembling in the host, in the *f* 1Sa 14:15
air, and to the beasts of the *f* 1Sa 17:44
my father in the *f* where thou art 1Sa 19:3
the *f* unto the third day at even 1Sa 20:5
Come, and let us go out into the *f* 1Sa 20:11
went out both of them into the *f* 1Sa 20:11
So David hid himself in the *f* 1Sa 20:24
the *f* at the time appointed with 1Sa 20:35
they found an Egyptian in the *f* 1Sa 30:11
were by themselves in the *f* 2Sa 10:8
and came out unto us into the *f* 2Sa 11:23
they two strove together in the *f* 2Sa 14:6
Joab's *f* is near mine, and he hath 2Sa 14:30
servants set the *f* on fire 2Sa 14:30
thy servants set my *f* on fire 2Sa 14:31
robbed of her whelps in the *f* 2Sa 17:8
out into the *f* against Israel 2Sa 18:6
out of the highway into the *f* 2Sa 20:12
nor the beasts of the *f* by night 2Sa 21:10
and they two were alone in the *f* 1Kin 11:29
him that dieth in the *f* shall the 1Kin 14:11
him that dieth in the *f* shall the 1Kin 21:24
out into the *f* to gather herbs 2Kin 4:39
camp to hide themselves in the *f* 2Kin 7:12
all the fruits of the *f* since the 2Kin 8:6
of the *f* of Naboth the Jezreelite 2Kin 9:25
the *f* in the portion of Jezreel 2Kin 9:37
in the highway of the fuller's *f* 2Kin 18:17
they were as the grass of the *f* 2Kin 19:26
smote Midian in the *f* of Moab 1Chr 1:46
come were by themselves in the *f* 1Chr 19:9
*f* for tillage of the ground was 1Chr 27:26
him with his fathers in the *f* of 2Chr 26:23
and of all the increase of the *f* 2Chr 31:5
were fled every one to his *f* Neh 13:10
league with the stones of the *f* Job 5:23
the beasts of the *f* shall be at Job 5:23
reap every one his corn in the *f* Job 24:6
all the beasts of the *f* play Job 40:20
oxen, yea, and the beasts of the *f* Ps 8:7
the wild beasts of the *f* are mine Ps 50:11
land of Egypt, in the *f* of Zoan Ps 78:12
and his wonders in the *f* of Zoan Ps 78:43
beast of the *f* doth devour it Ps 80:13
Let the *f* be joyful, and all that Ps 96:12
as a flower of the *f*, so he Ps 103:15
drink to every beast of the *f* Ps 104:11
make it fit for thyself in the *f* Prov 24:27
I went by the *f* of the slothful, Prov 24:30
the goats are the price of the *f* Prov 27:26
She considereth a *f*, and buyeth it Prov 31:16
king himself is served by the *f* Eccl 5:9
roes, and by the hinds of the *f* Song 2:7
roes, and by the hinds of the *f* Song 3:5
let us go forth into the *f* Song 7:11
to house, that lay *f* to *f* Is 5:8
to house, that lay *f* to *f* Is 5:8
in the highway of the fuller's *f* Is 7:3
his forest, and of his fruitful *f* Is 10:18
and joy out of the plentiful *f* Is 16:10
shall be turned into a fruitful *f* Is 29:17
the fruitful *f* shall be esteemed Is 29:17
and the wilderness be a fruitful *f* Is 32:15
the fruitful *f* be counted for a Is 32:15
remain in the fruitful *f* Is 32:16
in the highway of the fuller's *f* Is 36:2
they were as the grass of the *f* Is 37:27
thereof is as the flower of the *f* Is 40:6
beast of the *f* shall honour me Is 43:20
all the trees of the *f* shall clap Is 55:12
All ye beasts of the *f*, come to Is 56:9
As keepers of a *f*, are they Jer 4:17
Go not forth into the *f*, nor walk Jer 6:25
beast, and upon the trees of the *f* Jer 7:20
fall as dung upon the open *f* Jer 9:22
and the herbs of every *f* wither Jer 12:4
assemble all the beasts of the *f* Jer 12:9
the hind also calved in the *f* Jer 14:5
If I go forth into the *f*, then Jer 14:18
O my mountain in the *f*, I will Jer 17:3
cometh from the rock of the *f* Jer 18:14
Zion shall be plowed like a *f* Jer 26:18
the beasts of the *f* have I given Jer 27:6
him the beasts of the *f* also Jer 28:14
Buy thee my *f* that is in Anathoth Jer 32:7
LORD, and said unto me, Buy my *f* Jer 32:8
I bought the *f* of Hanameel my Jer 32:9
GOD, Buy thee the *f* for money Jer 32:25
neither have we vineyard, nor *f* Jer 35:9
for we have treasures in the *f* Jer 41:8
is taken from the plentiful *f* Jer 48:33
for want of the fruits of the *f* Lam 4:9
he that is in the *f* shall die Eze 7:15
thou wast cast out in the open *f* Eze 16:5
to multiply as the bud of the *f* Eze 16:7
and planted it in a fruitful *f* Eze 17:5
all the trees of the *f* shall know Eze 17:24
against the forest of the south *f* Eze 20:46
the *f* shall be slain by the sword Eze 26:6
the sword thy daughters in the *f* Eze 26:8
for meat to the beasts of the *f* Eze 29:5
unto all the trees of the *f* Eze 31:4
above all the trees of the *f* Eze 31:5
of the *f* bring forth their young Eze 31:6
all the beasts of the *f* shall be Eze 31:13
trees of the *f* fainted for him Eze 31:15
cast thee forth upon the open *f* Eze 32:4
him that is in the open *f* will I Eze 33:27
meat to all the beasts of the *f* Eze 34:5
meat to every beast of the *f* Eze 34:8
the tree of the *f* shall yield her Eze 34:27
tree, and the increase of the *f* Eze 36:30
heaven, and the beasts of the *f* Eze 38:20
beasts of the *f* to be devoured Eze 39:4
Thou shalt fall upon the open *f* Eze 39:5
shall take no wood out of the *f* Eze 39:10
fowl, and to every beast of the *f* Eze 39:17
of men dwell, the beasts of the *f* Dan 2:38
the beasts of the *f* had shadow Dan 4:12
in the tender grass of the *f* Dan 4:15
which the beasts of the *f* dwelt Dan 4:21
in the tender grass of the *f* Dan 4:23
be with the beasts of the *f* Dan 4:23
shall be with the beasts of the *f* Dan 4:25
shall be with the beasts of the *f* Dan 4:32
beasts of the *f* shall eat them Hos 2:12
for them with the beasts of the *f* Hos 2:18
with the beasts of the *f* Hos 4:3
hemlock in the furrows of the *f* Hos 10:4
The *f* is wasted, the land Joel 1:10
the harvest of the *f* is perished Joel 1:11
tree, even all the trees of the *f* Joel 1:12
burned all the trees of the *f* Joel 1:19
The beasts of the *f* cry also unto Joel 1:20
Be not afraid, ye beasts of the *f* Joel 2:22
make Samaria as an heap of the *f* Mic 1:6
for your sake be plowed as a *f* Mic 3:12
and thou shalt dwell in the *f* Mic 4:10
rain, to every one grass in the *f* Zec 10:1
fruit before the time in the *f* Mal 3:11
Consider the lilies of the *f* Mt 6:28
God so clothe the grass of the *f* Mt 6:30
which sowed good seed in his *f* Mt 13:24
not thou sow good seed in thy *f* Mt 13:27
a man took, and sowed in his *f* Mt 13:31
the parable of the tares of the *f* Mt 13:36
The *f* is the world Mt 13:38
is like unto treasure hid in a *f* Mt 13:44
that he hath, and buyeth that *f* Mt 13:44
*f* return back to take his clothes Mt 24:18
Then shall two be in the *f* Mt 24:40
bought with them the potter's *f* Mt 27:7
Wherefore that *f* was called Mt 27:8
The *f* of blood, unto this day Mt 27:8
And gave them for the potter's *f* Mt 27:10
let him that is in the *f* not turn Mk 13:16
shepherds abiding in the *f* Lk 2:8
grass, which is to day in the *f* Lk 12:28
Now his elder son was in the *f* Lk 15:25
and by, when he is come from the *f* Lk 17:7
and he that is in the *f*, let him Lk 17:31
Two men shall be in the *f* Lk 17:36
Now this man purchased a *f* with Acts 1:18
insomuch as that *f* is called in Acts 1:19
that is to say, The *f* of blood Acts 1:19

### FIELDS
of the villages, and out of the *f* Ex 8:13
out of the city into the open *f* Lev 14:53
counted as the *f* of the country Lev 25:31
is not of the *f* of his possession Lev 27:22
or given us inheritance of *f* Num 16:14
slain with a sword in the open *f* Num 19:16
we will not pass through the *f* Num 20:17
we will not turn into the *f* Num 21:22
grass in thy *f* for thy cattle Deut 11:15
might eat the increase of the *f* Deut 32:13
of Sodom, and of the *f* of Gomorrah Deut 32:32
But the *f* of the city, and the Josh 21:12
And they went out into the *f* Judg 9:27
all the people that were in the *f* Judg 9:44
And he will take your *f*, and your 1Sa 8:14
of Jesse give every one of you *f* 1Sa 22:7
with them, when we were in the *f* 1Sa 25:15
upon you, nor *f* of offerings 2Sa 1:21
lord, are encamped in the open *f* 2Sa 11:11
to Anathoth, unto thine own *f* 1Kin 2:26
him that dieth of his in the *f* 1Kin 16:4
Jerusalem in the *f* of Kidron 2Kin 23:4
But the *f* of the city, and the 1Chr 6:56

let the *f* rejoice, and all that is 1Chr 16:32
and over the storehouses in the *f* 1Chr 27:25
which were in the *f* of the 2Chr 31:19
And for the villages, with their *f* Neh 11:25
the *f* thereof, at Azekah, and in Neh 11:30
Gilgal, and out of the *f* of Geba Neh 12:29
*f* of the cities the portions of Neh 12:44
and sendeth waters upon the *f* Job 5:10
And sow the *f*, and plant vineyards, Ps 107:37
we found it in the *f* of the wood Ps 132:6
had not made the earth, nor the *f* Prov 8:26
not into the *f* of the fatherless Prov 23:10
For the *f* of Heshbon languish, and Is 16:8
for the teats, for the pleasant *f* Is 32:12
turned unto others, with their *f* Jer 6:12
their *f* to them that shall Jer 8:10
on the hills in the *f* Jer 13:27
all the *f* unto the brook of Jer 31:40
Houses and *f* and vineyards shall be Jer 32:15
*f* shall be bought in this land, Jer 32:43
Men shall buy *f* for money Jer 32:44
vineyards and *f* at the same time Jer 39:10
of the forces which were in the *f* Jer 40:7
of the forces that were in the *f* Jer 40:13
thou shalt fall upon the open *f* Eze 29:5
as heaps in the furrows of the *f* Hos 12:11
shall possess the *f* of Ephraim Obad 19
of Ephraim, and the *f* of Samaria Obad 19
And they covet *f*, and take them by Mic 2:2
away he hath divided our *f* Mic 2:4
the *f* shall yield no meat Hab 3:17
the corn *f* on the sabbath day Mk 2:23
that he went through the corn *f* Lk 6:1
sent him into his *f* to feed swine Lk 15:15
up your eyes, and look on the *f* Jn 4:35
who have reaped down your *f* Jas 5:4

### FIERCE

be their anger, for it was *f* Gen 49:7
Turn from thy *f* wrath, and repent Ex 32:12
that the *f* anger of the LORD may Num 25:4
to augment yet the *f* anger of the Num 32:14
A nation of *f* countenance Deut 28:50
arose from the table in *f* anger 1Sa 20:34
his *f* wrath upon Amalek, 1Sa 28:18
for the *f* wrath of the LORD is 2Chr 28:11
there is *f* wrath against Israel 2Chr 28:13
that his *f* wrath may turn away 2Chr 29:10
until the *f* wrath of our God for Ezr 10:14
lion, and the voice of the *f* lion Job 4:10
Thou huntest me as a *f* lion Job 10:16
nor the *f* lion passed by it Job 28:8
None is so *f* that dare stir him Job 41:10
Thy *f* wrath goeth over me Ps 88:16
for the *f* anger of Rezin with Is 7:4
*f* anger, to lay the land desolate Is 13:9
and in the day of his *f* anger Is 13:13
a *f* king shall rule over them, Is 19:4
Thou shalt not see a *f* people Is 33:19
for the *f* anger of the LORD is Jer 4:8
of the LORD, and by his *f* anger Jer 4:26
of the *f* anger of the LORD Jer 12:13
of the *f* anger of the LORD Jer 25:37
and because of his *f* anger Jer 25:38
The *f* anger of the LORD shall not Jer 30:24
evil upon them, even my *f* anger Jer 49:37
soul from the *f* anger of the LORD Jer 51:45
me in the day of his *f* anger Lam 1:12
He hath cut off in his *f* anger Lam 2:3
he hath poured out his *f* anger Lam 4:11
a king of *f* countenance, and Dan 8:23
and turn away from his *f* anger Jonah 3:9
are more *f* than the evening Hab 1:8
before the *f* anger of the LORD Zeph 2:2
indignation, even all my *f* anger Zeph 3:8
out of the tombs, exceeding *f* Mt 8:28
And they were the more *f*, saying, Lk 23:5
false accusers, incontinent, *f* 2Ti 3:3
great, and are driven of *f* winds Jas 3:4

### FIERCENESS

may turn from the *f* of his anger Deut 13:17
turned from the *f* of his anger Josh 7:26
not from the *f* of his great wrath 2Kin 23:26
that the *f* of his wrath may turn 2Chr 30:8
He swalloweth the ground with *f* Job 39:24
cast upon them the *f* of his anger Ps 78:49
thyself from the *f* of thine anger Ps 85:3
because of the *f* of the oppressor Jer 25:38
not execute the *f* of mine anger Hos 11:9
can abide in the *f* of his anger Nah 1:6
of the wine of the *f* of his wrath Rev 16:19
treadeth the winepress of the *f* Rev 19:15

### FIERCER

*f* than the words of the men of 2Sa 19:43

### FIERY

the LORD sent *f* serpents among Num 21:6
unto Moses, Make thee a *f* serpent Num 21:8
wherein were *f* serpents, and Deut 8:15
right hand went a *f* law for them Deut 33:2
Thou shalt make them as a *f* oven Ps 21:9
fruit shall be a *f* flying serpent Is 14:29
*f* flying serpent, they will carry Is 30:6
the midst of a burning *f* furnace Dan 3:6
the midst of a burning *f* furnace Dan 3:11
the midst of a burning *f* furnace Dan 3:15
us from the burning *f* furnace Dan 3:17
them into the burning *f* furnace Dan 3:20
midst of the burning *f* furnace Dan 3:21
midst of the burning *f* furnace Dan 3:23
mouth of the burning *f* furnace Dan 3:26
his throne was like the *f* flame Dan 7:9
A *f* stream issued and came forth Dan 7:10
all the *f* darts of the wicked Eph 6:16
*f* indignation, which shall devour Heb 10:27
the *f* trial which is to try you 1Pet 4:12

### FIFTEEN

*f* years, and begat sons and Gen 5:10
*F* cubits upward did the waters Gen 7:20
an hundred threescore and *f* years Gen 25:7
of the gate shall be *f* cubits Ex 27:14
side shall be hangings *f* cubits Ex 27:15
side of the gate were *f* cubits Ex 38:14
hand, were hangings of *f* cubits Ex 38:15
*f* shekels, after the shekel of Ex 38:25
thy estimation shall be *f* shekels Lev 27:7
six hundred and threescore and *f* Num 31:37
about *f* thousand men, all that Judg 8:10
Now Ziba had *f* sons and twenty 2Sa 9:10
his *f* sons and his twenty servants 2Sa 19:17
on forty five pillars, *f* in a row 1Kin 7:3
Jehoahaz king of Israel *f* years 2Kin 14:17
I will add unto thy days *f* years 2Kin 20:6
Jehoahaz king of Israel *f* years 2Chr 25:25
I will add unto thy days *f* years Is 38:5
*f* shekels, shall be your maneh Eze 45:12
her to me for *f* pieces of silver Hos 3:2
Jerusalem, about *f* furlongs off Jn 11:18
kindred, threescore and *f* souls Acts 7:14
again, and found it *f* fathoms Acts 27:28
Peter, and abode with him *f* days Gal 1:18

### FIFTEENTH

on the *f* day of the second month Ex 16:1
on the *f* day of the same month is Lev 23:6
The *f* day of this seventh month Lev 23:34
Also in the *f* day of the seventh Lev 23:39
in the *f* day of this month is the Num 28:17
on the *f* day of the seventh month Num 29:12
on the *f* day of the first month Num 33:3
on the *f* day of the month, like 1Kin 12:32
the *f* day of the eighth month 1Kin 12:33
In the *f* year of Amaziah the son 2Kin 14:23
The *f* to Bilgah, the sixteenth to 1Chr 24:14
The *f* to Jeremoth, he, his sons, 1Chr 25:22
in the *f* year of the reign of Asa 2Chr 15:10
on the *f* day of the same they Est 9:18
the *f* day of the same, yearly, Est 9:21
in the *f* day of the month, that Eze 32:17
in the *f* day of the month, shall Eze 45:25
Now in the *f* year of the reign of Lk 3:1

### FIFTH

and the morning were the *f* day Gen 1:23
and bare Jacob the *f* son Gen 30:17
take up the *f* part of the land of Gen 41:34
give the *f* part unto Pharaoh Gen 47:24
Pharaoh should have the *f* part Gen 47:26
and shall add the *f* part thereto Lev 5:16
shall add the *f* part more thereto Lev 6:5
in the *f* year shall ye eat of the Lev 19:25
put the *f* part thereof unto it Lev 22:14
then he shall add a *f* part Lev 27:13
then he shall add the *f* part of Lev 27:15
then he shall add the *f* part of Lev 27:19
shall add a *f* part of it thereto Lev 27:27
add thereto the *f* part thereof Lev 27:31
and add unto it the *f* part thereof Num 5:7
On the *f* day Shelumiel the son of Num 7:36
on the *f* day nine bullocks, two Num 29:26
in the first day of the *f* month Num 33:38
the *f* lot came out for the tribe Josh 19:24
morning on the *f* day to depart Judg 19:8
spear smote him under the *f* rib 2Sa 2:23
and the *f*, Shephatiah the son of 2Sa 3:4
smote him there under the *f* rib 2Sa 3:27
and they smote him under the *f* rib 2Sa 4:6
smote him therewith in the *f* rib 2Sa 20:10
posts were a *f* part of the wall 1Kin 6:31
in the *f* year of king Rehoboam 1Kin 14:25
in the *f* year of Joram the son of 2Kin 8:16
And in the *f* month, on the seventh 2Kin 25:8
the fourth, Raddai the *f*, 1Chr 2:14
The *f*, Shephatiah of Abital 1Chr 3:3
Nohah the fourth, and Rapha the *f* 1Chr 8:2
the fourth, Jeremiah the *f* 1Chr 12:10
The *f* to Malchijah, the sixth to 1Chr 24:9
The *f* to Nethaniah, he, his sons, 1Chr 25:12
Elam the *f*, Jehohanan the sixth, 1Chr 26:3
the fourth, and Nethaneel the *f* 1Chr 26:4
The *f* captain for the *f* month 1Chr 27:8
that in the *f* year of king 2Chr 12:2
came to Jerusalem in the *f* month Ezr 7:8
on the first day of the *f* month Ezr 7:9
unto me in like manner the *f* time Neh 6:5
*f* day of the month Elul, in fifty Neh 6:15
Jerusalem captive in the *f* month Jer 1:3
fourth year, and in the *f* month Jer 28:1
it came to pass in the *f* year of Jer 36:9
Now in the *f* month, in the tenth Jer 52:12
in the *f* day of the month, as I Eze 1:1
In the *f* day of the month Eze 1:2
which was the *f* year of king Eze 1:2
in the *f* day of the month, as I Eze 8:1
the seventh year, in the *f* month Eze 20:1
in the *f* day of the month, that Eze 33:21
Should I weep in the *f* month Zec 7:3
ye fasted and mourned in the *f* Zec 7:5
month, and the fast of the *f* Zec 8:19
And when he had opened the *f* seal Rev 6:9
the *f* angel sounded, and I saw a Rev 9:1
the *f* angel poured out his vial Rev 16:10
The *f*, sardonyx; the sixth Rev 21:20

### FIFTIES

rulers of hundreds, rulers of *f* Ex 18:21
rulers of hundreds, rulers of *f* Ex 18:25
over hundreds, and captains over *f* Deut 1:15
thousands, and captains over *f* 1Sa 8:12
the former *f* with their *f* 2Kin 1:14
in ranks, by hundreds, and by *f* Mk 6:40
them sit down by *f* in a company Lk 9:14

### FIFTIETH

And ye shall hallow the *f* year Lev 25:10
shall that *f* year be unto you Lev 25:11
In the *f* year of Azariah king of 2Kin 15:23
*f* year of Azariah king of Judah 2Kin 15:27

### FIFTY

the breadth of it *f* cubits Gen 6:15
the earth an hundred and *f* days Gen 7:24
*f* days the waters were abated Gen 8:3
flood three hundred and *f* years Gen 9:28
Noah were nine hundred and *f* years Gen 9:29
Peradventure there be *f* righteous Gen 18:24
the *f* righteous that are therein Gen 18:24
If I find in Sodom *f* righteous Gen 18:26
lack five of the *f* righteous Gen 18:28
*F* loops shalt thou make in the Ex 26:5
*f* loops shalt thou make in the Ex 26:5
thou shalt make *f* taches of gold Ex 26:6
thou shalt make *f* loops on the Ex 26:10
*f* loops in the edge of the Ex 26:10
thou shalt make *f* taches of brass Ex 26:11
shall be hangings of *f* cubits Ex 27:12
side eastward shall be *f* cubits Ex 27:13
and the breadth *f* every where Ex 27:18
*f* shekels, and of sweet calamus Ex 30:23
calamus two hundred and *f* shekels, Ex 30:23
*F* loops made he in one curtain, Ex 36:12
*f* loops made he in the edge of Ex 36:12
he made *f* taches of gold, and Ex 36:13
And he made *f* loops upon the Ex 36:17
*f* loops made he upon the edge of Ex 36:17
he made *f* taches of brass to Ex 36:18
side were hangings of *f* cubits Ex 38:12
the east side eastward *f* cubits Ex 38:13
thousand and five hundred and *f* men Ex 38:26
sabbath shall ye number *f* days Lev 23:16
shall be *f* shekels of silver Lev 27:3
be valued at *f* shekels of silver Lev 27:16
of the tribe of Simeon, were *f* Num 1:23
and five thousand six hundred and *f* Num 1:25
of the tribe of Issachar, were *f* Num 1:29
of the tribe of Zebulun, were *f* Num 1:31
of the tribe of Naphtali, were *f* Num 1:43
thousand and five hundred and *f* Num 1:46
were numbered thereof, were *f* Num 2:6
were numbered thereof, were *f* Num 2:8
were numbered of them, were *f* Num 2:13
five thousand and six hundred and *f* Num 2:15
were an hundred thousand and *f* Num 2:16
one thousand and four hundred and *f* Num 2:16
were numbered of them, were *f* Num 2:30
Dan were an hundred thousand and *f* Num 2:31
thousand and five hundred and *f* Num 2:32
and upward even until *f* years old Num 4:3
upward until *f* years old shalt Num 4:23
upward even unto *f* years old Num 4:30
and upward even unto *f* years old Num 4:35
two thousand seven hundred and *f* Num 4:36
and upward even unto *f* years old Num 4:39
and upward even unto *f* years old Num 4:43
and upward even unto *f* years old Num 4:47
from the age of *f* years they Num 8:25
*f* princes of the assembly, famous Num 16:2
censer, two hundred and *f* censers Num 16:17
*f* men that offered incense Num 16:35
devoured two hundred and *f* men Num 26:10
that were numbered of them, *f* Num 26:34
who were *f* and three thousand and Num 26:47
thou shalt take one portion of *f* Num 31:30
half, Moses took one portion of *f* Num 31:47
seven hundred and *f* shekels Num 31:52
father *f* shekels of silver Deut 22:29
wedge of gold of *f* shekels weight Josh 7:21
he smote of the people *f* thousand 1Sa 6:19
and *f* men to run before him 2Sa 15:1
the oxen for *f* shekels of silver 2Sa 24:24
and *f* men to run before him 1Kin 1:5
and the breadth thereof *f* cubits 1Kin 7:2
the length thereof was *f* cubits 1Kin 7:6
Solomon's work, five hundred and *f* 1Kin 9:23
and an horse for an hundred and *f* 1Kin 10:29
and hid them by *f* in a cave 1Kin 18:4
LORD's prophets by *f* in a cave 1Kin 18:13
of Baal four hundred and *f* 1Kin 18:19
are four hundred and *f* men 1Kin 18:22
him a captain of *f* with his *f* 2Kin 1:9
and said to the captain of *f* 2Kin 1:10
heaven, and consume thee and thy *f* 2Kin 1:10
heaven, and consumed him and his *f* 2Kin 1:10
captain of *f* with his *f* 2Kin 1:11
heaven, and consume thee and thy *f* 2Kin 1:12
heaven, and consumed him and his *f* 2Kin 1:12
of the third *f* with his *f* 2Kin 1:13
And the third captain of *f* went up 2Kin 1:13
the life of these *f* thy servants 2Kin 1:13
*f* men of the sons of the prophets 2Kin 2:7
be with thy servants *f* strong men 2Kin 2:16
They sent therefore *f* men 2Kin 2:17
people to Jehoahaz but *f* horsemen 2Kin 13:7

two and *f* years in Jerusalem 2Kin 15:2
of each man *f* shekels of silver, 2Kin 15:20
with him *f* men of the Gileadites 2Kin 15:25
he began to reign, and reigned *f* 2Kin 21:1
of their camels *f* thousand 1Chr 5:21
*f* thousand, and of asses two 1Chr 5:21
and sons' sons, an hundred and *f* 1Chr 8:40
generations, nine hundred and *f* 1Chr 9:9
*f* thousand, which could keep rank 1Chr 12:33
and an horse for an hundred and *f* 2Chr 1:17
*f* thousand and three thousand and 2Chr 2:17
the nails was *f* shekels of gold 2Chr 3:9
officers, even two hundred and *f* 2Chr 8:10
*f* talents of gold, and brought 2Chr 8:18
began to reign, and he reigned *f* 2Chr 26:3
began to reign, and he reigned *f* 2Chr 33:1
of Elam, a thousand two hundred *f* Ezr 2:7
of Bigvai, two thousand *f* Ezr 2:14
children of Adin, four hundred *f* Ezr 2:15
The men of Netophah, *f* and six Ezr 2:22
The children of Nebo, *f* and two Ezr 2:29
children of Magbish, an hundred *f* Ezr 2:30
Elam, a thousand two hundred *f* Ezr 2:31
children of Immer, a thousand *f* Ezr 2:37
children of Nekoda, six hundred *f* Ezr 2:60
of the males an hundred and *f* Ezr 8:3
of Jonathan, and with him *f* males Ezr 8:6
*f* talents of silver, and silver Ezr 8:26
*f* of the Jews and rulers, beside Neh 5:17
fifth day of the month Elul, in *f* Neh 6:15
children of Arah, six hundred *f* Neh 7:10
of Elam, a thousand two hundred *f* Neh 7:12
children of Adin, six hundred *f* Neh 7:20
The men of the other Nebo, *f* Neh 7:33
Elam, a thousand two hundred *f* Neh 7:34
children of Immer, a thousand *f* Neh 7:40
*f* basons, five hundred and thirty Neh 7:70
gallows be made of *f* cubits high Est 5:14
also, the gallows *f* cubits high Est 7:9
The captain of *f*, and the Is 3:3
of the inner gate were *f* cubits Eze 40:15
the length thereof was *f* cubits Eze 40:21
the length was *f* cubits, and the Eze 40:25
it was *f* cubits long, and five and Eze 40:29
it was *f* cubits long, and five and Eze 40:33
the length was *f* cubits, and the Eze 40:36
door, and the breadth was *f* cubits Eze 42:2
the length thereof was *f* cubits Eze 42:7
in the utter court was *f* cubits Eze 42:8
*f* cubits round about for the Eze 45:2
toward the north two hundred and *f* Eze 48:17
toward the south two hundred and *f* Eze 48:17
toward the east two hundred and *f* Eze 48:17
toward the west two hundred and *f* Eze 48:17
out *f* vessels out of the press Hag 2:16
hundred pence, and the other *f* Lk 7:41
and sit down quickly, and write *f* Lk 16:6
him, Thou art not yet *f* years old Jn 8:57
of great fishes, an hundred and *f* Jn 21:11
*f* years, until Samuel the prophet Acts 13:20
found it *f* thousand pieces of Acts 19:19

**FIG**
they sewed *f* leaves together, and Gen 3:7
and *f* trees, and pomegranates Deut 8:8
And the trees said to the *f* tree Judg 9:10
But the *f* tree said unto them, Judg 9:11
his vine and under his *f* tree 1Kin 4:25
vine, and every one of his *f* tree 2Kin 18:31
their vines also and their *f* trees Ps 105:33
Whoso keepeth the *f* tree shall Prov 27:18
The *f* tree putteth forth her Song 2:13
as a falling *f* from the *f* tree Is 34:4
vine, and every one of his *f* tree Is 36:16
eat up thy vines and thy *f* trees Jer 5:17
the vine, nor figs on the *f* tree Jer 8:13
her *f* trees, whereof she hath Hos 2:12
in the *f* tree at her first time Hos 9:10
vine waste, and barked my *f* tree Joel 1:7
up, and the *f* tree languisheth Joel 1:12
the *f* tree and the vine do yield Joel 2:22
your *f* trees and your olive trees Amos 4:9
his vine and under his *f* tree Mic 4:4
*f* trees with the firstripe figs Nah 3:12
Although the *f* tree shall not Hab 3:17
the *f* tree, and the pomegranate, Hag 2:19
the vine and under the *f* tree Zec 3:10
when he saw a *f* tree in the way, Mt 21:19
presently the *f* tree withered Mt 21:19
How soon is the *f* tree withered Mt 21:20
this which is done to the *f* tree Mt 21:21
Now learn a parable of the *f* tree Mt 24:32
seeing a *f* tree afar off having Mk 11:13
they saw the *f* tree dried up from Mk 11:20
the *f* tree which thou cursedst is Mk 11:21
Now learn a parable of the *f* tree Mk 13:28
A certain man had a *f* tree Lk 13:6
come seeking fruit on this *f* tree Lk 13:7
Behold the *f* tree, and all the Lk 21:29
when thou wast under the *f* tree Jn 1:48
thee, I saw thee under the *f* tree Jn 1:50
Can the *f* tree, my brethren, bear Jas 3:12
even as a *f* tree casteth her Rev 6:13

**FIGHT**
*f* against us, and so get them up Ex 1:10
The LORD shall *f* for you, and ye Ex 14:14
out men, and go out, *f* with Amalek Ex 17:9
before you, he shall *f* for you Deut 1:30
the LORD, we will go up and *f* Deut 1:41
unto them, Go not up, neither *f* Deut 1:42
and all his people, to *f* at Jahaz Deut 2:32
LORD your God he shall *f* for you Deut 3:22
to *f* for you against your enemies Deut 20:4
nigh unto a city to *f* against it Deut 20:10
to *f* with Joshua and with Israel, Josh 9:2
your enemies against whom ye *f* Josh 10:25
of Merom, to *f* against Israel Josh 11:5
Dan went up to *f* against Leshem Josh 19:47
first, to *f* against them Judg 1:1
that we may *f* against the Judg 1:3
down to *f* against the Canaanites Judg 1:9
wentest to *f* with the Midianites Judg 8:1
out, I pray now, and *f* with them Judg 9:38
Jordan to *f* also against Judah Judg 10:9
man is he that will begin to *f* Judg 10:18
that we may *f* with the children Judg 11:6
*f* against the children of Ammon, Judg 11:8
If ye bring me home again to *f* Judg 11:9
come against me to *f* in my land Judg 11:12
or did he ever *f* against them Judg 11:25
of Ammon to *f* against them Judg 11:32
*f* against the children of Ammon Judg 12:1
unto me this day, to *f* against me Judg 12:3
array to *f* against them at Gibeah Judg 20:20
quit yourselves like men, and *f* 1Sa 4:9
out before us, and *f* our battles 1Sa 8:20
together to *f* with Israel 1Sa 13:5
*f* against them until they be 1Sa 15:18
If he be able to *f* with me 1Sa 17:9
me a man, that we may *f* together 1Sa 17:10
the host was going forth to the *f* 1Sa 17:20
will go and *f* with this Philistine 1Sa 17:32
this Philistine to *f* with him 1Sa 17:33
for me, and *f* the LORD's battles 1Sa 18:17
the Philistines *f* against Keilah 1Sa 23:1
for warfare, to *f* with Israel 1Sa 28:1
that I may not go *f* against the 1Sa 29:8
nigh unto the city when ye did *f* 2Sa 11:20
to *f* against the house of Israel, 1Kin 12:21
nor *f* against your brethren the 1Kin 12:24
but let us *f* against them in the 1Kin 20:23
we will *f* against them in the 1Kin 20:25
up to Aphek, to *f* against Israel 1Kin 20:26
*F* neither with small nor great, 1Kin 22:31
turned aside to *f* against him 1Kin 22:32
were come up to *f* against them 2Kin 3:21
*f* for your master's house 2Kin 10:3
he is come out to *f* against thee 2Kin 19:9
to *f* against Israel, that he 2Chr 11:1
nor *f* against your brethren 2Chr 11:4
*f* ye not against the LORD God of 2Chr 13:12
*F* ye not with small or great, 2Chr 18:30
they compassed about him to *f* 2Chr 18:31
not need to *f* in this battle 2Chr 20:17
purposed to *f* against Jerusalem 2Chr 32:2
to help us, and to *f* our battles 2Chr 32:8
up to *f* against Charchemish by 2Chr 35:20
himself, that he might *f* with him 2Chr 35:22
came to *f* in the valley of 2Chr 35:22
to *f* against Jerusalem, and to Neh 4:8
*f* for your brethren, your sons, Neh 4:14
our God shall *f* for us Neh 4:20
*f* against them that *f* against Ps 35:1
they be many that *f* against me Ps 56:2
hands to war, and my fingers to *f* Ps 144:1
they shall *f* every one against Is 19:2
the nations that *f* against Ariel Is 29:7
even all that *f* against her Is 29:7
that *f* against mount Zion Is 29:8
of shaking will he *f* with it Is 30:32
come down to *f* for mount Zion Is 31:4
they shall *f* against thee Jer 1:19
they shall *f* against thee, but Jer 15:20
wherewith ye *f* against the king Jer 21:4
I myself will *f* against you with Jer 21:5
though ye *f* with the Chaldeans, Jer 32:5
that *f* against it, because of the Jer 32:24
that *f* against this city, shall Jer 32:29
They come to *f* with the Chaldeans Jer 33:5
and they shall *f* against it Jer 34:22
*f* against this city, and take it, Jer 37:8
the Chaldeans that *f* against you Jer 37:10
went to *f* with Ishmael the son of Jer 41:12
men of Babylon have forborn to *f* Jer 51:30
now will I return to *f* with the Dan 10:20
*f* with him, even with the king of Dan 11:11
and they shall *f*, because the LORD Zec 10:5
*f* against those nations, as when Zec 14:3
Judah also shall *f* at Jerusalem Zec 14:14
world, then would my servants *f* Jn 18:36
ye be found even to *f* against God Acts 5:39
to him, let us not *f* against God Acts 23:9
so *f* I, not as one that beateth 1Cor 9:26
*F* the good *f* of faith 1Ti 6:12
I have fought a good *f*, I have 2Ti 4:7
endured a great *f* of afflictions Heb 10:32
made strong, waxed valiant in *f* Heb 11:34
ye *f* and war, yet ye have not, Jas 4:2
will *f* against them with the Rev 2:16

**FIGHTETH**
for the LORD *f* for them against Ex 14:25
your God, he it is that *f* for you Josh 23:10
because my lord *f* the battles of 1Sa 25:28

**FIGHTING**
of Elah, *f* with the Philistines 1Sa 17:19
Uzziah had an host of *f* men 2Chr 26:11
he *f* daily oppresseth me Ps 56:1

**FIGHTINGS**
without were *f*, within were fears 2Cor 7:5
whence come wars and *f* among you Jas 4:1

**FIGS**
of the pomegranates, and of the *f* Num 13:23
it is no place of seed, or of *f* Num 20:5
and two hundred cakes of *f* 1Sa 25:18
gave him a piece of a cake of *f* 1Sa 30:12
And Isaiah said, Take a lump of *f* 2Kin 20:7
oxen, and meat, meal, cakes of *f* 1Chr 12:40
as also wine, grapes, and *f* Neh 13:15
tree putteth forth her green *f* Song 2:13
said, Let them take a lump of *f* Is 38:21
nor *f* on the fig tree, and the Jer 8:13
two baskets of *f* were set before Jer 24:1
One basket had very good *f* Jer 24:2
even like the *f* that are first Jer 24:2
other basket had very naughty *f* Jer 24:2
And I said, *F* Jer 24:3
the good *f*, very good Jer 24:3
Like these good *f*, so will I Jer 24:5
And as the evil *f*, which cannot be Jer 24:8
and will make them like vile *f* Jer 29:17
fig trees with the firstripe *f* Nah 3:12
of thorns, or *f* of thistles Mt 7:16
for the time of *f* was not yet Mk 11:13
For of thorns men do not gather *f* Lk 6:44
either a vine, *f*? Jas 3:12
a fig tree casteth her untimely *f* Rev 6:13

**FIGURE**
image, the similitude of any *f* Deut 4:16
and maketh it after the *f* of a man Is 44:13
who is the *f* of him that was to Rom 5:14
I have in a *f* transferred to 1Cor 4:6
Which was a *f* for the time then Heb 9:9
also he received him in a *f* Heb 11:19
The like *f* whereunto even baptism 1Pet 3:21

**FIGURES**
about with carved *f* of cherubims 1Kin 6:29
*f* which ye made to worship them Acts 7:43
which are the *f* of the true Heb 9:24

**FILE**
Yet they had a *f* for the mattocks 1Sa 13:21

**FILL**
*f* the waters in the seas, and let Gen 1:22
to *f* their sacks with corn Gen 42:25
*F* the men's sacks with food, as Gen 44:1
And they shall *f* thy houses Ex 10:6
*F* an omer of it to be kept for Ex 16:32
her fruit, and ye shall eat your *f* Lev 25:19
thy *f* at thine own pleasure Deut 23:24
*f* thine horn with oil, and go, I 1Sa 16:1
*F* four barrels with water, and 1Kin 18:33
Till he *f* thy mouth with laughing Job 8:21
*f* his belly with the east wind Job 15:2
When he is about to *f* his belly Job 20:23
*f* my mouth with arguments Job 23:4
or *f* the appetite of the young Job 38:39
Canst thou *f* his skin with barbed Job 41:7
thy mouth wide, and I will *f* it Ps 81:10
*F* their faces with shame Ps 83:16
he shall *f* the places with the Ps 110:6
we shall *f* our houses with spoil Prov 1:13
let us take our *f* of love until Prov 7:18
and I will *f* their treasures Prov 8:21
out of his wings shall *f* the Is 8:8
nor *f* the face of the world with Is 14:21
*f* the face of the world with Is 27:6
we will *f* ourselves with strong Is 56:12
I will *f* all the inhabitants of Jer 13:13
Do not I *f* heaven and earth Jer 23:24
but it is to *f* them with the dead Jer 33:5
Surely I will *f* thee with men Jer 51:14
*f* thy bowels with this roll that Eze 3:3
souls, neither *f* their bowels Eze 7:19
*f* the courts with the slain Eze 9:7
*f* thine hand with coals of fire Eze 10:2
*f* it with the choice bones Eze 24:4
*f* the land with the slain Eze 30:11
I will *f* the beasts of the whole Eze 32:4
*f* the valleys with thy height Eze 32:5
I will *f* his mountains with his Eze 35:8
which *f* their masters' houses Zeph 1:9
I will *f* this house with glory, Hag 2:7
for that which is put in to *f* it Mt 9:16
as to *f* so great a multitude Mt 15:33
*F* ye up then the measure of your Mt 23:32
*F* the waterpots with water Jn 2:7
God of hope *f* you with all joy Rom 15:13
that he might *f* all things Eph 4:10
*f* up that which is behind of the Col 1:24
saved, to *f* up their sins alway 1Th 2:16
she hath filled *f* to her double Rev 18:6

**FILLED**
and the earth was *f* with violence Gen 6:11
for the earth is *f* with violence Gen 6:13
*f* the bottle with water, and gave Gen 21:19
*f* her pitcher, and came up Gen 24:16
them, and *f* them with earth Gen 26:15
and the land was *f* with them Ex 1:7
*f* the troughs to water their Ex 2:16
morning ye shall be *f* with bread Ex 16:12
whom I have *f* with the spirit of Ex 28:3
I have *f* him with the spirit of Ex 31:3
he hath *f* him with the spirit of Ex 35:31
Them hath he *f* with wisdom of Ex 35:35
of the LORD *f* the tabernacle Ex 40:34
of the LORD *f* the tabernacle Ex 40:35
all the earth shall be *f* with the Num 14:21
may eat within thy gates, and be *f* Deut 26:12
*f* themselves, and waxen fat Deut 31:20
these bottles of wine, which we *f* Josh 9:13

and he was *f* with wisdom, and ... 1Kin 7:14
that the cloud *f* the house of the ... 1Kin 8:10
LORD had *f* the house of the LORD ... 1Kin 8:11
he *f* the trench also with water ... 1Kin 18:35
but the Syrians *f* the country ... 1Kin 20:27
that valley shall be *f* with water ... 2Kin 3:17
and the country was *f* with water ... 2Kin 3:20
cast every man his stone, and *f* it ... 2Kin 3:25
till he had *f* Jerusalem from one ... 2Kin 21:16
*f* their places with the bones of ... 2Kin 23:14
for he *f* Jerusalem with innocent ... 2Kin 24:4
then the house was *f* with a cloud ... 2Chr 5:13
the LORD had *f* the house of God ... 2Chr 5:14
the glory of the LORD *f* the house ... 2Chr 7:1
the LORD had *f* the LORD's house ... 2Chr 7:2
bed which was *f* with sweet odours .. 2Chr 16:14
which have *f* it from one end to ... Ezr 9:11
so they did eat, and were *f* ... Neh 9:25
who *f* their houses with silver ... Job 3:15
thou hast *f* me with wrinkles, ... Job 16:8
Yet he *f* their houses with good ... Job 22:18
For my loins are *f* with a ... Ps 38:7
Let my mouth be *f* with thy praise ... Ps 71:8
whole earth be *f* with his glory ... Ps 72:19
So they did eat, and were well *f* ... Ps 78:29
take deep root, and it *f* the land ... Ps 80:9
thine hand, they are *f* with good ... Ps 104:28
are exceedingly *f* with contempt ... Ps 123:3
Our soul is exceedingly *f* with ... Ps 123:4
was our mouth *f* with laughter ... Ps 126:2
be *f* with their own devices ... Prov 1:31
shall thy barns be *f* with plenty ... Prov 3:10
strangers be *f* with thy wealth ... Prov 5:10
wicked shall be *f* with mischief ... Prov 12:21
shall be *f* with his own ways ... Prov 14:14
of his lips shall he be *f* ... Prov 18:20
his mouth shall be *f* with gravel ... Prov 20:17
chambers be *f* with all precious ... Prov 24:4
thee, lest thou be *f* therewith ... Prov 25:16
earth that is not *f* with water ... Prov 30:16
and a fool when he is *f* with meat ... Prov 30:22
nor the ear *f* with hearing ... Eccl 1:8
and his soul be not *f* with good ... Eccl 6:3
and yet the appetite is not *f* ... Eccl 6:7
for my head is *f* with dew ... Song 5:2
up, and his train *f* the temple ... Is 6:1
and the house was *f* with smoke ... Is 6:4
are my loins *f* with pain ... Is 21:3
he hath *f* Zion with judgment and ... Is 33:5
sword of the LORD is *f* with blood ... Is 34:6
neither hast thou *f* me with the ... Is 43:24
old man that hath not *f* his days ... Is 65:20
Every bottle shall be *f* with wine ... Jer 13:12
every bottle shall be *f* with wine ... Jer 13:12
for thou hast *f* me with ... Jer 15:17
they have *f* mine inheritance with ... Jer 16:18
have *f* this place with the blood ... Jer 19:4
*f* it with them that were slain ... Jer 41:9
shame, and thy cry hath *f* the land ... Jer 46:12
though their land was *f* with sin ... Jer 51:5
he hath *f* his belly with my ... Jer 51:34
He hath *f* me with bitterness, he ... Lam 3:15
he is *f* full with reproach ... Lam 3:30
for they have *f* the land with ... Eze 8:17
the cloud *f* the inner court ... Eze 10:3
the house was *f* with the cloud, ... Eze 10:4
ye have *f* the streets thereof ... Eze 11:6
Thou shalt be *f* with drunkenness ... Eze 23:33
of thy merchandise they have *f* ... Eze 28:16
cities be *f* with flocks of men ... Eze 36:38
Thus ye shall be *f* at my table ... Eze 39:20
the glory of the LORD *f* the house ... Eze 43:5
the LORD *f* the house of the LORD ... Eze 44:4
mountain, and *f* the whole earth ... Dan 2:35
to their pasture, so were they *f* ... Hos 13:6
they were *f*, and their heart was ... Hos 13:6
*f* his holes with prey, and his ... Nah 2:12
For the earth shall be *f* with the ... Hab 2:14
Thou art *f* with shame for glory ... Hab 2:16
but ye are not *f* with drink ... Hag 1:6
*f* the bow with Ephraim, and raised ... Zec 9:13
and they shall be *f* like bowls ... Zec 9:15
for they shall be *f* ... Mt 5:6
And they did all eat, and were *f* ... Mt 14:20
And they did all eat, and were *f* ... Mt 15:37
*f* it with vinegar, and put it on a ... Mt 27:48
else the new piece that *f* it up ... Mk 2:21
And they did all eat, and were *f* ... Mk 6:42
her, Let the children first be *f* ... Mk 7:27
So they did eat, and were *f* ... Mk 8:8
*f* a spunge full of vinegar, and ... Mk 15:36
he shall be *f* with the Holy Ghost ... Lk 1:15
Elisabeth was *f* with the Holy ... Lk 1:41
He hath *f* the hungry with good ... Lk 1:53
was *f* with the Holy Ghost ... Lk 1:67
strong in spirit, *f* with wisdom ... Lk 2:40
Every valley shall be *f*, and every ... Lk 3:5
these things, were *f* with wrath, ... Lk 4:28
*f* both the ships, so that they ... Lk 5:7
were *f* with fear, saying, We have ... Lk 5:26
And they were *f* with madness ... Lk 6:11
for ye shall be *f* ... Lk 6:21
they were *f* with water, and were ... Lk 8:23
And they did eat, and were all *f* ... Lk 9:17
come in, that my house may be *f* ... Lk 14:23
he would fain have *f* his belly ... Lk 15:16
they *f* them up to the brim ... Jn 2:7
When they were *f*, he said unto ... Jn 6:12
*f* twelve baskets with the ... Jn 6:13
did eat of the loaves, and were *f* ... Jn 6:26
the house was *f* with the odour of ... Jn 12:3
you, sorrow hath *f* your heart ... Jn 16:6
they *f* a spunge with vinegar, and ... Jn 19:29
it *f* all the house where they ... Acts 2:2
they were all *f* with the Holy ... Acts 2:4
they were *f* with wonder and ... Acts 3:10
*f* with the Holy Ghost, said unto ... Acts 4:8
they were all *f* with the Holy ... Acts 4:31
why hath Satan *f* thine heart to ... Acts 5:3
and were *f* with indignation, ... Acts 5:17
ye have *f* Jerusalem with your ... Acts 5:28
and be *f* with the Holy Ghost ... Acts 9:17
*f* with the Holy Ghost, set his ... Acts 13:9
multitudes, they were *f* with envy ... Acts 13:45
And the disciples were *f* with joy ... Acts 13:52
whole city was *f* with confusion ... Acts 19:29
Being *f* with all unrighteousness, ... Rom 1:29
*f* with all knowledge, able also ... Rom 15:14
I be somewhat *f* with your company Rom 15:24
I am *f* with comfort, I am ... 2Cor 7:4
that ye might be *f* with all the ... Eph 3:19
but be *f* with the Spirit ... Eph 5:18
Being *f* with the fruits of ... Phil 1:11
to desire that ye might be *f* with ... Col 1:9
tears, that I may be *f* with joy ... 2Ti 1:4
in peace, be ye warmed and *f* ... Jas 2:16
*f* it with fire of the altar, and ... Rev 8:5
for in them is *f* up the wrath of ... Rev 15:1
the temple was *f* with smoke from ... Rev 15:8
she hath *f* fill to her double ... Rev 18:6
the fowls were *f* with their flesh ... Rev 19:21

**FILLEDST**
all good things, which thou *f* not ... Deut 6:11
of the seas, thou *f* many people ... Eze 27:33

**FILLEST**
whose belly thou *f* with thy hid ... Ps 17:14

**FILLET**
a *f* of twelve cubits did compass ... Jer 52:21

**FILLETED**
the court shall be *f* with silver ... Ex 27:17
of the court were *f* with silver ... Ex 38:17
their chapiters, and *f* them ... Ex 38:28

**FILLETH**
breath, but *f* me with bitterness ... Job 9:18
the rain also *f* the pools ... Ps 84:6
*f* the hungry soul with goodness ... Ps 107:9
the mower *f* not his hand ... Ps 129:7
*f* thee with the finest of the ... Ps 147:14
fulness of him that *f* all in all ... Eph 1:23

**FILLETS**
their *f* shall be of silver ... Ex 27:10
the pillars and their *f* of silver ... Ex 27:11
chapiters and their *f* with gold ... Ex 36:38
pillars and their *f* were of silver ... Ex 38:10
the pillars and their *f* of silver ... Ex 38:11
the pillars and their *f* of silver ... Ex 38:12
the pillars and their *f* of silver ... Ex 38:17
chapiters and their *f* of silver ... Ex 38:19

**FILLING**
*f* our hearts with food and ... Acts 14:17

**FILTH**
the *f* of the daughters of Zion ... Is 4:4
will cast abominable *f* upon thee ... Nah 3:6
we are made as the *f* of the world ... 1Cor 4:13
away of the *f* of the flesh ... 1Pet 3:21

**FILTHINESS**
carry forth the *f* out of the holy ... 2Chr 29:5
the *f* of the heathen of the land ... Ezr 6:21
the *f* of the people of the lands ... Ezr 9:11
and yet is not washed from their *f* ... Prov 30:12
all tables are full of vomit and *f* ... Is 28:8
Her *f* is in her skirts ... Lam 1:9
Because thy *f* was poured out, and ... Eze 16:36
and will consume thy *f* out of thee ... Eze 22:15
that the *f* of it may be molten in ... Eze 24:11
In thy *f* is lewdness ... Eze 24:13
not be purged from thy *f* any more ... Eze 24:13
from all your *f*, and from all your ... Eze 36:25
ourselves from all *f* of the flesh ... 2Cor 7:1
Neither *f*, nor foolish talking, ... Eph 5:4
Wherefore lay apart all *f* ... Jas 1:21
and *f* of her fornication ... Rev 17:4

**FILTHY**
*f* is man, which drinketh iniquity ... Job 15:16
they are all together become *f* ... Ps 14:3
they are altogether become *f* ... Ps 53:3
our righteousnesses are as *f* rags ... Is 64:6
Woe to her that is *f* and polluted, ... Zeph 3:1
was clothed with *f* garments ... Zec 3:3
Take away the *f* garments from him ... Zec 3:4
*f* communication out of your mouth ... Col 3:8
no striker, not greedy of *f* lucre ... 1Ti 3:3
much wine, not greedy of *f* lucre ... 1Ti 3:8
no striker, not given to *f* lucre ... Titus 1:7
ought not, for *f* lucre's sake ... Titus 1:11
not for *f* lucre, but of a ready ... 1Pet 5:2
vexed with the *f* conversation of ... 2Pet 2:7
Likewise also these *f* dreamers ... Jude 8
and he which is *f*, let him be ... Rev 22:11
let him be *f* still ... Rev 22:11

**FINALLY**
*F*, brethren, farewell ... 2Cor 13:11
*F*, my brethren, be strong in the ... Eph 6:10
*F*, my brethren, rejoice in the ... Phil 3:1
*F*, brethren, whatsoever things ... Phil 4:8
*F*, brethren, pray for us, that ... 2Th 3:1
*F*, be ye all of one mind, having ... 1Pet 3:8

**FIND**
If I *f* in Sodom fifty righteous ... Gen 18:26
If I *f* there forty and five, I ... Gen 18:28
not do it, if I *f* thirty there ... Gen 18:30
wearied themselves to *f* the door ... Gen 19:11
that I may *f* grace in thy sight ... Gen 32:5
ye speak unto Esau, when ye *f* him ... Gen 32:19
These are to *f* grace in the sight ... Gen 33:8
let me *f* grace in the sight of my ... Gen 33:15
Let me *f* grace in your eyes, and ... Gen 34:11
to Judah, and said, I cannot *f* her ... Gen 38:22
Can we *f* such a one as this is, a ... Gen 41:38
let us *f* grace in the sight of my ... Gen 47:25
get you straw where ye can *f* it ... Ex 5:11
ye shall not *f* it in the field ... Ex 16:25
that I may *f* grace in thy sight ... Ex 33:13
be sure your sin will *f* you out ... Num 32:23
the revenger of blood *f* him ... Num 35:27
LORD thy God, thou shalt *f* him ... Deut 4:29
a man *f* her in the city, and lie ... Deut 22:23
But if a man *f* a betrothed damsel ... Deut 22:25
If a man *f* a damsel that is a ... Deut 22:28
that she *f* no favour in his eyes ... Deut 24:1
nations shalt thou *f* no ease ... Deut 28:65
to them as thou shalt *f* occasion ... Judg 9:33
*f* it out, then I will give you ... Judg 14:12
sojourn where he could *f* a place ... Judg 17:8
to sojourn where I may *f* a place ... Judg 17:9
LORD grant you that ye may *f* rest ... Ruth 1:9
in whose sight I shall *f* grace ... Ruth 2:2
Let me *f* favour in thy sight, my ... Ruth 2:13
handmaid *f* grace in thy sight ... 1Sa 1:18
city, ye shall straightway *f* him ... 1Sa 9:13
about this time ye shall *f* him ... 1Sa 9:13
then thou shalt *f* two men by ... 1Sa 10:2
lad, saying, Go, *f* out the arrows ... 1Sa 20:21
*f* out now the arrows which I ... 1Sa 20:36
Saul my father shall not *f* thee ... 1Sa 23:17
For if a man *f* his enemy, will he ... 1Sa 24:19
young men *f* favour in thine eyes ... 1Sa 25:8
if I shall *f* favour in the eyes ... 2Sa 15:25
that I may *f* grace in thy sight ... 2Sa 16:4
had sought and could not *f* them ... 2Sa 17:20
peradventure we may *f* grass to ... 1Kin 18:5
and tell Ahab, and he cannot *f* thee .. 1Kin 18:12
to *f* out every device which shall ... 2Chr 2:14
ye shall *f* them at the end of the ... 2Chr 20:16
your children shall *f* compassion ... 2Chr 30:9
of Assyria come, and *f* much water ... 2Chr 32:4
so shalt thou *f* in the book of ... Ezr 4:15
gold that thou canst *f* in all the ... Ezr 7:16
glad, when they can *f* the grave ... Job 3:22
Canst thou by searching *f* out God ... Job 11:7
canst thou *f* out the Almighty ... Job 11:7
for I cannot *f* one wise man among ... Job 17:10
that I knew where I might *f* him ... Job 23:3
cause every man to *f* according to ... Job 34:11
the Almighty, we cannot *f* him out ... Job 37:23
his wickedness till thou *f* none ... Ps 10:15
hast tried me, and shalt *f* nothing ... Ps 17:3
Thine hand shall *f* out all thine ... Ps 21:8
thy right hand shall *f* out those ... Ps 21:8
Until I *f* out a place for the ... Ps 132:5
We shall *f* all precious substance ... Prov 1:13
me early, but they shall not *f* me ... Prov 1:28
LORD, and *f* the knowledge of God ... Prov 2:5
So shalt thou *f* favour and good ... Prov 3:4
are life unto those that *f* them ... Prov 4:22
and right to them that *f* knowledge ... Prov 8:9
and *f* out knowledge of witty ... Prov 8:12
that seek me early shall *f* me ... Prov 8:17
a matter wisely shall *f* good ... Prov 16:20
understanding shall *f* good ... Prov 19:8
but a faithful man who can *f* ... Prov 20:6
shall *f* more favour than he that ... Prov 28:23
Who can *f* a virtuous woman ... Prov 31:10
so that no man can *f* out the work ... Eccl 3:11
man should *f* nothing after him ... Eccl 7:14
exceeding deep, who can *f* it out ... Eccl 7:24
I *f* more bitter than death the ... Eccl 7:26
one by one, to *f* out the account ... Eccl 7:27
yet my soul seeketh, but I *f* not ... Eccl 7:28
that a man cannot *f* out the work ... Eccl 8:17
it out, yet he shall not *f* it ... Eccl 8:17
yet shall he not be able to *f* it ... Eccl 8:17
for thou shalt *f* it after many ... Eccl 11:1
sought to *f* out acceptable words ... Eccl 12:10
sought him, but I could not *f* him ... Song 5:6
if ye *f* my beloved, that ye tell ... Song 5:8
when I should *f* thee without ... Song 8:1
*f* for herself a place of rest ... Is 34:14
seek them, and shalt not *f* them ... Is 41:12
day of your fast ye *f* pleasure ... Is 58:3
in her month they shall *f* her ... Jer 2:24
places thereof, if ye can *f* a man ... Jer 5:1
ye shall *f* rest for your souls ... Jer 6:16
them, that they may *f* it so ... Jer 10:18
*f* me, when ye shall search for me ... Jer 29:13
in my sighing, and I *f* no rest ... Jer 45:3
like harts that *f* no pasture ... Lam 1:6
her prophets also *f* no vision ... Lam 2:9
princes sought to *f* occasion ... Dan 6:4
but they could *f* none occasion ... Dan 6:4
We shall not *f* any occasion ... Dan 6:5
except we *f* it against him ... Dan 6:5
that she shall not *f* her paths ... Hos 2:6
seek them, but shall not *f* them ... Hos 2:7

F

but they shall not *f* him Hos 5:6
in all my labours they shall *f* Hos 12:8
of the LORD, and shall not *f* it Amos 8:12
seek, and ye shall *f* Mt 7:7
life, and few there be that *f* it Mt 7:14
his life for my sake shall *f* it Mt 10:39
ye shall *f* rest unto your souls Mt 11:29
his life for my sake shall *f* it Mt 16:25
thou shalt *f* a piece of money Mt 17:27
And if so be that he *f* it, verily Mt 18:13
ye shall *f* an ass tied, and a colt Mt 21:2
and as many as ye shall *f* Mt 22:9
when he cometh shall *f* so doing Mt 24:46
ye shall *f* a colt tied, whereon Mk 11:2
he might *f* any thing thereon Mk 11:13
coming suddenly he *f* you sleeping Mk 13:36
Ye shall *f* the babe wrapped in Lk 2:12
when they could not *f* by what way Lk 5:19
that they might *f* an accusation Lk 6:7
seek, and ye shall *f* Lk 11:9
when he cometh shall *f* watching Lk 12:37
*f* them so, blessed are those Lk 12:38
when he cometh shall *f* so doing Lk 12:43
fruit on this fig tree, and *f* none Lk 13:7
that which is lost, until he *f* it Lk 15:4
and seek diligently till she *f* it Lk 15:8
shall he *f* faith on the earth Lk 18:8
entering ye shall *f* a colt tied Lk 19:30
could not *f* what they might do Lk 19:48
people, I *f* no fault in this man Lk 23:4
shall seek me, and shall not *f* me Jn 7:34
he go, that we shall not *f* him Jn 7:35
shall seek me, and shall not *f* me Jn 7:36
shall go in and out, and *f* pasture Jn 10:9
I *f* in him no fault at all Jn 18:38
may know that I *f* no fault in him Jn 19:4
for I *f* no fault in him Jn 19:6
side of the ship, and ye shall *f* Jn 21:6
desired to *f* a tabernacle for the Acts 7:46
*f* him, though he be not far from Acts 17:27
saying, We *f* no evil in this man Acts 23:9
that which is good I *f* not Rom 7:18
I *f* then a law, that, when I Rom 7:21
unto me, Why doth he yet *f* fault Rom 9:19
*f* you unprepared, we (that we say 2Cor 9:4
I shall not *f* you such as I would 2Cor 12:20
*f* mercy of the Lord in that day 2Ti 1:18
*f* grace to help in time of need Heb 4:16
men seek death, and shall not *f* it Rev 9:6
thou shalt *f* them no more at all Rev 18:14

**FINDEST**
With whomsoever thou *f* thy gods Gen 31:32
me, Son of man, eat that thou *f* Eze 3:1

**FINDETH**
every one that *f* me shall slay me Gen 4:14
he *f* occasions against me, he Job 33:10
word, as one that *f* great spoil Ps 119:162
Happy is the man that *f* wisdom Prov 3:13
For whoso *f* me *f* life Prov 8:35
seeketh wisdom, and *f* it not Prov 14:6
hath a froward heart *f* no good Prov 17:20
Whoso *f* a wife *f* a good Prov 18:22
his neighbour *f* no favour in his Prov 21:10
righteousness and mercy *f* life Prov 21:21
Whatsoever thy hand *f* to do Eccl 9:10
among the heathen, she *f* no rest Lam 1:3
in thee the fatherless *f* mercy Hos 14:3
and he that seeketh *f* Mt 7:8
He that *f* his life shall lose it Mt 10:39
places, seeking rest, and *f* none Mt 12:43
is come, he *f* it empty, swept, and Mt 12:44
*f* them asleep, and saith unto Mt 26:40
*f* them sleeping, and saith unto Mk 14:37
and he that seeketh *f* Lk 11:10
he *f* it swept and garnished Lk 11:25
He first *f* his own brother Simon, Jn 1:41
*f* Philip, and saith unto him, Jn 1:43
Philip *f* Nathanael, and saith unto Jn 1:45
Afterward Jesus *f* him in the Jn 5:14

**FINDING**
lest any *f* him should kill him Gen 4:15
doeth great things past *f* out Job 9:10
nor *f* thine own pleasure, nor Is 58:13
*f* none, he saith, I will return Lk 11:24
*f* nothing how they might punish Acts 4:21
and *f* certain disciples, Acts 19:1
*f* a ship sailing over unto Acts 21:2
*f* disciples, we tarried there Acts 21:4
judgments, and his ways past *f* out Rom 11:33
For *f* fault with them, he saith, Heb 8:8

**FINE**
quickly three measures of *f* meal Gen 18:6
him in vestures of *f* linen Gen 41:42
and *f* linen, and goats' hair, Ex 25:4
ten curtains of *f* twined linen Ex 26:1
*f* twined linen of cunning work Ex 26:31
*f* twined linen, wrought with Ex 26:36
of *f* twined linen of an hundred Ex 27:9
*f* twined linen, wrought with Ex 27:16
five cubits of *f* twined linen Ex 27:18
and purple, and scarlet, and *f* linen Ex 28:5
*f* twined linen, with cunning work Ex 28:6
and scarlet, and *f* twined linen Ex 28:8
of *f* twined linen, shalt thou Ex 28:15
embroider the coat of *f* linen Ex 28:39
shalt make the mitre of *f* linen Ex 28:39
and *f* linen, and goats' hair, Ex 35:6
*f* linen, and goats' hair, and red Ex 35:23
and of scarlet, and of *f* linen Ex 35:25
in *f* linen, and of the weaver, Ex 35:35
ten curtains of *f* twined linen Ex 36:8
and scarlet, and *f* twined linen Ex 36:35
*f* twined linen, of needlework Ex 36:37
the court were of *f* twined linen Ex 38:9
about were of *f* twined linen Ex 38:16
and scarlet, and *f* twined linen Ex 38:18
purple, and in scarlet, and *f* linen Ex 38:23
and scarlet, and *f* twined linen Ex 39:2
in the scarlet, and in the *f* linen Ex 39:3
and scarlet, and *f* twined linen Ex 39:5
and scarlet, and *f* twined linen Ex 39:8
they made coats of *f* linen of Ex 39:27
And a mitre of *f* linen Ex 39:28
and goodly bonnets of *f* linen Ex 39:28
linen breeches of *f* twined linen Ex 39:28
a girdle of *f* twined linen, and Ex 39:29
his offering shall be of *f* flour Lev 2:1
cakes of *f* flour mingled with oil Lev 2:4
it shall be of *f* flour unleavened Lev 2:5
shall be made of *f* flour with oil Lev 2:7
of *f* flour for a sin offering Lev 5:11
of *f* flour for a meat offering Lev 6:20
with oil, of *f* flour, fried Lev 7:12
three tenth deals of *f* flour for Lev 14:10
one tenth deal of *f* flour mingled Lev 14:21
deals of *f* flour mingled with oil Lev 23:13
they shall be of *f* flour Lev 23:17
And thou shalt take *f* flour Lev 24:5
cakes of *f* flour mingled with oil Num 6:15
both of them were full of *f* flour Num 7:13
both of them full of *f* flour Num 7:19
both of them full of *f* flour Num 7:25
both of them full of *f* flour Num 7:31
both of them full of *f* flour Num 7:37
both of them full of *f* flour Num 7:43
both of them full of *f* flour Num 7:49
both of them full of *f* flour Num 7:55
both of them full of *f* flour Num 7:61
both of them full of *f* flour Num 7:67
both of them full of *f* flour Num 7:73
both of them full of *f* flour Num 7:79
even *f* flour mingled with oil, and Num 8:8
was thirty measures of *f* flour 1Kin 4:22
of *f* flour be sold for a shekel 2Kin 7:1
So a measure of *f* flour was sold 2Kin 7:16
a measure of *f* flour for a shekel 2Kin 7:18
of them that wrought *f* linen 1Chr 4:21
the *f* flour, and the wine, and the 1Chr 9:29
clothed with a robe of *f* linen 1Chr 15:27
for the *f* flour for meat offering 1Chr 23:29
in *f* linen, and in crimson 2Chr 2:14
which he overlaid with *f* gold 2Chr 3:5
and he overlaid it with *f* gold 2Chr 3:8
*f* linen, and wrought cherubims 2Chr 3:14
and two vessels of *f* copper Ezr 8:27
fastened with cords of *f* linen Est 1:6
and with a garment of *f* linen Est 8:15
a place for gold where they *f* it Job 28:1
shall not be for jewels of *f* gold Job 28:17
hope, or have said to the *f* gold Job 31:24
than gold, yea, than much *f* gold Ps 19:10
yea, above *f* gold Ps 119:127
and the gain thereof than *f* gold Prov 3:14
works, with *f* linen of Egypt Prov 7:16
than gold, yea, than *f* gold Prov 8:19
of gold, and an ornament of *f* gold Prov 25:12
She maketh *f* linen, and selleth it Prov 31:24
His head is as the most *f* gold Song 5:11
set upon sockets of *f* gold Song 5:15
the *f* linen, and the hoods, and the Is 3:23
a man more precious than *f* gold Is 13:12
Moreover they that work in *f* flax Is 19:9
how is the most *f* gold changed Lam 4:1
of Zion, comparable to *f* gold Lam 4:2
I girded thee about with *f* linen Eze 16:10
and thy raiment was of *f* linen Eze 16:13
thou didst eat *f* flour, and honey, Eze 16:13
*f* flour, and oil, and honey, Eze 16:19
*F* linen with broidered work from Eze 27:7
*f* linen, and coral, and agate Eze 27:16
oil, to temper with the *f* flour Eze 46:14
This image's head was of *f* gold Dan 2:32
were girded with *f* gold of Uphaz Dan 10:5
*f* gold as the mire of the streets Zec 9:3
And he bought *f* linen, and took him Mk 15:46
*f* linen, and fared sumptuously Lk 16:19
And his feet like unto *f* brass Rev 1:15
and his feet are like *f* brass Rev 2:18
*f* linen, and purple, and silk, and Rev 18:12
*f* flour, and wheat, and beasts, and Rev 18:13
city, that was clothed in *f* linen Rev 18:16
she should be arrayed in *f* linen Rev 19:8
for the *f* linen is the Rev 19:8
white horses, clothed in *f* linen Rev 19:14

**FINER**
come forth a vessel for the *f* Prov 25:4

**FINEST**
them also with the *f* of the wheat Ps 81:16
thee with the *f* of the wheat Ps 147:14

**FINGER**
Pharaoh, This is the *f* of God Ex 8:19
the horns of the altar with thy *f* Ex 29:12
stone, written with the *f* of God Ex 31:18
shall dip his *f* in the blood Lev 4:6
dip his *f* in some of the blood Lev 4:17
of the sin offering with his *f* Lev 4:25
of the blood thereof with his *f* Lev 4:30
of the sin offering with his *f* Lev 4:34
the altar round about with his *f* Lev 8:15
and he dipped his *f* in the blood Lev 9:9
*f* in the oil that is in his left Lev 14:16
his *f* seven times before the LORD Lev 14:16
shall sprinkle with his right *f* Lev 14:27
sprinkle it with his *f* upon the Lev 16:14
the blood with his *f* seven times Lev 16:14
upon it with his *f* seven times Lev 16:19
take of her blood with his *f* Num 19:4
stone written with the *f* of God Deut 9:10
My little *f* shall be thicker than 1Kin 12:10
My little *f* shall be thicker than 2Chr 10:10
yoke, the putting forth of the *f* Is 58:9
But if I with the *f* of God cast Lk 11:20
may dip the tip of his *f* in water Lk 16:24
with his *f* wrote on the ground, Jn 8:6
put my *f* into the print of the Jn 20:25
he to Thomas, Reach hither thy *f* Jn 20:27

**FINGERS**
that had on every hand six *f* 2Sa 21:20
a man of great stature, whose *f* 1Chr 20:6
thy heavens, the work of thy *f* Ps 8:3
my hands to war, and my *f* to fight Ps 144:1
his feet, he teacheth with his *f* Prov 6:13
Bind them upon thy *f*, write them Prov 7:3
my *f* with sweet smelling myrrh, Song 5:5
that which their own *f* have made Is 2:8
that which his *f* have made Is 17:8
blood, and your *f* with iniquity Is 59:3
the thickness thereof was four *f* Jer 52:21
hour came forth of a man's hand Dan 5:5
not move them with one of their *f* Mt 23:4
put his *f* into his ears, and he Mk 7:33
the burdens with one of your *f* Lk 11:46

**FINING**
The *f* pot is for silver, and the Prov 17:3
As the *f* pot for silver, and the Prov 27:21

**FINISH**
in a cubit shalt thou *f* it above Gen 6:16
to *f* the transgression, and to Dan 9:24
his hands shall also *f* it Zec 4:9
he have sufficient to *f* it Lk 14:28
and is not able to *f* it, all that Lk 14:29
to build, and was not able to *f* Lk 14:30
that sent me, and to *f* his work Jn 4:34
the Father hath given me to *f* Jn 5:36
so that I might *f* my course with Acts 20:24
For he will *f* the work, and cut it Rom 9:28
so he would also *f* in you the 2Cor 8:6

**FINISHED**
the heavens and the earth were *f* Gen 2:1
of the tent of the congregation *f* Ex 39:32
So Moses *f* the work Ex 40:33
law in a book, until they were *f* Deut 31:24
until every thing was *f* that the Josh 4:10
until he have *f* the thing this Ruth 3:18
So he built the house, and *f* it 1Kin 6:9
Solomon built the house, and *f* it 1Kin 6:14
until he had *f* all the house 1Kin 6:22
was the house *f* throughout all 1Kin 6:38
years, and he *f* all his house 1Kin 7:1
so was the work of the pillars *f* 1Kin 7:22
when Solomon had *f* the building 1Kin 9:1
So he *f* the house 1Kin 9:25
began to number, but he *f* not 1Chr 27:24
until thou hast *f* all the work 1Chr 28:20
Huram *f* the work that he was to 2Chr 4:11
for the house of the LORD was *f* 2Chr 5:1
Thus Solomon *f* the house of the 2Chr 7:11
of the LORD, and until it was *f* 2Chr 8:16
And when they had *f* it, they 2Chr 24:14
until the burnt offering was *f* 2Chr 29:28
Now when all this was *f*, all 2Chr 31:1
*f* them in the seventh month 2Chr 31:7
in building, and yet it is not *f* Ezr 5:16
and *f* it, according to the Ezr 6:14
this house was *f* on the third day Ezr 6:15
So the wall was *f* in the twenty Neh 6:15
numbered thy kingdom, and *f* it Dan 5:26
all these things shall be *f* Dan 12:7
when Jesus had *f* these parables Mt 13:53
when Jesus had *f* these sayings Mt 19:1
when Jesus had *f* all these Mt 26:1
I have *f* the work which thou Jn 17:4
the vinegar, he said, It is *f* Jn 19:30
when we had *f* our course from Acts 21:7
I have *f* my course, I have kept 2Ti 4:7
although the works were *f* from Heb 4:3
and sin, when it is *f*, bringeth Jas 1:15
the mystery of God should be *f* Rev 10:7
they shall have *f* their testimony Rev 11:7
until the thousand years were *f* Rev 20:5

**FINISHER**
the author and *f* of our faith Heb 12:2

**FINS**
whatsoever hath *f* and scales in Lev 11:9
And all that have not *f* and scales Lev 11:10
Whatsoever hath no *f* nor scales Lev 11:12
all that have *f* and scales shall Deut 14:9
And whatsoever hath not *f* and Deut 14:10

**FIR**
of instruments made of *f* wood 2Sa 6:5
cedar, and concerning timber of *f* 1Kin 5:8
*f* trees according to all his 1Kin 5:10
of the house with planks of *f* 1Kin 6:15

And the two doors were of *f* tree 1Kin 6:34
*f* trees, and with gold, according 1Kin 9:11
the choice *f* trees thereof 2Kin 19:23
*f* trees, and algum trees, out of 2Chr 2:8
house he cieled with *f* tree 2Chr 3:5
the *f* trees are her house Ps 104:17
are cedar, and our rafters of *f* Song 1:17
the *f* trees rejoice at thee, and Is 14:8
the choice *f* trees thereof Is 37:24
will set in the desert the *f* tree Is 41:19
thorn shall come up the *f* tree Is 55:13
the *f* tree, the pine tree, and the Is 60:13
ship boards of *f* trees of Senir Eze 27:5
the *f* trees were not like his Eze 31:8
I am like a green *f* tree Hos 14:8
the *f* trees shall be terribly Nah 2:3
Howl, *f* tree Zec 11:2

**FIRE**

*f* from the LORD out of heaven Gen 19:24
and he took the *f* in his hand Gen 22:6
And he said, Behold the *f* and the Gen 22:7
of *f* out of the midst of a bush Ex 3:2
behold, the bush burned with *f* Ex 3:2
the *f* ran along upon the ground Ex 9:23
*f* mingled with the hail, very Ex 9:24
flesh in that night, roast with *f* Ex 12:8
all with water, but roast with *f* Ex 12:9
the morning ye shall burn with *f* Ex 12:10
and by night in a pillar of *f* Ex 13:21
day, nor the pillar of *f* by night Ex 13:22
Egyptians through the pillar of *f* Ex 14:24
the LORD descended upon it in *f* Ex 19:18
If *f* break out, and catch in Ex 22:6
he that kindled the *f* shall Ex 22:6
*f* on the top of the mount in the Ex 24:17
thou burn with *f* without the camp Ex 29:14
offering made by *f* unto the LORD Ex 29:18
offering made by *f* unto the LORD Ex 29:25
shalt burn the remainder with *f* Ex 29:34
offering made by *f* unto the LORD Ex 29:41
offering made by *f* unto the LORD Ex 30:20
had made, and burnt it in the *f* Ex 32:20
then I cast it into the *f* Ex 32:24
Ye shall kindle no *f* throughout Ex 35:3
*f* was on it by night, in the Ex 40:38
priest shall put *f* upon the altar Lev 1:7
lay the wood in order upon the *f* Lev 1:7
on the *f* which is upon the altar Lev 1:8
sacrifice, an offering made by *f* Lev 1:9
on the *f* which is upon the altar Lev 1:12
sacrifice, an offering made by *f* Lev 1:13
upon the wood that is upon the *f* Lev 1:17
sacrifice, an offering made by *f* Lev 1:17
to be an offering made by *f* Lev 2:2
offerings of the LORD made by *f* Lev 2:3
it is an offering made by *f* Lev 2:9
offerings of the LORD made by *f* Lev 2:10
offering of the LORD made by *f* Lev 2:11
green ears of corn dried by the *f* Lev 2:14
offering made by *f* unto the LORD Lev 2:16
offering made by *f* unto the LORD Lev 3:3
is upon the wood that is on the *f* Lev 3:5
it is an offering made by *f* Lev 3:5
offering made by *f* unto the LORD Lev 3:9
offering made by *f* unto the LORD Lev 3:11
offering made by *f* unto the LORD Lev 3:14
made by *f* for a sweet savour Lev 3:16
and burn him on the wood with *f* Lev 4:12
offerings made by *f* unto the LORD Lev 4:35
offerings made by *f* unto the LORD Lev 5:12
the *f* of the altar shall be Lev 6:9
take up the ashes which the *f* Lev 6:10
the *f* upon the altar shall be Lev 6:12
The *f* shall ever be burning upon Lev 6:13
portion of my offerings made by *f* Lev 6:17
offerings of the LORD made by *f* Lev 6:18
it shall be burnt in the *f* Lev 6:30
offering made by *f* unto the LORD Lev 7:5
third day shall be burnt with *f* Lev 7:17
it shall be burnt with *f* Lev 7:19
offering made by *f* unto the LORD Lev 7:25
offerings of the LORD made by *f* Lev 7:30
offerings of the LORD made by *f* Lev 7:35
he burnt with *f* without the camp Lev 8:17
offering made by *f* unto the LORD Lev 8:21
offering made by *f* unto the LORD Lev 8:28
of the bread shall ye burn with *f* Lev 8:32
he burnt with *f* without the camp Lev 9:11
there came a *f* out from before Lev 9:24
put *f* therein, and put incense Lev 10:1
offered strange *f* before the LORD Lev 10:1
And there went out *f* from the LORD Lev 10:2
offerings of the LORD made by *f* Lev 10:12
sacrifices of the LORD made by *f* Lev 10:13
offerings made by *f* of the fat Lev 10:15
it shall be burnt in the *f* Lev 13:52
thou shalt burn it in the *f* Lev 13:55
that wherein the plague is with *f* Lev 13:57
*f* from off the altar before the Lev 16:12
upon the *f* before the LORD Lev 16:13
shall burn in the *f* their skins Lev 16:27
seed pass through the *f* to Molech Lev 18:21
day, it shall be burnt in the *f* Lev 19:6
they shall be burnt with *f* Lev 20:14
offerings of the LORD made by *f* Lev 21:6
she shall be burnt with *f* Lev 21:9
offerings of the LORD made by *f* Lev 21:21
nor make an offering by *f* of them Lev 22:22
offering made by *f* unto the LORD Lev 22:27
by *f* unto the LORD seven days Lev 23:8
an offering made by *f* unto the Lev 23:13
even an offering made by *f* Lev 23:18
offering made by *f* unto the LORD Lev 23:25
offering made by *f* unto the LORD Lev 23:27
offering made by *f* unto the LORD Lev 23:36
offering made by *f* unto the LORD Lev 23:36
offering made by *f* unto the LORD Lev 23:37
offering made by *f* unto the LORD Lev 24:7
made by *f* by a perpetual statute Lev 24:9
offered strange *f* before the LORD Num 3:4
put it in the *f* which is under Num 6:18
as it were the appearance of *f* Num 9:15
and the appearance of *f* by night Num 9:16
the *f* of the LORD burnt among Num 11:1
unto the LORD, the *f* was quenched Num 11:2
because the *f* of the LORD burnt Num 11:3
and in a pillar of *f* by night Num 14:14
an offering by *f* unto the LORD Num 15:3
wine, for an offering made by *f* Num 15:10
in offering an offering made by *f* Num 15:13
will offer an offering made by *f* Num 15:14
sacrifice made by *f* unto the LORD Num 15:25
put *f* therein, and put incense in Num 16:7
put *f* in them, and laid incense Num 16:18
there came out a *f* from the LORD Num 16:35
and scatter thou the *f* yonder Num 16:37
put *f* therein from off the altar, Num 16:46
holy things, reserved from the *f* Num 18:9
fat for an offering made by *f* Num 18:17
For there is a *f* gone out of Num 21:28
what time the *f* devoured two Num 26:10
offered strange *f* before the LORD Num 26:61
bread for my sacrifices made by *f* Num 28:2
This is the offering made by *f* Num 28:3
sacrifice made by *f* unto the LORD Num 28:6
offer it, a sacrifice made by *f* Num 28:8
sacrifice made by *f* unto the LORD Num 28:13
*f* for a burnt offering unto the Num 28:19
meat of the sacrifice made by *f* Num 28:24
sacrifice made by *f* unto the LORD Num 29:6
offering, a sacrifice made by *f* Num 29:13
offering, a sacrifice made by *f* Num 29:36
all their goodly castles, with *f* Num 31:10
Every thing that may abide the *f* Num 31:23
ye shall make it go through the *f* Num 31:23
all that abideth not the *f* ye Num 31:23
in *f* by night, to shew you by Deut 1:33
with *f* unto the midst of heaven Deut 4:11
you out of the midst of the *f* Deut 4:12
Horeb out of the midst of the *f* Deut 4:15
the LORD thy God is a consuming *f* Deut 4:24
out of the midst of the *f* Deut 4:33
earth he shewed thee his great *f* Deut 4:36
words out of the midst of the *f* Deut 4:36
mount out of the midst of the *f* Deut 5:4
ye were afraid by reason of the *f* Deut 5:5
mount out of the midst of the *f* Deut 5:22
(for the mountain did burn with *f* Deut 5:23
voice out of the midst of the *f* Deut 5:24
for this great *f* will consume us Deut 5:25
out of the midst of the *f* Deut 5:26
burn their graven images with *f* Deut 7:5
their gods shall ye burn with *f* Deut 7:25
as a consuming *f* he shall destroy Deut 9:3
the *f* in the day of the assembly Deut 9:10
mount, and the mount burned with *f*. Deut 9:15
ye had made, and burnt it with *f* Deut 9:21
the *f* in the day of the assembly Deut 10:4
and burn their groves with *f* Deut 12:3
have burnt in the *f* to their gods Deut 12:31
and shalt burn with *f* the city Deut 13:16
offerings of the LORD made by *f* Deut 18:1
daughter to pass through the *f* Deut 18:10
let me see this great *f* any more Deut 18:16
For a *f* is kindled in mine anger, Deut 32:22
set on *f* the foundations of the Deut 32:22
And they burnt the city with *f* Josh 6:24
thing shall be burnt with *f* Josh 7:15
stones, and burned them with *f* Josh 7:25
that ye shall set the city on *f* Josh 8:8
and hasted and set the city on *f* Josh 8:19
and burn their chariots with *f* Josh 11:6
and burnt their chariots with *f* Josh 11:9
and he burnt Hazor with *f* Josh 11:11
made by *f* are their inheritance Josh 13:14
the sword, and set the city on *f* Judg 1:8
there rose up *f* out of the rock, Judg 6:21
let *f* come out of the bramble, and Judg 9:15
let *f* come out from Abimelech, and Judg 9:20
let *f* come out from the men of Judg 9:20
and set the hold on *f* upon them Judg 9:49
of the tower to burn it with *f* Judg 9:52
burn thine house upon thee with *f* Judg 12:1
thee and thy father's house with *f* Judg 14:15
when he had set the brands on *f* Judg 15:5
and burnt her and her father with *f* Judg 15:6
as flax that was burnt with *f* Judg 15:14
is broken when it toucheth the *f* Judg 16:9
sword, and burnt the city with *f* Judg 18:27
also they set on *f* all the cities Judg 20:48
by *f* of the children of Israel 1Sa 2:28
Ziklag, and burned it with *f* 1Sa 30:1
and, behold, it was burned with *f* 1Sa 30:3
and we burned Ziklag with *f* 1Sa 30:14
go and set it on *f* 2Sa 14:30
servants set the field on *f* 2Sa 14:30
thy servants set my field on *f* 2Sa 14:31
*f* out of his mouth devoured 2Sa 22:9
him were coals of *f* kindled 2Sa 22:13
burned with *f* in the same place 2Sa 23:7
taken Gezer, and burnt it with *f* 1Kin 9:16
the king's house over him with *f* 1Kin 16:18
lay it on wood, and put no *f* under 1Kin 18:23
lay it on wood, and put no *f* under 1Kin 18:23
and the God that answereth by *f* 1Kin 18:24
of your gods, but put no *f* under 1Kin 18:25
Then the *f* of the LORD fell, and 1Kin 18:38
And after the earthquake a *f* 1Kin 19:12
but the LORD was not in the *f* 1Kin 19:12
after the *f* a still small voice 1Kin 19:12
then let *f* come down from heaven, 2Kin 1:10
And there came down *f* from heaven 2Kin 1:10
let *f* come down from heaven, and 2Kin 1:12
the *f* of God came down from 2Kin 1:12
there came *f* down from heaven, and 2Kin 1:14
a chariot of *f*, and horses of *f* 2Kin 2:11
chariots of *f* round about Elisha 2Kin 6:17
strong holds wilt thou set on *f* 2Kin 8:12
his son to pass through the *f* 2Kin 16:3
daughters to pass through the *f* 2Kin 17:17
children in *f* to Adrammelech 2Kin 17:31
have cast their gods into the *f* 2Kin 19:18
made his son pass through the *f* 2Kin 21:6
to pass through the *f* to Molech 2Kin 23:10
the chariots of the sun with *f* 2Kin 23:11
great man's house burnt he with *f* 2Kin 25:9
and they were burned with *f* 1Chr 14:12
by *f* upon the altar of burnt 1Chr 21:26
the *f* came down from heaven, and 2Chr 7:1
of Israel saw how the *f* came down 2Chr 7:3
and burnt his children in the *f* 2Chr 28:3
the *f* in the valley of the son of 2Chr 33:6
with *f* according to the ordinance 2Chr 35:13
all the palaces thereof with *f* 2Chr 36:19
gates thereof are burned with *f* Neh 1:3
gates thereof are consumed with *f* Neh 2:3
thereof were consumed with *f* Neh 2:13
gates thereof are burned with *f* Neh 2:17
and in the night by a pillar of *f* Neh 9:12
neither the pillar of *f* by night Neh 9:19
The *f* of God is fallen from Job 1:16
*f* shall consume the tabernacles Job 15:34
spark of his *f* shall not shine Job 18:5
a *f* not blown shall consume him Job 20:26
remnant of them the *f* consumeth Job 22:20
it is turned up as it were *f* Job 28:5
For it is a *f* that consumeth to Job 31:12
lamps, and sparks of *f* leap out Job 41:19
wicked he shall rain snares, *f* Ps 11:6
*f* out of his mouth devoured Ps 18:8
passed, hail stones and coals of *f* Ps 18:12
hail stones and coals of *f* Ps 18:13
wrath, and the *f* shall devour them Ps 21:9
the LORD divideth the flames of *f* Ps 29:7
while I was musing the *f* burned Ps 39:3
he burneth the chariot in the *f* Ps 46:9
a *f* shall devour before him, and Ps 50:3
even among them that are set on *f* Ps 57:4
we went through *f* and through Ps 66:12
as wax melteth before the *f* Ps 68:2
They have cast *f* into thy Ps 74:7
all the night with a light of *f* Ps 78:14
so a *f* was kindled against Jacob, Ps 78:21
The *f* consumed their young men Ps 78:63
shall thy jealousy burn like *f* Ps 79:5
It is burned with *f*, it is cut Ps 80:16
As the *f* burneth a wood, and as Ps 83:14
flame setteth the mountains on *f* Ps 83:14
shall thy wrath burn like *f* Ps 89:46
A *f* goeth before him, and burneth Ps 97:3
his ministers a flaming *f* Ps 104:4
rain, and flaming *f* in their land Ps 105:32
*f* to give light in the night Ps 105:39
a *f* was kindled in their company Ps 106:18
are quenched as the *f* of thorns Ps 118:12
let them be cast into the *f* Ps 140:10
F, and hail; snow, and Ps 148:8
Can a man take *f* in his bosom Prov 6:27
his lips there is as a burning *f* Prov 16:27
heap coals of *f* upon his head Prov 25:22
no wood is, there the *f* goeth out Prov 26:20
to burning coals, and wood to *f* Prov 26:21
the *f* that saith not, It is Prov 30:16
the coals thereof are coals of *f* Song 8:6
your cities are burned with *f* Is 1:7
shining of a flaming *f* by night Is 4:5
Therefore as the *f* devoureth the Is 5:24
be with burning and fuel of *f* Is 9:5
For wickedness burneth as the *f* Is 9:18
shall be as the fuel of the *f* Is 9:19
a burning like the burning of a *f* Is 10:16
light of Israel shall be for a *f* Is 10:17
the *f* of thine enemies shall Is 26:11
the women come, and set them on *f* Is 27:11
and the flame of devouring *f* Is 29:6
a sherd to take *f* from the hearth Is 30:14
and his tongue as a devouring *f* Is 30:27
with the flame of a devouring *f* Is 30:30
the pile thereof is *f* and much Is 30:33
whose *f* is in Zion, and his Is 31:9
your breath, as *f*, shall devour Is 33:11
up shall they be burned in the *f* Is 33:12
shall dwell with the devouring *f* Is 33:14
have cast their gods into the *f* Is 37:19
it hath set him on *f* round about Is 42:25
when thou walkest through the *f* Is 43:2
He burneth part thereof in the *f* Is 44:16
Aha, I am warm, I have seen the *f* Is 44:16
I have burned part of it in the *f* Is 44:19
the *f* shall burn them Is 47:14

warm at, nor *f* to sit before it — Is 47:14
Behold, all ye that kindle a *f* — Is 50:11
walk in the light of your *f* — Is 50:11
that bloweth the coals in the *f* — Is 54:16
As when the melting *f* burneth — Is 64:2
the *f* causeth the waters to boil, — Is 64:2
praised thee, is burned up with *f* — Is 64:11
a *f* that burneth all the day — Is 65:5
behold, the LORD will come with *f* — Is 66:15
and his rebuke with flames of *f* — Is 66:15
For by *f* and by his sword will the — Is 66:16
neither shall their *f* be quenched — Is 66:24
lest my fury come forth like *f* — Jer 4:4
will make my words in thy mouth *f* — Jer 5:14
up a sign of *f* in Beth-haccerem — Jer 6:1
the lead is consumed of the *f* — Jer 6:29
wood, and the fathers kindle the *f* — Jer 7:18
sons and their daughters in the *f* — Jer 7:31
tumult he hath kindled *f* upon it — Jer 11:16
for a *f* is kindled in mine anger, — Jer 15:14
ye have kindled a *f* in mine anger — Jer 17:4
I kindle a *f* in the gates thereof — Jer 17:27
to burn their sons with *f* for — Jer 19:5
a burning *f* shut up in my bones — Jer 20:9
and he shall burn it with *f* — Jer 21:10
lest my fury go out like *f* — Jer 21:12
I will kindle a *f* in the forest — Jer 21:14
cedars, and cast them into the *f* — Jer 22:7
Is not my word like as a *f* — Jer 23:29
king of Babylon roasted in the *f* — Jer 29:22
set *f* on this city, and burn it — Jer 32:29
to pass through the *f* unto Molech — Jer 32:35
and he shall burn it with *f* — Jer 34:2
and and take it, and burn it with *f* — Jer 34:22
there was a *f* on the hearth — Jer 36:22
cast it into the *f* that was on — Jer 36:23
in the *f* that was on the hearth — Jer 36:23
king of Judah had burned in the *f* — Jer 36:32
and take it, and burn it with *f* — Jer 37:8
tent, and burn this city with *f* — Jer 37:10
city shall not be burned with *f* — Jer 38:17
and they shall burn it with *f* — Jer 38:18
this city to be burned with *f* — Jer 38:23
the houses of the people, with *f* — Jer 39:8
I will kindle a *f* in the houses — Jer 43:12
Egyptians shall he burn with *f* — Jer 43:13
but a *f* shall come forth out of — Jer 48:45
daughters shall be burned with *f* — Jer 49:2
I will kindle a *f* in the wall of — Jer 49:27
I will kindle a *f* in his cities — Jer 50:32
the reeds they have burned with *f* — Jer 51:32
high gates shall be burned with *f* — Jer 51:58
in vain, and the folk in the *f* — Jer 51:58
the great men, burned he with *f* — Jer 52:13
hath he sent *f* into my bones — Lam 1:13
against Jacob like a flaming *f* — Lam 2:3
he poured out his fury like *f* — Lam 2:4
and hath kindled a *f* in Zion — Lam 4:11
a *f* infolding itself, and a — Eze 1:4
amber, out of the midst of the *f* — Eze 1:4
was like burning coals of *f* — Eze 1:13
living creatures; and the *f* was bright — Eze 1:13
out of the *f* went forth lightning — Eze 1:13
as the appearance of *f* round — Eze 1:27
as it were the appearance of *f* — Eze 1:27
Thou shalt burn with *f* a third — Eze 5:2
cast them into the midst of the *f* — Eze 5:4
and burn them in the *f* — Eze 5:4
for thereof shall a *f* come forth — Eze 5:4
a likeness as the appearance of *f* — Eze 8:2
of his loins even downward, *f* — Eze 8:2
of *f* from between the cherubims — Eze 10:2
Take *f* from between the wheels, — Eze 10:6
*f* that was between the cherubims — Eze 10:7
it is cast into the *f* for fuel — Eze 15:4
the *f* devoureth both the ends of — Eze 15:4
when the *f* hath devoured it, and — Eze 15:5
I have given to the *f* for fuel — Eze 15:6
they shall go out from one *f* — Eze 15:7
another *f* shall devour them — Eze 15:7
to pass through the *f* for them — Eze 16:21
shall burn thine houses with *f* — Eze 16:41
the *f* consumed them — Eze 19:12
*f* is gone out of a rod of her — Eze 19:14
the *f* all that openeth the womb — Eze 20:26
your sons to pass through the *f* — Eze 20:31
Behold, I will kindle a *f* in thee — Eze 20:47
against thee in the *f* of my wrath — Eze 21:31
Thou shalt be for fuel to the *f* — Eze 21:32
furnace, to blow the *f* upon it — Eze 22:20
upon you in the *f* of my wrath — Eze 22:21
them with the *f* of my wrath — Eze 22:31
shall be devoured by the *f* — Eze 23:25
to pass for them through the *f* — Eze 23:37
and burn up their houses with *f* — Eze 23:47
even make the pile for *f* great — Eze 24:9
Heap on wood, kindle the *f* — Eze 24:10
her scum shall be in the *f* — Eze 24:12
in the midst of the stones of *f* — Eze 28:14
from the midst of the stones of *f* — Eze 28:16
forth a *f* from the midst of thee — Eze 28:18
when I have set a *f* in Egypt — Eze 30:8
desolate, and will set *f* in Zoan — Eze 30:14
And I will set *f* in Egypt — Eze 30:16
Surely in the *f* of my jealousy — Eze 36:5
in the *f* of my wrath have I — Eze 38:19
rain, and great hailstones, *f* — Eze 38:22
And I will send a *f* on Magog — Eze 39:6
shall go forth, and shall set on *f* — Eze 39:9
burn them with *f* seven years — Eze 39:9
shall burn the weapons with *f* — Eze 39:10
the flame of the *f* slew those men — Dan 3:22
men bound into the midst of the *f* — Dan 3:24
walking in the midst of the *f* — Dan 3:25
came forth of the midst of the *f* — Dan 3:26
whose bodies the *f* had no power — Dan 3:27
nor the smell of *f* had passed on — Dan 3:27
flame, and his wheels as burning *f* — Dan 7:9
and his eyes as lamps of *f* — Dan 10:6
morning it burneth as a flaming *f* — Hos 7:6
I will send a *f* upon his cities — Hos 8:14
for the *f* hath devoured the — Joel 1:19
the *f* hath devoured the pastures — Joel 1:20
A *f* devoureth before them — Joel 2:3
of *f* that devoureth the stubble — Joel 2:5
and in the earth, blood, and *f* — Joel 2:30
But I will send a *f* into the — Amos 1:4
But I will send a *f* on the wall — Amos 1:7
But I will send a *f* on the wall — Amos 1:10
But I will send a *f* upon Teman — Amos 1:12
But I will kindle a *f* in the wall — Amos 1:14
But I will send a *f* upon Moab — Amos 2:2
But I will send a *f* upon Judah — Amos 2:5
out like *f* in the house of Joseph — Amos 5:6
Lord GOD called to contend by *f* — Amos 7:4
the house of Jacob shall be a *f* — Obad 18
be cleft, as wax before the *f* — Mic 1:4
shall be burned with the *f* — Mic 1:7
his fury is poured out like *f* — Nah 1:6
the *f* shall devour thy bars — Nah 3:13
There shall the *f* devour thee — Nah 3:15
people shall labour in the very *f* — Hab 2:13
devoured by the *f* of his jealousy — Zeph 1:18
with the *f* of my jealousy — Zeph 3:8
unto her a wall of *f* round about — Zec 2:5
this a brand plucked out of the *f* — Zec 3:2
and she shall be devoured with *f* — Zec 9:4
that the *f* may devour thy cedars — Zec 11:1
an hearth of *f* among the wood — Zec 12:6
and like a torch of *f* in a sheaf — Zec 12:6
the third part through the *f* — Zec 13:9
neither do ye kindle *f* on mine — Mal 1:10
for he is like a refiner's *f* — Mal 3:2
is hewn down, and cast into the *f* — Mt 3:10
with the Holy Ghost, and with *f* — Mt 3:11
up the chaff with unquenchable *f* — Mt 3:12
shall be in danger of hell *f* — Mt 5:22
is hewn down, and cast into the *f* — Mt 7:19
are gathered and burned in the *f* — Mt 13:40
cast them into a furnace of *f* — Mt 13:42
cast them into the furnace of *f* — Mt 13:50
ofttimes he falleth into the *f* — Mt 17:15
to be cast into everlasting *f* — Mt 18:8
two eyes to be cast into hell *f* — Mt 18:9
me, ye cursed, into everlasting *f* — Mt 25:41
it hath cast him into the *f* — Mk 9:22
into the *f* that never shall be — Mk 9:43
not, and the *f* is not quenched — Mk 9:44
into the *f* that never shall be — Mk 9:45
not, and the *f* is not quenched — Mk 9:46
two eyes to be cast into hell *f* — Mk 9:47
not, and the *f* is not quenched — Mk 9:48
every one shall be salted with *f* — Mk 9:49
and warmed himself at the *f* — Mk 14:54
is hewn down, and cast into the *f* — Lk 3:9
you with the Holy Ghost and with *f* — Lk 3:16
he will burn with *f* unquenchable — Lk 3:17
*f* to come down from heaven — Lk 9:54
I am come to send *f* on the earth — Lk 12:49
Lot went out of Sodom it rained *f* — Lk 17:29
when they had kindled a *f* in the — Lk 22:55
beheld him as he sat by the *f* — Lk 22:56
them, and cast them into the *f* — Jn 15:6
there, who had made a *f* of coals — Jn 18:18
they saw a *f* of coals there, and — Jn 21:9
them cloven tongues like as of *f* — Acts 2:3
blood, and *f*, and vapour of smoke — Acts 2:19
Lord in a flame of *f* in a bush — Acts 7:30
for they kindled a *f*, and received — Acts 28:2
of sticks, and laid them on the *f* — Acts 28:3
he shook off the beast into the *f* — Acts 28:5
shalt heap coals of *f* on his head — Rom 12:20
because it shall be revealed by *f* — 1Cor 3:13
the *f* shall try every man's work — 1Cor 3:13
yet so as by *f* — 1Cor 3:15
In flaming *f* taking vengeance on — 2Th 1:8
and his ministers a flame of *f* — Heb 1:7
Quenched the violence of *f* — Heb 11:34
be touched, and that burned with *f* — Heb 12:18
For our God is a consuming *f* — Heb 12:29
a matter a little *f* kindleth — Jas 3:5
And the tongue is a *f*, a world of — Jas 3:6
setteth on *f* the course of nature — Jas 3:6
and it is set on *f* of hell — Jas 3:6
shall eat your flesh as it were *f* — Jas 5:3
though it be tried with *f* — 1Pet 1:7
reserved unto *f* against the day — 2Pet 3:7
being on *f* shall be dissolved — 2Pet 3:12
the vengeance of eternal *f* — Jude 7
fear, pulling them out of the *f* — Jude 23
and his eyes were as a flame of *f* — Rev 1:14
his eyes like unto a flame of *f* — Rev 2:18
to buy of me gold tried in the *f* — Rev 3:18
of *f* burning before the throne — Rev 4:5
and filled it with *f* of the altar — Rev 8:5
*f* mingled with blood, and they — Rev 8:7
with *f* was cast into the sea — Rev 8:8
on them, having breastplates of *f* — Rev 9:17
and out of their mouths issued *f* — Rev 9:17
part of men killed, by the *f* — Rev 9:18
sun, and his feet as pillars of *f* — Rev 10:1
*f* proceedeth out of their mouth, — Rev 11:5
so that he maketh *f* come down — Rev 13:13
and he shall be tormented with *f* — Rev 14:10
the altar, which had power over *f* — Rev 14:18
a sea of glass mingled with *f* — Rev 15:2
unto him to scorch men with *f* — Rev 16:8
eat her flesh, and burn her with *f* — Rev 17:16
shall be utterly burned with *f* — Rev 18:8
His eyes were as a flame of *f* — Rev 19:12
lake of *f* burning with brimstone — Rev 19:20
*f* came down from God out of — Rev 20:9
them was cast into the lake of *f* — Rev 20:10
hell were cast into the lake of *f* — Rev 20:14
life was cast into the lake of *f* — Rev 20:15
in the lake which burneth with *f* — Rev 21:8

**FIREBRAND**
put a *f* in the midst between two — Judg 15:4
ye were as a *f* plucked out of the — Amos 4:11

**FIREBRANDS**
three hundred foxes, and took *f* — Judg 15:4
As a mad man who casteth *f* — Prov 26:18
the two tails of these smoking *f* — Is 7:4

**FIREPANS**
and his fleshhooks, and his *f* — Ex 27:3
and the fleshhooks, and the *f* — Ex 38:3
And the *f*, and the bowls, and such — 2Kin 25:15
And the basons, and the *f*, and the — Jer 52:19

**FIRES**
glorify ye the LORD in the *f* — Is 24:15

**FIRKINS**
containing two or three *f* apiece — Jn 2:6

**FIRM**
*f* on dry ground in the midst of — Josh 3:17
where the priests' feet stood *f* — Josh 4:3
they are *f* in themselves — Job 41:23
His heart is as *f* as a stone — Job 41:24
but their strength is *f* — Ps 73:4
statute, and to make a *f* decree — Dan 6:7
of the hope *f* unto the end — Heb 3:6

**FIRMAMENT**
Let there be a *f* in the midst of — Gen 1:6
And God made the *f*, and divided the — Gen 1:7
the *f* from the waters which were — Gen 1:7
the waters which were above the *f* — Gen 1:7
And God called the *f* Heaven — Gen 1:8
Let there be lights in the *f* of — Gen 1:14
the *f* of the heaven to give light — Gen 1:15
God set them in the *f* of the — Gen 1:17
the earth in the open *f* of heaven — Gen 1:20
the *f* sheweth his handywork — Ps 19:1
praise him in the *f* of his power — Ps 150:1
the likeness of the *f* upon the — Eze 1:22
under the *f* were their wings — Eze 1:23
the *f* that was over their heads — Eze 1:25
above the *f* that was over their — Eze 1:26
in the *f* that was above the head — Eze 10:1
shine as the brightness of the *f* — Dan 12:3

**FIRST**
and the morning were the *f* day — Gen 1:5
The name of the *f* is Pison — Gen 2:11
on the *f* day of the month, were — Gen 8:5
and *f* year, in the *f* month — Gen 8:13
the *f* day of the month, the — Gen 8:13
which he had made there at the *f* — Gen 13:4
the *f* came out red, all over like — Gen 25:25
beside the *f* famine that was in — Gen 26:1
that city was called Luz at the *f* — Gen 28:19
thread, saying, This came out *f* — Gen 38:28
did eat up the *f* seven fat kine — Gen 41:20
at the *f* time are we brought in — Gen 43:18
down at the *f* time to buy food — Gen 43:20
to the voice of the *f* sign — Ex 4:8
it shall be the *f* month of the — Ex 12:2
blemish, a male of the *f* year — Ex 12:5
even the *f* day ye shall put away — Ex 12:15
the *f* day until the seventh day — Ex 12:15
in the *f* day there shall be an — Ex 12:16
In the *f* month, on the fourteenth — Ex 12:18
to offer the *f* of thy ripe fruits — Ex 22:29
The *f* of the firstfruits of thy — Ex 23:19
the *f* row shall be a sardius, a — Ex 28:17
this shall be the *f* row — Ex 28:17
two lambs of the *f* year day by — Ex 29:38
tables of stone like unto the *f* — Ex 34:1
words that were in the *f* tables — Ex 34:1
tables of stone like unto the *f* — Ex 34:4
The *f* of the firstfruits of thy — Ex 34:26
the *f* row was a sardius, a topaz, — Ex 39:10
this was the *f* row — Ex 39:10
On the *f* day of the *f* month — Ex 40:2
On the *f* day of the *f* month — Ex 40:2
it came to pass in the *f* month in — Ex 40:17
on the *f* day of the month, that — Ex 40:17
him as he burned the *f* bullock — Lev 4:21
which is for the sin offering *f* — Lev 5:8
and a lamb, both of the *f* year — Lev 9:3
and offered it for sin, as the *f* — Lev 9:15
the *f* year for a burnt offering — Lev 12:6
one ewe lamb of the *f* year — Lev 14:10
the *f* month at even is the LORD's — Lev 23:5
In the *f* day ye shall have an — Lev 23:7
*f* year for a burnt offering unto — Lev 23:12
without blemish of the *f* year — Lev 23:18
two lambs of the *f* year for a — Lev 23:19
the *f* fruits for a wave offering — Lev 23:20

in the *f* day of the month, shall ... Lev 23:24
On the *f* day shall be an holy ... Lev 23:35
on the *f* day shall be a sabbath, ... Lev 23:39
ye shall take you on the *f* day ... Lev 23:40
on the *f* day of the second month, ... Num 1:1
on the *f* day of the second month ... Num 1:18
These shall *f* set forth ... Num 2:9
shall bring a lamb of the *f* year ... Num 6:12
one he lamb of the *f* year without ... Num 6:14
one ewe lamb of the *f* year ... Num 6:14
the *f* day was Nahshon the son of ... Num 7:12
one ram, one lamb of the *f* year ... Num 7:15
goats, five lambs of the *f* year ... Num 7:17
one ram, one lamb of the *f* year ... Num 7:21
goats, five lambs of the *f* year ... Num 7:23
one ram, one lamb of the *f* year ... Num 7:27
goats, five lambs of the *f* year ... Num 7:29
one ram, one lamb of the *f* year ... Num 7:33
goats, five lambs of the *f* year ... Num 7:35
one ram, one lamb of the *f* year ... Num 7:39
goats, five lambs of the *f* year ... Num 7:41
one ram, one lamb of the *f* year ... Num 7:45
goats, five lambs of the *f* year ... Num 7:47
one ram, one lamb of the *f* year ... Num 7:51
goats, five lambs of the *f* year ... Num 7:53
one ram, one lamb of the *f* year ... Num 7:57
goats, five lambs of the *f* year ... Num 7:59
one ram, one lamb of the *f* year ... Num 7:63
goats, five lambs of the *f* year ... Num 7:65
one ram, one lamb of the *f* year ... Num 7:69
goats, five lambs of the *f* year ... Num 7:71
one ram, one lamb of the *f* year ... Num 7:75
goats, five lambs of the *f* year ... Num 7:77
one ram, one lamb of the *f* year ... Num 7:81
goats, five lambs of the *f* year ... Num 7:83
the lambs of the *f* year twelve ... Num 7:87
the lambs of the *f* year sixty ... Num 7:88
in the *f* month of the second year ... Num 9:1
on the fourteenth day of the *f* ... Num 9:5
they *f* took their journey ... Num 10:13
In the *f* place went the standard ... Num 10:14
the *f* of your dough for an heave ... Num 15:20
Of the *f* of your dough ye shall ... Num 15:21
of the *f* year for a sin offering ... Num 15:27
whatsoever is *f* ripe in the land, ... Num 18:13
the desert of Zin in the *f* month ... Num 20:1
Amalek was the *f* of the nations ... Num 24:20
two lambs of the *f* year without ... Num 28:3
lambs of the *f* year without spot ... Num 28:9
lambs of the *f* year without spot ... Num 28:11
*f* month is the passover of the ... Num 28:16
In the *f* day shall be an holy ... Num 28:18
ram, and seven lambs of the *f* year ... Num 28:19
ram, seven lambs of the *f* year ... Num 28:27
on the *f* day of the month, ye ... Num 29:1
seven lambs of the *f* year without ... Num 29:2
ram, and seven lambs of the *f* year ... Num 29:8
and fourteen lambs of the *f* year ... Num 29:13
lambs of the *f* year without spot ... Num 29:17
of the *f* year without blemish ... Num 29:20
of the *f* year without blemish ... Num 29:23
lambs of the *f* year without spot ... Num 29:26
of the *f* year without blemish ... Num 29:29
of the *f* year without blemish ... Num 29:32
seven lambs of the *f* year without ... Num 29:36
from Rameses in the *f* month ... Num 33:3
the fifteenth day of the *f* month ... Num 33:3
in the *f* day of the fifth month ... Num 33:38
on the *f* day of the month, that ... Deut 1:3
down before the LORD, as at the *f* ... Deut 9:18
nights, as I fell down at the *f* ... Deut 9:25
tables of stone like unto the *f* ... Deut 10:1
the *f* tables which thou brakest ... Deut 10:2
tables of stone like unto the *f* ... Deut 10:3
according to the *f* writing ... Deut 10:4
mount, according to the *f* time ... Deut 10:10
the *f* rain and the latter rain, ... Deut 11:14
thine hand shall be *f* upon him to ... Deut 13:9
sacrificedst the *f* day at even ... Deut 16:4
be *f* upon him to put him to death ... Deut 17:7
the *f* of the fleece of thy sheep, ... Deut 18:4
That thou shalt take of the *f* of ... Deut 26:2
he provided the *f* part for ... Deut 33:21
on the tenth day of the *f* month ... Josh 4:19
come out against us, as at the *f* ... Josh 8:5
They flee before us, as at the *f* ... Josh 8:6
for theirs was the *f* lot ... Josh 21:10
for us against the Canaanites *f* ... Judg 1:1
of the city was Laish at the *f* ... Judg 18:29
Which of us shall go up *f* to the ... Judg 20:18
LORD said, Judah shall go up *f* ... Judg 20:18
put themselves in array the *f* day ... Judg 20:22
down before us, as at the *f* ... Judg 20:32
before us, as in the *f* battle ... Judg 20:39
that *f* slaughter, which Jonathan ... 1Sa 14:14
the same was the *f* altar that he ... 1Sa 14:35
the battle were Eliab the *f* born ... 1Sa 17:13
except thou *f* bring Michal Saul's ... 2Sa 3:13
of them be overthrown at the *f* ... 2Sa 17:9
I am come the *f* this day of all ... 2Sa 19:20
*f* had in bringing back our king ... 2Sa 19:43
days of harvest, in the *f* days ... 2Sa 21:9
he attained not unto the *f* three ... 2Sa 23:19
he attained not to the *f* three ... 2Sa 23:23
*f* year of Asa king of Judah began ... 1Kin 16:23
make me thereof a little cake *f* ... 1Kin 17:13
for yourselves, and dress it *f* ... 1Kin 18:25
to thy servant at the *f* I will do ... 1Kin 20:9
of the provinces went out *f* ... 1Kin 20:17
Now the *f* inhabitants that dwelt ... 1Chr 9:2
the Jebusites *f* shall be chief ... 1Chr 11:6
Joab the son of Zeruiah went *f* up ... 1Chr 11:6
he attained not to the *f* three ... 1Chr 11:21
but attained not to the *f* three ... 1Chr 11:25
Ezer the *f*, Obadiah the second, ... 1Chr 12:9
went over Jordan in the *f* month ... 1Chr 12:15
because ye did it not at the *f* ... 1Chr 15:13
on that day David delivered *f* ... 1Chr 16:7
Jeriah the *f*, Amariah the second, ... 1Chr 23:19
Micah the *f*, and Jesiah the second ... 1Chr 23:20
Now the *f* lot came forth to ... 1Chr 24:7
of Rehabiah, the *f* was Isshiah ... 1Chr 24:21
Jeriah the *f*, Amariah the second, ... 1Chr 24:23
Now the *f* lot came forth for ... 1Chr 25:9
Over the *f* course for the *f* ... 1Chr 27:2
of the host for the *f* month ... 1Chr 27:3
Now the acts of David the king, *f* ... 1Chr 29:29
*f* measure was threescore cubits ... 2Chr 3:3
rest of the acts of Solomon, *f* ... 2Chr 9:29
Now the acts of Rehoboam, *f* ... 2Chr 12:15
And, behold, the acts of Asa, *f* ... 2Chr 16:11
in the *f* ways of his father David ... 2Chr 17:3
of the acts of Jehoshaphat, *f* ... 2Chr 20:34
rest of the acts of Amaziah, *f* ... 2Chr 25:26
the rest of the acts of Uzziah, *f* ... 2Chr 26:22
of his acts and of all his ways, *f* ... 2Chr 28:26
He in the *f* year of his reign, in ... 2Chr 29:3
year of his reign, in the *f* month ... 2Chr 29:3
Now they began on the *f* day of ... 2Chr 29:17
day of the *f* month to sanctify ... 2Chr 29:17
of the *f* month they made an end ... 2Chr 29:17
the fourteenth day of the *f* month ... 2Chr 35:1
And his deeds, *f* and last, behold, ... 2Chr 35:27
Now in the *f* year of Cyrus king ... 2Chr 36:22
Now in the *f* year of Cyrus king ... Ezr 1:1
From the *f* day of the seventh ... Ezr 3:6
men, that had seen the *f* house ... Ezr 3:12
But in the *f* year of Cyrus the ... Ezr 5:13
In the *f* year of Cyrus the king ... Ezr 6:3
the fourteenth day of the *f* month ... Ezr 6:19
For upon the *f* day of the ... Ezr 7:9
*f* month began he to go up from ... Ezr 7:9
on the *f* day of the fifth month ... Ezr 7:9
on the twelfth day of the *f* month ... Ezr 8:31
sat down in the *f* day of the ... Ezr 10:16
by the *f* day of the *f* month ... Ezr 10:17
by the *f* day of the *f* month ... Ezr 10:17
of them which came up at the *f* ... Neh 7:5
upon the *f* day of the seventh ... Neh 8:2
from the *f* day unto the last day, ... Neh 8:18
which sat the *f* in the kingdom ... Est 1:14
In the *f* month, that is, the ... Est 3:7
the thirteenth day of the *f* month ... Est 3:12
Art thou the *f* man that was born ... Job 15:7
And he called the name of the *f* ... Job 42:14
He that is *f* in his own cause ... Prov 18:17
restore thy judges as at the *f* ... Is 1:26
when at the *f* he lightly ... Is 9:1
I the LORD, the *f*, and with the ... Is 41:4
The *f* shall say to Zion, Behold, ... Is 41:27
Thy *f* father hath sinned, and thy ... Is 43:27
I am the *f*, and I am the last ... Is 44:6
I am the *f*, I also am the last ... Is 48:12
me, and the ships of Tarshish *f* ... Is 60:9
that bringeth forth her *f* child ... Jer 4:31
where I set my name at the *f* ... Jer 7:12
*f* I will recompense their ... Jer 16:18
like the figs that are *f* ripe ... Jer 24:2
of Judah, that was the *f* year of ... Jer 25:1
and will build them, as at the *f* ... Jer 33:7
of the land, as at the *f*, saith ... Jer 33:11
words that were in the *f* roll ... Jer 36:28
*f* the king of Assyria hath ... Jer 50:17
king of Babylon in the *f* year of ... Jer 52:31
the *f* face was the face of a ... Eze 10:14
in the *f* day of the month, that ... Eze 26:1
and twentieth year, in the *f* month ... Eze 29:17
in the *f* day of the month, the ... Eze 29:17
the eleventh year, in the *f* month ... Eze 30:20
in the *f* day of the month, that ... Eze 31:1
in the *f* day of the month, that ... Eze 32:1
after the measure of the *f* gate ... Eze 40:21
the *f* of all the firstfruits of ... Eze 44:30
the priest the *f* of your dough ... Eze 44:30
In the *f* month, in the ... Eze 45:18
in the *f* day of the month, thou ... Eze 45:18
In the *f* month, in the fourteenth ... Eze 45:21
of the *f* year without blemish ... Eze 46:13
unto the *f* year of king Cyrus ... Dan 1:21
of whom Daniel was *f* ... Dan 6:2
In the *f* year of Belshazzar king ... Dan 7:1
The *f* was like a lion, and had ... Dan 7:4
whom there were three of the *f* ... Dan 7:8
and he shall be diverse from the *f* ... Dan 7:24
which appeared unto me at the *f* ... Dan 8:1
is between his eyes is the *f* king ... Dan 8:21
In the *f* year of Darius the son ... Dan 9:1
In the *f* year of his reign I ... Dan 9:2
and twentieth day of the *f* month ... Dan 10:4
for from the *f* day that thou ... Dan 10:12
Also I in the *f* year of Darius ... Dan 11:1
will go and return to my *f* husband ... Hos 2:7
in the fig tree at her *f* time ... Hos 9:10
and the latter rain in the *f* month ... Joel 2:23
with the *f* that go captive ... Amos 6:7
it come, even the *f* dominion ... Mic 4:8
in the *f* day of the month, came ... Hag 1:1
saw this house in her *f* glory ... Hag 2:3
In the *f* chariot were red horses ... Zec 6:2
shall save the tents of Judah *f* ... Zec 12:7
gate unto the place of the *f* gate ... Zec 14:10
*f* be reconciled to thy brother, ... Mt 5:24
But seek ye *f* the kingdom of God, ... Mt 6:33
*f* cast out the beam out of thine ... Mt 7:5
unto him, Lord, suffer me *f* to go ... Mt 8:21
The *f*, Simon, who is called Peter ... Mt 10:2
except he *f* bind the strong man ... Mt 12:29
of that man is worse than the *f* ... Mt 12:45
Gather ye together *f* the tares ... Mt 13:30
scribes that Elias must *f* come ... Mt 17:10
them, Elias truly shall *f* come ... Mt 17:11
take up the fish that *f* cometh up ... Mt 17:27
But many that are *f* shall be last ... Mt 19:30
and the last shall be *f* ... Mt 19:30
from the last unto the *f* ... Mt 20:8
But when the *f* came, they ... Mt 20:10
shall be *f*, and the *f* last ... Mt 20:16
and he came to the *f*, and said, Son ... Mt 21:28
They say unto him, The *f* ... Mt 21:31
other servants more than the *f* ... Mt 21:36
and the *f*, when he had married a ... Mt 22:25
This is the *f* and great ... Mt 22:38
cleanse *f* that which is within ... Mt 23:26
Now the *f* day of the feast of ... Mt 26:17
error shall be worse than the *f* ... Mt 27:64
dawn toward the *f* day of the week ... Mt 28:1
except he will *f* bind the strong ... Mk 3:27
*f* the blade, then the ear, after ... Mk 4:28
her, Let the children *f* be filled ... Mk 7:27
scribes that Elias must *f* come ... Mk 9:11
told them, Elias verily cometh *f* ... Mk 9:12
them, If any man desire to be *f* ... Mk 9:35
But many that are *f* shall be last ... Mk 10:31
and the last *f* ... Mk 10:31
the *f* took a wife, and dying left ... Mk 12:20
Which is the *f* commandment of all ... Mk 12:28
The *f* of all the commandments is, ... Mk 12:29
this is the *f* commandment ... Mk 12:30
the gospel must *f* be published ... Mk 13:10
the *f* day of unleavened bread, ... Mk 14:12
the morning the *f* day of the week ... Mk 16:2
risen early the *f* day of the week ... Mk 16:9
he appeared *f* to Mary Magdalene, ... Mk 16:9
of all things from the very *f* ... Lk 1:3
this taxing was *f* made when ... Lk 2:2
on the second sabbath after the *f* ... Lk 6:1
cast out *f* the beam out of thine ... Lk 6:42
he said, Lord, suffer me *f* to go ... Lk 9:59
but let me *f* go bid them farewell ... Lk 9:61
*f* say, Peace be to this house ... Lk 10:5
of that man is worse than the *f* ... Lk 11:26
he had not *f* washed before dinner ... Lk 11:38
say unto his disciples *f* of all ... Lk 12:1
there are last which shall be *f* ... Lk 13:30
there are *f* which shall be last ... Lk 13:30
The *f* said unto him, I have ... Lk 14:18
build a tower, sitteth not down *f* ... Lk 14:28
another king, sitteth not down *f* ... Lk 14:31
unto him, and said unto the *f* ... Lk 16:5
But *f* must he suffer many things, ... Lk 17:25
Then came the *f*, saying, Lord, ... Lk 19:16
the *f* took a wife, and died ... Lk 20:29
these things must *f* come to pass ... Lk 21:9
Now upon the *f* day of the week, ... Lk 24:1
He *f* findeth his own brother ... Jn 1:41
whosoever then *f* after the ... Jn 5:4
let him *f* cast a stone at her ... Jn 8:7
place where John at *f* baptized ... Jn 10:40
not his disciples at the *f* ... Jn 12:16
And led him away to Annas *f* ... Jn 18:13
and brake the legs of the *f* ... Jn 19:32
which at the *f* came to Jesus by ... Jn 19:39
The *f* day of the week cometh Mary ... Jn 20:1
Peter, and came *f* to the sepulchre ... Jn 20:4
which came *f* to the sepulchre, and ... Jn 20:8
being the *f* day of the week, when ... Jn 20:19
Unto you *f* God, having raised up ... Acts 3:26
Egypt, he sent out our fathers *f* ... Acts 7:12
called Christians *f* in Antioch ... Acts 11:26
When they were past the *f* ... Acts 12:10
When John had *f* preached before ... Acts 13:24
should *f* have been spoken to you ... Acts 13:46
at the *f* did visit the Gentiles ... Acts 15:14
upon the *f* day of the week, when ... Acts 20:7
from the *f* day that I came into ... Acts 20:18
which was at the *f* among mine own ... Acts 26:4
But shewed *f* unto them of ... Acts 26:20
that he should be the *f* that ... Acts 26:23
cast themselves *f* into the sea ... Acts 27:43
*F*, I thank my God through Jesus ... Rom 1:8
to the Jew *f*, and also to the ... Rom 1:16
man that doeth evil, of the Jew *f* ... Rom 2:9
that worketh good, to the Jew *f* ... Rom 2:10
*F* Moses saith, I will provoke you ... Rom 10:19
Or who hath *f* given to him, and it ... Rom 11:35
if *f* I be somewhat filled with ... Rom 15:24
For *f* of all, when ye come ... 1Cor 11:18
*f* apostles, secondarily prophets, ... 1Cor 12:28
by, let the *f* hold his peace ... 1Cor 14:30
you *f* of all that which I also ... 1Cor 15:3
The *f* man Adam was made a living ... 1Cor 15:45
that was not *f* which is spiritual ... 1Cor 15:46
The *f* man is of the earth, earthy ... 1Cor 15:47
Upon the *f* day of the week let ... 1Cor 16:2
The *f* epistle to the Corinthians ... 1Cor s
but *f* gave their own selves to ... 2Cor 8:5
For if there be *f* a willing mind ... 2Cor 8:12
the gospel unto you at the *f* ... Gal 4:13
glory, who *f* trusted in Christ ... Eph 1:12
*f* into the lower parts of the ... Eph 4:9

which is the *f* commandment with ... Eph 6:2
gospel from the *f* day until now ... Phil 1:5
the dead in Christ shall rise *f* ... 1Th 4:16
The *f* epistle unto the ... 1Th s
there come a falling away *f* ... 2Th 2:3
that in me *f* Jesus Christ might ... 1Ti 1:16
*f* of all, supplications, prayers, ... 1Ti 2:1
For Adam was *f* formed, then Eve ... 1Ti 2:13
And let these also *f* be proved ... 1Ti 3:10
let them learn *f* to shew piety at ... 1Ti 5:4
they have cast off their *f* faith ... 1Ti 5:12
The *f* to Timothy was written from ... 1Ti s
which dwelt *f* in thy grandmother ... 2Ti 1:5
must be *f* partaker of the fruits ... 2Ti 2:6
At my *f* answer no man stood with ... 2Ti 4:16
ordained the *f* bishop of the ... 2Ti s
that is an heretick after the *f* ... Titus 3:10
ordained the *f* bishop of the ... Titus s
which at the *f* began to be spoken ... Heb 2:3
they to whom it was *f* preached ... Heb 4:6
*f* principles of the oracles of ... Heb 5:12
*f* being by interpretation King of ... Heb 7:2
*f* for his own sins, and then for ... Heb 7:27
For if that *f* covenant had been ... Heb 8:7
covenant, he hath made the *f* old ... Heb 8:13
Then verily the *f* covenant had ... Heb 9:1
the *f*, wherein was the ... Heb 9:2
went always into the *f* tabernacle ... Heb 9:6
while as the *f* tabernacle was yet ... Heb 9:8
that were under the *f* testament ... Heb 9:15
Whereupon neither the *f* testament ... Heb 9:18
He taketh away the *f*, that he may ... Heb 10:9
that is from above is *f* pure ... Jas 3:17
if it *f* begin at us, what shall ... 1Pet 4:17
Knowing this *f*, that no prophecy ... 2Pet 1:20
Knowing this *f*, that there shall ... 2Pet 3:3
love him, because he *f* loved us ... 1Jn 4:19
which kept not their *f* estate ... Jude 6
the *f* begotten of the dead, and ... Rev 1:5
I am Alpha and Omega, the *f* ... Rev 1:11
I am the *f* and the last ... Rev 1:17
because thou hast left thy *f* love ... Rev 2:4
and repent, and do the *f* works ... Rev 2:5
These things saith the *f* and the ... Rev 2:8
and the last to be more than the *f* ... Rev 2:19
the *f* voice which I heard was as ... Rev 4:1
the *f* beast was like a lion, and ... Rev 4:7
The *f* angel sounded, and there ... Rev 8:7
power of the *f* beast before him ... Rev 13:12
therein to worship the *f* beast ... Rev 13:12
the *f* went, and poured out his ... Rev 16:2
This is the *f* resurrection ... Rev 20:5
hath part in the *f* resurrection ... Rev 20:6
*f* heaven and the *f* earth ... Rev 21:1
The *f* foundation was jasper ... Rev 21:19
the beginning and the end, the *f* ... Rev 22:13

## FIRSTBEGOTTEN

bringeth in the *f* into the world ... Heb 1:6

## FIRSTBORN

And Canaan begat Sidon his *f* ... Gen 10:15
the *f* said unto the younger, Our ... Gen 19:31
the *f* went in, and lay with her ... Gen 19:33
that the *f* said unto the younger, ... Gen 19:34
the *f* bare a son, and called his ... Gen 19:37
Huz his *f*, and Buz his brother, and ... Gen 22:21
the *f* of Ishmael, Nebajoth ... Gen 25:13
unto his father, I am Esau thy *f* ... Gen 27:19
he said, I am thy son, thy *f* Esau ... Gen 27:32
to give the younger before the *f* ... Gen 29:26
Reuben, Jacob's *f*, and Simeon, and ... Gen 35:23
sons of Eliphaz the *f* son of Esau ... Gen 36:15
And Judah took a wife for Er his *f* ... Gen 38:6
And Er, Judah's *f*, was wicked in ... Gen 38:7
called the name of the *f* Manasseh ... Gen 41:51
the *f* according to his birthright ... Gen 43:33
Reuben, Jacob's *f* ... Gen 46:8
for Manasseh was the *f* ... Gen 48:14
for this is the *f* ... Gen 48:18
Reuben, thou art my *f*, my might, ... Gen 49:3
LORD, Israel is my son, even my *f* ... Ex 4:22
I will slay thy son, even thy *f* ... Ex 4:23
sons of Reuben the *f* of Israel ... Ex 6:14
all the *f* in the land of Egypt ... Ex 11:5
from the *f* of Pharaoh that ... Ex 11:5
throne, even unto the *f* of the ... Ex 11:5
and all the *f* of beasts ... Ex 11:5
will smite all the *f* in the land ... Ex 12:12
all the *f* in the land of Egypt ... Ex 12:29
from the *f* of Pharaoh that sat on ... Ex 12:29
*f* of the captive that was in the ... Ex 12:29
and all the *f* of cattle ... Ex 12:29
Sanctify unto me all the *f* ... Ex 13:2
all the *f* of man among thy ... Ex 13:13
all the *f* in the land of Egypt ... Ex 13:15
land of Egypt, both the *f* of man ... Ex 13:15
of man, and the *f* of beast ... Ex 13:15
but all the *f* of my children I ... Ex 13:15
the *f* of thy sons shalt thou give ... Ex 22:29
All the *f* of thy sons thou shalt ... Ex 34:20
Nadab the *f*, and Abihu, Eleazar, ... Num 3:2
of Israel instead of all the *f* ... Num 3:12
Because all the *f* are mine ... Num 3:13
*f* in the land of Egypt I hallowed ... Num 3:13
unto me all the *f* in Israel ... Num 3:13
Number all the *f* of the males of ... Num 3:40
*f* among the children of Israel ... Num 3:41
all the *f* among the children of ... Num 3:42
all the *f* males by the number of ... Num 3:43
*f* among the children of Israel ... Num 3:45
thirteen of the *f* of the children ... Num 3:46
Of the *f* of the children of ... Num 3:50
even instead of the *f* of all the ... Num 8:16
For all the *f* of the children of ... Num 8:17
every *f* in the land of Egypt I ... Num 8:17
the *f* of the children of Israel ... Num 8:18
nevertheless the *f* of man shalt ... Num 18:15
the Egyptians buried all their *f* ... Num 33:4
if the *f* son be hers that was ... Deut 21:15
*f* before the son of the hated ... Deut 21:16
which is indeed the *f* ... Deut 21:16
the son of the hated for the *f* ... Deut 21:17
the right of the *f* is his ... Deut 21:17
that the *f* which she beareth ... Deut 25:6
the foundation thereof in his *f* ... Josh 6:26
for he was the *f* of Joseph ... Josh 17:1
wit, for Machir the *f* of Manasseh ... Josh 17:1
And he said unto Jether his *f* ... Judg 8:20
Now the name of his *f* was Joel ... 1Sa 8:2
the name of the *f* Merab, and the ... 1Sa 14:49
his *f* was Amnon, of Ahinoam the ... 2Sa 3:2
thereof in Abiram his *f*, and set ... 1Kin 16:34
And Canaan begat Zidon his *f* ... 1Chr 1:13
The *f* of Ishmael, Nebaioth ... 1Chr 1:29
the *f* of Judah, was evil in the ... 1Chr 2:3
And Jesse begat his *f* Eliab ... 1Chr 2:13
of Jerahmeel the *f* of Hezron were ... 1Chr 2:25
Ram the *f*, and Bunah ... 1Chr 2:25
of Ram the *f* of Jerahmeel were ... 1Chr 2:27
of Jerahmeel were, Mesha his *f* ... 1Chr 2:42
the son of Hur, the *f* of Ephratah ... 1Chr 2:50
the *f* Amnon, of Ahinoam the ... 1Chr 3:1
the *f* Johanan, the second ... 1Chr 3:15
the *f* of Ephratah, the father of ... 1Chr 4:4
sons of Reuben the *f* of Israel ... 1Chr 5:1
(for he was the *f*; ... 1Chr 5:1
of Reuben the *f* of Israel were, ... 1Chr 5:3
the *f* Vashni, and Abiah ... 1Chr 6:28
Now Benjamin begat Bela his *f* ... 1Chr 8:1
his *f* son Abdon, and Zur, and Kish, ... 1Chr 8:30
his brother were, Ulam his *f* ... 1Chr 8:39
Asaiah the *f*, and his sons ... 1Chr 9:5
who was the *f* of Shallum the ... 1Chr 9:31
his *f* son Abdon, then Zur, and ... 1Chr 9:36
Meshelemiah were, Zechariah the *f* ... 1Chr 26:2
of Obed-edom were, Shemaiah the *f* ... 1Chr 26:4
(for though he was not the *f* ... 1Chr 26:10
because he was the *f* ... 2Chr 21:3
Also the *f* of our sons, and of our ... Neh 10:36
even the *f* of death shall devour ... Job 18:13
And smote all the *f* in Egypt ... Ps 78:51
Also I will make him my *f* ... Ps 89:27
also all the *f* in their land ... Ps 105:36
Who smote the *f* of Egypt, both of ... Ps 135:8
him that smote Egypt in their *f* ... Ps 136:10
the *f* of the poor shall feed, and ... Is 14:30
to Israel, and Ephraim is my *f* ... Jer 31:9
shall I give my *f* for my ... Mic 6:7
that is in bitterness for his *f* ... Zec 12:10
she had brought forth her *f* son ... Mt 1:25
And she brought forth her *f* son ... Lk 2:7
be the *f* among many brethren ... Rom 8:29
God, the *f* of every creature ... Col 1:15
beginning, the *f* from the dead ... Col 1:18
destroyed the *f* should touch them ... Heb 11:28
assembly and church of the *f* ... Heb 12:23

## FIRSTFRUIT

The *f* also of thy corn, of thy ... Deut 18:4
For if the *f* be holy, the lump is ... Rom 11:16

## FIRSTFRUITS

the *f* of thy labours, which thou ... Ex 23:16
The first of the *f* of thy land ... Ex 23:19
of the *f* of wheat harvest, and the ... Ex 34:22
The first of the *f* of thy land ... Ex 34:26
As for the oblation of the *f* ... Lev 2:12
offering of thy *f* unto the LORD ... Lev 2:14
for the meat offering of thy *f* ... Lev 2:14
ye shall bring a sheaf of the *f* ... Lev 23:10
they are the *f* unto the LORD ... Lev 23:17
the *f* of them which they shall ... Num 18:12
Also in the day of the *f*, when ye ... Num 28:26
I have brought the *f* of the land ... Deut 26:10
the man of God bread of the *f* ... 2Kin 4:42
in abundance the *f* of corn ... 2Chr 31:5
to bring the *f* of our ground, and ... Neh 10:35
the *f* of all fruit of all trees, ... Neh 10:35
should bring the *f* of our dough ... Neh 10:37
for the offerings, for the *f* ... Neh 12:44
at times appointed, and for the *f* ... Neh 13:31
with the *f* of all thine increase ... Prov 3:9
LORD, and the *f* of his increase ... Jer 2:3
the *f* of your oblations, with all ... Eze 20:40
first of all the *f* of all things ... Eze 44:30
nor alienate the *f* of the land ... Eze 48:14
which have the *f* of the Spirit ... Rom 8:23
who is the *f* of Achaia unto ... Rom 16:5
become the *f* of them that slept ... 1Cor 15:20
Christ the *f* ... 1Cor 15:23
that it is the *f* of Achaia ... 1Cor 16:15
be a kind of *f* of his creatures ... Jas 1:18
among men, being the *f* unto God ... Rev 14:4

## FIRSTLING

every *f* that cometh of a beast ... Ex 13:12
every *f* of an ass thou shalt ... Ex 13:13
every *f* among thy cattle, whether ... Ex 34:19
But the *f* of an ass thou shalt ... Ex 34:20
Only the *f* of the beasts, which ... Lev 27:26
which should be the LORD's *f* ... Lev 27:26
the *f* of unclean beasts shalt ... Num 18:15
*f* of a cow, or the *f* ... Num 18:17
or the *f* of a goat, thou shalt ... Num 18:17
All the *f* males that come of thy ... Deut 15:19
no work with the *f* of thy bullock ... Deut 15:19
nor shear the *f* of thy sheep ... Deut 15:19
is like the *f* of his bullock ... Deut 33:17

## FIRSTLINGS

brought of the *f* of his flock ... Gen 4:4
all the *f* among the cattle of the ... Num 3:41
the *f* of your herds and of your ... Deut 12:6
or the *f* of thy herds or of thy ... Deut 12:17
the *f* of thy herds and of thy ... Deut 14:23
the *f* of our herds and of our ... Neh 10:36

## FIRSTRIPE

time was the time of the *f* grapes ... Num 13:20
I saw your fathers as the *f* in ... Hos 9:10
my soul desired the *f* fruit ... Mic 7:1
be like fig trees with the *f* figs ... Nah 3:12

## FISH

dominion over the *f* of the sea ... Gen 1:26
dominion over the *f* of the sea ... Gen 1:28
the *f* that is in the river shall ... Ex 7:18
the *f* that was in the river died ... Ex 7:21
We remember the *f*, which we did ... Num 11:5
or shall all the *f* of the sea be ... Num 11:22
the likeness of any *f* that is in ... Deut 4:18
to the entering in at the *f* gate ... 2Chr 33:14
But the *f* gate did the sons of ... Neh 3:3
the old gate, and above the *f* gate ... Neh 12:39
also therein, which brought *f* ... Neh 13:16
or his head with *f* spears ... Job 41:7
the *f* of the sea, and whatsoever ... Ps 8:8
into blood, and slew their *f* ... Ps 105:29
that make sluices and ponds for *f* ... Is 19:10
their *f* stinketh, because there ... Is 50:2
the LORD, and they shall *f* them ... Jer 16:16
I will cause the *f* of thy rivers ... Eze 29:4
all the *f* of thy rivers shall ... Eze 29:4
thee and all the *f* of thy rivers ... Eze 29:5
be a very great multitude of *f* ... Eze 47:9
their *f* shall be according to ... Eze 47:10
as the *f* of the great sea, ... Eze 47:10
a great *f* to swallow up Jonah ... Jonah 1:17
in the belly of the *f* three days ... Jonah 1:17
And the LORD spake unto the *f* ... Jonah 2:10
noise of a cry from the *f* gate ... Zeph 1:10
Or if he ask a *f*, will he give ... Mt 7:10
take up the *f* that first cometh ... Mt 17:27
or if he ask a *f* ... Lk 11:11
will he for a *f* give him a ... Lk 11:11
gave him a piece of a broiled *f* ... Lk 24:42
and *f* laid thereon, and bread ... Jn 21:9
Bring of the *f* which ye have now ... Jn 21:10
and giveth them, and *f* likewise ... Jn 21:13

## FISHERMEN

but the *f* were gone out of them, ... Lk 5:2

## FISHER'S

he girt his *f* coat unto him, (for ... Jn 21:7

## FISHERS

The *f* also shall mourn, and all ... Is 19:8
Behold, I will send for many *f* ... Jer 16:16
that the *f* shall stand upon it ... Eze 47:10
for they were *f* ... Mt 4:18
me, and I will make you *f* of men ... Mt 4:19
for they were *f* ... Mk 1:16
will make you to become *f* of men ... Mk 1:17

## FISHES

and upon all the *f* of the sea ... Gen 9:2
and of creeping things, and of *f* ... 1Kin 4:33
the *f* of the sea shall declare ... Job 12:8
as the *f* that are taken in an ... Eccl 9:12
So that the *f* of the sea, and the ... Eze 38:20
the *f* of the sea also shall be ... Hos 4:3
And makest men as the *f* of the sea ... Hab 1:14
and the *f* of the sea, and the ... Zeph 1:3
here but five loaves, and two *f* ... Mt 14:17
the five loaves, and the two *f* ... Mt 14:19
said, Seven, and a few little *f* ... Mt 15:34
he took the seven loaves and the *f* ... Mt 15:36
knew, they say, Five, and two *f* ... Mk 6:38
the five loaves and the two *f* ... Mk 6:41
the two *f* divided he among them ... Mk 6:41
of the fragments, and of the *f* ... Mk 6:43
And they had a few small *f* ... Mk 8:7
inclosed a great multitude of *f* ... Lk 5:6
of the *f* which they had taken ... Lk 5:9
no more but five loaves and two *f* ... Lk 9:13
took the five loaves and the two *f* ... Lk 9:16
barley loaves, and two small *f* ... Jn 6:9
likewise of the *f* as much as they ... Jn 6:11
to draw it for the multitude of *f* ... Jn 21:6
cubits,) dragging the net with *f* ... Jn 21:8
the net to land full of great *f* ... Jn 21:11
flesh of beasts, another of *f* ... 1Cor 15:39

## FISHHOOKS

hooks, and your posterity with *f* ... Amos 4:2

## FISHING

Peter saith unto them, I go a *f* ... Jn 21:3

## FISHPOOLS

thine eyes like the *f* in Heshbon ... Song 7:4

## FISH'S

LORD his God out of the *f* belly ... Jonah 2:1

## FIST

with a stone, or with his *f* ... Ex 21:18
to smite with the *f* of wickedness ... Is 58:4

**FISTS**
hath gathered the wind in his *f* .......... Prov 30:4

**FIT**
of a *f* man into the wilderness .......... Lev 16:21
*f* to go out for war and battle .......... 1Chr 7:11
men of war *f* for the battle, that .......... 1Chr 12:8
Is it *f* to say to a king, Thou .......... Job 34:18
make it *f* for thyself in the .......... Prov 24:27
is *f* for the kingdom of God .......... Lk 9:62
It is neither *f* for the land .......... Lk 14:35
for it is not *f* that he should .......... Acts 22:22
husbands, as it is *f* in the Lord .......... Col 3:18

**FITCHES**
doth he not cast abroad the *f* .......... Is 28:25
For the *f* are not threshed with a .......... Is 28:27
but the *f* are beaten out with a .......... Is 28:27
and lentiles, and millet, and *f* .......... Eze 4:9

**FITLY**
A word *f* spoken is like apples of .......... Prov 25:11
washed with milk, and *f* set .......... Song 5:12
In whom all the building *f* framed .......... Eph 2:21
the whole body *f* joined together .......... Eph 4:16

**FITTED**
with gold *f* upon the carved work .......... 1Kin 6:35
shall withal be *f* in thy lips .......... Prov 22:18
vessels of wrath *f* to destruction .......... Rom 9:22

**FITTETH**
he *f* it with planes, and he .......... Is 44:13

**FIVE**
hundred and *f* years, and begat Enos .......... Gen 5:6
Enos were nine hundred and *f* years .......... Gen 5:11
sixty and *f* years, and begat Jared .......... Gen 5:15
eight hundred ninety and *f* years .......... Gen 5:17
*f* years, and begat Methuselah .......... Gen 5:21
three hundred sixty and *f* years .......... Gen 5:23
he begat Noah *f* hundred ninety .......... Gen 5:30
*f* years, and begat sons and .......... Gen 5:30
Noah was *f* hundred years old .......... Gen 5:32
he begat Arphaxad *f* hundred years .......... Gen 11:11
And Arphaxad lived *f* and thirty .......... Gen 11:12
Terah were two hundred and *f* years .......... Gen 11:32
*f* years old when he departed out .......... Gen 12:4
Ellasar; four kings with *f* .......... Gen 14:9
lack *f* of the fifty righteous .......... Gen 18:28
all the city for lack of *f* .......... Gen 18:28
said, If I find there forty and *f* .......... Gen 18:28
but Benjamin's mess was *f* times .......... Gen 43:34
and yet there are *f* years, in the .......... Gen 45:6
yet there are *f* years of famine .......... Gen 45:11
silver, and *f* changes of raiment .......... Gen 45:22
some of his brethren, even *f* men .......... Gen 47:2
he shall restore *f* oxen for an ox .......... Ex 22:1
The *f* curtains shall be coupled .......... Ex 26:3
other *f* curtains shall be coupled .......... Ex 26:3
thou shalt couple *f* curtains by .......... Ex 26:9
*f* for the boards of the one side .......... Ex 26:26
*f* bars for the boards of the .......... Ex 26:27
*f* bars for the boards of the side .......... Ex 26:27
hanging *f* pillars of shittim wood .......... Ex 26:37
thou shalt cast *f* sockets of .......... Ex 26:37
*f* cubits long, and *f* cubits .......... Ex 27:1
the height *f* cubits of fine .......... Ex 27:18
of pure myrrh *f* hundred shekels .......... Ex 30:23
of cassia *f* hundred shekels, .......... Ex 30:24
he coupled the *f* curtains one .......... Ex 36:10
the other *f* curtains he coupled .......... Ex 36:10
And he coupled *f* curtains by .......... Ex 36:16
*f* for the boards of the one side .......... Ex 36:31
*f* bars for the boards of the .......... Ex 36:32
*f* bars for the boards of the .......... Ex 36:32
the *f* pillars of it with their .......... Ex 36:38
but their *f* sockets were of brass .......... Ex 36:38
*f* cubits was the length thereof, .......... Ex 38:1
*f* cubits the breadth thereof .......... Ex 38:1
in the breadth was *f* cubits .......... Ex 38:18
and *f* hundred and fifty men .......... Ex 38:26
*f* shekels he made hooks for the .......... Ex 38:28
*f* of you shall chase an hundred, .......... Lev 26:8
if it be from *f* years old even .......... Lev 27:5
a month old even unto *f* years old .......... Lev 27:6
of the male *f* shekels of silver .......... Lev 27:6
and six thousand and *f* hundred .......... Num 1:21
*f* thousand six hundred and fifty .......... Num 1:25
were forty thousand and *f* hundred .......... Num 1:33
*f* thousand and four hundred .......... Num 1:37
and one thousand and *f* hundred .......... Num 1:41
thousand and *f* hundred and fifty .......... Num 1:46
and six thousand and *f* hundred .......... Num 2:11
*f* thousand and six hundred and .......... Num 2:15
were forty thousand and *f* hundred .......... Num 2:19
*f* thousand and four hundred .......... Num 2:23
and one thousand and *f* hundred .......... Num 2:28
thousand and *f* hundred and fifty .......... Num 2:32
were seven thousand and *f* hundred .......... Num 3:22
Thou shalt even take *f* shekels .......... Num 3:47
*f* shekels, after the shekel of .......... Num 3:50
and *f* hundred and fourscore .......... Num 4:48
*f* rams, *f* he goats, *f* lambs .......... Num 7:17
*f* rams, *f* he goats, *f* lambs .......... Num 7:23
*f* rams, *f* he goats, *f* lambs .......... Num 7:29
*f* rams, *f* he goats, *f* lambs .......... Num 7:35
*f* rams, *f* he goats, *f* lambs .......... Num 7:41
*f* rams, *f* he goats, *f* lambs .......... Num 7:47
*f* rams, *f* he goats, *f* lambs .......... Num 7:53
*f* rams, *f* he goats, *f* lambs .......... Num 7:59
*f* rams, *f* he goats, *f* lambs .......... Num 7:65
*f* rams, *f* he goats, *f* lambs .......... Num 7:71
*f* he goats, *f* lambs of the .......... Num 7:71
*f* rams, *f* he goats, *f* lambs .......... Num 7:77
*f* rams, *f* he goats, *f* lambs .......... Num 7:83
*f* years old and upward they shall .......... Num 8:24
nor *f* days, neither ten days, nor .......... Num 11:19
for the money of *f* shekels .......... Num 18:16
them, forty thousand and *f* hundred .......... Num 26:18
and sixteen thousand and *f* hundred .......... Num 26:22
threescore thousand and *f* hundred .......... Num 26:27
and two thousand and *f* hundred .......... Num 26:37
*f* thousand and six hundred .......... Num 26:41
*f* thousand and four hundred .......... Num 26:50
Hur, and Reba, *f* kings of Midian .......... Num 31:8
one soul of *f* hundred, both of .......... Num 31:28
thousand and *f* thousand sheep, .......... Num 31:32
thousand and *f* hundred sheep .......... Num 31:36
were thirty thousand and *f* hundred .......... Num 31:39
thousand and *f* hundred sheep, .......... Num 31:43
thousand asses and *f* hundred, .......... Num 31:45
And he took about *f* thousand men .......... Josh 8:12
Therefore the *f* kings of the .......... Josh 10:5
But these *f* kings fled, and hid .......... Josh 10:16
The *f* kings are found hid in a .......... Josh 10:17
bring out those *f* kings unto me .......... Josh 10:22
brought forth those *f* kings unto .......... Josh 10:23
them, and hanged them on *f* trees .......... Josh 10:26
*f* lords of the Philistines .......... Josh 13:3
*f* years, even since the LORD .......... Josh 14:10
this day fourscore and *f* years old .......... Josh 14:10
*f* lords of the Philistines, and .......... Judg 3:3
family *f* men from their coasts .......... Judg 18:2
Then the *f* men departed, and came .......... Judg 18:7
Then answered the *f* men that went .......... Judg 18:14
the *f* men that went to spy out .......... Judg 18:17
*f* thousand and an hundred men .......... Judg 20:35
in the highways *f* thousand men .......... Judg 20:45
*f* thousand men that drew the .......... Judg 20:46
F golden emerods, and *f* golden .......... 1Sa 6:4
*f* golden mice, according to the .......... 1Sa 6:4
And when the *f* lords of the .......... 1Sa 6:16
belonging to the *f* lords, both of .......... 1Sa 6:18
was *f* thousand shekels of brass .......... 1Sa 17:5
chose him *f* smooth stones out of .......... 1Sa 17:40
give me *f* loaves of bread in mine .......... 1Sa 21:3
*f* persons that did wear a linen .......... 1Sa 22:18
*f* sheep ready dressed, and .......... 1Sa 25:18
*f* measures of parched corn, and an .......... 1Sa 25:18
with *f* damsels of hers that went .......... 1Sa 25:42
He was *f* years old when the .......... 2Sa 4:4
the *f* sons of Michal the daughter .......... 2Sa 21:8
Judah were *f* hundred thousand men .......... 2Sa 24:9
and his songs were a thousand and *f* .......... 1Kin 4:32
chamber was *f* cubits broad .......... 1Kin 6:6
all the house, *f* cubits high .......... 1Kin 6:10
*f* cubits was the one wing of the .......... 1Kin 6:24
*f* cubits the other wing of the .......... 1Kin 6:24
that lay on forty *f* pillars .......... 1Kin 7:3
of the one chapiter was *f* cubits .......... 1Kin 7:16
the other chapiter was *f* cubits .......... 1Kin 7:16
about, and his height was *f* cubits .......... 1Kin 7:23
he put *f* bases on the right side .......... 1Kin 7:39
*f* on the left side of the house .......... 1Kin 7:39
*f* on the right side, and *f* on .......... 1Kin 7:49
*f* on the left, before the oracle, .......... 1Kin 7:49
*f* hundred and fifty, which bare .......... 1Kin 9:23
*f* years old when he began to .......... 1Kin 22:42
twenty and *f* years in Jerusalem .......... 1Kin 22:42
dung for *f* pieces of silver .......... 2Kin 6:25
*f* of the horses that remain, .......... 2Kin 7:13
have smitten *f* or six times .......... 2Kin 13:19
*f* years old when he began to .......... 2Kin 14:2
F and twenty years old was he when .......... 2Kin 15:33
*f* years old was he when he began .......... 2Kin 18:2
hundred fourscore and *f* thousand .......... 2Kin 19:35
fifty and *f* years in Jerusalem .......... 2Kin 21:1
*f* years old when he began to .......... 2Kin 23:36
*f* men of them that were in the .......... 2Kin 25:19
All the sons of Judah were *f* .......... 1Chr 2:4
*f* of them in all .......... 1Chr 2:6
and Hasadiah, Jushab-hesed, *f* .......... 1Chr 3:20
and Tochen, and Ashan, *f* cities .......... 1Chr 4:32
*f* hundred men, went to mount Seir .......... 1Chr 4:42
and Obadiah, and Joel, Ishiah, *f* .......... 1Chr 7:3
and Uzziel, and Jerimoth, and Iri, *f* .......... 1Chr 7:7
of great stature, *f* cubits high .......... 1Chr 11:23
of God of gold *f* thousand talents .......... 1Chr 29:7
of the one cherub was *f* cubits .......... 2Chr 3:11
other wing was likewise *f* cubits .......... 2Chr 3:11
of the other cherub was *f* cubits .......... 2Chr 3:12
the other wing was *f* cubits also .......... 2Chr 3:12
*f* cubits high, and the chapiter .......... 2Chr 3:15
top of each of them was *f* cubits .......... 2Chr 3:15
*f* cubits the height thereof .......... 2Chr 4:2
put *f* on the right hand, and .......... 2Chr 4:6
*f* on the left, to wash in them .......... 2Chr 4:6
*f* on the right hand, and *f* on .......... 2Chr 4:7
*f* on the right side, and *f* on .......... 2Chr 4:8
of *f* cubits long, and *f* cubits .......... 2Chr 6:13
*f* hundred thousand chosen men .......... 2Chr 13:17
there was no more war unto the *f* .......... 2Chr 15:19
*f* years old when he began to .......... 2Chr 20:31
twenty and *f* years in Jerusalem .......... 2Chr 20:31
*f* years old when he began to .......... 2Chr 25:1
*f* hundred, that made war with .......... 2Chr 26:13
*f* years old when he began to .......... 2Chr 27:1
He was *f* and twenty years old when .......... 2Chr 27:8
began to reign when he was *f* .......... 2Chr 29:1
fifty and *f* years in Jerusalem .......... 2Chr 33:1
offerings *f* thousand small cattle .......... 2Chr 35:9
small cattle, and *f* hundred oxen .......... 2Chr 35:9
*f* years old when he began to .......... 2Chr 36:5
gold and of silver were *f* thousand .......... Ezr 1:11
Arah, seven hundred seventy and *f* .......... Ezr 2:5
of Zattu, nine hundred forty and *f* .......... Ezr 2:8
children of Gibbar, ninety and *f* .......... Ezr 2:20
and Ono, seven hundred twenty and *f* .......... Ezr 2:33
Jericho, three hundred forty and *f* .......... Ezr 2:34
mules, two hundred forty and *f* .......... Ezr 2:66
camels, four hundred thirty and *f* .......... Ezr 2:67
*f* thousand pound of silver, and .......... Ezr 2:69
Zattu, eight hundred forty and *f* .......... Neh 7:13
of Adin, six hundred fifty and *f* .......... Neh 7:20
children of Gibeon, ninety and *f* .......... Neh 7:25
Jericho, three hundred forty and *f* .......... Neh 7:36
*f* singing men and singing women .......... Neh 7:67
mules, two hundred forty and *f* .......... Neh 7:68
camels, four hundred thirty and *f* .......... Neh 7:69
*f* hundred and thirty priests' .......... Neh 7:70
slew and destroyed *f* hundred men .......... Est 9:6
destroyed *f* hundred men in .......... Est 9:12
*f* thousand, but they laid not .......... Est 9:16
*f* hundred yoke of oxen, and *f* .......... Job 1:3
*f* hundred she asses, and a very .......... Job 1:3
*f* years shall Ephraim be broken, .......... Is 7:8
four or *f* in the outmost fruitful .......... Is 17:6
In that day shall *f* cities in the .......... Is 19:18
at the rebuke of *f* shall ye flee .......... Is 30:17
and fourscore and *f* thousand .......... Is 37:36
of one chapiter was *f* cubits .......... Jer 52:22
seven hundred forty and *f* persons .......... Jer 52:30
in the twelfth month, in the *f* .......... Jer 52:31
porch and the altar, were about *f* .......... Eze 8:16
behold at the door of the gate *f* .......... Eze 11:1
In the *f* and twentieth year of our .......... Eze 40:1
the little chambers were *f* cubits .......... Eze 40:7
the breadth was *f* and twenty .......... Eze 40:13
fifty cubits, and the breadth *f* .......... Eze 40:21
fifty cubits, and the breadth *f* .......... Eze 40:25
it was fifty cubits long, and *f* .......... Eze 40:29
And the arches round about were *f* .......... Eze 40:30
cubits long, and *f* cubits broad .......... Eze 40:30
it was fifty cubits long, and *f* .......... Eze 40:33
fifty cubits, and the breadth *f* .......... Eze 40:36
*f* cubits on this side .......... Eze 40:48
and *f* cubits on that side .......... Eze 40:48
were *f* cubits on the one side .......... Eze 41:2
*f* cubits on the other side .......... Eze 41:2
chamber without, was *f* cubits .......... Eze 41:9
was left was *f* cubits round about .......... Eze 41:11
was *f* cubits thick round about .......... Eze 41:12
*f* hundred reeds, with the .......... Eze 42:16
*f* hundred reeds, with the .......... Eze 42:17
*f* hundred reeds, with the .......... Eze 42:18
measured *f* hundred reeds with the .......... Eze 42:19
*f* hundred reeds long, and .......... Eze 42:20
*f* hundred broad, to make a .......... Eze 42:20
length shall be the length of *f* .......... Eze 45:1
the sanctuary *f* hundred in length .......... Eze 45:2
with *f* hundred in breadth, square .......... Eze 45:2
thou measure the length of *f* .......... Eze 45:3
And the *f* and twenty thousand of .......... Eze 45:5
city *f* thousand broad, and *f* .......... Eze 45:6
twenty shekels, *f* and twenty .......... Eze 45:12
which ye shall offer of *f* .......... Eze 48:8
offer unto the LORD shall be of *f* .......... Eze 48:9
toward the north *f* and twenty .......... Eze 48:10
in breadth, and toward the south *f* .......... Eze 48:10
priests the Levites shall have *f* .......... Eze 48:13
all the length shall be *f* .......... Eze 48:13
the *f* thousand, that are left in .......... Eze 48:15
in the breadth over against the *f* .......... Eze 48:15
*f* hundred, and the south side four .......... Eze 48:16
*f* hundred, and on the east side .......... Eze 48:16
*f* hundred, and the west side four .......... Eze 48:16
side four thousand and *f* hundred .......... Eze 48:16
be *f* and twenty thousand by *f* .......... Eze 48:20
of the city, over against the *f* .......... Eze 48:21
and westward over against the *f* .......... Eze 48:21
thousand and *f* hundred measures .......... Eze 48:30
side four thousand and *f* hundred .......... Eze 48:32
thousand and *f* hundred measures .......... Eze 48:33
*f* hundred, with their three gates .......... Eze 48:34
the thousand three hundred and *f* .......... Dan 12:12
him, We have here but *f* loaves .......... Mt 14:17
the grass, and took the *f* loaves .......... Mt 14:19
eaten were about *f* thousand men .......... Mt 14:21
neither remember the *f* loaves of .......... Mt 16:9
the *f* thousand, and how many baskets .......... Mt 16:9
*f* of them were wise, and *f* were .......... Mt 25:2
And unto one he gave *f* talents .......... Mt 25:15
had received the *f* talents went .......... Mt 25:16
and made them other *f* talents .......... Mt 25:16
that had received *f* talents came .......... Mt 25:20
came and brought other *f* talents .......... Mt 25:20
deliveredst unto me *f* talents .......... Mt 25:20
gained beside them *f* talents more .......... Mt 25:20
And when they knew, they say, *F* .......... Mk 6:38
And when he had taken the *f* loaves .......... Mk 6:41
loaves were about *f* thousand men .......... Mk 6:44
When I brake the *f* loaves among .......... Mk 8:19
*f* thousand, how many baskets .......... Mk 8:19
and hid herself *f* months, saying, .......... Lk 1:24
the one owed *f* hundred pence, and .......... Lk 7:41
We have no more but *f* loaves .......... Lk 9:13
they were about *f* thousand men .......... Lk 9:14
Then he took the *f* loaves .......... Lk 9:16
Are not *f* sparrows sold for two .......... Lk 12:6
shall be *f* in one house divided .......... Lk 12:52
I have bought *f* yoke of oxen .......... Lk 14:19
For I have *f* brethren .......... Lk 16:28
thy pound hath gained *f* pounds .......... Lk 19:18

him, Be thou also over *f* cities ... Lk 19:19
For thou hast had *f* husbands ... Jn 4:18
tongue Bethesda, having *f* porches ... Jn 5:2
which hath *f* barley loaves, and ... Jn 6:9
down, in number about *f* thousand ... Jn 6:10
fragments of the *f* barley loaves ... Jn 6:13
So when they had rowed about *f* ... Jn 6:19
of the men was about *f* thousand ... Acts 4:4
came unto them to Troas in *f* days ... Acts 20:6
after *f* days Ananias the high ... Acts 24:1
*f* words with my understanding ... 1Cor 14:19
he was seen of above *f* hundred ... 1Cor 15:6
Of the Jews *f* times received I ... 2Cor 11:24
they should be tormented *f* months ... Rev 9:5
power was to hurt men *f* months ... Rev 9:10
*f* are fallen, and one is, and the ... Rev 17:10

## FIXED
My heart is *f*, O God, my heart is ... Ps 57:7
is *f*, O God, my heart is *f* ... Ps 57:7
O God, my heart is *f* ... Ps 108:1
his heart is *f*, trusting in the ... Ps 112:7
us and you there is a great gulf *f* ... Lk 16:26

## FLAG
can the *f* grow without water ... Job 8:11

## FLAGON
piece of flesh, and a *f* of wine ... 2Sa 6:19
piece of flesh, and a *f* of wine ... 1Chr 16:3

## FLAGONS
Stay me with *f*, comfort me with ... Song 2:5
even to all the vessels of *f* ... Is 22:24
to other gods, and love *f* of wine ... Hos 3:1

## FLAGS
she laid it in the *f* by the ... Ex 2:3
when she saw the ark among the *f* ... Ex 2:5
the reeds and *f* shall wither ... Is 19:6

## FLAKES
The *f* of his flesh are joined ... Job 41:23

## FLAME
a *f* of fire out of the midst of a ... Ex 3:2
a *f* from the city of Sihon ... Num 21:28
when the *f* went up toward heaven ... Judg 13:20
ascended in the *f* of the altar ... Judg 13:20
*f* with smoke rise up out of the ... Judg 20:38
But when the *f* began to arise up ... Judg 20:40
the *f* of the city ascended up to ... Judg 20:40
the *f* shall dry up his branches, ... Job 15:30
a *f* goeth out of his mouth ... Job 41:21
as the *f* setteth the mountains on ... Ps 83:14
the *f* burned up the wicked ... Ps 106:18
which hath a most vehement *f* ... Song 8:6
the *f* consumeth the chaff, so ... Is 5:24
a fire, and his Holy One for a *f* ... Is 10:17
and the *f* of devouring fire ... Is 29:6
with the *f* of a devouring fire, ... Is 30:30
shall the *f* kindle upon thee ... Is 43:2
from the power of the *f* ... Is 47:14
a *f* from the midst of Sihon, and ... Jer 48:45
the flaming *f* shall not be ... Eze 20:47
the *f* of the fire slew those men ... Dan 3:22
his throne was like the fiery *f* ... Dan 7:9
and given to the burning *f* ... Dan 7:11
shall fall by the sword, and by *f* ... Dan 11:33
the *f* hath burned all the trees ... Joel 1:19
and behind them a *f* burneth ... Joel 2:3
like the noise of a *f* of fire ... Joel 2:5
fire, and the house of Joseph a *f* ... Obad 18
for I am tormented in this *f* ... Lk 16:24
the Lord in a *f* of fire in a bush ... Acts 7:30
and his ministers a *f* of fire ... Heb 1:7
and his eyes were as a *f* of fire ... Rev 1:14
his eyes like unto a *f* of fire ... Rev 2:18
His eyes were as a *f* of fire ... Rev 19:12

## FLAMES
the LORD divideth the *f* of fire ... Ps 29:7
their faces shall be as *f* ... Is 13:8
and his rebuke with *f* of fire ... Is 66:15

## FLAMING
a *f* sword which turned every way, ... Gen 3:24
his ministers a *f* fire ... Ps 104:4
for rain, and *f* fire in their land ... Ps 105:32
the shining of a *f* fire by night ... Is 4:5
against Jacob like a *f* fire ... Lam 2:3
the *f* flame shall not be quenched ... Eze 20:47
morning it burneth as a *f* fire ... Hos 7:6
with *f* torches in the day of his ... Nah 2:3
In *f* fire taking vengeance on ... 2Th 1:8

## FLANKS
is on them, which is by the *f* ... Lev 3:4
is upon them, which is by the *f* ... Lev 3:10
is upon them, which is by the *f* ... Lev 3:15
is upon them, which is by the *f* ... Lev 4:9
is on them, which is by the *f* ... Lev 7:4
and maketh collops of fat on his *f* ... Job 15:27

## FLASH
appearance of a *f* of lightning ... Eze 1:14

## FLAT
a lame, or he that hath a *f* nose ... Lev 21:18
his head, and fell *f* on his face ... Num 22:31
of the city shall fall down *f* ... Josh 6:5
shout, that the wall fell down *f* ... Josh 6:20

## FLATTER
they *f* with their tongue ... Ps 5:9
they did *f* him with their mouth ... Ps 78:36

## FLATTERETH
For he *f* himself in his own eyes, ... Ps 36:2
stranger which *f* with her words ... Prov 2:16
stranger which *f* with her words ... Prov 7:5
not with him that *f* with his lips ... Prov 20:19
than he that *f* with the tongue ... Prov 28:23
A man that *f* his neighbour ... Prov 29:5

## FLATTERIES
and obtain the kingdom by *f* ... Dan 11:21
covenant shall he corrupt by *f* ... Dan 11:32
many shall cleave to them with *f* ... Dan 11:34

## FLATTERING
let me give *f* titles unto man ... Job 32:21
For I know not to give *f* titles ... Job 32:22
with *f* lips and with a double ... Ps 12:2
The LORD shall cut off all *f* lips ... Ps 12:3
with the *f* of her lips she forced ... Prov 7:21
and a *f* mouth worketh ruin ... Prov 26:28
*f* divination within the house of ... Eze 12:24
at any time used we *f* words ... 1Th 2:5

## FLATTERY
He that speaketh *f* to his friends ... Job 17:5
from the *f* of the tongue of a ... Prov 6:24

## FLAX
And the *f* and the barley was ... Ex 9:31
in the ear, and the *f* was bolled ... Ex 9:31
and hid them with the stalks of *f* ... Josh 2:6
as *f* that was burnt with fire ... Judg 15:14
She seeketh wool, and *f*, and ... Prov 31:13
Moreover they that work in fine *f* ... Is 19:9
the smoking *f* shall he not quench ... Is 42:3
with a line of *f* in his hand ... Eze 40:3
and my water, my wool and my *f* ... Hos 2:5
my *f* given to cover her nakedness ... Hos 2:9
smoking *f* shall he not quench, ... Mt 12:20

## FLAY
he shall *f* the burnt offering, and ... Lev 1:6
so that they could not *f* all the ... 2Chr 29:34
*f* their skin from off them ... Mic 3:3

## FLAYED
hands, and the Levites *f* them ... 2Chr 35:11

## FLEA
after a dead dog, after a *f* ... 1Sa 24:14
of Israel is come out to seek a *f* ... 1Sa 26:20

## FLED
the kings of Sodom and Gomorrah *f* .. Gen 14:10
that remained *f* to the mountain ... Gen 14:10
with her, she *f* from her face ... Gen 16:6
in that he told him not that he *f* ... Gen 31:20
So he *f* with all that he had ... Gen 31:21
on the third day that Jacob was *f* ... Gen 31:22
when he *f* from the face of his ... Gen 35:7
his garment in her hand, and *f* ... Gen 39:12
in her hand, and was *f* forth, ... Gen 39:13
he left his garment with me, and *f* ... Gen 39:15
his garment with me, and *f* out ... Gen 39:18
But Moses *f* from the face of ... Ex 2:15
and Moses *f* from before it ... Ex 4:3
king of Egypt that the people *f* ... Ex 14:5
and the Egyptians *f* against it ... Ex 14:27
about them *f* at the cry of them ... Num 16:34
of his refuge, whither he was *f* ... Num 35:25
of his refuge, whither he was *f* ... Num 35:26
is *f* to the city of his refuge ... Num 35:32
they *f* before the men of Ai ... Josh 7:4
*f* by the way of the wilderness ... Josh 8:15
and the people that *f* to the ... Josh 8:20
as they *f* from before Israel, and ... Josh 10:11
But these five kings *f*, and hid ... Josh 10:16
unto the city from whence he *f* ... Josh 20:6
But Adoni-bezek *f* ... Judg 1:6
chariot, and *f* away on his feet ... Judg 4:15
Howbeit Sisera *f* away on his feet ... Judg 4:17
all the host ran, and cried, and *f* ... Judg 7:21
the host *f* to Beth-shittah in ... Judg 7:22
And when Zebah and Zalmunna *f* ... Judg 8:12
And Jotham ran away, and *f* ... Judg 9:21
he *f* before him, and many were ... Judg 9:40
thither *f* all the men and women, ... Judg 9:51
Then Jephthah *f* from his brethren ... Judg 11:3
*f* toward the wilderness unto the ... Judg 20:45
*f* to the wilderness unto the rock ... Judg 20:47
they *f* every man into his tent ... 1Sa 4:10
I *f* to day out of the army ... 1Sa 4:16
and said, Israel is *f* before the ... 1Sa 4:17
they heard that the Philistines *f* ... 1Sa 14:22
*f* from him, and were sore afraid ... 1Sa 17:24
their champion was dead, they *f* ... 1Sa 17:51
and they *f* from him ... 1Sa 19:8
and David *f*, and escaped that night ... 1Sa 19:10
and he went, and *f*, and escaped ... 1Sa 19:12
So David *f*, and escaped, and came ... 1Sa 19:18
David *f* from Naioth in Ramah, and ... 1Sa 20:1
*f* that day for fear of Saul, and ... 1Sa 21:10
and because they knew when he *f* ... 1Sa 22:17
escaped, and *f* after David ... 1Sa 22:20
of Ahimelech *f* to David to Keilah ... 1Sa 23:6
Saul that David was *f* to Gath ... 1Sa 27:4
men, which rode upon camels, and *f* ... 1Sa 30:17
the men of Israel *f* from before ... 1Sa 31:1
saw that the men of Israel *f* ... 1Sa 31:7
they forsook the cities, and *f* ... 1Sa 31:7
the people are *f* from the battle ... 2Sa 1:4
And the Beerothites *f* to Gittaim ... 2Sa 4:3
and his nurse took him up, and *f* ... 2Sa 4:4
and they *f* before him ... 2Sa 10:13
Ammon saw that the Syrians were *f* ... 2Sa 10:14
then *f* they also before Abishai, ... 2Sa 10:14
the Syrians *f* before Israel ... 2Sa 10:18
gat him up upon his mule, and *f* ... 2Sa 13:29
But Absalom *f*. And the young man ... 2Sa 13:34
But Absalom *f*, and went to Talmai, ... 2Sa 13:37
So Absalom *f*, and went to Geshur, ... 2Sa 13:38
all Israel *f* every one to his ... 2Sa 18:17
for Israel had *f* every man to his ... 2Sa 19:8
now he is *f* out of the land for ... 2Sa 19:9
the people *f* from the Philistines ... 2Sa 23:11
for so they came to me when I *f* ... 1Kin 2:7
Joab *f* unto the tabernacle of the ... 1Kin 2:28
*f* unto the tabernacle of the LORD ... 1Kin 2:29
That Hadad *f*, he and certain ... 1Kin 11:17
which *f* from his lord Hadadezer ... 1Kin 11:23
*f* into Egypt, unto Shishak king ... 1Kin 11:40
(for he was *f* from the presence ... 1Kin 12:2
and the Syrians *f* ... 1Kin 20:20
But the rest *f* to Aphek, into the ... 1Kin 20:30
And Ben-hadad *f*, and came into the. 1Kin 20:30
so that they *f* before them ... 2Kin 3:24
*f* in the twilight, and left their ... 2Kin 7:7
as it was, and *f* for their life ... 2Kin 7:7
the people *f* into their tents ... 2Kin 8:21
And he opened the door, and *f* ... 2Kin 9:10
And Joram turned his hands, and *f* ... 2Kin 9:23
he *f* by the way of the garden ... 2Kin 9:27
he *f* to Megiddo, and died there ... 2Kin 9:27
they *f* every man to their tents ... 2Kin 14:12
and he *f* to Lachish ... 2Kin 14:19
all the men of war *f* by night by ... 2Kin 25:4
the men of Israel *f* from before ... 1Chr 10:1
in the valley saw that they *f* ... 1Chr 10:7
they forsook their cities, and *f* ... 1Chr 10:7
the people *f* from before the ... 1Chr 11:13
and they *f* before him ... 1Chr 19:14
Ammon saw that the Syrians were *f*. 1Chr 19:15
they likewise *f* before Abishai ... 1Chr 19:15
But the Syrians *f* before Israel ... 1Chr 19:18
whither he had *f* from the ... 2Chr 10:2
children of Israel *f* before Judah ... 2Chr 13:16
and the Ethiopians *f* ... 2Chr 14:12
they *f* every man to his tent ... 2Chr 25:22
and he *f* to Lachish ... 2Chr 25:27
were *f* every one to his field ... Neh 13:10
when he *f* from Absalom his son ... Ps 3:*t*
that did see me without *f* from me ... Ps 31:11
when he *f* from Saul in the cave ... Ps 57:*t*
At thy rebuke they *f* ... Ps 104:7
The sea saw it, and *f* ... Ps 114:3
Gibeah of Saul is *f* ... Is 10:29
with their bread him that *f* ... Is 21:14
For they *f* from the swords, from ... Is 21:15
All thy rulers are *f* together ... Is 22:3
together, which have *f* from far ... Is 22:3
noise of the tumult the people *f* ... Is 33:3
the birds of the heavens were *f* ... Jer 4:25
of the heavens and the beast are *f* ... Jer 9:10
heard it, he was afraid, and *f* ... Jer 26:21
all the men of war, then they *f* ... Jer 39:4
are *f* apace, and look not back ... Jer 46:5
back, and are *f* away together ... Jer 46:21
They that *f* stood under the ... Jer 48:45
up, and all the men of war *f* ... Jer 52:7
when they *f* away and wandered, ... Lam 4:15
so that they *f* to hide themselves ... Dan 10:7
for they have *f* from me ... Hos 7:13
Jacob *f* into the country of Syria ... Hos 12:12
For the men knew that he *f* from ... Jonah 1:10
Therefore I *f* before unto ... Jonah 4:2
like as ye *f* from before the ... Zec 14:5
And they that kept them *f*, and went ... Mt 8:33
the disciples forsook him, and *f* ... Mt 26:56
And they that fed the swine *f* ... Mk 5:14
And they all forsook him, and *f* ... Mk 14:50
linen cloth, and *f* from them naked ... Mk 14:52
quickly, and *f* from the sepulchre ... Mk 16:8
them saw what was done, they *f* ... Lk 8:34
Then *f* Moses at this saying, and ... Acts 7:29
*f* unto Lystra and Derbe, cities of ... Acts 14:6
that the prisoners had been *f* ... Acts 16:27
so that they *f* out of that house ... Acts 19:16
who have *f* for refuge to lay hold ... Heb 6:18
the woman *f* into the wilderness, ... Rev 12:6
And every island *f* away, and the ... Rev 16:20
the earth and the heaven *f* away ... Rev 20:11

## FLEDDEST
thou *f* from the face of Esau thy ... Gen 35:1
thee, O thou sea, that thou *f* ... Ps 114:5

## FLEE
I *f* from the face of my mistress ... Gen 16:8
now, this city is near to *f* unto ... Gen 19:20
*f* thou to Laban my brother to ... Gen 27:43
didst thou *f* away secretly ... Gen 31:27
his cattle *f* into the houses ... Ex 9:20
Let us *f* from the face of Israel ... Ex 14:25
thee a place whither he shall *f* ... Ex 21:13
ye shall *f* when none pursueth you ... Lev 26:17
and they shall *f*, as fleeing from ... Lev 26:36
them that hate thee *f* before thee ... Num 10:35
Therefore now *f* thou to thy place ... Num 24:11
manslayer, that he may *f* thither ... Num 35:6
that the slayer may *f* thither ... Num 35:11
any person unawares may *f* thither .. Num 35:15
That the slayer might *f* thither ... Deut 4:42
that every slayer may *f* thither ... Deut 19:3
the slayer, which shall *f* thither ... Deut 19:4
he shall *f* unto one of those ... Deut 19:5

way, and *f* before thee seven ways ... Deut 28:7
them, and *f* seven ways before them ... Deut 28:25
first, that we will *f* before them ... Josh 8:5
They *f* before us, as at the first ... Josh 8:6
therefore we will *f* before them ... Josh 8:6
power to *f* this way or that way ... Josh 8:20
and unwittingly may *f* thither ... Josh 20:3
when he that doth *f* unto one of ... Josh 20:4
at unawares might *f* thither ... Josh 20:9
children of Israel said, Let us *f* ... Judg 20:32
to pass, as she made haste to *f* ... 2Sa 4:4
at Jerusalem, Arise, and let us *f* ... 2Sa 15:14
people that are with him shall *f* ... 2Sa 17:2
for if we *f* away, they will not ... 2Sa 18:3
steal away when they *f* in battle ... 2Sa 19:3
or wilt thou *f* three months ... 2Sa 24:13
to his chariot, to *f* to Jerusalem ... 1Kin 12:18
Then open the door, and *f*, and ... 2Kin 9:3
to his chariot, to *f* to Jerusalem ... 2Chr 10:18
I said, Should such a man as I *f* ... Neh 6:11
they *f* away, they see no good ... Job 9:25
He shall *f* from the iron weapon, ... Job 20:24
he would fain *f* out of his hand ... Job 27:22
they *f* far from me, and spare not ... Job 30:10
The arrow cannot make him *f* ... Job 41:28
*F* as a bird to your mountain ... Ps 11:1
all that see them shall *f* away ... Ps 64:8
also that hate him *f* before him ... Ps 68:1
Kings of armies did *f* apace ... Ps 68:12
shall I *f* from thy presence ... Ps 139:7
I *f* unto thee to hide me ... Ps 143:9
The wicked *f* when no man pursueth ... Prov 28:1
of any person shall *f* to the pit ... Prov 28:17
day break, and the shadows *f* away ... Song 2:17
day break, and the shadows *f* away ... Song 4:6
to whom will ye *f* for help ... Is 10:3
of Gebim gather themselves to *f* ... Is 10:31
*f* every one into his own land ... Is 13:14
his fugitives shall *f* unto Zoar ... Is 15:5
them, and they shall *f* far off ... Is 17:13
whither we *f* for help to be ... Is 20:6
for we will *f* upon horses ... Is 30:16
therefore shall ye *f* ... Is 30:16
One thousand shall *f* at the ... Is 30:17
at the rebuke of five shall ye *f* ... Is 30:17
but he shall *f* from the sword, and ... Is 31:8
and sorrow and sighing shall *f* away ... Is 35:10
*f* ye from the Chaldeans, with a ... Is 48:20
sorrow and mourning shall *f* away ... Is 51:11
The whole city shall *f* for the ... Jer 4:29
gather yourselves to *f* out of the ... Jer 6:1
shepherds shall have no way to *f* ... Jer 25:35
Let not the swift *f* away, nor the ... Jer 46:6
*F*, save your lives, and be like ... Jer 48:6
wings unto Moab, that it may *f* ... Jer 48:9
*F* ye, turn back, dwell deep, O ... Jer 49:8
feeble, and turneth herself to *f* ... Jer 49:24
*F*, get you far off, dwell deep, O ... Jer 49:30
they shall *f* every one to his own ... Jer 50:16
The voice of them that *f* and ... Jer 50:28
*F* out of the midst of Babylon, and ... Jer 51:6
shall *f* away naked in that day ... Amos 2:16
As if a man did *f* from a lion ... Amos 5:19
*f* thee away into the land of ... Amos 7:12
fleeth of them shall not *f* away ... Amos 9:1
But Jonah rose up to *f* unto ... Jonah 1:3
yet they shall *f* away ... Nah 2:8
look upon thee shall *f* from thee ... Nah 3:7
when the sun ariseth they *f* away ... Nah 3:17
*f* from the land of the north, ... Zec 2:6
ye shall *f* to the valley of the ... Zec 14:5
yea, ye shall *f*, like as ye fled ... Zec 14:5
*f* into Egypt, and be thou there ... Mt 2:13
you to *f* from the wrath to come ... Mt 3:7
in this city, *f* ye into another ... Mt 10:23
be in Judaea *f* into the mountains ... Mt 24:16
be in Judaea *f* to the mountains ... Mk 13:14
you to *f* from the wrath to come ... Lk 3:7
are in Judaea *f* to the mountains ... Lk 21:21
not follow, but will *f* from him ... Jn 10:5
were about to *f* out of the ship ... Acts 27:30
*F* fornication ... 1Cor 6:18
dearly beloved, *f* from idolatry ... 1Cor 10:14
O man of God, *f* these things ... 1Ti 6:11
*F* also youthful lusts ... 2Ti 2:22
the devil, and he will *f* from you ... Jas 4:7
die, and death shall *f* from them ... Rev 9:6

**FLEECE**

the first of the *f* of thy sheep ... Deut 18:4
I will put a *f* of wool in the ... Judg 6:37
and if the dew be on the *f* only ... Judg 6:37
morrow, and thrust the *f* together ... Judg 6:38
and wringed the dew out of the *f* ... Judg 6:38
thee, but this once with the *f* ... Judg 6:39
let it now be dry only upon the *f* ... Judg 6:39
for it was dry upon the *f* only ... Judg 6:40
not warmed with the *f* of my sheep ... Job 31:20

**FLEEING**

shall flee, as *f* from a sword ... Lev 26:36
that *f* unto one of these cities ... Deut 4:42
*f* into the wilderness in former ... Job 30:3

**FLEETH**

*f* into one of these cities ... Deut 19:11
he *f* also as a shadow, and ... Job 14:2
that he who *f* from the noise of ... Is 24:18
ask him that *f*, and her that ... Jer 48:19
He that *f* from the fear shall ... Jer 48:44
he that *f* of them shall not flee ... Amos 9:1
cankerworm spoileth, and *f* away ... Nah 3:16
and leaveth the sheep, and *f* ... Jn 10:12
The hireling *f*, because he is an ... Jn 10:13

**FLESH**

closed up the *f* instead thereof ... Gen 2:21
of my bones, and *f* of my *f* ... Gen 2:23
and they shall be one *f* ... Gen 2:24
with man, for that he also is *f* ... Gen 6:3
for all *f* had corrupted his way ... Gen 6:12
The end of all *f* is come before ... Gen 6:13
upon the earth, to destroy all *f* ... Gen 6:17
And of every living thing of all *f* ... Gen 6:19
into the ark, two and two of all *f* ... Gen 7:15
went in male and female of all *f* ... Gen 7:16
all *f* died that moved upon the ... Gen 7:21
thing that is with thee, of all *f* ... Gen 8:17
But *f* with the life thereof, ... Gen 9:4
neither shall all *f* be cut off ... Gen 9:11
and every living creature of all *f* ... Gen 9:15
become a flood to destroy all *f* ... Gen 9:15
of all *f* that is upon the earth ... Gen 9:16
all *f* that is upon the earth ... Gen 9:17
circumcise the *f* of your foreskin ... Gen 17:11
*f* for an everlasting covenant ... Gen 17:13
whose *f* of his foreskin is not ... Gen 17:14
circumcised the *f* of their ... Gen 17:23
in the *f* of his foreskin ... Gen 17:24
in the *f* of his foreskin ... Gen 17:25
Surely thou art my bone and my *f* ... Gen 29:14
for he is our brother and our *f* ... Gen 37:27
shall eat thy *f* from off thee ... Gen 40:19
was turned again as his other *f* ... Ex 4:7
shall eat the *f* in that night ... Ex 12:8
of the *f* abroad out of the house ... Ex 12:46
Egypt, when we sat by the *f* pots ... Ex 16:3
give you in the evening *f* to eat ... Ex 16:8
saying, At even ye shall eat *f* ... Ex 16:12
and his *f* shall not be eaten ... Ex 21:28
neither shall ye eat any *f* that ... Ex 22:31
But the *f* of the bullock, and his ... Ex 29:14
seethe his *f* in the holy place ... Ex 29:31
sons shall eat the *f* of the ram ... Ex 29:32
And if ought of the *f* of the ... Ex 29:34
Upon man's *f* shall it not be ... Ex 30:32
skin of the bullock, and all his *f* ... Lev 4:11
breeches shall he put upon his *f* ... Lev 6:10
touch the *f* thereof shall be holy ... Lev 6:27
the *f* of the sacrifice of his ... Lev 7:15
But the remainder of the *f* of the ... Lev 7:17
if any of the *f* of the sacrifice ... Lev 7:18
the *f* that toucheth any unclean ... Lev 7:19
and as for the *f*, all that be ... Lev 7:19
the *f* of the sacrifice of peace ... Lev 7:20
eat of the *f* of the sacrifice of ... Lev 7:21
the bullock, and his hide, his *f* ... Lev 8:17
Boil the *f* at the door of the ... Lev 8:31
And that which remaineth of the *f* ... Lev 8:32
And the *f* and the hide he burnt ... Lev 9:11
Of their *f* shall ye not eat, and ... Lev 11:8
ye shall not eat of their *f* ... Lev 11:11
in the eighth day the *f* of his ... Lev 12:3
in the skin of his *f* a rising ... Lev 13:2
it be in the skin of his *f* like ... Lev 13:2
the plague in the skin of the *f* ... Lev 13:3
be deeper than the skin of his *f* ... Lev 13:3
be white in the skin of his *f* ... Lev 13:4
be quick raw *f* in the rising ... Lev 13:10
old leprosy in the skin of his *f* ... Lev 13:11
leprosy have covered all his *f* ... Lev 13:13
But when raw *f* appeareth in him, ... Lev 13:14
And the priest shall see the raw *f* ... Lev 13:15
for the raw *f* is unclean ... Lev 13:15
Or if the raw *f* turn again ... Lev 13:16
The *f* also, in which, even in the ... Lev 13:18
Or if there be any *f*, in the skin ... Lev 13:24
the quick *f* that burneth have a ... Lev 13:24
the skin of their *f* bright spots ... Lev 13:38
skin of their *f* be darkish white ... Lev 13:39
appeareth in the skin of the *f* ... Lev 13:43
also he shall wash his *f* in water ... Lev 14:9
hath a running issue out of his *f* ... Lev 15:2
whether his *f* run with his issue, ... Lev 15:3
or his *f* be stopped from his ... Lev 15:3
he that toucheth the *f* of him ... Lev 15:7
bathe his *f* in running water, and ... Lev 15:13
he shall wash all his *f* in water ... Lev 15:16
and her issue in her *f* be blood ... Lev 15:19
the linen breeches upon his *f* ... Lev 16:4
shall he wash his *f* in water ... Lev 16:4
he shall wash his *f* with water in ... Lev 16:24
clothes, and bathe his *f* in water ... Lev 16:26
the fire their skins, and their *f* ... Lev 16:27
clothes, and bathe his *f* in water ... Lev 16:28
the life of the *f* is in the blood ... Lev 17:11
For it is the life of all *f* ... Lev 17:14
eat the blood of no manner of *f* ... Lev 17:14
for the life of all *f* is the ... Lev 17:14
he wash them not, nor bathe his *f* ... Lev 17:16
cuttings in your *f* for the dead ... Lev 19:28
nor make any cuttings in their *f* ... Lev 21:5
unless he wash his *f* with water ... Lev 22:6
ye shall eat the *f* of your sons ... Lev 26:29
the *f* of your daughters shall ye ... Lev 26:29
and let them shave all their *f* ... Num 8:7
said, Who shall give us *f* to eat ... Num 11:4
Whence should I have *f* to give ... Num 11:13
weep unto me, saying, Give us *f* ... Num 11:13
to morrow, and ye shall eat *f* ... Num 11:18
Who shall give us *f* to eat ... Num 11:18
the LORD will give you *f*, and ye ... Num 11:18
hast said, I will give them *f* ... Num 11:21
while the *f* was yet between their ... Num 11:33
of whom the *f* is half consumed ... Num 12:12
the God of the spirits of all *f* ... Num 16:22
that openeth the matrix in all *f* ... Num 18:15
the *f* of them shall be thine, as ... Num 18:18
her skin, and her *f*, and her blood, ... Num 19:5
and he shall bathe his *f* in water ... Num 19:7
in water, and bathe his *f* in water ... Num 19:8
the God of the spirits of all *f* ... Num 27:16
For who is there of all *f* ... Deut 5:26
kill and eat *f* in all thy gates, ... Deut 12:15
and thou shalt say, I will eat *f* ... Deut 12:20
because thy soul longeth to eat *f* ... Deut 12:20
thou mayest eat *f*, whatsoever thy ... Deut 12:20
not eat the life with the *f* ... Deut 12:23
offer thy burnt offerings, the *f* ... Deut 12:27
thy God, and thou shalt eat the *f* ... Deut 12:27
ye shall not eat of their *f* ... Deut 14:8
shall there any thing of the *f* ... Deut 16:4
the *f* of thy sons and of thy ... Deut 28:53
*f* of his children whom he shall ... Deut 28:55
blood, and my sword shall devour *f* ... Deut 32:42
the *f* he put in a basket, and he ... Judg 6:19
of God said unto him, Take the *f* ... Judg 6:20
was in his hand, and touched the *f* ... Judg 6:21
of the rock, and consumed the *f* ... Judg 6:21
then I will tear your *f* with the ... Judg 8:7
that I am your bone and your *f* ... Judg 9:2
while the *f* was in seething, with ... 1Sa 2:13
Give *f* to roast for the priest ... 1Sa 2:15
he will not have sodden *f* of thee ... 1Sa 2:15
I will give thy *f* unto the fowls ... 1Sa 17:44
my *f* that I have killed for my ... 1Sa 25:11
Behold, we are thy bone and thy *f* ... 2Sa 5:1
of bread, and a good piece of *f* ... 2Sa 6:19
brethren, ye are my bones and my *f* ... 2Sa 19:12
thou not of my bone, and of my *f* ... 2Sa 19:13
*f* in the morning, and bread and ... 1Kin 17:6
and bread and *f* in the evening ... 1Kin 17:6
them, and boiled their *f* with the ... 1Kin 19:21
and put sackcloth upon his *f* ... 1Kin 21:27
the *f* of the child waxed warm ... 2Kin 4:34
thy *f* shall come again to thee, ... 2Kin 5:10
his *f* came again like unto the ... 2Kin 5:14
like unto the *f* of a little child ... 2Kin 5:14
had sackcloth within upon his *f* ... 2Kin 6:30
shall dogs eat the *f* of Jezebel ... 2Kin 9:36
Behold, we are thy bone and thy *f* ... 1Chr 11:1
of bread, and a good piece of *f* ... 1Chr 16:3
With his is an arm of *f* ... 2Chr 32:8
*f* is as the *f* of our brethren ... Neh 5:5
now, and touch his bone and his *f* ... Job 2:5
the hair of my *f* stood up ... Job 4:15
or is my *f* of brass ... Job 6:12
My *f* is clothed with worms and ... Job 7:5
Hast thou eyes of *f* ... Job 10:4
hast clothed me with skin and *f* ... Job 10:11
do I take my *f* in my teeth ... Job 13:14
But his *f* upon him shall have ... Job 14:22
cleaveth to my skin and to my *f* ... Job 19:20
and are not satisfied with my *f* ... Job 19:22
yet in my *f* shall I see God ... Job 19:26
and trembling taketh hold on my *f* ... Job 21:6
said not, Oh that we had of his *f* ... Job 31:31
His *f* is consumed away, that it ... Job 33:21
His *f* shall be fresher than a ... Job 33:25
All *f* shall perish together, and ... Job 34:15
The flakes of his *f* are joined ... Job 41:23
my *f* also shall rest in hope ... Ps 16:9
foes, came upon me to eat up my *f* ... Ps 27:2
in my *f* because of thine anger ... Ps 38:3
and there is no soundness in my *f* ... Ps 38:7
Will I eat the *f* of bulls ... Ps 50:13
not fear what *f* can do unto me ... Ps 56:4
my *f* longeth for thee in a dry and ... Ps 63:1
unto thee shall all *f* come ... Ps 65:2
My *f* and my heart faileth ... Ps 73:26
can he provide *f* for his people ... Ps 78:20
He rained *f* also upon them as ... Ps 78:27
remembered that they were but *f* ... Ps 78:39
the *f* of thy saints unto the ... Ps 79:2
my *f* crieth out for the living ... Ps 84:2
and my *f* faileth of fatness ... Ps 109:24
My *f* trembleth for fear of thee ... Ps 119:120
Who giveth food to all *f* ... Ps 136:25
let all *f* bless his holy name for ... Ps 145:21
them, and health to all their *f* ... Prov 4:22
mourn at the last, when thy *f* ... Prov 5:11
that is cruel troubleth his own *f* ... Prov 11:17
sound heart is the life of the *f* ... Prov 14:30
among riotous eaters of *f* ... Prov 23:20
together, and eateth his own *f* ... Eccl 4:5
thy mouth to cause thy *f* to sin ... Eccl 5:6
and put away evil from thy *f* ... Eccl 11:10
study is a weariness of the *f* ... Eccl 12:12
every man the *f* of his own arm ... Is 9:20
fatness of his *f* shall wax lean ... Is 17:4
oxen, and killing sheep, eating *f* ... Is 22:13
and their horses *f*, and not spirit ... Is 31:3
all *f* shall see it together ... Is 40:5
All *f* is grass, and all the ... Is 40:6
with part thereof he eateth *f* ... Is 44:16
I have roasted *f*, and eaten it ... Is 44:19
oppress thee with their own *f* ... Is 49:26
all *f* shall know that I the LORD ... Is 49:26
hide not thyself from thine own *f* ... Is 58:7
monuments, which eat swine's *f* ... Is 65:4
will the LORD plead with all *f* ... Is 66:16
in the midst, eating swine's *f* ... Is 66:17
shall all *f* come to worship ... Is 66:23

shall be an abhorring unto all *f* Is 66:24
unto your sacrifices, and eat *f* Jer 7:21
the holy *f* is passed from thee Jer 11:15
no *f* shall have peace Jer 12:12
maketh *f* his arm, and whose heart Jer 17:5
them to eat the *f* of their sons Jer 19:9
the *f* of their daughters, and they Jer 19:9
the *f* of his friend in the siege Jer 19:9
nations, he will plead with all *f* Jer 25:31
I am the LORD, the God of all *f* Jer 32:27
I will bring evil upon all *f* Jer 45:5
to my *f* be upon Babylon, shall Jer 51:35
My *f* and my skin hath he made old Lam 3:4
there abominable *f* into my mouth Eze 4:14
is the caldron, and we be the *f* Eze 11:3
the midst of it, they are the *f* Eze 11:7
ye be the *f* in the midst thereof Eze 11:11
the stony heart out of their *f* Eze 11:19
and will give them an heart of *f* Eze 11:19
thy neighbours, great of *f* Eze 16:26
all *f* shall see that I the LORD Eze 20:48
all *f* from the south to the north Eze 21:4
That all *f* may know that I the Eze 21:5
whose *f* is as the *f* of asses, Eze 23:20
kindle the fire, consume the *f* Eze 24:10
I will lay thy *f* upon the Eze 32:5
the stony heart out of your *f* Eze 36:26
and I will give you an heart of *f* Eze 36:26
you, and will bring up *f* upon you Eze 37:6
the *f* came up upon them, and the Eze 37:8
of Israel, that ye may eat *f* Eze 39:17
Ye shall eat the *f* of the mighty Eze 39:18
tables was the *f* of the offering Eze 40:43
in heart, and uncircumcised in *f* Eze 44:7
in heart, nor uncircumcised in *f* Eze 44:9
fatter in *f* than all the children Dan 1:15
whose dwelling is not with *f* Dan 2:11
thereof, and all *f* was fed of it Dan 4:12
unto it, Arise, devour much *f* Dan 7:5
neither came *f* nor wine in my Dan 10:3
They sacrifice *f* for the Hos 8:13
pour out my spirit upon all *f* Joel 2:28
their *f* from off their bones Mic 3:2
Who also eat the *f* of my people Mic 3:3
pot, and as *f* within the caldron Mic 3:3
as dust, and their *f* as the dung Zeph 1:17
If one bear holy *f* in the skirt Hag 2:12
Be silent, O all *f*, before the Zec 2:13
eat every one the *f* of another Zec 11:9
but he shall eat the *f* of the fat Zec 11:16
Their *f* shall consume away while Zec 14:12
for *f* and blood hath not revealed Mt 16:17
and they twain shall be one *f* Mt 19:5
they are no more twain, but one *f* Mt 19:6
there should no *f* be saved Mt 24:22
is willing, but the *f* is weak Mt 26:41
And they twain shall be one *f* Mk 10:8
they are no more twain, but one *f* Mk 10:8
those days, no *f* should be saved Mk 13:20
truly is ready, but the *f* is weak Mk 14:38
all *f* shall see the salvation of Lk 3:6
for a spirit hath not *f* and bones, Lk 24:39
blood, nor of the will of the *f* Jn 1:13
And the Word was made *f*, and dwelt Jn 1:14
which is born of the *f* is *f* Jn 3:6
which is born of the *f* is *f* Jn 3:6
bread that I will give is my *f* Jn 6:51
can this man give us his *f* to eat Jn 6:52
ye eat the *f* of the Son of man Jn 6:53
Whoso eateth my *f*, and drinketh my Jn 6:54
For my *f* is meat indeed, and my Jn 6:55
He that eateth my *f*, and drinketh Jn 6:56
the *f* profiteth nothing Jn 6:63
Ye judge after the *f* Jn 8:15
hast given him power over all *f* Jn 17:2
pour out of my Spirit upon all *f* Acts 2:17
moreover also my *f* shall rest in Acts 2:26
of his loins, according to the *f* Acts 2:30
neither his *f* did see corruption Acts 2:31
seed of David according to the *f* Rom 1:3
which is outward in the *f* Rom 2:28
no *f* be justified in his sight Rom 3:20
father, as pertaining to the *f* Rom 4:1
of the infirmity of your *f* Rom 6:19
For when we were in the *f* Rom 7:5
know that in me (that is, in my *f* Rom 7:18
but with the *f* the law of sin Rom 7:25
Jesus, who walk not after the *f* Rom 8:1
in that it was weak through the *f* Rom 8:3
Son in the likeness of sinful *f* Rom 8:3
for sin, condemned sin in the *f* Rom 8:3
in us, who walk not after the *f* Rom 8:4
*f* do mind the things of the *f* Rom 8:5
are in the *f* cannot please God Rom 8:8
But ye are not in the *f*, but in Rom 8:9
to the *f*, to live after the *f* Rom 8:12
For if ye live after the *f* Rom 8:13
my kinsmen according to the *f* Rom 9:3
as concerning the *f* Christ came Rom 9:5
which are the children of the *f* Rom 9:8
to emulation them which are my *f* Rom 11:14
and make not provision for the *f* Rom 13:14
It is good neither to eat *f* Rom 14:21
not many wise men after the *f* 1Cor 1:26
That no *f* should glory in his 1Cor 1:29
for the destruction of the *f* 1Cor 5:5
for two, saith he, shall be one *f* 1Cor 6:16
such shall have trouble in the *f* 1Cor 7:28
I will eat no *f* while the world 1Cor 8:13
Behold Israel after the *f* 1Cor 10:18
All *f* is not the same *f* 1Cor 15:39
but there is one kind of *f* of men 1Cor 15:39
another *f* of beasts, another of 1Cor 15:39
Now this I say, brethren, that *f* 1Cor 15:50
do I purpose according to the *f* 2Cor 1:17
be made manifest in our mortal *f* 2Cor 4:11
know we no man after the *f* 2Cor 5:16
we have known Christ after the *f* 2Cor 5:16
from all filthiness of the *f* 2Cor 7:1
our *f* had no rest, but we were 2Cor 7:5
if we walked according to the *f* 2Cor 10:2
For though we walk in the *f* 2Cor 10:3
we do not war after the *f* 2Cor 10:3
that many glory after the *f* 2Cor 11:18
was given to me a thorn in the *f* 2Cor 12:7
I conferred not with *f* and blood Gal 1:16
the law shall no *f* be justified Gal 2:16
life which I now live in the *f* I Gal 2:20
are ye now made perfect by the *f* Gal 3:3
how through infirmity of the *f* I Gal 4:13
which was in my *f* ye despised not Gal 4:14
bondwoman was born after the *f* Gal 4:23
*f* persecuted him that was born Gal 4:29
liberty for an occasion to the *f* Gal 5:13
not fulfil the lust of the *f* Gal 5:16
For the *f* lusteth against the Gal 5:17
and the Spirit against the *f* Gal 5:17
the works of the *f* are manifest Gal 5:19
the *f* with the affections Gal 5:24
to his *f* shall of the *f* reap Gal 6:8
to make a fair shew in the *f* Gal 6:12
that they may glory in your *f* Gal 6:13
times past in the lusts of our *f* Eph 2:3
fulfilling the desires of the *f* Eph 2:3
in time past Gentiles in the *f* Eph 2:11
in the *f* made by hands Eph 2:11
abolished in his *f* the enmity Eph 2:15
no man ever yet hated his own *f* Eph 5:29
are members of his body, of his *f* Eph 5:30
wife, and they two shall be one *f* Eph 5:31
your masters according to the *f* Eph 6:5
For we wrestle not against *f* Eph 6:12
But if I live in the *f*, this is Phil 1:22
in the *f* is more needful for you Phil 1:24
and have no confidence in the *f* Phil 3:3
also have confidence in the *f* Phil 3:4
whereof he might trust in the *f* Phil 3:4
the body of his *f* through death Col 1:22
in my *f* for his body's sake Col 1:24
as have not seen my face in the *f* Col 2:1
For though I be absent in the *f* Col 2:5
*f* by the circumcision of Christ Col 2:11
and the uncircumcision of your *f* Col 2:13
honour to the satisfying of the *f* Col 2:23
your masters according to the *f* Col 3:22
God was manifest in the *f* 1Ti 3:16
more unto thee, both in the *f* Philem 16
the children are partakers of *f* Heb 2:14
Who in the days of his *f*, when he Heb 5:7
to the purifying of the *f* Heb 9:13
the veil, that is to say, his *f* Heb 10:20
of our *f* which corrected us Heb 12:9
shall eat your *f* as it were fire Jas 5:3
For all *f* is as grass, and all the 1Pet 1:24
God, being put to death in the *f* 1Pet 3:18
away of the filth of the *f* 1Pet 3:21
hath suffered for us in the *f* 1Pet 4:1
in the *f* hath ceased from sin 1Pet 4:1
time in the *f* to the lusts of men 1Pet 4:2
judged according to men in the *f* 1Pet 4:6
them that walk after the *f* in the 2Pet 2:10
allure through the lusts of the *f* 2Pet 2:18
in the world, the lust of the *f* 1Jn 2:16
Christ is come in the *f* is of God 1Jn 4:2
is come in the *f* is not of God 1Jn 4:3
Jesus Christ is come in the *f* 2Jn 7
and going after strange *f* Jude 7
filthy dreamers defile the *f* Jude 8
even the garment spotted by the *f* Jude 23
and naked, and shall eat her *f* Rev 17:16
That ye may eat the *f* of kings Rev 19:18
the *f* of captains, and the *f* Rev 19:18
the *f* of mighty men Rev 19:18
the *f* of horses, and of them that Rev 19:18
the *f* of all men, both free and Rev 19:18
fowls were filled with their *f* Rev 19:21

**FLESHHOOK**
with a *f* of three teeth in his 1Sa 2:13
all that the *f* brought up the 1Sa 2:14

**FLESHHOOKS**
shovels, and his basons, and his *f* Ex 27:3
shovels, and the basons, and the *f* Ex 38:3
about it, even the censers, the *f* Num 4:14
Also pure gold for the *f*, and the 1Chr 28:17
also, and the shovels, and the *f* 2Chr 4:16

**FLESHLY**
sincerity, not with *f* wisdom 2Cor 1:12
vainly puffed up by his *f* mind Col 2:18
and pilgrims, abstain from *f* lusts 1Pet 2:11

**FLESHY**
but in *f* tables of the heart 2Cor 3:3

**FLEW**
the people *f* upon the spoil, and 1Sa 14:32
Then *f* one of the seraphims unto Is 6:6

**FLIES**
I will send swarms of *f* upon thee Ex 8:21
shall be full of swarms of *f* Ex 8:21
no swarms of *f* shall be there Ex 8:22
of *f* into the house of Pharaoh Ex 8:24
by reason of the swarm of *f* Ex 8:24
of *f* may depart from Pharaoh Ex 8:29
the swarms of *f* from Pharaoh Ex 8:31
sent divers sorts of *f* among them Ps 78:45
and there came divers sorts of *f* Ps 105:31
Dead *f* cause the ointment of the Eccl 10:1

**FLIETH**
any winged fowl that *f* in the air Deut 4:17
thing that *f* is unclean unto you Deut 14:19
earth, as swift as the eagle *f* Deut 28:49
nor for the arrow that *f* by day Ps 91:5

**FLIGHT**
you shall put ten thousand to *f* Lev 26:8
and two put ten thousand to *f* Deut 32:30
they put to *f* all them of the 1Chr 12:15
go out with haste, nor go by *f* Is 52:12
Therefore the *f* shall perish from Amos 2:14
that your *f* be not in the winter Mt 24:20
pray ye that your *f* be not in the Mk 13:18
turned to *f* the armies of the Heb 11:34

**FLINT**
forth water out of the rock of *f* Deut 8:15
the *f* into a fountain of waters Ps 114:8
hoofs shall be counted like *f* Is 5:28
have I set my face like a *f* Is 50:7
than *f* have I made thy forehead Eze 3:9

**FLINTY**
rock, and oil out of the *f* rock Deut 32:13

**FLOATS**
I will convey them by sea in *f* 1Kin 5:9

**FLOCK**
of the firstlings of his *f* Gen 4:4
ewe lambs of the *f* by themselves Gen 21:28
Go now to the *f*, and fetch me from Gen 27:9
watered the *f* of Laban his Gen 29:10
I will again feed and keep thy *f* Gen 30:31
pass through all thy *f* to day Gen 30:32
all the brown in the *f* of Laban Gen 30:40
and Leah to the field unto his *f* Gen 31:4
the rams of thy *f* have I not Gen 31:38
them one day, all the *f* will die Gen 33:13
was feeding the *f* with his Gen 37:2
feed their father's *f* in Shechem Gen 37:12
brethren feed the *f* in Shechem Gen 37:13
I will send thee a kid from the *f* Gen 38:17
troughs to water their father's *f* Ex 2:16
helped them, and watered their *f* Ex 2:17
enough for us, and watered the *f* Ex 2:19
Now Moses kept the *f* of Jethro Ex 3:1
he led the *f* to the backside of Ex 3:1
even of the herd, and of the *f* Lev 1:2
unto the LORD be of the *f* Lev 3:6
hath sinned, a female from the *f* Lev 5:6
ram without blemish out of the *f* Lev 5:18
ram without blemish out of the *f* Lev 6:6
tithe of the herd, or of the *f* Lev 27:32
LORD, of the herd, or of the *f* Num 15:3
of thy herds or of thy *f*, nor any Deut 12:17
kill of thy herd and of thy *f* Deut 12:21
him liberally out of thy *f* Deut 15:14
of thy *f* thou shalt sanctify unto Deut 15:19
unto the LORD thy God, of the *f* Deut 16:2
bear, and took a lamb out of the *f* 1Sa 17:34
and he spared to take of his own *f* 2Sa 12:4
gave to the people, of the *f* 2Chr 35:7
a ram of the *f* for their trespass Ezr 10:19
forth their little ones like a *f* Job 21:11
to have set with the dogs of my *f* Job 30:1
like a *f* by the hand of Moses Ps 77:20
them in the wilderness like a *f* Ps 78:52
thou that leadest Joseph like a *f* Ps 80:1
and maketh him families like a *f* Ps 107:41
thou makest thy *f* to rest at noon Song 1:7
forth by the footsteps of the *f* Song 1:8
thy hair is as a *f* of goats Song 4:1
Thy teeth are like a *f* of sheep Song 4:2
thy hair is as a *f* of goats that Song 6:5
Thy teeth are as a *f* of sheep Song 6:6
shall feed his *f* like a shepherd Is 40:11
sea with the shepherd of his *f* Is 63:11
because the LORD's *f* is carried Jer 13:17
where is the *f* that was given Jer 13:20
was given thee, thy beautiful *f* Jer 13:20
Ye have scattered my *f*, and driven Jer 23:2
*f* out of all countries whither I Jer 23:3
the ashes, ye principal of the *f* Jer 25:34
the principal of the *f* to escape Jer 25:35
howling of the principal of the *f* Jer 25:36
him, as a shepherd doth his *f* Jer 31:10
oil, and for the young of the *f* Jer 31:12
of the *f* shall draw them out Jer 49:20
of the *f* shall draw them out Jer 50:45
with thee the shepherd and his *f* Jer 51:23
Take the choice of the *f*, and burn Eze 24:5
but ye feed not the *f* Eze 34:3
my *f* was scattered upon all the Eze 34:6
surely because my *f* became a prey Eze 34:8
my *f* became meat to every beast Eze 34:8
did my shepherds search for my *f* Eze 34:8
fed themselves, and fed not my *f* Eze 34:8
I will require my *f* at their hand Eze 34:10
them to cease from feeding the *f* Eze 34:10
deliver my *f* from their mouth Eze 34:10
As a shepherd seeketh out his *f* Eze 34:12
I will feed my *f*, and I will cause Eze 34:15

And as for you, O my *f*, thus saith Eze 34:17
And as for my *f*, they eat that Eze 34:19
Therefore will I save my *f* Eze 34:22
And ye my *f*, the *f* of my Eze 34:31
the *f* of my pasture, are men, and Eze 34:31
increase them with men like a *f* Eze 36:37
As the holy *f*, as the *f* of Eze 36:38
ram out of the *f* without blemish Eze 43:23
bullock, and a ram out of the *f* Eze 43:25
And one lamb out of the *f*, out of Eze 45:15
and eat the lambs out of the *f* Amos 6:4
LORD took me as I followed the *f* Amos 7:15
neither man nor beast, herd nor *f* Jonah 3:7
as the *f* in the midst of their Mic 2:12
And thou, O tower of the *f* Mic 4:8
the *f* of thine heritage, which Mic 7:14
the *f* shall be cut off from the Hab 3:17
that day as the *f* of his people Zec 9:16
they went their way as a *f* Zec 10:2
visited his *f* the house of Judah Zec 10:3
Feed the *f* of the slaughter Zec 11:4
And I will feed the *f* of slaughter Zec 11:7
even you, O poor of the *f* Zec 11:7
and I fed the *f* Zec 11:7
so the poor of the *f* that waited Zec 11:11
idol shepherd that leaveth the *f* Zec 11:17
which hath in his *f* a male Mal 1:14
the sheep of the *f* shall be Mt 26:31
watch over their *f* by night Lk 2:8
Fear not, little *f* Lk 12:32
unto yourselves, and to all the *f* Acts 20:28
in among you, not sparing the *f* Acts 20:29
or who feedeth a *f*, and eateth not 1Cor 9:7
eateth not of the milk of the *f* 1Cor 9:7
Feed the *f* of God which is among 1Pet 5:2
but being ensamples to the *f* 1Pet 5:3

## FLOCKS

which went with Abram, had *f* Gen 13:5
and he hath given him *f*, and herds, Gen 24:35
For he had possession of *f* Gen 26:14
there were three *f* of sheep lying Gen 29:2
of that well they watered the *f* Gen 29:2
thither were all the *f* gathered Gen 29:3
until all the *f* be gathered Gen 29:8
Jacob fed the rest of Laban's *f* Gen 30:36
*f* in the gutters in the watering Gen 30:38
troughs when the *f* came to drink Gen 30:38
the *f* conceived before the rods, Gen 30:39
set the faces of the *f* toward the Gen 30:40
and he put his own *f* by themselves Gen 30:40
And I have oxen, and asses, *f* Gen 32:5
that was with him, and the *f* Gen 32:7
the children are tender, and the *f* Gen 33:13
thy brethren, and well with the *f* Gen 37:14
thee, where they feed their *f* Gen 37:16
thy children's children, and thy *f* Gen 45:10
and they have brought their *f* Gen 46:32
father and my brethren, and their *f* Gen 47:1
have no pasture for their *f* Gen 47:4
exchange for horses, and for the *f* Gen 47:17
their little ones, and their *f* Gen 50:8
and with our daughters, with our *f* Ex 10:9
only let your *f* and your herds be Ex 10:24
Also take your *f* and your herds, Ex 12:32
and *f*, and herds, even very much Ex 12:38
neither let the *f* nor herds feed Ex 34:3
And if his offering be of the *f* Lev 1:10
ram without blemish out of the *f* Lev 5:15
Shall the *f* and the herds be slain Num 11:22
all their cattle, and all their *f* Num 31:9
beeves, of the asses, and of the *f* Num 31:30
Our little ones, our wives, our *f* Num 32:26
the *f* of thy sheep, in the land Deut 7:13
thy *f* multiply, and thy silver and Deut 8:13
of your herds and of your *f* Deut 12:6
of thy herds and of thy *f* Deut 14:23
thy kine, and the *f* of thy sheep Deut 28:4
thy kine, and the *f* of thy sheep Deut 28:18
or *f* of thy sheep, until he have Deut 28:51
to hear the bleatings of the *f* Judg 5:16
And David took all the *f* and the 1Sa 30:20
The rich man had exceeding many *f* 2Sa 12:2
them like two little *f* of kids 1Kin 20:27
to seek pasture for their *f* 1Chr 4:39
was pasture there for their *f* 1Chr 4:41
over the *f* was Jaziz the Hagerite 1Chr 27:31
and the Arabians brought him *f* 2Chr 17:11
manner of beasts, and cotes for *f* 2Chr 32:28
him cities, and possessions of *f* 2Chr 32:29
of our herds and of our *f*, to Neh 10:36
they violently take away *f* Job 24:2
The pastures are clothed with *f* Ps 65:13
their *f* to hot thunderbolts Ps 78:48
to know the state of thy *f* Prov 27:23
aside by the *f* of thy companions Song 1:7
they shall be for *f*, which shall Is 17:2
joy of wild asses, a pasture of *f* Is 32:14
All the *f* of Kedar shall be Is 60:7
shall stand and feed your *f* Is 61:5
And Sharon shall be a fold of *f* Is 65:10
their *f* and their herds, their Jer 3:24
they shall eat up thy *f* and thine Jer 5:17
with their *f* shall come unto her Jer 6:3
all their *f* shall be scattered Jer 10:21
and they that go forth with *f* Jer 31:24
causing their *f* to lie down Jer 33:12
shall the *f* pass again under the Jer 33:13
their *f* shall they take away Jer 49:29
be as the he goats before the *f* Jer 50:8
Ammonites a couchingplace for *f* Eze 25:5
not the shepherds feed the *f* Eze 34:2
cities be filled with *f* of men Eze 36:38
They shall go with their *f* Hos 5:6
the *f* of sheep are made desolate Joel 1:18
a young lion among the *f* of sheep Mic 5:8
for shepherds, and folds for *f* Zeph 2:6
*f* shall lie down in the midst of Zeph 2:14

## FLOOD

do bring a *f* of waters upon the Gen 6:17
*f* of waters was upon the earth Gen 7:6
because of the waters of the *f* Gen 7:7
of the *f* were upon the earth Gen 7:10
the *f* was forty days upon the Gen 7:17
off any more by the waters of a *f* Gen 9:11
more be a *f* to destroy the earth Gen 9:11
become a *f* to destroy all flesh Gen 9:15
lived after the *f* three hundred Gen 9:28
them were sons born after the *f* Gen 10:1
divided in the earth after the *f* Gen 10:32
Arphaxad two years after the *f* Gen 11:10
other side of the *f* in old time Josh 24:2
from the other side of the *f* Josh 24:3
served on the other side of the *f* Josh 24:14
were on the other side of the *f* Josh 24:15
the *f* decayeth and drieth up Job 14:11
foundation was overflown with a *f* Job 22:16
The *f* breaketh out from the Job 28:4
The LORD sitteth upon the *f* Ps 29:10
they went through the *f* on foot Ps 66:6
cleave the fountain and the *f* Ps 74:15
carriest them away as with a *f* Ps 90:5
storm, as a *f* of mighty waters Is 28:2
the enemy shall come in like a *f* Is 59:19
Who is this that cometh up as a *f* Jer 46:7
Egypt riseth up like a *f*, and his Jer 46:8
and shall be an overflowing *f* Jer 47:2
the end thereof shall be with a *f* Dan 9:26
with the arms of a *f* shall they Dan 11:22
and it shall rise up wholly as a *f* Amos 8:8
and drowned, as by the *f* of Egypt Amos 8:8
it shall rise up wholly like a *f* Amos 9:5
be drowned, as by the *f* of Egypt Amos 9:5
But with an overrunning *f* he will Nah 1:8
before the *f* they were eating Mt 24:38
And knew not until the *f* came Mt 24:39
and when the *f* arose, the stream Lk 6:48
the *f* came, and destroyed them all Lk 17:27
bringing in the *f* upon the world 2Pet 2:5
water as a *f* after the woman Rev 12:15
her to be carried away of the *f* Rev 12:15
swallowed up the *f* which the Rev 12:16

## FLOODS

the *f* stood upright as an heap, Ex 15:8
the *f* of ungodly men made me 2Sa 22:5
shall not see the rivers, the *f* Job 20:17
He bindeth the *f* from overflowing Job 28:11
the *f* of ungodly men made me Ps 18:4
and established it upon the *f* Ps 24:2
surely in the *f* of great waters Ps 32:6
waters, where the *f* overflow me Ps 69:2
and their *f*, that they could not Ps 78:44
The *f* have lifted up, O LORD, the Ps 93:3
the *f* have lifted up their voice Ps 93:3
the *f* lift up their waves Ps 93:3
Let the *f* clap their hands Ps 98:8
love, neither can the *f* drown it Song 8:7
thirsty, and *f* upon the dry ground Is 44:3
and I restrained the *f* thereof Eze 31:15
and the *f* compassed me about Jonah 2:3
the *f* came, and the winds blew, and Mt 7:25
the *f* came, and the winds blew, and Mt 7:27

## FLOOR

saw the mourning in the *f* of Atad Gen 50:11
of the dust that is in the *f* of Num 5:17
out of thy flock, and out of thy *f* Deut 15:14
put a fleece of wool in the *f* Judg 6:37
thee, and get thee down to the *f* Ruth 3:3
And she went down unto the *f* Ruth 3:6
that a woman came into the *f* Ruth 3:14
both the *f* of the house, and the 1Kin 6:15
covered the *f* of the house with 1Kin 6:15
sides of the house, both the *f* 1Kin 6:16
the *f* of the house he overlaid 1Kin 6:30
one side of the *f* to the other 1Kin 7:7
to *f* the houses which the kings 2Chr 34:11
my threshing, and the corn of my *f* Is 21:10
The *f* and the winepress shall not Hos 9:2
with the whirlwind out of the *f* Hos 13:3
them as the sheaves into the *f* Mic 4:12
and he will throughly purge his *f* Mt 3:12
and he will throughly purge his *f* Lk 3:17

## FLOORS

the *f* shall be full of wheat, and Joel 2:24

## FLOTES

it to thee in *f* by sea to Joppa 2Chr 2:16

## FLOUR

of wheaten *f* shalt thou make them Ex 29:2
the one lamb a tenth deal of *f* Ex 29:40
his offering shall be of fine *f* Lev 2:1
his handful of the *f* thereof Lev 2:2
cakes of fine *f* mingled with oil Lev 2:4
it shall be of fine *f* unleavened Lev 2:5
shall be made of fine *f* with oil Lev 2:7
of fine *f* for a sin offering Lev 5:11
of the *f* of the meat offering, and Lev 6:15
*f* for a meat offering perpetual Lev 6:20
cakes mingled with oil, of fine *f* Lev 7:12
of fine *f* for a meat offering Lev 14:10
one tenth deal of fine *f* mingled Lev 14:21
deals of fine *f* mingled with oil Lev 23:13
they shall be of fine *f* Lev 23:17
And thou shalt take fine *f* Lev 24:5
cakes of fine *f* mingled with oil, Num 6:15
*f* mingled with oil for a meat Num 7:13
both of them full of fine *f* Num 7:19
both of them full of fine *f* Num 7:25
both of them full of fine *f* Num 7:31
both of them full of fine *f* Num 7:37
both of them full of fine *f* Num 7:43
both of them full of fine *f* Num 7:49
both of them full of fine *f* Num 7:55
both of them full of fine *f* Num 7:61
both of them full of fine *f* Num 7:67
both of them full of fine *f* Num 7:73
both of them full of fine *f* Num 7:79
even fine *f* mingled with oil, and Num 8:8
offering of a tenth deal of *f* Num 15:4
offering two tenth deals of *f* Num 15:6
of three tenth deals of *f* mingled Num 15:9
an ephah of *f* for a meat offering Num 28:5
two tenth deals of *f* for a meat Num 28:9
deals of *f* for a meat offering Num 28:12
two tenth deals of *f* for a meat Num 28:12
a several tenth deal of *f* mingled Num 28:13
shall be of *f* mingled with oil Num 28:20
offering of *f* mingled with oil Num 28:28
shall be of *f* mingled with oil Num 29:3
shall be of *f* mingled with oil Num 29:9
shall be of *f* mingled with oil Num 29:14
unleavened cakes of an ephah of *f* Judg 6:19
three bullocks, and one ephah of *f* 1Sa 1:24
hasted, and killed it, and took *f* 1Sa 28:24
And she took *f*, and kneaded it, and 2Sa 13:8
and wheat, and barley, and *f* 2Sa 17:28
day was thirty measures of fine *f* 1Kin 4:22
of fine *f* be sold for a shekel 2Kin 7:1
So a measure of fine *f* was sold 2Kin 7:16
a measure of fine *f* for a shekel 2Kin 7:18
of the sanctuary, and the fine *f* 1Chr 9:29
for the fine *f* for meat offering, 1Chr 23:29
thou didst eat fine *f*, and honey, Eze 16:13
also which I gave thee, fine *f* Eze 16:19
of oil, to temper with the fine *f* Eze 46:14
and wine, and oil, and fine *f* Rev 18:13

## FLOURISH

In his days shall the righteous *f* Ps 72:7
they of the city shall *f* like Ps 72:16
all the workers of iniquity do *f* Ps 92:7
shall *f* like the palm tree Ps 92:12
shall *f* in the courts of our God Ps 92:13
upon himself shall his crown *f* Ps 132:18
the righteous shall *f* as a branch Prov 11:28
tabernacle of the upright shall *f* Prov 14:11
way, and the almond tree shall *f* Eccl 12:5
let us see if the vine *f*, whether Song 7:12
shalt thou make thy seed to *f* Is 17:11
your bones shall *f* like an herb Is 66:14
and have made the dry tree to *f* Eze 17:24

## FLOURISHED

and to see whether the vine *f* Song 6:11
last your care of me hath *f* again Phil 4:10

## FLOURISHETH

In the morning it *f*, and groweth Ps 90:6
as a flower of the field, so he *f* Ps 103:15

## FLOURISHING

they shall be fat and *f* Ps 92:14
in mine house, and *f* in my palace Dan 4:4

## FLOW

his goods shall *f* away in the day Job 20:28
his wind to blow, and the waters *f* Ps 147:18
that the spices thereof may *f* out Song 4:16
and all nations shall *f* unto it Is 2:2
he caused the waters to *f* out of Is 48:21
*f* together, and thine heart shall Is 60:5
might *f* down at thy presence Is 64:1
shall *f* together to the goodness Jer 31:12
the nations shall not *f* together Jer 51:44
and the hills shall *f* with milk Joel 3:18
of Judah shall *f* with waters Joel 3:18
and people shall *f* unto it Mic 4:1
shall *f* rivers of living water Jn 7:38

## FLOWED

*f* over all his banks, as they did Josh 4:18
the mountains *f* down at thy Is 64:3
Waters *f* over mine head Lam 3:54

## FLOWER

with a knop and a *f* in one branch Ex 25:33
other branch, with a knop and a *f* Ex 25:33
in one branch, a knop and a *f* Ex 37:19
in another branch, a knop and a *f* Ex 37:19
shall die in the *f* of their age 1Sa 2:33
He cometh forth like a *f*, and is Job 14:2
shall cast off his *f* as the olive Job 15:33
as a *f* of the field, so he Ps 103:15
sour grape is ripening in the *f* Is 18:5
glorious beauty is a fading *f* Is 28:1
fat valley, shall be a fading *f* Is 28:4
thereof is as the *f* of the field Is 40:6
The grass withereth, the *f* fadeth Is 40:7
The grass withereth, the *f* fadeth Is 40:8
the *f* of Lebanon languisheth Nah 1:4
if she pass the *f* of her age 1Cor 7:36
because as the *f* of the grass he Jas 1:10

F

the *f* thereof falleth, and the ... Jas 1:11
glory of man as the *f* of grass ... 1Pet 1:24
the *f* thereof falleth away ... 1Pet 1:24

### FLOWERS
his bowls, his knops, and his *f* ... Ex 25:31
with their knops and their *f* ... Ex 25:34
his bowls, his knops, and his *f* ... Ex 37:17
like almonds, his knops, and his *f* ... Ex 37:20
her *f* be upon him, he shall be ... Lev 15:24
And of her that is sick of her *f* ... Lev 15:33
shaft thereof, unto the *f* thereof ... Num 8:4
was carved with knops and open *f* ... 1Kin 6:18
cherubims and palm trees and open *f*. 1Kin 6:29
cherubims and palm trees and open *f*. 1Kin 6:32
cherubims and palm trees and open *f*. 1Kin 6:35
brim of a cup, with *f* of lilies ... 1Kin 7:26
before the oracle, with the *f* ... 1Kin 7:49
brim of a cup, with *f* of lilies ... 2Chr 4:5
And the *f*, and the lamps, and the ... 2Chr 4:21
The *f* appear on the earth ... Song 2:12
as a bed of spices, as sweet *f* ... Song 5:13

### FLOWETH
it, a land that *f* with milk ... Lev 20:24
us, and surely it *f* with milk ... Num 13:27
a land which *f* with milk and honey ... Num 14:8
up out of a land that *f* with milk ... Num 16:13
us into a land that *f* with milk ... Num 16:14
in the land that *f* with milk ... Deut 6:3
seed, a land that *f* with milk ... Deut 11:9
even a land that *f* with milk ... Deut 26:9
fathers, a land that *f* with milk ... Deut 26:15
thee, a land that *f* with milk ... Deut 27:3
that *f* with milk and honey ... Deut 31:20
give us, a land that *f* with milk ... Josh 5:6

### FLOWING
a large, unto a land *f* with milk ... Ex 3:8
unto a land *f* with milk and honey ... Ex 3:17
a land *f* with milk and honey, that ... Ex 13:5
Unto a land *f* with milk and honey ... Ex 33:3
wellspring of wisdom as a *f* brook ... Prov 18:4
of the Gentiles like a *f* stream ... Is 66:12
to give them a land *f* with milk ... Jer 11:5
or shall the cold *f* waters that ... Jer 18:14
a land *f* with milk and honey ... Jer 32:22
thy *f* valley, O backsliding ... Jer 49:4
*f* with milk and honey, which is ... Eze 20:6
*f* with milk and honey, which is ... Eze 20:15

### FLUTE
hear the sound of the cornet, *f* ... Dan 3:5
heard the sound of the cornet, *f* ... Dan 3:7
hear the sound of the cornet, *f* ... Dan 3:10
hear the sound of the cornet, *f* ... Dan 3:15

### FLUTTERETH
*f* over her young, spreadeth ... Deut 32:11

### FLUX
sick of a fever and of a bloody *f* ... Acts 28:8

### FLY
fowl that may *f* above the earth ... Gen 1:20
but didst *f* upon the spoil, and ... 1Sa 15:19
he rode upon a cherub, and did *f* ... 2Sa 22:11
trouble, as the sparks *f* upward ... Job 5:7
He shall *f* away as a dream, and ... Job 20:8
Doth the hawk *f* by thy wisdom ... Job 39:26
he rode upon a cherub, and did *f* ... Ps 18:10
he did *f* upon the wings of the ... Ps 18:10
for then would I *f* away, and be at ... Ps 55:6
it is soon cut off, and we *f* away ... Ps 90:10
they *f* away as an eagle toward ... Prov 23:5
his feet, and with twain he did *f* ... Is 6:2
the LORD shall hiss for the *f* ... Is 7:18
But they shall *f* upon the ... Is 11:14
Who are these that *f* as a cloud ... Is 60:8
he shall *f* as an eagle, and shall ... Jer 48:40
*f* as the eagle, and spread his ... Jer 49:22
hunt the souls to make them *f* ... Eze 13:20
souls that ye hunt to make them *f* ... Eze 13:20
being caused to *f* swiftly ... Dan 9:21
glory shall *f* away like a bird ... Hos 9:11
they shall *f* as the eagle that ... Hab 1:8
that she might *f* into the ... Rev 12:14
I saw another angel *f* in the ... Rev 14:6
that *f* in the midst of heaven ... Rev 19:17

### FLYING
Yet these may ye eat of every *f* ... Lev 11:21
But all other *f* creeping things, ... Lev 11:23
creeping things, and *f* fowl ... Ps 148:10
by wandering, as the swallow by *f* ... Prov 26:2
fruit shall be a fiery *f* serpent ... Is 14:29
fiery *f* serpent, they will carry ... Is 30:6
As birds *f*, so will the LORD of ... Is 31:5
and looked, and behold a *f* roll ... Zec 5:1
And I answered, I see a *f* roll ... Zec 5:2
fourth beast was like a *f* eagle ... Rev 4:7
heard an angel *f* through the ... Rev 8:13

### FOAL
Binding his *f* unto the vine, and ... Gen 49:11
and upon a colt the *f* of an ass ... Zec 9:9
an ass, and a colt the *f* of an ass ... Mt 21:5

### FOALS
bulls, twenty she asses, and ten *f* ... Gen 32:15

### FOAM
cut off as the *f* upon the water ... Hos 10:7

### FOAMETH
and he *f*, and gnasheth with his ... Mk 9:18
and it teareth him that he *f* again ... Lk 9:39

### FOAMING
fell on the ground, and wallowed *f* ... Mk 9:20
of the sea, *f* out their own shame ... Jude 13

### FODDER
or loweth the ox over his *f* ... Job 6:5

### FOES
to be destroyed before thy *f* ... 1Chr 21:12
and slew of their *f* seventy ... Est 9:16
wicked, even mine enemies and my *f* ... Ps 27:2
hast not made my *f* to rejoice ... Ps 30:1
beat down his *f* before his face ... Ps 89:23
a man's *f* shall be they of his ... Mt 10:36
Until I make thy *f* thy footstool ... Acts 2:35

### FOLD
the shepherds make their *f* there ... Is 13:20
And Sharon shall be a *f* of flocks ... Is 65:10
of Israel shall their *f* be ... Eze 34:14
there shall they lie in a good *f* ... Eze 34:14
the flock in the midst of their *f* ... Mic 2:12
flock shall be cut off from the *f* ... Hab 3:17
I have, which are not of this *f* ... Jn 10:16
and there shall be one *f*, and one ... Jn 10:16
as a vesture shalt thou *f* them up ... Heb 1:12

### FOLDEN
For while they be *f* together as ... Nah 1:10

### FOLDETH
The fool *f* his hands together, and ... Eccl 4:5

### FOLDING
two leaves of the one door were *f* ... 1Kin 6:34
leaves of the other door were *f* ... 1Kin 6:34
a little *f* of the hands to sleep ... Prov 6:10
a little *f* of the hands to sleep ... Prov 24:33

### FOLDS
little ones, and *f* for your sheep ... Num 32:24
and *f* of sheep ... Num 32:36
house, nor he goats out of thy *f* ... Ps 50:9
will bring them again to their *f* ... Jer 23:3
for shepherds, and *f* for flocks ... Zeph 2:6

### FOLK
some of the *f* that are with me ... Gen 33:15
The conies are but a feeble *f* ... Prov 30:26
the *f* in the fire, and they shall ... Jer 51:58
laid his hands upon a few sick *f* ... Mk 6:5
a great multitude of impotent *f* ... Jn 5:3

### FOLKS
unto Jerusalem, bringing sick *f* ... Acts 5:16

### FOLLOW
be willing to *f* me unto this land ... Gen 24:5
will not be willing to *f* thee ... Gen 24:8
the woman will not *f* me ... Gen 24:39
his steward, Up, *f* after the men ... Gen 44:4
and all the people that *f* thee ... Ex 11:8
heart, that he shall *f* after them ... Ex 14:4
Egyptians, and they shall *f* them ... Ex 14:17
from her, and yet no mischief *f* ... Ex 21:22
And if any mischief *f*, then thou ... Ex 21:23
Thou shalt not *f* a multitude to ... Ex 23:2
is altogether just shalt thou *f* ... Deut 16:20
of the LORD, if the thing *f* not ... Deut 18:22
And he said unto them, *F* after me ... Judg 3:28
bread unto the people that *f* me ... Judg 8:5
hearts inclined to *f* Abimelech ... Judg 9:3
unto the young men that *f* my lord ... 1Sa 25:27
faint that they could not *f* David ... 1Sa 30:21
among the people that *f* Absalom ... 2Sa 17:9
if the LORD be God, *f* him ... 1Kin 18:21
but if Baal, then *f* him ... 1Kin 18:21
my mother, and then I will *f* thee ... 1Kin 19:20
for all the people that *f* me ... 1Kin 20:10
*f* me, and I will bring you to the ... 2Kin 6:19
mercy shall *f* me all the days of ... Ps 23:6
because I *f* the thing that good ... Ps 38:20
*f* her shall be brought unto thee ... Ps 45:14
the upright in heart shall *f* it ... Ps 94:15
draw nigh that *f* after mischief ... Ps 119:150
that they may *f* strong drink ... Is 5:11
ye that *f* after righteousness, ye ... Is 51:1
from being a pastor to *f* thee ... Jer 17:16
shall *f* close after you there in ... Jer 42:16
that *f* their own spirit, and have ... Eze 13:3
she shall *f* after her lovers, but ... Hos 2:7
if we *f* on to know the LORD ... Hos 6:3
*F* me, and I will make you fishers ... Mt 4:19
I will *f* thee whithersoever thou ... Mt 8:19
But Jesus said unto him, *F* me ... Mt 8:22
and he saith unto him, *F* me ... Mt 9:9
and take up his cross, and *f* me ... Mt 16:24
and come and *f* me ... Mt 19:21
of custom, and said unto him, *F* me ... Mk 2:14
And he suffered no man to *f* him ... Mk 5:37
and his disciples *f* him ... Mk 6:1
and take up his cross, and *f* me ... Mk 8:34
come, take up the cross, and *f* me ... Mk 10:21
bearing a pitcher of water: *f* him ... Mk 14:13
signs shall *f* them that believe ... Mk 16:17
and he said unto him, *F* me ... Lk 5:27
take up his cross daily, and *f* me ... Lk 9:23
I will *f* thee whithersoever thou ... Lk 9:57
And he said unto another, *F* me ... Lk 9:59
also said, Lord, I will *f* thee ... Lk 9:61
go not after them, nor *f* them ... Lk 17:23
in heaven: and come, *f* me ... Lk 18:22
*f* him into the house where he ... Lk 22:10
were about him saw what would *f* ... Lk 22:49
Philip, and saith unto him, *F* me ... Jn 1:43
before them, and the sheep *f* him ... Jn 10:4
And a stranger will they not *f* ... Jn 10:5
and I know them, and they *f* me ... Jn 10:27
If any man serve me, let him *f* me ... Jn 12:26
I go, thou canst not *f* me now ... Jn 13:36
but thou shalt *f* me afterwards ... Jn 13:36
Lord, why cannot I *f* thee now ... Jn 13:37
this, he saith unto him, *F* me ... Jn 21:19
is that to thee? *f* thou me ... Jn 21:22
from Samuel and those that *f* after ... Acts 3:24
thy garment about thee, and *f* me ... Acts 12:8
Let us therefore *f* after the ... Rom 14:19
*F* after charity, and desire ... 1Cor 14:1
but I *f* after, if that I may ... Phil 3:12
but ever *f* that which is good, ... 1Th 5:15
know how ye ought to *f* us ... 2Th 3:7
an ensample unto you to *f* us ... 2Th 3:9
and some men they *f* after ... 1Ti 5:24
*f* after righteousness, godliness, ... 1Ti 6:11
but *f* righteousness, faith, ... 2Ti 2:22
*F* peace with all men, and holiness ... Heb 12:14
whose faith *f*, considering the ... Heb 13:7
and the glory that should *f* ... 1Pet 1:11
that ye should *f* his steps ... 1Pet 2:21
many shall *f* their pernicious ... 2Pet 2:2
*f* not that which is evil, but ... 3Jn 11
These are they which *f* the Lamb ... Rev 14:4
and their works do *f* them ... Rev 14:13

### FOLLOWED
upon the camels, and *f* the man ... Gen 24:61
all that *f* the droves, saying, On ... Gen 32:19
hath *f* me fully, him will I bring ... Num 14:24
and the elders of Israel *f* him ... Num 16:25
because they have not wholly *f* me .. Num 32:11
for they have wholly *f* the LORD ... Num 32:12
because he hath wholly *f* the LORD ... Deut 1:36
for all the men that *f* Baal-peor ... Deut 4:3
the covenant of the LORD *f* them ... Josh 6:8
but I wholly *f* the LORD my God ... Josh 14:8
hast wholly *f* the LORD my God ... Josh 14:9
wholly *f* the LORD God of Israel ... Josh 14:14
*f* other gods, of the gods of the ... Judg 2:12
and light persons, which *f* him ... Judg 9:4
*f* Abimelech, and put them to the ... Judg 9:49
and all the people *f* him trembling ... 1Sa 13:7
even they also *f* hard after them ... 1Sa 14:22
went and *f* Saul to the battle ... 1Sa 17:13
and the three eldest *f* Saul ... 1Sa 17:14
the Philistines *f* hard upon Saul ... 1Sa 31:2
horsemen *f* hard after him ... 2Sa 1:6
But the house of Judah *f* David ... 2Sa 2:10
And king David himself *f* the bier ... 2Sa 3:31
there *f* him a mess of meat from ... 2Sa 11:8
saw that his counsel was not *f* ... 2Sa 17:23
*f* Sheba the son of Bichri ... 2Sa 20:2
none that *f* the house of David ... 1Kin 12:20
who *f* me with all his heart, to ... 1Kin 14:8
half of the people *f* Tibni the ... 1Kin 16:21
and half *f* Omri ... 1Kin 16:21
But the people that *f* Omri ... 1Kin 16:22
that *f* Tibni the son of Ginath ... 1Kin 16:22
the LORD, and thou hast *f* Baalim ... 1Kin 18:18
city, and the army which *f* them ... 1Kin 20:19
and for the cattle that *f* them ... 2Kin 3:9
And he arose, and *f* her ... 2Kin 4:30
So Gehazi *f* after Naaman ... 2Kin 5:21
Jehu *f* after him, and said, Smite ... 2Kin 9:27
*f* the sins of Jeroboam the son of ... 2Kin 13:2
they *f* vanity, and became vain, and . 2Kin 17:15
the Philistines *f* hard after Saul ... 1Chr 10:2
the men of the guard which *f* me ... Neh 4:23
players on instruments *f* after ... Ps 68:25
whither the head looked they *f* it ... Eze 10:11
the LORD took me as I *f* the flock ... Amos 7:15
left their nets, and *f* him ... Mt 4:20
ship and their father, and *f* him ... Mt 4:22
there *f* him great multitudes of ... Mt 4:25
mountain, great multitudes *f* him ... Mt 8:1
marvelled, and said to them that *f* ... Mt 8:10
into a ship, his disciples *f* him ... Mt 8:23
And he arose, and *f* him ... Mt 9:9
*f* him, and so did his disciples ... Mt 9:19
thence, two blind men *f* him ... Mt 9:27
and great multitudes *f* him ... Mt 12:15
they *f* him on foot out of the ... Mt 14:13
And great multitudes *f* him ... Mt 19:2
we have forsaken all, and *f* thee ... Mt 19:27
unto you, That ye which have *f* me ... Mt 19:28
Jericho, a great multitude *f* him ... Mt 20:29
received sight, and they *f* him ... Mt 20:34
that went before, and that *f* ... Mt 21:9
But Peter *f* him afar off unto the ... Mt 26:58
which *f* Jesus from Galilee, ... Mt 27:55
that *f* the day of the preparation ... Mt 27:62
they forsook their nets, and *f* him ... Mk 1:18
that were with him *f* after him ... Mk 1:36
And he arose and *f* him ... Mk 2:14
there were many, and they *f* him ... Mk 2:15
multitude from Galilee *f* him ... Mk 3:7
and much people *f* him, and thronged ... Mk 5:24
we have left all, and have *f* thee ... Mk 10:28
and as they *f*, they were afraid ... Mk 10:32
his sight, and *f* Jesus in the way ... Mk 10:52
that went before, and they that *f* ... Mk 11:9
there *f* him a certain young man, ... Mk 14:51
Peter *f* him afar off, even into ... Mk 14:54
*f* him, and ministered unto him ... Mk 15:41
land, they forsook all, and *f* him ... Lk 5:11
And he left all, rose up, and *f* him ... Lk 5:28
said unto the people that *f* him ... Lk 7:9
people, when they knew it, *f* him ... Lk 9:11

Lo, we have left all, and *f* thee Lk 18:28
sight, and *f* him, glorifying God Lk 18:43
and his disciples also *f* him Lk 22:39
And Peter *f* afar off Lk 22:54
there *f* him a great company of Lk 23:27
the women that *f* him from Galilee Lk 23:49
*f* after, and beheld the sepulchre, Lk 23:55
heard him speak, and they *f* Jesus Jn 1:37
*f* him, was Andrew, Simon Peter's Jn 1:40
And a great multitude *f* him Jn 6:2
*f* her, saying, She goeth unto the Jn 11:31
And Simon Peter *f* Jesus, and so did Jn 18:15
And he went out, and *f* him Acts 12:9
and religious proselytes *f* Paul Acts 13:43
The same *f* Paul and us, and cried, Acts 16:17
multitude of the people *f* after Acts 21:36
which *f* not after righteousness, Rom 9:30
Israel, which *f* after the law of Rom 9:31
that spiritual Rock that *f* them 1Cor 10:4
have diligently *f* every good work 1Ti 5:10
For we have not *f* cunningly 2Pet 1:16
him was Death, and Hell *f* with him Rev 6:8
angel sounded, and there *f* hail Rev 8:7
there *f* another angel, saying, Rev 14:8
And the third angel *f* them Rev 14:9
in heaven *f* him upon white horses Rev 19:14

## FOLLOWEDST

inasmuch as thou *f* not young men Ruth 3:10

## FOLLOWERS

I beseech you, be ye *f* of me 1Cor 4:16
Be ye *f* of me, even as I also am 1Cor 11:1
Be ye therefore *f* of God, as dear Eph 5:1
be *f* together of me, and mark them Phil 3:17
And ye became *f* of us, and of the 1Th 1:6
became *f* of the churches of God 1Th 2:14
but *f* of them who through faith Heb 6:12
if ye be *f* of that which is good 1Pet 3:13

## FOLLOWETH

him that *f* her kill with the 2Kin 11:15
and whoso *f* her, let him be slain 2Chr 23:14
My soul *f* hard after thee Ps 63:8
but he that *f* vain persons is Prov 12:11
him that *f* after righteousness Prov 15:9
He that *f* after righteousness and Prov 21:21
but he that *f* after vain persons Prov 28:19
loveth gifts, and *f* after rewards Is 1:23
whereas none *f* thee to commit Eze 16:34
on wind, and *f* after the east wind Hos 12:1
*f* after me, is not worthy of me Mt 10:38
in thy name, and he *f* not us Mk 9:38
forbad him, because he *f* not us Mk 9:38
him, because he *f* not with us Lk 9:49
he that *f* me shall not walk in Jn 8:12

## FOLLOWING

land by reason of that famine *f* Gen 41:31
will turn away thy son from *f* me Deut 7:4
that thou be not snared by *f* them Deut 12:30
away this day from *f* the LORD Josh 22:16
away this day from *f* the LORD Josh 22:18
an altar to turn from *f* the LORD Josh 22:23
and turn this day from *f* the LORD Josh 22:29
in *f* other gods to serve them, and Judg 2:19
or to return from *f* after thee Ruth 1:16
you continue *f* the LORD your God 1Sa 12:14
turn not aside from *f* the LORD 1Sa 12:20
went up from *f* the Philistines 1Sa 14:46
for he is turned back from *f* me 1Sa 15:11
returned from *f* the Philistines 1Sa 24:1
hand nor to the left from *f* Abner 2Sa 2:19
not turn aside from *f* of him 2Sa 2:21
Asahel, Turn thee aside from *f* me 2Sa 2:22
return from *f* their brethren 2Sa 2:26
up every one from *f* his brother 2Sa 2:27
And Joab returned from *f* Abner 2Sa 2:30
from *f* the sheep, to be ruler 2Sa 7:8
they *f* Adonijah helped him 1Kin 1:7
if ye shall at all turn from *f* me 1Kin 9:6
he did very abominably in *f* idols 1Kin 21:26
drave Israel from *f* the LORD 2Kin 17:21
LORD, and departed not from *f* him 2Kin 18:6
sheepcote, even from *f* the sheep 1Chr 17:7
*f* the LORD they made a conspiracy 2Chr 25:27
they departed not from *f* the LORD 2Chr 34:33
may tell it to the generation *f* Ps 48:13
From *f* the ewes great with young Ps 78:71
in the generation *f* let their Ps 109:13
confirming the word with signs *f* Mk 16:20
day, and to morrow, and the day *f* Lk 13:33
Then Jesus turned, and saw them *f* Jn 1:38
The day *f* Jesus would go forth Jn 1:43
The day *f*, when the people which Jn 6:22
Then cometh Simon Peter *f* him Jn 20:6
the disciple whom Jesus loved *f* Jn 21:20
the day *f* unto Rhodes, and from Acts 21:1
the day *f* Paul went in with us Acts 21:18
the night *f* the Lord stood by him Acts 23:11
*f* the way of Balaam the son of 2Pet 2:15

## FOLLY

because he had wrought *f* in Gen 34:7
she hath wrought *f* in Israel Deut 22:21
he hath wrought *f* in Israel Josh 7:15
into mine house, do not this *f* Judg 19:23
committed lewdness and *f* in Israel Judg 20:6
according to all the *f* that they Judg 20:10
is his name, and *f* is with him 1Sa 25:25
do not thou this *f* 2Sa 13:12
and his angels he charged with *f* Job 4:18
yet God layeth not *f* to them Job 24:12
lest I deal with you after your *f* Job 42:8
This their way is their *f* Ps 49:13
but let them not turn again to *f* Ps 85:8
of his *f* he shall go astray Prov 5:23
but a fool layeth open his *f* Prov 13:16
but the *f* of fools is deceit Prov 14:8
The simple inherit *f* Prov 14:18
but the foolishness of fools is *f* Prov 14:24
is hasty of spirit exalteth *f* Prov 14:29
*F* is joy to him that is destitute Prov 15:21
but the instruction of fools is *f* Prov 16:22
man, rather than a fool in his *f* Prov 17:12
before he heareth it, it is *f* Prov 18:13
not a fool according to his *f* Prov 26:4
Answer a fool according to his *f* Prov 26:5
so a fool returneth to his *f* Prov 26:11
wisdom, and to know madness and *f* Eccl 1:17
and to lay hold on *f*, till I might Eccl 2:3
behold wisdom, and madness, and *f* Eccl 2:12
I saw that wisdom excelleth *f* Eccl 2:13
and to know the wickedness of *f* Eccl 7:25
so doth a little *f* him that is in Eccl 10:1
*F* is set in great dignity, and the Eccl 10:6
and every mouth speaketh *f* Is 9:17
I have seen *f* in the prophets of Jer 23:13
bear with me a little in my *f* 2Cor 11:1
for their *f* shall be manifest 2Ti 3:9

## FOOD

to the sight, and good for *f* Gen 2:9
saw that the tree was good for *f* Gen 3:6
unto thee of all *f* that is eaten Gen 6:21
and it shall be for *f* for thee Gen 6:21
let them gather all the *f* of Gen 41:35
and let them keep *f* in the cities Gen 41:35
that *f* shall be for store to the Gen 41:36
up all the *f* of the seven years Gen 41:48
laid up the *f* in the cities Gen 41:48
the *f* of the field, which was Gen 41:48
From the land of Canaan to buy *f* Gen 42:7
but to buy *f* are thy servants Gen 42:10
take *f* for the famine of your Gen 42:33
them, Go again, buy us a little *f* Gen 43:2
us, we will go down and buy thee *f* Gen 43:4
down at the first time to buy *f* Gen 43:20
down in our hands to buy *f* Gen 43:22
Fill the men's sacks with *f* Gen 44:1
Go again, and buy us a little *f* Gen 44:25
seed of the field, and for your *f* Gen 47:24
for *f* for your little ones Gen 47:24
her *f*, her raiment, and her duty Ex 21:10
it is the *f* of the offering made Lev 3:11
it is the *f* of the offering made Lev 3:16
planted all manner of trees for *f* Lev 19:23
because it is his *f* Lev 22:7
the stranger, in giving him *f* Deut 10:18
that eateth any *f* until evening 1Sa 14:24
none of the people tasted any *f* 1Sa 14:24
man that eateth any *f* this day 1Sa 14:28
master's son may have *f* to eat 2Sa 9:10
in giving *f* for my household 1Kin 5:9
of wheat for *f* to his household 1Kin 5:11
mouth more than my necessary *f* Job 23:12
wilderness yieldeth *f* for them Job 24:5
Who provideth for the raven his *f* Job 38:41
the mountains bring him forth *f* Job 40:20
Man did eat angels' *f* Ps 78:25
bring forth *f* out of the earth Ps 104:14
Who giveth *f* to all flesh Ps 136:25
which giveth *f* to the hungry Ps 146:7
He giveth to the beast his *f* Ps 147:9
gathereth her *f* in the harvest Prov 6:8
Much *f* is in the tillage of the Prov 13:23
have goats' milk enough for thy *f* Prov 27:27
for the *f* of thy household, and Prov 27:27
sweeping rain which leaveth no *f* Prov 28:3
feed me with *f* convenient for me Prov 30:8
she bringeth her *f* from afar Prov 31:14
have diminished thine ordinary *f* Eze 16:27
*f* unto them that serve the city Eze 48:18
filling our hearts with *f* Acts 14:17
both minister bread for your *f* 2Cor 9:10
And having *f* and raiment let us be 1Ti 6:8
be naked, and destitute of daily *f* Jas 2:15

## FOOL

behold, I have played the *f* 1Sa 26:21
and said, Died Abner as a *f* dieth 2Sa 3:33
The *f* hath said in his heart, Ps 14:1
that wise men die, likewise the *f* Ps 49:10
The *f* hath said in his heart, Ps 53:1
neither doth a *f* understand this Ps 92:6
or as a *f* to the correction of Prov 7:22
but a prating *f* shall fall Prov 10:8
but a prating *f* shall fall Prov 10:10
that uttereth a slander, is a *f* Prov 10:18
is as sport to a *f* to do mischief Prov 10:23
the *f* shall be servant to the Prov 11:29
The way of a *f* is right in his Prov 12:15
but a *f* layeth open his folly Prov 13:16
but the *f* rageth, and is confident Prov 14:16
A *f* despiseth his father's Prov 15:5
Excellent speech becometh not a *f* Prov 17:7
than an hundred stripes into a *f* Prov 17:10
man, rather than a *f* in his folly Prov 17:12
in the hand of a *f* to get wisdom Prov 17:16
He that begetteth a *f* doeth it to Prov 17:21
and the father of a *f* hath no joy Prov 17:21
but the eyes of a *f* are in the Prov 17:24
Even a *f*, when he holdeth his Prov 17:28
A *f* hath no delight in Prov 18:2
perverse in his lips, and is a *f* Prov 19:1
Delight is not seemly for a *f* Prov 19:10
but every *f* will be meddling Prov 20:3
Speak not in the ears of a *f* Prov 23:9
Wisdom is too high for a *f* Prov 24:7
so honour is not seemly for a *f* Prov 26:1
Answer not a *f* according to his Prov 26:4
Answer a *f* according to his folly Prov 26:5
hand of a *f* cutteth off the feet Prov 26:6
is he that giveth honour to a *f* Prov 26:8
all things both rewardeth the *f* Prov 26:10
so a *f* returneth to his folly Prov 26:11
is more hope of a *f* than of him Prov 26:12
Though thou shouldest bray a *f* in Prov 27:22
trusteth in his own heart is a *f* Prov 28:26
A *f* uttereth all his mind Prov 29:11
is more hope of a *f* than of him Prov 29:20
a *f* when he is filled with meat Prov 30:22
but the *f* walketh in darkness Eccl 2:14
heart, As it happeneth to the *f* Eccl 2:15
wise more than of the *f* for ever Eccl 2:16
the wise man? as the *f* Eccl 2:16
he shall be a wise man or a *f* Eccl 2:19
The *f* foldeth his hands together, Eccl 4:5
hath the wise more than the *f* Eccl 6:8
pot, so is the laughter of the *f* Eccl 7:6
when he that is a *f* walketh by Eccl 10:3
saith to every one that he is a *f* Eccl 10:3
but the lips of a *f* will swallow Eccl 10:12
A *f* also is full of words Eccl 10:14
days, and at his end shall be a *f* Jer 17:11
the prophet is a *f*, the spiritual Hos 9:7
but whosoever shall say, Thou *f* Mt 5:22
But God said unto him, Thou *f* Lk 12:20
in this world, let him become a *f* 1Cor 3:18
Thou *f*, that which thou sowest is 1Cor 15:36
again, Let no man think me a *f* 2Cor 11:16
yet as a *f* receive me, that I may 2Cor 11:16
(I speak as a *f*) I am more 2Cor 11:23
to glory, I shall not be a *f* 2Cor 12:6
I am become a *f* in glorying 2Cor 12:11

## FOOLISH

the LORD, O *f* people and unwise Deut 32:6
them to anger with a *f* nation Deut 32:21
as one of the *f* women speaketh Job 2:10
For wrath killeth the *f* man Job 5:2
I have seen the *f* taking root Job 5:3
The *f* shall not stand in thy Ps 5:5
make me not the reproach of the *f* Ps 39:8
For I was envious at the *f* Ps 73:3
So *f* was I, and ignorant Ps 73:22
that the *f* people have blasphemed Ps 74:18
remember how the *f* man Ps 74:22
Forsake the *f*, and live Prov 9:6
A *f* woman is clamorous Prov 9:13
but a *f* son is the heaviness of Prov 10:1
of the *f* is near destruction Prov 10:14
but the *f* plucketh it down with Prov 14:1
mouth of the *f* is a rod of pride Prov 14:3
Go from the presence of a *f* man Prov 14:7
the heart of the *f* doeth not so Prov 15:7
but a *f* man despiseth his mother Prov 15:20
A *f* son is a grief to his father, Prov 17:25
A *f* son is the calamity of his Prov 19:13
but a *f* man spendeth it up Prov 21:20
wise man contendeth with a *f* man Prov 29:9
*f* king, who will no more be Eccl 4:13
much wicked, neither be thou *f* Eccl 7:17
The labour of the *f* wearieth Eccl 10:15
and maketh their knowledge *f* Is 44:25
For my people is *f*, they have not Jer 4:22
these are poor; they are *f* Jer 5:4
now this, O *f* people, and without Jer 5:21
they are altogether brutish and *f* Jer 10:8
seen vain and *f* things for thee Lam 2:14
Woe unto the *f* prophets, that Eze 13:3
the instruments of a *f* shepherd Zec 11:15
shall be likened unto a *f* man Mt 7:26
of them were wise, and five were *f* Mt 25:2
They that were *f* took their lamps Mt 25:3
the *f* said unto the wise, Give us Mt 25:8
their *f* heart was darkened Rom 1:21
An instructor of the *f*, a teacher Rom 2:20
by a *f* nation I will anger you Rom 10:19
hath not God made *f* the wisdom of 1Cor 1:20
But God hath chosen the *f* things 1Cor 1:27
O *f* Galatians, who hath bewitched Gal 3:1
Are ye so *f*? Gal 3:3
nor *f* talking, nor jesting, which Eph 5:4
and a snare, and into many *f* 1Ti 6:9
But *f* and unlearned questions 2Ti 2:23
ourselves also were sometimes *f* Titus 3:3
But avoid *f* questions, and Titus 3:9
to silence the ignorance of *f* men 1Pet 2:15

## FOOLISHLY

thou hast now done *f* in so doing Gen 31:28
upon us, wherein we have done *f* Num 12:11
said to Saul, Thou hast done *f* 1Sa 13:13
for I have done very *f* 2Sa 24:10
for I have done very *f* 1Chr 21:8
Herein thou hast done *f* 2Chr 16:9
Job sinned not, nor charged God *f* Job 1:22
I said unto the fools, Deal not *f* Ps 75:4
He that is soon angry dealeth *f* Prov 14:17
If thou hast done *f* in lifting up Prov 30:32
after the Lord, but as it were *f* 2Cor 11:17
any is bold, (I speak *f*,) I am 2Cor 11:21

## FOOLISHNESS

the counsel of Ahithophel into *f* 2Sa 15:31
and are corrupt because of my *f* Ps 38:5

O God, thou knowest my *f* Ps 69:5
the heart of fools proclaimeth *f* Prov 12:23
but the *f* of fools is folly Prov 14:24
the mouth of fools poureth out *f* Prov 15:2
the mouth of fools feedeth on *f* Prov 15:14
The *f* of man perverteth his way Prov 19:3
*F* is bound in the heart of a Prov 22:15
The thought of *f* is sin Prov 24:9
will not his *f* depart from him Prov 27:22
wickedness of folly, even of *f* Eccl 7:25
of the words of his mouth is *f* Eccl 10:13
an evil eye, blasphemy, pride, *f* Mk 7:22
cross is to them that perish *f* 1Cor 1:18
it pleased God by the *f* of 1Cor 1:21
and unto the Greeks *f* 1Cor 1:23
Because the *f* of God is wiser 1Cor 1:25
for they are *f* unto him 1Cor 2:14
of this world is *f* with God 1Cor 3:19

**FOOL'S**
A *f* wrath is presently known Prov 12:16
A *f* lips enter into contention, Prov 18:6
A *f* mouth is his destruction, and Prov 18:7
the ass, and a rod for the *f* back Prov 26:3
but a *f* wrath is heavier than Prov 27:3
a *f* voice is known by multitude Eccl 5:3
but a *f* heart at his left Eccl 10:2

**FOOLS**
be as one of the *f* in Israel 2Sa 13:13
spoiled, and maketh the judges *f* Job 12:17
They were children of *f*, yea, Job 30:8
I said unto the *f*, Deal not Ps 75:4
and ye *f*, when will ye be wise Ps 94:8
*F*, because of their transgression Ps 107:17
but *f* despise wisdom and Prov 1:7
scorning, and *f* hate knowledge Prov 1:22
the prosperity of *f* shall destroy Prov 1:32
shame shall be the promotion of *f* Prov 3:35
and, ye *f*, be ye of an Prov 8:5
but *f* die for want of wisdom Prov 10:21
but the heart of *f* proclaimeth Prov 12:23
to *f* to depart from evil Prov 13:19
companion of *f* shall be destroyed Prov 13:20
but the folly of *f* is deceit Prov 14:8
*F* make a mock at sin Prov 14:9
but the foolishness of *f* is folly Prov 14:24
in the midst of *f* is made known Prov 14:33
but the mouth of *f* poureth out Prov 15:2
but the mouth of *f* feedeth on Prov 15:14
but the instruction of *f* is folly Prov 16:22
and stripes for the back of *f* Prov 19:29
so is a parable in the mouth of *f* Prov 26:7
so is a parable in the mouth of *f* Prov 26:9
than to give the sacrifice of *f* Eccl 5:1
for he hath no pleasure in *f* Eccl 5:4
but the heart of *f* is in the Eccl 7:4
for a man to hear the song of *f* Eccl 7:5
anger resteth in the bosom of *f* Eccl 7:9
cry of him that ruleth among *f* Eccl 9:17
Surely the princes of Zoan are *f* Is 19:11
The princes of Zoan are become *f* Is 19:13
the wayfaring men, though *f* Is 35:8
Ye *f* and blind Mt 23:17
Ye *f* and blind Mt 23:19
Ye *f*, did not he that made that Lk 11:40
Then he said unto them, O *f* Lk 24:25
to be wise, they became *f* Rom 1:22
We are *f* for Christ's sake, but 1Cor 4:10
For ye suffer *f* gladly, seeing ye 2Cor 11:19
ye walk circumspectly, not as *f* Eph 5:15

**FOOT**
no rest for the sole of her *f* Gen 8:9
or *f* in all the land of Egypt Gen 41:44
thousand on *f* that were men Ex 12:37
tooth, hand for hand, *f* for *f*, Ex 21:24
the great toe of their right *f* Ex 29:20
his *f* also of brass, to wash Ex 30:18
vessels, and the laver and his *f* Ex 30:28
furniture, and the laver and his *f* Ex 31:9
his vessels, the laver and his *f* Ex 35:16
the *f* of it of brass, of the Ex 38:8
his vessels, the laver and his *f* Ex 39:39
shalt anoint the laver and his *f* Ex 40:11
vessels, both the laver and his *f* Lev 8:11
upon the great toe of his right *f* Lev 8:23
from his head even to his *f* Lev 13:12
upon the great toe of his right *f* Lev 14:14
upon the great toe of his right *f* Lev 14:17
upon the great toe of his right *f* Lev 14:25
upon the great toe of his right *f* Lev 14:28
Balaam's *f* against the wall Num 22:25
thee, neither did thy *f* swell Deut 8:4
seed, and wateredst it with thy *f* Deut 11:10
tooth, hand for hand, *f* for *f* Deut 19:21
and loose his shoe from off his *f* Deut 25:9
from the sole of thy *f* unto the Deut 28:35
sole of her *f* upon the ground for Deut 28:56
shall the sole of thy *f* have rest Deut 28:65
shoe is not waxen old upon thy *f* Deut 29:5
their *f* shall slide in due time Deut 32:35
and let him dip his *f* in oil Deut 33:24
sole of your *f* shall tread upon Josh 1:3
Loose thy shoe from off thy *f* Josh 5:15
he was sent on *f* into the valley Judg 5:15
was as light of *f* as a wild roe 2Sa 2:18
from the sole of his *f* even to 2Sa 14:25
fingers, and on every *f* six toes 2Sa 21:20
and he trode her under *f* 2Kin 9:33
on each hand, and six on each *f* 1Chr 20:6
will I any more remove the *f* of 2Chr 33:8
the sole of his *f* unto his crown Job 2:7
My *f* hath held his steps, his way Job 23:11
the waters forgotten of the *f* Job 28:4
or if my *f* hath hasted to deceit Job 31:5
that the *f* may crush them Job 39:15
they hid is their own *f* taken Ps 9:15
My *f* standeth in an even place Ps 26:12
Let not the *f* of pride come Ps 36:11
when my *f* slippeth, they magnify Ps 38:16
they went through the flood on *f* Ps 66:6
That thy *f* may be dipped in the Ps 68:23
thou dash thy *f* against a stone Ps 91:12
When I said, My *f* slippeth Ps 94:18
will not suffer thy *f* to be moved Ps 121:3
refrain thy *f* from their path Prov 1:15
and thy *f* shall not stumble Prov 3:23
shall keep thy *f* from being taken Prov 3:26
remove thy *f* from evil Prov 4:27
Withdraw thy *f* from thy Prov 25:17
broken tooth, and a *f* out of joint Prov 25:19
Keep thy *f* when thou goest to the Eccl 5:1
From the sole of the *f* even unto Is 1:6
my mountains tread him under *f* Is 14:25
meted out and trodden under *f* Is 18:7
and put off thy shoe from thy *f* Is 20:2
The *f* shall tread it down, even Is 26:6
the east, called him to his *f* Is 41:2
turn away thy *f* from the sabbath Is 58:13
Withhold thy *f* from being unshod, Jer 2:25
have trodden my portion under *f* Jer 12:10
The Lord hath trodden under *f* all Lam 1:15
was like the sole of a calf's *f* Eze 1:7
thine hand, and stamp with thy *f* Eze 6:11
No *f* of man shall pass through it Eze 29:11
nor *f* of beast shall pass through Eze 29:11
neither shall the *f* of man Eze 32:13
and the host to be trodden under *f* Dan 8:13
he that is swift of *f* shall not Amos 2:15
thou dash thy *f* against a stone Mt 4:6
and to be trodden under *f* of men Mt 5:13
him on *f* out of the cities Mt 14:13
if thy hand or thy *f* offend thee Mt 18:8
the servants, Bind him hand and *f* Mt 22:13
if thy *f* offend thee, cut it off Mk 9:45
thou dash thy *f* against a stone Lk 4:11
bound hand and *f* with graveclothes Jn 11:44
not so much as to set his *f* on Acts 7:5
If the *f* shall say, Because I am 1Cor 12:15
trodden under *f* the Son of God Heb 10:29
with a garment down to the *f* Rev 1:13
he set his right *f* upon the sea Rev 10:2
and his left *f* on the earth Rev 10:2
shall they tread under *f* forty Rev 11:2

**FOOTBREADTH**
land, no, not so much as a *f* Deut 2:5

**FOOTMEN**
I am, are six hundred thousand *f* Num 11:21
thousand *f* that drew sword Judg 20:2
fell of Israel thirty thousand *f* 1Sa 4:10
in Telaim, two hundred thousand *f* 1Sa 15:4
unto the *f* that stood about him 1Sa 22:17
horsemen, and twenty thousand *f* 2Sa 8:4
of Zoba, twenty thousand *f* 2Sa 10:6
an hundred thousand *f* in one day 1Kin 20:29
ten chariots, and ten thousand *f* 2Kin 13:7
horsemen, and twenty thousand *f* 1Chr 18:4
in chariots, and forty thousand *f* 1Chr 19:18
If thou hast run with the *f* Jer 12:5

**FOOTSTEPS**
in thy paths, that my *f* slip not Ps 17:5
waters, and thy *f* are not known Ps 77:19
the *f* of thine anointed Ps 89:51
way forth by the *f* of the flock Song 1:8

**FOOTSTOOL**
for the *f* of our God, and had made 1Chr 28:2
with a *f* of gold, which were 2Chr 9:18
LORD our God, and worship at his *f* Ps 99:5
until I make thine enemies thy *f* Ps 110:1
we will worship at his *f* Ps 132:7
my throne, and the earth is my *f* Is 66:1
remembered not his *f* in the day Lam 2:1
for it is his *f* Mt 5:35
till I make thine enemies thy *f* Mt 22:44
till I make thine enemies thy *f* Mk 12:36
Till I make thine enemies thy *f* Lk 20:43
Until I make thy foes thy *f* Acts 2:35
is my throne, and earth is my *f* Acts 7:49
until I make thine enemies thy *f* Heb 1:13
till his enemies be made his *f* Heb 10:13
there, or sit here under my *f* Jas 2:3

**FOR** See PREFACE.

**FORASMUCH**
*F* as God hath shewed thee all Gen 41:39
*f* as thou knowest how we are to Num 10:31
*f* as he hath no part nor Deut 12:12
*f* as the LORD hath said unto you, Deut 17:16
*f* as the LORD hath blessed me Josh 17:14
*f* as the LORD hath taken Judg 11:36
*f* as we have sworn both of us in 1Sa 20:42
*f* as when the LORD had delivered 1Sa 24:18
*f* as my lord the king is come 2Sa 19:30
*F* as this is done of thee, and 1Kin 11:11
*F* as thou hast disobeyed the 1Kin 13:21
*F* as I exalted thee from among 1Kin 14:7
*F* as I exalted thee out of the 1Kin 16:2
*F* as thou hast sent messengers to 2Kin 1:16
*f* as he defiled his father's bed, 1Chr 5:1
*F* as it was in thine heart to 2Chr 6:8
*F* as thou art sent of the king, Ezr 7:14
*F* as this people refuseth the Is 8:6
*F* as this people draw near me Is 29:13
*F* as there is none like unto thee Jer 10:6
*f* as among all the wise men of Jer 10:7
*f* as iron breaketh in pieces and Dan 2:40
*f* as thou sawest the iron mixed Dan 2:41
*F* as thou sawest that the stone Dan 2:45
*f* as all the wise men of my Dan 4:18
*F* as an excellent spirit, and Dan 5:12
*f* as he was faithful, neither was Dan 6:4
*f* as before him innocency was Dan 6:22
*F* therefore as your treading is Amos 5:11
But *f* as he had not to pay, his Mt 18:25
*F* as many have taken in hand to Lk 1:1
*f* as Lydda was nigh to Joppa, and Acts 9:38
*F* then as God gave them the like Acts 11:17
*F* as we have heard, that certain Acts 15:24
*F* then as we are the offspring of Acts 17:29
*F* as I know that thou hast been Acts 24:10
*f* as he is the image and glory of 1Cor 11:7
*f* as ye are zealous of spiritual 1Cor 14:12
*f* as ye know that your labour is 1Cor 15:58
*f* as ye are manifestly declared 2Cor 3:3
*F* then as the children are Heb 2:14
*F* as ye know that ye were not 1Pet 1:18
*F* then as Christ hath suffered 1Pet 4:1

**FORBAD**
whatsoever the LORD our God *f* us Deut 2:37
But John *f* him, saying, I have Mt 3:14
we *f* him, because he followeth Mk 9:38
we *f* him, because he followeth Lk 9:49
*f* the madness of the prophet 2Pet 2:16

**FORBARE**
and he *f* to go forth 1Sa 23:13
Then the prophet *f*, and said, I 2Chr 25:16
So he *f*, and slew them not among Jer 41:8

**FORBEAR**
wouldest *f* to help him, thou Ex 23:5
But if thou shalt *f* to vow Deut 23:22
to battle, or shall I *f* 1Kin 22:6
to battle, or shall we *f* 1Kin 22:15
to battle, or shall I *f* 2Chr 18:5
to battle, or shall I *f* 2Chr 18:14
*f*; why shouldest thou be smitten 2Chr 25:16
*f* thee from meddling with God, 2Chr 35:21
Yet many years didst thou *f* them Neh 9:30
and though I *f*, what am I eased Job 16:6
If thou *f* to deliver them that Prov 24:11
to come with me into Babylon, *f* Jer 40:4
will hear, or whether they will *f* Eze 2:5
will hear, or whether they will *f* Eze 2:7
will hear, or whether they will *f* Eze 3:11
and he that forbeareth, let him *f* Eze 3:27
*F* to cry, make no mourning for Eze 24:17
my price; and if not, *f* Zec 11:12
have not we power to *f* working 1Cor 9:6
but now I *f*, lest any man should 2Cor 12:6
when we could no longer *f* 1Th 3:1
cause, when I could no longer *f* 1Th 3:5

**FORBEARANCE**
the riches of his goodness and *f* Rom 2:4
are past, through the *f* of God Rom 3:25

**FORBEARETH**
*f* to keep the passover, even the Num 9:13
and he that *f*, let him forbear Eze 3:27

**FORBEARING**
By long *f* is a prince persuaded, Prov 25:15
my bones, and I was weary with *f* Jer 20:9
*f* one another in love Eph 4:2
things unto them, *f* threatening Eph 6:9
*F* one another, and forgiving one Col 3:13

**FORBID**
God *f* that thy servants should do Gen 44:7
God *f* that I should do so Gen 44:17
and said, My lord Moses, *f* them Num 11:28
God *f* that we should rebel Josh 22:29
God *f* that we should forsake the Josh 24:16
God *f* that I should sin against 1Sa 12:23
God *f*: as the LORD liveth 1Sa 14:45
And he said unto him, God *f* 1Sa 20:2
The LORD *f* that I should do this 1Sa 24:6
The LORD *f* that I should stretch 1Sa 26:11
said to Ahab, The LORD *f* it me 1Kin 21:3
And said, My God *f* it me, that I 1Chr 11:19
God *f* that I should justify you Job 27:5
*f* them not, to come unto me Mt 19:14
But Jesus said, *F* him not Mk 9:39
to come unto me, and *f* them not Mk 10:14
cloke *f* not to take thy coat also Lk 6:29
And Jesus said unto him, *F* him not Lk 9:50
to come unto me, and *f* them not Lk 18:16
they heard it, they said, God *f* Lk 20:16
Can any man *f* water, that these Acts 10:47
that he should *f* none of his Acts 24:23
God *f*: yea, let God be true Rom 3:4
God *f*: for then how shall God Rom 3:6
God *f*: yea, we establish the law Rom 3:31
God *f*. How shall we Rom 6:2
but under grace? God *f* Rom 6:15
Is the law sin? God *f* Rom 7:7
good made death unto me? God *f* Rom 7:13
unrighteousness with God? God *f* Rom 9:14
God cast away his people? God *f* Rom 11:1
that they should fall? God *f* Rom 11:11

- members of an harlot? God *f* 1Cor 6:15
- *f* not to speak with tongues 1Cor 14:39
- the minister of sin? God *f* Gal 2:17
- the promises of God? God *f* Gal 3:21
- But God *f* that I should glory, Gal 6:14

### FORBIDDEN
- any of these things which are *f* Lev 5:17
- the LORD thy God hath *f* thee Deut 4:23
- were *f* of the Holy Ghost to Acts 16:6

### FORBIDDETH
- *f* them that would, and casteth 3Jn 10

### FORBIDDING
- *f* to give tribute to Caesar, Lk 23:2
- with all confidence, no man *f* him Acts 28:31
- *F* us to speak to the Gentiles 1Th 2:16
- *F* to marry, and commanding to 1Ti 4:3

### FORBORN
- men of Babylon have *f* to fight Jer 51:30

### FORCE
- take by *f* thy daughters from me Gen 31:31
- in the field, and the man *f* her Deut 22:25
- not dim, nor his natural *f* abated Deut 34:7
- and if not, I will take it by *f* 1Sa 2:16
- him, Nay, my brother, do not *f* me 2Sa 13:12
- Jews, and made them to cease by *f* Ezr 4:23
- Will he *f* the queen also before Est 7:8
- By the great *f* of my disease is Job 30:18
- his *f* is in the navel of his Job 40:16
- their blood by the *f* of the sword Jer 18:21
- is evil, and their *f* is not right Jer 23:10
- of Heshbon because of the *f* Jer 48:45
- but with *f* and with cruelty have Eze 34:4
- the *f* of the sword in the time of Eze 35:5
- strong shall not strengthen his *f* Amos 2:14
- and the violent take it by *f* Mt 11:12
- they would come and take him by *f* Jn 6:15
- to take him by *f* from among them, Acts 23:10
- is of *f* after men are dead Heb 9:17

### FORCED
- the Amorites *f* the children of Judg 1:34
- and my concubine have they *f* Judg 20:5
- I *f* myself therefore, and offered 1Sa 13:12
- than she, *f* her, and lay with her 2Sa 13:14
- because he had *f* his sister Tamar 2Sa 13:22
- day that he *f* his sister Tamar 2Sa 13:32
- flattering of her lips she *f* him Prov 7:21

### FORCES
- he placed *f* in all the fenced 2Chr 17:2
- gold, nor all the *f* of strength Job 36:19
- the *f* of the Gentiles shall come Is 60:5
- unto thee the *f* of the Gentiles Is 60:11
- of the *f* which were in the fields Jer 40:7
- of the *f* that were in the fields Jer 40:13
- of the *f* that were with him Jer 41:11
- of the *f* that were with him Jer 41:13
- of the *f* that were with him Jer 41:16
- Then all the captains of the *f* Jer 42:1
- of the *f* which were with him Jer 42:8
- and all the captains of the *f* Jer 43:4
- and all the captains of the *f* Jer 43:5
- assemble a multitude of great *f* Dan 11:10
- shall he honour the God of *f* Dan 11:38
- carried away captive his *f* Obad 11

### FORCIBLE
- How *f* are right words Job 6:25

### FORCING
- thereof by *f* an ax against them Deut 20:19
- so the *f* of wrath bringeth forth Prov 30:33

### FORD
- sons, and passed over the *f* Jabbok Gen 32:22

### FORDS
- them the way to Jordan unto the *f* Josh 2:7
- took the *f* of Jordan toward Moab, Judg 3:28
- Moab shall be at the *f* of Arnon Is 16:2

### FORECAST
- he shall *f* his devices against Dan 11:24
- for they shall *f* devices against Dan 11:25

### FOREFATHERS
- back to the iniquities of their *f* Jer 11:10
- from my *f* with pure conscience 2Ti 1:3

### FOREFRONT
- in the *f* of the tabernacle Ex 26:9
- upon the *f* of the mitre it shall Ex 28:37
- upon the mitre, even upon his *f* Lev 8:9
- The *f* of the one was situate 1Sa 14:5
- Set ye Uriah in the *f* of the 2Sa 11:15
- from the *f* of the house, from 2Kin 16:14
- and Jehoshaphat in the *f* of them 2Chr 20:27
- the *f* of the lower gate unto the Eze 40:19
- the *f* of the inner court without Eze 40:19
- for the *f* of the house stood Eze 47:1

### FOREHEAD
- And it shall be upon Aaron's *f* Ex 28:38
- and it shall be always upon his *f* Ex 28:38
- toward his face, he is *f* bald Lev 13:41
- be in the bald head, or bald *f* Lev 13:42
- in his bald head, or his bald *f* Lev 13:42
- his bald head, or in his bald *f* Lev 13:43
- and smote the Philistine in his *f* 1Sa 17:49
- that the stone sunk into his *f* 1Sa 17:49
- *f* before the priests in the house 2Chr 26:19
- behold, he was leprous in his *f* 2Chr 26:20
- and thou hadst a whore's *f* Jer 3:3
- thy *f* strong against their Eze 3:8
- than flint have I made thy *f* Eze 3:9
- And I put a jewel on thy *f* Eze 16:12
- and receive his mark in his *f* Rev 14:9
- upon her *f* was a name written, Rev 17:5

### FOREHEADS
- forehead strong against their *f* Eze 3:8
- set a mark upon the *f* of the men Eze 9:4
- servants of our God in their *f* Rev 7:3
- not the seal of God in their *f* Rev 9:4
- their right hand, or in their *f* Rev 13:16
- Father's name written in their *f* Rev 14:1
- received his mark upon their *f* Rev 20:4
- and his name shall be in their *f* Rev 22:4

### FOREIGNER
- A *f* and an hired servant shall not Ex 12:45
- Of a *f* thou mayest exact it again Deut 15:3

### FOREIGNERS
- *f* entered into his gates, and cast Obad 11
- ye are no more strangers and *f* Eph 2:19

### FOREKNEW
- cast away his people which he *f* Rom 11:2

### FOREKNOW
- For whom he did *f*, he also did Rom 8:29

### FOREKNOWLEDGE
- *f* of God, ye have taken, and by Acts 2:23
- to the *f* of God the Father 1Pet 1:2

### FOREMOST
- And he commanded the *f*, saying, Gen 32:17
- the handmaids and their children *f* Gen 33:2
- *f* is like the running of Ahimaaz 2Sa 18:27

### FOREORDAINED
- Who verily was *f* before the 1Pet 1:20

### FOREPART
- underneath, toward the *f* thereof Ex 28:27
- underneath, toward the *f* of it Ex 39:20
- the oracle in the *f* was twenty 1Kin 6:20
- court on the *f* of the chambers Eze 42:7
- the *f* stuck fast, and remained Acts 27:41

### FORERUNNER
- Whither the *f* is for us entered, Heb 6:20

### FORESAW
- I *f* the Lord always before my Acts 2:25

### FORESEEING
- *f* that God would justify the Gal 3:8

### FORESEETH
- A prudent man *f* the evil, and Prov 22:3
- A prudent man *f* the evil, and Prov 27:12

### FORESHIP
- have cast anchors out of the *f* Acts 27:30

### FORESKIN
- circumcise the flesh of your *f* Gen 17:11
- flesh of his *f* is not circumcised Gen 17:14
- of their *f* in the selfsame day Gen 17:23
- circumcised in the flesh of his *f* Gen 17:24
- circumcised in the flesh of his *f* Gen 17:25
- and cut off the *f* of her son Ex 4:25
- of his *f* shall be circumcised Lev 12:3
- therefore the *f* of your heart Deut 10:16
- also, and let thy *f* be uncovered Hab 2:16

### FORESKINS
- of Israel at the hill of the *f* Josh 5:3
- dowry, but an hundred *f* of the 1Sa 18:25
- and David brought their *f*, and they 1Sa 18:27
- an hundred *f* of the Philistines 2Sa 3:14
- and take away the *f* of your heart Jer 4:4

### FOREST
- and came into the *f* of Hareth 1Sa 22:5
- the house of the *f* of Lebanon 1Kin 7:2
- in the house of the *f* of Lebanon 1Kin 10:17
- *f* of Lebanon were of pure gold 1Kin 10:21
- and into the *f* of his Carmel 2Kin 19:23
- in the house of the *f* of Lebanon 2Chr 9:16
- *f* of Lebanon were of pure gold 2Chr 9:20
- Asaph the keeper of the king's *f* Neh 2:8
- For every beast of the *f* is mine Ps 50:10
- beasts of the *f* do creep forth Ps 104:20
- kindle in the thickets of the *f* Is 9:18
- shall consume the glory of his *f* Is 10:18
- the trees of his *f* shall be few Is 10:19
- the thickets of the *f* with iron Is 10:34
- In the *f* in Arabia shall ye lodge Is 21:13
- the armour of the house of the *f* Is 22:8
- field shall be esteemed as a *f* Is 29:17
- fruitful field be counted for a *f* Is 32:15
- shall hail, coming down on the *f* Is 32:19
- border, and the *f* of his Carmel Is 37:24
- himself among the trees of the *f* Is 44:14
- into singing, ye mountains, O *f* Is 44:23
- yea, all ye beasts in the *f* Is 56:9
- lion out of the *f* shall slay them Jer 5:6
- one cutteth a tree out of the *f* Jer 10:3
- is unto me as a lion in the *f* Jer 12:8
- kindle a fire in the *f* thereof Jer 21:14
- house as the high places of a *f* Jer 26:18
- They shall cut down her *f* Jer 46:23
- which is among the trees of the *f* Eze 15:2
- tree among the trees of the *f* Eze 15:6
- against the *f* of the south field Eze 20:46
- say to the *f* of the south, Hear Eze 20:47
- and I will make them a *f*, and the Hos 2:12
- Will a lion roar in the *f* Amos 3:4
- house as the high places of the *f* Mic 3:12
- a lion among the beasts of the *f* Mic 5:8
- for the *f* of the vintage is come Zec 11:2

### FORESTS
- in the *f* he built castles and 2Chr 27:4
- to calve, and discovereth the *f* Ps 29:9
- neither cut down any out of the *f* Eze 39:10

### FORETELL
- *f* you, as if I were present, the 2Cor 13:2

### FORETOLD
- behold, I have *f* you all things Mk 13:23
- have likewise *f* of these days Acts 3:24

### FOREWARN
- But I will *f* you whom ye shall Lk 12:5

### FOREWARNED
- all such, as we also have *f* you 1Th 4:6

### FORFEITED
- all his substance should be *f* Ezr 10:8

### FORGAT
- butler remember Joseph, but *f* him Gen 40:23
- *f* the LORD their God, and served Judg 3:7
- when they *f* the LORD their God, 1Sa 12:9
- *f* his works, and his wonders that Ps 78:11
- They soon *f* his works Ps 106:13
- They *f* God their saviour, which Ps 106:21
- I *f* prosperity Lam 3:17
- lovers, and *f* me, saith the LORD Hos 2:13

### FORGAVE
- *f* their iniquity, and destroyed Ps 78:38
- and loosed him, and *f* him the debt Mt 18:27
- I *f* thee all that debt, because Mt 18:32
- to pay, he frankly *f* them both Lk 7:42
- that he, to whom he *f* most Lk 7:43
- *f* any thing, to whom I *f* it 2Cor 2:10
- for your sakes *f* I it in the 2Cor 2:10
- even as Christ *f* you, so also do Col 3:13

### FORGAVEST
- thou *f* the iniquity of my sin Ps 32:5
- thou wast a God that *f* them Ps 99:8

### FORGED
- The proud have *f* a lie against me Ps 119:69

### FORGERS
- But ye are *f* of lies, ye are all Job 13:4

### FORGET
- he *f* that which thou hast done to Gen 27:45
- he, hath made me *f* all my toil Gen 41:51
- lest thou *f* the things which Deut 4:9
- lest ye *f* the covenant of the Deut 4:23
- nor *f* the covenant of thy fathers Deut 4:31
- Then beware lest thou *f* the LORD Deut 6:12
- Beware that thou *f* not the LORD Deut 8:11
- thou *f* the LORD thy God, which Deut 8:14
- thou do at all *f* the LORD thy God Deut 8:19
- *f* not, how thou provokedst the Deut 9:7
- thou shalt not *f* it Deut 25:19
- not *f* thine handmaid, but wilt 1Sa 1:11
- have made with you ye shall not *f* 2Kin 17:38
- are the paths of all that *f* God Job 8:13
- I will *f* my complaint, I will Job 9:27
- Because thou shalt *f* thy misery Job 11:16
- The womb shall *f* him Job 24:20
- and all the nations that *f* God Ps 9:17
- *f* not the humble Ps 10:12
- How long wilt thou *f* me, O LORD Ps 13:1
- *f* also thine own people, and thy Ps 45:10
- Now consider this, ye that *f* God Ps 50:22
- Slay them not, lest my people *f* Ps 59:11
- *f* not the congregation of thy Ps 74:19
- *F* not the voice of thine enemies Ps 74:23
- not *f* the works of God, but keep Ps 78:7
- so that I *f* to eat my bread Ps 102:4
- soul, and *f* not all his benefits Ps 103:2
- I will not *f* thy word Ps 119:16
- yet do I not *f* thy statutes Ps 119:83
- I will never *f* thy precepts Ps 119:93
- yet do I not *f* thy law Ps 119:109
- yet do not I *f* thy precepts Ps 119:141
- for I do not *f* thy law Ps 119:153
- for I do not *f* thy commandments Ps 119:176
- If I *f* thee, O Jerusalem Ps 137:5
- let my right hand *f* her cunning Ps 137:5
- My son, *f* not my law Prov 3:1
- get understanding: *f* it not Prov 4:5
- *f* the law, and pervert the Prov 31:5
- *f* his poverty, and remember his Prov 31:7
- Can a woman *f* her sucking child, Is 49:15
- yea, they may *f*, yet will I not Is 49:15
- may *f*, yet will I not *f* thee Is 49:15
- for thou shalt *f* the shame of thy Is 54:4
- that *f* my holy mountain, that Is 65:11
- Can a maid *f* her ornaments, or a Jer 2:32
- think to cause my people to *f* my Jer 23:27
- I, even I, will utterly *f* you Jer 23:39
- Wherefore dost thou *f* us for ever Lam 5:20
- I will also *f* thy children Hos 4:6
- I will never *f* any of their works Amos 8:7
- is not unrighteous to *f* your work Heb 6:10
- do good and to communicate *f* not Heb 13:16

### FORGETFUL
- Be not *f* to entertain strangers Heb 13:2
- therein, he being not a *f* hearer Jas 1:25

### FORGETFULNESS
righteousness in the land of *f* ... Ps 88:12

### FORGETTEST
face, and *f* our affliction and our ... Ps 44:24
*f* the LORD thy maker, that hath ... Is 51:13

### FORGETTETH
*f* that the foot may crush them, ... Job 39:15
he *f* not the cry of the humble ... Ps 9:12
*f* the covenant of her God ... Prov 2:17
straightway *f* what manner of man ... Jas 1:24

### FORGETTING
*f* those things which are behind, ... Phil 3:13

### FORGIVE
So shall ye say unto Joseph, *F* ... Gen 50:17
*f* the trespass of the servants of ... Gen 50:17
Now therefore *f*, I pray thee, my ... Ex 10:17
Yet now, if thou wilt *f* their sin ... Ex 32:32
and the LORD shall *f* her, because ... Num 30:5
and the LORD shall *f* her ... Num 30:8
and the LORD shall *f* her ... Num 30:12
he will not *f* your transgressions ... Josh 24:19
*f* the trespass of thine handmaid ... 1Sa 25:28
and when thou hearest, *f* ... 1Kin 8:30
*f* the sin of thy people Israel, ... 1Kin 8:34
*f* the sin of thy servants, and of ... 1Kin 8:36
heaven thy dwelling place, and *f* ... 1Kin 8:39
*f* thy people that have sinned ... 1Kin 8:50
and when thou hearest, *f* ... 2Chr 6:21
*f* the sin of thy people Israel, ... 2Chr 6:25
*f* the sin of thy servants, and of ... 2Chr 6:27
heaven thy dwelling place, and *f* ... 2Chr 6:30
*f* thy people which have sinned ... 2Chr 6:39
will *f* their sin, and will heal ... 2Chr 7:14
and *f* all my sins ... Ps 25:18
Lord, art good, and ready to *f* ... Ps 86:5
therefore *f* them not ... Is 2:9
*f* not their iniquity, neither ... Jer 18:23
for I will *f* their iniquity, and I ... Jer 31:34
that I may *f* their iniquity and ... Jer 36:3
O Lord, hear; O Lord, *f* ... Dan 9:19
land, then I said, O Lord GOD, *f* ... Amos 7:2
*f* us our debts, as we *f* our ... Mt 6:12
For if ye *f* men their trespasses, ... Mt 6:14
heavenly Father will also *f* you ... Mt 6:14
But if ye *f* not men their ... Mt 6:15
your Father *f* your trespasses ... Mt 6:15
man hath power on earth to *f* sins ... Mt 9:6
sin against me, and I *f* him ... Mt 18:21
if ye from your hearts *f* not ... Mt 18:35
who can *f* sins but God only ... Mk 2:7
man hath power on earth to *f* sins ... Mk 2:10
And when ye stand praying, *f* ... Mk 11:25
heaven may *f* you your trespasses ... Mk 11:25
But if ye do not *f*, neither will ... Mk 11:26
is in heaven *f* your trespasses ... Mk 11:26
Who can *f* sins, but God alone ... Lk 5:21
hath power upon earth to *f* sins ... Lk 5:24
*f*, and ye shall be forgiven ... Lk 6:37
And *f* us our sins ... Lk 11:4
for we also *f* every one that is ... Lk 11:4
and if he repent, *f* him ... Lk 17:3
thou shalt *f* him ... Lk 17:4
Then said Jesus, Father, *f* them ... Lk 23:34
ye ought rather to *f* him, and ... 2Cor 2:7
ye *f* any thing, I *f* also ... 2Cor 2:10
*f* me this wrong ... 2Cor 12:13
just to *f* us our sins, and to ... 1Jn 1:9

### FORGIVEN
for them, and it shall be *f* them ... Lev 4:20
his sin, and it shall be *f* him ... Lev 4:26
for him, and it shall be *f* him ... Lev 4:31
committed, and it shall be *f* him ... Lev 4:35
hath sinned, and it shall be *f* him ... Lev 5:10
of these, and it shall be *f* him ... Lev 5:13
offering, and it shall be *f* him ... Lev 5:16
wist it not, and it shall be *f* him ... Lev 5:18
it shall be *f* him for any thing ... Lev 6:7
which he hath done shall be *f* him ... Lev 19:22
and as thou hast *f* this people ... Num 14:19
of Israel, and it shall be *f* them ... Num 15:25
And it shall be *f* all the ... Num 15:26
and it shall be *f* him ... Num 15:28
And the blood shall be *f* them ... Deut 21:8
is he whose transgression is *f* ... Ps 32:1
Thou hast *f* the iniquity of thy ... Ps 85:2
therein shall be *f* their iniquity ... Is 33:24
thy sins be *f* thee ... Mt 9:2
to say, Thy sins be *f* thee ... Mt 9:5
and blasphemy shall be *f* unto men ... Mt 12:31
Ghost shall not be *f* unto men ... Mt 12:31
the Son of man, it shall be *f* him ... Mt 12:32
Holy Ghost, it shall not be *f* him ... Mt 12:32
palsy, Son, thy sins be *f* thee ... Mk 2:5
of the palsy, Thy sins be *f* thee ... Mk 2:9
All sins shall be *f* unto the sons ... Mk 3:28
and their sins should be *f* them ... Mk 4:12
him, Man, thy sins are *f* thee ... Lk 5:20
to say, Thy sins be *f* thee ... Lk 5:23
forgive, and ye shall be *f* ... Lk 6:37
Her sins, which are many, are *f* ... Lk 7:47
but to whom little is *f*, the same ... Lk 7:47
he said unto her, Thy sins are *f* ... Lk 7:48
the Son of man, it shall be *f* him ... Lk 12:10
the Holy Ghost it shall not be *f* ... Lk 12:10
of thine heart may be *f* thee ... Acts 8:22
are they whose iniquities are *f* ... Rom 4:7
God for Christ's sake hath *f* you ... Eph 4:32
having *f* you all trespasses ... Col 2:13
sins, they shall be *f* him ... Jas 5:15
because your sins are *f* you for ... 1Jn 2:12

### FORGIVENESS
But there is *f* with thee, that ... Ps 130:4
the Holy Ghost hath never *f* ... Mk 3:29
to Israel, and *f* of sins ... Acts 5:31
preached unto you the *f* of sins ... Acts 13:38
that they may receive *f* of sins ... Acts 26:18
the *f* of sins, according to the ... Eph 1:7
his blood, even the *f* of sins ... Col 1:14

### FORGIVENESSES
Lord our God belong mercies and *f* ... Dan 9:9

### FORGIVETH
Who *f* all thine iniquities ... Ps 103:3
Who is this that *f* sins also ... Lk 7:49

### FORGIVING
*f* iniquity and transgression and ... Ex 34:7
*f* iniquity and transgression, and ... Num 14:18
*f* one another, even as God for ... Eph 4:32
*f* one another, if any man have a ... Col 3:13

### FORGOT
hast *f* a sheaf in the field, thou ... Deut 24:19

### FORGOTTEN
shall be *f* in the land of Egypt ... Gen 41:30
neither have I *f* them ... Deut 26:13
for it shall not be *f* out of the ... Deut 31:21
hast *f* God that formed thee ... Deut 32:18
and my familiar friends have *f* me ... Job 19:14
even the waters *f* of the foot ... Job 28:4
the needy shall not alway be *f* ... Ps 9:18
said in his heart, God hath *f* ... Ps 10:11
I am *f* as a dead man out of mind ... Ps 31:12
God my rock, Why hast thou *f* me ... Ps 42:9
yet have we not *f* thee, neither ... Ps 44:17
If we have *f* the name of our God, ... Ps 44:20
Hath God *f* to be gracious ... Ps 77:9
but I have not *f* thy law ... Ps 119:61
mine enemies have *f* thy words ... Ps 119:139
the days to come shall all be *f* ... Eccl 2:16
they were *f* in the city where ... Eccl 8:10
for the memory of them is *f* ... Eccl 9:5
Because thou hast *f* the God of ... Is 17:10
Tyre shall be *f* seventy years ... Is 23:15
thou harlot that hast been *f* ... Is 23:16
Israel, thou shalt not be *f* of me ... Is 44:21
forsaken me, and my Lord hath *f* me ... Is 49:14
because the former troubles are *f* ... Is 65:16
yet my people have *f* me days ... Jer 2:32
they have *f* the LORD their God ... Jer 3:21
because thou hast *f* me, and ... Jer 13:25
Because my people hath *f* me ... Jer 18:15
confusion shall never be *f* ... Jer 20:11
fathers have *f* my name for Baal ... Jer 23:27
shame, which shall not be *f* ... Jer 23:40
All thy lovers have *f* thee ... Jer 30:14
Have ye *f* the wickedness of your ... Jer 44:9
covenant that shall not be *f* ... Jer 50:5
they have *f* their restingplace ... Jer 50:6
and sabbaths to be *f* in Zion ... Lam 2:6
by extortion, and hast *f* me ... Eze 22:12
Because thou hast *f* me, and cast ... Eze 23:35
seeing thou hast *f* the law of thy ... Hos 4:6
For Israel hath *f* his Maker ... Hos 8:14
therefore have they *f* me ... Hos 13:6
side, they had *f* to take bread ... Mt 16:5
the disciples had *f* to take bread ... Mk 8:14
not one of them is *f* before God ... Lk 12:6
ye have *f* the exhortation which ... Heb 12:5
hath *f* that he was purged from ... 2Pet 1:9

### FORKS
and for the coulters, and for the *f* ... 1Sa 13:21

### FORM
And the earth was without *f* ... Gen 1:2
he said unto her, What *f* is he of ... 1Sa 28:14
To fetch about this *f* of speech ... 2Sa 14:20
of gold according to their *f* ... 2Chr 4:7
I could not discern the *f* thereof ... Job 4:16
I *f* the light, and create darkness ... Is 45:7
his *f* more than the sons of men ... Is 52:14
he hath no *f* nor comeliness ... Is 53:2
earth, and, lo, it was without *f* ... Jer 4:23
And he put forth the *f* of an hand ... Eze 8:3
behold every *f* of creeping things ... Eze 8:10
the *f* of a man's hand under their ... Eze 10:8
shew them the *f* of the house ... Eze 43:11
they may keep the whole *f* thereof ... Eze 43:11
the *f* thereof was terrible ... Dan 2:31
the *f* of his visage was changed ... Dan 3:19
the *f* of the fourth is like the ... Dan 3:25
in another *f* unto two of them ... Mk 16:12
which hast the *f* of knowledge ... Rom 2:20
*f* of doctrine which was delivered ... Rom 6:17
Who, being in the *f* of God ... Phil 2:6
took upon him the *f* of a servant ... Phil 2:7
Hold fast the *f* of sound words, ... 2Ti 1:13
Having a *f* of godliness, but ... 2Ti 3:5

### FORMED
the LORD God *f* man of the dust of ... Gen 2:7
he put the man whom he had *f* ... Gen 2:8
God *f* every beast of the field ... Gen 2:19
and hast forgotten God that *f* thee ... Deut 32:18
of ancient times that I have *f* it ... 2Kin 19:25
Dead things are *f* from under the ... Job 26:5
his hand hath *f* the crooked ... Job 26:13
I also am *f* out of the clay ... Job 33:6
or ever thou hadst *f* the earth ... Ps 90:2
he that *f* the eye, shall he not ... Ps 94:9
and his hands *f* the dry land ... Ps 95:5
The great God that *f* all things ... Prov 26:10
he that *f* them will shew them no ... Is 27:11
ancient times, that I have *f* it ... Is 37:26
thee, O Jacob, and he that *f* thee ... Is 43:1
him for my glory, I have *f* him ... Is 43:7
before me there was no God *f* ... Is 43:10
This people have I *f* for myself ... Is 43:21
*f* thee from the womb, which will ... Is 44:2
Who hath *f* a god, or molten a ... Is 44:10
I have *f* thee ... Is 44:21
he that *f* thee from the womb, I ... Is 44:24
God himself that *f* the earth ... Is 45:18
in vain, he *f* it to be inhabited ... Is 45:18
saith the LORD that *f* me from the ... Is 49:5
No weapon that is *f* against thee ... Is 54:17
Before I *f* thee in the belly I ... Jer 1:5
maker thereof, the LORD that *f* it ... Jer 33:2
behold, he *f* grasshoppers in the ... Amos 7:1
Shall the thing *f* say to him that ... Rom 9:20
thing *f* say to him that *f* it ... Rom 9:20
again until Christ be *f* in you ... Gal 4:19
For Adam was first *f*, then Eve ... 1Ti 2:13

### FORMER
after the *f* manner when thou wast ... Gen 40:13
fought against the *f* king of Moab ... Num 21:26
Her *f* husband, which sent her ... Deut 24:4
in *f* time in Israel concerning ... Ruth 4:7
him again after the *f* manner ... 1Sa 17:30
the *f* fifties with their fifties ... 2Kin 1:14
day they do after the *f* manners ... 2Kin 17:34
but they did after their *f* manner ... 2Kin 17:40
But the *f* governors that had been ... Neh 5:15
I pray thee, of the *f* age ... Job 8:8
the wilderness in *f* time desolate ... Job 30:3
not against us *f* iniquities ... Ps 79:8
where are thy *f* lovingkindnesses, ... Ps 89:49
is no remembrance of *f* things ... Eccl 1:11
What is the cause that the *f* days ... Eccl 7:10
let them shew the *f* things ... Is 41:22
the *f* things are come to pass, and ... Is 42:9
declare this, and shew us *f* things ... Is 43:9
Remember ye not the *f* things ... Is 43:18
Remember the *f* things of old ... Is 46:9
I have declared the *f* things from ... Is 48:3
shall raise up the *f* desolations ... Is 61:4
their *f* work into their bosom ... Is 65:7
because the *f* troubles are ... Is 65:16
the *f* shall not be remembered, ... Is 65:17
God, that giveth rain, both the *f* ... Jer 5:24
for he is the *f* of all things ... Jer 10:16
the *f* kings which were before ... Jer 34:5
write in it all the *f* words that ... Jer 36:28
for he is the *f* of all things ... Jer 51:19
shall return to their *f* estate ... Eze 16:55
shall return to their *f* estate ... Eze 16:55
shall return to your *f* estate ... Eze 16:55
a multitude greater than the *f* ... Dan 11:13
but it shall not be as the *f* ... Dan 11:29
latter and *f* rain unto the earth ... Hos 6:3
given you the *f* rain moderately ... Joel 2:23
the *f* rain, and the latter rain in ... Joel 2:23
shall be greater than of the *f* ... Hag 2:9
unto whom the *f* prophets have ... Zec 1:4
LORD hath cried by the *f* prophets ... Zec 7:7
in his spirit by the *f* prophets ... Zec 7:12
of this people as in the *f* days ... Zec 8:11
half of them toward the *f* sea ... Zec 14:8
the days of old, and as in *f* years ... Mal 3:4
The *f* treatise have I made, O ... Acts 1:1
the *f* conversation the old man ... Eph 4:22
call to remembrance the *f* days ... Heb 10:32
to the *f* lusts in your ignorance ... 1Pet 1:14
for the *f* things are passed away ... Rev 21:4

### FORMETH
he that *f* the mountains, and ... Amos 4:13
*f* the spirit of man within him ... Zec 12:1

### FORMS
in thereof, and all the *f* thereof ... Eze 43:11
thereof, and all the *f* thereof ... Eze 43:11

### FORNICATION
of Jerusalem to commit *f*, and ... 2Chr 21:11
shall commit *f* with all the ... Is 23:17
*f* with the Egyptians thy ... Eze 16:26
thy *f* in the land of Canaan unto ... Eze 16:29
wife, saving for the cause of *f* ... Mt 5:32
away his wife, except it be for *f* ... Mt 19:9
they to him, We be not born of *f* ... Jn 8:41
pollutions of idols, and from *f* ... Acts 15:20
from things strangled, and from *f* ... Acts 15:29
and from strangled, and from *f* ... Acts 21:25
with all unrighteousness, *f* ... Rom 1:29
that there is *f* among you ... 1Cor 5:1
such *f* as is not so much as named ... 1Cor 5:1
Now the body is not for *f* ... 1Cor 6:13
Flee *f*. Every sin that ... 1Cor 6:18
but he that committeth *f* sinneth ... 1Cor 6:18
Nevertheless, to avoid *f*, let ... 1Cor 7:2
Neither let us commit *f*, as some ... 1Cor 10:8
repented of the uncleanness and *f* ... 2Cor 12:21
Adultery, *f*, uncleanness, ... Gal 5:19
But *f*, and all uncleanness, or ... Eph 5:3
*f*, uncleanness, inordinate ... Col 3:5
that ye should abstain from *f* ... 1Th 4:3
giving themselves over to *f* ... Jude 7
unto idols, and to commit *f* ... Rev 2:14

to seduce my servants to commit *f* ....... Rev 2:20
gave her space to repent of her *f* ....... Rev 2:21
their sorceries, nor of their *f* ....... Rev 9:21
of the wine of the wrath of her *f* ....... Rev 14:8
of the earth have committed *f* ....... Rev 17:2
made drunk with the wine of her *f* ....... Rev 17:2
and filthiness of her *f* ....... Rev 17:4
of the wine of the wrath of her *f* ....... Rev 18:3
earth have committed *f* with her ....... Rev 18:3
the earth, who have committed *f* ....... Rev 18:9
did corrupt the earth with her *f* ....... Rev 19:2

**FORNICATIONS**
pouredst out thy *f* on every one ....... Eze 16:15
thoughts, murders, adulteries, *f* ....... Mt 15:19
evil thoughts, adulteries, *f* ....... Mk 7:21

**FORNICATOR**
that is called a brother be a *f* ....... 1Cor 5:11
Lest there be any *f*, or profane ....... Heb 12:16

**FORNICATORS**
an epistle not to company with *f* ....... 1Cor 5:9
with the *f* of this world, or with ....... 1Cor 5:10
neither *f*, nor idolaters, nor ....... 1Cor 6:9

**FORSAKE**
he will not *f* thee, neither ....... Deut 4:31
*f* not the Levite as long as thou ....... Deut 12:19
thou shalt not *f* him ....... Deut 14:27
he will not fail thee, nor *f* thee ....... Deut 31:6
not fail thee, neither *f* thee ....... Deut 31:8
go to be among them, and will *f* me. Deut 31:16
in that day, and I will *f* them ....... Deut 31:17
I will not fail thee, nor *f* thee ....... Josh 1:5
forbid that we should *f* the LORD ....... Josh 24:16
If ye *f* the LORD, and serve ....... Josh 24:20
Should I *f* my sweetness, and my ....... Judg 9:11
For the LORD will not *f* his ....... 1Sa 12:22
will not *f* my people Israel ....... 1Kin 6:13
let him not leave us, nor *f* us ....... 1Kin 8:57
I will *f* the remnant of mine ....... 2Kin 21:14
but if thou *f* him, he will cast ....... 1Chr 28:9
nor *f* thee, until thou hast ....... 1Chr 28:20
*f* my statutes and my ....... 2Chr 7:19
if ye *f* him, he will *f* you ....... 2Chr 15:2
is against all them that *f* him ....... Ezr 8:22
utterly consume them, nor *f* them ....... Neh 9:31
we will not *f* the house of our ....... Neh 10:39
*f* it not, but keep it still ....... Job 20:13
leave me not, neither *f* me ....... Ps 27:9
When my father and my mother *f* me... Ps 27:10
Cease from anger, and *f* wrath ....... Ps 37:8
*F* me not, O LORD ....... Ps 38:21
*f* me not when my strength faileth ....... Ps 71:9
and greyheaded, O God, *f* me not ....... Ps 71:18
If his children *f* my law, and walk ....... Ps 89:30
neither will he *f* his inheritance ....... Ps 94:14
O *f* me not utterly ....... Ps 119:8
of the wicked that *f* thy law ....... Ps 119:53
*f* not the works of thine own ....... Ps 138:8
*f* not the law of thy mother ....... Prov 1:8
Let not mercy and truth *f* thee ....... Prov 3:3
good doctrine, *f* ye not my law ....... Prov 4:2
*F* her not, and she shall preserve ....... Prov 4:6
*f* not the law of thy mother ....... Prov 6:20
*F* the foolish, and live ....... Prov 9:6
and thy father's friend, *f* not ....... Prov 27:10
They that *f* the law praise the ....... Prov 28:4
they that *f* the LORD shall be ....... Is 1:28
the God of Israel will not *f* them ....... Is 41:17
I do unto them, and not *f* them ....... Is 42:16
Let the wicked *f* his way, and the ....... Is 55:7
But ye are they that *f* the LORD ....... Is 65:11
all that *f* thee shall be ashamed, ....... Jer 17:13
I will even *f* you, saith the LORD ....... Jer 23:33
forget you, and I will *f* you ....... Jer 23:39
*f* her, and let us go every one ....... Jer 51:9
us for ever, and *f* us so long time ....... Lam 5:20
neither did they *f* the idols of ....... Eze 20:8
them that *f* the holy covenant ....... Dan 11:30
lying vanities *f* their own mercy ....... Jonah 2:8
are among the Gentiles to *f* Moses ....... Acts 21:21
will never leave thee, nor *f* thee ....... Heb 13:5

**FORSAKEN**
doings, whereby thou hast *f* me ....... Deut 28:20
Because they have *f* the covenant ....... Deut 29:25
but now the LORD hath *f* us ....... Judg 6:13
both because we have *f* our God ....... Judg 10:10
Yet ye have *f* me, and served other... Judg 10:13
day, wherewith they have *f* me ....... 1Sa 8:8
because we have *f* the LORD ....... 1Sa 12:10
Because that they have *f* me ....... 1Kin 11:33
house, in that ye have *f* the ....... 1Kin 18:18
of Israel have *f* thy covenant ....... 1Kin 19:10
of Israel have *f* thy covenant ....... 1Kin 19:14
Because they have *f* me, and have ....... 2Kin 22:17
Thus saith the LORD, Ye have *f* me ....... 2Chr 12:5
is our God, and we have not *f* him ....... 2Chr 13:10
but ye have *f* him ....... 2Chr 13:11
because he had *f* the LORD God of ....... 2Chr 21:10
because ye have *f* the LORD ....... 2Chr 24:20
he hath also *f* you ....... 2Chr 24:20
because they had *f* the LORD God ....... 2Chr 24:24
because they had *f* the LORD God ....... 2Chr 28:6
the LORD our God, and have *f* him ....... 2Chr 29:6
Because they have *f* me, and have ....... 2Chr 34:25
God hath not *f* us in our bondage ....... Ezr 9:9
for we have *f* thy commandments, ....... Ezr 9:10
said, Why is the house of God *f* ....... Neh 13:11
shall the earth be *f* for thee ....... Job 18:4
hath oppressed and hath *f* the poor ....... Job 20:19
hast not *f* them that seek thee ....... Ps 9:10
God, my God, why hast thou *f* me ....... Ps 22:1
have I not seen the righteous *f* ....... Ps 37:25
Saying, God hath *f* him ....... Ps 71:11
they have *f* the LORD, they have ....... Is 1:4
Therefore thou hast *f* thy people ....... Is 2:6
shall be *f* of both her kings ....... Is 7:16
The cities of Aroer are *f* ....... Is 17:2
his strong cities be as a *f* bough ....... Is 17:9
be desolate, and the habitation *f* ....... Is 27:10
Because the palaces shall be *f* ....... Is 32:14
But Zion said, The LORD hath *f* me ....... Is 49:14
hath called thee as a woman *f* ....... Is 54:6
For a small moment have I *f* thee ....... Is 54:7
Whereas thou hast been *f* and hated ....... Is 60:15
Thou shalt no more be termed *F* ....... Is 62:4
called, Sought out, A city not *f* ....... Is 62:12
their wickedness, who have *f* me ....... Jer 1:16
they have *f* me the fountain of ....... Jer 2:13
that thou hast *f* the LORD thy God ....... Jer 2:17
that thou hast *f* the LORD thy God ....... Jer 2:19
every city shall be *f*, and not a ....... Jer 4:29
thy children have *f* me, and sworn ....... Jer 5:7
answer them, Like as ye have *f* me ....... Jer 5:19
*f* the generation of his wrath ....... Jer 7:29
Because they have *f* my law which ....... Jer 9:13
because we have *f* the land ....... Jer 9:19
I have *f* mine house, I have left ....... Jer 12:7
Thou hast *f* me, saith the LORD, ....... Jer 15:6
Because your fathers have *f* me ....... Jer 16:11
worshipped them, and have *f* me ....... Jer 16:11
because they have *f* the LORD ....... Jer 17:13
that come from another place be *f* ....... Jer 18:14
Because they have *f* me, and have ....... Jer 19:4
Because they have *f* the covenant ....... Jer 22:9
He hath *f* his covert, as the lion ....... Jer 25:38
For Israel hath not been *f* ....... Jer 51:5
the LORD hath *f* the earth ....... Eze 8:12
say, The LORD hath *f* the earth ....... Eze 9:9
and to the cities that are *f* ....... Eze 36:4
she is *f* upon her land ....... Amos 5:2
For Gaza shall be *f*, and Ashkelon ....... Zeph 2:4
unto him, Behold, we have *f* all ....... Mt 19:27
And every one that hath *f* houses ....... Mt 19:29
God, my God, why hast thou *f* me ....... Mt 27:46
God, my God, why hast thou *f* me ....... Mk 15:34
Persecuted, but not *f* ....... 2Cor 4:9
For Demas hath *f* me, having loved ....... 2Ti 4:10
Which have *f* the right way, and ....... 2Pet 2:15

**FORSAKETH**
but he *f* the fear of the Almighty ....... Job 6:14
judgment, and *f* not his saints ....... Ps 37:28
Which *f* the guide of her youth, ....... Prov 2:17
grievous unto him that *f* the way ....... Prov 15:10
and *f* them shall have mercy ....... Prov 28:13
you that *f* not all that he hath ....... Lk 14:33

**FORSAKING**
there be a great *f* in the midst ....... Is 6:12
Not *f* the assembling of ourselves ....... Heb 10:25

**FORSOMUCH**
*f* as he also is a son of Abraham ....... Lk 19:9

**FORSOOK**
then he *f* God which made him, and. Deut 32:15
they *f* the LORD God of their ....... Judg 2:12
they *f* the LORD, and served Baal ....... Judg 2:13
*f* the LORD, and served not him ....... Judg 10:6
they *f* the cities, and fled ....... 1Sa 31:7
Because they *f* the LORD their God ....... 1Kin 9:9
But he *f* the counsel of the old ....... 1Kin 12:8
*f* the old men's counsel that they ....... 1Kin 12:13
he *f* the LORD God of his fathers, ....... 2Kin 21:22
then they *f* their cities, and fled ....... 1Chr 10:7
Because they *f* the LORD God of ....... 2Chr 7:22
But he *f* the counsel which the ....... 2Chr 10:8
king Rehoboam *f* the counsel of ....... 2Chr 10:13
he *f* the law of the LORD, and all ....... 2Chr 12:1
So that he *f* the tabernacle of ....... Ps 78:60
but I *f* not thy precepts ....... Ps 119:87
*f* not the ordinance of their God ....... Is 58:2
*f* it, because there was no grass ....... Jer 14:5
Then all the disciples *f* him ....... Mt 26:56
And straightway they *f* their nets ....... Mk 1:18
And they all *f* him, and fled ....... Mk 14:50
their ships to land, they *f* all ....... Lk 5:11
stood with me, but all men *f* me ....... 2Ti 4:16
By faith he *f* Egypt, not fearing ....... Heb 11:27

**FORSOOKEST**
of great kindness, and *f* them not ....... Neh 9:17
*f* them not in the wilderness ....... Neh 9:19

**FORSWEAR**
time, Thou shalt not *f* thyself ....... Mt 5:33

**FORT**
So David dwelt in the *f*, and ....... 2Sa 5:9
the fortress of the high *f* of thy ....... Is 25:12
build a *f* against it, and cast a ....... Eze 4:2
to cast a mount, and to build a *f* ....... Eze 21:22
and he shall make a *f* against thee ....... Eze 26:8
face toward the *f* of his own land ....... Dan 11:19

**FORTH** See PREFACE.

**FORTHWITH**
*f* expences be given unto these ....... Ezr 6:8
*f* they sprung up, because they ....... Mt 13:5
*f* he came to Jesus, and said, Hail ....... Mt 26:49
*f*, when they were come out of the ....... Mk 1:29
charged him, and *f* sent him away ....... Mk 1:43
And *f* Jesus gave them leave ....... Mk 5:13
*f* came there out blood and water ....... Jn 19:34
and he received sight *f*, and arose, ....... Acts 9:18
*f* the angel departed from him ....... Acts 12:10
and *f* the doors were shut ....... Acts 21:30

**FORTIETH**
in the *f* year after the children ....... Num 33:38
And it came to pass in the *f* year ....... Deut 1:3
In the *f* year of the reign of ....... 1Chr 26:31
in the one and *f* year of his reign ....... 2Chr 16:13

**FORTIFIED**
he *f* the strong holds, and put ....... 2Chr 11:11
turning of the wall, and *f* them ....... 2Chr 26:9
they *f* Jerusalem unto the broad ....... Neh 3:8
Assyria, and from the *f* cities ....... Mic 7:12

**FORTIFY**
they *f* the city against thee ....... Judg 9:31
will they *f* themselves ....... Neh 4:2
have ye broken down to *f* the wall ....... Is 22:10
though she should *f* the height of ....... Jer 51:53
strong, *f* thy power mightily ....... Nah 2:1
for the siege, *f* thy strong holds ....... Nah 3:14

**FORTRESS**
The LORD is my rock, and my *f* ....... 2Sa 22:2
The LORD is my rock, and my *f* ....... Ps 18:2
For thou art my rock and my *f* ....... Ps 31:3
me, for thou art my rock and my *f* ....... Ps 71:3
the LORD, He is my refuge and my *f* ....... Ps 91:2
My goodness, and my *f* ....... Ps 144:2
The *f* also shall cease from ....... Is 17:3
the *f* of the high fort of thy ....... Is 25:12
a *f* among my people, that thou ....... Jer 6:27
the land, O inhabitant of the *f* ....... Jer 10:17
O LORD, my strength, and my *f* ....... Jer 16:19
shall enter into the *f* of the ....... Dan 11:7
and be stirred up, even to his *f* ....... Dan 11:10
spoiled shall come against the *f* ....... Amos 5:9
from the *f* even to the river, and ....... Mic 7:12

**FORTRESSES**
and brambles in the *f* thereof ....... Is 34:13
all thy *f* shall be spoiled, as ....... Hos 10:14

**FORTS**
they built *f* against it round ....... 2Kin 25:1
and I will raise *f* against thee ....... Is 29:3
the *f* and towers shall be for dens ....... Is 32:14
built *f* against it round about ....... Jer 52:4
casting up mounts, and building *f* ....... Eze 17:17
and they that be in the *f* ....... Eze 33:27

**FORTUNATUS** (*for-chu-na'-tus*) *A Christian acquaintance of Paul.*
of the coming of Stephanas and F ....... 1Cor 16:17
from Philippi by Stephanus, and F ....... 1Cor *s*

**FORTY**
*f* years, and begat sons and ....... Gen 5:13
it to rain upon the earth *f* days ....... Gen 7:4
the earth *f* days and *f* nights ....... Gen 7:4
the earth *f* days and *f* nights ....... Gen 7:12
the flood was *f* days upon the ....... Gen 7:17
came to pass at the end of *f* days ....... Gen 8:6
And he said, If I find there *f* ....... Gen 18:28
there shall be *f* found there ....... Gen 18:29
Isaac was *f* years old when he ....... Gen 25:20
Esau was *f* years old when he took ....... Gen 26:34
*f* kine, and ten bulls, twenty she ....... Gen 32:15
age of Jacob was an hundred *f* ....... Gen 47:28
*f* days were fulfilled for him ....... Gen 50:3
of Israel did eat manna *f* years ....... Ex 16:35
the mount *f* days and *f* nights ....... Ex 24:18
thou shalt make *f* sockets of ....... Ex 26:19
their *f* sockets of silver ....... Ex 26:21
the LORD *f* days and *f* nights ....... Ex 34:28
*f* sockets of silver he made under ....... Ex 36:24
their *f* sockets of silver ....... Ex 36:26
of years shall be unto thee *f* ....... Lev 25:8
of the tribe of Reuben, were *f* ....... Num 1:21
even of the tribe of Gad, were *f* ....... Num 1:25
were *f* thousand and five hundred ....... Num 1:33
of the tribe of Asher, were *f* ....... Num 1:41
were numbered thereof, were *f* ....... Num 2:11
were numbered of them, were *f* ....... Num 2:15
were *f* thousand and five hundred ....... Num 2:19
were numbered of them, were *f* ....... Num 2:28
of the land after *f* days ....... Num 13:25
wander in the wilderness *f* years ....... Num 14:33
ye searched the land, even *f* days ....... Num 14:34
even *f* years, and ye shall know my.. Num 14:34
that were numbered of them were *f* ... Num 26:7
*f* thousand and five hundred ....... Num 26:18
that were numbered of them were *f*. Num 26:41
that were numbered of them were *f*. Num 26:50
wander in the wilderness *f* years ....... Num 32:13
and to them ye shall add *f* ....... Num 35:6
give to the Levites shall be *f* ....... Num 35:7
these *f* years the LORD thy God ....... Deut 2:7
these *f* years in the wilderness ....... Deut 8:2
did thy foot swell, these *f* years ....... Deut 8:4
then I abode in the mount *f* days ....... Deut 9:9
*f* nights, I neither did eat bread ....... Deut 9:9
came to pass at the end of *f* days ....... Deut 9:11
*f* nights, that the LORD gave me ....... Deut 9:11
the first, *f* days and *f* nights ....... Deut 9:18
fell down before the LORD *f* days ....... Deut 9:25
*f* nights, as I fell down at the ....... Deut 9:25
time, *f* days and *f* nights ....... Deut 10:10
F stripes he may give him, and not ....... Deut 25:3
I have led you *f* years in the ....... Deut 29:5

About *f* thousand prepared for war...... Josh 4:13
walked *f* years in the wilderness............ Josh 5:6
*F* years old was I when Moses the....... Josh 14:7
me alive, as he said, these *f*................ Josh 14:10
of the children of Israel were *f*............. Josh 21:41
And the land had rest *f* years............... Judg 3:11
seen among *f* thousand in Israel .......... Judg 5:8
And the land had rest *f* years............... Judg 5:31
*f* years in the days of Gideon ............... Judg 8:28
at that time of the Ephraimites *f*......... Judg 12:6
And he had *f* sons and thirty .............. Judg 12:14
hand of the Philistines *f* years............... Judg 13:1
And he had judged Israel *f* years .......... 1Sa 4:18
and presented himself *f* days ............... 1Sa 17:16
was *f* years old when he began to.......... 2Sa 2:10
to reign, and he reigned *f* years................ 2Sa 5:4
*f* thousand horsemen, and smote............ 2Sa 10:18
And it came to pass after *f* years .......... 2Sa 15:7
reigned over Israel were *f* years.......... 1Kin 2:11
Solomon had *f* thousand stalls of......... 1Kin 4:26
before it, was *f* cubits long.................. 1Kin 6:17
that lay on *f* five pillars, ....................... 1Kin 7:3
one laver contained *f* baths ................. 1Kin 7:38
over all Israel was *f* years .................. 1Kin 11:42
Rehoboam was *f* and one years old... 1Kin 14:21
And *f* and one years reigned he in..... 1Kin 15:10
the strength of that meat *f* days........... 1Kin 19:8
*f* nights unto Horeb the mount of......... 1Kin 19:8
bears out of the wood, and tare *f*.......... 2Kin 2:24
*f* camels' burden, and came and............. 2Kin 8:9
shearing house, even two and *f* men. 2Kin 10:14
*f* years reigned he in Jerusalem............ 2Kin 12:1
to reign in Samaria, and reigned *f* ..... 2Kin 14:23
*f* thousand seven hundred and ............ 1Chr 5:18
battle, expert in war, *f* thousand........ 1Chr 12:36
*f* thousand footmen, and killed............ 1Chr 19:18
reigned over Israel was *f* years........... 1Chr 29:27
Jerusalem over all Israel *f* years........... 2Chr 9:30
*f* years old when he began to............... 2Chr 12:13
*F* and two years old was Ahaziah......... 2Chr 22:2
he reigned *f* years in Jerusalem......... 2Chr 24:1
children of Zattu, nine hundred *f*........... Ezr 2:8
children of Bani, six hundred *f*............... Ezr 2:10
The children of Azmaveth, *f*................... Ezr 2:24
and Beeroth, seven hundred and *f*.......... Ezr 2:25
of Jericho, three hundred *f*.................... Ezr 2:34
Pashur, a thousand two hundred *f*.......... Ezr 2:38
whole congregation together was *f*....... Ezr 2:64
their mules, two hundred *f*.................... Ezr 2:66
beside *f* shekels of silver...................... Neh 5:15
of Zattu, eight hundred *f*...................... Neh 7:13
children of Binnui, six hundred *f*.......... Neh 7:15
The men of Beth-azmaveth, *f*.................. Neh 7:28
and Beeroth, seven hundred *f*................ Neh 7:29
of Jericho, three hundred *f*.................... Neh 7:36
Pashur, a thousand two hundred *f*.......... Neh 7:41
children of Asaph, an hundred *f*.......... Neh 7:44
children of Nekoda, six hundred *f*.......... Neh 7:62
whole congregation together was *f*....... Neh 7:66
and they had two hundred *f*.................. Neh 7:67
their mules, two hundred *f*.................... Neh 7:68
*f* years didst thou sustain them ............ Neh 9:21
of the fathers, two hundred *f*............... Neh 11:13
*f* years, and saw his sons, and his......... Job 42:16
*F* years long was I grieved with............. Ps 95:10
of the Jews seven hundred *f*.................. Jer 52:30
of the house of Judah *f* days..................... Eze 4:6
shall it be inhabited *f* years.................. Eze 29:11
waste shall be desolate *f* years.............. Eze 29:12
At the end of *f* years will I .................. Eze 29:13
the length thereof, *f* cubits .................... Eze 41:2
courts joined of *f* cubits long ................ Eze 46:22
led you *f* years through the ................ Amos 2:10
in the wilderness *f* years...................... Amos 5:25
Yet *f* days, and Nineveh shall be ......... Jonah 3:4
And when he had fasted *f* days................. Mt 4:2
*f* nights, he was afterward an.................... Mt 4:2
there in the wilderness *f* days................. Mk 1:13
Being *f* days tempted of the devil .............. Lk 4:2
Then said the Jews, *F* and six.................... Jn 2:20
proofs, being seen of them *f* days.......... Acts 1:3
For the man was above *f* years old....... Acts 4:22
And when he was full *f* years old....... Acts 7:23
when *f* years were expired, there.......... Acts 7:30
sea, and in the wilderness *f* years......... Acts 7:36
of *f* years in the wilderness.................. Acts 7:42
about the time of *f* years .................... Acts 13:18
Benjamin, by the space of *f* years ...... Acts 13:21
they were more than *f* which had....... Acts 23:13
for him of them more than *f* men ...... Acts 23:21
received I *f* stripes save one.............. 2Cor 11:24
me, and saw my works *f* years.................. Heb 3:9
with whom was he grieved *f* years ....... Heb 3:17
there were sealed an hundred and *f*........ Rev 7:4
shall they tread under foot *f*................ Rev 11:2
was given unto him to continue *f*.......... Rev 13:5
Sion, and with him an hundred *f*.......... Rev 14:1
that song but the hundred and *f*............ Rev 14:3
the wall thereof, an hundred and *f*...... Rev 21:17

**FORTY'S**
said, I will not do it for *f* sake............. Gen 18:29

**FORUM**
came to meet us as far as Appii *f*....... Acts 28:15

**FORWARD**
man waxed great, and went *f*............... Gen 26:13
of Israel, that they go *f* .......................... Ex 14:15
And when the tabernacle setteth *f*..... Num 1:51
of the congregation shall set *f*............ Num 2:17
they encamp, so shall they set *f*........... Num 2:17
they shall go *f* in the third rank........... Num 2:24
their standards, and so they set *f*......... Num 2:34
And when the camp setteth *f* ................. Num 4:5
as the camp is to set *f*............................ Num 4:15
lie on the east parts shall go *f* ............ Num 10:5
and the sons of Merari set *f*................ Num 10:17
set *f* according to their armies........... Num 10:18
And the Kohathites set *f*, bearing....... Num 10:21
set *f* according to their armies........... Num 10:22
camp of the children of Dan set *f*....... Num 10:25
to their armies, when they set *f*......... Num 10:28
came to pass, when the ark set *f*....... Num 10:35
And the children of Israel set *f* .......... Num 21:10
And the children of Israel set *f* .......... Num 22:1
them on yonder side Jordan, or *f*...... Num 32:19
that was with him, rushed *f* ................. Judg 9:44
shalt thou go on *f* from thence.............. 1Sa 10:3
came upon David from that day *f*......... 1Sa 16:13
eyed David from that day and *f*.............. 1Sa 18:9
And it was so from that day *f*............. 1Sa 30:25
but they went *f* smiting the.................. 2Kin 3:24
to her servant, Drive, and go *f*............ 2Kin 4:24
shall the shadow go *f* ten degrees........ 2Kin 20:9
four thousand were to set *f* the........... 1Chr 23:4
of the Kohathites, to set it *f*............... 2Chr 34:12
to set *f* the work of the house of............. Ezr 3:8
to set *f* the workmen in the house .......... Ezr 3:9
Behold, I go *f*, but he is not .................... Job 23:8
they set *f* my calamity, they have......... Job 30:13
heart, and went backward, and not *f*..... Jer 7:24
they went every one straight *f*................... Eze 1:9
And they went every one straight *f*....... Eze 1:12
they went every one straight *f*............. Eze 10:22
LORD their God from that day and *f*.... Eze 39:22
that upon the eighth day, and so *f* ...... Eze 43:27
they helped *f* the affliction ..................... Zec 1:15
he went *f* a little, and fell on.............. Mk 14:35
multitude, the Jews putting him *f*....... Acts 19:33
do, but also to be *f* a year ago ............ 2Cor 8:10
but being more *f*, of his own............... 2Cor 8:17
the same which I also was *f* to do ......... Gal 2:10
whom if thou bring *f* on their....................... 3Jn 6

**FORWARDNESS**
by occasion of the *f* of others ................ 2Cor 8:8
For I know the *f* of your mind ............... 2Cor 9:2

**FOUGHT**
*f* with Israel in Rephidim ........................ Ex 17:8
had said to him, and *f* with Amalek ...... Ex 17:10
then he *f* against Israel, and took......... Num 21:1
to Jahaz, and *f* against Israel............... Num 21:23
who had *f* against the former king..... Num 21:26
for the LORD *f* for Israel....................... Josh 10:14
unto Libnah, and *f* against Libnah ...... Josh 10:29
against it, and *f* against it.................... Josh 10:31
against it, and *f* against it.................... Josh 10:34
and they *f* against it.............................. Josh 10:36
to Debir; and *f* against it....................... Josh 10:38
LORD God of Israel *f* for Israel ............ Josh 10:42
God is he that hath *f* for you................... Josh 23:3
and they *f* with you ................................. Josh 24:8
the men of Jericho *f* against you ......... Josh 24:11
they *f* against him, and they slew........... Judg 1:5
of Judah had *f* against Jerusalem........... Judg 1:8
The kings came and *f*............................... Judg 5:19
then *f* the kings of Canaan in.................. Judg 5:19
They *f* from heaven .................................. Judg 5:20
in their courses *f* against Sisera.............. Judg 5:20
(For my father *f* for you, and................. Judg 9:17
of Shechem, and *f* with Abimelech ...... Judg 9:39
Abimelech *f* against the city all.............. Judg 9:45
*f* against it, and went hard unto............. Judg 9:52
in Jahaz, and *f* against Israel ............. Judg 11:20
men of Gilead, and *f* with Ephraim ..... Judg 12:4
And the Philistines *f*, and Israel.............. 1Sa 4:10
of Moab, and they *f* against them .......... 1Sa 12:9
*f* against all his enemies on................. 1Sa 14:47
*f* with the Philistines, and slew .............. 1Sa 19:8
*f* with the Philistines, and........................ 1Sa 23:5
the Philistines *f* against Israel ................ 1Sa 31:1
no more, neither *f* they any more .......... 2Sa 2:28
him, because he had *f* against................... 2Sa 8:10
against David, and *f* with him.............. 2Sa 10:17
the city went out, and *f* with Joab........ 2Sa 11:17
Joab *f* against Rabbah of the.................. 2Sa 12:26
I have *f* against Rabbah, and have ...... 2Sa 12:27
and *f* against it, and took it .................. 2Sa 12:29
*f* against the Philistines........................ 2Sa 21:15
when he *f* against Hazael king of.......... 2Kin 8:29
when he *f* with Hazael king of............... 2Kin 9:15
*f* against Gath, and took it................... 2Kin 12:17
his might wherewith he *f* against....... 2Kin 13:12
how he *f* with Amaziah king of............ 2Kin 14:15
the Philistines *f* against Israel............... 1Chr 10:1
him, because he had *f* against............. 1Chr 18:10
the Syrians, they *f* with him................ 1Chr 19:17
thousand men which *f* in chariots ........ 1Chr 19:18
they had heard that the LORD *f*.......... 2Chr 20:29
when he *f* with Hazael king of............... 2Chr 22:6
He *f* also with the king of the............... 2Chr 27:5
*f* against me without a cause.................. Ps 109:3
*f* against Ashdod, and took it .................... Is 20:1
their enemy, and he *f* against them ........ Is 63:10
*f* against Jerusalem, and against............. Jer 34:1
army *f* against Jerusalem, and ................ Jer 34:7
as when he *f* in the day of battle ........... Zec 14:3
that have *f* against Jerusalem ............... Zec 14:12
I have *f* with beasts at Ephesus........ 1Cor 15:32
I have *f* a good fight, I have........................ 2Ti 4:7
his angels *f* against the dragon ............... Rev 12:7
and the dragon *f* and his angels,............ Rev 12:7

**FOUL**
My face is *f* with weeping, and on ....... Job 16:16
but ye must *f* the residue with............. Eze 34:18
It will be *f* weather to day......................... Mt 16:3
together, he rebuked the *f* spirit ............. Mk 9:25
and the hold of every *f* spirit .................. Rev 18:2

**FOULED**
which ye have *f* with your feet.............. Eze 34:19

**FOULEDST**
with thy feet, and *f* their rivers ............. Eze 32:2

**FOUND**
was not *f* an help meet for him ............. Gen 2:20
But Noah *f* grace in the eyes of.............. Gen 6:8
But the dove *f* no rest for the .................. Gen 8:9
that they *f* a plain in the land ................ Gen 11:2
the angel of the LORD *f* her by a ........... Gen 16:7
if now I have *f* favour in thy................... Gen 18:3
there shall be forty *f* there .................... Gen 18:29
there shall thirty be *f* there................... Gen 18:30
there shall be twenty *f* there .................. Gen 18:31
Peradventure ten shall be *f* there........ Gen 18:32
thy servant hath *f* grace in thy............ Gen 19:19
*f* there a well of springing water ......... Gen 26:19
and said unto him, We have *f* water .. Gen 26:32
it that thou hast *f* it so quickly............ Gen 27:20
*f* mandrakes in the field, and................ Gen 30:14
if I have *f* favour in thine eyes, ........... Gen 30:27
but he *f* them not .................................. Gen 31:33
all the tent, but *f* them not .................. Gen 31:34
he searched, but *f* not the images ....... Gen 31:35
what hast thou *f* of all thy.................... Gen 31:37
if now I have *f* grace in thy.................. Gen 33:10
this was that Anah that *f* the................ Gen 36:24
And a certain man *f* him, and,............... Gen 37:15
his brethren, and *f* them in Dothan.... Gen 37:17
and said, This have we *f*........................ Gen 37:32
but he *f* her not ..................................... Gen 38:20
this kid, and thou hast not *f* her.......... Gen 38:23
Joseph *f* grace in his sight, and............. Gen 39:4
which we *f* in our sacks' mouths,.......... Gen 44:8
of thy servants it be *f*, both let ............ Gen 44:9
he with whom it is *f* shall be my.......... Gen 44:10
the cup was *f* in Benjamin's sack ........ Gen 44:12
God hath *f* out the iniquity of .............. Gen 44:16
and he also with whom the cup is *f*.... Gen 44:16
man in whose hand the cup is *f*............ Gen 44:17
that was *f* in the land of Egypt............ Gen 47:14
If now I have *f* grace in thy ................. Gen 47:29
If now I have *f* grace in your............... Gen 50:4
which shall be *f* in the field ..................... Ex 9:19
be no leaven *f* in your houses................. Ex 12:19
in the wilderness, and *f* no water.......... Ex 15:22
day for to gather, and they *f* none......... Ex 16:27
him, or if he be *f* in his hand................. Ex 21:16
If a thief be *f* breaking up........................ Ex 22:2
be certainly *f* in his hand alive ................ Ex 22:4
if the thief be *f*, let him pay..................... Ex 22:7
If the thief be not *f*, then the.................... Ex 22:8
thou hast also *f* grace in my .................. Ex 33:12
if I have *f* grace in thy sight,................. Ex 33:13
thy people have *f* grace in thy............... Ex 33:16
for thou hast *f* grace in my sight ......... Ex 33:17
If now I have *f* grace in thy.................... Ex 34:9
every man, with whom was *f* blue......... Ex 35:23
with whom was *f* shittim wood for ....... Ex 35:24
Or have *f* that which was lost, and......... Lev 6:3
or the lost thing which he *f*...................... Lev 6:4
have I not *f* favour in thy sight.......... Num 11:11
if I have *f* favour in thy sight ............ Num 11:15
they *f* a man that gathered sticks........ Num 15:32
they that *f* him gathering sticks......... Num 15:33
if we have *f* grace in thy sight,............. Num 32:5
If there be *f* among you, within .......... Deut 17:2
There shall not be *f* among you ......... Deut 18:10
that all the people that is *f*................ Deut 20:11
If one be *f* slain in the land ................. Deut 21:1
he hath lost, and thou hast *f*.................. Deut 22:3
I came to her, I *f* her not a maid....... Deut 22:14
I *f* not thy daughter a maid ............... Deut 22:17
virginity be not *f* for the damsel ......... Deut 22:20
If a man be *f* lying with a woman..... Deut 22:22
For he *f* her in the field, and the........ Deut 22:27
and lie with her, and they be *f*............ Deut 22:28
his eyes, because he hath *f* some.......... Deut 24:1
If a man be *f* stealing any of his ......... Deut 24:7
He *f* him in a desert land, and in ....... Deut 32:10
shall be *f* liars unto thee ................... Deut 33:29
all the way, but *f* them not ................... Josh 2:22
The five kings are *f* hid in a............... Josh 10:17
they *f* Adoni-bezek in Bezek .................. Judg 1:5
If now I have *f* grace in thy................... Judg 6:17
ye had not *f* out my riddle ................... Judg 14:18
he *f* a new jawbone of an ass, and .... Judg 15:15
they *f* among the inhabitants of........... Judg 21:12
Why have I *f* grace in thine eyes, ....... Ruth 2:10
of Shalisha, but they *f* them not............... 1Sa 9:4
Benjamites, but they *f* them not............... 1Sa 9:4
they *f* young maidens going out to......... 1Sa 9:11
for they are *f*............................................ 1Sa 9:20
which thou wentest to seek are *f*............. 1Sa 10:2
us plainly that the asses were *f* ........... 1Sa 10:16
sought him, he could not be *f*................ 1Sa 10:21
ye have not *f* ought in my hand.............. 1Sa 12:5
Now there was no smith *f* ....................... 1Sa 13:19
spear *f* in the hand of any of the........... 1Sa 13:22
with Jonathan his son was there *f*....... 1Sa 13:22
of their enemies which they *f*.............. 1Sa 14:30

for he hath *f* favour in my sight 1Sa 16:22
that I have *f* grace in thine eyes 1Sa 20:3
if I have *f* favour in thine eyes, 1Sa 20:29
evil hath not been *f* in thee all 1Sa 25:28
If I have now *f* grace in thine 1Sa 27:5
I have *f* no fault in him since he 1Sa 29:3
for I have not *f* evil in thee 1Sa 29:6
what hast thou *f* in thy servant 1Sa 29:8
they *f* an Egyptian in the field, 1Sa 30:11
strip the slain, that they *f* Saul 1Sa 31:8
*f* in his heart to pray this 2Sa 7:27
that I have *f* grace in thy sight 2Sa 14:22
in some place where he shall be *f* 2Sa 17:12
be not one small stone *f* there 2Sa 17:13
*f* Abishag a Shunammite, and 1Kin 1:3
if wickedness shall be *f* in him 1Kin 1:52
was the weight of the brass *f* out 1Kin 7:47
Hadad *f* great favour in the sight 1Kin 11:19
the Shilonite *f* him in the way 1Kin 11:29
*f* him sitting under an oak 1Kin 13:14
*f* his carcase cast in the way, and 1Kin 13:28
because in him there is *f* some 1Kin 14:13
and nation, that they *f* thee not 1Kin 18:10
*f* Elisha the son of Shaphat, who 1Kin 19:19
departed from him, a lion *f* him 1Kin 20:36
Then he *f* another man, and said, 1Kin 20:37
said to Elijah, Hast thou *f* me 1Kin 21:20
And he answered, I have *f* thee 1Kin 21:20
sought three days, but *f* him not 2Kin 2:17
*f* a wild vine, and gathered 2Kin 4:39
but they *f* no more of her than 2Kin 9:35
wheresoever any breach shall be *f* 2Kin 12:5
told the money that was *f* in the 2Kin 12:10
all the gold that was *f* in the 2Kin 12:18
were *f* in the house of the LORD 2Kin 14:14
gold that was *f* in the house of 2Kin 16:8
the king of Assyria *f* conspiracy 2Kin 17:4
was *f* in the house of the LORD 2Kin 18:15
*f* the king of Assyria warring 2Kin 19:8
all that was *f* in his treasures 2Kin 20:13
I have *f* the book of the law in 2Kin 22:8
the money that was *f* in the house 2Kin 22:9
the words of this book that is *f* 2Kin 22:13
was *f* in the house of the LORD 2Kin 23:2
priest *f* in the house of the LORD 2Kin 23:24
which were *f* in the city, and the 2Kin 25:19
the land that were *f* in the city 2Kin 25:19
they *f* fat pasture and good, and 1Chr 4:40
the habitations that were *f* there 1Chr 4:41
strip the slain, that they *f* Saul 1Chr 10:8
therefore thy servant hath *f* in 1Chr 17:25
*f* it to weigh a talent of gold, 1Chr 20:2
there were more chief men *f* of 1Chr 24:4
there were *f* among them mighty 1Chr 26:31
seek him, he will be *f* of thee 1Chr 28:9
*f* gave them to the treasure of 1Chr 29:8
they were *f* an hundred and fifty 2Chr 2:17
of the brass could not be *f* out 2Chr 4:18
ye seek him, he will be *f* of you 2Chr 15:2
and sought him, he was *f* of them 2Chr 15:4
and he was *f* of them 2Chr 15:15
there are good things *f* in thee 2Chr 19:3
they *f* among them in abundance 2Chr 20:25
that was *f* in the king's house 2Chr 21:17
*f* the princes of Judah, and the 2Chr 22:8
*f* them three hundred thousand 2Chr 25:5
were *f* in the house of God with 2Chr 25:24
all the uncleanness that they *f* 2Chr 29:16
Hilkiah the priest *f* a book of 2Chr 34:14
I have *f* the book of the law in 2Chr 34:15
was *f* in the house of the LORD 2Chr 34:17
the words of the book that is *f* 2Chr 34:21
was *f* in the house of the LORD 2Chr 34:30
did, and that which was *f* in him 2Chr 36:8
by genealogy, but they were not *f* Ezr 2:62
it is *f* that this city of old Ezr 4:19
there was *f* at Achmetha, in the Ezr 6:2
*f* there none of the sons of Levi Ezr 8:15
*f* that had taken strange wives Ezr 10:18
have *f* favour in thy sight Neh 2:5
peace, and *f* nothing to answer Neh 5:8
I *f* a register of the genealogy Neh 7:5
the first, and *f* written therein, Neh 7:5
by genealogy, but it was not *f* Neh 7:64
they *f* written in the law which Neh 8:14
and therein was *f* written, that Neh 13:1
made of the matter, it was *f* out Est 2:23
If I have *f* favour in the sight Est 5:8
it was *f* written, that Mordecai Est 6:2
If I have *f* favour in thy sight, Est 7:3
if I have *f* favour in his sight, Est 8:5
the root of the matter is *f* in me Job 19:28
as a dream, and shall not be *f* Job 20:8
But where shall wisdom be *f* Job 28:12
neither is it *f* in the land of Job 28:13
lifted up myself when evil *f* him Job 31:29
because they had *f* no answer Job 32:3
should say, We have *f* out wisdom Job 32:13
I have *f* a ransom Job 33:24
in all the land were no women *f* Job 42:15
in a time when thou mayest be *f* Ps 32:6
his iniquity be *f* to be hateful Ps 36:2
sought him, but he could not be *f* Ps 37:36
and for comforters, but I *f* none Ps 69:20
men of might have *f* their hands Ps 76:5
Yea, the sparrow hath *f* an house Ps 84:3
I have *f* David my servant Ps 89:20
they *f* no city to dwell in Ps 107:4
I *f* trouble and sorrow Ps 116:3
we *f* it in the fields of the wood Ps 132:6
But if he be *f*, he shall restore Prov 6:31
seek thy face, and I have *f* thee Prov 7:15
hath understanding wisdom is *f* Prov 10:13
glory, if it be *f* in the way of Prov 16:31
when thou hast *f* it, then there Prov 24:14
Hast thou *f* honey Prov 25:16
reprove thee, and thou be *f* a liar Prov 30:6
curse thee, and thou be *f* guilty Prov 30:10
Behold, this have I *f*, saith the Eccl 7:27
one man among a thousand have I *f* Eccl 7:28
among all those have I not *f* Eccl 7:28
Lo, this only have I *f*, that God Eccl 7:29
Now there was *f* in it a poor wise Eccl 9:15
I sought him, but I *f* him not Song 3:1
I sought him, but I *f* him not Song 3:2
that go about the city *f* me Song 3:3
but I *f* him whom my soul loveth Song 3:4
that went about the city *f* me Song 5:7
in his eyes as one that *f* favour Song 8:10
As my hand hath *f* the kingdoms of Is 10:10
my hand hath *f* as a nest the Is 10:14
Every one that is *f* shall be Is 13:15
all that are *f* in thee are bound Is 22:3
so that there shall not be *f* in Is 30:14
thereon, it shall not be *f* there Is 35:9
*f* the king of Assyria warring Is 37:8
all that was *f* in his treasures Is 39:2
and gladness shall be *f* therein Is 51:3
ye the LORD while he may be *f* Is 55:6
thou hast *f* the life of thine Is 57:10
I am *f* of them that sought me not Is 65:1
the new wine is *f* in the cluster Is 65:8
have your fathers *f* in me Jer 2:5
the thief is ashamed when he is *f* Jer 2:26
Also in thy skirts is *f* the blood Jer 2:34
I have not *f* it by secret search, Jer 2:34
among my people are *f* wicked men Jer 5:26
A conspiracy is *f* among the men Jer 11:9
came to the pits, and *f* no water Jer 14:3
Thy words were *f*, and I did eat Jer 15:16
house have I *f* their wickedness Jer 23:11
And I will be *f* of you, saith the Jer 29:14
sword *f* grace in the wilderness Jer 31:2
the Chaldeans that were *f* there Jer 41:3
But ten men were *f* among them Jer 41:8
*f* him by the great waters that Jer 41:12
was he *f* among thieves Jer 48:27
All that *f* them have devoured Jer 50:7
of Judah, and they shall not be *f* Jer 50:20
thou art *f*, and also caught, Jer 50:24
person, which were *f* in the city Jer 52:25
that were *f* in the midst of the Jer 52:25
we have *f*, we have seen it Lam 2:16
not destroy it: but I *f* none Eze 22:30
yet shalt thou never be *f* again Eze 26:21
till iniquity was *f* in thee Eze 28:15
them all was *f* none like Daniel Dan 1:19
he *f* them ten times better than Dan 1:20
I have *f* a man of the captives of Dan 2:25
that no place was *f* for them Dan 2:35
wisdom of the gods, was *f* in him Dan 5:11
were *f* in the same Daniel, whom Dan 5:12
and excellent wisdom is *f* in thee Dan 5:14
in the balances, and art *f* wanting Dan 5:27
there any error or fault *f* in him Dan 6:4
*f* Daniel praying and making Dan 6:11
before him innocency was *f* in me Dan 6:22
no manner of hurt was *f* upon him Dan 6:23
stumble and fall, and not be *f* Dan 11:19
shall be *f* written in the book Dan 12:1
I *f* Israel like grapes in the Hos 9:10
now shall they be *f* faulty Hos 10:2
he *f* him in Beth-el, and there he Hos 12:4
I have *f* me out substance Hos 12:8
From me is thy fruit *f* Hos 14:8
he *f* a ship going to Tarshish Jonah 1:3
of Israel were *f* in thee Mic 1:13
tongue be *f* in their mouth Zeph 3:13
and place shall not be *f* for them Zec 10:10
and iniquity was not *f* in his lips Mal 2:6
she was *f* with child of the Holy Mt 1:18
and when ye have *f* him, bring me Mt 2:8
I have not *f* so great faith, no, Mt 8:10
the which when a man hath *f* Mt 13:44
when he had *f* one pearl of great Mt 13:46
*f* one of his fellowservants, Mt 18:28
*f* others standing idle, and saith Mt 20:6
*f* nothing thereon, but leaves Mt 21:19
together all as many as they *f* Mt 22:10
And he came and *f* them asleep again Mt 26:43
But *f* none: yea, though Mt 26:60
witnesses came, yet *f* they none Mt 26:60
they *f* a man of Cyrene, Simon by Mt 27:32
And when they had *f* him, they said Mk 1:37
unwashen, hands, they *f* fault Mk 7:2
she *f* the devil gone out, and her Mk 7:30
*f* the colt tied by the door Mk 11:4
to it, he *f* nothing but leaves Mk 11:13
*f* as he had said unto them Mk 14:16
he *f* them asleep again, (for Mk 14:40
and *f* none. Mk 14:55
for thou hast *f* favour with God Lk 1:30
*f* Mary, and Joseph, and the babe Lk 2:16
And when they *f* him not, they Lk 2:45
days they *f* him in the temple Lk 2:46
he *f* the place where it was Lk 4:17
I have not *f* so great faith, no, Lk 7:9
*f* the servant whole that had been Lk 7:10
*f* the man, out of whom the devils Lk 8:35
voice was past, Jesus was *f* alone Lk 9:36
sought fruit thereon, and *f* none Lk 13:6
And when he hath *f* it, he layeth Lk 15:5
for I have *f* my sheep which was Lk 15:6
And when she hath *f* it, she Lk 15:9
for I have *f* the piece which I Lk 15:9
he was lost, and is *f* Lk 15:24
and was lost, and is *f* Lk 15:32
There are not *f* that returned to Lk 17:18
*f* even as he had said unto them Lk 19:32
*f* as he had said unto them Lk 22:13
he *f* them sleeping for sorrow, Lk 22:45
We *f* this fellow perverting the Lk 23:2
have *f* no fault in this man Lk 23:14
I have *f* no cause of death in him Lk 23:22
they *f* the stone rolled away from Lk 24:2
*f* not the body of the Lord Jesus Lk 24:3
when they *f* not his body, they Lk 24:23
*f* it even so as the women had Lk 24:24
*f* the eleven gathered together, Lk 24:33
We have *f* the Messias, which is, Jn 1:41
and saith unto him, We have *f* him Jn 1:45
*f* in the temple those that sold Jn 2:14
when they had *f* him on the other Jn 6:25
and when he had *f* him, he said Jn 9:35
he *f* that he had lain in the Jn 11:17
Jesus, when he had *f* a young ass Jn 12:14
*f* her dead, and, carrying her Acts 5:10
*f* them not in the prison, they Acts 5:22
The prison truly *f* we shut with Acts 5:23
we had opened, we *f* no man within Acts 5:23
lest haply ye be *f* even to fight Acts 5:39
our fathers *f* no sustenance Acts 7:11
Who *f* favour before God, and Acts 7:46
But Philip was *f* at Azotus Acts 8:40
that if he *f* any of this way, Acts 9:2
there he *f* a certain man named Acts 9:33
*f* many that were come together Acts 10:27
And when he had *f* him, he brought Acts 11:26
*f* him not, he examined the Acts 12:19
they *f* a certain sorcerer, a Acts 13:6
I have *f* David the son of Jesse, Acts 13:22
though they *f* no cause of death Acts 13:28
And when they *f* them not, they Acts 17:6
devotions, I *f* an altar with this Acts 17:23
*f* a certain Jew named Aquila, Acts 18:2
*f* it fifty thousand pieces of Acts 19:19
For we have *f* this man a Acts 24:5
they neither *f* me in the temple Acts 24:12
certain Jews from Asia *f* me Acts 24:18
if they have *f* any evil doing in Acts 24:20
But when I *f* that he had Acts 25:25
there the centurion *f* a ship of Acts 27:6
sounded, and *f* it twenty fathoms Acts 27:28
again, and *f* it fifteen fathoms Acts 27:28
Where we *f* brethren, and were Acts 28:14
pertaining to the flesh, hath *f* Rom 4:1
to life, I *f* to be unto death Rom 7:10
I was *f* of them that sought me Rom 10:20
that a man be *f* faithful 1Cor 4:2
we are *f* false witnesses of God 1Cor 15:15
because I *f* not Titus my brother 2Cor 2:13
clothed we shall not be *f* naked 2Cor 5:3
I made before Titus, is *f* a truth 2Cor 7:14
glory, they may be *f* even as we 2Cor 11:12
that I shall be *f* unto you such 2Cor 12:20
we ourselves also are *f* sinners Gal 2:17
being *f* in fashion as a man, he Phil 2:8
be *f* in him, not having mine own Phil 3:9
of a deacon, being *f* blameless 1Ti 3:10
me out very diligently, and *f* me 2Ti 1:17
and was not *f*, because God had Heb 11:5
for he *f* no place of repentance, Heb 12:17
might be *f* unto praise and honour 1Pet 1:7
neither was guile *f* in his mouth 1Pet 2:22
that ye may be *f* of him in peace 2Pet 3:14
I rejoiced greatly that I *f* of 2Jn 4
and are not, and hast *f* them liars Rev 2:2
for I have not *f* thy works Rev 3:2
no man was *f* worthy to open Rev 5:4
their place *f* any more in heaven Rev 12:8
And in their mouth was *f* no guile Rev 14:5
away, and the mountains were not *f* Rev 16:20
shall be *f* no more at all Rev 18:21
shall be *f* any more in thee Rev 18:22
in her was *f* the blood of Rev 18:24
there was *f* no place for them Rev 20:11
whosoever was not *f* written in Rev 20:15

**FOUNDATION**

the *f* thereof even until now Ex 9:18
he shall lay the *f* thereof in his Josh 6:26
to lay the *f* of the house 1Kin 5:17
In the fourth year was the *f* of 1Kin 6:37
even from the *f* unto the coping, 1Kin 7:9
the *f* was of costly stones, even 1Kin 7:10
he laid the *f* thereof in Abiram 1Kin 16:34
of the *f* of the house of the LORD 2Chr 8:16
a third part at the gate of the *f* 2Chr 23:5
began to lay the *f* of the heaps 2Chr 31:7
But the *f* of the temple of the Ezr 3:6
the *f* of the temple of the LORD Ezr 3:10
because the *f* of the house of the Ezr 3:11
when the *f* of this house was laid Ezr 3:12
laid the *f* of the house of God Ezr 5:16
whose *f* is in the dust, which are Job 4:19
whose *f* was overflown with a Job 22:16
His *f* is in the holy mountains Ps 87:1
hast thou laid the *f* of the earth Ps 102:25
rase it, even to the *f* thereof Ps 137:7
the righteous is an everlasting *f* Prov 10:25
I lay in Zion for a *f* a stone Is 28:16

a precious corner stone, a sure *f* ... Is 28:16
the temple, Thy *f* shall be laid ... Is 44:28
also hath laid the *f* of the earth ... Is 48:13
so that the *f* thereof shall be ... Eze 13:14
discovering the *f* unto the neck ... Hab 3:13
even from the day that the *f* of ... Hag 2:18
have laid the *f* of this house ... Zec 4:9
the *f* of the house of the LORD of ... Zec 8:9
layeth the *f* of the earth, and ... Zec 12:1
secret from the *f* of the world ... Mt 13:35
for you from the *f* of the world ... Mt 25:34
deep, and laid the *f* on a rock ... Lk 6:48
is like a man that without a *f* ... Lk 6:49
was shed from the *f* of the world ... Lk 11:50
haply, after he hath laid the *f* ... Lk 14:29
me before the *f* of the world ... Jn 17:24
should build upon another man's *f* ... Rom 15:20
masterbuilder, I have laid the *f* ... 1Cor 3:10
For other *f* can no man lay than ... 1Cor 3:11
if any man build upon this *f* gold ... 1Cor 3:12
in him before the *f* of the world ... Eph 1:4
built upon the *f* of the apostles ... Eph 2:20
a good *f* against the time to come ... 1Ti 6:19
Nevertheless the *f* of God ... 2Ti 2:19
hast laid the *f* of the earth ... Heb 1:10
finished from the *f* of the world ... Heb 4:3
not laying again the *f* of ... Heb 6:1
suffered since the *f* of the world ... Heb 9:26
before the *f* of the world ... 1Pet 1:20
slain from the *f* of the world ... Rev 13:8
of life from the *f* of the world ... Rev 17:8
The first *f* was jasper ... Rev 21:19

**FOUNDATIONS**
and set on fire the *f* of the ... Deut 32:22
the *f* of heaven moved and shook, ... 2Sa 22:8
appeared, the *f* of the world were ... 2Sa 22:16
walls thereof, and joined the *f* ... Ezr 4:12
let the *f* thereof be strongly ... Ezr 6:3
when I laid the *f* of the earth ... Job 38:4
are the *f* thereof fastened ... Job 38:6
If the *f* be destroyed, what can ... Ps 11:3
the *f* also of the hills moved and ... Ps 18:7
seen, and the *f* of the world were ... Ps 18:15
all the *f* of the earth are out of ... Ps 82:5
Who laid the *f* of the earth ... Ps 104:5
he appointed the *f* of the earth ... Prov 8:29
for the *f* of Kir-hareseth shall ... Is 16:7
the *f* of the earth do shake ... Is 24:18
from the *f* of the earth ... Is 40:21
and laid the *f* of the earth ... Is 51:13
lay the *f* of the earth, and say ... Is 51:16
and lay thy *f* with sapphires ... Is 54:11
up the *f* of many generations ... Is 58:12
the *f* of the earth searched out ... Jer 31:37
her *f* are fallen, her walls are ... Jer 50:15
for a corner, nor a stone for *f* ... Jer 51:26
and it hath devoured the *f* thereof ... Lam 4:11
her *f* shall be broken down ... Eze 30:4
the *f* of the side chambers were a ... Eze 41:8
and I will discover the *f* thereof ... Mic 1:6
and ye strong *f* of the earth ... Mic 6:2
so that the *f* of the prison were ... Acts 16:26
he looked for a city which hath *f* ... Heb 11:10
the wall of the city had twelve *f* ... Rev 21:14
the *f* of the wall of the city ... Rev 21:19

**FOUNDED**
For he hath *f* it upon the seas, ... Ps 24:2
fulness thereof, thou hast *f* them ... Ps 89:11
place which thou hast *f* for them ... Ps 104:8
that thou hast *f* them for ever ... Ps 119:152
LORD by wisdom hath *f* the earth ... Prov 3:19
That the LORD hath *f* Zion ... Is 14:32
til the Assyrian *f* it for them ... Is 23:13
hath *f* his troop in the earth ... Amos 9:6
for it was *f* upon a rock ... Mt 7:25
for it was *f* upon a rock ... Lk 6:48

**FOUNDER**
of silver, and gave them to the *f* ... Judg 17:4
the *f* melteth in vain ... Jer 6:29
workman, and of the hands of the *f* ... Jer 10:9
every *f* is confounded by the ... Jer 10:14
every *f* is confounded by the ... Jer 51:17

**FOUNDEST**
*f* his heart faithful before thee, ... Neh 9:8

**FOUNTAIN**
by a *f* of water in the wilderness ... Gen 16:7
by the *f* in the way to Shur ... Gen 16:7
Nevertheless a *f* or pit, wherein ... Lev 11:36
he hath discovered her *f*, and she ... Lev 20:18
hath uncovered the *f* of her blood ... Lev 20:18
the *f* of Jacob shall be upon a ... Deut 33:28
the *f* of the water of Nephtoah ... Josh 15:9
by a *f* which is in Jezreel ... 1Sa 29:1
I went on to the gate of the *f* ... Neh 2:14
But the gate of the *f* repaired ... Neh 3:15
And at the *f* gate, which was over ... Neh 12:37
For with thee is the *f* of life ... Ps 36:9
the Lord, from the *f* of Israel ... Ps 68:26
Thou didst cleave the *f* and the ... Ps 74:15
the flint into a *f* of waters ... Ps 114:8
Let thy *f* be blessed ... Prov 5:18
law of the wise is a *f* of life ... Prov 13:14
fear of the LORD is a *f* of life ... Prov 14:27
the wicked is as a troubled *f* ... Prov 25:26
or the pitcher be broken at the *f* ... Eccl 12:6
a spring shut up, a *f* sealed ... Song 4:12
A *f* of gardens, a well of living ... Song 4:15
me the *f* of living waters ... Jer 2:13
As a *f* casteth out her waters, so ... Jer 6:7
waters, and mine eyes a *f* of tears ... Jer 9:1
the LORD, the *f* of living waters ... Jer 17:13
dry, and his *f* shall be dried up ... Hos 13:15
a *f* shall come forth of the house ... Joel 3:18
a *f* opened to the house of David ... Zec 13:1
straightway the *f* of her blood ... Mk 5:29
Doth a *f* send forth at the same ... Jas 3:11
so can no *f* both yield salt water ... Jas 3:12
the *f* of the water of life freely ... Rev 21:6

**FOUNTAINS**
the same day were all the *f* of ... Gen 7:11
The *f* also of the deep and the ... Gen 8:2
and in Elim were twelve *f* of water ... Num 33:9
a land of brooks of water, of *f* ... Deut 8:7
the land, unto all *f* of water ... 1Kin 18:5
the *f* which were without the city ... 2Chr 32:3
together, who stopped all the *f* ... 2Chr 32:4
Let thy *f* be dispersed abroad, and ... Prov 5:16
when there were no *f* abounding ... Prov 8:24
he strengthened the *f* of the deep ... Prov 8:28
*f* in the midst of the valleys ... Is 41:18
lead them unto living *f* of waters ... Rev 7:17
rivers, and upon the *f* of waters ... Rev 8:10
and the sea, and the *f* of waters ... Rev 14:7
upon the rivers and *f* of waters ... Rev 16:4

**FOUR**
parted, and became into *f* heads ... Gen 2:10
after he begat Salah *f* hundred ... Gen 11:13
after he begat Eber *f* hundred ... Gen 11:15
And Eber lived *f* and thirty years, ... Gen 11:16
after he begat Peleg *f* hundred ... Gen 11:17
*f* kings with five ... Gen 14:9
afflict them *f* hundred years ... Gen 15:13
the land is worth *f* hundred ... Gen 23:15
*f* hundred shekels of silver, ... Gen 23:16
thee, and *f* hundred men with him ... Gen 32:6
came, and with him *f* hundred men ... Gen 33:1
*f* parts shall be your own, for ... Gen 47:24
was *f* hundred and thirty years ... Ex 12:40
pass at the end of the *f* hundred ... Ex 12:41
for an ox, and *f* sheep for a sheep ... Ex 22:1
thou shalt cast *f* rings of gold ... Ex 25:12
put them in the *f* corners thereof ... Ex 25:12
shalt make for it *f* rings of gold ... Ex 25:26
put the rings in the *f* corners ... Ex 25:26
that are on the *f* feet thereof ... Ex 25:26
in the candlestick shall be *f* ... Ex 25:34
breadth of one curtain *f* cubits ... Ex 26:2
breadth of one curtain *f* cubits ... Ex 26:8
it upon *f* pillars of shittim wood ... Ex 26:32
upon the *f* sockets of silver ... Ex 26:32
of it upon the *f* corners thereof ... Ex 27:2
make *f* brasen rings in the *f* ... Ex 27:4
shall be *f*, and their sockets *f* ... Ex 27:16
of stones, even *f* rows of stones ... Ex 28:17
breadth of one curtain *f* cubits ... Ex 36:9
*f* cubits was the breadth of one ... Ex 36:15
he made thereunto *f* pillars of ... Ex 36:36
he cast for them *f* sockets of ... Ex 36:36
And he cast for it *f* rings of gold ... Ex 37:3
to be set by the *f* corners of it ... Ex 37:3
And he cast for it *f* rings of gold ... Ex 37:13
put the rings upon the *f* corners ... Ex 37:13
that were in the *f* feet thereof ... Ex 37:13
were *f* bowls made like almonds ... Ex 37:20
thereof on the *f* corners of it ... Ex 38:2
he cast *f* rings for the *f* ends ... Ex 38:5
And their pillars were *f* ... Ex 38:19
and their sockets of brass *f* ... Ex 38:19
two thousand and *f* hundred shekels ... Ex 38:29
they set in it *f* rows of stones ... Ex 39:10
that creep, going upon all *f* ... Lev 11:20
thing that goeth upon all *f* ... Lev 11:21
things, which have *f* feet ... Lev 11:23
manner of beasts that go on all *f* ... Lev 11:27
and whatsoever goeth upon all *f* ... Lev 11:42
and *f* thousand and *f* hundred ... Num 1:29
and seven thousand and *f* hundred ... Num 1:31
and five thousand and *f* hundred ... Num 1:37
and three thousand and *f* hundred ... Num 1:43
and *f* thousand and *f* hundred ... Num 2:6
and seven thousand and *f* hundred ... Num 2:8
*f* hundred, throughout their ... Num 2:9
*f* hundred and fifty, throughout ... Num 2:16
and five thousand and *f* hundred ... Num 2:23
and three thousand and *f* hundred ... Num 2:30
*f* oxen he gave unto the sons of ... Num 7:7
*f* wagons and eight oxen he gave ... Num 7:8
*f* hundred shekels, after the ... Num 7:85
*f* bullocks, the rams sixty, the ... Num 7:88
plague were twenty and *f* thousand ... Num 25:9
*f* thousand and three hundred ... Num 26:25
and *f* thousand and *f* hundred ... Num 26:43
and three thousand and *f* hundred ... Num 26:47
and five thousand and *f* hundred ... Num 26:50
*f* cubits the breadth of it, after ... Deut 3:11
the *f* quarters of thy vesture ... Deut 22:12
*f* cities and their villages ... Josh 19:7
Almon with her suburbs; *f* cities ... Josh 21:18
Beth-horon with her suburbs; *f* cities ... Josh 21:22
with her suburbs; *f* cities ... Josh 21:24
with her suburbs; *f* cities ... Josh 21:29
Rehob with her suburbs; *f* cities ... Josh 21:31
with her suburbs; *f* cities ... Josh 21:35
with her suburbs; *f* cities ... Josh 21:37
Jazer with her suburbs; *f* cities ... Josh 21:39
against Shechem in *f* companies ... Judg 9:34
the Gileadite *f* days in a year ... Judg 11:40
and was there *f* whole months ... Judg 19:2
*f* hundred thousand footmen that ... Judg 20:2
were numbered *f* hundred thousand ... Judg 20:17
abode in the rock Rimmon *f* months ... Judg 20:47
*f* hundred young virgins, that had ... Judg 21:12
in the field about *f* thousand men ... 1Sa 4:2
were with him about *f* hundred men ... 1Sa 22:2
after David about *f* hundred men ... 1Sa 25:13
was a full year and *f* months ... 1Sa 27:7
pursued, he and *f* hundred men ... 1Sa 30:10
save *f* hundred young men, which ... 1Sa 30:17
and on every foot six toes, *f* ... 2Sa 21:20
These *f* were born to the giant in ... 2Sa 21:22
it came to pass in the *f* hundred ... 1Kin 6:1
upon *f* rows of cedar pillars, ... 1Kin 7:2
lily work in the porch, *f* cubits ... 1Kin 7:19
*f* cubits was the length of one ... 1Kin 7:27
*f* cubits the breadth thereof, and ... 1Kin 7:27
And every base had *f* brasen wheels ... 1Kin 7:30
the *f* corners thereof had ... 1Kin 7:30
under the borders were *f* wheels ... 1Kin 7:32
there were *f* undersetters to the ... 1Kin 7:34
to the *f* corners of one base ... 1Kin 7:34
and every laver was *f* cubits ... 1Kin 7:38
*f* hundred pomegranates for the ... 1Kin 7:42
*f* hundred and twenty talents, and ... 1Kin 9:28
*f* hundred chariots, and twelve ... 1Kin 10:26
in Tirzah, twenty and *f* years ... 1Kin 15:33
and the prophets of Baal *f* hundred ... 1Kin 18:19
prophets of the groves *f* hundred ... 1Kin 18:19
but Baal's prophets are *f* hundred ... 1Kin 18:22
Fill *f* barrels with water, and ... 1Kin 18:33
about *f* hundred men, and said unto ... 1Kin 22:6
there were *f* leprous men at the ... 2Kin 7:3
the corner gate, *f* hundred cubits ... 2Kin 14:13
Shobab, and Nathan, and Solomon, *f* ... 1Chr 3:5
bow, and skilful in war, were *f* ... 1Chr 5:18
and Puah, Jashub, and Shimrom, *f* ... 1Chr 7:1
and two thousand and thirty and *f* ... 1Chr 7:7
In *f* quarters were the porters, ... 1Chr 9:24
the *f* chief porters, were in ... 1Chr 9:26
the children of Levi *f* thousand ... 1Chr 12:26
whose fingers and toes were *f* ... 1Chr 20:6
Judah was *f* hundred threescore and ... 1Chr 21:5
and his *f* sons with him hid ... 1Chr 21:20
*f* thousand were to set forward ... 1Chr 23:4
Moreover *f* thousand were porters ... 1Chr 23:5
*f* thousand praised the LORD with ... 1Chr 23:5
These *f* were the sons of Shimei ... 1Chr 23:10
Izhar, Hebron, and Uzziel, *f* ... 1Chr 23:12
and twentieth to Delaiah, the *f* ... 1Chr 24:18
The *f* and twentieth to ... 1Chr 25:31
*f* a day, southward *f* a day ... 1Chr 26:17
*f* at the causeway, and two at ... 1Chr 26:18
course were twenty and *f* thousand ... 1Chr 27:1
course were twenty and *f* thousand ... 1Chr 27:2
were twenty and *f* thousand ... 1Chr 27:4
course were twenty and *f* thousand ... 1Chr 27:5
course were twenty and *f* thousand ... 1Chr 27:7
course were twenty and *f* thousand ... 1Chr 27:8
course were twenty and *f* thousand ... 1Chr 27:9
course were twenty and *f* thousand ... 1Chr 27:10
course were twenty and *f* thousand ... 1Chr 27:11
course were twenty and *f* thousand ... 1Chr 27:12
course were twenty and *f* thousand ... 1Chr 27:13
course were twenty and *f* thousand ... 1Chr 27:14
course were twenty and *f* thousand ... 1Chr 27:15
*f* hundred chariots, and twelve ... 2Chr 1:14
*f* hundred pomegranates on the two ... 2Chr 4:13
Ophir, and took thence *f* hundred ... 2Chr 8:18
Solomon had *f* thousand stalls for ... 2Chr 9:25
even *f* hundred thousand chosen ... 2Chr 13:3
of prophets *f* hundred men ... 2Chr 18:5
the corner gate, *f* hundred cubits ... 2Chr 25:23
basons of a second sort *f* hundred ... Ezr 1:10
were five thousand and *f* hundred ... Ezr 1:11
a thousand two hundred fifty and *f* ... Ezr 2:7
of Adin, *f* hundred fifty and *f* ... Ezr 2:15
a thousand two hundred fifty and *f* ... Ezr 2:31
of Hodaviah, seventy and *f* ... Ezr 2:40
camels, *f* hundred thirty and five ... Ezr 2:67
two hundred rams, *f* hundred lambs ... Ezr 6:17
unto me *f* times after this sort ... Neh 6:4
a thousand two hundred fifty and *f* ... Neh 7:12
Bezai, three hundred twenty and *f* ... Neh 7:23
a thousand two hundred fifty and *f* ... Neh 7:34
children of Hodevah, seventy and *f* ... Neh 7:43
camels, *f* hundred thirty and five ... Neh 7:69
were *f* hundred threescore ... Neh 11:6
were two hundred fourscore and *f* ... Neh 11:18
smote the *f* corners of the house, ... Job 1:19
sons' sons, even *f* generations ... Job 42:16
*f* things say not, It is enough ... Prov 30:15
for me, yea, *f* which I know not ... Prov 30:18
for *f* which it cannot bear ... Prov 30:21
There be *f* things which are ... Prov 30:24
well, yea, *f* are comely in going ... Prov 30:29
from the *f* corners of the earth ... Is 11:12
*f* or five in the outmost fruitful ... Is 17:6
I will appoint over them *f* kinds ... Jer 15:3
Jehudi had read three or *f* leaves ... Jer 36:23
upon Elam will I bring the *f* ... Jer 49:36
from the *f* quarters of heaven ... Jer 49:36
thickness thereof was *f* fingers ... Jer 52:21
all the persons were *f* thousand ... Jer 52:30
likeness of *f* living creatures ... Eze 1:5
And every one had *f* faces ... Eze 1:6
and every one had *f* wings ... Eze 1:6
their wings on their *f* sides ... Eze 1:8
they *f* had their faces and their ... Eze 1:8

they *f* had the face of a man, and Eze 1:10
they *f* had the face of an ox on Eze 1:10
they *f* also had the face of an Eze 1:10
creatures, with his *f* faces Eze 1:15
and they *f* had one likeness Eze 1:16
they went upon their *f* sides Eze 1:17
full of eyes round about them *f* Eze 1:18
upon the *f* corners of the land Eze 7:2
behold the *f* wheels by the Eze 10:9
they *f* had one likeness, as if a Eze 10:10
they went upon their *f* sides Eze 10:11
even the wheels that they *f* had Eze 10:12
And every one had *f* faces Eze 10:14
Every one had *f* faces apiece Eze 10:21
and every one *f* wings Eze 10:21
How much more when I send my *f* Eze 14:21
Come from the *f* winds, O breath, Eze 37:9
*F* tables were on this side, and Eze 40:41
*f* tables on that side, by the Eze 40:41
the *f* tables were of hewn stone Eze 40:42
*f* cubits, round about the house Eze 41:5
He measured it by the *f* sides Eze 42:20
greater settle shall be *f* cubits Eze 43:14
So the altar shall be *f* cubits Eze 43:15
altar and upward shall be *f* horns Eze 43:15
square in the *f* squares thereof Eze 43:16
broad in the *f* squares thereof Eze 43:17
and put it on the *f* horns of it Eze 43:20
on the *f* corners of the settle, Eze 43:20
upon the *f* corners of the settle Eze 45:19
by the *f* corners of the court Eze 46:21
In the *f* corners of the court Eze 46:22
these *f* corners were of one Eze 46:22
about in them, round about them *f* Eze 46:23
the north side *f* thousand Eze 48:16
and the south side *f* thousand Eze 48:16
and on the east side *f* thousand Eze 48:16
and the west side *f* thousand Eze 48:16
*f* thousand and five hundred Eze 48:30
And at the east side *f* thousand Eze 48:32
And at the south side *f* thousand Eze 48:33
At the west side *f* thousand Eze 48:34
As for these *f* children, God gave Dan 1:17
I see *f* men loose, walking in the Dan 3:25
the *f* winds of the heaven strove Dan 7:2
*f* great beasts came up from the Dan 7:3
the back of it *f* wings of a fowl Dan 7:6
the beast had also *f* heads Dan 7:6
These great beasts, which are *f* Dan 7:17
are *f* kings, which shall arise Dan 7:17
for it came up *f* notable ones Dan 8:8
ones toward the *f* winds of heaven Dan 8:8
whereas *f* stood up for it Dan 8:22
*f* kingdoms shall stand up out of Dan 8:22
And in the *f* and twentieth day of Dan 10:4
toward the *f* winds of heaven Dan 11:4
of Damascus, and for *f*, I will not Amos 1:3
transgressions of Gaza, and for *f* Amos 1:6
transgressions of Tyrus, and for *f* Amos 1:9
transgressions of Edom, and for *f* Amos 1:11
the children of Ammon, and for *f* Amos 1:13
transgressions of Moab, and for *f* Amos 2:1
transgressions of Judah, and for *f* Amos 2:4
of Israel, and for *f*, I will not Amos 2:6
In the *f* and twentieth day of the Hag 1:15
In the *f* and twentieth day of the Hag 2:10
this day and upward, from the *f* Hag 2:18
LORD came unto Haggai in the *f* Hag 2:20
Upon the *f* and twentieth day of Zec 1:7
eyes, and saw, and behold *f* horns Zec 1:18
the LORD shewed me *f* carpenters Zec 1:20
as the *f* winds of the heaven Zec 2:6
there came *f* chariots out from Zec 6:1
These are the *f* spirits of the Zec 6:5
that did eat were *f* thousand men Mt 15:38
seven loaves of the *f* thousand Mt 16:10
his elect from the *f* winds Mt 24:31
the palsy, which was borne of *f* Mk 2:3
had eaten were about *f* thousand Mk 8:9
when the seven among *f* thousand Mk 8:20
his elect from the *f* winds Mk 13:27
*f* years, which departed not from Lk 2:37
not ye, There are yet *f* months Jn 4:35
lain in the grave *f* days already Jn 11:17
for he hath been dead *f* days Jn 11:39
made *f* parts, to every soldier a Jn 19:23
of men, about *f* hundred, joined Acts 5:36
entreat them evil *f* hundred years Acts 7:6
great sheet knit at the *f* corners Acts 10:11
*F* days ago I was fasting until Acts 10:30
let down from heaven by *f* corners Acts 11:5
delivered him to *f* quaternions of Acts 12:4
about the space of *f* hundred Acts 13:20
And the same man had *f* daughters Acts 21:9
We have *f* men which have Acts 21:23
*f* thousand men that were Acts 21:38
they cast *f* anchors out of the Acts 27:29
the law, which was *f* hundred Gal 3:17
And round about the throne were *f* Rev 4:4
and upon the seats I saw *f* Rev 4:4
were *f* beasts full of eyes before Rev 4:6
the *f* beasts had each of them six Rev 4:8
The *f* and twenty elders fall down Rev 4:10
of the throne and of the *f* beasts Rev 5:6
the *f* beasts and *f* and twenty Rev 5:8
And the *f* beasts said, Amen Rev 5:14
And the *f* and twenty elders fell Rev 5:14
one of the *f* beasts saying, Come Rev 6:1
in the midst of the *f* beasts say Rev 6:6
after these things I saw *f* angels Rev 7:1
on the *f* corners of the earth Rev 7:1
holding the *f* winds of the earth, Rev 7:1
with a loud voice to the *f* angels Rev 7:2
*f* thousand of all the tribes of Rev 7:4
the *f* beasts, and fell before the Rev 7:11
I heard a voice from the *f* horns Rev 9:13
Loose the *f* angels which are Rev 9:14
the *f* angels were loosed, which Rev 9:15
And the *f* and twenty elders, which Rev 11:16
*f* thousand, having his Father's Rev 14:1
throne, and before the *f* beasts Rev 14:3
*f* thousand, which were redeemed Rev 14:3
one of the *f* beasts gave unto the Rev 15:7
And the *f* and twenty elders and the Rev 19:4
the *f* beasts fell down and Rev 19:4
in the *f* quarters of the earth Rev 20:8
*f* cubits, according to the Rev 21:17

**FOURFOLD**

And he shall restore the lamb *f* 2Sa 12:6
false accusation, I restore him *f* Lk 19:8

**FOURFOOTED**

manner of *f* beasts of the earth Acts 10:12
saw *f* beasts of the earth, and Acts 11:6
*f* beasts, and creeping things Rom 1:23

**FOURSCORE**

And Abram was *f* and six years old, Gen 16:16
Isaac were an hundred and *f* years Gen 35:28
And Moses was *f* years old, and Ex 7:7
*f* years old, and Aaron *f* Ex 7:7
*f* thousand and six thousand and Num 2:9
thousand and five hundred and *f* Num 4:48
and now, lo, I am this day *f* Josh 14:10
And the land had rest *f* years Judg 3:30
priests, and slew on that day *f* 1Sa 22:18
a very aged man, even *f* years old 2Sa 19:32
I am this day *f* years old 2Sa 19:35
and *f* thousand hewers in the 1Kin 5:15
*f* thousand chosen men, which were 1Kin 12:21
was sold for *f* pieces of silver 2Kin 6:25
Jehu appointed *f* men without 2Kin 10:24
of the Assyrians an hundred *f* 2Kin 19:35
in all by their genealogies *f* 1Chr 7:5
the chief, and his brethren *f* 1Chr 15:9
were cunning, was two hundred *f* 1Chr 25:7
*f* thousand to hew in the mountain 2Chr 2:2
*f* thousand to be hewers in the 2Chr 2:18
*f* thousand chosen men, which were 2Chr 11:1
bows, two hundred and *f* thousand 2Chr 14:8
him two hundred and *f* thousand 2Chr 17:15
*f* thousand ready prepared for the 2Chr 17:18
with him *f* priests of the LORD, 2Chr 26:17
of Michael, and with him *f* males Ezr 8:8
and Netophah, an hundred *f* Neh 7:26
the holy city were two hundred *f* Neh 11:18
days, even an hundred and *f* days Est 1:4
of strength they be *f* years Ps 90:10
*f* concubines, and virgins without Song 6:8
of the Assyrians an hundred and *f* Is 37:36
and from Samaria, even *f* men Jer 41:5
And she was a widow of about *f* Lk 2:37
him, Take thy bill, and write *f* Lk 16:7

**FOURSQUARE**

the altar shall be *f* Ex 27:1
*F* it shall be being doubled Ex 28:16
breadth thereof; *f* shall it be Ex 30:2
of it a cubit; it was *f* Ex 37:25
the breadth thereof; it was *f* Ex 38:1
It was *f*; they made the Ex 39:9
gravings with their borders, *f* 1Kin 7:31
and an hundred cubits broad, *f* Eze 40:47
shall offer the holy oblation *f* Eze 48:20
And the city lieth *f*, and the Rev 21:16

**FOURTEEN**

I served thee *f* years for thy two Gen 31:41
all the souls were *f* Gen 46:22
*f* thousand and six hundred Num 1:27
*f* thousand and six hundred Num 2:4
in the plague were *f* thousand Num 16:49
*f* lambs of the first year Num 29:13
deal to each lamb of the *f* lambs Num 29:15
*f* lambs of the first year without Num 29:17
*f* lambs of the first year without Num 29:20
*f* lambs of the first year without Num 29:23
*f* lambs of the first year without Num 29:26
*f* lambs of the first year without Num 29:29
*f* lambs of the first year without Num 29:32
*f* cities with their villages Josh 15:36
*f* cities with their villages Josh 18:28
days and seven days, even *f* days 1Kin 8:65
And God gave to Heman *f* sons 1Chr 25:5
waxed mighty, and married *f* wives 2Chr 13:21
for he had *f* thousand sheep, and Job 42:12
the settle shall be *f* cubits long Eze 43:17
*f* broad in the four squares Eze 43:17
to David are *f* generations Mt 1:17
into Babylon are *f* generations Mt 1:17
unto Christ are *f* generations Mt 1:17
a man in Christ above *f* years ago 2Cor 12:2
Then *f* years after I went up Gal 2:1

**FOURTEENTH**

in the *f* year came Chedorlaomer, Gen 14:5
until the *f* day of the same month Ex 12:6
on the *f* day of the month at even Ex 12:18
In the *f* day of the first month Lev 23:5
In the *f* day of this month, at Num 9:3
they kept the passover on the *f* Num 9:5
The *f* day of the second month at Num 9:11
in the *f* day of the first month Num 28:16
kept the passover on the *f* day of Josh 5:10
Now in the *f* year of king 2Kin 18:13
to Huppah, the *f* to Jeshebeab, 1Chr 24:13
The *f* to Mattithiah, he, his sons 1Chr 25:21
on the *f* day of the second month 2Chr 30:15
on the *f* day of the first month 2Chr 35:1
upon the *f* day of the first month Ezr 6:19
the *f* day also of the month Adar Est 9:15
on the *f* day of the same rested Est 9:17
day thereof, and on the *f* thereof Est 9:18
made the *f* day of the month Adar Est 9:19
keep the *f* day of the month Adar Est 9:21
in the *f* year of king Hezekiah Is 36:1
in the *f* year after that the city Eze 40:1
in the *f* day of the month, ye Eze 45:21
But when the *f* night was come, as Acts 27:27
This day is the *f* day that ye Acts 27:33

**FOURTH**

and the morning were the *f* day Gen 1:19
And the *f* river is Euphrates Gen 2:14
But in the *f* generation they Gen 15:16
*f* generation of them that hate me Ex 20:5
the *f* row a beryl, and an onyx, and Ex 28:20
*f* part of an hin of beaten oil Ex 29:40
the *f* part of an hin of wine for Ex 29:40
the third and to the *f* generation Ex 34:7
And the *f* row, a beryl, an onyx, Ex 39:13
But in the *f* year all the fruit Lev 19:24
be of wine, the *f* part of a hin Lev 23:13
On the *f* day Elizur the son of Num 7:30
unto the third and *f* generation Num 14:18
with the *f* part of an hin of oil Num 15:4
the *f* part of an hin of wine for Num 15:5
number of the *f* part of Israel Num 23:10
mingled with the *f* part of an hin Num 28:5
offering thereof shall be the *f* Num 28:7
a *f* part of an hin unto a lamb Num 28:14
on the *f* day ten bullocks, two Num 29:23
*f* generation of them that hate me Deut 5:9
the *f* lot came out to Issachar, Josh 19:17
And it came to pass on the *f* day Judg 19:5
I have here at hand the *f* part of 1Sa 9:8
And the *f*, Adonijah the son of 2Sa 3:4
in the *f* year of Solomon's reign 1Kin 6:1
olive tree, a *f* part of the wall 1Kin 6:33
In the *f* year was the foundation 1Kin 6:37
to reign over Judah in the *f* year 1Kin 22:41
the *f* part of a cab of dove's 2Kin 6:25
thy children of the *f* generation 2Kin 10:30
of Israel unto the *f* generation 2Kin 15:12
in the *f* year of king Hezekiah 2Kin 18:9
on the ninth day of the *f* month 2Kin 25:3
Nethaneel the *f*, Raddai the fifth 1Chr 2:14
the *f*, Adonijah the son of 1Chr 3:2
the third Zedekiah, the *f* Shallum 1Chr 3:15
Nohah the *f*, and Rapha the fifth 1Chr 8:2
Mishmannah the *f*, Jeremiah the 1Chr 12:10
the third, and Jekameam the *f* 1Chr 23:19
third to Harim, the *f* to Seorim, 1Chr 24:8
the third, Jekameam the *f* 1Chr 24:23
The *f* to Izri, he, his sons, and 1Chr 25:11
the third, Jathniel the *f* 1Chr 26:2
Joah the third, and Sacar the *f* 1Chr 26:4
the third, Zechariah the *f* 1Chr 26:11
The *f* captain for the *f* 1Chr 27:7
The *f* captain for the *f* 1Chr 27:7
in the *f* year of his reign 2Chr 3:2
on the *f* day they assembled 2Chr 20:26
Now on the *f* day was the silver Ezr 8:33
*f* day of this month the children Neh 9:1
their God one *f* part of the day Neh 9:3
another *f* part they confessed, and Neh 9:3
*f* year of Jehoiakim the son of Jer 25:1
king of Judah, in the *f* year Jer 28:1
it came to pass in the *f* year of Jer 36:1
year of Zedekiah, in the *f* month Jer 39:2
in the *f* year of Jehoiakim the Jer 45:1
*f* year of Jehoiakim the son of Jer 46:2
in the *f* year of his reign Jer 51:59
And in the *f* month, in the ninth Jer 52:6
thirtieth year, in the *f* month Eze 1:1
the *f* the face of an eagle Eze 10:14
the *f* kingdom shall be strong as Dan 2:40
the form of the *f* is like the Son Dan 3:25
visions, and behold a *f* beast Dan 7:7
know the truth of the *f* beast Dan 7:19
The *f* beast shall be the *f* Dan 7:23
the *f* shall be far richer than Dan 11:2
in the *f* chariot grisled and bay Zec 6:3
pass in the *f* year of king Darius Zec 7:1
in the *f* day of the ninth month Zec 7:1
The fast of the *f* month, and the Zec 8:19
in the *f* watch of the night Jesus Mt 14:25
about the *f* watch of the night he Mk 6:48
the *f* beast was like a flying Rev 4:7
And when he had opened the *f* seal Rev 6:7
the voice of the *f* beast say Rev 6:7
them over the *f* part of the earth Rev 6:8
the *f* angel sounded, and the third Rev 8:12
the *f* angel poured out his vial Rev 16:8
the *f*, an emerald Rev 21:19

**FOWL**

*f* that may fly above the earth in Gen 1:20
every winged *f* after his kind Gen 1:21
let *f* multiply in the earth Gen 1:22
over the *f* of the air, and over Gen 1:26
over the *f* of the air, and over Gen 1:28
to every *f* of the air, and to Gen 1:30

F

the field, and every *f* of the air ... Gen 2:19
to the *f* of the air, and to every ... Gen 2:20
every *f* after his kind, every ... Gen 7:14
moved upon the earth, both of *f* ... Gen 7:21
things, and the *f* of the heaven ... Gen 7:23
thee, of all flesh, both of *f* ... Gen 8:17
every creeping thing, and every *f* ... Gen 8:19
clean beast, and of every clean *f* ... Gen 8:20
earth, and upon every *f* of the air ... Gen 9:2
that is with you, of the *f* ... Gen 9:10
whether it be of *f* or of beast ... Lev 7:26
law of the beasts, and of the *f* ... Lev 11:46
any beast or *f* that may be eaten ... Lev 17:13
abominable by beast, or by *f* ... Lev 20:25
winged *f* that flieth in the air ... Deut 4:17
and fallowdeer, and fatted *f* ... 1Kin 4:23
he spake also of beasts, and of *f* ... 1Kin 4:33
is a path which no *f* knoweth ... Job 28:7
The *f* of the air, and the fish of ... Ps 8:8
creeping things, and flying *f* ... Ps 148:10
both the *f* of the heavens and the ... Jer 9:10
shall dwell all *f* of every wing ... Eze 17:23
Speak unto every feathered *f* ... Eze 39:17
or torn, whether it be *f* or beast ... Eze 44:31
the back of it four wings of a *f* ... Dan 7:6

**FOWLER**
thee from the snare of the *f* ... Ps 91:3
as a bird from the hand of the *f* ... Prov 6:5
is a snare of a *f* in all his ways ... Hos 9:8

**FOWLERS**
a bird out of the snare of the *f* ... Ps 124:7

**FOWLS**
thing, and the *f* of the air ... Gen 6:7
Of *f* after their kind, and of ... Gen 6:20
Of *f* also of the air by sevens, ... Gen 7:3
that are not clean, and of *f* ... Gen 7:8
when the *f* came down upon the ... Gen 15:11
his offering to the LORD be of *f* ... Lev 1:14
have in abomination among the *f* ... Lev 11:13
All *f* that creep, going upon all ... Lev 11:20
and unclean, and between unclean *f* ... Lev 20:25
But of all clean *f* ye may eat ... Deut 14:20
be meat unto all *f* of the air ... Deut 28:26
thy flesh unto the *f* of the air ... 1Sa 17:44
this day unto the *f* of the air ... 1Sa 17:46
field shall the *f* of the air eat ... 1Kin 14:11
fields shall the *f* of the air eat ... 1Kin 16:4
field shall the *f* of the air eat ... 1Kin 21:24
also *f* were prepared for me, and ... Neh 5:18
the *f* of the air, and they shall ... Job 12:7
kept close from the *f* of the air ... Job 28:21
us wiser than the *f* of heaven ... Job 35:11
I know all the *f* of the mountains ... Ps 50:11
feathered *f* like as the sand of ... Ps 78:27
be meat unto the *f* of the heaven ... Ps 79:2
By them shall the *f* of the heaven ... Ps 104:12
unto the *f* of the mountains ... Is 18:6
the *f* shall summer upon them, and ... Is 18:6
be meat for the *f* of the heaven ... Jer 7:33
the *f* of the heaven, and the ... Jer 15:3
shall be meat for the *f* of heaven ... Jer 16:4
be meat for the *f* of the heaven ... Jer 19:7
for meat unto the *f* of the heaven ... Jer 34:20
field and to the *f* of the heaven ... Eze 29:5
All the *f* of heaven made their ... Eze 31:6
all the *f* of the heaven remain ... Eze 31:13
will cause all the *f* of the ... Eze 32:4
the *f* of the heaven, and the ... Eze 38:20
the *f* of the heaven hath he given ... Dan 2:38
the *f* of the heaven dwelt in the ... Dan 4:12
it, and the *f* from his branches ... Dan 4:14
the *f* of the heaven had their ... Dan 4:21
with the *f* of heaven, and with the ... Hos 2:18
field, and with the *f* of heaven ... Hos 4:3
them down as the *f* of the heaven ... Hos 7:12
will consume the *f* of the heaven ... Zeph 1:3
Behold the *f* of the air ... Mt 6:26
the *f* came and devoured them up ... Mt 13:4
the *f* of the air came and devoured ... Mk 4:4
so that the *f* of the air may ... Mk 4:32
the *f* of the air devoured it ... Lk 8:5
more are ye better than the *f* ... Lk 12:24
the *f* of the air lodged in the ... Lk 13:19
creeping things, and *f* of the air ... Acts 10:12
creeping things, and *f* of the air ... Acts 11:6
saying to all the *f* that fly in ... Rev 19:17
all the *f* were filled with their ... Rev 19:21

**FOX**
if a *f* go up, he shall even break ... Neh 4:3
unto them, Go ye, and tell that *f* ... Lk 13:32

**FOXES**
went and caught three hundred *f* ... Judg 15:4
they shall be a portion for *f* ... Ps 63:10
Take us the *f*, the little *f* ... Song 2:15
Take us the *f*, the little *f* ... Song 2:15
is desolate, the *f* walk upon it ... Lam 5:18
are like the *f* in the deserts ... Eze 13:4
The *f* have holes, and the birds of ... Mt 8:20
*F* have holes, and birds of the air ... Lk 9:58

**FRAGMENTS**
they took up of the *f* that ... Mt 14:20
up twelve baskets full of the *f* ... Mk 6:43
many baskets full of *f* took ye up ... Mk 8:19
many baskets full of *f* took ye up ... Mk 8:20
there was taken up of *f* that ... Lk 9:17
Gather up the *f* that remain ... Jn 6:12
the *f* of the five barley loaves ... Jn 6:13

**FRAIL**
that I may know how *f* I am ... Ps 39:4

**FRAME**
for he could not *f* to pronounce ... Judg 12:6
For he knoweth our *f* ... Ps 103:14
I *f* evil against you, and devise a ... Jer 18:11
by which was as the *f* of a city ... Eze 40:2
They will not *f* their doings to ... Hos 5:4

**FRAMED**
or shall the thing *f* say of him ... Is 29:16
thing *f* say of him that *f* it ... Is 29:16
*f* together groweth unto an holy ... Eph 2:21
worlds were *f* by the word of God ... Heb 11:3

**FRAMETH**
to evil, and thy tongue *f* deceit ... Ps 50:19
which *f* mischief by a law ... Ps 94:20

**FRANKINCENSE**
these sweet spices with pure *f* ... Ex 30:34
oil upon it, and put *f* thereon ... Lev 2:1
thereof, with all the *f* thereof ... Lev 2:2
put oil upon it, and lay *f* thereon ... Lev 2:15
thereof, with all the *f* thereof ... Lev 2:16
shall he put any *f* thereon ... Lev 5:11
all the *f* which is upon the meat ... Lev 6:15
shalt put pure *f* upon each row ... Lev 24:7
no oil upon it, nor put *f* thereon ... Num 5:15
and the wine, and the oil, and the *f* ... 1Chr 9:29
laid the meat offerings, the *f* ... Neh 13:5
with the meat offering and the *f* ... Neh 13:9
smoke, perfumed with myrrh and *f* ... Song 3:6
of myrrh, and to the hill of *f* ... Song 4:6
and cinnamon, with all trees of *f* ... Song 4:14
gold, and *f*, and myrrh ... Mt 2:11
and odours, and ointments, and *f* ... Rev 18:13

**FRANKLY**
to pay, he *f* forgave them both ... Lk 7:42

**FRAUD**
is full of cursing and deceit and *f* ... Ps 10:7
which is of you kept back by *f* ... Jas 5:4

**FRAY**
and no man shall *f* them away ... Deut 28:26
and none shall *f* them away ... Jer 7:33
but these are come to *f* them ... Zec 1:21

**FRECKLED**
it is a *f* spot that groweth in ... Lev 13:39

**FREE**
he shall go out *f* for nothing ... Ex 21:2
I will not go out *f* ... Ex 21:5
shall she go out *f* without money ... Ex 21:11
let him go *f* for his eye's sake ... Ex 21:26
he shall let him go *f* for his ... Ex 21:27
him *f* offerings every morning ... Ex 36:3
to death, because she was not *f* ... Lev 19:20
be thou *f* from this bitter water ... Num 5:19
then she shall be *f*, and shall ... Num 5:28
thou shalt let him go *f* from thee ... Deut 15:12
thou sendest him out *f* from thee ... Deut 15:13
thou sendest him away *f* from thee ... Deut 15:18
but he shall be *f* at home one ... Deut 24:5
his father's house *f* in Israel ... 1Sa 17:25
remaining in the chambers were *f* ... 1Chr 9:33
as many as were of a *f* heart ... 2Chr 29:31
the servant is *f* from his master ... Job 3:19
Who hath sent out the wild ass *f* ... Job 39:5
and uphold me with thy *f* spirit ... Ps 51:12
*F* among the dead, like the slain ... Ps 88:5
of the people, and let him go *f* ... Ps 105:20
and to let the oppressed go *f* ... Is 58:6
an Hebrew or an Hebrewess, go *f* ... Jer 34:9
every one his maidservant, go *f* ... Jer 34:10
handmaids, whom they had let go *f* ... Jer 34:11
thou shalt let him go *f* from thee ... Jer 34:14
and publish the *f* offerings ... Amos 4:5
or his mother, he shall be *f* ... Mt 15:6
unto him, Then are the children *f* ... Mt 17:26
he shall be *f* ... Mk 7:11
and the truth shall make you *f* ... Jn 8:32
sayest thou, Ye shall be made *f* ... Jn 8:33
Son therefore shall make you *f* ... Jn 8:36
ye shall be *f* indeed ... Jn 8:36
And Paul said, But I was *f* born ... Acts 22:28
offence, so also is the *f* gift ... Rom 5:15
but the *f* gift is of many ... Rom 5:16
the *f* gift came upon all men unto ... Rom 5:18
Being then made *f* from sin ... Rom 6:18
ye were *f* from righteousness ... Rom 6:20
But now being made *f* from sin ... Rom 6:22
be dead, she is *f* from that law ... Rom 7:3
made me *f* from the law of sin ... Rom 8:2
but if thou mayest be made *f* ... 1Cor 7:21
also he that is called, being *f* ... 1Cor 7:22
am I not *f*? ... 1Cor 9:1
For though I be *f* from all men ... 1Cor 9:19
Gentiles, whether we be bond or *f* ... 1Cor 12:13
there is neither bond nor *f* ... Gal 3:28
But Jerusalem which is above is *f* ... Gal 4:26
heir with the son of the *f* woman ... Gal 4:30
of the bondwoman, but of the *f* ... Gal 4:31
wherewith Christ hath made us *f* ... Gal 5:1
the Lord, whether he be bond or *f* ... Eph 6:8
Barbarian, Scythian, bond nor *f* ... Col 3:11
of the Lord may have *f* course ... 2Th 3:1
As *f*, and not using your liberty ... 1Pet 2:16
and every bondman, and every *f* man ... Rev 6:15
small and great, rich and poor, *f* ... Rev 13:16
and the flesh of all men, both *f* ... Rev 19:18

**FREED**
of you be *f* from being bondmen ... Josh 9:23
For he that is dead is *f* from sin ... Rom 6:7

**FREEDMEN** See LIBERTINES.

**FREEDOM**
at all redeemed, nor *f* given her ... Lev 19:20
a great sum obtained I this *f* ... Acts 22:28

**FREELY**
of the garden thou mayest *f* eat ... Gen 2:16
fish, which we did eat in Egypt *f* ... Num 11:5
*f* to day of the spoil of their ... 1Sa 14:30
offered *f* for the house of God to ... Ezr 2:68
his counsellors have *f* offered ... Ezr 7:15
I will *f* sacrifice unto thee ... Ps 54:6
backsliding, I will love them *f* ... Hos 14:4
*f* ye have received, *f* give ... Mt 10:8
*f* ye have received, *f* give ... Mt 10:8
let me *f* speak unto you of the ... Acts 2:29
before whom also I speak *f* ... Acts 26:26
Being justified *f* by his grace ... Rom 3:24
him also *f* give us all things ... Rom 8:32
that are *f* given to us of God ... 1Cor 2:12
to you the gospel of God *f* ... 2Cor 11:7
fountain of the water of life *f* ... Rev 21:6
let him take the water of life *f* ... Rev 22:17

**FREEMAN**
being a servant, is the Lord's *f* ... 1Cor 7:22

**FREEWILL**
vows, and for all his *f* offerings ... Lev 22:18
or a *f* offering in beeves or ... Lev 22:21
thou offer for a *f* offering ... Lev 22:23
and beside all your *f* offerings ... Lev 23:38
or in a *f* offering, or in your ... Num 15:3
your *f* offerings, for your burnt ... Num 29:39
vows, and your *f* offerings, and the ... Deut 12:6
nor thy *f* offerings, or heave ... Deut 12:17
of a *f* offering of thine hand ... Deut 16:10
even a *f* offering, according as ... Deut 23:23
was over the *f* offerings of God, ... 2Chr 31:14
beside the *f* offering for the ... Ezr 1:4
a *f* offering unto the LORD ... Ezr 3:5
their own *f* to go up to Jerusalem ... Ezr 7:13
with the *f* offering of the people ... Ezr 7:16
the gold are a *f* offering unto ... Ezr 8:28
the *f* offerings of my mouth, O ... Ps 119:108

**FREEWOMAN**
by a bondmaid, the other by a *f* ... Gal 4:22
but he of the *f* was by promise ... Gal 4:23

**FREQUENT**
above measure, in prisons more *f* ... 2Cor 11:23

**FRESH**
of it was as the taste of *f* oil ... Num 11:8
My glory was *f* in me, and my bow ... Job 29:20
I shall be anointed with *f* oil ... Ps 92:10
both yield salt water and *f* ... Jas 3:12

**FRESHER**
flesh shall be *f* than a child's ... Job 33:25

**FRET**
it is *f* inward, whether it be ... Lev 13:55
her sore, for to make her *f* ... 1Sa 1:6
*F* not thyself because of ... Ps 37:1
*f* not thyself because of him who ... Ps 37:7
*f* not thyself in any wise to do ... Ps 37:8
*F* not thyself because of evil men ... Prov 24:19
hungry, they shall *f* themselves ... Is 8:21

**FRETTED**
but hast *f* me in all these things ... Eze 16:43

**FRETTETH**
his heart *f* against the LORD ... Prov 19:3

**FRETTING**
the plague is a *f* leprosy ... Lev 13:51
for it is a *f* leprosy ... Lev 13:52
it is a *f* leprosy in the house ... Lev 14:44

**FRIED**
with oil, of fine flour, *f* ... Lev 7:12
the pan, and for that which is *f* ... 1Chr 23:29

**FRIEND**
his *f* Hirah the Adullamite ... Gen 38:12
the hand of his *f* the Adullamite ... Gen 38:20
as a man speaketh unto his *f* ... Ex 33:11
the wife of thy bosom, or thy *f* ... Deut 13:6
whom he had used as his *f* ... Judg 14:20
But Amnon had a *f*, whose name was ... 2Sa 13:3
So Hushai David's *f* came into the ... 2Sa 15:37
Hushai the Archite, David's *f* ... 2Sa 16:16
Is this thy kindness to thy *f* ... 2Sa 16:17
why wentest thou not with thy *f* ... 2Sa 16:17
officer, and the king's *f* ... 1Kin 4:5
seed of Abraham thy *f* for ever ... 2Chr 20:7
pity should be shewed from his *f* ... Job 6:14
and ye dig a pit for your *f* ... Job 6:27
he had been my *f* or brother ... Ps 35:14
Yea, mine own familiar *f*, in whom ... Ps 41:9
*f* hast thou put far from me, and ... Ps 88:18
son, if thou be surety for thy *f* ... Prov 6:1
art come into the hand of thy *f* ... Prov 6:3
thyself, and make sure thy *f* ... Prov 6:3
A *f* loveth at all times, and a ... Prov 17:17
surety in the presence of his *f* ... Prov 17:18
there is a *f* that sticketh closer ... Prov 18:24

every man is a *f* to him that Prov 19:6
his lips the king shall be his *f* Prov 22:11
Faithful are the wounds of a *f* Prov 27:6
of a man's *f* by hearty counsel Prov 27:9
Thine own *f*, and thy father's Prov 27:10
own *f*, and thy father's *f* Prov 27:10
blesseth his *f* with a loud voice Prov 27:14
the countenance of his *f* Prov 27:17
is my beloved, and this is my *f* Song 5:16
chosen, the seed of Abraham my *f* Is 41:8
neighbour and his *f* shall perish Jer 6:21
the flesh of his *f* in the siege Jer 19:9
love a woman beloved of her *f* Hos 3:1
Trust ye not in a *f*, put ye not Mic 7:5
a *f* of publicans and sinners Mt 11:19
answered one of them, and said, *F* Mt 20:13
And he saith unto him, *F*, how Mt 22:12
And Jesus said unto him, *F* Mt 26:50
a *f* of publicans and sinners Lk 7:34
them, Which of you shall have a *f* Lk 11:5
at midnight, and say unto him, *F* Lk 11:5
For a *f* of mine in his journey is Lk 11:6
and give him, because he is his *f* Lk 11:8
cometh, he may say unto thee, *F* Lk 14:10
but the *f* of the bridegroom, Jn 3:29
unto them, Our *f* Lazarus sleepeth Jn 11:11
man go, thou art not Caesar's *f* Jn 19:12
the king's chamberlain their *f* Acts 12:20
and he was called the *F* of God Jas 2:23
a *f* of the world is the enemy of Jas 4:4

**FRIENDLY**
after her, to speak *f* unto her Judg 19:3
hast spoken *f* unto thine handmaid Ruth 2:13
hath friends must shew himself *f* Prov 18:24

**FRIENDS**
Gerar, and Ahuzzath one of his *f* Gen 26:26
elders of Judah, even to his *f* 1Sa 30:26
to his brethren, and to his *f* 2Sa 3:8
thine enemies, and hatest thy *f* 2Sa 19:6
of his kinsfolks, nor of his *f* 1Kin 16:11
home, he sent and called for his *f* Est 5:10
all his *f* unto him, Let a gallows Est 5:14
all his *f* every thing that had Est 6:13
Now when Job's three *f* heard of Job 2:11
My *f* scorn me Job 16:20
that speaketh flattery to his *f* Job 17:5
my familiar *f* have forgotten me Job 19:14
All my inward *f* abhorred me Job 19:19
me, have pity upon me, O ye my *f* Job 19:21
his three *f* was his wrath kindled Job 32:3
thee, and against thy two *f* Job 42:7
of Job, when he prayed for his *f* Job 42:10
my *f* stand aloof from my sore Ps 38:11
but the rich hath many *f* Prov 14:20
and a whisperer separateth chief *f* Prov 16:28
a matter separateth very *f* Prov 17:9
A man that hath *f* must shew Prov 18:24
Wealth maketh many *f* Prov 19:4
more do his *f* go far from him Prov 19:7
eat, O *f*; drink, yea Song 5:1
to thyself, and to all thy *f* Jer 20:4
buried there, thou, and all thy *f* Jer 20:6
Thy *f* have set thee on, and have Jer 38:22
all her *f* have dealt Lam 1:2
was wounded in the house of my *f* Zec 13:6
when his *f* heard of it, they went Mk 3:21
saith unto him, Go home to thy *f* Mk 5:19
the centurion sent *f* to him Lk 7:6
And I say unto you my *f*, Be not Lk 12:4
or a supper, call not thy *f* Lk 14:12
home, he calleth together his *f* Lk 15:6
hath found it, she calleth her *f* Lk 15:9
that I might make merry with my *f* Lk 15:29
to yourselves *f* of the mammon of Lk 16:9
and brethren, and kinsfolks, and *f* Lk 21:16
and Herod were made *f* together Lk 23:12
a man lay down his life for his *f* Jn 15:13
Ye are my *f*, if ye do whatsoever Jn 15:14
but I have called you *f* Jn 15:15
together his kinsmen and near *f* Acts 10:24
chief of Asia, which were his *f* Acts 19:31
go unto his *f* to refresh himself Acts 27:3
Our *f* salute thee 3Jn 14
Greet the *f* by name 3Jn 14

**FRIENDSHIP**
Make no *f* with an angry man Prov 22:24
know ye not that the *f* of the Jas 4:4

**FRINGE**
that they put upon the *f* of the Num 15:38
And it shall be unto you for a *f* Num 15:39

**FRINGES**
them *f* in the borders of their Num 15:38
Thou shalt make thee *f* upon the Deut 22:12

**FRO**
a raven, which went forth to and *f* Gen 8:7
and walked in the house to and *f* 2Kin 4:35
*f* throughout the whole earth, to 2Chr 16:9
*f* in the earth, and from walking Job 1:7
*f* in the earth, and from walking Job 2:2
*f* unto the dawning of the day Job 7:4
thou break a leaf driven to and *f* Job 13:25
They reel to and *f*, and stagger Ps 107:27
*f* of them that seek death Prov 21:6
*f* like a drunkard, and shall be Is 24:20
*f* of locusts shall he run upon Is 33:4
a captive, and removing to and *f* Is 49:21
ye to and *f* through the streets of Jer 5:1
and run to and *f* by the hedges Jer 49:3
to and *f* occupied in thy fairs Eze 27:19
many shall run to and *f*, and Dan 12:4
shall run to and *f* in the city Joel 2:9
*f* to seek the word of the LORD, Amos 8:12
to walk to and *f* through the earth Zec 1:10
*f* through the earth, and, behold, Zec 1:11
*f* through the whole earth Zec 4:10
walk to and *f* through the earth Zec 6:7
walk to and *f* through the earth Zec 6:7
walked to and *f* through the earth Zec 6:7
no more children, tossed to and *f* Eph 4:14

**FROGS**
will smite all thy borders with *f* Ex 8:2
shall bring forth *f* abundantly Ex 8:3
the *f* shall come up both on thee, Ex 8:4
cause *f* to come up upon the land Ex 8:5
the *f* came up, and covered the Ex 8:6
brought up *f* upon the land of Ex 8:7
he may take away the *f* from me Ex 8:8
to destroy the *f* from thee Ex 8:9
the *f* shall depart from thee, and Ex 8:11
*f* which he had brought against Ex 8:12
the *f* died out of the houses, out Ex 8:13
and *f*, which destroyed them Ps 78:45
land brought forth *f* in abundance Ps 105:30
*f* come out of the mouth of the Rev 16:13

**FROM** See PREFACE.

**FRONT**
When Joab saw that the *f* of the 2Sa 10:9
that was in the *f* of the house 2Chr 3:4

**FRONTIERS**
his cities which are on his *f* Eze 25:9

**FRONTLETS**
hand, and for *f* between thine eyes Ex 13:16
they shall be as *f* between thine Deut 6:8
may be as *f* between your eyes Deut 11:18

**FROST**
consumed me, and the *f* by night Gen 31:40
small as the hoar *f* on the ground Ex 16:14
By the breath of God *f* is given Job 37:10
and the hoary *f* of heaven, who Job 38:29
and their sycomore trees with *f* Ps 78:47
scattereth the hoar *f* like ashes Ps 147:16
heat, and in the night to the *f* Jer 36:30

**FROWARD**
for they are a very *f* generation Deut 32:20
with the *f* thou wilt shew thyself 2Sa 22:27
the counsel of the *f* is carried Job 5:13
thyself pure; and with the *f* Ps 18:26
thou wilt shew thyself *f* Ps 18:26
A *f* heart shall depart from me Ps 101:4
the man that speaketh *f* things Prov 2:12
crooked, and they *f* in their paths Prov 2:15
For the *f* is abomination to the Prov 3:32
Put away from thee a *f* mouth Prov 4:24
man, walketh with a *f* mouth Prov 6:12
there is nothing *f* or perverse in Prov 8:8
way, and the *f* mouth, do I hate Prov 8:13
but the *f* tongue shall be cut out Prov 10:31
They that are of a *f* heart are Prov 11:20
A *f* man soweth strife Prov 16:28
his eyes to devise *f* things Prov 16:30
He that hath a *f* heart findeth no Prov 17:20
The way of man is *f* and strange Prov 21:8
and snares are in the way of the *f* Prov 22:5
good and gentle, but also to the *f* 1Pet 2:18

**FROWARDLY**
he went on *f* in the way of his Is 57:17

**FROWARDNESS**
and delight in the *f* of the wicked Prov 2:14
*F* is in his heart, he deviseth Prov 6:14
mouth of the wicked speaketh *f* Prov 10:32

**FROZEN**
and the face of the deep is *f* Job 38:30

**FRUIT**
the *f* tree yielding *f* after Gen 1:11
his kind, and the tree yielding *f* Gen 1:12
in the which is the *f* of a tree Gen 1:29
We may eat of the *f* of the trees Gen 3:2
But of the *f* of the tree which is Gen 3:3
wise, she took of the *f* thereof Gen 3:6
that Cain brought of the *f* of the Gen 4:3
from thee the *f* of the womb Gen 30:2
all the *f* of the trees which the Ex 10:15
so that her *f* depart from her, and Ex 21:22
then ye shall count the *f* thereof Lev 19:23
But in the fourth year all the *f* Lev 19:24
shall ye eat of the *f* thereof Lev 19:25
gathered in the *f* of the land Lev 23:39
and gather in the *f* thereof Lev 25:3
And the land shall yield her *f* Lev 25:19
bring forth *f* for three years Lev 25:21
eat yet of old *f* until the ninth Lev 25:22
of the field shall yield their *f* Lev 26:4
or of the *f* of the tree, is the Lev 27:30
and bring of the *f* of the land Num 13:20
and shewed them the *f* of the land Num 13:26
and this is the *f* of it Num 13:27
they took of the *f* of the land in Deut 1:25
will also bless the *f* of thy womb Deut 7:13
the *f* of thy land, thy corn, and Deut 7:13
and that the land yield not her *f* Deut 11:17
lest the *f* of thy seed which thou Deut 22:9
the *f* of thy vineyard, be defiled Deut 22:9
first of all the *f* of the earth Deut 26:2
shall be the *f* of thy body Deut 28:4
the *f* of thy ground, and the *f* Deut 28:4
the *f* of thy cattle, the increase Deut 28:4
in the *f* of thy body, and in the Deut 28:11
in the *f* of thy cattle, and in the Deut 28:11
in the *f* of thy ground, in the Deut 28:11
Cursed shall be the *f* of thy body Deut 28:18
the *f* of thy land, the increase Deut 28:18
The *f* of thy land, and all thy Deut 28:33
for thine olive shall cast his *f* Deut 28:40
*f* of thy land shall the locust Deut 28:42
he shall eat the *f* of thy cattle Deut 28:51
the *f* of thy land, until thou be Deut 28:51
shalt eat the *f* of thine own body Deut 28:53
in the *f* of thy body Deut 30:9
in the *f* of thy cattle Deut 30:9
in the *f* of thy land, for good Deut 30:9
but they did eat of the *f* of the Josh 5:12
my sweetness, and my good *f* Judg 9:11
summer *f* for the young men to eat 2Sa 16:2
root downward, and bear *f* upward 2Kin 19:30
and *f* trees in abundance Neh 9:25
our fathers to eat the *f* thereof Neh 9:36
firstfruits of all *f* of all trees Neh 10:35
the *f* of all manner of trees, of Neh 10:37
forth his *f* in his season Ps 1:3
Their *f* shalt thou destroy from Ps 21:10
the *f* thereof shall shake like Ps 72:16
still bring forth *f* in old age Ps 92:14
satisfied with the *f* of thy works Ps 104:13
devoured the *f* of their ground Ps 105:35
the *f* of the womb is his reward Ps 127:3
Of the *f* of thy body will I set Ps 132:11
eat of the *f* of their own way Prov 1:31
My *f* is better than gold, yea, Prov 8:19
the *f* of the wicked to sin Prov 10:16
The *f* of the righteous is a tree Prov 11:30
root of the righteous yieldeth *f* Prov 12:12
with good by the *f* of his mouth Prov 12:14
eat good by the *f* of his mouth Prov 13:2
satisfied with the *f* of his mouth Prov 18:20
love it shall eat the *f* thereof Prov 18:21
fig tree shall eat the *f* thereof Prov 27:18
with the *f* of her hands she Prov 31:16
Give her of the *f* of her hands Prov 31:31
his *f* was sweet to my taste Song 2:3
every one for the *f* thereof was Song 8:11
keep the *f* thereof two hundred Song 8:12
shall eat the *f* of their doings Is 3:10
the *f* of the earth shall be Is 4:2
I will punish the *f* of the stout Is 10:12
have no pity on the *f* of the womb Is 13:18
his *f* shall be a fiery flying Is 14:29
fill the face of the world with *f* Is 27:6
this is all the *f* to take away Is 27:9
as the hasty *f* before the summer Is 28:4
vineyards, and eat the *f* thereof Is 37:30
root downward, and bear *f* upward Is 37:31
I create the *f* of the lips Is 57:19
vineyards, and eat the *f* of them Is 65:21
country, to eat the *f* thereof Jer 2:7
even the *f* of their thoughts, Jer 6:19
and upon the *f* of the ground Jer 7:20
olive tree, fair, and of goodly *f* Jer 11:16
the tree with the *f* thereof Jer 11:19
grow, yea, they bring forth *f* Jer 12:2
shall cease from yielding *f* Jer 17:8
according to the *f* of his doings Jer 17:10
according to the *f* of your doings Jer 21:14
gardens, and eat the *f* of them Jer 29:5
gardens, and eat the *f* of them Jer 29:28
according to the *f* of his doings Jer 32:19
Shall the women eat their *f* Lam 2:20
branches, and that it might bear *f* Eze 17:8
thereof, and cut off the *f* thereof Eze 17:9
bring forth boughs, and bear *f* Eze 17:23
and the east wind dried up her *f* Eze 19:12
which hath devoured her *f* Eze 19:14
they shall eat thy *f*, and they Eze 25:4
of the field shall yield her *f* Eze 34:27
yield your *f* to my people of Eze 36:8
and they shall increase and bring *f* Eze 36:11
I will multiply the *f* of the tree Eze 36:30
neither shall the *f* thereof be Eze 47:12
new *f* according to his months Eze 47:12
the *f* thereof shall be for meat, Eze 47:12
the *f* thereof much, and in it was Dan 4:12
off his leaves, and scatter his *f* Dan 4:14
the *f* thereof much, and in it was Dan 4:21
is dried up, they shall bear no *f* Hos 9:16
even the beloved *f* of their womb Hos 9:16
he bringeth forth *f* unto himself Hos 10:1
to the multitude of his *f* he hath Hos 10:1
ye have eaten the *f* of lies Hos 10:13
From me is thy *f* found Hos 14:8
for the tree beareth her *f* Joel 2:22
yet I destroyed his *f* from above Amos 2:9
the *f* of righteousness into Amos 6:12
and a gatherer of sycomore *f* Amos 7:14
and behold a basket of summer *f* Amos 8:1
And I said, A basket of summer *f* Amos 8:2
gardens, and eat the *f* of them Amos 9:14
the *f* of my body for the sin of Mic 6:7
my soul desired the firstripe *f* Mic 7:1
for the *f* of their doings Mic 7:13
neither shall *f* be in the vines Hab 3:17
and the earth is stayed from her *f* Hag 1:10
the vine shall give her *f* Zec 8:12

the *f* thereof, even his meat, is Mal 1:12
shall your vine cast her *f* before Mal 3:11
not forth good *f* is hewn down Mt 3:10
good tree bringeth forth good *f* Mt 7:17
tree bringeth forth evil *f* Mt 7:17
tree cannot bring forth evil *f* Mt 7:18
a corrupt tree bring forth good *f* Mt 7:18
not forth good *f* is hewn down Mt 7:19
make the tree good, and his *f* good Mt 12:33
tree corrupt, and his *f* corrupt Mt 12:33
for the tree is known by his *f* Mt 12:33
good ground, and brought forth *f* Mt 13:8
which also beareth *f*, and bringeth Mt 13:23
was sprung up, and brought forth *f* Mt 13:26
unto it, Let no *f* grow on thee Mt 21:19
when the time of the *f* drew near Mt 21:34
henceforth of this *f* of the vine Mt 26:29
and choked it, and it yielded no *f* Mk 4:7
did yield *f* that sprang up and Mk 4:8
and receive it, and bring forth *f* Mk 4:20
earth bringeth forth *f* of herself Mk 4:28
But when the *f* is brought forth, Mk 4:29
No man eat *f* of thee hereafter Mk 11:14
of the *f* of the vineyard Mk 12:2
no more of the *f* of the vine Mk 14:25
and blessed is the *f* of thy womb Lk 1:42
not forth good *f* is hewn down Lk 3:9
tree bringeth not forth corrupt *f* Lk 6:43
a corrupt tree bring forth good *f* Lk 6:43
every tree is known by his own *f* Lk 6:44
up, and bare *f* an hundredfold Lk 8:8
life, and bring no *f* to perfection Lk 8:14
bring forth *f* with patience Lk 8:15
sought *f* thereon, and found none Lk 13:6
I come seeking *f* on this fig tree Lk 13:7
And if it bear *f*, well Lk 13:9
give him of the *f* of the vineyard Lk 20:10
not drink of the *f* of the vine Lk 22:18
gathereth *f* unto life eternal Jn 4:36
it die, it bringeth forth much *f* Jn 12:24
that beareth not *f* he taketh away Jn 15:2
and every branch that beareth *f* Jn 15:2
that it may bring forth more *f* Jn 15:2
branch cannot bear *f* of itself Jn 15:4
the same bringeth forth much *f* Jn 15:5
glorified, that ye bear much *f* Jn 15:8
ye should go and bring forth *f* Jn 15:16
that your *f* should remain Jn 15:16
that of the *f* of his loins, Acts 2:30
might have some *f* among you also Rom 1:13
What *f* had ye then in those Rom 6:21
ye have your *f* unto holiness, and Rom 6:22
we should bring forth *f* unto God Rom 7:4
to bring forth *f* unto death Rom 7:5
and have sealed to them this *f* Rom 15:28
and eateth not of the *f* thereof 1Cor 9:7
But the *f* of the Spirit is love, Gal 5:22
(For the *f* of the Spirit is in Eph 5:9
this is the *f* of my labour Phil 1:22
but I desire *f* that may abound to Phil 4:17
and bringeth forth *f*, as it doth Col 1:6
it yieldeth the peaceable *f* of Heb 12:11
the *f* of our lips giving thanks Heb 13:15
the *f* of righteousness is sown in Jas 3:18
for the precious *f* of the earth Jas 5:7
and the earth brought forth her *f* Jas 5:18
trees whose *f* withereth, without Jude 12
whose *f* withereth, without *f* Jude 12
and yielded her *f* every month Rev 22:2

**FRUITFUL**

And God blessed them, saying, Be *f* Gen 1:22
them, and God said unto them, Be *f* Gen 1:28
abundantly in the earth, and be *f* Gen 8:17
his sons, and said unto them, Be *f* Gen 9:1
And you, be ye *f*, and multiply Gen 9:7
And I will make thee exceeding *f* Gen 17:6
blessed him, and will make him *f* Gen 17:20
us, and we shall be *f* in the land Gen 26:22
bless thee, and make thee *f* Gen 28:3
be *f* and multiply Gen 35:11
be *f* in the land of my affliction Gen 41:52
me, Behold, I will make thee *f* Gen 48:4
Joseph is a *f* bough Gen 49:22
even a *f* bough by a well Gen 49:22
And the children of Israel were *f* Ex 1:7
respect unto you, and make you *f* Lev 26:9
A *f* land into barrenness, for the Ps 107:34
Thy wife shall be as a *f* vine by Ps 128:3
*f* trees, and all cedars Ps 148:9
hath a vineyard in a very *f* hill Is 5:1
of his forest, and of his *f* field Is 10:18
in the outmost *f* branches thereof Is 17:6
shall be turned into a *f* field Is 29:17
the *f* field shall be esteemed as Is 29:17
pleasant fields, for the *f* vine Is 32:12
and the wilderness be a *f* field Is 32:15
the *f* field be counted for a Is 32:15
remain in the *f* field Is 32:16
the *f* place was a wilderness, and Jer 4:26
and they shall be *f* and increase Jer 23:3
land, and planted it in a *f* field Eze 17:5
she was *f* and full of branches by Eze 19:10
Though he be *f* among his brethren Hos 13:15
*f* seasons, filling our hearts Acts 14:17
being *f* in every good work, and Col 1:10

**FRUITS**

take of the best *f* in the land in Gen 43:11
to offer the first of thy ripe *f* Ex 22:29
and shalt gather in the *f* thereof Ex 23:10
with the bread of the first *f* for Lev 23:20
of the *f* he shall sell unto thee Lev 25:15
of the *f* doth he sell unto thee Lev 25:16
until her *f* come in ye shall eat Lev 25:22
trees of the land yield their *f* Lev 26:20
for the precious *f* brought forth Deut 33:14
him, and thou shalt bring in the *f* 2Sa 9:10
and an hundred of summer *f* 2Sa 16:1
all the *f* of the field since the 2Kin 8:6
vineyards, and eat the *f* thereof 2Kin 19:29
If I have eaten the *f* thereof Job 31:39
which may yield *f* of increase Ps 107:37
trees in them of all kind of *f* Eccl 2:5
of pomegranates, with pleasant *f* Song 4:13
his garden, and eat his pleasant *f* Song 4:16
nuts to see the *f* of the valley Song 6:11
are all manner of pleasant *f* Song 7:13
for the shouting for thy summer *f* Is 16:9
and Carmel shake off their *f* Is 33:9
ye, gather ye wine, and summer *f* Jer 40:10
wine and summer *f* very much Jer 40:12
is fallen upon thy summer *f* Jer 48:32
for want of the *f* of the field Lam 4:9
they have gathered the summer *f* Mic 7:1
not destroy the *f* of your ground Mal 3:11
therefore *f* meet for repentance Mt 3:8
Ye shall know them by their *f* Mt 7:16
by their *f* ye shall know them Mt 7:20
they might receive the *f* of it Mt 21:34
render him the *f* in their seasons Mt 21:41
bringing forth the *f* thereof Mt 21:43
therefore *f* worthy of repentance Lk 3:8
have no room where to bestow my *f* Lk 12:17
and there will I bestow all my *f* Lk 12:18
sown, and increase the *f* of your 2Cor 9:10
with the *f* of righteousness Phil 1:11
must be first partaker of the *f* 2Ti 2:6
full of mercy and good *f*, without Jas 3:17
the *f* that thy soul lusted after Rev 18:14
which bare twelve manner of *f* Rev 22:2

**FRUSTRATE**

to *f* their purpose, all the days Ezr 4:5
I do not *f* the grace of God Gal 2:21

**FRUSTRATETH**

That *f* the tokens of the liars, Is 44:25

**FRYING**

meat offering baken in the *f* pan Lev 2:7

**FRYINGPAN**

and all that is dressed in the *f* Lev 7:9

**FUEL**

be with burning and *f* of fire Is 9:5
shall be as the *f* of the fire Is 9:19
it is cast into the fire for *f* Eze 15:4
I have given to the fire for *f* Eze 15:6
Thou shalt be for *f* to the fire Eze 21:32

**FUGITIVE**

a *f* and a vagabond shalt thou be Gen 4:12
and I shall be a *f* and a vagabond Gen 4:14

**FUGITIVES**

Ye Gileadites are *f* of Ephraim Judg 12:4
the *f* that fell away to the king 2Kin 25:11
his *f* shall flee unto Zoar, an Is 15:5
all his *f* with all his bands Eze 17:21

**FULFIL**

*F* her week, and we will give thee Gen 29:27
*F* your works, your daily tasks, Ex 5:13
the number of thy days I will *f* Ex 23:26
that he might *f* the word of the 1Kin 2:27
takest heed to *f* the statutes 1Chr 22:13
To *f* the word of the LORD by the 2Chr 36:21
to *f* threescore and ten years 2Chr 36:21
number the months that they *f* Job 39:2
own heart, and *f* all thy counsel Ps 20:4
the LORD *f* all thy petitions Ps 20:5
He will *f* the desire of them that Ps 145:19
us to *f* all righteousness Mt 3:15
am not come to destroy, but to *f* Mt 5:17
heart, which shall *f* all my will Acts 13:22
if it *f* the law, judge thee, who Rom 2:27
the flesh, to *f* the lusts thereof Rom 13:14
ye shall not *f* the lust of the Gal 5:16
and so *f* the law of Christ Gal 6:2
*F* ye my joy, that ye be Phil 2:2
me for you, to *f* the word of God Col 1:25
in the Lord, that thou *f* it Col 4:17
*f* all the good pleasure of his 2Th 1:11
If ye *f* the royal law according Jas 2:8
put in their hearts to *f* his will Rev 17:17

**FULFILLED**

her days to be delivered were *f* Gen 25:24
me my wife, for my days are *f* Gen 29:21
And Jacob did so, and *f* her week Gen 29:28
And forty days were *f* for him Gen 50:3
for so are *f* the days of those Gen 50:3
Wherefore have ye not *f* your task Ex 5:14
And seven days were *f*, after that Ex 7:25
the days of her purifying be *f* Lev 12:4
the days of her purifying are *f* Lev 12:6
until the days be *f*, in the which Num 6:5
the days of his separation are *f* Num 6:13
And when thy days be *f*, and thou 2Sa 7:12
in that the king hath *f* the 2Sa 14:22
and hath with his hand *f* it 1Kin 8:15
hast *f* it with thine hand, as it 1Kin 8:24
who hath with his hands *f* that 2Chr 6:4
hast *f* it with thine hand, as it 2Chr 6:15
the mouth of Jeremiah might be *f* Ezr 1:1
But thou hast *f* the judgment of Job 36:17
*f* with your hand, saying, We will Jer 44:25
he hath *f* his word that he had Lam 2:17
our end is near, our days are *f* Lam 4:18
when the days of the siege are *f* Eze 5:2
the thing *f* upon Nebuchadnezzar Dan 4:33
till three whole weeks were *f* Dan 10:3
that it might be *f* which was Mt 1:22
that it might be *f* which was Mt 2:15
Then was *f* that which was spoken Mt 2:17
that it might be *f* which was Mt 2:23
That it might be *f* which was Mt 4:14
pass from the law, till all be *f* Mt 5:18
That it might be *f* which was Mt 8:17
That it might be *f* which was Mt 12:17
in them is *f* the prophecy of Mt 13:14
That it might be *f* which was Mt 13:35
that it might be *f* which was Mt 21:4
pass, till all these things be *f* Mt 24:34
then shall the scriptures be *f* Mt 26:54
of the prophets might be *f* Mt 26:56
Then was *f* that which was spoken Mt 27:9
that it might be *f* which was Mt 27:35
And saying, The time is *f*, and the Mk 1:15
when all these things shall be *f* Mk 13:4
but the scriptures must be *f* Mk 14:49
And the scripture was *f*, which Mk 15:28
which shall be *f* in their season Lk 1:20
And when they had *f* the days Lk 2:43
is this scripture *f* in your ears Lk 4:21
things which are written may be *f* Lk 21:22
the times of the Gentiles be *f* Lk 21:24
not pass away, till all be *f* Lk 21:32
until it be *f* in the kingdom of Lk 22:16
you, that all things must be *f* Lk 24:44
this my joy therefore is *f* Jn 3:29
of Esaias the prophet might be *f* Jn 12:38
but that the scripture may be *f* Jn 13:18
that the word might be *f* that is Jn 15:25
that the scripture might be *f* Jn 17:12
might have my joy *f* in themselves Jn 17:13
That the saying might be *f* Jn 18:9
the saying of Jesus might be *f* Jn 18:32
that the scripture might be *f* Jn 19:24
that the scripture might be *f* Jn 19:28
that the scripture should be *f* Jn 19:36
scripture must needs have been *f* Acts 1:16
should suffer, he hath so *f* Acts 3:18
And after that many days were *f* Acts 9:23
when they had *f* their ministry, Acts 12:25
as John *f* his course, he said, Acts 13:25
they have *f* them in condemning Acts 13:27
when they had *f* all that was Acts 13:29
God hath *f* the same unto us their Acts 13:33
of God for the work which they *f* Acts 14:26
of the law might be *f* in us Rom 8:4
loveth another hath *f* the law Rom 13:8
when your obedience is *f* 2Cor 10:6
For all the law is *f* in one word Gal 5:14
the scripture was *f* which saith Jas 2:23
killed as they were, should be *f* Rev 6:11
of the seven angels were *f* Rev 15:8
until the words of God shall be *f* Rev 17:17
the thousand years should be *f* Rev 20:3

**FULFILLING**

stormy wind *f* his word Ps 148:8
love is the *f* of the law Rom 13:10
*f* the desires of the flesh and of Eph 2:3

**FULL**

vale of Siddim was *f* of slimepits Gen 14:10
of the Amorites is not yet *f* Gen 15:16
age, an old man, and *f* of years Gen 25:8
people, being old and *f* of days Gen 35:29
to pass at the end of two *f* years Gen 41:1
devoured the seven rank and *f* ears Gen 41:7
ears came up in one stalk, *f* Gen 41:22
his sack, our money in *f* weight Gen 43:21
shall be *f* of swarms of flies Ex 8:21
and when we did eat bread to the *f* Ex 16:3
and in the morning bread to the *f* Ex 16:8
put an omer *f* of manna therein, Ex 16:33
for he should make *f* restitution Ex 22:3
even corn beaten out of *f* ears Lev 2:14
he shall take a censer *f* of Lev 16:12
his hands *f* of sweet incense Lev 16:12
the land become *f* of wickedness Lev 19:29
within a *f* year may he redeem it Lev 25:29
within the space of a *f* year Lev 25:30
ye shall eat your bread to the *f* Lev 26:5
both of them were *f* of fine flour Num 7:13
ten shekels of gold, *f* of incense Num 7:14
both of them *f* of fine flour Num 7:19
gold of ten shekels, *f* of incense Num 7:20
both of them *f* of fine flour Num 7:25
of ten shekels, *f* of incense Num 7:26
both of them *f* of fine flour Num 7:31
of ten shekels, *f* of incense Num 7:32
both of them *f* of fine flour Num 7:37
of ten shekels, *f* of incense Num 7:38
both of them *f* of fine flour Num 7:43
of ten shekels, *f* of incense Num 7:44
both of them *f* of fine flour Num 7:49
of ten shekels, *f* of incense Num 7:50
both of them *f* of fine flour Num 7:55
of ten shekels, *f* of incense Num 7:56
both of them *f* of fine flour Num 7:61
of ten shekels, *f* of incense Num 7:62

both of them *f* of fine flour ... Num 7:67
of ten shekels, *f* of incense ... Num 7:68
both of them *f* of fine flour ... Num 7:73
of ten shekels, *f* of incense ... Num 7:74
both of them *f* of fine flour ... Num 7:79
of ten shekels, *f* of incense ... Num 7:80
*f* of incense, weighing ten ... Num 7:86
give me his house *f* of silver ... Num 22:18
give me his house *f* of silver ... Num 24:13
houses *f* of all good things, ... Deut 6:11
thou shalt have eaten and be *f* ... Deut 6:11
When thou hast eaten and art *f* ... Deut 8:10
when thou hast eaten and art *f* ... Deut 8:12
that thou mayest eat and be *f* ... Deut 11:15
father and her mother a *f* month ... Deut 21:13
*f* with the blessing of the LORD, ... Deut 33:23
Nun was *f* of the spirit of wisdom ... Deut 34:9
of the fleece, a bowl *f* of water ... Judg 6:38
Now the house was *f* of men ... Judg 16:27
I went out *f*, and the LORD hath ... Ruth 1:21
a *f* reward be given thee of the ... Ruth 2:12
They that were *f* have hired out ... 1Sa 2:5
gave them in *f* tale to the king ... 1Sa 18:27
of the Philistines was a *f* year ... 1Sa 27:7
with one *f* line to keep alive ... 2Sa 8:2
it came to pass after two *f* years ... 2Sa 13:23
dwelt two *f* years in Jerusalem ... 2Sa 14:28
a piece of ground *f* of lentiles ... 2Sa 23:11
Make this valley *f* of ditches ... 2Kin 3:16
shalt set aside that which is *f* ... 2Kin 4:4
to pass, when the vessels were *f* ... 2Kin 4:6
thereof wild gourds his lap *f* ... 2Kin 4:39
*f* ears of corn in the husk ... 2Kin 4:42
the mountain was *f* of horses ... 2Kin 6:17
lo, all the way was *f* of garments ... 2Kin 7:15
drew a bow with his *f* strength ... 2Kin 9:24
the house of Baal was *f* from one ... 2Kin 10:21
he reigned a *f* month in Samaria ... 2Kin 15:13
a parcel of ground *f* of barley ... 1Chr 11:13
shalt grant it me for the *f* price ... 1Chr 21:22
verily buy it for the *f* price ... 1Chr 21:24
*f* of days, he made Solomon his ... 1Chr 23:1
*f* of days, riches, and honour ... 1Chr 29:28
was *f* of days when he died ... 2Chr 24:15
possessed houses *f* of all goods ... Neh 9:25
then was Haman *f* of wrath ... Est 3:5
he was *f* of indignation against ... Est 5:9
come to thy grave in a *f* age ... Job 5:26
I am *f* of tossings to and fro unto ... Job 7:4
I am *f* of confusion ... Job 10:15
should a man *f* of talk be ... Job 11:2
is of few days, and *f* of trouble ... Job 14:1
His bones are *f* of the sin of his ... Job 20:11
One dieth in his *f* strength ... Job 21:23
His breasts are *f* of milk ... Job 21:24
For I am *f* of matter ... Job 32:18
thy table should be *f* of fatness ... Job 36:16
Job died, being old and *f* of days ... Job 42:17
His mouth is *f* of cursing ... Ps 10:7
they are *f* of children, and leave ... Ps 17:14
their right hand is *f* of bribes ... Ps 26:10
voice of the LORD is *f* of majesty ... Ps 29:4
the earth is *f* of the goodness of ... Ps 33:5
right hand is *f* of righteousness ... Ps 48:10
river of God, which is *f* of water ... Ps 65:9
and I am *f* of heaviness ... Ps 69:20
waters of a *f* cup are wrung out ... Ps 73:10
dark places of the earth are *f* of ... Ps 74:20
it is *f* of mixture ... Ps 75:8
he sent them meat to the *f* ... Ps 78:25
being *f* of compassion, forgave ... Ps 78:38
art a God *f* of compassion, and ... Ps 86:15
For my soul is *f* of troubles ... Ps 88:3
trees of the LORD are *f* of sap ... Ps 104:16
the earth is *f* of thy riches ... Ps 104:24
is gracious and *f* of compassion ... Ps 111:4
*f* of compassion, and righteous ... Ps 112:4
earth, O LORD, is *f* of thy mercy ... Ps 119:64
that hath his quiver *f* of them ... Ps 127:5
That our garners may be *f* ... Ps 144:13
is gracious, and *f* of compassion ... Ps 145:8
than an house *f* of sacrifices ... Prov 17:1
The *f* soul loatheth an honeycomb ... Prov 27:7
Hell and destruction are never *f* ... Prov 27:20
Lest I be *f*, and deny thee, and say ... Prov 30:9
yet the sea is not *f* ... Eccl 1:7
All things are *f* of labour ... Eccl 1:8
both the hands *f* with travail ... Eccl 4:6
of the sons of men is *f* of evil ... Eccl 9:3
A fool also is *f* of words ... Eccl 10:14
If the clouds be *f* of rain ... Eccl 11:3
I am *f* of the burnt offerings of ... Is 1:11
your hands are *f* of blood ... Is 1:15
it was *f* of judgment ... Is 1:21
Their land also is *f* of silver ... Is 2:7
their land is also *f* of horses ... Is 2:7
Their land also is *f* of idols ... Is 2:8
the whole earth is *f* of his glory ... Is 6:3
for the earth shall be *f* of the ... Is 11:9
shall be *f* of doleful creatures ... Is 13:21
of Dimon shall be *f* of blood ... Is 15:9
Thou that art *f* of stirs, a ... Is 22:2
valleys shall be *f* of chariots ... Is 22:7
lees, of fat things *f* of marrow ... Is 25:6
For all tables are *f* of vomit ... Is 28:8
his lips are *f* of indignation, and ... Is 30:27
they are *f* of the fury of the ... Is 51:20
Even a *f* wind from those places ... Jer 4:12
yet will I not make a *f* end ... Jer 4:27
when I had fed them to the *f* ... Jer 5:7
but make not a *f* end ... Jer 5:10
I will not make a *f* end with you ... Jer 5:18
As a cage is *f* of birds, so are ... Jer 5:27
so are their houses *f* of deceit ... Jer 5:27
Therefore I am *f* of the fury of ... Jer 6:11
aged with him that is *f* of days ... Jer 6:11
For the land is *f* of adulterers ... Jer 23:10
Within two *f* years will I bring ... Jer 28:3
within the space of two *f* years ... Jer 28:11
though I make a *f* end of all ... Jer 30:11
will I not make a *f* end of thee ... Jer 30:11
of the Rechabites pots *f* of wine ... Jer 35:5
for I will make a *f* end of all ... Jer 46:28
I will not make a *f* end of thee ... Jer 46:28
solitary, that was *f* of people ... Lam 1:1
he is filled *f* with reproach ... Lam 3:30
their rings were *f* of eyes round ... Eze 1:18
for the land is *f* of bloody ... Eze 7:23
and the city is *f* of violence ... Eze 7:23
great, and the land is *f* of blood ... Eze 9:9
the city *f* of perverseness ... Eze 9:9
the court was *f* of the brightness ... Eze 10:4
were *f* of eyes round about, even ... Eze 10:12
wilt thou make a *f* end of the ... Eze 11:13
*f* of feathers, which had divers ... Eze 17:3
*f* of branches by reason of many ... Eze 19:10
*f* of wisdom, and perfect in beauty ... Eze 28:12
and the rivers shall be *f* of thee ... Eze 32:6
of that whereof it was *f*, when I ... Eze 32:15
the valley which was *f* of bones ... Eze 37:1
And ye shall eat fat till ye be *f* ... Eze 39:19
were a *f* reed of six great cubits ... Eze 41:8
Then was Nebuchadnezzar *f* of fury ... Dan 3:19
transgressors are come to the *f* ... Dan 8:23
Daniel was mourning three *f* weeks ... Dan 10:2
And the floors shall be *f* of wheat ... Joel 2:24
for the press is *f*, the fats ... Joel 3:13
is pressed that is *f* of sheaves ... Amos 2:13
But truly I am *f* of power by the ... Mic 3:8
men thereof are *f* of violence ... Mic 6:12
it is all *f* of lies and robbery ... Nah 3:1
and the earth was *f* of his praise ... Hab 3:3
of the city shall be *f* of boys ... Zec 8:5
whole body shall be *f* of light ... Mt 6:22
whole body shall be *f* of darkness ... Mt 6:23
Which, when it was *f*, they drew ... Mt 13:48
that remained twelve baskets *f* ... Mt 14:20
that was left seven baskets *f* ... Mt 15:37
within they are *f* of extortion ... Mt 23:25
but are within *f* of dead men's ... Mt 23:27
but within ye are *f* of hypocrisy ... Mt 23:28
after that the *f* corn in the ear ... Mk 4:28
the ship, so that it was now *f* ... Mk 4:37
twelve baskets *f* of the fragments ... Mk 6:43
*F* well ye reject the commandment ... Mk 7:9
how many baskets *f* of fragments ... Mk 8:19
how many baskets *f* of fragments ... Mk 8:20
and filled a spunge *f* of vinegar ... Mk 15:36
Now Elisabeth's *f* time came that ... Lk 1:57
Jesus being *f* of the Holy Ghost ... Lk 4:1
city, behold a man *f* of leprosy ... Lk 5:12
Woe unto you that are *f* ... Lk 6:25
thy whole body also is *f* of light ... Lk 11:34
thy body also is *f* of darkness ... Lk 11:34
body therefore be *f* of light ... Lk 11:36
the whole shall be *f* of light ... Lk 11:36
your inward part is *f* of ravening ... Lk 11:39
was laid at his gate, *f* of sores, ... Lk 16:20
the Father,) *f* of grace and truth ... Jn 1:14
for my time is not yet *f* come ... Jn 7:8
you, and that your joy might be *f* ... Jn 15:11
receive, that your joy may be *f* ... Jn 16:24
was set a vessel *f* of vinegar ... Jn 19:29
the net to land *f* of great fishes ... Jn 21:11
said, These men are *f* of new wine ... Acts 2:13
thou shalt make me *f* of joy with ... Acts 2:28
*f* of the Holy Ghost and wisdom, ... Acts 6:3
a man *f* of faith and of the Holy ... Acts 6:5
*f* of faith and power, did great ... Acts 6:8
when he was *f* forty years old, it ... Acts 7:23
being *f* of the Holy Ghost, looked ... Acts 7:55
this woman was *f* of good works ... Acts 9:36
*f* of the Holy Ghost and of faith ... Acts 11:24
O *f* of all subtilty and all ... Acts 13:10
sayings, they were *f* of wrath ... Acts 19:28
*f* of envy, murder, debate, deceit ... Rom 1:29
Whose mouth is *f* of cursing ... Rom 3:14
that ye also are *f* of goodness ... Rom 15:14
Now ye are *f*, now ye are rich, ye ... 1Cor 4:8
was *f* of heaviness, because that ... Phil 2:26
I am instructed both to be *f* ... Phil 4:12
I am *f*, having received of ... Phil 4:18
love, and unto all riches of the *f* ... Col 2:2
make *f* proof of thy ministry ... 2Ti 4:5
to them that are of *f* age ... Heb 5:14
*f* assurance of hope unto the end ... Heb 6:11
heart in *f* assurance of faith ... Heb 10:22
unruly evil, *f* of deadly poison ... Jas 3:8
*f* of mercy and good fruits, ... Jas 3:17
joy unspeakable and *f* of glory ... 1Pet 1:8
Having eyes *f* of adultery ... 2Pet 2:14
unto you, that your joy may be *f* ... 1Jn 1:4
but that we receive a *f* reward ... 2Jn 8
to face, that our joy may be *f* ... 2Jn 12
were four beasts *f* of eyes before ... Rev 4:6
they were *f* of eyes within ... Rev 4:8
and golden vials *f* of odours ... Rev 5:8
vials *f* of the wrath of God ... Rev 15:7
and his kingdom was *f* of darkness ... Rev 16:10
*f* of names of blasphemy, having ... Rev 17:3
cup in her hand *f* of abominations ... Rev 17:4
vials *f* of the seven last plagues ... Rev 21:9

**FULLER**
so as no *f* on earth can white ... Mk 9:3

**FULLER'S**
is in the highway of the *f* field ... 2Kin 18:17
in the highway of the *f* field ... Is 7:3
in the highway of the *f* field ... Is 36:2

**FULLERS'**
a refiner's fire, and like *f* sope ... Mal 3:2

**FULLY**
Moses had *f* set up the tabernacle ... Num 7:1
with him, and hath followed me *f* ... Num 14:24
It hath *f* been shewed me, all ... Ruth 2:11
went not *f* after the LORD, as did ... 1Kin 11:6
men is *f* set in them to do evil ... Eccl 8:11
be devoured as stubble *f* dry ... Nah 1:10
the day of Pentecost was *f* come ... Acts 2:1
being *f* persuaded that, what he ... Rom 4:21
Let every man be *f* persuaded in ... Rom 14:5
I have *f* preached the gospel of ... Rom 15:19
But thou hast *f* known my doctrine ... 2Ti 3:10
me the preaching might be *f* known ... 2Ti 4:17
for her grapes are *f* ripe ... Rev 14:18

**FULNESS**
as the *f* of the winepress ... Num 18:27
*f* thereof, and for the good will ... Deut 33:16
the sea roar, and the *f* thereof ... 1Chr 16:32
In the *f* of his sufficiency he ... Job 20:22
in thy presence is *f* of joy ... Ps 16:11
is the LORD's, and the *f* thereof ... Ps 24:1
world is mine, and the *f* thereof ... Ps 50:12
the *f* thereof, thou hast founded ... Ps 89:11
the sea roar, and the *f* thereof ... Ps 96:11
the sea roar, and the *f* thereof ... Ps 98:7
*f* of bread, and abundance of ... Eze 16:49
the *f* thereof, by the noise of ... Eze 19:7
of his *f* have all we received, and ... Jn 1:16
how much more their *f* ... Rom 11:12
until the *f* of the Gentiles be ... Rom 11:25
I shall come in the *f* of the ... Rom 15:29
is the Lord's, and the *f* thereof ... 1Cor 10:26
is the Lord's, and the *f* thereof ... 1Cor 10:28
But when the *f* of the time was ... Gal 4:4
of the *f* of times he might gather ... Eph 1:10
the *f* of him that filleth all in ... Eph 1:23
be filled with all the *f* of God ... Eph 3:19
of the stature of the *f* of Christ ... Eph 4:13
that in him should all *f* dwell ... Col 1:19
all the *f* of the Godhead bodily ... Col 2:9

**FURBISH**
*f* the spears, and put on the ... Jer 46:4

**FURBISHED**
a sword is sharpened, and also *f* ... Eze 21:9
it is *f* that it may glitter ... Eze 21:10
And he hath given it to be *f* ... Eze 21:11
sword is sharpened, and it is *f* ... Eze 21:11
for the slaughter it is *f* ... Eze 21:28

**FURIOUS**
with a *f* man thou shalt not go ... Prov 22:24
strife, and a *f* man aboundeth in ... Prov 29:22
anger and in fury and in *f* rebukes ... Eze 5:15
upon them with *f* rebukes ... Eze 25:17
the king was angry and very *f* ... Dan 2:12
the LORD revengeth, and is *f* ... Nah 1:2

**FURIOUSLY**
for he driveth *f* ... 2Kin 9:20
and they shall deal *f* with thee ... Eze 23:25

**FURLONGS**
from Jerusalem about threescore *f* ... Lk 24:13
about five and twenty or thirty *f* ... Jn 6:19
Jerusalem, about fifteen *f* off ... Jn 11:18
of a thousand and six hundred *f* ... Rev 14:20
with the reed, twelve thousand *f* ... Rev 21:16

**FURNACE**
it was dark, behold a smoking *f* ... Gen 15:17
went up as the smoke of a *f* ... Gen 19:28
to you handfuls of ashes of the *f* ... Ex 9:8
And they took ashes of the *f* ... Ex 9:10
ascended as the smoke of a *f* ... Ex 19:18
you forth out of the iron *f* ... Deut 4:20
from the midst of the *f* of iron ... 1Kin 8:51
as silver tried in a *f* of earth ... Ps 12:6
is for silver, and the *f* for gold ... Prov 17:3
pot for silver, and the *f* for gold ... Prov 27:21
is in Zion, and his *f* in Jerusalem ... Is 31:9
thee in the *f* of affliction ... Is 48:10
land of Egypt, from the iron *f* ... Jer 11:4
and lead, in the midst of the *f* ... Eze 22:18
and tin, into the midst of the *f* ... Eze 22:20
is melted in the midst of the *f* ... Eze 22:22
the midst of a burning fiery *f* ... Dan 3:6
the midst of a burning fiery *f* ... Dan 3:11
the midst of a burning fiery *f* ... Dan 3:15
us from the burning fiery *f* ... Dan 3:17
that they should heat the *f* one ... Dan 3:19
them into the burning fiery *f* ... Dan 3:20
the midst of the burning fiery *f* ... Dan 3:21
the *f* exceeding hot, the flame of ... Dan 3:22
the midst of the burning fiery *f* ... Dan 3:23
the mouth of the burning fiery *f* ... Dan 3:26
shall cast them into a *f* of fire ... Mt 13:42
cast them into the *f* of fire ... Mt 13:50
brass, as if they burned in a *f* ... Rev 1:15

F

pit, as the smoke of a great *f* ............ Rev 9:2

**FURNACES**
piece, and the tower of the *f* ............ Neh 3:11
of the *f* even unto the broad wall ............ Neh 12:38

**FURNISH**
Thou shalt *f* him liberally out of ............ Deut 15:14
said, Can God *f* a table in the ............ Ps 78:19
that *f* the drink offering unto ............ Is 65:11
*f* thyself to go into captivity ............ Jer 46:19

**FURNISHED**
had *f* Solomon with cedar trees ............ 1Kin 9:11
she hath also *f* her table ............ Prov 9:2
and the wedding was *f* with guests ............ Mt 22:10
shew you a large upper room *f* ............ Mk 14:15
shew you a large upper room *f* ............ Lk 22:12
throughly *f* unto all good works ............ 2Ti 3:17

**FURNITURE**
and put them in the camel's *f* ............ Gen 31:34
all the *f* of the tabernacle, ............ Ex 31:7
And the table and his *f*, and the ............ Ex 31:8
pure candlestick with all his *f* ............ Ex 31:8
of burnt offering with all his *f* ............ Ex 31:9
also for the light, and his *f* ............ Ex 35:14
Moses, the tent, and all his *f* ............ Ex 39:33
glory out of all the pleasant *f* ............ Nah 2:9

**FURROW**
unicorn with his band in the *f* ............ Job 39:10

**FURROWS**
or that the *f* likewise thereof ............ Job 31:38
thou settlest the *f* thereof ............ Ps 65:10
they made long their *f* ............ Ps 129:3
it by the *f* of her plantation ............ Eze 17:7
wither in the *f* where it grew ............ Eze 17:10
as hemlock in the *f* of the field ............ Hos 10:4
bind themselves in their two *f* ............ Hos 10:10
as heaps in the *f* of the fields ............ Hos 12:11

**FURTHER**
And the angel of the LORD went *f* ............ Num 22:26
shall speak *f* unto the people ............ Deut 20:8
they enquired of the LORD *f* ............ 1Sa 10:22
or what is thy request *f* ............ Est 9:12
shalt thou come, but no *f* ............ Job 38:11
but I will proceed no *f* ............ Job 40:5
*f* not his wicked device ............ Ps 140:8
yea *f*; though a wise man think to ............ Eccl 8:17
And *f*, by these, my son, be ............ Eccl 12:12
what *f* need have we of witnesses ............ Mt 26:65
troublest thou the Master any *f* ............ Mk 5:35
What need we any *f* witnesses ............ Mk 14:63
said, What need we any *f* witness ............ Lk 22:71
as though he would have gone *f* ............ Lk 24:28
it spread no *f* among the people ............ Acts 4:17
when they had *f* threatened them ............ Acts 4:21
he proceeded *f* to take Peter also ............ Acts 12:3
*f* brought Greeks also into the ............ Acts 21:28
that I be not *f* tedious unto thee ............ Acts 24:4
and when they had gone a little *f* ............ Acts 27:28
But they shall proceed no *f* ............ 2Ti 3:9
what *f* need was there that ............ Heb 7:11

**FURTHERANCE**
rather unto the *f* of the gospel ............ Phil 1:12
continue with you all for your *f* ............ Phil 1:25

**FURTHERED**
they *f* the people, and the house ............ Ezr 8:36

**FURTHERMORE**
And the LORD said *f* unto him ............ Ex 4:6
*F* the LORD was angry with me for ............ Deut 4:21
*F* the LORD spake unto me, saying, ............ Deut 9:13
David said *f*, As the LORD liveth, ............ 1Sa 26:10
*F* I tell thee that the LORD will ............ 1Chr 17:10
*F* over the tribes of Israel ............ 1Chr 27:16
*F* David the king said unto all ............ 1Chr 29:1
*F* he made the court of the ............ 2Chr 4:9
*F* Elihu answered and said, ............ Job 34:1
He said *f* unto me, Son of man, ............ Eze 8:6
And *f*, that ye have sent for men ............ Eze 23:40
*F*, when I came to Troas to preach ............ 2Cor 2:12
*F* then we beseech you, brethren, ............ 1Th 4:1
*F* we have had fathers of our ............ Heb 12:9

**FURY**
until thy brother's *f* turn away ............ Gen 27:44
walk contrary unto you also in *f* ............ Lev 26:28
God shall cast the *f* of his wrath ............ Job 20:23
*F* is not in me ............ Is 27:4
his *f* upon all their armies ............ Is 34:2
upon him the *f* of his anger ............ Is 42:25
because of the *f* of the oppressor ............ Is 51:13
where is the *f* of the oppressor ............ Is 51:13
hand of the LORD the cup of his *f* ............ Is 51:17
are full of the *f* of the LORD ............ Is 51:20
even the dregs of the cup of my *f* ............ Is 51:22
*f* to his adversaries, recompence ............ Is 59:18
anger, and trample them in my *f* ............ Is 63:3
and my *f*, it upheld me ............ Is 63:5
anger, and make them drunk in my *f* ............ Is 63:6
to render his anger with *f* ............ Is 66:15
lest my *f* come forth like fire, ............ Jer 4:4
I am full of the *f* of the LORD ............ Jer 6:11
my *f* shall be poured out upon ............ Jer 7:20
Pour out thy *f* upon the heathen ............ Jer 10:25
arm, even in anger, and in *f* ............ Jer 21:5
lest my *f* go out like fire, and ............ Jer 21:12
of the LORD is gone forth in *f* ............ Jer 23:19
the wine cup of this *f* at my hand ............ Jer 25:15
of the LORD goeth forth with *f* ............ Jer 30:23
of my *f* from the day that they ............ Jer 32:31
them in mine anger, and in my *f* ............ Jer 32:37
slain in mine anger and in my *f* ............ Jer 33:5
anger and the *f* that the LORD hath ............ Jer 36:7
my *f* hath been poured forth upon ............ Jer 42:18
so shall my *f* be poured forth ............ Jer 42:18
Wherefore my *f* and mine anger was ............ Jer 44:6
he poured out his *f* like fire ............ Lam 2:4
The LORD hath accomplished his *f* ............ Lam 4:11
I will cause my *f* to rest upon ............ Eze 5:13
I have accomplished my *f* in them ............ Eze 5:13
in thee in anger and in *f* and in ............ Eze 5:15
will I accomplish my *f* upon them ............ Eze 6:12
I shortly pour out my *f* upon thee ............ Eze 7:8
Therefore will I also deal in *f* ............ Eze 8:18
out of thy *f* upon Jerusalem ............ Eze 9:8
it with a stormy wind in my *f* ............ Eze 13:13
hailstones in my *f* to consume it ............ Eze 13:13
pour out my *f* upon it in blood, ............ Eze 14:19
and I will give thee blood in *f* ............ Eze 16:38
So will I make my *f* toward thee ............ Eze 16:42
But she was plucked up in *f* ............ Eze 19:12
I will pour out my *f* upon them ............ Eze 20:8
I would pour out my *f* upon them ............ Eze 20:13
I would pour out my *f* upon them ............ Eze 20:21
with *f* poured out, will I rule ............ Eze 20:33
out arm, and with *f* poured out ............ Eze 20:34
and I will cause my *f* to rest ............ Eze 21:17
you in mine anger and in my *f* ............ Eze 22:20
have poured out my *f* upon you ............ Eze 22:22
That it might cause *f* to come up ............ Eze 24:8
caused my *f* to rest upon thee ............ Eze 24:13
mine anger and according to my *f* ............ Eze 25:14
And I will pour my *f* upon Sin ............ Eze 30:15
spoken in my jealousy and in my *f* ............ Eze 36:6
Wherefore I poured my *f* upon them ............ Eze 36:18
that my *f* shall come up in my ............ Eze 38:18
*f* commanded to bring Shadrach, ............ Dan 3:13
Then was Nebuchadnezzar full of *f* ............ Dan 3:19
unto him in the *f* of his power ............ Dan 8:6
thy *f* be turned away from thy ............ Dan 9:16
go forth with great *f* to destroy ............ Dan 11:44
*f* upon the heathen, such as they ............ Mic 5:15
his *f* is poured out like fire, and ............ Nah 1:6
was jealous for her with great *f* ............ Zec 8:2

# G

**GAAL** (*ga'-al*) *A son of Ebed.*
G the son of Ebed came with his ............ Judg 9:26
G the son of Ebed said, Who is ............ Judg 9:28
the words of G the son of Ebed ............ Judg 9:30
G the son of Ebed and his brethren ............ Judg 9:31
G the son of Ebed went out, and ............ Judg 9:35
when G saw the people, he said to ............ Judg 9:36
G spake again and said, See there ............ Judg 9:37
G went out before the men of ............ Judg 9:39
and Zebul thrust out G and his ............ Judg 9:41

**GAASH** (*ga'-ash*) *A mountain near Mt. Ephraim.*
the north side of the hill of G ............ Josh 24:30
on the north side of the hill G ............ Judg 2:9
Hiddai of the brooks of G ............ 2Sa 23:30
Hurai of the brooks of G, Abiel ............ 1Chr 11:32

**GABA** (*ga'-bah*) See GEBA. *A Levitical city in Benjamin.*
and Ophni, and G ............ Josh 18:24
The children of Ramah and G ............ Ezr 2:26
The men of Ramah and G, six ............ Neh 7:30

**GABBAI** (*gab'-bahee*) *A family of exiles.*
And after him G, Sallai, nine ............ Neh 11:8

**GABBATHA** (*gab'-ba-thah*) *Place where Pilate judged.*
Pavement, but in the Hebrew, G ............ Jn 19:13

**GABRIEL** (*ga'-bre-el*) *An angel.*
of Ulai, which called, and said, G ............ Dan 8:16
in prayer, even the man G ............ Dan 9:21
answering said unto him, I am G ............ Lk 1:19
in the sixth month the angel G ............ Lk 1:26

**GAD** (*gad*)
*1. A son of Jacob.*
and she called his name G ............ Gen 30:11
Leah's handmaid; G, and Asher ............ Gen 35:26
And the sons of G ............ Gen 46:16
G, a troop shall overcome him ............ Gen 49:19
Dan, and Naphtali, G, and Asher ............ Ex 1:4
the children of G dwelt over ............ 1Chr 5:11
*2. The tribe descended from Gad 1.*
Of G; Eliasaph the son ............ Num 1:14
Of the children of G, by their ............ Num 1:24
of them, even of the tribe of G ............ Num 1:25
Then the tribe of G ............ Num 2:14
the captain of the sons of G ............ Num 2:14
prince of the children of G ............ Num 7:42
G was Eliasaph the son of Deuel ............ Num 10:20
Of the tribe of G, Geuel the son ............ Num 13:15
The children of G after their ............ Num 26:15
of G according to those that were ............ Num 26:18
the children of G had a very ............ Num 32:1
The children of G and the children ............ Num 32:2
Moses said unto the children of G ............ Num 32:6
And the children of G and the ............ Num 32:25
unto them, If the children of G ............ Num 32:29
And the children of G and the ............ Num 32:31
them, even to the children of G ............ Num 32:33
And the children of G built Dibon ............ Num 32:34
the tribe of the children of G ............ Num 34:14
Reuben, G, and Asher, and Zebulun, ............ Deut 27:13
of G he said, Blessed be he that ............ Deut 33:20
Blessed be he that enlargeth G ............ Deut 33:20
of Reuben, and the children of G ............ Josh 4:12
inheritance unto the tribe of G ............ Josh 13:24
of G according their families ............ Josh 13:24
of G after their families ............ Josh 13:28
and G, and Reuben, and half the ............ Josh 18:7
in Gilead out of the tribe of G ............ Josh 20:8
Reuben, and out of the tribe of G ............ Josh 21:7
And out of the tribe of G, Ramoth ............ Josh 21:38
of Reuben and the children of G ............ Josh 22:9
of Reuben and the children of G ............ Josh 22:10
of Reuben and the children of G ............ Josh 22:11
Reuben, and to the children of G ............ Josh 22:13
Reuben, and to the children of G ............ Josh 22:15
of Reuben and the children of G ............ Josh 22:21
of Reuben and children of G ............ Josh 22:25
of Reuben and the children of G ............ Josh 22:30
Reuben, and to the children of G ............ Josh 22:31
Reuben, and from the children of G ............ Josh 22:32
the children of Reuben and G dwelt ............ Josh 22:33
the children of G called the ............ Josh 22:34
went over Jordan to the land of G ............ 1Sa 13:7
in the midst of the river of G ............ 2Sa 24:5
Joseph, and Benjamin, Naphtali, G ............ 1Chr 2:2
Reuben, and out of the tribe of G ............ 1Chr 6:63
And out of the tribe of G ............ 1Chr 6:80
These were of the sons of G ............ 1Chr 12:14
then doth their king inherit G ............ Jer 49:1
unto the west side, G a portion ............ Eze 48:27
And by the border of G, at the ............ Eze 48:28
one gate of G, one gate of Asher, ............ Eze 48:34
Of the tribe of G were sealed ............ Rev 7:5
*3. A prophet who assisted David.*
the prophet G said unto David, ............ 1Sa 22:5
the LORD came unto the prophet G ............ 2Sa 24:11
So G came to David, and told him, ............ 2Sa 24:13
And David said unto G, I am in a ............ 2Sa 24:14
G came that day to David, and said ............ 2Sa 24:18
according to the saying of G ............ 2Sa 24:19
And the LORD spake unto G, David's ............ 1Chr 21:9
So G came to David, and said unto ............ 1Chr 21:11
And David said unto G, I am in a ............ 1Chr 21:13
LORD commanded G to say to David. ............ 1Chr 21:18
David went up at the saying of G ............ 1Chr 21:19
and in the book of G the seer ............ 1Chr 29:29
of G the king's seer, and Nathan ............ 2Chr 29:25

**GADARENES** (*gad-a-renes'*) *Inhabitants of Gadara.*
sea, into the country of the G ............ Mk 5:1
arrived at the country of the G ............ Lk 8:26
the G round about besought him to ............ Lk 8:37

**GADDEST**
Why *g* thou about so much to ............ Jer 2:36

**GADDI** (*gad'-di*) *One of the twelve spies.*
of Manasseh, G the son of Susi ............ Num 13:11

**GADDIEL** (*gad'-de-el*) *One of the twelve spies.*
of Zebulun, G the son of Sodi ............ Num 13:10

**GADI** (*ga'-di*) *Father of Menahem.*
the son of G went up from Tirzah ............ 2Kin 15:14
the son of G to reign over Israel ............ 2Kin 15:17

**GADITE** (*gad'-ite*) See GADITES. *A member of the tribe of Dan.*
of Nathan of Zobah, Bani the G ............ 2Sa 23:36

**GADITES** (*gad'-ites*)
I unto the Reubenites and to the G ............ Deut 3:12
unto the G I gave from Gilead ............ Deut 3:16
and Ramoth in Gilead, of the G ............ Deut 4:43
unto the Reubenites, and to the G ............ Deut 29:8
And to the Reubenites, and to the G ............ Josh 1:12
unto the Reubenites, and the G ............ Josh 12:6
the G have received their ............ Josh 13:8
called the Reubenites, and the G ............ Josh 22:1
all the land of Gilead, the G ............ 2Kin 10:33
The sons of Reuben, and the G ............ 1Chr 5:18
even the Reubenites, and the G ............ 1Chr 5:26
And of the G there separated ............ 1Chr 12:8
of the Reubenites, and the G ............ 1Chr 12:37
rulers over the Reubenites, the G ............ 1Chr 26:32

**GAHAM** (*ga'-ham*) *A son of Nahor.*
Reumah, she bare also Tebah, and G. ............ Gen 22:24

**GAHAR** (*ga'-har*) *A family of exiles.*
of Giddel, the children of G ............ Ezr 2:47
of Giddel, the children of G ............ Neh 7:49

**GAHER**

**GAIN**
they took no *g* of money ............ Judg 5:19
or is it *g* to him, that thou ............ Job 22:3
of every one that is greedy of *g* ............ Prov 1:19
the *g* thereof than fine gold ............ Prov 3:14
He that is greedy of *g* troubleth ............ Prov 15:27
unjust *g* increaseth his substance ............ Prov 28:8
despiseth the *g* of oppressions ............ Is 33:15
own way, every one for his *g* ............ Is 56:11
dishonest *g* which thou hast made ............ Eze 22:13
destroy souls, to get dishonest *g* ............ Eze 22:27
that ye would *g* the time, because ............ Dan 2:8

and shall divide the land for g ............ Dan 11:39
consecrate their g unto the LORD .......... Mic 4:13
if he shall g the whole world, and ......... Mt 16:26
if he shall g the whole world, and .......... Mk 8:36
if he g the whole world, and lose ........... Lk 9:25
her masters much g by soothsaying ... Acts 16:16
brought no small g unto the ............... Acts 19:24
unto all, that I might g the more ......... 1Cor 9:19
as a Jew, that I might g the Jews ........ 1Cor 9:20
that I might g them that are ............... 1Cor 9:20
that I might g them that are ............... 1Cor 9:21
as weak, that I might g the weak .......... 1Cor 9:22
Did I make a g of you by any of ........ 2Cor 12:17
Did Titus make a g of you ................. 2Cor 12:18
to live is Christ, and to die is g ............. Phil 1:21
But what things were g to me ................. Phil 3:7
supposing that g is godliness ..................... 1Ti 6:5
with contentment is great g ....................... 1Ti 6:6
a year, and buy and sell, and get g ......... Jas 4:13

**GAINED**
the hypocrite, though he hath g .............. Job 27:8
thou hast greedily g of thy ..................... Eze 22:12
thee, thou hast g thy brother .................. Mt 18:15
received two, he also g other two ........... Mt 25:17
I have g beside them five talents ........... Mt 25:20
I have g two other talents beside ........... Mt 25:22
much every man had g by trading ............ Lk 19:15
Lord, thy pound hath g ten pounds ......... Lk 19:16
thy pound hath g five pounds .................. Lk 19:18
to have g this harm and loss ................ Acts 27:21

**GAINS**
that the hope of their g was gone ...... Acts 16:19

**GAINSAY**
shall not be able to g nor resist ............ Lk 21:15

**GAINSAYERS**
to exhort and to convince the g ............. Titus 1:9

**GAINSAYING**
came I unto you without g .................. Acts 10:29
unto a disobedient and g people ......... Rom 10:21
and perished in the g of Core .................. Jude 11

**GAIUS** (*gah'-yus*)
*1. A native of Macedonia.*
and having caught G ........................... Acts 19:29
*2. A native of Derbe.*
and G of Derbe, and Timotheus ............ Acts 20:4
*3. A native of Corinth.*
G mine host, and of the whole ............... Rom 16:23
none of you, but Crispus and G ............ 1Cor 1:14
*4. Addressee of John's third epistle.*
The elder unto the wellbeloved G ...................... 3Jn 1

**GALAL** (*ga'-lal*)
*1. Son of Jeduthun.*
And Bakbakkar, Heresh, and G ............ 1Chr 9:15
*2. A Levite exile.*
the son of Shemaiah, the son of G ...... 1Chr 9:16
the son of Shammua, the son of G ..... Neh 11:17

**GALATIA** (*ga-la'-she-ah*) See GALATIANS. *A Roman province in Asia Minor.*
Phrygia and the region of G .................. Acts 16:6
and went over all the country of G .... Acts 18:23
given order to the churches of G ......... 1Cor 16:1
with me, unto the churches of G ................ Gal 1:2
Crescens to G, Titus unto ..................... 2Ti 4:10
scattered throughout Pontus, G .............. 1Pet 1:1

**GALATIANS** (*ga-la'-she-uns*) *Inhabitants of Galatia.*
O foolish G, who hath bewitched ............ Gal 3:1
Unto the G written from Rome ................... Gal s

**GALBANUM**
spices, stacte, and onycha, and g .......... Ex 30:34

**GALEED** (*ga'-le-ed*) See JAGAR-SAHADUTHA. *A memorial mound of stones.*
but Jacob called it G ............................. Gen 31:47
was the name of it called G ................. Gen 31:48

**GALILAEAN** (*gal-i-le'-un*) See GALILAEANS. *An inhabitant of Galilee.*
for thou art a G, and thy speech .......... Mk 14:70
for he is a G ........................................ Lk 22:59
he asked whether the man were a G ...... Lk 23:6

**GALILAEANS** (*gal-i-le-uns*)
some that told him of the G ...................... Lk 13:1
Suppose ye that these G were .................. Lk 13:2
were sinners above all the G .................... Lk 13:2
the G received him, having seen ............. Jn 4:45
are not all these which speak G ............ Acts 2:7

**GALILEE** (*gal'-i-lee*) See GALILAEAN. *A district north of Samaria.*
Kedesh in G in mount Naphtali ........... Josh 20:7
Kedesh in G with her suburbs, to ....... Josh 21:32
twenty cities in the land of G ............... 1Kin 9:11
Hazor, and Gilead, and G .................. 2Kin 15:29
Kedesh in G with her suburbs, and ..... 1Chr 6:76
Jordan, in G of the nations ........................ Is 9:1
turned aside into the parts of G .............. Mt 2:22
Jesus from G to Jordan unto John ........... Mt 3:13
into prison, he departed into G ............... Mt 4:12
beyond Jordan, G of the Gentiles ............ Mt 4:15
And Jesus, walking by the sea of G ......... Mt 4:18
And Jesus went about all G ..................... Mt 4:23
great multitudes of people from G ........... Mt 4:25
and came nigh unto the sea of G .......... Mt 15:29
And while they abode in G, Jesus .......... Mt 17:22
these sayings, he departed from G .......... Mt 19:1
the prophet of Nazareth of G ................. Mt 21:11
I will go before you into G .................... Mt 26:32
Thou also wast with Jesus of G .............. Mt 26:69
off, which followed Jesus from G ............ Mt 27:55
he goeth before you into G ...................... Mt 28:7
my brethren that they go into G ............ Mt 28:10
eleven disciples went away into G ......... Mt 28:16
Jesus came from Nazareth of G ................. Mk 1:9
put in prison, Jesus came into G ............. Mk 1:14
Now as he walked by the sea of G .......... Mk 1:16
all the region round about G .................... Mk 1:28
their synagogues throughout all G .......... Mk 1:39
multitude from G followed him .................. Mk 3:7
captains, and chief estates of G ................ Mk 6:21
Sidon, he came unto the sea of G ............. Mk 7:31
thence, and passed through G ................... Mk 9:30
I will go before you into G ..................... Mk 14:28
(Who also, when he was in G .................. Mk 15:41
that he goeth before you into G ............... Mk 16:7
sent from God unto a city of G ................. Lk 1:26
And Joseph also went up from G ............... Lk 2:4
of the Lord, they returned into G ............. Lk 2:39
and Herod being tetrarch of G ..................... Lk 3:1
in the power of the Spirit into G ............... Lk 4:14
down to Capernaum, a city of G ............... Lk 4:31
preached in the synagogues of G .............. Lk 4:44
were come out of every town of G ............. Lk 5:17
which is over against G ............................. Lk 8:26
through the midst of Samaria and G ..... Lk 17:11
beginning from G to this place .................. Lk 23:5
When Pilate heard of G, he asked .............. Lk 23:6
women that followed him from G .......... Lk 23:49
also, which came with him from G ......... Lk 23:55
unto you when he was yet in G ................. Lk 24:6
Jesus would go forth into G ....................... Jn 1:43
there was a marriage in Cana of G ............. Jn 2:1
miracles did Jesus in Cana of G ................. Jn 2:11
Judaea, and departed again into G ............. Jn 4:3
departed thence, and went into G .............. Jn 4:43
Then when he was come into G ................. Jn 4:45
Jesus came again into Cana of G .............. Jn 4:46
was come out of Judaea into G ................. Jn 4:47
he was come out of Judaea into G ............. Jn 4:54
Jesus went over the sea of G ...................... Jn 6:1
these things Jesus walked in G ................... Jn 7:1
unto them, he abode still in G ..................... Jn 7:9
said, Shall Christ come out of G ................ Jn 7:41
said unto him, Art thou also of G .............. Jn 7:52
for out of G ariseth no prophet ................. Jn 7:52
which was of Bethsaida of G ................... Jn 12:21
and Nathanael of Cana in G ....................... Jn 21:2
Which also said, Ye men of G .............. Acts 1:11
of G in the days of the taxing ............... Acts 5:37
rest throughout all Judaea and G .......... Acts 9:31
all Judaea, and began from G ............. Acts 10:37
up with him from G to Jerusalem ...... Acts 13:31

**GALL**
among you a root that beareth g ....... Deut 29:18
their grapes are grapes of g ............... Deut 32:32
poureth out my g upon the ground ...... Job 16:13
it is the g of asps within him ............. Job 20:14
sword cometh out of his g .................. Job 20:25
They gave me also g for my meat .......... Ps 69:21
and given us water of g to drink ............ Jer 8:14
and give them water of g to drink .......... Jer 9:15
and make them drink the water of g .... Jer 23:15
me, and compassed me with g ................ Lam 3:5
my misery, the wormwood and the g .. Lam 3:19
ye have turned judgment into g .......... Amos 6:12
vinegar to drink mingled with g ........... Mt 27:34
thou art in the g of bitterness ............. Acts 8:23

**GALLANT**
neither shall g ship pass thereby ............ Is 33:21

**GALLERIES**
the king is held in the g .......................... Song 7:5
the g thereof on the one side and ......... Eze 41:15
the g round about on their three .......... Eze 41:16
for the g were higher than these, .......... Eze 42:5

**GALLERY**
was g against g in three ............................ Eze 42:3

**GALLEY**
wherein shall go no g with oars .............. Is 33:21

**GALLIM** (*gal'-lim*) *A city in Benjamin.*
the son of Laish, which was of G ......... 1Sa 25:44
up thy voice, O daughter of G ............... Is 10:30

**GALLIO** (*gal'-le-o*) *A Roman proconsul of Achaia.*
when G was the deputy of Achaia, .... Acts 18:12
G said unto the Jews, If it were .......... Acts 18:14
G cared for none of those things ......... Acts 18:17

**GALLOWS**
Let a g be made of fifty cubits ................. Est 5:14
and he caused the g to be made .............. Est 5:14
g that he had prepared for him ................. Est 6:4
the g fifty cubits high, which .................... Est 7:9
on the g that he had prepared for ........... Est 7:10
him they have hanged upon the g ............. Est 8:7
ten sons be hanged upon the g ................ Est 9:13
sons should be hanged on the g ............... Est 9:25

**GAMAD** See GAMMADIMS.

**GAMALIEL** (*gam-a'-le-el*)
*1. A chief of Manasseh.*
G the son of Pedahzur ........................... Num 1:10
shall be G the son of Pedahzur ................ Num 2:20
day offered G the son of Pedahzur ...... Num 7:54
offering of G the son of Pedahzur ........ Num 7:59
was G the son of Pedahzur .................. Num 10:23
*2. A noted Rabbinic teacher.*
the council, a Pharisee, named G .......... Acts 5:34
up in this city at the feet of G .............. Acts 22:3

**GAMMAD** See GAMMADIMS.

**GAMMADIM** See GAMMADIMS.

**GAMMADIMS** (*gam'-ma-dims*) *Defenders of Tyre.*
and the G were in thy towers .............. Eze 27:11

**GAMUL** (*ga'-mul*) See BETH-GAMUL. *A sanctuary servant in David's time.*
Jachin, the two and twentieth to G... 1Chr 24:17

**GAP**
stand in the g before me for the .......... Eze 22:30

**GAPED**
They have g upon me with their .......... Job 16:10
They g upon me with their mouths, ....... Ps 22:13

**GAPS**
Ye have not gone up into the g .............. Eze 13:5

**GARDEN**
God planted a g eastward in Eden .......... Gen 2:8
life also in the midst of the g .................. Gen 2:9
went out of Eden to water the g ........... Gen 2:10
put him into the g of Eden to ................. Gen 2:15
Of every tree of the g thou ..................... Gen 2:16
not eat of every tree of the g ................... Gen 3:1
the fruit of the trees of the g .................. Gen 3:2
which is in the midst of the g .................. Gen 3:3
in the g in the cool of the day .................. Gen 3:8
God amongst the trees of the g ................. Gen 3:8
said, I heard thy voice in the g .............. Gen 3:10
sent him forth from the g of Eden .......... Gen 3:23
east of the g of Eden Cherubim .............. Gen 3:24
even as the g of the LORD ..................... Gen 13:10
it with thy foot, as a g of herbs ........... Deut 11:10
I may have it for a g of herbs ............... 1Kin 21:2
he fled by the way of the g house ......... 2Kin 9:27
buried in the g of his own house ........ 2Kin 21:18
his own house, in the g of Uzza ......... 2Kin 21:18
in his sepulchre in the g of Uzza ......... 2Kin 21:26
walls, which is by the king's g ............. 2Kin 25:4
pool of Siloah by the king's g ................ Neh 3:15
in the court of the g of the ...................... Est 1:5
his wrath went into the palace g .............. Est 7:7
g into the place of the banquet ................ Est 7:8
branch shooteth forth in his g ................ Job 8:16
A g inclosed is my sister, my .............. Song 4:12
blow upon my g, that the spices .......... Song 4:16
Let my beloved come into his g ............ Song 4:16
I am come into my g, my sister, ............. Song 5:1
beloved is gone down into his g .............. Song 6:2
I went down into the g of nuts to ....... Song 6:11
as a lodge in a g of cucumbers ..................... Is 1:8
as a g that hath no water ......................... Is 1:30
her desert like the g of the LORD ............. Is 51:3
and thou shalt be like a watered g ........... Is 58:11
as the g causeth the things that .............. Is 61:11
soul shall be as a watered g ................. Jer 31:12
night, by the way of the king's g ............. Jer 39:4
walls, which was by the king's g .............. Jer 52:7
tabernacle, as if it were of a g ................. Lam 2:6
hast been in Eden the g of God ............ Eze 28:13
The cedars in the g of God could ............ Eze 31:8
nor any tree in the g of God was ............ Eze 31:8
Eden, that were in the g of God ............ Eze 31:9
is become like the g of Eden ................ Eze 36:35
the land is as the g of Eden ..................... Joel 2:3
a man took, and cast into his g ............. Lk 13:19
the brook Cedron, where was a g .............. Jn 18:1
not I see thee in the g with him .............. Jn 18:26
he was crucified there was a g ............... Jn 19:41
in the g a new sepulchre, wherein ........... Jn 19:41

**GARDENER**
She, supposing him to be the g .............. Jn 20:15

**GARDENS**
as g by the river's side, as the ............... Num 24:6
I made me g and orchards, and I ............ Eccl 2:5
A fountain of g, a well of living ........... Song 4:15
beds of spices, to feed in the g ................ Song 6:2
Thou that dwellest in the g ................... Song 8:13
for the g that ye have chosen ..................... Is 1:29
that sacrificeth in g, and burneth ............... Is 65:3
purify themselves in the g behind ............ Is 66:17
and plant g, and eat the fruit of ............... Jer 29:5
and plant g, and eat the fruit of ............. Jer 29:28
when your g and your vineyards and .. Amos 4:9
they shall also make g, and eat ............ Amos 9:14

**GAREB** (*ga'-reb*)
*1. A "mighty man" of David.*
Ira an Ithrite, G an Ithrite, .................... 2Sa 23:38
Ira the Ithrite, G the Ithrite, .................. 1Chr 11:40
*2. A hill near Jerusalem.*
over against it upon the hill G ................ Jer 31:39

**GARLANDS**
g unto the gates, and would have ...... Acts 14:13

**GARLICK**
leeks, and the onions, and the g .......... Num 11:5

**GARMENT**
And Shem and Japheth took a g ............. Gen 9:23
out red, all over like an hairy g ............. Gen 25:25
And she caught him by his g ................. Gen 39:12
and he left his g in her hand ................ Gen 39:12

he had left his g in her hand Gen 39:13
cried, that he left his g with me Gen 39:15
And she laid up his g by her Gen 39:16
cried, that he left his g with me Gen 39:18
priest shall put on his linen g Lev 6:10
of the blood thereof upon any g Lev 6:27
The g also that the plague of Lev 13:47
a woollen g, or a linen g Lev 13:47
be greenish or reddish in the g Lev 13:49
if the plague be spread in the g Lev 13:51
He shall therefore burn that g Lev 13:52
the plague be not spread in the g Lev 13:53
he shall rend it out of the g Lev 13:56
And if it appear still in the g Lev 13:57
And the g, either warp, or woof, Lev 13:58
in a g of woollen or linen Lev 13:59
And for the leprosy of a g Lev 14:55
And every g, and every skin, Lev 15:17
neither shall a g mingled of Lev 19:19
shall a man put on a woman's g Deut 22:5
not wear a g of divers sorts Deut 22:11
the spoils a goodly Babylonish g Josh 7:21
of Zerah, and the silver, and the g Josh 7:24
And they spread a g, and did cast Judg 8:25
she had a g of divers colours 2Sa 13:18
rent her g of divers colours that 2Sa 13:19
Joab's g that he had put on was 2Sa 20:8
he had clad himself with a new g 1Kin 11:29
caught the new g that was on him 1Kin 11:30
hasted, and took every man his g 2Kin 9:13
I heard this thing, I rent my g Ezr 9:3
and having rent my g and my mantle, Ezr 9:5
with a g of fine linen and purple Est 8:15
as a g that is moth eaten Job 13:28
of my disease is my g changed Job 30:18
I made the cloud the g thereof Job 38:9
and they stand as a g Job 38:14
can discover the face of his g Job 41:13
I made sackcloth also my g Ps 69:11
violence covereth them as a g Ps 73:6
of them shall wax old like a g Ps 102:26
thyself with light as with a g Ps 104:2
it with the deep as with a g Ps 104:6
with cursing like as with his g Ps 109:18
him as the g which covereth him Ps 109:19
Take his g that is surety for a Prov 20:16
taketh away a g in cold weather Prov 25:20
Take his g that is surety for a Prov 27:13
who hath bound the waters in a g Prov 30:4
lo, they all shall wax old as a g Is 50:9
the earth shall wax old like a g Is 51:6
moth shall eat them up like a g Is 51:8
the g of praise for the spirit of Is 61:3
as a shepherd putteth on his g Jer 43:12
hath covered the naked with a g Eze 18:7
hath covered the naked with a g Eze 18:16
whose g was white as snow, and the Dan 7:9
ye pull off the robe with the g Mic 2:8
holy flesh in the skirt of his g Hag 2:12
they wear a rough g to deceive Zec 13:4
one covereth violence with his g Mal 2:16
piece of new cloth unto an old g Mt 9:16
to fill it up taketh from the g Mt 9:16
him, and touched the hem of his g Mt 9:20
herself, If I may but touch his g Mt 9:21
might only touch the hem of his g Mt 14:36
man which had not on a wedding g Mt 22:11
in hither not having a wedding g Mt 22:12
a piece of new cloth on an old g Mk 2:21
press behind, and touched his g Mk 5:27
it were but the border of his g Mk 6:56
And he, casting away his g Mk 10:50
back again for to take up his g Mk 13:16
side, clothed in a long white g Mk 16:5
a piece of a new g upon an old Lk 5:36
and touched the border of his g Lk 8:44
hath no sword, let him sell his g Lk 22:36
Cast thy g about thee, and follow Acts 12:8
all shall wax old as doth a g Heb 1:11
hating even the g spotted by the Jude 23
clothed with a g down to the foot Rev 1:13

**GARMENTS**

and be clean, and change your g Gen 35:2
put her widow's g off from her Gen 38:14
put on the g of her widowhood Gen 38:19
he washed his g in wine, and his Gen 49:11
thou shalt make holy g for Aaron Ex 28:2
make Aaron's g to consecrate him Ex 28:3
these are the g which they shall Ex 28:4
they shall make holy g for Aaron Ex 28:4
And thou shalt take the g, and put Ex 29:5
it upon Aaron, and upon his g Ex 29:21
upon the g of his sons with him Ex 29:21
and he shall be hallowed, and his g Ex 29:21
his sons, and his sons' g with him Ex 29:21
the holy g of Aaron shall be his Ex 29:29
the holy g for Aaron the priest, Ex 31:10
the g of his sons, to minister in Ex 31:10
the holy g for Aaron the priest, Ex 35:19
the g of his sons, to minister in Ex 35:19
his service, and for the holy g Ex 35:21
and made the holy g for Aaron Ex 39:1
the holy g for Aaron the priest, Ex 39:41
Aaron the priest, and his sons' g Ex 39:41
shalt put upon Aaron the holy g Ex 40:13
his g, and put on other g Lev 6:11
and his sons with him, and the g Lev 8:2
it upon Aaron, and upon his g Lev 8:30
and upon his sons' g with him Lev 8:30
and sanctified Aaron, and his g Lev 8:30
his sons, and his sons' g with him Lev 8:30
these are holy g Lev 16:4
and shall put off the linen g Lev 16:23
the holy place, and put on his g Lev 16:24
linen clothes, even the holy g Lev 16:32
is consecrated to put on the g Lev 21:10
g throughout their generations Num 15:38
And strip Aaron of his g, and put Num 20:26
And Moses stripped Aaron of his g ... Num 20:28
their feet, and old g upon them Josh 9:5
and these our g and our shoes are Josh 9:13
sheets and thirty change of g Judg 14:12
sheets and thirty change of g Judg 14:13
gave change of g unto them which ... Judg 14:19
and gave it to David, and his g 1Sa 18:4
and cut off their g in the middle 2Sa 10:4
the king arose, and tare his g 2Sa 13:31
silver, and vessels of gold, and g 1Kin 10:25
of silver, and two changes of g 2Kin 5:22
two bags, with two changes of g 2Kin 5:23
to receive money, and to receive g 2Kin 5:26
and, lo, all the way was full of g 2Kin 7:15
And changed his prison g 2Kin 25:29
cut off their g in the midst hard 1Chr 19:4
silver, and one hundred priests' g Ezr 2:69
five hundred and thirty priests' g Neh 7:70
and threescore and seven priests' g Neh 7:72
How thy g are warm, when he Job 37:17
They part my g among them Ps 22:18
All thy g smell of myrrh, and Ps 45:8
went down to the skirts of his g Ps 133:2
Let thy g be always white Eccl 9:8
the smell of thy g is like the Song 4:11
noise, and g rolled in blood Is 9:5
put on thy beautiful g, O Is 52:1
Their webs shall not become g Is 59:6
he put on the g of vengeance for Is 59:17
me with the g of salvation Is 61:10
Edom, with dyed g from Bozrah Is 63:1
thy g like him that treadeth in Is 63:2
shall be sprinkled upon my g Is 63:3
were not afraid, nor rent their g Jer 36:24
And changed his prison g Jer 52:33
that men could not touch their g Lam 4:14
of thy g thou didst take, and Eze 16:16
And tookest thy broidered g Eze 16:18
and put off their broidered g Eze 26:16
lay their g wherein they minister Eze 42:14
and shall put on other g, and shall Eze 42:14
shall be clothed with linen g Eze 44:17
their g wherein they ministered Eze 44:19
and they shall put on other g Eze 44:19
sanctify the people with their g Eze 44:19
and their hats, and their other g Dan 3:21
And rend your heart, and not your g Joel 2:13
Joshua was clothed with filthy g Zec 3:3
Take away the filthy g from him Zec 3:4
his head, and clothed him with g Zec 3:5
spread their g in the way Mt 21:8
and enlarge the borders of their g Mt 23:5
crucified him, and parted his g Mt 27:35
They parted my g among them Mt 27:35
to Jesus, and cast their g on him Mk 11:7
And many spread their g in the way Mk 11:8
crucified him, they parted his g Mk 15:24
they cast their g upon the colt Lk 19:35
men stood by them in shining g Lk 24:4
from supper, and laid aside his g Jn 13:4
their feet, and had taken his g Jn 13:12
had crucified Jesus, took his g Jn 19:23
g which Dorcas made, while she Acts 9:39
and your g are motheaten Jas 5:2
which have not defiled their g Rev 3:4
that watcheth, and keepeth his g Rev 16:15

**GARMITE** (*gar'-mite*) *A descendant of Judah.*
Naham, the father of Keilah the G 1Chr 4:19

**GARNER**
and gather his wheat into the g Mt 3:12
will gather the wheat into his g Lk 3:17

**GARNERS**
That our g may be full, affording Ps 144:13
the g are laid desolate, the Joel 1:17

**GARNISH**
g the sepulchres of the righteous Mt 23:29

**GARNISHED**
he g the house with precious 2Chr 3:6
his spirit he hath g the heavens Job 26:13
he findeth it empty, swept, and g Mt 12:44
cometh, he findeth it swept and g Lk 11:25
g with all manner of precious Rev 21:19

**GARRISON**
where is the g of the Philistines 1Sa 10:5
Jonathan smote the g of the 1Sa 13:3
smitten a g of the Philistines 1Sa 13:4
the g of the Philistines went out 1Sa 13:23
us go over to the Philistines' g 1Sa 14:1
go over unto the Philistines' g 1Sa 14:4
unto the g of these uncircumcised 1Sa 14:6
unto the g of the Philistines 1Sa 14:11
the men of the g answered 1Sa 14:12
the g, and the spoilers, they also 1Sa 14:15
the g of the Philistines was then 2Sa 23:14
the Philistines' g was then at 1Chr 11:16
city of the Damascenes with a g 2Cor 11:32

**GARRISONS**
Then David put g in Syria of 2Sa 8:6
And he put g in Edom 2Sa 8:14
throughout all Edom put he g 2Sa 8:14
Then David put g in 1Chr 18:6
And he put g in Edom 1Chr 18:13
set g in the land of Judah, and in 2Chr 17:2
thy strong g shall go down to the Eze 26:11

**GASHMU** (*gash'-mu*) See GESHEM. *A Samaritan in Nehemiah's time.*
G saith it, that thou and the Jews Neh 6:6

**GAT**
Abraham g up early in the morning ... Gen 19:27
cloud, and g him up into the mount Ex 24:18
Moses g him into the camp, he and .. Num 11:30
g them up into the top of the Num 14:40
So they g up from the tabernacle Num 16:27
Abimelech g him up to mount Judg 9:48
g them up to the top of the tower Judg 9:51
rose up, and g him unto his place Judg 19:28
g him up from Gilgal unto Gibeah 1Sa 13:15
his men g them up unto the hold 1Sa 24:22
they g them away, and no man saw 1Sa 26:12
g them away through the plain all 2Sa 4:7
David g him a name when he 2Sa 8:13
every man g him up upon his mule, 2Sa 13:29
g him home to his house, to his 2Sa 17:23
the people g them by stealth that 2Sa 19:3
with clothes, but he g no heat 1Kin 1:1
the pains of hell g hold upon me Ps 116:3
I g me men singers and women Eccl 2:8
We g our bread with the peril of Lam 5:9

**GATAM** (*ga'-tam*) *A son of Eliphaz.*
were Teman, Omar, Zepho, and G Gen 36:11
Duke Korah, duke G, and duke Gen 36:16
Teman, and Omar, Zephi, and G 1Chr 1:36

**GATE**
and Lot sat in the g of Sodom Gen 19:1
possess the g of his enemies Gen 22:17
that went in at the g of his city Gen 23:10
that went in at the g of his city Gen 23:18
the g of those which hate them Gen 24:60
God, and this is the g of heaven Gen 28:17
son came unto the g of their city Gen 34:20
went out of the g of his city Gen 34:24
went out of the g of his city Gen 34:24
of the g shall be fifteen cubits Ex 27:14
for the g of the court shall be Ex 27:16
Moses stood in the g of the camp Ex 32:26
out from g to g throughout the Ex 32:27
side of the g were fifteen cubits Ex 38:14
for the other side of the court g Ex 38:15
the hanging for the g of the Ex 38:18
and the sockets of the court g Ex 38:31
and the hanging for the court g Ex 39:40
up the hanging at the court g Ex 40:8
set up the hanging of the court g Ex 40:33
the door of the g of the court Num 4:26
city, and unto the g of his place Deut 21:19
the elders of the city in the g Deut 22:15
both out unto the g of that city Deut 22:24
go up to the g unto the elders Deut 25:7
the time of shutting of the g Josh 2:5
were gone out, they shut the g Josh 2:7
before the g even unto Shebarim Josh 7:5
the entering of the g of the city Josh 8:29
the entering of the g of the city Josh 20:4
the entering of the g of the city Judg 9:35
even unto the entering of the g Judg 9:40
the entering of the g of the city Judg 9:44
all night in the g of the city Judg 16:2
the doors of the g of the city Judg 16:3
stood by the entering of the g Judg 18:16
stood in the entering of the g Judg 18:17
Then went Boaz up to the g Ruth 4:1
and from the g of his place Ruth 4:10
all the people that were in the g Ruth 4:11
backward by the side of the g 1Sa 4:18
Saul drew near to Samuel in the g 1Sa 9:18
scrabbled on the doors of the g 1Sa 21:13
the g to speak with him quietly 2Sa 3:27
array at the entering in of the g 2Sa 10:8
even unto the entering of the g 2Sa 11:23
and stood beside the way of the g 2Sa 15:2
And the king stood by the g side 2Sa 18:4
the roof over the g unto the wall 2Sa 18:24
went up to the chamber over the g 2Sa 18:33
the king arose, and sat in the g 2Sa 19:8
the king doth sit in the g 2Sa 19:8
of Beth-lehem, which is by the g 2Sa 23:15
of Beth-lehem, that was by the g 2Sa 23:16
when he came to the g of the city 1Kin 17:10
the entrance of the g of Samaria 1Kin 22:10
for a shekel, in the g of Samaria 2Kin 7:1
men at the entering in of the g 2Kin 7:3
to have the charge of the g 2Kin 7:17
people trode upon him in the g 2Kin 7:17
this time in the g of Samaria 2Kin 7:18
people trode upon him in the g 2Kin 7:20
And as Jehu entered in at the g 2Kin 9:31
in of the g until the morning 2Kin 10:8
part shall be at the g of Sur 2Kin 11:6
part at the g behind the guard 2Kin 11:6
came by the way of the g of the 2Kin 11:19
g of Ephraim unto the corner g 2Kin 14:13
He built the higher g of the 2Kin 15:35
g of Joshua the governor of the 2Kin 23:8
left hand at the g of the city 2Kin 23:8

way of the g between two walls 2Kin 25:4
waited in the king's g eastward 1Chr 9:18
of Beth-lehem, that is at the g 1Chr 11:17
of Beth-lehem, that was by the g 1Chr 11:18
in array before the g of the city 1Chr 19:9
of their fathers, for every g 1Chr 26:13
with the g Shallecheth, by the 1Chr 26:16
also by their courses at every g 2Chr 8:14
entering in of the g of Samaria 2Chr 18:9
part at the g of the foundation 2Chr 23:5
the horse g by the king's house 2Chr 23:15
the high g into the king's house 2Chr 23:20
set it without at the g of the 2Chr 24:8
g of Ephraim to the corner g 2Chr 25:23
corner g, and at the valley g 2Chr 26:9
He built the high g of the house 2Chr 27:3
the street of the g of the city 2Chr 32:6
to the entering in at the fish g 2Chr 33:14
and the porters waited at every g 2Chr 35:15
by night by the g of the valley Neh 2:13
went on to the g of the fountain Neh 2:14
and entered by the g of the valley Neh 2:15
and they builded the sheep g Neh 3:1
But the fish g did the sons of Neh 3:3
Moreover the old g repaired Neh 3:6
The valley g repaired Hanun, and Neh 3:13
on the wall unto the dung g Neh 3:13
But the dung g repaired Malchiah Neh 3:14
But the g of the fountain Neh 3:15
the water g toward the east Neh 3:26
the horse g repaired the priests Neh 3:28
the keeper of the east g Neh 3:29
over against the g Miphkad Neh 3:31
sheep g repaired the goldsmiths Neh 3:32
that was before the water g Neh 8:1
that was before the water g from Neh 8:3
and in the street of the water g Neh 8:16
in the street of the g of Ephraim Neh 8:16
upon the wall toward the dung g Neh 12:31
And at the fountain g, which was Neh 12:37
even unto the water g eastward Neh 12:37
And from above the g of Ephraim Neh 12:39
the old g, and above the fish g Neh 12:39
of Meah, even unto the sheep g Neh 12:39
they stood still in the prison g Neh 12:39
then Mordecai sat in the king's g Est 2:19
Mordecai sat in the king's g Est 2:21
that were in the king's g Est 3:2
which were in the king's g Est 3:3
And came even before the king's g Est 4:2
king's g clothed with sackcloth Est 4:2
which was before the king's g Est 4:6
over against the g of the house Est 5:1
saw Mordecai in the king's g Est 5:9
the Jew sitting at the king's g Est 5:13
Jew, that sitteth at the king's g Est 6:10
came again to the king's g Est 6:12
and they are crushed in the g Job 5:4
out to the g through the city Job 29:7
when I saw my help in the g Job 31:21
sit in the g speak against me Ps 69:12
This g of the LORD, into which Ps 118:20
speak with the enemies in the g Ps 127:5
his g seeketh destruction Prov 17:19
oppress the afflicted in the g Prov 22:22
he openeth not his mouth in the g Prov 24:7
Heshbon, by the g of Bath-rabbim Song 7:4
Howl, O g; cry, O city Is 14:31
set themselves in array at the g Is 22:7
the g is smitten with destruction Is 24:12
that turn the battle to the g Is 28:6
for him that reproveth in the g Is 29:21
Stand in the g of the LORD's Jer 7:2
stand in the g of the children of Jer 17:19
is by the entry of the east g Jer 19:2
were in the high g of Benjamin Jer 20:2
of the new g of the LORD's house Jer 26:10
Hananeel unto the g of the corner Jer 31:38
of the horse g toward the east Jer 31:40
of the new g of the LORD's house Jer 36:10
when he was in the g of Benjamin Jer 37:13
then sitting in the g of Benjamin Jer 38:7
came in, and sat in the middle g Jer 39:3
by the g betwixt the two walls Jer 39:4
of the g between the two walls Jer 52:7
The elders have ceased from the g Lam 5:14
to the door of the inner g Eze 8:3
behold northward at the g of the Eze 8:5
g of the LORD's house which was Eze 8:14
came from the way of the higher g Eze 9:2
of the east g of the LORD's house Eze 10:19
the east g of the LORD's house Eze 11:1
behold at the door of the g five Eze 11:1
and he stood in the g Eze 40:3
Then came he unto the g which Eze 40:6
measured the threshold of the g Eze 40:6
and the other threshold of the g Eze 40:6
the threshold of the g by the Eze 40:7
of the g within was one reed Eze 40:7
also the porch of the g within Eze 40:8
measured he the porch of the g Eze 40:9
and the porch of the g was inward Eze 40:9
the little chambers of the g Eze 40:10
the breadth of the entry of the g Eze 40:11
and the length of the g, thirteen Eze 40:11
He measured then the g from the Eze 40:13
of the court round about the g Eze 40:14
from the face of the g of the Eze 40:15
of the inner g were fifty cubits Eze 40:15
posts within the g round about Eze 40:16
g unto the forefront of the inner Eze 40:19
the g of the outward court that Eze 40:20
after the measure of the first g Eze 40:21
g that looketh toward the east Eze 40:22
the g of the inner court was over Eze 40:23
against the g toward the north Eze 40:23
from g to g an hundred cubits Eze 40:23
behold a g toward the south Eze 40:24
there was a g in the inner court Eze 40:27
he measured from g to g toward Eze 40:27
to the inner court by the south g Eze 40:28
he measured the south g according Eze 40:28
he measured the g according to Eze 40:32
And he brought me to the north g Eze 40:35
in the porch of the g were two Eze 40:39
up to the entry of the north g Eze 40:40
which was at the porch of the g Eze 40:40
that side, by the side of the g Eze 40:41
without the inner g were the Eze 40:44
was at the side of the north g Eze 40:44
one at the side of the east g Eze 40:44
the breadth of the g was three Eze 40:48
g whose prospect is toward the Eze 42:15
Afterward he brought me to the g Eze 43:1
even the g that looketh toward Eze 43:1
the house by the way of the g Eze 43:4
g of the outward sanctuary which Eze 44:1
This g shall be shut, it shall Eze 44:2
by the way of the porch of that g Eze 44:3
of the north g before the house Eze 44:4
posts of the g of the inner court Eze 45:19
The g of the inner court that Eze 46:1
of the porch of that g without Eze 46:2
shall stand by the post of the g Eze 46:2
worship at the threshold of the g Eze 46:2
but the g shall not be shut until Eze 46:2
worship at the door of this g Eze 46:3
by the way of the porch of that g Eze 46:8
in by the way of the north g to Eze 46:9
go out by the way of the south g Eze 46:9
by the way of the south g shall Eze 46:9
forth by the way of the north g Eze 46:9
way of the g whereby he came in Eze 46:9
one shall then open him the g Eze 46:12
going forth one shall shut the g Eze 46:12
which was at the side of the g Eze 46:19
out of the way of the g northward Eze 47:2
utter g by the way that looketh Eze 47:2
one g of Reuben Eze 48:31
one g of Judah, one g of Levi Eze 48:31
one g of Joseph Eze 48:32
g of Benjamin, one g of Dan Eze 48:32
one g of Simeon Eze 48:33
of Issachar, one g of Zebulun Eze 48:33
one g of Gad Eze 48:34
g of Asher, one g of Naphtali Eze 48:34
Daniel sat in the g of the king Dan 2:49
hate him that rebuketh in the g Amos 5:10
poor in the g from their right Amos 5:12
and establish judgment in the g Amos 5:15
not have entered into the g of my Obad 13
is come unto the g of my people Mic 1:9
the LORD unto the g of Jerusalem Mic 1:12
up, and have passed through the g Mic 2:13
noise of a cry from the fish g Zeph 1:10
from Benjamin's g unto the place Zec 14:10
the first g, unto the corner g Zec 14:10
Enter ye in at the strait g Mt 7:13
for wide is the g, and broad is Mt 7:13
Because strait is the g, and Mt 7:14
he came nigh to the g of the city Lk 7:12
to enter in at the strait g Lk 13:24
Lazarus, which was laid at his g Lk 16:20
whom they laid daily at the g of Acts 3:2
at the Beautiful g of the temple Acts 3:10
house, and stood before the g Acts 10:17
they came unto the iron g that Acts 12:10
knocked at the door of the g Acts 12:13
she opened not the g for gladness Acts 12:14
told how Peter stood before the g Acts 12:14
own blood, suffered without the g Heb 13:12
every several g was of one pearl Rev 21:21

**GATES**

thy stranger that is within thy g Ex 20:10
were fenced with high walls, g Deut 3:5
thy stranger that is within thy g Deut 5:14
posts of thy house, and on thy g Deut 6:9
of thine house, and upon thy g Deut 11:20
the Levite that is within your g Deut 12:12
kill and eat flesh in all thy g Deut 12:15
thy g the tithe of thy corn Deut 12:17
the Levite that is within thy g Deut 12:18
thee, and thou shalt eat in thy g Deut 12:21
the stranger that is in thy g Deut 14:21
the Levite that is within thy g Deut 14:27
and shalt lay it up within thy g Deut 14:28
the widow, which are within thy g Deut 14:29
g in thy land which the LORD thy Deut 15:7
Thou shalt eat it within thy g Deut 15:22
the passover within any of thy g Deut 16:5
the Levite that is within thy g Deut 16:11
the widow, that are within thy g Deut 16:14
shalt thou make thee in all thy g Deut 16:18
within any of thy g which the Deut 17:2
that wicked thing, unto thy g Deut 17:5
of controversy within thy g Deut 17:8
any of thy g out of all Israel Deut 18:6
he shall choose in one of thy g Deut 23:16
that are in thy land within thy g Deut 24:14
that they may eat within thy g Deut 26:12
shall besiege thee in all thy g Deut 28:52
all thy g throughout all thy land Deut 28:52
shall distress thee in all thy g Deut 28:55
shall distress thee in thy g Deut 28:57
thy stranger that is within thy g Deut 31:12
son shall he set up the g of it Josh 6:26
then was war in the g Judg 5:8
of the LORD go down to the g Judg 5:11
the valley, and to the g of Ekron 1Sa 17:52
entering into a town that hath g 1Sa 23:7
And David sat between the two g 2Sa 18:24
set up the g thereof in his 1Kin 16:34
down the high places of the g 2Kin 23:8
service, keepers of the g of the 1Chr 9:19
porters in the g were two hundred 1Chr 9:22
of the g of the house of the LORD 1Chr 9:23
the nails for the doors of the g 1Chr 22:3
fenced cities, with walls, g 2Chr 8:5
about them walls, and towers, g 2Chr 14:7
at the g of the house of the LORD 2Chr 23:19
to praise in the g of the tents 2Chr 31:2
the g thereof are burned with Neh 1:3
the g thereof are consumed with Neh 2:3
g of the palace which appertained Neh 2:8
the g thereof were consumed with Neh 2:13
the g thereof are burned with Neh 2:17
not set up the doors upon the g Neh 6:1
Let not the g of Jerusalem be Neh 7:3
and their brethren that kept the g Neh 11:19
ward at the thresholds of the g Neh 12:25
and purified the people, and the g Neh 12:30
that when the g of Jerusalem Neh 13:19
that the g should be shut Neh 13:19
of my servants set I at the g Neh 13:19
they should come and keep the g Neh 13:22
Have the g of death been opened Job 38:17
liftest me up from the g of death Ps 9:13
in the g of the daughter of Zion Ps 9:14
Lift up your heads, O ye g Ps 24:7
Lift up your heads, O ye g Ps 24:9
The LORD loveth the g of Zion Ps 87:2
Enter into his g with Ps 100:4
For he hath broken the g of brass Ps 107:16
draw near unto the g of death Ps 107:18
Open to me the g of righteousness Ps 118:19
Our feet shall stand within thy g Ps 122:2
strengthened the bars of thy g Ps 147:13
in the openings of the g Prov 1:21
She crieth at the g, at the entry Prov 8:3
me, watching daily at my g Prov 8:34
wicked at the g of the righteous Prov 14:19
Her husband is known in the g Prov 31:23
her own works praise her in the g Prov 31:31
at our g are all manner of Song 7:13
her g shall lament and mourn Is 3:26
may go into the g of the nobles Is 13:2
Open ye the g, that the righteous Is 26:2
I shall go to the g of the grave Is 38:10
open before him the two leaved g Is 45:1
and the g shall not be shut Is 45:1
break in pieces the g of brass Is 45:2
thy g of carbuncles, and all thy Is 54:12
Therefore thy g shall be open Is 60:11
walls Salvation, and thy g Praise Is 60:18
Go through, go through the g Is 62:10
entering of the g of Jerusalem Jer 1:15
in at these g to worship the LORD Jer 7:2
and the g thereof languish Jer 14:2
with a fan in the g of the land Jer 15:7
in all the g of Jerusalem Jer 17:19
that enter in by these g Jer 17:20
bring it in by the g of Jerusalem Jer 17:21
bring in no burden through the g Jer 17:24
into the g of this city kings Jer 17:25
even entering in at the g of Jer 17:27
I kindle a fire in the g thereof Jer 17:27
people that enter in by these g Jer 22:2
the g of this house kings sitting Jer 22:4
forth beyond the g of Jerusalem Jer 22:19
which have neither g nor bars Jer 49:31
her high g shall be burned with Jer 51:58
all her g are desolate Lam 1:4
Her g are sunk into the ground Lam 2:9
entered into the g of Jerusalem Lam 4:12
of the sword against all their g Eze 21:15
battering rams against the g Eze 21:22
that was the g of the people Eze 26:2
when he shall enter into thy g Eze 26:10
and having neither bars nor g Eze 38:11
g over against the length of the Eze 40:18
of the g was the lower pavement Eze 40:18
were by the posts of the g Eze 40:38
charge at the g of the house Eze 44:11
in at the g of the inner court Eze 44:17
in the g of the inner court Eze 44:17
the g of the city shall be after Eze 48:31
three g northward Eze 48:31
five hundred: and three g Eze 48:32
measures: and three g Eze 48:33
five hundred, with their three g Eze 48:34
and foreigners entered into his g Obad 11
The g of the rivers shall be Nah 2:6
the g of thy land shall be set Nah 3:13
of truth and peace in your g Zec 8:16
the g of hell shall not prevail Mt 16:18
And they watched the g day Acts 9:24
oxen and garlands unto the g Acts 14:13
great and high, and had twelve g Rev 21:12
at the g twelve angels, and names Rev 21:12
On the east three g Rev 21:13

on the north three g ... Rev 21:13
on the south three g ... Rev 21:13
and on the west three g ... Rev 21:13
the g thereof, and the wall ... Rev 21:15
the twelve g were twelve pearls ... Rev 21:21
the g of it shall not be shut at ... Rev 21:25
in through the g into the city ... Rev 22:14

**GATH** (*gath*) See GATH-HEPHER, GATH-RIMMON, GITTITE, MORESHETH-GATH. *A royal Philistine city.*
only in Gaza, in G, and in Ashdod, ... Josh 11:22
of Israel be carried about unto G ... 1Sa 5:8
one, for Askelon one, for G one ... 1Sa 6:17
to Israel, from Ekron even unto G ... 1Sa 7:14
Philistines, named Goliath, of G ... 1Sa 17:4
the champion, the Philistine of G ... 1Sa 17:23
the way to Shaaraim, even unto G ... 1Sa 17:52
and went to Achish the king of G ... 1Sa 21:10
afraid of Achish the king of G ... 1Sa 21:12
the son of Maoch, king of G ... 1Sa 27:2
And David dwelt with Achish at G ... 1Sa 27:3
Saul that David was fled to G ... 1Sa 27:4
alive, to bring tidings to G ... 1Sa 27:11
Tell it not in G, publish it not ... 2Sa 1:20
men which came after him from G ... 2Sa 15:18
And there was yet a battle in G ... 2Sa 21:20
four were born to the giant in G ... 2Sa 21:22
Achish son of Maachah king of G ... 1Kin 2:39
Behold, thy servants be in G ... 1Kin 2:39
went to G to Achish to seek his ... 1Kin 2:40
and brought his servants from G ... 1Kin 2:40
had gone from Jerusalem to G ... 1Kin 2:41
went up, and fought against G ... 2Kin 12:17
whom the men of G that were born ... 1Chr 7:21
drove away the inhabitants of G ... 1Chr 8:13
and subdued them, and took G ... 1Chr 18:1
And yet again there was war at G ... 1Chr 20:6
were born unto the giant in G ... 1Chr 20:8
And G, and Mareshah, and Ziph, ... 2Chr 11:8
and brake down the wall of G ... 2Chr 26:6
the Philistines took him in G ... Ps 56:*t*
then go down to G of the ... Amos 6:2
Declare ye it not at G, weep ye ... Mic 1:10

**GATHER**
eaten, and thou shalt g it to thee ... Gen 6:21
said unto his brethren, G stones ... Gen 31:46
they shall g themselves together ... Gen 34:30
let them g all the food of those ... Gen 41:35
G yourselves together, that I may ... Gen 49:1
G yourselves together, and hear, ... Gen 49:2
g the elders of Israel together, ... Ex 3:16
them go and g straw for themselves ... Ex 5:7
to g stubble instead of straw ... Ex 5:12
g thy cattle, and all that thou ... Ex 9:19
g a certain rate every day, that ... Ex 16:4
be twice as much as they g daily ... Ex 16:5
G of it every man according to ... Ex 16:16
Six days ye shall g it ... Ex 16:26
on the seventh day for to g ... Ex 16:27
shalt g in the fruits thereof ... Ex 23:10
g thou all the congregation ... Lev 8:3
field, neither shalt thou g the ... Lev 19:9
neither shalt thou g every grape ... Lev 19:10
neither shalt thou g any gleaning ... Lev 23:22
and g in the fruit thereof ... Lev 25:3
neither g the grapes of thy vine ... Lev 25:5
nor g the grapes in it of thy ... Lev 25:11
not sow, nor g in our increase ... Lev 25:20
thou shalt g the whole assembly ... Num 8:9
shall g themselves unto thee ... Num 10:4
G unto me seventy men of the ... Num 11:16
a man that is clean shall g up ... Num 19:9
g thou the assembly together, ... Num 20:8
G the people together, and I will ... Num 21:16
G me the people together, and I ... Deut 4:10
that thou mayest g in thy corn ... Deut 11:14
thou shalt g all the spoil of it ... Deut 13:16
shalt not g the grapes thereof ... Deut 28:30
field, and shalt g but little in ... Deut 28:38
of the wine, nor g the grapes ... Deut 28:39
g thee from all the nations, ... Deut 30:3
will the LORD thy God g thee ... Deut 30:4
G the people together, men, and ... Deut 31:12
G unto me all the elders of your ... Deut 31:28
g after the reapers among the ... Ruth 2:7
G all Israel to Mizpeh, and I will ... 1Sa 7:5
will g all Israel unto my lord ... 2Sa 3:21
Now therefore g the rest of the ... 2Sa 12:28
g to me all Israel unto mount ... 1Kin 18:19
out into the field to g herbs ... 2Kin 4:39
I will g thee unto thy fathers, ... 2Kin 22:20
that they may g themselves unto ... 1Chr 13:2
g us together, and deliver us from ... 1Chr 16:35
David commanded to g together the ... 1Chr 22:2
g of all Israel money to repair ... 2Chr 24:5
I will g thee to thy fathers, and ... 2Chr 34:28
that they should g themselves ... Ezr 10:7
yet will I g them from thence, and ... Neh 1:9
heart to g together the nobles ... Neh 7:5
to g into them out of the fields ... Neh 12:44
that they may g together all the ... Est 2:3
g together all the Jews that are ... Est 4:16
city to g themselves together ... Est 8:11
or g together, then who can ... Job 11:10
they g the vintage of the wicked ... Job 24:6
if he g unto himself his spirit ... Job 34:14
thy seed, and g it into thy barn ... Job 39:12
G not my soul with sinners, nor ... Ps 26:9
and knoweth not who shall g them ... Ps 39:6
G my saints together unto me ... Ps 50:5
They g themselves together, they ... Ps 56:6
They g themselves together ... Ps 94:21
they g themselves together, and ... Ps 104:22
That thou givest them they g ... Ps 104:28
g us from among the heathen, to ... Ps 106:47
he shall g it for him that will ... Prov 28:8
sinner he giveth travail, to g ... Eccl 2:26
a time to g stones together ... Eccl 3:5
in the gardens, and to g lilies ... Song 6:2
of Gebim g themselves to flee ... Is 10:31
g together the dispersed of Judah ... Is 11:12
and hatch, and g under her shadow ... Is 34:15
he shall g the lambs with his arm ... Is 40:11
the east, and g thee from the west ... Is 43:5
all these g themselves together, ... Is 49:18
with great mercies will I g thee ... Is 54:7
they shall surely g together ... Is 54:15
whosoever shall g together ... Is 54:15
Yet will I g others to him, ... Is 56:8
all they g themselves together, ... Is 60:4
g out the stones ... Is 62:10
come, that I will g all nations ... Is 66:18
g together, and say, Assemble ... Jer 4:5
g yourselves to flee out of the ... Jer 6:1
The children g wood, and the ... Jer 7:18
harvestman, and none shall g them ... Jer 9:22
G up thy wares out of the land, O ... Jer 10:17
I will g the remnant of my flock ... Jer 23:3
I will g you from all the nations ... Jer 29:14
g them from the coasts of the ... Jer 31:8
that scattered Israel will g him ... Jer 31:10
Behold, I will g them out of all ... Jer 32:37
g ye wine, and summer fruits, and ... Jer 40:10
and none shall g up him that ... Jer 49:5
G ye together, and come against ... Jer 49:14
bright the arrows; g the shields ... Jer 51:11
I will even g you from the people ... Eze 11:17
therefore I will g all thy lovers ... Eze 16:37
I will even g them round about ... Eze 16:37
will g you out of the countries ... Eze 20:34
g you out of the countries ... Eze 20:41
therefore I will g you into the ... Eze 22:19
As they g silver, and brass, and ... Eze 22:20
so will I g you in mine anger and ... Eze 22:20
Yea, I will g you, and blow upon ... Eze 22:21
G the pieces thereof into it, ... Eze 24:4
I g the Egyptians from the people ... Eze 29:13
g them from the countries, and ... Eze 34:13
g you out of all countries, and ... Eze 36:24
will g them on every side, and ... Eze 37:21
g yourselves on every side to my ... Eze 39:17
sent to g together the princes ... Dan 3:2
the nations, now will I g them ... Hos 8:10
Egypt shall g them up, Memphis ... Hos 9:6
assembly, g the elders and all the ... Joel 1:14
all faces shall g blackness ... Joel 2:6
G the people, sanctify the ... Joel 2:16
g the children, and those that ... Joel 2:16
I will also g all nations ... Joel 3:2
g yourselves together round about ... Joel 3:11
I will surely g the remnant of ... Mic 2:12
I will g her that is driven out, ... Mic 4:6
for he shall g them as the ... Mic 4:12
Now g thyself in troops, O ... Mic 5:1
the faces of them all g blackness ... Nah 2:10
they shall g the captivity as the ... Hab 1:9
net, and g them in their drag ... Hab 1:15
G yourselves together, yea, ... Zeph 2:1
g together, O nation not desired ... Zeph 2:1
determination is to g the nations ... Zeph 3:8
I will g them that are sorrowful ... Zeph 3:18
g her that was driven out ... Zeph 3:19
even in the time that I g you ... Zeph 3:20
I will hiss for them, and g them ... Zec 10:8
Egypt, and g them out of Assyria ... Zec 10:10
For I will g all nations against ... Zec 14:2
g his wheat into the garner ... Mt 3:12
do they reap, nor g into barns ... Mt 6:26
Do men g grapes of thorns, or ... Mt 7:16
thou then that we go and g them up ... Mt 13:28
lest while ye g up the tares ... Mt 13:29
G ye together first the tares, and ... Mt 13:30
but g the wheat into my barn ... Mt 13:30
they shall g out of his kingdom ... Mt 13:41
they shall g together his elect ... Mt 24:31
g where I have not strawed ... Mt 25:26
shall g together his elect from ... Mk 13:27
will g the wheat into his garner ... Lk 3:17
For of thorns men do not g figs ... Lk 6:44
of a bramble bush g they grapes ... Lk 6:44
as a hen doth g her brood under ... Lk 13:34
G up the fragments that remain, ... Jn 6:12
but that also he should g ... Jn 11:52
men g them, and cast them into the ... Jn 15:6
g together in one all things in ... Eph 1:10
g the clusters of the vine of the ... Rev 14:18
to g them to the battle of that ... Rev 16:14
g yourselves together unto the ... Rev 19:17
to g them together to battle ... Rev 20:8

**GATHERED**
be g together unto one place ... Gen 1:9
their substance that they had g ... Gen 12:5
and was g to his people ... Gen 25:8
and was g unto his people ... Gen 25:17
And thither were all the flocks g ... Gen 29:3
the cattle should be g together ... Gen 29:7
all the flocks be g together ... Gen 29:8
Laban g together all the men of ... Gen 29:22
was g unto his people, being old ... Gen 35:29
he g up all the food of the seven ... Gen 41:48
Joseph g corn as the sand of the ... Gen 41:49
Joseph g up all the money that ... Gen 47:14
I am to be g unto my people ... Gen 49:29
he g up his feet into the bed, and ... Gen 49:33
ghost, and was g unto his people ... Gen 49:33
g together all the elders of the ... Ex 4:29
they g them together upon heaps ... Ex 8:14
the waters were g together ... Ex 15:8
children of Israel did so, and g ... Ex 16:17
he that g much had nothing over, ... Ex 16:18
he that g little had no lack ... Ex 16:18
they g every man according to his ... Ex 16:18
they g it every morning, every ... Ex 16:21
day they g twice as much bread ... Ex 16:22
when thou hast g in thy labours ... Ex 23:16
the people g themselves together ... Ex 32:1
all the sons of Levi g themselves ... Ex 32:26
Moses g all the congregation of ... Ex 35:1
the assembly was g together unto ... Lev 8:4
when ye have g in the fruit of ... Lev 23:39
when ye are g together within ... Lev 26:25
congregation is to be g together ... Num 10:7
g it, and ground it in mills, or ... Num 11:8
of the sea be g together for them ... Num 11:22
g the seventy men of the elders ... Num 11:24
next day, and they g the quails ... Num 11:32
that g least g ten homers ... Num 11:32
that are g together against me ... Num 14:35
they found a man that g sticks ... Num 15:32
they g themselves together ... Num 16:3
all thy company are g together ... Num 16:11
Korah g all the congregation ... Num 16:19
congregation was g against Moses ... Num 16:42
they g themselves together ... Num 20:2
Aaron g the congregation together ... Num 20:10
Aaron shall be g unto his people ... Num 20:24
Aaron shall be g unto his people, ... Num 20:26
but Sihon g all his people ... Num 21:23
g themselves together against the ... Num 27:3
also shalt be g unto thy people ... Num 27:13
as Aaron thy brother was g ... Num 27:13
shalt thou be g unto thy people ... Num 31:2
that thou hast g in thy corn ... Deut 16:13
goest up, and be g unto thy people ... Deut 32:50
Hor, and was g unto his people ... Deut 32:50
tribes of Israel were g together ... Deut 33:5
That they g themselves together, ... Josh 9:2
g themselves together, and went up ... Josh 10:5
are g together against us ... Josh 10:6
of the children of Israel g ... Josh 22:12
Joshua g all the tribes of Israel ... Josh 24:1
g their meat under my table ... Judg 1:7
were g unto their fathers ... Judg 2:10
he g unto him the children of ... Judg 3:13
Sisera g together all his ... Judg 4:13
of the east were g together ... Judg 6:33
and Abi-ezer was g after him ... Judg 6:34
who also was g after him ... Judg 6:35
the men of Israel g themselves ... Judg 7:23
of Ephraim g themselves together ... Judg 7:24
all the men of Shechem g together ... Judg 9:6
g their vineyards, and trode the ... Judg 9:27
tower of Shechem were g together ... Judg 9:47
children of Ammon were g together ... Judg 10:17
there were g vain men to Jephthah ... Judg 11:3
but Sihon g all his people ... Judg 11:20
the men of Ephraim g themselves ... Judg 12:1
Then Jephthah g together all the ... Judg 12:4
g them together for to offer a ... Judg 16:23
to Micah's house were g together ... Judg 18:22
was g together as one man ... Judg 20:1
of Israel were g against the city ... Judg 20:11
But the children of Benjamin g ... Judg 20:14
and g all the lords of the ... 1Sa 5:8
g together all the lords of the ... 1Sa 5:11
they g together to Mizpeh, and ... 1Sa 7:6
Israel were g together to Mizpeh ... 1Sa 7:7
of Israel g themselves together ... 1Sa 8:4
the Philistines g themselves ... 1Sa 13:5
that the Philistines g themselves ... 1Sa 13:11
he g an host, and smote the ... 1Sa 14:48
Saul g the people together, and ... 1Sa 15:4
Now the Philistines g together ... 1Sa 17:1
were g together at Shochoh, which ... 1Sa 17:1
the men of Israel were g together ... 1Sa 17:2
And Jonathan's lad g up the arrows ... 1Sa 20:38
g themselves unto him ... 1Sa 22:2
the Israelites were g together ... 1Sa 25:1
that the Philistines g their ... 1Sa 28:1
the Philistines g themselves ... 1Sa 28:4
Saul g all Israel together, and ... 1Sa 28:4
Now the Philistines g together ... 1Sa 29:1
the children of Benjamin g ... 2Sa 2:25
when he had g all the people ... 2Sa 2:30
David g together all the chosen ... 2Sa 6:1
they g themselves together ... 2Sa 10:15
he g all Israel together, and ... 2Sa 10:17
David g all the people together, ... 2Sa 12:29
which cannot be g up again ... 2Sa 14:14
Israel be generally g unto thee ... 2Sa 17:11
and they were g together, and went ... 2Sa 20:14
they g the bones of them that ... 2Sa 21:13
were there g together to battle ... 2Sa 23:9
the Philistines were g together ... 2Sa 23:11
Solomon g together chariots and ... 1Kin 10:26
he g men unto him, and became ... 1Kin 11:24
g the prophets together unto ... 1Kin 18:20
of Syria g all his host together ... 1Kin 20:1
of Israel g the prophets together ... 1Kin 22:6

they g all that were able to put 2Kin 3:21
g thereof wild gourds his lap 2Kin 4:39
king of Syria g all his host 2Kin 6:24
Jehu g all the people together, 2Kin 10:18
of the door have g of the people 2Kin 22:4
Thy servants have g the money 2Kin 22:9
thou shalt be g into thy grave in 2Kin 22:20
they g unto him all the elders of 2Kin 23:1
Then all Israel g themselves to 1Chr 11:1
were g together to battle 1Chr 11:13
So David g all Israel together, 1Chr 13:5
David g all Israel together to 1Chr 15:3
And the children of Ammon g 1Chr 19:7
he g all Israel, and passed over 1Chr 19:17
he g together all the princes of 1Chr 23:2
Solomon g chariots and horsemen 2Chr 1:14
he g of the house of Judah and 2Chr 11:1
that were g together to Jerusalem 2Chr 12:5
there are g unto him vain men, 2Chr 13:7
he g all Judah and Benjamin, and 2Chr 15:9
So they g themselves together at 2Chr 15:10
g together of prophets four 2Chr 18:5
Judah g themselves together, to 2Chr 20:4
g the Levites out of all the 2Chr 23:2
he g together the priests and the 2Chr 24:5
by day, and g money in abundance 2Chr 24:11
Moreover Amaziah g Judah together 2Chr 25:5
Ahaz g together the vessels of 2Chr 28:24
g them together into the east 2Chr 29:4
they g their brethren, and 2Chr 29:15
g the rulers of the city, and went 2Chr 29:20
people g themselves together to 2Chr 30:3
So there was g much people 2Chr 32:4
g them together to him in the 2Chr 32:6
had g of the hand of Manasseh 2Chr 34:9
they have g together the money 2Chr 34:17
thou shalt be g to thy grave in 2Chr 34:28
g together all the elders of 2Chr 34:29
the people g themselves together Ezr 3:1
I g together out of Israel chief Ezr 7:28
I g them together to the river Ezr 8:15
Benjamin g themselves together Ezr 10:9
all my servants were g thither Neh 5:16
all the people g themselves Neh 8:1
on the second day were g together Neh 8:13
the singers g themselves together Neh 12:28
I g them together, and set them in Neh 13:11
when many maidens were g together Est 2:8
when the virgins were g together Est 2:19
The Jews g themselves together in Est 9:2
g themselves together on the Est 9:15
provinces g themselves together Est 9:16
they have g themselves together Job 16:10
lie down, but he shall not be g Job 27:19
the nettles they were g together Job 30:7
and g themselves together Ps 35:15
the abjects g themselves together Ps 35:15
of the people are g together Ps 47:9
the mighty are g against me Ps 59:3
When the people are g together Ps 102:22
g them out of the lands, from the Ps 107:3
are they g together for war Ps 140:2
and herbs of the mountains are g Prov 27:25
who hath g the wind in his fists Prov 30:4
I g me also silver and gold, and Eccl 2:8
I have g my myrrh with my spice Song 5:1
g out the stones thereof, and Is 5:2
are left, have I g all the earth Is 10:14
kingdoms of nations g together Is 13:4
ye g together the waters of the Is 22:9
And they shall be g together Is 24:22
as prisoners are g in the pit Is 24:22
and ye shall be g one by one Is 27:12
your spoil shall be g like the Is 33:4
shall the vultures also be g Is 34:15
and his spirit it hath g them Is 34:16
Let all the nations be g together Is 43:9
let them all be g together Is 44:11
to him, Though Israel be not g Is 49:5
beside those that are g unto him Is 56:8
shall be g together unto thee Is 60:7
they that have g it shall eat it Is 62:9
the nations shall be g unto it Jer 3:17
they shall not be g, nor be Jer 8:2
shall not be lamented, neither g Jer 25:33
all the people were g against Jer 26:9
g wine and summer fruits very much Jer 40:12
that all the Jews which are g Jer 40:15
When I shall have g the house of Eze 28:25
nor be brought together, nor g Eze 29:5
is g out of many people, against Eze 38:8
that are g out of the nations Eze 38:12
hast thou g thy company to take a Eze 38:13
g them out of their enemies' Eze 39:27
but I have g them unto their own Eze 39:28
were g together unto the Dan 3:3
being g together, saw these men, Dan 3:27
children of Israel be g together Hos 1:11
people shall be g against them Hos 10:10
for she g it of the hire of an Mic 1:7
many nations are g against thee Mic 4:11
they have g the summer fruits Mic 7:1
earth be g together against it Zec 12:3
round about shall be g together Zec 14:14
when he had g all the chief Mt 2:4
were g together unto him, so that Mt 13:2
As therefore the tares are g Mt 13:40
into the sea, and g of every kind Mt 13:47
g the good into vessels, but cast Mt 13:48
three are g together in my name Mt 18:20
g together all as many as they Mt 22:10
to silence, they were g together Mt 22:34
the Pharisees were g together Mt 22:41
I have g thy children together Mt 23:37
will the eagles be g together Mt 24:28
before him shall be g all nations Mt 25:32
when they were g together Mt 27:17
g unto him the whole band of Mt 27:27
all the city was g together at Mk 1:33
straightway many were g together Mk 2:2
there was g unto him a great Mk 4:1
side, much people g unto him Mk 5:21
the apostles g themselves Mk 6:30
when much people were g together Lk 8:4
the people were g thick together Lk 11:29
when there were g together an Lk 12:1
I have g thy children together Lk 13:34
the younger son g all together Lk 15:13
will the eagles be g together Lk 17:37
and found the eleven g together Lk 24:33
Therefore they g them together Jn 6:13
Then g the chief priests and the Jn 11:47
were g together at Jerusalem Acts 4:6
the rulers were g together Acts 4:26
of Israel, were g together, Acts 4:27
where many were g together Acts 12:12
had g the church together, they Acts 14:27
when they had g the multitude Acts 15:30
g a company, and set all the city Acts 17:5
where they were g together Acts 20:8
when Paul had g a bundle of Acts 28:3
Christ, when ye are g together 1Cor 5:4
He that had g much had nothing 2Cor 8:15
he that had g little had no lack 2Cor 8:15
g the vine of the earth, and cast Rev 14:19
he g them together into a place Rev 16:16
g together to make war against Rev 19:19

## GATHERER
herdman, and a g of sycomore fruit Amos 7:14

## GATHEREST
When thou g the grapes of thy Deut 24:21

## GATHERETH
he that g the ashes of the heifer Num 19:10
He g the waters of the sea Ps 33:7
his heart g iniquity to itself Ps 41:6
he g together the outcasts of Ps 147:2
g her food in the harvest Prov 6:8
He that g in summer is a wise son Prov 10:5
but he that g by labour shall Prov 13:11
as one g eggs that are left, have Is 10:14
as when the harvestman g the corn Is 17:5
it shall be as he that g ears in Is 17:5
The Lord GOD which g the outcasts Is 56:8
the mountains, and no man g them Nah 3:18
but g unto him all nations, and Hab 2:5
he that g not with me scattereth Mt 12:30
even as a hen g her chickens Mt 23:37
he that g not with me scattereth Lk 11:23
g fruit unto life eternal Jn 4:36

## GATHERING
the g together of the waters Gen 1:10
him shall the g of the people be Gen 49:10
they that found him g sticks Num 15:33
widow woman was there g of sticks 1Kin 17:10
I am g two sticks, that I may go 1Kin 17:12
were three days in g of the spoil 2Chr 20:25
shall fail, the g shall not come Is 32:10
like the g of the caterpiller Is 33:4
g where thou hast not strawed Mt 25:24
assuredly g that the Lord had Acts 16:10
by our g together unto him, 2Th 2:1

## GATHERINGS
that there be no g when I come 1Cor 16:2

## GATH-HEPHER (*gath-he'-fer*) See GITTAH-HEPHER. *A town in Zebulun.*
the prophet, which was of G 2Kin 14:25

## GATH-RIMMON (*gath-rim'-mon*)
*1. A Levitical town in Dan.*
And Jehud, and Bene-berak, and G Josh 19:45
*2. A Levitical town in Manasseh.*
her suburbs, G with her suburbs Josh 21:24
suburbs, and G with her suburbs Josh 21:25
suburbs, and G with her suburbs 1Chr 6:69

## GAVE
Adam g names to all cattle, and to Gen 2:20
g also unto her husband with her Gen 3:6
she g me of the tree, and I did Gen 3:12
And he g him tithes of all Gen 14:20
g her to her husband Abram to be Gen 16:3
and good, and g it unto a young man Gen 18:7
g them unto Abraham, and restored Gen 20:14
g it unto Hagar, putting it on Gen 21:14
with water, and g the lad drink Gen 21:19
g them unto Abimelech Gen 21:27
upon her hand, and g him drink Gen 24:18
g straw and provender for the Gen 24:32
and raiment, and g them to Rebekah Gen 24:53
he g also to her brother and to Gen 24:53
Abraham g all that he had unto Gen 25:5
Abraham had, Abraham g gifts Gen 25:6
Then Abraham g up the ghost Gen 25:8
he g up the ghost and died Gen 25:17
Then Jacob g Esau bread and Gen 25:34
she g the savoury meat and the Gen 27:17
which God g unto Abraham Gen 28:4
he blessed him he g him a charge Gen 28:6
Laban g unto his daughter Leah Gen 29:24
he g him Rachel his daughter to Gen 29:28
Laban g to Rachel his daughter Gen 29:29
she g him Bilhah her handmaid to Gen 30:4
her maid, and g her Jacob to wife Gen 30:9
g them into the hand of his sons Gen 30:35
they g unto Jacob all the strange Gen 35:4
And the land which I g Abraham Gen 35:12
Isaac g up the ghost, and died, and Gen 35:29
he g it her, and came in unto her, Gen 38:18
because that I g her not to Gen 38:26
g him favour in the sight of the Gen 39:21
I g the cup into Pharaoh's hand Gen 40:11
he g the cup into Pharaoh's hand Gen 40:21
he g him to wife Asenath the Gen 41:45
g them water, and they washed Gen 43:24
he g their asses provender Gen 43:24
Joseph g them wagons, according Gen 45:21
g them provision for the way Gen 45:21
To all of them he g each man Gen 45:22
but to Benjamin he g three Gen 45:22
whom Laban g to Leah his daughter Gen 46:18
which Laban g unto Rachel his Gen 46:25
g them a possession in the land Gen 47:11
Joseph g them bread in exchange Gen 47:17
portion which Pharaoh g them Gen 47:22
he g Moses Zipporah his daughter Ex 2:21
g them a charge unto the children Ex 6:13
the LORD g the people favour in Ex 11:3
the LORD g the people favour in Ex 12:36
but it g light by night to these Ex 14:20
he g unto Moses, when he had made Ex 31:18
So they g it me Ex 32:24
he g them in commandment all that Ex 34:32
Moses g commandment, and they Ex 36:6
Moses g the money of them that Num 3:51
oxen, and g them unto the Levites Num 7:6
four oxen he g unto the sons of Num 7:7
eight oxen he g unto the sons of Num 7:8
unto the sons of Kohath he g none Num 7:9
g it unto the seventy elders Num 11:25
their princes g him a rod apiece Num 17:6
g him a charge, as the LORD Num 27:23
Moses g the tribute, which was Num 31:41
g them unto the Levites, which Num 31:47
Moses g unto them, even to the Num 32:33
g other names unto the cities Num 32:38
Moses g Gilead unto Machir the Num 32:40
which the LORD g unto them Deut 2:12
g I unto the Reubenites and to the Deut 3:12
g I unto the half tribe of Deut 3:13
And I g Gilead unto Machir Deut 3:15
unto the Gadites I g from Gilead Deut 3:16
that the LORD g me the two tables Deut 9:11
and the LORD g them unto me Deut 10:4
I g my daughter unto this man to Deut 22:16
g it for an inheritance unto the Deut 29:8
he g Joshua the son of Nun a Deut 31:23
Moses g you on this side Jordan Josh 1:14
g you on this side Jordan toward Josh 1:15
Joshua g it for an inheritance Josh 11:23
g it for a possession unto the Josh 12:6
which Joshua g unto the tribes of Josh 12:7
inheritance, which Moses g them Josh 13:8
the servant of the LORD g them Josh 13:8
of Levi he g none inheritance Josh 13:14
Moses g unto the tribe of the Josh 13:15
Moses g inheritance unto the Josh 13:24
Moses g inheritance unto the half Josh 13:29
Levi Moses g not any inheritance Josh 13:33
but unto the Levites he g none Josh 14:3
therefore they g no part unto the Josh 14:4
g unto Caleb the son of Jephunneh Josh 14:13
he g a part among the children of Josh 15:13
he g him Achsah his daughter to Josh 15:17
he g her the upper springs, and Josh 15:19
g them an inheritance among the Josh 17:4
the servant of the LORD g them Josh 18:7
the children of Israel g an Josh 19:49
g him the city which he asked Josh 19:50
the children of Israel g unto the Josh 21:3
the children of Israel g by lot Josh 21:8
they g out of the tribe of the Josh 21:9
they g them the city of Arba the Josh 21:11
g they to Caleb the son of Josh 21:12
Thus they g to the children of Josh 21:13
For they g them Shechem with her Josh 21:21
they g Golan in Bashan with her Josh 21:27
the LORD g unto Israel all the Josh 21:43
the LORD g them rest round about, Josh 21:44
g you on the other side Jordan Josh 22:4
g Joshua among their brethren on Josh 22:7
his seed, and g him Isaac Josh 24:3
I g unto Isaac Jacob and Esau Josh 24:4
I g unto Esau mount Seir, to Josh 24:4
I g them into your hand, that ye Josh 24:8
he g him Achsah his daughter to Judg 1:13
Caleb g her the upper springs and Judg 1:15
they g Hebron unto Caleb, as Judg 1:20
g their daughters to their sons, Judg 3:6
g him drink, and covered him Judg 4:19
He asked water, and she g him milk Judg 5:25
before you, and g you their land Judg 6:9
they g him threescore and ten Judg 9:4
and g them, and they did eat Judg 14:9
g change of garments unto them Judg 14:19
therefore I g her to thy Judg 15:2
g them to the founder, who made Judg 17:4
g provender unto the asses Judg 19:21
for the men of Israel g place to Judg 20:36

they g them wives which they had ... Judg 21:14
g to her that she had reserved ... Ruth 2:18
six measures of barley g he me ... Ruth 3:17
shoe, and g it to his neighbour ... Ruth 4:7
the LORD g her conception, and she ... Ruth 4:13
women her neighbours g it a name ... Ruth 4:17
he g to Peninnah his wife, and to ... 1Sa 1:4
unto Hannah he g a worthy portion ... 1Sa 1:5
g her son suck until she weaned ... 1Sa 1:23
Bring the portion which I g thee ... 1Sa 9:23
Samuel, God g him another heart ... 1Sa 10:9
g it to David, and his garments, ... 1Sa 18:4
they g them in full tale to the ... 1Sa 18:27
Saul g him Michal his daughter to ... 1Sa 18:27
Jonathan g his artillery unto his ... 1Sa 20:40
So the priest g him hallowed ... 1Sa 21:6
g him victuals, and g him the ... 1Sa 22:10
Then Achish g him Ziklag that day ... 1Sa 27:6
g him bread, and he did eat ... 1Sa 30:11
they g him a piece of a cake of ... 1Sa 30:12
I g thee thy master's house, and ... 2Sa 12:8
g thee the house of Israel and of ... 2Sa 12:8
king g all the captains charge ... 2Sa 18:5
Joab g up the sum of the number ... 2Sa 24:9
And God g Solomon wisdom and ... 1Kin 4:29
So Hiram g Solomon cedar trees and .. 1Kin 5:10
Solomon g Hiram twenty thousand ... 1Kin 5:11
thus g Solomon to Hiram year by ... 1Kin 5:11
the LORD g Solomon wisdom, as he ... 1Kin 5:12
that then king Solomon g Hiram ... 1Kin 9:11
she g the king an hundred and ... 1Kin 10:10
queen of Sheba g to king Solomon ... 1Kin 10:10
king Solomon g unto the queen of ... 1Kin 10:13
Solomon g her of his royal bounty ... 1Kin 10:13
which g him an house, and ... 1Kin 11:18
him victuals, and g him land ... 1Kin 11:18
so that he g him to wife the ... 1Kin 11:19
old men's counsel that they g him ... 1Kin 12:13
he g a sign the same day, saying, ... 1Kin 13:3
the house of David, and g it thee ... 1Kin 14:8
which he g to their fathers, and ... 1Kin 14:15
g unto the people, and they did ... 1Kin 19:21
And he g him his hand ... 2Kin 10:15
upon him, and g him the testimony ... 2Kin 11:12
they g the money, being told, ... 2Kin 12:11
But they g that to the workmen, ... 2Kin 12:14
the LORD g Israel a saviour, so ... 2Kin 13:5
Menahem g Pul a thousand talents ... 2Kin 15:19
his servant, and g him presents ... 2Kin 17:3
Hezekiah g him all the silver ... 2Kin 18:15
g it to the king of Assyria ... 2Kin 18:16
the land which I g their fathers ... 2Kin 21:8
Hilkiah g the book to Shaphan, and ... 2Kin 22:8
Jehoiakim g the silver and the ... 2Kin 23:35
and they g judgment upon him ... 2Kin 25:6
Sheshan g his daughter to Jarha ... 1Chr 2:35
they g them Hebron in the land of ... 1Chr 6:55
they g to Caleb the son of ... 1Chr 6:56
Aaron they g the cities of Judah ... 1Chr 6:57
the children of Israel g to the ... 1Chr 6:64
they g by lot out of the tribe of ... 1Chr 6:65
they g unto them, of the cities ... 1Chr 6:67
they g also Gezer with her ... 1Chr 6:67
David g a commandment, and they ... 1Chr 14:12
Joab g the sum of the number of ... 1Chr 21:5
So David g to Ornan for the place ... 1Chr 21:25
God g to Heman fourteen sons and ... 1Chr 25:5
Then David g to Solomon his son ... 1Chr 28:11
He g of gold by weight for things ... 1Chr 28:14
by weight he g gold for the ... 1Chr 28:16
for the golden basons he g gold ... 1Chr 28:17
g for the service of the house of ... 1Chr 29:7
g them to the treasure of the ... 1Chr 29:8
she g the king an hundred and ... 2Chr 9:9
the queen of Sheba g king Solomon ... 2Chr 9:9
king Solomon g to the queen of ... 2Chr 9:12
counsel which the old men g him ... 2Chr 10:8
he g them victual in abundance ... 2Chr 11:23
g the kingdom over Israel to ... 2Chr 13:5
Then the men of Judah g a shout ... 2Chr 13:15
the LORD g them rest round about ... 2Chr 15:15
for his God g him rest round ... 2Chr 20:30
their father g them great gifts ... 2Chr 21:3
but the kingdom g he to Jehoram ... 2Chr 21:3
g him the testimony, and made him .. 2Chr 23:11
Jehoiada g it to such as did the ... 2Chr 24:12
the Ammonites g gifts to Uzziah ... 2Chr 26:8
the children of Ammon g him the ... 2Chr 27:5
g them to eat and to drink, and ... 2Chr 28:15
g it unto the king of Assyria ... 2Chr 28:21
who therefore g them up to ... 2Chr 30:7
the princes g to the congregation ... 2Chr 30:24
unto him, and he g him a sign ... 2Chr 32:24
they g it to the workmen that ... 2Chr 34:10
artificers and builders g they it ... 2Chr 34:11
Josiah g to the people, of the ... 2Chr 35:7
his princes g willingly unto the ... 2Chr 35:8
g unto the priests for the ... 2Chr 35:8
g unto the Levites for passover ... 2Chr 35:9
he g them all into his hand ... 2Chr 36:17
They g after their ability unto ... Ezr 2:69
They g money also unto the masons ... Ezr 3:7
he g them into the hand of ... Ezr 5:12
Artaxerxes g unto Ezra the priest ... Ezr 7:11
they g their hands that they ... Ezr 10:19
the wine, and g it unto the king ... Neh 2:1
g them the king's letters ... Neh 2:9
That I g my brother Hanani, and ... Neh 7:2
of the fathers g unto the work ... Neh 7:70
The Tirshatha g to the treasure a ... Neh 7:70
g to the treasure of the work ... Neh 7:71
g was twenty thousand drams of ... Neh 7:72
g the sense, and caused them to ... Neh 8:8
companies of them that g thanks ... Neh 12:31
g thanks went over against them ... Neh 12:38
that g thanks in the house of God ... Neh 12:40
g the portions of the singers and ... Neh 12:47
they g them drink in vessels of ... Est 1:7
he speedily g her her things for ... Est 2:9
g gifts, according to the state ... Est 2:18
g it unto Haman the son of ... Est 3:10
g him a commandment to Mordecai, ... Est 4:5
Also he g him the copy of the ... Est 4:8
g him commandment unto Mordecai ... Est 4:10
from Haman, and g it unto Mordecai ... Est 8:2
the LORD g, and the LORD hath ... Job 1:21
my servant, and he g me no answer ... Job 19:16
eye saw me, it g witness to me ... Job 29:11
Unto me men g ear, and waited, and ... Job 29:21
I g ear to your reasons, whilst ... Job 32:11
also the LORD g Job twice as much ... Job 42:10
every man also g him a piece of ... Job 42:11
their father g them inheritance ... Job 42:15
and the Highest g his voice ... Ps 18:13
The Lord g the word ... Ps 68:11
They g me also gall for my meat ... Ps 69:21
in my thirst they g me vinegar to ... Ps 69:21
and he g ear unto me ... Ps 77:1
g them drink as out of the great ... Ps 78:15
for he g them their own desire ... Ps 78:29
He g also their increase unto the ... Ps 78:46
He g up their cattle also to the ... Ps 78:48
but g their life over to the ... Ps 78:50
He g his people over also unto ... Ps 78:62
So I g them up unto their own ... Ps 81:12
and the ordinance that he g them ... Ps 99:7
He g them hail for rain, and ... Ps 105:32
g them the lands of the heathen ... Ps 105:44
And he g them their request ... Ps 106:15
he g them into the hand of the ... Ps 106:41
g their land for an heritage, an ... Ps 135:12
g their land for an heritage ... Ps 136:21
When he g to the sea his decree, ... Prov 8:29
I g my heart to seek and search ... Eccl 1:13
I g my heart to know wisdom, and ... Eccl 1:17
shall return unto God who g it ... Eccl 12:7
he g good heed, and sought out, and ... Eccl 12:9
called him, but he g me no answer ... Song 5:6
g the nations before him, and made ... Is 41:2
he g them as the dust to his ... Is 41:2
Who g Jacob for a spoil, and ... Is 42:24
I g Egypt for thy ransom, ... Is 43:3
I g my back to the smiters, and my ... Is 50:6
the land that I g to your fathers ... Jer 7:7
unto the place which I g to you ... Jer 7:14
land that I g unto their fathers ... Jer 16:15
from thine heritage that I g thee ... Jer 17:4
you, and the city that I g you ... Jer 23:39
off the land that I g unto them ... Jer 24:10
land that I g to their fathers ... Jer 30:3
I g the evidence of the purchase ... Jer 32:12
g it to Baruch the scribe, the ... Jer 36:32
where he g judgment upon him ... Jer 39:5
g them vineyards and fields at the ... Jer 39:10
g charge concerning Jeremiah to ... Jer 39:11
of the guard g him victuals ... Jer 40:5
as I g Zedekiah king of Judah ... Jer 44:30
where he g judgment upon him ... Jer 52:9
mine elders g up the ghost in the ... Lam 1:19
My meat also which I g thee ... Eze 16:19
I g them my statutes, and shewed ... Eze 20:11
Moreover also I g them my ... Eze 20:12
Wherefore I g them also statutes ... Eze 20:25
the land that I g to your fathers ... Eze 36:28
g them into the hand of their ... Eze 39:23
the Lord g Jehoiakim king of ... Dan 1:2
the prince of the eunuchs g names ... Dan 1:7
for he g unto Daniel the name of ... Dan 1:7
and g them pulse ... Dan 1:16
God g them knowledge and skill in ... Dan 1:17
g him many great gifts, and made ... Dan 2:48
O thou king, the most high God g ... Dan 5:18
And for the majesty that he g him ... Dan 5:19
g thanks before his God, as he ... Dan 6:10
did not know that I g her corn ... Hos 2:8
I g thee a king in mine anger, and ... Hos 13:11
But ye g the Nazarites wine to ... Amos 2:12
I g them to him for the fear ... Mal 2:5
he g commandment to depart unto ... Mt 8:18
he g them power against unclean ... Mt 10:1
g the loaves to his disciples, and ... Mt 14:19
g thanks, and brake them ... Mt 15:36
g to his disciples, and the ... Mt 15:36
who g thee this authority ... Mt 21:23
unto one he g five talents, to ... Mt 25:15
I was an hungred, and ye g me meat ... Mt 25:35
I was thirsty, and ye g me drink ... Mt 25:35
or thirsty, and g thee drink ... Mt 25:37
an hungred, and ye g me no meat ... Mt 25:42
was thirsty, and ye g me no drink ... Mt 25:42
g it to the disciples, and said, ... Mt 26:26
g thanks, and g it to them, ... Mt 26:27
that betrayed him g them a sign ... Mt 26:48
g them for the potter's field, as ... Mt 27:10
They g him vinegar to drink ... Mt 27:34
it on a reed, and g him to drink ... Mt 27:48
they g large money unto the ... Mt 28:12
g also to them which were with ... Mk 2:26
And forthwith Jesus g them leave ... Mk 5:13
g them power over unclean spirits ... Mk 6:7
a charger, and g it to the damsel ... Mk 6:28
the damsel g it to her mother ... Mk 6:28
g them to his disciples to set ... Mk 6:41
g thanks, and brake ... Mk 8:6
g to his disciples to set before ... Mk 8:6
who g thee this authority to do ... Mk 11:28
g authority to his servants, and ... Mk 13:34
g to them, and said, Take, eat ... Mk 14:22
had given thanks, he g it to them ... Mk 14:23
they g him to drink wine mingled ... Mk 15:23
g him to drink, saying, Let alone ... Mk 15:36
a loud voice, and g up the ghost ... Mk 15:37
g up the ghost, he said, Truly ... Mk 15:39
he g the body to Joseph ... Mk 15:45
she coming in that instant g ... Lk 2:38
he g it again to the minister, and ... Lk 4:20
g also to them that were with him ... Lk 6:4
many that were blind he g sight ... Lk 7:21
g them power and authority over ... Lk 9:1
g to the disciples to set before ... Lk 9:16
g them to the host, and said unto ... Lk 10:35
and no man g unto him ... Lk 15:16
they saw it, g praise unto God ... Lk 18:43
or who is he that g thee this ... Lk 20:2
g thanks, and said, Take this, and ... Lk 22:17
g thanks, and brake it ... Lk 22:19
g unto them, saying, This is my ... Lk 22:19
Pilate g sentence that it should ... Lk 23:24
and the paps which never g suck ... Lk 23:29
said thus, he g up the ghost ... Lk 23:46
it, and brake, and g to them ... Lk 24:30
they g him a piece of a broiled ... Lk 24:42
to them g he power to become the ... Jn 1:12
that he g his only begotten Son, ... Jn 3:16
that Jacob g to his son Joseph ... Jn 4:5
which g us the well, and drank ... Jn 4:12
He g them bread from heaven to ... Jn 6:31
Moses g you not that bread from ... Jn 6:32
Moses therefore g unto you ... Jn 7:22
which g them me, is greater than ... Jn 10:29
he g me a commandment, what I ... Jn 12:49
he g it to Judas Iscariot, the ... Jn 13:26
as the Father g me commandment, ... Jn 14:31
which g counsel to the Jews, that ... Jn 18:14
But Jesus g him no answer ... Jn 19:9
bowed his head, and g up the ghost ... Jn 19:30
and Pilate g him leave ... Jn 19:38
And they g forth their lots ... Acts 1:26
as the Spirit g them utterance ... Acts 2:4
he g heed unto them, expecting to ... Acts 3:5
with great power g the apostles ... Acts 4:33
fell down, and g up the ghost ... Acts 5:5
he g him none inheritance in it, ... Acts 7:5
And he g him the covenant of ... Acts 7:8
g him favour and wisdom in the ... Acts 7:10
g them up to worship the host of ... Acts 7:42
the people with one accord g heed ... Acts 8:6
To whom they all g heed, from the ... Acts 8:10
he g her his hand, and lifted her ... Acts 9:41
which g much alms to the people, ... Acts 10:2
Forasmuch then as God g them the ... Acts 11:17
And the people g a shout, saying, ... Acts 12:22
because he g not God the glory ... Acts 12:23
eaten of worms, and g up the ghost ... Acts 12:23
after that he g unto them judges ... Acts 13:20
God g unto them Saul the son of ... Acts 13:21
to whom also he g testimony ... Acts 13:22
which g testimony unto the word ... Acts 14:3
g us rain from heaven, and ... Acts 14:17
g audience to Barnabas and Paul, ... Acts 15:12
we g no such commandment ... Acts 15:24
they g him audience unto this ... Acts 22:22
g commandment to his accusers ... Acts 23:30
I g my voice against them ... Acts 26:10
g him liberty to go unto his ... Acts 27:3
g thanks to God in presence of ... Acts 27:35
Wherefore God also g them up to ... Rom 1:24
For this cause God g them up unto ... Rom 1:26
God g them over to a reprobate ... Rom 1:28
even as the Lord g to every man ... 1Cor 3:5
but God g the increase ... 1Cor 3:6
but first g their own selves to ... 2Cor 8:5
Who g himself for our sins, that ... Gal 1:4
To whom we g place by subjection, ... Gal 2:5
they g to me and Barnabas the ... Gal 2:9
who loved me, and g himself for me ... Gal 2:20
but God g it to Abraham by ... Gal 3:18
g him to be the head over all ... Eph 1:22
captive, and g gifts unto men ... Eph 4:8
And he g some, apostles ... Eph 4:11
the church, and g himself for it ... Eph 5:25
we g you by the Lord Jesus ... 1Th 4:2
Who g himself a ransom for all, ... 1Ti 2:6
Who g himself for us, that he ... Titus 2:14
Abraham g a tenth part of all ... Heb 7:2
Abraham g the tenth of the spoils ... Heb 7:4
of which no man g attendance at ... Heb 7:13
g commandment concerning his ... Heb 11:22
us, and we g them reverence ... Heb 12:9
again, and the heaven g rain ... Jas 5:18
up from the dead, and g him glory ... 1Pet 1:21
another, as he g us commandment ... 1Jn 3:23
the record that God g of his Son ... 1Jn 5:10
when I g all diligence to write ... Jude 3
Christ, which God g unto him ... Rev 1:1
I g her space to repent of her ... Rev 2:21
g glory to the God of heaven ... Rev 11:13
the dragon g him his power, and ... Rev 13:2
which g power unto the beast ... Rev 13:4
one of the four beasts g unto the ... Rev 15:7

the sea g up the dead which were ....... Rev 20:13

**GAVEST**
woman whom thou g to be with me .... Gen 3:12
which thou g unto their fathers ........... 1Kin 8:34
which thou g unto our fathers ............. 1Kin 8:40
which thou g unto their fathers, .......... 1Kin 8:48
the land which thou g to them ............ 2Chr 6:25
which thou g unto our fathers ............. 2Chr 6:31
which thou g unto their fathers, ......... 2Chr 6:38
g it to the seed of Abraham thy .......... 2Chr 20:7
g him the name of Abraham .................... Neh 9:7
g them right judgments, and true ......... Neh 9:13
g them bread from heaven for .............. Neh 9:15
Thou g also thy good spirit to ............... Neh 9:20
g them water for their thirst ................... Neh 9:20
Moreover thou g them kingdoms .......... Neh 9:22
g them into their hands, with ................ Neh 9:24
mercies thou g them saviours ................ Neh 9:27
therefore g thou them into the ............. Neh 9:30
great goodness that thou g them ............ Neh 9:35
fat land which thou g before them ....... Neh 9:35
for the land that thou g unto our .......... Neh 9:36
G thou the goodly wings unto the ....... Job 39:13
thou g it him, even length of ..................... Ps 21:4
g him to be meat to the people .............. Ps 74:14
thou g me no water for my feet .............. Lk 7:44
Thou g me no kiss .................................... Lk 7:45
and yet thou never g me a kid .............. Lk 15:29
Wherefore then g not thou my ............... Lk 19:23
the work which thou g me to do .............. Jn 17:4
which thou g me out of the world ............ Jn 17:6
they were, and thou g them me ............... Jn 17:6
them the words which thou g me ............. Jn 17:8
those that thou g me I have kept ........... Jn 17:12
which thou g me I have given them ...... Jn 17:22
Of them which thou g me have I ............ Jn 18:9

**GAY**
him that weareth the g clothing ................ Jas 2:3

**GAZA** (*ga'-zah*) See Azzah, Gazites.
*1. A royal Philistine city.*
as thou comest to Gerar, unto G ......... Gen 10:19
from Kadesh-barnea even unto G ....... Josh 10:41
only in G, in Gath, and in Ashdod, ...... Josh 11:22
G with her towns and her villages, ..... Josh 15:47
Also Judah took G with the coast ......... Judg 1:18
Then went Samson to G, and saw ......... Judg 16:1
eyes, and brought him down to G ...... Judg 16:21
for Ashdod one, for G one ....................... 1Sa 6:17
the Philistines, even unto G .................. 2Kin 18:8
before that Pharaoh smote G ................. Jer 47:1
Baldness is come upon G ......................... Jer 47:5
For three transgressions of G ............... Amos 1:6
will send a fire on the wall of G ............. Amos 1:7
For G shall be forsaken, and .................. Zeph 2:4
G also shall see it, and be very ............... Zec 9:5
and the king shall perish from G ............. Zec 9:5
goeth down from Jerusalem unto G ..... Acts 8:26
*2. A city in Ephraim.*
the earth, till thou come unto G ............ Judg 6:4
also and the towns thereof, unto G ..... 1Chr 7:28

**GAZATHITES** (*ga'-zath-ites*) See Gazites.
*Inhabitants of Gaza.*
the G, and the Ashdothites, the ............ Josh 13:3

**GAZE**
break through unto the LORD to g ......... Ex 19:21

**GAZER** (*ga'-zur*) See Gezer. *A Canaanite city.*
from Geba until thou come to G ............ 2Sa 5:25
Philistines from Gibeon even to G ..... 1Chr 14:16

**GAZEZ** (*ga'-zez*) *A son of Caleb.*
bare Haran, and Moza, and G ............... 1Chr 2:46
and Haran begat G ................................ 1Chr 2:46

**GAZING**
why stand ye g up into heaven ............. Acts 1:11

**GAZINGSTOCK**
vile, and will set thee as a g ...................... Nah 3:6
were made a g both by reproaches ..... Heb 10:33

**GAZITES** (*ga'-zites*) See Gazathites.
*Inhabitants of Gaza.*
And it was told the G, saying, ............... Judg 16:2

**GAZZAM** (*gaz'-zam*) *A family of exiles.*
of Nekoda, the children of G ................... Ezr 2:48
The children of G, the children .............. Neh 7:51

**GEBA** (*ghe'-bah*) See Gaba, Gibeah, Gibeon. *A Levitical city in Benjamin.*
her suburbs, G with her suburbs, ......... Josh 21:17
of the Philistines that was in G ................ 1Sa 13:3
from G until thou come to Gazer ........... 2Sa 5:25
Asa built with them G of Benjamin ... 1Kin 15:22
from G to Beer-sheba, and brake ........... 2Kin 23:8
G with her suburbs, and Alemeth ........ 1Chr 6:60
fathers of the inhabitants of G ............... 1Chr 8:6
and he built therewith G and Mizpah . 2Chr 16:6
Benjamin from G dwelt at Michmash . Neh 11:31
Gilgal, and out of the fields of G ......... Neh 12:29
have taken up their lodging at G ........... Is 10:29
G to Rimmon south of Jerusalem ........ Zec 14:10

**GEBAL** (*ghe'-bal*) See Giblites.
*1. An Edomite territory.*
G, and Ammon, and Amalek ...................... Ps 83:7
*2. A Phoenician trade city.*
The ancients of G and the wise men ..... Eze 27:9

**GEBALITES** See Giblites.

**GEBER** See Ezion-geber.
*1. Father of an officer of Solomon.*
The son of G, in Ramoth-gilead ........... 1Kin 4:13
*2. The son of Uri.*
G the son of Uri was in the .................. 1Kin 4:19

**GEBIM** (*ghe'-bim*) *A city in Benjamin.*
the inhabitants of G gather ....................... Is 10:31

**GEDALIAH** (*ghed-a-li'-ah*)
*1. Son of Ahikam.*
them he made G the son of Ahikam . 2Kin 25:22
of Babylon had made G governor ....... 2Kin 25:23
there came to G to Mizpah .................. 2Kin 25:23
G sware to them, and to their men, ... 2Kin 25:24
and ten men with him, and smote G . 2Kin 25:25
committed him unto G the son of ......... Jer 39:14
Go back also to G the son of ................... Jer 40:5
Then went Jeremiah unto G the son ...... Jer 40:6
the king of Babylon had made G ............ Jer 40:7
Then they came to G to Mizpah .............. Jer 40:8
G the son of Ahikam the son of ............. Jer 40:9
that he had set over them G the ........... Jer 40:11
came to the land of Judah, to G ........... Jer 40:12
the fields, came to G to Mizpah, ........... Jer 40:13
But G the son of Ahikam believed ........ Jer 40:14
spake to G in Mizpah secretly ............... Jer 40:15
But G the son of Ahikam said unto ...... Jer 40:16
came unto G the son of Ahikam to ........ Jer 41:1
smote G the son of Ahikam the son ........ Jer 41:2
that were with him, even with G ........... Jer 41:3
second day after he had slain G ............ Jer 41:4
Come to G the son of Ahikam ................. Jer 41:6
whom he had slain because of G ............ Jer 41:9
committed to G the son of Ahikam ...... Jer 41:10
he had slain G the son of Ahikam ......... Jer 41:16
had slain G the son of Ahikam .............. Jer 41:18
of the guard had left with G the ............. Jer 43:6
*2. A son of Jeduthun.*
G, and Zeri, and Jeshaiah, .................... 1Chr 25:3
the second to G, who with his ............... 1Chr 25:9
*3. Priest who married a foreigner.*
and Eliezer, and Jarib, and G ............... Ezr 10:18
*4. Grandfather of Zephaniah.*
the son of Cushi, the son of G ................ Zeph 1:1
*5. A prince who had Jeremiah imprisoned.*
G the son of Pashur, and Jucal the ........ Jer 38:1

**GEDEON** (*ghed'-e-on*) See Gideon. *Greek form of Gideon.*
time would fail me to tell of G ............ Heb 11:32

**GEDER** (*ghe'-dur*) See Beth-gader, Gederite, Gedor. *A Canaanite city.*
the king of G, one ................................. Josh 12:13

**GEDERAH** (*ghed'-e-rah*) See Gederathite. *A city in Judah.*
And Sharaim, and Adithaim, and G ... Josh 15:36

**GEDERATHITE** (*ghed'-e-rath-ite*) *An inhabitant of Gederah.*
and Johanan, and Josabad the G ......... 1Chr 12:4

**GEDERITE** (*ghed'-e-rite*) *An inhabitant of Geder.*
low plains was Baal-hanan the G ....... 1Chr 27:28

**GEDEROTH** (*ghed'-e-roth*) *A town in Judah.*
And G, Beth-dagon ............................... Josh 15:41
Beth-shemesh, and Ajalon, and G ...... 2Chr 28:18

**GEDEROTHAIM** (*ghed-e-ro-tha'-im*) *A town in Judah.*
and Adithaim, and Gederah, and G .... Josh 15:36

**GEDOR** (*ghe'-dor*) See Geder.
*1. A city in Judah.*
Halhul, Beth-zur, and G, ...................... Josh 15:58
*2. Hometown of Jeroham.*
the sons of Jeroham of G ....................... 1Chr 12:7
*3. Son of Jehiel.*
And G, and Ahio, and Zacher ............... 1Chr 8:31
And G, and Ahio, and Zechariah, and. 1Chr 9:37
*4. A descendant of Judah.*
And Penuel the father of G ...................... 1Chr 4:4
bare Jered the father of G ..................... 1Chr 4:18
*5. A place in Judah.*
And they went to the entrance of G ... 1Chr 4:39

**GE-HARASHIM** See Charashim.

**GEHAZI** (*ghe-ha'-zi*) *A servant of Elijah.*
he said to G his servant, Call ............... 2Kin 4:12
G answered, Verily she hath no ........... 2Kin 4:14
that he said to G his servant ................. 2Kin 4:25
but G came near to thrust her .............. 2Kin 4:27
Then he said to G, Gird up thy ............. 2Kin 4:29
G passed on before them, and laid ....... 2Kin 4:31
And he called G, and said, Call ............ 2Kin 4:36
But G, the servant of Elisha the .......... 2Kin 5:20
So G followed after Naaman ................ 2Kin 5:21
unto him, Whence comest thou, G ...... 2Kin 5:25
the king talked with G the ..................... 2Kin 8:4
G said, My lord, O king, this is ............. 2Kin 8:5

**GELILOTH** (*ghel'-il-oth*) *Place on boundary of Benjamin and Judah.*
and went forth toward G, which is .... Josh 18:17

**GEMALLI** (*ghe-mal'-li*) *One of the twelve spies.*
tribe of Dan, Ammiel the son of G .... Num 13:12

**GEMARIAH** (*ghem-a-ri'-ah*)
*1. Son of Shaphan.*
in the chamber of G the son of ............... Jer 36:10
When Michaiah the son of G ................. Jer 36:11
G the son of Shaphan, and Zedekiah ... Jer 36:12
G had made intercession to the ........... Jer 36:25
*2. Son of Hilkiah.*
G the son of Hilkiah, (whom ................... Jer 29:3

**GENDER**
thy cattle g with a diverse kind ........... Lev 19:19
knowing that they do g strifes ................. 2Ti 2:23

**GENDERED**
frost of heaven, who hath g it ............... Job 38:29

**GENDERETH**
Their bull g, and faileth not .................. Job 21:10
which g to bondage, which is Agar ........ Gal 4:24

**GENEALOGIES**
All these were reckoned by g in ........... 1Chr 5:17
in all by their g fourscore ...................... 1Chr 7:5
were reckoned by their g twenty ........... 1Chr 7:7
So all Israel were reckoned by g ............ 1Chr 9:1
and of Iddo the seer concerning g ..... 2Chr 12:15
reckoned by g among the Levites ...... 2Chr 31:19
give heed to fables and endless g ............ 1Ti 1:4
But avoid foolish questions, and g .......... Titus 3:9

**GENEALOGY**
their habitations, and their g ................. 1Chr 4:33
the g is not to be reckoned after ........... 1Chr 5:1
when the g of their generations ............. 1Chr 5:7
of them, after their g by their ................ 1Chr 7:9
the number throughout the g of ......... 1Chr 7:40
by their g in their villages .................... 1Chr 9:22
Beside their g of males, from .............. 2Chr 31:16
Both to the g of the priests by ............ 2Chr 31:17
to the g of all their little ones ............ 2Chr 31:18
those that were reckoned by g ................. Ezr 2:62
this is the g of them that went ................ Ezr 8:1
by g of the males an hundred ................. Ezr 8:3
that they might be reckoned by g ............ Neh 7:5
I found a register of the g of ................... Neh 7:5
those that were reckoned by g ............... Neh 7:64

**GENERAL**
the g of the king's army was Joab ..... 1Chr 27:34
To the g assembly and church of ........ Heb 12:23

**GENERALLY**
Israel be g gathered unto thee ............. 2Sa 17:11
There shall be lamentation g upon ........ Jer 48:38

**GENERATION**
righteous before me in this g ................... Gen 7:1
But in the fourth g they shall ............... Gen 15:16
Ephraim's children of the third g ......... Gen 50:23
all his brethren, and all that g ..................... Ex 1:6
with Amalek from g to g ......................... Ex 17:16
fourth g of them that hate me ................... Ex 20:5
unto the third and to the fourth g .......... Ex 34:7
unto the third and fourth g ................. Num 14:18
forty years, until all the g .................... Num 32:13
of this evil g see that good land .......... Deut 1:35
until all the g of the men of war .......... Deut 2:14
fourth g of them that hate me, .............. Deut 5:9
even to his tenth g shall he not ............. Deut 23:2
even to their tenth g shall they ............ Deut 23:3
of the LORD in their third g .................. Deut 23:8
So that the g to come of your ............. Deut 29:22
they are a perverse and crooked g ....... Deut 32:5
for they are a very froward g .............. Deut 32:20
also all that g were gathered ................ Judg 2:10
there arose another g after them ........ Judg 2:10
g shall sit on the throne of .................. 2Kin 10:30
of Israel unto the fourth g .................. 2Kin 15:12
and kept throughout every g .................. Est 9:28
them from this g for ever ......................... Ps 12:7
God is in the g of the righteous ................ Ps 14:5
be accounted to the Lord for a g ............ Ps 22:30
This is the g of them that seek ................. Ps 24:6
ye may tell it to the g following ............ Ps 48:13
shall go to the g of his fathers ............... Ps 49:19
shewed thy strength unto this g ............. Ps 71:18
against the g of thy children .................. Ps 73:15
shewing to the g to come the .................... Ps 78:4
That the g to come might know ................ Ps 78:6
a stubborn and rebellious g ...................... Ps 78:8
a g that set not their heart ....................... Ps 78:8
long was I grieved with this g ................ Ps 95:10
be written for the g to come .................. Ps 102:18
in the g following let their name ......... Ps 109:13
the g of the upright shall be ................. Ps 112:2
One g shall praise thy works to ............. Ps 145:4
doth the crown endure to every g ....... Prov 27:24
There is a g that curseth their .......... Prov 30:11
There is a g that are pure in ............. Prov 30:12
There is a g, O how lofty are ............. Prov 30:13
There is a g, whose teeth are as ......... Prov 30:14
passeth away, and another g cometh ..... Eccl 1:4
be dwelt in from g to g ........................... Is 13:20
from g to g it shall lie ........................... Is 34:10
from g to g shall they ............................ Is 34:17
my salvation from g to g ........................... Is 51:8
and who shall declare his g ...................... Is 53:8
O g, see ye the word of the LORD ............ Jer 2:31
and forsaken the g of his wrath ............... Jer 7:29
be dwelt in from g to g .......................... Jer 50:39
thy throne from g to g ............................ Lam 5:19
dominion is from g to g ........................... Dan 4:3
kingdom is from g to g ............................ Dan 4:34
and their children another g .................... Joel 1:3

and Jerusalem from *g* to *g* — Joel 3:20
The book of the *g* of Jesus Christ — Mt 1:1
O *g* of vipers, who hath warned — Mt 3:7
whereunto shall I liken this *g* — Mt 11:16
O *g* of vipers, how can ye, being — Mt 12:34
adulterous *g* seeketh after a sign — Mt 12:39
rise in judgment with this *g* — Mt 12:41
up in the judgment with this *g* — Mt 12:42
it be also unto this wicked *g* — Mt 12:45
adulterous *g* seeketh after a sign — Mt 16:4
said, O faithless and perverse *g* — Mt 17:17
ye *g* of vipers, how can ye escape — Mt 23:33
things shall come upon this *g* — Mt 23:36
This *g* shall not pass, till all — Mt 24:34
Why doth this *g* seek after a sign — Mk 8:12
no sign be given unto this *g* — Mk 8:12
in this adulterous and sinful *g* — Mk 8:38
him, and saith, O faithless *g* — Mk 9:19
that this *g* shall not pass, till — Mk 13:30
fear him from *g* to *g* — Lk 1:50
O *g* of vipers, who hath warned — Lk 3:7
shall I liken the men of this *g* — Lk 7:31
said, O faithless and perverse *g* — Lk 9:41
began to say, This is an evil *g* — Lk 11:29
also the Son of man be to this *g* — Lk 11:30
judgment with the men of this *g* — Lk 11:31
up in the judgment with this *g* — Lk 11:32
world, may be required of this *g* — Lk 11:50
It shall be required of this *g* — Lk 11:51
*g* wiser than the children of — Lk 16:8
things, and be rejected of this *g* — Lk 17:25
This *g* shall not pass away, till — Lk 21:32
yourselves from this untoward *g* — Acts 2:40
and who shall declare his *g* — Acts 8:33
his own *g* by the will of God — Acts 13:36
I was grieved with that *g* — Heb 3:10
But ye are a chosen *g*, a royal — 1Pet 2:9

**GENERATIONS**
These are the *g* of the heavens and — Gen 2:4
This is the book of the *g* of Adam — Gen 5:1
These are the *g* of Noah — Gen 6:9
a just man and perfect in his *g* — Gen 6:9
that is with you, for perpetual *g* — Gen 9:12
Now these are the *g* of the sons — Gen 10:1
the sons of Noah, after their *g* — Gen 10:32
These are the *g* of Shem — Gen 11:10
Now these are the *g* of Terah — Gen 11:27
*g* for an everlasting covenant — Gen 17:7
and thy seed after thee in their *g* — Gen 17:9
you, every man child in your *g* — Gen 17:12
Now these are the *g* of Ishmael — Gen 25:12
their names, according to their *g* — Gen 25:13
And these are the *g* of Isaac — Gen 25:19
Now these are the *g* of Esau — Gen 36:1
these are the *g* of Esau the — Gen 36:9
These are the *g* of Jacob — Gen 37:2
and this is my memorial unto all *g* — Ex 3:15
sons of Levi according to their *g* — Ex 6:16
of Levi according to their *g* — Ex 6:19
to the LORD throughout your *g* — Ex 12:14
your *g* by an ordinance for ever — Ex 12:17
the children of Israel in their *g* — Ex 12:42
omer of it to be kept for your *g* — Ex 16:32
the LORD, to be kept for your *g* — Ex 16:33
*g* on the behalf of the children — Ex 27:21
*g* at the door of the tabernacle — Ex 29:42
before the LORD throughout your *g* — Ex 30:8
upon it throughout your *g* — Ex 30:10
and to his seed throughout their *g* — Ex 30:21
oil unto me throughout your *g* — Ex 30:31
me and you throughout your *g* — Ex 31:13
the sabbath throughout their *g* — Ex 31:16
priesthood throughout their *g* — Ex 40:15
*g* throughout all your dwellings — Lev 3:17
be a statute for ever in your *g* — Lev 6:18
for ever throughout their *g* — Lev 7:36
for ever throughout your *g* — Lev 10:9
ever unto them throughout their *g* — Lev 17:7
in their *g* that hath any blemish — Lev 21:17
be of all your seed among your *g* — Lev 22:3
your *g* in all your dwellings — Lev 23:14
your dwellings throughout your *g* — Lev 23:21
your *g* in all your dwellings — Lev 23:31
be a statute for ever in your *g* — Lev 23:41
That your *g* may know that I made — Lev 23:43
be a statute for ever in your *g* — Lev 24:3
that bought it throughout his *g* — Lev 25:30
Israel's eldest son, by their *g* — Num 1:20
children of Simeon, by their *g* — Num 1:22
the children of Gad, by their *g* — Num 1:24
the children of Judah, by their *g* — Num 1:26
children of Issachar, by their *g* — Num 1:28
children of Zebulun, by their *g* — Num 1:30
children of Ephraim, by their *g* — Num 1:32
children of Manasseh, by their *g* — Num 1:34
children of Benjamin, by their *g* — Num 1:36
the children of Dan, by their *g* — Num 1:38
the children of Asher, by their *g* — Num 1:40
of Naphtali, throughout their *g* — Num 1:42
These also are the *g* of Aaron — Num 3:1
for ever throughout your *g* — Num 10:8
whosoever be among you in your *g* — Num 15:14
an ordinance for ever in your *g* — Num 15:15
LORD an heave offering in your *g* — Num 15:21
and henceforward among your *g* — Num 15:23
their garments throughout their *g* — Num 15:38
for ever throughout your *g* — Num 18:23
your *g* in all your dwellings — Num 35:29
his commandments to a thousand *g* — Deut 7:9
old, consider the years of many *g* — Deut 32:7
our *g* after us, that we might do — Josh 22:27
to us or to our *g* in time to come — Josh 22:28
Only that the *g* of the children — Judg 3:2
Now these are the *g* of Pharez — Ruth 4:18
These are their *g* — 1Chr 1:29
genealogy of their *g* was reckoned — 1Chr 5:7
valiant men of might in their *g* — 1Chr 7:2
And with them, by their *g*, after — 1Chr 7:4
after their genealogy by their *g* — 1Chr 7:9
heads of the fathers, by their *g* — 1Chr 8:28
brethren, according to their *g* — 1Chr 9:9
were chief throughout their *g* — 1Chr 9:34
he commanded to a thousand *g* — 1Chr 16:15
according to the *g* of his fathers — 1Chr 26:31
and his sons' sons, even four *g* — Job 42:16
thoughts of his heart to all *g* — Ps 33:11
name to be remembered in all *g* — Ps 45:17
and their dwelling places to all *g* — Ps 49:11
and his years as many *g* — Ps 61:6
and moon endure, throughout all *g* — Ps 72:5
shew forth thy praise to all *g* — Ps 79:13
draw out thine anger to all *g* — Ps 85:5
known thy faithfulness to all *g* — Ps 89:1
and build up thy throne to all *g* — Ps 89:4
been our dwelling place in all *g* — Ps 90:1
and his truth endureth to all *g* — Ps 100:5
and thy remembrance unto all *g* — Ps 102:12
thy years are throughout all *g* — Ps 102:24
he commanded to a thousand *g* — Ps 105:8
unto all *g* for evermore — Ps 106:31
Thy faithfulness is unto all *g* — Ps 119:90
O LORD, throughout all *g* — Ps 135:13
endureth throughout all *g* — Ps 145:13
even thy God, O Zion, unto all *g* — Ps 146:10
calling the *g* from the beginning — Is 41:4
the ancient days, in the *g* of old — Is 51:9
up the foundations of many *g* — Is 58:12
excellency, a joy of many *g* — Is 60:15
cities, the desolations of many *g* — Is 61:4
it, even to the years of many *g* — Joel 2:2
So all the *g* from Abraham to — Mt 1:17
Abraham to David are fourteen *g* — Mt 1:17
away into Babylon are fourteen *g* — Mt 1:17
unto Christ are fourteen *g* — Mt 1:17
from henceforth all *g* shall call — Lk 1:48
hath been hid from ages and from *g* — Col 1:26

**GENNESARET** (*ghen-nes'-a-ret*) See CHINNERETH. *Same as Galilee.*
they came into the land of *G* — Mt 14:34
they came into the land of *G* — Mk 6:53
of God, he stood by the lake of *G* — Lk 5:1

**GENTILE** (*jen'-tile*) See GENTILES. *A non-Jew.*
the Jew first, and also of the *G* — Rom 2:9
the Jew first, and also to the *G* — Rom 2:10

**GENTILES**
of the *G* divided in their lands — Gen 10:5
which dwelt in Harosheth of the *G* — Judg 4:2
from Harosheth of the *G* unto the — Judg 4:13
the host, unto Harosheth of the *G* — Judg 4:16
to it shall the *G* seek — Is 11:10
bring forth judgment to the *G* — Is 42:1
the people, for a light of the *G* — Is 42:6
give thee for a light to the *G* — Is 49:6
I will lift up mine hand to the *G* — Is 49:22
and thy seed shall inherit the *G* — Is 54:3
the *G* shall come to thy light, and — Is 60:3
the forces of the *G* shall come — Is 60:5
unto thee the forces of the *G* — Is 60:11
shalt also suck the milk of the *G* — Is 60:16
ye shall eat the riches of the *G* — Is 61:6
seed shall be known among the *G* — Is 61:9
the *G* shall see thy righteousness — Is 62:2
the glory of the *G* like a flowing — Is 66:12
declare my glory among the *G* — Is 66:19
destroyer of the *G* is on his way — Jer 4:7
of the *G* that can cause rain — Jer 14:22
the *G* shall come unto thee from — Jer 16:19
the prophet against the *G* — Jer 46:1
and her princes are among the *G* — Lam 2:9
their defiled bread among the *G* — Eze 4:13
the *G* as a vessel wherein is no — Hos 8:8
Proclaim ye this among the *G* — Joel 3:9
of Jacob shall be among the *G* in — Mic 5:8
to cast out the horns of the *G* — Zec 1:21
name shall be great among the *G* — Mal 1:11
beyond Jordan, Galilee of the *G* — Mt 4:15
all these things do the *G* seek — Mt 6:32
Go not into the way of the *G* — Mt 10:5
a testimony against them and the *G* — Mt 10:18
he shall shew judgment to the *G* — Mt 12:18
And in his name shall the *G* trust — Mt 12:21
deliver him to the *G* to mock — Mt 20:19
the *G* exercise dominion over them — Mt 20:25
and shall deliver him to the *G* — Mk 10:33
the *G* exercise lordship over them — Mk 10:42
A light to lighten the *G*, and the — Lk 2:32
he shall be delivered unto the *G* — Lk 18:32
shall be trodden down of the *G* — Lk 21:24
the times of the *G* be fulfilled — Lk 21:24
The kings of the *G* exercise — Lk 22:25
go unto the dispersed among the *G* — Jn 7:35
the *G*, and teach the *G* — Jn 7:35
and Pontius Pilate, with the *G* — Acts 4:27
into the possession of the *G* — Acts 7:45
me, to bear my name before the *G* — Acts 9:15
because that on the *G* also was — Acts 10:45
*G* had also received the word of — Acts 11:1
Then hath God also to the *G* — Acts 11:18
the *G* besought that these words — Acts 13:42
life, lo, we turn to the *G* — Acts 13:46
set thee to be a light of the *G* — Acts 13:47
when the *G* heard this, they were — Acts 13:48
unbelieving Jews stirred up the *G* — Acts 14:2
was an assault made both of the *G* — Acts 14:5
the door of faith unto the *G* — Acts 14:27
declaring the conversion of the *G* — Acts 15:3
that the *G* by my mouth should — Acts 15:7
had wrought among the *G* by them — Acts 15:12
God at the first did visit the *G* — Acts 15:14
seek after the Lord, and all the *G* — Acts 15:17
among the *G* are turned to God — Acts 15:19
which are of the *G* in Antioch — Acts 15:23
henceforth I will go unto the *G* — Acts 18:6
him into the hands of the *G* — Acts 21:11
among the *G* by his ministry — Acts 21:19
are among the *G* to forsake Moses — Acts 21:21
As touching the *G* which believe — Acts 21:25
send thee far hence unto the *G* — Acts 22:21
from the people, and from the *G* — Acts 26:17
of Judaea, and then to the *G* — Acts 26:20
unto the people, and to the *G* — Acts 26:23
of God is sent unto the *G* — Acts 28:28
you also, even as among other *G* — Rom 1:13
For when the *G*, which have not — Rom 2:14
among the *G* through you, as it is — Rom 2:24
have before proved both Jews and *G* — Rom 3:9
is he not also of the *G* — Rom 3:29
Yes, of the *G* also — Rom 3:29
the Jews only, but also of the *G* — Rom 9:24
That the *G*, which followed not — Rom 9:30
fall salvation is come unto the *G* — Rom 11:11
of them the riches of the *G* — Rom 11:12
For I speak to you *G*, inasmuch as — Rom 11:13
as I am the apostle of the *G* — Rom 11:13
the fulness of the *G* be come in — Rom 11:25
that the *G* might glorify God for — Rom 15:9
will confess to thee among the *G* — Rom 15:9
And again he saith, Rejoice, ye *G* — Rom 15:10
again, Praise the Lord, all ye *G* — Rom 15:11
shall rise to reign over the *G* — Rom 15:12
in him shall the *G* trust — Rom 15:12
minister of Jesus Christ to the *G* — Rom 15:16
up of the *G* might be acceptable — Rom 15:16
by me, to make the *G* obedient — Rom 15:18
For if the *G* have been made — Rom 15:27
also all the churches of the *G* — Rom 16:4
not so much as named among the *G* — 1Cor 5:1
the things which the *G* sacrifice — 1Cor 10:20
neither to the Jews, nor to the *G* — 1Cor 10:32
Ye know that ye were *G*, carried — 1Cor 12:2
one body, whether we be Jews or *G* — 1Cor 12:13
gospel which I preach among the *G* — Gal 2:2
was mighty in me toward the *G* — Gal 2:8
from James, he did eat with the *G* — Gal 2:12
Jew, livest after the manner of *G* — Gal 2:14
thou the *G* to live as do the Jews — Gal 2:14
nature, and not sinners of the *G* — Gal 2:15
on the *G* through Jesus Christ — Gal 3:14
being in time past *G* in the flesh — Eph 2:11
of Jesus Christ for you *G* — Eph 3:1
That the *G* should be fellowheirs — Eph 3:6
the *G* the unsearchable riches of — Eph 3:8
walk not as other *G* walk, in the — Eph 4:17
glory of this mystery among the *G* — Col 1:27
to the *G* that they might be saved — 1Th 2:16
even as the *G* which know not God — 1Th 4:5
a teacher of the *G* in faith — 1Ti 2:7
of angels, preached unto the *G* — 1Ti 3:16
an apostle, and a teacher of the *G* — 2Ti 1:11
and that all the *G* might hear — 2Ti 4:17
conversation honest among the *G* — 1Pet 2:12
to have wrought the will of the *G* — 1Pet 4:3
forth, taking nothing of the *G* — 3Jn 7
for it is given unto the *G* — Rev 11:2

**GENTLE**
But we were *g* among you, even as — 1Th 2:7
but be *g* unto all men, apt to — 2Ti 2:24
no man, to be no brawlers, but *g* — Titus 3:2
is first pure, then peaceable, *g* — Jas 3:17
not only to the good and *g* — 1Pet 2:18

**GENTLENESS**
and thy *g* hath made me great — 2Sa 22:36
up, and thy *g* hath made me great — Ps 18:35
*g* of Christ, who in presence am — 2Cor 10:1
joy, peace, longsuffering, *g* — Gal 5:22

**GENTLY**
Deal *g* for my sake with the young — 2Sa 18:5
shall *g* lead those that are with — Is 40:11

**GENUBATH** (*ghen'-u-bath*) *Son of Hadad.*
of Tahpenes bare him *G* his son — 1Kin 11:20
*G* was in Pharaoh's household — 1Kin 11:20

**GERA** (*ghe'-rah*) *A son of Bela.*
Belah, and Becher, and Ashbel, *G* — Gen 46:21
up a deliverer, Ehud the son of *G* — Judg 3:15
name was Shimei, the son of *G* — 2Sa 16:5
And Shimei the son of *G*, a — 2Sa 19:16
Shimei the son of *G* fell down — 2Sa 19:18
with thee Shimei the son of *G* — 1Kin 2:8
sons of Bela were, Addar, and *G* — 1Chr 8:3
And *G*, and Shephuphan, and Huram — 1Chr 8:5
And Naaman, and Ahiah, and *G* — 1Chr 8:7

**GERAHS**
(a shekel is twenty *g* — Ex 30:13
twenty *g* shall be the shekel — Lev 27:25
(the shekel is twenty *g* — Num 3:47
the sanctuary, which is twenty *g* — Num 18:16

And the shekel shall be twenty g ......... Eze 45:12

**GERAR** (*ghe'-rar*) *A city in Gaza.*
from Sidon, as thou comest to G ......... Gen 10:19
Kadesh and Shur, and sojourned in G . Gen 20:1
and Abimelech king of G sent ......... Gen 20:2
king of the Philistines unto G ......... Gen 26:1
And Isaac dwelt in G ......... Gen 26:6
his tent in the valley of G ......... Gen 26:17
the herdmen of G did strive with ......... Gen 26:20
Then Abimelech went to him from G. Gen 26:26
were with him pursued them unto G 2Chr 14:13
all the cities round about G ......... 2Chr 14:14

**GERGESENES** (*ghur'-ghes-enes'*) *Inhabitants of an area near Sea of Galilee.*
side into the country of the G ......... Mt 8:28

**GERIZIM** (*gher'-iz-im*) *A mountain in central Palestine.*
put the blessing upon mount G ......... Deut 11:29
upon mount G to bless the people ..... Deut 27:12
half of them over against mount G ......... Josh 8:33
and stood in the top of mount G ......... Judg 9:7

**GERSHOM** (*ghur'-shom*) See GERSHON.
*1. Firstborn son of Moses.*
a son, and he called his name G ......... Ex 2:22
which the name of the one was G ......... Ex 18:3
The sons of Moses were, G ......... 1Chr 23:15
Of the sons of G, Shebuel was the ..... 1Chr 23:16
And Shebuel the son of G, the son .... 1Chr 26:24
*2. A son of Levi.*
G, Kohath, and Merari ......... 1Chr 6:16
be the names of the sons of G ......... 1Chr 6:17
Of G ......... 1Chr 6:20
The son of Jahath, the son of G ......... 1Chr 6:43
to the sons of G throughout their ......... 1Chr 6:62
Unto the sons of G were given out ..... 1Chr 6:71
Of the sons of G ......... 1Chr 15:7
*3. A descendant of Phinehas.*
G ......... Ezr 8:2
*4. Father of Jonathan.*
and Jonathan, the son of G ......... Judg 18:30

**GERSHON** (*ghur'-shon*) See GERSHOM, GERSHONITE. *A form of Gershom 2.*
G, Kohath, and Merari ......... Gen 46:11
G, and Kohath, and Merari ......... Ex 6:16
The sons of G ......... Ex 6:17
G, and Kohath, and Merari ......... Num 3:17
the sons of G by their families ......... Num 3:18
Of G was the family of the ......... Num 3:21
of G in the tabernacle of the ......... Num 3:25
also the sum of the sons of G ......... Num 4:22
of G in the tabernacle of the ......... Num 4:28
were numbered of the sons of G ......... Num 4:38
of the families of the sons of G ......... Num 4:41
oxen he gave unto the sons of G ......... Num 7:7
and the sons of G and the sons of ..... Num 10:17
of G, the family of the ......... Num 26:57
the children of G had by lot out ......... Josh 21:6
And unto the children of G ......... Josh 21:27
G, Kohath, and Merari ......... 1Chr 6:1
among the sons of Levi, namely, G ..... 1Chr 23:6

**GERSHONITE** (*ghur'-shon-ites*) See GERSHONITES. *Descendant of Gershom 2.*
the sons of the G Laadan, chief ......... 1Chr 26:21
fathers, even of Laadan the G ......... 1Chr 26:21
LORD, by the hand of Jehiel the G ....... 1Chr 29:8

**GERSHONITES** (*ghur'-shon-ites*)
these are the families of the G ......... Num 3:21
The families of the G shall pitch ......... Num 3:23
G shall be Eliasaph the son of ......... Num 3:24
service of the families of the G ......... Num 4:24
the service of the sons of the G ......... Num 4:27
of Gershon, the family of the G ......... Num 26:57
All the cities of the G according ......... Josh 21:33
Of the G were, Laadan, and Shimei ..... 1Chr 23:7
and of the G ......... 2Chr 29:12

**GERUTH** See CHIMHAM.

**GERUTH KIMHAM** See CHIMHAM.

**GESHAM** (*ghe'-sham*) *A son of Jahdai.*
Regem, and Jotham, and G ......... 1Chr 2:47

**GESHAN** See GESHAM.

**GESHEM** (*ghe'-shem*) See GASHMU. *An opponent of Nehemiah.*
G the Arabian, heard it, they ......... Neh 2:19
G the Arabian, and the rest of our ......... Neh 6:1
G sent unto me, saying, Come, let ......... Neh 6:2

**GESHUR** (*ghe'-shur*) See GESHURITES. *A kingdom in Bashan.*
the daughter of Talmai king of G ......... 2Sa 3:3
the son of Ammihud, king of G ......... 2Sa 13:37
So Absalom fled, and went to G ......... 2Sa 13:38
So Joab arose and went to G ......... 2Sa 14:23
say, Wherefore am I come from G ......... 2Sa 14:32
a vow while I abode at G in Syria ......... 2Sa 15:8
And he took G, and Aram, with the .... 1Chr 2:23
the daughter of Talmai king of G ......... 1Chr 3:2

**GESHURI** (*ghesh'-u-ri*) See GESHURITES.
*1. Inhabitants of Geshur.*
of Argob unto the coasts of G ......... Deut 3:14
*2. A people dwelling between Arabia and Philistia.*
of the Philistines, and all G ......... Josh 13:2

**GESHURITES** (*ghesh'-u-rites*)
*1. Inhabitants of Geshur.*
Bashan, unto the border of the G ......... Josh 12:5
And Gilead, and the border of the G.. Josh 13:11
of Israel expelled not the G ......... Josh 13:13
but the G and the Maachathites ......... Josh 13:13
*2. Same as Geshuri 2.*
his men went up, and invaded the G ..... 1Sa 27:8

**GET**
G thee out of thy country, and ......... Gen 12:1
said, Up, g you out of this place ......... Gen 19:14
g thee into the land of Moriah ......... Gen 22:2
g thee out from this land, and ......... Gen 31:13
saying, G me this damsel to wife ......... Gen 34:4
g you possessions therein ......... Gen 34:10
g you down thither, and buy for us ...... Gen 42:2
g you up in peace unto your ......... Gen 44:17
g you unto the land of Canaan ......... Gen 45:17
so g them up out of the land ......... Ex 1:10
g you unto your burdens ......... Ex 5:4
g you straw where ye can find it ......... Ex 5:11
G thee unto Pharaoh in the ......... Ex 7:15
G thee from me, take heed to ......... Ex 10:28
G thee out, and all the people ......... Ex 11:8
g you forth from among my people, ..... Ex 12:31
I will g me honour upon Pharaoh, ......... Ex 14:17
g thee down, and thou shalt come ......... Ex 19:24
said unto Moses, Go, g thee down ......... Ex 32:7
he be poor, and cannot g so much ....... Lev 14:21
pigeons, such as he is able to g ......... Lev 14:22
young pigeons, such as he can g ......... Lev 14:30
Even such as he is able to g ......... Lev 14:31
whose hand is not able to g that ......... Lev 14:32
beside that that his hand shall g ......... Num 6:21
G you up this way southward, and .... Num 13:17
g you into the wilderness by the ......... Num 14:25
saying, G you up from about the ....... Num 16:24
G you up from among this ......... Num 16:45
of Balak, G you into your land ......... Num 22:13
thee, I will g me back again ......... Num 22:34
G thee up into this mount Abarim, ... Num 27:12
g you over the brook Zered ......... Deut 2:13
G thee up into the top of Pisgah, ......... Deut 3:27
G you into your tents again ......... Deut 5:30
giveth thee power to g wealth ......... Deut 8:18
g thee down quickly from hence ......... Deut 9:12
g thee up into the place which ......... Deut 17:8
shall g up above thee very high ......... Deut 28:43
G thee up into this mountain ......... Deut 32:49
G you to the mountain, lest the ......... Josh 2:16
LORD said unto Joshua, G thee up ......... Josh 7:10
then g thee up to the wood ......... Josh 17:15
g you unto your tents, and unto ......... Josh 22:4
g thee down unto the host ......... Judg 7:9
now therefore g her for me to ......... Judg 14:2
unto his father, G her for me ......... Judg 14:3
to morrow g you early on your way .... Judg 19:9
thee, and g thee down to the floor ......... Ruth 3:3
Now therefore g you up ......... 1Sa 9:13
g you down from among the ......... 1Sa 15:6
in thine eyes, let me g away ......... 1Sa 20:29
g thee into the land of Judah ......... 1Sa 22:5
David made haste to g away for ......... 1Sa 23:26
G you up to Carmel, and go to ......... 1Sa 25:5
lest he g him fenced cities, and ......... 2Sa 20:6
that my lord the king may g heat ......... 1Kin 1:2
g thee in unto king David, and say ...... 1Kin 1:13
G thee to Anathoth, unto thine ......... 1Kin 2:26
speed to g him up to his chariot ......... 1Kin 12:18
and g thee to Shiloh ......... 1Kin 14:2
g thee to thine own house ......... 1Kin 14:12
G thee hence, and turn thee ......... 1Kin 17:3
g thee to Zarephath, which ......... 1Kin 17:9
Ahab, G thee up, eat and drink ......... 1Kin 18:41
g thee down, that the rain stop ......... 1Kin 18:44
g thee to the prophets of thy ......... 2Kin 3:13
them alive, and g into the city ......... 2Kin 7:12
speed to g him up to his chariot ......... 2Chr 10:18
So didst thou g thee a name ......... Neh 9:10
thy precepts I g understanding ......... Ps 119:104
G wisdom, g understanding ......... Prov 4:5
therefore g wisdom ......... Prov 4:7
all thy getting g understanding ......... Prov 4:7
A wound and dishonour shall he g ...... Prov 6:33
is it to g wisdom than gold ......... Prov 16:16
to g understanding rather to be ......... Prov 16:16
in the hand of a fool to g wisdom ...... Prov 17:16
ways, and g a snare to thy soul ......... Prov 22:25
A time to g, and a time to lose ......... Eccl 3:6
I will g me to the mountain of ......... Song 4:6
Let us g up early to the ......... Song 7:12
g thee unto this treasurer, even ......... Is 22:15
G you out of the way, turn aside ......... Is 30:11
shalt say unto it, G thee hence ......... Is 30:22
g thee up into the high mountain ......... Is 40:9
g thee into darkness, O daughter ......... Is 47:5
I will g me unto the great men, ......... Jer 5:5
g thee a linen girdle, and put it ......... Jer 13:1
g a potter's earthen bottle, and ......... Jer 19:1
g up, ye horsemen, and stand forth ......... Jer 46:4
Moab, that it may flee and g away ......... Jer 48:9
g you far off, dwell deep, O ye ......... Jer 49:30
g you up unto the wealthy nation, ......... Jer 49:31
me about, that I cannot g out ......... Lam 3:7
g thee unto the house of Israel, ......... Eze 3:4
g thee to them of the captivity, ......... Eze 3:11
said, G you far from the LORD ......... Eze 11:15
souls, to g dishonest gain ......... Eze 22:27
let the beasts g away from under ......... Dan 4:14
come, g you down ......... Joel 3:13
I will g them praise and fame in ......... Zeph 3:19
G you hence, walk to and fro ......... Zec 6:7
unto him, G thee hence, Satan ......... Mt 4:10
his disciples to g into a ship ......... Mt 14:22
Peter, G thee behind me, Satan ......... Mt 16:23
his disciples to g into the ship ......... Mk 6:45
saying, G thee behind me, Satan ......... Mk 8:33
unto him, G thee behind me, Satan ......... Lk 4:8
about, and lodge, and g victuals ......... Lk 9:12
G thee out, and depart hence ......... Lk 13:31
G thee out of thy country, and ......... Acts 7:3
g thee down, and go with them, ......... Acts 10:20
g thee quickly out of Jerusalem ......... Acts 22:18
first into the sea, and g to land ......... Acts 27:43
Lest Satan should g an advantage ....... 2Cor 2:11
a year, and buy and sell, and g gain ....... Jas 4:13

**GETHER** (*ghe'-ther*) *A son of Aram.*
Uz, and Hul, and G, and Mash ......... Gen 10:23
and Uz, and Hul, and G ......... 1Chr 1:17

**GETHSEMANE** (*gheth-sem'-a-ne*) *A garden near Jerusalem.*
with them unto a place called G ......... Mt 26:36
came to a place which was named G... Mk 14:32

**GETTETH**
Whosoever g up to the gutter, and ......... 2Sa 5:8
the man that g understanding ......... Prov 3:13
a scorner g to himself shame ......... Prov 9:7
a wicked man g himself a blot ......... Prov 9:7
heareth reproof g understanding ......... Prov 15:32
heart of the prudent g knowledge ...... Prov 18:15
He that g wisdom loveth his own ......... Prov 19:8
so he that g riches, and not by ......... Jer 17:11
he that g up out of the pit shall ......... Jer 48:44

**GETTING**
had gotten, the cattle of his g ......... Gen 31:18
with all thy g get understanding ......... Prov 4:7
The g of treasures by a lying ......... Prov 21:6

**GEUEL** (*ghe-u'-el*) *A son of Machri.*
tribe of Gad, G the son of Machi ....... Num 13:15

**GEZER** (*ghe'-zur*) See GAZER, GEZRITES. *A Canaanite city.*
Then Horam king of G came up to .... Josh 10:33
the king of G, one ......... Josh 12:12
of Beth-horon the nether, and to G ...... Josh 16:3
the Canaanites that dwelt in G ......... Josh 16:10
and G with her suburbs, ......... Josh 21:21
the Canaanites that dwelt in G ......... Judg 1:29
Canaanites dwelt in G among them .... Judg 1:29
and Hazor, and Megiddo, and G ......... 1Kin 9:15
of Egypt had gone up, and taken G ..... 1Kin 9:16
And Solomon built G, and Beth-horon 1Kin 9:17
they gave also G with her suburbs ...... 1Chr 6:67
Naaran, and westward G ......... 1Chr 7:28
war at G with the Philistines ......... 1Chr 20:4

**GEZRITES** (*ghez'-rites*) *Inhabitants of Gezer.*
invaded the Geshurites, and the G ......... 1Sa 27:8

**GHOST**
Then Abraham gave up the g ......... Gen 25:8
and he gave up the g and died ......... Gen 25:17
And Isaac gave up the g and died, ..... Gen 35:29
into the bed, and yielded up the g ....... Gen 49:33
why did I not give up the g when ......... Job 3:11
Oh that I had given up the g ......... Job 10:18
be as the giving up of the g ......... Job 11:20
my tongue, I shall give up the g ......... Job 13:19
yea, man giveth up the g, and ......... Job 14:10
she hath given up the g ......... Jer 15:9
elders gave up the g in the city ......... Lam 1:19
found with child of the Holy G ......... Mt 1:18
conceived in her is of the Holy G ......... Mt 1:20
shall baptize you with the Holy G ......... Mt 3:11
G shall not be forgiven unto men ......... Mt 12:31
speaketh against the Holy G ......... Mt 12:32
a loud voice, yielded up the g ......... Mt 27:50
and of the Son, and of the Holy G ......... Mt 28:19
shall baptize you with the Holy G ......... Mk 1:8
the Holy G hath never forgiveness ......... Mk 3:29
David himself said by the Holy G ......... Mk 12:36
not ye that speak, but the Holy G ......... Mk 13:11
a loud voice, and gave up the g ......... Mk 15:37
he so cried out, and gave up the g ....... Mk 15:39
shall be filled with the Holy G ......... Lk 1:15
The Holy G shall come upon thee, ......... Lk 1:35
was filled with the Holy G ......... Lk 1:41
was filled with the Holy G ......... Lk 1:67
and the Holy G was upon him ......... Lk 2:25
revealed unto him by the Holy G ......... Lk 2:26
shall baptize you with the Holy G ......... Lk 3:16
the Holy G descended in a bodily ......... Lk 3:22
the Holy G returned from Jordan ......... Lk 4:1
Holy G it shall not be forgiven ......... Lk 12:10
For the Holy G shall teach you in ......... Lk 12:12
said thus, he gave up the g ......... Lk 23:46
which baptizeth with the Holy G ......... Jn 1:33
for the Holy G was not yet given ......... Jn 7:39
Comforter, which is the Holy G ......... Jn 14:26
bowed his head, and gave up the g ......... Jn 19:30
unto them, Receive ye the Holy G ......... Jn 20:22
after that he through the Holy G ......... Acts 1:2
the Holy G not many days hence ......... Acts 1:5
that the Holy G is come upon you ......... Acts 1:8
which the Holy G by the mouth of ..... Acts 1:16
were all filled with the Holy G ......... Acts 2:4
Father the promise of the Holy G ......... Acts 2:33
receive the gift of the Holy G ......... Acts 2:38
Peter, filled with the Holy G ......... Acts 4:8

were all filled with the Holy G ... Acts 4:31
thine heart to lie to the Holy G ... Acts 5:3
words fell down, and gave up the g ... Acts 5:5
at his feet, and yielded up the g ... Acts 5:10
and so is also the Holy G, whom ... Acts 5:32
honest report, full of the Holy G ... Acts 6:3
full of faith and of the Holy G ... Acts 6:5
ye do always resist the Holy G ... Acts 7:51
But he, being full of the Holy G ... Acts 7:55
they might receive the Holy G ... Acts 8:15
them, and they received the Holy G ... Acts 8:17
hands the Holy G was given ... Acts 8:18
hands, he may receive the Holy G ... Acts 8:19
and be filled with the Holy G ... Acts 9:17
and in the comfort of the Holy G ... Acts 9:31
Jesus of Nazareth with the Holy G ... Acts 10:38
the Holy G fell on all them which ... Acts 10:44
poured out the gift of the Holy G ... Acts 10:45
received the Holy G as well as we ... Acts 10:47
the Holy G fell on them, as on us ... Acts 11:15
shall be baptized with the Holy G ... Acts 11:16
a good man, and full of the Holy G ... Acts 11:24
eaten of worms, and gave up the g ... Acts 12:23
Lord, and fasted, the Holy G said ... Acts 13:2
being sent forth by the Holy G ... Acts 13:4
Paul,) filled with the Holy G ... Acts 13:9
with joy, and with the Holy G ... Acts 13:52
witness, giving them the Holy G ... Acts 15:8
For it seemed good to the Holy G ... Acts 15:28
Holy G to preach the word in Asia ... Acts 16:6
the Holy G since ye believed ... Acts 19:2
heard whether there be any Holy G ... Acts 19:2
them, the Holy G came on them ... Acts 19:6
Save that the Holy G witnesseth ... Acts 20:23
Holy G hath made you overseers ... Acts 20:28
and said, Thus saith the Holy G ... Acts 21:11
Well spake the Holy G by Esaias ... Acts 28:25
the Holy G which is given unto us ... Rom 5:5
bearing me witness in the Holy G ... Rom 9:1
and peace, and joy in the Holy G ... Rom 14:17
through the power of the Holy G ... Rom 15:13
being sanctified by the Holy G ... Rom 15:16
but which the Holy G teacheth ... 1Cor 2:13
of the Holy G which is in you ... 1Cor 6:19
is the Lord, but by the Holy G ... 1Cor 12:3
by kindness, by the Holy G ... 2Cor 6:6
and the communion of the Holy G ... 2Cor 13:14
also in power, and in the Holy G ... 1Th 1:5
with joy of the Holy G ... 1Th 1:6
the Holy G which dwelleth in us ... 2Ti 1:14
and renewing of the Holy G ... Titus 3:5
miracles, and gifts of the Holy G ... Heb 2:4
Wherefore (as the Holy G saith ... Heb 3:7
were made partakers of the Holy G ... Heb 6:4
The Holy G this signifying, that ... Heb 9:8
Whereof the Holy G also is a ... Heb 10:15
the Holy G sent down from heaven ... 1Pet 1:12
as they were moved by the Holy G ... 2Pet 1:21
Father, the Word, and the Holy G ... 1Jn 5:7
holy faith, praying in the Holy G ... Jude 20

**GIAH** (*ghi'-ah*) *A place near the wilderness of Gibeon.*
that lieth before G by the way of ... 2Sa 2:24

**GIANT**
which was of the sons of the g ... 2Sa 21:16
which was of the sons of the g ... 2Sa 21:18
and he also was born to the g ... 2Sa 21:20
four were born to the g in Gath ... 2Sa 21:22
that was of the children of the g ... 1Chr 20:4
and he also was the son of the g ... 1Chr 20:6
were born unto the g in Gath ... 1Chr 20:8
he runneth upon me like a g ... Job 16:14

**GIANTS**
There were g in the earth in ... Gen 6:4
And there we saw the g ... Num 13:33
sons of Anak, which come of the g ... Num 13:33
Which also were accounted g ... Deut 2:11
also was accounted a land of g ... Deut 2:20
g dwelt therein in old time ... Deut 2:20
remained of the remnant of g ... Deut 3:11
which was called the land of g ... Deut 3:13
which was of the remnant of the g ... Josh 12:4
remained of the remnant of the g ... Josh 13:12
of the valley of the g northward ... Josh 15:8
of the Perizzites and of the g ... Josh 17:15
the valley of the g on the north ... Josh 18:16

**GIBALITES** See GIBLITES.

**GIBBAR** (*ghib'-bar*) See GIBEON. *A family of exiles.*
The children of G, ninety and five ... Ezr 2:20

**GIBBETHON** (*ghib'-be-thon*) *A town in Dan.*
And Eltekeh, and G, and Baalath ... Josh 19:44
her suburbs, G with her suburbs ... Josh 21:23
and Baasha smote him at G, which ... 1Kin 15:27
and all Israel laid siege to G ... 1Kin 15:27
people were encamped against G ... 1Kin 16:15
And Omri went up from G, and all ... 1Kin 16:17

**GIBEA** (*ghib'-e-ah*) See GIBEAH. *Son of Sheva.*
of Machbenah, and the father of G ... 1Chr 2:49

**GIBEAH** (*ghib'-e-ah*) *A city in Judah.*
Cain, G, and Timnah ... Josh 15:57
we will pass over to G ... Judg 19:12
places to lodge all night, in G ... Judg 19:13
upon them when they were by G ... Judg 19:14
to go in and to lodge in G ... Judg 19:15
and he sojourned in G ... Judg 19:16
I came into G that belongeth to ... Judg 20:4
the men of G rose against me, and ... Judg 20:5
the thing which we will do to G ... Judg 20:9
when they come to G of Benjamin ... Judg 20:10
of Belial, which are in G ... Judg 20:13
together out of the cities unto G ... Judg 20:14
beside the inhabitants of G ... Judg 20:15
morning, and encamped against G ... Judg 20:19
array to fight against them at G ... Judg 20:20
of Benjamin came forth out of G ... Judg 20:21
them out of G the second day ... Judg 20:25
set liers in wait round about G ... Judg 20:29
put themselves in array against G ... Judg 20:30
and the other to G in the field ... Judg 20:31
even out of the meadows of G ... Judg 20:33
there came against G ten thousand ... Judg 20:34
wait which they had set beside G ... Judg 20:36
in wait hasted, and rushed upon G ... Judg 20:37
against G toward the sunrising ... Judg 20:43
And Saul also went home to G ... 1Sa 10:26
came the messengers to G of Saul ... 1Sa 11:4
with Jonathan in G of Benjamin ... 1Sa 13:2
up from Gilgal unto G of Benjamin ... 1Sa 13:15
with them, abode in G of Benjamin ... 1Sa 13:16
in the uttermost part of G under ... 1Sa 14:2
other southward over against G ... 1Sa 14:5
of Saul in G of Benjamin looked ... 1Sa 14:16
went up to his house to G of Saul ... 1Sa 15:34
(now Saul abode in G under a tree ... 1Sa 22:6
came up the Ziphites to Saul to G ... 1Sa 23:19
the Ziphites came unto Saul to G ... 1Sa 26:1
house of Abinadab that was in G ... 2Sa 6:3
house of Abinadab which was at G ... 2Sa 6:4
up unto the LORD in G of Saul ... 2Sa 21:6
of G of the children of Benjamin ... 2Sa 23:29
Ithai the son of Ribai of G ... 1Chr 11:31
the daughter of Uriel of G ... 2Chr 13:2
G of Saul is fled ... Is 10:29
Blow ye the cornet in G, and the ... Hos 5:8
themselves, as in the days of G ... Hos 9:9
hast sinned from the days of G ... Hos 10:9
the battle in G against the ... Hos 10:9

**GIBEATH** (*ghib'-e-ath*) See GIBEAH, GIBEATHITE. *Same as Gibeah.*
and Jebusi, which is Jerusalem, G ... Josh 18:28

**GIBEATH-HAARALOTH** See GIBEATH.

**GIBEATHITE** (*ghib'-e-ath-ite*) *An inhabitant of Gibeah.*
Joash, the sons of Shemaah the G ... 1Chr 12:3

**GIBEON** (*ghib'-e-on*) See GEBA, GIBEAH, GIBEONITE.
*1. A Hivite city.*
when the inhabitants of G heard ... Josh 9:3
Now their cities were G, and ... Josh 9:17
how the inhabitants of G had made ... Josh 10:1
because G was a great city, as ... Josh 10:2
and help me, that we may smite G ... Josh 10:4
their hosts, and encamped before G ... Josh 10:5
the men of G sent unto Joshua to ... Josh 10:6
them with a great slaughter at G ... Josh 10:10
Sun, stand thou still upon G ... Josh 10:12
country of Goshen, even unto G ... Josh 10:41
the Hivites the inhabitants of G ... Josh 11:19
*2. A city in Benjamin.*
G, and Ramah, and Beeroth ... Josh 18:25
G with her suburbs, Geba with her ... Josh 21:17
Saul, went out from Mahanaim to G ... 2Sa 2:12
and met together by the pool of G ... 2Sa 2:13
Helkath-hazzurim, which is in G ... 2Sa 2:16
by the way of the wilderness of G ... 2Sa 2:24
brother Asahel at G in the battle ... 2Sa 3:30
at the great stone which is in G ... 2Sa 20:8
the king went to G to sacrifice ... 1Kin 3:4
In G the LORD appeared to Solomon ... 1Kin 3:5
as he had appeared unto him at G ... 1Kin 9:2
at G dwelt the father of Gibeon ... 1Chr 8:29
in G dwelt the father of Gibeon ... 1Chr 9:35
Philistines from G even to Gazer ... 1Chr 14:16
in the high place that was at G ... 1Chr 16:39
season in the high place at G ... 1Chr 21:29
to the high place that was at G ... 2Chr 1:3
place that was at G to Jerusalem ... 2Chr 1:13
the Meronothite, the men of G ... Neh 3:7
The children of G, ninety and five ... Neh 7:25
be wroth as in the valley of G ... Is 28:21
Azur the prophet, which was of G ... Jer 28:1
by the great waters that are in G ... Jer 41:12
whom he had brought again from G ... Jer 41:16

**GIBEONITE** (*ghib'-e-on-ite*) See GIBEONITES. *An inhabitant of Gibeon.*
And Ismaiah the G, a mighty man ... 1Chr 12:4
unto them repaired Melatiah the G ... Neh 3:7

**GIBEONITES** (*ghib'-e-on-ites*)
house, because he slew the G ... 2Sa 21:1
And the king called the G, and said ... 2Sa 21:2
(now the G were not of the ... 2Sa 21:2
Wherefore David said unto the G ... 2Sa 21:3
the G said unto him, We will have ... 2Sa 21:4
them into the hands of the G ... 2Sa 21:9

**GIBLITES** (*ghib'-lites*) *Inhabitants of Gebal.*
And the land of the G, and all ... Josh 13:5

**GIDDALTI** (*ghid-dal'-ti*) *A son of Heman.*
Hananiah, Hanani, Eliathah, G ... 1Chr 25:4
The two and twentieth to G ... 1Chr 25:29

**GIDDEL** (*ghid'-del*)
*1. A family of exiles.*
The children of G, the children ... Ezr 2:47
of Hanan, the children of G ... Neh 7:49
*2. Servants of Solomon.*
of Darkon, the children of G ... Ezr 2:56
of Darkon, the children of G ... Neh 7:58

**GIDEON** (*ghid'-e-on*) See GEDEON, JERUBBAAL. *A judge of Israel.*
his son G threshed wheat by the ... Judg 6:11
G said unto him, Oh my Lord, if ... Judg 6:13
G went in, and made ready a kid ... Judg 6:19
when G perceived that he was an ... Judg 6:22
LORD, G said, Alas, O Lord GOD ... Judg 6:22
Then G built an altar there unto ... Judg 6:24
Then G took ten men of his ... Judg 6:27
G the son of Joash hath done this ... Judg 6:29
Spirit of the LORD came upon G ... Judg 6:34
G said unto God, If thou wilt ... Judg 6:36
G said unto God, Let not thine ... Judg 6:39
Then Jerubbaal, who is G, and all ... Judg 7:1
And the LORD said unto G, The ... Judg 7:2
And the LORD said unto G, The ... Judg 7:4
and the LORD said unto G, Every ... Judg 7:5
And the LORD said unto G, By the ... Judg 7:7
when G was come, behold, there ... Judg 7:13
the sword of G the son of Joash ... Judg 7:14
when G heard the telling of the ... Judg 7:15
The sword of the LORD, and of G ... Judg 7:18
So G, and the hundred men that ... Judg 7:19
The sword of the LORD, and of G ... Judg 7:20
G sent messengers throughout all ... Judg 7:24
Zeeb to G on the other side ... Judg 7:25
G came to Jordan, and passed over ... Judg 8:4
G said, Therefore when the LORD ... Judg 8:7
G went up by the way of them that ... Judg 8:11
G the son of Joash returned from ... Judg 8:13
G arose, and slew Zebah and ... Judg 8:21
the men of Israel said unto G ... Judg 8:22
G said unto them, I will not rule ... Judg 8:23
G said unto them, I would desire ... Judg 8:24
G made an ephod thereof, and put ... Judg 8:27
which thing became a snare unto G ... Judg 8:27
forty years in the days of G ... Judg 8:28
G had threescore and ten sons of ... Judg 8:30
G the son of Joash died in a good ... Judg 8:32
to pass, as soon as G was dead ... Judg 8:33
the house of Jerubbaal, namely, G ... Judg 8:35

**GIDEONI** (*ghid-e-o'-ni*) *A Benjamite who counted the people.*
Abidan the son of G ... Num 1:11
shall be Abidan the son of G ... Num 2:22
the ninth day Abidan the son of G ... Num 7:60
offering of Abidan the son of G ... Num 7:65
Benjamin was Abidan the son of G ... Num 10:24

**GIDOM** (*ghi'-dom*) *A place near Bethel.*
and pursued hard after them unto G. Judg 20:45

**GIER**
and the pelican, and the g eagle ... Lev 11:18
the g eagle, and the cormorant ... Deut 14:17

**GIFT**
Ask me never so much dowry and g ... Gen 34:12
And thou shalt take no g ... Ex 23:8
for the g blindeth the wise, and ... Ex 23:8
given the Levites as a g to Aaron ... Num 8:19
are given as a g for the LORD ... Num 18:6
office unto you as a service of g ... Num 18:7
the heave offering of their g ... Num 18:11
respect persons, neither take a g ... Deut 16:19
for a g doth blind the eyes of ... Deut 16:19
or hath he given us any g ... 2Sa 19:42
of Tyre shall be there with a g ... Ps 45:12
A g is as a precious stone in the ... Prov 17:8
A wicked man taketh a g out of ... Prov 17:23
A man's g maketh room for ... Prov 18:16
A g in secret pacifieth anger ... Prov 21:14
of a false g is like clouds ... Prov 25:14
his labour, it is the g of God ... Eccl 3:13
this is the g of God ... Eccl 5:19
and a g destroyeth the heart ... Eccl 7:7
give a g unto any of his sons ... Eze 46:16
But if he give a g of his ... Eze 46:17
if thou bring thy g to the altar ... Mt 5:23
Leave there thy g before the ... Mt 5:24
and then come and offer thy g ... Mt 5:24
offer the g that Moses commanded ... Mt 8:4
father or his mother, It is a g ... Mt 15:5
sweareth by the g that is upon it ... Mt 23:18
for whether is greater, the g ... Mt 23:19
the altar that sanctifieth the g ... Mt 23:19
It is Corban, that is to say, a g ... Mk 7:11
her, If thou knewest the g of God ... Jn 4:10
receive the g of the Holy Ghost ... Acts 2:38
thou hast thought that the g of ... Acts 8:20
out the g of the Holy Ghost ... Acts 10:45
them the like g as he did unto us ... Acts 11:17
impart unto you some spiritual g ... Rom 1:11
offence, so also is the free g ... Rom 5:15
the g by grace, which is by one ... Rom 5:15
by one that sinned, so is the g ... Rom 5:16
but the free g is of many ... Rom 5:16
of the g of righteousness shall ... Rom 5:17
the free g came upon all men unto ... Rom 5:18
but the g of God is eternal life ... Rom 6:23
So that ye come behind in no g ... 1Cor 1:7
man hath his proper g of God ... 1Cor 7:7
though I have the g of prophecy ... 1Cor 13:2
that for the g bestowed upon us ... 2Cor 1:11

that we would receive the g ........ 2Cor 8:4
be unto God for his unspeakable g ........ 2Cor 9:15
it is the g of God........ Eph 2:8
according to the g of the grace........ Eph 3:7
to the measure of the g of Christ........ Eph 4:7
Not because I desire a g........ Phil 4:17
Neglect not the g that is in thee........ 1Ti 4:14
that thou stir up the g of God........ 2Ti 1:6
and have tasted of the heavenly g ........ Heb 6:4
good g and every perfect g ........ Jas 1:17
As every man hath received the g........ 1Pet 4:10

**GIFTS**
which Abraham had, Abraham gave g. Gen 25:6
shall hallow in all their holy g ........ Ex 28:38
of the LORD, and beside your g........ Lev 23:38
Out of all your g ye shall offer........ Num 18:29
David's servants, and brought g........ 2Sa 8:2
servants to David, and brought g........ 2Sa 8:6
David's servants, and brought g........ 1Chr 18:2
David's servants, and brought g........ 1Chr 18:6
of persons, nor taking of g........ 2Chr 19:7
gave them great g of silver........ 2Chr 21:3
And the Ammonites gave g to Uzziah 2Chr 26:8
many brought g unto the LORD to..... 2Chr 32:23
to the provinces, and gave g........ Est 2:18
one to another, and g to the poor........ Est 9:22
thou hast received g for men........ Ps 68:18
of Sheba and Seba shall offer g........ Ps 72:10
though thou givest many g........ Prov 6:35
but he that hateth g shall live........ Prov 15:27
is a friend to him that giveth g........ Prov 19:6
that receiveth g overthroweth it........ Prov 29:4
every one loveth g, and followeth........ Is 1:23
They give g to all whores........ Eze 16:33
givest thy g to all thy lovers........ Eze 16:33
And I polluted them in their own g..... Eze 20:26
For when ye offer your g, when ye........ Eze 20:31
my holy name no more with your g.... Eze 20:39
have they taken g to shed blood........ Eze 22:12
thereof, ye shall receive of me g........ Dan 2:6
man, and gave him many great g........ Dan 2:48
Let thy g be to thyself, and give........ Dan 5:17
they presented unto him g........ Mt 2:11
to give good g unto your children........ Mt 7:11
to give good g unto your children........ Lk 11:13
casting their g into the treasury........ Lk 21:1
adorned with goodly stones and g........ Lk 21:5
For the g and calling of God are........ Rom 11:29
Having then g differing according........ Rom 12:6
Now concerning spiritual g........ 1Cor 12:1
Now there are diversities of g........ 1Cor 12:4
to another the g of healing by........ 1Cor 12:9
then g of healings, helps,........ 1Cor 12:28
Have all the g of healing........ 1Cor 12:30
But covet earnestly the best g........ 1Cor 12:31
charity, and desire spiritual g........ 1Cor 14:1
as ye are zealous of spiritual g........ 1Cor 14:12
captive, and gave g unto men........ Eph 4:8
g of the Holy Ghost, according to........ Heb 2:4
to God, that he may offer both g........ Heb 5:1
priest is ordained to offer g........ Heb 8:3
that offer g according to the law........ Heb 8:4
in which were offered both g........ Heb 9:9
God testifying of his g........ Heb 11:4
shall send g one to another........ Rev 11:10

**GIHON** (*ghi'-hon*)
*1. A river in the Garden of Eden.*
the name of the second river is G........ Gen 2:13
*2. A place near Jerusalem.*
own mule, and bring him down to G... 1Kin 1:33
David's mule, and brought him to G... 1Kin 1:38
have anointed him king in G........ 1Kin 1:45
the upper watercourse of G........ 2Chr 32:30
of David, on the west side of G........ 2Chr 33:14

**GILALAI** (*ghil'-a-lahee*) *A priest who dedicated the wall.*
Shemaiah, and Azarael, Milalai, G...... Neh 12:36

**GILBOA** (*ghil-bo'-ah*)
*1. A district in Manasseh.*
together, and they pitched in G........ 1Sa 28:4
Philistines had slain Saul in G........ 2Sa 21:12
*2. A mountain near the valley Jezreel.*
and fell down slain in mount G........ 1Sa 31:1
his three sons fallen in mount G........ 1Sa 31:8
I happened by chance upon mount G..... 2Sa 1:6
Ye mountains of G, let there be........ 2Sa 1:21
and fell down slain in mount G........ 1Chr 10:1
and his sons fallen in mount G........ 1Chr 10:8

**GILEAD** (*ghil'-e-ad*) See GILEADITE, GILEAD'S, JABESH-GILEAD, RAMOTH-GILEAD.
*1. District east of the Jordan River.*
of Ishmeelites came from G with........ Gen 37:25
land of Jazer, and the land of G........ Num 32:1
shall be there in the cities of G........ Num 32:26
the land of G for a possession........ Num 32:29
the son of Manasseh went to G........ Num 32:39
Moses gave G unto Machir the son... Num 32:40
that is by the river, even unto G........ Deut 2:36
the cities of the plain, and all G........ Deut 3:10
And the rest of G, and all Bashan,........ Deut 3:13
And I gave G unto Machir........ Deut 3:15
unto the Gadites I gave from G........ Deut 3:16
and Ramoth in G, of the Gadites........ Deut 4:43
LORD shewed him all the land of G..... Deut 34:1
of the river, and from half G........ Josh 12:2
and the Maachathites, and half G........ Josh 12:5
And G, and the border of the........ Josh 13:11
was Jazer, and all the cities of G........ Josh 13:25
And half G, and Ashtaroth........ Josh 13:31
a man of war, therefore he had G........ Josh 17:1
to Manasseh, beside the land of G........ Josh 17:5
Manasseh's sons had the land of G...... Josh 17:6
Ramoth in G out of the tribe of........ Josh 20:8
Ramoth in G with her suburbs, to...... Josh 21:38
to go unto the country of G........ Josh 22:9
of Manasseh, into the land of G........ Josh 22:13
of Manasseh, unto the land of G........ Josh 22:15
of Gad, out of the land of G........ Josh 22:32
G abode beyond Jordan........ Judg 5:17
day, which are in the land of G........ Judg 10:4
of the Amorites, which is in G........ Judg 10:8
together, and encamped in G........ Judg 10:17
princes of G said one to another,........ Judg 10:18
over all the inhabitants of G........ Judg 10:18
the elders of G went to fetch........ Judg 11:5
said unto the elders of G........ Judg 11:7
the elders of G said unto........ Judg 11:8
over all the inhabitants of G........ Judg 11:8
said unto the elders of G........ Judg 11:9
the elders of G said unto........ Judg 11:10
went with the elders of G........ Judg 11:11
Jephthah, and he passed over G........ Judg 11:29
and passed over Mizpeh of G........ Judg 11:29
from Mizpeh of G he passed over........ Judg 11:29
together all the men of G........ Judg 12:4
the men of G smote Ephraim,........ Judg 12:4
that the men of G said unto him........ Judg 12:5
buried in one of the cities of G........ Judg 12:7
to Beer-sheba, with the land of G........ Judg 20:1
Jordan to the land of Gad and G........ 1Sa 13:7
And made him king over G, and over..... 2Sa 2:9
Absalom pitched in the land of G........ 2Sa 17:26
Then they came to G, and to the........ 2Sa 24:6
son of Manasseh, which are in G........ 1Kin 4:13
of Uri was in the country of G........ 1Kin 4:19
who was of the inhabitants of G........ 1Kin 17:1
Know ye that Ramoth in G is ours...... 1Kin 22:3
eastward, all the land of G........ 2Kin 10:33
is by the river Arnon, even G........ 2Kin 10:33
Kedesh, and Hazor, and G........ 2Kin 15:29
and twenty cities in the land of G........ 1Chr 2:22
were multiplied in the land of G........ 1Chr 5:9
throughout all the east land of G........ 1Chr 5:10
And they dwelt in G in Bashan........ 1Chr 5:16
Ramoth in G with her suburbs, and.... 1Chr 6:80
men of valour at Jazer of G........ 1Chr 26:31
the half tribe of Manasseh in G........ 1Chr 27:21
G is mine, and Manasseh is mine........ Ps 60:7
G is mine........ Ps 108:8
flock of goats that appear from G........ Song 6:5
Is there no balm in G........ Jer 8:22
Thou art G unto me, and the head........ Jer 22:6
Go up into G, and take balm, O........ Jer 46:11
satisfied upon mount Ephraim and G... Jer 50:19
and from Damascus, and from G........ Eze 47:18
G is a city of them that work........ Hos 6:8
Is there iniquity in G........ Hos 12:11
because they have threshed G with..... Amos 1:3
up the women with child of G........ Amos 1:13
and Benjamin shall possess G........ Obad 19
let them feed in Bashan and G........ Mic 7:14
bring them into the land of G........ Zec 10:10
*2. A mountain range in Gilead 1.*
set his face toward the mount G........ Gen 31:21
they overtook him in the mount G..... Gen 31:23
pitched in the mount of G........ Gen 31:25
the river Arnon, and half mount G........ Deut 3:12
and depart early from mount G........ Judg 7:3
goats, that appear from mount G........ Song 4:1
*3. Son of Machir.*
and Machir begat G........ Num 26:29
of G come the family of the........ Num 26:29
These are the sons of G........ Num 26:30
the son of Hepher, the son of G........ Num 27:1
the families of the children of G........ Num 36:1
of Manasseh, the father of G........ Josh 17:1
the son of Hepher, the son of G........ Josh 17:3
of Machir the father of G........ 1Chr 2:21
sons of Machir the father of G........ 1Chr 2:23
bare Machir the father of G........ 1Chr 7:14
These were the sons of G, the son........ 1Chr 7:17
*4. Father of Jephthah.*
and G begat Jephthah........ Judg 11:1
*5. A chief of Gad.*
the son of Jaroah, the son of G........ 1Chr 5:14

**GILEADITE** (*ghil'-e-ad-ite*) See GILEADITES. *A descendant of Gilead.*
And after him arose Jair, a G........ Judg 10:3
Now Jephthah the G was a mighty..... Judg 11:1
the G four days in a year........ Judg 11:40
Then died Jephthah the G, and was..... Judg 12:7
and Barzillai the G of Rogelim........ 2Sa 17:27
Barzillai the G came down from........ 2Sa 19:31
unto the sons of Barzillai the G........ 1Kin 2:7
the daughters of Barzillai the G........ Ezr 2:61
of Barzillai the G to wife........ Neh 7:63

**GILEADITES** (*ghil'-e-ad-ites*)
Gilead come the family of the G........ Num 26:29
Ye G are fugitives of Ephraim........ Judg 12:4
the G took the passages of Jordan........ Judg 12:5
and with him fifty men of the G........ 2Kin 15:25

**GILEAD'S** (*ghil'-e-ads*) *Refers to Gilead 4.*
And G wife bare him sons........ Judg 11:2

**GILGAL** (*ghil'-gal*)
*1. A place near Jericho.*
in the champaign over against G....... Deut 11:30
the first month, and encamped in G.... Josh 4:19
of Jordan, did Joshua pitch in G........ Josh 4:20
place is called G unto this day........ Josh 5:9
children of Israel encamped in G........ Josh 5:10
sent unto Joshua to the camp to G...... Josh 10:6
So Joshua ascended from G........ Josh 10:7
and went up from G all night........ Josh 10:9
with him, unto the camp to G........ Josh 10:15
with him, unto the camp to G........ Josh 10:43
of Judah came unto Joshua in G........ Josh 14:6
and so northward, looking toward G... Josh 15:7
the LORD came up from G to Bochim... Judg 2:1
from the quarries that were by G........ Judg 3:19
year in circuit to Beth-el, and G........ 1Sa 7:16
thou shalt go down before me to G...... 1Sa 10:8
people, Come, and let us go to G........ 1Sa 11:14
And all the people went to G........ 1Sa 11:15
Saul king before the LORD in G........ 1Sa 11:15
called together after Saul to G........ 1Sa 13:4
As for Saul, he was yet in G........ 1Sa 13:7
but Samuel came not to G........ 1Sa 13:8
will come down now upon me to G..... 1Sa 13:12
gat him up from G unto Gibeah of...... 1Sa 13:15
and passed on, and gone down to G.... 1Sa 15:12
unto the LORD thy God in G........ 1Sa 15:21
in pieces before the LORD in G........ 1Sa 15:33
And Judah came to G, to go to meet.. 2Sa 19:15
Then the king went on to G........ 2Sa 19:40
Also from the house of G, and out...... Neh 12:29
and come not ye unto G, neither go..... Hos 4:15
All their wickedness is in G........ Hos 9:15
they sacrifice bullocks in G........ Hos 12:11
at G multiply transgression........ Amos 4:4
not Beth-el, nor enter into G........ Amos 5:5
for G shall surely go into........ Amos 5:5
answered him from Shittim unto G........ Mic 6:5
*2. A city between Dor and Tirsa.*
the king of the nations of G........ Josh 12:23
*3. A city north of Joppa.*
went to Joshua unto the camp at G....... Josh 9:6
*4. A place south of Ebal and Gerizim.*
Elijah went with Elisha from G........ 2Kin 2:1
And Elisha came again to G........ 2Kin 4:38

**GILO** See GILOH.

**GILOH** (*ghi'-loh*) See GILONITE. *A town in Judah.*
And Goshen, and Holon, and G........ Josh 15:51
from his city, even from G........ 2Sa 15:12

**GILONITE** (*ghi'-lo-nite*) *An inhabitant of Giloh.*
Absalom sent for Ahithophel the G..... 2Sa 15:12
Eliam the son of Ahithophel the G..... 2Sa 23:34

**GIMZO** (*ghim'-zo*) *A city in Judah.*
G also and the villages thereof........ 2Chr 28:18

**GIN**
The g shall take him by the heel,........ Job 18:9
the houses of Israel, for a g........ Is 8:14
the earth, where no g is for him........ Amos 3:5

**GINATH** (*ghi'-nath*) *Father of Tibni.*
followed Tibni the son of G........ 1Kin 16:21
that followed Tibni the son of G........ 1Kin 16:22

**GINNETHO** (*ghin'-ne-tho*) See GINNETHON. *A priest who renewed the covenant.*
Iddo, G, Abijah,........ Neh 12:4

**GINNETHOI** See GINNETHO.

**GINNETHON** (*ghin'-ne-thon*) See GINNETHO. *Same as Ginnetho.*
Daniel, G, Baruch,........ Neh 10:6
of G, Meshullam........ Neh 12:16

**GINS**
they have set g for me........ Ps 140:5
the g of the workers of iniquity........ Ps 141:9

**GIRD**
g him with the curious girdle of........ Ex 29:5
thou shalt g them with girdles,........ Ex 29:9
he did g it under his raiment........ Judg 3:16
G ye on every man his sword........ 1Sa 25:13
g you with sackcloth, and mourn........ 2Sa 3:31
G up thy loins, and take my staff........ 2Kin 4:29
G up thy loins, and take this box........ 2Kin 9:1
G up now thy loins like a man........ Job 38:3
G up thy loins now like a man........ Job 40:7
G thy sword upon thy thigh, O........ Ps 45:3
g yourselves, and ye shall be........ Is 8:9
g yourselves, and ye shall be........ Is 8:9
shall g themselves with sackcloth........ Is 15:3
g sackcloth upon your loins........ Is 32:11
Thou therefore g up thy loins........ Jer 1:17
For this g you with sackcloth,........ Jer 4:8
g thee with sackcloth, and wallow........ Jer 6:26
of Rabbah, g you with sackcloth........ Jer 49:3
They shall also g themselves with........ Eze 7:18
g them with sackcloth, and they........ Eze 27:31
they shall not g themselves with........ Eze 44:18
G yourselves, and lament, ye........ Joel 1:13
unto you, that he shall g himself........ Lk 12:37
g thyself, and serve me, till I........ Lk 17:8
hands, and another shall g thee........ Jn 21:18
G thyself, and bind on thy sandals........ Acts 12:8
Wherefore g up the loins of your........ 1Pet 1:13

**GIRDED**
with your loins g, your shoes on........ Ex 12:11
g him with the girdle, and clothed........ Lev 8:7
he g him with the curious girdle........ Lev 8:7

g them with girdles, and put .......... Lev 8:13
shall be g with a linen girdle, .......... Lev 16:4
when ye had g on every man his .......... Deut 1:41
that stumbled are g with strength .......... 1Sa 2:4
a child, g with a linen ephod .......... 1Sa 2:18
David g his sword upon his armour .......... 1Sa 17:39
they g on every man his sword .......... 1Sa 25:13
David also g on his sword .......... 1Sa 25:13
David was g with a linen ephod .......... 2Sa 6:14
that he had put on was g unto him .......... 2Sa 20:8
he being g with a new sword, .......... 2Sa 21:16
For thou hast g me with strength .......... 2Sa 22:40
he g up his loins, and ran before .......... 1Kin 18:46
So they g sackcloth on their .......... 1Kin 20:32
one had his sword g by his side .......... Neh 4:18
For thou hast g me with strength .......... Ps 18:39
sackcloth, and g me with gladness .......... Ps 30:11
being g with power .......... Ps 65:6
wherewith he hath g himself .......... Ps 93:1
wherewith he is g continually .......... Ps 109:19
I g thee, though thou hast not .......... Is 45:5
they have g themselves with .......... Lam 2:10
I g thee about with fine linen, .......... Eze 16:10
G with girdles upon their loins, .......... Eze 23:15
whose loins were g with fine gold .......... Dan 10:5
Lament like a virgin g with .......... Joel 1:8
Let your loins be g about .......... Lk 12:35
and took a towel, and g himself .......... Jn 13:4
with the towel wherewith he was g .......... Jn 13:5
breasts g with golden girdles .......... Rev 15:6

**GIRDEDST**
thou g thyself, and walkedst .......... Jn 21:18

**GIRDETH**
Let not him that g on his harness .......... 1Kin 20:11
g their loins with a girdle .......... Job 12:18
It is God that g me with strength .......... Ps 18:32
She g her loins with strength, and .......... Prov 31:17

**GIRDING**
of a stomacher a g of sackcloth .......... Is 3:24
baldness, and to g with sackcloth .......... Is 22:12

**GIRDLE**
a broidered coat, a mitre, and a g .......... Ex 28:4
the curious g of the ephod, which .......... Ex 28:8
above the curious g of the ephod .......... Ex 28:27
above the curious g of the ephod .......... Ex 28:28
shalt make the g of needlework .......... Ex 28:39
with the curious g of the ephod .......... Ex 29:5
the curious g of his ephod, that .......... Ex 39:5
above the curious g of the ephod .......... Ex 39:20
above the curious g of the ephod .......... Ex 39:21
a g of fine twined linen, and blue .......... Ex 39:29
coat, and girded him with the g .......... Lev 8:7
with the curious g of the ephod .......... Lev 8:7
and shall be girded with a linen g .......... Lev 16:4
sword, and to his bow, and to his g .......... 1Sa 18:4
ten shekels of silver, and a g .......... 2Sa 18:11
upon it a g with a sword fastened .......... 2Sa 20:8
his g that was about his loins .......... 1Kin 2:5
girt with a g of leather about .......... 2Kin 1:8
and girdeth their loins with a g .......... Job 12:18
for a g wherewith he is girded .......... Ps 109:19
and instead of a g a rent .......... Is 3:24
neither shall the g of their .......... Is 5:27
shall be the g of his loins .......... Is 11:5
faithfulness the g of his reins .......... Is 11:5
and strengthen him with thy g .......... Is 22:21
unto me, Go and get thee a linen g .......... Jer 13:1
So I got a g according to the .......... Jer 13:2
Take the g that thou hast got, .......... Jer 13:4
take the g from thence, which I .......... Jer 13:6
took the g from the place where I .......... Jer 13:7
behold, the g was marred, it was .......... Jer 13:7
them, shall even be as this g .......... Jer 13:10
For as the g cleaveth to the .......... Jer 13:11
a leathern g about his loins .......... Mt 3:4
with a g of a skin about his .......... Mk 1:6
come unto us, he took Paul's g .......... Acts 21:11
bind the man that owneth this g .......... Acts 21:11
about the paps with a golden g .......... Rev 1:13

**GIRDLES**
and thou shalt make for them g .......... Ex 28:40
And thou shalt gird them with g .......... Ex 29:9
upon them, and girded them with g .......... Lev 8:13
delivereth g unto the merchant .......... Prov 31:24
Girded with g upon their loins, .......... Eze 23:15
breasts girded with golden g .......... Rev 15:6

**GIRGASHITE** (*ghur'-gash-ite*) See GIRGASHITES, GIRGASITE. *A Canaanite tribe.*
also, and the Amorite, and the G .......... 1Chr 1:14

**GIRGASHITES** (*ghur'-gash-ites*)
and the Canaanites, and the G .......... Gen 15:21
thee, the Hittites, and the G .......... Deut 7:1
and the Perizzites, and the G .......... Josh 3:10
and the Hittites, and the G .......... Josh 24:11
and the Jebusites, and the G .......... Neh 9:8

**GIRGASITE** (*ghur'-ga-site*) See GIRGASHITE. *Same as Girgashite.*
and the Amorite, and the G .......... Gen 10:16

**GIRL**
sold a g for wine, that they .......... Joel 3:3

**GIRLS**
g playing in the streets thereof .......... Zec 8:5

**GIRT**
g with a girdle of leather about .......... 2Kin 1:8
he g his fisher's coat unto him, ( .......... Jn 21:7
your loins g about with truth .......... Eph 6:14
g about the paps with a golden .......... Rev 1:13

**GIRZITES** See GEZRITES.

**GISHPA** See GISPA.

**GISPA** (*ghis'-pah*) *An overseer of the Nethinim.*
G were over the Nethinims .......... Neh 11:21

**GISPHA** See GISPA.

**GITTAH-HEPHER** (*ghit''-tah-he'-fer*) See GATH-HEPHER. *A town in Zebulun.*
passeth on along on the east to G .......... Josh 19:13

**GITTAIM** (*ghit-ta'-im*)
*1. A city of refuge.*
And the Beerothites fled to G .......... 2Sa 4:3
*2. A Benjamite city.*
Hazor, Ramah, G, .......... Neh 11:33

**GITTITE** (*ghit'-tite*) See GITTITES, GITTITH. *An inhabitant of Gath.*
into the house of Obed-edom the G .......... 2Sa 6:10
of Obed-edom the G three months .......... 2Sa 6:11
Then said the king to Ittai the G .......... 2Sa 15:19
Ittai the G passed over, and all .......... 2Sa 15:22
under the hand of Ittai the G .......... 2Sa 18:2
slew the brother of Goliath the G .......... 2Sa 21:19
into the house of Obed-edom the G .. 1Chr 13:13
the brother of Goliath the G .......... 1Chr 20:5

**GITTITES**
the Eshkalonites, the G, and the .......... Josh 13:3
all the Pelethites, and all the G .......... 2Sa 15:18

**GITTITH** (*ghit'-tith*) *A musical instrument.*
To the chief Musician upon G .......... Ps 8:t
To the chief Musician upon G .......... Ps 81:t
To the chief Musician upon G .......... Ps 84:t

**GIVE** See PREFACE.
of all that thou shalt g me I .......... Gen 28:22
Every man shall g as he is able .......... Deut 16:17
O g thanks unto the LORD .......... 1Chr 16:34
I shall g thee the heathen for .......... Ps 2:8
he shall g thee the desires of .......... Ps 37:4
O God, do we g .......... Ps 75:1
unto thee do we g thanks .......... Ps 75:1
For he shall g his angels charge .......... Ps 91:11
g me thine heart, and let thine .......... Prov 23:26
lambs as he shall be able to g .......... Eze 46:5
to the lambs as he is able to g .......... Eze 46:11
He shall g his angels charge .......... Mt 4:6
G us this day our daily bread .......... Mt 6:11
or what shall a man g in exchange .......... Mt 16:26
Or what shall a man g in exchange .......... Mk 8:37
g to the poor, and thou shalt have .......... Mk 10:21
G, and it shall be given unto you .......... Lk 6:38
G us day by day our daily bread .......... Lk 11:3
I shall g him shall never thirst .......... Jn 4:14
but the water that I shall g him .......... Jn 4:14
the Son of man shall g unto you .......... Jn 6:27
with you, my peace I g unto you .......... Jn 14:27
but such as I have g I thee .......... Acts 3:6
more blessed to g than to receive .......... Acts 20:35
him also freely g us all things .......... Rom 8:32
shall g account of himself to God .......... Rom 14:12
in his heart, so let him g .......... 2Cor 9:7
In every thing g thanks .......... 1Th 5:18
I will g thee a crown of life .......... Rev 2:10
to g every man according as his .......... Rev 22:12

**GIVEN** See PREFACE.

**GIVER**
so with the g of usury to him .......... Is 24:2
for God loveth a cheerful g .......... 2Cor 9:7

**GIVEST**
brother, and thou g him nought .......... Deut 15:9
be grieved when thou g unto him .......... Deut 15:10
be righteous, what g thou him .......... Job 35:7
Thou g thy mouth to evil, and thy .......... Ps 50:19
g them tears to drink in great .......... Ps 80:5
That thou g them they gather .......... Ps 104:28
thou g them their meat in due .......... Ps 145:15
content, though thou g many gifts .......... Prov 6:35
thou g him not warning, nor .......... Eze 3:18
but thou g thy gifts to all thy .......... Eze 16:33
and in that thou g a reward .......... Eze 16:34
For thou verily g thanks well .......... 1Cor 14:17

**GIVETH**
he g goodly words .......... Gen 49:21
therefore he g you on the sixth .......... Ex 16:29
which the LORD thy God g thee .......... Ex 20:12
of every man that g it willingly .......... Ex 25:2
that g any of his seed unto .......... Lev 20:2
when he g of his seed unto Molech .......... Lev 20:4
all that any man g of such unto .......... Lev 27:9
whatsoever any man g the priest .......... Num 5:10
land which the LORD our God g us .......... Deut 2:29
LORD God of your fathers g you .......... Deut 4:1
which the LORD thy God g thee for .......... Deut 4:21
which the LORD thy God g thee .......... Deut 4:40
which the LORD thy God g thee .......... Deut 5:16
for it is he that g thee power to .......... Deut 8:18
that the LORD thy God g thee not .......... Deut 9:6
good land which the LORD g you .......... Deut 11:17
which the LORD your God g you .......... Deut 11:31
thy fathers g thee to possess it .......... Deut 12:1
which the LORD your God g you .......... Deut 12:9
LORD your God g you to inherit .......... Deut 12:10
when he g you rest from all your .......... Deut 12:10
g thee a sign or a wonder, .......... Deut 13:1
God g thee for an inheritance to .......... Deut 15:4
which the LORD thy God g thee .......... Deut 15:7
which the LORD thy God g thee .......... Deut 16:5
which the LORD thy God g thee .......... Deut 16:18
which the LORD thy God g thee .......... Deut 16:20
which the LORD thy God g thee .......... Deut 17:2
which the LORD thy God g thee .......... Deut 17:14
which the LORD thy God g thee .......... Deut 18:9
land the LORD thy God g thee .......... Deut 19:1
LORD thy God g thee to possess it .......... Deut 19:2
LORD thy God g thee to inherit .......... Deut 19:3
which the LORD thy God g thee for .. Deut 19:10
LORD thy God g thee to possess it .......... Deut 19:14
LORD thy God g thee to possess it .......... Deut 21:1
which the LORD thy God g thee for .. Deut 21:23
g it in her hand, and sendeth her .......... Deut 24:3
which the LORD thy God g thee for .......... Deut 24:4
which the LORD thy God g thee .......... Deut 25:15
God g thee for an inheritance to .......... Deut 25:19
thy God g thee for an inheritance .......... Deut 26:1
land that the LORD thy God g thee .......... Deut 26:2
which the LORD thy God g thee .......... Deut 27:2
which the LORD thy God g thee .......... Deut 27:3
which the LORD thy God g thee .......... Deut 28:8
LORD your God g you to possess it .......... Josh 1:11
which the LORD your God g them .......... Josh 1:15
Chemosh thy god g thee to possess .. Judg 11:24
Cursed be he that g a wife to .......... Judg 21:18
Who g rain upon the earth, and .......... Job 5:10
man g up the ghost, and where is .......... Job 14:10
the Almighty g them understanding .......... Job 32:8
for he g not account of any of .......... Job 33:13
When he g quietness, who then can .......... Job 34:29
maker, who g songs in the night .......... Job 35:10
There they cry, but none g answer .......... Job 35:12
but g right to the poor .......... Job 36:6
he g meat in abundance .......... Job 36:31
deliverance g he to his king .......... Ps 18:50
the righteous sheweth mercy, and g .......... Ps 37:21
of Israel is he that g strength .......... Ps 68:35
The entrance of thy words g light .......... Ps 119:130
it g understanding unto the .......... Ps 119:130
for so he g his beloved sleep .......... Ps 127:2
Who g food to all flesh .......... Ps 136:25
It is he that g salvation unto .......... Ps 144:10
which g food to the hungry .......... Ps 146:7
He g to the beast his food, and to .......... Ps 147:9
He g snow like wool .......... Ps 147:16
For the LORD g wisdom .......... Prov 2:6
but he g grace unto the lowly .......... Prov 3:34
Good understanding g favour .......... Prov 13:15
A wicked doer g heed to false .......... Prov 17:4
a liar g ear to a naughty tongue .......... Prov 17:4
is a friend to him that g gifts .......... Prov 19:6
but the righteous g and spareth .......... Prov 21:26
for he g of his bread to the poor .......... Prov 22:9
he that g to the rich, shall .......... Prov 22:16
when it g his colour in the cup, .......... Prov 23:31
his lips that g a right answer .......... Prov 24:26
so is he that g honour to a fool .......... Prov 26:8
He that g unto the poor shall not .......... Prov 28:27
g meat to her household, and a .......... Prov 31:15
For God g to a man that is good .......... Eccl 2:26
but to the sinner he g travail .......... Eccl 2:26
days of his life, which God g him .......... Eccl 5:18
yet God g him not power to eat .......... Eccl 6:2
that wisdom g life to them that .......... Eccl 7:12
which God g him under the sun .......... Eccl 8:15
He g power to the faint .......... Is 40:29
he that g breath unto the people .......... Is 42:5
the LORD our God, that g rain .......... Jer 5:24
wages, and g him not for his work .......... Jer 22:13
which g the sun for a light by .......... Jer 31:35
He g his cheek to him that .......... Lam 3:30
he g wisdom unto the wise, and .......... Dan 2:21
g it to whomsoever he will, and .......... Dan 4:17
g it to whomsoever he will .......... Dan 4:25
g it to whomsoever he will .......... Dan 4:32
Woe unto him that g his neighbour .......... Hab 2:15
it g light unto all that are in .......... Mt 5:15
for God g not the Spirit by .......... Jn 3:34
but my Father g you the true .......... Jn 6:32
heaven, and g life unto the world .......... Jn 6:33
the Father g me shall come to me .......... Jn 6:37
the good shepherd g his life for .......... Jn 10:11
not as the world g, give I unto .......... Jn 14:27
and g them, and fish likewise .......... Jn 21:13
seeing he g to all life, and .......... Acts 17:25
he that g, let him do it with .......... Rom 12:8
to the Lord, for he g God thanks .......... Rom 14:6
he eateth not, and g God thanks .......... Rom 14:6
but God that g the increase .......... 1Cor 3:7
So then he that g her in marriage .......... 1Cor 7:38
but he that g her not in marriage .......... 1Cor 7:38
But God g it a body as it hath .......... 1Cor 15:38
which g us the victory through .......... 1Cor 15:57
killeth, but the spirit g life .......... 2Cor 3:6
who g us richly all things to .......... 1Ti 6:17
that g to all men liberally, and .......... Jas 1:5
But he g more grace .......... Jas 4:6
but g grace unto the humble .......... Jas 4:6
it as of the ability which God g .......... 1Pet 4:11
proud, and g grace to the humble .......... 1Pet 5:5
for the Lord God g them light .......... Rev 22:5

**GIVING**
And when she had done g him drink . Gen 24:19
in g him food and raiment .......... Deut 10:18
by g him a double portion of all .......... Deut 21:17
his people in g them bread .......... Ruth 1:6
in g food for my household .......... 1Kin 5:9
by g him according to his .......... 2Chr 6:23

and g thanks unto the LORD ..... Ezr 3:11
shall be as the g up of the ghost..... Job 11:20
g in marriage, until the day that..... Mt 24:38
face at his feet, g him thanks..... Lk 17:16
g out that himself was some great..... Acts 8:9
g them the Holy Ghost, even as he..... Acts 15:8
strong in faith, g glory to God..... Rom 4:20
the g of the law, and the service..... Rom 9:4
even things without life g sound..... 1Cor 14:7
say Amen at thy g of thanks..... 1Cor 14:16
G no offence in any thing, that..... 2Cor 6:3
but rather g of thanks..... Eph 5:4
G thanks always for all things..... Eph 5:20
with me as concerning g and..... Phil 4:15
G thanks unto the Father, which..... Col 1:12
g thanks to God and the Father by..... Col 3:17
g of thanks, be made for all men..... 1Ti 2:1
g heed to seducing spirits, and..... 1Ti 4:1
Not g heed to Jewish fables, and..... Titus 1:14
of our lips g thanks to his name..... Heb 13:15
g honour unto the wife, as unto..... 1Pet 3:7
g all diligence, add to your..... 2Pet 1:5
g themselves over to fornication,..... Jude 7

**GIZONITE** (*ghi'-zo-nite*) *A bodyguard of David.*
The sons of Hashem the G, ..... 1Chr 11:34

**GLAD**
he will be g in his heart..... Ex 4:14
And the priest's heart was g..... Judg 18:20
and they were g..... 1Sa 11:9
g of heart for all the goodness..... 1Kin 8:66
Let the heavens be g, and let the..... 1Chr 16:31
people away into their tents, g..... 2Chr 7:10
that day joyful and with a g heart..... Est 5:9
city of Shushan rejoiced and was g..... Est 8:15
rejoice exceedingly, and are g..... Job 3:22
The righteous see it, and are g..... Job 22:19
I will be g and rejoice in thee..... Ps 9:2
rejoice, and Israel shall be g..... Ps 14:7
Therefore my heart is g, and my..... Ps 16:9
exceeding g with thy countenance..... Ps 21:6
I will be g and rejoice in thy..... Ps 31:7
Be g in the LORD, and rejoice, ye..... Ps 32:11
shall hear thereof, and be g..... Ps 34:2
Let them shout for joy, and be g..... Ps 35:27
seek thee rejoice and be g in thee..... Ps 40:16
whereby they have made thee g..... Ps 45:8
shall make g the city of God..... Ps 46:4
let the daughters of Judah be g..... Ps 48:11
rejoice, and Israel shall be g..... Ps 53:6
righteous shall be g in the LORD..... Ps 64:10
O let the nations be g and sing..... Ps 67:4
But let the righteous be g..... Ps 68:3
humble shall see this, and be g..... Ps 69:32
seek thee rejoice and be g in thee..... Ps 70:4
may rejoice and be g all our days..... Ps 90:14
Make us g according to the days..... Ps 90:15
hast made me g through thy work..... Ps 92:4
rejoice, and let the earth be g..... Ps 96:11
multitude of isles be g thereof..... Ps 97:1
Zion heard, and was g..... Ps 97:8
that maketh g the heart of man..... Ps 104:15
I will be g in the LORD..... Ps 104:34
Egypt was g when they departed..... Ps 105:38
Then are they g because they be..... Ps 107:30
we will rejoice and be g in it..... Ps 118:24
thee will be g when they see me..... Ps 119:74
I was g when they said unto me,..... Ps 122:1
whereof we are g..... Ps 126:3
A wise son maketh a g father..... Prov 10:1
but a good word maketh it g..... Prov 12:25
A wise son maketh a g father..... Prov 15:20
he that is g at calamities shall..... Prov 17:5
father and thy mother shall be g..... Prov 23:25
heart be g when he stumbleth..... Prov 24:17
son, be wise, and make my heart g..... Prov 27:11
we will be g and rejoice in thee,..... Song 1:4
have waited for him, we will be g..... Is 25:9
place shall be g for them..... Is 35:1
And Hezekiah was g of them..... Is 39:2
But be ye g and rejoice for ever..... Is 65:18
be g with her, all ye that love..... Is 66:10
making him very g..... Jer 20:15
were with him, then they were g..... Jer 41:13
Because ye were g, because ye..... Jer 50:11
they are g that thou hast done it..... Lam 1:21
Rejoice and be g, O daughter of..... Lam 4:21
was the king exceeding g for him..... Dan 6:23
They make the king g with their..... Hos 7:3
be g and rejoice..... Joel 2:21
Be g then, ye children of Zion,..... Joel 2:23
was exceeding g of the gourd..... Jonah 4:6
therefore they rejoice and are g..... Hab 1:15
be g and rejoice with all the..... Zeph 3:14
children shall see it, and be g..... Zec 10:7
Rejoice, and be exceeding g..... Mt 5:12
when they heard it, they were g..... Mk 14:11
and to shew thee these g tidings..... Lk 1:19
shewing the g tidings of the..... Lk 8:1
we should make merry, and be g..... Lk 15:32
And they were g, and covenanted to..... Lk 22:5
saw Jesus, he was exceeding g..... Lk 23:8
and he saw it, and was g..... Jn 8:56
I am g for your sakes that I was..... Jn 11:15
Then were the disciples g..... Jn 20:20
heart rejoice, and my tongue was g..... Acts 2:26
had seen the grace of God, was g..... Acts 11:23
And we declare unto you g tidings..... Acts 13:32
Gentiles heard this, they were g..... Acts 13:48
bring g tidings of good things..... Rom 10:15
I am g therefore on your behalf..... Rom 16:19
I am g of the coming of Stephanas..... 1Cor 16:17
who is he then that maketh me g..... 2Cor 2:2
For we are g, when we are weak,..... 2Cor 13:9
ye may be g also with exceeding..... 1Pet 4:13
Let us be g and rejoice, and give..... Rev 19:7

**GLADLY**
did many things, and heard him g..... Mk 6:20
And the common people heard him g..... Mk 12:37
the people g received him..... Lk 8:40
Then they that g received his..... Acts 2:41
the brethren received us g..... Acts 21:17
For ye suffer fools g, seeing ye..... 2Cor 11:19
Most g therefore will I rather..... 2Cor 12:9
And I will very g spend and be..... 2Cor 12:15

**GLADNESS**
Also in the day of your g..... Num 10:10
and with g of heart, for the..... Deut 28:47
into the city of David with g..... 2Sa 6:12
strength and g are in his place..... 1Chr 16:27
the LORD on that day with great g..... 1Chr 29:22
And they sang praises with g..... 2Chr 29:30
bread seven days with great g..... 2Chr 30:21
they kept other seven days with g..... 2Chr 30:23
And there was very great g..... Neh 8:17
to keep the dedication with g..... Neh 12:27
The Jews had light, and g, and joy,..... Est 8:16
came, the Jews had joy and g..... Est 8:17
and made it a day of feasting and g..... Est 9:17
and made it a day of feasting and g..... Est 9:18
day of the month Adar a day of g..... Est 9:19
Thou hast put g in my heart..... Ps 4:7
my sackcloth, and girded me with g..... Ps 30:11
the oil of g above thy fellows..... Ps 45:7
With g and rejoicing shall they be..... Ps 45:15
Make me to hear joy and g..... Ps 51:8
g for the upright in heart..... Ps 97:11
Serve the LORD with g..... Ps 100:2
with joy, and his chosen with g..... Ps 105:43
rejoice in the g of thy nation..... Ps 106:5
hope of the righteous shall be g..... Prov 10:28
in the day of the g of his heart..... Song 3:11
g is taken away, and joy out of..... Is 16:10
And behold joy and g, slaying oxen,..... Is 22:13
g of heart, as when one goeth..... Is 30:29
they shall obtain joy and g..... Is 35:10
g shall be found therein,..... Is 51:3
they shall obtain g and joy..... Is 51:11
voice of mirth, and the voice of g..... Jer 7:34
voice of mirth, and the voice of g..... Jer 16:9
voice of mirth, and the voice of g..... Jer 25:10
Sing with g for Jacob, and shout..... Jer 31:7
voice of joy, and the voice of g..... Jer 33:11
g is taken from the plentiful..... Jer 48:33
g from the house of our God..... Joel 1:16
be to the house of Judah joy and g..... Zec 8:19
immediately receive it with g..... Mk 4:16
And thou shalt have joy and g..... Lk 1:14
house, did eat their meat with g..... Acts 2:46
she opened not the gate for g..... Acts 12:14
filling our hearts with food and g..... Acts 14:17
therefore in the Lord with all g..... Phil 2:29
the oil of g above thy fellows..... Heb 1:9

**GLASS**
strong, and as a molten looking g..... Job 37:18
For now we see through a g..... 1Cor 13:12
as in a g the glory of the Lord..... 2Cor 3:18
beholding his natural face in a g..... Jas 1:23
was a sea of g like unto crystal..... Rev 4:6
were a sea of g mingled with fire..... Rev 15:2
his name, stand on the sea of g..... Rev 15:2
was pure gold, like unto clear g..... Rev 21:18
gold, as it were transparent g..... Rev 21:21

**GLASSES**
The g, and the fine linen, and the..... Is 3:23

**GLEAN**
And thou shalt not g thy vineyard..... Lev 19:10
thou shalt not g it afterward..... Deut 24:21
g ears of corn after him in whose..... Ruth 2:2
And she said, I pray you, let me g..... Ruth 2:7
Go not to g in another field,..... Ruth 2:8
And when she was risen up to g..... Ruth 2:15
Let her g even among the sheaves,..... Ruth 2:15
leave them, that she may g them..... Ruth 2:16
g unto the end of barley harvest..... Ruth 2:23
They shall throughly g the..... Jer 6:9

**GLEANED**
they g of them in the highways..... Judg 20:45
g in the field after the reapers..... Ruth 2:3
So she g in the field until even,..... Ruth 2:17
even, and beat out that she had g..... Ruth 2:17
mother in law saw what she had g..... Ruth 2:18
her, Where hast thou g to day..... Ruth 2:19

**GLEANING**
thou gather any g of thy harvest..... Lev 23:22
Is not the g of the grapes of..... Judg 8:2
Yet g grapes shall be left in it,..... Is 17:6
as the g grapes when the vintage..... Is 24:13
they not leave some g grapes..... Jer 49:9

**GLEANINGS**
thou gather the g of thy harvest..... Lev 19:9

**GLEDE**
And the g, and the kite, and the..... Deut 14:13

**GLISTERING**
g stones, and of divers colours,..... 1Chr 29:2
and his raiment was white and g..... Lk 9:29

**GLITTER**
it is furbished that it may g..... Eze 21:10

**GLITTERING**
If I whet my g sword, and mine..... Deut 32:41
the g sword cometh out of his..... Job 20:25
the g spear and the shield..... Job 39:23
to consume because of the g..... Eze 21:28
the bright sword and the g spear..... Nah 3:3
and at the shining of thy g spear..... Hab 3:11

**GLOOMINESS**
A day of darkness and of g..... Joel 2:2
a day of darkness and g, a day of..... Zeph 1:15

**GLORIEST**
Wherefore g thou in the valleys,..... Jer 49:4

**GLORIETH**
But let him that g glory in this..... Jer 9:24
as it is written, He that g..... 1Cor 1:31
But he that g, let him glory in..... 2Cor 10:17

**GLORIFIED**
before all the people I will be g..... Lev 10:3
thou art g..... Is 26:15
Jacob, and g himself in Israel..... Is 44:23
O Israel, in whom I will be g..... Is 49:3
for he hath g thee..... Is 55:5
of Israel, because he hath g thee..... Is 60:9
work of my hands, that I may be g..... Is 60:21
of the LORD, that he might be g..... Is 61:3
sake, said, Let the LORD be g..... Is 66:5
I will be g in the midst of thee..... Eze 28:22
renown the day that I shall be g..... Eze 39:13
are all thy ways, hast thou not g..... Dan 5:23
pleasure in it, and I will be g..... Hag 1:8
g God, which had given such power..... Mt 9:8
and they g the God of Israel..... Mt 15:31
g God, saying, We never saw it on..... Mk 2:12
their synagogues, being g of all..... Lk 4:15
were all amazed, and they g God..... Lk 5:26
and they g God, saying, That a..... Lk 7:16
she was made straight, and g God..... Lk 13:13
back, and with a loud voice g God..... Lk 17:15
he g God, saying, Certainly this..... Lk 23:47
because that Jesus was not yet g..... Jn 7:39
the Son of God might be g thereby..... Jn 11:4
but when Jesus was g, then..... Jn 12:16
that the Son of man should be g..... Jn 12:23
heaven, saying, I have both g it..... Jn 12:28
said, Now is the Son of man g..... Jn 13:31
man g, and God is g in him..... Jn 13:31
If God be g in him, God shall..... Jn 13:32
the Father may be g in the Son..... Jn 14:13
Herein is my Father g, that ye..... Jn 15:8
I have g thee on the earth..... Jn 17:4
and I am g in them..... Jn 17:10
our fathers, hath g his Son Jesus..... Acts 3:13
for all men g God for that which..... Acts 4:21
g God, saying, Then hath God also..... Acts 11:18
glad, and g the word of the Lord..... Acts 13:48
they g the Lord, and said unto him..... Acts 21:20
they g him not as God, neither..... Rom 1:21
that we may be also g together..... Rom 8:17
whom he justified, them he also g..... Rom 8:30
And they g God in me..... Gal 1:24
shall come to be g in his saints..... 2Th 1:10
Lord Jesus Christ may be g in you..... 2Th 1:12
may have free course, and be g..... 2Th 3:1
So also Christ g not himself to..... Heb 5:5
may be g through Jesus Christ..... 1Pet 4:11
of, but on your part he is g..... 1Pet 4:14
How much she hath g herself..... Rev 18:7

**GLORIFIETH**
Whoso offereth praise g me..... Ps 50:23

**GLORIFY**
all ye the seed of Jacob, g him..... Ps 22:23
deliver thee, and thou shalt g me..... Ps 50:15
and shall g thy name..... Ps 86:9
I will g thy name for evermore..... Ps 86:12
Wherefore g ye the LORD in the..... Is 24:15
shall the strong people g thee..... Is 25:3
I will g the house of my glory..... Is 60:7
I will also g them, and they shall..... Jer 30:19
g your Father which is in heaven..... Mt 5:16
Father, g thy name..... Jn 12:28
glorified it, and will g it again..... Jn 12:28
God shall also g him in himself..... Jn 13:32
and shall straightway g him..... Jn 13:32
He shall g me..... Jn 16:14
the hour is come; g thy Son..... Jn 17:1
that thy Son also may g thee..... Jn 17:1
g thou me with thine own self..... Jn 17:5
by what death he should g God..... Jn 21:19
with one mind and one mouth g God..... Rom 15:6
might g God for his mercy..... Rom 15:9
therefore g God in your body, and..... 1Cor 6:20
they g God for your professed..... 2Cor 9:13
g God in the day of visitation..... 1Pet 2:12
but let him g God on this behalf..... 1Pet 4:16
fear thee, O Lord, and g thy name..... Rev 15:4

**GLORIFYING**
And the shepherds returned, g..... Lk 2:20
departed to his own house, g God..... Lk 5:25
his sight, and followed him, g God..... Lk 18:43

**GLORIOUS**
O LORD, is become g in power..... Ex 15:6
g in holiness, fearful in praises..... Ex 15:11
that thou mayest fear this g..... Deut 28:58
How g was the king of Israel..... 2Sa 6:20

thank thee, and praise thy g name .... 1Chr 29:13
and blessed be thy g name, which .... Neh 9:5
the riches of his g kingdom .... Est 1:4
king's daughter is all g within .... Ps 45:13
make his praise g .... Ps 66:2
And blessed be his g name for ever .... Ps 72:19
Thou art more g and excellent than .... Ps 76:4
G things are spoken of thee, O .... Ps 87:3
His work is honourable and g .... Ps 111:3
I will speak of the g honour of .... Ps 145:5
the g majesty of his kingdom .... Ps 145:12
of the LORD be beautiful and g .... Is 4:2
and his rest shall be g .... Is 11:10
he shall be for a g throne to his .... Is 22:23
whose g beauty is a fading flower .... Is 28:1
the g beauty, which is on the .... Is 28:4
cause his g voice to be heard .... Is 30:30
But there the g LORD will be unto .... Is 33:21
yet shall I be g in the eyes of .... Is 49:5
will make the place of my feet g .... Is 60:13
this that is g in his apparel, .... Is 63:1
hand of Moses with his g arm .... Is 63:12
people, to make thyself a g name .... Is 63:14
A g high throne from the .... Jer 17:12
made very g in the midst of the .... Eze 27:25
and he shall stand in the g land .... Dan 11:16
shall enter also into the g land .... Dan 11:41
the seas in the g holy mountain .... Dan 11:45
g things that were done by him .... Lk 13:17
g liberty of the children of God .... Rom 8:21
and engraven in stones, was g .... 2Cor 3:7
of the spirit be rather g .... 2Cor 3:8
g had no glory in this respect .... 2Cor 3:10
if that which is done away was g .... 2Cor 3:11
more that which remaineth is g .... 2Cor 3:11
light of the g gospel of Christ .... 2Cor 4:4
present it to himself a g church .... Eph 5:27
be fashioned like unto his g body .... Phil 3:21
might, according to his g power .... Col 1:11
According to the g gospel of the .... 1Ti 1:11
the g appearing of the great God .... Titus 2:13

## GLORIOUSLY

the LORD, for he hath triumphed g .... Ex 15:1
the LORD, for he hath triumphed g .... Ex 15:21
and before his ancients g .... Is 24:23

## GLORY

hath he gotten all this g .... Gen 31:1
my father of all my g in Egypt .... Gen 45:13
said unto Pharaoh, G over me .... Ex 8:9
ye shall see the g of the LORD .... Ex 16:7
the g of the LORD appeared in the .... Ex 16:10
the g of the LORD abode upon .... Ex 24:16
the sight of the g of the LORD .... Ex 24:17
for Aaron thy brother for g .... Ex 28:2
shalt thou make for them, for g .... Ex 28:40
shall be sanctified by my g .... Ex 29:43
I beseech thee, shew me thy g .... Ex 33:18
while my g passeth by, that I .... Ex 33:22
the g of the LORD filled the .... Ex 40:34
the g of the LORD filled the .... Ex 40:35
the g of the LORD shall appear .... Lev 9:6
the g of the LORD appeared unto .... Lev 9:23
the g of the LORD appeared in the .... Num 14:10
be filled with the g of the LORD .... Num 14:21
those men which have seen my g .... Num 14:22
the g of the LORD appeared unto .... Num 16:19
the g of the LORD appeared .... Num 16:42
the g of the LORD appeared unto .... Num 20:6
LORD our God hath shewed us his g .... Deut 5:24
His g is like the firstling of .... Deut 33:17
g to the LORD God of Israel, and .... Josh 7:19
make them inherit the throne of g .... 1Sa 2:8
The g is departed from Israel .... 1Sa 4:21
The g is departed from Israel .... 1Sa 4:22
ye shall give g unto the God of .... 1Sa 6:5
for the g of the LORD had filled .... 1Kin 8:11
g of this, and tarry at home .... 2Kin 14:10
G ye in his holy name .... 1Chr 16:10
Declare his g among the heathen .... 1Chr 16:24
G and honour are in his presence .... 1Chr 16:27
the people, give unto the LORD g .... 1Chr 16:28
the LORD the g due unto his name .... 1Chr 16:29
thy holy name, and g in thy praise .... 1Chr 16:35
of g throughout all countries .... 1Chr 22:5
greatness, and the power, and the g .. 1Chr 29:11
for the g of the LORD had filled .... 2Chr 5:14
the g of the LORD filled the .... 2Chr 7:1
because the g of the LORD had .... 2Chr 7:2
the g of the LORD upon the house, .... 2Chr 7:3
told them of the g of his riches .... Est 5:11
He hath stripped me of my g .... Job 19:9
My g was fresh in me, and my bow .... Job 29:20
the g of his nostrils is terrible .... Job 39:20
and array thyself with g and beauty .... Job 40:10
my g, and the lifter up of mine .... Ps 3:3
long will ye turn my g into shame .... Ps 4:2
who hast set thy g above the .... Ps 8:1
and hast crowned him with g .... Ps 8:5
heart is glad, and my g rejoiceth .... Ps 16:9
The heavens declare the g of God .... Ps 19:1
His g is great in thy salvation .... Ps 21:5
the King of g shall come in .... Ps 24:7
Who is this King of g .... Ps 24:8
the King of g shall come in .... Ps 24:9
Who is this King of g .... Ps 24:10
of hosts, he is the King of g .... Ps 24:10
O ye mighty, give unto the LORD g .... Ps 29:1
the LORD the g due unto his name .... Ps 29:2
the God of g thundereth .... Ps 29:3
doth every one speak of his g .... Ps 29:9
To the end that my g may sing .... Ps 30:12
thigh, O most mighty, with thy g .... Ps 45:3
when the g of his house is .... Ps 49:16
his g shall not descend after him .... Ps 49:17
let thy g be above all the earth .... Ps 57:5
Awake up, my g .... Ps 57:8
let thy g be above all the earth .... Ps 57:11
In God is my salvation and my g .... Ps 62:7
To see thy power and thy g .... Ps 63:2
one that sweareth by him shall g .... Ps 63:11
all the upright in heart shall g .... Ps 64:10
whole earth be filled with his g .... Ps 72:19
and afterward receive me to g .... Ps 73:24
his g into the enemy's hand .... Ps 78:61
salvation, for the g of thy name .... Ps 79:9
the LORD will give grace and g .... Ps 84:11
that g may dwell in our land .... Ps 85:9
For thou art the g of their .... Ps 89:17
Thou hast made his g to cease .... Ps 89:44
thy g unto their children .... Ps 90:16
Declare his g among the heathen, .... Ps 96:3
the people, give unto the LORD g .... Ps 96:7
the LORD the g due unto his name .... Ps 96:8
and all the people see his g .... Ps 97:6
all the kings of the earth thy g .... Ps 102:15
up Zion, he shall appear in his g .... Ps 102:16
The g of the LORD shall endure .... Ps 104:31
G ye in his holy name .... Ps 105:3
nation, that I may g with thine .... Ps 106:5
Thus they changed their g into .... Ps 106:20
and give praise, even with my g .... Ps 108:1
thy g above all the earth .... Ps 108:5
and his g above the heavens .... Ps 113:4
unto us, but unto thy name give g .... Ps 115:1
for great is the g of the LORD .... Ps 138:5
speak of the g of thy kingdom .... Ps 145:11
his g is above the earth and .... Ps 148:13
Let the saints be joyful in g .... Ps 149:5
The wise shall inherit g .... Prov 3:35
a crown of g shall she deliver to .... Prov 4:9
The hoary head is a crown of g .... Prov 16:31
the g of children are their .... Prov 17:6
it is his g to pass over a .... Prov 19:11
The g of young men is their .... Prov 20:29
It is the g of God to conceal a .... Prov 25:2
search their own g is not g .... Prov 25:27
men do rejoice, there is great g .... Prov 28:12
LORD, and for the g of his majesty .... Is 2:10
for the g of his majesty, when he .... Is 2:19
for the g of his majesty, when he .... Is 2:21
to provoke the eyes of his g .... Is 3:8
for upon all the g shall be a .... Is 4:5
and their g, and their multitude, .... Is 5:14
the whole earth is full of his g .... Is 6:3
the king of Assyria, and all his g .... Is 8:7
and where will ye leave your g .... Is 10:3
and the g of his high looks .... Is 10:12
under his g he shall kindle a .... Is 10:16
shall consume the g of his forest .... Is 10:18
the g of kingdoms, the beauty of .... Is 13:19
even all of them, lie in g .... Is 14:18
the g of Moab shall be contemned, .... Is 16:14
they shall be as the g of the .... Is 17:3
that the g of Jacob shall be made .... Is 17:4
expectation, and of Egypt their g .... Is 20:5
all the g of Kedar shall fail .... Is 21:16
thy g shall be the shame of thy .... Is 22:18
all the g of his father's house .... Is 22:24
it, to stain the pride of all g .... Is 23:9
songs, even g to the righteous .... Is 24:16
LORD of hosts be for a crown of g .... Is 28:5
the g of Lebanon shall be given .... Is 35:2
they shall see the g of the LORD .... Is 35:2
the g of the LORD shall be .... Is 40:5
shalt g in the Holy One of Israel .... Is 41:16
my g will I not give to another, .... Is 42:8
Let them give g unto the LORD .... Is 42:12
for I have created him for my g .... Is 43:7
Israel be justified, and shall g .... Is 45:25
salvation in Zion for Israel my g .... Is 46:13
I will not give my g unto another .... Is 48:11
the g of the LORD shall be thy .... Is 58:8
his g from the rising of the sun .... Is 59:19
the g of the LORD is risen upon .... Is 60:1
his g shall be seen upon thee .... Is 60:2
I will glorify the house of my g .... Is 60:7
The g of Lebanon shall come unto .... Is 60:13
light, and thy God thy g .... Is 60:19
in their g shall ye boast .... Is 61:6
righteousness, and all kings thy g .... Is 62:2
of g in the hand of the LORD .... Is 62:3
of thy holiness and of thy g .... Is 63:15
with the abundance of her g .... Is 66:11
the g of the Gentiles like a .... Is 66:12
and they shall come, and see my g .... Is 66:18
my fame, neither have seen my g .... Is 66:19
declare my g among the Gentiles .... Is 66:19
my people have changed their g .... Jer 2:11
in him, and in him shall they g .... Jer 4:2
not the wise man g in his wisdom .... Jer 9:23
let the mighty man g in his might .... Jer 9:23
not the rich man g in his riches .... Jer 9:23
let him that glorieth g in this .... Jer 9:24
name, and for a praise, and for a g .... Jer 13:11
Give g to the LORD your God, .... Jer 13:16
down, even the crown of your g .... Jer 13:18
not disgrace the throne of thy g .... Jer 14:21
Ah lord! or, Ah his g! .... Jer 22:18
Dibon, come down from thy g .... Jer 48:18
the likeness of the g of the LORD .... Eze 1:28
Blessed be the g of the LORD from .... Eze 3:12
the g of the LORD stood there, as .... Eze 3:23
as the g which I saw by the river .... Eze 3:23
the g of the God of Israel was .... Eze 8:4
the g of the God of Israel was .... Eze 9:3
Then the g of the LORD went up .... Eze 10:4
of the brightness of the LORD's g .... Eze 10:4
Then the g of the LORD departed .... Eze 10:18
the g of the God of Israel was .... Eze 10:19
the g of the God of Israel was .... Eze 11:22
the g of the LORD went up from .... Eze 11:23
which is the g of all lands .... Eze 20:6
which is the g of all lands .... Eze 20:15
strength, the joy of their g .... Eze 24:25
frontiers, the g of the country, .... Eze 25:9
I shall set g in the land of the .... Eze 26:20
To whom art thou thus like in g .... Eze 31:18
I will set my g among the heathen .... Eze 39:21
the g of the God of Israel came .... Eze 43:2
and the earth shined with his g .... Eze 43:2
the g of the LORD came into the .... Eze 43:4
the g of the LORD filled the .... Eze 43:5
the g of the LORD filled the .... Eze 44:4
kingdom, power, and strength, and g .... Dan 2:37
for the g of my kingdom, mine .... Dan 4:36
father a kingdom and majesty, and g .... Dan 5:18
and they took his g from him .... Dan 5:20
was given him dominion, and g .... Dan 7:14
of taxes in the g of the kingdom .... Dan 11:20
acknowledge and increase with g .... Dan 11:39
will I change their g into shame .... Hos 4:7
their g shall fly away like a .... Hos 9:11
rejoiced on it, for the g thereof .... Hos 10:5
come unto Adullam the g of Israel .... Mic 1:15
have ye taken away my g for ever .... Mic 2:9
g out of all the pleasant .... Nah 2:9
knowledge of the g of the LORD .... Hab 2:14
Thou art filled with shame for g .... Hab 2:16
spewing shall be on thy g .... Hab 2:16
His g covered the heavens, and the .... Hab 3:3
saw this house in her first g .... Hag 2:3
and I will fill this house with g .... Hag 2:7
The g of this latter house shall .... Hag 2:9
will be the g in the midst of her .... Zec 2:5
After the g hath he sent me unto .... Zec 2:8
and he shall bear the g, and shall .... Zec 6:13
for their g is spoiled .... Zec 11:3
that the g of the house of David .... Zec 12:7
the g of the inhabitants of .... Zec 12:7
to give g unto my name, saith the .... Mal 2:2
of the world, and the g of them .... Mt 4:8
that they may have g of men .... Mt 6:2
kingdom, and the power, and the g .... Mt 6:13
his g was not arrayed like one of .... Mt 6:29
Son of man shall come in the g of .... Mt 16:27
shall sit in the throne of his g .... Mt 19:28
of heaven with power and great g .... Mt 24:30
Son of man shall come in his g .... Mt 25:31
he sit upon the throne of his g .... Mt 25:31
when he cometh in the g of his .... Mk 8:38
other on thy left hand, in thy g .... Mk 10:37
the clouds with great power and g .... Mk 13:26
the g of the Lord shone round .... Lk 2:9
G to God in the highest, and on .... Lk 2:14
the g of thy people Israel .... Lk 2:32
I give thee, and the g of them .... Lk 4:6
when he shall come in his own g .... Lk 9:26
Who appeared in g, and spake of .... Lk 9:31
they were awake, they saw his g .... Lk 9:32
that Solomon in all his g was not .... Lk 12:27
that returned to give g to God .... Lk 17:18
in heaven, and g in the highest .... Lk 19:38
in a cloud with power and great g .... Lk 21:27
things, and to enter into his g .... Lk 24:26
among us, (and we beheld his g .... Jn 1:14
the g as of the only begotten of .... Jn 1:14
and manifested forth his g .... Jn 2:11
of himself seeketh his own g .... Jn 7:18
that seeketh his g that sent him .... Jn 7:18
And I seek not mine own g .... Jn 8:50
unto death, but for the g of God .... Jn 11:4
thou shouldest see the g of God .... Jn 11:40
said Esaias, when he saw his g .... Jn 12:41
g which I had with thee before .... Jn 17:5
the g which thou gavest me I have .... Jn 17:22
that they may behold my g .... Jn 17:24
The God of g appeared unto our .... Acts 7:2
into heaven, and saw the g of God .... Acts 7:55
because he gave not God the g .... Acts 12:23
not see for the g of that light .... Acts 22:11
And changed the g of the .... Rom 1:23
in well doing seek for g and .... Rom 2:7
But g, honour, and peace, to every .... Rom 2:10
through my lie unto his g .... Rom 3:7
and come short of the g of God .... Rom 3:23
by works, he hath whereof to g .... Rom 4:2
strong in faith, giving g to God .... Rom 4:20
rejoice in hope of the g of God .... Rom 5:2
but we g in tribulations also .... Rom 5:3
the dead by the g of the Father .... Rom 6:4
g which shall be revealed in us .... Rom 8:18
pertaineth the adoption, and the g .... Rom 9:4
of his g on the vessels of mercy .... Rom 9:23
he had afore prepared unto g .... Rom 9:23
to whom be g for ever .... Rom 11:36
also received us to the g of God .... Rom 15:7
g through Jesus Christ in those .... Rom 15:17
be g through Jesus Christ for .... Rom 16:27
no flesh should g in his presence .... 1Cor 1:29

glorieth, let him g in the Lord 1Cor 1:31
before the world unto our g 1Cor 2:7
not have crucified the Lord of g 1Cor 2:8
Therefore let no man g in men 1Cor 3:21
didst receive it, why dost thou g 1Cor 4:7
gospel, I have nothing to g of 1Cor 9:16
ye do, do all to the g of God 1Cor 10:31
as he is the image and g of God 1Cor 11:7
but the woman is the g of the man 1Cor 11:7
have long hair, it is a g to her 1Cor 11:15
but the g of the celestial is one 1Cor 15:40
the g of the terrestrial is 1Cor 15:40
There is one g of the sun 1Cor 15:41
another g of the moon 1Cor 15:41
and another g of the stars 1Cor 15:41
differeth from another star in g 1Cor 15:41
it is raised in g 1Cor 15:43
him Amen, unto the g of God by us 2Cor 1:20
for the g of his countenance 2Cor 3:7
which g was to be done away 2Cor 3:7
ministration of condemnation be g 2Cor 3:9
of righteousness exceed in g 2Cor 3:9
glorious had no g in this respect 2Cor 3:10
by reason of the g that excelleth 2Cor 3:10
as in a glass the g of the Lord 2Cor 3:18
the same image from g to g 2Cor 3:18
the g of God in the face of Jesus 2Cor 4:6
of many redound to the g of God 2Cor 4:15
exceeding and eternal weight of g 2Cor 4:17
you occasion to g on our behalf 2Cor 5:12
answer them which g in appearance 2Cor 5:12
by us to the g of the same Lord 2Cor 8:19
the churches, and the g of Christ 2Cor 8:23
glorieth, let him g in the Lord 2Cor 10:17
that wherein they g, they may be 2Cor 11:12
g after the flesh, I will g also 2Cor 11:18
If I must needs g, I will g 2Cor 11:30
expedient for me doubtless to g 2Cor 12:1
Of such an one will I g 2Cor 12:5
yet of myself I will not g 2Cor 12:5
For though I would desire to g 2Cor 12:6
will I rather g in my infirmities 2Cor 12:9
To whom be g for ever and ever Gal 1:5
Let us not be desirous of vain g Gal 5:26
that they may g in your flesh Gal 6:13
But God forbid that I should g Gal 6:14
the praise of the g of his grace Eph 1:6
should be to the praise of his g Eph 1:12
unto the praise of his g Eph 1:14
Jesus Christ, the Father of g Eph 1:17
what the riches of the g of his Eph 1:18
for you, which is your g Eph 3:13
according to the riches of his g Eph 3:16
Unto him be g in the church by Eph 3:21
are by Jesus Christ, unto the g Phil 1:11
to the g of God the Father Phil 2:11
whose g is in their shame, who Phil 3:19
his riches in g by Christ Jesus Phil 4:19
God and our Father be g for ever Phil 4:20
the g of this mystery among the Col 1:27
is Christ in you, the hope of g Col 1:27
ye also appear with him in g Col 3:4
Nor of men sought we g, neither 1Th 2:6
called you unto his kingdom and g 1Th 2:12
For ye are our g and joy 1Th 2:20
So that we ourselves g in you in 2Th 1:4
Lord, and from the g of his power 2Th 1:9
to the obtaining of the g of our 2Th 2:14
be honour and g for ever and ever 1Ti 1:17
in the world, received up into g 1Ti 3:16
is in Christ Jesus with eternal g 2Ti 2:10
to whom be g for ever and ever 2Ti 4:18
Who being the brightness of his g Heb 1:3
thou crownedst him with g Heb 2:7
of death, crowned with g and Heb 2:9
in bringing many sons unto g Heb 2:10
worthy of more g than Moses Heb 3:3
of g shadowing the mercyseat Heb 9:5
to whom be g for ever and ever Heb 13:21
Lord Jesus Christ, the Lord of g Jas 2:1
g not, and lie not against the Jas 3:14
g at the appearing of Jesus 1Pet 1:7
with joy unspeakable and full of g 1Pet 1:8
and the g that should follow 1Pet 1:11
up from the dead, and gave him g 1Pet 1:21
all the g of man as the flower of 1Pet 1:24
For what g is it, if, when ye be 1Pet 2:20
when his g shall be revealed, ye 1Pet 4:13
for the spirit of g and of God 1Pet 4:14
of the g that shall be revealed 1Pet 5:1
a crown of g that fadeth not away 1Pet 5:4
his eternal g by Christ Jesus 1Pet 5:10
To him be g and dominion for ever 1Pet 5:11
of him that hath called us to g 2Pet 1:3
from God the Father honour and g 2Pet 1:17
voice to him from the excellent g 2Pet 1:17
To him be g both now and for ever 2Pet 3:18
of his g with exceeding joy Jude 24
only wise God our Saviour, be g Jude 25
to him be g and dominion for ever Rev 1:6
And when those beasts give g Rev 4:9
art worthy, O Lord, to receive g Rev 4:11
and strength, and honour, and g Rev 5:12
saying, Blessing, and honour, and g Rev 5:13
Blessing, and g, and wisdom, and Rev 7:12
gave g to the God of heaven Rev 11:13
voice, Fear God, and give g to him Rev 14:7
with smoke from the g of God Rev 15:8
they repented not to give him g Rev 16:9
earth was lightened with his g Rev 18:1
Salvation, and g, and honour, and Rev 19:1
Having the g of God Rev 21:11
for the g of God did lighten it, Rev 21:23
of the earth do bring their g Rev 21:24
And they shall bring the g Rev 21:26

**GLORYING**
Your g is not good 1Cor 5:6
any man should make my g void 1Cor 9:15
toward you, great is my g of you 2Cor 7:4
I am become a fool in g 2Cor 12:11

**GLUTTON**
he is a g, and a drunkard Deut 21:20
the g shall come to poverty Prov 23:21

**GLUTTONOUS**
and they say, Behold a man g Mt 11:19
and ye say, Behold a g man Lk 7:34

**GNASH**
he shall g with his teeth, and Ps 112:10
they hiss and g the teeth Lam 2:16

**GNASHED**
they g upon me with their teeth Ps 35:16
they g on him with their teeth Acts 7:54

**GNASHETH**
he g upon me with his teeth Job 16:9
g upon him with his teeth Ps 37:12
g with his teeth, and pineth away Mk 9:18

**GNASHING**
shall be weeping and g of teeth Mt 8:12
shall be wailing and g of teeth Mt 13:42
shall be wailing and g of teeth Mt 13:50
shall be weeping and g of teeth Mt 22:13
shall be weeping and g of teeth Mt 24:51
shall be weeping and g of teeth Mt 25:30
g of teeth, when ye shall see Lk 13:28

**GNAT**
blind guides, which strain at a g Mt 23:24

**GNAW**
they g not the bones till the Zeph 3:3

**GNAWED**
they g their tongues for pain, Rev 16:10

**GO** See PREFACE.

**GOAD**
six hundred men with an ox g Judg 3:31

**GOADS**
for the axes, and to sharpen the g 1Sa 13:21
The words of the wise are as g Eccl 12:11

**GOAH** See GOATH.

**GOAT**
a she g of three years old, and a Gen 15:9
And if his offering be a g Lev 3:12
his hand upon the head of the g Lev 4:24
fat, of ox, or of sheep, or of g Lev 7:23
people's offering, and took the g Lev 9:15
sought the g of the sin offering Lev 10:16
Aaron shall bring the g upon Lev 16:9
But the g, on which the lot fell Lev 16:10
he kill the g of the sin offering Lev 16:15
bullock, and of the blood of the g Lev 16:18
altar, he shall bring the live g Lev 16:20
hands upon the head of the live g Lev 16:21
them upon the head of the g Lev 16:21
the g shall bear upon him all Lev 16:22
let go the g in the wilderness Lev 16:22
he that let go the g for the Lev 16:26
the g for the sin offering, whose Lev 16:27
that killeth an ox, or lamb, or g Lev 17:3
a bullock, or a sheep, or a g Lev 22:27
then he shall bring a she g of Num 15:27
a sheep, or the firstling of a g Num 18:17
one g for a sin offering, to make Num 28:22
And one g for a sin offering Num 29:22
And one g for a sin offering Num 29:28
And one g for a sin offering Num 29:31
And one g for a sin offering Num 29:34
And one g for a sin offering Num 29:38
the ox, the sheep, and the g Deut 14:4
and the fallow deer, and the wild g Deut 14:5
an he g also Prov 30:31
every day a g for a sin offering Eze 43:25
an he g came from the west on the Dan 8:5
the g had a notable horn between Dan 8:5
the he g waxed very great Dan 8:8
the rough g is the king of Grecia Dan 8:21

**GOATH** (*go'-ath*) *A place near Jerusalem.*
and shall compass about to G Jer 31:39

**GOATS**
thence two good kids of the g Gen 27:9
the kids of the g upon his hands Gen 27:16
spotted and speckled among the g Gen 30:32
speckled and spotted among the g Gen 30:33
the he g that were ringstraked Gen 30:35
all the she g that were speckled Gen 30:35
thy she g have not cast their Gen 31:38
Two hundred she g Gen 32:14
and twenty he g Gen 32:14
coat, and killed a kid of the g Gen 37:31
out from the sheep, or from the g Ex 12:5
namely, of the sheep, or of the g Lev 1:10
his offering, a kid of the g Lev 4:23
his offering, a kid of the g Lev 4:28
flock, a lamb or a kid of the g Lev 5:6
a kid of the g for a sin offering Lev 9:3
kids of the g for a sin offering Lev 16:5
And he shall take the two g Lev 16:7
shall cast lots upon the two g Lev 16:8
beeves, of the sheep, or of the g Lev 22:19
kid of the g for a sin offering Lev 23:19
One kid of the g for a sin Num 7:16
two oxen, five rams, five he g Num 7:17
One kid of the g for a sin Num 7:22
two oxen, five rams, five he g Num 7:23
One kid of the g for a sin Num 7:28
two oxen, five rams, five he g Num 7:29
One kid of the g for a sin Num 7:34
two oxen, five rams, five he g Num 7:35
One kid of the g for a sin Num 7:40
two oxen, five rams, five he g Num 7:41
One kid of the g for a sin Num 7:46
two oxen, five rams, five he g Num 7:47
One kid of the g for a sin Num 7:52
two oxen, five rams, five he g Num 7:53
One kid of the g for a sin Num 7:58
two oxen, five rams, five he g Num 7:59
One kid of the g for a sin Num 7:64
two oxen, five rams, five he g Num 7:65
One kid of the g for a sin Num 7:70
two oxen, five rams, five he g Num 7:71
One kid of the g for a sin Num 7:76
two oxen, five rams, five he g Num 7:77
One kid of the g for a sin Num 7:82
two oxen, five rams, five he g Num 7:83
the kids of the g for sin Num 7:87
the rams sixty, the he g sixty Num 7:88
one kid of the g for a sin Num 15:24
one kid of the g for a sin Num 28:15
And one kid of the g, to make an Num 28:30
one kid of the g for a sin Num 29:5
One kid of the g for a sin Num 29:11
one kid of the g for a sin Num 29:16
one kid of the g for a sin Num 29:19
one kid of the g for a sin Num 29:25
rams of the breed of Bashan, and g Deut 32:14
men upon the rocks of the wild g 1Sa 24:2
thousand sheep, and a thousand g 1Sa 25:2
thousand and seven hundred he g 2Chr 17:11
and seven lambs, and seven he g 2Chr 29:21
they brought forth the he g for 2Chr 29:23
for all Israel, twelve he g Ezr 6:17
twelve he g for a sin offering Ezr 8:35
wild g of the rock bring forth Job 39:1
nor he g out of thy folds Ps 50:9
of bulls, or drink the blood of g Ps 50:13
I will offer bullocks with g Ps 66:15
hills are a refuge for the wild g Ps 104:18
the g are the price of the field Prov 27:26
thy hair is as a flock of g Song 4:1
of g that appear from Gilead Song 6:5
bullocks, or of lambs, or of he g Is 1:11
and with the blood of lambs and g Is 34:6
be as the he g before the flocks Jer 50:8
slaughter, like rams with he g Jer 51:40
with thee in lambs, and rams, and g Eze 27:21
between the rams and the he g Eze 34:17
earth, of rams, of lambs, and of g Eze 39:18
the g without blemish for a sin Eze 43:22
a kid of the g daily for a sin Eze 45:23
shepherds, and I punished the g Zec 10:3
divideth his sheep from the g Mt 25:32
right hand, but the g on the left Mt 25:33
Neither by the blood of g Heb 9:12
For if the blood of bulls and of g Heb 9:13
took the blood of calves and of g Heb 9:19
of g should take away sins Heb 10:4

**GOATS'**
and fine linen, and g hair, Ex 25:4
thou shalt make curtains of g Ex 26:7
and fine linen, and g hair, Ex 35:6
g hair, and red skins of rams, and Ex 35:23
them up in wisdom spun g hair Ex 35:26
he made curtains of g hair for Ex 36:14
of skins, and all work of g hair Num 31:20
put a pillow of g hair for his 1Sa 19:13
with a pillow of g hair for his 1Sa 19:16
thou shalt have g milk enough for Prov 27:27

**GOATSKINS**
wandered about in sheepskins and g Heb 11:37

**GOB** (*gob*) *A place where David battled the Philistines.*
battle with the Philistines at G 2Sa 21:18
battle in G with the Philistines 2Sa 21:19

**GOBLET**
Thy navel is like a round g Song 7:2

**GOD** (*god*) See PREFACE. See also GODDESS, GODHEAD, GOD'S, GODS, GOD-WARD. *Creator and Ruler of the world, Israel, and the church.*
G called the dry land Earth Gen 1:10
and G saw that it was good Gen 1:10
Enoch walked with G after he Gen 5:22
And Enoch walked with G Gen 5:24
for G took him Gen 5:24
spake unto her, Thou G seest me Gen 16:13
G said unto Moses, I AM THAT I AM Ex 3:14
G is not a man, that he should Num 23:19
For the LORD thy G is a consuming Deut 4:24
The LORD our G is one LORD Deut 6:4
LORD thy G with all thine heart Deut 6:5
the LORD your G is G of gods Deut 10:17
The eternal G is thy refuge, and Deut 33:27

G

For who is G, save the LORD 2Sa 22:32
and who is a rock, save our G 2Sa 22:32
if the LORD be G, follow him 1Kin 18:21
they said, The LORD, he is the G 1Kin 18:39
O LORD G of Israel, which 2Kin 19:15
O LORD G of our fathers 2Chr 20:6
art not thou G in heaven 2Chr 20:6
And thou sayest, How doth G know Job 22:13
said in his heart, There is no G Ps 14:1
For who is G save the LORD Ps 18:31
or who is a rock save our G Ps 18:31
heavens declare the glory of G Ps 19:1
My G, my G, why hast thou Ps 22:1
My soul thirsteth for G Ps 42:2
for the living G Ps 42:2
G is our refuge and strength, a Ps 46:1
Be still, and know that I am G Ps 46:10
Create in me a clean heart, O G Ps 51:10
said in his heart, There is no G Ps 53:1
In G I will praise his word Ps 56:4
in G I have put my trust Ps 56:4
Blessed be G, which hath not Ps 66:20
a doorkeeper in the house of my G Ps 84:10
to everlasting, thou art G Ps 90:2
For the LORD is a great G Ps 95:3
Know ye that the LORD he is G Ps 100:3
the courts of the house of our G Ps 135:2
O give thanks unto the G of gods Ps 136:2
Search me, O G, and know my heart Ps 139:23
that people, whose G is the LORD Ps 144:15
hath the G of Jacob for his help Ps 146:5
whose hope is in the LORD his G Ps 146:5
and take the name of my G in vain Prov 30:9
hasty to utter any thing before G Eccl 5:2
Fear G, and keep his commandments Eccl 12:13
Behold, G is my salvation Is 12:2
for I am thy G Is 41:10
and beside me there is no G Is 44:6
for I am G, and there is none else Is 45:22
Spirit of the Lord G is upon me Is 61:1
Let us now fear the LORD our G Jer 5:24
and will be their G, and they shall Jer 31:33
I am the LORD your G Eze 20:19
know that I am the LORD your G Eze 20:20
for I am G, and not man Hos 11:9
arise, call upon thy G Jonah 1:6
and to walk humbly with thy G Mic 6:8
Will a man rob G Mal 3:8
being interpreted is, G with us Mt 1:23
Ye cannot serve G and mammon Mt 6:24
is none good but one, that is, G Mt 19:17
I am the G of Abraham Mt 22:32
the Lord thy G with all thy heart Mt 22:37
that is to say, My G, my G Mt 27:46
for there is one G Mk 12:32
being interpreted, My G, my G Mk 15:34
For with G nothing shall be Lk 1:37
Glory to G in the highest, and on Lk 2:14
the Lord thy G with all thy heart Lk 10:27
Ye cannot serve G and mammon Lk 16:13
all, Art thou then the Son of G Lk 22:70
was with G, and the Word was G Jn 1:1
G is a Spirit Jn 4:24
we have one Father, even G Jn 8:41
ask of G, G will give it thee Jn 11:22
ye believe in G, believe also in Jn 14:1
might know thee the only true G Jn 17:3
and said unto him, My Lord and my G Jn 20:28
ought to obey G rather than men Acts 5:29
heaven, and saw the glory of G Acts 7:55
standing on the right hand of G Acts 7:55
because he gave not G the glory Acts 12:23
inscription, TO THE UNKNOWN G Acts 17:23
because the love of G is shed Rom 5:5
But G commendeth his love toward Rom 5:8
G forbid. How shall we Rom 6:2
but the gift of G is eternal life Rom 6:23
as are led by the Spirit of G Rom 8:14
they are the sons of G Rom 8:14
If G be for us, who can be Rom 8:31
give account of himself to G Rom 14:12
But to us there is but one G 1Cor 8:6
him, that G may be all in all 1Cor 15:28
Blessed be G, even the Father of 2Cor 1:3
mercies, and the G of all comfort 2Cor 1:3
For we are unto G a sweet savour 2Cor 2:15
we have a building of G, an 2Cor 5:1
that G was in Christ, reconciling 2Cor 5:19
for G loveth a cheerful giver 2Cor 9:7
Thanks be unto G for his 2Cor 9:15
G is not mocked Gal 6:7
For it is G which worketh in you Phil 2:13
But my G shall supply all your Phil 4:19
let the peace of G rule in your Col 3:15
not as pleasing men, but G 1Th 2:4
and one mediator between G 1Ti 2:5
G was manifest in the flesh, 1Ti 3:16
glorious appearing of the great G Titus 2:13
therefore G, even thy G Heb 1:9
but he that built all things is G Heb 3:4
not ashamed to be called their G Heb 11:16
For our G is a consuming fire Heb 12:29
believest that there is one G Jas 2:19
that G is light, and in him is no 1Jn 1:5
is born of G doth not commit sin 1Jn 3:9
sin, because he is born of G 1Jn 3:9
the children of G are manifest 1Jn 3:10
not righteousness is not of G 1Jn 3:10
for love is of G 1Jn 4:7
because that G sent his only 1Jn 4:9
No man hath seen G at any time 1Jn 4:12
G is love 1Jn 4:16
love dwelleth in G, and G in him 1Jn 4:16
Jesus is the Christ is born of G 1Jn 5:1
that G hath given to us eternal 1Jn 5:11
not the Son of G hath not life 1Jn 5:12
on the name of the Son of G 1Jn 5:13
G shall wipe away all tears from Rev 7:17
Saying with a loud voice, Fear G Rev 14:7
G shall wipe away all tears from Rev 21:4
and I will be his G, and he shall Rev 21:7

## GODDESS

Ashtoreth the g of the Zidonians 1Kin 11:5
Ashtoreth the g of the Zidonians 1Kin 11:33
great g Diana should be despised Acts 19:27
a worshipper of the great g Diana Acts 19:35
nor yet blasphemers of your g Acts 19:37

## GODHEAD *That which is divine.*

that the G is like unto gold Acts 17:29
made, even his eternal power and G Rom 1:20
all the fulness of the G bodily Col 2:9

## GODLINESS

quiet and peaceable life in all g 1Ti 2:2
professing g) with good works 1Ti 2:10
great is the mystery of g 1Ti 3:16
and exercise thyself rather unto g 1Ti 4:7
but g is profitable unto all 1Ti 4:8
doctrine which is according to g 1Ti 6:3
truth, supposing that gain is g 1Ti 6:5
But g with contentment is great 1Ti 6:6
and follow after righteousness, g 1Ti 6:11
Having a form of g, but denying 2Ti 3:5
of the truth which is after g Titus 1:1
that pertain unto life and g 2Pet 1:3
and to patience g 2Pet 1:6
And to g brotherly kindness 2Pet 1:7
be in all holy conversation and g 2Pet 3:11

## GODLY

apart him that is g for himself Ps 4:3
for the g man ceaseth Ps 12:1
this shall every one that is g Ps 32:6
That he might seek a g seed Mal 2:15
g sincerity, not with fleshly 2Cor 1:12
were made sorry after a g manner 2Cor 7:9
For g sorrow worketh repentance 2Cor 7:10
that ye sorrowed after a g sort 2Cor 7:11
jealous over you with g jealousy 2Cor 11:2
rather than g edifying which is 1Ti 1:4
all that will live g in Christ 2Ti 3:12
live soberly, righteously, and g Titus 2:12
with reverence and g fear Heb 12:28
deliver the g out of temptations 2Pet 2:9
on their journey after a g sort 3Jn 6

## GOD'S *Refers to God 1.*

for a pillar, shall be G house Gen 28:22
and he said, Am I in G stead Gen 30:2
saw them, he said, This is G host Gen 32:2
G anger was kindled because he Num 22:22
for the judgment is G Deut 1:17
the battle is not yours, but G 2Chr 20:15
and into an oath, to walk in G law Neh 10:29
according to thy wish in G stead Job 33:6
My righteousness is more than G Job 35:2
I have yet to speak on G behalf Job 36:2
for it is G throne Mt 5:34
and unto God the things that are G Mt 22:21
and to God the things that are G Mk 12:17
for the kingdom of G sake Lk 18:29
and unto God the things which be G Lk 20:25
He that is of God heareth G words Jn 8:47
said, Revilest thou G high priest Acts 23:4
thing to the charge of G elect Rom 8:33
being ignorant of G righteousness Rom 10:3
for they are G ministers, Rom 13:6
ye are G husbandry, ye are G 1Cor 3:9
and Christ is G 1Cor 3:23
and in your spirit, which are G 1Cor 6:20
according to the faith of G elect Titus 1:1
as being lords over G heritage 1Pet 5:3

## GODS

be opened, and ye shall be as g Gen 3:5
wherefore hast thou stolen my g Gen 31:30
whomsoever thou findest thy g Gen 31:32
the strange g that are among you Gen 35:2
g which were in their hand Gen 35:4
against all the g of Egypt I will Ex 12:12
unto thee, O LORD, among the g Ex 15:11
the LORD is greater than all g Ex 18:11
shalt have no other g before me Ex 20:3
not make with me g of silver Ex 20:23
shall ye make unto you g of gold Ex 20:23
Thou shalt not revile the g Ex 22:28
no mention of the name of other g Ex 23:13
shalt not bow down to their g Ex 23:24
with them, nor with their g Ex 23:32
for if thou serve their g Ex 23:33
and said unto him, Up, make us g Ex 32:1
and they said, These be thy g Ex 32:4
and said, These be thy g, O Ex 32:8
For they said unto me, Make us g Ex 32:23
sin, and have made them g of gold Ex 32:31
they go a whoring after their g Ex 34:15
and do sacrifice unto their g Ex 34:15
go a whoring after their g Ex 34:16
sons go a whoring after their g Ex 34:16
Thou shalt make thee no molten g Ex 34:17
nor make to yourselves molten g Lev 19:4
unto the sacrifices of their g Num 25:2
did eat, and bowed down to their g Num 25:2
upon their g also the LORD Num 33:4
And there ye shall serve g Deut 4:28
shalt have none other g before me Deut 5:7
Ye shall not go after other g Deut 6:14
of the g of the people which are Deut 6:14
me, that they may serve other g Deut 7:4
neither shalt thou serve their g Deut 7:16
their g shall ye burn with fire Deut 7:25
thy God, and walk after other g Deut 8:19
For the LORD your God is God of g Deut 10:17
ye turn aside, and serve other g Deut 11:16
you this day, to go after other g Deut 11:28
ye shall possess served their g Deut 12:2
down the graven images of their g Deut 12:3
thou enquire not after their g Deut 12:30
did these nations serve their g Deut 12:30
have they done unto their g Deut 12:31
have burnt in the fire to their g Deut 12:31
saying, Let us go after other g Deut 13:2
Let us go and serve other g Deut 13:6
of the g of the people which are Deut 13:7
Let us go and serve other g Deut 13:13
And hath gone and served other g Deut 17:3
speak in the name of other g Deut 18:20
which they have done unto their g Deut 20:18
to go after other g to serve them Deut 28:14
and there shalt thou serve other g Deut 28:36
and there thou shalt serve other g Deut 28:64
serve the g of these nations Deut 29:18
For they went and served other g Deut 29:26
g whom they knew not Deut 29:26
be drawn away, and worship other g Deut 30:17
go a whoring after the g of the Deut 31:16
that they are turned unto other g Deut 31:18
then will they turn unto other g Deut 31:20
him to jealousy with strange g Deut 32:16
to g whom they knew not Deut 32:17
to new g that came newly up, whom Deut 32:17
he shall say, Where are their g Deut 32:37
God of g, the LORD God of g Josh 22:22
mention of the names of their g Josh 23:7
and have gone and served other g Josh 23:16
and they served other g Josh 24:2
put away the g which your fathers Josh 24:14
whether the g which your fathers Josh 24:15
or the g of the Amorites, in Josh 24:15
the LORD, to serve other g Josh 24:16
the LORD, and serve strange g Josh 24:20
the strange g which are among you Josh 24:23
their g shall be a snare unto you Judg 2:3
of Egypt, and followed other g Judg 2:12
of the g of the people that were Judg 2:12
they went a whoring after other g Judg 2:17
following other g to serve them Judg 2:19
to their sons, and served their g Judg 3:6
They chose new g Judg 5:8
fear not the g of the Amorites, Judg 6:10
the g of Syria Judg 10:6
the g of Zidon Judg 10:6
the g of Moab Judg 10:6
the g of the children of Ammon Judg 10:6
the g of the Philistines, and Judg 10:6
forsaken me, and served other g Judg 10:13
cry unto the g which ye have Judg 10:14
the strange g from among them Judg 10:16
the man Micah had an house of g Judg 17:5
have taken away my g Judg 18:24
unto her people, and unto her g Ruth 1:15
out of the hand of these mighty G 1Sa 4:8
these are the G that smote the 1Sa 4:8
from off you, and from off your g 1Sa 6:5
then put away the strange g 1Sa 7:3
forsaken me, and served other g 1Sa 8:8
Philistine cursed David by his g 1Sa 17:43
LORD, saying, Go, serve other g 1Sa 26:19
I saw g ascending out of the 1Sa 28:13
from the nations and their g 2Sa 7:23
you, but go and serve other g 1Kin 9:6
and have taken hold upon other g 1Kin 9:9
away your heart after their g 1Kin 11:2
away his heart after other g 1Kin 11:4
and sacrificed unto their g 1Kin 11:8
he should not go after other g 1Kin 11:10
behold thy g, O Israel, which 1Kin 12:28
hast gone and made thee other g 1Kin 14:9
And call ye on the name of your g 1Kin 18:24
and call on the name of your g 1Kin 18:25
saying, So let the g do to me 1Kin 19:2
The g do so unto me, and more also 1Kin 20:10
Their g are g of the hills 1Kin 20:23
Their g are g of the hills 1Kin 20:23
nor sacrifice unto other g 2Kin 5:17
of Egypt, and had feared other g 2Kin 17:7
every nation made g of their own 2Kin 17:29
Anammelech, the g of Sepharvaim 2Kin 17:31
the LORD, and served their own g 2Kin 17:33
saying, Ye shall not fear other g 2Kin 17:35
and ye shall not fear other g 2Kin 17:37
neither shall ye fear other g 2Kin 17:38
Hath any of the g of the nations 2Kin 18:33
Where are the g of Hamath 2Kin 18:34
where are the g of Sepharvaim 2Kin 18:34
among all the g of the countries 2Kin 18:35
Have the g of the nations 2Kin 19:12
have cast their g into the fire 2Kin 19:18
for they were no g, but the work 2Kin 19:18
have burned incense unto other g 2Kin 22:17
went a whoring after the g of the 1Chr 5:25

armour in the house of their g ... 1Chr 10:10
when they had left their g there ... 1Chr 14:12
also is to be feared above all g ... 1Chr 16:25
For all the g of the people are ... 1Chr 16:26
for great is our God above all g ... 2Chr 2:5
you, and shall go and serve other g ... 2Chr 7:19
of Egypt, and laid hold on other g ... 2Chr 7:22
which Jeroboam made you for g ... 2Chr 13:8
be a priest of them that are no g ... 2Chr 13:9
away the altars of the strange g ... 2Chr 14:3
that he brought the g of the ... 2Chr 25:14
Seir, and set them up to be his g ... 2Chr 25:14
sought after the g of the people ... 2Chr 25:15
they sought after the g of Edom ... 2Chr 25:20
sacrificed unto the g of Damascus ... 2Chr 28:23
Because the g of the kings of ... 2Chr 28:23
to burn incense unto other g ... 2Chr 28:25
were the g of the nations of ... 2Chr 32:13
the g of those nations that my ... 2Chr 32:14
As the g of the nations of other ... 2Chr 32:17
as against the g of the people of ... 2Chr 32:19
And he took away the strange g ... 2Chr 33:15
have burned incense unto other g ... 2Chr 34:25
put them in the house of his g ... Ezr 1:7
he judgeth among the g ... Ps 82:1
I have said, Ye are g ... Ps 82:6
Among the g there is none like ... Ps 86:8
God, and a great King above all g ... Ps 95:3
he is to be feared above all g ... Ps 96:4
For all the g of the nations are ... Ps 96:5
worship him, all ye g ... Ps 97:7
thou art exalted far above all g ... Ps 97:9
and that our Lord is above all g ... Ps 135:5
O give thanks unto the God of g ... Ps 136:2
before the g will I sing praise ... Ps 138:1
all the graven images of her g he ... Is 21:9
Hath any of the g of the nations ... Is 36:18
Where are the g of Hamath ... Is 36:19
where are the g of Sepharvaim ... Is 36:19
among all the g of these lands ... Is 36:20
Have the g of the nations ... Is 37:12
have cast their g into the fire ... Is 37:19
for they were no g, but the work ... Is 37:19
that we may know that ye are g ... Is 41:23
the molten images, Ye are our g ... Is 42:17
have burned incense unto other g ... Jer 1:16
their g, which are yet no g ... Jer 2:11
But where are thy g that thou ... Jer 2:28
number of thy cities are thy g ... Jer 2:28
and sworn by them that are no g ... Jer 5:7
and served strange g in your land ... Jer 5:19
walk after other g to your hurt ... Jer 7:6
after other g whom ye know not ... Jer 7:9
out drink offerings unto other g ... Jer 7:18
The g that have not made the ... Jer 10:11
went after other g to serve them ... Jer 11:10
cry unto the g unto whom they ... Jer 11:12
number of thy cities were thy g ... Jer 11:13
heart, and walk after other g ... Jer 13:10
and have walked after other g ... Jer 16:11
there shall ye serve other g day ... Jer 16:13
Shall a man make g unto himself ... Jer 16:20
and they are no g ... Jer 16:20
burned incense in it unto other g ... Jer 19:4
out drink offerings unto other g ... Jer 19:13
their God, and worshipped other g ... Jer 22:9
not after other g to serve them ... Jer 25:6
out drink offerings unto other g ... Jer 32:29
not after other g to serve them ... Jer 35:15
in the houses of the g of Egypt ... Jer 43:12
the houses of the g of the ... Jer 43:13
burn incense, and to serve other g ... Jer 44:3
to burn no incense unto other g ... Jer 44:5
unto other g in the land of Egypt ... Jer 44:8
had burned incense unto other g ... Jer 44:15
Pharaoh, and Egypt, with their g ... Jer 46:25
him that burneth incense to his g ... Jer 48:35
it before the king, except the g ... Dan 2:11
is, that your God is a God of g ... Dan 2:47
they serve not thy g, nor worship ... Dan 3:12
Abed-nego, do not ye serve my g ... Dan 3:14
that we will not serve thy g ... Dan 3:18
whom is the spirit of the holy g ... Dan 4:8
spirit of the holy g is in thee ... Dan 4:9
spirit of the holy g is in thee ... Dan 4:18
wine, and praised the g of gold ... Dan 5:4
whom is the spirit of the holy g ... Dan 5:11
wisdom, like the wisdom of the g ... Dan 5:11
the spirit of the g is in thee ... Dan 5:14
thou hast praised the g of silver ... Dan 5:23
carry captives into Egypt their g ... Dan 11:8
things against the God of g ... Dan 11:36
of Israel, who look to other g ... Hos 3:1
work of our hands, Ye are our g ... Hos 14:3
out of the house of thy g will I ... Nah 1:14
famish all the g of the earth ... Zeph 2:11
in your law, I said, Ye are g ... Jn 10:34
If he called them g, unto whom ... Jn 10:35
Make us g to go before us ... Acts 7:40
The g are come down to us in the ... Acts 14:11
to be a setter forth of strange g ... Acts 17:18
people, saying that they be no g ... Acts 19:26
though there be that are called g ... 1Cor 8:5
or in earth, (as there be g many ... 1Cor 8:5
them which by nature are no g ... Gal 4:8

## GOD-WARD

Be thou for the people to G ... Ex 18:19
trust have we through Christ to G ... 2Cor 3:4
your faith to G is spread abroad ... 1Th 1:8

## GOEST

as thou g, unto Sodom, and ... Gen 10:19
as thou g unto Sephar a mount of ... Gen 10:30
Egypt, as thou g toward Assyria ... Gen 25:18
thee in all places whither thou g ... Gen 28:15
and whither g thou ... Gen 32:17
When thou g to return into Egypt, ... Ex 4:21
is it not in that thou g with us ... Ex 33:16
of the land whither thou g ... Ex 34:12
that thou g before them, by ... Num 14:14
land whither thou g to possess it ... Deut 7:1
whither thou g in to possess it, ... Deut 11:10
land whither thou g to possess it ... Deut 11:29
whither thou g to possess them, ... Deut 12:29
When thou g out to battle against ... Deut 20:1
When thou g forth to war against ... Deut 21:10
land whither thou g to possess it ... Deut 23:20
shalt thou be when thou g out ... Deut 28:6
shalt thou be when thou g out ... Deut 28:19
whither thou g to possess it ... Deut 28:21
land whither thou g to possess it ... Deut 28:63
land whither thou g to possess it ... Deut 30:16
in the mount whither thou g up ... Deut 32:50
prosper whithersoever thou g ... Josh 1:7
is with thee whithersoever thou g ... Josh 1:9
that thou g to take a wife of the ... Judg 14:3
the old man said, Whither g thou ... Judg 19:17
for whither thou g, I will go ... Ruth 1:16
of the land, as thou g to Shur ... 1Sa 27:8
strength, when thou g on thy way ... 1Sa 28:22
Wherefore g thou also with us ... 2Sa 15:19
be, that on the day thou g out ... 1Kin 2:37
a certain, on the day thou g out ... 1Kin 2:42
g not forth with our armies ... Ps 44:9
When thou g, thy steps shall not ... Prov 4:12
When thou g, it shall lead thee ... Prov 6:22
when thou g to the house of God ... Eccl 5:1
in the grave, whither thou g ... Eccl 9:10
prey in all places whither thou g ... Jer 45:5
Then said I, Whither g thou ... Zec 2:2
follow thee whithersoever thou g ... Mt 8:19
follow thee whithersoever thou g ... Lk 9:57
When thou g with thine adversary ... Lk 12:58
and g thou thither again ... Jn 11:8
unto him, Lord, whither g thou ... Jn 13:36
Lord, we know not whither thou g ... Jn 14:5
of you asketh me, Whither g thou ... Jn 16:5

## GOETH

that is it which g toward the ... Gen 2:14
with the present that g before me ... Gen 32:20
as the cattle that g before me ... Gen 33:14
Behold thy father in law g up to ... Gen 38:13
lo, he g out unto the water ... Ex 7:15
unto him by that the sun g down ... Ex 22:26
when he g in unto the holy place, ... Ex 28:29
when he g in before the LORD ... Ex 28:30
sound shall be heard when he g in ... Ex 28:35
thing that g upon all four ... Lev 11:21
whatsoever g upon his paws, among ... Lev 11:27
Whatsoever g upon the belly, and ... Lev 11:42
whatsoever g upon all four, or ... Lev 11:42
Moreover he that g into the house ... Lev 14:46
and of him whose seed g from him ... Lev 15:32
of the congregation when he g in ... Lev 16:17
that g unto the holy things, ... Lev 22:3
or a man whose seed g from him ... Lev 22:4
when it g out in the jubile, ... Lev 27:21
when a wife g aside to another ... Num 5:29
that g down to the dwelling of Ar ... Num 21:15
LORD your God which g before you ... Deut 1:30
is he which g over before thee ... Deut 9:3
by the way where the sun g down ... Deut 11:30
As when a man g into the wood ... Deut 19:5
your God is he that g with you ... Deut 20:4
When the host g forth against ... Deut 23:9
pledge again when the sun g down ... Deut 24:13
the way that g up to Beth-horon ... Josh 10:10
that g up to Seir, even unto ... Josh 11:17
mount Halak, that g up to Seir ... Josh 12:7
to the wilderness that g up from ... Josh 16:1
g out from Beth-el to Luz, and ... Josh 16:2
g down westward to the coast of ... Josh 16:3
then g out to Daberath, and g ... Josh 19:12
g out to Remmon-methoar to Neah ... Josh 19:13
g out to Cabul on the left hand, ... Josh 19:27
g out from thence to Hukkok, and ... Josh 19:34
sun when he g forth in his might ... Judg 5:31
of which one g up to the house of ... Judg 20:31
that g up from Beth-el to Shechem ... Judg 21:19
if it g up by the way of his own ... 1Sa 6:9
law, and g at thy bidding, and is ... 1Sa 22:14
part is that g down to the battle ... 1Sa 30:24
that when my master g into the ... 2Kin 5:18
be ye with the king as he g out ... 2Kin 11:8
of Millo, which g down to Silla ... 2Kin 12:20
he cometh in, and when he g out ... 2Chr 23:7
the walls, and this work g fast on ... Ezr 5:8
so he that g down to the grave ... Job 7:9
he g by me, and I see him not ... Job 9:11
Which g in company with the ... Job 34:8
the sound that g out of his mouth ... Job 37:2
he g on to meet the armed men ... Job 39:21
Out of his nostrils g smoke ... Job 41:20
a flame g out of his mouth ... Job 41:21
that g not out of feigned lips ... Ps 17:1
when he g abroad, he telleth it ... Ps 41:6
as g on still in his trespasses ... Ps 68:21
Thy fierce wrath g over me ... Ps 88:16
A fire g before him, and burneth ... Ps 97:3
Man g forth unto his work and to ... Ps 104:23
He that g forth and weepeth, ... Ps 126:6
His breath g forth, he returneth ... Ps 146:4
So he that g in to his ... Prov 6:29
He g after her straightway ... Prov 7:22
as an ox g to the slaughter, or ... Prov 7:22
When it g well with the righteous ... Prov 11:10
Pride g before destruction, and an ... Prov 16:18
He that g about as a talebearer ... Prov 20:19
As a thorn g up into the hand of ... Prov 26:9
no wood is, there the fire g out ... Prov 26:20
her candle g not out by night ... Prov 31:18
also ariseth, and the sun g down ... Eccl 1:5
The wind g toward the south, and ... Eccl 1:6
the spirit of man that g upward ... Eccl 3:21
that g downward to the earth ... Eccl 3:21
because man g to his long home, ... Eccl 12:5
that g down sweetly, causing the ... Song 7:9
From the time that it g forth it ... Is 28:19
as when one g with a pipe to come ... Is 30:29
be that g forth out of my mouth ... Is 55:11
whosoever g therein shall not ... Is 59:8
As a beast g down into the valley ... Is 63:14
every one that g out thence shall ... Jer 5:6
for the day g away, for the ... Jer 6:4
but he that g out, and falleth to ... Jer 21:9
but weep sore for him that g away ... Jer 22:10
of the LORD g forth with fury ... Jer 30:23
but he that g forth to the ... Jer 38:2
g forth out of our own mouth ... Jer 44:17
every one that g by it shall be ... Jer 49:17
every one that g by Babylon shall ... Jer 50:13
but none g to the battle ... Eze 7:14
but their heart g after their ... Eze 33:31
as one g up to the entry of the ... Eze 40:40
as one g into them from the utter ... Eze 42:9
day that he g into the sanctuary ... Eze 44:27
as one g to Hamath, Hazar-enan, ... Eze 48:1
and as the early dew it g away ... Hos 6:4
are as the light that g forth ... Hos 6:5
This is the curse that g forth ... Zec 5:3
and see what is this that g forth ... Zec 5:5
This is an ephah that g forth ... Zec 5:6
and I say to this man, Go, and he g ... Mt 8:9
Then g he, and taketh with himself ... Mt 12:45
he hideth, and for joy thereof g ... Mt 13:44
Not that which g into the mouth ... Mt 15:11
in at the mouth g into the belly ... Mt 15:17
Howbeit this kind g not out but ... Mt 17:21
g into the mountains, and seeketh ... Mt 18:12
The Son of man g as it is written ... Mt 26:24
he g before you into Galilee ... Mt 28:7
he g up into a mountain, and ... Mk 3:13
g out into the draught, purging ... Mk 7:19
The Son of man indeed g, as it is ... Mk 14:21
he g straightway to him, and saith ... Mk 14:45
Peter that he g before you into ... Mk 16:7
and I say unto one, Go, and he g ... Lk 7:8
Then g he, and taketh to him seven ... Lk 11:26
And truly the Son of man g ... Lk 22:22
whence it cometh, and whither it g ... Jn 3:8
who g about to kill thee ... Jn 7:20
he g before them, and the sheep ... Jn 10:4
She g unto the grave to weep ... Jn 11:31
darkness knoweth not whither he g ... Jn 12:35
the south unto the way that g ... Acts 8:26
But brother g to law with brother ... 1Cor 6:6
Who g a warfare any time at his ... 1Cor 9:7
g his way, and straightway ... Jas 1:24
and knoweth not whither he g ... 1Jn 2:11
the Lamb whithersoever he g ... Rev 14:4
of the seven, and g into perdition ... Rev 17:11
out of his mouth g a sharp sword ... Rev 19:15

## GOG See HAMON-GOG, MAGOG.

*1. Son of Shemarah.*

G his son, Shimei his son, ... 1Chr 5:4

*2. A prince of Scythia.*

of man, set thy face against G ... Eze 38:2
Behold, I am against thee, O G ... Eze 38:3
of man, prophesy and say unto G ... Eze 38:14
shall be sanctified in thee, O G ... Eze 38:16
to pass at the same time when G ... Eze 38:18
son of man, prophesy against G ... Eze 39:1
Behold, I am against thee, O G ... Eze 39:1
that I will give unto G a place ... Eze 39:11
and there shall they bury G ... Eze 39:11
the four quarters of the earth, G ... Rev 20:8

## GOIIM See NATIONS.

## GOING

g on still toward the south ... Gen 12:9
And when the sun was g down ... Gen 15:12
g to carry it down to Egypt ... Gen 37:25
until the g down of the sun ... Ex 17:12
enemy's ox or his ass g astray ... Ex 23:4
six branches g out of the sides ... Ex 37:18
branches g out of the candlestick ... Ex 37:19
to the six branches g out of it ... Ex 37:21
g upon all four, shall be an ... Lev 11:20
g over into the land which the ... Num 32:7
the g forth thereof shall be from ... Num 34:4
at the g down of the sun, at the ... Deut 16:6
Rejoice, Zebulun, in thy g out ... Deut 33:18
sea toward the g down of the sun ... Josh 1:4
after the ark, the priests g on ... Josh 6:9
the city, g about it once ... Josh 6:11
ark of the LORD, the priests g on ... Josh 6:13
and smote them in the g down ... Josh 7:5
were in the g down to Beth-horon, ... Josh 10:11
the time of the g down of the sun ... Josh 10:27
is before the g up to Adummim ... Josh 15:7

G

over against the *g* up of Adummim ... Josh 18:17
this day I am *g* the way of all ... Josh 23:14
was from the *g* up to Akrabbim ... Judg 1:36
but I am now *g* to the house of ... Judg 19:18
said unto her, Up, and let us be *g* ... Judg 19:28
young maidens *g* out to draw water ... 1Sa 9:11
as they were *g* down to the end of ... 1Sa 9:27
three men *g* up to God to Beth-el ... 1Sa 10:3
as the host was *g* forth to the ... 1Sa 17:20
hast been upright, and thy *g* out ... 1Sa 29:6
in *g* he turned not to the right ... 2Sa 2:19
thee, and to know thy *g* out ... 2Sa 3:25
a *g* in the tops of the mulberry ... 2Sa 5:24
as she was *g* to fetch it, he ... 1Kin 17:11
host about the *g* down of the sun ... 1Kin 22:36
as he was *g* up by the way, there ... 2Kin 2:23
And they did so at the *g* up to Gur ... 2Kin 9:27
I know thy abode, and thy *g* out ... 2Kin 19:27
of *g* in the tops of the mulberry ... 1Chr 14:15
by the causeway of the *g* up ... 1Chr 26:16
returned from *g* against Jeroboam ... 2Chr 11:4
time of the sun *g* down he died ... 2Chr 18:34
the *g* up to the armoury at the ... Neh 3:19
to the *g* up of the corner ... Neh 3:31
between the *g* up of the corner ... Neh 3:32
at the *g* up of the wall, above ... Neh 12:37
the LORD, and said, From *g* to ... Job 1:7
the LORD, and said, From *g* to ... Job 2:2
him from *g* down to the pit ... Job 33:24
his soul from *g* into the pit ... Job 33:28
His *g* forth is from the end of ... Ps 19:6
the sun unto the *g* down thereof ... Ps 50:1
the sun knoweth his *g* down ... Ps 104:19
the *g* down of the same the LORD's ... Ps 113:3
The LORD shall preserve thy *g* out ... Ps 121:8
be no breaking in, nor *g* out ... Ps 144:14
*g* down to the chambers of death ... Prov 7:27
prudent man looketh well to his *g* ... Prov 14:15
well, yea, four are comely in *g* ... Prov 30:29
shall be darkened in his *g* forth ... Is 13:10
I know thy abode, and thy *g* out ... Is 37:28
For in the *g* up of Luhith ... Jer 48:5
for in the *g* down of Horonaim the ... Jer 48:5
the children of Judah together, *g* ... Jer 50:4
Dan also and Javan *g* to and fro ... Eze 27:19
the *g* up to it had eight steps ... Eze 40:31
the *g* up to it had eight steps ... Eze 40:34
the *g* up to it had eight steps ... Eze 40:37
with every *g* forth of the ... Eze 44:5
after his *g* forth one shall shut ... Eze 46:12
he laboured till the *g* down of ... Dan 6:14
that from the *g* forth of the ... Dan 9:25
his *g* forth is prepared as the ... Hos 6:3
and he found a ship *g* to Tarshish ... Jonah 1:3
*g* down of the same my name shall ... Mal 1:11
*g* on from thence, he saw other ... Mt 4:21
Jesus *g* up to Jerusalem took the ... Mt 20:17
Rise, let us be *g* ... Mt 26:46
Now when they were *g*, behold, ... Mt 28:11
for there were many coming and *g* ... Mk 6:31
were in the way *g* up to Jerusalem ... Mk 10:32
*g* to make war against another ... Lk 14:31
And as he was now *g* down, his ... Jn 4:51
*g* through the midst of them, and ... Jn 8:59
coming in and *g* out at Jerusalem ... Acts 9:28
These *g* before tarried for us at ... Acts 20:5
*g* about to establish their own ... Rom 10:3
beforehand, *g* before to judgment ... 1Ti 5:24
*g* before for the weakness ... Heb 7:18
For ye were as sheep *g* astray ... 1Pet 2:25
*g* after strange flesh, are set ... Jude 7

**GOINGS**

Moses wrote their *g* out according ... Num 33:2
journeys according to their *g* out ... Num 33:2
the *g* out of it shall be at the ... Num 34:5
the *g* forth of the border shall ... Num 34:8
the *g* out of it shall be at ... Num 34:9
the *g* out of it shall be at the ... Num 34:12
the *g* out of that coast were at ... Josh 15:4
the *g* out thereof were at ... Josh 15:7
the *g* out of the border were at ... Josh 15:11
the *g* out thereof are at the sea ... Josh 16:3
the *g* out thereof were at the sea ... Josh 16:8
the *g* out thereof were at the ... Josh 18:12
the *g* out thereof were at ... Josh 18:14
of man, and he seeth all his *g* ... Job 34:21
Hold up my *g* in thy paths, that ... Ps 17:5
upon a rock, and established my *g* ... Ps 40:2
They have seen thy *g*, O God ... Ps 68:24
even the *g* of my God, my King, in ... Ps 68:24
have purposed to overthrow my *g* ... Ps 140:4
LORD, and he pondereth all his *g* ... Prov 5:21
Man's *g* are of the LORD ... Prov 20:24
there is no judgment in their *g* ... Is 59:8
all their *g* out were both ... Eze 42:11
the *g* out thereof, and the comings ... Eze 43:11
these are the *g* out of the city ... Eze 48:30
whose *g* forth have been from of ... Mic 5:2

**GOLAN** (*go'-lan*) *A Levitical city in Manasseh.*

G in Bashan, of the Manassites ... Deut 4:43
G in Bashan out of the tribe of ... Josh 20:8
gave G in Bashan with her suburbs ... Josh 21:27
G in Bashan with her suburbs, and ... 1Chr 6:71

**GOLD**

land of Havilah, where there is *g* ... Gen 2:11
the *g* of that land is good ... Gen 2:12
in cattle, in silver, and in *g* ... Gen 13:2
hands of ten shekels weight of *g* ... Gen 24:22
flocks, and herds, and silver, and *g* ... Gen 24:35
jewels of silver, and jewels of *g* ... Gen 24:53
put a *g* chain about his neck ... Gen 41:42
of thy lord's house silver or *g* ... Gen 44:8
jewels of silver, and jewels of *g* ... Ex 3:22
jewels of silver, and jewels of *g* ... Ex 11:2
jewels of silver, and jewels of *g* ... Ex 12:35
shall ye make unto you gods of *g* ... Ex 20:23
*g*, and silver, and brass, ... Ex 25:3
thou shalt overlay it with pure *g* ... Ex 25:11
upon it a crown of *g* round about ... Ex 25:11
shalt cast four rings of *g* for it ... Ex 25:12
wood, and overlay them with *g* ... Ex 25:13
shalt make a mercy seat of pure *g* ... Ex 25:17
shalt make two cherubims of *g* ... Ex 25:18
thou shalt overlay it with pure *g* ... Ex 25:24
thereto a crown of *g* round about ... Ex 25:24
shalt make for it four rings of *g* ... Ex 25:26
wood, and overlay them with *g* ... Ex 25:28
of pure *g* shalt thou make them ... Ex 25:29
make a candlestick of pure *g* ... Ex 25:31
be one beaten work of pure *g* ... Ex 25:36
thereof, shall be of pure *g* ... Ex 25:38
talent of pure *g* shall he make it ... Ex 25:39
thou shalt make fifty taches of *g* ... Ex 26:6
shalt overlay the boards with *g* ... Ex 26:29
make their rings of *g* for places ... Ex 26:29
shalt overlay the bars with *g* ... Ex 26:29
of shittim wood overlaid with *g* ... Ex 26:32
their hooks shall be of *g* ... Ex 26:32
wood, and overlay them with *g* ... Ex 26:37
and their hooks shall be of *g* ... Ex 26:37
And they shall take *g*, and blue, and ... Ex 28:5
And they shall make the ephod of *g* ... Ex 28:6
even of *g*, of blue, and purple, and ... Ex 28:8
them to be set in ouches of *g* ... Ex 28:11
And thou shalt make ouches of *g* ... Ex 28:13
two chains of pure *g* at the ends ... Ex 28:14
of *g*, of blue, and of purple, and ... Ex 28:15
be set in *g* in their inclosings ... Ex 28:20
ends of wreathen work of pure *g* ... Ex 28:22
the breastplate two rings of *g* ... Ex 28:23
*g* in the two rings which are on ... Ex 28:24
And thou shalt make two rings of *g* ... Ex 28:26
other rings of *g* thou shalt make ... Ex 28:27
bells of *g* between them round ... Ex 28:33
thou shalt make a plate of pure *g* ... Ex 28:36
thou shalt overlay it with pure *g* ... Ex 30:3
unto it a crown of *g* round about ... Ex 30:3
wood, and overlay them with *g* ... Ex 30:5
cunning works, to work in *g* ... Ex 31:4
unto them, Whosoever hath any *g* ... Ex 32:24
sin, and have made them gods of *g* ... Ex 32:31
*g*, and silver, and brass, ... Ex 35:5
and tablets, all jewels of *g* ... Ex 35:22
an offering of *g* unto the LORD ... Ex 35:22
curious works, to work in *g* ... Ex 35:32
And he made fifty taches of *g* ... Ex 36:13
And he overlaid the boards with *g* ... Ex 36:34
made their rings of *g* to be ... Ex 36:34
bars, and overlaid the bars with *g* ... Ex 36:34
wood, and overlaid them with *g* ... Ex 36:36
their hooks were of *g* ... Ex 36:36
chapiters and their fillets with *g* ... Ex 36:38
he overlaid it with pure *g* within ... Ex 37:2
made a crown of *g* to it round ... Ex 37:2
And he cast for it four rings of *g* ... Ex 37:3
wood, and overlaid them with *g* ... Ex 37:4
he made the mercy seat of pure *g* ... Ex 37:6
And he made two cherubims of *g* ... Ex 37:7
And he overlaid it with pure *g* ... Ex 37:11
a crown of *g* round about ... Ex 37:11
made a crown of *g* for the border ... Ex 37:12
And he cast for it four rings of *g* ... Ex 37:13
wood, and overlaid them with *g* ... Ex 37:15
covers to cover withal, of pure *g* ... Ex 37:16
he made the candlestick of pure *g* ... Ex 37:17
it was one beaten work of pure *g* ... Ex 37:22
and his snuffdishes, of pure *g* ... Ex 37:23
Of a talent of pure *g* made he it ... Ex 37:24
And he overlaid it with pure *g* ... Ex 37:26
unto it a crown of *g* round about ... Ex 37:26
he made two rings of *g* for it ... Ex 37:27
wood, and overlaid them with *g* ... Ex 37:28
All the *g* that was occupied for ... Ex 38:24
even the *g* of the offering, was ... Ex 38:24
And he made the ephod of *g* ... Ex 39:2
did beat the *g* into thin plates ... Ex 39:3
of *g*, blue, and purple, and scarlet ... Ex 39:5
stones inclosed in ouches of *g* ... Ex 39:6
of *g*, blue, and purple, and scarlet ... Ex 39:8
ouches of *g* in their inclosings ... Ex 39:13
ends, of wreathen work of pure *g* ... Ex 39:15
And they made two ouches of *g* ... Ex 39:16
ouches of *g*, and two *g* rings ... Ex 39:16
put the two wreathen chains of *g* ... Ex 39:17
And they made two rings of *g* ... Ex 39:19
And they made bells of pure *g* ... Ex 39:25
plate of the holy crown of pure *g* ... Ex 39:30
thou shalt set the altar of *g* for ... Ex 40:5
One spoon of ten shekels of *g* ... Num 7:14
One spoon of *g* of ten shekels, ... Num 7:20
silver bowls, twelve spoons of *g* ... Num 7:84
all the *g* of the spoons was an ... Num 7:86
the candlestick was of beaten *g* ... Num 8:4
me his house full of silver and *g* ... Num 22:18
me his house full of silver and *g* ... Num 24:13
Only the *g*, and the silver, the ... Num 31:22
man hath gotten, of jewels of *g* ... Num 31:50
the priest took the *g* of them ... Num 31:51
all the *g* of the offering that ... Num 31:52
Eleazar the priest took the *g* of ... Num 31:54
the silver or *g* that is on them ... Deut 7:25
thy *g* is multiplied, and all that ... Deut 8:13
multiply to himself silver and *g* ... Deut 17:17
idols, wood and stone, silver and *g* ... Deut 29:17
But all the silver, and *g*, and ... Josh 6:19
only the silver, and the *g* ... Josh 6:24
a wedge of *g* of fifty shekels ... Josh 7:21
and the garment, and the wedge of *g* ... Josh 7:24
cattle, with silver, and with *g* ... Josh 22:8
and seven hundred shekels of *g* ... Judg 8:26
and put the jewels of *g*, which ye ... 1Sa 6:8
and the coffer with the mice of *g* ... 1Sa 6:11
it, wherein the jewels of *g* were ... 1Sa 6:15
ornaments of *g* upon your apparel ... 2Sa 1:24
David took the shields of *g* that ... 2Sa 8:7
of silver, and vessels of *g* ... 2Sa 8:10
*g* that he had dedicated of all ... 2Sa 8:11
of *g* with the precious stones ... 2Sa 12:30
will have no silver nor *g* of Saul ... 2Sa 21:4
and he overlaid it with pure *g* ... 1Kin 6:20
the house within with pure *g* ... 1Kin 6:21
the chains of *g* before the oracle ... 1Kin 6:21
and he overlaid it with *g* ... 1Kin 6:21
whole house he overlaid with *g* ... 1Kin 6:22
by the oracle he overlaid with *g* ... 1Kin 6:22
he overlaid the cherubims with *g* ... 1Kin 6:28
of the house he overlaid with *g* ... 1Kin 6:30
flowers, and overlaid them with *g* ... 1Kin 6:32
spread *g* upon the cherubims, and ... 1Kin 6:32
covered them with *g* fitted upon ... 1Kin 6:35
altar of *g*, and the table of *g* ... 1Kin 7:48
And the candlesticks of pure *g* ... 1Kin 7:49
and the lamps, and the tongs of *g* ... 1Kin 7:49
spoons, and the censers of pure *g* ... 1Kin 7:50
and the hinges of *g*, both for the ... 1Kin 7:50
even the silver, and the *g* ... 1Kin 7:51
trees and fir trees, and with *g* ... 1Kin 9:11
to the king sixscore talents of *g* ... 1Kin 9:14
Ophir, and fetched from thence *g* ... 1Kin 9:28
that bare spices, and very much *g* ... 1Kin 10:2
an hundred and twenty talents of *g* ... 1Kin 10:10
Hiram, that brought *g* from Ophir ... 1Kin 10:11
Now the weight of *g* that came to ... 1Kin 10:14
threescore and six talents of *g* ... 1Kin 10:14
two hundred targets of beaten *g* ... 1Kin 10:16
shekels of *g* went to one target ... 1Kin 10:16
three hundred shields of beaten *g* ... 1Kin 10:17
three pound of *g* went to one ... 1Kin 10:17
and overlaid it with the best *g* ... 1Kin 10:18
drinking vessels were of *g* ... 1Kin 10:21
forest of Lebanon were of pure *g* ... 1Kin 10:21
the navy of Tharshish, bringing *g* ... 1Kin 10:22
of silver, and vessels of *g* ... 1Kin 10:25
counsel, and made two calves of *g* ... 1Kin 12:28
of *g* which Solomon had made ... 1Kin 14:26
house of the LORD, silver, and *g* ... 1Kin 15:15
the *g* that were left in the ... 1Kin 15:18
thee a present of silver and *g* ... 1Kin 15:19
Thy silver and thy *g* is mine ... 1Kin 20:3
deliver me thy silver, and thy *g* ... 1Kin 20:5
and for my silver, and for my *g* ... 1Kin 20:7
of Tharshish to go to Ophir for *g* ... 1Kin 22:48
and six thousand pieces of *g* ... 2Kin 5:5
and carried thence silver, and *g* ... 2Kin 7:8
trumpets, any vessels of *g* ... 2Kin 12:13
all the *g* that was found in the ... 2Kin 12:18
And he took all the *g* and silver, ... 2Kin 14:14
*g* that was found in the house of ... 2Kin 16:8
of silver and thirty talents of *g* ... 2Kin 18:14
time did Hezekiah cut off the *g* ... 2Kin 18:16
things, the silver, and the *g* ... 2Kin 20:13
of silver, and a talent of *g* ... 2Kin 23:33
the silver and the *g* to Pharaoh ... 2Kin 23:35
the *g* of the people of the land, ... 2Kin 23:35
of *g* which Solomon king of Israel ... 2Kin 24:13
such things as were of *g*, in *g* ... 2Kin 25:15
David took the shields of *g* that ... 1Chr 18:7
him all manner of vessels of *g* ... 1Chr 18:10
the *g* that he brought from all ... 1Chr 18:11
found it to weigh a talent of *g* ... 1Chr 20:2
hundred shekels of *g* by weight ... 1Chr 21:25
an hundred thousand talents of *g* ... 1Chr 22:14
Of the *g*, the silver, and the ... 1Chr 22:16
of *g* by weight for things of *g* ... 1Chr 28:14
weight for the candlesticks of *g* ... 1Chr 28:15
and for their lamps of *g* ... 1Chr 28:15
by weight he gave *g* for the ... 1Chr 28:16
Also pure *g* for the fleshhooks, ... 1Chr 28:17
gave *g* by weight for every bason ... 1Chr 28:17
of incense refined *g* by weight ... 1Chr 28:18
*g* for the pattern of the chariot ... 1Chr 28:18
*g* for things to be made of *g* ... 1Chr 29:2
of mine own proper good, of *g* ... 1Chr 29:3
Even three thousand talents of *g* ... 1Chr 29:4
of the *g* of Ophir, and seven ... 1Chr 29:4
The *g* for things of *g*, and the ... 1Chr 29:5
of God of *g* five thousand talents ... 1Chr 29:7
*g* at Jerusalem as plenteous as ... 2Chr 1:15
a man cunning to work in *g* ... 2Chr 2:7
man of Tyre, skilful to work in *g* ... 2Chr 2:14
he overlaid it within with pure *g* ... 2Chr 3:4
which he overlaid with fine *g* ... 2Chr 3:5
and the *g* was *g* of Parvaim ... 2Chr 3:6
and the doors thereof, with *g* ... 2Chr 3:7
and he overlaid it with fine *g* ... 2Chr 3:8
the nails was fifty shekels of *g* ... 2Chr 3:9
the upper chambers with *g* ... 2Chr 3:9
work, and overlaid them with *g* ... 2Chr 3:10
of *g* according to their form ... 2Chr 4:7

And he made an hundred basons of g .. 2Chr 4:8
before the oracle, of pure g 2Chr 4:20
he of g, and that perfect g 2Chr 4:21
spoons, and the censers, of pure g 2Chr 4:22
house of the temple, were of g 2Chr 4:22
and the silver, and the g, and all 2Chr 5:1
hundred and fifty talents of g 2Chr 8:18
g in abundance, and precious 2Chr 9:1
an hundred and twenty talents of g 2Chr 9:9
which brought g from Ophir 2Chr 9:10
Now the weight of g that came to 2Chr 9:13
and threescore and six talents of g 2Chr 9:13
of the country brought g and 2Chr 9:14
two hundred targets of beaten g 2Chr 9:15
of beaten g went to one target 2Chr 9:15
shields made he of beaten g 2Chr 9:16
shekels of g went to one shield 2Chr 9:16
ivory, and overlaid it with pure g 2Chr 9:17
the throne, with a footstool of g 2Chr 9:18
vessels of king Solomon were of g 2Chr 9:20
forest of Lebanon were of pure g 2Chr 9:20
the ships of Tarshish bringing g 2Chr 9:21
of silver, and vessels of g 2Chr 9:24
of g which Solomon had made 2Chr 12:9
the candlestick of g with the 2Chr 13:11
had dedicated, silver, and g 2Chr 15:18
g out of the treasures of the 2Chr 16:2
I have sent thee silver and g 2Chr 16:3
great gifts of silver, and of g 2Chr 21:3
and spoons, and vessels of g 2Chr 24:14
And he took all the g and the 2Chr 25:24
treasuries for silver, and for g 2Chr 32:27
of silver and a talent of g 2Chr 36:3
help him with silver, and with g Ezr 1:4
with vessels of silver, with g Ezr 1:6
thirty chargers of g, a thousand Ezr 1:9
Thirty basons of g, silver basons Ezr 1:10
All the vessels of g and of silver Ezr 1:11
and one thousand drams of g Ezr 2:69
And the vessels also of g and Ezr 5:14
And to carry the silver and g Ezr 7:15
g that thou canst find in all the Ezr 7:16
the rest of the silver and the g Ezr 7:18
unto them the silver, and the g Ezr 8:25
and of g an hundred talents Ezr 8:26
Also twenty basons of g, of a Ezr 8:27
of fine copper, precious as g Ezr 8:27
the g are a freewill offering Ezr 8:28
weight of the silver, and the g Ezr 8:30
day was the silver and the g Ezr 8:33
treasure a thousand drams of g Neh 7:70
work twenty thousand drams of g Neh 7:71
was twenty thousand drams of g Neh 7:72
the beds were of g and silver, Est 1:6
gave them drink in vessels of g Est 1:7
white, and with a great crown of g Est 8:15
Or with princes that had g Job 3:15
Then shalt thou lay up g as dust Job 22:24
the g of Ophir as the stones of Job 22:24
tried me, I shall come forth as g Job 23:10
a place for g where they fine it Job 28:1
and it hath dust of g Job 28:6
It cannot be gotten for g Job 28:15
be valued with the g of Ophir Job 28:16
The g and the crystal cannot equal Job 28:17
shall not be for jewels of fine g Job 28:17
shall it be valued with pure g Job 28:19
If I have made g my hope Job 31:24
or have said to the fine g Job 31:24
no, not g, nor all the forces of Job 36:19
and every one an earring of g Job 42:11
to be desired are they than g Ps 19:10
yea, than much fine g Ps 19:10
a crown of pure g on his head Ps 21:3
did stand the queen in g of Ophir Ps 45:9
her clothing is of wrought g Ps 45:13
and her feathers with yellow g Ps 68:13
shall be given of the g of Sheba Ps 72:15
them forth also with silver and g Ps 105:37
Their idols are silver and g Ps 115:4
unto me than thousands of g Ps 119:72
I love thy commandments above g Ps 119:127
yea, above fine g Ps 119:127
of the heathen are silver and g Ps 135:15
and the gain thereof than fine g Prov 3:14
and knowledge rather than choice g Prov 8:10
My fruit is better than g Prov 8:19
yea, than fine g Prov 8:19
As a jewel of g in a swine's Prov 11:22
better is it to get wisdom than g Prov 16:16
for silver, and the furnace for g Prov 17:3
There is g, and a multitude of Prov 20:15
favour rather than silver and g Prov 22:1
apples of g in pictures of silver Prov 25:11
As an earring of g, and an Prov 25:12
of g, and an ornament of fine g Prov 25:12
for silver, and the furnace for g Prov 27:21
I gathered me also silver and g Eccl 2:8
jewels, thy neck with chains of g Song 1:10
borders of g with studs of silver Song 1:11
silver, the bottom thereof of g Song 3:10
His head is as the most fine g Song 5:11
His hands are as g rings set with Song 5:14
set upon sockets of fine g Song 5:15
land also is full of silver and g Is 2:7
of silver, and his idols of g Is 2:20
a man more precious than fine g Is 13:12
and as for g, they shall not Is 13:17
of thy molten images of g Is 30:22
of silver, and his idols of g Is 31:7
things, the silver, and the g Is 39:2
spreadeth it over with g, and Is 40:19
They lavish g out of the bag, and Is 46:6
they shall bring g and incense Is 60:6
their g with them, unto the name Is 60:9
For brass I will bring g, and for Is 60:17
deckest thee with ornaments of g Jer 4:30
deck it with silver and with g Jer 10:4
g from Uphaz, the work of the Jer 10:9
that which was of g in g Jer 52:19
How is the g become dim Lam 4:1
how is the most fine g changed Lam 4:1
of Zion, comparable to fine g Lam 4:2
and their g shall be removed Eze 7:19
their g shall not be able to Eze 7:19
Thus wast thou decked with g Eze 16:13
taken thy fair jewels of my g Eze 16:17
and with all precious stones, and g Eze 27:22
thee riches, and hast gotten g Eze 28:4
emerald, and the carbuncle, and g Eze 28:13
to carry away silver and g Eze 38:13
This image's head was of fine g Dan 2:32
the brass, the silver, and the g Dan 2:35
Thou art this head of g Dan 2:38
the clay, the silver, and the g Dan 2:45
the king made an image of g Dan 3:1
wine, and praised the gods of g Dan 5:4
have a chain of g about his neck Dan 5:7
have a chain of g about thy neck Dan 5:16
praised the gods of silver, and g Dan 5:23
put a chain of g about his neck Dan 5:29
were girded with fine g of Uphaz Dan 10:5
vessels of silver and of g Dan 11:8
knew not shall he honour with g Dan 11:38
power over the treasures of g Dan 11:43
and multiplied her silver and g Hos 2:8
their g have they made them idols Hos 8:4
ye have taken my silver and my g Joel 3:5
of silver, take the spoil of g Nah 2:9
Behold, it is laid over with g Hab 2:19
g shall be able to deliver them Zeph 1:18
the g is mine, saith the LORD of Hag 2:8
and behold a candlestick all of g Zec 4:2
Then take silver and g, and make Zec 6:11
fine g as the mire of the streets Zec 9:3
and will try them as g is tried Zec 13:9
shall be gathered together, g Zec 14:14
sons of Levi, and purge them as g Mal 3:3
g, and frankincense, and myrrh Mt 2:11
Provide neither g, nor silver, Mt 10:9
swear by the g of the temple Mt 23:16
for whether is greater, the g Mt 23:17
the temple that sanctifieth the g Mt 23:17
said, Silver and g have I none Acts 3:6
that the Godhead is like unto g Acts 17:29
coveted no man's silver, or g Acts 20:33
man build upon this foundation g 1Cor 3:12
not with broided hair, or g 1Ti 2:9
there are not only vessels of g 2Ti 2:20
overlaid round about with g Heb 9:4
your assembly a man with a g ring Jas 2:2
Your g and silver is cankered Jas 5:3
precious than of g that perisheth 1Pet 1:7
things, as silver and g, from your 1Pet 1:18
the hair, and of wearing of g 1Pet 3:3
to buy of me g tried in the fire Rev 3:18
had on their heads crowns of g Rev 4:4
were as it were crowns like g Rev 9:7
not worship devils, and idols of g Rev 9:20
scarlet colour, and decked with g Rev 17:4
The merchandise of g, and silver, Rev 18:12
and scarlet, and decked with g Rev 18:16
and the city was pure g, like unto Rev 21:18
the street of the city was pure g Rev 21:21

**GOLDEN**

that the man took a g earring of Gen 24:22
thou shalt make a g crown to the Ex 25:25
A g bell and a pomegranate Ex 28:34
a g bell and a pomegranate, upon Ex 28:34
two g rings shalt thou make to it Ex 30:4
them, Break off the g earrings Ex 32:2
g earrings which were in their Ex 32:3
And they made two other g rings Ex 39:20
the g altar, and the anointing oil Ex 39:38
he put the g altar in the tent of Ex 40:26
forefront, did he put the g plate Lev 8:9
upon the g altar they shall Num 4:11
One g spoon of ten shekels, full Num 7:26
One g spoon of ten shekels, full Num 7:32
One g spoon of ten shekels, full Num 7:38
One g spoon of ten shekels, full Num 7:44
One g spoon of ten shekels, full Num 7:50
One g spoon of ten shekels, full Num 7:56
One g spoon of ten shekels, full Num 7:62
One g spoon of ten shekels, full Num 7:68
One g spoon of ten shekels, full Num 7:74
One g spoon of ten shekels, full Num 7:80
The g spoons were twelve, full of Num 7:86
(For they had g earrings, because Judg 8:24
the weight of the g earrings that Judg 8:26
g emerods, and five g mice 1Sa 6:4
these are the g emerods which the 1Sa 6:17
the g mice, according to the 1Sa 6:18
the g calves that were in Beth-el 2Kin 10:29
for the g basons he gave gold by 1Chr 28:17
the g altar also, and the tables 2Chr 4:19
and there are with you g calves 2Chr 13:8
And also let the g and silver Ezr 6:5
king shall hold out the g sceptre Est 4:11
g sceptre that was in his hand Est 5:2
out the g sceptre toward Esther Est 8:4
or the g bowl be broken, or the Eccl 12:6
a man than the g wedge of Ophir Is 13:12
the g city ceased Is 14:4
Babylon hath been a g cup in the Jer 51:7
down and worship the g image that Dan 3:5
worshipped the g image that Dan 3:7
fall down and worship the g image Dan 3:10
nor worship the g image which Dan 3:12
nor worship the g image which I Dan 3:14
nor worship the g image which Dan 3:18
wine, commanded to bring the g Dan 5:2
Then they brought the g vessels Dan 5:3
g pipes empty the g oil out Zec 4:12
Which had the g censer, and the Heb 9:4
wherein was the g pot that had Heb 9:4
I saw seven g candlesticks Rev 1:12
about the paps with a g girdle Rev 1:13
hand, and the seven g candlesticks Rev 1:20
midst of the seven g candlesticks Rev 2:1
g vials full of odours, which are Rev 5:8
at the altar, having a g censer Rev 8:3
the g altar which was before the Rev 8:3
the g altar which is before God Rev 9:13
man, having on his head a g crown Rev 14:14
breasts girded with g girdles Rev 15:6
unto the seven angels seven g Rev 15:7
having a g cup in her hand full Rev 17:4
had a g reed to measure the city Rev 21:15

**GOLDSMITH**

the g spreadeth it over with gold Is 40:19
So the carpenter encouraged the g Is 41:7
in the balance, and hire a g Is 46:6

**GOLDSMITH'S**

the g son unto the place of the Neh 3:31

**GOLDSMITHS**

the son of Harhaiah, of the g Neh 3:8
the sheep gate repaired the g Neh 3:32

**GOLGOTHA** (*gol'-go-thah*) See CALVARY. *Hill where Jesus was crucified.*

were come unto a place called G Mt 27:33
they bring him unto the place G Mk 15:22
which is called in the Hebrew G Jn 19:17

**GOLIATH** (*go-li'-ath*) *Philistine warrior killed by David.*

camp of the Philistines, named G 1Sa 17:4
G by name, out of the armies of 1Sa 17:23
The sword of G the Philistine, 1Sa 21:9
him the sword of G the Philistine 1Sa 22:10
slew the brother of G the Gittite 2Sa 21:19
the brother of G the Gittite 1Chr 20:5

**GOMER** (*go'-mer*)

*1. Son of Japheth.*
G, and Magog, and Madai, and Javan, Gen 10:2
And the sons of G Gen 10:3
G, and Magog, and Madai, and Javan, 1Chr 1:5
And the sons of G 1Chr 1:6
*2. Descendants of Gomer 1.*
G, and all his bands Eze 38:6
*3. Wife of Hosea.*
took G the daughter of Diblaim Hos 1:3

**GOMORRAH** (*go-mor'-rah*) See GOMORRHA. *City destroyed by God.*

as thou goest, unto Sodom, and G Gen 10:19
the LORD destroyed Sodom and G Gen 13:10
Sodom, and with Birsha king of G Gen 14:2
king of Sodom, and the king of G Gen 14:8
of Sodom and G fled, and fell there Gen 14:10
took all the goods of Sodom and G Gen 14:11
G is great, and because their sin Gen 18:20
upon G brimstone and fire from the Gen 19:24
And he looked toward Sodom and G Gen 19:28
like the overthrow of Sodom, and G. Deut 29:23
of Sodom, and of the fields of G Deut 32:32
we should have been like unto G Is 1:9
law of our God, ye people of G Is 1:10
as when God overthrew Sodom and G Is 13:19
and the inhabitants thereof as G Jer 23:14
As in the overthrow of Sodom and G Jer 49:18
As God overthrew Sodom and G Jer 50:40
you, as God overthrew Sodom and G Amos 4:11
and the children of Ammon as G Zeph 2:9
G into ashes condemned them with 2Pet 2:6

**GOMORRHA** (*go-mor'-rah*) See GOMORRAH. *Greek form of Gomorrah.*

G in the day of judgment, than Mt 10:15
G in the day of judgment, than Mk 6:11
Sodoma, and been made like unto G Rom 9:29
Even as Sodom and G, and the cities Jude 7

**GONE**

Jacob was yet scarce g out from Gen 27:30
mother, and was g to Padan-aram Gen 28:7
though thou wouldest needs be g Gen 31:30
our daughter, and we will be g Gen 34:17
of your households, and be g Gen 42:33
when they were g out of the city, Gen 44:4
the prey, my son, thou art g up Gen 49:9
As soon as I am g out of the city Ex 9:29
herds, as ye have said, and be g Ex 12:32
And when the dew that lay was g up Ex 16:14
the children of Israel were g Ex 19:1
Moses, until he was g into the Ex 33:8
after whom they have g a whoring Lev 17:7
if thou hast not g aside to Num 5:19
But if thou hast g aside to Num 5:20

when Moses was g into the Num 7:89
which we have g to search it Num 13:32
is wrath g out from the LORD Num 16:46
there is a fire g out of Heshbon Num 21:28
When I was g up into the mount to Deut 9:9
are g out from among you, and have Deut 13:13
And hath g and served other gods, Deut 17:3
That which is g out of thy lips Deut 23:23
shall be when ye be g over Jordan Deut 27:4
he seeth that their power is g Deut 32:36
pursued after them were g out Josh 2:7
before us, until we were g over Josh 4:23
commanded you, and have g Josh 23:16
When he was g out, his servants Judg 3:24
Abinoam was g up to mount Tabor Judg 4:12
is not the LORD g out before thee Judg 4:14
and the priest, and ye are g away Judg 18:24
of Israel were g up to Mizpeh Judg 20:3
of the LORD is g out against me Ruth 1:13
in law is g back unto her people Ruth 1:15
knew not that Jonathan was g 1Sa 14:3
now, and see who is g from us 1Sa 14:17
is g about, and passed on 1Sa 15:12
and g down to Gilgal 1Sa 15:12
have g the way which the LORD 1Sa 15:20
And as soon as the lad was g 1Sa 20:41
when the wine was g out of Nabal 1Sa 25:37
in the morning the people had g 2Sa 2:27
Wherefore hast thou g in unto my 2Sa 3:7
him away, and he was g in peace 2Sa 3:22
him away, and he is g in peace 2Sa 3:23
sent him away, and he is quite g 2Sa 3:24
ark of the LORD had g six paces 2Sa 6:13
Amnon said unto her, Arise, be g 2Sa 13:15
They be g over the brook of water 2Sa 17:20
them that was not g over Jordan 2Sa 17:22
and the men of Israel were g away 2Sa 23:9
So when they had g through all 2Sa 24:8
For he is g down this day, and 1Kin 1:25
had g from Jerusalem to Gath 1Kin 2:41
Pharaoh king of Egypt had g up 1Kin 9:16
host was g up to bury the slain 1Kin 11:15
And when he was g, a lion met him 1Kin 13:24
for thou hast g and made thee 1Kin 14:9
away dung, till it be all g 1Kin 14:10
pass, as soon as I am g from thee 1Kin 18:12
was busy here and there, he was g 1Kin 20:40
whither he is g down to possess 1Kin 21:18
the messenger that was g to call 1Kin 22:13
that bed on which thou art g up 2Kin 1:4
that bed on which thou art g up 2Kin 1:6
that bed on which thou art g up 2Kin 1:16
to pass, when they were g over 2Kin 2:9
And the Syrians had g out by 2Kin 5:2
and g forth, behold, an host 2Kin 6:15
therefore are they g out of the 2Kin 7:12
afore Isaiah was g out into the 2Kin 20:4
by which it had g down in the 2Kin 20:11
for God is g forth before thee to 1Chr 14:15
but have g from tent to tent, and 1Chr 17:5
of their feasting were g about Job 1:5
shall I arise, and the night be g Job 7:4
me on every side, and I am g Job 19:10
Neither have I g back from the Job 23:12
for a little while, but are g Job 24:24
up, they are g away from men Job 28:4
They are all g aside, they are Ps 14:3
Their line is g out through all Ps 19:4
iniquities are g over mine head Ps 38:4
mine eyes, it also is g from me Ps 38:10
for I had g with the multitude, I Ps 42:4
and thy billows are g over me Ps 42:7
God is g up with a shout, the Ps 47:5
after he had g in to Bath-sheba Ps 51:t
Every one of them is g back Ps 53:3
as for me, my feet were almost g Ps 73:2
Is his mercy clean g for ever Ps 77:8
thing that is g out of my lips Ps 89:34
wind passeth over it, and it is g Ps 103:16
I am g like the shadow when it Ps 109:23
I have g astray like a lost sheep Ps 119:176
the stream had g over our soul Ps 124:4
proud waters had g over our soul Ps 124:5
at home, he is g a long journey Prov 7:19
but when he is g his way, then he Prov 20:14
g from the place of the holy, and Eccl 8:10
is past, the rain is over and g Song 2:11
had withdrawn himself, and was g Song 5:6
Whither is thy beloved g, O thou Song 6:1
My beloved is g down into his Song 6:2
anger, they are g away backward Is 1:4
my people are g into captivity Is 5:13
They are g over the passage Is 10:29
He is g up to Bajith, and to Dibon Is 15:2
For the cry is g round about the Is 15:8
out, they are g over the sea Is 16:8
art wholly g up to the housetops Is 22:1
the mirth of the land is g Is 24:11
which is g down in the sun dial Is 38:8
by which degrees it was g down Is 38:8
that he had not g with his feet Is 41:3
the word is g out of my mouth in Is 45:23
themselves are g into captivity Is 46:2
my salvation is g forth, and mine Is 51:5
All we like sheep have g astray Is 53:6
to another than me, and art g up Is 57:8
me, that they are g far from me Jer 2:5
I have not g after Baalim Jer 2:23
she is g up upon every high Jer 3:6
he is g forth from his place to Jer 4:7
they are revolted and g Jer 5:23
beast are fled; they are g Jer 9:10
my children are g forth of me Jer 10:20
and the cry of Jerusalem is g up Jer 14:2
the LORD, thou art g backward Jer 15:6
her sun is g down while it was Jer 15:9
g forth into all the land Jer 23:15
of the LORD is g forth in fury Jer 23:19
g forth with you into captivity Jer 29:16
army, which are g up from you Jer 34:21
Now while he was not yet g back Jer 40:5
Egypt, whither ye be g to dwell Jer 44:8
which are g into the land of Jer 44:14
that are g into the land of Egypt Jer 44:28
neither hath he g into captivity Jer 48:11
g up out of her cities, and his Jer 48:15
men are g down to the slaughter Jer 48:15
thy plants are g over the sea Jer 48:32
they have g from mountain to hill Jer 50:6
Judah is g into captivity because Lam 1:3
her children are g into captivity Lam 1:5
they are g without strength Lam 1:6
my young men are g into captivity Lam 1:18
the morning is g forth Eze 7:10
Israel was g up from the cherub Eze 9:3
Ye have not g up into the gaps, Eze 13:5
fire is g out of a rod of her Eze 19:14
because thou hast g a whoring Eze 23:30
and whose scum is not g out of it Eze 24:6
earth are g down from his shadow Eze 31:12
they are g down, they lie Eze 32:21
which are g down uncircumcised Eze 32:24
which are g down to hell with Eze 32:27
which are g down with the slain Eze 32:30
are g forth out of his land Eze 36:20
the heathen, whither they be g Eze 37:21
that are g away far from me Eze 44:10
Chaldeans, The thing is g from me Dan 2:5
ye see the thing is g from me Dan 2:8
which was g forth to slay the Dan 2:14
and when I am g forth, lo, the Dan 10:20
they have g a whoring from under Hos 4:12
For they are g up to Assyria, a Hos 8:9
for thou hast g a whoring from Hos 9:1
they are g because of destruction Hos 9:6
When will the new moon be g Amos 8:5
But Jonah was g down into the Jonah 1:5
for they are g into captivity Mic 1:16
the gate, and are g out by it Mic 2:13
are g away from mine ordinances Mal 3:7
Ye shall not have g over the Mt 10:23
unclean spirit is g out of a man Mt 12:43
And when they were g over, they Mt 14:34
sheep, and one of them be g astray Mt 18:12
and seeketh that which is g astray Mt 18:12
for our lamps are g out Mt 25:8
when he was g out into the porch, Mt 26:71
when he had g a little farther Mk 1:19
that virtue had g out of him Mk 5:30
the devil is g out of thy Mk 7:29
house, she found the devil g out Mk 7:30
when he was g forth into the way, Mk 10:17
as the angels were g away from Lk 2:15
the fishermen were g out of them Lk 5:2
that virtue is g out of me Lk 8:46
to pass, when the devil was g out Lk 11:14
unclean spirit is g out of a man Lk 11:24
That he was g to be guest with a Lk 19:7
as though he would have g further Lk 24:28
(For his disciples were g away Jn 4:8
his disciples were g away alone Jn 6:22
But when his brethren were g up Jn 7:10
behold, the world is g after him Jn 12:19
Therefore, when he was g out Jn 13:31
when they had g through the isle Acts 13:6
when the Jews were g out of the Acts 13:42
Now when they had g throughout Acts 16:6
the hope of their gains was g Acts 16:19
g up, and saluted the church, he Acts 18:22
when he had g over those parts, Acts 20:2
among whom I have g preaching the Acts 20:25
Who also hath g about to profane Acts 24:6
And when they were g aside Acts 26:31
when they had g a little further, Acts 27:28
They are all g out of the way, Rom 3:12
Who is g into heaven, and is on 1Pet 3:22
are g astray, following the way 2Pet 2:15
prophets are g out into the world 1Jn 4:1
for they have g in the way of Jude 11

**GOOD** See PREFACE.

**GOODLIER**
of Israel a g person than he 1Sa 9:2

**GOODLIEST**
your g young men, and your asses, 1Sa 8:16
also and thy children, even the g 1Kin 20:3

**GOODLINESS**
all the g thereof is as the Is 40:6

**GOODLY**
Rebekah took g raiment of her Gen 27:15
And Joseph was a g person, and well Gen 39:6
he giveth g words Gen 49:21
she saw him that he was a g child Ex 2:2
g bonnets of fine linen, and linen Ex 39:28
first day the boughs of g trees Lev 23:40
How g are thy tents, O Jacob, and Num 24:5
dwelt, and all their g castles Num 31:10
that g mountain, and Lebanon Deut 3:25
g cities, which thou buildedst Deut 6:10
art full, and hast built g houses Deut 8:12
the spoils a g Babylonish garment Josh 7:21
Saul, a choice young man, and a g 1Sa 9:2
countenance, and g to look to 1Sa 16:12
And he slew an Egyptian, a g man 2Sa 23:21
and he also was a very g man 1Kin 1:6
with the g vessels of the house 2Chr 36:10
all the g vessels thereof 2Chr 36:19
Gavest thou the g wings unto the Job 39:13
yea, I have a g heritage Ps 16:6
thereof were like the g cedars Ps 80:10
a g heritage of the hosts of Jer 3:19
olive tree, fair, and of g fruit Jer 11:16
fruit, that it might be a g vine Eze 17:8
and bear fruit, and be a g cedar Eze 17:23
his land they have made g images Hos 10:1
your temples my g pleasant things Joel 3:5
them as his g horse in the battle Zec 10:3
a g price that I was prised at of Zec 11:13
a merchant man, seeking g pearls Mt 13:45
how it was adorned with g stones Lk 21:5
in g apparel, and there come in Jas 2:2
g are departed from thee, and thou Rev 18:14

**GOODMAN**
For the g is not at home, he is Prov 7:19
against the g of the house Mt 20:11
that if the g of the house had Mt 24:43
in, say ye to the g of the house Mk 14:14
that if the g of the house had Lk 12:39
shall say unto the g of the house Lk 22:11

**GOODNESS**
the g which the LORD had done to Ex 18:9
make all my g pass before thee Ex 33:19
longsuffering, and abundant in g Ex 34:6
that what g the LORD shall do Num 10:32
according to all the g which he Judg 8:35
promised this g unto thy servant 2Sa 7:28
glad of heart for all the g that 1Kin 8:66
promised this g unto thy servant 1Chr 17:26
and let thy saints rejoice in g 2Chr 6:41
merry in heart for the g that the 2Chr 7:10
of the acts of Hezekiah, and his g 2Chr 32:32
of the acts of Josiah, and his g 2Chr 35:26
themselves in thy great g Neh 9:25
in thy great g that thou gavest Neh 9:35
my g extendeth not to thee Ps 16:2
him with the blessings of g Ps 21:3
Surely g and mercy shall follow me Ps 23:6
I had believed to see the g of Ps 27:13
Oh how great is thy g, which thou Ps 31:19
is full of the g of the LORD Ps 33:5
the g of God endureth continually Ps 52:1
satisfied with the g of thy house Ps 65:4
Thou crownest the year with thy g Ps 65:11
prepared of thy g for the poor Ps 68:10
would praise the LORD for his g Ps 107:8
and filleth the hungry soul with g Ps 107:9
would praise the LORD for his g Ps 107:15
would praise the LORD for his g Ps 107:21
would praise the LORD for his g Ps 107:31
My g, and my fortress Ps 144:2
utter the memory of thy great g Ps 145:7
will proclaim every one his own g Prov 20:6
the great g toward the house of Is 63:7
fruit thereof and the g thereof Jer 2:7
together to the g of the LORD Jer 31:12
shall be satisfied with my g Jer 31:14
fear and tremble for all the g Jer 33:9
LORD and his g in the latter days Hos 3:5
for your g is as a morning cloud, Hos 6:4
according to the g of his land Hos 10:1
For how great is his g, and how Zec 9:17
thou the riches of his g and Rom 2:4
not knowing that the g of God Rom 2:4
Behold therefore the g and Rom 11:22
but toward thee, g Rom 11:22
if thou continue in his g Rom 11:22
that ye also are full of g Rom 15:14
longsuffering, gentleness, g Gal 5:22
fruit of the Spirit is in all g Eph 5:9
all the good pleasure of his g 2Th 1:11

**GOODNESS'**
remember thou me for thy g sake Ps 25:7

**GOODS**
And they took all the g of Sodom Gen 14:11
son, who dwelt in Sodom, and his g Gen 14:12
And he brought back all the g Gen 14:16
again his brother Lot, and his g Gen 14:16
persons, and take the g to thyself Gen 14:21
for all the g of his master were Gen 24:10
all his g which he had gotten, Gen 31:18
took their cattle, and their g Gen 46:6
his hand unto his neighbour's g Ex 22:8
his hand unto his neighbour's g Ex 22:11
unto Korah, and all their g Num 16:32
all their flocks, and all their g Num 31:9
for their cattle, and for their g Num 35:3
shall make thee plenteous in g Deut 28:11
and thy wives, and all thy g 2Chr 21:14
silver, and with gold, and with g Ezr 1:4
of silver, with gold, with g Ezr 1:6
that of the king's g, even of the Ezr 6:8
or to confiscation of g, or to Ezr 7:26
and possessed houses full of all g Neh 9:25
his hands shall restore their g Job 20:10
shall no man look for his g Job 20:21
his g shall flow away in the day Job 20:28
When g increase, they are Eccl 5:11

which have gotten cattle and g ... Eze 38:12
and gold, to take away cattle and g ... Eze 38:13
Therefore their g shall become a ... Zeph 1:13
man's house, and spoil his g ... Mt 12:29
make him ruler over all his g ... Mt 24:47
and delivered unto them his g ... Mt 25:14
man's house, and spoil his g ... Mk 3:27
away thy g ask them not again ... Lk 6:30
his palace, his g are in peace ... Lk 11:21
I bestow all my fruits and my g ... Lk 12:18
thou hast much g laid up for many ... Lk 12:19
portion of g that falleth to me ... Lk 15:12
unto him that he had wasted his g ... Lk 16:1
the half of my g I give to the ... Lk 19:8
And sold their possessions and g ... Acts 2:45
bestow all my g to feed the poor ... 1Cor 13:3
joyfully the spoiling of your g ... Heb 10:34
I am rich, and increased with g ... Rev 3:17

### GOPHER
Make thee an ark of g wood ... Gen 6:14

### GORE
If an ox g a man or a woman, that ... Ex 21:28

### GORED
Whether he have g a son ... Ex 21:31
or have g a daughter, according ... Ex 21:31

### GORGEOUS
him, and arrayed him in a g robe ... Lk 23:11

### GORGEOUSLY
captains and rulers clothed most g ... Eze 23:12
they which are g apparelled ... Lk 7:25

### GOSHEN (*go'-shen*)
*1. A district of Egypt.*
thou shalt dwell in the land of G ... Gen 45:10
Joseph, to direct his face unto G ... Gen 46:28
and they came into the land of G ... Gen 46:28
to meet Israel his father, to G ... Gen 46:29
ye may dwell in the land of G ... Gen 46:34
behold, they are in the land of G ... Gen 47:1
servants dwell in the land of G ... Gen 47:4
in the land of G let them dwell ... Gen 47:6
of Egypt, in the country of G ... Gen 47:27
herds, they left in the land of G ... Gen 50:8
sever in that day the land of G ... Ex 8:22
Only in the land of G, where the ... Ex 9:26
*2. A district in southern Palestine.*
Gaza, and all the country of G ... Josh 10:41
country, and all the land of G ... Josh 11:16
*3. A town in Judea.*
And G, and Holon, and Giloh ... Josh 15:51

### GOSPEL
preaching the g of the kingdom, ... Mt 4:23
preaching the g of the kingdom, ... Mt 9:35
poor have the g preached to them ... Mt 11:5
this g of the kingdom shall be ... Mt 24:14
Wheresoever this g shall be ... Mt 26:13
of the g of Jesus Christ, the Son ... Mk 1:1
preaching the g of the kingdom of ... Mk 1:14
repent ye, and believe the g ... Mk 1:15
the g must first be published ... Mk 13:10
Wheresoever this g shall be ... Mk 14:9
preach the g to every creature ... Mk 16:15
me to preach the g to the poor ... Lk 4:18
to the poor the g is preached ... Lk 7:22
the towns, preaching the g ... Lk 9:6
in the temple, and preached the g ... Lk 20:1
preached the g in many villages ... Acts 8:25
And there they preached the g ... Acts 14:7
had preached the g to that city ... Acts 14:21
should hear the word of the g ... Acts 15:7
us for to preach the g unto them ... Acts 16:10
to testify the g of the grace of ... Acts 20:24
separated unto the g of God ... Rom 1:1
my spirit in the g of his Son ... Rom 1:9
I am ready to preach the g to you ... Rom 1:15
am not ashamed of the g of Christ ... Rom 1:16
by Jesus Christ according to my g ... Rom 2:16
them that preach the g of peace ... Rom 10:15
they have not all obeyed the g ... Rom 10:16
As concerning the g, they are ... Rom 11:28
ministering the g of God ... Rom 15:16
fully preached the g of Christ ... Rom 15:19
so have I strived to preach the g ... Rom 15:20
the blessing of the g of Christ ... Rom 15:29
to stablish you according to my g ... Rom 16:25
to baptize, but to preach the g ... 1Cor 1:17
I have begotten you through the g ... 1Cor 4:15
we should hinder the g of Christ ... 1Cor 9:12
the g should live of the g ... 1Cor 9:14
For though I preach the g ... 1Cor 9:16
is unto me, if I preach not the g ... 1Cor 9:16
of the g is committed unto me ... 1Cor 9:17
Verily that, when I preach the g ... 1Cor 9:18
I may make the g of Christ ... 1Cor 9:18
I abuse not my power in the g ... 1Cor 9:18
I declare unto you the g which I ... 1Cor 15:1
to Troas to preach Christ's g ... 2Cor 2:12
But if our g be hid, it is hid to ... 2Cor 4:3
light of the glorious g of Christ ... 2Cor 4:4
brother, whose praise is in the g ... 2Cor 8:18
subjection unto the g of Christ ... 2Cor 9:13
also in preaching the g of Christ ... 2Cor 10:14
To preach the g in the regions ... 2Cor 10:16
have not received, or another g ... 2Cor 11:4
to you the g of God freely ... 2Cor 11:7
grace of Christ unto another g ... Gal 1:6
and would pervert the g of Christ ... Gal 1:7
preach any other g unto you than ... Gal 1:8
g unto you than that ye have ... Gal 1:9
that the g which was preached of ... Gal 1:11
that g which I preach among the ... Gal 2:2
that the truth of the g might ... Gal 2:5
when they saw that the g of the ... Gal 2:7
as the g of the circumcision was ... Gal 2:7
according to the truth of the g ... Gal 2:14
before the g unto Abraham ... Gal 3:8
the g unto you at the first ... Gal 4:13
of truth, the g of your salvation ... Eph 1:13
of his promise in Christ by the g ... Eph 3:6
the preparation of the g of peace ... Eph 6:15
make known the mystery of the g ... Eph 6:19
For your fellowship in the g from ... Phil 1:5
defence and comfirmation of the g ... Phil 1:7
unto the furtherance of the g ... Phil 1:12
I am set for the defence of the g ... Phil 1:17
be as it becometh the g of Christ ... Phil 1:27
together for the faith of the g ... Phil 1:27
he hath served with me in the g ... Phil 2:22
which laboured with me in the g ... Phil 4:3
that in the beginning of the g ... Phil 4:15
in the word of the truth of the g ... Col 1:5
moved away from the hope of the g ... Col 1:23
For our g came not unto you in ... 1Th 1:5
the g of God with much contention ... 1Th 2:2
God to be put in trust with the g ... 1Th 2:4
not the g of God only, but also ... 1Th 2:8
we preached unto you the g of God ... 1Th 2:9
fellowlabourer in the g of Christ ... 1Th 3:2
that obey not the g of our Lord ... 2Th 1:8
Whereunto he called you by our g ... 2Th 2:14
the glorious g of the blessed God ... 1Ti 1:11
of the afflictions of the g ... 2Ti 1:8
to light through the g ... 2Ti 1:10
from the dead according to my g ... 2Ti 2:8
unto me in the bonds of the g ... Philem 13
For unto us was the g preached ... Heb 4:2
g unto you with the Holy Ghost ... 1Pet 1:12
by the g is preached unto you ... 1Pet 1:25
For for this cause was the g ... 1Pet 4:6
them that obey not the g of God ... 1Pet 4:17
having the everlasting g to ... Rev 14:6

### GOSPEL'S
his life for my sake and the g ... Mk 8:35
or lands, for my sake, and the g ... Mk 10:29
And this I do for the g sake ... 1Cor 9:23

### GOT
which he had g in the land of ... Gen 36:6
her hand, and fled, and g him out ... Gen 39:12
with me, and fled, and g him out ... Gen 39:15
For they g not the land in ... Ps 44:3
I g me servants and maidens, and ... Eccl 2:7
So I g a girdle according to the ... Jer 13:2
Take the girdle that thou hast g ... Jer 13:4

### GOTTEN
I have g a man from the LORD ... Gen 4:1
souls that they had g in Haran ... Gen 12:5
father's hath he g all this glory ... Gen 31:1
and all his goods which he had g ... Gen 31:18
which he had g in Padan-aram, for ... Gen 31:18
which they had g in the land of ... Gen 46:6
when I have g me honour upon ... Ex 14:18
thing which he hath deceitfully g ... Lev 6:4
the LORD, what every man hath g ... Num 31:50
mine hand hath g me this wealth ... Deut 8:17
if he be g into a city, then ... 2Sa 17:13
It cannot be g for gold, neither ... Job 28:15
and because mine hand had g much ... Job 31:25
holy arm, hath g him the victory ... Ps 98:1
Wealth g by vanity shall be ... Prov 13:11
An inheritance may be g hastily ... Prov 20:21
have g more wisdom than all they ... Eccl 1:16
the abundance they have g ... Is 15:7
that he hath g are perished ... Jer 48:36
thou hast g thee riches, and hast ... Eze 28:4
thee riches, and hast g gold ... Eze 28:4
the nations, which have g cattle ... Eze 38:12
hast g thee renown, as at this ... Dan 9:15
that after we were g from them ... Acts 21:1
them that had g the victory over ... Rev 15:2

### GOURD
And the LORD God prepared a g ... Jonah 4:6
Jonah was exceeding glad of the g ... Jonah 4:6
it smote the g that it withered ... Jonah 4:7
thou well to be angry for the g ... Jonah 4:9
LORD, Thou hast had pity on the g ... Jonah 4:10

### GOURDS
thereof wild g his lap full ... 2Kin 4:39

### GOVERN
Dost thou now g the kingdom of ... 1Kin 21:7
Shall even he that hateth right g ... Job 34:17
and g the nations upon earth ... Ps 67:4

### GOVERNMENT
the g shall be upon his shoulder ... Is 9:6
Of the increase of his g and peace ... Is 9:7
I will commit thy g into his hand ... Is 22:21
lust of uncleanness, and despise g ... 2Pet 2:10

### GOVERNMENTS
then gifts of healings, helps, g ... 1Cor 12:28

### GOVERNOR
And Joseph was the g over the land ... Gen 42:6
he is g over all the land of ... Gen 45:26
which was the g of his house ... 1Kin 18:3
back unto Amon the g of the city ... 1Kin 22:26
gate of Joshua the g of the city ... 2Kin 23:8
of Babylon had made Gedaliah g ... 2Kin 25:23
unto the LORD to be the chief g ... 1Chr 29:22
to every g in all Israel, the ... 2Chr 1:2
back to Amon the g of the city ... 2Chr 18:25
Azrikam the g of the house, and ... 2Chr 28:7
and Maaseiah the g of the city ... 2Chr 34:8
g on this side the river, and ... Ezr 5:3
g on this side the river, and ... Ezr 5:6
Sheshbazzar, whom he had made g ... Ezr 5:14
Tatnai, g beyond the river, ... Ezr 6:6
let the g of the Jews and the ... Ezr 6:7
g on this side the river, ... Ezr 6:13
of the g on this side the river ... Neh 3:7
be their g in the land of Judah ... Neh 5:14
have not eaten the bread of the g ... Neh 5:14
required not I the bread of the g ... Neh 5:18
and in the days of Nehemiah the g ... Neh 12:26
he is the g among the nations ... Ps 22:28
who was also chief g in the house ... Jer 20:1
their g shall proceed from the ... Jer 30:21
made g over the cities of Judah ... Jer 40:5
the son of Ahikam g in the land ... Jer 40:7
Babylon had made g over the land ... Jer 41:2
of Babylon made g in the land ... Jer 41:18
g of Judah, and to Joshua the son ... Hag 1:1
g of Judah, and the spirit of ... Hag 1:14
g of Judah, and to Joshua the son ... Hag 2:2
g of Judah, saying, I will shake ... Hag 2:21
and he shall be as a g in Judah ... Zec 9:7
offer it now unto thy g ... Mal 1:8
for out of thee shall come a G ... Mt 2:6
him to Pontius Pilate the g ... Mt 27:2
And Jesus stood before the g ... Mt 27:11
the g asked him, saying, Art thou ... Mt 27:11
that the g marvelled greatly ... Mt 27:14
Now at that feast the g was wont ... Mt 27:15
The g answered and said unto them, ... Mt 27:21
the g said, Why, what evil hath ... Mt 27:23
Then the soldiers of the g took ... Mt 27:27
made when Cyrenius was g of Syria ... Lk 2:2
Pontius Pilate being g of Judaea ... Lk 3:1
the power and authority of the g ... Lk 20:20
and bear unto the g of the feast ... Jn 2:8
the g of the feast called the ... Jn 2:9
and he made him g over Egypt ... Acts 7:10
bring him safe unto Felix the g ... Acts 23:24
g Felix sendeth greeting ... Acts 23:26
and delivered the epistle to the g ... Acts 23:33
when the g had read the letter, ... Acts 23:34
who informed the g against Paul ... Acts 24:1
after that the g had beckoned ... Acts 24:10
the king rose up, and the g ... Acts 26:30
In Damascus the g under Aretas ... 2Cor 11:32
helm, whithersoever the g listeth ... Jas 3:4

### GOVERNOR'S
And if this come to the g ears ... Mt 28:14

### GOVERNORS
heart is toward the g of Israel ... Judg 5:9
out of Machir came down g ... Judg 5:14
and of the g of the country ... 1Kin 10:15
for the g of the sanctuary, and ... 1Chr 24:5
g of the house of God, were of ... 1Chr 24:5
g of the country brought gold and ... 2Chr 9:14
the g of the people, and all the ... 2Chr 23:20
to the g on this side the river ... Ezr 8:36
me to the g beyond the river ... Neh 2:7
I came to the g beyond the river ... Neh 2:9
But the former g that had been ... Neh 5:15
to the g that were over every ... Est 3:12
chief of the g over all the wise ... Dan 2:48
together the princes, the g ... Dan 3:2
Then the princes, the g, and ... Dan 3:3
And the princes, g, and captains, ... Dan 3:27
presidents of the kingdom, the g ... Dan 6:7
the g of Judah shall say in their ... Zec 12:5
In that day will I make the g of ... Zec 12:6
And ye shall be brought before g ... Mt 10:18
g until the time appointed of the ... Gal 4:2
Or unto g, as unto them that are ... 1Pet 2:14

### GOYIM See NATIONS.

### GOZAN (*go'-zan*) *An Assyrian city.*
and in Habor by the river of G ... 2Kin 17:6
and in Habor by the river of G ... 2Kin 18:11
G, and Haran, and Rezeph ... 2Kin 19:12
Habor, and Hara, and to the river G ... 1Chr 5:26
my fathers have destroyed, as G ... Is 37:12

### GRACE
But Noah found g in the eyes of ... Gen 6:8
servant hath found g in thy sight ... Gen 19:19
that I may find g in thy sight ... Gen 32:5
These are to find g in the sight ... Gen 33:8
now I have found g in thy sight ... Gen 33:10
let me find g in the sight of my ... Gen 33:15
Let me find g in your eyes, and ... Gen 34:11
And Joseph found g in his sight ... Gen 39:4
let us find g in the sight of my ... Gen 47:25
now I have found g in thy sight ... Gen 47:29
now I have found g in your eyes ... Gen 50:4
hast also found g in my sight ... Ex 33:12
if I have found g in thy sight ... Ex 33:13
that I may find g in thy sight ... Ex 33:13
people have found g in thy sight ... Ex 33:16
for thou hast found g in my sight ... Ex 33:17
now I have found g in thy sight ... Ex 34:9
if we have found g in thy sight ... Num 32:5
now I have found g in thy sight ... Judg 6:17

him in whose sight I shall find g ... Ruth 2:2
Why have I found g in thine eyes ... Ruth 2:10
handmaid find g in thy sight ... 1Sa 1:18
that I have found g in thine eyes ... 1Sa 20:3
I have now found g in thine eyes ... 1Sa 27:5
that I have found g in thy sight ... 2Sa 14:22
that I may find g in thy sight ... 2Sa 16:4
now for a little space g hath ... Ezr 9:8
all the women, and she obtained g ... Est 2:17
g is poured into thy lips ... Ps 45:2
the LORD will give g and glory ... Ps 84:11
be an ornament of g unto thy head ... Prov 1:9
unto thy soul, and g to thy neck ... Prov 3:22
but he giveth g unto the lowly ... Prov 3:34
to thine head an ornament of g ... Prov 4:9
for the g of his lips the king ... Prov 22:11
sword found g in the wilderness ... Jer 31:2
crying, G, g unto it ... Zec 4:7
of Jerusalem, the spirit of g ... Zec 12:10
the g of God was upon him ... Lk 2:40
of the Father,) full of g ... Jn 1:14
all we received, and g for g ... Jn 1:16
the law was given by Moses, but g ... Jn 1:17
great g was upon them all ... Acts 4:33
he came, and had seen the g of God.. Acts 11:23
them to continue in the g of God ... Acts 13:43
testimony unto the word of his g ... Acts 14:3
had been recommended to the g of ... Acts 14:26
the g of the Lord Jesus Christ we ... Acts 15:11
by the brethren unto the g of God ... Acts 15:40
much which had believed through g.. Acts 18:27
the gospel of the g of God ... Acts 20:24
to God, and to the word of his g ... Acts 20:32
By whom we have received g ... Rom 1:5
G to you and peace from God our ... Rom 1:7
Being justified freely by his g ... Rom 3:24
is the reward not reckoned of g ... Rom 4:4
of faith, that it might be by g ... Rom 4:16
into this g wherein we stand ... Rom 5:2
g of God, and the gift by g ... Rom 5:15
they which receive abundance of g ... Rom 5:17
abounded, g did much more abound ... Rom 5:20
even so might g reign through ... Rom 5:21
in sin, that g may abound ... Rom 6:1
not under the law, but under g ... Rom 6:14
not under the law, but under g ... Rom 6:15
according to the election of g ... Rom 11:5
And if by g, then is it no more of ... Rom 11:6
otherwise g is no more g ... Rom 11:6
be of works, then is it no more g ... Rom 11:6
through the g given unto me, to ... Rom 12:3
to the g that is given to us ... Rom 12:6
because of the g that is given to ... Rom 15:15
The g of our Lord Jesus Christ be ... Rom 16:20
The g of our Lord Jesus Christ be ... Rom 16:24
G be unto you, and peace, from God ... 1Cor 1:3
for the g of God which is given ... 1Cor 1:4
According to the g of God which ... 1Cor 3:10
For if I by g be a partaker, why ... 1Cor 10:30
But by the g of God I am what I ... 1Cor 15:10
his g which was bestowed upon me .. 1Cor 15:10
but the g of God which was with ... 1Cor 15:10
The g of our Lord Jesus Christ be ... 1Cor 16:23
G be to you and peace from God our ... 2Cor 1:2
wisdom, but by the g of God ... 2Cor 1:12
that the abundant g might through ... 2Cor 4:15
receive not the g of God in vain ... 2Cor 6:1
we do you to wit of the g of God ... 2Cor 8:1
finish in you the same g also ... 2Cor 8:6
see that ye abound in this g also ... 2Cor 8:7
For ye know the g of our Lord ... 2Cor 8:9
to travel with us with this g ... 2Cor 8:19
to make all g abound toward you ... 2Cor 9:8
for the exceeding g of God in you ... 2Cor 9:14
My g is sufficient for thee ... 2Cor 12:9
The g of the Lord Jesus Christ, ... 2Cor 13:14
G be to you and peace from God the ... Gal 1:3
him that called you into the g of ... Gal 1:6
womb, and called me by his g ... Gal 1:15
perceived the g that was given ... Gal 2:9
I do not frustrate the g of God ... Gal 2:21
ye are fallen from g ... Gal 5:4
the g of our Lord Jesus Christ be ... Gal 6:18
G be to you, and peace, from God ... Eph 1:2
the praise of the glory of his g ... Eph 1:6
according to the riches of his g ... Eph 1:7
with Christ, (by g ye are saved ... Eph 2:5
his g in his kindness toward us ... Eph 2:7
For by g are ye saved through ... Eph 2:8
of the dispensation of the g of ... Eph 3:2
the g of God given unto me by the ... Eph 3:7
of all saints, is this g given ... Eph 3:8
unto every one of us is given g ... Eph 4:7
may minister g unto the hearers ... Eph 4:29
G be with all them that love our ... Eph 6:24
G be unto you, and peace, from God ... Phil 1:2
ye all are partakers of my g ... Phil 1:7
The g of our Lord Jesus Christ be ... Phil 4:23
G be unto you, and peace, from God ... Col 1:2
knew the g of God in truth ... Col 1:6
singing with g in your hearts to ... Col 3:16
Let your speech be alway with g ... Col 4:6
G be with you ... Col 4:18
G be unto you, and peace, from God ... 1Th 1:1
The g of our Lord Jesus Christ be ... 1Th 5:28
G unto you, and peace, from God ... 2Th 1:2
according to the g of our God ... 2Th 1:12
and good hope through g, ... 2Th 2:16
The g of our Lord Jesus Christ be ... 2Th 3:18
G, mercy, and peace, from God our ... 1Ti 1:2
the g of our Lord was exceeding ... 1Ti 1:14
G be with thee ... 1Ti 6:21
G, mercy, and peace, from God the ... 2Ti 1:2
according to his own purpose and g ... 2Ti 1:9
be strong in the g that is in ... 2Ti 2:1
G be with you ... 2Ti 4:22
G, mercy, and peace, from God the ... Titus 1:4
For the g of God that bringeth ... Titus 2:11
That being justified by his g ... Titus 3:7
G be with you all ... Titus 3:15
G to you, and peace, from God our ... Philem 3
The g of our Lord Jesus Christ be ... Philem 25
that he by the g of God should ... Heb 2:9
come boldly unto the throne of g ... Heb 4:16
find g to help in time of need ... Heb 4:16
done despite unto the Spirit of g ... Heb 10:29
lest any man fail of the g of God ... Heb 12:15
cannot be moved, let us have g ... Heb 12:28
the heart be established with g ... Heb 13:9
G be with you all ... Heb 13:25
the g of the fashion of it ... Jas 1:11
But he giveth more g ... Jas 4:6
but giveth g unto the humble ... Jas 4:6
G unto you, and peace, be ... 1Pet 1:2
who prophesied of the g that ... 1Pet 1:10
hope to the end for the g that is ... 1Pet 1:13
heirs together of the g of life ... 1Pet 3:7
stewards of the manifold g of God ... 1Pet 4:10
proud, and giveth g to the humble ... 1Pet 5:5
But the God of all g, who hath ... 1Pet 5:10
that this is the true g of God ... 1Pet 5:12
G and peace be multiplied unto you ... 2Pet 1:2
But grow in g, and in the ... 2Pet 3:18
G be with you, mercy, and peace, ... 2Jn 3
turning the g of our God into ... Jude 4
G be unto you, and peace, from him ... Rev 1:4
The g of our Lord Jesus Christ be ... Rev 22:21

### GRACIOUS

God be g unto thee, my son ... Gen 43:29
for I am g ... Ex 22:27
be g to whom I will be g ... Ex 33:19
LORD, The LORD God, merciful and g ... Ex 34:6
upon thee, and be g unto thee ... Num 6:25
tell whether GOD will be g to me ... 2Sa 12:22
And the LORD was g unto them ... 2Kin 13:23
for the LORD your God is g ... 2Chr 30:9
thou art a God ready to pardon, g ... Neh 9:17
for thou art a g and merciful God ... Neh 9:31
Then he is g unto him, and saith, ... Job 33:24
Hath God forgotten to be g ... Ps 77:9
a God full of compassion, and g ... Ps 86:15
The LORD is merciful and g ... Ps 103:8
the LORD is g and full of ... Ps 111:4
he is g, and full of compassion, ... Ps 112:4
G is the LORD, and righteous ... Ps 116:5
The LORD is g, and full of ... Ps 145:8
A g woman retaineth honour ... Prov 11:16
words of a wise man's mouth are g ... Eccl 10:12
wait, that he may be g unto you ... Is 30:18
he will be very g unto thee at ... Is 30:19
O LORD, be g unto us ... Is 33:2
how g shalt thou be when pangs ... Jer 22:23
for he is g and merciful, slow to ... Joel 2:13
be g unto the remnant of Joseph ... Amos 5:15
for I knew that thou art a g God ... Jonah 4:2
God that he will be g unto us ... Mal 1:9
wondered at the g words which ... Lk 4:22
ye have tasted that the Lord is g ... 1Pet 2:3

### GRACIOUSLY

God hath g given thy servant ... Gen 33:5
because God hath dealt g with me ... Gen 33:11
and grant me thy law g ... Ps 119:29
all iniquity, and receive us g ... Hos 14:2

### GRAFF

God is able to g them in again ... Rom 11:23

### GRAFFED

wert g in among them, and with ... Rom 11:17
broken off, that I might be g in ... Rom 11:19
still in unbelief, shall be g in ... Rom 11:23
wert g contrary to nature into a ... Rom 11:24
be g into their own olive tree ... Rom 11:24

### GRAIN

the least g fall upon the earth ... Amos 9:9
is like to a g of mustard seed ... Mt 13:31
have faith as a g of mustard seed ... Mt 17:20
It is like a g of mustard seed, ... Mk 4:31
It is like a g of mustard seed, ... Lk 13:19
had faith as a g of mustard seed ... Lk 17:6
body that shall be, but bare g ... 1Cor 15:37
of wheat, or of some other g ... 1Cor 15:37

### GRANDMOTHER

which dwelt first in thy g Lois ... 2Ti 1:5

### GRANT

shall g a redemption for the land ... Lev 25:24
The LORD g you that ye may find ... Ruth 1:9
the God of Israel g thee thy ... 1Sa 1:17
to Ornan, G me the place of this ... 1Chr 21:22
thou shalt g it me for the full ... 1Chr 21:22
them, but I will g them some ... 2Chr 12:7
according to the g that they had ... Ezr 3:7
g him mercy in the sight of this ... Neh 1:11
please the king to g my petition ... Est 5:8
that God would g me the thing ... Job 6:8
G thee according to thine own ... Ps 20:4
O LORD, and g us thy salvation ... Ps 85:7
and g me thy law graciously ... Ps 119:29
G not, O LORD, the desires of the ... Ps 140:8
G that these my two sons may sit, ... Mt 20:21
G unto us that we may sit, one on ... Mk 10:37
That he would g unto us, that we, ... Lk 1:74
g unto thy servants, that with ... Acts 4:29
and consolation g you to be ... Rom 15:5
That he would g you, according to ... Eph 3:16
The Lord g unto him that he may ... 2Ti 1:18
I g to sit with me in my throne ... Rev 3:21

### GRANTED

God g him that which he requested ... 1Chr 4:10
and knowledge is g unto thee ... 2Chr 1:12
the king g him all his request, ... Ezr 7:6
And the king g me, according to ... Neh 2:8
and it shall be g thee ... Est 5:6
and it shall be g thee ... Est 7:2
Wherein the king g the Jews which ... Est 8:11
and it shall be g thee ... Est 9:12
let it be g to the Jews which are ... Est 9:13
Thou hast g me life and favour, and ... Job 10:12
of the righteous shall be g ... Prov 10:24
a murderer to be g unto you ... Acts 3:14
Gentiles g repentance unto life ... Acts 11:18
g signs and wonders to be done by ... Acts 14:3
to her was g that she should be ... Rev 19:8

### GRAPE

gather every g of thy vineyard ... Lev 19:10
drink the pure blood of the g ... Deut 32:14
off his unripe g as the vine ... Job 15:33
the tender g give a good smell ... Song 2:13
whether the tender g appear ... Song 7:12
the sour g is ripening in the ... Is 18:5
The fathers have eaten a sour g ... Jer 31:29
every man that eateth the sour g ... Jer 31:30

### GRAPEGATHERER

hand as a g into the baskets ... Jer 6:9

### GRAPEGATHERERS

If g come to thee, would they not ... Jer 49:9
if the g came to thee, would they ... Obad 5

### GRAPEGLEANINGS

fruits, as the g of the vintage ... Mic 7:1

### GRAPES

thereof brought forth ripe g ... Gen 40:10
and I took the g, and pressed them ... Gen 40:11
and his clothes in the blood of g ... Gen 49:11
neither gather the g of thy vine ... Lev 25:5
nor gather the g in it of thy ... Lev 25:11
liquor of g, nor eat moist g ... Num 6:3
was the time of the firstripe g ... Num 13:20
a branch with one cluster of g ... Num 13:23
because of the cluster of g which ... Num 13:24
then thou mayest eat g thy fill ... Deut 23:24
gatherest the g of thy vineyard ... Deut 24:21
and shalt not gather the g thereof ... Deut 28:30
of the wine, nor gather the g ... Deut 28:39
their g are g of gall ... Deut 32:32
the g of Ephraim better than the ... Judg 8:2
their vineyards, and trode the g ... Judg 9:27
as also wine, g, and figs, and all ... Neh 13:15
for our vines have tender g ... Song 2:15
and thy breasts to clusters of g ... Song 7:7
that it should bring forth g ... Is 5:2
and it brought forth wild g ... Is 5:2
that it should bring forth g ... Is 5:4
brought it forth wild g ... Is 5:4
Yet gleaning g shall be left in ... Is 17:6
as the gleaning g when the ... Is 24:13
there shall be no g on the vine ... Jer 8:13
a shout, as they that tread the g ... Jer 25:30
they not leave some gleaning g ... Jer 49:9
The fathers have eaten sour g ... Eze 18:2
Israel like g in the wilderness ... Hos 9:10
the treader of g him that soweth ... Amos 9:13
thee, would they not leave some g ... Obad 5
Do men gather g of thorns ... Mt 7:16
of a bramble bush gather they g ... Lk 6:44
for her g are fully ripe ... Rev 14:18

### GRASS

said, Let the earth bring forth g ... Gen 1:11
And the earth brought forth g ... Gen 1:12
ox licketh up the g of the field ... Num 22:4
I will send g in thy fields for ... Deut 11:15
nor any g groweth therein, like ... Deut 29:23
and as the showers upon the g ... Deut 32:2
as the tender g springing out of ... 2Sa 23:4
we may find g to save the horses ... 1Kin 18:5
they were as the g of the field ... 2Kin 19:26
as the g on the house tops, and as ... 2Kin 19:26
offspring as the g of the earth ... Job 5:25
the wild ass bray when he hath g ... Job 6:5
he eateth g as an ox ... Job 40:15
shall soon be cut down like the g ... Ps 37:2
down like rain upon the mown g ... Ps 72:6
flourish like g of the earth ... Ps 72:16
they are like g which groweth up ... Ps 90:5
When the wicked spring as the g ... Ps 92:7
is smitten, and withered like g ... Ps 102:4
and I am withered like g ... Ps 102:11
As for man, his days are as g ... Ps 103:15
He causeth the g to grow for the ... Ps 104:14
similitude of an ox that eateth g ... Ps 106:20
be as the g upon the housetops ... Ps 129:6
who maketh g to grow upon the ... Ps 147:8
his favour is as dew upon the g ... Prov 19:12
the tender g sheweth itself, and ... Prov 27:25
the g faileth, there is no green ... Is 15:6

shall be g with reeds and rushes Is 35:7
they were as the g of the field Is 37:27
as the g on the housetops, and as Is 37:27
All flesh is g, and all the Is 40:6
The g withereth, the flower Is 40:7
surely the people is g Is 40:7
The g withereth, the flower Is 40:8
shall spring up as among the g Is 44:4
of man which shall be made as g Is 51:12
it, because there was no g Jer 14:5
did fail, because there was no g Jer 14:6
are grown fat as the heifer at g Jer 50:11
in the tender g of the field Dan 4:15
the beasts in the g of the earth Dan 4:15
in the tender g of the field Dan 4:23
shall make thee to eat g as oxen Dan 4:25
shall make thee to eat g as oxen Dan 4:32
from men, and did eat g as oxen Dan 4:33
they fed him with g like oxen Dan 5:21
end of eating the g of the land Amos 7:2
LORD, as the showers upon the g Mic 5:7
rain, to every one g in the field Zec 10:1
God so clothe the g of the field Mt 6:30
multitude to sit down on the g Mt 14:19
by companies upon the green g Mk 6:39
If then God so clothe the g Lk 12:28
Now there was much g in the place Jn 6:10
of the g he shall pass away Jas 1:10
heat, but it withereth the g Jas 1:11
For all flesh is as g, and all the 1Pet 1:24
glory of man as the flower of g 1Pet 1:24
The g withereth, and the flower 1Pet 1:24
up, and all green g was burnt up Rev 8:7
not hurt the g of the earth Rev 9:4

### GRASSHOPPER
his kind, and the g after his kind Lev 11:22
Canst thou make him afraid as a g Job 39:20
the g shall be a burden, and Eccl 12:5

### GRASSHOPPERS
and we were in our own sight as g Num 13:33
they came as g for multitude Judg 6:5
the valley like g for multitude Judg 7:12
the inhabitants thereof are as g Is 40:22
because they are more than the g Jer 46:23
he formed g in the beginning of Amos 7:1
and thy captains as the great g Nah 3:17

### GRATE
for it a g of network of brass Ex 27:4
burnt offering, with his brasen g Ex 35:16
g of network under the compass Ex 38:4
the four ends of the g of brass Ex 38:5
altar, and the brasen g for it Ex 38:30
his g of brass, his staves, and Ex 39:39

### GRAVE
And Jacob set a pillar upon her g Gen 35:20
of Rachel's g unto this day Gen 35:20
into the g unto my son mourning Gen 37:35
gray hairs with sorrow to the g Gen 42:38
gray hairs with sorrow to the g Gen 44:29
our father with sorrow to the g Gen 44:31
in my g which I have digged for Gen 50:5
g on them the names of the Ex 28:9
g upon it, like the engravings of Ex 28:36
body, or a bone of a man, or a g Num 19:16
or one slain, or one dead, or a g Num 19:18
he bringeth down to the g 1Sa 2:6
voice, and wept at the g of Abner 2Sa 3:32
be buried by the g of my father 2Sa 19:37
head go down to the g in peace 1Kin 2:6
thou down to the g with blood 1Kin 2:9
he laid his carcase in his own g 1Kin 13:30
of Jeroboam shall come to the g 1Kin 14:13
be gathered into thy g in peace 2Kin 22:20
that can skill to g with the 2Chr 2:7
also to g any manner of graving, 2Chr 2:14
be gathered to thy g in peace 2Chr 34:28
glad, when they can find the g Job 3:22
shalt come to thy g in a full age Job 5:26
to the g shall come up no more Job 7:9
carried from the womb to the g Job 10:19
thou wouldest hide me in the g Job 14:13
If I wait, the g is mine house Job 17:13
and in a moment go down to the g Job 21:13
Yet shall he be brought to the g Job 21:32
so doth the g those which have Job 24:19
not stretch out his hand to the g Job 30:24
his soul draweth near unto the g Job 33:22
in the g who shall give thee Ps 6:5
brought up my soul from the g Ps 30:3
and let them be silent in the g Ps 31:17
Like sheep they are laid in the g Ps 49:14
in the g from their dwelling Ps 49:14
my soul from the power of the g Ps 49:15
my life draweth nigh unto the g Ps 88:3
like the slain that lie in the g Ps 88:5
be declared in the g Ps 88:11
his soul from the hand of the g Ps 89:48
us swallow them up alive as the g Prov 1:12
The g; and the barren Prov 30:16
knowledge, nor wisdom, in the g Eccl 9:10
jealousy is cruel as the g Song 8:6
Thy pomp is brought down to the g Is 14:11
thy g like an abominable branch Is 14:19
I shall go to the gates of the g Is 38:10
For the g cannot praise thee, Is 38:18
he made his g with the wicked, and Is 53:9
my mother might have been my g Jer 20:17
down to the g I caused a mourning Eze 31:15
her company is round about her g Eze 32:23
her multitude round about her g Eze 32:24
them from the power of the g Hos 13:14
O g, I will be thy destruction Hos 13:14
I will make thy g Nah 1:14
lain in the g four days already Jn 11:17
goeth unto the g to weep there Jn 11:31
in himself cometh to the g Jn 11:38
he called Lazarus out of his g Jn 12:17
O g, where is thy victory 1Cor 15:55
Likewise must the deacons be g 1Ti 3:8
Even so must their wives be g 1Ti 3:11
That the aged men be sober, g Titus 2:2

### GRAVECLOTHES
forth, bound hand and foot with g Jn 11:44

### GRAVED
he g cherubims, lions, and palm 1Kin 7:36
and g cherubims on the walls 2Chr 3:7

### GRAVEL
his mouth shall be filled with g Prov 20:17
of thy bowels like the g thereof Is 48:19
broken my teeth with g stones Lam 3:16

### GRAVEN
not make unto thee any g image Ex 20:4
writing of God, g upon the tables Ex 32:16
inclosed in ouches of gold, g Ex 39:6
of gold, g, as signets are g Ex 39:6
make you no idols nor g image Lev 26:1
yourselves, and make you a g image Deut 4:16
with you, and make you a g image Deut 4:23
yourselves, and make a g image Deut 4:25
shalt not make thee any g image Deut 5:8
burn their g images with fire Deut 7:5
The g images of their gods shall Deut 7:25
down the g images of their gods Deut 12:3
that maketh any g or molten image Deut 27:15
for my son, to make a g image Judg 17:3
who made thereof a g image Judg 17:4
a g image, and a molten image Judg 18:14
in thither, and took the g image Judg 18:17
the g image, and went in the midst Judg 18:20
of Dan set up the g image Judg 18:30
they set them up Micah's g image Judg 18:31
LORD, and served their g images 2Kin 17:41
he set a g image of the grove 2Kin 21:7
g images, before he was humbled 2Chr 33:19
had beaten the g images into 2Chr 34:7
That they were g with an iron pen Job 19:24
to jealousy with their g images Ps 78:58
be all they that serve g images Ps 97:7
whose g images did excel them of Is 10:10
all the g images of her gods he Is 21:9
of thy g images of silver Is 30:22
The workman melteth a g image Is 40:19
workman to prepare a g image Is 40:20
neither my praise to g images Is 42:8
ashamed, that trust in g images Is 42:17
They that make a g image are all Is 44:9
or molten a g image that is Is 44:10
he maketh it a g image, and Is 44:15
he maketh a god, even his g image Is 44:17
set up the wood of their g image Is 45:20
my g image, and my molten image, Is 48:5
I have g thee upon the palms of Is 49:16
me to anger with their g images Jer 8:19
is confounded by the g image Jer 10:14
it is g upon the table of their Jer 17:1
for it is the land of g images Jer 50:38
is confounded by the g image Jer 51:17
upon the g images of Babylon Jer 51:47
do judgment upon her g images Jer 51:52
and burned incense to g images Hos 11:2
all the g images thereof shall be Mic 1:7
Thy g images also will I cut off, Mic 5:13
gods will I cut off the g image Nah 1:14
What profiteth the g image that Hab 2:18
that the maker thereof hath g it Hab 2:18
stone, g by art and man's device Acts 17:29

### GRAVE'S
are scattered at the g mouth Ps 141:7

### GRAVES
Because there were no g in Egypt Ex 14:11
the powder thereof upon the g of 2Kin 23:6
strowed it upon the g of them 2Chr 34:4
extinct, the g are ready for me Job 17:1
Which remain among the g, and Is 65:4
of Jerusalem, out of their g Jer 8:1
into the g of the common people Jer 26:23
his g are about him Eze 32:22
Whose g are set in the sides of Eze 32:23
her g are round about him Eze 32:25
her g are round about him Eze 32:26
O my people, I will open your g Eze 37:12
you to come up out of your g Eze 37:12
LORD, when I have opened your g Eze 37:13
and brought you up out of your g Eze 37:13
Gog a place there of g in Israel Eze 39:11
And the g were opened Mt 27:52
came out of the g after his Mt 27:53
for ye are as g which appear not, Lk 11:44
are in the g shall hear his voice Jn 5:28
their dead bodies to be put in g Rev 11:9

### GRAVETH
that g an habitation for himself Is 22:16

### GRAVING
and fashioned it with a g tool Ex 32:4
also to grave any manner of g 2Chr 2:14
I will engrave the g thereof Zec 3:9

### GRAVINGS
of it were g with their borders 1Kin 7:31

### GRAVITY
children in subjection with all g 1Ti 3:4
doctrine shewing uncorruptness, g Titus 2:7

### GRAY
then shall ye bring down my g Gen 42:38
ye shall bring down my g hairs Gen 44:29
servants shall bring down the g Gen 44:31
also with the man of g hairs Deut 32:25
g hairs are here and there upon Hos 7:9

### GRAYHEADED
and I am old and g 1Sa 12:2
With us are both the g and very Job 15:10

### GREASE
Their heart is as fat as g Ps 119:70

### GREAT See PREFACE.

### GREATER
the g light to rule the day, and Gen 1:16
punishment is g than I can bear Gen 4:13
There is none g in this house Gen 39:9
the throne will I be g than thou Gen 41:40
brother shall be g than he Gen 48:19
that the LORD is g than all gods Ex 18:11
and will make of thee a g nation Num 14:12
heart, saying, The people is g Deut 1:28
out nations from before thee g Deut 4:38
and the Jebusites, seven nations g Deut 7:1
to go in to possess nations g Deut 9:1
a nation mightier and g than they Deut 9:14
and ye shall possess g nations Deut 11:23
and because it was g than Ai Josh 10:2
had there not been now a much g 1Sa 14:30
wherewith he hated her was g than 2Sa 13:15
g than the other that thou didst 2Sa 13:16
make his throne g than the throne 1Kin 1:37
make his throne g than thy throne 1Kin 1:47
So David waxed g and g 1Chr 11:9
So David waxed g and g 1Chr 11:9
the g house he cieled with fir 2Chr 3:5
man Mordecai waxed g and g Est 9:4
thee, that God is g than man Job 33:12
g than the punishment of the sin Lam 4:6
and thou shalt see g abominations Eze 8:6
thou shalt see g abominations Eze 8:13
thou shalt see g abominations Eze 8:15
the g settle shall be four cubits Eze 43:14
a multitude g than the former Dan 11:13
or their border g than your Amos 6:2
shall be g than of the former Hag 2:9
risen a g than John the Baptist Mt 11:11
kingdom of heaven is g than he Mt 11:11
place is one g than the temple Mt 12:6
behold, a g than Jonas is here Mt 12:41
behold, a g than Solomon is here Mt 12:42
ye shall receive the g damnation Mt 23:14
for whether is g, the gold, or Mt 23:17
for whether is g, the gift, or Mt 23:19
becometh g than all herbs, and Mk 4:32
other commandment g than these Mk 12:31
these shall receive g damnation Mk 12:40
born of women there is not a g Lk 7:28
the kingdom of God is g than he Lk 7:28
behold, a g than Solomon is here Lk 11:31
behold, a g than Jonas is here Lk 11:32
pull down my barns, and build g Lk 12:18
same shall receive g damnation Lk 20:47
For whether is g, he that sitteth Lk 22:27
thou shalt see g things than Jn 1:50
Art thou g than our father Jacob, Jn 4:12
will shew him g works than these Jn 5:20
But I have g witness than that of Jn 5:36
Art thou g than our father Jn 8:53
which gave them me, is g than all Jn 10:29
servant is not g than his lord Jn 13:16
is sent g than he that sent him Jn 13:16
g works than these shall he do Jn 14:12
for my Father is g than I Jn 14:28
G love hath no man than this, Jn 15:13
servant is not g than his lord Jn 15:20
me unto thee hath the g sin Jn 19:11
to lay upon you no g burden than Acts 15:28
for g is he that prophesieth than 1Cor 14:5
of whom the g part remain unto 1Cor 15:6
because he could swear by no g Heb 6:13
For men verily swear by the g Heb 6:16
of good things to come, by a g Heb 9:11
the reproach of Christ g riches Heb 11:26
shall receive the g condemnation Jas 3:1
angels, which are g in power 2Pet 2:11
God is g than our heart, and 1Jn 3:20
because g is he that is in you, 1Jn 4:4
of men, the witness of God is g 1Jn 5:9
I have no g joy than to hear that 3Jn 4

### GREATEST
hundred, and the g over a thousand 1Chr 12:14
for hitherto the g part of them 1Chr 12:29
so that this man was the g of all Job 1:3
g of them every one is given to Jer 6:13
the g is given to covetousness Jer 8:10
least of them unto the g of them Jer 31:34
from the least even unto the g Jer 42:1
from the least even to the g Jer 42:8
from the least even unto the g Jer 44:12
from the g of them even to the Jonah 3:5
it is the g among herbs, and Mt 13:32

Who is the g in the kingdom of.............. Mt 18:1
the same is g in the kingdom of.............. Mt 18:4
But he that is g among you shall.......... Mt 23:11
themselves, who should be the g............ Mk 9:34
them, which of them should be g............ Lk 9:46
of them should be accounted the g....... Lk 22:24
but he that is g among you.................... Lk 22:26
heed, from the least to the g................. Acts 8:10
but the g of these is charity................. 1Cor 13:13
know me, from the least to the g.......... Heb 8:11

**GREATLY**
I will g multiply thy sorrow and........... Gen 3:16
were increased g upon the earth........... Gen 7:18
And he pressed upon them g................. Gen 19:3
the LORD hath blessed my master g.... Gen 24:35
Then Jacob was g afraid and................ Gen 32:7
and the whole mount quaked g............. Ex 19:18
anger of the LORD was kindled g....... Num 11:10
and the people mourned g.................... Num 14:39
for the LORD shall g bless thee............ Deut 15:4
neither shall he g multiply to.............. Deut 17:17
That they feared g, because.................. Josh 10:2
and they were g distressed................... Judg 2:15
Israel was g impoverished because........ Judg 6:6
and his anger was kindled g................. 1Sa 11:6
all the men of Israel rejoiced g............ 1Sa 11:15
all the people g feared the LORD........... 1Sa 12:18
and he loved him g................................ 1Sa 16:21
they were dismayed, and g afraid.......... 1Sa 17:11
afraid, and his heart g trembled............ 1Sa 28:5
And David was g distressed................... 1Sa 30:6
because the men were g ashamed.......... 2Sa 10:5
David's anger was g kindled.................. 2Sa 12:5
I have sinned g in that I have............... 2Sa 24:10
and his kingdom was established g...... 1Kin 2:12
of Solomon, that he rejoiced g............. 1Kin 5:7
(Now Obadiah feared the LORD g.......... 1Kin 18:3
of their fathers increased g.................. 1Chr 4:38
is the LORD, and g to be praised........... 1Chr 16:25
for the men were g ashamed................ 1Chr 19:5
said unto God, I have sinned g............. 1Chr 21:8
anger was g kindled against Judah...... 2Chr 25:10
humbled himself g before the God..... 2Chr 33:12
For the thing which I g feared is........... Job 3:25
thy latter end should g increase............. Job 8:7
salvation how g shall he rejoice............. Ps 21:1
therefore my heart g rejoiceth............... Ps 28:7
I am bowed down g................................. Ps 38:6
the king g desire thy beauty.................. Ps 45:11
he is g exalted....................................... Ps 47:9
g to be praised in the city of.................. Ps 48:1
I shall not be g moved............................ Ps 62:2
thou g enrichest it with the.................... Ps 65:9
My lips shall g rejoice when I................ Ps 71:23
was wroth, and g abhorred Israel.......... Ps 78:59
God is g to be feared in the................... Ps 89:7
LORD is great, and g to be praised........... Ps 96:4
And he increased his people g.............. Ps 105:24
so that they are multiplied g................. Ps 107:38
I will g praise the LORD with my.......... Ps 109:30
LORD, that delighteth g in his................ Ps 112:1
I was g afflicted.................................... Ps 116:10
proud have had me g in derision.......... Ps 119:51
is the LORD, and g to be praised........... Ps 145:3
of the righteous shall g rejoice........... Prov 23:24
back, they shall be g ashamed............... Is 42:17
I will g rejoice in the LORD, my............. Is 61:10
shall not that land be g polluted............. Jer 3:1
surely thou hast g deceived this............ Jer 4:10
we are g confounded, because we.......... Jer 9:19
they shall be g ashamed....................... Jer 20:11
and my sabbaths they g polluted.......... Eze 20:13
hath g offended, and revenged............. Eze 25:12
was king Belshazzar g troubled............. Dan 5:9
for thou art g beloved........................... Dan 9:23
a man g beloved, understand the.......... Dan 10:11
O man g beloved, fear not................... Dan 10:19
thou art g despised............................... Obad 2
is near, it is near, and hasteth g......... Zeph 1:14
Rejoice g, O daughter of Zion................... Zec 9:9
that the governor marvelled g............... Mt 27:14
that were done, they feared g.............. Mt 27:54
And besought him g, saying, My........... Mk 5:23
and them that wept and wailed g........... Mk 5:38
were g amazed, and running to him...... Mk 9:15
ye therefore do g err............................. Mk 12:27
rejoiceth g because of the..................... Jn 3:29
is called Solomon's, g wondering.......... Acts 3:11
multiplied in Jerusalem g....................... Acts 6:7
I g desired him to come unto you...... 1Cor 16:12
how g I long after you all in the.............. Phil 1:8
But I rejoiced in the Lord g................... Phil 4:10
desiring g to see us, as we also.............. 1Th 3:6
G desiring to see thee, being................. 2Ti 1:4
for he hath g withstood our words....... 2Ti 4:15
Wherein ye g rejoice, though now........ 1Pet 1:6
I rejoiced g that I found of thy................. 2Jn 4
For I rejoiced g, when the......................... 3Jn 3

**GREATNESS**
in the g of thine excellency thou............ Ex 15:7
by the g of thine arm they shall............ Ex 15:16
according unto the g of thy mercy.... Num 14:19
begun to shew thy servant thy g........ Deut 3:24
hath shewed us his glory and his g..... Deut 5:24
thou hast redeemed through thy g...... Deut 9:26
of the LORD your God, his g.................. Deut 11:2
ascribe ye g unto our God..................... Deut 32:3
heart, hast thou done all this g........... 1Chr 17:19
people, to make thee a name of g...... 1Chr 17:21
Thine, O LORD, is the g, and the......... 1Chr 29:11
the one half of the g of thy.................. 2Chr 9:6
the g of the burdens laid upon........... 2Chr 24:27
according to the g of thy mercy.......... Neh 13:22
declaration of the g of Mordecai........... Est 10:2
through the g of thy power shall............ Ps 66:3
Thou shalt increase my g, and............. Ps 71:21
according to the g of thy power............ Ps 79:11
and his g is unsearchable.................... Ps 145:3
and I will declare thy g......................... Ps 145:6
him according to his excellent g.......... Ps 150:2
in the g of his folly he shall go............ Prov 5:23
by names by the g of his might............. Is 40:26
art wearied in the g of thy way............. Is 57:10
in the g of his strength............................. Is 63:1
For the g of thine iniquity are.............. Jer 13:22
Whom art thou like in thy g................... Eze 31:2
Thus was he fair in his g...................... Eze 31:7
in g among the trees of Eden.............. Eze 31:18
for thy g is grown, and reacheth.......... Dan 4:22
the g of the kingdom under the............ Dan 7:27
what is the exceeding g of his............. Eph 1:19

**GREAVES**
he had g of brass upon his legs,............. 1Sa 17:6

**GRECIA** See GRECIANS, GREECE. *Latin form of Greece.*
the rough goat is the king of G............. Dan 8:21
lo, the prince of G shall come............. Dan 10:20
up all against the realm of G................ Dan 11:2

**GRECIANS** See GREEKS.
*1. Inhabitants of Greece.*
Jerusalem have ye sold unto the G......... Joel 3:6
*2. Hellenistic Jews.*
of the G against the Hebrews................ Acts 6:1
Jesus, and disputed against the G......... Acts 9:29
come to Antioch, spake unto the G... Acts 11:20

**GREECE** See GRECIA. *Peninsula south of the Balkans.*
O Zion, against thy sons, O G.............. Zec 9:13
much exhortation, he came into G........ Acts 20:2

**GREEDILY**
He coveteth g all the day long........... Prov 21:26
thou hast g gained of thy.................... Eze 22:12
ran g after the error of Balaam............... Jude 11

**GREEDINESS**
to work all uncleanness with g............. Eph 4:19

**GREEDY**
as a lion that is g of his prey............... Ps 17:12
of every one that is g of gain.............. Prov 1:19
He that is g of gain troubleth.............. Prov 15:27
they are g dogs which can never.......... Is 56:11
no striker, not g of filthy lucre.................. 1Ti 3:3
much wine, not g of filthy lucre............... 1Ti 3:8

**GREEK** See GREEKS.
*1. A native of Greece.*
written over him in letters of G............. Lk 23:38
and it was written in Hebrew, and G..... Jn 19:20
but his father was a G.......................... Acts 16:1
knew all that his father was a G........... Acts 16:3
the Jew first, and also to the G............ Rom 1:16
between the Jew and the G.................. Rom 10:12
Titus, who was with me, being a G.......... Gal 2:3
There is neither Jew nor G................... Gal 3:28
Where there is neither G nor Jew.......... Col 3:11
*2. A language.*
Who said, Canst thou speak G............ Acts 21:37
but in the G tongue hath his name....... Rev 9:11
*3. A female.*
The woman was a G, a........................... Mk 7:26

**GREEKS** See GRECIANS. *Plural of Greek 1.*
there were certain G among them......... Jn 12:20
Jews and also of the G believed........... Acts 14:1
of the devout G a great multitude......... Acts 17:4
of honourable women which were G. Acts 17:12
and persuaded the Jews and the G........ Acts 18:4
Then all the G took Sosthenes,............. Acts 18:17
of the Lord Jesus, both Jews and G... Acts 19:10
G also dwelling at Ephesus................. Acts 19:17
to the Jews, and also to the G............. Acts 20:21
further brought G also into the............ Acts 21:28
I am debtor both to the G..................... Rom 1:14
sign, and the G seek after wisdom......... 1Cor 1:22
and unto the G foolishness.................. 1Cor 1:23
which are called, both Jews and G...... 1Cor 1:24

**GREEN**
have given every g herb for meat......... Gen 1:30
even as the g herb have I given.............. Gen 9:3
Jacob took him rods of g poplar.......... Gen 30:37
not any g thing in the trees................... Ex 10:15
offering of thy firstfruits g...................... Lev 2:14
nor g ears, until the selfsame.............. Lev 23:14
the hills, and under every g tree........... Deut 12:2
If they bind me with seven g................. Judg 16:7
brought up to her seven g withs........... Judg 16:8
high hill, and under every g tree........ 1Kin 14:23
the hills, and under every g tree............ 2Kin 16:4
high hill, and under every g tree......... 2Kin 17:10
of the field, and as the g herb............ 2Kin 19:26
the hills, and under every g tree.......... 2Chr 28:4
Where were white, g, and blue,................. Est 1:6
He is g before the sun, and his.............. Job 8:16
and his branch shall not be g.............. Job 15:32
he searcheth after every g thing........... Job 39:8
me to lie down in g pastures.................... Ps 23:2
grass, and wither as the g herb.............. Ps 37:2
himself like a g bay tree....................... Ps 37:35
But I am like a g olive tree in................. Ps 52:8
also our bed is g.................................. Song 1:16
fig tree putteth forth her g figs........... Song 2:13
faileth, there is no g thing..................... Is 15:6
of the field, and as the g herb............... Is 37:27
with idols under every g tree................. Is 57:5
under every g tree thou wanderest........ Jer 2:20
mountain and under every g tree............. Jer 3:6
the strangers under every g tree............ Jer 3:13
A g olive tree, fair, and of................. Jer 11:16
their groves by the g trees upon............. Jer 17:2
cometh, but her leaf shall be g............... Jer 17:8
mountains, and under every g tree........ Eze 6:13
tree, have dried up the g tree.............. Eze 17:24
shall devour every g tree in thee......... Eze 20:47
I am like a g fir tree.............................. Hos 14:8
by companies upon the g grass.............. Mk 6:39
they do these things in a g tree............. Lk 23:31
up, and all g grass was burnt up............. Rev 8:7
of the earth, neither any g thing............. Rev 9:4

**GREENISH**
if the plague be g or reddish in............ Lev 13:49
g or reddish, which in sight are........... Lev 14:37

**GREENNESS**
Whilst it is yet in his g.......................... Job 8:12

**GREET**
go to Nabal, and g him in my name...... 1Sa 25:5
G Priscilla and Aquila my helpers......... Rom 16:3
Likewise g the church that is in........... Rom 16:5
G Mary, who bestowed much labour... Rom 16:6
G Amplias my beloved in the Lord....... Rom 16:8
G them that be of the household....... Rom 16:11
All the brethren g you........................ 1Cor 16:20
G ye one another with an holy............ 1Cor 16:20
G one another with an holy kiss........ 2Cor 13:12
brethren which are with me g you........... Phil 4:21
physician, and Demas, g you................... Col 4:14
G all the brethren with an holy.............. 1Th 5:26
G them that love us in the faith.......... Titus 3:15
G ye one another with a kiss of........... 1Pet 5:14
of thy elect sister g thee.......................... 2Jn 13
G the friends by name.............................. 3Jn 14

**GREETETH**
Eubulus g thee, and Pudens, and............ 2Ti 4:21

**GREETING**
brethren send g unto the brethren..... Acts 15:23
governor Felix sendeth g.................. Acts 23:26
which are scattered abroad, g.................... Jas 1:1

**GREETINGS**
g in the markets, and to be called........... Mt 23:7
synagogues, and g in the markets.......... Lk 11:43
love g in the markets, and the............... Lk 20:46

**GREW**
herb of the field before it g.................. Gen 2:5
that which g upon the ground.............. Gen 19:25
And the child g, and was weaned.......... Gen 21:8
and he g, and dwelt in the................... Gen 21:20
And the boys g...................................... Gen 25:27
g until he became very great................ Gen 26:13
had possessions therein, and g............ Gen 47:27
the more they multiplied and g................ Ex 1:12
And the child g, and she brought............ Ex 2:10
and his wife's sons g up, and they......... Judg 11:2
and the child g, and the LORD............ Judg 13:24
child Samuel g before the LORD............ 1Sa 2:21
And the child Samuel g on, and was....... 1Sa 2:26
And Samuel g, and the LORD was with. 1Sa 3:19
g great, and the LORD God of hosts........ 2Sa 5:10
it g up together with him, and.............. 2Sa 12:3
And it g, and became a spreading......... Eze 17:6
wither in the furrows where it g........... Eze 17:10
The tree g, and was strong, and the..... Dan 4:11
tree that thou sawest, which g.............. Dan 4:20
among thorns, and the thorns g up.......... Mk 4:7
bettered, but rather g worse.................. Mk 5:26
And the child g, and waxed strong.......... Lk 1:80
And the child g, and waxed strong.......... Lk 2:40
and it g, and waxed a great tree............ Lk 13:19
sworn to Abraham, the people g............ Acts 7:17
But the word of God g and.................. Acts 12:24
So mightily g the word of God and.... Acts 19:20

**GREY**
beauty of old men is the g head......... Prov 20:29

**GREYHEADED**
Now also when I am old and g................ Ps 71:18

**GREYHOUND**
A g Prov 30:31

**GRIEF**
Which were a g of mind unto Isaac.... Gen 26:35
and g have I spoken hitherto............... 1Sa 1:16
That this shall be no g unto thee........ 1Sa 25:31
know his own sore and his own g........ 2Chr 6:29
saw that his g was very great................ Job 2:13
O that my g were throughly.................... Job 6:2
of my lips should asswage your g........... Job 16:5
I speak, my g is not asswaged............... Job 16:6
Mine eye is consumed because of g........... Ps 6:7
mine eye is consumed with g.................... Ps 31:9
For my life is spent with g..................... Ps 31:10
they talk to the g of those whom........... Ps 69:26
foolish son is a g to his father............... Prov 17:25
For in much wisdom is much g............... Eccl 1:18
are sorrows, and his travail g................ Eccl 2:23

shall be a heap in the day of g ... Is 17:11
of sorrows, and acquainted with g ... Is 53:3
he hath put him to g ... Is 53:10
before me continually is g ... Jer 6:7
but I said, Truly this is a g ... Jer 10:19
LORD hath added g to my sorrow ... Jer 45:3
But though he cause g, yet will ... Lam 3:32
head, to deliver him from his g ... Jonah 4:6
But if any have caused g, he hath ... 2Cor 2:5
may do it with joy, and not with g ... Heb 13:17
conscience toward God endure g ... 1Pet 2:19

**GRIEFS**
Surely he hath borne our g ... Is 53:4

**GRIEVANCE**
iniquity, and cause me to behold g ... Hab 1:3

**GRIEVE**
thine eyes, and to g thine heart ... 1Sa 2:33
from evil, that it may not g me ... 1Chr 4:10
and g him in the desert ... Ps 78:40
nor g the children of men ... Lam 3:33
g not the holy Spirit of God, ... Eph 4:30

**GRIEVED**
earth, and it g him at his heart ... Gen 6:6
and the men were g, and they were ... Gen 34:7
Now therefore be not g, nor angry ... Gen 45:5
The archers have sorely g him ... Gen 49:23
they were g because of the ... Ex 1:12
thine heart shall not be g when ... Deut 15:10
his soul was g for the misery of ... Judg 10:16
and why is thy heart g ... 1Sa 1:8
And it g Samuel ... 1Sa 15:11
Jonathan know this, lest he be g ... 1Sa 20:3
for he was g for David, because ... 1Sa 20:34
the soul of all the people was g ... 1Sa 30:6
how the king was g for his son ... 2Sa 19:2
it g them exceedingly that there ... Neh 2:10
neither be ye g ... Neh 8:11
And it g me sore ... Neh 13:8
Then was the queen exceedingly g ... Est 4:4
commune with thee, wilt thou be g ... Job 4:2
was not my soul g for the poor ... Job 30:25
Thus my heart was g, and I was ... Ps 73:21
long was I g with this generation ... Ps 95:10
The wicked shall see it, and be g ... Ps 112:10
the transgressors, and was g ... Ps 119:158
am not I g with those that rise ... Ps 139:21
g in spirit, and a wife of youth, ... Is 54:6
therefore thou wast not g ... Is 57:10
them, but they have not g ... Jer 5:3
I Daniel was g in my spirit in ... Dan 7:15
therefore he shall be g, and ... Dan 11:30
but they are not g for the ... Amos 6:6
being g for the hardness of their ... Mk 3:5
at that saying, and went away g ... Mk 10:22
Peter was g because he said unto ... Jn 21:17
Being g that they taught the ... Acts 4:2
But Paul, being g, turned and said ... Acts 16:18
if thy brother be g with thy meat ... Rom 14:15
not that ye should be g, but that ... 2Cor 2:4
caused grief, he hath not g me ... 2Cor 2:5
Wherefore I was g with that ... Heb 3:10
with whom was he g forty years ... Heb 3:17

**GRIEVETH**
for it g me much for your sakes ... Ruth 1:13
it g him to bring it again to his ... Prov 26:15

**GRIEVING**
nor any g thorn of all that are ... Eze 28:24

**GRIEVOUS**
for the famine was g in the land ... Gen 12:10
and because their sin is very g ... Gen 18:20
the thing was very g in Abraham's ... Gen 21:11
Let it not be g in thy sight ... Gen 21:12
for it shall be very g ... Gen 41:31
This is a g mourning to the ... Gen 50:11
there came a g swarm of flies ... Ex 8:24
there shall be a very g murrain ... Ex 9:3
cause it to rain a very g hail ... Ex 9:18
mingled with the hail, very g ... Ex 9:24
very g were they ... Ex 10:14
which cursed me with a g curse in ... 1Kin 2:8
Thy father made our yoke g ... 1Kin 12:4
thou the g service of thy father ... 1Kin 12:4
Thy father made our yoke g ... 2Chr 10:4
ease thou somewhat the g ... 2Chr 10:4
His ways are always g ... Ps 10:5
which speak g things proudly and ... Ps 31:18
but g words stir up anger ... Prov 15:1
Correction is g unto him that ... Prov 15:10
under the sun is g unto me ... Eccl 2:17
his life shall be g unto him ... Is 15:4
A g vision is declared unto me ... Is 21:2
They are all g revolters, walking ... Jer 6:28
my wound is g ... Jer 10:19
great breach, with a very g blow ... Jer 14:17
They shall die of g deaths ... Jer 16:4
forth in fury, even a g whirlwind ... Jer 23:19
is incurable, and thy wound is g ... Jer 30:12
thy wound is g ... Nah 3:19
g to be borne, and lay them on ... Mt 23:4
men with burdens g to be borne ... Lk 11:46
shall g wolves enter in among you ... Acts 20:29
g complaints against Paul, which ... Acts 25:7
to you, to me indeed is not g ... Phil 3:1
seemeth to be joyous, but g ... Heb 12:11
and his commandments are not g ... 1Jn 5:3
g sore upon the men which had the ... Rev 16:2

**GRIEVOUSLY**
afterward did more g afflict her ... Is 9:1
it shall fall g upon the head of ... Jer 23:19
Jerusalem hath g sinned ... Lam 1:8
for I have g rebelled ... Lam 1:20
against me by trespassing g ... Eze 14:13
sick of the palsy, g tormented ... Mt 8:6
my daughter is g vexed with a ... Mt 15:22

**GRIEVOUSNESS**
that write g which they have ... Is 10:1
bent bow, and from the g of war ... Is 21:15

**GRIND**
he did g in the prison house ... Judg 16:21
Then let my wife g unto another ... Job 31:10
and g the faces of the poor ... Is 3:15
Take the millstones, and g meal ... Is 47:2
They took the young men to g ... Lam 5:13
fall, it will g him to powder ... Mt 21:44
fall, it will g him to powder ... Lk 20:18

**GRINDERS**
the g cease because they are few, ... Eccl 12:3

**GRINDING**
when the sound of the g is low ... Eccl 12:4
Two women shall be g at the mill ... Mt 24:41
Two women shall be g together ... Lk 17:35

**GRISLED**
were ringstraked, speckled, and g ... Gen 31:10
are ringstraked, speckled, and g ... Gen 31:12
and in the fourth chariot g ... Zec 6:3
the g go forth toward the south ... Zec 6:6

**GROAN**
Men g from out of the city, and ... Job 24:12
all her land the wounded shall g ... Jer 51:52
he shall g before him with the ... Eze 30:24
How do the beasts g ... Joel 1:18
we ourselves g within ourselves ... Rom 8:23
For in this we g, earnestly ... 2Cor 5:2
that are in this tabernacle do g ... 2Cor 5:4

**GROANED**
he g in the spirit, and was ... Jn 11:33

**GROANETH**
we know that the whole creation g ... Rom 8:22

**GROANING**
And God heard their g, and God ... Ex 2:24
I have also heard the g of the ... Ex 6:5
my stroke is heavier than my g ... Job 23:2
I am weary with my g ... Ps 6:6
my g is not hid from thee ... Ps 38:9
my g my bones cleave to my skin ... Ps 102:5
To hear the g of the prisoner ... Ps 102:20
Jesus therefore again g in ... Jn 11:38
in Egypt, and I have heard their g ... Acts 7:34

**GROANINGS**
of their g by reason of them that ... Judg 2:18
the g of a deadly wounded man ... Eze 30:24
us with g which cannot be uttered ... Rom 8:26

**GROPE**
And thou shalt g at noonday ... Deut 28:29
g in the noonday as in the night ... Job 5:14
They g in the dark without light, ... Job 12:25
We g for the wall like the blind, ... Is 59:10
we g as if we had no eyes ... Is 59:10

**GROPETH**
as the blind g in darkness ... Deut 28:29

**GROSS**
earth, and g darkness the people ... Is 60:2
of death, and make it g darkness ... Jer 13:16
this people's heart is waxed g ... Mt 13:15
heart of this people is waxed g ... Acts 28:27

**GROUND**
there was not a man to till the g ... Gen 2:5
watered the whole face of the g ... Gen 2:6
formed man of the dust of the g ... Gen 2:7
out of the g made the LORD God to ... Gen 2:9
out of the g the LORD God formed ... Gen 2:19
cursed is the g for thy sake ... Gen 3:17
till thou return unto the g ... Gen 3:19
to till the g from whence he was ... Gen 3:23
but Cain was a tiller of the g ... Gen 4:2
the g an offering unto the LORD ... Gen 4:3
blood crieth unto me from the g ... Gen 4:10
When thou tillest the g, it shall ... Gen 4:12
because of the g which the LORD ... Gen 5:29
which was upon the face of the g ... Gen 7:23
abated from off the face of the g ... Gen 8:8
behold, the face of the g was dry ... Gen 8:13
the g any more for man's sake ... Gen 8:21
and bowed himself toward the g ... Gen 18:2
with his face toward the g ... Gen 19:1
and that which grew upon the g ... Gen 19:25
himself to the g seven times ... Gen 33:3
wife, that he spilled it on the g ... Gen 38:9
down every man his sack to the g ... Gen 44:11
and they fell before him on the g ... Gen 44:14
whereon thou standest is holy g ... Ex 3:5
And he said, Cast it on the g ... Ex 4:3
And he cast it on the g, and it ... Ex 4:3
also the g whereon they are ... Ex 8:21
and the fire ran along upon the g ... Ex 9:23
of Israel shall go on dry g ... Ex 14:16
midst of the sea upon the dry g ... Ex 14:22
small as the hoar frost on the g ... Ex 16:14
g it to powder, and strawed it ... Ex 32:20
thing that creepeth on the g ... Lev 20:25
g it in mills, or beat it in a ... Num 11:8
that the g clave asunder that was ... Num 16:31
any thing that creepeth on the g ... Deut 4:18
g it very small, even until it ... Deut 9:21
shalt pour it upon the g as water ... Deut 15:23
the way in any tree, or on the g ... Deut 22:6
thy body, and the fruit of thy g ... Deut 28:4
cattle, and in the fruit of thy g ... Deut 28:11
foot upon the g for delicateness ... Deut 28:56
on dry g in the midst of Jordan ... Josh 3:17
Israelites passed over on dry g ... Josh 3:17
in a parcel of g which Jacob ... Josh 24:32
and fastened it into the g ... Judg 4:21
upon all the g let there be dew ... Judg 6:39
and there was dew on all the g ... Judg 6:40
and fell on their faces to the g ... Judg 13:20
destroyed down to the g of the ... Judg 20:21
destroyed down to the g of the ... Judg 20:25
face, and bowed herself to the g ... Ruth 2:10
none of his words fall to the g ... 1Sa 3:19
the g before the ark of the LORD ... 1Sa 5:4
and will set them to ear his g ... 1Sa 8:12
and there was honey upon the g ... 1Sa 14:25
and calves, and slew them on the g ... 1Sa 14:32
hair of his head fall to the g ... 1Sa 14:45
son of Jesse liveth upon the g ... 1Sa 20:31
and fell on his face to the g ... 1Sa 20:41
face, and bowed herself to the g ... 1Sa 25:23
stuck in the g at his bolster ... 1Sa 26:7
he stooped with his face to the g ... 1Sa 28:14
should I smite thee to the g ... 2Sa 2:22
line, casting them down to the g ... 2Sa 8:2
she fell on her face to the g ... 2Sa 14:4
and are as water spilt on the g ... 2Sa 14:14
And Joab fell to the g on his face ... 2Sa 14:22
his face to the g before the king ... 2Sa 14:33
him as the dew falleth on the g ... 2Sa 17:12
mouth, and spread g corn thereon ... 2Sa 17:19
thou not smite him there to the g ... 2Sa 18:11
and shed out his bowels to the g ... 2Sa 20:10
was a piece of g full of lentiles ... 2Sa 23:11
he stood in the midst of the g ... 2Sa 23:12
the king on his face upon the g ... 2Sa 24:20
the king with his face to the g ... 1Kin 1:23
in the clay g between Succoth and ... 1Kin 7:46
that they two went over on dry g ... 2Kin 2:8
themselves to the g before him ... 2Kin 2:15
water is naught, and the g barren ... 2Kin 2:19
feet, and bowed herself to the g ... 2Kin 4:37
and cast him into the plat of g ... 2Kin 9:26
king of Israel, Smite upon the g ... 2Kin 13:18
was a parcel of g full of barley ... 1Chr 11:13
to David with his face to the g ... 1Chr 21:21
the g was Ezri the son of Chelub ... 1Chr 27:26
in the clay g between Succoth and ... 2Chr 4:17
faces to the g upon the pavement ... 2Chr 7:3
his head with his face to the g ... 2Chr 20:18
LORD with their faces to the g ... Neh 8:6
to bring the firstfruits of our g ... Neh 10:35
tithes of our g unto the Levites ... Neh 10:37
his head, and fell down upon the g ... Job 1:20
with him upon the g seven days ... Job 2:13
doth trouble spring out of the g ... Job 5:6
and the stock thereof die in the g ... Job 14:8
he poureth out my gall upon the g ... Job 16:13
snare is laid for him in the g ... Job 18:10
satisfy the desolate and waste g ... Job 38:27
swalloweth the g with fierceness ... Job 39:24
place of thy name to the g ... Ps 74:7
his crown by casting it to the g ... Ps 89:39
and cast his throne down to the g ... Ps 89:44
and devoured the fruit of their g ... Ps 105:35
and the watersprings into dry g ... Ps 107:33
water, and dry g into watersprings ... Ps 107:35
smitten my life down to the g ... Ps 143:3
casteth the wicked down to the g ... Ps 147:6
desolate shall sit upon the g ... Is 3:26
how art thou cut down to the g ... Is 14:12
gods he hath broken unto the g ... Is 21:9
down, lay low, and bring to the g ... Is 25:12
he layeth it low, even to the g ... Is 26:5
open and break the clods of his g ... Is 28:24
down, and shalt speak out of the g ... Is 29:4
a familiar spirit, out of the g ... Is 29:4
that thou shalt sow the g withal ... Is 30:23
the g shall eat clean provender ... Is 30:24
the parched g shall become a pool ... Is 35:7
thirsty, and floods upon the dry g ... Is 44:3
daughter of Babylon, sit on the g ... Is 47:1
thou hast laid thy body as the g ... Is 51:23
and as a root out of a dry g ... Is 53:2
Jerusalem, Break up your fallow g ... Jer 4:3
field, and upon the fruit of the g ... Jer 7:20
they are black unto the g ... Jer 14:2
Because the g is chapt, for there ... Jer 14:4
they shall be dung upon the g ... Jer 25:33
and the beast that are upon the g ... Jer 27:5
hath brought them down to the g ... Lam 2:2
Her gates are sunk into the g ... Lam 2:9
daughter of Zion sit upon the g ... Lam 2:10
hang down their heads to the g ... Lam 2:10
old lie on the g in the streets ... Lam 2:21
thy face, that thou see not the g ... Eze 12:6
he see not the g with his eyes ... Eze 12:12
morter, and bring it down to the g ... Eze 13:14
fury, she was cast down to the g ... Eze 19:12
wilderness, in a dry and thirsty g ... Eze 19:13
she poured it not upon the g ... Eze 24:7
garrisons shall go down to the g ... Eze 26:11

they shall sit upon the g ........ Eze 26:16
I will cast thee to the g ........ Eze 28:17
and every wall shall fall to the g ........ Eze 38:20
from the g up to the windows, and ........ Eze 41:16
From the g unto above the door ........ Eze 41:20
and the middlemost from the g ........ Eze 42:6
from the bottom upon the g even ........ Eze 43:14
whole earth, and touched not the g ........ Dan 8:5
but he cast him down to the g ........ Dan 8:7
the host and of the stars to the g ........ Dan 8:10
it cast down the truth to the g ........ Dan 8:12
sleep on my face toward the g ........ Dan 8:18
my face, and my face toward the g ........ Dan 10:9
me, I set my face toward the g ........ Dan 10:15
with the creeping things of the g ........ Hos 2:18
break up your fallow g ........ Hos 10:12
be cut off, and fall to the g ........ Amos 3:14
Who shall bring me down to the g ........ Obad 3
that which the g bringeth forth ........ Hag 1:11
the g shall give her increase, and ........ Zec 8:12
not destroy the fruits of your g ........ Mal 3:11
fall on the g without your Father ........ Mt 10:29
But other fell into good g ........ Mt 13:8
g is he that heareth the word ........ Mt 13:23
multitude to sit down on the g ........ Mt 15:35
And some fell on stony g, where it ........ Mk 4:5
And other fell on good g, and did ........ Mk 4:8
which are sown on stony g ........ Mk 4:16
are they which are sown on good g ........ Mk 4:20
a man should cast seed into the g ........ Mk 4:26
the people to sit down on the g ........ Mk 8:6
and he fell on the g, and wallowed ........ Mk 9:20
a little, and fell on the g ........ Mk 14:35
And other fell on good g, and ........ Lk 8:8
But that on the good g are they ........ Lk 8:15
The g of a certain rich man ........ Lk 12:16
why cumbereth it the g ........ Lk 13:7
him, I have bought a piece of g ........ Lk 14:18
And shall lay thee even with the g ........ Lk 19:44
of blood falling down to the g ........ Lk 22:44
near to the parcel of g that ........ Jn 4:5
and with his finger wrote on the g ........ Jn 8:6
stooped down, and wrote on the g ........ Jn 8:8
had thus spoken, he spat on the g ........ Jn 9:6
a corn of wheat fall into the g ........ Jn 12:24
went backward, and fell to the g ........ Jn 18:6
where thou standest is holy g ........ Acts 7:33
And I fell unto the g, and heard a ........ Acts 22:7
God, the pillar and g of the truth ........ 1Ti 3:15

### GROUNDED

where the g staff shall pass ........ Is 30:32
ye, being rooted and g in love, ........ Eph 3:17
If ye continue in the faith g ........ Col 1:23

### GROVE

Abraham planted a g in Beer-sheba ........ Gen 21:33
a g of any trees near unto the ........ Deut 16:21
cut down the g that is by it ........ Judg 6:25
the g which thou shalt cut down ........ Judg 6:26
the g was cut down that was by it ........ Judg 6:28
cut down the g that was by it ........ Judg 6:30
she had made an idol in a g ........ 1Kin 15:13
And Ahab made a g ........ 1Kin 16:33
remained the g also in Samaria ........ 2Kin 13:6
even two calves, and made a g ........ 2Kin 17:16
up altars for Baal, and made a g ........ 2Kin 21:3
he set a graven image of the g ........ 2Kin 21:7
were made for Baal, and for the g ........ 2Kin 23:4
he brought out the g from the ........ 2Kin 23:6
the women wove hangings for the g ... 2Kin 23:7
small to powder, and burned the g .... 2Kin 23:15
she had made an idol in a g ........ 2Chr 15:16

### GROVES

their images, and cut down their g ........ Ex 34:13
their images, and cut down their g ........ Deut 7:5
and burn their g with fire ........ Deut 12:3
God, and served Baalim and the g ........ Judg 3:7
because they have made their g ........ 1Kin 14:15
them high places, and images, and g. 1Kin 14:23
prophets of the g four hundred ........ 1Kin 18:19
g in every high hill, and under ........ 2Kin 17:10
the images, and cut down the g ........ 2Kin 18:4
the images, and cut down the g ........ 2Kin 23:14
the images, and cut down the g ........ 2Chr 14:3
the high places and g out of Judah ........ 2Chr 17:6
taken away the g out of the land ........ 2Chr 19:3
God of their fathers, and served g ........ 2Chr 24:18
in pieces, and cut down the g ........ 2Chr 31:1
up altars for Baalim, and made g ........ 2Chr 33:3
he built high places, and set up g ........ 2Chr 33:19
from the high places, and the g ........ 2Chr 34:3
and the g, and the carved images, ........ 2Chr 34:4
broken down the altars and the g ........ 2Chr 34:7
fingers have made, either the g ........ Is 17:8
that are beaten in sunder, the g ........ Is 27:9
their g by the green trees upon ........ Jer 17:2
I will pluck up thy g out of the ........ Mic 5:14

### GROW

g every tree that is pleasant to ........ Gen 2:9
let them g into a multitude in ........ Gen 48:16
locks of the hair of his head g ........ Num 6:5
to g again after he was shaven ........ Judg 16:22
although he make it not to g ........ 2Sa 23:5
such things as g of themselves ........ 2Kin 19:29
why should damage g to the hurt ........ Ezr 4:22
Can the rush g up without mire ........ Job 8:11
can the flag g without water ........ Job 8:11
out of the earth shall others g ........ Job 8:19
g out of the dust of the earth ........ Job 14:19
Let thistles g instead of wheat, ........ Job 31:40
good liking, they g up with corn ........ Job 39:4
he shall g like a cedar in ........ Ps 92:12
the grass to g for the cattle ........ Ps 104:14
grass to g upon the mountains ........ Ps 147:8
nor how the bones do g in the ........ Eccl 11:5
a Branch shall g out of his roots ........ Is 11:1
shalt thou make thy plant to g ........ Is 17:11
For he shall g up before him as a ........ Is 53:2
they g, yea, they bring forth ........ Jer 12:2
righteousness to g up unto David ........ Jer 33:15
nor suffer their locks to g long ........ Eze 44:20
shall g all trees for meat, whose ........ Eze 47:12
he shall g as the lily, and cast ........ Hos 14:5
as the corn, and g as the vine ........ Hos 14:7
not laboured, neither madest it g ........ Jonah 4:10
he shall g up out of his place, ........ Zec 6:12
g up as calves of the stall ........ Mal 4:2
lilies of the field, how they g ........ Mt 6:28
Let both g together until the ........ Mt 13:30
unto it, Let no fruit g on thee ........ Mt 21:19
and g up, he knoweth not how ........ Mk 4:27
Consider the lilies how they g ........ Lk 12:27
of them whereunto this would g ........ Acts 5:24
may g up into him in all things, ........ Eph 4:15
the word, that ye may g thereby ........ 1Pet 2:2
But g in grace, and in the ........ 2Pet 3:18

### GROWETH

which g for you out of the field ........ Ex 10:5
freckled spot that g in the skin ........ Lev 13:39
That which g of its own accord of ........ Lev 25:5
reap that which g of itself in it ........ Lev 25:11
beareth, nor any grass g therein ........ Deut 29:23
the day g to an end, lodge here, ........ Judg 19:9
When the dust g into hardness ........ Job 38:38
they are like grass which g up ........ Ps 90:5
morning it flourisheth, and g up ........ Ps 90:6
which withereth afore it g up ........ Ps 129:6
eat this year such as g of itself ........ Is 37:30
But when it is sown, it g up ........ Mk 4:32
building fitly framed together g ........ Eph 2:21
that your faith g exceedingly ........ 2Th 1:3

### GROWN

house, till Shelah my son be g ........ Gen 38:11
for she saw that Shelah was g ........ Gen 38:14
in those days, when Moses was g ........ Ex 2:11
for they were not g up ........ Ex 9:32
there is black hair g up therein ........ Lev 13:37
art waxen fat, thou art g thick ........ Deut 32:15
tarry for them till they were g ........ Ruth 1:13
at Jericho until your beards be g ........ 2Sa 10:5
young men that were g up with him ... 1Kin 12:8
the young men that were g up with .. 1Kin 12:10
And when the child was g, it fell ........ 2Kin 4:18
as corn blasted before it be g up ........ 2Kin 19:26
at Jericho until your beards be g ........ 1Chr 19:5
our trespass is g up unto the ........ Ezr 9:6
be as plants g up in their youth ........ Ps 144:12
it was all g over with thorns, and ........ Prov 24:31
as corn blasted before it be g up ........ Is 37:27
because ye are g fat as the ........ Jer 50:11
are fashioned, and thine hair is g ........ Eze 16:7
It is thou, O king, that art g ........ Dan 4:22
for thy greatness is g, and ........ Dan 4:22
till his hairs were g like ........ Dan 4:33
but when it is g, it is the ........ Mt 13:32

### GROWTH

the shooting up of the latter g ........ Amos 7:1
it was the latter g after the ........ Amos 7:1

### GRUDGE

nor bear any g against the ........ Lev 19:18
g if they be not satisfied ........ Ps 59:15
G not one against another, ........ Jas 5:9

### GRUDGING

one to another without g ........ 1Pet 4:9

### GRUDGINGLY

not g, or of necessity ........ 2Cor 9:7

### GUARD

of Pharaoh's, and captain of the g ........ Gen 37:36
of Pharaoh, captain of the g ........ Gen 39:1
the house of the captain of the g ........ Gen 40:3
the captain of the g charged ........ Gen 40:4
servant to the captain of the g ........ Gen 41:12
And David set him over his g ........ 2Sa 23:23
the hands of the chief of the g ........ 1Kin 14:27
that the g bare them, and brought ........ 1Kin 14:28
them back into the g chamber ........ 1Kin 14:28
offering, that Jehu said to the g ........ 2Kin 10:25
and the g and the captains cast ........ 2Kin 10:25
with the captains and the g ........ 2Kin 11:4
part at the gate behind the g ........ 2Kin 11:6
the g stood, every man with his ........ 2Kin 11:11
Athaliah heard the noise of the g ........ 2Kin 11:13
and the captains, and the g ........ 2Kin 11:19
gate of the g to the king's house ........ 2Kin 11:19
Nebuzar-adan, captain of the g ........ 2Kin 25:8
were with the captain of the g ........ 2Kin 25:10
the captain of the g carry away ........ 2Kin 25:11
But the captain of the g left of ........ 2Kin 25:12
the captain of the g took away ........ 2Kin 25:15
the captain of the g took Seraiah ........ 2Kin 25:18
captain of the g took these ........ 2Kin 25:20
and David set him over his g ........ 1Chr 11:25
the hands of the chief of the g ........ 2Chr 12:10
the g came and fetched them, and ........ 2Chr 12:11
them again into the g chamber ........ 2Chr 12:11
the night they may be a g to us ........ Neh 4:22
men of the g which followed me ........ Neh 4:23
the g carried away captive into ........ Jer 39:9
g left of the poor of the people ........ Jer 39:10
Nebuzar-adan the captain of the g ........ Jer 39:11
the captain of the g sent ........ Jer 39:13
the g had let him go from Ramah ........ Jer 40:1
captain of the g took Jeremiah ........ Jer 40:2
of the g gave him victuals ........ Jer 40:5
g had committed to Gedaliah the ........ Jer 41:10
g had left with Gedaliah the son ........ Jer 43:6
Nebuzar-adan, captain of the g ........ Jer 52:12
were with the captain of the g ........ Jer 52:14
g carried away captive certain of ........ Jer 52:15
g left certain of the poor of the ........ Jer 52:16
took the captain of the g away ........ Jer 52:19
the captain of the g took Seraiah ........ Jer 52:24
the captain of the g took them ........ Jer 52:26
the g carried away captive of the ........ Jer 52:30
thee, and be thou a g unto them ........ Eze 38:7
the captain of the king's g ........ Dan 2:14
prisoners to the captain of the g ........ Acts 28:16

### GUARD'S

in the captain of the g house ........ Gen 41:10

### GUDGODAH (*gud-go'-dah*) See HOR-HAGIDGAD. *A wilderness encampment of Israel.*

From thence they journeyed unto G... Deut 10:7
from G to Jotbath, a land of ........ Deut 10:7

### GUEST

That he was gone to be g with a ........ Lk 19:7

### GUESTCHAMBER

The Master saith, Where is the g ........ Mk 14:14
saith unto thee, Where is the g ........ Lk 22:11

### GUESTS

all the g that were with him ........ 1Kin 1:41
all the g that were with Adonijah ........ 1Kin 1:49
that her g are in the depths of ........ Prov 9:18
a sacrifice, he hath bid his g ........ Zeph 1:7
the wedding was furnished with g ........ Mt 22:10
the king came in to see the g ........ Mt 22:11

### GUIDE

or canst thou g Arcturus with his ........ Job 38:32
The meek will he g in judgment ........ Ps 25:9
thy name's sake lead me, and g me ........ Ps 31:3
I will g thee with mine eye ........ Ps 32:8
he will be our g even unto death ........ Ps 48:14
was thou, a man mine equal, my g ........ Ps 55:13
Thou shalt g me with thy counsel, ........ Ps 73:24
he will g his affairs with ........ Ps 112:5
forsaketh the g of her youth ........ Prov 2:17
Which having no g, overseer, or ........ Prov 6:7
of the upright shall g them ........ Prov 11:3
wise, and g thine heart in the way ..... Prov 23:19
springs of water shall he g them ........ Is 49:10
There is none to g her among all ........ Is 51:18
the LORD shall g thee continually ........ Is 58:11
thou art the g of my youth ........ Jer 3:4
put ye not confidence in a g ........ Mic 7:5
to g our feet into the way of ........ Lk 1:79
he will g you into all truth ........ Jn 16:13
which was g to them that took ........ Acts 1:16
I, except some man should g me ........ Acts 8:31
thou thyself art a g of the blind ........ Rom 2:19
g the house, give none occasion ........ 1Ti 5:14

### GUIDED

thou hast g them in thy strength ........ Ex 15:13
other, and g them on every side ........ 2Chr 32:22
I have g her from my mother's ........ Job 31:18
g them in the wilderness like a ........ Ps 78:52
g them by the skilfulness of his ........ Ps 78:72

### GUIDES

Woe unto you, ye blind g, which ........ Mt 23:16
Ye blind g, which strain at a ........ Mt 23:24

### GUIDING

head, g his hands wittingly ........ Gen 48:14

### GUILE

his neighbour, to slay him with g ........ Ex 21:14
and in whose spirit there is no g ........ Ps 32:2
evil, and thy lips from speaking g ........ Ps 34:13
g depart not from her streets ........ Ps 55:11
Israelite indeed, in whom is no g ........ Jn 1:47
being crafty, I caught you with g ........ 2Cor 12:16
nor of uncleanness, nor in g ........ 1Th 2:3
laying aside all malice, and all g ........ 1Pet 2:1
neither was g found in his mouth ........ 1Pet 2:22
and his lips that they speak no g ........ 1Pet 3:10
And in their mouth was found no g ........ Rev 14:5

### GUILT

but thou shalt put away the g of ........ Deut 19:13
So shalt thou put away the g of ........ Deut 21:9

### GUILTINESS

shouldest have brought g upon us ........ Gen 26:10

### GUILTLESS

g that taketh his name in vain ........ Ex 20:7
shall the man be g from iniquity ........ Num 5:31
be g before the LORD, and before ........ Num 32:22
g that taketh his name in vain ........ Deut 5:11
be upon his head, and we will be g ........ Josh 2:19
the LORD's anointed, and be g ........ 1Sa 26:9
my kingdom are g before the LORD ........ 2Sa 3:28
and the king and his throne be g ........ 2Sa 14:9
Now therefore hold him not g ........ 1Kin 2:9

ye would not have condemned the *g*...... Mt 12:7

**GUILTY**
We are verily *g* concerning our.......... Gen 42:21
that will by no means clear the *g*.............. Ex 34:7
should not be done, and are *g*................ Lev 4:13
which should not be done, and is *g*....... Lev 4:22
ought not to be done, and be *g*............. Lev 4:27
he also shall be unclean, and *g*............... Lev 5:2
knoweth of it, then he shall be *g*.............. Lev 5:3
he shall be *g* in one of these.................... Lev 5:4
when he shall be *g* in one of...................... Lev 5:5
he wist it not, yet is he *g*......................... Lev 5:17
because he hath sinned, and is *g*............. Lev 6:4
the LORD, and that person be *g*............... Num 5:6
and by no means clearing the *g*.......... Num 14:18
he shall not be *g* of blood......................... Num 35:27
a murderer, which is *g* of death............ Num 35:31
at this time, that ye should be *g*........ Judg 21:22
and being *g*, they offered a ram of...... Ezr 10:19
he curse thee, and thou be found *g*... Prov 30:10
Thou art become *g* in thy blood............. Eze 22:4
them, and hold themselves not *g*............. Zec 11:5
the gift that is upon it, he is *g*.............. Mt 23:18
and said, He is *g* of death......................... Mt 26:66
condemned him to be *g* of death.......... Mk 14:64
the world may become *g* before God... Rom 3:19
shall be *g* of the body and blood....... 1Cor 11:27
in one point, he is *g* of all......................... Jas 2:10

**GULF**
and you there is a great *g* fixed............. Lk 16:26

**GUNI** (*gu'-ni*) See GUNITES.
*1. A son of Naphtali.*
Jahzeel, and G, and Jezer, and............. Gen 46:24
of G, the family of the Gunites.......... Num 26:48
Jahziel, and G, and Jezer, and............. 1Chr 7:13
*2. Father of Abdiel.*
the son of Abdiel, the son of G............ 1Chr 5:15

**GUNITES** (*gu'-nites*) *Descendants of Guni 1.*
of Guni, the family of the G.............. Num 26:48

**GUR** (*gur*) See GUR-BAAL. *A hill near Ibleam.*
they did so at the going up to G.......... 2Kin 9:27

**GUR-BAAL** (*gur-ba'-al*) *Place in western Arabia.*
the Arabians that dwelt in G................ 2Chr 26:7

**GUSH**
our eyelids *g* out with waters................... Jer 9:18

**GUSHED**
till the blood *g* out upon them............ 1Kin 18:28
the rock, that the waters *g* out.............. Ps 78:20
the rock, and the waters *g* out............ Ps 105:41
rock also, and the waters *g* out.............. Is 48:21
midst, and all his bowels *g* out............ Acts 1:18

**GUTTER**
Whosoever getteth up to the *g*.................. 2Sa 5:8

**GUTTERS**
*g* in the watering troughs when.......... Gen 30:38
the eyes of the cattle in the *g*............ Gen 30:41

# H

**HA**
saith among the trumpets, H, *h*........... Job 39:25

**HAAHASHTARI** (*ha-a-hash'-te-ri*) *A son of Naarah.*
and Hepher, and Temeni, and H............. 1Chr 4:6

**HABAIAH** (*hab-ah'-yah*) *A family of exiles.*
the children of H, the children................ Ezr 2:61
the children of H, the children.............. Neh 7:63

**HABAKKUK** (*hab'-ak-kuk*) *A prophet of Judah.*
The burden which H the prophet............ Hab 1:1
A prayer of H the prophet upon............. Hab 3:1

**HABAZINIAH** (*hab-az-in-i'-ah*) *Head of a Rechabite family.*
the son of Jeremiah, the son of H........... Jer 35:3

**HABAZZINIAH** See HABAZINIAH.

**HABERGEON**
it, as it were the hole of an *h*................... Ex 28:32
of the robe, as the hole of an *h*............... Ex 39:23
the spear, the dart, nor the *h*................ Job 41:26

**HABERGEONS**
and spears, and helmets, and *h*.......... 2Chr 26:14
shields, and the bows, and the *h*........... Neh 4:16

**HABITABLE**
Rejoicing in the *h* part of his................ Prov 8:31

**HABITATION**
God, and I will prepare him an *h*............ Ex 15:2
in thy strength unto thy holy *h*.............. Ex 15:13
without the camp shall his *h* be.......... Lev 13:46
even unto his *h* shall ye seek................. Deut 12:5
Look down from thy holy *h*................... Deut 26:15
which I have commanded in my *h*........ 1Sa 2:29
thou shalt see an enemy in my *h*........... 1Sa 2:32
and shew me both it, and his *h*.......... 2Sa 15:25
have built an house of *h* for thee.......... 2Chr 6:2
faces from the *h* of the LORD................. 2Chr 29:6
Israel, whose *h* is in Jerusalem,............... Ezr 7:15
but suddenly I cursed his *h*...................... Job 5:3
and thou shalt visit thy *h*....................... Job 5:24
make the *h* of thy righteousness.............. Job 8:6
shall be scattered upon his *h*.................. Job 18:15
I have loved the *h* of thy house.............. Ps 26:8
From the place of his *h* he...................... Ps 33:14
the widows, is God in his holy *h*............. Ps 68:5
Let their *h* be desolate.......................... Ps 69:25
Be thou my strong *h*, whereunto I........... Ps 71:3
judgment are the *h* of thy throne.......... Ps 89:14
refuge, even the most High, thy *h*.......... Ps 91:9
judgment are the *h* of his throne............ Ps 97:2
fowls of the heaven have their *h*........ Ps 104:12
that they might go to a city of *h*........... Ps 107:7
they may prepare a city for *h*............... Ps 107:36
an *h* for the mighty God of Jacob........... Ps 132:5
he hath desired it for his *h*................ Ps 132:13
but he blesseth the *h* of the just.......... Prov 3:33
that graveth an *h* for himself in.............. Is 22:16
the *h* forsaken, and left like a................. Is 27:10
shall dwell in a peaceable *h*.................... Is 32:18
shall see Jerusalem a quiet *h*.................. Is 33:20
and it shall be an *h* of dragons................ Is 34:13
in the *h* of dragons, where each................ Is 35:7
behold from the *h* of thy holiness............ Is 63:15
Thine *h* is in the midst of deceit................ Jer 9:6
him, and have made his *h* desolate....... Jer 10:25
utter his voice from his holy *h*................ Jer 25:30
he shall mightily roar upon his *h*.......... Jer 25:30
O *h* of justice, and mountain of.............. Jer 31:23
shall be an *h* of shepherds.................... Jer 33:12
and dwelt in the *h* of Chimham.............. Jer 41:17
against the *h* of the strong.................... Jer 49:19
the *h* of justice, even the LORD,.............. Jer 50:7
will bring Israel again to his *h*.............. Jer 50:19
Jordan unto the *h* of the strong............ Jer 50:44
make their *h* desolate with them.......... Jer 50:45
Pathros, into the land of their *h*.......... Eze 29:14
fowls of the heaven had their *h*............. Dan 4:21
of the rock, whose *h* is high.................... Obad 3
and moon stood still in their *h*.............. Hab 3:11
he is raised up out of his holy *h*............ Zec 2:13
Let his *h* be desolate, and let no........... Acts 1:20
and the bounds of their *h*.................... Acts 17:26
an *h* of God through the Spirit................ Eph 2:22
estate, but left their own *h*...................... Jude 6
and is become the *h* of devils................. Rev 18:2

**HABITATIONS**
according to their *h* in the land.......... Gen 36:43
of cruelty are in their *h*........................ Gen 49:5
in all your *h* shall ye eat...................... Ex 12:20
your *h* upon the sabbath day.................. Ex 35:3
Ye shall bring out of your *h* two.......... Lev 23:17
be come into the land of your *h*............. Num 15:2
These were their *h*, and their................ 1Chr 4:33
the *h* that were found there, and.......... 1Chr 4:41
*h* were, Beth-el and the towns............. 1Chr 7:28
are full of the *h* of cruelty..................... Ps 74:20
their camp, round about their *h*.............. Ps 78:28
forth the curtains of thine *h*.................. Is 54:2
for the *h* of the wilderness a.................. Jer 9:10
or who shall enter into our *h*................ Jer 21:13
the peaceable *h* are cut down................ Jer 25:37
make their *h* desolate with them........... Jer 49:20
swallowed up all the *h* of Jacob............. Lam 2:2
toward Diblath, in all their *h*.................. Eze 6:14
the *h* of the shepherds shall.................. Amos 1:2
receive you into everlasting *h*................. Lk 16:9

**HABOR** (*ha'-bor*) *A Mesopotamian district.*
in H by the river of Gozan, and in....... 2Kin 17:6
in H by the river of Gozan, and in....... 2Kin 18:11
and brought them unto Halah, and H. 1Chr 5:26

**HACALIAH** See HACHILAH.

**HACHALIAH** (*hak-a-li'-ah*) *Father of Nehemiah.*
words of Nehemiah the son of H............. Neh 1:1
the Tirshatha, the son of H................... Neh 10:1

**HACHILAH** (*hak'-i-lah*) *A hill in Judah.*
in the wood, in the hill of H................. 1Sa 23:19
hide himself in the hill of H................... 1Sa 26:1
And Saul pitched in the hill of H.......... 1Sa 26:3

**HACHMONI** (*hak'-mo-ni*) See HACHMONITE.
*Father of Jehiel.*
Jehiel the son of H was with the........ 1Chr 27:32

**HACHMONITE** (*hak'-mo-nite*) See TACHMONITE. *A descendant of Hachmoni.*
Jashobeam, a H, the chief of the........ 1Chr 11:11

**HAD** See PREFACE.

**HADAD** (*ha'-dad*) See BEN-HADAD, HADADRIMMON, HADAR.
*1. A son of Bedad.*
H the son of Bedad, who smote............ Gen 36:35
H died, and Samlah of Masrekah......... Gen 36:36
H the son of Bedad, which smote.......... 1Chr 1:46
when H was dead, Samlah of................ 1Chr 1:47
*2. A royal Edomite.*
unto Solomon, H the Edomite.............. 1Kin 11:14
That H fled, he and certain................. 1Kin 11:17
H being yet a little child...................... 1Kin 11:17
H found great favour in the sight......... 1Kin 11:19
when H heard in Egypt that David....... 1Kin 11:21
H said to Pharaoh, Let me depart,...... 1Kin 11:21
beside the mischief that H did............. 1Kin 11:25
*3. A son of Ishmael.*
Mishma, and Dumah, Massa, H............. 1Chr 1:30
*4. An early king of Edom.*
was dead, H reigned in his stead.......... 1Chr 1:50
H died also.............................................. 1Chr 1:51

**HADADEZER** (*had-a-de'-zer*) See HADAREZER.
*King of Zobah.*
David smote also H, the son of................. 2Sa 8:3
came to succour H king of Zobah........... 2Sa 8:5
that were on the servants of H............... 2Sa 8:7
and from Berothai, cities of H................. 2Sa 8:8
had smitten all the host of H................... 2Sa 8:9
because he had fought against H.......... 2Sa 8:10
for H had wars with Toi.......................... 2Sa 8:10
of Amalek, and of the spoil of H............ 2Sa 8:12
from his lord H king of Zobah........... 1Kin 11:23

**HADADRIMMON** (*ha''-dad-rim'-mom*) *A place in the valley of Megiddo.*
as the mourning of H in the.................. Zec 12:11

**HADAR** (*ha'-dar*) See HADAD.
*1. A son of Ishmael.*
H, and Tema, Jetur, Naphish, and....... Gen 25:15
*2. An early king of Edom.*
died, and H reigned in his stead........... Gen 36:39

**HADAREZER** (*had-a-re'-zer*) See HADADEZER.
*Another name for Hadadezer.*
H sent, and brought out the................. 2Sa 10:16
of the host of H went before them........ 2Sa 10:16
to H saw that they were smitten.......... 2Sa 10:19
David smote H king of Zobah unto....... 1Chr 18:3
came to help H king of Zobah.............. 1Chr 18:5
that were on the servants of H............. 1Chr 18:7
and from Chun, cities of H.................... 1Chr 18:8
all the host of H king of Zobah............. 1Chr 18:9
because he had fought against H....... 1Chr 18:10
(for H had war with Tou...................... 1Chr 18:10
of the host of H went before them.... 1Chr 19:16
when the servants of H saw that....... 1Chr 19:19

**HADASHAH** (*had'-a-shah*) *A town in Judah.*
Zenan, and H, and Migdal-gad,........... Josh 15:37

**HADASSAH** (*ha-das'-sah*) See ESTHER.
*Another name for Esther.*
And he brought up H, that is,................. Est 2:7

**HADATTAH** (*ha-dat'-tah*) See HAZOR-HADATTAH. *Another name for Hazor.*
And Hazor, H, and Kerioth, and......... Josh 15:25

**HADES**

**HADID** (*ha'-did*) *A city in Benjamin.*
The children of Lod, H, and Ono,........... Ezr 2:33
The children of Lod, H, and Ono,.......... Neh 7:37
H, Zeboim, Neballat,............................ Neh 11:34

**HADLAI** (*had'-la-i*) *Father of Amasa.*
of Shallum, and Amasa the son of H 2Chr 28:12

**HADORAM** (*ha-do'-ram*) See ADORAM.
*1. A son of Joktan.*
And H, and Uzal, and Diklah,.............. Gen 10:27
H also, and Uzal, and Diklah,................ 1Chr 1:21
*2. A son of Tou.*
He sent H his son to king David,....... 1Chr 18:10
*3. An officer of Rehoboam.*
Then king Rehoboam sent H that...... 2Chr 10:18

**HADRACH** (*ha'-drak*) *A district in Syria.*
word of the LORD in the land of H........... Zec 9:1

**HADST**
little which thou *h* before I came......... Gen 30:30
surely thou *h* sent me away now......... Gen 31:42
that thou *h* utterly hated her.............. Judg 15:2
thee, except thou *h* hasted................. 1Sa 25:34
God liveth, unless thou *h* spoken.......... 2Sa 2:27
then *h* thou smitten Syria till.............. 2Kin 13:19
Syria till thou *h* consumed it.............. 2Kin 13:19
with us till thou *h* consumed us............. Ezr 9:14
which thou *h* sworn to give them......... Neh 9:15
concerning which thou *h* promised....... Neh 9:23
because thou *h* a favour unto them......... Ps 44:3
thou, O God, which *h* cast us off............ Ps 60:10
or ever thou *h* formed the earth............. Ps 90:2
thou *h* removed it far unto all................ Is 26:15
O that thou *h* hearkened to my............... Is 48:18
thou *h* a whore's forehead, thou.............. Jer 3:3
For thou *h* cast me into the deep,........ Jonah 2:3
Saying, If thou *h* known, even.............. Lk 19:42
if thou *h* been here, my brother.............. Jn 11:21
if thou *h* been here, my brother.............. Jn 11:32
as if thou *h* not received it.................... 1Cor 4:7
neither *h* pleasure therein...................... Heb 10:8

**HA-ELEPH** See ELEPH.

**HAFT**
the *h* also went in after the.................... Judg 3:22

**HAGAB** (*ha'-gab*) See HAGABA. *A family of exiles.*
The children of H, the children.............. Ezr 2:46

**HAGABA** (*hag'-a-bah*) *Same as Hagab.*
of Lebana, the children of H.................. Neh 7:48

**HAGABAH** (*hag'-a-bah*) See HAGABA. *Same as Hagab.*
of Lebanah, the children of H................. Ezr 2:45

**HAGAR** (*ha'-gar*) *Sarah's handmaid.*
an Egyptian, whose name was H........... Gen 16:1
wife took H her maid the Egyptian...... Gen 16:3

And he went in unto *H*, and she .......... Gen 16:4
And he said, *H*, Sarai's maid, .......... Gen 16:8
And *H* bare Abram a son .......... Gen 16:15
his son's name, which *H* bare .......... Gen 16:15
when *H* bare Ishmael to Abram .......... Gen 16:16
saw the son of *H* the Egyptian .......... Gen 21:9
of water, and gave it unto *H* .......... Gen 21:14
of God called to *H* out of heaven .......... Gen 21:17
unto her, What aileth thee, *H* .......... Gen 21:17
whom *H* the Egyptian, Sarah's .......... Gen 25:12

**HAGARENES** (*haga-renes'*) See HAGARITES. *A people east of the Jordan.*
of Moab, and the *H* .......... Ps 83:6

**HAGARITES** (*hag'-a-rites*) *Same as Hagarenes.*
of Saul they made war with the *H* .......... 1Chr 5:10
And they made war with the *H* .......... 1Chr 5:19
the *H* were delivered into their .......... 1Chr 5:20

**HAGERITE** (*hag'-e-rite*) See HAGARITES, HAGGERI. *Family of David's herdsmen.*
over the flocks was Jaziz the *H* .......... 1Chr 27:31

**HAGGAI** (*hag'-ga-i*) *A prophet.*
*H* the prophet, and Zechariah the .......... Ezr 5:1
the prophesying of *H* the prophet .......... Ezr 6:14
came the word of the LORD by *H* .......... Hag 1:1
word of the LORD by *H* the prophet .......... Hag 1:3
and the words of *H* the prophet .......... Hag 1:12
Then spake *H* the LORD's messenger .......... Hag 1:13
word of the LORD by the prophet *H* .......... Hag 2:1
word of the LORD by *H* the prophet .......... Hag 2:10
Then said *H*, If one that is .......... Hag 2:13
Then answered *H*, and said, So is .......... Hag 2:14
the LORD came unto *H* in the four .......... Hag 2:20

**HAGGEDOLIM** See NEH 12:14

**HAGGERI** (*hag'-gher-i*) See HAGERITE. *Father of Mibhar.*
of Nathan, Mibhar the son of *H* .......... 1Chr 11:38

**HAGGI** (*hag'-ghi*) See HAGGITES. *A son of Gad.*
Ziphion, and *H*, Shuni, and Ezbon, .......... Gen 46:16
of *H*, the family of the Haggites .......... Num 26:15

**HAGGIAH** (*hag-ghi'-ah*) *A descendant of Merari.*
*H* his son, Asaiah his son .......... 1Chr 6:30

**HAGGITES** (*hag'-ghites*) See HAGGI. *Descendants of Haggi.*
of Haggi, the family of the *H* .......... Num 26:15

**HAGGITH** (*hag'-ghith*) *A wife of David.*
the fourth, Adonijah the son of *H* .......... 2Sa 3:4
the son of *H* exalted himself .......... 1Kin 1:5
Adonijah the son of *H* doth reign .......... 1Kin 1:11
Adonijah the son of *H* came to .......... 1Kin 2:13
the fourth, Adonijah the son of *H* .......... 1Chr 3:2

**HAGRI** See HAGGERI.

**HAGRITE** See HAGERITE.

**HAGRITES** See HAGARITES.

**HAI** (*ha'-i*) See AI. *A form of Ai.*
on the west, and *H* on the east .......... Gen 12:8
beginning, between Beth-el and *H* .......... Gen 13:3

**HAIL**
it to rain a very grievous *h* .......... Ex 9:18
the *h* shall come down upon them, .......... Ex 9:19
that there may be *h* in all the .......... Ex 9:22
and the LORD sent thunder and *h* .......... Ex 9:23
the LORD rained *h* upon the land .......... Ex 9:23
*h*, and fire mingled with the *h* .......... Ex 9:24
the *h* smote throughout all the .......... Ex 9:25
the *h* smote every herb of the .......... Ex 9:25
of Israel were, was there no *h* .......... Ex 9:26
no more mighty thunderings and *h* .......... Ex 9:28
neither shall there be any more *h* .......... Ex 9:29
*h* ceased, and the rain was not .......... Ex 9:33
saw that the rain and the *h* .......... Ex 9:34
remaineth unto you from the *h* .......... Ex 10:5
even all that the *h* hath left .......... Ex 10:12
of the trees which the *h* had left .......... Ex 10:15
thou seen the treasures of the *h* .......... Job 38:22
*h* stones and coals of fire .......... Ps 18:12
*h* stones and coals of fire .......... Ps 18:13
He destroyed their vines with *h* .......... Ps 78:47
up their cattle also to the *h* .......... Ps 78:48
He gave them *h* for rain, and .......... Ps 105:32
Fire, and *h*; snow, and vapours .......... Ps 148:8
one, which as a tempest of *h* .......... Is 28:2
the *h* shall sweep away the refuge .......... Is 28:17
When it shall *h*, coming down on .......... Is 32:19
with *h* in all the labours of your .......... Hag 2:17
he came to Jesus, and said, *H* .......... Mt 26:49
him, and mocked him, saying, *H* .......... Mt 27:29
Jesus met them, saying, All *h* .......... Mt 28:9
And began to salute him, *H* .......... Mk 15:18
came in unto her, and said, *H* .......... Lk 1:28
And said, *H*, King of the Jews .......... Jn 19:3
sounded, and there followed *h* .......... Rev 8:7
and an earthquake, and great *h* .......... Rev 11:19
upon men a great *h* out of heaven .......... Rev 16:21
because of the plague of the *h* .......... Rev 16:21

**HAILSTONES**
*h* than they whom the children of .......... Josh 10:11
with scattering, and tempest, and *h* .......... Is 30:30
and ye, O great *h*, shall fall .......... Eze 13:11
great *h* in my fury to consume it .......... Eze 13:13
and overflowing rain, and great *h* .......... Eze 38:22

**HAIR**
and fine linen, and goats' *h* .......... Ex 25:4
*h* to be a covering upon the .......... Ex 26:7
and fine linen, and goats' *h* .......... Ex 35:6
and fine linen, and goats' *h* .......... Ex 35:23
them up in wisdom spun goats' *h* .......... Ex 35:26
of goats' *h* for the tent over the .......... Ex 36:14
when the *h* in the plague is .......... Lev 13:3
the *h* thereof be not turned white .......... Lev 13:4
and it have turned the *h* white .......... Lev 13:10
the *h* thereof be turned white .......... Lev 13:20
if the *h* in the bright spot be .......... Lev 13:25
there be no white *h* in the bright .......... Lev 13:26
and there be in it a yellow thin *h* .......... Lev 13:30
and that there is no black *h* in it .......... Lev 13:31
and there be in it no yellow *h* .......... Lev 13:32
shall not seek for yellow *h* .......... Lev 13:36
there is black *h* grown up therein .......... Lev 13:37
the man whose *h* is fallen off his .......... Lev 13:40
he that hath his *h* fallen off .......... Lev 13:41
clothes, and shave off all his *h* .......... Lev 14:8
shave all his *h* off his head .......... Lev 14:9
even all his *h* he shall shave off .......... Lev 14:9
locks of the *h* of his head grow .......... Num 6:5
shall take the *h* of the head of .......... Num 6:18
after the *h* of his separation is .......... Num 6:19
of skins, and all work of goats' *h* .......... Num 31:20
Howbeit the *h* of his head began .......... Judg 16:22
sling stones at an *h* breadth .......... Judg 20:16
there shall not one *h* of his head .......... 1Sa 14:45
of goats' *h* for his bolster .......... 1Sa 19:13
of goats' *h* for his bolster .......... 1Sa 19:16
there shall not one *h* of thy son .......... 2Sa 14:11
because the *h* was heavy on him, .......... 2Sa 14:26
he weighed the *h* of his head at .......... 2Sa 14:26
there shall not an *h* of him fall .......... 1Kin 1:52
and plucked off the *h* of my head .......... Ezr 9:3
of them, and plucked off their *h* .......... Neh 13:25
the *h* of my flesh stood up .......... Job 4:15
thy *h* is as a flock of goats, .......... Song 4:1
thy *h* is as a flock of goats that .......... Song 6:5
the *h* of thine head like purple .......... Song 7:5
and instead of well set *h* baldness .......... Is 3:24
the head, and the *h* of the feet .......... Is 7:20
to them that plucked off the *h* .......... Is 50:6
Cut off thine *h*, O Jerusalem, and .......... Jer 7:29
to weigh, and divide the *h* .......... Eze 5:1
thine *h* is grown, whereas thou .......... Eze 16:7
nor was an *h* of their head singed .......... Dan 3:27
the *h* of his head like the pure .......... Dan 7:9
John had his raiment of camel's *h* .......... Mt 3:4
not make one *h* white or black .......... Mt 5:36
John was clothed with camel's *h* .......... Mk 1:6
not an *h* of your head perish .......... Lk 21:18
and wiped his feet with her *h* .......... Jn 11:2
and wiped his feet with her *h* .......... Jn 12:3
for there shall not an *h* fall .......... Acts 27:34
you, that, if a man have long *h* .......... 1Cor 11:14
But if a woman have long *h* .......... 1Cor 11:15
for her *h* is given her for a .......... 1Cor 11:15
not with broided *h*, or gold, or .......... 1Ti 2:9
adorning of plaiting the *h* .......... 1Pet 3:3
became black as sackcloth of *h* .......... Rev 6:12
they had *h* as the *h* of women, .......... Rev 9:8

**HAIRS**
gray *h* with sorrow to the grave .......... Gen 42:38
gray *h* with sorrow to the grave .......... Gen 44:29
shall bring down the gray *h* of .......... Gen 44:31
there be no white *h* therein .......... Lev 13:21
also with the man of gray *h* .......... Deut 32:25
are more than the *h* of mine head .......... Ps 40:12
are more than the *h* of mine head .......... Ps 69:4
even to hoar *h* will I carry you .......... Is 46:4
till his *h* were grown like .......... Dan 4:33
gray *h* are here and there upon him .......... Hos 7:9
But the very *h* of your head are .......... Mt 10:30
wipe them with the *h* of her head .......... Lk 7:38
wiped them with the *h* of her head .......... Lk 7:44
But even the very *h* of your head .......... Lk 12:7
his *h* were white like wool, as .......... Rev 1:14

**HAIRY**
red, all over like an *h* garment .......... Gen 25:25
Esau my brother is a *h* man .......... Gen 27:11
him not, because his hands were *h* .......... Gen 27:23
answered him, He was an *h* man .......... 2Kin 1:8
the *h* scalp of such an one as .......... Ps 68:21

**HAKELDAMA** See ACELDAMA.

**HAKKATAN** (*hak'-ka-tan*) *A family of exiles.*
Johanan the son of *H*, and with him .......... Ezr 8:12

**HAKKOZ** (*hak'-koz*) See KOZ. *A sanctuary servant.*
The seventh to *H*, the eighth to .......... 1Chr 24:10

**HAKUPHA** (*ha-ku'-fah*) *A family of exiles.*
of Bakbuk, the children of *H* .......... Ezr 2:51
of Bakbuk, the children of *H* .......... Neh 7:53

**HALAH** (*ha'-lah*) *An Assyrian district.*
into Assyria, and placed them in *H* .......... 2Kin 17:6
unto Assyria, and put them in *H* .......... 2Kin 18:11
Manasseh, and brought them unto *H*. 1Chr 5:26

**HALAK** (*ha'-lak*) *A mountain in southern Canaan.*
Even from the mount *H*, that goeth .. Josh 11:17
of Lebanon even unto the mount *H* .......... Josh 12:7

**HALE**
lest he *h* thee to the judge, and .......... Lk 12:58

**HALF**
earring of *h* a shekel weight .......... Gen 24:22
Moses took *h* of the blood, and put .......... Ex 24:6
*h* of the blood he sprinkled on .......... Ex 24:6
a *h* shall be the length thereof, .......... Ex 25:10
a *h* the breadth thereof .......... Ex 25:10
a cubit and a *h* the height thereof .......... Ex 25:10
a *h* shall be the length thereof, .......... Ex 25:17
cubit and a *h* the breadth thereof .......... Ex 25:17
a cubit and a *h* the height thereof .......... Ex 25:23
the *h* curtain that remaineth, .......... Ex 26:12
a *h* shall be the breadth of one .......... Ex 26:16
*h* a shekel after the shekel of .......... Ex 30:13
an *h* shekel shall be the .......... Ex 30:13
not give less than *h* a shekel .......... Ex 30:15
and of sweet cinnamon *h* so much .......... Ex 30:23
of a board one cubit and a *h* .......... Ex 36:21
a *h* was the length of it, and a .......... Ex 37:1
a *h* the breadth of it .......... Ex 37:1
a cubit and a *h* the height of it .......... Ex 37:1
a *h* was the length thereof, and .......... Ex 37:6
cubit and a *h* the breadth thereof .......... Ex 37:6
a cubit and a *h* the height thereof .......... Ex 37:10
*h* a shekel, after the shekel of .......... Ex 38:26
*h* of it in the morning, and *h* .......... Lev 6:20
of whom the flesh is *h* consumed .......... Num 12:12
mingled with *h* an hin of oil .......... Num 15:9
a drink offering *h* an hin of wine .......... Num 15:10
*h* an hin of wine unto a bullock .......... Num 28:14
Take it of their *h*, and give it .......... Num 31:29
And of the children of Israel's *h* .......... Num 31:30
And the *h*, which was the portion .......... Num 31:36
And of the children of Israel's *h* .......... Num 31:42
(Now the *h* that pertained unto .......... Num 31:43
of the children of Israel's *h* .......... Num 31:47
unto *h* the tribe of Manasseh the .......... Num 32:33
nine tribes, and to the *h* tribe .......... Num 34:13
*h* the tribe of Manasseh have .......... Num 34:14
the *h* tribe have received their .......... Num 34:15
*h* mount Gilead, and the cities .......... Deut 3:12
gave I unto the *h* tribe of .......... Deut 3:13
unto the river Arnon *h* the valley .......... Deut 3:16
to the *h* tribe of Manasseh .......... Deut 29:8
to *h* the tribe of Manasseh, spake .......... Josh 1:12
*h* the tribe of Manasseh, passed .......... Josh 4:12
*h* of them over against mount .......... Josh 8:33
*h* of them over against mount Ebal .......... Josh 8:33
from *h* Gilead, even unto the .......... Josh 12:2
*h* Gilead, the border of Sihon .......... Josh 12:5
and the *h* tribe of Manasseh .......... Josh 12:6
and the *h* tribe of Manasseh, .......... Josh 13:7
*h* the land of the children of .......... Josh 13:25
unto the *h* tribe of Manasseh .......... Josh 13:29
of the *h* tribe of the children of .......... Josh 13:29
*h* Gilead, and Ashtaroth, and Edrei, .......... Josh 13:31
even to the one *h* of the children .......... Josh 13:31
nine tribes, and for the *h* tribe .......... Josh 14:2
an *h* tribe on the other side .......... Josh 14:3
*h* the tribe of Manasseh, have .......... Josh 18:7
out of the *h* tribe of Manasseh, .......... Josh 21:5
out of the *h* tribe of Manasseh in .......... Josh 21:6
out of the *h* tribe of Manasseh, .......... Josh 21:25
out of the other *h* tribe of .......... Josh 21:27
and the *h* tribe of Manasseh, .......... Josh 22:1
Now to the one *h* of the tribe of .......... Josh 22:7
but unto the other *h* thereof gave .......... Josh 22:7
the *h* tribe of Manasseh returned, .......... Josh 22:9
the *h* tribe of Manasseh built .......... Josh 22:10
the *h* tribe of Manasseh have .......... Josh 22:11
to the *h* tribe of Manasseh, into .......... Josh 22:13
to the *h* tribe of Manasseh, unto .......... Josh 22:15
the *h* tribe of Manasseh answered, .......... Josh 22:21
as it were an *h* acre of land .......... 1Sa 14:14
off the one *h* of their beards .......... 2Sa 10:4
neither if *h* of us die, will they .......... 2Sa 18:3
also *h* the people of Israel .......... 2Sa 19:40
give *h* to the one, and *h* to the .......... 1Kin 3:25
work of the base, a cubit and an *h* .......... 1Kin 7:31
a wheel was a cubit and *h* a cubit .......... 1Kin 7:32
a round compass of *h* a cubit high .......... 1Kin 7:35
and, behold, the *h* was not told me .......... 1Kin 10:7
thou wilt give me *h* thine house .......... 1Kin 13:8
captain of *h* his chariots, .......... 1Kin 16:9
*h* of the people followed Tibni .......... 1Kin 16:21
and *h* followed Omri .......... 1Kin 16:21
Haroeh, and *h* of the Manahethites .......... 1Chr 2:52
*h* of the Manahethites, the .......... 1Chr 2:54
*h* the tribe of Manasseh, of .......... 1Chr 5:18
the children of the *h* tribe of .......... 1Chr 5:23
the *h* tribe of Manasseh, and .......... 1Chr 5:26
cities given out of the *h* tribe .......... 1Chr 6:61
out of the *h* tribe of Manasseh, .......... 1Chr 6:61
out of the *h* tribe of Manasseh .......... 1Chr 6:70
family of the *h* tribe of Manasseh .......... 1Chr 6:71
of the *h* tribe of Manasseh .......... 1Chr 12:31
of the *h* tribe of Manasseh, with .......... 1Chr 12:37
the *h* tribe of Manasseh, for .......... 1Chr 26:32
of the *h* tribe of Manasseh, Joel .......... 1Chr 27:20
Of the *h* tribe of Manasseh in .......... 1Chr 27:21
the one *h* of the greatness of thy .......... 2Chr 9:6
the ruler of the *h* part of .......... Neh 3:9
the ruler of the *h* part of .......... Neh 3:12
ruler of the *h* part of Beth-zur .......... Neh 3:16
the ruler of the *h* part of Keilah .......... Neh 3:17
the ruler of the *h* part of Keilah .......... Neh 3:18
together unto the *h* thereof .......... Neh 4:6
that the *h* of my servants wrought .......... Neh 4:16
the other *h* of them held both the .......... Neh 4:16

*h* of them held the spears from Neh 4:21
*h* of the princes of Judah, Neh 12:32
the *h* of the people upon the wall Neh 12:38
the *h* of the rulers with me Neh 12:40
their children spake *h* in the Neh 13:24
thee to the *h* of the kingdom Est 5:3
even to the *h* of the kingdom it Est 5:6
even to the *h* of the kingdom Est 7:2
shall not live out *h* their days Ps 55:23
Samaria committed *h* of thy sins Eze 16:51
an *h* long, and a cubit and an *h* Eze 40:42
about it shall be *h* a cubit Eze 43:17
be for a time, times, and an *h* Dan 12:7
barley, and an *h* homer of barley Hos 3:2
*h* of the city shall go forth into Zec 14:2
*h* of the mountain shall remove Zec 14:4
and *h* of it toward the south Zec 14:4
*h* of them toward the former sea, Zec 14:8
*h* of them toward the hinder sea Zec 14:8
it thee, unto the *h* of my kingdom Mk 6:23
and departed, leaving him *h* dead Lk 10:30
the *h* of my goods I give to the Lk 19:8
about the space of *h* an hour Rev 8:1
dead bodies three days and an *h* Rev 11:9
an *h* the Spirit of life from God Rev 11:11
*h* a time, from the face of the Rev 12:14

**HALHUL** (*hal'-hul*) *A city in Judah.*
*H*, Beth-zur, and Gedor, Josh 15:58

**HALI** (*ha'-li*) *A town in Asher.*
And their border was Helkath, and *H* Josh 19:25

**HALING**
*h* men and women committed them to Acts 8:3

**HALL**
took Jesus into the common *h* Mt 27:27
soldiers led him away into the *h* Mk 15:16
a fire in the midst of the *h* Lk 22:55
Caiaphas unto the *h* of judgment Jn 18:28
went not into the judgment *h* Jn 18:28
entered into the judgment *h* again Jn 18:33
And went again into the judgment *h* Jn 19:9
to be kept in Herod's judgment *h* Acts 23:35

**HALLOHESH** (*hal-lo'-hesh*) See HALOHESH. *Father of Shallum.*
*H*, Pileha, Shobek, Neh 10:24

**HALLOW**
shall *h* in all their holy gifts Ex 28:38
thou shalt do unto them to *h* them Ex 29:1
that is therein, and shalt *h* it Ex 40:9
*h* it from the uncleanness of the Lev 16:19
those things which they *h* unto me Lev 22:2
of Israel *h* unto the LORD Lev 22:3
I am the LORD which *h* you Lev 22:32
ye shall *h* the fiftieth year, and Lev 25:10
shall *h* his head that same day Num 6:11
The same day did the king *h* the 1Kin 8:64
but *h* ye the sabbath day, as I Jer 17:22
but *h* the sabbath day, to do no Jer 17:24
unto me to *h* the sabbath day Jer 17:27
And *h* my sabbaths Eze 20:20
and they shall *h* my sabbaths Eze 44:24

**HALLOWED**
blessed the sabbath day, and *h* it Ex 20:11
and he shall be *h*, and his garments Ex 29:21
she shall touch no *h* thing Lev 12:4
profaned the *h* thing of the LORD Lev 19:8
but I will be *h* among the Lev 22:32
in the land of Egypt I *h* unto me Num 3:13
every man's *h* things shall be his Num 5:10
for they are *h* Num 16:37
the LORD, therefore they are *h* Num 16:38
the *h* things of the children of Num 18:8
even the *h* part thereof out of it Num 18:29
I have brought away the *h* things Deut 26:13
mine hand, but there is *h* bread 1Sa 21:4
So the priest gave him *h* bread 1Sa 21:6
I have *h* this house, which thou 1Kin 9:3
house, which I have *h* for my name 1Kin 9:7
all the *h* things that Jehoshaphat 2Kin 12:18
dedicated, and his own *h* things 2Kin 12:18
Moreover Solomon *h* the middle of 2Chr 7:7
LORD which he had *h* in Jerusalem 2Chr 36:14
art in heaven, *H* be thy name Mt 6:9
art in heaven, *H* be thy name Lk 11:2

**HALOHESH** (*ha-lo'-hesh*) See HALLOHESH. *Same as Hallohesh.*
him repaired Shallum the son of *H* Neh 3:12

**HALT**
How long *h* ye between two 1Kin 18:21
For I am ready to *h*, and my sorrow Ps 38:17
to enter into life *h* or maimed Mt 18:8
for thee to enter *h* into life Mk 9:45
the poor, and the maimed, and the *h* Lk 14:21
of impotent folk, of blind, *h* Jn 5:3

**HALTED**
upon him, and he *h* upon his thigh Gen 32:31
I will make her that *h* a remnant Mic 4:7

**HALTETH**
LORD, will I assemble her that *h* Mic 4:6
and I will save her that *h* Zeph 3:19

**HALTING**
All my familiars watched for my *h* Jer 20:10

**HAM** (*ham*)
*1. A son of Noah.*
and Noah begat Shem, *H*, and Japheth Gen 5:32
And Noah begat three sons, Shem, *H* Gen 6:10
day entered Noah, and Shem, and *H* Gen 7:13
forth of the ark, were Shem, and *H* Gen 9:18
*H* is the father of Canaan Gen 9:18
And *H*, the father of Canaan, saw Gen 9:22
of the sons of Noah, Shem, *H* Gen 10:1
And the sons of *H* Gen 10:6
These are the sons of *H*, after Gen 10:20
Karnaim, and the Zuzims in *H* Gen 14:5
Noah, Shem, *H*, and Japheth 1Chr 1:4
The sons of *H* 1Chr 1:8
*2. Descendants and land of Ham.*
for they of *H* had dwelt there of 1Chr 4:40
strength in the tabernacles of *H* Ps 78:51
Jacob sojourned in the land of *H* Ps 105:23
them, and wonders in the land of *H* Ps 105:27
Wondrous works in the land of *H* Ps 106:22

**HAMAN** (*ha'-man*) See HAMAN'S. *Prime minister under King Ahasuerus.*
*H* the son of Hammedatha the Est 3:1
gate, bowed, and reverenced *H* Est 3:2
not unto them, that they told *H* Est 3:4
when *H* saw that Mordecai bowed Est 3:5
then was *H* full of wrath Est 3:5
wherefore *H* sought to destroy all Est 3:6
before *H* from day to day, and from Est 3:7
*H* said unto king Ahasuerus, There Est 3:8
gave it unto *H* the son of Est 3:10
And the king said unto *H*, The Est 3:11
*H* had commanded unto the king's Est 3:12
the king and *H* sat down to drink Est 3:15
that *H* had promised to pay to the Est 4:7
*H* come this day unto the banquet Est 5:4
Cause *H* to make haste, that he Est 5:5
*H* came to the banquet that Esther Est 5:5
*H* come to the banquet that I Est 5:8
Then went *H* forth that day joyful Est 5:9
but when *H* saw Mordecai in the Est 5:9
Nevertheless *H* refrained himself Est 5:10
*H* told them of the glory of his Est 5:11
*H* said moreover, Yea, Esther the Est 5:12
And the thing pleased *H* Est 5:14
Now *H* was come into the outward Est 6:4
Behold, *H* standeth in the court Est 6:5
So *H* came in Est 6:6
Now *H* thought in his heart, To Est 6:6
*H* answered the king, For the man Est 6:7
Then the king said to *H*, Make Est 6:10
Then took *H* the apparel and the Est 6:11
But *H* hasted to his house Est 6:12
*H* told Zeresh his wife and all his Est 6:13
hasted to bring *H* unto the Est 6:14
*H* came to banquet with Esther the Est 7:1
and enemy is this wicked *H* Est 7:6
Then *H* was afraid before the king Est 7:6
*H* stood up to make request for Est 7:7
*H* was fallen upon the bed whereon Est 7:8
which *H* had made for Mordecai, Est 7:9
king, standeth in the house of *H* Est 7:9
So they hanged *H* on the gallows Est 7:10
Ahasuerus give the house of *H* the Est 8:1
ring, which he had taken from *H* Est 8:2
set Mordecai over the house of *H* Est 8:2
the mischief of *H* the Agagite Est 8:3
by *H* the son of Hammedatha the Est 8:5
have given Esther the house of *H* Est 8:7
The ten sons of *H* the son of Est 9:10
the palace, and the ten sons of *H* Est 9:12
Because *H* the son of Hammedatha, Est 9:24

**HAMAN'S** (*ha'-mans*)
king's mouth, they covered *H* face Est 7:8
let *H* ten sons be hanged upon the Est 9:13
and they hanged *H* ten sons Est 9:14

**HAMATH** (*ha'-math*) See HAMATHITE, HAMATH-ZOBAH, HEMATH. *A capital of Syria.*
Zin unto Rehob, as men come to *H* Num 13:21
border unto the entrance of *H* Num 34:8
Hermon unto the entering into *H* Josh 13:5
unto the entering in of *H* Judg 3:3
When Toi king of *H* heard that 2Sa 8:9
in of *H* unto the river of Egypt 1Kin 8:65
of *H* unto the sea of the plain 2Kin 14:25
how he recovered Damascus, and *H* 2Kin 14:28
Cuthah, and from Ava, and from *H* 2Kin 17:24
the men of *H* made Ashima, 2Kin 17:30
Where are the gods of *H*, and of 2Kin 18:34
Where is the king of *H*, and the 2Kin 19:13
bands at Riblah in the land of *H* 2Kin 23:33
them at Riblah in the land of *H* 2Kin 25:21
Hadarezer king of Zobah unto *H* 1Chr 18:3
Now when Tou king of *H* heard how 1Chr 18:9
in of *H* unto the river of Egypt 2Chr 7:8
store cities, which he built in *H* 2Chr 8:4
is not *H* as Arpad Is 10:9
Elam, and from Shinar, and from *H* Is 11:11
Where are the gods of *H* and Arphad Is 36:19
Where is the king of *H*, and the Is 37:13
to Riblah in the land of *H* Jer 39:5
*H* is confounded, and Arpad Jer 49:23
to Riblah in the land of *H* Jer 52:9
death in Riblah in the land of *H* Jer 52:27
*H*, Berothah, Sibraim, which is Eze 47:16
of Damascus and the border of *H* Eze 47:16
northward, and the border of *H* Eze 47:17
till a man come over against *H* Eze 47:20
way of Hethlon, as one goeth to *H* Eze 48:1
northward, to the coast of *H* Eze 48:1
from thence go ye to *H* the great Amos 6:2
*H* also shall border thereby Zec 9:2

**HAMATHITE**
and the Zemarite, and the *H* Gen 10:18
and the Zemarite, and the *H* 1Chr 1:16

**HAMATH-ZOBAH** (*ha''-math-zo'-bah*) *Full name of Hamath.*
And Solomon went to *H*, and 2Chr 8:3

**HAMITES** See HAM.

**HAMMATH** (*ham'-math*) *A city in Naphtali.*
cities are Ziddim, Zer, and *H* Josh 19:35

**HAMMEDATHA** (*ham-med'a-thah*) *Father of Haman.*
Haman the son of *H* the Agagite Est 3:1
Haman the son of *H* the Agagite Est 3:10
by Haman the son of *H* the Agagite Est 8:5
ten sons of Haman the son of *H* Est 9:10
Because Haman the son of *H* Est 9:24

**HAMMELECH** (*ham'-me-lek*) *Father of Jerahmeel*
commanded Jerahmeel the son of *H* Jer 36:26
dungeon of Malchiah the son of *H* Jer 38:6

**HAMMER**
took an *h* in her hand, and went Judg 4:21
her right hand to the workmen's *h* Judg 5:26
with the *h* she smote Sisera, she Judg 5:26
so that there was neither *h* nor 1Kin 6:7
the *h* him that smote the anvil Is 41:7
like a *h* that breaketh the rock Jer 23:29
How is the *h* of the whole earth Jer 50:23

**HAMMERS**
thereof at once with axes and *h* Ps 74:6
coals, and fashioneth it with *h* Is 44:12
fasten it with nails and with *h* Jer 10:4

**HAMMOLEKETH** (*ham-mol'-e-keth*) *Daughter of Machir.*
And his sister *H* bare Ishod 1Chr 7:18

**HAMMON** (*ham'-mon*)
*1. A city in Asher.*
And Hebron, and Rehob, and *H* Josh 19:28
*2. A city in Naphtali.*
*H* with her suburbs, and Kirjathaim 1Chr 6:76

**HAMMOTH-DOR** (*ham''-moth-dor'*) *Same as Hammon 2.*
*H* with her suburbs, and Kartan Josh 21:32

**HAMMUEL** See HAMUEL.

**HAMONAH** (*ha-mo'-nah*) *Place where Gog is buried.*
the name of the city shall be *H* Eze 39:16

**HAMON-GOG** (*ha''-mon-gog*) *Same as Hamonah.*
shall call it The valley of *H* Eze 39:11
have buried it in the valley of *H* Eze 39:15

**HAMOR** (*ha'-mor*) See EMMOR, HAMOR'S. *Father of Shechem.*
at the hand of the children of *H* Gen 33:19
Shechem the son of *H* the Hivite Gen 34:2
Shechem spake unto his father *H* Gen 34:4
*H* the father of Shechem went out Gen 34:6
*H* communed with them, saying, The Gen 34:8
*H* his father deceitfully, and said Gen 34:13
And their words pleased *H*, and Gen 34:18
*H* and Shechem his son came Gen 34:20
unto *H* and unto Shechem Gen 34:24
And they slew *H* and Shechem Gen 34:26
Jacob bought of the sons of *H* the Josh 24:32
serve the men of *H* the father of Judg 9:28

**HAMOR'S** (*ha'-mors*)
pleased Hamor, and Shechem *H* son Gen 34:18

**HAMRAN** See AMRAN.

**HAMUEL** (*ha-mu'-el*) *Son of Mishma.*
*H* his son, Zacchur his son, 1Chr 4:26

**HAMUL** (*ha'-mul*) See HAMULITES. *A son of Pharez.*
sons of Pharez were Hezron and *H* Gen 46:12
of *H*, the family of the Hamulites Num 26:21
Hezron, and *H* 1Chr 2:5

**HAMULITES** (*ha'-mu-lites*) *Descendants of Hamul.*
of Hamul, the family of the *H* Num 26:21

**HAMUTAL** (*ha-mu'-tal*) *Mother of King Jehoahaz.*
And his mother's name was *H* 2Kin 23:31
And his mother's name was *H* 2Kin 24:18
his mother's name was *H* the Jer 52:1

**HANAMEAL** See HANAMEEL.

**HANAMEEL** (*ha-nam'-e-el*) *Son of Shallum.*
*H* the son of Shallum thine uncle Jer 32:7
So *H* mine uncle's son came to me Jer 32:8
the field of *H* my uncle's son Jer 32:9
in the sight of *H* mine uncle's Jer 32:12

**HANAMEL** See HANAMEEL.

**HANAN** (*ha'-nan*) See BAAL-HANAN, BEN-HANAN, ELON-BETH-HANAN.
*1. A son of Shashak.*
And Abdon, and Zichri, and *H* 1Chr 8:23
*2. A son of Azel.*
and Sheariah, and Obadiah, and *H* 1Chr 8:38
and Sheariah, and Obadiah, and *H* 1Chr 9:44

*3. A "mighty man" of David.*
H the son of Maachah, and 1Chr 11:43
*4. Family of exiles.*
of Shalmai, the children of H Ezr 2:46
The children of H, the children Neh 7:49
*5. A priest who assisted Ezra.*
Kelita, Jozabad, H Neh 8:7
*6. A Levite who renewed the covenant.*
Hodijah, Kelita, Pelaiah, H Neh 10:10
next to them was H the son of Neh 13:13
*7. A chief who renewed the covenant.*
Pelatiah, H, Anaiah, Neh 10:22
*8. Another chief who renewed the covenant.*
And Ahijah, H, Anan, Neh 10:26
*9. Son of Igdaliah.*
into the chamber of the sons of H Jer 35:4

**HANANEAL** See HANANEEL.

**HANANEEL** (*ha-nan'-e-el*) *A tower on Jerusalem's wall.*
it, unto the tower of H Neh 3:1
the fish gate, and the tower of H Neh 12:39
of H unto the gate of the corner Jer 31:38
from the tower of H unto the Zec 14:10

**HANANEL** See HANANEEL.

**HANANI** (*ha-na'-ni*)
*1. A son of Heman.*
Shebuel, and Jerimoth, Hananiah, H... 1Chr 25:4
The eighteenth to H, he, his sons 1Chr 25:25
*2. A prophet.*
at that time H the seer came to 2Chr 16:7
*3. Father of Jehu.*
Jehu the son of H against Baasha 1Kin 16:1
of H came the word of the LORD 1Kin 16:7
Jehu the son of H the seer went 2Chr 19:2
in the book of Jehu the son of H 2Chr 20:34
*4. Married a foreigner in exile.*
of Immer; H, and Zebadiah Ezr 10:20
*5. Brother of Nehemiah.*
That H, one of my brethren, came, Neh 1:2
That I gave my brother H, and Neh 7:2
*6. A priest.*
Maai, Nethaneel, and Judah, H Neh 12:36

**HANANIAH** (*han-a-ni'-ah*) See SHADRACH.
*1. A son of Heman.*
Uzziel, Shebuel, and Jerimoth, H 1Chr 25:4
The sixteenth to H, he, his sons, 1Chr 25:23
Meraiah; of Jeremiah, H Neh 12:12
Hear now, H; The LORD hath Jer 28:15
*2. A captain of King Uzziah.*
the ruler, under the hand of H 2Chr 26:11
*3. Father of Zedekiah.*
Shaphan, and Zedekiah the son of H... Jer 36:12
*4. A false prophet.*
that H the son of Azur the Jer 28:1
H in the presence of the priests Jer 28:5
Then H the prophet took the yoke Jer 28:10
H spake in the presence of all Jer 28:11
after that H the prophet had Jer 28:12
Go and tell H, saying, Thus saith Jer 28:13
Jeremiah unto H the prophet Jer 28:15
So H the prophet died the same Jer 28:17
*5. Grandfather of Irijah.*
son of Shelemiah, the son of H Jer 37:13
*6. Son of Shashak.*
And H, and Elam, and Antothijah, 1Chr 8:24
*7. Hebrew form of Shadrach.*
the children of Judah, Daniel, H Dan 1:6
and to H, of Shadrach Dan 1:7
eunuchs had set over Daniel, H Dan 1:11
all was found none like Daniel, H Dan 1:19
and made the thing known to H Dan 2:17
*8. A son of Zerubbabel.*
Meshullam, and H, and Shelomith 1Chr 3:19
And the sons of H 1Chr 3:21
*9. Married a foreigner in exile.*
Jehohanan, H, Zabbai, and Athlai Ezr 10:28
*10. A rebuilder of Jerusalem's wall.*
repaired H the son of one of the Neh 3:8
*11. Another rebuilder of Jerusalem's wall.*
After him repaired H the son of Neh 3:30
*12. A palace servant of Nehemiah.*
H the ruler of the palace, charge Neh 7:2
*13. An Israelite who renewed the covenant.*
Hoshea, H, Hashub, Neh 10:23
*14. A priest.*
Elioenai, Zechariah, and H Neh 12:41

**HAND** See PREFACE.

**HANDBREADTH**
a border of an h round about Ex 37:12
And the thickness of it was an h 2Chr 4:5
thou hast made my days as an h Ps 39:5

**HANDED**
him while he is weary and weak h 2Sa 17:2

**HANDFUL**
his h of the flour thereof Lev 2:2
the priest shall take his h of it Lev 5:12
And he shall take of it his h Lev 6:15
offering, and took an h thereof Lev 9:17
shall take an h of the offering Num 5:26
but an h of meal in a barrel, and 1Kin 17:12
There shall be an h of corn in Ps 72:16
Better is an h with quietness, Eccl 4:6
as the h after the harvestman, and Jer 9:22

**HANDFULS**
the earth brought forth by h Gen 41:47
Take to you h of ashes of the Ex 9:8
some of the h of purpose for her Ruth 2:16
of Samaria shall suffice for h 1Kin 20:10
among my people for h of barley Eze 13:19

**HANDKERCHIEFS**
brought unto the sick h or aprons Acts 19:12

**HANDLE**
father of all such as h the harp Gen 4:21
they that h the pen of the writer Judg 5:14
the battle, that could h shield 1Chr 12:8
forth to war, that could h spear 2Chr 25:5
They have hands, but they h not Ps 115:7
they that h the law knew me not Jer 2:8
and the Libyans, that h the shield Jer 46:9
and the Lydians, that h and bend Jer 46:9
And all that h the oar, the Eze 27:29
h me, and see Lk 24:39
taste not; h not Col 2:21

**HANDLED**
to be furbished, that it may be h Eze 21:11
and sent him away shamefully h Mk 12:4
looked upon, and our hands have h 1Jn 1:1

**HANDLES**
myrrh, upon the h of the lock Song 5:5

**HANDLETH**
He that h a matter wisely shall Prov 16:20
him that h the sickle in the time Jer 50:16
shall he stand that h the bow Amos 2:15

**HANDLING**
and shields, all of them h swords Eze 38:4
nor h the word of God deceitfully 2Cor 4:2

**HANDMAID**
and she had an h, an Egyptian, Gen 16:1
Hagar the Egyptian, Sarah's h Gen 25:12
Leah Zilpah his maid for an h Gen 29:24
Bilhah his h to be her maid Gen 29:29
she gave him Bilhah her h to wife Gen 30:4
And the sons of Bilhah, Rachel's h Gen 35:25
And the sons of Zilpah, Leah's h Gen 35:26
ass may rest, and the son of thy h Ex 23:12
and wine also for me, and for thy h.. Judg 19:19
hast spoken friendly unto thine h Ruth 2:13
she answered, I am Ruth thine h Ruth 3:9
therefore thy skirt over thine h Ruth 3:9
look on the affliction of thine h 1Sa 1:11
me, and not forget thine h 1Sa 1:11
give unto thine h a man child 1Sa 1:11
Count not thine h for a daughter 1Sa 1:16
Let thine h find grace in thy 1Sa 1:18
and let thine h, I pray thee, 1Sa 25:24
and hear the words of thine h 1Sa 25:24
but I thine h saw not the young 1Sa 25:25
thine h hath brought unto my lord 1Sa 25:27
forgive the trespass of thine h 1Sa 25:28
my lord, then remember thine h 1Sa 25:31
let thine h be a servant to wash 1Sa 25:41
thine h hath obeyed thy voice, and 1Sa 28:21
also unto the voice of thine h 1Sa 28:22
thy h had two sons, and they two 2Sa 14:6
family is risen against thine h 2Sa 14:7
Then the woman said, Let thine h 2Sa 14:12
thy h said, I will now speak unto 2Sa 14:15
will perform the request of his h 2Sa 14:15
to deliver his h out of the hand 2Sa 14:16
Then thine h said, The word of my 2Sa 14:17
words in the mouth of thine h 2Sa 14:19
him, Hear the words of thine h 2Sa 20:17
lord, O king, swear unto thine h 1Kin 1:13
by the LORD thy God unto thine h 1Kin 1:17
beside me, while thine h slept 1Kin 3:20
Thine h hath not any thing in the 2Kin 4:2
of God, do not lie unto thine h 2Kin 4:16
and save the son of thine h Ps 86:16
servant, and the son of thine h Ps 116:16
an h that is heir to her mistress Prov 30:23
his servant, and every man his h Jer 34:16
said, Behold the h of the Lord Lk 1:38

**HANDMAIDEN**
regarded the low estate of his h Lk 1:48

**HANDMAIDENS**
Then the h came near, they and Gen 33:6
I be not like unto one of thine h Ruth 2:13
on my h I will pour out in those Acts 2:18

**HANDMAIDS**
and unto Rachel, and unto the two h.. Gen 33:1
And he put the h and their children Gen 33:2
the eyes of the h of his servants 2Sa 6:20
of the LORD for servants and h Is 14:2
and caused the servants and the h Jer 34:11
subjection for servants and for h Jer 34:11
be unto you for servants and for h Jer 34:16
upon the h in those days will I Joel 2:29

**HANDS**
our work and toil of our h Gen 5:29
and submit thyself under her h Gen 16:9
innocency of my h have I done Gen 20:5
two bracelets for her h of ten Gen 24:22
and bracelets upon his sister's h Gen 24:30
face, and the bracelets upon her h Gen 24:47
the kids of the goats upon his h Gen 27:16
but the h are the h of Esau Gen 27:22
him not, because his h were hairy Gen 27:23
as his brother Esau's h Gen 27:23
affliction and the labour of my h Gen 31:42
he delivered him out of their h Gen 37:21
he might rid him out of their h Gen 37:22
bought him of the h of the Gen 39:1
brought down in our h to buy food Gen 43:22
head, guiding his h wittingly Gen 48:14
the arms of his h were made Gen 49:24
the h of the mighty God of Jacob Gen 49:24
spread abroad my h unto the LORD Ex 9:29
spread abroad his h unto the LORD Ex 9:33
which thy h have established Ex 15:17
But Moses' h were heavy Ex 17:12
and Aaron and Hur stayed up his h Ex 17:12
his h were steady until the going Ex 17:12
his sons shall put their h upon Ex 29:10
their h upon the head of the ram Ex 29:15
their h upon the head of the ram Ex 29:19
shalt put all in the h of Aaron Ex 29:24
and in the h of his sons Ex 29:24
shalt receive them of their h Ex 29:25
and his sons shall wash their h Ex 30:19
So they shall wash their h Ex 30:21
he cast the tables out of his h Ex 32:19
hearted did spin with their h Ex 35:25
Aaron and his sons washed their h Ex 40:31
h upon the head of the bullock Lev 4:15
His own h shall bring the Lev 7:30
his sons laid their h upon the Lev 8:14
his sons laid their h upon the Lev 8:18
his sons laid their h upon the Lev 8:22
upon the thumbs of their right h Lev 8:24
And he put all upon Aaron's h Lev 8:27
and upon his sons' h Lev 8:27
Moses took them from off their h Lev 8:28
and hath not rinsed his h in water Lev 15:11
his h full of sweet incense Lev 16:12
Aaron shall lay both his h upon Lev 16:21
him lay their h upon his head Lev 24:14
the offering of memorial in her h Num 5:18
them upon the h of the Nazarite Num 6:19
put their h upon the Levites Num 8:10
the Levites shall lay their h Num 8:12
and he smote his h together Num 24:10
And he laid his h upon him Num 27:23
the fruit of the land in their h Deut 1:25
God delivered into our h Og also Deut 3:3
serve gods, the work of men's h Deut 4:28
of the covenant were in my two h Deut 9:15
and cast them out of my two h Deut 9:17
that thou puttest thine h unto Deut 12:18
and in all the works of thine h Deut 16:15
The h of the witnesses shall be Deut 17:7
afterward the h of all the people Deut 17:7
hath delivered it into thine h Deut 20:13
shall wash their h over the Deut 21:6
Our h have not shed this blood, Deut 21:7
hath delivered them into thine h Deut 21:10
thee in all the work of thine h Deut 24:19
LORD, the work of the h of the Deut 27:15
anger through the work of your h Deut 31:29
let his h be sufficient for him Deut 33:7
and accept the work of his h Deut 33:11
for Moses had laid his h upon him Deut 34:9
delivered into our h all the land Josh 2:24
he delivered them into the h of Judg 2:14
he sold them into the h of their Judg 2:14
us into the h of the Midianites Judg 6:13
give the Midianites into their h Judg 7:2
afterward shall thine h be Judg 7:11
the pitchers that were in their h Judg 7:19
and held the lamps in their left h Judg 7:20
in their right h to blow withal Judg 7:20
into your h the princes of Midian Judg 8:3
Are the h of Zebah and Zalmunna Judg 8:6
Are the h of Zebah and Zalmunna Judg 8:15
h of all their enemies on every Judg 8:34
to the deserving of his h Judg 9:16
into the h of the Philistines Judg 10:7
into the h of the children of Judg 10:7
the children of Ammon into mine h.. Judg 11:30
LORD delivered them into his h Judg 11:32
delivered me not out of their h Judg 12:2
me not, I put my life in my h Judg 12:3
and a meat offering at our h Judg 13:23
And he took thereof in his h Judg 14:9
his bands loosed from off his h Judg 15:14
delivered into our h our enemy Judg 16:24
for God hath given it into your h Judg 18:10
her h were upon the threshold Judg 19:27
both the palms of his h were cut 1Sa 5:4
out of the h of the Philistines 1Sa 7:14
thou shalt receive of their h 1Sa 10:4
of Israel by the h of messengers 1Sa 11:7
And Jonathan climbed up upon his h.. 1Sa 14:13
the h of them that spoiled them 1Sa 14:48
and he will give you into our h 1Sa 17:47
and feigned himself mad in their h 1Sa 21:13
me into the h of my master 1Sa 30:15
now let your h be strengthened 2Sa 2:7
Thy h were not bound, nor thy 2Sa 3:34
his h were feeble, and all the 2Sa 4:1
slew them, and cut off their h 2Sa 4:12
then shall the h of all that are 2Sa 16:21
them into the h of the Gibeonites 2Sa 21:9
of my h hath he recompensed me 2Sa 22:21
He teacheth my h to war 2Sa 22:35
they cannot be taken with h 2Sa 23:6
spread forth his h toward heaven 1Kin 8:22
spread forth his h toward this 1Kin 8:38

with his *h* spread up to heaven 1Kin 8:54
committed them unto the *h* of the 1Kin 14:27
to anger with the work of his *h* 1Kin 16:7
poured water on the *h* of Elijah 2Kin 3:11
his eyes, and his *h* upon his *h* 2Kin 4:34
at his *h* that which he brought 2Kin 5:20
And Joram turned his *h*, and fled, 2Kin 9:23
the feet, and the palms of her *h* 2Kin 9:35
I have brought into your *h* escape 2Kin 10:24
and they clapped their *h*, and said, 2Kin 11:12
And they laid *h* on her 2Kin 11:16
into the *h* of them that did the 2Kin 12:11
put his *h* upon the king's *h* 2Kin 13:16
no gods, but the work of men's *h* 2Kin 19:18
with all the works of their *h* 2Kin 22:17
there is no wrong in mine *h* 1Chr 12:17
of Asaph under the *h* of Asaph 1Chr 25:2
under the *h* of their father 1Chr 25:3
All these were under the *h* of 1Chr 25:6
to be made by the *h* of artificers 1Chr 29:5
who hath with his *h* fulfilled 2Chr 6:4
of Israel, and spread forth his *h* 2Chr 6:12
spread forth his *h* toward heaven 2Chr 6:13
spread forth his *h* in this house 2Chr 6:29
by the *h* of his servants ships 2Chr 8:18
committed them to the *h* of the 2Chr 12:10
and let not your *h* be weak 2Chr 15:7
So they laid *h* on her 2Chr 23:15
and they laid their *h* upon them 2Chr 29:23
were the work of the *h* of man 2Chr 32:19
with all the works of their *h* 2Chr 34:25
sprinkled the blood from their *h* 2Chr 35:11
their *h* with vessels of silver Ezr 1:6
the *h* of the people of Judah Ezr 4:4
fast on, and prospereth in their *h* Ezr 5:8
to strengthen their *h* in the work Ezr 6:22
spread out my *h* unto the LORD my Ezr 9:5
they gave their *h* that they would Ezr 10:19
their *h* for this good work Neh 2:18
one of his *h* wrought in the work Neh 4:17
Their *h* shall be weakened from Neh 6:9
therefore, O God, strengthen my *h* Neh 6:9
Amen, with lifting up their *h* Neh 8:6
and gavest them into their *h* Neh 9:24
do so again, I will lay *h* on you Neh 13:21
scorn to lay *h* on Mordecai alone Est 3:6
talents of silver to the *h* of Est 3:9
they laid not their *h* on the prey Est 9:16
hast blessed the work of his *h* Job 1:10
thou hast strengthened the weak *h* Job 4:3
so that their *h* cannot perform Job 5:12
he woundeth, and his *h* make whole Job 5:18
and make my *h* never so clean Job 9:30
despise the work of thine *h* Job 10:3
Thine *h* have made me and fashioned Job 10:8
and stretch out thine *h* toward him Job 11:13
a desire to the work of thine *h* Job 14:15
me over into the *h* of the wicked Job 16:11
Not for any injustice in mine *h* Job 16:17
is he that will strike *h* with me Job 17:3
hath clean *h* shall be stronger Job 17:9
his *h* shall restore their goods Job 20:10
by the pureness of thine *h* Job 22:30
Men shall clap their *h* at him Job 27:23
the strength of their *h* profit me Job 30:2
any blot hath cleaved to mine *h* Job 31:7
they all are the work of his *h* Job 34:19
sin, he clappeth his *h* among us Job 34:37
if there be iniquity in my *h* Ps 7:3
dominion over the works of thy *h* Ps 8:6
snared in the work of his own *h* Ps 9:16
of my *h* hath he recompensed me Ps 18:20
cleanness of my *h* in his eyesight Ps 18:24
He teacheth my *h* to war, so that Ps 18:34
they pierced my *h* and my feet Ps 22:16
He that hath clean *h*, and a pure Ps 24:4
I will wash mine *h* in innocency Ps 26:6
In whose *h* is mischief, and their Ps 26:10
when I lift up my *h* toward thy Ps 28:2
them after the work of their *h* Ps 28:4
LORD, nor the operation of his *h* Ps 28:5
out our *h* to a strange god Ps 44:20
O clap your *h*, all ye people Ps 47:1
He hath put forth his *h* against Ps 55:20
violence of your *h* in the earth Ps 58:2
I will lift up my *h* in thy name Ps 63:4
soon stretch out her *h* unto God Ps 68:31
vain, and washed my *h* in innocency Ps 73:13
men of might have found their *h* Ps 76:5
them by the skilfulness of his *h* Ps 78:72
his *h* were delivered from the Ps 81:6
have stretched out my *h* unto thee Ps 88:9
thou the work of our *h* upon us Ps 90:17
the work of our *h* establish thou Ps 90:17
shall bear thee up in their *h* Ps 91:12
triumph in the works of thy *h* Ps 92:4
his *h* formed the dry land Ps 95:5
Let the floods clap their *h* Ps 98:8
the heavens are the work of thy *h* Ps 102:25
The works of his *h* are verity Ps 111:7
and gold, the work of men's *h* Ps 115:4
They have *h*, but they handle not Ps 115:7
My *h* also will I lift up unto thy Ps 119:48
Thy *h* have made me and fashioned Ps 119:73
put forth their *h* unto iniquity Ps 125:3
shalt eat the labour of thine *h* Ps 128:2
Lift up your *h* in the sanctuary, Ps 134:2
and gold, the work of men's *h* Ps 135:15
not the works of thine own *h* Ps 138:8
O LORD, from the *h* of the wicked Ps 140:4

the lifting up of my *h* as the Ps 141:2
I muse on the work of thy *h* Ps 143:5
I stretch forth my *h* unto thee Ps 143:6
which teacheth my *h* to war Ps 144:1
little folding of the *h* to sleep Prov 6:10
*h* that shed innocent blood, Prov 6:17
the recompence of a man's *h* shall Prov 12:14
plucketh it down with her *h* Prov 14:1
void of understanding striketh *h* Prov 17:18
for his *h* refuse to labour Prov 21:25
thou one of them that strike *h* Prov 22:26
little folding of the *h* to sleep Prov 24:33
The spider taketh hold with her *h* Prov 30:28
and worketh willingly with her *h* Prov 31:13
with the fruit of her *h* she Prov 31:16
She layeth her *h* to the spindle Prov 31:19
and her *h* hold the distaff Prov 31:19
reacheth forth her *h* to the needy Prov 31:20
Give her of the fruit of her *h* Prov 31:31
the works that my *h* had wrought Eccl 2:11
The fool foldeth his *h* together Eccl 4:5
than both the *h* full with travail Eccl 4:6
and destroy the work of thine *h* Eccl 5:6
snares and nets, and her *h* as bands Eccl 7:26
through idleness of the *h* the Eccl 10:18
my *h* dropped with myrrh, and my Song 5:5
His *h* are as gold rings set with Song 5:14
the work of the *h* of a cunning Song 7:1
And when ye spread forth your *h* Is 1:15
your *h* are full of blood Is 1:15
worship the work of their own *h* Is 2:8
of his *h* shall be given him Is 3:11
consider the operation of his *h* Is 5:12
Therefore shall all *h* be faint Is 13:7
to the altars, the work of his *h* Is 17:8
and Assyria the work of my *h* Is 19:25
forth his *h* in the midst of them Is 25:11
spreadeth forth his *h* to swim Is 25:11
with the spoils of their *h* Is 25:11
his children, the work of mine *h* Is 29:23
which your own *h* have made unto Is 31:7
that shaketh his *h* from holding Is 33:15
Strengthen ye the weak *h*, and Is 35:3
no gods, but the work of men's *h* Is 37:19
or thy work, He hath no *h* Is 45:9
the work of my *h* command ye me Is 45:11
I, even my *h*, have stretched out Is 45:12
thee upon the palms of my *h* Is 49:16
of the field shall clap their *h* Is 55:12
For your *h* are defiled with blood Is 59:3
the act of violence is in their *h* Is 59:6
of my planting, the work of my *h* Is 60:21
I have spread out my *h* all the Is 65:2
long enjoy the work of their *h* Is 65:22
the works of their own *h* Jer 1:16
him, and thine *h* upon thine head Jer 2:37
herself, that spreadeth her *h* Jer 4:31
our *h* wax feeble Jer 6:24
the work of the *h* of the workman Jer 10:3
and of the *h* of the founder Jer 10:9
by the *h* of them that seek their Jer 19:7
weapons of war that are in your *h* Jer 21:4
also the *h* of evildoers, that Jer 23:14
to anger with the works of your *h* Jer 25:6
works of your *h* to your own hurt Jer 25:7
to the works of their own *h* Jer 25:14
every man with his *h* on his loins Jer 30:6
to anger with the work of their *h* Jer 32:30
the *h* of him that telleth them Jer 33:13
for thus he weakeneth the *h* of Jer 38:4
the *h* of all the people, in Jer 38:4
wrath with the works of your *h* Jer 44:8
children for feebleness of *h* Jer 47:3
upon all the *h* shall be cuttings, Jer 48:37
of them, and his *h* waxed feeble Jer 50:43
hath delivered me into their *h* Lam 1:14
Zion spreadeth forth her *h* Lam 1:17
that pass by clap their *h* at thee Lam 2:15
lift up thy *h* toward him for the Lam 2:19
our *h* unto God in the heavens Lam 3:41
according to the work of their *h* Lam 3:64
the work of the *h* of the potter Lam 4:2
a moment, and no *h* stayed on her Lam 4:6
The *h* of the pitiful women have Lam 4:10
they had the *h* of a man under Eze 1:8
All *h* shall be feeble, and all Eze 7:17
I will give it into the *h* of the Eze 7:21
the *h* of the people of the land Eze 7:27
put it into the *h* of him that was Eze 10:7
body, and their backs, and their *h* Eze 10:12
the likeness of the *h* of a man Eze 10:21
you into the *h* of strangers Eze 11:9
strengthened the *h* of the wicked Eze 13:22
and I put bracelets upon thy *h* Eze 16:11
all *h* shall be feeble, and every Eze 21:7
and smite thine *h* together Eze 21:14
I will also smite mine *h* together Eze 21:17
endure, or can thine *h* be strong Eze 22:14
adultery, and blood is in their *h* Eze 23:37
which put bracelets upon their *h* Eze 23:42
and blood is in their *h* Eze 23:45
Because thou hast clapped thine *h* Eze 25:6
a stone was cut out without *h* Dan 2:34
cut out of the mountain without *h* Dan 2:45
shall deliver you out of my *h* Dan 3:15
knees and upon the palms of my *h* Dan 10:10
say any more to the work of our *h* Hos 14:3
nor have laid *h* on their Obad 13
the violence that is in their *h* Jonah 3:8
more worship the work of thine *h* Mic 5:13

may do evil with both *h* earnestly Mic 7:3
thee shall clap the *h* over thee Nah 3:19
voice, and lifted up his *h* on high Hab 3:10
to Zion, Let not thine *h* be slack Zeph 3:16
and upon all the labour of the *h* Hag 1:11
and so is every work of their *h* Hag 2:14
hail in all the labours of your *h* Hag 2:17
The *h* of Zerubbabel have laid the Zec 4:9
his *h* shall also finish it Zec 4:9
Let your *h* be strong, ye that Zec 8:9
not, but let your *h* be strong Zec 8:13
What are these wounds in thine *h* Zec 13:6
in their *h* they shall bear thee Mt 4:6
not their *h* when they eat bread Mt 15:2
unwashen *h* defileth not a man Mt 15:20
be betrayed into the *h* of men Mt 17:22
rather than having two *h* or two Mt 18:8
and he laid *h* on him, and took him Mt 18:28
that he should put his *h* on them Mt 19:13
And he laid his *h* on them, and Mt 19:15
when they sought to lay *h* on him Mt 21:46
is betrayed into the *h* of sinners Mt 26:45
laid *h* on Jesus, and took him Mt 26:50
him with the palms of their *h* Mt 26:67
washed his *h* before the multitude Mt 27:24
thee, come and lay thy *h* on her Mk 5:23
mighty works are wrought by his *h* Mk 6:2
laid his *h* upon a few sick folk Mk 6:5
that is to say, with unwashen, *h* Mk 7:2
except they wash their *h* oft Mk 7:3
but eat bread with unwashen *h* Mk 7:5
put his *h* upon him, he asked him Mk 8:23
he put his *h* again upon his eyes Mk 8:25
is delivered into the *h* of men Mk 9:31
than having two *h* to go into hell Mk 9:43
put his *h* upon them, and blessed Mk 10:16
is betrayed into the *h* of sinners Mk 14:41
And they laid their *h* on him Mk 14:46
this temple that is made with *h* Mk 14:58
will build another made without *h* Mk 14:58
him with the palms of their *h* Mk 14:65
they shall lay *h* on the sick Mk 16:18
in their *h* they shall bear thee Lk 4:11
he laid his *h* on every one of Lk 4:40
did eat, rubbing them in their *h* Lk 6:1
be delivered into the *h* of men Lk 9:44
And he laid his *h* on her Lk 13:13
same hour sought to lay *h* on him Lk 20:19
they shall lay their *h* on you Lk 21:12
stretched forth no *h* against me Lk 22:53
into thy *h* I commend my spirit Lk 23:46
into the *h* of sinful men, and be Lk 24:7
Behold my *h* and my feet, that it Lk 24:39
thus spoken, he shewed them his *h* Lk 24:40
to Bethany, and he lifted up his *h* Lk 24:50
but no man laid *h* on him, because Jn 7:30
but no man laid *h* on him Jn 7:44
and no man laid *h* on him Jn 8:20
had given all things into his *h* Jn 13:3
not my feet only, but also my *h* Jn 13:9
and they smote him with their *h* Jn 19:3
said, he shewed unto them his *h* Jn 20:20
in his *h* the print of the nails Jn 20:25
hither thy finger, and behold my *h* Jn 20:27
thou shalt stretch forth thy *h* Jn 21:18
by wicked *h* have crucified and Acts 2:23
And they laid *h* on them, and put Acts 4:3
by the *h* of the apostles were Acts 5:12
laid their *h* on the apostles, and Acts 5:18
prayed, they laid their *h* on them Acts 6:6
in the works of their own *h* Acts 7:41
not in temples made with *h* Acts 7:48
Then laid they their *h* on them Acts 8:17
*h* the Holy Ghost was given Acts 8:18
power, that on whomsoever I lay *h* Acts 8:19
and putting his *h* on him said Acts 9:17
the elders by the *h* of Barnabas Acts 11:30
*h* to vex certain of the church Acts 12:1
And his chains fell off from his *h* Acts 12:7
prayed, and laid their *h* on them Acts 13:3
and wonders to be done by their *h* Acts 14:3
not in temples made with *h* Acts 17:24
is worshipped with men's *h* Acts 17:25
Paul had laid his *h* upon them Acts 19:6
special miracles by the *h* of Paul Acts 19:11
be no gods, which are made with *h* Acts 19:26
that these *h* have ministered unto Acts 20:34
Paul's girdle, and bound his own *h* Acts 21:11
him into the *h* of the Gentiles Acts 21:11
all the people, and laid *h* on him, Acts 21:27
took him away out of our *h* Acts 24:7
own *h* the tackling of the ship Acts 27:19
and prayed, and laid his *h* on him Acts 28:8
into the *h* of the Romans Acts 28:17
forth my *h* unto a disobedient Rom 10:21
And labour, working with our own *h* 1Cor 4:12
of God, an house not made with *h* 2Cor 5:1
by the wall, and escaped his *h* 2Cor 11:33
the right *h* of fellowship Gal 2:9
in the flesh made by *h* Eph 2:11
working with his *h* the thing Eph 4:28
the circumcision made without *h* Col 2:11
and to work with your own *h* 1Th 4:11
every where, lifting up holy *h* 1Ti 2:8
on of the *h* of the presbytery 1Ti 4:14
Lay *h* suddenly on no man, neither 1Ti 5:22
in thee by the putting on of my *h* 2Ti 1:6
heavens are the works of thine *h* Heb 1:10
set him over the works of thy *h* Heb 2:7
of baptisms, and of laying on of *h* Heb 6:2

tabernacle, not made with *h* Heb 9:11
into the holy places made with *h* Heb 9:24
fall into the *h* of the living God Heb 10:31
lift up the *h* which hang down Heb 12:12
Cleanse your *h*, ye sinners Jas 4:8
our *h* have handled, of the Word 1Jn 1:1
white robes, and palms in their *h* Rev 7:9
not of the works of their *h* Rev 9:20
their foreheads, or in their *h* Rev 20:4

**HANDSTAVES**
the bows and the arrows, and the *h* Eze 39:9

**HANDWRITING**
Blotting out the *h* of ordinances Col 2:14

**HANDYWORK**
and the firmament sheweth his *h* Ps 19:1

**HANES** (*ha'-nees*) See TAHPANES. *A place in Egypt.*
and his ambassadors came to *H* Is 30:4

**HANG**
thee, and shall *h* thee on a tree Gen 40:19
shall *h* over the backside of the Ex 26:12
it shall *h* over the sides of the Ex 26:13
thou shalt *h* it upon four pillars Ex 26:32
thou shalt *h* up the vail under Ex 26:33
*h* up the hanging at the court Ex 40:8
*h* them up before the LORD against Num 25:4
to death, and thou *h* him on a tree Deut 21:22
thy life shall *h* in doubt before Deut 28:66
we will *h* them up unto the LORD 2Sa 21:6
to speak unto the king to *h* Est 6:4
Then the king said, *H* him thereon Est 7:9
whereon there *h* a thousand Song 4:4
they shall *h* upon him all the Is 22:24
the virgins of Jerusalem *h* down Lam 2:10
pin of it to *h* any vessel thereon Eze 15:3
two commandments *h* all the law Mt 22:40
the venomous beast *h* on his hand Acts 28:4
lift up the hands which *h* down Heb 12:12

**HANGED**
But he *h* the chief baker Gen 40:22
unto mine office, and him he *h* Gen 41:13
(for he that is *h* is accursed of Deut 21:23
the king of Ai he *h* on a tree Josh 8:29
them, and *h* them on five trees Josh 10:26
*h* them up over the pool in Hebron 2Sa 4:12
*h* himself, and died, and was buried 2Sa 17:23
Behold, I saw Absalom *h* in an oak 2Sa 18:10
they *h* them in the hill before 2Sa 21:9
where the Philistines had *h* them 2Sa 21:12
the bones of them that were *h* 2Sa 21:13
set up, let him be *h* thereon Ezr 6:11
they were both *h* on a tree Est 2:23
that Mordecai may be *h* thereon Est 5:14
So they *h* Haman on the gallows Est 7:10
him they have *h* upon the gallows, Est 8:7
ten sons be *h* upon the gallows Est 9:13
and they *h* Haman's ten sons Est 9:14
sons should be *h* on the gallows Est 9:25
We *h* our harps upon the willows Ps 137:2
Princes are *h* up by their hand Lam 5:12
they *h* the shield and helmet in Eze 27:10
they *h* their shields upon thy Eze 27:11
a millstone were *h* about his neck Mt 18:6
and departed, and went and *h* himself Mt 27:5
a millstone were *h* about his neck Mk 9:42
a millstone were *h* about his neck Lk 17:2
which were *h* railed on him Lk 23:39
whom ye slew and *h* on a tree Acts 5:30
whom they slew and *h* on a tree Acts 10:39

**HANGETH**
and *h* the earth upon nothing Job 26:7
is every one that *h* on a tree Gal 3:13

**HANGING**
thou shalt make an *h* for the door Ex 26:36
thou shalt make for the *h* five Ex 26:37
shall be an *h* of twenty cubits Ex 27:16
the *h* for the door at the Ex 35:15
the *h* for the door of the court, Ex 35:17
he made an *h* for the tabernacle Ex 36:37
the *h* for the gate of the court Ex 38:18
the *h* for the tabernacle door, Ex 39:38
the *h* for the court gate, his Ex 39:40
put the *h* of the door to the Ex 40:5
hang up the *h* at the court gate Ex 40:8
he set up the *h* at the door of Ex 40:28
set up the *h* of the court gate Ex 40:33
the *h* for the door of the Num 3:25
wherewith they minister, and the *h* Num 3:31
the *h* for the door of the Num 4:25
the *h* for the door of the gate of Num 4:26
they were *h* upon the trees until Josh 10:26

**HANGINGS**
be *h* for the court of fine twined Ex 27:9
be *h* of an hundred cubits long Ex 27:11
side shall be *h* of fifty cubits Ex 27:12
The *h* of one side of the gate Ex 27:14
side shall be *h* fifteen cubits Ex 27:15
The *h* of the court, his pillars, Ex 35:17
the *h* of the court were of fine Ex 38:9
side the *h* were an hundred cubits Ex 38:11
west side were *h* of fifty cubits Ex 38:12
The *h* of the one side of the gate Ex 38:14
hand, were *h* of fifteen cubits Ex 38:15
All the *h* of the court round Ex 38:16
answerable to the *h* of the court Ex 38:18
The *h* of the court, his pillars, Ex 39:40
the *h* of the court, and the Num 3:26
the *h* of the court, and the Num 4:26
the women wove *h* for the grove 2Kin 23:7
were white, green, and blue, *h* Est 1:6

**HANIEL** (*ha'-ne-el*) See HANNIEL. *A son of Ulla.*
Arah, and *H*, and Rezia 1Chr 7:39

**HANNAH** (*han'-nah*) *Mother of Samuel.*
the name of the one was *H* 1Sa 1:2
children, but *H* had no children 1Sa 1:2
But unto *H* he gave a worthy 1Sa 1:5
for he loved *H* 1Sa 1:5
Elkanah her husband to her, *H* 1Sa 1:8
So *H* rose up after they had eaten 1Sa 1:9
Now *H*, she spake in her heart 1Sa 1:13
*H* answered and said, No, my lord, 1Sa 1:15
and Elkanah knew *H* his wife 1Sa 1:19
come about after *H* had conceived 1Sa 1:20
But *H* went not up 1Sa 1:22
*H* prayed, and said, My heart 1Sa 2:1
And the LORD visited *H*, so that 1Sa 2:21

**HANNATHON** (*han'-na-thon*) *A city in Zebulun.*
it on the north side to *H* Josh 19:14

**HANNIEL** (*han'-ne-el*) See HANIEL. *A prince of Manasseh.*
of Manasseh, *H* the son of Ephod Num 34:23

**HANOCH** (*ha'-nok*) See HANOCHITES, HENOCH.
*1. A son of Midian.*
Ephah, and Epher, and *H*, and Abidah, Gen 25:4
*2. A son of Reuben.*
*H*, and Phallu, and Hezron, and Carmi Gen 46:9
*H*, and Pallu, Hezron, and Carmi Ex 6:14
*H*, of whom cometh the family of Num 26:5
the firstborn of Israel were, *H* 1Chr 5:3

**HANOCHITES** (*ha'-nok-ites*) *Descendants of Hanoch 2.*
whom cometh the family of the *H* Num 26:5

**HANUN** (*ha'-nun*)
*1. A king of Ammon.*
*H* his son reigned in his stead 2Sa 10:1
kindness unto *H* the son of Nahash 2Sa 10:2
of Ammon said unto *H* their lord 2Sa 10:3
Wherefore *H* took David's servants 2Sa 10:4
kindness unto *H* the son of Nahash 1Chr 19:2
of the children of Ammon to *H* 1Chr 19:2
the children of Ammon said to *H* 1Chr 19:3
Wherefore *H* took David's servants 1Chr 19:4
themselves odious to David, *H* 1Chr 19:6
*2. A son of Zalaph.*
*H* the sixth son of Zalaph, Neh 3:30
*3. A rebuilder of Jerusalem's wall.*
The valley gate repaired *H* Neh 3:13

**HAP**
her *h* was to light on a part of Ruth 2:3

**HAPHRAIM** (*haf-ra'-im*) *A city in Issachar.*
And *H*, and Shihon, and Anaharath, Josh 19:19

**HAPLY**
if *h* the people had eaten freely 1Sa 14:30
if *h* he might find any thing Mk 11:13
Lest *h*, after he hath laid the Lk 14:29
lest *h* ye be found even to fight Acts 5:39
if *h* they might feel after him, Acts 17:27
Lest *h* if they of Macedonia come 2Cor 9:4

**HAPPEN**
*h* to thee for this thing 1Sa 28:10
There shall no evil *h* to the just Prov 12:21
forth, and shew us what shall *h* Is 41:22
what things should *h* unto him Mk 10:32

**HAPPENED**
it was a chance that *h* to us 1Sa 6:9
As I *h* by chance upon mount 2Sa 1:6
there *h* to be there a man of 2Sa 20:1
him of all that had *h* unto him Est 4:7
therefore this evil is *h* unto you Jer 44:23
of all these things which had *h* Lk 24:14
at that which had *h* unto him Acts 3:10
blindness in part is *h* to Israel Rom 11:25
Now all these things *h* unto them 1Cor 10:11
that the things which *h* unto me Phil 1:12
some strange thing *h* unto you 1Pet 4:12
But it is *h* unto them according 2Pet 2:22

**HAPPENETH**
also that one event *h* to them all Eccl 2:14
As it *h* to the fool Eccl 2:15
so it *h* even to me Eccl 2:15
unto whom it *h* according to the Eccl 8:14
to whom it *h* according to the Eccl 8:14
but time and chance *h* to them all Eccl 9:11

**HAPPIER**
But she is *h* if she so abide, 1Cor 7:40

**HAPPIZZEZ** See APHSES.

**HAPPY**
*H* am I, for the daughters will Gen 30:13
*H* art thou, O Israel Deut 33:29
*H* are thy men, *h* are these 1Kin 10:8
*H* are thy men, and *h* are these 2Chr 9:7
*h* is the man whom God correcteth Job 5:17
*H* is the man that hath his quiver Ps 127:5
*h* shalt thou be, and it shall be Ps 128:2
*h* shall he be, that rewardeth Ps 137:8
*H* shall he be, that taketh and Ps 137:9
*H* is that people, that is in such Ps 144:15
*h* is that people, whose God is Ps 144:15
*H* is he that hath the God of Ps 146:5
*H* is the man that findeth wisdom, Prov 3:13
*h* is every one that retaineth her Prov 3:18
hath mercy on the poor, *h* is he Prov 14:21
trusteth in the LORD, *h* is he Prov 16:20
*H* is the man that feareth alway Prov 28:14
he that keepeth the law, *h* is he Prov 29:18
wherefore are all they *h* that Jer 12:1
And now we call the proud *h* Mal 3:15
things, *h* are ye if ye do them Jn 13:17
I think myself *h*, king Agrippa, Acts 26:2
*H* is he that condemneth not Rom 14:22
we count them *h* which endure Jas 5:11
for righteousness' sake, *h* are ye 1Pet 3:14
for the name of Christ, *h* are ye 1Pet 4:14

**HARA** (*ha'-rah*) *An Assyrian province.*
them unto Halah, and Habor, and *H* 1Chr 5:26

**HARADAH** (*har'-a-dah*) *A Hebrew encampment in the wilderness.*
mount Shapher, and encamped in *H*. Num 33:24
And they removed from *H*, and Num 33:25

**HARAN** (*ha'-ran*) See BETH-HARAN, CHARRAN.
*1. A son of Terah.*
and begat Abram, Nahor, and *H* Gen 11:26
Terah begat Abram, Nahor, and *H* Gen 11:27
and *H* begat Lot Gen 11:27
*H* died before his father Terah in Gen 11:28
wife, Milcah, the daughter of *H* Gen 11:29
and Lot the son of *H* his son's son Gen 11:31
*2. A Levite.*
Shelomith, and Haziel, and *H* 1Chr 23:9
*3. A son of Caleb.*
Ephah, Caleb's concubine, bare *H* 1Chr 2:46
and *H* begat Gazez 1Chr 2:46
*4. A city in northern Mesopotamia.*
and they came unto *H*, and dwelt Gen 11:31
and Terah died in *H* Gen 11:32
old when he departed out of *H* Gen 12:4
souls that they had gotten in *H* Gen 12:5
thou to Laban my brother to *H* Gen 27:43
from Beer-sheba, and went toward *H*. Gen 28:10
And they said, Of *H* are we Gen 29:4
Gozan, and *H*, and Rezeph 2Kin 19:12
have destroyed, as Gozan, and *H* Is 37:12
*H*, and Canneh, and Eden, the Eze 27:23

**HARARITE** (*har'-a-rite*) *Native of the hill country of Judah.*
was Shammah the son of Agee the *H*. 2Sa 23:11
Shammah the *H*, Ahiam the son of 2Sa 23:33
Ahiam the son of Sharar the *H* 2Sa 23:33
Jonathan the son of Shage the *H* 1Chr 11:34
Ahiam the son of Sacar the *H* 1Chr 11:35

**HARBONA** (*har-bo'-nah*) See HARBONAH. *A servant of King Ahasuerus.*
he commanded Mehuman, Biztha, *H* Est 1:10

**HARBONAH** (*har-bo'-nah*) See HARBONA. *Same as Harbona.*
And *H*, one of the chamberlains, Est 7:9

**HARD**
Is any thing too *h* for the LORD Gen 18:14
travailed, and she had *h* labour Gen 35:16
to pass, when she was in *h* labour Gen 35:17
their lives bitter with *h* bondage Ex 1:14
the *h* causes they brought unto Ex 18:26
he take off *h* by the backbone Lev 3:9
the cause that is too *h* for you Deut 1:17
It shall not seem *h* unto thee Deut 15:18
matter too *h* for thee in judgment Deut 17:8
us, and laid upon us *h* bondage Deut 26:6
went *h* unto the door of the tower Judg 9:52
pursued *h* after them unto Gidom, Judg 20:45
even they also followed *h* after 1Sa 14:22
Philistines followed *h* upon Saul 1Sa 31:2
and horsemen followed *h* after him 2Sa 1:6
sons of Zeruiah be too *h* for me 2Sa 3:39
Amnon thought it *h* for him to do 2Sa 13:2
to prove him with *h* questions 1Kin 10:1
*h* by the palace of Ahab king of 1Kin 21:1
said, Thou hast asked a *h* thing 2Kin 2:10
Philistines followed *h* after Saul 1Chr 10:2
in the midst *h* by their buttocks 1Chr 19:4
with *h* questions at Jerusalem 2Chr 9:1
as *h* as a piece of the nether Job 41:24
hast shewed thy people *h* things Ps 60:3
My soul followeth *h* after thee Ps 63:8
Thy wrath lieth *h* upon me Ps 88:7
they utter and speak *h* things Ps 94:4
but the way of transgressors is *h* Prov 13:15
from the *h* bondage wherein thou Is 14:3
there is nothing too *h* for thee Jer 32:17
is there any thing too *h* for me Jer 32:27
of an *h* language, but to the Eze 3:5
of an *h* language, whose words Eze 3:6
dreams, and shewing of *h* sentences Dan 5:12
rowed *h* to bring it to the land Jonah 1:13
knew thee that thou art an *h* man Mt 25:24
how *h* is it for them that trust Mk 10:24
this, said, This is an *h* saying Jn 6:60
it is *h* for thee to kick against Acts 9:5
house joined *h* to the synagogue Acts 18:7
it is *h* for thee to kick against Acts 26:14
*h* to be uttered, seeing ye are Heb 5:11
some things *h* to be understood 2Pet 3:16

of all their *h* speeches which .................... Jude 15

**HARDEN**
but I will *h* his heart, that he .................... Ex 4:21
I will *h* Pharaoh's heart, and .................... Ex 7:3
I will *h* Pharaoh's heart, that he .................... Ex 14:4
I will *h* the hearts of the .................... Ex 14:17
thou shalt not *h* thine heart .................... Deut 15:7
was of the LORD to *h* their hearts .................... Josh 11:20
then do ye *h* your hearts, as the .................... 1Sa 6:6
I would *h* myself in sorrow .................... Job 6:10
*H* not your heart, as in the .................... Ps 95:8
*H* not your hearts, as in the .................... Heb 3:8
*h* not your hearts, as in the .................... Heb 3:15
hear his voice, *h* not your hearts .................... Heb 4:7

**HARDENED**
he *h* Pharaoh's heart, that he .................... Ex 7:13
unto Moses, Pharaoh's heart is *h* .................... Ex 7:14
and Pharaoh's heart was *h*, neither .................... Ex 7:22
he *h* his heart, and hearkened not .................... Ex 8:15
and Pharaoh's heart was *h*, and he .................... Ex 8:19
Pharaoh *h* his heart at this time .................... Ex 8:32
And the heart of Pharaoh was *h* .................... Ex 9:7
the LORD *h* the heart of Pharaoh, .................... Ex 9:12
*h* his heart, he and his servants .................... Ex 9:34
And the heart of Pharaoh was *h* .................... Ex 9:35
for I have *h* his heart, and the .................... Ex 10:1
But the LORD *h* Pharaoh's heart, .................... Ex 10:20
But the LORD *h* Pharaoh's heart, .................... Ex 10:27
the LORD *h* Pharaoh's heart, so .................... Ex 11:10
the LORD *h* the heart of Pharaoh .................... Ex 14:8
for the LORD thy God *h* his spirit .................... Deut 2:30
and Pharaoh *h* their hearts .................... 1Sa 6:6
but *h* their necks, like to the .................... 2Kin 17:14
*h* his heart from turning unto the .................... 2Chr 36:13
*h* their necks, and hearkened not .................... Neh 9:16
but *h* their necks, and in their .................... Neh 9:17
*h* their neck, and would not hear .................... Neh 9:29
who hath *h* himself against him, .................... Job 9:4
She is *h* against her young ones, .................... Job 39:16
*h* our heart from thy fear .................... Is 63:17
their ear, but *h* their neck .................... Jer 7:26
because they have *h* their necks .................... Jer 19:15
lifted up, and his mind *h* in pride .................... Dan 5:20
for their heart was *h* .................... Mk 6:52
have ye your heart yet *h* .................... Mk 8:17
their eyes, and *h* their heart .................... Jn 12:40
But when divers were *h*, and .................... Acts 19:9
lest any of you be *h* through the .................... Heb 3:13

**HARDENETH**
A wicked man *h* his face .................... Prov 21:29
but he that *h* his heart shall .................... Prov 28:14
being often reproved *h* his neck .................... Prov 29:1
have mercy, and whom he will he *h* .... Rom 9:18

**HARDER**
A brother offended is *h* to be won .... Prov 18:19
made their faces *h* than a rock .................... Jer 5:3
As an adamant *h* than flint have I .................... Eze 3:9

**HARDHEARTED**
house of Israel are impudent and *h* .................... Eze 3:7

**HARDLY**
And when Sarai dealt *h* with her .................... Gen 16:6
when Pharaoh would *h* let us go .................... Ex 13:15
through it, *h* bestead and hungry .................... Is 8:21
That a rich man shall *h* enter .................... Mt 19:23
How *h* shall they that have riches .................... Mk 10:23
bruising him *h* departeth from him .................... Lk 9:39
How *h* shall they that have riches .................... Lk 18:24
*h* passing it, came unto a place .................... Acts 27:8

**HARDNESS**
When the dust groweth into *h* .................... Job 38:38
Moses because of the *h* of your .................... Mt 19:8
grieved for the *h* of their hearts .................... Mk 3:5
For the *h* of your heart he wrote .................... Mk 10:5
*h* of heart, because they believed .................... Mk 16:14
But after thy *h* and impenitent .................... Rom 2:5
Thou therefore endure *h*, as a .................... 2Ti 2:3

**HARE**
And the *h*, because he cheweth the .................... Lev 11:6
as the camel, and the *h*, and the .................... Deut 14:7

**HAREPH** (*ha'-ref*) *A son of Caleb.*
*H* the father of Beth-gader .................... 1Chr 2:51

**HARETH** (*ha'-reth*) *Forest land in Judah.*
and came into the forest of *H* .................... 1Sa 22:5

**HARHAIAH** (*har-ha-i'-ah*) *Father of Uzziel.*
him repaired Uzziel the son of *H* .................... Neh 3:8

**HARHAS** (*har'-has*) See HASRAH. *Grandfather of Shallum.*
the son of Tikvah, the son of *H* .................... 2Kin 22:14

**HARHUR** (*har'-hur*) *A family in exile.*
of Hakupha, the children of *H* .................... Ezr 2:51
of Hakupha, the children of *H* .................... Neh 7:53

**HARIM** (*ha'-rim*)
*1. A priest.*
The third to *H*, the fourth to .................... 1Chr 24:8
The children of *H*, a thousand and .................... Ezr 2:39
And of the sons of *H* .................... Ezr 10:21
Malchijah the son of *H*, and Hashub .... Neh 3:11
The children of *H*, a thousand and .................... Neh 7:42
Of *H*, Adna; of Meraioth .................... Neh 12:15
*2. A family in exile.*
The children of *H*, three hundred .................... Ezr 2:32
The children of *H*, three hundred .................... Neh 7:35
*3. Married a foreigner in exile.*
And of the sons of *H* .................... Ezr 10:31
*4. An Israelite who renewed the covenant.*
*H*, Meremoth, Obadiah, .................... Neh 10:5
*5. A family who renewed the covenant.*
Malluch, *H*, Baanah .................... Neh 10:27

**HARIPH** (*ha'-rif*) See JORAH.
*1. A family of exiles.*
The children of *H*, an hundred and .................... Neh 7:24
*2. A family who renewed the covenant.*
*H*, Anathoth, Nebai, .................... Neh 10:19

**HARLOT**
deal with our sister as with an *h* .................... Gen 34:31
her, he thought her to be an *h* .................... Gen 38:15
place, saying, Where is the *h* .................... Gen 38:21
There was no *h* in this place .................... Gen 38:21
that there was no *h* in this place .................... Gen 38:22
daughter in law hath played the *h* .................... Gen 38:24
woman, or profane, or an *h* .................... Lev 21:14
only Rahab the *h* shall live .................... Josh 6:17
And Joshua saved Rahab the *h* alive ... Josh 6:25
valour, and he was the son of an *h* .... Judg 11:1
Samson to Gaza, and saw there an *h* .. Judg 16:1
a woman with the attire of an *h* .................... Prov 7:10
is the faithful city become an *h* .................... Is 1:21
years shall Tyre sing as an *h* .................... Is 23:15
thou *h* that hast been forgotten .................... Is 23:16
thou wanderest, playing the *h* .................... Jer 2:20
played the *h* with many lovers .................... Jer 3:1
tree, and there hath played the *h* .................... Jer 3:6
but went and played the *h* also .................... Jer 3:8
playedst the *h* because of thy .................... Eze 16:15
and playedst the *h* thereupon .................... Eze 16:16
thou hast played the *h* with them .................... Eze 16:28
and hast not been as an *h*, in that .................... Eze 16:31
Wherefore, O *h*, hear the word of .................... Eze 16:35
thee to cease from playing the *h* .................... Eze 16:41
played the *h* when she was mine .................... Eze 23:5
played the *h* in the land of Egypt .................... Eze 23:19
unto a woman that playeth the *h* .................... Eze 23:44
their mother hath played the *h* .................... Hos 2:5
thou shalt not play the *h* .................... Hos 3:3
Though thou, Israel, play the *h* .................... Hos 4:15
and have given a boy for an *h* .................... Joel 3:3
wife shall be an *h* in the city .................... Amos 7:17
gathered it of the hire of an *h* .................... Mic 1:7
shall return to the hire of an *h* .................... Mic 1:7
whoredoms of the wellfavoured *h* .................... Nah 3:4
and make them the members of an *h*. 1Cor 6:15
is joined to an *h* is one body .................... 1Cor 6:16
By faith the *h* Rahab perished not .... Heb 11:31
Rahab the *h* justified by works .................... Jas 2:25

**HARLOT'S**
went, and came into an *h* house .................... Josh 2:1
the country, Go into the *h* house .................... Josh 6:22

**HARLOTS**
came there two women, that were *h*... 1Kin 3:16
with *h* spendeth his substance .................... Prov 29:3
whores, and they sacrifice with *h* .................... Hos 4:14
the *h* go into the kingdom of God .................... Mt 21:31
publicans and the *h* believed him .................... Mt 21:32
hath devoured thy living with *h* .................... Lk 15:30
THE GREAT, THE MOTHER OF *H* .................... Rev 17:5

**HARLOTS'**
by troops in the *h* houses .................... Jer 5:7

**HARM**
and this pillar unto me, for *h* .................... Gen 31:52
he shall make amends for the *h* .................... Lev 5:16
his enemy, neither sought his *h* .................... Num 35:23
for I will no more do thee *h* .................... 1Sa 26:21
do us more *h* than did Absalom .................... 2Sa 20:6
And there was no *h* in the pot .................... 2Kin 4:41
anointed, and do my prophets no *h* .. 1Chr 16:22
anointed, and do my prophets no *h* .... Ps 105:15
cause, if he have done thee no *h* .................... Prov 3:30
look well to him, and do him no *h* .................... Jer 39:12
voice, saying, Do thyself no *h* .................... Acts 16:28
Crete, and to have gained this *h* .................... Acts 27:21
beast into the fire, and felt no *h* .................... Acts 28:5
saw no *h* come to him, they .................... Acts 28:6
shewed or spake any *h* of thee .................... Acts 28:21
And who is he that will *h* you .................... 1Pet 3:13

**HAR-MAGEDON** See ARMAGEDDON.

**HARMLESS**
wise as serpents, and *h* as doves .................... Mt 10:16
That ye may be blameless and *h* .................... Phil 2:15
priest became us, who is holy, *h* .................... Heb 7:26

**HARNEPHER** (*har-ne'-fur*) *A son of Zophah.*
*H*, and Shual, and Beri .................... 1Chr 7:36

**HARNESS**
on his *h* boast himself as he that .................... 1Kin 20:11
between the joints of the *h* .................... 1Kin 22:34
and vessels of gold, and raiment, *h* .... 2Chr 9:24
between the joints of the *h* .................... 2Chr 18:33
*H* the horses .................... Jer 46:4

**HARNESSED**
up *h* out of the land of Egypt .................... Ex 13:18

**HAROD** (*ha'-rod*) See HARODITE. *A spring of water.*
and pitched beside the well of *H* .................... Judg 7:1

**HARODITE** (*ha-ro'-dite*) See HARORITE. *Family name of two of David's "mighty men."*
Shammah the *H*, Elika the *H* .................... 2Sa 23:25

**HAROEH** (*ha-ro'-eh*) See REAIAH. *A son of Shobal.*
*H*, and half of the Manahethites .................... 1Chr 2:52

**HARORITE** (*ha'-ro-rite*) *Family name of a "mighty man."*
Shammoth the *H*, Helez the .................... 1Chr 11:27

**HAROSHETH** (*har'o-sheth*) *A city in Galilee.*
which dwelt in *H* of the Gentiles .................... Judg 4:2
from *H* of the Gentiles unto the .................... Judg 4:13
the host, unto *H* of the Gentiles .................... Judg 4:16

**HARP**
of all such as handle the *h* .................... Gen 4:21
songs, with tabret, and with *h* .................... Gen 31:27
and a tabret, and a pipe, and a *h* .................... 1Sa 10:5
who is a cunning player on an *h* .................... 1Sa 16:16
upon Saul, that David took an *h* .................... 1Sa 16:23
Jeduthun, who prophesied with a *h* .... 1Chr 25:3
They take the timbrel and *h* .................... Job 21:12
My *h* also is turned to mourning, .................... Job 30:31
Praise the LORD with *h* .................... Ps 33:2
upon the *h* will I praise thee, O .................... Ps 43:4
open my dark saying upon the *h* .................... Ps 49:4
awake, psaltery and *h* .................... Ps 57:8
unto thee will I sing with the *h* .................... Ps 71:22
the pleasant *h* with the psaltery .................... Ps 81:2
upon the *h* with a solemn sound .................... Ps 92:3
Sing unto the LORD with the *h* .................... Ps 98:5
with the *h*, and the voice of a .................... Ps 98:5
Awake, psaltery and *h* .................... Ps 108:2
praise upon the *h* unto our God .................... Ps 147:7
unto him with the timbrel and *h* .................... Ps 149:3
praise him with the psaltery and *h* .................... Ps 150:3
And the *h*, and the viol, the tabret .................... Is 5:12
shall sound like an *h* for Moab .................... Is 16:11
Take an *h*, go about the city, .................... Is 23:16
endeth, the joy of the *h* ceaseth .................... Is 24:8
the sound of the cornet, flute, *h* .................... Dan 3:5
the sound of the cornet, flute, *h* .................... Dan 3:7
the sound of the cornet, flute, *h* .................... Dan 3:10
the sound of the cornet, flute, *h* .................... Dan 3:15
giving sound, whether pipe or *h* .................... 1Cor 14:7

**HARPED**
it be known what is piped or *h* .................... 1Cor 14:7

**HARPERS**
I heard the voice of *h* harping .................... Rev 14:2
And the voice of *h*, and musicians, .... Rev 18:22

**HARPING**
of harpers *h* with their harps .................... Rev 14:2

**HARPS**
made of fir wood, even on *h* .................... 2Sa 6:5
*h* also and psalteries for singers .................... 1Kin 10:12
might, and with singing, and with *h* .... 1Chr 13:8
of musick, psalteries and *h* .................... 1Chr 15:16
with *h* on the Sheminith to excel .................... 1Chr 15:21
a noise with psalteries and *h* .................... 1Chr 15:28
Jeiel with psalteries and with *h* .................... 1Chr 16:5
who should prophesy with *h* .................... 1Chr 25:1
with cymbals, psalteries, and *h* .................... 1Chr 25:6
having cymbals and psalteries and *h*... 2Chr 5:12
and to the king's palace, and *h* .................... 2Chr 9:11
to Jerusalem with psalteries and *h* .... 2Chr 20:28
with psalteries, and with *h* .................... 2Chr 29:25
cymbals, psalteries, and with *h* .................... Neh 12:27
We hanged our *h* upon the willows .................... Ps 137:2
it shall be with tabrets and *h* .................... Is 30:32
the sound of thy *h* shall be no .................... Eze 26:13
Lamb, having every one of them *h* .................... Rev 5:8
of harpers harping with their *h* .................... Rev 14:2
sea of glass, having the *h* of God .................... Rev 15:2

**HARROW**
or will he *h* the valleys after .................... Job 39:10

**HARROWS**
under *h* of iron, and under axes of .................... 2Sa 12:31
with *h* of iron, and with axes .................... 1Chr 20:3

**HARSHA** (*har'-shah*) *A family of exiles.*
of Mehida, the children of *H* .................... Ezr 2:52
of Mehida, the children of *H* .................... Neh 7:54

**HART**
as of the roebuck, and as of the *h* .... Deut 12:15
the *h* is eaten, so thou shalt eat .................... Deut 12:22
The *h*, and the roebuck, and the .................... Deut 14:5
as the roebuck, and as the *h* .................... Deut 15:22
As the *h* panteth after the water .................... Ps 42:1
is like a roe or a young *h* .................... Song 2:9
*h* upon the mountains of Bether .................... Song 2:17
like to a roe or to a young *h* .................... Song 8:14
shall the lame man leap as an *h* .................... Is 35:6

**HARTS**
and an hundred sheep, beside *h* .................... 1Kin 4:23
like *h* that find no pasture .................... Lam 1:6

**HARUM** (*ha'-rum*) *Father of Aharhel.*
families of Aharhel the son of *H* .................... 1Chr 4:8

**HARUMAPH** (*ha-ru'-maf*) *Father of Jedaiah.*
repaired Jedaiah the son of *H* .................... Neh 3:10

**HARUPHITE** (*ha'-ru-fite*) *A Korhite soldier.*
and Shephatiah the *H* .................... 1Chr 12:5

**HARUZ** (*ha'ruz*) *Father of Meshullemeth.*
the daughter of *H* of Jotbah .................... 2Kin 21:19

**HARVEST**
earth remaineth, seedtime and *h* .................... Gen 8:22
went in the days of wheat *h* .................... Gen 30:14

shall neither be earing nor *h* .................. Gen 45:6
And the feast of *h*, the ............................. Ex 23:16
time and in *h* thou shalt rest..................... Ex 34:21
of the firstfruits of wheat *h* ..................... Ex 34:22
when ye reap the *h* of your land............ Lev 19:9
gather the gleanings of thy *h*.................. Lev 19:9
you, and shall reap the *h* thereof ......... Lev 23:10
of your *h* unto the priest.......................... Lev 23:10
when ye reap the *h* of your land............ Lev 23:22
thou gather any gleaning of thy *h*....... Lev 23:22
of thy *h* thou shalt not reap.................... Lev 25:5
cuttest down thine *h* in thy field........ Deut 24:19
all his banks all the time of *h*............... Josh 3:15
after, in the time of wheat *h* ................. Judg 15:1
in the beginning of barley *h*.................. Ruth 1:22
until they have ended all my *h*.............. Ruth 2:21
of barley *h* and of wheat *h*..................... Ruth 2:23
their wheat *h* in the valley...................... 1Sa 6:13
ear his ground, and to reap his *h*........... 1Sa 8:12
Is it not wheat *h* to day............................ 1Sa 12:17
put to death in the days of *h*................... 2Sa 21:9
in the beginning of barley *h* ................... 2Sa 21:9
from the beginning of *h* until................. 2Sa 21:10
came to David in the *h* time unto ........ 2Sa 23:13
Whose *h* the hungry eateth up, and ........ Job 5:5
and gathereth her food in the *h*.............. Prov 6:8
but he that sleepeth in *h* is a................. Prov 10:5
therefore shall he beg in *h* ..................... Prov 20:4
the cold of snow in the time of *h*....... Prov 25:13
snow in summer, and as rain in *h*........ Prov 26:1
thee according to the joy in *h*.................... Is 9:3
fruits and for thy *h* is fallen..................... Is 16:9
but the *h* shall be a heap in the............... Is 17:11
a cloud of dew in the heat of *h*.................. Is 18:4
For afore the *h*, when the bud is .............. Is 18:5
the *h* of the river, is her........................... Is 23:3
And they shall eat up thine *h*.................... Jer 5:17
us the appointed weeks of the *h*.............. Jer 5:24
The *h* is past, the summer is..................... Jer 8:20
the sickle in the time of *h* ....................... Jer 50:16
and the time of her *h* shall come........... Jer 51:33
Judah, he hath set an *h* for thee ............. Hos 6:11
because the *h* of the field is ..................... Joel 1:11
in the sickle, for the *h* is ripe.................. Joel 3:13
were yet three months to the *h*............... Amos 4:7
The *h* truly is plenteous, but the............. Mt 9:37
ye therefore the Lord of the *h*................... Mt 9:38
send forth labourers into his *h* ................ Mt 9:38
both grow together until the *h*................ Mt 13:30
in the time of *h* I will say to................... Mt 13:30
the *h* is the end of the world.................. Mt 13:39
the sickle, because the *h* is come............. Mk 4:29
The *h* truly is great, but the.................... Lk 10:2
ye therefore the Lord of the *h* .................. Lk 10:2
send forth labourers into his *h*................ Lk 10:2
yet four months, and then cometh *h*........ Jn 4:35
for they are white already to *h* ................ Jn 4:35
for the *h* of the earth is ripe................. Rev 14:15

**HARVESTMAN**
as when the *h* gathereth the corn............. Is 17:5
and as the handful after the *h*................... Jer 9:22

**HAS**
the words which thou *h* heard........... 2Kin 22:18

**HASADIAH** (*has-a-di'-ah*) *A son of Zerubbabel.*
and Ohel, and Berechiah, and *H*............. 1Chr 3:20

**HASENUAH** (*has-e-nu'-ah*) See SENUAH. *Father of Hodaviah.*
the son of Hodaviah, the son of *H*......... 1Chr 9:7

**HASHABIAH** (*hash-a-bi'-ah*)
*1. Son of Amaziah.*
The son of *H*, the son of Amaziah,...... 1Chr 6:45
*2. A Merarite Levite.*
the son of Azrikam, the son of *H*......... 1Chr 9:14
*3. A son of Jeduthun.*
Gedaliah, and Zeri, and Jeshaiah, *H*.... 1Chr 25:3
The twelfth to *H*, he, his sons,........... 1Chr 25:19
*4. A descendant of Hebron.*
And of the Hebronites, *H* and his ...... 1Chr 26:30
*5. Son of Kemuel.*
the Levites, *H* the son of Kemuel ...... 1Chr 27:17
*6. A Levite chief.*
and Nethaneel, his brethren, and *H*..... 2Chr 35:9
*7. A Levite in exile.*
And *H*, and with him Jeshaiah of the.... Ezr 8:19
*8. A chief priest.*
of the priests, Sherebiah, *H*................. Ezr 8:24
*9. A rebuilder of Jerusalem's wall.*
Next unto him repaired *H*, the.............. Neh 3:17
*10. A Levite who renewed the covenant.*
Micha, Rehob, *H*,................................... Neh 10:11
*11. Son of Bunni.*
the son of Azrikam, the son of *H*........ Neh 11:15
*12. Another Levite.*
the son of Bani, the son of *H*................ Neh 11:22
*13. A priest in Joiakim's time.*
Of Hilkiah, *H* ......................................... Neh 12:21
*14. A chief Levite.*
*H*, Sherebiah, and Jeshua the son ....... Neh 12:24

**HASHABNAH** (*hash-ab'-nah*) *A clan leader who renewed the covenant.*
Rehum, *H*, Maaseiah,............................... Neh 10:25

**HASHABNEIAH** See HASHABNIAH.

**HASHABNIAH** (*hash-ab-ni'-ah*)
*1. Father of Hattush.*
him repaired Hattush the son of *H* ....... Neh 3:10
*2. A Levite.*
Jeshua, and Kadmiel, Bani, *H*.................. Neh 9:5

**HASHBADANA** (*hash-bad'-a-nah*) *A priest.*
and Malchiah, and Hashum, and *H*......... Neh 8:4

**HASHBADDANAH** See HASHBADANA.

**HASHEM** (*ha'-shem*) *Father of several "mighty men."*
The sons of *H* the Gizonite,................. 1Chr 11:34

**HASHMONAH** (*hash-mo'-nah*) *A Hebrew encampment in the wilderness.*
from Mithcah, and pitched in *H*......... Num 33:29
And they departed from *H*, and.......... Num 33:30

**HASHUB** (*ha'-shub*) See HASSHUB.
*1. Father of Shemaiah.*
Shemaiah the son of *H*, the son of...... Neh 11:15
*2. Son of Pahath-moab.*
*H* the son of Pahath-moab,................... Neh 3:11
*3. A rebuilder of Jerusalem's wall.*
*H* over against their house..................... Neh 3:23
*4. A clan leader who renewed the covenant.*
Hoshea, Hananiah, *H*,............................ Neh 10:23

**HASHUBAH** (*hash-u'-bah*) *A son of Zerubbabel.*
And *H*, and Ohel, and Berechiah, and. 1Chr 3:20

**HASHUM** (*ha'-shum*)
*1. A family of exiles.*
The children of *H*, two hundred.............. Ezr 2:19
Of the sons of *H*...................................... Ezr 10:33
The children of *H*, three hundred.......... Neh 7:22
*2. A priest.*
and Mishael, and Malchiah, and *H*.......... Neh 8:4
*3. A clan leader who renewed the covenant.*
Hodijah, *H*, Bezai,................................... Neh 10:18

**HASHUPHA** (*hash-u'-fah*) See HASUPHA. *A family of exiles.*
of Ziha, the children of *H*....................... Neh 7:46

**HASRAH** (*has'-rah*) See HARHAS. *Same as Harhas.*
the son of Tikvath, the son of *H*........ 2Chr 34:22

**HASSENAAH** (*has-se-na'-ah*) See SENAAH. *Father of some rebuilders of Jerusalem's wall.*
fish gate did the sons of *H* build.............. Neh 3:3

**HASSENUAH** See SENUAH.

**HASSHUB** (*hash'-ub*) See HASHUB. *Father of Shemaiah.*
Shemaiah the son of *H*, the son of ...... 1Chr 9:14

**HASSPHERETH** See SOPHERETH.

**HAST** See PREFACE.

**HASTE**
*H* thee, escape thither ........................... Gen 19:22
And she made *h*, and let down her ...... Gen 24:46
And Joseph made *h*................................ Gen 43:30
*H* ye, and go up to my father, and........ Gen 45:9
and ye shall *h* and bring down my........ Gen 45:13
called for Moses and Aaron in *h* ........... Ex 10:16
and ye shall eat it in *h*............................. Ex 12:11
send them out of the land in *h* ............... Ex 12:33
And Moses made *h*, and bowed his ......... Ex 34:8
out of the land of Egypt in *h* ................ Deut 16:3
that shall come upon them make *h*... Deut 32:35
What ye have seen me do, make *h*....... Judg 9:48
the woman made *h*, and ran................ Judg 13:10
make *h* now, for he came to day to....... 1Sa 9:12
after the lad, Make speed, *h*.................. 1Sa 20:38
the king's business required *h*............... 1Sa 21:8
David made *h* to get away for fear........ 1Sa 23:26
Saul, saying, *H* thee, and come............. 1Sa 23:27
Then Abigail made *h*, and took two ..... 1Sa 25:18
to pass, as she made *h* to flee................... 2Sa 4:4
Syrians had cast away in their *h*.......... 2Kin 7:15
for God commanded me to make *h*... 2Chr 35:21
they went up in *h* to Jerusalem ............. Ezr 4:23
king said, Cause Haman to make *h*........... Est 5:5
the king said to Haman, Make *h*............. Est 6:10
to answer, and for this I make *h* ........... Job 20:2
O my strength, *h* thee to help me.......... Ps 22:19
For I said in my *h*, I am cut off ............. Ps 31:22
Make *h* to help me, O Lord my............... Ps 38:22
O LORD, make *h* to help me .................... Ps 40:13
Make *h*, O God, to deliver me ................... Ps 70:1
make *h* to help me, O LORD ..................... Ps 70:1
make *h* unto me, O God............................ Ps 70:5
O my God, make *h* for my help .............. Ps 71:12
I said in my *h*, All men are liars........... Ps 116:11
I made *h*, and delayed not to keep....... Ps 119:60
make *h* unto me....................................... Ps 141:1
to evil, and make *h* to shed blood......... Prov 1:16
but he that maketh *h* to be rich ......... Prov 28:20
Make *h*, my beloved, and be thou ....... Song 8:14
that believeth shall not make *h* ............. Is 28:16
Thy children shall make *h*....................... Is 49:17
For ye shall not go out with *h* ............... Is 52:12
they make *h* to shed innocent.................. Is 59:7
And let them make *h*, and take up a...... Jer 9:18
in Daniel before the king in *h* .............. Dan 2:25
was astonied, and rose up in *h*............... Dan 3:24
went in *h* unto the den of lions ............. Dan 6:19
they shall make *h* to the wall................... Nah 2:5
straightway with *h* unto the king.......... Mk 6:25
went into the hill country with *h*........... Lk 1:39
And they came with *h*, and found .......... Lk 2:16
said unto him, Zacchaeus, make *h* ......... Lk 19:5
And he made *h*, and came down, and..... Lk 19:6
saying unto me, Make *h* ...................... Acts 22:18

**HASTED**
and he *h* to dress it ................................. Gen 18:7
and she *h*, and let down her pitcher... Gen 24:18
And she *h*, and emptied her pitcher.... Gen 24:20
And the taskmasters *h* them..................... Ex 5:13
and the people *h* and passed over.......... Josh 4:10
king of Ai saw it, that they *h* ................. Josh 8:14
into the city, and took it, and *h*............. Josh 8:19
*h* not to go down about a whole.......... Josh 10:13
And the liers in wait *h*, and rushed ... Judg 20:37
nigh to meet David, that David *h*......... 1Sa 17:48
And when Abigail saw David, she *h*.... 1Sa 25:23
hurting thee, except thou hadst *h* ....... 1Sa 25:34
And Abigail *h*, and arose, and rode...... 1Sa 25:42
and she *h*, and killed it, and took......... 1Sa 28:24
which was of Bahurim, *h* and came...... 2Sa 19:16
And he *h*, and took the ashes away .. 1Kin 20:41
Then they *h*, and took every man......... 2Kin 9:13
himself *h* also to go out, because....... 2Chr 26:20
But Haman *h* to his house mourning..... Est 6:12
*h* to bring Haman unto the banquet ...... Est 6:14
or if my foot hath *h* to deceit ............... Job 31:5
they were troubled, and *h* away ............. Ps 48:5
voice of thy thunder they *h* away .......... Ps 104:7
for he *h*, if it were possible for ............ Acts 20:16

**HASTEN**
*H* hither Micaiah the son of Imlah ...... 1Kin 22:9
year, and see that ye *h* the matter....... 2Chr 24:5
that *h* after another god ............................ Ps 16:4
I would *h* my escape from the................. Ps 55:8
eat, or who else can *h* hereunto ............ Eccl 2:25
*h* his work, that we may see it................. Is 5:19
I the LORD will *h* it in his time............... Is 60:22
for I will *h* my word to perform .............. Jer 1:12

**HASTENED**
Abraham *h* into the tent unto................ Gen 18:6
arose, then the angels *h* Lot ................. Gen 19:15
Howbeit the Levites *h* it not ................. 2Chr 24:5
being *h* by the king's commandment...... Est 3:15
mules and camels went out, being *h*...... Est 8:14
I have not *h* from being a pastor .......... Jer 17:16

**HASTENETH**
The captive exile *h* that he may ............. Is 51:14

**HASTETH**
as the eagle that *h* to the prey ................ Job 9:26
he drinketh up a river, and *h* not ......... Job 40:23
as a bird *h* to the snare, and.................. Prov 7:23
he that *h* with his feet sinneth.............. Prov 19:2
He that *h* to be rich hath an evil........ Prov 28:22
*h* to his place where he arose.................. Eccl 1:5
to come, and his affliction *h* fast .......... Jer 48:16
fly as the eagle that *h* to eat..................... Hab 1:8
*h* greatly, even the voice of the ............ Zeph 1:14

**HASTILY**
they brought him *h* out of the............. Gen 41:14
without driving them out *h* ................... Judg 2:23
Then he called *h* unto the young .......... Judg 9:54
And the man came in *h*, and told Eli........ 1Sa 4:14
come from him, and did *h* catch it...... 1Kin 20:33
may be gotten *h* at the beginning...... Prov 20:21
Go not forth *h* to strive, lest.................. Prov 25:8
they saw Mary, that she rose up *h*.......... Jn 11:31

**HASTING**
judgment, and *h* righteousness................. Is 16:5
*h* unto the coming of the day of ........... 2Pet 3:12

**HASTY**
but he that is *h* of spirit....................... Prov 14:29
every one that is *h* only to want ........ Prov 21:5
thou a man that is *h* in his words....... Prov 29:20
let not thine heart be *h* to utter ............. Eccl 5:2
Be not *h* in thy spirit to be ..................... Eccl 7:9
Be not *h* to go out of his sight.............. Eccl 8:3
as the *h* fruit before the summer............ Is 28:4
is the decree so *h* from the king............ Dan 2:15
*h* nation, which shall march ..................... Hab 1:6

**HASUPHA** (*has-u'-fah*) *A family of exiles.*
of Ziha, the children of *H*....................... Ezr 2:43

**HATACH** (*ha'-tak*) *A servant of King Ahasuerus.*
Then called Esther for *H*, one of.............. Est 4:5
So *H* went forth to Mordecai unto ............ Est 4:6
*H* came and told Esther the words ........... Est 4:9
Again Esther spake unto *H* ..................... Est 4:10

**HATCH**
owl make her nest, and lay, and *h* ........... Is 34:15
They *h* cockatrice' eggs, and weave ......... Is 59:5

**HATCHETH**
sitteth on eggs, and *h* them not.............. Jer 17:11

**HATE**
the gate of those which *h* them........... Gen 24:60
come ye to me, seeing ye *h* me............ Gen 26:27
Joseph will peradventure *h* us.............. Gen 50:15
generation of them that *h* me.................. Ex 20:5
Thou shalt not *h* thy brother in........... Lev 19:17
they that *h* you shall reign over.......... Lev 26:17
let them that *h* thee flee before.......... Num 10:35
generation of them that *h* me............... Deut 5:9
them that *h* him to their face ............... Deut 7:10
them upon all them that *h* thee ........... Deut 7:15
But if any man *h* his neighbour ......... Deut 19:11
and go in unto her, and *h* her,............ Deut 22:13

And if the latter husband *h* her... Deut 24:3
enemies, and on them that *h* thee... Deut 30:7
and will reward them that *h* me... Deut 32:41
him, and of them that *h* him... Deut 33:11
elders of Gilead, Did not ye *h* me... Judg 11:7
him, and said, Thou dost but *h* me... Judg 14:16
I might destroy them that *h* me... 2Sa 22:41
but I *h* him... 1Kin 22:8
but I *h* him... 2Chr 18:7
and love them that *h* the LORD... 2Chr 19:2
They that *h* thee shall be clothed... Job 8:22
which I suffer of them that *h* me... Ps 9:13
I might destroy them that *h* me... Ps 18:40
shall find out those that *h* thee... Ps 21:8
they *h* me with cruel hatred... Ps 25:19
they that *h* the righteous shall... Ps 34:21
the eye that *h* me without a cause... Ps 35:19
they that *h* me wrongfully are... Ps 38:19
All that *h* me whisper together... Ps 41:7
they which *h* us spoil for... Ps 44:10
upon me, and in wrath they *h* me... Ps 55:3
let them also that *h* him flee... Ps 68:1
They that *h* me without a cause... Ps 69:4
be delivered from them that *h* me... Ps 69:14
they that *h* thee have lifted up... Ps 83:2
that they which *h* me may see it... Ps 86:17
face, and plague them that *h* him... Ps 89:23
Ye that love the LORD, *h* evil... Ps 97:10
I *h* the work of them that turn... Ps 101:3
their heart to *h* his people... Ps 105:25
see my desire upon them that *h* me... Ps 118:7
therefore I *h* every false way... Ps 119:104
I *h* vain thoughts... Ps 119:113
and I *h* every false way... Ps 119:128
I *h* and abhor lying... Ps 119:163
and turned back that *h* Zion... Ps 129:5
I *h* them, O LORD, that *h* thee... Ps 139:21
I *h* them with perfect hatred... Ps 139:22
scorning, and fools *h* knowledge... Prov 1:22
These six things doth the LORD *h*... Prov 6:16
The fear of the LORD is to *h* evil... Prov 8:13
way, and the froward mouth, do I *h*... Prov 8:13
all they that *h* me love death... Prov 8:36
not a scorner, lest he *h* thee... Prov 9:8
the brethren of the poor do *h* him... Prov 19:7
he be weary of thee, and so *h* thee... Prov 25:17
The bloodthirsty *h* the upright... Prov 29:10
A time to love, and a time to *h*... Eccl 3:8
I *h* robbery for burnt offering... Is 61:8
this abominable thing that I *h*... Jer 44:4
unto the will of them that *h* thee... Eze 16:27
the dream be to them that *h* thee... Dan 4:19
They *h* him that rebuketh in the... Amos 5:10
*H* the evil, and love the good, and... Amos 5:15
I *h*, I despise your feast days... Amos 5:21
of Jacob, and *h* his palaces... Amos 6:8
Who *h* the good, and love the evil... Mic 3:2
for all these are things that I *h*... Zec 8:17
thy neighbour, and *h* thine enemy... Mt 5:43
you, do good to them that *h* you... Mt 5:44
for either he will *h* the one... Mt 6:24
another, and shall *h* one another... Mt 24:10
and from the hand of all that *h* us... Lk 1:71
are ye, when men shall *h* you... Lk 6:22
do good to them which *h* you... Lk 6:27
*h* not his father, and mother, and... Lk 14:26
for either he will *h* the one... Lk 16:13
The world cannot *h* you... Jn 7:7
If the world *h* you, ye know that... Jn 15:18
but what I *h*, that do I... Rom 7:15
my brethren, if the world *h* you... 1Jn 3:13
the Nicolaitanes, which I also *h*... Rev 2:6
the Nicolaitanes, which thing I *h*... Rev 2:15
beast, these shall *h* the whore... Rev 17:16

**HATED**
Esau *h* Jacob because of the... Gen 27:41
when the LORD saw that Leah was *h*. Gen 29:31
the LORD hath heard that I was *h*... Gen 29:33
than all his brethren, they *h* him... Gen 37:4
and they *h* him yet the more... Gen 37:5
they *h* him yet the more for his... Gen 37:8
him, and shot at him, and *h* him... Gen 49:23
and said, Because the LORD *h* us... Deut 1:27
and *h* him not in times past... Deut 4:42
them, and because he *h* them... Deut 9:28
whom he *h* not in time past... Deut 19:4
inasmuch as he *h* him not in time... Deut 19:6
wives, one beloved, and another *h*... Deut 21:15
both the beloved and the *h*... Deut 21:15
firstborn son be hers that was *h*... Deut 21:15
firstborn before the son of the *h*... Deut 21:16
son of the *h* for the firstborn... Deut 21:17
and *h* him not beforetime... Josh 20:5
that thou hadst utterly *h* her... Judg 15:2
that are *h* of David's soul, he... 2Sa 5:8
Then Amnon *h* her exceedingly... 2Sa 13:15
*h* her was greater than the love... 2Sa 13:15
for Absalom *h* Amnon, because he... 2Sa 13:22
enemy, and from them that *h* me... 2Sa 22:18
had rule over them that *h* them... Est 9:1
they would unto those that *h* them... Est 9:5
the destruction of him that *h* me... Job 31:29
enemy, and from them which *h* me... Ps 18:17
I have *h* the congregation of... Ps 26:5
I have *h* them that regard lying... Ps 31:6
hast put them to shame that *h* us... Ps 44:7
neither was it he that *h* me that... Ps 55:12
from the hand of him that *h* them... Ps 106:10
they that *h* them ruled over them... Ps 106:41
For that they *h* knowledge... Prov 1:29

How have I *h* instruction, and my... Prov 5:12
and a man of wicked devices is *h*... Prov 14:17
The poor is *h* even of his own... Prov 14:20
Therefore I *h* life... Eccl 2:17
I *h* all my labour which I had... Eccl 2:18
thou hast been forsaken and *h*... Is 60:15
Your brethren that *h* you, that... Is 66:5
therefore have I *h* it... Jer 12:8
with all them that thou hast *h*... Eze 16:37
sith thou hast not *h* blood... Eze 35:6
for there I *h* them... Hos 9:15
I *h* Esau, and laid his mountains... Mal 1:3
ye shall be *h* of all men for my... Mt 10:22
ye shall be *h* of all nations for... Mt 24:9
ye shall be *h* of all men for my... Mk 13:13
But his citizens *h* him, and sent a... Lk 19:14
ye shall be *h* of all men for my... Lk 21:17
ye know that it *h* me before it... Jn 15:18
me before it *h* you... Jn 15:18
seen and *h* both me and my Father... Jn 15:24
They *h* me without a cause... Jn 15:25
and the world hath *h* them, because... Jn 17:14
have I loved, but Esau have I *h*... Rom 9:13
no man ever yet *h* his own flesh... Eph 5:29
righteousness, and *h* iniquity... Heb 1:9

**HATEFUL**
his iniquity be found to be *h*... Ps 36:2
living in malice and envy, *h*... Titus 3:3
a cage of every unclean and *h* bird... Rev 18:2

**HATEFULLY**
And they shall deal with thee *h*... Eze 23:29

**HATERS**
The *h* of the LORD should have... Ps 81:15
*h* of God, despiteful, proud,... Rom 1:30

**HATEST**
thine enemies, and *h* thy friends... 2Sa 19:6
thou *h* all workers of iniquity... Ps 5:5
righteousness, and *h* wickedness... Ps 45:7
Seeing thou *h* instruction... Ps 50:17
into the hand of them whom thou *h*... Eze 23:28
that thou *h* the deeds of the... Rev 2:6

**HATETH**
*h* thee lying under his burden... Ex 23:5
not be slack to him that *h* him... Deut 7:10
to the LORD, which he *h*, have... Deut 12:31
which the LORD thy God *h*... Deut 16:22
this man to wife, and he *h* her... Deut 22:16
teareth me in his wrath, who *h* me... Job 16:9
Shall even he that *h* right govern... Job 34:17
that loveth violence his soul *h*... Ps 11:5
long dwelt with him that *h* peace... Ps 120:6
he that *h* suretiship is sure... Prov 11:15
but he that *h* reproof is brutish... Prov 12:1
A righteous man *h* lying... Prov 13:5
He that spareth his rod *h* his son... Prov 13:24
he that *h* reproof shall die... Prov 15:10
but he that *h* gifts shall live... Prov 15:27
He that *h* dissembleth with his... Prov 26:24
A lying tongue *h* those that are... Prov 26:28
but he that *h* covetousness shall... Prov 28:16
with a thief *h* his own soul... Prov 29:24
your appointed feasts my soul *h*... Is 1:14
saith that he *h* putting away... Mal 2:16
one that doeth evil *h* the light... Jn 3:20
but me it *h*, because I testify of... Jn 7:7
he that *h* his life in this world... Jn 12:25
world, therefore the world *h* you... Jn 15:19
He that *h* me *h* my Father... Jn 15:23
*h* his brother, is in darkness... 1Jn 2:9
But he that *h* his brother is in... 1Jn 2:11
Whosoever *h* his brother is a... 1Jn 3:15
*h* his brother, he is a liar... 1Jn 4:20

**HATH** See PREFACE.

**HATHACH** See HATACH.

**HATHATH** (*ha'-thath*) *Son of Othniel.*
sons of Othniel; *H*... 1Chr 4:13

**HATING**
God, men of truth, *h* covetousness... Ex 18:21
envy, hateful, and *h* one another... Titus 3:3
*h* even the garment spotted by the... Jude 23

**HATIPHA** (*hat'-if-ah*) *A family of exiles.*
of Neziah, the children of *H*... Ezr 2:54
of Neziah, the children of *H*... Neh 7:56

**HATITA** (*hat'-it-ah*) *A family of exiles.*
of Akkub, the children of *H*... Ezr 2:42
of Akkub, the children of *H*... Neh 7:45

**HATRED**
But if he thrust him of *h*... Num 35:20
so that the *h* wherewith he hated... 2Sa 13:15
and they hate me with cruel *h*... Ps 25:19
me about also with words of *h*... Ps 109:3
evil for good, and *h* for my love... Ps 109:5
I hate them with perfect *h*... Ps 139:22
*H* stirreth up strifes... Prov 10:12
He that hideth *h* with lying lips... Prov 10:18
than a stalled ox and *h* therewith... Prov 15:17
Whose *h* is covered by deceit, his... Prov 26:26
or *h* by all that is before them... Eccl 9:1
Also their love, and their *h*... Eccl 9:6
to destroy it for the old *h*... Eze 25:15
thou hast had a perpetual *h*... Eze 35:5
used out of thy *h* against them... Eze 35:11
of thine iniquity, and the great *h*... Hos 9:7
*h* in the house of his God... Hos 9:8

Idolatry, witchcraft, *h*, variance... Gal 5:20

**HATS**
coats, their hosen, and their *h*... Dan 3:21

**HATTIL** (*hat'-til*) *A family of exiles.*
of Shephatiah, the children of *H*... Ezr 2:57
of Shephatiah, the children of *H*... Neh 7:59

**HATTUSH** (*hat'-tush*)
*1. A son of Shemaiah.*
*H*, and Igeal, and Bariah, and... 1Chr 3:22
the sons of David; *H*... Ezr 8:2
*3. A priest.*
Amariah, Malluch, *H*,... Neh 12:2
*4. A rebuilder of Jerusalem's wall.*
repaired *H* the son of Hashabniah... Neh 3:10
*5. Renewed the covenant.*
*H*, Shebaniah, Malluch,... Neh 10:4

**HAUGHTILY**
neither shall ye go *h*... Mic 2:3

**HAUGHTINESS**
the *h* of men shall be bowed down,... Is 2:11
the *h* of men shall be made low... Is 2:17
lay low the *h* of the terrible... Is 13:11
even of his *h*, and his pride, and... Is 16:6
his pride, and the *h* of his heart... Jer 48:29

**HAUGHTY**
but thine eyes are upon the *h*... 2Sa 22:28
Lord, my heart is not *h*, nor mine... Ps 131:1
an *h* spirit before a fall... Prov 16:18
destruction the heart of man is *h*... Prov 18:12
*h* scorner is his name, who... Prov 21:24
the daughters of Zion are *h*... Is 3:16
down, and the *h* shall be humbled... Is 10:33
the *h* people of the earth do... Is 24:4
And they were *h*, and committed... Eze 16:50
thou shalt no more be *h* because... Zeph 3:11

**HAUNT**
and see his place where his *h* is... 1Sa 23:22
himself and his men were wont to *h*... 1Sa 30:31
terror to be on all that *h* it... Eze 26:17

**HAURAN** (*hau'-ran*) *A province south of Damascus.*
which is by the coast of *H*... Eze 47:16
east side ye shall measure from *H*... Eze 47:18

**HAVE** See PREFACE.

**HAVEN**
shall dwell at the *h* of the sea... Gen 49:13
and he shall be for an *h* of ships... Gen 49:13
them unto their desired *h*... Ps 107:30
because the *h* was not commodious... Acts 27:12
which is an *h* of Crete, and lieth... Acts 27:12

**HAVENS**
place which is called The fair *h*... Acts 27:8

**HAVILAH** (*hav'-il-ah*)
*1. A son of Cush.*
Seba, and *H*, and Sabtah... Gen 10:7
Seba, and *H*, and Sabta, and Raamah,... 1Chr 1:9
*2. A son of Joktan.*
And Ophir, and *H*, and Jobab... Gen 10:29
And Ophir, and *H*, and Jobab... 1Chr 1:23
*3. A land west of Ural.*
compasseth the whole land of *H*... Gen 2:11
*4. A district east of Amalek.*
And they dwelt from *H* unto Shur... Gen 25:18
from *H* until thou comest to Shur... 1Sa 15:7

**HAVING**
*h* Beth-el on the west, and Hai on... Gen 12:8
*h* his uncleanness upon him, even... Lev 7:20
lie with a woman *h* her sickness... Lev 20:18
*h* his uncleanness upon him, that... Lev 22:3
or *h* a wen, or scurvy, or scabbed... Lev 22:22
a trance, but *h* his eyes open... Num 24:4
a trance, but *h* his eyes open... Num 24:16
*h* the two tables in mine hand... Deut 10:3
*h* their thumbs and their great... Judg 1:7
*h* his servant with him, and a... Judg 19:3
ye stay for them from *h* husbands... Ruth 1:13
*h* his spear in his hand, and all... 1Sa 22:6
*h* three thousand chosen men of... 1Sa 26:2
*h* put on their robes, in a void... 1Kin 22:10
*h* for their captains Pelatiah, and... 1Chr 4:42
*h* a drawn sword in his hand... 1Chr 21:16
*h* wards one against another, to... 1Chr 26:12
*h* cymbals and psalteries and harps,... 2Chr 5:12
*h* Judah and Benjamin on his side... 2Chr 11:12
every man *h* his weapon in his... 2Chr 23:10
*h* rent my garment and my mantle, I... Ezr 9:5
*h* knowledge, and *h* understanding... Neh 10:28
*h* the oversight of the chamber of... Neh 13:4
mourning, and *h* his head covered... Est 6:12
*h* sorrow in my heart daily... Ps 13:2
Which *h* no guide, overseer, or... Prov 6:7
*h* separated himself, seeketh and... Prov 18:1
*h* a live coal in his hand, which... Is 6:6
threshing instrument *h* teeth... Is 41:15
*h* their beards shaven, and their... Jer 41:5
*h* cut themselves, with offerings... Jer 41:5
*h* neither bars nor gates,... Eze 38:11
at the side of the east gate *h*... Eze 40:44
*h* charge at the gates of the... Eze 44:11
The ram which thou sawest *h* two... Dan 8:20
of Saphir, *h* thy shame naked... Mic 1:11
he is just, and *h* salvation... Zec 9:9
he taught them as one *h* authority... Mt 7:29

authority, *h* soldiers under me.......... Mt 8:9
abroad, as sheep *h* no shepherd.......... Mt 9:36
*h* with them those that were lame,....... Mt 15:30
rather than *h* two hands or two.......... Mt 18:8
rather than *h* two eyes to be cast.......... Mt 18:9
in hither not *h* a wedding garment....... Mt 22:12
*h* no children, his brother shall.......... Mt 22:24
*h* no issue, left his wife unto.......... Mt 22:25
woman *h* an alabaster box of very.......... Mt 26:7
were as sheep not *h* a shepherd.......... Mk 6:34
*h* nothing to eat, Jesus called.......... Mk 8:1
*H* eyes, see ye not.......... Mk 8:18
and *h* ears, hear ye not.......... Mk 8:18
than *h* two hands to go into hell,.......... Mk 9:43
than *h* two feet to be cast into.......... Mk 9:45
than *h* two eyes to be cast into.......... Mk 9:47
a fig tree afar off *h* leaves.......... Mk 11:13
*H* yet therefore one son, his.......... Mk 12:6
*h* heard them reasoning together,.......... Mk 12:28
there came a woman *h* an alabaster...... Mk 14:3
*h* a linen cloth cast about his.......... Mk 14:51
*h* had perfect understanding of.......... Lk 1:3
No man also *h* drunk old wine.......... Lk 5:39
*h* under me soldiers, and I say.......... Lk 7:8
*h* heard the word, keep it, and.......... Lk 8:15
a woman *h* an issue of blood.......... Lk 8:43
*h* put his hand to the plough, and.......... Lk 9:62
*h* no part dark, the whole shall.......... Lk 11:36
*h* an hundred sheep, if he lose.......... Lk 15:4
Either what woman *h* ten pieces of.......... Lk 15:8
*h* a servant plowing or feeding.......... Lk 17:7
*h* received the kingdom, then he.......... Lk 19:15
*h* a wife, and he die without.......... Lk 20:28
*h* examined him before you, have.......... Lk 23:14
*h* said thus, he gave up the ghost.......... Lk 23:46
*h* seen all the things that he did.......... Jn 4:45
tongue Bethesda, *h* five porches.......... Jn 5:2
this man letters, *h* never learned.......... Jn 7:15
*h* loved his own which were in the.......... Jn 13:1
the devil *h* now put into the.......... Jn 13:2
He then *h* received the sop went.......... Jn 13:30
*h* received a band of men and.......... Jn 18:3
Simon Peter *h* a sword drew it.......... Jn 18:10
*h* loosed the pains of death.......... Acts 2:24
*h* received of the Father the.......... Acts 2:33
*h* favour with all the people.......... Acts 2:47
*h* raised up his Son Jesus, sent.......... Acts 3:26
*H* land, sold it, and brought the.......... Acts 4:37
*h* made Blastus the king's.......... Acts 12:20
*h* stoned Paul, drew him out of.......... Acts 14:19
*h* received such a charge, thrust.......... Acts 16:24
*h* shorn his head in Cenchrea.......... Acts 18:18
Paul *h* passed through the upper.......... Acts 19:1
*h* caught Gaius and Aristarchus,.......... Acts 19:29
*h* a good report of all the Jews.......... Acts 22:12
*h* understood that he was a Roman... Acts 23:27
*h* more perfect knowledge of that...... Acts 24:22
*h* received authority from the.......... Acts 26:10
*H* therefore obtained help of God,...... Acts 26:22
fasting, *h* taken nothing.......... Acts 27:33
*h* not the law, are a law unto.......... Rom 2:14
neither *h* done any good or evil,.......... Rom 9:11
*H* then gifts differing according.......... Rom 12:6
But now *h* no more place in these..... Rom 15:23
*h* a great desire these many years...... Rom 15:23
*h* a matter against another, go to.......... 1Cor 6:1
*h* no necessity, but hath power.......... 1Cor 7:37
*h* his head covered, dishonoureth.......... 1Cor 11:4
*h* given more abundant honour to...... 1Cor 12:24
*h* confidence in you all, that my.......... 2Cor 2:3
We *h* the same spirit of faith,.......... 2Cor 4:13
as *h* nothing, and yet possessing.......... 2Cor 6:10
*H* therefore these promises dearly.......... 2Cor 7:1
always *h* all sufficiency in all.......... 2Cor 9:8
*h* in a readiness to revenge all.......... 2Cor 10:6
but *h* hope, when your faith is.......... 2Cor 10:15
*h* begun in the Spirit, are ye now.......... Gal 3:3
*H* predestinated us unto the.......... Eph 1:5
*H* made known unto us the mystery...... Eph 1:9
*h* no hope, and without God in the...... Eph 2:12
*H* abolished in his flesh the.......... Eph 2:15
*h* slain the enmity thereby.......... Eph 2:16
*H* the understanding darkened,.......... Eph 4:18
not *h* spot, or wrinkle, or any.......... Eph 5:27
evil day, and *h* done all, to stand.......... Eph 6:13
*h* your loins girt about with.......... Eph 6:14
truth, and *h* on the breastplate of.......... Eph 6:14
*h* a desire to depart, and to be.......... Phil 1:23
*h* this confidence, I know that I.......... Phil 1:25
*H* the same conflict which ye saw.......... Phil 1:30
*h* the same love, being of one.......... Phil 2:2
not *h* mine own righteousness,.......... Phil 3:9
*h* received of Epaphroditus the.......... Phil 4:18
*h* made peace through the blood of...... Col 1:20
*h* forgiven you all trespasses.......... Col 2:13
*h* spoiled principalities and.......... Col 2:15
bands *h* nourishment ministered,.......... Col 2:19
*h* received the word in much.......... 1Th 1:6
From which some *h* swerved have.......... 1Ti 1:6
which some *h* put away concerning...... 1Ti 1:19
*h* his children in subjection with.......... 1Ti 3:4
*h* their conscience seared with a.......... 1Ti 4:2
*h* promise of the life that now is.......... 1Ti 4:8
*h* been the wife of one man,.......... 1Ti 5:9
*H* damnation, because they have.......... 1Ti 5:12
*h* food and raiment let us be.......... 1Ti 6:8
*h* this seal, The Lord knoweth.......... 2Ti 2:19
*H* a form of godliness, but.......... 2Ti 3:5
teachers, *h* itching ears.......... 2Ti 4:3
*h* loved this present world, and is.......... 2Ti 4:10
*h* faithful children not accused.......... Titus 1:6
*h* no evil thing to say of you.......... Titus 2:8
*H* confidence in thy obedience I.......... Philem 21
*h* neither beginning of days, nor.......... Heb 7:3
*h* obtained eternal redemption for.......... Heb 9:12
For the law *h* a shadow of good.......... Heb 10:1
*H* therefore, brethren, boldness.......... Heb 10:19
*h* an high priest over the house.......... Heb 10:21
*h* our hearts sprinkled from an.......... Heb 10:22
not *h* received the promises.......... Heb 11:13
but *h* seen them afar off, and were..... Heb 11:13
*h* obtained a good report through...... Heb 11:39
God *h* provided some better thing...... Heb 11:40
Whom *h* not seen, ye love.......... 1Pet 1:8
*H* your conversation honest among..... 1Pet 2:12
*h* compassion one of another, love.......... 1Pet 3:8
*H* a good conscience.......... 1Pet 3:16
*h* escaped the corruption that is.......... 2Pet 1:4
*H* eyes full of adultery, and that.......... 2Pet 2:14
*H* many things to write unto you,.......... 2Jn 12
*h* saved the people out of the.......... Jude 5
*h* men's persons in admiration.......... Jude 16
sensual, *h* not the Spirit.......... Jude 19
*h* seven horns and seven eyes,.......... Rev 5:6
*h* every one of them harps, and.......... Rev 5:8
*h* the seal of the living God.......... Rev 7:2
at the altar, *h* a golden censer.......... Rev 8:3
*h* breastplates of fire, and of.......... Rev 9:17
*h* seven heads and ten horns, and.......... Rev 12:3
*h* great wrath, because he knoweth.... Rev 12:12
*h* seven heads and ten horns, and.......... Rev 13:1
*h* his Father's name written in.......... Rev 14:1
*h* the everlasting gospel to.......... Rev 14:6
*h* on his head a golden crown, and...... Rev 14:14
heaven, he also *h* a sharp sickle.......... Rev 14:17
seven angels *h* the seven last.......... Rev 15:1
sea of glass, *h* the harps of God.......... Rev 15:2
*h* the seven plagues, clothed in.......... Rev 15:6
*h* their breasts girded with.......... Rev 15:6
*h* seven heads and ten horns.......... Rev 17:3
*h* a golden cup in her hand full.......... Rev 17:4
down from heaven, *h* great power.......... Rev 18:1
*h* the key of the bottomless pit.......... Rev 20:1
*H* the glory of God.......... Rev 21:11

**HAVOCK**
he made *h* of the church, entering.......... Acts 8:3

**HAVOTH-JAIR** (*ha''-voth-ja'-ir*) See BASHAN-HAVOTH. *Villages in Gilead.*
towns thereof, and called them *H*...... Num 32:41
which are called *H* unto this day.......... Judg 10:4

**HAWK**
And the owl, and the night *h*.......... Lev 11:16
cuckow, and the *h* after his kind,.......... Lev 11:16
And the owl, and the night *h*.......... Deut 14:15
cuckow, and the *h* after his kind,...... Deut 14:15
Doth the *h* fly by thy wisdom, and...... Job 39:26

**HAY**
The *h* appeareth, and the tender.......... Prov 27:25
for the *h* is withered away, the.......... Is 15:6
silver, precious stones, wood, *h*.......... 1Cor 3:12

**HAZAEL** (*ha'-za-el*) *A king of Syria.*
anoint *H* to be king over Syria.......... 1Kin 19:15
the sword of *H* shall Jehu slay.......... 1Kin 19:17
And the king said unto *H*, Take a.......... 2Kin 8:8
So *H* went to meet him, and took a...... 2Kin 8:9
*H* said, Why weepeth my lord.......... 2Kin 8:12
*H* said, But what, is thy servant.......... 2Kin 8:13
and *H* reigned in his stead.......... 2Kin 8:15
*H* king of Syria in Ramoth-gilead.......... 2Kin 8:28
he fought against *H* king of Syria.......... 2Kin 8:29
because of *H* king of Syria.......... 2Kin 9:14
he fought with *H* king of Syria.......... 2Kin 9:15
*H* smote them in all the coasts of...... 2Kin 10:32
Then *H* king of Syria went up, and... 2Kin 12:17
*H* set his face to go up to.......... 2Kin 12:17
sent it to *H* king of Syria.......... 2Kin 12:18
into the hand of *H* king of Syria.......... 2Kin 13:3
hand of Ben-hadad the son of *H*.......... 2Kin 13:3
But *H* king of Syria oppressed.......... 2Kin 13:22
So *H* king of Syria died.......... 2Kin 13:24
Ben-hadad the son of *H* the cities...... 2Kin 13:25
king of Israel to war against *H*.......... 2Chr 22:5
he fought with *H* king of Syria.......... 2Chr 22:6
send a fire into the house of *H*.......... Amos 1:4

**HAZAIAH** (*ha-za-i'-ah*) *Son of Adaiah.*
the son of Colhozeh, the son of *H*.......... Neh 11:5

**HAZAR-ADDAR** (*ha''-zar-ad'-dar*) See ADDAR. *A place in southern Palestine.*
and shall go on to *H*, and pass on.......... Num 34:4

**HAZARDED**
Men that have *h* their lives for.......... Acts 15:26

**HAZAR-ENAN** (*ha''-zar-e'-nan*) *A village in northeastern Palestine.*
goings out of it shall be at *H*.......... Num 34:9
east border from *H* to Shepham.......... Num 34:10
border from the sea shall be *H*.......... Eze 47:17
as one goeth to Hamath, *H*.......... Eze 48:1

**HAZAR-GADDAH** (*ha''-zar-gad'-dah*) *A town in Judah.*
And *H*, and Heshmon.......... Josh 15:27

**HAZAR-HATTICON** (*ha''-zar-hat'-ti-con*) *A place in Hauran.*
*H*, which is by the coast of.......... Eze 47:16

**HAZARMAVETH** (*ha-zar-ma'-veth*) *A son of Joktan.*
begat Almodad, and Sheleph, and *H*... Gen 10:26
begat Almodad, and Sheleph, and *H*... 1Chr 1:20

**HAZAR-SHUAL** (*ha''-zar-shoo'-al*) *A town in Judah.*
And *H*, and Beer-sheba, and.......... Josh 15:28
And *H*, and Balah, and Azem,.......... Josh 19:3
at Beer-sheba, and Moladah, and *H*..... 1Chr 4:28
And at *H*, and at Beer-sheba, and in... Neh 11:27

**HAZAR-SUSAH** (*ha''-zar-soo'-sah*) See HAZAR-SUSIM. *A city in Judah.*
Ziklag, and Beth-marcaboth, and *H*..... Josh 19:5

**HAZAR-SUSIM** (*ha''-zar-soo'-sim*) See HAZAR-SUSAH. *Same as Hazar-susah.*
And at Beth-marcaboth, and *H*.......... 1Chr 4:31

**HAZAZON-TAMAR** (*haz''-a-zon-ta'-mar*) See HAZEZON-TAMAR. *A name for En-gedi.*
and, behold, they be in *H*, which.......... 2Chr 20:2

**HAZEL**
rods of green poplar, and of the *h*....... Gen 30:37

**HAZELELPONI** (*haz-el-el-po'-ni*) *Sister of the sons of Etam.*
and the name of their sister was *H*....... 1Chr 4:3

**HAZER-HATTICON** See HAZAR-HATTICON.

**HAZERIM** (*haz'-e-rim*) *A district near Gaza.*
And the Avims which dwelt in *H*.......... Deut 2:23

**HAZEROTH** (*haz'-e-roth*) *A Hebrew encampment in the wilderness.*
from Kibroth-hattaavah unto *H*.......... Num 11:35
and abode at *H*.......... Num 11:35
the people removed from *H*.......... Num 12:16
and encamped at *H*.......... Num 33:17
And they departed from *H*, and.......... Num 33:18
Paran, and Tophel, and Laban, and *H*.. Deut 1:1

**HAZEZON-TAMAR** (*haz''-e-zon-ta'-mar*) See EN-GEDI, HAZAZON-TAMAR. *Same as Hazazon-tamar.*
the Amorites, that dwelt in *H*.......... Gen 14:7

**HAZIEL** (*ha'-ze-el*) *A Levite.*
Shelomith, and *H*, and Haran, three.... 1Chr 23:9

**HAZO** (*ha'-zo*) *A son of Nahor.*
And Chesed, and *H*, and Pildash, and. Gen 22:22

**HAZOBEBAH** See HAZELELPONI.

**HAZOR** (*ha'-zor*) See BAAL-HAZOR, EN-HAZOR, HEZRON.
*1. A fortified city in Naphtali.*
when Jabin king of *H* had heard.......... Josh 11:1
that time turned back, and took *H*...... Josh 11:10
for *H* beforetime was the head of...... Josh 11:10
and he burnt *H* with fire.......... Josh 11:11
burned none of them, save *H* only..... Josh 11:13
the king of *H*, one.......... Josh 12:19
And Adamah, and Ramah, and *H*....... Josh 19:36
king of Canaan, that reigned in *H*.......... Judg 4:2
peace between Jabin the king of *H*...... Judg 4:17
Sisera, captain of the host of *H*.......... 1Sa 12:9
and the wall of Jerusalem, and *H*.......... 1Kin 9:15
*H*, Ramah, Gittaim,.......... Neh 11:33
*2. A city in Judah.*
And Kedesh, and *H*, and Ithnan,.......... Josh 15:23
and Janoah, and Kedesh, and *H*.......... 2Kin 15:29
*3. Another town in Judah.*
And *H*, Hadattah, and Kerioth, and... Josh 15:25
and Kerioth, and Hezron, which is *H* Josh 15:25
*4. Where the Benjamites lived after the Exile.*
and concerning the kingdoms of *H*....... Jer 49:28
*5. An area in eastern Arabia.*
dwell deep, O ye inhabitants of *H*.......... Jer 49:30
*H* shall be a dwelling for dragons.......... Jer 49:33

**HAZZELELPONI** See HAZELELPONI.

**HE** (*hay*) See PREFACE. *A Hebrew letter.*

**HEAD**
it shall bruise thy *h*, and thou.......... Gen 3:15
And the man bowed down his *h*.......... Gen 24:26
And I bowed down my *h*, and.......... Gen 24:48
shall Pharaoh lift up thine *h*.......... Gen 40:13
I had three white baskets on my *h*...... Gen 40:16
them out of the basket upon my *h*..... Gen 40:17
lift up thy *h* from off thee.......... Gen 40:19
he lifted up the *h* of the chief.......... Gen 40:20
bowed himself upon the bed's *h*.......... Gen 47:31
hand, and laid it upon Ephraim's *h*..... Gen 48:14
his left hand upon Manasseh's *h*.......... Gen 48:14
right hand upon the *h* of Ephraim.......... Gen 48:17
Ephraim's *h* unto Manasseh's *h*.......... Gen 48:17
put thy right hand upon his *h*.......... Gen 48:18
they shall be on the *h* of Joseph.......... Gen 49:26
on the crown of the *h* of him that...... Gen 49:26
his *h* with his legs, and with the.......... Ex 12:9
And the people bowed the *h*.......... Ex 12:27
above the *h* of it unto one ring.......... Ex 26:24
shalt put the mitre upon his *h*.......... Ex 29:6
oil, and pour it upon his *h*.......... Ex 29:7
hands upon the *h* of the bullock.......... Ex 29:10
their hands upon the *h* of the ram.......... Ex 29:15
unto his pieces, and unto his *h*.......... Ex 29:17
their hands upon the *h* of the ram.......... Ex 29:19
bowed his *h* toward the earth, and.......... Ex 34:8
coupled together at the *h* thereof.......... Ex 36:29
upon the *h* of the burnt offering.......... Lev 1:4

sons, shall lay the parts, the *h* Lev 1:8
it into his pieces, with his *h* Lev 1:12
the altar, and wring off his *h* Lev 1:15
hand upon the *h* of his offering Lev 3:2
hand upon the *h* of his offering Lev 3:8
lay his hand upon the *h* of it Lev 3:13
lay his hand upon the bullock's *h* Lev 4:4
and all his flesh, with his *h* Lev 4:11
*h* of the bullock before the LORD Lev 4:15
his hand upon the *h* of the goat Lev 4:24
upon the *h* of the sin offering Lev 4:29
upon the *h* of the sin offering Lev 4:33
and wring off his *h* from his neck Lev 5:8
And he put the mitre upon his *h* Lev 8:9
the anointing oil upon Aaron's *h* Lev 8:12
the *h* of the bullock for the sin Lev 8:14
their hands upon the *h* of the ram Lev 8:18
and Moses burnt the *h*, and the Lev 8:20
their hands upon the *h* of the ram Lev 8:22
with the pieces thereof, and the *h* Lev 9:13
from his *h* even to his foot Lev 13:12
a plague upon the *h* or the beard Lev 13:29
a leprosy upon the *h* or beard Lev 13:30
whose hair is fallen off his *h* Lev 13:40
the part of his *h* toward his face Lev 13:41
And if there be in the bald *h* Lev 13:42
a leprosy sprung up in his bald *h* Lev 13:42
be white reddish in his bald *h* Lev 13:43
his plague is in his *h* Lev 13:44
his *h* bare, and he shall put a Lev 13:45
shave all his hair off his *h* Lev 14:9
hand he shall pour upon the *h* of Lev 14:18
hand he shall put upon the *h* of Lev 14:29
hands upon the *h* of the live goat Lev 16:21
them upon the *h* of the goat Lev 16:21
shalt rise up before the hoary *h* Lev 19:32
not make baldness upon their *h* Lev 21:5
upon whose *h* the anointing oil Lev 21:10
garments, shall not uncover his *h* Lev 21:10
him lay their hands upon his *h* Lev 24:14
every one *h* of the house of his Num 1:4
LORD, and uncover the woman's *h* Num 5:18
shall no razor come upon his *h* Num 6:5
locks of the hair of his *h* grow Num 6:5
of his God is upon his *h* Num 6:7
defiled the *h* of his consecration Num 6:9
then he shall shave his *h* in the Num 6:9
shall hallow his *h* that same day Num 6:11
the Nazarite shall shave the *h* of Num 6:18
hair of the *h* of his separation Num 6:18
for one rod shall be for the *h* of Num 17:3
and he bowed down his *h*, and fell Num 22:31
he was *h* over a people, and of a Num 25:15
the *h* slippeth from the helve, and Deut 19:5
and she shall shave her *h*, and pare Deut 21:12
And the LORD shall make thee the *h* Deut 28:13
that is over thy *h* shall be brass Deut 28:23
of thy foot unto the top of thy *h* Deut 28:35
he shall be the *h*, and thou shalt Deut 28:44
come upon the *h* of Joseph Deut 33:16
upon the top of the *h* of him that Deut 33:16
the arm with the crown of the *h* Deut 33:20
his blood shall be upon his *h* Josh 2:19
his blood shall be on our *h* Josh 2:19
was the *h* of all those kingdoms Josh 11:10
each one was an *h* of the house of Josh 22:14
smote Sisera, she smote off his *h* Judg 5:26
of a millstone upon Abimelech's *h* Judg 9:53
he shall be *h* over all the Judg 10:18
be our *h* over all the inhabitants Judg 11:8
them before me, shall I be your *h* Judg 11:9
Gilead, and the people made him *h* Judg 11:11
and no razor shall come on his *h* Judg 13:5
seven locks of my *h* with the web Judg 16:13
hath not come a razor upon mine *h* Judg 16:17
off the seven locks of his *h* Judg 16:19
Howbeit the hair of his *h* began Judg 16:22
shall no razor come upon his *h* 1Sa 1:11
rent, and with earth upon his *h* 1Sa 4:12
the *h* of Dagon and both the palms 1Sa 5:4
of oil, and poured it upon his *h* 1Sa 10:1
hair of his *h* fall to the ground 1Sa 14:45
wast thou not made the *h* of the 1Sa 15:17
had an helmet of brass upon his *h* 1Sa 17:5
his spear's *h* weighed six hundred 1Sa 17:7
put an helmet of brass upon his *h* 1Sa 17:38
thee, and take thine *h* from thee 1Sa 17:46
him, and cut off his *h* therewith 1Sa 17:51
And David took the *h* of the 1Sa 17:54
him before Saul with the *h* of the 1Sa 17:57
of Nabal upon his own *h* 1Sa 25:39
thee keeper of mine *h* for ever 1Sa 28:2
And they cut off his *h*, and 1Sa 31:9
clothes rent, and earth upon his *h* 2Sa 1:2
the crown that was upon his *h* 2Sa 1:10
unto him, Thy blood be upon thy *h* 2Sa 1:16
every one his fellow by the *h* 2Sa 2:16
and said, Am I a dog's *h*, which 2Sa 3:8
Let it rest on the *h* of Joab 2Sa 3:29
and beheaded him, and took his *h* 2Sa 4:7
they brought the *h* of Ish-bosheth 2Sa 4:8
Behold the *h* of Ish-bosheth the 2Sa 4:8
they took the *h* of Ish-bosheth 2Sa 4:12
their king's crown from off his *h* 2Sa 12:30
and it was set on David's *h* 2Sa 12:30
And Tamar put ashes on her *h* 2Sa 13:19
on her, and laid her hand on her *h* 2Sa 13:19
his *h* there was no blemish in him 2Sa 14:25
And when he polled his *h*, (for it 2Sa 14:26
he weighed the hair of his *h* at 2Sa 14:26

he went up, and had his *h* covered 2Sa 15:30
with him covered every man his *h* 2Sa 15:30
coat rent, and earth upon his *h* 2Sa 15:32
I pray thee, and take off his *h* 2Sa 16:9
his *h* caught hold of the oak, and 2Sa 18:9
his *h* shall be thrown to thee 2Sa 20:21
they cut off the *h* of Sheba the 2Sa 20:22
kept me to be *h* of the heathen 2Sa 22:44
let not his hoar *h* go down to the 1Kin 2:6
but his hoar *h* bring thou down to 1Kin 2:9
return his blood upon his own *h* 1Kin 2:32
return upon the *h* of Joab 1Kin 2:33
upon the *h* of his seed for ever 1Kin 2:33
blood shall be upon thine own *h* 1Kin 2:37
thy wickedness upon thine own *h* 1Kin 2:44
to bring his way upon his *h* 1Kin 8:32
and a cruse of water at his *h* 1Kin 19:6
away thy master from thy *h* to day 2Kin 2:3
away thy master from thy *h* to day 2Kin 2:5
said unto him, Go up, thou bald *h* 2Kin 2:23
go up, thou bald *h* 2Kin 2:23
unto his father, My *h*, my *h* 2Kin 4:19
the ax *h* fell into the water 2Kin 6:5
until an ass's *h* was sold for 2Kin 6:25
if the *h* of Elisha the son of 2Kin 6:31
hath sent to take away mine *h* 2Kin 6:32
box of oil, and pour it on his *h* 2Kin 9:3
and he poured the oil on his *h* 2Kin 9:6
painted her face, and tired her *h* 2Kin 9:30
hath shaken her *h* at thee 2Kin 19:21
began to reign did lift up the *h* 2Kin 25:27
had stripped him, they took his *h* 1Chr 10:9
fastened his *h* in the temple of 1Chr 10:10
of their king from off his *h* 1Chr 20:2
and it was set upon David's *h* 1Chr 20:2
thou art exalted as *h* above all 1Chr 29:11
his way upon his own *h* 2Chr 6:23
Jehoshaphat bowed his *h* with his 2Chr 20:18
and plucked off the hair of my *h* Ezr 9:3
are increased over our *h*, and our Ezr 9:6
their reproach upon their own *h* Neh 4:4
he set the royal crown upon her *h* Est 2:17
royal which is set upon his *h* Est 6:8
mourning, and having his *h* covered Est 6:12
should return upon his own *h* Est 9:25
rent his mantle, and shaved his *h* Job 1:20
yet will I not lift up my *h* Job 10:15
you, and shake mine *h* at you Job 16:4
and taken the crown from my *h* Job 19:9
his *h* reach unto the clouds Job 20:6
When his candle shined upon my *h* Job 29:3
or his *h* with fish spears Job 41:7
glory, and the lifter up of mine *h* Ps 3:3
shall return upon his own *h* Ps 7:16
hast made me the *h* of the heathen Ps 18:43
a crown of pure gold on his *h* Ps 21:3
out the lip, they shake the *h* Ps 22:7
thou anointest my *h* with oil Ps 23:5
now shall mine *h* be lifted up Ps 27:6
iniquities are gone over mine *h* Ps 38:4
are more than the hairs of mine *h* Ps 40:12
shaking of the *h* among the people Ps 44:14
also is the strength of mine *h* Ps 60:7
shall wound the *h* of his enemies Ps 68:21
are more than the hairs of mine *h* Ps 69:4
hate thee have lifted up the *h* Ps 83:2
also is the strength of mine *h* Ps 108:8
therefore shall he lift up the *h* Ps 110:7
become the *h* stone of the corner Ps 118:22
the precious ointment upon the *h* Ps 133:2
covered my *h* in the day of battle Ps 140:7
As for the *h* of those that Ps 140:9
oil, which shall not break my *h* Ps 141:5
an ornament of grace unto thy *h* Prov 1:9
to thine *h* an ornament of grace Prov 4:9
are upon the *h* of the just Prov 10:6
upon the *h* of him that selleth it Prov 11:26
The hoary *h* is a crown of glory, Prov 16:31
beauty of old men is the grey *h* Prov 20:29
heap coals of fire upon his *h* Prov 25:22
The wise man's eyes are in his *h* Eccl 2:14
let thy *h* lack no ointment Eccl 9:8
His left hand is under my *h* Song 2:6
for my *h* is filled with dew, and Song 5:2
His *h* is as the most fine gold, Song 5:11
Thine *h* upon thee is like Carmel, Song 7:5
the hair of thine *h* like purple Song 7:5
left hand should be under my *h* Song 8:3
the whole *h* is sick, and the whole Is 1:5
the *h* there is no soundness in it Is 1:6
of the *h* of the daughters of Zion Is 3:17
For the *h* of Syria is Damascus, Is 7:8
the *h* of Damascus is Rezin Is 7:8
the *h* of Ephraim is Samaria, and Is 7:9
the *h* of Samaria is Remaliah's Is 7:9
by the king of Assyria, the *h* Is 7:20
LORD will cut off from Israel *h* Is 9:14
and honourable, he is the *h* Is 9:15
for Egypt, which the *h* or tail Is 19:15
which are on the *h* of the fat Is 28:1
which is on the *h* of the fat Is 28:4
hath shaken her *h* at thee Is 37:22
joy shall be upon their *h* Is 51:11
they lie at the *h* of all the Is 51:20
it to bow down his *h* as a bulrush Is 58:5
an helmet of salvation upon his *h* Is 59:17
have broken the crown of thy *h* Jer 2:16
him, and thine hands upon thine *h* Jer 2:37
Oh that my *h* were waters, and mine Jer 9:1
shall be astonished, and wag his *h* Jer 18:16

unto me, and the *h* of Lebanon Jer 22:6
upon the *h* of the wicked Jer 23:19
pain upon the *h* of the wicked Jer 30:23
For every *h* shall be bald, and Jer 48:37
the crown of the *h* of the Jer 48:45
the *h* of Jehoiachin king of Judah Jer 52:31
wag their *h* at the daughter of Lam 2:15
Waters flowed over mine *h* Lam 3:54
The crown is fallen from our *h* Lam 5:16
and cause it to pass upon thine *h* Eze 5:1
and took me by a lock of mine *h* Eze 8:3
recompense their way upon their *h* Eze 9:10
firmament that was above the *h* of Eze 10:1
the *h* looked they followed it Eze 10:11
make kerchiefs upon the *h* of Eze 13:18
and a beautiful crown upon thine *h* Eze 16:12
high place at every *h* of the way Eze 16:25
place in the *h* of every way Eze 16:31
recompense thy way upon thine *h* Eze 16:43
will I recompense upon his own *h* Eze 17:19
choose it at the *h* of the way to Eze 21:19
at the *h* of the two ways, to use Eze 21:21
the tire of thine *h* upon thee Eze 24:17
every *h* was made bald, and every Eze 29:18
his blood shall be upon his own *h* Eze 33:4
was a door in the *h* of the way Eze 42:12
make me endanger my *h* to the king Dan 1:10
the visions of thy *h* upon thy bed Dan 2:28
This image's *h* was of fine gold, Dan 2:32
Thou art this *h* of gold Dan 2:38
nor was an hair of their *h* singed Dan 3:27
the visions of my *h* troubled me Dan 4:5
the visions of mine *h* in my bed Dan 4:10
the visions of my *h* upon my bed Dan 4:13
and visions of his *h* upon his bed Dan 7:1
the hair of his *h* like the pure Dan 7:9
the visions of my *h* troubled me Dan 7:15
the ten horns that were in his *h* Dan 7:20
and appoint themselves one *h* Hos 1:11
your recompence upon your own *h* Joel 3:4
your recompence upon your own *h* Joel 3:7
of the earth on the *h* of the poor Amos 2:7
loins, and baldness upon every *h* Amos 8:10
and cut them in the *h*, all of them Amos 9:1
shall return upon thine own *h* Obad 15
the weeds were wrapped about my *h* Jonah 2:5
it might be a shadow over his *h* Jonah 4:6
the sun beat upon the *h* of Jonah Jonah 4:8
and the LORD on the *h* of them Mic 2:13
thou woundedst the *h* out of the Hab 3:13
his staves the *h* of his villages Hab 3:14
so that no man did lift up his *h* Zec 1:21
them set a fair mitre upon his *h* Zec 3:5
they set a fair mitre upon his *h* Zec 3:5
set them upon the *h* of Joshua the Zec 6:11
Neither shalt thou swear by thy *h* Mt 5:36
when thou fastest, anoint thine *h* Mt 6:17
man hath not where to lay his *h* Mt 8:20
hairs of your *h* are all numbered Mt 10:30
John Baptist's *h* in a charger Mt 14:8
his *h* was brought in a charger, Mt 14:11
is become the *h* of the corner Mt 21:42
ointment, and poured it on his *h* Mt 26:7
of thorns, they put it upon his *h* Mt 27:29
the reed, and smote him on the *h* Mt 27:30
set up over his *h* his accusation Mt 27:37
The *h* of John the Baptist Mk 6:24
charger the *h* of John the Baptist Mk 6:25
and commanded his *h* to be brought Mk 6:27
brought his *h* in a charger, and Mk 6:28
stones, and wounded him in the *h* Mk 12:4
is become the *h* of the corner Mk 12:10
the box, and poured it on his *h* Mk 14:3
of thorns, and put it about his *h* Mk 15:17
smote him on the *h* with a reed Mk 15:19
wipe them with the hairs of her *h* Lk 7:38
them with the hairs of her *h* Lk 7:44
My *h* with oil thou didst not Lk 7:46
man hath not where to lay his *h* Lk 9:58
hairs of your *h* are all numbered Lk 12:7
is become the *h* of the corner Lk 20:17
not an hair of your *h* perish Lk 21:18
only, but also my hands and my *h* Jn 13:9
of thorns, and put it on his *h* Jn 19:2
and he bowed his *h*, and gave up the Jn 19:30
the napkin, that was about his *h* Jn 20:7
white sitting, the one at the *h* Jn 20:12
is become the *h* of the corner Acts 4:11
having shorn his *h* in Cenchrea Acts 18:18
fall from the *h* of any of you Acts 27:34
shalt heap coals of fire on his *h* Rom 12:20
that the *h* of every man is Christ 1Cor 11:3
the *h* of the woman is the man 1Cor 11:3
and the *h* of Christ is God 1Cor 11:3
prophesying, having his *h* covered 1Cor 11:4
*h* uncovered dishonoureth her *h* 1Cor 11:5
indeed ought not to cover his *h* 1Cor 11:7
on her *h* because of the angels 1Cor 11:10
nor again the *h* to the feet 1Cor 12:21
gave him to be the *h* over all Eph 1:22
him in all things, which is the *h* Eph 4:15
the husband is the *h* of the wife Eph 5:23
as Christ is the *h* of the church Eph 5:23
he is the *h* of the body, the Col 1:18
in him, which is the *h* of all Col 2:10
And not holding the *H*, from which Col 2:19
same is made the *h* of the corner 1Pet 2:7
His *h* and his hairs were white Rev 1:14
and a rainbow was upon his *h* Rev 10:1
upon her *h* a crown of twelve Rev 12:1

having on his *h* a golden crown, ... Rev 14:14
on his *h* were many crowns ... Rev 19:12

### HEADBANDS
ornaments of the legs, and the *h* ... Is 3:20

### HEADLONG
of the froward is carried *h* ... Job 5:13
that they might cast him down *h* ... Lk 4:29
and falling *h*, he burst asunder in ... Acts 1:18

### HEADS
was parted, and became into four *h* ... Gen 2:10
And they bowed down their *h* ... Gen 43:28
then they bowed their *h* and ... Ex 4:31
These be the *h* of their fathers' ... Ex 6:14
these are the *h* of the fathers of ... Ex 6:25
made them *h* over the people, ... Ex 18:25
his sons, Uncover not your *h* ... Lev 10:6
not round the corners of your *h* ... Lev 19:27
fathers, *h* of thousands in Israel ... Num 1:16
*h* of the house of their fathers, ... Num 7:2
hands upon the *h* of the bullocks ... Num 8:12
which are *h* of the thousands of ... Num 10:4
all those men were *h* of the ... Num 13:3
Take all the *h* of the people, and ... Num 25:4
Moses spake unto the *h* of the ... Num 30:1
and made them *h* over you ... Deut 1:15
even all the *h* of your tribes, and ... Deut 5:23
when the *h* of the people and the ... Deut 33:5
he came with the *h* of the people ... Deut 33:21
Israel, and put dust upon their *h* ... Josh 7:6
the *h* of the fathers of the ... Josh 14:1
the *h* of the fathers of the ... Josh 19:51
Then came near the *h* of the ... Josh 21:1
unto the *h* of the fathers of the ... Josh 21:1
said unto the *h* of the thousands ... Josh 22:21
*h* of the thousands of Israel ... Josh 22:30
for their elders, and for their *h* ... Josh 23:2
elders of Israel, and for their *h* ... Josh 24:1
Midian, and brought the *h* of Oreb ... Judg 7:25
they lifted up their *h* no more ... Judg 8:28
did God render upon their *h* ... Judg 9:57
it not be with the *h* of these men ... 1Sa 29:4
all the *h* of the tribes, the ... 1Kin 8:1
on our loins, and ropes upon our *h* ... 1Kin 20:31
loins, and put ropes on their *h* ... 1Kin 20:32
take ye the *h* of the men your ... 2Kin 10:6
put their *h* in baskets, and sent ... 2Kin 10:7
brought the *h* of the king's sons ... 2Kin 10:8
these were the *h* of the house of ... 1Chr 5:24
*h* of the house of their fathers ... 1Chr 5:24
*h* of their father's house, to wit ... 1Chr 7:2
*h* of the house of their fathers, ... 1Chr 7:7
*h* of the house of their fathers, ... 1Chr 7:9
by the *h* of their fathers, mighty ... 1Chr 7:11
*h* of their father's house, choice ... 1Chr 7:40
these are the *h* of the fathers of ... 1Chr 8:6
were his sons, *h* of the fathers ... 1Chr 8:10
who were *h* of the fathers of the ... 1Chr 8:13
These were *h* of the fathers, by ... 1Chr 8:28
*h* of the house of their fathers, ... 1Chr 9:13
Saul to the jeopardy of our *h* ... 1Chr 12:19
the *h* of them were two hundred ... 1Chr 12:32
fathers, and bowed down their *h* ... 1Chr 29:20
put them on the *h* of the pillars ... 2Chr 3:16
all the *h* of the tribes, the ... 2Chr 5:2
Then certain of the *h* of the ... 2Chr 28:12
gladness, and they bowed their *h* ... 2Chr 29:30
and they bowed their *h*, and ... Neh 8:6
dust upon their *h* toward heaven ... Job 2:12
Lift up your *h*, O ye gates ... Ps 24:7
Lift up your *h*, O ye gates ... Ps 24:9
caused men to ride over our *h* ... Ps 66:12
thou brakest the *h* of the dragons ... Ps 74:13
Thou brakest the *h* of leviathan ... Ps 74:14
upon me they shaked their *h* ... Ps 109:25
he shall wound the *h* over many ... Ps 110:6
on all their *h* shall be baldness, ... Is 15:2
and everlasting joy upon their *h* ... Is 35:10
and confounded, and covered their *h* ... Jer 14:3
ashamed, they covered their *h* ... Jer 14:4
have cast up dust upon their *h* ... Lam 2:10
hang down their *h* to the ground ... Lam 2:10
of the firmament upon the *h* of ... Eze 1:22
forth over their *h* above ... Eze 1:22
firmament that was over their *h* ... Eze 1:25
*h* was the likeness of a throne ... Eze 1:26
and baldness upon all their *h* ... Eze 7:18
their way upon their own *h* ... Eze 11:21
have I recompensed upon their *h* ... Eze 22:31
in dyed attire upon their *h* ... Eze 23:15
and beautiful crowns upon their *h* ... Eze 23:42
your tires shall be upon your *h* ... Eze 24:23
shall cast up dust upon their *h* ... Eze 27:30
laid their swords under their *h* ... Eze 32:27
have linen bonnets upon their *h* ... Eze 44:18
Neither shall they shave their *h* ... Eze 44:20
they shall only poll their *h* ... Eze 44:20
the beast had also four *h* ... Dan 7:6
O *h* of Jacob, and ye princes of ... Mic 3:1
ye *h* of the house of Jacob, and ... Mic 3:9
The *h* thereof judge for reward, ... Mic 3:11
by reviled him, wagging their *h* ... Mt 27:39
by railed on him, wagging their *h* ... Mk 15:29
then look up, and lift up your *h* ... Lk 21:28
Your blood be upon your own *h* ... Acts 18:6
them, that they may shave their *h* ... Acts 21:24
had on their *h* crowns of gold ... Rev 4:4
on their *h* were as it were crowns ... Rev 9:7
the *h* of the horses were as the ... Rev 9:17
the horses were as the *h* of lions ... Rev 9:17
were like unto serpents, and had *h* ... Rev 9:19
great red dragon, having seven *h* ... Rev 12:3
horns, and seven crowns upon his *h* ... Rev 12:3
up out of the sea, having seven *h* ... Rev 13:1
upon his *h* the name of blasphemy ... Rev 13:1
I saw one of his *h* as it were ... Rev 13:3
of blasphemy, having seven *h* ... Rev 17:3
her, which hath the seven *h* ... Rev 17:7
The seven *h* are seven mountains, ... Rev 17:9
And they cast dust on their *h* ... Rev 18:19

### HEADSTONE
the *h* thereof with shoutings ... Zec 4:7

### HEADY
Traitors, *h*, highminded, lovers ... 2Ti 3:4

### HEAL
*H* her now, O God, I beseech thee ... Num 12:13
I wound, and I *h* ... Deut 32:39
behold, I will *h* thee ... 2Kin 20:5
the sign that the LORD will *h* me ... 2Kin 20:8
their sin, and will *h* their land ... 2Chr 7:14
O LORD, *h* me ... Ps 6:2
*h* my soul ... Ps 41:4
*h* the breaches thereof ... Ps 60:2
A time to kill, and a time to *h* ... Eccl 3:3
he shall smite and *h* it ... Is 19:22
of them, and shall *h* them ... Is 19:22
have seen his ways, and will *h* him ... Is 57:18
and I will *h* him ... Is 57:19
I will *h* your backslidings ... Jer 3:22
*H* me, O LORD, and I shall be ... Jer 17:14
I will *h* thee of thy wounds, ... Jer 30:17
who can *h* thee? ... Lam 2:13
yet could he not *h* you, nor cure ... Hos 5:13
for he hath torn, and he will *h* us ... Hos 6:1
I will *h* their backsliding, I ... Hos 14:4
nor *h* that that is broken, nor ... Zec 11:16
unto him, I will come and *h* him ... Mt 8:7
to *h* all manner of sickness and ... Mt 10:1
*H* the sick, cleanse the lepers, ... Mt 10:8
Is it lawful to *h* on the sabbath ... Mt 12:10
be converted, and I should *h* them ... Mt 13:15
whether he would *h* him on the ... Mk 3:2
And to have power to *h* sicknesses ... Mk 3:15
sent me to *h* the brokenhearted ... Lk 4:18
proverb, Physician, *h* thyself ... Lk 4:23
of the Lord was present to *h* them ... Lk 5:17
whether he would *h* on the sabbath ... Lk 6:7
he would come and *h* his servant ... Lk 7:3
kingdom of God, and to *h* the sick ... Lk 9:2
*h* the sick that are therein, and ... Lk 10:9
Is it lawful to *h* on the sabbath ... Lk 14:3
he would come down, and *h* his son ... Jn 4:47
be converted, and I should *h* them ... Jn 12:40
stretching forth thine hand to *h* ... Acts 4:30
be converted, and I should *h* them ... Acts 28:27

### HEALED
God *h* Abimelech, and his wife, and ... Gen 20:17
cause him to be thoroughly *h* ... Ex 21:19
skin thereof, was a boil, and is *h* ... Lev 13:18
the scall is *h*, he is clean ... Lev 13:37
of leprosy be *h* in the leper ... Lev 14:3
clean, because the plague is *h* ... Lev 14:48
itch, whereof thou canst not be *h* ... Deut 28:27
a sore botch that cannot be *h* ... Deut 28:35
then ye shall be *h*, and it shall ... 1Sa 6:3
the LORD, I have *h* these waters ... 2Kin 2:21
the waters were *h* unto this day ... 2Kin 2:22
king Joram went back to be *h* in ... 2Kin 8:29
king Joram was returned to be *h* ... 2Kin 9:15
he returned to be *h* in Jezreel ... 2Chr 22:6
to Hezekiah, and *h* the people ... 2Chr 30:20
unto thee, and thou hast *h* me ... Ps 30:2
*h* them, and delivered them from ... Ps 107:20
their heart, and convert, and be *h* ... Is 6:10
and with his stripes we are *h* ... Is 53:5
They have *h* also the hurt of the ... Jer 6:14
For they have *h* the hurt of the ... Jer 8:11
incurable, which refuseth to be *h* ... Jer 15:18
Heal me, O LORD, and I shall be *h* ... Jer 17:14
her pain, if so be she may be *h* ... Jer 51:8
*h* Babylon, but she is not *h* ... Jer 51:9
it shall not be bound up to be *h* ... Eze 30:21
neither have ye *h* that which was ... Eze 34:4
the sea, the waters shall be *h* ... Eze 47:8
for they shall be *h* ... Eze 47:9
marishes thereof shall not be *h* ... Eze 47:11
When I would have *h* Israel ... Hos 7:1
but they knew not that I *h* them ... Hos 11:3
and he *h* them ... Mt 4:24
only, and my servant shall be *h* ... Mt 8:8
his servant was *h* in the selfsame ... Mt 8:13
his word, and *h* all that were sick ... Mt 8:16
followed him, and he *h* them all ... Mt 12:15
he *h* him, insomuch that the blind ... Mt 12:22
toward them, and he *h* their sick ... Mt 14:14
and he *h* them ... Mt 15:30
and he *h* them there ... Mt 19:2
and he *h* them ... Mt 21:14
he *h* many that were sick of ... Mk 1:34
For he had *h* many ... Mk 3:10
hands on her, that she may be *h* ... Mk 5:23
that she was *h* of that plague ... Mk 5:29
upon a few sick folk, and *h* them ... Mk 6:5
many that were sick, and *h* them ... Mk 6:13
on every one of them, and *h* them ... Lk 4:40
hear, and to be *h* by him of their ... Lk 5:15
to be *h* of their diseases ... Lk 6:17
and they were *h* ... Lk 6:18
virtue out of him, and *h* them all ... Lk 6:19
a word, and my servant shall be *h* ... Lk 7:7
which had been *h* of evil spirits ... Lk 8:2
was possessed of the devils was *h* ... Lk 8:36
neither could be *h* of any ... Lk 8:43
him, and how she was *h* immediately ... Lk 8:47
*h* them that had need of healing ... Lk 9:11
*h* the child, and delivered him ... Lk 9:42
Jesus had *h* on the sabbath day ... Lk 13:14
in them therefore come and be *h* ... Lk 13:14
took him, and *h* him, and let him go ... Lk 14:4
them, when he saw that he was *h* ... Lk 17:15
And he touched his ear, and *h* him ... Lk 22:51
he that was *h* wist not who it was ... Jn 5:13
lame man which was *h* held Peter ... Acts 3:11
which was *h* standing with them ... Acts 4:14
and they were *h* every one ... Acts 5:16
and that were lame, were *h* ... Acts 8:7
that he had faith to be *h* ... Acts 14:9
laid his hands on him, and *h* him ... Acts 28:8
in the island, came, and were *h* ... Acts 28:9
but let it rather be *h* ... Heb 12:13
one for another, that ye may be *h* ... Jas 5:16
by whose stripes ye were *h* ... 1Pet 2:24
and his deadly wound was *h* ... Rev 13:3
beast, whose deadly wound was *h* ... Rev 13:12

### HEALER
swear, saying, I will not be an *h* ... Is 3:7

### HEALETH
for I am the LORD that *h* thee ... Ex 15:26
who *h* all thy diseases ... Ps 103:3
He *h* the broken in heart, and ... Ps 147:3
*h* the stroke of their wound ... Is 30:26

### HEALING
us, and there is no *h* for us ... Jer 14:19
and for the time of *h*, and behold ... Jer 14:19
thou hast no *h* medicines ... Jer 30:13
There is no *h* of thy bruise ... Nah 3:19
arise with *h* in his wings ... Mal 4:2
*h* all manner of sickness and all ... Mt 4:23
*h* every sickness and every disease ... Mt 9:35
the gospel, and *h* every where ... Lk 9:6
and healed them that had need of *h* ... Lk 9:11
whom this miracle of *h* was shewed ... Acts 4:22
*h* all that were oppressed of the ... Acts 10:38
the gifts of *h* by the same Spirit ... 1Cor 12:9
Have all the gifts of *h* ... 1Cor 12:30
were for the *h* of the nations ... Rev 22:2

### HEALINGS
that miracles, then gifts of *h* ... 1Cor 12:28

### HEALTH
servant our father is in good *h* ... Gen 43:28
Joab said to Amasa, Art thou in *h* ... 2Sa 20:9
who is the *h* of my countenance, ... Ps 42:11
who is the *h* of my countenance, ... Ps 43:5
thy saving *h* among all nations ... Ps 67:2
It shall be *h* to thy navel, and ... Prov 3:8
them, and *h* to all their flesh ... Prov 4:22
but the tongue of the wise is *h* ... Prov 12:18
but a faithful ambassador is *h* ... Prov 13:17
to the soul, and *h* to the bones ... Prov 16:24
thine *h* shall spring forth ... Is 58:8
and for a time of *h*, and behold ... Jer 8:15
why then is not the *h* of the ... Jer 8:22
For I will restore *h* unto thee ... Jer 30:17
Behold, I will bring it *h* ... Jer 33:6
for this is for your *h* ... Acts 27:34
thou mayest prosper and be in *h* ... 3Jn 2

### HEAP
and they took stones, and made an *h* ... Gen 31:46
and they did eat there upon the *h* ... Gen 31:46
This *h* is a witness between me and ... Gen 31:48
said to Jacob, Behold this *h* ... Gen 31:51
This *h* be witness, and this pillar ... Gen 31:52
will not pass over this *h* to thee ... Gen 31:52
thou shalt not pass over this *h* ... Gen 31:52
the floods stood upright as an *h* ... Ex 15:8
and it shall be an *h* for ever ... Deut 13:16
I will *h* mischiefs upon them ... Deut 32:23
and they shall stand upon an *h* ... Josh 3:13
rose up upon an *h* very far from ... Josh 3:16
a great *h* of stones unto this day ... Josh 7:26
Ai, and made it an *h* for ever ... Josh 8:28
raise thereon a great *h* of stones ... Josh 8:29
down at the end of the *h* of corn ... Ruth 3:7
laid a very great *h* of stones ... 2Sa 18:17
His roots are wrapped about the *h* ... Job 8:17
I could *h* up words against you, ... Job 16:4
Though he *h* up silver as the dust ... Job 27:16
hypocrites in heart *h* up wrath ... Job 36:13
of the sea together as an *h* ... Ps 33:7
made the waters to stand as an *h* ... Ps 78:13
For thou shalt *h* coals of fire ... Prov 25:22
travail, to gather and to *h* up ... Eccl 2:26
thy belly is like an *h* of wheat ... Song 7:2
city, and it shall be a ruinous *h* ... Is 17:1
shall be a *h* in the day of grief ... Is 17:11
For thou hast made of a city an *h* ... Is 25:2
shall be builded upon her own *h* ... Jer 30:18
and it shall be a desolate *h* ... Jer 49:2
*H* on wood, kindle the fire, ... Eze 24:10
make Samaria as an *h* of the field ... Mic 1:6
for they shall *h* dust, and take it ... Hab 1:10
through the *h* of great waters ... Hab 3:15
came to an *h* of twenty measures ... Hag 2:16
shalt *h* coals of fire on his head ... Rom 12:20
they *h* to themselves teachers ... 2Ti 4:3

**HEAPED**
*h* up silver as the dust, and fine ... Zec 9:3
Ye have *h* treasure together for ... Jas 5:3

**HEAPETH**
he *h* up riches, and knoweth not ... Ps 39:6
nations, and *h* unto him all people ... Hab 2:5

**HEAPS**
gathered them together upon *h* ... Ex 8:14
*h* upon *h*, with the jaw of an ... Judg 15:16
Lay ye them in two *h* at the ... 2Kin 10:8
fenced cities into ruinous *h* ... 2Kin 19:25
LORD their God, and laid them by *h* ... 2Chr 31:6
to lay the foundation of the *h* ... 2Chr 31:7
and the princes came and saw the *h* ... 2Chr 31:8
and the Levites concerning the *h* ... 2Chr 31:9
revive the stones out of the *h* of ... Neh 4:2
which are ready to become *h* ... Job 15:28
they have laid Jerusalem on *h* ... Ps 79:1
defenced cities into ruinous *h* ... Is 37:26
And I will make Jerusalem *h* ... Jer 9:11
and Jerusalem shall become *h* ... Jer 26:18
up waymarks, make thee high *h* ... Jer 31:21
cast her up as *h*, and destroy her ... Jer 50:26
And Babylon shall become *h* ... Jer 51:37
their altars are as *h* in the ... Hos 12:11
and Jerusalem shall become *h* ... Mic 3:12

**HEAR** See PREFACE.
and I will make them *h* my words ... Deut 4:10
have not known any thing, may *h* ... Deut 31:13
when ye *h* the sound of the ... Josh 6:5
for I *h* of your evil dealings by ... 1Sa 2:23
until noon, saying, O Baal, *h* us ... 1Kin 18:26
then will I *h* from heaven ... 2Chr 7:14
*H* my words, O ye wise men ... Job 34:2
The LORD *h* thee in the day of ... Ps 20:1
*H*, O LORD, when I cry with my ... Ps 27:7
for who, say they, doth *h* ... Ps 59:7
Come and *h*, all ye that fear God, ... Ps 66:16
I will *h* what God the LORD will ... Ps 85:8
A wise man will *h*, and will ... Prov 1:5
*H* instruction, and be wise, and ... Prov 8:33
Let us *h* the conclusion of the ... Eccl 12:13
*H* ye indeed, but understand not ... Is 6:9
*H*, ye that are far off, what I ... Is 33:13
*h*, and your soul shall live ... Is 55:3
He that heareth, let him *h* ... Eze 3:27
*h* the prayer of thy servant, and ... Dan 9:17
that hath ears to *h*, let him *h* ... Mt 11:15
*h* ye him ... Mt 17:5
And ye shall *h* of wars and rumours ... Mt 24:6
and hearing they may *h*, and not ... Mk 4:12
such as *h* the word, and receive it ... Mk 4:20
he maketh both the deaf to *h* ... Mk 7:37
But when ye shall *h* of wars ... Lk 21:9
when the dead shall *h* the voice ... Jn 5:25
and they that *h* shall live ... Jn 5:25
and the sheep *h* his voice ... Jn 10:3
My sheep *h* my voice, and I know ... Jn 10:27
And if any man *h* my words, and ... Jn 12:47
how *h* we every man in our own ... Acts 2:8
we do *h* them speak in our tongues ... Acts 2:11
together to *h* the word of God ... Acts 13:44
to tell, or to *h* some new thing ... Acts 17:21
how shall they *h* without a ... Rom 10:14
let every man be swift to *h* ... Jas 1:19
if any man *h* my voice, and open ... Rev 3:20

**HEARD** See PREFACE.
they *h* the voice of the LORD God ... Gen 3:8
God *h* their groaning, and God ... Ex 2:24
have *h* their cry by reason of ... Ex 3:7
and the LORD *h* it ... Num 11:1
And the LORD *h* it ... Num 12:2
that hath *h* the voice of the ... Deut 5:26
all that we have *h* with our ears ... 2Sa 7:22
I sought the LORD, and he *h* me ... Ps 34:4
But I, as a deaf man, *h* not ... Ps 38:13
Zion *h*, and was glad ... Ps 97:8
of the turtle is *h* in our land ... Song 2:12
have ye not *h*? ... Is 40:21
had not *h* shall they consider ... Is 52:15
unto the LORD, and he *h* me ... Jonah 2:2
Ye have *h* that it was said by ... Mt 5:21
for thy prayer is *h* ... Lk 1:13
darkness shall be *h* in the light ... Lk 12:3
And what he hath seen and *h* ... Jn 3:32
for we have *h* him ourselves, and ... Jn 4:42
because that every man *h* them ... Acts 2:6
of them which *h* the word believed ... Acts 4:4
*h* a voice saying unto him, Saul, ... Acts 9:4
*h* a voice saying unto me, Saul, ... Acts 22:7
but they *h* not the voice of him ... Acts 22:9
I *h* a voice speaking unto me, and ... Acts 26:14
in him of whom they have not *h* ... Rom 10:14
Eye hath not seen, nor ear *h* ... 1Cor 2:9
If so be that ye have *h* him ... Eph 4:21
with faith in them that *h* it ... Heb 4:2
Ye have *h* of the patience of Job, ... Jas 5:11
the beginning, which we have *h* ... 1Jn 1:1
*h* declare we unto you, that ye ... 1Jn 1:3
how thou hast received and *h* ... Rev 3:3
John saw these things, and *h* them ... Rev 22:8
And when I had *h* and seen, I fell ... Rev 22:8

**HEARDEST**
thou *h* his words out of the midst ... Deut 4:36
for thou *h* in that day how the ... Josh 14:12
when thou *h* what I spake against ... 2Kin 22:19
when thou *h* his words against ... 2Chr 34:27
*h* their cry by the Red sea ... Neh 9:9
thee, thou *h* them from heaven ... Neh 9:27
thee, thou *h* them from heaven ... Neh 9:28
nevertheless thou *h* the voice of ... Ps 31:22
declared my ways, and thou *h* me ... Ps 119:26
the day when thou *h* them not ... Is 48:7
Yea, thou *h* not ... Is 48:8
hell cried I, and thou *h* my voice ... Jonah 2:2

**HEARER**
For if any be a *h* of the word ... Jas 1:23
he being not a forgetful *h* ... Jas 1:25

**HEARERS**
(For not the *h* of the law are ... Rom 2:13
it may minister grace unto the *h* ... Eph 4:29
but to the subverting of the *h* ... 2Ti 2:14
not *h* only, deceiving your own ... Jas 1:22

**HEAREST**
Ruth, *H* thou not, my daughter ... Ruth 2:8
Wherefore *h* thou men's words, ... 1Sa 24:9
when thou *h* the sound of a going ... 2Sa 5:24
and when thou *h*, forgive ... 1Kin 8:30
and when thou *h*, forgive ... 2Chr 6:21
in the daytime, but thou *h* not ... Ps 22:2
O thou that *h* prayer, unto thee ... Ps 65:2
unto him, *H* thou what these say ... Mt 21:16
*H* thou not how many things they ... Mt 27:13
thou *h* the sound thereof, but ... Jn 3:8
And I knew that thou *h* me always ... Jn 11:42

**HEARETH**
for that he *h* your murmurings ... Ex 16:7
for that the LORD *h* your ... Ex 16:8
disallow her in the day that he *h* ... Num 30:5
when he *h* the words of this curse ... Deut 29:19
for thy servant *h* ... 1Sa 3:9
for thy servant *h* ... 1Sa 3:10
every one that *h* it shall tingle ... 1Sa 3:11
that whosoever *h* it will say ... 2Sa 17:9
and Judah, that whosoever *h* of it ... 2Kin 21:12
he *h* the cry of the afflicted ... Job 34:28
The righteous cry, and the LORD *h* ... Ps 34:17
Thus I was as a man that *h* not ... Ps 38:14
For the LORD *h* the poor, and ... Ps 69:33
Blessed is the man that *h* me ... Prov 8:34
A wise son *h* his father's ... Prov 13:1
but a scorner *h* not rebuke ... Prov 13:1
but the poor *h* not rebuke ... Prov 13:8
but he *h* the prayer of the ... Prov 15:29
The ear that *h* the reproof of ... Prov 15:31
but he that *h* reproof getteth ... Prov 15:32
answereth a matter before he *h* it ... Prov 18:13
but the man that *h* speaketh ... Prov 21:28
Lest he that *h* it put thee to ... Prov 25:10
he *h* cursing, and bewrayeth it not ... Prov 29:24
there is none that *h* your words ... Is 41:26
opening the ears, but he *h* not ... Is 42:20
this place, the which whosoever *h* ... Jer 19:3
He that *h*, let him hear ... Eze 3:27
Then whosoever *h* the sound of the ... Eze 33:4
Therefore whosoever *h* these ... Mt 7:24
every one that *h* these sayings of ... Mt 7:26
When any one *h* the word of the ... Mt 13:19
the same is he that *h* the word ... Mt 13:20
the thorns is he that *h* the word ... Mt 13:22
good ground is he that *h* the word ... Mt 13:23
*h* my sayings, and doeth them, I ... Lk 6:47
But he that *h*, and doeth not, is ... Lk 6:49
He that *h* you *h* me ... Lk 10:16
*h* him, rejoiceth greatly because ... Jn 3:29
I say unto you, He that *h* my word ... Jn 5:24
He that is of God *h* God's words ... Jn 8:47
we know that God *h* not sinners ... Jn 9:31
God, and doeth his will, him he *h* ... Jn 9:31
that is of the truth *h* my voice ... Jn 18:37
me to be, or that he *h* of me ... 2Cor 12:6
of the world, and the world *h* them ... 1Jn 4:5
he that knoweth God *h* us ... 1Jn 4:6
he that is not of God *h* not us ... 1Jn 4:6
according to his will, he *h* us ... 1Jn 5:14
And let him that *h* say, Come ... Rev 22:17
*h* the words of the prophecy of ... Rev 22:18

**HEARING**
law before all Israel in their *h* ... Deut 31:11
for in our *h* the king charged ... 2Sa 18:12
there was neither voice, nor *h* ... 2Kin 4:31
Surely thou hast spoken in mine *h* ... Job 33:8
heard of thee by the *h* of the ear ... Job 42:5
The *h* ear, and the seeing eye, the ... Prov 20:12
away his ear from *h* the law ... Prov 28:9
seeing, nor the ear filled with *h* ... Eccl 1:8
reprove after the *h* of his ears ... Is 11:3
I was bowed down at the *h* of it ... Is 21:3
stoppeth his ears from *h* of blood ... Is 33:15
to the others he said in mine *h* ... Eze 9:5
it was cried unto them in my *h* ... Eze 10:13
but of *h* the words of the LORD ... Amos 8:11
*h* they hear not, neither do they ... Mt 13:13
By *h* ye shall hear, and shall not ... Mt 13:14
and their ears are dull of *h* ... Mt 13:15
and *h* they may hear, and not ... Mk 4:12
many *h* him were astonished, ... Mk 6:2
midst of the doctors, both *h* them ... Lk 2:46
*h* they might not understand ... Lk 8:10
*h* the multitude pass by, he asked ... Lk 18:36
Ananias *h* these words fell down, ... Acts 5:5
things which Philip spake, *h* ... Acts 8:6
*h* a voice, but seeing no man ... Acts 9:7
of the Corinthians *h* believed ... Acts 18:8
reserved unto the *h* of Augustus ... Acts 25:21
was entered into the place of *h* ... Acts 25:23
*H* ye shall hear, and shall not ... Acts 28:26
and their ears are dull of *h* ... Acts 28:27
So then faith cometh by *h* ... Rom 10:17
and *h* by the word of God ... Rom 10:17
were an eye, where were the *h* ... 1Cor 12:17
If the whole were *h*, where were ... 1Cor 12:17
of the law, or by the *h* of faith ... Gal 3:2
of the law, or by the *h* of faith ... Gal 3:5
*H* of thy love and faith, which ... Philem 5
uttered, seeing ye are dull of *h* ... Heb 5:11
among them, in seeing and *h* ... 2Pet 2:8

**HEARKEN**
wives of Lamech, *h* unto my speech ... Gen 4:23
said unto thee, *h* unto her voice ... Gen 21:12
My lord, *h* unto me ... Gen 23:15
But if ye will not *h* unto us ... Gen 34:17
*h* unto Israel your father ... Gen 49:2
they shall *h* to thy voice ... Ex 3:18
believe me, nor *h* unto my voice ... Ex 4:1
neither *h* to the voice of the ... Ex 4:8
neither *h* unto thy voice, that ... Ex 4:9
and how shall Pharaoh *h* unto me ... Ex 6:30
But Pharaoh shall not *h* unto you ... Ex 7:4
neither did he *h* unto them ... Ex 7:22
Pharaoh shall not *h* unto you ... Ex 11:9
If thou wilt diligently *h* to the ... Ex 15:26
*H* now unto my voice, I will give ... Ex 18:19
But if ye will not *h* unto me ... Lev 26:14
not yet for all this *h* unto me ... Lev 26:18
unto me, and will not *h* unto me ... Lev 26:21
will not for all this *h* unto me ... Lev 26:27
*h* unto me, thou son of Zippor ... Num 23:18
LORD would not *h* to your voice ... Deut 1:45
Now therefore *h*, O Israel, unto ... Deut 4:1
if ye *h* to these judgments, and ... Deut 7:12
if ye shall *h* diligently unto my ... Deut 11:13
Thou shalt not *h* unto the words ... Deut 13:3
consent unto him, nor *h* unto him ... Deut 13:8
When thou shalt *h* to the voice of ... Deut 13:18
Only if thou carefully *h* unto the ... Deut 15:5
will not *h* unto the priest that ... Deut 17:12
unto him ye shall *h* ... Deut 18:15
that whosoever will not *h* unto my ... Deut 18:19
him, will not *h* unto them ... Deut 21:18
thy God would not *h* unto Balaam ... Deut 23:5
judgments, and to *h* unto his voice ... Deut 26:17
Israel, saying, Take heed, and *h* ... Deut 27:9
if thou shalt *h* diligently unto ... Deut 28:1
if thou shalt *h* unto the voice of ... Deut 28:2
if that thou *h* unto the ... Deut 28:13
if thou wilt not *h* unto the voice ... Deut 28:15
If thou shalt *h* unto the voice of ... Deut 30:10
things, so will we *h* unto thee ... Josh 1:17
will not *h* unto thy words in all ... Josh 1:18
But I would not *h* unto Balaam ... Josh 24:10
would not *h* unto their judges ... Judg 2:17
to know whether they would *h* unto ... Judg 3:4
*H* unto me, ye men of Shechem, ... Judg 9:7
that God may *h* unto you ... Judg 9:7
king of Edom would not *h* thereto ... Judg 11:17
But the men would not *h* to him ... Judg 19:25
*h* to the voice of their brethren ... Judg 20:13
*H* unto the voice of the people in ... 1Sa 8:7
Now therefore *h* unto their voice ... 1Sa 8:9
*H* unto their voice, and make them ... 1Sa 8:22
now therefore *h* thou unto the ... 1Sa 15:1
to *h* than the fat of rams ... 1Sa 15:22
*h* thou also unto the voice of ... 1Sa 28:22
For who will *h* unto you in this ... 1Sa 30:24
he would not *h* unto our voice ... 2Sa 12:18
he would not *h* unto her voice ... 2Sa 13:14
But he would not *h* unto her ... 2Sa 13:16
to *h* unto the cry and to the ... 1Kin 8:28
that thou mayest *h* unto the ... 1Kin 8:29
*h* thou to the supplication of thy ... 1Kin 8:30
to *h* unto them in all that they ... 1Kin 8:52
if thou wilt *h* unto all that I ... 1Kin 11:38
*H* not unto him, nor consent ... 1Kin 20:8
And he said, *H*, O people, every ... 1Kin 22:28
if ye will *h* unto my voice, take ... 2Kin 10:6
Howbeit they did not *h*, but they ... 2Kin 17:40
*H* not to Hezekiah ... 2Kin 18:31
*h* not unto Hezekiah, when he ... 2Kin 18:32
to *h* unto the cry and the prayer ... 2Chr 6:19
to *h* unto the prayer which thy ... 2Chr 6:20
*H* therefore unto the ... 2Chr 6:21
the king would not *h* unto them ... 2Chr 10:16
And he said, *H*, all ye people ... 2Chr 18:27
he said, *H* ye, all Judah, and ye ... 2Chr 20:15
but they would not *h* ... 2Chr 33:10
Shall we then *h* unto you to do ... Neh 13:27
*h* to the pleadings of my lips ... Job 13:6
Therefore I said, *H* to me ... Job 32:10
my speeches, and *h* to all my words ... Job 33:1
Mark well, O Job, *h* unto me ... Job 33:31
If not, *h* unto me ... Job 33:33
Therefore *h* unto me, ye men of ... Job 34:10
*h* to the voice of my words ... Job 34:16
me, and let a wise man *h* unto me ... Job 34:34
*H* unto this, O Job ... Job 37:14
*H* unto the voice of my cry, my ... Ps 5:2
Come, ye children, *h* unto me ... Ps 34:11
*H*, O daughter, and consider, and ... Ps 45:10
Which will not *h* to the voice of ... Ps 58:5
O Israel, if thou wilt *h* unto me ... Ps 81:8
my people would not *h* to my voice ... Ps 81:11
*H* unto me now therefore, O ye ... Prov 7:24
Now therefore *h* unto me, O ye ... Prov 8:32
*H* unto thy father that begat thee ... Prov 23:22
If a ruler *h* to lies, all his ... Prov 29:12

the companions *h* to thy voice .... Song 8:13
*h*, and hear my speech .... Is 28:23
ears of them that hear shall *h* .... Is 32:3
and *h*, ye people .... Is 34:1
*H* not to Hezekiah .... Is 36:16
who will *h* and hear for the time .... Is 42:23
*H* unto me, O house of Jacob, and .... Is 46:3
*H* unto me, ye stouthearted, that .... Is 46:12
*H* unto me, O Jacob and Israel, my .... Is 48:12
and *h*, ye people, from far .... Is 49:1
*H* to me, ye that follow after .... Is 51:1
*H* unto me, my people .... Is 51:4
*H* unto me, ye that know .... Is 51:7
*h* diligently unto me, and eat ye .... Is 55:2
uncircumcised, and they cannot *h* .... Jer 6:10
*H* to the sound of the trumpet .... Jer 6:17
But they said, We will not *h* .... Jer 6:17
but they will not *h* to thee .... Jer 7:27
unto me, I will not *h* unto them .... Jer 11:11
that they may not *h* unto me .... Jer 16:12
pass, if ye diligently *h* unto me .... Jer 17:24
But if ye will not *h* unto me to .... Jer 17:27
*h* to the voice of them that .... Jer 18:19
*H* not unto the words of the .... Jer 23:16
If so be they will *h*, and turn .... Jer 26:3
If ye will not *h* to me, to walk .... Jer 26:4
To *h* to the words of my servants .... Jer 26:5
Therefore *h* not ye to your .... Jer 27:9
Therefore *h* not unto the words of .... Jer 27:14
*H* not to the words of your .... Jer 27:16
*H* not unto them .... Jer 27:17
neither *h* to your dreams which ye .... Jer 29:8
unto me, and I will *h* unto you .... Jer 29:12
instruction to *h* to my words .... Jer 35:13
did *h* unto the words of the LORD, .... Jer 37:2
counsel, wilt thou not *h* unto me .... Jer 38:15
the LORD, we will not *h* unto thee .... Jer 44:16
of Israel will not *h* unto thee .... Eze 3:7
for they will not *h* unto me .... Eze 3:7
me, and would not *h* unto me .... Eze 20:8
also, if ye will not *h* unto me .... Eze 20:39
O Lord, *h* and do .... Dan 9:19
and *h*, ye house of Israel .... Hos 5:1
because they did not *h* unto him .... Hos 9:17
*h*, O earth, and all that therein .... Mic 1:2
nor *h* unto me, saith the LORD .... Zec 1:4
But they refused to *h*, and pulled .... Zec 7:11
*H*; Behold, there went .... Mk 4:3
*H* unto me every one of you, and .... Mk 7:14
known unto you, and *h* to my words .. Acts 2:14
to *h* unto you more than unto God .... Acts 4:19
Men, brethren, and fathers, *h* .... Acts 7:2
of the gate, a damsel came to *h* .... Acts 12:13
Men and brethren, *h* unto me .... Acts 15:13
*H*, my beloved brethren, Hath not .... Jas 2:5

## HEARKENED

Because thou hast *h* unto the .... Gen 3:17
Abram *h* to the voice of Sarai .... Gen 16:2
And Abraham *h* unto Ephron .... Gen 23:16
God *h* unto Leah, and she conceived . Gen 30:17
God *h* to her, and opened her womb .. Gen 30:22
unto Shechem his son *h* all that .... Gen 34:24
that he *h* not unto her, to lie by .... Gen 39:10
but they *h* not unto Moses for .... Ex 6:9
of Israel have not *h* unto me .... Ex 6:12
heart, that he *h* not unto them .... Ex 7:13
his heart, and *h* not unto them .... Ex 8:15
hardened, and he *h* not unto them .... Ex 8:19
of Pharaoh, and he *h* not unto them .... Ex 9:12
they *h* not unto Moses .... Ex 16:20
So Moses *h* to the voice of his .... Ex 18:24
times, and have not *h* to my voice .... Num 14:22
the LORD *h* to the voice of Israel .... Num 21:3
But the LORD *h* unto me at that .... Deut 9:19
him not, nor *h* to his voice .... Deut 9:23
the LORD *h* unto me at that time .... Deut 10:10
*h* unto observers of times, and .... Deut 18:14
but I have *h* to the voice of the .... Deut 26:14
the children of Israel *h* unto him .... Deut 34:9
According as we *h* unto Moses in .... Josh 1:17
that the LORD *h* unto the voice of .... Josh 10:14
and have not *h* unto my voice .... Judg 2:20
king of the children of Ammon *h* .... Judg 11:28
God *h* to the voice of Manoah .... Judg 13:9
Notwithstanding they *h* not unto .... 1Sa 2:25
I have *h* unto your voice in all .... 1Sa 12:1
Saul *h* unto the voice of Jonathan .... 1Sa 19:6
I have *h* to thy voice, and have .... 1Sa 25:35
have *h* unto thy words which thou .... 1Sa 28:21
and he *h* unto their voice .... 1Sa 28:23
Wherefore the king *h* not unto the .... 1Kin 12:15
saw that the king *h* not unto them ... 1Kin 12:16
They *h* therefore to the word of .... 1Kin 12:24
So Ben-hadad *h* unto king Asa, and .. 1Kin 15:20
he *h* unto their voice, and did so .... 1Kin 20:25
the LORD, and the LORD *h* unto him .... 2Kin 13:4
And the king of Assyria *h* unto him .... 2Kin 16:9
Hezekiah *h* unto them, and shewed .. 2Kin 20:13
But they *h* not .... 2Kin 21:9
not *h* unto the words of this book .... 2Kin 22:13
So the king *h* not unto the people .... 2Chr 10:15
Ben-hadad *h* unto king Asa, and .... 2Chr 16:4
Then the king *h* unto them .... 2Chr 24:17
hast not *h* unto my counsel .... 2Chr 25:16
the LORD *h* to Hezekiah, and healed . 2Chr 30:20
*h* not unto the words of Necho .... 2Chr 35:22
*h* not to thy commandments, .... Neh 9:16
*h* not unto thy commandments, but .... Neh 9:29
nor *h* unto thy commandments and .... Neh 9:34
he *h* not unto them, that they .... Est 3:4
that he had *h* unto my voice .... Job 9:16
Oh that my people had *h* unto me .... Ps 81:13
*h* not unto the voice of the LORD .... Ps 106:25
he *h* diligently with much heed .... Is 21:7
O that thou hadst *h* to my .... Is 48:18
they have not *h* unto my words .... Jer 6:19
But they *h* not, nor inclined .... Jer 7:24
Yet they *h* not unto me, nor .... Jer 7:26
I *h* and heard, but they spake not .... Jer 8:6
but ye have not *h* .... Jer 25:3
but ye have not *h*, nor inclined .... Jer 25:4
Yet ye have not *h* unto me .... Jer 25:7
sending them, but ye have not *h* .... Jer 26:5
they have not *h* to my words .... Jer 29:19
yet they have not *h* to receive .... Jer 32:33
but your fathers *h* not unto me .... Jer 34:14
Ye have not *h* unto me, in .... Jer 34:17
but ye *h* not unto me .... Jer 35:14
inclined your ear, nor *h* unto me .... Jer 35:15
this people hath not *h* unto me .... Jer 35:16
but they *h* not .... Jer 36:31
But he *h* not to him .... Jer 37:14
But they *h* not, nor inclined .... Jer 44:5
them, they would have *h* unto thee .... Eze 3:6
Neither have we *h* unto thy .... Dan 9:6
and the LORD *h*, and heard it, and a .... Mal 3:16
Sirs, ye should have *h* unto me .... Acts 27:21

## HEARKENEDST

because thou *h* not unto the voice .... Deut 28:45

## HEARKENETH

But whoso *h* unto me shall dwell .... Prov 1:33
but he that *h* unto counsel is .... Prov 12:15

## HEARKENING

*h* unto the voice of his word .... Ps 103:20

## HEART See PREFACE.

of the thoughts of his *h* was only .... Gen 6:5
hath he filled with wisdom of *h* .... Ex 35:35
and to serve him with all your *h* .... Deut 11:13
and to serve him with all your *h* .... Josh 22:5
My *h* rejoiceth in the LORD, mine .... 1Sa 2:1
Samuel, God gave him another *h* .... 1Sa 10:9
serve the LORD with all your *h* .... 1Sa 12:20
but the LORD looketh on the *h* .... 1Sa 16:7
and who followed me with all his *h* .... 1Kin 14:8
and said to him, Is thine *h* right .... 2Kin 10:15
they were not of double *h* .... 1Chr 12:33
let the *h* of them rejoice that .... 1Chr 16:10
my God, that thou triest the *h* .... 1Chr 29:17
of their fathers with all their *h* .... 2Chr 15:12
his God, he did it with all his *h* .... 2Chr 31:21
is nothing else but sorrow of *h* .... Neh 2:2
He is wise in *h*, and mighty in .... Job 9:4
the widow's *h* to sing for joy .... Job 29:13
hath given understanding to the *h* .... Job 38:36
The fool hath said in his *h* .... Ps 14:1
hath clean hands, and a pure *h* .... Ps 24:4
against me, my *h* shall not fear .... Ps 27:3
unto them that are of a broken *h* .... Ps 34:18
he knoweth the secrets of the *h* .... Ps 44:21
Create in me a clean *h*, O God .... Ps 51:10
of every one of them, and the *h* .... Ps 64:6
they have more than *h* could wish .... Ps 73:7
For their *h* was not right with .... Ps 78:37
let the *h* of them rejoice that .... Ps 105:3
Search me, O God, and know my *h* .... Ps 139:23
Keep thy *h* with all diligence .... Prov 4:23
The *h* knoweth his own bitterness .... Prov 14:10
For as he thinketh in his *h* .... Prov 23:7
My son, give me thine *h*, and let .... Prov 23:26
a wise man's *h* discerneth both .... Eccl 8:5
and drink thy wine with a merry *h* .... Eccl 9:7
and gladness of *h*, as when one .... Is 30:29
and no man layeth it to *h* .... Is 57:1
to revive the *h* of the contrite .... Is 57:15
my *h* maketh a noise in me .... Jer 4:19
that triest the reins and the *h* .... Jer 11:20
The *h* is deceitful above all .... Jer 17:9
I will give them an *h* to know me .... Jer 24:7
return unto me with their whole *h* .... Jer 24:7
And I will give them one *h* .... Jer 32:39
Give them sorrow of *h*, thy curse .... Lam 3:65
And I will give them one *h* .... Eze 11:19
and make you a new *h* and a new .... Eze 18:31
A new *h* also will I give you, and .... Eze 36:26
strangers, uncircumcised in *h* .... Eze 44:7
And rend your *h*, and not your .... Joel 2:13
he shall turn the *h* of the .... Mal 4:6
Blessed are the pure in *h* .... Mt 5:8
is, there will your *h* be also .... Mt 6:21
for I am meek and lowly in *h* .... Mt 11:29
of the *h* the mouth speaketh .... Mt 12:34
For out of the *h* proceed evil .... Mt 15:19
the Lord thy God with all thy *h* .... Mt 22:37
from within, out of the *h* of men .... Mk 7:21
For the hardness of your *h* he .... Mk 10:5
the Lord thy God with all thy *h* .... Mk 12:30
*h* bringeth forth that which is .... Lk 6:45
the Lord thy God with all thy *h* .... Lk 10:27
is, there will your *h* be also .... Lk 12:34
slow of *h* to believe all that the .... Lk 24:25
Let not your *h* be troubled .... Jn 14:1
Let not your *h* be troubled .... Jn 14:27
with gladness and singleness of *h* .... Acts 2:46
stiffnecked and uncircumcised in *h* .... Acts 7:51
shalt believe in thine *h* that God .... Rom 10:9
For with the *h* man believeth unto .... Rom 10:10
have entered into the *h* of man .... 1Cor 2:9
but in singleness of *h*, fearing .... Col 3:22
is charity out of a pure *h* .... 1Ti 1:5
the thoughts and intents of the *h* .... Heb 4:12
true *h* in full assurance of faith .... Heb 10:22
For if our *h* condemn .... 1Jn 3:20
God is greater than our *h* .... 1Jn 3:20

## HEARTED

speak unto all that are wise *h* .... Ex 28:3
that are wise *h* I have put wisdom .... Ex 31:6
every wise *h* among you shall come .... Ex 35:10
women, as many as were willing *h* .... Ex 35:22
wise *h* did spin with their hands .... Ex 35:25
and Aholiab, and every wise *h* man .... Ex 36:1
and Aholiab, and every wise *h* man .... Ex 36:2
every wise *h* man among them that .... Ex 36:8

## HEARTH

it, and make cakes upon the *h* .... Gen 18:6
and my bones are burned as an *h* .... Ps 102:3
a sherd to take fire from the *h* .... Is 30:14
fire on the *h* burning before him .... Jer 36:22
into the fire that was on the *h* .... Jer 36:23
in the fire that was on the *h* .... Jer 36:23
like an *h* of fire among the wood .... Zec 12:6

## HEARTILY

And whatsoever ye do, do it *h* .... Col 3:23

## HEART'S

wicked boasteth of his *h* desire .... Ps 10:3
Thou hast given him his *h* desire .... Ps 21:2
my *h* desire and prayer to God for .... Rom 10:1

## HEARTS

of bread, and comfort ye your *h* .... Gen 18:5
harden the *h* of the Egyptians .... Ex 14:17
in the *h* of all that are wise .... Ex 31:6
send a faintness into their *h* in .... Lev 26:36
their uncircumcised *h* be humbled .... Lev 26:41
let not your *h* faint, fear not, .... Deut 20:3
Set your *h* unto all the words .... Deut 32:46
our *h* did melt, neither did there .... Josh 2:11
wherefore the *h* of the people .... Josh 7:5
was of the LORD to harden their *h* .... Josh 11:20
and ye know in all your *h* and in .... Josh 23:14
their *h* inclined to follow .... Judg 9:3
to pass, when their *h* were merry .... Judg 16:25
as they were making their *h* merry ... Judg 19:22
then do ye harden your *h*, as the .... 1Sa 6:6
and Pharaoh hardened their *h* .... 1Sa 6:6
unto the LORD with all your *h* .... 1Sa 7:3
prepare your *h* unto the LORD, and .... 1Sa 7:3
of men, whose *h* God had touched .... 1Sa 10:26
stole the *h* of the men of Israel .... 2Sa 15:6
The *h* of the men of Israel are .... 2Sa 15:13
knowest the *h* of all the children .... 1Kin 8:39
he may incline our *h* unto him .... 1Kin 8:58
for the LORD searcheth all *h* .... 1Chr 28:9
walk before thee with all their *h* .... 2Chr 6:14
the *h* of the children of men .... 2Chr 6:30
of Israel such as set their *h* to .... 2Chr 11:16
*h* unto the God of their fathers .... 2Chr 20:33
sinned, and cursed God in their *h* .... Job 1:5
the righteous God trieth the *h* .... Ps 7:9
but mischief is in their *h* .... Ps 28:3
He fashioneth their *h* alike .... Ps 33:15
Let them not say in their *h* .... Ps 35:25
They said in their *h*, Let us .... Ps 74:8
we may apply our *h* unto wisdom .... Ps 90:12
them that are upright in their *h* .... Ps 125:4
then the *h* of the children of men .... Prov 15:11
but the LORD trieth the *h* .... Prov 17:3
but the LORD pondereth the *h* .... Prov 21:2
unto those that be of heavy *h* .... Prov 31:6
and their *h*, that they cannot .... Is 44:18
parts, and write it in their *h* .... Jer 31:33
but I will put my fear in their *h* .... Jer 32:40
For ye dissembled in your *h* .... Jer 42:20
the mighty men's *h* in Moab at .... Jer 48:41
that prophesy out of their own *h* .... Eze 13:2
also vex the *h* of many people .... Eze 32:9
both these kings' *h* shall be to .... Dan 11:27
their *h* that I remember all their .... Hos 7:2
they made their *h* as an adamant .... Zec 7:12
in your *h* against his neighbour .... Zec 8:17
Wherefore think ye evil in your *h* .... Mt 9:4
if ye from your *h* forgive not .... Mt 18:35
*h* suffered you to put away your .... Mt 19:8
there, and reasoning in their *h* .... Mk 2:6
reason ye these things in your *h* .... Mk 2:8
for the hardness of their *h* .... Mk 3:5
the word that was sown in their *h* .... Mk 4:15
to turn the *h* of the fathers to .... Lk 1:17
in the imagination of their *h* .... Lk 1:51
them laid them up in their *h* .... Lk 1:66
of many *h* may be revealed .... Lk 2:35
all men mused in their *h* of John .... Lk 3:15
them, What reason ye in your *h* .... Lk 5:22
away the word out of their *h* .... Lk 8:12
but God knoweth your *h* .... Lk 16:15
Settle it therefore in your *h* .... Lk 21:14
Men's *h* failing them for fear, and .... Lk 21:26
lest at any time your *h* be .... Lk 21:34
why do thoughts arise in your *h* .... Lk 24:38
which knowest the *h* of all men .... Acts 1:24
in their *h* turned back again into .... Acts 7:39
seasons, filling our *h* with food .... Acts 14:17
And God, which knoweth the *h* .... Acts 15:8
them, purifying their *h* by faith .... Acts 15:9
through the lusts of their own *h* .... Rom 1:24
of the law written in their *h* .... Rom 2:15
our *h* by the Holy Ghost which is .... Rom 5:5
he that searcheth the *h* knoweth .... Rom 8:27

deceive the *h* of the simple Rom 16:18
manifest the counsels of the *h* 1Cor 4:5
earnest of the Spirit in our *h* 2Cor 1:22
are our epistle written in our *h* 2Cor 3:2
of darkness, hath shined in our *h* 2Cor 4:6
that ye are in our *h* to die 2Cor 7:3
the Spirit of his Son into your *h* Gal 4:6
may dwell in your *h* by faith Eph 3:17
and that he might comfort your *h* Eph 6:22
understanding, shall keep your *h* Phil 4:7
That their *h* might be comforted, Col 2:2
the peace of God rule in your *h* Col 3:15
with grace in your *h* to the Lord Col 3:16
your estate, and comfort your *h* Col 4:8
men, but God, which trieth our *h* 1Th 2:4
*h* unblameable in holiness before 1Th 3:13
Comfort your *h*, and stablish you 2Th 2:17
your *h* into the love of God 2Th 3:5
Harden not your *h*, as in the Heb 3:8
hear his voice, harden not your *h* Heb 3:15
hear his voice, harden not your *h* Heb 4:7
mind, and write them in their *h* Heb 8:10
I will put my laws into their *h* Heb 10:16
having our *h* sprinkled from an Heb 10:22
envying and strife in your *h* Jas 3:14
and purify your *h*, ye double Jas 4:8
ye have nourished your *h*, as in a Jas 5:5
ye also patient; stablish your *h* Jas 5:8
sanctify the Lord God in your *h* 1Pet 3:15
and the day star arise in your *h* 2Pet 1:19
and shall assure our *h* before him 1Jn 3:19
he which searcheth the reins and *h* Rev 2:23
put in their *h* to fulfil his will Rev 17:17

**HEARTS'**
them up unto their own *h* lust Ps 81:12

**HEARTY**
of a man's friend by *h* counsel Prov 27:9

**HEAT**
seedtime and harvest, and cold and *h* Gen 8:22
the tent door in the *h* of the day Gen 18:1
what meaneth the *h* of this great Deut 29:24
and devoured with burning *h* Deut 32:24
Ammonites until the *h* of the day 1Sa 11:11
came about the *h* of the day to 2Sa 4:5
him with clothes, but he gat no *h* 1Kin 1:1
that my lord the king may get *h* 1Kin 1:2
*h* consume the snow waters Job 24:19
me, and my bones are burned with *h* Job 30:30
is nothing hid from the *h* thereof Ps 19:6
lie together, then they have *h* Eccl 4:11
shadow in the daytime from the *h* Is 4:6
place like a clear *h* upon herbs Is 18:4
cloud of dew in the *h* of harvest Is 18:4
the storm, a shadow from the *h* Is 25:4
as the *h* in a dry place Is 25:5
even the *h* with the shadow of a Is 25:5
neither shall the *h* nor sun smite Is 49:10
and shall not see when *h* cometh Jer 17:8
be cast out in the day to the *h* Jer 36:30
In their *h* I will make their Jer 51:39
bitterness, in the *h* of my spirit Eze 3:14
commanded that they should *h* the Dan 3:19
borne the burden and *h* of the day Mt 20:12
blow, ye say, There will be *h* Lk 12:55
there came a viper out of the *h* Acts 28:3
no sooner risen with a burning *h* Jas 1:11
shall melt with fervent *h* 2Pet 3:10
shall melt with fervent *h* 2Pet 3:12
the sun light on them, nor any *h* Rev 7:16
And men were scorched with great *h* Rev 16:9

**HEATED**
more than it was wont to be *h* Dan 3:19
as an oven *h* by the baker, who Hos 7:4

**HEATH**
shall be like the *h* in the desert Jer 17:6
be like the *h* in the wilderness Jer 48:6

**HEATHEN**
shall be of the *h* that are round Lev 25:44
And I will scatter you among the *h* Lev 26:33
And ye shall perish among the *h* Lev 26:38
of Egypt in the sight of the *h* Lev 26:45
be left few in number among the *h* Deut 4:27
hast kept me to be head of the *h* 2Sa 22:44
unto thee, O LORD, among the *h* 2Sa 22:50
to the abominations of the *h* 2Kin 16:3
walked in the statutes of the *h* 2Kin 17:8
as did the *h* whom the LORD 2Kin 17:11
went after the *h* that were round 2Kin 17:15
after the abominations of the *h* 2Kin 21:2
Declare his glory among the *h* 1Chr 16:24
and deliver us from the *h* 1Chr 16:35
over all the kingdoms of the *h* 2Chr 20:6
the *h* whom the LORD had cast out 2Chr 28:3
unto the abominations of the *h* 2Chr 33:2
to err, and to do worse than the *h* 2Chr 33:9
all the abominations of the *h* 2Chr 36:14
filthiness of the *h* of the land Ezr 6:21
Jews, which were sold unto the *h* Neh 5:8
the reproach of the *h* our enemies Neh 5:9
among the *h* that are about us Neh 5:17
It is reported among the *h* Neh 6:6
all the *h* that were about us saw Neh 6:16
Why do the *h* rage, and the people Ps 2:1
thee the *h* for thine inheritance Ps 2:8
Thou hast rebuked the *h*, thou Ps 9:5
The *h* are sunk down in the pit Ps 9:15
let the *h* be judged in thy sight Ps 9:19
the *h* are perished out of his Ps 10:16
hast made me the head of the *h* Ps 18:43
unto thee, O LORD, among the *h* Ps 18:49
the counsel of the *h* to nought Ps 33:10
drive out the *h* with thy hand Ps 44:2
and hast scattered us among the *h* Ps 44:11
makest us a byword among the *h* Ps 44:14
The *h* raged, the kingdoms were Ps 46:6
I will be exalted among the *h* Ps 46:10
God reigneth over the *h* Ps 47:8
Israel, awake to visit all the *h* Ps 59:5
shalt have all the *h* in derision Ps 59:8
He cast out the *h* also before Ps 78:55
the *h* are come into thine Ps 79:1
the *h* that have not known thee Ps 79:6
Wherefore should the *h* say Ps 79:10
let him be known among the *h* in Ps 79:10
thou hast cast out the *h*, and Ps 80:8
He that chastiseth the *h*, shall Ps 94:10
Declare his glory among the *h* Ps 96:3
Say among the *h* that the LORD Ps 96:10
shewed in the sight of the *h* Ps 98:2
So the *h* shall fear the name of Ps 102:15
And gave them the lands of the *h* Ps 105:44
But were mingled among the *h* Ps 106:35
gave them into the hand of the *h* Ps 106:41
and gather us from among the *h* Ps 106:47
He shall judge among the *h* Ps 110:6
give them the heritage of the *h* Ps 111:6
Wherefore should the *h* say Ps 115:2
then said they among the *h* Ps 126:2
The idols of the *h* are silver Ps 135:15
To execute vengeance upon the *h* Ps 149:7
the lords of the *h* have broken Is 16:8
scatter them also among the *h* Jer 9:16
LORD, Learn not the way of the *h* Jer 10:2
for the *h* are dismayed at them Jer 10:2
upon the *h* that know thee not Jer 10:25
Ask ye now among the *h*, who hath Jer 18:13
an ambassador is sent unto the *h* Jer 49:14
will make thee small among the *h* Jer 49:15
she dwelleth among the *h*, she Lam 1:3
the *h* entered into her sanctuary Lam 1:10
wandered, they said among the *h* Lam 4:15
shadow we shall live among the *h* Lam 4:20
I will bring the worst of the *h* Eze 7:24
of the *h* that are round about you Eze 11:12
cast them far off among the *h* Eze 11:16
among the *h* whither they come Eze 12:16
forth among the *h* for thy beauty Eze 16:14
not be polluted before the *h* Eze 20:9
not be polluted before the *h* Eze 20:14
be polluted in the sight of the *h* Eze 20:22
I would scatter them among the *h* Eze 20:23
that ye say, We will be as the *h* Eze 20:32
be sanctified in you before the *h* Eze 20:41
I made thee a reproach unto the *h* Eze 22:4
I will scatter thee among the *h* Eze 22:15
in thyself in the sight of the *h* Eze 22:16
hast gone a whoring after the *h* Eze 23:30
deliver thee for a spoil to the *h* Eze 25:7
of Judah is like unto all the *h* Eze 25:8
in them in the sight of the *h* Eze 28:25
it shall be the time of the *h* Eze 30:3
hand of the mighty one of the *h* Eze 31:11
his shadow in the midst of the *h* Eze 31:17
shall no more be a prey to the *h* Eze 34:28
bear the shame of the *h* any more Eze 34:29
unto the residue of the *h* Eze 36:3
of the *h* that are round about Eze 36:4
against the residue of the *h* Eze 36:5
ye have borne the shame of the *h* Eze 36:6
Surely the *h* that are about you, Eze 36:7
thee the shame of the *h* any more Eze 36:15
And I scattered them among the *h* Eze 36:19
And when they entered unto the *h* Eze 36:20
Israel had profaned among the *h* Eze 36:21
ye have profaned among the *h* Eze 36:22
which was profaned among the *h* Eze 36:23
the *h* shall know that I am the Eze 36:23
I will take you from among the *h* Eze 36:24
reproach of famine among the *h* Eze 36:30
Then the *h* that are left round Eze 36:36
of Israel from among the *h* Eze 37:21
the *h* shall know that I the LORD Eze 37:28
that the *h* may know me, when I Eze 38:16
the *h* shall know that I am the Eze 39:7
I will set my glory among the *h* Eze 39:21
all the *h* shall see my judgment Eze 39:21
the *h* shall know that the house Eze 39:23
be led into captivity among the *h* Eze 39:28
that the *h* should rule over them Joel 2:17
make you a reproach among the *h* Joel 2:19
yourselves, and come, all ye *h* Joel 3:11
Let the *h* be wakened, and come up Joel 3:12
to judge all the *h* round about Joel 3:12
remnant of Edom, and of all the *h* Amos 9:12
an ambassador is sent among the *h* Obad 1
have made thee small among the *h* Obad 2
the LORD is near upon all the *h* Obad 15
so shall all the *h* drink Obad 16
in anger and fury upon the *h* Mic 5:15
Behold ye among the *h*, and regard, Hab 1:5
thou didst thresh the *h* in anger Hab 3:12
even all the isles of the *h* Zeph 2:11
strength of the kingdoms of the *h* Hag 2:22
with the *h* that are at ease Zec 1:15
as ye were a curse among the *h* Zec 8:13
he shall speak peace unto the *h* Zec 9:10
the wealth of all the *h* round Zec 14:14
the LORD will smite the *h* that Zec 14:18
name shall be great among the *h* Mal 1:11
my name is dreadful among the *h* Mal 1:14
not vain repetitions, as the *h* do Mt 6:7
let him be unto thee as an *h* man Mt 18:17
hast said, Why did the *h* rage Acts 4:25
countrymen, in perils by the *h* 2Cor 11:26
I might preach him among the *h* Gal 1:16
that we should go unto the *h* Gal 2:9
would justify the *h* through faith Gal 3:8

**HEAVE**
and the shoulder of the *h* offering Ex 29:27
for it is an *h* offering Ex 29:28
it shall be an *h* offering from Ex 29:28
even their *h* offering unto the Ex 29:28
for an *h* offering unto the LORD Lev 7:14
*h* offering of the sacrifices of Lev 7:32
the *h* shoulder have I taken of Lev 7:34
*h* shoulder shall ye eat in a Lev 10:14
The *h* shoulder and the wave breast Lev 10:15
the wave breast and *h* shoulder Num 6:20
ye shall offer up an *h* offering Num 15:19
of your dough for an *h* offering Num 15:20
as ye do the *h* offering of the Num 15:20
threshingfloor, so shall ye *h* it Num 15:20
an *h* offering in your generations Num 15:21
*h* offerings of all the hallowed Num 18:8
the *h* offering of their gift, Num 18:11
All the *h* offerings of the holy Num 18:19
as an *h* offering unto the LORD Num 18:24
then ye shall offer up an *h* Num 18:26
this your *h* offering shall be Num 18:27
Thus ye also shall offer an *h* Num 18:28
*h* offering to Aaron the priest Num 18:28
every *h* offering of the LORD Num 18:29
for an *h* offering of the LORD Num 31:29
which was the LORD's *h* offering Num 31:41
*h* offerings of your hand, and your Deut 12:6
the *h* offering of your hand, and Deut 12:11
or *h* offering of thine hand Deut 12:17

**HEAVED**
which is waved, and which is *h* up Ex 29:27
When ye have *h* the best thereof Num 18:30
when ye have *h* from it the best Num 18:32

**HEAVEN** See PREFACE.
the beginning God created the *h* Gen 1:1
And God called the firmament *H* Gen 1:8
of God, and this is the gate of *h* Gen 28:17
I have talked with you from *h* Ex 20:22
Behold, the *h* and the *h* of Deut 10:14
for the precious things of *h* Deut 33:13
behold, the *h* and *h* of 1Kin 8:27
the LORD would make windows in *h* 2Kin 7:2
then will I hear from *h*, and will 2Chr 7:14
and he walketh in the circuit of *h* Job 22:14
Whom have I in *h* but thee Ps 73:25
For who in the *h* can be compared Ps 89:6
For as the *h* is high above the Ps 103:11
The *h*, even the heavens, are the Ps 115:16
time to every purpose under the *h* Eccl 3:1
for God is in *h*, and thou upon Eccl 5:2
meted out *h* with the span, and Is 40:12
The *h* is my throne, and the earth Is 66:1
Do not I fill *h* and earth Jer 23:24
If *h* above can be measured, and Jer 31:37
out the *h* by his understanding Jer 51:15
put thee out, I will cover the *h* Eze 32:7
to his will in the army of *h* Dan 4:35
of man came with the clouds of *h* Dan 7:13
Therefore the *h* over you is Hag 1:10
not open you the windows of *h* Mal 3:10
for the kingdom of *h* is at hand Mt 3:2
for great is your reward in *h* Mt 5:12
For verily I say unto you, Till *h* Mt 5:18
Swear not at all; neither by *h* Mt 5:34
Our Father which art in *h* Mt 6:9
thee the keys of the kingdom of *h* Mt 16:19
the sign of the Son of man in *h* Mt 24:30
*H* and earth shall pass away, but Mt 24:35
and coming in the clouds of *h* Mt 26:64
earth to the uttermost part of *h* Mk 13:27
and coming in the clouds of *h* Mk 14:62
and praying, the *h* was opened, Lk 3:21
Father, I have sinned against *h* Lk 15:18
Hereafter ye shall see *h* open Jn 1:51
He gave them bread from *h* to eat Jn 6:31
Whom the *h* must receive until the Acts 3:21
name under *h* given among men Acts 4:12
*H* is my throne, and earth is my Acts 7:49
from *h* against all ungodliness Rom 1:18
whether in *h* or in earth, (as 1Cor 8:5
the second man is the Lord from *h* 1Cor 15:47
an one caught up to the third *h* 2Cor 12:2
Of whom the whole family in *h* Eph 3:15
knee should bow, of things in *h* Phil 2:10
all things created, that are in *h* Col 1:16
firstborn, which are written in *h* Heb 12:23
are three that bear record in *h* 1Jn 5:7
behold, a door was opened in *h* Rev 4:1
there was silence in *h* about the Rev 8:1
the temple of God was opened in *h* Rev 11:19
appeared a great wonder in *h* Rev 12:1
for the first *h* and the first Rev 21:1

**HEAVENLY**
your *h* Father will also forgive Mt 6:14
yet your *h* Father feedeth them Mt 6:26
for your *h* Father knoweth that Mt 6:32
which my *h* Father hath not Mt 15:13

So likewise shall my *h* Father do ... Mt 18:35
of the *h* host praising God ... Lk 2:13
how much more shall your *h* Father ... Lk 11:13
if I tell you of *h* things ... Jn 3:12
not disobedient unto the *h* vision ... Acts 26:19
and as is the *h*, such are they ... 1Cor 15:48
such are they also that are *h* ... 1Cor 15:48
also bear the image of the *h* ... 1Cor 15:49
blessings in *h* places in Christ ... Eph 1:3
own right hand in the *h* places ... Eph 1:20
in *h* places in Christ Jesus ... Eph 2:6
powers in *h* places might be known ... Eph 3:10
preserve me unto his *h* kingdom ... 2Ti 4:18
partakers of the *h* calling ... Heb 3:1
and have tasted of the *h* gift ... Heb 6:4
the example and shadow of *h* things ... Heb 8:5
but the *h* things themselves with ... Heb 9:23
a better country, that is, an *h* ... Heb 11:16
the *h* Jerusalem, and to an ... Heb 12:22

**HEAVEN'S**
eunuchs for the kingdom of *h* sake ... Mt 19:12

**HEAVENS**
Thus the *h* and the earth were ... Gen 2:1
are the generations of the *h* ... Gen 2:4
LORD God made the earth and the *h* ... Gen 2:4
the heaven of *h* is the LORD's thy ... Deut 10:14
Give ear, O ye *h*, and I will speak ... Deut 32:1
also his *h* shall drop down dew ... Deut 33:28
the *h* dropped, the clouds also ... Judg 5:4
He bowed the *h* also, and came down. 2Sa 22:10
heaven of *h* cannot contain thee ... 1Kin 8:27
but the LORD made the *h* ... 1Chr 16:26
Let the *h* be glad, and let the ... 1Chr 16:31
Israel like to the stars of the *h* ... 1Chr 27:23
heaven of *h* cannot contain him ... 2Chr 2:6
the heaven of *h* cannot contain ... 2Chr 6:18
Then hear thou from the *h* ... 2Chr 6:25
Then hear thou from the *h* ... 2Chr 6:33
hear thou from the *h* their prayer ... 2Chr 6:35
Then hear thou from the *h* ... 2Chr 6:39
trespass is grown up unto the *h* ... Ezr 9:6
hast made heaven, the heaven of *h* ... Neh 9:6
Which alone spreadeth out the *h* ... Job 9:8
till the *h* be no more, they shall ... Job 14:12
the *h* are not clean in his sight ... Job 15:15
his excellency mount up to the *h* ... Job 20:6
spirit he hath garnished the *h* ... Job 26:13
Look unto the *h*, and see ... Job 35:5
that sitteth in the *h* shall laugh ... Ps 2:4
hast set thy glory above the *h* ... Ps 8:1
When I consider thy *h*, the work ... Ps 8:3
He bowed the *h* also, and came down ... Ps 18:9
The LORD also thundered in the *h* ... Ps 18:13
The *h* declare the glory of God ... Ps 19:1
word of the LORD were the *h* made ... Ps 33:6
Thy mercy, O LORD, is in the *h* ... Ps 36:5
He shall call to the *h* from above ... Ps 50:4
And the *h* shall declare his ... Ps 50:6
thou exalted, O God, above the *h* ... Ps 57:5
For thy mercy is great unto the *h* ... Ps 57:10
thou exalted, O God, above the *h* ... Ps 57:11
rideth upon the *h* by his name JAH ... Ps 68:4
the *h* also dropped at the ... Ps 68:8
that rideth upon the *h* of *h* ... Ps 68:33
set their mouth against the *h* ... Ps 73:9
thou establish in the very *h* ... Ps 89:2
the *h* shall praise thy wonders, O ... Ps 89:5
The *h* are thine, the earth also ... Ps 89:11
but the LORD made the *h* ... Ps 96:5
Let the *h* rejoice, and let the ... Ps 96:11
The *h* declare his righteousness ... Ps 97:6
the *h* are the work of thy hands ... Ps 102:25
hath prepared his throne in the *h* ... Ps 103:19
out the *h* like a curtain ... Ps 104:2
thy mercy is great above the *h* ... Ps 108:4
thou exalted, O God, above the *h* ... Ps 108:5
nations, and his glory above the *h* ... Ps 113:4
But our God is in the *h* ... Ps 115:3
The heaven, even the *h*, are the ... Ps 115:16
O thou that dwellest in the *h* ... Ps 123:1
To him that by wisdom made the *h* ... Ps 136:5
Bow thy *h*, O LORD, and come down ... Ps 144:5
Praise ye the LORD from the *h* ... Ps 148:1
Praise him, ye *h* of *h* ... Ps 148:4
and ye waters that be above the *h* ... Ps 148:4
hath he established the *h* ... Prov 3:19
When he prepared the *h*, I was ... Prov 8:27
Hear, O *h*, and give ear, O earth ... Is 1:2
is darkened in the *h* thereof ... Is 5:30
Therefore I will shake the *h* ... Is 13:13
the *h* shall be rolled together as ... Is 34:4
stretcheth out the *h* as a curtain ... Is 40:22
the LORD, he that created the *h* ... Is 42:5
Sing, O ye *h* ... Is 44:23
that stretcheth forth the *h* alone ... Is 44:24
Drop down, ye *h*, from above, and ... Is 45:8
hands, have stretched out the *h* ... Is 45:12
saith the LORD that created the *h* ... Is 45:18
my right hand hath spanned the *h* ... Is 48:13
Sing, O *h* ... Is 49:13
I clothe the *h* with blackness, and ... Is 50:3
Lift up your eyes to the *h* ... Is 51:6
for the *h* shall vanish away like ... Is 51:6
that hath stretched forth the *h* ... Is 51:13
mine hand, that I may plant the *h* ... Is 51:16
For as the *h* are higher than the ... Is 55:9
Oh that thou wouldest rend the *h* ... Is 64:1
For, behold, I create new *h* ... Is 65:17
For as the new *h* and the new earth ... Is 66:22
Be astonished, O ye *h*, at this ... Jer 2:12
and the *h*, and they had no light ... Jer 4:23
all the birds of the *h* were fled ... Jer 4:25
mourn, and the *h* above be black ... Jer 4:28
both the fowl of the *h* and the ... Jer 9:10
The gods that have not made the *h* ... Jer 10:11
the earth, and from under these *h* ... Jer 10:11
out the *h* by his discretion ... Jer 10:12
is a multitude of waters in the *h* ... Jer 10:13
or can the *h* give showers ... Jer 14:22
is a multitude of waters in the *h* ... Jer 51:16
with our hands unto God in the *h* ... Lam 3:41
from under the *h* of the LORD ... Lam 3:66
that the *h* were opened, and I saw ... Eze 1:1
have known that the *h* do rule ... Dan 4:26
saith the LORD, I will hear the *h* ... Hos 2:21
the *h* shall tremble ... Joel 2:10
And I will shew wonders in the *h* ... Joel 2:30
and the *h* and the earth shall shake ... Joel 3:16
His glory covered the *h*, and the ... Hab 3:3
while, and I will shake the *h* ... Hag 2:6
Judah, saying, I will shake the *h* ... Hag 2:21
are the four spirits of the *h* ... Zec 6:5
the *h* shall give their dew ... Zec 8:12
which stretcheth forth the *h* ... Zec 12:1
the *h* were opened unto him, and he ... Mt 3:16
powers of the *h* shall be shaken ... Mt 24:29
of the water, he saw the *h* opened ... Mk 1:10
in the *h* that faileth not ... Lk 12:33
David is not ascended into the *h* ... Acts 2:34
said, Behold, I see the *h* opened ... Acts 7:56
made with hands, eternal in the *h* ... 2Cor 5:1
that ascended up far above all *h* ... Eph 4:10
the *h* are the works of thine ... Heb 1:10
priest, that is passed into the *h* ... Heb 4:14
and made higher than the *h* ... Heb 7:26
throne of the Majesty in the *h* ... Heb 8:1
*h* should be purified with these ... Heb 9:23
the word of God the *h* were of old ... 2Pet 3:5
But the *h* and the earth, which are ... 2Pet 3:7
in the which the *h* shall pass ... 2Pet 3:10
wherein the *h* being on fire shall ... 2Pet 3:12
to his promise, look for new *h* ... 2Pet 3:13
Therefore rejoice, ye *h*, and ye ... Rev 12:12

**HEAVIER**
For now it would be *h* than the ... Job 6:3
my stroke is *h* than my groaning ... Job 23:2
fool's wrath is *h* than them both ... Prov 27:3

**HEAVILY**
wheels, that they drave them *h* ... Ex 14:25
I bowed down *h*, as one that ... Ps 35:14
hast thou very *h* laid thy yoke ... Is 47:6

**HEAVINESS**
sacrifice I arose up from my *h* ... Ezr 9:5
complaint, I will leave off my *h* ... Job 9:27
and I am full of *h* ... Ps 69:20
My soul melteth for *h* ... Ps 119:28
son is the *h* of his mother ... Prov 10:1
*H* in the heart of man maketh it ... Prov 12:25
and the end of that mirth is *h* ... Prov 14:13
Ariel, and there shall be *h* ... Is 29:2
of praise for the spirit of *h* ... Is 61:3
That I have great *h* and continual ... Rom 9:2
would not come again to you in *h* ... 2Cor 2:1
after you all, and was full of *h* ... Phil 2:26
to mourning, and your joy to *h* ... Jas 4:9
ye are in *h* through manifold ... 1Pet 1:6

**HEAVY**
But Moses' hands were *h* ... Ex 17:12
for this thing is too *h* for thee ... Ex 18:18
alone, because it is too *h* for me ... Num 11:14
for he was an old man, and *h* ... 1Sa 4:18
LORD was *h* upon them of Ashdod ... 1Sa 5:6
the hand of God was very *h* there ... 1Sa 5:11
because the hair was *h* on him ... 2Sa 14:26
his *h* yoke which he put upon us ... 1Kin 12:4
Thy father made our yoke *h* ... 1Kin 12:10
father did lade you with a *h* yoke ... 1Kin 12:11
My father made your yoke *h* ... 1Kin 12:14
I am sent to thee with *h* tidings ... 1Kin 14:6
of Israel went to his house *h* ... 1Kin 20:43
And Ahab came into his house *h* ... 1Kin 21:4
his *h* yoke that he put upon us ... 2Chr 10:4
Thy father made our yoke *h* ... 2Chr 10:10
my father put a *h* yoke upon you ... 2Chr 10:11
My father made your yoke *h* ... 2Chr 10:14
bondage was *h* upon this people ... Neh 5:18
shall my hand be *h* upon thee ... Job 33:7
and night thy hand was *h* upon me ... Ps 32:4
as an *h* burden they are too *h* ... Ps 38:4
burden they are too *h* for me ... Ps 38:4
that singeth songs to an *h* heart ... Prov 25:20
A stone is *h*, and the sand weighty ... Prov 27:3
unto those that be of *h* hearts ... Prov 31:6
people fat, and make their ears *h* ... Is 6:10
thereof shall be *h* upon it ... Is 24:20
anger, and the burden thereof is *h* ... Is 30:27
your carriages were *h* loaden ... Is 46:1
wickedness, to undo the *h* burdens ... Is 58:6
neither his ear *h*, that it cannot ... Is 59:1
he hath made my chain *h* ... Lam 3:7
are *h* laden, and I will give you ... Mt 11:28
For they bind *h* burdens and ... Mt 23:4
began to be sorrowful and very *h* ... Mt 26:37
for their eyes were *h* ... Mt 26:43
be sore amazed, and to be very *h* ... Mk 14:33
again, (for their eyes were *h* ... Mk 14:40
were with him were *h* with sleep ... Lk 9:32

**HEBER** (*he'-bur*) See EBER, HEBER'S, HEBERITES.
*1. A son of Beriah.*
*H*, and Malchiel ... Gen 46:17
of *H*, the family of the Heberites ... Num 26:45
*H*, and Malchiel, who is the father ... 1Chr 7:31
*H* begat Japhlet, and Shomer, and ... 1Chr 7:32
of Phalec, which was the son of *H* ... Lk 3:35
*2. Husband of Jael.*
Now *H* the Kenite, which was of ... Judg 4:11
of Jael the wife of *H* the Kenite ... Judg 4:17
and the house of *H* the Kenite ... Judg 4:17
Jael the wife of *H* the Kenite be ... Judg 5:24
*3. A son of Ezra.*
*H* the father of Socho, and ... 1Chr 4:18
*4. A son of Elpaal.*
and Meshullam, and Hezeki, and *H* ... 1Chr 8:17
*5. A head of a Gadite family.*
and Jachan, and Zia, and *H* ... 1Chr 5:13
*6. A son of Shashak.*
And Ishpan, and *H*, and Eliel ... 1Chr 8:22

**HEBERITES** (*he'-bur-ites*) *Descendants of Heber.*
of Heber, the family of the *H* ... Num 26:45

**HEBER'S** (*he'-burs*) *Refers to Heber 2.*
Then Jael *H* wife took a nail of ... Judg 4:21

**HEBREW** (*he'-broo*) See HEBREWESS, HEBREWS.
*1. Descendants of Jacob.*
had escaped, and told Abram the *H* ... Gen 14:13
in an *H* unto us to mock us ... Gen 39:14
The *H* servant, which thou hast ... Gen 39:17
there with us a young man, an *H* ... Gen 41:12
of Egypt spake to the *H* midwives ... Ex 1:15
of a midwife to the *H* women ... Ex 1:16
Because the *H* women are not as ... Ex 1:19
to thee a nurse of the *H* women ... Ex 2:7
he spied an Egyptian smiting an *H* ... Ex 2:11
If thou buy an *H* servant, six ... Ex 21:2
an *H* man, or an *H* woman, be ... Deut 15:12
being an *H* or an Hebrewess, go ... Jer 34:9
ye go every man his brother an *H* ... Jer 34:14
And he said unto them, I am an *H* ... Jonah 1:9
of Benjamin, an *H* of the Hebrews ... Phil 3:5
*2. A language.*
letters of Greek, and Latin, and *H* ... Lk 23:38
called in the *H* tongue Bethesda ... Jn 5:2
called the Pavement, but in the *H* ... Jn 19:13
which is called in the *H* Golgotha ... Jn 19:17
and it was written in *H*, and Greek ... Jn 19:20
spake unto them in the *H* tongue ... Acts 21:40
he spake in the *H* tongue to them ... Acts 22:2
me, and saying in the *H* tongue ... Acts 26:14
name in the *H* tongue is Abaddon ... Rev 9:11
called in the *H* tongue Armageddon ... Rev 16:16

**HEBREWESS** (*he'-broo-ess*)
being an Hebrew or an *H*, go free ... Jer 34:9

**HEBREWS** (*he'-brooz*) See HEBREWS'.
away out of the land of the *H* ... Gen 40:15
might not eat bread with the *H* ... Gen 43:32
two men of the *H* strove together ... Ex 2:13
God of the *H* hath met with us ... Ex 3:18
The God of the *H* hath met with us ... Ex 5:3
The LORD God of the *H* hath sent ... Ex 7:16
Thus saith the LORD God of the *H* ... Ex 9:1
Thus saith the LORD God of the *H* ... Ex 9:13
Thus saith the LORD God of the *H* ... Ex 10:3
great shout in the camp of the *H* ... 1Sa 4:6
ye be not servants unto the *H* ... 1Sa 4:9
the land, saying, Let the *H* hear ... 1Sa 13:3
some of the *H* went over Jordan to ... 1Sa 13:7
Lest the *H* make them swords or ... 1Sa 13:19
the *H* come forth out of the holes ... 1Sa 14:11
Moreover the *H* that were with the ... 1Sa 14:21
Philistines, What do these *H* here ... 1Sa 29:3
of the Grecians against the *H* ... Acts 6:1
Are they *H* ... 2Cor 11:22
of Benjamin, an Hebrew of the *H* ... Phil 3:5
Written to the *H* from Italy by ... Heb s

**HEBREWS'** (*he'-brooz*)
This is one of the *H* children ... Ex 2:6

**HEBRON** (*he'-brun*) See HEBRONITES.
*1. A city in Asher.*
And *H*, and Rehob ... Josh 19:28
*2. A city in Judah.*
the plain of Mamre, which is in *H* ... Gen 13:18
the same is *H* in the land of ... Gen 23:2
the same is *H* in the land of ... Gen 23:19
the city of Arbah, which is *H* ... Gen 35:27
he sent him out of the vale of *H* ... Gen 37:14
by the south, and came unto *H* ... Num 13:22
(Now *H* was built seven years ... Num 13:22
sent unto Hoham king of *H* ... Josh 10:3
king of Jerusalem, the king of *H* ... Josh 10:5
king of Jerusalem, the king of *H* ... Josh 10:23
and all Israel with him, unto *H* ... Josh 10:36
as he had done to *H*, so he did to ... Josh 10:39
from the mountains, from *H* ... Josh 11:21
the king of *H*, one ... Josh 12:10
of Jephunneh *H* for an inheritance ... Josh 14:13
*H* therefore became the ... Josh 14:14
And the name of *H* before was ... Josh 14:15
father of Anak, which city is *H* ... Josh 15:13
and Kirjath-arba, which is *H* ... Josh 15:54
and Kirjath-arba, which is *H* ... Josh 20:7
father of Anak, which city is *H* ... Josh 21:11
the priest *H* with her suburbs ... Josh 21:13

the Canaanites that dwelt in *H*............ Judg 1:10
(now the name of *H* before was............ Judg 1:10
they gave *H* unto Caleb, as Moses....... Judg 1:20
top of an hill that is before *H*............ Judg 16:3
And to them which were in *H*............... 1Sa 30:31
And he said, Unto *H*.......................... 2Sa 2:1
and they dwelt in the cities of *H*.......... 2Sa 2:3
in *H* over the house of Judah was.......... 2Sa 2:11
they came to *H* at break of day............. 2Sa 2:32
And unto David were sons born in *H*...... 2Sa 3:2
These were born to David in *H*.............. 2Sa 3:5
speak in the ears of David in *H*............ 2Sa 3:19
So Abner came to David to *H*................ 2Sa 3:20
but Abner was not with David in *H*........ 2Sa 3:22
And when Abner was returned to *H*...... 2Sa 3:27
And they buried Abner in *H*................. 2Sa 3:32
heard that Abner was dead in *H*............ 2Sa 4:1
of Ish-bosheth unto David to *H*............. 2Sa 4:8
hanged them up over the pool in *H*....... 2Sa 4:12
it in the sepulchre of Abner in *H*.......... 2Sa 4:12
tribes of Israel to David unto *H*............ 2Sa 5:1
of Israel came to the king to *H*............. 2Sa 5:3
with them in *H* before the LORD.............. 2Sa 5:3
In *H* he reigned over Judah seven.......... 2Sa 5:5
after he was come from *H*..................... 2Sa 5:13
I have vowed unto the LORD, in *H*......... 2Sa 15:7
So he arose, and went to *H*.................. 2Sa 15:9
shall say, Absalom reigneth in *H*.......... 2Sa 15:10
seven years reigned he in *H*................. 1Kin 2:11
which were born unto him in *H*............. 1Chr 3:1
Amram, Izhar, and *H*, and Uzziel.......... 1Chr 6:2
they gave them *H* in the land of........... 1Chr 6:55
the cities of Judah, namely, *H*.............. 1Chr 6:57
themselves to David unto *H*.................. 1Chr 11:1
elders of Israel to the king to *H*........... 1Chr 11:3
with them in *H* before the LORD............ 1Chr 11:3
to the war, and came to David to *H*.. 1Chr 12:23
came with a perfect heart to *H*............ 1Chr 12:38
seven years reigned he in *H*................ 1Chr 29:27
And Zorah, and Aijalon, and *H*............ 2Chr 11:10
*3. A son of Kohath.*
Amram, and Izhar, and *H*, and Uzziel.... Ex 6:18
Amram, and Izehar, *H*, and Uzziel...... Num 3:19
These six were born unto him in *H*....... 1Chr 3:4
were, Amram, and Izhar, and *H*............ 1Chr 6:18
Amram, Izhar, *H*, and Uzziel, four........ 1Chr 23:12
Of the sons of *H*................................ 1Chr 23:19
And the sons of *H*.............................. 1Chr 24:23
*4. A son of Mareshah.*
sons of Mareshah the father of *H*......... 1Chr 2:42
And the sons of *H*.............................. 1Chr 2:43
Of the sons of *H*................................ 1Chr 15:9

**HEBRONITES** (*he'-brun-ites*) *Descendants of Hebron 3.*
and the family of the *H*, and the.......... Num 3:27
the Libnites, the family of the *H*........ Num 26:58
and the Izharites, the *H*, and the........ 1Chr 26:23
And of the *H*, Hashabiah and his......... 1Chr 26:30
Among the *H* was Jerijah the chief... 1Chr 26:31
even among the *H*, according to the. 1Chr 26:31

**HEDGE**
Hast not thou made an *h* about him..... Job 1:10
slothful man is as an *h* of thorns........ Prov 15:19
and whoso breaketh an *h*, a serpent.... Eccl 10:8
I will take away the *h* thereof.................. Is 5:5
neither made up the *h* for the.............. Eze 13:5
them, that should make up the *h*........ Eze 22:30
I will *h* up thy way with thorns,............ Hos 2:6
upright is sharper than a thorn *h*.......... Mic 7:4
set an *h* about it, and digged a............. Mk 12:1

**HEDGED**
way is hid, and whom God hath *h* in.... Job 3:23
He hath *h* me about, that I cannot........ Lam 3:7
*h* it round about, and digged a.............. Mt 21:33

**HEDGES**
that dwelt among plants and *h*............ 1Chr 4:23
hast thou then broken down her *h*......... Ps 80:12
Thou hast broken down all his *h*.......... Ps 89:40
lament, and run to and fro by the *h*........ Jer 49:3
camp in the *h* in the cold day............... Nah 3:17
Go out into the highways and *h*............ Lk 14:23

**HEED**
Take *h* that thou speak not to............. Gen 31:24
Take thou *h* that thou speak not.......... Gen 31:29
take *h* to thyself, see my face no.......... Ex 10:28
Take *h* to yourselves, that ye go............ Ex 19:12
Take *h* to thyself, lest thou make.......... Ex 34:12
Must I not take *h* to speak that........ Num 23:12
take ye good *h* unto yourselves............ Deut 2:4
Only take *h* to thyself, and keep........... Deut 4:9
therefore good *h* unto yourselves......... Deut 4:15
Take *h* unto yourselves, lest ye........... Deut 4:23
Take *h* to yourselves, that your........... Deut 11:16
Take *h* to thyself that thou offer......... Deut 12:13
Take *h* to thyself that thou............... Deut 12:19
Take *h* to thyself that thou be............ Deut 12:30
Take *h* in the plague of leprosy,........... Deut 24:8
unto all Israel, saying, Take *h*............. Deut 27:9
But take diligent *h* to do the.............. Josh 22:5
Take good *h* therefore unto................ Josh 23:11
take *h* to thyself until the..................... 1Sa 19:2
But Amasa took no *h* to the sword...... 2Sa 20:10
thy children take *h* to their way............. 1Kin 2:4
thy children take *h* to their way............ 1Kin 8:25
But Jehu took no *h* to walk in the....... 2Kin 10:31
if thou takest *h* to fulfil the............. 1Chr 22:13
Take *h* now....................................... 1Chr 28:10
yet so that thy children take *h*.............. 2Chr 6:16
to the judges, Take *h* what ye do........ 2Chr 19:6
take *h* and do it.................................. 2Chr 19:7
so that they will take *h* to do.............. 2Chr 33:8
Take *h* now that ye fail not to do......... Ezr 4:22
Take *h*, regard not iniquity.................... Job 36:21
I said, I will take *h* to my ways.............. Ps 39:1
by taking *h* thereto according to............ Ps 119:9
doer giveth *h* to false lips...................... Prov 17:4
Also take no *h* unto all words................. Eccl 7:21
yea, he gave good *h*, and sought............. Eccl 12:9
And say unto him, Take *h*, and be............ Is 7:4
hearkened diligently with much *h*........... Is 21:7
Take ye *h* every one of his...................... Jer 9:4
Take *h* to yourselves, and bear no.......... Jer 17:21
let us not give *h* to any of his.................. Jer 18:18
Give *h* to me, O LORD, and hearken...... Jer 18:19
left off to take *h* to the LORD.................. Hos 4:10
Therefore take *h* to your spirit.............. Mal 2:15
therefore take *h* to your spirit............... Mal 2:16
Take *h* that ye do not your alms............... Mt 6:1
Then Jesus said unto them, Take *h*........ Mt 16:6
Take *h* that ye despise not one of......... Mt 18:10
Take *h* that no man deceive you............ Mt 24:4
unto them, Take *h* what ye hear............ Mk 4:24
he charged them, saying, Take *h*........... Mk 8:15
Take *h* lest any man deceive you............ Mk 13:5
But take *h* to yourselves........................ Mk 13:9
But take ye *h*..................................... Mk 13:23
Take ye *h*, watch and pray..................... Mk 13:33
Take *h* therefore how ye hear................ Lk 8:18
Take *h* therefore that the light.............. Lk 11:35
And he said unto them, Take *h*............. Lk 12:15
Take *h* to yourselves.............................. Lk 17:3
Take *h* that ye be not deceived.............. Lk 21:8
take *h* to yourselves, lest at any............ Lk 21:34
he gave *h* unto them, expecting to.......... Acts 3:5
take *h* to yourselves what ye................ Acts 5:35
*h* unto those things which Philip............ Acts 8:6
To whom they all gave *h*, from the....... Acts 8:10
Take *h* therefore unto yourselves,....... Acts 20:28
saying, Take *h* what thou doest........ Acts 22:26
take *h* lest he also spare not............... Rom 11:21
But let every man take *h* how he......... 1Cor 3:10
But take *h* lest by any means this......... 1Cor 8:9
he standeth take *h* lest he fall............ 1Cor 10:12
take *h* that ye be not consumed............ Gal 5:15
Take *h* to the ministry which thou......... Col 4:17
Neither give *h* to fables and................... 1Ti 1:4
giving *h* to seducing spirits, and.............. 1Ti 4:1
Take *h* unto thyself, and unto the......... 1Ti 4:16
Not giving *h* to Jewish fables, and...... Titus 1:14
*h* to the things which we have................ Heb 2:1
Take *h*, brethren, lest there be.............. Heb 3:12
ye do well that ye take *h*...................... 2Pet 1:19

**HEEL**
head, and thou shalt bruise his *h*.......... Gen 3:15
and his hand took hold on Esau's *h*.... Gen 25:26
The gin shall take him by the *h*............. Job 18:9
hath lifted up his *h* against me.............. Ps 41:9
his brother by the *h* in the womb.......... Hos 12:3
hath lifted up his *h* against me............. Jn 13:18

**HEELS**
the path, that biteth the horse *h*......... Gen 49:17
a print upon the *h* of my feet............... Job 13:27
of my *h* shall compass me about............. Ps 49:5
discovered, and thy *h* made bare........... Jer 13:22

**HEGAI** (*he'-gahee*) See HEGE. *Servant of King Ahasuerus.*
the palace, to the custody of *H*............. Est 2:8
king's house, to the custody of *H*.......... Est 2:8
but what *H* the king's chamberlain........ Est 2:15

**HEGE** (*he'-ghe*) See HEGAI. *Same as Hegai.*
unto the custody of *H* the king's............. Est 2:3

**HEIFER**
Take me an *h* of three years old,........... Gen 15:9
bring thee a red *h* without spot............ Num 19:2
one shall burn the *h* in his sight........... Num 19:5
the midst of the burning of the *h*.......... Num 19:6
gather up the ashes of the *h*............... Num 19:9
of the *h* shall wash his clothes............ Num 19:10
burnt *h* of purification for sin............. Num 19:17
of that city shall take an *h*.................. Deut 21:3
down the *h* unto a rough valley............ Deut 21:4
*h* that is beheaded in the valley........... Deut 21:6
If ye had not plowed with my *h*........... Judg 14:18
Take an *h* with thee, and say, I am....... 1Sa 16:2
Zoar, an *h* of three years old.................. Is 15:5
Egypt is like a very fair *h*..................... Jer 46:20
as an *h* of three years old..................... Jer 48:34
are grown fat as the *h* at grass............... Jer 50:11
slideth back as a backsliding *h*............... Hos 4:16
Ephraim is as an *h* that is taught.......... Hos 10:11
the ashes of an *h* sprinkling the............. Heb 9:13

**HEIFER'S**
shall strike off the *h* neck there............ Deut 21:4

**HEIGHT**
the *h* of it thirty cubits......................... Gen 6:15
a cubit and a half the *h* thereof............. Ex 25:10
a cubit and a half the *h* thereof............. Ex 25:23
the *h* thereof shall be three.................... Ex 27:1
the *h* five cubits of fine twined............... Ex 27:18
two cubits shall be the *h* thereof............ Ex 30:2
and a cubit and a half the *h* of it............ Ex 37:1
a cubit and a half the *h* thereof............. Ex 37:10
and two cubits was the *h* of it............... Ex 37:25
and three cubits the *h* thereof............... Ex 38:1
the *h* in the breadth was five.................. Ex 38:18
or on the *h* of his stature........................ 1Sa 16:7
whose *h* was six cubits and a span.......... 1Sa 17:4
the *h* thereof thirty cubits....................... 1Kin 6:2
and twenty cubits in the *h* thereof...... 1Kin 6:20
The *h* of the one cherub was ten........... 1Kin 6:26
the *h* thereof thirty cubits, upon........... 1Kin 7:2
the *h* of the one chapiter was............... 1Kin 7:16
the *h* of the other chapiter was............. 1Kin 7:16
about, and his *h* was five cubits............ 1Kin 7:23
and three cubits the *h* of it................... 1Kin 7:27
the *h* of a wheel was a cubit and........... 1Kin 7:32
come up to the *h* of the mountains... 2Kin 19:23
The *h* of the one pillar was............... 2Kin 25:17
the *h* of the chapiter three................. 2Kin 25:17
the *h* was an hundred and twenty.......... 2Chr 3:4
and ten cubits the *h* thereof.................. 2Chr 4:1
and five cubits the *h* thereof................. 2Chr 4:2
and raised it up a very great *h*.......... 2Chr 33:14
the *h* thereof threescore cubits,................ Ezr 6:3
Is not God in the *h* of heaven.............. Job 22:12
behold the *h* of the stars, how............. Job 22:12
down from the *h* of his sanctuary......... Ps 102:19
The heaven for *h*, and the earth........... Prov 25:3
in the depth, or in the *h* above................ Is 7:11
come up to the *h* of the mountains........ Is 37:24
enter into the *h* of his border................ Is 37:24
come and sing in the *h* of Zion............ Jer 31:12
that holdest the *h* of the hill................. Jer 49:16
fortify the *h* of her strength.................. Jer 51:53
the *h* of one pillar was eighteen............ Jer 52:21
the *h* of one chapiter was five............... Jer 52:22
In the mountain of the *h* of.................. Eze 17:23
she appeared in her *h* with the............ Eze 19:11
the mountain of the *h* of Israel............ Eze 20:40
Therefore his *h* was exalted above........ Eze 31:5
thou hast lifted up thyself in *h*............ Eze 31:10
his heart is lifted up in his *h*............... Eze 31:10
exalt themselves for their *h*................. Eze 31:14
their trees stand up in their *h*............. Eze 31:14
and fill the valleys with thy *h*............... Eze 32:5
and the *h*, one reed.............................. Eze 40:5
I saw also the *h* of the house................. Eze 41:8
whose *h* was threescore cubits, and....... Dan 3:1
earth, and the *h* thereof was great......... Dan 4:10
the *h* thereof reached unto heaven......... Dan 4:11
whose *h* reached unto the heaven,.......... Dan 4:20
whose *h* was like the *h* of.................... Amos 2:9
was like the *h* of the cedars.................. Amos 2:9
Nor *h*, nor depth, nor any other........... Rom 8:39
and length, and depth, and *h*................ Eph 3:18
breadth and the *h* of it are equal......... Rev 21:16

**HEIGHTS**
praise him in the *h*............................ Ps 148:1
ascend above the *h* of the clouds............ Is 14:14

**HEINOUS**
For this is an *h* crime.......................... Job 31:11

**HEIR**
one born in my house is mine *h*............ Gen 15:3
saying, This shall not be thine *h*........... Gen 15:4
thine own bowels shall be thine *h*......... Gen 15:4
shall not be *h* with my son................... Gen 21:10
and we will destroy the *h* also.............. 2Sa 14:7
that is *h* to her mistress....................... Prov 30:23
hath he no *h*?...................................... Jer 49:1
then shall Israel be *h* unto them............ Jer 49:2
Yet will I bring an *h* unto thee............... Mic 1:15
among themselves, This is the *h*............ Mt 21:38
among themselves, This is the *h*............ Mk 12:7
themselves, saying, This is the *h*........... Lk 20:14
he should be the *h* of the world........... Rom 4:13
Now I say, That the *h*, as long as............ Gal 4:1
then an *h* of God through Christ.............. Gal 4:7
of the bondwoman shall not be *h*............ Gal 4:30
he hath appointed *h* of all things............ Heb 1:2
became *h* of the righteousness............... Heb 11:7

**HEIRS**
be heir unto them that were his *h*........... Jer 49:2
if they which are of the law be *h*.......... Rom 4:14
And if children, then *h*....................... Rom 8:17
*h* of God, and joint-heirs with................ Rom 8:17
*h* according to the promise.................... Gal 3:29
we should be made *h* according to........ Titus 3:7
them who shall be *h* of salvation............ Heb 1:14
abundantly to shew unto the *h* of........... Heb 6:17
the *h* with him of the same.................... Heb 11:9
*h* of the kingdom which he hath................ Jas 2:5
as being *h* together of the grace............ 1Pet 3:7

**HELAH** (*he'-lah*) *A wife of Asher.*
father of Tekoa had two wives, *H*.......... 1Chr 4:5
And the sons of *H* were, Zereth, and.... 1Chr 4:7

**HELAM** (*he'-lam*) *A place east of the Jordan.*
and they came to *H*............................ 2Sa 10:16
passed over Jordan, and came to *H*..... 2Sa 10:17

**HELBAH** (*hel'-bah*) *A town in Asher.*
of Ahlab, nor of Achzib, nor of *H*......... Judg 1:31

**HELBON** (*hel'-bon*) *A city near Damascus.*
in the wine of *H*, and white wool.......... Eze 27:18

**HELD**
man wondering at her *h* his peace....... Gen 24:21
Jacob *h* his peace until they were.......... Gen 34:5
he *h* up his father's hand, to................ Gen 48:17
when Moses *h* up his hand, that............ Ex 17:11
the loops *h* one curtain to..................... Ex 36:12
And Aaron *h* his peace.......................... Lev 10:3

H

*h* his peace at her in the day ................ Num 30:7
*h* his peace at her, and disallowed ..... Num 30:11
because he *h* his peace at her in ........ Num 30:14
*h* the lamps in their left hands, ........... Judg 7:20
the lad that *h* him by the hand .......... Judg 16:26
And when she *h* it, he measured six ... Ruth 3:15
But he *h* his peace ................................ 1Sa 10:27
he *h* a feast in his house, like ............... 1Sa 25:36
for Joab *h* back the people .................... 2Sa 18:16
And at that time Solomon *h* a feast .... 1Kin 8:65
But the people *h* their peace ................ 2Kin 18:36
and *h* three thousand baths .................... 2Chr 4:5
half of them *h* both the spears .............. Neh 4:16
and with the other hand *h* a weapon ... Neh 4:17
half of them *h* the spears from ............. Neh 4:21
Then *h* they their peace, and found ........ Neh 5:8
the king *h* out to Esther the ..................... Est 5:2
I had *h* my tongue, although the ............. Est 7:4
Then the king *h* out the golden ............... Est 8:4
My foot hath *h* his steps, his way ....... Job 23:11
The nobles *h* their peace, and ............... Job 29:10
whose mouth must be *h* in with bit ......... Ps 32:9
I *h* my peace, even from good .................. Ps 39:2
thy mercy, O LORD, *h* me up .................... Ps 94:18
I *h* him, and would not let him go, ....... Song 3:4
the king is *h* in the galleries .................. Song 7:5
But they *h* their peace, and ..................... Is 36:21
have not I *h* my peace even of old .......... Is 57:11
took them captives *h* them fast ............... Jer 50:33
when he *h* up his right hand and ............ Dan 12:7
*h* a council against him, how they ........ Mt 12:14
But Jesus *h* his peace ............................ Mt 26:63
*h* him by the feet, and worshipped .......... Mt 28:9
But they *h* their peace ............................... Mk 3:4
But they *h* their peace ............................... Mk 9:34
But he *h* his peace, and answered ........ Mk 14:61
the morning the chief priests *h* a ........... Mk 15:1
And they *h* their peace ............................ Lk 14:4
at his answer, and *h* their peace ............ Lk 20:26
the men that *h* Jesus mocked him, ......... Lk 22:63
lame man which was healed *h* Peter ... Acts 3:11
they *h* their peace, and glorified ......... Acts 11:18
part *h* with the Jews, and part ............ Acts 14:4
And after they had *h* their peace ........ Acts 15:13
that being dead wherein we were *h* .......... Rom 7:6
and for the testimony which they *h* ........ Rev 6:9

**HELDAI** (*hel'-dahee*) See HELED, HELEM.
*1. A sanctuary servant.*
month was *H* the Netophathite .......... 1Chr 27:15
*2. An honored exile.*
them of the captivity, even of *H* ............ Zec 6:10

**HELEB** (*he'-leb*) See HELED. *A 'mighty man' of David.*
*H* the son of Baanah, a ........................... 2Sa 23:29

**HELECH** See HELEK.

**HELED** (*he'-led*) See HELEB, HELDAI. *Same as Heleb.*
*H* the son of Baanah the ...................... 1Chr 11:30

**HELEK** (*he'-lek*) See HELEKITES. *A son of Gilead.*
of *H*, the family of the Helekites ........ Num 26:30
Abiezer, and for the children of *H* ........ Josh 17:2

**HELEKITES** (*he'-lek-ites*) *Descendants of Helek.*
of Helek, the family of the *H* ............. Num 26:30

**HELEM** (*he'-lem*)
*1. A descendant of Asher.*
And the sons of his brother *H* ............. 1Chr 7:35
*2. Same as Heldai.*
And the crowns shall be to *H* ................ Zec 6:14

**HELEPH** (*he'-lef*) *A town in Naphtali.*
And their coast was from *H* ................ Josh 19:33

**HELEZ** (*he'-lez*)
*1. A 'mighty man' of David.*
*H* the Paltite, Ira the son of ................ 2Sa 23:26
the Harorite, *H* the Pelonite, ............... 1Chr 11:27
seventh month was *H* the Pelonite .... 1Chr 27:10
*2. A son of Azariah.*
And Azariah begat *H*, and Helez .......... 1Chr 2:39
begat Helez, and *H* begat Eleasah, ....... 1Chr 2:39

**HELI** (*he'-li*) See ELI. *Father of Joseph; ancestor of Jesus.*
of Joseph, which was the son of *H* .......... Lk 3:23

**HELKAI** (*hel'-kahee*) *A priest.*
Adna; of Meraioth, *H* ............................. Neh 12:15

**HELKATH** (*hel'-kath*) See HELKATH-HAZZURIM, HUKOK. *A town in Asher.*
And their border was *H*, and Hali, ........ Josh 19:25
*H* with her suburbs, and Rehob with . Josh 21:31

**HELKATH-HAZZURIM** (*hel''-kath-haz'zu-rim*) *A plain near the pool of Gibeon.*
wherefore that place was called *H* ........ 2Sa 2:16

**HELL**
and shall burn unto the lowest *h* ....... Deut 32:22
The sorrows of *h* compassed me ............ 2Sa 22:6
deeper than *h* ........................................... Job 11:8
*H* is naked before him, and ..................... Job 26:6
The wicked shall be turned into *h* ............ Ps 9:17
thou wilt not leave my soul in *h* ............ Ps 16:10
The sorrows of *h* compassed me ............... Ps 18:5
and let them go down quick into *h* ........ Ps 55:15
my soul from the lowest *h* ..................... Ps 86:13
the pains of *h* gat hold upon me ............ Ps 116:3
if I make my bed in *h*, behold, ............... Ps 139:8
her steps take hold on *h* ........................... Prov 5:5
Her house is the way to *h* ....................... Prov 7:27
her guests are in the depths of *h* .......... Prov 9:18
*H* and destruction are before the ........ Prov 15:11
that he may depart from *h* beneath ... Prov 15:24
and shalt deliver his soul from *h* ........ Prov 23:14
*H* and destruction are never full .......... Prov 27:20
Therefore *h* hath enlarged herself ............ Is 5:14
*H* from beneath is moved for thee ............ Is 14:9
thou shalt be brought down to *h* ............ Is 14:15
with *h* are we at agreement ....................... Is 28:15
agreement with *h* shall not stand ............ Is 28:18
didst debase thyself even unto *h* ............ Is 57:9
when I cast him down to *h* with .......... Eze 31:16
They also went down into *h* with ......... Eze 31:17
of *h* with them that help him ............... Eze 32:21
which are gone down to *h* with ............ Eze 32:27
Though they dig into *h*, thence ............ Amos 9:2
out of the belly of *h* cried I ................ Jonah 2:2
who enlargeth his desire as *h* .................. Hab 2:5
shall be in danger of *h* fire ...................... Mt 5:22
whole body should be cast into *h* ............. Mt 5:29
whole body should be cast into *h* ............. Mt 5:30
to destroy both soul and body in *h* ...... Mt 10:28
shalt be brought down to *h* .................... Mt 11:23
the gates of *h* shall not prevail .............. Mt 16:18
two eyes to be cast into *h* fire ................. Mt 18:9
the child of *h* than yourselves ............... Mt 23:15
can ye escape the damnation of *h* .......... Mt 23:33
having two hands to go into *h* ................. Mk 9:43
having two feet to be cast into *h* ............ Mk 9:45
two eyes to be cast into *h* fire ................ Mk 9:47
heaven, shalt be thrust down to *h* .......... Lk 10:15
killed hath power to cast into *h* ............. Lk 12:5
in *h* he lift up his eyes, being ................ Lk 16:23
thou wilt not leave my soul in *h* .......... Acts 2:27
that his soul was not left in *h* ............. Acts 2:31
and it is set on fire of *h* ........................... Jas 3:6
sinned, but cast them down to *h* ............. 2Pet 2:4
and have the keys of *h* and of death .... Rev 1:18
was Death, and *H* followed with him ...... Rev 6:8
*h* delivered up the dead which ............. Rev 20:13
*h* were cast into the lake of fire .......... Rev 20:14

**HELLENISTS** See GRECIANS.

**HELM**
turned about with a very small *h* ............. Jas 3:4

**HELMET**
he had an *h* of brass upon his ............... 1Sa 17:5
he put an *h* of brass upon his .............. 1Sa 17:38
an *h* of salvation upon his head .............. Is 59:17
and shield and *h* round about .............. Eze 23:24
hanged the shield and *h* in thee .......... Eze 27:10
all of them with shield and *h* ................ Eze 38:5
take the *h* of salvation, and the ............ Eph 6:17
and for an *h*, the hope of ........................ 1Th 5:8

**HELMETS**
the host shields, and spears, and *h* .... 2Chr 26:14
and stand forth with your *h* ..................... Jer 46:4

**HELON** (*he'-lon*) *Father of Eliab.*
Eliab the son of *H* ................................... Num 1:9
Eliab the son of *H* shall be ..................... Num 2:7
the third day Eliab the son of *H* .......... Num 7:24
offering of Eliab the son of *H* ............... Num 7:29
of Zebulun was Eliab the son of *H* .... Num 10:16

**HELP**
I will make him an *h* meet for him ....... Gen 2:18
was not found an *h* meet for him ........ Gen 2:20
of thy father, who shall *h* thee ........... Gen 49:25
of my father, said he, was mine *h* .......... Ex 18:4
and wouldest forbear to *h* him ................ Ex 23:5
thou shalt surely *h* with him .................. Ex 23:5
thou shalt surely *h* him to lift ............. Deut 22:4
*h* you, and be your protection ........... Deut 32:38
be thou an *h* to him from his ............... Deut 33:7
rideth upon the heaven in thy *h* .......... Deut 33:26
by the LORD, the shield of thy *h* .......... Deut 33:29
mighty men of valour, and *h* them ....... Josh 1:14
*h* me, that we may smite Gibeon ......... Josh 10:4
us quickly, and save us, and *h* us ......... Josh 10:6
of Gezer came up to *h* Lachish ........... Josh 10:33
came not to the *h* of the LORD ............. Judg 5:23
to the *h* of the LORD against the ........... Judg 5:23
the sun be hot, ye shall have *h* ............. 1Sa 11:9
for me, then thou shalt *h* me .............. 2Sa 10:11
thee, then I will come and *h* thee ........ 2Sa 10:11
So the Syrians feared to *h* the ............ 2Sa 10:19
and did obeisance, and said, *H* ............... 2Sa 14:4
cried a woman unto him, saying, *H* .... 2Kin 6:26
*h* thee, whence shall I *h* thee ............... 2Kin 6:27
be come peaceably unto me to *h* me. 1Chr 12:17
day there came to David to *h* him ..... 1Chr 12:22
came to *h* Hadarezer king of Zobah .... 1Chr 18:5
for me, then thou shalt *h* me ............. 1Chr 19:12
for thee, then I will *h* thee ................. 1Chr 19:12
neither would the Syrians *h* the ........ 1Chr 19:19
of Israel to *h* Solomon his son ............ 1Chr 22:17
it is nothing with thee to *h* ................. 2Chr 14:11
*h* us, O LORD our God ........................... 2Chr 14:11
Shouldest thou *h* the ungodly .............. 2Chr 19:2
together, to ask *h* of the LORD .............. 2Chr 20:4
then thou wilt hear and *h* ...................... 2Chr 20:9
for God hath power to *h*, and to .......... 2Chr 25:8
to *h* the king against the enemy ......... 2Chr 26:13
the kings of Assyria to *h* him ............. 2Chr 28:16
gods of the kings of Syria *h* them ..... 2Chr 28:23
to them, that they may *h* me .............. 2Chr 28:23
brethren the Levites did *h* them ........ 2Chr 29:34
and they did *h* him ............................... 2Chr 32:3
us is the LORD our God to *h* us ............ 2Chr 32:8
of his place *h* him with silver .................... Ezr 1:4
horsemen to *h* us against the ................. Ezr 8:22
Is not my *h* in me ..................................... Job 6:13
neither will he *h* the evil doers .............. Job 8:20
and him that had none to *h* him ........... Job 29:12
when I saw my *h* in the gate ................. Job 31:21
There is no *h* for him in God ...................... Ps 3:2
*H*, LORD; for the godly ............................. Ps 12:1
Send thee *h* from the sanctuary, ............... Ps 20:2
for there is none to *h* ............................. Ps 22:11
O my strength, haste thee to *h* me ......... Ps 22:19
thou hast been my *h* ................................. Ps 27:9
he is our *h* and our shield ........................ Ps 33:20
buckler, and stand up for mine *h* ............... Ps 35:2
And the LORD shall *h* them, and ............. Ps 37:40
Make haste to *h* me, O Lord my .............. Ps 38:22
O LORD, make haste to *h* me .................. Ps 40:13
thou art my *h* and my deliverer ............... Ps 40:17
him for the *h* of his countenance ............... Ps 42:5
Arise for our *h*, and redeem us for ......... Ps 44:26
a very present *h* in trouble ....................... Ps 46:1
God shall *h* her, and that right ................... Ps 46:5
awake to *h* me, and behold ........................ Ps 59:4
Give us *h* from trouble ............................. Ps 60:11
for vain is the *h* of man .......................... Ps 60:11
Because thou hast been my *h* ....................... Ps 63:7
make haste to *h* me, O LORD ....................... Ps 70:1
thou art my *h* and my deliverer ................. Ps 70:5
O my God, make haste for my *h* .............. Ps 71:12
*H* us, O God of our salvation, for ............. Ps 79:9
I have laid *h* upon one that is .................. Ps 89:19
Unless the LORD had been my *h* ............... Ps 94:17
fell down, and there was none to *h* ...... Ps 107:12
Give us *h* from trouble ........................... Ps 108:12
for vain is the *h* of man ......................... Ps 108:12
*H* me, O LORD my God ............................. Ps 109:26
he is their *h* and their shield ..................... Ps 115:9
he is their *h* and their shield ................... Ps 115:10
he is their *h* and their shield ................... Ps 115:11
my part with them that *h* me ..................... Ps 118:7
*h* thou me .............................................. Ps 119:86
Let thine hand *h* me ............................. Ps 119:173
and let thy judgments *h* me ................... Ps 119:175
hills, from whence cometh my *h* ............. Ps 121:1
My *h* cometh from the LORD, which ...... Ps 121:2
Our *h* is in the name of the LORD, ........... Ps 124:8
son of man, in whom there is no *h* ......... Ps 146:3
hath the God of Jacob for his *h* ............. Ps 146:5
he hath not another to *h* him up .......... Eccl 4:10
to whom will ye flee for *h* ......................... Is 10:3
whither we flee for *h* to be ....................... Is 20:6
nor be an *h* nor profit, but a ...................... Is 30:5
For the Egyptians shall *h* in vain ............. Is 30:7
them that go down to Egypt for *h* ............. Is 31:1
against the *h* of them that work ................ Is 31:2
yea, I will *h* thee ...................................... Is 41:10
I will *h* thee ............................................. Is 41:13
I will *h* thee, saith the LORD, and ............ Is 41:14
from the womb, which will *h* thee ............ Is 44:2
For the Lord GOD will *h* me ....................... Is 50:7
Behold, the Lord GOD will *h* me ............... Is 50:9
I looked, and there was none to *h* ............. Is 63:5
which is come forth to *h* you .................. Jer 37:7
of the enemy, and none did *h* her ............ Lam 1:7
eyes as yet failed for our vain *h* ........... Lam 4:17
all that are about him to *h* him ............ Eze 12:14
of hell with them that *h* him ................. Eze 32:21
the chief princes, came to *h* me ........... Dan 10:13
shall be holpen with a little *h* ................ Dan 11:34
to his end, and none shall *h* him .......... Dan 11:45
but in me is thine *h* .................................. Hos 13:9
him, saying, Lord, *h* me .......................... Mt 15:25
have compassion on us, and *h* us ............ Mk 9:22
*h* thou mine unbelief ................................. Mk 9:24
that they should come and *h* them ............ Lk 5:7
bid her therefore that she *h* me .............. Lk 10:40
Come over into Macedonia, and *h* us .. Acts 16:9
Crying out, Men of Israel, *h* ................. Acts 21:28
therefore obtained *h* of God ................ Acts 26:22
*h* those women which laboured with ...... Phil 4:3
find grace to *h* in time of need .............. Heb 4:16

**HELPED**
*h* them, and watered their flock ................ Ex 2:17
Hitherto hath the LORD *h* us ................... 1Sa 7:12
and they following Adonijah *h* him ...... 1Kin 1:7
thirty and two kings that *h* him ......... 1Kin 20:16
they were *h* against them, and the ....... 1Chr 5:20
but they *h* them not ............................. 1Chr 12:19
they *h* David against the band of ....... 1Chr 12:21
when God *h* the Levites that bare ..... 1Chr 15:26
cried out, and the LORD *h* him ........... 2Chr 18:31
every one *h* to destroy another .......... 2Chr 20:23
God *h* him against the Philistines ........ 2Chr 26:7
for he was marvellously *h* .................... 2Chr 26:15
but he *h* him not .................................. 2Chr 28:21
and Shabbethai the Levite *h* them ....... Ezr 10:15
officers of the king, *h* the Jews ................ Est 9:3
How hast thou *h* him that is .................... Job 26:2
heart trusted in him, and I am *h* ............... Ps 28:7
I was brought low, and he *h* me ............ Ps 116:6
but the LORD *h* me ............................... Ps 118:13
They *h* every one his neighbour ................ Is 41:6
a day of salvation have I *h* thee ................ Is 49:8
they *h* forward the affliction .................. Zec 1:15
*h* them much which had believed ......... Acts 18:27
And the earth *h* the woman, and the . Rev 12:16

**HELPER**
any left, nor any *h* for Israel ............ 2Kin 14:26
my calamity, they have no *h* ............ Job 30:13
thou art the *h* of the fatherless ............ Ps 10:14
LORD, be thou my *h* ............ Ps 30:10
Behold, God is mine *h* ............ Ps 54:4
poor also, and him that hath no *h* ............ Ps 72:12
Zidon every *h* that remaineth ............ Jer 47:4
our *h* in Christ, and Stachys my ............ Rom 16:9
may boldly say, The Lord is my *h* ............ Heb 13:6

**HELPERS**
the mighty men, *h* of the war ............ 1Chr 12:1
unto thee, and peace be to thine *h* ............ 1Chr 12:18
the proud *h* do stoop under him ............ Job 9:13
when all her *h* shall be destroyed ............ Eze 30:8
Put and Lubim were thy *h* ............ Nah 3:9
Aquila my *h* in Christ Jesus ............ Rom 16:3
your faith, but are *h* of your joy ............ 2Cor 1:24

**HELPETH**
for thy God *h* thee ............ 1Chr 12:18
hand, both he that *h* shall fall ............ Is 31:3
the Spirit also *h* our infirmities ............ Rom 8:26
and to every one that *h* with us ............ 1Cor 16:16

**HELPING**
were the prophets of God *h* them ............ Ezr 5:2
why art thou so far from *h* me ............ Ps 22:1
Ye also *h* together by prayer for ............ 2Cor 1:11

**HELPS**
they had taken up, they used *h* ............ Acts 27:17
then gifts of healings, *h* ............ 1Cor 12:28

**HELVE**
and the head slippeth from the *h* ............ Deut 19:5

**HEM**
beneath upon the *h* of it thou ............ Ex 28:33
round about the *h* thereof ............ Ex 28:33
upon the *h* of the robe round ............ Ex 28:34
upon the *h* of the robe, round ............ Ex 39:25
round about the *h* of the robe to ............ Ex 39:26
touched the *h* of his garment ............ Mt 9:20
only touch the *h* of his garment ............ Mt 14:36

**HEMAM** (*he'-mam*) See HOMAM. *A son of Lotan.*
children of Lotan were Hori and *H* ............ Gen 36:22

**HEMAN** (*he'-man*)
*1. A son of Zerah.*
than Ethan the Ezrahite, and *H* ............ 1Kin 4:31
Zimri, and Ethan, and *H*, and Calcol, ............ 1Chr 2:6
Of *H*: the sons of *H* ............ 1Chr 25:4
*2. A son of Joel.*
*H* a singer, the son of Joel, the ............ 1Chr 6:33
appointed *H* the son of Joel ............ 1Chr 15:17
So the singers, *H*, Asaph, and ............ 1Chr 15:19
And with them *H* and Jeduthun, and ............ 1Chr 16:41
with them *H* and Jeduthun ............ 1Chr 16:42
of the sons of Asaph, and of *H* ............ 1Chr 25:1
All these were the sons of *H* the ............ 1Chr 25:5
God gave to *H* fourteen sons and ............ 1Chr 25:5
order to Asaph, Jeduthun, and *H* ............ 1Chr 25:6
all of them of Asaph, of *H* ............ 2Chr 5:12
And of the sons of *H* ............ 2Chr 29:14
of David, and Asaph, and *H*, and ............ 2Chr 35:15
Maschil of *H* the Ezrahite ............ Ps 88:*t*

**HEMATH** (*he'-math*) See HAMATH.
*1. Same as Hamath.*
Egypt even unto the entering of *H* ............ 1Chr 13:5
in of *H* unto the river of the ............ Amos 6:14
*2. Father of the Kenites and Rechabites.*
are the Kenites that came of *H* ............ 1Chr 2:55

**HEMDAN** (*hem'-dan*) See AMRAM. *Son of Dishon.*
*H*, and Eshban, and Ithran, and ............ Gen 36:26

**HEMLOCK**
as *h* in the furrows of the field ............ Hos 10:4
the fruit of righteousness into *h* ............ Amos 6:12

**HEMS**
they made upon the *h* of the robe ............ Ex 39:24

**HEN** (*hen*) *A son of Zephaniah.*
to *H* the son of Zephaniah, for a ............ Zec 6:14
even as a *h* gathereth her ............ Mt 23:37
as a *h* doth gather her brood ............ Lk 13:34

**HENA** (*he'-nah*) *A city on the Euphrates.*
are the gods of Sepharvaim, *H* ............ 2Kin 18:34
of the city of Sepharvaim, of *H* ............ 2Kin 19:13
king of the city of Sepharvaim, *H* ............ Is 37:13

**HENADAD** (*hen'-a-dad*) *A Levite.*
the sons of *H*, with their sons and ............ Ezr 3:9
brethren, Bavai the son of *H* ............ Neh 3:18
Binnui the son of *H* another piece ............ Neh 3:24
Azaniah, Binnui of the sons of *H* ............ Neh 10:9

**HENCE**
the man said, They are departed *h* ............ Gen 37:17
Pharaoh ye shall not go forth *h* ............ Gen 42:15
ye shall carry up my bones from *h* ............ Gen 50:25
afterwards he will let you go *h* ............ Ex 11:1
thrust you out *h* altogether ............ Ex 11:1
carry up my bones away *h* with you ............ Ex 13:19
unto Moses, Depart, and go up *h* ............ Ex 33:1
go not with me, carry us not up *h* ............ Ex 33:15
get thee down quickly from *h* ............ Deut 9:12
Take you *h* out of the midst of ............ Josh 4:3
Depart not *h*, I pray thee, until ............ Judg 6:18
another field, neither go from *h* ............ Ruth 2:8
Get thee *h*, and turn thee eastward ............ 1Kin 17:3
recover strength, before I go *h* ............ Ps 39:13
shalt say unto it, Get thee *h* ............ Is 30:22
Take from *h* thirty men with thee, ............ Jer 38:10
and he said, Get you *h*, walk to and ............ Zec 6:7
saith Jesus unto him, Get thee *h* ............ Mt 4:10
Remove *h* to yonder place ............ Mt 17:20
of God, cast thyself down from *h* ............ Lk 4:9
him, Get thee out, and depart *h* ............ Lk 13:31
would pass from *h* to you cannot ............ Lk 16:26
sold doves, Take these things *h* ............ Jn 2:16
therefore said unto him, Depart *h* ............ Jn 7:3
Arise, let us go *h* ............ Jn 14:31
but now is my kingdom not from *h* ............ Jn 18:36
Sir, if thou have borne him *h* ............ Jn 20:15
the Holy Ghost not many days *h* ............ Acts 1:5
send thee far *h* unto the Gentiles ............ Acts 22:21
come they not *h*, even of your ............ Jas 4:1

**HENCEFORTH**
it shall not *h* yield unto thee ............ Gen 4:12
must the children of Israel *h* ............ Num 18:22
Ye shall *h* return no more that ............ Deut 17:16
shall *h* commit no more any such ............ Deut 19:20
I also will not *h* drive out any ............ Judg 2:21
for thy servant will *h* offer ............ 2Kin 5:17
therefore from *h* thou shalt have ............ 2Chr 16:9
his people from *h* even for ever ............ Ps 125:2
Israel hope in the LORD from *h* ............ Ps 131:3
with justice from *h* even for ever ............ Is 9:7
for *h* there shall no more come ............ Is 52:1
seed, saith the LORD, from *h* ............ Is 59:21
thou shalt no more *h* bereave them ............ Eze 36:12
over them in mount Zion from *h* ............ Mic 4:7
unto you, Ye shall not see me *h* ............ Mt 23:39
I will not drink *h* of this fruit ............ Mt 26:29
from *h* all generations shall call ............ Lk 1:48
from *h* thou shalt catch men ............ Lk 5:10
For from *h* there shall be five in ............ Lk 12:52
from *h* ye know him, and have seen ............ Jn 14:7
*H* I call you not servants ............ Jn 15:15
that they speak *h* to no man in ............ Acts 4:17
from *h* I will go unto the ............ Acts 18:6
that *h* we should not serve sin ............ Rom 6:6
should not *h* live unto themselves ............ 2Cor 5:15
Wherefore *h* know we no man after ............ 2Cor 5:16
yet now *h* know we him no more ............ 2Cor 5:16
From *h* let no man trouble me ............ Gal 6:17
That we *h* be no more children, ............ Eph 4:14
that ye *h* walk not as other ............ Eph 4:17
*H* there is laid up for me a crown ............ 2Ti 4:8
From *h* expecting till his enemies ............ Heb 10:13
dead which die in the Lord from *h* ............ Rev 14:13

**HENCEFORWARD**
and *h* among your generations ............ Num 15:23
no fruit grow on thee *h* for ever ............ Mt 21:19

**HENNA** See CAMPHIRE.

**HENOCH** (*he'-nok*) See ENOCH. *Same as Enoch.*
*H*, Methuselah, Lamech, ............ 1Chr 1:3
Ephah, and Epher, and *H*, and Abida, ............ 1Chr 1:33

**HEPHER** (*he'-fer*) See GATH-HEPHER, HEPHERITES.
*1. A son of Gilead.*
and of *H*, the family of the ............ Num 26:32
the son of *H* had no sons, but ............ Num 26:33
of Zelophehad, the son of *H* ............ Num 27:1
Shechem, and for the children of *H* ............ Josh 17:2
But Zelophehad, the son of *H* ............ Josh 17:3
*2. A son of Naarah.*
And Naarah bare him Ahuzam, and *H* ............ 1Chr 4:6
*3. A mighty man of David.*
*H* the Mecherathite, Ahijah the... ............ 1Chr 11:36
*4. A Canaanite city.*
the king of *H*, one ............ Josh 12:17
Sochoh, and all the land of *H* ............ 1Kin 4:10

**HEPHERITES** (*he'-fer-ites*) *Descendants of Hepher 1.*
and of Hepher, the family of the *H* ............ Num 26:32

**HEPHZI-BAH** (*hef'-zi-bah*)
*1. Wife of King Hezekiah.*
And his mother's name was *H* ............ 2Kin 21:1
*2. A symbolic name for Jerusalem.*
but thou shalt be called *H* ............ Is 62:4

**HER** See PREFACE.

**HERALD**
Then an *h* cried aloud, To you it ............ Dan 3:4

**HERB**
the *h* yielding seed, and the fruit ............ Gen 1:11
*h* yielding seed after his kind, ............ Gen 1:12
given you every *h* bearing seed ............ Gen 1:29
have given every green *h* for meat ............ Gen 1:30
every *h* of the field before it ............ Gen 2:5
thou shalt eat the *h* of the field ............ Gen 3:18
even as the green *h* have I given ............ Gen 9:3
upon every *h* of the field, ............ Ex 9:22
hail smote every *h* of the field ............ Ex 9:25
eat every *h* of the land, even all ............ Ex 10:12
they did eat every *h* of the land ............ Ex 10:15
the small rain upon the tender *h* ............ Deut 32:2
of the field, and as the green *h* ............ 2Kin 19:26
it withereth before any other *h* ............ Job 8:12
of the tender *h* to spring forth ............ Job 38:27
grass, and wither as the green *h* ............ Ps 37:2
and *h* for the service of man ............ Ps 104:14
of the field, and as the green *h* ............ Is 37:27
bones shall flourish like an *h* ............ Is 66:14

**HERBS**
or in the *h* of the field, through ............ Ex 10:15
with bitter *h* they shall eat it ............ Ex 12:8
with unleavened bread and bitter *h* ............ Num 9:11
with thy foot, as a garden of *h* ............ Deut 11:10
I may have it for a garden of *h* ............ 1Kin 21:2
out into the field to gather *h* ............ 2Kin 4:39
eat up all the *h* in their land ............ Ps 105:35
is a dinner of *h* where love is ............ Prov 15:17
*h* of the mountains are gathered ............ Prov 27:25
place like a clear heat upon *h* ............ Is 18:4
for thy dew is as the dew of *h* ............ Is 26:19
and hills, and dry up all their *h* ............ Is 42:15
the *h* of every field wither, for ............ Jer 12:4
grown, it is the greatest among *h* ............ Mt 13:32
and becometh greater than all *h* ............ Mk 4:32
mint and rue and all manner of *h* ............ Lk 11:42
another, who is weak, eateth *h* ............ Rom 14:2
bringeth forth *h* meet for them by ............ Heb 6:7

**HERD**
And Abraham ran unto the *h* ............ Gen 18:7
of the cattle, even of the *h* ............ Lev 1:2
be a burnt sacrifice of the *h* ............ Lev 1:3
offering, if he offer it of the *h* ............ Lev 3:1
And concerning the tithe of the *h* ............ Lev 27:32
savour unto the LORD, of the *h* ............ Num 15:3
then thou shalt kill of thy *h* ............ Deut 12:21
males that come of thy *h* and of ............ Deut 15:19
thy God, of the flock and the *h* ............ Deut 16:2
came after the *h* out of the field ............ 1Sa 11:5
of his own flock and of his own *h* ............ 2Sa 12:4
young of the flock and of the *h* ............ Jer 31:12
*h* nor flock, taste any thing ............ Jonah 3:7
there shall be no *h* in the stalls ............ Hab 3:17
them an *h* of many swine feeding ............ Mt 8:30
us to go away into the *h* of swine ............ Mt 8:31
they went into the *h* of swine ............ Mt 8:32
behold, the whole *h* of swine ran ............ Mt 8:32
a great *h* of swine feeding ............ Mk 5:11
the *h* ran violently down a steep ............ Mk 5:13
there was there an *h* of many ............ Lk 8:32
the *h* ran violently down a steep ............ Lk 8:33

**HERDMAN**
but I was an *h*, and a gatherer of ............ Amos 7:14

**HERDMEN**
between the *h* of Abram's cattle ............ Gen 13:7
cattle and the *h* of Lot's cattle ............ Gen 13:7
and between my *h* and thy *h* ............ Gen 13:8
the *h* of Gerar did strive with ............ Gen 26:20
Gerar did strive with Isaac's *h* ............ Gen 26:20
the chiefest of the *h* that ............ 1Sa 21:7
who was among the *h* of Tekoa ............ Amos 1:1

**HERDS**
went with Abram, had flocks, and *h* ............ Gen 13:5
and he hath given him flocks, and *h* ............ Gen 24:35
of flocks, and possession of *h* ............ Gen 26:14
was with him, and the flocks, and *h* ............ Gen 32:7
and *h* with young are with me ............ Gen 33:13
children, and thy flocks, and thy *h* ............ Gen 45:10
brought their flocks, and their *h* ............ Gen 46:32
and their flocks, and their *h* ............ Gen 47:1
and for the cattle of the *h* ............ Gen 47:17
my lord also hath our *h* of cattle ............ Gen 47:18
ones, and their flocks, and their *h* ............ Gen 50:8
flocks and with our *h* will we go ............ Ex 10:9
your flocks and your *h* be stayed ............ Ex 10:24
Also take your flocks and your *h* ............ Ex 12:32
and flocks, and *h*, even very much ............ Ex 12:38
nor *h* feed before that mount ............ Ex 34:3
the *h* be slain for them, to ............ Num 11:22
And when thy *h* and thy flocks ............ Deut 8:13
and the firstlings of your *h* ............ Deut 12:6
of thy *h* or of thy flock, nor any ............ Deut 12:17
oil, and the firstlings of thy *h* ............ Deut 14:23
took all the flocks and the *h* ............ 1Sa 30:20
had exceeding many flocks and *h* ............ 2Sa 12:2
over the *h* that fed in Sharon was ............ 1Chr 27:29
over the *h* that were in the ............ 1Chr 27:29
of flocks and *h* in abundance ............ 2Chr 32:29
law, and the firstlings of our *h* ............ Neh 10:36
thy flocks, and look well to thy *h* ............ Prov 27:23
a place for the *h* to lie down in ............ Is 65:10
their flocks and their *h*, their ............ Jer 3:24
eat up thy flocks and thine *h* ............ Jer 5:17
with their *h* to seek the LORD ............ Hos 5:6
the *h* of cattle are perplexed, ............ Joel 1:18

**HERE**
Have I also *h* looked after him ............ Gen 16:13
unto Lot, Hast thou *h* any besides ............ Gen 19:12
and thy two daughters, which are *h* ............ Gen 19:15
Now therefore swear unto me *h* by ............ Gen 21:23
and he said, Behold, *h* I am ............ Gen 22:1
men, Abide ye *h* with the ass ............ Gen 22:5
and he said, *H* am I, my son ............ Gen 22:7
and he said, *H* am I ............ Gen 22:11
I stand *h* by the well of water ............ Gen 24:13
he said unto him, Behold, *h* am I ............ Gen 27:1
and he said, *H* am I ............ Gen 27:18
And I said, *H* am I ............ Gen 31:11
set it *h* before my brethren and ............ Gen 31:37
And he said to him, *H* am I ............ Gen 37:13
*h* also have I done nothing that ............ Gen 40:15
one of your brethren *h* with me ............ Gen 42:33
And he said, *H* am I ............ Gen 46:2
*h* is seed for you, and ye shall ............ Gen 47:23

H

And he said, H am I Ex 3:4
the elders, Tarry ye h for us Ex 24:14
shall it be known h that I Ex 33:16
the mountain, saying, Lo, we be h Num 14:40
Lodge h this night, and I will Num 22:8
you, tarry ye also h this night Num 22:19
Build me h seven altars, and Num 23:1
and prepare me h seven oxen Num 23:1
Stand h by thy burnt offering, Num 23:15
Build me h seven altars, and Num 23:29
prepare me h seven bullocks and Num 23:29
go to war, and shall ye sit h Num 32:6
build sheepfolds h for our cattle Num 32:16
are all of us h alive this day Deut 5:3
as for thee, stand thou h by me Deut 5:31
the things that we do h this day Deut 12:8
But with him that standeth h with Deut 29:15
that is not h with us this day Deut 29:15
for you h before the LORD our God Josh 18:6
that I may h cast lots for you Josh 18:8
which are h mentioned by name Josh 21:9
thee, and say, Is there any man h Judg 4:20
and what hast thou h Judg 18:3
day groweth to an end, lodge h Judg 19:9
h is my daughter a maiden, and his Judg 19:24
give h your advice and counsel Judg 20:7
but abide h fast by my maidens Ruth 2:8
turn aside, sit down h Ruth 4:1
the city, and said, Sit ye down h Ruth 4:2
am the woman that stood by thee h 1Sa 1:26
and he answered, H am I 1Sa 3:4
he ran unto Eli, and said, H am I 1Sa 3:5
and went to Eli, and said, H am I 1Sa 3:6
and went to Eli, and said, H am I 1Sa 3:8
And he answered, H am I 1Sa 3:16
I have h at hand the fourth part 1Sa 9:8
and said unto them, Is the seer h 1Sa 9:11
Behold, h I am 1Sa 12:3
man his sheep, and slay them h 1Sa 14:34
Jesse, Are h all thy children 1Sa 16:11
is there not h under thine hand 1Sa 21:8
it is h wrapped in a cloth behind 1Sa 21:9
for there is no other save that h 1Sa 21:9
And he answered, H I am, my lord 1Sa 22:12
Behold, we be afraid h in Judah 1Sa 23:3
What do these Hebrews h 1Sa 29:3
And I answered, H am I 2Sa 1:7
Tarry h to day also, and to morrow 2Sa 11:12
h am I, let him do to me as 2Sa 15:26
unto him, Turn aside, and stand h 2Sa 18:30
three days, and be thou h present 2Sa 20:4
h be oxen for burnt sacrifice, and 2Sa 24:22
but I will die h 1Kin 2:30
thy lord, Behold, Elijah is h 1Kin 18:8
thy lord, Behold, Elijah is h 1Kin 18:11
thy lord, Behold, Elijah is h 1Kin 18:14
said unto him, What doest thou h 1Kin 19:9
him, and said, What doest thou h 1Kin 19:13
And as thy servant was busy h 1Kin 20:40
Is there not h a prophet of the 1Kin 22:7
Elijah said unto Elisha, Tarry h 2Kin 2:2
said unto him, Elisha, tarry h 2Kin 2:4
unto him, Tarry, I pray thee, h 2Kin 2:6
Is there not h a prophet of the 2Kin 3:11
H is Elisha the son of Shaphat, 2Kin 3:11
Why sit we h until we die 2Kin 7:3
and if we sit still h, we die also 2Kin 7:4
look that there be h with you 2Kin 10:23
thy people, which are present h 1Chr 29:17
Is there not h a prophet of the 2Chr 18:6
h shall thy proud waves be stayed Job 38:11
go, and say unto thee, H we are Job 38:35
h will I dwell Ps 132:14
Then said I, H am I Is 6:8
h cometh a chariot of men, with a Is 21:9
What hast thou h Is 22:16
and whom hast thou h, that thou Is 22:16
hast hewed thee out a sepulchre h Is 22:16
h a little, and there a little Is 28:10
h a little, and there a little Is 28:13
Now therefore, what have I h Is 52:5
cry, and he shall say, H I am Is 58:9
the house of Israel committeth h Eze 8:6
abominations that they do h Eze 8:9
abominations which they commit h Eze 8:17
yea, gray hairs are h and there Hos 7:9
behold, a greater than Jonas is h Mt 12:41
a greater than Solomon is h Mt 12:42
Give me h John Baptist's head in Mt 14:8
We have h but five loaves, and two Mt 14:17
you, There be some standing h Mt 16:28
Lord, it is good for us to be h Mt 17:4
let us make h three tabernacles Mt 17:4
Why stand ye h all the day idle Mt 20:6
be left h one stone upon another Mt 24:2
you, Lo, h is Christ, or there Mt 24:23
unto the disciples, Sit ye h Mt 26:36
tarry ye h, and watch with me Mt 26:38
He is not h Mt 28:6
and are not his sisters h with us Mk 6:3
with bread h in the wilderness Mk 8:4
be some of them that stand h Mk 9:1
Master, it is good for us to be h Mk 9:5
of stones and what buildings are h Mk 13:1
shall say to you, Lo, h is Christ Mk 13:21
saith to his disciples, Sit ye h Mk 14:32
tarry ye h, and watch Mk 14:34
he is not h Mk 16:6
do also h in thy country Lk 4:23
for we are h in a desert place Lk 9:12
a truth, there be some standing h Lk 9:27
Master, it is good for us to be h Lk 9:33
a greater than Solomon is h Lk 11:31
behold, a greater than Jonas is h Lk 11:32
Neither shall they say, Lo h Lk 17:21
And they shall say to you, See h Lk 17:23
h is thy pound, which I have kept Lk 19:20
Lord, behold, h are two swords Lk 22:38
He is not h, but is risen Lk 24:6
unto them, Have ye h any meat Lk 24:41
There is a lad h, which hath five Jn 6:9
Jesus, Lord, if thou hadst been h Jn 11:21
him, Lord, if thou hadst been h Jn 11:32
this man stand h before you whole Acts 4:10
the eunuch said, See, h is water Acts 8:36
And he said, Behold, I am h Acts 9:10
h he hath authority from the Acts 9:14
are we all h present before God Acts 10:33
for we are all h Acts 16:28
ought to have been h before thee Acts 24:19
Or else let these same h say Acts 24:20
men which are h present with us Acts 25:24
me, both at Jerusalem, and also h Acts 25:24
you all things which are done h Col 4:9
h men that die receive tithes Heb 7:8
For h have we no continuing city, Heb 13:14
Sit thou h in a good place Jas 2:3
or sit h under my footstool Jas 2:3
time of your sojourning h in fear 1Pet 1:17
H is the patience and the faith of Rev 13:10
H is wisdom Rev 13:18
H is the patience of the saints Rev 14:12
h are they that keep the Rev 14:12
h is the mind which hath wisdom Rev 17:9

**HEREAFTER**
the things that are to come h Is 41:23
h also, if ye will not hearken Eze 20:39
bed, what should come to pass h Dan 2:29
king what shall come to pass h Dan 2:45
H shall ye see the Son of man Mt 26:64
man eat fruit of thee h for ever Mk 11:14
H shall the Son of man sit on the Lk 22:69
H ye shall see heaven open, and Jn 1:51
but thou shalt know h Jn 13:7
H I will not talk much with you Jn 14:30
should h believe on him to life 1Ti 1:16
and the things which shall be h Rev 1:19
shew thee things which must be h Rev 4:1
there come two woes more h Rev 9:12

**HEREBY**
H ye shall be proved Gen 42:15
H shall I know that ye are true Gen 42:33
H ye shall know that the LORD Num 16:28
H ye shall know that the living Josh 3:10
yet am I not h justified 1Cor 4:4
h we do know that we know him, if 1Jn 2:3
h know we that we are in him 1Jn 2:5
H perceive we the love of God, 1Jn 3:16
h we know that we are of the 1Jn 3:19
h we know that he abideth in us, 1Jn 3:24
H know ye the Spirit of God 1Jn 4:2
H know we the spirit of truth, and 1Jn 4:6
H know we that we dwell in him, 1Jn 4:13

**HEREIN**
Only h will the men consent unto Gen 34:22
H thou hast done foolishly 2Chr 16:9
h is that saying true, One soweth Jn 4:37
Why h is a marvellous thing, that Jn 9:30
H is my Father glorified, that ye Jn 15:8
h do I exercise myself, to have Acts 24:16
And h I give my advice 2Cor 8:10
H is love, not that we loved God, 1Jn 4:10
H is our love made perfect, that 1Jn 4:17

**HEREOF**
the fame h went abroad into all Mt 9:26
And by reason h he ought, as for Heb 5:3

**HERES** (*he'-res*) See KIR-HERES, TIMMATH-HERES. *A mountain in Judah.*
would dwell in mount H in Aijalon Judg 1:35

**HERESH** (*he'-resh*) *A Levite.*
And Bakbakkar, H, and Galal, and 1Chr 9:15

**HERESIES**
there must be also h among you 1Cor 11:19
wrath, strife, seditions, h Gal 5:20
privily shall bring in damnable h 2Pet 2:1

**HERESY**
after the way which they call h Acts 24:14

**HERETH** See HARETH.

**HERETICK**
man that is an h after the first Titus 3:10

**HERETOFORE**
I am not eloquent, neither h Ex 4:10
people straw to make brick, as h Ex 5:7
the bricks, which they did make h Ex 5:8
both yesterday and to day, as h Ex 5:14
for ye have not passed this way h Josh 3:4
a people which thou knewest not h Ruth 2:11
hath not been such a thing h 1Sa 4:7
write to them which h have sinned 2Cor 13:2

**HEREUNTO**
can eat, or who else can hasten h Eccl 2:25
For even h were ye called 1Pet 2:21

**HEREWITH**
and yet thou wast not satisfied h Eze 16:29
in mine house, and prove me now h Mal 3:10

**HERITAGE**
and I will give it you for an h Ex 6:8
the h appointed unto him by God Job 20:29
the h of oppressors, which they Job 27:13
yea, I have a goodly h Ps 16:6
thou hast given me the h of those Ps 61:5
O LORD, and afflict thine h Ps 94:5
give them the h of the heathen Ps 111:6
have I taken as an h for ever Ps 119:111
Lo, children are an h of the LORD Ps 127:3
And gave their land for an h Ps 135:12
an h unto Israel his people Ps 135:12
And gave their land for an h Ps 136:21
Even an h unto Israel his servant Ps 136:22
This is the h of the servants of Is 54:17
feed thee with the h of Jacob thy Is 58:14
made mine h an abomination Jer 2:7
a goodly h of the hosts of Jer 3:19
mine house, I have left mine h Jer 12:7
Mine h is unto me as a lion in Jer 12:8
Mine h is unto me as a speckled Jer 12:9
them again, every man to his h Jer 12:15
from thine h that I gave thee Jer 17:4
O ye destroyers of mine h Jer 50:11
and give not thine h to reproach Joel 2:17
for my people and for my h Israel Joel 3:2
and his house, even a man and his h Mic 2:2
thy rod, the flock of thine h Mic 7:14
of the remnant of his h Mic 7:18
his h waste for the dragons of Mal 1:3
as being lords over God's h 1Pet 5:3

**HERITAGES**
cause to inherit the desolate h Is 49:8

**HERMAS** (*her'-mas*) *A Christian acquaintance of Paul.*
Salute Asyncritus, Phlegon, H Rom 16:14

**HERMES** (*her'-mees*) *A Christian acquaintance of Paul.*
Phlegon, Hermas, Patrobas, H Rom 16:14

**HERMOGENES** (*her-mof'-e-nees*) *A false Christian teacher.*
of whom are Phygellus and H 2Ti 1:15

**HERMON**
the river of Arnon unto mount H Deut 3:8
(Which H the Sidonians call Deut 3:9
even unto mount Sion which is H Deut 4:48
to the Hivite under H in the land Josh 11:3
valley of Lebanon under mount H Josh 11:17
from the river Arnon unto mount H Josh 12:1
And reigned in mount H, and in Josh 12:5
from Baal-gad under mount H unto Josh 13:5
and Maachathites, and all mount H Josh 13:11
and Senir, and unto mount H 1Chr 5:23
H shall rejoice in thy name Ps 89:12
As the dew of H, and as the dew Ps 133:3
from the top of Shenir and H Song 4:8

**HERMONITES** (*her'-mon-ites*) See HERMON. *Inhabitants of Mt. Hermon.*
the land of Jordan, and of the H Ps 42:6

**HEROD** (*her'-od*) See HERODIANS, HEROD'S.
*1. Herod the Great.*
Judaea in the days of H the king Mt 2:1
When H the king had heard these Mt 2:3
Then H, when he had privily Mt 2:7
that they should not return to H Mt 2:12
for H will seek the young child Mt 2:13
And was there until the death of H Mt 2:15
Then H, when he saw that he was Mt 2:16
But when H was dead, behold, an Mt 2:19
in the room of his father H Mt 2:22
There was in the days of H Lk 1:5
No, nor yet H: for I sent Lk 23:15
*2. Herod Antipas.*
At that time H the tetrarch heard Mt 14:1
For H had laid hold on John, and Mt 14:3
danced before them, and pleased H Mt 14:6
And king H heard of him Mk 6:14
But when H heard thereof, he said Mk 6:16
For H himself had sent forth and Mk 6:17
For John had said unto H, It is Mk 6:18
For H feared John, knowing that Mk 6:20
that H on his birthday made a Mk 6:21
came in, and danced, and pleased H Mk 6:22
Pharisees, and of the leaven of H Mk 8:15
H being tetrarch of Galilee, and Lk 3:1
But H the tetrarch, being Lk 3:19
all the evils which H had done Lk 3:19
Now H the tetrarch heard of all Lk 9:7
H said, John have I beheaded Lk 9:9
for H will kill thee Lk 13:31
jurisdiction, he sent him to H Lk 23:7
And when H saw Jesus, he was Lk 23:8
H with his men of war set him at Lk 23:11
H were made friends together Lk 23:12
whom thou hast anointed, both H Acts 4:27
brought up with H the tetrarch Acts 13:1
*3. Herod Agrippa I.*
Now about that time H the king Acts 12:1
when H would have brought him Acts 12:6
delivered me out of the hand of H Acts 12:11
when H had sought for him, and Acts 12:19
H was highly displeased with them Acts 12:20
And upon a set day H, arrayed in Acts 12:21

**HERODIANS** (*he-ro'-de-uns*) *Hellenizing Jews.*
him their disciples with the *H* .......... Mt 22:16
counsel with the *H* against him .......... Mk 3:6
of the Pharisees and of the *H* .......... Mk 12:13

**HERODIAS** (*he-ro'-de-as*) See HERODIAS'. *Granddaughter of Herod 1.*
the daughter of *H* danced before .......... Mt 14:6
Therefore *H* had a quarrel against .......... Mk 6:19
daughter of the said *H* came in .......... Mk 6:22
for *H* his brother Philip's wife .......... Lk 3:19

**HERODIAS'** (*he-ro'-de-as*)
and put him in prison for *H* sake .......... Mt 14:3
and bound him in prison for *H* sake .......... Mk 6:17

**HERODION** (*he-ro'-de-on*) *A relative of Paul.*
Salute *H* my kinsman .......... Rom 16:11

**HEROD'S** (*her'-ods*)
*1. Refers to Herod 2.*
But when *H* birthday was kept, the .......... Mt 14:6
the wife of Chuza *H* steward .......... Lk 8:3
he belonged unto *H* jurisdiction .......... Lk 23:7
*2. Refers to Herod 3.*
him to be kept in *H* judgment hall .......... Acts 23:35

**HERON**
the *h* after her kind, and the .......... Lev 11:19
the *h* after her kind, and the .......... Deut 14:18

**HERS**
firstborn son be *h* that was hated .......... Deut 21:15
damsels of *h* that went after her .......... 1Sa 25:42
saying, Restore all that was *h* .......... 2Kin 8:6
ones, as though they were not *h* .......... Job 39:16

**HERSELF**
Therefore Sarah laughed within *h* .......... Gen 18:12
and she, even she *h* said, He is my .......... Gen 20:5
she took a vail, and covered *h* .......... Gen 24:65
her with a vail, and wrapped *h* .......... Gen 38:14
came down to wash *h* at the river .......... Ex 2:5
she shall number to *h* seven days .......... Lev 15:28
if she profane *h* by playing the .......... Lev 21:9
she thrust *h* unto the wall, and .......... Num 22:25
bind *h* by a bond, being in her .......... Num 30:3
yea, she returned answer to *h* .......... Judg 5:29
bowed *h* to the ground, and said .......... Ruth 2:10
husband were dead, she bowed *h* .......... 1Sa 4:19
face, and bowed *h* to the ground, .......... 1Sa 25:23
bowed *h* on her face to the earth, .......... 1Sa 25:41
the roof he saw a woman washing *h* .......... 2Sa 11:2
shall feign *h* to be another woman .......... 1Kin 14:5
bowed *h* to the ground, and took up .......... 2Kin 4:37
time she lifteth up *h* on high .......... Job 39:18
and the swallow a nest for *h* .......... Ps 84:3
She maketh *h* coverings of .......... Prov 31:22
Therefore hell hath enlarged *h* .......... Is 5:14
find for *h* a place of rest .......... Is 34:14
bride adorneth *h* with her jewels .......... Is 61:10
Israel hath justified *h* more than .......... Jer 3:11
of Zion, that bewaileth *h* .......... Jer 4:31
feeble, and turneth *h* to flee .......... Jer 49:24
idols against *h* to defile *h* .......... Eze 22:3
all their idols she defiled *h* .......... Eze 23:7
She hath wearied *h* with lies .......... Eze 24:12
she decked *h* with her earrings and .......... Hos 2:13
Tyrus did build *h* a strong hold .......... Zec 9:3
For she said within *h*, If I may .......... Mt 9:21
earth bringeth forth fruit of *h* .......... Mk 4:28
hid *h* five months, saying, .......... Lk 1:24
and could in no wise lift up *h* .......... Lk 13:11
had thus said, she turned *h* back .......... Jn 20:14
She turned *h*, and saith unto him, .......... Jn 20:16
Through faith also Sara *h* .......... Heb 11:11
which calleth *h* a prophetess .......... Rev 2:20
How much she hath glorified *h* .......... Rev 18:7
and his wife hath made *h* ready .......... Rev 19:7

**HESED** (*he'-sed*) See JUSHAB-HESED. *Father of an officer of Solomon.*
The son of *H*, in Aruboth .......... 1Kin 4:10

**HESHBON** (*hesh'-bon*) *A Levitical city in Reuben and Gad.*
the cities of the Amorites, in *H* .......... Num 21:25
For *H* was the city of Sihon the .......... Num 21:26
in proverbs say, Come into *H* .......... Num 21:27
For there is a fire gone out of *H* .......... Num 21:28
*H* is perished even unto Dibon, and .......... Num 21:30
of the Amorites, which dwelt at *H* .......... Num 21:34
Dibon, and Jazer, and Nimrah, and *H*. .......... Num 32:3
And the children of Reuben built *H* .......... Num 32:37
of the Amorites, which dwelt in *H* .......... Deut 1:4
hand Sihon the Amorite, king of *H* .......... Deut 2:24
king of *H* with words of peace .......... Deut 2:26
But Sihon king of *H* would not let .......... Deut 2:30
of the Amorites, which dwelt at *H* .......... Deut 3:2
as we did unto Sihon king of *H* .......... Deut 3:6
of the Amorites, who dwelt at *H* .......... Deut 4:46
this place, Sihon the king of *H* .......... Deut 29:7
beyond Jordan, to Sihon king of *H* .......... Josh 9:10
of the Amorites, who dwelt in *H* .......... Josh 12:2
the border of Sihon king of *H* .......... Josh 12:5
the Amorites, which reigned in *H* .......... Josh 13:10
*H*, and all her cities that are in .......... Josh 13:17
the Amorites, which reigned in *H* .......... Josh 13:21
from *H* unto Ramath-mizpeh, and .......... Josh 13:26
of the kingdom of Sihon king of *H* .......... Josh 13:27
*H* with her suburbs, Jazer with .......... Josh 21:39
of the Amorites, the king of *H* .......... Judg 11:19
While Israel dwelt in *H* and her .......... Judg 11:26
*H* with her suburbs, and Jazer with .......... 1Chr 6:81
and the land of the king of *H* .......... Neh 9:22
eyes like the fishpools in *H* .......... Song 7:4
And *H* shall cry, and Elealeh .......... Is 15:4
For the fields of *H* languish .......... Is 16:8
water thee with my tears, O *H* .......... Is 16:9
in *H* they have devised evil .......... Jer 48:2
From the cry of *H* even unto .......... Jer 48:34
shadow of *H* because of the force .......... Jer 48:45
a fire shall come forth out of *H* .......... Jer 48:45
Howl, O *H*, for Ai is spoiled .......... Jer 49:3

**HESHMON** (*hesh'-mon*) See AZMON. *A town in Judah.*
And Hazar-gaddah, and *H*, and .......... Josh 15:27

**HESLI** See ESLI.

**HETH** (*heth*) *Son of Canaan.*
begat Sidon his firstborn, and *H* .......... Gen 10:15
dead, and spake unto the sons of *H* .......... Gen 23:3
the children of *H* answered .......... Gen 23:5
land, even to the children of *H* .......... Gen 23:7
dwelt among the children of *H* .......... Gen 23:10
the audience of the children of *H* .......... Gen 23:10
in the audience of the sons of *H* .......... Gen 23:16
the presence of the children of *H* .......... Gen 23:18
a buryingplace by the sons of *H* .......... Gen 23:20
purchased of the sons of *H* .......... Gen 25:10
because of the daughters of *H* .......... Gen 27:46
take a wife of the daughters of *H* .......... Gen 27:46
was from the children of *H* .......... Gen 49:32
begat Zidon his firstborn, and *H* .......... 1Chr 1:13

**HETHLON** (*heth'-lon*) *A place in northern Palestine.*
from the great sea, the way of *H* .......... Eze 47:15
end to the coast of the way of *H* .......... Eze 48:1

**HEW**
*H* thee two tables of stone like .......... Ex 34:1
*H* thee two tables of stone like .......... Deut 10:1
ye shall *h* down the graven images .......... Deut 12:3
wood with his neighbour to *h* wood .......... Deut 19:5
command thou that they *h* me cedar .......... 1Kin 5:6
*h* timber like unto the Sidonians .......... 1Kin 5:6
and Hiram's builders did *h* them .......... 1Kin 5:18
he set masons to *h* wrought stones .......... 1Chr 22:2
thousand to *h* in the mountain .......... 2Chr 2:2
*H* ye down trees, and cast a mount .......... Jer 6:6
*H* down the tree, and cut off his .......... Dan 4:14
*H* the tree down, and destroy it .......... Dan 4:23

**HEWED**
he *h* two tables of stone like .......... Ex 34:4
*h* two tables of stone like unto .......... Deut 10:3
*h* them in pieces, and sent them .......... 1Sa 11:7
Samuel *h* Agag in pieces before .......... 1Sa 15:33
*h* stones, to lay the foundation .......... 1Kin 5:17
court with three rows of *h* stone .......... 1Kin 6:36
to the measures of *h* stones .......... 1Kin 7:9
after the measures of *h* stones .......... 1Kin 7:11
was with three rows of *h* stones .......... 1Kin 7:12
*h* stone to repair the breaches of .......... 2Kin 12:12
that thou hast *h* thee out a .......... Is 22:16
*h* them out cisterns, broken .......... Jer 2:13
Therefore have I *h* them by the .......... Hos 6:5

**HEWER**
from the *h* of thy wood unto the .......... Deut 29:11

**HEWERS**
but let them be *h* of wood .......... Josh 9:21
*h* of wood and drawers of water for .......... Josh 9:23
made them that day *h* of wood .......... Josh 9:27
thousand *h* in the mountains .......... 1Kin 5:15
*h* of stone, and to buy timber and .......... 2Kin 12:12
workmen with thee in abundance, *h*. .......... 1Chr 22:15
the *h* that cut timber, twenty .......... 2Chr 2:10
thousand to be *h* in the mountain .......... 2Chr 2:18
her with axes, as *h* of wood .......... Jer 46:22

**HEWETH**
against him that *h* therewith .......... Is 10:15
as he that *h* him out an sepulchre .......... Is 22:16
He *h* him down cedars, and taketh .......... Is 44:14

**HEWN**
shalt not build it of *h* stone .......... Ex 20:25
*h* stone to repair the house .......... 2Kin 22:6
gave they it, to buy *h* stone .......... 2Chr 34:11
she hath *h* out her seven pillars .......... Prov 9:1
but we will build with *h* stones .......... Is 9:10
ones of stature shall be *h* down .......... Is 10:33
Lebanon is ashamed and *h* down .......... Is 33:9
unto the rock whence ye are *h* .......... Is 51:1
inclosed my ways with *h* stone .......... Lam 3:9
the four tables were of *h* stone .......... Eze 40:42
ye have built houses of *h* stone .......... Amos 5:11
not forth good fruit is *h* down .......... Mt 3:10
not forth good fruit is *h* down .......... Mt 7:19
which he had *h* out in the rock .......... Mt 27:60
which was *h* out of a rock .......... Mk 15:46
not forth good fruit is *h* down .......... Lk 3:9
a sepulchre that was *h* in stone .......... Lk 23:53

**HEZEKI** (*hez'-e-ki*) *A Benjamite.*
And Zebadiah, and Meshullam, and *H* .......... 1Chr 8:17

**HEZEKIAH** (*hez-e-ki'-ah*) See EZEKIAS, HIZKIAH.
*1. Son of King Ahaz.*
*H* his son reigned in his stead .......... 2Kin 16:20
that *H* the son of Ahaz king of .......... 2Kin 18:1
pass in the fourth year of king *H* .......... 2Kin 18:9
even in the sixth year of *H* .......... 2Kin 18:10
in the fourteenth year of king *H* .......... 2Kin 18:13
*H* king of Judah sent to the king .......... 2Kin 18:14
*H* king of Judah three hundred .......... 2Kin 18:14
*H* gave him all the silver that .......... 2Kin 18:15
At that time did *H* cut off the .......... 2Kin 18:16
from the pillars which *H* king of .......... 2Kin 18:16
king *H* with a great host against .......... 2Kin 18:17
said unto them, Speak ye now to *H* .......... 2Kin 18:19
whose altars *H* hath taken away, .......... 2Kin 18:22
the king, Let not *H* deceive you .......... 2Kin 18:29
Neither let *H* make you trust in .......... 2Kin 18:30
Hearken not to *H* .......... 2Kin 18:31
and hearken not unto *H*, when he .......... 2Kin 18:32
to *H* with their clothes rent, and .......... 2Kin 18:37
to pass, when king *H* heard it .......... 2Kin 19:1
they said unto him, Thus saith *H* .......... 2Kin 19:3
servants of king *H* came to Isaiah .......... 2Kin 19:5
he sent messengers again unto *H* .......... 2Kin 19:9
shall ye speak to *H* king of Judah .......... 2Kin 19:10
*H* received the letter of the hand .......... 2Kin 19:14
*H* went up into the house of the .......... 2Kin 19:14
*H* prayed before the LORD, and said .......... 2Kin 19:15
Isaiah the son of Amoz sent to *H* .......... 2Kin 19:20
those days was *H* sick unto death .......... 2Kin 20:1
And *H* wept sore .......... 2Kin 20:3
tell *H* the captain of my people, .......... 2Kin 20:5
*H* said unto Isaiah, What shall be .......... 2Kin 20:8
*H* answered, It is a light thing .......... 2Kin 20:10
sent letters and a present unto *H* .......... 2Kin 20:12
he had heard that *H* had been sick .......... 2Kin 20:12
*H* hearkened unto them, and shewed .......... 2Kin 20:13
dominion, that *H* shewed them not .......... 2Kin 20:13
Isaiah the prophet unto king *H* .......... 2Kin 20:14
*H* said, They are come from a far .......... 2Kin 20:14
*H* answered, All the things that .......... 2Kin 20:15
And Isaiah said unto *H*, Hear the .......... 2Kin 20:16
Then said *H* unto Isaiah, Good is .......... 2Kin 20:19
And the rest of the acts of *H* .......... 2Kin 20:20
And *H* slept with his fathers .......... 2Kin 20:21
which *H* his father had destroyed .......... 2Kin 21:3
*H* his son, Manasseh his son, .......... 1Chr 3:13
in the days of *H* king of Judah .......... 1Chr 4:41
*H* his son reigned in his stead .......... 2Chr 28:27
*H* began to reign when he was five .......... 2Chr 29:1
Then they went in to *H* the king .......... 2Chr 29:18
Then *H* the king rose early, and .......... 2Chr 29:20
*H* commanded to offer the burnt .......... 2Chr 29:27
Moreover *H* the king and the .......... 2Chr 29:30
Then *H* answered and said, Now ye .......... 2Chr 29:31
*H* rejoiced, and all the people, .......... 2Chr 29:36
*H* sent to all Israel and Judah, and .......... 2Chr 30:1
But *H* prayed for them, saying, .......... 2Chr 30:18
And the LORD hearkened to *H* .......... 2Chr 30:20
*H* spake comfortably unto all the .......... 2Chr 30:22
For *H* king of Judah did give to .......... 2Chr 30:24
*H* appointed the courses of the .......... 2Chr 31:2
when *H* and the princes came .......... 2Chr 31:8
Then *H* questioned with the .......... 2Chr 31:9
Then *H* commanded to prepare .......... 2Chr 31:11
at the commandment of *H* the king .......... 2Chr 31:13
thus did *H* throughout all Judah, .......... 2Chr 31:20
when *H* saw that Sennacherib was .......... 2Chr 32:2
upon the words of *H* king of Judah .......... 2Chr 32:8
unto *H* king of Judah, and unto .......... 2Chr 32:9
Doth not *H* persuade you to give .......... 2Chr 32:11
Hath not the same *H* taken away .......... 2Chr 32:12
therefore let not *H* deceive you .......... 2Chr 32:15
God, and against his servant *H* .......... 2Chr 32:16
so shall not the God of *H* deliver .......... 2Chr 32:17
And for this cause *H* the king .......... 2Chr 32:20
Thus the LORD saved *H* and the .......... 2Chr 32:22
presents to *H* king of Judah .......... 2Chr 32:23
In those days *H* was sick to the .......... 2Chr 32:24
But *H* rendered not again .......... 2Chr 32:25
Notwithstanding *H* humbled himself. .......... 2Chr 32:26
not upon them in the days of *H* .......... 2Chr 32:26
*H* had exceeding much riches and .......... 2Chr 32:27
This same *H* also stopped the .......... 2Chr 32:30
*H* prospered in all his works .......... 2Chr 32:30
Now the rest of the acts of *H* .......... 2Chr 32:32
*H* slept with his fathers, and they .......... 2Chr 32:33
*H* his father had broken down .......... 2Chr 33:3
which the men of *H* king of Judah .......... Prov 25:1
of Uzziah, Jotham, Ahaz, and *H* .......... Is 1:1
in the fourteenth year of king *H* .......... Is 36:1
unto king *H* with a great army .......... Is 36:2
said unto them, Say ye now to *H* .......... Is 36:4
whose altars *H* hath taken away, .......... Is 36:7
the king, Let not *H* deceive you .......... Is 36:14
Neither let *H* make you trust in .......... Is 36:15
Hearken not to *H* .......... Is 36:16
Beware lest *H* persuade you, .......... Is 36:18
to *H* with their clothes rent, and .......... Is 36:22
to pass, when king *H* heard it .......... Is 37:1
they said unto him, Thus saith *H* .......... Is 37:3
servants of king *H* came to Isaiah .......... Is 37:5
heard it, he sent messengers to *H* .......... Is 37:9
shall ye speak to *H* king of Judah .......... Is 37:10
*H* received the letter from the .......... Is 37:14
*H* went up unto the house of the .......... Is 37:14
*H* prayed unto the LORD, saying, .......... Is 37:15
the son of Amoz sent unto *H* .......... Is 37:21
those days was *H* sick unto death .......... Is 38:1
Then *H* turned his face toward the .......... Is 38:2
And *H* wept sore .......... Is 38:3
Go, and say to *H*, Thus saith the .......... Is 38:5
The writing of *H* king of Judah .......... Is 38:9
*H* also had said, What is the sign .......... Is 38:22
sent letters and a present to *H* .......... Is 39:1
*H* was glad of them, and shewed .......... Is 39:2
dominion, that *H* shewed them not .......... Is 39:2

H

Isaiah the prophet unto king *H* Is 39:3
*H* said, They are come from a far Is 39:3
*H* answered, All that is in mine Is 39:4
Then said Isaiah to *H*, Hear the Is 39:5
Then said *H* to Isaiah, Good is Is 39:8
the son of *H* king of Judah Jer 15:4
in the days of *H* king of Judah Jer 26:18
Did *H* king of Judah and all Judah Jer 26:19
of Uzziah, Jotham, Ahaz, and *H* Hos 1:1
in the days of Jotham, Ahaz, and *H* Mic 1:1
*2. A son of Neariah.*
Elioenai, and *H*, and Azrikam, three 1Chr 3:23
*3. A family of exiles.*
The children of Ater of *H* Ezr 2:16
The children of Ater of *H* Neh 7:21

**HEZION** (*he'-zi-on*) *Grandfather of King Benhadad of Syria.*
the son of Tabrimon, the son of *H* 1Kin 15:18

**HEZIR** (*he'-zir*)
*1. A sanctuary servant.*
The seventeenth to *H*, the 1Chr 24:15
*2. An Israelite who renewed the covenant.*
Magpiash, Meshullam, *H*, Neh 10:20

**HEZRAI** (*hez'-rahee*) See HEZRO. *A mighty man of David.*
*H* the Carmelite, Paarai the 2Sa 23:35

**HEZRO** (*hez'-ro*) See HEZRAI. *Same as Hezrai.*
*H* the Carmelite, Naarai the son 1Chr 11:37

**HEZRON** (*hez'-ron*) See HAZOR, HEZRONITES, HEZBON'S.
*1. Son of Pharez.*
And the sons of Pharez were *H* Gen 46:12
Of *H*, the family of the Num 26:6
of *H*, the family of the Num 26:21
Pharez begat *H*, Ruth 4:18
*H* begat Ram, and Ram begat Ruth 4:19
of Pharez; *H*, and Hamul 1Chr 2:5
The sons also of *H*, that were 1Chr 2:9
Caleb the son of *H* begat children 1Chr 2:18
afterward *H* went in to the 1Chr 2:21
And after that *H* was dead in 1Chr 2:24
Jerahmeel the firstborn of *H* were 1Chr 2:25
Pharez, *H*, and Carmi, and Hur, and 1Chr 4:1
*2. A son of Reuben.*
Hanoch, and Phallu, and *H*, and Carmi Gen 46:9
Hanoch, and Pallu, *H*, and Carmi Ex 6:14
Israel were, Hanoch, and Pallu, *H* 1Chr 5:3
*3. A town in Judah.*
and passed along to *H*, and went up Josh 15:3
Hazor, Hadattah, and Kerioth, and *H* Josh 15:25

**HEZRONITES** (*hez'-ron-ites*) *Descendants of Hezron 2.*
Of Hezron, the family of the *H* Num 26:6
of Hezron, the family of the *H* Num 26:21

**HEZRON'S** (*hez'-ronz*) *Refers to Hezron 2.*
then Abiah *H* wife bare him Ashur 1Chr 2:24

**HID**
his wife *h* themselves from the Gen 3:8
and I *h* myself Gen 3:10
and from thy face shall I be *h* Gen 4:14
Jacob *h* them under the oak which Gen 35:4
child, she *h* him three months Ex 2:2
Egyptian, and *h* him in the sand Ex 2:12
And Moses *h* his face Ex 3:6
the thing be *h* from the eyes of Lev 4:13
withal, and it be *h* from him Lev 5:3
with an oath, and it be *h* from him Lev 5:4
it be *h* from the eyes of her Num 5:13
and of treasures *h* in the sand Deut 33:19
*h* them, and said thus, There came Josh 2:4
*h* them with the stalks of flax, Josh 2:6
because she *h* the messengers that Josh 6:17
because she *h* the messengers, Josh 6:25
they are *h* in the earth in the Josh 7:21
it was *h* in his tent, and the Josh 7:22
*h* themselves in a cave at Josh 10:16
are found *h* in a cave at Makkedah Josh 10:17
the cave wherein they had been *h* Josh 10:27
for he *h* himself Judg 9:5
every whit, and *h* nothing from him 1Sa 3:18
he hath *h* himself among the stuff 1Sa 10:22
holes where they had *h* themselves 1Sa 14:11
had *h* themselves in mount Ephraim 1Sa 14:22
So David *h* himself in the field 1Sa 20:24
he is *h* now in some pit, or in 2Sa 17:9
is no matter *h* from the king 2Sa 18:13
was not any thing *h* from the king 1Kin 10:3
*h* them by fifty in a cave, and fed 1Kin 18:4
how I *h* an hundred men of the 1Kin 18:13
and the LORD hath *h* it from me 2Kin 4:27
and she hath *h* her son 2Kin 6:29
gold, and raiment, and went and *h* it 2Kin 7:8
thence also, and went and *h* it 2Kin 7:8
and they *h* him, even him and his 2Kin 11:2
he was with her *h* in the house of 2Kin 11:3
four sons with him *h* themselves 1Chr 21:20
there was nothing *h* from Solomon 2Chr 9:2
him, (for he was *h* in Samaria 2Chr 22:9
*h* him from Athaliah, so that she 2Chr 22:11
he was with them *h* in the house 2Chr 22:12
nor *h* sorrow from mine eyes Job 3:10
for it more than for *h* treasures Job 3:21
given to a man whose way is *h* Job 3:23
Thou shalt be *h* from the scourge Job 5:21
the ice, and wherein the snow is *h* Job 6:16
things hast thou *h* in thine heart Job 10:13
their fathers, and have not *h* it Job 15:18
For thou hast *h* their heart from Job 17:4
shall be *h* in his secret places Job 20:26
the thing that is *h* bringeth he Job 28:11
Seeing it is *h* from the eyes of Job 28:21
young men saw me, and *h* themselves Job 29:8
The waters are *h* as with a stone, Job 38:30
in the net which they *h* is their Ps 9:15
thou fillest with thy *h* treasure Ps 17:14
there is nothing *h* from the heat Ps 19:6
neither hath he *h* his face from Ps 22:24
and mine iniquity have I not *h* Ps 32:5
they *h* for me their net in a pit Ps 35:7
net that he hath *h* catch himself Ps 35:8
and my groaning is not *h* from thee Ps 38:9
I have not *h* thy righteousness Ps 40:10
I would have *h* myself from him Ps 55:12
and my sins are not *h* from thee Ps 69:5
Thy word have I *h* in mine heart Ps 119:11
My substance was not *h* from thee Ps 139:15
The proud have *h* a snare for me Ps 140:5
for her as for *h* treasures Prov 2:4
falsehood have we *h* ourselves Is 28:15
of their prudent men shall be *h* Is 29:14
My way is *h* from the LORD, and my Is 40:27
they are *h* in prison houses Is 42:22
shadow of his hand hath he *h* me Is 49:2
in his quiver hath he *h* me Is 49:2
I *h* not my face from shame and Is 50:6
we *h* as it were our faces from Is 53:3
In a little wrath I *h* my face Is 54:8
I *h* me, and was wroth, and he went Is 57:17
your sins have *h* his face from Is 59:2
for thou hast *h* thy face from us, Is 64:7
because they are *h* from mine eyes Is 65:16
*h* it by Euphrates, as the LORD Jer 13:5
from the place where I had *h* it Jer 13:7
they are not *h* from my face Jer 16:17
their iniquity *h* from mine eyes Jer 16:17
take me, and *h* snares for my feet Jer 18:22
I have *h* my face from this city Jer 33:5
but the LORD *h* them Jer 36:26
upon these stones that I have *h* Jer 43:10
have *h* their eyes from my Eze 22:26
therefore *h* I my face from them, Eze 39:23
unto them, and *h* my face from them Eze 39:24
and Israel is not *h* from me Hos 5:3
his sin is *h* Hos 13:12
shall be *h* from mine eyes Hos 13:14
though they be *h* from my sight in Amos 9:3
thou shalt be *h*, thou also shalt Nah 3:11
it may be ye shall be *h* in the Zeph 2:3
is set on an hill cannot be *h* Mt 5:14
and *h*, that shall not be known Mt 10:26
because thou hast *h* these things Mt 11:25
*h* in three measures of meal, till Mt 13:33
like unto treasure *h* in a field Mt 13:44
the earth, and *h* his lord's money Mt 25:18
*h* thy talent in the earth Mt 25:25
For there is nothing *h*, which Mk 4:22
but he could not be *h* Mk 7:24
*h* herself five months, saying, Lk 1:24
neither any thing *h*, that shall Lk 8:17
the woman saw that she was not *h* Lk 8:47
it was *h* from them, that they Lk 9:45
that thou hast *h* these things Lk 10:21
neither *h*, that shall not be Lk 12:2
*h* in three measures of meal, till Lk 13:21
and this saying was *h* from them Lk 18:34
now they are *h* from thine eyes Lk 19:42
but Jesus *h* himself, and went out Jn 8:59
But if our gospel be *h*, it is *h* 2Cor 4:3
of the world hath been *h* in God Eph 3:9
which hath been *h* from ages Col 1:26
In whom are *h* all the treasures Col 2:3
your life is *h* with Christ in God Col 3:3
that are otherwise cannot be *h* 1Ti 5:25
was *h* three months of his parents Heb 11:23
*h* themselves in the dens and in Rev 6:15

**HIDDAI** (*hid'-dahee*) See HURAI. *A mighty man of David.*
*H* of the brooks of Gaash, 2Sa 23:30

**HIDDEKEL** (*hid'-de-kel*) *A name for the Tigris River.*
the name of the third river is *H* Gen 2:14
of the great river, which is *H* Dan 10:4

**HIDDEN**
things, and if it be *h* from him Lev 5:2
this day, it is not *h* from thee Deut 30:11
Or as an *h* untimely birth I had Job 3:16
of years is *h* to the oppressor Job 15:20
times are not *h* from the Almighty Job 24:1
in the *h* part thou shalt make me Ps 51:6
and consulted against thy *h* ones Ps 83:3
when the wicked rise, a man is *h* Prov 28:12
*h* riches of secret places, that Is 45:3
even *h* things, and thou didst not Is 48:6
how are his *h* things sought up Obad 6
of these things are *h* from him Acts 26:26
in a mystery, even the *h* wisdom 1Cor 2:7
to light the *h* things of darkness 1Cor 4:5
the *h* things of dishonesty 2Cor 4:2
let it be the *h* man of the heart 1Pet 3:4
will I give to eat of the *h* manna Rev 2:17

**HIDE**
Shall I *h* from Abraham that thing Gen 18:17
We will not *h* it from my lord, Gen 47:18
when she could not longer *h* him Ex 2:3
But the bullock, and his *h* Lev 8:17
the *h* he burnt with fire without Lev 9:11
ways *h* their eyes from the man Lev 20:4
*h* themselves from thee, be Deut 7:20
go astray, and *h* thyself from them Deut 22:1
thou mayest not *h* thyself Deut 22:3
the way, and *h* thyself from them Deut 22:4
I will *h* my face from them, and Deut 31:17
I will surely *h* my face in that Deut 31:18
I will *h* my face from them, I Deut 32:20
*h* yourselves there three days, Josh 2:16
*h* it not from me Josh 7:19
to *h* it from the Midianites Judg 6:11
I pray thee *h* it not from me 1Sa 3:17
if thou *h* any thing from me of 1Sa 3:17
people did *h* themselves in caves 1Sa 13:6
in a secret place, and *h* thyself 1Sa 19:2
my father *h* this thing from me 1Sa 20:2
that I may *h* myself in the field 1Sa 20:5
*h* thyself when the business was 1Sa 20:19
Doth not David *h* himself with us 1Sa 23:19
Doth not David *h* himself in the 1Sa 26:1
*H* not from me, I pray thee, the 2Sa 14:18
*h* thyself by the brook Cherith, 1Kin 17:3
an inner chamber to *h* thyself 1Kin 22:25
camp to *h* themselves in the field 2Kin 7:12
an inner chamber to *h* thyself 2Chr 18:24
then I will not *h* myself from Job 13:20
thou wouldest *h* me in the grave Job 14:13
though he *h* it under his tongue Job 20:12
the earth *h* themselves together Job 24:4
his purpose, and *h* pride from man Job 33:17
of iniquity may *h* themselves Job 34:22
*H* them in the dust together Job 40:13
long wilt thou *h* thy face from me Ps 13:1
*h* me under the shadow of thy Ps 17:8
he shall *h* me in his pavilion Ps 27:5
of his tabernacle shall he *h* me Ps 27:5
*H* not thy face far from me Ps 27:9
thou didst *h* thy face, and I was Ps 30:7
Thou shalt *h* them in the secret Ps 31:20
*H* thy face from my sins, and blot Ps 51:9
Doth not David *h* himself with us Ps 54:*t*
and *h* not thyself from my Ps 55:1
they *h* themselves, they mark my Ps 56:6
*H* me from the secret counsel of Ps 64:2
*h* not thy face from thy servant Ps 69:17
We will not *h* them from their Ps 78:4
wilt thou *h* thyself for ever Ps 89:46
*H* not thy face from me in the day Ps 102:2
*h* not thy commandments from me Ps 119:19
*h* not thy face from me, lest I be Ps 143:7
I flee unto thee to *h* me Ps 143:9
*h* my commandments with thee Prov 2:1
the wicked rise, men *h* themselves Prov 28:28
I will *h* mine eyes from you Is 1:15
*h* thee in the dust, for fear of Is 2:10
their sin as Sodom, they *h* it not Is 3:9
*h* the outcasts Is 16:3
*h* thyself as it were for a little Is 26:20
to *h* their counsel from the LORD Is 29:15
that thou *h* not thyself from Is 58:7
*h* it there in a hole of the rock Jer 13:4
which I commanded thee to *h* there Jer 13:6
Can any *h* himself in secret Jer 23:24
Go, *h* thee, thou and Jeremiah Jer 36:19
*h* nothing from me Jer 38:14
*h* it not from us, and we will not Jer 38:25
*h* them in the clay in the Jer 43:9
he shall not be able to *h* himself Jer 49:10
*h* not thine ear at my breathing, Lam 3:56
secret that they can *h* from thee Eze 28:3
the garden of God could not *h* him Eze 31:8
Neither will I *h* my face any more Eze 39:29
so that they fled to *h* themselves Dan 10:7
though they *h* themselves in the Amos 9:3
he will even *h* his face from them Mic 3:4
and did *h* himself from them Jn 12:36
shall *h* a multitude of sins Jas 5:20
*h* us from the face of him that Rev 6:16

**HIDEST**
Wherefore *h* thou thy face, and Job 13:24
why *h* thou thyself in times of Ps 10:1
Wherefore *h* thou thy face, and Ps 44:24
why *h* thou thy face from me Ps 88:14
Thou *h* thy face, they are Ps 104:29
thou art a God that *h* thyself Is 45:15

**HIDETH**
lurking places where he *h* himself 1Sa 23:23
he *h* himself on the right hand, Job 23:9
when he *h* his face, who then can Job 34:29
Who is he that *h* counsel without Job 42:3
he *h* his face Ps 10:11
the darkness *h* not from thee Ps 139:12
He that *h* hatred with lying lips, Prov 10:18
A slothful man *h* his hand in his Prov 19:24
foreseeth the evil, and *h* himself Prov 22:3
The slothful *h* his hand in his Prov 26:15
foreseeth the evil, and *h* himself Prov 27:12
Whosoever *h* her *h* the wind, Prov 27:16
but he that *h* his eyes shall have Prov 28:27
that *h* his face from the house of Is 8:17
which when a man hath found, he *h* Mt 13:44

**HIDING**
by *h* mine iniquity in my bosom Job 31:33
Thou art my *h* place Ps 32:7
Thou art my *h* place and my shield Ps 119:114
waters shall overflow the *h* place Is 28:17
be as an *h* place from the wind Is 32:2

and there was the *h* of his power........... Hab 3:4

**HIEL** (*hi'-el*) *A Bethelite.*
In his days did *H* the Beth-elite.......... 1Kin 16:34

**HIERAPOLIS** (*hi-e-rap'-o-lis*) *A city in Phrygia.*
are in Laodicea, and them in *H*............... Col 4:13

**HIGGAION** (*hig-gah'-yon*) *A musical notation.*
work of his own hands. *H*. ......................... Ps 9:16

**HIGH** See PREFACE.

**HIGHER**
and his king shall be *h* than Agag....... Num 24:7
upward he was *h* than any of the........... 1Sa 9:2
he was *h* than any of the people............ 1Sa 10:23
He built the *h* gate of the house......... 2Kin 15:35
the wall, and on the *h* places.................. Neh 4:13
the clouds which are *h* than thou.......... Job 35:5
me to the rock that is *h* than I................. Ps 61:2
*h* than the kings of the earth.................. Ps 89:27
for he that is *h* than the highest........... Eccl 5:8
and there be *h* than they......................... Eccl 5:8
the heavens are *h* than the earth............ Is 55:9
so are my ways *h* than your ways............ Is 55:9
the scribe, in the *h* court......................... Jer 36:10
came from the way of the *h* gate............ Eze 9:2
the galleries were *h* than these.............. Eze 42:5
this shall be the *h* place of the.............. Eze 43:13
but one was *h* than the other.................. Dan 8:3
and the *h* came up last ........................... Dan 8:3
say unto thee, Friend, go up *h*................ Lk 14:10
soul be subject unto the *h* powers.......... Rom 13:1
and made *h* than the heavens................. Heb 7:26

**HIGHEST**
heavens, and the *H* gave his voice......... Ps 18:13
the *h* himself shall establish her.............. Ps 87:5
nor the *h* part of the dust of the........... Prov 8:26
upon the *h* places of the city.................. Prov 9:3
is higher than the *h* regardeth................. Eccl 5:8
took the *h* branch of the cedar................ Eze 17:3
I will also take of the *h* branch.............. Eze 17:22
chamber to the *h* by the midst............... Eze 41:7
Hosanna in the *h*...................................... Mt 21:9
Hosanna in the *h*....................................... Mk 11:10
shall be called the Son of the *H*.............. Lk 1:32
thee, and the power of the *H* shall.......... Lk 1:35
be called the prophet of the *H*................. Lk 1:76
Glory to God in the *h*, and on.................. Lk 2:14
ye shall be the children of the *H*............. Lk 6:35
sit not down in the *h* room....................... Lk 14:8
in heaven, and glory in the *h*.................... Lk 19:38
the *h* seats in the synagogues, and......... Lk 20:46

**HIGHLY**
Hail, thou that art *h* favoured.................. Lk 1:28
for that which is *h* esteemed.................... Lk 16:15
Herod was *h* displeased with them........ Acts 12:20
more *h* than he ought to think................. Rom 12:3
God also hath *h* exalted him..................... Phil 2:9
to esteem them very *h* in love for.......... 1Th 5:13

**HIGHMINDED**
Be not *h*, but fear.................................... Rom 11:20
in this world, that they be not *h*.............. 1Ti 6:17
Traitors, heady, *h*, lovers of...................... 2Ti 3:4

**HIGHNESS**
by reason of his *h* I could not................ Job 31:23
even them that rejoice in my *h*................. Is 13:3

**HIGHWAY**
on the east side of the *h* that.................. Judg 21:19
Beth-shemesh, and went along the *h*..... 1Sa 6:12
in blood in the midst of the *h*................... 2Sa 20:12
Amasa out of the *h* into the field............. 2Sa 20:12
When he was removed out of the *h*........ 2Sa 20:13
which is in the *h* of the fuller's............. 2Kin 18:17
The *h* of the upright is to depart............ Prov 16:17
in the *h* of the fuller's field.................... Is 7:3
there shall be an *h* for the..................... Is 11:16
be a *h* out of Egypt to Assyria................ Is 19:23
an *h* shall be there, and a way, and....... Is 35:8
in the *h* of the fuller's field.................... Is 36:2
in the desert a *h* for our God.................. Is 40:3
set thine heart toward the *h*................... Jer 31:21
sat by the *h* side begging........................ Mk 10:46

**HIGHWAYS**
the *h* were unoccupied, and the............. Judg 5:6
kill, as at other times, in the *h*............... Judg 20:31
them from the city unto the *h*................. Judg 20:32
them in the *h* five thousand men........... Judg 20:45
The *h* lie waste, the wayfaring................. Is 33:8
a way, and my *h* shall be exalted............ Is 49:11
cast up, cast up the *h*.............................. Is 62:10
and they shall say in all the *h*................ Amos 5:16
Go ye therefore into the *h*....................... Mt 22:9
servants went out into the *h*................... Mt 22:10
the servant, Go out into the *h*................ Lk 14:23

**HILEN** (*hi'-len*) See HOLON. *A Levitical city in Judah.*
*H* with her suburbs, Debir with.............. 1Chr 6:58

**HILKIAH** (*hil-ki'-ah*) See HELKAI, HILKIAH'S.
*1. Father of Eliakim.*
out to them Eliakim the son of *H*........ 2Kin 18:18
Then said Eliakim the son of *H*............. 2Kin 18:26
Then came Eliakim the son of *H*............ 2Kin 18:37
And Shallum begat *H*.............................. 1Chr 6:13
and *H* begat Azariah ............................... 1Chr 6:13
Of *H*, Hashabiah; of Jedaiah.................. Neh 12:21
my servant Eliakim the son of *H*............. Is 22:20
Then came Eliakim, the son of *H*............ Is 36:22
*2. A High Priest.*
Go up to *H* the high priest, that........... 2Kin 22:4
*H* the high priest said unto..................... 2Kin 22:8
*H* gave the book to Shaphan, and he.. 2Kin 22:8
*H* the priest hath delivered me a........ 2Kin 22:10
the king commanded *H* the priest......... 2Kin 22:12
So *H* the priest, and Ahikam, and........ 2Kin 22:14
king commanded *H* the high priest....... 2Kin 23:4
*H* the priest found in the house........... 2Kin 23:24
And Azariah the son of *H*, the son........ 1Chr 9:11
they came to *H* the high priest.............. 2Chr 34:9
*H* the priest found a book of the........... 2Chr 34:14
*H* answered and said to Shaphan the 2Chr 34:15
*H* delivered the book to Shaphan......... 2Chr 34:15
*H* the priest hath given me a book...... 2Chr 34:18
And the king commanded *H*, and......... 2Chr 34:20
And *H*, and they that the king had ... 2Chr 34:22
*H* and Zechariah and Jehiel, rulers...... 2Chr 35:8
the son of Azariah, the son of *H*.............. Ezr 7:1
Shaphan, and Gemariah the son of *H*.... Jer 29:3
*3. A descendant of Merari.*
the son of Amaziah, the son of *H*........ 1Chr 6:45
*4. A son of Hosah.*
*H* the second, Tebaliah the third,....... 1Chr 26:11
*5. A priest who assisted Ezra.*
Shema, and Anaiah, and Urijah, and *H*. Neh 8:4
Seraiah the son of *H*, the son of.......... Neh 11:11
Sallu, Amok, *H*, Jedaiah......................... Neh 12:7
*6. Father of Jeremiah.*
words of Jeremiah the son of *H*................ Jer 1:1

**HILKIAH'S** (*hil-ki'-ahs*) *Refers to Hilkiah 1.*
*H* son, which was over the house,............ Is 36:3

**HILL**
the *h* with the rod of God in mine.......... Ex 17:9
Hur went up to the top of the *h*............. Ex 17:10
and builded an altar under the *h*............ Ex 24:4
presumed to go up unto the *h* top..... Num 14:44
Canaanites which dwelt in that *h*...... Num 14:45
ye were ready to go up into the *h*........ Deut 1:41
went presumptuously up into the *h*..... Deut 1:43
Israel at the *h* of the foreskins............... Josh 5:3
the *h* country from Lebanon unto.......... Josh 13:6
was drawn from the top of the *h*........... Josh 15:9
The *h* is not enough for us.................... Josh 17:16
near the *h* that lieth on the.................. Josh 18:13
from the *h* that lieth before.................. Josh 18:14
in the *h* country of Judah, with............. Josh 21:11
the north side of the *h* of Gaash.......... Josh 24:30
they buried him in a *h* that................... Josh 24:33
on the north side of the *h* Gaash.......... Judg 2:9
by the *h* of Moreh, in the valley............ Judg 7:1
top of an *h* that is before Hebron......... Judg 16:3
the house of Abinadab in the *h*............. 1Sa 7:1
as they went up the *h* to the city.......... 1Sa 9:11
thou shalt come to the *h* of God............ 1Sa 10:5
when they came thither to the *h*........... 1Sa 10:10
in the *h* of Hachilah, which is on.......... 1Sa 23:19
came down by the covert of the *h*....... 1Sa 25:20
hide himself in the *h* of Hachilah.......... 1Sa 26:1
Saul pitched in the *h* of Hachilah.......... 1Sa 26:3
stood on the top of an *h* afar off.......... 1Sa 26:13
they were come to the *h* of Ammah...... 2Sa 2:24
and stood on the top of an *h*................. 2Sa 2:25
the way of the *h* side behind him.......... 2Sa 13:34
a little past the top of the *h*................. 2Sa 16:1
them in the *h* before the LORD.............. 2Sa 21:9
in the *h* that is before Jerusalem.......... 1Kin 11:7
and groves, on every high *h*.................. 1Kin 14:23
he bought the *h* Samaria of Shemer.. 1Kin 16:24
of silver, and built on the *h*................... 1Kin 16:24
name of Shemer, owner of the *h*......... 1Kin 16:24
behold, he sat on the top of an *h*......... 2Kin 1:9
came to the man of God to the *h*.......... 2Kin 4:27
images and groves in every high *h*...... 2Kin 17:10
my king upon my holy *h* of Zion.............. Ps 2:6
and he heard me out of his holy *h*.......... Ps 3:4
who shall dwell in thy holy *h*................... Ps 15:1
ascend into the *h* of the LORD................ Ps 24:3
the Hermonites, from the *h* Mizar.......... Ps 42:6
let them bring me unto thy holy *h*.......... Ps 43:3
*h* of God is as the *h* of Bashan............... Ps 68:15
an high *h* as the *h* of Bashan................. Ps 68:15
this is the *h* which God desireth............ Ps 68:16
our God, and worship at his holy *h*.......... Ps 99:9
and to the *h* of frankincense.................. Song 4:6
a vineyard in a very fruitful *h*.................. Is 5:1
of Zion, the *h* of Jerusalem...................... Is 10:32
mountain, and as an ensign on an *h*....... Is 30:17
mountain, and upon every high *h*........... Is 30:25
mount Zion, and for the *h* thereof.......... Is 31:4
mountain and *h* shall be made low.......... Is 40:4
when upon every high *h* and under......... Jer 2:20
every mountain, and from every *h*......... Jer 16:16
over against it upon the *h* Gareb.......... Jer 31:39
that holdest the height of the *h*............ Jer 49:16
they have gone from mountain to *h*....... Jer 50:6
their altars, upon every high *h*.............. Eze 6:13
them, then they saw every high *h*......... Eze 20:28
mountains, and upon every high *h*......... Eze 34:6
round about my *h* a blessing.................. Eze 34:26
that is set on an *h* cannot be hid........... Mt 5:14
went into the *h* country with.................. Lk 1:39
all the *h* country of Judaea..................... Lk 1:65
and *h* shall be brought low..................... Lk 3:5
*h* whereon their city was built................. Lk 4:29
they were come down from the *h*............ Lk 9:37
stood in the midst of Mars' *h*................. Acts 17:22

**HILLEL** (*hil'-lel*) *Father of Abdon.*
And after him Abdon the son of *H*.... Judg 12:13
And Abdon the son of *H* the.............. Judg 12:15

**HILL'S**
on the *h* side over against him.............. 2Sa 16:13

**HILLS**
and all the high *h*, that were.................. Gen 7:19
utmost bound of the everlasting *h*...... Gen 49:26
him, and from the *h* I behold him....... Num 23:9
thereunto, in the plain, in the *h*............ Deut 1:7
that spring out of valleys and *h*............ Deut 8:7
out of whose *h* thou mayest dig.......... Deut 8:9
go to possess it, is a land of *h*............. Deut 11:11
the high mountains, and upon the *h*... Deut 12:2
precious things of the lasting *h*.......... Deut 33:15
on this side Jordan, in the *h*................. Josh 9:1
smote all the country of the *h*............. Josh 10:40
Joshua took all that land, the *h*........... Josh 11:16
him, Their gods are gods of the *h*...... 1Kin 20:23
said, The LORD is God of the *h*........... 1Kin 20:28
all Israel scattered upon the *h*............. 1Kin 22:17
in the high places, and on the *h*.......... 2Kin 16:4
in the high places, and on the *h*........... 2Chr 28:4
or wast thou made before the *h*.............. Job 15:7
foundations also of the *h* moved............. Ps 18:7
and the cattle upon a thousand *h*........... Ps 50:10
the little *h* rejoice on every.................. Ps 65:12
Why leap ye, ye high *h*.......................... Ps 68:16
to the people, and the little *h*................ Ps 72:3
The *h* were covered with the.................. Ps 80:10
the strength of the *h* is his also............. Ps 95:4
The *h* melted like wax at the.................. Ps 97:5
let the *h* be joyful together...................... Ps 98:8
valleys, which run among the *h*........... Ps 104:10
He watereth the *h* from his................... Ps 104:13
The high *h* are a refuge for the............ Ps 104:18
he toucheth the *h*, and they smoke..... Ps 104:32
rams, and the little *h* like lambs.......... Ps 114:4
and ye little *h*, like lambs.................... Ps 114:6
will lift up mine eyes unto the *h*.......... Ps 121:1
Mountains, and all *h*............................. Ps 148:9
before the *h* was I brought forth.......... Prov 8:25
mountains, skipping upon the *h*............ Song 2:8
and shall be exalted above the *h*................ Is 2:2
upon all the *h* that are lifted up............ Is 2:14
the *h* did tremble, and their..................... Is 5:25
on all *h* that shall be digged.................... Is 7:25
in scales, and the *h* in a balance............ Is 40:12
and shalt make the *h* as chaff................ Is 41:15
I will make waste mountains and *h*......... Is 42:15
shall depart, and the *h* be removed........ Is 54:10
the *h* shall break forth before.................. Is 55:12
and blasphemed me upon the *h*.................. Is 65:7
is salvation hoped for from the *h*............ Jer 3:23
and all the *h* moved lightly..................... Jer 4:24
on the *h* in the fields.............................. Jer 13:27
the green trees upon the high *h*.............. Jer 17:2
GOD to the mountains, and to the *h*........ Eze 6:3
in thy *h*, and in thy valleys, and............. Eze 35:8
GOD to the mountains, and to the *h*....... Eze 36:4
unto the mountains, and to the *h*........... Eze 36:6
and burn incense upon the *h*................... Hos 4:13
and to the *h*, Fall on us.......................... Hos 10:8
the *h* shall flow with milk, and.............. Joel 3:18
wine, and all the *h* shall melt.............. Amos 9:13
it shall be exalted above the *h*................. Mic 4:1
and let the *h* hear thy voice.................... Mic 6:1
the *h* melt, and the earth is....................... Nah 1:5
the perpetual *h* did bow.......................... Hab 3:6
and a great crashing from the *h*........... Zeph 1:10
and to the *h*, Cover us.............................. Lk 23:30

**HIM** See PREFACE.

**HIMSELF** See PREFACE.

**HIN**
fourth part of an *h* of beaten oil............ Ex 29:40
the fourth part of an *h* of wine.............. Ex 29:40
sanctuary, and of oil olive an *h*.............. Ex 30:24
a just ephah, and a just *h*..................... Lev 19:36
of wine, the fourth part of a *h*.............. Lev 23:13
the fourth part of an *h* of oil................ Num 15:4
the fourth part of an *h* of wine............. Num 15:5
the third part of an *h* of oil.................. Num 15:6
the third part of an *h* of wine................ Num 15:7
mingled with half an *h* of oil................. Num 15:9
drink offering half an *h* of wine........... Num 15:10
fourth part of an *h* of beaten oil.......... Num 28:5
part of an *h* for the one lamb................ Num 28:7
half an *h* of wine unto a bullock.......... Num 28:14
the third part of an *h* unto a ram......... Num 28:14
a fourth part of an *h* unto a lamb...... Num 28:14
measure, the sixth part of an *h*............ Eze 4:11
ram, and an *h* of oil for an ephah........ Eze 45:24
give, and an *h* of oil to an ephah......... Eze 46:5
unto, and an *h* of oil to an ephah......... Eze 46:7
give, and an *h* of oil to an ephah........ Eze 46:11
and the third part of an *h* of oil.......... Eze 46:14

**HIND**
Naphtali is a *h* let loose........................ Gen 49:21
Let her be as the loving *h*....................... Prov 5:19
the *h* also calved in the field,................... Jer 14:5

**HINDER**
*H* me not, seeing the LORD hath.......... Gen 24:56
*h* thee from coming unto me............. Num 22:16
wherefore Abner with the *h* end of....... 2Sa 2:23
all their *h* parts were inward................ 1Kin 7:25
all their *h* parts were inward................ 2Chr 4:4

against Jerusalem, and to *h* it ........ Neh 4:8
he taketh away, who can *h* him ........ Job 9:12
together, then who can *h* him ........ Job 11:10
smote his enemies in the *h* parts ........ Ps 78:66
his *h* part toward the utmost sea, ........ Joel 2:20
and half of them toward the *h* sea ........ Zec 14:8
he was in the *h* part of the ship, ........ Mk 4:38
what doth *h* me to be baptized ........ Acts 8:36
but the *h* part was broken with ........ Acts 27:41
lest we should *h* the gospel of ........ 1Cor 9:12
who did *h* you that ye should not ........ Gal 5:7

**HINDERED**
these men, that they be not *h* ........ Ezr 6:8
them that were entering in ye *h* ........ Lk 11:52
been much *h* from coming to you ........ Rom 15:22
but Satan *h* us ........ 1Th 2:18
that your prayers be not *h* ........ 1Pet 3:7

**HINDERETH**
anger, is persecuted, and none *h* ........ Is 14:6

**HINDERMOST**
after, and Rachel and Joseph *h* ........ Gen 33:2
the *h* of the nations shall be a ........ Jer 50:12

**HINDMOST**
They shall go *h* with their ........ Num 2:31
the way, and smote the *h* of thee ........ Deut 25:18
enemies, and smite the *h* of them ........ Josh 10:19

**HINDS**
thou mark when the *h* do calve ........ Job 39:1
of the LORD maketh the *h* to calve ........ Ps 29:9
by the *h* of the field, that ye ........ Song 2:7
by the *h* of the field, that ye ........ Song 3:5

**HINDS'**
He maketh my feet like *h* feet ........ 2Sa 22:34
He maketh my feet like *h* feet ........ Ps 18:33
he will make my feet like *h* feet ........ Hab 3:19

**HINGES**
the *h* of gold, both for the doors ........ 1Kin 7:50
As the door turneth upon his *h* ........ Prov 26:14

**HINNOM** (*hin'-nom*) *A valley near Jerusalem.*
of *H* unto the south side of the ........ Josh 15:8
before the valley of *H* westward ........ Josh 15:8
before the valley of the son of *H* ........ Josh 18:16
and descended to the valley of *H* ........ Josh 18:16
the valley of the children of *H* ........ 2Kin 23:10
in the valley of the son of *H* ........ 2Chr 28:3
in the valley of the son of *H* ........ 2Chr 33:6
Beer-sheba unto the valley of *H* ........ Neh 11:30
is in the valley of the son of *H* ........ Jer 7:31
nor the valley of the son of *H* ........ Jer 7:32
unto the valley of the son of *H* ........ Jer 19:2
nor The valley of the son of *H* ........ Jer 19:6
are in the valley of the son of *H* ........ Jer 32:35

**HIP**
And he smote them *h* and thigh with. Judg 15:8

**HIRAH** (*hi'-rah*) *A friend of Judah.*
Adullamite, whose name was *H* ........ Gen 38:1
his friend *H* the Adullamite ........ Gen 38:12

**HIRAM** (*hi'-ram*) See HIRAM'S, HURAM.
*1. A king of Tyre.*
*H* king of Tyre sent messengers to ........ 2Sa 5:11
*H* king of Tyre sent his servants ........ 1Kin 5:1
for *H* was ever a lover of David ........ 1Kin 5:1
And Solomon sent to *H*, saying, ........ 1Kin 5:2
when *H* heard the words of Solomon ........ 1Kin 5:7
*H* sent to Solomon, saying, I have ........ 1Kin 5:8
So *H* gave Solomon cedar trees and ........ 1Kin 5:10
Solomon gave *H* twenty thousand ........ 1Kin 5:11
gave Solomon to *H* year by year ........ 1Kin 5:11
and there was peace between *H* ........ 1Kin 5:12
(Now *H* the king of Tyre had ........ 1Kin 9:11
*H* twenty cities in the land of ........ 1Kin 9:11
*H* came out from Tyre to see the ........ 1Kin 9:12
*H* sent to the king sixscore ........ 1Kin 9:14
*H* sent in the navy his servants, ........ 1Kin 9:27
And the navy also of *H*, that ........ 1Kin 10:11
of Tharshish with the navy of *H* ........ 1Kin 10:22
Now *H* king of Tyre sent ........ 1Chr 14:1
*2. An architect.*
sent and fetched *H* out of Tyre ........ 1Kin 7:13
*H* made the lavers, and the shovels ........ 1Kin 7:40
So *H* made an end of doing all the ........ 1Kin 7:40
which *H* made to king Solomon for ........ 1Kin 7:45

**HIRAM'S** (*hi'-rams*) *Refers to Hiram 1.*
*H* builders did hew them, and the ........ 1Kin 5:18

**HIRE**
Leah said, God hath given me my *h* ... Gen 30:18
and of such shall be my *h* ........ Gen 30:32
come for my *h* before thy face ........ Gen 30:33
The ringstraked shall be thy *h* ........ Gen 31:8
an hired thing, it came for his *h* ........ Ex 22:15
shalt not bring the *h* of a whore ........ Deut 23:18
his day thou shalt give him his *h* ........ Deut 24:15
unto thee will I give *h* for thy ........ 1Kin 5:6
of silver to *h* them chariots ........ 1Chr 19:6
Tyre, and she shall turn to her *h* ........ Is 23:17
her *h* shall be holiness to the ........ Is 23:18
in the balance, and *h* a goldsmith ........ Is 46:6
harlot, in that thou scornest *h* ........ Eze 16:31
also shalt give no *h* any more ........ Eze 16:41
gathered it of the *h* of an harlot ........ Mic 1:7
return to the *h* of an harlot ........ Mic 1:7
the priests thereof teach for *h* ........ Mic 3:11
*h* for man, nor any *h* for beast ........ Zec 8:10
to *h* labourers into his vineyard ........ Mt 20:1
labourers, and give them their *h* ........ Mt 20:8
the labourer is worthy of his *h* ........ Lk 10:7
the *h* of the labourers who have ........ Jas 5:4

**HIRED**
for surely I have *h* thee with my ........ Gen 30:16
an *h* servant shall not eat ........ Ex 12:45
if it be an *h* thing, it came for ........ Ex 22:15
the wages of him that is *h* shall ........ Lev 19:13
or an *h* servant, shall not eat of ........ Lev 22:10
thy maid, and for thy *h* servant ........ Lev 25:6
But as an *h* servant, and as a ........ Lev 25:40
according to the time of an *h* ........ Lev 25:50
as a yearly *h* servant shall he be ........ Lev 25:53
worth a double *h* servant to thee ........ Deut 15:18
because they *h* against thee ........ Deut 23:4
oppress an *h* servant that is poor ........ Deut 24:14
wherewith Abimelech *h* vain ........ Judg 9:4
Micah with me, and hath *h* me ........ Judg 18:4
have *h* out themselves for bread ........ 1Sa 2:5
*h* the Syrians of Beth-rehob, and ........ 2Sa 10:6
the king of Israel hath *h* against ........ 2Kin 7:6
So they *h* thirty and two thousand ........ 1Chr 19:7
*h* masons and carpenters to repair ........ 2Chr 24:12
He *h* also an hundred thousand ........ 2Chr 25:6
*h* counsellors against them, to ........ Ezr 4:5
for Tobiah and Sanballat had *h* him ........ Neh 6:12
Therefore was he *h*, that I should ........ Neh 6:13
but *h* Balaam against them, that ........ Neh 13:2
Lord shave with a razor that is *h* ........ Is 7:20
Also her *h* men are in the midst ........ Jer 46:21
Ephraim hath *h* lovers ........ Hos 8:9
though they have *h* among the ........ Hos 8:10
him, Because no man hath *h* us ........ Mt 20:7
were *h* about the eleventh hour ........ Mt 20:9
in the ship with the *h* servants ........ Mk 1:20
How many *h* servants of my ........ Lk 15:17
make me as one of thy *h* servants ........ Lk 15:19
whole years in his own *h* house ........ Acts 28:30

**HIRELING**
days also like the days of a *h* ........ Job 7:1
as a *h* looketh for the reward of ........ Job 7:2
till he shall accomplish, as an *h* ........ Job 14:6
three years, as the years of an *h* ........ Is 16:14
according to the years of an *h* ........ Is 21:16
that oppress the *h* in his wages ........ Mal 3:5
But he that is an *h*, and not the ........ Jn 10:12
*h* fleeth, because he is an *h* ........ Jn 10:13

**HIRES**
all the *h* thereof shall be burned ........ Mic 1:7

**HIREST**
*h* them, that they may come unto ........ Eze 16:33

**HIS** See PREFACE.

**HISS**
shall be astonished, and shall *h* ........ 1Kin 9:8
shall *h* him out of his place ........ Job 27:23
will *h* unto them from the end of ........ Is 5:26
that the LORD shall *h* for the fly ........ Is 7:18
*h* because of all the plagues ........ Jer 19:8
shall *h* at all the plagues ........ Jer 49:17
and *h* at all her plagues ........ Jer 50:13
they *h* and wag their head at the ........ Lam 2:15
they *h* and gnash the teeth ........ Lam 2:16
among the people shall *h* at thee ........ Eze 27:36
one that passeth by her shall *h* ........ Zeph 2:15
I will *h* for them, and gather them ........ Zec 10:8

**HISSING**
trouble, to astonishment, and to *h* ........ 2Chr 29:8
land desolate, and a perpetual *h* ........ Jer 18:16
make this city desolate, and an *h* ........ Jer 19:8
them an astonishment, and an *h* ........ Jer 25:9
desolation, an astonishment, an *h* ........ Jer 25:18
and an astonishment, and an *h* ........ Jer 29:18
dragons, an astonishment, and an *h* ........ Jer 51:37
and the inhabitants thereof an *h* ........ Mic 6:16

**HIT**
Saul, and the archers *h* him ........ 1Sa 31:3
Saul, and the archers *h* him ........ 1Chr 10:3

**HITHER**
they shall come *h* again ........ Gen 15:16
your youngest brother come *h* ........ Gen 42:15
yourselves, that ye sold me *h* ........ Gen 45:5
now it was not you that sent me *h* ........ Gen 45:8
haste and bring down my father *h* ........ Gen 45:13
And he said, Draw not nigh *h* ........ Ex 3:5
there came men in *h* to night of ........ Josh 2:2
the children of Israel, Come *h* ........ Josh 3:9
and bring the description *h* to me ........ Josh 18:6
Gazites, saying, Samson is come *h* ........ Judg 16:2
said unto him, Who brought thee *h* ........ Judg 18:3
We will not turn aside *h* into the ........ Judg 19:12
unto her, At mealtime come thou *h* ........ Ruth 2:14
Bring *h* a burnt offering to me, ........ 1Sa 13:9
Ahiah, Bring *h* the ark of God ........ 1Sa 14:18
Bring me *h* every man his ox, and ........ 1Sa 14:34
Let us draw near *h* unto God ........ 1Sa 14:36
And Saul said, Draw ye near *h* ........ 1Sa 14:38
Bring ye *h* to me Agag the king of ........ 1Sa 15:32
will not sit down till he come *h* ........ 1Sa 16:11
he said, Why camest thou down *h* ........ 1Sa 17:28
the priest, Bring *h* the ephod ........ 1Sa 23:9
I pray thee, bring me *h* the ephod ........ 1Sa 30:7
have brought them *h* unto my lord ........ 2Sa 1:10
lame, thou shalt not come in *h* ........ 2Sa 5:6
I sent unto thee, saying, Come *h* ........ 2Sa 14:32
pray you, unto Joab, Come near *h* ........ 2Sa 20:16
Hasten *h* Micaiah the son of Imlah ........ 1Kin 22:9
waters, and they were divided *h* ........ 2Kin 2:8
smitten the waters, they parted *h* ........ 2Kin 2:14
saying, The man of God is come *h* ........ 2Kin 8:7
to David, Thou shalt not come *h* ........ 1Chr 11:5
shall not bring in the captives *h* ........ 2Chr 28:13
of Assur, which brought us up *h* ........ Ezr 4:2
Therefore his people return *h* ........ Ps 73:10
bring *h* the timbrel, the pleasant ........ Ps 81:2
is simple, let him turn in *h* ........ Prov 9:4
is simple, let him turn in *h* ........ Prov 9:16
it be said unto thee, Come up *h* ........ Prov 25:7
But draw near *h*, ye sons of the ........ Is 57:3
them unto thee art thou brought *h* ........ Eze 40:4
high God, come forth, and come *h* ........ Dan 3:26
art thou come *h* to torment us ........ Mt 8:29
He said, Bring them *h* to me ........ Mt 14:18
bring him *h* to me ........ Mt 17:17
how camest thou in *h* not having a ........ Mt 22:12
and straightway he will send him *h* ........ Mk 11:3
Bring thy son *h* ........ Lk 9:41
the city, and bring in *h* the poor ........ Lk 14:21
bring *h* the fatted calf, and kill ........ Lk 15:23
I should reign over them, bring *h* ........ Lk 19:27
loose him, and bring him *h* ........ Lk 19:30
not, neither come *h* to draw ........ Jn 4:15
Go, call thy husband, and come *h* ........ Jn 4:16
him, Rabbi, when camest thou *h* ........ Jn 6:25
Reach *h* thy finger, and behold my ........ Jn 20:27
reach *h* thy hand, and thrust it ........ Jn 20:27
came *h* for that intent, that he ........ Acts 9:21
call *h* Simon, whose surname is ........ Acts 10:32
world upside down are come *h* also ........ Acts 17:6
For ye have brought *h* these men ........ Acts 19:37
Therefore, when they were come *h* ........ Acts 25:17
which said, Come up *h*, and I will ........ Rev 4:1
saying unto them, Come up *h* ........ Rev 11:12
with me, saying unto me, Come *h* ........ Rev 17:1
and talked with me, saying, Come *h* ........ Rev 21:9

**HITHERTO**
behold, *h* thou wouldest not hear ........ Ex 7:16
as the LORD hath blessed me *h* ........ Josh 17:14
*H* thou hast mocked me ........ Judg 16:13
and grief have I spoken *h* ........ 1Sa 1:16
*H* hath the LORD helped us ........ 1Sa 7:12
that thou hast brought me *h* ........ 2Sa 7:18
have been thy father's servant *h* ........ 2Sa 15:34
Who *h* waited in the king's gate ........ 1Chr 9:18
for *h* the greatest part of them ........ 1Chr 12:29
that thou hast brought me *h* ........ 1Chr 17:16
*H* shalt thou come, but no further ........ Job 38:11
*h* have I declared thy wondrous ........ Ps 71:17
terrible from their beginning *h* ........ Is 18:2
terrible from their beginning *h* ........ Is 18:7
*H* is the end of the matter ........ Dan 7:28
them, My Father worketh *h* ........ Jn 5:17
*H* have ye asked nothing in my ........ Jn 16:24
to come unto you, (but was let *h* ........ Rom 1:13
for *h* ye were not able to bear it ........ 1Cor 3:2

**HITTITE** (*hit'-tite*) See HITTITES. *A descendant of Heth.*
Ephron the *H* answered Abraham in .. Gen 23:10
of Ephron the son of Zohar the *H* ........ Gen 25:9
the daughter of Beeri the *H* ........ Gen 26:34
the daughter of Elon the *H* ........ Gen 26:34
Adah the daughter of Elon the *H* ........ Gen 36:2
is in the field of Ephron the *H* ........ Gen 49:29
the *H* for a possession of a ........ Gen 49:30
of a buryingplace of Ephron the *H* ........ Gen 50:13
Hivite, the Canaanite, and the *H* ........ Ex 23:28
Canaanite, the Amorite, and the *H* ........ Ex 33:2
and the Canaanite, and the *H* ........ Ex 34:11
sea over against Lebanon, the *H* ........ Josh 9:1
west, and to the Amorite, and the *H* ... Josh 11:3
David and said to Ahimelech the *H* ........ 1Sa 26:6
of Eliam, the wife of Uriah the *H* ........ 2Sa 11:3
Joab, saying, Send me Uriah the *H* ........ 2Sa 11:6
and Uriah the *H* died also ........ 2Sa 11:17
servant Uriah the *H* is dead also ........ 2Sa 11:21
servant Uriah the *H* is dead also ........ 2Sa 11:24
killed Uriah the *H* with the sword ........ 2Sa 12:9
of Uriah the *H* to be thy wife ........ 2Sa 12:10
Uriah the *H*: thirty and seven ........ 2Sa 23:39
only in the matter of Uriah the *H* ........ 1Kin 15:5
Uriah the *H*, Zabad the son of ........ 1Chr 11:41
an Amorite, and thy mother an *H* ........ Eze 16:3
your mother was an *H*, and your ........ Eze 16:45

**HITTITES** (*hit'-tites*)
And the *H*, and the Perizzites, and ........ Gen 15:20
place of the Canaanites, and the *H* ........ Ex 3:8
land of the Canaanites, and the *H* ........ Ex 3:17
land of the Canaanites, and the *H* ........ Ex 13:5
in unto the Amorites, and the *H* ........ Ex 23:23
and the *H*, and the Jebusites, and ........ Num 13:29
many nations before thee, the *H* ........ Deut 7:1
namely, the *H*, and the Amorites, ........ Deut 20:17
Euphrates, all the land of the *H* ........ Josh 1:4
you the Canaanites, and the *H* ........ Josh 3:10
the *H*, the Amorites, and the ........ Josh 12:8
and the Canaanites, and the *H* ........ Josh 24:11
man went into the land of the *H* ........ Judg 1:26
dwelt among the Canaanites, *H* ........ Judg 3:5
that were left of the Amorites, *H* ........ 1Kin 9:20
and so for all the kings of the *H* ........ 1Kin 10:29
Edomites, Zidonians, and *H* ........ 1Kin 11:1
against us the kings of the *H* ........ 2Kin 7:6
horses for all the kings of the *H* ........ 2Chr 1:17
people that were left of the *H* ........ 2Chr 8:7

even of the Canaanites, the *H* ... Ezr 9:1
the land of the Canaanites, the *H* ... Neh 9:8

**HIVITE** (*hi'-vite*) *A descendant of Canaan.*
And the *H*, and the Arkite, and the ... Gen 10:17
Shechem the son of Hamor the *H* ... Gen 34:2
Anah the daughter of Zibeon the *H* ... Gen 36:2
thee, which shall drive out the *H* ... Ex 23:28
Hittite, and the Perizzite, the *H* ... Ex 33:2
and the Perizzite, and the *H* ... Ex 34:11
Canaanite, the Perizzite, the *H* ... Josh 9:1
to the *H* under Hermon in the land ... Josh 11:3
And the *H*, and the Arkite, and the ... 1Chr 1:15

**HIVITES** (*hi'-vites*)
and the Perizzites, and the *H* ... Ex 3:8
and the Perizzites, and the *H* ... Ex 3:17
and the Amorites, and the *H* ... Ex 13:5
and the Canaanites, the *H* ... Ex 23:23
and the Perizzites, and the *H* ... Deut 7:1
and the Perizzites, the *H* ... Deut 20:17
and the Hittites, and the *H* ... Josh 3:10
the men of Israel said unto the *H* ... Josh 9:7
save the *H* the inhabitants of ... Josh 11:19
Canaanites, the Perizzites, the *H* ... Josh 12:8
and the Girgashites, the *H* ... Josh 24:11
the *H* that dwelt in mount Lebanon ... Judg 3:3
and Amorites, and Perizzites, and *H* ... Judg 3:5
and to all the cities of the *H* ... 2Sa 24:7
Amorites, Hittites, Perizzites, *H* ... 1Kin 9:20
and the Perizzites, and the *H* ... 2Chr 8:7

**HIZKI** See HEZEKI.

**HIZKIAH** (*hiz-ki'-ah*) See HEZEKIAH, HIZKIJAH. *An ancestor of Zephaniah.*
the son of Amariah, the son of *H* ... Zeph 1:1

**HIZKIJAH** (*hiz-ki'-jah*) See HIZKIAH. *An Israelite who renewed the covenant.*
Ater, *H*, Azzur, ... Neh 10:17

**HO**
unto whom he said, *H*, such a one ... Ruth 4:1
*H*, every one that thirsteth, come ... Is 55:1
*H*, *h*, come forth, and flee from ... Zec 2:6

**HOAR**
as small as the *h* frost on the ... Ex 16:14
let not his *h* head go down to the ... 1Kin 2:6
but his *h* head bring thou down to ... 1Kin 2:9
scattereth the *h* frost like ashes ... Ps 147:16
even to *h* hairs will I carry you ... Is 46:4

**HOARY**
shalt rise up before the *h* head ... Lev 19:32
the *h* frost of heaven, who hath ... Job 38:29
one would think the deep to be *h* ... Job 41:32
The *h* head is a crown of glory, ... Prov 16:31

**HOBAB** (*ho'-bab*) See JETHRO. *Another name for Jethro.*
And Moses said unto *H*, the son of ... Num 10:29
of *H* the father in law of Moses ... Judg 4:11

**HOBAH** (*ho'-bah*) *Place where Abraham pursued the five kings.*
them, and pursued them unto *H* ... Gen 14:15

**HOBAIAH** See HABAIAH.

**HOD** (*hod*) *A son of Zophah.*
Bezer, and *H*, and Shamma, and ... 1Chr 7:37

**HODAIAH** (*ho-da-i'-ah*) See HODAVIAH. *A royal descendant of Judah.*
And the sons of Elioenai were, *H* ... 1Chr 3:24

**HODAVIAH** (*ho-da-vi'-ah*) See HODAIAH, HODEVAH.
*1. A chief of Manasseh.*
and Azriel, and Jeremiah, and *H* ... 1Chr 5:24
*2. Son of Hassenuah.*
son of Meshullam, the son of *H* ... 1Chr 9:7
*3. A family of exiles.*
and Kadmiel, of the children of *H* ... Ezr 2:40

**HODESH** (*ho'-desh*) *Wife of Shaharaim.*
And he begat of *H* his wife ... 1Chr 8:9

**HODEVAH** (*ho-de'-vah*) See HODAVIAH. *A family of exiles.*
Kadmiel, and of the children of *H* ... Neh 7:43

**HODIAH** (*ho-di'-ah*) See HODIJAH. *A wife of Mered.*
of his wife *H* the sister of Naham ... 1Chr 4:19

**HODIJAH** (*ho-di'-jah*) See HODIAH.
*1. A Levite.*
Jamin, Akkub, Shabbethai, *H* ... Neh 8:7
Bani, Hashabniah, Sherebiah, *H* ... Neh 9:5
And their brethren, Shebaniah, *H* ... Neh 10:10
*H*, Bani, Beninu ... Neh 10:13
*2. A leader of the people.*
*H*, Hashum, Bezai, ... Neh 10:18

**HOGLAH** (*hog'-lah*) See BETH-HOGLAH. *A daughter of Zelophehad.*
were Mahlah, and Noah, *H*, Milcah, .. Num 26:33
Noah, and *H*, and Milcah ... Num 27:1
For Mahlah, Tirzah, and *H*, and ... Num 36:11
his daughters, Mahlah, and Noah, *H* ... Josh 17:3

**HOHAM** (*ho'-ham*) *An Amorite king.*
sent unto *H* king of Hebron ... Josh 10:3

**HOISED**
*h* up the mainsail to the wind, and ... Acts 27:40

**HOLD**
the men laid *h* upon his hand, and ... Gen 19:16
the lad, and *h* him in thine hand ... Gen 21:18
his hand took *h* on Esau's heel ... Gen 25:26
that they may *h* a feast unto me ... Ex 5:1
them go, and wilt *h* them still, ... Ex 9:2
for we must *h* a feast unto the ... Ex 10:9
for you, and ye shall *h* your peace ... Ex 14:14
sorrow shall take *h* on the ... Ex 15:14
trembling shall take *h* upon them ... Ex 15:15
for the LORD will not *h* him ... Ex 20:7
loops may take *h* one of another ... Ex 26:5
father shall *h* his peace at her ... Num 30:4
*h* his peace at her from day to ... Num 30:14
for the LORD will not *h* him ... Deut 5:11
father and his mother lay *h* on him .. Deut 21:19
lay *h* on her, and lie with her, and ... Deut 22:28
and mine hand take *h* on judgment .. Deut 32:41
they entered into an *h* of the ... Judg 9:46
Abimelech, and put them to the *h* ... Judg 9:49
set the *h* on fire upon them ... Judg 9:49
Samson took *h* of the two middle ... Judg 16:29
*H* thy peace, lay thine hand upon ... Judg 18:19
laid *h* on his concubine, and ... Judg 19:29
that thou hast upon thee, and *h* it ... Ruth 3:15
he laid *h* upon the skirt of his ... 1Sa 15:27
the while that David was in the *h* ... 1Sa 22:4
unto David, Abide not in the *h* ... 1Sa 22:5
and his men gat them up unto the *h* ... 1Sa 24:22
Then David took *h* on his clothes ... 2Sa 1:11
lay thee *h* on one of the young ... 2Sa 2:21
how then should I *h* up my face to ... 2Sa 2:22
good tidings, I took *h* of him ... 2Sa 4:10
David took the strong *h* of Zion ... 2Sa 5:7
of it, and went down to the *h* ... 2Sa 5:17
the ark of God, and took *h* of it ... 2Sa 6:6
unto him to eat, he took *h* of her ... 2Sa 13:11
but *h* now thy peace, my sister ... 2Sa 13:20
and his head caught *h* of the oak ... 2Sa 18:9
And David was then in an *h* ... 2Sa 23:14
And came to the strong *h* of Tyre ... 2Sa 24:7
caught *h* on the horns of the ... 1Kin 1:50
he hath caught *h* on the horns of ... 1Kin 1:51
Now therefore *h* him not guiltless ... 1Kin 2:9
caught *h* on the horns of the ... 1Kin 2:28
have taken *h* upon other gods, and ... 1Kin 9:9
the altar, saying, Lay *h* on him ... 1Kin 13:4
*h* ye your peace ... 2Kin 2:3
*h* ye your peace ... 2Kin 2:5
he took *h* of his own clothes, and ... 2Kin 2:12
door, and *h* him fast at the door ... 2Kin 6:32
good tidings, and we *h* our peace ... 2Kin 7:9
And David was then in the *h* ... 1Chr 11:16
*h* to the wilderness men of might ... 1Chr 12:8
and Judah to the *h* unto David ... 1Chr 12:16
put forth his hand to *h* the ark ... 1Chr 13:9
and laid *h* on other gods, and ... 2Chr 7:22
*H* your peace, for the day is holy ... Neh 8:11
shall *h* out the golden sceptre ... Est 4:11
Teach me, and I will *h* my tongue ... Job 6:24
he shall *h* it fast, but it shall ... Job 8:15
that thou wilt not *h* me innocent ... Job 9:28
thy lies make men *h* their peace ... Job 11:3
ye would altogether *h* your peace ... Job 13:5
*H* your peace, let me alone, that ... Job 13:13
if I *h* my tongue, I shall give up ... Job 13:19
righteous also shall *h* on his way ... Job 17:9
and trembling taketh *h* on my flesh ... Job 21:6
My righteousness I *h* fast ... Job 27:6
Terrors take *h* on him as waters, ... Job 27:20
affliction have taken *h* upon me ... Job 30:16
*h* thy peace, and I will speak ... Job 33:31
*h* thy peace, and I shall teach ... Job 33:33
and justice take *h* on thee ... Job 36:17
That it might take *h* of the ends ... Job 38:13
him that layeth at him cannot *h* ... Job 41:26
*H* up my goings in thy paths, that ... Ps 17:5
Take *h* of shield and buckler, and ... Ps 35:2
*h* not thy peace at my tears ... Ps 39:12
iniquities have taken *h* upon me ... Ps 40:12
Fear took *h* upon them there, and ... Ps 48:6
thy wrathful anger take *h* of them ... Ps 69:24
*h* not thy peace, and be not still, ... Ps 83:1
*H* not thy peace, O God of my ... Ps 109:1
the pains of hell gat *h* upon me ... Ps 116:3
Horror hath taken *h* upon me ... Ps 119:53
*H* thou me up, and I shall be safe ... Ps 119:117
and anguish have taken *h* on me ... Ps 119:143
me, and thy right hand shall *h* me ... Ps 139:10
neither take they *h* of the paths ... Prov 2:19
life to them that lay *h* upon her ... Prov 3:18
Take fast *h* of instruction ... Prov 4:13
her steps take *h* on hell ... Prov 5:5
spider taketh *h* with her hands ... Prov 30:28
and her hands *h* the distaff ... Prov 31:19
to lay *h* on folly, till I might ... Eccl 2:3
thou shouldest take *h* of this ... Eccl 7:18
They all *h* swords, being expert ... Song 3:8
I will take *h* of the boughs ... Song 7:8
When a man shall take *h* of his ... Is 3:6
women shall take *h* of one man ... Is 4:1
lay *h* of the prey, and shall carry ... Is 5:29
and sorrows shall take *h* of them ... Is 13:8
pangs have taken *h* upon me ... Is 21:3
Or let him take *h* of my strength ... Is 27:5
over to his strong *h* for fear ... Is 31:9
thy God will *h* thy right hand ... Is 41:13
will *h* thine hand, and will keep ... Is 42:6
son of man that layeth *h* on it ... Is 56:2
me, and take *h* of my covenant ... Is 56:4
it, and taketh *h* of my covenant ... Is 56:6
Zion's sake will I not *h* my peace ... Is 62:1
which shall never *h* their peace ... Is 62:6
up himself to take *h* of thee ... Is 64:7
wilt thou *h* thy peace, and afflict ... Is 64:12
cisterns, that can *h* no water ... Jer 2:13
I cannot *h* my peace, because thou ... Jer 4:19
They shall lay *h* on bow and spear ... Jer 6:23
anguish hath taken *h* of us ... Jer 6:24
they *h* fast deceit, they refuse ... Jer 8:5
astonishment hath taken *h* on me ... Jer 8:21
They shall *h* the bow and the lance ... Jer 50:42
anguish took *h* of him, and pangs ... Jer 50:43
When they took *h* of thee by thy ... Eze 29:7
to make it strong to *h* the sword ... Eze 30:21
about, that they might have *h* ... Eze 41:6
but they had not *h* in the wall of ... Eze 41:6
Then shall he say, *H* thy tongue ... Amos 6:10
the strong *h* of the daughter of ... Mic 4:8
and thou shalt take *h*, but shalt ... Mic 6:14
a strong *h* in the day of trouble ... Nah 1:7
they shall deride every strong *h* ... Hab 1:10
*H* thy peace at the presence of ... Zeph 1:7
they not take *h* of your fathers ... Zec 1:6
that ten men shall take *h* out of ... Zec 8:23
even shall take *h* of the skirt of ... Zec 8:23
did build herself a strong *h* ... Zec 9:3
Turn you to the strong *h*, ye ... Zec 9:12
them, and *h* themselves not guilty ... Zec 11:5
they shall lay *h* every one on the ... Zec 14:13
or else he will *h* to the one ... Mt 6:24
day, will he not lay *h* on it ... Mt 12:11
For Herod had laid *h* on John ... Mt 14:3
because they should *h* their peace ... Mt 20:31
for all *h* John as a prophet ... Mt 21:26
same is he: *h* him fast ... Mt 26:48
the temple, and ye laid no *h* on me ... Mt 26:55
they that had laid *h* on Jesus led ... Mt 26:57
*H* thy peace, and come out of him ... Mk 1:25
it, they went out to lay *h* on him ... Mk 3:21
laid *h* upon John, and bound him in ... Mk 6:17
be, which they have received to *h* ... Mk 7:4
ye *h* the tradition of men, as the ... Mk 7:8
him that he should *h* his peace ... Mk 10:48
And they sought to lay *h* on him ... Mk 12:12
and the young men laid *h* on him ... Mk 14:51
*H* thy peace, and come out of him ... Lk 4:35
or else he will *h* to the one ... Lk 16:13
him, that he should *h* his peace ... Lk 18:39
if these should *h* their peace ... Lk 19:40
they might take *h* of his words ... Lk 20:20
they could not take *h* of his ... Lk 20:26
they laid *h* upon one Simon, a ... Lk 23:26
put them in *h* unto the next day ... Acts 4:3
with the hand to *h* their peace ... Acts 12:17
but speak, and *h* not thy peace ... Acts 18:9
of men, who *h* the truth in ... Rom 1:18
by, let the first *h* his peace ... 1Cor 14:30
and *h* such in reputation ... Phil 2:29
*h* fast that which is good ... 1Th 5:21
*h* the traditions which ye have ... 2Th 2:15
lay *h* on eternal life, whereunto ... 1Ti 6:12
they may lay *h* on eternal life ... 1Ti 6:19
*H* fast the form of sound words, ... 2Ti 1:13
if we *h* fast the confidence and ... Heb 3:6
if we *h* the beginning of our ... Heb 3:14
let us *h* fast our profession ... Heb 4:14
lay *h* upon the hope set before us ... Heb 6:18
Let us *h* fast the profession of ... Heb 10:23
that *h* the doctrine of Balaam ... Rev 2:14
them that *h* the doctrine of the ... Rev 2:15
have already *h* fast till I come ... Rev 2:25
and heard, and *h* fast, and repent ... Rev 3:3
*h* that fast which thou hast, that ... Rev 3:11
the *h* of every foul spirit, and a ... Rev 18:2
he laid *h* on the dragon, that old ... Rev 20:2

**HOLDEN**
Surely there was not *h* such a ... 2Kin 23:22
was *h* to the LORD in Jerusalem ... 2Kin 23:23
be *h* in cords of affliction ... Job 36:8
and thy right hand hath *h* me up ... Ps 18:35
have I been *h* up from the womb ... Ps 71:6
thou hast *h* me by my right hand ... Ps 73:23
he shall be *h* with the cords of ... Prov 5:22
I have long time *h* my peace ... Is 42:14
Cyrus, whose right hand I have *h* ... Is 45:1
But their eyes were *h* that they ... Lk 24:16
that he should be *h* of it ... Acts 2:24
Yea, he shall be *h* up ... Rom 14:4

**HOLDEST**
*h* thy peace at this time, then ... Est 4:14
thy face, and *h* me for thine enemy ... Job 13:24
Thou *h* mine eyes waking ... Ps 77:4
that *h* the height of the hill ... Jer 49:16
*h* thy tongue when the wicked ... Hab 1:13
thou *h* fast my name, and hast not ... Rev 2:13

**HOLDETH**
still he *h* fast his integrity, ... Job 2:3
He *h* back the face of his throne, ... Job 26:9
Which *h* our soul in life, and ... Ps 66:9
man of understanding *h* his peace ... Prov 11:12
when he *h* his peace, is counted ... Prov 17:28
there is none that *h* with me in ... Dan 10:21
him that *h* the sceptre from the ... Amos 1:5

him that *h* the sceptre from ... Amos 1:8
These things saith he that *h* the ... Rev 2:1

**HOLDING**
his hands from *h* of bribes ... Is 33:15
I am weary with *h* in ... Jer 6:11
*h* the tradition of the elders ... Mk 7:3
*H* forth the word of life ... Phil 2:16
not *h* the Head, from which all ... Col 2:19
*H* faith, and a good conscience ... 1Ti 1:19
*H* the mystery of the faith in a ... 1Ti 3:9
*H* fast the faithful word as he ... Titus 1:9
*h* the four winds of the earth, ... Rev 7:1

**HOLDS**
whether in tents, or in strong *h* ... Num 13:19
mountains, and caves, and strong *h* ... Judg 6:2
in the wilderness in strong *h* ... 1Sa 23:14
with us in strong *h* in the wood ... 1Sa 23:19
and dwelt in strong *h* at En-gedi ... 1Sa 23:29
their strong *h* wilt thou set on ... 2Kin 8:12
And he fortified the strong *h* ... 2Chr 11:11
hast brought his strong *h* to ruin ... Ps 89:40
to destroy the strong *h* thereof ... Is 23:11
and he shall destroy thy strong *h* ... Jer 48:18
the strong *h* are surprised, and ... Jer 48:41
they have remained in their *h* ... Jer 51:30
strong *h* of the daughter of Judah ... Lam 2:2
he hath destroyed his strong *h* ... Lam 2:5
they brought him into *h*, that his ... Eze 19:9
his devices against the strong *h* ... Dan 11:24
most strong *h* with a strange god ... Dan 11:39
and throw down all thy strong *h* ... Mic 5:11
All thy strong *h* shall be like ... Nah 3:12
the siege, fortify thy strong *h* ... Nah 3:14
to the pulling down of strong *h* ... 2Cor 10:4

**HOLE**
shall be an *h* in the top of it ... Ex 28:32
work round about the *h* of it ... Ex 28:32
as it were the *h* of an habergeon, ... Ex 28:32
there was an *h* in the midst of ... Ex 39:23
as the *h* of an habergeon, with a ... Ex 39:23
with a band round about the *h* ... Ex 39:23
bored a *h* in the lid of it, and ... 2Kin 12:9
in his hand by the *h* of the door ... Song 5:4
shall play on the *h* of the asp ... Is 11:8
to the *h* of the pit whence ye are ... Is 51:1
hide it there in a *h* of the rock ... Jer 13:4
I looked, behold a *h* in the wall ... Eze 8:7

**HOLE'S**
nest in the sides of the *h* mouth ... Jer 48:28

**HOLES**
*h* where they had hid themselves ... 1Sa 14:11
shall go into the *h* of the rocks ... Is 2:19
in the *h* of the rocks, and upon ... Is 7:19
they are all of them snared in *h* ... Is 42:22
out of the *h* of the rocks ... Jer 16:16
their *h* like worms of the earth ... Mic 7:17
and filled his *h* with prey ... Nah 2:12
wages to put it into a bag with *h* ... Hag 1:6
shall consume away in their *h* ... Zec 14:12
saith unto him, The foxes have *h* ... Mt 8:20
Jesus said unto him, Foxes have *h* ... Lk 9:58

**HOLIER**
for I am *h* than thou ... Is 65:5

**HOLIEST**
which is called the *H* of all ... Heb 9:3
that the way into the *h* of all ... Heb 9:8
into the *h* by the blood of Jesus ... Heb 10:19

**HOLILY**
are witnesses, and God also, how *h* ... 1Th 2:10

**HOLINESS**
Who is like thee, glorious in *h* ... Ex 15:11
of a signet, *H* TO THE LORD ... Ex 28:36
of a signet, *H* TO THE LORD ... Ex 39:30
the LORD in the beauty of *h* ... 1Chr 16:29
should praise the beauty of *h* ... 2Chr 20:21
they sanctified themselves in *h* ... 2Chr 31:18
the LORD in the beauty of *h* ... Ps 29:2
at the remembrance of his *h* ... Ps 30:4
sitteth upon the throne of his *h* ... Ps 47:8
our God, in the mountain of his *h* ... Ps 48:1
God hath spoken in his *h* ... Ps 60:6
Once have I sworn by my *h* that I ... Ps 89:35
*h* becometh thine house, O LORD, ... Ps 93:5
the LORD in the beauty of *h* ... Ps 96:9
at the remembrance of his *h* ... Ps 97:12
God hath spoken in his *h* ... Ps 108:7
in the beauties of *h* from the ... Ps 110:3
her hire shall be *h* to the LORD ... Is 23:18
it shall be called The way of *h* ... Is 35:8
drink it in the courts of my *h* ... Is 62:9
from the habitation of thy *h* ... Is 63:15
The people of thy *h* have ... Is 63:18
Israel was *h* unto the LORD, and ... Jer 2:3
and because of the words of his *h* ... Jer 23:9
of justice, and mountain of *h* ... Jer 31:23
The Lord GOD hath sworn by his *h* ... Amos 4:2
deliverance, and there shall be *h* ... Obad 17
of the horses, *H* UNTO THE LORD ... Zec 14:20
in Judah shall be *h* unto the LORD ... Zec 14:21
of the LORD which he loved ... Mal 2:11
In *h* and righteousness before him, ... Lk 1:75
or *h* we had made this man to walk ... Acts 3:12
according to the spirit of *h* ... Rom 1:4
servants to righteousness unto *h* ... Rom 6:19
to God, ye have your fruit unto *h* ... Rom 6:22
perfecting *h* in the fear of God ... 2Cor 7:1
in righteousness and true *h* ... Eph 4:24
unblameable in *h* before God ... 1Th 3:13
us unto uncleanness, but unto *h* ... 1Th 4:7
and charity and *h* with sobriety ... 1Ti 2:15
be in behaviour as becometh *h* ... Titus 2:3
we might be partakers of his *h* ... Heb 12:10
Follow peace with all men, and *h* ... Heb 12:14

**HOLLOW**
he touched the *h* of his thigh ... Gen 32:25
the *h* of Jacob's thigh was out of ... Gen 32:25
which is upon the *h* of the thigh ... Gen 32:32
because he touched the *h* of ... Gen 32:32
*H* with boards shalt thou make it ... Ex 27:8
he made the altar *h* with boards ... Ex 38:7
walls of the house with *h* strakes ... Lev 14:37
But God clave an *h* place that was ... Judg 15:19
the waters in the *h* of his hand ... Is 40:12
was four fingers: it was *h* ... Jer 52:21

**HOLON** (*ho'-lon*) See HILEN.
*1. A Levitical city in Judah.*
And Goshen, and *H*, and Giloh ... Josh 15:51
*H* with her suburbs, and Debir with ... Josh 21:15
*2. A Moabite city.*
upon *H*, and upon Jahazah, and upon .. Jer 48:21

**HOLPEN**
they have *h* the children of Lot ... Ps 83:8
because thou, LORD, hast *h* me ... Ps 86:17
he that is *h* shall fall down, and ... Is 31:3
they shall be *h* with a little ... Dan 11:34
He hath *h* his servant Israel, in ... Lk 1:54

**HOLY** See PREFACE.
whereon thou standest is *h* ground ... Ex 3:5
the sabbath day, to keep it *h* ... Ex 20:8
for it is *h* unto you ... Ex 31:14
ye may put difference between *h* ... Lev 10:10
yourselves, and ye shall be *h* ... Lev 11:44
yourselves therefore, and be ye *h* ... Lev 20:7
place whereon thou standest is *h* ... Josh 5:15
There is none *h* as the LORD ... 1Sa 2:2
that this is an *h* man of God ... 2Kin 4:9
he will hear him from his *h* ... Ps 20:6
his ways, and *h* in all his works ... Ps 145:17
another, and said, *H*, *h*, *h* ... Is 6:3
LORD in the *h* mount at Jerusalem ... Is 27:13
his *h* arm in the eyes of all the ... Is 52:10
doing thy pleasure on my *h* day ... Is 58:13
put no difference between the *h* ... Eze 22:26
in her is of the *H* Ghost ... Mt 1:20
baptize you with the *H* Ghost ... Mt 3:11
not that which is *h* unto the dogs ... Mt 7:6
baptize you with the *H* Ghost ... Mk 1:8
of his Father with the *h* angels ... Mk 8:38
shall be filled with the *H* Ghost ... Lk 1:15
The *H* Ghost shall come upon thee, ... Lk 1:35
therefore also that *h* thing which ... Lk 1:35
baptize you with the *H* Ghost ... Lk 3:16
Jesus being full of the *H* Ghost ... Lk 4:1
the *H* One of God ... Lk 4:34
his Father's, and of the *h* angels ... Lk 9:26
which baptizeth with the *H* Ghost ... Jn 1:33
for the *H* Ghost was not yet given ... Jn 7:39
unto them, Receive ye the *H* Ghost ... Jn 20:22
the *H* Ghost not many days hence ... Acts 1:5
were all filled with the *H* Ghost ... Acts 2:4
receive the gift of the *H* Ghost ... Acts 2:38
thine heart to lie to the *H* Ghost ... Acts 5:3
where thou standest is *h* ground ... Acts 7:33
ye do always resist the *H* Ghost ... Acts 7:51
of Nazareth with the *H* Ghost ... Acts 10:38
For it seemed good to the *H* Ghost ... Acts 15:28
Have ye received the *H* Ghost ... Acts 19:2
be *h*, the lump is also *h* ... Rom 11:16
your bodies a living sacrifice, *h* ... Rom 12:1
and peace, and joy in the *H* Ghost ... Rom 14:17
of the world, that we should be *h* ... Eph 1:4
but that it should be *h* and ... Eph 5:27
through death, to present you *h* ... Col 1:22
every where, lifting up *h* hands ... 1Ti 2:8
and called us with an *h* calling ... 2Ti 1:9
high priest became us, who is *h* ... Heb 7:26
so be ye *h* in all manner of ... 1Pet 1:15
an *h* priesthood, to offer up ... 1Pet 2:5
ye to be in all *h* conversation ... 2Pet 3:11
These things saith he that is *h* ... Rev 3:7
that is *h*, let him be *h* still ... Rev 22:11

**HOLYDAY**
with a multitude that kept *h* ... Ps 42:4
in drink, or in respect of an *h* ... Col 2:16

**HOMAM** (*ho'-mam*) See HEMAM. *A son of Lotan.*
of Lotan; Hori, and *H* ... 1Chr 1:39

**HOME**
by her, until his lord came *h* ... Gen 39:16
of his house, Bring these men *h* ... Gen 43:16
And when Joseph came *h*, they ... Gen 43:26
field, and shall not be brought *h* ... Ex 9:19
mother, whether she be born at *h* ... Lev 18:9
shalt bring her *h* to thine house ... Deut 21:12
he shall be free at *h* one year ... Deut 24:5
father's household, *h* unto thee ... Josh 2:18
If ye bring me *h* again to fight ... Judg 11:9
your way, that thou mayest go *h* ... Judg 19:9
hath brought me *h* again empty ... Ruth 1:21
And they went unto their own *h* ... 1Sa 2:20
and bring their calves *h* from them ... 1Sa 6:7
and shut up their calves at *h* ... 1Sa 6:10
And Saul also went *h* to Gibeah ... 1Sa 10:26
no more *h* to his father's house ... 1Sa 18:2
And Saul went *h* ... 1Sa 24:22
Then David sent *h* to Tamar ... 2Sa 13:7
not fetch *h* again his banished ... 2Sa 14:13
gat him *h* to his house, to his ... 2Sa 17:23
in Lebanon, and two months at *h* ... 1Kin 5:14
Come *h* with me, and refresh ... 1Kin 13:7
Come *h* with me, and eat bread ... 1Kin 13:15
glory of this, and tarry at *h* ... 2Kin 14:10
I bring the ark of God *h* to me ... 1Chr 13:12
So David brought not the ark *h* to ... 1Chr 13:13
him out of Ephraim, to go *h* again ... 2Chr 25:10
they returned *h* in great anger ... 2Chr 25:10
abide now at *h* ... 2Chr 25:19
and when he came *h*, he sent and ... Est 5:10
that he will bring *h* thy seed ... Job 39:12
tarried at *h* divided the spoil ... Ps 68:12
For the goodman is not at *h* ... Prov 7:19
will come *h* at the day appointed ... Prov 7:20
because man goeth to his long *h* ... Eccl 12:5
that he should carry him *h* ... Jer 39:14
bereaveth, at *h* there is as death ... Lam 1:20
a proud man, neither keepeth at *h* ... Hab 2:5
and when ye brought it *h*, I did ... Hag 1:9
lieth at *h* sick of the palsy ... Mt 8:6
Go *h* to thy friends, and tell them ... Mk 5:19
which are at *h* at my house ... Lk 9:61
And when he cometh *h*, he calleth ... Lk 15:6
disciple took her unto his own *h* ... Jn 19:27
went away again unto their own *h* ... Jn 20:10
and they returned *h* again ... Acts 21:6
any man hunger, let him eat at *h* ... 1Cor 11:34
let them ask their husbands at *h* ... 1Cor 14:35
whilst we are at *h* in the body ... 2Cor 5:6
learn first to shew piety at *h* ... 1Ti 5:4
be discreet, chaste, keepers at *h* ... Titus 2:5

**HOMEBORN**
One law shall be to him that is *h* ... Ex 12:49
is he a *h* slave? ... Jer 2:14

**HOMER**
a *h* of barley seed shall be ... Lev 27:16
the seed of an *h* shall yield an ... Is 5:10
contain the tenth part of an *h* ... Eze 45:11
the ephah the tenth part of an *h* ... Eze 45:11
thereof shall be after the *h* ... Eze 45:11
part of an ephah of an *h* of wheat ... Eze 45:13
of an ephah of an *h* of barley ... Eze 45:13
which is an *h* of ten baths ... Eze 45:14
for ten baths are an *h* ... Eze 45:14
an *h* of barley, and an half *h* ... Hos 3:2

**HOMERS**
gathered least gathered ten *h* ... Num 11:32

**HONEST**
ground are they, which in an *h* ... Lk 8:15
among you seven men of *h* report ... Acts 6:3
Provide things *h* in the sight of ... Rom 12:17
Providing for *h* things, not only ... 2Cor 8:21
that ye should do that which is *h* ... 2Cor 13:7
are true, whatsoever things are *h* ... Phil 4:8
conversation *h* among the Gentiles ... 1Pet 2:12

**HONESTLY**
Let us walk *h*, as in the day ... Rom 13:13
That ye may walk *h* toward them ... 1Th 4:12
in all things willing to live *h* ... Heb 13:18

**HONESTY**
life in all godliness and *h* ... 1Ti 2:2

**HONEY**
a little balm, and a little *h* ... Gen 43:11
a land flowing with milk and *h* ... Ex 3:8
a land flowing with milk and *h* ... Ex 3:17
a land flowing with milk and *h* ... Ex 13:5
of it was like wafers made with *h* ... Ex 16:31
a land flowing with milk and *h* ... Ex 33:3
shall burn no leaven, nor any *h* ... Lev 2:11
land that floweth with milk and *h* ... Lev 20:24
surely it floweth with milk and *h* ... Num 13:27
land which floweth with milk and *h* ... Num 14:8
land that floweth with milk and *h* ... Num 16:13
land that floweth with milk and *h* ... Num 16:14
land that floweth with milk and *h* ... Deut 6:3
a land of oil olive, and *h* ... Deut 8:8
land that floweth with milk and *h* ... Deut 11:9
land that floweth with milk and *h* ... Deut 26:9
land that floweth with milk and *h* ... Deut 26:15
land that floweth with milk and *h* ... Deut 27:3
that floweth with milk and *h* ... Deut 31:20
him to suck *h* out of the rock ... Deut 32:13
land that floweth with milk and *h* ... Josh 5:6
*h* in the carcase of the lion ... Judg 14:8
*h* out of the carcase of the lion ... Judg 14:9
went down, What is sweeter than *h* .. Judg 14:18
there was *h* upon the ground ... 1Sa 14:25
the wood, behold, the *h* dropped ... 1Sa 14:26
I tasted a little of this *h* ... 1Sa 14:29
I did but taste a little *h* with ... 1Sa 14:43
And *h*, and butter, and sheep, and ... 2Sa 17:29
and cracknels, and a cruse of *h* ... 1Kin 14:3
a land of oil olive and of *h* ... 2Kin 18:32
of corn, wine, and oil, and *h* ... 2Chr 31:5
the floods, the brooks of *h* ... Job 20:17
sweeter also than *h* and the ... Ps 19:10
with *h* out of the rock should I ... Ps 81:16
yea, sweeter than *h* to my mouth ... Ps 119:103
My son, eat thou *h*, because it is ... Prov 24:13

Hast thou found *h*? Prov 25:16
It is not good to eat much *h* Prov 25:27
*h* and milk are under thy tongue Song 4:11
have eaten my honeycomb with my *h*. Song 5:1
*h* shall he eat, that he may know Is 7:15
*h* shall every one eat that is Is 7:22
a land flowing with milk and *h* Jer 11:5
a land flowing with milk and *h* Jer 32:22
and of barley, and of oil, and of *h* Jer 41:8
in my mouth as *h* for sweetness Eze 3:3
thou didst eat fine flour, and *h* Eze 16:13
thee, fine flour, and oil, and *h* Eze 16:19
for them, flowing with milk and *h* Eze 20:6
them, flowing with milk and *h* Eze 20:15
wheat of Minnith, and Pannag, and *h*. Eze 27:17
and his meat was locusts and wild *h* Mt 3:4
and he did eat locusts and wild *h* Mk 1:6
shall be in thy mouth sweet as *h* Rev 10:9
and it was in my mouth sweet as *h* Rev 10:10

## HONEYCOMB

in his hand, and dipped it in an *h* 1Sa 14:27
sweeter also than honey and the *h* Ps 19:10
of a strange woman drop as an *h* Prov 5:3
Pleasant words are as an *h* Prov 16:24
and the *h*, which is sweet to thy Prov 24:13
The full soul loatheth an *h* Prov 27:7
lips, O my spouse, drop as the *h* Song 4:11
I have eaten my *h* with my honey Song 5:1
of a broiled fish, and of an *h* Lk 24:42

## HONOUR

unto their assembly, mine *h* Gen 49:6
and I will get me *h* upon Pharaoh Ex 14:17
I have gotten me *h* upon Pharaoh Ex 14:18
*H* thy father and thy mother Ex 20:12
nor *h* the person of the mighty Lev 19:15
*h* the face of the old man, and Lev 19:32
promote thee unto very great *h* Num 22:17
able indeed to promote thee to *h* Num 22:37
to promote thee unto great *h* Num 24:11
LORD hath kept thee back from *h* Num 24:11
put some of thine *h* upon him Num 27:20
*H* thy father and thy mother, as Deut 5:16
in praise, and in name, and in *h* Deut 26:19
takest shall not be for thine *h* Judg 4:9
wherewith by me they *h* God Judg 9:9
come to pass we may do thee *h* Judg 13:17
for them that *h* me I will *h*, 1Sa 2:30
yet *h* me now, I pray thee, before 1Sa 15:30
of, of them shall I be had in *h* 2Sa 6:22
thou that David doth *h* thy father 2Sa 10:3
hast not asked, both riches, and *h* 1Kin 3:13
Glory and *h* are in his presence 1Chr 16:27
to thee for the *h* of thy servant 1Chr 17:18
thou that David doth *h* thy father 1Chr 19:3
*h* come of thee, and thou reignest 1Chr 29:12
age, full of days, riches, and *h* 1Chr 29:28
not asked riches, wealth, or *h* 2Chr 1:11
give thee riches, and wealth, and *h* 2Chr 1:12
he had riches and *h* in abundance 2Chr 17:5
*h* in abundance, and joined 2Chr 18:1
be for thine *h* from the LORD God 2Chr 26:18
had exceeding much riches and *h* 2Chr 32:27
Jerusalem did him *h* at his death 2Chr 32:33
the *h* of his excellent majesty Est 1:4
shall give to their husbands *h* Est 1:20
And the king said, What *h* and Est 6:3
man whom the king delighteth to *h* Est 6:6
to do *h* more than to myself Est 6:6
man whom the king delighteth to *h* Est 6:7
whom the king delighteth to *h* Est 6:9
man whom the king delighteth to *h* Est 6:9
man whom the king delighteth to *h* Est 6:11
light, and gladness, and joy, and *h* Est 8:16
His sons come to *h*, and he knoweth Job 14:21
earth, and lay mine *h* in the dust Ps 7:5
hast crowned him with glory and *h* Ps 8:5
*h* and majesty hast thou laid upon Ps 21:5
the place where thine *h* dwelleth Ps 26:8
man being in *h* abideth not Ps 49:12
Man that is in *h*, and Ps 49:20
Sing forth the *h* of his name Ps 66:2
praise and with thy *h* all the day Ps 71:8
I will deliver him, and *h* him Ps 91:15
*H* and majesty are before him Ps 96:6
thou art clothed with *h* and Ps 104:1
his horn shall be exalted with *h* Ps 112:9
of the glorious *h* of thy majesty Ps 145:5
this *h* have all his saints Ps 149:9
*H* the LORD with thy substance, and Prov 3:9
and in her left hand riches and *h* Prov 3:16
she shall bring thee to *h* Prov 4:8
thou give thine *h* unto others Prov 5:9
Riches and *h* are with me Prov 8:18
A gracious woman retaineth *h* Prov 11:16
of people is the king's *h* Prov 14:28
and before *h* is humility Prov 15:33
and before *h* is humility Prov 18:12
It is an *h* for a man to cease Prov 20:3
findeth life, righteousness, and *h* Prov 21:21
fear of the LORD are riches, and *h* Prov 22:4
but the *h* of kings is to search Prov 25:2
so *h* is not seemly for a fool Prov 26:1
so is he that giveth *h* to a fool Prov 26:8
but *h* shall uphold the humble in Prov 29:23
Strength and *h* are her clothing Prov 31:25
hath given riches, wealth, and *h* Eccl 6:2
is in reputation for wisdom and *h* Eccl 10:1
mouth, and with their lips do *h* me Is 29:13
The beast of the field shall *h* me Is 43:20
and shalt *h* him, not doing thine Is 58:13
an *h* before all the nations of Jer 33:9
of me gifts and rewards and great *h* Dan 2:6
power, and for the *h* of my majesty Dan 4:30
the glory of my kingdom, mine *h* Dan 4:36
*h* the King of heaven, all whose Dan 4:37
and majesty, and glory, and *h* Dan 5:18
not give the *h* of the kingdom Dan 11:21
shall he *h* the God of forces Dan 11:38
knew not shall he *h* with gold Dan 11:38
I be a father, where is mine *h* Mal 1:6
them, A prophet is not without *h* Mt 13:57
saying, *H* thy father and mother Mt 15:4
*h* not his father or his mother, Mt 15:6
*H* thy father and thy mother Mt 19:19
them, A prophet is not without *h* Mk 6:4
*H* thy father and thy mother Mk 7:10
not, *H* thy father and mother Mk 10:19
*H* thy father and thy mother Lk 18:20
hath no *h* in his own country Jn 4:44
That all men should *h* the Son Jn 5:23
even as they *h* the Father Jn 5:23
I receive not *h* from men Jn 5:41
which receive *h* one of another, Jn 5:44
seek not the *h* that cometh from Jn 5:44
but I *h* my Father, and ye do Jn 8:49
I *h* myself, my *h* is nothing Jn 8:54
serve me, him will my Father *h* Jn 12:26
in well doing seek for glory and *h* Rom 2:7
But glory, *h*, and peace, to every Rom 2:10
lump to make one vessel unto *h* Rom 9:21
in *h* preferring one another Rom 12:10
to whom fear; *h* to whom *h* Rom 13:7
these we bestow more abundant *h* 1Cor 12:23
*h* to that part which lacked 1Cor 12:24
By *h* and dishonour, by evil report 2Cor 6:8
*H* thy father and mother Eph 6:2
not in any *h* to the satisfying of Col 2:23
his vessel in sanctification and *h* 1Th 4:4
the only wise God, be *h* and glory 1Ti 1:17
*H* widows that are widows indeed 1Ti 5:3
be counted worthy of double *h* 1Ti 5:17
their own masters worthy of all *h* 1Ti 6:1
to whom be *h* and power everlasting 1Ti 6:16
and some to *h*, and some to 2Ti 2:20
he shall be a vessel unto *h* 2Ti 2:21
crownedst him with glory and *h* Heb 2:7
of death, crowned with glory and *h* Heb 2:9
house hath more *h* than the house Heb 3:3
no man taketh this *h* unto himself Heb 5:4
might be found unto praise and *h* 1Pet 1:7
*H* all men 1Pet 2:17
*H* the king 1Pet 2:17
giving *h* unto the wife, as unto 1Pet 3:7
he received from God the Father *h* 2Pet 1:17
when those beasts give glory and *h* Rev 4:9
O Lord, to receive glory and *h* Rev 4:11
and wisdom, and strength, and *h* Rev 5:12
heard I saying, Blessing, and *h* Rev 5:13
and wisdom, and thanksgiving, and *h* Rev 7:12
Salvation, and glory, and *h* Rev 19:1
glad and rejoice, and give *h* to him Rev 19:7
do bring their glory and *h* into it Rev 21:24
glory and *h* of the nations into it Rev 21:26

## HONOURABLE

he was more *h* than all the house Gen 34:19
more, and more *h* than they Num 22:15
a man of God, and he is an *h* man 1Sa 9:6
bidding, and is *h* in thine house 1Sa 22:14
Was he not most *h* of three 2Sa 23:19
He was more *h* than the thirty, 2Sa 23:23
a great man with his master, and *h* 2Kin 5:1
Jabez was more *h* than his 1Chr 4:9
he was more *h* than the two 1Chr 11:21
he was *h* among the thirty, but 1Chr 11:25
and the *h* man dwelt in it Job 22:8
daughters were among thy *h* women Ps 45:9
His work is *h* and glorious Ps 111:3
captain of fifty, and the *h* man Is 3:3
and the base against the *h* Is 3:5
their *h* men are famished, and Is 5:13
The ancient and *h*, he is the head Is 9:15
are the *h* of the earth Is 23:8
contempt all the *h* of the earth Is 23:9
magnify the law, and make it *h* Is 42:21
in my sight, thou hast been *h* Is 43:4
delight, the holy of the LORD, *h* Is 58:13
and they cast lots for her *h* men Nah 3:10
an *h* counsellor, which also Mk 15:43
lest a more *h* man than thou be Lk 14:8
*h* women, and the chief men of the Acts 13:50
also of *h* women which were Greeks. Acts 17:12
ye are *h*, but we are despised 1Cor 4:10
body, which we think to be less *h* 1Cor 12:23
Marriage is *h* in all, and the bed Heb 13:4

## HONOURED

I will be *h* upon Pharaoh, and upon Ex 14:4
that regardeth reproof shall be *h* Prov 13:18
waiteth on his master shall be *h* Prov 27:18
neither hast thou *h* me with thy Is 43:23
all that *h* her despise her, Lam 1:8
the faces of elders were not *h* Lam 5:12
*h* him that liveth for ever, whose Dan 4:34
Who also *h* us with many honours Acts 28:10
or one member be *h*, all the 1Cor 12:26

## HONOUREST

*h* thy sons above me, to make 1Sa 2:29

## HONOURETH

but he *h* them that fear the LORD Ps 15:4
is better than he that *h* himself Prov 12:9
but he that *h* him hath mercy on Prov 14:31
A son *h* his father, and a servant Mal 1:6
mouth, and *h* me with their lips Mt 15:8
This people *h* me with their lips, Mk 7:6
He that *h* not the Son *h* not Jn 5:23
it is my Father that *h* me Jn 8:54

## HONOURS

Who also honoured us with many *h*. Acts 28:10

## HOODS

and the fine linen, and the *h* Is 3:23

## HOOF

shall not an *h* be left behind Ex 10:26
Whatsoever parteth the *h*, and is Lev 11:3
cud, or of them that divide the *h* Lev 11:4
the cud, but divideth not the *h* Lev 11:4
the cud, but divideth not the *h* Lev 11:5
the cud, but divideth not the *h* Lev 11:6
the swine, though he divide the *h* Lev 11:7
every beast which divideth the *h* Lev 11:26
And every beast that parteth the *h* Deut 14:6
of them that divide the cloven *h* Deut 14:7
the cud, but divide not the *h* Deut 14:7
swine, because it divideth the *h* Deut 14:8

## HOOFS

or bullock that hath horns and *h* Ps 69:31
their horses' *h* shall be counted Is 5:28
of the *h* of his strong horses Jer 47:3
With the *h* of his horses shall he Eze 26:11
nor the *h* of beasts trouble them Eze 32:13
iron, and I will make thy *h* brass Mic 4:13



## HOOK

I will put my *h* in thy nose 2Kin 19:28
thou draw out leviathan with an *h* Job 41:1
Canst thou put an *h* into his nose Job 41:2
will I put my *h* in thy nose Is 37:29
go thou to the sea, and cast an *h* Mt 17:27

## HOOKS

their *h* shall be of gold, upon Ex 26:32
gold, and their *h* shall be of gold Ex 26:37
the *h* of the pillars and their Ex 27:10
the *h* of the pillars and their Ex 27:11
their *h* shall be of silver, and Ex 27:17
their *h* were of gold Ex 36:36
five pillars of it with their *h* Ex 36:38
the *h* of the pillars and their Ex 38:10
the *h* of the pillars and their Ex 38:11
the *h* of the pillars and their Ex 38:12
the *h* of the pillars and their Ex 38:17
their *h* of silver, and the Ex 38:19
shekels he made *h* for the pillars Ex 38:28
But I will put *h* in thy jaws Eze 29:4
put *h* into thy jaws, and I will Eze 38:4
And within were *h*, an hand broad, Eze 40:43
that he will take you away with *h* Amos 4:2

## HOPE

If I should say, I have *h* Ruth 1:12
yet now there is *h* in Israel Ezr 10:2
thy fear, thy confidence, thy *h* Job 4:6
So the poor hath *h*, and iniquity Job 5:16
is my strength, that I should *h* Job 6:11
shuttle, and are spent without *h* Job 7:6
and the hypocrite's *h* shall perish Job 8:13
Whose *h* shall be cut off, and Job 8:14
be secure, because there is *h* Job 11:18
their *h* shall be as the giving up Job 11:20
For there is *h* of a tree, if it Job 14:7
and thou destroyest the *h* of man Job 14:19
And where is now my *h* Job 17:15
as for my *h*, who shall see it Job 17:15
mine *h* hath he removed like a Job 19:10
For what is the *h* of the Job 27:8
If I have made gold my *h*, or have Job 31:24
Behold, the *h* of him is in vain Job 41:9
my flesh also shall rest in *h* Ps 16:9
thou didst make me *h* when I was Ps 22:9
heart, all ye that *h* in the LORD Ps 31:24
upon them that *h* in his mercy Ps 33:18
us, according as we *h* in thee Ps 33:22
For in thee, O LORD, do I *h* Ps 38:15
my *h* is in thee Ps 39:7
*h* thou in God Ps 42:5
*h* thou in God Ps 42:11
*h* in God Ps 43:5
For thou art my *h*, O Lord GOD Ps 71:5
But I will *h* continually, and will Ps 71:14
they might set their *h* in God Ps 78:7
which thou hast caused me to *h* Ps 119:49
but I *h* in thy word Ps 119:81
I *h* in thy word Ps 119:114
and let me not be ashamed of my *h* Ps 119:116
doth wait, and in his word do I *h* Ps 130:5
Let Israel *h* in the LORD Ps 130:7
Let Israel *h* in the LORD from Ps 131:3
whose *h* is in the LORD his God Ps 146:5
him, in those that *h* in his mercy Ps 147:11
The *h* of the righteous shall be Prov 10:28
the *h* of unjust men perisheth Prov 11:7
*H* deferred maketh the heart sick, Prov 13:12
the righteous hath *h* in his death Prov 14:32
Chasten thy son while there is *h* Prov 19:18
there is more *h* of a fool than of Prov 26:12
there is more *h* of a fool than of Prov 29:20
to all the living there is *h* Eccl 9:4
the pit cannot *h* for thy truth Is 38:18
saidst thou not, There is no *h* Is 57:10
but thou saidst, There is no *h* Jer 2:25
O the *h* of Israel, the saviour Jer 14:8

the LORD, and whose *h* the LORD is ... Jer 17:7
the *h* of Israel, all that forsake ... Jer 17:13
thou art my *h* in the day of evil ... Jer 17:17
And they said, There is no *h* ... Jer 18:12
there is *h* in thine end, saith ... Jer 31:17
the LORD, the *h* of their fathers ... Jer 50:7
my *h* is perished from the LORD ... Lam 3:18
to my mind, therefore have I *h* ... Lam 3:21
therefore will I *h* in him ... Lam 3:24
is good that a man should both *h* ... Lam 3:26
if so be there may be *h* ... Lam 3:29
they have made others to *h* that ... Eze 13:6
her *h* was lost, then she took ... Eze 19:5
bones are dried, and our *h* is lost ... Eze 37:11
valley of Achor for a door of *h* ... Hos 2:15
LORD will be the *h* of his people ... Joel 3:16
strong hold, ye prisoners of *h* ... Zec 9:12
to them of whom ye *h* to receive ... Lk 6:34
also my flesh shall rest in *h* ... Acts 2:26
the *h* of their gains was gone ... Acts 16:19
of the *h* and resurrection of the ... Acts 23:6
have *h* toward God, which they ... Acts 24:15
am judged for the *h* of the ... Acts 26:6
God day and night, *h* to come ... Acts 26:7
all *h* that we should be saved was ... Acts 27:20
because that for the *h* of Israel ... Acts 28:20
Who against *h* believed in *h*, ... Rom 4:18
Who against *h* believed in *h*, ... Rom 4:18
rejoice in *h* of the glory of God ... Rom 5:2
experience; and experience, *h* ... Rom 5:4
And *h* maketh not ashamed ... Rom 5:5
who hath subjected the same in *h* ... Rom 8:20
For we are saved by *h* ... Rom 8:24
but *h* that is seen is not *h* ... Rom 8:24
man seeth, why doth he yet *h* for ... Rom 8:24
But if we *h* for that we see not, ... Rom 8:25
Rejoicing in *h* ... Rom 12:12
of the scriptures might have *h* ... Rom 15:4
Now the God of *h* fill you with ... Rom 15:13
that ye may abound in *h*, through ... Rom 15:13
he that ploweth should plow in *h* ... 1Cor 9:10
that he that thresheth in *h* ... 1Cor 9:10
*h* should be partaker of his *h* ... 1Cor 9:10
And now abideth faith, *h*, charity, ... 1Cor 13:13
life only we have *h* in Christ ... 1Cor 15:19
our *h* of you is stedfast, knowing ... 2Cor 1:7
Seeing then that we have such *h* ... 2Cor 3:12
but having *h*, when your faith is ... 2Cor 10:15
the *h* of righteousness by faith ... Gal 5:5
know what is the *h* of his calling ... Eph 1:18
covenants of promise, having no *h* ... Eph 2:12
called in one *h* of your calling ... Eph 4:4
to my earnest expectation and my *h* ... Phil 1:20
Him therefore I *h* to send ... Phil 2:23
For the *h* which is laid up for ... Col 1:5
away from the *h* of the gospel ... Col 1:23
is Christ in you, the *h* of glory ... Col 1:27
patience of *h* in our Lord Jesus ... 1Th 1:3
For what is our *h*, or joy, or ... 1Th 2:19
even as others which have no *h* ... 1Th 4:13
for an helmet, the *h* of salvation ... 1Th 5:8
and good *h* through grace, ... 2Th 2:16
Lord Jesus Christ, which is our *h* ... 1Ti 1:1
In *h* of eternal life, which God, ... Titus 1:2
Looking for that blessed *h* ... Titus 2:13
to the *h* of eternal life ... Titus 3:7
of the *h* firm unto the end ... Heb 3:6
full assurance of *h* unto the end ... Heb 6:11
lay hold upon the *h* set before us ... Heb 6:18
Which *h* we have as an anchor of ... Heb 6:19
the bringing in of a better *h* did ... Heb 7:19
*h* by the resurrection of Jesus ... 1Pet 1:3
*h* to the end for the grace that ... 1Pet 1:13
your faith and *h* might be in God ... 1Pet 1:21
*h* that is in you with meekness ... 1Pet 3:15
this *h* in him purifieth himself ... 1Jn 3:3

### HOPED
Jews *h* to have power over them ... Est 9:1
confounded because they had *h* ... Job 6:20
for I have *h* in thy judgments ... Ps 119:43
because I have *h* in thy word ... Ps 119:74
I *h* in thy word ... Ps 119:147
I have *h* for thy salvation, and ... Ps 119:166
is salvation *h* for from the hills ... Jer 3:23
he *h* to have seen some miracle ... Lk 23:8
He *h* also that money should have ... Acts 24:26
And this they did, not as we *h* ... 2Cor 8:5
is the substance of things *h* for ... Heb 11:1

### HOPE'S
For which *h* sake, king Agrippa, I ... Acts 26:7

### HOPETH
*h* all things, endureth all things ... 1Cor 13:7

### HOPHNI (*hof'-ni*) *A son of Eli.*
And the two sons of Eli, *H* ... 1Sa 1:3
come upon thy two sons, on *H* ... 1Sa 2:34
and the two sons of Eli, *H* ... 1Sa 4:4
and the two sons of Eli, *H* ... 1Sa 4:11
people, and thy two sons also, *H* ... 1Sa 4:17

### HOPING
and lend, *h* for nothing again ... Lk 6:35
*h* to come unto thee shortly ... 1Ti 3:14

### HOR (*hor*) See HOR-HAGIDGAD.
*1. A mountain in Moab.*
and came unto mount *H* ... Num 20:22
unto Moses and Aaron in mount *H* ... Num 20:23
and bring them up unto mount *H* ... Num 20:25
mount *H* in the sight of all the ... Num 20:27
mount *H* by the way of the Red sea ... Num 21:4
Kadesh, and pitched in mount *H* ... Num 33:37
the priest went up into mount *H* ... Num 33:38
years old when he died in mount *H* ... Num 33:39
And they departed from mount *H* ... Num 33:41
Aaron thy brother died in mount *H* ... Deut 32:50
*2. A hill in northern Israel.*
shall point out for you mount *H* ... Num 34:7
From mount *H* ye shall point out ... Num 34:8

### HORAM (*ho'-ram*) *A Canaanite king.*
Then *H* king of Gezer came up to ... Josh 10:33

### HOREB (*ho'-reb*) See SINAI. *A mountain range in Sinai.*
to the mountain of God, even to *H* ... Ex 3:1
thee there upon the rock in *H* ... Ex 17:6
of their ornaments by the mount *H* ... Ex 33:6
*H* by the way of mount Seir unto ... Deut 1:2
LORD our God spake unto us in *H* ... Deut 1:6
And when we departed from *H* ... Deut 1:19
before the LORD thy God in *H* ... Deut 4:10
in *H* out of the midst of the fire ... Deut 4:15
God made a covenant with us in *H* ... Deut 5:2
Also in *H* ye provoked the LORD to ... Deut 9:8
of the LORD thy God in *H* in the ... Deut 18:16
which he made with them in *H* ... Deut 29:1
stone, which Moses put there at *H* ... 1Kin 8:9
nights unto *H* the mount of God ... 1Kin 19:8
which Moses put therein at *H* ... 2Chr 5:10
They made a calf in *H*, and ... Ps 106:19
unto him in *H* for all Israel ... Mal 4:4

### HOREM (*ho'-rem*) *A city in Naphtali.*
And Iron, and Migdal-el, *H*, and ... Josh 19:38

### HORESH See ZIPH.

### HOR-HAGIDGAD (*hor-hag-id'-gad*) *An encampment of Israel in the wilderness.*
Bene-jaakan, and encamped at *H* ... Num 33:32
And they went from *H*, and pitched ... Num 33:33

### HORI (*ho'-ri*) See HORITE.
*1. Son of Lotan.*
And the children of Lotan were *H* ... Gen 36:22
are the dukes that came of *H* ... Gen 36:30
*H*, and Homam ... 1Chr 1:39
*2. Father of Shapat.*
of Simeon, Shaphat the son of *H* ... Num 13:5

### HORIMS (*ho'-rims*) See HORITES. *Inhabitants of Mt. Seir.*
The *H* also dwelt in Seir ... Deut 2:12
destroyed the *H* from before them ... Deut 2:22

### HORITE (*ho'-rite*) See HORI, HORITES. *An inhabitant of Mt. Seir.*
These are the sons of Seir the *H* ... Gen 36:20

### HORITES (*ho'-rites*) See HORIMS. *Same as Horims.*
the *H* in their mount Seir, unto ... Gen 14:6
these are the dukes of the *H* ... Gen 36:21
are the dukes that came of the *H* ... Gen 36:29

### HORMAH (*hor'-mah*) See ZEPHATH. *A Canaanite royal town.*
and discomfited them, even unto *H* ... Num 14:45
he called the name of the place *H* ... Num 21:3
you in Seir, even unto *H* ... Deut 1:44
The king of *H*, one ... Josh 12:14
And Eltolad, and Chesil, and *H* ... Josh 15:30
And Eltolad, and Bethul, and *H* ... Josh 19:4
the name of the city was called *H* ... Judg 1:17
And to them which were in *H* ... 1Sa 30:30
And at Bethuel, and at *H*, and at ... 1Chr 4:30

### HORN
to push with his *h* in time past ... Ex 21:29
a long blast with the ram's *h* ... Josh 6:5
mine *h* is exalted in the LORD ... 1Sa 2:1
exalt the *h* of his anointed ... 1Sa 2:10
fill thine *h* with oil, and go, I ... 1Sa 16:1
Then Samuel took the *h* of oil ... 1Sa 16:13
the *h* of my salvation, my high ... 2Sa 22:3
Zadok the priest took an *h* of oil ... 1Kin 1:39
words of God, to lift up the *h* ... 1Chr 25:5
skin, and defiled my *h* in the dust ... Job 16:15
the *h* of my salvation, and my high ... Ps 18:2
to the wicked, Lift not up the *h* ... Ps 75:4
Lift not up your *h* on high ... Ps 75:5
thy favour our *h* shall be exalted ... Ps 89:17
in my name shall his *h* be exalted ... Ps 89:24
But my *h* shalt thou exalt like ... Ps 92:10
exalt like the *h* of an unicorn ... Ps 92:10
his *h* shall be exalted with ... Ps 112:9
will I make the *h* of David to bud ... Ps 132:17
also exalteth the *h* of his people ... Ps 148:14
The *h* of Moab is cut off, and his ... Jer 48:25
fierce anger all the *h* of Israel ... Lam 2:3
he hath set up the *h* of thine ... Lam 2:17
In that day will I cause the *h* of ... Eze 29:21
up among them another little *h* ... Dan 7:8
in this *h* were eyes like the eyes ... Dan 7:8
the great words which the *h* spake ... Dan 7:11
even of that *h* that had eyes, and ... Dan 7:20
the same *h* made war with the ... Dan 7:21
had a notable *h* between his eyes ... Dan 8:5
strong, the great *h* was broken ... Dan 8:8
one of them came forth a little *h* ... Dan 8:9
the great *h* that is between his ... Dan 8:21
for I will make thine *h* iron ... Mic 4:13
which lifted up their *h* over the ... Zec 1:21
hath raised up an *h* of salvation ... Lk 1:69

### HORNET
God will send the *h* among them ... Deut 7:20
And I sent the *h* before you ... Josh 24:12

### HORNETS
And I will send *h* before thee ... Ex 23:28

### HORNS
ram caught in a thicket by his *h* ... Gen 22:13
thou shalt make the *h* of it upon ... Ex 27:2
his *h* shall be of the same ... Ex 27:2
put it upon the *h* of the altar ... Ex 29:12
the *h* thereof shall be of the same ... Ex 30:2
round about, and the *h* thereof ... Ex 30:3
make an atonement upon the *h* of ... Ex 30:10
the *h* thereof were of the same ... Ex 37:25
round about, and the *h* of it ... Ex 37:26
he made the *h* thereof on the four ... Ex 38:2
the *h* thereof were of the same ... Ex 38:2
*h* of the altar of sweet incense ... Lev 4:7
*h* of the altar which is before ... Lev 4:18
put it upon the *h* of the altar of ... Lev 4:25
put it upon the *h* of the altar of ... Lev 4:30
put it upon the *h* of the altar of ... Lev 4:34
put it upon the *h* of the altar ... Lev 8:15
and put it upon the *h* of the altar ... Lev 9:9
put it upon the *h* of the altar ... Lev 16:18
*h* are like the *h* of unicorns ... Deut 33:17
the ark seven trumpets of rams' *h* ... Josh 6:4
*h* before the ark of the LORD ... Josh 6:6
rams' *h* passed on before the LORD ... Josh 6:8
*h* before the ark of the LORD went ... Josh 6:13
caught hold on the *h* of the altar ... 1Kin 1:50
caught hold on the *h* of the altar ... 1Kin 1:51
caught hold on the *h* of the altar ... 1Kin 2:28
of Chenaanah made him *h* of iron ... 1Kin 22:11
Chenaanah had made him *h* of iron ... 2Chr 18:10
me from the *h* of the unicorns ... Ps 22:21
than an ox or bullock that hath *h* ... Ps 69:31
All the *h* of the wicked also will ... Ps 75:10
but the *h* of the righteous shall ... Ps 75:10
even unto the *h* of the altar ... Ps 118:27
upon the *h* of your altars ... Jer 17:1
thee for a present *h* of ivory ... Eze 27:15
all the diseased with your *h* ... Eze 34:21
altar and upward shall be four *h* ... Eze 43:15
and put it on the four *h* of it ... Eze 43:20
and it had ten *h* ... Dan 7:7
I considered the *h*, and, behold, ... Dan 7:8
first *h* plucked up by the roots ... Dan 7:8
of the ten *h* that were in his ... Dan 7:20
the ten *h* out of this kingdom are ... Dan 7:24
the river a ram which had two *h* ... Dan 8:3
and the two *h* were high ... Dan 8:3
he came to the ram that had two *h* ... Dan 8:6
smote the ram, and brake his two *h* ... Dan 8:7
two *h* are the kings of Media ... Dan 8:20
the *h* of the altar shall be cut ... Amos 3:14
taken to us *h* by our own strength ... Amos 6:13
he had *h* coming out of his hand ... Hab 3:4
eyes, and saw, and behold four *h* ... Zec 1:18
These are the *h* which have ... Zec 1:19
These are the *h* which have ... Zec 1:21
to cast out the *h* of the Gentiles ... Zec 1:21
it had been slain, having seven *h* ... Rev 5:6
*h* of the golden altar which is ... Rev 9:13
having seven heads and ten *h* ... Rev 12:3
sea, having seven heads and ten *h* ... Rev 13:1
upon his *h* ten crowns, and upon ... Rev 13:1
he had two *h* like a lamb, and he ... Rev 13:11
having seven heads and ten *h* ... Rev 17:3
hath the seven heads and ten *h* ... Rev 17:7
the ten *h* which thou sawest are ... Rev 17:12
the ten *h* which thou sawest upon ... Rev 17:16

### HORONAIM (*hor-o-na'-im*) See HOLON. *A Moabite city.*
for in the way of *H* they shall ... Is 15:5
A voice of crying shall be from *H* ... Jer 48:3
for in the going down of *H* the ... Jer 48:5
voice, from Zoar even unto *H* ... Jer 48:34

### HORONITE (*ho'-ron-ite*) *A native of Horonaim.*
When Sanballat the *H*, and Tobiah ... Neh 2:10
But when Sanballat the *H*, and ... Neh 2:19
was son in law to Sanballat the *H* ... Neh 13:28

### HORRIBLE
and brimstone, and an *h* tempest ... Ps 11:6
me up also out of an *h* pit ... Ps 40:2
*h* thing is committed in the land ... Jer 5:30
Israel hath done a very *h* thing ... Jer 18:13
prophets of Jerusalem an *h* thing ... Jer 23:14
I have seen an *h* thing in the ... Hos 6:10

### HORRIBLY
be *h* afraid, be ye very desolate, ... Jer 2:12
kings shall be *h* afraid for thee ... Eze 32:10

### HORROR
an *h* of great darkness fell upon ... Gen 15:12
upon me, and *h* hath overwhelmed me ... Ps 55:5
*H* hath taken hold upon me because ... Ps 119:53
sackcloth, and *h* shall cover them ... Eze 7:18

### HORSE
the path, that biteth the *h* heels ... Gen 49:17
the *h* and his rider hath he thrown ... Ex 15:1
For the *h* of Pharaoh went in with ... Ex 15:19
the *h* and his rider hath he thrown ... Ex 15:21
an *h* for an hundred and fifty ... 1Kin 10:29
escaped on an *h* with the horsemen ... 1Kin 20:20
*h* for *h*, and chariot for ... 1Kin 20:25

that thou hast lost, *h* for *h* 1Kin 20:25
an *h* for an hundred and fifty 2Chr 1:17
of the *h* gate by the king's house 2Chr 23:15
From above the *h* gate repaired Neh 3:28
the *h* that the king rideth upon, Est 6:8
*h* be delivered to the hand of one Est 6:9
and take the apparel and the *h* Est 6:10
took Haman the apparel and the *h* Est 6:11
on high, she scorneth the *h* Job 39:18
Hath thou given the *h* strength Job 39:19
Be ye not as the *h*, or as the Ps 32:9
An *h* is a vain thing for safety Ps 33:17
*h* are cast into a dead sleep Ps 76:6
not in the strength of the *h* Ps 147:10
The *h* is prepared against the day Prov 21:31
A whip for the *h*, a bridle for Prov 26:3
bringeth forth the chariot and *h* Is 43:17
as an *h* in the wilderness, that Is 63:13
as the *h* rusheth into the battle Jer 8:6
of the *h* gate toward the east Jer 31:40
thee will I break in pieces the *h* Jer 51:21
that rideth the *h* deliver himself Amos 2:15
behold a man riding upon a red *h* Zec 1:8
the *h* from Jerusalem, and the Zec 9:10
as his goodly *h* in the battle Zec 10:3
smite every *h* with astonishment Zec 12:4
will smite every *h* of the people Zec 12:4
so shall be the plague of the *h* Zec 14:15
And I saw, and behold a white *h* Rev 6:2
went out another *h* that was red Rev 6:4
And I beheld, and lo a black *h* Rev 6:5
And I looked, and behold a pale *h* Rev 6:8
even unto the *h* bridles, by the Rev 14:20
opened, and behold a white *h* Rev 19:11
war against him that sat on the *h* Rev 19:19
sword of him that sat upon the *h* Rev 19:21

**HORSEBACK**
there went one on *h* to meet him 2Kin 9:18
Then he sent out a second on *h* 2Kin 9:19
bring him on *h* through the street Est 6:9
brought him on *h* through the Est 6:11
and sent letters by posts on *h* Est 8:10

**HORSEHOOFS**
Then were the *h* broken by the Judg 5:22

**HORSELEACH**
The *h* hath two daughters, crying, Prov 30:15

**HORSEMAN**
And Joram said, Take an *h*, and send 2Kin 9:17
The *h* lifteth up both the bright Nah 3:3

**HORSEMEN**
up with him both chariots and *h* Gen 50:9
and chariots of Pharaoh, and his *h* Ex 14:9
upon his chariots, and upon his *h* Ex 14:17
upon his chariots, and upon his *h* Ex 14:18
horses, his chariots, and his *h* Ex 14:23
their chariots, and upon their *h* Ex 14:26
and covered the chariots, and the *h* Ex 14:28
with his *h* into the sea, and the Ex 15:19
chariots and *h* unto the Red sea Josh 24:6
for his chariots, and to be his *h* 1Sa 8:11
chariots, and six thousand *h* 1Sa 13:5
*h* followed hard after him 2Sa 1:6
chariots, and seven hundred *h* 2Sa 8:4
the Syrians, and forty thousand *h* 2Sa 10:18
and he prepared him chariots and *h* 1Kin 1:5
chariots, and twelve thousand *h* 1Kin 4:26
his chariots, and cities for his *h* 1Kin 9:19
rulers of his chariots, and his *h* 1Kin 9:22
gathered together chariots and *h* 1Kin 10:26
chariots, and twelve thousand *h* 1Kin 10:26
escaped on an horse with the *h* 1Kin 20:20
of Israel, and the *h* thereof 2Kin 2:12
people to Jehoahaz but fifty *h* 2Kin 13:7
of Israel, and the *h* thereof 2Kin 13:14
on Egypt for chariots and for *h* 2Kin 18:24
chariots, and seven thousand *h* 1Chr 18:4
*h* out of Mesopotamia, and out of 1Chr 19:6
Solomon gathered chariots and *h* 2Chr 1:14
chariots, and twelve thousand *h* 2Chr 1:14
cities, and the cities of the *h* 2Chr 8:6
and captains of his chariots and *h* 2Chr 8:9
and chariots, and twelve thousand *h* 2Chr 9:25
and threescore thousand *h* 2Chr 12:3
with very many chariots and *h* 2Chr 16:8
*h* to help us against the enemy in Ezr 8:22
captains of the army and *h* with me Neh 2:9
saw a chariot with a couple of *h* Is 21:7
of men, with a couple of *h* Is 21:9
quiver with chariots of men and *h* Is 22:6
the *h* shall set themselves in Is 22:7
cart, nor bruise it with his *h* Is 28:28
and in *h*, because they are very Is 31:1
on Egypt for chariots and for *h* Is 36:9
shall flee for the noise of the *h* Jer 4:29
and get up, ye *h*, and stand forth Jer 46:4
young men, *h* riding upon horses Eze 23:6
*h* riding upon horses, all of them Eze 23:12
and with chariots, and with *h* Eze 26:7
shall shake at the noise of the *h* Eze 26:10
in thy fairs with horses and *h* Eze 27:14
and all thine army, horses and *h* Eze 38:4
with chariots, and with *h* Dan 11:40
by battle, by horses, nor by *h* Hos 1:7
and as *h*, so shall they run Joel 2:4
their *h* shall spread themselves, Hab 1:8
their *h* shall come from far Hab 1:8
*h* threescore and ten, and spearmen Acts 23:23
they left the *h* to go with him Acts 23:32

the *h* were two hundred thousand Rev 9:16

**HORSES**
gave them bread in exchange for *h* Gen 47:17
which is in the field, upon the *h* Ex 9:3
pursued after them, all the *h* Ex 14:9
of the sea, even all Pharaoh's *h* Ex 14:23
the army of Egypt, unto their *h* Deut 11:4
shall not multiply *h* to himself Deut 17:16
the end that he should multiply *h* Deut 17:16
against thine enemies, and seest *h* Deut 20:1
sea shore in multitude, with *h* Josh 11:4
thou shalt hough their *h*, and burn Josh 11:6
he houghed their *h*, and burnt Josh 11:9
David houghed all the chariot *h* 2Sa 8:4
prepared him chariots and *h* 2Sa 15:1
stalls of *h* for his chariots 1Kin 4:26
Barley also and straw for the *h* 1Kin 4:28
garments, and armour, and spices, *h* 1Kin 10:25
Solomon had *h* brought out of 1Kin 10:28
we may find grass to save the *h* 1Kin 18:5
and two kings with him, and *h* 1Kin 20:1
Israel went out, and smote the *h* 1Kin 20:21
as thy people, my *h* as thy *h* 1Kin 22:4
*h* of fire, and parted them both 2Kin 2:11
thy people, and my *h* as thy *h* 2Kin 3:7
So Naaman came with his *h* 2Kin 5:9
Therefore sent he thither *h* 2Kin 6:14
compassed the city both with *h* 2Kin 6:15
the mountain was full of *h* 2Kin 6:17
of chariots, and a noise of *h* 2Kin 7:6
and left their tents, and their *h* 2Kin 7:7
but *h* tied, and asses tied, and the 2Kin 7:10
thee, five of the *h* that remain 2Kin 7:13
They took therefore two chariot *h* 2Kin 7:14
on the wall, and on the *h* 2Kin 9:33
there are with you chariots and *h* 2Kin 10:2
the *h* came into the king's house 2Kin 11:16
And they brought him on *h* 2Kin 14:20
will deliver thee two thousand *h* 2Kin 18:23
he took away the *h* that the kings 2Kin 23:11
also houghed all the chariot *h* 1Chr 18:4
Solomon had *h* brought out of 2Chr 1:16
so brought they out *h* for all the 2Chr 1:17
and raiment, harness, and spices, *h* 2Chr 9:24
had four thousand stalls for *h* 2Chr 9:25
unto Solomon *h* out of Egypt 2Chr 9:28
And they brought him upon *h* 2Chr 25:28
Their *h* were seven hundred thirty Ezr 2:66
Their *h*, seven hundred thirty and Neh 7:68
trust in chariots, and some in *h* Ps 20:7
I have seen servants upon *h* Eccl 10:7
to a company of *h* in Pharaoh's Song 1:9
their land is also full of *h* Is 2:7
for we will flee upon *h* Is 30:16
and stay on *h*, and trust in Is 31:1
and their *h* flesh, and not spirit Is 31:3
I will give thee two thousand *h* Is 36:8
LORD out of all nations upon *h* Is 66:20
his *h* are swifter than eagles Jer 4:13
They were as fed *h* in the morning Jer 5:8
and they ride upon *h*, set in array Jer 6:23
of his *h* was heard from Dan Jer 8:16
how canst thou contend with *h* Jer 12:5
David, riding in chariots and on *h* Jer 17:25
David, riding in chariots and on *h* Jer 22:4
Harness the *h* Jer 46:4
Come up, ye *h* Jer 46:9
of the hoofs of his strong *h* Jer 47:3
A sword is upon their *h*, and upon Jer 50:37
sea, and they shall ride upon *h* Jer 50:42
cause the *h* to come up as the Jer 51:27
Egypt, that they might give him *h* Eze 17:15
young men, horsemen riding upon *h* Eze 23:6
horsemen riding upon *h*, all of Eze 23:12
issue is like the issue of *h* Eze 23:20
all of them riding upon *h* Eze 23:23
of kings, from the north, with *h* Eze 26:7
his *h* their dust shall cover thee Eze 26:10
With the hoofs of his *h* shall he Eze 26:11
traded in thy fairs with *h* Eze 27:14
thee forth, and all thine army, *h* Eze 38:4
thee, all of them riding upon *h* Eze 38:15
be filled at my table with *h* Eze 39:20
nor by sword, nor by battle, by *h* Hos 1:7
we will not ride upon *h* Hos 14:3
of them is as the appearance of *h* Joel 2:4
sword, and have taken away your *h* Amos 4:10
Shall *h* run upon the rock Amos 6:12
that I will cut off thy *h* out of Mic 5:10
the wheels, and of the pransing *h* Nah 3:2
Their *h* also are swifter than the Hab 1:8
that thou didst ride upon thine *h* Hab 3:8
walk through the sea with thine *h* Hab 3:15
and the *h* and their riders shall Hag 2:22
and behind him were there red *h* Zec 1:8
In the first chariot were red *h* Zec 6:2
and in the second chariot black *h* Zec 6:2
And in the third chariot white *h* Zec 6:3
fourth chariot grisled and bay *h* Zec 6:3
The black *h* which are therein go Zec 6:6
them, and the riders on *h* shall be Zec 10:5
there be upon the bells of the *h* Zec 14:20
like unto *h* prepared unto battle Rev 9:7
of many *h* running to battle Rev 9:9
And thus I saw the *h* in the vision Rev 9:17
the heads of the *h* were as the Rev 9:17
wheat, and beasts, and sheep, and *h* Rev 18:13
heaven followed him upon white *h* Rev 19:14
of mighty men, and the flesh of *h* Rev 19:18

**HORSES'**
their *h* hoofs shall be counted Is 5:28
we put bits in the *h* mouths Jas 3:3

**HOSAH** (*ho'-sah*)
*1. A city in Asher.*
and the coast turneth to *H* Josh 19:29
*2. A Levite.*
of Jeduthun and *H* to be porters 1Chr 16:38
Also *H*, of the children of Merari 1Chr 26:10
brethren of *H* were thirteen 1Chr 26:11
*H* the lot came forth westward, 1Chr 26:16

**HOSANNA**
saying, *H* to the son of David Mt 21:9
*H* in the highest Mt 21:9
and saying, *H* to the son of David Mt 21:15
that followed, cried, saying, *H* Mk 11:9
*H* in the highest Mk 11:10
forth to meet him, and cried, *H* Jn 12:13

**HOSEA** (*ho-se'-ah*) See HOSHEA, OSEE, OSHEA.
*A prophet.*
word of the LORD that came unto *H* Hos 1:1
of the word of the LORD by *H* Hos 1:2
And the LORD said to *H*, Go, take Hos 1:2

**HOSEN**
bound in their coats, their *h* Dan 3:21

**HOSHAIAH** (*ho-sha-i'-ah*)
*1. Helped dedicate the wall.*
And after them went *H*, and half of Neh 12:32
*2. Father of Jezaniah.*
Kareah, and Jezaniah the son of *H* Jer 42:1
Then spake Azariah the son of *H* Jer 43:2

**HOSHAMA** (*ho-sha'-mah*) *Father of Jeconiah.*
Pedaiah, and Shenazar, Jecamiah, *H* 1Chr 3:18

**HOSHEA** (*ho-she'-ah*) See HOSEA.
*1. Original name of Joshua.*
people, he, and *H* the son of Nun Deut 32:44
*2. An Ephramite ruler.*
of Ephraim, *H* the son of Azaziah 1Chr 27:20
*3. Last king of Israel.*
And *H* the son of Elah made a 2Kin 15:30
*H* the son of Elah to reign in 2Kin 17:1
*H* became his servant, and gave him 2Kin 17:3
of Assyria found conspiracy in *H* 2Kin 17:4
In the ninth year of *H* the king 2Kin 17:6
of *H* son of Elah king of Israel 2Kin 18:1
of *H* son of Elah king of Israel 2Kin 18:9
ninth year of *H* king of Israel 2Kin 18:10
*4. An Israelite who renewed the covenant.*
*H*, Hananiah, Hashub, Neh 10:23

**HOSPITALITY**
given to *h* Rom 12:13
of good behaviour, given to *h* 1Ti 3:2
But a lover of *h*, a lover of good Titus 1:8
Use *h* one to another without 1Pet 4:9

**HOST**
finished, and all the *h* of them Gen 2:1
of his *h* spake unto Abraham Gen 21:22
the chief captain of his *h* Gen 21:32
them, he said, This is God's *h* Gen 32:2
upon Pharaoh, and upon all his *h* Ex 14:4
upon Pharaoh, and upon all his *h* Ex 14:17
*h* of the Egyptians through the Ex 14:24
troubled the *h* of the Egyptians, Ex 14:24
all the *h* of Pharaoh that came Ex 14:28
his *h* hath he cast into the sea Ex 15:4
the dew lay round about the *h* Ex 16:13
And his *h*, and those that were Num 2:4
And his *h*, and those that were Num 2:6
And his *h*, and those that were Num 2:8
And his *h*, and those that were Num 2:11
And his *h*, and those that were Num 2:13
And his *h*, and those that were Num 2:15
And his *h*, and those that were Num 2:19
And his *h*, and those that were Num 2:21
And his *h*, and those that were Num 2:23
And his *h*, and those that were Num 2:26
And his *h*, and those that were Num 2:28
And his *h*, and those that were Num 2:30
old, all that enter into the *h* Num 4:3
over his *h* was Nahshon the son of Num 10:14
over the *h* of the tribe of the Num 10:15
over the *h* of the tribe of the Num 10:16
over his *h* was Elizur the son of Num 10:18
over the *h* of the tribe of the Num 10:19
over the *h* of the tribe of the Num 10:20
over his *h* was Elishama the son Num 10:22
over the *h* of the tribe of the Num 10:23
over the *h* of the tribe of the Num 10:24
over his *h* was Ahiezer the son of Num 10:25
over the *h* of the tribe of the Num 10:26
over the *h* of the tribe of the Num 10:27
wroth with the officers of the *h* Num 31:14
were over thousands of the *h* Num 31:48
were wasted out from among the *h* Deut 2:14
to destroy them from among the *h* Deut 2:15
stars, even all the *h* of heaven Deut 4:19
moon, or any of the *h* of heaven Deut 17:3
When the *h* goeth forth against Deut 23:9
Pass through the *h*, and command Josh 1:11
the officers went through the *h* Josh 3:2
but as captain of the *h* of the Josh 5:14
of the LORD's *h* said unto Joshua Josh 5:15
even all the *h* that was on the Josh 8:13
to Joshua to the *h* at Shiloh Josh 18:9
the captain of whose *h* was Sisera Judg 4:2

H

and all his chariots, and all his *h* Judg 4:15
the chariots, and after the *h* Judg 4:16
all the *h* of Sisera fell upon the Judg 4:16
so that the *h* of the Midianites Judg 7:1
the *h* of Midian was beneath him Judg 7:8
Arise, get thee down unto the *h* Judg 7:9
Phurah thy servant down to the *h* Judg 7:10
to go down unto the *h* Judg 7:11
the armed men that were in the *h* Judg 7:11
tumbled into the *h* of Midian Judg 7:13
delivered Midian, and all the *h* Judg 7:14
and returned into the *h* of Israel Judg 7:15
into your hand the *h* of Midian Judg 7:15
and all the *h* ran, and cried, and Judg 7:21
fellow, even throughout all the *h* Judg 7:22
the *h* fled to Beth-shittah in Judg 7:22
Jogbehah, and smote the *h* Judg 8:11
for the *h* was secure Judg 8:11
and discomfited all the *h* Judg 8:12
of the *h* in the morning watch 1Sa 11:11
Sisera, captain of the *h* of Hazor 1Sa 12:9
And there was trembling in the *h* 1Sa 14:15
the *h* of the Philistines went on 1Sa 14:19
And he gathered an *h*, and smote the. 1Sa 14:48
of the captain of his *h* was Abner 1Sa 14:50
as the *h* was going forth to the 1Sa 17:20
the *h* of the Philistines this day 1Sa 17:46
unto Abner, the captain of the *h* 1Sa 17:55
son of Ner, the captain of his *h* 1Sa 26:5
when Saul saw the *h* of the 1Sa 28:5
*h* of Israel into the hand of the 1Sa 28:19
me in the *h* is good in my sight 1Sa 29:6
son of Ner, captain of Saul's *h* 2Sa 2:8
all the *h* that was with him were 2Sa 3:23
to smite the *h* of the Philistines 2Sa 5:24
smitten all the *h* of Hadadezer 2Sa 8:9
the son of Zeruiah was over the *h* 2Sa 8:16
all the *h* of the mighty men 2Sa 10:7
Shobach the captain of the *h* of 2Sa 10:16
Shobach the captain of their *h* 2Sa 10:18
captain of the *h* instead of Joab 2Sa 17:25
*h* before me continually in the 2Sa 19:13
Joab was over all the *h* of Israel 2Sa 20:23
through the *h* of the Philistines 2Sa 23:16
said to Joab the captain of the *h* 2Sa 24:2
and against the captains of the *h* 2Sa 24:4
the captains of the *h* went out 2Sa 24:4
and Joab the captain of the *h* 1Kin 1:19
sons, and the captains of the *h* 1Kin 1:25
Ner, captain of the *h* of Israel 1Kin 2:32
Jether, captain of the *h* of Judah 1Kin 2:32
Jehoiada in his room over the *h* 1Kin 2:35
son of Jehoiada was over the *h* 1Kin 4:4
Joab the captain of the *h* was 1Kin 11:15
the captain of the *h* was dead 1Kin 11:21
made Omri, the captain of the *h* 1Kin 16:16
Syria gathered all his *h* together 1Kin 20:1
all the *h* of heaven standing by 1Kin 22:19
hand, and carry me out of the *h* 1Kin 22:34
a proclamation throughout the *h* 1Kin 22:36
and there was no water for the *h* 2Kin 3:9
king, or to the captain of the *h* 2Kin 4:13
captain of the *h* of the king of 2Kin 5:1
horses, and chariots, and a great *h* 2Kin 6:14
an *h* compassed the city both with 2Kin 6:15
king of Syria gathered all his *h* 2Kin 6:24
us fall unto the *h* of the Syrians 2Kin 7:4
For the LORD had made the *h* of 2Kin 7:6
even the noise of a great *h* 2Kin 7:6
sent after the *h* of the Syrians 2Kin 7:14
captains of the *h* were sitting 2Kin 9:5
hundreds, the officers of the *h* 2Kin 11:15
and worshipped all the *h* of heaven... 2Kin 17:16
with a great *h* against Jerusalem 2Kin 18:17
and worshipped all the *h* of heaven 2Kin 21:3
he built altars for all the *h* of 2Kin 21:5
grove, and for all the *h* of heaven 2Kin 23:4
and to all the *h* of heaven 2Kin 23:5
of Babylon came, he, and all his *h* 2Kin 25:1
and the principal scribe of the *h* 2Kin 25:19
being over the *h* of the LORD 1Chr 9:19
the *h* of the Philistines encamped 1Chr 11:15
through the *h* of the Philistines 1Chr 11:18
sons of Gad, captains of the *h* 1Chr 12:14
valour, and were captains in the *h* 1Chr 12:21
a great *h*, like the *h* of God 1Chr 12:22
to smite the *h* of the Philistines 1Chr 14:15
and they smote the *h* of the 1Chr 14:16
the *h* of Hadarezer king of Zobah 1Chr 18:9
the son of Zeruiah was over the *h* 1Chr 18:15
all the *h* of the mighty men 1Chr 19:8
Shophach the captain of the *h* of 1Chr 19:16
Shophach the captain of the *h* 1Chr 19:18
the captains of the *h* separated 1Chr 25:1
and the captains of the *h* 1Chr 26:26
of the *h* for the first month 1Chr 27:3
The third captain of the *h* for 1Chr 27:5
with an *h* of a thousand thousand 2Chr 14:9
before the LORD, and before his *h* 2Chr 14:13
therefore is the *h* of the king of 2Chr 16:7
Ethiopians and the Lubims a huge *h* 2Chr 16:8
all the *h* of heaven standing on 2Chr 18:18
thou mayest carry me out of the *h* 2Chr 18:33
hundreds that were set over the *h* 2Chr 23:14
that the *h* of Syria came up 2Chr 24:23
a very great *h* into their hand 2Chr 24:24
Uzziah had an *h* of fighting men 2Chr 26:11
them throughout all the *h* shields 2Chr 26:14
before the *h* that came to Samaria 2Chr 28:9
and worshipped all the *h* of heaven 2Chr 33:3
he built altars for all the *h* of 2Chr 33:5
of the *h* of the king of Assyria 2Chr 33:11
of heavens, with all their *h* Neh 9:6
the *h* of heaven worshippeth thee Neh 9:6
Though an *h* should encamp against Ps 27:3
all the *h* of them by the breath Ps 33:6
saved by the multitude of an *h* Ps 33:16
Pharaoh and his *h* in the Red sea Ps 136:15
mustereth the *h* of the battle Is 13:4
*h* of the high ones that are on Is 24:21
all the *h* of heaven shall be Is 34:4
all their *h* shall fall down, as Is 34:4
bringeth out their *h* by number Is 40:26
all their *h* have I commanded Is 45:12
all the *h* of heaven, whom they Jer 8:2
incense unto all the *h* of heaven Jer 19:13
As the *h* of heaven cannot be Jer 33:22
destroy ye utterly all her *h* Jer 51:3
and the principal scribe of the *h* Jer 52:25
of speech, as the noise of an *h* Eze 1:24
great, even to the *h* of heaven Dan 8:10
and it cast down some of the *h* Dan 8:10
even to the prince of the *h* Dan 8:11
an *h* was given him against the Dan 8:12
the *h* to be trodden under foot Dan 8:13
the captivity of this *h* of the Obad 20
them that worship the *h* of heaven Zeph 1:5
of the heavenly *h* praising God Lk 2:13
two pence, and gave them to the *h* Lk 10:35
up to worship the *h* of heaven Acts 7:42
Gaius mine *h*, and of the whole Rom 16:23

## HOSTAGES

of the king's house, and *h* 2Kin 14:14
the *h* also, and returned to 2Chr 25:24

## HOSTS

that all the *h* of the LORD went Ex 12:41
own standard, throughout their *h* Num 1:52
their *h* were six hundred thousand Num 2:32
all the camps throughout their *h* Num 10:25
and went up, they and all their *h* Josh 10:5
they and all their *h* with them Josh 11:4
their *h* with them, about fifteen Judg 8:10
the *h* of the children of the east Judg 8:10
unto the LORD of *h* in Shiloh 1Sa 1:3
vowed a vow, and said, O LORD of *h* 1Sa 1:11
of the covenant of the LORD of *h* 1Sa 4:4
Thus saith the LORD of *h*, I 1Sa 15:2
thee in the name of the LORD of *h* 1Sa 17:45
and the LORD God of *h* was with him... 2Sa 5:10
of *h* that dwelleth between the 2Sa 6:2
in the name of the LORD of *h* 2Sa 6:18
David, Thus saith the LORD of *h* 2Sa 7:8
The LORD of *h* is the God over 2Sa 7:26
For thou, O LORD of *h*, God of 2Sa 7:27
two captains of the *h* of Israel 1Kin 2:5
sent the captains of the *h* which 1Kin 15:20
said, As the LORD of *h* liveth 1Kin 18:15
jealous for the LORD God of *h* 1Kin 19:10
jealous for the LORD God of *h* 1Kin 19:14
said, As the LORD of *h* liveth 2Kin 3:14
of the LORD of *h* shall do this 2Kin 19:31
for the LORD of *h* was with him 1Chr 11:9
David, Thus saith the LORD of *h* 1Chr 17:7
The LORD of *h* is the God of 1Chr 17:24
The LORD of *h*, he is the King of Ps 24:10
The LORD of *h* is with us Ps 46:7
The LORD of *h* is with us Ps 46:11
seen in the city of the LORD of *h* Ps 48:8
Thou therefore, O LORD God of *h* Ps 59:5
wait on thee, O Lord GOD of *h* Ps 69:6
O LORD God of *h*, how long wilt Ps 80:4
Turn us again, O God of *h* Ps 80:7
we beseech thee, O God of *h* Ps 80:14
Turn us again, O LORD God of *h* Ps 80:19
are thy tabernacles, O LORD of *h* Ps 84:1
even thine altars, O LORD of *h* Ps 84:3
O LORD God of *h*, hear my prayer Ps 84:8
O LORD of *h*, blessed is the man Ps 84:12
O LORD God of *h*, who is a strong Ps 89:8
Bless ye the LORD, all ye his *h* Ps 103:21
thou, O God, go forth with our *h* Ps 108:11
praise ye him, all his *h* Ps 148:2
Except the LORD of *h* had left Is 1:9
saith the Lord, the LORD of *h* Is 1:24
For the day of the LORD of *h* Is 2:12
behold, the Lord, the LORD of *h* Is 3:1
saith the Lord GOD of *h* Is 3:15
LORD of *h* is the house of Israel Is 5:7
In mine ears said the LORD of *h* Is 5:9
But the LORD of *h* shall be Is 5:16
away the law of the LORD of *h* Is 5:24
holy, holy, is the LORD of *h* Is 6:3
have seen the King, the LORD of *h* Is 6:5
Sanctify the LORD of *h* himself Is 8:13
in Israel from the LORD of *h* Is 8:18
the LORD of *h* will perform this Is 9:7
do they seek the LORD of *h* Is 9:13
LORD of *h* is the land darkened Is 9:19
shall the Lord, the Lord of *h* Is 10:16
For the Lord GOD of *h* shall make Is 10:23
thus saith the Lord GOD of *h* Is 10:24
the LORD of *h* shall stir up a Is 10:26
Behold, the Lord, the LORD of *h* Is 10:33
the LORD of *h* mustereth the host Is 13:4
in the wrath of the LORD of *h* Is 13:13
against them, saith the LORD of *h* Is 14:22
destruction, saith the LORD of *h* Is 14:23
The LORD of *h* hath sworn, saying, Is 14:24
For the LORD of *h* hath purposed Is 14:27
of Israel, saith the LORD of *h* Is 17:3
LORD of *h* of a people scattered Is 18:7
of the name of the LORD of *h* Is 18:7
saith the Lord, the LORD of *h* Is 19:4
of *h* hath purposed upon Egypt Is 19:12
of the hand of the LORD of *h* Is 19:16
of the counsel of the LORD of *h* Is 19:17
Canaan, and swear to the LORD of *h* Is 19:18
LORD of *h* in the land of Egypt Is 19:20
Whom the LORD of *h* shall bless Is 19:25
I have heard of the LORD of *h* Is 21:10
GOD of *h* in the valley of vision Is 22:5
the Lord GOD of *h* call to weeping Is 22:12
in mine ears by the LORD of *h* Is 22:14
ye die, saith the Lord GOD of *h* Is 22:14
Thus saith the Lord GOD of *h* Is 22:15
In that day, saith the LORD of *h* Is 22:25
The LORD of *h* hath purposed it, Is 23:9
when the LORD of *h* shall reign in Is 24:23
*h* make unto all people a feast of Is 25:6
LORD of *h* be for a crown of glory Is 28:5
the Lord GOD of *h* a consumption Is 28:22
cometh forth from the LORD of *h* Is 28:29
of the LORD of *h* with thunder Is 29:6
so shall the LORD of *h* come down Is 31:4
the LORD of *h* defend Jerusalem Is 31:5
O LORD of *h*, God of Israel, that Is 37:16
of the LORD of *h* shall do this Is 37:32
Hear the word of the LORD of *h* Is 39:5
and his redeemer the LORD of *h* Is 44:6
nor reward, saith the LORD of *h* Is 45:13
the LORD of *h* is his name Is 47:4
The LORD of *h* is his name Is 48:2
The LORD of *h* is his name Is 51:15
the LORD of *h* is his name Is 54:5
in thee, saith the Lord GOD of *h* Jer 2:19
heritage of the *h* of nations Jer 3:19
thus saith the LORD God of *h* Jer 5:14
For thus hath the LORD of *h* said Jer 6:6
Thus saith the LORD of *h*, They Jer 6:9
Thus saith the LORD of *h*, the God Jer 7:3
Thus saith the LORD of *h*, the God Jer 7:21
driven them, saith the LORD of *h* Jer 8:3
thus saith the LORD of *h*, Behold, Jer 9:7
thus saith the LORD of *h*, the God Jer 9:15
Thus saith the LORD of *h*, Jer 9:17
The LORD of *h* is his name Jer 10:16
For the LORD of *h*, that planted Jer 11:17
But, O LORD of *h*, that judgest Jer 11:20
thus saith the LORD of *h*, Behold, Jer 11:22
by thy name, O LORD God of *h* Jer 15:16
For thus saith the LORD of *h* Jer 16:9
Thus saith the LORD of *h*, the God Jer 19:3
them, Thus saith the LORD of *h* Jer 19:11
Thus saith the LORD of *h*, the God Jer 19:15
But, O LORD of *h*, that triest the Jer 20:12
thus saith the LORD of *h* Jer 23:15
Thus saith the LORD of *h*, Hearken Jer 23:16
God, of the LORD of *h* our God Jer 23:36
thus saith the LORD of *h* Jer 25:8
them, Thus saith the LORD of *h* Jer 25:27
them, Thus saith the LORD of *h* Jer 25:28
of the earth, saith the LORD of *h* Jer 25:29
Thus saith the LORD of *h*, Behold, Jer 25:32
saying, Thus saith the LORD of *h* Jer 26:18
masters, Thus saith the LORD of *h* Jer 27:4
intercession to the LORD of *h* Jer 27:18
LORD of *h* concerning the pillars Jer 27:19
Yea, thus saith the LORD of *h* Jer 27:21
Thus speaketh the LORD of *h* Jer 28:2
For thus saith the LORD of *h* Jer 28:14
Thus saith the LORD of *h*, the God Jer 29:4
For thus saith the LORD of *h* Jer 29:8
Thus saith the LORD of *h* Jer 29:17
Thus saith the LORD of *h*, the God Jer 29:21
Thus speaketh the LORD of *h* Jer 29:25
in that day, saith the LORD of *h* Jer 30:8
Thus saith the LORD of *h*, the God Jer 31:23
The LORD of *h* is his name Jer 31:35
Thus saith the LORD of *h*, the God Jer 32:14
For thus saith the LORD of *h* Jer 32:15
the Mighty God, the LORD of *h* Jer 32:18
shall say, Praise the LORD of *h* Jer 33:11
Thus saith the LORD of *h* Jer 33:12
Thus saith the LORD of *h*, the God Jer 35:13
thus saith the LORD God of *h* Jer 35:17
Thus saith the LORD of *h* Jer 35:18
thus saith the LORD of *h*, the God Jer 35:19
Thus saith the LORD, the God of *h* Jer 38:17
saying, Thus saith the LORD of *h* Jer 39:16
Thus saith the LORD of *h*, the God Jer 42:15
For thus saith the LORD of *h* Jer 42:18
them, Thus saith the LORD of *h* Jer 43:10
Thus saith the LORD of *h*, the God Jer 44:2
thus saith the LORD, the God of *h* Jer 44:7
thus saith the LORD of *h*, the God Jer 44:11
Thus saith the LORD of *h*, the God Jer 44:25
is the day of the Lord GOD of *h* Jer 46:10
for the Lord GOD of *h* hath a Jer 46:10
King, whose name is the LORD of *h* Jer 46:18
The LORD of *h*, the God of Israel, Jer 46:25
Moab thus saith the LORD of *h* Jer 48:1
King, whose name is the LORD of *h* Jer 48:15
thee, saith the Lord GOD of *h* Jer 49:5
Edom, thus saith the LORD of *h* Jer 49:7
in that day, saith the LORD of *h* Jer 49:26
Thus saith the LORD of *h* Jer 49:35
thus saith the LORD of *h*, the God Jer 50:18
of *h* in the land of the Chaldeans Jer 50:25
proud, saith the Lord GOD of *h* Jer 50:31

Thus saith the LORD of *h* — Jer 50:33
the LORD of *h* is his name — Jer 50:34
of his God, of the LORD of *h* — Jer 51:5
The LORD of *h* hath sworn by — Jer 51:14
the LORD of *h* is his name — Jer 51:19
For thus saith the LORD of *h* — Jer 51:33
King, whose name is the LORD of *h* — Jer 51:57
Thus saith the LORD of *h* — Jer 51:58
Even the LORD God of *h* — Hos 12:5
saith the Lord GOD, the God of *h* — Amos 3:13
the earth, The LORD, The God of *h* — Amos 4:13
and so the LORD, the God of *h* — Amos 5:14
of *h* will be gracious unto the — Amos 5:15
Therefore the LORD, the God of *h* — Amos 5:16
LORD, whose name is The God of *h* — Amos 5:27
saith the LORD the God of *h* — Amos 6:8
saith the LORD the God of *h* — Amos 6:14
the Lord GOD of *h* is he that — Amos 9:5
of the LORD of *h* hath spoken it — Mic 4:4
against thee, saith the LORD of *h* — Nah 2:13
against thee, saith the LORD of *h* — Nah 3:5
is it not of the LORD of *h* that — Hab 2:13
as I live, saith the LORD of *h* — Zeph 2:9
the people of the LORD of *h* — Zeph 2:10
Thus speaketh the LORD of *h* — Hag 1:2
thus saith the LORD of *h* — Hag 1:5
Thus saith the LORD of *h* — Hag 1:7
saith the LORD of *h* — Hag 1:9
in the house of the LORD of *h* — Hag 1:14
am with you, saith the LORD of *h* — Hag 2:4
For thus saith the LORD of *h* — Hag 2:6
with glory, saith the LORD of *h* — Hag 2:7
gold is mine, saith the LORD of *h* — Hag 2:8
the former, saith the LORD of *h* — Hag 2:9
I give peace, saith the LORD of *h* — Hag 2:9
Thus saith the LORD of *h* — Hag 2:11
In that day, saith the LORD of *h* — Hag 2:23
chosen thee, saith the LORD of *h* — Hag 2:23
them, Thus saith the LORD of *h* — Zec 1:3
ye unto me, saith the LORD of *h* — Zec 1:3
unto you, saith the LORD of *h* — Zec 1:3
saying, Thus saith the LORD of *h* — Zec 1:4
Like as the LORD of *h* thought to — Zec 1:6
answered and said, O LORD of *h* — Zec 1:12
saying, Thus saith the LORD of *h* — Zec 1:14
built in it, saith the LORD of *h* — Zec 1:16
saying, Thus saith the LORD of *h* — Zec 1:17
For thus saith the LORD of *h* — Zec 2:8
that the LORD of *h* hath sent me — Zec 2:9
LORD of *h* hath sent me unto thee — Zec 2:11
Thus saith the LORD of *h* — Zec 3:7
thereof, saith the LORD of *h* — Zec 3:9
In that day, saith the LORD of *h* — Zec 3:10
by my spirit, saith the LORD of *h* — Zec 4:6
LORD of *h* hath sent me unto you — Zec 4:9
it forth, saith the LORD of *h* — Zec 5:4
Thus speaketh the LORD of *h* — Zec 6:12
LORD of *h* hath sent me unto you — Zec 6:15
in the house of the LORD of *h* — Zec 7:3
the word of the LORD of *h* unto me — Zec 7:4
Thus speaketh the LORD of *h* — Zec 7:9
the words which the LORD of *h* — Zec 7:12
a great wrath from the LORD of *h* — Zec 7:12
not hear, saith the LORD of *h* — Zec 7:13
word of the LORD of *h* came to me — Zec 8:1
Thus saith the LORD of *h* — Zec 8:2
the LORD of *h* the holy mountain — Zec 8:3
Thus saith the LORD of *h* — Zec 8:4
Thus saith the LORD of *h* — Zec 8:6
saith the LORD of *h* — Zec 8:6
Thus saith the LORD of *h* — Zec 8:7
Thus saith the LORD of *h* — Zec 8:9
house of the LORD of *h* was laid — Zec 8:9
former days, saith the LORD of *h* — Zec 8:11
For thus saith the LORD of *h* — Zec 8:14
me to wrath, saith the LORD of *h* — Zec 8:14
of the LORD of *h* came unto me — Zec 8:18
Thus saith the LORD of *h* — Zec 8:19
Thus saith the LORD of *h* — Zec 8:20
LORD, and to seek the LORD of *h* — Zec 8:21
seek the LORD of *h* in Jerusalem — Zec 8:22
Thus saith the LORD of *h* — Zec 8:23
The LORD of *h* shall defend them — Zec 9:15
for the LORD of *h* hath visited — Zec 10:3
in the LORD of *h* their God — Zec 12:5
in that day, saith the LORD of *h* — Zec 13:2
is my fellow, saith the LORD of *h* — Zec 13:7
worship the King, the LORD of *h* — Zec 14:16
worship the King, the LORD of *h* — Zec 14:17
be holiness unto the LORD of *h* — Zec 14:21
in the house of the LORD of *h* — Zec 14:21
thus saith the LORD of *h*, They — Mal 1:4
saith the LORD of *h* unto you — Mal 1:6
saith the LORD of *h* — Mal 1:8
saith the LORD of *h* — Mal 1:9
in you, saith the LORD of *h* — Mal 1:10
the heathen, saith the LORD of *h* — Mal 1:11
at it, saith the LORD of *h* — Mal 1:13
a great King, saith the LORD of *h* — Mal 1:14
unto my name, saith the LORD of *h* — Mal 2:2
be with Levi, saith the LORD of *h* — Mal 2:4
is the messenger of the LORD of *h* — Mal 2:7
of Levi, saith the LORD of *h* — Mal 2:8
an offering unto the LORD of *h* — Mal 2:12
his garment, saith the LORD of *h* — Mal 2:16
shall come, saith the LORD of *h* — Mal 3:1
fear not me, saith the LORD of *h* — Mal 3:5
unto you, saith the LORD of *h* — Mal 3:7
now herewith, saith the LORD of *h* — Mal 3:10
in the field, saith the LORD of *h* — Mal 3:11
land, saith the LORD of *h* — Mal 3:12
mournfully before the LORD of *h* — Mal 3:14
be mine, saith the LORD of *h* — Mal 3:17
burn them up, saith the LORD of *h* — Mal 4:1
do this, saith the LORD of *h* — Mal 4:3

### HOT
and when the sun waxed *h*, it — Ex 16:21
And my wrath shall wax *h*, and I — Ex 22:24
my wrath may wax *h* against them — Ex 32:10
wrath wax *h* against thy people — Ex 32:11
and Moses' anger waxed *h*, and he — Ex 32:19
not the anger of my lord wax *h* — Ex 32:22
skin whereof there is a *h* burning — Lev 13:24
*h* displeasure, wherewith the LORD — Deut 9:19
the slayer, while his heart is *h* — Deut 19:6
This our bread we took *h* for our — Josh 9:12
of the LORD was *h* against Israel — Judg 2:14
of the LORD was *h* against Israel — Judg 2:20
of the LORD was *h* against Israel — Judg 3:8
not thine anger be *h* against me — Judg 6:39
of the LORD was *h* against Israel — Judg 10:7
morrow, by that time the sun be *h* — 1Sa 11:9
to put *h* bread in the day when it — 1Sa 21:6
be opened until the sun be *h* — Neh 7:3
when it is *h*, they are consumed — Job 6:17
chasten me in thy *h* displeasure — Ps 6:1
chasten me in thy *h* displeasure — Ps 38:1
My heart was *h* within me — Ps 39:3
and their flocks to *h* thunderbolts — Ps 78:48
Can one go upon *h* coals, and his — Prov 6:28
that the brass of it may be *h* — Eze 24:11
and the furnace exceeding *h* — Dan 3:22
They are all *h* as an oven — Hos 7:7
conscience seared with a *h* iron — 1Ti 4:2
that thou art neither cold nor *h* — Rev 3:15
I would thou wert cold or *h* — Rev 3:15
lukewarm, and neither cold nor *h* — Rev 3:16

**HOTHAM** (*ho'-tham*) See HOTHAN. *A son of Heber.*
begat Japhlet, and Shomer, and *H* — 1Chr 7:32

**HOTHAN** (*ho'-than*) See HOTHAM. *Father of Shama and Jehiel.*
Jehiel the sons of *H* the Aroerite — 1Chr 11:44

**HOTHIR** (*ho'-thir*) *A son of Heman.*
Joshbekashah, Mallothi, *H* — 1Chr 25:4
The one and twentieth to *H* — 1Chr 25:28

### HOTLY
thou hast so *h* pursued after me — Gen 31:36

### HOTTEST
in the forefront of the *h* battle — 2Sa 11:15

### HOUGH
thou shalt *h* their horses, and — Josh 11:6

### HOUGHED
he *h* their horses, and burnt their — Josh 11:9
David *h* all the chariot horses, — 2Sa 8:4
David also *h* all the chariot — 1Chr 18:4

### HOUR
worshippeth shall the same *h* be — Dan 3:6
ye shall be cast the same *h* into — Dan 3:15
was astonied for one *h*, and his — Dan 4:19
The same *h* was the thing — Dan 4:33
In the same *h* came forth fingers — Dan 5:5
was healed in the selfsame *h* — Mt 8:13
woman was made whole from that *h* — Mt 9:22
that same *h* what ye shall speak — Mt 10:19
was made whole from that very *h* — Mt 15:28
child was cured from that very *h* — Mt 17:18
And he went out about the third *h* — Mt 20:3
out about the sixth and ninth *h* — Mt 20:5
about the eleventh *h* he went out — Mt 20:6
were hired about the eleventh *h* — Mt 20:9
These last have wrought but one *h* — Mt 20:12
*h* knoweth no man, no, not the — Mt 24:36
not what *h* your Lord doth come — Mt 24:42
for in such an *h* as ye think not — Mt 24:44
in an *h* that he is not aware of, — Mt 24:50
*h* wherein the Son of man cometh — Mt 25:13
could ye not watch with me one *h* — Mt 26:40
the *h* is at hand, and the Son of — Mt 26:45
In that same *h* said Jesus to the — Mt 26:55
Now from the sixth *h* there was — Mt 27:45
all the land unto the ninth *h* — Mt 27:45
about the ninth *h* Jesus cried — Mt 27:46
shall be given you in that *h* — Mk 13:11
that *h* knoweth no man, no, not — Mk 13:32
the *h* might pass from him — Mk 14:35
couldest not thou watch one *h* — Mk 14:37
it is enough, the *h* is come — Mk 14:41
And it was the third *h*, and they — Mk 15:25
And when the sixth *h* was come — Mk 15:33
the whole land until the ninth *h* — Mk 15:33
at the ninth *h* Jesus cried with a — Mk 15:34
in that same *h* he cured many of — Lk 7:21
In that *h* Jesus rejoiced in — Lk 10:21
the same *h* what ye ought to say — Lk 12:12
known what *h* the thief would come — Lk 12:39
cometh at an *h* when ye think not — Lk 12:40
at an *h* when he is not aware, and — Lk 12:46
the scribes the same *h* sought to — Lk 20:19
And when the *h* was come, he sat — Lk 22:14
but this is your *h*, and the power — Lk 22:53
about the space of one *h* after — Lk 22:59
And it was about the sixth *h* — Lk 23:44
all the earth until the ninth *h* — Lk 23:44
And they rose up the same *h* — Lk 24:33
for it was about the tenth *h* — Jn 1:39
mine *h* is not yet come — Jn 2:4
and it was about the sixth *h* — Jn 4:6
the *h* cometh, when ye shall — Jn 4:21
But the *h* cometh, and now is, when — Jn 4:23
them the *h* when he began to amend — Jn 4:52
the seventh *h* the fever left him — Jn 4:52
knew that it was at the same *h* — Jn 4:53
The *h* is coming, and now is, when — Jn 5:25
for the *h* is coming, in the which — Jn 5:28
because his *h* was not yet come — Jn 7:30
for his *h* was not yet come — Jn 8:20
The *h* is come, that the Son of — Jn 12:23
Father, save me from this *h* — Jn 12:27
for this cause came I unto this *h* — Jn 12:27
when Jesus knew that his *h* was — Jn 13:1
sorrow, because her *h* is come — Jn 16:21
the *h* cometh, yea, is now come, — Jn 16:32
and said, Father, the *h* is come — Jn 17:1
passover, and about the sixth *h* — Jn 19:14
from that *h* that disciple took — Jn 19:27
it is but the third *h* of the day — Acts 2:15
*h* of prayer, being the ninth *h* — Acts 3:1
evidently about the ninth *h* of — Acts 10:3
to pray about the sixth *h* — Acts 10:9
ago I was fasting until this *h* — Acts 10:30
at the ninth *h* I prayed in my — Acts 10:30
And he came out the same *h* — Acts 16:18
took them the same *h* of the night — Acts 16:33
the same *h* I looked up upon him — Acts 22:13
at the third *h* of the night — Acts 23:23
this present *h* we both hunger — 1Cor 4:11
of the idol unto this *h* eat it as — 1Cor 8:7
why stand we in jeopardy every *h* — 1Cor 15:30
by subjection, no, not for an *h* — Gal 2:5
know what *h* I will come upon thee — Rev 3:3
thee from the *h* of temptation — Rev 3:10
about the space of half an *h* — Rev 8:1
which were prepared for an *h* — Rev 9:15
the same *h* was there a great — Rev 11:13
for the *h* of his judgment is come — Rev 14:7
as kings one *h* with the beast — Rev 17:12
for in one *h* is thy judgment come — Rev 18:10
For in one *h* so great riches is — Rev 18:17
for in one *h* is she made desolate — Rev 18:19

### HOURS
Are there not twelve *h* in the day — Jn 11:9
about the space of three *h* after — Acts 5:7
the space of two *h* cried out — Acts 19:34

**HOUSE** See PREFACE.
kindred, and from thy father's *h* — Gen 12:1
is none other but the *h* of God — Gen 28:17
Egypt, out of the *h* of bondage — Ex 13:3
shalt not covet thy neighbour's *h* — Ex 20:17
thou covet thy neighbour's *h* — Deut 5:21
Why is the *h* of God forsaken — Neh 13:11
to the *h* appointed for all living — Job 30:23
I will dwell in the *h* of the LORD — Ps 23:6
walked unto the *h* of God in — Ps 55:14
zeal of thine *h* hath eaten me up — Ps 69:9
Yea, the sparrow hath found an *h* — Ps 84:3
Let us go into the *h* of the LORD — Ps 122:1
Wisdom hath builded her *h* — Prov 9:1
but the *h* of the righteous shall — Prov 12:7
The *h* of the wicked shall be — Prov 14:11
better to go to the *h* of mourning — Eccl 7:2
keepers of the *h* shall tremble — Eccl 12:3
unto them that join *h* to *h* — Is 5:8
for mine *h* shall be called an — Is 56:7
Our holy and our beautiful *h* — Is 64:11
winter *h* with the summer *h* — Amos 3:15
to the *h* of the God of Jacob — Mic 4:2
houses, and this *h* lie waste — Hag 1:4
light unto all that are in the *h* — Mt 5:15
which built his *h* upon a rock — Mt 7:24
winds blew, and beat upon that *h* — Mt 7:27
And when ye come into an *h* — Mt 10:12
every city or *h* divided against — Mt 12:25
one enter into a strong man's *h* — Mt 12:29
My *h* shall be called the *h* of — Mt 21:13
your *h* is left unto you desolate — Mt 23:38
at thy *h* with my disciples — Mt 26:18
if a *h* be divided against itself, — Mk 3:25
He is like a man which built an *h* — Lk 6:48
Go not from *h* to *h* — Lk 10:7
*h* divided against a *h* falleth — Lk 11:17
come in, that my *h* may be filled — Lk 14:23
light a candle, and sweep the *h* — Lk 15:8
this man went down to his *h* — Lk 18:14
*h* an *h* of merchandise — Jn 2:16
zeal of thine *h* hath eaten me up — Jn 2:17
the *h* was filled with the odour — Jn 12:3
In my Father's *h* are many — Jn 14:2
it filled all the *h* where they — Acts 2:2
and breaking bread from *h* to *h* — Acts 2:46
earthly *h* of this tabernacle were — 2Cor 5:1
an *h* not made with hands, eternal — 2Cor 5:1
wandering about from *h* to *h* — 1Ti 5:13
But in a great *h* there are not — 2Ti 2:20
must begin at the *h* of God — 1Pet 4:17

### HOUSEHOLD
his *h* after him, and they shall — Gen 18:19
thou found of all thy *h* stuff — Gen 31:37
Then Jacob said unto his *h* — Gen 35:2
lest thou, and thy *h*, and all that — Gen 45:11
brethren, and all his father's *h* — Gen 47:12
man and his *h* came with Jacob — Ex 1:1
if the *h* be too little for the — Ex 12:4
for himself, and for his *h* — Lev 16:17

upon Pharaoh, and upon all his *h* — Deut 6:22
shalt rejoice, thou, and thine *h* — Deut 14:26
LORD shall choose, thou and thy *h* — Deut 15:20
brethren, and all thy father's *h* — Josh 2:18
harlot alive, and her father's *h* — Josh 6:25
the *h* which the LORD shall take — Josh 7:14
And he brought his *h* man by man — Josh 7:18
because he feared his father's *h* — Judg 6:27
thy life, with the lives of thy *h* — Judg 18:25
our master, and against all his *h* — 1Sa 25:17
and his men, every man with his *h* — 1Sa 27:3
bring up, every man with his *h* — 2Sa 2:3
blessed Obed-edom, and all his *h* — 2Sa 6:11
David returned to bless his *h* — 2Sa 6:20
forth, and all his *h* after him — 2Sa 15:16
be for the king's *h* to ride on — 2Sa 16:2
put his *h* in order, and hanged — 2Sa 17:23
boat to carry over the king's *h* — 2Sa 19:18
have brought the king, and his *h* — 2Sa 19:41
And Ahishar was over the *h* — 1Kin 4:6
victuals for the king and his *h* — 1Kin 4:7
desire, in giving food for my *h* — 1Kin 5:9
of wheat for food to his *h* — 1Kin 5:11
*h* among the sons of Pharaoh — 1Kin 11:20
we may go and tell the king's *h* — 2Kin 7:9
Arise, and go thou and thine *h* — 2Kin 8:1
and she went with her *h*, and — 2Kin 8:2
of Hilkiah, which was over the *h* — 2Kin 18:18
of Hilkiah, which was over the *h* — 2Kin 18:37
Eliakim, which was over the *h* — 2Kin 19:2
one principal *h* being taken for — 1Chr 24:6
the *h* stuff of Tobiah out of the — Neh 13:8
she asses, and a very great *h* — Job 1:3
thy food, for the food of thy *h* — Prov 27:27
night, and giveth meat to her *h* — Prov 31:15
not afraid of the snow for her *h* — Prov 31:21
for all her *h* are clothed with — Prov 31:21
looketh well to the ways of her *h* — Prov 31:27
of Hilkiah, that was over the *h* — Is 36:22
sent Eliakim, who was over the *h* — Is 37:2
shall they call them of his *h* — Mt 10:25
foes shall be they of his own *h* — Mt 10:36
lord hath made ruler over his *h* — Mt 24:45
lord shall make ruler over his *h* — Lk 12:42
he called two of his *h* servants — Acts 10:7
when she was baptized, and her *h* — Acts 16:15
them which are of Aristobulus' *h* — Rom 16:10
that be of the *h* of Narcissus — Rom 16:11
baptized also the *h* of Stephanas — 1Cor 1:16
them who are of the *h* of faith — Gal 6:10
the saints, and of the *h* of God — Eph 2:19
they that are of Caesar's *h* — Phil 4:22
Aquila, and the *h* of Onesiphorus — 2Ti 4:19

## HOUSEHOLDER
So the servants of the *h* came — Mt 13:27
is like unto a man that is an *h* — Mt 13:52
is like unto a man that is an *h* — Mt 20:1
There was a certain *h*, which — Mt 21:33

## HOUSEHOLDS
food for the famine of your *h* — Gen 42:33
And take your father and your *h* — Gen 45:18
your food, and for them of your *h* — Gen 47:24
it in every place, ye and your *h* — Num 18:31
and swallowed them up, and their *h* — Deut 11:6
put your hand unto, ye and your *h* — Deut 12:7
LORD shall take shall come by *h* — Josh 7:14

## HOUSES
corn for the famine of your *h* — Gen 42:19
feared God, that he made them *h* — Ex 1:21
be the heads of their fathers' *h* — Ex 6:14
the frogs from thee and thy *h* — Ex 8:9
depart from thee, and from thy *h* — Ex 8:11
and the frogs died out of the *h* — Ex 8:13
and upon thy people, and into thy *h* — Ex 8:21
the *h* of the Egyptians shall be — Ex 8:21
Pharaoh, and into his servants' *h* — Ex 8:24
and his cattle flee into the *h* — Ex 9:20
And they shall fill thy *h* — Ex 10:6
the *h* of all thy servants — Ex 10:6
the *h* of all the Egyptians — Ex 10:6
on the upper door post of the *h* — Ex 12:7
a token upon the *h* where ye are — Ex 12:13
put away leaven out of your *h* — Ex 12:15
be no leaven found in your *h* — Ex 12:19
come in unto your *h* to smite you — Ex 12:23
who passed over the *h* of the — Ex 12:27
the Egyptians, and delivered our *h* — Ex 12:27
But the *h* of the villages which — Lev 25:31
the *h* of the cities of their — Lev 25:32
for the *h* of the cities of the — Lev 25:33
throughout the *h* of their fathers — Num 4:22
and swallowed them up, and their *h* — Num 16:32
according to their fathers' *h* — Num 17:6
We will not return unto our *h* — Num 32:18
*h* full of all good things, which — Deut 6:11
art full, and hast built goodly *h* — Deut 8:12
in their cities, and in their *h* — Deut 19:1
for our provision out of our *h* on — Josh 9:12
that there is in these *h* an ephod — Judg 18:14
the men that were in the *h* near — Judg 18:22
when Solomon had built the two *h* — 1Kin 9:10
against all the *h* of the high — 1Kin 13:32
house, and the *h* of thy servants — 1Kin 20:6
put them in the *h* of the high — 2Kin 17:29
them in the *h* of the high places — 2Kin 17:32
brake down the *h* of the sodomites — 2Kin 23:7
all the *h* also of the high places — 2Kin 23:19
all the *h* of Jerusalem, and every — 2Kin 25:9
David made him *h* in the city of — 1Chr 15:1
of the *h* thereof, and of the — 1Chr 28:11
overlay the walls of the *h* withal — 1Chr 29:4
to the *h* of their fathers — 2Chr 25:5
to floor the *h* which the kings of — 2Chr 34:11
by the *h* of your fathers, after — 2Chr 35:4
daughters, your wives, and your *h* — Neh 4:14
our lands, vineyards, and *h* — Neh 5:3
their oliveyards, and their *h* — Neh 5:11
and the *h* were not builded — Neh 7:4
possessed *h* full of all goods, — Neh 9:25
after the *h* of our fathers, at — Neh 10:34
sons went and feasted in their *h* — Job 1:4
who filled their *h* with silver — Job 3:15
in them that dwell in *h* of clay — Job 4:19
in *h* which no man inhabiteth, — Job 15:28
Their *h* are safe from fear, — Job 21:9
filled their *h* with good things — Job 22:18
In the dark they dig through *h* — Job 24:16
that their *h* shall continue for — Ps 49:11
the *h* of God in possession — Ps 83:12
we shall fill our *h* with spoil — Prov 1:13
make they their *h* in the rocks — Prov 30:26
I builded me *h* — Eccl 2:4
spoil of the poor is in your *h* — Is 3:14
Of a truth many *h* shall be — Is 5:9
the *h* without man, and the land be — Is 6:11
offence to both the *h* of Israel — Is 8:14
their *h* shall be spoiled, and — Is 13:16
their *h* shall be full of doleful — Is 13:21
shall cry in their desolate *h* — Is 13:22
on the tops of their *h*, and in — Is 15:3
have numbered the *h* of Jerusalem — Is 22:10
the *h* have ye broken down to — Is 22:10
upon all the *h* of joy in the — Is 32:13
and they are hid in prison *h* — Is 42:22
And they shall build *h*, and inhabit — Is 65:21
by troops in the harlots' *h* — Jer 5:7
so are their *h* full of deceit — Jer 5:27
their *h* shall be turned unto — Jer 6:12
out of your *h* on the sabbath day — Jer 17:22
Let a cry be heard from their *h* — Jer 18:22
the *h* of Jerusalem — Jer 19:13
the *h* of the kings of Judah, — Jer 19:13
because of all the *h* upon whose — Jer 19:13
Build ye *h*, and dwell in them — Jer 29:5
build ye *h*, and dwell in them — Jer 29:28
*H* and fields and vineyards shall be — Jer 32:15
this city, and burn it with the *h* — Jer 32:29
concerning the *h* of this city — Jer 33:4
concerning the *h* of the kings of — Jer 33:4
Nor to build *h* for us to dwell in — Jer 35:9
the *h* of the people, with fire, — Jer 39:8
in the *h* of the gods of Egypt — Jer 43:12
and the *h* of the gods of the — Jer 43:13
all the *h* of Jerusalem, and all — Jer 52:13
all the *h* of the great men, — Jer 52:13
to strangers, our *h* to aliens — Lam 5:2
and they shall possess their *h* — Eze 7:24
let us build *h* — Eze 11:3
they shall burn thine *h* with fire — Eze 16:41
and burn up their *h* with fire — Eze 23:47
walls, and destroy thy pleasant *h* — Eze 26:12
safely therein, and shall build *h* — Eze 28:26
walls and in the doors of the *h* — Eze 33:30
it shall be a place for their *h* — Eze 45:4
your *h* shall be made a dunghill — Dan 2:5
their *h* shall be made a dunghill — Dan 3:29
and I will place them in their *h* — Hos 11:11
they shall climb up upon the *h* — Joel 2:9
the *h* of ivory shall perish, and — Amos 3:15
the great *h* shall have an end, — Amos 3:15
ye have built *h* of hewn stone — Amos 5:11
the *h* of Achzib shall be a lie to — Mic 1:14
and *h*, and take them away — Mic 2:2
ye cast out from their pleasant *h* — Mic 2:9
their masters' *h* with violence — Zeph 1:9
a booty, and their *h* a desolation — Zeph 1:13
they shall also build *h*, but not — Zeph 1:13
in the *h* of Ashkelon shall they — Zeph 2:7
O ye, to dwell in your cieled *h* — Hag 1:4
the *h* rifled, and the women — Zec 14:2
soft clothing are in kings' *h* — Mt 11:8
And every one that hath forsaken *h* — Mt 19:29
for ye devour widows' *h*, and for a — Mt 23:14
them away fasting to their own *h* — Mk 8:3
hundredfold now in this time, *h* — Mk 10:30
Which devour widows' *h*, and for a — Mk 12:40
they may receive me into their *h* — Lk 16:4
Which devour widows' *h*, and for a — Lk 20:47
of lands or *h* sold them, and — Acts 4:34
have ye not *h* to eat and to drink — 1Cor 11:22
children and their own *h* well — 1Ti 3:12
sort are they which creep into *h* — 2Ti 3:6
be stopped, who subvert whole *h* — Titus 1:11

## HOUSETOP
to dwell in a corner of the *h* — Prov 21:9
to dwell in the corner of the *h* — Prov 25:24
Let him which is on the *h* not — Mt 24:17
let him that is on the *h* not go — Mk 13:15
multitude, they went upon the *h* — Lk 5:19
day, he which shall be upon the *h* — Lk 17:31
Peter went up upon the *h* to pray — Acts 10:9

## HOUSETOPS
them be as the grass upon the *h* — Ps 129:6
thou art wholly gone up to the *h* — Is 22:1
green herb, as the grass on the *h* — Is 37:27
generally upon all the *h* of Moab — Jer 48:38
the host of heaven upon the *h* — Zeph 1:5
ear, that preach ye upon the *h* — Mt 10:27
shall be proclaimed upon the *h* — Lk 12:3

**HOW** See PREFACE.

## HOWBEIT
*H* Sisera fled away on his feet to — Judg 4:17
*H* the king of the children of — Judg 11:28
*H* the hair of his head began to — Judg 16:22
*h* the name of the city was Laish — Judg 18:29
*H* we may not give them wives of — Judg 21:18
*h* there is a kinsman nearer than — Ruth 3:12
*h* yet protest solemnly unto them, — 1Sa 8:9
*H* he refused to turn aside — 2Sa 2:23
*H*, because by this deed thou hast — 2Sa 12:14
*H* he would not hearken unto her — 2Sa 13:14
*h* he would not go, but blessed — 2Sa 13:25
*h* he attained not unto the first — 2Sa 23:19
*h* the kingdom is turned about, and — 1Kin 2:15
*H* I believed not the words, until — 1Kin 10:7
*H* I will not rend away all the — 1Kin 11:13
*h* let me go in any wise — 1Kin 11:22
*H* I will not take the whole — 1Kin 11:34
*h* the slingers went about it, and — 2Kin 3:25
*h* the LORD hath shewed me that he — 2Kin 8:10
*H* from the sins of Jeroboam the — 2Kin 10:29
*H* there were not made for the — 2Kin 12:13
*H* the high places were not taken — 2Kin 14:4
*H* the high places were not — 2Kin 15:35
*H* every nation made gods of their — 2Kin 17:29
*H* they did not hearken, but they — 2Kin 17:40
*H* there was no reckoning made — 2Kin 22:7
*h* he attained not to the first — 1Chr 11:21
*H* the LORD God of Israel chose me — 1Chr 28:4
*H* I believed not their words, — 2Chr 9:6
*h* the king of Israel stayed — 2Chr 18:34
*H* the high places were not taken — 2Chr 20:33
*H* the LORD would not destroy the — 2Chr 21:7
*H* they buried him in the city of — 2Chr 21:20
*H* the Levites hastened it not — 2Chr 24:5
*h* he entered not into the temple — 2Chr 27:2
*H* in the business of the — 2Chr 32:31
*H* thou art just in all that is — Neh 9:33
*h* our God turned the curse into a — Neh 13:2
*H* he will not stretch out his — Job 30:24
*H* he meaneth not so, neither doth — Is 10:7
*H* I sent unto you all my servants — Jer 44:4
*H* this kind goeth not out but by — Mt 17:21
*H* Jesus suffered him not, but — Mk 5:19
*H* in vain do they worship me, — Mk 7:7
(*H* there came other boats from — Jn 6:23
*H* no man spake openly of him for — Jn 7:13
*H* we know this man whence he is — Jn 7:27
*H* Jesus spake of his death — Jn 11:13
*H* when he, the Spirit of truth, — Jn 16:13
*H* many of them which heard the — Acts 4:4
*H* the most High dwelleth not in — Acts 7:48
*H*, as the disciples stood round — Acts 14:20
*H* certain men clave unto him, and — Acts 17:34
*H* we must be cast upon a certain — Acts 27:26
*H* they looked when he should have — Acts 28:6
*H* we speak wisdom among them that — 1Cor 2:6
*H* there is not in every man that — 1Cor 8:7
*h* in the spirit he speaketh — 1Cor 14:2
*h* in malice be ye children, but — 1Cor 14:20
*H* that was not first which is — 1Cor 15:46
*H* whereinsoever any is bold, (I — 2Cor 11:21
*H* then, when ye knew not God, ye — Gal 4:8
*H* for this cause I obtained mercy — 1Ti 1:16
*h* not all that came out of Egypt — Heb 3:16

## HOWL
*H* ye; for the day of the LORD — Is 13:6
*H*, O gate — Is 14:31
Moab shall *h* over Nebo, and over — Is 15:2
their streets, every one shall *h* — Is 15:3
*h* for Moab, every one shall *h* — Is 16:7
*H*, ye ships of Tarshish — Is 23:1
*h*, ye inhabitants of the isle — Is 23:6
*H*, ye ships of Tarshish — Is 23:14
rule over them make them to *h* — Is 52:5
shall *h* for vexation of spirit — Is 65:14
you with sackcloth, lament and *h* — Jer 4:8
*H*, ye shepherds, and cry — Jer 25:34
inhabitants of the land shall *h* — Jer 47:2
*h* and cry; tell ye it — Jer 48:20
Therefore will I *h* for Moab — Jer 48:31
They shall *h*, saying, How is it — Jer 48:39
*H*, O Heshbon, for Ai is spoiled — Jer 49:3
*h* for her; take balm — Jer 51:8
Cry and *h*, son of man — Eze 21:12
*H* ye, Woe worth the day — Eze 30:2
and *h*, all ye drinkers of wine, — Joel 1:5
*h*, O ye vinedressers, for the — Joel 1:11
*h*, ye ministers of the altar — Joel 1:13
Therefore I will wail and *h* — Mic 1:8
*H*, ye inhabitants of Maktesh, for — Zeph 1:11
*H*, fir tree; for the cedar — Zec 11:2
*h*, O ye oaks of Bashan — Zec 11:2
*h* for your miseries that shall — Jas 5:1

## HOWLED
when they *h* upon their beds — Hos 7:14

## HOWLING
and in the waste *h* wilderness — Deut 32:10
the *h* thereof unto Eglaim, and the — Is 15:8
the *h* thereof unto Beer-elim — Is 15:8
an *h* of the principal of the — Jer 25:36
an *h* from the second, and a great — Zeph 1:10
a voice of the *h* of the shepherds — Zec 11:3

**HOWLINGS**
the temple shall be *h* in that day ... Amos 8:3

**HOWSOEVER**
*h* let all thy wants lie upon me ... Judg 19:20
of Zadok yet again to Joab, But *h* ... 2Sa 18:22
But *h*, said he, let me run ... 2Sa 18:23
not be cut off, *h* I punished them ... Zeph 3:7

**HOZAI** See SEERS.

**HUBBAH** See JUHUBBAH.

**HUGE**
Ethiopians and the Lubims a *h* host ... 2Chr 16:8

**HUKKOK** (*huk'-kok*) See HELKATH, HUKOK. *A place in Naphtali.*
and goeth out from thence to *H* ... Josh 19:34

**HUKOK** (*hu'-kok*) See HUKKOK. *A city in Asher.*
*H* with her suburbs, and Rehob with .. 1Chr 6:75

**HUL** (*hul*) *A son of Aram.*
Uz, and *H*, and Gether, and Mash ... Gen 10:23
and Lud, and Aram, and Uz, and *H* ... 1Chr 1:17

**HULDAH** (*hul'-dah*) *A prophetess.*
went unto *H* the prophetess, the ... 2Kin 22:14
went to *H* the prophetess, the ... 2Chr 34:22

**HUMBLE**
refuse to *h* thyself before me ... Ex 10:3
to *h* thee, and to prove thee, to ... Deut 8:2
knew not, that he might *h* thee ... Deut 8:16
*h* ye them, and do with them what ... Judg 19:24
shall *h* themselves, and pray, and ... 2Chr 7:14
thou didst *h* thyself before God, ... 2Chr 34:27
and he shall save the *h* person ... Job 22:29
forgetteth not the cry of the *h* ... Ps 9:12
forget not the *h* ... Ps 10:12
hast heard the desire of the *h* ... Ps 10:17
the *h* shall hear thereof, and be ... Ps 34:2
The *h* shall see this, and be glad ... Ps 69:32
*h* thyself, and make sure thy ... Prov 6:3
be of an *h* spirit with the lowly ... Prov 16:19
shall uphold the *h* in spirit ... Prov 29:23
that is of a contrite and *h* spirit ... Is 57:15
to revive the spirit of the *h* ... Is 57:15
the queen, *H* yourselves, sit down ... Jer 13:18
Whosoever therefore shall *h* ... Mt 18:4
he that shall *h* himself shall be ... Mt 23:12
my God will *h* me among you, and ... 2Cor 12:21
but giveth grace unto the *h* ... Jas 4:6
*H* yourselves in the sight of the ... Jas 4:10
proud, and giveth grace to the *h* ... 1Pet 5:5
*H* yourselves therefore under the ... 1Pet 5:6

**HUMBLED**
their uncircumcised hearts be *h* ... Lev 26:41
he *h* thee, and suffered thee to ... Deut 8:3
of her, because thou hast *h* her ... Deut 21:14
because he hath *h* his neighbour's ... Deut 22:24
because he hath *h* her, he may not ... Deut 22:29
thou hast *h* thyself before the ... 2Kin 22:19
Israel and the king *h* themselves ... 2Chr 12:6
LORD saw that they *h* themselves ... 2Chr 12:7
saying, They have *h* themselves ... 2Chr 12:7
And when he *h* himself, the wrath ... 2Chr 12:12
and of Zebulun *h* themselves ... 2Chr 30:11
Notwithstanding Hezekiah *h* ... 2Chr 32:26
*h* himself greatly before the God ... 2Chr 33:12
and graven images, before he was *h* . 2Chr 33:19
*h* not himself before the LORD, as ... 2Chr 33:23
Manasseh his father had *h* himself ... 2Chr 33:23
*h* not himself before Jeremiah the ... 2Chr 36:12
I *h* my soul with fasting ... Ps 35:13
The lofty looks of man shall be *h* ... Is 2:11
and the mighty man shall be *h* ... Is 5:15
the eyes of the lofty shall be *h* ... Is 5:15
down, and the haughty shall be *h* ... Is 10:33
They are not *h* even unto this day ... Jer 44:10
in remembrance, and is *h* in me ... Lam 3:20
in thee have they *h* her that was ... Eze 22:10
another in thee hath *h* his sister ... Eze 22:11
hast not *h* thine heart, though ... Dan 5:22
he *h* himself, and became obedient ... Phil 2:8

**HUMBLEDST**
*h* thyself before me, and didst ... 2Chr 34:27

**HUMBLENESS**
kindness, *h* of mind, meekness, ... Col 3:12

**HUMBLETH**
thou how Ahab *h* himself before me . 1Kin 21:29
because he *h* himself before me, I ... 1Kin 21:29
*h* himself, that the poor may fall ... Ps 10:10
Who *h* himself to behold the ... Ps 113:6
down, and the great man *h* himself ... Is 2:9
he that *h* himself shall be ... Lk 14:11
he that *h* himself shall be ... Lk 18:14

**HUMBLY**
I *h* beseech thee that I may find ... 2Sa 16:4
mercy, and to walk *h* with thy God ... Mic 6:8

**HUMILIATION**
In his *h* his judgment was taken ... Acts 8:33

**HUMILITY**
and before honour is *h* ... Prov 15:33
and before honour is *h* ... Prov 18:12
By *h* and the fear of the LORD are ... Prov 22:4
the Lord with all *h* of mind ... Acts 20:19
of your reward in a voluntary *h* ... Col 2:18
of wisdom in will worship, and *h* ... Col 2:23
to another, and be clothed with *h* ... 1Pet 5:5

**HUMTAH** (*hum'-tah*) *A city in Judah.*
And *H*, and Kirjath-arba, which is ... Josh 15:54

**HUNDRED** See PREFACE.

**HUNDREDFOLD**
and received in the same year an *h* ... Gen 26:12
how many soever they be, an *h* ... 2Sa 24:3
and brought forth fruit, some an *h* ... Mt 13:8
and bringeth forth, some an *h* ... Mt 13:23
name's sake, shall receive an *h* ... Mt 19:29
receive an *h* now in this time ... Mk 10:30
and sprang up, and bare fruit an *h* ... Lk 8:8

**HUNDREDS**
of thousands, and rulers of *h* ... Ex 18:21
rulers of thousands, rulers of *h* ... Ex 18:25
thousands, and captains over *h* ... Num 31:14
of thousands, and captains of *h* ... Num 31:48
and of the captains of *h*, was ... Num 31:52
the captains of thousands and of *h* ... Num 31:54
thousands, and captains over *h* ... Deut 1:15
of thousands, and captains of *h* ... 1Sa 22:7
of the Philistines passed on by *h* ... 1Sa 29:2
and captains of *h* over them ... 2Sa 18:1
and all the people came out by *h* ... 2Sa 18:4
sent and fetched the rulers over *h* ... 2Kin 11:4
the captains over the *h* did ... 2Kin 11:9
to the captains over *h* did the ... 2Kin 11:10
commanded the captains of the *h* ... 2Kin 11:15
And he took the rulers over *h* ... 2Kin 11:19
the captains of thousands and *h* ... 1Chr 13:1
the captains over thousands and *h* ... 1Chr 26:26
and captains of thousands and *h* ... 1Chr 27:1
thousands, and captains over the *h* ... 1Chr 28:1
the captains of thousands and of *h* ... 1Chr 29:6
the captains of thousands and of *h* ... 2Chr 1:2
and took the captains of *h* ... 2Chr 23:1
to the captains of *h* spears ... 2Chr 23:9
of *h* that were set over the host ... 2Chr 23:14
And he took the captains of *h* ... 2Chr 23:20
thousands, and captains over *h* ... 2Chr 25:5
And they sat down in ranks, by *h* ... Mk 6:40

**HUNDREDTH**
In the six *h* year of Noah's life, ... Gen 7:11
And it came to pass in the six *h* ... Gen 8:13
also the *h* part of the money, and ... Neh 5:11

**HUNGER**
kill this whole assembly with *h* ... Ex 16:3
thee, and suffered thee to *h* ... Deut 8:3
shall send against thee, in *h* ... Deut 28:48
They shall be burnt with *h* ... Deut 32:24
bread from heaven for their *h* ... Neh 9:15
young lions do lack, and suffer *h* ... Ps 34:10
and an idle soul shall suffer *h* ... Prov 19:15
They shall not *h* nor thirst ... Is 49:10
he is like to die for *h* in the ... Jer 38:9
the trumpet, nor have *h* of bread ... Jer 42:14
that faint for *h* in the top of ... Lam 2:19
than they that be slain with *h* ... Lam 4:9
more consumed with *h* in the land ... Eze 34:29
Blessed are they which do *h* ... Mt 5:6
Blessed are ye that *h* now ... Lk 6:21
for ye shall *h* ... Lk 6:25
and to spare, and I perish with *h* ... Lk 15:17
that cometh to me shall never *h* ... Jn 6:35
Therefore if thine enemy *h* ... Rom 12:20
unto this present hour we both *h* ... 1Cor 4:11
And if any man *h*, let him eat at ... 1Cor 11:34
in watchings often, in *h* ... 2Cor 11:27
to kill with sword, and with *h* ... Rev 6:8
They shall *h* no more, neither ... Rev 7:16

**HUNGERBITTEN**
His strength shall be *h*, and ... Job 18:12

**HUNGERED**
he returned into the city, he *h* ... Mt 21:18
they were ended, he afterward *h* ... Lk 4:2

**HUNGRED**
nights, he was afterward an *h* ... Mt 4:2
and his disciples were an *h* ... Mt 12:1
what David did, when he was an *h* ... Mt 12:3
For I was an *h*, and ye gave me ... Mt 25:35
Lord, when saw we thee an *h* ... Mt 25:37
For I was an *h*, and ye gave me no ... Mt 25:42
Lord, when saw we thee an *h* ... Mt 25:44
when he had need, and was an *h* ... Mk 2:25
David did, when himself was an *h* ... Lk 6:3

**HUNGRY**
and they that were *h* ceased ... 1Sa 2:5
for they said, The people is *h* ... 2Sa 17:29
They know that we be *h* ... 2Kin 7:12
Whose harvest the *h* eateth up ... Job 5:5
hast withholden bread from the *h* ... Job 22:7
take away the sheaf from the *h* ... Job 24:10
If I were *h*, I would not tell ... Ps 50:12
*H* and thirsty, their soul fainted ... Ps 107:5
filleth the *h* soul with goodness ... Ps 107:9
And there he maketh the *h* to dwell ... Ps 107:36
which giveth food to the *h* ... Ps 146:7
to satisfy his soul when he is *h* ... Prov 6:30
If thine enemy be *h*, give him ... Prov 25:21
but to the *h* soul every bitter ... Prov 27:7
through it, hardly bestead and *h* ... Is 8:21
pass, that when they shall be *h* ... Is 8:21
snatch on the right hand, and be *h* ... Is 9:20
even be as when an *h* man dreameth ... Is 29:8
to make empty the soul of the *h* ... Is 32:6
yea, he is *h*, and his strength ... Is 44:12
it not to deal thy bread to the *h* ... Is 58:7
thou draw out thy soul to the *h* ... Is 58:10
shall eat, but ye shall be *h* ... Is 65:13
hath given his bread to the *h* ... Eze 18:7
but hath given his bread to the *h* ... Eze 18:16
were come from Bethany, he was *h* ... Mk 11:12
filled the *h* with good things ... Lk 1:53
And he became very *h*, and would ... Acts 10:10
and one is *h*, and another is ... 1Cor 11:21
both to be full and to be *h* ... Phil 4:12

**HUNT**
to the field to *h* for venison ... Gen 27:5
as when one doth *h* a partridge in ... 1Sa 26:20
Wilt thou *h* the prey for the lion ... Job 38:39
evil shall *h* the violent man to ... Ps 140:11
the adulteress will *h* for the ... Prov 6:26
they shall *h* them from every ... Jer 16:16
They *h* our steps, that we cannot ... Lam 4:18
head of every stature to *h* souls ... Eze 13:18
Will ye *h* the souls of my people, ... Eze 13:18
wherewith ye there *h* the souls to ... Eze 13:20
souls that ye *h* to make them fly ... Eze 13:20
they *h* every man his brother with ... Mic 7:2

**HUNTED**
be no more in your hand to be *h* ... Eze 13:21

**HUNTER**
He was a mighty *h* before the LORD ... Gen 10:9
the mighty *h* before the LORD ... Gen 10:9
and Esau was a cunning *h*, a man of . Gen 25:27
as a roe from the hand of the *h* ... Prov 6:5

**HUNTERS**
and after will I send for many *h* ... Jer 16:16

**HUNTEST**
yet thou *h* my soul to take it ... 1Sa 24:11
Thou *h* me as a fierce lion ... Job 10:16

**HUNTETH**
that sojourn among you, which *h* ... Lev 17:13

**HUNTING**
his brother came in from his *h* ... Gen 27:30
not that which he took in *h* ... Prov 12:27

**HUPHAM** (*hu'-fam*) See HUPPIM, HUPHAMITES. *A son of Benjamin.*
of *H*, the family of the ... Num 26:39

**HUPHAMITES** (*hu'-fam-ites*) *Descendants of hupham.*
of Hupham, the family of the *H* ... Num 26:39

**HUPPAH** (*hup'-pah*) *A priest.*
The thirteenth to *H*, the ... 1Chr 24:13

**HUPPIM** (*hup'-pim*) See HUPHAM. *Head of a Benjamite family.*
Ehi, and Rosh, Muppim, and *H* ... Gen 46:21
Shuppim also, and *H*, the children ... 1Chr 7:12
took to wife the sister of *H* ... 1Chr 7:15

**HUPPITES** See HUPPIM.

**HUR** (*hur*)
*1. Assisted Moses at Rephidim.*
*H* went up to the top of the hill ... Ex 17:10
*H* stayed up his hands, the one on ... Ex 17:12
behold, Aaron and *H* are with you ... Ex 24:14
*2. A son of Caleb.*
the son of Uri, the son of *H* ... Ex 31:2
the son of Uri, the son of *H* ... Ex 35:30
the son of Uri, the son of *H* ... Ex 38:22
him Ephrath, which bare him *H* ... 1Chr 2:19
*H* begat Uri, and Uri begat ... 1Chr 2:20
the son of Uri, the son of *H* ... 2Chr 1:5
*3. A Midianite king.*
Evi, and Rekem, and Zur, and *H* ... Num 31:8
Evi, and Rekem, and Zur, and *H* ... Josh 13:21
*4. An officer of Solomon.*
The son of *H*, in mount Ephraim ... 1Kin 4:8
*5. Father of Caleb.*
the sons of Caleb the son of *H* ... 1Chr 2:50
These are the sons of *H*, the ... 1Chr 4:4
*6. A descendant of Judah.*
Pharez, Hezron, and Carmi, and *H* ... 1Chr 4:1
*7. A rebuilder of Jerusalem's wall.*
repaired Rephaiah the son of *H* ... Neh 3:9

**HURAI** (*hu'-rahee*) See HIDDAI. *A mighty man of David.*
*H* of the brooks of Gaash, Abiel ... 1Chr 11:32

**HURAM** (*hu'-ram*) See HIRAM.
*1. Son of Bela.*
And Gera, and Shephuphan, and *H* ... 1Chr 8:5
*2. Same as Hiram 1.*
Solomon sent to *H* the king of ... 2Chr 2:3
Then *H* the king of Tyre answered ... 2Chr 2:11
*H* said moreover, Blessed be the ... 2Chr 2:12
understanding, of *H* my father's, ... 2Chr 2:13
That the cities which *H* had ... 2Chr 8:2
*H* sent him by the hands of his ... 2Chr 8:18
And the servants also of *H* ... 2Chr 9:10
Tarshish with the servants of *H* ... 2Chr 9:21
*3. Same as Hiram 2.*
*H* made the pots, and the shovels, ... 2Chr 4:11
*H* finished the work that he was ... 2Chr 4:11
did *H* his father make to king ... 2Chr 4:16

**HURAM-ABI** See Huram.

**HURI** (*hu'-ri*) *Father of Abihail.*
children of Abihail the son of *H* ... 1Chr 5:14

**HURL**
or *h* at him by laying of wait, ... Num 35:20

**HURLETH**
as a storm *h* him out of his place ... Job 27:21

**HURLING**
hand and the left in *h* stones ... 1Chr 12:2

**HURT**
wounding, and a young man to my *h* ... Gen 4:23
That thou wilt do us no *h* ... Gen 26:29
but God suffered him not to *h* me ... Gen 31:7
the power of my hand to do you *h* ... Gen 31:29
*h* a woman with child, so that her ... Ex 21:22
And if one man's ox *h* another's ... Ex 21:35
and it die, or be *h*, or driven ... Ex 22:10
of his neighbour, and it be *h* ... Ex 22:14
neither have I *h* one of them ... Num 16:15
then he will turn and do you *h* ... Josh 24:20
there is peace to thee, and no *h* ... 1Sa 20:21
Behold, David seeketh thy *h* ... 1Sa 24:9
we *h* them not, neither was there ... 1Sa 25:7
good unto us, and we were not *h* ... 1Sa 25:15
rise against thee to do thee *h* ... 2Sa 18:32
shouldest thou meddle to thy *h* ... 2Kin 14:10
shouldest thou meddle to thine *h* ... 2Chr 25:19
damage grow to the *h* of the kings ... Ezr 4:22
hand on such as sought their *h* ... Est 9:2
may *h* a man as thou art ... Job 35:8
He that sweareth to his own *h* ... Ps 15:4
to confusion that devise my *h* ... Ps 35:4
together that rejoice at mine *h* ... Ps 35:26
they that seek my *h* speak ... Ps 38:12
against me do they devise my *h* ... Ps 41:7
to confusion, that desire my *h* ... Ps 70:2
and dishonour that seek my *h* ... Ps 71:13
unto shame, that seek my *h* ... Ps 71:24
Whose feet they *h* with fetters ... Ps 105:18
for the owners thereof to their *h* ... Eccl 5:13
ruleth over another to his own *h* ... Eccl 8:9
stones shall be *h* therewith ... Eccl 10:9
They shall not *h* nor destroy in ... Is 11:9
lest any *h* it, I will keep it ... Is 27:3
They shall not *h* nor destroy in ... Is 65:25
They have healed also the *h* of ... Jer 6:14
walk after other gods to your *h* ... Jer 7:6
For they have healed the *h* of the ... Jer 8:11
For the *h* of the daughter of my ... Jer 8:21
the daughter of my people am I *h* ... Jer 8:21
Woe is me for my *h* ... Jer 10:19
kingdoms of the earth for their *h* ... Jer 24:9
and I will do you no *h* ... Jer 25:6
works of your hands to your own *h* ... Jer 25:7
welfare of this people, but the *h* ... Jer 38:4
of the fire, and they have no *h* ... Dan 3:25
mouths, that they have not *h* me ... Dan 6:22
thee, O king, have I done no *h* ... Dan 6:22
no manner of *h* was found upon him ... Dan 6:23
deadly thing, it shall not *h* them ... Mk 16:18
he came out of him, and *h* him not ... Lk 4:35
nothing shall by any means *h* you ... Lk 10:19
man shall set on thee to *h* thee ... Acts 18:10
that this voyage will be with *h* ... Acts 27:10
not be *h* of the second death ... Rev 2:11
see thou *h* not the oil and the ... Rev 6:6
whom it was given to *h* the earth ... Rev 7:2
*H* not the earth, neither the sea, ... Rev 7:3
not *h* the grass of the earth ... Rev 9:4
power was to *h* men five months ... Rev 9:10
had heads, and with them they do *h* ... Rev 9:19
And if any man will *h* them ... Rev 11:5
and if any man will *h* them ... Rev 11:5

**HURTFUL**
*h* unto kings and provinces, and ... Ezr 4:15
his servant from the *h* sword ... Ps 144:10
*h* lusts, which drown men in ... 1Ti 6:9

**HURTING**
hath kept me back from *h* thee ... 1Sa 25:34

**HUSBAND**
and gave also unto her *h* with her ... Gen 3:6
and thy desire shall be to thy *h* ... Gen 3:16
gave her to her *h* Abram to be his ... Gen 16:3
now therefore my *h* will love me ... Gen 29:32
time will my *h* be joined unto me ... Gen 29:34
matter that thou hast taken my *h* ... Gen 30:15
I have given my maiden to my *h* ... Gen 30:18
now will my *h* dwell with me, ... Gen 30:20
Surely a bloody *h* art thou to me ... Ex 4:25
she said, A bloody *h* thou art ... Ex 4:26
the woman's *h* will lay upon him ... Ex 21:22
is a bondmaid, betrothed to an *h* ... Lev 19:20
unto him, which hath had no *h* ... Lev 21:3
take a woman put away from her *h* ... Lev 21:7
it be hid from the eyes of her *h* ... Num 5:13
with another instead of thy *h* ... Num 5:19
aside to another instead of thy *h* ... Num 5:20
lain with thee beside thine *h* ... Num 5:20
have done trespass against her *h* ... Num 5:27
aside to another instead of her *h* ... Num 5:29
And if she had at all an *h* ... Num 30:6
her *h* heard it, and held his peace ... Num 30:7
But if her *h* disallowed her on ... Num 30:8
her *h* heard it, and held his peace ... Num 30:11
But if her *h* hath utterly made ... Num 30:12
her *h* hath made them void ... Num 30:12
her *h* may establish it ... Num 30:13
or her *h* may make it void ... Num 30:13
But if her *h* altogether hold his ... Num 30:14
shalt go in unto her, and be her *h* ... Deut 21:13
with a woman married to an *h* ... Deut 22:22
a virgin be betrothed unto an *h* ... Deut 22:23
And if the latter *h* hate her ... Deut 24:3
or if the latter *h* die, which ... Deut 24:3
Her former *h*, which sent her away ... Deut 24:4
her *h* out of the hand of him that ... Deut 25:11
be evil toward the *h* of her bosom ... Deut 28:56
Then the woman came and told her *h* ... Judg 13:6
but Manoah her *h* was not with her ... Judg 13:9
haste, and ran, and shewed her *h* ... Judg 13:10
unto Samson's wife, Entice thy *h* ... Judg 14:15
her *h* arose, and went after her, ... Judg 19:3
the *h* of the woman that was slain ... Judg 20:4
And Elimelech Naomi's *h* died ... Ruth 1:3
was left of her two sons and her *h* ... Ruth 1:5
each of you in the house of her *h* ... Ruth 1:9
for I am too old to have an *h* ... Ruth 1:12
I should have an *h* also to night ... Ruth 1:12
in law since the death of thine *h* ... Ruth 2:11
Then said Elkanah her *h* to her ... 1Sa 1:8
for she said unto her *h*, I will ... 1Sa 1:22
Elkanah her *h* said unto her, Do ... 1Sa 1:23
when she came up with her *h* to ... 1Sa 2:19
her *h* were dead, she bowed ... 1Sa 4:19
of her father in law and her *h* ... 1Sa 4:21
But she told not her *h* Nabal ... 1Sa 25:19
sent, and took her from her *h* ... 2Sa 3:15
her *h* went with her along weeping ... 2Sa 3:16
heard that Uriah her *h* was dead ... 2Sa 11:26
she mourned for her *h* ... 2Sa 11:26
a widow woman, and mine *h* is dead ... 2Sa 14:5
shall not leave to my *h* neither ... 2Sa 14:7
saying, Thy servant my *h* is dead ... 2Kin 4:1
And she said unto her *h*, Behold ... 2Kin 4:9
hath no child, and her *h* is old ... 2Kin 4:14
And she called unto her *h*, and said ... 2Kin 4:22
is it well with thy *h* ... 2Kin 4:26
woman is a crown to her *h* ... Prov 12:4
The heart of her *h* doth safely ... Prov 31:11
Her *h* is known in the gates, when ... Prov 31:23
her *h* also, and he praiseth her ... Prov 31:28
For thy Maker is thine *h* ... Is 54:5
departeth from her *h*, so have ye ... Jer 3:20
for even the *h* with the wife ... Jer 6:11
although I was an *h* unto them ... Jer 31:32
taketh strangers instead of her *h* ... Eze 16:32
daughter, that lotheth her *h* ... Eze 16:45
or for sister that hath had no *h* ... Eze 44:25
not my wife, neither am I her *h* ... Hos 2:2
I will go and return to my first *h* ... Hos 2:7
sackcloth for the *h* of her youth ... Joel 1:8
Jacob begat Joseph the *h* of Mary ... Mt 1:16
Then Joseph her *h*, being a just ... Mt 1:19
if a woman shall put away her *h* ... Mk 10:12
had lived with an *h* seven years ... Lk 2:36
from her *h* committeth adultery ... Lk 16:18
saith unto her, Go, call thy *h* ... Jn 4:16
answered and said, I have no *h* ... Jn 4:17
Thou hast well said, I have no *h* ... Jn 4:17
whom thou now hast is not thy *h* ... Jn 4:18
have buried thy *h* are at the door ... Acts 5:9
her forth, buried her by her *h* ... Acts 5:10
an *h* is bound by the law to her ... Rom 7:2
law to her *h* so long as he liveth ... Rom 7:2
but if the *h* be dead, she is ... Rom 7:2
is loosed from the law of her *h* ... Rom 7:2
So then if, while her *h* liveth ... Rom 7:3
but if her *h* be dead, she is free ... Rom 7:3
and let every woman have her own *h* ... 1Cor 7:2
Let the *h* render unto the wife ... 1Cor 7:3
likewise also the wife unto the *h* ... 1Cor 7:3
power of her own body, but the *h* ... 1Cor 7:4
likewise also the *h* hath not ... 1Cor 7:4
not the wife depart from her *h* ... 1Cor 7:10
or be reconciled to her *h* ... 1Cor 7:11
let not the *h* put away his wife ... 1Cor 7:11
hath an *h* that believeth not ... 1Cor 7:13
For the unbelieving *h* is ... 1Cor 7:14
wife is sanctified by the *h* ... 1Cor 7:14
whether thou shalt save thy *h* ... 1Cor 7:16
world, how she may please her *h* ... 1Cor 7:34
the law as long as her *h* liveth ... 1Cor 7:39
but if her *h* be dead, she is at ... 1Cor 7:39
for I have espoused you to one *h* ... 2Cor 11:2
children than she which hath a *h* ... Gal 4:27
For the *h* is the head of the wife ... Eph 5:23
wife see that she reverence her *h* ... Eph 5:33
the *h* of one wife, vigilant, ... 1Ti 3:2
the *h* of one wife, having ... Titus 1:6
as a bride adorned for her *h* ... Rev 21:2

**HUSBANDMAN**
And Noah began to be an *h*, and he ... Gen 9:20
thee will I break in pieces the *h* ... Jer 51:23
they shall call the *h* to mourning ... Amos 5:16
say, I am no prophet, I am an *h* ... Zec 13:5
true vine, and my Father is the *h* ... Jn 15:1
The *h* that laboureth must be ... 2Ti 2:6
the *h* waiteth for the precious ... Jas 5:7

**HUSBANDMEN**
the land to be vinedressers and *h* ... 2Kin 25:12
*h* also, and vine dressers in the ... 2Chr 26:10
the cities thereof together, *h* ... Jer 31:24
land for vinedressers and for *h* ... Jer 52:16
Be ye ashamed, O ye *h* ... Joel 1:11
built a tower, and let it out to *h* ... Mt 21:33
he sent his servants to the *h* ... Mt 21:34
the *h* took his servants, and beat ... Mt 21:35
But when the *h* saw the son ... Mt 21:38
what will he do unto those *h* ... Mt 21:40
let out his vineyard unto other *h* ... Mt 21:41
built a tower, and let it out to *h* ... Mk 12:1
season he sent to the *h* a servant ... Mk 12:2
*h* of the fruit of the vineyard ... Mk 12:2
But those *h* said among themselves ... Mk 12:7
he will come and destroy the *h* ... Mk 12:9
a vineyard, and let it forth to *h* ... Lk 20:9
season he sent a servant to the *h* ... Lk 20:10
but the *h* beat him, and sent him ... Lk 20:10
But when the *h* saw him, they ... Lk 20:14
He shall come and destroy these *h* ... Lk 20:16

**HUSBANDRY**
for he loved *h* ... 2Chr 26:10
ye are God's *h*, ye are God's ... 1Cor 3:9

**HUSBAND'S**
And if she vowed in her *h* house ... Num 30:10
her *h* brother shall go in unto ... Deut 25:5
the duty of an *h* brother unto her ... Deut 25:5
My *h* brother refuseth to raise up ... Deut 25:7
perform the duty of my *h* brother ... Deut 25:7
And Naomi had a kinsman of her *h* ... Ruth 2:1

**HUSBANDS**
my womb, that they may be your *h* ... Ruth 1:11
ye stay for them from having *h* ... Ruth 1:13
despise their *h* in their eyes ... Est 1:17
shall give to their *h* honour ... Est 1:20
sons, and give your daughters to *h* ... Jer 29:6
thy sisters, which lothed their *h* ... Eze 16:45
For thou hast had five *h* ... Jn 4:18
let them ask their *h* at home ... 1Cor 14:35
submit yourselves unto your own *h* ... Eph 5:22
be to their own *h* in every thing ... Eph 5:24
*H*, love your wives, even as ... Eph 5:25
submit yourselves unto your own *h* ... Col 3:18
*H*, love your wives, and be not ... Col 3:19
the deacons be the *h* of one wife ... 1Ti 3:12
to be sober, to love their *h* ... Titus 2:4
good, obedient to their own *h* ... Titus 2:5
be in subjection to your own *h* ... 1Pet 3:1
in subjection unto their own *h* ... 1Pet 3:5
Likewise, ye *h*, dwell with them ... 1Pet 3:7

**HUSHAH** (*hu'-shah*) See Hushathite, Shuah.
*A son of Ezer.*
of Gedor, and Ezer the father of *H* ... 1Chr 4:4

**HUSHAI** (*hu'-shahee*) *Friend and advisor of David.*
*H* the Archite came to meet him ... 2Sa 15:32
So *H* David's friend came into the ... 2Sa 15:37
when *H* the Archite, David's ... 2Sa 16:16
that *H* said unto Absalom, God ... 2Sa 16:16
And Absalom said to *H*, Is this thy ... 2Sa 16:17
And *H* said unto Absalom, Nay ... 2Sa 16:18
Call now *H* the Archite also, and ... 2Sa 17:5
when *H* was come to Absalom, ... 2Sa 17:6
*H* said unto Absalom, The counsel ... 2Sa 17:7
For, said *H*, thou knowest thy ... 2Sa 17:8
The counsel of *H* the Archite is ... 2Sa 17:14
Then said *H* unto Zadok and to ... 2Sa 17:15
Baanah the son of *H* was in Asher ... 1Kin 4:16
*H* the Archite was the king's ... 1Chr 27:33

**HUSHAM** (*hu'-sham*) *A king of Edom.*
*H* of the land of Temani reigned ... Gen 36:34
*H* died, and Hadad the son of Bedad ... Gen 36:35
*H* of the land of the Temanites ... 1Chr 1:45
when *H* was dead, Hadad the son of ... 1Chr 1:46

**HUSHATHITE** (*hu'-shath-ite*) *A descendant of Hushah.*
then Sibbechai the *H* slew Saph ... 2Sa 21:18
the Anethothite, Mebunnai the *H* ... 2Sa 23:27
Sibbecai the *H*, Ilai the Ahohite, ... 1Chr 11:29
time Sibbechai the *H* slew Sippai ... 1Chr 20:4
eighth month was Sibbecai the *H* ... 1Chr 27:11

**HUSHIM** (*hu'-shim*) See Shuham.
*1. A son of Dan.*
the sons of Dan; *H* ... Gen 46:23
*2. Son of Aher.*
Huppim, the children of Ir, and *H* ... 1Chr 7:12
*3. A wife of Shaharaim.*
*H* and Baara were his wives ... 1Chr 8:8
of *H* he begat Abitub, and Elpaal ... 1Chr 8:11

**HUSHITES** See Hushim.

**HUSK**
from the kernels even to the *h* ... Num 6:4
ears of corn in the *h* thereof ... 2Kin 4:42

**HUSKS**
with the *h* that the swine did eat ... Lk 15:16

**HUZ**
*H* his firstborn, and Buz his ... Gen 22:21

**HUZZAB** (*huz'-zab*) *A region in Assyria.*
*H* shall be led away captive, she ... Nah 2:7

**HYMENAEUS** (*hy-men-e'-us*) *A false Christian teacher.*
Of whom is *H* and Alexander ... 1Ti 1:20
of whom is *H* and Philetus ... 2Ti 2:17

**HYMN**
And when they had sung an *h* ... Mt 26:30
And when they had sung an *h* ... Mk 14:26

**HYMNS**
to yourselves in psalms and *h* ... Eph 5:19
one another in psalms and *h* ... Col 3:16

**HYPOCRISIES**
all malice, and all guile, and *h* ... 1Pet 2:1

**HYPOCRISY**
will work iniquity, to practise *h* ... Is 32:6
men, but within ye are full of *h* ... Mt 23:28
But he, knowing their *h*, said ... Mk 12:15
of the Pharisees, which is *h* ... Lk 12:1
Speaking lies in *h* ... 1Ti 4:2
without partiality, and without *h* ... Jas 3:17

**HYPOCRITE**
for an *h* shall not come before ... Job 13:16
stir up himself against the *h* ... Job 17:8
the joy of the *h* but for a moment ... Job 20:5
For what is the hope of the *h* ... Job 27:8
That the *h* reign not, lest the ... Job 34:30
An *h* with his mouth destroyeth ... Prov 11:9
for every one is an *h* and an ... Is 9:17
Thou *h*, first cast out the beam ... Mt 7:5
Thou *h*, cast out first the beam ... Lk 6:42
answered him, and said, Thou *h* ... Lk 13:15

**HYPOCRITE'S**
and the *h* hope shall perish ... Job 8:13

**HYPOCRITES**
of *h* shall be desolate, and fire ... Job 15:34
But the *h* in heart heap up wrath ... Job 36:13
fearfulness hath surprised the *h* ... Is 33:14
as the *h* do in the synagogues and ... Mt 6:2
thou shalt not be as the *h* are ... Mt 6:5
when ye fast, be not, as the *h* ... Mt 6:16
Ye *h*, well did Esaias prophesy of ... Mt 15:7
O ye *h*, ye can discern the face ... Mt 16:3
and said, Why tempt ye me, ye *h* ... Mt 22:18
unto you, scribes and Pharisees, *h* ... Mt 23:13
unto you, scribes and Pharisees, *h* ... Mt 23:14
unto you, scribes and Pharisees, *h* ... Mt 23:15
unto you, scribes and Pharisees, *h* ... Mt 23:23
unto you, scribes and Pharisees, *h* ... Mt 23:25
unto you, scribes and Pharisees, *h* ... Mt 23:27
unto you, scribes and Pharisees, *h* ... Mt 23:29
him his portion with the *h* ... Mt 24:51
hath Esaias prophesied of you *h* ... Mk 7:6
unto you, scribes and Pharisees, *h* ... Lk 11:44
Ye *h*, ye can discern the face of ... Lk 12:56

**HYPOCRITICAL**
With *h* mockers in feasts, they ... Ps 35:16
will send him against an *h* nation ... Is 10:6

**HYSSOP**
And ye shall take a bunch of *h* ... Ex 12:22
and cedar wood, and scarlet, and *h* ... Lev 14:4
wood, and the scarlet, and the *h* ... Lev 14:6
and cedar wood, and scarlet, and *h* ... Lev 14:49
take the cedar wood, and the *h* ... Lev 14:51
the cedar wood, and with the *h* ... Lev 14:52
shall take cedar wood, and *h* ... Num 19:6
And a clean person shall take *h* ... Num 19:18
is in Lebanon even unto the *h* ... 1Kin 4:33
Purge me with *h*, and I shall be ... Ps 51:7
with vinegar, and put it upon *h* ... Jn 19:29
with water, and scarlet wool, and *h* ... Heb 9:19

# I

**I** See PREFACE.

**IBHAR** (*ib'-har*) *A son of David.*
*I* also, and Elishua, and Nepheg, and ... 2Sa 5:15
*I* also, and Elishama, and Eliphelet ... 1Chr 3:6
And *I*, and Elishua, and Elpalet, ... 1Chr 14:5

**IBLEAM** (*ib'-le-am*) *A city in Asher.*
Beth-shean and her towns, and *I* ... Josh 17:11
towns, nor the inhabitants of *I* ... Judg 1:27
going up to Gur, which is by *I* ... 2Kin 9:27

**IBNEIAH** (*ib-ne-i'-ah*) *A son of Jeroham.*
*I* the son of Jeroham, and Elah the ... 1Chr 9:8

**IBNIJAH** (*ib-ni'-jah*) *A family of exiles.*
the son of Reuel, the son of *I* ... 1Chr 9:8

**IBRI** (*ib'-ri*) *A descendant of Levi.*
Shoham, and Zaccur, and *I* ... 1Chr 24:27

**IBSAM** See JIBSAM.

**IBZAN** (*ib'-zan*) *A judge of Israel.*
after him *I* of Beth-lehem judged ... Judg 12:8
Then died *I*, and was buried at ... Judg 12:10

**ICE**
are blackish by reason of the *i* ... Job 6:16
Out of whose womb came the *i* ... Job 38:29
casteth forth his *i* like morsels ... Ps 147:17

**I-CHABOD** (*ik'-a-bod*) See I-CHABOD'S. *Son of Phinehas.*
And she named the child *I*, saying ... 1Sa 4:21

**ICHABOD** See I-CHABOD.

**I-CHABOD'S** (*ik'-a-bods*)
*I* brother, the son of Phinehas, ... 1Sa 14:3

**ICONIUM** (*i-co'-ne-um*) *A city in Asia Minor.*
feet against them, and came unto *I* ... Acts 13:51
And it came to pass in *I*, that ... Acts 14:1
certain Jews from Antioch and *I* ... Acts 14:19
returned again to Lystra, and to *I* ... Acts 14:21
brethren that were at Lystra and *I* ... Acts 16:2
came unto me at Antioch, at *I* ... 2Ti 3:11

**IDALAH** (*id'-a-lah*) *A town in Zebulun.*
and Nahallal, and Shimron, and *I* ... Josh 19:15

**IDBASH** (*id'-bash*) *A son of Abi-etam.*
Jezreel, and Ishma, and *I* ... 1Chr 4:3

**IDDO** (*id'-do*)
*1. Father of Ahinadab.*
the son of *I* had Mahanaim ... 1Kin 4:14
*2. A descendant of Gershom.*
*I* his son, Zerah his son, ... 1Chr 6:21
*3. A son of Zechariah.*
in Gilead, *I* the son of Zechariah ... 1Chr 27:21
*4. A seer.*
in the visions of *I* the seer ... 2Chr 9:29
and of *I* the seer concerning ... 2Chr 12:15
in the story of the prophet *I* ... 2Chr 13:22
*5. An ancestor of Zechariah.*
and Zechariah the son of *I* ... Ezr 5:1
prophet and Zechariah the son of *I* ... Ezr 6:14
the son of *I* the prophet, saying, ... Zec 1:1
the son of *I* the prophet, saying, ... Zec 1:7
*6. A Nethinim chief in exile.*
*I* the chief at the place Casiphia ... Ezr 8:17
them what they should say unto *I* ... Ezr 8:17
*7. A priest.*
*I*, Ginnetho, Abijah, ... Neh 12:4
Of *I*, Zechariah ... Neh 12:16

**IDLE**
for they be *i* ... Ex 5:8
he said, Ye are *i*, ye are *i* ... Ex 5:17
an *i* soul shall suffer hunger ... Prov 19:15
That every *i* word that men shall ... Mt 12:36
standing *i* in the marketplace ... Mt 20:3
out, and found others standing *i* ... Mt 20:6
Why stand ye here all the day *i* ... Mt 20:6
words seemed to them as *i* tales ... Lk 24:11
And withal they learn to be *i* ... 1Ti 5:13
and not only *i*, but tattlers also ... 1Ti 5:13

**IDLENESS**
and eateth not the bread of *i* ... Prov 31:27
through *i* of the hands the house ... Eccl 10:18
and abundance of *i* was in her ... Eze 16:49

**IDOL**
she had made an *i* in a grove ... 1Kin 15:13
and Asa destroyed her *i*, and burnt ... 1Kin 15:13
she had made an *i* in a grove ... 2Chr 15:16
and Asa cut down her *i* ... 2Chr 15:16
the *i* which he had made, in the ... 2Chr 33:7
the *i* out of the house of the ... 2Chr 33:15
Mine *i* hath done them, and my ... Is 48:5
incense, as if he blessed an *i* ... Is 66:3
man Coniah a despised broken *i* ... Jer 22:28
Woe to the *i* shepherd that ... Zec 11:17
and offered sacrifice unto the *i* ... Acts 7:41
we know that an *i* is nothing in ... 1Cor 8:4
the *i* unto this hour eat it as a ... 1Cor 8:7
it as a thing offered unto an *i* ... 1Cor 8:7
that the *i* is any thing, or that ... 1Cor 10:19

**IDOLATER**
fornicator, or covetous, or an *i* ... 1Cor 5:11
nor covetous man, who is an *i* ... Eph 5:5

**IDOLATERS**
or extortioners, or with *i* ... 1Cor 5:10
neither fornicators, nor *i* ... 1Cor 6:9
Neither be ye *i*, as were some of ... 1Cor 10:7
whoremongers, and sorcerers, and *i* ... Rev 21:8
whoremongers, and murderers, and *i* .. Rev 22:15

**IDOLATRIES**
banquetings, and abominable *i* ... 1Pet 4:3

**IDOLATROUS**
And he put down the *i* priests ... 2Kin 23:5

**IDOLATRY**
stubbornness is as iniquity and *i* ... 1Sa 15:23
he saw the city wholly given to *i* ... Acts 17:16
my dearly beloved, flee from *i* ... 1Cor 10:14
*I*, witchcraft, hatred, variance, ... Gal 5:20
and covetousness, which is *i* ... Col 3:5

**IDOL'S**
sit at meat in the *i* temple ... 1Cor 8:10

**IDOLS**
Turn ye not unto *i*, nor make to ... Lev 19:4
make you no *i* nor graven image ... Lev 26:1
upon the carcases of your *i* ... Lev 26:30
their abominations, and their *i* ... Deut 29:17
it in the house of their *i* ... 1Sa 31:9
removed all the *i* that his ... 1Kin 15:12
very abominably in following *i* ... 1Kin 21:26
For they served *i*, whereof the ... 2Kin 17:12
made Judah also to sin with his *i* ... 2Kin 21:11
served the *i* that his father ... 2Kin 21:21
wizards, and the images, and the *i* ... 2Kin 23:24
to carry tidings unto their *i* ... 1Chr 10:9
all the gods of the people are *i* ... 1Chr 16:26
put away the abominable *i* out of ... 2Chr 15:8
fathers, and served groves and *i* ... 2Chr 24:18
cut down all the *i* throughout all ... 2Chr 34:7
all the gods of the nations are *i* ... Ps 96:5
that boast themselves of *i* ... Ps 97:7
And they served their *i* ... Ps 106:36
sacrificed unto the *i* of Canaan ... Ps 106:38
Their *i* are silver and gold, the ... Ps 115:4
The *i* of the heathen are silver ... Ps 135:15
Their land also is full of *i* ... Is 2:8
the *i* he shall utterly abolish ... Is 2:18
a man shall cast his *i* of silver ... Is 2:20
his *i* of gold, which they made ... Is 2:20
hath found the kingdoms of the *i* ... Is 10:10
I have done unto Samaria and her *i* ... Is 10:11
so do to Jerusalem and her *i* ... Is 10:11
the *i* of Egypt shall be moved at ... Is 19:1
and they shall seek to the *i* ... Is 19:3
shall cast away his *i* of silver ... Is 31:7
his *i* of gold, which your own ... Is 31:7
together that are makers of *i* ... Is 45:16
their *i* were upon the beasts, and ... Is 46:1
with *i* under every green tree ... Is 57:5
her *i* are confounded, her images ... Jer 50:2
and they are mad upon their *i* ... Jer 50:38
down your slain men before your *i* ... Eze 6:4
children of Israel before their *i* ... Eze 6:5
your *i* may be broken and cease, and ... Eze 6:6
which go a whoring after their *i* ... Eze 6:9
their *i* round about their altars ... Eze 6:13
offer sweet savour to all their *i* ... Eze 6:13
all the *i* of the house of Israel, ... Eze 8:10
set up their *i* in their heart ... Eze 14:3
setteth up his *i* in his heart ... Eze 14:4
to the multitude of his *i* ... Eze 14:4
estranged from me through their *i* ... Eze 14:5
and turn yourselves from your *i* ... Eze 14:6
and setteth up his *i* in his heart ... Eze 14:7
lovers, and with all the *i* of thy ... Eze 16:36
to the *i* of the house of Israel ... Eze 18:6
hath lifted up his eyes to the *i* ... Eze 18:12
to the *i* of the house of Israel ... Eze 18:15
yourselves with the *i* of Egypt ... Eze 20:7
did they forsake the *i* of Egypt ... Eze 20:8
their heart went after their *i* ... Eze 20:16
defile yourselves with their *i* ... Eze 20:18
eyes were after their fathers' *i* ... Eze 20:24
yourselves with all your *i* ... Eze 20:31
Go ye, serve ye every one his *i* ... Eze 20:39
with your gifts, and with your *i* ... Eze 20:39
maketh *i* against herself to ... Eze 22:3
in thine *i* which thou hast made ... Eze 22:4
with all their *i* she defiled ... Eze 23:7
thou art polluted with their *i* ... Eze 23:30
with their *i* have they committed ... Eze 23:37
slain their children to their *i* ... Eze 23:39
ye shall bear the sins of your *i* ... Eze 23:49
I will also destroy the *i* ... Eze 30:13
lift up your eyes toward your *i* ... Eze 33:25
for their *i* wherewith they had ... Eze 36:18
filthiness, and from all your *i* ... Eze 36:25
themselves any more with their *i* ... Eze 37:23
astray away from me after their *i* ... Eze 44:10
unto them before their *i*, and ... Eze 44:12
Ephraim is joined to *i* ... Hos 4:17
their gold have they made them *i* ... Hos 8:4
and *i* according to their own ... Hos 13:2
What have I to do any more with *i* ... Hos 14:8
all the *i* thereof will I lay ... Mic 1:7
trusteth therein, to make dumb *i* ... Hab 2:18
For the *i* have spoken vanity, and ... Zec 10:2
names of the *i* out of the land ... Zec 13:2
they abstain from pollutions of *i* ... Acts 15:20
abstain from meats offered to *i* ... Acts 15:29
from things offered to *i*, and from ... Acts 21:25
thou that abhorrest *i*, dost thou ... Rom 2:22
as touching things offered unto *i* ... 1Cor 8:1
are offered in sacrifice unto *i* ... 1Cor 8:4
things which are offered to *i* ... 1Cor 8:10
in sacrifice to *i* is any thing ... 1Cor 10:19
is offered in sacrifice unto *i* ... 1Cor 10:28
carried away unto these dumb *i* ... 1Cor 12:2
hath the temple of God with *i* ... 2Cor 6:16
to God from *i* to serve the living ... 1Th 1:9
children, keep yourselves from *i* ... 1Jn 5:21
to eat things sacrificed unto *i* ... Rev 2:14
to eat things sacrificed unto *i* ... Rev 2:20
*i* of gold, and silver, and brass, ... Rev 9:20

**IDUMAEA** (*i-doo-me'-ah*) See IDUMEA. *Greek form of Edom.*
And from Jerusalem, and from *I* ... Mk 3:8

**IDUMEA** (*i-doo-me'-ah*) See EDOM, IDUMAEA. *Same as Edom.*
behold, it shall come down upon *I* ... Is 34:5
great slaughter in the land of *I* ... Is 34:6
desolate, O mount Seir, and all *I* ... Eze 35:15
of the heathen, and against all *I* ... Eze 36:5

**IEZERITES**

**IF** See PREFACE.

**IGAL** (*i'-gal*) See IGEAL.
*1. One of the twelve spies.*
of Issachar, *I* the son of Joseph ... Num 13:7
*2. A mighty man of David.*
*I* the son of Nathan of Zobah, ... 2Sa 23:36

**IGDALIAH** (*ig-da-li'-ah*) *Father of Hanan.*
the sons of Hanan, the son of *I* ... Jer 35:4

**IGEAL** (*ig'-e-al*) See IGAL. *A royal descendant of Judah.*
Hattush, and *I*, and Bariah, and ... 1Chr 3:22

**IGNOMINY**
also contempt, and with *i* reproach ..... Prov 18:3

**IGNORANCE**
If a soul shall sin through *i*........................ Lev 4:2
of Israel sin through *i*, and the.............. Lev 4:13
done somewhat through *i* against........... Lev 4:22
the common people sin through *i* .......... Lev 4:27
a trespass, and sin through *i* .............. Lev 5:15
concerning his *i* wherein he erred.......... Lev 5:18
if ought be committed by *i* .................. Num 15:24
for it is *i*.................................................. Num 15:25
before the LORD, for their *i*................... Num 15:25
seeing all the people were in *i* ............ Num 15:26
And if any soul sin through *i*............... Num 15:27
he sinneth by *i* before the LORD.......... Num 15:28
for him that sinneth through *i*............. Num 15:29
I wot that through *i* ye did it .............. Acts 3:17
the times of this *i* God winked at....... Acts 17:30
God through the *i* that is in them ......... Eph 4:18
to the former lusts in your *i*.................. 1Pet 1:14
to silence the *i* of foolish men............... 1Pet 2:15

**IGNORANT**
So foolish was I, and *i*............................. Ps 73:22
they are all *i*, they are all dumb.............. Is 56:10
father, though Abraham be *i* of us......... Is 63:16
and *i* men, they marvelled...................... Acts 4:13
Now I would not have you *i*..................... Rom 1:13
For they being *i* of God's........................ Rom 10:3
ye should be *i* of this mystery................. Rom 11:25
I would not that ye should be *i*............ 1Cor 10:1
brethren, I would not have you *i*.......... 1Cor 12:1
any man be *i*, let him be *i*.................... 1Cor 14:38
have you *i* of our trouble which............. 2Cor 1:8
for we are not *i* of his devices................ 2Cor 2:11
But I would not have you to be *i*.............. 1Th 4:13
Who can have compassion on the *i* ........ Heb 5:2
For this they willingly are *i* of................ 2Pet 3:5
be not *i* of this one thing, that.............. 2Pet 3:8

**IGNORANTLY**
for the soul that sinneth *i*..................... Num 15:28
Whoso killeth his neighbour *i*............... Deut 19:4
Whom therefore ye *i* worship................ Acts 17:23
because I did it *i* in unbelief.................... 1Ti 1:13

**IIM** (*i'-im*) See IJE-ABARIM.
*1. A Hebrew encampment in the wilderness.*
And they departed from I, and........... Num 33:45
*2. A town in Judah.*
Baalah, and I, and Azem,........................ Josh 15:29

**IJE-ABARIM** (*i'-je-ab'-a-rim*) See IIM. *Same as Iim 1.*
from Oboth, and pitched at *I* ............. Num 21:11
from Oboth, and pitched in *I*............... Num 33:44

**IJON** (*i'-jon*) *A town in Naphtali.*
the cities of Israel, and smote *I*.......... 1Kin 15:20
king of Assyria, and took *I* .................. 2Kin 15:29
and they smote *I*, and Dan, and........... 2Chr 16:4

**IKKESH** (*ik'-kesh*) *Father of Ira.*
Ira the son of *I* the Tekoite................... 2Sa 23:26
Ira the son of *I* the Tekoite.................. 1Chr 11:28
was Ira the son of *I* the Tekoite........... 1Chr 27:9

**ILAI** (*i'-lahee*) See ZALMON. *A "mighty man" of David.*
the Hushathite, *I* the Ahohite,........... 1Chr 11:29

**ILL**
*i* favoured and leanfleshed...................... Gen 41:3
the *i* favoured and leanfleshed.............. Gen 41:4
very *i* favoured and leanfleshed,........... Gen 41:19
the *i* favoured kine did eat up............... Gen 41:20
but they were still *i* favoured................ Gen 41:21
*i* favoured kine that came up................. Gen 41:27
Wherefore dealt ye so *i* with me............. Gen 43:6
or blind, or have any *i* blemish.............. Deut 15:21
it shall go *i* with him that is.................. Job 20:26
so that it went *i* with Moses for............. Ps 106:32
it shall be *i* with him.................................. Is 3:11
but if it seem *i* unto thee to................... Jer 40:4
his *i* savour shall come up,..................... Joel 2:20
themselves *i* in their doings...................... Mic 3:4
Love worketh no *i* to his........................ Rom 13:10

**ILLUMINATED**
days, in which, after ye were *i* ............ Heb 10:32

**ILLYRICUM** (*il-lir'-ic-um*) *A Roman Adriatic province.*
Jerusalem, and round about unto *I*.... Rom 15:19

**IMAGE**
said, Let us make man in our *i* ............. Gen 1:26
So God created man in his own *i* ........... Gen 1:27
in the *i* of God created he him............... Gen 1:27
in his own likeness, after his *i*................ Gen 5:3
for in the *i* of God made he man.............. Gen 9:6
not make unto thee any graven *i*.............. Ex 20:4
make you no idols nor graven *i*.............. Lev 26:1
neither rear you up a standing *i*............ Lev 26:1
up any *i* of stone in your land.................. Lev 26:1
and make you a graven *i*, the................ Deut 4:16
with you, and make you a graven *i*........ Deut 4:23
yourselves, and make a graven *i*........... Deut 4:25
shalt not make thee any graven *i*............ Deut 5:8
they have made them a molten *i*............ Deut 9:12
shalt thou set thee up any *i* ................ Deut 16:22
maketh any graven or molten *i*.......... Deut 27:15
make a graven *i* and a molten *i*............ Judg 17:3
a graven *i* and a molten *i*....................... Judg 17:4
and a graven *i*, and a molten *i*........... Judg 18:14
in thither, and took the graven *i*......... Judg 18:17
and the teraphim, and the molten *i*.... Judg 18:17
house, and fetched the carved *i*.......... Judg 18:18
and the teraphim, and the molten *i*... Judg 18:18
and the teraphim, and the graven *i*... Judg 18:20
of Dan set up the graven *i*.................... Judg 18:30
they set them up Micah's graven *i*...... Judg 18:31
And Michal took an *i*, and laid it.......... 1Sa 19:13
behold, there was an *i* in the bed .......... 1Sa 19:16
for he put away the *i* of Baal ................. 2Kin 3:2
And they brake down the *i* of Baal.... 2Kin 10:27
he set a graven *i* of the grove .............. 2Kin 21:7
he made two cherubims of *i* work ....... 2Chr 3:10
And he set a carved *i*, the idol............. 2Chr 33:7
an *i* was before mine eyes, there ............ Job 4:16
thou shalt despise their *i*........................ Ps 73:20
Horeb, and worshipped the molten *i*.... Ps 106:19
The workman melteth a graven *i*............ Is 40:19
workman to prepare a graven *i*............... Is 40:20
a graven *i* are all of them vanity .............. Is 44:9
or molten a graven *i* that is.................... Is 44:10
he maketh it a graven *i*, and................... Is 44:15
maketh a god, even his graven *i*............. Is 44:17
set up the wood of their graven *i*............ Is 45:20
hath done them, and my graven *i* ............. Is 48:5
my graven *i*, and my molten *i* .................. Is 48:5
is confounded by the graven *i*............... Jer 10:14
for his molten *i* is falsehood................... Jer 10:14
is confounded by the graven *i*............... Jer 51:17
for his molten *i* is falsehood.................. Jer 51:17
was the seat of the *i* of jealousy.............. Eze 8:3
this *i* of jealousy in the entry .................. Eze 8:5
king, sawest, and behold a great *i*......... Dan 2:31
This great *i*, whose brightness............... Dan 2:31
which smote the *i* upon his feet ............ Dan 2:34
the *i* became a great mountain ............... Dan 2:35
the king made an *i* of gold......................... Dan 3:1
*i* which Nebuchadnezzar the king............ Dan 3:2
unto the dedication of the *i* that ............ Dan 3:3
they stood before the *i* that..................... Dan 3:3
worship the golden *i* that.......................... Dan 3:5
worshipped the golden *i* that.................. Dan 3:7
fall down and worship the golden *i*...... Dan 3:10
golden *i* which thou hast set up............. Dan 3:12
the golden *i* which I have set up............ Dan 3:14
worship the *i* which I have made............ Dan 3:15
golden *i* which thou hast set up............. Dan 3:18
a sacrifice, and without an *i*..................... Hos 3:4
gods will I cut off the graven *i*............... Nah 1:14
the graven *i* and the molten *i*................. Nah 1:14
What profiteth the graven *i* that ............. Hab 2:18
the molten *i*, and a teacher of................. Hab 2:18
saith unto them, Whose is this *i* ............ Mt 22:20
saith unto them, Whose is this *i* ............ Mk 12:16
Whose *i* and superscription hath it......... Lk 20:24
of the *i* which fell down from............... Acts 19:35
an *i* made like to corruptible man.......... Rom 1:23
be conformed to the *i* of his Son........... Rom 8:29
bowed the knee to the *i* of Baal............ Rom 11:4
head, forasmuch as he is the *i*.............. 1Cor 11:7
we have borne the *i* of the earthy...... 1Cor 15:49
also bear the *i* of the heavenly........... 1Cor 15:49
the same *i* from glory to glory............. 2Cor 3:18
of Christ, who is the *i* of God............... 2Cor 4:4
Who is the *i* of the invisible God ............ Col 1:15
the *i* of him that created him.................. Col 3:10
the express *i* of his person, and................ Heb 1:3
not the very *i* of the things, can ............ Heb 10:1
should make an *i* to the beast ............... Rev 13:14
give life unto the *i* of the beast ............ Rev 13:15
that the *i* of the beast should................. Rev 13:15
*i* of the beast should be killed................ Rev 13:15
man worship the beast and his *i* ............. Rev 14:9
who worship the beast and his *i* ........... Rev 14:11
over the beast, and over his *i*................... Rev 15:2
upon them which worshipped his *i*.......... Rev 16:2
and them that worshipped his *i*............. Rev 19:20
the beast, neither his *i*, neither.............. Rev 20:4

**IMAGERY**
man in the chambers of his *i*.................. Eze 8:12

**IMAGE'S**
This *i* head was of fine gold, his ........... Dan 2:32

**IMAGES**
Rachel had stolen the *i* that were ....... Gen 31:19
Now Rachel had taken the *i*.................. Gen 31:34
he searched, but found not the *i*.......... Gen 31:35
them, and quite break down their *i*....... Ex 23:24
their altars, break their *i* ....................... Ex 34:13
high places, and cut down your *i* ......... Lev 26:30
and destroy all their molten *i*............. Num 33:52
altars, and break down their *i*................... Deut 7:5
and burn their graven *i* with fire............ Deut 7:5
The graven *i* of their gods shall............ Deut 7:25
down the graven *i* of their gods ............ Deut 12:3
ye shall make *i* of your emerods.............. 1Sa 6:5
*i* of your mice that mar the land .............. 1Sa 6:5
of gold and the *i* of their emerods.......... 1Sa 6:11
And there they left their *i*....................... 2Sa 5:21
made thee other gods, and molten *i* .... 1Kin 14:9
also built them high places, and *i*....... 1Kin 14:23
they brought forth the *i* out of............. 2Kin 10:26
his *i* brake they in pieces...................... 2Kin 11:18
And they set them up *i* and groves....... 2Kin 17:10
their God, and made them molten *i*...... 2Kin 17:16
LORD, and served their graven *i*........... 2Kin 17:41
the high places, and brake the *i*............ 2Kin 18:4
And he brake in pieces the *i*.................. 2Kin 23:14
spirits, and the wizards, and the *i* ...... 2Kin 23:24
high places, and brake down the *i*....... 2Chr 14:3
of Judah the high places and the *i*....... 2Chr 14:5
his *i* in pieces, and slew Mattan .......... 2Chr 23:17
and made also molten *i* for Baalim...... 2Chr 28:2
Judah, and brake the *i* in pieces .......... 2Chr 31:1
and set up groves and graven *i*........... 2Chr 33:19
*i* which Manasseh his father had ....... 2Chr 33:22
carved *i*, and the molten *i*...................... 2Chr 34:3
and the *i*, that were on high above...... 2Chr 34:4
carved *i*, and the molten *i*...................... 2Chr 34:4
beaten the graven *i* into powder .......... 2Chr 34:7
to jealousy with their graven *i*................ Ps 78:58
be all they that serve graven *i*................... Ps 97:7
whose graven *i* did excel them of............ Is 10:10
made, either the groves, or the *i*................ Is 17:8
all the graven *i* of her gods he .................. Is 21:9
groves and *i* shall not stand up................ Is 27:9
of thy graven *i* of silver.......................... Is 30:22
ornament of thy molten *i* of gold ........... Is 30:22
their molten *i* are wind and ..................... Is 41:29
neither my praise to graven *i* ................... Is 42:8
ashamed, that trust in graven *i*.............. Is 42:17
*i*, that say to the molten *i*....................... Is 42:17
me to anger with their graven *i*.............. Jer 8:19
break also the *i* of Beth-shemesh .......... Jer 43:13
her *i* are broken in pieces........................ Jer 50:2
for it is the land of graven *i*................... Jer 50:38
upon the graven *i* of Babylon................. Jer 51:47
do judgment upon her graven *i* .............. Jer 51:52
and your *i* shall be broken ......................... Eze 6:4
your *i* may be cut down, and your........... Eze 6:6
but they made the *i* of their ..................... Eze 7:20
and madest to thyself *i* of men ............. Eze 16:17
bright, he consulted with *i*..................... Eze 21:21
the *i* of the Chaldeans pourtrayed........ Eze 23:14
I will cause their *i* to cease out............ Eze 30:13
his land they have made goodly *i* .......... Hos 10:1
altars, he shall spoil their *i*...................... Hos 10:2
and burned incense to graven *i*............... Hos 11:2
them molten *i* of their silver .................. Hos 13:2
of your Moloch and Chiun your *i*...... Amos 5:26
all the graven *i* thereof shall be................ Mic 1:7
Thy graven *i* also will I cut off,............... Mic 5:13
thy standing *i* out of the midst................ Mic 5:13

**IMAGINATION**
that every *i* of the thoughts of................. Gen 6:5
for the *i* of man's heart is evil.............. Gen 8:21
I walk in the *i* of mine heart.............. Deut 29:19
for I know their *i* which they go.......... Deut 31:21
keep this for ever in the *i* of............. 1Chr 29:18
after the *i* of their evil heart.................. Jer 3:17
in the *i* of their evil heart, and.............. Jer 7:24
after the *i* of their own heart................. Jer 9:14
one in the *i* of their evil heart............... Jer 11:8
walk in the *i* of their heart.................. Jer 13:10
one after the *i* of his evil heart ........... Jer 16:12
one do the *i* of his evil heart................. Jer 18:12
after the *i* of his own heart.................. Jer 23:17
proud in the *i* of their hearts................... Lk 1:51

**IMAGINATIONS**
all the *i* of the thoughts......................... 1Chr 28:9
An heart that deviseth wicked *i* ............. Prov 6:18
and all their *i* against me........................ Lam 3:60
O LORD, and all their *i* against me......... Lam 3:61
but became vain in their *i*....................... Rom 1:21
Casting down *i*, and every high.............. 2Cor 10:5

**IMAGINE**
Do ye *i* to reprove words, and the........... Job 6:26
which ye wrongfully *i* against me ........ Job 21:27
the people *i* a vain thing .............................. Ps 2:1
*i* deceits all the day long ........................... Ps 38:12
How long will ye *i* mischief....................... Ps 62:3
Which *i* mischiefs in their heart............. Ps 140:2
in the heart of them that *i* evil ............ Prov 12:20
yet do they *i* mischief against me........... Hos 7:15
What do ye *i* against the LORD ................. Nah 1:9
let none of you *i* evil against..................... Zec 7:10
let none of you *i* evil in your................... Zec 8:17
rage, and the people *i* vain things.......... Acts 4:25

**IMAGINED**
them, which they have *i* to do ............... Gen 11:6
in the devices that they have *i*.................. Ps 10:2
they *i* a mischievous device,.................... Ps 21:11

**IMAGINETH**
that *i* evil against the LORD, a................... Nah 1:11

**IMLA** (*im'-lah*) See IMLAH. *Father of Michaiah.*
the same is Micaiah the son of *I* ........... 2Chr 18:7
quickly Micaiah the son of *I*.............. 2Chr 18:8

**IMLAH** (*im'-lah*) See IMLA. *Same as Imla.*
yet one man, Micaiah the son of *I* ....... 1Kin 22:8
hither Micaiah the son of *I* .................. 1Kin 22:9

**IMMANUEL** (*im-man'-u-el*) See EMMANUEL. *A Messianic name.*
a son, and shall call his name *I*.................. Is 7:14
fill the breadth of thy land, O *I*.................... Is 8:8

**IMMEDIATELY**
they *i* left the ship and their ....................... Mt 4:22
*i* his leprosy was cleansed............................ Mt 8:3
*i* Jesus stretched forth his hand,.............. Mt 14:31
*i* their eyes received sight, and.............. Mt 20:34
*I* after the tribulation of those............... Mt 24:29
And *i* the cock crew.................................. Mt 26:74
*i* the spirit driveth him into the.................. Mk 1:12
And *i* his fame spread abroad..................... Mk 1:28
*i* the fever left her, and she....................... Mk 1:31
*i* the leprosy departed from him,.............. Mk 1:42

*i* when Jesus perceived in his... Mk 2:8
*i* he arose, took up the bed, and... Mk 2:12
*i* it sprang up, because it had no... Mk 4:5
they have heard, Satan cometh *i*... Mk 4:15
*i* receive it with gladness... Mk 4:16
word's sake, *i* they are offended... Mk 4:17
*i* he putteth in the sickle,... Mk 4:29
*i* there met him out of the tombs... Mk 5:2
*i* knowing in himself that virtue... Mk 5:30
*i* the king sent an executioner,... Mk 6:27
*i* he talked with them, and saith... Mk 6:50
*i* he received his sight, and... Mk 10:52
And *i*, while he yet spake, cometh... Mk 14:43
And his mouth was opened *i*... Lk 1:64
*i* she arose and ministered unto... Lk 4:39
*i* the leprosy departed from him... Lk 5:13
*i* he rose up before them, and took... Lk 5:25
did beat vehemently, and *i* it fell... Lk 6:49
*i* her issue of blood stanched... Lk 8:44
him, and how she was healed *i*... Lk 8:47
they may open unto him *i*... Lk 12:36
*i* she was made straight, and... Lk 13:13
*i* he received his sight, and... Lk 18:43
kingdom of God should *i* appear... Lk 19:11
peace, the stones would *i* cry out... Lk 19:40
And *i*, while he yet spake, the... Lk 22:60
*i* the man was made whole, and took... Jn 5:9
*i* the ship was at the land... Jn 6:21
received the sop went *i* out... Jn 13:30
and *i* the cock crew... Jn 18:27
forth, and entered into a ship *i*... Jn 21:3
*i* his feet and ancle bones... Acts 3:7
*i* there fell from his eyes as it... Acts 9:18
And he arose *i*... Acts 9:34
*I* therefore I sent to thee... Acts 10:33
*i* there were three men already... Acts 11:11
*i* the angel of the Lord smote him... Acts 12:23
*i* there fell on him a mist and a... Acts 13:11
*i* we endeavoured to go into... Acts 16:10
*i* all the doors were opened, and... Acts 16:26
the brethren *i* sent away Paul and... Acts 17:10
then *i* the brethren sent away... Acts 17:14
Who *i* took soldiers and centurions... Acts 21:32
*i* I conferred not with flesh and... Gal 1:16
And *i* I was in the spirit... Rev 4:2

**IMMER** (*im'-mur*)
*1. Father of Meshillemeth.*
son of Meshillemith, the son of *I*... 1Chr 9:12
The children of *I*, a thousand... Ezr 2:37
And of the sons of *I*... Ezr 10:20
The children of *I*, a thousand... Neh 7:40
son of Meshillemoth, the son of *I*... Neh 11:13
*2. A sanctuary servant.*
to Bilgah, the sixteenth to *I*... 1Chr 24:14
*3. An exile.*
Tel-harsa, Cherub, Addan, and *I*... Ezr 2:59
Tel-haresha, Cherub, Addon, and *I*... Neh 7:61
*4. Father of Zadok.*
son of *I* over against his house... Neh 3:29
*5. A priest.*
Pashur the son of *I* the priest... Jer 20:1

**IMMORTAL**
Now unto the King eternal, *i*... 1Ti 1:17

**IMMORTALITY**
seek for glory and honour and *i*... Rom 2:7
and this mortal must put on *i*... 1Cor 15:53
this mortal shall have put on *i*... 1Cor 15:54
Who only hath *i*, dwelling in the... 1Ti 6:16
*i* to light through the gospel... 2Ti 1:10

**IMMUTABILITY**
of promise the *i* of his counsel... Heb 6:17

**IMMUTABLE**
That by two *i* things, in which it... Heb 6:18

**IMNA** (*im'-nah*) See IMNAH, JIMNA. *A son of Helem.*
*I*, and Shelesh, and Amal... 1Chr 7:35

**IMNAH** (*im'-nah*) See IMNA, JIMNAH.
*1. Son of Asher.*
*I*, and Isuah, and Ishuai, and Beriah... 1Chr 7:30
*2. Father of Kore.*
And Kore the son of *I* the Levite... 2Chr 31:14

**IMPART**
let him *i* to him that hath none... Lk 3:11
that I may *i* unto you some... Rom 1:11

**IMPARTED**
wisdom, neither hath he *i* to her... Job 39:17
were willing to have *i* unto you... 1Th 2:8

**IMPEDIMENT**
deaf, and had an *i* in his speech... Mk 7:32

**IMPENITENT**
*i* heart treasurest up unto... Rom 2:5

**IMPERIOUS**
the work of an *i* whorish woman... Eze 16:30

**IMPLACABLE**
without natural affection, *i*... Rom 1:31

**IMPLEAD**
let them *i* one another... Acts 19:38

**IMPORTUNITY**
yet because of his *i* he will rise... Lk 11:8

**IMPOSE**
it shall not be lawful to *i* toll... Ezr 7:24

**IMPOSED**
*i* on them until the time of... Heb 9:10

**IMPOSSIBLE**
and nothing shall be *i* unto you... Mt 17:20
unto them, With men this is *i*... Mt 19:26
upon them saith, With men it is *i*... Mk 10:27
For with God nothing shall be *i*... Lk 1:37
It is *i* but that offences will... Lk 17:1
The things which are *i* with men... Lk 18:27
For it is *i* for those who were... Heb 6:4
in which it was *i* for God to lie... Heb 6:18
faith it is *i* to please him... Heb 11:6

**IMPOTENT**
lay a great multitude of *i* folk... Jn 5:3
The *i* man answered him, Sir, I... Jn 5:7
the good deed done to the *i* man... Acts 4:9
*i* in his feet, being a cripple... Acts 14:8

**IMPOVERISH**
they shall *i* thy fenced cities,... Jer 5:17

**IMPOVERISHED**
Israel was greatly *i* because of... Judg 6:6
He that is so *i* that he hath no... Is 40:20
Whereas Edom saith, We are *i*... Mal 1:4

**IMPRISONED**
I said, Lord, they know that I *i*... Acts 22:19

**IMPRISONMENT**
to confiscation of goods, or to *i*... Ezr 7:26
yea, moreover of bonds and *i*... Heb 11:36

**IMPRISONMENTS**
In stripes, in *i*, in tumults, in... 2Cor 6:5

**IMPUDENT**
with an *i* face said unto him,... Prov 7:13
For they are *i* children and... Eze 2:4
for all the house of Israel are *i*... Eze 3:7

**IMPUTE**
let not the king *i* any thing unto... 1Sa 22:15
Let not my lord *i* iniquity unto... 2Sa 19:19
to whom the Lord will not *i* sin... Rom 4:8

**IMPUTED**
neither shall it be *i* unto him... Lev 7:18
blood shall be *i* unto that man... Lev 17:4
might be *i* unto them also... Rom 4:11
therefore it was *i* to him for... Rom 4:22
sake alone, that it was *i* to him... Rom 4:23
us also, to whom it shall be *i*... Rom 4:24
but sin is not *i* when there is no... Rom 5:13
God, and it was *i* unto him for... Jas 2:23

**IMPUTETH**
unto whom the LORD *i* not iniquity... Ps 32:2
unto whom God *i* righteousness... Rom 4:6

**IMPUTING**
*i* this his power unto his god... Hab 1:11
not *i* their trespasses unto them... 2Cor 5:19

**IMRAH** (*im'-rah*) *A chief of Asher.*
and Shual, and Beri, and *I*,... 1Chr 7:36

**IMRI** (*im'-ri*)
*1. Son of Bani.*
the son of Omri, the son of *I*... 1Chr 9:4
*2. Father of Zaccur.*
them builded Zaccur the son of *I*... Neh 3:2

**IN** See PREFACE.

**INASMUCH**
*i* as he hated him not in time... Deut 19:6
*i* as thou followedst not young... Ruth 3:10
*I* as ye have done it unto one of... Mt 25:40
*I* as ye did it not to one of the... Mt 25:45
*i* as I am the apostle of the... Rom 11:13
*i* as both in my bonds, and in the... Phil 1:7
*i* as he who hath builded the... Heb 3:3
*i* as not without an oath he was... Heb 7:20
*i* as ye are partakers of Christ's... 1Pet 4:13

**INCENSE**
for anointing oil, and for sweet *i*... Ex 25:6
make an altar to burn *i* upon... Ex 30:1
thereon sweet *i* every morning... Ex 30:7
lamps, he shall burn *i* upon it... Ex 30:7
at even, he shall burn *i* upon it... Ex 30:8
a perpetual *i* before the LORD... Ex 30:8
shall offer no strange *i* thereon... Ex 30:9
and his vessels, and the altar of *i*... Ex 30:27
his furniture, and the altar of *i*... Ex 31:8
sweet *i* for the holy place... Ex 31:11
anointing oil, and for the sweet *i*... Ex 35:8
the *i* altar, and his staves, and... Ex 35:15
the anointing oil, and the sweet *i*... Ex 35:15
anointing oil, and for the sweet *i*... Ex 35:28
he made the *i* altar of shittim... Ex 37:25
the pure *i* of sweet spices,... Ex 37:29
the anointing oil, and the sweet *i*... Ex 39:38
set the altar of gold for the *i*... Ex 40:5
And he burnt sweet *i* thereon... Ex 40:27
altar of sweet *i* before the LORD... Lev 4:7
put *i* thereon, and offered strange... Lev 10:1
full of sweet *i* beaten small... Lev 16:12
he shall put the *i* upon the fire... Lev 16:13
that the cloud of the *i* may cover... Lev 16:13
oil for the light, and the sweet *i*... Num 4:16
of ten shekels of gold, full of *i*... Num 7:14
of gold of ten shekels, full of *i*... Num 7:20
spoon of ten shekels, full of *i*... Num 7:26
spoon of ten shekels, full of *i*... Num 7:32
spoon of ten shekels, full of *i*... Num 7:38
spoon of ten shekels, full of *i*... Num 7:44
spoon of ten shekels, full of *i*... Num 7:50
spoon of ten shekels, full of *i*... Num 7:56
spoon of ten shekels, full of *i*... Num 7:62
spoon of ten shekels, full of *i*... Num 7:68
spoon of ten shekels, full of *i*... Num 7:74
spoon of ten shekels, full of *i*... Num 7:80
spoons were twelve, full of *i*... Num 7:86
put *i* in them before the LORD to... Num 16:7
put *i* in them, and bring ye before... Num 16:17
laid *i* thereon, and stood in the... Num 16:18
and fifty men that offered *i*... Num 16:35
near to offer *i* before the LORD... Num 16:40
from off the altar, and put on *i*... Num 16:46
and he put on *i*, and made an... Num 16:47
they shall put *i* before thee... Deut 33:10
offer upon mine altar, to burn *i*... 1Sa 2:28
and burnt *i* in high places... 1Kin 3:3
he burnt *i* upon the altar that... 1Kin 9:25
his strange wives, which burnt *i*... 1Kin 11:8
upon the altar, and burnt *i*... 1Kin 12:33
stood by the altar to burn *i*... 1Kin 13:1
high places that burn *i* upon thee... 1Kin 13:2
burnt *i* yet in the high places... 1Kin 22:43
burnt *i* in the high places... 2Kin 12:3
burnt *i* on the high places... 2Kin 14:4
burnt *i* still on the high places... 2Kin 15:4
burned *i* still in the high places... 2Kin 15:35
burnt *i* in the high places, and on... 2Kin 16:4
there they burnt *i* in all the... 2Kin 17:11
of Israel did burn *i* to it... 2Kin 18:4
have burned *i* unto other gods,... 2Kin 22:17
burn *i* in the high places in the... 2Kin 23:5
them also that burned *i* unto Baal... 2Kin 23:5
where the priests had burned *i*... 2Kin 23:8
offering, and on the altar of *i*... 1Chr 6:49
to burn *i* before the LORD, to... 1Chr 23:13
for the altar of *i* refined gold... 1Chr 28:18
and to burn before him sweet *i*... 2Chr 2:4
burnt sacrifices and sweet *i*... 2Chr 13:11
them, and burned *i* unto them... 2Chr 25:14
burn *i* upon the altar of *i*... 2Chr 26:16
to burn *i* unto the LORD, but to... 2Chr 26:18
that are consecrated to burn *i*... 2Chr 26:18
a censer in his hand to burn *i*... 2Chr 26:19
the LORD, from beside the *i* altar... 2Chr 26:19
Moreover he burnt *i* in the valley... 2Chr 28:3
burnt *i* in the high places, and on... 2Chr 28:4
places to burn *i* unto other gods... 2Chr 28:25
have not burned *i* nor offered... 2Chr 29:7
minister unto him, and burn *i*... 2Chr 29:11
the altars for *i* took they away... 2Chr 30:14
one altar, and burn *i* upon it... 2Chr 32:12
have burned *i* unto other gods,... 2Chr 34:25
of fatlings, with the *i* of rams... Ps 66:15
be set forth before thee as *i*... Ps 141:2
*i* is an abomination unto me... Is 1:13
offering, nor wearied thee with *i*... Is 43:23
they shall bring gold and *i*... Is 60:6
burneth *i* upon altars of brick... Is 65:3
which have burned *i* upon the... Is 65:7
he that burneth *i*, as if he... Is 66:3
have burned *i* unto other gods, and... Jer 1:16
cometh there to me *i* from Sheba... Jer 6:20
burn *i* unto Baal, and walk after... Jer 7:9
the gods unto whom they offer *i*... Jer 11:12
even altars to burn *i* unto Baal... Jer 11:13
to anger in offering *i* unto Baal... Jer 11:17
and meat offerings, and *i*, and... Jer 17:26
me, they have burned *i* to vanity... Jer 18:15
have burned *i* in it unto other... Jer 19:4
*i* unto all the host of heaven... Jer 19:13
they have offered *i* unto Baal... Jer 32:29
*i* in their hand, to bring them to... Jer 41:5
in that they went to burn *i*... Jer 44:3
to burn no *i* unto other gods... Jer 44:5
burning *i* unto other gods in the... Jer 44:8
had burned *i* unto other gods... Jer 44:15
to burn *i* unto the queen of... Jer 44:17
to burn *i* to the queen of heaven... Jer 44:18
when we burned *i* to the queen of... Jer 44:19
The *i* that ye burned in the... Jer 44:21
Because ye have burned *i*, and... Jer 44:23
to burn *i* to the queen of heaven,... Jer 44:25
and him that burneth *i* to his gods... Jer 48:35
and a thick cloud of *i* went up... Eze 8:11
mine oil and mine *i* before them... Eze 16:18
whereupon thou hast set mine *i*... Eze 23:41
wherein she burned *i* to them... Hos 2:13
burn *i* upon the hills, under oaks... Hos 4:13
burned *i* to graven images... Hos 11:2
net, and burn *i* unto their drag... Hab 1:16
in every place *i* shall be offered... Mal 1:11
his lot was to burn *i* when he... Lk 1:9
praying without at the time of *i*... Lk 1:10
the right side of the altar of *i*... Lk 1:11
there was given unto him much *i*... Rev 8:3
And the smoke of the *i*, which came... Rev 8:4

**INCENSED**
all they that were *i* against thee... Is 41:11
all that are *i* against him shall... Is 45:24

**INCLINE**
*i* your heart unto the LORD God of... Josh 24:23
That he may *i* our hearts unto him... 1Kin 8:58
*i* thine ear unto me, and hear my... Ps 17:6
and consider, and *i* thine ear... Ps 45:10
I will *i* mine ear to a parable... Ps 49:4
*i* thine ear unto me, and save me... Ps 71:2
*i* your ears to the words of my... Ps 78:1
*i* thine ear unto my cry... Ps 88:2
*i* thine ear unto me... Ps 102:2
*I* my heart unto thy testimonies,... Ps 119:36
*I* not my heart to any evil thing,... Ps 141:4
So that thou *i* thine ear unto... Prov 2:2
*i* thine ear unto my sayings... Prov 4:20

*I* thine ear, O LORD, and hear Is 37:17
*I* your ear, and come unto me Is 55:3
O my God, *i* thine ear, and hear Dan 9:18

## INCLINED
and their hearts *i* to follow Judg 9:3
he *i* unto me, and heard my cry Ps 40:1
Because he hath *i* his ear unto me Ps 116:2
I have *i* mine heart to perform Ps 119:112
nor *i* mine ear to them that Prov 5:13
nor *i* their ear, but walked in Jer 7:24
nor *i* their ear, but hardened Jer 7:26
nor *i* their ear, but walked every Jer 11:8
neither *i* their ear, but made Jer 17:23
hearkened, nor *i* your ear to hear Jer 25:4
not unto me, neither *i* their ear Jer 34:14
but ye have not *i* your ear Jer 35:15
nor *i* their ear to turn from Jer 44:5

## INCLINETH
For her house *i* unto death Prov 2:18

## INCLOSE
we will *i* her with boards of Song 8:9

## INCLOSED
onyx stones *i* in ouches of gold Ex 39:6
they were *i* in ouches of gold in Ex 39:13
Thus they *i* the Benjamites round Judg 20:43
They are *i* in their own fat Ps 17:10
assembly of the wicked have *i* me Ps 22:16
A garden *i* is my sister, my Song 4:12
He hath *i* my ways with hewn stone Lam 3:9
they *i* a great multitude of Lk 5:6

## INCLOSINGS
shall be set in gold in their *i* Ex 28:20
in ouches of gold in their *i* Ex 39:13

## INCONTINENCY
Satan tempt you not for your *i* 1Cor 7:5

## INCONTINENT
trucebreakers, false accusers, *i* 2Ti 3:3

## INCORRUPTIBLE
but we an *i* 1Cor 9:25
and the dead shall be raised *i* 1Cor 15:52
To an inheritance *i*, and undefiled 1Pet 1:4
not of corruptible seed, but of *i* 1Pet 1:23

## INCORRUPTION
it is raised in *i* 1Cor 15:42
neither doth corruption inherit *i* 1Cor 15:50
this corruptible must put on *i* 1Cor 15:53
corruptible shall have put on *i* 1Cor 15:54

## INCREASE
And it shall come to pass in the *i* Gen 47:24
may yield unto you the *i* thereof Lev 19:25
shall all the *i* thereof be meat Lev 25:7
ye shall eat the *i* thereof out of Lev 25:12
thou shalt *i* the price thereof Lev 25:16
not sow, nor gather in our *i* Lev 25:20
Take thou no usury of him, or *i* Lev 25:36
nor lend him thy victuals for *i* Lev 25:37
and the land shall yield her *i* Lev 26:4
your land shall not yield her *i* Lev 26:20
as the *i* of the threshingfloor Num 18:30
as the *i* of the winepress Num 18:30
an *i* of sinful men, to augment Num 32:14
thee, and that ye may *i* mightily Deut 6:3
the *i* of thy kine, and the flocks Deut 7:13
beasts of the field *i* upon thee Deut 7:22
truly tithe all the *i* of thy seed Deut 14:22
tithe of thine *i* the same year Deut 14:28
shall bless thee in all thine *i* Deut 16:15
tithes of thine *i* the third year Deut 26:12
the *i* of thy kine, and the flocks Deut 28:4
the *i* of thy kine, and the flocks Deut 28:18
or the *i* of thy kine, or flocks Deut 28:51
he might eat the *i* of the fields Deut 32:13
consume the earth with her *i* Deut 32:22
and destroyed the *i* of the earth Judg 6:4
*I* thine army, and come out Judg 9:29
all the *i* of thine house shall 1Sa 2:33
the LORD had said he would *i* 1Chr 27:23
over the *i* of the vineyards for 1Chr 27:27
of all the *i* of the field 2Chr 31:5
also for the *i* of corn, and wine, 2Chr 32:28
to *i* the trespass of Israel Ezr 10:10
it yieldeth much *i* unto the kings Neh 9:37
thy latter end should greatly *i* Job 8:7
The *i* of his house shall depart, Job 20:28
and would root out all mine *i* Job 31:12
dost not *i* thy wealth by their Ps 44:12
if riches *i*, set not your heart Ps 62:10
Then shall the earth yield her *i* Ps 67:6
Thou shalt *i* my greatness, and Ps 71:21
they *i* in riches Ps 73:12
He gave also their *i* unto the Ps 78:46
and our land shall yield her *i* Ps 85:12
which may yield fruits of *i* Ps 107:37
The LORD shall *i* you more Ps 115:14
man will hear, and will *i* learning Prov 1:5
the firstfruits of all thine *i* Prov 3:9
man, and he will *i* in learning Prov 9:9
that gathereth by labour shall *i* Prov 13:11
but much *i* is by the strength of Prov 14:4
with the *i* of his lips shall he Prov 18:20
the poor to *i* his riches, and he Prov 22:16
when they perish, the righteous *i* Prov 28:28
he that loveth abundance with *i* Eccl 5:10
When goods *i*, they are increased Eccl 5:11
be many things that *i* vanity Eccl 6:11
Of the *i* of his government and Is 9:7
The meek also shall *i* their joy Is 29:19
and bread of the *i* of the earth Is 30:23
didst *i* thy perfumes, and didst Is 57:9
LORD, and the firstfruits of his *i* Jer 2:3
and they shall be fruitful and *i* Jer 23:3
I will *i* the famine upon you, and Eze 5:16
usury, neither hath taken any *i* Eze 18:8
forth upon usury, and hath taken *i* Eze 18:13
hath not received usury nor *i* Eze 18:17
thou hast taken usury and *i* Eze 22:12
and the earth shall yield her *i* Eze 34:27
and they shall *i* and bring fruit Eze 36:11
call for the corn, and will *i* it Eze 36:29
the *i* of the field, that ye shall Eze 36:30
I will *i* them with men like a Eze 36:37
the *i* thereof shall be for food Eze 48:18
shall acknowledge and *i* with glory Dan 11:39
commit whoredom, and shall not *i* Hos 4:10
and the ground shall give her *i* Zec 8:12
they shall *i* as they have Zec 10:8
said unto the Lord, *I* our faith Lk 17:5
He must *i*, but I must decrease Jn 3:30
but God gave the *i* 1Cor 3:6
but God that giveth the *i* 1Cor 3:7
sown, and *i* the fruits of your 2Cor 9:10
maketh *i* of the body unto the Eph 4:16
increaseth with the *i* of God Col 2:19
And the Lord make you to *i* 1Th 3:12
you, brethren, that ye *i* more 1Th 4:10
for they will *i* unto more 2Ti 2:16

## INCREASED
and the waters *i*, and bare up the Gen 7:17
were *i* greatly upon the earth Gen 7:18
it is now *i* unto a multitude Gen 30:30
the man *i* exceedingly, and had Gen 30:43
*i* abundantly, and multiplied, and Ex 1:7
from before thee, until thou be *i* Ex 23:30
of the Philistines went on and *i* 1Sa 14:19
for the people *i* continually with 2Sa 15:12
And the battle *i* that day 1Kin 22:35
house of their fathers *i* greatly 1Chr 4:38
they *i* from Bashan unto 1Chr 5:23
And the battle *i* that day 2Chr 18:34
iniquities are *i* over our head Ezr 9:6
and his substance is *i* in the land Job 1:10
how are they *i* that trouble me Ps 3:1
that their corn and their wine *i* Ps 4:7
when the glory of his house is *i* Ps 49:16
And he *i* his people greatly Ps 105:24
the years of thy life shall be *i* Prov 9:11
*i* more than all that were before Eccl 2:9
they are *i* that eat them Eccl 5:11
the nation, and not *i* the joy Is 9:3
Thou hast *i* the nation, O LORD, Is 26:15
thou hast *i* the nation Is 26:15
alone, and blessed him, and *i* him Is 51:2
*i* in the land, in those days, Jer 3:16
many, and their backslidings are *i* Jer 5:6
Their widows are *i* to me above Jer 15:8
that ye may be *i* there, and not Jer 29:6
because thy sins were *i* Jer 30:14
because thy sins were *i*, I have Jer 30:15
hath *i* in the daughter of Judah Lam 2:5
bud of the field, and thou hast *i* Eze 16:7
hast *i* thy whoredoms, to provoke Eze 16:26
And that she *i* her whoredoms Eze 23:14
traffick hast thou *i* thy riches Eze 28:5
so *i* from the lowest chamber to Eze 41:7
and fro, and knowledge shall be *i* Dan 12:4
As they were *i*, so they sinned Hos 4:7
of his fruit he hath *i* the altars Hos 10:1
fig trees and your olive trees *i* Amos 4:9
shall increase as they have *i* Zec 10:8
yield fruit that sprang up and *i* Mk 4:8
Jesus *i* in wisdom and stature, and Lk 2:52
And the word of God *i* Acts 6:7
But Saul *i* the more in strength, Acts 9:22
the faith, and *i* in number daily Acts 16:5
having hope, when your faith is *i* 2Cor 10:15
*i* with goods, and have need of Rev 3:17

## INCREASEST
*i* thine indignation upon me Job 10:17

## INCREASETH
For it *i*. Thou huntest me Job 10:16
He *i* the nations, and destroyeth Job 12:23
up against thee *i* continually Ps 74:23
is that scattereth, and yet *i* Prov 11:24
sweetness of the lips *i* learning Prov 16:21
*i* the transgressors among men Prov 23:28
a man of knowledge *i* strength Prov 24:5
unjust gain *i* his substance, he Prov 28:8
are multiplied, transgression *i* Prov 29:16
he that *i* knowledge *i* sorrow Eccl 1:18
that have no might he *i* strength Is 40:29
he daily *i* lies and desolation Hos 12:1
Woe to him that *i* that which is Hab 2:6
*i* with the increase of God Col 2:19

## INCREASING
*i* in the knowledge of God Col 1:10

## INCREDIBLE
it be thought a thing *i* with you Acts 26:8

## INCURABLE
in his bowels with an *i* disease 2Chr 21:18
my wound is *i* without Job 34:6
my pain perpetual, and my wound *i* Jer 15:18
saith the LORD, Thy bruise is *i* Jer 30:12
thy sorrow is *i* for the multitude Jer 30:15
For her wound is *i* Mic 1:9

## INDEBTED
forgive every one that is *i* to us Lk 11:4

## INDEED
thy wife shall bear thee a son *i* Gen 17:19
And yet *i* she is my sister Gen 20:12
Shalt thou *i* reign over us Gen 37:8
or shalt thou *i* have dominion Gen 37:8
thy brethren *i* come to bow down Gen 37:10
For *i* I was stolen away out of Gen 40:15
we came *i* down at the first time Gen 43:20
and whereby *i* he divineth Gen 44:5
if ye will obey my voice *i* Ex 19:5
if thou shalt *i* obey his voice Ex 23:22
ye should *i* have eaten it in the Lev 10:18
Hath the LORD *i* spoken only by Num 12:2
If thou wilt *i* deliver this Num 21:2
am I not able *i* to promote thee Num 22:37
For *i* the hand of the LORD was Deut 2:15
hated, which is *i* the firstborn Deut 21:16
*I* I have sinned against the LORD Josh 7:20
if thou wilt *i* look on the 1Sa 1:11
I said *i* that thy house, and the 1Sa 2:30
I am *i* a widow woman, and mine 2Sa 14:5
bring me again *i* to Jerusalem 2Sa 15:8
But will God *i* dwell on the earth 1Kin 8:27
Thou hast *i* smitten Edom, and 2Kin 14:10
Oh that thou wouldest bless me *i* 1Chr 4:10
that have sinned and done evil *i* 1Chr 21:17
be it *i* that I have erred, mine Job 19:4
If *i* ye will magnify yourselves Job 19:5
Do ye *i* speak righteousness, O Ps 58:1
and tell this people, Hear ye *i* Is 6:9
and see ye *i*, but perceive not Is 6:9
For if ye do this thing *i* Jer 22:4
I *i* baptize you with water unto Mt 3:11
Which *i* is the least of all seeds Mt 13:32
them, Ye shall drink *i* of my cup Mt 20:23
which *i* appear beautiful outward, Mt 23:27
the spirit *i* is willing, but the Mt 26:41
I *i* have baptized you with water Mk 1:8
unto you, That Elias is *i* come Mk 9:13
Ye shall *i* drink of the cup that Mk 10:39
John, that he was a prophet *i* Mk 11:32
The Son of man *i* goeth, as it is Mk 14:21
I *i* baptize you with water Lk 3:16
for they *i* killed them, and ye Lk 11:48
And we *i* justly; for we Lk 23:41
Saying, The Lord is risen *i* Lk 24:34
of him, Behold an Israelite *i* Jn 1:47
and know that this is *i* the Christ Jn 4:42
For my flesh is meat *i* Jn 6:55
and my blood is drink *i* Jn 6:55
Do the rulers know *i* that this is Jn 7:26
word, then are ye my disciples *i* Jn 8:31
make you free, ye shall be free *i* Jn 8:36
for that *i* a notable miracle hath Acts 4:16
John *i* baptized with water Acts 11:16
that were with me saw *i* the light Acts 22:9
yourselves to be dead *i* unto sin Rom 6:11
the law of God, neither *i* can be Rom 8:7
All things *i* are pure Rom 14:20
For a man *i* ought not to cover 1Cor 11:7
For *i* he accepted the exhortation 2Cor 8:17
and *i* bear with me 2Cor 11:1
Some *i* preach Christ even of envy Phil 1:15
For *i* he was sick nigh unto death Phil 2:27
to me *i* is not grievous, but for Phil 3:1
Which things have *i* a shew of Col 2:23
*i* ye do it toward all the 1Th 4:10
Honour widows that are widows *i* 1Ti 5:3
Now she that is a widow *i* 1Ti 5:5
relieve them that are widows *i* 1Ti 5:16
living stone, disallowed *i* of men 1Pet 2:4

## INDIA
(*in'-de-ah*) *Eastern boundary of the Persian Empire.*
reigned from *I* even unto Ethiopia Est 1:1
which are from *I* unto Ethiopia Est 8:9

## INDIGNATION
anger, and in wrath, and in great *i* Deut 29:28
there was great *i* against Israel 2Kin 3:27
he was wroth, and took great *i* Neh 4:1
he was full of *i* against Mordecai Est 5:9
me, and increasest thine *i* upon me Job 10:17
Pour out thine *i* upon them Ps 69:24
of his anger, wrath, and *i* Ps 78:49
Because of thine *i* and thy wrath Ps 102:10
the staff in their hand is mine *i* Is 10:5
the *i* shall cease, and mine anger Is 10:25
the LORD, and the weapons of his *i* Is 13:5
moment, until the *i* be overpast Is 26:20
his lips are full of *i*, and his Is 30:27
with the *i* of his anger, and with Is 30:30
For the *i* of the LORD is upon all Is 34:2
and his *i* toward his enemies Is 66:14
shall not be able to abide his *i* Jer 10:10
for thou hast filled me with *i* Jer 15:17
forth the weapons of his *i* Jer 50:25
hath despised in the *i* of his Lam 2:6
I will pour out mine *i* upon thee Eze 21:31
nor rained upon in the day of *i* Eze 22:24
I poured out mine *i* upon them Eze 22:31
shall be in the last end of the *i* Dan 8:19
have *i* against the holy covenant Dan 11:30
till the *i* be accomplished Dan 11:36
I will bear the *i* of the LORD Mic 7:9
Who can stand before his *i* Nah 1:6

- didst march through the land in *i* Hab 3:12
- to pour upon them mine *i* Zeph 3:8
- thou hast had *i* these threescore Zec 1:12
- whom the LORD hath *i* for ever Mal 1:4
- they were moved with *i* against Mt 20:24
- his disciples saw it, they had *i* Mt 26:8
- some that had *i* within themselves Mk 14:4
- of the synagogue answered with *i* Lk 13:14
- Sadducees,) and were filled with *i* Acts 5:17
- but obey unrighteousness, *i* Rom 2:8
- of yourselves, yea, what *i* 2Cor 7:11
- for of judgment and fiery *i* Heb 10:27
- mixture into the cup of his *i* Rev 14:10

**INDITING**

- My heart is *i* a good matter Ps 45:1

**INDUSTRIOUS**

- the young man that he was *i* 1Kin 11:28

**INEXCUSABLE**

- Therefore thou art *i*, O man, Rom 2:1

**INFALLIBLE**

- his passion by many *i* proofs Acts 1:3

**INFAMOUS**

- shall mock thee, which art *i* Eze 22:5

**INFAMY**

- shame, and thine *i* turn not away Prov 25:10
- and are an *i* of the people Eze 36:3

**INFANT**

- but slay both man and woman, *i* 1Sa 15:3
- be no more thence an *i* of days Is 65:20

**INFANTS**

- as *i* which never saw light Job 3:16
- their *i* shall be dashed in pieces Hos 13:16
- And they brought unto him also *i* Lk 18:15

**INFERIOR**

- I am not *i* to you Job 12:3
- I am not *i* unto you Job 13:2
- arise another kingdom *i* to thee Dan 2:39
- ye were *i* to other churches 2Cor 12:13

**INFIDEL**

- hath he that believeth with an *i* 2Cor 6:15
- the faith, and is worse than an *i* 1Ti 5:8

**INFINITE**

- and thine iniquities *i* Job 22:5
- his understanding is *i* Ps 147:5
- were her strength, and it was *i* Nah 3:9

**INFIRMITIES**

- saying, Himself took our *i* Mt 8:17
- and to be healed by him of their *i* Lk 5:15
- hour he cured many of their *i* Lk 7:21
- been healed of evil spirits and *i* Lk 8:2
- the Spirit also helpeth our *i* Rom 8:26
- ought to bear the *i* of the weak Rom 15:1
- the things which concern mine *i* 2Cor 11:30
- I will not glory, but in mine *i* 2Cor 12:5
- will I rather glory in my *i* 2Cor 12:9
- Therefore I take pleasure in *i* 2Cor 12:10
- stomach's sake and thine often *i* 1Ti 5:23
- touched with the feeling of our *i* Heb 4:15

**INFIRMITY**

- for her *i* shall she be unclean Lev 12:2
- And I said, This is my *i* Ps 77:10
- of a man will sustain his *i* Prov 18:14
- had a spirit of *i* eighteen years Lk 13:11
- thou art loosed from thine *i* Lk 13:12
- was there, which had an *i* thirty Jn 5:5
- because of the *i* of your flesh Rom 6:19
- Ye know how through *i* of the Gal 4:13
- himself also is compassed with *i* Heb 5:2
- men high priests which have *i* Heb 7:28

**INFLAME**

- until night, till wine *i* them Is 5:11

**INFLAMMATION**

- for it is an *i* of the burning Lev 13:28
- and with a fever, and with an *i* Deut 28:22

**INFLICTED**

- punishment, which was *i* of many 2Cor 2:6

**INFLUENCES**

- thou bind the sweet *i* of Pleiades Job 38:31

**INFOLDING**

- a great cloud, and a fire *i* itself Eze 1:4

**INFORM**

- according to all that they *i* thee Deut 17:10

**INFORMED**

- And he *i* me, and talked with me, and Dan 9:22
- And they are *i* of thee, that thou Acts 21:21
- they were *i* concerning thee Acts 21:24
- who *i* the governor against Paul Acts 24:1
- of the Jews *i* him against Paul Acts 25:2
- and the elders of the Jews *i* me Acts 25:15

**INGATHERING**

- and the feast of *i*, which is in Ex 23:16
- the feast of *i* at the year's end Ex 34:22

**INHABIT**

- the land which ye shall *i* Num 35:34
- the wicked shall not *i* the earth Prov 10:30
- the villages that Kedar doth *i* Is 42:11
- shall build houses, and *i* them Is 65:21
- shall not build, and another *i* Is 65:22
- but shall *i* the parched places in Jer 17:6
- Thou daughter that dost *i* Dibon Jer 48:18
- they that *i* those wastes of the Eze 33:24
- build the waste cities, and *i* them Amos 9:14
- also build houses, but not *i* them Zeph 1:13

**INHABITANT**

- The flood breaketh out from the *i* Job 28:4
- even great and fair, without *i* Is 5:9
- the cities be wasted without *i* Is 6:11
- the *i* of Samaria, that say in the Is 9:9
- Cry out and shout, thou *i* of Zion Is 12:6
- the *i* of this isle shall say in Is 20:6
- are upon thee, O *i* of the earth Is 24:17
- the *i* shall not say, I am sick Is 33:24
- his cities are burned without *i* Jer 2:15
- shall be laid waste, without an *i* Jer 4:7
- of Judah desolate, without an *i* Jer 9:11
- of the land, O *i* of the fortress Jer 10:17
- O *i* of the valley, and rock of the Jer 21:13
- O *i* of Lebanon, that makest thy Jer 22:23
- shall be desolate without an *i* Jer 26:9
- without man, and without *i* Jer 33:10
- Judah a desolation without an *i* Jer 34:22
- and a curse, without an *i* Jer 44:22
- be waste and desolate without an *i* Jer 46:19
- O *i* of Aroer, stand by the way, Jer 48:19
- O *i* of Moab, saith the LORD Jer 48:43
- Babylon a desolation without an *i* Jer 51:29
- Babylon, shall the *i* of Zion say Jer 51:35
- and an hissing, without an *i* Jer 51:37
- cut off the *i* from the plain of Amos 1:5
- I will cut off the *i* from Ashdod Amos 1:8
- thou *i* of Saphir, having thy Mic 1:11
- the *i* of Zaanan came not forth in Mic 1:11
- For the *i* of Maroth waited Mic 1:12
- O thou *i* of Lachish, bind the Mic 1:13
- heir unto thee, O *i* of Mareshah Mic 1:15
- thee, that there shall be no *i* Zeph 2:5
- is no man, that there is none *i* Zeph 3:6

**INHABITANTS**

- all the *i* of the cities, and that Gen 19:25
- to stink among the *i* of the land Gen 34:30
- when the *i* of the land, the Gen 50:11
- take hold on the *i* of Palestina Ex 15:14
- all the *i* of Canaan shall melt Ex 15:15
- for I will deliver the *i* of the Ex 23:31
- thou make a covenant with the *i* Ex 34:12
- a covenant with the *i* of the land Ex 34:15
- land itself vomiteth out her *i* Lev 18:25
- the land unto all the *i* thereof Lev 25:10
- land that eateth up the *i* thereof Num 13:32
- tell it to the *i* of this land Num 14:14
- because of the *i* of the land Num 32:17
- the *i* of the land from before you Num 33:52
- dispossess the *i* of the land Num 33:53
- the *i* of the land from before you Num 33:55
- withdrawn the *i* of their city Deut 13:13
- Thou shalt surely smite the *i* of Deut 13:15
- that all the *i* of the land faint Josh 2:9
- for even all the *i* of the country Josh 2:24
- all the *i* of the land shall hear Josh 7:9
- all the *i* of Ai in the field Josh 8:24
- utterly destroyed all the *i* of Ai Josh 8:26
- when the *i* of Gibeon heard what Josh 9:3
- all the *i* of our country spake to Josh 9:11
- to destroy all the *i* of the land Josh 9:24
- how the *i* of Gibeon had made Josh 10:1
- save the Hivites the *i* of Gibeon Josh 11:19
- All the *i* of the hill country Josh 13:6
- went up thence to the *i* of Debir Josh 15:15
- the Jebusites the *i* of Jerusalem Josh 15:63
- hand unto the *i* of En-tappuah Josh 17:7
- the *i* of Dor and her towns Josh 17:11
- the *i* of En-dor and her towns, and Josh 17:11
- the *i* of Taanach and her towns, and. Josh 17:11
- the *i* of Megiddo and her towns, Josh 17:11
- drive out the *i* of those cities Josh 17:12
- he went against the *i* of Debir Judg 1:11
- drave out the *i* of the mountain Judg 1:19
- not drive out the *i* of the valley Judg 1:19
- drive out the *i* of Beth-shean Judg 1:27
- and her towns, nor the *i* of Dor Judg 1:27
- nor the *i* of Ibleam and her towns, Judg 1:27
- nor the *i* of Megiddo and her towns Judg 1:27
- Zebulun drive out the *i* of Kitron Judg 1:30
- nor the *i* of Nahalol Judg 1:30
- Asher drive out the *i* of Accho Judg 1:31
- nor the *i* of Zidon, nor of Ahlab, Judg 1:31
- the Canaanites, the *i* of the land Judg 1:32
- drive out the *i* of Beth-shemesh Judg 1:33
- nor the *i* of Beth-anath Judg 1:33
- the Canaanites, the *i* of the land Judg 1:33
- the *i* of Beth-shemesh and of Judg 1:33
- no league with the *i* of this land Judg 2:2
- The *i* of the villages ceased, Judg 5:7
- the *i* of his villages in Israel Judg 5:11
- curse ye bitterly the *i* thereof Judg 5:23
- be head over all the *i* of Gilead Judg 10:18
- our head over all the *i* of Gilead Judg 11:8
- Amorites, the *i* of that country Judg 11:21
- sword, beside the *i* of Gibeah Judg 20:15
- of the *i* of Jabesh-gilead there Judg 21:9
- smite the *i* of Jabesh-gilead with Judg 21:10
- they found among the *i* of Judg 21:12
- thee, saying, Buy it before the *i* Ruth 4:4
- to the *i* of Kirjath-jearim 1Sa 6:21
- So David saved the *i* of Keilah 1Sa 23:5
- were of old the *i* of the land 1Sa 27:8
- when the *i* of Jabesh-gilead heard 1Sa 31:11
- the Jebusites, the *i* of the land 2Sa 5:6
- who was of the *i* of Gilead 1Kin 17:1
- nobles who were the *i* in his city 1Kin 21:11
- Therefore their *i* were of small 2Kin 19:26
- this place, and upon the *i* thereof 2Kin 22:16
- place, and against the *i* thereof 2Kin 22:19
- all the *i* of Jerusalem with him, 2Kin 23:2
- of the fathers of the *i* of Geba 1Chr 8:6
- the fathers of the *i* of Aijalon 1Chr 8:13
- who drove away the *i* of Gath 1Chr 8:13
- Now the first *i* that dwelt in 1Chr 9:2
- Jebusites were, the *i* of the land 1Chr 11:4
- the *i* of Jebus said to David, 1Chr 11:5
- for he hath given the *i* of the 1Chr 22:18
- upon all the *i* of the countries 2Chr 15:5
- who didst drive out the *i* of this 2Chr 20:7
- ye *i* of Jerusalem, and thou king 2Chr 20:15
- the *i* of Jerusalem fell before 2Chr 20:18
- me, O Judah, and ye *i* of Jerusalem 2Chr 20:20
- up against the *i* of mount Seir 2Chr 20:23
- had made an end of the *i* of Seir 2Chr 20:23
- caused the *i* of Jerusalem to 2Chr 21:11
- the *i* of Jerusalem to go a 2Chr 21:13
- the *i* of Jerusalem made Ahaziah 2Chr 22:1
- the *i* of Jerusalem from the hand 2Chr 32:22
- the *i* of Jerusalem, so that the 2Chr 32:26
- the *i* of Jerusalem did him honour 2Chr 32:33
- the *i* of Jerusalem to err, and to 2Chr 33:9
- this place, and upon the *i* thereof 2Chr 34:24
- place, and against the *i* thereof 2Chr 34:27
- place, and upon the *i* of the same 2Chr 34:28
- the *i* of Jerusalem, and the 2Chr 34:30
- the *i* of Jerusalem did according 2Chr 34:32
- present, and the *i* of Jerusalem 2Chr 35:18
- accusation against the *i* of Judah Ezr 4:6
- Hanun, and the *i* of Zanoah Neh 3:13
- watches of the *i* of Jerusalem Neh 7:3
- before them the *i* of the land Neh 9:24
- the waters, and the *i* thereof Job 26:5
- let all the *i* of the world stand Ps 33:8
- upon all the *i* of the earth Ps 33:14
- give ear, all ye *i* of the world Ps 49:1
- all the *i* thereof are dissolved Ps 75:3
- Philistines with the *i* of Tyre Ps 83:7
- O *i* of Jerusalem, and men of Judah Is 5:3
- for a snare to the *i* of Jerusalem Is 8:14
- put down the *i* like a valiant man Is 10:13
- the *i* of Gebim gather themselves Is 10:31
- All ye *i* of the world, and Is 18:3
- The *i* of the land of Tema brought Is 21:14
- be a father to the *i* of Jerusalem Is 22:21
- Be still, ye *i* of the isle Is 23:2
- howl, ye *i* of the isle Is 23:6
- scattereth abroad the *i* thereof Is 24:1
- is defiled under the *i* thereof Is 24:5
- therefore the *i* of the earth are Is 24:6
- the *i* of the world will learn Is 26:9
- neither have the *i* of the world Is 26:18
- out of his place to punish the *i* Is 26:21
- Therefore their *i* were of small Is 37:27
- no more with the *i* of the world Is 38:11
- the *i* thereof are as grasshoppers Is 40:22
- the isles, and the *i* thereof Is 42:10
- let the *i* of the rock sing, let Is 42:11
- be too narrow by reason of the *i* Is 49:19
- forth upon all the *i* of the land Jer 1:14
- ye men of Judah and *i* of Jerusalem Jer 4:4
- my hand upon the *i* of the land Jer 6:12
- the bones of the *i* of Jerusalem Jer 8:1
- I will sling out the *i* of the Jer 10:18
- Judah, and to the *i* of Jerusalem Jer 11:2
- and among the *i* of Jerusalem Jer 11:9
- *i* of Jerusalem go, and cry unto Jer 11:12
- will fill all the *i* of this land Jer 13:13
- all the *i* of Jerusalem, with Jer 13:13
- all the *i* of Jerusalem, that Jer 17:20
- of Judah, and the *i* of Jerusalem Jer 17:25
- to the *i* of Jerusalem, saying, Jer 18:11
- kings of Judah, and *i* of Jerusalem Jer 19:3
- to the *i* thereof, and even make Jer 19:12
- I will smite the *i* of this city Jer 21:6
- the *i* thereof as Gomorrah Jer 23:14
- to all the *i* of Jerusalem, saying Jer 25:2
- land, and against the *i* thereof Jer 25:9
- sword upon all the *i* of the earth Jer 25:29
- against all the *i* of the earth Jer 25:30
- this city, and upon the *i* thereof Jer 26:15
- of Judah, and the *i* of Jerusalem Jer 32:32
- the *i* of Jerusalem, Will ye not Jer 35:13
- upon all the *i* of Jerusalem all Jer 35:17
- upon the *i* of Jerusalem, and upon Jer 36:31
- forth upon the *i* of Jerusalem Jer 42:18
- destroy the city and the *i* thereof Jer 46:8
- all the *i* of the land shall howl Jer 47:2
- back, dwell deep, O *i* of Dedan Jer 49:8
- purposed against the *i* of Teman Jer 49:20
- O ye *i* of Hazor, saith the LORD Jer 49:30
- it, and against the *i* of Pekod Jer 50:21
- and disquiet the *i* of Babylon Jer 50:34
- upon the *i* of Babylon, and upon Jer 50:35
- he spake against the *i* of Babylon Jer 51:12
- to all the *i* of Chaldea all their Jer 51:24
- and my blood upon the *i* of Chaldea Jer 51:35
- all the *i* of the world, would not Lam 4:12
- whom the *i* of Jerusalem have said Eze 11:15
- Lord GOD of the *i* of Jerusalem Eze 12:19
- so will I give the *i* of Jerusalem Eze 15:6
- strong in the sea, she and her *i* Eze 26:17
- The *i* of Zidon and Arvad were thy Eze 27:8
- All the *i* of the isles shall be Eze 27:35

all the *i* of Egypt shall know ... Eze 29:6
all the *i* of the earth are ... Dan 4:35
and among the *i* of the earth ... Dan 4:35
to the *i* of Jerusalem, and unto ... Dan 9:7
with the *i* of the land, because ... Hos 4:1
The *i* of Samaria shall fear ... Hos 10:5
and give ear, all ye *i* of the land ... Joel 1:2
all the *i* of the land into the ... Joel 1:14
let all the *i* of the land tremble ... Joel 2:1
the *i* thereof have spoken lies, ... Mic 6:12
and the *i* thereof an hissing ... Mic 6:16
and upon all the *i* of Jerusalem ... Zeph 1:4
ye *i* of Maktesh, for all the ... Zeph 1:11
Woe unto the *i* of the sea coast, ... Zeph 2:5
people, and the *i* of many cities ... Zec 8:20
the *i* of one city shall go to ... Zec 8:21
no more pity the *i* of the land ... Zec 11:6
The *i* of Jerusalem shall be my ... Zec 12:5
the glory of the *i* of Jerusalem ... Zec 12:7
LORD defend the *i* of Jerusalem ... Zec 12:8
upon the *i* of Jerusalem, the ... Zec 12:10
to the *i* of Jerusalem for sin and ... Zec 13:1
the *i* of the earth have been made ... Rev 17:2

**INHABITED**

Seir the Horite, who *i* the land ... Gen 36:20
until they came to a land *i* ... Ex 16:35
iniquities unto a land not *i* ... Lev 16:22
the Canaanites that *i* Zephath ... Judg 1:17
the Jebusites that *i* Jerusalem ... Judg 1:21
eastward he *i* unto the entering ... 1Chr 5:9
It shall never be *i*, neither ... Is 13:20
to Jerusalem, Thou shalt be *i* ... Is 44:26
not in vain, he formed it to be *i* ... Is 45:18
make the desolate cities to be *i* ... Is 54:3
make thee desolate, a land not *i* ... Jer 6:8
in a salt land and not *i* ... Jer 17:6
and cities which are not *i* ... Jer 22:6
and afterward it shall be *i* ... Jer 46:26
of the LORD it shall not be *i* ... Jer 50:13
and it shall be no more *i* for ever ... Jer 50:39
that are *i* shall be laid waste ... Eze 12:20
that wast *i* of seafaring men, the ... Eze 26:17
like the cities that are not *i* ... Eze 26:19
to the pit, that thou be not *i* ... Eze 26:20
neither shall it be *i* forty years ... Eze 29:11
in all the *i* places of the ... Eze 34:13
and the cities shall be *i*, and the ... Eze 36:10
are become fenced, and are *i* ... Eze 36:35
desolate places that are now *i* ... Eze 38:12
Jerusalem shall be *i* as towns ... Zec 2:4
prophets, when Jerusalem was *i* ... Zec 7:7
when men *i* the south and the plain ... Zec 7:7
Gaza, and Ashkelon shall not be *i* ... Zec 9:5
Jerusalem shall be *i* again in her ... Zec 12:6
*i* in her place, from Benjamin's ... Zec 14:10
but Jerusalem shall be safely *i* ... Zec 14:11

**INHABITERS**

to the *i* of the earth by reason ... Rev 8:13
Woe to the *i* of the earth and of ... Rev 12:12

**INHABITEST**

O thou that *i* the praises of ... Ps 22:3

**INHABITETH**

and in houses which no man *i* ... Job 15:28
high and lofty One that *i* eternity ... Is 57:15

**INHABITING**

to the people *i* the wilderness ... Ps 74:14

**INHERIT**

to give thee this land to *i* it ... Gen 15:7
shall I know that I shall *i* it ... Gen 15:8
that thou mayest *i* the land ... Gen 28:4
thou be increased, and *i* the land ... Ex 23:30
seed, and they shall *i* it for ever ... Ex 32:13
Ye shall *i* their land, and I will ... Lev 20:24
to *i* them for a possession ... Lev 25:46
I have given to the Levites to *i* ... Num 18:24
of their fathers they shall *i* ... Num 26:55
For we will not *i* with them on ... Num 32:19
tribes of your fathers ye shall *i* ... Num 33:54
the land which ye shall *i* by lot ... Num 34:13
for he shall cause Israel to *i* it ... Deut 1:38
that thou mayest *i* his land ... Deut 2:31
he shall cause them to *i* the land ... Deut 3:28
the LORD your God giveth you to *i* ... Deut 12:10
*i* the land which the LORD thy God ... Deut 16:20
the LORD thy God giveth thee to *i* ... Deut 19:3
which thou shalt *i* in the land ... Deut 19:14
his sons to *i* that which he hath ... Deut 21:16
and thou shalt cause them to *i* it ... Deut 31:7
but one lot and one portion to *i* ... Josh 17:14
Thou shalt not *i* in our father's ... Judg 11:2
to make them *i* the throne of ... 1Sa 2:8
which thou hast given us to *i* ... 2Chr 20:11
and his seed shall *i* the earth ... Ps 25:13
the LORD, they shall *i* the earth ... Ps 37:9
But the meek shall *i* the earth ... Ps 37:11
blessed of him shall *i* the earth ... Ps 37:22
The righteous shall *i* the land ... Ps 37:29
he shall exalt thee to *i* the land ... Ps 37:34
also of his servants shall *i* it ... Ps 69:36
for thou shalt *i* all nations ... Ps 82:8
The wise shall *i* glory ... Prov 3:35
those that love me to *i* substance ... Prov 8:21
his own house shall *i* the wind ... Prov 11:29
The simple *i* folly ... Prov 14:18
to cause to *i* the desolate ... Is 49:8
and thy seed shall *i* the Gentiles ... Is 54:3
land, and shall *i* my holy mountain ... Is 57:13
they shall *i* the land for ever, ... Is 60:21
and mine elect shall *i* it, and my ... Is 65:9
fields to them that shall *i* them ... Jer 8:10
have caused my people Israel to *i* ... Jer 12:14
why then doth their king *i* Gad ... Jer 49:1
whereby ye shall *i* the land ... Eze 47:13
And ye shall *i* it, one as well as ... Eze 47:14
the LORD shall *i* Judah his ... Zec 2:12
for they shall *i* the earth ... Mt 5:5
and shall *i* everlasting life ... Mt 19:29
*i* the kingdom prepared for you ... Mt 25:34
I do that I may *i* eternal life ... Mk 10:17
what shall I do to *i* eternal life ... Lk 10:25
what shall I do to *i* eternal life ... Lk 18:18
shall not *i* the kingdom of God ... 1Cor 6:9
shall *i* the kingdom of God ... 1Cor 6:10
blood cannot *i* the kingdom of God ... 1Cor 15:50
doth corruption *i* incorruption ... 1Cor 15:50
shall not *i* the kingdom of God ... Gal 5:21
faith and patience *i* the promises ... Heb 6:12
that ye should *i* a blessing ... 1Pet 3:9
overcometh shall *i* all things ... Rev 21:7

**INHERITANCE**

Is there yet any portion or *i* for ... Gen 31:14
name of their brethren in their *i* ... Gen 48:6
them in the mountain of thine *i* ... Ex 15:17
our sin, and take us for thine *i* ... Ex 34:9
ye shall take them as an *i* for ... Lev 25:46
and honey, or given us *i* of fields ... Num 16:14
shalt have no *i* in their land ... Num 18:20
thine *i* among the children of ... Num 18:20
all the tenth in Israel for an *i* ... Num 18:21
children of Israel they have no *i* ... Num 18:23
of Israel they shall have no *i* ... Num 18:24
given you from them for your *i* ... Num 18:26
an *i* according to the number of ... Num 26:53
many thou shalt give the more *i* ... Num 26:54
to few thou shalt give the less *i* ... Num 26:54
to every one shall his *i* be given ... Num 26:54
because there was no *i* given them ... Num 26:62
give them a possession of an *i* ... Num 27:7
thou shalt cause the *i* of their ... Num 27:7
then ye shall cause his *i* to pass ... Num 27:8
give his *i* unto his brethren ... Num 27:9
then ye shall give his *i* unto his ... Num 27:10
then ye shall give his *i* unto his ... Num 27:11
have inherited every man his *i* ... Num 32:18
because our *i* is fallen to us on ... Num 32:19
that the possession of our *i* on ... Num 32:32
lot for an *i* among your families ... Num 33:54
the more ye shall give the more *i* ... Num 33:54
fewer ye shall give the less *i* ... Num 33:54
every man's *i* shall be in the ... Num 33:54
that shall fall unto you for an *i* ... Num 34:2
fathers, have received their *i* ... Num 34:14
of Manasseh have received their *i* ... Num 34:14
their *i* on this side Jordan near ... Num 34:15
tribe, to divide the land by *i* ... Num 34:18
LORD commanded to divide the *i* ... Num 34:29
give unto the Levites of the *i* of ... Num 35:2
to his *i* which he inheriteth ... Num 35:8
an *i* by lot to the children of ... Num 36:2
by the LORD to give the *i* of ... Num 36:2
then shall their *i* be taken from ... Num 36:3
taken from the *i* of our fathers ... Num 36:3
shall be put to the *i* of the ... Num 36:3
it be taken from the lot of our *i* ... Num 36:3
*i* be put unto the *i* of ... Num 36:4
so shall their *i* be taken away ... Num 36:4
be taken away from the *i* of the ... Num 36:4
So shall not the *i* of the ... Num 36:7
shall keep himself to the *i* of ... Num 36:7
that possesseth an *i* in any tribe ... Num 36:8
every man the *i* of his fathers ... Num 36:8
Neither shall the *i* remove from ... Num 36:9
shall keep himself to his own *i* ... Num 36:9
their *i* remained in the tribe of ... Num 36:12
to be unto him a people of *i* ... Deut 4:20
LORD thy God giveth thee for an *i* ... Deut 4:21
to give thee their land for an *i* ... Deut 4:38
destroy not thy people and thine *i* ... Deut 9:26
they are thy people and thine *i* ... Deut 9:29
no part nor *i* with his brethren ... Deut 10:9
the LORD is his *i*, according as ... Deut 10:9
yet come to the rest and to the *i* ... Deut 12:9
as he hath no part nor *i* with you ... Deut 12:12
he hath no part nor *i* with thee ... Deut 14:27
he hath no part nor *i* with thee ... Deut 14:29
thee for an *i* to possess it ... Deut 15:4
have no part nor *i* with Israel ... Deut 18:1
the LORD made by fire, and his *i* ... Deut 18:1
have no *i* among their brethren ... Deut 18:2
the LORD is their *i*, as he hath ... Deut 18:2
LORD thy God giveth thee for an *i* ... Deut 19:10
of old time have set in thine *i* ... Deut 19:14
thy God doth give thee for an *i* ... Deut 20:16
LORD thy God giveth thee for an *i* ... Deut 21:23
LORD thy God giveth thee for an *i* ... Deut 24:4
thee for an *i* to possess it ... Deut 25:19
LORD thy God giveth thee for an *i* ... Deut 26:1
gave it for an *i* unto the ... Deut 29:8
divided to the nations their *i* ... Deut 32:8
Jacob is the lot of his *i* ... Deut 32:9
even the *i* of the congregation of ... Deut 33:4
thou divide for an *i* the land ... Josh 1:6
Joshua gave it for an *i* unto ... Josh 11:23
lot unto the Israelites for an *i* ... Josh 13:6
for an *i* unto the nine tribes ... Josh 13:7
the Gadites have received their *i* ... Josh 13:8
the tribe of Levi he gave none *i* ... Josh 13:14
Israel made by fire are their *i* ... Josh 13:14
*i* according to their families ... Josh 13:15
This was the *i* of the children of ... Josh 13:23
Moses gave *i* unto the tribe of ... Josh 13:24
This is the *i* of the children of ... Josh 13:28
Moses gave *i* unto the half tribe ... Josh 13:29
for *i* in the plains of Moab ... Josh 13:32
of Levi Moses gave not any *i* ... Josh 13:33
LORD God of Israel was their *i* ... Josh 13:33
Israel, distributed for *i* to them ... Josh 14:1
By lot was their *i*, as the LORD ... Josh 14:2
had given the *i* of two tribes ... Josh 14:3
Levites he gave none *i* among them ... Josh 14:3
have trodden shall be thine *i* ... Josh 14:9
son of Jephunneh Hebron for an *i* ... Josh 14:13
Hebron therefore became the *i* of ... Josh 14:14
This is the *i* of the tribe of the ... Josh 15:20
Manasseh and Ephraim, took their *i* ... Josh 16:4
of their *i* on the east side was ... Josh 16:5
This is the *i* of the tribe of the ... Josh 16:8
of Ephraim were among the *i* of ... Josh 16:9
give us an *i* among our brethren ... Josh 17:4
an *i* among the brethren of their ... Josh 17:4
Manasseh had an *i* among his sons ... Josh 17:6
had not yet received their *i* ... Josh 18:2
it according to the *i* of them ... Josh 18:4
priesthood of the LORD is their *i* ... Josh 18:7
have received their *i* beyond ... Josh 18:7
This was the *i* of the children of ... Josh 18:20
This is the *i* of the children of ... Josh 18:28
and their *i* was within the ... Josh 19:1
the *i* of the children of Judah ... Josh 19:1
And they had in their *i* Beer-sheba ... Josh 19:2
This is the *i* of the tribe of the ... Josh 19:8
the *i* of the children of Simeon ... Josh 19:9
*i* within the *i* of them ... Josh 19:9
border of their *i* was unto Sarid ... Josh 19:10
This is the *i* of the children of ... Josh 19:16
This is the *i* of the tribe of the ... Josh 19:23
This is the *i* of the tribe of the ... Josh 19:31
This is the *i* of the tribe of the ... Josh 19:39
And the coast of their *i* was Zorah ... Josh 19:41
This is the *i* of the tribe of the ... Josh 19:48
the land for *i* by their coasts ... Josh 19:49
*i* to Joshua the son of Nun among ... Josh 19:49
divided for an *i* by lot in Shiloh ... Josh 19:51
unto the Levites out of their *i* ... Josh 21:3
to be an *i* for your tribes, from ... Josh 23:4
depart, every man unto his *i* ... Josh 24:28
border of his *i* in Timnath-serah ... Josh 24:30
it became the *i* of the children ... Josh 24:32
unto his *i* to possess the land ... Judg 2:6
border of his *i* in Timnath-heres ... Judg 2:9
sought them an *i* to dwell in ... Judg 18:1
for unto that day all their *i* had ... Judg 18:1
the country of the *i* of Israel ... Judg 20:6
There must be an *i* for them that ... Judg 21:17
went and returned unto their *i* ... Judg 21:23
from thence every man to his *i* ... Judg 21:24
the name of the dead upon his *i* ... Ruth 4:5
for myself, lest I mar mine own *i* ... Ruth 4:6
the name of the dead upon his *i* ... Ruth 4:10
thee to be captain over his *i* ... 1Sa 10:1
from abiding in the *i* of the LORD ... 1Sa 26:19
son together out of the *i* of God ... 2Sa 14:16
neither have we *i* in the son of ... 2Sa 20:1
thou swallow up the *i* of the LORD ... 2Sa 20:19
ye may bless the *i* of the LORD ... 2Sa 21:3
hast given to thy people for an *i* ... 1Kin 8:36
they be thy people, and thine *i* ... 1Kin 8:51
of the earth, to be thine *i* ... 1Kin 8:53
neither have we *i* in the son of ... 1Kin 12:16
that I should give the *i* of my ... 1Kin 21:3
not give thee the *i* of my fathers ... 1Kin 21:4
forsake the remnant of mine *i* ... 2Kin 21:14
land of Canaan, the lot of your *i* ... 1Chr 16:18
leave it for an *i* for your ... 1Chr 28:8
given unto thy people for an *i* ... 2Chr 6:27
we have none *i* in the son of ... 2Chr 10:16
leave it for an *i* to your ... Ezr 9:12
of Judah, every one in his *i* ... Neh 11:20
what *i* of the Almighty from on ... Job 31:2
gave them *i* among their brethren ... Job 42:15
give thee the heathen for thine *i* ... Ps 2:8
The LORD is the portion of mine *i* ... Ps 16:5
Save thy people, and bless thine *i* ... Ps 28:9
whom he hath chosen for his own *i* ... Ps 33:12
their *i* shall be for ever ... Ps 37:18
He shall choose our *i* for us ... Ps 47:4
thou didst confirm thine *i* ... Ps 68:9
the rod of thine *i*, which thou ... Ps 74:2
and divided them an *i* by line ... Ps 78:55
and was wroth with his *i* ... Ps 78:62
Jacob his people, and Israel his *i* ... Ps 78:71
the heathen are come into thine *i* ... Ps 79:1
neither will he forsake his *i* ... Ps 94:14
land of Canaan, the lot of your *i* ... Ps 105:11
that I may glory with thine *i* ... Ps 106:5
that he abhorred his own *i* ... Ps 106:40
A good man leaveth an *i* to his ... Prov 13:22
part of the *i* among the brethren ... Prov 17:2
and riches are the *i* of fathers ... Prov 19:14
An *i* may be gotten hastily at the ... Prov 20:21
Wisdom is good with an *i* ... Eccl 7:11
of my hands, and Israel mine *i* ... Is 19:25
my people, I have polluted mine *i* ... Is 47:6
sake, the tribes of thine *i* ... Is 63:17
given for an *i* unto your fathers ... Jer 3:18
and Israel is the rod of his *i* ... Jer 10:16
that touch the *i* which I have ... Jer 12:14

they have filled mine *i* with the ... Jer 16:18
for the right of *i* is thine ... Jer 32:8
and Israel is the rod of his *i* ... Jer 51:19
Our *i* is turned to strangers, our ... Lam 5:2
thou shalt take thine *i* in ... Eze 22:16
the land is given us for *i* ... Eze 33:24
at the *i* of the house of Israel ... Eze 35:15
thee, and thou shalt be their *i* ... Eze 36:12
And it shall be unto them for an *i* ... Eze 44:28
I am their *i* ... Eze 44:28
divide by lot the land for *i* ... Eze 45:1
the *i* thereof shall be his sons' ... Eze 46:16
it shall be their possession by *i* ... Eze 46:16
of his *i* to one of his servants ... Eze 46:17
but his *i* shall be his sons' for ... Eze 46:17
of the people's *i* by oppression ... Eze 46:18
sons *i* out of his own possession ... Eze 46:18
land shall fall unto you for *i* ... Eze 47:14
it by lot for an *i* unto you ... Eze 47:22
they shall have *i* with you among ... Eze 47:22
there shall ye give him his *i* ... Eze 47:23
unto the tribes of Israel for *i* ... Eze 48:29
him, and let us seize on his *i* ... Mt 21:38
kill him, and the *i* shall be ours ... Mk 12:7
that he divide the *i* with me ... Lk 12:13
kill him, that the *i* may be ours ... Lk 20:14
And he gave him none *i* in it ... Acts 7:5
to give you an *i* among all them ... Acts 20:32
*i* among them which are sanctified ... Acts 26:18
For if the *i* be of the law, it is ... Gal 3:18
whom also we have obtained an *i* ... Eph 1:11
our *i* until the redemption of the ... Eph 1:14
the glory of his *i* in the saints ... Eph 1:18
hath any *i* in the kingdom of ... Eph 5:5
of the *i* of the saints in light ... Col 1:12
shall receive the reward of the *i* ... Col 3:24
as he hath by *i* obtained a more ... Heb 1:4
receive the promise of eternal *i* ... Heb 9:15
he should after receive for an *i* ... Heb 11:8
To an *i* incorruptible, and ... 1Pet 1:4

**INHERITANCES**
These are the *i*, which Eleazar ... Josh 19:51

**INHERITED**
have *i* every man his inheritance ... Num 32:18
of Israel *i* in the land of Canaan ... Josh 14:1
they *i* the labour of the people ... Ps 105:44
Surely our fathers have *i* lies ... Jer 16:19
Abraham was one, and he *i* the land ... Eze 33:24
when he would have *i* the blessing ... Heb 12:17

**INHERITETH**
to his inheritance which he *i* ... Num 35:8

**INHERITOR**
out of Judah an *i* of my mountains ... Is 65:9

**INIQUITIES**
confess over him all the *i* of the ... Lev 16:21
their *i* unto a land not inhabited ... Lev 16:22
also in the *i* of their fathers ... Lev 26:39
for a year, shall ye bear your *i* ... Num 14:34
for our *i* are increased over our ... Ezr 9:6
and for our *i* have we, our kings, ... Ezr 9:7
us less than our *i* deserve ... Ezr 9:13
sins, and the *i* of their fathers ... Neh 9:2
How many are mine *i* and sins ... Job 13:23
me to possess the *i* of my youth ... Job 13:26
and thine *i* infinite ... Job 22:5
For mine *i* are gone over mine ... Ps 38:4
mine *i* have taken hold upon me, ... Ps 40:12
my sins, and blot out all mine *i* ... Ps 51:9
They search out *i* ... Ps 64:6
*I* prevail against me ... Ps 65:3
remember not against us former *i* ... Ps 79:8
Thou hast set our *i* before thee ... Ps 90:8
Who forgiveth all thine *i* ... Ps 103:3
rewarded us according to our *i* ... Ps 103:10
and because of their *i*, are ... Ps 107:17
If thou, LORD, shouldest mark *i* ... Ps 130:3
redeem Israel from all his *i* ... Ps 130:8
His own *i* shall take the wicked ... Prov 5:22
thou hast wearied me with thine *i* ... Is 43:24
Behold, for your *i* have ye sold ... Is 50:1
he was bruised for our *i* ... Is 53:5
for he shall bear their *i* ... Is 53:11
But your *i* have separated between ... Is 59:2
and as for our *i*, we know them ... Is 59:12
and our *i*, like the wind, have ... Is 64:6
consumed us, because of our *i* ... Is 64:7
Your *i*, and the *i* of your ... Is 65:7
Your *i* have turned away these ... Jer 5:25
to the *i* of their forefathers ... Jer 11:10
though our *i* testify against us, ... Jer 14:7
and I will pardon all their *i* ... Jer 33:8
the *i* of her priests, that have ... Lam 4:13
and we have borne their *i* ... Lam 5:7
but ye shall pine away for your *i* ... Eze 24:23
by the multitude of thine *i* ... Eze 28:18
but their *i* shall be upon their ... Eze 32:27
in your own sight for your *i* ... Eze 36:31
*i* I will also cause you to dwell ... Eze 36:33
they may be ashamed of their *i* ... Eze 43:10
thine *i* by shewing mercy to the ... Dan 4:27
that we might turn from our *i* ... Dan 9:13
for the *i* of our fathers, ... Dan 9:16
I will punish you for all your *i* ... Amos 3:2
he will subdue our *i* ... Mic 7:19
away every one of you from his *i* ... Acts 3:26
are they whose *i* are forgiven ... Rom 4:7
their *i* will I remember no more ... Heb 8:12
*i* will I remember no more ... Heb 10:17

and God hath remembered her *i* ... Rev 18:5

**INIQUITY**
for the *i* of the Amorites is not ... Gen 15:16
be consumed in the *i* of the city ... Gen 19:15
found out the *i* of thy servants ... Gen 44:16
visiting the *i* of the fathers ... Ex 20:5
may bear the *i* of the holy things ... Ex 28:38
that they bear not *i*, and die ... Ex 28:43
mercy for thousands, forgiving *i* ... Ex 34:7
visiting the *i* of the fathers ... Ex 34:7
and pardon our *i* and our sin, and ... Ex 34:9
it, then he shall bear his *i* ... Lev 5:1
is he guilty, and shall bear his *i* ... Lev 5:17
eateth of it shall bear his *i* ... Lev 7:18
to bear the *i* of the congregation ... Lev 10:17
then he shall bear his *i* ... Lev 17:16
I do visit the *i* thereof upon it ... Lev 18:25
that eateth it shall bear his *i* ... Lev 19:8
he shall bear his *i* ... Lev 20:17
they shall bear their *i* ... Lev 20:19
them to bear the *i* of trespass ... Lev 22:16
in their *i* in your enemies' lands ... Lev 26:39
If they shall confess their *i* ... Lev 26:40
the *i* of their fathers, with ... Lev 26:40
of the punishment of their *i* ... Lev 26:41
of the punishment of their *i* ... Lev 26:43
bringing *i* to remembrance ... Num 5:15
shall the man be guiltless from *i* ... Num 5:31
and this woman shall bear her *i* ... Num 5:31
and of great mercy, forgiving *i* ... Num 14:18
visiting the *i* of the fathers ... Num 14:18
the *i* of this people according ... Num 14:19
his *i* shall be upon him ... Num 15:31
shall bear the *i* of the sanctuary ... Num 18:1
bear the *i* of your priesthood ... Num 18:1
and they shall bear their *i* ... Num 18:23
He hath not beheld *i* in Jacob ... Num 23:21
then he shall bear her *i* ... Num 30:15
visiting the *i* of the fathers ... Deut 5:9
rise up against a man for any *i* ... Deut 19:15
a God of truth and without *i* ... Deut 32:4
Is the *i* of Peor too little for ... Josh 22:17
man perished not alone in his *i* ... Josh 22:20
ever for the *i* which he knoweth ... 1Sa 3:13
that the *i* of Eli's house shall ... 1Sa 3:14
and stubbornness is as *i* and ... 1Sa 15:23
what is mine *i*? ... 1Sa 20:1
if there be in me *i*, slay me ... 1Sa 20:8
my lord, upon me let this *i* be ... 1Sa 25:24
If he commit *i*, I will chasten ... 2Sa 7:14
the *i* be on me, and on my father's ... 2Sa 14:9
and if there be any *i* in me ... 2Sa 14:32
Let not my lord impute *i* unto me ... 2Sa 19:19
and have kept myself from mine *i* ... 2Sa 22:24
take away the *i* of thy servant ... 2Sa 24:10
do away the *i* of thy servant ... 1Chr 21:8
for there is no *i* with the LORD ... 2Chr 19:7
And cover not their *i*, and let not ... Neh 4:5
as I have seen, they that plow *i* ... Job 4:8
hope, and *i* stoppeth her mouth ... Job 5:16
I pray you, let it not be *i* ... Job 6:29
Is there *i* in my tongue ... Job 6:30
and take away mine *i* ... Job 7:21
That thou enquirest after mine *i* ... Job 10:6
wilt not acquit me from mine *i* ... Job 10:14
thee less than thine *i* deserveth ... Job 11:6
If *i* be in thine hand, put it far ... Job 11:14
a bag, and thou sewest up mine *i* ... Job 14:17
For thy mouth uttereth thine *i* ... Job 15:5
man, which drinketh *i* like water ... Job 15:16
The heaven shall reveal his *i* ... Job 20:27
layeth up his *i* for his children ... Job 21:19
thou shalt put away *i* far from ... Job 22:23
punishment to the workers of *i* ... Job 31:3
it is an *i* to be punished by the ... Job 31:11
This also were an *i* to be ... Job 31:28
by hiding mine *i* in my bosom ... Job 31:33
neither is there *i* in me ... Job 33:9
in company with the workers of *i* ... Job 34:8
Almighty, that he should commit *i* ... Job 34:10
workers of *i* may hide themselves ... Job 34:22
if I have done *i*, I will do no ... Job 34:32
that they return from *i* ... Job 36:10
Take heed, regard not *i* ... Job 36:21
who can say, Thou hast wrought *i* ... Job 36:23
thou hatest all workers of *i* ... Ps 5:5
from me, all ye workers of *i* ... Ps 6:8
if there be *i* in my hands ... Ps 7:3
Behold, he travaileth with *i* ... Ps 7:14
all the workers of *i* no knowledge ... Ps 14:4
him, and I kept myself from mine *i* ... Ps 18:23
sake, O LORD, pardon mine *i* ... Ps 25:11
wicked, and with the workers of *i* ... Ps 28:3
faileth because of mine *i* ... Ps 31:10
unto whom the LORD imputeth not *i* ... Ps 32:2
thee, and mine *i* have I not hid ... Ps 32:5
and thou forgavest the *i* of my sin ... Ps 32:5
until his *i* be found to be ... Ps 36:2
The words of his mouth are *i* ... Ps 36:3
There are the workers of *i* fallen ... Ps 36:12
envious against the workers of *i* ... Ps 37:1
For I will declare mine *i* ... Ps 38:18
rebukes dost correct man for *i* ... Ps 39:11
his heart gathereth *i* to itself ... Ps 41:6
when the *i* of my heels shall ... Ps 49:5
Wash me throughly from mine *i* ... Ps 51:2
Behold, I was shapen in *i* ... Ps 51:5
they, and have done abominable *i* ... Ps 53:1
the workers of *i* no knowledge ... Ps 53:4
for they cast *i* upon me, and in ... Ps 55:3

Shall they escape by *i* ... Ps 56:7
Deliver me from the workers of *i* ... Ps 59:2
insurrection of the workers of *i* ... Ps 64:2
If I regard *i* in my heart ... Ps 66:18
Add *i* unto their *i* ... Ps 69:27
of compassion, forgave their *i* ... Ps 78:38
hast forgiven the *i* of thy people ... Ps 85:2
the rod, and their *i* with stripes ... Ps 89:32
all the workers of *i* do flourish ... Ps 92:7
workers of *i* shall be scattered ... Ps 92:9
the workers of *i* boast themselves ... Ps 94:4
for me against the workers of *i* ... Ps 94:16
Shall the throne of *i* have ... Ps 94:20
shall bring upon them their own *i* ... Ps 94:23
our fathers, we have committed *i* ... Ps 106:6
and were brought low for their *i* ... Ps 106:43
all *i* shall stop her mouth ... Ps 107:42
Let the *i* of his fathers be ... Ps 109:14
They also do no *i* ... Ps 119:3
let not any *i* have dominion over ... Ps 119:133
put forth their hands unto *i* ... Ps 125:3
them forth with the workers of *i* ... Ps 125:5
wicked works with men that work *i* ... Ps 141:4
and the gins of the workers of *i* ... Ps 141:9
shall be to the workers of *i* ... Prov 10:29
By mercy and truth *i* is purged ... Prov 16:6
mouth of the wicked devoureth *i* ... Prov 19:28
shall be to the workers of *i* ... Prov 21:15
He that soweth *i* shall reap ... Prov 22:8
righteousness, that *i* was there ... Eccl 3:16
nation, a people laden with *i* ... Is 1:4
it is *i*, even the solemn meeting ... Is 1:13
that draw *i* with cords of vanity ... Is 5:18
thine *i* is taken away, and thy sin ... Is 6:7
evil, and the wicked for their *i* ... Is 13:11
for the *i* of their fathers ... Is 14:21
Surely this *i* shall not be purged ... Is 22:14
of the earth for their *i* ... Is 26:21
shall the *i* of Jacob be purged ... Is 27:9
all that watch for *i* are cut off ... Is 29:20
Therefore this *i* shall be to you ... Is 30:13
the help of them that work *i* ... Is 31:2
villany, and his heart will work *i* ... Is 32:6
therein shall be forgiven their *i* ... Is 33:24
that her *i* is pardoned ... Is 40:2
hath laid on him the *i* of us all ... Is 53:6
For the *i* of his covetousness was ... Is 57:17
blood, and your fingers with *i* ... Is 59:3
mischief, and bring forth *i* ... Is 59:4
their works are works of *i* ... Is 59:6
their thoughts are thoughts of *i* ... Is 59:7
LORD, neither remember *i* for ever ... Is 64:9
What *i* have your fathers found in ... Jer 2:5
yet thine *i* is marked before me, ... Jer 2:22
Only acknowledge thine *i*, that ... Jer 3:13
and weary themselves to commit *i* ... Jer 9:5
thine *i* are thy skirts discovered ... Jer 13:22
he will now remember their *i* ... Jer 14:10
and the *i* of our fathers ... Jer 14:20
or what is our *i* ... Jer 16:10
neither is their *i* hid from mine ... Jer 16:17
first I will recompense their *i* ... Jer 16:18
forgive not their *i*, neither blot ... Jer 18:23
saith the LORD, for their *i* ... Jer 25:12
one, for the multitude of thine *i* ... Jer 30:14
for the multitude of thine *i* ... Jer 30:15
every one shall die for his own *i* ... Jer 31:30
for I will forgive their *i* ... Jer 31:34
recompensest the *i* of the fathers ... Jer 32:18
cleanse them from all their *i* ... Jer 33:8
that I may forgive their *i* ... Jer 36:3
seed and his servants for their *i* ... Jer 36:31
the *i* of Israel shall be sought ... Jer 50:20
be not cut off in her *i* ... Jer 51:6
they have not discovered thine *i* ... Lam 2:14
For the punishment of the *i* of ... Lam 4:6
of thine *i* is accomplished ... Lam 4:22
he will visit thine *i*, O daughter ... Lam 4:22
wicked man shall die in his *i* ... Eze 3:18
wicked way, he shall die in his *i* ... Eze 3:19
his righteousness, and commit *i* ... Eze 3:20
lay the *i* of the house of Israel ... Eze 4:4
upon it thou shalt bear their *i* ... Eze 4:4
upon thee the years of their *i* ... Eze 4:5
bear the *i* of the house of Israel ... Eze 4:5
thou shalt bear the *i* of the ... Eze 4:6
and consume away for their *i* ... Eze 4:17
himself in the *i* of his life ... Eze 7:13
mourning, every one for his *i* ... Eze 7:16
is the stumblingblock of their *i* ... Eze 7:19
The *i* of the house of Israel and ... Eze 9:9
of their *i* before their face ... Eze 14:3
of his *i* before his face, and ... Eze 14:4
of his *i* before his face, and ... Eze 14:7
bear the punishment of their *i* ... Eze 14:10
this was the *i* of thy sister ... Eze 16:49
hath withdrawn his hand from *i* ... Eze 18:8
not die for the *i* of his father ... Eze 18:17
lo, even he shall die in his *i* ... Eze 18:18
the son bear the *i* of the father ... Eze 18:19
not bear the *i* of the father ... Eze 18:20
the father bear the *i* of the son ... Eze 18:20
righteousness, and committeth *i* ... Eze 18:24
righteousness, and committeth *i* ... Eze 18:26
for his *i* that he hath done shall ... Eze 18:26
so *i* shall not be your ruin ... Eze 18:30
he will call to remembrance the *i* ... Eze 21:23
have made your *i* to be remembered ... Eze 21:24
when *i* shall have an end, ... Eze 21:25
when their *i* shall have an end ... Eze 21:29

I

created, till *i* was found in thee ... Eze 28:15
by the *i* of thy traffick ... Eze 28:18
bringeth their *i* to remembrance ... Eze 29:16
them, he is taken away in his *i* ... Eze 33:6
wicked man shall die in his *i* ... Eze 33:8
his way, he shall die in his *i* ... Eze 33:9
own righteousness, and commit *i* ... Eze 33:13
but for his *i* that he hath ... Eze 33:13
of life, without committing *i* ... Eze 33:15
righteousness, and committeth *i* ... Eze 33:18
the time that their *i* had an end ... Eze 35:5
went into captivity for their *i* ... Eze 39:23
they shall even bear their *i* ... Eze 44:10
house of Israel to fall into *i* ... Eze 44:12
GOD, and they shall bear their *i* ... Eze 44:12
have sinned, and have committed *i* ... Dan 9:5
and to make reconciliation for *i* ... Dan 9:24
they set their heart on their *i* ... Hos 4:8
Israel and Ephraim fall in their *i* ... Hos 5:5
is a city of them that work *i* ... Hos 6:8
then the *i* of Ephraim was ... Hos 7:1
now will he remember their *i* ... Hos 8:13
mad, for the multitude of thine *i* ... Hos 9:7
he will remember their *i*, he will ... Hos 9:9
of *i* did not overtake them ... Hos 10:9
wickedness, ye have reaped *i* ... Hos 10:13
find none *i* in me that were sin ... Hos 12:8
Is there *i* in Gilead ... Hos 12:11
The *i* of Ephraim is bound up ... Hos 13:12
for thou hast fallen by thine *i* ... Hos 14:1
say unto him, Take away all *i* ... Hos 14:2
Woe to them that devise *i* ... Mic 2:1
with blood, and Jerusalem with *i* ... Mic 3:10
like unto thee, that pardoneth *i* ... Mic 7:18
Why dost thou shew me *i*, and cause ... Hab 1:3
evil, and canst not look on *i* ... Hab 1:13
blood, and stablisheth a city by *i* ... Hab 2:12
he will not do *i* ... Zeph 3:5
remnant of Israel shall not do *i* ... Zeph 3:13
caused thine *i* to pass from thee ... Zec 3:4
I will remove the *i* of that land ... Zec 3:9
*i* was not found in his lips ... Mal 2:6
and did turn many away from *i* ... Mal 2:6
depart from me, ye that work *i* ... Mt 7:23
that offend, and them which do *i* ... Mt 13:41
ye are full of hypocrisy and *i* ... Mt 23:28
because *i* shall abound, the love ... Mt 24:12
from me, all ye workers of *i* ... Lk 13:27
a field with the reward of *i* ... Acts 1:18
bitterness, and in the bond of *i* ... Acts 8:23
uncleanness and to *i* unto *i* ... Rom 6:19
Rejoiceth not in *i*, but rejoiceth ... 1Cor 13:6
mystery of *i* doth already work ... 2Th 2:7
the name of Christ depart from *i* ... 2Ti 2:19
he might redeem us from all *i* ... Titus 2:14
loved righteousness, and hated *i* ... Heb 1:9
tongue is a fire, a world of *i* ... Jas 3:6
But was rebuked for his *i* ... 2Pet 2:16

## INJURED
ye have not *i* me at all ... Gal 4:12

## INJURIOUS
blasphemer, and a persecutor, and *i* ... 1Ti 1:13

## INJUSTICE
Not for any *i* in mine hands ... Job 16:17

## INK
I wrote them with *i* in the book ... Jer 36:18
by us, written not with *i* ... 2Cor 3:3
I would not write with paper and *i* ... 2Jn 12
to write, but I will not with *i* ... 3Jn 13

## INKHORN
with a writer's *i* by his side ... Eze 9:2
had the writer's *i* by his side ... Eze 9:3
which had the *i* by his side ... Eze 9:11

## INN
give his ass provender in the *i* ... Gen 42:27
to pass, when we came to the *i* ... Gen 43:21
came to pass by the way in the *i* ... Ex 4:24
was no room for them in the *i* ... Lk 2:7
own beast, and brought him to an *i* ... Lk 10:34

## INNER
the cherubims within the *i* house ... 1Kin 6:27
he built the *i* court with three ... 1Kin 6:36
both for the *i* court of the house ... 1Kin 7:12
both for the doors of the *i* house ... 1Kin 7:50
into the city, into an *i* chamber ... 1Kin 20:30
into an *i* chamber to hide thyself ... 1Kin 22:25
and carry him to an *i* chamber ... 2Kin 9:2
of the *i* parlours thereof, and of ... 1Chr 28:11
the *i* doors thereof for the most ... 2Chr 4:22
into an *i* chamber to hide thyself ... 2Chr 18:24
the priests went into the *i* part ... 2Chr 29:16
unto the king into the *i* court ... Est 4:11
stood in the *i* court of the ... Est 5:1
to the door of the *i* gate ... Eze 8:3
he brought me into the *i* court of ... Eze 8:16
and the cloud filled the *i* court ... Eze 10:3
of the *i* gate were fifty cubits ... Eze 40:15
forefront of the *i* court without ... Eze 40:19
the gate of the *i* court was over ... Eze 40:23
in the *i* court toward the south ... Eze 40:27
he brought me to the *i* court by ... Eze 40:28
into the *i* court toward the east ... Eze 40:32
without the *i* gate were the ... Eze 40:44
of the singers in the *i* court ... Eze 40:44
hundred cubits, with the *i* temple ... Eze 41:15
the door, even unto the *i* house ... Eze 41:17
cubits which were for the *i* court ... Eze 42:3
an end of measuring the *i* house ... Eze 42:15
and brought me into the *i* court ... Eze 43:5
in at the gates of the *i* court ... Eze 44:17
in the gates of the *i* court ... Eze 44:17
when they enter into the *i* court ... Eze 44:21
the sanctuary, unto the *i* court ... Eze 44:27
posts of the gate of the *i* court ... Eze 45:19
The gate of the *i* court that ... Eze 46:1
thrust them into the *i* prison ... Acts 16:24
might by his Spirit in the *i* man ... Eph 3:16

## INNERMOST
into the *i* parts of the belly ... Prov 18:8
into the *i* parts of the belly ... Prov 26:22

## INNOCENCY
*i* of my hands have I done this ... Gen 20:5
I will wash mine hands in *i* ... Ps 26:6
in vain, and washed my hands in *i* ... Ps 73:13
as before him *i* was found in me ... Dan 6:22
will it be ere they attain to *i* ... Hos 8:5

## INNOCENT
and the *i* and righteous slay thou ... Ex 23:7
That *i* blood be not shed in thy ... Deut 19:10
the guilt of *i* blood from Israel ... Deut 19:13
lay not *i* blood unto thy people ... Deut 21:8
guilt of *i* blood from among you ... Deut 21:9
taketh reward to slay an *i* person ... Deut 27:25
wilt thou sin against *i* blood ... 1Sa 19:5
thou mayest take away the *i* blood ... 1Kin 2:31
Manasseh shed *i* blood very much ... 2Kin 21:16
also for the *i* blood that he shed ... 2Kin 24:4
he filled Jerusalem with *i* blood ... 2Kin 24:4
thee, who ever perished, being *i* ... Job 4:7
will laugh at the trial of the *i* ... Job 9:23
know that thou wilt not hold me *i* ... Job 9:28
the *i* shall stir up himself ... Job 17:8
the *i* laugh them to scorn ... Job 22:19
shall deliver the island of the *i* ... Job 22:30
the *i* shall divide the silver ... Job 27:17
without transgression, I am *i* ... Job 33:9
places doth he murder the *i* ... Ps 10:8
nor taketh reward against the *i* ... Ps 15:5
I shall be *i* from the great ... Ps 19:13
righteous, and condemn the *i* blood ... Ps 94:21
shed *i* blood, even the blood of ... Ps 106:38
privily for the *i* without cause ... Prov 1:11
and hands that shed *i* blood ... Prov 6:17
toucheth her shall not be *i* ... Prov 6:29
haste to be rich shall not be *i* ... Prov 28:20
they make haste to shed *i* blood ... Is 59:7
Yet thou sayest, Because I am *i* ... Jer 2:35
shed not *i* blood in this place, ... Jer 7:6
neither shed *i* blood in this ... Jer 22:3
and for to shed *i* blood, and for ... Jer 22:17
bring *i* blood upon yourselves ... Jer 26:15
have shed *i* blood in their land ... Joel 3:19
life, and lay not upon us *i* blood ... Jonah 1:14
that I have betrayed the *i* blood ... Mt 27:4
I am *i* of the blood of this just ... Mt 27:24

## INNOCENTS
blood of the souls of the poor *i* ... Jer 2:34
this place with the blood of *i* ... Jer 19:4

## INNUMERABLE
him, as there are *i* before him ... Job 21:33
For *i* evils have compassed me ... Ps 40:12
wherein are things creeping *i* ... Ps 104:25
than the grasshoppers, and are *i* ... Jer 46:23
together an *i* multitude of people ... Lk 12:1
sand which is by the sea shore *i* ... Heb 11:12
to an *i* company of angels, ... Heb 12:22

## INORDINATE
corrupt in her *i* love than she ... Eze 23:11
*i* affection, evil concupiscence, ... Col 3:5

## INQUISITION
the judges shall make diligent *i* ... Deut 19:18
when *i* was made of the matter, it ... Est 2:23
When he maketh *i* for blood ... Ps 9:12

## INSCRIPTION
I found an altar with this *i* ... Acts 17:23

## INSIDE
covered them on the *i* with wood ... 1Kin 6:15

## INSOMUCH
*i* that he abhorred his own ... Ps 106:40
*i* that he regardeth not the ... Mal 2:13
*i* that the ship was covered with ... Mt 8:24
*i* that the blind and dumb both ... Mt 12:22
*i* that they were astonished, and ... Mt 13:54
*I* that the multitude wondered, ... Mt 15:31
*i* that, if it were possible, they ... Mt 24:24
*i* that the governor marvelled ... Mt 27:14
*i* that they questioned among ... Mk 1:27
*i* that Jesus could no more openly ... Mk 1:45
*i* that there was no room to ... Mk 2:2
*i* that they were all amazed, and ... Mk 2:12
*i* that they pressed upon him for ... Mk 3:10
*i* that many said, He is dead ... Mk 9:26
*i* that they trode one upon ... Lk 12:1
*i* as that field is called in ... Acts 1:19
*I* that they brought forth the ... Acts 5:15
*i* that we despaired even of life ... 2Cor 1:8
*I* that we desired Titus, that as ... 2Cor 8:6
*i* that Barnabas also was carried ... Gal 2:13

## INSPIRATION
the *i* of the Almighty giveth them ... Job 32:8
scripture is given by *i* of God ... 2Ti 3:16

## INSTANT
yea, it shall be at an *i* suddenly ... Is 29:5
breaking cometh suddenly at an *i* ... Is 30:13
At what *i* I shall speak ... Jer 18:7
And at what *i* I shall speak ... Jer 18:9
she coming in that *i* gave thanks ... Lk 2:38
they were *i* with loud voices, ... Lk 23:23
continuing *i* in prayer ... Rom 12:12
be *i* in season, out of season ... 2Ti 4:2

## INSTANTLY
to Jesus, they besought him *i* ... Lk 7:4
*i* serving God day and night, hope ... Acts 26:7

## INSTEAD
and closed up the flesh *i* thereof ... Gen 2:21
me another seed *i* of Abel ... Gen 4:25
let thy servant abide *i* of the ... Gen 44:33
he shall be to thee *i* of a mouth ... Ex 4:16
and thou shalt be to him *i* of God ... Ex 4:16
to gather stubble *i* of straw ... Ex 5:12
*i* of all the firstborn that ... Num 3:12
*i* of all the firstborn among the ... Num 3:41
the cattle of the Levites *i* of ... Num 3:41
Take the Levites *i* of all the ... Num 3:45
of the Levites *i* of their cattle ... Num 3:45
with another *i* of thy husband ... Num 5:19
aside to another *i* of thy husband ... Num 5:20
aside to another *i* of her husband ... Num 5:29
*i* of such as open every womb, ... Num 8:16
even *i* of the firstborn of all ... Num 8:16
and thou mayest be to us *i* of eyes ... Num 10:31
take her, I pray thee, *i* of her ... Judg 15:2
captain of the host *i* of Joab ... 2Sa 17:25
servant king *i* of David my father ... 1Kin 3:7
made him king *i* of his father ... 2Kin 14:21
*i* of the children of Israel ... 2Kin 17:24
as king *i* of David his father ... 1Chr 29:23
*I* of which king Rehoboam made ... 2Chr 12:10
the king be queen *i* of Vashti ... Est 2:4
and made her queen *i* of Vashti ... Est 2:17
Let thistles grow *i* of wheat ... Job 31:40
and cockle *i* of barley ... Job 31:40
*I* of thy fathers shall be thy ... Ps 45:16
that *i* of sweet smell there shall ... Is 3:24
and *i* of a girdle a rent ... Is 3:24
*i* of well set hair baldness ... Is 3:24
*i* of a stomacher a girding of ... Is 3:24
and burning *i* of beauty ... Is 3:24
*I* of the the thorn shall come up ... Is 55:13
*i* of the brier shall come up the ... Is 55:13
which reigned *i* of Josiah his ... Jer 22:11
the son of Josiah reigned *i* of ... Jer 37:1
taketh strangers *i* of her husband ... Eze 16:32

## INSTRUCT
his voice, that he might *i* thee ... Deut 4:36
also thy good spirit to *i* them ... Neh 9:20
with the Almighty *i* him ... Job 40:2
my reins also *i* me in the night ... Ps 16:7
I will *i* thee and teach thee in ... Ps 32:8
my mother's house, who would *i* me ... Song 8:2
For his God doth *i* him to ... Is 28:26
among the people shall *i* many ... Dan 11:33
of the Lord, that he may *i* him ... 1Cor 2:16

## INSTRUCTED
he *i* him, he kept him as the ... Deut 32:10
wherein Jehoiada the priest *i* him ... 2Kin 12:2
he *i* about the song, because he ... 1Chr 15:22
were *i* in the songs of the LORD ... 1Chr 25:7
*i* for the building of the house ... 2Chr 3:3
Behold, thou hast *i* many, and thou ... Job 4:3
be *i*, ye judges of the earth ... Ps 2:10
mine ear to them that *i* me ... Prov 5:13
and when the wise is *i*, he ... Prov 21:11
*i* me that I should not walk in ... Is 8:11
took he counsel, and who *i* him ... Is 40:14
Be thou *i*, O Jerusalem, lest my ... Jer 6:8
and after that I was *i*, I smote ... Jer 31:19
*i* unto the kingdom of heaven is ... Mt 13:52
being before *i* of her mother, ... Mt 14:8
things, wherein thou hast been *i* ... Lk 1:4
This man was *i* in the way of the ... Acts 18:25
excellent, being *i* out of the law ... Rom 2:18
all things I am *i* both to be full ... Phil 4:12

## INSTRUCTER
an *i* of every artificer in brass ... Gen 4:22

## INSTRUCTERS
ye have ten thousand *i* in Christ ... 1Cor 4:15

## INSTRUCTING
In meekness *i* those that oppose ... 2Ti 2:25

## INSTRUCTION
ears of men, and sealeth their *i* ... Job 33:16
Seeing thou hatest *i*, and castest ... Ps 50:17
To know wisdom and *i* ... Prov 1:2
To receive the *i* of wisdom ... Prov 1:3
but fools despise wisdom and *i* ... Prov 1:7
hear the *i* of thy father, and ... Prov 1:8
the *i* of a father, and attend to ... Prov 4:1
Take fast hold of *i* ... Prov 4:13
And say, How have I hated *i* ... Prov 5:12
He shall die without *i* ... Prov 5:23
reproofs of *i* are the way of life ... Prov 6:23
Receive my *i*, and not silver ... Prov 8:10
Hear *i*, and be wise, and refuse it ... Prov 8:33

- Give *i* to a wise man, and he will ... Prov 9:9
- in the way of life that keepeth *i* ... Prov 10:17
- Whoso loveth *i* loveth knowledge ... Prov 12:1
- A wise son heareth his father's *i* ... Prov 13:1
- shall be to him that refuseth *i* ... Prov 13:18
- A fool despiseth his father's *i* ... Prov 15:5
- He that refuseth *i* despiseth his ... Prov 15:32
- of the LORD is the *i* of wisdom ... Prov 15:33
- but the *i* of fools is folly ... Prov 16:22
- Hear counsel, and receive *i* ... Prov 19:20
- to hear the *i* that causeth to err ... Prov 19:27
- Apply thine heart unto *i*, and ... Prov 23:12
- also wisdom, and *i*, and ... Prov 23:23
- I looked upon it, and received *i* ... Prov 24:32
- might not hear, nor receive *i* ... Jer 17:23
- have not hearkened to receive *i* ... Jer 32:33
- Will ye not receive *i* to hearken ... Jer 35:13
- be a reproach and a taunt, an *i* ... Eze 5:15
- wilt fear me, thou wilt receive *i* ... Zeph 3:7
- for *i* in righteousness ... 2Ti 3:16

### INSTRUCTOR
- An *i* of the foolish, a teacher of ... Rom 2:20

### INSTRUMENT
- if he smite him with an *i* of iron ... Num 35:16
- psaltery and an *i* of ten strings ... Ps 33:2
- Upon an *i* of ten strings, and upon ... Ps 92:3
- an *i* of ten strings will I sing ... Ps 144:9
- not threshed with a threshing *i* ... Is 28:27
- sharp threshing *i* having teeth ... Is 41:15
- bringeth forth an *i* for his work ... Is 54:16
- voice, and can play well on an *i* ... Eze 33:32

### INSTRUMENTS
- *i* of cruelty are in their ... Gen 49:5
- the pattern of all the *i* thereof ... Ex 25:9
- they shall keep all the *i* of the ... Num 3:8
- shall take all the *i* of ministry ... Num 4:12
- all the *i* of their service, and ... Num 4:26
- and their cords, with all their *i* ... Num 4:32
- by name ye shall reckon the *i* of ... Num 4:32
- it, and all the *i* thereof, both ... Num 7:1
- to the war, with the holy *i* ... Num 31:6
- harvest, and to make his *i* of war ... 1Sa 8:12
- and *i* of his chariots ... 1Sa 8:12
- with joy, and with *i* of musick ... 1Sa 18:6
- all manner of *i* made of fir wood ... 2Sa 6:5
- burnt sacrifice, and threshing *i* ... 2Sa 24:22
- other *i* of the oxen for wood ... 2Sa 24:22
- flesh with the *i* of the oxen ... 1Kin 19:21
- all the *i* of the sanctuary, and ... 1Chr 9:29
- expert in war, with all *i* of war ... 1Chr 12:33
- with all manner of *i* of war for ... 1Chr 12:37
- be the singers with *i* of musick ... 1Chr 15:16
- a sound, and with musical *i* of God ... 1Chr 16:42
- and the threshing *i* for wood ... 1Chr 21:23
- the LORD with the *i* which I made ... 1Chr 23:5
- for all *i* of all manner of ... 1Chr 28:14
- for all *i* of silver by weight ... 1Chr 28:14
- for all *i* of every kind of ... 1Chr 28:14
- and the fleshhooks, and all their *i* ... 2Chr 4:16
- silver, and the gold, and all the *i* ... 2Chr 5:1
- *i* of musick, and praised the LORD, ... 2Chr 5:13
- also with *i* of musick of the LORD ... 2Chr 7:6
- also the singers with *i* of musick ... 2Chr 23:13
- Levites stood with the *i* of David ... 2Chr 29:26
- with the *i* ordained by David king ... 2Chr 29:27
- singing with loud *i* unto the LORD ... 2Chr 30:21
- that could skill of *i* of musick ... 2Chr 34:12
- with the musical *i* of David the ... Neh 12:36
- prepared for him the *i* of death ... Ps 7:13
- the players on *i* followed after ... Ps 68:25
- the players on *i* shall be there ... Ps 87:7
- praise him with stringed *i* ... Ps 150:4
- of the sons of men, as musical *i* ... Eccl 2:8
- The *i* also of the churl are evil ... Is 32:7
- sing my songs to the stringed *i* ... Is 38:20
- whereupon also they laid the *i* ... Eze 40:42
- neither were *i* of musick brought ... Dan 6:18
- Gilead with threshing *i* of iron ... Amos 1:3
- invent to themselves *i* of musick ... Amos 6:5
- the chief singer on my stringed *i* ... Hab 3:19
- yet the *i* of a foolish shepherd ... Zec 11:15
- yield ye your members as *i* of ... Rom 6:13
- the dead, and your members as *i* of ... Rom 6:13

### INSURRECTION
- time hath made *i* against kings ... Ezr 4:19
- from the *i* of the workers of ... Ps 64:2
- them that had made *i* with him ... Mk 15:7
- who had committed murder in the *i* ... Mk 15:7
- the Jews made *i* with one accord ... Acts 18:12

### INTEGRITY
- in the *i* of my heart and innocency ... Gen 20:5
- didst this in the *i* of thy heart ... Gen 20:6
- in *i* of heart, and in uprightness, ... 1Kin 9:4
- and still he holdeth fast his *i* ... Job 2:3
- Dost thou still retain thine *i* ... Job 2:9
- I will not remove mine *i* from me ... Job 27:5
- balance, that God may know mine *i* ... Job 31:6
- according to mine *i* that is in me ... Ps 7:8
- Let *i* and uprightness preserve me ... Ps 25:21
- for I have walked in mine *i* ... Ps 26:1
- as for me, I will walk in mine *i* ... Ps 26:11
- me, thou upholdest me in mine *i* ... Ps 41:12
- according to the *i* of his heart ... Ps 78:72
- The *i* of the upright shall guide ... Prov 11:3
- is the poor that walketh in his *i* ... Prov 19:1
- The just man walketh in his *i* ... Prov 20:7

### INTELLIGENCE
- have *i* with them that forsake the ... Dan 11:30

### INTEND
- did not *i* to go up against them ... Josh 22:33
- ye *i* to add more to our sins and ... 2Chr 28:13
- *i* to bring this man's blood upon ... Acts 5:28
- ye *i* to do as touching these men ... Acts 5:35

### INTENDED
- For they *i* evil against thee ... Ps 21:11

### INTENDEST
- *i* thou to kill me, as thou ... Ex 2:14

### INTENDING
- *i* to build a tower, sitteth not ... Lk 14:28
- *i* after Easter to bring him forth ... Acts 12:4
- Assos, there *i* to take in Paul ... Acts 20:13

### INTENT
- to the *i* that the LORD might ... 2Sa 17:14
- to the *i* that he might destroy ... 2Kin 10:19
- to the *i* that he might let none ... 2Chr 16:1
- for to the *i* that I might shew ... Eze 40:4
- to the *i* that the living may know ... Dan 4:17
- there, to the *i* ye may believe ... Jn 11:15
- for what *i* he spake this unto him ... Jn 13:28
- and came hither for that *i* ... Acts 9:21
- for what *i* ye have sent for me ... Acts 10:29
- to the *i* we should not lust after ... 1Cor 10:6
- To the *i* that now unto the ... Eph 3:10

### INTENTS
- have performed the *i* of his heart ... Jer 30:24
- of the thoughts and *i* of the heart ... Heb 4:12

### INTERCESSION
- made *i* for the transgressors ... Is 53:12
- for them, neither make *i* to me ... Jer 7:16
- let them now make *i* to the LORD ... Jer 27:18
- Gemariah had made *i* to the king ... Jer 36:25
- *i* for us with groanings which ... Rom 8:26
- because he maketh *i* for the ... Rom 8:27
- of God, who also maketh *i* for us ... Rom 8:34
- how he maketh *i* to God against ... Rom 11:2
- he ever liveth to make *i* for them ... Heb 7:25

### INTERCESSIONS
- of all, supplications, prayers, *i* ... 1Ti 2:1

### INTERCESSOR
- and wondered that there was no *i* ... Is 59:16

### INTERMEDDLE
- stranger doth not *i* with his joy ... Prov 14:10

### INTERMEDDLETH
- seeketh and *i* with all wisdom ... Prov 18:1

### INTERMISSION
- and ceaseth not, without any *i* ... Lam 3:49

### INTERPRET
- that could *i* them unto Pharaoh ... Gen 41:8
- according to his dream he did *i* ... Gen 41:12
- and there is none that can *i* it ... Gen 41:15
- canst understand a dream to *i* it ... Gen 41:15
- do all *i*? ... 1Cor 12:30
- with tongues, except he *i* ... 1Cor 14:5
- unknown tongue pray that he may *i*. 1Cor 14:13
- and let one *i* ... 1Cor 14:27

### INTERPRETATION
- according to the *i* of his dream ... Gen 40:5
- unto him, This is the *i* of it ... Gen 40:12
- baker saw that the *i* was good ... Gen 40:16
- and said, This is the *i* thereof ... Gen 40:18
- according to the *i* of his dream ... Gen 41:11
- the *i* thereof, that he worshipped ... Judg 7:15
- To understand a proverb, and the *i* ... Prov 1:6
- and who knoweth the *i* of a thing ... Eccl 8:1
- the dream, and we will shew the *i* ... Dan 2:4
- me the dream, with the *i* thereof ... Dan 2:5
- the *i* thereof, ye shall receive ... Dan 2:6
- me the dream, and the *i* thereof ... Dan 2:6
- and we will shew the *i* of it ... Dan 2:7
- that ye can shew me the *i* thereof ... Dan 2:9
- that he would shew the king the *i* ... Dan 2:16
- I will shew unto the king the *i* ... Dan 2:24
- make known unto the king the *i* ... Dan 2:25
- I have seen, and the *i* thereof ... Dan 2:26
- make known the *i* to the king ... Dan 2:30
- we will tell the *i* thereof before ... Dan 2:36
- is certain, and the *i* thereof sure ... Dan 2:45
- known unto me the *i* of the dream ... Dan 4:6
- make known unto me the *i* thereof ... Dan 4:7
- I have seen, and the *i* thereof ... Dan 4:9
- declare the *i* thereof, forasmuch ... Dan 4:18
- able to make known unto me the *i* ... Dan 4:18
- or the *i* thereof, trouble thee ... Dan 4:19
- the *i* thereof to thine enemies ... Dan 4:19
- This is the *i*, O king, and this is ... Dan 4:24
- writing, and shew me the *i* thereof ... Dan 5:7
- known to the king the *i* thereof ... Dan 5:8
- be called, and he will shew the *i* ... Dan 5:12
- make known unto me the *i* thereof ... Dan 5:15
- could not shew the *i* of the thing ... Dan 5:15
- and make known to me the *i* thereof ... Dan 5:16
- king, and make known to him the *i* ... Dan 5:17
- This is the *i* of the thing ... Dan 5:26
- made me know the *i* of the things ... Dan 7:16
- be called Cephas, which is by *i* ... Jn 1:42
- pool of Siloam, (which is by *i* ... Jn 9:7
- which by *i* is called Dorcas ... Acts 9:36
- is his name by *i*) withstood them ... Acts 13:8
- to another the *i* of tongues ... 1Cor 12:10
- hath a revelation, hath an *i* ... 1Cor 14:26
- first being by *i* King of ... Heb 7:2
- the scripture is of any private *i* ... 2Pet 1:20

### INTERPRETATIONS
- unto them, Do not *i* belong to God ... Gen 40:8
- of thee, that thou canst make *i* ... Dan 5:16

### INTERPRETED
- as Joseph had *i* to them ... Gen 40:22
- him, and he *i* to us our dreams ... Gen 41:12
- And it came to pass, as he *i* to us ... Gen 41:13
- tongue, and *i* in the Syrian tongue ... Ezr 4:7
- name Emmanuel, which being *i* is ... Mt 1:23
- which is, being *i*, Damsel, I say ... Mk 5:41
- place Golgotha, which is, being *i* ... Mk 15:22
- which is, being *i*, My God, my God ... Mk 15:34
- Rabbi, (which is to say, being *i* ... Jn 1:38
- the Messias, which is, being *i* ... Jn 1:41
- Barnabas, (which is, being *i* ... Acts 4:36

### INTERPRETER
- a dream, and there is no *i* of it ... Gen 40:8
- for he spake unto them by an *i* ... Gen 42:23
- be a messenger with him, an *i* ... Job 33:23
- But if there be no *i*, let him ... 1Cor 14:28

### INTERPRETING
- *i* of dreams, and shewing of hard ... Dan 5:12

**INTO** See PREFACE.

### INTREAT
- *i* for me to Ephron the son of ... Gen 23:8
- *I* the LORD, that he may take away ... Ex 8:8
- when shall I *i* for thee, and for ... Ex 8:9
- very far away: *i* for me ... Ex 8:28
- I will *i* the LORD that the swarms ... Ex 8:29
- *I* the LORD (for it is enough) ... Ex 9:28
- *i* the LORD your God, that he may ... Ex 10:17
- *I* me not to leave thee, or to ... Ruth 1:16
- the LORD, who shall *i* for him ... 1Sa 2:25
- *I* now the face of the LORD thy ... 1Kin 13:6
- the people shall *i* thy favour ... Ps 45:12
- Many will *i* the favour of the ... Prov 19:6
- Being defamed, we *i* ... 1Cor 4:13
- I *i* thee also, true yokefellow, ... Phil 4:3
- an elder, but *i* him as a father ... 1Ti 5:1

### INTREATED
- Isaac *i* the LORD for his wife, ... Gen 25:21
- and the LORD was *i* of him, and ... Gen 25:21
- out from Pharaoh, and *i* the LORD ... Ex 8:30
- out from Pharaoh, and *i* the LORD ... Ex 10:18
- Then Manoah *i* the LORD, and said, ... Judg 13:8
- after that God was *i* for the land ... 2Sa 21:14
- So the LORD was *i* for the land ... 2Sa 24:25
- the battle, and he was *i* of them ... 1Chr 5:20
- and he was *i* of him, and heard his ... 2Chr 33:13
- also, and how God was *i* of him ... 2Chr 33:19
- and he was *i* of us ... Ezr 8:23
- I *i* him with my mouth ... Job 19:16
- though I *i* for the children's ... Job 19:17
- I *i* thy favour with my whole ... Ps 119:58
- LORD, and he shall be *i* of them ... Is 19:22
- came his father out, and *i* him ... Lk 15:28
- *i* that the word should not be ... Heb 12:19
- gentle, and easy to be *i*, full of ... Jas 3:17

### INTREATIES
- The poor useth *i* ... Prov 18:23

### INTREATY
- Praying us with much *i* that we ... 2Cor 8:4

### INTRUDING
- *i* into those things which he hath ... Col 2:18

### INVADE
- thou wouldest not let Israel *i* ... 2Chr 20:10
- he will *i* them with his troops ... Hab 3:16

### INVADED
- the Philistines have *i* the land ... 1Sa 23:27
- *i* the Geshurites, and the Gezrites ... 1Sa 27:8
- the Amalekites had *i* the south ... 1Sa 30:1
- the bands of the Moabites *i* the ... 2Kin 13:20
- The Philistines also had *i* the ... 2Chr 28:18

### INVASION
- We made an *i* upon the south of ... 1Sa 30:14

### INVENT
- *i* to themselves instruments of ... Amos 6:5

### INVENTED
- *i* by cunning men, to be on the ... 2Chr 26:15

### INVENTIONS
- thou tookest vengeance of their *i* ... Ps 99:8
- him to anger with their *i* ... Ps 106:29
- went a whoring with their own *i* ... Ps 106:39
- and find out knowledge of witty *i* ... Prov 8:12
- but they have sought out many *i* ... Eccl 7:29

### INVENTORS
- *i* of evil things, disobedient to ... Rom 1:30

### INVISIBLE
- For the *i* things of him from the ... Rom 1:20
- Who is the image of the *i* God ... Col 1:15
- that are in earth, visible and *i* ... Col 1:16
- the King eternal, immortal, *i* ... 1Ti 1:17
- endured, as seeing him who is *i* ... Heb 11:27

### INVITED
- since I said, I have *i* the people ... 1Sa 9:24
- Absalom *i* all the king's sons ... 2Sa 13:23
- to morrow am I *i* unto her also ... Est 5:12

**INWARD**
is in the side of the ephod *i* Ex 28:26
was on the side of the ephod *i* Ex 39:19
it is fret *i*, whether it be bare Lev 13:55
built round about from Millo and *i* 2Sa 5:9
and all their hinder parts were *i* 1Kin 7:25
their feet, and their faces were *i* 2Chr 3:13
and all their hinder parts were *i* 2Chr 4:4
All my *i* friends abhorred me Job 19:19
hath put wisdom in the *i* parts Job 38:36
their *i* part is very wickedness Ps 5:9
Their *i* thought is, that their Ps 49:11
desirest truth in the *i* parts Ps 51:6
both the *i* thought of every one Ps 64:6
searching all the *i* parts of the Prov 20:27
so do stripes the *i* parts of the Prov 20:30
mine *i* parts for Kir-haresh Is 16:11
will put my law in their *i* parts Jer 31:33
and the porch of the gate was *i* Eze 40:9
and windows were round about *i* Eze 40:16
Then went he *i*, and measured the Eze 41:3
a walk of ten cubits breadth *i* Eze 42:4
but your *i* part is full of Lk 11:39
in the law of God after the *i* man Rom 7:22
yet the *i* man is renewed day by 2Cor 4:16
his *i* affection is more abundant 2Cor 7:15

**INWARDLY**
their mouth, but they curse *i* Ps 62:4
but *i* they are ravening wolves Mt 7:15
But he is a Jew, which is one *i* Rom 2:29

**INWARDS**
all the fat that covereth the *i* Ex 29:13
in pieces, and wash the *i* of him Ex 29:17
and the fat that covereth the *i* Ex 29:22
But his *i* and his legs shall he Lev 1:9
But he shall wash the *i* and the Lev 1:13
the fat that covereth the *i* Lev 3:3
and all the fat that is upon the *i* Lev 3:3
and the fat that covereth the *i* Lev 3:9
and all the fat that is upon the *i* Lev 3:9
the fat that covereth the *i* Lev 3:14
and all the fat that is upon the *i* Lev 3:14
the fat that covereth the *i* Lev 4:8
and all the fat that is upon the *i* Lev 4:8
head, and with his legs, and his *i* Lev 4:11
and the fat that covereth the *i* Lev 7:3
all the fat that was upon the *i* Lev 8:16
And he washed the *i* and the legs in Lev 8:21
all the fat that was upon the *i* Lev 8:25
And he did wash the *i* and the legs, Lev 9:14
and that which covereth the *i* Lev 9:19

**IOB** See Job.

**IPHEDEIAH** (*if-e-di'-ah*) *A son of Shashak.*
And *I*, and Penuel, the sons of 1Chr 8:25

**IPHTAH** See Jiphtah.

**IPHTAH EL** See Jiphthah-el.

**IR** (*ur*) See Ir-nahash, Ir-shemesh. *Father of Machir.*
and Huppim, the children of *I* 1Chr 7:12

**IRA** (*i'-rah*)
*1. An officer of David.*
*I* also the Jairite was a chief 2Sa 20:26
*2. A mighty man of David.*
*I* the son of Ikkesh the Tekoite, 2Sa 23:26
*I* an Ithrite, Gareb an Ithrite, 2Sa 23:38
*I* the son of Ikkesh the Tekoite, 1Chr 11:28
*I* the Ithrite, Gareb the Ithrite, 1Chr 11:40
*I* the son of Ikkesh the Tekoite 1Chr 27:9

**IRAD** (*i'-rad*) *Son of Enoch.*
And unto Enoch was born *I* Gen 4:18
and *I* begat Mehujael Gen 4:18

**IRAM** (*i'-ram*) *An Edomite leader.*
Duke Magdiel, duke *I* Gen 36:43
Duke Magdiel, duke *I* 1Chr 1:54

**IRI** (*i'-ri*) *A son of Bela.*
and Uzziel, and Jerimoth, and *I* 1Chr 7:7

**IRIJAH** (*i-ri'-jah*) *A captain of the guard.*
ward was there, whose name was *I* Jer 37:13
so *I* took Jeremiah, and brought Jer 37:14

**IR-NAHASH** (*ur-na'-hash*) *A descendant of Chelub.*
and Tehinnah the father of *I* 1Chr 4:12

**IRON** (*i'-ron*) *A city in Naphtali.*
And *I*, and Migdal-el, Horem, and Josh 19:38
*A metal.*
of every artificer in brass and *i* Gen 4:22
and I will make your heaven as *i* Lev 26:19
and the silver, the brass, the *i* Num 31:22
smite him with an instrument of *i* Num 35:16
his bedstead was a bedstead of *i* Deut 3:11
you forth out of the *i* furnace Deut 4:20
a land whose stones are *i* Deut 8:9
not lift up any *i* tool upon them Deut 27:5
that is under thee shall be *i* Deut 28:23
put a yoke of *i* upon thy neck Deut 28:48
Thy shoes shall be *i* and brass Deut 33:25
and gold, and vessels of brass and *i* Josh 6:19
and the vessels of brass and of *i* Josh 6:24
which no man hath lift up any *i* Josh 8:31
of the valley have chariots of *i* Josh 17:16
though they have *i* chariots Josh 17:18
gold, and with brass, and with *i* Josh 22:8
because they had chariots of *i* Judg 1:19
he had nine hundred chariots of *i* Judg 4:3
even nine hundred chariots of *i* Judg 4:13
weighed six hundred shekels of *i* 1Sa 17:7
of iron, and under axes of *i* 2Sa 12:31
touch them must be fenced with *i* 2Sa 23:7
any tool of *i* heard in the house 1Kin 6:7
the midst of the furnace of *i* 1Kin 8:51
of Chenaanah made him horns of *i* 1Kin 22:11
and the *i* did swim 2Kin 6:6
with saws, and with harrows of *i* 1Chr 20:3
David prepared *i* in abundance for 1Chr 22:3
and of brass and *i* without weight 1Chr 22:14
silver, and the brass, and the *i* 1Chr 22:16
the *i* for things of iron, and wood 1Chr 29:2
brass, the iron for things of *i* 1Chr 29:2
one hundred thousand talents of *i* 1Chr 29:7
in silver, and in brass, and in *i* 2Chr 2:7
and in silver, in brass, in *i* 2Chr 2:14
Chenaanah had made him horns of *i* 2Chr 18:10
Lord, and also such as wrought *i* 2Chr 24:12
they were graven with an *i* pen Job 19:24
He shall flee from the *i* weapon Job 20:24
*I* is taken out of the earth, and Job 28:2
his bones are like bars of *i* Job 40:18
He esteemeth *i* as straw, and brass Job 41:27
shalt break them with a rod of *i* Ps 2:9
he was laid in *i* Ps 105:18
being bound in affliction and *i* Ps 107:10
and cut the bars of *i* in sunder Ps 107:16
and their nobles with fetters of *i* Ps 149:8
*I* sharpeneth iron Prov 27:17
Iron sharpeneth *i* Prov 27:17
If the *i* be blunt, and he do not Eccl 10:10
the thickets of the forest with *i* Is 10:34
and cut in sunder the bars of *i* Is 45:2
and thy neck is an *i* sinew Is 48:4
for *i* I will bring silver, and for Is 60:17
for wood brass, and for stones *i* Is 60:17
an *i* pillar, and brasen walls Jer 1:18
they are brass and *i* Jer 6:28
land of Egypt, from the *i* furnace Jer 11:4
Shall *i* break the northern iron Jer 15:12
Shall iron break the northern *i* Jer 15:12
Judah is written with a pen of *i* Jer 17:1
shalt make for them yokes of *i* Jer 28:13
I have put a yoke of *i* upon the Jer 28:14
take thou unto thee an *i* pan Eze 4:3
it for a wall of *i* between thee Eze 4:3
all they are brass, and tin, and *i* Eze 22:18
gather silver, and brass, and *i* Eze 22:20
with silver, *i*, tin, and lead, Eze 27:12
bright *i*, cassia, and calamus, Eze 27:19
legs of iron, his feet part of *i* Dan 2:33
upon his feet that were of *i* Dan 2:34
Then was the *i*, the clay, the Dan 2:35
kingdom shall be strong as *i* Dan 2:40
forasmuch as *i* breaketh in pieces Dan 2:40
as *i* that breaketh all these, Dan 2:40
of potters' clay, and part of *i* Dan 2:41
be in it of the strength of the *i* Dan 2:41
sawest the *i* mixed with miry clay Dan 2:41
toes of the feet were part of *i* Dan 2:42
whereas thou sawest *i* mixed with Dan 2:43
even as *i* is not mixed with clay Dan 2:43
and that it brake in pieces the *i* Dan 2:45
the earth, even with a band of *i* Dan 4:15
the earth, even with a band of *i* Dan 4:23
and of silver, of brass, of *i* Dan 5:4
of silver, and gold, of brass, *i* Dan 5:23
and it had great *i* teeth Dan 7:7
dreadful, whose teeth were of *i* Dan 7:19
with threshing instruments of *i* Amos 1:3
for I will make thine horn *i* Mic 4:13
they came unto the *i* gate that Acts 12:10
conscience seared with a hot *i* 1Ti 4:2
shall rule them with a rod of *i* Rev 2:27
as it were breastplates of *i* Rev 9:9
rule all nations with a rod of *i* Rev 12:5
precious wood, and of brass, and *i* Rev 18:12
shall rule them with a rod of *i* Rev 19:15

**IRONS**
thou fill his skin with barbed *i* Job 41:7

**IRPEEL** (*ur'-pe-el*) *A city in Benjamin.*
And Rekem, and *I*, and Taralah, Josh 18:27

**IR-SHEMESH** (*ur-she'-mesh*) *A city in Dan.*
was Zorah, and Eshtaol, and *I* Josh 19:41

**IRU** (*i'-ru*) *A son of Caleb.*
*I*, Elah, and Naam 1Chr 4:15

**IS** See PREFACE.

**ISAAC** (*i'-za-ak*) See Isaac's. *Son of Abraham and Sarah.*
and thou shalt call his name *I* Gen 17:19
covenant will I establish with *I* Gen 17:21
him, whom Sarah bare to him, *I* Gen 21:3
his son *I* being eight days old Gen 21:4
when his son *I* was born unto him Gen 21:5
the same day that *I* was weaned Gen 21:8
be heir with my son, even with *I* Gen 21:10
for in *I* shall thy seed be called Gen 21:12
now thy son, thine only son *I* Gen 22:2
*I* his son, and clave the wood for Gen 22:3
and laid it upon *I* his son Gen 22:6
*I* spake unto Abraham his father, Gen 22:7
bound *I* his son, and laid him on Gen 22:9
and take a wife unto my son *I* Gen 24:4
hast appointed for thy servant *I* Gen 24:14
*I* came from the way of the well Gen 24:62
*I* went out to meditate in the Gen 24:63
up her eyes, and when she saw *I* Gen 24:64
the servant told *I* all things Gen 24:66
*I* brought her into his mother Gen 24:67
*I* was comforted after his Gen 24:67
gave all that he had unto *I* Gen 25:5
and sent them away from *I* his son Gen 25:6
And his sons *I* and Ishmael buried Gen 25:9
that God blessed his son *I* Gen 25:11
*I* dwelt by the well Lahai-roi Gen 25:11
And these are the generations of *I* Gen 25:19
Abraham begat *I* Gen 25:19
*I* was forty years old when he Gen 25:20
*I* intreated the Lord for his wife Gen 25:21
*I* was threescore years old when Gen 25:26
*I* loved Esau, because he did eat Gen 25:28
*I* went unto Abimelech king of the Gen 26:1
And *I* dwelt in Gerar Gen 26:6
*I* was sporting with Rebekah his Gen 26:8
And Abimelech called *I*, and said, Gen 26:9
*I* said unto him, Because I said, Gen 26:9
Then *I* sowed in that land, and Gen 26:12
And Abimelech said unto *I*, Go from Gen 26:16
*I* departed thence, and pitched his Gen 26:17
*I* digged again the wells of water Gen 26:18
*I* said unto them, Wherefore come Gen 26:27
*I* sent them away, and they Gen 26:31
Which were a grief of mind unto *I* Gen 26:35
came to pass, that when *I* was old Gen 27:1
Rebekah heard when *I* spake to Gen 27:5
*I* said unto his son, How is it Gen 27:20
*I* said unto Jacob, Come near, I Gen 27:21
Jacob went near unto *I* his father Gen 27:22
his father *I* said unto him, Come Gen 27:26
as soon as *I* had made an end of Gen 27:30
from the presence of *I* his father Gen 27:30
*I* his father said unto him, Who Gen 27:32
*I* trembled very exceedingly, and Gen 27:33
*I* answered and said unto Esau, Gen 27:37
*I* his father answered and said Gen 27:39
And Rebekah said to *I*, I am weary Gen 27:46
*I* called Jacob, and blessed him, Gen 28:1
And *I* sent away Jacob Gen 28:5
Esau saw that *I* had blessed Jacob Gen 28:6
Canaan pleased not *I* his father Gen 28:8
thy father, and the God of *I* Gen 28:13
for to go to *I* his father in the Gen 31:18
God of Abraham, and the fear of *I* Gen 31:42
sware by the fear of his father *I* Gen 31:53
Abraham, and God of my father *I* Gen 32:9
land which I gave Abraham and *I* Gen 35:12
Jacob came unto *I* his father unto Gen 35:27
where Abraham and *I* sojourned Gen 35:27
the days of *I* were an hundred and Gen 35:28
*I* gave up the ghost, and died, and Gen 35:29
unto the God of his father *I* Gen 46:1
*I* did walk, the God which fed me Gen 48:15
name of my fathers Abraham and *I* Gen 48:16
there they buried *I* and Rebekah Gen 49:31
which he sware to Abraham, to *I* Gen 50:24
his covenant with Abraham, with *I* Ex 2:24
the God of Abraham, the God of *I* Ex 3:6
the God of Abraham, the God of *I* Ex 3:15
fathers, the God of Abraham, the God of *I* Ex 3:16
the God of Abraham, the God of *I* Ex 4:5
I appeared unto Abraham, unto *I* Ex 6:3
swear to give it to Abraham, to *I* Ex 6:8
Remember Abraham, *I*, and Israel, Ex 32:13
which I sware unto Abraham, to *I* Ex 33:1
Jacob, and also my covenant with *I* Lev 26:42
I sware unto Abraham, unto *I* Num 32:11
unto your fathers, Abraham, *I* Deut 1:8
thy fathers, to Abraham, to *I* Deut 6:10
unto thy fathers, Abraham, *I* Deut 9:5
Remember thy servants, Abraham, *I* Deut 9:27
thy fathers, to Abraham, to *I* Deut 29:13
thy fathers, to Abraham, to *I* Deut 30:20
I sware unto Abraham, unto *I* Deut 34:4
his seed, and gave him *I* Josh 24:3
And I gave unto *I* Jacob and Esau Josh 24:4
and said, Lord God of Abraham, *I* 1Kin 18:36
of his covenant with Abraham, *I* 2Kin 13:23
*I*, and Ishmael 1Chr 1:28
And Abraham begat *I* 1Chr 1:34
The sons of *I* 1Chr 1:34
Abraham, and of his oath unto *I* 1Chr 16:16
O Lord God of Abraham, *I*, and of 1Chr 29:18
unto the Lord God of Abraham, *I* 2Chr 30:6
with Abraham, and his oath unto *I* Ps 105:9
over the seed of Abraham, *I* Jer 33:26
places of *I* shall be desolate Amos 7:9
thy word against the house of *I* Amos 7:16
Abraham begat *I* Mt 1:2
and *I* begat Jacob Mt 1:2
shall sit down with Abraham, and *I* Mt 8:11
God of Abraham, and the God of *I* Mt 22:32
God of Abraham, and the God of *I* Mk 12:26
of Jacob, which was the son of *I* Lk 3:34
when ye shall see Abraham, and *I* Lk 13:28
God of Abraham, and the God of *I* Lk 20:37
The God of Abraham, and of *I* Acts 3:13
and so Abraham begat *I* Acts 7:8
and *I* begat Jacob Acts 7:8
God of Abraham, and the God of *I* Acts 7:32
In *I* shall thy seed be called Rom 9:7
by one, even by our father *I* Rom 9:10
as *I* was, are the children of Gal 4:28
dwelling in tabernacles with *I* Heb 11:9
when he was tried, offered up *I* Heb 11:17
That in *I* shall thy seed be Heb 11:18
By faith *I* blessed Jacob and Esau Heb 11:20

when he had offered *I* his son ............ Jas 2:21

**ISAAC'S** (*i'-za-aks*)
*I* servants digged in the valley, ............ Gen 26:19
Gerar did strive with *I* herdmen ............ Gen 26:20
there *I* servants digged a well ............ Gen 26:25
that *I* servants came, and told him ..... Gen 26:32

**ISAIAH** (*i-za'-yah*) See ESAIAS. *A prophet.*
to *I* the prophet the son of Amoz ......... 2Kin 19:2
of king Hezekiah came to *I* ............ 2Kin 19:5
*I* said unto them, Thus shall ye ............ 2Kin 19:6
Then *I* the son of Amoz sent to ............ 2Kin 19:20
the prophet *I* the son of Amoz ............ 2Kin 20:1
afore *I* was gone out into the ............ 2Kin 20:4
*I* said, Take a lump of figs ............ 2Kin 20:7
And Hezekiah said unto *I*, What ............ 2Kin 20:8
*I* said, This sign shalt thou have ............ 2Kin 20:9
*I* the prophet cried unto the LORD ..... 2Kin 20:11
Then came *I* the prophet unto king... 2Kin 20:14
*I* said unto Hezekiah, Hear the ............ 2Kin 20:16
Then said Hezekiah unto *I* ............ 2Kin 20:19
did *I* the prophet, the son of ............ 2Chr 26:22
the prophet *I* the son of Amoz, ............ 2Chr 32:20
in the vision of *I* the prophet ............ 2Chr 32:32
The vision of *I* the son of Amoz, ............ Is 1:1
The word that *I* the son of Amoz ............ Is 2:1
Then said the LORD unto *I* ............ Is 7:3
which *I* the son of Amoz did see ............ Is 13:1
the LORD by *I* the son of Amoz ............ Is 20:2
as my servant *I* hath walked naked ............ Is 20:3
unto *I* the prophet the son of ............ Is 37:2
of king Hezekiah came to *I* ............ Is 37:5
*I* said unto them, Thus shall ye ............ Is 37:6
Then *I* the son of Amoz sent unto ............ Is 37:21
*I* the prophet the son of Amoz ............ Is 38:1
came the word of the LORD to *I* ............ Is 38:4
For *I* had said, Let them take a ............ Is 38:21
Then came *I* the prophet unto king ............ Is 39:3
Then said *I* to Hezekiah, Hear the ............ Is 39:5
Then said Hezekiah to *I*, Good is ............ Is 39:8

**ISCAH** (*is'-cah*) See SARAH. *A daughter of Haran.*
of Milcah, and the father of *I* ............ Gen 11:29

**ISCARIOT** (*is-car'-e-ot*) See JUDAS. *Disciple who betrayed Jesus.*
Simon the Canaanite, and Judas *I* ............ Mt 10:4
one of the twelve, called Judas *I* ............ Mt 26:14
And Judas *I*, which also betrayed ............ Mk 3:19
And Judas *I*, one of the twelve, ............ Mk 14:10
the brother of James, and Judas *I* ............ Lk 6:16
Satan into Judas surnamed *I* ............ Lk 22:3
spake of Judas *I* the son of Simon ............ Jn 6:71
one of his disciples, Judas *I* ............ Jn 12:4
now put into the heart of Judas *I* ............ Jn 13:2
the sop, he gave it to Judas *I* ............ Jn 13:26
Judas saith unto him, not *I* ............ Jn 14:22

**ISHBAH** (*ish'-bah*) *Father of Eshtemoa.*
and *I* the father of Eshtemoa ............ 1Chr 4:17

**ISHBAK** (*ish'-bak*) *A son of Abraham.*
and Medan, and Midian, and *I* ............ Gen 25:2
and Medan, and Midian, and *I* ............ 1Chr 1:32

**ISHBI-BENOB** (*ish'-bi-be'-nob*) *A Philistine giant.*
And *I*, which was of the sons of ............ 2Sa 21:16

**ISH-BOSHETH** (*ish-bo'-sheth*) See ESH-BAAL. *Son of Saul.*
took *I* the son of Saul, and ............ 2Sa 2:8
*I* Saul's son was forty years old ............ 2Sa 2:10
the servants of *I* the son of Saul ............ 2Sa 2:12
pertained to *I* the son of Saul ............ 2Sa 2:15
*I* said to Abner, Wherefore hast ............ 2Sa 3:7
very wroth for the words of *I* ............ 2Sa 3:8
sent messengers to *I* Saul's son ............ 2Sa 3:14
*I* sent, and took her from her ............ 2Sa 3:15
heat of the day to the house of *I* ............ 2Sa 4:5
head of *I* unto David to Hebron ............ 2Sa 4:8
Behold the head of *I* the son of ............ 2Sa 4:8
But they took the head of *I* ............ 2Sa 4:12

**ISHI** (*i'-shi*)
*1. A descendant of Pharez.*
*I* ............ 1Chr 2:31
And the sons of *I* ............ 1Chr 2:31
*2. A descendant of Judah.*
And the sons of *I* were, Zoheth, and... 1Chr 4:20
*3. A Simeonite.*
and Uzziel, the sons of *I* ............ 1Chr 4:42
*4. A chief of Manasseh.*
their fathers, even Epher, and *I* ............ 1Chr 5:24
*5. A symbolic name for Israel.*
LORD, that thou shalt call me *I* ............ Hos 2:16

**ISHIAH** (*i-shi'-ah*) See ISHIJAH, ISSHIAH. *A son of Izrahiah.*
Michael, and Obadiah, and Joel, *I* ............ 1Chr 7:3

**ISHIJAH** (*i-shi'-jah*) See ISHIAH, JESIAH. *Married a foreigner in exile.*
Eliezer, *I*, Malchiah, Shemaiah, ............ Ezr 10:31

**ISHMA** (*ish'-mah*) *A descendant of Caleb.*
Jezreel, and *I*, and Idbash ............ 1Chr 4:3

**ISHMAEL** (*ish'-ma-el*) See ISHMAELITE, ISHMAEL'S.
*1. Son of Abraham and Hagar.*
a son, and shalt call his name *I* ............ Gen 16:11
son's name, which Hagar bare, *I* ............ Gen 16:15
old, when Hagar bare *I* to Abram ............ Gen 16:16
O that *I* might live before thee ............ Gen 17:18
And as for *I*, I have heard thee ............ Gen 17:20
And Abraham took *I* his son ............ Gen 17:23
*I* his son was thirteen years old, ............ Gen 17:25
Abraham circumcised, and *I* his son... Gen 17:26
*I* buried him in the cave of ............ Gen 25:9
these are the generations of *I* ............ Gen 25:12
are the names of the sons of *I* ............ Gen 25:13
the firstborn of *I*, Nebajoth ............ Gen 25:13
These are the sons of *I*, and these ............ Gen 25:16
are the years of the life of *I* ............ Gen 25:17
Then went Esau unto *I*, and took ............ Gen 28:9
the daughter of *I* Abraham's son ............ Gen 28:9
Isaac, and *I* ............ 1Chr 1:28
The firstborn of *I*, Nebaioth ............ 1Chr 1:29
These are the sons of *I* ............ 1Chr 1:31
*2. A ruler of Judah.*
and Zebadiah the son of *I*, the ............ 2Chr 19:11
*3. Son of Azel.*
are these, Azrikam, Bocheru, and *I* ..... 1Chr 8:38
are these, Azrikam, Bocheru, and *I* ..... 1Chr 9:44
*4. A captain who aided Joash.*
*I* the son of Jehohanan, and ............ 2Chr 23:1
*5. Married a foreigner in exile.*
Elioenai, Maaseiah, *I*, Nethaneel, ............ Ezr 10:22
*6. The son of Nethaniah.*
even *I* the son of Nethaniah, and ............ 2Kin 25:23
that *I* the son of Nethaniah, the ............ 2Kin 25:25
even *I* the son of Nethaniah, and ............ Jer 40:8
*I* the son of Nethaniah to slay ............ Jer 40:14
thee, and I will slay *I* the son of ............ Jer 40:15
for thou speakest falsely of *I* ............ Jer 40:16
that *I* the son of Nethaniah the ............ Jer 41:1
Then arose *I* the son of Nethaniah ............ Jer 41:2
*I* also slew all the Jews that ............ Jer 41:3
*I* the son of Nethaniah went forth ............ Jer 41:6
that *I* the son of Nethaniah slew ............ Jer 41:7
found among them that said unto *I* ............ Jer 41:8
Now the pit wherein *I* had cast ............ Jer 41:9
*I* the son of Nethaniah filled it ............ Jer 41:9
Then *I* carried away captive all ............ Jer 41:10
*I* the son of Nethaniah carried ............ Jer 41:10
heard of all the evil that *I* the ............ Jer 41:11
went to fight with *I* the son of ............ Jer 41:12
*I* saw Johanan the son of Kareah ............ Jer 41:13
So all the people that *I* had ............ Jer 41:14
But *I* the son of Nethaniah ............ Jer 41:15
from *I* the son of Nethaniah ............ Jer 41:16
because *I* the son of Nethaniah ............ Jer 41:18

**ISHMAELITE** (*ish'-ma-el-ite*) *Descendants of Ishmael 1.*
the camels also was Obil the *I* ............ 1Chr 27:30

**ISHMAELITES** (*ish'-ma-el-lites*) See ISHMEELITES.
earrings, because they were *I* ............ Judg 8:24
The tabernacles of Edom, and the *I* ............ Ps 83:6

**ISHMAEL'S** (*ish'-ma-els*) *Refers to Ishmael 1.*
And Bashemath *I* daughter, sister ............ Gen 36:3

**ISHMAIAH** (*ish-ma-i'-ah*) See ISMAIAH. *A prince of Zebulun.*
Of Zebulun, *I* the son of Obadiah ...... 1Chr 27:19

**ISHMEELITE** (*ish'-me-el-ite*) See ISHMAELITE, ISHMEELITES. *Same as Ishmaelite.*
father of Amasa was Jether the *I* ............ 1Chr 2:17

**ISHMEELITES** (*ish'-me-el-ites*) See ISHMAELITES.
a company of *I* came from Gilead ....... Gen 37:25
Come, and let us sell him to the *I* ............ Gen 37:27
sold Joseph to the *I* for twenty ............ Gen 37:28
bought him of the hands of the *I* ............ Gen 39:1

**ISHMERAI** (*ish'-me-rahee*) *A chief of Benjamin.*
*I* also, and Jezliah, and Jobab, the ....... 1Chr 8:18

**ISHOD** (*i'-shod*) *A son of Hammoleketh.*
And his sister Hammoleketh bare *I* ..... 1Chr 7:18

**ISHPAH** See ISPAH.

**ISHPAN** (*ish'-pan*) *A son of Shashak.*
And *I*, and Heber, and Eliel, ............ 1Chr 8:22

**ISH-TOB** (*ish'-tob*) *A district of Aram.*
men, and of *I* twelve thousand men ...... 2Sa 10:6
of Zoba, and of Rehob, and *I* ............ 2Sa 10:8

**ISHUAH** (*ish'-u-ah*) See ISUAH. *A son of Asher.*
Jimnah, and *I*, and Isui, and Beriah,... Gen 46:17

**ISHUAI**
Imnah, and Isuah, and *I*, and Beriah,.. 1Chr 7:30

**ISHUI** (*ish'-u-i*) See ISHUAI, JESUI. *A son of Saul.*
sons of Saul were Jonathan, and *I* ....... 1Sa 14:49

**ISLAND**
deliver the *i* of the innocent ............ Job 22:30
with the wild beasts of the *i* ............ Is 34:14
certain *i* which is called Clauda ............ Acts 27:16
we must be cast upon a certain *i* ............ Acts 27:26
knew that the *i* was called Melita ............ Acts 28:1
of the chief man of the *i* ............ Acts 28:7
also, which had diseases in the *i* ............ Acts 28:9
*i* were moved out of their places ............ Rev 6:14
every *i* fled away, and the ............ Rev 16:20

**ISLANDS**
Hamath, and from the *i* of the sea ............ Is 11:11
the wild beasts of the *i* shall ............ Is 13:22
Keep silence before me, O *i* ............ Is 41:1
and declare his praise in the *i* ............ Is 42:12
and I will make the rivers *i* ............ Is 42:15
to the *i* he will repay recompence ............ Is 59:18
beasts of the *i* shall dwell there ............ Jer 50:39

**ISLE**
of this *i* shall say in that day ............ Is 20:6
Be still, ye inhabitants of the *i* ............ Is 23:2
howl, ye inhabitants of the *i* ............ Is 23:6
gone through the *i* unto Paphos ............ Acts 13:6
which had wintered in the *i* ............ Acts 28:11
was in the *i* that is called ............ Rev 1:9

**ISLES**
By these were the *i* of the ............ Gen 10:5
land, and upon the *i* of the sea ............ Est 10:1
of the *i* shall bring presents ............ Ps 72:10
multitude of *i* be glad thereof ............ Ps 97:1
God of Israel in the *i* of the sea ............ Is 24:15
he taketh up the *i* as a very ............ Is 40:15
The *i* saw it, and feared ............ Is 41:5
the *i* shall wait for his law ............ Is 42:4
the *i*, and the inhabitants thereof ............ Is 42:10
Listen, O *i*, unto me ............ Is 49:1
the *i* shall wait upon me, and on ............ Is 51:5
Surely the *i* shall wait for me, ............ Is 60:9
to the *i* afar off, that have not ............ Is 66:19
For pass over the *i* of Chittim ............ Jer 2:10
the kings of the *i* which are ............ Jer 25:22
and declare it in the *i* afar off ............ Jer 31:10
Shall not the *i* shake at the ............ Eze 26:15
Now shall the *i* tremble in the ............ Eze 26:18
the *i* that are in the sea shall ............ Eze 26:18
merchant of the people for many *i* ....... Eze 27:3
brought out of the *i* of Chittim ............ Eze 27:6
purple from the *i* of Elishah was ............ Eze 27:7
many *i* were the merchandise of ............ Eze 27:15
All the inhabitants of the *i* ............ Eze 27:35
that dwell carelessly in the *i* ............ Eze 39:6
shall he turn his face unto the *i* ............ Dan 11:18
even all the *i* of the heathen ............ Zeph 2:11

**ISMACHIAH** (*is-ma-ki'-ah*) *A temple servant.*
and Jozabad, and Eliel, and *I* ............ 2Chr 31:13

**ISMAIAH** (*is-ma-i'-ah*) See ISHMAIAH. *A warrior in David's army.*
*I* the Gibeonite, a mighty man ............ 1Chr 12:4

**ISPAH** (*is'-pah*) *A son of Beriah.*
And Michael, and *I*, and Joha, the ....... 1Chr 8:16

**ISRAEL** (*iz'-ra-el*) See PREFACE. SEE ALSO EL-ELOHE-ISRAEL, ISRAELITE, ISRAEL'S, JACOB, JESHURUN.
*1. Name given to Jacob.*
be called no more Jacob, but *I* ............ Gen 32:28
Jacob, but *I* shall be thy name ............ Gen 35:10
and he called his name *I* ............ Gen 35:10
*2. People descended from Jacob.*
these are the twelve tribes of *I* ............ Gen 49:28
*I* is my son, even my firstborn ............ Ex 4:22
should obey his voice to let *I* go ............ Ex 5:2
the LORD, neither will I let *I* go ............ Ex 5:2
not let the children of *I* go ............ Ex 10:20
Thus did all the children of *I* ............ Ex 12:50
pursued after the children of *I* ............ Ex 14:8
the children of *I* went into the ............ Ex 14:22
Thus the LORD saved *I* that day ............ Ex 14:30
Moses brought *I* from the Red sea ............ Ex 15:22
shalt say unto the children of *I* ............ Ex 20:22
a covenant with thee and with *I* ............ Ex 34:27
the children of *I* did according ............ Num 1:54
my name upon the children of *I* ............ Num 6:27
*I* vowed a vow unto the LORD, and ..... Num 21:2
*I* joined himself unto Baal-peor ............ Num 25:3
of the LORD was kindled against *I* ....... Num 25:3
Hear, O *I*: The LORD our God ............ Deut 6:4
And his name shall be called in *I* ....... Deut 25:10
Happy art thou, O *I* ............ Deut 33:29
the LORD God of *I* in mount Ebal ............ Josh 8:30
the LORD gave unto *I* all the land ....... Josh 21:43
the children of *I* again did evil ............ Judg 4:1
If thou wilt save *I* by mine hand ............ Judg 6:36
Behold, ye are all children of *I* ............ Judg 20:7
The glory is departed from *I* ............ 1Sa 4:21
So the LORD saved *I* that day ............ 1Sa 14:23
thee, Thou shalt feed my people *I* ............ 2Sa 5:2
and thou shalt be a captain over *I* ............ 2Sa 5:2
dwell among the children of *I* ............ 1Kin 6:13
and will not forsake my people *I* ............ 1Kin 6:13
And he said, LORD God of *I* ............ 1Kin 8:23
O ye seed of *I* his servant ............ 1Chr 16:13
Jerusalem over all *I* forty years ............ 2Chr 9:30
to *I* for an everlasting covenant ............ Ps 105:10
O *I*, trust thou in the LORD ............ Ps 115:9
he that keepeth *I* shall neither ............ Ps 121:4
that shall rule my people *I* ............ Mt 2:6
the lost sheep of the house of *I* ............ Mt 10:6
the lost sheep of the house of *I* ............ Mt 15:24
many of the children of *I* shall ............ Lk 1:16
thou art the King of *I* ............ Jn 1:49
Blessed is the King of *I* that ............ Jn 12:13
promise raised unto *I* a Saviour ............ Acts 13:23
of *I* I am bound with this chain ............ Acts 28:20
Esaias also crieth concerning *I* ............ Rom 9:27
*I* hath not obtained that which he ....... Rom 11:7
And so all *I* shall be saved ............ Rom 11:26
new covenant with the house of *I* ............ Heb 8:8
*3. The ten northern tribes.*
not the army of *I* go with thee ............ 2Chr 25:7
for the LORD is not with *I* ............ 2Chr 25:7

**ISRAELITE** (*iz'-ra-el-ite*) See ISRAELITES, ISRAELITISH. *A member of Israel 3.*
the name of the I that was slain ... Num 25:14
son, whose name was Ithra an I ... 2Sa 17:25
saith of him, Behold an I indeed ... Jn 1:47
For I also am an I, of the seed ... Rom 11:1

**ISRAELITES** (*iz'-ra-el-ites*)
one of the cattle of the I dead ... Ex 9:7
all that are I born shall dwell ... Lev 23:42
all the I passed over on dry ... Josh 3:17
that all the I returned unto Ai, ... Josh 8:24
lot unto the I for an inheritance ... Josh 13:6
dwell among the I until this day ... Josh 13:13
ground of the I that day twenty ... Judg 20:21
unto all the I that came thither ... 1Sa 2:14
But all the I went down to the ... 1Sa 13:20
be with the I that were with Saul ... 1Sa 14:21
all the I were gathered together, ... 1Sa 25:1
the I pitched by a fountain which ... 1Sa 29:1
and all the I were troubled ... 2Sa 4:1
the I rose up and smote the ... 2Kin 3:24
of the I that are consumed ... 2Kin 7:13
in their cities were, the I ... 1Chr 9:2
Who are I ... Rom 9:4
Are they I ... 2Cor 11:22

**ISRAELITISH**
And the son of an I woman, whose ... Lev 24:10
and this son of the I woman ... Lev 24:10
the I woman's son blasphemed the ... Lev 24:11

**ISRAEL'S** (*iz'-ra-els*)
*1. Refers to Israel 1.*
his right hand toward I left hand ... Gen 48:13
his left hand toward I right hand ... Gen 48:13
of Reuben, I eldest son, by their ... Num 1:20
*2. Refers to Israel 2.*
and to the Egyptians for I sake ... Ex 18:8
And of the children of I half ... Num 31:30
And of the children of I half ... Num 31:42
Even of the children of I half ... Num 31:47
blood unto thy people of I charge ... Deut 21:8
his kingdom for his people I sake ... 2Sa 5:12
*3. Refers to Israel 3.*
the king of I servants answered ... 2Kin 3:11

**ISSACHAR** (*is'-sa-kar*)
*1. A son of Jacob.*
and she called his name I ... Gen 30:18
Simeon, and Levi, and Judah, and I ... Gen 35:23
And the sons of I ... Gen 46:13
I is a strong ass couching down ... Gen 49:14
I, Zebulun, and Benjamin, ... Ex 1:3
Reuben, Simeon, Levi, and Judah, I ... 1Chr 2:1
Now the sons of I were, Tola, and ... 1Chr 7:1
*2. Descendants of Issachar 1.*
Of I ... Num 1:8
Of the children of I, by their ... Num 1:28
of them, even of the tribe of I ... Num 1:29
unto him shall be the tribe of I ... Num 2:5
be captain of the children of I ... Num 2:5
the son of Zuar, prince of I ... Num 7:18
I was Nethaneel the son of Zuar ... Num 10:15
Of the tribe of I, Igal the son ... Num 13:7
Of the sons of I after their ... Num 26:23
These are the families of I ... Num 26:25
of the tribe of the children of I ... Num 34:26
Simeon, and Levi, and Judah, and I ... Deut 27:12
and, I, in thy tents ... Deut 33:18
on the north, and in I on the east ... Josh 17:10
And Manasseh had in I and in Asher ... Josh 17:11
And the fourth lot came out to I ... Josh 19:17
for the children of I according ... Josh 19:17
of I according to their families ... Josh 19:23
of the families of the tribe of I ... Josh 21:6
And out of the tribe of I, Kishon ... Josh 21:28
the princes of I were with ... Judg 5:15
even I, and also Barak ... Judg 5:15
Puah, the son of Dodo, a man of I ... Judg 10:1
the son of Paruah, in I ... 1Kin 4:17
son of Ahijah, of the house of I ... 1Kin 15:27
families out of the tribe of I ... 1Chr 6:62
And out of the tribe of I ... 1Chr 6:72
of I were valiant men of might ... 1Chr 7:5
And of the children of I, which ... 1Chr 12:32
that were nigh them, even unto I ... 1Chr 12:40
of I, Omri the son of Michael ... 1Chr 27:18
many of Ephraim, and Manasseh, I ... 2Chr 30:18
unto the west side, I a portion ... Eze 48:25
And by the border of I, from the ... Eze 48:26
one gate of Simeon, one gate of I ... Eze 48:33
Of the tribe of I were sealed ... Rev 7:7
*3. A porter of the tabernacle.*
I the seventh, Peulthai the ... 1Chr 26:5

**ISSHIAH** (*is-shi'-ah*) See ISAIAH, JESIAH.
*1. A descendant of Moses.*
sons of Rehabiah, the first was I ... 1Chr 24:21
*2. A Levite.*
The brother of Michah was I ... 1Chr 24:25
of the sons of I ... 1Chr 24:25

**ISSHIJAH** See ISHIJAH.

**ISSHOD** See ISHOD.

**ISSUE**
And thy i, which thou begettest ... Gen 48:6
cleansed from the i of her blood ... Lev 12:7
hath a running i out of his flesh ... Lev 15:2
because of his i he is unclean ... Lev 15:2
shall be his uncleanness in his i ... Lev 15:3
whether his flesh run with his i ... Lev 15:3
his flesh be stopped from his i ... Lev 15:3
whereon he lieth that hath the i ... Lev 15:4
hath the i shall wash his clothes ... Lev 15:6
hath the i shall wash his clothes ... Lev 15:7
if he that hath the i spit upon ... Lev 15:8
that hath the i shall be unclean ... Lev 15:9
he toucheth that hath the i ... Lev 15:11
that he toucheth which hath the i ... Lev 15:12
when he that hath an i is ... Lev 15:13
an i is cleansed of his i ... Lev 15:13
for him before the LORD for his i ... Lev 15:15
And if a woman have an i ... Lev 15:19
her i in her flesh be blood, she ... Lev 15:19
if a woman have an i of her blood ... Lev 15:25
all the days of the i of her ... Lev 15:25
she lieth all the days of her i ... Lev 15:26
But if she be cleansed of her i ... Lev 15:28
LORD for the i of her uncleanness ... Lev 15:30
is the law of him that hath an i ... Lev 15:32
flowers, and of him that hath an i ... Lev 15:33
is a leper, or hath a running i ... Lev 22:4
and every one that hath an i ... Num 5:2
house of Joab one that hath an i ... 2Sa 3:29
thy sons that shall i from thee ... 2Kin 20:18
house, the offspring and the i ... Is 22:24
thy sons that shall i from thee ... Is 39:7
i is like the i of horses ... Eze 23:20
These waters i out toward the ... Eze 47:8
with an i of blood twelve years ... Mt 9:20
a wife, deceased, and, having no i ... Mt 22:25
which had an i of blood twelve ... Mk 5:25
a woman having an i of blood ... Lk 8:43
immediately her i of blood ... Lk 8:44

**ISSUED**
the other i out of the city ... Josh 8:22
as if it had i out of the womb ... Job 38:8
waters i out from under the ... Eze 47:1
they they i out of the sanctuary ... Eze 47:12
A fiery stream i and came forth ... Dan 7:10
and out of their mouths i fire ... Rev 9:17
which i out of their mouths ... Rev 9:18

**ISSUES**
the Lord belong the i from death ... Ps 68:20
for out of it are the i of life ... Prov 4:23

**ISUAH** (*is'-u-ah*) See ISHUAH. *A son of Asher.*
Imnah, and I, and Ishuai, and Beriah ... 1Chr 7:30

**ISUI** (*is'-u-i*) See ISHUI. *A son of Asher.*
Jimnah, and Ishuah, and I, and ... Gen 46:17

**IT** See PREFACE.

**ITALIAN** (*it-al'-yan*)
of the band called the I band ... Acts 10:1

**ITALY** (*it'-a-lee*) *Homeland of most Roman citizens.*
in Pontus, lately come from I ... Acts 18:2
that we should sail into I ... Acts 27:1
ship of Alexandria sailing into I ... Acts 27:6
They of I salute you ... Heb 13:24
to the Hebrews from I by Timothy ... Heb s

**ITCH**
and with the scab, and with the i ... Deut 28:27

**ITCHING**
teachers, having i ears ... 2Ti 4:3

**ITHAI** (*ith'-a-i*) See ITTAI. *A mighty man of David.*
I the son of Ribai of Gibeah, ... 1Chr 11:31

**ITHAMAR** (*ith'-a-mar*) *A son of Aaron.*
Nadab, and Abihu, Eleazar, and I ... Ex 6:23
Nadab and Abihu, Eleazar and I ... Ex 28:1
of the Levites, by the hand of I ... Ex 38:21
Aaron, and unto Eleazar and unto I ... Lev 10:6
Aaron, and unto Eleazar and unto I ... Lev 10:12
and he was angry with Eleazar and I ... Lev 10:16
and Abihu, Eleazar, and I ... Num 3:2
I ministered in the priest's ... Num 3:4
shall be under the hand of I the ... Num 4:28
under the hand of I the son of ... Num 4:33
under the hand of I the son of ... Num 7:8
Nadab, and Abihu, Eleazar, and I ... Num 26:60
Nadab, and Abihu, Eleazar, and I ... 1Chr 6:3
Nadab, and Abihu, Eleazar, and I ... 1Chr 24:1
I executed the priest's office ... 1Chr 24:2
and Ahimelech of the sons of I ... 1Chr 24:3
of Eleazar than of the sons of I ... 1Chr 24:4
eight among the sons of I ... 1Chr 24:4
of Eleazar, and of the sons of I ... 1Chr 24:5
for Eleazar, and one taken for I ... 1Chr 24:6
of the sons of I ... Ezr 8:2

**ITHIEL** (*ith'-e-el*)
*1. Son of Jesaiah.*
the son of Maaseiah, the son of I ... Neh 11:7
*2. Person mentioned in Proverbs.*
the man spake unto I, even unto ... Prov 30:1
spake unto Ithiel, even unto I ... Prov 30:1

**ITHLAH** See JETHLAH.

**ITHMAH** (*ith'-mah*) *A mighty man of David.*
sons of Elnaam, and I the Moabite, ... 1Chr 11:46

**ITHNAN** (*ith'-nan*) *A town in Judah.*
And Kedesh, and Hazor, and I ... Josh 15:23

**ITHRA** (*ith'-rah*) See JETHER. *Father of Amasa.*
whose name was I an Israelite ... 2Sa 17:25

**ITHRAN** (*ith'-ran*)
*1. A son of Dishon.*
Hemdan, and Eshban, and I, and ... Gen 36:26
Amram, and Eshban, and I ... 1Chr 1:41
*2. A son of Zophah.*
Shamma, and Shilshah, and I ... 1Chr 7:37

**ITHREAM** (*ith'-re-am*) *A son of David.*
And the sixth, I, by Eglah David's ... 2Sa 3:5
the sixth, I by Eglah his wife ... 1Chr 3:3

**ITHRITE** (*ith'-rite*) See ITHRITES. *A descendant of Jether.*
Ira an I, Gareb an I, ... 2Sa 23:38
Ira an I, Gareb an I ... 2Sa 23:38
Ira the I, Gareb the I, ... 1Chr 11:40
Ira the I, Gareb the I ... 1Chr 11:40

**ITHRITES** (*ith'-rites*)
the I, and the Puhites, and the ... 1Chr 2:53

**ITS**
That which groweth of i own ... Lev 25:5

**ITSELF**
his kind, whose seed is in i ... Gen 1:11
fruit, whose seed was in i ... Gen 1:12
fat of the beast that dieth of i ... Lev 7:24
that eateth that which died of i ... Lev 17:15
the land i vomiteth out her ... Lev 18:25
That which dieth of i, or is torn ... Lev 22:8
that which groweth of i in it ... Lev 25:11
eat of any thing that dieth of i ... Deut 14:21
were of the very base i ... 1Kin 7:34
A land of darkness, as darkness i ... Job 10:22
his heart gathereth iniquity to i ... Ps 41:6
even Sinai i was moved at the ... Ps 68:8
but that his heart may discover i ... Prov 18:2
the cup, when it moveth i aright ... Prov 23:31
his right hand, which bewrayeth i ... Prov 27:16
and the tender grass sheweth i ... Prov 27:25
Shall the ax boast i against him ... Is 10:15
or shall the saw magnify i ... Is 10:15
as if the rod should shake i ... Is 10:15
as if the staff should lift up i ... Is 10:15
this year such as groweth of i ... Is 37:30
your soul delight i in fatness ... Is 55:2
neither shall thy moon withdraw i ... Is 60:20
And there shall dwell in Judah i ... Jer 31:24
cloud, and a fire infolding i ... Eze 1:4
eaten of that which dieth of i ... Eze 4:14
base, that it might not lift i up ... Eze 17:14
neither shall it exalt i any more ... Eze 29:15
of any thing that is dead of i ... Eze 44:31
and it raised up i on one side ... Dan 7:5
take thought for the things of i ... Mt 6:34
i is brought to desolation ... Mt 12:25
divided against i shall not stand ... Mt 12:25
if a kingdom be divided against i ... Mk 3:24
if a house be divided against i ... Mk 3:25
i is brought to desolation ... Lk 11:17
the branch cannot bear fruit of i ... Jn 15:4
wrapped together in a place by i ... Jn 20:7
i could not contain the books ... Jn 21:25
The Spirit i beareth witness with ... Rom 8:16
Because the creature i also shall ... Rom 8:21
but the Spirit i maketh ... Rom 8:26
there is nothing unclean of i ... Rom 14:14
Doth not even nature i teach you ... 1Cor 11:14
charity vaunteth not i, is not ... 1Cor 13:4
Doth not behave i unseemly ... 1Cor 13:5
i against the knowledge of God ... 2Cor 10:5
unto the edifying of i in love ... Eph 4:16
but into heaven i, now to appear ... Heb 9:24
of all men, and of the truth i ... 3Jn 12

**ITTAH-KAZIN** (*it'-tah-ka'-zin*) *A city in Zebulun.*
the east to Gittah-hepher, to I ... Josh 19:13

**ITTAI** (*it'-ta-i*) See ITHAI.
*1. A Philistine in David's army.*
said the king to I the Gittite ... 2Sa 15:19
I answered the king, and said, As ... 2Sa 15:21
And David said to I, Go and pass ... 2Sa 15:22
I the Gittite passed over, and all ... 2Sa 15:22
under the hand of I the Gittite ... 2Sa 18:2
commanded Joab and Abishai and I ... 2Sa 18:5
king charged thee and Abishai and I ... 2Sa 18:12
*2. A mighty man of David.*
I the son of Ribai out of Gibeah ... 2Sa 23:29

**ITURAEA** (*i-tu-re'-ah*) *A province near Mt. Hermon.*
his brother Philip tetrarch of I ... Lk 3:1

**IVAH** (*i'-vah*) See AHAVA, AVA. *A Mesopotamian district.*
gods of Sepharvaim, Hena, and I ... 2Kin 18:34
city of Sepharvaim, of Hena, and I ... 2Kin 19:13
city of Sepharvaim, Hena, and I ... Is 37:13

**IVORY**
the king made a great throne of i ... 1Kin 10:18
bringing gold, and silver, i ... 1Kin 10:22
the i house which he made, and all ... 1Kin 22:39
the king made a great throne of i ... 2Chr 9:17
bringing gold, and silver, i ... 2Chr 9:21
and cassia, out of the i palaces ... Ps 45:8
his belly is as bright i overlaid ... Song 5:14
Thy neck is as a tower of i ... Song 7:4
have made thy benches of i ... Eze 27:6
thee for a present horns of i ... Eze 27:15
and the houses of i shall perish ... Amos 3:15
That lie upon beds of i, and ... Amos 6:4
wood, and all manner vessels of i ... Rev 18:12

**IZEHAR** (*iz'-e-har*) See IZEHARITES, IZHAR. *A son of Kohath.*
Amram, and I, Hebron, and Uzziel ... Num 3:19

**IZEHARITES** (*iz'-e-har-ites*) See IZHARITE.
*Descendants of Izehar.*
Amramites, and the family of the I ..... Num 3:27

**IZHAR** (*iz'-har*) See IZEHAB, IZHARITES. *Same as Izehar.*
Amram, and I, and Hebron, and Uzziel .. Ex 6:18
And the sons of I ..... Ex 6:21
Now Korah, the son of I, the son ..... Num 16:1
Amram, I, and Hebron, and Uzziel ..... 1Chr 6:2
sons of Kohath were, Amram, and I ... 1Chr 6:18
The son of I, the son of Kohath, ..... 1Chr 6:38
Amram, I, Hebron, and Uzziel, four .. 1Chr 23:12
Of the sons of I ..... 1Chr 23:18

**IZHARITES** (*iz'-har-ites*) See IZEHARITES.
*Same as Izeharites.*
Of the I; Shelomoth ..... 1Chr 24:22
Of the Amramites, and the I ..... 1Chr 26:23
Of the I, Chenaniah and his sons ..... 1Chr 26:29

**IZLIAH** See JEZLIAH.

**IZRAHIAH** (*iz-ra-hi'-ah*) See JEZRAHIAH.
*Grandson of Tola.*
the sons of Uzzi; I ..... 1Chr 7:3
and the sons of I ..... 1Chr 7:3

**IZRAHITE** (*iz'-ra-hite*) See EZRAHITE. *Family name of Shamhuth.*
fifth month was Shamhuth the I ..... 1Chr 27:8

**IZRI** (*iz'-ri*) See ZERI. *A sanctuary servant.*
The fourth to I, he, his sons, and ..... 1Chr 25:11

**IZZIAH** See JEZIAH.

# J

**JAAKAN** (*ja'-a-kan*) See AKAN, BENE-JAAKAN. *A son of Ezer.*
of the children of J to Mosera ..... Deut 10:6

**JAAKOBAH** (*ja-ak'-o-bah*) *A descendant of Simeon.*
And Elioenai, and J, and Jeshohaiah, .. 1Chr 4:36

**JAALA** (*ja'-a-lah*) See JAALAH. *A family of exiles.*
The children of J, the children ..... Neh 7:58

**JAALAH** (*ja'-a-lah*) See JAALA. *Same as Jaala.*
The children of J, the children ..... Ezr 2:56

**JAALAM** (*ja'-a-lam*) *A son of Esau.*
And Aholibamah bare Jeush, and J ..... Gen 36:5
and she bare to Esau Jeush, and J ..... Gen 36:14
duke Jeush, duke J, duke Korah ..... Gen 36:18
Eliphaz, Reuel, and Jeush, and J ..... 1Chr 1:35

**JAANAI** (*ja'-a-nahee*) *A Gadite.*
chief, and Shapham the next, and J .... 1Chr 5:12

**JAAR** See WOOD.

**JAARE-OREGIM** (*ja'-a-re-or'-eg-im*) See JAIR. *Father of Elhanan.*
where Elhanan the son of J ..... 2Sa 21:19

**JAASAU** (*ja-a'-saw*) *Married a foreigner in exile.*
Mattaniah, Mattenai, and J ..... Ezr 10:37

**JAASIEL** (*ja-a'-se-el*) *A son of Abner.*
of Benjamin, J the son of Abner ..... 1Chr 27:21

**JAASU** See JAASAU.

**JAAZANIAH** (*ja-az-a-ni'-ah*) See JEZANIAH.
*1. A son of a Maachathite.*
J the son of a Maachathite, they ..... 2Kin 25:23
*2. A chief Rechabite.*
Then I took J the son of Jeremiah ..... Jer 35:3
*3. Son of Shaphan.*
them stood J the son of Shaphan ..... Eze 8:11
*4. Son of Azur.*
whom I saw J the son of Azur ..... Eze 11:1

**JAAZER** (*ja-a'-zer*) See JAZER. *A city in Gilead.*
And Moses sent to spy out J ..... Num 21:32
And Atroth, Shophan, and J, and ..... Num 32:35

**JAAZIAH** (*ja-a-zi'-ah*) *A descendant of Merari.*
the sons of J; Beno ..... 1Chr 24:26
The sons of Merari by J ..... 1Chr 24:27

**JA-AZIEL** See BEN.

**JAAZIEL** (*ja-a'-ze-el*) See AZIEL. *A priest.*
degree, Zechariah, Ben, and J ..... 1Chr 15:18

**JABAL** (*ja'-bal*) *A son of Adah.*
And Adah bare J ..... Gen 4:20

**JABBOK** (*jab'-bok*) *A brook in Bashan.*
sons, and passed over the ford J ..... Gen 32:22
his land from Arnon unto J ..... Num 21:24
nor unto any place of the river J ..... Deut 2:37
the border even unto the river J ..... Deut 3:16
Gilead, even unto the river J ..... Josh 12:2
of Egypt, from Arnon even unto J ..... Judg 11:13
Amorites, from Arnon even unto J .... Judg 11:22

**JABESH** (*ja'-besh*) See JABESH-GILEAD.
*1. A city in Gad.*
all the men of J said unto Nahash ..... 1Sa 11:1
And the elders of J said unto him ..... 1Sa 11:3
him the tidings of the men of J ..... 1Sa 11:5
came and shewed it to the men of J ..... 1Sa 11:9
Therefore the men of J said ..... 1Sa 11:10
wall of Beth-shan, and came to J ..... 1Sa 31:12
and buried them under a tree at J ..... 1Sa 31:13
of his sons, and brought them to J .... 1Chr 10:12
their bones under the oak in J ..... 1Chr 10:12
*2. Father of Shallum.*
Shallum the son of J conspired ..... 2Kin 15:10
Shallum the son of J began to ..... 2Kin 15:13
Shallum the son of J in Samaria ..... 2Kin 15:14

**JABESH-GILEAD** (*ja''-besh-ghil'-e-ad*) *Same as Jabesh 1.*
the camp from J to the assembly ..... Judg 21:8
of the inhabitants of J there ..... Judg 21:9
smite the inhabitants of J with ..... Judg 21:10
of J four hundred young virgins ..... Judg 21:12
had saved alive of the women of J .... Judg 21:14
came up, and encamped against J ..... 1Sa 11:1
shall ye say unto the men of J ..... 1Sa 11:9
of J heard of that which the ..... 1Sa 31:11
That the men of J were they that ..... 2Sa 2:4
sent messengers unto the men of J ..... 2Sa 2:5
his son from the men of J ..... 2Sa 21:12
when all J heard all that the ..... 1Chr 10:11

**JABEZ** (*ja'-bez*)
*1. A city in Judah.*
of the scribes which dwelt at J ..... 1Chr 2:55
*2. Head of a family of Judah.*
J was more honourable than his ..... 1Chr 4:9
and his mother called his name J ..... 1Chr 4:9
J called on the God of Israel, ..... 1Chr 4:10

**JABIN** (*ja'-bin*) See JABIN'S.
*1. A king of Hazor.*
when J king of Hazor had heard ..... Josh 11:1
*2. Another king of Hazor.*
into the hand of J king of Canaan ..... Judg 4:2
peace between J the king of Hazor ..... Judg 4:17
So God subdued on that day J the ..... Judg 4:23
prevailed against J the king of ..... Judg 4:24
had destroyed J king of Canaan ..... Judg 4:24
as to Sisera, as to J, at the ..... Ps 83:9

**JABIN'S**
Sisera, the captain of J army ..... Judg 4:7

**JABNEEL** (*jab'-ne-el*) See JABNEH.
*1. A city in Judah.*
mount Baalah, and went out unto J .. Josh 15:11
*2. A city in Naphtali.*
and Adami, Nekeb, and J ..... Josh 19:33

**JABNEH** (*jab'-neh*) See JABNEEL. *A Philistine city.*
wall of Gath, and the wall of J ..... 2Chr 26:6

**JACAN** See JACHAN.

**JACHAN** (*ja'-kan*) See AKAN. *Head of a Gadite family.*
and Sheba, and Jorai, and J ..... 1Chr 5:13

**JACHIN** (*ja'-kin*) See JACHINITES, JARIB.
*1. A son of Simeon.*
Jemuel, and Jamin, and Ohad, and J .. Gen 46:10
Jemuel, and Jamin, and Ohad, and J ..... Ex 6:15
of J, the family of the ..... Num 26:12
*2. A pillar of Solomon's Temple.*
and called the name thereof J ..... 1Kin 7:21
name of that on the right hand J ..... 2Chr 3:17
*3. A family of exiles.*
Jedaiah, and Jehoiarib, and J ..... 1Chr 9:10
Jedaiah the son of Joiarib, J ..... Neh 11:10
*4. A sanctuary servant.*
The one and twentieth to J ..... 1Chr 24:17

**JACHINITES** (*ja'-kin-ites*) *Descendants of Jachin 1.*
of Jachin, the family of the J ..... Num 26:12

**JACINTH**
breastplates of fire, and of j ..... Rev 9:17
the eleventh, a j ..... Rev 21:20

**JACOB** (*ja'-cub*) See ISRAEL, JACOB'S, JAMES.
*1. Son of Isaac and Rebekah.*
and his name was called J ..... Gen 25:26
J was a plain man, dwelling in ..... Gen 25:27
but Rebekah loved J ..... Gen 25:28
And J sod pottage ..... Gen 25:29
And Esau said to J, Feed me, I ..... Gen 25:30
J said, Sell me this day thy ..... Gen 25:31
J said, Swear to me this day ..... Gen 25:33
and he sold his birthright unto J ..... Gen 25:33
Then J gave Esau bread and pottage.. Gen 25:34
And Rebekah spake unto J her son ..... Gen 27:6
J said to Rebekah his mother, ..... Gen 27:11
put them upon J her younger son ..... Gen 27:15
into the hand of her son J ..... Gen 27:17
J said unto his father, I am Esau ..... Gen 27:19
And Isaac said unto J, Come near, ..... Gen 27:21
J went near unto Isaac his father ..... Gen 27:22
had made an end of blessing J ..... Gen 27:30
J was yet scarce gone out from ..... Gen 27:30
said, Is not he rightly named J ..... Gen 27:36
Esau hated J because of the ..... Gen 27:41
then will I slay my brother J ..... Gen 27:41
called J her younger son, and said ..... Gen 27:42
if J take a wife of the daughters ..... Gen 27:46
And Isaac called J, and blessed him ..... Gen 28:1
And Isaac sent away J ..... Gen 28:5
Esau saw that Isaac had blessed J ..... Gen 28:6
that J obeyed his father and his ..... Gen 28:7
J went out from Beer-sheba, and ..... Gen 28:10
J awaked out of his sleep, and he ..... Gen 28:16
J rose up early in the morning, ..... Gen 28:18
J vowed a vow, saying, If God ..... Gen 28:20
Then J went on his journey, and ..... Gen 29:1
J said unto them, My brethren, ..... Gen 29:4
when J saw Rachel the daughter of ... Gen 29:10
that J went near, and rolled the ..... Gen 29:10
J kissed Rachel, and lifted up his ..... Gen 29:11
J told Rachel that he was her ..... Gen 29:12
the tidings of J his sister's son ..... Gen 29:13
And Laban said unto J, Because ..... Gen 29:15
And J loved Rachel ..... Gen 29:18
J served seven years for Rachel ..... Gen 29:20
J said unto Laban, Give me my ..... Gen 29:21
J did so, and fulfilled her week ..... Gen 29:28
saw that she bare J no children ..... Gen 30:1
and said unto J, Give me children, ..... Gen 30:1
and J went in unto her ..... Gen 30:4
Bilhah conceived, and bare J a son ..... Gen 30:5
again, and bare J a second son ..... Gen 30:7
her maid, and gave her J to wife ..... Gen 30:9
Zilpah Leah's maid bare J a son ..... Gen 30:10
Leah's maid bare J a second son ..... Gen 30:12
J came out of the field in the ..... Gen 30:16
and bare J the fifth son ..... Gen 30:17
again, and bare J the sixth son ..... Gen 30:19
that J said unto Laban, Send me ..... Gen 30:25
J said, Thou shalt not give me ..... Gen 30:31
journey betwixt himself and J ..... Gen 30:36
J fed the rest of Laban's flocks ..... Gen 30:36
J took him rods of green poplar, ..... Gen 30:37
J did separate the lambs, and set ..... Gen 30:40
that J laid the rods before the ..... Gen 30:41
J hath taken away all that was ..... Gen 31:1
J beheld the countenance of Laban ..... Gen 31:2
And the LORD said unto J, Return ..... Gen 31:3
J sent and called Rachel and Leah ..... Gen 31:4
unto me in a dream, saying, J ..... Gen 31:11
Then J rose up, and set his sons ..... Gen 31:17
J stole away unawares to Laban ..... Gen 31:20
on the third day that J was fled ..... Gen 31:22
speak not to J either good or bad ..... Gen 31:24
Then Laban overtook J ..... Gen 31:25
Now J had pitched his tent in the ..... Gen 31:25
And Laban said to J, What hast ..... Gen 31:26
speak not to J either good or bad ..... Gen 31:29
J answered and said to Laban, ..... Gen 31:31
For J knew not that Rachel had ..... Gen 31:32
J was wroth, and chode with Laban ..... Gen 31:36
J answered and said to Laban, What.. Gen 31:36
And Laban answered and said unto J Gen 31:43
J took a stone, and set it up for ..... Gen 31:45
J said unto his brethren, Gather ..... Gen 31:46
but J called it Galeed ..... Gen 31:47
And Laban said to J, Behold this ..... Gen 31:51
J sware by the fear of his father ..... Gen 31:53
Then J offered sacrifice upon the ..... Gen 31:54
J went on his way, and the angels ..... Gen 32:1
when J saw them, he said, This is ..... Gen 32:2
J sent messengers before him to ..... Gen 32:3
Thy servant J saith thus, I have ..... Gen 32:4
And the messengers returned to J ..... Gen 32:6
Then J was greatly afraid and ..... Gen 32:7
J said, O God of my father ..... Gen 32:9
thy servant J is behind us ..... Gen 32:20
And J was left alone ..... Gen 32:24
And he said, J ..... Gen 32:27
name shall be called no more J ..... Gen 32:28
J asked him, and said, Tell me, I ..... Gen 32:29
J called the name of the place ..... Gen 32:30
J lifted up his eyes, and looked, ..... Gen 33:1
J said, Nay, I pray thee, if now ..... Gen 33:10
J journeyed to Succoth, and built ..... Gen 33:17
J came to Shalem, a city of ..... Gen 33:18
of Leah, which she bare unto J ..... Gen 34:1
unto Dinah the daughter of J ..... Gen 34:3
J heard that he had defiled Dinah ..... Gen 34:5
J held his peace until they were ..... Gen 34:5
out unto J to commune with him ..... Gen 34:6
the sons of J came out of the ..... Gen 34:7
the sons of J answered Shechem and. Gen 34:13
sore, that two of the sons of J ..... Gen 34:25
The sons of J came upon the slain ..... Gen 34:27
J said to Simeon and Levi, Ye have ..... Gen 34:30
And God said unto J, Arise, go up ..... Gen 35:1
Then J said unto his household, ..... Gen 35:2
they gave unto J all the strange ..... Gen 35:4
J hid them under the oak which ..... Gen 35:4
not pursue after the sons of J ..... Gen 35:5
So J came to Luz, which is in the ..... Gen 35:6
And God appeared unto J again ..... Gen 35:9
God said unto him, Thy name is J ..... Gen 35:10
shall not be called any more J ..... Gen 35:10
J set up a pillar in the place ..... Gen 35:14
J called the name of the place ..... Gen 35:15
J set a pillar upon her grave ..... Gen 35:20
Now the sons of J were twelve ..... Gen 35:22
these are the sons of J, which ..... Gen 35:26
J came unto Isaac his father unto ..... Gen 35:27
and his sons Esau and J buried him ..... Gen 35:29
from the face of his brother J ..... Gen 36:6
J dwelt in the land wherein his ..... Gen 37:1
These are the generations of J ..... Gen 37:2
J rent his clothes, and put ..... Gen 37:34
Now when J saw that there was ..... Gen 42:1
J said unto his sons, Why do ye ..... Gen 42:1
J sent not with his brethren ..... Gen 42:4
they came unto J their father ..... Gen 42:29
J their father said unto them, Me ..... Gen 42:36
of Canaan unto J their father ..... Gen 45:25
the spirit of J their father ..... Gen 45:27

of the night, and said, J, J ... Gen 46:2
J rose up from Beer-sheba ... Gen 46:5
of Israel carried J their father ... Gen 46:5
of Canaan, and came into Egypt, J ... Gen 46:6
Israel, which came into Egypt, J ... Gen 46:8
she bare unto J in Padan-aram ... Gen 46:15
and these she bare unto J ... Gen 46:18
of Rachel, which were born to J ... Gen 46:22
and she bare these unto J ... Gen 46:25
souls that came with J into Egypt ... Gen 46:26
all the souls of the house of J ... Gen 46:27
And Joseph brought in J his father ... Gen 47:7
and J blessed Pharaoh ... Gen 47:7
And Pharaoh said unto J, How old ... Gen 47:8
J said unto Pharaoh, The days of ... Gen 47:9
J blessed Pharaoh, and went out ... Gen 47:10
J lived in the land of Egypt ... Gen 47:28
so the whole age of J was an ... Gen 47:28
And one told J, and said, Behold, ... Gen 48:2
J said unto Joseph, God Almighty ... Gen 48:3
J called unto his sons, and said, ... Gen 49:1
together, and hear, ye sons of J ... Gen 49:2
I will divide them in J, and ... Gen 49:7
the hands of the mighty God of J ... Gen 49:24
when J had made an end of ... Gen 49:33
to Abraham, to Isaac, and to J ... Gen 50:24
man and his household came with J ... Ex 1:1
the loins of J were seventy souls ... Ex 1:5
Abraham, with Isaac, and with J ... Ex 2:24
the God of Isaac, and the God of J ... Ex 3:6
the God of Isaac, and the God of J ... Ex 3:15
God of Abraham, of Isaac, and of J ... Ex 3:16
the God of Isaac, and the God of J ... Ex 4:5
Abraham, unto Isaac, and unto J ... Ex 6:3
it to Abraham, to Isaac, and to J ... Ex 6:8
shalt thou say to the house of J ... Ex 19:3
unto Abraham, to Isaac, and to J ... Ex 33:1
I remember my covenant with J ... Lev 26:42
Abraham, unto Isaac, and unto J ... Num 32:11
fathers, Abraham, Isaac, and J ... Deut 1:8
to Abraham, to Isaac, and to J ... Deut 6:10
thy fathers, Abraham, Isaac, and J ... Deut 9:5
servants, Abraham, Isaac, and J ... Deut 9:27
to Abraham, to Isaac, and to J ... Deut 29:13
to Abraham, to Isaac, and to J ... Deut 30:20
Abraham, unto Isaac, and unto J ... Deut 34:4
And I gave unto Isaac J and Esau ... Josh 24:4
but J and his children went down ... Josh 24:4
in a parcel of ground which J ... Josh 24:32
When J was come into Egypt, and ... 1Sa 12:8
with Abraham, Isaac, and J ... 2Kin 13:23
yet I loved J, ... Mal 1:2
and Isaac begat J ... Mt 1:2
J begat Judas and his brethren ... Mt 1:2
down with Abraham, and Isaac, and J ... Mt 8:11
the God of Isaac, and the God of J ... Mt 22:32
the God of Isaac, and the God of J ... Mk 12:26
over the house of J for ever ... Lk 1:33
Which was the son of J, which was ... Lk 3:34
shall see Abraham, and Isaac, and J ... Lk 13:28
the God of Isaac, and the God of J ... Lk 20:37
that J gave to his son Joseph ... Jn 4:5
thou greater than our father J ... Jn 4:12
of Abraham, and of Isaac, and of J ... Acts 3:13
and Isaac begat J ... Acts 7:8
J begat the twelve patriarchs ... Acts 7:8
But when J heard that there was ... Acts 7:12
and called his father J to him ... Acts 7:14
So J went down into Egypt, and ... Acts 7:15
the God of Isaac, and the God of J ... Acts 7:32
a tabernacle for the God of J ... Acts 7:46
J have I loved, but Esau have I ... Rom 9:13
turn away ungodliness from J ... Rom 11:26
in tabernacles with Isaac and J ... Heb 11:9
By faith Isaac blessed J and Esau ... Heb 11:20
By faith J, when he was a dying, ... Heb 11:21
*2. Father of Joseph; ancestor of Jesus.*
and Matthan begat J ... Mt 1:15
J begat Joseph the husband of ... Mt 1:16
*3. Descendants of Jacob.*
east, saying, Come, curse me J ... Num 23:7
Who can count the dust of J ... Num 23:10
He hath not beheld iniquity in J ... Num 23:21
there is no enchantment against J ... Num 23:23
this time it shall be said of J ... Num 23:23
How goodly are thy tents, O J ... Num 24:5
there shall come a Star out of J ... Num 24:17
Out of J shall come he that shall ... Num 24:19
J is the lot of his inheritance ... Deut 32:9
of the congregation of J ... Deut 33:4
They shall teach J thy judgments ... Deut 33:10
the fountain of J shall be upon a ... Deut 33:28
the anointed of the God of J ... 2Sa 23:1
of the tribes of the sons of J ... 1Kin 18:31
LORD commanded the children of J ... 2Kin 17:34
his servant, ye children of J ... 1Chr 16:13
confirmed the same to J for a law ... 1Chr 16:17
J shall rejoice, and Israel shall ... Ps 14:7
name of the God of J defend thee ... Ps 20:1
all ye the seed of J, glorify him ... Ps 22:23
seek him, that seek thy face, O J ... Ps 24:6
command deliverances for J ... Ps 44:4
the God of J is our refuge ... Ps 46:7
the God of J is our refuge ... Ps 46:11
the excellency of J whom he loved ... Ps 47:4
J shall rejoice, and Israel shall ... Ps 53:6
in J unto the ends of the earth ... Ps 59:13
will sing praises to the God of J ... Ps 75:9
At thy rebuke, O God of J ... Ps 76:6
thy people, the sons of J ... Ps 77:15
he established a testimony in J ... Ps 78:5
so a fire was kindled against J ... Ps 78:21
brought him to feed J his people ... Ps 78:71
For they have devoured J, and laid ... Ps 79:7
a joyful noise unto the God of J ... Ps 81:1
Israel, and a law of the God of J ... Ps 81:4
give ear, O God of J ... Ps 84:8
brought back the captivity of J ... Ps 85:1
more than all the dwellings of J ... Ps 87:2
shall the God of J regard it ... Ps 94:7
judgment and righteousness in J ... Ps 99:4
ye children of J his chosen ... Ps 105:6
the same unto J for a law ... Ps 105:10
J sojourned in the land of Ham ... Ps 105:23
the house of J from a people of ... Ps 114:1
at the presence of the God of J ... Ps 114:7
and vowed unto the mighty God of J ... Ps 132:2
for the mighty God of J ... Ps 132:5
LORD hath chosen J unto himself ... Ps 135:4
hath the God of J for his help ... Ps 146:5
He sheweth his word unto J ... Ps 147:19
to the house of the God of J ... Is 2:3
O house of J, come ye, and let us ... Is 2:5
thy people the house of J ... Is 2:6
his face from the house of J ... Is 8:17
The Lord sent a word into J ... Is 9:8
as are escaped of the house of J ... Is 10:20
return, even the remnant of J ... Is 10:21
For the LORD will have mercy on J ... Is 14:1
shall cleave to the house of J ... Is 14:1
that the glory of J shall be made ... Is 17:4
them that come of J to take root ... Is 27:6
shall the iniquity of J be purged ... Is 27:9
concerning the house of J ... Is 29:22
J shall not now be ashamed, ... Is 29:22
and sanctify the Holy One of J ... Is 29:23
Why sayest thou, O J, and speakest ... Is 40:27
J whom I have chosen, the seed of ... Is 41:8
Fear not, thou worm J, and ye men ... Is 41:14
reasons, saith the King of J ... Is 41:21
Who gave J for a spoil, and Israel ... Is 42:24
the LORD that created thee, O J ... Is 43:1
thou hast not called upon me, O J ... Is 43:22
have given J to the curse, and ... Is 43:28
Yet now hear, O J my servant ... Is 44:1
Fear not, O J, my servant ... Is 44:2
call himself by the name of J ... Is 44:5
Remember these, O J and Israel ... Is 44:21
for the LORD hath redeemed J ... Is 44:23
For J my servant's sake, and ... Is 45:4
I said not unto the seed of J ... Is 45:19
Hearken unto me, O house of J ... Is 46:3
Hear ye this, O house of J ... Is 48:1
Hearken unto me, O J and Israel, ... Is 48:12
LORD hath redeemed his servant J ... Is 48:20
to bring J again to him, Though ... Is 49:5
to raise up the tribes of J ... Is 49:6
thy Redeemer, the mighty One of J ... Is 49:26
and the house of J their sins ... Is 58:1
with the heritage of J thy father ... Is 58:14
that turn from transgression in J ... Is 59:20
thy Redeemer, the mighty One of J ... Is 60:16
will bring forth a seed out of J ... Is 65:9
word of the LORD, O house of J ... Jer 2:4
Declare this in the house of J ... Jer 5:20
The portion of J is not like them ... Jer 10:16
for they have eaten up J, and ... Jer 10:25
fear thou not, O my servant J ... Jer 30:10
J shall return, and shall be in ... Jer 30:10
Sing with gladness for J, and ... Jer 31:7
For the LORD hath redeemed J ... Jer 31:11
will I cast away the seed of J ... Jer 33:26
the seed of Abraham, Isaac, and J ... Jer 33:26
But fear not thou, O my servant J ... Jer 46:27
J shall return, and be in rest and ... Jer 46:27
O J my servant, saith the LORD ... Jer 46:28
The portion of J is not like them ... Jer 51:19
LORD hath commanded concerning J ... Lam 1:17
up all the habitations of J ... Lam 2:2
he burned against J like a ... Lam 2:3
unto the seed of the house of J ... Eze 20:5
that I have given to my servant J ... Eze 28:25
I have given unto J my servant ... Eze 37:25
I bring again the captivity of J ... Eze 39:25
plow, and J shall break his clods ... Hos 10:11
will punish J according to his ... Hos 12:2
J fled into the country of Syria, ... Hos 12:12
ye, and testify in the house of J ... Amos 3:13
I abhor the excellency of J ... Amos 6:8
by whom shall J arise ... Amos 7:2
by whom shall J arise ... Amos 7:5
hath sworn by the excellency of J ... Amos 8:7
utterly destroy the house of J ... Amos 9:8
brother J shame shall cover thee ... Obad 10
the house of J shall possess ... Obad 17
the house of J shall be a fire, ... Obad 18
transgression of J is all this ... Mic 1:5
What is the transgression of J ... Mic 1:5
that art named the house of J ... Mic 2:7
I will surely assemble, O J ... Mic 2:12
Hear, I pray you, O heads of J ... Mic 3:1
of might, to declare unto J his ... Mic 3:8
you, ye heads of the house of J ... Mic 3:9
and to the house of the God of J ... Mic 4:2
the remnant of J shall be in the ... Mic 5:7
the remnant of J shall be among ... Mic 5:8
Thou wilt perform the truth to J ... Mic 7:20
turned away the excellency of J ... Nah 2:2
out of the tabernacles of J ... Mal 2:12
ye sons of J are not consumed ... Mal 3:6

**JACOB'S** (*ja'-cubs*)
*1. Refers to Jacob 1.*
and said, The voice is J voice ... Gen 27:22
Syrian, the brother of Rebekah, J ... Gen 28:5
J anger was kindled against ... Gen 30:2
were Laban's, and the stronger J ... Gen 30:42
And Laban went into J tent ... Gen 31:33
shalt say, They be thy servant J ... Gen 32:18
the hollow of J thigh was out of ... Gen 32:25
he touched the hollow of J thigh ... Gen 32:32
Israel in lying with J daughter ... Gen 34:7
he had delight in J daughter ... Gen 34:19
J firstborn, and Simeon, and Levi, ... Gen 35:23
J heart fainted, for he believed ... Gen 45:26
Reuben, J firstborn ... Gen 46:8
The sons of Rachel J wife ... Gen 46:19
besides J sons' wives, all the ... Gen 46:26
Was not Esau J brother ... Mal 1:2
Now J well was there ... Jn 4:6
*2. Refers to Jacob 3.*
it is even the time of J trouble ... Jer 30:7
again the captivity of J tents ... Jer 30:18

**JADA** (*ja'-dah*) *A grandson of Jerahmeel.*
sons of Onam were, Shammai, and J ... 1Chr 2:28
the sons of J the brother of ... 1Chr 2:32

**JADAH** See JARAH.

**JADAI** See JADAU.

**JADAU** (*ja'-daw*) *Married a foreigner in exile.*
Mattithiah, Zabad, Zebina, J ... Ezr 10:43

**JADDAI** See JADAU.

**JADDUA** (*jad'-du-ah*)
*1. A Levite.*
Meshezabeel, Zadok, J, ... Neh 10:21
*2. A priest.*
Jonathan, and Jonathan begat J ... Neh 12:11
Joiada, and Johanan, and J ... Neh 12:22

**JADON** (*ja'-don*) *A repairer of Jerusalem's wall.*
J the Meronothite, the men of ... Neh 3:7

**JAEL** (*ja'-el*) *The wife of Heber.*
of J the wife of Heber the Kenite ... Judg 4:17
J went out to meet Sisera, and ... Judg 4:18
Then J Heber's wife took a nail ... Judg 4:21
J came out to meet him, and said ... Judg 4:22
son of Anath, in the days of J ... Judg 5:6
Blessed above women shall J the ... Judg 5:24

**JAGUR** (*ja'-gur*) *A town in Judah.*
were Kabzeel, and Eder, and J ... Josh 15:21

**JAH** (*jah*) See JEHOVAH. *A shortened form of Jehovah.*
upon the heavens by his name J ... Ps 68:4

**JAHALALEEL** See JAHEEL.

**JAHATH** (*ja'-hath*)
*1. A descendant of Shobal.*
Reaiah the son of Shobal begat J ... 1Chr 4:2
and J begat Ahumai, and Lahad ... 1Chr 4:2
*2. A descendant of Gershom.*
J his son, Zimmah his son, ... 1Chr 6:20
The son of J, the son of Gershom, ... 1Chr 6:43
*3. Another descendant of Gershom.*
And the sons of Shimei were, J ... 1Chr 23:10
J was the chief, and Zizah the ... 1Chr 23:11
*4. A descendant of Kohath.*
of the sons of Shelomoth; J ... 1Chr 24:22
*5. A descendant of Merari.*
and the overseers of them were J ... 2Chr 34:12

**JAHAZ** (*ja'-haz*) See JAHAZA, JAHAZAH, JAHZAH. *A Levitical city in Reuben.*
and he came to J, and fought ... Num 21:23
and all his people, to fight at J ... Deut 2:32
people together, and pitched in J ... Judg 11:20
voice shall be heard even unto J ... Is 15:4
even unto Elealeh, and even unto J ... Jer 48:34

**JAHAZA** (*ja-ha'-zah*) See JAHAZ. *Same as Jahaz.*
And J, and Kedemoth ... Josh 13:18

**JAHAZAH** (*ja-ha'-zah*) See JAHAZ. *Same as Jahaz.*
suburbs, and J with her suburbs, ... Josh 21:36
upon Holon, and upon J, and upon ... Jer 48:21

**JAHAZIAH** (*ja-ha-zi'-ah*) *Son of Tikvah.*
J the son of Tikvah were employed ... Ezr 10:15

**JAHAZIEL** (*ja-ha'-ze-el*)
*1. A captain in David's army.*
and J, and Johanan, and ... 1Chr 12:4
*2. A priest.*
J the priests with trumpets ... 1Chr 16:6
*3. A son of Hebron.*
J the third, and Jekameam the ... 1Chr 23:19
J the third, Jekameam the fourth ... 1Chr 24:23
*4. A Levite.*
Then upon J the son of Zechariah, ... 2Chr 20:14
*5. A family of exiles.*
the son of J, and with him three ... Ezr 8:5

**JAHDAI** (*jah'-dahee*) *A descendant of Caleb.*
And the sons of J ... 1Chr 2:47

**JAHDIEL** (*jah'-de-el*) *Head of a family of Manasseh.*
and Jeremiah, and Hodaviah, and J ... 1Chr 5:24

**JAHDO** (*jah'-do*) *Son of Buz.*
son of Jeshishai, the son of J ............... 1Chr 5:14

**JAHLEEL** (*jah'-le-el*) See JAHLEELITES. *A son of Zebulun.*
Sered, and Elon, and J ........................ Gen 46:14
of J, the family of the ........................ Num 26:26

**JAHLEELITES** (*jah'-le-el-ites*) *Descendants of Jahleel.*
of Jahleel, the family of the J ............ Num 26:26

**JAHMAI** (*jah'-mahee*) *A son of Tola.*
and Rephaiah, and Jeriel, and J............. 1Chr 7:2

**JAHZAH** (*jah'-zah*) See JAHAZ. *A Levitical city in Reuben.*
suburbs, and J with her suburbs, ......... 1Chr 6:78

**JAHZEEL** (*jah'-ze-el*) See JAHZEELITES, JAHZIEL. *A son of Naphtali.*
J, and Guni, and Jezer, and Shillem.... Gen 46:24
of J, the family of the ........................ Num 26:48

**JAHZEELITES** (*jah'-ze-el-ites*) *Descendants of Jahzeel.*
of Jahzeel, the family of the J............ Num 26:48

**JAHZEIAH** See JAHAZIAH.

**JAHZERAH** (*jah'-ze-rah*) See AHAZAI. *The son of Meshullam.*
the son of Adiel, the son of J ............... 1Chr 9:12

**JAHZIEL** (*jah'-ze-el*) See JAHZEEL. *Same as Jahzeel.*
J, and Guni, and Jezer, and Shallum,.. 1Chr 7:13

**JAILER**
charging the *j* to keep them................ Acts 16:23

**JAIR** (*ja'-ur*) See HAVOTH-JAIR, JAARE-OREGIM, JAIRITE.
*1. A descendant of Judah and Manasseh.*
J the son of Manasseh went and........ Num 32:41
J the son of Manasseh took all............ Deut 3:14
towns of J the son of Manasseh .......... 1Kin 4:13
And Segub begat J, who had three....... 1Chr 2:22
*2. A judge.*
And after him arose J, a Gileadite ....... Judg 10:3
J died, and was buried in Camon ......... Judg 10:5
*3. A district in Bashan.*
of Bashan, and all the towns of J ....... Josh 13:30
and Aram, with the towns of J........... 1Chr 2:23
*4. Father of Mordecai.*
name was Mordecai, the son of J............ Est 2:5
*5. Father of Elhanan.*
Elhanan the son of J slew Lahmi ......... 1Chr 20:5

**JAIRITE** (*ja'-ur-ite*) *A descendant of Jair 1.*
Ira also the J was a chief ruler ............ 2Sa 20:26

**JAIRUS** (*ja-i'-rus*) *A ruler of a synagogue.*
of the synagogue, J by name .................. Mk 5:22
behold, there came a man named J......... Lk 8:41

**JAKAN** (*ja'-kan*) See AKAN, JAAKAN. *A son of Ezer.*
Bilhan, and Zavan, and J...................... 1Chr 1:42

**JAKEH** (*ja'-keh*) *Father of Agur.*
The words of Agur the son of J............ Prov 30:1

**JAKIM** (*ja'-kim*)
*1. Son of Shimhi.*
And J, and Zichri, and Zabdi,............... 1Chr 8:19
*2. A sanctuary servant.*
to Eliashib, the twelfth to J .............. 1Chr 24:12

**JAKIN** See JACHINITES.

**JAKINITE** See JACHINITES.

**JALAM** See JAALAM.

**JALON** (*ja'-lon*) *A son of Ezra.*
Jether, and Mered, and Epher, and J... 1Chr 4:17

**JAMBRES** (*jam'-brees*) *An opponent of Moses.*
J withstood Moses, so do these................. 2Ti 3:8

**JAMES** (*james*) See JACOB.
*1. Son of Zebedee.*
J the son of Zebedee, and John his......... Mt 4:21
J the son of Zebedee, and John his......... Mt 10:2
six days Jesus taketh Peter, J.............. Mt 17:1
he saw J the son of Zebedee, and........... Mk 1:19
house of Simon and Andrew, with J...... Mk 1:29
And J the son of.................................. Mk 3:17
and John the brother of J..................... Mk 3:17
J, and John the brother of J................. Mk 5:37
Jesus taketh with him Peter, and J.......... Mk 9:2
And J and John, the sons of Zebedee.. Mk 10:35
to be much displeased with J.............. Mk 10:41
against the temple, Peter and J............. Mk 13:3
And he taketh with him Peter and J.... Mk 14:33
And so was also J, and John, the............ Lk 5:10
Peter,) and Andrew his brother, J.......... Lk 6:14
no man to go in, save Peter, and J......... Lk 8:51
he took Peter and John and J............... Lk 9:28
And when his disciples J and John......... Lk 9:54
where abode both Peter, and J............ Acts 1:13
he killed J the brother of John ........... Acts 12:2
*2. Son of Alphaeus.*
J the son of Alphaeus, and...................... Mt 10:3
J the son of Alphaeus, and..................... Mk 3:18
J the son of Alphaeus, and Simon ........... Lk 6:15
J the son of Alphaeus, and Simon ......... Acts 1:13
*3. Brother of Jesus.*
and his brethren, J, and Joses, and....... Mt 13:55
and Mary the mother of J and Joses..... Mt 27:56
the son of Mary, the brother of J ............ Mk 6:3
and Mary the mother of J the less ....... Mk 15:40
and Mary the mother of J, and............... Mk 16:1
And Judas the brother of J.................... Lk 6:16
Joanna, and Mary the mother of J ........ Lk 24:10
and Judas the brother of J ................. Acts 1:13
said, Go shew these things unto J...... Acts 12:17
J answered, saying, Men and............. Acts 15:13
Paul went in with us unto J................ Acts 21:18
After that, he was seen of J............... 1Cor 15:7
save J the Lord's brother ....................... Gal 1:19
And when J, Cephas, and John, who........ Gal 2:9
before that certain came from J ............ Gal 2:12
J, a servant of God and of the ................... Jas 1:1
of Jesus Christ, and brother of J............... Jude 1

**JAMIN** (*ja'-min*) See JAMINITES.
*1. A son of Simeon.*
Jemuel, and J, and Ohad, and Jachin, Gen 46:10
Jemuel, and J, and Ohad, and Jachin,..... Ex 6:15
of J, the family of the Jaminites......... Num 26:12
sons of Simeon were, Nemuel, and J... 1Chr 4:24
*2. A descendant of Hezron.*
of Jerahmeel were, Maaz, and J .......... 1Chr 2:27
*3. A priest.*
Jeshua, and Bani, and Sherebiah, J......... Neh 8:7

**JAMINITES** (*ja'-min-ites*) *Descendants of Jamin.*
of Jamin, the family of the J.............. Num 26:12

**JAMLECH** (*jam'-lek*) *A royal descendant of Simeon.*
and J, and Joshah the........................... 1Chr 4:34

**JANAI** See JAANAI.

**JANGLING**
have turned aside unto vain *j* .................... 1Ti 1:6

**JANIM** See JANUM.

**JANNA** (*jan'-nah*) *Father of Melchi; ancestor of Jesus.*
of Melchi, which was the son of J ........... Lk 3:24

**JANNAI** See JANNA.

**JANNES** (*jan'-nees*) *An opponent of Moses.*
Now as J and Jambres withstood.............. 2Ti 3:8

**JANOAH** (*ja-no'-ah*) See JANOHAH. *A city in Naphtali.*
Ijon, and Abel-beth-maachah, and J.. 2Kin 15:29

**JANOHAH** (*ja-no'-hah*) See JANOAH. *A city between Ephraim and Manasseh.*
and passed by it on the east to J.......... Josh 16:6
And it went down from J to Ataroth... Josh 16:7

**JANUM** (*ja'-num*) *A city in Judah.*
And J, and Beth-tappuah ..................... Josh 15:53

**JAPHETH** (*ja'-feth*) *A son of Noah.*
and Noah begat Shem, Ham, and J....... Gen 5:32
begat three sons, Shem, Ham, and J..... Gen 6:10
Noah, and Shem, and Ham, and J.......... Gen 7:13
the ark, were Shem, and Ham, and J ... Gen 9:18
J took a garment, and laid it upon........ Gen 9:23
God shall enlarge J, and he shall.......... Gen 9:27
the sons of Noah, Shem, Ham, and J.... Gen 10:1
The sons of J; Gomer ........................... Gen 10:2
Eber, the brother of J the elder............ Gen 10:21
Noah, Shem, Ham, and J........................ 1Chr 1:4
The sons of J; Gomer ........................... 1Chr 1:5

**JAPHIA** (*ja-fi'-ah*)
*1. An Amorite king.*
unto J king of Lachish, and unto.......... Josh 10:3
*2. A town in Zebulun.*
out to Daberath, and goeth up to J.... Josh 19:12
*3. A son of David.*
also, and Elishua, and Nepheg, and J .... 2Sa 5:15
And Nogah, and Nepheg, and J............ 1Chr 3:7
And Nogah, and Nepheg, and J.......... 1Chr 14:6

**JAPHLET** (*jaf'-let*) See JAPHLETI. *A grandson of Beriah.*
And Heber begat J, and Shomer, and . 1Chr 7:32
And the sons of J................................. 1Chr 7:33
These are the children of J.................. 1Chr 7:33

**JAPHLETI** (*jaf'-let-i*) See JAPHLET. *A landmark in Ephraim.*
down westward to the coast of J.......... Josh 16:3

**JAPHLETITES** See JAPHLETI.

**JAPHO** (*ja'-fo*) See JOPPA. *A city in Dan.*
Rakkon, with the border before J....... Josh 19:46

**JARAH** (*ja'-rah*) See JEHOADAH. *A son of Ahaz.*
And Ahaz begat J ................................ 1Chr 9:42
J begat Alemeth, and Azmaveth, and. 1Chr 9:42

**JAREB** (*ja'-reb*) *An Assyrian king.*
the Assyrian, and sent to king J ........... Hos 5:13
Assyria for a present to king J ............. Hos 10:6

**JARED** (*ja'-red*) See JERED.
*1. A descendant of Seth.*
sixty and five years, and begat J ........... Gen 5:15
after he begat J eight hundred............... Gen 5:16
J lived an hundred sixty and two.......... Gen 5:18
J lived after he begat Enoch ................ Gen 5:19
all the days of J were nine.................... Gen 5:20
*2. Father of Enoch; ancestor of Jesus.*
of Enoch, which was the son of J ............ Lk 3:37

**JARESIAH** *A descendant of Benjamin.*
And J, and Eliah, and Zichri, the ......... 1Chr 8:27

**JARHA** (*jar'-hah*) *An Egyptian servant.*
an Egyptian, whose name was J .......... 1Chr 2:34
daughter to J his servant to wife......... 1Chr 2:35

**JARIB** (*ja'-rib*) See JACHIN.
*1. A son of Simeon.*
Simeon were, Nemuel, and Jamin, J.... 1Chr 4:24
*2. A family of exiles.*
and for Elnathan, and for J ................... Ezr 8:16
*3. Married a foreigner.*
Maaseiah, and Eliezer, and J................. Ezr 10:18

**JARMUTH** (*jar'-muth*) See REMETH.
*1. A city in Judah.*
Hebron, and unto Piram king of J......... Josh 10:3
the king of Hebron, the king of J ......... Josh 10:5
the king of Hebron, the king of J ....... Josh 10:23
The king of J, one............................... Josh 12:11
J, and Adullam, Socoh, and Azekah,.. Josh 15:35
J with her suburbs, En-gannim ........... Josh 21:29
En-rimmon, and at Zareah, and at J... Neh 11:29

**JAROAH** (*ja-ro'-ah*) *A descendant of Gad.*
the son of Huri, the son of J ................ 1Chr 5:14

**JASHAR** See JASHER.

**JASHEN** (*ja'-shen*) See HASHEM. *Father of several "mighty men" of David.*
the Shaalbonite, of the sons of J .......... 2Sa 23:32

**JASHER** (*ja'-shur*) *A book of songs.*
not this written in the book of J......... Josh 10:13
it is written in the book of J................... 2Sa 1:18

**JASHOBEAM** (*jash-o'-be-am*)
*1. A "mighty man" of David.*
J, a Hachmonite, the chief of the....... 1Chr 11:11
month was J the son of Zabdiel ........... 1Chr 27:2
*2. Another "mighty man" of David.*
and Azareel, and Joezer, and J ............ 1Chr 12:6

**JASHUB** (*ja'-shub*) See JASHUBI-LEHEM, JOB, JASHUBITES, SHEAR-JASHUB.
*1. A son of Issachar.*
Of J, the family of the........................ Num 26:24
Issachar were, Tola, and Puah, J............ 1Chr 7:1
*2. Married a foreigner in exile.*
Meshullam, Malluch, and Adaiah, J ..... Ezr 10:29

**JASHUBI-LAHEM** See JASHUBI-LEHEM.

**JASHUBI-LEHEM** (*jash'-u-bi-le'-hem*) *A descendant of Shelah.*
had the dominion in Moab, and J ........ 1Chr 4:22

**JASHUBITES** (*jash'-u-bites*) *Descendants of Jashub.*
Of Jashub, the family of the J............. Num 26:24

**JASIEL** (*ja'-se-el*) *A 'mighty man' of David.*
and Obed, and J the Mesobaite........... 1Chr 11:47

**JASON** (*ja'-sun*)
*1. A Christian in Thessalonica.*
and assaulted the house of J................. Acts 17:5
they found them not, they drew J.......... Acts 17:6
Whom J hath received: ........................ Acts 17:7
when they had taken security of J....... Acts 17:9
*2. A relative of Paul.*
my workfellow, and Lucius, and J ..... Rom 16:21

**JASPER**
row a beryl, and an onyx, and a *j* .......... Ex 28:20
row, a beryl, an onyx, and a *j* ............... Ex 39:13
the beryl, the onyx, and the *j* ............... Eze 28:13
sat was to look upon like a *j*.................... Rev 4:3
precious, even like a *j* stone.................. Rev 21:11
of the wall of it was of *j*....................... Rev 21:18
The first foundation was *j* ..................... Rev 21:19

**JATHNIEL** (*jath'-ne-el*) *A son of Meshelemiah.*
Zebadiah the third, J the fourth,.......... 1Chr 26:2

**JATTIR** (*jat'-tur*) *A Levitical city in Judah.*
And in the mountains, Shamir, and J Josh 15:48
J with her suburbs, and Eshtemoa ..... Josh 21:14
and to them which were in J................. 1Sa 30:27
and Libnah with her suburbs, and J.... 1Chr 6:57

**JAVAN** (*ja'-van*)
*1. A son of Japheth.*
Gomer, and Magog, and Madai, and J.. Gen 10:2
And the sons of J ................................. Gen 10:4
Gomer, and Magog, and Madai, and J.. 1Chr 1:5
And the sons of J................................... 1Chr 1:7
*2. Descendants of Javan 1.*
that draw the bow, to Tubal, and J......... Is 66:19
*3. A city in southern Arabia.*
J, Tubal, and Meshech, they were.......... Eze 27:13
J going to and fro occupied in thy........ Eze 27:19

**JAVELIN**
and took a *j* in his hand ........................ Num 25:7
there was a *j* in Saul's hand................. 1Sa 18:10
And Saul cast the *j* .............................. 1Sa 18:11
his house with his *j* in his hand.............. 1Sa 19:9
David even to the wall with the *j*.......... 1Sa 19:10
he smote the *j* into the wall.................. 1Sa 19:10
Saul cast a *j* at him to smite him ......... 1Sa 20:33

**JAW**
with the *j* of an ass have I slain......... Judg 15:16
an hollow place that was in the *j* ........ Judg 15:19
or bore his *j* through with a.................... Job 41:2
their *j* teeth as knives, to ................... Prov 30:14

J

**JAWBONE**
And he found a new *j* of an ass.......... Judg 15:15
With the *j* of an ass, heaps upon........ Judg 15:16
cast away the *j* out of his hand.......... Judg 15:17

**JAWS**
I brake the *j* of the wicked, and.......... Job 29:17
and my tongue cleaveth to my *j*............ Ps 22:15
a bridle in the *j* of the people.................. Is 30:28
But I will put hooks in thy *j*................ Eze 29:4
back, and put hooks into thy *j*............... Eze 38:4
that take off the yoke on their *j*............ Hos 11:4

**JAZER** (*ja'-zur*) See JAAZER. *A Levitical city in Gad.*
and when they saw the land of *J*........... Num 32:1
Ataroth, and Dibon, and *J*, and........... Num 32:3
And their coast was *J*, and all the...... Josh 13:25
her suburbs, *J* with her suburbs.......... Josh 21:39
of the river of Gad, and toward *J*........... 2Sa 24:5
suburbs, and *J* with her suburbs.......... 1Chr 6:81
men of valour at *J* of Gilead................ 1Chr 26:31
they are come even unto *J*....................... Is 16:8
weeping of *J* the vine of Sibmah.............. Is 16:9
for thee with the weeping of *J*.............. Jer 48:32
they reach even to the sea of *J*.............. Jer 48:32

**JAZIZ** (*ja'-ziz*) *Overseer of David's flocks.*
the flocks was *J* the Hagerite.............. 1Chr 27:31

**JEALOUS**
for I the LORD thy God am a *j* God........ Ex 20:5
whose name is *J*, is a *j* God.................... Ex 34:14
he be *j* of his wife, and she be............. Num 5:14
he be *j* of his wife, and she be............. Num 5:14
he be *j* over his wife, and shall............ Num 5:30
is a consuming fire, even a *j* God.......... Deut 4:24
for I the LORD thy God am a *j* God........ Deut 5:9
(For the LORD thy God is a *j* God....... Deut 6:15
he is a *j* God........................................ Josh 24:19
I have been very *j* for the LORD......... 1Kin 19:10
I have been very *j* for the LORD......... 1Kin 19:14
will be *j* for my holy name................... Eze 39:25
will the LORD be *j* for his land.............. Joel 2:18
God is *j*, and the LORD revengeth........... Nah 1:2
I am *j* for Jerusalem and for Zion......... Zec 1:14
I was *j* for Zion with great..................... Zec 8:2
I was *j* for her with great fury................ Zec 8:2
For I am *j* over you with godly............ 2Cor 11:2

**JEALOUSIES**
This is the law of *j*, when a wife.......... Num 5:29

**JEALOUSY**
And the spirit of *j* come upon him...... Num 5:14
if the spirit of *j* come upon him........... Num 5:14
for it is an offering of *j*......................... Num 5:15
hands, which is the *j* offering................ Num 5:18
the *j* offering out of the woman's.......... Num 5:25
the spirit of *j* cometh upon him.......... Num 5:30
the children of Israel in my *j*................. Num 25:11
his *j* shall smoke against that............. Deut 29:20
him to *j* with strange gods.................. Deut 32:16
They have moved me to *j* with that.. Deut 32:21
I will move them to *j* with those....... Deut 32:21
they provoked him to *j* with their...... 1Kin 14:22
moved him to *j* with their graven.......... Ps 78:58
shall thy *j* burn like fire........................... Ps 79:5
For *j* is the rage of a man.................... Prov 6:34
*j* is cruel as the grave.......................... Song 8:6
he shall stir up *j* like a man of............. Is 42:13
of *j*, which provoketh to *j*....................... Eze 8:3
this image of *j* in the entry..................... Eze 8:5
will give thee blood in fury and *j*.......... Eze 16:38
my *j* shall depart from thee, and I....... Eze 16:42
And I will set my *j* against thee........... Eze 23:25
Surely in the fire of my *j* have I............ Eze 36:5
Behold, I have spoken in my *j*.................. Eze 36:6
For in my *j* and in the fire of my.......... Eze 38:19
be devoured by the fire of his *j*............ Zeph 1:18
be devoured with the fire of my *j*.......... Zeph 3:8
and for Zion with a great *j*..................... Zec 1:14
was jealous for Zion with great *j*............. Zec 8:2
I will provoke you to *j* by them.......... Rom 10:19
for to provoke them to *j*....................... Rom 11:11
Do we provoke the Lord to *j*.............. 1Cor 10:22
am jealous over you with godly *j*.......... 2Cor 11:2

**JEARIM** (*je'-a-rim*) See KIRJATH-JEARIM. *A mountain in Judah.*
along unto the side of mount *J*.......... Josh 15:10

**JEATERAI** (*je-at'-e-rahee*) *A descendant of Gershom.*
his son, Zerah his son, *J* his son........... 1Chr 6:21

**JEATHERAI** See JEATERAI.

**JEBERECHIAH** (*je-ber'-e-ki'-ah*) *Father of Zechariah.*
priest, and Zechariah the son of *J*............... Is 8:2

**JEBEREKIAH** See JEBERECHIAH.

**JEBUS** (*je'-bus*) See JEBUSI, JEBUSITE, JERUSALEM. *Original name of Jerusalem.*
departed, and came over against *J*....... Judg 19:10
And when they were by *J*, the day..... Judg 19:11
went to Jerusalem, which is *J*................. 1Chr 11:4
inhabitants of *J* said to David.............. 1Chr 11:5

**JEBUSI** (*jeb'-u-si*) See JEBUSITE. *Same as Jebus.*
to the side of *J* on the south................ Josh 18:16
And Zelah, Eleph, and *J*, which is....... Josh 18:28

**JEBUSITE** (*jeb'-u-site*) See JEBUSITES. *Descendant of Canaan.*
And the *J*, and the Amorite, and the.. Gen 10:16
Perizzite, the Hivite, and the *J*................. Ex 33:2
and the Hivite, and the *J*....................... Ex 34:11
Perizzite, the Hivite, and the *J*............... Josh 9:1
the *J* in the mountains, and to the....... Josh 11:3
unto the south side of the *J*................. Josh 15:8
threshingplace of Araunah the *J*.......... 2Sa 24:16
threshingfloor of Araunah the *J*.......... 2Sa 24:18
The *J* also, and the Amorite, and.......... 1Chr 1:14
the threshingfloor of Ornan the *J*...... 1Chr 21:15
the threshingfloor of Ornan the *J*...... 1Chr 21:18
the threshingfloor of Ornan the *J*...... 1Chr 21:28
the threshingfloor of Ornan the *J*.......... 2Chr 3:1
in Judah, and Ekron as a *J*........................ Zec 9:7

**JEBUSITES** (*jeb'-u-sites*)
and the Girgashites, and the *J*............ Gen 15:21
and the Hivites, and the *J*........................ Ex 3:8
and the Hivites, and the *J*...................... Ex 3:17
and the Hivites, and the *J*...................... Ex 13:5
Canaanites, the Hivites, and the *J*......... Ex 23:23
and the Hittites, and the *J*.................. Num 13:29
and the Hivites, and the *J*...................... Deut 7:1
Perizzites, the Hivites, and the *J*.......... Deut 20:17
and the Amorites, and the *J*................ Josh 3:10
Perizzites, the Hivites, and the *J*.......... Josh 12:8
As for the *J* the inhabitants of............ Josh 15:63
but the *J* dwell with the children........ Josh 15:63
the Hivites, and the *J*........................... Josh 24:11
the *J* that inhabited Jerusalem............. Judg 1:21
but the *J* dwell with the children......... Judg 1:21
and Perizzites, and Hivites, and *J*........... Judg 3:5
turn in into this city of the *J*............. Judg 19:11
men went to Jerusalem unto the *J*........... 2Sa 5:6
to the gutter, and smiteth the *J*.............. 2Sa 5:8
Perizzites, Hivites, and *J*.................... 1Kin 9:20
where the *J* were, the inhabitants........ 1Chr 11:4
the *J* first shall be chief....................... 1Chr 11:6
and the Hivites, and the *J*...................... 2Chr 8:7
Hittites, the Perizzites, the *J*................... Ezr 9:1
and the Perizzites, and the *J*................. Neh 9:8

**JECAMIAH** (*jek-a-mi'-ah*) See JEKAMIAH. *A son of Jeconiah.*
also, and Pedaiah, and Shenazar, *J*...... 1Chr 3:18

**JECHILIAH** See JECHOLIAH.

**JECHOLIAH** (*jek-o-li'-ah*) See JECOLIAH. *Mother of Uzziah.*
mother's name was *J* of Jerusalem...... 2Kin 15:2

**JECHONIAS** (*jek-o-ni'-as*) See JECONIAH. *Greek form of Jeconiah.*
And Josias begat *J* and his brethren.......... Mt 1:11
to Babylon, *J* begat Salathiel.................. Mt 1:12

**JECOLIAH** (*jek-o-li'-ah*) See JECHOLIAH. *Same as Jecholiah.*
name also was *J* of Jerusalem............... 2Chr 26:3

**JECONIAH** (*jek-o-ni'-ah*) See CONIAH, JECHONIAS, JEHOIACHIN. *A king of Judah.*
*J* his son, Zedekiah his son.................... 1Chr 3:16
And the sons of *J*................................... 1Chr 3:17
carried away with *J* king of Judah............ Est 2:6
had carried away captive *J* the.............. Jer 24:1
*J* the son of Jehoiakim king of............ Jer 27:20
*J* the son of Jehoiakim king of............... Jer 28:4
(After that *J* the king, and the.............. Jer 29:2

**JEDAIAH** (*jed-a-i'-ah*)
*1. A descendant of Simeon.*
the son of Allon, the son of *J*............... 1Chr 4:37
*2. A rebuilder of Jerusalem's wall.*
repaired *J* the son of Harumaph............ Neh 3:10
*3. A priest in Jerusalem.*
*J*, and Jehoiarib, and Jachin,................. 1Chr 9:10
to Jehoiarib, the second to *J*................ 1Chr 24:7
the children of *J*, of the house................. Ezr 2:36
the children of *J*, of the house................ Neh 7:39
*4. A family of exiles.*
*J* the son of Joiarib, Jachin.................. Neh 11:10
Shemaiah, and Joiarib, *J*,........................ Neh 12:6
Mattenai; of *J*, Uzzi............................... Neh 12:19
of Heldai, of Tobijah, and of *J*................. Zec 6:10
to Helem, and to Tobijah, and to *J*........ Zec 6:14
*5. A priest.*
Sallu, Amok, Hilkiah, *J*............................ Neh 12:7
of *J*, Nethaneel...................................... Neh 12:21

**JEDIAEL** (*jed-e-a'-el*)
*1. A son of Benjamin.*
Bela, and Becher, and *J*, three................. 1Chr 7:6
The sons also of *J*.................................... 1Chr 7:10
All these the sons of *J*, by the................ 1Chr 7:11
*2. A 'mighty man' of David.*
*J* the son of Shimri, and Joha his....... 1Chr 11:45
*3. A warrior in David's army.*
Adnah, and Jozabad, and *J*................. 1Chr 12:20
*4. Son of Meshelemiah.*
*J* the second, Zebadiah the third,......... 1Chr 26:2

**JEDIDAH** (*je-di'-dah*) *Mother of King Josiah.*
And his mother's name was *J*.............. 2Kin 22:1

**JEDIDIAH** (*jed-id-i'-ah*) *Another name for Solomon.*
and he called his name *J*, because........ 2Sa 12:25

**JEDUTHUN** (*jed'-u-thun*) *A Levite.*
the son of Galal, the son of *J*................ 1Chr 9:16
Obed-edom also the son of *J*............... 1Chr 16:38
with them Heman and *J*...................... 1Chr 16:41
*J* with trumpets and cymbals for......... 1Chr 16:42
the sons of *J* were porters.................... 1Chr 16:42
of Asaph, and of Heman, and of *J*........ 1Chr 25:1
Of *J*: the sons of *J*................................. 1Chr 25:3
under the hands of their father *J*......... 1Chr 25:3
to the king's order to Asaph, *J*............. 1Chr 25:6
of them of Asaph, of Heman, of *J*......... 2Chr 5:12
and of the sons of *J*............................. 2Chr 29:14
and Heman, and *J* the king's seer...... 2Chr 35:15
the son of Galal, the son of *J*............... Neh 11:17
To the chief Musician, even to *J*............. Ps 39:*t*
To the chief Musician, to *J*..................... Ps 62:*t*
To the chief Musician, to *J*..................... Ps 77:*t*

**JEEZER** (*je-e'-zur*) See ABIEZER, JEEZERITES. *A son of Gilead.*
of *J*, the family of the.......................... Num 26:30

**JEEZERITES** (*je-e'-zur-ites*) *Descendants of Jeezer.*
of Jeezer, the family of the *J*.............. Num 26:30

**JEGAR-SAHADUTHA**
And Laban called it *J*............................ Gen 31:47

**JEHALELEEL** (*je-hal-e'-le-el*) See JEHALELEL. *A descendant of Judah.*
And the sons of *J*.................................... 1Chr 4:16

**JEHALELEL** (*je-hal'-e-lel*) See JEHALELEEL. *A descendant of Merari.*
of Abdi, and Azariah the son of *J*...... 2Chr 29:12

**JEHALLELEL** See JEHALELEL.

**JEHDEIAH** (*jeh-di'-ah*)
*1. A sanctuary servant.*
the sons of Shubael; *J*.......................... 1Chr 24:20
*2. A herdsman of David.*
the asses was *J* the Meronothite........ 1Chr 27:30

**JEHEZEKEL** (*je-hez'-e-kel*) See EZEKIEL. *A sanctuary servant.*
to Pethahiah, the twentieth to *J*........ 1Chr 24:16

**JEHEZEL** See JEHEZEKEL.

**JEHIAH** (*je-hi'-ah*) See JEHIEL. *A priest.*
*J* were doorkeepers for the ark........... 1Chr 15:24

**JEHIEL** (*je-hi'-el*) See JEHIAH, JEIEL, JEHIELI.
*1. A Levite.*
and Jaaziel, and Shemiramoth, and *J* 1Chr 15:18
and Aziel, and Shemiramoth, and *J*... 1Chr 15:20
Jeiel, and Shemiramoth, and *J*.............. 1Chr 16:5
*2. A Gershonite.*
the chief was *J*, and Zetham, and.......... 1Chr 23:8
by the hand of *J* the Gershonite........... 1Chr 29:8
*3. A friend of David's son.*
*J* the son of Hachmoni was with........ 1Chr 27:32
*4. Son of King Jehoshaphat.*
of Jehoshaphat, Azariah, and *J*............. 2Chr 21:2
*5. A son of Heman.*
sons of Heman; *J*, and Shimei............ 2Chr 29:14
*6. A Levite in Hezekiah's time.*
*J*, and Azaziah, and Nahath................ 2Chr 31:13
*7. A chief priest.*
Hilkiah and Zechariah and *J*................. 2Chr 35:8
*8. A family of exiles.*
Obadiah the son of *J*, and with him......... Ezr 8:9
*9. The father of Shechaniah.*
And Shechaniah the son of *J*................... Ezr 10:2
*10. A son of Harim.*
and Elijah, and Shemaiah, and *J*........... Ezr 10:21
*11. A man of Elam's family who married a foreigner.*
Mattaniah, Zechariah, and *J*................. Ezr 10:26
*12. Father of Gibeon.*
dwelt the father of Gibeon, *J*................ 1Chr 9:35
*13. A 'mighty man' of David.*
*J* the sons of Hothan the Aroerite..... 1Chr 11:44

**JEHIELI** (*je-hi'-el-i*) See JEHIEL. *A sanctuary servant.*
of Laadan the Gershonite, were *J*...... 1Chr 26:21
The sons of *J*; Zetham, and.................. 1Chr 26:22

**JEHIELITES** See JEHIEL.

**JEHIZKIAH** (*je-hiz-ki'-ah*) See HEZEKIAH. *A son of Shallum.*
*J* the son of Shallum, and Amasa.......... 2Chr 28:12

**JEHOADAH** (*je-ho'-a-dah*) See JARAH. *Son of Ahaz.*
And Ahaz begat *J*.................................. 1Chr 8:36
*J* begat Alemeth, and Azmaveth, and. 1Chr 8:36

**JEHOADDAH** See JEHOADAH.

**JEHOADDAN** (*je-ho-ad'-dan*) *Mother of King Amaziah.*
mother's name was *J* of Jerusalem...... 2Kin 14:2
mother's name was *J* of Jerusalem...... 2Chr 25:1

**JEHOADDIN** See JEHOADDAN.

**JEHOAHAZ** (*je-ho'-a-haz*) See AHAZIAH, JOAHAZ, SHALLUM.
*1. Son of King Jehu.*
*J* his son reigned in his stead.............. 2Kin 10:35
son of Ahaziah king of Judah *J*............ 2Kin 13:1
*J* besought the LORD, and the LORD..... 2Kin 13:4
people to *J* but fifty horsemen.............. 2Kin 13:7
Now the rest of the acts of *J*................ 2Kin 13:8
And *J* slept with his fathers.................. 2Kin 13:9
Judah began Jehoash the son of *J*...... 2Kin 13:10
Israel all the days of *J*......................... 2Kin 13:22
Jehoash the son of *J* took again......... 2Kin 13:25

the hand of J his father by war .......... 2Kin 13:25
J king of Israel reigned Amaziah ......... 2Kin 14:1
the son of J son of Jehu, king of.......... 2Kin 14:8
the death of Jehoash son of J............ 2Kin 14:17
and sent to Joash, the son of J............ 2Chr 25:17
of J king of Israel fifteen years........... 2Chr 25:25
*2. Son of King Josiah.*
the land took J the son of Josiah ....... 2Kin 23:30
J was twenty and three years old....... 2Kin 23:31
name to Jehoiakim, and took J away 2Kin 23:34
J was twenty and three years old ........ 2Chr 36:2
Necho took J his brother, and ............ 2Chr 36:4
*3. A son of King Jehoram.*
was never a son left him, save J ........ 2Chr 21:17
the son of Joash, the son of J............. 2Chr 25:23

**JEHOASH** (*je-ho'-ash*) See JOASH.
*1. A king of Judah.*
Seven years old was J when he .......... 2Kin 11:21
year of Jehu J began to reign.............. 2Kin 12:1
J did that which was right in the........... 2Kin 12:2
J said to the priests, All the.................. 2Kin 12:4
twentieth year of king J the.................. 2Kin 12:6
Then king J called for Jehoiada............ 2Kin 12:7
J king of Judah took all the................. 2Kin 12:18
the son of J the son of Ahaziah,.......... 2Kin 14:13
*2. A king of Israel.*
J the son of Jehoahaz to reign............ 2Kin 13:10
J the son of Jehoahaz took again....... 2Kin 13:25
Then Amaziah sent messengers to J ... 2Kin 14:8
J the king of Israel sent to.................... 2Kin 14:9
Therefore J king of Israel went .......... 2Kin 14:11
J king of Israel took Amaziah.............. 2Kin 14:13
of the acts of J which he did................ 2Kin 14:15
J slept with his fathers, and was ........ 2Kin 14:16
J son of Jehoahaz king of Israel......... 2Kin 14:17

**JEHOHANAN** (*je-ho'-ha-nan*)
*1. A sanctuary servant.*
J the sixth, Elioenai the seventh .......... 1Chr 26:3
*2. A chief captain.*
And next to him was J the captain ... 2Chr 17:15
*3. Father of Ishmael.*
Jeroham, and Ishmael the son of J...... 2Chr 23:1
*4. Married a foreigner in exile.*
J, Hananiah, Zabbai, and Athlai............ Ezr 10:28
*5. A priest in exile.*
Meshullam; of Amariah, J.......................... Neh 12:13
*6. A priest who dedicated the wall.*
and Eleazar, and Uzzi, and J................. Neh 12:42

**JEHOIACHIN** (*je-hoy'-a-kin*) See CONIAH, JECONIAH, JECONIAS, JEHOIACHIN'S. *A king of Judah.*
J his son reigned in his stead ................ 2Kin 24:6
J was eighteen years old when he......... 2Kin 24:8
J the king of Judah went out to.......... 2Kin 24:12
And he carried away J to Babylon...... 2Kin 24:15
the captivity of J king of Judah.......... 2Kin 25:27
of J king of Judah out of prison .......... 2Kin 25:27
J his son reigned in his stead .............. 2Chr 36:8
J was eight years old when he.............. 2Chr 36:9
the captivity of J king of Judah............ Jer 52:31
up the head of J king of Judah.............. Jer 52:31

**JEHOIACHIN'S** (*je-hoy'-a-kins*)
fifth year of king J captivity....................... Eze 1:2

**JEHOIADA** (*je-hoy'-a-dah*) See BERECHIAS, JOIADA.
*1. Father of Benaiah.*
Benaiah the son of J was over ................ 2Sa 8:18
Benaiah the son of J was over the....... 2Sa 20:23
And Benaiah the son of J, the son ....... 2Sa 23:20
things did Benaiah the son of J............. 2Sa 23:22
priest, and Benaiah the son of J ............... 1Kin 1:8
priest, and Benaiah the son of J ........... 1Kin 1:26
prophet, and Benaiah the son of J ....... 1Kin 1:32
the son of J answered the king............. 1Kin 1:36
prophet, and Benaiah the son of J ....... 1Kin 1:38
prophet, and Benaiah the son of J ....... 1Kin 1:44
the hand of Benaiah the son of J.......... 1Kin 2:25
Solomon sent Benaiah the son of J...... 1Kin 2:29
So Benaiah the son of J went up........ 1Kin 2:34
of J in his room over the host............. 1Kin 2:35
commanded Benaiah the son of J ......... 1Kin 2:46
the son of J was over the host................ 1Kin 4:4
Benaiah the son of J, the son of.......... 1Chr 11:22
things did Benaiah the son of J........... 1Chr 11:24
Benaiah the son of J was over the..... 1Chr 18:17
month was Benaiah the son of J........... 1Chr 27:5
*2. A high priest.*
And the seventh year J sent.................. 2Kin 11:4
that J the priest commanded.................. 2Kin 11:9
sabbath, and came to J the priest ........ 2Kin 11:9
But J the priest commanded the......... 2Kin 11:15
J made a covenant between the.......... 2Kin 11:17
J the priest instructed him..................... 2Kin 12:2
Jehoash called for J the priest.............. 2Kin 12:7
But J the priest took a chest, and ........ 2Kin 12:9
Jehoram, the wife of J the priest........ 2Chr 22:11
And in the seventh year J.................... 2Chr 23:1
that J the priest had commanded .......... 2Chr 23:8
for J the priest dismissed not.............. 2Chr 23:8
Moreover J the priest delivered.......... 2Chr 23:9
J and his sons anointed him............... 2Chr 23:11
Then J the priest brought out the...... 2Chr 23:14
J made a covenant between ............. 2Chr 23:16
Also J appointed the offices of.............. 2Chr 23:18
LORD all the days of J the priest........... 2Chr 24:2
And J took for him two wives ............... 2Chr 24:3
the king called for J the chief.............. 2Chr 24:6
J gave it to such as did the work....... 2Chr 24:12
of the money before the king and J .. 2Chr 24:14
continually all the days of J ................ 2Chr 24:14
But J waxed old, and was full of........ 2Chr 24:15
Now after the death of J came the.... 2Chr 24:17
Zechariah the son of J the priest ....... 2Chr 24:20
not the kindness which J his............... 2Chr 24:22
blood of the sons of J the priest ......... 2Chr 24:25
*3. A captain in David's army.*
J was the leader of the Aaronites ...... 1Chr 12:27
*4. Son of Benaiah.*
was J the son of Benaiah, and............ 1Chr 27:34
*5. A rebuilder of Jerusalem's wall.*
gate repaired J the son of Paseah........... Neh 3:6
*6. A pre-exilic priest.*
in the stead of J the priest ...................... Jer 29:26

**JEHOIAKIM** (*je-hoy'-a-kim*) See ELIAKIM, JOIAKIM. *A king of Judah.*
father, and turned his name to J........ 2Kin 23:34
J gave the silver and the gold to........ 2Kin 23:35
J was twenty and five years old .......... 2Kin 23:36
J became his servant three years ......... 2Kin 24:1
Now the rest of the acts of J................. 2Kin 24:5
So J slept with his fathers..................... 2Kin 24:6
according to all that J had done......... 2Kin 24:19
firstborn Johanan, the second J.......... 1Chr 3:15
And the sons of J...................................... 1Chr 3:16
and turned his name to J ....................... 2Chr 36:4
J was twenty and five years old............ 2Chr 36:5
Now the rest of the acts of J................ 2Chr 36:8
It came also in the days of J the ............... Jer 1:3
thus saith the LORD concerning J.......... Jer 22:18
though Coniah the son of J king............ Jer 22:24
the son of J king of Judah ........................ Jer 24:1
of Judah in the fourth year of J................. Jer 25:1
the beginning of the reign of J.................. Jer 26:1
when J the king, with all his ................... Jer 26:21
J the king sent men into Egypt, ............ Jer 26:22
and brought him unto J the king.......... Jer 26:23
the beginning of the reign of J.................. Jer 27:1
captive Jeconiah the son of J ................. Jer 27:20
the son of J king of Judah ....................... Jer 28:4
from the LORD in the days of J ................. Jer 35:1
to pass in the fourth year of J................... Jer 36:1
to pass in the fifth year of J...................... Jer 36:9
which J the king of Judah hath............ Jer 36:28
thou shalt say to J king of Judah.......... Jer 36:29
saith the LORD of J king of Judah ......... Jer 36:30
J king of Judah had burned in the........ Jer 36:32
instead of Coniah the son of J ................... Jer 37:1
in the fourth year of J the son................. Jer 45:1
smote in the fourth year of J the ............ Jer 46:2
according to all that J had done................ Jer 52:2
the reign of J king of Judah came .......... Dan 1:1
the Lord gave J king of Judah................. Dan 1:2

**JEHOIARIB** (*je-hoy'-a-rib*) See JOIARIB.
*1. A priest.*
Jedaiah, and J, and Jachin,.................... 1Chr 9:10
*2. A sanctuary servant.*
Now the first lot came forth to J ......... 1Chr 24:7

**JEHONADAB** (*je-hon'-a-dab*) See JONADAB. *A son of Rechab.*
he lighted on J the son of Rechab...... 2Kin 10:15
And J answered, It is........................... 2Kin 10:15
J the son of Rechab, into the ............. 2Kin 10:23

**JEHONATHAN** (*je-hon'-a-than*) See JONATHAN.
*1. A storehouse servant.*
castles, was J the son of Uzziah......... 1Chr 27:25
*2. A Levite teacher.*
and Asahel, and Shemiramoth, and J.. 2Chr 17:8
*3. A priest.*
of Shemaiah, J......................................... Neh 12:18

**JEHORAM** (*je-ho'-ram*) See HADORAM, JORAM.
*1. A king of Judah.*
J his son reigned in his stead ............. 1Kin 22:50
J the son of Jehoshaphat king of......... 2Kin 1:17
J the son of Jehoshaphat king of......... 2Kin 8:16
of J king of Judah begin to reign.......... 2Kin 8:25
Ahaziah the son of J king of................. 2Kin 8:29
things that Jehoshaphat, and J......... 2Kin 12:18
J his son reigned in his stead............... 2Chr 21:1
but the kingdom gave he to J................ 2Chr 21:3
Now when J was risen up to the.......... 2Chr 21:4
J was thirty and two years old ............ 2Chr 21:5
Then J went forth with his................... 2Chr 21:9
the LORD stirred up against J the....... 2Chr 21:16
son of J king of Judah reigned ............ 2Chr 22:1
Azariah the son of J king of................. 2Chr 22:6
the daughter of king J, the wife.......... 2Chr 22:11
*2. A son of Ahab.*
J reigned in his stead in the................... 2Kin 1:17
Now J the son of Ahab began to.............. 2Kin 3:1
king J went out of Samaria the............. 2Kin 3:6
smote J between his arms, and the...... 2Kin 9:24
went with J the son of Ahab king ....... 2Chr 22:5
see J the son of Ahab at Jezreel.......... 2Chr 22:6
he went out with J against Jehu .......... 2Chr 22:7
*3. A priest.*
and with them Elishama and J............. 2Chr 17:8

**JEHOSHABEATH** (*je-ho-shab'-e-ath*) See JEHOSHEBA. *A daughter of King Jehoram.*
But J, the daughter of the king,......... 2Chr 22:11
So J, the daughter of king .................. 2Chr 22:11

**JEHOSHAPHAT** (*je-hosh'-a-fat*) See JOSAPHAT, JOSHAPHAT.
*1. David's recorder.*
J the son of Ahilud was recorder............ 2Sa 8:16
J the son of Ahilud was recorder.......... 2Sa 20:24
J the son of Ahilud, the recorder.......... 1Kin 4:3
J the son of Ahilud, recorder.............. 1Chr 18:15
*2. An officer of Solomon.*
J the son of Paruah, in Issachar ........... 1Kin 4:17
*3. A king of Judah.*
J his son reigned in his stead ............. 1Kin 15:24
that J the king of Judah came .............. 1Kin 22:2
And he said unto J, Wilt thou go ......... 1Kin 22:4
J said to the king of Israel, I ................ 1Kin 22:4
J said unto the king of Israel,................. 1Kin 22:5
J said, Is there not here a...................... 1Kin 22:7
And the king of Israel said unto J....... 1Kin 22:8
J said, Let not the king say so ............. 1Kin 22:8
J the king of Judah sat each on ......... 1Kin 22:10
And the king of Israel said unto J..... 1Kin 22:18
J the king of Judah went up to .......... 1Kin 22:29
And the king of Israel said unto J..... 1Kin 22:30
captains of the chariots saw J............ 1Kin 22:32
and J cried out....................................... 1Kin 22:32
J the son of Asa began to reign.......... 1Kin 22:41
J was thirty and five years old............ 1Kin 22:42
J made peace with the king of............ 1Kin 22:44
Now the rest of the acts of J.............. 1Kin 22:45
J made ships of Tharshish to go......... 1Kin 22:48
Ahaziah the son of Ahab unto J......... 1Kin 22:49
But J would not...................................... 1Kin 22:49
J slept with his fathers, and was ........ 1Kin 22:50
year of J king of Judah, and............... 1Kin 22:51
the son of J king of Judah ..................... 2Kin 1:17
year of J king of Judah, and...................... 2Kin 3:1
sent to J the king of Judah,....................... 2Kin 3:7
But J said, Is there not here a.............. 2Kin 3:11
J said, The word of the LORD is ........... 2Kin 3:12
So the king of Israel and J.................... 2Kin 3:12
presence of J the king of Judah............ 2Kin 3:14
J being then king of Judah,.................. 2Kin 8:16
Jehoram the son of J king of................ 2Kin 8:16
all the hallowed things that J............. 2Kin 12:18
his son, Asa his son, J his son,............. 1Chr 3:10
J his son reigned in his stead,.............. 2Chr 17:1
And the LORD was with J, because...... 2Chr 17:3
all Judah brought to J presents............ 2Chr 17:5
that they made no war against J...... 2Chr 17:10
Philistines brought J presents............ 2Chr 17:11
J waxed great exceedingly................ 2Chr 17:12
Now J had riches and honour in.......... 2Chr 18:1
Israel said unto J king of Judah........... 2Chr 18:3
J said unto the king of Israel,............... 2Chr 18:4
But J said, Is there not here a ............. 2Chr 18:6
And the king of Israel said unto J...... 2Chr 18:7
J said, Let not the king say so............. 2Chr 18:7
J king of Judah sat either of ................. 2Chr 18:9
And the king of Israel said to J.......... 2Chr 18:17
J the king of Judah went up to.......... 2Chr 18:28
And the king of Israel said unto J..... 2Chr 18:29
captains of the chariots saw J........... 2Chr 18:31
but J cried out, and the LORD ............ 2Chr 18:31
J the king of Judah returned to............. 2Chr 19:1
to meet him, and said to king J............ 2Chr 19:2
And J dwelt at Jerusalem.................... 2Chr 19:4
did J set of the Levites, and of.............. 2Chr 19:8
came against J to battle ...................... 2Chr 20:1
Then there came some that told J....... 2Chr 20:2
J feared, and set himself to seek ......... 2Chr 20:3
J stood in the congregation of.............. 2Chr 20:5
of Jerusalem, and thou king J............ 2Chr 20:15
J bowed his head with his face to...... 2Chr 20:18
J stood and said, Hear me, O Judah... 2Chr 20:20
And when J and his people came to.. 2Chr 20:25
J in the forefront of them, to go ........ 2Chr 20:27
So the realm of J was quiet............... 2Chr 20:30
And J reigned over Judah................... 2Chr 20:31
Now the rest of the acts of J............... 2Chr 20:34
after this did J king of Judah ............ 2Chr 20:35
of Mareshah prophesied against J...... 2Chr 20:37
Now J slept with his fathers, and......... 2Chr 21:1
And he had brethren the sons of J...... 2Chr 21:2
were the sons of J king of Israel.......... 2Chr 21:2
in the ways of J thy father.................. 2Chr 21:12
said they, he is the son of J.................. 2Chr 22:9
*4. Father of Jehu.*
the son of J the son of Nimshi................ 2Kin 9:2
So Jehu the son of J the son of ........... 2Kin 9:14
*5. A priest.*
Shebaniah, and J, and........................... 1Chr 15:24
*6. A valley near Jerusalem.*
them down into the valley of J................ Joel 3:2
and come up to the valley of J.............. Joel 3:12

**JEHOSHEBA** (*je-hosh'-e-bah*) See JEHOSHABEATH. *Same as Jehoshabeath.*
But J, the daughter of king Joram....... 2Kin 11:2

**JEHOSHUA** (*je-hosh'-u-ah*) See JEHOSHUAH, JOSHUA. *Same as Joshua, son of Nun.*
called Oshea the son of Nun J............ Num 13:16

**JEHOSHUAH** (*je-hosh'-u-ah*) *Same as Joshua, son of Nun.*
Non his son, J his son ............................. 1Chr 7:27

**JEHOVAH** (*je-ho'-vah*) See GOD, JAH, JEHOVAH-JIREH, JEHOVAH-NISSI, JEHOVAH-SHALOM, LORD. *A name for God.*
but by my name J was I not known......... Ex 6:3
that thou, whose name alone is J........... Ps 83:18
for the LORD J is my strength and............. Is 12:2
for in the LORD J is everlasting ................. Is 26:4

**JEHOVAH-JIREH** (*je-ho'-vah-ji'-reh*) *Mt. Moriah.*
called the name of that place J............ Gen 22:14

**JEHOVAH-NISSI** *(je-ho'-vah-nis'-si) An altar built by Moses.*
altar, and called the name of it J .......... Ex 17:15

**JEHOVAH-SHALOM** *(je-ho'-vah-sha'-lom) An altar built by Gideon.*
unto the LORD, and called it J .......... Judg 6:24

**JEHOZABAD** *(je-hoz'-a-bad)* See JOZABAD.
*1. Son of Shomer.*
J the son of Shomer, his servants ...... 2Kin 12:21
J the son of Shimrith a Moabitess ..... 2Chr 24:26
*2. A son of Obed-edom.*
J the second, Joah the third, and......... 1Chr 26:4
*3. A general of Jehoshaphat.*
And next him was J .......................... 2Chr 17:18

**JEHOZADAK** *(je-hoz'-a-dak) Great-grandson of Hilkiah.*
begat Seraiah, and Seraiah begat J...... 1Chr 6:14
J went into captivity, when the............ 1Chr 6:15

**JEHU** *(je-hu)*
*1. A son of Hanani.*
to J the son of Hanani against............. 1Kin 16:1
J the son of Hanani came the word..... 1Kin 16:7
against Baasha by J the prophet ....... 1Kin 16:12
J the son of Hanani the seer went....... 2Chr 19:2
the book of J the son of Hanani......... 2Chr 20:34
*2. A king of Israel.*
J the son of Nimshi shalt thou............ 1Kin 19:16
the sword of Hazael shall J slay ......... 1Kin 19:17
the sword of J shall Elisha slay.......... 1Kin 19:17
look out there J the son of .................... 2Kin 9:2
J said, Unto which of all us ................. 2Kin 9:5
Then J came forth to the servants....... 2Kin 9:11
with trumpets, saying, J is king........... 2Kin 9:13
So J the son of Jehoshaphat the......... 2Kin 9:14
J said, If it be your minds, then........... 2Kin 9:15
So J rode in a chariot, and went ......... 2Kin 9:16
spied the company of J as he came...... 2Kin 9:17
J said, What hast thou to do with....... 2Kin 9:18
J answered, What hast thou to do....... 2Kin 9:19
driving of J the son of Nimshi.............. 2Kin 9:20
and they went out against J................ 2Kin 9:21
it came to pass, when Joram saw J ..... 2Kin 9:22
that he said, Is it peace, J ................... 2Kin 9:22
J drew a bow with his full..................... 2Kin 9:24
Then said J to Bidkar his captain......... 2Kin 9:25
J followed after him, and said,............ 2Kin 9:27
when J was come to Jezreel,............... 2Kin 9:30
as J entered in at the gate, she........... 2Kin 9:31
J wrote letters, and sent to.................. 2Kin 10:1
up of the children, sent to J................. 2Kin 10:5
So J slew all that remained of............. 2Kin 10:11
J met with the brethren of.................. 2Kin 10:13
J gathered all the people .................... 2Kin 10:18
but J shall serve him much.................. 2Kin 10:18
But J did it in subtilty, to the.............. 2Kin 10:19
J said, Proclaim a solemn .................... 2Kin 10:20
J sent through all Israel........................ 2Kin 10:21
J went, and Jehonadab the son of...... 2Kin 10:23
J appointed fourscore men without... 2Kin 10:24
that J said to the guard and to ............ 2Kin 10:25
Thus J destroyed Baal out of............... 2Kin 10:28
J departed not from after them, .......... 2Kin 10:29
And the LORD said unto J, Because.... 2Kin 10:30
But J took no heed to walk in the.... 2Kin 10:31
Now the rest of the acts of J............... 2Kin 10:34
And J slept with his fathers................. 2Kin 10:35
the time that J reigned over................ 2Kin 10:36
year of J Jehoash began to reign........ 2Kin 12:1
of Judah Jehoahaz the son of J........... 2Kin 13:1
the son of Jehoahaz son of J............... 2Kin 14:8
of the LORD which he spake unto J... 2Kin 15:12
against J the son of Nimshi.................. 2Chr 22:7
when J was executing judgment.......... 2Chr 22:8
in Samaria,) and brought him to J....... 2Chr 22:9
the son of Jehoahaz, the son of J ...... 2Chr 25:17
of Jezreel upon the house of J................ Hos 1:4
*3. A son of Obed.*
begat Jehu, and J begat Azariah,......... 1Chr 2:38
*4. A son of Josibiah.*
J the son of Josibiah, the son of........... 1Chr 4:35
*5. A warrior in David's army.*
and Berachah, and J the Antothite,..... 1Chr 12:3

**JEHUBBAH** *(je-hub'-bah) A descendant of Shamer.*
Ahi, and Rohgah, J, and Aram............... 1Chr 7:34

**JEHUCAL** *(je-hu'-kal)* See JUCAL. *A son of Shelemiah.*
king sent J the son of Shelemiah ........... Jer 37:3

**JEHUD** *(je'-hud) A city in Dan.*
And J, and Bene-berak, and .................. Josh 19:45

**JEHUDI** *(je-hu'-di) Son of Nethaniah.*
sent J the son of Nethaniah..................... Jer 36:14
So the king sent J to fetch the.............. Jer 36:21
J read it in the ears of the king .............. Jer 36:21
that when J had read three or .............. Jer 36:23

**JEHUDIJAH** *(je-hu-di'-jah)* See HODIAH. *A descendant of Judah.*
his wife J bare Jered the father............ 1Chr 4:18

**JEHUSH** *(je'-hush)* See JEUSH. *A descendant of King Saul.*
J the second, and Eliphelet the............ 1Chr 8:39

**JEIEL** *(je-i'-el)* See JEHIEL, JEUEL.
*1. A chief Reubenite.*
was reckoned, were the chief, J ............ 1Chr 5:7
*2. A Levite gatekeeper.*
and Obed-edom, and J ......................... 1Chr 15:18
and Obed-edom, and J ......................... 1Chr 15:21
and next to him Zechariah, J................ 1Chr 16:5
J with psalteries and with harps........... 1Chr 16:5
*3. A Levite of the Asaph family.*
the son of Benaiah, the son of J........ 2Chr 20:14
*4. A scribe.*
by the hand of J the scribe.................. 2Chr 26:11
*5. A Levite in Hezekiah's time.*
Shimri, and J: and of the sons ............ 2Chr 29:13
*6. A chief Levite.*
his brethren, and Hashabiah and J...... 2Chr 35:9
*7. An exile.*
names are these, Eliphelet, J................. Ezr 8:13
*8. Married a foreigner in exile.*
J, Mattithiah, Zabad, Zebina,................ Ezr 10:43

**JEKABZEEL** *(je-kab'-ze-el)* See KABZEEL. *A city in Judah.*
in the villages thereof, and at J........... Neh 11:25

**JEKAMEAM** *(je-kam'-e-am) Son of Hebron.*
the third, and J the fourth................... 1Chr 23:19
Jahaziel the third, J the fourth ........... 1Chr 24:23

**JEKAMIAH** *(jek-a-mi'-ah)* See JECAMIAH. *A descendant of Shallum.*
And Shallum begat J.............................. 1Chr 2:41
and J begat Elishama ............................ 1Chr 2:41

**JEKUTHIEL** *(je-ku'-the-el) A descendant of Ezra.*
Socho, and J the father of Zanoah ...... 1Chr 4:18

**JEMIMA** *(je-mi'-mah) A daughter of Job.*
called the name of the first, J............... Job 42:14

**JEMIMAH** See JEMIMA.

**JEMUEL** *(je-mu'-el)* See NEMUEL. *A son of Simeon.*
J, and Jamin, and Ohad, and Jachin,.. Gen 46:10
J, and Jamin, and Ohad, and Jachin,....... Ex 6:15

**JEOPARDED**
Naphtali were a people that j............... Judg 5:18

**JEOPARDY**
men that went in j of their lives........... 2Sa 23:17
that have put their lives in j................ 1Chr 11:19
for with the j of their lives .................. 1Chr 11:19
master Saul to the j of our heads....... 1Chr 12:19
filled with water, and were in j................... Lk 8:23
And why stand we in j every hour.... 1Cor 15:30

**JEPHTHAE** *(jef'-thah-e)* See JEPHTHAH. *Same as Jephthah.*
of Barak, and of Samson, and of J...... Heb 11:32

**JEPHTHAH** *(jef'-thah)* See JEPHTHAE, JIPHTHAH-EL. *A judge.*
Now J the Gileadite was a mighty....... Judg 11:1
and Gilead begat J................................ Judg 11:1
grew up, and they thrust out J............. Judg 11:2
Then J fled from his brethren, and...... Judg 11:3
there were gathered vain men to J....... Judg 11:3
to fetch J out of the land of Tob......... Judg 11:5
And they said unto J, Come, and be... Judg 11:6
J said unto the elders of Gilead, ........... Judg 11:7
the elders of Gilead said unto J............ Judg 11:8
J said unto the elders of Gilead,........... Judg 11:9
the elders of Gilead said unto J........... Judg 11:10
Then J went with the elders of............ Judg 11:11
J uttered all his words before............. Judg 11:11
J sent messengers unto the king.......... Judg 11:12
answered unto the messengers of J... Judg 11:13
J sent messengers again unto the...... Judg 11:14
And said unto him, Thus saith J.......... Judg 11:15
the words of J which he sent him...... Judg 11:28
Spirit of the LORD came upon J.......... Judg 11:29
J vowed a vow unto the LORD, and... Judg 11:30
So J passed over unto the.................... Judg 11:32
J came to Mizpeh unto his house,...... Judg 11:34
to lament the daughter of J the.......... Judg 11:40
and went northward, and said unto J. Judg 12:1
J said unto them, I and my people ...... Judg 12:2
Then J gathered together all the ....... Judg 12:4
J judged Israel six years...................... Judg 12:7
Then died J the Gileadite, and was...... Judg 12:7
sent Jerubbaal, and Bedan, and J ......... 1Sa 12:11

**JEPHUNNEH** *(je-fun'-neh)*
*1. Father of Caleb.*
of Judah, Caleb the son of J................. Num 13:6
son of Nun, and Caleb the son of J..... Num 14:6
therein, save Caleb the son of J......... Num 14:30
son of Nun, and Caleb the son of J... Num 14:38
of them, save Caleb the son of J........ Num 26:65
Caleb the son of J the Kenezite ......... Num 32:12
of Judah, Caleb the son of J ............. Num 34:19
Save Caleb the son of J........................ Deut 1:36
Caleb the son of J the Kenezite............ Josh 14:6
of J Hebron for an inheritance............ Josh 14:13
of J the Kenezite unto this day........... Josh 14:14
unto Caleb the son of J he gave a....... Josh 15:13
the son of J for his possession............ Josh 21:12
And the sons of Caleb the son of J...... 1Chr 4:15
they gave to Caleb the son of J........... 1Chr 6:56
*2. Head of an Asherite family.*
J, and Pispah, and Ara .......................... 1Chr 7:38

**JERAH** *(je'-rah) A son of Joktan.*
and Hazarmaveth, and J...................... Gen 10:26
and Sheleph, and Hazarmaveth, and J 1Chr 1:20

**JERAHMEEL** *(je-rah'-me-el)* See JERAHMEELITES.
*1. A son of Hezron.*
J, and Ram, and Chelubai ....................... 1Chr 2:9
the sons of J the firstborn of................. 1Chr 2:25
J had also another wife, whose............ 1Chr 2:26
of Ram the firstborn of J were ............ 1Chr 2:27
These were the sons of J..................... 1Chr 2:33
of Caleb the brother of J were............. 1Chr 2:42
*2. A son of Kish.*
the son of Kish was J.......................... 1Chr 24:29
*3. An officer of Jehoiakim.*
commanded J the son of Hammelech... Jer 36:26

**JERAHMEELITES** *(je-rah'-me-el-ites) Descendants of Jerahmeel.*
and against the south of the J ............ 1Sa 27:10
which were in the cities of the J ......... 1Sa 30:29

**JERED** *(je'-red)* See JARED.
*1. A descendant of Seth.*
Kenan, Mahalaleel, J, ................................ 1Chr 1:2
*2. A descendant of Ezra.*
bare J the father of Gedor ..................... 1Chr 4:18

**JEREMAI** *(jer'-e-mahee) Married a foreigner in exile.*
Mattathah, Zabad, Eliphelet, J ............. Ezr 10:33

**JEREMIAH** *(jer-e-mi'-ah)* See JEREMIAH'S, JEREMIAS, JEREMY.
*1. Father of Hamutal.*
the daughter of J of Libnah.................. 2Kin 23:31
the daughter of J of Libnah.................. 2Kin 24:18
the daughter of J of Libnah ...................... Jer 52:1
*2. Head of a Manassite family.*
Ishi, and Eliel, and Azriel, and J........... 1Chr 5:24
*3. A warrior in David's army.*
J, and Jahaziel, and Johanan................. 1Chr 12:4
*4. A Gadite warrior.*
the fourth, J the fifth, .......................... 1Chr 12:10
*5. Another Gadite warrior.*
J the tenth, Machbanai the................... 1Chr 12:13
*6. A prophet.*
And J lamented for Josiah .................. 2Chr 35:25
humbled not himself before J the ...... 2Chr 36:12
of the LORD by the mouth of J .......... 2Chr 36:21
mouth of J might be accomplished.... 2Chr 36:22
the mouth of J might be fulfilled.............. Ezr 1:1
The words of J the son of Hilkiah............. Jer 1:1
the LORD came unto me, saying, J ......... Jer 1:11
word that came to J from the LORD .......... Jer 7:1
word that came to J from the LORD ....... Jer 11:1
came to J concerning the dearth............ Jer 14:1
which came to J from the LORD ............. Jer 18:1
let us devise devices against J............... Jer 18:18
Then came J from Tophet, whither ...... Jer 19:14
heard that J prophesied these ................ Jer 20:1
Then Pashur smote J the prophet ........... Jer 20:2
brought forth J out of the stocks........... Jer 20:3
Then said J unto him, The LORD ............ Jer 20:3
which came unto J from the LORD.......... Jer 21:1
Then said J unto them, Thus shall......... Jer 21:3
LORD unto me, What seest thou, J.......... Jer 24:3
The word that came to J ......................... Jer 25:1
The which J the prophet spake................ Jer 25:2
which J hath prophesied against .......... Jer 25:13
all the people heard J speaking.............. Jer 26:7
when J had made an end of.................... Jer 26:8
J in the house of the LORD....................... Jer 26:9
Then spake J unto all the princes ......... Jer 26:12
according to all the words of J............. Jer 26:20
the son of Shaphan was with J.............. Jer 26:24
this word unto J from the LORD ............... Jer 27:1
Then the prophet J said unto the............ Jer 28:5
Even the prophet J said, Amen............... Jer 28:6
the prophet J went his way .................... Jer 28:11
the LORD came unto J the prophet .......... Jer 28:12
off the neck of the prophet J................. Jer 28:12
Then said the prophet J unto ................ Jer 28:15
the words of the letter that J .................. Jer 29:1
thou not reproved J of Anathoth .......... Jer 29:27
in the ears of J the prophet ................... Jer 29:29
came the word of the LORD unto J ....... Jer 29:30
word that came to J from the LORD ........ Jer 30:1
The word that came to J from the.......... Jer 32:1
J the prophet was shut up in the............ Jer 32:2
J said, The word of the LORD came........ Jer 32:6
came the word of the LORD unto J ....... Jer 32:26
LORD came unto J the second time......... Jer 33:1
the word of the LORD came unto J ....... Jer 33:19
the word of the LORD came to J ........... Jer 33:23
which came unto J from the LORD.......... Jer 34:1
Then J the prophet spake all ................ Jer 34:6
that came unto J from the LORD ............ Jer 34:8
the LORD came to J from the LORD....... Jer 34:12
The word which came unto J from.......... Jer 35:1
I took Jaazaniah the son of J .................. Jer 35:3
came the word of the LORD unto J ....... Jer 35:12
J said unto the house of the................. Jer 35:18
word came unto J from the LORD ............ Jer 36:1
Then J called Baruch the son of............ Jer 36:4
of J all the words of the LORD................. Jer 36:4
J commanded Baruch, saying, I am......... Jer 36:5
that J the prophet commanded him........ Jer 36:8
of J in the house of the LORD................ Jer 36:10
Baruch, Go, hide thee, thou and J......... Jer 36:19
the scribe and J the prophet.................. Jer 36:26
the word of the LORD came to J ............ Jer 36:27
Baruch wrote at the mouth of J ........... Jer 36:27
Then took J another roll, and gave....... Jer 36:32
J all the words of the book which.......... Jer 36:32

which he spake by the prophet J ... Jer 37:2
the priest to the prophet J ... Jer 37:3
Now J came in and went out among ... Jer 37:4
of the LORD unto the prophet J ... Jer 37:6
Then J went forth out of ... Jer 37:12
he took J the prophet, saying, ... Jer 37:13
Then said J, It is false ... Jer 37:14
so Irijah took J, and brought him ... Jer 37:14
the princes were wroth with J ... Jer 37:15
When J was entered into the ... Jer 37:16
J had remained there many days ... Jer 37:16
And J said, There is ... Jer 37:17
Moreover J said unto king ... Jer 37:18
that they should commit J into ... Jer 37:21
Thus J remained in the court of ... Jer 37:21
heard the words that J had spoken ... Jer 38:1
Then took they J, and cast him ... Jer 38:6
and they let down J with cords ... Jer 38:6
so J sunk in the mire ... Jer 38:6
they had put J in the dungeon ... Jer 38:7
they have done to J the prophet ... Jer 38:9
take up J the prophet out of the ... Jer 38:10
by cords into the dungeon to J ... Jer 38:11
the Ethiopian said unto J ... Jer 38:12
And J did so ... Jer 38:12
So they drew up J with cords ... Jer 38:13
J remained in the court of the ... Jer 38:13
took J the prophet unto him into ... Jer 38:14
and the king said unto J, I will ... Jer 38:14
Then J said unto Zedekiah, If I ... Jer 38:15
the king sware secretly unto J ... Jer 38:16
Then said J unto Zedekiah, Thus ... Jer 38:17
And Zedekiah the king said unto J ... Jer 38:19
But J said, They shall not ... Jer 38:20
Then said Zedekiah unto J ... Jer 38:24
Then came all the princes unto J ... Jer 38:27
So J abode in the court of the ... Jer 38:28
J to Nebuzar-adan the captain of ... Jer 39:11
took J out of the court of the ... Jer 39:14
the word of the LORD came unto J ... Jer 39:15
word that came to J from the LORD ... Jer 40:1
the captain of the guard took J ... Jer 40:2
Then went J unto Gedaliah the son ... Jer 40:6
said unto J the prophet, Let, we ... Jer 42:2
Then J the prophet said unto them ... Jer 42:4
Then they said to J, The LORD be ... Jer 42:5
the word of the LORD came unto J ... Jer 42:7
that when J had made an end of ... Jer 43:1
all the proud men, saying unto J ... Jer 43:2
J the prophet, and Baruch the son ... Jer 43:6
of the LORD unto J in Tahpanhes ... Jer 43:8
The word that came to J ... Jer 44:1
of Egypt, in Pathros, answered J ... Jer 44:15
Then J said unto all the people, ... Jer 44:20
Moreover J said unto all the ... Jer 44:24
The word that J the prophet spake ... Jer 45:1
words in a book at the mouth of J ... Jer 45:1
came to J the prophet against the ... Jer 46:1
the LORD spake to J the prophet ... Jer 46:13
came to J the prophet against the ... Jer 47:1
word of the LORD that came to J ... Jer 49:34
of the Chaldeans by J the prophet ... Jer 50:1
The word which J the prophet ... Jer 51:59
So J wrote in a book all the evil ... Jer 51:60
J said to Seraiah, When thou ... Jer 51:61
Thus far are the words of J ... Jer 51:64
of the LORD came to J the prophet ... Dan 9:2
7. *A priest.*
Seraiah, Azariah, J, ... Neh 10:2
Seraiah, J, Ezra, ... Neh 12:1
of J, Hananiah ... Neh 12:12
and Benjamin, and Shemaiah, and J ... Neh 12:34

**JEREMIAH'S** (*jer-e-mi'-ahz*) *Refers to Jeremiah 6.*
yoke from off the prophet J neck ... Jer 28:10

**JEREMIAS** (*jer-e-mi'-as*) See JEREMIAH. *Greek form of Jeremiah.*
and others, J, or one of the ... Mt 16:14

**JEREMOTH** (*jer'-e-moth*) See JERIMOTH.
1. *A son of Beriah.*
And Ahio, Shashak, and J, ... 1Chr 8:14
2. *A son of Elam.*
and Jehiel, and Abdi, and J ... Ezr 10:26
3. *Another who married a foreigner in exile.*
Eliashib, Mattaniah, and J ... Ezr 10:27
4. *A son of Mushi.*
Mahli, and Eder, and J, three ... 1Chr 23:23
5. *A sanctuary servant.*
The fifteenth to J, he, his sons, ... 1Chr 25:22

**JEREMY** (*jer'-e-mee*) See JEREMIAH. *Latin form of Jeremiah.*
which was spoken by J the prophet ... Mt 2:17
which was spoken by J the prophet ... Mt 27:9

**JERIAH** (*je-ri'-ah*) See JERIJAH. *A descendant of Hebron.*
J the first, Amariah the second, ... 1Chr 23:19
J the first, Amariah the second, ... 1Chr 24:23

**JERIBAI** (*jer'-ib-ahee*) *A 'mighty man' of David.*
Eliel the Mahavite, and J, and ... 1Chr 11:46

**JERICHO** (*jer'-ik-o*) *A city in Benjamin.*
of Moab on this side Jordan by J ... Num 22:1
plains of Moab by Jordan near J ... Num 26:3
plains of Moab by Jordan near J ... Num 26:63
Moab, which are by Jordan near J ... Num 31:12
plains of Moab by Jordan near J ... Num 33:48
plains of Moab by Jordan, near J ... Num 33:50
this side Jordan near J eastward ... Num 34:15
plains of Moab by Jordan near J ... Num 35:1
plains of Moab by Jordan near J ... Num 36:13
of Moab, that is over against J ... Deut 32:49
of Pisgah, that is over against J ... Deut 34:1
and the plain of the valley of J ... Deut 34:3
saying, Go view the land, even J ... Josh 2:1
And it was told the king of J ... Josh 2:2
the king of J sent unto Rahab, ... Josh 2:3
passed over right against J ... Josh 3:16
unto battle, to the plains of J ... Josh 4:13
Gilgal, in the east border of J ... Josh 4:19
month at even in the plains of J ... Josh 5:10
to pass, when Joshua was by J ... Josh 5:13
Now J was straitly shut up ... Josh 6:1
I have given into thine hand J ... Josh 6:2
which Joshua sent to spy out J ... Josh 6:25
riseth up and buildeth this city J ... Josh 6:26
And Joshua sent men from J to Ai ... Josh 7:2
and her king as thou didst unto J ... Josh 8:2
heard what Joshua had done unto J ... Josh 9:3
as he had done to J and her king, ... Josh 10:1
as he did unto the king of J ... Josh 10:28
as he did unto the king of J ... Josh 10:30
The king of J, one ... Josh 12:9
on the other side Jordan, by J ... Josh 13:32
of Joseph fell from Jordan by J ... Josh 16:1
unto the water of J on the east ... Josh 16:1
from J throughout mount Beth-el ... Josh 16:1
and to Naarath, and came to J ... Josh 16:7
the side of J on the north side ... Josh 18:12
to their families were J, and ... Josh 18:21
other side Jordan by J eastward ... Josh 20:8
went over Jordan, and came unto J ... Josh 24:11
the men of J fought against you, ... Josh 24:11
Tarry at J until your beards be ... 2Sa 10:5
did Hiel the Beth-elite build J ... 1Kin 16:34
for the LORD hath sent me to J ... 2Kin 2:4
So they came to J ... 2Kin 2:4
that were at J came to Elisha ... 2Kin 2:5
which were to view at J saw him ... 2Kin 2:15
to him, (for he tarried at J ... 2Kin 2:18
overtook him in the plains of J ... 2Kin 25:5
And on the other side Jordan by J ... 1Chr 6:78
Tarry at J until your beards be ... 1Chr 19:5
upon asses, and brought them to J ... 2Chr 28:15
The children of J, three hundred ... Ezr 2:34
unto him builded the men of J ... Neh 3:2
The children of J, three hundred ... Neh 7:36
Zedekiah in the plains of J ... Jer 39:5
Zedekiah in the plains of J ... Jer 52:8
And as they departed from J ... Mt 20:29
And they came to J ... Mk 10:46
as he went out of J with his ... Mk 10:46
man went down from Jerusalem to J ... Lk 10:30
that as he was come nigh unto J ... Lk 18:35
Jesus entered and passed through J ... Lk 19:1
By faith the walls of J fell down ... Heb 11:30

**JERIEL** (*je-ri'-el*) *A son of Tola.*
Uzzi, and Rephaiah, and J, and ... 1Chr 7:2

**JERIJAH** (*je-ri'-jah*) *Same as Jeriah.*
the Hebronites was J the chief ... 1Chr 26:31

**JERIMOTH** (*jer'-im-oth*) See JEREMOTH.
1. *A son of Bela.*
Ezbon, and Uzzi, and Uzziel, and J ... 1Chr 7:7
2. *A son of Becher.*
and Elioenai, and Omri, and J ... 1Chr 7:8
3. *A warrior in David's army.*
Eluzai, and J, and Bealiah, and ... 1Chr 12:5
4. *A son of Mushi.*
Mahli, and Eder, and J ... 1Chr 24:30
5. *A sanctuary servant.*
Mattaniah, Uzziel, Shebuel, and J ... 1Chr 25:4
6. *A Naphtalite ruler.*
of Naphtali, J the son of Azriel ... 1Chr 27:19
7. *A son of David.*
of J the son of David to wife ... 2Chr 11:18
8. *A Temple servant.*
and Nahath, and Asahel, and J ... 2Chr 31:13

**JERIOTH** (*je'-re-oth*) *A wife of Caleb.*
of Azubah his wife, and of J ... 1Chr 2:18

**JEROBOAM** (*jer-o-bo'-am*) See JEROBOAM'S.
1. *A king of Israel.*
J the son of Nebat, an Ephrathite ... 1Kin 11:26
the man J was a mighty man of ... 1Kin 11:28
time when J went out of Jerusalem ... 1Kin 11:29
And he said to J, Take thee ten ... 1Kin 11:31
sought therefore to kill J ... 1Kin 11:40
J arose, and fled into Egypt, unto ... 1Kin 11:40
when J the son of Nebat, who was ... 1Kin 12:2
king Solomon, and J dwelt in Egypt ... 1Kin 12:2
And J and all the congregation of ... 1Kin 12:3
So J and all the people came to ... 1Kin 12:12
Shilonite unto J the son of Nebat ... 1Kin 12:15
heard that J was come again ... 1Kin 12:20
Then J built Shechem in mount ... 1Kin 12:25
J said in his heart, Now shall ... 1Kin 12:26
J ordained a feast in the eighth ... 1Kin 12:32
J stood by the altar to burn ... 1Kin 13:1
when king J heard the saying of ... 1Kin 13:4
After this thing J returned not ... 1Kin 13:33
became sin unto the house of J ... 1Kin 13:34
Abijah the son of J fell sick ... 1Kin 14:1
J said to his wife, Arise, I pray ... 1Kin 14:2
be not known to be the wife of J ... 1Kin 14:2
the wife of J cometh to ask a ... 1Kin 14:5
he said, Come in, thou wife of J ... 1Kin 14:6
Go, tell J, Thus saith the LORD ... 1Kin 14:7
bring evil upon the house of J ... 1Kin 14:10
will cut off from J him that ... 1Kin 14:10
the remnant of the house of J ... 1Kin 14:10
Him that dieth of J in the city ... 1Kin 14:11
for he only of J shall come to ... 1Kin 14:13
God of Israel in the house of J ... 1Kin 14:13
cut off the house of J that day ... 1Kin 14:14
up because of the sins of J ... 1Kin 14:16
And the rest of the acts of J ... 1Kin 14:19
the days which J reigned were two ... 1Kin 14:20
Rehoboam and J all their days ... 1Kin 14:30
in the eighteenth year of king J ... 1Kin 15:1
J all the days of his life ... 1Kin 15:6
there was war between Abijam and J. 1Kin 15:7
in the twentieth year of J king ... 1Kin 15:9
Nadab the son of J began to reign ... 1Kin 15:25
that he smote all the house of J ... 1Kin 15:29
he left not to J any that ... 1Kin 15:29
of the sins of J which he sinned ... 1Kin 15:30
LORD, and walked in the way of J ... 1Kin 15:34
thou hast walked in the way of J ... 1Kin 16:2
the house of J the son of Nebat ... 1Kin 16:3
in being like the house of J ... 1Kin 16:7
LORD, in walking in the way of J ... 1Kin 16:19
all the way of J the son of Nebat ... 1Kin 16:26
in the sins of J the son of Nebat ... 1Kin 16:31
the house of J the son of Nebat ... 1Kin 21:22
in the way of J the son of Nebat, ... 1Kin 22:52
the sins of J the son of Nebat ... 2Kin 3:3
the house of J the son of Nebat ... 2Kin 9:9
the sins of J the son of Nebat ... 2Kin 10:29
departed not from the sins of J ... 2Kin 10:31
the sins of J the son of Nebat ... 2Kin 13:2
from the sins of the house of J ... 2Kin 13:6
the sins of J the son of Nebat ... 2Kin 13:11
the sins of J the son of Nebat ... 2Kin 14:24
the sins of J the son of Nebat ... 2Kin 15:9
the sins of J the son of Nebat ... 2Kin 15:18
the sins of J the son of Nebat ... 2Kin 15:24
the sins of J the son of Nebat ... 2Kin 15:28
they made J the son of Nebat king ... 2Kin 17:21
J drave Israel from following the ... 2Kin 17:21
in all the sins of J which he did ... 2Kin 17:22
place which J the son of Nebat ... 2Kin 23:15
seer against J the son of Nebat ... 2Chr 9:29
when J the son of Nebat, who was ... 2Chr 10:2
that J returned out of Egypt ... 2Chr 10:2
So J and all Israel came and spake ... 2Chr 10:3
So J and all the people came to ... 2Chr 10:12
Shilonite to J the son of Nebat ... 2Chr 10:15
and returned from going against J ... 2Chr 11:4
for J and his sons had cast them ... 2Chr 11:14
Rehoboam and J continually ... 2Chr 12:15
king J began Abijah to reign over ... 2Chr 13:1
there was war between Abijah and J.. 2Chr 13:2
J also set the battle in array ... 2Chr 13:3
Ephraim, and said, Hear me, thou J ... 2Chr 13:4
Yet J the son of Nebat, the ... 2Chr 13:6
which J made you for gods ... 2Chr 13:8
But J caused an ambushment to ... 2Chr 13:13
it came to pass, that God smote J ... 2Chr 13:15
And Abijah pursued after J ... 2Chr 13:19
Neither did J recover strength ... 2Chr 13:20
2. *Another king of Israel, son of Jehoash.*
and J sat upon his throne ... 2Kin 13:13
J his son reigned in his stead ... 2Kin 14:16
the son of Joash king of Judah J ... 2Kin 14:23
by the hand of J the son of Joash ... 2Kin 14:27
Now the rest of the acts of J ... 2Kin 14:28
J slept with his fathers, even ... 2Kin 14:29
seventh year of J king of Israel ... 2Kin 15:1
of J reign over Israel in Samaria ... 2Kin 15:8
in the days of J king of Israel ... 1Chr 5:17
in the days of J the son of Joash ... Hos 1:1
in the days of J the son of Joash ... Amos 1:1
the house of J with the sword ... Amos 7:9
Beth-el sent to J king of Israel ... Amos 7:10
J shall die by the sword, and ... Amos 7:11

**JEROBOAM'S** (*jer-o-bo'-ams*) *Refers to Jeroboam 1.*
J wife did so, and arose, and went ... 1Kin 14:4
J wife arose, and departed, and ... 1Kin 14:17

**JEROHAM** (*je-ro'-ham*)
1. *Grandfather of Samuel.*
name was Elkanah, the son of J ... 1Sa 1:1
J his son, Elkanah his son ... 1Chr 6:27
The son of Elkanah, the son of J ... 1Chr 6:34
2. *Head of a Benjamite family.*
Eliah, and Zichri, the sons of J ... 1Chr 8:27
3. *A descendant of Benjamin.*
And Ibneiah the son of J, and Elah ... 1Chr 9:8
4. *A family of exiles.*
And Adaiah the son of J, the son ... 1Chr 9:12
and Adaiah the son of J, the son ... Neh 11:12
5. *A warrior in David's army.*
Zebadiah, the sons of J of Gedor ... 1Chr 12:7
6. *Father of Azareel.*
Of Dan, Azareel the son of J ... 1Chr 27:22
7. *Father of Azariah.*
of hundreds, Azariah the son of J ... 2Chr 23:1

**JERUBBAAL** (*je-rub'-ba-al*) See GIDEON, JERUBBESHETH. *Another name for Gideon.*
on that day he called him J ... Judg 6:32
Then J, who is Gideon, and all the ... Judg 7:1
J the son of Joash went and dwelt ... Judg 8:29
they kindness to the house of J ... Judg 8:35
Abimelech the son of J went to ... Judg 9:1
either that all the sons of J ... Judg 9:2

slew his brethren the sons of J .............. Judg 9:5
the youngest son of J was left .............. Judg 9:5
and if ye have dealt well with J .............. Judg 9:16
dealt truly and sincerely with J .............. Judg 9:19
and ten sons of J might come .............. Judg 9:24
is not he the son of J .............. Judg 9:28
the curse of Jotham the son of J .............. Judg 9:57
And the LORD sent J, and Bedan, and. 1Sa 12:11

**JERUBBESHETH** (*je-rub'-be-sheth*) See JERUBBAAL. *Another name for Gideon.*
Who smote Abimelech the son of J .... 2Sa 11:21

**JERUEL** (*je-ru'-el*) *A wilderness in Judah.*
brook, before the wilderness of J ....... 2Chr 20:16

**JERUSALEM** (*je-ru'-sa-lem*) See PREFACE. SEE ALSO JERUSALEM'S, SALEM. *City where the Temple was located.*
carried the ark of God again to J ........ 2Sa 15:29
said, In J will I put my name .............. 2Kin 21:4
his son, In this house, and in J .............. 2Kin 21:7
And he carried away all J, and all ....... 2Kin 24:14
built the house of the LORD in J .............. 1Chr 6:32
that they may dwell in J for ever ....... 1Chr 23:25
But I have chosen J, that my name ...... 2Chr 6:6
me to build him an house at J .............. Ezr 1:2
house of the LORD which is at J .............. Ezr 2:68
the house of God which is at J .............. Ezr 5:2
So I came to J, and was there .............. Neh 2:11
out of Zion, which dwelleth at J .............. Ps 135:21
For J is ruined, and Judah is .............. Is 3:8
on thy beautiful garments, O J .............. Is 52:1
is a wilderness, J a desolation .............. Is 64:10
O J, wash thine heart from .............. Jer 4:14
be saved, and J shall dwell safely .......... Jer 33:16
and brake down the walls of J .............. Jer 39:8
from J eight hundred thirty .............. Jer 52:29
J remembered in the days of her .......... Lam 1:7
J hath grievously sinned .............. Lam 1:8
came wise men from the east to J .......... Mt 2:1
was troubled, and all J with him .............. Mt 2:3
O J, J, thou that killest .............. Mt 23:37
they brought him to J, to .............. Lk 2:22
they went up to J after the .............. Lk 2:42
child Jesus tarried behind in J .............. Lk 2:43
O J, J, which killest the .............. Lk 13:34
among all nations, beginning at J .......... Lk 24:47
but tarry ye in the city of J .............. Lk 24:49
be witnesses unto me both in J .............. Acts 1:8
And there were dwelling at J Jews ........ Acts 2:5
against the church which was at J .......... Acts 8:1
and elders which were at J .............. Acts 16:4
But now I go unto J to minister .......... Rom 15:25
But J which is above is free, .............. Gal 4:26
of the living God, the heavenly J .......... Heb 12:22
city of my God, which is new J .......... Rev 3:12
I John saw the holy city, new J .......... Rev 21:2
me that great city, the holy J .............. Rev 21:10

**JERUSALEM'S** (*je-ru'-sa-lems*)
for J sake which I have chosen .......... 1Kin 11:13
for J sake, the city which I have .......... 1Kin 11:32
for J sake I will not rest, until .............. Is 62:1

**JERUSHA** (*je-ru'-shah*) See JERUSHAH. *Mother of King Jotham of Judah.*
And his mother's name was J .............. 2Kin 15:33

**JERUSHAH** (*je-ru'-shah*) See JERUSHA. *Same as Jerusha.*
His mother's name also was J .............. 2Chr 27:1

**JESAIAH** (*jes-a-i'-ah*) See ISAIAH, JESHAIAH.
*1. Grandson of Zerubbabel.*
Hananiah; Pelatiah, and J .............. 1Chr 3:21
*2. A family of exiles.*
the son of Ithiel, the son of J .............. Neh 11:7

**JESHAIAH** (*jesh-a-i'-ah*) See JESAIAH.
*1. A sanctuary servant.*
Gedaliah, and Zeri, and J, .............. 1Chr 25:3
The eighth to J, he, his sons, and ....... 1Chr 25:15
*2. A grandson of Eliezer.*
J his son, and Joram his son, and ...... 1Chr 26:25
*3. An Elamite exile.*
J the son of Athaliah, and with .............. Ezr 8:7
*4. A Merarite exile.*
with him J of the sons of Merari, .......... Ezr 8:19

**JESHANAH** (*je-sha'-nah*) *A city near Bethel.*
J with the towns thereof, and .............. 2Chr 13:19

**JESHARELAH** (*je-shar'-e-lah*) See ASARELAH. *A sanctuary servant.*
The seventh to J, he, his sons, .............. 1Chr 25:14

**JESHEBEAB** (*je-sheb'-e-ab*) *A sanctuary servant.*
to Huppah, the fourteenth to J .............. 1Chr 24:13

**JESHER** (*je'-shur*) *A son of Caleb.*
J, and Shobab, and Ardon .............. 1Chr 2:18

**JESHIMON** (*jesh'-im-on*)
*1. A place in the Sinai.*
of Pisgah, which looketh toward J .... Num 21:20
of Peor, that looketh toward J .......... Num 23:28
*2. A place in the wilderness of Judah.*
which is on the south of J .............. 1Sa 23:19
in the plain on the south of J .............. 1Sa 23:24
of Hachilah, which is before J .............. 1Sa 26:1
of Hachilah, which is before J .............. 1Sa 26:3

**JESHISHAI** (*jesh'-i-shahee*) *Ancestor of a Gadite family.*
the son of Michael, the son of J .......... 1Chr 5:14

**JESHOHAIAH** (*je-sho-ha-i'-ah*) *A descendant of Simeon.*
And Elioenai, and Jaakobah, and J ...... 1Chr 4:36

**JESHUA** (*jesh'-u-ah*) See JESHUAH, JOSHUA.
*1. A sanctuary servant.*
of Jedaiah, of the house of J .............. Ezr 2:36
of Jedaiah, of the house of J .............. Neh 7:39
*2. A Levite in Hezekiah's time.*
The ninth to J, the tenth to .............. 1Chr 24:11
him were Eden, and Miniamin, and J 2Chr 31:15
the children of J and Kadmiel, of .......... Ezr 2:40
the children of J, of Kadmiel, and .......... Neh 7:43
*3. A priest in exile.*
J, Nehemiah, Seraiah, Reelaiah, .............. Ezr 2:2
Then stood up J the son of .............. Ezr 3:2
J the son of Jozadak, and the .............. Ezr 3:8
Then stood J with his sons and his .......... Ezr 3:9
But Zerubbabel, and J, and the rest .......... Ezr 4:3
J the son of Jozadak, and began to .......... Ezr 5:2
of the sons of J the son of .............. Ezr 10:18
Who came with Zerubbabel, J .............. Neh 7:7
the son of Shealtiel, and J .............. Neh 12:1
their brethren in the days of J .............. Neh 12:7
J begat Joiakim, Joiakim also .............. Neh 12:10
the days of Joiakim the son of J .......... Neh 12:26
*4. Father of Jozabad.*
them was Jozabad the son of J .............. Ezr 8:33
*5. A family of exiles.*
Pahath-moab, of the children of J .......... Ezr 2:6
Pahath-moab, of the children of J .......... Neh 7:11
*6. Father of Ezer.*
to him repaired Ezer the son of J .......... Neh 3:19
*7. A priest who assisted Ezra.*
Also J, and Bani, and Sherebiah, .......... Neh 8:7
the stairs, of the Levites, J .............. Neh 9:4
Then the Levites, J, and Kadmiel, .......... Neh 9:5
J, Binnui, Kadmiel, Sherebiah, .............. Neh 12:8
J the son of Kadmiel, with their .......... Neh 12:24
*8. Same as Joshua, son of Nun.*
for since the days of J the son .............. Neh 8:17
*9. A Levite who renewed the covenant.*
both J the son of Azaniah, Binnui .......... Neh 10:9
*10. A city in Benjamin.*
And at J, and at Moladah, and at .......... Neh 11:26

**JESHURUN** (*jesh'-u-run*) *Another name for the people Israel.*
But J waxed fat, and kicked .............. Deut 32:15
And he was king in J, when the .......... Deut 33:5
is none like unto the God of J .......... Deut 33:26

**JESIAH** (*je-si'-ah*) See ISHIAH.
*1. A warrior in David's army.*
Elkanah, and J, and Azareel, and .......... 1Chr 12:6
*2. A descendant of Uzziel.*
Micah the first, and J the second ....... 1Chr 23:20

**JESIMIEL** (*je-sim'-e-el*) *A descendant of Simeon.*
and Asaiah, and Adiel, and J .............. 1Chr 4:36

**JESSE** (*jes'-se*) *Father of David.*
he is the father of J, the father .......... Ruth 4:17
begat J, and J begat David .............. Ruth 4:22
send thee to J the Beth-lehemite .......... 1Sa 16:1
call J to the sacrifice, and I .............. 1Sa 16:3
And he sanctified J and his sons, .......... 1Sa 16:5
Then J called Abinadab, and made .......... 1Sa 16:8
Then J made Shammah to pass by .......... 1Sa 16:9
J made seven of his sons to pass .......... 1Sa 16:10
And Samuel said unto J, The LORD .......... 1Sa 16:10
And Samuel said unto J, Are here .......... 1Sa 16:11
And Samuel said unto J, Send and .......... 1Sa 16:11
seen a son of J the Beth-lehemite .......... 1Sa 16:18
Saul sent messengers unto J .............. 1Sa 16:19
J took an ass laden with bread, .......... 1Sa 16:20
And Saul sent to J, saying, Let .......... 1Sa 16:22
whose name was J; and he had .......... 1Sa 17:12
the three eldest sons of J went .......... 1Sa 17:13
J said unto David his son, Take .......... 1Sa 17:17
and went, as J had commanded him ... 1Sa 17:20
thy servant J the Beth-lehemite .......... 1Sa 17:58
cometh not the son of J to meat .......... 1Sa 20:27
son of J to thine own confusion .......... 1Sa 20:30
son of J liveth upon the ground .......... 1Sa 20:31
will the son of J give every one .......... 1Sa 22:7
made a league with the son of J .......... 1Sa 22:8
I saw the son of J coming to Nob .......... 1Sa 22:9
against me, thou and the son of J .......... 1Sa 22:13
and who is the son of J .............. 1Sa 25:10
we inheritance in the son of J .............. 2Sa 20:1
David the son of J said, and the .......... 2Sa 23:1
we inheritance in the son of J .............. 1Kin 12:16
Boaz begat Obed, and Obed begat J .... 1Chr 2:12
J begat his firstborn Eliab, and .......... 1Chr 2:13
kingdom unto David the son of J ...... 1Chr 10:14
and on thy side, thou son of J .......... 1Chr 12:18
Thus David the son of J reigned .......... 1Chr 29:26
none inheritance in the son of J .......... 2Chr 10:16
daughter of Eliab the son of J .......... 2Chr 11:18
of David the son of J are ended .......... Ps 72:20
forth a rod out of the stem of J .......... Is 11:1
day there shall be a root of J .............. Is 11:10
and Obed begat J .............. Mt 1:5
And J begat David the king .............. Mt 1:6
Which was the son of J, which was ........ Lk 3:32
I have found David the son of J .......... Acts 13:22
saith, There shall be a root of J .......... Rom 15:12

**JESSHIAH** See JESIAH.

**JESTING**
nor foolish talking, nor *j* .............. Eph 5:4

**JESUI** (*jes'-u-i*) See ISHUI, JESUITES. *A descendant of Asher.*
of J, the family of the Jesuites .......... Num 26:44

**JESUITES** (*jes'-u-ites*) *Descendants of Jesui.*
of Jesui, the family of the J .............. Num 26:44

**JESURUN** (*jes'-u-run*) See JESHURUN. *Same as Jeshurun.*
and thou, J, whom I have chosen .......... Is 44:2

**JESUS** (*je'-zus*) See PREFACE. SEE ALSO BAR-JESUS, CHRIST, JESUS', JUSTUS.
*1. The Christ.*
of the generation of J Christ .............. Mt 1:1
and thou shalt call his name J .............. Mt 1:21
and he called his name J .............. Mt 1:25
Then saith J unto him, Get thee .......... Mt 4:10
But J said unto him, Follow me .......... Mt 8:22
What have we to do with thee, J .......... Mt 8:29
But J said unto them, A prophet .......... Mt 13:57
J to shew unto his disciples .............. Mt 16:21
And J rebuked the devil .............. Mt 17:18
J called a little child unto him, .......... Mt 18:2
But J said, Suffer little .............. Mt 19:14
J said unto him, If thou wilt be .......... Mt 19:21
This is J the prophet of Nazareth .......... Mt 21:11
J took bread, and blessed it, and .......... Mt 26:26
was also with J of Nazareth .............. Mt 26:71
J stood before the governor .............. Mt 27:11
J said unto him, Thou sayest .............. Mt 27:11
with J which is called Christ .............. Mt 27:22
THIS IS J THE KING OF THE JEWS .. Mt 27:37
for I know that ye seek J .............. Mt 28:5
J met them, saying, All hail .............. Mt 28:9
J came and spake unto them, saying .... Mt 28:18
What have I to do with thee, J .............. Mk 5:7
But J said unto them, A prophet .......... Mk 6:4
And J said, I am .............. Mk 14:62
thou also wast with J of Nazareth ....... Mk 14:67
a son, and shalt call his name J .......... Lk 1:31
do with thee, thou J of Nazareth .......... Lk 4:34
What have I to do with thee, J .............. Lk 8:28
And J, perceiving the thought of .......... Lk 9:47
Then said J unto him, Go, and do .......... Lk 10:37
J said unto him, Receive thy .............. Lk 18:42
Then said J, Father, forgive them .......... Lk 23:34
And he said unto J, Lord, remember .... Lk 23:42
grace and truth came by J Christ .......... Jn 1:17
J saith unto them, My meat is to .......... Jn 4:34
Then said J unto him, Except ye .......... Jn 4:48
J answered and said unto them, .......... Jn 6:29
J said unto them, I am the bread .......... Jn 6:35
J answered, Ye neither know me, .......... Jn 8:19
J said unto her, I am the .............. Jn 11:25
J wept .............. Jn 11:35
him, saying, Sir, we would see J .......... Jn 12:21
J cried and said, He that .............. Jn 12:44
J knowing that the Father had .............. Jn 13:3
J said, Now is the Son of man .............. Jn 13:31
J saith unto him, I am the way, .......... Jn 14:6
J answered, I have told you that .......... Jn 18:8
J answered, My kingdom is not of .......... Jn 18:36
J answered, Thou sayest that I am ........ Jn 18:37
But J gave him no answer .............. Jn 19:9
saw J standing, and knew not that .......... Jn 20:14
and knew not that it was J .............. Jn 20:14
believe that J is the Christ .............. Jn 20:31
this same J, which is taken up .......... Acts 1:11
This J hath God raised up, .............. Acts 2:32
God, having raised up his Son J .......... Acts 3:26
I believe that J Christ is the .............. Acts 8:37
the scriptures that J was Christ .......... Acts 18:28
I am J of Nazareth, whom thou .......... Acts 22:8
confess with thy mouth the Lord J .......... Rom 10:9
the body the dying of the Lord J .......... 2Cor 4:10
that the life also of J might be .......... 2Cor 4:10
by him, as the truth is in J .............. Eph 4:21
That at the name of J every knee .......... Phil 2:10
confess that J Christ is Lord .............. Phil 2:11
do all in the name of the Lord J .......... Col 3:17
For if we believe that J died .............. 1Th 4:14
that Christ J came into the world .......... 1Ti 1:15
confess that J is the Son of God .......... 1Jn 4:15
Whosoever believeth that J is the .......... 1Jn 5:1
who confess not that J Christ is .......... 2Jn 7
Even so, come, Lord J .............. Rev 22:20
*2. Joshua, son of Nun.*
For if J had given them rest, .............. Heb 4:8
*3. Justus, a Roman Christian.*
And J, which is called Justus, who .......... Col 4:11

**JESUS'** (*je'-zus*) *Refers to the Christ.*
and cast them down at J feet .............. Mt 15:30
who also himself was J disciple .......... Mt 27:57
saw it, he fell down at J knees .......... Lk 5:8
and he fell down at J feet .............. Lk 8:41
Mary, which also sat at J feet .............. Lk 10:39
and they came not for J sake only .......... Jn 12:9
Now there was leaning on J bosom .......... Jn 13:23
He then lying on J breast saith .......... Jn 13:25
your servants for J sake .............. 2Cor 4:5
delivered unto death for J sake .......... 2Cor 4:11

**JETHER** (*je'-thur*) See HOBAB, ITHRA, ITHRITES, JETHRO, RAGUEL.
*1. A son of Gideon.*

he said unto J his firstborn, Up, Judg 8:20
*2. Father of Amasa.*
Ner, and unto Amasa the son of J 1Kin 2:5
of Israel, and Amasa the son of J 1Kin 2:32
of Amasa was J the Ishmeelite 1Chr 2:17
*3. A son of Jerahmeel.*
J, and Jonathan 1Chr 2:32
and J died without children 1Chr 2:32
*4. A son of Ezra.*
And the sons of Ezra were, J 1Chr 4:17
*5. A descendant of Asher.*
And the sons of J 1Chr 7:38

**JETHETH** (*je'-theth*) *A prince of Edom.*
duke Timnah, duke Alvah, duke J Gen 36:40
duke Timnah, duke Aliah, duke J 1Chr 1:51

**JETHLAH** (*jeth'-lah*) *A city in Dan.*
And Shaalabbin, and Ajalon, and J Josh 19:42

**JETHRO** (*je'-thro*) See JETHER. *Father-in-law of Moses.*
the flock of J his father in law Ex 3:1
returned to J his father in law, Ex 4:18
J said to Moses, Go in peace Ex 4:18
When J, the priest of Midian, Ex 18:1
Then J, Moses' father in law, Ex 18:2
And J, Moses' father in law, came Ex 18:5
father in law J am come unto thee Ex 18:6
J rejoiced for all the goodness Ex 18:9
J said, Blessed be the LORD, who Ex 18:10
And J, Moses' father in law, took Ex 18:12

**JETUR** (*je'-tur*)
*1. A son of Ishmael.*
Hadar, and Tema, J, Naphish, and Gen 25:15
J, Naphish, and Kedemah 1Chr 1:31
*2. Descendants of Jetur.*
war with the Hagarites, with J 1Chr 5:19

**JEUEL** (*je-u'-el*) See JEIEL. *A descendant of Zerah.*
J, and their brethren, six hundred 1Chr 9:6

**JEUSH** (*je'-ush*) See JEHUSH.
*1. A son of Esau.*
And Aholibamah bare J, and Jaalam, Gen 36:5
and she bare to Esau J, and Jaalam, Gen 36:14
duke J, duke Jaalam, duke Korah Gen 36:18
Eliphaz, Reuel, and J, and Jaalam, 1Chr 1:35
*2. Grandson of Jediael.*
J, and Benjamin, and Ehud, and 1Chr 7:10
*3. A sanctuary servant.*
Shimei were, Jahath, Zina, and J 1Chr 23:10
but J and Beriah had not many sons 1Chr 23:11
*4. A son of Rehoboam.*
J, and Shamariah, and Zaham 2Chr 11:19

**JEUZ** (*je'-uz*) *Son of Shaharaim.*
And J, and Shachia, and Mirma 1Chr 8:10

**JEW** (*jew*) See JEWESS, JEWISH, JEWS. *Post-exilic term for the Israelites.*
the palace there was a certain J Est 2:5
he had told them that he was a J Est 3:4
the J sitting at the king's gate Est 5:13
and do even so to Mordecai the J Est 6:10
the queen and to Mordecai the J Est 8:7
of Abihail, and Mordecai the J Est 9:29
according as Mordecai the J Est 9:31
For Mordecai the J was next unto Est 10:3
them, to wit, of a J his brother Jer 34:9
of the skirt of him that is a J Zec 8:23
How is it that thou, being a J Jn 4:9
Pilate answered, Am I a J Jn 18:35
a man that is a J to keep company Acts 10:28
sorcerer, a false prophet, a J Acts 13:6
And found a certain J named Aquila Acts 18:2
a certain J named Apollos, born Acts 18:24
were seven sons of one Sceva, a J Acts 19:14
when they knew that he was a J Acts 19:34
I am a man which am a J of Tarsus Acts 21:39
I am verily a man which am a J Acts 22:3
to the J first, and also to the Rom 1:16
that doeth evil, of the J first Rom 2:9
that worketh good, to the J first Rom 2:10
Behold, thou art called a J Rom 2:17
For he is not a J, which is one Rom 2:28
But he is a J, which is one Rom 2:29
What advantage then hath the J Rom 3:1
is no difference between the J Rom 10:12
And unto the Jews I became as a J 1Cor 9:20
them all, If thou, being a J Gal 2:14
There is neither J nor Greek Gal 3:28
there is neither Greek nor J Col 3:11

**JEWEL**
As a *j* of gold in a swine's snout Prov 11:22
of knowledge are a precious *j* Prov 20:15
I put a *j* on thy forehead, and Eze 16:12

**JEWELS**
servant brought forth *j* of silver Gen 24:53
*j* of gold, and raiment, and gave Gen 24:53
*j* of silver, and *j* of gold, Ex 3:22
*j* of silver, and *j* of gold Ex 11:2
of the Egyptians *j* of silver Ex 12:35
and *j* of gold, and raiment Ex 12:35
rings, and tablets, all *j* of gold Ex 35:22
gotten, of *j* of gold, chains, and Num 31:50
gold of them, even all wrought *j* Num 31:51
and put the *j* of gold, which ye 1Sa 6:8
wherein the *j* of gold were, and 1Sa 6:15
the dead bodies, and precious *j* 2Chr 20:25
and for all manner of pleasant *j* 2Chr 32:27
shall not be for *j* of fine gold Job 28:17
cheeks are comely with rows of *j* Song 1:10
joints of thy thighs are like *j* Song 7:1
The rings, and nose *j*, Is 3:21
bride adorneth herself with her *j* Is 61:10
also taken thy fair *j* of my gold Eze 16:17
clothes, and shall take thy fair *j* Eze 16:39
clothes, and take away thy fair *j* Eze 23:26
with her earrings and her *j* Hos 2:13
in that day when I make up my *j* Mal 3:17

**JEWESS** (*jew'-ess*) *A female Jew.*
of a certain woman, which was a J Acts 16:1
his wife Drusilla, which was a J Acts 24:24

**JEWISH** (*jew'-ish*) *Of or relating to the Jews.*
Not giving heed to J fables Titus 1:14

**JEWRY** (*jew'-ree*) See JUDEA. *Of or relating to the Jews.*
king my father brought out of J Dan 5:13
people, teaching throughout all J Lk 23:5
for he would not walk in J Jn 7:1

**JEWS** (*jews*) See JEWS'.
Syria, and drave the J from Elath 2Kin 16:6
Gedaliah, that he died, and the J 2Kin 25:25
that the J which came up from Ezr 4:12
in haste to Jerusalem unto the J Ezr 4:23
unto the J that were in Judah Ezr 5:1
God was upon the elders of the J Ezr 5:5
let the governor of the J Ezr 6:7
the elders of the J build this Ezr 6:7
J for the building of this house Ezr 6:8
And the elders of the J builded Ezr 6:14
concerning the J that had escaped Neh 1:2
had I as yet told it to the J Neh 2:16
indignation, and mocked the J Neh 4:1
and said, What do these feeble J Neh 4:2
that when the J which dwelt by Neh 4:12
against their brethren the J Neh 5:1
have redeemed our brethren the J Neh 5:8
an hundred and fifty of the J Neh 5:17
that thou and the J think to rebel Neh 6:6
In those days also saw I J that Neh 13:23
J that were throughout the whole Est 3:6
and to cause to perish, all J Est 3:13
was great mourning among the J Est 4:3
the king's treasuries for the J Est 4:7
king's house, more than all the J Est 4:13
arise to the J from another place Est 4:14
gather together all the J that Est 4:16
Mordecai be of the seed of the J Est 6:13
that he had devised against the J Est 8:3
the J which are in all the king's Est 8:5
he laid his hand upon the J Est 8:7
Write ye also for the J, as it Est 8:8
Mordecai commanded unto the J Est 8:9
to the J according to their Est 8:9
the J which were in every city to Est 8:11
that the J should be ready Est 8:13
The J had light, and gladness, and Est 8:16
the J had joy and gladness, a Est 8:17
the people of the land became J Est 8:17
the fear of the J fell upon them Est 8:17
J hoped to have power over them Est 9:1
that the J had rule over them Est 9:1
The J gathered themselves Est 9:2
of the king, helped the J Est 9:3
Thus the J smote all their Est 9:5
in Shushan the palace the J slew Est 9:6
of Hammedatha, the enemy of the J Est 9:10
The J have slain and destroyed Est 9:12
let it be granted to the J which Est 9:13
For the J that were in Shushan Est 9:15
But the other J that were in the Est 9:16
But the J that were at Shushan Est 9:18
Therefore the J of the villages, Est 9:19
sent letters unto all the J that Est 9:20
As the days wherein the J rested Est 9:22
the J undertook to do as they had Est 9:23
Agagite, the enemy of all the J Est 9:24
against the J to destroy them Est 9:24
which he devised against the J Est 9:25
The J ordained, and took upon them Est 9:27
should not fail from among the J Est 9:28
sent the letters unto all the J Est 9:30
Ahasuerus, and great among the J Est 10:3
before all the J that sat in the Jer 32:12
I am afraid of the J that are Jer 38:19
when all the J that were in Moab Jer 40:11
Even all the J returned out of Jer 40:12
that all the J which are gathered Jer 40:15
slew all the J that were with him Jer 41:3
the J which dwell in the land of Jer 44:1
the seventh year three thousand J Jer 52:28
of the J seven hundred forty Jer 52:30
came near, and accused the J Dan 3:8
There are certain J whom thou Dan 3:12
is he that is born King of the J Mt 2:2
Art thou the King of the J Mt 27:11
him, saying, Hail, King of the J Mt 27:29
THIS IS JESUS THE KING OF THE J. Mt 27:37
among the J until this day Mt 28:15
For the Pharisees, and all the J Mk 7:3
him, Art thou the King of the J Mk 15:2
unto you the King of the J Mk 15:9
whom ye call the King of the J Mk 15:12
salute him, Hail, King of the J Mk 15:18
written over, THE KING OF THE J Mk 15:26
sent unto him the elders of the J Lk 7:3
Art thou the King of the J Lk 23:3
If thou be the king of the J Lk 23:37
THE KING OF THE J Lk 23:38
of Arimathaea, a city of the J Lk 23:51
when the J sent priests and Jn 1:19
manner of the purifying of the J Jn 2:6
Then answered the J and said unto Jn 2:18
Then said the J, Forty and six Jn 2:20
named Nicodemus, a ruler of the J Jn 3:1
and the J about purifying Jn 3:25
for the J have no dealings with Jn 4:9
for salvation is of the J Jn 4:22
this there was a feast of the J Jn 5:1
The J therefore said unto him Jn 5:10
told the J that it was Jesus, Jn 5:15
did the J persecute Jesus Jn 5:16
Therefore the J sought the more Jn 5:18
And the passover, a feast of the J Jn 6:4
The J then murmured at him, Jn 6:41
The J therefore strove among Jn 6:52
because the J sought to kill him Jn 7:1
Then the J sought him at the Jn 7:11
openly of him for fear of the J Jn 7:13
the J marvelled, saying, How Jn 7:15
Then said the J among themselves, Jn 7:35
Then said the J, Will he kill Jn 8:22
to those J which believed on him Jn 8:31
Then answered the J, and said unto Jn 8:48
Then said the J unto him, Now we Jn 8:52
Then said the J unto him, Thou Jn 8:57
But the J did not believe Jn 9:18
because they feared the J Jn 9:22
for the J had agreed already, Jn 9:22
among the J for these sayings Jn 10:19
Then came the J round about him, Jn 10:24
Then the J took up stones again Jn 10:31
The J answered him, saying, For a Jn 10:33
the J of late sought to stone Jn 11:8
many of the J came to Martha and Jn 11:19
The J then which were with her in Jn 11:31
the J also weeping which came Jn 11:33
Then said the J, Behold how he Jn 11:36
Then many of the J which came to Jn 11:45
walked no more openly among the J Jn 11:54
Much people of the J therefore Jn 12:9
of him many of the J went away Jn 12:11
and as I said unto the J, Whither Jn 13:33
and officers of the J took Jesus Jn 18:12
he, which gave counsel to the J Jn 18:14
whither the J always resort Jn 18:20
The J therefore said unto him, It Jn 18:31
him, Art thou the King of the J Jn 18:33
should not be delivered to the J Jn 18:36
he went out again unto the J Jn 18:38
unto you the King of the J Jn 18:39
And said, Hail, King of the J Jn 19:3
The J answered him, We have a law Jn 19:7
but the J cried out, saying, If Jn 19:12
and he saith unto the J, Behold Jn 19:14
OF NAZARETH THE KING OF THE J Jn 19:19
title then read many of the J Jn 19:20
chief priests of the J to Pilate Jn 19:21
Write not, The King of the J Jn 19:21
that he said, I am King of the J Jn 19:21
The J therefore, because it was Jn 19:31
but secretly for fear of the J Jn 19:38
as the manner of the J is to bury Jn 19:40
were assembled for fear of the J Jn 20:19
were dwelling at Jerusalem J Acts 2:5
Cyrene, and strangers of Rome, J Acts 2:10
confounded the J which dwelt at Acts 9:22
the J took counsel to kill him Acts 9:23
among all the nation of the J Acts 10:22
he did both in the land of the J Acts 10:39
word to none but unto the J only Acts 11:19
because he saw it pleased the J Acts 12:3
of the people of the J Acts 12:11
of God in the synagogues of the J Acts 13:5
when the J were gone out of the Acts 13:42
was broken up, many of the J Acts 13:43
But when the J saw the multitudes Acts 13:45
But the J stirred up the devout Acts 13:50
into the synagogue of the J Acts 14:1
a great multitude both of the J Acts 14:1
But the unbelieving J stirred up Acts 14:2
and part held with the J, and part Acts 14:4
also of the J with their rulers, Acts 14:5
thither certain J from Antioch Acts 14:19
J which were in those quarters Acts 16:3
saying, These men, being J Acts 16:20
where was a synagogue of the J Acts 17:1
But the J which believed not, Acts 17:5
went into the synagogue of the J Acts 17:10
But when the J of Thessalonica Acts 17:13
he in the synagogue with the J Acts 17:17
all J to depart from Rome Acts 18:2
every sabbath, and persuaded the J Acts 18:4
testified to the J that Jesus was Acts 18:5
the J made insurrection with one Acts 18:12
his mouth, Gallio said unto the J Acts 18:14
wrong or wicked lewdness, O ye J Acts 18:14
synagogue, and reasoned with the J Acts 18:19
For he mightily convinced the J Acts 18:28
word of the Lord Jesus, both J Acts 19:10
Then certain of the vagabond J Acts 19:13
And this was known to all the J Acts 19:17
the J putting him forward Acts 19:33
when the J laid wait for him, as Acts 20:3
me by the lying in wait of the J Acts 20:19
Testifying both to the J, and also Acts 20:21
So shall the J at Jerusalem bind Acts 21:11

how many thousands of *J* there are... Acts 21:20
that thou teachest all the *J*... Acts 21:21
the *J* which were of Asia, when... Acts 21:27
of all the *J* which dwelt there... Acts 22:12
wherefore he was accused of the *J*... Acts 22:30
certain of the *J* banded together,... Acts 23:12
The *J* have agreed to desire thee... Acts 23:20
This man was taken of the *J*... Acts 23:27
that the *J* laid wait for the man... Acts 23:30
all the *J* throughout the world... Acts 24:5
the *J* also assented, saying that... Acts 24:9
Whereupon certain *J* from Asia... Acts 24:18
willing to shew the *J* a pleasure... Acts 24:27
the chief of the *J* informed him... Acts 25:2
the *J* which came down from... Acts 25:7
Neither against the law of the *J*... Acts 25:8
willing to do the *J* a pleasure... Acts 25:9
to the *J* have I done no wrong, as... Acts 25:10
the elders of the *J* informed me... Acts 25:15
of the *J* have dealt with me... Acts 25:24
whereof I am accused of the *J*... Acts 26:2
questions which are among the *J*... Acts 26:3
at Jerusalem, know all the *J*... Acts 26:4
Agrippa, I am accused of the *J*... Acts 26:7
For these causes the *J* caught me... Acts 26:21
the chief of the *J* together... Acts 28:17
But when the *J* spake against it,... Acts 28:19
the *J* departed, and had great... Acts 28:29
for we have before proved both *J*... Rom 3:9
Is he the God of the *J* only... Rom 3:29
he hath called, not of the *J* only... Rom 9:24
For the *J* require a sign, and the... 1Cor 1:22
unto the *J* a stumblingblock, and... 1Cor 1:23
them which are called, both *J*... 1Cor 1:24
unto the *J* I became as a Jew,... 1Cor 9:20
as a Jew, that I might gain the *J*... 1Cor 9:20
none offence, neither to the *J*... 1Cor 10:32
body, whether we be *J* or Gentiles... 1Cor 12:13
Of the *J* five times received I... 2Cor 11:24
the other *J* dissembled likewise... Gal 2:13
of Gentiles, and not as do the *J*... Gal 2:14
the Gentiles to live as do the *J*... Gal 2:14
We who are *J* by nature, and not... Gal 2:15
even as they have of the *J*... 1Th 2:14
of them which say they are *J*... Rev 2:9
of Satan, which say they are *J*... Rev 3:9

**JEWS'** (*jews*)
talk not with us in the *J*... 2Kin 18:26
a loud voice in the *J* language... 2Kin 18:28
the *J* speech unto the people of... 2Chr 32:18
could not speak in the *J* language... Neh 13:24
the Agagite, the *J* enemy... Est 3:10
the *J* enemy unto Esther the queen... Est 8:1
speak not to us in the *J* language... Is 36:11
a loud voice in the *J* language... Is 36:13
the *J* passover was at hand, and... Jn 2:13
Now the *J* feast of tabernacles... Jn 7:2
the *J* passover was nigh at hand... Jn 11:55
because of the *J* preparation day... Jn 19:42
in time past in the *J* religion... Gal 1:13
profited in the *J* religion above... Gal 1:14

**JEZANIAH** (*jez-a-ni'-ah*) See JAAZANIAH. *A Jewish captain.*
*J* the son of a Maachathite, they... Jer 40:8
*J* the son of Hoshaiah, and all the... Jer 42:1

**JEZEBEL** (*jez'-e-bel*) See JEZEBEL'S. *Wife of King Ahab.*
that he took to wife *J* the... 1Kin 16:31
when *J* cut off the prophets of... 1Kin 18:4
told my lord what I did when *J*... 1Kin 18:13
Ahab told *J* all that Elijah had... 1Kin 19:1
Then *J* sent a messenger unto... 1Kin 19:2
But *J* his wife came to him, and... 1Kin 21:5
*J* his wife said unto him, Dost... 1Kin 21:7
did as *J* had sent unto them, and... 1Kin 21:11
Then they sent to *J*, saying,... 1Kin 21:14
when *J* heard that Naboth was... 1Kin 21:15
that *J* said to Ahab, Arise, take... 1Kin 21:15
of *J* also spake the LORD, saying,... 1Kin 21:23
The dogs shall eat *J* by the wall... 1Kin 21:23
whom *J* his wife stirred up... 1Kin 21:25
of the LORD, at the hand of *J*... 2Kin 9:7
the dogs shall eat *J* in the... 2Kin 9:10
as the whoredoms of thy mother *J*... 2Kin 9:22
come to Jezreel, *J* heard of it... 2Kin 9:30
shall dogs eat the flesh of *J*... 2Kin 9:36
the carcase of *J* shall be as dung... 2Kin 9:37
they shall not say, This is *J*... 2Kin 9:37
thou sufferest that woman *J*... Rev 2:20

**JEZEBEL'S** (*jez'-e-bels*)
hundred, which eat at *J* table... 1Kin 18:19

**JEZER** (*je'-zur*) See JEZERITES. *A son of Naphtali.*
Jahzeel, and Guni, and *J*, and... Gen 46:24
Of *J*, the family of the Jezerites... Num 26:49
Jahziel, and Guni, and *J*, and... 1Chr 7:13

**JEZERITES** (*je'-zur-ites*) *Descendants of Jezer.*
Of Jezer, the family of the *J*... Num 26:49

**JEZIAH** (*je-zi'-ah*) *Married a foreigner in exile.*
Ramiah, and *J*, and Malchiah, and... Ezr 10:25

**JEZIEL** (*je'-ze-el*) *A warrior in David's army.*
and *J*, and Pelet, the sons of... 1Chr 12:3

**JEZLIAH** (*jez-li'-ah*) *A son of Elpaal.*
Ishmerai also, and *J*, and Jobab,... 1Chr 8:18

**JEZOAR** (*je-zo'-ar*) See ZOAR. *A son of Helah.*
sons of Helah were, Zereth, and *J*... 1Chr 4:7

**JEZRAHIAH** (*jez-ra-hi'-ah*) See IZRAHIAH. *A priest.*
sang loud, with *J* their overseer... Neh 12:42

**JEZREEL** (*jez'-re-el*) See JEZREELITE.
*1. A city in Judah.*
And *J*, and Jokdeam, and Zanoah,... Josh 15:56
and pitched in the valley of *J*... Judg 6:33
David also took Ahinoam of *J*... 1Sa 25:43
by a fountain which is in *J*... 1Sa 29:1
And the Philistines went up to *J*... 1Sa 29:11
*2. A city in Issachar.*
And their border was toward *J*... Josh 19:18
and over the Ashurites, and over *J*... 2Sa 2:9
came of Saul and Jonathan out of *J*... 2Sa 4:4
which is by Zartanah beneath *J*... 1Kin 4:12
And Ahab rode, and went to *J*... 1Kin 18:45
before Ahab to the entrance of *J*... 1Kin 18:46
had a vineyard, which was in *J*... 1Kin 21:1
eat Jezebel by the wall of *J*... 1Kin 21:23
*J* of the wounds which the Syrians... 2Kin 8:29
to see Joram the son of Ahab in *J*... 2Kin 8:29
eat Jezebel in the portion of *J*... 2Kin 9:10
was returned to be healed in *J* of... 2Kin 9:15
of the city to go to tell it in *J*... 2Kin 9:15
rode in a chariot, and went to *J*... 2Kin 9:16
a watchman on the tower in *J*... 2Kin 9:17
And when Jehu was come to *J*... 2Kin 9:30
In the portion of *J* shall dogs... 2Kin 9:36
of the field in the portion of *J*... 2Kin 9:37
to Samaria, unto the rulers of *J*... 2Kin 10:1
come to me to *J* by to morrow this... 2Kin 10:6
in baskets, and sent him them to *J*... 2Kin 10:7
of the house of Ahab in *J*... 2Kin 10:11
in *J* because of the wounds which... 2Chr 22:6
see Jehoram the son of Ahab at *J*... 2Chr 22:6
*3. A plain.*
they who are of the valley of *J*... Josh 17:16
bow of Israel in the valley of *J*... Hos 1:5
and they shall hear *J*... Hos 2:22
*4. A descendant of Etam.*
*J*, and Ishma, and Idbash... 1Chr 4:3
*5. Symbolic name for Hosea's eldest son.*
said unto him, Call his name *J*... Hos 1:4
*6. Symbolic name for Hosea's eldest son.*
blood of *J* upon the house of Jehu... Hos 1:4
for great shall be the day of *J*... Hos 1:11

**JEZREELITE** (*jez'-re-el-ite*) See JEZREELITESS. *An inhabitant of Jezreel.*
that Naboth the *J* had a vineyard... 1Kin 21:1
Naboth the *J* had spoken to him... 1Kin 21:4
Because I spake unto Naboth the *J*... 1Kin 21:6
thee the vineyard of Naboth the *J*... 1Kin 21:7
of the vineyard of Naboth the *J*... 1Kin 21:15
to the vineyard of Naboth the *J*... 1Kin 21:16
in the portion of Naboth the *J*... 2Kin 9:21
of the field of Naboth the *J*... 2Kin 9:25

**JEZREELITESS** (*jez'-re-el-i-tess*) *A female Jezreelite.*
with his two wives, Ahinoam the *J*... 1Sa 27:3
taken captives, Ahinoam the *J*... 1Sa 30:5
his two wives also, Ahinoam the *J*... 2Sa 2:2
was Amnon, of Ahinoam the *J*... 2Sa 3:2
firstborn Amnon, of Ahinoam the *J*... 1Chr 3:1

**JIBSAM** (*jib'-sam*) *A son of Tola.*
and Jeriel, and Jahmai, and *J*... 1Chr 7:2

**JIDLAPH** (*jid'-laf*) *A son of Nahor.*
Chesed, and Hazo, and Pildash, and *J* Gen 22:22

**JIMNA** (*jim'-nah*) See IMNA, JIMNAH, JIMNITES. *A son of Asher.*
of *J*, the family of the Jimnites... Num 26:44

**JIMNAH** (*jim'-nah*) See JIMNA. *Same as Jimna.*
*J*, and Ishuah, and Isui, and Beriah,... Gen 46:17

**JIMNITES** (*jim'-nites*) *Descendants of Jimna.*
of Jimna, the family of the *J*... Num 26:44

**JIPHTAH** (*jif'-tah*) See JEPHTHAH, JIPHTHAH-EL. *A city in Judah.*
And *J*, and Ashnah, and Nezib,... Josh 15:43

**JIPHTHAH-EL** (*jif'-thah-el*) *A valley in Zebulun.*
thereof are in the valley of *J*... Josh 19:14
to the valley of *J* toward the... Josh 19:27

**JOAB** (*jo'-ab*) See ATAROTH, HOUSE, JOAB'S.
*1. Commander of David's army.*
the son of Zeruiah, brother to *J*... 1Sa 26:6
*J* the son of Zeruiah, and the... 2Sa 2:13
And Abner said to *J*, Let the young... 2Sa 2:14
And *J* said, Let them arise... 2Sa 2:14
three sons of Zeruiah there, *J*... 2Sa 2:18
hold up my face to *J* thy brother... 2Sa 2:22
*J* also and Abishai pursued after... 2Sa 2:24
Then Abner called to *J*, and said,... 2Sa 2:26
*J* said, As God liveth, unless... 2Sa 2:27
So *J* blew a trumpet, and all the... 2Sa 2:28
*J* returned from following Abner... 2Sa 2:30
And *J* and his men went all night,... 2Sa 2:32
*J* came from pursuing a troop, and... 2Sa 3:22
When *J* and all the host that was... 2Sa 3:23
with him were come, they told *J*... 2Sa 3:23
Then *J* came to the king, and said,... 2Sa 3:24
when *J* was come out from David,... 2Sa 3:26
*J* took him aside in the gate to... 2Sa 3:27
Let it rest on the head of *J*... 2Sa 3:29
house of *J* one that hath an issue... 2Sa 3:29
So *J* and Abishai his brother slew... 2Sa 3:30
And David said to *J*, and to all the... 2Sa 3:31
*J* the son of Zeruiah was over the... 2Sa 8:16
when David heard of it, he sent *J*... 2Sa 10:7
When *J* saw that the front of the... 2Sa 10:9
*J* drew nigh, and the people that... 2Sa 10:13
So *J* returned from the children... 2Sa 10:14
to battle, that David sent *J*... 2Sa 11:1
And David sent to *J*, saying, Send... 2Sa 11:6
And *J* sent Uriah to David... 2Sa 11:6
David demanded of him how *J* did... 2Sa 11:7
and my lord *J*, and the servants of... 2Sa 11:11
that David wrote a letter to *J*... 2Sa 11:14
when *J* observed the city, that he... 2Sa 11:16
city went out, and fought with *J*... 2Sa 11:17
Then *J* sent and told David all the... 2Sa 11:18
David all that *J* had sent him for... 2Sa 11:22
Thus shalt thou say unto *J*... 2Sa 11:25
*J* fought against Rabbah of the... 2Sa 12:26
*J* sent messengers to David, and... 2Sa 12:27
Now *J* the son of Zeruiah... 2Sa 14:1
*J* sent to Tekoah, and fetched... 2Sa 14:2
So *J* put the words in her mouth... 2Sa 14:3
Is not the hand of *J* with thee in... 2Sa 14:19
for thy servant *J*, he bade me, and... 2Sa 14:19
thy servant *J* done this thing... 2Sa 14:20
And the king said unto *J*, Behold... 2Sa 14:21
*J* fell to the ground on his face,... 2Sa 14:22
*J* said, Today thy servant knoweth... 2Sa 14:22
So *J* arose and went to Geshur, and... 2Sa 14:23
Therefore Absalom sent for *J*... 2Sa 14:29
Then *J* arose, and came to Absalom... 2Sa 14:31
And Absalom answered *J*, Behold, I... 2Sa 14:32
So *J* came to the king, and told... 2Sa 14:33
captain of the host instead of *J*... 2Sa 17:25
of the people under the hand of *J*... 2Sa 18:2
And the king commanded *J* and... 2Sa 18:5
a certain man saw it, and told *J*... 2Sa 18:10
*J* said unto the man that told him... 2Sa 18:11
And the man said unto *J*, Though I... 2Sa 18:12
Then said *J*, I may not tarry thus... 2Sa 18:14
*J* blew the trumpet, and the people... 2Sa 18:16
for *J* held back the people... 2Sa 18:16
*J* said unto him, Thou shalt not... 2Sa 18:20
Then said *J* to Cushi, Go tell the... 2Sa 18:21
And Cushi bowed himself unto *J*... 2Sa 18:21
the son of Zadok yet again to *J*... 2Sa 18:22
*J* said, Wherefore wilt thou run,... 2Sa 18:22
When *J* sent the king's servant,... 2Sa 18:29
And it was told *J*, Behold, the... 2Sa 19:1
*J* came into the house to the king... 2Sa 19:5
me continually in the room of *J*... 2Sa 19:13
*J* said to Amasa, Art thou in... 2Sa 20:9
*J* took Amasa, by the beard with... 2Sa 20:9
So *J* and Abishai his brother... 2Sa 20:10
him, and said, He that favoureth *J*... 2Sa 20:11
is for David, let him go after *J*... 2Sa 20:11
all the people went on after *J*... 2Sa 20:13
were with *J* battered the wall... 2Sa 20:15
say, I pray you, unto *J*, Come... 2Sa 20:16
her, the woman said, Art thou *J*... 2Sa 20:17
*J* answered and said, Far be it,... 2Sa 20:20
And the woman said unto *J*, Behold,... 2Sa 20:21
of Bichri, and cast it out to *J*... 2Sa 20:22
*J* returned to Jerusalem unto the... 2Sa 20:22
Now *J* was over all the host of... 2Sa 20:23
And Abishai, the brother of *J*... 2Sa 23:18
of *J* was one of the thirty... 2Sa 23:24
armourbearer to *J* the son of... 2Sa 23:37
For the king said to *J* the... 2Sa 24:2
*J* said unto the king, Now the... 2Sa 24:3
king's word prevailed against *J*... 2Sa 24:4
And *J* and the captains of the host... 2Sa 24:4
*J* gave up the sum of the number... 2Sa 24:9
he conferred with *J* the son of... 1Kin 1:7
*J* the captain of the host... 1Kin 1:19
when *J* heard the sound of the... 1Kin 1:41
*J* the son of Zeruiah did to me... 1Kin 2:5
and for *J* the son of Zeruiah... 1Kin 2:22
Then tidings came to *J*... 1Kin 2:28
for *J* had turned after Adonijah,... 1Kin 2:28
*J* fled unto the tabernacle of the... 1Kin 2:28
it was told king Solomon that *J*... 1Kin 2:29
word again, saying, Thus said *J*... 1Kin 2:30
the innocent blood, which *J* shed... 1Kin 2:31
return upon the head of *J*... 1Kin 2:33
*J* the captain of the host was... 1Kin 11:15
(For six months did *J* remain... 1Kin 11:16
that *J* the captain of the host... 1Kin 11:21
Abishai, and *J*, and Asahel, three... 1Chr 2:16
So *J* the son of Zeruiah went... 1Chr 11:6
*J* repaired the rest of the city... 1Chr 11:8
And Abishai the brother of *J*... 1Chr 11:20
were, Asahel the brother of *J*... 1Chr 11:26
of *J* the son of Zeruiah,... 1Chr 11:39
*J* the son of Zeruiah was over the... 1Chr 18:15
when David heard of it, he sent *J*... 1Chr 19:8
Now when *J* saw that the battle... 1Chr 19:10

So J and the people that were with... 1Chr 19:14
Then J came to Jerusalem 1Chr 19:15
J led forth the power of the army 1Chr 20:1
J smote Rabbah, and destroyed it 1Chr 20:1
And David said to J and to the 1Chr 21:2
J answered, The LORD make his 1Chr 21:3
king's word prevailed against J 1Chr 21:4
Wherefore J departed, and went 1Chr 21:4
J gave the sum of the number of 1Chr 21:5
king's word was abominable to J 1Chr 21:6
J the son of Zeruiah, had 1Chr 26:28
month was Asahel the brother of J 1Chr 27:7
J the son of Zeruiah began to 1Chr 27:24
general of the king's army was J 1Chr 27:34
when J returned, and smote of Edom Ps 60:*t*
*2. A descendant of Caleb.*
Ataroth, the house of J, and half 1Chr 2:54
*3. A grandson of Kenaz.*
and Seraiah begat J, the father of 1Chr 4:14
*4. A family of exiles with Zerubbabel.*
of the children of Jeshua and J Ezr 2:6
of the children of Jeshua and J Neh 7:11
*5. A family of exiles with Ezra.*
Of the sons of J Ezr 8:9

**JOAB'S** *(jo'-abs) Refers to Joab 1.*
J field is near mine, and he hath 2Sa 14:30
sister to Zeruiah J mother 2Sa 17:25
J brother, and a third part under 2Sa 18:2
bare J armour compassed about 2Sa 18:15
And there went out after him J men 2Sa 20:7
J garment that he had put on was 2Sa 20:8
to the sword that was in J hand 2Sa 20:10
one of J men stood by him, and 2Sa 20:11

**JOAH** *(jo'-ah)* See ETHAN.
*1. A son of Asaph.*
J the son of Asaph the recorder 2Kin 18:18
son of Hilkiah, and Shebna, and J 2Kin 18:26
J the son of Asaph the recorder, 2Kin 18:37
house, and Shebna the scribe, and J Is 36:3
J unto Rabshakeh, Speak, I pray Is 36:11
and Shebna the scribe, and J Is 36:22
*2. A descendant of Gershom.*
J his son, Iddo his son, Zerah 1Chr 6:21
J the son of Zimmah 2Chr 29:12
and Eden the son of J 2Chr 29:12
*3. A sanctuary servant.*
J the third, and Sacar the fourth, 1Chr 26:4
*4. A Levite.*
J the son of Joahaz the recorder, 2Chr 34:8

**JOAHAZ** *(jo'-a-haz)* See JEHOAHAZ. *Father of Joah.*
and Joah the son of J the recorder 2Chr 34:8

**JOANAN** See JOANNA.

**JOANNA** *(jo-an'-nah)*
*1. A female disciple.*
J the wife of Chuza Herod's Lk 8:3
It was Mary Magdalene, and J Lk 24:10
*2. An ancestor of Jesus.*
Which was the son of J, which was Lk 3:27

**JOASH** *(jo'-ash)* See JEHOASH.
*1. A son of Becher.*
Zemira, and J, and Eliezer, and 1Chr 7:8
*2. A sanctuary servant.*
and over the cellars of oil was J 1Chr 27:28
*3. Father of Gideon.*
pertained unto J the Abi-ezrite Judg 6:11
Gideon the son of J hath done Judg 6:29
the men of the city said unto J Judg 6:30
J said unto all that stood Judg 6:31
the sword of Gideon the son of J Judg 7:14
Gideon the son of J returned from Judg 8:13
And Jerubbaal the son of J went Judg 8:29
Gideon the son of J died in a Judg 8:32
in the sepulchre of J his father Judg 8:32
*4. A son of King Ahab.*
the city, and to J the king's son 1Kin 22:26
the city, and to J the king's son 2Chr 18:25
*5. A son of King Ahaziah.*
took J the son of Ahaziah, and 2Kin 11:2
And the rest of the acts of J 2Kin 12:19
slew J in the house of Millo, 2Kin 12:20
twentieth year of J the son of 2Kin 13:1
seventh year of J king of Judah 2Kin 13:10
the son of J king of Judah 2Kin 14:1
to all things as J his father did 2Kin 14:3
Amaziah the son of J king of 2Kin 14:17
year of Amaziah the son of J king 2Kin 14:23
son, Ahaziah his son, J his son, 1Chr 3:11
took J the son of Ahaziah, and 2Chr 22:11
J was seven years old when he 2Chr 24:1
J did that which was right in the 2Chr 24:2
that J was minded to repair the 2Chr 24:4
Thus J the king remembered not 2Chr 24:22
they executed judgment against J 2Chr 24:24
king of Judah, the son of J 2Chr 25:23
Amaziah the son of J king of 2Chr 25:25
*6. A king of Israel.*
J his son reigned in his stead 2Kin 13:9
And the rest of the acts of J 2Kin 13:12
And J slept with his fathers 2Kin 13:13
J was buried in Samaria with the 2Kin 13:13
J the king of Israel came down 2Kin 13:14
Three times did J beat him 2Kin 13:25
In the second year of J son of 2Kin 14:1
of Judah Jeroboam the son of J 2Kin 14:23
the hand of Jeroboam the son of J 2Kin 14:27
Judah took advice, and sent to J 2Chr 25:17
J king of Israel sent to Amaziah 2Chr 25:18
So J the king of Israel went up 2Chr 25:21
J the king of Israel took Amaziah 2Chr 25:23
J son of Jehoahaz king of Israel 2Chr 25:25
the days of Jeroboam the son of J Hos 1:1
the son of J king of Israel Amos 1:1
*7. A descendant of Shelah.*
and the men of Chozeba, and J 1Chr 4:22
*8. A captain in David's army.*
The chief was Ahiezer, then J 1Chr 12:3

**JOATHAM** *(jo'-a-tham)* See JOTHAM. *Ancestor of Joseph, husband of Mary.*
And Ozias begat J Mt 1:9
and J begat Achaz Mt 1:9

**JOAZCAR** See JOZACHAR.

**JOB** *(jobe)* See JASHUB, JOB'S.
*1. A descendant of Issachar.*
Tola, and Phuvah, and J Gen 46:13
*2. A righteous sufferer.*
the land of Uz, whose name was J Job 1:1
were gone about, that J sent Job 1:5
for J said, It may be that my Job 1:5
Thus did J continually Job 1:5
Hast thou considered my servant J Job 1:8
Doth J fear God for nought Job 1:9
And there came a messenger unto J Job 1:14
Then J arose, and rent his mantle, Job 1:20
In all this J sinned not, nor Job 1:22
Hast thou considered my servant J Job 2:3
smote J with sore boils from the Job 2:7
this did not J sin with his lips Job 2:10
After this opened J his mouth Job 3:1
And J spake, and said, Job 3:2
But J answered and said, Job 6:1
Then J answered and said, Job 9:1
And J answered and said, Job 12:1
Then J answered and said, Job 16:1
Then J answered and said, Job 19:1
But J answered and said, Job 21:1
Then J answered and said, Job 23:1
But J answered and said, Job 26:1
Moreover J continued his parable, Job 27:1
Moreover J continued his parable, Job 29:1
The words of J are ended Job 31:40
three men ceased to answer J Job 32:1
against J was his wrath kindled, Job 32:2
no answer, and yet had condemned J Job 32:3
had waited till J had spoken Job 32:4
was none of you that convinced J Job 32:12
Wherefore, J, I pray thee, hear Job 33:1
Mark well, O J, hearken unto me Job 33:31
For J hath said, I am righteous Job 34:5
What man is like J, who drinketh Job 34:7
J hath spoken without knowledge, Job 34:35
My desire is that J may be tried Job 34:36
Therefore doth J open his mouth Job 35:16
Hearken unto this, O J Job 37:14
answered J out of the whirlwind Job 38:1
Moreover the LORD answered J Job 40:1
Then J answered the LORD, and said Job 40:3
LORD unto J out of the whirlwind Job 40:6
Then J answered the LORD, and said Job 42:1
had spoken these words unto J Job 42:7
is right, as my servant J hath Job 42:7
seven rams, and go to my servant J Job 42:8
my servant J shall pray for you Job 42:8
which is right, like my servant J Job 42:8
the LORD also accepted J Job 42:9
LORD turned the captivity of J Job 42:10
also the LORD gave J twice as Job 42:10
end of J more than his beginning Job 42:12
so fair as the daughters of J Job 42:15
After this lived J an hundred Job 42:16
So J died, being old and full of Job 42:17
three men, Noah, Daniel, and J Eze 14:14
Though Noah, Daniel, and J Eze 14:20
have heard of the patience of J Jas 5:11

**JOBAB** *(jo'-bab)*
*1. A son of Joktan.*
And Ophir, and Havilah, and J Gen 10:29
And Ophir, and Havilah, and J 1Chr 1:23
*2. A king of Edom.*
J the son of Zerah of Bozrah Gen 36:33
J died, and Husham of the land of Gen 36:34
J the son of Zerah of Bozrah 1Chr 1:44
when J was dead, Husham of the 1Chr 1:45
*3. A Canaanite king.*
that he sent to J king of Madon Josh 11:1
*4. A son of Shaharaim.*
And he begat of Hodesh his wife, J 1Chr 8:9
*5. A son of Elpaal.*
Ishmerai also, and Jezliah, and J 1Chr 8:18

**JOB'S** *(jobes) Refers to Job 2.*
Now when J three friends heard of Job 2:11

**JOCHEBED** *(jok'-e-bed) Wife of Amram.*
Amram took him J his father's Ex 6:20
of Amram's wife was J Num 26:59

**JODA** See JUDA.

**JOED** *(jo'-ed) A son of Pedaiah.*
son of Meshullam, the son of J Neh 11:7

**JOEL** *(jo'-el)*
*1. A son of Samuel.*
the name of his firstborn was J 1Sa 8:2
Heman a singer, the son of J 1Chr 6:33
appointed Heman the son of J 1Chr 15:17
*2. A Simeonite.*
And J, and Jehu the son of Josibiah 1Chr 4:35
*3. Father of Shemaiah.*
The sons of J 1Chr 5:4
the son of Shema, the son of J 1Chr 5:8
*4. A chief Gadite.*
J the chief, and Shapham the next, 1Chr 5:12
*5. A Kohathite.*
The son of Elkanah, the son of J 1Chr 6:36
*6. A descendant of Tola.*
Michael, and Obadiah, and J 1Chr 7:3
*7. A 'mighty man' of David.*
J the brother of Nathan, Mibhar 1Chr 11:38
*8. A Gershomite.*
J the chief, and his brethren an 1Chr 15:7
Levites, for Uriel, Asaiah, and J 1Chr 15:11
chief was Jehiel, and Zetham, and J 1Chr 23:8
*9. A treasurer of the Temple.*
J his brother, which were over 1Chr 26:22
*10. A prince of Manasseh.*
of Manasseh, J the son of Pedaiah 1Chr 27:20
*11. A Kohathite who cleansed the Temple.*
J the son of Azariah, of the sons 2Chr 29:12
*12. Married a foreigner in exile.*
Zabad, Zebina, Jadau, and J Ezr 10:43
*13. An overseer of the Benjamites.*
J the son of Zichri was their Neh 11:9
*14. A prophet.*
that came to J the son of Pethuel Joel 1:1
which was spoken by the prophet J Acts 2:16

**JOELAH** *(jo-e'-lah) A member of David's band.*
And J, and Zebadiah, the sons of 1Chr 12:7

**JOEZER** *(jo-e'-zer) A warrior in David's army.*
and Jesiah, and Azareel, and J 1Chr 12:6

**JOGBEHAH** *(jog'-be-hah) A place in Gad.*
Atroth, Shophan, and Jaazer, and J Num 32:35
tents on the east of Nobah and J Judg 8:11

**JOGLI** *(jog'-li) A Danite prince.*
of Dan, Bukki the son of J Num 34:22

**JOHA** *(jo'-hah)*
*1. Son of Beriah.*
And Michael, and Ispah, and J 1Chr 8:16
*2. A 'mighty man' of David.*
J his brother, the Tizite, 1Chr 11:45

**JOHANAN** *(jo-ha'-nan)* See JEHOHANAN, JOHN.
*1. A son of Kareah.*
J the son of Careah, and Seraiah 2Kin 25:23
the son of Nethaniah, and J Jer 40:8
Moreover J the son of Kareah, and Jer 40:13
Then J the son of Kareah spake to Jer 40:15
said unto J the son of Kareah Jer 40:16
But when J the son of Kareah, and Jer 41:11
Ishmael saw J the son of Kareah Jer 41:13
went unto J the son of Kareah Jer 41:14
escaped from J with eight men Jer 41:15
Then took J the son of Kareah, and Jer 41:16
J the son of Kareah, and Jezaniah Jer 42:1
Then called he J the son of Jer 42:8
J the son of Kareah, and all the Jer 43:2
So J the son of Kareah, and all Jer 43:4
But J the son of Kareah, and all Jer 43:5
*2. A son of King Josiah.*
of Josiah were, the firstborn J 1Chr 3:15
*3. A son of Elioenai.*
and Pelaiah, and Akkub, and J 1Chr 3:24
*4. A grandson of Ahimaaz.*
begat Azariah, and Azariah begat J 1Chr 6:9
J begat Azariah, (he it is that 1Chr 6:10
*5. A warrior in David's army.*
and Jeremiah, and Jahaziel, and J 1Chr 12:4
*6. A Gadite warrioer in David's army.*
J the eighth, Elzabad the ninth, 1Chr 12:12
*7. An Ephraimite.*
of Ephraim, Azariah the son of J 2Chr 28:12
*8. An exile with Ezra.*
J the son of Hakkatan, and with Ezr 8:12
*9. A priest in exile with Ezra.*
chamber of J the son of Eliashib Ezr 10:6
*10. A son of Tobiah.*
his son J had taken the daughter Neh 6:18
*11. A priest in exile with Zerubbabel.*
days of Eliashib, Joiada, and J Neh 12:22
the days of J the son of Eliashib Neh 12:23

**JOHN** *(jon)* See BAPTIST, JEHOHANAN, JOHN'S, MARK.
*1. The Baptizer.*
In those days came J the Baptist Mt 3:1
the same J had his raiment of Mt 3:4
from Galilee to Jordan unto J Mt 3:13
But J forbad him, saying, I have Mt 3:14
heard that J was cast into prison Mt 4:12
came to him the disciples of J Mt 9:14
Now when J had heard in the Mt 11:2
shew J again those things which Mt 11:4
unto the multitudes concerning J Mt 11:7
a greater than J the Baptist Mt 11:11
from the days of J the Baptist Mt 11:12
and the law prophesied until J Mt 11:13
For J came neither eating nor Mt 11:18
servants, This is J the Baptist Mt 14:2
For Herod had laid hold on J Mt 14:3
For J said unto him, It is not Mt 14:4
Give me here J Baptist's head in Mt 14:8
sent, and beheaded J in the prison Mt 14:10
say that thou art J the Baptist Mt 16:14
spake unto them of J the Baptist Mt 17:13

J

The baptism of J, whence was it Mt 21:25
for all hold J as a prophet Mt 21:26
For J came unto you in the way of Mt 21:32
J did baptize in the wilderness, Mk 1:4
J was clothed with camel's hair, Mk 1:6
and was baptized of J in Jordan Mk 1:9
Now after that J was put in Mk 1:14
And the disciples of J and of the Mk 2:18
him, Why do the disciples of J Mk 2:18
That J the Baptist was risen from Mk 6:14
heard thereof, he said, It is J Mk 6:16
sent forth and laid hold upon J Mk 6:17
For J had said unto Herod, It is Mk 6:18
For Herod feared J, knowing that Mk 6:20
said, The head of J the Baptist Mk 6:24
charger the head of J the Baptist Mk 6:25
And they answered, J the Baptist Mk 8:28
The baptism of J, was it from Mk 11:30
for all men counted J, that he Mk 11:32
and thou shalt call his name J Lk 1:13
but he shall be called J Lk 1:60
and wrote, saying, His name is J Lk 1:63
the word of God came unto J the Lk 3:2
men mused in their hearts of J Lk 3:15
J answered, saying unto them all, Lk 3:16
all, that he shut up J in prison Lk 3:20
do the disciples of J fast often Lk 5:33
the disciples of J shewed him of Lk 7:18
J calling unto him two of his Lk 7:19
J Baptist hath sent us unto thee, Lk 7:20
tell J what things ye have seen Lk 7:22
the messengers of J were departed Lk 7:24
unto the people concerning J Lk 7:24
prophet than J the Baptist Lk 7:28
baptized with the baptism of J Lk 7:29
For J the Baptist came neither Lk 7:33
that J was risen from the dead Lk 9:7
And Herod said, J have I beheaded Lk 9:9
answering said, J the Baptist Lk 9:19
as J also taught his disciples Lk 11:1
law and the prophets were until J Lk 16:16
The baptism of J, was it from Lk 20:4
be persuaded that J was a prophet Lk 20:6
sent from God, whose name was J Jn 1:6
J bare witness of him, and cried, Jn 1:15
And this is the record of J Jn 1:19
J answered them, saying, I Jn 1:26
Jordan, where J was baptizing Jn 1:28
The next day J seeth Jesus coming Jn 1:29
J bare record, saying, I saw the Jn 1:32
Again the next day after J stood Jn 1:35
of the two which heard J speak Jn 1:40
J also was baptizing in Aenon Jn 3:23
For J was not yet cast into Jn 3:24
And they came unto J, and said unto Jn 3:26
J answered and said, A man can Jn 3:27
and baptized more disciples than J Jn 4:1
Ye sent unto J, and he bare Jn 5:33
greater witness than that of J Jn 5:36
place where J at first baptized Jn 10:40
him, and said, J did no miracle Jn 10:41
but all things that J spake of Jn 10:41
For J truly baptized with water Acts 1:5
Beginning from the baptism of J Acts 1:22
the baptism which J preached Acts 10:37
J indeed baptized with water Acts 11:16
When J had first preached before Acts 13:24
as J fulfilled his course, he Acts 13:25
knowing only the baptism of J Acts 18:25
J verily baptized with the Acts 19:4

*2. Son of Zebedee.*

J his brother, in a ship with Mt 4:21
son of Zebedee, and J his brother Mt 10:2
J his brother, and bringeth them Mt 17:1
J his brother, who also were in Mk 1:19
Simon and Andrew, with James and J Mk 1:29
and J the brother of James Mk 3:17
James, and J the brother of James Mk 5:37
with him Peter, and James, and J Mk 9:2
J answered him, saying, Master, Mk 9:38
And James and J, the sons of Mk 10:35
much displeased with James and J Mk 10:41
the temple, Peter and James and J Mk 13:3
with him Peter and James and J Mk 14:33
And so was also James, and J Lk 5:10
and Andrew his brother, James and J Lk 6:14
go in, save Peter, and James, and J Lk 8:51
these sayings, he took Peter and J Lk 9:28
J answered and said, Master, we Lk 9:49
J saw this, they said, Lord, wilt Lk 9:54
And he sent Peter and J, saying, Go Lk 22:8
abode both Peter, and James, and J Acts 1:13
J went up together into the Acts 3:1
J about to go into the temple Acts 3:3
his eyes upon him with J, said, Acts 3:4
which was healed held Peter and J Acts 3:11
saw the boldness of Peter and J Acts 4:13
J answered and said unto them, Acts 4:19
they sent unto them Peter and J Acts 8:14
the brother of J with the sword Acts 12:2
And when James, Cephas, and J Gal 2:9
by his angel unto his servant J Rev 1:1
J to the seven churches which are Rev 1:4
I J, who also am your brother, and Rev 1:9
I J saw the holy city, new Rev 21:2
I J saw these things, and heard Rev 22:8

*3. A relative of Annas the priest.*

high priest, and Caiaphas, and J Acts 4:6

*4. Surnamed Mark.*

the house of Mary the mother of J Acts 12:12
ministry, and took with them J Acts 12:25
they had also J to their minister Acts 13:5
J departing from them returned to Acts 13:13
determined to take with them J Acts 15:37

**JOHN'S** (*jonz*) *Refers to John 1.*

between some of J disciples Jn 3:25
And they said, Unto J baptism Acts 19:3

**JOIADA** (*joy'-a-dah*) See JEHOIADA. *A priest with Zerubbabel.*

Eliashib, and Eliashib begat J Neh 12:10
J begat Jonathan, and Jonathan Neh 12:11
in the days of Eliashib, J Neh 12:22
And one of the sons of J, the son Neh 13:28

**JOIAKIM** (*joy'-a-kim*) See JEHOIAKIM. *Another priest with Zerubbabel.*

And Jeshua begat J Neh 12:10
J also begat Eliashib Neh 12:10
And in the days of J were priests Neh 12:12
the days of J the son of Jeshua Neh 12:26

**JOIARIB** (*joy'-a-rib*) See JEHOIARIB.

*1. A messenger for Ezra.*

also for J, and for Elnathan, men Ezr 8:16

*2. A descendant of Perez.*

the son of Adaiah, the son of J Neh 11:5

*3. Father of Jedaiah.*

Jedaiah the son of J, Jachin Neh 11:10
Shemaiah, and J, Jedaiah, Neh 12:6
And of J, Mattenai Neh 12:19

**JOIN**

they *j* also unto our enemies, and Ex 1:10
*j* himself with Ahaziah king of 2Chr 20:35
*j* in affinity with the people of Ezr 9:14
Though hand *j* in hand, the wicked Prov 11:21
though hand *j* in hand, he shall Prov 16:5
unto them that *j* house to house Is 5:8
him, and *j* his enemies together Is 9:11
that *j* themselves to the LORD, to Is 56:6
let us *j* ourselves to the LORD in Jer 50:5
*j* them one to another into one Eze 37:17
they shall *j* themselves together Dan 11:6
durst no man *j* himself to them Acts 5:13
*j* thyself to this chariot Acts 8:29
he assayed to *j* himself to the Acts 9:26

**JOINED**

All these were *j* together in the Gen 14:3
they *j* battle with them in the Gen 14:8
time will my husband be *j* unto me Gen 29:34
*j* at the two edges thereof Ex 28:7
and so it shall be *j* together Ex 28:7
that they may be *j* unto thee Num 18:2
And they shall be *j* unto thee Num 18:4
Israel *j* himself unto Baal-peor Num 25:3
men that were *j* unto Baal-peor Num 25:5
and when they *j* battle, Israel was 1Sa 4:2
of the wheels were *j* to the base 1Kin 7:32
the seventh day the battle was *j* 1Kin 20:29
and *j* affinity with Ahab 2Chr 18:1
he *j* himself with him to make 2Chr 20:36
Because thou hast *j* thyself with 2Chr 20:37
thereof, and *j* the foundations Ezr 4:12
all the wall was *j* together unto Neh 4:6
upon all such as *j* themselves Est 9:27
let it not be *j* unto the days of Job 3:6
They are *j* one to another, they Job 41:17
of his flesh are *j* together Job 41:23
Assur also is *j* with them Ps 83:8
They *j* themselves also unto Ps 106:28
For to him that is *j* to all the Eccl 9:4
every one that is *j* unto them Is 13:15
strangers shall be *j* with them Is 14:1
Thou shalt not be *j* with them in Is 14:20
that hath *j* himself to the LORD, Is 56:3
Their wings were *j* one to another Eze 1:9
every one were *j* one to another Eze 1:11
courts *j* of forty cubits long Eze 46:22
Ephraim is *j* to idols Hos 4:17
many nations shall be *j* to the Zec 2:11
therefore God hath *j* together Mt 19:6
therefore God hath *j* together Mk 10:9
*j* himself to a citizen of that Lk 15:15
about four hundred, *j* themselves Acts 5:36
whose house *j* hard to the Acts 18:7
but that ye be perfectly *j* 1Cor 1:10
is *j* to an harlot is one body 1Cor 6:16
But he that is *j* unto the Lord is 1Cor 6:17
the whole body fitly *j* together Eph 4:16
shall be *j* unto his wife, and they Eph 5:31

**JOINING**

*j* to the wing of the other cherub 2Chr 3:12

**JOININGS**

doors of the gates, and for the *j* 1Chr 22:3

**JOINT**

of Jacob's thigh was out of *j* Gen 32:25
and all my bones are out of *j* Ps 22:14
broken tooth, and a foot out of *j* Prov 25:19
by that which every *j* supplieth Eph 4:16

**JOINT-HEIRS**

heirs of God, and *j* with Christ Rom 8:17

**JOINTS**

between the *j* of the harness 1Kin 22:34
between the *j* of the harness 2Chr 18:33
the *j* of thy thighs are like Song 7:1
so that the *j* of his loins were Dan 5:6
from which all the body by *j* Col 2:19
of soul and spirit, and of the *j* Heb 4:12

**JOKDEAM** (*jok'-de-am*) *A city in Judah.*

And Jezreel, and J, and Zanoah, Josh 15:56

**JOKIM** (*jo'-kim*) *A descendant of Shelah.*

And J, and the men of Chozeba, and 1Chr 4:22

**JOKMEAM** (*jok'-me-am*) See JOKNEAM. *A Levitical city in Ephraim.*

J with her suburbs, and Beth-horon 1Chr 6:68

**JOKNEAM** (*jok'-ne-am*) See JOKMEAM, KIBZAIM.

*1. A Levitical city in Zebulun.*

the king of J of Carmel, one Josh 12:22
to the river that is before J Josh 19:11
J with her suburbs, and Kartah Josh 21:34

*2. A Levitical city in Ephraim.*

unto the place that is beyond J 1Kin 4:12

**JOKSHAN** (*jok'-shan*) *A son of Abraham.*

And she bare him Zimran, and J Gen 25:2
And J begat Sheba, and Dedan Gen 25:3
she bare Zimran, and J, and Medan, 1Chr 1:32
And the sons of J 1Chr 1:32

**JOKTAN** (*jok'-tan*) *A son of Eber.*

and his brother's name was J Gen 10:25
J begat Almodad, and Sheleph, and Gen 10:26
all these were the sons of J Gen 10:29
and his brother's name was J 1Chr 1:19
J begat Almodad, and Sheleph, and 1Chr 1:20
All these were the sons of J 1Chr 1:23

**JOKTHEEL** (*jok'-the-el*) See SELAH.

*1. A city in Judah.*

And Dilean, and Mizpeh, and J Josh 15:38

*2. Another name for Petra in Edom.*

the name of it J unto this day 2Kin 14:7

**JONA** (*jo'-nah*) See BAR-JONA, JONAH, JONAS. *Greek form of Jonah.*

said, Thou art Simon the son of J Jn 1:42

**JONADAB** (*jon'-a-dab*) See JEHONADAB.

*1. A son of Shimeah.*

had a friend, whose name was J 2Sa 13:3
and J was a very subtil man 2Sa 13:3
J said unto him, Lay thee down on 2Sa 13:5
And J, the son of Shimeah David's 2Sa 13:32
J said unto the king, Behold, the 2Sa 13:35

*2. A son of Rechab.*

for J the son of Rechab our Jer 35:6
have we obeyed the voice of J the Jer 35:8
that J our father commanded us Jer 35:10
The words of J the son of Rechab, Jer 35:14
Because the sons of J the son of Jer 35:16
the commandment of J your father Jer 35:18
J the son of Rechab shall not Jer 35:19

**JONAH** (*jo'-nah*) See JONA, JONAS. *A prophet.*

by the hand of his servant J 2Kin 14:25
came unto J the son of Amittai Jonah 1:1
But J rose up to flee unto Jonah 1:3
But J was gone down into the Jonah 1:5
cast lots, and the lot fell upon J Jonah 1:7
So they took up J, and cast him Jonah 1:15
a great fish to swallow up J Jonah 1:17
J was in the belly of the fish Jonah 1:17
Then J prayed unto the LORD his Jonah 2:1
it vomited out J upon the dry Jonah 2:10
LORD came unto J the second time Jonah 3:1
So J arose, and went unto Nineveh, Jonah 3:3
J began to enter into the city a Jonah 3:4
But it displeased J exceedingly Jonah 4:1
So J went out of the city, and sat Jonah 4:5
and made it to come up over J Jonah 4:6
So J was exceeding glad of the Jonah 4:6
the sun beat upon the head of J Jonah 4:8
And God said to J, Doest thou well Jonah 4:9

**JONAM** See JONAN.

**JONAN** (*jo'-nan*) *Ancestor of Joseph, husband of Mary.*

of Joseph, which was the son of J Lk 3:30

**JONAS** (*jo'-nas*) See JONA, JONAH.

*1. Same as Jonah.*

it, but the sign of the prophet J Mt 12:39
For as J was three days and three Mt 12:40
repented at the preaching of J Mt 12:41
behold, a greater than J is here Mt 12:41
it, but the sign of the prophet J Mt 16:4
it, but the sign of J the prophet Lk 11:29
For as J was a sign unto the Lk 11:30
repented at the preaching of J Lk 11:32
behold, a greater than J is here Lk 11:32

*2. Father of Peter.*

to Simon Peter, Simon, son of J Jn 21:15
the second time, Simon, son of J Jn 21:16
the third time, Simon, son of J Jn 21:17

**JONATHAN** (*jon'-a-than*) See JEHONATHAN, JONATHAN'S.

*1. A Levite.*

and J, the son of Gershom, the son Judg 18:30

*2. Son of Saul.*

a thousand were with J in Gibeah 1Sa 13:2
J smote the garrison of the 1Sa 13:3
J his son, and the people that 1Sa 13:16
people that were with Saul and J 1Sa 13:22
with J his son was there found 1Sa 13:22
that J the son of Saul said unto 1Sa 14:1
people knew not that J was gone 1Sa 14:3
by which J sought to go over unto 1Sa 14:4

J said to the young man that bare ... 1Sa 14:6
Then said J, Behold, we will pass ... 1Sa 14:8
men of the garrison answered J... 1Sa 14:12
J said unto his armourbearer,... 1Sa 14:12
J climbed up upon his hands and ... 1Sa 14:13
and they fell before J... 1Sa 14:13
And that first slaughter, which J... 1Sa 14:14
when they had numbered, behold, J.... 1Sa 14:17
that were with Saul and J... 1Sa 14:21
But J heard not when his father... 1Sa 14:27
Then said J, My father hath ... 1Sa 14:29
Israel, though it be in J my son ... 1Sa 14:39
J my son will be on the other... 1Sa 14:40
And Saul and J were taken... 1Sa 14:41
Cast lots between me and J my son .... 1Sa 14:42
And J was taken... 1Sa 14:42
Then Saul said to J, Tell me what... 1Sa 14:43
J told him, and said, I did but ... 1Sa 14:43
for thou shalt surely die, J ... 1Sa 14:44
said unto Saul, Shall J die... 1Sa 14:45
So the people rescued J, that he... 1Sa 14:45
Now the sons of Saul were J... 1Sa 14:49
that the soul of J was knit with... 1Sa 18:1
J loved him as his own soul... 1Sa 18:1
Then J and David made a covenant, ..... 1Sa 18:3
J stripped himself of the robe... 1Sa 18:4
And Saul spake to J his son... 1Sa 19:1
But J Saul's son delighted much... 1Sa 19:2
J told David, saying, Saul my... 1Sa 19:2
J spake good of David unto Saul... 1Sa 19:4
hearkened unto the voice of J... 1Sa 19:6
J called David, and Jonathan... 1Sa 19:7
J shewed him all those things... 1Sa 19:7
J brought David to Saul, and he... 1Sa 19:7
Ramah, and came and said before J ... 1Sa 20:1
Let not J know this, lest he be... 1Sa 20:3
Then said J unto David,... 1Sa 20:4
And David said unto J, Behold, to... 1Sa 20:5
J said, Far be it from thee... 1Sa 20:9
Then said David to J, Who shall... 1Sa 20:10
J said unto David, Come, and let... 1Sa 20:11
J said unto David, O LORD God of... 1Sa 20:12
The LORD do so and much more to J.. 1Sa 20:13
So J made a covenant with the ... 1Sa 20:16
J caused David to swear again,... 1Sa 20:17
Then J said to David, To morrow... 1Sa 20:18
J arose, and Abner sat by Saul's... 1Sa 20:25
and Saul said unto J his son... 1Sa 20:27
J answered Saul, David earnestly... 1Sa 20:28
anger was kindled against J... 1Sa 20:30
J answered Saul his father, and... 1Sa 20:32
whereby J knew that it was ... 1Sa 20:33
So J arose from the table in... 1Sa 20:34
that J went out into the field at ... 1Sa 20:35
of the arrow which J had shot... 1Sa 20:37
J cried after the lad, and said,... 1Sa 20:37
J cried after the lad, Make speed... 1Sa 20:38
only J and David knew the matter ... 1Sa 20:39
J gave his artillery unto his lad... 1Sa 20:40
J said to David, Go in peace,... 1Sa 20:42
and J went into the city... 1Sa 20:42
J Saul's son arose, and went to... 1Sa 23:16
the wood, and J went to his house... 1Sa 23:18
and the Philistines slew J ... 1Sa 31:2
Saul and J his son are dead also... 2Sa 1:4
that Saul and J his son be dead... 2Sa 1:5
for J his son, and for the people... 2Sa 1:12
over Saul and over J his son... 2Sa 1:17
the bow of J turned not back, and... 2Sa 1:22
J were lovely and pleasant in... 2Sa 1:23
O J, thou wast slain in thine... 2Sa 1:25
distressed for thee, my brother J... 2Sa 1:26
And J, Saul's son, had a son that ... 2Sa 4:4
J out of Jezreel, and his nurse... 2Sa 4:4
J hath yet a son, which is lame ... 2Sa 9:3
when Mephibosheth, the son of J... 2Sa 9:6
kindness for J thy father's sake ... 2Sa 9:7
the son of J the son of Saul,... 2Sa 21:7
David and J the son of Saul,... 2Sa 21:7
the bones of J his son from the ... 2Sa 21:12
of Saul and the bones of J his son ... 2Sa 21:13
J his son buried they in the ... 2Sa 21:14
Kish begat Saul, and Saul begat J ... 1Chr 8:33
the son of J was Merib-baal ... 1Chr 8:34
and Saul begat J, and Malchi-shua,... 1Chr 9:39
the son of J was Merib-baal ... 1Chr 9:40
and the Philistines slew J... 1Chr 10:2
*3. A son of Abiathar.*
thy son, and J the son of Abiathar... 2Sa 15:27
Zadok's son, and J Abiathar's son... 2Sa 15:36
Now J and Ahimaaz stayed by... 2Sa 17:17
they said, Where is Ahimaaz and J... 2Sa 17:20
J the son of Abiathar the priest... 1Kin 1:42
J answered and said to Adonijah, ... 1Kin 1:43
*4. A son of Shimea.*
J the son of Shimeah the brother... 2Sa 21:21
J the son of Shimea David's... 1Chr 20:7
*5. A 'mighty man' of David.*
of the sons of Jashen, J... 2Sa 23:32
J the son of Shage the Hararite,... 1Chr 11:34
*6. A son of Jada.*
Shammai; Jether, and J ... 1Chr 2:32
And the sons of J... 1Chr 2:33
*7. An uncle of David.*
Also J David's uncle was a ... 1Chr 27:32
*8. A family of exiles.*
Ebed the son of J, and with him... Ezr 8:6
*9. Son of Asahel.*
Only J the son of Asahel and... Ezr 10:15
*10. A descendant of Jeshua.*
And Joiada begat J... Neh 12:11
and J begat Jaddua ... Neh 12:11
*11. A priest descended from Melicu.*
Of Melicu, J... Neh 12:14
*12. A priest descended from Shemaiah.*
namely, Zechariah the son of J... Neh 12:35
*13. A scribe.*
in the house of J the scribe... Jer 37:15
to the house of J the scribe ... Jer 37:20
*14. A son of Kareah.*
J the sons of Kareah, and Seraiah... Jer 40:8

**JONATHAN'S** (*jon'-a-thans*) *Refers to Jonathan 2.*
J lad gathered up the arrows, and... 1Sa 20:38
may shew him kindness for J sake ... 2Sa 9:1
not cause me to return to J house ... Jer 38:26

**JONATH-ELEM-RECHOKIM** (*jo''-nath-e''-lem-re-ko'-kim*) *A musical notation.*
To the chief Musician upon J... Ps 56:t

**JOPPA** (*jop'-pah*) *A seaport in Dan.*
it to thee in flotes by sea to J ... 2Chr 2:16
from Lebanon to the sea of J... Ezr 3:7
of the LORD, and went down to J... Jonah 1:3
Now there was at J a certain... Acts 9:36
forasmuch as Lydda was nigh to J... Acts 9:38
And it was known throughout all J ... Acts 9:42
days in J with one Simon a tanner... Acts 9:43
And now send men to J, and call for... Acts 10:5
unto them, he sent them to J ... Acts 10:8
brethren from J accompanied him... Acts 10:23
Send therefore to J, and call... Acts 10:32
I was in the city of J praying ... Acts 11:5
and said unto him, Send men to J... Acts 11:13

**JORAH** (*jo'-rah*) See HARIPH. *A family of exiles.*
The children of J, an hundred and ... Ezr 2:18

**JORAI** (*jo'-rahee*) *Head of a Gadite family.*
and Meshullam, and Sheba, and J... 1Chr 5:13

**JORAM** (*jo'-ram*) See JEHORAM.
*1. A son of Toi.*
Then Toi sent J his son unto king... 2Sa 8:10
J brought with him vessels of ... 2Sa 8:10
*2. Same as Jehoram.*
So J went over to Zair, and all ... 2Kin 8:21
And the rest of the acts of J... 2Kin 8:23
J slept with his fathers, and was ... 2Kin 8:24
Jehosheba, the daughter of king J ... 2Kin 11:2
J his son, Ahaziah his son, Joash ... 1Chr 3:11
and Josaphat begat J ... Mt 1:8
and J begat Ozias... Mt 1:8
*3. A son of Ahab.*
in the fifth year of J the son of... 2Kin 8:16
In the twelfth year of J the son... 2Kin 8:25
he went with J the son of Ahab to ... 2Kin 8:28
and the Syrians wounded J... 2Kin 8:28
king J went back to be healed in ... 2Kin 8:29
see J the son of Ahab in Jezreel ... 2Kin 8:29
son of Nimshi conspired against J... 2Kin 9:14
(Now J had kept Ramoth-gilead, he ... 2Kin 9:14
But king J was returned to be... 2Kin 9:15
for J lay there... 2Kin 9:16
of Judah was come down to see J... 2Kin 9:16
J said, Take an horseman, and send ... 2Kin 9:17
And J said, Make ready ... 2Kin 9:21
J king of Israel and Ahaziah king ... 2Kin 9:21
when J saw Jehu, that he said, Is ... 2Kin 9:22
J turned his hands, and fled, and... 2Kin 9:23
in the eleventh year of J the son... 2Kin 9:29
and the Syrians smote J... 2Chr 22:5
Ahaziah was of God by coming to J ... 2Chr 22:7
*4. A descendant of Eliezer.*
J his son, and Zichri his son, and... 1Chr 26:25

**JORDAN** (*jor'-dan*) *A river that runs from the Sea of Galilee to the Dead Sea.*
and beheld all the plain of J... Gen 13:10
Lot chose him all the plain of J ... Gen 13:11
my staff I passed over this J... Gen 32:10
of Atad, which is beyond J... Gen 50:10
Abel-mizraim, which is beyond J... Gen 50:11
by the sea, and by the coast of J ... Num 13:29
of Moab on this side J by Jericho ... Num 22:1
plains of Moab by J near Jericho ... Num 26:3
plains of Moab by J near Jericho ... Num 26:63
Moab, which are by J near Jericho.... Num 31:12
and bring us not over J... Num 32:5
with them on yonder side J... Num 32:19
to us on this side J eastward... Num 32:19
you armed over J before the LORD .... Num 32:21
Reuben will pass with you over J... Num 32:29
on this side J may be ours... Num 32:32
plains of Moab by J near Jericho ... Num 33:48
And they pitched by J, from ... Num 33:49
Moses in the plains of Moab by J ... Num 33:50
over J into the land of Canaan... Num 33:51
And the border shall go down to J.... Num 34:12
this side J near Jericho eastward ... Num 34:15
plains of Moab by J near Jericho ... Num 35:1
When ye be come over J into the... Num 35:10
give three cities on this side J... Num 35:14
plains of Moab by J near Jericho ... Num 36:13
on this side J in the wilderness... Deut 1:1
On this side J, in the land of... Deut 1:5
until I shall pass over J into... Deut 2:29
the land that was on this side J ... Deut 3:8
The plain also, and J, and the... Deut 3:17
your God hath given them beyond J.. Deut 3:20
the good land that is beyond J ... Deut 3:25
for thou shalt not go over this J ... Deut 3:27
sware that I should not go over J... Deut 4:21
this land, I must not go over J... Deut 4:22
ye go over J to possess it ... Deut 4:26
this side J toward the sunrising... Deut 4:41
On this side J, in the valley ... Deut 4:46
this side J toward the sunrising... Deut 4:47
the plain on this side J eastward... Deut 4:49
Thou art to pass over J this day ... Deut 9:1
Are they not on the other side J ... Deut 11:30
For ye shall pass over J to go in ... Deut 11:31
But when ye go over J, and dwell... Deut 12:10
J unto the land which the LORD... Deut 27:2
shall be when ye be gone over J ... Deut 27:4
people, when ye are come over J... Deut 27:12
over J to go to possess it... Deut 30:18
me, Thou shalt not go over this J... Deut 31:2
ye go over J to possess it... Deut 31:13
ye go over J to possess it ... Deut 32:47
therefore arise, go over this J ... Josh 1:2
days ye shall pass over this J... Josh 1:11
Moses gave you on this side J... Josh 1:14
this side J toward the sunrising ... Josh 1:15
them the way to J unto the fords... Josh 2:7
that were on the other side J... Josh 2:10
from Shittim, and came to J... Josh 3:1
to the brink of the water of J... Josh 3:8
J, ye shall stand still in J... Josh 3:8
passeth over before you into J ... Josh 3:11
shall rest in the waters of J... Josh 3:13
that the waters of J shall be cut ... Josh 3:13
from their tents, to pass over J ... Josh 3:14
bare the ark were come unto J... Josh 3:15
(for J overfloweth all his banks... Josh 3:15
on dry ground in the midst of J... Josh 3:17
people were passed clean over J... Josh 3:17
people were clean passed over J ... Josh 4:1
you hence out of the midst of J... Josh 4:3
LORD your God into the midst of J... Josh 4:5
That the waters of J were cut off... Josh 4:7
when it passed over J ... Josh 4:7
the waters of J were cut off... Josh 4:7
stones out of the midst of J ... Josh 4:8
twelve stones in the midst of J... Josh 4:9
the ark stood in the midst of J... Josh 4:10
that they come up out of J... Josh 4:16
saying, Come ye up out of J ... Josh 4:17
come up out of the midst of J ... Josh 4:18
that the waters of J returned... Josh 4:18
the people came up out of J on... Josh 4:19
stones, which they took out of J ... Josh 4:20
came over this J on dry land ... Josh 4:22
the waters of J from before you... Josh 4:23
were on the side of J westward... Josh 5:1
of J from before the children of... Josh 5:1
at all brought this people over J ... Josh 7:7
and dwelt on the other side J ... Josh 7:7
kings which were on this side J... Josh 9:1
the Amorites, that were beyond J ... Josh 9:10
J toward the rising of the sun ... Josh 12:1
smote on this side J on the west... Josh 12:7
beyond J eastward, even as Moses ... Josh 13:8
of the children of Reuben was J ... Josh 13:23
of Sihon king of Heshbon, J... Josh 13:27
on the other side J eastward... Josh 13:27
of Moab, on the other side J... Josh 13:32
an half tribe on the other side J... Josh 14:3
salt sea, even unto the end of J ... Josh 15:5
sea at the uttermost part of J... Josh 15:5
of Joseph fell from J by Jericho ... Josh 16:1
came to Jericho, and went out at J..... Josh 16:7
which were on the other side J... Josh 17:5
inheritance beyond J on the east... Josh 18:7
on the north side was from J... Josh 18:12
salt sea at the south end of J... Josh 18:19
J was the border of it on the ... Josh 18:20
of their border were at J... Josh 19:22
the outgoings thereof were at J... Josh 19:33
to Judah upon J toward the... Josh 19:34
on the other side J by Jericho ... Josh 20:8
LORD gave you on the other side J... Josh 22:4
brethren on this side J westward... Josh 22:7
they came unto the borders of J... Josh 22:10
built there an altar by J ... Josh 22:10
of Canaan, in the borders of J... Josh 22:11
hath made J a border between us... Josh 22:25
for your tribes, from J, with all... Josh 23:4
which dwelt on the other side J... Josh 24:8
And ye went over J, and came unto.. Josh 24:11
took the fords of J toward Moab... Judg 3:28
Gilead abode beyond J... Judg 5:17
the waters unto Beth-barah and J ... Judg 7:24
the waters unto Beth-barah and J ... Judg 7:24
to Gideon on the other side J... Judg 7:25
And Gideon came to J, and passed... Judg 8:4
J in the land of the Amorites ... Judg 10:8
J to fight also against Judah... Judg 10:9
Arnon even unto Jabbok, and unto J Judg 11:13
from the wilderness even unto J ... Judg 11:22
of J before the Ephraimites... Judg 12:5
and slew him at the passages of J... Judg 12:6
went over J to the land of Gad... 1Sa 13:7
that were on the other side J ... 1Sa 31:7
the plain, and passed over J ... 2Sa 2:29
Israel together, and passed over J... 2Sa 10:17
with him, and they passed over J... 2Sa 17:22
of them that was not gone over J... 2Sa 17:22
And Absalom passed over J, he and.... 2Sa 17:24
the king returned, and came to J ... 2Sa 19:15
king, to conduct the king over J ... 2Sa 19:15

J

they went over J before the king ......... 2Sa 19:17
the king, as he was come over J.......... 2Sa 19:18
went over J with the king.......... 2Sa 19:31
to conduct him over J.......... 2Sa 19:31
a little way over J with the king .......... 2Sa 19:36
And all the people went over J.......... 2Sa 19:39
all David's men with him, over J.......... 2Sa 19:41
king, from J even to Jerusalem.......... 2Sa 20:2
And they passed over J, and pitched..... 2Sa 24:5
but he came down to meet me at J ....... 1Kin 2:8
In the plain of J did the king .......... 1Kin 7:46
brook Cherith, that is before J.......... 1Kin 17:3
brook Cherith, that is before J.......... 1Kin 17:5
for the LORD hath sent me to J.......... 2Kin 2:6
and they two stood by J.......... 2Kin 2:7
back, and stood by the bank of J.......... 2Kin 2:13
wash in J seven times, and thy.......... 2Kin 5:10
dipped himself seven times in J.......... 2Kin 5:14
Let us go, we pray thee, unto J.......... 2Kin 6:2
And when they came to J, they cut ...... 2Kin 6:4
And they went after them unto J.......... 2Kin 7:15
From J eastward, all the land of.......... 2Kin 10:33
And on the other side J by Jericho...... 1Chr 6:78
on the east side of J.......... 1Chr 6:78
went over J in the first month.......... 1Chr 12:15
And on the other side of J.......... 1Chr 12:37
all Israel, and passed over J.......... 1Chr 19:17
them of Israel on this side J.......... 1Chr 26:30
In the plain of J did the king .......... 2Chr 4:17
he can draw up J into his mouth.......... Job 40:23
remember thee from the land of J.......... Ps 42:6
J was driven back.......... Ps 114:3
thou J, that thou wast driven.......... Ps 114:5
by the way of the sea, beyond J.......... Is 9:1
wilt thou do in the swelling of J.......... Jer 12:5
a lion from the swelling of J.......... Jer 49:19
of J unto the habitation of the.......... Jer 50:44
and from the land of Israel by J.......... Eze 47:18
for the pride of J is spoiled.......... Zec 11:3
and all the region round about J.......... Mt 3:5
And were baptized of him in J.......... Mt 3:6
Jesus from Galilee to J unto John.......... Mt 3:13
by the way of the sea, beyond J.......... Mt 4:15
and from Judaea, and from beyond J..... Mt 4:25
the coasts of Judaea beyond J.......... Mt 19:1
baptized of him in the river of J.......... Mk 1:5
and was baptized of John in J.......... Mk 1:9
and from Idumaea, and from beyond J... Mk 3:8
Judaea by the farther side of J.......... Mk 10:1
came into all the country about J.......... Lk 3:3
of the Holy Ghost returned from J.......... Lk 4:1
were done in Bethabara beyond J.......... Jn 1:28
he that was with thee beyond J.......... Jn 3:26
went away again beyond J into the....... Jn 10:40

**JORIM** (*jo'-rim*) *Son of Matthat; ancestor of Jesus.*
Eliezer, which was the son of J.......... Lk 3:29

**JORKEAM** See JORKOAM.

**JORKOAM** (*jor'-ko-am*) *A descendant of Hebron.*
begat Raham, the father of J.......... 1Chr 2:44

**JOSABAD** (*jos'-a-bad*) See JOZABAD. *A warrior in David's army.*
and Johanan, and J the Gederathite,... 1Chr 12:4

**JOSAPHAT** (*jos'-a-fat*) See JEHOSHAPHAT. *Son of Asa; ancestor of Jesus.*
And Asa begat J.......... Mt 1:8
and J begat Joram.......... Mt 1:8

**JOSE** (*jo'-ze*) See JOSES. *Son of Eliezer; ancestor of Jesus.*
Which was the son of J, which was....... Lk 3:29

**JOSECH** See JOSEPH.

**JOSEDECH** (*jos'-e-dek*) See JOZADAK. *Father of Joshua, the priest.*
Judah, and to Joshua the son of J.......... Hag 1:1
Shealtiel, and Joshua the son of J.......... Hag 1:12
the spirit of Joshua the son of J.......... Hag 1:14
Judah, and to Joshua the son of J.......... Hag 2:2
and be strong, O Joshua, son of J.......... Hag 2:4
the head of Joshua the son of J.......... Zec 6:11

**JOSEPH** (*jo'-zef*) See BARSABAS, JOSEPH'S.
*1. Son of Jacob and Rachel.*
And she called his name J.......... Gen 30:24
to pass, when Rachel had born J.......... Gen 30:25
after, and Rachel and J hindermost....... Gen 33:2
and after came J near and Rachel,....... Gen 33:7
sons of Rachel; J, and Benjamin.......... Gen 35:24
J, being seventeen years old, was.......... Gen 37:2
J brought unto his father their.......... Gen 37:2
Now Israel loved J more than all.......... Gen 37:3
J dreamed a dream, and he told it.......... Gen 37:5
And Israel said unto J, Do not thy...... Gen 37:13
J went after his brethren, and.......... Gen 37:17
when J was come unto his brethren... Gen 37:23
they stript J out of his coat.......... Gen 37:23
lifted up J out of the pit, and.......... Gen 37:28
sold J to the Ishmeelites for.......... Gen 37:28
and they brought J into Egypt.......... Gen 37:28
and, behold, J was not in the pit.......... Gen 37:29
J is without doubt rent in pieces.......... Gen 37:33
J was brought down to Egypt.......... Gen 39:1
And the LORD was with J, and he was. Gen 39:2
J found grace in his sight, and he.......... Gen 39:4
J was a goodly person, and well.......... Gen 39:6
wife cast her eyes upon J.......... Gen 39:7
as she spake to J day by day.......... Gen 39:10
that J went into the house to do.......... Gen 39:11
But the LORD was with J, and.......... Gen 39:21
the place where J was bound.......... Gen 40:3
of the guard charged J with them.......... Gen 40:4
J came in unto them in the.......... Gen 40:6
And J said unto them, Do not.......... Gen 40:8
chief butler told his dream to J.......... Gen 40:9
J said unto him, This is the.......... Gen 40:12
was good, he said unto J, I also.......... Gen 40:16
J answered and said, This is the.......... Gen 40:18
as J had interpreted to them.......... Gen 40:22
not the chief butler remember J.......... Gen 40:23
Then Pharaoh sent and called J.......... Gen 41:14
And Pharaoh said unto J, I have.......... Gen 41:15
J answered Pharaoh, saying, It is.......... Gen 41:16
And Pharaoh said unto J, In my.......... Gen 41:17
J said unto Pharaoh, The dream of..... Gen 41:25
And Pharaoh said unto J, Forasmuch Gen 41:39
And Pharaoh said unto J, See, I.......... Gen 41:41
And Pharaoh said unto J, I am.......... Gen 41:44
J went out over all the land of.......... Gen 41:45
J was thirty years old when he.......... Gen 41:46
J went out from the presence of.......... Gen 41:46
J gathered corn as the sand of.......... Gen 41:49
unto J were born two sons before....... Gen 41:50
And J called the name of the.......... Gen 41:51
to come, according as J had said.......... Gen 41:54
unto all the Egyptians, Go unto J....... Gen 41:55
J opened all the storehouses, and.......... Gen 41:56
into Egypt to J for to buy corn.......... Gen 41:57
J was the governor over the land,.......... Gen 42:6
J saw his brethren, and he knew.......... Gen 42:7
J knew his brethren, but they.......... Gen 42:8
J remembered the dreams which he..... Gen 42:9
J said unto them, That is it that.......... Gen 42:14
J said unto them the third day,.......... Gen 42:18
knew not that J understood them....... Gen 42:23
Then J commanded to fill their.......... Gen 42:25
J is not, and Simeon is not, and ye..... Gen 42:36
down to Egypt, and stood before J..... Gen 43:15
when J saw Benjamin with them, he . Gen 43:16
And the man did as J bade.......... Gen 43:17
present against J came at noon.......... Gen 43:25
when J came home, they brought.......... Gen 43:26
And J made haste.......... Gen 43:30
to the word that J had spoken.......... Gen 44:2
J said unto his steward, Up,.......... Gen 44:4
J said unto them, What deed is.......... Gen 44:15
Then J could not refrain himself.......... Gen 45:1
while J made himself known unto.......... Gen 45:1
J said unto his brethren.......... Gen 45:3
I am J; doth my father yet.......... Gen 45:3
J said unto his brethren, Come.......... Gen 45:4
I am J your brother, whom ye sold....... Gen 45:4
unto him, Thus saith thy son J.......... Gen 45:9
And Pharaoh said unto J, Say unto..... Gen 45:17
J gave them wagons, according to..... Gen 45:21
J is yet alive, and he is governor.......... Gen 45:26
they told him all the words of J.......... Gen 45:27
which J had sent to carry him.......... Gen 45:27
J my son is yet alive.......... Gen 45:28
J shall put his hand upon thine.......... Gen 46:4
Jacob's wife; J, and Benjamin.......... Gen 46:19
unto J in the land of Egypt were.......... Gen 46:20
And the sons of J, which were born..... Gen 46:27
he sent Judah before him unto J.......... Gen 46:28
J made ready his chariot, and went..... Gen 46:29
And Israel said unto J, Now let me..... Gen 46:30
J said unto his brethren, and unto....... Gen 46:31
Then J came and told Pharaoh, and..... Gen 47:1
And Pharaoh spake unto J, saying,....... Gen 47:5
J brought in Jacob his father, and.......... Gen 47:7
J placed his father and his.......... Gen 47:11
J nourished his father, and his.......... Gen 47:12
J gathered up all the money that.......... Gen 47:14
and J brought the money into.......... Gen 47:14
all the Egyptians came unto J.......... Gen 47:15
And J said, Give your cattle.......... Gen 47:16
they brought their cattle unto J.......... Gen 47:17
J gave them bread in exchange for..... Gen 47:17
J bought all the land of Egypt.......... Gen 47:20
Then J said unto the people,.......... Gen 47:23
J made it a law over the land of.......... Gen 47:26
and he called his son J, and said.......... Gen 47:29
these things, that one told J.......... Gen 48:1
thy son J cometh unto thee.......... Gen 48:2
And Jacob said unto J, God.......... Gen 48:3
J said unto his father, They are.......... Gen 48:9
And Israel said unto J, I had not.......... Gen 48:11
J brought them out from between.......... Gen 48:12
J took them both, Ephraim in his.......... Gen 48:13
And he blessed J, and said, God,.......... Gen 48:15
when J saw that his father laid.......... Gen 48:17
J said unto his father, Not so,.......... Gen 48:18
And Israel said unto J, Behold, I.......... Gen 48:21
J is a fruitful bough, even a.......... Gen 49:22
they shall be on the head of J.......... Gen 49:26
J fell upon his father's face, and.......... Gen 50:1
J commanded his servants the.......... Gen 50:2
J spake unto the house of Pharaoh.......... Gen 50:4
J went up to bury his father.......... Gen 50:7
And all the house of J, and his.......... Gen 50:8
J returned into Egypt, he, and his....... Gen 50:14
J will peradventure hate us, and.......... Gen 50:15
And they sent a messenger unto J....... Gen 50:16
So shall ye say unto J, Forgive,.......... Gen 50:17
J wept when they spake unto him....... Gen 50:17
J said unto them, Fear not.......... Gen 50:19
J dwelt in Egypt, he, and his.......... Gen 50:22
J lived an hundred and ten years.......... Gen 50:22
J saw Ephraim's children of the.......... Gen 50:23
J said unto his brethren, I die.......... Gen 50:24
J took an oath of the children of.......... Gen 50:25
So J died, being an hundred and.......... Gen 50:26
for J was in Egypt already.......... Ex 1:5
J died, and all his brethren, and.......... Ex 1:6
king over Egypt, which knew not J.......... Ex 1:8
took the bones of J with him.......... Ex 13:19
families of Manasseh the son of J....... Num 27:1
tribe of Manasseh the son of J.......... Num 32:33
The prince of the children of J.......... Num 34:23
the sons of Manasseh the son of J....... Num 36:12
Levi, and Judah, and Issachar, and J Deut 27:12
the children of J were two tribes.......... Josh 14:4
the lot of the children of J fell.......... Josh 16:1
So the children of J, Manasseh and..... Josh 16:4
for he was the firstborn of J.......... Josh 17:1
the son of J by their families.......... Josh 17:2
the children of J spake unto.......... Josh 17:14
And the children of J said.......... Josh 17:16
And the bones of J, which the.......... Josh 24:32
Dan, J, and Benjamin, Naphtali,.......... 1Chr 2:2
He sent a man before them, even J..... Ps 105:17
that Jacob gave to his son J.......... Jn 4:5
with envy, sold J into Egypt.......... Acts 7:9
at the second time J was made.......... Acts 7:13
Then sent J, and called his father.......... Acts 7:14
king arose, which knew not J.......... Acts 7:18
dying, blessed both the sons of J.......... Heb 11:21
By faith J, when he died, made.......... Heb 11:22
*2. Descendants of Joseph 1.*
Of the children of J.......... Num 1:10
Of the children of J, namely, of.......... Num 1:32
Of the tribe of J, namely, of the.......... Num 13:11
The sons of J after their.......... Num 26:28
sons of J after their families.......... Num 26:37
of the families of the sons of J.......... Num 36:1
of the sons of J hath said well.......... Num 36:5
of J he said, Blessed of the LORD.......... Deut 33:13
blessing come upon the head of J.......... Deut 33:16
Joshua spake unto the house of J...... Josh 17:17
the house of J shall abide in.......... Josh 18:5
of Judah and the children of J.......... Josh 18:11
inheritance of the children of J.......... Josh 24:32
And the house of J, they also went..... Judg 1:22
the house of J sent to descry.......... Judg 1:23
hand of the house of J prevailed.......... Judg 1:35
this day of all the house of J to.......... 2Sa 19:20
all the charge of the house of J.......... 1Kin 11:28
the sons of J the son of Israel.......... 1Chr 5:1
children of J the son of Israel.......... 1Chr 7:29
people, the sons of Jacob and J.......... Ps 77:15
he refused the tabernacle of J.......... Ps 78:67
thou that leadest J like a flock.......... Ps 80:1
he ordained in J for a testimony.......... Ps 81:5
stick, and write upon it, For J.......... Eze 37:16
I will take the stick of J.......... Eze 37:19
J shall have two portions.......... Eze 47:13
and one gate of J, one gate of.......... Eze 48:32
out like fire in the house of J.......... Amos 5:6
be gracious unto the remnant of J..... Amos 5:15
grieved for the affliction of J.......... Amos 6:6
a fire, and the house of J a flame.......... Obad 18
and I will save the house of J.......... Zec 10:6
Of the tribe of J were sealed.......... Rev 7:8
*3. A spy sent to the Promised Land.*
of Issachar, Igal the son of J.......... Num 13:7
*4. A son of Asaph.*
Zaccur, and J, and Nethaniah, and...... 1Chr 25:2
lot came forth for Asaph to J.......... 1Chr 25:9
*5. Married a foreigner in exile.*
Shallum, Amariah, and J.......... Ezr 10:42
*6. A priest.*
Jonathan; of Shebaniah, J.......... Neh 12:14
*7. Husband of Mary, the mother of Jesus.*
Jacob begat J the husband of Mary.......... Mt 1:16
his mother Mary was espoused to J.......... Mt 1:18
Then J her husband, being a just.......... Mt 1:19
unto him in a dream, saying, J.......... Mt 1:20
Then J being raised from sleep.......... Mt 1:24
Lord appeareth to J in a dream.......... Mt 2:13
in a dream to J in Egypt,.......... Mt 2:19
to a man whose name was J.......... Lk 1:27
J also went up from Galilee, out.......... Lk 2:4
with haste, and found Mary, and J.......... Lk 2:16
And J and his mother marvelled at.......... Lk 2:33
and J and his mother knew not of it.......... Lk 2:43
(as was supposed) the son of J.......... Lk 3:23
Jesus of Nazareth, the son of J.......... Jn 1:45
Is not this Jesus, the son of J.......... Jn 6:42
*8. A disciple of Jesus.*
a rich man of Arimathaea, named J...... Mt 27:57
when J had taken the body, he.......... Mt 27:59
J of Arimathaea, an honourable.......... Mk 15:43
centurion, he gave the body to J.......... Mk 15:45
behold, there was a man named J.......... Lk 23:50
after this J of Arimathaea, being.......... Jn 19:38
*9. Son of Mattathias; ancestor of Jesus.*
of Janna, which was the son of J.......... Lk 3:24
*10. Son of Juda; ancestor of Jesus.*
of Semei, which was the son of J.......... Lk 3:26
*11. Son of Jonan; ancestor of Jesus.*
of Juda, which was the son of J.......... Lk 3:30
*12. A nominee for Judas' apostleship.*
J called Barsabas, who was.......... Acts 1:23

**JOSEPH'S** (*jo'-zefs*)
*1. Refers to Joseph 1.*
And they took J coat, and killed a...... Gen 37:31
the Egyptian's house for J sake.......... Gen 39:5

he left all that he had in J hand .......... Gen 39:6
J master took him, and put him .......... Gen 39:20
of the prison committed to J hand.......... Gen 39:22
his hand, and put it upon J hand.......... Gen 41:42
And Pharaoh called J name.......... Gen 41:45
J ten brethren went down to buy.......... Gen 42:3
J brother, Jacob sent not with .......... Gen 42:4
J brethren came, and bowed down .......... Gen 42:6
man brought the men into J house.......... Gen 43:17
they were brought into J house.......... Gen 43:18
near to the steward of J house.......... Gen 43:19
man brought the men into J house.......... Gen 43:24
and his brethren came to J house .......... Gen 44:14
saying, J brethren are come.......... Gen 45:16
And Israel beheld J sons, and said, .......... Gen 48:8
when J brethren saw that their .......... Gen 50:15
were brought up upon J knees.......... Gen 50:23
but the birthright was J.......... 1Chr 5:2
J kindred was made known unto.......... Acts 7:13
*2. Refers to Joseph 7.*
And they said, Is not this J son.......... Lk 4:22

**JOSES** (*jo'-zez*) See JOSE.
*1. A brother of Jesus.*
and his brethren, James, and J.......... Mt 13:55
Mary, the brother of James, and J.......... Mk 6:3
*2. Same as Barnabas.*
and Mary the mother of James and J... Mt 27:56
mother of James the less and of J.......... Mk 15:40
Mary the mother of J beheld where.......... Mk 15:47
And J, who by the apostles was.......... Acts 4:36

**JOSHAH** (*jo'-shah*) *A descendant of Simeon.*
Jamlech, and J the son of Amaziah,.... 1Chr 4:34

**JOSHAPHAT** (*josh'-a-fat*) See JEHOSHAPHAT, JOSAPHAT. *A 'mighty man' of David.*
of Maachah, and J the Mithnite,.......... 1Chr 11:43

**JOSHAVIAH** (*josh-a-vi'-ah*) *A 'mighty man' of David.*
the Mahavite, and Jeribai, and J .......... 1Chr 11:46

**JOSHBEKASHAH** (*josh-bek'-a-shah*) *A sanctuary servant.*
Giddalti, and Romamti-ezer, J.......... 1Chr 25:4
The seventeenth to J, he, his .......... 1Chr 25:24

**JOSHEB-BASSHEBETH** See ADINO.

**JOSHUA** (*josh'-u-ah*) See HOSEA, HOSHEA, JEHOSHUAH, JESHUA, JESHUAH, JESUS, OSEA, OSHEA.
*1. Son of Nun.*
And Moses said unto J, Choose us .......... Ex 17:9
So J did as Moses had said to him.......... Ex 17:10
J discomfited Amalek and his.......... Ex 17:13
and rehearse it in the ears of J.......... Ex 17:14
Moses rose up, and his minister J.......... Ex 24:13
when J heard the noise of the.......... Ex 32:17
but his servant J, the son of Nun.......... Ex 33:11
J the son of Nun, the servant of .......... Num 11:28
J the son of Nun, and Caleb the .......... Num 14:6
of Jephunneh, and J the son of Nun. Num 14:30
But J the son of Nun, and Caleb.......... Num 14:38
of Jephunneh, and J the son of Nun. Num 26:65
Take thee J the son of Nun, a man... Num 27:18
and he took J, and set him before .... Num 27:22
the Kenezite, and J the son of Nun.... Num 32:12
J the son of Nun, and the chief.......... Num 32:28
the priest, and J the son of Nun.......... Num 34:17
But J the son of Nun, which.......... Deut 1:38
I commanded J at that time,.......... Deut 3:21
But charge J, and encourage him, .......... Deut 3:28
and J, he shall go over before.......... Deut 31:3
And Moses called unto J, and said.......... Deut 31:7
call J, and present yourselves in.......... Deut 31:14
J went, and presented themselves .......... Deut 31:14
he gave J the son of Nun a charge.... Deut 31:23
J the son of Nun was full of the.......... Deut 34:9
LORD spake unto J the son of Nun.......... Josh 1:1
Then J commanded the officers of .......... Josh 1:10
the tribe of Manasseh, spake J.......... Josh 1:12
And they answered J, saying, All.......... Josh 1:16
J the son of Nun sent out of.......... Josh 2:1
came to J the son of Nun, and told.......... Josh 2:23
And they said unto J, Truly the.......... Josh 2:24
J rose early in the morning.......... Josh 3:1
J said unto the people, Sanctify.......... Josh 3:5
J spake unto the priests, saying,.......... Josh 3:6
And the LORD said unto J, This day.......... Josh 3:7
J said unto the children of.......... Josh 3:9
J said, Hereby ye shall know that.......... Josh 3:10
that the LORD spake unto J.......... Josh 4:1
Then J called the twelve men,.......... Josh 4:4
J said unto them, Pass over .......... Josh 4:5
of Israel did so as J commanded.......... Josh 4:8
Jordan, as the LORD spake unto J.......... Josh 4:8
J set up twelve stones in the .......... Josh 4:9
that the LORD commanded J to.......... Josh 4:10
to all that Moses commanded J .......... Josh 4:10
J in the sight of all Israel.......... Josh 4:14
And the LORD spake unto J, saying,.......... Josh 4:15
J therefore commanded the priests .......... Josh 4:17
of Jordan, did J pitch in Gilgal.......... Josh 4:20
At that time the LORD said unto J.......... Josh 5:2
J made him sharp knives, and.......... Josh 5:3
is the cause why J did circumcise .......... Josh 5:4
their stead, them J circumcised.......... Josh 5:7
And the LORD said unto J, This day.......... Josh 5:9
when J was by Jericho, that he.......... Josh 5:13
J went unto him, and said unto him.... Josh 5:13
J fell on his face to the earth,.......... Josh 5:14
of the LORD's host said unto J.......... Josh 5:15
And J did so.......... Josh 5:15
And the LORD said unto J, See, I .......... Josh 6:2
J the son of Nun called the.......... Josh 6:6
when J had spoken unto the people .......... Josh 6:8
J had commanded the people,.......... Josh 6:10
J rose early in the morning, and.......... Josh 6:12
J said unto the people, Shout .......... Josh 6:16
But J had said unto the two men .......... Josh 6:22
J saved Rahab the harlot alive,.......... Josh 6:25
which J sent to spy out Jericho .......... Josh 6:25
J adjured them at that time,.......... Josh 6:26
So the LORD was with J .......... Josh 6:27
J sent men from Jericho to Ai,.......... Josh 7:2
And they returned to J, and said.......... Josh 7:3
J rent his clothes, and fell to.......... Josh 7:6
J said, Alas, O Lord GOD,.......... Josh 7:7
And the LORD said unto J, Get thee..... Josh 7:10
So J rose up early in the morning .......... Josh 7:16
J said unto Achan, My son, give,.......... Josh 7:19
And Achan answered J, and said,.......... Josh 7:20
So J sent messengers, and they ran .......... Josh 7:22
the tent, and brought them unto J.......... Josh 7:23
And J, and all Israel with him,.......... Josh 7:24
J said, Why hast thou troubled us.......... Josh 7:25
And the LORD said unto J, Fear not .......... Josh 8:1
So J arose, and all the people of .......... Josh 8:3
J chose out thirty thousand .......... Josh 8:3
J therefore sent them forth.......... Josh 8:9
but J lodged that night among the.......... Josh 8:9
J rose up early in the morning,.......... Josh 8:10
J went that night into the midst.......... Josh 8:13
And J and all Israel made as if.......... Josh 8:15
and they pursued after J, and were...... Josh 8:16
And the LORD said unto J, Stretch .......... Josh 8:18
J stretched out the spear that he.......... Josh 8:18
And when J and all Israel saw that .......... Josh 8:21
took alive, and brought him to J .......... Josh 8:23
For J drew not his hand back,.......... Josh 8:26
of the LORD which he commanded J.......... Josh 8:27
J burnt Ai, and made it an heap .......... Josh 8:28
J commanded that they should take.... Josh 8:29
Then J built an altar unto the.......... Josh 8:30
which J read not before all the .......... Josh 8:35
together, to fight with J.......... Josh 9:2
of Gibeon heard what J had done .......... Josh 9:3
they went to J unto the camp at .......... Josh 9:6
And they said unto J, We are thy.......... Josh 9:8
J said unto them, Who are ye.......... Josh 9:8
J made peace with them, and made a . Josh 9:15
J called for them, and he spake.......... Josh 9:22
And they answered J, and said,.......... Josh 9:24
J made them that day hewers of .......... Josh 9:27
had heard how J had taken Ai .......... Josh 10:1
for it hath made peace with J.......... Josh 10:4
sent unto J to the camp to Gilgal.......... Josh 10:6
So J ascended from Gilgal, he, and .......... Josh 10:7
And the LORD said unto J, Fear .......... Josh 10:8
J therefore came unto them.......... Josh 10:9
Then spake J to the LORD in the.......... Josh 10:12
J returned, and all Israel with .......... Josh 10:15
And it was told J, saying, The.......... Josh 10:17
J said, Roll great stones upon.......... Josh 10:18
And it came to pass, when J.......... Josh 10:20
camp to J at Makkedah in peace.......... Josh 10:21
Then said J, Open the mouth of.......... Josh 10:22
brought out those kings unto J.......... Josh 10:24
that J called for all the men of.......... Josh 10:24
J said unto them, Fear not, nor.......... Josh 10:25
afterward J smote them, and slew.......... Josh 10:26
that J commanded, and they took.......... Josh 10:27
that day J took Makkedah, and.......... Josh 10:28
Then J passed from Makkedah, and .. Josh 10:29
J passed from Libnah, and all.......... Josh 10:31
J smote him and his people, until.......... Josh 10:33
from Lachish J passed unto Eglon,.......... Josh 10:34
J went up from Eglon, and all .......... Josh 10:36
J returned, and all Israel with .......... Josh 10:38
So J smote all the country of the .......... Josh 10:40
J smote them from Kadesh-barnea .......... Josh 10:41
their land did J take at one time.......... Josh 10:42
J returned, and all Israel with .......... Josh 10:43
And the LORD said unto J, Be not.......... Josh 11:6
So J came, and all the people of .......... Josh 11:7
J did unto them as the LORD bade.......... Josh 11:9
J at that time turned back, and .......... Josh 11:10
did J take, and smote them with .......... Josh 11:12
that did J burn.......... Josh 11:13
Moses command J, and so did J.......... Josh 11:15
So J took all that land, the.......... Josh 11:16
J made war a long time with all .......... Josh 11:18
And at that time came J, and cut.......... Josh 11:21
J destroyed them utterly with .......... Josh 11:21
So J took the whole land,.......... Josh 11:23
J gave it for an inheritance unto .......... Josh 11:23
the kings of the country which J.......... Josh 12:7
which J gave unto the tribes of .......... Josh 12:7
Now J was old and stricken in.......... Josh 13:1
J the son of Nun, and the heads of.......... Josh 14:1
of Judah came unto J in Gilgal .......... Josh 14:6
J blessed him, and gave unto Caleb... Josh 14:13
the commandment of the LORD to J .. Josh 15:13
before J the son of Nun, and .......... Josh 17:4
children of Joseph spake unto J.......... Josh 17:14
J answered them, If thou be a.......... Josh 17:15
J spake unto the house of Joseph,.......... Josh 17:17
J said unto the children of.......... Josh 18:3
J charged them that went to .......... Josh 18:8
came again to J to the host at.......... Josh 18:9
J cast lots for them in Shiloh.......... Josh 18:10
there J divided the land unto the.......... Josh 18:10
to J the son of Nun among them.......... Josh 19:49
J the son of Nun, and the heads of.... Josh 19:51
The LORD also spake unto J.......... Josh 20:1
unto J the son of Nun, and unto .......... Josh 21:1
Then J called the Reubenites, and.......... Josh 22:1
So J blessed them, and sent them.......... Josh 22:6
the other half thereof gave J.......... Josh 22:7
when J sent them away also unto.......... Josh 22:7
that J waxed old and stricken in .......... Josh 23:1
J called for all Israel, and for.......... Josh 23:2
J gathered all the tribes of.......... Josh 24:1
J said unto all the people, Thus .......... Josh 24:2
J said unto the people, Ye cannot .......... Josh 24:19
And the people said unto J.......... Josh 24:21
J said unto the people, Ye are.......... Josh 24:22
And the people said unto J.......... Josh 24:24
So J made a covenant with the.......... Josh 24:25
J wrote these words in the book.......... Josh 24:26
J said unto all the people,.......... Josh 24:27
So J let the people depart, every.......... Josh 24:28
that J the son of Nun, the.......... Josh 24:29
served the LORD all the days of J.......... Josh 24:31
of the elders that overlived J.......... Josh 24:31
the death of J it came to pass.......... Judg 1:1
when J had let the people go, the.......... Judg 2:6
served the LORD all the days of J.......... Judg 2:7
of the elders that outlived J.......... Judg 2:7
J the son of Nun, the servant of.......... Judg 2:8
nations which J left when he died.......... Judg 2:21
he them into the hand of J.......... Judg 2:23
he spake by J the son of Nun.......... 1Kin 16:34
*2. A Bethshemite.*
the cart came into the field of J.......... 1Sa 6:14
unto this day in the field of J.......... 1Sa 6:18
*3. A governor of Jerusalem.*
of J the governor of the city.......... 2Kin 23:8
*4. A High Priest.*
to J the son of Josedech, the.......... Hag 1:1
J the son of Josedech, the high.......... Hag 1:12
the spirit of J the son of.......... Hag 1:14
to J the son of Josedech, the.......... Hag 2:2
and be strong, O J, son of.......... Hag 2:4
he shewed me J the high priest.......... Zec 3:1
Now J was clothed with filthy.......... Zec 3:3
of the LORD protested unto J.......... Zec 3:6
O J the high priest, thou, and thy.......... Zec 3:8
stone that I have laid before J.......... Zec 3:9
the head of J the son of Josedech.......... Zec 6:11

**JOSIAH** (*jo-si'-ah*) See JOSIAS.
*1. A king of Judah.*
the house of David, J by name.......... 1Kin 13:2
made J his son king in his stead.......... 2Kin 21:24
J his son reigned in his stead.......... 2Kin 21:26
J was eight years old when he.......... 2Kin 22:1
in the eighteenth year of king J.......... 2Kin 22:3
as J turned himself, he spied the.......... 2Kin 23:16
J took away, and did to them.......... 2Kin 23:19
in the eighteenth year of king J.......... 2Kin 23:23
did J put away, that he might.......... 2Kin 23:24
Now the rest of the acts of J.......... 2Kin 23:28
and king J went against him.......... 2Kin 23:29
land took Jehoahaz the son of J.......... 2Kin 23:30
made Eliakim the son of J king in..... 2Kin 23:34
king in the room of J his father.......... 2Kin 23:34
Amon his son, J his son.......... 1Chr 3:14
And the sons of J were, the.......... 1Chr 3:15
made J his son king in his stead.......... 2Chr 33:25
J was eight years old when he.......... 2Chr 34:1
J took away all the abominations.......... 2Chr 34:33
Moreover J kept a passover unto.......... 2Chr 35:1
J gave to the people, of the.......... 2Chr 35:7
to the commandment of king J.......... 2Chr 35:16
keep such a passover as J kept.......... 2Chr 35:18
reign of J was this passover kept.......... 2Chr 35:19
when J had prepared the temple,.......... 2Chr 35:20
and J went out against him.......... 2Chr 35:20
Nevertheless J would not turn his..... 2Chr 35:22
And the archers shot at king J.......... 2Chr 35:23
Judah and Jerusalem mourned for J. 2Chr 35:24
And Jeremiah lamented for J.......... 2Chr 35:25
the singing women spake of J in.......... 2Chr 35:25
Now the rest of the acts of J.......... 2Chr 35:26
land took Jehoahaz the son of J.......... 2Chr 36:1
J the son of Amon king of Judah.......... Jer 1:2
the son of J king of Judah.......... Jer 1:3
the son of J king of Judah.......... Jer 1:3
unto me in the days of J the king.......... Jer 3:6
the son of J king of Judah.......... Jer 22:11
reigned instead of J his father.......... Jer 22:11
the son of J king of Judah.......... Jer 22:18
the son of J king of Judah.......... Jer 25:1
From the thirteenth year of J the.......... Jer 25:3
of J king of Judah came this word.......... Jer 26:1
of J king of Judah came this word.......... Jer 27:1
the son of J king of Judah.......... Jer 35:1
the son of J king of Judah.......... Jer 36:1
unto thee, from the days of J.......... Jer 36:2
the son of J king of Judah.......... Jer 36:9
king Zedekiah the son of J.......... Jer 37:1
the son of J king of Judah.......... Jer 45:1
the son of J king of Judah.......... Jer 46:2
in the days of J the son of Amon,.......... Zeph 1:1
*2. A son of Zephaniah.*
house of J the son of Zephaniah.......... Zec 6:10

**JOSIAS** (*jo-si'-as*) See JOSIAH. *Son of Amon; ancestor of Jesus.*
and Amon begat J.......... Mt 1:10
J begat Jechonias and his brethren.......... Mt 1:11

**JOSIBIAH** (*jos-ib-i'-ah*) *A Simeonite.*
And Joel, and Jehu the son of *J* ... 1Chr 4:35

**JOSIPHIAH** (*jos-if-i'-ah*) *A family of exiles.*
the son of *J*, and with him an ... Ezr 8:10

**JOT**
one *j* or one tittle shall in no ... Mt 5:18

**JOTBAH** (*jot'-bah*) *A place near Hebron.*
the daughter of Haruz of *J* ... 2Kin 21:19

**JOTBATH** (*jot'-bath*) See JOTBATHAH. *An encampment during the Exodus.*
and from Gudgodah to *J*, a land of ... Deut 10:7

**JOTBATHAH** (*jot'-ba-thah*) See JOTBATH. *Same as Jotbath.*
Hor-hagidgad, and pitched in *J* ... Num 33:33
And they removed from *J*, and ... Num 33:34

**JOTHAM** (*jo'-tham*) See JOATHAM.
*1. A son of Gideon.*
notwithstanding yet *J* the ... Judg 9:5
And when they told it to *J* ... Judg 9:7
*J* ran away, and fled, and went to ... Judg 9:21
curse of *J* the son of Jerubbaal ... Judg 9:57
*2. Father of King Ahaz.*
*J* the king's son was over the ... 2Kin 15:5
*J* his son reigned in his stead ... 2Kin 15:7
year of *J* the son of Uzziah ... 2Kin 15:30
Remaliah king of Israel began *J* ... 2Kin 15:32
Now the rest of the acts of *J* ... 2Kin 15:36
*J* slept with his fathers, and was ... 2Kin 15:38
of *J* king of Judah began to reign ... 2Kin 16:1
son, Azariah his son, *J* his son, ... 1Chr 3:12
in the days of *J* king of Judah ... 1Chr 5:17
*J* his son was over the king's ... 2Chr 26:21
*J* his son reigned in his stead ... 2Chr 26:23
*J* was twenty and five years old ... 2Chr 27:1
So *J* became mighty, because he ... 2Chr 27:6
Now the rest of the acts of *J* ... 2Chr 27:7
*J* slept with his fathers, and they ... 2Chr 27:9
in the days of Uzziah, *J*, Ahaz, ... Is 1:1
in the days of Ahaz the son of *J* ... Is 7:1
Beeri, in the days of Uzziah, *J* ... Hos 1:1
the Morasthite in the days of *J* ... Mic 1:1
*3. A descendant of Caleb.*
and *J*, and Gesham, and Pelet ... 1Chr 2:47

**JOURNEY**
had made his *j* prosperous or not ... Gen 24:21
Then Jacob went on his *j*, and came ... Gen 29:1
set three days' *j* betwixt himself ... Gen 30:36
pursued after him seven days' *j* ... Gen 31:23
And he said, Let us take our *j* ... Gen 33:12
Israel took his *j* with all that ... Gen 46:1
three days' *j* into the wilderness ... Ex 3:18
three days' *j* into the desert, and ... Ex 5:3
three days' *j* into the wilderness ... Ex 8:27
And they took their *j* from Succoth ... Ex 13:20
And they took their *j* from Elim ... Ex 16:1
dead body, or be in a *j* afar off ... Num 9:10
that is clean, and is not in a *j* ... Num 9:13
the south side shall take their *j* ... Num 10:6
they first took their *j* according ... Num 10:13
mount of the LORD three days' *j* ... Num 10:33
before them in the three days' *j* ... Num 10:33
as it were a day's *j* on this side ... Num 11:31
were a day's *j* on the other side ... Num 11:31
went three days' *j* in the ... Num 33:8
they took their *j* out of the ... Num 33:12
(There are eleven days' *j* from ... Deut 1:2
Turn you, and take your *j*, and go ... Deut 1:7
take your *j* into the wilderness ... Deut 1:40
took our *j* into the wilderness by ... Deut 2:1
Rise ye up, take your *j*, and pass ... Deut 2:24
children of Israel took their *j* ... Deut 10:6
take thy *j* before the people, ... Deut 10:11
Take victuals with you for the *j* ... Josh 9:11
old by reason of the very long *j* ... Josh 9:13
notwithstanding the *j* that thou ... Judg 4:9
And the LORD sent thee on a *j* ... 1Sa 15:18
Uriah, Camest thou not from thy *j* ... 2Sa 11:10
he is pursuing, or he is in a *j* ... 1Kin 18:27
a day's *j* into the wilderness ... 1Kin 19:4
because the *j* is too great for ... 1Kin 19:7
a compass of seven days' *j* ... 2Kin 3:9
Then Solomon came from his *j* to ... 2Chr 1:13
him,) For how long shall thy *j* be ... Neh 2:6
not at home, he is gone a long *j* ... Prov 7:19
great city of three days' *j* ... Jonah 3:3
to enter into the city a day's *j* ... Jonah 3:4
Nor scrip for your *j*, neither two ... Mt 10:10
and straightway took his *j* ... Mt 25:15
should take nothing for their *j* ... Mk 6:8
of man is as a man taking a far *j* ... Mk 13:34
in the company, went a day's *j* ... Lk 2:44
them, Take nothing for your *j* ... Lk 9:3
of mine in his *j* is come to me ... Lk 11:6
took his *j* into a far country, and ... Lk 15:13
being wearied with his *j* ... Jn 4:6
from Jerusalem a sabbath day's *j* ... Acts 1:12
morrow, as they went on their *j* ... Acts 10:9
to pass, that, as I made my *j* ... Acts 22:6
I might have a prosperous *j* by ... Rom 1:10
Whensoever I take my *j* into Spain ... Rom 15:24
for I trust to see you in my *j* ... Rom 15:24
me on my *j* whithersoever I go ... 1Cor 16:6
and Apollos on their *j* diligently ... Titus 3:13
on their *j* after a godly sort ... 3Jn 6

**JOURNEYED**
as they *j* from the east, that ... Gen 11:2
And Abram *j*, going on still toward ... Gen 12:9
and Lot *j* east ... Gen 13:11
Abraham *j* from thence toward the ... Gen 20:1
Jacob *j* to Succoth, and built him ... Gen 33:17
And they *j*: and the terror ... Gen 35:5
And they *j* from Beth-el ... Gen 35:16
And Israel *j*, and spread his tent ... Gen 35:21
the children of Israel *j* from ... Ex 12:37
of the children of Israel *j* from ... Ex 17:1
then they *j* not till the day that ... Ex 40:37
that the children of Israel *j* ... Num 9:17
the LORD the children of Israel *j* ... Num 9:18
the charge of the LORD, and *j* not ... Num 9:19
commandment of the LORD they *j* ... Num 9:20
up in the morning, then they *j* ... Num 9:21
the cloud was taken up, they *j* ... Num 9:21
abode in their tents, and *j* not ... Num 9:22
but when it was taken up, they *j* ... Num 9:22
commandment of the LORD they *j* ... Num 9:23
And the people *j* from ... Num 11:35
the people *j* not till Miriam was ... Num 12:15
*j* from Kadesh, and came unto ... Num 20:22
they *j* from mount Hor by the way ... Num 21:4
they *j* from Oboth, and pitched at ... Num 21:11
they *j* from Rissah, and pitched in ... Num 33:22
From thence they *j* unto Gudgodah ... Deut 10:7
And the children of Israel *j* ... Josh 9:17
to the house of Micah, as he *j* ... Judg 17:8
But a certain Samaritan, as he *j* ... Lk 10:33
And as he *j*, he came near Damascus ... Acts 9:3
the men which *j* with him stood ... Acts 9:7
about me and them which *j* with me. Acts 26:13

**JOURNEYING**
and for the *j* of the camps ... Num 10:2
We are *j* unto the place of which ... Num 10:29
teaching, and *j* toward Jerusalem ... Lk 13:22

**JOURNEYINGS**
Thus were the *j* of the children ... Num 10:28
In *j* often, in perils of waters, ... 2Cor 11:26

**JOURNEYS**
he went on his *j* from the south ... Gen 13:3
wilderness of Sin, after their *j* ... Ex 17:1
Israel went onward in all their *j* ... Ex 40:36
of Israel, throughout all their *j* ... Ex 40:38
shall blow an alarm for their *j* ... Num 10:6
children of Israel took their *j* ... Num 10:12
These are the *j* of the children ... Num 33:1
goings out according to their *j* ... Num 33:2
these are their *j* according to ... Num 33:2

**JOY**
king Saul, with tabrets, with *j* ... 1Sa 18:6
pipes, and rejoiced with great *j* ... 1Kin 1:40
for there was *j* in Israel ... 1Chr 12:40
by lifting up the voice with *j* ... 1Chr 15:16
of the house of Obed-edom with *j* ... 1Chr 15:25
king also rejoiced with great *j* ... 1Chr 29:9
now have I seen with *j* thy people ... 1Chr 29:17
to go again to Jerusalem with *j* ... 2Chr 20:27
So there was great *j* in Jerusalem ... 2Chr 30:26
and many shouted aloud for *j* ... Ezr 3:12
the noise of the shout of *j* from ... Ezr 3:13
of this house of God with *j* ... Ezr 6:16
bread seven days with *j* ... Ezr 6:22
for the *j* of the LORD is your ... Neh 8:10
made them rejoice with great *j* ... Neh 12:43
so that the *j* of Jerusalem was ... Neh 12:43
Jews had light, and gladness, and *j* ... Est 8:16
his decree came, the Jews had *j* ... Est 8:17
turned unto them from sorrow to *j* ... Est 9:22
make them days of feasting and *j* ... Est 9:22
Behold, this is the *j* of his way ... Job 8:19
the *j* of the hypocrite but for a ... Job 20:5
the widow's heart to sing for *j* ... Job 29:13
and he shall see his face with *j* ... Job 33:26
all the sons of God shouted for *j* ... Job 38:7
is turned into *j* before him ... Job 41:22
let them ever shout for *j* ... Ps 5:11
in thy presence is fulness of *j* ... Ps 16:11
The king shall *j* in thy strength, ... Ps 21:1
in his tabernacle sacrifices of *j* ... Ps 27:6
but *j* cometh in the morning ... Ps 30:5
and shout for *j*, all ye that are ... Ps 32:11
Let them shout for *j*, and be glad, ... Ps 35:27
house of God, with the voice of *j* ... Ps 42:4
of God, unto God my exceeding *j* ... Ps 43:4
the *j* of the whole earth, is ... Ps 48:2
Make me to hear *j* and gladness ... Ps 51:8
unto me the *j* of thy salvation ... Ps 51:12
they shout for *j*, they also sing ... Ps 65:13
the nations be glad and sing for *j* ... Ps 67:4
brought forth his people with *j* ... Ps 105:43
that sow in tears shall reap in *j* ... Ps 126:5
and let thy saints shout for *j* ... Ps 132:9
saints shall shout aloud for *j* ... Ps 132:16
not Jerusalem above my chief *j* ... Ps 137:6
to the counsellors of peace is *j* ... Prov 12:20
doth not intermeddle with his *j* ... Prov 14:10
Folly is *j* to him that is ... Prov 15:21
A man hath *j* by the answer of his ... Prov 15:23
and the father of a fool hath no *j* ... Prov 17:21
It is *j* to the just to do ... Prov 21:15
a wise child shall have *j* of him ... Prov 23:24
withheld not my heart from any *j* ... Eccl 2:10
sight wisdom, and knowledge, and *j* ... Eccl 2:26
him in the *j* of his heart ... Eccl 5:20
Go thy way, eat thy bread with *j* ... Eccl 9:7
nation, and not increased the *j* ... Is 9:3
they *j* before thee according to ... Is 9:3
according to the *j* in harvest ... Is 9:3
have no *j* in their young men ... Is 9:17
Therefore with *j* shall ye draw ... Is 12:3
*j* out of the plentiful field ... Is 16:10
And behold *j* and gladness, slaying ... Is 22:13
the *j* of the harp ceaseth ... Is 24:8
all *j* is darkened, the mirth of ... Is 24:11
increase their *j* in the LORD ... Is 29:19
houses of *j* in the joyous city ... Is 32:13
a *j* of wild asses, a pasture of ... Is 32:14
and rejoice even with *j* and ... Is 35:2
everlasting *j* upon their heads ... Is 35:10
they shall obtain *j* and gladness, ... Is 35:10
*j* and gladness shall be found ... Is 51:3
everlasting *j* shall be upon their ... Is 51:11
they shall obtain gladness and *j* ... Is 51:11
Break forth into *j*, sing together ... Is 52:9
For ye shall go out with *j* ... Is 55:12
a *j* of many generations ... Is 60:15
the oil of *j* for mourning, the ... Is 61:3
everlasting *j* shall be unto them ... Is 61:7
shall sing for *j* of heart ... Is 65:14
a rejoicing, and her people a *j* ... Is 65:18
in Jerusalem, and *j* in my people ... Is 65:19
but he shall appear to your *j* ... Is 66:5
rejoice for *j* with her, all ye ... Is 66:10
and thy word was unto me the *j* ... Jer 15:16
I will turn their mourning into *j* ... Jer 31:13
And it shall be to me a name of *j* ... Jer 33:9
The voice of *j*, and the voice of ... Jer 33:11
of him, thou skippedst for *j* ... Jer 48:27
And *j* and gladness is taken from ... Jer 48:33
praise not left, the city of my *j* ... Jer 49:25
beauty, The *j* of the whole earth ... Lam 2:15
The *j* of our heart is ceased ... Lam 5:15
the *j* of their glory, the desire ... Eze 24:25
with the *j* of all their heart ... Eze 36:5
Rejoice not, O Israel, for *j* ... Hos 9:1
because *j* is withered away from ... Joel 1:12
cut off before our eyes, yea, *j* ... Joel 1:16
I will *j* in the God of my ... Hab 3:18
he will rejoice over thee with *j* ... Zeph 3:17
he will *j* over thee with singing ... Zeph 3:17
shall be to the house of Judah *j* ... Zec 8:19
rejoiced with exceeding great *j* ... Mt 2:10
word, and anon with *j* receiveth it ... Mt 13:20
for *j* thereof goeth and selleth ... Mt 13:44
enter thou into the *j* of thy lord ... Mt 25:21
enter thou into the *j* of thy lord ... Mt 25:23
sepulchre with fear and great *j* ... Mt 28:8
And thou shalt have *j* and gladness ... Lk 1:14
the babe leaped in my womb for *j* ... Lk 1:44
bring you good tidings of great *j* ... Lk 2:10
ye in that day, and leap for *j* ... Lk 6:23
hear, receive the word with *j* ... Lk 8:13
the seventy returned again with *j* ... Lk 10:17
that likewise *j* shall be in ... Lk 15:7
there is *j* in the presence of the ... Lk 15:10
while they yet believed not for *j* ... Lk 24:41
to Jerusalem with great *j* ... Lk 24:52
this my *j* therefore is fulfilled ... Jn 3:29
that my *j* might remain in you, and ... Jn 15:11
that your *j* might be full ... Jn 15:11
sorrow shall be turned into *j* ... Jn 16:20
for *j* that a man is born into the ... Jn 16:21
your *j* no man taketh from you ... Jn 16:22
receive, that your *j* may be full ... Jn 16:24
have my *j* fulfilled in themselves ... Jn 17:13
me full of *j* with thy countenance ... Acts 2:28
And there was great *j* in that city ... Acts 8:8
the disciples were filled with *j* ... Acts 13:52
they caused great *j* unto all the ... Acts 15:3
I might finish my course with *j* ... Acts 20:24
but we also *j* in God through our ... Rom 5:11
and peace, and *j* in the Holy Ghost ... Rom 14:17
God of hope fill you with all *j* ... Rom 15:13
you with *j* by the will of God ... Rom 15:32
faith, but are helpers of your *j* ... 2Cor 1:24
that my *j* is the *j* of you all ... 2Cor 2:3
that my *j* is the *j* of you all ... 2Cor 2:3
more joyed we for the *j* of Titus ... 2Cor 7:13
the abundance of their *j* and their ... 2Cor 8:2
fruit of the Spirit is love, *j* ... Gal 5:22
for you all making request with *j* ... Phil 1:4
your furtherance and *j* of faith ... Phil 1:25
Fulfil ye my *j*, that ye be ... Phil 2:2
and service of your faith, I *j* ... Phil 2:17
For the same cause also do ye *j* ... Phil 2:18
beloved and longed for, my *j* ... Phil 4:1
with *j* of the Holy Ghost ... 1Th 1:6
For what is our hope, or *j* ... 1Th 2:19
For ye are our glory and *j* ... 1Th 2:20
for all the *j* wherewith we *j* ... 1Th 3:9
for all the *j* wherewith we *j* ... 1Th 3:9
that I may be filled with *j* ... 2Ti 1:4
For we have great *j* and ... Philem 7
let me have *j* of thee in the Lord ... Philem 20
who for the *j* that was set before ... Heb 12:2
that they may do it with *j* ... Heb 13:17
count it all *j* when ye fall into ... Jas 1:2
mourning, and your *j* to heaviness ... Jas 4:9
ye rejoice with *j* unspeakable ... 1Pet 1:8
may be glad also with exceeding *j* ... 1Pet 4:13
unto you, that your *j* may be full ... 1Jn 1:4
to face, that our *j* may be full ... 2Jn 12
I have no greater *j* than to hear ... 3Jn 4
of his glory with exceeding *j* ... Jude 24

**JOYED**
exceedingly the more *j* we for the ....... 2Cor 7:13

**JOYFUL**
king, and went unto their tents *j* ......... 1Kin 8:66
for the LORD had made them *j* ................ Ezr 6:22
Then went Haman forth that day *j* ......... Est 5:9
let no *j* voice come therein ..................... Job 3:7
that love thy name be *j* in thee................. Ps 5:11
And my soul shall be *j* in the LORD......... Ps 35:9
shall praise thee with *j* lips...................... Ps 63:5
Make a *j* noise unto God, all ye .............. Ps 66:1
make a *j* noise unto the God of ............... Ps 81:1
the people that know the *j* sound.......... Ps 89:15
let us make a *j* noise to the rock............. Ps 95:1
make a *j* noise unto him with................... Ps 95:2
Let the field be *j*, and all that................. Ps 96:12
Make a *j* noise unto the LORD, all.......... Ps 98:4
make a *j* noise before the LORD .............. Ps 98:6
let the hills be *j* together......................... Ps 98:8
Make a *j* noise unto the LORD, all.......... Ps 100:1
to be a *j* mother of children ..................... Ps 113:9
of Zion be *j* in their King......................... Ps 149:2
Let the saints be *j* in glory ....................... Ps 149:5
In the day of prosperity be *j*..................... Eccl 7:14
and be *j*, O earth ......................................... Is 49:13
make them *j* in my house of prayer.......... Is 56:7
my soul shall be *j* in my God.................... Is 61:10
I am exceeding *j* in all our ....................... 2Cor 7:4

**JOYFULLY**
Live *j* with the wife whom thou ............. Eccl 9:9
and came down, and received him *j*......... Lk 19:6
took *j* the spoiling of your goods......... Heb 10:34

**JOYFULNESS**
not the LORD thy God with *j*.............. Deut 28:47
patience and longsuffering with *j* .......... Col 1:11

**JOYING**
am I with you in the spirit, *j*...................... Col 2:5

**JOYOUS**
a tumultuous city, a *j* city .......................... Is 22:2
Is this your *j* city, whose ............................ Is 23:7
the houses of joy in the *j* city .................... Is 32:13
for the present seemeth to be *j*........... Heb 12:11

**JOZABAD/1**
*2. Another warrior in David's army.*
to him of Manasseh, Adnah, and J.... 1Chr 12:20
and Jediael, and Michael, and J.......... 1Chr 12:20
*3. A Chief Levite in Josiah's time.*
and Asahel, and Jerimoth, and J.......... 2Chr 31:13
*4. An exile with Ezra.*
and Hashabiah and Jeiel and J............. 2Chr 35:9
*5. A priest.*
with them was J the son of Jeshua........ Ezr 8:33
*6. A Levite.*
Maaseiah, Ishmael, Nethaneel, J.......... Ezr 10:22
*7. A priest who helped Ezra.*
J, and Shimei, and Kelaiah, (the .......... Ezr 10:23
*8. A chief Levite in exile.*
Maaseiah, Kelita, Azariah, J ................... Neh 8:7
*9. A chief Levite in exile.*
And Shabbethai and J, of the chief..... Neh 11:16

**JOZACHAR** (*joz'-a-kar*) See ZABAD. *Son of Shimeath.*
For J the son of Shimeath, and........... 2Kin 12:21

**JOZADAK** (*joz'-a-dak*) See JEHOZADAK, JOSEDECH. *A priest with Zerubbabel.*
Then stood up Jeshua the son of J........... Ezr 3:2
Shealtiel, and Jeshua the son of J........... Ezr 3:8
Shealtiel, and Jeshua the son of J ........... Ezr 5:2
the sons of Jeshua the son of J.............. Ezr 10:18
the son of Jeshua, the son of J.............. Neh 12:26

**JUBAL** (*ju'-bal*) *Son of Adah.*
And his brother's name was J ................ Gen 4:21

**JUBILE**
*j* to sound on the tenth day of................. Lev 25:9
it shall be a *j* unto you............................. Lev 25:10
A *j* shall that fiftieth year be................... Lev 25:11
For it is the *j* ............................................. Lev 25:12
In the year of this *j* ye shall .................... Lev 25:13
the number of years after the *j*................. Lev 25:15
bought it until the year of *j*...................... Lev 25:28
in the *j* it shall go out, and he.................. Lev 25:28
it shall not go out in the *j* ........................ Lev 25:30
and they shall go out in the *j*.................... Lev 25:31
shall go out in the year of *j* ..................... Lev 25:33
serve thee unto the year of *j* .................... Lev 25:40
sold to him unto the year of *j*.................... Lev 25:50
but few years unto the year of *j*............... Lev 25:52
he shall go out in the year of *j* ................ Lev 25:54
his field from the year of *j* ....................... Lev 27:17
he sanctify his field after the *j* ................ Lev 27:18
even unto the year of the *j*......................... Lev 27:18
field, when it goeth out in the *j* ................ Lev 27:21
even unto the year of the *j* ........................ Lev 27:23
In the year of the *j* the field...................... Lev 27:24
when the *j* of the children of..................... Num 36:4

**JUCAL** (*ju'-kal*) See JEHUCAL. *An enemy of Jeremiah.*
J the son of Shelemiah, and Pashur........ Jer 38:1

**JUCE**
wine of the *j* of my pomegranate .......... Song 8:2

**JUDA** (*ju'-dah*) See JUDAH.
*1. Greek form of Judah, the tribe.*
thou Bethlehem, in the land of J .............. Mt 2:6
the least among the princes of J................ Mt 2:6
with haste, into a city of J........................ Lk 1:39
that our Lord sprang out of J.................. Heb 7:14
the Lion of the tribe of J......................... Rev 5:5
Of the tribe of J were sealed.................... Rev 7:5
*2. A brother of Jesus.*
of James, and Joses, and of J..................... Mk 6:3
*3. Son of Jacob; an ancestor of Jesus.*
of Phares, which was the son of J .......... Lk 3:33

**JUDAEA** *A Roman province.*
J in the days of Herod the king ................. Mt 2:1
said unto him, In Bethlehem of J .............. Mt 2:5
that Archelaus did reign in J in................. Mt 2:22
preaching in the wilderness of J ............... Mt 3:1
out to him Jerusalem, and all J................. Mt 3:5
and from Jerusalem, and from J ............... Mt 4:25
the coasts of J beyond Jordan .................. Mt 19:1
be in J flee into the mountains.............. Mt 24:16
out unto him all the land of J................... Mk 1:5
Galilee followed him, and from J ............. Mk 3:7
cometh into the coasts of J by ................ Mk 10:1
be in J flee to the mountains ................. Mk 13:14
the days of Herod, the king of J................. Lk 1:5
all the hill country of J.............................. Lk 1:65
of the city of Nazareth, into J.................... Lk 2:4
Pilate being governor of J ......................... Lk 3:1
of every town of Galilee, and J................. Lk 5:17
multitude of people out of all J ............... Lk 6:17
him went forth throughout all J................. Lk 7:17
are in J flee to the mountains.................. Lk 21:21
his disciples into the land of J.................. Jn 3:22
He left J, and departed again into ............. Jn 4:3
was come out of J into Galilee.................. Jn 4:47
he was come out of J into Galilee ............. Jn 4:54
him, Depart hence, and go into J ............... Jn 7:3
disciples, Let us go into J again................. Jn 11:7
me both in Jerusalem, and in all J............. Acts 1:8
dwellers in Mesopotamia, and in J ........... Acts 2:9
and said unto them, Ye men of J.............. Acts 2:14
throughout the regions of J ..................... Acts 8:1
churches rest throughout all J ............... Acts 9:31
was published throughout all J ............. Acts 10:37
brethren that were in J heard................. Acts 11:1
the brethren which dwelt in J ................ Acts 11:29
he went down from J to Caesarea........ Acts 12:19
down from J taught the brethren ............ Acts 15:1
down from J a certain prophet ............ Acts 21:10
and throughout all the coasts of J........ Acts 26:20
letters out of J concerning thee ............ Acts 28:21
them that do not believe in J............... Rom 15:31
to be brought on my way toward J....... 2Cor 1:16
of J which were in Christ ........................ Gal 1:22
which in J are in Christ Jesus............... 1Th 2:14

**JUDAH** (*ju'-dah*) See PREFACE. SEE ALSO BETHLEHEM-JUDAH, JUDA, JUDAH'S, JUDAS, JUDEA, JUDE.
*1. Son of Jacob and Leah.*
therefore she called his name J............ Gen 29:35
J said unto Israel his father, .................. Gen 43:8
J, thou art he whom thy brethren.......... Gen 49:8
*2. The tribe and its land.*
And this is the blessing of J ................. Deut 33:7
of J according to their families........... Josh 15:20
David king over the house of J................ 2Sa 2:4
In J is God known........................................ Ps 76:1
of Israel and with the house of J ............. Heb 8:8
*3. The southern kingdom after the revolt of the ten northern tribes.*
of David, but the tribe of J only ......... 1Kin 12:20
that dwelt in the cities of J.................. 2Chr 10:17
the wrath of the LORD was upon J....... 2Chr 29:8
is ruined, and J is fallen ............................. Is 3:8
the word of the LORD, all ye of J................ Jer 7:2
concerning Israel and concerning J ........ Jer 30:4
In those days shall J be saved................ Jer 33:16
Thus J was carried away captive............ Jer 52:27
J is gone into captivity because ............... Lam 1:3
For three transgressions of J................. Amos 2:4

**JUDAH'S** (*ju'-dahs*)
*1. Refers to Judah 1.*
J firstborn, was wicked in the ............... Gen 38:7
the daughter of Shuah J wife died.......... Gen 38:12
which was in the king of J house........... Jer 32:2
that are left in the king of J.................. Jer 38:22

**JUDAISM** See JEWS.

**JUDAS** (*ju'-das*) See BARSABAS, ISCARIOT, JUDAH, JUDE, LEBBAEUS, THADDAEUS.
*1. Betrayer of Jesus.*
J Iscariot, who also betrayed him............ Mt 10:4
called J Iscariot, went unto the............. Mt 26:14
Then J, which betrayed him,..................... Mt 26:25
And while he yet spake, lo, J.................. Mt 26:47
Then J, which had betrayeth him,............. Mt 27:3
J Iscariot, which also betrayed ................. Mk 3:19
J Iscariot, one of the twelve,.................. Mk 14:10
while he yet spake, cometh J.................. Mk 14:43
J Iscariot, which also was the.................... Lk 6:16
Satan into J surnamed Iscariot................ Lk 22:3
and he that was called J, one of.............. Lk 22:47
But Jesus said unto him, J........................ Lk 22:48
He spake of J Iscariot the son of............. Jn 6:71
J Iscariot, Simon's son, which ................. Jn 12:4
put into the heart of J Iscariot................ Jn 13:2
the sop, he gave it to J Iscariot ............... Jn 13:26
because J had the bag, that Jesus ........... Jn 13:29
J also, which betrayed him, knew ............ Jn 18:2
J then, having received a band of............. Jn 18:3
J also, which betrayed him, stood .......... Jn 18:5
David spake before concerning J.......... Acts 1:16
from which J by transgression .............. Acts 1:25
*2. A brother of Jesus.*
James, and Joses, and Simon, and J...... Mt 13:55
*3. A disciple of Jesus.*
J the brother of James, and Judas ........... Lk 6:16
J saith unto him, not Iscariot,.................. Jn 14:22
and J the brother of James..................... Acts 1:13
*4. A seditious Galilean.*
After this man rose up J of ..................... Acts 5:37
*5. Lodged Paul in Damascus.*
house of J for one called Saul............... Acts 9:11
*6. Surnamed Barsabas.*
J surnamed Barsabas, and Silas,.......... Acts 15:22
We have sent therefore J and Silas.... Acts 15:27
And J and Silas, being prophets.......... Acts 15:32
and Jacob begat J and his brethren ......... Mt 1:2
J begat Phares and Zara of Thamar.......... Mt 1:3

**JUDE** (*jood*) See JUDAS. *A brother of Jesus.*
J, the servant of Jesus Christ, ........................ Jude 1

**JUDEA** (*ju-de'-ah*) See JEWRY, JUDAH. *Southern portion of Israel.*
we went into the province of J ................. Ezr 5:8

**JUDEAN** See JUDEA.

**JUDGE**
whom they shall serve, will I *j*............ Gen 15:14
the LORD *j* between me and thee........... Gen 16:5
Shall not the J of all the earth ............. Gen 18:25
sojourn, and he will needs be a *j*............. Gen 19:9
that they may *j* betwixt us both ........... Gen 31:37
God of their father, *j* betwixt us........... Gen 31:53
Dan shall *j* his people, as one of ......... Gen 49:16
made thee a prince and a *j* over us ......... Ex 2:14
The LORD look upon you, and *j*................. Ex 5:21
that Moses sat to *j* the people.............. Ex 18:13
I *j* between one and another, and I ........ Ex 18:16
let them *j* the people at all.................... Ex 18:22
every small matter they shall *j* .............. Ex 18:22
shalt thou *j* thy neighbour .................. Lev 19:15
shall *j* between the slayer .................. Num 35:24
*j* righteously between every man......... Deut 1:16
they shall *j* the people with just......... Deut 16:18
unto the *j* that shall be in those.......... Deut 17:9
the LORD thy God, or unto the *j* ......... Deut 17:12
that the judges may *j* them.................. Deut 25:1
that the *j* shall cause him to lie........... Deut 25:2
For the LORD shall *j* his people............ Deut 32:36
then the LORD was with the *j*................. Judg 2:18
enemies all the days of the *j*................... Judg 2:18
came to pass, when the *j* was dead..... Judg 2:19
the LORD the J be *j* this day .............. Judg 11:27
the LORD shall *j* the ends of the............ 1Sa 2:10
another, the *j* shall *j* him ...................... 1Sa 2:25
will *j* his house for ever for the.............. 1Sa 3:13
now make us a king to *j* us like ............. 1Sa 8:5
they said, Give us a king to *j* us.............. 1Sa 8:6
and that our king may *j* us......................... 1Sa 8:20
The LORD *j* between me and thee, and 1Sa 24:12
The LORD therefore be *j*........................ 1Sa 24:15
*j* between me and thee, and see, and... 1Sa 24:15
Oh that I were made *j* in the land ........ 2Sa 15:4
heart to *j* thy people, that I may .......... 1Kin 3:9
for who is able to *j* this thy so.............. 1Kin 3:9
for the throne where he might *j*............. 1Kin 7:7
*j* thy servants, condemning the ............ 1Kin 8:32
because he cometh to *j* the earth....... 1Chr 16:33
for who can *j* this thy people,.............. 2Chr 1:10
that thou mayest *j* my people............. 2Chr 1:11
*j* thy servants, by requiting the ........... 2Chr 6:23
for ye *j* not for man, but for the............ 2Chr 19:6
O our God, wilt thou not *j* them ....... 2Chr 20:12
which may *j* all the people that ........... Ezr 7:25
I would make supplication to my *j* ......... Job 9:15
can he *j* through the dark cloud.......... Job 22:13
I be delivered for ever from my *j*............ Job 23:7
iniquity to be punished by the *j*........... Job 31:28
The LORD shall *j* the people..................... Ps 7:8
*j* me, O LORD, according to my.................. Ps 7:8
And he shall *j* the world in......................... Ps 9:8
To *j* the fatherless and the....................... Ps 10:18
J me, O LORD ............................................. Ps 26:1
J me, O LORD my God, according to...... Ps 35:24
J me, O God, and plead my cause.............. Ps 43:1
earth, that he may *j* his people................. Ps 50:4
for God is *j* himself...................................... Ps 50:6
thy name, and *j* me by thy strength ......... Ps 54:1
do ye *j* uprightly, O ye sons of ................... Ps 58:1
for thou shalt *j* the people .......................... Ps 67:4
a *j* of the widows, is God in his.................... Ps 68:5
He shall *j* thy people with.......................... Ps 72:2
He shall *j* the poor of the people................ Ps 72:4
congregation I will *j* uprightly.................... Ps 75:2
But God is the *j* ........................................... Ps 75:7
How long will ye *j* unjustly ......................... Ps 82:2
Arise, O God, *j* the earth............................. Ps 82:8
up thyself, thou *j* of the earth ..................... Ps 94:2
he shall *j* the people righteously ............. Ps 96:10
for he cometh to *j* the earth ...................... Ps 96:13
he shall *j* the world with........................... Ps 96:13
for he cometh to *j* the earth ........................ Ps 98:9
shall he *j* the world, and the ....................... Ps 98:9
He shall *j* among the heathen, he.............. Ps 110:6
For the LORD will *j* his people.................. Ps 135:14
*j* righteously, and plead the cause.......... Prov 31:9
God shall *j* the righteous and the.......... Eccl 3:17
*j* the fatherless, plead for the...................... Is 1:17
they *j* not the fatherless,............................ Is 1:23
he shall *j* among the nations, and .............. Is 2:4

man, and the man of war, the j ... Is 3:2
and standeth to j the people ... Is 3:13
of Jerusalem, and men of Judah, j ... Is 5:3
he shall not j after the sight of ... Is 11:3
righteousness shall he j the poor ... Is 11:4
For the LORD is our j, the LORD ... Is 33:22
and mine arms shall j the people ... Is 51:5
they j not the cause, the cause ... Jer 5:28
right of the needy do they not j ... Jer 5:28
j thou my cause ... Lam 3:59
will j thee according to thy ways ... Eze 7:3
I will j thee according to thy ... Eze 7:8
to their deserts will I j them ... Eze 7:27
I will j you in the border of ... Eze 11:10
but I will j you in the border of ... Eze 11:11
And I will j thee, as women that ... Eze 16:38
Therefore I will j you, O house ... Eze 18:30
Wilt thou j them, son of man, ... Eze 20:4
son of man, wilt thou j them ... Eze 20:4
I will j thee in the place where ... Eze 21:30
Now, thou son of man, wilt thou j ... Eze 22:2
wilt thou j the bloody city ... Eze 22:2
they shall j thee according to ... Eze 23:24
Son of man, wilt thou j Aholah ... Eze 23:36
they shall j them after the ... Eze 23:45
to thy doings, shall they j thee ... Eze 24:14
I will j you every one after his ... Eze 33:20
I j between cattle and cattle, ... Eze 34:17
will j between the fat cattle and ... Eze 34:20
I will j between cattle and cattle ... Eze 34:22
they shall j it according to my ... Eze 44:24
for there will I sit to j all the ... Joel 3:12
I will cut off the j from the ... Amos 2:3
mount Zion to j the mount of Esau ... Obad 21
The heads thereof j for reward ... Mic 3:11
he shall j among many people, and ... Mic 4:3
they shall smite the j of Israel ... Mic 5:1
the j asketh for a reward ... Mic 7:3
then thou shalt also j my house ... Zec 3:7
adversary deliver thee to the j ... Mt 5:25
the j deliver thee to the officer ... Mt 5:25
J not, that ye be not judged ... Mt 7:1
For with what judgment ye j ... Mt 7:2
J not, and ye shall not be judged ... Lk 6:37
who made me a j or a divider over ... Lk 12:14
yourselves j ye not what is right ... Lk 12:57
lest he hale thee to the j ... Lk 12:58
the j deliver thee to the officer ... Lk 12:58
Saying, There was in a city a j ... Lk 18:2
Hear what the unjust j saith ... Lk 18:6
of thine own mouth will I j thee ... Lk 19:22
as I hear, I j ... Jn 5:30
J not according to the appearance ... Jn 7:24
but j righteous judgment ... Jn 7:24
Doth our law j any man, before it ... Jn 7:51
Ye j after the flesh ... Jn 8:15
I j no man ... Jn 8:15
And yet if I j, my judgment is ... Jn 8:16
many things to say and to j of you ... Jn 8:26
and believe not, I j him not ... Jn 12:47
for I came not to j the world ... Jn 12:47
the same shall j him in the last ... Jn 12:48
j him according to your law ... Jn 18:31
unto you more than unto God, j ye ... Acts 4:19
they shall be in bondage will I j ... Acts 7:7
made thee a ruler and a j over us ... Acts 7:27
Who made thee a ruler and a j ... Acts 7:35
of God to be the J of quick ... Acts 10:42
you, and j yourselves unworthy of ... Acts 13:46
in the which he will j the world ... Acts 17:31
I will be no j of such matters ... Acts 18:15
thou to j me after the law ... Acts 23:3
many years a j unto this nation ... Acts 24:10
In the day when God shall j the ... Rom 2:16
j thee, who by the letter and ... Rom 2:27
then how shall God j the world ... Rom 3:6
eateth not j him that eateth ... Rom 14:3
But why dost thou j thy brother ... Rom 14:10
therefore j one another any more ... Rom 14:13
but j this rather, that no man ... Rom 14:13
yea, I j not mine own self ... 1Cor 4:3
Therefore j nothing before the ... 1Cor 4:5
For what have I to do to j them ... 1Cor 5:12
do not ye j them that are within ... 1Cor 5:12
that the saints shall j the world ... 1Cor 6:2
are ye unworthy to j the smallest ... 1Cor 6:2
ye not that we shall j angels ... 1Cor 6:3
set them to j who are least ... 1Cor 6:4
be able to j between his brethren ... 1Cor 6:5
j ye what I say ... 1Cor 10:15
J in yourselves ... 1Cor 11:13
For if we would j ourselves ... 1Cor 11:31
two or three, and let the other j ... 1Cor 14:29
because we thus j, that if one ... 2Cor 5:14
no man therefore j you in meat ... Col 2:16
Christ, who shall j the quick ... 2Ti 4:1
which the Lord, the righteous j ... 2Ti 4:8
The Lord shall j his people ... Heb 10:30
in heaven, and to God the J of all ... Heb 12:23
and adulterers God will j ... Heb 13:4
but if thou j the law, thou art ... Jas 4:11
not a doer of the law, but a j ... Jas 4:11
the j standeth before the door ... Jas 5:9
him that is ready to j the quick ... 1Pet 4:5
holy and true, dost thou not j ... Rev 6:10
and in righteousness he doth j ... Rev 19:11

## JUDGED

And Rachel said, God hath j me ... Gen 30:6
they j the people at all seasons ... Ex 18:26
small matter they j themselves ... Ex 18:26
he j Israel, and went out to war ... Judg 3:10
she j Israel at that time ... Judg 4:4
he j Israel twenty and three years ... Judg 10:2
j Israel twenty and two years ... Judg 10:3
Jephthah j Israel six years ... Judg 12:7
him Ibzan of Beth-lehem j Israel ... Judg 12:8
And he j Israel seven years ... Judg 12:9
him Elon, a Zebulonite, j Israel ... Judg 12:11
and he j Israel ten years ... Judg 12:11
Hillel, a Pirathonite, j Israel ... Judg 12:13
and he j Israel eight years ... Judg 12:14
he j Israel in the days of the ... Judg 15:20
And he j Israel twenty years ... Judg 16:31
he had j Israel forty years ... 1Sa 4:18
Samuel j the children of Israel ... 1Sa 7:6
Samuel j Israel all the days of ... 1Sa 7:15
j Israel in all those places ... 1Sa 7:16
and there he j Israel ... 1Sa 7:17
the judgment which the king had j ... 1Kin 3:28
days of the judges that j Israel ... 2Kin 23:22
let the heathen be j in thy sight ... Ps 9:19
nor condemn him when he is j ... Ps 37:33
When he shall be j, let him be ... Ps 109:7
He j the cause of the poor and ... Jer 22:16
break wedlock and shed blood are j ... Eze 16:38
which hast j thy sisters, bear ... Eze 16:52
the wounded shall be j in the ... Eze 28:23
among them, when I have j thee ... Eze 35:11
to their doings I j them ... Eze 36:19
and against our judges that j us ... Dan 9:12
Judge not, that ye be not j ... Mt 7:1
judgment ye judge, ye shall be j ... Mt 7:2
Judge not, and ye shall not be j ... Lk 6:37
unto him, Thou hast rightly j ... Lk 7:43
the prince of this world is j ... Jn 16:11
If ye have j me to be faithful to ... Acts 16:15
would have j according to our law ... Acts 24:6
there be j of these things before ... Acts 25:9
seat, where I ought to be j ... Acts 25:10
there be j of these matters ... Acts 25:20
am j for the hope of the promise ... Acts 26:6
in the law shall be j by the law ... Rom 2:12
mightest overcome when thou art j ... Rom 3:4
why yet am I also j as a sinner ... Rom 3:7
yet he himself is j of no man ... 1Cor 2:15
thing that I should be j of you ... 1Cor 4:3
have j already, as though I were ... 1Cor 5:3
and if the world shall be j by you ... 1Cor 6:2
for why is my liberty j of ... 1Cor 10:29
ourselves, we should not be j ... 1Cor 11:31
But when we are j, we are ... 1Cor 11:32
convinced of all, he is j of all ... 1Cor 14:24
because she j him faithful who ... Heb 11:11
shall be j by the law of liberty ... Jas 2:12
that they might be j according to ... 1Pet 4:6
the dead, that they should be j ... Rev 11:18
be, because thou hast j thus ... Rev 16:5
for he hath j the great whore, ... Rev 19:2
the dead were j out of those ... Rev 20:12
they were j every man according ... Rev 20:13

## JUDGES

master shall bring him unto the j ... Ex 21:6
he shall pay as the j determine ... Ex 21:22
house shall be brought unto the j ... Ex 22:8
parties shall come before the j ... Ex 22:9
whom the j shall condemn, he ... Ex 22:9
Moses said unto the j of Israel ... Num 25:5
And I charged your j at that time ... Deut 1:16
J and officers shalt thou make ... Deut 16:18
LORD, before the priests and the j ... Deut 19:17
the j shall make diligent ... Deut 19:18
thy j shall come forth, and they ... Deut 21:2
that the j may judge them ... Deut 25:1
our enemies themselves being j ... Deut 32:31
elders, and officers, and their j ... Josh 8:33
for their heads, and for their j ... Josh 23:2
for their heads, and for their j ... Josh 24:1
Nevertheless the LORD raised up j ... Judg 2:16
would not hearken unto their j ... Judg 2:17
And when the LORD raised them up j. Judg 2:18
pass in the days when the j ruled ... Ruth 1:1
he made his sons j over Israel ... 1Sa 8:1
they were j in Beer-sheba ... 1Sa 8:2
j to be over my people Israel ... 2Sa 7:11
days of the j that judged Israel ... 2Kin 23:22
a word to any of the j of Israel ... 1Chr 17:6
j to be over my people Israel ... 1Chr 17:10
six thousand were officers and j ... 1Chr 23:4
over Israel, for officers and j ... 1Chr 26:29
and of hundreds, and to the j ... 2Chr 1:2
he set j in the land throughout ... 2Chr 19:5
And said to the j, Take heed what ... 2Chr 19:6
thine hand, set magistrates and j ... Ezr 7:25
the j thereof, until the fierce ... Ezr 10:14
the faces of the j thereof ... Job 9:24
spoiled, and maketh the j fools ... Job 12:17
iniquity to be punished by the j ... Job 31:11
be instructed, ye j of the earth ... Ps 2:10
When their j are overthrown in ... Ps 141:6
princes, and all j of the earth ... Ps 148:11
even all the j of the earth ... Prov 8:16
restore thy j as at the first ... Is 1:26
he maketh the j of the earth as ... Is 40:23
governors, and the captains, the j ... Dan 3:2
the governors, and captains, the j ... Dan 3:3
against our j that judged us, by ... Dan 9:12
an oven, and have devoured their j ... Hos 7:7
thy j of whom thou saidst, Give ... Hos 13:10
her j are evening wolves ... Zeph 3:3
therefore they shall be your j ... Mt 12:27
therefore shall they be your j ... Lk 11:19
after that he gave unto them j ... Acts 13:20
are become j of evil thoughts ... Jas 2:4

## JUDGEST

speakest, and be clear when thou j ... Ps 51:4
that j righteously, that triest ... Jer 11:20
O man, whosoever thou art that j ... Rom 2:1
for wherein thou j another ... Rom 2:1
for thou that j doest the same ... Rom 2:1
that j them which do such things, ... Rom 2:3
Who art thou that j another man's ... Rom 14:4
who art thou that j another ... Jas 4:12

## JUDGETH

seeing he j those that are high ... Job 21:22
For by them j he the people ... Job 36:31
God j the righteous, and God is ... Ps 7:11
he is a God that j in the earth ... Ps 58:11
he j among the gods ... Ps 82:1
king that faithfully j the poor ... Prov 29:14
For the Father j no man, but hath ... Jn 5:22
there is one that seeketh and j ... Jn 8:50
not my words, hath one that j him ... Jn 12:48
he that is spiritual j all things ... 1Cor 2:15
but he that j me is the Lord ... 1Cor 4:4
But them that are without God j ... 1Cor 5:13
j his brother, speaketh evil of ... Jas 4:11
evil of the law, and j the law ... Jas 4:11
j according to every man's work ... 1Pet 1:17
himself to him that j righteously ... 1Pet 2:23
strong is the Lord God who j her ... Rev 18:8

## JUDGING

house, j the people of the land ... 2Kin 15:5
house, j the people of the land ... 2Chr 26:21
thou satest in the throne j right ... Ps 9:4
in the tabernacle of David, j ... Is 16:5
j the twelve tribes of Israel ... Mt 19:28
sit on thrones j the twelve ... Lk 22:30

## JUDGMENT

of the LORD, to do justice and j ... Gen 18:19
gods of Egypt I will execute j ... Ex 12:12
according to this j shall it be ... Ex 21:31
to decline after many to wrest j ... Ex 23:2
the j of thy poor in his cause ... Ex 23:6
of j with cunning work ... Ex 28:15
breastplate of j upon his heart ... Ex 28:29
in the breastplate of j the Urim ... Ex 28:30
Aaron shall bear the j of the ... Ex 28:30
shall do no unrighteousness in j ... Lev 19:15
shall do no unrighteousness in j ... Lev 19:35
children of Israel a statute of j ... Num 27:11
the j of Urim before the LORD ... Num 27:21
before the congregation in j ... Num 35:12
of j unto you throughout your ... Num 35:29
Ye shall not respect persons in j ... Deut 1:17
for the j is God's ... Deut 1:17
execute the j of the fatherless ... Deut 10:18
judge the people with just j ... Deut 16:18
Thou shalt not wrest j ... Deut 16:19
a matter too hard for thee in j ... Deut 17:8
shall shew thee the sentence of j ... Deut 17:9
according to the j which they ... Deut 17:11
not pervert the j of the stranger ... Deut 24:17
between men, and they come unto j ... Deut 25:1
perverteth the j of the stranger ... Deut 27:19
for all his ways are j ... Deut 32:4
and mine hand take hold on j ... Deut 32:41
before the congregation for j ... Josh 20:6
of Israel came up to her for j ... Judg 4:5
on white asses, ye that sit in j ... Judg 5:10
and took bribes, and perverted j ... 1Sa 8:3
and David executed j and justice ... 2Sa 8:15
came to the king for j, then ... 2Sa 15:2
that came to the king for j ... 2Sa 15:6
understanding to discern j ... 1Kin 3:11
all Israel heard of the j which ... 1Kin 3:28
wisdom of God was in him, to do j ... 1Kin 3:28
might judge, even the porch of j ... 1Kin 7:7
made he thee king, to do j ... 1Kin 10:9
said unto him, So shall thy j be ... 1Kin 20:40
and they gave j upon him ... 2Kin 25:6
over all Israel, and executed j ... 1Chr 18:14
he thee king over them, to do j ... 2Chr 9:8
LORD, who is with you in the j ... 2Chr 19:6
for the j of the LORD, and for ... 2Chr 19:8
cometh upon us, as the sword, j ... 2Chr 20:9
j upon the house of Ahab, and ... 2Chr 22:8
So they executed j against Joash ... 2Chr 24:24
let j be executed speedily upon ... Ezr 7:26
toward all that knew law and j ... Est 1:13
Doth God pervert j? ... Job 8:3
and if of j, who shall set me a ... Job 9:19
and we should come together in j ... Job 9:32
and bringest me into j with thee ... Job 14:3
I cry aloud, but there is no j ... Job 19:7
that ye may know there is a j ... Job 19:29
will he enter with thee into j ... Job 22:4
liveth, who hath taken away my j ... Job 27:2
my j was as a robe and a diadem ... Job 29:14
neither do the aged understand j ... Job 32:9
Let us choose to us j ... Job 34:4
and God hath taken away my j ... Job 34:5
will the Almighty pervert j ... Job 34:12
he should enter into j with God ... Job 34:23
not see him, yet j is before him ... Job 35:14
fulfilled the j of the wicked ... Job 36:17
j and justice take hold on thee ... Job 36:17
he is excellent in power, and in j ... Job 37:23
Wilt thou also disannul my j ... Job 40:8

ungodly shall not stand in the j ... Ps 1:5
awake for me to the j that thou ... Ps 7:6
he hath prepared his throne for j ... Ps 9:7
he shall minister j to the people ... Ps 9:8
known by the j which he executeth ... Ps 9:16
The meek will he guide in j ... Ps 25:9
He loveth righteousness and j ... Ps 33:5
Stir up thyself, and awake to my j ... Ps 35:23
light, and thy j as the noonday ... Ps 37:6
For the LORD loveth j, and ... Ps 37:28
and his tongue talketh of j ... Ps 37:30
righteousness and thy poor with j ... Ps 72:2
Thou didst cause j to be heard ... Ps 76:8
When God arose to j, to save all ... Ps 76:9
j are the habitation of thy ... Ps 89:14
But j shall return unto ... Ps 94:15
j are the habitation of his ... Ps 97:2
The king's strength also loveth j ... Ps 99:4
equity, thou executest j and ... Ps 99:4
I will sing of mercy and j ... Ps 101:1
j for all that are oppressed ... Ps 103:6
Blessed are they that keep j ... Ps 106:3
stood up Phinehas, and executed j ... Ps 106:30
of his hands are verity and j ... Ps 111:7
Teach me good j and knowledge ... Ps 119:66
when wilt thou execute j on them ... Ps 119:84
I have done j and justice ... Ps 119:121
quicken me according to thy j ... Ps 119:149
For there are set thrones of j ... Ps 122:5
enter not into j with thy servant ... Ps 143:2
Which executeth j for the ... Ps 146:7
execute upon them the j written ... Ps 149:9
of wisdom, justice, and j, and ... Prov 1:3
He keepeth the paths of j ... Prov 2:8
understand righteousness, and j ... Prov 2:9
in the midst of the paths of j ... Prov 8:20
that is destroyed for want of j ... Prov 13:23
his mouth transgresseth not in j ... Prov 16:10
bosom to pervert the ways of j ... Prov 17:23
to overthrow the righteous in j ... Prov 18:5
An ungodly witness scorneth j ... Prov 19:28
j scattereth away all evil with ... Prov 20:8
j is more acceptable to the LORD ... Prov 21:3
because they refuse to do j ... Prov 21:7
It is joy to the just to do j ... Prov 21:15
to have respect of persons in j ... Prov 24:23
Evil men understand not j ... Prov 28:5
The king by j establisheth the ... Prov 29:4
but every man's j cometh from the ... Prov 29:26
pervert the j of any of the ... Prov 31:5
saw under the sun the place of j ... Eccl 3:16
poor, and violent perverting of j ... Eccl 5:8
heart discerneth both time and j ... Eccl 8:5
every purpose there is time and j ... Eccl 8:6
things God will bring thee into j ... Eccl 11:9
God shall bring every work into j ... Eccl 12:14
seek j, relieve the oppressed, ... Is 1:17
it was full of j ... Is 1:21
Zion shall be redeemed with j ... Is 1:27
The LORD will enter into j with ... Is 3:14
midst thereof by the spirit of j ... Is 4:4
and he looked for j, but behold ... Is 5:7
of hosts shall be exalted in j ... Is 5:16
it, and to establish it with j ... Is 9:7
To turn aside the needy from j ... Is 10:2
Take counsel, execute j ... Is 16:3
of David, judging, and seeking j ... Is 16:5
j to him that sitteth in j ... Is 28:6
err in vision, they stumble in j ... Is 28:7
J also will I lay to the line, and ... Is 28:17
for the LORD is a God of j ... Is 30:18
and princes shall rule in j ... Is 32:1
Then j shall dwell in the ... Is 32:16
he hath filled Zion with j ... Is 33:5
upon the people of my curse, to j ... Is 34:5
and taught him in the path of j ... Is 40:14
my j is passed over from my God ... Is 40:27
let us come near together to j ... Is 41:1
bring forth j to the Gentiles ... Is 42:1
he shall bring forth j unto truth ... Is 42:3
till he have set j in the earth ... Is 42:4
yet surely my j is with the LORD, ... Is 49:4
I will make my j to rest for a ... Is 51:4
was taken from prison and from j ... Is 53:8
thee in j thou shalt condemn ... Is 54:17
Thus saith the LORD, Keep ye j ... Is 56:1
there is no j in their goings ... Is 59:8
Therefore is j far from us ... Is 59:9
we look for j, but there is none ... Is 59:11
j is turned away backward, and ... Is 59:14
him that there was no j ... Is 59:15
For I the LORD love j, I hate ... Is 61:8
The LORD liveth, in truth, in j ... Jer 4:2
if there be any that executeth j ... Jer 5:1
the LORD, nor the j of their God ... Jer 5:4
the LORD, and the j of their God ... Jer 5:5
throughly execute j between a man ... Jer 7:5
people know not the j of the LORD ... Jer 8:7
which exercise lovingkindness, j ... Jer 9:24
O LORD, correct me, but with j ... Jer 10:24
Execute j in the morning, and ... Jer 21:12
Execute ye j and righteousness, and ... Jer 22:3
thy father eat and drink, and do j ... Jer 22:15
and prosper, and shall execute j ... Jer 23:5
and he shall execute j and ... Jer 33:15
Hamath, where he gave j upon him ... Jer 39:5
j is come upon the plain country ... Jer 48:21
Thus far is the j of Moab ... Jer 48:47
they whose j was not to drink of ... Jer 49:12
for her j reacheth unto heaven, ... Jer 51:9
that I will do j upon the graven ... Jer 51:47
that I will do j upon her graven ... Jer 51:52
where he gave j upon him ... Jer 52:9
hath executed true j between man ... Eze 18:8
for they had executed j upon her ... Eze 23:10
I will set j before them, and they ... Eze 23:24
I will feed them with j ... Eze 34:16
see my j that I have executed ... Eze 39:21
controversy they shall stand in j ... Eze 44:24
violence and spoil, and execute j ... Eze 45:9
works are truth, and his ways j ... Dan 4:37
the j was set, and the books were ... Dan 7:10
j was given to the saints of the ... Dan 7:22
But the j shall sit, and they ... Dan 7:26
unto me in righteousness, and in j ... Hos 2:19
for j is toward you, because ye ... Hos 5:1
is oppressed and broken in j ... Hos 5:11
thus j springeth up as hemlock in ... Hos 10:4
keep mercy and j, and wait on thy ... Hos 12:6
Ye who turn j to wormwood ... Amos 5:7
good, and establish j in the gate ... Amos 5:15
But let j run down as waters, and ... Amos 5:24
for ye have turned j into gall ... Amos 6:12
Is it not for you to know j ... Mic 3:1
the spirit of the LORD, and of j ... Mic 3:8
the house of Israel, that abhor j ... Mic 3:9
my cause, and execute j for me ... Mic 7:9
slacked, and j doth never go forth ... Hab 1:4
therefore wrong j proceedeth ... Hab 1:4
their j and their dignity shall ... Hab 1:7
thou hast ordained them for j ... Hab 1:12
earth, which have wrought his j ... Zeph 2:3
doth he bring his j to light ... Zeph 3:5
of hosts, saying, Execute true j ... Zec 7:9
execute the j of truth and peace ... Zec 8:16
or, Where is the God of j ... Mal 2:17
And I will come near to you to j ... Mal 3:5
kill shall be in danger of the j ... Mt 5:21
cause shall be in danger of the j ... Mt 5:22
For with what j ye judge, ye ... Mt 7:2
Sodom and Gomorrha in the day of j ... Mt 10:15
for Tyre and Sidon at the day of j ... Mt 11:22
the land of Sodom in the day of j ... Mt 11:24
he shall shew j to the Gentiles ... Mt 12:18
till he send forth j unto victory ... Mt 12:20
account thereof in the day of j ... Mt 12:36
rise in j with this generation ... Mt 12:41
up in the j with this generation ... Mt 12:42
weightier matters of the law, j ... Mt 23:23
he was set down on the j seat ... Mt 27:19
Sodom and Gomorrha in the day of j ... Mk 6:11
for Tyre and Sidon at the j ... Lk 10:14
the south shall rise up in the j ... Lk 11:31
up in the j with this generation ... Lk 11:32
manner of herbs, and pass over j ... Lk 11:42
hath committed all j unto the Son ... Jn 5:22
him authority to execute j also ... Jn 5:27
and my j is just ... Jn 5:30
appearance, but judge righteous j ... Jn 7:24
And yet if I judge, my j is true ... Jn 8:16
For j I am come into this world, ... Jn 9:39
Now is the j of this world ... Jn 12:31
sin, and of righteousness, and of j ... Jn 16:8
Of j, because the prince of this ... Jn 16:11
from Caiaphas unto the hall of j ... Jn 18:28
went not into the j hall, lest ... Jn 18:28
entered into the j hall again ... Jn 18:33
And went again into the j hall ... Jn 19:9
sat down in the j seat in a place ... Jn 19:13
humiliation his j was taken away ... Acts 8:33
and brought him to the j seat ... Acts 18:12
And he drave them from the j seat ... Acts 18:16
and beat him before the j seat ... Acts 18:17
him to be kept in Herod's j hall ... Acts 23:35
j to come, Felix trembled, and ... Acts 24:25
the j seat commanded Paul to be ... Acts 25:6
Paul, I stand at Caesar's j seat ... Acts 25:10
desiring to have j against him ... Acts 25:15
on the morrow I sat on the j seat ... Acts 25:17
Who knowing the j of God, that ... Rom 1:32
But we are sure that the j of God ... Rom 2:2
thou shalt escape the j of God ... Rom 2:3
of the righteous j of God ... Rom 2:5
for the j was by one to ... Rom 5:16
of one j came upon all men to ... Rom 5:18
stand before the j seat of Christ ... Rom 14:10
in the same mind and in the same j ... 1Cor 1:10
be judged of you, or of man's j ... 1Cor 4:3
yet I give my j, as one that hath ... 1Cor 7:25
if she so abide, after my j ... 1Cor 7:40
before the j seat of Christ ... 2Cor 5:10
troubleth you shall bear his j ... Gal 5:10
and more in knowledge and in all j ... Phil 1:9
token of the righteous j of God ... 2Th 1:5
beforehand, going before to j ... 1Ti 5:24
of the dead, and of eternal j ... Heb 6:2
once to die, but after this the j ... Heb 9:27
certain fearful looking for of j ... Heb 10:27
and draw you before the j seats ... Jas 2:6
For he shall have j without mercy ... Jas 2:13
and mercy rejoiceth against j ... Jas 2:13
For the time is come that j must ... 1Pet 4:17
whose j now of a long time ... 2Pet 2:3
darkness, to be reserved unto j ... 2Pet 2:4
unto the day of j to be punished ... 2Pet 2:9
unto fire against the day of j ... 2Pet 3:7
may have boldness in the day of j ... 1Jn 4:17
unto the j of the great day ... Jude 6
To execute j upon all, and to ... Jude 15
for the hour of his j is come ... Rev 14:7
I will shew unto thee the j of ... Rev 17:1
for in one hour is thy j come ... Rev 18:10
them, and j was given unto them ... Rev 20:4

## JUDGMENTS

out arm, and with great j ... Ex 6:6
of the land of Egypt by great j ... Ex 7:4
Now these are the j which thou ... Ex 21:1
words of the LORD, and all the j ... Ex 24:3
Ye shall do my j, and keep mine ... Lev 18:4
keep my statutes, and my j ... Lev 18:5
keep my statutes and my j, and ... Lev 18:26
all my statutes, and all my j ... Lev 19:37
keep all my statutes, and all my j ... Lev 20:22
do my statutes, and keep my j ... Lev 25:18
or if your soul abhor my j ... Lev 26:15
even because they despised my j ... Lev 26:43
These are the statutes and j ... Lev 26:46
gods also the LORD executed j ... Num 33:4
of blood according to these j ... Num 35:24
are the commandments and the j ... Num 36:13
unto the statutes and unto the j ... Deut 4:1
I have taught you statutes and j ... Deut 4:5
j so righteous as all this law, ... Deut 4:8
time to teach you statutes and j ... Deut 4:14
and the statutes, and the j ... Deut 4:45
j which I speak in your ears this ... Deut 5:1
and the statutes, and the j ... Deut 5:31
the statutes, and the j, which ... Deut 6:1
and the statutes, and the j ... Deut 6:20
and the statutes, and the j ... Deut 7:11
to pass, if ye hearken to these j ... Deut 7:12
his commandments, and his j ... Deut 8:11
charge, and his statutes, and his j ... Deut 11:1
j which I set before you this day ... Deut 11:32
These are the statutes and j ... Deut 12:1
thee to do these statutes and j ... Deut 26:16
and his commandments, and his j ... Deut 26:17
and his statutes and his j, that ... Deut 30:16
They shall teach Jacob thy j ... Deut 33:10
of the LORD, and his j with Israel ... Deut 33:21
For all his j were before me ... 2Sa 22:23
and his commandments, and his j ... 1Kin 2:3
in my statutes, and execute my j ... 1Kin 6:12
and his statutes, and his j ... 1Kin 8:58
and wilt keep my statutes and my j ... 1Kin 9:4
and to keep my statutes and my j ... 1Kin 11:33
wonders, and the j of his mouth ... 1Chr 16:12
his j are in all the earth ... 1Chr 16:14
j which the LORD charged Moses ... 1Chr 22:13
to do my commandments and my j ... 1Chr 28:7
shalt observe my statutes and my j ... 2Chr 7:17
commandment, statutes and j ... 2Chr 19:10
to teach in Israel statutes and j ... Ezr 7:10
nor the statutes, nor the j ... Neh 1:7
heaven, and gavest them right j ... Neh 9:13
but sinned against thy j ... Neh 9:29
of the LORD our Lord, and his j ... Neh 10:29
thy j are far above out of his ... Ps 10:5
For all his j were before me, and ... Ps 18:22
the j of the LORD are true and ... Ps 19:9
thy j are a great deep ... Ps 36:6
Judah be glad, because of thy j ... Ps 48:11
Give the king thy j, O God, and ... Ps 72:1
my law, and walk not in my j ... Ps 89:30
Judah rejoiced because of thy j ... Ps 97:8
wonders, and the j of his mouth ... Ps 105:5
his j are in all the earth ... Ps 105:7
have learned thy righteous j ... Ps 119:7
I declared all the j of thy mouth ... Ps 119:13
it hath unto thy j at all times ... Ps 119:20
thy j have I laid before me ... Ps 119:30
for thy j are good ... Ps 119:39
for I have hoped in thy j ... Ps 119:43
I remembered thy j of old ... Ps 119:52
thee because of thy righteous j ... Ps 119:62
that thy j are right, and that ... Ps 119:75
I have not departed from thy j ... Ps 119:102
that I will keep thy righteous j ... Ps 119:106
mouth, O LORD, and teach me thy j ... Ps 119:108
and I am afraid of thy j ... Ps 119:120
O LORD, and upright are thy j ... Ps 119:137
quicken me according to thy j ... Ps 119:156
thy righteous j endureth for ever ... Ps 119:160
thee because of thy righteous j ... Ps 119:164
and let thy j help me ... Ps 119:175
his statutes and his j unto Israel ... Ps 147:19
and as for his j, they have not ... Ps 147:20
J are prepared for scorners, and ... Prov 19:29
Yea, in the way of thy j, O LORD, ... Is 26:8
for when thy j are in the earth, ... Is 26:9
I will utter my j against them ... Jer 1:16
let me talk with thee of thy j ... Jer 12:1
she hath changed my j into ... Eze 5:6
for they have refused my j ... Eze 5:6
statutes, neither have kept my j ... Eze 5:7
have done according to the j of ... Eze 5:7
will execute j in the midst of ... Eze 5:8
and I will execute j in thee ... Eze 5:10
shall execute j in thee in anger ... Eze 5:15
and will execute j among you ... Eze 11:9
statutes, neither executed my j ... Eze 11:12
my four sore j upon Jerusalem ... Eze 14:21
execute j upon thee in the sight ... Eze 16:41
in my statutes, and hath kept my j ... Eze 18:9
nor increase, hath executed my j ... Eze 18:17
my statutes, and shewed them my j ... Eze 20:11
statutes, and they despised my j ... Eze 20:13
Because they despised my j ... Eze 20:16
fathers, neither observe their j ... Eze 20:18
walk in my statutes, and keep my j ... Eze 20:19

neither kept my *j* to do them Eze 20:21
they had not executed my *j* Eze 20:24
*j* whereby they should not live Eze 20:25
judge thee according to their *j* Eze 23:24
And I will execute *j* upon Moab Eze 25:11
I shall have executed *j* in her Eze 28:22
when I have executed *j* upon all Eze 28:26
in Zoan, and will execute *j* in No Eze 30:14
Thus will I execute *j* in Egypt Eze 30:19
statutes, and ye shall keep my *j* Eze 36:27
they shall also walk in my *j* Eze 37:24
shall judge it according to my *j* Eze 44:24
from thy precepts and from thy *j* Dan 9:5
thy *j* are as the light that goeth Hos 6:5
The LORD hath taken away thy *j* Zeph 3:15
Israel, with the statutes and *j* Mal 4:4
how unsearchable are his *j* Rom 11:33
If then ye have *j* of things 1Cor 6:4
for thy *j* are made manifest Rev 15:4
true and righteous are thy *j* Rev 16:7
For true and righteous are his *j* Rev 19:2

**JUDITH** (*ju'-dith*) *A wife of Esau.*
wife *J* the daughter of Beeri the Gen 26:34

**JULIA** (*ju'-le-ah*) *A Christian acquaintance of Paul.*
Salute Philologus, and *J*, Nereus, Rom 16:15

**JULIUS** (*ju'-le-us*) *A Roman centurion.*
other prisoners unto one named *J* Acts 27:1
*J* courteously entreated Paul, and Acts 27:3

**JUMPING**
horses, and of the *j* chariots Nah 3:2

**JUNIA** (*ju'-ne-ah*) *A Christian acquaintance of Paul.*
Salute Andronicus and *J*, my Rom 16:7

**JUNIPER**
came and sat down under a *j* tree 1Kin 19:4
as he lay and slept under a *j* tree 1Kin 19:5
bushes, and *j* roots for their meat Job 30:4
of the mighty, with coals of *j* Ps 120:4

**JUPITER** (*ju'-pit-ur*) *Chief god of the Romans.*
And they called Barnabas, *J* Acts 14:12
Then the priest of *J*, which was Acts 14:13
the image which fell down from *J* Acts 19:35

**JURISDICTION**
that he belonged unto Herod's *j* Lk 23:7

**JUSHAB-HESED** (*ju''-shab-he'-sed*) *A son of Zerubbabel.*
and Berechiah, and Hasadiah, *J* 1Chr 3:20

**JUST**
Noah was a *j* man and perfect in Gen 6:9
*J* balances, *j* weights Lev 19:36
a *j* ephah, and a *j* hin, shall Lev 19:36
judge the people with *j* judgment Deut 16:18
is altogether *j* shalt thou follow Deut 16:20
*j* weight, a perfect and Deut 25:15
*j* measure shalt thou have Deut 25:15
of truth and without iniquity, *j* Deut 32:4
He that ruleth over men must be *j* 2Sa 23:3
Howbeit thou art *j* in all that is Neh 9:33
mortal man be more *j* than God Job 4:17
but how should man be *j* with God Job 9:2
the *j* upright man is laughed to Job 12:4
but the *j* shall put it on, and the Job 27:17
Behold, in this thou art not *j* Job 33:12
thou condemn him that is most *j* Job 34:17
but establish the *j* Ps 7:9
The wicked plotteth against the *j* Ps 37:12
blesseth the habitation of the *j* Prov 3:33
But the path of the *j* is as the Prov 4:18
teach a *j* man, and he will Prov 9:9
are upon the head of the *j* Prov 10:6
The memory of the *j* is blessed Prov 10:7
The tongue of the *j* is as choice Prov 10:20
The mouth of the *j* bringeth forth Prov 10:31
but a *j* weight is his delight Prov 11:1
shall the *j* be delivered Prov 11:9
but the *j* shall come out of Prov 12:13
shall no evil happen to the *j* Prov 12:21
the sinner is laid up for the *j* Prov 13:22
A *j* weight and balance are the Prov 16:11
and he that condemneth the *j* Prov 17:15
Also to punish the *j* is not good Prov 17:26
first in his own cause seemeth *j* Prov 18:17
The *j* man walketh in his Prov 20:7
It is joy to the *j* to do judgment Prov 21:15
For a *j* man falleth seven times, Prov 24:16
but the *j* seek his soul Prov 29:10
man is an abomination to the *j* Prov 29:27
there is a *j* man that perisheth Eccl 7:15
there is not a *j* man upon earth Eccl 7:20
that there be *j* men, unto whom it Eccl 8:14
The way of the *j* is uprightness Is 26:7
dost weigh the path of the *j* Is 26:7
turn aside the *j* for a thing of Is 29:21
a *j* God and a Saviour Is 45:21
of the *j* in the midst of her Lam 4:13
But if a man be *j*, and do that Eze 18:5
he is *j*, he shall surely live, Eze 18:9
Ye shall have *j* balances, and a Eze 45:10
a *j* ephah, and a *j* bath Eze 45:10
and the *j* shall walk in them Hos 14:9
they afflict the *j*, they take a Amos 5:12
but the *j* shall live by his faith Hab 2:4
The *j* LORD is in the midst Zeph 3:5
he is *j*, and having salvation Zec 9:9
Joseph her husband, being a *j* man Mt 1:19
good, and sendeth rain on the *j* Mt 5:45
sever the wicked from among the *j* Mt 13:49
nothing to do with that *j* man Mt 27:19
of the blood of this *j* person Mt 27:24
John, knowing that he was a *j* man Mk 6:20
to the wisdom of the *j* Lk 1:17
and the same man was *j* and devout, Lk 2:25
at the resurrection of the *j* Lk 14:14
nine *j* persons, which need no Lk 15:7
should feign themselves *j* men Lk 20:20
and he was a good man, and a *j* Lk 23:50
and my judgment is *j* Jn 5:30
ye denied the Holy One and the *J* Acts 3:14
before of the coming of the *J* One Acts 7:52
a *j* man, and one that feareth God, Acts 10:22
know his will, and see that *J* One Acts 22:14
of the dead, both of the *j* Acts 24:15
The *j* shall live by faith Rom 1:17
of the law are *j* before God Rom 2:13
whose damnation is *j* Rom 3:8
that he might be *j*, and the Rom 3:26
and the commandment holy, and *j* Rom 7:12
The *j* shall live by faith Gal 3:11
honest, whatsoever things are *j* Phil 4:8
your servants that which is *j* Col 4:1
a lover of good men, sober, *j* Titus 1:8
received a *j* recompence of reward Heb 2:2
Now the *j* shall live by faith Heb 10:38
the spirits of *j* men made perfect Heb 12:23
Ye have condemned and killed the *j* Jas 5:6
the *j* for the unjust, that he 1Pet 3:18
And delivered *j* Lot, vexed with 2Pet 2:7
*j* to forgive us our sins, and to 1Jn 1:9
*j* and true are thy ways, thou King Rev 15:3

**JUSTICE**
keep the way of the LORD, to do *j* Gen 18:19
he executed the *j* of the LORD Deut 33:21
judgment and *j* unto all his people 2Sa 8:15
come unto me, and I would do him *j* 2Sa 15:4
he thee king, to do judgment and *j* 1Kin 10:9
and *j* among all his people 1Chr 18:14
over them, to do judgment and *j* 2Chr 9:8
or doth the Almighty pervert *j* Job 8:3
judgment and *j* take hold on thee Job 36:17
and in judgment, and in plenty of *j* Job 37:23
do *j* to the afflicted and needy Ps 82:3
*J* and judgment are the habitation Ps 89:14
I have done judgment and *j* Ps 119:121
the instruction of wisdom, *j* Prov 1:3
kings reign, and princes decree *j* Prov 8:15
To do *j* and judgment is more Prov 21:3
*j* in a province, marvel not at Eccl 5:8
with *j* from henceforth even for Is 9:7
LORD, Keep ye judgment, and do *j* Is 56:1
ask of me the ordinances of *j* Is 58:2
None calleth for *j*, nor any Is 59:4
us, neither doth *j* overtake us Is 59:9
backward, and *j* standeth afar off Is 59:14
eat and drink, and do judgment and *j* Jer 22:15
judgment and *j* in the earth Jer 23:5
bless thee, O habitation of *j* Jer 31:23
the LORD, the habitation of *j* Jer 50:7
spoil, and execute judgment and *j* Eze 45:9

**JUSTIFICATION**
and was raised again for our *j* Rom 4:25
gift is of many offences unto *j* Rom 5:16
came upon all men unto *j* of life Rom 5:18

**JUSTIFIED**
and should a man full of talk be *j* Job 11:2
I know that I shall be *j* Job 13:18
How then can man be *j* with God Job 25:4
because he *j* himself rather than Job 32:2
mightest be *j* when thou speakest Ps 51:4
sight shall no man living be *j* Ps 143:2
witnesses, that they may be *j* Is 43:9
thou, that thou mayest be *j* Is 43:26
shall all the seed of Israel be *j* Is 45:25
The backsliding Israel hath *j* Jer 3:11
hast *j* thy sisters in all thine Eze 16:51
in that thou hast *j* thy sisters Eze 16:52
But wisdom is *j* of her children Mt 11:19
For by thy words thou shalt be *j* Mt 12:37
*j* God, being baptized with the Lk 7:29
But wisdom is *j* of all her Lk 7:35
his house *j* rather than the other Lk 18:14
believe are *j* from all things Acts 13:39
not be *j* by the law of Moses Acts 13:39
the doers of the law shall be *j* Rom 2:13
thou mightest be *j* in thy sayings Rom 3:4
shall no flesh be *j* in his sight Rom 3:20
Being *j* freely by his grace Rom 3:24
we conclude that a man is *j* by Rom 3:28
For if Abraham were *j* by works Rom 4:2
Therefore being *j* by faith Rom 5:1
being now *j* by his blood, we Rom 5:9
and whom he called, them he also *j* Rom 8:30
and whom he *j*, them he also Rom 8:30
yet am I not hereby *j* 1Cor 4:4
but ye are *j* in the name of the 1Cor 6:11
is not *j* by the works of the law Gal 2:16
that we might be *j* by the faith Gal 2:16
of the law shall no flesh be *j* Gal 2:16
while we seek to be *j* by Christ Gal 2:17
But that no man is *j* by the law Gal 3:11
that we might be *j* by faith Gal 3:24
whosoever of you are *j* by the law Gal 5:4
*j* in the Spirit, seen of angels, 1Ti 3:16
That being *j* by his grace, we Titus 3:7
not Abraham our father *j* by works Jas 2:21
then how that by works a man is *j* Jas 2:24
not Rahab the harlot *j* by works Jas 2:25

**JUSTIFIER**
the *j* of him which believeth in Rom 3:26

**JUSTIFIETH**
He that *j* the wicked, and he that Prov 17:15
He is near that *j* me Is 50:8
on him that *j* the ungodly Rom 4:5
It is God that *j* Rom 8:33

**JUSTIFY**
for I will not *j* the wicked Ex 23:7
then they shall *j* the righteous Deut 25:1
If I *j* myself, mine own mouth Job 9:20
God forbid that I should *j* you Job 27:5
speak, for I desire to *j* thee Job 33:32
Which *j* the wicked for reward, and Is 5:23
shall my righteous servant *j* many Is 53:11
But he, willing to *j* himself Lk 10:29
Ye are they which *j* yourselves Lk 16:15
which shall *j* the circumcision by Rom 3:30
would *j* the heathen through faith Gal 3:8

**JUSTIFYING**
*j* the righteous, to give him 1Kin 8:32
by *j* the righteous, by giving him 2Chr 6:23

**JUSTLE**
they shall *j* one against another Nah 2:4

**JUSTLY**
LORD require of thee, but to do *j* Mic 6:8
And we indeed *j*; for we receive Lk 23:41
and God also, how holily and *j* 1Th 2:10

**JUSTUS** (*jus'-tus*) See BARSABAS, JESUS.
1. *Surname for Barsabas.*
Barsabas, who was surnamed *J* Acts 1:23
2. *A Corinthian Christian.*
a certain man's house, named *J* Acts 18:7
3. *A Christian acquaintance of Paul.*
And Jesus, which is called *J* Col 4:11

**JUTTAH** (*jut'-tah*) *A city in Judah.*
Maon, Carmel, and Ziph, and *J* Josh 15:55
and *J* with her suburbs, and Josh 21:16

# K

**KABZEEL** (*kab'-ze-el*) See JEKABZEEL. *A city in Judah.*
coast of Edom southward were *K* Josh 15:21
the son of a valiant man, of *K* 2Sa 23:20
the son of a valiant man of *K* 1Chr 11:22

**KADESH** (*ka'-desh*) See EN-MISHPAT, KADESH-BARNEA, KEDESH. *A place in the wilderness, south of Judah.*
and came to En-mishpat, which is *K* Gen 14:7
behold, it is between *K* and Bered Gen 16:14
country, and dwelled between *K* Gen 20:1
the wilderness of Paran, to *K* Num 13:26
and the people abode in *K* Num 20:1
from *K* unto the king of Edom Num 20:14
and, behold, we are in *K*, a city Num 20:16
congregation, journeyed from *K* Num 20:22
in *K* in the wilderness of Zin Num 27:14
the wilderness of Zin, which is *K* Num 33:36
And they removed from *K*, and Num 33:37
So ye abode in *K* many days Deut 1:46
unto the Red sea, and came to *K* Judg 11:16
and Israel abode in *K* Judg 11:17
LORD shaketh the wilderness of *K* Ps 29:8
even to the waters of strife in *K* Eze 47:19
unto the waters of strife in *K* Eze 48:28

**KADESH-BARNEA** (*ka''-desh-bar'-ne-ah*) See KADESH. *Same as Kadesh.*
sent them from *K* to see the land Num 32:8
shall be from the south to *K* Num 34:4
by the way of mount Seir unto *K* Deut 1:2
and we came to *K* Deut 1:19
the space in which we came from *K* Deut 2:14
when the LORD sent you from *K* Deut 9:23
smote them from *K* even unto Gaza Josh 10:41
of God concerning me and thee in *K* Josh 14:6
me from *K* to espy out the land Josh 14:7
up on the south side unto *K* Josh 15:3

**KADMIEL** (*kad'-me-el*)
1. *An exile.*
the children of Jeshua and *K* Ezr 2:40
the children of Jeshua, of *K* Neh 7:43
2. *A rebuilder of the Temple.*
with his sons and his brethren, *K* Ezr 3:9
3. *A Levite with Nehemiah.*
the Levites, Jeshua, and Bani, *K* Neh 9:4
Then the Levites, Jeshua, and *K* Neh 9:5
Binnui of the sons of Henadad, *K* Neh 10:9
Jeshua, Binnui, *K*, Sherebiah, Neh 12:8
Sherebiah, and Jeshua the son of *K* Neh 12:24

**KADMONITES** (*kad'-mo-nites*) *A Phoenician tribe.*
and the Kenizzites, and the *K* Gen 15:19

**KAIN** See CAIN.

**KAIWAN** See CHIUN.

**KALLAI** (*kal'-la-i*) *A priest.*
Of Sallai, *K*; of Amok ... Neh 12:20

**KAMON** See CAMON.

**KANAH** (*ka'-nah*)
*1. A brook between Ephraim and Manasseh.*
Tappuah westward unto the river *K*... Josh 16:8
coast descended unto the river *K*... Josh 17:9
*2. A city in Asher.*
Rehob, and Hammon, and *K*... Josh 19:28

**KAREAH** (*ka'-re-ah*) See CAREAH. *A captain of the Jews.*
Johanan and Jonathan the sons of *K*... Jer 40:8
Moreover Johanan the son of *K*... Jer 40:13
Then Johanan the son of *K* spake... Jer 40:15
said unto Johanan the son of *K*... Jer 40:16
But when Johanan the son of *K*... Jer 41:11
Ishmael saw Johanan the son of *K*... Jer 41:13
and went unto Johanan the son of *K*... Jer 41:14
Then took Johanan the son of *K*... Jer 41:16
forces, and Johanan the son of *K*... Jer 42:1
called he Johanan the son of *K*... Jer 42:8
Hoshaiah, and Johanan the son of *K*... Jer 43:2
So Johanan the son of *K*, and all... Jer 43:4
But Johanan the son of *K*, and all... Jer 43:5

**KARKA** See KARKAA.

**KARKAA** (*kar'-ka-ah*) *A city in Judah.*
Adar, and fetched a compass to *K*... Josh 15:3

**KARKOR** (*kar'-kor*) *A Gadite city.*
Now Zebah and Zalmunna were in *K*. Judg 8:10

**KARNAIM** (*kar'-na-im*) See ASHTEROTH. *A city in Og.*
smote the Rephaims in Ashteroth *K*... Gen 14:5

**KARTAH** (*kar'-tah*) See KATTATH. *A Levitical city in Zebulun.*
suburbs, and *K* with her suburbs,... Josh 21:34

**KARTAN** (*kar'-tan*) See KIRJATHAIM. *A Levitical city in Naphtali.*
suburbs, and *K* with her suburbs... Josh 21:32

**KATTATH** (*kat'-tath*) See KARTAH, KITRON. *A city in Zebulun.*
And *K*, and Nahallal... Josh 19:15

**KEBAR** See CHEBAR.

**KEDAR** (*ke'-dar*)
*1. A son of Ishmael.*
and *K*, and Adbeel, and Mibsam,... Gen 25:13
then *K*, and Adbeel, and Mibsam,... 1Chr 1:29
*2. The tribe.*
that I dwell in the tents of *K*... Ps 120:5
of Jerusalem, as the tents of *K*... Song 1:5
and all the glory of *K* shall fail... Is 21:16
mighty men of the children of *K*... Is 21:17
the villages that *K* doth inhabit... Is 42:11
All the flocks of *K* shall be... Is 60:7
and send unto *K*, and consider... Jer 2:10
Concerning *K*, and concerning the... Jer 49:28
Arise ye, go up to *K*, and spoil... Jer 49:28
Arabia, and all the princes of *K*... Eze 27:21

**KEDEMAH** (*ked'-e-mah*) *A son of Ishmael.*
and Tema, Jetur, Naphish, and *K*... Gen 25:15
Jetur, Naphish, and *K*... 1Chr 1:31

**KEDEMOTH** (*ked'-e-moth*)
*1. A wilderness in Reuben.*
out of the wilderness of *K* unto... Deut 2:26
*2. A Levitical city in Reuben.*
And Jahaza, and *K*, and Mephaath,... Josh 13:18
*K* with her suburbs, and Mephaath... Josh 21:37
*K* also with her suburbs, and... 1Chr 6:79

**KEDESH** (*ke'-desh*) See KADESH, KEDESH-NAPHTALI, KISHION.
*1. A Canaanite city.*
The king of *K*, one... Josh 12:22
And *K*, and Edrei, and En-hazor,... Josh 19:37
*2. A city of refuge in Naphtali.*
they appointed *K* in Galilee in... Josh 20:7
*K* in Galilee with her suburbs, to... Josh 21:32
arose, and went with Barak to *K*... Judg 4:9
called Zebulun and Naphtali to *K*... Judg 4:10
plain of Zaanaim, which is by *K*... Judg 4:11
and Janoah, and *K*, and Hazor, and... 2Kin 15:29
*K* in Galilee with her suburbs, and... 1Chr 6:76
*3. A Levitical city in Naphtali.*
*K* with her suburbs, Daberath with... 1Chr 6:72
*4. A city in Judah.*
And *K*, and Hazor, and Ithnan,... Josh 15:23

**KEDESH-NAPHTALI** (*ke''-desh-naf'-ta-li*)
*Same as Kedesh 2.*
Barak the son of Abinoam out of *K*... Judg 4:6

**KEDOLAOMER** See CHEDORLAOMER.

**KEEP**
of Eden to dress it and to *k* it... Gen 2:15
to *k* the way of the tree of life... Gen 3:24
to *k* them alive with thee... Gen 6:19
come unto thee, to *k* them alive... Gen 6:20
to *k* seed alive upon the face of... Gen 7:3
Abraham, Thou shalt *k* my covenant... Gen 17:9
is my covenant, which ye shall *k*... Gen 17:10
they shall *k* the way of the LORD,... Gen 18:19
will *k* thee in all places whither... Gen 28:15
will *k* me in this way that I go,... Gen 28:20
I will again feed and *k* thy flock... Gen 30:31
*k* that thou hast unto thyself... Gen 33:9
let them *k* food in the cities... Gen 41:35
whom the Egyptians *k* in bondage... Ex 6:5
ye shall *k* it up until the... Ex 12:6
ye shall *k* it a feast to the LORD... Ex 12:14
ye shall *k* it a feast by an... Ex 12:14
that ye shall *k* this service... Ex 12:25
congregation of Israel shall *k* it... Ex 12:47
will *k* the passover to the LORD,... Ex 12:48
and then let him come near and *k* it... Ex 12:48
that thou shalt *k* this service in... Ex 13:5
Thou shalt therefore *k* this... Ex 13:10
*k* all his statutes, I will put... Ex 15:26
refuse ye to *k* my commandments... Ex 16:28
*k* my covenant, then ye shall be a... Ex 19:5
love me, and *k* my commandments... Ex 20:6
the sabbath day, to *k* it holy... Ex 20:8
his neighbour money or stuff to *k*... Ex 22:7
or a sheep, or any beast, to *k*... Ex 22:10
*K* thee far from a false matter... Ex 23:7
Three times thou shalt *k* a feast... Ex 23:14
Thou shalt *k* the feast of... Ex 23:15
to *k* thee in the way, and to bring... Ex 23:20
Verily my sabbaths ye shall *k*... Ex 31:13
Ye shall *k* the sabbath therefore... Ex 31:14
of Israel shall *k* the sabbath... Ex 31:16
of unleavened bread shalt thou *k*... Ex 34:18
that which was delivered him to *k*... Lev 6:2
that which was delivered him to *k*... Lev 6:4
*k* the charge of the LORD, that ye... Lev 8:35
*k* mine ordinances, to walk... Lev 18:4
Ye shall therefore *k* my statutes... Lev 18:5
Ye shall therefore *k* my statutes... Lev 18:26
shall ye *k* mine ordinance... Lev 18:30
and his father, and *k* my sabbaths... Lev 19:3
Ye shall *k* my statutes... Lev 19:19
Ye shall *k* my sabbaths, and... Lev 19:30
ye shall *k* my statutes, and do... Lev 20:8
shall therefore *k* all my statutes... Lev 20:22
shall therefore *k* mine ordinance... Lev 22:9
shall ye *k* my commandments... Lev 22:31
ye shall *k* a feast unto the LORD... Lev 23:39
ye shall *k* it a feast unto the... Lev 23:41
then shall the land *k* a sabbath... Lev 25:2
*k* my judgments, and do them... Lev 25:18
Ye shall *k* my sabbaths, and... Lev 26:2
*k* my commandments, and do them... Lev 26:3
the Levites shall *k* the charge of... Num 1:53
And they shall *k* his charge... Num 3:7
they shall *k* all the instruments... Num 3:8
*k* the charge of the sanctuary... Num 3:32
The LORD bless thee, and *k* thee... Num 6:24
to *k* the charge, and shall do no... Num 8:26
*k* the passover at his appointed... Num 9:2
ye shall *k* it in his appointed... Num 9:3
ceremonies thereof, shall ye *k* it... Num 9:3
that they should *k* the passover... Num 9:4
that they could not *k* the... Num 9:6
yet he shall *k* the passover unto... Num 9:10
month at even they shall *k* it... Num 9:11
of the passover they shall *k* it... Num 9:12
and forbeareth to *k* the passover... Num 9:13
will *k* the passover unto the LORD... Num 9:14
And they shall *k* thy charge... Num 18:3
*k* the charge of the tabernacle of... Num 18:4
ye shall *k* the charge of the... Num 18:5
thy sons with thee shall *k* your... Num 18:7
ye shall *k* a feast unto the LORD... Num 29:12
with him, *k* alive for yourselves... Num 31:18
which *k* the charge of the... Num 31:30
*k* himself to the inheritance of... Num 36:7
*k* himself to his own inheritance... Num 36:9
that ye may *k* the commandments of... Deut 4:2
*K* therefore and do them... Deut 4:6
*k* thy soul diligently, lest thou... Deut 4:9
Thou shalt *k* therefore his... Deut 4:40
day, that ye may learn them, and *k*... Deut 5:1
me and *k* my commandments... Deut 5:10
*K* the sabbath day to sanctify it,... Deut 5:12
thee to *k* the sabbath day... Deut 5:15
*k* all my commandments always,... Deut 5:29
to *k* all his statutes and his... Deut 6:2
Ye shall diligently *k* the... Deut 6:17
because he would *k* the oath which... Deut 7:8
*k* his commandments to a thousand... Deut 7:9
therefore *k* the commandments... Deut 7:11
hearken to these judgments, and *k*... Deut 7:12
shall *k* unto thee the covenant... Deut 7:12
thou wouldest *k* his commandments... Deut 8:2
Therefore thou shalt *k* the... Deut 8:6
To *k* the commandments... Deut 10:13
*k* his charge, and his statutes, and... Deut 11:1
Therefore shall ye *k* all the... Deut 11:8
For if ye shall diligently *k* all... Deut 11:22
*k* his commandments, and obey his... Deut 13:4
to *k* all his commandments which I.. Deut 13:18
*k* the passover unto the LORD thy... Deut 16:1
thou shalt *k* the feast of weeks... Deut 16:10
Seven days shalt thou *k* a solemn... Deut 16:15
to *k* all the words of this law and... Deut 17:19
If thou shalt *k* all these... Deut 19:9
then *k* thee from every wicked... Deut 23:9
gone out of thy lips thou shalt *k*... Deut 23:23
thou shalt therefore *k* and do them.. Deut 26:16
to *k* his statutes, and his... Deut 26:17
that thou shouldest *k* all his... Deut 26:18
*K* all the commandments which I... Deut 27:1
if thou shalt *k* the commandments... Deut 28:9
to *k* his commandments and his... Deut 28:45
*K* therefore the words of this... Deut 29:9
to *k* his commandments and his... Deut 30:10
to *k* his commandments and his... Deut 30:16
in any wise *k* yourselves from the... Josh 6:18
and set men by it for to *k* them... Josh 10:18
to *k* his commandments, and to... Josh 22:5
ye therefore very courageous to *k*... Josh 23:6
whether they will *k* the way of... Judg 2:22
as their fathers did *k* it... Judg 2:22
who said, *K* silence... Judg 3:19
Thou shalt *k* fast by my young men... Ruth 2:21
He will *k* the feet of his saints,... 1Sa 2:9
his son to *k* the ark of the LORD... 1Sa 7:1
and with one full line to *k* alive... 2Sa 8:2
were concubines, to *k* the house... 2Sa 15:16
which he hath left to *k* the house... 2Sa 16:21
I have no son to *k* my name in... 2Sa 18:18
whom he had left to *k* the house... 2Sa 20:3
*k* the charge of the LORD thy God,... 1Kin 2:3
to *k* his statutes, and his... 1Kin 2:3
my ways, to *k* my statutes and my... 1Kin 3:14
*k* all my commandments to walk in... 1Kin 6:12
*k* with thy servant David my... 1Kin 8:25
to *k* his commandments, and his... 1Kin 8:58
to *k* his commandments, as at this... 1Kin 8:61
thee, and wilt *k* my statutes and my... 1Kin 9:4
will not *k* my commandments and my. 1Kin 9:6
to *k* my statutes and my judgments,. 1Kin 11:33
my sight, to *k* my statutes and my... 1Kin 11:38
man unto me, and said, *K* this man... 1Kin 20:39
so shall ye *k* the watch of the... 2Kin 11:6
even they shall *k* the watch of... 2Kin 11:7
*k* my commandments... 2Kin 17:13
to *k* his commandments and his... 2Kin 23:3
*K* the passover unto the LORD your... 2Kin 23:21
that thou wouldest *k* me from evil... 1Chr 4:10
thousand, which could *k* rank... 1Chr 12:33
men of war, that could *k* rank... 1Chr 12:38
that thou mayest *k* the law of the... 1Chr 22:12
that they should *k* the charge of... 1Chr 23:32
and in the audience of our God, *k*... 1Chr 28:8
fathers, *k* this for ever in the... 1Chr 29:18
to *k* thy commandments, thy... 1Chr 29:19
*k* with thy servant David my... 2Chr 6:16
for we *k* the charge of the LORD... 2Chr 13:11
no power to *k* still the kingdom... 2Chr 22:9
shall *k* the watch of the LORD... 2Chr 23:6
now ye purpose to *k* under the... 2Chr 28:10
to *k* the passover unto the LORD... 2Chr 30:1
to *k* the passover in the second... 2Chr 30:2
they could not *k* it at that time... 2Chr 30:3
that they should come to *k* the... 2Chr 30:5
at Jerusalem much people to *k* the... 2Chr 30:13
counsel to *k* other seven days... 2Chr 30:23
to *k* his commandments, and his... 2Chr 34:31
to *k* the passover, and to offer... 2Chr 35:16
did all the kings of Israel *k*... 2Chr 35:18
*k* them, until ye weigh them... Ezr 8:29
*k* my commandments, and do them... Neh 1:9
to *k* the dedication with gladness... Neh 12:27
*k* the gates, to sanctify the... Neh 13:22
neither *k* they the king's laws... Est 3:8
that they should *k* the fourteenth... Est 9:21
that they would *k* these two days... Est 9:27
that thou wouldest *k* me secret... Job 14:13
but *k* it still within his mouth... Job 20:13
Thou shalt *k* them, O LORD, thou... Ps 12:7
*K* me as the apple of the eye... Ps 17:8
*K* back thy servant also from... Ps 19:13
none can *k* alive his own soul... Ps 22:29
truth unto such as *k* his covenant... Ps 25:10
O *k* my soul, and deliver me... Ps 25:20
thou shalt *k* them secretly in a... Ps 31:20
to *k* them alive in famine... Ps 33:19
*K* thy tongue from evil, and thy... Ps 34:13
*k* not silence... Ps 35:22
*k* his way, and he shall exalt thee... Ps 37:34
I will *k* my mouth with a bridle,... Ps 39:1
will preserve him, and *k* him alive... Ps 41:2
come, and shall not *k* silence... Ps 50:3
of God, but *k* his commandments... Ps 78:7
*K* not thou silence, O God... Ps 83:1
My mercy will I *k* for him for... Ps 89:28
and *k* not my commandments... Ps 89:31
to *k* thee in all thy ways... Ps 91:11
neither will he *k* his anger for... Ps 103:9
To such as *k* his covenant, and to... Ps 103:18
his statutes, and *k* his laws... Ps 105:45
Blessed are they that *k* judgment... Ps 106:3
the barren woman to *k* house... Ps 113:9
are they that *k* his testimonies... Ps 119:2
us to *k* thy precepts diligently... Ps 119:4
were directed to *k* thy statutes... Ps 119:5
I will *k* thy statutes... Ps 119:8
that I may live, and *k* thy word... Ps 119:17
I shall *k* it unto the end... Ps 119:33
and I shall *k* thy law... Ps 119:34
So shall I *k* thy law continually... Ps 119:44
said that I would *k* thy words... Ps 119:57
delayed not to *k* thy commandments.. Ps 119:60
and of them that *k* thy precepts... Ps 119:63
but I will *k* thy precepts with my... Ps 119:69
so shall I *k* the testimony of thy... Ps 119:88
because I *k* thy precepts... Ps 119:100
evil way, that I might *k* thy word... Ps 119:101
that I will *k* thy righteous... Ps 119:106
for I will *k* the commandments of... Ps 119:115
therefore doth my soul *k* them... Ps 119:129

so will I *k* thy precepts ... Ps 119:134
eyes, because they *k* not thy law ... Ps 119:136
I will *k* thy statutes ... Ps 119:145
I shall *k* thy testimonies ... Ps 119:146
except the LORD *k* the city ... Ps 127:1
thy children will *k* my covenant ... Ps 132:12
*K* me, O LORD, from the hands of ... Ps 140:4
*K* the door of my lips ... Ps 141:3
*K* me from the snares which they ... Ps 141:9
thee, understanding shall *k* thee ... Prov 2:11
*k* the paths of the righteous ... Prov 2:20
let thine heart *k* my commandments ... Prov 3:1
*k* sound wisdom and discretion ... Prov 3:21
shall *k* thy foot from being taken ... Prov 3:26
*k* my commandments, and live ... Prov 4:4
love her, and she shall *k* thee ... Prov 4:6
let her not go: *k* her ... Prov 4:13
*k* them in the midst of thine ... Prov 4:21
*K* thy heart with all diligence ... Prov 4:23
and that thy lips may *k* knowledge ... Prov 5:2
*k* thy father's commandment, and ... Prov 6:20
thou sleepest, it shall *k* thee ... Prov 6:22
To *k* thee from the evil woman, ... Prov 6:24
My son, *k* my words, and lay up my ... Prov 7:1
*K* my commandments, and live ... Prov 7:2
That they may *k* thee from the ... Prov 7:5
blessed are they that *k* my ways ... Prov 8:32
he that doth *k* his soul shall be ... Prov 22:5
thing if thou *k* them within thee ... Prov 22:18
but such as *k* the law contend ... Prov 28:4
a time to *k*, and a time to cast ... Eccl 3:6
a time to *k* silence, and a time to ... Eccl 3:7
*K* thy foot when thou goest to the ... Eccl 5:1
I counsel thee to *k* the king's ... Eccl 8:2
Fear God, and *k* his commandments .. Eccl 12:13
those that *k* the fruit thereof ... Song 8:12
Thou wilt *k* him in perfect peace, ... Is 26:3
I the LORD do *k* it ... Is 27:3
hurt it, I will *k* it night and day ... Is 27:3
*K* silence before me, O islands ... Is 41:1
hold thine hand, and will *k* thee ... Is 42:6
and to the south, *K* not back ... Is 43:6
*K* ye judgment, and do justice ... Is 56:1
the eunuchs that *k* my sabbaths ... Is 56:4
of the LORD, *k* not silence, ... Is 62:6
I will not *k* silence, but will ... Is 65:6
will he *k* it to the end ... Jer 3:5
I will not *k* anger for ever ... Jer 3:12
*k* him, as a shepherd doth his ... Jer 31:10
I will *k* nothing back from you ... Jer 42:4
sit upon the ground, and *k* silence ... Lam 2:10
*k* mine ordinances, and do them ... Eze 11:20
*k* all my statutes, and do that ... Eze 18:21
*k* my judgments, and do them ... Eze 20:19
ye shall *k* my judgments, and do ... Eze 36:27
that they may *k* the whole form ... Eze 43:11
me, and they shall *k* my charge ... Eze 44:16
and they shall *k* my laws and my ... Eze 44:24
to them that *k* his commandments ... Dan 9:4
*k* mercy and judgment, and wait on ... Hos 12:6
shall *k* silence in that time ... Amos 5:13
*k* the doors of thy mouth from her ... Mic 7:5
*k* thy solemn feasts, perform thy ... Nah 1:15
*k* the munition, watch the way, ... Nah 2:1
let all the earth *k* silence ... Hab 2:20
ways, and if thou wilt *k* my charge ... Zec 3:7
house, and shalt also *k* my courts ... Zec 3:7
me to *k* cattle from my youth ... Zec 13:5
to *k* the feast of tabernacles ... Zec 14:16
up to *k* the feast of tabernacles ... Zec 14:18
up to *k* the feast of tabernacles ... Zec 14:19
priest's lips should *k* knowledge ... Mal 2:7
into life, *k* the commandments ... Mt 19:17
I will *k* the passover at thy ... Mt 26:18
that ye may *k* your own tradition ... Mk 7:9
charge over thee, to *k* thee ... Lk 4:10
*k* it, and bring forth fruit with ... Lk 8:15
hear the word of God, and *k* it ... Lk 11:28
and *k* thee in on every side, ... Lk 19:43
If a man *k* my saying, he shall ... Jn 8:51
If a man *k* my saying, he shall ... Jn 8:52
but I know him, and *k* his saying ... Jn 8:55
shall *k* it unto life eternal ... Jn 12:25
If ye love me, *k* my commandments ... Jn 14:15
a man love me, he will *k* my words ... Jn 14:23
If ye *k* my commandments, ye shall ... Jn 15:10
my saying, they will *k* yours also ... Jn 15:20
*k* through thine own name those ... Jn 17:11
shouldest *k* them from the evil ... Jn 17:15
to *k* back part of the price of ... Acts 5:3
a man that is a Jew to *k* company ... Acts 10:28
quaternions of soldiers to *k* him ... Acts 12:4
them to *k* the law of Moses ... Acts 15:5
must be circumcised, and *k* the law ... Acts 15:24
from which if ye *k* yourselves ... Acts 15:29
them the decrees for to *k* ... Acts 16:4
the jailer to *k* them safely ... Acts 16:23
I must by all means *k* this feast ... Acts 18:21
save only that they *k* themselves ... Acts 21:25
commanded a centurion to *k* Paul ... Acts 24:23
profiteth, if thou *k* the law ... Rom 2:25
*k* the righteousness of the law ... Rom 2:26
Therefore let us *k* the feast ... 1Cor 5:8
written unto you not to *k* company ... 1Cor 5:11
heart that he will *k* his virgin ... 1Cor 7:37
But I *k* under my body, and bring ... 1Cor 9:27
*k* the ordinances, as I delivered ... 1Cor 11:2
let him *k* silence in the church ... 1Cor 14:28
Let your women *k* silence in the ... 1Cor 14:34
if ye *k* in memory what I preached ... 1Cor 15:2
unto you, and so will I *k* myself ... 2Cor 11:9
who are circumcised *k* the law ... Gal 6:13
Endeavouring to *k* the unity of ... Eph 4:3
shall *k* your hearts and minds ... Phil 4:7
stablish you, and *k* you from evil ... 2Th 3:3
*k* thyself pure ... 1Ti 5:22
That thou *k* this commandment ... 1Ti 6:14
*k* that which is committed to thy ... 1Ti 6:20
to *k* that which I have committed ... 2Ti 1:12
thee *k* by the Holy Ghost which ... 2Ti 1:14
to *k* himself unspotted from the ... Jas 1:27
whosoever shall *k* the whole law ... Jas 2:10
him, if we *k* his commandments ... 1Jn 2:3
because we *k* his commandments, and . 1Jn 3:22
love God, and *k* his commandments ... 1Jn 5:2
that we *k* his commandments ... 1Jn 5:3
children, *k* yourselves from idols ... 1Jn 5:21
*K* yourselves in the love of God, .. Jude 21
is able to *k* you from falling ... Jude 24
*k* those things which are written ... Rev 1:3
I also will *k* thee from the hour ... Rev 3:10
which *k* the commandments of God, .. Rev 12:17
here are they that *k* the ... Rev 14:12
of them which *k* the sayings of ... Rev 22:9

**KEEPER**

And Abel was a *k* of sheep, but ... Gen 4:2
Am I my brother's *k* ... Gen 4:9
the sight of the *k* of the prison ... Gen 39:21
the *k* of the prison committed to ... Gen 39:22
The *k* of the prison looked not to ... Gen 39:23
and left the sheep with a *k* ... 1Sa 17:20
the hand of the *k* of the carriage ... 1Sa 17:22
make thee *k* of mine head for ever ... 1Sa 28:2
son of Harhas, *k* of the wardrobe ... 2Kin 22:14
son of Hasrah, *k* of the wardrobe ... 2Chr 34:22
Asaph the *k* of the king's forest ... Neh 2:8
the *k* of the east gate ... Neh 3:29
chamberlain, *k* of the women ... Est 2:3
custody of Hegai, *k* of the women ... Est 2:8
the *k* of the women, appointed ... Est 2:15
and as a booth that the *k* maketh ... Job 27:18
The LORD is thy *k* ... Ps 121:5
made me the *k* of the vineyards ... Song 1:6
son of Shallum, the *k* of the door ... Jer 35:4
the *k* of the prison awaking out ... Acts 16:27
the *k* of the prison told this ... Acts 16:36

**KEEPERS**

be *k* of the watch of the king's ... 2Kin 11:5
which the *k* of the door have ... 2Kin 22:4
the *k* of the door, to bring forth ... 2Kin 23:4
and the three *k* of the door ... 2Kin 25:18
*k* of the gates of the tabernacle ... 1Chr 9:19
of the LORD, were *k* of the entry ... 1Chr 9:19
the *k* of the door, who sought to ... Est 6:2
In the day when the *k* of the ... Eccl 12:3
the *k* of the walls took away my ... Song 5:7
he let out the vineyard unto *k* ... Song 8:11
As *k* of a field, are they against ... Jer 4:17
and the three *k* of the door ... Jer 52:24
the *k* of the charge of the house ... Eze 40:45
the *k* of the charge of the altar ... Eze 40:46
but ye have set *k* of my charge in ... Eze 44:8
But I will make them *k* of the ... Eze 44:14
for fear of him the *k* did shake ... Mt 28:4
the *k* standing without before the ... Acts 5:23
the *k* before the door kept the ... Acts 12:6
found him not, he examined the *k* ... Acts 12:19
*k* at home, good, obedient to ... Titus 2:5

**KEEPEST**

who *k* covenant and mercy with thy .. 1Kin 8:23
which *k* covenant, and shewest ... 2Chr 6:14
who *k* covenant and mercy, let not ... Neh 9:32
walkest orderly, and *k* the law ... Acts 21:24

**KEEPETH**

and he die not, but *k* his bed ... Ex 21:18
which *k* covenant and mercy with ... Deut 7:9
and, behold, he *k* the sheep ... 1Sa 16:11
that *k* covenant and mercy for them ... Neh 1:5
He *k* back his soul from the pit, ... Job 33:18
He *k* all his bones ... Ps 34:20
he that *k* thee will not slumber ... Ps 121:3
he that *k* Israel shall neither ... Ps 121:4
which *k* truth for ever ... Ps 146:6
He *k* the paths of judgment, and ... Prov 2:8
way of life that *k* instruction ... Prov 10:17
He that *k* his mouth *k* his ... Prov 13:3
that *k* his mouth *k* his life ... Prov 13:3
Righteousness *k* him that is ... Prov 13:6
he that *k* his way preserveth his ... Prov 16:17
he that *k* understanding shall ... Prov 19:8
He that *k* the commandment *k* ... Prov 19:16
Whoso *k* his mouth and his tongue ... Prov 21:23
his tongue *k* his soul from ... Prov 21:23
he that *k* thy soul, doth not he ... Prov 24:12
Whoso *k* the fig tree shall eat ... Prov 27:18
Whoso *k* the law is a wise son ... Prov 28:7
but he that *k* company with ... Prov 29:3
but a wise man *k* it in till ... Prov 29:11
but he that *k* the law, happy is ... Prov 29:18
Whoso *k* the commandment shall ... Eccl 8:5
which *k* the truth may enter in ... Is 26:2
that *k* the sabbath from polluting ... Is 56:2
*k* his hand from doing any evil ... Is 56:2
every one that *k* the sabbath from ... Is 56:6
cursed be he that *k* back his ... Jer 48:10
*k* silence, because he hath borne ... Lam 3:28
is a proud man, neither *k* at home ... Hab 2:5
a strong man armed *k* his palace ... Lk 11:21
law, and yet none of you *k* the law ... Jn 7:19
because he *k* not the sabbath day ... Jn 9:16
*k* them, he it is that loveth me ... Jn 14:21
loveth me not *k* not my sayings ... Jn 14:24
*k* not his commandments, is a liar ... 1Jn 2:4
But whoso *k* his word, in him ... 1Jn 2:5
he that *k* his commandments ... 1Jn 3:24
that is begotten of God *k* himself ... 1Jn 5:18
*k* my works unto the end, to him ... Rev 2:26
*k* his garments, lest he walk ... Rev 16:15
blessed is he that *k* the sayings ... Rev 22:7

**KEEPING**

*K* mercy for thousands, forgiving ... Ex 34:7
*k* the charge of the sanctuary ... Num 3:28
*k* the charge of the sanctuary for ... Num 3:38
in not *k* his commandments, and his .. Deut 8:11
we were with them *k* the sheep ... 1Sa 25:16
were porters *k* the ward at the ... Neh 12:25
in *k* of them there is great ... Ps 19:11
but that by *k* of his covenant it ... Eze 17:14
*k* the covenant and mercy to them ... Dan 9:4
*k* watch over their flock by night ... Lk 2:8
but the *k* of the commandments of ... 1Cor 7:19
*k* of their souls to him in well ... 1Pet 4:19

**KEHELATHAH** (*ke-hel'-a-thah*) *An Israelites encampment in the wilderness.*
from Rissah, and pitched in *K* ... Num 33:22
And they went from *K*, and pitched.. Num 33:23

**KEILAH** (*ki'-lah*)
*1. A city in Judah.*
And *K*, and Achzib, and Mareshah ... Josh 15:44
the Philistines fight against *K* ... 1Sa 23:1
smite the Philistines, and save *K* ... 1Sa 23:2
to *K* against the armies of the ... 1Sa 23:3
him and said, Arise, go down to *K* ... 1Sa 23:4
So David and his men went to *K* ... 1Sa 23:5
David saved the inhabitants of *K* ... 1Sa 23:5
of Ahimelech fled to David to *K* ... 1Sa 23:6
Saul that David was come to *K* ... 1Sa 23:7
together to war, to go down to *K* ... 1Sa 23:8
that Saul seeketh to come to *K* ... 1Sa 23:10
Will the men of *K* deliver me up ... 1Sa 23:11
Will the men of *K* deliver me ... 1Sa 23:12
arose and departed out of *K* ... 1Sa 23:13
that David was escaped from *K* ... 1Sa 23:13
the ruler of the half part of *K* ... Neh 3:17
the ruler of the half part of *K* ... Neh 3:18
*2. A descendant of Caleb.*
the father of *K* the Garmite ... 1Chr 4:19

**KELAIAH** (*kel-ah'-yah*) See KELITA. *Married a foreigner in exile.*
Jozabad, and Shimei, and *K*, (the ... Ezr 10:23

**KELAL** See CHELAL.

**KELITA** (*kel'-i-tah*) See KELAIAH.
*1. Married a foreigner in exile.*
and Kelaiah, (the same is *K* ... Ezr 10:23
*2. A priest who assisted Ezra.*
Shabbethai, Hodijah, Maaseiah, *K* ... Neh 8:7
*3. A Levite who renewed the covenant.*
brethren, Shebaniah, Hodijah, *K* ... Neh 10:10

**KELUB** See CHELUB.

**KELUHI** See CHELLUH.

**KEMUEL** (*kem-u'-el*)
*1. A son of Nahor.*
brother, and *K* the father of Aram, ... Gen 22:21
*2. An Ephraimite prince.*
of Ephraim, *K* the son of Shiphtan ... Num 34:24
*3. Father of Hashabiah.*
Levites, Hashabiah the son of *K* ... 1Chr 27:17

**KENAANAH** See CHENAANAH.

**KENAN** (*ke'-nan*) See CAINAN. *Son of Enosh.*
*K*, Mahalaleel, Jered, ... 1Chr 1:2

**KENANI** See CHENANI.

**KENANIAH** See CHENANIAH.

**KENATH** (*ke'-nath*) See NOBAH. *A city in Bashan.*
And Nobah went and took *K* ... Num 32:42
towns of Jair, from them, with *K* ... 1Chr 2:23

**KENAZ** (*ke'-naz*) See KENEZITE.
*1. A son of Eliphaz.*
Omar, Zepho, and Gatam, and *K* ... Gen 36:11
duke Omar, duke Zepho, duke *K* ... Gen 36:15
and Omar, Zephi, and Gatam, *K* ... 1Chr 1:36
*2. A duke of Edom.*
Duke *K*, duke Teman, duke Mibzar, ... Gen 36:42
Duke *K*, duke Teman, duke Mibzar, ... 1Chr 1:53
*3. Brother of Caleb.*
And Othniel the son of *K*, the ... Josh 15:17
And Othniel the son of *K*, Caleb's ... Judg 1:13
them, even Othniel the son of *K* ... Judg 3:9
And Othniel the son of *K* died ... Judg 3:11
And the sons of *K* ... 1Chr 4:13
*4. A grandson of Caleb.*
and the sons of Elah, even *K* ... 1Chr 4:15

**KENEZITE** (*ken'-e-zite*) See KENIZZITES.
*Descendants of Jephunneh.*
Caleb the son of Jephunneh the *K* ... Num 32:12
of Jephunneh the *K* said unto him ... Josh 14:6
of Jephunneh the *K* unto this day ... Josh 14:14

**KENITE** (*ken'-ite*) See KENITES. *A member of a Canaanite tribe.*
the *K* shall be wasted, until... Num 24:22
And the children of the *K*, Moses'... Judg 1:16
Now Heber the *K*, which was of the... Judg 4:11
of Jael the wife of Heber the *K*... Judg 4:17
Hazor and the house of Heber the *K*.. Judg 4:17
Jael the wife of Heber the *K* be... Judg 5:24

**KENITES** (*ken'-ites*) See MIDIANITES.
The *K*, and the Kenizzites, and the... Gen 15:19
And he looked on the *K*... Num 24:21
had severed himself from the *K*... Judg 4:11
And Saul said unto the *K*, Go,... 1Sa 15:6
So the *K* departed from among the... 1Sa 15:6
and against the south of the *K*... 1Sa 27:10
which were in the cities of the *K*... 1Sa 30:29
These are the *K* that came of... 1Chr 2:55

**KENIZZITE** See KENIZZITES.

**KENIZZITES** (*ken'-iz-zites*) See KENEZITE. *A Canaanite tribe in Abraham's time.*
The Kenites, and the *K*, and the... Gen 15:19

**KENNIZZITE** See KENIZZITES.

**KEPHER AMMONI** See CHEPHAR-HAAMMONAI.

**KEPHIRAH** See CHEPHIRAH.

**KEPT**
*k* my charge, my commandments, my. Gen 26:5
father's sheep: for she *k* them... Gen 29:9
neither hath he *k* back any thing... Gen 39:9
and ye shall be *k* in prison... Gen 42:16
Now Moses *k* the flock of Jethro... Ex 3:1
for you to be *k* until the morning... Ex 16:23
it to be *k* for your generations... Ex 16:32
to be *k* for your generations... Ex 16:33
up before the Testimony, to be *k*... Ex 16:34
owner, and he hath not *k* him in... Ex 21:29
and his owner hath not *k* him in... Ex 21:36
be *k* close, and she be defiled, and... Num 5:13
they *k* the passover on the... Num 9:5
wherefore are we *k* back, that we... Num 9:7
Israel *k* the charge of the LORD... Num 9:19
they *k* the charge of the LORD, at... Num 9:23
to be *k* for a token against the... Num 17:10
place, and it shall be *k* for the... Num 19:9
the LORD hath *k* thee back from... Num 24:11
which *k* the charge of the... Num 31:47
he *k* him as the apple of his eye... Deut 32:10
thy word, and *k* thy covenant... Deut 33:9
*k* the passover on the fourteenth... Josh 5:10
behold, the LORD hath *k* me alive... Josh 14:10
Ye have *k* all that Moses the... Josh 22:2
but have *k* the charge of the... Josh 22:3
So she *k* fast by the maidens of... Ruth 2:23
it been *k* for thee since I said... 1Sa 9:24
thou hast not *k* the commandment... 1Sa 13:13
because thou hast not *k* that... 1Sa 13:14
Thy servant *k* his father's sheep,... 1Sa 17:34
if the young men have *k*... 1Sa 21:4
Of a truth women have been *k* from... 1Sa 21:5
Surely in vain have I *k* all that... 1Sa 25:21
which hast *k* me this day from... 1Sa 25:33
which hath *k* me back from hurting... 1Sa 25:34
hath *k* his servant from evil... 1Sa 25:39
hast thou not *k* thy lord the king... 1Sa 26:15
because ye have not *k* your master... 1Sa 26:16
the young man that *k* the watch... 2Sa 13:34
For I have *k* the ways of the LORD... 2Sa 22:22
have *k* myself from mine iniquity... 2Sa 22:24
thou hast *k* me to be head of the... 2Sa 22:44
thou not *k* the oath of the LORD... 1Kin 2:43
thou hast *k* for him this great... 1Kin 3:6
Who hast *k* with thy servant David... 1Kin 8:24
but he *k* not that which the LORD... 1Kin 11:10
and thou hast not *k* my covenant... 1Kin 11:11
he *k* my commandments... 1Kin 11:34
hast not *k* the commandment which. 1Kin 13:21
who *k* my commandments, and who... 1Kin 14:8
which *k* the door of the king's... 1Kin 14:27
(Now Joram had *k* Ramoth-gilead... 2Kin 9:14
the priests that *k* the door put... 2Kin 12:9
*k* not the commandments... 2Kin 17:19
but *k* his commandments, which the.. 2Kin 18:6
word of the LORD, which he *k* not... 1Chr 10:13
while he yet *k* himself close... 1Chr 12:1
*k* the ward of the house of Saul... 1Chr 12:29
Thou which hast *k* with thy... 2Chr 6:15
Solomon *k* the feast seven days... 2Chr 7:8
for they *k* the dedication of the... 2Chr 7:9
that *k* the entrance of the king's... 2Chr 12:10
*k* the feast of unleavened bread... 2Chr 30:21
they *k* other seven days with... 2Chr 30:23
which the Levites that *k* the... 2Chr 34:9
have not *k* the word of the LORD... 2Chr 34:21
Moreover Josiah *k* a passover unto... 2Chr 35:1
*k* the passover at that time... 2Chr 35:17
that *k* in Israel from the days of... 2Chr 35:18
keep such a passover as Josiah *k*... 2Chr 35:18
of Josiah was this passover *k*... 2Chr 35:19
as she lay desolate she *k* sabbath... 2Chr 36:21
They *k* also the feast of... Ezr 3:4
*k* the dedication of this house of... Ezr 6:16
captivity *k* the passover upon the... Ezr 6:19
*k* the feast of unleavened bread... Ezr 6:22
have not *k* the commandments, nor... Neh 1:7
they *k* the feast seven days... Neh 8:18
*k* thy law, nor hearkened unto thy... Neh 9:34
their brethren that *k* the gates... Neh 11:19
the porters *k* the ward of their... Neh 12:45
which *k* the concubines... Est 2:14
Teresh, of those which *k* the door... Est 2:21
*k* throughout every generation,... Est 9:28
held his steps, his way have I *k*... Job 23:11
*k* close from the fowls of the air... Job 28:21
and *k* silence at my counsel... Job 29:21
that I *k* silence, and went not out... Job 31:34
I have *k* me from the paths of the... Ps 17:4
For I have *k* the ways of the LORD... Ps 18:21
I *k* myself from mine iniquity... Ps 18:23
thou hast *k* me alive, that I... Ps 30:3
When I *k* silence, my bones waxed... Ps 32:3
with a multitude that *k* holyday... Ps 42:4
hast thou done, and I *k* silence... Ps 50:21
They *k* not the covenant of God,... Ps 78:10
God, and *k* not his testimonies... Ps 78:56
they *k* his testimonies, and the... Ps 99:7
for I have *k* thy testimonies... Ps 119:22
in the night, and have *k* thy law... Ps 119:55
I had, because I *k* thy precepts... Ps 119:56
but now have I *k* thy word... Ps 119:67
because they *k* not thy word... Ps 119:158
My soul hath *k* thy testimonies... Ps 119:167
I have *k* thy precepts and thy... Ps 119:168
eyes desired I *k* not from them... Eccl 2:10
riches *k* for the owners thereof... Eccl 5:13
mine own vineyard have I not *k*... Song 1:6
night when a holy solemnity is *k*... Is 30:29
forsaken me, and have not *k* my law... Jer 16:11
*k* all his precepts, and done... Jer 35:18
neither have *k* my judgments... Eze 5:7
hath *k* my judgments, to deal... Eze 18:9
hath *k* all my statutes, and hath... Eze 18:19
neither *k* my judgments to do them... Eze 20:21
ye have not *k* the charge of mine... Eze 44:8
that *k* the charge of my sanctuary... Eze 44:15
which have *k* my charge, which... Eze 48:11
and whom he would he *k* alive... Dan 5:19
but I *k* the matter in my heart... Dan 7:28
a wife, and for a wife he *k* sheep... Hos 12:12
and he *k* his wrath for ever... Amos 1:11
have not *k* his commandments, and... Amos 2:4
For the statutes of Omri are *k*... Mic 6:16
as ye have not *k* my ways, but... Mal 2:9
ordinances, and have not *k* them... Mal 3:7
it that we have *k* his ordinance... Mal 3:14
And they that *k* them fled, and went... Mt 8:33
utter things which have been *k*... Mt 13:35
But when Herod's birthday was *k*... Mt 14:6
things have I *k* from my youth up... Mt 19:20
neither was any thing *k* secret... Mk 4:22
And they *k* that saying with... Mk 9:10
But Mary *k* all these things, and... Lk 2:19
but his mother *k* all these... Lk 2:51
he was *k* bound with chains and in... Lk 8:29
they *k* it close, and told no man... Lk 9:36
these have I *k* from my youth up... Lk 18:21
which I have *k* laid up in a... Lk 19:20
but thou hast *k* the good wine... Jn 2:10
day of my burying hath she *k* this... Jn 12:7
even as I have *k* my Father's... Jn 15:10
if they have *k* my saying, they... Jn 15:20
and they have *k* thy word... Jn 17:6
the world, I *k* them in thy name... Jn 17:12
that thou gavest me I have *k*... Jn 17:12
and spake unto her that *k* the door... Jn 18:16
damsel that *k* the door unto Peter... Jn 18:17
*k* back part of the price, his... Acts 5:2
of angels, and have not *k* it... Acts 7:53
which had *k* his bed eight years,... Acts 9:33
Peter therefore was *k* in prison... Acts 12:5
before the door *k* the prison... Acts 12:6
Then all the multitude *k* silence... Acts 15:12
how I *k* back nothing that was... Acts 20:20
to them, they *k* the more silence... Acts 22:2
*k* the raiment of them that slew... Acts 22:20
he commanded him to be *k* in... Acts 23:35
that Paul should be *k* at Caesarea... Acts 25:4
I commanded him to be *k* till I... Acts 25:21
*k* them from their purpose... Acts 27:43
himself with a soldier that *k* him... Acts 28:16
which was *k* secret since the... Rom 16:25
in all things I have *k* myself... 2Cor 11:9
governor under Aretas the king *k*... 2Cor 11:32
we were *k* under the law, shut up... Gal 3:23
my course, I have *k* the faith... 2Ti 4:7
Through faith he *k* the passover... Heb 11:28
which is of you *k* back by fraud... Jas 5:4
Who are *k* by the power of God... 1Pet 1:5
by the same word are *k* in store... 2Pet 3:7
the angels which *k* not their... Jude 6
hast *k* my word, and hast not... Rev 3:8
Because thou hast *k* the word of... Rev 3:10

**KERAN** See CHERAN.

**KERCHIEFS**
make *k* upon the head of every... Eze 13:18
Your *k* also will I tear, and... Eze 13:21

**KEREN-HAPPUCH** (*ke''-ren-hap'-puk*) *A daughter of Job.*
and the name of the third, *K*... Job 42:14

**KERETHITE** See CHERETHITES.

**KERETHITES** See CHERETHITES.

**KERIOTH** (*ke'-re-oth*) See ISCARIOT, KIRIOTH.
*1. A city in Judah.*
And Hazor, Hadattah, and *K*, and... Josh 15:25
*2. A city in Moab.*
And upon *K*, and upon Bozrah, and... Jer 48:24
*K* is taken, and the strong holds... Jer 48:41

**KERIOTH HEZRON**

**KERITH** See CHERITH.

**KERNELS**
from the *k* even to the husk... Num 6:4

**KEROS** (*ke'-ros*) *A family of exiles.*
The children of *K*, the children... Ezr 2:44
The children of *K*, the children... Neh 7:47

**KERUB** See CHERUB.

**KESALON** See CHESALON.

**KESED** See CHESED.

**KESIL** See CHESIL.

**KESULLOTH** See CHESULLOTH.

**KETTLE**
he struck it into the pan, or *k*... 1Sa 2:14

**KETURAH** (*ket-u'-rah*) *A wife of Abraham.*
took a wife, and her name was *K*... Gen 25:1
All these were the children of *K*... Gen 25:4
Now the sons of *K*, Abraham's... 1Chr 1:32
All these are the sons of *K*... 1Chr 1:33

**KEY**
therefore they took a *k*, and... Judg 3:25
the *k* of the house of David will... Is 22:22
taken away the *k* of knowledge... Lk 11:52
true, he that hath the *k* of David... Rev 3:7
to him was given the *k* of the... Rev 9:1
having the *k* of the bottomless... Rev 20:1

**KEYS**
the *k* of the kingdom of heaven... Mt 16:19
and have the *k* of hell and of death... Rev 1:18

**KEZIA** (*ke-zi'-ah*) *A daughter of Job.*
and the name of the second, *K*... Job 42:14



**KEZIAH** See KEZIA.

**KEZIB** See CHEZIB.

**KEZIZ** (*ke'-ziz*) *A valley in Benjamin.*
Beth-hoglah, and the valley of *K*... Josh 18:21

**KIBROTH-HATTAAVAH** (*kib'-roth-hat-ta'-a-vah*) *A Hebrew encampment in the wilderness.*
called the name of that place *K*... Num 11:34
journeyed from *K* unto Hazeroth... Num 11:35
desert of Sinai, and pitched at *K*... Num 33:16
And they departed from *K*, and... Num 33:17
at Taberah, and at Massah, and at *K*.. Deut 9:22

**KIBZAIM** (*kib-za'-im*) See JOKMEAM. *A Levitical city in Ephraim.*
*K* with her suburbs, and Beth-horon. Josh 21:22

**KICK**
Wherefore *k* ye at my sacrifice and... 1Sa 2:29
for thee to *k* against the pricks... Acts 9:5
for thee to *k* against the pricks... Acts 26:14

**KICKED**
But Jeshurun waxed fat, and *k*... Deut 32:15

**KID**
killed a *k* of the goats, and... Gen 37:31
will send thee a *k* from the flock... Gen 38:17
Judah sent the *k* by the hand of... Gen 38:20
behold, I sent this *k*, and thou... Gen 38:23
seethe a *k* in his mother's milk... Ex 23:19
seethe a *k* in his mother's milk... Ex 34:26
a *k* of the goats, a male without... Lev 4:23
a *k* of the goats, a female... Lev 4:28
a lamb or a *k* of the goats, for a... Lev 5:6
Take ye a *k* of the goats for a... Lev 9:3
Then ye shall sacrifice one *k* of... Lev 23:19
One *k* of the goats for a sin... Num 7:16
One *k* of the goats for a sin... Num 7:22
One *k* of the goats for a sin... Num 7:28
One *k* of the goats for a sin... Num 7:34
One *k* of the goats for a sin... Num 7:40
One *k* of the goats for a sin... Num 7:46
One *k* of the goats for a sin... Num 7:52
One *k* of the goats for a sin... Num 7:58
One *k* of the goats for a sin... Num 7:64
One *k* of the goats for a sin... Num 7:70
One *k* of the goats for a sin... Num 7:76
One *k* of the goats for a sin... Num 7:82
one ram, or for a lamb, or a *k*... Num 15:11
one *k* of the goats for a sin... Num 15:24
one *k* of the goats for a sin... Num 28:15
one *k* of the goats, to make an... Num 28:30
one *k* of the goats for a sin... Num 29:5
One *k* of the goats for a sin... Num 29:11
one *k* of the goats for a sin... Num 29:16
one *k* of the goats for a sin... Num 29:19
one *k* of the goats for a sin... Num 29:25
seethe a *k* in his mother's milk... Deut 14:21
Gideon went in, and made ready a *k*.. Judg 6:19
have made ready a *k* for thee... Judg 13:15
So Manoah took a *k* with a meat... Judg 13:19
him as he would have rent a *k*... Judg 14:6
Samson visited his wife with a *k*... Judg 15:1
and a bottle of wine, and a *k*... 1Sa 16:20
leopard shall lie down with the *k*... Is 11:6
a *k* of the goats without blemish... Eze 43:22

a *k* of the goats daily for a sin ........ Eze 45:23
and yet thou never gavest me a *k* ........ Lk 15:29

**KIDNEYS**
is above the liver, and the two *k* ........ Ex 29:13
above the liver, and the two *k* ........ Ex 29:22
And the two *k*, and the fat that is ........ Lev 3:4
caul above the liver, with the *k* ........ Lev 3:4
And the two *k*, and the fat that is ........ Lev 3:10
caul above the liver, with the *k* ........ Lev 3:10
And the two *k*, and the fat that is ........ Lev 3:15
caul above the liver, with the *k* ........ Lev 3:15
And the two *k*, and the fat that is ........ Lev 4:9
caul above the liver, with the *k* ........ Lev 4:9
And the two *k*, and the fat that is ........ Lev 7:4
is above the liver, with the *k* ........ Lev 7:4
above the liver, and the two *k* ........ Lev 8:16
above the liver, and the two *k* ........ Lev 8:25
But the fat, and the *k*, and the ........ Lev 9:10
covereth the inwards, and the *k* ........ Lev 9:19
goats, with the fat of *k* of wheat ........ Deut 32:14
with the fat of the *k* of rams ........ Is 34:6

**KIDON**

**KIDRON** (*kid'-ron*) *A brook near Jerusalem.*
himself passed over the brook *K* ........ 2Sa 15:23
out, and passest over the brook *K* ........ 1Kin 2:37
idol, and burnt it by the brook *K* ........ 1Kin 15:13
Jerusalem in the fields of *K* ........ 2Kin 23:4
Jerusalem, unto the brook *K* ........ 2Kin 23:6
and burned it at the brook *K* ........ 2Kin 23:6
the dust of them into the brook *K* ........ 2Kin 23:12
it, and burnt it at the brook *K* ........ 2Chr 15:16
it out abroad into the brook *K* ........ 2Chr 29:16
and cast them into the brook *K* ........ 2Chr 30:14
the fields unto the brook of *K* ........ Jer 31:40

**KIDS**
thence two good *k* of the goats ........ Gen 27:9
she put the skins of the *k* of the ........ Gen 27:16
of the children of Israel two *k* ........ Lev 16:5
the *k* of the goats for sin ........ Num 7:87
to Beth-el, one carrying three *k* ........ 1Sa 10:3
them like two little flocks of *k* ........ 1Kin 20:27
people, of the flock, lambs and *k* ........ 2Chr 35:7
feed thy *k* beside the shepherds' ........ Song 1:8

**KILEAB** See CHILEAB.

**KILION** See CHILION.

**KILION'S** See CHILION'S.

**KILL**
lest any finding him should *k* him ........ Gen 4:15
and they will *k* me, but they will ........ Gen 12:12
the place should *k* me for Rebekah ........ Gen 26:7
himself, purposing to *k* thee ........ Gen 27:42
and said, Let us not *k* him ........ Gen 37:21
it be a son, then ye shall *k* him ........ Ex 1:16
intendest thou to *k* me, as thou ........ Ex 2:14
LORD met him, and sought to *k* him ........ Ex 4:24
Israel shall *k* it in the evening ........ Ex 12:6
your families, and *k* the passover ........ Ex 12:21
to *k* this whole assembly with ........ Ex 16:3
us up out of Egypt, to *k* us ........ Ex 17:3
Thou shalt not *k* ........ Ex 20:13
or a sheep, and *k* it, or sell it ........ Ex 22:1
I will *k* you with the sword ........ Ex 22:24
thou shalt *k* the bullock before ........ Ex 29:11
Then shalt thou *k* the ram ........ Ex 29:20
he shall *k* the bullock before the ........ Lev 1:5
he shall *k* it on the side of the ........ Lev 1:11
and *k* it at the door of the ........ Lev 3:2
*k* it before the tabernacle of the ........ Lev 3:8
*k* it before the tabernacle of the ........ Lev 3:13
*k* the bullock before the LORD ........ Lev 4:4
*k* it in the place where they *k* ........ Lev 4:24
where they *k* the burnt offering ........ Lev 4:33
In the place where they *k* the ........ Lev 7:2
they *k* the trespass offering ........ Lev 7:2
where he shall *k* the sin offering ........ Lev 14:13
he shall *k* the burnt offering ........ Lev 14:19
he shall *k* the lamb of the ........ Lev 14:25
he shall *k* the one of the birds ........ Lev 14:50
shall *k* the bullock of the sin ........ Lev 16:11
Then shall he *k* the goat of the ........ Lev 16:15
seed unto Molech, and *k* him not ........ Lev 20:4
thereto, thou shalt *k* the woman ........ Lev 20:16
be cow or ewe, ye shall not *k* it ........ Lev 22:28
*k* me, I pray thee, out of hand, ........ Num 11:15
Now if thou shalt *k* all this ........ Num 14:15
to *k* us in the wilderness, except ........ Num 16:13
mine hand, for now would I *k* thee... Num 22:29
Now therefore *k* every male among.. Num 31:17
*k* every woman that hath ........ Num 31:17
revenger of blood *k* the slayer ........ Num 35:27
which should *k* his neighbour ........ Deut 4:42
Thou shalt not *k* ........ Deut 5:17
Notwithstanding thou mayest *k* ........ Deut 12:15
then thou shalt *k* of thy herd ........ Deut 12:21
But thou shalt surely *k* him ........ Deut 13:9
I *k*, and I make alive ........ Deut 32:39
If the LORD were pleased to *k* us ........ Judg 13:23
but surely we will not *k* thee ........ Judg 15:13
when it is day, we shall *k* him ........ Judg 16:2
to smite of the people, and *k* ........ Judg 20:31
*k* of the men of Israel about ........ Judg 20:39
if Saul hear it, he will *k* me ........ 1Sa 16:2
able to fight with me, and to *k* me ........ 1Sa 17:9
*k* him, then shall ye be our ........ 1Sa 17:9
that they should *k* David ........ 1Sa 19:1
Saul my father seeketh to *k* thee ........ 1Sa 19:2
why should I *k* thee ........ 1Sa 19:17
and some bade me *k* thee ........ 1Sa 24:10
God, that thou wilt neither *k* me ........ 1Sa 30:15
then *k* him, fear not ........ 2Sa 13:28
his brother, that we may *k* him ........ 2Sa 14:7
any iniquity in me, let him *k* me ........ 2Sa 14:32
us shalt thou *k* any man in Israel ........ 2Sa 21:4
sought therefore to *k* Jeroboam ........ 1Kin 11:40
king of Judah, and they shall *k* me.... 1Kin 12:27
clothes, and said, Am I God, to *k* ........ 2Kin 5:7
and if they *k* us, we shall but die ........ 2Kin 7:4
followeth her *k* with the sword ........ 2Kin 11:15
So *k* the passover, and sanctify ........ 2Chr 35:6
provinces, to destroy, to *k* ........ Est 3:13
they watched the house to *k* him ........ Ps 59:*t*
A time to *k*, and a time to heal ........ Eccl 3:3
I will *k* thy root with famine, and ........ Is 14:30
let them *k* sacrifices ........ Is 29:1
the wool, ye *k* them that are fed ........ Eze 34:3
of old time, Thou shalt not *k* ........ Mt 5:21
whosoever shall *k* shall be in ........ Mt 5:21
And fear not them which *k* the body ... Mt 10:28
but are not able to *k* the soul ........ Mt 10:28
And they shall *k* him, and the third ........ Mt 17:23
come, let us *k* him, and let us ........ Mt 21:38
and some of them ye shall *k* ........ Mt 23:34
to be afflicted, and shall *k* you ........ Mt 24:9
take Jesus by subtilty, and *k* him ........ Mt 26:4
to save life, or to *k* ........ Mk 3:4
hands of men, and they shall *k* him ........ Mk 9:31
Do not commit adultery, Do not *k* ........ Mk 10:19
spit upon him, and shall *k* him ........ Mk 10:34
come, let us *k* him, and the ........ Mk 12:7
afraid of them that *k* the body ........ Lk 12:4
for Herod will *k* thee ........ Lk 13:31
hither the fatted calf, and *k* it ........ Lk 15:23
Do not commit adultery, Do not *k* ........ Lk 18:20
come, let us *k* him, that the ........ Lk 20:14
sought how they might *k* him ........ Lk 22:2
the Jews sought the more to *k* him ........ Jn 5:18
because the Jews sought to *k* him ........ Jn 7:1
Why go ye about to *k* me ........ Jn 7:19
who goeth about to *k* thee ........ Jn 7:20
not this he, whom they seek to *k* ........ Jn 7:25
said the Jews, Will he *k* himself ........ Jn 8:22
but ye seek to *k* me, because my ........ Jn 8:37
But now ye seek to *k* me, a man ........ Jn 8:40
not, but for to steal, and to *k* ........ Jn 10:10
Wilt thou *k* me, as thou diddest ........ Acts 7:28
the Jews took counsel to *k* him ........ Acts 9:23
the gates day and night to *k* him ........ Acts 9:24
Rise, Peter; *k*, and eat ........ Acts 10:13
And as they went about to *k* him ........ Acts 21:31
he come near, are ready to *k* him ........ Acts 23:15
laying wait in the way to *k* him ........ Acts 25:3
the temple, and went about to *k* me.. Acts 26:21
counsel was to *k* the prisoners ........ Acts 27:42
commit adultery, Thou shalt not *k* ........ Rom 13:9
adultery, said also, Do not *k* ........ Jas 2:11
commit no adultery, yet if thou *k* ........ Jas 2:11
ye *k*, and desire to have, and ........ Jas 4:2
I will *k* her children with death ........ Rev 2:23
and that they should *k* one another ........ Rev 6:4
to *k* with sword, and with hunger, ........ Rev 6:8
given that they should not *k* them ........ Rev 9:5
and shall overcome them, and *k* them . Rev 11:7

**KILLED**
*k* a kid of the goats, and dipped ........ Gen 37:31
that he hath *k* a man or a woman ........ Ex 21:29
shall be *k* before the LORD ........ Lev 4:15
is *k* shall the sin offering be ........ Lev 6:25
sin offering be *k* before the LORD ........ Lev 6:25
And he *k* it; and Moses ........ Lev 8:19
that one of the birds be *k* in an ........ Lev 14:5
that was *k* over the running water ........ Lev 14:6
Ye have *k* the people of the LORD ........ Num 16:41
whosoever hath *k* any person ........ Num 31:19
*k* thee not, know thou and see that ........ 1Sa 24:11
that I have *k* for my shearers ........ 1Sa 25:11
*k* it, and took flour, and kneaded ........ 1Sa 28:24
thou hast *k* Uriah the Hittite ........ 2Sa 12:9
and smote the Philistine, and *k* him .... 2Sa 21:17
and because he *k* him ........ 1Kin 16:7
*k* him, in the twenty and seventh ........ 1Kin 16:10
Thus saith the LORD, Hast thou *k* ........ 1Kin 21:19
he *k* him, and reigned in his room ........ 2Kin 15:25
*k* Shophach the captain of the ........ 1Chr 19:18
Ahab *k* sheep and oxen for him in ........ 2Chr 18:2
that had *k* the king his father ........ 2Chr 25:3
So they *k* the bullocks, and the ........ 2Chr 29:22
when they had *k* the rams ........ 2Chr 29:22
they *k* also the lambs, and they ........ 2Chr 29:22
And the priests *k* them, and they ........ 2Chr 29:24
Then they *k* the passover on the ........ 2Chr 30:15
they *k* the passover on the ........ 2Chr 35:1
they *k* the passover, and the ........ 2Chr 35:11
*k* the passover for all the ........ Ezr 6:20
sake are we *k* all the day long ........ Ps 44:22
She hath *k* her beasts ........ Prov 9:2
thou hast *k*, and not pitied ........ Lam 2:21
chief priests and scribes, and be *k* ........ Mt 16:21
*k* another, and stoned another ........ Mt 21:35
my oxen and my fatlings are *k* ........ Mt 22:4
of them which *k* the prophets ........ Mt 23:31
against him, and would have *k* him ........ Mk 6:19
priests, and scribes, and be *k* ........ Mk 8:31
and after that he is *k*, he shall ........ Mk 9:31
and him they *k*, and many others ........ Mk 12:5
*k* him, and cast him out of the ........ Mk 12:8
when they *k* the passover, his ........ Mk 14:12
prophets, and your fathers *k* them ........ Lk 11:47
for they indeed *k* them, and ye ........ Lk 11:48
which after he hath *k* hath power ........ Lk 12:5
thy father hath *k* the fatted calf ........ Lk 15:27
thou hast *k* for him the fatted ........ Lk 15:30
him out of the vineyard, and *k* him ........ Lk 20:15
when the passover must be *k* ........ Lk 22:7
*k* the Prince of life, whom God ........ Acts 3:15
he *k* James the brother of John ........ Acts 12:2
sword, and would have *k* himself ........ Acts 16:27
nor drink till they had *k* Paul ........ Acts 23:12
nor drink till they have *k* him ........ Acts 23:21
and should have been *k* of them ........ Acts 23:27
sake we are *k* all the day long ........ Rom 8:36
they have *k* thy prophets, and ........ Rom 11:3
as chastened, and not *k* ........ 2Cor 6:9
Who both *k* the Lord Jesus, and ........ 1Th 2:15
Ye have condemned and *k* the just ........ Jas 5:6
that should be *k* as they were ........ Rev 6:11
three was the third part of men *k* ........ Rev 9:18
*k* by these plagues yet repented ........ Rev 9:20
them, he must in this manner be *k* ........ Rev 11:5
sword must be *k* with the sword ........ Rev 13:10
image of the beast should be *k* ........ Rev 13:15

**KILLEDST**
kill me, as thou *k* the Egyptian ........ Ex 2:14
me into thine hand, thou *k* me not ........ 1Sa 24:18

**KILLEST**
thou that *k* the prophets, and ........ Mt 23:37
which *k* the prophets, and stonest ........ Lk 13:34

**KILLETH**
that *k* an ox, or lamb, or goat, ........ Lev 17:3
or that *k* it out of the camp, ........ Lev 17:3
he that *k* any man shall surely be ........ Lev 24:17
he that *k* a beast shall make it ........ Lev 24:18
And he that *k* a beast, he shall ........ Lev 24:21
and he that *k* a man, he shall be ........ Lev 24:21
which *k* any person at unawares ........ Num 35:11
that every one that *k* any person ........ Num 35:15
Whoso *k* any person, the murderer ... Num 35:30
Whoso *k* his neighbour ignorantly, ........ Deut 19:4
slayer that *k* any person unawares ........ Josh 20:3
that whosoever *k* any person at ........ Josh 20:9
The LORD *k*, and maketh alive ........ 1Sa 2:6
shall be, that the man who *k* him ........ 1Sa 17:25
to the man that *k* this Philistine ........ 1Sa 17:26
it be done to the man that *k* him ........ 1Sa 17:27
For wrath *k* the foolish man, and ........ Job 5:2
rising with the light *k* the poor ........ Job 24:14
The desire of the slothful *k* him ........ Prov 21:25
He that *k* an ox is as if he slew ........ Is 66:3
that whosoever *k* you will think ........ Jn 16:2
for the letter *k*, but the spirit ........ 2Cor 3:6
he that *k* with the sword must be ........ Rev 13:10

**KILLING**
him in the *k* of his brethren ........ Judg 9:24
Levites had the charge of the *k* ........ 2Chr 30:17
*k* sheep, eating flesh, and ........ Is 22:13
By swearing, and lying, and *k* ........ Hos 4:2
beating some, and *k* some ........ Mk 12:5

**KILMAD** See CHILMAD.

**KIMHAM** See CHIMHAM.

**KIN**
to any that is near of *k* to him ........ Lev 18:6
for he uncovereth his near *k* ........ Lev 20:19
But for his *k*, that is near unto ........ Lev 21:2
if any of his *k* come to redeem it ........ Lev 25:25
or any that is nigh of *k* unto him ........ Lev 25:49
her, The man is near of *k* unto us ........ Ruth 2:20
the king is near of *k* to us ........ 2Sa 19:42
own country, and among his own *k* ........ Mk 6:4

**KINAH** (*ki'-nah*) *A city in Judah.*
And *K*, and Dimonah, and Adadah, ... Josh 15:22

**KIND**
tree yielding fruit after his *k* ........ Gen 1:11
and herb yielding seed after his *k* ........ Gen 1:12
seed was in itself, after his *k* ........ Gen 1:12
forth abundantly, after their *k* ........ Gen 1:21
and every winged fowl after his *k* ........ Gen 1:21
the living creature after his *k* ........ Gen 1:24
and beast of the earth after his *k* ........ Gen 1:24
his *k*, and cattle after their *k* ........ Gen 1:25
upon the earth after his *k* ........ Gen 1:25
Of fowls after their *k* ........ Gen 6:20
and of cattle after their *k* ........ Gen 6:20
thing of the earth after his *k* ........ Gen 6:20
They, and every beast after his *k* ........ Gen 7:14
and all the cattle after their *k* ........ Gen 7:14
upon the earth after his *k* ........ Gen 7:14
and every fowl after his *k* ........ Gen 7:14
vulture, and the kite after his *k* ........ Lev 11:14
Every raven after his *k* ........ Lev 11:15
cuckow, and the hawk after his *k* ........ Lev 11:16
the stork, the heron after her *k* ........ Lev 11:19
the locust after his *k* ........ Lev 11:22
and the bald locust after his *k* ........ Lev 11:22
and the beetle after his *k* ........ Lev 11:22
and the grasshopper after his *k* ........ Lev 11:22
and the tortoise after his *k* ........ Lev 11:29
cattle gender with a diverse *k* ........ Lev 19:19
kite, and the vulture after his *k* ........ Deut 14:13
And every raven after his *k* ........ Deut 14:14
cuckow, and the hawk after his *k* ........ Deut 14:15
stork, and the heron after her *k* ........ Deut 14:18
instruments of every *k* of service ........ 1Chr 28:14

If thou be *k* to this people, and 2Chr 10:7
sellers of all *k* of ware lodged Neh 13:20
trees in them of all *k* of fruits Eccl 2:5
the multitude of all *k* of riches Eze 27:12
the sea, and gathered of every *k* Mt 13:47
Howbeit this *k* goeth not out but Mt 17:21
This *k* can come forth by nothing, Mk 9:29
for he is *k* unto the unthankful Lk 6:35
Charity suffereth long, and is *k* 1Cor 13:4
there is one *k* of flesh of men 1Cor 15:39
And be ye *k* one to another, Eph 4:32
truth, that we should be a *k* of Jas 1:18
For every *k* of beasts, and of Jas 3:7

**KINDLE**
Ye shall *k* no fire throughout Ex 35:3
is a contentious man to *k* strife Prov 26:21
shall *k* in the thickets of the Is 9:18
under his glory he shall *k* a Is 10:16
a stream of brimstone, doth *k* it Is 30:33
shall the flame *k* upon thee Is 43:2
Behold, all ye that *k* a fire Is 50:11
wood, and the fathers *k* the fire Jer 7:18
then will I *k* a fire in the gates Jer 17:27
I will *k* a fire in the forest Jer 21:14
to *k* meat offerings, and to do Jer 33:18
I will *k* a fire in the houses of Jer 43:12
I will *k* a fire in the wall of Jer 49:27
I will *k* a fire in his cities, and Jer 50:32
I will *k* a fire in thee, and it Eze 20:47
*k* the fire, consume the flesh, and Eze 24:10
But I will *k* a fire in the wall Amos 1:14
stubble, and they shall *k* in them Obad 18
neither do ye *k* fire on mine Mal 1:10

**KINDLED**
anger was *k* against Rachel Gen 30:2
that his wrath was *k* Gen 39:19
of the LORD was *k* against Moses Ex 4:14
he that *k* the fire shall surely Ex 22:6
the burning which the LORD hath *k* Lev 10:6
and his anger was *k* Num 11:1
anger of the LORD was *k* greatly Num 11:10
the LORD was *k* against the people Num 11:33
of the LORD was *k* against them Num 12:9
God's anger was *k* because he went Num 22:22
and Balaam's anger was *k*, and he Num 22:27
anger was *k* against Balaam Num 24:10
of the LORD was *k* against Israel Num 25:3
LORD's anger was *k* the same time Num 32:10
LORD's anger was *k* against Israel Num 32:13
LORD thy God be *k* against thee Deut 6:15
of the LORD be *k* against you Deut 7:4
the LORD's wrath be *k* against you Deut 11:17
the LORD was *k* against this land Deut 29:27
Then my anger shall be *k* against Deut 31:17
For a fire is *k* in mine anger Deut 32:22
the anger of the LORD was *k* Josh 7:1
of the LORD be *k* against you Josh 23:16
the son of Ebed, his anger was *k* Judg 9:30
And his anger was *k* Judg 14:19
and his anger was *k* greatly 1Sa 11:6
Eliab's anger was *k* against David 1Sa 17:28
anger was *k* against Jonathan 1Sa 20:30
of the LORD was *k* against Uzzah 2Sa 6:7
was greatly *k* against the man 2Sa 12:5
coals were *k* by it 2Sa 22:9
before him were coals of fire *k* 2Sa 22:13
of the LORD was *k* against Israel 2Sa 24:1
of the LORD was *k* against Israel 2Kin 13:3
of the LORD that is *k* against us 2Kin 22:13
shall be *k* against this place 2Kin 22:17
his anger was *k* against Judah 2Kin 23:26
of the LORD was *k* against Uzza 1Chr 13:10
anger was greatly *k* against Judah 2Chr 25:10
of the LORD was *k* against Amaziah 2Chr 25:15
He hath also *k* his wrath against Job 19:11
Then was *k* the wrath of Elihu the Job 32:2
against Job was his wrath *k* Job 32:2
his three friends was his wrath *k* Job 32:3
three men, then his wrath was *k* Job 32:5
My wrath is *k* against thee, and Job 42:7
when his wrath is *k* but a little Ps 2:12
coals were *k* by it Ps 18:8
so a fire was *k* against Jacob Ps 78:21
a fire was *k* in their company Ps 106:18
of the LORD *k* against his people Ps 106:40
when their wrath was *k* against us Ps 124:3
of the LORD *k* against his people Is 5:25
and in the sparks that ye have *k* Is 50:11
tumult he hath *k* fire upon it Jer 11:16
for a fire is *k* in mine anger Jer 15:14
for ye have *k* a fire in mine Jer 17:4
was *k* in the cities of Judah and Jer 44:6
hath *k* a fire in Zion, and it hath Lam 4:11
see that I the LORD have *k* it Eze 20:48
mine anger is *k* against them Hos 8:5
me, my repentings are *k* together Hos 11:8
Mine anger was *k* against the Zec 10:3
what will I, if it be already *k* Lk 12:49
when they had *k* a fire in the Lk 22:55
for they *k* a fire, and received us Acts 28:2

**KINDLETH**
His breath *k* coals, and a flame Job 41:21
yea, he *k* it, and baketh bread Is 44:15
great a matter a little fire *k* Jas 3:5

**KINDLY**
And now if ye will deal *k* and truly Gen 24:49
and spake *k* unto the damsel Gen 34:3
hand under my thigh, and deal *k* Gen 47:29
them, and spake *k* unto them Gen 50:21
us the land, that we will deal *k* Josh 2:14
the LORD deal *k* with you, as ye Ruth 1:8
shalt deal *k* with thy servant 1Sa 20:8
And he spake *k* to him, and set his 2Kin 25:28
spake *k* unto him, and set his Jer 52:32
Be *k* affectioned one to another Rom 12:10

**KINDNESS**
This is thy *k* which thou shalt Gen 20:13
but according to the *k* that I Gen 21:23
shew *k* unto my master Abraham Gen 24:12
thou hast shewed *k* unto my master Gen 24:14
be well with thee, and shew *k* Gen 40:14
LORD, since I have shewed you *k* Josh 2:12
shew *k* unto my father's house Josh 2:12
Neither shewed they *k* to the Judg 8:35
not left off his *k* to the living Ruth 2:20
for thou hast shewed more *k* in Ruth 3:10
for ye shewed *k* to all the 1Sa 15:6
I live shew me the *k* of the LORD 1Sa 20:14
off thy *k* from my house for ever 1Sa 20:15
have shewed this *k* unto your lord 2Sa 2:5
And now the LORD shew *k* and truth 2Sa 2:6
and I also will requite you this *k* 2Sa 2:6
which against Judah do shew *k* 2Sa 3:8
shew him *k* for Jonathan's sake 2Sa 9:1
I may shew the *k* of God unto him 2Sa 9:3
for I will surely shew thee *k* for 2Sa 9:7
I will shew *k* unto Hanun the son 2Sa 10:2
as his father shewed *k* unto me 2Sa 10:2
Is this thy *k* to thy friend 2Sa 16:17
But shew *k* unto the sons of 1Kin 2:7
hast kept for him this great *k* 1Kin 3:6
I will shew *k* unto Hanun the son 1Chr 19:2
because his father shewed *k* to me 1Chr 19:2
the king remembered not the *k* 2Chr 24:22
slow to anger, and of great *k* Neh 9:17
him, and she obtained *k* of him Est 2:9
his marvellous *k* in a strong city Ps 31:21
For his merciful *k* is great Ps 117:2
thy merciful *k* be for my comfort, Ps 119:76
it shall be a *k* Ps 141:5
The desire of a man is his *k* Prov 19:22
and in her tongue is the law of *k* Prov 31:26
but with everlasting *k* will I Is 54:8
but my *k* shall not depart from Is 54:10
the *k* of thy youth, the love of Jer 2:2
slow to anger, and of great *k* Joel 2:13
slow to anger, and of great *k* Jonah 4:2
people shewed us no little *k* Acts 28:2
knowledge, by longsuffering, by *k* 2Cor 6:6
riches of his grace in his *k* Eph 2:7
and beloved, bowels of mercies, *k* Col 3:12
But after that the *k* and love of Titus 3:4
And to godliness brotherly *k* 2Pet 1:7
and to brotherly *k* charity 2Pet 1:7

**KINDRED**
out of thy country, and from thy *k* Gen 12:1
go unto my country, and to my *k* Gen 24:4
house, and from the land of my *k* Gen 24:7
my father's house, and to my *k* Gen 24:38
take a wife for my son of my *k* Gen 24:40
my oath, when thou comest to my *k* Gen 24:41
land of thy fathers, and to thy *k* Gen 31:3
and return unto the land of thy *k* Gen 31:13
unto thy country, and to thy *k* Gen 32:9
of our state, and of our *k* Gen 43:7
to mine own land, and to my *k* Num 10:30
and they brought out all her *k* Josh 6:23
who was of the *k* of Elimelech Ruth 2:3
And now is not Boaz of our *k* Ruth 3:2
the *k* of Saul, three thousand 1Chr 12:29
not shewed her people nor her *k* Est 2:10
yet shewed her *k* nor her people Est 2:20
to see the destruction of my *k* Est 8:6
the Buzite, of the *k* of Ram Job 32:2
thy brethren, the men of thy *k* Eze 11:15
There is none of thy *k* that is Lk 1:61
were of the *k* of the high priest Acts 4:6
out of thy country, and from thy *k* Acts 7:3
Joseph's *k* was made known unto Acts 7:13
father Jacob to him, and all his *k* Acts 7:14
same dealt subtilly with our *k* Acts 7:19
God by thy blood out of every *k* Rev 5:9
earth, and to every nation, and *k* Rev 14:6

**KINDREDS**
ye *k* of the people, give unto the 1Chr 16:28
all the *k* of the nations shall Ps 22:27
O ye *k* of the people, give unto Ps 96:7
all the *k* of the earth be blessed Acts 3:25
all *k* of the earth shall wail Rev 1:7
number, of all nations, and *k* Rev 7:9
And they of the people and *k* Rev 11:9
and power was given him over all *k* Rev 13:7

**KINDS**
upon the earth, after their *k* Gen 8:19
divers *k* of spices prepared by 2Chr 16:14
I will appoint over them four *k* Jer 15:3
shall be according to their *k* Eze 47:10
all *k* of musick, ye fall down and Dan 3:5
all *k* of musick, all the people, Dan 3:7
all *k* of musick, shall fall down Dan 3:10
all *k* of musick, ye fall down and Dan 3:15
to another divers *k* of tongues 1Cor 12:10
so many *k* of voices in the world, 1Cor 14:10

**KINE**
camels with their colts, forty *k* Gen 32:15
the river seven well favoured *k* Gen 41:2
seven other *k* came up after them Gen 41:3
stood by the other *k* upon the Gen 41:3
leanfleshed *k* did eat up the Gen 41:4
the seven well favoured and fat *k* Gen 41:4
came up out of the river seven *k* Gen 41:18
seven other *k* came up after them, Gen 41:19
the ill favoured *k* did eat up the Gen 41:20
did eat up the first seven fat *k* Gen 41:20
The seven good *k* are seven years Gen 41:26
ill favoured *k* that came up after Gen 41:27
thine oil, the increase of thy *k* Deut 7:13
thy cattle, the increase of thy *k* Deut 28:4
thy land, the increase of thy *k* Deut 28:18
or oil, or the increase of thy *k* Deut 28:51
Butter of *k*, and milk of sheep, Deut 32:14
a new cart, and take two milch *k* 1Sa 6:7
tie the *k* to the cart, and bring 1Sa 6:7
and took two milch *k*, and tied them 1Sa 6:10
the *k* took the straight way to 1Sa 6:12
offered the *k* a burnt offering 1Sa 6:14
butter, and sheep, and cheese of *k* 2Sa 17:29
ye *k* of Bashan, that are in the Amos 4:1

**KING** See PREFACE.
and the shout of a *k* is among them Num 23:21
now make us a *k* to judge us like 1Sa 8:5
the people that asked of him a *k* 1Sa 8:10
shouted, and said, God save the *k* 1Sa 10:24
there they made Saul *k* before the 1Sa 11:15
David *k* over the house of Judah 2Sa 2:4
God save the *k*, God save the *k* 2Sa 16:16
and say, God save *k* Solomon 1Kin 1:34
come to Shechem to make him *k* 1Kin 12:1
and they made him *k*, and anointed 2Kin 11:12
hands, and said, God save the *k* 2Kin 11:12
Nebuchadnezzar *k* of Babylon came 2Kin 25:1
and with all Israel, to make him *k* 1Chr 11:10
Now the acts of David the *k* 1Chr 29:29
for thou hast made me *k* over a 2Chr 1:9
so the *k* and all the people 2Chr 7:5
all Israel come to make him *k* 2Chr 10:1
to the commandment of the *k* 2Chr 29:15
bring him to the *k* of terrors Job 18:14
Yet have I set my *k* upon my holy Ps 2:6
The LORD is *K* for ever and ever Ps 10:16
the *K* of glory shall come in Ps 24:7
Who is this *K* of glory Ps 24:8
of hosts, he is the *K* of glory Ps 24:10
For God is my *K* of old, working Ps 74:12
of Zion be joyful in their *K* Ps 149:2
son, fear thou the LORD and the *k* Prov 24:21
man do that cometh after the *k* Eccl 2:12
when thy *k* is a child, and thy Eccl 10:16
Curse not the *k*, no not in thy Eccl 10:20
for mine eyes have seen the *K* Is 6:5
living God, and an everlasting *k* Jer 10:10
the LORD shall be *k* over all the Zec 14:9
year to year to worship the *K* Zec 14:16
is he that is born *K* of the Jews Mt 2:2
for it is the city of the great *K* Mt 5:35
thy *K* cometh unto thee, meek, and Mt 21:5
Art thou the *K* of the Jews Mt 27:11
Or what *k*, going to make war Lk 14:31
Blessed be the *K* that cometh in Lk 19:38
that he himself is Christ a *K* Lk 23:2
him by force, to make him a *k* Jn 6:15
said unto him, Art thou a *k* then Jn 18:37
Thou sayest that I am a *k* Jn 18:37
unto the Jews, Behold your *K* Jn 19:14
saying that there is another *k* Acts 17:7
Now unto the *K* eternal, immortal, 1Ti 1:17
the *K* of kings, and Lord of lords 1Ti 6:15
*K* OF KINGS Rev 19:16

**KINGDOM**
the beginning of his *k* was Babel Gen 10:10
on me and on my *k* a great sin Gen 20:9
shall be unto me a *k* of priests Ex 19:6
Agag, and his *k* shall be exalted Num 24:7
the *k* of Sihon king of the Num 32:33
the *k* of Og king of Bashan, the Num 32:33
of Argob, the *k* of Og in Bashan Deut 3:4
cities of the *k* of Og in Bashan Deut 3:10
and all Bashan, being the *k* of Og Deut 3:13
sitteth upon the throne of his *k* Deut 17:18
he may prolong his days in his *k* Deut 17:20
All the *k* of Og in Bashan, which Josh 13:12
all the *k* of Sihon king of the Josh 13:21
the rest of the *k* of Sihon king Josh 13:27
all the *k* of Og king of Bashan, Josh 13:30
cities of the *k* of Og in Bashan, Josh 13:31
But of the matter of the *k* 1Sa 10:16
the people the manner of the *k* 1Sa 10:25
to Gilgal, and renew the *k* there 1Sa 11:14
thy *k* upon Israel for ever 1Sa 13:13
But now thy *k* shall not continue 1Sa 13:14
So Saul took the *k* over Israel 1Sa 14:47
The LORD hath rent the *k* of 1Sa 15:28
what can he have more but the *k* 1Sa 18:8
not be established, nor thy *k* 1Sa 20:31
that the *k* of Israel shall be 1Sa 24:20
hath rent the *k* out of thine hand 1Sa 28:17
To translate the *k* from the house 2Sa 3:10
my *k* are guiltless before the 2Sa 3:28
that he had exalted his *k* for his 2Sa 5:12
bowels, and I will establish his *k* 2Sa 7:12
the throne of his *k* for ever 2Sa 7:13
thy *k* shall be established for 2Sa 7:16
restore me the *k* of my father 2Sa 16:3
the LORD hath delivered the *k* 2Sa 16:8
sitteth on the throne of the *k* 1Kin 1:46

his *k* was established greatly ... 1Kin 2:12
Thou knowest that the *k* was mine ... 1Kin 2:15
howbeit the *k* is turned about, and ... 1Kin 2:15
ask for him the *k* also ... 1Kin 2:22
the *k* was established in the hand ... 1Kin 2:46
of thy *k* upon Israel for ever ... 1Kin 9:5
was not the like made in any *k* ... 1Kin 10:20
will surely rend the *k* from thee ... 1Kin 11:11
I will not rend away all the *k* ... 1Kin 11:13
I will rend the *k* out of the hand ... 1Kin 11:31
take the whole *k* out of his hand ... 1Kin 11:34
But I will take the *k* out of his ... 1Kin 11:35
to bring the *k* again to Rehoboam ... 1Kin 12:21
Now shall the *k* return to the ... 1Kin 12:26
rent the *k* away from the house of ... 1Kin 14:8
liveth, there is no nation or *k* ... 1Kin 18:10
he took an oath of the *k* and ... 1Kin 18:10
thou now govern the *k* of Israel ... 1Kin 21:7
as soon as the *k* was confirmed in ... 2Kin 14:5
him to confirm the *k* in his hand ... 2Kin 15:19
turned the *k* unto David the son ... 1Chr 10:14
themselves with him in his *k* ... 1Chr 11:10
to turn the *k* of Saul to him, ... 1Chr 12:23
for his *k* was lifted up on high, ... 1Chr 14:2
from one *k* to another people ... 1Chr 16:20
and I will establish his *k* ... 1Chr 17:11
in mine house and in my *k* for ever ... 1Chr 17:14
of his *k* over Israel for ever ... 1Chr 22:10
of the *k* of the LORD over Israel ... 1Chr 28:5
I will establish his *k* for ever ... 1Chr 28:7
thine is the *k*, O LORD, and thou ... 1Chr 29:11
David was strengthened in his *k* ... 2Chr 1:1
the LORD, and an house for his *k* ... 2Chr 2:1
the LORD, and an house for his *k* ... 2Chr 2:12
I stablish the throne of thy *k* ... 2Chr 7:18
was not the like made in any *k* ... 2Chr 9:19
bring the *k* again to Rehoboam ... 2Chr 11:1
they strengthened the *k* of Judah ... 2Chr 11:17
Rehoboam had established the *k* ... 2Chr 12:1
*k* over Israel to David for ever ... 2Chr 13:5
now ye think to withstand the *k* ... 2Chr 13:8
the *k* was quiet before him ... 2Chr 14:5
LORD stablished the *k* in his hand ... 2Chr 17:5
but the *k* gave he to Jehoram ... 2Chr 21:3
risen up to the *k* of his father ... 2Chr 21:4
had no power to keep still the *k* ... 2Chr 22:9
the king upon the throne of the *k* ... 2Chr 23:20
when the *k* was established to him ... 2Chr 25:3
for a sin offering for the *k* ... 2Chr 29:21
for no god of any nation or *k* was ... 2Chr 32:15
him again to Jerusalem into his *k* ... 2Chr 33:13
the reign of the *k* of Persia ... 2Chr 36:20
proclamation throughout all his *k* ... 2Chr 36:22
proclamation throughout all his *k* ... Ezr 1:1
have not served thee in their *k* ... Neh 9:35
sat on the throne of his *k* ... Est 1:2
the riches of his glorious *k* ... Est 1:4
and which sat the first in the *k* ... Est 1:14
in all the provinces of his *k* ... Est 2:3
the whole *k* of Ahasuerus, even ... Est 3:6
in all the provinces of thy *k* ... Est 3:8
to the *k* for such a time as this ... Est 4:14
given thee to the half of the *k* ... Est 5:3
of the *k* it shall be performed ... Est 5:6
even to the half of the *k* ... Est 7:2
provinces of the *k* of Ahasuerus ... Est 9:30
For the *k* is the LORD's ... Ps 22:28
of thy *k* is a right sceptre ... Ps 45:6
and his *k* ruleth over all ... Ps 103:19
from one *k* to another people ... Ps 105:13
shall speak of the glory of thy *k* ... Ps 145:11
and the glorious majesty of his *k* ... Ps 145:12
Thy *k* is an everlasting *k*, ... Ps 145:13
is born in his *k* becometh poor ... Eccl 4:14
throne of David, and upon his *k* ... Is 9:7
the *k* from Damascus, and the ... Is 17:3
city, and *k* against *k* ... Is 19:2
call the nobles thereof to the *k* ... Is 34:12
*k* that will not serve thee shall ... Is 60:12
a nation, and concerning a *k* ... Jer 18:7
a nation, and concerning a *k* ... Jer 18:9
*k* which will not serve the same ... Jer 27:8
he hath polluted the *k* and the ... Lam 2:2
and thou didst prosper into a *k* ... Eze 16:13
That the *k* might be base, that it ... Eze 17:14
and they shall be there a base *k* ... Eze 29:14
God of heaven hath given thee a *k* ... Dan 2:37
arise another *k* inferior to thee ... Dan 2:39
and another third *k* of brass ... Dan 2:39
the fourth *k* shall be strong as ... Dan 2:40
of iron, the *k* shall be divided ... Dan 2:41
so the *k* shall be partly strong, ... Dan 2:42
the God of heaven set up a *k* ... Dan 2:44
the *k* shall not be left to other ... Dan 2:44
his *k* is an everlasting *k*, ... Dan 4:3
most High ruleth in the *k* of men ... Dan 4:17
as all the wise men of my *k* are ... Dan 4:18
most High ruleth in the *k* of men ... Dan 4:25
thy *k* shall be sure unto thee, ... Dan 4:26
in the palace of the *k* of Babylon ... Dan 4:29
of the *k* by the might of my power ... Dan 4:30
The *k* is departed from thee ... Dan 4:31
most High ruleth in the *k* of men ... Dan 4:32
his *k* is from generation to ... Dan 4:34
and for the glory of my *k*, mine ... Dan 4:36
and I was established in my *k* ... Dan 4:36
shall be the third ruler in the *k* ... Dan 5:7
There is a man in thy *k*, in whom ... Dan 5:11
shalt be the third ruler in the *k* ... Dan 5:16
Nebuchadnezzar thy father a *k* ... Dan 5:18
high God ruled in the *k* of men ... Dan 5:21
God hath numbered thy *k*, and ... Dan 5:26
Thy *k* is divided, and given to the ... Dan 5:28
be the third ruler in the *k* ... Dan 5:29
And Darius the Median took the *k* ... Dan 5:31
to set over the *k* an hundred ... Dan 6:1
which should be over the whole *k* ... Dan 6:1
against Daniel concerning the *k* ... Dan 6:4
All the presidents of the *k* ... Dan 6:7
dominion of my *k* men tremble ... Dan 6:26
his *k* that which shall not be ... Dan 6:26
him dominion, and glory, and a *k* ... Dan 7:14
his *k* that which shall not be ... Dan 7:14
of the most High shall take the *k* ... Dan 7:18
and possess the *k* for ever ... Dan 7:18
that the saints possessed the *k* ... Dan 7:22
shall be the fourth *k* upon earth ... Dan 7:23
the ten horns out of this *k* are ... Dan 7:24
And the *k* and dominion ... Dan 7:27
the greatness of the *k* under the ... Dan 7:27
whose *k* is an everlasting *k* ... Dan 7:27
And in the latter time of their *k* ... Dan 8:23
But the prince of the *k* of Persia ... Dan 10:13
his *k* shall be broken, and shall ... Dan 11:4
for his *k* shall be plucked up, ... Dan 11:4
the south shall come into his *k* ... Dan 11:9
with the strength of his whole *k* ... Dan 11:17
of taxes in the glory of the *k* ... Dan 11:20
not give the honour of the *k* ... Dan 11:21
obtain the *k* by flatteries ... Dan 11:21
the *k* of the house of Israel ... Hos 1:4
Lord GOD are upon the sinful *k* ... Amos 9:8
the *k* shall be the LORD's ... Obad 21
the *k* shall come to the daughter ... Mic 4:8
for the *k* of heaven is at hand ... Mt 3:2
for the *k* of heaven is at hand ... Mt 4:17
and preaching the gospel of the *k* ... Mt 4:23
for theirs is the *k* of heaven ... Mt 5:3
for theirs is the *k* of heaven ... Mt 5:10
the least in the *k* of heaven ... Mt 5:19
called great in the *k* of heaven ... Mt 5:19
case enter into the *k* of heaven ... Mt 5:20
Thy *k* come ... Mt 6:10
For thine is the *k*, and the power, ... Mt 6:13
But seek ye first the *k* of God ... Mt 6:33
shall enter into the *k* of heaven ... Mt 7:21
and Jacob, in the *k* of heaven ... Mt 8:11
But the children of the *k* shall ... Mt 8:12
and preaching the gospel of the *k* ... Mt 9:35
The *k* of heaven is at hand ... Mt 10:7
he that is least in the *k* of ... Mt 11:11
*k* of heaven suffereth violence ... Mt 11:12
Every *k* divided against itself is ... Mt 12:25
how shall then his *k* stand ... Mt 12:26
then the *k* of God is come unto ... Mt 12:28
the mysteries of the *k* of heaven ... Mt 13:11
any one heareth the word of the *k* ... Mt 13:19
The *k* of heaven is likened unto a ... Mt 13:24
The *k* of heaven is like to a ... Mt 13:31
The *k* of heaven is like unto ... Mt 13:33
seed are the children of the *k* ... Mt 13:38
of his *k* all things that offend ... Mt 13:41
the sun in the *k* of their Father ... Mt 13:43
the *k* of heaven is like unto ... Mt 13:44
the *k* of heaven is like unto a ... Mt 13:45
the *k* of heaven is like unto a ... Mt 13:47
*k* of heaven is like unto a man ... Mt 13:52
thee the keys of the *k* of heaven ... Mt 16:19
the Son of man coming in his *k* ... Mt 16:28
the greatest in the *k* of heaven ... Mt 18:1
not enter into the *k* of heaven ... Mt 18:3
is greatest in the *k* of heaven ... Mt 18:4
Therefore is the *k* of heaven ... Mt 18:23
for the *k* of heaven's sake ... Mt 19:12
for of such is the *k* of heaven ... Mt 19:14
hardly enter into the *k* of heaven ... Mt 19:23
man to enter into the *k* of God ... Mt 19:24
For the *k* of heaven is like unto ... Mt 20:1
the other on the left, in thy *k* ... Mt 20:21
go into the *k* of God before you ... Mt 21:31
The *k* of God shall be taken from ... Mt 21:43
The *k* of heaven is like unto a ... Mt 22:2
for ye shut up the *k* of heaven ... Mt 23:13
nation, and *k* against *k* ... Mt 24:7
this gospel of the *k* shall be ... Mt 24:14
Then shall the *k* of heaven be ... Mt 25:1
For the *k* of heaven is as a man ... Mt 25:14
inherit the *k* prepared for you ... Mt 25:34
it new with you in my Father's *k* ... Mt 26:29
the gospel of the *k* of God ... Mk 1:14
and the *k* of God is at hand ... Mk 1:15
if a *k* be divided against itself, ... Mk 3:24
that *k* cannot stand ... Mk 3:24
know the mystery of the *k* of God ... Mk 4:11
And he said, So is the *k* of God ... Mk 4:26
shall we liken the *k* of God ... Mk 4:30
it thee, unto the half of my *k* ... Mk 6:23
seen the *k* of God come with power ... Mk 9:1
into the *k* of God with one eye ... Mk 9:47
for of such is the *k* of God ... Mk 10:14
the *k* of God as a little child ... Mk 10:15
riches enter into the *k* of God ... Mk 10:23
riches to enter into the *k* of God ... Mk 10:24
man to enter into the *k* of God ... Mk 10:25
Blessed be the *k* of our father ... Mk 11:10
art not far from the *k* of God ... Mk 12:34
nation, and *k* against *k* ... Mk 13:8
I drink it new in the *k* of God ... Mk 14:25
also waited for the *k* of God ... Mk 15:43
of his *k* there shall be no end ... Lk 1:33
I must preach the *k* of God to ... Lk 4:43
for yours is the *k* of God ... Lk 6:20
the *k* of God is greater than he ... Lk 7:28
the glad tidings of the *k* of God ... Lk 8:1
the mysteries of the *k* of God ... Lk 8:10
sent them to preach the *k* of God ... Lk 9:2
spake unto them of the *k* of God ... Lk 9:11
death, till they see the *k* of God ... Lk 9:27
go thou and preach the *k* of God ... Lk 9:60
back, is fit for the *k* of God ... Lk 9:62
The *k* of God is come nigh unto ... Lk 10:9
that the *k* of God is come nigh ... Lk 10:11
Thy *k* come ... Lk 11:2
Every *k* divided against itself is ... Lk 11:17
himself, how shall his *k* stand ... Lk 11:18
no doubt the *k* of God is come ... Lk 11:20
But rather seek ye the *k* of God ... Lk 12:31
good pleasure to give you the *k* ... Lk 12:32
Unto what is the *k* of God like ... Lk 13:18
shall I liken the *k* of God ... Lk 13:20
all the prophets, in the *k* of God ... Lk 13:28
and shall sit down in the *k* of God ... Lk 13:29
shall eat bread in the *k* of God ... Lk 14:15
time the *k* of God is preached ... Lk 16:16
when the *k* of God should come, he ... Lk 17:20
The *k* of God cometh not with ... Lk 17:20
the *k* of God is within you ... Lk 17:21
for of such is the *k* of God ... Lk 18:16
*k* of God as a little child shall ... Lk 18:17
riches enter into the *k* of God ... Lk 18:24
man to enter into the *k* of God ... Lk 18:25
for the *k* of God's sake, ... Lk 18:29
the *k* of God should immediately ... Lk 19:11
to receive for himself a *k* ... Lk 19:12
returned, having received the *k* ... Lk 19:15
nation, and *k* against *k* ... Lk 21:10
know ye that the *k* of God is nigh ... Lk 21:31
it be fulfilled in the *k* of God ... Lk 22:16
until the *k* of God shall come ... Lk 22:18
And I appoint unto you a *k* ... Lk 22:29
eat and drink at my table in my *k* ... Lk 22:30
me when thou comest into thy *k* ... Lk 23:42
himself waited for the *k* of God ... Lk 23:51
again, he cannot see the *k* of God ... Jn 3:3
he cannot enter into the *k* of God ... Jn 3:5
My *k* is not of this world ... Jn 18:36
if my *k* were of this world, then ... Jn 18:36
but now is my *k* not from hence ... Jn 18:36
things pertaining to the *k* of God ... Acts 1:3
restore again the *k* to Israel ... Acts 1:6
things concerning the *k* of God ... Acts 8:12
enter into the *k* of God ... Acts 14:22
things concerning the *k* of God ... Acts 19:8
have gone preaching the *k* of God ... Acts 20:25
and testified the *k* of God ... Acts 28:23
Preaching the *k* of God, and ... Acts 28:31
For the *k* of God is not meat and ... Rom 14:17
For the *k* of God is not in word, ... 1Cor 4:20
shall not inherit the *k* of God ... 1Cor 6:9
shall inherit the *k* of God ... 1Cor 6:10
have delivered up the *k* to God ... 1Cor 15:24
blood cannot inherit the *k* of God ... 1Cor 15:50
shall not inherit the *k* of God ... Gal 5:21
inheritance in the *k* of Christ ... Eph 5:5
us into the *k* of his dear Son ... Col 1:13
fellow workers unto the *k* of God ... Col 4:11
who hath called you unto his *k* ... 1Th 2:12
be counted worthy of the *k* of God ... 2Th 1:5
dead at his appearing and his *k* ... 2Ti 4:1
preserve me unto his heavenly *k* ... 2Ti 4:18
is the sceptre of thy *k* ... Heb 1:8
a *k* which cannot be moved ... Heb 12:28
heirs of the *k* which he hath ... Jas 2:5
the everlasting *k* of our Lord ... 2Pet 1:11
in tribulation, and in the *k* ... Rev 1:9
the *k* of our God, and the power of ... Rev 12:10
his *k* was full of darkness ... Rev 16:10
which have received no *k* as yet ... Rev 17:12
give their *k* unto the beast, ... Rev 17:17

**KINGDOMS**

all the *k* whither thou passest ... Deut 3:21
into all the *k* of the earth ... Deut 28:25
was the head of all those *k* ... Josh 11:10
and out of the hand of all *k* ... 1Sa 10:18
Solomon reigned over all *k* from ... 1Kin 4:21
of all the *k* of the earth ... 2Kin 19:15
that all the *k* of the earth may ... 2Kin 19:19
over all the *k* of the countries ... 1Chr 29:30
service of the *k* of the countries ... 2Chr 12:8
*k* of the lands that were round ... 2Chr 17:10
over all the *k* of the heathen ... 2Chr 20:6
on all the *k* of those countries ... 2Chr 20:29
All the *k* of the earth hath the ... 2Chr 36:23
given me all the *k* of the earth ... Ezr 1:2
Moreover thou gavest them *k* ... Neh 9:22
heathen raged, the *k* were moved ... Ps 46:6
Sing unto God, ye *k* of the earth ... Ps 68:32
upon the *k* that have not called ... Ps 79:6
are gathered together, and the *k* ... Ps 102:22
of Bashan, and all the *k* of Canaan ... Ps 135:11
hath found the *k* of the idols ... Is 10:10
a tumultuous noise of the *k* of ... Is 13:4
And Babylon, the glory of *k* ... Is 13:19
to tremble, that did shake *k* ... Is 14:16
hand over the sea, he shook the *k* ... Is 23:11
*k* of the world upon the face of ... Is 23:17
of all the *k* of the earth ... Is 37:16
that all the *k* of the earth may ... Is 37:20
no more be called, The lady of *k* ... Is 47:5
over the nations and over the *k* ... Jer 1:10

families of the *k* of the north Jer 1:15
of the nations, and in all their *k* Jer 10:7
removed into all *k* of the earth Jer 15:4
the *k* of the earth for their hurt Jer 24:9
all the *k* of the world, which are Jer 25:26
countries, and against great *k* Jer 28:8
removed to all the *k* of the earth Jer 29:18
all the *k* of the earth of his Jer 34:1
into all the *k* of the earth Jer 34:17
and concerning the *k* of Hazor Jer 49:28
and with thee will I destroy *k* Jer 51:20
against her the *k* of Ararat Jer 51:27
It shall be the basest of the *k* Eze 29:15
into two *k* any more at all Eze 37:22
in pieces and consume all these *k* Dan 2:44
which shall be diverse from all *k* Dan 7:23
four *k* shall stand up out of the Dan 8:22
be they better than these *k* Amos 6:2
thy nakedness, and the *k* thy shame Nah 3:5
that I may assemble the *k* Zeph 3:8
I will overthrow the throne of *k* Hag 2:22
strength of the *k* of the heathen Hag 2:22
him all the *k* of the world Mt 4:8
shewed unto him all the *k* of the Lk 4:5
Who through faith subdued *k* Heb 11:33
The *k* of this world are become Rev 11:15
are become the *k* of our Lord Rev 11:15

**KINGLY**
he was deposed from his *k* throne Dan 5:20

**KING'S**
of Shaveh, which is the *k* dale Gen 14:17
a place where the *k* prisoners Gen 39:20
we will go by the *k* high way Num 20:17
will go along by the *k* high way Num 21:22
now therefore be the *k* son in law 1Sa 18:22
light thing to be a *k* son in law 1Sa 18:23
to be avenged of the *k* enemies 1Sa 18:25
David well to be the *k* son in law 1Sa 18:26
that he might be the *k* son in law 1Sa 18:27
he cometh not unto the *k* table 1Sa 20:29
because the *k* business required 1Sa 21:8
David, which is the *k* son in law 1Sa 22:14
be to deliver him into the *k* hand 1Sa 23:20
And now see where the *k* spear is 1Sa 26:16
and said, Behold the *k* spear 1Sa 26:22
at my table, as one of the *k* sons 2Sa 9:11
eat continually at the *k* table 2Sa 9:13
upon the roof of the *k* house 2Sa 11:2
Uriah departed out of the *k* house 2Sa 11:8
*k* house with all the servants of 2Sa 11:9
if so be that the *k* wrath arise 2Sa 11:20
some of the *k* servants be dead, 2Sa 11:24
he took their *k* crown from off 2Sa 12:30
Why art thou, being the *k* son 2Sa 13:4
the *k* daughters that were virgins 2Sa 13:18
and Absalom invited all the *k* sons 2Sa 13:23
all the *k* sons go with him 2Sa 13:27
Then all the *k* sons arose 2Sa 13:29
Absalom hath slain all the *k* sons 2Sa 13:30
all the young men the *k* sons 2Sa 13:32
that all the *k* sons are dead 2Sa 13:33
the king, Behold, the *k* sons come 2Sa 13:35
the *k* sons came, and lifted up 2Sa 13:36
the *k* heart was toward Absalom 2Sa 14:1
own house, and saw not the *k* face 2Sa 14:24
shekels after the *k* weight 2Sa 14:26
Jerusalem, and saw not the *k* face 2Sa 14:28
therefore let me see the *k* face 2Sa 14:32
the *k* servants said unto the king 2Sa 15:15
shalt hear out of the *k* house 2Sa 15:35
be for the *k* household to ride on 2Sa 16:2
forth mine hand against the *k* son 2Sa 18:12
a pillar, which is in the *k* dale 2Sa 18:18
because the *k* son is dead 2Sa 18:20
When Joab sent the *k* servant 2Sa 18:29
to carry over the *k* household 2Sa 19:18
we eaten at all of the *k* cost 2Sa 19:42
Notwithstanding the *k* word 2Sa 24:4
all his brethren the *k* sons 1Kin 1:9
the men of Judah the *k* servants 1Kin 1:9
and hath called all the *k* sons 1Kin 1:25
And she came into the *k* presence 1Kin 1:28
him to ride upon the *k* mule 1Kin 1:44
moreover the *k* servants came to 1Kin 1:47
a seat to be set for the *k* mother 1Kin 2:19
officer, and the *k* friend 1Kin 4:5
the *k* house, and all Solomon's 1Kin 9:1
of the LORD, and the *k* house, 1Kin 9:10
of the LORD, and for the *k* house 1Kin 10:12
the *k* merchants received the 1Kin 10:28
he was of the *k* seed in Edom 1Kin 11:14
the *k* hand was restored him again 1Kin 13:6
and the treasures of the *k* house 1Kin 14:26
kept the door of the *k* house 1Kin 14:27
and the treasures of the *k* house 1Kin 15:18
into the palace of the *k* house 1Kin 16:18
burnt the *k* house over him with 1Kin 16:18
shall deliver it into the *k* hand 1Kin 22:12
the city, and to Joash the *k* son 1Kin 22:26
we may go and tell the *k* household 2Kin 7:9
told it to the *k* house within 2Kin 7:11
for she is a *k* daughter 2Kin 9:34
Now the *k* sons, being seventy 2Kin 10:6
them, that they took the *k* sons 2Kin 10:7
brought the heads of the *k* sons 2Kin 10:8
among the *k* sons which were slain 2Kin 11:2
LORD, and shewed them the *k* son 2Kin 11:4
of the watch of the *k* house 2Kin 11:5
And he brought forth the *k* son 2Kin 11:12
the horses came into the *k* house 2Kin 11:16
gate of the guard to the *k* house 2Kin 11:19
with the sword beside the *k* house 2Kin 11:20
in the chest, that the *k* scribe 2Kin 12:10
of the LORD, and in the *k* house 2Kin 12:18
put his hands upon the *k* hands 2Kin 13:16
in the treasures of the *k* house 2Kin 14:14
Jotham the *k* son was over the 2Kin 15:5
in the palace of the *k* house 2Kin 15:25
in the treasures of the *k* house 2Kin 16:8
the *k* burnt sacrifice, and his 2Kin 16:15
the *k* entry without, turned he 2Kin 16:18
in the treasures of the *k* house 2Kin 18:15
for the *k* commandment was, saying 2Kin 18:36
and Asahiah a servant of the *k* 2Kin 22:12
and the treasures of the *k* house 2Kin 24:13
the *k* mother, and the *k* wives 2Kin 24:15
walls, which is by the *k* garden 2Kin 25:4
the *k* house, and all the houses of 2Kin 25:9
them that were in the *k* presence 2Kin 25:19
waited in the *k* gate eastward 1Chr 9:18
Nevertheless the *k* word prevailed 1Chr 21:4
for the *k* word was abominable to 1Chr 21:6
the *k* seer in the words of God 1Chr 25:5
according to the *k* order to Asaph 1Chr 25:6
over the *k* treasures was Azmaveth 1Chr 27:25
of Hachmoni was with the *k* sons 1Chr 27:32
Ahithophel was the *k* counsellor 1Chr 27:33
the Archite was the *k* companion 1Chr 27:33
general of the *k* army was Joab 1Chr 27:34
with the rulers of the *k* work 1Chr 29:6
the *k* merchants received the 2Chr 1:16
house of the LORD, and the *k* house 2Chr 7:11
of the LORD, and to the *k* palace 2Chr 9:11
For the *k* ships went to Tarshish 2Chr 9:21
and the treasures of the *k* house 2Chr 12:9
kept the entrance of the *k* house 2Chr 12:10
of the LORD and of the *k* house 2Chr 16:2
will deliver it into the *k* hand 2Chr 18:5
the city, and to Joash the *k* son 2Chr 18:25
of Judah, for all the *k* matters 2Chr 19:11
that was found in the *k* house 2Chr 21:17
among the *k* sons that were slain 2Chr 22:11
the *k* son shall reign, as the 2Chr 23:3
part shall be at the *k* house 2Chr 23:5
Then they brought out the *k* son 2Chr 23:11
of the horse gate by the *k* house 2Chr 23:15
the high gate into the *k* house 2Chr 23:20
at the *k* commandment they made a 2Chr 24:8
the *k* office by the hand of the 2Chr 24:11
the *k* scribe and the high priest's 2Chr 24:11
Art thou made of the *k* counsel 2Chr 25:16
and the treasures of the *k* house 2Chr 25:24
Hananiah, one of the *k* captains 2Chr 26:11
his son was over the *k* house 2Chr 26:21
Ephraim, slew Maaseiah the *k* son 2Chr 28:7
of David, and of Gad the *k* seer 2Chr 29:25
He appointed also the *k* portion 2Chr 31:3
and Asaiah a servant of the *k* 2Chr 34:20
these were of the *k* substance 2Chr 35:7
according to the *k* commandment 2Chr 35:10
and Jeduthun the *k* seer 2Chr 35:15
maintenance from the *k* palace Ezr 4:14
for us to see the *k* dishonour Ezr 4:14
made in the *k* treasure house Ezr 5:17
be given out of the *k* house Ezr 6:4
that of the *k* goods, even of the Ezr 6:8
it out of the *k* treasure house Ezr 7:20
a thing as this in the *k* heart Ezr 7:27
before all the *k* mighty princes Ezr 7:28
they delivered the *k* commissions Ezr 8:36
unto the *k* lieutenants, and to the Ezr 8:36
For I was the *k* cupbearer Neh 1:11
Asaph the keeper of the *k* forest Neh 2:8
river, and gave them the *k* letters Neh 2:9
of the fountain, and to the *k* pool Neh 2:14
as also the *k* words that he had Neh 2:18
pool of Siloah by the *k* garden Neh 3:15
lieth out from the *k* high house Neh 3:25
borrowed money for the *k* tribute Neh 5:4
For it was the *k* commandment Neh 11:23
was at the *k* hand in all matters Neh 11:24
of the garden of the *k* palace Est 1:5
Vashti refused to come at the *k* Est 1:12
(for so was the *k* manner toward Est 1:13
and Media, which saw the *k* face Est 1:14
this day unto all the *k* princes Est 1:18
when the *k* decree which he shall Est 1:20
letters into all the *k* provinces Est 1:22
Then said the *k* servants that Est 2:2
custody of Hege the *k* chamberlain Est 2:3
when the *k* commandment and his Est 2:8
was brought also unto the *k* house Est 2:8
be given her, out of the *k* house Est 2:9
of the women unto the *k* house Est 2:13
the *k* chamberlain, which kept the Est 2:14
but what Hegai the *k* chamberlain Est 2:15
then Mordecai sat in the *k* gate Est 2:19
while Mordecai sat in the *k* gate Est 2:21
two of the *k* chamberlains, Est 2:21
all the *k* servants, that were in Est 3:2
servants, that were in the *k* gate Est 3:2
Then the *k* servants, which were Est 3:3
which were in the *k* gate Est 3:3
thou the *k* commandment Est 3:3
neither keep they the *k* laws Est 3:8
for the *k* profit to suffer them Est 3:8
to bring it into the *k* treasuries Est 3:9
Then were the *k* scribes called on Est 3:12
commanded unto the *k* lieutenants Est 3:12
and sealed with the *k* ring Est 3:12
by posts into all the *k* provinces Est 3:13
hastened by the *k* commandment Est 3:15
And came even before the *k* gate Est 4:2
the *k* gate clothed with sackcloth Est 4:2
whithersoever the *k* commandment Est 4:3
one of the *k* chamberlains, whom Est 4:5
city, which was before the *k* gate Est 4:6
to the *k* treasuries for the Jews Est 4:7
All the *k* servants, and the people Est 4:11
and the people of the *k* provinces Est 4:11
thou shalt escape in the *k* house Est 4:13
in the inner court of the *k* house Est 5:1
over against the *k* house Est 5:1
Haman saw Mordecai in the *k* gate Est 5:9
the Jew sitting at the *k* gate Est 5:13
two of the *k* chamberlains, the Est 6:2
Then said the *k* servants that Est 6:3
the outward court of the *k* house Est 6:4
the *k* servants said unto him, Est 6:5
one of the *k* most noble princes Est 6:9
Jew, that sitteth at the *k* gate Est 6:10
Mordecai came again to the *k* gate Est 6:12
came the *k* chamberlains, and Est 6:14
not countervail the *k* damage Est 7:4
the word went out of the *k* mouth Est 7:8
Then was the *k* wrath pacified Est 7:10
which are in all the *k* provinces Est 8:5
as it liketh you, in the *k* name Est 8:8
and seal it with the *k* ring Est 8:8
which is written in the *k* name Est 8:8
and sealed with the *k* ring Est 8:8
Then were the *k* scribes called at Est 8:9
and sealed it with the *k* ring Est 8:10
pressed on by the *k* commandment Est 8:14
whithersoever the *k* commandment Est 8:17
when the *k* commandment and his Est 9:1
Mordecai was great in the *k* house Est 9:4
in the rest of the *k* provinces Est 9:12
*k* provinces gathered themselves Est 9:16
in the heart of the *k* enemies Ps 45:5
The *k* daughter is all glorious Ps 45:13
shall enter into the *k* palace Ps 45:15
Thou wilt prolong the *k* life Ps 61:6
thy righteousness unto the *k* son Ps 72:1
The *k* strength also loveth Ps 99:4
of people is the *k* honour Prov 14:28
The *k* favour is toward a wise Prov 14:35
of the *k* countenance is life Prov 16:15
The *k* wrath is as the roaring of Prov 19:12
The *k* heart is in the hand of the Prov 21:1
thee to keep the *k* commandment Eccl 8:2
for the *k* commandment was, saying Is 36:21
LORD unto the *k* house of Judah Jer 22:6
then they came up from the *k* Jer 26:10
he went down into the *k* house Jer 36:12
eunuchs which was in the *k* house Jer 38:7
went forth out of the *k* house Jer 38:8
night, by the way of the *k* garden Jer 39:4
the Chaldeans burned the *k* house Jer 39:8
even the *k* daughters, and all the Jer 41:10
the *k* daughters, and every person Jer 43:6
walls, which was by the *k* garden Jer 52:7
house of the LORD, and the *k* house Jer 52:13
them that were near the *k* person Jer 52:25
And hath taken of the *k* seed Eze 17:13
of Israel, and of the *k* seed Dan 1:3
in them to stand in the *k* palace Dan 1:4
a daily provision of the *k* meat Dan 1:5
with the portion of the *k* meat Dan 1:8
eat of the portion of the *k* meat Dan 1:13
did eat the portion of the *k* meat Dan 1:15
earth that can shew the *k* matter Dan 2:10
Arioch the captain of the *k* guard Dan 2:14
and said to Arioch the *k* captain Dan 2:15
made known unto us the *k* matter Dan 2:23
Therefore because the *k* Dan 3:22
the *k* counsellors, being gathered Dan 3:27
him, and have changed the *k* word Dan 3:28
While the word was in the *k* mouth Dan 4:31
of the wall of the *k* palace Dan 5:5
Then the *k* countenance was Dan 5:6
Then came in all the *k* wise men Dan 5:8
the king concerning the *k* decree Dan 6:12
I rose up, and did the *k* business Dan 8:27
for the *k* daughter of the south Dan 11:6
latter growth after the *k* mowings Amos 7:1
for it is the *k* chapel Amos 7:13
and it is the *k* court Amos 7:13
the *k* children, and all such as Zeph 1:8
Hananeel unto the *k* winepresses Zec 14:10
having made Blastus the *k* Acts 12:20
was nourished by the *k* country Acts 12:20
not afraid of the *k* commandment Heb 11:23

**KINGS**
the *k* that were with him, and Gen 14:5
four *k* with five Gen 14:9
the *k* of Sodom and Gomorrah fled, Gen 14:10
of the *k* that were with him, at Gen 14:17
thee, and *k* shall come out of thee Gen 17:6
*k* of people shall be of her Gen 17:16
*k* shall come out of thy loins Gen 35:11
these are the *k* that reigned in Gen 36:31
And they slew the *k* of Midian Num 31:8
and Hur, and Reba, five *k* of Midian Num 31:8
*k* of the Amorites the land that Deut 3:8
God hath done unto these two *k* Deut 3:21
two *k* of the Amorites, which were Deut 4:47
deliver their *k* into thine hand Deut 7:24
*k* of the Amorites, and unto the Deut 31:4

unto the two *k* of the Amorites Josh 2:10
when all the *k* of the Amorites, Josh 5:1
all the *k* of the Canaanites, Josh 5:1
when all the *k* which were on this Josh 9:1
did to the two *k* of the Amorites Josh 9:10
the five *k* of the Amorites Josh 10:5
for all the *k* of the Amorites Josh 10:6
But these five *k* fled, and hid Josh 10:16
The five *k* are found hid in a Josh 10:17
bring out those five *k* unto me Josh 10:22
five *k* unto him out of the cave Josh 10:23
brought out those *k* unto Joshua Josh 10:24
feet upon the necks of these *k* Josh 10:24
and of the springs, and all their *k* Josh 10:40
And all these *k* and their land did Josh 10:42
to the *k* that were on the north Josh 11:2
when all these *k* were met Josh 11:5
those *k*, and all the *k* of them Josh 11:12
and all their *k* he took, and smote Josh 11:17
war a long time with all those *k* Josh 11:18
Now these are the *k* of the land Josh 12:1
these are the *k* of the country Josh 12:7
all the *k* thirty and one Josh 12:24
even the two *k* of the Amorites Josh 24:12
said, Threescore and ten *k* Judg 1:7
Hear, O ye *k* Judg 5:3
The *k* came and fought Judg 5:19
then fought the *k* of Canaan in Judg 5:19
Zebah and Zalmunna, *k* of Midian Judg 8:5
them, and took the two *k* of Midian Judg 8:12
that was on the *k* of Midian Judg 8:26
Edom, and against the *k* of Zobah 1Sa 14:47
unto the *k* of Judah unto this day 1Sa 27:6
when all the *k* that were servants 2Sa 10:19
at the time when *k* go forth to 2Sa 11:1
shall not be any among the *k* like 1Kin 3:13
over all the *k* on this side the 1Kin 4:24
from all *k* of the earth, which 1Kin 4:34
and of all the *k* of Arabia 1Kin 10:15
all the *k* of the earth for riches 1Kin 10:23
so for all the *k* of the Hittites, 1Kin 10:29
for the *k* of Syria, did they 1Kin 10:29
the chronicles of the *k* of Israel 1Kin 14:19
the chronicles of the *k* of Judah 1Kin 14:29
the chronicles of the *k* of Judah 1Kin 15:7
the chronicles of the *k* of Judah 1Kin 15:23
the chronicles of the *k* of Israel 1Kin 15:31
the chronicles of the *k* of Israel 1Kin 16:5
the chronicles of the *k* of Israel 1Kin 16:14
the chronicles of the *k* of Israel 1Kin 16:20
the chronicles of the *k* of Israel 1Kin 16:27
*k* of Israel that were before him 1Kin 16:33
two *k* with him, and horses, and 1Kin 20:1
the *k* in the pavilions, that he 1Kin 20:12
in the pavilions, he and the *k* 1Kin 20:16
thirty and two *k* that helped him 1Kin 20:16
And do this thing, Take the *k* away 1Kin 20:24
we have heard that the *k* of the 1Kin 20:31
house of Israel are merciful *k* 1Kin 20:31
the chronicles of the *k* of Israel 1Kin 22:39
the chronicles of the *k* of Judah 1Kin 22:45
the chronicles of the *k* of Israel 2Kin 1:18
called these three *k* together 2Kin 3:10
called these three *k* together 2Kin 3:13
*k* were come up to fight against 2Kin 3:21
the *k* are surely slain, and they 2Kin 3:23
against us the *k* of the Hittites 2Kin 7:6
the *k* of the Egyptians, to come 2Kin 7:6
in the way of the *k* of Israel 2Kin 8:18
the chronicles of the *k* of Judah 2Kin 8:23
two *k* stood not before him 2Kin 10:4
the chronicles of the *k* of Israel 2Kin 10:34
And he sat on the throne of the *k* 2Kin 11:19
*k* of Judah, had dedicated, and his 2Kin 12:18
the chronicles of the *k* of Judah 2Kin 12:19
the chronicles of the *k* of Israel 2Kin 13:8
the chronicles of the *k* of Israel 2Kin 13:12
in Samaria with the *k* of Israel 2Kin 13:13
the chronicles of the *k* of Israel 2Kin 14:15
in Samaria with the *k* of Israel 2Kin 14:16
the chronicles of the *k* of Judah 2Kin 14:18
the chronicles of the *k* of Israel 2Kin 14:28
even with the *k* of Israel 2Kin 14:29
the chronicles of the *k* of Judah 2Kin 15:6
the chronicles of the *k* of Israel 2Kin 15:11
the chronicles of the *k* of Israel 2Kin 15:15
the chronicles of the *k* of Israel 2Kin 15:21
the chronicles of the *k* of Israel 2Kin 15:26
the chronicles of the *k* of Israel 2Kin 15:31
the chronicles of the *k* of Judah 2Kin 15:36
in the way of the *k* of Israel 2Kin 16:3
the chronicles of the *k* of Judah 2Kin 16:19
but not as the *k* of Israel that 2Kin 17:2
of the *k* of Israel, which they 2Kin 17:8
like him among all the *k* of Judah 2Kin 18:5
thou hast heard what the *k* of 2Kin 19:11
the *k* of Assyria have destroyed 2Kin 19:17
the chronicles of the *k* of Judah 2Kin 20:20
the chronicles of the *k* of Judah 2Kin 21:17
the chronicles of the *k* of Judah 2Kin 21:25
whom the *k* of Judah had ordained 2Kin 23:5
*k* of Judah had given to the sun 2Kin 23:11
which the *k* of Judah had made, and 2Kin 23:12
which the *k* of Israel had made to 2Kin 23:19
all the days of the *k* of Israel 2Kin 23:22
nor of the *k* of Judah 2Kin 23:22
the chronicles of the *k* of Judah 2Kin 23:28
the chronicles of the *k* of Judah 2Kin 24:5
*k* that were with him in Babylon 2Kin 25:28
Now these are the *k* that reigned 1Chr 1:43
in the book of the *k* of Israel 1Chr 9:1
he reproved *k* for their sakes, 1Chr 16:21
the *k* that were come were by 1Chr 19:9
the time that *k* go out to battle 1Chr 20:1
such as none of the *k* have had 2Chr 1:12
for all the *k* of the Hittites 2Chr 1:17
for the *k* of Syria, by their 2Chr 1:17
all the *k* of Arabia and governors 2Chr 9:14
all the *k* of the earth in riches 2Chr 9:22
all the *k* of the earth sought the 2Chr 9:23
he reigned over all the *k* from 2Chr 9:26
in the book of the *k* of Judah 2Chr 16:11
in the book of the *k* of Israel 2Chr 20:34
in the way of the *k* of Israel 2Chr 21:6
in the way of the *k* of Israel 2Chr 21:13
not in the sepulchres of the *k* 2Chr 21:20
in the city of David among the *k* 2Chr 24:16
not in the sepulchres of the *k* 2Chr 24:25
in the story of the book of the *k* 2Chr 24:27
in the book of the *k* of Judah 2Chr 25:26
burial which belonged to the *k* 2Chr 26:23
in the book of the *k* of Israel 2Chr 27:7
in the ways of the *k* of Israel 2Chr 28:2
unto the *k* of Assyria to help him 2Chr 28:16
gods of the *k* of Syria help them 2Chr 28:23
in the book of the *k* of Judah 2Chr 28:26
the sepulchres of the *k* of Israel 2Chr 28:27
of the hand of the *k* of Assyria 2Chr 30:6
Why should the *k* of Assyria come, 2Chr 32:4
and in the book of the *k* of Judah 2Chr 32:32
in the book of the *k* of Israel 2Chr 33:18
the *k* of Judah had destroyed 2Chr 34:11
neither did all the *k* of Israel 2Chr 35:18
in the book of the *k* of Israel 2Chr 35:27
in the book of the *k* of Israel 2Chr 36:8
endamage the revenue of the *k* Ezr 4:13
city, and hurtful unto *k* and Ezr 4:15
hath made insurrection against *k* Ezr 4:19
been mighty *k* also over Jerusalem Ezr 4:20
damage grow to the hurt of the *k* Ezr 4:22
name to dwell there destroy all *k* Ezr 6:12
Artaxerxes, king of *k*, unto Ezra Ezr 7:12
for our iniquities have we, our *k* Ezr 9:7
the hand of the *k* of the lands Ezr 9:7
in the sight of the *k* of Persia Ezr 9:9
into their hands, with their *k* Neh 9:24
that hath come upon us, on our *k* Neh 9:32
since the time of the *k* of Neh 9:32
Neither have our *k*, our princes, Neh 9:34
the *k* whom thou hast set over us Neh 9:37
the chronicles of the *k* of Media Est 10:2
With *k* and counsellors of the Job 3:14
He looseth the bond of *k*, and Job 12:18
but with *k* are they on the throne Job 36:7
The *k* of the earth set themselves Ps 2:2
Be wise now therefore, O ye *k* Ps 2:10
the *k* were assembled, they passed Ps 48:4
*K* of armies did flee apace Ps 68:12
the Almighty scattered *k* in it Ps 68:14
shall *k* bring presents unto thee Ps 68:29
The *k* of Tarshish and of the isles Ps 72:10
the *k* of Sheba and Seba shall Ps 72:10
all *k* shall fall down before him Ps 72:11
is terrible to the *k* of the earth Ps 76:12
higher than the *k* of the earth Ps 89:27
all the *k* of the earth thy glory Ps 102:15
he reproved *k* for their sakes Ps 105:14
in the chambers of their *k* Ps 105:30
through *k* in the day of his wrath Ps 110:5
of thy testimonies also before *k* Ps 119:46
great nations, and slew mighty *k* Ps 135:10
To him which smote great *k* Ps 136:17
And slew famous *k* Ps 136:18
All the *k* of the earth shall Ps 138:4
he that giveth salvation unto *k* Ps 144:10
*K* of the earth, and all people Ps 148:11
To bind their *k* with chains Ps 149:8
By me *k* reign, and princes decree Prov 8:15
to *k* to commit wickedness Prov 16:12
lips are the delight of *k* Prov 16:13
he shall stand before *k* Prov 22:29
but the honour of *k* is to search Prov 25:2
the heart of *k* is unsearchable Prov 25:3
ways to that which destroyeth *k* Prov 31:3
It is not for *k*, O Lemuel, it is Prov 31:4
it is not for *k* to drink wine Prov 31:4
and the peculiar treasure of *k* Eccl 2:8
Ahaz, and Hezekiah, *k* of Judah Is 1:1
shall be forsaken of both her *k* Is 7:16
Are not my princes altogether *k* Is 10:8
thrones all the *k* of the nations Is 14:9
All the *k* of the nations, even Is 14:18
of the wise, the son of ancient *k* Is 19:11
the *k* of the earth upon the earth Is 24:21
thou hast heard what the *k* of Is 37:11
the *k* of Assyria have laid waste Is 37:18
him, and made him rule over *k* Is 41:2
and I will loose the loins of *k* Is 45:1
*K* shall see and arise, princes Is 49:7
*k* shall be thy nursing fathers, Is 49:23
the *k* shall shut their mouths at Is 52:15
*k* to the brightness of thy rising Is 60:3
their *k* shall minister unto thee Is 60:10
that their *k* may be brought Is 60:11
and shalt suck the breast of *k* Is 60:16
righteousness, and all *k* thy glory Is 62:2
land, against the *k* of Judah Jer 1:18
they, their *k*, their princes, and Jer 2:26
out the bones of the *k* of Judah Jer 8:1
even the *k* that sit upon David's Jer 13:13
whereby the *k* of Judah come in, Jer 17:19
ye *k* of Judah, and all Judah, and Jer 17:20
into the gates of this city *k* Jer 17:25
O *k* of Judah, and inhabitants of Jer 19:3
nor the *k* of Judah, and have Jer 19:4
and the houses of the *k* of Judah Jer 19:13
all the treasures of the *k* of Jer 20:5
*k* sitting upon the throne of Jer 22:4
great *k* shall serve themselves of Jer 25:14
the *k* thereof, and the princes Jer 25:18
all the *k* of the land of Uz, and Jer 25:20
all the *k* of the land of the Jer 25:20
all the *k* of Tyrus Jer 25:22
all the *k* of Zidon Jer 25:22
the *k* of the isles which are Jer 25:22
all the *k* of Arabia Jer 25:24
all the *k* of the mingled people Jer 25:24
all the *k* of Zimri Jer 25:25
and all the *k* of Elam Jer 25:25
and all the *k* of the Medes Jer 25:25
all the *k* of the north, far and Jer 25:26
great *k* shall serve themselves of Jer 27:7
me to anger, they, their *k* Jer 32:32
the houses of the *k* of Judah Jer 33:4
the former *k* which were before Jer 34:5
the wickedness of the *k* of Judah Jer 44:9
done, we, and our fathers, our *k* Jer 44:17
ye, and your fathers, your *k* Jer 44:21
with their gods, and their *k* Jer 46:25
many *k* shall be raised up from Jer 50:41
the spirit of the *k* of the Medes Jer 51:11
nations with the *k* of the Medes Jer 51:28
*k* that were with him in Babylon Jer 52:32
The *k* of the earth, and all the Lam 4:12
king of Babylon, a king of *k* Eze 26:7
thou didst enrich the *k* of the Eze 27:33
their *k* shall be sore afraid, Eze 27:35
ground, I will lay thee before *k* Eze 28:17
their *k* shall be horribly afraid Eze 32:10
There is Edom, her *k*, and all her Eze 32:29
defile, neither they, nor their *k* Eze 43:7
of their *k* in their high places Eze 43:7
and the carcases of their *k* Eze 43:9
removeth *k*, and setteth up *k* Dan 2:21
Thou, O king, art a king of *k* Dan 2:37
in the days of these *k* shall the Dan 2:44
is a God of gods, and a LORD of *k* Dan 2:47
which are four, are four *k* Dan 7:17
are ten *k* that shall arise Dan 7:24
first, and he shall subdue three *k* Dan 7:24
two horns are the *k* of Media Dan 8:20
which spake in thy name to our *k* Dan 9:6
confusion of face, to our *k* Dan 9:8
there with the *k* of Persia Dan 10:13
stand up yet three *k* in Persia Dan 11:2
*k* of Judah, and in the days of Hos 1:1
all their *k* are fallen Hos 7:7
They have set up *k*, but not by me Hos 8:4
*k* of Judah, which he saw Mic 1:1
shall be a lie to the *k* of Israel Mic 1:14
And they shall scoff at the *k* Hab 1:10
*k* for my sake, for a testimony Mt 10:18
of whom do the *k* of the earth Mt 17:25
*k* for my sake, for a testimony Mk 13:9
*k* have desired to see those Lk 10:24
prisons, being brought before *k* Lk 21:12
The *k* of the Gentiles exercise Lk 22:25
The *k* of the earth stood up, and Acts 4:26
my name before the Gentiles, and *k* Acts 9:15
ye have reigned as *k* without us 1Cor 4:8
For *k*, and for all that are in 1Ti 2:2
and only Potentate, the King of *k* 1Ti 6:15
from the slaughter of the *k* Heb 7:1
the prince of the *k* of the earth Rev 1:5
And hath made us *k* and priests unto Rev 1:6
And hast made us unto our God *k* Rev 5:10
the *k* of the earth, and the great Rev 6:15
and nations, and tongues, and *k* Rev 10:11
that the way of the *k* of the east Rev 16:12
go forth unto the *k* of the earth Rev 16:14
With whom the *k* of the earth have Rev 17:2
And there are seven *k* Rev 17:10
horns which thou sawest are ten *k* Rev 17:12
but receive power as *k* one hour Rev 17:12
he is Lord of lords, and King of *k* Rev 17:14
reigneth over the *k* of the earth Rev 17:18
the *k* of the earth have committed Rev 18:3
the *k* of the earth, who have Rev 18:9
thigh a name written, KING OF *K* Rev 19:16
That ye may eat the flesh of *k* Rev 19:18
the *k* of the earth, and their Rev 19:19
the *k* of the earth do bring their Rev 21:24

**KINGS'**
*K* daughters were among thy Ps 45:9
her hands, and is in *k* palaces Prov 30:28
both these *k* hearts shall be to Dan 11:27
soft clothing are in *k* houses Mt 11:8
live delicately, are in *k* courts Lk 7:25

**KINNERETH** See CINNEROTH.

**KINSFOLK**
My *k* have failed, and my familiar Job 19:14
and they sought him among their *k* Lk 2:44

**KINSFOLKS**
against a wall, neither of his *k* 1Kin 16:11
and all his great men, and his *k* 2Kin 10:11
by parents, and brethren, and *k* Lk 21:16

**KINSMAN**
But if the man have no *k* to ... Num 5:8
his *k* that is next to him of his ... Num 27:11
Naomi had a *k* of her husband's, a ... Ruth 2:1
for thou art a near *k* ... Ruth 3:9
it is true that I am thy near *k* ... Ruth 3:12
there is a *k* nearer than I ... Ruth 3:12
perform unto thee the part of a *k* ... Ruth 3:13
not do the part of a *k* to thee ... Ruth 3:13
will I do the part of a *k* to thee ... Ruth 3:13
the *k* of whom Boaz spake came by ... Ruth 4:1
And he said unto the *k*, Naomi, ... Ruth 4:3
the *k* said, I cannot redeem it ... Ruth 4:6
Therefore the *k* said unto Boaz, ... Ruth 4:8
left thee this day without a *k* ... Ruth 4:14
being his *k* whose ear Peter cut ... Jn 18:26
Salute Herodion my *k* ... Rom 16:11

**KINSMAN'S**
let him do the *k* part ... Ruth 3:13

**KINSMEN**
of kin unto us, one of our next *k* ... Ruth 2:20
and my *k* stand afar off ... Ps 38:11
nor thy brethren, neither thy *k* ... Lk 14:12
and had called together his *k* ... Acts 10:24
my *k* according to the flesh ... Rom 9:3
Salute Andronicus and Junia, my *k* ... Rom 16:7
and Jason, and Sosipater, my *k* ... Rom 16:21

**KINSWOMAN**
she is thy father's near *k* ... Lev 18:12
for she is thy mother's near *k* ... Lev 18:13
and call understanding thy *k* ... Prov 7:4

**KINSWOMEN**
for they are her near *k* ... Lev 18:17

**KIOS** See CHIOS.

**KIR** (*kur*) See KIR-HARESH.
*1. An Assyrian district on the Kur River.*
the people of it captive to *K* ... 2Kin 16:9
shall go into captivity unto *K* ... Amos 1:5
Caphtor, and the Syrians from *K* ... Amos 9:7
*2. A Moabite city.*
because in the night *K* of Moab is ... Is 15:1
*3. Inhabitants of Kir 1.*
and *K* uncovered the shield ... Is 22:6

**KIR-HARASETH** (*kur-har'-a-seth*) See KIR-HARESETH. *A Moabite city.*
only in *K* left they the stones ... 2Kin 3:25

**KIR-HARESETH** (*kur-har'-e-seth*) See KIR-HARESH. *Same as Kir-haraseth.*
foundations of *K* shall ye mourn ... Is 16:7

**KIR-HARESH** (*kur-ha'-resh*) See KIR-HARASETH, KIR-HARESETH, KIR-HERES. *Same as Kir-haraseth.*
Moab, and mine inward parts for *K* ... Is 16:11

**KIR-HERES** (*kur-he'-res*) See KIR-HARESH. *Same as Kir-haraseth.*
shall mourn for the men of *K* ... Jer 48:31
sound like pipes for the men of *K* ... Jer 48:36

**KIRIATH** See KIRJATH.

**KIRIATHAIM** (*kir-e-a-thay'-im*) See KIRTAN, KIRJATHAIM.
*1. A town east of the Jordan.*
in Ham, and the Emims in Shaveh *K* ... Gen 14:5
*2. A city in Reuben.*
*K* is confounded and taken ... Jer 48:1
And upon *K*, and upon ... Jer 48:23
Beth-jeshimoth, Baal-meon, and *K* ... Eze 25:9

**KIRIATH ARBA** See KIRJATH-ARBA.

**KIRIATH-ARBA** See KIRJATH-ARBA.

**KIRIATH-ARIM** See KIRJATH-ARIM.

**KIRIATH-BAAL** See KIRJATH-BAAL.

**KIRIATH-JEARIM** See KIRJATH.

**KIRIATH-SANNAH** See KIRJATH-SANNAH.

**KIRIATH-SEPHER** See KIRJATH-SEPHER.

**KIRIOTH** (*kir'-e-oth*) See KERIOTH. *A Moabite city.*
it shall devour the palaces of *K* ... Amos 2:2

**KIRJATH** (*kur'-jath*) See KIRJATH-ARIM, KIRJATH-BAAL, KIRJATH-JEARIM. *Short form of Kirjath-jearim.*
which is Jerusalem, Gibeath, and *K* ... Josh 18:28

**KIRJATHAIM** (*jur'-jath-a'-im*)
*1. A city in Reuben.*
built Heshbon, and Elealeh, and *K* ... Num 32:37
And *K*, and Sibmah ... Josh 13:19
*2. A Levitical city in Naphtali.*
suburbs, and *K* with her suburbs ... 1Chr 6:76

**KIRJATH-ARBA** (*kur'-jath-ar'-bah*) See HERBON. *A city in Judah.*
And Sarah died in *K* ... Gen 23:2
the name of Hebron before was *K* ... Josh 14:15
And Humtah, and *K*, which ... Josh 15:54
in mount Ephraim, and *K* ... Josh 20:7
the name of Hebron before was *K* ... Judg 1:10
the children of Judah dwelt at *K* ... Neh 11:25

**KIRJATH-ARIM** (*kur'-jath-a'-rim*) See KIRJATH-JEARIM. *Same as Kirjath-jearim.*
The children of *K*, Chephirah, and ... Ezr 2:25

**KIRJATH-BAAL** (*kur'-jath-ba'-al*) See BAALAH, KIRJATH-JEARIM. *Same as Kirjath-jearim.*
*K*, which is Kirjath-jearim, and ... Josh 15:60
the goings out thereof were at *K* ... Josh 18:14

**KIRJATH-HUZOTH** (*kur'-jath-hu'-zoth*) *Residence of Balak, king of Edom.*
with Balak, and they came unto *K* ... Num 22:39

**KIRJATH-JEARIM** (*kur'-jath-je'-a-rim*) See KIRJATH, KIRJATH-ARIM, KIRJATH-BAAL.
*1. A city in Judah.*
and Chephirah, and Beeroth, and *K* ... Josh 9:17
was drawn to Baalah, which is *K* ... Josh 15:9
Kirjath-baal, which is *K*, and ... Josh 15:60
were at Kirjath-baal, which is *K* ... Josh 18:14
quarter was from the end of *K* ... Josh 18:15
And they went up, and pitched in *K*. Judg 18:12
behold, it is behind *K* ... Judg 18:12
to the inhabitants of *K*, saying, ... 1Sa 6:21
And the men of *K* came, and brought ... 1Sa 7:1
to pass, while the ark abode in *K* ... 1Sa 7:2
to bring the ark of God from *K* ... 1Chr 13:5
Israel, to Baalah, that is, to *K* ... 1Chr 13:6
*K* to the place which David had ... 2Chr 1:4
The men of *K*, Chephirah, and ... Neh 7:29
Urijah the son of Shemaiah of *K* ... Jer 26:20
*2. A descendant of Caleb.*
Shobal the father of *K*, ... 1Chr 2:50
Shobal the father of *K* had sons ... 1Chr 2:52
And the families of *K* ... 1Chr 2:53

**KIRJATH-SANNAH** (*kur'-jath-san'-nah*) *A city in Judah.*
And Dannah, and *K*, which is Debir,. Josh 15:49

**KIRJATH-SEPHER** (*kur'-jath-se'-fer*) See DEBIR, KIRJATH-SANNAH. *Same as Kirjath-sannah.*
and the name of Debir before was *K*. Josh 15:15
And Caleb said, He that smiteth *K* ... Josh 15:16
and the name of Debir before was *K* .. Judg 1:11
And Caleb said, He that smiteth *K* ... Judg 1:12

**KISH** (*kish*)
*1. Father of King Saul.*
man of Benjamin, whose name was *K* ... 1Sa 9:1
the asses of *K* Saul's father were ... 1Sa 9:3
*K* said to Saul his son, Take now ... 1Sa 9:3
that is come unto the son of *K* ... 1Sa 10:11
and Saul the son of *K* was taken ... 1Sa 10:21
And *K* was the father of Saul ... 1Sa 14:51
in the sepulchre of *K* his father ... 2Sa 21:14
And Ner begat *K* ... 1Chr 8:33
*K* begat Saul ... 1Chr 8:33
And Ner begat *K* ... 1Chr 9:39
and *K* begat Saul ... 1Chr 9:39
because of Saul the son of *K* ... 1Chr 12:1
the seer, and Saul the son of *K* ... 1Chr 26:28
*2. Son of Abi-Gibeon.*
firstborn son Abdon, and Zur, and *K* .. 1Chr 8:30
son Abdon, then Zur, and *K* ... 1Chr 9:36
*3. A sanctuary servant.*
of Mahli; Eleazar, and *K* ... 1Chr 23:21
brethren the sons of *K* took them ... 1Chr 23:22
Concerning *K*: the son of Kish ... 1Chr 24:29
*4. A Levite.*
*K* the son of Abdi, and Azariah the ... 2Chr 29:12
*5. An ancestor of Mordecai.*
the son of Shimei, the son of *K* ... Est 2:5

**KISHI** (*kish'-i*) See KUSHAIAH. *Father of Ethan.*
Ethan the son of *K*, the son of ... 1Chr 6:44

**KISHION** (*kish'-e-on*) See KEDESH, KISHON. *A Levitical city in Issachar.*
And Rabbith, and *K*, and Abez, ... Josh 19:20

**KISHON** (*ki'-shon*) See KISHION, KISON.
*1. Same as Kishion.*
*K* with her suburbs, Dabareh with ... Josh 21:28
the Gentiles unto the river of *K* ... Judg 4:13
The river of *K* swept them away, ... Judg 5:21
that ancient river, the river *K* ... Judg 5:21
brought them down to the brook *K* .. 1Kin 18:40
*2. A brook near Mt. Tabor.*
draw unto thee to the river *K* ... Judg 4:7

**KISLEV** See CHISLEU.

**KISLON** See CHISLON.

**KISLOTH TABOR** See CHISLOTH-TABOR.

**KISON** (*ki'-son*) See KISHON. *Same as Kishon 2.*
as to Jabin, at the brook of *K* ... Ps 83:9

**KISS**
Come near now, and *k* me, my son ... Gen 27:26
hast not suffered me to *k* my sons ... Gen 31:28
with the right hand to *k* him ... 2Sa 20:9
*k* my father and my mother ... 1Kin 19:20
*K* the Son, lest he be angry, and ... Ps 2:12
Every man shall *k* his lips that ... Prov 24:26
Let him *k* me with the kisses of ... Song 1:2
find thee without, I would *k* thee ... Song 8:1
men that sacrifice *k* the calves ... Hos 13:2
saying, Whomsoever I shall *k* ... Mt 26:48
saying, Whomsoever I shall *k* ... Mk 14:44
Thou gavest me no *k* ... Lk 7:45
in hath not ceased to *k* my feet ... Lk 7:45
and drew near unto Jesus to *k* him ... Lk 22:47
thou the Son of man with a *k* ... Lk 22:48
Salute one another with an holy *k* ... Rom 16:16
ye one another with an holy *k* ... 1Cor 16:20
Greet one another with an holy *k* ... 2Cor 13:12
all the brethren with an holy *k* ... 1Th 5:26
one another with a *k* of charity ... 1Pet 5:14

**KISSED**
And he came near, and *k* him ... Gen 27:27
Jacob *k* Rachel, and lifted up his ... Gen 29:11
*k* him, and brought him to his ... Gen 29:13
*k* his sons and his daughters, and ... Gen 31:55
and fell on his neck, and *k* him ... Gen 33:4
Moreover he *k* all his brethren, ... Gen 45:15
he *k* them, and embraced them ... Gen 48:10
face, and wept upon him, and *k* him ... Gen 50:1
him in the mount of God, and *k* him ... Ex 4:27
law, and did obeisance, and *k* him ... Ex 18:7
Then she *k* them ... Ruth 1:9
Orpah *k* her mother in law ... Ruth 1:14
*k* him, and said, Is it not because ... 1Sa 10:1
they *k* one another, and wept one ... 1Sa 20:41
and the king *k* Absalom ... 2Sa 14:33
his hand, and took him, and *k* him ... 2Sa 15:5
the king *k* Barzillai, and blessed ... 2Sa 19:39
every mouth which hath not *k* him ... 1Kin 19:18
or my mouth hath *k* my hand ... Job 31:27
and peace have *k* each other ... Ps 85:10
*k* him, and with an impudent face ... Prov 7:13
master; and *k* him ... Mt 26:49
Master, master; and *k* him ... Mk 14:45
*k* his feet, and anointed them with ... Lk 7:38
and fell on his neck, and *k* him ... Lk 15:20
and fell on Paul's neck, and *k* him, ... Acts 20:37

**KISSES**
but the *k* of an enemy are ... Prov 27:6
kiss me with the *k* of his mouth ... Song 1:2

**KITE**
vulture, and the *k* after his kind ... Lev 11:14
And the glede, and the *k*, and the ... Deut 14:13

**KITHLISH** (*kith'-lish*) *A city in Judah.*
And Cabbon, and Lahmam, and *K* ... Josh 15:40

**KITRON** (*ki'-tron*) See KATTAH. *A city in Zebulun.*
drive out the inhabitants of *K* ... Judg 1:30

K

**KITTIM** (*kit'-tim*) See CHITTIM. *A son of Javan.*
Elishah, and Tarshish, *K*, and ... Gen 10:4
Elishah, and Tarshish, *K*, and ... 1Chr 1:7

**KIYYUN** See CHIUN.

**KNEAD**
*k* it, and make cakes upon the ... Gen 18:6
the women *k* their dough, to make ... Jer 7:18

**KNEADED**
*k* it, and did bake unleavened ... 1Sa 28:24
*k* it, and made cakes in his sight, ... 2Sa 13:8
raising after he hath *k* the dough ... Hos 7:4

**KNEADINGTROUGHS**
into thine ovens, and into thy *k* ... Ex 8:3
their *k* being bound up in their ... Ex 12:34

**KNEE**
they cried before him, Bow the *k* ... Gen 41:43
That unto me every *k* shall bow ... Is 45:23
and they bowed the *k* before him ... Mt 27:29
bowed the *k* to the image of Baal ... Rom 11:4
every *k* shall bow to me, and every ... Rom 14:11
name of Jesus every *k* should bow ... Phil 2:10

**KNEEL**
he made his camels to *k* down ... Gen 24:11
let us *k* before the LORD our ... Ps 95:6

**KNEELED**
*k* down upon his knees before all ... 2Chr 6:13
he *k* upon his knees three times a ... Dan 6:10
*k* to him, and asked him, Good ... Mk 10:17
cast, and *k* down, and prayed, ... Lk 22:41
he *k* down, and cried with a loud ... Acts 7:60
all forth, and *k* down, and prayed ... Acts 9:40
he *k* down, and prayed with them ... Acts 20:36
we *k* down on the shore, and prayed ... Acts 21:5

**KNEELING**
from *k* on his knees with his ... 1Kin 8:54
*k* down to him, and saying, ... Mt 17:14
*k* down to him, and saying unto him ... Mk 1:40

**KNEES**
and she shall bear upon my *k* ... Gen 30:3
them out from between his *k* ... Gen 48:12
were brought up upon Joseph's *k* ... Gen 50:23
LORD shall smite thee in the *k* ... Deut 28:35
boweth down upon his *k* to drink ... Judg 7:5
down upon their *k* to drink water ... Judg 7:6
And she made him sleep upon her *k*. Judg 16:19
from kneeling on his *k* with his ... 1Kin 8:54
and put his face between his *k* ... 1Kin 18:42
all the *k* which have not bowed ... 1Kin 19:18
fell on his *k* before Elijah, and ... 2Kin 1:13
mother, he sat on her *k* till noon ... 2Kin 4:20
kneeled down upon his *k* before ... 2Chr 6:13
and my mantle, I fell upon my *k* ... Ezr 9:5
Why did the *k* prevent me ... Job 3:12
hast strengthened the feeble *k* ... Job 4:4
My *k* are weak through fasting ... Ps 109:24
hands, and confirm the feeble *k* ... Is 35:3
sides, and be dandled upon her *k* ... Is 66:12
all *k* shall be weak as water ... Eze 7:17
all *k* shall be weak as water ... Eze 21:7
the waters were to the *k* ... Eze 47:4
his *k* smote one against another ... Dan 5:6

upon his *k* three times a day ... Dan 6:10
me, which set me upon my *k* ... Dan 10:10
the *k* smite together, and much ... Nah 2:10
bowing their *k* worshipped him ... Mk 15:19
saw it, he fell down at Jesus' *k* ... Lk 5:8
For this cause I bow my *k* unto ... Eph 3:14
which hang down, and the feeble *k* ... Heb 12:12

## KNEW

they *k* that they were naked ... Gen 3:7
And Adam *k* Eve his wife ... Gen 4:1
And Cain *k* his wife ... Gen 4:17
And Adam *k* his wife again ... Gen 4:25
so Noah *k* that the waters were ... Gen 8:11
*k* what his younger son had done ... Gen 9:24
and I *k* it not ... Gen 28:16
For Jacob *k* not that Rachel had ... Gen 31:32
And he *k* it, and said, It is my ... Gen 37:33
Onan *k* that the seed should not ... Gen 38:9
(for he *k* not that she was his ... Gen 38:16
And he *k* her again no more ... Gen 38:26
he *k* not ought he had, save the ... Gen 39:6
he *k* them, but made himself ... Gen 42:7
Joseph *k* his brethren ... Gen 42:8
his brethren, but they *k* not him ... Gen 42:8
they *k* not that Joseph understood ... Gen 42:23
over Egypt, which *k* not Joseph ... Ex 1:8
for I *k* not that thou stoodest in ... Num 22:34
*k* the knowledge of the most High, ... Num 24:16
manna, which thy fathers *k* not ... Deut 8:16
LORD from the day that I *k* you ... Deut 9:24
them, gods whom they *k* not ... Deut 29:26
to gods whom they *k* not, to new ... Deut 32:17
brethren, nor *k* his own children ... Deut 33:9
whom the LORD *k* face to face ... Deut 34:10
which *k* not the LORD, nor yet the ... Judg 2:10
such as before *k* nothing thereof ... Judg 3:2
and she *k* no man ... Judg 11:39
For Manoah *k* not that he was an ... Judg 13:16
Then Manoah *k* that he was an ... Judg 13:21
his mother *k* not that it was of ... Judg 14:4
they *k* the voice of the young man ... Judg 18:3
and they *k* her, and abused her all ... Judg 19:25
but they *k* not that evil was near ... Judg 20:34
Elkanah *k* Hannah his wife ... 1Sa 1:19
they *k* not the LORD ... 1Sa 2:12
from Dan even to Beer-sheba *k* ... 1Sa 3:20
when all that *k* him beforetime ... 1Sa 10:11
the people *k* not that Jonathan ... 1Sa 14:3
*k* that the LORD was with David, ... 1Sa 18:28
for if I *k* certainly that evil ... 1Sa 20:9
whereby Jonathan *k* that it was ... 1Sa 20:33
But the lad *k* not any thing ... 1Sa 20:39
Jonathan and David *k* the matter ... 1Sa 20:39
for thy servant *k* nothing of all ... 1Sa 22:15
and because they *k* when he fled ... 1Sa 22:17
I *k* it that day, when Doeg the ... 1Sa 22:22
David *k* that Saul secretly ... 1Sa 23:9
away, and no man saw it, nor *k* it ... 1Sa 26:12
Saul *k* David's voice, and said, Is ... 1Sa 26:17
but David *k* it not ... 2Sa 3:26
where he *k* that valiant men were ... 2Sa 11:16
*k* ye not that they would shoot ... 2Sa 11:20
and they *k* not any thing ... 2Sa 15:11
tumult, but I *k* not what it was ... 2Sa 18:29
a people which I *k* not shall ... 2Sa 22:44
but the king *k* her not ... 1Kin 1:4
he *k* him, and fell on his face, and ... 1Kin 18:7
for they *k* them not ... 2Kin 4:39
Then Manasseh *k* that the LORD he .. 2Chr 33:13
the rulers *k* not whither I went, ... Neh 2:16
which *k* the times, (for so was ... Est 1:13
manner toward all that *k* law ... Est 1:13
*k* him not, they lifted up their ... Job 2:12
Oh that I *k* where I might find ... Job 23:3
the cause which I *k* not I ... Job 29:16
wonderful for me, which I *k* not ... Job 42:3
to my charge things that I *k* not ... Ps 35:11
against me, and I *k* it not ... Ps 35:15
thou sayest, Behold, we *k* it not ... Prov 24:12
blind by a way that they *k* not ... Is 42:16
on fire round about, yet he *k* not ... Is 42:25
Because I *k* that thou art ... Is 48:4
shouldest say, Behold, I *k* them ... Is 48:7
for I *k* that thou wouldest deal ... Is 48:8
nations that *k* not thee shall run ... Is 55:5
formed thee in the belly I *k* thee ... Jer 1:5
they that handle the law *k* me not ... Jer 2:8
I *k* not that they had devised ... Jer 11:19
Then I *k* that this was the word ... Jer 32:8
slain Gedaliah, and no man *k* it ... Jer 41:4
serve other gods, whom they *k* not ... Jer 44:3
Then all the men which *k* that ... Jer 44:15
I *k* that they were the cherubims ... Eze 10:20
he *k* their desolate palaces, and ... Eze 19:7
till he *k* that the most high God ... Dan 5:21
Now when Daniel *k* that the ... Dan 6:10
a god whom his fathers *k* not ... Dan 11:38
have made princes, and I *k* it not ... Hos 8:4
but they *k* not that I healed them ... Hos 11:3
For the men *k* that he fled from ... Jonah 1:10
for I *k* that thou art a gracious ... Jonah 4:2
all the nations whom they *k* not ... Zec 7:14
me *k* that it was the word of the ... Zec 11:11
*k* her not till she had brought ... Mt 1:25
profess unto them, I never *k* you ... Mt 7:23
But when Jesus *k* it, he withdrew ... Mt 12:15
Jesus *k* their thoughts, and said ... Mt 12:25
they *k* him not, but have done ... Mt 17:12
*k* not until the flood came, and ... Mt 24:39
I *k* thee that thou art an hard ... Mt 25:24
For he *k* that for envy they had ... Mt 27:18
to speak, because they *k* him ... Mk 1:34
saw them departing, and many *k* him ... Mk 6:33
And when they *k*, they say, Five, ... Mk 6:38
the ship, straightway they *k* him ... Mk 6:54
And when Jesus *k* it, he saith unto ... Mk 8:17
for they *k* that he had spoken the ... Mk 12:12
For he *k* that the chief priests ... Mk 15:10
when he *k* it of the centurion, he ... Mk 15:45
Joseph and his mother *k* not of it ... Lk 2:43
for they *k* that he was Christ ... Lk 4:41
But he *k* their thoughts, and said ... Lk 6:8
when she *k* that Jesus sat at meat ... Lk 7:37
And the people, when they *k* it ... Lk 9:11
which *k* his lord's will, and ... Lk 12:47
But he that *k* not, and did commit ... Lk 12:48
neither *k* they the things which ... Lk 18:34
as soon as he *k* that he belonged ... Lk 23:7
eyes were opened, and they *k* him ... Lk 24:31
by him, and the world *k* him not ... Jn 1:10
And I *k* him not ... Jn 1:31
And I *k* him not ... Jn 1:33
made wine, and *k* not whence it was ... Jn 2:9
servants which drew the water *k* ... Jn 2:9
unto them, because he *k* all men ... Jn 2:24
for he *k* what was in man ... Jn 2:25
When therefore the Lord *k* how the ... Jn 4:1
So the father *k* that it was at ... Jn 4:53
*k* that he had been now a long ... Jn 5:6
for he himself *k* what he would do ... Jn 6:6
When Jesus *k* in himself that his ... Jn 6:61
For Jesus *k* from the beginning ... Jn 6:64
I *k* that thou hearest me always ... Jn 11:42
if any man *k* where he were, he ... Jn 11:57
therefore *k* that he was there ... Jn 12:9
when Jesus *k* that his hour was ... Jn 13:1
For he *k* who should betray him ... Jn 13:11
Now no man at the table *k* for ... Jn 13:28
Now Jesus *k* that they were ... Jn 16:19
which betrayed him, *k* the place ... Jn 18:2
For as yet they *k* not the ... Jn 20:9
and *k* not that it was Jesus ... Jn 20:14
but the disciples *k* not that it ... Jn 21:4
they *k* that it was he which sat ... Acts 3:10
king arose, which *k* not Joseph ... Acts 7:18
Which when the brethren *k*, ... Acts 9:30
when she *k* Peter's voice, she ... Acts 12:14
rulers, because they *k* him not ... Acts 13:27
for they *k* all that his father ... Acts 16:3
the more part *k* not wherefore ... Acts 19:32
But when they *k* that he was a Jew .. Acts 19:34
after he *k* that he was a Roman, ... Acts 22:29
Which *k* me from the beginning, if ... Acts 26:5
it was day, they *k* not the land ... Acts 27:39
then they *k* that the island was ... Acts 28:1
Because that, when they *k* God ... Rom 1:21
God the world by wisdom *k* not God .. 1Cor 1:21
of the princes of this world *k* ... 1Cor 2:8
to be sin for us, who *k* no sin ... 2Cor 5:21
I *k* a man in Christ above ... 2Cor 12:2
I *k* such a man, (whether in the ... 2Cor 12:3
Howbeit then, when ye *k* not God ... Gal 4:8
*k* the grace of God in truth ... Col 1:6
For I would that ye *k* what great ... Col 2:1
us not, because it *k* him not ... 1Jn 3:1
though ye once *k* this, how that ... Jude 5
had a name written, that no man *k* ... Rev 19:12

## KNEWEST

thee with manna, which thou *k* not ... Deut 8:3
which thou *k* not heretofore ... Ruth 2:11
for thou *k* that they dealt ... Neh 9:10
within me, then thou *k* my path ... Ps 142:3
yea, thou *k* not ... Is 48:8
heart, though thou *k* all this ... Dan 5:22
thou *k* that I reap where I sowed ... Mt 25:26
Thou *k* that I was an austere man, ... Lk 19:22
because thou *k* not the time of ... Lk 19:44
If thou *k* the gift of God, and who ... Jn 4:10

## KNIFE

took the fire in his hand, and a *k* ... Gen 22:6
took the *k* to slay his son ... Gen 22:10
come into his house, he took a *k* ... Judg 19:29
put a *k* to thy throat, if thou be ... Prov 23:2
son of man, take thee a sharp *k* ... Eze 5:1
part, and smite about it with a *k* ... Eze 5:2

## KNIT

the city, *k* together as one man ... Judg 20:11
was *k* with the soul of David ... 1Sa 18:1
mine heart shall be *k* unto you ... 1Chr 12:17
great sheet *k* at the four corners ... Acts 10:11
being *k* together in love, and unto ... Col 2:2
*k* together, increaseth with the ... Col 2:19

## KNIVES

unto Joshua, Make thee sharp *k* ... Josh 5:2
And Joshua made him sharp *k* ... Josh 5:3
after their manner with *k* ... 1Kin 18:28
of silver, nine and twenty *k* ... Ezr 1:9
swords, and their jaw teeth as *k* ... Prov 30:14

## KNOCK

*k*, and it shall be opened unto you ... Mt 7:7
*k*, and it shall be opened unto you ... Lk 11:9
to *k* at the door, saying, Lord, ... Lk 13:25
Behold, I stand at the door, and *k* ... Rev 3:20

## KNOCKED

as Peter *k* at the door of the ... Acts 12:13

## KNOCKETH

is the voice of my beloved that *k* ... Song 5:2
to him that *k* it shall be opened ... Mt 7:8
to him that *k* it shall be opened ... Lk 11:10
that when he cometh and *k*, they ... Lk 12:36

## KNOCKING

But Peter continued *k* ... Acts 12:16

## KNOP

made like unto almonds, with a *k* ... Ex 25:33
in the other branch, with a *k* ... Ex 25:33
there shall be a *k* under two ... Ex 25:35
a *k* under two branches of the ... Ex 25:35
a *k* under two branches of the ... Ex 25:35
of almonds in one branch, a *k* ... Ex 37:19
almonds in another branch, a *k* ... Ex 37:19
a *k* under two branches of the ... Ex 37:21
a *k* under two branches of the ... Ex 37:21
a *k* under two branches of the ... Ex 37:21

## KNOPS

and his branches, his bowls, his *k* ... Ex 25:31
like unto almonds, with their *k* ... Ex 25:34
Their *k* and their branches shall ... Ex 25:36
and his branch, his bowls, his *k* ... Ex 37:17
bowls made like almonds, his *k* ... Ex 37:20
Their *k* and their branches were of ... Ex 37:22
house within was carved with *k* ... 1Kin 6:18
about there were *k* compassing it ... 1Kin 7:24
the *k* were cast in two rows, when ... 1Kin 7:24

## KNOW See PREFACE.

as one of us, to *k* good and evil ... Gen 3:22
for now I *k* that thou fearest God ... Gen 22:12
that thou mightest *k* that the ... Deut 4:35
to *k* whether ye love the LORD ... Deut 13:3
Now Samuel did not yet *k* the LORD ... 1Sa 3:7
I *k* thy pride, and the naughtiness ... 1Sa 17:28
earth may *k* that the LORD is God ... 1Kin 8:60
For I *k* that my redeemer liveth, ... Job 19:25
And thou sayest, How doth God *k* ... Job 22:13
Be still, and *k* that I am God ... Ps 46:10
And they say, How doth God *k* ... Ps 73:11
*K* ye that the LORD he is God ... Ps 100:3
Search me, O God, and *k* my heart ... Ps 139:23
But I *k* thy abode, and thy going ... Is 37:28
my people shall *k* my name ... Is 52:6
therefore they shall *k* in that ... Is 52:6
ye shall *k* that I am the LORD ... Eze 6:7
and thou shalt *k* the LORD ... Hos 2:20
let not thy left hand *k* what thy ... Mt 6:3
Ye shall *k* them by their fruits ... Mt 7:16
by their fruits ye shall *k* them ... Mt 7:20
for ye *k* not what hour your Lord ... Mt 24:42
for ye *k* neither the day nor the ... Mt 25:13
with an oath, I do not *k* the man ... Mt 26:72
him, saying, Woman, I *k* him not ... Lk 22:57
for they *k* not what they do ... Lk 23:34
*k* that this is indeed the Christ, ... Jn 4:42
I *k* them, and they follow me ... Jn 10:27
*K* ye what I have done to you ... Jn 13:12
If ye *k* these things, happy are ... Jn 13:17
I go ye *k*, and the way ye *k* ... Jn 14:4
It is not for you to *k* the times ... Acts 1:7
we *k* that all things work ... Rom 8:28
neither can he *k* them, because ... 1Cor 2:14
For we *k* in part, and we prophesy ... 1Cor 13:9
but then shall I *k* even as also I ... 1Cor 13:12
for I *k* whom I have believed, and ... 2Ti 1:12
Whereas ye *k* not what shall be on ... Jas 4:14
hereby we do *k* that we *k* him ... 1Jn 2:3
hereby *k* we that we are in him ... 1Jn 2:5
that ye may *k* that ye have ... 1Jn 5:13
We *k* that whosoever is born of ... 1Jn 5:18

## KNOWEST

for thou *k* my service which I ... Gen 30:26
Thou *k* how I have served thee, and .. Gen 30:29
if thou *k* any men of activity ... Gen 47:6
*k* thou not yet that Egypt is ... Ex 10:7
thou *k* the people, that they are ... Ex 32:22
forasmuch as thou *k* how we are to . Num 10:31
whom thou *k* to be the elders of ... Num 11:16
Thou *k* all the travel that hath ... Num 20:14
diseases of Egypt, which thou *k* ... Deut 7:15
of the Anakims, whom thou *k* ... Deut 9:2
Only the trees which thou *k* that ... Deut 20:20
a nation which thou *k* not eat up ... Deut 28:33
Thou *k* the thing that the LORD ... Josh 14:6
*K* thou not that the Philistines ... Judg 15:11
thou *k* what Saul hath done, how ... 1Sa 28:9
How *k* thou that Saul and Jonathan ... 2Sa 1:5
*k* thou not that it will be ... 2Sa 2:26
Thou *k* Abner the son of Ner, that ... 2Sa 3:25
for thou, Lord GOD, *k* thy servant ... 2Sa 7:20
thou *k* thy father and his men, ... 2Sa 17:8
my lord the king, thou *k* it not ... 1Kin 1:18
Moreover thou *k* also what Joab ... 1Kin 2:5
*k* what thou oughtest to do unto ... 1Kin 2:9
Thou *k* that the kingdom was mine, ... 1Kin 2:15
Thou *k* all the wickedness which ... 1Kin 2:44
Thou *k* how that David my father ... 1Kin 5:3
for thou *k* that there is not ... 1Kin 5:6
to his ways, whose heart thou *k* ... 1Kin 8:39
*k* the hearts of all the children ... 1Kin 8:39
*K* thou that the LORD will take ... 2Kin 2:3
*K* thou that the LORD will take ... 2Kin 2:5
thou *k* that thy servant did fear ... 2Kin 4:1
for thou *k* thy servant ... 1Chr 17:18
all his ways, whose heart thou *k* ... 2Chr 6:30
(for thou only *k* the hearts of ... 2Chr 6:30
Thou *k* that I am not wicked ... Job 10:7
What *k* thou, that we know not ... Job 15:9
*K* thou not this of old, since man ... Job 20:4
therefore speak what thou *k* ... Job 34:33
the measures thereof, if thou *k* ... Job 38:5

declare if thou *k* it all ... Job 38:18
*K* thou it, because thou wast then ... Job 38:21
*K* thou the ordinances of heaven ... Job 38:33
*K* thou the time when the wild ... Job 39:1
or *k* thou the time when they ... Job 39:2
refrained my lips, O LORD, thou *k* ... Ps 40:9
O God, thou *k* my foolishness ... Ps 69:5
Thou *k* my downsitting and mine ... Ps 139:2
lo, O LORD, thou *k* it altogether ... Ps 139:4
for thou *k* not what a day may ... Prov 27:1
for thou *k* not what evil shall be ... Eccl 11:2
As thou *k* not what is the way of ... Eccl 11:5
even so thou *k* not the works of ... Eccl 11:5
for thou *k* not whether shall ... Eccl 11:6
call a nation that thou *k* not ... Is 55:5
nation whose language thou *k* not ... Jer 5:15
But thou, O LORD, *k* me ... Jer 12:3
into a land which thou *k* not ... Jer 15:14
O LORD, thou *k* ... Jer 15:15
in the land which thou *k* not ... Jer 17:4
thou *k*: that which came ... Jer 17:16
thou *k* all their counsel against ... Jer 18:23
mighty things, which thou *k* not ... Jer 33:3
And I answered, O Lord GOD, thou *k* ... Eze 37:3
*K* thou wherefore I come unto thee ... Dan 10:20
unto me, *K* thou not what these be ... Zec 4:5
and said, *K* thou not what these be ... Zec 4:13
*K* thou that the Pharisees were ... Mt 15:12
Thou *k* the commandments, Do not ... Mk 10:19
Thou *k* the commandments, Do not ... Lk 18:20
shalt thrice deny that thou *k* me ... Lk 22:34
saith unto him, Whence *k* thou me ... Jn 1:48
of Israel, and *k* not these things ... Jn 3:10
him, What I do thou *k* not now ... Jn 13:7
we sure that thou *k* all things ... Jn 16:30
*k* thou not that I have power to ... Jn 19:10
thou *k* that I love thee ... Jn 21:15
thou *k* that I love thee ... Jn 21:16
unto him, Lord, thou *k* all things ... Jn 21:17
thou *k* that I love thee ... Jn 21:17
which *k* the hearts of all men, ... Acts 1:24
no wrong, as thou very well *k* ... Acts 25:10
*k* his will, and approvest the ... Rom 2:18
For what *k* thou, O wife, whether ... 1Cor 7:16
or how *k* thou, O man, whether ... 1Cor 7:16
This thou *k*, that all they which ... 2Ti 1:15
me at Ephesus, thou *k* very well ... 2Ti 1:18
*k* not that thou art wretched, and ... Rev 3:17
And I said unto him, Sir, thou *k* ... Rev 7:14

**KNOWETH**

My lord *k* that the children are ... Gen 33:13
when he *k* of it, then he shall be ... Lev 5:3
when he *k* of it, then he shall be ... Lev 5:4
he *k* thy walking through this ... Deut 2:7
but no man *k* of his sepulchre ... Deut 34:6
gods, the LORD God of gods, he *k* ... Josh 22:22
ever for the iniquity which he *k* ... 1Sa 3:13
Thy father certainly *k* that I ... 1Sa 20:3
and that also Saul my father *k* ... 1Sa 23:17
Today thy servant *k* that I have ... 2Sa 14:22
for all Israel *k* that thy father ... 2Sa 17:10
reign, and David our lord *k* it not ... 1Kin 1:11
who *k* whether thou art come to ... Est 4:14
For he *k* vain men ... Job 11:11
who *k* not such things as these ... Job 12:3
Who *k* not in all these that the ... Job 12:9
come to honour, and he *k* it not ... Job 14:21
he *k* that the day of darkness is ... Job 15:23
the place of him that *k* not God ... Job 18:21
But he *k* the way that I take ... Job 23:10
There is a path which no fowl *k* ... Job 28:7
Man *k* not the price thereof ... Job 28:13
and he *k* the place thereof ... Job 28:23
Therefore he *k* their works ... Job 34:25
yet he *k* it not in great ... Job 35:15
For the LORD *k* the way of the ... Ps 1:6
The LORD *k* the days of the ... Ps 37:18
*k* not who shall gather them ... Ps 39:6
for he *k* the secrets of the heart ... Ps 44:21
among us any that *k* how long ... Ps 74:9
Who *k* the power of thine anger ... Ps 90:11
A brutish man *k* not ... Ps 92:6
The LORD *k* the thoughts of man, ... Ps 94:11
For he *k* our frame ... Ps 103:14
the sun *k* his going down ... Ps 104:19
but the proud he *k* afar off ... Ps 138:6
and that my soul *k* right well ... Ps 139:14
*k* not that it is for his life ... Prov 7:23
she is simple, and *k* nothing ... Prov 9:13
But he *k* not that the dead are ... Prov 9:18
The heart *k* his own bitterness ... Prov 14:10
who *k* the ruin of them both ... Prov 24:22
who *k* whether he shall be a wise ... Eccl 2:19
Who *k* the spirit of man that ... Eccl 3:21
that *k* to walk before the living ... Eccl 6:8
For who *k* what is good for man in ... Eccl 6:12
*k* that thou thyself likewise hast ... Eccl 7:22
who *k* the interpretation of a ... Eccl 8:1
For he *k* not that which shall be ... Eccl 8:7
no man *k* either love or hatred by ... Eccl 9:1
For man also *k* not his time ... Eccl 9:12
because he *k* not how to go to the ... Eccl 10:15
The ox *k* his owner, and the ass ... Is 1:3
and who *k* us? ... Is 29:15
the heaven *k* her appointed times ... Jer 8:7
*k* me, that I am the LORD which ... Jer 9:24
he *k* what is in the darkness, and ... Dan 2:22
his strength, and he *k* it not ... Hos 7:9
and there upon him, yet he *k* not ... Hos 7:9
Who *k* if he will return and repent ... Joel 2:14
he *k* them that trust in him ... Nah 1:7
but the unjust *k* no shame ... Zeph 3:5
for your Father *k* what things ye ... Mt 6:8
for your heavenly Father *k* that ... Mt 6:32
no man *k* the Son, but the Father ... Mt 11:27
neither *k* any man the Father, ... Mt 11:27
hour *k* no man, no, not the angels ... Mt 24:36
spring and grow up, he *k* not how ... Mk 4:27
of that day and that hour *k* no man ... Mk 13:32
no man *k* who the Son is, but the ... Lk 10:22
your Father *k* that ye have need ... Lk 12:30
but God *k* your hearts ... Lk 16:15
How *k* this man letters, having ... Jn 7:15
cometh, no man *k* whence he is ... Jn 7:27
But this people who *k* not the law ... Jn 7:49
As the Father *k* me, even so know ... Jn 10:15
darkness *k* not whither he goeth ... Jn 12:35
it seeth him not, neither *k* him ... Jn 14:17
for the servant *k* not what his ... Jn 15:15
he *k* that he saith true, that ye ... Jn 19:35
which *k* the hearts, bare them ... Acts 15:8
what man is there that *k* not how ... Acts 19:35
For the king *k* of these things, ... Acts 26:26
he that searcheth the hearts *k* ... Rom 8:27
For what man *k* the things of a ... 1Cor 2:11
so the things of God *k* no man ... 1Cor 2:11
The Lord *k* the thoughts of the ... 1Cor 3:20
any man think that he *k* any thing ... 1Cor 8:2
he *k* nothing yet as he ought to ... 1Cor 8:2
I love you not? God *k* ... 2Cor 11:11
for evermore, *k* that I lie not ... 2Cor 11:31
I cannot tell: God *k* ... 2Cor 12:2
I cannot tell: God *k* ... 2Cor 12:3
The Lord *k* them that are his ... 2Ti 2:19
to him that *k* to do good, and ... Jas 4:17
The Lord *k* how to deliver the ... 2Pet 2:9
*k* not whither he goeth, because ... 1Jn 2:11
therefore the world *k* us not ... 1Jn 3:1
than our heart, and *k* all things ... 1Jn 3:20
he that *k* God heareth us ... 1Jn 4:6
loveth is born of God, and *k* God ... 1Jn 4:7
He that loveth not *k* not God ... 1Jn 4:8
which no man *k* saving he that ... Rev 2:17
because he *k* that he hath but a ... Rev 12:12

**KNOWING**

shall be as gods, *k* good and evil ... Gen 3:5
my father David not *k* thereof ... 1Kin 2:32
Jesus *k* their thoughts said, ... Mt 9:4
not *k* the scriptures, nor the ... Mt 22:29
immediately *k* in himself that ... Mk 5:30
*k* what was done in her, came and ... Mk 5:33
*k* that he was a just man and an ... Mk 6:20
*k* their hypocrisy, said unto them ... Mk 12:15
him to scorn, *k* that she was dead ... Lk 8:53
not *k* what he said ... Lk 9:33
*k* their thoughts, said unto them, ... Lk 11:17
Jesus *k* that the Father had given ... Jn 13:3
*k* all things that should come ... Jn 18:4
Jesus *k* that all things were now ... Jn 19:28
*k* that it was the Lord ... Jn 21:12
*k* that God had sworn with an oath ... Acts 2:30
not *k* what was done, came in ... Acts 5:7
*k* only the baptism of John ... Acts 18:25
not *k* the things that shall ... Acts 20:22
Who *k* the judgment of God, that ... Rom 1:32
not *k* that the goodness of God ... Rom 2:4
*k* that tribulation worketh ... Rom 5:3
*K* this, that our old man is ... Rom 6:6
*K* that Christ being raised from ... Rom 6:9
*k* the time, that now it is high ... Rom 13:11
And our hope of you is stedfast, *k* ... 2Cor 1:7
*K* that he which raised up the ... 2Cor 4:14
*k* that, whilst we are at home in ... 2Cor 5:6
*K* therefore the terror of the ... 2Cor 5:11
*K* that a man is not justified by ... Gal 2:16
*K* that whatsoever good thing any ... Eph 6:8
*k* that your Master also is in ... Eph 6:9
*k* that I am set for the defence ... Phil 1:17
*K* that of the Lord ye shall ... Col 3:24
*k* that ye also have a Master in ... Col 4:1
*K*, brethren beloved, your ... 1Th 1:4
*K* this, that the law is not made ... 1Ti 1:9
*k* nothing, but doting about ... 1Ti 6:4
*k* that they do gender strifes ... 2Ti 2:23
*k* of whom thou hast learned them ... 2Ti 3:14
*K* that he that is such is ... Titus 3:11
*k* that thou wilt also do more ... Philem 21
*k* in yourselves that ye have in ... Heb 10:34
went out, not *k* whither he went ... Heb 11:8
*K* this, that the trying of your ... Jas 1:3
*k* that we shall receive the ... Jas 3:1
*k* that ye are thereunto called, ... 1Pet 3:9
*k* that the same afflictions are ... 1Pet 5:9
*K* that shortly I must put off ... 2Pet 1:14
*K* this first, that no prophecy of ... 2Pet 1:20
*K* this first, that there shall ... 2Pet 3:3

**KNOWLEDGE**

garden, and the tree of *k* of good ... Gen 2:9
But of the tree of the *k* of good ... Gen 2:17
and in understanding, and in *k* ... Ex 31:3
wisdom, in understanding, and in *k* ... Ex 35:31
he hath sinned, come to his *k* ... Lev 4:23
he hath sinned, come to his *k* ... Lev 4:28
without the *k* of the congregation ... Num 15:24
knew the *k* of the most High, ... Num 24:16
in that day had no *k* between good ... Deut 1:39
that thou shouldest take *k* of me ... Ruth 2:10
be he that did take *k* of thee ... Ruth 2:19
for the LORD is a God of *k* ... 1Sa 2:3
take *k* of all the lurking places ... 1Sa 23:23
shipmen that had *k* of the sea ... 1Kin 9:27
Give me now wisdom and *k*, that I ... 2Chr 1:10
*k* for thyself, that thou mayest ... 2Chr 1:11
Wisdom and *k* is granted unto thee ... 2Chr 1:12
and servants that had *k* of the sea ... 2Chr 8:18
taught the good *k* of the LORD ... 2Chr 30:22
daughters, every one having *k* ... Neh 10:28
Should a wise man utter vain *k* ... Job 15:2
we desire not the *k* of thy ways ... Job 21:14
Shall any teach God *k* ... Job 21:22
and my lips shall utter *k* clearly ... Job 33:3
give ear unto me, ye that have *k* ... Job 34:2
Job hath spoken without *k* ... Job 34:35
he multiplieth words without *k* ... Job 35:16
I will fetch my *k* from afar ... Job 36:3
that is perfect in *k* is with thee ... Job 36:4
and they shall die without *k* ... Job 36:12
of him which is perfect in *k* ... Job 37:16
counsel by words without *k* ... Job 38:2
he that hideth counsel without *k* ... Job 42:3
all the workers of iniquity no *k* ... Ps 14:4
and night unto night sheweth *k* ... Ps 19:2
Have the workers of iniquity no *k* ... Ps 53:4
is there *k* in the most High ... Ps 73:11
he that teacheth man *k*, shall not ... Ps 94:10
Teach me good judgment and *k* ... Ps 119:66
Such *k* is too wonderful for me ... Ps 139:6
is man, that thou takest *k* of him ... Ps 144:3
to the simple, to the young man *k* ... Prov 1:4
of the LORD is the beginning of *k* ... Prov 1:7
their scorning, and fools hate *k* ... Prov 1:22
For that they hated *k*, and did not ... Prov 1:29
Yea, if thou criest after *k* ... Prov 2:3
of the LORD, and find the *k* of God ... Prov 2:5
out of his mouth cometh *k* ... Prov 2:6
*k* is pleasant unto thy soul ... Prov 2:10
By his *k* the depths are broken up ... Prov 3:20
and that thy lips may keep *k* ... Prov 5:2
and right to them that find *k* ... Prov 8:9
*k* rather than choice gold ... Prov 8:10
find out *k* of witty inventions ... Prov 8:12
and the *k* of the holy is ... Prov 9:10
Wise men lay up *k* ... Prov 10:14
but through *k* shall the just be ... Prov 11:9
Whoso loveth instruction loveth *k* ... Prov 12:1
A prudent man concealeth *k* ... Prov 12:23
Every prudent man dealeth with *k* ... Prov 13:16
but *k* is easy unto him that ... Prov 14:6
not in him the lips of *k* ... Prov 14:7
the prudent are crowned with *k* ... Prov 14:18
tongue of the wise useth *k* aright ... Prov 15:2
The lips of the wise disperse *k* ... Prov 15:7
that hath understanding seeketh *k* ... Prov 15:14
He that hath *k* spareth his words ... Prov 17:27
heart of the prudent getteth *k* ... Prov 18:15
and the ear of the wise seeketh *k* ... Prov 18:15
Also, that the soul be without *k* ... Prov 19:2
and he will understand *k* ... Prov 19:25
to err from the words of *k* ... Prov 19:27
but the lips of *k* are a precious ... Prov 20:15
is instructed, he receiveth *k* ... Prov 21:11
The eyes of the LORD preserve *k* ... Prov 22:12
and apply thine heart unto my *k* ... Prov 22:17
excellent things in counsels and *k* ... Prov 22:20
and thine ears to the words of *k* ... Prov 23:12
by *k* shall the chambers be filled ... Prov 24:4
a man of *k* increaseth strength ... Prov 24:5
So shall the *k* of wisdom be unto ... Prov 24:14
*k* the state thereof shall be ... Prov 28:2
nor have the *k* of the holy ... Prov 30:3
great experience of wisdom and *k* ... Eccl 1:16
increaseth *k* increaseth sorrow ... Eccl 1:18
labour is in wisdom, and in *k* ... Eccl 2:21
is good in his sight wisdom, and *k* ... Eccl 2:26
but the excellency of *k* is ... Eccl 7:12
is no work, nor device, nor *k* ... Eccl 9:10
he still taught the people *k* ... Eccl 12:9
captivity, because they have no *k* ... Is 5:13
the child shall have *k* to cry ... Is 8:4
counsel and might, the spirit of *k* ... Is 11:2
be full of the *k* of the LORD ... Is 11:9
Whom shall he teach *k* ... Is 28:9
of the rash shall understand *k* ... Is 32:4
*k* shall be the stability of thy ... Is 33:6
path of judgment, and taught him *k* ... Is 40:14
his heart, neither is there *k* nor ... Is 44:19
and maketh their *k* foolish ... Is 44:25
they have no *k* that set up the ... Is 45:20
Thy wisdom and thy *k*, it hath ... Is 47:10
by his *k* shall my righteous ... Is 53:11
our soul, and thou takest no *k* ... Is 58:3
which shall feed you with *k* ... Jer 3:15
but to do good they have no *k* ... Jer 4:22
Every man is brutish in his *k* ... Jer 10:14
And the LORD hath given me *k* of it ... Jer 11:18
Every man is brutish by his *k* ... Jer 51:17
in all wisdom, and cunning in *k* ... Dan 1:4
four children, God gave them *k* ... Dan 1:17
*k* to them that know understanding ... Dan 2:21
as an excellent spirit, and *k* ... Dan 5:12
and fro, and *k* shall be increased ... Dan 12:4
mercy, nor *k* of God in the land ... Hos 4:1
are destroyed for lack of *k* ... Hos 4:6
because thou hast rejected *k* ... Hos 4:6
the *k* of God more than burnt ... Hos 6:6
the *k* of the glory of the LORD ... Hab 2:14
the priest's lips should keep *k* ... Mal 2:7
men of that place had *k* of him ... Mt 14:35
To give *k* of salvation unto his ... Lk 1:77

ye have taken away the key of *k* ... Lk 11:52
and they took *k* of them, that they ... Acts 4:13
had *k* that the word of God was ... Acts 17:13
mayest take *k* of all these things ... Acts 24:8
having more perfect *k* of that way ... Acts 24:22
not like to retain God in their *k* ... Rom 1:28
babes, which hast the form of *k* ... Rom 2:20
for by the law is the *k* of sin ... Rom 3:20
of God, but not according to *k* ... Rom 10:2
both of the wisdom and *k* of God ... Rom 11:33
of goodness, filled with all *k* ... Rom 15:14
in all utterance, and in all *k* ... 1Cor 1:5
idols, we know that we all have *k* ... 1Cor 8:1
*K* puffeth up, but charity ... 1Cor 8:1
there is not in every man that *k* ... 1Cor 8:7
hast *k* sit at meat in the idol's ... 1Cor 8:10
through thy *k* shall the weak ... 1Cor 8:11
the word of *k* by the same Spirit ... 1Cor 12:8
all mysteries, and all *k* ... 1Cor 13:2
whether there be *k*, it shall ... 1Cor 13:8
you either by revelation, or by *k* ... 1Cor 14:6
for some have not the *k* of God ... 1Cor 15:34
of his *k* by us in every place ... 2Cor 2:14
to give the light of the *k* of the ... 2Cor 4:6
By pureness, by *k*, by ... 2Cor 6:6
in faith, and utterance, and *k* ... 2Cor 8:7
itself against the *k* of God ... 2Cor 10:5
I be rude in speech, yet not in *k* ... 2Cor 11:6
and revelation in the *k* of him ... Eph 1:17
ye may understand my *k* in the ... Eph 3:4
love of Christ, which passeth *k* ... Eph 3:19
of the *k* of the Son of God, unto ... Eph 4:13
may abound yet more and more in *k* ... Phil 1:9
of the *k* of Christ Jesus my Lord ... Phil 3:8
the *k* of his will in all wisdom ... Col 1:9
and increasing in the *k* of God ... Col 1:10
all the treasures of wisdom and *k* ... Col 2:3
which is renewed in *k* after the ... Col 3:10
to come unto the *k* of the truth ... 1Ti 2:4
to come to the *k* of the truth ... 2Ti 3:7
have received the *k* of the truth ... Heb 10:26
man and endued with *k* among you ... Jas 3:13
dwell with them according to *k* ... 1Pet 3:7
unto you through the *k* of God ... 2Pet 1:2
through the *k* of him that hath ... 2Pet 1:3
and to virtue *k* ... 2Pet 1:5
And to *k* temperance ... 2Pet 1:6
in the *k* of our Lord Jesus Christ ... 2Pet 1:8
world through the *k* of the Lord ... 2Pet 2:20
in the *k* of our Lord and Saviour ... 2Pet 3:18

**KNOWN**

daughters which have not *k* man ... Gen 19:8
virgin, neither had any man *k* her ... Gen 24:16
it could not be *k* that they had ... Gen 41:21
the plenty shall not be *k* in the ... Gen 41:31
made himself *k* unto his brethren ... Gen 45:1
and said, Surely this thing is *k* ... Ex 2:14
name JEHOVAH was I not *k* to them ... Ex 6:3
Or if it be *k* that the ox hath ... Ex 21:36
wherein shall it be *k* here that I ... Ex 33:16
they have sinned against it, is *k* ... Lev 4:14
whether he hath seen or *k* of it ... Lev 5:1
myself *k* unto him in a vision ... Num 12:6
that hath *k* man by lying with him ... Num 31:17
that have not *k* a man by lying ... Num 31:18
had not *k* man by lying with him ... Num 31:35
*k* among your tribes, and I will ... Deut 1:13
of your tribes, wise men, and *k* ... Deut 1:15
your children which have not *k* ... Deut 11:2
other gods, which ye have not *k* ... Deut 11:28
other gods, which thou hast not *k* ... Deut 13:2
other gods, which thou hast not *k* ... Deut 13:6
other gods, which ye have not *k* ... Deut 13:13
it be not *k* who hath slain him ... Deut 21:1
thou nor thy fathers have *k* ... Deut 28:36
thou nor thy fathers have *k* ... Deut 28:64
which have not *k* any thing ... Deut 31:13
which had *k* all the works of the ... Josh 24:31
had not *k* all the wars of Canaan ... Judg 3:1
So his strength was not *k* ... Judg 16:9
that had *k* no man by lying with ... Judg 21:12
make not thyself *k* unto the man ... Ruth 3:3
Let it not be *k* that a woman came ... Ruth 3:14
it shall be *k* to you why his hand ... 1Sa 6:3
that thou mayest make *k* unto me ... 1Sa 28:15
and the thing was not *k* ... 2Sa 17:19
that thou be not *k* to be the wife ... 1Kin 14:2
let it be *k* this day that thou ... 1Kin 18:36
make *k* his deeds among the people ... 1Chr 16:8
in making *k* all these great ... 1Chr 17:19
Be it *k* unto the king, that the ... Ezr 4:12
Be it *k* now unto the king, that, ... Ezr 4:13
Be it *k* unto the king, that we ... Ezr 5:8
heard that it was *k* unto us ... Neh 4:15
madest *k* unto them thy holy ... Neh 9:14
And the thing was *k* to Mordecai ... Est 2:22
The LORD is *k* by the judgment ... Ps 9:16
whom I have not *k* shall serve me ... Ps 18:43
thou hast *k* my soul in ... Ps 31:7
God is *k* in her palaces for a ... Ps 48:3
That thy way may be *k* upon earth ... Ps 67:2
Thou hast *k* my reproach, and my ... Ps 69:19
In Judah is God *k* ... Ps 76:1
and thy footsteps are not *k* ... Ps 77:19
Which we have heard and *k*, and our ... Ps 78:3
make them *k* to their children ... Ps 78:5
the heathen that have not *k* thee ... Ps 79:6
let him be *k* among the heathen in ... Ps 79:10
thy wonders be *k* in the dark ... Ps 88:12
I make *k* thy faithfulness to all ... Ps 89:1
high, because he hath *k* my name ... Ps 91:14
heart, and they have not *k* my ways ... Ps 95:10
LORD hath made *k* his salvation ... Ps 98:2
He made *k* his ways unto Moses, ... Ps 103:7
make *k* his deeds among the people ... Ps 105:1
make his mighty power to be *k* ... Ps 106:8
those that have *k* thy testimonies ... Ps 119:79
I have *k* of old that thou hast ... Ps 119:152
thou hast searched me, and *k* me ... Ps 139:1
To make *k* to the sons of men his ... Ps 145:12
judgments, they have not *k* them ... Ps 147:20
I will make *k* my words unto you ... Prov 1:23
perverteth his ways shall be *k* ... Prov 10:9
A fool's wrath is presently *k* ... Prov 12:16
in the midst of fools is made *k* ... Prov 14:33
Even a child is *k* by his doings ... Prov 20:11
I have made *k* to thee this day, ... Prov 22:19
Her husband is *k* in the gates ... Prov 31:23
a fool's voice is *k* by multitude ... Eccl 5:3
not seen the sun, nor *k* any thing ... Eccl 6:5
and it is *k* that it is man ... Eccl 6:10
this is *k* in all the earth ... Is 12:5
And the LORD shall be *k* to Egypt ... Is 19:21
children shall make *k* thy truth ... Is 38:19
Have ye not *k*? ... Is 40:21
Hast thou not *k*? ... Is 40:28
in paths that they have not *k* ... Is 42:16
They have not *k* nor understood ... Is 44:18
thee, though thou hast not *k* me ... Is 45:4
thee, though thou hast not *k* me ... Is 45:5
shall be *k* among the Gentiles ... Is 61:9
to make thy name *k* to thine ... Is 64:2
shall be *k* toward his servants ... Is 66:14
is foolish, they have not *k* me ... Jer 4:22
for they have *k* the way of the ... Jer 5:5
they nor their fathers have *k* ... Jer 9:16
they nor their fathers have *k* ... Jer 19:4
pass, then shall the prophet be *k* ... Jer 28:9
they are not *k* in the streets ... Lam 4:8
made myself *k* unto them in the ... Eze 20:5
sight I made myself *k* unto them ... Eze 20:9
countries which thou hast not *k* ... Eze 32:9
I will make myself *k* among them ... Eze 35:11
the Lord GOD, be it *k* unto you ... Eze 36:32
I will be *k* in the eyes of many ... Eze 38:23
name *k* in the midst of my people ... Eze 39:7
will not make *k* unto me the dream ... Dan 2:5
will not make *k* unto me the dream ... Dan 2:9
Arioch made the thing *k* to Daniel ... Dan 2:15
and made the thing *k* to Hananiah ... Dan 2:17
hast made *k* unto me now what we ... Dan 2:23
for thou hast now made *k* unto us ... Dan 2:23
that will make *k* unto the king ... Dan 2:25
Art thou able to make *k* unto me ... Dan 2:26
secrets, and maketh *k* to the king ... Dan 2:28
that revealeth secrets maketh *k* ... Dan 2:29
*k* the interpretation to the king ... Dan 2:30
the great God hath made *k* to the ... Dan 2:45
be it *k* unto thee, O king, that ... Dan 3:18
that they might make *k* unto me ... Dan 4:6
but they did not make *k* unto me ... Dan 4:7
make *k* unto me the interpretation ... Dan 4:18
have *k* that the heavens do rule ... Dan 4:26
nor make *k* to the king the ... Dan 5:8
make *k* unto me the interpretation ... Dan 5:15
make *k* to me the interpretation ... Dan 5:16
make *k* to him the interpretation ... Dan 5:17
them, and they have not *k* the LORD ... Hos 5:4
made *k* that which shall surely be ... Hos 5:9
You only have I *k* of all the ... Amos 3:2
place is not *k* where they are ... Nah 3:17
in the midst of the years make *k* ... Hab 3:2
day which shall be *k* to the LORD ... Zec 14:7
and hid, that shall not be *k* ... Mt 10:26
But if ye had *k* what this meaneth ... Mt 12:7
that they should not make him *k* ... Mt 12:16
for the tree is *k* by his fruit ... Mt 12:33
*k* in what watch the thief would ... Mt 24:43
that they should not make him *k* ... Mk 3:12
the Lord hath made *k* unto us ... Lk 2:15
they made *k* abroad the saying ... Lk 2:17
every tree is *k* by his own fruit ... Lk 6:44
were a prophet, would have *k* who ... Lk 7:39
thing hid, that shall not be *k* ... Lk 8:17
neither hid, that shall not be *k* ... Lk 12:2
*k* what hour the thief would come ... Lk 12:39
Saying, If thou hadst *k*, even ... Lk 19:42
hast not *k* the things which are ... Lk 24:18
how he was *k* of them in breaking ... Lk 24:35
he himself seeketh to be *k* openly ... Jn 7:4
if ye had *k* me, ye should have ... Jn 8:19
ye should have *k* my Father also ... Jn 8:19
Yet ye have not *k* him ... Jn 8:55
and know my sheep, and am *k* of mine ... Jn 10:14
If ye had *k* me, ye should have ... Jn 14:7
ye should have *k* my Father also ... Jn 14:7
you, and yet hast thou not *k* me ... Jn 14:9
my Father I have made *k* unto you ... Jn 15:15
they have not *k* the Father ... Jn 16:3
Now they have *k* that all things ... Jn 17:7
have *k* surely that I came out ... Jn 17:8
Father, the world hath not *k* thee ... Jn 17:25
but I have *k* thee, and these have ... Jn 17:25
these have *k* that thou hast sent ... Jn 17:25
that disciple was *k* unto the high ... Jn 18:15
which was *k* unto the high priest, ... Jn 18:16
it was *k* unto all the dwellers at ... Acts 1:19
be this *k* unto you, and hearken to ... Acts 2:14
Thou hast made *k* to me the ways ... Acts 2:28
Be it *k* unto you all, and to all ... Acts 4:10
Joseph was made *k* to his brethren ... Acts 7:13
kindred was made *k* unto Pharaoh ... Acts 7:13
their laying await was *k* of Saul ... Acts 9:24
it was *k* throughout all Joppa ... Acts 9:42
Be it *k* unto you therefore, men ... Acts 13:38
*K* unto God are all his works from ... Acts 15:18
this was *k* to all the Jews and ... Acts 19:17
because he would have *k* the ... Acts 22:30
when I would have *k* the cause ... Acts 23:28
Be it *k* therefore unto you, that ... Acts 28:28
Because that which may be *k* of ... Rom 1:19
the way of peace have they not *k* ... Rom 3:17
Nay, I had not *k* sin, but by the ... Rom 7:7
for I had not *k* lust, except the ... Rom 7:7
his wrath, and to make his power *k* ... Rom 9:22
that he might make *k* the riches ... Rom 9:23
For who hath *k* the mind of the ... Rom 11:34
made *k* to all nations for the ... Rom 16:26
for had they *k* it, they would not ... 1Cor 2:8
For who hath *k* the mind of the ... 1Cor 2:16
love God, the same is *k* of him ... 1Cor 8:3
shall I know even as also I am *k* ... 1Cor 13:12
how shall it be *k* what is piped ... 1Cor 14:7
how shall it be *k* what is spoken ... 1Cor 14:9
epistle written in our hearts, *k* ... 2Cor 3:2
though we have *k* Christ after the ... 2Cor 5:16
As unknown, and yet well *k* ... 2Cor 6:9
But now, after that ye have *k* God ... Gal 4:9
or rather are *k* of God ... Gal 4:9
Having made *k* unto us the mystery ... Eph 1:9
he made *k* unto me the mystery ... Eph 3:3
not made *k* unto the sons of men ... Eph 3:5
be *k* by the church the manifold ... Eph 3:10
to make *k* the mystery of the ... Eph 6:19
shall make *k* to you all things ... Eph 6:21
your moderation be *k* unto all men ... Phil 4:5
your requests be made *k* unto God ... Phil 4:6
To whom God would make *k* what is ... Col 1:27
They shall make *k* unto you all ... Col 4:9
But thou hast fully *k* my doctrine ... 2Ti 3:10
thou hast *k* the holy scriptures ... 2Ti 3:15
me the preaching might be fully *k* ... 2Ti 4:17
and they have not *k* my ways ... Heb 3:10
when we made *k* unto you the power ... 2Pet 1:16
have *k* the way of righteousness ... 2Pet 2:21
than, after they have *k* it ... 2Pet 2:21
because ye have *k* him that is ... 1Jn 2:13
because ye have *k* the Father ... 1Jn 2:13
because ye have *k* him that is ... 1Jn 2:14
hath not seen him, neither *k* him ... 1Jn 3:6
And we have *k* and believed the love ... 1Jn 4:16
all they that have *k* the truth ... 2Jn 1
which have not *k* the depths of ... Rev 2:24

**KOA** (*ko'-ah*) *An obscure tribe.*
Chaldeans, Pekod, and Shoa, and *K* ... Eze 23:23

**KOHATH** (*ko'-hath*) See KOHATHITES. *A son of Levi.*
Gershon, *K*, and Merari ... Gen 46:11
Gershon, and *K*, and Merari ... Ex 6:16
And the sons of *K* ... Ex 6:18
life of *K* were an hundred thirty ... Ex 6:18
Gershon, and *K*, and Merari ... Num 3:17
the sons of *K* by their families ... Num 3:19
of *K* was the family of the ... Num 3:27
The families of the sons of *K* ... Num 3:29
of *K* from among the sons of Levi ... Num 4:2
of *K* in the tabernacle of the ... Num 4:4
the sons of *K* shall come to bear ... Num 4:15
of *K* in the tabernacle of the ... Num 4:15
unto the sons of *K* he gave none ... Num 7:9
the son of Izhar, the son of *K* ... Num 16:1
of *K*, the family of the ... Num 26:57
And *K* begat Amram ... Num 26:58
the rest of the children of *K* had ... Josh 21:5
the families of the children of *K* ... Josh 21:20
remained of the children of *K* ... Josh 21:20
the children of *K* that remained ... Josh 21:26
Gershon, *K*, and Merari ... 1Chr 6:1
And the sons of *K* ... 1Chr 6:2
Gershom, *K*, and Merari ... 1Chr 6:16
And the sons of *K* were, Amram, and ... 1Chr 6:18
The sons of *K* ... 1Chr 6:22
The son of Izhar, the son of *K* ... 1Chr 6:38
And unto the sons of *K*, which were ... 1Chr 6:61
*K* had cities of their coasts out ... 1Chr 6:66
of the remnant of the sons of *K* ... 1Chr 6:70
Of the sons of *K* ... 1Chr 15:5
sons of Levi, namely, Gershon, *K* ... 1Chr 23:6
The sons of *K* ... 1Chr 23:12

**KOHATHITES** (*ko'-hath-ites*) *Descendants of Kohath.*
these are the families of the *K* ... Num 3:27
*K* shall be Elizaphan the son of ... Num 3:30
of the *K* from among the Levites ... Num 4:18
of the *K* after their families ... Num 4:34
numbered of the families of the *K* ... Num 4:37
the *K* set forward, bearing the ... Num 10:21
of Kohath, the family of the *K* ... Num 26:57
out for the families of the *K* ... Josh 21:4
being of the families of the *K* ... Josh 21:10
Of the sons of the *K* ... 1Chr 6:33
Aaron, of the families of the *K* ... 1Chr 6:54
brethren, of the sons of the *K* ... 1Chr 9:32
Levites, of the children of the *K* ... 2Chr 20:19
of Azariah, of the sons of the *K* ... 2Chr 29:12
Meshullam, of the sons of the *K* ... 2Chr 34:12

**KOLAIAH** (*ko-la-i'-ah*)
*1. A family of exiles.*
the son of Pedaiah, the son of *K* ... Neh 11:7

*2. Father of Ahab.*
of Israel, of Ahab the son of K ... Jer 29:21

**KORAH** (*ko'-rah*) See CORE, KORAHITE, KORE.
*1. A son of Esau.*
bare Jeush, and Jaalam, and K ... Gen 36:5
to Esau Jeush, and Jaalam, and K ... Gen 36:14
duke Jeush, duke Jaalam, duke K ... Gen 36:18
Reuel, and Jeush, and Jaalam, and K .. 1Chr 1:35
*2. A son of Eliphaz.*
Duke K, duke Gatam, and duke ... Gen 36:16
*3. A conspirator against Moses.*
K, and Nepheg, and Zichri ... Ex 6:21
And the sons of K ... Ex 6:24
Now K, the son of Izhar, the son ... Num 16:1
And he spake unto K and unto all ... Num 16:5
Take you censers, K, and all his ... Num 16:6
And Moses said unto K, Hear, I ... Num 16:8
And Moses said unto K ... Num 16:16
K gathered all the congregation ... Num 16:19
up from about the tabernacle of K ... Num 16:24
gat up from the tabernacle of K ... Num 16:27
the men that appertained unto K ... Num 16:32
that he be not as K, and as his ... Num 16:40
that died about the matter of K ... Num 16:49
against Aaron in the company of K ... Num 26:9
swallowed them up together with K. Num 26:10
the children of K died not ... Num 26:11
the LORD in the company of K ... Num 27:3
the son of Ebiasaph, the son of K ... 1Chr 6:37
the son of Ebiasaph, the son of K ... 1Chr 9:19
*4. A son of Hebron.*
K, and Tappuah, and Rekem ... 1Chr 2:43
*5. A grandson of Kohath.*
K his son, Assir his son, ... 1Chr 6:22
Maschil, for the sons of K ... Ps 42:t
chief Musician for the sons of K ... Ps 44:t
Shoshannim, for the sons of K ... Ps 45:t
chief Musician for the sons of K ... Ps 46:t
A Psalm for the sons of K ... Ps 47:t
A Song and Psalm for the sons of K ... Ps 48:t
A Psalm for the sons of K ... Ps 49:t
A Psalm for the sons of K ... Ps 84:t
A Psalm for the sons of K ... Ps 85:t
A Psalm or Song for the sons of K ... Ps 87:t
of K to the chief Musician upon ... Ps 88:t

**KORAHITE** (*ko'-ra-hite*) See KORAHITES, KORE.
*A descendant of Korah.*
the firstborn of Shallum the K ... 1Chr 9:31

**KORAHITES** (*ko'-ra-hites*) See KORATHITES, KORHITES.
of the house of his father, the K ... 1Chr 9:19

**KORATHITES** (*ko'-ra-thites*) See KORAHITES.
*Same as Korahites.*
the Mushites, the family of the K ... Num 26:58

**KORAZIN** See CHORAZIN.

**KORE** (*ko'-re*) See KORAH, KORAHITE.
*1. Father of Shallum.*
And Shallum the son of K, the son ... 1Chr 9:19
was Meshelemiah the son of K ... 1Chr 26:1
the porters among the sons of K ... 1Chr 26:19
*2. A Temple servant.*
K the son of Imnah the Levite, ... 2Chr 31:14

**KORHITES** (*kor'-hites*) See KORAHITES. *Same as Korahites.*
these are the families of the K ... Ex 6:24
and Joezer, and Jashobeam, the K ... 1Chr 12:6
Of the K was Meshelemiah the son ... 1Chr 26:1
and of the children of the K ... 2Chr 20:19

**KOUM** See CUMI.

**KOZ** (*coz*) See HAKKOZ.
*1. A family of exiles.*
of Habaiah, the children of K ... Ezr 2:61
of Habaiah, the children of K ... Neh 7:63
*2. Father of two rebuilders of the wall.*
the son of Urijah, the son of K ... Neh 3:4
Urijah the son of K another piece ... Neh 3:21

**KUSHAIAH** (*cu-shah'-yah*) See KISHI. *Father of Ethan.*
brethren, Ethan the son of K ... 1Chr 15:17

# L

**LAADAH** (*la'-a-dah*) *Son of Shelah.*
L the father of Mareshah, and the ... 1Chr 4:21

**LAADAN** (*la'-a-dan*) See LIBNI.
*1. A descendant of Ephraim.*
L his son, Ammihud his son, ... 1Chr 7:26
*2. A descendant of Gershon.*
Of the Gershonites were, L ... 1Chr 23:7
The sons of L ... 1Chr 23:8
the chief of the fathers of L ... 1Chr 23:9
As concerning the sons of L ... 1Chr 26:21
the sons of the Gershonite L ... 1Chr 26:21
even of L the Gershonite, were ... 1Chr 26:21

**LABAN** (*la'-ban*) See LABAN'S, LIBNAH.
*1. Father of Rachel.*
had a brother, and his name was L ... Gen 24:29
L ran out unto the man, unto the ... Gen 24:29
Then L and Bethuel answered and ... Gen 24:50
the sister to L the Syrian ... Gen 25:20
flee thou to L my brother to ... Gen 27:43
of L thy mother's brother ... Gen 28:2
and he went to Padan-aram unto L ... Gen 28:5
Know ye L the son of Nahor ... Gen 29:5
of L his mother's brother ... Gen 29:10
the sheep of L his mother's ... Gen 29:10
flock of L his mother's brother ... Gen 29:10
when L heard the tidings of Jacob ... Gen 29:13
he told L all these things ... Gen 29:13
L said to him, Surely thou art my ... Gen 29:14
L said unto Jacob, Because thou ... Gen 29:15
And L had two daughters ... Gen 29:16
L said, It is better that I give ... Gen 29:19
And Jacob said unto L, Give me my ... Gen 29:21
L gathered together all the men ... Gen 29:22
L gave unto his daughter Leah ... Gen 29:24
and he said to L, What is this ... Gen 29:25
L said, It must not be so done in ... Gen 29:26
L gave to Rachel his daughter ... Gen 29:29
Joseph, that Jacob said unto L ... Gen 30:25
L said unto him, I pray thee, if ... Gen 30:27
L said, Behold, I would it might ... Gen 30:34
all the brown in the flock of L ... Gen 30:40
Jacob beheld the countenance of L ... Gen 31:2
seen all that L doeth unto thee ... Gen 31:12
L went to shear his sheep ... Gen 31:19
away unawares to L the Syrian ... Gen 31:20
it was told L on the third day ... Gen 31:22
God came to L the Syrian in a ... Gen 31:24
Then L overtook Jacob ... Gen 31:25
L with his brethren pitched in ... Gen 31:25
L said to Jacob, What hast thou ... Gen 31:26
And Jacob answered and said to L ... Gen 31:31
L went into Jacob's tent, and into ... Gen 31:33
L searched all the tent, but ... Gen 31:34
Jacob was wroth, and chode with L ... Gen 31:36
and Jacob answered and said to L ... Gen 31:36
L answered and said unto Jacob, ... Gen 31:43
L called it Jegar-sahadutha ... Gen 31:47
L said, This heap is a witness ... Gen 31:48
L said to Jacob, Behold this heap ... Gen 31:51
And early in the morning L rose up ... Gen 31:55
L departed, and returned unto his ... Gen 31:55
thus, I have sojourned with L ... Gen 32:4
whom L gave to Leah his daughter, ... Gen 46:18
which L gave unto Rachel his ... Gen 46:25
*2. A Hebrew encampment in the wilderness.*
between Paran, and Tophel, and L ... Deut 1:1

**LABAN'S** (*la'-bans*) *Refers to Laban 1.*
and Jacob fed the rest of L flocks ... Gen 30:36
and put them not unto L cattle ... Gen 30:40
so the feebler were L, and the ... Gen 30:42
And he heard the words of L sons ... Gen 31:1

**LABOUR**
the l of my hands, and rebuked ... Gen 31:42
travailed, and she had hard l ... Gen 35:16
to pass, when she was in hard l ... Gen 35:17
the men, that they may l therein ... Ex 5:9
Six days shalt thou l, and do all ... Ex 20:9
Six days thou shalt l, and do all ... Deut 5:13
on our affliction, and our l ... Deut 26:7
not all the people to l thither ... Josh 7:3
you a land for which ye did not l ... Josh 24:13
be a guard to us, and l on the day ... Neh 4:22
man from his house, and from his l ... Neh 5:13
I be wicked, why then l I in vain ... Job 9:29
or wilt thou leave thy l to him ... Job 39:11
her l is in vain without fear ... Job 39:16
and their l unto the locust ... Ps 78:46
years, yet is their strength l ... Ps 90:10
to his l until the evening ... Ps 104:23
inherited the l of the people ... Ps 105:44
brought down their heart with l ... Ps 107:12
and let the strangers spoil his l ... Ps 109:11
they l in vain that build it ... Ps 127:1
shalt eat the l of thine hands ... Ps 128:2
That our oxen may be strong to l ... Ps 144:14
The l of the righteous tendeth to ... Prov 10:16
gathereth by l shall increase ... Prov 13:11
In all l there is profit ... Prov 14:23
for his hands refuse to l ... Prov 21:25
L not to be rich ... Prov 23:4
profit hath a man of all his l ... Eccl 1:3
All things are full of l ... Eccl 1:8
for my heart rejoiced in all my l ... Eccl 2:10
this was my portion of all my l ... Eccl 2:10
on the l that I had laboured to ... Eccl 2:11
I hated all my l which I had ... Eccl 2:18
all my l wherein I have laboured ... Eccl 2:19
the l which I took under the sun ... Eccl 2:20
is a man whose l is in wisdom ... Eccl 2:21
For what hath man of all his l ... Eccl 2:22
make his soul enjoy good in his l ... Eccl 2:24
and enjoy the good of all his l ... Eccl 3:13
yet is there no end of all his l ... Eccl 4:8
neither saith he, For whom do I l ... Eccl 4:8
have a good reward for their l ... Eccl 4:9
and shall take nothing of his l ... Eccl 5:15
l that he taketh under the sun ... Eccl 5:18
portion, and to rejoice in his l ... Eccl 5:19
All the l of man is for his mouth ... Eccl 6:7
him of his l the days of his life ... Eccl 8:15
though a man l to seek it out ... Eccl 8:17
in thy l which thou takest under ... Eccl 9:9
The l of the foolish wearieth ... Eccl 10:15
l not to comfort me, because of ... Is 22:4
The l of Egypt, and merchandise of ... Is 45:14
your l for that which satisfieth ... Is 55:2
They shall not l in vain, nor ... Is 65:23
For shame hath devoured the l of ... Jer 3:24
I forth out of the womb to see l ... Jer 20:18
and the people shall l in vain ... Jer 51:58
we l, and have no rest ... Lam 5:5
and shall take away all thy l ... Eze 23:29
him the land of Egypt for his l ... Eze 29:20
l to bring forth, O daughter of ... Mic 4:10
people shall l in the very fire ... Hab 2:13
the l of the olive shall fail, and ... Hab 3:17
and upon all the l of the hands ... Hag 1:11
Come unto me, all ye that l ... Mt 11:28
that whereon ye bestowed no l ... Jn 4:38
L not for the meat which ... Jn 6:27
Mary, who bestowed much l on us ... Rom 16:6
and Tryphosa, who l in the Lord ... Rom 16:12
own reward according to his own l ... 1Cor 3:8
And l, working with our own hands ... 1Cor 4:12
your l is not in vain in the Lord ... 1Cor 15:58
Wherefore we l, that, whether ... 2Cor 5:9
have bestowed upon you l in vain ... Gal 4:11
but rather let him l, working ... Eph 4:28
flesh, this is the fruit of my l ... Phil 1:22
my brother, and companion in l ... Phil 2:25
Whereunto I also l, striving ... Col 1:29
l of love, and patience of hope in ... 1Th 1:3
For ye remember, brethren, our l ... 1Th 2:9
tempted you, and our l be in vain ... 1Th 3:5
to know them which l among you ... 1Th 5:12
but wrought with l and travail ... 2Th 3:8
For therefore we both l and suffer ... 1Ti 4:10
especially they who l in the word ... 1Ti 5:17
Let us l therefore to enter into ... Heb 4:11
l of love, which ye have shewed ... Heb 6:10
I know thy works, and thy l ... Rev 2:2

**LABOURED**
So we l in the work ... Neh 4:21
That which he l for shall he ... Job 20:18
on the labour that I had l to do ... Eccl 2:11
all my labour wherein I have l ... Eccl 2:19
yet to a man that hath not l ... Eccl 2:21
wherein he hath l under the sun ... Eccl 2:22
hath he that hath l for the wind ... Eccl 5:16
thou hast l from thy youth ... Is 47:12
unto thee with whom thou hast l ... Is 47:15
I have l in vain, I have spent my ... Is 49:4
wine, for the which thou hast l ... Is 62:8
he l till the going down of the ... Dan 6:14
for the which thou hast not l ... Jonah 4:10
other men l, and ye are entered ... Jn 4:38
Persis, which l much in the Lord ... Rom 16:12
but I l more abundantly than they ... 1Cor 15:10
run in vain, neither l in vain ... Phil 2:16
which l with me in the gospel ... Phil 4:3
and for my name's sake hast l ... Rev 2:3

**LABOURER**
for the l is worthy of his hire ... Lk 10:7
The l is worthy of his reward ... 1Ti 5:18

**LABOURERS**
is plenteous, but the l are few ... Mt 9:37
send forth l into his harvest ... Mt 9:38
to hire l into his vineyard ... Mt 20:1
with the l for a penny a day ... Mt 20:2
unto his steward, Call the l ... Mt 20:8
truly is great, but the l are few ... Lk 10:2
send forth l into his harvest ... Lk 10:2
For we are l together with God ... 1Cor 3:9
the hire of the l who have reaped ... Jas 5:4

**LABOURETH**
He that l l for himself ... Prov 16:26
He that l l for himself ... Prov 16:26
that worketh in that wherein he l ... Eccl 3:9
one that helpeth with us, and l ... 1Cor 16:16
The husbandman that l must be ... 2Ti 2:6

**LABOURING**
The sleep of a l man is sweet ... Eccl 5:12
how that so l ye ought to support ... Acts 20:35
always l fervently for you in ... Col 4:12
for l night and day, because we ... 1Th 2:9

**LABOURS**
harvest, the firstfruits of thy l ... Ex 23:16
in thy l out of the field ... Ex 23:16
fruit of thy land, and all thy l ... Deut 28:33
thy l be in the house of a ... Prov 5:10
pleasure, and exact all your l ... Is 58:3
this city, and all the l thereof ... Jer 20:5
in all my l they shall find none ... Hos 12:8
hail in all the l of your hands ... Hag 2:17
and ye are entered into their l ... Jn 4:38
imprisonments, in tumults, in l ... 2Cor 6:5
that is, of other men's l ... 2Cor 10:15
in l more abundant, in stripes ... 2Cor 11:23
that they may rest from their l ... Rev 14:13

**LACE**
of the ephod with a l of blue ... Ex 28:28
And thou shalt put it on a blue l ... Ex 28:37
of the ephod with a l of blue ... Ex 39:21
And they tied unto it a l of blue ... Ex 39:31

**LACHISH** (*la'-kish*) *An Amorite city.*
Jarmuth, and unto Japhia king of L ... Josh 10:3
king of Jarmuth, the king of L ... Josh 10:5
king of Jarmuth, the king of L ... Josh 10:23
and all Israel with him, unto L ... Josh 10:31
the LORD delivered L into the ... Josh 10:32
king of Gezer came up to help L ... Josh 10:33
from L Joshua passed unto Eglon, ... Josh 10:34
to all that he had done to L ... Josh 10:35

the king of *L*, one ........ Josh 12:11
*L*, and Bozkath, and Eglon, ........ Josh 15:39
and he fled to *L* ........ 2Kin 14:19
but they sent after him to *L* ........ 2Kin 14:19
sent to the king of Assyria to *L* ........ 2Kin 18:14
Rab-shakeh from *L* to king ........ 2Kin 18:17
heard that he was departed from *L* ........ 2Kin 19:8
And Adoraim, and *L*, and Azekah, ........ 2Chr 11:9
and he fled to *L* ........ 2Chr 25:27
but they sent to *L* after him ........ 2Chr 25:27
he himself laid siege against *L* ........ 2Chr 32:9
and in their villages, at *L* ........ Neh 11:30
of Assyria sent Rabshakeh from *L* ........ Is 36:2
heard that he was departed from *L* ........ Is 37:8
Judah that were left, against *L* ........ Jer 34:7
O thou inhabitant of *L*, bind the ........ Mic 1:13

**LACK**
Peradventure there shall *l* five ........ Gen 18:28
all the city for *l* of five ........ Gen 18:28
he that gathered little had no *l* ........ Ex 16:18
thou shalt not *l* any thing in it ........ Deut 8:9
old lion perisheth for *l* of prey ........ Job 4:11
God, they wander for *l* of meat ........ Job 38:41
The young lions do *l*, and suffer ........ Ps 34:10
giveth unto the poor shall not *l* ........ Prov 28:27
and let thy head *l* no ointment ........ Eccl 9:8
are destroyed for *l* of knowledge ........ Hos 4:6
what *l* I yet ........ Mt 19:20
that had gathered little had no *l* ........ 2Cor 8:15
to supply your *l* of service ........ Phil 2:30
and that ye may have *l* of nothing ........ 1Th 4:12
If any of you *l* wisdom, let him ........ Jas 1:5

**LACKED**
thou hast *l* nothing ........ Deut 2:7
there *l* of David's servants ........ 2Sa 2:30
by the morning light there *l* not ........ 2Sa 17:22
they *l* nothing ........ 1Kin 4:27
him, But what hast thou *l* with me ........ 1Kin 11:22
so that they *l* nothing ........ Neh 9:21
away, because it *l* moisture ........ Lk 8:6
scrip, and shoes, *l* ye any thing ........ Lk 22:35
was there any among them that *l* ........ Acts 4:34
honour to that part which *l* ........ 1Cor 12:24
careful, but ye *l* opportunity ........ Phil 4:10

**LACKEST**
said unto him, One thing thou *l* ........ Mk 10:21
unto him, Yet *l* thou one thing ........ Lk 18:22

**LACKETH**
there *l* not one man of us ........ Num 31:49
on the sword, or that *l* bread ........ 2Sa 3:29
with a woman *l* understanding ........ Prov 6:32
honoureth himself, and *l* bread ........ Prov 12:9
But he that *l* these things is ........ 2Pet 1:9

**LACKING**
to be *l* from thy meat offering ........ Lev 2:13
superfluous or *l* in his parts ........ Lev 22:23
be to day one tribe *l* in Israel ........ Judg 21:3
And there was nothing *l* to them ........ 1Sa 30:19
dismayed, neither shall they be *l* ........ Jer 23:4
for that which was *l* on your part ........ 1Cor 16:17
for that which was *l* to me the ........ 2Cor 11:9
that which is *l* in your faith ........ 1Th 3:10

**LAD**
in thy sight because of the *l* ........ Gen 21:12
And God heard the voice of the *l* ........ Gen 21:17
the voice of the *l* where he is ........ Gen 21:17
Arise, lift up the *l*, and hold him ........ Gen 21:18
with water, and gave the *l* drink ........ Gen 21:19
And God was with the *l* ........ Gen 21:20
the *l* will go yonder and worship, ........ Gen 22:5
Lay not thine hand upon the *l* ........ Gen 22:12
the *l* was with the sons of Bilhah ........ Gen 37:2
his father, Send the *l* with me ........ Gen 43:8
The *l* cannot leave his father ........ Gen 44:22
father, and the *l* be not with us ........ Gen 44:30
seeth that the *l* is not with us ........ Gen 44:31
surety for the *l* unto my father ........ Gen 44:32
of the *l* a bondman to my lord ........ Gen 44:33
let the *l* go up with his brethren ........ Gen 44:33
father, and the *l* be not with me ........ Gen 44:34
Samson said unto the *l* that held ........ Judg 16:26
And, behold, I will send a *l* ........ 1Sa 20:21
If I expressly say unto the *l* ........ 1Sa 20:21
David, and a little *l* with him ........ 1Sa 20:35
And he said unto his *l*, Run, find ........ 1Sa 20:36
And as the *l* ran, he shot an arrow ........ 1Sa 20:36
when the *l* was come to the place ........ 1Sa 20:37
shot, Jonathan cried after the *l* ........ 1Sa 20:37
And Jonathan cried after the *l* ........ 1Sa 20:38
Jonathan's *l* gathered up the ........ 1Sa 20:38
But the *l* knew not any thing ........ 1Sa 20:39
gave his artillery unto his *l* ........ 1Sa 20:40
And as soon as the *l* was gone ........ 1Sa 20:41
Nevertheless a *l* saw them ........ 2Sa 17:18
And he said to a *l*, Carry him to ........ 2Kin 4:19
There is a *l* here, which hath ........ Jn 6:9

**LADAN** See LAADAN.

**LADDER**
behold a *l* set up on the earth, ........ Gen 28:12

**LADE**
*l* your beasts, and go, get you ........ Gen 45:17
did *l* you with a heavy yoke ........ 1Kin 12:11
for ye *l* men with burdens ........ Lk 11:46

**LADED**
they *l* their asses with the corn, ........ Gen 42:26
*l* every man his ass, and returned ........ Gen 44:13
bare burdens, with those that *l* ........ Neh 4:17
they *l* us with such things as ........ Acts 28:10

**LADEN**
ten asses *l* with the good things ........ Gen 45:23
and ten she asses *l* with corn ........ Gen 45:23
And Jesse took an ass *l* with bread ........ 1Sa 16:20
a people *l* with iniquity, a seed ........ Is 1:4
all ye that labour and are heavy *l* ........ Mt 11:28
captive silly women *l* with sins ........ 2Ti 3:6

**LADETH**
to him that *l* himself with thick ........ Hab 2:6

**LADIES**
Her wise *l* answered her, yea, she ........ Judg 5:29
Likewise shall the *l* of Persia ........ Est 1:18

**LADING**
bringing in sheaves, and *l* asses ........ Neh 13:15
and much damage, not only of the *l* ........ Acts 27:10

**LAD'S**
life is bound up in the *l* life ........ Gen 44:30

**LADS**
me from all evil, bless the *l* ........ Gen 48:16

**LADY**
more be called, The *l* of kingdoms ........ Is 47:5
saidst, I shall be a *l* for ever ........ Is 47:7
The elder unto the elect *l* ........ 2Jn 1
And now I beseech thee, *l*, not as ........ 2Jn 5

**LAEL** (*la'-el*) *A Levite.*
shall be Eliasaph the son of *L* ........ Num 3:24

**LAHAD** (*la'-had*) *Great-grandson of Shobal.*
and Jahath begat Ahumai, and *L* ........ 1Chr 4:2

**LAHAI-ROI** (*la-hah'-ee-roy*) See BEER-LAHAIROI. *A well in Paran.*
came from the way of the well *L* ........ Gen 24:62
and Isaac dwelt by the well *L* ........ Gen 25:11

**LAHMAM** (*lah'-mam*) *A city in Judah.*
And Cabbon, and *L*, and Kithlish, ........ Josh 15:40

**LAHMAS** See LAHMAM.

**LAHMI** (*lah'-mi*) See BETHLEHEMITE. *A brother of Goliath.*
slew *L* the brother of Goliath the ........ 1Chr 20:5

**LAID**
*l* it upon both their shoulders, ........ Gen 9:23
*l* each piece one against another ........ Gen 15:10
the men *l* hold upon his hand, and ........ Gen 19:16
and *l* it upon Isaac his son ........ Gen 22:6
*l* the wood in order, and bound ........ Gen 22:9
*l* him on the altar upon the wood ........ Gen 22:9
that Jacob *l* the rods before the ........ Gen 30:41
*l* by her vail from her, and put on ........ Gen 38:19
she *l* up his garment by her, ........ Gen 39:16
*l* up the food in the cities ........ Gen 41:48
every city, *l* he up in the same ........ Gen 41:48
*l* it upon Ephraim's head, who was ........ Gen 48:14
*l* his right hand upon the head of ........ Gen 48:17
she *l* it in the flags by the ........ Ex 2:3
there more work be *l* upon the men ........ Ex 5:9
they *l* it up till the morning, as ........ Ex 16:24
so Aaron *l* it up before the ........ Ex 16:34
*l* before their faces all these ........ Ex 19:7
If there be *l* on him a sum of ........ Ex 21:30
his life whatsoever is *l* upon him ........ Ex 21:30
of Israel he *l* not his hand ........ Ex 24:11
his sons *l* their hands upon the ........ Lev 8:14
his sons *l* their hands upon the ........ Lev 8:18
his sons *l* their hands upon the ........ Lev 8:22
*l* incense thereon, and stood in ........ Num 16:18
Moses *l* up the rods before the ........ Num 17:7
we have *l* them waste even unto ........ Num 21:30
he *l* his hands upon him, and gave ........ Num 27:23
us, and *l* upon us hard bondage ........ Deut 26:6
which the LORD hath *l* upon it ........ Deut 29:22
Is not this *l* up in store with me ........ Deut 32:34
for Moses had *l* his hands upon ........ Deut 34:9
which she had *l* in order upon the ........ Josh 2:6
And before they were *l* down ........ Josh 2:8
they lodged, and *l* them down there ........ Josh 4:8
*l* them out before the LORD ........ Josh 7:23
*l* great stones in the cave's ........ Josh 10:27
their blood be *l* upon Abimelech ........ Judg 9:24
they *l* wait against Shechem in ........ Judg 9:34
*l* wait in the field, and looked, ........ Judg 9:43
*l* it on his shoulder, and said ........ Judg 9:48
*l* wait for him all night in the ........ Judg 16:2
*l* hold on his concubine, and ........ Judg 19:29
uncovered his feet, and *l* her down ........ Ruth 3:7
of barley, and *l* it on her ........ Ruth 3:15
*l* it in her bosom, and became ........ Ruth 4:16
when Eli was *l* down in his place, ........ 1Sa 3:2
Samuel was *l* down to sleep ........ 1Sa 3:3
they *l* the ark of the LORD upon ........ 1Sa 6:11
book, and *l* it up before the LORD ........ 1Sa 10:25
how he *l* wait for him in the way, ........ 1Sa 15:2
Amalek, and *l* wait in the valley ........ 1Sa 15:5
he *l* hold upon the skirt of his ........ 1Sa 15:27
*l* it in the bed, and put a pillow ........ 1Sa 19:13
David *l* up these words in his ........ 1Sa 21:12
cakes of figs, and *l* them on asses ........ 1Sa 25:18
and he was *l* down ........ 2Sa 13:8
*l* her hand on her head, and went ........ 2Sa 13:19
*l* a very great heap of stones ........ 2Sa 18:17
*l* it in her bosom ........ 1Kin 3:20
*l* her dead child in my bosom ........ 1Kin 3:20
of the house of the LORD *l* ........ 1Kin 6:37
an oath be *l* upon him to cause ........ 1Kin 8:31
*l* it upon the ass, and brought it ........ 1Kin 13:29
he *l* his carcase in his own grave ........ 1Kin 13:30
all Israel *l* siege to Gibbethon ........ 1Kin 15:27
he *l* the foundation thereof in ........ 1Kin 16:34
abode, and *l* him upon his own bed ........ 1Kin 17:19
*l* him on the wood, and said, Fill ........ 1Kin 18:33
eat and drink, and *l* him down again ........ 1Kin 19:6
he *l* him down upon his bed, and ........ 1Kin 21:4
*l* him on the bed of the man of ........ 2Kin 4:21
*l* the staff upon the face of the ........ 2Kin 4:31
child was dead, and *l* upon his bed ........ 2Kin 4:32
*l* them upon two of his servants ........ 2Kin 5:23
the LORD *l* this burden upon him ........ 2Kin 9:25
And they *l* hands on her ........ 2Kin 11:16
they *l* it out to the carpenters ........ 2Kin 12:11
for all that was *l* out for the ........ 2Kin 12:12
*l* it on the boil, and he recovered ........ 2Kin 20:7
have *l* up in store unto this day ........ 2Kin 20:17
an oath be *l* upon him to make him ........ 2Chr 6:22
and *l* hold on other gods, and ........ 2Chr 7:22
*l* him in the bed which was filled ........ 2Chr 16:14
So they *l* hands on her ........ 2Chr 23:15
*l* upon Israel in the wilderness ........ 2Chr 24:9
of the burdens *l* upon him ........ 2Chr 24:27
they *l* their hands upon them ........ 2Chr 29:23
their God, and *l* them by heaps ........ 2Chr 31:6
(but he himself *l* siege against ........ 2Chr 32:9
temple of the LORD was not yet *l* ........ Ezr 3:6
And when the builders *l* the ........ Ezr 3:10
of the house of the LORD was *l* ........ Ezr 3:11
house was *l* before their eyes ........ Ezr 3:12
timber is *l* in the walls, and this ........ Ezr 5:8
*l* the foundation of the house of ........ Ezr 5:16
treasures were *l* up in Babylon ........ Ezr 6:1
foundations thereof be strongly *l* ........ Ezr 6:3
who also *l* the beams thereof, and ........ Neh 3:3
they *l* the beams thereof, and set ........ Neh 3:6
they *l* the meat offerings ........ Neh 13:5
because he *l* his hand upon the ........ Est 8:7
but on the spoil *l* they not their ........ Est 9:10
on the prey they *l* not their hand ........ Est 9:15
but they *l* not their hands on the ........ Est 9:16
the king Ahasuerus *l* a tribute ........ Est 10:1
my calamity *l* in the balances ........ Job 6:2
The snare is *l* for him in the ........ Job 18:10
*l* their hand on their mouth ........ Job 29:9
or if I have *l* wait at my ........ Job 31:9
Where wast thou when I *l* the ........ Job 38:4
Who hath *l* the measures thereof, ........ Job 38:5
or who *l* the corner stone thereof ........ Job 38:6
I *l* me down and slept ........ Ps 3:5
and majesty hast thou *l* upon him ........ Ps 21:5
that they have *l* privily for me ........ Ps 31:4
which thou hast *l* up for them ........ Ps 31:19
they *l* to my charge things that I ........ Ps 35:11
sheep they are *l* in the grave ........ Ps 49:14
to be *l* in the balance, they are ........ Ps 62:9
they have *l* Jerusalem on heaps ........ Ps 79:1
*l* waste his dwelling place ........ Ps 79:7
Thou hast *l* me in the lowest pit, ........ Ps 88:6
I have *l* help upon one that is ........ Ps 89:19
Of old hast thou *l* the foundation ........ Ps 102:25
Who *l* the foundations of the ........ Ps 104:5
he was *l* in iron ........ Ps 105:18
thy judgments have I *l* before me ........ Ps 119:30
The wicked have *l* a snare for me ........ Ps 119:110
before, and *l* thine hand upon me ........ Ps 139:5
snares which they have *l* for me ........ Ps 141:9
they privily *l* a snare for me ........ Ps 142:3
the sinner is *l* up for the just ........ Prov 13:22
old, which I have *l* up for thee ........ Song 7:13
he *l* it upon my mouth, and said, ........ Is 6:7
he hath *l* up his carriages ........ Is 10:28
saying, Since thou art *l* down ........ Is 14:8
the night Ar of Moab is *l* waste ........ Is 15:1
the night Kir of Moab is *l* waste ........ Is 15:1
and that which they have *l* up ........ Is 15:7
for it is *l* waste, so that there ........ Is 23:1
for your strength is *l* waste ........ Is 23:14
shall not be treasured nor *l* up ........ Is 23:18
have *l* waste all the nations ........ Is 37:18
have *l* up in store until this day ........ Is 39:6
him, yet he *l* it not to heart ........ Is 42:25
temple, Thy foundation shall be *l* ........ Is 44:28
hast thou very heavily *l* thy yoke ........ Is 47:6
Mine hand also hath *l* the ........ Is 48:13
*l* the foundations of the earth ........ Is 51:13
thou hast *l* thy body as the ........ Is 51:23
the LORD hath *l* on him the ........ Is 53:6
me, nor *l* it to thy heart ........ Is 57:11
our pleasant things are *l* waste ........ Is 64:11
and thy cities shall be *l* waste ........ Jer 4:7
should this city be *l* waste ........ Jer 27:17
but they *l* up the roll in the ........ Jer 36:20
I have *l* a snare for thee, and ........ Jer 50:24
they *l* wait for us in the ........ Lam 4:19
For I have *l* upon thee the years ........ Eze 4:5
the cities shall be *l* waste ........ Eze 6:6
that your altars may be *l* waste ........ Eze 6:6
whom ye have *l* in the midst of it ........ Eze 11:7
are inhabited shall be *l* waste ........ Eze 12:20
and he *l* waste their cities ........ Eze 19:7
replenished, now she is *l* waste ........ Eze 26:2
among the cities that are *l* waste ........ Eze 29:12
be thou *l* with the uncircumcised ........ Eze 32:19
they have *l* their swords under ........ Eze 32:27

which with their might are *l* by Eze 32:29
he shall be *l* in the midst of the Eze 32:32
when I have *l* the land most Eze 33:29
saying, They are *l* desolate Eze 35:12
my hand that I have *l* upon them Eze 39:21
whereupon also they *l* the Eze 40:42
*l* upon the mouth of the den Dan 6:17
their jaws, and I *l* meat unto them Hos 11:4
He hath *l* my vine waste, and Joel 1:7
clods, the garners are *l* desolate Joel 1:17
*l* to pledge by every altar Amos 2:8
of Israel shall be *l* waste Amos 7:9
bread have *l* a wound under thee Obad 7
nor have *l* hands on their Obad 13
he *l* his robe from him, and Jonah 3:6
he hath *l* siege against us Mic 5:1
thee, and say, Nineveh is *l* waste Nah 3:7
it is *l* over with gold and silver, Hab 2:19
from before a stone was *l* upon a Hag 2:15
of the LORD's temple was *l* Hag 2:18
stone that I have *l* before Joshua Zec 3:9
*l* the foundation of this house Zec 4:9
for they *l* the pleasant land Zec 7:14
house of the LORD of hosts was *l* Zec 8:9
*l* his mountains and his heritage Mal 1:3
now also the ax is *l* unto the Mt 3:10
house, he saw his wife's mother *l* Mt 8:14
For Herod had *l* hold on John Mt 14:3
he *l* hands on him, and took him by Mt 18:28
he *l* his hands on them, and Mt 19:15
*l* hands on Jesus, and took him Mt 26:50
the temple, and ye *l* no hold on me Mt 26:55
they that had *l* hold on Jesus led Mt 26:57
*l* it in his own new tomb, which Mt 27:60
save that he *l* his hands upon a Mk 6:5
*l* hold upon John, and bound him in Mk 6:17
up his corpse, and *l* it in a tomb Mk 6:29
they *l* the sick in the streets, Mk 6:56
and her daughter *l* upon the bed Mk 7:30
they *l* their hands on him, and Mk 14:46
and the young men *l* hold on him Mk 14:51
*l* him in a sepulchre which was Mk 15:46
of Joses beheld where he was *l* Mk 15:47
behold the place where they *l* him Mk 16:6
them *l* them up in their hearts Lk 1:66
clothes, and *l* him in a manger Lk 2:7
now also the axe is *l* unto the Lk 3:9
he *l* his hands on every one of Lk 4:40
*l* the foundation on a rock Lk 6:48
much goods *l* up for many years Lk 12:19
And he *l* his hands on her Lk 13:13
after he hath *l* the foundation, Lk 14:29
which was *l* at his gate, full of Lk 16:20
I have kept *l* up in a napkin Lk 19:20
man, taking up that I *l* not down Lk 19:22
they *l* hold upon one Simon, a Lk 23:26
and on him they *l* the cross Lk 23:26
*l* it in a sepulchre that was hewn Lk 23:53
wherein never man before was *l* Lk 23:53
sepulchre, and how his body was *l* Lk 23:55
the linen clothes *l* by themselves Lk 24:12
but no man *l* hands on him, Jn 7:30
but no man *l* hands on him Jn 7:44
and no man *l* hands on him Jn 8:20
And said, Where have ye *l* him Jn 11:34
the place where the dead was *l* Jn 11:41
supper, and *l* aside his garments Jn 13:4
wherein was never man yet *l* Jn 19:41
There *l* they Jesus therefore Jn 19:42
we know not where they have *l* him Jn 20:2
I know not where they have *l* him Jn 20:13
tell me where thou hast *l* him Jn 20:15
and fish *l* thereon, and bread Jn 21:9
whom they *l* daily at the gate of Acts 3:2
they *l* hands on them, and put them Acts 4:3
*l* them down at the apostles' feet Acts 4:35
*l* it at the apostles' feet Acts 4:37
*l* it at the apostles' feet Acts 5:2
*l* them on beds and couches, that Acts 5:15
*l* their hands on the apostles, and Acts 5:18
they *l* their hands on them Acts 6:6
*l* in the sepulchre that Abraham Acts 7:16
the witnesses *l* down their Acts 7:58
Then *l* they their hands on them, Acts 8:17
they *l* her in an upper chamber Acts 9:37
*l* their hands on them, they sent Acts 13:3
the tree, and *l* him in a sepulchre Acts 13:29
was *l* unto his fathers, and saw Acts 13:36
when they had *l* many stripes upon Acts 16:23
when Paul had *l* his hands upon Acts 19:6
And when the Jews *l* wait for him Acts 20:3
the people, and *l* hands on him, Acts 21:27
but to have nothing *l* to his Acts 23:29
that the Jews *l* wait for the man Acts 23:30
*l* many and grievous complaints Acts 25:7
the crime *l* against him Acts 25:16
signify the crimes *l* against him Acts 25:27
*l* them on the fire, there came a Acts 28:3
*l* his hands on him, and healed him Acts 28:8
my life *l* down their own necks Rom 16:4
I have *l* the foundation, and 1Cor 3:10
can no man lay than that is *l* 1Cor 3:11
for necessity is *l* upon me 1Cor 9:16
which is *l* up for you in heaven Col 1:5
Henceforth there is *l* up for me a 2Ti 4:8
it may not be *l* to their charge 2Ti 4:16
in the beginning hast *l* the Heb 1:10
because he *l* down his life for us 1Jn 3:16
he *l* his right hand upon me, Rev 1:17
he *l* hold on the dragon, that old Rev 20:2

**LAIDST**
thou *l* affliction upon our loins Ps 66:11

**LAIN**
woman, If no man have *l* with thee Num 5:19
some man have *l* with thee beside Num 5:20
woman that hath *l* by man Judg 21:11
For now should I have *l* still Job 3:13
he found that he had *l* in the Jn 11:17
where the body of Jesus had *l* Jn 20:12

**LAISH** (*la'-ish*) See DAN, LESHEM.
*1. Same as the city of Dan.*
five men departed, and came to *L* Judg 18:7
went to spy out the country of *L* Judg 18:14
which he had, and came unto *L* Judg 18:27
of the city was *L* at the first Judg 18:29
cause it to be heard unto *L* Is 10:30
*2. Father of Phaltiel.*
wife, to Phalti the son of *L* 1Sa 25:44
even from Phaltiel the son of *L* 2Sa 3:15

**LAKE**
he stood by the *l* of Gennesaret Lk 5:1
saw two ships standing by the *l* Lk 5:2
over unto the other side of the *l* Lk 8:22
down a storm of wind on the *l* Lk 8:23
down a steep place into the *l* Lk 8:33
both were cast alive into a *l* of Rev 19:20
them was cast into the *l* of fire Rev 20:10
hell were cast into the *l* of fire Rev 20:14
life was cast into the *l* of fire Rev 20:15
in the *l* which burneth with fire Rev 21:8

**LAKKUM** See LAKUM.

**LAKUM** (*la'-kum*) *A city in Naphtali.*
Adami, Nekeb, and Jabneel, unto *L* Josh 19:33

**LAMA**
saying, Eli, Eli, *l* sabachthani Mt 27:46
saying, Eloi, Eloi, *l* sabachthani Mk 15:34

**LAMB**
but where is the *l* for a burnt Gen 22:7
himself a *l* for a burnt offering Gen 22:8
shall take to them every man a *l* Ex 12:3
their fathers, a *l* for an house Ex 12:3
household be too little for the *l* Ex 12:4
shall make your count for the *l* Ex 12:4
Your *l* shall be without blemish, Ex 12:5
take you a *l* according to your Ex 12:21
an ass thou shalt redeem with a *l* Ex 13:13
The one *l* thou shalt offer in the Ex 29:39
the other *l* thou shalt offer at Ex 29:39
with the one *l* a tenth deal of Ex 29:40
the other *l* thou shalt offer at Ex 29:41
an ass thou shalt redeem with a *l* Ex 34:20
If he offer a *l* for his offering, Lev 3:7
if he bring a *l* for a sin Lev 4:32
as the fat of the *l* is taken away Lev 4:35
a *l* or a kid of the goats, for a Lev 5:6
And if he be not able to bring a *l* Lev 5:7
and a calf and a *l*, both of the Lev 9:3
she shall bring a *l* of the first Lev 12:6
if she be not able to bring a *l* Lev 12:8
one ewe *l* of the first year Lev 14:10
And the priest shall take one he *l* Lev 14:12
he shall slay the *l* in the place Lev 14:13
then he shall take one *l* for a Lev 14:21
the *l* of the trespass offering Lev 14:24
he shall kill the *l* of the Lev 14:25
Israel, that killeth an ox, or *l* Lev 17:3
Either a bullock or a *l* that hath Lev 22:23
he *l* without blemish of the first Lev 23:12
shall bring a *l* of the first year Num 6:12
one he *l* of the first year Num 6:14
one ewe *l* of the first year Num 6:14
one *l* of the first year, for a Num 7:15
one *l* of the first year, for a Num 7:21
one *l* of the first year, for a Num 7:27
one *l* of the first year, for a Num 7:33
one *l* of the first year, for a Num 7:39
one *l* of the first year, for a Num 7:45
one *l* of the first year, for a Num 7:51
one *l* of the first year, for a Num 7:57
one *l* of the first year, for a Num 7:63
one *l* of the first year, for a Num 7:69
one *l* of the first year, for a Num 7:75
one *l* of the first year, for a Num 7:81
offering or sacrifice, for one *l* Num 15:5
or for one ram, or for a *l* Num 15:11
The one *l* shalt thou offer in the Num 28:4
the other *l* shalt thou offer at Num 28:4
part of an hin for the one *l* Num 28:7
the other *l* shalt thou offer at Num 28:8
for a meat offering unto one *l* Num 28:13
a fourth part of an hin unto a *l* Num 28:14
deal shalt thou offer for every *l* Num 28:21
A several tenth deal unto one *l* Num 28:29
And one tenth deal for one *l* Num 29:4
A several tenth deal for one *l* Num 29:10
to each *l* of the fourteen lambs Num 29:15
And Samuel took a sucking *l* 1Sa 7:9
took a *l* out of the flock 1Sa 17:34
nothing, save one little ewe *l* 2Sa 12:3
but took the poor man's *l* 2Sa 12:4
he shall restore the *l* fourfold 2Sa 12:6
wolf also shall dwell with the *l* Is 11:6
Send ye the *l* to the ruler of the Is 16:1
brought as a *l* to the slaughter Is 53:7
the *l* shall feed together, and the Is 65:25
he that sacrificeth a *l*, as if he Is 66:3
But I was like a *l* or an ox that Jer 11:19
one *l* out of the flock, out of Eze 45:15
of a *l* of the first year without Eze 46:13
Thus shall they prepare the *l* Eze 46:15
feed them as a *l* in a large place Hos 4:16
and saith, Behold the *L* of God Jn 1:29
he saith, Behold the *L* of God Jn 1:36
like a *l* dumb before his shearer, Acts 8:32
as of a *l* without blemish and 1Pet 1:19
stood a *L* as it had been slain, Rev 5:6
elders fell down before the *L* Rev 5:8
Worthy is the *L* that was slain to Rev 5:12
throne, and unto the *L* for ever Rev 5:13
I saw when the *L* opened one of Rev 6:1
and from the wrath of the *L* Rev 6:16
the throne, and before the *L* Rev 7:9
upon the throne, and unto the *L* Rev 7:10
them white in the blood of the *L* Rev 7:14
For the *L* which is in the midst Rev 7:17
him by the blood of the *L* Rev 12:11
in the book of life of the *L* Rev 13:8
and he had two horns like a *l* Rev 13:11
a *L* stood on the mount Sion, and Rev 14:1
the *L* whithersoever he goeth Rev 14:4
firstfruits unto God and to the *L* Rev 14:4
and in the presence of the *L* Rev 14:10
of God, and the song of the *L* Rev 15:3
These shall make war with the *L* Rev 17:14
the *L* shall overcome them Rev 17:14
for the marriage of the *L* is come Rev 19:7
unto the marriage supper of the *L* Rev 19:9
of the twelve apostles of the *L* Rev 21:14
the *L* are the temple of it Rev 21:22
the *L* is the light thereof Rev 21:23
of the throne of God and of the *L* Rev 22:1
of God and of the *L* shall be in it Rev 22:3

**LAMB'S**
shew thee the bride, the *L* wife Rev 21:9
are written in the *L* book of life Rev 21:27

**LAMBS**
Abraham set seven ewe *l* of the Gen 21:28
ewe *l* which thou hast set by Gen 21:29
For these seven ewe *l* shalt thou Gen 21:30
And Jacob did separate the *l* Gen 30:40
two *l* of the first year day by Ex 29:38
take two he *l* without blemish Lev 14:10
offer with the bread seven *l* Lev 23:18
two *l* of the first year for a Lev 23:19
before the LORD, with the two *l* Lev 23:20
goats, five *l* of the first year Num 7:17
goats, five *l* of the first year Num 7:23
goats, five *l* of the first year Num 7:29
goats, five *l* of the first year Num 7:35
goats, five *l* of the first year Num 7:41
goats, five *l* of the first year Num 7:47
goats, five *l* of the first year Num 7:53
goats, five *l* of the first year Num 7:59
goats, five *l* of the first year Num 7:65
goats, five *l* of the first year Num 7:71
goats, five *l* of the first year Num 7:77
goats, five *l* of the first year Num 7:83
the *l* of the first year twelve, Num 7:87
the *l* of the first year sixty Num 7:88
two *l* of the first year without Num 28:3
on the sabbath day two *l* of the Num 28:9
seven *l* of the first year without Num 28:11
seven *l* of the first year Num 28:19
lamb, throughout the seven *l* Num 28:21
seven *l* of the first year Num 28:27
one lamb, throughout the seven *l* Num 28:29
seven *l* of the first year without Num 29:2
one lamb, throughout the seven *l* Num 29:4
seven *l* of the first year Num 29:8
one lamb, throughout the seven *l* Num 29:10
fourteen *l* of the first year Num 29:13
to each lamb of the fourteen *l* Num 29:15
fourteen *l* of the first year Num 29:17
for the rams, and for the *l* Num 29:18
fourteen *l* of the first year Num 29:20
for the rams, and for the *l* Num 29:21
fourteen *l* of the first year Num 29:23
for the rams, and for the *l* Num 29:24
fourteen *l* of the first year Num 29:26
for the rams, and for the *l* Num 29:27
fourteen *l* of the first year Num 29:29
for the rams, and for the *l* Num 29:30
fourteen *l* of the first year Num 29:32
for the rams, and for the *l* Num 29:33
seven *l* of the first year without Num 29:36
for the ram, and for the *l* Num 29:37
and milk of sheep, with fat of *l* Deut 32:14
and of the fatlings, and the *l* 1Sa 15:9
of Israel an hundred thousand *l* 2Kin 3:4
a thousand rams, and a thousand *l* 1Chr 29:21
and seven rams, and seven *l* 2Chr 29:21
they killed also the *l*, and they 2Chr 29:22
an hundred rams, and two hundred *l* 2Chr 29:32
to the people, of the flock, *l* 2Chr 35:7
young bullocks, and rams, and *l* Ezr 6:9
two hundred rams, four hundred *l* Ezr 6:17
with this money bullocks, rams, *l* Ezr 7:17
and six rams, seventy and seven *l* Ezr 8:35
the LORD shall be as the fat of *l* Ps 37:20
rams, and the little hills like *l* Ps 114:4
and ye little hills, like *l* Ps 114:6
The *l* are for thy clothing, and Prov 27:26
in the blood of bullocks, or of *l* Is 1:11
Then shall the *l* feed after their Is 5:17
fatness, and with the blood of *l* Is 34:6

shall gather the *l* with his arm ... Is 40:11
them down like *l* to the slaughter ... Jer 51:40
they occupied with thee in *l* ... Eze 27:21
of the earth, of rams, of *l* ... Eze 39:18
shall be six *l* without blemish ... Eze 46:4
the meat offering for the *l* as he ... Eze 46:5
bullock without blemish, and six *l* ... Eze 46:6
for the *l* according as his hand ... Eze 46:7
to the *l* as he is able to give, ... Eze 46:11
eat the *l* out of the flock, and ... Amos 6:4
send you forth as *l* among wolves ... Lk 10:3
He saith unto him, Feed my *l* ... Jn 21:15

**LAME**
a blind man, or a *l*, or he that ... Lev 21:18
blemish therein, as if it be *l* ... Deut 15:21
had a son that was *l* of his feet ... 2Sa 4:4
flee, that he fell, and became *l* ... 2Sa 4:4
thou take away the blind and the *l* ... 2Sa 5:6
smiteth the Jebusites, and the *l* ... 2Sa 5:8
the *l* shall not come into the ... 2Sa 5:8
yet a son, which is *l* on his feet ... 2Sa 9:3
and was *l* on both his feet ... 2Sa 9:13
because thy servant is *l* ... 2Sa 19:26
the blind, and feet was I to the *l* ... Job 29:15
The legs of the *l* are not equal ... Prov 26:7
the *l* take the prey ... Is 33:23
Then shall the *l* man leap as an ... Is 35:6
and with them the blind and the *l* ... Jer 31:8
and if ye offer the *l* and sick, is ... Mal 1:8
that which was torn, and the *l* ... Mal 1:13
the *l* walk, the lepers are ... Mt 11:5
with them those that were *l* ... Mt 15:30
the *l* to walk, and the blind to ... Mt 15:31
the *l* came to him in the temple ... Mt 21:14
the *l* walk, the lepers are ... Lk 7:22
call the poor, the maimed, the *l* ... Lk 14:13
a certain man *l* from his mother's ... Acts 3:2
as the *l* man which was healed ... Acts 3:11
with palsies, and that were *l* ... Acts 8:7
lest that which is *l* be turned ... Heb 12:13

**LAMECH** (*la'-mek*) *A son of Methuselah.*
and Methusael begat *L* ... Gen 4:18
*L* took unto him two wives ... Gen 4:19
*L* said unto his wives, Adah and ... Gen 4:23
ye wives of *L*, hearken unto my ... Gen 4:23
truly *L* seventy and sevenfold ... Gen 4:24
eighty and seven years, and begat *L* ... Gen 5:25
he begat *L* seven hundred eighty ... Gen 5:26
*L* lived an hundred eighty and two ... Gen 5:28
*L* lived after he begat Noah five ... Gen 5:30
all the days of *L* were seven ... Gen 5:31
Henoch, Methuselah, *L*, ... 1Chr 1:3
of Noe, which was the son of *L* ... Lk 3:36

**LAMENT**
of Israel went yearly to *l* the ... Judg 11:40
And her gates shall *l* and mourn ... Is 3:26
angle into the brooks shall *l* ... Is 19:8
They shall *l* for the teats, for ... Is 32:12
this gird you with sackcloth, *l* ... Jer 4:8
neither go to *l* nor bemoan them ... Jer 16:5
neither shall men *l* for them ... Jer 16:6
They shall not *l* for him, saying, ... Jer 22:18
they shall not *l* for him, saying, ... Jer 22:18
and they will *l* thee, saying, Ah ... Jer 34:5
*l*, and run to and fro by the hedges ... Jer 49:3
made the rampart and the wall to *l* ... Lam 2:8
*l* over thee, saying, What city is ... Eze 27:32
wherewith they shall *l* her ... Eze 32:16
of the nations shall *l* her ... Eze 32:16
they shall *l* for her, even for ... Eze 32:16
*L* like a virgin girded with ... Joel 1:8
Gird yourselves, and *l*, ye priests ... Joel 1:13
*l* with a doleful lamentation, and ... Mic 2:4
unto you, That ye shall weep and *l* ... Jn 16:20
*l* for her, when they shall see ... Rev 18:9

**LAMENTABLE**
he cried with a *l* voice unto ... Dan 6:20

**LAMENTATION**
with a great and very sore *l* ... Gen 50:10
lamented with this *l* over Saul ... 2Sa 1:17
and their widows made no *l* ... Ps 78:64
as for an only son, most bitter *l* ... Jer 6:26
take up a *l* on high places ... Jer 7:29
habitations of the wilderness a *l* ... Jer 9:10
and every one her neighbour *l* ... Jer 9:20
A voice was heard in Ramah, *l* ... Jer 31:15
There shall be *l* generally upon ... Jer 48:38
daughter of Judah mourning and *l* ... Lam 2:5
Moreover take thou up a *l* for the ... Eze 19:1
is a *l*, and shall be for a *l* ... Eze 19:14
they shall take up a *l* for thee ... Eze 26:17
son of man, take up a *l* for Tyrus ... Eze 27:2
they shall take up a *l* for thee ... Eze 27:32
take up a *l* upon the king of ... Eze 28:12
take up a *l* for Pharaoh king of ... Eze 32:2
This is the *l* wherewith they ... Eze 32:16
I take up against you, even a *l* ... Amos 5:1
as are skilful of *l* to wailing ... Amos 5:16
and all your songs into *l* ... Amos 8:10
you, and lament with a doleful *l* ... Mic 2:4
Rama was there a voice heard, *l* ... Mt 2:18
burial, and made great *l* over him ... Acts 8:2

**LAMENTATIONS**
of Josiah in their *l* to this day ... 2Chr 35:25
behold, they are written in the *l* ... 2Chr 35:25
and there was written therein *l* ... Eze 2:10

**LAMENTED**
and the people *l*, because the LORD ... 1Sa 6:19
house of Israel *l* after the LORD ... 1Sa 7:2
*l* him, and buried him in his house ... 1Sa 25:1
was dead, and all Israel had *l* him ... 1Sa 28:3
David *l* with this lamentation ... 2Sa 1:17
the king *l* over Abner, and said, ... 2Sa 3:33
And Jeremiah *l* for Josiah ... 2Chr 35:25
they shall not be *l* ... Jer 16:4
they shall not be *l*, neither ... Jer 25:33
unto you, and ye have not *l* ... Mt 11:17
which also bewailed and *l* him ... Lk 23:27

**LAMP**
a burning *l* that passed between ... Gen 15:17
to cause the *l* to burn always ... Ex 27:20
ere the *l* of God went out in the ... 1Sa 3:3
For thou art my *l*, O LORD ... 2Sa 22:29
his God give him a *l* in Jerusalem ... 1Kin 15:4
to slip with his feet is as a *l* ... Job 12:5
Thy word is a *l* unto my feet ... Ps 119:105
ordained a *l* for mine anointed ... Ps 132:17
For the commandment is a *l* ... Prov 6:23
but the *l* of the wicked shall be ... Prov 13:9
his *l* shall be put out in obscure ... Prov 20:20
thereof as a *l* that burneth ... Is 62:1
heaven, burning as it were a *l* ... Rev 8:10

**LAMPS**
shalt make the seven *l* thereof ... Ex 25:37
and they shall light the *l* thereof ... Ex 25:37
when he dresseth the *l*, he shall ... Ex 30:7
when Aaron lighteth the *l* at even ... Ex 30:8
light, and his furniture, and his *l* ... Ex 35:14
And he made his seven *l*, and his ... Ex 37:23
candlestick, with the *l* thereof ... Ex 39:37
even with the *l* to be set in ... Ex 39:37
and light the *l* thereof ... Ex 40:4
he lighted the *l* before the LORD ... Ex 40:25
the light, to cause the *l* to burn ... Lev 24:2
He shall order the *l* upon the ... Lev 24:4
of the light, and his *l*, and his ... Num 4:9
him, When thou lightest the *l* ... Num 8:2
the seven *l* shall give light over ... Num 8:2
he lighted the *l* thereof over ... Num 8:3
and *l* within the pitchers ... Judg 7:16
held the *l* in their left hands, ... Judg 7:20
with the flowers, and the *l* ... 1Kin 7:49
of gold, and for their *l* of gold ... 1Chr 28:15
candlestick, and for the *l* thereof ... 1Chr 28:15
and also for the *l* thereof ... 1Chr 28:15
the candlesticks with their *l* ... 2Chr 4:20
And the flowers, and the *l*, and the ... 2Chr 4:21
of gold with the *l* thereof ... 2Chr 13:11
of the porch, and put out the *l* ... 2Chr 29:7
Out of his mouth go burning *l* ... Job 41:19
fire, and like the appearance of *l* ... Eze 1:13
and his eyes as *l* of fire ... Dan 10:6
top of it, and his seven *l* thereon ... Zec 4:2
and seven pipes to the seven *l* ... Zec 4:2
ten virgins, which took their *l* ... Mt 25:1
that were foolish took their *l* ... Mt 25:3
oil in their vessels with their *l* ... Mt 25:4
virgins arose, and trimmed their *l* ... Mt 25:7
for our *l* are gone out ... Mt 25:8
there were seven *l* of fire ... Rev 4:5

**LANCE**
They shall hold the bow and the *l* ... Jer 50:42

**LANCETS**
their manner with knives and *l* ... 1Kin 18:28

**LAND** See PREFACE.

**LANDED**
And when he had *l* at Caesarea ... Acts 18:22
sailed into Syria, and *l* at Tyre ... Acts 21:3

**LANDING**
*l* at Syracuse, we tarried there ... Acts 28:12

**LANDMARK**
not remove thy neighbour's *l* ... Deut 19:14
that removeth his neighbour's *l* ... Deut 27:17
Remove not the ancient *l*, which ... Prov 22:28
Remove not the old *l* ... Prov 23:10

**LANDMARKS**
Some remove the *l* ... Job 24:2

**LANDS**
the Gentiles divided in their *l* ... Gen 10:5
after their tongues, in their *l* ... Gen 10:31
and the dearth was in all *l* ... Gen 41:54
the famine was so sore in all *l* ... Gen 41:57
my lord, but our bodies, and our *l* ... Gen 47:18
wherefore they sold not their *l* ... Gen 47:22
hearts in the *l* of their enemies ... Lev 26:36
their iniquity in your enemies' *l* ... Lev 26:39
restore those *l* again peaceably ... Judg 11:13
of Assyria have done to all *l* ... 2Kin 19:11
destroyed the nations and their *l* ... 2Kin 19:17
fame of David went out into all *l* ... 1Chr 14:17
out of Egypt, and out of all *l* ... 2Chr 9:28
manner of the nations of other *l* ... 2Chr 13:9
the *l* that were round about Judah ... 2Chr 17:10
unto all the people of other *l* ... 2Chr 32:13
gods of the nations of those *l* ... 2Chr 32:13
deliver their *l* out of mine hand ... 2Chr 32:13
gods of the nations of other *l* ... 2Chr 32:17
from the people of the *l*, doing ... Ezr 9:1
with the people of those *l* ... Ezr 9:2
the hand of the kings of the *l* ... Ezr 9:7
filthiness of the people of the *l* ... Ezr 9:11
said, We have mortgaged our *l* ... Neh 5:3
tribute, and that upon our *l* ... Neh 5:4
for other men have our *l* and ... Neh 5:5
to them, even this day, their *l* ... Neh 5:11
the hand of the people of the *l* ... Neh 9:30
of the *l* unto the law of God ... Neh 10:28
they call their *l* after their own ... Ps 49:11
a joyful noise unto God, all ye *l* ... Ps 66:1
noise unto the LORD, all ye *l* ... Ps 100:1
gave them the *l* of the heathen ... Ps 105:44
and to scatter them in the *l* ... Ps 106:27
And gathered them out of the *l* ... Ps 107:3
among all the gods of these *l* ... Is 36:20
all *l* by destroying them utterly ... Is 37:11
from all the *l* whither he had ... Jer 16:15
now have I given all these *l* into ... Jer 27:6
which is the glory of all *l* ... Eze 20:6
which is the glory of all *l* ... Eze 20:15
them out of their enemies' *l* ... Eze 39:27
or wife, or children, or *l* ... Mt 19:29
or wife, or children, or *l* ... Mk 10:29
and mothers, and children, and *l* ... Mk 10:30
of *l* or houses sold them, and ... Acts 4:34

**LANES**
*l* of the city, and bring in hither ... Lk 14:21

**LANGUAGE**
And the whole earth was of one *l* ... Gen 11:1
is one, and they have all one *l* ... Gen 11:6
down, and there confound their *l* ... Gen 11:7
confound the *l* of all the earth ... Gen 11:9
to thy servants in the Syrian *l* ... 2Kin 18:26
talk not with us in the Jews' *l* ... 2Kin 18:26
with a loud voice in the Jews' *l* ... 2Kin 18:28
and could not speak in the Jews' *l* ... Neh 13:24
according to the *l* of each people ... Neh 13:24
and to every people after their *l* ... Est 1:22
to the *l* of every people ... Est 1:22
and to every people after their *l* ... Est 3:12
unto every people after their *l* ... Est 8:9
writing, and according to their *l* ... Est 8:9
There is no speech nor *l*, where ... Ps 19:3
where I heard a *l* that I ... Ps 81:5
Jacob from a people of strange *l* ... Ps 114:1
of Egypt speak the *l* of Canaan ... Is 19:18
unto thy servants in the Syrian *l* ... Is 36:11
and speak not to us in the Jews' *l* ... Is 36:11
with a loud voice in the Jews' *l* ... Is 36:13
a nation whose *l* thou knowest not ... Jer 5:15
a strange speech and of an hard *l* ... Eze 3:5
a strange speech and of an hard *l* ... Eze 3:6
That every people, nation, and *l* ... Dan 3:29
I turn to the people a pure *l* ... Zeph 3:9
man heard them speak in his own *l* ... Acts 2:6

**LANGUAGES**
O people, nations, and *l*, ... Dan 3:4
the people, the nations, and the *l* ... Dan 3:7
unto all people, nations, and *l* ... Dan 4:1
him, all people, nations, and *l* ... Dan 5:19
unto all people, nations, and *l* ... Dan 6:25
that all people, nations, and *l* ... Dan 7:14
hold out of all *l* of the nations ... Zec 8:23

**LANGUISH**
For the fields of Heshbon *l* ... Is 16:8
nets upon the waters shall *l* ... Is 19:8
haughty people of the earth do *l* ... Is 24:4
mourneth, and the gates thereof *l* ... Jer 14:2
one that dwelleth therein shall *l* ... Hos 4:3

**LANGUISHED**
they *l* together ... Lam 2:8

**LANGUISHETH**
and fadeth away, the world *l* ... Is 24:4
The new wine mourneth, the vine *l* ... Is 24:7
The earth mourneth and *l* ... Is 33:9
She that hath borne seven *l* ... Jer 15:9
new wine is dried up, the oil *l* ... Joel 1:10
is dried up, and the fig tree *l* ... Joel 1:12
Bashan *l*, and Carmel ... Nah 1:4
and the flower of Lebanon *l* ... Nah 1:4

**LANGUISHING**
strengthen him upon the bed of *l* ... Ps 41:3

**LANTERNS**
Pharisees, cometh thither with *l* ... Jn 18:3

**LAODICEA** (*la-od-i-se'-ah*) *Chief city of Phrygia.*
I have for you, and for them at *L* ... Col 2:1
for you, and them that are in *L* ... Col 4:13
the brethren which are in *L* ... Col 4:15
likewise read the epistle from *L* ... Col 4:16
to Timothy was written from *L* ... 1Ti s
and unto Philadelphia, and unto *L* ... Rev 1:11

**LAODICEANS** (*la-od-i-se'-uns*) *Inhabitants of Laodicea.*
read also in the church of the *L* ... Col 4:16
of the church of the *L* write ... Rev 3:14

**LAP**
thereof wild gourds his *l* full ... 2Kin 4:39
Also I shook my *l*, and said, So ... Neh 5:13
The lot is cast into the *l* ... Prov 16:33

**LAPIDOTH** (*lap'-i-doth*) *Husband of Deborah.*
a prophetess, the wife of *L* ... Judg 4:4

**LAPPED**
And the number of them that *l* ... Judg 7:6
men that *l* will I save you ... Judg 7:7

**LAPPETH**
Every one that *l* of the water...... Judg 7:5
water with his tongue, as a dog *l*...... Judg 7:5

**LAPPIDOTH** See LAPIDOTH.

**LAPWING**
heron after her kind, and the *l*...... Lev 11:19
heron after her kind, and the *l*...... Deut 14:18

**LARGE**
behold, it is *l* enough for them...... Gen 34:21
that land unto a good land and a *l*...... Ex 3:8
a people secure, and to a *l* land...... Judg 18:10
me forth also into a *l* place...... 2Sa 22:20
people, The work is great and *l*...... Neh 4:19
Now the city was *l* and great...... Neh 7:4
thou gavest them, and in the *l*...... Neh 9:35
me forth also into a *l* place...... Ps 18:19
thou hast set my feet in a *l* room...... Ps 31:8
me, and set me in a *l* place...... Ps 118:5
thee like a ball into a *l* country...... Is 22:18
thy cattle feed in *l* pastures...... Is 30:23
he hath made it deep and *l*...... Is 30:33
*l* chambers, and cutteth him out...... Jer 22:14
of thy sister's cup deep and *l*...... Eze 23:32
feed them as a lamb in a *l* place...... Hos 4:16
they gave *l* money unto the...... Mt 28:12
he will shew you a *l* upper room...... Mk 14:15
he shall shew you a *l* upper room...... Lk 22:12
Ye see how *l* a letter I have...... Gal 6:11
the length is as *l* as the breadth...... Rev 21:16

**LARGENESS**
*l* of heart, even as the sand that...... 1Kin 4:29

**LASCIVIOUSNESS**
wickedness, deceit, *l*, an evil...... Mk 7:22
*l* which they have committed...... 2Cor 12:21
fornication, uncleanness, *l*...... Gal 5:19
have given themselves over unto *l*...... Eph 4:19
the Gentiles, when we walked in *l*...... 1Pet 4:3
the grace of our God into *l*...... Jude 4

**LASEA** (*la-se'-ah*) *A city on Crete.*
nigh whereunto was the city of *L*...... Acts 27:8

**LASHA** (*la'-shah*) *A place in southern Canaan.*
and Zeboim, even unto *L*...... Gen 10:19

**LASHARON** (*lash'-ar-on*) *A Canaanite town.*
the king of *L*, one...... Josh 12:18

**LAST**
shall befall you in the *l* days...... Gen 49:1
but he shall overcome at the *l*...... Gen 49:19
and let my *l* end be like his...... Num 23:10
Why are ye the *l* to bring the...... 2Sa 19:11
ye the *l* to bring back the king...... 2Sa 19:12
Now these be the *l* words of David...... 2Sa 23:1
For by the *l* words of David the...... 1Chr 23:27
of David the king, first and *l*...... 1Chr 29:29
the acts of Solomon, first and *l*...... 2Chr 9:29
the acts of Rehoboam, first and *l*...... 2Chr 12:15
the acts of Asa, first and *l*...... 2Chr 16:11
acts of Jehoshaphat, first and *l*...... 2Chr 20:34
the acts of Amaziah, first and *l*...... 2Chr 25:26
of the acts of Uzziah, first and *l*...... 2Chr 26:22
and of all his ways, first and *l*...... 2Chr 28:26
And his deeds, first and *l*, behold,...... 2Chr 35:27
of the *l* sons of Adonikam, whose...... Ezr 8:13
from the first day unto the *l* day...... Neh 8:18
And thou mourn at the *l*, when thy...... Prov 5:11
At the *l* it biteth like a serpent...... Prov 23:32
shall come to pass in the *l* days...... Is 2:2
LORD, the first, and with the *l*...... Is 41:4
I am the first, and I am the *l*...... Is 44:6
I am the first, I also am the *l*...... Is 48:12
said, He shall not see our *l* end...... Jer 12:4
*l* this Nebuchadrezzar king of...... Jer 50:17
she remembereth not her *l* end...... Lam 1:9
But at the *l* Daniel came in...... Dan 4:8
other, and the higher came up *l*...... Dan 8:3
in the *l* end of the indignation...... Dan 8:19
I will slay the *l* of them with...... Amos 9:1
But in the *l* days it shall come...... Mic 4:1
the *l* state of that man is worse...... Mt 12:45
many that are first shall be *l*...... Mt 19:30
and the *l* shall be first...... Mt 19:30
from the *l* unto the first...... Mt 20:8
These *l* have wrought but one hour...... Mt 20:12
I will give unto this *l*, even as...... Mt 20:14
So the *l* shall be first...... Mt 20:16
shall be first, and the first *l*...... Mt 20:16
But *l* of all he sent unto them...... Mt 21:37
*l* of all the woman died also...... Mt 22:27
At the *l* came two false witnesses...... Mt 26:60
so the *l* error shall be worse...... Mt 27:64
first, the same shall be *l* of all...... Mk 9:35
many that are first shall be *l*...... Mk 10:31
and the *l* first...... Mk 10:31
he sent him also *l* unto them...... Mk 12:6
*l* of all the woman died also...... Mk 12:22
the *l* state of that man is worse...... Lk 11:26
thou hast paid the very *l* mite...... Lk 12:59
there are *l* which shall be first,...... Lk 13:30
there are first which shall be *l*...... Lk 13:30
*L* of all the woman died also...... Lk 20:32
raise it up again at the *l* day...... Jn 6:39
I will raise him up at the *l* day...... Jn 6:40
I will raise him up at the *l* day...... Jn 6:44
I will raise him up at the *l* day...... Jn 6:54
In the *l* day, that great day of...... Jn 7:37
at the eldest, even unto the *l*...... Jn 8:9
in the resurrection at the *l* day...... Jn 11:24
same shall judge him in the *l* day...... Jn 12:48
shall come to pass in the *l* days...... Acts 2:17
hath set forth us the apostles *l*...... 1Cor 4:9
*l* of all he was seen of me also,...... 1Cor 15:8
The *l* enemy that shall be...... 1Cor 15:26
the *l* Adam was made a quickening...... 1Cor 15:45
of an eye, at the *l* trump...... 1Cor 15:52
that now at the *l* your care of me...... Phil 4:10
that in the *l* days perilous times...... 2Ti 3:1
Hath in these *l* days spoken unto...... Heb 1:2
treasure together for the *l* days...... Jas 5:3
to be revealed in the *l* time...... 1Pet 1:5
manifest in these *l* times for you...... 1Pet 1:20
shall come in the *l* days scoffers...... 2Pet 3:3
Little children, it is the *l* time...... 1Jn 2:18
we know that it is the *l* time...... 1Jn 2:18
should be mockers in the *l* time...... Jude 18
and Omega, the first and the *l*...... Rev 1:11
I am the first and the *l*...... Rev 1:17
things saith the first and the *l*...... Rev 2:8
the *l* to be more than the first...... Rev 2:19
angels having the seven *l* plagues...... Rev 15:1
vials full of the seven *l* plagues...... Rev 21:9
and the end, the first and the *l*...... Rev 22:13

**LASTED**
seven days, while their feast *l*...... Judg 14:17

**LASTING**
precious things of the *l* hills...... Deut 33:15

**LATCHET**
nor the *l* of their shoes be...... Is 5:27
the *l* of whose shoes I am not...... Mk 1:7
the *l* of whose shoes I am not...... Lk 3:16
whose shoe's *l* I am not worthy to...... Jn 1:27

**LATE**
you to rise up early, to sit up *l*...... Ps 127:2
Even of *l* my people is risen up...... Mic 2:8
the Jews of *l* sought to stone...... Jn 11:8

**LATELY**
*l* come from Italy, with his wife...... Acts 18:2

**LATIN** (*lat'-in*) *Language spoken by the Romans.*
him in letters of Greek, and *L*...... Lk 23:38
written in Hebrew, and Greek, and *L*...... Jn 19:20

**LATTER**
believe the voice of the *l* sign...... Ex 4:8
do to thy people in the *l* days...... Num 24:14
but his *l* end shall be that he...... Num 24:20
upon thee, even in the *l* days...... Deut 4:30
to do thee good at thy *l* end...... Deut 8:16
the *l* rain, that thou mayest...... Deut 11:14
if the *l* husband hate her, and...... Deut 24:3
or if the *l* husband die, which...... Deut 24:3
will befall you in the *l* days...... Deut 31:29
they would consider their *l* end...... Deut 32:29
the *l* end than at the beginning...... Ruth 3:10
will be bitterness in the *l* end...... 2Sa 2:26
yet thy *l* end should greatly...... Job 8:7
stand at the *l* day upon the earth...... Job 19:25
mouth wide as for the *l* rain...... Job 29:23
So the LORD blessed the *l* end of...... Job 42:12
is as a cloud of the *l* rain...... Prov 16:15
thou mayest be wise in thy *l* end...... Prov 19:20
them, and know the *l* end of them...... Is 41:22
didst remember the *l* end of it...... Is 47:7
and there hath been no *l* rain...... Jer 3:3
rain, both the former and the *l*...... Jer 5:24
in the *l* days ye shall consider...... Jer 23:20
in the *l* days ye shall consider...... Jer 30:24
captivity of Moab in the *l* days...... Jer 48:47
shall come to pass in the *l* days...... Jer 49:39
in the *l* years thou shalt come...... Eze 38:8
it shall be in the *l* days...... Eze 38:16
what shall be in the *l* days...... Dan 2:28
in the *l* time of their kingdom,...... Dan 8:23
befall thy people in the *l* days...... Dan 10:14
not be as the former, or as the *l*...... Dan 11:29
and his goodness in the *l* days...... Hos 3:5
unto us as the rain, as the *l*...... Hos 6:3
the *l* rain in the first month...... Joel 2:23
the shooting up of the *l* growth...... Amos 7:1
it was the *l* growth after the...... Amos 7:1
The glory of this *l* house shall...... Hag 2:9
rain in the time of the *l* rain...... Zec 10:1
that in the *l* times some shall...... 1Ti 4:1
he receive the early and *l* rain...... Jas 5:7
the *l* end is worse with them than...... 2Pet 2:20

**LATTICE**
a window, and cried through the *l*...... Judg 5:28
Ahaziah fell down through a *l* in...... 2Kin 1:2
shewing himself through the *l*...... Song 2:9

**LAUD**
and *l* him, all ye people...... Rom 15:11

**LAUGH**
Abraham, Wherefore did Sarah *l*...... Gen 18:13
but thou didst *l*...... Gen 18:15
Sarah said, God hath made me to *l*...... Gen 21:6
that all that hear will *l* with me...... Gen 21:6
and famine thou shalt *l*...... Job 5:22
he will *l* at the trial of the...... Job 9:23
the innocent *l* them to scorn...... Job 22:19
sitteth in the heavens shall *l*...... Ps 2:4
they that see me *l* me to scorn...... Ps 22:7
The LORD shall *l* at him...... Ps 37:13
see, and fear, and shall *l* at him...... Ps 52:6
But thou, O LORD, shalt *l* at them...... Ps 59:8
our enemies *l* among themselves...... Ps 80:6
I also will *l* at your calamity...... Prov 1:26
foolish man, whether he rage or *l*...... Prov 29:9
A time to weep, and a time to *l*...... Eccl 3:4
for ye shall *l*...... Lk 6:21
Woe unto you that *l* now...... Lk 6:25

**LAUGHED**
Abraham fell upon his face, and *l*...... Gen 17:17
Therefore Sarah *l* within herself...... Gen 18:12
Sarah denied, saying, I *l* not...... Gen 18:15
despised thee, and *l* thee to scorn...... 2Kin 19:21
but they *l* them to scorn, and...... 2Chr 30:10
they *l* us to scorn, and despised...... Neh 2:19
just upright man is *l* to scorn...... Job 12:4
If I *l* on them, they believed it...... Job 29:24
despised thee, and *l* thee to scorn...... Is 37:22
thou shalt be *l* to scorn and had...... Eze 23:32
And they *l* him to scorn...... Mt 9:24
And they *l* him to scorn...... Mk 5:40
they *l* him to scorn, knowing that...... Lk 8:53

**LAUGHETH**
he *l* at the shaking of a spear...... Job 41:29

**LAUGHING**
Till he fill thy mouth with *l*...... Job 8:21

**LAUGHTER**
Then was our mouth filled with *l*...... Ps 126:2
Even in *l* the heart is sorrowful...... Prov 14:13
I said of *l*, It is mad...... Eccl 2:2
Sorrow is better than *l*...... Eccl 7:3
a pot, so is the *l* of the fool...... Eccl 7:6
A feast is made for *l*, and wine...... Eccl 10:19
let your *l* be turned to mourning,...... Jas 4:9

**LAUNCH**
*L* out into the deep, and let down...... Lk 5:4

**LAUNCHED**
And they *l* forth...... Lk 8:22
were gotten from them, and had *l*...... Acts 21:1
into a ship of Adramyttium, we *l*...... Acts 27:2
And when we had *l* from thence...... Acts 27:4

**LAVER**
Thou shalt also make a *l* of brass...... Ex 30:18
with all his vessels, and the *l*...... Ex 30:28
with all his furniture, and the *l*...... Ex 31:9
staves, and all his vessels, the *l*...... Ex 35:16
And he made the *l* of brass...... Ex 38:8
staves, and all his vessels, the *l*...... Ex 39:39
thou shalt set the *l* between the...... Ex 40:7
And thou shalt anoint the *l*...... Ex 40:11
he set the *l* between the tent of...... Ex 40:30
and all his vessels, both the *l*...... Lev 8:11
under the *l* were undersetters...... 1Kin 7:30
one *l* contained forty baths...... 1Kin 7:38
and every *l* was four cubits...... 1Kin 7:38
every one of the ten bases one *l*...... 1Kin 7:38
removed the *l* from off them...... 2Kin 16:17

**LAVERS**
Then made he ten *l* of brass...... 1Kin 7:38
And Hiram made the *l*, and the...... 1Kin 7:40
ten bases, and ten *l* on the bases...... 1Kin 7:43
He made also ten *l*, and put five...... 2Chr 4:6
and *l* made he upon the bases...... 2Chr 4:14

**LAVISH**
They *l* gold out of the bag, and...... Is 46:6

**LAW**
son, and Sarai his daughter in *l*...... Gen 11:31
son in *l*, and thy sons, and thy...... Gen 19:12
out, and spake unto his sons in *l*...... Gen 19:14
that mocked unto his sons in *l*...... Gen 19:14
Judah to Tamar his daughter in *l*...... Gen 38:11
Behold thy father in *l* goeth up...... Gen 38:13
that she was his daughter in *l*...... Gen 38:16
Tamar thy daughter in *l* hath...... Gen 38:24
she sent to her father in *l*...... Gen 38:25
Joseph made it a *l* over the land...... Gen 47:26
flock of Jethro his father in *l*...... Ex 3:1
to Jethro his father in *l*...... Ex 4:18
One *l* shall be to him that is...... Ex 12:49
that the LORD's *l* may be in thy...... Ex 13:9
whether they will walk in my *l*...... Ex 16:4
of Midian, Moses' father in *l*...... Ex 18:1
Then Jethro, Moses' father in *l*...... Ex 18:2
And Jethro, Moses' father in *l*...... Ex 18:5
I thy father in *l* Jethro am come...... Ex 18:6
went out to meet his father in *l*...... Ex 18:7
Moses told his father in *l* all...... Ex 18:8
And Jethro, Moses' father in *l*...... Ex 18:12
Moses' father in *l* before God...... Ex 18:12
when Moses' father in *l* saw all...... Ex 18:14
Moses said unto his father in *l*...... Ex 18:15
Moses' father in *l* said unto him...... Ex 18:17
to the voice of his father in *l*...... Ex 18:24
Moses let his father in *l* depart...... Ex 18:27
give thee tables of stone, and a *l*...... Ex 24:12
This is the *l* of the burnt...... Lev 6:9
this is the *l* of the meat...... Lev 6:14
This is the *l* of the sin offering...... Lev 6:25
Likewise this is the *l* of the...... Lev 7:1
there is one *l* for them...... Lev 7:7
this is the *l* of the sacrifice of...... Lev 7:11
This is the *l* of the burnt...... Lev 7:37
This is the *l* of the beasts, and...... Lev 11:46
This is the *l* for her that hath...... Lev 12:7
This is the *l* of the plague of...... Lev 13:59
This shall be the *l* of the leper...... Lev 14:2

L

This is the *l* of him in whom is... Lev 14:32
This is the *l* for all manner of... Lev 14:54
this is the *l* of leprosy... Lev 14:57
This is the *l* of him that hath an... Lev 15:32
nakedness of thy daughter in *l*... Lev 18:15
a man lie with his daughter in *l*... Lev 20:12
Ye shall have one manner of *l*... Lev 24:22
This is the *l* of jealousies, when... Num 5:29
shall execute upon her all this *l*... Num 5:30
this is the *l* of the Nazarite,... Num 6:13
This is the *l* of the Nazarite who... Num 6:21
do after the *l* of his separation... Num 6:21
the Midianite, Moses' father in *l*... Num 10:29
One *l* and one manner shall be for... Num 15:16
Ye shall have one *l* for him that... Num 15:29
This is the ordinance of the *l*... Num 19:2
This is the *l*, when a man dieth... Num 19:14
This is the ordinance of the *l*... Num 31:21
began Moses to declare this *l*... Deut 1:5
so righteous as all this *l*... Deut 4:8
this is the *l* which Moses set... Deut 4:44
to the sentence of the *l* which... Deut 17:11
*l* in a book out of that which is... Deut 17:18
to keep all the words of this *l*... Deut 17:19
upon them all the words of this *l*... Deut 27:3
the words of this *l* very plainly... Deut 27:8
that lieth with his mother in *l*... Deut 27:23
the words of this *l* to do them... Deut 27:26
to do all the words of this *l*... Deut 28:58
not written in the book of this *l*... Deut 28:61
are written in this book of the *l*... Deut 29:21
we may do all the words of this *l*... Deut 29:29
are written in this book of the *l*... Deut 30:10
And Moses wrote this *l*, and... Deut 31:9
thou shalt read this *l* before all... Deut 31:11
to do all the words of this *l*... Deut 31:12
the words of this *l* in a book... Deut 31:24
Take this book of the *l*, and put... Deut 31:26
to do, all the words of this *l*... Deut 32:46
hand went a fiery *l* for them... Deut 33:2
Moses commanded us a *l*, even the... Deut 33:4
thy judgments, and Israel thy *l*... Deut 33:10
to do according to all the *l*... Josh 1:7
This book of the *l* shall not... Josh 1:8
in the book of the *l* of Moses... Josh 8:31
stones a copy of the *l* of Moses... Josh 8:32
he read all the words of the *l*... Josh 8:34
is written in the book of the *l*... Josh 8:34
to do the commandment and the *l*... Josh 22:5
in the book of the *l* of Moses... Josh 23:6
words in the book of the *l* of God... Josh 24:26
of the Kenite, Moses' father in *l*... Judg 1:16
of Hobab the father in *l* of Moses... Judg 4:11
the son in *l* of the Timnite,... Judg 15:6
And his father in *l*, the damsel's... Judg 19:4
father said unto his son in *l*... Judg 19:5
depart, his father in *l* urged him... Judg 19:7
and his servant, his father in *l*... Judg 19:9
she arose with her daughters in *l*... Ruth 1:6
her two daughters in *l* with her... Ruth 1:7
said unto her two daughters in *l*... Ruth 1:8
and Orpah kissed her mother in *l*... Ruth 1:14
thy sister in *l* is gone back unto... Ruth 1:15
return thou after thy sister in *l*... Ruth 1:15
the Moabitess, her daughter in *l*... Ruth 1:22
in *l* since the death of thine... Ruth 2:11
her mother in *l* saw what she had... Ruth 2:18
And her mother in *l* said unto her... Ruth 2:19
she shewed her mother in *l* with... Ruth 2:19
Naomi said unto her daughter in *l*... Ruth 2:20
said unto Ruth her daughter in *l*... Ruth 2:22
and dwelt with her mother in *l*... Ruth 2:23
her mother in *l* said unto her... Ruth 3:1
all that her mother in *l* bade her... Ruth 3:6
when she came to her mother in *l*... Ruth 3:16
Go not empty unto thy mother in *l*... Ruth 3:17
for thy daughter in *l*, which... Ruth 4:15
And his daughter in *l*, Phinehas'... 1Sa 4:19
taken, and that her father in *l*... 1Sa 4:19
and because of her father in *l*... 1Sa 4:21
I should be son in *l* to the king... 1Sa 18:18
son in *l* in the one of the twain... 1Sa 18:21
therefore be the king's son in *l*... 1Sa 18:22
thing to be a king's son in *l*... 1Sa 18:23
well to be the king's son in *l*... 1Sa 18:26
he might be the king's son in *l*... 1Sa 18:27
which is the king's son in *l*... 1Sa 22:14
it is written in the *l* of Moses... 1Kin 2:3
the son in *l* of the house of Ahab... 2Kin 8:27
took no heed to walk in the *l* of... 2Kin 10:31
in the book of the *l* of Moses... 2Kin 14:6
according to all the *l* which I... 2Kin 17:13
their ordinances, or after the *l*... 2Kin 17:34
and the ordinances, and the *l*... 2Kin 17:37
according to all the *l* that my... 2Kin 21:8
of the *l* in the house of the LORD... 2Kin 22:8
the words of the book of the *l*... 2Kin 22:11
*l* which were written in the book... 2Kin 23:24
according to all the *l* of Moses... 2Kin 23:25
his daughter in *l* bare him Pharez... 1Chr 2:4
the same to Jacob for a *l*... 1Chr 16:17
is written in the *l* of the LORD... 1Chr 16:40
keep the *l* of the LORD thy God... 1Chr 22:12
heed to their way to walk in my *l*... 2Chr 6:16
he forsook the *l* of the LORD... 2Chr 12:1
of their fathers, and to do the *l*... 2Chr 14:4
a teaching priest, and without *l*... 2Chr 15:3
had the book of the *l* of the LORD... 2Chr 17:9
between blood and blood, between *l*. 2Chr 19:10
it is written in the *l* of Moses... 2Chr 23:18
in the *l* in the book of Moses... 2Chr 25:4
according to the *l* of Moses the... 2Chr 30:16
is written in the *l* of the LORD... 2Chr 31:3
encouraged in the *l* of the LORD... 2Chr 31:4
of the house of God, and in the *l*... 2Chr 31:21
them, according to the whole *l*... 2Chr 33:8
the *l* of the LORD given by Moses... 2Chr 34:14
of the *l* in the house of the LORD... 2Chr 34:15
king had heard the words of the *l*... 2Chr 34:19
was written in the *l* of the LORD... 2Chr 35:26
in the *l* of Moses the man of God... Ezr 3:2
a ready scribe in the *l* of Moses... Ezr 7:6
heart to seek the *l* of the LORD... Ezr 7:10
a scribe of the *l* of the God of... Ezr 7:12
according to the *l* of thy God... Ezr 7:14
the scribe of the *l* of the God of... Ezr 7:21
will not do the *l* of thy God... Ezr 7:26
the *l* of the king, let judgment... Ezr 7:26
let it be done according to the *l*... Ezr 10:3
because he was the son in *l* of... Neh 6:18
bring the book of the *l* of Moses... Neh 8:1
Ezra the priest brought the *l*... Neh 8:2
attentive unto the book of the *l*... Neh 8:3
the people to understand the *l*... Neh 8:7
book in the *l* of God distinctly... Neh 8:8
they heard the words of the *l*... Neh 8:9
to understand the words of the *l*... Neh 8:13
they found written in the *l* which... Neh 8:14
read in the book of the *l* of God... Neh 8:18
read in the book of the *l* of the... Neh 9:3
cast thy *l* behind their backs, and... Neh 9:26
bring them again unto thy *l*... Neh 9:29
nor our fathers, kept thy *l*... Neh 9:34
of the lands unto the *l* of God... Neh 10:28
into an oath, to walk in God's *l*... Neh 10:29
God, as it is written in the *l*... Neh 10:34
cattle, as it is written in the *l*... Neh 10:36
portions of the *l* for the priests... Neh 12:44
pass, when they had heard the *l*... Neh 13:3
was son in *l* to Sanballat the... Neh 13:28
drinking was according to the *l*... Est 1:8
manner toward all that knew *l*... Est 1:13
the queen Vashti according to *l*... Est 1:15
there is one *l* of his to put him... Est 4:11
which is not according to the *l*... Est 4:16
the *l* from his mouth, and lay up... Job 22:22
delight is in the *l* of the LORD... Ps 1:2
in his *l* doth he meditate day and... Ps 1:2
The *l* of the LORD is perfect,... Ps 19:7
The *l* of his God is in his heart... Ps 37:31
yea, thy *l* is within my heart... Ps 40:8
Give ear, O my people, to my *l*... Ps 78:1
Jacob, and appointed a *l* in Israel... Ps 78:5
God, and refused to walk in his *l*... Ps 78:10
and a *l* of the God of Jacob... Ps 81:4
If his children forsake my *l*... Ps 89:30
and teachest him out of thy *l*... Ps 94:12
which frameth mischief by a *l*... Ps 94:20
the same unto Jacob for a *l*... Ps 105:10
who walk in the *l* of the LORD... Ps 119:1
wondrous things out of thy *l*... Ps 119:18
and grant me thy *l* graciously... Ps 119:29
and I shall keep thy *l*... Ps 119:34
So shall I keep thy *l* continually... Ps 119:44
have I not declined from thy *l*... Ps 119:51
of the wicked that forsake thy *l*... Ps 119:53
in the night, and have kept thy *l*... Ps 119:55
but I have not forgotten thy *l*... Ps 119:61
but I delight in thy *l*... Ps 119:70
The *l* of thy mouth is better unto... Ps 119:72
for thy *l* is my delight... Ps 119:77
for me, which are not after thy *l*... Ps 119:85
Unless thy *l* had been my delights... Ps 119:92
O how love I thy *l*... Ps 119:97
yet do I not forget thy *l*... Ps 119:109
but thy *l* do I love... Ps 119:113
for they have made void thy *l*... Ps 119:126
eyes, because they keep not thy *l*... Ps 119:136
and thy *l* is the truth... Ps 119:142
they are far from thy *l*... Ps 119:150
for I do not forget thy *l*... Ps 119:153
but thy *l* do I love... Ps 119:163
peace have they which love thy *l*... Ps 119:165
and thy *l* is my delight... Ps 119:174
forsake not the *l* of thy mother... Prov 1:8
My son, forget not my *l*... Prov 3:1
doctrine, forsake ye not my *l*... Prov 4:2
forsake not the *l* of thy mother... Prov 6:20
and the *l* is light... Prov 6:23
my *l* as the apple of thine eye... Prov 7:2
The *l* of the wise is a fountain... Prov 13:14
forsake the *l* praise the wicked... Prov 28:4
as keep the *l* contend with them... Prov 28:4
Whoso keepeth the *l* is a wise son... Prov 28:7
away his ear from hearing the *l*... Prov 28:9
but he that keepeth the *l*... Prov 29:18
Lest they drink, and forget the *l*... Prov 31:5
her tongue is the *l* of kindness... Prov 31:26
give ear unto the *l* of our God... Is 1:10
out of Zion shall go forth the *l*... Is 2:3
away the *l* of the LORD of hosts... Is 5:24
seal the *l* among my disciples... Is 8:16
To the *l* and to the testimony... Is 8:20
will not hear the *l* of the LORD... Is 30:9
and the isles shall wait for his *l*... Is 42:4
he will magnify the *l*, and make it... Is 42:21
were they obedient unto his *l*... Is 42:24
for a *l* shall proceed from me, and... Is 51:4
the people in whose heart is my *l*... Is 51:7
that handle the *l* knew me not... Jer 2:8
unto my words, nor to my *l*... Jer 6:19
the *l* of the LORD is with us... Jer 8:8
my *l* which I set before them... Jer 9:13
me, and have not kept my *l*... Jer 16:11
for the *l* shall not perish from... Jer 18:18
hearken to me, to walk in my *l*... Jer 26:4
I will put my *l* in their inward... Jer 31:33
was sealed according to the *l*... Jer 32:11
voice, neither walked in thy *l*... Jer 32:23
they feared, nor walked in my *l*... Jer 44:10
of the LORD, nor walked in his *l*... Jer 44:23
the *l* is no more... Lam 2:9
but the *l* shall perish from the... Eze 7:26
lewdly defiled his daughter in *l*... Eze 22:11
Her priests have violated my *l*... Eze 22:26
This is the *l* of the house... Eze 43:12
this is the *l* of the house... Eze 43:12
him concerning the *l* of his God... Dan 6:5
according to the *l* of the Medes... Dan 6:8
according to the *l* of the Medes... Dan 6:12
that the *l* of the Medes and... Dan 6:15
Israel have transgressed thy *l*... Dan 9:11
the *l* of Moses the servant of God... Dan 9:11
it is written in the *l* of Moses... Dan 9:13
hast forgotten the *l* of thy God... Hos 4:6
and trespassed against my *l*... Hos 8:1
to him the great things of my *l*... Hos 8:12
have despised the *l* of the LORD... Amos 2:4
for the *l* shall go forth of Zion,... Mic 4:2
the daughter in *l* against her... Mic 7:6
against her mother in *l*... Mic 7:6
Therefore the *l* is slacked... Hab 1:4
they have done violence to the *l*... Zeph 3:4
now the priests concerning the *l*... Hag 2:11
lest they should hear the *l*... Zec 7:12
The *l* of truth was in his mouth,... Mal 2:6
should seek the *l* at his mouth... Mal 2:7
caused many to stumble at the *l*... Mal 2:8
but have been partial in the *l*... Mal 2:9
Remember ye the *l* of Moses my... Mal 4:4
that I am come to destroy the *l*... Mt 5:17
shall in no wise pass from the *l*... Mt 5:18
if any man will sue thee at the *l*... Mt 5:40
for this is the *l* and the prophets... Mt 7:12
the daughter in *l* against her... Mt 10:35
against her mother in *l*... Mt 10:35
the *l* prophesied until John... Mt 11:13
Or have ye not read in the *l*... Mt 12:5
is the great commandment in the *l*... Mt 22:36
two commandments hang all the *l*... Mt 22:40
the weightier matters of the *l*... Mt 23:23
the *l* of Moses were accomplished... Lk 2:22
is written in the *l* of the Lord... Lk 2:23
is said in the *l* of the Lord... Lk 2:24
for him after the custom of the *l*... Lk 2:27
according to the *l* of the Lord... Lk 2:39
and doctors of the *l* sitting by... Lk 5:17
him, What is written in the *l*... Lk 10:26
the mother in *l* against her... Lk 12:53
against her daughter in *l*... Lk 12:53
the daughter in *l* against her... Lk 12:53
against her mother in *l*... Lk 12:53
The *l* and the prophets were until... Lk 16:16
than one tittle of the *l* to fail... Lk 16:17
were written in the *l* of Moses... Lk 24:44
For the *l* was given by Moses, but... Jn 1:17
found him, of whom Moses in the *l*... Jn 1:45
Did not Moses give you the *l*... Jn 7:19
and yet none of you keepeth the *l*... Jn 7:19
that the *l* of Moses should not be... Jn 7:23
who knoweth not the *l* are cursed... Jn 7:49
Doth our *l* judge any man, before... Jn 7:51
Now Moses in the *l* commanded us... Jn 8:5
It is also written in your *l*... Jn 8:17
them, Is it not written in your *l*... Jn 10:34
We have heard out of the *l* that... Jn 12:34
that is written in their *l*... Jn 15:25
he was father in *l* to Caiaphas... Jn 18:13
and judge him according to your *l*... Jn 18:31
Jews answered him, We have a *l*... Jn 19:7
by our *l* he ought to die, because... Jn 19:7
named Gamaliel, a doctor of the *l*... Acts 5:34
against this holy place, and the *l*... Acts 6:13
Who have received the *l* by the... Acts 7:53
And after the reading of the *l*... Acts 13:15
be justified by the *l* of Moses... Acts 13:39
them to keep the *l* of Moses... Acts 15:5
be circumcised, and keep the *l*... Acts 15:24
to worship God contrary to the *l*... Acts 18:13
of words and names, and of your *l*... Acts 18:15
the *l* is open, and there are... Acts 19:38
and they are all zealous of the *l*... Acts 21:20
walkest orderly, and keepest the *l*... Acts 21:24
against the people, and the *l*... Acts 21:28
manner of the *l* of the fathers... Acts 22:3
a devout man according to the *l*... Acts 22:12
thou to judge me after the *l*... Acts 23:3
to be smitten contrary to the *l*... Acts 23:3
accused of questions of their *l*... Acts 23:29
have judged according to our *l*... Acts 24:6
things which are written in the *l*... Acts 24:14
Neither against the *l* of the Jews... Acts 25:8
Jesus, both out of the *l* of Moses... Acts 28:23
*l* shall also perish without *l*... Rom 2:12
the *l* shall be judged by the *l*... Rom 2:12
of the *l* are just before God... Rom 2:13
doers of the *l* shall be justified... Rom 2:13
Gentiles, which have not the *l*... Rom 2:14
the things contained in the *l*... Rom 2:14
these, having not the *l*... Rom 2:14

the *l*, are a *l* unto themselves Rom 2:14
of the *l* written in their hearts Rom 2:15
called a Jew, and restest in the *l* Rom 2:17
being instructed out of the *l* Rom 2:18
and of the truth in the *l* Rom 2:20
that makest thy boast of the *l* Rom 2:23
through breaking the *l* Rom 2:23
profiteth, if thou keep the *l* Rom 2:25
but if thou be a breaker of the *l* Rom 2:25
keep the righteousness of the *l* Rom 2:26
is by nature, if it fulfil the *l* Rom 2:27
dost transgress the *l* Rom 2:27
what things soever the *l* saith Rom 3:19
saith to them who are under the *l* Rom 3:19
of the *l* there shall no flesh be Rom 3:20
for by the *l* is the knowledge of Rom 3:20
God without the *l* is manifested Rom 3:21
being witnessed by the *l* Rom 3:21
By what *l*? Rom 3:27
but by the *l* of faith Rom 3:27
faith without the deeds of the *l* Rom 3:28
make void the *l* through faith Rom 3:31
yea, we establish the *l* Rom 3:31
or to his seed, through the *l* Rom 4:13
they which are of the *l* be heirs Rom 4:14
Because the *l* worketh wrath Rom 4:15
for where no *l* is, there is no Rom 4:15
to that only which is of the *l* Rom 4:16
(For until the *l* sin was in the Rom 5:13
is not imputed when there is no *l* Rom 5:13
Moreover the *l* entered, that the Rom 5:20
for ye are not under the *l* Rom 6:14
because we are not under the *l* Rom 6:15
I speak to them that know the *l* Rom 7:1
how that the *l* hath dominion Rom 7:1
*l* to her husband so long as he Rom 7:2
loosed from the *l* of her husband Rom 7:2
be dead, she is free from that *l* Rom 7:3
to the *l* by the body of Christ Rom 7:4
of sins, which were by the *l* Rom 7:5
now we are delivered from the *l* Rom 7:6
Is the *l* sin Rom 7:7
I had not known sin, but by the *l* Rom 7:7
known lust, except the *l* had said Rom 7:7
For without the *l* sin was dead Rom 7:8
I was alive without the *l* once Rom 7:9
Wherefore the *l* is holy, and the Rom 7:12
we know that the *l* is spiritual Rom 7:14
unto the *l* that it is good Rom 7:16
I find then a *l*, that, when I Rom 7:21
For I delight in the *l* of God Rom 7:22
But I see another *l* in my members Rom 7:23
warring against the *l* of my mind Rom 7:23
me into captivity to the *l* of sin Rom 7:23
mind I myself serve the *l* of God Rom 7:25
but with the flesh the *l* of sin Rom 7:25
For the *l* of the the Spirit of Rom 8:2
made me free from the *l* of sin Rom 8:2
For what the *l* could not do Rom 8:3
of the *l* might be fulfilled in us Rom 8:4
it is not subject to the *l* of God Rom 8:7
covenants, and the giving of the *l* Rom 9:4
after the *l* of righteousness Rom 9:31
to the *l* of righteousness Rom 9:31
as it were by the works of the *l* Rom 9:32
For Christ is the end of the *l* Rom 10:4
righteousness which is of the *l* Rom 10:5
another hath fulfilled the *l* Rom 13:8
love is the fulfilling of the *l* Rom 13:10
go to *l* before the unjust, and not 1Cor 6:1
brother goeth to *l* with brother 1Cor 6:6
ye go to *l* one with another 1Cor 6:7
The wife is bound by the *l* as 1Cor 7:39
or saith not the *l* the same also 1Cor 9:8
it is written in the *l* of Moses 1Cor 9:9
are under the *l*, as under the *l* 1Cor 9:20
gain them that are under the *l* 1Cor 9:20
are without *l*, as without *l* 1Cor 9:21
*l*, (being not without *l* to God 1Cor 9:21
but under the *l* to Christ 1Cor 9:21
gain them that are without *l* 1Cor 9:21
In the *l* it is written, With men 1Cor 14:21
obedience, as also saith the *l* 1Cor 14:34
and the strength of sin is the *l* 1Cor 15:56
justified by the works of the *l* Gal 2:16
and not by the works of the *l* Gal 2:16
for by the works of the *l* shall Gal 2:16
For I through the *l* am dead to Gal 2:19
through the *l* am dead to the *l* Gal 2:19
if righteousness come by the *l* Gal 2:21
the Spirit by the works of the *l* Gal 3:2
doeth he it by the works of the *l* Gal 3:5
of the *l* are under the curse Gal 3:10
in the book of the *l* to do them Gal 3:10
by the *l* in the sight of God Gal 3:11
And the *l* is not of faith Gal 3:12
us from the curse of the *l* Gal 3:13
before of God in Christ, the *l* Gal 3:17
if the inheritance be of the *l* Gal 3:18
Wherefore then serveth the *l* Gal 3:19
Is the *l* then against the Gal 3:21
for if there had been a *l* given Gal 3:21
should have been by the *l* Gal 3:21
came, we were kept under the *l* Gal 3:23
Wherefore the *l* was our Gal 3:24
made of a woman, made under the *l* Gal 4:4
redeem them that were under the *l* Gal 4:5
ye that desire to be under the *l* Gal 4:21
do ye not hear the *l* Gal 4:21
he is a debtor to do the whole *l* Gal 5:3
of you are justified by the *l* Gal 5:4
For all the *l* is fulfilled in one Gal 5:14
Spirit, ye are not under the *l* Gal 5:18
against such there is no *l* Gal 5:23
and so fulfil the *l* of Christ Gal 6:2
who are circumcised keep the *l* Gal 6:13
even the *l* of commandments Eph 2:15
as touching the *l*, a Pharisee Phil 3:5
righteousness which is in the *l* Phil 3:6
righteousness, which is of the *l* Phil 3:9
Desiring to be teachers of the *l* 1Ti 1:7
But we know that the *l* is good 1Ti 1:8
that the *l* is not made for a 1Ti 1:9
and strivings about the *l* Titus 3:9
of the people according to the *l* Heb 7:5
it the people received the *l* Heb 7:11
necessity a change also of the *l* Heb 7:12
not after the *l* of a carnal Heb 7:16
For the *l* made nothing perfect, Heb 7:19
For the *l* maketh men high priests Heb 7:28
the oath, which was since the *l* Heb 7:28
offer gifts according to the *l* Heb 8:4
all the people according to the *l* Heb 9:19
are by the *l* purged with blood Heb 9:22
For the *l* having a shadow of good Heb 10:1
which are offered by the *l* Heb 10:8
He that despised Moses' *l* died Heb 10:28
into the perfect *l* of liberty Jas 1:25
If ye fulfil the royal *l* Jas 2:8
of the *l* as transgressors Jas 2:9
whosoever shall keep the whole *l* Jas 2:10
become a transgressor of the *l* Jas 2:11
be judged by the *l* of liberty Jas 2:12
evil of the *l*, and judgeth the *l* Jas 4:11
but if thou judge the *l* Jas 4:11
thou art not a doer of the *l* Jas 4:11
sin transgresseth also the *l* 1Jn 3:4
sin is the transgression of the *l* 1Jn 3:4

## LAWFUL
it shall not be *l* to impose toll Ezr 7:24
or the *l* captive delivered Is 49:24
be just, and do that which is *l* Eze 18:5
the son hath done that which is *l* Eze 18:19
statutes, and do that which is *l* Eze 18:21
and doeth that which is *l* Eze 18:27
his sin, and do that which is *l* Eze 33:14
he hath done that which is *l* Eze 33:16
wickedness, and do that which is *l* Eze 33:19
not *l* to do upon the sabbath day Mt 12:2
which was not *l* for him to eat, Mt 12:4
Is it *l* to heal on the sabbath Mt 12:10
Wherefore it is *l* to do well on Mt 12:12
It is not *l* for thee to have her Mt 14:4
Is it *l* for a man to put away his Mt 19:3
Is it not *l* for me to do what I Mt 20:15
Is it *l* to give tribute unto Mt 22:17
It is not *l* for to put them into Mt 27:6
sabbath day that which is not *l* Mk 2:24
which is not *l* to eat but for the Mk 2:26
Is it *l* to do good on the sabbath Mk 3:4
It is not *l* for thee to have thy Mk 6:18
Is it *l* for a man to put away his Mk 10:2
Is it *l* to give tribute to Caesar Mk 12:14
not *l* to do on the sabbath days Lk 6:2
which it is not *l* to eat but for Lk 6:4
Is it *l* on the sabbath days to do Lk 6:9
Is it *l* to heal on the sabbath Lk 14:3
Is it *l* for us to give tribute Lk 20:22
it is not *l* for thee to carry thy Jn 5:10
It is not *l* for us to put any man Jn 18:31
which are not *l* for us to receive Acts 16:21
be determined in a *l* assembly Acts 19:39
Is it *l* for you to scourge a man Acts 22:25
All things are *l* unto me, but all 1Cor 6:12
all things are *l* for me, but I 1Cor 6:12
All things are *l* for me, but all 1Cor 10:23
all things are *l* for me, but all 1Cor 10:23
which it is not *l* for a man to 2Cor 12:4

## LAWFULLY
law is good, if a man use it *l* 1Ti 1:8
not crowned, except he strive *l* 2Ti 2:5

## LAWGIVER
nor a *l* from between his feet, Gen 49:10
it, by the direction of the *l* Num 21:18
there, in a portion of the *l* Deut 33:21
Judah is my *l* Ps 60:7
Judah is my *l* Ps 108:8
is our judge, the LORD is our *l* Is 33:22
There is one *l*, who is able to Jas 4:12

## LAWLESS
a righteous man, but for the *l* 1Ti 1:9

## LAWS
my statutes, and my *l* Gen 26:5
to keep my commandments and my *l* Ex 16:28
the statutes of God, and his *l* Ex 18:16
shalt teach them ordinances and *l* Ex 18:20
the statutes and judgments and *l* Lev 26:46
all such as know the *l* of thy God Ezr 7:25
them right judgments, and true *l* Neh 9:13
them precepts, statutes, and *l* Neh 9:14
among the *l* of the Persians Est 1:19
their *l* are diverse from all Est 3:8
neither keep they the king's *l* Est 3:8
his statutes, and keep his *l* Ps 105:45
they have transgressed the *l* Is 24:5
thereof, and all the *l* thereof Eze 43:11
of the LORD, and all the *l* thereof Eze 44:5
and they shall keep my *l* and my Eze 44:24
and think to change times and *l* Dan 7:25
LORD our God, to walk in his *l* Dan 9:10
I will put my *l* into their mind, Heb 8:10
I will put my *l* into their hearts Heb 10:16

## LAWYER
Then one of them, which was a *l* Mt 22:35
And, behold, a certain *l* stood up Lk 10:25
Bring Zenas the *l* and Apollos on Titus 3:13

## LAWYERS
*l* rejected the counsel of God Lk 7:30
Then answered one of the *l* Lk 11:45
he said, Woe unto you also, ye *l* Lk 11:46
Woe unto you, *l* Lk 11:52
Jesus answering spake unto the *l* Lk 14:3

## LAY
But before they *l* down, the men Gen 19:4
went in, and *l* with her father Gen 19:33
he perceived not when she *l* down Gen 19:33
I *l* yesternight with my father Gen 19:34
the younger arose, and *l* with him Gen 19:35
he perceived not when she *l* down Gen 19:35
*L* not thine hand upon the lad, Gen 22:12
*l* down in that place to sleep Gen 28:11
And he *l* with her that night Gen 30:16
*l* with her, and defiled her Gen 34:2
*l* with Bilhah his father's Gen 35:22
wilderness, and *l* no hand upon him Gen 37:22
*l* up corn under the hand of Gen 41:35
heretofore, ye shall *l* upon them Ex 5:8
that I may *l* my hand upon Egypt, Ex 7:4
the dew *l* round about the host Ex 16:13
when the dew that *l* was gone up Ex 16:14
there *l* a small round thing Ex 16:14
that which remaineth over *l* up Ex 16:23
*l* it up before the LORD, to be Ex 16:33
woman's husband will *l* upon him Ex 21:22
shalt thou *l* upon him usury Ex 22:25
*l* the wood in order upon the fire Lev 1:7
shall *l* the parts, the head, and Lev 1:8
the priest shall *l* them in order Lev 1:12
it, and *l* frankincense thereon Lev 2:15
he shall *l* his hand upon the head Lev 3:2
he shall *l* his hand upon the head Lev 3:8
he shall *l* his hand upon the head Lev 3:13
shall *l* his hand upon the Lev 4:4
of the congregation shall *l* their Lev 4:15
he shall *l* his hand upon the head Lev 4:24
he shall *l* his hand upon the head Lev 4:29
he shall *l* his hand upon the head Lev 4:33
*l* the burnt offering in order Lev 6:12
Aaron shall *l* both his hands upon Lev 16:21
let all that heard him *l* their Lev 24:14
the Levites shall *l* their hands Num 8:12
*l* not the sin upon us, wherein we Num 12:11
thou shalt *l* them up in the Num 17:4
*l* them up without the camp in a Num 19:9
he *l* down as a lion, and as a Num 24:9
spirit, and *l* thine hand upon him Num 27:18
but will *l* them upon all them Deut 7:15
Therefore shall ye *l* up these my Deut 11:18
your God shall *l* the fear of you Deut 11:25
shalt *l* it up within thy gates Deut 14:28
*l* not innocent blood unto thy Deut 21:8
his mother *l* hold on him, and Deut 21:19
the man that *l* with the woman Deut 22:22
only that *l* with her shall die Deut 22:25
*l* hold on her, and lie with her, Deut 22:28
Then the man that *l* with her Deut 22:29
he shall *l* the foundation thereof Josh 6:26
*l* thee an ambush for the city Josh 8:2
all that *l* near Ashdod, with Josh 15:46
her tent, behold, Sisera *l* dead Judg 4:22
feet he bowed, he fell, he *l* down Judg 5:27
*l* them upon this rock, and pour Judg 6:20
east *l* along in the valley like Judg 7:12
it, that the tent *l* along Judg 7:13
because she *l* sore upon him Judg 14:17
Samson *l* till midnight, and arose Judg 16:3
*l* thine hand upon thy mouth, and Judg 18:19
uncover his feet, and *l* thee down Ruth 3:4
and, behold, a woman *l* at his feet Ruth 3:8
she *l* at his feet until the Ruth 3:14
how they *l* with the women that 1Sa 2:22
And he went and *l* down 1Sa 3:5
went and *l* down in his place 1Sa 3:9
Samuel *l* until the morning, and 1Sa 3:15
the LORD, and *l* it upon the cart 1Sa 6:8
*l* it for a reproach upon all 1Sa 11:2
*l* down naked all that day and all 1Sa 19:24
beheld the place where Saul *l* 1Sa 26:5
Saul *l* in the trench, and the 1Sa 26:5
Saul *l* sleeping within the trench 1Sa 26:7
the people *l* round about him 1Sa 26:7
*l* thee hold on one of the young 2Sa 2:21
who *l* on a bed at noon 2Sa 4:5
he *l* on his bed in his bedchamber 2Sa 4:7
in unto him, and he *l* with her 2Sa 11:4
*l* in his bosom, and was unto him 2Sa 12:3
*l* all night upon the earth 2Sa 12:16
went in unto her, and *l* with her 2Sa 12:24
*L* thee down on thy bed, and make 2Sa 13:5
So Amnon *l* down, and made himself 2Sa 13:6
she, forced her, and *l* with her 2Sa 13:14
his garments, and *l* on the earth 2Sa 13:31
sustenance while he *l* at Mahanaim 2Sa 19:32
to *l* the foundation of the house 1Kin 5:17
that *l* on forty five pillars, 1Kin 7:3
the altar, saying, *L* hold on him 1Kin 13:4
*l* my bones beside his bones 1Kin 13:31

l it on wood, and put no fire................ 1Kin 18:23
l it on wood, and put no fire................ 1Kin 18:23
And as he l and slept under a .......... 1Kin 19:5
l in sackcloth, and went softly........... 1Kin 21:27
into the chamber, and l there.............. 2Kin 4:11
l my staff upon the face of the............. 2Kin 4:29
l upon the child, and put his............... 2Kin 4:34
for Joram l there.................................. 2Kin 9:16
L ye them in two heaps at the.............. 2Kin 10:8
be to l waste fenced cities into .......... 2Kin 19:25
to l the foundation of the heaps.......... 2Chr 31:7
for as long as she l desolate she......... 2Chr 36:21
of such as l in wait by the way.............. Ezr 8:31
so again, I will l hands on you............. Neh 13:21
sought to l hand on the king.................. Est 2:21
he thought scorn to l hands on .............. Est 3:6
many l in sackcloth and ashes................ Est 4:3
who sought to l hand on the king ............ Est 6:2
to l hand on such as sought their............ Est 9:2
that might l his hand upon us.............. Job 9:33
L down now, put me in a surety.......... Job 17:3
l your hand upon your mouth............... Job 21:5
l up his words in thine heart.............. Job 22:22
Then shalt thou l up gold as dust......... Job 22:24
the dew l all night upon my................. Job 29:19
For he will not l upon man more.......... Job 34:23
I will l mine hand upon my mouth ........ Job 40:4
L thine hand upon him, remember......... Job 41:8
I will both l me down in peace,................. Ps 4:8
l mine honour in the dust......................... Ps 7:5
after my life l snares for me................... Ps 38:12
they that l wait for my soul take............ Ps 71:10
where she may l her young........................ Ps 84:3
l them down in their dens ..................... Ps 104:22
let us l wait for blood, let us.................. Prov 1:11
they l wait for their own blood............... Prov 1:18
life to them that l hold upon her............. Prov 3:18
l up my commandments with thee......... Prov 7:1
Wise men l up knowledge .................... Prov 10:14
L not wait, O wicked man, against.... Prov 24:15
l thine hand upon thy mouth................. Prov 30:32
to l hold on folly, till I might................... Eccl 2:3
the living will l it to his heart.................. Eccl 7:2
And I will l it waste ................................... Is 5:6
that l field to field, till there.................... Is 5:8
l hold of the prey, and shall ...................... Is 5:29
they shall l their hand upon Edom.......... Is 11:14
anger, to l the land desolate...................... Is 13:9
will l low the haughtiness of the............ Is 13:11
David will I l upon his shoulder.............. Is 22:22
l low, and bring to the ground,................ Is 25:12
I l in Zion for a foundation a................... Is 28:16
also will I l to the line ........................... Is 28:17
will l siege against thee with a.................. Is 29:3
l a snare for him that reproveth .............. Is 29:21
which the LORD shall l upon him.............. Is 30:32
the great owl make her nest, and l.......... Is 34:15
of dragons, where each l, shall................... Is 35:7
that thou shouldest be to l waste............. Is 37:26
l it for a plaister upon the boil ................ Is 38:21
so that thou didst not l these ..................... Is 47:7
l the foundations of the earth,................ Is 51:16
I will l thy stones with fair..................... Is 54:11
l thy foundations with sapphires ............ Is 54:11
they l wait, as he that setteth ................. Jer 5:26
I will l stumblingblocks before................ Jer 6:21
They shall l hold on bow and spear........ Jer 6:23
I l a stumblingblock before him,............. Eze 3:20
l it before thee, and pourtray .................... Eze 4:1
l siege against it, and build a .................. Eze 4:2
thou shalt l siege against it...................... Eze 4:3
l the iniquity of the house of.................... Eze 4:4
I will l bands upon thee, and thou .......... Eze 4:8
I will l the dead carcases of the................ Eze 6:5
she l down among lions, she..................... Eze 19:2
for in her youth they l with her............... Eze 23:8
I will l my vengeance upon Edom......... Eze 25:14
when I shall l my vengeance upon ...... Eze 25:17
and they shall l thy stones................... Eze 26:12
l away their robes, and put off.............. Eze 26:16
I will l thee before kings, that.............. Eze 28:17
I will l thy flesh upon the....................... Eze 32:5
For I will l the land most ..................... Eze 33:28
I will l thy cities waste, and.................. Eze 35:4
it, and l no famine upon you ................ Eze 36:29
whereas it l desolate in the................... Eze 36:34
I will l sinews upon you, and will............ Eze 37:6
there shall they l the most holy.............. Eze 42:13
but there they shall l their ................... Eze 42:14
l them in the holy chambers, and......... Eze 44:19
they l themselves down upon................. Amos 2:8
and he l, and was fast asleep ............... Jonah 1:5
l not upon us innocent blood............... Jonah 1:14
idols thereof will I l desolate.................... Mic 1:7
they shall l their hand upon ................... Mic 7:16
they shall l hold every one on............... Zec 14:13
and if ye will not l it to heart.................. Mal 2:2
because ye do not l it to heart.................. Mal 2:2
L not up for yourselves treasures............ Mt 6:19
But l up for yourselves treasures............ Mt 6:20
man hath not where to l his head ............ Mt 8:20
l thy hand upon her, and she shall........... Mt 9:18
day, will he not l hold on it................... Mt 12:11
they sought to l hands on him .............. Mt 21:46
l them on men's shoulders........................ Mt 23:4
see the place where the Lord l .................. Mt 28:6
wife's mother l sick of a fever ................. Mk 1:30
wherein the sick of the palsy l ................... Mk 2:4
they went out to l hold on him ................. Mk 3:21
l thy hands on her, that she may............ Mk 5:23
And they sought to l hold on him ........ Mk 12:12
which l bound with them that had.......... Mk 15:7
they shall l hands on the sick,.............. Mk 16:18
him in, and to l him before him................ Lk 5:18
and took up that whereon he l................ Lk 5:25
years of age, and she l a dying ................ Lk 8:42
man hath not where to l his head............ Lk 9:58
shall l thee even with the ground ........... Lk 19:44
hour sought to l hands on him ............... Lk 20:19
they shall l their hands on you,.............. Lk 21:12
In these l a great multitude of ........................ Jn 5:3
I l down my life for the sheep ................ Jn 10:15
because I l down my life, that I.............. Jn 10:17
but I l it down of myself......................... Jn 10:18
I have power to l it down ....................... Jn 10:18
was a cave, and a stone l upon it ........... Jn 11:38
I will l down my life for thy..................... Jn 13:37
Wilt thou l down thy life for my............... Jn 13:38
that a man l down his life for.................. Jn 15:13
l not this sin to their charge ................. Acts 7:60
that on whomsoever I l hands................. Acts 8:19
to l upon you no greater burden......... Acts 15:28
and no small tempest l on us............... Acts 27:20
of Publius l sick of a fever..................... Acts 28:8
Who shall l any thing to the................... Rom 8:33
I l in Sion a stumblingstone and............ Rom 9:33
can no man l than that is laid.............. 1Cor 3:11
one of you l by him in store .................. 1Cor 16:2
ought not to l up for the parents ....... 2Cor 12:14
L hands suddenly on no man,.................... 1Ti 5:22
l hold on eternal life, whereunto ............. 1Ti 6:12
that they may l hold on eternal ................ 1Ti 6:19
who have fled for refuge to l ................... Heb 6:18
let us l aside every weight, and.............. Heb 12:1
Wherefore l apart all filthiness.................. Jas 1:21
I l in Sion a chief corner stone,............... 1Pet 2:6
we ought to l down our lives for ........... 1Jn 3:16

## LAYEDST

takest up that thou l not down ............. Lk 19:21

## LAYEST

that thou l the burden of all................ Num 11:11
wherefore then l thou a snare for ......... 1Sa 28:9

## LAYETH

God l up his iniquity for his.................. Job 21:19
yet God l not folly to them ................... Job 24:12
of him that l at him cannot hold .......... Job 41:26
he l up the depth in storehouses............... Ps 33:7
Who l the beams of his chambers ........... Ps 104:3
He l up sound wisdom for the.................. Prov 2:7
but a fool l open his folly ................... Prov 13:16
lips, and l up deceit within him.......... Prov 26:24
She l her hands to the spindle,............ Prov 31:19
the lofty city, he l it low ......................... Is 26:5
he l it low, even to the ground.................. Is 26:5
the son of man that l hold on it.................. Is 56:2
and no man l it to heart............................ Is 57:1
mouth, but in heart he l his wait............... Jer 9:8
because no man l it to heart................... Jer 12:11
l the foundation of the earth, and.......... Zec 12:1
So is he that l up treasure for................ Lk 12:21
he l it on his shoulders, ......................... Lk 15:5

## LAYING

or hurl at him by l of wait................... Num 35:20
him any thing without l of wait........ Num 35:22
they commune of l snares privily .............. Ps 64:5
For l aside the commandment of............... Mk 7:8
L wait for him, and seeking to............... Lk 11:54
when Simon saw that through l on....... Acts 8:18
But their l await was known of............. Acts 9:24
l wait in the way to kill him ................ Acts 25:3
with the l on of the hands of the ............ 1Ti 4:14
L up in store for themselves a ............... 1Ti 6:19
not l again the foundation of.................. Heb 6:1
and of l on of hands, and of.................... Heb 6:2
Wherefore l aside all malice, and ........... 1Pet 2:1

## LAZARUS (*laz'-a-rus*)

*1. Name for a beggar in a parable of Jesus.*

was a certain beggar named L................ Lk 16:20
afar off, and L in his bosom.................. Lk 16:23
have mercy on me, and send L............... Lk 16:24
things, and likewise L evil things........... Lk 16:25

*2. Man raised from the dead by Jesus.*

a certain man was sick, named L ............ Jn 11:1
hair, whose brother L was sick ................ Jn 11:2
loved Martha, and her sister, and L ......... Jn 11:5
unto them, Our friend L sleepeth ........... Jn 11:11
unto them plainly, L is dead .................. Jn 11:14
he cried with a loud voice, L .................. Jn 11:43
where L was which had been dead, ......... Jn 12:1
but L was one of them that sat at............ Jn 12:2
but that they might see L also ................ Jn 12:9
they might put L also to death............... Jn 12:10
when he called L out of his grave .......... Jn 12:17

## LEAD

I will l on softly, according as............. Gen 33:14
of a cloud, to l them the way................ Ex 13:21
they sank as l in the mighty.................. Ex 15:10
l the people unto the place of ............... Ex 32:34
them, and which may l them out........... Num 27:17
the iron, the tin, and the l.................. Num 31:22
whither the LORD shall l you............... Deut 4:27
of the armies to l the people ................. Deut 20:9
whither the LORD shall l thee.............. Deut 28:37
So the LORD alone did l him.................. Deut 32:12
l thy captivity captive, thou son............ Judg 5:12
that they may l them away.................... 1Sa 30:22
before them that l them captive........... 2Chr 30:9
them by day, to l them in the way........ Neh 9:19
pen and l in the rock for ever............... Job 19:24
L me, O LORD, in thy ................................ Ps 5:8
L me in thy truth, and teach me............ Ps 25:5
l me in a plain path, because of ............ Ps 27:11
for thy name's sake l me, and.................. Ps 31:3
let them l me............................................ Ps 43:3
who will l me into Edom........................... Ps 60:9
l me to the rock that is higher ................. Ps 61:2
who will l me into Edom......................... Ps 108:10
the LORD shall l them forth with ............ Ps 125:5
Even there shall thy hand l me ............. Ps 139:10
l me in the way everlasting .................. Ps 139:24
l me into the land of uprightness.......... Ps 143:10
When thou goest, it shall l thee............ Prov 6:22
I l in the way of righteousness, ............ Prov 8:20
I would l thee, and bring thee .............. Song 8:2
they which l thee cause thee to................. Is 3:12
and a little child shall l them ................. Is 11:6
l away the Egyptians prisoners ................ Is 20:4
shall gently l those that are .................... Is 40:11
I will l them in paths that they.............. Is 42:16
hath mercy on them shall l them ............ Is 49:10
I will l him also, and restore ................. Is 57:18
so didst thou l thy people ...................... Is 63:14
the l is consumed of the fire .................. Jer 6:29
with supplications will I l them ............... Jer 31:9
he shall l Zedekiah to Babylon,................ Jer 32:5
are brass, and tin, and iron, and l......... Eze 22:18
silver, and brass, and iron, and l.......... Eze 22:20
with silver, iron, tin, and l.................. Eze 27:12
her maids shall l her as with the ............ Nah 2:7
there was lifted up a talent of l ............... Zec 5:7
he cast the weight of l upon the .............. Zec 5:8
l us not into temptation, but.................... Mt 6:13
And if the blind l the blind.................... Mt 15:14
But when they shall l you....................... Mk 13:11
take him, and l him away safely ............ Mk 14:44
them, Can the blind l the blind................. Lk 6:39
And l us not into temptation.................... Lk 11:4
stall, and l him away to watering........... Lk 13:15
seeking some to l him by the hand .... Acts 13:11
we not power to l about a sister............. 1Cor 9:5
that we may l a quiet and.......................... 1Ti 2:2
l captive silly women laden with .............. 2Ti 3:6
l them out of the land of Egypt .............. Heb 8:9
them, and shall l them unto living.......... Rev 7:17

## LEADER

was the l of the Aaronites.................... 1Chr 12:27
and hundreds, and with every l............ 1Chr 13:1
for a witness to the people, a l................. Is 55:4

## LEADERS

mighty men of valour, and the l......... 2Chr 32:21
For the l of this people cause .................... Is 9:16
they be blind l of the blind .................... Mt 15:14

## LEADEST

thou that l Joseph like a flock.................... Ps 80:1

## LEADETH

unto the way that l to Ophrah .............. 1Sa 13:17
He l counsellors away spoiled, and....... Job 12:17
He l princes away spoiled, and............. Job 12:19
he l me beside the still waters .................. Ps 23:2
he l me in the paths of ............................ Ps 23:3
l him into the way that is not .............. Prov 16:29
which l thee by the way that thou............. Is 48:17
that l to destruction, and many.............. Mt 7:13
which l unto life, and few there .............. Mt 7:14
l them up into an high mountain.............. Mk 9:2
own sheep by name, and l them out......... Jn 10:3
iron gate that l unto the city ............... Acts 12:10
of God l thee to repentance..................... Rom 2:4
He that l into captivity shall go ........... Rev 13:10

## LEAF

mouth was an olive l pluckt off............ Gen 8:11
of a shaken l shall chase them............ Lev 26:36
Wilt thou break a l driven to................ Job 13:25
his l also shall not wither............................ Ps 1:3
shall be as an oak whose l fadeth............. Is 1:30
as the l falleth off from the ..................... Is 34:4
and we all do fade as a l ........................ Is 64:6
the fig tree, and the l shall fade .............. Jer 8:13
cometh, but her l shall be green .............. Jer 17:8
whose l shall not fade, neither .............. Eze 47:12
the l thereof for medicine..................... Eze 47:12

## LEAGUE

now therefore make ye a l with us ........ Josh 9:6
and how shall we make a l with you........ Josh 9:7
therefore now make ye a l with us ...... Josh 9:11
made a l with them, to let them .......... Josh 9:15
after they had made a l with them....... Josh 9:16
ye shall make no l with the................... Judg 2:2
made a l with the son of Jesse .............. 1Sa 22:8
saying also, Make thy l with me............ 2Sa 3:12
I will make a l with thee ...................... 2Sa 3:13
that they may make a l with thee ........ 2Sa 3:21
king David made a l with them in ........... 2Sa 5:3
and they two made a l together ............ 1Kin 5:12
There is a l between me and thee, ..... 1Kin 15:19
break thy l with Baasha king of......... 1Kin 15:19
There is a l between me and thee, ....... 2Chr 16:3
break thy l with Baasha king of........... 2Chr 16:3
For thou shalt be in l with the............... Job 5:23
the men of the land that is in l.............. Eze 30:5
after the l made with him he............... Dan 11:23

**LEAH** (*le'-ah*) See LEAH's. *Wife of Jacob.*
the name of the elder was *L* Gen 29:16
*L* was tender eyed Gen 29:17
that he took *L* his daughter Gen 29:23
Laban gave unto his daughter *L* Gen 29:24
in the morning, behold, it was *L* Gen 29:25
he loved also Rachel more than *L* Gen 29:30
the LORD saw that *L* was hated Gen 29:31
*L* conceived, and bare a son, and Gen 29:32
When *L* saw that she had left Gen 30:9
And *L* said, A troop cometh Gen 30:11
*L* said, Happy am I, for the Gen 30:13
and brought them unto his mother *L*. Gen 30:14
Then Rachel said to *L*, Give me, I Gen 30:14
*L* went out to meet him, and said, Gen 30:16
And God hearkened unto *L*, and she.. Gen 30:17
*L* said, God hath given me my hire Gen 30:18
*L* conceived again, and bare Jacob Gen 30:19
*L* said, God hath endued me with a Gen 30:20
*L* to the field unto his flock, Gen 31:4
*L* answered and said unto him, Is Gen 31:14
And he divided the children unto *L* Gen 33:1
and their children foremost, and *L* Gen 33:2
*L* also with her children came Gen 33:7
And Dinah the daughter of *L* Gen 34:1
The sons of *L*; Reuben Gen 35:23
These be the sons of *L*, which she Gen 46:15
whom Laban gave to *L* his daughter.. Gen 46:18
and there I buried *L* Gen 49:31
thine house like Rachel and like *L* Ruth 4:11

**LEAH'S** (*le'-ahs*)
Zilpah *L* maid bare Jacob a son Gen 30:10
Zilpah *L* maid bare Jacob a second Gen 30:12
into Jacob's tent, and into *L* tent Gen 31:33
Then went he out of *L* tent Gen 31:33
And the sons of Zilpah, *L* handmaid .. Gen 35:26

**LEAN**
And the *l* and the ill favoured kine Gen 41:20
land is, whether it be fat or *l* Num 13:20
standeth, that I may *l* upon them Judg 16:26
the king's son, *l* from day to day 2Sa 13:4
upon Egypt, on which if a man *l* 2Kin 18:21
He shall *l* upon his house, but it Job 8:15
and *l* not unto thine own Prov 3:5
fatness of his flesh shall wax *l* Is 17:4
whereon if a man *l*, it will go Is 36:6
cattle and between the *l* cattle Eze 34:20
yet will they *l* upon the LORD Mic 3:11

**LEANED**
behold, Saul *l* upon his spear 2Sa 1:6
king *l* answered the man of God 2Kin 7:2
the lord on whose hand he *l* to 2Kin 7:17
and when they *l* upon thee, thou Eze 29:7
*l* his hand on the wall, and a Amos 5:19
which also *l* on his breast at Jn 21:20

**LEANETH**
or that *l* on a staff, or that 2Sa 3:29
he *l* on my hand, and I bow myself 2Kin 5:18

**LEANFLESHED**
of the river, ill favoured and *l* Gen 41:3
*l* kine did eat up the seven well Gen 41:4
poor and very ill favoured and *l* Gen 41:19

**LEANING**
wilderness, *l* upon her beloved Song 8:5
Now there was *l* on Jesus' bosom Jn 13:23
*l* upon the top of his staff Heb 11:21

**LEANNESS**
my *l* rising up in me beareth Job 16:8
but sent *l* into their soul Ps 106:15
hosts, send among his fat ones *l* Is 10:16
But I said, My *l*, my *l*, Is 24:16

**LEANNOTH** (*le-an'-noth*) *A musical choir.*
chief Musician upon Mahalath *L* Ps 88:t

**LEAP**
all the rams which *l* upon the Gen 31:12
to *l* withal upon the earth Lev 11:21
he shall *l* from Bashan Deut 33:22
lamps, and sparks of fire *l* out Job 41:19
Why *l* ye, ye high hills Ps 68:16
shall the lame man *l* as an hart Is 35:6
tops of mountains shall they *l* Joel 2:5
all those that *l* on the threshold Zeph 1:9
ye in that day, and *l* for joy Lk 6:23

**LEAPED**
the rams which *l* upon the cattle Gen 31:10
by my God have I *l* over a wall 2Sa 22:30
they *l* upon the altar which was 1Kin 18:26
and by my God have I *l* over a wall Ps 18:29
of Mary, the babe *l* in her womb Lk 1:41
the babe *l* in my womb for joy Lk 1:44
And he *l* and walked Acts 14:10
the evil spirit was *l* on them Acts 19:16

**LEAPING**
a window, and saw king David *l* 2Sa 6:16
he cometh *l* upon the mountains, Song 2:8
he *l* up stood, and walked, and Acts 3:8
into the temple, walking, and *l* Acts 3:8

**LEARN**
that they may *l* to fear me all Deut 4:10
ears this day, that ye may *l* them Deut 5:1
that thou mayest *l* to fear the Deut 14:23
that he may *l* to fear the LORD Deut 17:19
thou shalt not *l* to do after the Deut 18:9
they may hear, and that they may *l*.. Deut 31:12
*l* to fear the LORD your God, as Deut 31:13
that I might *l* thy statutes Ps 119:71
that I may *l* thy commandments Ps 119:73
Lest thou *l* his ways, and get a Prov 22:25
*L* to do well Is 1:17
neither shall they *l* war any more Is 2:4
of the world will *l* righteousness Is 26:9
yet will he not *l* righteousness Is 26:10
that murmured shall *l* doctrine Is 29:24
*L* not the way of the heathen, and Jer 10:2
*l* the ways of my people, to swear Jer 12:16
neither shall they *l* war any more Mic 4:3
*l* what that meaneth, I will have Mt 9:13
Take my yoke upon you, and *l* of me... Mt 11:29
Now *l* a parable of the fig tree Mt 24:32
Now *l* a parable of the fig tree Mk 13:28
that ye might *l* in us not to 1Cor 4:6
one by one, that all may *l* 1Cor 14:31
And if they will *l* any thing 1Cor 14:35
This only would I *l* of you Gal 3:2
that they may *l* not to blaspheme 1Ti 1:20
Let the woman *l* in silence with 1Ti 2:11
let them *l* first to shew piety at 1Ti 5:4
And withal they *l* to be idle 1Ti 5:13
let ours also *l* to maintain good Titus 3:14
no man could *l* that song but the Rev 14:3

**LEARNED**
for I have *l* by experience that Gen 30:27
the heathen, and *l* their works Ps 106:35
when I shall have *l* thy righteous Ps 119:7
I neither *l* wisdom, nor have the Prov 30:3
men deliver to one that is *l* Is 29:11
is delivered to him that is not *l* Is 29:12
and he saith, I am not *l* Is 29:12
hath given me the tongue of the *l* Is 50:4
mine ear to hear as the *l* Is 50:4
lion, and it *l* to catch the prey Eze 19:3
*l* to catch the prey, and devoured Eze 19:6
hath *l* of the Father, cometh unto Jn 6:45
this man letters, having never *l* Jn 7:15
Moses was *l* in all the wisdom of Acts 7:22
to the doctrine which ye have *l* Rom 16:17
But ye have not so *l* Christ Eph 4:20
things, which ye have both *l* Phil 4:9
for I have *l*, in whatsoever state Phil 4:11
As ye also *l* of Epaphras our dear Col 1:7
in the things which thou hast *l* 2Ti 3:14
knowing of whom thou hast *l* them 2Ti 3:14
yet *l* he obedience by the things Heb 5:8

**LEARNING**
man will hear, and will increase *l* Prov 1:5
man, and he will increase in *l* Prov 9:9
of the lips increaseth *l* Prov 16:21
mouth, and addeth *l* to his lips Prov 16:23
and whom they might teach the *l* Dan 1:4
them knowledge and skill in all *l* Dan 1:17
much *l* doth make thee mad Acts 26:24
aforetime were written for our *l* Rom 15:4
Ever *l*, and never able to come to 2Ti 3:7

**LEASING**
ye love vanity, and seek after *l* Ps 4:2
shalt destroy them that speak *l* Ps 5:6

**LEAST**
with us a few days, at the *l* ten Gen 24:55
of the *l* of all the mercies Gen 32:10
he that gathered *l* gathered ten Num 11:32
at the *l* such as before knew Judg 3:2
I am the *l* in my father's house Judg 6:15
my family the *l* of all the 1Sa 9:21
kept themselves at *l* from women 1Sa 21:4
of the *l* of my master's servants 2Kin 18:24
one of the *l* was over an hundred, 1Chr 12:14
of the *l* of my master's servants Is 36:9
For from the *l* of them even unto Jer 6:13
for every one from the *l* even Jer 8:10
from the *l* of them unto the Jer 31:34
from the *l* even unto the greatest Jer 42:1
from the *l* even to the greatest Jer 42:8
from the *l* even unto the greatest Jer 44:12
Surely the *l* of the flock shall Jer 49:20
Surely the *l* of the flock shall Jer 50:45
yet shall not the *l* grain fall Amos 9:9
of them even to the *l* of them Jonah 3:5
art not the *l* among the princes Mt 2:6
break one of these *l* commandments Mt 5:19
he shall be called the *l* in the Mt 5:19
notwithstanding he that is *l* in Mt 11:11
indeed is the *l* of all seeds Mt 13:32
one of the *l* of these my brethren Mt 25:40
it not to one of the *l* of these Mt 25:45
but he that is *l* in the kingdom Lk 7:28
for he that is *l* among you all Lk 9:48
able to do that thing which is *l* Lk 12:26
is *l* is faithful also in much Lk 16:10
in the *l* is unjust also in much Lk 16:10
at *l* in this thy day, the things Lk 19:42
that at the *l* the shadow of Peter Acts 5:15
from the *l* to the greatest, Acts 8:10
who are *l* esteemed in the church 1Cor 6:4
For I am the *l* of the apostles, 1Cor 15:9
am less than the *l* of all saints Eph 3:8
from the *l* to the greatest Heb 8:11

**LEATHER**
a girdle of *l* about his loins 2Kin 1:8

**LEATHERN**
a *l* girdle about his loins Mt 3:4

**LEAVE**
shall a man *l* his father and his Gen 2:24
for I will not *l* thee, until I Gen 28:15
Let me now *l* with thee some of Gen 33:15
*l* one of your brethren here with Gen 42:33
lord, The lad cannot *l* his father Gen 44:22
for if he should *l* his father Gen 44:22
Let no man *l* of it till the Ex 16:19
what they *l* the beasts of the Ex 23:11
he shall not *l* any of it until Lev 7:15
holy place, and shall *l* them there Lev 16:23
thou shalt *l* them for the poor and Lev 19:10
ye shall *l* none of it until the Lev 22:30
thou shalt *l* them unto the poor, Lev 23:22
They shall *l* none of it unto the Num 9:12
And he said, *L* us not, I pray thee Num 10:31
to give me *l* to go with you Num 22:13
he will yet again *l* them in the Num 32:15
also shall not *l* thee either corn Deut 28:51
of his children which he shall *l* Deut 28:54
*l* them in the lodging place, Josh 4:3
Should I *l* my fatness, wherewith Judg 9:9
unto them, Should I *l* my wine Judg 9:13
said, Intreat me not to *l* thee Ruth 1:16
*l* them, that she may glean them, Ruth 2:16
lest my father *l* caring for the 1Sa 9:5
let us not *l* a man of them 1Sa 14:36
David earnestly asked *l* of me 1Sa 20:6
David earnestly asked *l* of me to 1Sa 20:28
if I *l* of all that pertain to him 1Sa 25:22
shall not *l* to my husband neither 2Sa 14:7
let him not *l* us, nor forsake us 1Kin 8:57
soul liveth, I will not *l* thee 2Kin 2:2
soul liveth, I will not *l* thee 2Kin 2:4
soul liveth, I will not *l* thee 2Kin 2:6
soul liveth, I will not *l* thee 2Kin 4:30
shall eat, and shall *l* thereof 2Kin 4:43
Neither did he *l* of the people to 2Kin 13:7
*l* it for an inheritance for your 1Chr 28:8
to *l* us a remnant to escape, and Ezr 9:8
*l* it for an inheritance to your Ezr 9:12
pray you, let us *l* off this usury Neh 5:10
the work cease, whilst I *l* it Neh 6:3
that we would *l* the seventh year, Neh 10:31
days obtained I *l* of the king Neh 13:6
I will *l* off my heaviness, and Job 9:27
I will *l* my complaint upon myself Job 10:1
or wilt thou *l* thy labour to him Job 39:11
thou wilt not *l* my soul in hell Ps 16:10
*l* the rest of their substance to Ps 17:14
*l* me not, neither forsake me, O Ps 27:9
LORD will not *l* him in his hand Ps 37:33
and *l* their wealth to others Ps 49:10
*l* me not to mine oppressors Ps 119:121
*l* not my soul destitute Ps 141:8
Who *l* the paths of uprightness, Prov 2:13
therefore *l* off contention, Prov 17:14
because I should *l* it unto the Eccl 2:18
shall he *l* it for his portion Eccl 2:21
up against thee, *l* not thy place Eccl 10:4
and where will ye *l* your glory Is 10:3
ye shall *l* your name for a curse Is 65:15
that I might *l* my people, and go Jer 9:2
*l* us not Jer 14:9
shall *l* them in the midst of his Jer 17:11
Will a man *l* the snow of Lebanon Jer 18:14
will not *l* thee altogether Jer 30:11
of Judah, to *l* you none to remain Jer 44:7
yet will I not *l* thee wholly Jer 46:28
*l* the cities, and dwell in the Jer 48:28
would they not *l* some gleaning Jer 49:9
*L* thy fatherless children, I will Jer 49:11
Yet will I *l* a remnant, that ye Eze 6:8
But I will *l* a few men of them Eze 12:16
jewels, and *l* thee naked and bare Eze 16:39
I will *l* you there, and melt you Eze 22:20
shall *l* thee naked and bare Eze 23:29
I will *l* thee thrown into the Eze 29:5
Then will I *l* thee upon the land, Eze 32:4
*l* but the sixth part of thee, and Eze 39:2
Nevertheless *l* the stump of his Dan 4:15
yet *l* the stump of the roots Dan 4:23
whereas they commanded to *l* the Dan 4:26
shall he *l* his blood upon him Hos 12:14
and *l* a blessing behind him Joel 2:14
by a thousand shall *l* an hundred Amos 5:3
forth by an hundred shall *l* ten Amos 5:3
*l* off righteousness in the earth, Amos 5:7
would they not *l* some grapes Obad 5
I will also *l* in the midst of Zeph 3:12
that it shall *l* them neither root Mal 4:1
*L* there thy gift before the altar Mt 5:24
astray, doth he not *l* the ninety Mt 18:12
this cause shall a man *l* father Mt 19:5
not to *l* the other undone Mt 23:23
And forthwith Jesus gave them *l* Mk 5:13
cause shall a man *l* his father Mk 10:7
*l* his wife behind him Mk 12:19
*l* no children, that his brother Mk 12:19
not to *l* the other undone Lk 11:42
doth not *l* the ninety and nine in Lk 15:4
they shall not *l* in thee one Lk 19:44
I will not *l* you comfortless Jn 14:18
Peace I *l* with you, my peace I Jn 14:27
I *l* the world, and go to the Jn 16:28
to his own, and shall *l* me alone Jn 16:32
and Pilate gave him *l* Jn 19:38
thou wilt not *l* my soul in hell Acts 2:27
that we should *l* the word of God Acts 6:2
then took his *l* of the brethren, Acts 18:18
we had taken our *l* one of another Acts 21:6
dwell with her, let her not *l* him 1Cor 7:13
but taking my *l* of them, I went 2Cor 2:13

L

cause shall a man *l* his father........ Eph 5:31
he hath said, I will never *l* thee........ Heb 13:5
which is without the temple *l* out........ Rev 11:2

**LEAVED**
open before him the two *l* gates........ Is 45:1

**LEAVEN**
put away *l* out of your houses........ Ex 12:15
be no *l* found in your houses........ Ex 12:19
neither shall there be *l* seen........ Ex 13:7
the blood of my sacrifice with *l*........ Ex 34:25
the LORD, shall be made with *l*........ Lev 2:11
for ye shall burn no *l*, nor any........ Lev 2:11
It shall not be baken with *l*........ Lev 6:17
eat it without *l* beside the altar........ Lev 10:12
they shall be baken with *l*........ Lev 23:17
sacrifice of thanksgiving with *l*........ Amos 4:5
kingdom of heaven is like unto *l*........ Mt 13:33
beware of the *l* of the Pharisees........ Mt 16:6
beware of the *l* of the Pharisees........ Mt 16:11
them not beware of the *l* of bread........ Mt 16:12
beware of the *l* of the Pharisees,........ Mk 8:15
and of the *l* of Herod........ Mk 8:15
ye of the *l* of the Pharisees........ Lk 12:1
It is like *l*, which a woman took........ Lk 13:21
little *l* leaveneth the whole lump........ 1Cor 5:6
Purge out therefore the old *l*........ 1Cor 5:7
us keep the feast, not with old *l*........ 1Cor 5:8
neither with the *l* of malice........ 1Cor 5:8
A little *l* leaveneth the whole........ Gal 5:9

**LEAVENED**
for whosoever eateth *l* bread from........ Ex 12:15
whosoever eateth that which is *l*........ Ex 12:19
Ye shall eat nothing *l*........ Ex 12:20
took their dough before it was *l*........ Ex 12:34
out of Egypt, for it was not *l*........ Ex 12:39
there shall no *l* bread be eaten........ Ex 13:3
there shall no *l* bread be seen........ Ex 13:7
of my sacrifice with *l* bread........ Ex 23:18
*l* bread with the sacrifice of........ Lev 7:13
Thou shalt eat no *l* bread with it........ Deut 16:3
there shall be no *l* bread seen........ Deut 16:4
kneaded the dough, until it be *l*........ Hos 7:4
of meal, till the whole was *l*........ Mt 13:33
of meal, till the whole was *l*........ Lk 13:21

**LEAVENETH**
a little leaven *l* the whole lump........ 1Cor 5:6
A little leaven *l* the whole lump........ Gal 5:9

**LEAVES**
and they sewed fig *l* together........ Gen 3:7
the two *l* of the one door were........ 1Kin 6:34
the two *l* of the other door were........ 1Kin 6:34
in them, when they cast their *l*........ Is 6:13
Jehudi had read three or four *l*........ Jer 36:23
wither in all the *l* of her spring........ Eze 17:9
two *l* apiece, two turning *l*........ Eze 41:24
two *l* for the one door........ Eze 41:24
and two *l* for the other door........ Eze 41:24
The *l* thereof were fair, and the........ Dan 4:12
off his branches, shake off his *l*........ Dan 4:14
Whose *l* were fair, and the fruit........ Dan 4:21
but *l* only, and said unto it, Let........ Mt 21:19
is yet tender, and putteth forth *l*........ Mt 24:32
a fig tree afar off having *l*........ Mk 11:13
to it, he found nothing but *l*........ Mk 11:13
is yet tender, and putteth forth *l*........ Mk 13:28
the *l* of the tree were for the........ Rev 22:2

**LEAVETH**
Which *l* her eggs in the earth, and........ Job 39:14
A good man *l* an inheritance to........ Prov 13:22
a sweeping rain which *l* no food........ Prov 28:3
idol shepherd that *l* the flock........ Zec 11:17
Then the devil *l* him, and, behold,........ Mt 4:11
coming, and *l* the sheep, and fleeth........ Jn 10:12

**LEAVING**
*l* Nazareth, he came and dwelt in........ Mt 4:13
him, and departed, *l* him half dead........ Lk 10:30
*l* the natural use of the woman,........ Rom 1:27
Therefore *l* the principles of the........ Heb 6:1
*l* us an example, that ye should........ 1Pet 2:21

**LEBANA** (*leb'-a-nah*) See LEBANAH. *A family of exiles.*
The children of L, the children........ Neh 7:48

**LEBANAH** (*leb'-a-nah*) *Same as Lebana.*
The children of L, the children........ Ezr 2:45

**LEBANON** (*leb'-a-non*) *Chief mountain range in Syria.*
land of the Canaanites, and unto L........ Deut 1:7
that goodly mountain, and L........ Deut 3:25
from the wilderness and L, from........ Deut 11:24
this L even unto the great river,........ Josh 1:4
of the great sea over against L........ Josh 9:1
valley of L under mount Hermon........ Josh 11:17
of L even unto the mount Halak........ Josh 12:7
land of the Giblites, and all L........ Josh 13:5
from L unto Misrephoth-maim........ Josh 13:6
the Hivites that dwelt in mount L........ Judg 3:3
and devour the cedars of L........ Judg 9:15
is in L even unto the hyssop that........ 1Kin 4:33
they hew me cedar trees out of L........ 1Kin 5:6
them down from L unto the sea........ 1Kin 5:9
And he sent them to L, ten........ 1Kin 5:14
a month they were in L, and two........ 1Kin 5:14
also the house of the forest of L........ 1Kin 7:2
to build in Jerusalem, and in L........ 1Kin 9:19
in the house of the forest of L........ 1Kin 10:17
the forest of L were of pure gold........ 1Kin 10:21
The thistle that was in L sent to........ 2Kin 14:9
sent to the cedar that was in L........ 2Kin 14:9
by a wild beast that was in L........ 2Kin 14:9
the mountains, to the sides of L........ 2Kin 19:23
trees, and algum trees, out of L........ 2Chr 2:8
can skill to cut timber in L........ 2Chr 2:8
And we will cut wood out of L........ 2Chr 2:16
to build in Jerusalem, and in L........ 2Chr 8:6
in the house of the forest of L........ 2Chr 9:16
the forest of L were of pure gold........ 2Chr 9:20
The thistle that was in L sent to........ 2Chr 25:18
sent to the cedar that was in L........ 2Chr 25:18
by a wild beast that was in L........ 2Chr 25:18
trees from L to the sea of Joppa........ Ezr 3:7
the LORD breaketh the cedars of L........ Ps 29:5
L and Sirion like a young unicorn........ Ps 29:6
fruit thereof shall shake like L........ Ps 72:16
he shall grow like a cedar in L........ Ps 92:12
the cedars of L, which he hath........ Ps 104:16
a chariot of the wood of L........ Song 3:9
Come with me from L, my spouse,........ Song 4:8
with me from L........ Song 4:8
garments is like the smell of L........ Song 4:11
living waters, and streams from L........ Song 4:15
his countenance is as L,........ Song 5:15
thy nose is as the tower of L........ Song 7:4
And upon all the cedars of L........ Is 2:13
L shall fall by a mighty one........ Is 10:34
at thee, and the cedars of L........ Is 14:8
L shall be turned into a fruitful........ Is 29:17
L is ashamed and hewn down........ Is 33:9
the glory of L shall be given........ Is 35:2
the mountains, to the sides of L........ Is 37:24
L is not sufficient to burn, nor........ Is 40:16
The glory of L shall come unto........ Is 60:13
Will a man leave the snow of L........ Jer 18:14
Gilead unto me, and the head of L........ Jer 22:6
Go up to L, and cry........ Jer 22:20
O inhabitant of L, that makest........ Jer 22:23
had divers colours, came unto L........ Eze 17:3
from L to make masts for thee........ Eze 27:5
a cedar in L with fair branches........ Eze 31:3
I caused L to mourn for him, and........ Eze 31:15
of Eden, the choice and best of L........ Eze 31:16
and cast forth his roots as L........ Hos 14:5
the olive tree, and his smell as L........ Hos 14:6
thereof shall be as the wine of L........ Hos 14:7
and the flower of L languisheth........ Nah 1:4
violence of L shall cover thee........ Hab 2:17
them into the land of Gilead and L........ Zec 10:10
Open thy doors, O L, that the........ Zec 11:1

**LEBAOTH** (*leb'-a-oth*) See BETH-LEBAOTH. *A city in Judah.*
And L, and Shilhim, and Ain, and........ Josh 15:32

**LEBBAEUS** (*leb-be'-us*) See JUDAS, THADDAEUS. *Same as Thaddaeus.*
James the son of Alphaeus, and L........ Mt 10:3

**LEB-KAMAI** See MIDST.

**LEBONAH** (*le-bo'-nah*) *A city in Ephraim.*
to Shechem, and on the south of L........ Judg 21:19

**LECAH** (*le'-cah*) *Son of Er.*
of Judah were, Er the father of L........ 1Chr 4:21

**LED**
the LORD *l* me to the house of my........ Gen 24:27
which had *l* me in the right way........ Gen 24:48
he *l* the flock to the backside of........ Ex 3:1
that God *l* them not through the........ Ex 13:17
But God *l* the people about,........ Ex 13:18
Thou in thy mercy hast *l* forth........ Ex 15:13
*l* thee these forty years in the........ Deut 8:2
Who *l* thee through that great and........ Deut 8:15
I have *l* you forty years in the........ Deut 29:5
he *l* him about, he instructed him........ Deut 32:10
*l* him throughout all the land of........ Josh 24:3
which *l* them away captive, and........ 1Kin 8:48
But he *l* them to Samaria........ 2Kin 6:19
Joab *l* forth the power of the........ 1Chr 20:1
*l* forth his people, and went to........ 2Chr 25:11
thou hast *l* captivity captive........ Ps 68:18
also he *l* them with a cloud........ Ps 78:14
he *l* them on safely, so that they........ Ps 78:53
so he *l* them through the depths,........ Ps 106:9
he *l* them forth by the right way,........ Ps 107:7
To him which *l* his people through........ Ps 136:16
I have *l* thee in right paths........ Prov 4:11
they that are *l* of them are........ Is 9:16
he *l* them through the deserts........ Is 48:21
joy, and be *l* forth with peace........ Is 55:12
That *l* them by the right hand of........ Is 63:12
That *l* them through the deep, as........ Is 63:13
that *l* us through the wilderness,........ Jer 2:6
when he *l* thee by the way........ Jer 2:17
whither they have *l* him captive........ Jer 22:12
which *l* the seed of the house of........ Jer 23:8
He hath *l* me, and brought me into........ Lam 3:2
*l* them with him to Babylon........ Eze 17:12
which caused them to be *l* into........ Eze 39:28
*l* me about the way without unto........ Eze 47:2
*l* you forty years through the........ Amos 2:10
Israel shall surely be *l* away........ Amos 7:11
And Huzzab shall be *l* away captive........ Nah 2:7
Then was Jesus *l* up of the spirit........ Mt 4:1
that had laid hold on Jesus *l* him........ Mt 26:57
they *l* him away, and delivered him........ Mt 27:2
*l* him away to crucify him........ Mt 27:31
hand, and *l* him out of the town........ Mk 8:23
they *l* Jesus away to the high........ Mk 14:53
the soldiers *l* him away into the........ Mk 15:16
him, and *l* him out to crucify him........ Mk 15:20
was *l* by the Spirit into the........ Lk 4:1
*l* him unto the brow of the hill........ Lk 4:29
shall be *l* away captive into all........ Lk 21:24
*l* him, and brought him into the........ Lk 22:54
*l* him into their council, saying,........ Lk 22:66
them arose, and *l* him unto Pilate........ Lk 23:1
as they *l* him away, they laid........ Lk 23:26
*l* with him to be put to death........ Lk 23:32
he *l* them out as far as to........ Lk 24:50
*l* him away to Annas first........ Jn 18:13
Then *l* they Jesus from Caiaphas........ Jn 18:28
And they took Jesus, and *l* him away... Jn 19:16
He was *l* as a sheep to the........ Acts 8:32
but they *l* him by the hand, and........ Acts 9:8
Paul was to be *l* into the castle........ Acts 21:37
being *l* by the hand of them that........ Acts 22:11
For as many as are *l* by the........ Rom 8:14
dumb idols, even as ye were *l*........ 1Cor 12:2
But if ye be *l* of the Spirit, ye........ Gal 5:18
he *l* captivity captive, and gave........ Eph 4:8
*l* away with divers lusts,........ 2Ti 3:6
being *l* away with the error of........ 2Pet 3:17

**LEDDEST**
over us, thou wast he that *l* out........ 2Sa 5:2
was king, thou wast he that *l* out........ 1Chr 11:2
Moreover thou *l* them in the day........ Neh 9:12
Thou *l* thy people like a flock by........ Ps 77:20
*l* out into the wilderness four........ Acts 21:38

**LEDGES**
and the borders were between the *l*.... 1Kin 7:28
were between the *l* were lions........ 1Kin 7:29
upon the *l* there was a base above........ 1Kin 7:29
the top of the base the *l* thereof........ 1Kin 7:35
on the plates of the *l* thereof........ 1Kin 7:36

**LEEKS**
and the melons, and the *l*, and the........ Num 11:5

**LEES**
things, a feast of wines on the *l*........ Is 25:6
of wines on the *l* well refined........ Is 25:6
and he hath settled on his *l*........ Jer 48:11
men that are settled on their *l*........ Zeph 1:12

**LEFT**
they *l* off to build the city........ Gen 11:8
if thou wilt take the *l* hand........ Gen 13:9
hand, then I will go to the *l*........ Gen 13:9
which is on the *l* hand of........ Gen 14:15
he *l* off talking with him, and God........ Gen 17:22
as soon as he had *l* communing........ Gen 18:33
who hath not *l* destitute my........ Gen 24:27
to the right hand, or to the *l*........ Gen 24:49
and *l* bearing........ Gen 29:35
Leah saw that she had *l* bearing........ Gen 30:9
company which is *l* shall escape........ Gen 32:8
And Jacob was *l* alone........ Gen 32:24
he *l* all that he had in Joseph's........ Gen 39:6
he *l* his garment in her hand, and........ Gen 39:12
he had *l* his garment in her hand........ Gen 39:13
that he *l* his garment with me, and........ Gen 39:15
that he *l* his garment with me, and........ Gen 39:18
very much, until he *l* numbering........ Gen 41:49
brother is dead, and he is *l* alone........ Gen 42:38
the eldest, and *l* at the youngest........ Gen 44:12
he alone is *l* of his mother, and........ Gen 44:20
there is not ought *l* in the sight........ Gen 47:18
right hand toward Israel's *l* hand........ Gen 48:13
Manasseh in his *l* hand toward........ Gen 48:13
his *l* hand upon Manasseh's head,........ Gen 48:14
they *l* in the land of Goshen........ Gen 50:8
why is it that ye have *l* the man........ Ex 2:20
word of the LORD *l* his servants........ Ex 9:21
even all that the hail hath *l*........ Ex 10:12
of the trees which the hail had *l*........ Ex 10:15
shall not an hoof be *l* behind........ Ex 10:26
their right hand, and on their *l*........ Ex 14:22
their right hand, and on their *l*........ Ex 14:29
but some of them *l* of it until........ Ex 16:20
passover be *l* unto the morning........ Ex 34:25
that which is *l* of the meat........ Lev 2:10
Ithamar, his sons that were *l*........ Lev 10:12
sons of Aaron which were *l* alive........ Lev 10:16
into the palm of his own *l* hand........ Lev 14:15
in the oil that is in his *l* hand........ Lev 14:16
into the palm of his own *l* hand........ Lev 14:26
his *l* hand seven times before the........ Lev 14:27
upon them that are *l* alive of you........ Lev 26:36
they that are *l* of you shall pine........ Lev 26:39
The land also shall be *l* of them........ Lev 26:43
to the right hand nor to the *l*........ Num 20:17
until there was none *l* him alive........ Num 21:35
to the right hand or to the *l*........ Num 22:26
And there was not *l* a man of them.. Num 26:65
unto the right hand nor to the *l*........ Deut 2:27
every city, we *l* none to remain........ Deut 2:34
until none was *l* to him remaining........ Deut 3:3
ye shall be *l* few in number among..... Deut 4:27
to the right hand or to the *l*........ Deut 5:32
among them, until they that are *l*........ Deut 7:20
to the right hand, nor to the *l*........ Deut 17:11
to the right hand, or to the *l*........ Deut 17:20
to the right hand, or to the *l*........ Deut 28:14
hath nothing *l* him in the siege........ Deut 28:55
ye shall be *l* few in number,........ Deut 28:62
and there is none shut up, or *l*........ Deut 32:36
it to the right hand or to the *l*........ Josh 1:7
*l* them without the camp of Israel........ Josh 6:23

was not a man l in Ai or Beth-el ... Josh 8:17
they l the city open, and pursued ... Josh 8:17
until he had l him none remaining ... Josh 10:33
he l none remaining, according to ... Josh 10:37
he l none remaining ... Josh 10:39
he l none remaining, but utterly ... Josh 10:40
until they l them none remaining ... Josh 11:8
there was not any l to breathe ... Josh 11:11
neither l they any to breathe ... Josh 11:14
he l nothing undone of all that ... Josh 11:15
There was none of the Anakims l ... Josh 11:22
goeth out to Cabul on the l hand ... Josh 19:27
Ye have not l your brethren these ... Josh 22:3
to the right hand or to the l ... Josh 23:6
which Joshua l when he died ... Judg 2:21
the LORD l those nations, without ... Judg 2:23
are the nations which the LORD l ... Judg 3:1
And Ehud put forth his l hand ... Judg 3:21
and there was not a man l ... Judg 4:16
l no sustenance for Israel, ... Judg 6:4
held the lamps in their l hands ... Judg 7:20
all that were l of all the hosts ... Judg 8:10
youngest son of Jerubbaal was l ... Judg 9:5
hand, and of the other with his l ... Judg 16:29
and she was l, and her two sons ... Ruth 1:3
the woman was l of her two sons ... Ruth 1:5
then she l speaking unto her ... Ruth 1:18
and how thou hast l thy father ... Ruth 2:11
did eat, and was sufficed, and l ... Ruth 2:14
who hath not l off his kindness ... Ruth 2:20
which hath not l thee this day ... Ruth 4:14
that every one that is l in thine ... 1Sa 2:36
the stump of Dagon was l to him ... 1Sa 5:4
to the right hand or to the l ... 1Sa 6:12
said, Behold that which is l ... 1Sa 9:24
thy father hath l the care of the ... 1Sa 10:2
two of them were not l together ... 1Sa 11:11
l the sheep with a keeper, and ... 1Sa 17:20
David l his carriage in the hand ... 1Sa 17:22
with whom hast thou l those few ... 1Sa 17:28
surely there had not been l unto ... 1Sa 25:34
l neither man nor woman alive, and ... 1Sa 27:9
those that were l behind stayed ... 1Sa 30:9
and my master l me, because three ... 1Sa 30:13
nor to the l from following Abner ... 2Sa 2:19
to thy right hand or to thy l ... 2Sa 2:21
there they l their images, and ... 2Sa 5:21
that is l of the house of Saul ... 2Sa 9:1
and there is not one of them l ... 2Sa 13:30
shall quench my coal which is l ... 2Sa 14:7
the l from ought that my lord the ... 2Sa 14:19
the king l ten women, which were ... 2Sa 15:16
on his right hand and on his l ... 2Sa 16:6
which he hath l to keep the house ... 2Sa 16:21
shall not be l so much as one ... 2Sa 17:12
whom he had l to keep the house, ... 2Sa 20:3
and he set up the l pillar ... 1Kin 7:21
five on the l side of the house ... 1Kin 7:39
Solomon l all the vessels ... 1Kin 7:47
the right side, and five on the l ... 1Kin 7:49
that were l of the Amorites ... 1Kin 9:20
were l after them in the land ... 1Kin 9:21
l in Israel, and will take away ... 1Kin 14:10
the gold that were l in the ... 1Kin 15:18
that he l off building of Ramah, ... 1Kin 15:21
he l not to Jeroboam any that ... 1Kin 15:29
he l him not one that pisseth ... 1Kin 16:11
that there was no breath l in him ... 1Kin 17:17
to Judah, and l his servant there ... 1Kin 19:3
and I, even I only, am l ... 1Kin 19:10
and I, even I only, am l ... 1Kin 19:14
Yet I have l me seven thousand in ... 1Kin 19:18
he l the oxen, and ran after ... 1Kin 19:20
thousand of the men that were l ... 1Kin 20:30
that is shut up and l in Israel, ... 1Kin 21:21
him on his right hand and on his l ... 1Kin 22:19
only in Kir-haraseth l they the ... 2Kin 3:25
l thereof, according to the word ... 2Kin 4:44
l their tents, and their horses, ... 2Kin 7:7
which are l in the city, (behold, ... 2Kin 7:13
of Israel that are l in it ... 2Kin 7:13
since the day that she l the land ... 2Kin 8:6
that is shut up and l in Israel ... 2Kin 9:8
until he l him none remaining ... 2Kin 10:11
neither l he any of them ... 2Kin 10:14
was not a man l that came not ... 2Kin 10:21
to the l corner of the temple ... 2Kin 11:11
was not any shut up, nor any l ... 2Kin 14:26
they l all the commandments of ... 2Kin 17:16
there was none l but the tribe of ... 2Kin 17:18
prayer for the remnant that are l ... 2Kin 19:4
nothing shall be l, saith the ... 2Kin 20:17
to the right hand or to the l ... 2Kin 22:2
which were on a man's l hand at ... 2Kin 23:8
people that were l in the city ... 2Kin 25:11
But the captain of the guard l of ... 2Kin 25:12
king of Babylon had l, even over ... 2Kin 25:22
of Merari stood on the l hand ... 1Chr 6:44
which were l of the family of ... 1Chr 6:61
the l in hurling stones and ... 1Chr 12:2
that are l in all the land of ... 1Chr 13:2
when they had l their gods there, ... 1Chr 14:12
So he l there before the ark of ... 1Chr 16:37
right hand, and the other on the l ... 2Chr 3:17
and the name of that on the l Boaz ... 2Chr 3:17
the right hand, and five on the l ... 2Chr 4:6
the right hand, and five on the l ... 2Chr 4:7
the right side, and five on the l ... 2Chr 4:8
that were l of the Hittites ... 2Chr 8:7
who were l after them in the land ... 2Chr 8:8
For the Levites l their suburbs ... 2Chr 11:14
therefore have I also l you in ... 2Chr 12:5
that he l off building of Ramah, ... 2Chr 16:5
on his right hand and on his l ... 2Chr 18:18
that there was never a son l him ... 2Chr 21:17
to the l side of the temple ... 2Chr 23:10
they l the house of the LORD God ... 2Chr 24:18
(for they l him in great diseases ... 2Chr 24:25
other ten thousand l alive did ... 2Chr 25:12
So the armed men l the captives ... 2Chr 28:14
enough to eat, and have l plenty ... 2Chr 31:10
that which is l is this great ... 2Chr 31:10
was done in the land, God l him ... 2Chr 32:31
to the right hand, nor to the l ... 2Chr 34:2
and for them that are l in Israel ... 2Chr 34:21
which were l of the captivity, and ... Neh 1:2
The remnant that are l of the ... Neh 1:3
there was no breach l therein ... Neh 6:1
and on his l hand, Pedaiah, and ... Neh 8:4
There shall none of his meat be l ... Job 20:21
him that is l in his tabernacle ... Job 20:26
On the l hand, where he doth work ... Job 23:9
they l off speaking ... Job 32:15
he hath l off to be wise, and to ... Ps 36:3
there was not one of them l ... Ps 106:11
in her l hand riches and honour ... Prov 3:16
to the right hand nor to the l ... Prov 4:27
but a child l to himself bringeth ... Prov 29:15
but a fool's heart at his l ... Eccl 10:2
His l hand is under my head, and ... Song 2:6
His l hand should be under my ... Song 8:3
the daughter of Zion is l as a ... Is 1:8
l unto us a very small remnant ... Is 1:9
pass, that he that is l in Zion ... Is 4:3
one eat that is l in the land ... Is 7:22
and he shall eat on the l hand ... Is 9:20
as one gathereth eggs that are l ... Is 10:14
of his people, which shall be l ... Is 11:11
of his people, which shall be l ... Is 11:16
gleaning grapes shall be l in it ... Is 17:6
which they l because of the ... Is 17:9
They shall be l together unto the ... Is 18:6
earth are burned, and few men l ... Is 24:6
In the city is l desolation ... Is 24:12
forsaken, and l like a wilderness ... Is 27:10
till ye be l as a beacon upon the ... Is 30:17
hand, and when ye turn to the l ... Is 30:21
multitude of the city shall be l ... Is 32:14
prayer for the remnant that is l ... Is 37:4
nothing shall be l, saith the ... Is 39:6
Behold, I was l alone ... Is 49:21
on the right hand and on the l ... Is 54:3
house, I have l mine heritage ... Jer 12:7
such as are l in this city from ... Jer 21:7
are l in the house of the LORD ... Jer 27:18
The people which were l of the ... Jer 31:2
the cities of Judah that were l ... Jer 34:7
all the women that are l in the ... Jer 38:22
So they l off speaking with him ... Jer 38:27
the captain of the guard l of the ... Jer 39:10
people that were l in the land ... Jer 40:6
Babylon had l a remnant of Judah ... Jer 40:11
(for we are l but a few of many, ... Jer 42:2
the captain of the guard had l ... Jer 43:6
But since we l off to burn ... Jer 44:18
How is the city of praise not l ... Jer 49:25
let nothing of her be l ... Jer 50:26
the captain of the guard l ... Jer 52:16
the face of an ox on the l side ... Eze 1:10
Lie thou also upon thy l side ... Eze 4:4
were slaying them, and I was l ... Eze 9:8
therein shall be l a remnant that ... Eze 14:22
that dwell at thy l hand ... Eze 16:46
on the right hand, or on the l ... Eze 21:16
Neither l she her whoredoms ... Eze 23:8
ye have l shall fall by the sword ... Eze 24:21
have cut him off, and have l him ... Eze 31:12
from his shadow, and have l him ... Eze 31:12
Then the heathen that are l round ... Eze 36:36
smite thy bow out of thy l hand ... Eze 39:3
have l none of them any more ... Eze 39:28
that which was l was the place of ... Eze 41:9
were toward the place that was l ... Eze 41:11
was l was five cubits round about ... Eze 41:11
that are l in the breadth over ... Eze 48:15
shall not be l to other people ... Dan 2:44
Therefore I was l alone, and saw ... Dan 10:8
neither is there breath l in me ... Dan 10:17
his l hand unto heaven, and sware ... Dan 12:7
because they have l off to take ... Hos 4:10
that there shall not be a man l ... Hos 9:12
hath l hath the locust eaten ... Joel 1:4
hath l hath the cankerworm eaten ... Joel 1:4
hath l hath the caterpiller eaten ... Joel 1:4
their right hand and their l hand ... Jonah 4:11
Who is l among you that saw this ... Hag 2:3
the other upon the l side thereof ... Zec 4:3
and upon the l side thereof ... Zec 4:11
on the right hand and on the l ... Zec 12:6
but the third shall be l therein ... Zec 13:8
that every one that is l of all ... Zec 14:16
And they straightway l their nets ... Mt 4:20
And they immediately l the ship ... Mt 4:22
let not thy l hand know what thy ... Mt 6:3
her hand, and the fever l her ... Mt 8:15
that was l seven baskets full ... Mt 15:37
And he l them, and departed ... Mt 16:4
right hand, and the other on the l ... Mt 20:21
sit on my right hand, and on my l ... Mt 20:23
he l them, and went out of the ... Mt 21:17
and l him, and went their way ... Mt 22:22
l his wife unto his brother ... Mt 22:25
your house is l unto you desolate ... Mt 23:38
There shall not be l here one ... Mt 24:2
shall be taken, and the other l ... Mt 24:40
shall be taken, and the other l ... Mt 24:41
hand, but the goats on the l ... Mt 25:33
say also unto them on the l hand ... Mt 25:41
he l them, and went away again, and ... Mt 26:44
right hand, and another on the l ... Mt 27:38
they l their father Zebedee in ... Mk 1:20
and immediately the fever l her ... Mk 1:31
meat that was l seven baskets ... Mk 8:8
he l them, and entering into the ... Mk 8:13
say unto him, Lo, we have l all ... Mk 10:28
There is no man that hath l house ... Mk 10:29
hand, and the other on thy l hand ... Mk 10:37
on my l hand is not mine to give ... Mk 10:40
and they l him, and went their way ... Mk 12:12
took a wife, and dying l no seed ... Mk 12:20
and died, neither l he any seed ... Mk 12:21
the seven had her, and l no seed ... Mk 12:22
there shall not be l one stone ... Mk 13:2
journey, who l his house, and gave ... Mk 13:34
he l the linen cloth, and fled ... Mk 14:52
right hand, and the other on his l ... Mk 15:27
and it l her ... Lk 4:39
Now when he had l speaking ... Lk 5:4
he l all, rose up, and followed ... Lk 5:28
sister hath l me to serve alone ... Lk 10:40
your house is l unto you desolate ... Lk 13:35
be taken, and the other shall be l ... Lk 17:34
shall be taken, and the other l ... Lk 17:35
shall be taken, and the other l ... Lk 17:36
Peter said, Lo, we have l all ... Lk 18:28
There is no man that hath l house ... Lk 18:29
they l no children, and died ... Lk 20:31
not be l one stone upon another ... Lk 21:6
right hand, and the other on the l ... Lk 23:33
He l Judaea, and departed again ... Jn 4:3
The woman then l her waterpot ... Jn 4:28
the seventh hour the fever l him ... Jn 4:52
and Jesus was l alone, and the ... Jn 8:9
the Father hath not l me alone ... Jn 8:29
that his soul was not l in hell ... Acts 2:31
Nevertheless he l not himself ... Acts 14:17
came to Ephesus, and l them there ... Acts 18:19
we l it on the l hand, and ... Acts 21:3
Cyprus, we l it on the l hand ... Acts 21:3
soldiers, they l beating of Paul ... Acts 21:32
On the morrow they l the horsemen ... Acts 23:32
the Jews a pleasure, l Paul bound ... Acts 24:27
a certain man l in bonds by Felix ... Acts 25:14
Lord of Sabaoth had l us a seed ... Rom 9:29
I am l alone, and they seek my ... Rom 11:3
on the right hand and on the l ... 2Cor 6:7
it good to be l at Athens alone ... 1Th 3:1
The cloke that I l at Troas with ... 2Ti 4:13
have I l at Miletum sick ... 2Ti 4:20
For this cause l I thee in Crete, ... Titus 1:5
he l nothing that is not put ... Heb 2:8
a promise being l us of entering ... Heb 4:1
but l their own habitation, he ... Jude 6
thou hast l thy first love ... Rev 2:4
sea, and his l foot on the earth, ... Rev 10:2

**LEFTEST**
therefore l thou them in the hand ... Neh 9:28

**LEFTHANDED**
son of Gera, a Benjamite, a man l ... Judg 3:15
were seven hundred chosen men l ... Judg 20:16

**LEG**
thy locks, make bare the l ... Is 47:2

**LEGION**
he answered, saying, My name is L ... Mk 5:9
with the devil, and had the l ... Mk 5:15
And he said, L ... Lk 8:30

**LEGIONS**
me more than twelve l of angels ... Mt 26:53

**LEGS**
his head with his l, and with the ... Ex 12:9
wash the inwards of him, and his l ... Ex 29:17
his l shall he wash in water ... Lev 1:9
the inwards and the l with water ... Lev 1:13
with his head, and with his l ... Lev 4:11
the inwards and the l in water ... Lev 8:21
he did wash the inwards and the l ... Lev 9:14
which have l above their feet, to ... Lev 11:21
thee in the knees, and in the l ... Deut 28:35
had greaves of brass upon his l ... 1Sa 17:6
not pleasure in the l of a man ... Ps 147:10
The l of the lame are not equal ... Prov 26:7
His l are as pillars of marble, ... Song 5:15
and the ornaments of the l ... Is 3:20
His l of iron, his feet part of ... Dan 2:33
of the mouth of the lion two l ... Amos 3:12
that their l might be broken ... Jn 19:31
brake the l of the first, and of ... Jn 19:32
already, they brake not his l ... Jn 19:33

**LEHAB**

**LEHABIM** (*le'-ha-bim*) *A son of Mizraim.*
begat Ludim, and Anamim, and L ... Gen 10:13
begat Ludim, and Anamim, and L ... 1Chr 1:11

**LEHABITES** See LEHABIM.

**LEHI** (*le'-hi*) See RAMATH-LEHI. *A district near Jerusalem.*
Judah, and spread themselves in L ... Judg 15:9

And when he came unto *L*, the ........ Judg 15:14
which is in *L* unto this day ........ Judg 15:19

**LEISURE**
they had no *l* so much as to eat ........ Mk 6:31

**LEMUEL** (*lem'-u-el*) *A king mentioned in Proverbs.*
The words of king *L*, the prophecy ...... Prov 31:1
It is not for kings, O *L*, it is ........ Prov 31:4

**LEND**
If thou *l* money to any of my ........ Ex 22:25
nor *l* him thy victuals for ........ Lev 25:37
thou shalt *l* unto many nations, ........ Deut 15:6
shalt surely *l* him sufficient for ........ Deut 15:8
Thou shalt not *l* upon usury to ........ Deut 23:19
stranger thou mayest *l* upon usury ... Deut 23:20
thou shalt not *l* upon usury ........ Deut 23:20
When thou dost *l* thy brother any ..... Deut 24:10
the man to whom thou dost *l* shall ..... Deut 24:11
thou shalt *l* unto many nations, ........ Deut 28:12
He shall *l* to thee, and thou shalt ...... Deut 28:44
and thou shalt not *l* to him ........ Deut 28:44
if ye *l* to them of whom ye hope ........ Lk 6:34
for sinners also *l* to sinners ........ Lk 6:34
ye your enemies, and do good, and *l* ....... Lk 6:35
him, Friend, *l* me three loaves ........ Lk 11:5

**LENDER**
the borrower is servant to the *l* ........ Prov 22:7
as with the *l*, so with the ........ Is 24:2

**LENDETH**
Every creditor that *l* ought unto ........ Deut 15:2
He is ever merciful, and *l* ........ Ps 37:26
A good man sheweth favour, and *l* ........ Ps 112:5
upon the poor *l* unto the LORD ........ Prov 19:17

**LENGTH**
The *l* of the ark shall be three ........ Gen 6:15
through the land in the *l* of it ........ Gen 13:17
and a half shall be the *l* thereof ........ Ex 25:10
and a half shall be the *l* thereof ........ Ex 25:17
two cubits shall be the *l* thereof ........ Ex 25:23
The *l* of one curtain shall be ........ Ex 26:2
The *l* of one curtain shall be ........ Ex 26:8
the *l* of the curtains of the tent ........ Ex 26:13
cubits shall be the *l* of a board ........ Ex 26:16
*l* there shall be hangings of an ........ Ex 27:11
The *l* of the court shall be an ........ Ex 27:18
a span shall be the *l* thereof ........ Ex 28:16
A cubit shall be the *l* thereof ........ Ex 30:2
The *l* of one curtain was twenty ........ Ex 36:9
The *l* of one curtain was thirty ........ Ex 36:15
The *l* of a board was ten cubits, ........ Ex 36:21
cubits and a half was the *l* of it ........ Ex 37:1
and a half was the *l* thereof ........ Ex 37:6
two cubits was the *l* thereof ........ Ex 37:10
the *l* of it was a cubit, and the ........ Ex 37:25
five cubits was the *l* thereof ........ Ex 38:1
and twenty cubits was the *l* ........ Ex 38:18
a span was the *l* thereof, and a ........ Ex 39:9
nine cubits was the *l* thereof ........ Deut 3:11
is thy life, and the *l* of thy days ........ Deut 30:20
which had two edges, of a cubit *l* ........ Judg 3:16
the *l* thereof was threescore ........ 1Kin 6:2
twenty cubits was the *l* thereof ........ 1Kin 6:3
forepart was twenty cubits in *l* ........ 1Kin 6:20
the *l* thereof was an hundred ........ 1Kin 7:2
the *l* thereof was fifty cubits, ........ 1Kin 7:6
four cubits was the *l* of one base ........ 1Kin 7:27
The *l* by cubits after the first ........ 2Chr 3:3
the *l* of it was according to the ........ 2Chr 3:4
the *l* whereof was according to ........ 2Chr 3:8
twenty cubits the *l* thereof ........ 2Chr 4:1
in *l* of days understanding ........ Job 12:12
even *l* of days for ever and ever ........ Ps 21:4
For *l* of days, and long life, and ........ Prov 3:2
*L* of days is in her right hand ........ Prov 3:16
have him become his son at the *l* ....... Prov 29:21
in the *l* of his branches ........ Eze 31:7
the *l* of the gate, thirteen ........ Eze 40:11
the *l* of the gates was the lower ........ Eze 40:18
north, he measured the *l* thereof ........ Eze 40:20
the *l* thereof was fifty cubits, ........ Eze 40:21
the *l* was fifty cubits, and the ........ Eze 40:25
the *l* was fifty cubits, and the ........ Eze 40:36
The *l* of the porch was twenty ........ Eze 40:49
and he measured the *l* thereof ........ Eze 41:2
So he measured the *l* thereof ........ Eze 41:4
the *l* thereof ninety cubits ........ Eze 41:12
he measured the *l* of the building ........ Eze 41:15
high, and the *l* thereof two cubits ........ Eze 41:22
the *l* thereof, and the walls ........ Eze 41:22
Before the *l* of an hundred cubits ........ Eze 42:2
the *l* thereof was fifty cubits ........ Eze 42:7
For the *l* of the chambers that ........ Eze 42:8
the *l* shall be the *l* of five ........ Eze 45:1
the sanctuary five hundred in *l* ........ Eze 45:2
shalt thou measure the *l* of five ........ Eze 45:3
the five and twenty thousand of *l* ........ Eze 45:5
the *l* shall be over against one ........ Eze 45:7
in *l* as one of the other parts, ........ Eze 48:8
of five and twenty thousand in *l* ........ Eze 48:9
five and twenty thousand in *l* ........ Eze 48:10
five and twenty thousand in *l* ........ Eze 48:10
have five and twenty thousand in *l* ..... Eze 48:13
all the *l* shall be five and twenty ........ Eze 48:13
the residue in *l* over against the ........ Eze 48:18
thereof, and what is the *l* thereof ........ Zec 2:2
the *l* thereof is twenty cubits, ........ Zec 5:2
if by any means now at *l* I might ........ Rom 1:10

saints what is the breadth, and *l* ........ Eph 3:18
the *l* is as large as the breadth ........ Rev 21:16
The *l* and the breadth and the ........ Rev 21:16

**LENGTHEN**
did walk, then I will *l* thy days ........ 1Kin 3:14
*l* thy cords, and strengthen thy ........ Is 54:2

**LENGTHENED**
that thy days may be *l* in the ........ Deut 25:15

**LENGTHENING**
if it may be a *l* of thy ........ Dan 4:27

**LENT**
so that they *l* unto them such ........ Ex 12:36
of any thing that is *l* upon usury ........ Deut 23:19
also I have *l* him to the LORD ........ 1Sa 1:28
liveth he shall be *l* to the LORD ........ 1Sa 1:28
the loan which is *l* to the LORD ........ 1Sa 2:20
I have neither *l* on usury ........ Jer 15:10
nor men have *l* to me on usury ........ Jer 15:10

**LENTILES**
gave Esau bread and pottage of *l* ........ Gen 25:34
and parched corn, and beans, and *l* ..... 2Sa 17:28
was a piece of ground full of *l* ........ 2Sa 23:11
wheat, and barley, and beans, and *l* ........ Eze 4:9

**LEOPARD**
the *l* shall lie down with the kid ........ Is 11:6
a *l* shall watch over their cities ........ Jer 5:6
his skin, or the *l* his spots ........ Jer 13:23
I beheld, and lo another, like a *l* ........ Dan 7:6
as a *l* by the way will I observe ........ Hos 13:7
which I saw was like unto a *l* ........ Rev 13:2

**LEOPARDS**
dens, from the mountains of the *l* ........ Song 4:8
also are swifter than the *l* ........ Hab 1:8

**LEPER**
the *l* in whom the plague is, his ........ Lev 13:45
the *l* in the day of his cleansing ........ Lev 14:2
of leprosy be healed in the *l* ........ Lev 14:3
of the seed of Aaron is a *l* ........ Lev 22:4
they put out of the camp every *l* ........ Num 5:2
hath an issue, or that is a *l* ........ 2Sa 3:29
man in valour, but he was a *l* ........ 2Kin 5:1
over the place, and recover the *l* ........ 2Kin 5:11
his presence a *l* as white as snow ........ 2Kin 5:27
so that he was a *l* unto the day ........ 2Kin 15:5
Uzziah the king was a *l* unto the ....... 2Chr 26:21
in a several house, being a *l* ........ 2Chr 26:21
for they said, He is a *l* ........ 2Chr 26:23
And, behold, there came a *l* ........ Mt 8:2
in the house of Simon the *l* ........ Mt 26:6
And there came a *l* to him, ........ Mk 1:40
in the house of Simon the *l* ........ Mk 14:3

**LEPERS**
And when these *l* came to the ........ 2Kin 7:8
Heal the sick, cleanse the *l* ........ Mt 10:8
the *l* are cleansed, and the deaf ........ Mt 11:5
many *l* were in Israel in the time ........ Lk 4:27
the *l* are cleansed, the deaf hear ........ Lk 7:22
there met him ten men that were *l* ....... Lk 17:12

**LEPROSY**
of his flesh like the plague of *l* ........ Lev 13:2
of his flesh, it is a plague of *l* ........ Lev 13:3
it is a *l* ........ Lev 13:8
When the plague of *l* is in a man ........ Lev 13:9
It is an old *l* in the skin of his ........ Lev 13:11
if a *l* break out abroad in the ........ Lev 13:12
the *l* cover all the skin of him ........ Lev 13:12
if the *l* have covered all his ........ Lev 13:13
it is a *l* ........ Lev 13:15
it is a plague of *l* broken out of ........ Lev 13:20
it is a *l* broken out of the ........ Lev 13:25
it is the plague of *l* ........ Lev 13:25
it is the plague of *l* ........ Lev 13:27
even a *l* upon the head or beard ........ Lev 13:30
it is a *l* sprung up in his bald ........ Lev 13:42
as the *l* appeareth in the skin of ........ Lev 13:43
also that the plague of *l* is in ........ Lev 13:47
it is a plague of *l*, and shall be ........ Lev 13:49
the plague is a fretting *l* ........ Lev 13:51
for it is a fretting *l* ........ Lev 13:52
of *l* in a garment of woollen or ........ Lev 13:59
if the plague of *l* be healed in ........ Lev 14:3
cleansed from the *l* seven times ........ Lev 14:7
of him in whom is the plague of *l* ........ Lev 14:32
I put the plague of *l* in a house ........ Lev 14:34
it is a fretting *l* in the house ........ Lev 14:44
law for all manner of plague of *l* ........ Lev 14:54
for the *l* of a garment, and of a ........ Lev 14:55
this is the law of *l* ........ Lev 14:57
Take heed in the plague of *l* ........ Deut 24:8
for he would recover him of his *l* ........ 2Kin 5:3
thou mayest recover him of his *l* ........ 2Kin 5:6
unto me to recover a man of his *l* ........ 2Kin 5:7
The *l* therefore of Naaman shall ........ 2Kin 5:27
the *l* even rose up in his ........ 2Chr 26:19
And immediately his *l* was cleansed ........ Mt 8:3
immediately the *l* departed from ........ Mk 1:42
city, behold a man full of *l* ........ Lk 5:12
immediately the *l* departed from ........ Lk 5:13

**LEPROUS**
behold, his hand was *l* as snow ........ Ex 4:6
He is a *l* man, he is unclean ........ Lev 13:44
and, behold, Miriam became *l* ........ Num 12:10
Miriam, and, behold, she was *l* ........ Num 12:10
there were four *l* men at the ........ 2Kin 7:3

he was *l* in his forehead, and they ..... 2Chr 26:20

**LESHEM** (*le'-shem*) See LAISH. *Same as Laish.*
of Dan went up to fight against *L* ..... Josh 19:47
it, and dwelt therein, and called *L* ..... Josh 19:47

**LESS**
and gathered, some more, some *l* ........ Ex 16:17
not give *l* than half a shekel ........ Ex 30:15
the LORD my God, to do *l* or more ..... Num 22:18
thou shalt give the *l* inheritance ........ Num 26:54
ye shall give the *l* inheritance ........ Num 33:54
nothing of all this, *l* or more ........ 1Sa 22:15
*l* or more, until the morning ........ 1Sa 25:36
how much *l* this house that I have ...... 1Kin 8:27
how much *l* this house which I ........ 2Chr 6:18
how much *l* shall your God deliver .... 2Chr 32:15
us *l* than our iniquities deserve ........ Ezr 9:13
How much *l* in them that dwell in ........ Job 4:19
How much *l* shall I answer him, and ..... Job 9:14
that God exacteth of thee *l* than ........ Job 11:6
How much *l* man, that is a worm ........ Job 25:6
How much *l* to him that accepteth ...... Job 34:19
much *l* do lying lips a prince ........ Prov 17:7
much *l* for a servant to have rule ....... Prov 19:10
are counted to him *l* than nothing ........ Is 40:17
how much *l* shall it be meet yet ........ Eze 15:5
is *l* than all the seeds that be ........ Mk 4:31
and Mary the mother of James the *l* .... Mk 15:40
which we think to be *l* honourable .... 1Cor 12:23
I love you, the *l* I be loved ........ 2Cor 12:15
who am *l* than the least of all ........ Eph 3:8
and that I may be the *l* sorrowful ........ Phil 2:28
the *l* is blessed of the better ........ Heb 7:7

**LESSER**
the *l* light to rule the night ........ Gen 1:16
and for the treading of *l* cattle ........ Is 7:25
from the *l* settle even to the ........ Eze 43:14

**LEST**
shall ye touch it, *l* ye die ........ Gen 3:3
*l* he put forth his hand, and take ........ Gen 3:22
*l* any finding him should kill him ........ Gen 4:15
*l* we be scattered abroad upon the ........ Gen 11:4
*l* thou shouldest say, I have made ...... Gen 14:23
*l* thou be consumed in the ........ Gen 19:15
the mountain, *l* thou be consumed ..... Gen 19:17
*l* some evil take me, and I die ........ Gen 19:19
*l*, said he, the men of the place ........ Gen 26:7
Because I said, *L* I die for her ........ Gen 26:9
*l* he will come and smite me, and ........ Gen 32:11
*l* that he should give seed to his ........ Gen 38:9
*L* peradventure he die also, as ........ Gen 38:11
take it to her, *l* we be shamed ........ Gen 38:23
*L* peradventure mischief befall ........ Gen 42:4
*l* peradventure I see the evil ........ Gen 44:34
*l* thou, and thy household, and all ....... Gen 45:11
*l* they multiply, and it come to ........ Ex 1:10
*l* he fall upon us with pestilence ........ Ex 5:3
*L* peradventure the people repent ........ Ex 13:17
*l* they break through unto the ........ Ex 19:21
*l* the LORD break forth upon them ........ Ex 19:22
*l* he break forth upon them ........ Ex 19:24
not God speak with us, *l* we die ........ Ex 20:19
*l* the land become desolate, and ........ Ex 23:29
*l* they make thee sin against me ........ Ex 23:33
*l* I consume thee in the way ........ Ex 33:3
*l* thou make a covenant with the ........ Ex 34:12
*l* it be for a snare in the midst ........ Ex 34:12
*L* thou make a covenant with the ........ Ex 34:15
*l* ye die, and *l* wrath come upon ........ Lev 10:6
*l* wrath come upon all the people ........ Lev 10:6
of the congregation, *l* ye die ........ Lev 10:7
of the congregation, *l* ye die ........ Lev 10:9
*l* the land fall to whoredom, and ........ Lev 19:29
*l* they bear sin for it, and die ........ Lev 22:9
touch any holy thing, *l* they die ........ Num 4:15
things are covered, *l* they die ........ Num 4:20
*l* ye be consumed in all their ........ Num 16:26
*L* the earth swallow us up also ........ Num 16:34
*l* they bear sin, and die ........ Num 18:22
the children of Israel, *l* ye die ........ Num 18:32
*l* I come out against thee with ........ Num 20:18
*l* ye be smitten before your ........ Deut 1:42
*l* thou forget the things which ........ Deut 4:9
*l* they depart from thy heart all ........ Deut 4:9
*L* ye corrupt yourselves, and make ...... Deut 4:16
*l* thou lift up thine eyes unto ........ Deut 4:19
*l* ye forget the covenant of the ........ Deut 4:23
Then beware *l* thou forget the ........ Deut 6:12
*l* the anger of the LORD thy God ........ Deut 6:15
*l* the beasts of the field ........ Deut 7:22
thee, *l* thou be snared therein ........ Deut 7:25
*l* thou be a cursed thing like it ........ Deut 7:26
*L* when thou hast eaten and art ........ Deut 8:12
*L* the land whence thou broughtest .... Deut 9:28
*l* ye perish quickly from off the ........ Deut 11:17
*L* the avenger of the blood pursue ...... Deut 19:6
*l* he die in the battle, and ........ Deut 20:5
*l* he die in the battle, and ........ Deut 20:6
*l* he die in the battle, and ........ Deut 20:7
*l* his brethren's heart faint as ........ Deut 20:8
*l* the fruit of thy seed which ........ Deut 22:9
*l* he cry against thee unto the ........ Deut 24:15
*l*, if he should exceed, and beat ........ Deut 25:3
*L* there should be among you man, ... Deut 29:18
*l* there should be among you a ........ Deut 29:18
*l* their adversaries should behave ........ Deut 32:27
*l* they should say, Our hand is ........ Deut 32:27
mountain, *l* the pursuers meet you ...... Josh 2:16
*l* ye make yourselves accursed, ........ Josh 6:18

*l* wrath be upon us, because of ... Josh 9:20
unto you, *l* ye deny your God ... Josh 24:27
*l* Israel vaunt themselves against ... Judg 7:2
*l* we burn thee and thy father's ... Judg 14:15
*l* angry fellows run upon thee, and ... Judg 18:25
*l* I mar mine own inheritance ... Ruth 4:6
*l* my father leave caring for the ... 1Sa 9:5
*L* the Hebrews make them swords or.. 1Sa 13:19
*l* I destroy you with them ... 1Sa 15:6
know this, *l* he be grieved ... 1Sa 20:3
*L* they should tell on us, saying, ... 1Sa 27:11
battle, *l* in the battle he be an ... 1Sa 29:4
*l* these uncircumcised come and ... 1Sa 31:4
*l* the daughters of the ... 2Sa 1:20
rejoice, *l* the daughters of the ... 2Sa 1:20
*l* I take the city, and it be ... 2Sa 12:28
*l* we be chargeable unto thee ... 2Sa 13:25
any more, *l* they destroy my son ... 2Sa 14:11
*l* he overtake us suddenly, and ... 2Sa 15:14
*l* the king be swallowed up, and ... 2Sa 17:16
*l* he get him fenced cities, and ... 2Sa 20:6
*l* peradventure the Spirit of the ... 2Kin 2:16
*l* these uncircumcised come and ... 1Chr 10:4
*L* ye should say, We have found ... Job 32:13
not, *l* the people be ensnared ... Job 34:30
beware *l* he take thee away with ... Job 36:18
*l* I deal with you after your ... Job 42:8
*l* he be angry, and ye perish from ... Ps 2:12
*L* he tear my soul like a lion, ... Ps 7:2
*l* I sleep the sleep of death ... Ps 13:3
*L* mine enemy say, I have ... Ps 13:4
*l*, if thou be silent to me, I ... Ps 28:1
*l* they come near unto thee ... Ps 32:9
*l* otherwise they should rejoice ... Ps 38:16
*l* I tear you in pieces, and there ... Ps 50:22
Slay them not, *l* my people forget ... Ps 59:11
*l* thou dash thy foot against a ... Ps 91:12
wrath, *l* he should destroy them ... Ps 106:23
*l* the righteous put forth their ... Ps 125:3
*l* they exalt themselves ... Ps 140:8
*l* I be like unto them that go ... Ps 143:7
*L* thou shouldest ponder the path ... Prov 5:6
*L* thou give thine honour unto ... Prov 5:9
*L* strangers be filled with thy ... Prov 5:10
not a scorner, *l* he hate thee ... Prov 9:8
not sleep, *l* thou come to poverty ... Prov 20:13
*L* thou learn his ways, and get a ... Prov 22:25
*L* the LORD see it, and it ... Prov 24:18
*l* thou know not what to do in the ... Prov 25:8
*L* he that heareth it put thee to ... Prov 25:10
*l* thou be filled therewith, and ... Prov 25:16
*l* he be weary of thee, and so hate ... Prov 25:17
*l* thou also be like unto him ... Prov 26:4
*l* he be wise in his own conceit ... Prov 26:5
*l* he reprove thee, and thou be ... Prov 30:6
*L* I be full, and deny thee, and say ... Prov 30:9
or *l* I be poor, and steal, and take ... Prov 30:9
*l* he curse thee, and thou be found ... Prov 30:10
*L* they drink, and forget the law, ... Prov 31:5
*l* thou hear thy servant curse ... Eccl 7:21
*l* they see with their eyes, and ... Is 6:10
*l* any hurt it, I will keep it ... Is 27:3
*l* your bands be made strong ... Is 28:22
Beware *l* Hezekiah persuade you, ... Is 36:18
*l* thou shouldest say, Mine idol ... Is 48:5
*l* thou shouldest say, Behold, I ... Is 48:7
*l* I confound thee before them ... Jer 1:17
*l* my fury come forth like fire, ... Jer 4:4
*l* my soul depart from thee ... Jer 6:8
*l* I make thee desolate, a land ... Jer 6:8
*l* thou bring me to nothing ... Jer 10:24
*l* my fury go out like fire, and ... Jer 21:12
the scribe, *l* I die there ... Jer 37:20
*l* they deliver me into their hand ... Jer 38:19
*l* your heart faint, and ye fear ... Jer 51:46
*L* I strip her naked, and set her ... Hos 2:3
*l* he break out like fire in the ... Amos 5:6
*l* they should hear the law, and ... Zec 7:12
*l* I come and smite the earth with ... Mal 4:6
*l* at any time thou dash thy foot ... Mt 4:6
*l* at any time the adversary ... Mt 5:25
*l* they trample them under their ... Mt 7:6
*l* at any time they should see ... Mt 13:15
*l* while ye gather up the tares, ... Mt 13:29
fasting, *l* they faint in the way ... Mt 15:32
*l* we should offend them, go thou ... Mt 17:27
*l* there be not enough for us and ... Mt 25:9
*l* there be an uproar among the ... Mt 26:5
*l* his disciples come by night, and ... Mt 27:64
*l* they should throng him ... Mk 3:9
*l* at any time they should be ... Mk 4:12
Take heed *l* any man deceive you ... Mk 13:5
*L* coming suddenly he find you ... Mk 13:36
*l* there be an uproar of the ... Mk 14:2
*l* ye enter into temptation ... Mk 14:38
*l* at any time thou dash thy foot ... Lk 4:11
*l* they should believe and be saved ... Lk 8:12
*l* he hale thee to the judge, and ... Lk 12:58
*l* a more honourable man than thou ... Lk 14:8
*l* they also bid thee again, and a ... Lk 14:12
*L* haply, after he hath laid the ... Lk 14:29
*l* they also come into this place ... Lk 16:28
*l* by her continual coming she ... Lk 18:5
*l* at any time your hearts be ... Lk 21:34
*l* ye enter into temptation ... Lk 22:46
*l* his deeds should be reproved ... Jn 3:20
*l* a worse thing come unto thee ... Jn 5:14
light, *l* darkness come upon you ... Jn 12:35
*l* they should be put out of the ... Jn 12:42
hall, *l* they should be defiled ... Jn 18:28
*l* they should have been stoned ... Acts 5:26
*l* haply ye be found even to fight ... Acts 5:39
*l* that come upon you, which is ... Acts 13:40
fearing *l* Paul should have been ... Acts 23:10
fearing *l* they should fall into ... Acts 27:17
Then fearing *l* we should have ... Acts 27:29
*l* any of them should swim out, and... Acts 27:42
*l* they should see with their eyes ... Acts 28:27
take heed *l* he also spare not ... Rom 11:21
*l* ye should be wise in your own ... Rom 11:25
*l* I should build upon another ... Rom 15:20
*L* any should say that I had ... 1Cor 1:15
*l* the cross of Christ should be ... 1Cor 1:17
But take heed *l* by any means this ... 1Cor 8:9
*l* I make my brother to offend ... 1Cor 8:13
*l* we should hinder the gospel of ... 1Cor 9:12
*l* that by any means, when I have ... 1Cor 9:27
he standeth take heed *l* he fall ... 1Cor 10:12
And I wrote this same unto you, *l* ... 2Cor 2:3
*l* perhaps such a one should be ... 2Cor 2:7
*L* Satan should get an advantage ... 2Cor 2:11
*l* the light of the glorious ... 2Cor 4:4
*l* our boasting of you should be ... 2Cor 9:3
*L* haply if they of Macedonia come ... 2Cor 9:4
*l* by any means, as the serpent ... 2Cor 11:3
*l* any man should think of me ... 2Cor 12:6
*l* I should be exalted above ... 2Cor 12:7
*l* I should be exalted above ... 2Cor 12:7
For I fear, *l*, when I come, I ... 2Cor 12:20
*l* there be debates, envyings, ... 2Cor 12:20
And *l*, when I come again, my God... 2Cor 12:21
*l* being present I should use ... 2Cor 13:10
*l* by any means I should run, or ... Gal 2:2
*l* I have bestowed upon you labour ... Gal 4:11
thyself, *l* thou also be tempted ... Gal 6:1
only *l* they should suffer ... Gal 6:12
of works, *l* any man should boast ... Eph 2:9
*l* I should have sorrow upon ... Phil 2:27
*l* any man should beguile you with ... Col 2:4
Beware *l* any man spoil you ... Col 2:8
to anger, *l* they be discouraged ... Col 3:21
*l* by some means the tempter have ... 1Th 3:5
*l* being lifted up with pride he ... 1Ti 3:6
*l* he fall into reproach and the ... 1Ti 3:7
*l* at any time we should let them ... Heb 2:1
*l* there be in any of you an evil ... Heb 3:12
*l* any of you be hardened through ... Heb 3:13
Let us therefore fear, *l*, a ... Heb 4:1
*l* any man fall after the same ... Heb 4:11
*l* he that destroyed the firstborn ... Heb 11:28
*l* ye be wearied and faint in your ... Heb 12:3
*l* that which is lame be turned ... Heb 12:13
Looking diligently *l* any man fail ... Heb 12:15
*l* any root of bitterness ... Heb 12:15
*L* there be any fornicator, or ... Heb 12:16
brethren, *l* ye be condemned ... Jas 5:9
*l* ye fall into condemnation ... Jas 5:12
beware *l* ye also, being led away ... 2Pet 3:17
*l* he walk naked, and they see his ... Rev 16:15

**LET** See PREFACE.

**LETHEK** See HOMER.

**LETTER**
that David wrote a *l* to Joab ... 2Sa 11:14
And he wrote in the *l*, saying, Set ... 2Sa 11:15
I will send a *l* unto the king of ... 2Kin 5:5
he brought the *l* to the king of ... 2Kin 5:6
Now when this *l* is come unto thee ... 2Kin 5:6
the king of Israel had read the *l* ... 2Kin 5:7
as soon as this *l* cometh to you ... 2Kin 10:2
Then he wrote a *l* the second time ... 2Kin 10:6
when the *l* came to them, that ... 2Kin 10:7
Hezekiah received the *l* of the ... 2Kin 19:14
the writing of the *l* was written ... Ezr 4:7
Shimshai the scribe wrote a *l* ... Ezr 4:8
of the *l* that they sent unto him ... Ezr 4:11
The *l* which ye sent unto us hath ... Ezr 4:18
*l* was read before Rehum, and ... Ezr 4:23
by *l* concerning this matter ... Ezr 5:5
The copy of the *l* that Tatnai ... Ezr 5:6
They sent a *l* unto him, wherein ... Ezr 5:7
Now this is the copy of the *l* ... Ezr 7:11
a *l* unto Asaph the keeper of the ... Neh 2:8
time with an open *l* in his hand ... Neh 6:5
for all the words of this *l* ... Est 9:26
to confirm this second *l* of Purim ... Est 9:29
Hezekiah received the *l* from the ... Is 37:14
*l* that Jeremiah the prophet sent ... Jer 29:1
*l* in the ears of Jeremiah the ... Jer 29:29
he wrote a *l* after this manner ... Acts 23:25
when the governor had read the *l* ... Acts 23:34
the law, judge thee, who by the *l* ... Rom 2:27
in the spirit, and not in the *l* ... Rom 2:29
and not in the oldness of the *l* ... Rom 7:6
not of the *l*, but of the spirit ... 2Cor 3:6
for the *l* killeth, but the spirit ... 2Cor 3:6
though I made you sorry with a *l* ... 2Cor 7:8
Ye see how large a *l* I have ... Gal 6:11
nor by *l* as from us, as that the ... 2Th 2:2
for I have written a *l* unto you ... Heb 13:22

**LETTERS**
So she wrote *l* in Ahab's name, and ... 1Kin 21:8
sent the *l* unto the elders and to ... 1Kin 21:8
And she wrote in the *l*, saying, ... 1Kin 21:9
as it was written in the *l* which ... 1Kin 21:11
And Jehu wrote *l*, and sent to ... 2Kin 10:1
Baladan, king of Babylon, sent *l* ... 2Kin 20:12
wrote *l* also to Ephraim and ... 2Chr 30:1
went with the *l* from the king ... 2Chr 30:6
He wrote also *l* to rail on the ... 2Chr 32:17
king, let *l* be given me to the ... Neh 2:7
river, and gave them the king's *l* ... Neh 2:9
of Judah sent many *l* unto Tobiah ... Neh 6:17
the *l* of Tobiah came unto them ... Neh 6:17
Tobiah sent *l* to put me in fear ... Neh 6:19
For he sent *l* into all the king's ... Est 1:22
the *l* were sent by posts into all ... Est 3:13
the *l* devised by Haman the son of ... Est 8:5
sent *l* by posts on horseback, and ... Est 8:10
sent *l* unto all the Jews that ... Est 9:20
he commanded by *l* that his wicked ... Est 9:25
he sent the *l* unto all the Jews, ... Est 9:30
Baladan, king of Babylon, sent *l* ... Is 39:1
Because thou hast sent *l* in thy ... Jer 29:25
written over him in *l* of Greek ... Lk 23:38
saying, How knoweth this man *l* ... Jn 7:15
desired of him *l* to Damascus to ... Acts 9:2
they wrote *l* by them after this ... Acts 15:23
I received *l* unto the brethren ... Acts 22:5
We neither received *l* out of ... Acts 28:21
ye shall approve by your *l* ... 1Cor 16:3
or *l* of commendation from you ... 2Cor 3:1
as if I would terrify you by *l* ... 2Cor 10:9
For his *l*, say they, are weighty ... 2Cor 10:10
in word by *l* when we are absent ... 2Cor 10:11

**LETTEST**
*l* such words go out of thy mouth ... Job 15:13
with a cord which thou *l* down ... Job 41:1
now *l* thou thy servant depart in ... Lk 2:29

**LETTETH**
hands escape, he that *l* him go ... 2Kin 10:24
strife is as when one *l* out water ... Prov 17:14
only he who now *l* will let ... 2Th 2:7

**LETTING**
deceitfully any more in not *l* the ... Ex 8:29

**LETUSHIM** (*le-tu'-shim*) *A son of Dedan.*
sons of Dedan were Asshurim, and *L*... Gen 25:3

**LETUSHITES** See LETUSHIM.

**LEUMMIM** (*le-um'-mim*) *A son of Dedan.*
were Asshurim, and Letushim, and *L*... Gen 25:3

**LEVI** (*le'-vi*) See LEVITE, LEVITICAL, MATTHEW.
*1. A son of Jacob.*
therefore was his name called *L* ... Gen 29:34
of the sons of Jacob, Simeon and *L* ... Gen 34:25
And Jacob said to Simeon and *L* ... Gen 34:30
firstborn, and Simeon, and *L* ... Gen 35:23
Simeon and *L* are brethren ... Gen 49:5
Reuben, Simeon, *L*, and Judah, ... Ex 1:2
are the names of the sons of *L* ... Ex 6:16
life of *L* were an hundred thirty ... Ex 6:16
were the sons of *L* by their names ... Num 3:17
the son of Kohath, the son of *L* ... Num 16:1
was Jochebed, the daughter of *L* ... Num 26:59
her mother bare to *L* in Egypt ... Num 26:59
the son of Kohath, the son of *L* ... 1Chr 6:38
the son of Gershom, the son of *L* ... 1Chr 6:43
the son of Merari, the son of *L* ... 1Chr 6:47
the sons of Mahli, the son of *L* ... Ezr 8:18
*2. The tribe.*
And the sons of *L* ... Gen 46:11
went a man of the house of *L* ... Ex 2:1
and took to wife a daughter of *L* ... Ex 2:1
these are the families of *L* ... Ex 6:19
all the sons of *L* gathered ... Ex 32:26
the children of *L* did according ... Ex 32:28
shalt not number the tribe of *L* ... Num 1:49
Bring the tribe of *L* near ... Num 3:6
Number the children of *L* after ... Num 3:15
Kohath from among the sons of *L* ... Num 4:2
too much upon you, ye sons of *L* ... Num 16:7
Hear, I pray you, ye sons of *L* ... Num 16:8
brethren the sons of *L* with thee ... Num 16:10
Aaron's name upon the rod of *L* ... Num 17:3
for the house of *L* was budded ... Num 17:8
brethren also of the tribe of *L* ... Num 18:2
I have given the children of *L* ... Num 18:21
the LORD separated the tribe of *L* ... Deut 10:8
Wherefore *L* hath no part nor ... Deut 10:9
Levites, and all the tribe of *L* ... Deut 18:1
the sons of *L* shall come near ... Deut 21:5
Simeon, and *L*, and Judah, and ... Deut 27:12
it unto the priests the sons of *L* ... Deut 31:9
of *L* he said, Let thy Thummim and... Deut 33:8
Only unto the tribe of *L* he gave ... Josh 13:14
But unto the tribe of *L* Moses ... Josh 13:33
who were of the children of *L* ... Josh 21:10
which were not of the sons of *L* ... 1Kin 12:31
Reuben, Simeon, *L*, and Judah, ... 1Chr 2:1
The sons of *L*; Gershon ... 1Chr 6:1
The sons of *L*; Gershom ... 1Chr 6:16
companies of the children of *L* ... 1Chr 9:18
the children of *L* four thousand ... 1Chr 12:26
But *L* and Benjamin counted he not... 1Chr 21:6
into courses among the sons of *L* ... 1Chr 23:6
sons were named of the tribe of *L* ... 1Chr 23:14
These were the sons of *L* after ... 1Chr 23:24
rest of the sons of *L* were these ... 1Chr 24:20
found there none of the sons of *L* ... Ezr 8:15
the children of *L* shall bring the ... Neh 10:39
The sons of *L*, the chief of the ... Neh 12:23
Bless the LORD, O house of *L* ... Ps 135:20
sons of Zadok among the sons of *L* ... Eze 40:46
one gate of Judah, one gate of *L* ... Eze 48:31
family of the house of *L* apart ... Zec 12:13
that my covenant might be with *L* ... Mal 2:4

have corrupted the covenant of *L* Mal 2:8
and he shall purify the sons of *L* Mal 3:3
they that are of the sons of *L* Heb 7:5
*L* also, who receiveth tithes, Heb 7:9
Of the tribe of *L* were sealed Rev 7:7
*3. Same as Matthew the apostle.*
he saw *L* the son of Alphaeus Mk 2:14
forth, and saw a publican, named *L* Lk 5:27
*L* made him a great feast in his Lk 5:29
*4. Father of Matthat; ancestor of Jesus.*
Matthat, which was the son of *L* Lk 3:24
*5. Father of another Matthat; ancestor of Jesus.*
Matthat, which was the son of *L* Lk 3:29

**LEVIATHAN**
thou draw out *l* with an hook Job 41:1
brakest the heads of *l* in pieces Ps 74:14
there is that *l*, whom thou hast Ps 104:26
punish *l* the piercing serpent Is 27:1
even *l* that crooked serpent Is 27:1

**LEVITE** (*le'-vite*) See LEVITES, LEVITICAL. *A descendant of Levi.*
Is not Aaron the *L* thy brother Ex 4:14
the *L* that is within your gates Deut 12:12
the *L* that is within thy gates Deut 12:18
that thou forsake not the *L* as Deut 12:19
the *L* that is within thy gates Deut 14:27
And the *L*, (because he hath no Deut 14:29
the *L* that is within thy gates, Deut 16:11
and thy maidservant, and the *L* Deut 16:14
if a *L* come from any of thy gates Deut 18:6
unto thine house, thou, and the *L* Deut 26:11
and hast given it unto the *L* Deut 26:12
also have given them unto the *L* Deut 26:13
the family of Judah, who was a *L* Judg 17:7
I am a *L* of Beth-lehem-judah, and Judg 17:9
So the *L* went in Judg 17:10
the *L* was content to dwell with Judg 17:11
And Micah consecrated the *L* Judg 17:12
seeing I have a *L* to my priest Judg 17:13
the voice of the young man the *L* Judg 18:3
the house of the young man the *L* Judg 18:15
that there was a certain *L* Judg 19:1
And the *L*, the husband of the Judg 20:4
a *L* of the sons of Asaph, came 2Chr 20:14
which Cononiah the *L* was ruler 2Chr 31:12
And Kore the son of Imnah the *L* 2Chr 31:14
and Shabbethai the *L* helped them Ezr 10:15
And likewise a *L*, when he was at Lk 10:32
The son of consolation,) a *L* Acts 4:36

**LEVITES**
the *L* according to their families Ex 6:25
Moses, for the service of the *L* Ex 38:21
the cities of the *L*, and the Lev 25:32
may the *L* redeem at any time Lev 25:32
And if a man purchase of the *L* Lev 25:33
*L* are their possession among the Lev 25:33
But the *L* after the tribe of Num 1:47
the *L* over the tabernacle of Num 1:50
forward, the *L* shall take it down Num 1:51
be pitched, the *L* shall set it up Num 1:51
But the *L* shall pitch round about Num 1:53
the *L* shall keep the charge of Num 1:53
of the *L* in the midst of the camp Num 2:17
But the *L* were not numbered among Num 2:33
thou shalt give the *L* unto Aaron Num 3:9
I have taken the *L* from among the Num 3:12
therefore the *L* shall be mine Num 3:12
These are the families of the *L* Num 3:20
be chief over the chief of the *L* Num 3:32
All that were numbered of the *L* Num 3:39
thou shalt take the *L* for me (I Num 3:41
the cattle of the *L* instead of Num 3:41
Take the *L* instead of all the Num 3:45
the cattle of the *L* instead of Num 3:45
and the *L* shall be mine Num 3:45
Israel, which are more than the *L* Num 3:46
them that were redeemed by the *L* Num 3:49
the Kohathites from among the *L* Num 4:18
those that were numbered of the *L* Num 4:46
thou shalt give them unto the *L* Num 7:5
the oxen, and gave them unto the *L* Num 7:6
Take the *L* from among the Num 8:6
thou shalt bring the *L* before the Num 8:9
shalt bring the *L* before the LORD Num 8:10
shall put their hands upon the *L* Num 8:10
Aaron shall offer the *L* before Num 8:11
the *L* shall lay their hands upon Num 8:12
to make an atonement for the *L* Num 8:12
thou shalt set the *L* before Aaron Num 8:13
the *L* from among the children of Num 8:14
and the *L* shall be mine Num 8:14
after that shall the *L* go in to Num 8:15
I have taken the *L* for all the Num 8:18
I have given the *L* as a gift to Num 8:19
did to the *L* according unto all Num 8:20
commanded Moses concerning the *L* Num 8:20
the *L* were purified, and they Num 8:21
after that went the *L* in to do Num 8:22
commanded Moses concerning the *L* Num 8:22
is it that belongeth unto the *L* Num 8:24
unto the *L* touching their charge Num 8:26
the *L* from among the children of Num 18:6
But the *L* shall do the service of Num 18:23
I have given to the *L* to inherit Num 18:24
Thus speak unto the *L*, and say Num 18:26
unto the *L* as the increase of the Num 18:30
of the *L* after their families Num 26:57
These are the families of the *L* Num 26:58
beasts, and give them unto the *L* Num 31:30
of beast, and gave them unto the *L* Num 31:47
that they give unto the *L* of the Num 35:2
ye shall give also unto the *L* Num 35:2
which ye shall give unto the *L* Num 35:4
which ye shall give unto the *L* Num 35:6
give to the *L* shall be forty Num 35:7
give of his cities unto the *L* Num 35:8
shalt come unto the priests the *L* Deut 17:9
which is before the priests the *L* Deut 17:18
The priests the *L*, and all the Deut 18:1
God, as all his brethren the *L* do Deut 18:7
the priests the *L* shall teach you Deut 24:8
the priests the *L* spake unto all Deut 27:9
the *L* shall speak, and say unto Deut 27:14
That Moses commanded the *L* Deut 31:25
and the priests the *L* bearing it Josh 3:3
side before the priests the *L* Josh 8:33
but unto the *L* he gave none Josh 14:3
no part unto the *L* in the land Josh 14:4
But the *L* have no part among you Josh 18:7
of the *L* unto Eleazar the priest Josh 21:1
of Israel gave unto the *L* out of Josh 21:3
the priest, which were of the *L* Josh 21:4
of Israel gave by lot unto the *L* Josh 21:8
the *L* which remained of the Josh 21:20
Gershon, of the families of the *L* Josh 21:27
of Merari, the rest of the *L* Josh 21:34
of the families of the *L*, were by Josh 21:40
All the cities of the *L* within Josh 21:41
the *L* took down the ark of the 1Sa 6:15
all the *L* were with him, bearing 2Sa 15:24
did the priests and the *L* bring up 1Kin 8:4
the *L* according to their fathers 1Chr 6:19
Their brethren also the *L* were 1Chr 6:48
children of Israel gave to the *L* 1Chr 6:64
the Israelites, the priests, *L* 1Chr 9:2
And of the *L* 1Chr 9:14
For these *L*, the four chief 1Chr 9:26
And Mattithiah, one of the *L* 1Chr 9:31
chief of the fathers of the *L* 1Chr 9:33
These chief fathers of the *L* were 1Chr 9:34
*L* which are in their cities and 1Chr 13:2
to carry the ark of God but the *L* 1Chr 15:2
the children of Aaron, and the *L* 1Chr 15:4
the priests, and for the *L* 1Chr 15:11
the chief of the fathers of the *L* 1Chr 15:12
the *L* sanctified themselves to 1Chr 15:14
the children of the *L* bare the 1Chr 15:15
*L* to appoint their brethren to be 1Chr 15:16
So the *L* appointed Heman the son 1Chr 15:17
And Chenaniah, chief of the *L* 1Chr 15:22
when God helped the *L* that bare 1Chr 15:26
all the *L* that bare the ark, and 1Chr 15:27
he appointed certain of the *L* to 1Chr 16:4
Israel, with the priests and the *L* 1Chr 23:2
Now the *L* were numbered from the 1Chr 23:3
And also unto the *L* 1Chr 23:26
by the last words of David the *L* 1Chr 23:27
the scribe, one of the *L*, wrote 1Chr 24:6
the fathers of the priests and *L* 1Chr 24:6
of the *L* after the house of their 1Chr 24:30
the fathers of the priests and *L* 1Chr 24:31
Eastward were six *L*, northward 1Chr 26:17
And of the *L*, Ahijah was over the 1Chr 26:20
Of the *L*, Hashabiah the son of 1Chr 27:17
courses of the priests and the *L* 1Chr 28:13
courses of the priests and the *L* 1Chr 28:21
and the *L* took up the ark 2Chr 5:4
did the priests and the *L* bring up 2Chr 5:5
Also the *L* which were the singers 2Chr 5:12
the *L* also with instruments of 2Chr 7:6
the *L* to their charges, to praise 2Chr 8:14
*L* concerning any matter, or 2Chr 8:15
the *L* that were in all Israel 2Chr 11:13
For the *L* left their suburbs and 2Chr 11:14
LORD, the sons of Aaron, and the *L* 2Chr 13:9
the *L* wait upon their business 2Chr 13:10
And with them he sent *L*, even 2Chr 17:8
and Tobijah, and Tob-adonijah, *L* 2Chr 17:8
did Jehoshaphat set of the *L* 2Chr 19:8
also the *L* shall be officers 2Chr 19:11
And the *L*, of the children of the 2Chr 20:19
gathered the *L* out of all the 2Chr 23:2
of the priests and of the *L* 2Chr 23:4
and they that minister of the *L* 2Chr 23:6
the *L* shall compass the king 2Chr 23:7
So the *L* and all Judah did 2Chr 23:8
by the hand of the priests the *L* 2Chr 23:18
together the priests and the *L* 2Chr 24:5
Howbeit the *L* hastened it not 2Chr 24:5
of the *L* to bring in out of Judah 2Chr 24:6
office by the hand of the *L* 2Chr 24:11
brought in the priests and the *L* 2Chr 29:4
And said unto them, Hear me, ye *L* 2Chr 29:5
Then the *L* arose, Mahath the son 2Chr 29:12
the *L* took it, to carry it out 2Chr 29:16
he set the *L* in the house of the 2Chr 29:25
the *L* stood with the instruments 2Chr 29:26
the princes commanded the *L* to 2Chr 29:30
brethren the *L* did help them 2Chr 29:34
for the *L* were more upright in 2Chr 29:34
the *L* were ashamed, and sanctified 2Chr 30:15
received of the hand of the *L* 2Chr 30:16
therefore the *L* had the charge of 2Chr 30:17
and the *L* and the priests praised 2Chr 30:21
*L* that taught the good knowledge 2Chr 30:22
Judah, with the priests and the *L* 2Chr 30:25
Then the priests the *L* arose 2Chr 30:27
the *L* after their courses, every 2Chr 31:2
*L* for burnt offerings and for 2Chr 31:2
portion of the priests and the *L* 2Chr 31:4
the *L* concerning the heaps 2Chr 31:9
the *L* from twenty years old and 2Chr 31:17
by genealogies among the *L* 2Chr 31:19
which the *L* that kept the doors 2Chr 34:9
were Jahath and Obadiah, the *L* 2Chr 34:12
and other of the *L*, all that could 2Chr 34:12
of the *L* there were scribes, and 2Chr 34:13
and the priests, and the *L* 2Chr 34:30
said unto the *L* that taught all 2Chr 35:3
division of the families of the *L* 2Chr 35:5
to the priests, and to the *L* 2Chr 35:8
Jeiel and Jozabad, chief of the *L* 2Chr 35:9
gave unto the *L* for passover 2Chr 35:9
the *L* in their courses, according 2Chr 35:10
their hands, and the *L* flayed them 2Chr 35:11
therefore the *L* prepared for 2Chr 35:14
brethren the *L* prepared for them 2Chr 35:15
kept, and the priests, and the *L* 2Chr 35:18
and the priests, and the *L* Ezr 1:5
The *L*: the children Ezr 2:40
So the priests, and the *L*, and some Ezr 2:70
brethren the priests and the *L* Ezr 3:8
and appointed the *L*, from twenty Ezr 3:8
sons and their brethren the *L* Ezr 3:9
the *L* the sons of Asaph with Ezr 3:10
But many of the priests and *L* Ezr 3:12
of Israel, the priests, and the *L* Ezr 6:16
the *L* in their courses, for the Ezr 6:18
the *L* were purified together, all Ezr 6:20
and of the priests, and the *L* Ezr 7:7
of Israel, and of his priests and *L* Ezr 7:13
touching any of the priests and *L* Ezr 7:24
for the service of the *L*, two Ezr 8:20
the chief of the priests and the *L* Ezr 8:29
the *L* the weight of the silver, Ezr 8:30
and Noadiah the son of Binnui, *L* Ezr 8:33
Israel, and the priests, and the *L* Ezr 9:1
and made the chief priests, the *L* Ezr 10:5
Also of the *L* Ezr 10:23
After him repaired the *L*, Rehum Neh 3:17
singers and the *L* were appointed, Neh 7:1
The *L*: the children Neh 7:43
So the priests, and the *L*, and the Neh 7:73
Jozabad, Hanan, Pelaiah, and the *L* Neh 8:7
the *L* that taught the people, Neh 8:9
So the *L* stilled all the people, Neh 8:11
the people, the priests, and the *L* Neh 8:13
up upon the stairs, of the *L* Neh 9:4
Then the *L*, Jeshua, and Kadmiel, Neh 9:5
and our princes, *L*, and priests, Neh 9:38
And the *L*: both Jeshua Neh 10:9
of the people, the priests, the *L* Neh 10:28
the lots among the priests, the *L* Neh 10:34
tithes of our ground unto the *L* Neh 10:37
that the same *L* might have the Neh 10:37
son of Aaron shall be with the *L* Neh 10:38
when the *L* take tithes Neh 10:38
the *L* shall bring up the tithe of Neh 10:38
Israel, the priests, and the *L* Neh 11:3
Also of the *L* Neh 11:15
and Jozabad, of the chief of the *L* Neh 11:16
All the *L* in the holy city were Neh 11:18
Israel, of the priests, and the *L* Neh 11:20
The overseer also of the *L* at Neh 11:22
of the *L* were divisions in Judah, Neh 11:36
and the *L* that went up with Neh 12:1
Moreover the *L*: Jeshua, Neh 12:8
The *L* in the days of Eliashib, Neh 12:22
And the chief of the *L* Neh 12:24
the *L* out of all their places Neh 12:27
the *L* purified themselves, and Neh 12:30
of the law for the priests and *L* Neh 12:44
priests and for the *L* that waited Neh 12:44
sanctified holy things unto the *L* Neh 12:47
the *L* sanctified them unto the Neh 12:47
commanded to be given to the *L* Neh 13:5
of the *L* had not been given them Neh 13:10
for the *L* and the singers, that Neh 13:10
and Zadok the scribe, and of the *L* Neh 13:13
I commanded the *L* that they Neh 13:22
of the priesthood, and of the *L* Neh 13:29
the wards of the priests and the *L* Neh 13:30
take of them for priests and for *L* Is 66:21
*L* want a man before me to offer Jer 33:18
with the *L* the priests, my Jer 33:21
the *L* that minister unto me Jer 33:22
*L* that be of the seed of Zadok Eze 43:19
the *L* that are gone away far from Eze 44:10
But the priests the *L*, the sons Eze 44:15
of breadth, shall also the *L* Eze 45:5
went astray, as the *L* went astray Eze 48:11
most holy by the border of the *L* Eze 48:12
the priests the *L* shall have five Eze 48:13
from the possession of the *L* Eze 48:22
*L* from Jerusalem to ask him, Who Jn 1:19

**LEVITICAL** (*le-vit'-i-cal*) *Belonging to the Levites.*
were by the *L* priesthood, (for Heb 7:11

**LEVY**
*l* a tribute unto the LORD of the Num 31:28
raised a *l* out of all Israel 1Kin 5:13
the *l* was thirty thousand men 1Kin 5:13
and Adoniram was over the *l* 1Kin 5:14
the *l* which king Solomon raised 1Kin 9:15
upon those did Solomon *l* a 1Kin 9:21

**LEWD**
which are ashamed of thy *l* way Eze 16:27
and unto Aholibah, the *l* women Eze 23:44

took unto them certain *l* fellows Acts 17:5

## LEWDLY
another hath *l* defiled his Eze 22:11

## LEWDNESS
for they have committed *l* Judg 20:6
she hath wrought *l* with many Jer 11:15
the *l* of thy whoredom, and thine Jer 13:27
thou shalt not commit this *l* Eze 16:43
Thou hast borne thy *l* and thine Eze 16:58
the midst of thee they commit *l* Eze 22:9
to remembrance the *l* of thy youth Eze 23:21
I make thy *l* to cease from thee Eze 23:27
shall be discovered, both thy *l* Eze 23:29
therefore bear thou also thy *l* Eze 23:35
Thus will I cause *l* to cease out Eze 23:48
be taught not to do after your *l* Eze 23:48
shall recompense your *l* upon you Eze 23:49
In thy filthiness is *l* Eze 24:13
now will I discover her *l* in the Hos 2:10
for they commit *l* Hos 6:9
a matter of wrong or wicked *l* Acts 18:14

## LIAR
not so now, who will make me a *l* Job 24:25
a *l* giveth ear to a naughty Prov 17:4
and a poor man is better than a *l* Prov 19:22
thee, and thou be found a *l* Prov 30:6
thou be altogether unto me as a *l* Jer 15:18
for he is a *l*, and the father of Jn 8:44
I shall be a *l* like unto you Jn 8:55
God be true, but every man a *l* Rom 3:4
have not sinned, we make him a *l* 1Jn 1:10
not his commandments, is a *l* 1Jn 2:4
Who is a *l* but he that denieth 1Jn 2:22
and hateth his brother, he is a *l* 1Jn 4:20
not God hath made him a *l* 1Jn 5:10

## LIARS
shall be found *l* unto thee Deut 33:29
I said in my haste, All men are *l* Ps 116:11
frustrateth the tokens of the *l* Is 44:25
A sword is upon the *l* Jer 50:36
mankind, for menstealers, for *l* 1Ti 1:10
said, The Cretians are alway *l* Titus 1:12
and are not, and hast found them *l* Rev 2:2
sorcerers, and idolaters, and all *l* Rev 21:8

## LIBERAL
The *l* soul shall be made fat Prov 11:25
person shall be no more called *l* Is 32:5
But the *l* deviseth *l* things Is 32:8
by *l* things shall he stand Is 32:8
for your *l* distribution unto them 2Cor 9:13

## LIBERALITY
to bring your *l* unto Jerusalem 1Cor 16:3
unto the riches of their *l* 2Cor 8:2

## LIBERALLY
furnish him *l* out of thy flock Deut 15:14
of God, that giveth to all men *l* Jas 1:5

## LIBERTINES (*lib'-ur-tins*) *Former Jewish slaves.*
is called the synagogue of the *L* Acts 6:9

## LIBERTY
proclaim *l* throughout all the Lev 25:10
And I will walk at *l* Ps 119:45
to proclaim *l* to the captives, and Is 61:1
to proclaim *l* unto them Jer 34:8
in proclaiming *l* every man to his Jer 34:15
he had set at *l* at their pleasure Jer 34:16
unto me, in proclaiming *l* Jer 34:17
behold, I proclaim a *l* for you Jer 34:17
it shall be his to the year of *l* Eze 46:17
to set at *l* them that are bruised Lk 4:18
keep Paul, and to let him have *l* Acts 24:23
This man might have been set at *l* Acts 26:32
gave him *l* to go unto his friends Acts 27:3
glorious *l* of the children of God Rom 8:21
she is at *l* to be married to whom 1Cor 7:39
means this *l* of yours become a 1Cor 8:9
for why is my *l* judged of another 1Cor 10:29
Spirit of the Lord is, there is *l* 2Cor 3:17
*l* which we have in Christ Jesus Gal 2:4
Stand fast therefore in the *l* Gal 5:1
ye have been called unto *l* Gal 5:13
only use not *l* for an occasion to Gal 5:13
our brother Timothy is set at *l* Heb 13:23
looketh into the perfect law of *l* Jas 1:25
shall be judged by the law of *l* Jas 2:12
not using your *l* for a cloke of 1Pet 2:16
While they promise them *l* 2Pet 2:19

## LIBNAH (*lib'-nah*) See LABAN.
*1. A Hebrew encampment in the wilderness.*
Rimmon-parez, and pitched in *L* Num 33:20
And they removed from *L*, and Num 33:21
*2. A Levitical city in Judah.*
and all Israel with him, unto *L* Josh 10:29
unto Libnah, and fought against *L* Josh 10:29
And Joshua passed from *L*, and all Josh 10:31
to all that he had done to *L* Josh 10:32
as he had done also to *L*, and to Josh 10:39
The king of *L*, one Josh 12:15
*L*, and Ether, and Ashan, Josh 15:42
and *L* with her suburbs, Josh 21:13
Then *L* revolted at the same time 2Kin 8:22
king of Assyria warring against *L* 2Kin 19:8
the daughter of Jeremiah of *L* 2Kin 23:31
the daughter of Jeremiah of *L* 2Kin 24:18
*L* with her suburbs, and Jattir, and 1Chr 6:57
The same time also did *L* revolt 2Chr 21:10
king of Assyria warring against *L* Is 37:8
the daughter of Jeremiah of *L* Jer 52:1

## LIBNI (*lib'-ni*) See LAADAN, LIBNITES.
*1. Son of Gershon.*
*L*, and Shimi, according to their Ex 6:17
their families; *L*, and Shimei Num 3:18
of Gershom; *L*, and Shimei 1Chr 6:17
*L* his son, Jahath his son, Zimmah 1Chr 6:20
*2. Grandson of Merari.*
*L* his son, Shimei his son, Uzza 1Chr 6:29

## LIBNITES (*lib'-nites*) *Descendants of Libni 1.*
Gershon was the family of the *L* Num 3:21
the family of the *L*, the family Num 26:58

## LIBYA (*lib'-e-ah*) See LIBYANS. *A land in north Africa.*
Ethiopia, and *L*, and Lydia, and all Eze 30:5
Persia, Ethiopia, and *L* with them Eze 38:5
and in the parts of *L* about Cyrene Acts 2:10

## LIBYANS (*lib'-e-uns*) See LEHABIM. *Inhabitants of Libya.*
the Ethiopians and the *L*, that Jer 46:9
and the *L* and the Ethiopians shall Dan 11:43

## LICE
that it may become *l* throughout Ex 8:16
the earth, and it became *l* in man Ex 8:17
*l* throughout all the land of Ex 8:17
enchantments to bring forth *l* Ex 8:18
so there were *l* upon man, and upon Ex 8:18
flies, and *l* in all their coasts Ps 105:31

## LICENCE
And when he had given him *l* Acts 21:40
have *l* to answer for himself Acts 25:16

## LICK
Now shall this company *l* up all Num 22:4
of Naboth shall dogs *l* thy blood 1Kin 21:19
and his enemies shall *l* the dust Ps 72:9
*l* up the dust of thy feet Is 49:23
They shall *l* the dust like a Mic 7:17

## LICKED
*l* up the water that was in the 1Kin 18:38
In the place where dogs *l* the 1Kin 21:19
and the dogs *l* up his blood 1Kin 22:38
the dogs came and *l* his sores Lk 16:21

## LICKETH
as the ox *l* up the grass of the Num 22:4

## LID
and bored a hole in the *l* of it 2Kin 12:9

## LIE
we will *l* with him, that we may Gen 19:32
*l* with him, that we may preserve Gen 19:34
Therefore he shall *l* with thee to Gen 30:15
and she said, *L* with me Gen 39:7
to *l* by her, or to be with her Gen 39:10
by his garment, saying, *L* with me Gen 39:12
he came in unto me to *l* with me Gen 39:14
But I will *l* with my fathers, and Gen 47:30
if a man *l* not in wait, but God Ex 21:13
*l* with her, he shall surely endow Ex 22:16
thou shalt let it rest and *l* still Ex 23:11
*l* unto his neighbour in that Lev 6:2
shall *l* with seed of copulation Lev 15:18
if any man *l* with her at all, and Lev 15:24
Moreover thou shalt not *l* Lev 18:20
Thou shalt not *l* with mankind Lev 18:22
Neither shalt thou *l* with any Lev 18:23
before a beast to *l* down thereto Lev 18:23
falsely, neither *l* one to another Lev 19:11
if a man *l* with his daughter in Lev 20:12
If a man also *l* with mankind Lev 20:13
if a man *l* with a beast, he shall Lev 20:15
*l* down thereto, thou shalt kill Lev 20:16
if a man shall *l* with a woman Lev 20:18
if a man shall *l* with his uncle's Lev 20:20
in the land, and ye shall *l* down Lev 26:6
a man *l* with her carnally, and it Num 5:13
then the camps that *l* on the east Num 10:5
then the camps that *l* on the Num 10:6
is not a man, that he should *l* Num 23:19
he shall not *l* down until he eat Num 23:24
*l* in wait for him, and rise up Deut 19:11
her in the city, and *l* with her Deut 22:23
the man force her, and *l* with her Deut 22:25
*l* with her, and they be found Deut 22:28
judge shall cause him to *l* down Deut 25:2
and another man shall *l* with her Deut 28:30
in this book shall *l* upon him Deut 29:20
ye shall *l* in wait against the Josh 8:4
and they went to *l* in ambush Josh 8:9
set them to *l* in ambush between Josh 8:12
thee, and *l* in wait in the field Judg 9:32
let all thy wants *l* upon me Judg 19:20
*l* in wait in the vineyards Judg 21:20
mark the place where he shall *l* Ruth 3:4
he went to *l* down at the end of Ruth 3:7
*l* down until the morning Ruth 3:13
*l* down again 1Sa 3:5
*l* down again 1Sa 3:6
Eli said unto Samuel, Go, *l* down 1Sa 3:9
of Israel will not *l* nor repent 1Sa 15:29
to *l* in wait, as at this day 1Sa 22:8
to *l* in wait, as at this day 1Sa 22:13
and to drink, and to *l* with my wife 2Sa 11:11
at even he went out to *l* on his 2Sa 11:13
he shall *l* with thy wives in the 2Sa 12:11
Come *l* with me, my sister 2Sa 13:11
let her *l* in thy bosom, that my 1Kin 1:2
do not *l* unto thine handmaid 2Kin 4:16
for it is evident unto you if I *l* Job 6:28
When I *l* down, I say, When shall Job 7:4
Also thou shalt *l* down, and none Job 11:19
which shall *l* down with him in Job 20:11
They shall *l* down alike in the Job 21:26
The rich man shall *l* down Job 27:19
Should I *l* against my right Job 34:6
abide in the covert to *l* in wait Job 38:40
He maketh me to *l* down in green Ps 23:2
I *l* even among them that are set Ps 57:4
they *l* in wait for my soul Ps 59:3
and men of high degree are a *l* Ps 62:9
the slain that *l* in the grave Ps 88:5
that I will not *l* unto David Ps 89:35
proud have forged a *l* against me Ps 119:69
yea, thou shalt *l* down, and thy Prov 3:24
wicked are to *l* in wait for blood Prov 12:6
A faithful witness will not *l* Prov 14:5
if two *l* together, then they have Eccl 4:11
he shall *l* all night betwixt my Song 1:13
leopard shall *l* down with the kid Is 11:6
young ones shall *l* down together Is 11:7
of the desert shall *l* there Is 13:21
*l* in glory, every one in his own Is 14:18
the needy shall *l* down in safety Is 14:30
be for flocks, which shall *l* down Is 17:2
feed, and there shall he *l* down Is 27:10
The highways *l* waste, the Is 33:8
to generation it shall *l* waste Is 34:10
they shall *l* down together, they Is 43:17
Is there not a *l* in my right hand Is 44:20
ye shall *l* down in sorrow Is 50:11
they *l* at the head of all the Is 51:20
people, children that will not *l* Is 63:8
place for the herds to *l* down in Is 65:10
We *l* down in our shame, and our Jer 3:25
For they prophesy a *l* unto you Jer 27:10
for they prophesy a *l* unto you Jer 27:14
yet they prophesy a *l* in my name Jer 27:15
for they prophesy a *l* unto you Jer 27:16
this people to trust in a *l* Jer 28:15
which prophesy a *l* unto you in my Jer 29:21
and he caused you to trust in a *l* Jer 29:31
causing their flocks to *l* down Jer 33:12
the old *l* on the ground in the Lam 2:21
*L* thou also upon thy left side, Eze 4:4
of the days that thou shalt *l* Eze 4:4
*l* again on thy right side, and Eze 4:6
that thou shalt *l* upon thy side Eze 4:9
whiles they divine a *l* unto thee Eze 21:29
thou shalt *l* in the midst of the Eze 31:18
they *l* uncircumcised, slain by Eze 32:21
they shall not *l* with the mighty Eze 32:27
shalt *l* with them that are slain Eze 32:28
they shall *l* with the Eze 32:29
they *l* uncircumcised with them Eze 32:30
there shall they *l* in a good fold Eze 34:14
and I will cause them to *l* down Eze 34:15
will make them to *l* down safely Hos 2:18
an oven, whiles they *l* in wait Hos 7:6
*l* all night in sackcloth, ye Joel 1:13
That *l* upon beds of ivory, and Amos 6:4
be a *l* to the kings of Israel Mic 1:14
in the spirit and falsehood do *l* Mic 2:11
they all *l* in wait for blood Mic 7:2
the end it shall speak, and not *l* Hab 2:3
shall they *l* down in the evening Zeph 2:7
flocks shall *l* down in the midst Zeph 2:14
a place for beasts to *l* down in Zeph 2:15
*l* down, and none shall make them Zeph 3:13
houses, and this house *l* waste Hag 1:4
and the diviners have seen a *l* Zec 10:2
When Jesus saw him *l*, and knew Jn 5:6
When he speaketh a *l*, he speaketh Jn 8:44
and seeth the linen clothes *l* Jn 20:6
heart to *l* to the Holy Ghost Acts 5:3
for there *l* in wait for him of Acts 23:21
changed the truth of God into a *l* Rom 1:25
through my *l* unto his glory Rom 3:7
I *l* not, my conscience also Rom 9:1
evermore, knoweth that I *l* not 2Cor 11:31
you, behold, before God, I *l* not Gal 1:20
whereby they *l* in wait to deceive Eph 4:14
*L* not one to another, seeing that Col 3:9
that they should believe a *l* 2Th 2:11
the truth in Christ, and *l* not 1Ti 2:7
life, which God, that cannot *l* Titus 1:2
it was impossible for God to *l* Heb 6:18
not, and *l* not against the truth Jas 3:14
him, and walk in darkness, we *l* 1Jn 1:6
that no *l* is of the truth 1Jn 2:21
things, and is truth, and is no *l* 1Jn 2:27
are Jews, and are not, but do *l* Rev 3:9
their dead bodies shall *l* in the Rev 11:8
abomination, or maketh a *l* Rev 21:27
and whosoever loveth and maketh a *l* Rev 22:15

## LIED
But he *l* unto him 1Kin 13:18
they *l* unto him with their Ps 78:36
or feared, that thou hast *l* Is 57:11
thou hast not *l* unto men, but Acts 5:4

## LIEN
lightly have *l* with thy wife Gen 26:10
Though ye have *l* among the pots Ps 68:13
where thou hast not been *l* with Jer 3:2

## LIERS
their *l* in wait on the west of Josh 8:13
*l* in ambush against him behind Josh 8:14

the men of Shechem set *l* in wait ........ Judg 9:25
there were *l* in wait abiding in........... Judg 16:12
Israel set *l* in wait round about .......... Judg 20:29
the *l* in wait of Israel came.............. Judg 20:33
the *l* in wait which they had set.......... Judg 20:36
the *l* in wait hasted, and rushed ......... Judg 20:37
the *l* in wait drew themselves ............ Judg 20:37
the *l* in wait, that they should............ Judg 20:38

**LIES**

thou hast mocked me, and told me *l*. Judg 16:10
thou hast mocked me, and told me *l*. Judg 16:13
Should thy *l* make men hold their.......... Job 11:3
But ye are forgers of *l*, ye are................. Job 13:4
nor such as turn aside to *l*........................ Ps 40:4
soon as they be born, speaking *l*.............. Ps 58:3
they delight in *l*....................................... Ps 62:4
that speak *l* shall be stopped.................. Ps 63:11
he that telleth *l* shall not tarry................ Ps 101:7
A false witness that speaketh *l*............. Prov 6:19
but a false witness will utter *l*.............. Prov 14:5
a deceitful witness speaketh *l*............. Prov 14:25
that speaketh *l* shall not escape............ Prov 19:5
he that speaketh *l* shall perish ............ Prov 19:9
If a ruler hearken to *l*, all his ............. Prov 29:12
Remove far from me vanity and *l* ........ Prov 30:8
and the prophet that teacheth *l*................. Is 9:15
but his *l* shall not be so.......................... Is 16:6
for we have made *l* our refuge................. Is 28:15
shall sweep away the refuge of *l* ............. Is 28:17
your lips have spoken *l*, your ................... Is 59:3
they trust in vanity, and speak *l*.............. Is 59:4
tongues like their bow for *l*...................... Jer 9:3
taught their tongue to speak *l* ................. Jer 9:5
prophets prophesy *l* in my name .......... Jer 14:14
our fathers have inherited *l* ................. Jer 16:19
to whom thou hast prophesied *l*............... Jer 20:6
commit adultery, and walk in *l*............. Jer 23:14
said, that prophesy *l* in my name .......... Jer 23:25
of the prophets that prophesy *l*............. Jer 23:26
cause my people to err by their *l*.......... Jer 23:32
his *l* shall not so effect it ..................... Jer 48:30
ye have spoken vanity, and seen *l*......... Eze 13:8
that see vanity, and that divine *l*.......... Eze 13:9
to my people that hear your *l*.............. Eze 13:19
Because with *l* ye have made the......... Eze 13:22
divining *l* unto them, saying,................ Eze 22:28
She hath wearied herself with *l*............ Eze 24:12
they shall speak *l* at one table ............. Dan 11:27
and the princes with their *l*..................... Hos 7:3
yet they have spoken *l* against me........ Hos 7:13
ye have eaten the fruit of *l*.................. Hos 10:13
compasseth me about with *l*.................. Hos 11:12
he daily increaseth *l* and ........................ Hos 12:1
their *l* caused them to err, after............ Amos 2:4
inhabitants thereof have spoken *l*.......... Mic 6:12
it is all full of *l* and robbery ..................... Nah 3:1
molten image, and a teacher of *l*............ Hab 2:18
not do iniquity, nor speak *l*................. Zeph 3:13
for thou speakest *l* in the name............. Zec 13:3
Speaking *l* in hypocrisy ............................ 1Ti 4:2

**LIEST**

the land whereon thou *l*, to thee......... Gen 28:13
by the way, and when thou *l* down....... Deut 6:7
by the way, when thou *l* down........... Deut 11:19
wherefore *l* thou thus upon thy........... Josh 7:10
When thou *l* down, thou shalt not....... Prov 3:24

**LIETH**

doest not well, sin *l* at the door................ Gen 4:7
of the deep that *l* under,....................... Gen 49:25
Whosoever *l* with a beast shall.............. Ex 22:19
*l* concerning it, and sweareth.................... Lev 6:3
he that *l* in the house shall wash ......... Lev 14:47
whereon he *l* that hath the issue,.......... Lev 15:4
every thing that she *l* upon in.............. Lev 15:20
bed whereon he *l* shall be unclean....... Lev 15:24
Every bed whereon she *l* all the ........... Lev 15:26
of him that *l* with her that is............... Lev 15:33
whosoever *l* carnally with a woman.... Lev 19:20
the man that *l* with his father's.............. Lev 20:11
as he *l* with a woman, both of............. Lev 20:13
as long as it *l* desolate........................ Lev 26:34
As long as it *l* desolate it shall........... Lev 26:35
while she *l* desolate without them ...... Lev 26:43
*l* upon the border of Moab.................. Num 21:15
Cursed be he that *l* with his................ Deut 27:20
Cursed be he that *l* with any .............. Deut 27:21
be he that *l* with his sister.................. Deut 27:22
Cursed be he that *l* with his................ Deut 27:23
*l* before the valley of Hinnom................ Josh 15:8
Michmethah, that *l* before Shechem.... Josh 17:7
near the hill that *l* on the south.......... Josh 18:13
from the hill that *l* before.................. Josh 18:14
*l* before the valley of the son of........... Josh 18:16
which *l* in the south of Arad................. Judg 1:16
see wherein his great strength *l* ........... Judg 16:5
wherein thy great strength *l*.................... Judg 16:6
me wherein thy great strength *l*........... Judg 16:15
the valley that *l* by Beth-rehob............ Judg 18:28
And it shall be, when he *l* down ............. Ruth 3:4
that *l* before Giah by the way of............ 2Sa 2:24
*l* in the midst of the river of................. 2Sa 24:5
*l* waste, and the gates thereof are .......... Neh 2:3
we are in, how Jerusalem *l* waste.......... Neh 2:17
the tower which *l* out from the ............ Neh 3:25
the east, and the tower that *l* out ......... Neh 3:26
the great tower that *l* out.................... Neh 3:27
So man *l* down, and riseth not............. Job 14:12
He *l* under the shady trees, in ............ Job 40:21
He *l* in wait secretly as a lion ................. Ps 10:9
he *l* in wait to catch the poor.................. Ps 10:9
now that he *l* he shall rise up no .............. Ps 41:8
Thy wrath *l* hard upon me, and thou ...... Ps 88:7
*l* in wait at every corner...................... Prov 7:12
She also *l* in wait as for a prey, ......... Prov 23:28
thou shalt be as he that *l* down ........... Prov 23:34
or as he that *l* upon the top of a ........ Prov 23:34
which *l* toward the north, and.................. Eze 9:2
the great dragon that *l* in the................. Eze 29:3
from her that *l* in thy bosom..................... Mic 7:5
my servant *l* at home sick of the................ Mt 8:6
My little daughter *l* at the point .............. Mk 5:23
the region that *l* round about ............... Acts 14:6
*l* toward the south west and north...... Acts 27:12
be possible, as much as *l* in you ......... Rom 12:18
the whole world *l* in wickedness ............ 1Jn 5:19
the city *l* foursquare, and the .............. Rev 21:16

**LIEUTENANTS**

commissions unto the king's *l*................ Ezr 8:36
had commanded unto the king's *l*.......... Est 3:12
unto the Jews, and to the *l*...................... Est 8:9
rulers of the provinces, and the *l* ........... Est 9:3

**LIFE**

the moving creature that hath *l* ........... Gen 1:20
the earth, wherein there is *l*.................. Gen 1:30
into his nostrils the breath of *l*............... Gen 2:7
the tree of *l* also in the midst ................ Gen 2:9
thou eat all the days of thy *l*................ Gen 3:14
eat of it all the days of thy *l*................ Gen 3:17
and take also of the tree of *l* ................ Gen 3:22
to keep the way of the tree of *l* ............ Gen 3:24
flesh, wherein is the breath of *l* ............ Gen 6:17
six hundredth year of Noah's *l*................ Gen 7:11
flesh, wherein is the breath of *l* ............ Gen 7:15
nostrils was the breath of *l* ................... Gen 7:22
But flesh with the *l* thereof..................... Gen 9:4
will I require the *l* of man ........................ Gen 9:5
thee according to the time of *l*............ Gen 18:10
thee, according to the time of *l*........... Gen 18:14
that he said, Escape for thy *l*.............. Gen 19:17
shewed unto me in saving my *l*............. Gen 19:19
were the years of the *l* of Sarah ........... Gen 23:1
of Abraham's *l* which he lived................ Gen 25:7
are the years of the *l* of Ishmael.......... Gen 25:17
I am weary of my *l* because of the ..... Gen 27:46
land, what good shall my *l* do me ....... Gen 27:46
to face, and my *l* is preserved.............. Gen 32:30
By the *l* of Pharaoh ye shall not .......... Gen 42:15
or else by the *l* of Pharaoh.................... Gen 42:16
seeing that his *l* is bound up in............ Gen 44:30
is bound up in the lad's *l* ..................... Gen 44:30
send me before you to preserve *l*.......... Gen 45:5
days of the years of my *l* been ............. Gen 47:9
*l* of my fathers in the days of................. Gen 47:9
me all my *l* long unto this day ............. Gen 48:15
men are dead which sought thy *l*.............. Ex 4:19
the years of the *l* of Levi were................ Ex 6:16
the years of the *l* of Kohath were............ Ex 6:18
the years of the *l* of Amram were............ Ex 6:20
then thou shalt give *l* for *l*.................... Ex 21:23
give for the ransom of his *l* .................. Ex 21:30
For the *l* of the flesh is in the ............. Lev 17:11
For it is the *l* of all flesh ..................... Lev 17:14
blood of it is for the *l* thereof............... Lev 17:14
for the *l* of all flesh is the..................... Lev 17:14
beside the other in her *l* time................. Lev 18:18
for the *l* of a murderer, which is ........ Num 35:31
thy heart all the days of thy *l*............... Deut 4:9
son's son, all the days of thy *l* ............. Deut 6:2
for the blood is the *l*.......................... Deut 12:23
not eat the *l* with the flesh ................. Deut 12:23
of Egypt all the days of thy *l* ............... Deut 16:3
therein all the days of his *l*.................. Deut 17:19
but *l* shall go for *l*, eye for.................. Deut 19:21
*l*) to employ them in the siege............... Deut 20:19
for he taketh a man's *l* to pledge........... Deut 24:6
thy *l* shall hang in doubt before......... Deut 28:66
have none assurance of thy *l*.............. Deut 28:66
I have set before thee this day *l*.......... Deut 30:15
you, that I have set before you *l*........ Deut 30:19
therefore choose *l*, that both............... Deut 30:19
for he is thy *l*, and the length of ....... Deut 30:20
because it is your *l*............................. Deut 32:47
before thee all the days of thy *l* .............. Josh 1:5
Our *l* for yours, if ye utter not ............. Josh 2:14
Moses, all the days of his *l* ................... Josh 4:14
for you, and adventured his *l* far.......... Judg 9:17
I put my *l* in my hands, and passed...... Judg 12:3
than they which he slew in his *l* ......... Judg 16:30
run upon thee, and thou lose thy *l* .... Judg 18:25
be unto thee a restorer of thy *l*.......... Ruth 4:15
be the LORD all the days of his *l*.................. 1Sa 1:11
Israel all the days of his *l* ........................ 1Sa 7:15
and what is my *l*, or my father's............ 1Sa 18:18
For he did put his *l* in his hand.............. 1Sa 19:5
thy father, that he seeketh my *l* ............ 1Sa 20:1
seeketh my *l* seeketh thy *l*................... 1Sa 22:23
Saul was come out to seek his *l* .......... 1Sa 23:15
bundle of *l* with the LORD thy God ....... 1Sa 25:29
as thy *l* was much set by this day....... 1Sa 26:24
so let my *l* be much set by in the......... 1Sa 26:24
then layest thou a snare for my *l* ........ 1Sa 28:9
and I have put my *l* in my hand........... 1Sa 28:21
because my *l* is yet whole in me.............. 2Sa 1:9
thine enemy, which sought thy *l*.............. 2Sa 4:8
for the *l* of his brother whom he ............ 2Sa 14:7
shall be, whether in death or *l* ............ 2Sa 15:21
forth of my bowels, seeketh my *l*......... 2Sa 16:11
falsehood against mine own *l* .............. 2Sa 18:13
which this day have saved thy *l* ............. 2Sa 19:5
that thou mayest save thine own *l* ...... 1Kin 1:12
and the *l* of thy son Solomon ............... 1Kin 1:12
this word against his own *l*.................. 1Kin 2:23
hast not asked for thyself long *l*........... 1Kin 3:11
hast asked the *l* of thine enemies......... 1Kin 3:11
Solomon all the days of his *l*.............. 1Kin 4:21
his *l* for David my servant's sake ....... 1Kin 11:34
him all the days of his *l*...................... 1Kin 15:5
and Jeroboam all the days of his *l* ....... 1Kin 15:6
if I make not thy *l* as the *l*................. 1Kin 19:2
that, he arose, and went for his *l* ........ 1Kin 19:3
now, O LORD, take away my *l*................. 1Kin 19:4
and they seek my *l*, to take it ............ 1Kin 19:10
and they seek my *l*, to take it ............ 1Kin 19:14
peradventure he will save thy *l*............ 1Kin 20:31
then shall thy *l* be for his *l*,.............. 1Kin 20:39
thy *l* shall go for his *l*....................... 1Kin 20:42
man of God, I pray thee, let my *l*......... 2Kin 1:13
the *l* of these fifty thy servants............. 2Kin 1:13
therefore let my *l* now be..................... 2Kin 1:14
according to the time of *l*.................... 2Kin 4:16
her, according to the time of *l*............. 2Kin 4:17
as it was, and fled for their *l*................. 2Kin 7:7
whose son he had restored to *l*.................. 2Kin 8:1
he had restored a dead body to *l* ............. 2Kin 8:5
whose son he had restored to *l*................ 2Kin 8:5
son, whom Elisha restored to *l*............... 2Kin 8:5
his *l* shall be for the *l* of...................... 2Kin 10:24
*l* shall be for the *l* of him....................... 2Kin 10:24
before him all the days of his *l*........... 2Kin 25:29
every day, all the days of his *l* ............ 2Kin 25:30
nor the *l* of thine enemies,..................... 2Chr 1:11
neither yet hast asked long *l*................. 2Chr 1:11
and pray for the *l* of the king.................. Ezr 6:10
go into the temple to save his *l*.............. Neh 6:11
let my *l* be given me at my......................... Est 7:3
for his *l* to Esther the queen........................ Est 7:7
together, and to stand for their *l*................ Est 8:11
a man hath will he give for his *l*................. Job 2:4
but save his *l*............................................. Job 2:6
*l* unto the bitter in soul............................ Job 3:20
end, that I should prolong my *l* ................ Job 6:11
O remember that my *l* is wind ..................... Job 7:7
and death rather than my *l*...................... Job 7:15
I would despise my *l*................................... Job 9:21
My soul is weary of my *l* ............................. Job 10:1
Thou hast granted me *l* and favour, .... Job 10:12
teeth, and put my *l* in mine hand......... Job 13:14
riseth up, and no man is sure of *l*......... Job 24:22
owners thereof to lose their *l*............... Job 31:39
of the Almighty hath given me *l*............... Job 33:4
his *l* from perishing by the sword......... Job 33:18
So that his *l* abhorreth bread, and........ Job 33:20
grave, and his *l* to the destroyers ......... Job 33:22
his *l* shall see the light......................... Job 33:28
not the *l* of the wicked.............................. Job 36:6
their *l* is among the unclean................. Job 36:14
tread down my *l* upon the earth........................ Ps 7:5
Thou wilt shew me the path of *l*............ Ps 16:11
have their portion in this *l*..................... Ps 17:14
He asked *l* of thee, and thou..................... Ps 21:4
follow me all the days of my *l*................. Ps 23:6
sinners, nor my *l* with bloody men........... Ps 26:9
the LORD is the strength of my *l*............... Ps 27:1
of the LORD all the days of my *l*............... Ps 27:4
in his favour is *l*............................................ Ps 30:5
For my *l* is spent with grief, and............. Ps 31:10
they devised to take away my *l*............... Ps 31:13
What man is he that desireth *l*............... Ps 34:12
with thee is the fountain of *l*.................... Ps 36:9
seek after my *l* lay snares for me.......... Ps 38:12
and my prayer unto the God of my *l*......... Ps 42:8
Thou wilt prolong the king's *l*.................... Ps 61:6
lovingkindness is better than *l* ................. Ps 63:3
preserve my *l* from fear of the................. Ps 64:1
Which holdeth our soul in *l* ....................... Ps 66:9
but gave their *l* over to the..................... Ps 78:50
my *l* draweth nigh unto the grave............. Ps 88:3
With long *l* will I satisfy him,................. Ps 91:16
redeemeth thy *l* from destruction........... Ps 103:4
Jerusalem all the days of thy *l* ................ Ps 128:5
the blessing, even *l* for evermore ........... Ps 133:3
smitten my *l* down to the ground............ Ps 143:3
away the *l* of the owners thereof .......... Prov 1:19
take they hold of the paths of *l* ............ Prov 2:19
For length of days, and long *l*................. Prov 3:2
She is a tree of *l* to them that............... Prov 3:18
So shall they be *l* unto thy soul............. Prov 3:22
the years of thy *l* shall be many ........... Prov 4:10
for she is thy *l*...................................... Prov 4:13
For they are *l* unto those that............... Prov 4:22
for out of it are the issues of *l*............. Prov 4:23
shouldest ponder the path of *l*.................. Prov 5:6
of instruction are the way of *l* ............... Prov 6:23
will hunt for the precious *l* ................... Prov 6:26
knoweth not that it is for his *l*............... Prov 7:23
For whoso findeth me findeth *l*............... Prov 8:35
the years of thy *l* shall be...................... Prov 9:11
of a righteous man is a well of *l*.......... Prov 10:11
of the righteous tendeth to *l*................. Prov 10:16
He is in the way of *l* that ..................... Prov 10:17
As righteousness tendeth to *l* ................ Prov 11:19
of the righteous is a tree of *l*............... Prov 11:30
man regardeth the *l* of his beast............ Prov 12:10
In the way of righteousness is *l*............. Prov 12:28
keepeth his mouth keepeth his *l* ............. Prov 13:3
of a man's *l* are his riches ...................... Prov 13:8
desire cometh, it is a tree of *l* ............. Prov 13:12
of the wise is a fountain of *l*................. Prov 13:14

of the LORD is a fountain of *l* Prov 14:27
sound heart is the *l* of the flesh Prov 14:30
A wholesome tongue is a tree of *l* Prov 15:4
The way of *l* is above to the wise Prov 15:24
of *l* abideth among the wise Prov 15:31
of the king's countenance is *l* Prov 16:15
is a wellspring of *l* unto him Prov 16:22
*l* are in the power of the tongue Prov 18:21
The fear of the LORD tendeth to *l* Prov 19:23
righteousness and mercy findeth *l* Prov 21:21
LORD are riches, and honour, and *l* Prov 22:4
and not evil all the days of her *l* Prov 31:12
heaven all the days of their *l* Eccl 2:3
Therefore I hated *l* Eccl 2:17
rejoice, and to do good in his *l* Eccl 3:12
the sun all the days of his *l* Eccl 5:18
much remember the days of his *l* Eccl 5:20
what is good for man in this *l* Eccl 6:12
all the days of his vain *l* which Eccl 6:12
that wisdom giveth *l* to them that Eccl 7:12
his *l* in his wickedness Eccl 7:15
of his labour the days of his *l* Eccl 8:15
the days of the *l* of thy vanity Eccl 9:9
for that is thy portion in this *l* Eccl 9:9
his *l* shall be grievous unto him Is 15:4
I have cut off like a weaver my *l* Is 38:12
things is the *l* of my spirit Is 38:16
of our *l* in the house of the LORD Is 38:20
men for thee, and people for thy *l* Is 43:4
hast found the *l* of thine hand Is 57:10
thee, they will seek thy *l* Jer 4:30
shall be chosen rather than *l* by Jer 8:3
men of Anathoth, that seek thy *l* Jer 11:21
hand of those that seek their *l* Jer 21:7
I set before you the way of *l* Jer 21:8
his *l* shall be unto him for a Jer 21:9
the hand of them that seek thy *l* Jer 22:25
hand of them that seek their *l* Jer 34:20
hand of them that seek their *l* Jer 34:21
he shall have his *l* for a prey Jer 38:2
hand of these men that seek thy *l* Jer 38:16
but thy *l* shall be for a prey Jer 39:18
the hand of them that seek his *l* Jer 44:30
his enemy, and that sought his *l* Jer 44:30
but thy *l* will I give unto thee Jer 45:5
and before them that seek their *l* Jer 49:37
before him all the days of his *l* Jer 52:33
his death, all the days of his *l* Jer 52:34
for the *l* of thy young children Lam 2:19
have cut off my *l* in the dungeon Lam 3:53
thou hast redeemed my *l* Lam 3:58
his wicked way, to save his *l* Eze 3:18
himself in the iniquity of his *l* Eze 7:13
wicked way, by promising him *l* Eze 13:22
moment, every man for his own *l* Eze 32:10
robbed, walk in the statutes of *l* Eze 33:15
awake, some to everlasting *l* Dan 12:2
us not perish for this man's *l* Jonah 1:14
brought up my *l* from corruption Jonah 2:6
I beseech thee, my *l* from me Jonah 4:3
My covenant was with him of *l* Mal 2:5
which sought the young child's *l* Mt 2:20
you, Take no thought for your *l* Mt 6:25
Is not the *l* more than meat, and Mt 6:25
is the way, which leadeth unto *l* Mt 7:14
that findeth his *l* shall lose it Mt 10:39
he that loseth his *l* for my sake Mt 10:39
will save his *l* shall lose it Mt 16:25
whosoever will lose his *l* for my Mt 16:25
to enter into *l* halt or maimed Mt 18:8
thee to enter into *l* with one eye Mt 18:9
I do, that I may have eternal *l* Mt 19:16
but if thou wilt enter into *l* Mt 19:17
and shall inherit everlasting *l* Mt 19:29
to give his *l* a ransom for many Mt 20:28
but the righteous into *l* eternal Mt 25:46
to save *l*, or to kill Mk 3:4
will save his *l* shall lose it Mk 8:35
shall lose his *l* for my sake Mk 8:35
for thee to enter into *l* maimed Mk 9:43
for thee to enter halt into *l* Mk 9:45
I do that I may inherit eternal *l* Mk 10:17
and in the world to come eternal *l* Mk 10:30
to give his *l* a ransom for many Mk 10:45
before him, all the days of our *l* Lk 1:75
to save *l*, or to destroy it Lk 6:9
and riches and pleasures of this *l* Lk 8:14
will save his *l* shall lose it Lk 9:24
will lose his *l* for my sake Lk 9:24
shall I do to inherit eternal *l* Lk 10:25
for a man's *l* consisteth not in Lk 12:15
you, Take no thought for your *l* Lk 12:22
The *l* is more than meat, and the Lk 12:23
sisters, yea, and his own *l* also Lk 14:26
seek to save his *l* shall lose it Lk 17:33
lose his *l* shall preserve it Lk 17:33
shall I do to inherit eternal *l* Lk 18:18
the world to come *l* everlasting Lk 18:30
drunkenness, and cares of this *l* Lk 21:34
In him was *l* Jn 1:4
the *l* was the light of men Jn 1:4
not perish, but have eternal *l* Jn 3:15
perish, but have everlasting *l* Jn 3:16
on the Son hath everlasting *l* Jn 3:36
not the Son shall not see *l* Jn 3:36
springing up into everlasting *l* Jn 4:14
and gathereth fruit unto *l* eternal Jn 4:36
that sent me, hath everlasting *l* Jn 5:24
but is passed from death unto *l* Jn 5:24
as the Father hath *l* in himself Jn 5:26
to the Son to have *l* in himself Jn 5:26
good, unto the resurrection of *l* Jn 5:29
them ye think ye have eternal *l* Jn 5:39
come to me, that ye might have *l* Jn 5:40
which endureth unto everlasting *l* Jn 6:27
and giveth *l* unto the world Jn 6:33
unto them, I am the bread of *l* Jn 6:35
on him, may have everlasting *l* Jn 6:40
on me hath everlasting *l* Jn 6:47
I am that bread of *l* Jn 6:48
will give for the *l* of the world Jn 6:51
his blood, ye have no *l* in you Jn 6:53
drinketh my blood, hath eternal *l* Jn 6:54
they are spirit, and they are *l* Jn 6:63
thou hast the words of eternal *l* Jn 6:68
but shall have the light of *l* Jn 8:12
I am come that they might have *l* Jn 10:10
giveth his *l* for the sheep Jn 10:11
and I lay down my *l* for the sheep Jn 10:15
love me, because I lay down my *l* Jn 10:17
And I give unto them eternal *l* Jn 10:28
I am the resurrection, and the *l* Jn 11:25
that loveth his *l* shall lose it Jn 12:25
he that hateth his *l* in this Jn 12:25
shall keep it unto *l* eternal Jn 12:25
his commandment is *l* everlasting Jn 12:50
I will lay down my *l* for thy sake Jn 13:37
thou lay down thy *l* for my sake Jn 13:38
I am the way, the truth, and the *l* Jn 14:6
lay down his *l* for his friends Jn 15:13
that he should give eternal *l* to Jn 17:2
And this is *l* eternal, that they Jn 17:3
ye might have *l* through his name Jn 20:31
made known to me the ways of *l* Acts 2:28
And killed the Prince of *l* Acts 3:15
people all the words of this *l* Acts 5:20
for his *l* is taken from the earth Acts 8:33
granted repentance unto *l* Acts 11:18
unworthy of everlasting *l* Acts 13:46
ordained to eternal *l* believed Acts 13:48
thing, seeing he giveth to all *l* Acts 17:25
for his *l* is in him Acts 20:10
count I my *l* dear unto myself Acts 20:24
My manner of *l* from my youth, Acts 26:4
no loss of any man's *l* among you Acts 27:22
honour and immortality, eternal *l* Rom 2:7
we shall be saved by his *l* Rom 5:10
shall reign in *l* by one, Jesus Rom 5:17
all men unto justification of *l* Rom 5:18
*l* by Jesus Christ our Lord Rom 5:21
also should walk in newness of *l* Rom 6:4
and the end everlasting *l* Rom 6:22
*l* through Jesus Christ our Lord Rom 6:23
which was ordained to *l*, I found Rom 7:10
of *l* in Christ Jesus hath made me Rom 8:2
but to be spiritually minded is *l* Rom 8:6
but the Spirit is *l* because of Rom 8:10
that neither death, nor *l* Rom 8:38
am left alone, and they seek my *l* Rom 11:3
of them be, but *l* from the dead Rom 11:15
Who have for my *l* laid down their Rom 16:4
or Cephas, or the world, or *l* 1Cor 3:22
things that pertain to this *l* 1Cor 6:3
of things pertaining to this *l* 1Cor 6:4
things without *l* giving sound 1Cor 14:7
If in this *l* only we have hope in 1Cor 15:19
that we despaired even of *l* 2Cor 1:8
other the savour of *l* unto *l* 2Cor 2:16
killeth, but the spirit giveth *l* 2Cor 3:6
that the *l* also of Jesus might be 2Cor 4:10
that the *l* also of Jesus might be 2Cor 4:11
death worketh in us, but *l* in you 2Cor 4:12
might be swallowed up of *l* 2Cor 5:4
the *l* which I now live in the Gal 2:20
given which could have given *l* Gal 3:21
of the Spirit reap *l* everlasting Gal 6:8
being alienated from the *l* of God Eph 4:18
in my body, whether it be by *l* Phil 1:20
Holding forth the word of *l* Phil 2:16
unto death, not regarding his *l* Phil 2:30
whose names are in the book of *l* Phil 4:3
your *l* is hid with Christ in God Col 3:3
When Christ, who is our *l* Col 3:4
believe on him to *l* everlasting 1Ti 1:16
peaceable *l* in all godliness and 1Ti 2:2
promise of the *l* that now is 1Ti 4:8
of faith, lay hold on eternal *l* 1Ti 6:12
they may lay hold on eternal *l* 1Ti 6:19
of *l* which is in Christ Jesus 2Ti 1:1
death, and hath brought *l* and 2Ti 1:10
with the affairs of this *l* 2Ti 2:4
known my doctrine, manner of *l* 2Ti 3:10
In hope of eternal *l*, which God, Titus 1:2
to the hope of eternal *l* Titus 3:7
beginning of days, nor end of *l* Heb 7:3
after the power of an endless *l* Heb 7:16
their dead raised to *l* again Heb 11:35
he shall receive the crown of *l* Jas 1:12
For what is your *l* Jas 4:14
heirs together of the grace of *l* 1Pet 3:7
For he that will love *l*, and see 1Pet 3:10
For the time past of our *l* may 1Pet 4:3
us all things that pertain unto *l* 2Pet 1:3
have handled, of the Word of *l* 1Jn 1:1
(For the *l* was manifested, and we 1Jn 1:2
and shew unto you that eternal *l* 1Jn 1:2
of the eyes, and the pride of *l* 1Jn 2:16
hath promised us, even eternal *l* 1Jn 2:25
we have passed from death unto *l* 1Jn 3:14
hath eternal *l* abiding in him 1Jn 3:15
because he laid down his *l* for us 1Jn 3:16
God hath given to us eternal *l* 1Jn 5:11
and this *l* is in his Son 1Jn 5:11
He that hath the Son hath *l* 1Jn 5:12
not the Son of God hath not *l* 1Jn 5:12
may know that ye have eternal *l* 1Jn 5:13
he shall give him *l* for them that 1Jn 5:16
is the true God, and eternal *l* 1Jn 5:20
Lord Jesus Christ unto eternal *l* Jude 21
I give to eat of the tree of *l* Rev 2:7
and I will give thee a crown of *l* Rev 2:10
out his name out of the book of *l* Rev 3:5
which were in the sea, and had *l* Rev 8:9
an half the Spirit of *l* from God Rev 11:11
of *l* of the Lamb slain from the Rev 13:8
he had power to give *l* unto the Rev 13:15
of *l* from the foundation of the Rev 17:8
opened, which is the book of *l* Rev 20:12
found written in the book of *l* Rev 20:15
fountain of the water of *l* freely Rev 21:6
written in the Lamb's book of *l* Rev 21:27
me a pure river of water of *l* Rev 22:1
river, was there the tree of *l* Rev 22:2
may have right to the tree of *l* Rev 22:14
him take the water of *l* freely Rev 22:17
his part out of the book of *l* Rev 22:19

**LIFETIME**

Now Absalom in his *l* had taken 2Sa 18:18
remember that thou in thy *l* Lk 16:25
all their *l* subject to bondage Heb 2:15

**LIFT**

it was *l* up above the earth Gen 7:17
*L* up now thine eyes, and look from Gen 13:14
I have *l* up mine hand unto the Gen 14:22
he *l* up his eyes and looked, and, Gen 18:2
him, and *l* up her voice, and wept Gen 21:16
*l* up the lad, and hold him in Gen 21:18
*L* up now thine eyes, and see, all Gen 31:12
shall Pharaoh *l* up thine head Gen 40:13
*l* up thy head from off thee Gen 40:19
without thee shall no man *l* up Gen 41:44
But *l* thou up thy rod, and stretch Ex 14:16
for if thou *l* up thy tool upon it Ex 20:25
The LORD *l* up his countenance Num 6:26
wherefore then *l* ye up yourselves Num 16:3
*l* up himself as a young lion Num 23:24
*l* up thine eyes westward, and Deut 3:27
lest thou *l* up thine eyes unto Deut 4:19
help him to *l* them up again Deut 22:4
thou shalt not *l* up any iron tool Deut 27:5
For I *l* up my hand to heaven, and Deut 32:40
which no man hath *l* up any iron Josh 8:31
he *l* up his spear against eight 2Sa 23:8
wherefore *l* up thy prayer for the 2Kin 19:4
*l* up the head of Jehoiachin king 2Kin 25:27
words of God, to *l* up the horn 1Chr 25:5
blush to *l* up my face to thee, my Ezr 9:6
yet will I not *l* up my head Job 10:15
For then shalt thou *l* up thy face Job 11:15
shalt *l* up thy face unto God Job 22:26
Canst thou *l* up thy voice to the Job 38:34
*l* thou up the light of thy Ps 4:6
*l* up thyself because of the rage Ps 7:6
O God, *l* up thine hand Ps 10:12
*L* up your heads, O ye gates Ps 24:7
*L* up your heads, O ye gates Ps 24:9
even *l* them up, ye everlasting Ps 24:9
thee, O LORD, do I *l* up my soul Ps 25:1
when I *l* up my hands toward thy Ps 28:2
them also, and *l* them up for ever Ps 28:9
I will *l* up my hands in thy name Ps 63:4
*L* up thy feet unto the perpetual Ps 74:3
to the wicked, *L* not up the horn Ps 75:4
*L* not up your horn on high Ps 75:5
thee, O Lord, do I *l* up my soul Ps 86:4
the floods *l* up their waves Ps 93:3
*L* up thyself, thou judge of the Ps 94:2
therefore shall he *l* up the head Ps 110:7
My hands also will I *l* up unto Ps 119:48
I will *l* up mine eyes unto the Ps 121:1
Unto thee *l* I up mine eyes, O Ps 123:1
*L* up your hands in the sanctuary, Ps 134:2
for I *l* up my soul unto thee Ps 143:8
the one will *l* up his fellow Eccl 4:10
nation shall not *l* up sword Is 2:4
he will *l* up an ensign to the Is 5:26
itself against them that *l* it up Is 10:15
if the staff should *l* up itself Is 10:15
shall *l* up his staff against thee Is 10:24
so shall he *l* it up after the Is 10:26
*L* up thy voice, O daughter of Is 10:30
*L* ye up a banner upon the high Is 13:2
They shall *l* up their voice, they Is 24:14
now will I *l* up myself Is 33:10
wherefore *l* up thy prayer for the Is 37:4
*l* up thy voice with strength Is 40:9
*l* it up, be not afraid Is 40:9
*L* up your eyes on high, and behold Is 40:26
He shall not cry, nor *l* up Is 42:2
cities thereof *l* up their voice Is 42:11
*L* up thine eyes round about, and Is 49:18
I will *l* up mine hand to the Is 49:22
*L* up your eyes to the heavens, and Is 51:6
Thy watchmen shall *l* up the voice Is 52:8
*l* up thy voice like a trumpet, and Is 58:1
shall *l* up a standard against him Is 59:19
*L* up thine eyes round about, and Is 60:4
*l* up a standard for the people Is 62:10
*L* up thine eyes unto the high Jer 3:2

L

neither *l* up cry nor prayer for Jer 7:16
neither *l* up a cry or prayer for Jer 11:14
*L* up your eyes, and behold them Jer 13:20
*l* up thy voice in Bashan, and cry Jer 22:20
they shall *l* up a shout against Jer 51:14
*l* up thy hands toward him for the Lam 2:19
Let us *l* up our heart with our Lam 3:41
*l* up thine eyes now the way Eze 8:5
the cherubims *l* up their wings Eze 11:22
that it might not *l* itself up Eze 17:14
to *l* up the voice with shouting, Eze 21:22
so that thou shalt not *l* up thine Eze 23:27
*l* up the buckler against thee Eze 26:8
*l* up your eyes toward your idols, Eze 33:25
nation shall not *l* up a sword Mic 4:3
so that no man did *l* up his head Zec 1:21
*L* up now thine eyes, and see what Zec 5:5
not lay hold on it, and *l* it out Mt 12:11
and could in no wise *l* up herself Lk 13:11
in hell he *l* up his eyes, being Lk 16:23
would not *l* up so much as his Lk 18:13
then look up, and *l* up your heads Lk 21:28
*L* up your eyes, and look on the Jn 4:35
Wherefore *l* up the hands which Heb 12:12
of the Lord, and he shall *l* you up Jas 4:10

## LIFTED
Lot *l* up his eyes, and beheld all Gen 13:10
third day Abraham *l* up his eyes Gen 22:4
Abraham *l* up his eyes, and looked, Gen 22:13
he *l* up his eyes, and saw, and, Gen 24:63
Rebekah *l* up her eyes, and when Gen 24:64
Esau *l* up his voice, and wept Gen 27:38
and *l* up his voice, and wept Gen 29:11
that I *l* up mine eyes, and saw in Gen 31:10
Jacob *l* up his eyes, and looked, Gen 33:1
he *l* up his eyes, and saw the Gen 33:5
they *l* up their eyes and looked, Gen 37:25
*l* up Joseph out of the pit, and Gen 37:28
he heard that I *l* up my voice Gen 39:15
as I *l* up my voice and cried, that Gen 39:18
he *l* up the head of the chief Gen 40:20
he *l* up his eyes, and saw his Gen 43:29
he *l* up the rod, and smote the Ex 7:20
of Israel *l* up their eyes Ex 14:10
Aaron *l* up his hand toward the Lev 9:22
the congregation *l* up their voice Num 14:1
Moses *l* up his hand, and with his Num 20:11
Balaam *l* up his eyes, and he saw Num 24:2
Then thine heart be *l* up, and thou Deut 8:14
be not *l* up above his brethren Deut 17:20
feet were *l* up unto the dry land Josh 4:18
that he *l* up his eyes and looked, Josh 5:13
that the people *l* up their voice Judg 2:4
so that they *l* up their heads no Judg 8:28
*l* up his voice, and cried, and said Judg 9:7
And when he had *l* up his eyes Judg 19:17
*l* up their voices, and wept sore Judg 21:2
they *l* up their voice, and wept Ruth 1:9
they *l* up their voice, and wept Ruth 1:14
they *l* up their eyes, and saw the 1Sa 6:13
all the people *l* up their voices, 1Sa 11:4
Saul *l* up his voice, and wept 1Sa 24:16
were with him *l* up their voice 1Sa 30:4
the king *l* up his voice, and wept 2Sa 3:32
that kept the watch *l* up his eyes 2Sa 13:34
came, and *l* up their voice and wept 2Sa 13:36
*l* up his eyes, and looked, and 2Sa 18:24
*l* up their hand against my lord 2Sa 18:28
hath *l* up his hand against the 2Sa 20:21
thou also hast *l* me up on high 2Sa 22:49
he *l* up his spear against three 2Sa 23:18
even he *l* up his hand against the 1Kin 11:26
this was the cause that he *l* up 1Kin 11:27
he *l* up his face to the window, 2Kin 9:32
and thine heart hath *l* thee up 2Kin 14:10
voice, and *l* up thine eyes on high 2Kin 19:22
he *l* up his spear against three 1Chr 11:11
for his kingdom was *l* up on high 1Chr 14:2
David *l* up his eyes, and saw the 1Chr 21:16
when they *l* up their voice with 2Chr 5:13
his heart was *l* up in the ways of 2Chr 17:6
his heart was *l* up to his 2Chr 26:16
for his heart was *l* up 2Chr 32:25
when they *l* up their eyes afar Job 2:12
they *l* up their voice, and wept Job 2:12
If I have *l* up my hand against Job 31:21
or *l* up myself when evil found Job 31:29
who hath not *l* up his soul unto Ps 24:4
and be ye *l* up, ye everlasting Ps 24:7
now shall mine head be *l* up above Ps 27:6
for thou hast *l* me up, and hast Ps 30:1
hath *l* up his heel against me Ps 41:9
*l* up axes upon the thick trees Ps 74:5
that hate thee have *l* up the head Ps 83:2
The floods have *l* up, O LORD, the Ps 93:3
the floods have *l* up their voice Ps 93:3
for thou hast *l* me up, and cast me Ps 102:10
Therefore he *l* up his hand Ps 106:26
and their eyelids are *l* up Prov 30:13
and upon every one that is *l* up Is 2:12
*l* up, and upon all the oaks of Is 2:13
upon all the hills that are *l* up Is 2:14
*l* up, and his train filled the Is 6:1
LORD, when thy hand is *l* up Is 26:11
voice, and *l* up thine eyes on high Is 37:23
is *l* up even to the skies Jer 51:9
*l* up the head of Jehoiachin king Jer 52:31
were *l* up from the earth, the Eze 1:19
the earth, the wheels were *l* up Eze 1:19
the wheels were *l* up over against Eze 1:20
when those were *l* up from the Eze 1:21
the wheels were *l* up over against Eze 1:21
So the spirit *l* me up, and took me Eze 3:14
the spirit *l* me up between the Eze 8:3
So I *l* up mine eyes the way Eze 8:5
And the cherubims were *l* up Eze 10:15
when the cherubims *l* up their Eze 10:16
and when they were *l* up Eze 10:17
these *l* up themselves also Eze 10:17
the cherubims *l* up their wings, Eze 10:19
Moreover the spirit *l* me up Eze 11:1
neither hath *l* up his eyes to the Eze 18:6
hath *l* up his eyes to the idols, Eze 18:12
neither hath *l* up his eyes to the Eze 18:15
*l* up mine hand unto the seed of Eze 20:5
when I *l* up mine hand unto them, Eze 20:5
In the day that I *l* up mine hand Eze 20:6
Yet also I *l* up my hand unto them Eze 20:15
I *l* up mine hand unto them also Eze 20:23
for the which I *l* up mine hand to Eze 20:28
the country for the which I *l* up Eze 20:42
Because thine heart is *l* up Eze 28:2
thine heart is *l* up because of Eze 28:5
Thine heart was *l* up because of Eze 28:17
Because thou hast *l* up thyself in Eze 31:10
his heart is *l* up in his height Eze 31:10
I have *l* up mine hand, Surely the Eze 36:7
therefore have I *l* up mine hand Eze 44:12
concerning the which I *l* up mine Eze 47:14
*l* up mine eyes unto heaven Dan 4:34
But when his heart was *l* up Dan 5:20
But hast *l* up thyself against the Dan 5:23
it was *l* up from the earth, and Dan 7:4
Then I *l* up mine eyes, and saw, and Dan 8:3
Then I *l* up mine eyes, and looked, Dan 10:5
his heart shall be *l* up Dan 11:12
Thine hand shall be *l* up upon Mic 5:9
his soul which is *l* up is not Hab 2:4
voice, and *l* up his hands on high Hab 3:10
Then I *l* up mine eyes, and saw, and Zec 1:18
which *l* up their horn over the Zec 1:21
I *l* up mine eyes again, and looked Zec 2:1
*l* up mine eyes, and looked, and Zec 5:1
there was *l* up a talent of lead Zec 5:7
Then I *l* up mine eyes, and looked, Zec 5:9
they *l* up the ephah between the Zec 5:9
*l* up mine eyes, and looked, and, Zec 6:1
*l* up as an ensign upon his land Zec 9:16
and it shall be *l* up, and inhabited Zec 14:10
And when they had *l* up their eyes Mt 17:8
took her by the hand, and *l* her up Mk 1:31
took him by the hand, and *l* him up Mk 9:27
he *l* up his eyes on his disciples Lk 6:20
of the company *l* up her voice Lk 11:27
they *l* up their voices, and said, Lk 17:13
he *l* up his hands, and blessed Lk 24:50
as Moses *l* up the serpent in the Jn 3:14
so must the Son of man be *l* up Jn 3:14
When Jesus then *l* up his eyes Jn 6:5
he *l* up himself, and said unto Jn 8:7
When Jesus had *l* up himself Jn 8:10
When ye have *l* up the Son of man, Jn 8:28
Jesus *l* up his eyes, and said, Jn 11:41
if I be *l* up from the earth, will Jn 12:32
thou, The Son of man must be *l* up Jn 12:34
me hath *l* up his heel against me Jn 13:18
*l* up his eyes to heaven, and said, Jn 17:1
*l* up his voice, and said unto them Acts 2:14
by the right hand, and *l* him up Acts 3:7
they *l* up their voice to God with Acts 4:24
*l* her up, and when he had called Acts 9:41
they *l* up their voices, saying in Acts 14:11
then *l* up their voices, and said, Acts 22:22
lest being *l* up with pride he 1Ti 3:6
upon the earth *l* up his hand to Rev 10:5

## LIFTER
glory, and the *l* up of mine head Ps 3:3

## LIFTEST
Thou *l* me up to the wind Job 30:22
thou that *l* me up from the gates Ps 9:13
thou *l* me up above those that Ps 18:48
*l* up thy voice for understanding Prov 2:3

## LIFTETH
he bringeth low, and *l* up 1Sa 2:7
*l* up the beggar from the dunghill 1Sa 2:8
thine heart *l* thee up to boast 2Chr 25:19
What time she *l* up herself on Job 39:18
which *l* up the waves thereof Ps 107:25
*l* the needy out of the dunghill Ps 113:7
The LORD *l* up the meek Ps 147:6
when he *l* up an ensign on the Is 18:3
against him that *l* himself up in Jer 51:3
The horseman *l* up both the bright Nah 3:3

## LIFTING
for *l* up his spear against three 1Chr 11:20
by *l* up the voice with joy 1Chr 15:16
Amen, Amen, with *l* up their hands Neh 8:6
thou shalt say, There is *l* up Job 22:29
the *l* up of my hands as the Ps 141:2
done foolishly in *l* up thyself Prov 30:32
mount up like the *l* up of smoke Is 9:18
at the *l* up of thyself the Is 33:3
*l* up holy hands, without wrath and 1Ti 2:8

## LIGHT
And God said, Let there be *l* Gen 1:3
and there was *l* Gen 1:3
And God saw the *l*, that it was Gen 1:4
God divided the *l* from the Gen 1:4
And God called the *l* Day, and the Gen 1:5
heaven to give *l* upon the earth Gen 1:15
the greater *l* to rule the day, and Gen 1:16
the lesser *l* to rule the night Gen 1:16
heaven to give *l* upon the earth Gen 1:17
to divide the *l* from the darkness Gen 1:18
As soon as the morning was *l* Gen 44:3
Israel had *l* in their dwellings Ex 10:23
a pillar of fire, to give them *l* Ex 13:21
but it gave *l* by night to these Ex 14:20
Oil for the *l*, spices for Ex 25:6
they shall *l* the lamps thereof, Ex 25:37
they may give *l* over against it Ex 25:37
pure oil olive beaten for the *l* Ex 27:20
And oil for the *l*, and spices for Ex 35:8
The candlestick also for the *l* Ex 35:14
his lamps, with the oil for the *l* Ex 35:14
And spice, and oil for the *l* Ex 35:28
vessels thereof, and the oil for *l* Ex 39:37
and *l* the lamps thereof Ex 40:4
pure oil olive beaten for the *l* Lev 24:2
and cover the candlestick of the *l* Num 4:9
pertaineth the oil for the *l* Num 4:16
the seven lamps shall give *l* over Num 8:2
and our soul loatheth this *l* bread Num 21:5
Cursed be he that setteth *l* by Deut 27:16
*l* persons, which followed him Judg 9:4
where her lord was, till it was *l* Judg 19:26
her hap was to *l* on a part of the Ruth 2:3
and spoil them until the morning *l* 1Sa 14:36
Seemeth it to you a *l* thing to be 1Sa 18:23
*l* any that pisseth against the 1Sa 25:22
*l* any that pisseth against the 1Sa 25:34
less or more, until the morning *l* 1Sa 25:36
early in the morning, and have *l* 1Sa 29:10
Asahel was as *l* of foot as a wild 2Sa 2:18
we will *l* upon him as the dew 2Sa 17:12
by the morning *l* there lacked not 2Sa 17:22
thou quench not the *l* of Israel 2Sa 21:17
shall be as the *l* of the morning 2Sa 23:4
*l* was against *l* in three 1Kin 7:4
*l* was against *l* in three 1Kin 7:5
was against *l* in three ranks 1Kin 7:5
David my servant may have a *l* 1Kin 11:36
as if it had been a *l* thing for 1Kin 16:31
this is but a *l* thing in the 2Kin 3:18
if we tarry till the morning *l* 2Kin 7:9
him to give him alway a *l* 2Kin 8:19
It is a *l* thing for the shadow to 2Kin 20:10
as he promised to give a *l* to him 2Chr 21:7
to give them *l* in the way wherein Neh 9:12
of fire by night, to shew them *l* Neh 9:19
The Jews had *l*, and gladness, and Est 8:16
neither let the *l* shine upon it Job 3:4
let it look for *l*, but have none Job 3:9
as infants which never saw *l* Job 3:16
Wherefore is *l* given to him that Job 3:20
Why is *l* given to a man whose way Job 3:23
where the *l* is as darkness Job 10:22
bringeth out to *l* the shadow of Job 12:22
They grope in the dark without *l* Job 12:25
the *l* is short because of Job 17:12
the *l* of the wicked shall be put Job 18:5
The *l* shall be dark in his Job 18:6
be driven from *l* into darkness Job 18:18
the *l* shall shine upon thy ways Job 22:28
of those that rebel against the *l* Job 24:13
with the *l* killeth the poor Job 24:14
they know not the *l* Job 24:16
and upon whom doth not his *l* arise Job 25:3
is hid bringeth he forth to *l* Job 28:11
when by his *l* I walked through Job 29:3
the *l* of my countenance they cast Job 29:24
and when I waited for *l*, there Job 30:26
pit, and his life shall see the *l* Job 33:28
with the *l* of the living Job 33:30
he spreadeth his *l* upon it Job 36:30
With clouds he covereth the *l* Job 36:32
caused the *l* of his cloud to Job 37:15
bright *l* which is in the clouds Job 37:21
the wicked their *l* is withholden Job 38:15
Where is the way where *l* dwelleth Job 38:19
By what way is the *l* parted Job 38:24
By his neesings a *l* doth shine Job 41:18
lift thou up the *l* of thy Ps 4:6
For thou wilt *l* my candle Ps 18:28
The LORD is my *l* and my salvation Ps 27:1
in thy *l* shall we see *l* Ps 36:9
in thy *l* shall we see *l* Ps 36:9
forth thy righteousness as the *l* Ps 37:6
as for the *l* of mine eyes, it Ps 38:10
O send out thy *l* and thy truth Ps 43:3
the *l* of thy countenance, because Ps 44:3
they shall never see *l* Ps 49:19
before God in the *l* of the living Ps 56:13
thou hast prepared the *l* and the Ps 74:16
and all the night with a *l* of fire Ps 78:14
in the *l* of thy countenance Ps 89:15
sins in the *l* of thy countenance Ps 90:8
*L* is sown for the righteous, and Ps 97:11
thyself with *l* as with a garment Ps 104:2
and fire to give *l* in the night Ps 105:39
there ariseth *l* in the darkness Ps 112:4
the LORD, which hath shewed us *l* Ps 118:27
unto my feet, and a *l* unto my path Ps 119:105
entrance of thy words giveth *l* Ps 119:130
the night shall be *l* about me Ps 139:11
the *l* are both alike to thee Ps 139:12
praise him, all ye stars of *l* Ps 148:3
of the just is as the shining *l* Prov 4:18

and the law is *l* Prov 6:23
The *l* of the righteous rejoiceth Prov 13:9
The *l* of the eyes rejoiceth the Prov 15:30
In the *l* of the king's Prov 16:15
as far as *l* excelleth darkness Eccl 2:13
Truly the *l* is sweet, and a Eccl 11:7
While the sun, or the *l*, or the Eccl 12:2
let us walk in the *l* of the LORD Is 2:5
for *l*, and *l* for darkness Is 5:20
the *l* is darkened in the heavens Is 5:30
is because there is no *l* in them Is 8:20
in darkness have seen a great *l* Is 9:2
upon them hath the *l* shined Is 9:2
the *l* of Israel shall be for a Is 10:17
thereof shall not give their *l* Is 13:10
shall not cause her *l* to shine Is 13:10
Moreover the *l* of the moon shall Is 30:26
moon shall be as the *l* of the sun Is 30:26
the *l* of the sun shall be Is 30:26
as the *l* of seven days, in the Is 30:26
people, for a *l* of the Gentiles Is 42:6
will make darkness *l* before them Is 42:16
I form the *l*, and create darkness Is 45:7
It is a *l* thing that thou Is 49:6
give thee for a *l* to the Gentiles Is 49:6
walketh in darkness, and hath no *l* Is 50:10
walk in the *l* of your fire, and in Is 50:11
to rest for a *l* of the people Is 51:4
Then shall thy *l* break forth as Is 58:8
then shall thy *l* rise in Is 58:10
we wait for *l*, but behold Is 59:9
for thy *l* is come, and the glory Is 60:1
the Gentiles shall come to thy *l* Is 60:3
sun shall be no more thy *l* by day Is 60:19
shall the moon give *l* unto thee Is 60:19
be unto thee an everlasting *l* Is 60:19
LORD shall be thine everlasting *l* Is 60:20
and the heavens, and they had no *l* Jer 4:23
and, while ye look for *l*, he turn Jer 13:16
and the *l* of the candle Jer 25:10
giveth the sun for a *l* by day Jer 31:35
and of the stars for a *l* by night Jer 31:35
me into darkness, but not into *l* Lam 3:2
Is it a *l* thing to the house of Eze 8:17
In thee have they set *l* by father Eze 22:7
and the moon shall not give her *l* Eze 32:7
and the *l* dwelleth with him Dan 2:22
and in the days of thy father *l* Dan 5:11
of the gods is in thee, and that *l* Dan 5:14
are as the *l* that goeth forth Hos 6:5
of the LORD is darkness, and not *l* Amos 5:18
of the LORD be darkness, and not *l* Amos 5:20
when the morning is *l*, they Mic 2:1
the LORD shall be a *l* unto me Mic 7:8
he will bring me forth to the *l* Mic 7:9
And his brightness was as the *l* Hab 3:4
at the *l* of thine arrows they Hab 3:11
Her prophets are *l* and treacherous Zeph 3:4
doth he bring his judgment to *l* Zeph 3:5
that the *l* shall not be clear, Zec 14:6
at evening time it shall be *l* Zec 14:7
which sat in darkness saw great *l* Mt 4:16
and shadow of death *l* is sprung up Mt 4:16
Ye are the *l* of the world Mt 5:14
Neither do men *l* a candle Mt 5:15
it giveth *l* unto all that are in Mt 5:15
Let your *l* so shine before men, Mt 5:16
The *l* of the body is the eye Mt 6:22
thy whole body shall be full of *l* Mt 6:22
If therefore the *l* that is in Mt 6:23
in darkness, that speak ye in *l* Mt 10:27
yoke is easy, and my burden is *l* Mt 11:30
and his raiment was white as the *l* Mt 17:2
But they made *l* of it, and went Mt 22:5
and the moon shall not give her *l* Mt 24:29
and the moon shall not give her *l* Mk 13:24
To give *l* to them that sit in Lk 1:79
A *l* to lighten the Gentiles, and Lk 2:32
they which enter in may see the *l* Lk 8:16
they which come in may see the *l* Lk 11:33
The *l* of the body is the eye Lk 11:34
thy whole body also is full of *l* Lk 11:34
the *l* which is in thee be not Lk 11:35
whole body therefore be full of *l* Lk 11:36
the whole shall be full of *l* Lk 11:36
of a candle doth give thee *l* Lk 11:36
darkness shall be heard in the *l* Lk 12:3
one piece, doth not *l* a candle Lk 15:8
wiser than the children of *l* Lk 16:8
and the life was the *l* of men Jn 1:4
the *l* shineth in darkness Jn 1:5
witness, to bear witness of the *L* Jn 1:7
He was not that *L*, but was sent Jn 1:8
sent to bear witness of that *L* Jn 1:8
That was the true *L*, which Jn 1:9
that *l* is come into the world, and Jn 3:19
men loved darkness rather than *l* Jn 3:19
one that doeth evil hateth the *l* Jn 3:20
neither cometh to the *l* Jn 3:20
that doeth truth cometh to the *l* Jn 3:21
He was a burning and a shining *l* Jn 5:35
for a season to rejoice in his *l* Jn 5:35
saying, I am the *l* of the world Jn 8:12
but shall have the *l* of life Jn 8:12
world, I am the *l* of the world Jn 9:5
he seeth the *l* of this world Jn 11:9
because there is no *l* in him Jn 11:10
a little while is the *l* with you Jn 12:35
Walk while ye have the *l*, lest Jn 12:35
ye have *l*, believe in the *l* Jn 12:36
that ye may be the children of *l* Jn 12:36
I am come a *l* into the world, Jn 12:46
round about him a *l* from heaven Acts 9:3
him, and a *l* shined in the prison Acts 12:7
thee to be a *l* of the Gentiles Acts 13:47
Then he called for a *l*, and sprang Acts 16:29
heaven a great *l* round about me Acts 22:6
were with me saw indeed the *l* Acts 22:9
not see for the glory of that *l* Acts 22:11
I saw in the way a *l* from heaven Acts 26:13
to turn them from darkness to *l* Acts 26:18
should shew *l* unto the people, and Acts 26:23
a *l* of them which are in darkness Rom 2:19
and let us put on the armour of *l* Rom 13:12
who both will bring to *l* the 1Cor 4:5
lest the *l* of the glorious gospel 2Cor 4:4
who commanded the *l* to shine out 2Cor 4:6
to give the *l* of the knowledge of 2Cor 4:6
For our *l* affliction, which is 2Cor 4:17
communion hath *l* with darkness 2Cor 6:14
is transformed into an angel of *l* 2Cor 11:14
but now are ye *l* in the Lord Eph 5:8
walk as children of *l* Eph 5:8
are made manifest by the *l* Eph 5:13
doth make manifest is *l* Eph 5:13
dead, and Christ shall give thee *l* Eph 5:14
inheritance of the saints in *l* Col 1:12
Ye are all the children of *l* 1Th 5:5
dwelling in the *l* which no man 1Ti 6:16
immortality to *l* through the 2Ti 1:10
of darkness into his marvellous *l* 1Pet 2:9
as unto a *l* that shineth in a 2Pet 1:19
declare unto you, that God is *l* 1Jn 1:5
in the *l*, as he is in the *l* 1Jn 1:7
past, and the true *l* now shineth 1Jn 2:8
He that saith he is in the *l* 1Jn 2:9
his brother abideth in the *l* 1Jn 2:10
neither shall the sun *l* on them Rev 7:16
the *l* of a candle shall shine no Rev 18:23
her *l* was like unto a stone most Rev 21:11
it, and the Lamb is the *l* thereof Rev 21:23
saved shall walk in the *l* of it Rev 21:24
no candle, neither *l* of the sun Rev 22:5
for the Lord God giveth them *l* Rev 22:5

### LIGHTED
saw Isaac, she *l* off the camel Gen 24:64
he *l* upon a certain place, and Gen 28:11
he *l* the lamps before the LORD Ex 40:25
he *l* the lamps thereof over Num 8:3
and she *l* off her ass Josh 15:18
and she *l* from off her ass Judg 1:14
so that Sisera *l* down off his Judg 4:15
*l* off the ass, and fell before 1Sa 25:23
he *l* down from the chariot to 2Kin 5:21
he *l* on Jehonadab the son of 2Kin 10:15
Jacob, and it hath *l* upon Israel Is 9:8
No man, when he hath *l* a candle Lk 8:16
No man, when he hath *l* a candle Lk 11:33

### LIGHTEN
peradventure he will *l* his hand 1Sa 6:5
and the LORD will *l* my darkness 2Sa 22:29
that our God may *l* our eyes Ezr 9:8
*l* mine eyes, lest I sleep the Ps 13:3
into the sea, to *l* it of them Jonah 1:5
A light to *l* the Gentiles, and the Lk 2:32
for the glory of God did *l* it Rev 21:23

### LIGHTENED
They looked unto him, and were *l* Ps 34:5
the lightnings *l* the world Ps 77:18
the next day they *l* the ship Acts 27:18
they *l* the ship, and cast out the Acts 27:38
the earth was *l* with his glory Rev 18:1

### LIGHTENETH
the LORD *l* both their eyes Prov 29:13
that *l* out of the one part under Lk 17:24

### LIGHTER
yoke which he put upon us, *l* 1Kin 12:4
thy father did put upon us *l* 1Kin 12:9
heavy, but make thou it *l* unto us 1Kin 12:10
make thou it somewhat *l* for us 2Chr 10:10
they are altogether *l* than vanity Ps 62:9

### LIGHTEST
unto him, When thou *l* the lamps Num 8:2

### LIGHTETH
when Aaron *l* the lamps at even, Ex 30:8
*l* upon his neighbour, that he die Deut 19:5
which *l* every man that cometh Jn 1:9

### LIGHTING
shall shew the *l* down of his arm, Is 30:30
like a dove, and *l* upon him Mt 3:16

### LIGHTLY
might *l* have lien with thy wife Gen 26:10
*l* esteemed the Rock of his Deut 32:15
despise me shall be *l* esteemed 1Sa 2:30
I am a poor man, and *l* esteemed 1Sa 18:23
when at the first he *l* afflicted Is 9:1
and all the hills moved *l* Jer 4:24
that can *l* speak evil of me Mk 9:39

### LIGHTNESS
through the *l* of her whoredom Jer 3:9
err by their lies, and by their *l* Jer 23:32
was thus minded, did I use *l* 2Cor 1:17

### LIGHTNING
*l*, and discomfited them 2Sa 22:15
a way for the *l* of the thunder Job 28:26
his *l* unto the ends of the earth Job 37:3
or a way for the *l* of thunder Job 38:25
Cast forth *l*, and scatter them Ps 144:6
and out of the fire went forth *l* Eze 1:13
as the appearance of a flash of *l* Eze 1:14
his face as the appearance of *l* Dan 10:6
his arrow shall go forth as the *l* Zec 9:14
For as the *l* cometh out of the Mt 24:27
His countenance was like *l* Mt 28:3
Satan as *l* fall from heaven Lk 10:18
For as the *l*, that lighteneth out Lk 17:24

### LIGHTNINGS
that there were thunders and *l* Ex 19:16
saw the thunderings, and the *l* Ex 20:18
Canst thou send *l*, that they may Job 38:35
and he shot out *l*, and discomfited Ps 18:14
the *l* lightened the world Ps 77:18
His *l* enlightened the world Ps 97:4
he maketh *l* for the rain Ps 135:7
he maketh *l* with rain, and Jer 10:13
he maketh *l* with rain, and Jer 51:16
they shall run like the *l* Nah 2:4
And out of the throne proceeded *l* Rev 4:5
were voices, and thunderings, and *l* Rev 8:5
and there were *l*, and voices, and Rev 11:19
were voices, and thunders, and *l* Rev 16:18

### LIGHTS
Let there be *l* in the firmament Gen 1:14
And let them be for *l* in the Gen 1:15
And God made two great *l* Gen 1:16
house he made windows of narrow *l* 1Kin 6:4
To him that made great *l* Ps 136:7
All the bright *l* of heaven will I Eze 32:8
girded about, and your *l* burning Lk 12:35
there were many *l* in the upper Acts 20:8
whom ye shine as *l* in the world Phil 2:15
cometh down from the Father of *l* Jas 1:17

### LIGN
as the trees of *l* aloes which the Num 24:6

### LIGURE
And the third row a *l*, an agate, Ex 28:19
And the third row, a *l*, an agate, Ex 39:12

**LIKE** See PREFACE.

### LIKED
he *l* me to make me king over all 1Chr 28:4

### LIKEMINDED
consolation grant you to be *l* one Rom 15:5
Fulfil ye my joy, that ye be *l* Phil 2:2
For I have no man *l*, who will Phil 2:20

### LIKEN
To whom then will ye *l* God Is 40:18
To whom then will ye *l* me Is 40:25
To whom will ye *l* me, and make me Is 46:5
what thing shall I *l* to thee Lam 2:13
I will *l* him unto a wise man, Mt 7:24
shall I *l* this generation Mt 11:16
shall we *l* the kingdom of God Mk 4:30
Whereunto then shall I *l* the men Lk 7:31
Whereunto shall I *l* the kingdom Lk 13:20

### LIKENED
the mighty can be *l* unto the LORD Ps 89:6
I have *l* the daughter of Zion to Jer 6:2
shall be *l* unto a foolish man, Mt 7:26
The kingdom of heaven is *l* unto a Mt 13:24
of heaven *l* unto a certain king Mt 18:23
of heaven be *l* unto ten virgins Mt 25:1

### LIKENESS
man in our image, after our *l* Gen 1:26
in the *l* of God made he him Gen 5:1
and begat a son in his own *l* Gen 5:3
or any *l* of any thing that is in Ex 20:4
figure, the *l* of male or female, Deut 4:16
The *l* of any beast that is on the Deut 4:17
the *l* of any winged fowl that Deut 4:17
The *l* of any thing that creepeth Deut 4:18
the *l* of any fish that is in the Deut 4:18
or the *l* of any thing, which the Deut 4:23
or the *l* of any thing, and shall Deut 4:25
or any *l* of any thing that is in Deut 5:8
when I awake, with thy *l* Ps 17:15
or what *l* will ye compare unto Is 40:18
the *l* of four living creatures Eze 1:5
they had the *l* of a man Eze 1:5
As for the *l* of their faces, they Eze 1:10
As for the *l* of the living Eze 1:13
and they four had one *l* Eze 1:16
the *l* of the firmament upon the Eze 1:22
their heads was the *l* of a throne Eze 1:26
upon the *l* of the throne was the Eze 1:26
the *l* as the appearance of a man Eze 1:26
of the *l* of the glory of the LORD Eze 1:28
lo a *l* as the appearance of fire Eze 8:2
appearance of the *l* of a throne Eze 10:1
appearances, they four had one *l* Eze 10:10
the *l* of the hands of a man was Eze 10:21
the *l* of their faces was the same Eze 10:22
come down to us in the *l* of men Acts 14:11
together in the *l* of his death Rom 6:5
also in the *l* of his resurrection Rom 6:5
own Son in the *l* of sinful flesh Rom 8:3
and was made in the *l* of men Phil 2:7

**LIKETH**
of thy gates, where it *l* him best ... Deut 23:16
ye also for the Jews, as it *l* you ... Est 8:8
for this *l* you, O ye children of ... Amos 4:5

**LIKEWISE**
*L* shalt thou do with thine oxen, ... Ex 22:30
and *l* shalt thou make in the ... Ex 26:4
*l* for the north side in length ... Ex 27:11
*l* he made in the uttermost side ... Ex 36:11
*L* this is the law of the trespass ... Lev 7:1
*L* when the LORD sent you from ... Deut 9:23
even so will I do *l* ... Deut 12:30
thy maidservant thou shalt do *l* ... Deut 15:17
thou hast found, shalt thou do *l* ... Deut 22:3
I *l* will go with thee into thy ... Judg 1:3
*l* every one that boweth down upon ... Judg 7:5
unto them, Look on me, and do *l* ... Judg 7:17
to Penuel, and spake unto them *l* ... Judg 8:8
all the people *l* cut down every ... Judg 9:49
*L* all the men of Israel which had ... 1Sa 14:22
messengers, and they prophesied *l* ... 1Sa 19:21
he fell *l* upon his sword, and died ... 1Sa 31:5
*l* all the men that were with him ... 2Sa 1:11
let us hear *l* what he saith ... 2Sa 17:5
*l* did he for all his strange ... 1Kin 11:8
he fell *l* on the sword, and died ... 1Chr 10:5
*L* from Tibhath, and from Chun, ... 1Chr 18:8
they *l* fled before Abishai his ... 1Chr 19:15
and praise the LORD, and *l* at even ... 1Chr 23:30
These *l* cast lots over against ... 1Chr 24:31
in his course *l* were twenty ... 1Chr 27:4
*l* silver for the tables of silver ... 1Chr 28:16
*l* silver by weight for every ... 1Chr 28:17
all the sons *l* of king David, ... 1Chr 29:24
the other wing was *l* five cubits ... 2Chr 3:11
*l*, when they had killed the rams, ... 2Chr 29:22
*L* at the same time said I unto ... Neh 4:22
I *l*, and my brethren, and my ... Neh 5:10
*L* shall the ladies of Persia and ... Est 1:18
I also and my maidens will fast *l* ... Est 4:16
the furrows *l* thereof complain ... Job 31:38
*l* to the small rain, and to the ... Job 37:6
*l* the fool and the brutish person ... Ps 49:10
God shall *l* destroy thee for ever ... Ps 52:5
thou thyself *l* hast cursed others ... Eccl 7:22
The oxen *l* and the young asses ... Is 30:24
*L* when all the Jews that were in ... Jer 40:11
*L*, thou son of man, set thy face ... Eze 13:17
round about, and *l* to the arches ... Eze 40:16
*L* the people of the land shall ... Eze 46:3
*l* many, yet thus shall they be ... Nah 1:12
*L* shall also the Son of man ... Mt 17:12
So *l* shall my heavenly Father do ... Mt 18:35
the sixth and ninth hour, and did *l* ... Mt 20:5
they *l* received every man a penny ... Mt 20:10
he came to the second, and said *l* ... Mt 21:30
and they did unto them *l* ... Mt 21:36
*L* the second also, and the third, ... Mt 22:26
So *l* ye, when ye shall see all ... Mt 24:33
*l* he that had received two, he ... Mt 25:17
*L* also said all the disciples ... Mt 26:35
*L* also the chief priests mocking ... Mt 27:41
these are they *l* which are sown ... Mk 4:16
and the third *l* ... Mk 12:21
*L* also said they all ... Mk 14:31
*L* also the chief priests mocking ... Mk 15:31
gave thanks *l* unto the Lord ... Lk 2:38
he that hath meat, let him do *l* ... Lk 3:11
the soldiers *l* demanded of him, ... Lk 3:14
*l* the disciples of the Pharisees ... Lk 5:33
do to you, do ye also to them *l* ... Lk 6:31
*l* a Levite, when he was at the ... Lk 10:32
Jesus unto him, Go, and do thou *l* ... Lk 10:37
ye repent, ye shall all *l* perish ... Lk 13:3
ye repent, ye shall all *l* perish ... Lk 13:5
So *l*, whosoever he be of you that ... Lk 14:33
that *l* joy shall be in heaven ... Lk 15:7
*L*, I say unto you, there is joy ... Lk 15:10
things, and *l* Lazarus evil things ... Lk 16:25
So *l* ye, when ye shall have done ... Lk 17:10
*L* also as it was in the days of ... Lk 17:28
let him *l* not return back ... Lk 17:31
And he said *l* to him, Be thou also ... Lk 19:19
So *l* ye, when ye see these things ... Lk 21:31
*L* also the cup after supper, ... Lk 22:20
let him take it, and *l* his scrip ... Lk 22:36
doeth, these also doeth the Son *l* ... Jn 5:19
*l* of the fishes as much as they ... Jn 6:11
bread, and giveth them, and fish *l* ... Jn 21:13
have *l* foretold of these days ... Acts 3:24
*l* also the men, leaving the ... Rom 1:27
*L* reckon ye also yourselves to be ... Rom 6:11
*L* the Spirit also helpeth our ... Rom 8:26
*L* greet the church that is in ... Rom 16:5
*l* also the wife unto the husband ... 1Cor 7:3
*l* also the husband hath not power ... 1Cor 7:4
*l* also he that is called, being ... 1Cor 7:22
So *l* ye, except ye utter by the ... 1Cor 14:9
other Jews dissembled *l* with him ... Gal 2:13
that ye *l* read the epistle from ... Col 4:16
*L* must the deacons be grave, not ... 1Ti 3:8
*L* also the good works of some are ... 1Ti 5:25
The aged women *l*, that they be in ... Titus 2:3
Young men *l* exhort to be sober ... Titus 2:6
he also himself *l* took part of ... Heb 2:14
*L* also was not Rahab the harlot ... Jas 2:25
*L*, ye wives, be in subjection to ... 1Pet 3:1
*L*, ye husbands, dwell with them ... 1Pet 3:7
arm yourselves *l* with the same ... 1Pet 4:1
*L*, ye younger, submit yourselves ... 1Pet 5:5
*L* also these filthy dreamers ... Jude 8
third part of it, and the night *l* ... Rev 8:12

**LIKHI** (*lik'-hi*) *Son of Shemidah.*
were, Ahian, and Shechem, and *L* ... 1Chr 7:19

**LIKING**
Their young ones are in good *l* ... Job 39:4
*l* than the children which are of ... Dan 1:10

**LILIES**
brim of a cup, with flowers of *l* ... 1Kin 7:26
brim of a cup, with flowers of *l* ... 2Chr 4:5
he feedeth among the *l* ... Song 2:16
are twins, which feed among the *l* ... Song 4:5
his lips like *l*, dropping sweet ... Song 5:13
in the gardens, and to gather *l* ... Song 6:2
he feedeth among the *l* ... Song 6:3
an heap of wheat set about with *l* ... Song 7:2
Consider the *l* of the field ... Mt 6:28
Consider the *l* how they grow ... Lk 12:27

**LILY**
were of *l* work in the porch ... 1Kin 7:19
the top of the pillars was *l* work ... 1Kin 7:22
Sharon, and the *l* of the valleys ... Song 2:1
As the *l* among thorns, so is my ... Song 2:2
he shall grow as the *l*, and cast ... Hos 14:5

**LIME**
shall be as the burnings of *l* ... Is 33:12
bones of the king of Edom into *l* ... Amos 2:1

**LIMIT**
*l* thereof round about shall be ... Eze 43:12

**LIMITED**
God, and *l* the Holy One of Israel ... Ps 78:41

**LIMITETH**
he *l* a certain day, saying in ... Heb 4:7

**LINE**
thou shalt bind this *l* of scarlet ... Josh 2:18
bound the scarlet *l* in the window ... Josh 2:21
Moab, and measured them with a *l* ... 2Sa 8:2
and with one full *l* to keep alive ... 2Sa 8:2
a *l* of twelve cubits did compass ... 1Kin 7:15
a *l* of thirty cubits did compass ... 1Kin 7:23
over Jerusalem the *l* of Samaria ... 2Kin 21:13
a *l* of thirty cubits did compass ... 2Chr 4:2
who hath stretched the *l* upon it ... Job 38:5
Their *l* is gone out through all ... Ps 19:4
divided them an inheritance by *l* ... Ps 78:55
*l* upon *l*, *l* upon *l* ... Is 28:10
*l* upon *l*, *l* upon *l* ... Is 28:13
Judgment also will I lay to the *l* ... Is 28:17
out upon it the *l* of confusion ... Is 34:11
hath divided it unto them by *l* ... Is 34:17
he marketh it out with a *l* ... Is 44:13
the measuring *l* shall yet go ... Jer 31:39
he hath stretched out a *l* ... Lam 2:8
with a *l* of flax in his hand, and ... Eze 40:3
when the man that had the *l* in ... Eze 47:3
and thy land shall be divided by *l* ... Amos 7:17
a *l* shall be stretched forth upon ... Zec 1:16
with a measuring *l* in his hand ... Zec 2:1
*l* of things made ready to our ... 2Cor 10:16

**LINEAGE**
he was of the house and *l* of David ... Lk 2:4

**LINEN**
arrayed him in vestures of fine *l* ... Gen 41:42
and purple, and scarlet, and fine *l* ... Ex 25:4
ten curtains of fine twined *l* ... Ex 26:1
fine twined *l* of cunning work ... Ex 26:31
and scarlet, and fine twined *l* ... Ex 26:36
for the court of fine twined *l* of ... Ex 27:9
and scarlet, and fine twined *l* ... Ex 27:16
five cubits of fine twined *l* ... Ex 27:18
and purple, and scarlet, and fine *l* ... Ex 28:5
of scarlet, and fine twined *l* ... Ex 28:6
and scarlet, and fine twined *l* ... Ex 28:8
of scarlet, and of fine twined *l* ... Ex 28:15
embroider the coat of fine *l* ... Ex 28:39
shalt make the mitre of fine *l* ... Ex 28:39
thou shalt make them *l* breeches ... Ex 28:42
and purple, and scarlet, and fine *l* ... Ex 35:6
and purple, and scarlet, and fine *l* ... Ex 35:23
and of scarlet, and of fine *l* ... Ex 35:25
purple, in scarlet, and in fine *l* ... Ex 35:35
ten curtains of fine twined *l* ... Ex 36:8
and scarlet, and fine twined *l* ... Ex 36:35
and scarlet, and fine twined *l* ... Ex 36:37
the court were of fine twined *l* ... Ex 38:9
round about were of fine twined *l* ... Ex 38:16
and scarlet, and fine twined *l* ... Ex 38:18
purple, and in scarlet, and fine *l* ... Ex 38:23
and scarlet, and fine twined *l* ... Ex 39:2
in the scarlet, and in the fine *l* ... Ex 39:3
and scarlet, and fine twined *l* ... Ex 39:5
and scarlet, and fine twined *l* ... Ex 39:8
purple, and scarlet, and twined *l* ... Ex 39:24
of fine *l* of woven work for Aaron ... Ex 39:27
And a mitre of fine *l* ... Ex 39:28
and goodly bonnets of fine *l* ... Ex 39:28
*l* breeches of fine twined *l*, ... Ex 39:28
*l* breeches of fine twined *l* ... Ex 39:28
And a girdle of fine twined *l* ... Ex 39:29
priest shall put on his *l* garment ... Lev 6:10
his *l* breeches shall he put upon ... Lev 6:10
a woollen garment, or a *l* garment ... Lev 13:47
of *l*, or of woollen ... Lev 13:48
warp or woof, in woollen or in *l* ... Lev 13:52
in a garment of woollen or *l* ... Lev 13:59
He shall put on the holy *l* coat ... Lev 16:4
he shall have the *l* breeches upon ... Lev 16:4
shall be girded with a *l* girdle ... Lev 16:4
with the *l* mitre shall he be ... Lev 16:4
and shall put off the *l* garments ... Lev 16:23
and shall put on the *l* clothes ... Lev 16:32
shall a garment mingled of *l* ... Lev 19:19
as of woollen and *l* together ... Deut 22:11
a child, girded with a *l* ephod ... 1Sa 2:18
persons that did wear a *l* ephod ... 1Sa 22:18
David was girded with a *l* ephod ... 2Sa 6:14
brought out of Egypt, and *l* yarn ... 1Kin 10:28
received the *l* yarn at a price ... 1Kin 10:28
house of them that wrought fine *l* ... 1Chr 4:21
was clothed with a robe of fine *l* ... 1Chr 15:27
also had upon him an ephod of *l* ... 1Chr 15:27
brought out of Egypt, and *l* yarn ... 2Chr 1:16
received the *l* yarn at a price ... 2Chr 1:16
in purple, in blue, and in fine *l* ... 2Chr 2:14
and purple, and crimson, and fine *l* ... 2Chr 3:14
being arrayed in white *l* ... 2Chr 5:12
fastened with cords of fine *l* ... Est 1:6
gold, and with a garment of fine *l* ... Est 8:15
works, with fine *l* of Egypt ... Prov 7:16
She maketh fine *l*, and selleth it ... Prov 31:24
The glasses, and the fine *l* ... Is 3:23
me, Go and get thee a *l* girdle ... Jer 13:1
man among them was clothed with *l* ... Eze 9:2
called to the man clothed with *l* ... Eze 9:3
behold, the man clothed with *l* ... Eze 9:11
spake unto the man clothed with *l* ... Eze 10:2
commanded the man clothed with *l* ... Eze 10:6
of him that was clothed with *l* ... Eze 10:7
I girded thee about with fine *l* ... Eze 16:10
and thy raiment was of fine *l* ... Eze 16:13
Fine *l* with broidered work from ... Eze 27:7
and broidered work, and fine *l* ... Eze 27:16
shall be clothed with *l* garments ... Eze 44:17
They shall have *l* bonnets upon ... Eze 44:18
shall have *l* breeches upon their ... Eze 44:18
behold a certain man clothed in *l* ... Dan 10:5
one said to the man clothed in *l* ... Dan 12:6
And I heard the man clothed in *l* ... Dan 12:7
he wrapped it in a clean *l* cloth ... Mt 27:59
having a *l* cloth cast about his ... Mk 14:51
And he left the *l* cloth, and fled ... Mk 14:52
And he bought fine *l*, and took him ... Mk 15:46
him down, and wrapped him in the *l* ... Mk 15:46
was clothed in purple and fine *l* ... Lk 16:19
took it down, and wrapped it in *l* ... Lk 23:53
he beheld the *l* clothes laid by ... Lk 24:12
wound it in *l* clothes with the ... Jn 19:40
in, saw the *l* clothes lying ... Jn 20:5
and seeth the *l* clothes lie, ... Jn 20:6
not lying with the *l* clothes ... Jn 20:7
clothed in pure and white *l* ... Rev 15:6
stones, and of pearls, and fine *l* ... Rev 18:12
city, that was clothed in fine *l* ... Rev 18:16
she should be arrayed in fine *l* ... Rev 19:8
for the fine *l* is the ... Rev 19:8
white horses, clothed in fine *l* ... Rev 19:14

**LINES**
even with two *l* measured he to ... 2Sa 8:2
The *l* are fallen unto me in ... Ps 16:6

**LINGERED**
And while he *l*, the men laid hold ... Gen 19:16
For except we had *l*, surely now ... Gen 43:10

**LINGERETH**
judgment now of a long time *l* not ... 2Pet 2:3

**LINTEL**
is in the bason, and strike the *l* ... Ex 12:22
he seeth the blood upon the *l* ... Ex 12:23
the *l* and side posts were a fifth ... 1Kin 6:31
Smite the *l* of the door, that the ... Amos 9:1

**LINTELS**
shall lodge in the upper *l* of it ... Zeph 2:14

**LINUS** (*li'-nus*) *A Christian at Rome.*
greeteth thee, and Pudens, and *L* ... 2Ti 4:21

**LION**
stooped down, he couched as a *l* ... Gen 49:9
and as an old *l* ... Gen 49:9
people shall rise up as a great *l* ... Num 23:24
and lift up himself as a young *l* ... Num 23:24
He couched, he lay down as a *l* ... Num 24:9
and as a great *l* ... Num 24:9
he dwelleth as a *l*, and teareth ... Deut 33:20
a young *l* roared against him ... Judg 14:5
aside to see the carcase of the *l* ... Judg 14:8
and honey in the carcase of the *l* ... Judg 14:8
honey out of the carcase of the *l* ... Judg 14:9
And what is stronger than a *l* ... Judg 14:18
father's sheep, and there came a *l* ... 1Sa 17:34
Thy servant slew both the *l* ... 1Sa 17:36
me out of the paw of the *l* ... 1Sa 17:37
heart is as the heart of a *l* ... 2Sa 17:10
slew a *l* in the midst of a pit in ... 2Sa 23:20
a *l* met him by the way, and slew ... 1Kin 13:24
the *l* also stood by the carcase ... 1Kin 13:24
the *l* standing by the carcase ... 1Kin 13:25
hath delivered him unto the *l* ... 1Kin 13:26
the *l* standing by the carcase ... 1Kin 13:28
the *l* had not eaten the carcase, ... 1Kin 13:28
from me, a *l* shall slay thee ... 1Kin 20:36
a *l* found him, and slew him ... 1Kin 20:36
slew a *l* in a pit in a snowy day ... 1Chr 11:22

The roaring of the *l* .......... Job 4:10
and the voice of the fierce *l* .......... Job 4:10
The old *l* perisheth for lack of .......... Job 4:11
Thou huntest me as a fierce *l* .......... Job 10:16
it, nor the fierce *l* passed by it .......... Job 28:8
Wilt thou hunt the prey for the *l* .......... Job 38:39
Lest he tear my soul like a *l* .......... Ps 7:2
wait secretly as a *l* in his den .......... Ps 10:9
Like as a *l* that is greedy of his .......... Ps 17:12
as it were a young *l* lurking in .......... Ps 17:12
as a ravening and a roaring *l* .......... Ps 22:13
Thou shalt tread upon the *l* .......... Ps 91:13
the young *l* and the dragon shalt .......... Ps 91:13
wrath is as the roaring of a *l* .......... Prov 19:12
a king is as the roaring of a *l* .......... Prov 20:2
man saith, There is a *l* without .......... Prov 22:13
saith, There is a *l* in the way .......... Prov 26:13
a *l* is in the streets .......... Prov 26:13
but the righteous are bold as a *l* .......... Prov 28:1
As a roaring *l*, and a ranging bear .......... Prov 28:15
A *l* which is strongest among .......... Prov 30:30
dog is better than a dead *l* .......... Eccl 9:4
Their roaring shall be like a *l* .......... Is 5:29
and the calf and the young *l* .......... Is 11:6
the *l* shall eat straw like the ox .......... Is 11:7
And he cried, A *l* .......... Is 21:8
whence come the young and old *l* .......... Is 30:6
spoken unto me, Like as the *l* .......... Is 31:4
the young *l* roaring on his prey, .......... Is 31:4
No *l* shall be there, nor any .......... Is 35:9
till morning, that, as a *l* .......... Is 38:13
the *l* shall eat straw like the .......... Is 65:25
prophets, like a destroying *l* .......... Jer 2:30
The *l* is come up from his thicket .......... Jer 4:7
Wherefore a *l* out of the forest .......... Jer 5:6
is unto me as a *l* in the forest .......... Jer 12:8
forsaken his covert, as the *l* .......... Jer 25:38
he shall come up like a *l* from .......... Jer 49:19
he shall come up like a *l* from .......... Jer 50:44
wait, and as a *l* in secret places .......... Lam 3:10
face of a man, and the face of a *l* .......... Eze 1:10
man, and the third the face of a *l* .......... Eze 10:14
it became a young *l*, and it .......... Eze 19:3
her whelps, and made him a young *l* .......... Eze 19:5
the lions, he became a young *l* .......... Eze 19:6
like a roaring *l* ravening the .......... Eze 22:25
art like a young *l* of the nations .......... Eze 32:2
the face of a young *l* toward the .......... Eze 41:19
The first was like a *l*, and had .......... Dan 7:4
For I will be unto Ephraim as a *l* .......... Hos 5:14
as a young *l* to the house of .......... Hos 5:14
he shall roar like a *l* .......... Hos 11:10
I will be unto them as a *l* .......... Hos 13:7
there will I devour them like a *l* .......... Hos 13:8
whose teeth are the teeth of a *l* .......... Joel 1:6
hath the cheek teeth of a great *l* .......... Joel 1:6
Will a *l* roar in the forest, when .......... Amos 3:4
will a young *l* cry out of his den .......... Amos 3:4
The *l* hath roared, who will not .......... Amos 3:8
of the mouth of the *l* two legs .......... Amos 3:12
As if a man did flee from a *l* .......... Amos 5:19
the midst of many people as a *l* .......... Mic 5:8
as a young *l* among the flocks of .......... Mic 5:8
of the young lions, where the *l* .......... Nah 2:11
even the old *l* .......... Nah 2:11
The *l* did tear in pieces enough .......... Nah 2:12
out of the mouth of the *l* .......... 2Ti 4:17
the devil, as a roaring *l* .......... 1Pet 5:8
And the first beast was like a *l* .......... Rev 4:7
the *L* of the tribe of Juda, the .......... Rev 5:5
a loud voice, as when a *l* roareth .......... Rev 10:3
and his mouth as the mouth of a *l* .......... Rev 13:2

## LIONESS

A *l* .......... Eze 19:2

## LIONESSES

whelps, and strangled for his *l* .......... Nah 2:12

## LIONLIKE

acts, he slew two *l* men of Moab .......... 2Sa 23:20
he slew two *l* men of Moab .......... 1Chr 11:22

## LION'S

Judah is a *l* whelp .......... Gen 49:9
of Dan he said, Dan is a *l* whelp .......... Deut 33:22
the stout *l* whelps are scattered .......... Job 4:11
The *l* whelps have not trodden it, .......... Job 28:8
Save me from the *l* mouth .......... Ps 22:21
the *l* whelp, and none made them .......... Nah 2:11

## LIONS

eagles, they were stronger than *l* .......... 2Sa 1:23
were between the ledges were *l* .......... 1Kin 7:29
and beneath the *l* and oxen were .......... 1Kin 7:29
thereof, he graved cherubims, *l* .......... 1Kin 7:36
two *l* stood beside the stays .......... 1Kin 10:19
twelve *l* stood there on the one .......... 1Kin 10:20
the LORD sent *l* among them .......... 2Kin 17:25
he hath sent *l* among them .......... 2Kin 17:26
faces were like the faces of *l* .......... 1Chr 12:8
two *l* standing by the stays .......... 2Chr 9:18
twelve *l* stood there on the one .......... 2Chr 9:19
lion, and the teeth of the young *l* .......... Job 4:10
fill the appetite of the young *l* .......... Job 38:39
The young *l* do lack, and suffer .......... Ps 34:10
my darling from the *l* .......... Ps 35:17
My soul is among *l* .......... Ps 57:4
the great teeth of the young *l* .......... Ps 58:6
The young *l* roar after their prey .......... Ps 104:21
they shall roar like young *l* .......... Is 5:29
*l* upon him that escapeth of Moab, .......... Is 15:9
The young *l* roared upon him, and .......... Jer 2:15
the *l* have driven him away .......... Jer 50:17
They shall roar together like *l* .......... Jer 51:38
she lay down among *l*, she .......... Eze 19:2
her whelps among young *l* .......... Eze 19:2
up and down among the *l* .......... Eze 19:6
with all the young *l* thereof .......... Eze 38:13
shall be cast into the den of *l* .......... Dan 6:7
shall be cast into the den of *l* .......... Dan 6:12
and cast him into the den of *l* .......... Dan 6:16
went in haste unto the den of *l* .......... Dan 6:19
able to deliver thee from the *l* .......... Dan 6:20
they cast them into the den of *l* .......... Dan 6:24
the *l* had the mastery of them, and .......... Dan 6:24
Daniel from the power of the *l* .......... Dan 6:27
Where is the dwelling of the *l* .......... Nah 2:11
the feeding place of the young *l* .......... Nah 2:11
sword shall devour thy young *l* .......... Nah 2:13
princes within her are roaring *l* .......... Zeph 3:3
a voice of the roaring of young *l* .......... Zec 11:3
promises, stopped the mouths of *l* .......... Heb 11:33
teeth were as the teeth of *l* .......... Rev 9:8
the horses were as the heads of *l* .......... Rev 9:17

## LIONS'

Shenir and Hermon, from the *l* dens .......... Song 4:8
they shall yell as *l* whelps .......... Jer 51:38
angel, and hath shut the *l* mouths .......... Dan 6:22

## LIP

put a covering upon his upper *l* .......... Lev 13:45
they shoot out the *l*, they shake .......... Ps 22:7
The *l* of truth shall be .......... Prov 12:19

## LIPS

me, who am of uncircumcised *l* .......... Ex 6:12
Behold, I am of uncircumcised *l* .......... Ex 6:30
pronouncing with his *l* to do evil .......... Lev 5:4
or uttered ought out of her *l* .......... Num 30:6
that which she uttered with her *l* .......... Num 30:8
out of her *l* concerning her vows .......... Num 30:12
gone out of thy *l* thou shalt keep .......... Deut 23:23
only her *l* moved, but her voice .......... 1Sa 1:13
thy nose, and my bridle in thy *l* .......... 2Kin 19:28
this did not Job sin with his *l* .......... Job 2:10
laughing, and thy *l* with rejoicing .......... Job 8:21
speak, and open his *l* against thee .......... Job 11:5
hearken to the pleadings of my *l* .......... Job 13:6
thine own *l* testify against thee .......... Job 15:6
the moving of my *l* should asswage .......... Job 16:5
from the commandment of his *l* .......... Job 23:12
My *l* shall not speak wickedness, .......... Job 27:4
I will open my *l* and answer .......... Job 32:20
my *l* shall utter knowledge .......... Job 33:3
with flattering *l* and with a .......... Ps 12:2
shall cut off all flattering *l* .......... Ps 12:3
our *l* are our own .......... Ps 12:4
nor take up their names into my *l* .......... Ps 16:4
that goeth not out of feigned *l* .......... Ps 17:1
by the word of thy *l* I have kept .......... Ps 17:4
withholden the request of his *l* .......... Ps 21:2
Let the lying *l* be put to silence .......... Ps 31:18
thy *l* from speaking guile .......... Ps 34:13
lo, I have not refrained my *l* .......... Ps 40:9
grace is poured into thy *l* .......... Ps 45:2
O Lord, open thou my *l* .......... Ps 51:15
swords are in their *l* .......... Ps 59:7
the words of their *l* let them .......... Ps 59:12
than life, my *l* shall praise thee .......... Ps 63:3
shall praise thee with joyful *l* .......... Ps 63:5
Which my *l* have uttered, and my .......... Ps 66:14
My *l* shall greatly rejoice when I .......... Ps 71:23
thing that is gone out of my *l* .......... Ps 89:34
he spake unadvisedly with his *l* .......... Ps 106:33
With my *l* have I declared all the .......... Ps 119:13
My *l* shall utter praise, when .......... Ps 119:171
my soul, O LORD, from lying *l* .......... Ps 120:2
adders' poison is under their *l* .......... Ps 140:3
of their own *l* cover them .......... Ps 140:9
Keep the door of my *l* .......... Ps 141:3
perverse *l* put far from thee .......... Prov 4:24
that thy *l* may keep knowledge .......... Prov 5:2
For the *l* of a strange woman drop .......... Prov 5:3
of her *l* she forced him .......... Prov 7:21
the opening of my *l* shall be .......... Prov 8:6
is an abomination to my *l* .......... Prov 8:7
In the *l* of him that hath .......... Prov 10:13
that hideth hatred with lying *l* .......... Prov 10:18
he that refraineth his *l* is wise .......... Prov 10:19
The *l* of the righteous feed many .......... Prov 10:21
The *l* of the righteous know what .......... Prov 10:32
by the transgression of his *l* .......... Prov 12:13
Lying *l* are abomination to the .......... Prov 12:22
wide his *l* shall have destruction .......... Prov 13:3
but the *l* of the wise shall .......... Prov 14:3
not in him the *l* of knowledge .......... Prov 14:7
but the talk of the *l* tendeth .......... Prov 14:23
The *l* of the wise disperse .......... Prov 15:7
sentence is in the *l* of the king .......... Prov 16:10
Righteous *l* are the delight of .......... Prov 16:13
of the *l* increaseth learning .......... Prov 16:21
and addeth learning to his *l* .......... Prov 16:23
in his *l* there is as a burning .......... Prov 16:27
moving his *l* he bringeth evil to .......... Prov 16:30
doer giveth heed to false *l* .......... Prov 17:4
much less do lying *l* a prince .......... Prov 17:7
his *l* is esteemed a man of .......... Prov 17:28
A fool's *l* enter into contention, .......... Prov 18:6
his *l* are the snare of his soul .......... Prov 18:7
of his *l* shall he be filled .......... Prov 18:20
than he that is perverse in his *l* .......... Prov 19:1
but the *l* of knowledge are a .......... Prov 20:15
him that flattereth with his *l* .......... Prov 20:19
for the grace of his *l* the king .......... Prov 22:11
shall withal be fitted in thy *l* .......... Prov 22:18
when thy *l* speak right things .......... Prov 23:16
and their *l* talk of mischief .......... Prov 24:2
Every man shall kiss his *l* that .......... Prov 24:26
and deceive not with thy *l* .......... Prov 24:28
Burning *l* and a wicked heart are .......... Prov 26:23
hateth dissembleth with his *l* .......... Prov 26:24
a stranger, and not thine own *l* .......... Prov 27:2
but the *l* of a fool will swallow .......... Eccl 10:12
Thy *l* are like a thread of .......... Song 4:3
Thy *l*, O my spouse, drop as the .......... Song 4:11
his *l* like lilies, dropping sweet .......... Song 5:13
causing the *l* of those that are .......... Song 7:9
because I am a man of unclean *l* .......... Is 6:5
midst of a people of unclean *l* .......... Is 6:5
said, Lo, this hath touched thy *l* .......... Is 6:7
with the breath of his *l* shall he .......... Is 11:4
For with stammering *l* and another .......... Is 28:11
with their *l* do honour me, but .......... Is 29:13
his *l* are full of indignation, and .......... Is 30:27
thy nose, and my bridle in thy *l* .......... Is 37:29
I create the fruit of the *l* .......... Is 57:19
your *l* have spoken lies, your .......... Is 59:3
out of my *l* was right before thee .......... Jer 17:16
The *l* of those that rose up .......... Lam 3:62
upon thy feet, and cover not thy *l* .......... Eze 24:17
ye shall not cover your *l* .......... Eze 24:22
are taken up in the *l* of talkers .......... Eze 36:3
of the sons of men touched my *l* .......... Dan 10:16
we render the calves of our *l* .......... Hos 14:2
yea, they shall all cover their *l* .......... Mic 3:7
my *l* quivered at the voice .......... Hab 3:16
iniquity was not found in his *l* .......... Mal 2:6
For the priest's *l* should keep .......... Mal 2:7
and honoureth me with their *l* .......... Mt 15:8
people honoureth me with their *l* .......... Mk 7:6
poison of asps is under their *l* .......... Rom 3:13
other *l* will I speak unto this .......... 1Cor 14:21
the fruit of our *l* giving thanks .......... Heb 13:15
his *l* that they speak no guile .......... 1Pet 3:10

## LIQUOR

shall he drink any *l* of grapes .......... Num 6:3
round goblet, which wanteth not *l* .......... Song 7:2

## LIQUORS

of thy ripe fruits, and of thy *l* .......... Ex 22:29

## LISTED

done unto him whatsoever they *l* .......... Mt 17:12
done unto him whatsoever they *l* .......... Mk 9:13

## LISTEN

*L*, O isles, unto me .......... Is 49:1

## LISTETH

The wind bloweth where it *l* .......... Jn 3:8
whithersoever the governor *l* .......... Jas 3:4

## LITTERS

horses, and in chariots, and in *l* .......... Is 66:20

## LITTLE

Let a *l* water, I pray you, be .......... Gen 18:4
to flee unto, and it is a *l* one .......... Gen 19:20
thither, (is it not a *l* one .......... Gen 19:20
drink a *l* water of thy pitcher .......... Gen 24:17
a *l* water of thy pitcher to drink .......... Gen 24:43
For it was *l* which thou hadst .......... Gen 30:30
their wealth, and all their *l* ones .......... Gen 34:29
there was but a *l* way to come to .......... Gen 35:16
them, Go again, buy us a *l* food .......... Gen 43:2
we, and thou, and also our *l* ones .......... Gen 43:8
a *l* balm, and a *l* honey, .......... Gen 43:11
a child of his old age, a *l* one .......... Gen 44:20
Go again, and buy us a *l* food .......... Gen 44:25
the land of Egypt for your *l* ones .......... Gen 45:19
their father, and their *l* ones .......... Gen 46:5
and for food for your *l* ones .......... Gen 47:24
but a *l* way to come unto Ephrath .......... Gen 48:7
only their *l* ones, and their .......... Gen 50:8
will nourish you, and your *l* ones .......... Gen 50:21
I will let you go, and your *l* ones .......... Ex 10:10
let your *l* ones also go with you .......... Ex 10:24
household be too *l* for the lamb .......... Ex 12:4
and he that gathered *l* had no lack .......... Ex 16:18
By *l* and *l* I will drive them .......... Ex 23:30
And the *l* owl, and the cormorant, .......... Lev 11:17
But your *l* ones, which ye said .......... Num 14:31
their sons, and their *l* children .......... Num 16:27
Midian captives, and their *l* ones .......... Num 31:9
kill every male among the *l* ones .......... Num 31:17
cattle, and cities for our *l* ones .......... Num 32:16
our *l* ones shall dwell in the .......... Num 32:17
Build you cities for your *l* ones .......... Num 32:24
Our *l* ones, our wives, our flocks .......... Num 32:26
Moreover your *l* ones, which ye .......... Deut 1:39
the *l* ones, of every city, we .......... Deut 2:34
But your wives, and your *l* ones .......... Deut 3:19
before thee by *l* and *l* .......... Deut 7:22
The *l* owl, and the great owl, and .......... Deut 14:16
the *l* ones, and the cattle, and all .......... Deut 20:14
field, and shalt gather but *l* in .......... Deut 28:38
Your *l* ones, your wives, and thy .......... Deut 29:11
Your wives, your *l* ones, and your .......... Josh 1:14
the *l* ones, and the strangers that .......... Josh 8:35
of Dan went out too *l* for them .......... Josh 19:47
the iniquity of Peor too *l* for us .......... Josh 22:17
I pray thee, a *l* water to drink .......... Judg 4:19
and departed, and put the *l* ones .......... Judg 18:21
that she tarried a *l* in the house .......... Ruth 2:7
his mother made him a *l* coat .......... 1Sa 2:19

L

I tasted a *l* of this honey 1Sa 14:29
I did but taste a *l* honey with 1Sa 14:43
When thou wast *l* in thine own 1Sa 15:17
with David, and a *l* lad with him 1Sa 20:35
had nothing, save one *l* ewe lamb 2Sa 12:3
and if that had been too *l* 2Sa 12:8
all the *l* ones that were with him 2Sa 15:22
when David was a *l* past the top 2Sa 16:1
Thy servant will go a *l* way over 2Sa 19:36
and I am but a *l* child 1Kin 3:7
was before the LORD was too *l* to 1Kin 8:64
Hadad being yet a *l* child 1Kin 11:17
My *l* finger shall be thicker than 1Kin 12:10
a *l* water in a vessel, that I may 1Kin 17:10
a barrel, and a *l* oil in a cruse 1Kin 17:12
make me thereof a *l* cake first 1Kin 17:13
there ariseth a *l* cloud out of 1Kin 18:44
them like two *l* flocks of kids 1Kin 20:27
there came forth *l* children out 2Kin 2:23
Let us make a *l* chamber, I pray 2Kin 4:10
of the land of Israel a *l* maid 2Kin 5:2
like unto the flesh of a *l* child 2Kin 5:14
So he departed from him a *l* way 2Kin 5:19
unto them, Ahab served Baal a *l* 2Kin 10:18
My *l* finger shall be thicker than 2Chr 10:10
the LORD, with their *l* ones 2Chr 20:13
the genealogy of all their *l* ones 2Chr 31:18
way for us, and for our *l* ones Ezr 8:21
now for a *l* space grace hath been Ezr 9:8
give us a *l* reviving in our Ezr 9:8
the trouble seem *l* before thee Neh 9:32
*l* children and women, in one day, Est 3:13
would assault them, both *l* ones Est 8:11
and mine ear received a *l* thereof Job 4:12
that I may take comfort a *l* Job 10:20
forth their *l* ones like a flock Job 21:11
They are exalted for a *l* while Job 24:24
but how *l* a portion is heard of Job 26:14
Suffer me a *l*, and I will shew Job 36:2
when his wrath is kindled but a *l* Ps 2:12
him a *l* lower than the angels Ps 8:5
For yet a *l* while, and the wicked Ps 37:10
A *l* that a righteous man hath is Ps 37:16
the *l* hills rejoice on every side Ps 65:12
There is *l* Benjamin with their Ps 68:27
the *l* hills, by righteousness Ps 72:3
rams, and the *l* hills like lambs Ps 114:4
and ye *l* hills, like lambs Ps 114:6
dasheth thy *l* ones against the Ps 137:9
Yet a *l* sleep, a *l* slumber, Prov 6:10
a *l* folding of the hands to sleep Prov 6:10
heart of the wicked is *l* worth Prov 10:20
Better is *l* with the fear of the Prov 15:16
Better is a *l* with righteousness Prov 16:8
Yet a *l* sleep, a *l* slumber, Prov 24:33
a *l* folding of the hands to sleep Prov 24:33
things which are *l* upon the earth Prov 30:24
sweet, whether he eat *l* or much Eccl 5:12
There was a *l* city, and few men Eccl 9:14
so doth a *l* folly him that is in Eccl 10:1
the *l* foxes, that spoil the vines Song 2:15
It was but a *l* that I passed from Song 3:4
We have a *l* sister, and she hath Song 8:8
For yet a very *l* while, and the Is 10:25
a *l* child shall lead them Is 11:6
thyself as it were for a *l* moment Is 26:20
here a *l*, and there a *l* Is 28:10
here a *l*, and there a *l* Is 28:13
Is it not yet a very *l* while Is 29:17
up the isles as a very *l* thing Is 40:15
In a *l* wrath I hid my face from Is 54:8
A *l* one shall become a thousand, Is 60:22
have possessed it but a *l* while Is 63:18
sent their *l* ones to the waters Jer 14:3
her *l* ones have caused a cry to Jer 48:4
yet a *l* while, and the time of her Jer 51:33
maids, and *l* children, and women Eze 9:6
as a *l* sanctuary in the countries Eze 11:16
as if that were a very *l* thing Eze 16:47
sent out her *l* rivers unto all Eze 31:4
every *l* chamber was one reed long Eze 40:7
between the *l* chambers were five Eze 40:7
the *l* chambers of the gate Eze 40:10
The space also before the *l* Eze 40:12
the *l* chambers were six cubits on Eze 40:12
the gate from the roof of one *l* Eze 40:13
narrow windows to the *l* chambers Eze 40:16
the *l* chambers thereof were three Eze 40:21
the *l* chambers thereof, and the Eze 40:29
the *l* chambers thereof, and the Eze 40:33
The *l* chambers thereof, the posts Eze 40:36
came up among them another *l* horn Dan 7:8
one of them came forth a *l* horn Dan 8:9
shall be holpen with a *l* help Dan 11:34
for yet a *l* while, and I will Hos 1:4
they shall sorrow a *l* for the Hos 8:10
and the *l* house with clefts Amos 6:11
though thou be *l* among the Mic 5:2
Ye have sown much, and bring in *l* Hag 1:6
for much, and, lo, it came to *l* Hag 1:9
Yet once, it is a *l* while Hag 2:6
for I was but a *l* displeased Zec 1:15
turn mine hand upon the *l* ones Zec 13:7
more clothe you, O ye of *l* faith Mt 6:30
are ye fearful, O ye of *l* faith Mt 8:26
*l* ones a cup of cold water only Mt 10:42
said unto him, O thou of *l* faith Mt 14:31
said, Seven, and a few *l* fishes Mt 15:34
said unto them, O ye of *l* faith Mt 16:8
Jesus called a *l* child unto him Mt 18:2
and become as *l* children, ye Mt 18:3
humble himself as this *l* child Mt 18:4
whoso shall receive one such *l* Mt 18:5
these *l* ones which believe in me Mt 18:6
despise not one of these *l* ones Mt 18:10
that one of these *l* ones should Mt 18:14
there brought unto him *l* children Mt 19:13
Suffer *l* children, and forbid them Mt 19:14
And he went a *l* farther, and fell Mt 26:39
he had gone a *l* farther thence Mk 1:19
were also with him other *l* ships Mk 4:36
My *l* daughter lieth at the point Mk 5:23
these *l* ones that believe in me Mk 9:42
Suffer the *l* children to come Mk 10:14
the kingdom of God as a *l* child Mk 10:15
And he went forward a *l*, and fell Mk 14:35
a *l* after, they that stood by Mk 14:70
thrust out a *l* from the land Lk 5:3
but to whom *l* is forgiven Lk 7:47
is forgiven, the same loveth *l* Lk 7:47
he clothe you, O ye of *l* faith Lk 12:28
Fear not, *l* flock Lk 12:32
should offend one of these *l* ones Lk 17:2
Suffer *l* children to come unto me Lk 18:16
a *l* child shall in no wise enter Lk 18:17
because he was *l* of stature Lk 19:3
hast been faithful in a very *l* Lk 19:17
after a *l* while another saw him, Lk 22:58
every one of them may take a *l* Jn 6:7
Yet a *l* while am I with you, and Jn 7:33
Yet a *l* while is the light with Jn 12:35
*L* children, yet a *l* while I Jn 13:33
Yet a *l* while, and the world seeth Jn 14:19
A *l* while, and ye shall not see me Jn 16:16
a *l* while, and ye shall see me, Jn 16:16
A *l* while, and ye shall not see me Jn 16:17
a *l* while, and ye shall see me Jn 16:17
is this that he saith, A *l* while Jn 16:18
A *l* while, and ye shall not see me Jn 16:19
a *l* while, and ye shall see me Jn 16:19
other disciples came in a *l* ship Jn 21:8
put the apostles forth a *l* space Acts 5:34
alive, and were not a *l* comforted Acts 20:12
and when they had gone a *l* further Acts 27:28
people shewed us no *l* kindness Acts 28:2
Know ye not that a *l* leaven 1Cor 5:6
that had gathered *l* had no lack 2Cor 8:15
bear with me a *l* in my folly 2Cor 11:1
me, that I may boast myself a *l* 2Cor 11:16
My *l* children, of whom I travail Gal 4:19
A *l* leaven leaveneth the whole Gal 5:9
For bodily exercise profiteth *l* 1Ti 4:8
water, but use a *l* wine for thy 1Ti 5:23
Thou madest him a *l* lower than Heb 2:7
who was made a *l* lower than the Heb 2:9
For yet a *l* while, and he that Heb 10:37
Even so the tongue is a *l* member Jas 3:5
great a matter a *l* fire kindleth Jas 3:5
that appeareth for a *l* time Jas 4:14
My *l* children, these things write 1Jn 2:1
*l* children, because your sins are 1Jn 2:12
*l* children, because ye have known 1Jn 2:13
*L* children, it is the last time 1Jn 2:18
And now, *l* children, abide in him 1Jn 2:28
*L* children, let no man deceive 1Jn 3:7
My *l* children, let us not love in 1Jn 3:18
*l* children, and have overcome them 1Jn 4:4
*L* children, keep yourselves from 1Jn 5:21
for thou hast a *l* strength Rev 3:8
should rest yet for a *l* season Rev 6:11
he had in his hand a *l* book open Rev 10:2
take the *l* book which is open in Rev 10:8
said unto him, Give me the *l* book Rev 10:9
I took the *l* book out of the Rev 10:10
that he must be loosed a *l* season Rev 20:3

## LIVE

of life, and eat, and *l* for ever Gen 3:22
my soul shall *l* because of thee Gen 12:13
that Ishmael might *l* before thee Gen 17:18
and my soul shall *l* Gen 19:20
pray for thee, and thou shalt *l* Gen 20:7
And by thy sword shalt thou *l* Gen 27:40
findest thy gods, let him not *l* Gen 31:32
that we may *l*, and not die Gen 42:2
them the third day, This do, and *l* Gen 42:18
that we may *l*, and not die, both Gen 43:8
doth my father yet *l* Gen 45:3
and give us seed, that we may *l* Gen 47:19
be a daughter, then she shall *l* Ex 1:16
be beast or man, it shall not *l* Ex 19:13
then they shall sell the *l* ox Ex 21:35
shalt not suffer a witch to *l* Ex 22:18
there shall no man see me, and *l* Ex 33:20
altar, he shall bring the *l* goat Lev 16:20
hands upon the head of the *l* goat Lev 16:21
if a man do, he shall *l* in them Lev 18:5
that he may *l* with thee Lev 25:35
that thy brother may *l* with thee Lev 25:36
do unto them, that they may *l* Num 4:19
But as truly as I *l*, all the Num 14:21
Say unto them, As truly as I *l* Num 14:28
when he looketh upon it, shall *l* Num 21:8
who shall *l* when God doeth this Num 24:23
for to do them, that ye may *l* Deut 4:1
that they shall *l* upon the earth Deut 4:10
fire, as thou hast heard, and *l* Deut 4:33
one of these cities he might *l* Deut 4:42
hath commanded you, that ye may *l* Deut 5:33
ye observe to do, that ye may *l* Deut 8:1
that man doth not *l* by bread only Deut 8:3
the mouth of the LORD doth man *l* Deut 8:3
the days that ye *l* upon the earth Deut 12:1
thou follow, that thou mayest *l* Deut 16:20
shall flee thither, that he may *l* Deut 19:4
unto one of those cities, and *l* Deut 19:5
all thy soul, that thou mayest *l* Deut 30:6
his judgments, that thou mayest *l* Deut 30:16
that both thou and thy seed may *l* Deut 30:19
as long as ye *l* in the land Deut 31:13
to heaven, and say, I *l* for ever Deut 32:40
Let Reuben *l*, and not die Deut 33:6
only Rahab the harlot shall *l* Josh 6:17
a league with them, to let them *l* Josh 9:15
we will even let them *l*, lest Josh 9:20
said unto them, Let them *l* Josh 9:21
I *l* shew me the kindness of the 1Sa 20:14
not *l* after that he was fallen 2Sa 1:10
to me, that the child may *l* 2Sa 12:22
the king, How long have I to *l* 2Sa 19:34
Let my lord king David *l* for ever 1Kin 1:31
thee all the days that they *l* in 1Kin 8:40
saith, I pray thee, let me *l* 1Kin 20:32
*l* thou and thy children of the 2Kin 4:7
if they save us alive, we shall *l* 2Kin 7:4
shall be wanting, he shall not *l* 2Kin 10:19
olive and of honey, that ye may *l* 2Kin 18:32
for thou shalt die, and not *l* 2Kin 20:1
so long as they *l* in the land 2Chr 6:31
the king, Let the king *l* for ever Neh 2:3
for them, that we may eat, and *l* Neh 5:2
if a man do, he shall *l* in them Neh 9:29
the golden sceptre, that he may *l* Est 4:11
I would not *l* alway Job 7:16
If a man die, shall he *l* again Job 14:14
Wherefore do the wicked *l* Job 21:7
not reproach me so long as I *l* Job 27:6
your heart shall *l* for ever Ps 22:26
That he should still *l* for ever Ps 49:9
shall not *l* out half their days Ps 55:23
Thus will I bless thee while I *l* Ps 63:4
your heart shall *l* that seek God Ps 69:32
And he shall *l*, and to him shall be Ps 72:15
sing unto the LORD as long as I *l* Ps 104:33
I call upon him as long as I *l* Ps 116:2
I shall not die, but *l*, and Ps 118:17
with thy servant, that I may *l* Ps 119:17
come unto me, that I may *l* Ps 119:77
unto thy word, that I may *l* Ps 119:116
me understanding, and I shall *l* Ps 119:144
Let my soul *l*, and it shall praise Ps 119:175
While I *l* will I praise the LORD Ps 146:2
keep my commandments, and *l* Prov 4:4
Keep my commandments, and *l* Prov 7:2
Forsake the foolish, and *l* Prov 9:6
but he that hateth gifts shall *l* Prov 15:27
*l* many years, so that the days of Eccl 6:3
though he *l* a thousand years Eccl 6:6
is in their heart while they *l* Eccl 9:3
*L* joyfully with the wife whom Eccl 9:9
But if a man *l* many years Eccl 11:8
having a *l* coal in his hand, Is 6:6
They are dead, they shall not *l* Is 26:14
Thy dead men shall *l*, together Is 26:19
for thou shalt die, and not *l* Is 38:1
O Lord, by these things men *l* Is 38:16
thou recover me, and make me to *l* Is 38:16
As I *l*, saith the LORD, thou Is 49:18
hear, and your soul shall *l* Is 55:3
that besiege you, he shall *l* Jer 21:9
As I *l*, saith the LORD, though Jer 22:24
and serve him and his people, and *l* Jer 27:12
serve the king of Babylon, and *l* Jer 27:17
that ye may *l* many days in the Jer 35:7
forth to the Chaldeans shall *l* Jer 38:2
his life for a prey, and shall *l* Jer 38:2
princes, then thy soul shall *l* Jer 38:17
and thou shalt *l*, and thine house Jer 38:17
unto thee, and thy soul shall *l* Jer 38:20
As I *l*, saith the King, whose Jer 46:18
we shall *l* among the heathen Lam 4:20
doth not sin, he shall surely *l* Eze 3:21
Wherefore, as I *l*, saith the Lord Eze 5:11
the souls alive that should not *l* Eze 13:19
three men were in it, as I *l* Eze 14:16
three men were in it, as I *l* Eze 14:18
and Job, were in it, as I *l* Eze 14:20
when thou wast in thy blood, *L* Eze 16:6
when thou wast in thy blood, *L* Eze 16:6
As I *l*, saith the Lord GOD, Sodom Eze 16:48
As I *l*, saith the Lord GOD, Eze 17:16
As I *l*, surely mine oath that he Eze 17:19
As I *l*, saith the Lord GOD, ye Eze 18:3
he is just, he shall surely *l* Eze 18:9
shall he then *l* Eze 18:13
he shall not *l* Eze 18:13
of his father, he shall surely *l* Eze 18:17
hath done them, he shall surely *l* Eze 18:19
and right, he shall surely *l* Eze 18:21
that he hath done he shall *l* Eze 18:22
should return from his ways, and *l* Eze 18:23
the wicked man doeth, shall he *l* Eze 18:24
hath committed, he shall surely *l* Eze 18:28
turn yourselves, and *l* ye Eze 18:32
As I *l*, saith the Lord GOD, I Eze 20:3
a man do, he shall even *l* in them Eze 20:11
a man do, he shall even *l* in them Eze 20:13
a man do, he shall even *l* in them Eze 20:21
whereby they should not *l* Eze 20:25
As I *l*, saith the Lord GOD, I Eze 20:31
As I *l*, saith the Lord GOD, Eze 20:33

in them, how should we then *l* ... Eze 33:10
Say unto them, As I *l*, saith the ... Eze 33:11
the wicked turn from his way and *l* ... Eze 33:11
to *l* for his righteousness in the ... Eze 33:12
righteous, that he shall surely *l* ... Eze 33:13
he shall surely *l*, he shall not ... Eze 33:15
he shall surely *l* ... Eze 33:16
and right, he shall *l* thereby ... Eze 33:19
As I *l*, surely they that are in ... Eze 33:27
As I *l* saith the Lord GOD, surely ... Eze 34:8
Therefore, as I *l*, saith the Lord ... Eze 35:6
Therefore, as I *l*, saith the Lord ... Eze 35:11
me, Son of man, can these bones *l* ... Eze 37:3
to enter into you, and ye shall *l* ... Eze 37:5
put breath in you, and ye shall *l* ... Eze 37:6
upon these slain, that they may *l* ... Eze 37:9
my spirit in you, and ye shall *l* ... Eze 37:14
the rivers shall come, shall *l* ... Eze 47:9
every thing shall *l* whither the ... Eze 47:9
in Syriack, O king, *l* for ever ... Dan 2:4
O king, *l* for ever ... Dan 3:9
spake and said, O king, *l* for ever ... Dan 5:10
unto him, King Darius, *l* for ever ... Dan 6:6
unto the king, O king, *l* for ever ... Dan 6:21
us up, and we shall *l* in his sight ... Hos 6:2
Israel, Seek ye me, and ye shall *l* ... Amos 5:4
Seek the LORD, and ye shall *l* ... Amos 5:6
good, and not evil, that ye may *l* ... Amos 5:14
is better for me to die than to *l* ... Jonah 4:3
is better for me to die than to *l* ... Jonah 4:8
but the just shall *l* by his faith ... Hab 2:4
Therefore as I *l*, saith the LORD ... Zeph 2:9
the prophets, do they *l* for ever ... Zec 1:5
they shall *l* with their children, ... Zec 10:9
say unto him, Thou shalt not *l* ... Zec 13:3
Man shall not *l* by bread alone, ... Mt 4:4
thy hand upon her, and she shall *l* ... Mt 9:18
and she shall *l* ... Mk 5:23
man shall not *l* by bread alone ... Lk 4:4
*l* delicately, are in kings' ... Lk 7:25
this do, and thou shalt *l* ... Lk 10:28
for all *l* unto him ... Lk 20:38
and they that hear shall *l* ... Jn 5:25
this bread, he shall *l* for ever ... Jn 6:51
sent me, and I *l* by the Father ... Jn 6:57
eateth me, even he shall *l* by me ... Jn 6:57
of this bread shall *l* for ever ... Jn 6:58
he were dead, yet shall he *l* ... Jn 11:25
because I *l*, ye shall *l* also ... Jn 14:19
to the end they might not *l* ... Acts 7:19
For in him we *l*, and move, and have ... Acts 17:28
it is not fit that he should *l* ... Acts 22:22
that he ought not to *l* any longer ... Acts 25:24
yet vengeance suffereth not to *l* ... Acts 28:4
The just shall *l* by faith ... Rom 1:17
dead to sin, *l* any longer therein ... Rom 6:2
that we shall also *l* with him ... Rom 6:8
the flesh, to *l* after the flesh ... Rom 8:12
For if ye *l* after the flesh, ye ... Rom 8:13
the deeds of the body, ye shall *l* ... Rom 8:13
those things shall *l* by them ... Rom 10:5
in you, *l* peaceably with all men ... Rom 12:18
we *l*, we *l* unto the Lord ... Rom 14:8
whether we *l* therefore, or die, ... Rom 14:8
For it is written, As I *l* ... Rom 14:11
minister about holy things *l* of ... 1Cor 9:13
the gospel should *l* of the gospel ... 1Cor 9:14
For we which *l* are alway ... 2Cor 4:11
that they which *l* should not ... 2Cor 5:15
not henceforth *l* unto themselves ... 2Cor 5:15
as dying, and, behold, we *l* ... 2Cor 6:9
our hearts to die and *l* with you ... 2Cor 7:3
but we shall *l* with him by the ... 2Cor 13:4
be of one mind, *l* in peace ... 2Cor 13:11
the Gentiles to *l* as do the Jews ... Gal 2:14
the law, that I might *l* unto God ... Gal 2:19
nevertheless I *l* ... Gal 2:20
the life which I now *l* in the ... Gal 2:20
*l* by the faith of the Son of God ... Gal 2:20
for, The just shall *l* by faith ... Gal 3:11
that doeth them shall *l* in them ... Gal 3:12
If we *l* in the Spirit, let us ... Gal 5:25
thou mayest *l* long on the earth ... Eph 6:3
For to me to *l* is Christ, and to ... Phil 1:21
But if I *l* in the flesh, this is ... Phil 1:22
For now we *l*, if ye stand fast in ... 1Th 3:8
we should *l* together with him ... 1Th 5:10
him, we shall also *l* with him ... 2Ti 2:11
all that will *l* godly in Christ ... 2Ti 3:12
lusts, we should *l* soberly ... Titus 2:12
Now the just shall *l* by faith ... Heb 10:38
unto the Father of spirits, and *l* ... Heb 12:9
all things willing to *l* honestly ... Heb 13:18
say, If the Lord will, we shall *l* ... Jas 4:15
should *l* unto righteousness ... 1Pet 2:24
That he no longer should *l* the ... 1Pet 4:2
but *l* according to God in the ... 1Pet 4:6
those that after should *l* ungodly ... 2Pet 2:6
escaped from them who *l* in error ... 2Pet 2:18
that we might *l* through him ... 1Jn 4:9
the wound by a sword, and did *l* ... Rev 13:14

**LIVED**

Adam *l* an hundred and thirty years ... Gen 5:3
that Adam *l* were nine hundred ... Gen 5:5
Seth *l* an hundred and five years, ... Gen 5:6
Seth *l* after he begat Enos eight ... Gen 5:7
Enos *l* ninety years, and begat ... Gen 5:9
Enos *l* after he begat Cainan ... Gen 5:10
Cainan *l* seventy years, and begat ... Gen 5:12
And Cainan *l* after he begat ... Gen 5:13
And Mahalaleel *l* sixty and five ... Gen 5:15
Mahalaleel *l* after he begat Jared ... Gen 5:16
Jared *l* an hundred sixty and two ... Gen 5:18
Jared *l* after he begat Enoch ... Gen 5:19
And Enoch *l* sixty and five years, ... Gen 5:21
Methuselah *l* an hundred eighty and ... Gen 5:25
Methuselah *l* after he begat ... Gen 5:26
Lamech *l* an hundred eighty and two ... Gen 5:28
Lamech *l* after he begat Noah five ... Gen 5:30
Noah *l* after the flood three ... Gen 9:28
Shem *l* after he begat Arphaxad ... Gen 11:11
And Arphaxad *l* five and thirty ... Gen 11:12
Arphaxad *l* after he begat Salah ... Gen 11:13
Salah *l* thirty years, and begat ... Gen 11:14
Salah *l* after he begat Eber four ... Gen 11:15
And Eber *l* four and thirty years, ... Gen 11:16
Eber *l* after he begat Peleg four ... Gen 11:17
Peleg *l* thirty years, and begat ... Gen 11:18
Peleg *l* after he begat Reu two ... Gen 11:19
And Reu *l* two and thirty years, and ... Gen 11:20
Reu *l* after he begat Serug two ... Gen 11:21
Serug *l* thirty years, and begat ... Gen 11:22
Serug *l* after he begat Nahor two ... Gen 11:23
And Nahor *l* nine and twenty years, ... Gen 11:24
Nahor *l* after he begat Terah an ... Gen 11:25
Terah *l* seventy years, and begat ... Gen 11:26
Isaac his son, while he yet *l* ... Gen 25:6
of Abraham's life which he *l* ... Gen 25:7
Jacob *l* in the land of Egypt ... Gen 47:28
Joseph *l* an hundred and ten years ... Gen 50:22
went to search the land, *l* still ... Num 14:38
beheld the serpent of brass, he *l* ... Num 21:9
of the fire, as we have, and *l* ... Deut 5:26
I perceive, that if Absalom had *l* ... 2Sa 19:6
Solomon his father while he yet *l* ... 1Kin 12:6
*l* after the death of Jehoash son ... 2Kin 14:17
Solomon his father while he yet *l* ... 2Chr 10:6
the son of Joash king of Judah *l* ... 2Chr 25:25
After this *l* Job an hundred and ... Job 42:16
Though while he *l* he blessed his ... Ps 49:18
breath came into them, and they *l* ... Eze 37:10
had *l* with an husband seven years ... Lk 2:36
I have *l* in all good conscience ... Acts 23:1
of our religion I *l* a Pharisee ... Acts 26:5
some time, when ye *l* in them ... Col 3:7
Ye have *l* in pleasure on the ... Jas 5:5
*l* deliciously, so much torment and ... Rev 18:7
*l* deliciously with her, shall ... Rev 18:9
and they *l* and reigned with Christ ... Rev 20:4
But the rest of the dead *l* not ... Rev 20:5

**LIVELY**

for they are *l*, and are delivered ... Ex 1:19
But mine enemies are *l*, and they ... Ps 38:19
who received the *l* oracles to ... Acts 7:38
a *l* hope by the resurrection of ... 1Pet 1:3
as *l* stones, are built up a ... 1Pet 2:5

**LIVER**

and the caul that is above the *l* ... Ex 29:13
inwards, and the caul above the *l* ... Ex 29:22
flanks, and the caul above the *l* ... Lev 3:4
flanks, and the caul above the *l* ... Lev 3:10
flanks, and the caul above the *l* ... Lev 3:15
flanks, and the caul above the *l* ... Lev 4:9
and the caul that is above the *l* ... Lev 7:4
inwards, and the caul above the *l* ... Lev 8:16
inwards, and the caul above the *l* ... Lev 8:25
the caul above the *l* of the sin ... Lev 9:10
kidneys, and the caul above the *l* ... Lev 9:19
Till a dart strike through his *l* ... Prov 7:23
my *l* is poured upon the earth, ... Lam 2:11
with images, he looked in the *l* ... Eze 21:21

**LIVES**

blood of your *l* will I require ... Gen 9:5
to save your *l* by a great ... Gen 45:7
they said, Thou hast saved our *l* ... Gen 47:25
they made their *l* bitter with ... Ex 1:14
have, and deliver our *l* from death ... Josh 2:13
afraid of our *l* because of you ... Josh 9:24
*l* unto the death in the high ... Judg 5:18
with the *l* of thy household ... Judg 18:25
lovely and pleasant in their *l* ... 2Sa 1:23
the *l* of thy sons and of thy ... 2Sa 19:5
the *l* of thy wives ... 2Sa 19:5
and the *l* of thy concubines ... 2Sa 19:5
that went in jeopardy of their *l* ... 2Sa 23:17
that have put their *l* in jeopardy ... 1Chr 11:19
of their *l* they brought it ... 1Chr 11:19
together, and stood for their *l* ... Est 9:16
they lurk privily for their own *l* ... Prov 1:18
hands of them that seek their *l* ... Jer 19:7
and they that seek their *l* ... Jer 19:9
hand of those that seek their *l* ... Jer 46:26
Flee, save your *l*, and be like the ... Jer 48:6
our *l* because of the sword of the ... Lam 5:9
yet their *l* were prolonged for a ... Dan 7:12
is not come to destroy men's *l* ... Lk 9:56
Men that have hazarded their *l* ... Acts 15:26
lading and ship, but also of our *l* ... Acts 27:10
lay down our *l* for the brethren ... 1Jn 3:16
loved not their *l* unto the death ... Rev 12:11

**LIVEST**

as long as thou *l* upon the earth ... Deut 12:19
as thou *l*, and as thy soul liveth, ... 2Sa 11:11
*l* after the manner of Gentiles, ... Gal 2:14
that thou hast a name that thou *l* ... Rev 3:1

**LIVETH**

that *l* shall be meat for you ... Gen 9:3
God doth talk with man, and he *l* ... Deut 5:24
as the LORD *l*, if ye had saved ... Judg 8:19
a kinsman to thee, as the LORD *l* ... Ruth 3:13
said, Oh my lord, as thy soul *l* ... 1Sa 1:26
as long as he *l* he shall be lent ... 1Sa 1:28
For, as the LORD *l*, which saveth ... 1Sa 14:39
as the LORD *l*, there shall not ... 1Sa 14:45
And Abner said, As thy soul *l* ... 1Sa 17:55
and Saul sware, As the LORD *l* ... 1Sa 19:6
the LORD *l*, and as thy soul *l* ... 1Sa 20:3
as the LORD *l* ... 1Sa 20:21
son of Jesse *l* upon the ground ... 1Sa 20:31
say to him that *l* in prosperity ... 1Sa 25:6
the LORD *l*, and as thy soul *l* ... 1Sa 25:26
deed, as the LORD God of Israel *l* ... 1Sa 25:34
said furthermore, As the LORD *l* ... 1Sa 26:10
As the LORD *l*, ye are worthy to ... 1Sa 26:16
the LORD, saying, As the LORD *l* ... 1Sa 28:10
unto him, Surely, as the LORD *l* ... 1Sa 29:6
And Joab said, As God *l*, unless ... 2Sa 2:27
and said unto them, As the LORD *l* ... 2Sa 4:9
as thou livest, and as thy soul *l* ... 2Sa 11:11
he said to Nathan, As the LORD *l* ... 2Sa 12:5
And he said, As the LORD *l* ... 2Sa 14:11
answered and said, As thy soul *l* ... 2Sa 14:19
the king, and said, As the LORD *l* ... 2Sa 15:21
and as my lord the king *l* ... 2Sa 15:21
The LORD *l* ... 2Sa 22:47
sware, and said, As the LORD *l* ... 1Kin 1:29
Now therefore, as the LORD *l* ... 1Kin 2:24
one saith, This is my son that *l* ... 1Kin 3:23
Ahab, As the LORD God of Israel *l* ... 1Kin 17:1
she said, As the LORD thy God *l* ... 1Kin 17:12
and Elijah said, See, thy son *l* ... 1Kin 17:23
As the LORD thy God *l*, there is ... 1Kin 18:10
said, As the LORD of hosts *l* ... 1Kin 18:15
And Micaiah said, As the LORD *l* ... 1Kin 22:14
the LORD *l*, and as thy soul *l* ... 2Kin 2:2
the LORD *l*, and as thy soul *l* ... 2Kin 2:4
the LORD *l*, and as thy soul *l* ... 2Kin 2:6
said, As the LORD of hosts *l* ... 2Kin 3:14
the LORD *l*, and as thy soul *l* ... 2Kin 4:30
But he said, As the LORD *l* ... 2Kin 5:16
but, as the LORD *l*, I will run ... 2Kin 5:20
And Micaiah said, As the LORD *l* ... 2Chr 18:13
For I know that my redeemer *l* ... Job 19:25
As God *l*, who hath taken away my ... Job 27:2
The LORD *l* ... Ps 18:46
What man is he that *l*, and shall ... Ps 89:48
And thou shalt swear, The LORD *l* ... Jer 4:2
And though they say, The LORD *l* ... Jer 5:2
to swear by my name, The LORD *l* ... Jer 12:16
shall no more be said, The LORD *l* ... Jer 16:14
But, The LORD *l*, that brought up ... Jer 16:15
shall no more say, The LORD *l* ... Jer 23:7
But, The LORD *l*, which brought up ... Jer 23:8
Jeremiah, saying, As the LORD *l* ... Jer 38:16
of Egypt, saying, The Lord GOD *l* ... Jer 44:26
to pass, that every thing that *l* ... Eze 47:9
and honoured him that *l* for ever ... Dan 4:34
sware by him that *l* for ever that ... Dan 12:7
Beth-aven, nor swear, The LORD *l* ... Hos 4:15
and say, Thy god, O Dan, *l* ... Amos 8:14
and, The manner of Beer-sheba *l* ... Amos 8:14
thy son *l* ... Jn 4:50
and told him, saying, Thy son *l* ... Jn 4:51
Jesus said unto him, Thy son *l* ... Jn 4:53
And whosoever *l* and believeth in me ... Jn 11:26
in that he *l*, he *l* unto God ... Rom 6:10
over a man as long as he *l* ... Rom 7:1
to her husband so long as he *l* ... Rom 7:2
So then if, while her husband *l* ... Rom 7:3
For none of us *l* to himself ... Rom 14:7
the law as long as her husband *l* ... 1Cor 7:39
yet he *l* by the power of God ... 2Cor 13:4
yet not I, but Christ *l* in me ... Gal 2:20
But she that *l* in pleasure is ... 1Ti 5:6
in pleasure is dead while she *l* ... 1Ti 5:6
of whom it is witnessed that he *l* ... Heb 7:8
by him, seeing he ever *l* to make ... Heb 7:25
at all while the testator *l* ... Heb 9:17
by the word of God, which *l* ... 1Pet 1:23
I am he that *l*, and was dead ... Rev 1:18
throne, who *l* for ever and ever, ... Rev 4:9
and worship him that *l* for ever ... Rev 4:10
and worshipped him that *l* for ever ... Rev 5:14
And sware by him that *l* for ever ... Rev 10:6
of God, who *l* for ever and ever ... Rev 15:7

**LIVING**

every *l* creature that moveth, ... Gen 1:21
the *l* creature after his kind ... Gen 1:24
over every *l* thing that moveth ... Gen 1:28
and man became a *l* soul ... Gen 2:7
Adam called every *l* creature ... Gen 2:19
she was the mother of all *l* ... Gen 3:20
of every *l* thing of all flesh, ... Gen 6:19
every *l* substance that I have ... Gen 7:4
every *l* substance was destroyed ... Gen 7:23
remembered Noah, and every *l* thing ... Gen 8:1
every *l* thing that is with thee ... Gen 8:17
smite any more every thing *l* ... Gen 8:21
with every *l* creature that is ... Gen 9:10
every *l* creature that is with you ... Gen 9:12
every *l* creature of all flesh ... Gen 9:15
every *l* creature of all flesh ... Gen 9:16
of any *l* thing which is in the ... Lev 11:10
of every *l* creature that moveth ... Lev 11:46
As for the *l* bird, he shall take ... Lev 14:6
the *l* bird in the blood of the ... Lev 14:6
shall let the *l* bird loose into ... Lev 14:7
the *l* bird, and dip them in the ... Lev 14:51

running water, and with the *l* bird Lev 14:52
But he shall let go the *l* bird Lev 14:53
or by any manner of *l* thing that Lev 20:25
stood between the dead and the *l* Num 16:48
hath heard the voice of the *l* God Deut 5:26
know that the *l* God is among you Josh 3:10
left off his kindness to the *l* Ruth 2:20
defy the armies of the *l* God 1Sa 17:26
defied the armies of the *l* God 1Sa 17:36
of their death, *l* in widowhood 2Sa 20:3
but the *l* is my son, and the dead 1Kin 3:22
is thy son, and the *l* is my son 1Kin 3:22
is the dead, and my son is the *l* 1Kin 3:23
Divide the *l* child in two, and 1Kin 3:25
the *l* child was unto the king 1Kin 3:26
O my lord, give her the *l* child 1Kin 3:26
and said, Give her the *l* child 1Kin 3:27
hath sent to reproach the *l* God 2Kin 19:4
sent him to reproach the *l* God 2Kin 19:16
hand is the soul of every *l* thing Job 12:10
is it found in the land of the *l* Job 28:13
it is hid from the eyes of all *l* Job 28:21
to the house appointed for all *l* Job 30:23
with the light of the *l* Job 33:30
of the LORD in the land of the *l* Ps 27:13
thirsteth for God, for the *l* God Ps 42:2
thee out of the land of the *l* Ps 52:5
before God in the light of the *l* Ps 56:13
away as with a whirlwind, both *l* Ps 58:9
blotted out of the book of the *l* Ps 69:28
my flesh crieth out for the *l* God Ps 84:2
the LORD in the land of the *l* Ps 116:9
my portion in the land of the *l* Ps 142:5
sight shall no man *l* be justified Ps 143:2
the desire of every *l* thing Ps 145:16
than the *l* which are yet alive Eccl 4:2
I considered all the *l* which walk Eccl 4:15
that knoweth to walk before the *l* Eccl 6:8
the *l* will lay it to his heart Eccl 7:2
joined to all the *l* there is hope Eccl 9:4
for a *l* dog is better than a dead Eccl 9:4
For the *l* know that they shall Eccl 9:5
of gardens, a well of *l* waters Song 4:15
written among the *l* in Jerusalem Is 4:3
for the *l* to the dead Is 8:19
hath sent to reproach the *l* God Is 37:4
hath sent to reproach the *l* God Is 37:17
the LORD, in the land of the *l* Is 38:11
The *l*, the *l*, he shall Is 38:19
cut off out of the land of the *l* Is 53:8
me the fountain of *l* waters Jer 2:13
is the true God, he is the *l* God Jer 10:10
him off from the land of the *l* Jer 11:19
LORD, the fountain of *l* waters Jer 17:13
perverted the words of the *l* God Jer 23:36
Wherefore doth a *l* man complain Lam 3:39
the likeness of four *l* creatures Eze 1:5
the likeness of the *l* creatures Eze 1:13
up and down among the *l* creatures Eze 1:13
the *l* creatures ran and returned Eze 1:14
Now as I beheld the *l* creatures Eze 1:15
upon the earth by the *l* creatures Eze 1:15
when the *l* creatures went, the Eze 1:19
when the *l* creatures were lifted Eze 1:19
for the spirit of the *l* creature Eze 1:20
for the spirit of the *l* creature Eze 1:21
*l* creature was as the colour of Eze 1:22
the *l* creatures that touched one Eze 3:13
This is the *l* creature that I saw Eze 10:15
of the *l* creature was in them Eze 10:17
This is the *l* creature that I saw Eze 10:20
set glory in the land of the *l* Eze 26:20
terror in the land of the *l* Eze 32:23
their terror in the land of the *l* Eze 32:24
was caused in the land of the *l* Eze 32:25
their terror in the land of the *l* Eze 32:26
the mighty in the land of the *l* Eze 32:27
my terror in the land of the *l* Eze 32:32
that I have more than any *l* Dan 2:30
to the intent that the *l* may know Dan 4:17
O Daniel, servant of the *l* God Dan 6:20
for he is the *l* God, and stedfast Dan 6:26
Ye are the sons of the *l* God Hos 1:10
that *l* waters shall go out from Zec 14:8
the Christ, the Son of the *l* God Mt 16:16
the God of the dead, but of the *l* Mt 22:32
him, I adjure thee by the *l* God Mt 26:63
of the dead, but the God of the *l* Mk 12:27
all that she had, even all her *l* Mk 12:44
spent all her *l* upon physicians Lk 8:43
And he divided unto them his *l* Lk 15:12
his substance with riotous *l* Lk 15:13
hath devoured thy *l* with harlots Lk 15:30
a God of the dead, but of the *l* Lk 20:38
cast in all the *l* that she had Lk 21:4
Why seek ye the *l* among the dead Lk 24:5
he would have given thee *l* water Jn 4:10
then hast thou that *l* water Jn 4:11
I am the *l* bread which came down Jn 6:51
As the *l* Father hath sent me, and Jn 6:57
that Christ, the Son of the *l* God Jn 6:69
shall flow rivers of *l* water Jn 7:38
these vanities unto the *l* God Acts 14:15
called the children of the *l* God Rom 9:26
present your bodies a *l* sacrifice Rom 12:1
be Lord both of the dead and *l* Rom 14:9
first man Adam was made a *l* soul 1Cor 15:45
but with the Spirit of the *l* God 2Cor 3:3
ye are the temple of the *l* God 2Cor 6:16
as though *l* in the world, are ye Col 2:20
to God from idols to serve the *l* 1Th 1:9
which is the church of the *l* God 1Ti 3:15
because we trust in the *l* God 1Ti 4:10
riches, but in the *l* God, who 1Ti 6:17
*l* in malice and envy, hateful, and Titus 3:3
in departing from the *l* God Heb 3:12
dead works to serve the *l* God Heb 9:14
*l* way, which he hath consecrated Heb 10:20
fall into the hands of the *l* God Heb 10:31
and unto the city of the *l* God Heb 12:22
To whom coming, as unto a *l* stone 1Pet 2:4
having the seal of the *l* God Rev 7:2
them unto *l* fountains of waters Rev 7:17
every *l* soul died in the sea Rev 16:3

### LIZARD

and the chameleon, and the *l* Lev 11:30

### LO

and, *l*, in her mouth was an olive Gen 8:11
and, *l*, one born in my house is Gen 15:3
and, *l*, an horror of great Gen 15:12
lift up his eyes and looked, and, *l* Gen 18:2
and, *l*, Sarah thy wife shall have Gen 18:10
of the plain, and beheld, and, *l* Gen 19:28
behold a well in the field, and, *l* Gen 29:2
And he said, *L*, it is yet high day Gen 29:7
sheaves in the field, and, *l* Gen 37:7
and, *l*, it is even in my sack Gen 42:28
*l*, here is seed for you, and ye Gen 47:23
and, *l*, God hath shewed me also Gen 48:11
father made me swear, saying, *L* Gen 50:5
*l*, he goeth out unto the water Ex 7:15
*l*, he cometh forth to the water Ex 8:20
*l*, shall we sacrifice the Ex 8:26
And the LORD said unto Moses, *L* Ex 19:9
top of the mountain, saying, *L* Num 14:40
And Balaam said unto Balak, *L* Num 22:38
And he returned unto him and, *l* Num 23:6
*l*, the people shall dwell alone, Num 23:9
but, *l*, the LORD hath kept thee Num 24:11
And, *l*, he hath given occasions of Deut 22:17
and now, *l*, I am this day Josh 14:10
Behold, I dreamed a dream, and, *l* Judg 7:13
For, *l*, thou shalt conceive, and Judg 13:5
And when he came, *l*, Eli sat upon 1Sa 4:13
and, *l*, thy father hath left the 1Sa 10:2
rod that was in mine hand, and, *l* 1Sa 14:43
said Achish unto his servants, *L* 1Sa 21:14
and, *l*, the chariots and horsemen 2Sa 1:6
*l* Zadok also, and all the Levites 2Sa 15:24
that smote the people, and said, *L* 2Sa 24:17
And, *l*, while she yet talked with 1Kin 1:22
for, *l*, he hath caught hold on 1Kin 1:51
*l*, I have given thee a wise and an 1Kin 3:12
and they said one to another, *L* 2Kin 7:15
and, *l*, all the way was full of 2Kin 7:15
said to Nathan the prophet, *L* 1Chr 17:1
*l*, I give thee the oxen also for 1Chr 21:23
the acts of Asa, first and last, *l* 2Chr 16:11
Thou sayest, *L*, thou hast smitten 2Chr 25:19
and all his wars, and his ways, *l* 2Chr 27:7
For, *l*, our fathers have fallen 2Chr 29:9
and, *l*, we bring into bondage our Neh 5:5
And, *l*, I perceived that God had Neh 6:12
*L*, let that night be solitary Job 3:7
*L* this, we have searched it, so Job 5:27
*L*, he goeth by me, and I see him Job 9:11
If I speak of strength, *l* Job 9:19
*L*, mine eye hath seen all this, Job 13:1
*L*, their good is not in their Job 21:16
*L*, these are parts of his ways Job 26:14
*L*, all these things worketh God Job 33:29
*L* now, his strength is in his Job 40:16
For, *l*, the wicked bend their bow Ps 11:2
Yet he passed away, and, *l* Ps 37:36
Then said I, *L*, I come Ps 40:7
*l*, I have not refrained my lips, Ps 40:9
For, *l*, the kings were assembled, Ps 48:4
*L*, this is the man that made not Ps 52:7
*L*, then would I wander far off, Ps 55:7
For, *l*, they lie in wait for my Ps 59:3
*l*, he doth send out his voice, and Ps 68:33
For, *l*, they that are far from Ps 73:27
For, *l*, thine enemies make a Ps 83:2
*l*, thine enemies, O LORD, for, *l* Ps 92:9
*L*, children are an heritage of Ps 127:3
*L*, we heard of it at Ephratah Ps 132:6
not a word in my tongue, but, *l* Ps 139:4
And, *l*, it was all grown over with Prov 24:31
with mine own heart, saying, *L* Eccl 1:16
*L*, this only have I found, that Eccl 7:29
For, *l*, the winter is past, the Song 2:11
laid it upon my mouth, and said, *L* Is 6:7
it shall be said in that day, *L* Is 25:9
*L*, thou trustest in the staff of Is 36:6
and, *l*, these from the north and Is 49:12
*l*, they all shall wax old as a Is 50:9
For, *l*, I will call all the Jer 1:15
I beheld the earth, and, *l* Jer 4:23
I beheld the mountains, and, *l* Jer 4:24
I beheld, and, *l*, there was no man Jer 4:25
I beheld, and, *l*, the fruitful Jer 4:26
*L*, I will bring a nation upon you Jer 5:15
*L*, certainly in vain made he it Jer 8:8
*l*, they have rejected the word of Jer 8:9
For, *l*, I begin to bring evil on Jer 25:29
For, *l*, the days come, saith the Jer 30:3
for, *l*, I will save thee from Jer 30:10
and, *l*, all the princes sat there, Jer 36:12
For, *l*, I will make thee small Jer 49:15
For, *l*, I will raise and cause to Jer 50:9
and, *l*, a roll of a book was Eze 2:9
Then he said unto me, *L*, I have Eze 4:15
*l* a likeness as the appearance of Eze 8:2
and, *l*, they put the branch to Eze 8:17
and one built up a wall, and, *l* Eze 13:10
*L*, when the wall is fallen, shall Eze 13:12
by breaking the covenant, when, *l* Eze 17:18
Now, *l*, if he beget a son, that Eze 18:14
is not good among his people, *l* Eze 18:18
and, *l*, thus have they done in the Eze 23:39
and, *l*, they came Eze 23:40
for, *l*, it cometh Eze 30:9
and, *l*, it shall not be bound up Eze 30:21
And, *l*, thou art unto them as a Eze 33:32
And when this cometh to pass, (*l* Eze 33:33
and, *l*, they were very dry Eze 37:2
And when I beheld, *l*, the sinews Eze 37:8
me into the outward court, and, *l* Eze 40:17
and, *l*, before the temple were an Eze 42:8
He answered and said, *L*, I see Dan 3:25
*l* another, like a leopard, which Dan 7:6
but, *l*, Michael, one of the chief Dan 10:13
and when I am gone forth, *l* Dan 10:20
For, *l*, they are gone because of Hos 9:6
sworn by his holiness, that, *l* Amos 4:2
For, *l*, he that formeth the Amos 4:13
and, *l*, it was the latter growth Amos 7:1
For, *l*, I will command, and I will Amos 9:9
For, *l*, I raise up the Chaldeans, Hab 1:6
Ye looked for much, and, *l* Hag 1:9
for, *l*, I come, and I will dwell Zec 2:10
but, *l*, I will deliver the men Zec 11:6
For, *l*, I will raise up a Zec 11:16
and, *l*, the star, which they saw Mt 2:9
and, *l*, the heavens were opened Mt 3:16
*l* a voice from heaven, saying, Mt 3:17
if any man shall say unto you, *L* Mt 24:23
*l*, there thou hast that is thine Mt 25:25
And while he yet spake, *l*, Judas, Mt 26:47
*l*, I have told you Mt 28:7
and, *l*, I am with you alway, even Mt 28:20
Peter began to say unto him, *L* Mk 10:28
if any man shall say to you, *L* Mk 13:21
or, *l*, he is there Mk 13:21
*l*, he that betrayeth me is at Mk 14:42
For, *l*, as soon as the voice of Lk 1:44
And, *l*, the angel of the Lord came Lk 2:9
And, *l*, a spirit taketh him, and he Lk 9:39
Abraham, whom Satan hath bound, *l* Lk 13:16
answering said to his father, *L* Lk 15:29
Neither shall they say, *L* here Lk 17:21
or, *l* there Lk 17:21
Then Peter said, *L*, we have left Lk 18:28
and, *l*, nothing worthy of death is Lk 23:15
But, *l*, he speaketh boldly, and Jn 7:26
His disciples said unto him, *L* Jn 16:29
unworthy of everlasting life, *l* Acts 13:46
and, *l*, God hath given thee all Acts 27:24
Then said I, *L*, I come (in the Heb 10:7
Then said he, *L*, I come to do thy Heb 10:9
And I beheld, and, *l*, in the midst Rev 5:6
And I beheld, and *l* a black horse Rev 6:5
had opened the sixth seal, and, *l* Rev 6:12
After this I beheld, and, *l* Rev 7:9
And I looked, and, *l*, a Lamb stood Rev 14:1

### LOADEN

your carriages were heavy *l* Is 46:1

### LOADETH

who daily *l* us with benefits, Ps 68:19

### LOAF

one *l* of bread, and one cake of Ex 29:23
woman, to every one a *l* of bread 1Chr 16:3
ship with them more than one *l* Mk 8:14

### LO-AMMI

*(lo-am'-mi) Symbolic name meaning 'Not My People.'*
Then said God, Call his name *L* Hos 1:9

### LOAN

the *l* which is lent to the LORD 1Sa 2:20

### LOATHE

I *l* it Job 7:16

### LOATHETH

our soul *l* this light bread Num 21:5
The full soul *l* an honeycomb Prov 27:7

### LOATHSOME

nostrils, and it be *l* unto you Num 11:20
my skin is broken, and become *l* Job 7:5
loins are filled with a *l* disease Ps 38:7
but a wicked man is *l*, and cometh Prov 13:5

### LOAVES

two wave *l* of two tenth deals Lev 23:17
*l* of bread unto the people that Judg 8:5
another carrying three *l* of bread 1Sa 10:3
thee, and give thee two *l* of bread 1Sa 10:4
this parched corn, and these ten *l* 1Sa 17:17
give me five *l* of bread in mine 1Sa 21:3
made haste, and took two hundred *l* 1Sa 25:18
upon them two hundred *l* of bread 2Sa 16:1
And take with thee ten *l*, and 1Kin 14:3
twenty *l* of barley, and full ears 2Kin 4:42
unto him, We have here but five *l* Mt 14:17
on the grass, and took the five *l* Mt 14:19
gave the *l* to his disciples, and Mt 14:19
unto them, How many *l* have ye Mt 15:34
And he took the seven *l* and the Mt 15:36

the five l of the five thousand ... Mt 16:9
Neither the seven l of the four ... Mt 16:10
unto them, How many l have ye ... Mk 6:38
And when he had taken the five l ... Mk 6:41
and blessed, and brake the l ... Mk 6:41
they that did eat of the l were ... Mk 6:44
not the miracle of the l ... Mk 6:52
he asked them, How many l have ye ... Mk 8:5
and he took the seven l, and gave ... Mk 8:6
the five l among five thousand ... Mk 8:19
said, We have no more but five l ... Lk 9:13
Then he took the five l and the ... Lk 9:16
unto him, Friend, lend me three l ... Lk 11:5
here, which hath five barley l ... Jn 6:9
And Jesus took the l ... Jn 6:11
fragments of the five barley l ... Jn 6:13
but because ye did eat of the l ... Jn 6:26

**LOCK**
myrrh, upon the handles of the l ... Song 5:5
and took me by a l of mine head ... Eze 8:3

**LOCKED**
the parlour upon him, and l them ... Judg 3:23
the doors of the parlour were l ... Judg 3:24

**LOCKS**
shall let the l of the hair of ... Num 6:5
seven l of my head with the web ... Judg 16:13
shave off the seven l of his head ... Judg 16:19
the l thereof, and the bars ... Neh 3:3
the l thereof, and the bars ... Neh 3:6
the l thereof, and the bars ... Neh 3:13
the l thereof, and the bars ... Neh 3:14
the l thereof, and the bars ... Neh 3:15
hast doves' eyes within thy l ... Song 4:1
of a pomegranate within thy l ... Song 4:3
my l with the drops of the night ... Song 5:2
his l are bushy, and black as a ... Song 5:11
are thy temples within thy l ... Song 6:7
uncover thy l, make bare the leg, ... Is 47:2
nor suffer their l to grow long ... Eze 44:20

**LOCUST**
there remained not one l in all ... Ex 10:19
the l after his kind, and the bald ... Lev 11:22
the bald l after his kind, and the ... Lev 11:22
for the l shall consume it ... Deut 28:38
of thy land shall the l consume ... Deut 28:42
pestilence, blasting, mildew, l ... 1Kin 8:37
and their labour unto the l ... Ps 78:46
I am tossed up and down as the l ... Ps 109:23
hath left hath the l eaten ... Joel 1:4
that which the l hath left hath ... Joel 1:4
the years that the l hath eaten ... Joel 2:25

**LOCUSTS**
will I bring the l into thy coast ... Ex 10:4
over the land of Egypt for the l ... Ex 10:12
the east wind brought the l ... Ex 10:13
the l went up over all the land ... Ex 10:14
them there were no such l as they ... Ex 10:14
west wind, which took away the l ... Ex 10:19
there be blasting, or mildew, l ... 2Chr 6:28
command the l to devour the land ... 2Chr 7:13
the l came, and caterpillers, and ... Ps 105:34
The l have no king, yet go they ... Prov 30:27
fro of l shall he run upon them ... Is 33:4
make thyself many as the l ... Nah 3:15
Thy crowned are as the l, and thy ... Nah 3:17
and his meat was l and wild honey ... Mt 3:4
and he did eat l and wild honey ... Mk 1:6
out of the smoke l upon the earth ... Rev 9:3
the shapes of the l were like ... Rev 9:7

**LOD** *A city in Benjamin.*
and Shamed, who built Ono, and L ... 1Chr 8:12
The children of L, Hadid, and Ono, ... Ezr 2:33
The children of L, Hadid, and Ono, ... Neh 7:37
L, and Ono, the valley of ... Neh 11:35

**LO-DEBAR** (*lo-de'-bar*) *A city in Manasseh.*
Machir, the son of Ammiel, in L ... 2Sa 9:4
Machir, the son of Ammiel, from L ... 2Sa 9:5
and Machir the son of Ammiel of L ... 2Sa 17:27

**LODGE**
thy father's house for us to l in ... Gen 24:23
provender enough, and room to l in ... Gen 24:25
L here this night, and I will ... Num 22:8
where ye shall l this night ... Josh 4:3
l here, that thine heart may be ... Judg 19:9
city of the Jebusites, and l in it ... Judg 19:11
of these places to l all night ... Judg 19:13
to go in and to l in Gibeah ... Judg 19:15
only l not in the street ... Judg 19:20
Benjamin, I and my concubine, to l ... Judg 20:4
and where thou lodgest, I will l ... Ruth 1:16
will not l with the people ... 2Sa 17:8
L not this night in the plains of ... 2Sa 17:16
his servant l within Jerusalem ... Neh 4:22
them, Why l ye about the wall ... Neh 13:21
the naked to l without clothing ... Job 24:7
stranger did not l in the street ... Job 31:32
let us l in the villages ... Song 7:11
as a l in a garden of cucumbers, ... Is 1:8
the forest in Arabia shall ye l ... Is 21:13
l in the monuments, which eat ... Is 65:4
thy vain thoughts l within thee ... Jer 4:14
the bittern shall l in the upper ... Zeph 2:14
l in the branches thereof ... Mt 13:32
air may l under the shadow of it ... Mk 4:32
and country round about, and l ... Lk 9:12
disciple, with whom we should l ... Acts 21:16

**LODGED**
he l there that same night ... Gen 32:13
himself l that night in the ... Gen 32:21
house, named Rahab, and l there ... Josh 2:1
l there before they passed over ... Josh 3:1
them unto the place where they l ... Josh 4:8
into the camp, and l in the camp ... Josh 6:11
but Joshua l that night among the ... Josh 8:9
the house of Micah, they l there ... Judg 18:2
they did eat and drink, and l there ... Judg 19:4
therefore he l there again ... Judg 19:7
thither unto a cave, and l there ... 1Kin 19:9
they l round about the house of ... 1Chr 9:27
sellers of all kind of ware l ... Neh 13:20
righteousness l in it ... Is 1:21
and he l there ... Mt 21:17
the fowls of the air l in the ... Lk 13:19
was surnamed Peter, were l there ... Acts 10:18
Then called he them in, and l them ... Acts 10:23
he is l in the house of one Simon ... Acts 10:32
l us three days courteously ... Acts 28:7
children, if she have l strangers ... 1Ti 5:10

**LODGEST**
and where thou l, I will lodge ... Ruth 1:16

**LODGETH**
He l with one Simon a tanner, ... Acts 10:6

**LODGING**
you, and leave them in the l place ... Josh 4:3
took them into his house to l ... Judg 19:15
have taken up their l at Geba ... Is 10:29
a l place of wayfaring men ... Jer 9:2
there came many to him into his l ... Acts 28:23
But withal prepare me also a l ... Philem 22

**LODGINGS**
enter into the l of his borders ... 2Kin 19:23

**LOFT**
bosom, and carried him up into a l ... 1Kin 17:19
and fell down from the third l ... Acts 20:9

**LOFTILY**
they speak l ... Ps 73:8

**LOFTINESS**
the l of man shall be bowed down, ... Is 2:17
(he is exceeding proud) his l ... Jer 48:29

**LOFTY**
is not haughty, nor mine eyes l ... Ps 131:1
O how l are their eyes ... Prov 30:13
The l looks of man shall be ... Is 2:11
upon every one that is proud and l ... Is 2:12
the eyes of the l shall be ... Is 5:15
the l city, he layeth it low ... Is 26:5
Upon a l and high mountain hast ... Is 57:7
l One that inhabiteth eternity, ... Is 57:15

**LOG**
mingled with oil, and one l of oil ... Lev 14:10
the l of oil, and wave them for a ... Lev 14:12
shall take some of the l of oil ... Lev 14:15
a meat offering, and a l of oil ... Lev 14:21
the l of oil, and the priest shall ... Lev 14:24

**LOINS**
and kings shall come out of thy l ... Gen 35:11
and put sackcloth upon his l ... Gen 37:34
Egypt, which came out of his l ... Gen 46:26
the l of Jacob were seventy souls ... Ex 1:5
with your l girded, your shoes on ... Ex 12:11
from the l even unto the thighs ... Ex 28:42
smite through the l of them that ... Deut 33:11
upon his l in the sheath thereof ... 2Sa 20:8
his girdle that was about his l ... 1Kin 2:5
shall come forth out of thy l ... 1Kin 8:19
be thicker than my father's l ... 1Kin 12:10
and he girded up his l, and ran ... 1Kin 18:46
pray thee, put sackcloth on our l ... 1Kin 20:31
they girded sackcloth on their l ... 1Kin 20:32
a girdle of leather about his l ... 2Kin 1:8
he said to Gehazi, Gird up thy l ... 2Kin 4:29
and said unto him, Gird up thy l ... 2Kin 9:1
shall come forth out of thy l ... 2Chr 6:9
be thicker than my father's l ... 2Chr 10:10
and girdeth their l with a girdle ... Job 12:18
If his l have not blessed me, and ... Job 31:20
Gird up now thy l like a man ... Job 38:3
Gird up thy l now like a man ... Job 40:7
Lo now, his strength is in his l ... Job 40:16
For my l are filled with a ... Ps 38:7
thou laidst affliction upon our l ... Ps 66:11
make their l continually to shake ... Ps 69:23
She girdeth her l with strength ... Prov 31:17
the girdle of their l be loosed ... Is 5:27
shall be the girdle of his l ... Is 11:5
the sackcloth from off thy l ... Is 20:2
are my l filled with pain ... Is 21:3
and gird sackcloth upon your l ... Is 32:11
and I will loose the l of kings ... Is 45:1
Thou therefore gird up thy l ... Jer 1:17
girdle, and put it upon thy l ... Jer 13:1
of the LORD, and put it on my l ... Jer 13:2
hast got, which is upon thy l ... Jer 13:4
girdle cleaveth to the l of a man ... Jer 13:11
every man with his hands on his l ... Jer 30:6
cuttings, and upon the l sackcloth ... Jer 48:37
appearance of his l even upward ... Eze 1:27
appearance of his l even downward ... Eze 1:27
appearance of his l even downward ... Eze 8:2
from his l even upward, as the ... Eze 8:2
man, with the breaking of thy l ... Eze 21:6
Girded with girdles upon their l ... Eze 23:15
all their l to be at a stand ... Eze 29:7
have linen breeches upon their l ... Eze 44:18
the waters were to the l ... Eze 47:4
the joints of his l were loosed ... Dan 5:6
whose l were girded with fine ... Dan 10:5
bring up sackcloth upon all l ... Amos 8:10
watch the way, make thy l strong ... Nah 2:1
and much pain is in all l ... Nah 2:10
and a leathern girdle about his l ... Mt 3:4
a girdle of a skin about his l ... Mk 1:6
Let your l be girded about, and ... Lk 12:35
him, that of the fruit of his l ... Acts 2:30
having your l girt about with ... Eph 6:14
they come out of the l of Abraham ... Heb 7:5
he was yet in the l of his father ... Heb 7:10
gird up the l of your mind ... 1Pet 1:13

**LOIS** (*lo'-is*) *Grandmother of Timothy.*
dwelt first in thy grandmother L ... 2Ti 1:5

**LONG**
when he had been there a l time ... Gen 26:8
me all my life l unto this day ... Gen 48:15
How l wilt thou refuse to humble ... Ex 10:3
How l shall this man be a snare ... Ex 10:7
How l refuse ye to keep my ... Ex 16:28
when the trumpet soundeth l ... Ex 19:13
voice of the trumpet sounded l ... Ex 19:19
that thy days may be l upon the ... Ex 20:12
of shittim wood, five cubits l ... Ex 27:1
an hundred cubits l for one side ... Ex 27:9
hangings of an hundred cubits l ... Ex 27:11
as l as she is put apart for her ... Lev 18:19
as l as it lieth desolate, and ye ... Lev 26:34
As l as it lieth desolate it ... Lev 26:35
as l as the cloud abode upon the ... Num 9:18
when the cloud tarried l upon the ... Num 9:19
How l will this people provoke me ... Num 14:11
how l will it be ere they believe ... Num 14:11
How l shall I bear with this evil ... Num 14:27
we have dwelt in Egypt a l time ... Num 20:15
Ye have dwelt l enough in this ... Deut 1:6
compassed this mountain l enough ... Deut 2:3
shall have remained l in the land ... Deut 4:25
l as thou livest upon the earth ... Deut 12:19
And if the way be too l for thee ... Deut 14:24
him, because the way is l ... Deut 19:6
shalt besiege a city a l time ... Deut 20:19
longing for them all the day l ... Deut 28:32
of l continuance, and sore ... Deut 28:59
sicknesses, and of l continuance ... Deut 28:59
as l as ye live in the land ... Deut 31:13
shall cover him all the day l ... Deut 33:12
that when they make a l blast ... Josh 6:5
by reason of the very l journey ... Josh 9:13
Joshua made war a l time with all ... Josh 11:18
How l are ye slack to go to ... Josh 18:3
it came to pass a l time after ... Josh 23:1
in the wilderness a l season ... Josh 24:7
Why is his chariot so l in coming ... Judg 5:28
How l wilt thou be drunken ... 1Sa 1:14
as l as he liveth he shall be ... 1Sa 1:28
that the time was l ... 1Sa 7:2
How l wilt thou mourn for Saul, ... 1Sa 16:1
For as l as the son of Jesse ... 1Sa 20:31
as l as we were conversant with ... 1Sa 25:15
thou found in thy servant so l as ... 1Sa 29:8
how l shall it be then, ere thou ... 2Sa 2:26
Now there was l war between the ... 2Sa 3:1
had a l time mourned for the dead ... 2Sa 14:2
How l have I to live, that I ... 2Sa 19:34
hast not asked for thyself l life ... 1Kin 3:11
before it, was forty cubits l ... 1Kin 6:17
How l halt ye between two ... 1Kin 18:21
so l as the whoredoms of thy ... 2Kin 9:22
Hast thou not heard l ago how I ... 2Kin 19:25
neither yet hast asked l life ... 2Chr 1:11
cherubims were twenty cubits l ... 2Chr 3:11
brasen scaffold, of five cubits l ... 2Chr 6:13
so l as they live in the land ... 2Chr 6:31
Now for a l season Israel hath ... 2Chr 15:3
as l as he sought the LORD, God ... 2Chr 26:5
a l time in such sort as it was ... 2Chr 30:5
for as l as she lay desolate she ... 2Chr 36:21
For how l shall thy journey be ... Neh 2:6
so l as I see Mordecai the Jew ... Est 5:13
Which l for death, but it cometh ... Job 3:21
grant me the thing that I l for ... Job 6:8
How l wilt thou not depart from ... Job 7:19
How l wilt thou speak these ... Job 8:2
how l shall the words of thy ... Job 8:2
How l will it be ere ye make an ... Job 18:2
How l will ye vex my soul, and ... Job 19:2
not reproach me so l as I live ... Job 27:6
how l will ye turn my glory into ... Ps 4:2
how l will ye love vanity, and ... Ps 4:2
but thou, O LORD, how l ... Ps 6:3
How l wilt thou forget me, O LORD ... Ps 13:1
how l wilt thou hide thy face ... Ps 13:1
How l shall I take counsel in my ... Ps 13:2
how l shall mine enemy be exalted ... Ps 13:2
through my roaring all the day l ... Ps 32:3
LORD, how l wilt thou look on ... Ps 35:17
and of thy praise all the day l ... Ps 35:28
I go mourning all the day l ... Ps 38:6
and imagine deceits all the day l ... Ps 38:12
In God we boast all the day l ... Ps 44:8
sake are we killed all the day l ... Ps 44:22
How l will ye imagine mischief ... Ps 62:3
thy righteousness all the day l ... Ps 71:24

shall fear thee as *l* as the sun ..... Ps 72:5
peace so *l* as the moon endureth ..... Ps 72:7
be continued as *l* as the sun ..... Ps 72:17
For all the day *l* have I been ..... Ps 73:14
among us any that knoweth how *l* ..... Ps 74:9
how *l* shall the adversary ..... Ps 74:10
How *l*, LORD ..... Ps 79:5
how *l* wilt thou be angry against ..... Ps 80:4
How *l* will ye judge unjustly, and ..... Ps 82:2
How *l*, LORD¿ ..... Ps 89:46
Return, O LORD, how *l* ..... Ps 90:13
With *l* life will I satisfy him, ..... Ps 91:16
how *l* shall the wicked ..... Ps 94:3
how *l* shall the wicked triumph ..... Ps 94:3
How *l* shall they utter and speak ..... Ps 94:4
Forty years *l* was I grieved with ..... Ps 95:10
sing unto the LORD as *l* as I live ..... Ps 104:33
I call upon him as *l* as I live ..... Ps 116:2
My soul hath *l* dwelt with him ..... Ps 120:6
they made *l* their furrows ..... Ps 129:3
as those that have been *l* dead ..... Ps 143:3
How *l*, ye simple ones, will ye ..... Prov 1:22
*l* life, and peace, shall they add ..... Prov 3:2
How *l* wilt thou sleep, O sluggard ..... Prov 6:9
at home, he is gone a *l* journey ..... Prov 7:19
coveteth greedily all the day *l* ..... Prov 21:26
fear of the LORD all the day *l* ..... Prov 23:17
They that tarry *l* at the wine ..... Prov 23:30
By *l* forbearing is a prince ..... Prov 25:15
because man goeth to his *l* home ..... Eccl 12:5
Then said I, Lord, how *l* ..... Is 6:11
unto him that fashioned it *l* ago ..... Is 22:11
Hast thou not heard *l* ago ..... Is 37:26
I have *l* time holden my peace ..... Is 42:14
mine elect shall *l* enjoy the work ..... Is 65:22
How *l* shall thy vain thoughts ..... Jer 4:14
How *l* shall I see the standard, ..... Jer 4:21
How *l* shall the land mourn, and ..... Jer 12:4
How *l* shall this be in the heart ..... Jer 23:26
saying, This captivity is *l* ..... Jer 29:28
How *l* wilt thou go about, O thou ..... Jer 31:22
how *l* wilt thou cut thyself ..... Jer 47:5
how *l* will it be ere thou be ..... Jer 47:6
fruit, and children of a span *l* ..... Lam 2:20
for ever, and forsake us so *l* time ..... Lam 5:20
his branches became *l* because of ..... Eze 31:5
reed of six cubits *l* by the cubit ..... Eze 40:5
little chamber was one reed *l* ..... Eze 40:7
it was fifty cubits *l*, and five and ..... Eze 40:29
were five and twenty cubits *l* ..... Eze 40:30
it was fifty cubits *l*, and five and ..... Eze 40:33
offering, of a cubit and an half *l* ..... Eze 40:42
the court, an hundred cubits *l* ..... Eze 40:47
the house, an hundred cubits *l* ..... Eze 41:13
thereof, an hundred cubits *l* ..... Eze 41:13
as *l* as they, and as broad as they ..... Eze 42:11
round about, five hundred reeds *l* ..... Eze 42:20
altar shall be twelve cubits *l* ..... Eze 43:16
settle shall be fourteen cubits *l* ..... Eze 43:17
nor suffer their locks to grow *l* ..... Eze 44:20
and five and twenty thousand *l* ..... Eze 45:6
courts joined of forty cubits *l* ..... Eze 46:22
How *l* shall be the vision ..... Dan 8:13
but the time appointed was *l* ..... Dan 10:1
How *l* shall it be to the end of ..... Dan 12:6
how *l* will it be ere they attain ..... Hos 8:5
for he should not stay *l* in the ..... Hos 13:13
how *l* shall I cry, and thou wilt ..... Hab 1:2
which is not his! how *l*? ..... Hab 2:6
how *l* wilt thou not have mercy on ..... Zec 1:12
as *l* as the bridegroom is with ..... Mt 9:15
have repented *l* ago in sackcloth ..... Mt 11:21
how *l* shall I be with you ..... Mt 17:17
how *l* shall I suffer you ..... Mt 17:17
and for a pretence make *l* prayer ..... Mt 23:14
After a *l* time the lord of those ..... Mt 25:19
as *l* as they have the bridegroom ..... Mk 2:19
how *l* shall I be with you ..... Mk 9:19
how *l* shall I suffer you ..... Mk 9:19
How *l* is it ago since this came ..... Mk 9:21
which love to go in *l* clothing ..... Mk 12:38
and for a pretence make *l* prayers ..... Mk 12:40
clothed in a *l* white garment ..... Mk 16:5
he tarried so *l* in the temple ..... Lk 1:21
man, which had devils *l* time ..... Lk 8:27
how *l* shall I be with you, and ..... Lk 9:41
him, though he bear *l* with them ..... Lk 18:7
into a far country for a *l* time ..... Lk 20:9
which desire to walk in *l* robes ..... Lk 20:46
and for a shew make *l* prayers ..... Lk 20:47
desirous to see him of a *l* season ..... Lk 23:8
been now a *l* time in that case ..... Jn 5:6
As *l* as I am in the world, I am ..... Jn 9:5
How *l* dost thou make us to doubt ..... Jn 10:24
Have I been so *l* time with you ..... Jn 14:9
because that of *l* time he had ..... Acts 8:11
*L* time therefore abode they ..... Acts 14:3
there they abode *l* time with the ..... Acts 14:28
and as Paul was *l* preaching ..... Acts 20:9
and eaten, and talked a *l* while ..... Acts 20:11
But not *l* after there arose ..... Acts 27:14
But after *l* abstinence Paul stood ..... Acts 27:21
For I *l* to see you, that I may ..... Rom 1:11
over a man as *l* as he liveth ..... Rom 7:1
to her husband so *l* as he liveth ..... Rom 7:2
sake we are killed all the day *l* ..... Rom 8:36
All day *l* I have stretched forth ..... Rom 10:21
law as *l* as her husband liveth ..... 1Cor 7:39
you, that, if a man have *l* hair ..... 1Cor 11:14
But if a woman have *l* hair ..... 1Cor 11:15

Charity suffereth *l*, and is kind ..... 1Cor 13:4
which *l* after you for the ..... 2Cor 9:14
as *l* as he is a child, differeth ..... Gal 4:1
thou mayest live *l* on the earth ..... Eph 6:3
how greatly I *l* after you all in ..... Phil 1:8
But if I tarry *l*, that thou ..... 1Ti 3:15
David, To day, after so *l* a time ..... Heb 4:7
hath *l* patience for it, until he ..... Jas 5:7
as *l* as ye do well, and are not ..... 1Pet 3:6
as *l* as I am in this tabernacle, ..... 2Pet 1:13
now of a *l* time lingereth not ..... 2Pet 2:3
with a loud voice, saying, How *l* ..... Rev 6:10

### LONGED

the soul of king David *l* to go ..... 2Sa 13:39
And David *l*, and said, Oh that one ..... 2Sa 23:15
And David *l*, and said, Oh that one ... 1Chr 11:17
I have *l* after thy precepts ..... Ps 119:40
for I *l* for thy commandments ..... Ps 119:131
I have *l* for thy salvation, O ..... Ps 119:174
For he *l* after you all, and was ..... Phil 2:26
*l* for, my joy and crown, so stand ..... Phil 4:1

### LONGEDST

because thou sore *l* after thy ..... Gen 31:30

### LONGER

And when she could not *l* hide him ..... Ex 2:3
let you go, and ye shall stay no *l* ..... Ex 9:28
any *l* stand before their enemies ..... Judg 2:14
but he tarried *l* than the set ..... 2Sa 20:5
should I wait for the LORD any *l* ..... 2Kin 6:33
thereof is *l* than the earth ..... Job 11:9
So that the LORD could no *l* bear ..... Jer 44:22
for thou mayest be no *l* steward ..... Lk 16:2
him to tarry *l* time with them ..... Acts 18:20
that he ought not to live any *l* ..... Acts 25:24
dead to sin, live any *l* therein ..... Rom 6:2
we are no *l* under a schoolmaster ..... Gal 3:25
when we could no *l* forbear ..... 1Th 3:1
cause, when I could no *l* forbear ..... 1Th 3:5
Drink no *l* water, but use a ..... 1Ti 5:23
That he no *l* should live the rest ..... 1Pet 4:2
that there should be time no *l* ..... Rev 10:6

### LONGETH

son Shechem *l* for your daughter ..... Gen 34:8
because thy soul *l* to eat flesh ..... Deut 12:20
my flesh *l* for thee in a dry and ..... Ps 63:1
My soul *l*, yea, even fainteth for ..... Ps 84:2

### LONGING

fail with *l* for them all the day ..... Deut 28:32
For he satisfieth the *l* soul ..... Ps 107:9
My soul breaketh for the *l* that ..... Ps 119:20

### LONGSUFFERING

LORD God, merciful and gracious, *l* ..... Ex 34:6
The LORD is *l*, and of great mercy, ..... Num 14:18
of compassion, and gracious, *l* ..... Ps 86:15
take me not away in thy *l* ..... Jer 15:15
his goodness and forbearance and *l* ..... Rom 2:4
endured with much *l* the vessels ..... Rom 9:22
By pureness, by knowledge, by *l* ..... 2Cor 6:6
the Spirit is love, joy, peace, *l* ..... Gal 5:22
all lowliness and meekness, with *l* ..... Eph 4:2
all patience and *l* with joyfulness ..... Col 1:11
humbleness of mind, meekness, *l* ..... Col 3:12
Christ might shew forth all *l* ..... 1Ti 1:16
manner of life, purpose, faith, *l* ..... 2Ti 3:10
rebuke, exhort with all *l* ..... 2Ti 4:2
when once the *l* of God waited in ..... 1Pet 3:20
but is *l* to us-ward, not willing ..... 2Pet 3:9
account that the *l* of our Lord is ..... 2Pet 3:15

### LONGWINGED

A great eagle with great wings, *l* ..... Eze 17:3

### LOOK

I will *l* upon it, that I may ..... Gen 9:16
thou art a fair woman to *l* upon ..... Gen 12:11
*l* from the place where thou art ..... Gen 13:14
*L* now toward heaven, and tell the ..... Gen 15:5
*l* not behind thee, neither stay ..... Gen 19:17
damsel was very fair to *l* upon ..... Gen 24:16
because she was fair to *l* upon ..... Gen 26:7
Wherefore *l* ye so sadly to day ..... Gen 40:7
let Pharaoh *l* out a man discreet ..... Gen 41:33
Why do ye *l* one upon another ..... Gen 42:1
for he was afraid to *l* upon God ..... Ex 3:6
unto them, The LORD *l* upon you ..... Ex 5:21
*l* to it ..... Ex 10:10
faces shall *l* one to another ..... Ex 25:20
*l* that thou make them after their ..... Ex 25:40
Moses did *l* upon all the work, and ..... Ex 39:43
the priest shall *l* on the plague ..... Lev 13:3
and the priest shall *l* on him ..... Lev 13:3
the priest shall *l* on him the ..... Lev 13:5
the priest shall *l* on him again ..... Lev 13:6
But if the priest *l* on it ..... Lev 13:21
Then the priest shall *l* upon it ..... Lev 13:25
But if the priest *l* on it ..... Lev 13:26
the priest shall *l* upon him the ..... Lev 13:27
if the priest *l* on the plague of ..... Lev 13:31
the priest shall *l* on the plague ..... Lev 13:32
the priest shall *l* on the scall ..... Lev 13:34
Then the priest shall *l* on him ..... Lev 13:36
Then the priest shall *l* ..... Lev 13:39
Then the priest shall *l* upon it ..... Lev 13:43
priest shall *l* upon the plague ..... Lev 13:50
he shall *l* on the plague on the ..... Lev 13:51
And if the priest shall *l*, and, ..... Lev 13:53
the priest shall *l* on the plague ..... Lev 13:55
And if the priest *l*, and, behold, ..... Lev 13:56

and the priest shall *l*, and, behold ..... Lev 14:3
he shall *l* on the plague, and, ..... Lev 14:37
again the seventh day, and shall *l* ..... Lev 14:39
Then the priest shall come and *l* ..... Lev 14:44
*l* upon it, and, behold, the plague ..... Lev 14:48
a fringe, that ye may *l* upon it ..... Num 15:39
*l* not unto the stubbornness of ..... Deut 9:27
*L* down from thy holy habitation, ..... Deut 26:15
people, and thine eyes shall *l* ..... Deut 28:32
them, *L* on me, and do likewise ..... Judg 7:17
if thou wilt indeed *l* on the ..... 1Sa 1:11
*L* not on his countenance, or on ..... 1Sa 16:7
countenance, and goodly to *l* to ..... 1Sa 16:12
*l* how thy brethren fare, and take ..... 1Sa 17:18
that thou shouldest *l* upon such a ..... 2Sa 9:8
was very beautiful to *l* upon ..... 2Sa 11:2
LORD will *l* on mine affliction ..... 2Sa 16:12
Go up now, *l* toward the sea ..... 1Kin 18:43
Judah, I would not *l* toward thee ..... 2Kin 3:14
*l*, when the messenger cometh, ..... 2Kin 6:32
*l* out there Jehu the son of ..... 2Kin 9:2
*L* even out the best and meetest of ..... 2Kin 10:3
*l* that there be here with you ..... 2Kin 10:23
let us *l* one another in the face ..... 2Kin 14:8
the God of our fathers *l* thereon ..... 1Chr 12:17
died, he said, The LORD *l* upon it ..... 2Chr 24:22
for she was fair to *l* on ..... Est 1:11
let it *l* for light, but have none ..... Job 3:9
therefore be content, *l* upon me ..... Job 6:28
shall no man *l* for his goods ..... Job 20:21
*L* unto the heavens, and see ..... Job 35:5
*L* on every one that is proud, and ..... Job 40:12
my prayer unto thee, and will *l* up ..... Ps 5:3
they *l* and stare upon me ..... Ps 22:17
*L* upon mine affliction and my pain ..... Ps 25:18
LORD, how long wilt thou *l* on ..... Ps 35:17
me, so that I am not able to *l* up ..... Ps 40:12
*l* down from heaven, and behold, and ..... Ps 80:14
*l* upon the face of thine anointed ..... Ps 84:9
shall *l* down from heaven ..... Ps 85:11
him that hath an high *l* and a ..... Ps 101:5
*L* thou upon me, and be merciful ..... Ps 119:132
as the eyes of servants *l* unto ..... Ps 123:2
Let thine eyes *l* right on ..... Prov 4:25
let thine eyelids *l* straight ..... Prov 4:25
A proud *l*, a lying tongue, and ..... Prov 6:17
An high *l*, and a proud heart, and ..... Prov 21:4
*L* not thou upon the wine when it ..... Prov 23:31
flocks, and *l* well to thy herds ..... Prov 27:23
those that *l* out of the windows ..... Eccl 12:3
*L* not upon me, because I am black ..... Song 1:6
*l* from the top of Amana, from the ..... Song 4:8
return, that we may *l* upon thee ..... Song 6:13
if one *l* unto the land, behold ..... Is 5:30
of Jacob, and I will *l* for him ..... Is 8:17
king and their God, and *l* upward ..... Is 8:21
they shall *l* unto the earth ..... Is 8:22
thee shall narrowly *l* upon thee ..... Is 14:16
day shall a man *l* to his Maker ..... Is 17:7
he shall not *l* to the altars, the ..... Is 17:8
Therefore said I, *L* away from me ..... Is 22:4
thou didst *l* in that day to the ..... Is 22:8
but they *l* not unto the Holy One ..... Is 31:1
*L* upon Zion, the city of our ..... Is 33:20
and *l*, ye blind, that ye may see ..... Is 42:18
*L* unto me, and be ye saved, all ..... Is 45:22
*l* unto the rock whence ye are ..... Is 51:1
*L* unto Abraham your father, and ..... Is 51:2
and *l* upon the earth beneath ..... Is 51:6
they all *l* to their own way, ..... Is 56:11
we *l* for judgment, but there is ..... Is 59:11
*L* down from heaven, and behold ..... Is 63:15
but to this man will I *l*, even to ..... Is 66:2
*l* upon the carcases of the men ..... Is 66:24
while ye *l* for light, he turn it ..... Jer 13:16
*l* well to him, and do him no harm ..... Jer 39:12
and I will *l* well unto thee ..... Jer 40:4
and are fled apace, and *l* not back ..... Jer 46:5
the fathers shall not *l* back to ..... Jer 47:3
Till the LORD *l* down, and behold ..... Lam 3:50
all of them princes to *l* to ..... Eze 23:15
when they shall *l* after them ..... Eze 29:16
stairs shall *l* toward the east ..... Eze 43:17
whose *l* was more stout than his ..... Dan 7:20
who *l* to other gods, and love ..... Hos 3:1
yet I will *l* again toward thy ..... Jonah 2:4
and let our eye *l* upon Zion ..... Mic 4:11
Therefore I will *l* unto the LORD ..... Mic 7:7
but none shall *l* back ..... Nah 2:8
that all they that *l* upon thee ..... Nah 3:7
evil, and canst not *l* on iniquity ..... Hab 1:13
that thou mayest *l* on their ..... Hab 2:15
they shall *l* upon me whom they ..... Zec 12:10
come, or do we *l* for another ..... Mt 11:3
upon his eyes, and made him *l* up ..... Mk 8:25
or *l* we for another ..... Lk 7:19
or *l* we for another ..... Lk 7:20
I beseech thee, *l* upon my son ..... Lk 9:38
begin to come to pass, then *l* up ..... Lk 21:28
up your eyes, and *l* on the fields ..... Jn 4:35
Search, and *l* ..... Jn 7:52
They shall *l* on him whom they ..... Jn 19:37
upon him with John, said, *L* on us ..... Acts 3:4
or why *l* ye so earnestly on us, ..... Acts 3:12
*l* ye out among you seven men of ..... Acts 6:3
names, and of your law, *l* ye to it ..... Acts 18:15
for I *l* for him with the brethren ..... 1Cor 16:11
*l* to the end of that which is ..... 2Cor 3:13
While we *l* not at the things ..... 2Cor 4:18
Do ye *l* on things after the ..... 2Cor 10:7

*L* not every man on his own things ........ Phil 2:4
whence also we *l* for the Saviour ........ Phil 3:20
unto them that *l* for him shall he ........ Heb 9:28
the angels desire to *l* into ........ 1Pet 1:12
*l* for new heavens and a new earth, ..... 2Pet 3:13
seeing that ye *l* for such things, ........ 2Pet 3:14
*L* to yourselves, that we lose not ........ 2Jn 8
sat was to *l* upon like a jasper ........ Rev 4:3
the book, neither to *l* thereon ........ Rev 5:3
the book, neither to *l* thereon ........ Rev 5:4

**LOOKED**

God *l* upon the earth, and, behold, ........ Gen 6:12
the covering of the ark, and *l* ........ Gen 8:13
Have I also here *l* after him that ........ Gen 16:13
And he lift up his eyes and *l* ........ Gen 18:2
up from thence, and *l* toward Sodom. Gen 18:16
But his wife *l* back from behind ........ Gen 19:26
*l* toward Sodom and Gomorrah ........ Gen 19:28
Abraham lifted up his eyes, and *l* ........ Gen 22:13
the Philistines *l* out at a window ........ Gen 26:8
And he *l*, and behold a well in the ........ Gen 29:2
LORD hath *l* upon my affliction ........ Gen 29:32
And Jacob lifted up his eyes, and *l* ........ Gen 33:1
and they lifted up their eyes and *l* ........ Gen 37:25
The keeper of the prison *l* not to ........ Gen 39:23
*l* upon them, and, behold, they ........ Gen 40:6
brethren, and *l* on their burdens ........ Ex 2:11
he *l* this way and that way, and ........ Ex 2:12
God *l* upon the children of Israel ........ Ex 2:25
and he *l*, and, behold, the bush ........ Ex 3:2
and that he had *l* upon their ........ Ex 4:31
in the morning watch the LORD *l* ........ Ex 14:24
that they *l* toward the wilderness ........ Ex 16:10
*l* after Moses, until he was gone ........ Ex 33:8
Aaron *l* upon Miriam, and, behold, .... Num 12:10
that they *l* toward the tabernacle ........ Num 16:42
and they *l*, and took every man his..... Num 17:9
when he *l* on Amalek, he took up ..... Num 24:20
he *l* on the Kenites, and took up ........ Num 24:21
And I *l*, and, behold, ye had sinned ........ Deut 9:16
*l* on our affliction, and our ........ Deut 26:7
that he lifted up his eyes and *l* ........ Josh 5:13
when the men of Ai *l* behind them ...... Josh 8:20
of Sisera *l* out at a window ........ Judg 5:28
And the LORD *l* upon him, and said, .... Judg 6:14
and laid wait in the field, and *l* ........ Judg 9:43
and Manoah and his wife *l* on ........ Judg 13:19
And Manoah and his wife *l* on it ........ Judg 13:20
the Benjamites *l* behind them ........ Judg 20:40
because they had *l* into the ark ........ 1Sa 6:19
for I have *l* upon my people, ........ 1Sa 9:16
of Saul in Gibeah of Benjamin *l* ........ 1Sa 14:16
that he *l* on Eliab, and said, ........ 1Sa 16:6
And when the Philistine *l* about ........ 1Sa 17:42
when Saul *l* behind him, David ........ 1Sa 24:8
when he *l* behind him, he saw me, ........ 2Sa 1:7
Then Abner *l* behind him, and said, ........ 2Sa 2:20
daughter *l* through a window ........ 2Sa 6:16
watch lifted up his eyes, and *l* ........ 2Sa 13:34
wall, and lifted up his eyes, and *l* ........ 2Sa 18:24
They *l*, but there was none to ........ 2Sa 22:42
And Araunah *l*, and saw the king and 2Sa 24:20
And he went up, and *l*, and said, ........ 1Kin 18:43
And he *l*, and, behold, there was a ........ 1Kin 19:6
*l* on them, and cursed them in the ........ 2Kin 2:24
by upon the wall, and the people *l* ........ 2Kin 6:30
her head, and *l* out at a window ........ 2Kin 9:30
there *l* out to him two or three ........ 2Kin 9:32
And when she *l*, behold, the king ........ 2Kin 11:14
Amaziah king of Judah *l* one ........ 2Kin 14:11
as David came to Ornan, Ornan *l* ........ 1Chr 21:21
And when Judah *l* back, behold, the. 2Chr 13:14
they *l* unto the multitude, and, ........ 2Chr 20:24
And she *l*, and, behold, the king ........ 2Chr 23:13
*l* upon him, and, behold, he was ........ 2Chr 26:20
And I *l*, and rose up, and said unto ........ Neh 4:14
sight of all them that *l* upon her ........ Est 2:15
The troops of Tema *l*, the ........ Job 6:19
When I *l* for good, then evil came ........ Job 30:26
The LORD *l* down from heaven upon ........ Ps 14:2
They *l* unto him, and were ........ Ps 34:5
God *l* down from heaven upon the ........ Ps 53:2
I *l* for some to take pity, but ........ Ps 69:20
For he hath *l* down from the ........ Ps 102:19
when they *l* upon me they shaked ........ Ps 109:25
I *l* on my right hand, and beheld, ........ Ps 142:4
my house I *l* through my casement ........ Prov 7:6
I *l* upon it, and received ........ Prov 24:32
Then I *l* on all the works that my ........ Eccl 2:11
because the sun hath *l* upon me ........ Song 1:6
he *l* that it should bring forth ........ Is 5:2
when I *l* that it should bring ........ Is 5:4
he *l* for judgment, but behold ........ Is 5:7
but ye have not *l* unto the maker ........ Is 22:11
And I *l*, and there was none to help ........ Is 63:5
things which we *l* not for ........ Is 64:3
We *l* for peace, but no good came ........ Jer 8:15
we *l* for peace, and there is no ........ Jer 14:19
this is the day that we *l* for ........ Lam 2:16
And I *l*, and, behold, a whirlwind ........ Eze 1:4
And when I *l*, behold, an hand was ........ Eze 2:9
and when I *l*, behold a hole in the ........ Eze 8:7
Then I *l*, and, behold, in the ........ Eze 10:1
And when I *l*, behold the four ........ Eze 10:9
the head *l* they followed it ........ Eze 10:11
*l* upon thee, behold, thy time was ........ Eze 16:8
with images, he *l* in the liver ........ Eze 21:21
court that *l* toward the north ........ Eze 40:20
and I *l*, and, behold, the glory of ........ Eze 44:4
priests, which *l* toward the north ........ Eze 46:19
be *l* upon before thee, and the ........ Dan 1:13
Then I lifted up mine eyes, and *l* ........ Dan 10:5
Then I Daniel *l*, and, behold, ........ Dan 12:5
But thou shouldest not have *l* on ........ Obad 12
thou shouldest not have *l* on ........ Obad 13
Ye *l* for much, and, lo, it came to ........ Hag 1:9
I lifted up mine eyes again, and *l* ........ Zec 2:1
And I said, I have *l*, and behold a ........ Zec 4:2
and lifted up mine eyes, and *l* ........ Zec 5:1
Then lifted I up mine eyes, and *l* ........ Zec 5:9
and lifted up mine eyes, and *l* ........ Zec 6:1
when he had *l* round about on them ........ Mk 3:5
he *l* round about on them which ........ Mk 3:34
he *l* round about to see her that ........ Mk 5:32
he *l* up to heaven, and blessed, and ........ Mk 6:41
And he *l* up, and said, I see men as ........ Mk 8:24
*l* on his disciples, he rebuked ........ Mk 8:33
when they had *l* round about ........ Mk 9:8
Jesus *l* round about, and saith ........ Mk 10:23
when he had *l* round about upon ........ Mk 11:11
she *l* upon him, and said, And thou ........ Mk 14:67
And when they *l*, they saw that the ........ Mk 16:4
me in the days wherein he *l* on me ........ Lk 1:25
*l* for redemption in Jerusalem ........ Lk 2:38
*l* on him, and passed by on the ........ Lk 10:32
Jesus came to the place, he *l* up ........ Lk 19:5
And he *l* up, and saw the rich men ........ Lk 21:1
the fire, and earnestly *l* upon him ........ Lk 22:56
the Lord turned, and *l* upon Peter ........ Lk 22:61
the disciples *l* one on another ........ Jn 13:22
down, and *l* into the sepulchre, ........ Jn 20:11
while they *l* stedfastly toward ........ Acts 1:10
*l* up stedfastly into heaven, and ........ Acts 7:55
And when he *l* on him, he was ........ Acts 10:4
And the same hour I *l* up upon him .. Acts 22:13
Howbeit they *l* when he should ........ Acts 28:6
after they had *l* a great while ........ Acts 28:6
For he *l* for a city which hath ........ Heb 11:10
our eyes, which we have *l* upon ........ 1Jn 1:1
After this I *l*, and, behold, a ........ Rev 4:1
And I *l*, and behold a pale horse ........ Rev 6:8
And I *l*, and, lo, a Lamb stood on ........ Rev 14:1
And I *l*, and behold a white cloud, ...... Rev 14:14
And after that I *l*, and, behold, ........ Rev 15:5

**LOOKEST**

*l* narrowly unto all my paths ........ Job 13:27
wherefore *l* thou upon them that ........ Hab 1:13

**LOOKETH**

foot, wheresoever the priest *l* ........ Lev 13:12
that is bitten, when he *l* upon it ........ Num 21:8
Pisgah, which *l* toward Jeshimon ........ Num 21:20
of Peor, that *l* toward Jeshimon ........ Num 23:28
from the bay that *l* southward ........ Josh 15:2
to the way of the border that *l* ........ 1Sa 13:18
for man *l* on the outward ........ 1Sa 16:7
but the LORD *l* on the heart ........ 1Sa 16:7
as a hireling *l* for the reward of ........ Job 7:2
For he *l* to the ends of the earth ........ Job 28:24
He *l* upon men, and if any say, I ........ Job 33:27
The LORD *l* from heaven ........ Ps 33:13
the place of his habitation he *l* ........ Ps 33:14
He *l* on the earth, and it ........ Ps 104:32
prudent man *l* well to his going ........ Prov 14:15
She *l* well to the ways of her ........ Prov 31:27
he *l* forth at the windows, ........ Song 2:9
Who is she that *l* forth as the ........ Song 6:10
Lebanon which *l* toward Damascus ...... Song 7:4
when he that *l* upon it seeth ........ Is 28:4
gate, that *l* toward the north ........ Eze 8:3
LORD's house, which *l* eastward ........ Eze 11:1
the gate which *l* toward the east ........ Eze 40:6
the gate that *l* toward the east ........ Eze 40:22
the gate that *l* toward the east ........ Eze 43:1
sanctuary which *l* toward the east ........ Eze 44:1
gate of the inner court that *l* ........ Eze 46:1
the gate that *l* toward the east ........ Eze 46:12
gate by the way that *l* eastward ........ Eze 47:2
That whosoever *l* on a woman to ........ Mt 5:28
in a day when he *l* not for him ........ Mt 24:50
in a day when he *l* not for him ........ Lk 12:46
But whoso *l* into the perfect law ........ Jas 1:25

**LOOKING**

*l* toward Gilgal, that is before ........ Josh 15:7
three *l* toward the north, and ........ 1Kin 7:25
three *l* toward the west ........ 1Kin 7:25
three *l* toward the south ........ 1Kin 7:25
and three *l* toward the east ........ 1Kin 7:25
Michal the daughter of Saul *l* out ...... 1Chr 15:29
three *l* toward the north, and ........ 2Chr 4:4
three *l* toward the west ........ 2Chr 4:4
three *l* toward the south ........ 2Chr 4:4
and three *l* toward the east ........ 2Chr 4:4
is strong, and as a molten *l* glass ........ Job 37:18
mine eyes fail with *l* upward ........ Is 38:14
*l* up to heaven, he blessed, and ........ Mt 14:19
*l* up to heaven, he sighed, and ........ Mk 7:34
Jesus *l* upon them saith, With men ........ Mk 10:27
were also women *l* on afar off ........ Mk 15:40
*l* round about upon them all, he ........ Lk 6:10
*l* up to heaven, he blessed them, ........ Lk 9:16
*l* back, is fit for the kingdom of ........ Lk 9:62
for *l* after those things which ........ Lk 21:26
*l* upon Jesus as he walked, he ........ Jn 1:36
*l* in, saw the linen clothes lying ........ Jn 20:5
*l* stedfastly on him, saw his face ........ Acts 6:15
*l* for a promise from thee ........ Acts 23:21
*L* for that blessed hope, and the ........ Titus 2:13
certain fearful *l* for of judgment ........ Heb 10:27
*L* unto Jesus the author and ........ Heb 12:2
*L* diligently lest any man fail of ........ Heb 12:15
*L* for and hasting unto the coming ........ 2Pet 3:12
*l* for the mercy of our Lord Jesus ........ Jude 21

**LOOKINGGLASSES**

of the *l* of the women assembling, ........ Ex 38:8

**LOOKS**

but wilt bring down high *l* ........ Ps 18:27
The lofty *l* of man shall be ........ Is 2:11
and the glory of his high *l* ........ Is 10:12
words, nor be dismayed at their *l* ........ Eze 2:6
neither be dismayed at their *l* ........ Eze 3:9

**LOOPS**

thou shalt make *l* of blue upon ........ Ex 26:4
Fifty *l* shalt thou make in the ........ Ex 26:5
fifty *l* shalt thou make in the ........ Ex 26:5
that the *l* may take hold one of ........ Ex 26:5
thou shalt make fifty *l* on the ........ Ex 26:10
fifty *l* in the edge of the ........ Ex 26:10
and put the taches into the *l* ........ Ex 26:11
he made *l* of blue on the edge of ........ Ex 36:11
Fifty *l* made he in one curtain, ........ Ex 36:12
fifty *l* made he in the edge of ........ Ex 36:12
the *l* held one curtain to another ........ Ex 36:12
And he made fifty *l* upon the ........ Ex 36:17
fifty *l* made he upon the edge of ........ Ex 36:17

**LOOSE**

Naphtali is a hind let *l* ........ Gen 49:21
living bird *l* into the open field ........ Lev 14:7
*l* his shoe from off his foot, and ........ Deut 25:9
*L* thy shoe from off thy foot ........ Josh 5:15
that he would let *l* his hand ........ Job 6:9
they have also let *l* the bridle ........ Job 30:11
Pleiades, or *l* the bands of Orion ........ Job 38:31
to *l* those that are appointed to ........ Ps 102:20
*l* the sackcloth from off thy ........ Is 20:2
I will *l* the loins of kings, to ........ Is 45:1
*l* thyself from the bands of thy ........ Is 52:2
to *l* the bands of wickedness, to ........ Is 58:6
I *l* thee this day from the chains ........ Jer 40:4
and said, Lo, I see four men *l* ........ Dan 3:25
whatsoever thou shalt *l* on earth ........ Mt 16:19
whatsoever ye shall *l* on earth ........ Mt 18:18
*l* them, and bring them unto me ........ Mt 21:2
*l* him, and bring him ........ Mk 11:2
and they *l* him ........ Mk 11:4
*l* his ox or his ass from the ........ Lk 13:15
*l* him, and bring him hither ........ Lk 19:30
any man ask you, Why do ye *l* him ........ Lk 19:31
said unto them, Why *l* ye the colt ........ Lk 19:33
unto them, *L* him, and let him go ........ Jn 11:44
of his feet I am not worthy to *l* ........ Acts 13:25
him of Paul, that he might *l* him ........ Acts 24:26
book, and to *l* the seals thereof ........ Rev 5:2
to *l* the seven seals thereof ........ Rev 5:5
*L* the four angels which are bound ........ Rev 9:14

**LOOSED**

be not *l* from the ephod ........ Ex 28:28
might not be *l* from the ephod ........ Ex 39:21
house of him that hath his shoe *l* ...... Deut 25:10
his bands *l* from off his hands ........ Judg 15:14
Because he hath *l* my cord ........ Job 30:11
or who hath *l* the bands of the ........ Job 39:5
The king sent and *l* him ........ Ps 105:20
thou hast *l* my bonds ........ Ps 116:16
Or ever the silver cord be *l* ........ Eccl 12:6
the girdle of their loins be *l* ........ Is 5:27
Thy tacklings are *l* ........ Is 33:23
exile hasteneth that he may be *l* ........ Is 51:14
the joints of his loins were *l* ........ Dan 5:6
on earth shall be *l* in heaven ........ Mt 16:19
on earth shall be *l* in heaven ........ Mt 18:18
*l* him, and forgave him the debt ........ Mt 18:27
and the string of his tongue was *l* ........ Mk 7:35
immediately, and his tongue *l* ........ Lk 1:64
thou art *l* from thine infirmity ........ Lk 13:12
be *l* from this bond on the ........ Lk 13:16
having *l* the pains of death ........ Acts 2:24
Paul and his company *l* from Paphos Acts 13:13
and every one's bands were *l* ........ Acts 16:26
he *l* him from his bands, and ........ Acts 22:30
not have *l* from Crete, and to have ........ Acts 27:21
*l* the rudder bands, and hoised up ........ Acts 27:40
she is *l* from the law of her ........ Rom 7:2
seek not to be *l* ........ 1Cor 7:27
Art thou *l* from a wife ........ 1Cor 7:27
And the four angels were *l* ........ Rev 9:15
that he must be *l* a little season ........ Rev 20:3
Satan shall be *l* out of his ........ Rev 20:7

**LOOSETH**

He *l* the bond of kings, and ........ Job 12:18
The LORD *l* the prisoners ........ Ps 146:7

**LOOSING**

unto them, What do ye, *l* the colt ........ Mk 11:5
And as they were *l* the colt ........ Lk 19:33
Therefore *l* from Troas, we came ........ Acts 16:11
*l* thence, they sailed close by ........ Acts 27:13

**LOP**

shall *l* the bough with terror ........ Is 10:33

**LORD** See PREFACE.

*1. God.*

Now the *L* had said unto Abram, ........ Gen 12:1
Is any thing too hard for the *L* ........ Gen 18:14
then shall the *L* be my God ........ Gen 28:21
the name of the *L* thy God in vain ........ Ex 20:7
for the *L* will not hold him ........ Ex 20:7

proclaimed, The *L*, The *L* God ... Ex 34:6
know that the *L* he is God ... Deut 4:35
The *L* our God is one *L* ... Deut 6:4
thou forget not the *L* thy God ... Deut 8:11
to know whether ye love the *L* ... Deut 13:3
seem evil unto you to serve the *L* ... Josh 24:15
and my house, we will serve the *L* ... Josh 24:15
There is none holy as the *L* ... 1Sa 2:2
And he said, It is the *L* ... 1Sa 3:18
For the *L* will not forsake his ... 1Sa 12:22
But the *L* said unto Samuel, Look ... 1Sa 16:7
for the *L* seeth not as man seeth ... 1Sa 16:7
but the *L* looketh on the heart ... 1Sa 16:7
the *L*, he is the God ... 1Kin 18:39
For the eyes of the *L* run to ... 2Chr 16:9
Thou, even thou, art *L* alone ... Neh 9:6
For who is God save the *L* ... Ps 18:31
The *L* is my light and my salvation ... Ps 27:1
the *L* is the strength of my life ... Ps 27:1
Wait on the *L* ... Ps 27:14
wait, I say, on the *L* ... Ps 27:14
is the nation whose God is the *L* ... Ps 33:12
Know ye that the *L* he is God ... Ps 100:3
Bless the *L*, O my soul ... Ps 103:1
God is the *L*, which hath shewed ... Ps 118:27
The fear of the *L* is the ... Prov 1:7
For whom the *L* loveth he ... Prov 3:12
These six things doth the *L* hate ... Prov 6:16
The fear of the *L* is the ... Prov 9:10
may know that thou art the *L* ... Is 37:20
I, even I, am the *L* ... Is 43:11
I am the *L*, your Holy One, the ... Is 43:15
I am the *L*, and there is none else ... Is 45:5
The *L* hath made bare his holy arm ... Is 52:10
whom is the arm of the *L* revealed ... Is 53:1
the *L* hath laid on him the ... Is 53:6
Seek ye the *L* while he may be ... Is 55:6
Spirit of the *L* God is upon me ... Is 61:1
the *L* shall be king over all the ... Zec 14:9
in that day shall there be one *L* ... Zec 14:9
Prepare ye the way of the *L* ... Mt 3:3
one that saith unto me, *L*, *L* ... Mt 7:21
Prepare ye the way of the *L* ... Mk 1:3
of man is *L* also of the sabbath ... Mk 2:28
cried out, and said with tears, *L* ... Mk 9:24
The *L* our God is one *L* ... Mk 12:29
thou shalt love the *L* thy God ... Mk 12:30
the angel of the *L* came upon them ... Lk 2:9
the glory of the *L* shone round ... Lk 2:9
a Saviour, which is Christ the *L* ... Lk 2:11
The Spirit of the *L* is upon me ... Lk 4:18
of man is *L* also of the sabbath ... Lk 6:5
And he said unto him, *L*, I am ... Lk 22:33
Make straight the way of the *L* ... Jn 1:23
Then Simon Peter answered him, *L* ... Jn 6:68
Ye call me Master and *L* ... Jn 13:13
said unto him, We have seen the *L* ... Jn 20:25
answered and said unto him, My *L* ... Jn 20:28
saith unto Peter, It is the *L* ... Jn 21:7
Peter heard that it was the *L* ... Jn 21:7
seeing him saith to Jesus, *L* ... Jn 21:21
whom ye have crucified, both *L* ... Acts 2:36
And he said, Who art thou, *L* ... Acts 9:5
the *L* said, I am Jesus whom thou ... Acts 9:5
saying, The will of the *L* be done ... Acts 21:14
And I said, Who art thou, *L* ... Acts 26:15
life through Jesus Christ our *L* ... Rom 6:23
with thy mouth the *L* Jesus ... Rom 10:9
for the same *L* over all is rich ... Rom 10:12
I will repay, saith the *L* ... Rom 12:19
he might be *L* both of the dead ... Rom 14:9
written, As I live, saith the *L* ... Rom 14:11
not have crucified the *L* of glory ... 1Cor 2:8
man can say that Jesus is the *L* ... 1Cor 12:3
second man is the *L* from heaven ... 1Cor 15:47
One *L*, one faith, one baptism, ... Eph 4:5
confess that Jesus Christ is *L* ... Phil 2:11
worthy of the *L* unto all pleasing ... Col 1:10
do, do it heartily, as to the *L* ... Col 3:23
For the *L* himself shall descend ... 1Th 4:16
clouds, to meet the *L* in the air ... 1Th 4:17
and so shall we ever be with the *L* ... 1Th 4:17
the *L* so cometh as a thief in the ... 1Th 5:2
the coming of our *L* Jesus Christ ... 2Th 2:1
the King of kings, and *L* of lords ... 1Ti 6:15
The *L* shall judge his people ... Heb 10:30
ye ought to say, If the *L* will ... Jas 4:15
that the *L* is very pitiful, and of ... Jas 5:11
him with oil in the name of the *L* ... Jas 5:14
sick, and the *L* shall raise him up ... Jas 5:15
word of the *L* endureth for ever ... 1Pet 1:25
is with the *L* as a thousand years ... 2Pet 3:8
The *L* is not slack concerning his ... 2Pet 3:9
But the day of the *L* will come as ... 2Pet 3:10
the *L* cometh with ten thousands ... Jude 14
*L* God Almighty, which was, and is, ... Rev 4:8
for the *L* God omnipotent reigneth ... Rev 19:6
AND *L* OF LORDS ... Rev 19:16
Even so, come, *L* Jesus ... Rev 22:20

*2. A human title of honor.*

His *l* said unto him, Well done, ... Mt 25:21
enter thou into the joy of thy *l* ... Mt 25:21

## LORDLY

brought forth butter in a *l* dish ... Judg 5:25

## LORD'S

*1. Refers to Lord 1.*

know how that the earth is the *L* ... Ex 9:29
it is the *L* passover ... Ex 12:11
the sacrifice of the *L* passover ... Ex 12:27
that the *L* law may be in thy ... Ex 13:9
the males shall be the *L* ... Ex 13:12
and said, Who is on the *L* side ... Ex 32:26
they brought the *L* offering to ... Ex 35:21
and brass brought the *L* offering ... Ex 35:24
all the fat is the *L* ... Lev 3:16
goat upon which the *L* lot fell ... Lev 16:9
month at even is the *L* passover ... Lev 23:5
which should be the *L* firstling ... Lev 27:26
it is the *L* ... Lev 27:26
the fruit of the tree, is the *L* ... Lev 27:30
Is the *L* hand waxed short ... Num 11:23
all the *L* people were prophets ... Num 11:29
ye shall give thereof the *L* heave ... Num 18:28
the *L* tribute of the sheep was ... Num 31:37
of which the *L* tribute was ... Num 31:38
of which the *L* tribute was ... Num 31:39
of which the *L* tribute was thirty ... Num 31:40
which was the *L* heave offering, ... Num 31:41
the *L* anger was kindled the same ... Num 32:10
the *L* anger was kindled against ... Num 32:13
of heavens is the *L* thy God ... Deut 10:14
then the *L* wrath be kindled ... Deut 11:17
it is called the *L* release ... Deut 15:2
For the *L* portion is his people ... Deut 32:9
which Moses the *L* servant gave ... Josh 1:15
the captain of the *L* host said ... Josh 5:15
wherein the *L* tabernacle dwelleth ... Josh 22:19
of Ammon, shall surely be the *L* ... Judg 11:31
pillars of the earth are the *L* ... 1Sa 2:8
ye make the *L* people to ... 1Sa 2:24
the *L* priest in Shiloh, wearing ... 1Sa 14:3
Surely the *L* anointed is before ... 1Sa 16:6
for the battle is the *L*, and he ... 1Sa 17:47
for me, and fight the *L* battles ... 1Sa 18:17
that Saul had slain the *L* priests ... 1Sa 22:21
the *L* anointed, to stretch forth ... 1Sa 24:6
for he is the *L* anointed ... 1Sa 24:10
his hand against the *L* anointed ... 1Sa 26:9
mine hand against the *L* anointed ... 1Sa 26:11
kept your master, the *L* anointed ... 1Sa 26:16
mine hand against the *L* anointed ... 1Sa 26:23
hand to destroy the *L* anointed ... 2Sa 1:14
I have slain the *L* anointed ... 2Sa 1:16
because he cursed the *L* anointed ... 2Sa 19:21
because of the *L* oath that was ... 2Sa 21:7
the *L* prophets by fifty in a cave ... 1Kin 18:13
that they should be the *L* people ... 2Kin 11:17
The arrow of the *L* deliverance ... 2Kin 13:17
the Lord had filled the *L* house ... 2Chr 7:2
that they should be the *L* people ... 2Chr 23:16
the *L* throne is in heaven ... Ps 11:4
For the kingdom is the *L* ... Ps 22:28
The earth is the *L*, and the ... Ps 24:1
same the *L* name is to be praised ... Ps 113:3
even the heavens, are the *L* ... Ps 115:16
In the courts of the *L* house ... Ps 116:19
This is the *L* doing ... Ps 118:23
How shall we sing the *L* song in a ... Ps 137:4
just weight and balance are the *L* ... Prov 16:11
that the mountain of the *L* house ... Is 2:2
it is the day of the *L* vengeance ... Is 34:8
*L* hand double for all her sins ... Is 40:2
and blind as the *L* servant ... Is 42:19
One shall say, I am the *L* ... Is 44:5
the *L* hand is not shortened, that ... Is 59:1
for they are not the *L* ... Jer 5:10
Stand in the gate of the *L* house ... Jer 7:2
because the *L* flock is carried ... Jer 13:17
stood in the court of the *L* house ... Jer 19:14
Then took I the cup at the *L* hand ... Jer 25:17
Stand in the court of the *L* house ... Jer 26:2
come to worship in the *L* house ... Jer 26:2
of the new gate of the *L* house ... Jer 26:10
the vessels of the *L* house shall ... Jer 27:16
all the vessels of the *L* house ... Jer 28:3
again the vessels of the *L* house ... Jer 28:6
the *L* house upon the fasting day ... Jer 36:6
words of the Lord in the *L* house ... Jer 36:8
of the new gate of the *L* house ... Jer 36:10
is the time of the *L* vengeance ... Jer 51:6
been a golden cup in the *L* hand ... Jer 51:7
the sanctuaries of the *L* house ... Jer 51:51
so that in the day of the *L* anger ... Lam 2:22
It is of the *L* mercies that we ... Lam 3:22
the *L* house which was toward the ... Eze 8:14
the inner court of the *L* house ... Eze 8:16
of the brightness of the *L* glory ... Eze 10:4
of the east gate of the *L* house ... Eze 10:19
unto the east gate of the *L* house ... Eze 11:1
that is desolate, for the *L* sake ... Dan 9:17
shall not dwell in the *L* land ... Hos 9:3
priests, the *L* ministers, mourn ... Joel 1:9
and the kingdom shall be the *L* ... Obad 21
the *L* controversy, and ye strong ... Mic 6:2
The *L* voice crieth unto the city, ... Mic 6:9
the cup of the *L* right hand shall ... Hab 2:16
in the day of the *L* sacrifice ... Zeph 1:8
them in the day of the *L* wrath ... Zeph 1:18
day of the *L* anger come upon you ... Zeph 2:2
be hid in the day of the *L* anger ... Zeph 2:3
the time that the *L* house should ... Hag 1:2
Then spake Haggai the *L* messenger ... Hag 1:13
in the *L* message unto the people ... Hag 1:13
of the *L* temple was laid, ... Hag 2:18
the pots in the *L* house shall be ... Zec 14:20
this is the *L* doing, and it is ... Mt 21:42
This was the *L* doing, and it is ... Mk 12:11
before he had seen the *L* Christ ... Lk 2:26
therefore, or die, we are the *L* ... Rom 14:8
being a servant, is the *L* freeman ... 1Cor 7:22
be partakers of the *L* table ... 1Cor 10:21
For the earth is the *L*, and the ... 1Cor 10:26
for the earth is the *L*, and the ... 1Cor 10:28
this is not to eat the *L* supper ... 1Cor 11:20
ye do shew the *L* death till he ... 1Cor 11:26
not discerning the *L* body ... 1Cor 11:29
I none, save James the *L* brother ... Gal 1:19
ordinance of man for the *L* sake ... 1Pet 2:13
I was in the Spirit on the *L* day ... Rev 1:10

## LORDS

And he said, Behold now, my *l* ... Gen 19:2
the *l* of the high places of Arnon ... Num 21:28
God is God of gods, and Lord of *l* ... Deut 10:17
five *l* of the Philistines ... Josh 13:3
five *l* of the Philistines, and all ... Judg 3:3
the *l* of the Philistines came up ... Judg 16:5
Then the *l* of the Philistines ... Judg 16:8
sent and called for the *l* of the ... Judg 16:18
Then the *l* of the Philistines ... Judg 16:18
Then the *l* of the Philistines ... Judg 16:23
all the *l* of the Philistines were ... Judg 16:27
and the house fell upon the *l* ... Judg 16:30
gathered all the *l* of the ... 1Sa 5:8
all the *l* of the Philistines ... 1Sa 5:11
of the *l* of the Philistines ... 1Sa 6:4
was on you all, and on your *l* ... 1Sa 6:4
the *l* of the Philistines went ... 1Sa 6:12
And when the five *l* of the ... 1Sa 6:16
belonging to the five *l*, both of ... 1Sa 6:18
the *l* of the Philistines went up ... 1Sa 7:7
the *l* of the Philistines passed ... 1Sa 29:2
the *l* favour thee not ... 1Sa 29:6
not the *l* of the Philistines ... 1Sa 29:7
for the *l* of the Philistines upon ... 1Chr 12:19
and his counsellors, and his *l* ... Ezr 8:25
O give thanks to the Lord of *l* ... Ps 136:3
the *l* of the heathen have broken ... Is 16:8
other *l* besides thee have had ... Is 26:13
wherefore say my people, We are *l* ... Jer 2:31
men, captains and rulers, great *l* ... Eze 23:23
and my *l* sought unto me ... Dan 4:36
feast to a thousand of his *l* ... Dan 5:1
in him, and his *l* were astonied ... Dan 5:9
of the words of the king and his *l* ... Dan 5:10
before thee, and thou, and thy *l* ... Dan 5:23
and with the signet of his *l* ... Dan 6:17
birthday made a supper to his *l* ... Mk 6:21
there be gods many, and *l* many,) ... 1Cor 8:5
the King of kings, and Lord of *l* ... 1Ti 6:15
Neither as being *l* over God's ... 1Pet 5:3
for he is Lord of *l*, and King of ... Rev 17:14
KING OF KINGS, AND LORD OF *L* ... Rev 19:16

## LORD'S/1

*2. Refers to Lord 2.*

him in the ward of his *l* house ... Gen 40:7
out of thy *l* house silver or gold ... Gen 44:8
and we also will be my *l* bondmen ... Gen 44:9
behold, we are my *l* servants ... Gen 44:16
thee, speak a word in my *l* ears ... Gen 44:18
take thou thy *l* servants, and ... 2Sa 20:6
are they not all my *l* servants ... 1Chr 21:3
shall be the shame of thy *l* house ... Is 22:18
in the earth, and hid his *l* money ... Mt 25:18
servant, which knew his *l* will ... Lk 12:47
one of his *l* debtors unto him ... Lk 16:5

## LORDSHIP

the Gentiles exercise *l* over them ... Mk 10:42
the Gentiles exercise *l* over them ... Lk 22:25

## LO-RUHAMAH (*lo-ru-ha'-mah*) *Symbolic name meaning 'Not pitied.'*

said unto him, Call her name *L* ... Hos 1:6
Now when she had weaned *L* ... Hos 1:8

## LOSE

thou *l* thy life, with the lives ... Judg 18:25
that we *l* not all the beasts ... 1Kin 18:5
owners thereof to *l* their life ... Job 31:39
vomit up, and *l* thy sweet words ... Prov 23:8
A time to get, and a time to *l* ... Eccl 3:6
that findeth his life shall *l* it ... Mt 10:39
he shall in no wise *l* his reward ... Mt 10:42
will save his life shall *l* it ... Mt 16:25
whosoever will *l* his life for my ... Mt 16:25
whole world, and *l* his own soul ... Mt 16:26
will save his life shall *l* it ... Mk 8:35
but whosoever shall *l* his life ... Mk 8:35
whole world, and *l* his own soul ... Mk 8:36
you, he shall not *l* his reward ... Mk 9:41
will save his life shall *l* it ... Lk 9:24
but whosoever will *l* his life for ... Lk 9:24
*l* himself, or be cast away ... Lk 9:25
if he *l* one of them, doth not ... Lk 15:4
if she *l* one piece, doth not ... Lk 15:8
seek to save his life shall *l* it ... Lk 17:33
whosoever shall *l* his life shall ... Lk 17:33
hath given me I should *l* nothing ... Jn 6:39
that loveth his life shall *l* it ... Jn 12:25
that we *l* not those things which ... 2Jn 8

## LOSETH

he that *l* his life for my sake ... Mt 10:39

## LOSS

I bare the *l* of it ... Gen 31:39
shall pay for the *l* of his time ... Ex 21:19
shall I know the *l* of children ... Is 47:8
the *l* of children, and widowhood ... Is 47:9
and to have gained this harm and *l* ... Acts 27:21

for there shall be no *l* of any ... Acts 27:22
be burned, he shall suffer *l* ... 1Cor 3:15
me, those I counted *l* for Christ ... Phil 3:7
I count all things but *l* for the ... Phil 3:8
have suffered the *l* of all things ... Phil 3:8

**LOST**
or for any manner of *l* thing ... Ex 22:9
Or have found that which was *l* ... Lev 6:3
or the *l* thing which he found, ... Lev 6:4
days that were before shall be *l* ... Num 6:12
and with all *l* things of thy ... Deut 22:3
of thy brother's, which he hath *l* ... Deut 22:3
of Kish Saul's father were *l* ... 1Sa 9:3
asses that were *l* three days ago ... 1Sa 9:20
like the army that thou hast *l* ... 1Kin 20:25
I have gone astray like a *l* sheep ... Ps 119:176
have, after thou hast *l* the other ... Is 49:20
seeing I have *l* my children ... Is 49:21
My people hath been *l* sheep ... Jer 50:6
she had waited, and her hope was *l* ... Eze 19:5
have ye sought that which was *l* ... Eze 34:4
I will seek that which was *l* ... Eze 34:16
bones are dried, and our hope is *l* ... Eze 37:11
but if the salt have *l* his savour ... Mt 5:13
But go rather to the *l* sheep of ... Mt 10:6
I am not sent but unto the *l* ... Mt 15:24
is come to save that which was *l* ... Mt 18:11
if the salt have *l* his saltness ... Mk 9:50
but if the salt have *l* his savour ... Lk 14:34
and go after that which is *l* ... Lk 15:4
I have found my sheep which was *l* ... Lk 15:6
found the piece which I had *l* ... Lk 15:9
he was *l*, and is found ... Lk 15:24
and was *l*, and is found ... Lk 15:32
seek and to save that which was *l* ... Lk 19:10
that remain, that nothing be *l* ... Jn 6:12
I have kept, and none of them is *l* ... Jn 17:12
thou gavest me have I *l* none ... Jn 18:9
hid, it is hid to them that are *l* ... 2Cor 4:3

**LOT** (*lot*) See LOT'S. *Abraham's nephew.*
and Haran begat *L* ... Gen 11:27
*L* the son of Haran his son's son, ... Gen 11:31
and *L* went with him ... Gen 12:4
*L* his brother's son, and all their ... Gen 12:5
*L* with him, into the south ... Gen 13:1
*L* also, which went with Abram, ... Gen 13:5
And Abram said unto *L*, Let there ... Gen 13:8
*L* lifted up his eyes, and beheld ... Gen 13:10
Then *L* chose him all the plain of ... Gen 13:11
and *L* journeyed east ... Gen 13:11
*L* dwelled in the cities of the ... Gen 13:12
after that *L* was separated from ... Gen 13:14
And they took *L*, Abram's brother's ... Gen 14:12
also brought again his brother *L* ... Gen 14:16
*L* sat in the gate of Sodom ... Gen 19:1
*L* seeing them rose up to meet ... Gen 19:1
And they called unto *L*, and said ... Gen 19:5
*L* went out at the door unto them, ... Gen 19:6
pressed sore upon the man, even *L* ... Gen 19:9
pulled *L* into the house to them, ... Gen 19:10
And the men said unto *L*, Hast thou .. Gen 19:12
*L* went out, and spake unto his ... Gen 19:14
arose, then the angels hastened *L* ... Gen 19:15
*L* said unto them, Oh, not so, my ... Gen 19:18
earth when *L* entered into Zoar ... Gen 19:23
sent *L* out of the midst of the ... Gen 19:29
the cities in the which *L* dwelt ... Gen 19:29
*L* went up out of Zoar, and dwelt ... Gen 19:30
of *L* with child by their father ... Gen 19:36
one *l* for the LORD, and the other ... Lev 16:8
the other *l* for the scapegoat ... Lev 16:8
goat upon which the LORD's *l* fell ... Lev 16:9
on which the *l* fell to be the ... Lev 16:10
the land shall be divided by *l* ... Num 26:55
According to the *l* shall the ... Num 26:56
ye shall divide the land by *l* for ... Num 33:54
in the place where his *l* falleth ... Num 33:54
land which ye shall inherit by *l* ... Num 34:13
by *l* to the children of Israel ... Num 36:2
from the *l* of our inheritance ... Num 36:3
children of *L* for a possession ... Deut 2:9
children of *L* for a possession ... Deut 2:19
Jacob is the *l* of his inheritance ... Deut 32:9
only divide thou it by *l* unto the ... Josh 13:6
By *l* was their inheritance, as ... Josh 14:2
This then was the *l* of the tribe ... Josh 15:1
the *l* of the children of Joseph ... Josh 16:1
There was also a *l* for the tribe ... Josh 17:1
There was also a *l* for the rest ... Josh 17:2
Why hast thou given me but one *l* ... Josh 17:14
thou shalt not have one *l* only ... Josh 17:17
the *l* of the tribe of the ... Josh 18:11
the coast of their *l* came forth ... Josh 18:11
the second *l* came forth to Simeon ... Josh 19:1
the third *l* came up for the ... Josh 19:10
the fourth *l* came out to Issachar ... Josh 19:17
the fifth *l* came out for the ... Josh 19:24
The sixth *l* came out to the ... Josh 19:32
the seventh *l* came out for the ... Josh 19:40
by *l* in Shiloh before the LORD ... Josh 19:51
the *l* came out for the families ... Josh 21:4
had by *l* out of the tribe of ... Josh 21:4
by *l* out of the families of the ... Josh 21:5
by *l* out of the families of the ... Josh 21:6
*l* unto the Levites these cities ... Josh 21:8
for theirs was the first *l* ... Josh 21:10
*l* out of the tribe of Ephraim ... Josh 21:20
were by their *l* twelve cities ... Josh 21:40
by *l* these nations that remain ... Josh 23:4
Come up with me into my *l* ... Judg 1:3
will go with thee into thy *l* ... Judg 1:3
we will go up by *l* against it ... Judg 20:9
God of Israel, Give a perfect *l* ... 1Sa 14:41
for theirs was the *l* ... 1Chr 6:54
the half tribe of Manasseh, by *l* ... 1Chr 6:61
sons of Merari were given by *l* ... 1Chr 6:63
they gave by *l* out of the tribe ... 1Chr 6:65
the *l* of your inheritance ... 1Chr 16:18
Thus were they divided by *l* ... 1Chr 24:5
Now the first *l* came forth to ... 1Chr 24:7
Now the first *l* came forth for ... 1Chr 25:9
the *l* eastward fell to Shelemiah ... 1Chr 26:14
and his *l* came out northward ... 1Chr 26:14
Hosah the *l* came forth westward, ... 1Chr 26:16
they cast Pur, that is, the *l* ... Est 3:7
and had cast Pur, that is, the *l* ... Est 9:24
thou maintainest my *l* ... Ps 16:5
have holpen the children of *L* ... Ps 83:8
the *l* of your inheritance ... Ps 105:11
rest upon the *l* of the righteous ... Ps 125:3
Cast in thy *l* among us ... Prov 1:14
The *l* is cast into the lap ... Prov 16:33
The *l* causeth contentions to ... Prov 18:18
the *l* of them that rob us ... Is 17:14
And he hath cast the *l* for them ... Is 34:17
they, they are thy *l* ... Is 57:6
This is thy *l*, the portion of thy ... Jer 13:25
let no *l* fall upon it ... Eze 24:6
when ye shall divide by *l* the ... Eze 45:1
that ye shall divide it by *l* for ... Eze 47:22
*l* unto the tribes of Israel for ... Eze 48:29
stand in thy *l* at the end of the ... Dan 12:13
lots, and the *l* fell upon Jonah ... Jonah 1:7
none that shall cast a cord by *l* ... Mic 2:5
his *l* was to burn incense when he ... Lk 1:9
also as it was in the days of *L* ... Lk 17:28
But the same day that *L* went out ... Lk 17:29
and the *l* fell upon Matthias ... Acts 1:26
neither part nor *l* in this matter ... Acts 8:21
divided their land to them by *l* ... Acts 13:19
And delivered just *L*, vexed with ... 2Pet 2:7

**LOTAN** (*lo'-tan*) See LOTAN'S. *Son of Seir.*
*L*, and Shobal, and Zibeon ... Gen 36:20
And the children of *L* were Hori ... Gen 36:22
duke *L*, duke Shobal, duke Zibeon, ... Gen 36:29
*L*, and Shobal, and Zibeon, and Anah, 1Chr 1:38
And the sons of *L* ... 1Chr 1:39

**LOTAN'S** (*lo'-tans*)
and *L* sister was Timna ... Gen 36:22
and Timna was *L* sister ... 1Chr 1:39

**LOTHE**
the Egyptians shall *l* to drink of ... Ex 7:18
they shall *l* themselves for the ... Eze 6:9
ye shall *l* yourselves in your own ... Eze 20:43
shall *l* yourselves in your own ... Eze 36:31

**LOTHED**
hath thy soul *l* Zion ... Jer 14:19
which *l* their husbands and their ... Eze 16:45
and my soul *l* them, and their soul ... Zec 11:8

**LOTHETH**
that *l* her husband and her ... Eze 16:45

**LOTHING**
to the *l* of thy person, in the ... Eze 16:5

**LOT'S** (*lots*)
cattle and the herdmen of *L* cattle ... Gen 13:7
Remember *L* wife ... Lk 17:32

**LOTS**
Aaron shall cast *l* upon the two ... Lev 16:8
that I may cast *l* for you here ... Josh 18:6
that I may here cast *l* for you ... Josh 18:8
Joshua cast *l* for them in Shiloh ... Josh 18:10
Cast *l* between me and Jonathan my .. 1Sa 14:42
These likewise cast *l* over ... 1Chr 24:31
And they cast *l*, ward against ward ... 1Chr 25:8
And they cast *l*, as well the small ... 1Chr 26:13
a wise counsellor, they cast *l* ... 1Chr 26:14
we cast the *l* among the priests, ... Neh 10:34
rest of the people also cast *l* ... Neh 11:1
them, and cast *l* upon my vesture ... Ps 22:18
And they have cast *l* for my people ... Joel 3:3
cast *l* upon Jerusalem, even thou ... Obad 11
fellow, Come, and let us cast *l* ... Jonah 1:7
So they cast *l*, and the lot fell ... Jonah 1:7
they cast *l* for her honourable ... Nah 3:10
and parted his garments, casting *l* ... Mt 27:35
upon my vesture did they cast *l* ... Mt 27:35
casting *l* upon them, what every ... Mk 15:24
parted his raiment, and cast *l* ... Lk 23:34
us not rend it, but cast *l* for it ... Jn 19:24
and for my vesture they did cast *l* ... Jn 19:24
And they gave forth their *l* ... Acts 1:26

**LOUD**
me, and I cried with a *l* voice ... Gen 39:14
voice of the trumpet exceeding *l* ... Ex 19:16
the men of Israel with a *l* voice ... Deut 27:14
Samuel, she cried with a *l* voice ... 1Sa 28:12
the country wept with a *l* voice ... 2Sa 15:23
and the king cried with a *l* voice ... 2Sa 19:4
of Israel with a *l* voice, saying, ... 1Kin 8:55
cried with a *l* voice in the Jews' ... 2Kin 18:28
unto the LORD with a *l* voice ... 2Chr 15:14
of Israel with a *l* voice on high ... 2Chr 20:19
singing with *l* instruments unto ... 2Chr 30:21
Then they cried with a *l* voice in ... 2Chr 32:18
their eyes, wept with a *l* voice ... Ezr 3:12
the people shouted with a *l* shout ... Ezr 3:13
answered and said with a *l* voice ... Ezr 10:12
cried with a *l* voice unto the ... Neh 9:4
And the singers sang *l*, with ... Neh 12:42
of the city, and cried with a *l* ... Est 4:1
play skilfully with a *l* noise ... Ps 33:3
make a *l* noise, and rejoice, and ... Ps 98:4
Praise him upon the *l* cymbals ... Ps 150:5
(She is *l* and stubborn ... Prov 7:11
his friend with a *l* voice ... Prov 27:14
cried with a *l* voice in the Jews' ... Is 36:13
cry in mine ears with a *l* voice ... Eze 8:18
also in mine ears with a *l* voice ... Eze 9:1
my face, and cried with a *l* voice ... Eze 11:13
hour Jesus cried with a *l* voice ... Mt 27:46
he had cried again with a *l* voice ... Mt 27:50
torn him, and cried with a *l* voice ... Mk 1:26
And cried with a *l* voice, and said, ... Mk 5:7
hour Jesus cried with a *l* voice ... Mk 15:34
And Jesus cried with a *l* voice ... Mk 15:37
And she spake out with a *l* voice ... Lk 1:42
and cried out with a *l* voice ... Lk 4:33
with a *l* voice said, What have I ... Lk 8:28
with a *l* voice glorified God, ... Lk 17:15
praise God with a *l* voice for all ... Lk 19:37
they were instant with *l* voices ... Lk 23:23
Jesus had cried with a *l* voice ... Lk 23:46
spoken, he cried with a *l* voice ... Jn 11:43
they cried out with a *l* voice ... Acts 7:57
down, and cried with a *l* voice ... Acts 7:60
spirits, crying with *l* voice ... Acts 8:7
Said with a *l* voice, Stand ... Acts 14:10
But Paul cried with a *l* voice ... Acts 16:28
Festus said with a *l* voice ... Acts 26:24
angel proclaiming with a *l* voice ... Rev 5:2
Saying with a *l* voice, Worthy is ... Rev 5:12
And they cried with a *l* voice ... Rev 6:10
he cried with a *l* voice to the ... Rev 7:2
And cried with a *l* voice, saying, ... Rev 7:10
of heaven, saying with a *l* voice ... Rev 8:13
And cried with a *l* voice, as when ... Rev 10:3
I heard a *l* voice saying in ... Rev 12:10
Saying with a *l* voice, Fear God, ... Rev 14:7
them, saying with a *l* voice ... Rev 14:9
crying with a *l* voice to him that ... Rev 14:15
cried with a *l* cry to him that ... Rev 14:18
and he cried with a *l* voice ... Rev 19:17

**LOUDER**
long, and waxed *l* and *l* ... Ex 19:19

**LOVE**
make me savoury meat, such as I *l* ... Gen 27:4
few days, for the *l* he had to her ... Gen 29:20
therefore my husband will *l* me ... Gen 29:32
unto thousands of them that *l* me ... Ex 20:6
I *l* my master, my wife, and my ... Ex 21:5
but thou shalt *l* thy neighbour as ... Lev 19:18
thou shalt *l* him as thyself ... Lev 19:34
unto thousands of them that *l* me ... Deut 5:10
thou shalt *l* the LORD thy God ... Deut 6:5
LORD did not set his *l* upon you ... Deut 7:7
and mercy with them that *l* him ... Deut 7:9
And he will *l* thee, and bless thee, ... Deut 7:13
to *l* him, and to serve the LORD ... Deut 10:12
delight in thy fathers to *l* them ... Deut 10:15
*L* ye therefore the stranger ... Deut 10:19
thou shalt *l* the LORD thy God ... Deut 11:1
to *l* the LORD your God, and to ... Deut 11:13
to *l* the LORD your God, to walk ... Deut 11:22
to know whether ye *l* the LORD ... Deut 13:3
to *l* the LORD thy God, and to walk ... Deut 19:9
to *l* the LORD thy God with all ... Deut 30:6
this day to *l* the LORD thy God ... Deut 30:16
thou mayest *l* the LORD thy God ... Deut 30:20
to *l* the LORD your God, and to ... Josh 22:5
that ye *l* the LORD your God ... Josh 23:11
but let them that *l* him be as the ... Judg 5:31
I *l* thee, when thine heart is not ... Judg 16:15
thee, and all his servants *l* thee ... 1Sa 18:22
thy *l* to me was wonderful, ... 2Sa 1:26
passing the *l* of women ... 2Sa 1:26
I *l* Tamar, my brother Absalom's ... 2Sa 13:4
the *l* wherewith he had loved her ... 2Sa 13:15
Solomon clave unto these in *l* ... 1Kin 11:2
*l* them that hate the LORD ... 2Chr 19:2
and mercy for them that *l* him ... Neh 1:5
how long will ye *l* vanity ... Ps 4:2
let them also that *l* thy name be ... Ps 5:11
I will *l* thee, O LORD, my ... Ps 18:1
O *l* the LORD, all ye his saints ... Ps 31:23
let such as *l* thy salvation say ... Ps 40:16
they that *l* his name shall dwell ... Ps 69:36
let such as *l* thy salvation say ... Ps 70:4
Because he hath set his *l* upon me ... Ps 91:14
Ye that *l* the LORD, hate evil ... Ps 97:10
For my *l* they are my adversaries ... Ps 109:4
evil for good, and hatred for my *l* ... Ps 109:5
I *l* the LORD, because he hath ... Ps 116:1
O how *l* I thy law ... Ps 119:97
but thy law do I *l* ... Ps 119:113
therefore I *l* thy testimonies ... Ps 119:119
Therefore I *l* thy commandments ... Ps 119:127
to do unto those that *l* thy name ... Ps 119:132
Consider how I *l* thy precepts ... Ps 119:159
but thy law do I *l* ... Ps 119:163
peace have they which *l* thy law ... Ps 119:165
and I *l* them exceedingly ... Ps 119:167
they shall prosper that *l* thee ... Ps 122:6
preserveth all them that *l* him ... Ps 145:20

simple ones, will ye *l* simplicity Prov 1:22
*l* her, and she shall keep thee Prov 4:6
thou ravished always with her *l* Prov 5:19
our fill of *l* until the morning Prov 7:18
I *l* them that *l* me Prov 8:17
that *l* me to inherit substance Prov 8:21
all they that hate me *l* death Prov 8:36
a wise man, and he will *l* thee Prov 9:8
but *l* covereth all sins Prov 10:12
is a dinner of herbs where *l* is Prov 15:17
they *l* him that speaketh right Prov 16:13
a transgression seeketh *l* Prov 17:9
they that *l* it shall eat the Prov 18:21
*L* not sleep, lest thou come to Prov 20:13
rebuke is better than secret *l* Prov 27:5
A time to *l*, and a time to hate Eccl 3:8
no man knoweth either *l* or hatred Eccl 9:1
Also their *l*, and their hatred, and Eccl 9:6
for thy *l* is better than wine Song 1:2
therefore do the virgins *l* thee Song 1:3
remember thy *l* more than wine Song 1:4
the upright *l* thee Song 1:4
I have compared thee, O my *l* Song 1:9
Behold, thou art fair, my *l* Song 1:15
so is my *l* among the daughters Song 2:2
and his banner over me was *l* Song 2:4
for I am sick of *l* Song 2:5
ye stir not up, nor awake my *l* Song 2:7
and said unto me, Rise up, my *l* Song 2:10
Arise, my *l*, my fair one, and come Song 2:13
ye stir not up, nor awake my *l* Song 3:5
midst thereof being paved with *l* Song 3:10
Behold, thou art fair, my *l* Song 4:1
Thou art all fair, my *l* Song 4:7
How fair is thy *l*, my sister, my Song 4:10
much better is thy *l* than wine Song 4:10
Open to me, my sister, my *l* Song 5:2
ye tell him, that I am sick of *l* Song 5:8
Thou art beautiful, O my *l* Song 6:4
and how pleasant art thou, O *l* Song 7:6
ye stir not up, nor awake my *l* Song 8:4
for *l* is strong as death Song 8:6
Many waters cannot quench *l* Song 8:7
the substance of his house for *l* Song 8:7
but thou hast in *l* to my soul Is 38:17
to *l* the name of the LORD, to be Is 56:6
For I the LORD *l* judgment Is 61:8
in his *l* and in his pity he Is 63:9
glad with her, all ye that *l* her Is 66:10
the *l* of thine espousals, when Jer 2:2
trimmest thou thy way to seek *l* Jer 2:33
my people *l* to have it so Jer 5:31
loved thee with an everlasting *l* Jer 31:3
thy time was the time of *l* Eze 16:8
in her inordinate *l* than she Eze 23:11
came to her into the bed of *l* Eze 23:17
with their mouth they shew much *l* Eze 33:31
tender *l* with the prince of the Dan 1:9
and mercy to them that *l* him Dan 9:4
*l* a woman beloved of her friend, Hos 3:1
according to the *l* of the LORD Hos 3:1
other gods, and *l* flagons of wine Hos 3:1
her rulers with shame do *l* Hos 4:18
mine house, I will *l* them no more Hos 9:15
cords of a man, with bands of *l* Hos 11:4
backsliding, I will *l* them freely Hos 14:4
*l* the good, and establish judgment Amos 5:15
Who hate the good, and *l* the evil Mic 3:2
to *l* mercy, and to walk humbly Mic 6:8
he will rest in his *l*, he will Zeph 3:17
and *l* no false oath Zec 8:17
therefore *l* the truth and peace Zec 8:19
Thou shalt *l* thy neighbour, and Mt 5:43
*L* your enemies, bless them that Mt 5:44
For if ye *l* them which *l* you, Mt 5:46
for they *l* to pray standing in Mt 6:5
will hate the one, and *l* the other Mt 6:24
Thou shalt *l* thy neighbour as Mt 19:19
Thou shalt *l* the Lord thy God Mt 22:37
Thou shalt *l* thy neighbour as Mt 22:39
*l* the uppermost rooms at feasts, Mt 23:6
the *l* of many shall wax cold Mt 24:12
thou shalt *l* the Lord thy God Mk 12:30
Thou shalt *l* thy neighbour as Mk 12:31
to *l* him with all the heart, and Mk 12:33
to *l* his neighbour as himself, is Mk 12:33
which *l* to go in long clothing, Mk 12:38
*l* salutations in the marketplaces Mk 12:38
*L* your enemies, do good to them Lk 6:27
For if ye *l* them which *l* you Lk 6:32
also *l* those that *l* them Lk 6:32
But *l* ye your enemies, and do good Lk 6:35
which of them will *l* him most Lk 7:42
Thou shalt *l* the Lord thy God Lk 10:27
over judgment and the *l* of God Lk 11:42
for ye *l* the uppermost seats in Lk 11:43
will hate the one, and *l* the other Lk 16:13
*l* greetings in the markets, and Lk 20:46
ye have not the *l* of God in you Jn 5:42
were your Father, ye would *l* me Jn 8:42
Therefore doth my Father *l* me Jn 10:17
unto you, That ye *l* one another Jn 13:34
you, that ye also *l* one another Jn 13:34
if ye have *l* one to another Jn 13:35
If ye *l* me, keep my commandments Jn 14:15
of my Father, and I will *l* him Jn 14:21
and said unto him, If a man *l* me Jn 14:23
and my Father will *l* him, and we Jn 14:23
may know that I *l* the Father Jn 14:31
continue ye in my *l* Jn 15:9
ye shall abide in my *l* Jn 15:10
commandments, and abide in his *l* Jn 15:10
That ye *l* one another, as I have Jn 15:12
Greater *l* hath no man than this, Jn 15:13
you, that ye *l* one another Jn 15:17
world, the world would *l* his own Jn 15:19
that the *l* wherewith thou hast Jn 17:26
thou knowest that I *l* thee Jn 21:15
thou knowest that I *l* thee Jn 21:16
thou knowest that I *l* thee Jn 21:17
because the *l* of God is shed Rom 5:5
God commendeth his *l* toward us Rom 5:8
for good to them that *l* God Rom 8:28
separate us from the *l* of Christ Rom 8:35
to separate us from the *l* of God Rom 8:39
Let *l* be without dissimulation Rom 12:9
one to another with brotherly *l* Rom 12:10
any thing, but to *l* one another Rom 13:8
Thou shalt *l* thy neighbour as Rom 13:9
*L* worketh no ill to his neighbour Rom 13:10
therefore *l* is the fulfilling of Rom 13:10
for the *l* of the Spirit, that ye Rom 15:30
hath prepared for them that *l* him 1Cor 2:9
come unto you with a rod, or in *l* 1Cor 4:21
But if any man *l* God, the same is 1Cor 8:3
If any man *l* not the Lord Jesus 1Cor 16:22
My *l* be with you all in Christ 1Cor 16:24
but that ye might know the *l* 2Cor 2:4
would confirm your *l* toward him 2Cor 2:8
For the *l* of Christ constraineth 2Cor 5:14
the Holy Ghost, by *l* unfeigned, 2Cor 6:6
all diligence, and in your *l* to us 2Cor 8:7
to prove the sincerity of your *l* 2Cor 8:8
the churches, the proof of your *l* 2Cor 8:24
because I *l* you not 2Cor 11:11
the more abundantly I *l* you 2Cor 12:15
and the God of *l* and peace shall be 2Cor 13:11
the *l* of God, and the communion of 2Cor 13:14
but faith which worketh by *l* Gal 5:6
but by *l* serve one another Gal 5:13
Thou shalt *l* thy neighbour as Gal 5:14
But the fruit of the Spirit is *l* Gal 5:22
and without blame before him in *l* Eph 1:4
Jesus, and *l* unto all the saints, Eph 1:15
for his great *l* wherewith he Eph 2:4
ye, being rooted and grounded in *l* Eph 3:17
And to know the *l* of Christ Eph 3:19
forbearing one another in *l* Eph 4:2
But speaking the truth in *l* Eph 4:15
unto the edifying of itself in *l* Eph 4:16
And walk in *l*, as Christ also hath Eph 5:2
*l* your wives, even as Christ also Eph 5:25
So ought men to *l* their wives as Eph 5:28
so *l* his wife even as himself Eph 5:33
*l* with faith, from God the Father Eph 6:23
that *l* our Lord Jesus Christ in Eph 6:24
that your *l* may abound yet more Phil 1:9
But the other of *l*, knowing that Phil 1:17
in Christ, if any comfort of *l* Phil 2:1
be likeminded, having the same *l* Phil 2:2
of the *l* which ye have to all the Col 1:4
unto us your *l* in the Spirit Col 1:8
being knit together in *l* Col 2:2
*l* your wives, and be not bitter Col 3:19
work of faith, and labour of *l* 1Th 1:3
abound in *l* one toward another, 1Th 3:12
But as touching brotherly *l* ye 1Th 4:9
taught of God to *l* one another 1Th 4:9
on the breastplate of faith and *l* 1Th 5:8
highly in *l* for their work's sake 1Th 5:13
received not the *l* of the truth 2Th 2:10
your hearts into the *l* of God 2Th 3:5
*l* which is in Christ Jesus 1Ti 1:14
For the *l* of money is the root of 1Ti 6:10
godliness, faith, *l*, patience, 1Ti 6:11
but of power, and of *l*, and of a 2Ti 1:7
*l* which is in Christ Jesus 2Ti 1:13
them also that *l* his appearing 2Ti 4:8
be sober, to *l* their husbands Titus 2:4
to *l* their children Titus 2:4
*l* of God our Saviour toward man Titus 3:4
Greet them that *l* us in the faith Titus 3:15
Hearing of thy *l* and faith, which Philem 5
great joy and consolation in thy *l* Philem 7
forget your work and labour of *l* Heb 6:10
one another to provoke unto *l* Heb 10:24
Let brotherly *l* continue Heb 13:1
hath promised to them that *l* him Jas 1:12
hath promised to them that *l* him Jas 2:5
Thou shalt *l* thy neighbour as Jas 2:8
Whom having not seen, ye *l* 1Pet 1:8
unto unfeigned *l* of the brethren 1Pet 1:22
see that ye *l* one another with a 1Pet 1:22
*L* the brotherhood 1Pet 2:17
*l* as brethren, be pitiful, be 1Pet 3:8
For he that will *l* life, and see 1Pet 3:10
verily is the *l* of God perfected 1Jn 2:5
*L* not the world, neither the 1Jn 2:15
If any man *l* the world 1Jn 2:15
the *l* of the Father is not in him 1Jn 2:15
what manner of *l* the Father hath 1Jn 3:1
that we should *l* one another 1Jn 3:11
because we *l* the brethren 1Jn 3:14
Hereby perceive we the *l* of God 1Jn 3:16
how dwelleth the *l* of God in him 1Jn 3:17
children, let us not *l* in word 1Jn 3:18
*l* one another, as he gave us 1Jn 3:23
Beloved, let us *l* one another 1Jn 4:7
for *l* is of God 1Jn 4:7
for God is *l* 1Jn 4:8
manifested the *l* of God toward us 1Jn 4:9
Herein is *l*, not that we loved 1Jn 4:10
we ought also to *l* one another 1Jn 4:11
If we *l* one another, God dwelleth 1Jn 4:12
us, and his *l* is perfected in us 1Jn 4:12
believed the *l* that God hath to 1Jn 4:16
God is *l* 1Jn 4:16
dwelleth in *l* dwelleth in God 1Jn 4:16
Herein is our *l* made perfect 1Jn 4:17
There is no fear in *l* 1Jn 4:18
but perfect *l* casteth out fear 1Jn 4:18
feareth is not made perfect in *l* 1Jn 4:18
We *l* him, because he first loved 1Jn 4:19
I *l* God, and hateth his brother, 1Jn 4:20
how can he *l* God whom he hath not 1Jn 4:20
who loveth God *l* his brother also 1Jn 4:21
that we *l* the children of God 1Jn 5:2
children of God, when we *l* God 1Jn 5:2
For this is the *l* of God, that we 1Jn 5:3
children, whom I *l* in the truth 2Jn 1
Son of the Father, in truth and *l* 2Jn 3
beginning, that we *l* one another 2Jn 5
And this is *l*, that we walk after 2Jn 6
Gaius, whom I *l* in the truth 3Jn 1
Mercy unto you, and peace, and *l* Jude 2
Keep yourselves in the *l* of God Jude 21
thou hast left thy first *l* Rev 2:4
As many as I *l*, I rebuke and Rev 3:19

## LOVED

his wife; and he *l* her Gen 24:67
And Isaac *l* Esau, because he did Gen 25:28
but Rebekah *l* Jacob Gen 25:28
meat, such as his father *l* Gen 27:14
And Jacob *l* Rachel Gen 29:18
he *l* also Rachel more than Leah, Gen 29:30
he *l* the damsel, and spake kindly Gen 34:3
Now Israel *l* Joseph more than all Gen 37:3
*l* him more than all his brethren Gen 37:4
because he *l* thy fathers, Deut 4:37
But because the LORD *l* you Deut 7:8
because the LORD thy God *l* thee Deut 23:5
Yea, he *l* the people Deut 33:3
that he *l* a woman in the valley Judg 16:4
for he *l* Hannah 1Sa 1:5
and he *l* him greatly 1Sa 16:21
Jonathan *l* him as his own soul 1Sa 18:1
because he *l* him as his own soul 1Sa 18:3
But all Israel and Judah *l* David 1Sa 18:16
And Michal Saul's daughter *l* David 1Sa 18:20
that Michal Saul's daughter *l* him 1Sa 18:28
to swear again, because he *l* him 1Sa 20:17
for he *l* him as he 1Sa 20:17
him as he *l* his own soul 1Sa 20:17
and the LORD *l* him 2Sa 12:24
and Amnon the son of David *l* her 2Sa 13:1
the love wherewith he had *l* her 2Sa 13:15
Solomon *l* the LORD, walking in 1Kin 3:3
the LORD *l* Israel for ever 1Kin 10:9
But king Solomon *l* many strange 1Kin 11:1
the LORD hath *l* his people 2Chr 2:11
because thy God *l* Israel, to 2Chr 9:8
Rehoboam *l* Maachah the daughter 2Chr 11:21
for he *l* husbandry 2Chr 26:10
the king *l* Esther above all the Est 2:17
they whom I *l* are turned against Job 19:19
I have *l* the habitation of thy Ps 26:8
the excellency of Jacob whom he *l* Ps 47:4
Judah, the mount Zion which he *l* Ps 78:68
As he *l* cursing, so let it come Ps 109:17
thy commandments, which I have *l* Ps 119:47
thy commandments, which I have *l* Ps 119:48
been honourable, and I have *l* thee Is 43:4
The LORD hath *l* him Is 48:14
for I have *l* strangers, and after Jer 2:25
host of heaven, whom they have *l* Jer 8:2
Thus have they *l* to wander Jer 14:10
I have *l* thee with an everlasting Jer 31:3
and all them that thou hast *l* Eze 16:37
thou hast *l* a reward upon every Hos 9:1
were according as they *l* Hos 9:10
Israel was a child, then I *l* him Hos 11:1
I have *l* you, saith the LORD Mal 1:2
ye say, Wherein hast thou *l* us Mal 1:2
yet I *l* Jacob, Mal 1:2
holiness of the LORD which he *l* Mal 2:11
Then Jesus beholding him *l* him Mk 10:21
for she *l* much Lk 7:47
For God so *l* the world, that he Jn 3:16
men *l* darkness rather than light, Jn 3:19
Now Jesus *l* Martha, and her sister Jn 11:5
the Jews, Behold how he *l* him Jn 11:36
For they *l* the praise of men more Jn 12:43
having *l* his own which were in Jn 13:1
the world, he *l* them unto the end Jn 13:1
of his disciples, whom Jesus *l* Jn 13:23
as I have *l* you, that ye also Jn 13:34
loveth me shall be *l* of my Father Jn 14:21
If ye *l* me, ye would rejoice, Jn 14:28
hath *l* me, so have I *l* you Jn 15:9
love one another, as I have *l* you Jn 15:12
loveth you, because ye have *l* me Jn 16:27
thou hast sent me, and hast *l* them Jn 17:23
as thou hast *l* me Jn 17:23
thou hast *l* me may be in them Jn 17:26
disciple standing by, whom he *l* Jn 19:26
the other disciple, whom Jesus *l* Jn 20:2
whom Jesus *l* saith unto Peter Jn 21:7
disciple whom Jesus *l* following Jn 21:20
conquerors through him that *l* us Rom 8:37
As it is written, Jacob have I *l* Rom 9:13

I love you, the less I be l ... 2Cor 12:15
faith of the Son of God, who l me ... Gal 2:20
his great love wherewith he l us ... Eph 2:4
in love, as Christ also hath l us ... Eph 5:2
even as Christ also l the church ... Eph 5:25
even our Father, which hath l us ... 2Th 2:16
having l this present world, and ... 2Ti 4:10
Thou hast l righteousness, and ... Heb 1:9
son of Bosor, who l the wages of ... 2Pet 2:15
Herein is love, not that we l God ... 1Jn 4:10
but that he l us ... 1Jn 4:10
Beloved, if God so l us, we ought ... 1Jn 4:11
love him, because he first l us ... 1Jn 4:19
Unto him that l us, and washed us ... Rev 1:5
and to know that I have l thee ... Rev 3:9
they l not their lives unto the ... Rev 12:11

**LOVEDST**
thou l their bed where thou ... Is 57:8
for thou l me before the ... Jn 17:24

**LOVELY**
Saul and Jonathan were l and ... 2Sa 1:23
yea, he is altogether l ... Song 5:16
a very l song of one that hath a ... Eze 33:32
are pure, whatsoever things are l ... Phil 4:8

**LOVER**
for Hiram was ever a l of David ... 1Kin 5:1
L and friend hast thou put far ... Ps 88:18
But a l of hospitality ... Titus 1:8
a l of good men, sober, just, ... Titus 1:8

**LOVERS**
My l and my friends stand aloof ... Ps 38:11
played the harlot with many l ... Jer 3:1
thy l will despise thee, they ... Jer 4:30
for all thy l are destroyed ... Jer 22:20
thy l shall go into captivity ... Jer 22:22
All thy l have forgotten thee ... Jer 30:14
among all her l she hath none to ... Lam 1:2
I called for my l, but they ... Lam 1:19
givest thy gifts to all thy l ... Eze 16:33
through thy whoredoms with thy l ... Eze 16:36
therefore I will gather all thy l ... Eze 16:37
and she doted on her l, on the ... Eze 23:5
her into the hand of her l ... Eze 23:9
will raise up thy l against thee ... Eze 23:22
she said, I will go after my l ... Hos 2:5
And she shall follow after her l ... Hos 2:7
lewdness in the sight of her l ... Hos 2:10
rewards that my l have given me ... Hos 2:12
jewels, and she went after her l ... Hos 2:13
Ephraim hath hired l ... Hos 8:9
For men shall be l of their own ... 2Ti 3:2
l of pleasures more than ... 2Ti 3:4
of pleasures more than l of God ... 2Ti 3:4

**LOVE'S**
Yet for l sake I rather beseech ... Philem 9

**LOVES**
of Korah, A Maschil, A Song of l ... Ps 45:t
let us solace ourselves with l ... Prov 7:18
there will I give thee my l ... Song 7:12

**LOVEST**
thine only son Isaac, whom thou l ... Gen 22:2
dost but hate me, and l me not ... Judg 14:16
In that thou l thine enemies, and ... 2Sa 19:6
Thou l righteousness, and hatest ... Ps 45:7
Thou l evil more than good ... Ps 52:3
Thou l all devouring words, O ... Ps 52:4
with the wife whom thou l all the ... Eccl 9:9
behold, he whom thou l is sick ... Jn 11:3
l thou me more than these ... Jn 21:15
Simon, son of Jonas, l thou me ... Jn 21:16
Simon, son of Jonas, l thou me ... Jn 21:17
him the third time, L thou me ... Jn 21:17

**LOVETH**
meat for thy father, such as he l ... Gen 27:9
his mother, and his father l him ... Gen 44:20
l the stranger, in giving him ... Deut 10:18
because he l thee and thine house, ... Deut 15:16
thy daughter in law, which l thee ... Ruth 4:15
him that l violence his soul ... Ps 11:5
righteous LORD l righteousness ... Ps 11:7
He l righteousness and judgment ... Ps 33:5
l many days, that he may see good ... Ps 34:12
For the LORD l judgment, and ... Ps 37:28
The LORD l the gates of Zion more ... Ps 87:2
king's strength also l judgment ... Ps 99:4
therefore thy servant l it ... Ps 119:140
the LORD l the righteous ... Ps 146:8
For whom the LORD l he correcteth ... Prov 3:12
l instruction l knowledge ... Prov 12:1
but he that l him chasteneth him ... Prov 13:24
but he l him that followeth after ... Prov 15:9
A scorner l not one that ... Prov 15:12
A friend l at all times, and a ... Prov 17:17
He l transgression that ... Prov 17:19
transgression that l strife ... Prov 17:19
getteth wisdom l his own soul ... Prov 19:8
He that l pleasure shall be a ... Prov 21:17
he that l wine and oil shall not ... Prov 21:17
He that l pureness of heart, for ... Prov 22:11
Whoso l wisdom rejoiceth his ... Prov 29:3
He that l silver shall not be ... Eccl 5:10
nor he that l abundance with ... Eccl 5:10
Tell me, O thou whom my soul l ... Song 1:7
bed I sought him whom my soul l ... Song 3:1
I will seek him whom my soul l ... Song 3:2
I said, Saw ye him whom my soul l ... Song 3:3
but I found him whom my soul l ... Song 3:4
every one l gifts, and followeth ... Is 1:23
and l to tread out the corn ... Hos 10:11
he l to oppress ... Hos 12:7
He that l father or mother more ... Mt 10:37
he that l son or daughter more ... Mt 10:37
For he l our nation, and he hath ... Lk 7:5
is forgiven, the same l little ... Lk 7:47
The Father l the Son, and hath ... Jn 3:35
For the Father l the Son, and ... Jn 5:20
He that l his life shall lose it ... Jn 12:25
keepeth them, he it is that l me ... Jn 14:21
he that l me shall be loved of my ... Jn 14:21
He that l me not keepeth not my ... Jn 14:24
For the Father himself l you ... Jn 16:27
for he that l another hath ... Rom 13:8
for God l a cheerful giver ... 2Cor 9:7
He that l his wife l himself ... Eph 5:28
For whom the Lord l he chasteneth ... Heb 12:6
He that l his brother abideth in ... 1Jn 2:10
neither he that l not his brother ... 1Jn 3:10
He that l not his brother abideth ... 1Jn 3:14
every one that l is born of God ... 1Jn 4:7
He that l not knoweth not God ... 1Jn 4:8
for he that l not his brother ... 1Jn 4:20
That he who l God love his ... 1Jn 4:21
every one that l him that begat ... 1Jn 5:1
l him also that is begotten of ... 1Jn 5:1
who l to have the preeminence ... 3Jn 9
and idolaters, and whosoever l ... Rev 22:15

**LOVING**
Let her be as the l hind and ... Prov 5:19
l favour rather than silver and ... Prov 22:1
lying down, l to slumber ... Is 56:10

**LOVINGKINDNESS**
Shew thy marvellous l, O thou ... Ps 17:7
For thy l is before mine eyes ... Ps 26:3
How excellent is thy l, O God ... Ps 36:7
O continue thy l unto them that ... Ps 36:10
I have not concealed thy l ... Ps 40:10
let thy l and thy truth ... Ps 40:11
will command his l in the daytime ... Ps 42:8
We have thought of thy l, O God, ... Ps 48:9
me, O God, according to thy l ... Ps 51:1
Because thy l is better than life ... Ps 63:3
for thy l is good ... Ps 69:16
Shall thy l be declared in the ... Ps 88:11
Nevertheless my l will I not ... Ps 89:33
shew forth thy l in the morning ... Ps 92:2
who crowneth thee with l and ... Ps 103:4
understand the l of the LORD ... Ps 107:43
Quicken me after thy l ... Ps 119:88
my voice according unto thy l ... Ps 119:149
me, O LORD, according to thy l ... Ps 119:159
and praise thy name for thy l ... Ps 138:2
me to hear thy l in the morning ... Ps 143:8
I am the LORD which exercise l ... Jer 9:24
people, saith the LORD, even l ... Jer 16:5
therefore with l have I drawn ... Jer 31:3
Thou shewest l unto thousands, and ... Jer 32:18
and in judgment, and in l, and in ... Hos 2:19

**LOVINGKINDNESSES**
LORD, thy tender mercies and thy l ... Ps 25:6
Lord, where are thy former l ... Ps 89:49
I will mention the l of the LORD ... Is 63:7
to the multitude of his l ... Is 63:7

**LOW**
and thou shalt come down very l ... Deut 28:43
thou hast brought me very l ... Judg 11:35
he bringeth l, and lifteth up ... 1Sa 2:7
the l plains was Baal-hanan the ... 1Chr 27:28
are in the l plains in abundance ... 2Chr 9:27
cattle, both in the l country ... 2Chr 26:10
the cities of the l country ... 2Chr 28:18
For the LORD brought Judah l ... 2Chr 28:19
To set up on high those that be l ... Job 5:11
and they are brought l, but he ... Job 14:21
while, but are gone and brought l ... Job 24:24
one that is proud, and bring him l ... Job 40:12
Both l and high, rich and poor, ... Ps 49:2
Surely men of l degree are vanity ... Ps 62:9
for we are brought very l ... Ps 79:8
were brought l for their iniquity ... Ps 106:43
brought l through oppression, ... Ps 107:39
I was brought l, and he helped me ... Ps 116:6
Who remembered us in our l estate ... Ps 136:23
for I am brought very l ... Ps 142:6
A man's pride shall bring him l ... Prov 29:23
and the rich sit in l place ... Eccl 10:6
the sound of the grinding is l ... Eccl 12:4
of musick shall be brought l ... Eccl 12:4
and he shall be brought l ... Is 2:12
of men shall be made l ... Is 2:17
will lay l the haughtiness of the ... Is 13:11
terrible ones shall be brought l ... Is 25:5
walls shall he bring down, lay l ... Is 25:12
the lofty city, he layeth it l ... Is 26:5
he layeth it l, even to the ... Is 26:5
speech shall be l out of the dust ... Is 29:4
city shall be l in a l place ... Is 32:19
city shall be l in a l place ... Is 32:19
mountain and hill shall be made l ... Is 40:4
O LORD, out of the l dungeon ... Lam 3:55
a spreading vine of l stature ... Eze 17:6
tree, have exalted the l tree ... Eze 17:24
exalt him that is l, and abase him ... Eze 21:26
thee in the l parts of the earth ... Eze 26:20
the l estate of his handmaiden ... Lk 1:48
and exalted them of l degree ... Lk 1:52
and hill shall be brought l ... Lk 3:5
but condescend to men of l estate ... Rom 12:16
Let the brother of l degree ... Jas 1:9
the rich, in that he is made l ... Jas 1:10

**LOWER**
with l, second, and third stories ... Gen 6:16
it be in sight l than the skin ... Lev 13:20
if it be not l than the skin, but ... Lev 13:21
it be no l than the other skin, ... Lev 13:26
in sight are l than the wall ... Lev 14:37
I in the l places behind the wall ... Neh 4:13
him a little l than the angels ... Ps 8:5
shall go into the l parts of the ... Ps 63:9
l in the presence of the prince ... Prov 25:7
together the waters of the l pool ... Is 22:9
shout, ye l parts of the earth ... Is 44:23
of the gates was the l pavement ... Eze 40:18
from the forefront of the l gate ... Eze 40:19
higher than these, than the l ... Eze 42:5
the l settle shall be two cubits ... Eze 43:14
into the l parts of the earth ... Eph 4:9
him a little l than the angels ... Heb 2:7
who was made a little l than the ... Heb 2:9

**LOWEST**
and shall burn unto the l hell ... Deut 32:22
priests of the l of the people ... 1Kin 12:31
but made again of the l of the ... 1Kin 13:33
the l of them priests of the high ... 2Kin 17:32
delivered my soul from the l hell ... Ps 86:13
Thou hast laid me in the l pit ... Ps 88:6
in the l parts of the earth ... Ps 139:15
so increased from the l chamber ... Eze 41:7
was straitened more than the l ... Eze 42:6
with shame to take the l room ... Lk 14:9
go and sit down in the l room ... Lk 14:10

**LOWETH**
or l the ox over his fodder ... Job 6:5

**LOWINESS**
but in l of mind let each esteem ... Phil 2:3

**LOWING**
l as they went, and turned not ... 1Sa 6:12
the l of the oxen which I hear ... 1Sa 15:14

**LOWLINESS**
With all l and meekness, with ... Eph 4:2

**LOWLY**
yet hath he respect unto the l ... Ps 138:6
but he giveth grace unto the l ... Prov 3:34
but with the l is wisdom ... Prov 11:2
be of an humble spirit with the l ... Prov 16:19
l, and riding upon an ass, and upon ... Zec 9:9
for I am meek and l in heart ... Mt 11:29

**LOWRING**
for the sky is red and l ... Mt 16:3

**LUBIM** (*lu'-bim*) See LUBIMS. *An African race.*
the L, the Sukkiims, and the ... 2Chr 12:3
Put and L were thy helpers ... Nah 3:9

**LUBIMS** (*lu'-bims*) See LEHABIM, LUBIM. *Same as Lubim.*
the L a huge host, with very many ... 2Chr 16:8

**LUCAS** (*lu'-cas*) See LUKE. *Same as Luke.*
city of Macedonia, by Titus and L ... 2Cor s
Marcus, Aristarchus, Demas, L ... Philem 24

**LUCIFER** (*lu'-sif-ur*) *Title applied to king of Babylon.*
art thou fallen from heaven, O L ... Is 14:12

**LUCIUS** (*lu'-she-us*)
*1. A Christian from Cyrene.*
L of Cyrene, and Manaen, which had ... Acts 13:1
*2. A relative of Paul.*
Timotheus my workfellow, and L ... Rom 16:21

**LUCRE**
ways, but turned aside after l ... 1Sa 8:3
striker, not greedy of filthy l ... 1Ti 3:3
much wine, not greedy of filthy l ... 1Ti 3:8
no striker, not given to filthy l ... Titus 1:7
not for filthy l, but of a ready ... 1Pet 5:2

**LUCRE'S**
they ought not, for filthy l sake ... Titus 1:11

**LUD** (*lud*) See LUDIM, LYDIA.
*1. Son of Shem.*
and Asshur, and Arphaxad, and L ... Gen 10:22
and Asshur, and Arphaxad, and L ... 1Chr 1:17
*2. Descendants of Lud 1.*
nations, to Tarshish, Pul, and L ... Is 66:19
They of Persia and of L and of Phut ... Eze 27:10

**LUDIM** (*lu'-dim*) See LUD. *Son of Mizraim.*
And Mizraim begat L ... Gen 10:13
And Mizraim begat L ... 1Chr 1:11

**LUHITH** (*lu'-hith*) *A Moabite city.*
for by the mounting up of L with ... Is 15:5
For in the going up of L ... Jer 48:5

**LUKE** (*luke*) See LUCAS. *A companion of Paul.*
L, the beloved physician, and ... Col 4:14
Only L is with me ... 2Ti 4:11

L

**LUKEWARM**
So then because thou art *l* ... Rev 3:16

**LUMP**
And Isaiah said, Take a *l* of figs ... 2Kin 20:7
said, Let them take a *l* of figs ... Is 38:21
of the same *l* to make one vessel ... Rom 9:21
be holy, the *l* is also holy ... Rom 11:16
leaven leaveneth the whole *l* ... 1Cor 5:6
leaven, that ye may be a new *l* ... 1Cor 5:7
leaven leaveneth the whole *l* ... Gal 5:9

**LUNATICK**
devils, and those which were *l* ... Mt 4:24
for he is *l*, and sore vexed ... Mt 17:15

**LURK**
let us *l* privily for the innocent ... Prov 1:11
they *l* privily for their own ... Prov 1:18

**LURKING**
take knowledge of all the *l* ... 1Sa 23:23
He sitteth in the *l* places of the ... Ps 10:8
a young lion *l* in secret places ... Ps 17:12

**LUST**
my *l* shall be satisfied upon them ... Ex 15:9
heart by asking meat for their *l* ... Ps 78:18
were not estranged from their *l* ... Ps 78:30
them up unto their own hearts' *l* ... Ps 81:12
*L* not after her beauty in thine ... Prov 6:25
to *l* after her hath committed ... Mt 5:28
burned in their *l* one toward ... Rom 1:27
for I had not known *l*, except the ... Rom 7:7
we should not *l* after evil things ... 1Cor 10:6
not fulfil the *l* of the flesh ... Gal 5:16
Not in the *l* of concupiscence, ... 1Th 4:5
he is drawn away of his own *l* ... Jas 1:14
Then when *l* hath conceived, it ... Jas 1:15
Ye *l*, and have not ... Jas 4:2
that is in the world through *l* ... 2Pet 1:4
the flesh in the *l* of uncleanness ... 2Pet 2:10
the *l* of the flesh ... 1Jn 2:16
the *l* of the eyes, and the pride ... 1Jn 2:16
passeth away, and the *l* thereof ... 1Jn 2:17

**LUSTED**
they buried the people that *l* ... Num 11:34
But *l* exceedingly in the ... Ps 106:14
after evil things, as they also *l* ... 1Cor 10:6
the fruits that thy soul *l* after ... Rev 18:14

**LUSTETH**
whatsoever thy soul *l* after ... Deut 12:15
whatsoever thy soul *l* after ... Deut 12:20
gates whatsoever thy soul *l* after ... Deut 12:21
for whatsoever thy soul *l* after ... Deut 14:26
For the flesh *l* against the ... Gal 5:17
that dwelleth in us *l* to envy ... Jas 4:5

**LUSTING**
that was among them fell a *l* ... Num 11:4

**LUSTS**
the *l* of other things entering in ... Mk 4:19
the *l* of your father ye will do ... Jn 8:44
through the *l* of their own hearts ... Rom 1:24
should obey it in the *l* thereof ... Rom 6:12
flesh, to fulfil the *l* thereof ... Rom 13:14
flesh with the affections and *l* ... Gal 5:24
times past in the *l* of our flesh ... Eph 2:3
according to the deceitful *l* ... Eph 4:22
and into many foolish and hurtful *l* ... 1Ti 6:9
Flee also youthful *l* ... 2Ti 2:22
with sins, led away with divers *l* ... 2Ti 3:6
but after their own *l* shall they ... 2Ti 4:3
denying ungodliness and worldly *l* ... Titus 2:12
deceived, serving divers *l* ... Titus 3:3
even of your *l* that war in your ... Jas 4:1
ye may consume it upon your *l* ... Jas 4:3
to the former *l* in your ignorance ... 1Pet 1:14
pilgrims, abstain from fleshly *l* ... 1Pet 2:11
time in the flesh to the *l* of men ... 1Pet 4:2
we walked in lasciviousness, *l* ... 1Pet 4:3
allure through the *l* of the flesh ... 2Pet 2:18
walking after their own *l* ... 2Pet 3:3
walking after their own *l* ... Jude 16
walk after their own ungodly *l* ... Jude 18

**LUSTY**
about ten thousand men, all *l* ... Judg 3:29

**LUZ** (*luz*) See BETH-EL.
*1. A Canaanite city.*
city was called *L* at the first ... Gen 28:19
So Jacob came to *L*, which is in ... Gen 35:6
me at *L* in the land of Canaan ... Gen 48:3
And goeth out from Beth-el to *L* ... Josh 16:2
toward *L*, to the side of *L* ... Josh 18:13
the name of the city before was *L* ... Judg 1:23
*2. A Hittite city.*
and called the name thereof *L* ... Judg 1:26

**LYCAONIA** (*li-ca-o'-ne-ah*) *A Roman province in Asia Minor.*
unto Lystra and Derbe, cities of *L* ... Acts 14:6
voices, saying in the speech of *L* ... Acts 14:11

**LYCAONIAN**

**LYCIA** (*lish'-e-ah*) *A Roman province in Asia Minor.*
we came to Myra, a city of *L* ... Acts 27:5

**LYDDA** (*lid'-dah*) See LOD. *A city in Judea.*
to the saints which dwelt at *L* ... Acts 9:32
And all that dwelt at *L* and Saron ... Acts 9:35
forasmuch as *L* was nigh to Joppa, ... Acts 9:38

**LYDIA** (*lid'-e-ah*) See LUDIM, LYDIANS.
*1. A people in North Africa.*
Ethiopia, and Libya, and *L*, and all ... Eze 30:5
*2. A Christian woman.*
And a certain woman named *L* ... Acts 16:14
and entered into the house of *L* ... Acts 16:40

**LYDIANS** (*lid'-e-uns*) *Same as Lydia 1.*
and the *L*, that handle and bend the ... Jer 46:9

**LYING**
three flocks of sheep *l* by it ... Gen 29:2
Israel in *l* with Jacob's daughter ... Gen 34:7
hateth thee *l* under his burden ... Ex 23:5
that hath known man by *l* with him. Num 31:17
not known a man by *l* with him ... Num 31:18
had not known man by *l* with him ... Num 31:35
*l* in the field, and it be not ... Deut 21:1
If a man be found *l* with a woman ... Deut 22:22
were with him, from *l* in wait ... Judg 9:35
Now there were men *l* in wait ... Judg 16:9
known no man by *l* with any male ... Judg 21:12
I will be a *l* spirit in the mouth ... 1Kin 22:22
the LORD hath put a *l* spirit in ... 1Kin 22:23
be a *l* spirit in the mouth of all ... 2Chr 18:21
the LORD hath put a *l* spirit in ... 2Chr 18:22
hated them that regard *l* vanities ... Ps 31:6
Let the *l* lips be put to silence ... Ps 31:18
and *l* rather than to speak ... Ps 52:3
for cursing and *l* which they speak ... Ps 59:12
spoken against me with a *l* tongue ... Ps 109:2
Remove from me the way of *l* ... Ps 119:29
I hate and abhor *l* ... Ps 119:163
my soul, O LORD, from *l* lips ... Ps 120:2
my *l* down, and art acquainted with ... Ps 139:3
a *l* tongue, and hands that shed ... Prov 6:17
He that hideth hatred with *l* lips ... Prov 10:18
but a *l* tongue is but for a ... Prov 12:19
*L* lips are abomination to the ... Prov 12:22
A righteous man hateth *l* ... Prov 13:5
much less do *l* lips a prince ... Prov 17:7
a *l* tongue is a vanity tossed to ... Prov 21:6
A *l* tongue hateth those that are ... Prov 26:28
*l* children, children that will ... Is 30:9
to destroy the poor with *l* words ... Is 32:7
*l* down, loving to slumber ... Is 56:10
*l* against the LORD, and departing ... Is 59:13
Trust ye not in *l* words, saying, ... Jer 7:4
Behold, ye trust in *l* words ... Jer 7:8
have spoken *l* words in my name, ... Jer 29:23
was unto me as a bear *l* in wait ... Lam 3:10
*l* divination, saying, The LORD ... Eze 13:6
have ye not spoken a *l* divination ... Eze 13:7
by your *l* to my people that hear ... Eze 13:19
for ye have prepared *l* and corrupt ... Dan 2:9
By swearing, and *l*, and killing, and ... Hos 4:2
They that observe *l* vanities ... Jonah 2:8
man sick of the palsy, *l* on a bed ... Mt 9:2
in where the damsel was *l* ... Mk 5:40
swaddling clothes, *l* in a manger ... Lk 2:12
Joseph, and the babe *l* in a manger ... Lk 2:16
He then *l* on Jesus' breast saith ... Jn 13:25
in, saw the linen clothes *l* ... Jn 20:5
not *l* with the linen clothes, but ... Jn 20:7
me by the *l* in wait of the Jews ... Acts 20:19
son heard of their *l* in wait ... Acts 23:16
Wherefore putting away *l*, speak ... Eph 4:25
all power and signs and *l* wonders, ... 2Th 2:9

**LYSANIAS** (*li-sa'-ne-as*) *Governor of Abilene.*
*L* the tetrarch of Abilene, ... Lk 3:1

**LYSIAS** (*lis'-e-as*) *A Roman commander.*
Claudius *L* unto the most ... Acts 23:26
the chief captain *L* came upon us ... Acts 24:7
When *L* the chief captain shall ... Acts 24:22

**LYSTRA** (*lis'-trah*) *A city in Lycaonia.*
were ware of it, and fled unto *L* ... Acts 14:6
And there sat a certain man at *L* ... Acts 14:8
many, they returned again to *L* ... Acts 14:21
Then came he to Derbe and *L* ... Acts 16:1
of by the brethren that were at *L* ... Acts 16:2
me at Antioch, at Iconium, at *L* ... 2Ti 3:11

# M

**MAACAH** (*ma'-a-kah*) See MAACHAH.
*1. A wife of David.*
Absalom the son of *M* the daughter ... 2Sa 3:3
*2. A king of Maacah 3.*
of king *M* a thousand men, and of ... 2Sa 10:6
*3. A district of Syria.*
and of Rehob, and Ish-tob, and *M* ... 2Sa 10:8

**MAACATHITE** See MAACHATHITE.

**MAACHAH** (*ma'-a-kah*) See BETH-MAACHAH, MAACAH, MAACHATHITE, SYRIA-MAACHAH.
*1. A son of Nahor.*
and Gaham, and Thahash, and *M* ... Gen 22:24
*2. Father of Achish.*
unto Achish son of *M* king of Gath ... 1Kin 2:39
*3. Wife of King Rehoboam.*
And his mother's name was *M* ... 1Kin 15:2
And his mother's name was *M* ... 1Kin 15:10
after her he took *M* the daughter ... 2Chr 11:20
Rehoboam loved *M* the daughter of .. 2Chr 11:21
Abijah the son of *M* the chief ... 2Chr 11:22
*4. Mother of King Asa.*
also *M* his mother, even her he ... 1Kin 15:13
also concerning *M* the mother of ... 2Chr 15:16
*5. Concubine of Caleb.*
*M*, Caleb's concubine, bare Sheber ... 1Chr 2:48
*6. A wife of David.*
Absalom the son of *M* the daughter ... 1Chr 3:2
*7. A wife of Machir.*
whose sister's name was *M* ... 1Chr 7:15
*M* the wife of Machir bare a son, ... 1Chr 7:16
*8. Wife of Jehiel.*
whose wife's name was *M* ... 1Chr 8:29
Jehiel, whose wife's name was *M* ... 1Chr 9:35
*9. Father of Hanan.*
Hanan the son of *M*, and Joshaphat .. 1Chr 11:43
*10.A district of Syria.*
chariots, and the king of *M* ... 1Chr 19:7
*11. Father of Shephatiah.*
Shephatiah the son of *M* ... 1Chr 27:16

**MAACHATHI** (*ma-ak'-a-thi*) See MAACHATHITE. *Inhabitants of Maachah 10.*
unto the coasts of Geshuri and *M* ... Deut 3:14

**MAACHATHITE** (*ma-ak'-a-thite*) See MAACHATHI, MAACHATHITES. *Same as Maachathi.*
son of Ahasbai, the son of the *M* ... 2Sa 23:34
and Jaazaniah the son of a *M* ... 2Kin 25:23
the Garmite, and Eshtemoa the *M* ... 1Chr 4:19
and Jezaniah the son of a *M* ... Jer 40:8

**MAACHATHITES**
border of the Geshurites and the *M* ... Josh 12:5
the border of the Geshurites and *M* ... Josh 13:11
not the Geshurites, nor the *M* ... Josh 13:13
the *M* dwell among the Israelites ... Josh 13:13

**MAADAI** (*ma'-a-dahee*) *Married a foreigner in exile.*
*M*, Amram, and Uel, ... Ezr 10:34

**MAADIAH** (*ma-a-di'-ah*) See MOADIAH. *A priest with Zerubbabel.*
Miamin, *M*, Bilgah, ... Neh 12:5

**MAAI** (*ma'-ahee*) *A priest.*
and Azarael, Milalai, Gilalai, *M* ... Neh 12:36

**MAALEH-ACRABBIM** (*ma'-a-leh-ac-rab'-bim*) See AKRABBIM. *A pass on Judah's southern border.*
went out to the south side to *M* ... Josh 15:3

**MAARATH** (*ma'-a-rath*) *A city in Judah.*
And *M*, and Beth-anoth, and Eltekon Josh 15:59

**MAAREH-GEBA**

**MAASAI** See MAASIAI.

**MAASEIAH** (*ma-a-si'-ah*)
*1. A priest who relocated the Ark.*
and Unni, Eliab, and Benaiah, and *M* 1Chr 15:18
Jehiel, and Unni, and Eliab, and *M* ... 1Chr 15:20
*2. Son of Adaiah.*
Obed, and *M* the son of Adaiah, and ... 2Chr 23:1
*3. An officer of King Uzziah.*
*M* the ruler, under the hand of ... 2Chr 26:11
*4. A son of King Ahaz.*
slew *M* the king's son, and Azrikam ... 2Chr 28:7
*5. A governor of Jerusalem.*
*M* the governor of the city, and ... 2Chr 34:8
*6. A priest who married a foreigner.*
*M*, and Eliezer, and Jarib, and ... Ezr 10:18
*7. A priest of the Harim family.*
*M*, and Elijah, and Shemaiah, and ... Ezr 10:21
*8. A priest of the Pashur family.*
Elioenai, *M*, Ishmael, Nethaneel, ... Ezr 10:22
*9. A priest of the Pahath-moab family.*
Adna, and Chelal, Benaiah, *M* ... Ezr 10:30
*10. Father of Azariah.*
*M* the son of Ananiah by his house ... Neh 3:23
*11. A priest with Ezra.*
and Urijah, and Hilkiah, and *M* ... Neh 8:4
*12. Another priest with Ezra.*
Akkub, Shabbethai, Hodijah, *M* ... Neh 8:7
*13. An Israelite who renewed the covenant.*
Rehum, Hashabnah, *M*, ... Neh 10:25
*14. A family of exiles.*
*M* the son of Baruch, the son of ... Neh 11:5
*15. A descendant of Benjamin.*
the son of Kolaiah, the son of *M* ... Neh 11:7
*16. A priest who dedicated the wall.*
Eliakim, *M*, Miniamin, Michaiah, ... Neh 12:41
*17. Another priest who dedicated the wall.*
*M*, and Shemaiah ... Neh 12:42
*18. Father of Zephaniah.*
Zephaniah the son of *M* the priest ... Jer 21:1
Zephaniah the son of *M* the priest ... Jer 29:25
Zephaniah the son of *M* the priest ... Jer 37:3
*19. Father of Zedekiah.*
and of Zedekiah the son of *M* ... Jer 29:21
*20. A Temple officer.*
chamber of *M* the son of Shallum ... Jer 35:4
*21. Grandfather of Baruch.*
the son of Neriah, the son of *M* ... Jer 32:12
the son of Neriah, the son of *M* ... Jer 51:59

**MAASIAI** (*ma-a'-see-ahee*) *A family of exiles.*
*M* the son of Adiel, the son of ............. 1Chr 9:12

**MAATH** (*ma'-ath*) *Father of Nagge; ancestor of Jesus.*
Which was the son of *M*, which was ...... Lk 3:26

**MAAZ** (*ma'-az*) *A son of Ram.*
firstborn of Jerahmeel were, *M*............ 1Chr 2:27

**MAAZIAH** (*ma-a-zi'-ah*)
*1. A sanctuary servant.*
the four and twentieth to *M*............... 1Chr 24:18
*2. A priest who renewed the covenant.*
*M*, Bilgai, Shemaiah ............................ Neh 10:8

**MACBENNAH** See MACHBENAH.

**MACEDONIA** (*mas-e-do'-nee-ah*) See MACEDONIAN. *A Roman province north of Greece.*
There stood a man of *M*, and prayed... Acts 16:9
him, saying, Come over into *M*............ Acts 16:9
we endeavoured to go into *M*............... Acts 16:10
the chief city of that part of *M*.......... Acts 16:12
and Timotheus were come from *M*...... Acts 18:5
when he had passed through *M*.......... Acts 19:21
So he sent into *M* two of them .......... Acts 19:22
Gaius and Aristarchus, men of *M*....... Acts 19:29
and departed for to go into *M*............ Acts 20:1
he purposed to return through *M*........ Acts 20:3
For it hath pleased them of *M*........... Rom 15:26
you, when I shall pass through *M*........ 1Cor 16:5
for I do pass through *M*....................... 1Cor 16:5
And to pass by you into *M*.................. 2Cor 1:16
to come again out of *M* unto you ....... 2Cor 1:16
them, I went from thence into *M*.......... 2Cor 2:13
For, when we were come into *M*........... 2Cor 7:5
God bestowed on the churches of *M*...... 2Cor 8:1
which I boast of you to them of *M*....... 2Cor 9:2
haply if they of *M* come with me.......... 2Cor 9:4
which came from *M* supplied.............. 2Cor 11:9
from Philippi, a city of *M*........................ 2Cor *s*
gospel, when I departed from *M*........... Phil 4:15
to all that believe in *M* and ..................... 1Th 1:7
word of the Lord not only in *M*.................. 1Th 1:8
the brethren which are in all *M*............. 1Th 4:10
at Ephesus, when I went into *M*.................. 1Ti 1:3
the Cretians, from Nicopolis of *M*.......... Titus *s*

**MACEDONIAN** (*mas-e-do'-nee-an*) *An inhabitant of Macedonia.*
a *M* of Thessalonica, being with .......... Acts 27:2

**MACHBANAI** (*mak'-ba-nahee*) *A warrior in David's army.*
the tenth, *M* the eleventh .................... 1Chr 12:13

**MACHBANNAI** See MACEBANAI.

**MACHBENA** See MACHBENAH.

**MACHBENAH** (*mak'-be-nah*) *A descendant of Caleb.*
Madmannah, Sheva the father of *M*.... 1Chr 2:49

**MACHI** (*ma'-ki*) *Father of Geuel.*
tribe of Gad, Geuel the son of *M*......... Num 13:15

**MACHIR** (*ma'-kur*) See MACHIRITE.
*1. Son of Manasseh.*
the children also of *M* the son of......... Gen 50:23
of *M*, the family of the......................... Num 26:29
and *M* begat Gilead .............................. Num 26:29
the son of Gilead, the son of *M*............ Num 27:1
the children of *M* the son of................ Num 32:39
Gilead unto *M* the son of Manasseh.. Num 32:40
children of Gilead, the son of *M*.......... Num 36:1
And I gave Gilead unto *M*................... Deut 3:15
children of *M* the son of Manasseh.... Josh 13:31
children of *M* by their families........... Josh 13:31
for *M* the firstborn of Manasseh,.......... Josh 17:1
the son of Gilead, the son of *M*............. Josh 17:3
out of *M* came down governors, and... Judg 5:14
of *M* the father of Gilead ..................... 1Chr 2:21
sons of *M* the father of Gilead ............ 1Chr 2:23
bare *M* the father of Gilead ................. 1Chr 7:14
*M* took to wife the sister of.................. 1Chr 7:15
Maachah the wife of *M* bare a son...... 1Chr 7:16
the sons of Gilead, the son of *M*.......... 1Chr 7:17
*2. Son of Ammiel.*
Behold, he is in the house of *M*.................. 2Sa 9:4
fetched him out of the house of *M*.............. 2Sa 9:5
*M* the son of Ammiel of Lo-debar,......... 2Sa 17:27

**MACHIRITES** (*ma'-kur-ites*) *Descendants of Machir 1.*
of Machir, the family of the *M*........... Num 26:29

**MACHNADEBAI** (*mak-nad'-e-bahee*) *Married a foreigner in exile.*
*M*, Shashai, Sharai,............................. Ezr 10:40

**MACHPELAH** (*mak-pe'-lah*) *Burial place of Abraham.*
That he may give me the cave of *M*..... Gen 23:9
field of Ephron, which was in *M*.......... Gen 23:17
of the field of *M* before Mamre........... Gen 23:19
buried him in the cave of *M*................ Gen 25:9
cave that is in the field of *M*.............. Gen 49:30
him in the cave of the field of *M*.......... Gen 50:13

**MAD**
So that thou shalt be *m* for the.......... Deut 28:34
feigned himself *m* in their hands......... 1Sa 21:13
servants, Lo, ye see the man is *m*........... 1Sa 21:14
Have I need of *m* men, that ye............. 1Sa 21:15
to play the *m* man in my presence....... 1Sa 21:15
came this *m* fellow to thee..................... 2Kin 9:11
they that are *m* against me are.............. Ps 102:8
As a *m* man who casteth firebrands.. Prov 26:18
I said of laughter, It is *m*....................... Eccl 2:2
oppression maketh a wise man *m*........... Eccl 7:7
the liars, and maketh diviners *m*............. Is 44:25
shall drink, and be moved, and be *m*.... Jer 25:16
the LORD, for every man that is *m*........ Jer 29:26
they are *m* upon their idols................... Jer 50:38
therefore the nations are *m*........................ Jer 51:7
is a fool, the spiritual man is *m*............... Hos 9:7
said, He hath a devil, and is *m*................ Jn 10:20
And they said unto her, Thou art *m*.. Acts 12:15
being exceedingly *m* against them...... Acts 26:11
much learning doth make thee *m*....... Acts 26:24
But he said, I am not *m*, most............ Acts 26:25
will they not say that ye are *m*............ 1Cor 14:23

**MADAI** (*ma'-dahee*) See MEDE, MEDIA. *Son of Japheth.*
Gomer, and Magog, and *M*..................... Gen 10:2
Gomer, and Magog, and *M*, and Javan, 1Chr 1:5

**MADE** See PREFACE.

**MADEST**
*m* a covenant with him to give the......... Neh 9:8
*m* known unto them thy holy................ Neh 9:14
Thou *m* him to have dominion over........... Ps 8:6
that thou *m* strong for thyself................ Ps 80:15
whom thou *m* strong for thyself.............. Ps 80:17
*m* to thyself images of men, and.......... Eze 16:17
*m* all their loins to be at a..................... Eze 29:7
not laboured, neither *m* it grow .......... Jonah 4:10
before these days *m* an uproar........... Acts 21:38
Thou *m* him a little lower than............... Heb 2:7

**MADIAN** (*ma'-de-an*) See MIDIAN. *Same as Midian 2.*
was a stranger in the land of *M*............ Acts 7:29

**MADMANNAH** (*mad-man'-nah*)
*1. A city in Judah.*
And Ziklag, and *M*, and Sansannah,.. Josh 15:31
*2. Grandson of Caleb.*
bare also Shaaph the father of *M*......... 1Chr 2:49

**MADMEN** (*mad'-men*) See MADMENAH. *A Moabite city.*
Also thou shalt be cut down, O *M*........... Jer 48:2

**MADMENAH** (*mad-me'-nah*) See MADMEN. *A city in Benjamin.*
*M* is removed............................................ Is 10:31

**MADNESS**
The LORD shall smite thee with *m*..... Deut 28:28
to know wisdom, and to know *m*............. Eccl 1:17
myself to behold wisdom, and *m*............ Eccl 2:12
folly, even of foolishness and *m*.............. Eccl 7:25
*m* is in their heart while they.................... Eccl 9:3
end of his talk is mischievous *m*.......... Eccl 10:13
astonishment, and his rider with *m*....... Zec 12:4
And they were filled with *m*........................ Lk 6:11
voice forbad the *m* of the prophet........ 2Pet 2:16

**MADON** (*ma'-don*) *A Canaanite city.*
that he sent to Jobab king of *M*............. Josh 11:1
The king of *M*, one.............................. Josh 12:19

**MAGADAN** See MAGDALA.

**MAGBISH** (*mag'-bish*) *A family of exiles.*
The children of *M*, an hundred................ Ezr 2:30

**MAGDALA** (*mag'-da-lah*) See MAGDALENE. *A city in Galilee.*
and came into the coasts of *M*.............. Mt 15:39

**MAGDALENE** (*mag'-da-leen*) *A woman acquaintance of Jesus.*
Among which was Mary *M*, and Mary. Mt 27:56
And there was Mary *M*, and the other. Mt 27:61
day of the week, came Mary *M*............... Mt 28:1
among whom was Mary *M*, and Mary. Mk 15:40
And Mary *M* and Mary the mother of. Mk 15:47
when the sabbath was past, Mary *M*...... Mk 16:1
week, he appeared first to Mary *M*........ Mk 16:9
and infirmities, Mary called *M*...................... Lk 8:2
It was Mary *M*, and Joanna, and Mary Lk 24:10
the wife of Cleophas, and Mary *M*.......... Jn 19:25
of the week cometh Mary *M* early............ Jn 20:1
Mary *M* came and told the disciples...... Jn 20:18

**MAGDIEL** (*mag'-de-el*) *A duke of Edom.*
Duke *M*, duke Iram ............................. Gen 36:43
Duke *M*, duke Iram ............................... 1Chr 1:54

**MAGICIAN**
that asked such things at any *m*........... Dan 2:10

**MAGICIANS**
and called for all the *m* of Egypt............ Gen 41:8
and I told this unto the *m*...................... Gen 41:24
now the *m* of Egypt, they also did............ Ex 7:11
the *m* of Egypt did so with their............. Ex 7:22
And the *m* did so with their ....................... Ex 8:7
And the *m* did so with their....................... Ex 8:18
Then the *m* said unto Pharaoh,................ Ex 8:19
the *m* could not stand before..................... Ex 9:11
for the boil was upon the *m*........................ Ex 9:11
ten times better than all the *m*................ Dan 1:20
the king commanded to call the *m*.......... Dan 2:2
wise men, the astrologers, the *m*............ Dan 2:27
Then came in the *m*, the ........................... Dan 4:7
O Belteshazzar, master of the *m*............. Dan 4:9
thy father, made master of the *m*......... Dan 5:11

**MAGISTRATE**
and there was no *m* in the land........... Judg 18:7
with thine adversary to the *m*................. Lk 12:58

**MAGISTRATES**
God, that is in thine hand, set *m*........... Ezr 7:25
unto the synagogues, and unto *m*............ Lk 12:11
And brought them to the *m*, saying,.. Acts 16:20
the *m* rent off their clothes, and......... Acts 16:22
the *m* sent the serjeants, saying,........ Acts 16:35
The *m* have sent to let you go ........... Acts 16:36
told these words unto the *m*................ Acts 16:38
and powers, to obey *m*, to be ready...... Titus 3:1

**MAGNIFICAL**
for the LORD must be exceeding *m*...... 1Chr 22:5

**MAGNIFICENCE**
her *m* should be destroyed, whom...... Acts 19:27

**MAGNIFIED**
sight, and thou hast *m* thy mercy....... Gen 19:19
On that day the LORD *m* Joshua in...... Josh 4:14
And let thy name be *m* for ever ............. 2Sa 7:26
that thy name may be *m* for ever...... 1Chr 17:24
the LORD *m* Solomon exceedingly in. 1Chr 29:25
with him, and *m* him exceedingly.......... 2Chr 1:1
so that he was *m* in the sight of ........ 2Chr 32:23
continually, Let the LORD be *m*................. Ps 35:27
say continually, The LORD be *m*................ Ps 40:16
say continually, Let God be *m*................... Ps 70:4
for thou hast *m* thy word above............. Ps 138:2
for he *m* himself against the LORD........ Jer 48:26
because he hath *m* himself against....... Jer 48:42
for the enemy hath *m* himself................. Lam 1:9
he *m* himself even to the prince........... Dan 8:11
*m* themselves against their border ....... Zeph 2:8
*m* themselves against the people ........ Zeph 2:10
The LORD will be *m* from the.................... Mal 1:5
but the people *m* them ........................ Acts 5:13
the name of the Lord Jesus was *m*..... Acts 19:17
also Christ shall be *m* in my body ......... Phil 1:20

**MAGNIFY**
This day will I begin to *m* thee ............. Josh 3:7
is man, that thou shouldest *m* him ........ Job 7:17
If indeed ye will *m* yourselves.................. Job 19:5
Remember that thou *m* his work ......... Job 36:24
O *m* the LORD with me, and let us ........... Ps 34:3
dishonour that *m* themselves................... Ps 35:26
they *m* themselves against me ............... Ps 38:16
me that did *m* himself against me.......... Ps 55:12
will *m* him with thanksgiving.................. Ps 69:30
or shall the saw *m* itself against .............. Is 10:15
he will *m* the law, and make it.................. Is 42:21
Thus will I *m* myself, and sanctify........ Eze 38:23
he shall *m* himself in his heart,.............. Dan 8:25
*m* himself above every god, and.......... Dan 11:36
for he shall *m* himself above all.......... Dan 11:37
do not *m* themselves against Judah....... Zec 12:7
said, My soul doth *m* the Lord.................. Lk 1:46
with tongues, and *m* God.................... Acts 10:46
of the Gentiles, I *m* mine office ........... Rom 11:13

**MAGOG** (*ma'-gog*)
*1. A son of Japheth.*
Gomer, and *M*, and Madai, and Javan,. Gen 10:2
Gomer, and *M*, and Madai, and Javan,. 1Chr 1:5
*2. Descendants of Magog.*
face against Gog, the land of *M*............. Eze 38:2
And I will send a fire on *M*.................... Eze 39:6
quarters of the earth, Gog and *M*.......... Rev 20:8

**MAGOR-MISSABIB** (*ma''-gor-mis'-sa-bib*) *A symbolic name of Pashur.*
not called thy name Pashur, but *M*......... Jer 20:3

**MAGPIASH** (*mag'-pe-ash*) *A chief Israelite who renewed the covenant.*
*M*, Meshullam, Hezir,.............................. Neh 10:20

**MAHALAH** (*ma'-ha-lah*) See MAHLAH. *Great-grandson of Manasseh.*
bare Ishod, and Abiezer, and *M*............ 1Chr 7:18

**MAHALALEEL** (*ma-hal'-a-le-el*) See MALELEEL.
*1. Son of Cainan.*
lived seventy years, and begat *M*.......... Gen 5:12
after he begat *M* eight hundred............. Gen 5:13
*M* lived sixty and five years, and............ Gen 5:15
*M* lived after he begat Jared................... Gen 5:16
all the days of *M* were eight.................. Gen 5:17
Kenan, *M*, Jered,...................................... 1Chr 1:2
*2. A family of exiles.*
son of Shephatiah, the son of *M*............ Neh 11:4

**MAHALALEL**

**MAHALATH** (*ma'-ha-lath*) See BASHEMATH.
*1. A daughter of Ishmael.*
he had *M* the daughter of Ishmael........ Gen 28:9
*2. A granddaughter of David.*
Rehoboam took him *M* the daughter 2Chr 11:18
*3. A musical choir.*
To the chief Musician upon *M*..................... Ps 53:*t*
chief Musician upon *M* Leannoth............. Ps 88:*t*

**MAHALI** (*ma'-ha-li*) See MAHLI. *Same as Lahli 1.*
sons of Merari; *M* and Mushi..................... Ex 6:19

**MAHANAIM** (*ma-ha-na'-im*) *A town east of the Jordan.*
called the name of that place *M*............ Gen 32:2

M

from *M* unto the border of Debir........ Josh 13:26
And their coast was from *M*................ Josh 13:30
and *M* with her suburbs,...................... Josh 21:38
of Saul, and brought him over to *M*........ 2Sa 2:8
Saul, went out from *M* to Gibeon............ 2Sa 2:12
all Bithron, and they came to *M*............ 2Sa 2:29
Then David came to *M*........................ 2Sa 17:24
to pass, when David was come to *M*... 2Sa 17:27
of sustenance while he lay at *M*........... 2Sa 19:32
curse in the day when I went to *M*....... 1Kin 2:8
Ahinadab the son of Iddo had *M*.......... 1Kin 4:14
suburbs, and *M* with her suburbs,........ 1Chr 6:80

**MAHANEH-DAN** (*ma'-ha-neh-dan*) *A place in Judah.*
called that place *M* unto this day....... Judg 18:12

**MAHARAI** (*ma'-ha-rahee*) *A warrior of David.*
the Ahohite, *M* the Netophathite, ........ 2Sa 23:28
*M* the Netophathite, Heled the son..... 1Chr 11:30
month was *M* the Netophathite.......... 1Chr 27:13

**MAHATH** (*ma'-hath*)
*1. A descendant of Kohath.*
the son of Elkanah, the son of *M*......... 1Chr 6:35
*M* the son of Amasai, and Joel the.... 2Chr 29:12
*2. A Temple servant.*
and Eliel, and Ismachiah, and *M*........ 2Chr 31:13

**MAHAVITE** (*ma'-ha-vite*) *Family name of Eliel.*
Eliel the *M*, and Jeribai, and................ 1Chr 11:46

**MAHAZIOTH** (*ma-ha'-ze-oth*) *A sanctuary servant.*
Mallothi, Hothir, and *M*.......................... 1Chr 25:4
The three and twentieth to *M*............. 1Chr 25:30

**MAHER-SHALAL-HASH-BAZ** (*ma''-her-sha''-lal-hash'-baz*) *A son of Isaiah.*
it with a man's pen concerning *M*.............. Is 8:1
the LORD to me, Call his name *M*.............. Is 8:3

**MAHLAH** (*mah'-lah*) *A daughter of Zelophehad.*
daughters of Zelophehad were *M*...... Num 26:33
*M*, Noah, and Hoglah.............................. Num 27:1
For *M*, Tirzah, and Hoglah, and......... Num 36:11
are the names of his daughters, *M*....... Josh 17:3

**MAHLI** (*mah'-li*) See MAHALI, MAHLITES.
*1. Son of Merari.*
their families; *M*, and Mushi................. Num 3:20
of Merari; *M*, and Mushi......................... 1Chr 6:19
*M*, Libni his son, Shimei his son,.......... 1Chr 6:29
*M*, and Mushi. The sons of *M*.............. 1Chr 23:21
The sons of Merari were *M*.................. 1Chr 24:26
Of *M* came Eleazar, who had no........ 1Chr 24:28
understanding, of the sons of *M*............ Ezr 8:18
*2. Son of Mushi.*
The son of *M*, the son of Mushi,.......... 1Chr 6:47
*M*, and Eder, and Jeremoth, three...... 1Chr 23:23
*M*, and Eder, and Jerimoth................. 1Chr 24:30

**MAHLITES** (*mah'-lites*) *Descendants of Mahli 1.*
Of Merari was the family of the *M*...... Num 3:33
Hebronites, the family of the *M*......... Num 26:58

**MAHLON** (*mah'-lon*) See MAHLON'S. *A son of Naomi.*
and the name of his two sons *M*........... Ruth 1:2
And *M* and Chilion died also both of.... Ruth 1:5
Ruth the Moabitess, the wife of *M*...... Ruth 4:10

**MAHLON'S** (*mah'-lons*)
and all that was Chilion's and *M*............ Ruth 4:9

**MAHOL** (*ma'-hol*) *Father of some wise men.*
Chalcol, and Darda, the sons of *M*...... 1Kin 4:31

**MAHSEIAH** See MASEIAH.

**MAID**
I pray thee, go in unto my *m*................ Gen 16:2
took Hagar her *m* the Egyptian............ Gen 16:3
I have given my *m* into thy bosom....... Gen 16:5
Behold, thy *m* is in thy hand............... Gen 16:6
And he said, Hagar, Sarai's *m*............... Gen 16:8
Leah Zilpah his *m* for an handmaid..... Gen 29:24
Bilhah his handmaid to be her *m*......... Gen 29:29
And she said, Behold my *m* Bilhah....... Gen 30:3
Bilhah Rachel's *m* conceived again....... Gen 30:7
bearing, she took Zilpah her *m*............ Gen 30:9
Zilpah Leah's *m* bare Jacob a son....... Gen 30:10
Zilpah Leah's *m* bare Jacob a.............. Gen 30:12
flags, she sent her *m* to fetch it............. Ex 2:5
the *m* went and called the child's............ Ex 2:8
a man smite his servant, or his *m*.......... Ex 21:20
his servant, or the eye of his *m*.............. Ex 21:26
if a man entice a *m* that is not.............. Ex 22:16
But if she bear a *m* child...................... Lev 12:5
and for thy servant, and for thy *m*.......... Lev 25:6
came to her, I found her not a *m*....... Deut 22:14
I found not thy daughter a *m*.............. Deut 22:17
of the land of Israel a little *m*............... 2Kin 5:2
thus said the *m* that is of the............... 2Kin 5:4
the *m* was fair and beautiful...................... Est 2:7
why then should I think upon a *m*........... Job 31:1
and the way of a man with a *m*.......... Prov 30:19
as with the *m*, so with her.......................... Is 24:2
Can a *m* forget her ornaments, or.......... Jer 2:32
in pieces the young man and the *m*....... Jer 51:22
father will go in unto the same *m*........ Amos 2:7
for the *m* is not dead, but..................... Mt 9:24
her by the hand, and the *m* arose.......... Mt 9:25
into the porch, another *m* saw him....... Mt 26:71
a *m* saw him again, and began to......... Mk 14:69
by the hand, and called, saying, *M*.......... Lk 8:54
But a certain *m* beheld him as he.......... Lk 22:56

**MAIDEN**
I have given my *m* to my husband..... Gen 30:18
Behold, here is my daughter a *m*....... Judg 19:24
upon young man or *m*........................ 2Chr 36:17
let the *m* which pleaseth the king........... Est 2:4
the *m* pleased him, and she...................... Est 2:9
thus came every *m* unto the king........... Est 2:13
as the eyes of a *m* unto the hand.......... Ps 123:2
the father and the mother of the *m*........ Lk 8:51

**MAIDENS**
her *m* walked along by the river's............. Ex 2:5
but abide here fast by my *m*.................. Ruth 2:8
that thou go out with his *m*.................. Ruth 2:22
So she kept fast by the *m* of Boaz....... Ruth 2:23
kindred, with whose *m* thou wast.......... Ruth 3:2
they found young *m* going out to.......... 1Sa 9:11
when many *m* were gathered................. Est 2:8
as belonged to her, and seven *m*............... Est 2:9
I also and my *m* will fast likewise.......... Est 4:16
or wilt thou bind him for thy *m*............. Job 41:5
their *m* were not given to...................... Ps 78:63
Both young men, and *m*........................ Ps 148:12
She hath sent forth her *m*...................... Prov 9:3
and for the maintenance for thy *m*.... Prov 27:27
household, and a portion to her *m*..... Prov 31:15
I got me servants and *m*, and had......... Eccl 2:7
but they shall take *m* of the seed......... Eze 44:22
to beat the menservants and *m*............. Lk 12:45

**MAID'S**
Now when every *m* turn was come to... Est 2:12

**MAIDS**
Beside their servants and their *m*........... Ezr 2:65
her *m* unto the best place of the.............. Est 2:9
So Esther's *m* and her chamberlains......... Est 4:4
that dwell in mine house, and my *m*... Job 19:15
the *m* in the cities of Judah.................. Lam 5:11
Slay utterly old and young, both *m*......... Eze 9:6
her *m* shall lead her as with the............. Nah 2:7
men cheerful, and new wine the *m*......... Zec 9:17
one of the *m* of the high priest.............. Mk 14:66

**MAIDSERVANT**
of the *m* that is behind the mill................ Ex 11:5
thy manservant, nor thy *m*................... Ex 20:10
nor his manservant, nor his *m*.............. Ex 20:17
a man sell his daughter to be a *m*........... Ex 21:7
ox shall push a manservant or a *m*....... Ex 21:32
nor thy manservant, nor thy *m*............. Deut 5:14
thy *m* may rest as well as thou............. Deut 5:14
or his manservant, or his *m*................ Deut 5:21
and thy manservant, and thy *m*.......... Deut 12:18
also unto thy *m* thou shalt do............ Deut 15:17
and thy manservant, and thy *m*.......... Deut 16:11
and thy manservant, and thy *m*.......... Deut 16:14
made Abimelech, the son of his *m*....... Judg 9:18
cause of my manservant or of my *m*..... Job 31:13
manservant, and every man his *m*........ Jer 34:9
manservant, and every one his *m*......... Jer 34:10

**MAIDSERVANT'S**
tooth, or his *m* tooth.............................. Ex 21:27

**MAIDSERVANTS**
and menservants, and *m*..................... Gen 12:16
Abimelech, and his wife, and his *m*.... Gen 20:17
and gold, and menservants, and *m*....... Gen 24:35
and had much cattle, and *m*................. Gen 30:43
and your menservants, and your *m*... Deut 12:12
take your menservants, and your *m*........ 1Sa 8:16
of the *m* which thou hast spoken........... 2Sa 6:22
and oxen, and menservants, and *m*..... 2Kin 5:26
their manservants and their *m*............... Neh 7:67

**MAIDSERVANTS'**
tent, and into the two *m* tents............ Gen 31:33

**MAIL**
and he was armed with a coat of *m*...... 1Sa 17:5
he armed him with a coat of *m*............ 1Sa 17:38

**MAIMED**
Blind, or broken, or *m*, or having......... Lev 22:22
that were lame, blind, dumb, *m*............ Mt 15:30
the *m* to be whole, the lame to.............. Mt 15:31
thee to enter into life halt or *m*............... Mt 18:8
for thee to enter into life *m*.................... Mk 9:43
a feast, call the poor, the *m*................... Lk 14:13
in hither the poor, and the *m*.................. Lk 14:21

**MAINSAIL**
and hoised up the *m* to the wind........ Acts 27:40

**MAINTAIN**
supplication, and *m* their cause............ 1Kin 8:45
dwelling place, and *m* their cause,....... 1Kin 8:49
that he *m* the cause of his.................... 1Kin 8:59
to *m* the house of the LORD.................. 1Chr 26:27
supplication, and *m* their cause........... 2Chr 6:35
*m* their cause, and forgive thy............. 2Chr 6:39
but I will *m* mine own ways before..... Job 13:15
I know that the LORD will *m* the.......... Ps 140:12
might be careful to *m* good works........ Titus 3:8
let ours also learn to *m* good.............. Titus 3:14

**MAINTAINED**
For thou hast *m* my right and my............. Ps 9:4

**MAINTAINEST**
thou *m* my lot........................................ Ps 16:5

**MAINTENANCE**
Now because we have *m* from the......... Ezr 4:14
for the *m* for thy maidens.................. Prov 27:27

**MAJESTY**
glory, and the victory, and the *m*...... 1Chr 29:11
*m* as had not been on any king.......... 1Chr 29:25
of his excellent *m* many days.................. Est 1:4
with God is terrible *m*.......................... Job 37:22
Deck thyself now with *m* and.............. Job 40:10
*m* hast thou laid upon him...................... Ps 21:5
voice of the LORD is full of *m*................. Ps 29:4
mighty, with thy glory and thy *m*........... Ps 45:3
in thy *m* ride prosperously...................... Ps 45:4
reigneth, he is clothed with *m*............... Ps 93:1
Honour and *m* are before him................. Ps 96:6
thou art clothed with honour and *m*..... Ps 104:1
of the glorious honour of thy *m*.............. Ps 145:5
the glorious *m* of his kingdom.............. Ps 145:12
LORD, and for the glory of his *m*.............. Is 2:10
LORD, and for the glory of his *m*.............. Is 2:19
LORD, and for the glory of his *m*.............. Is 2:21
shall sing for the *m* of the LORD............. Is 24:14
will not behold the *m* of the LORD........... Is 26:10
of his ornament, he set it in *m*.............. Eze 7:20
power, and for the honour of my *m*..... Dan 4:30
excellent *m* was added unto me............ Dan 4:36
thy father a kingdom and *m*................. Dan 5:18
for the *m* that he gave him, all............. Dan 5:19
in the *m* of the name of the LORD.......... Mic 5:4
the right hand of the *M* on high.............. Heb 1:3
throne of the *M* in the heavens............... Heb 8:1
but were eyewitnesses of his *m*............ 2Pet 1:16
God our Saviour, be glory and *m*............ Jude 25

**MAKAZ** (*ma'-kaz*) *A town in Judah.*
The son of Dekar, in *M*, and in.............. 1Kin 4:9

**MAKE** See PREFACE.

**MAKER**
a man be more pure than his *m*.............. Job 4:17
in so doing my *m* would soon take...... Job 32:22
But none saith, Where is God my *m*.... Job 35:10
ascribe righteousness to my *M*............. Job 36:3
us kneel before the LORD our *m*.............. Ps 95:6
the poor reproacheth his *M*............... Prov 14:31
the poor reproacheth his *M*................ Prov 17:5
the LORD is the *m* of them all............. Prov 22:2
the *m* of it as a spark, and they............... Is 1:31
day shall a man look to his *M*................ Is 17:7
not looked unto the *m* thereof.............. Is 22:11
unto him that striveth with his *M*........... Is 45:9
the Holy One of Israel, and his *M*.......... Is 45:11
And forgettest the LORD thy *m*.............. Is 51:13
For thy *M* is thine husband.................... Is 54:5
Thus saith the LORD the *m* thereof......... Jer 33:2
For Israel hath forgotten his *M*............ Hos 8:14
that the *m* thereof hath graven it.......... Hab 2:18
that the *m* of his work trusteth............. Hab 2:18
whose builder and *m* is God................. Heb 11:10

**MAKERS**
together that are *m* of idols................... Is 45:16

**MAKEST**
what *m* thou in this place..................... Judg 18:3
*m* me to possess the iniquities of.......... Job 13:26
that thou *m* thy ways perfect................. Job 22:3
only *m* me dwell in safety........................ Ps 4:8
thou *m* his beauty to consume away..... Ps 39:11
Thou *m* us to turn back from the........... Ps 44:10
Thou *m* us a reproach to our................ Ps 44:13
Thou *m* us a byword among the............. Ps 44:14
thou *m* the outgoings of the.................... Ps 65:8
thou *m* it soft with showers................... Ps 65:10
Thou *m* us a strife unto our................... Ps 80:6
Thou *m* darkness, and it is night.......... Ps 104:20
that thou *m* account of him.................. Ps 144:3
where thou *m* thy flock to rest at......... Song 1:7
that fashioneth it, What *m* thou.............. Is 45:9
that *m* thy nest in the cedars,............... Jer 22:23
but thou *m* this people to trust.............. Jer 28:15
*m* thine high place in every................ Eze 16:31
*m* men as the fishes of the sea,............... Hab 1:14
*m* him drunken also, that thou.............. Hab 2:15
When thou *m* a dinner or a supper,...... Lk 14:12
But when thou *m* a feast, call the.......... Lk 14:13
whom *m* thou thyself............................. Jn 8:53
thou, being a man, *m* thyself God.......... Jn 10:33
the law, and *m* thy boast of God,.......... Rom 2:17
Thou that *m* thy boast of the law,........ Rom 2:23

**MAKETH**
or who *m* the dumb, or deaf, or............. Ex 4:11
the priest that *m* atonement.................... Lev 7:7
the priest that *m* him clean shall........... Lev 14:11
for it is the blood that *m* an.................. Lev 17:11
*m* his son or his daughter to pass...... Deut 18:10
the city that *m* war with thee.............. Deut 20:20
when he *m* his sons to inherit............. Deut 21:16
*m* merchandise of him, or selleth.......... Deut 24:7
Cursed be the man that *m* any............ Deut 27:15
Cursed be he that *m* the blind to......... Deut 27:18
LORD thy God *m* with thee this day.. Deut 29:12
The LORD killeth, and *m* alive................. 1Sa 2:6
The LORD *m* poor, and *m* rich................. 1Sa 2:7
and he *m* my way perfect...................... 2Sa 22:33
He *m* my feet like hinds' feet.................. 2Sa 22:34
For he *m* sore, and bindeth up................ Job 5:18
Which *m* Arcturus, Orion, and.................. Job 9:9
spoiled, and *m* the judges fools............. Job 12:17
he *m* them to stagger like a.................. Job 12:25
*m* collops of fat on his flanks................ Job 15:27
For God *m* my heart soft, and the......... Job 23:16
he *m* peace in his high places............... Job 25:2
and as a booth that the keeper *m*.......... Job 27:18
*m* us wiser than the fowls of................ Job 35:11

For he *m* small the drops of water ....... Job 36:27
He *m* the deep to boil like a pot ........... Job 41:31
he *m* the sea like a pot of ...................... Job 41:31
He *m* a path to shine after him ............ Job 41:32
When he *m* inquisition for blood, .............. Ps 9:12
strength, and *m* my way perfect ............. Ps 18:32
He *m* my feet like hinds' feet, and ........... Ps 18:33
He *m* me to lie down in green ................... Ps 23:2
He *m* them also to skip like a .................. Ps 29:6
of the LORD *m* the hinds to calve .............. Ps 29:9
he *m* the devices of the people of ........... Ps 33:10
man that *m* the LORD his trust .................. Ps 40:4
He *m* wars to cease unto the end ............. Ps 46:9
who *m* the clouds his chariot .................. Ps 104:3
Who *m* his angels spirits ......................... Ps 104:4
wine that *m* glad the heart of man ...... Ps 104:15
He *m* the storm a calm, so that ............. Ps 107:29
there he *m* the hungry to dwell, ........... Ps 107:36
*m* him families like a flock ...................... Ps 107:41
He *m* the barren woman to keep ............ Ps 113:9
he *m* lightnings for the rain ................... Ps 135:7
who *m* grass to grow upon the ................ Ps 147:8
He *m* peace in thy borders, and ........... Ps 147:14
A wise son *m* a glad father ..................... Prov 10:1
the hand of the diligent *m* rich ............. Prov 10:4
it *m* rich, and he addeth no sorrow ... Prov 10:22
but she that *m* ashamed is as ................. Prov 12:4
in the heart of man *m* it stoop ............ Prov 12:25
but a good word *m* it glad ..................... Prov 12:25
There is that *m* himself rich ................... Prov 13:7
there is that *m* himself poor ................... Prov 13:7
Hope deferred *m* the heart sick, ......... Prov 13:12
A merry heart *m* a cheerful ................... Prov 15:13
A wise son *m* a glad father ................... Prov 15:20
and a good report *m* the bones fat ....... Prov 15:30
he *m* even his enemies to be at ............ Prov 16:7
A man's gift *m* room for him .................. Prov 18:16
Wealth *m* many friends ........................... Prov 19:4
but he that *m* haste to be rich ............ Prov 28:20
She *m* herself coverings of ..................... Prov 31:22
She *m* fine linen, and selleth it ............ Prov 31:24
*m* from the beginning to the end .......... Eccl 3:11
oppression *m* a wise man mad ................. Eccl 7:7
a man's wisdom *m* his face to .................. Eccl 8:1
for laughter, and wine *m* merry ........... Eccl 10:19
not the works of God who *m* all ............. Eccl 11:5
every one that *m* mention thereof .......... Is 19:17
the LORD *m* the earth empty, and ............ Is 24:1
*m* it waste, and turneth it upside .............. Is 24:1
when he *m* all the stones of the ............... Is 27:9
he *m* the judges of the earth as .............. Is 40:23
which *m* a way in the sea, and a ............ Is 43:16
*m* it after the figure of a man, ................. Is 44:13
he *m* a god, and worshippeth it ............... Is 44:15
he *m* it a graven image, and ..................... Is 44:15
And the residue thereof he *m* a god ....... Is 44:17
I am the LORD that *m* all things ............. Is 44:24
of the liars, and *m* diviners mad ............ Is 44:25
*m* their knowledge foolish ........................ Is 44:25
and he *m* it a god ........................................ Is 46:6
*m* it bring forth and bud, that it ............. Is 55:10
from evil *m* himself a prey ........................ Is 59:15
my heart *m* a noise in me ........................... Jer 4:19
he *m* lightnings with rain, and ............... Jer 10:13
*m* flesh his arm, and whose heart ............ Jer 17:5
king of Babylon *m* war against us ............ Jer 21:2
*m* himself a prophet, that thou ............... Jer 29:26
which *m* himself a prophet to you ......... Jer 29:27
be like the dove that *m* her nest ............ Jer 48:28
he *m* lightnings with rain, and ............... Jer 51:16
*m* idols against herself to defile ............ Eze 22:3
secrets, and *m* known to the king .......... Dan 2:28
he that revealeth secrets *m* known ........ Dan 2:29
but *m* his petition three times a ............ Dan 6:13
the abomination that *m* desolate ........... Dan 11:31
that *m* desolate set up, there ................ Dan 12:11
that *m* the morning darkness, and ..... Amos 4:13
Seek him that *m* the seven stars .......... Amos 5:8
*m* the day dark with night ...................... Amos 5:8
*m* it dry, and drieth up all the ................ Nah 1:4
for he *m* his sun to rise on the ................. Mt 5:45
he *m* both the deaf to hear, and ............... Mk 7:37
then both the new *m* a rent ........................ Lk 5:36
whosoever *m* himself a king ................... Jn 19:12
Aeneas, Jesus Christ *m* thee whole ...... Acts 9:34
And hope *m* not ashamed .......................... Rom 5:5
but the Spirit itself *m* .............................. Rom 8:26
because he *m* intercession for the ........ Rom 8:27
who also *m* intercession for us ............. Rom 8:34
how he *m* intercession to God ............... Rom 11:2
For who *m* thee to differ from ................ 1Cor 4:7
who is he then that *m* me glad .............. 2Cor 2:2
*m* manifest the savour of his ................ 2Cor 2:14
they were, it *m* no matter to me ............... Gal 2:6
*m* increase of the body unto the ............ Eph 4:16
Who *m* his angels spirits, and his ............. Heb 1:7
For the law *m* men high priests ............. Heb 7:28
*m* the Son, who is consecrated for ........ Heb 7:28
so that he *m* fire come down from ...... Rev 13:13
worketh abomination, or *m* a lie .......... Rev 21:27
and whosoever loveth and *m* a lie ....... Rev 22:15

**MAKHELOTH** (*mak'-he-loth*) *An Israelite encampment in the wilderness.*
from Haradah, and pitched in *M* ........ Num 33:25
And they removed from *M*, and ......... Num 33:26

**MAKI** See MACHI.

**MAKING**
task in *m* brick both yesterday .................. Ex 5:14
in *m* war against it to take it, ............ Deut 20:19
Now as they were *m* their hearts ....... Judg 19:22
eating and drinking, and *m* merry ....... 1Kin 4:20
*m* a noise with psalteries and ............ 1Chr 15:28
in *m* known all these great things ..... 1Chr 17:19
*m* confession to the LORD God of ......... 2Chr 30:22
LORD is sure, *m* wise the simple ................ Ps 19:7
of *m* many books there is no end ........ Eccl 12:12
*m* a tinkling with their feet ........................ Is 3:16
*m* him very glad ........................................ Jer 20:15
multitude of the wares of thy *m* ........... Eze 27:16
multitude of the wares of thy *m* ........... Eze 27:18
*m* supplication before his God ................ Dan 6:11
swearing falsely in *m* a covenant ............. Hos 10:4
*m* the ephah small, and the shekel ....... Amos 8:5
in *m* thee desolate because of thy ........... Mic 6:13
minstrels and the people *m* a noise .......... Mt 9:23
*M* the word of God of none effect .......... Mk 7:13
Father, *m* himself equal with God ............ Jn 5:18
*M* request, if by any means now at ...... Rom 1:10
as poor, yet *m* many rich ....................... 2Cor 6:10
*m* mention of you in my prayers ............ Eph 1:16
of twain one new man, so *m* peace ....... Eph 2:15
*m* melody in your heart to the ............... Eph 5:19
for you all *m* request with joy .................. Phil 1:4
*m* mention of you in our prayers .............. 1Th 1:2
*m* mention of thee always in my ............ Philem 4
*m* them an ensample unto those ............. 2Pet 2:6
have compassion, *m* a difference ............. Jude 22

**MAKIR** See MACHIR.

**MAKIRITE** See MACHIRITES.

**MAKKEDAH** (*mak'-ke-dah*) *A city in Judah.*
smote them to Azekah, and unto *M* .. Josh 10:10
and hid themselves in a cave at *M* ..... Josh 10:16
are found hid in a cave at *M* ............... Josh 10:17
the camp to Joshua at *M* in peace ...... Josh 10:21
And that day Joshua took *M* ............... Josh 10:28
he did to the king of *M* as he did ....... Josh 10:28
Then Joshua passed from *M* ................. Josh 10:29
The king of *M*, one .............................. Josh 12:16
Beth-dagon, and Naamah, and *M* ....... Josh 15:41

**MAKTESH** (*mak'-tesh*) *A district near Jerusalem.*
Howl, ye inhabitants of *M* .................... Zeph 1:11

**MALACHI** (*mal'-a-ki*) *A prophet.*
word of the LORD to Israel by *M* ............. Mal 1:1

**MALCAM** See MALCHAM.

**MALCHAM** (*mal'-kam*) See MILCOM.
*1. Son of Shaharaim.*
Jobab, and Zibia, and Mesha, and *M* ..... 1Chr 8:9
*2. An Ammonite idol.*
by the LORD, and that swear by *M* ...... Zeph 1:5

**MALCHIAH** (*mal-ki'-ah*) See MALCHIJAH, MELCHIAH.
*1. Father of Baaseiah.*
the son of Baaseiah, the son of *M* ........ 1Chr 6:40
*2. A descendant of Parosh.*
Ramiah, and Jeziah, and *M*, and ........... Ezr 10:25
the son of Pashur, the son of *M* ............ Neh 11:12
*3. Another descendant of Parosh.*
Eliezer, Ishijah, *M*, Shemaiah, ............... Ezr 10:31
*4. A repairer of Jerusalem's wall.*
gate repaired *M* the son of Rechab ....... Neh 3:14
*5. Another repairer of Jerusalem's wall.*
After him repaired *M* the ....................... Neh 3:31
*6. A priest who aided Ezra.*
hand, Pedaiah, and Mishael, and *M* ........ Neh 8:4
*7. A priest who dedicated the wall.*
Shelemiah, and Pashur the son of *M* ......... Jer 38:1
dungeon of *M* the son of Hammelech .... Jer 38:6

**MALCHIEL** (*mal'-ke-el*) See MALCHIELITES. *A son of Beriah.*
Heber, and *M* ......................................... Gen 46:17
of *M*, the family of the ........................... Num 26:45
Heber, and *M*, who is the father of ...... 1Chr 7:31

**MALCHIELITES** (*mal'-ke-el-ites*) *Descendants of Malchiel.*
of Malchiel, the family of the *M* ......... Num 26:45

**MALCHIJAH** (*mal-ki'-jah*) See MALCHIAH.
*1. A family of exiles.*
the son of Pashur, the son of *M* ........... 1Chr 9:12
*2. A sanctuary servant.*
The fifth to *M*, the sixth to ................... 1Chr 24:9
*3. Married a foreigner in exile.*
and Miamin, and Eleazar, and *M* .......... Ezr 10:25
*4. A rebuilder of Jerusalem's wall.*
*M* the son of Harim, and Hashub the ... Neh 3:11
*5. A priest who dedicated the wall.*
Pashur, Amariah, *M*, ............................... Neh 10:3
and Uzzi, and Jehohanan, and *M* ........ Neh 12:42

**MALCHIRAM** (*mal'-ki-ram*) *A descendant of King Jehoiakim.*
*M* also, and Pedaiah, and Shenazar, .... 1Chr 3:18

**MALCHI-SHUA** (*mal''-ki-shu'-ah*) See MELCHISHUA. *A son of King Saul.*
and Saul begat Jonathan, and *M* .......... 1Chr 8:33
and Saul begat Jonathan, and *M* .......... 1Chr 9:39
slew Jonathan, and Abinadab, and *M*. 1Chr 10:2

**MALCHUS** (*mal'-kus*) *A servant wounded by Simon Peter.*
The servant's name was *M* ...................... Jn 18:10

**MALE**
*m* and female created he them ................ Gen 1:27
*M* and female created he them .................. Gen 5:2
they shall be *m* and female ..................... Gen 6:19
take to thee by sevens, the *m* ................... Gen 7:2
that are not clean by two, the *m* ............. Gen 7:2
also of the air by sevens, the *m* ............... Gen 7:3
two unto Noah into the ark, the *m* ......... Gen 7:9
And they that went in, went in *m* ......... Gen 7:16
money, every *m* among the men of .... Gen 17:23
as we be, that every *m* of you be ........ Gen 34:15
people, if every *m* among us be .......... Gen 34:22
every *m* was circumcised, all that ........ Gen 34:24
blemish, a *m* of the first year ..................... Ex 12:5
whether ox or sheep, that is *m* .............. Ex 34:19
let him offer a *m* without blemish ............ Lev 1:3
bring it a *m* without blemish .................. Lev 1:10
whether it be a *m* or female ..................... Lev 3:1
*m* or female, he shall offer it .................... Lev 3:6
of the goats, a *m* without blemish ......... Lev 4:23
Every *m* among the priests shall ............... Lev 7:6
that hath born a *m* or a female ............... Lev 12:7
your own will a *m* without blemish ..... Lev 22:19
thy estimation shall be of the *m* .............. Lev 27:3
shall be of the *m* twenty shekels ............. Lev 27:5
of the *m* five shekels of silver ................. Lev 27:6
if it be a *m*, then thy estimation ............ Lev 27:7
names, every *m* by their polls .................. Num 1:2
every *m* from twenty years old and .... Num 1:20
every *m* from twenty years old and .... Num 1:22
every *m* from a month old and .............. Num 3:15
Both *m* and female shall ye put out ...... Num 5:3
every *m* shall eat it ............................... Num 18:10
every *m* among the little ones .............. Num 31:17
the likeness of *m* or female .................... Deut 4:16
there shall not be *m* or female ............... Deut 7:14
thou shalt smite every *m* thereof ....... Deut 20:13
these were the *m* children of ................. Josh 17:2
Ye shall utterly destroy every *m* ........ Judg 21:11
known no man by lying with any *m*. Judg 21:12
he had smitten every *m* in Edom ....... 1Kin 11:15
he had cut off every *m* in Edom ........ 1Kin 11:16
which hath in his flock a *m* ..................... Mal 1:14
them at the beginning made them *m* ..... Mt 19:4
of the creation God made them *m* ......... Mk 10:6
Every *m* that openeth the womb ............... Lk 2:23
there is neither *m* nor female ................... Gal 3:28

**MALEFACTOR**
said unto him, If he were not a *m* .......... Jn 18:30

**MALEFACTORS**
And there were also two others, *m* ....... Lk 23:32
they crucified him, and the *m* ................ Lk 23:33
one of the *m* which were hanged ............ Lk 23:39

**MALELEEL** (*mal'-e-le-el*) See MAHALALEEL.
*Son of Cainan; ancestor of Jesus.*
of Jared, which was the son of *M* ............ Lk 3:37

**MALES**
city boldly, and slew all the *m* ............. Gen 34:25
let all his *m* be circumcised, and ............ Ex 12:48
the *m* shall be the LORD's .......................... Ex 13:12
that openeth the matrix, being *m* ........... Ex 13:15
*m* shall appear before the Lord ............... Ex 23:17
All the *m* among the children of ............ Lev 6:18
All the *m* among the priests shall .......... Lev 6:29
to the number of all the *m* ................... Num 3:22
In the number of all the *m* ................... Num 3:28
to the number of all the *m* ................... Num 3:34
all the *m* from a month old and ........... Num 3:39
*m* of the children of Israel from ............ Num 3:40
all the firstborn *m* by the number ......... Num 3:43
all *m* from a month old and upward . Num 26:62
and they slew all the *m* ............................ Num 31:7
All the firstling *m* that come of .......... Deut 15:19
times in a year shall all thy *m* ............. Deut 16:16
came out of Egypt, that were *m* ............... Josh 5:4
Beside their genealogy of *m* ................. 2Chr 31:16
to all the *m* among the priests ............. 2Chr 31:19
by genealogy of the *m* an hundred .......... Ezr 8:3
and with him two hundred *m* .................... Ezr 8:4
and with him three hundred *m* ................. Ezr 8:5
of Jonathan, and with him fifty *m* ............. Ezr 8:6
Athaliah, and with him seventy *m* ............ Ezr 8:7
Michael, and with him fourscore *m* .......... Ezr 8:8
him two hundred and eighteen *m* ............. Ezr 8:9
him an hundred and threescore *m* ......... Ezr 8:10
and with him twenty and eight *m* ........... Ezr 8:11
and with him an hundred and ten *m* ..... Ezr 8:12
and with them threescore *m* ................... Ezr 8:13
and Zabbud, and with them seventy *m*. Ezr 8:14

**MALICE**
neither with the leaven of *m* .................... 1Cor 5:8
howbeit in *m* be ye children, but ........ 1Cor 14:20
be put away from you, with all *m* ......... Eph 4:31
anger, wrath, *m*, blasphemy, ..................... Col 3:8
lusts and pleasures, living in *m* .............. Titus 3:3
Wherefore laying aside all *m* ................... 1Pet 2:1

**MALICIOUS**
prating against us with *m* words .............. 3Jn 10

**MALICIOUSNESS**
wickedness, covetousness, *m*, ............... Rom 1:29
your liberty for a cloke of *m* ................. 1Pet 2:16

**MALIGNITY**
envy, murder, debate, deceit, *m* ............ Rom 1:29

**MALLOTHI** (*mal'-lo-thi*) *A son of Heman.*
and Romamti-ezer, Joshbekashah, *M*.. 1Chr 25:4
The nineteenth to *M*, he, his sons ...... 1Chr 25:26

**MALLOWS**
Who cut up *m* by the bushes, and ......... Job 30:4

**MALLUCH** (*mal'-luk*) See MELICU.
*1. Ancestor of Ethan.*
the son of Abdi, the son of *M* ............... 1Chr 6:44

*2. A son of Bani.*
Meshullam, M, and Adaiah, Jashub,..... Ezr 10:29
*3. A descendant of Harim.*
Benjamin, M, and Shemariah................. Ezr 10:32
*4. A priest who renewed the covenant.*
Hattush, Shebaniah, M,........................... Neh 10:4
Amariah, M, Hattush,............................. Neh 12:2
*5. A clan leader who renewed the covenant.*
M, Harim, Baanah .................................. Neh 10:27

**MALLUCHI** See MELICU.

**MALTA** See MELITA.

**MAMMON**
Ye cannot serve God and *m*..................... Mt 6:24
of the *m* of unrighteousness..................... Lk 16:9
faithful in the unrighteous *m*.................. Lk 16:11
Ye cannot serve God and *m*..................... Lk 16:13

**MAMRE** (*mam'-re*)
*1. A place near Hebron.*
came and dwelt in the plain of *M*........ Gen 13:18
unto him in the plains of *M*.................... Gen 18:1
in Machpelah, which was before *M*..... Gen 23:17
the field of Machpelah before *M*.......... Gen 23:19
the Hittite, which is before *M*............... Gen 25:9
came unto Isaac his father unto *M*..... Gen 35:27
of Machpelah, which is before *M*......... Gen 49:30
of Ephron the Hittite, before *M*........... Gen 50:13
*2. An Amorite ally of Abraham.*
in the plain of *M* the Amorite ............. Gen 14:13
went with me, Aner, Eshcol, and *M*.... Gen 14:24

**MAN** See PREFACE.

**MANAEN** (*man'-a-en*) *A Christian teacher at Antioch.*
Niger, and Lucius of Cyrene, and *M*.... Acts 13:1

**MANAHATH** (*man'-a-hath*)
*1. A son of Shobal.*
Alvan, and *M*, and Ebal, Shepho, and. Gen 36:23
Alian, and *M*, and Ebal, Shephi, and ... 1Chr 1:40
*2. A city in Benjamin.*
Geba, and they removed them to *M*...... 1Chr 8:6

**MANAHETHITES** (*man'-a-heth-ites*)
*Descendants of Shobal.*
Haroeh, and half of the *M*..................... 1Chr 2:52
house of Joab, and half of the *M*.......... 1Chr 2:54

**MANASSEH** (*ma-nas'-seh*) See MANASSEH'S, MANASSES, MANASSITES.
*1. A son of Joseph.*
the name of the firstborn *M*................. Gen 41:51
in the land of Egypt were born *M*....... Gen 46:20
he took with him his two sons, *M*......... Gen 48:1
two sons, Ephraim and *M*..................... Gen 48:5
*M* in his left hand toward..................... Gen 48:13
for *M* was the firstborn......................... Gen 48:14
God make thee as Ephraim and as *M*. Gen 48:20
and he set Ephraim before *M*................ Gen 48:20
also of Machir the son of *M* were.......... Gen 50:23
after their families were *M*.................. Num 26:28
Of the sons of *M*.................................... Num 26:29
the son of Machir, the son of *M*........... Num 27:1
families of *M* the son of Joseph........... Num 27:1
the son of *M* went to Gilead ............... Num 32:39
Gilead unto Machir the son of *M*....... Num 32:40
And Jair the son of *M* went ............... Num 32:41
the son of Machir, the son of *M*............ Num 36:1
Jair the son of *M* took all the .............. Deut 3:14
children of Machir the son of *M*.......... Josh 13:31
for Machir the firstborn of *M*................. Josh 17:1
of *M* the son of Joseph by their ............ Josh 17:2
the son of Machir, the son of *M*............. Josh 17:3
the towns of Jair the son of *M*............... 1Kin 4:13
The ......................................................... 1Chr 7:14
the son of Machir, the son of *M*............ 1Chr 7:17
*2. Descendants and land of Manasseh 1.*
of *M*; Gamaliel the son ........................ Num 1:10
Of the children of *M*, by their............... Num 1:34
of them, even of the tribe of *M*............. Num 1:35
And by him shall be the tribe of *M*....... Num 2:20
of *M* shall be Gamaliel the son of......... Num 2:20
prince of the children of *M*................... Num 7:54
of *M* was Gamaliel the son of............. Num 10:23
Joseph, namely, of the tribe of *M*....... Num 13:11
These are the families of *M*................. Num 26:34
the tribe of *M* the son of Joseph.......... Num 32:33
half the tribe of *M* have received........ Num 34:14
the tribe of the children of *M*............. Num 34:23
the sons of *M* the son of Joseph.......... Num 36:12
gave I unto the half tribe of *M*............. Deut 3:13
and to the half tribe of *M*.................... Deut 29:8
and they are the thousands of *M*....... Deut 33:17
and the land of Ephraim, and *M*.......... Deut 34:2
and to half the tribe of *M*..................... Josh 1:12
of Gad, and half the tribe of *M*............. Josh 4:12
Gadites, and the half tribe of *M*............ Josh 12:6
tribes, and the half tribe of *M*.............. Josh 13:7
unto the half tribe of *M*...................... Josh 13:29
children of *M* by their families........... Josh 13:29
of Joseph were two tribes, *M*................ Josh 14:4
So the children of Joseph, *M*................ Josh 16:4
inheritance of the children of *M*.......... Josh 16:9
was also a lot for the tribe of *M*.......... Josh 17:1
children of *M* by their families............. Josh 17:2
And there fell ten portions to *M*.......... Josh 17:5
Because the daughters of *M* had an...... Josh 17:6
the coast of *M* was from Asher to........ Josh 17:7
Now *M* had the land of Tappuah........... Josh 17:8
of *M* belonged to the children of .......... Josh 17:8
Ephraim are among the cities of *M*...... Josh 17:9
the coast of *M* also was on the ............ Josh 17:9
*M* had in Issachar and in Asher.......... Josh 17:11
Yet the children of *M* could not.......... Josh 17:12
Joseph, even to Ephraim and to *M*..... Josh 17:17
and Reuben, and half the tribe of *M*.... Josh 18:7
in Bashan out of the tribe of *M*............ Josh 20:8
and out of the half tribe of *M*................ Josh 21:5
of the half tribe of *M* in Bashan........... Josh 21:6
And out of the half tribe of *M*............ Josh 21:25
*M* they gave Golan in Bashan with.... Josh 21:27
Gadites, and the half tribe of *M*.......... Josh 22:1
*M* Moses had given possession in......... Josh 22:7
and the half tribe of *M* returned.......... Josh 22:9
the half tribe of *M* built there............ Josh 22:10
the half tribe of *M* have built an.......... Josh 22:11
of Gad, and to the half tribe of *M*....... Josh 22:13
of Gad, and to the half tribe of *M*....... Josh 22:15
and the half tribe of *M* answered........ Josh 22:21
of Gad and the children of *M* spake... Josh 22:30
of Gad, and to the children of *M*......... Josh 22:31
Neither did *M* drive out the................. Judg 1:27
behold, my family is poor in *M*............ Judg 6:15
sent messengers throughout all *M*...... Judg 6:35
and out of Asher, and out of all *M*...... Judg 7:23
and he passed over Gilead, and *M*..... Judg 11:29
Gadites, and half the tribe of *M*......... 1Chr 5:18
half tribe of *M* dwelt in the land.......... 1Chr 5:23
Gadites, and the half tribe of *M*.......... 1Chr 5:26
out of the half tribe of *M*..................... 1Chr 6:61
out of the tribe of *M* in Bashan............ 1Chr 6:62
And out of the half tribe of *M*............. 1Chr 6:70
the family of the half tribe of *M*.......... 1Chr 6:71
the borders of the children of *M*.......... 1Chr 7:29
of the children of Ephraim, and *M*........ 1Chr 9:3
And there fell some of *M* to David .... 1Chr 12:19
to Ziklag, there fell to him of *M*.......... 1Chr 12:20
of the thousands that were of *M*......... 1Chr 12:20
half tribe of *M* eighteen thousand....... 1Chr 12:31
and of the half tribe of *M*................... 1Chr 12:37
Gadites, and the half tribe of *M*........ 1Chr 26:32
of the half tribe of *M*, Joel the........... 1Chr 27:20
Of the half tribe of *M* in Gilead.......... 1Chr 27:21
with them out of Ephraim and *M*......... 2Chr 15:9
letters also to Ephraim and *M*............. 2Chr 30:1
Ephraim and *M* even unto.................... 2Chr 30:10
Nevertheless divers of Asher and *M*.. 2Chr 30:11
even many of Ephraim, and *M*............ 2Chr 30:18
and Benjamin, in Ephraim also and *M* 2Chr 31:1
And so did he in the cities of *M*........... 2Chr 34:6
had gathered of the hand of *M*............. 2Chr 34:9
Gilead is mine, and *M* is mine ................ Ps 60:7
*M* stir up thy strength, and come............ Ps 80:2
*M* is mine................................................ Ps 108:8
*M*, Ephraim; and Ephraim ........................... Is 9:21
and Ephraim, *M* ........................................... Is 9:21
the west side, a portion for *M*............... Eze 48:4
And by the border of *M*, from the........... Eze 48:5
*3. Grandfather of Jonathan.*
the son of Gershom, the son of *M*...... Judg 18:30
*4. Son of King Hezekiah.*
*M* his son reigned in his stead........... 2Kin 20:21
*M* was twelve years old when he .......... 2Kin 21:1
*M* seduced them to do more evil........... 2Kin 21:9
Because *M* king of Judah hath done . 2Kin 21:11
Moreover *M* shed innocent blood......... 2Kin 21:16
Now the rest of the acts of *M*............... 2Kin 21:17
*M* slept with his fathers, and was......... 2Kin 21:18
of the LORD, as his father *M* did........... 2Kin 21:20
the altars which *M* had made in.......... 2Kin 23:12
that *M* had provoked him withal........... 2Kin 23:26
of his sight, for the sins of *M*............... 2Kin 24:3
son, Hezekiah his son, *M* his son, ........ 1Chr 3:13
*M* his son reigned in his stead .......... 2Chr 32:33
*M* was twelve years old when he......... 2Chr 33:1
So *M* made Judah and the.................... 2Chr 33:9
the LORD spake to *M*............................. 2Chr 33:10
took *M* among the thorns..................... 2Chr 33:11
Then *M* knew that the LORD he was. 2Chr 33:13
Now the rest of the acts of *M*............... 2Chr 33:18
So *M* slept with his fathers, and......... 2Chr 33:20
of the LORD, as did *M* his father......... 2Chr 33:22
which *M* his father had made ............. 2Chr 33:22
as *M* his father had humbled............... 2Chr 33:23
because of *M* the son of Hezekiah .......... Jer 15:4
*5. Married a foreigner in exile.*
Bezaleel, and Binnui, and *M*................... Ezr 10:30
*6. A descendant of Hashum.*
Zabad, Eliphelet, Jeremai, *M*.................. Ezr 10:33

**MANASSEH'S** (*ma-nas'-sez*)
*1. Refers to Manasseh 1.*
and his left hand upon *M* head............ Gen 48:14
from Ephraim's head unto *M* head........ Gen 48:17
the rest of *M* sons had the land ............ Josh 17:6
*2. Refers to Manasseh 2.*
Ephraim's, and northward it was *M*... Josh 17:10

**MANASSES** (*ma-nas'-seez*) See MANASSEH.
*1. Greek form of Manasseh; ancestor of Jesus.*
And Ezekias begat *M*................................ Mt 1:10
and *M* begat Amon...................................... Mt 1:10
*2. Greek form of Manasseh 2.*
Of the tribe of *M* were sealed .................... Rev 7:6

**MANASSITES** (*ma-nas'-sites*) *Same as Manasseh 2.*
and Golan in Bashan, of the *M*............. Deut 4:43
the Ephraimites, and among the *M*........ Judg 12:4
and the Reubenites, and the *M*........... 2Kin 10:33

**MANDRAKES**
found *m* in the field, and brought ....... Gen 30:14
me, I pray thee, of thy son's *m*.............. Gen 30:14
thou take away my son's *m* also ......... Gen 30:15
thee to night for thy son's *m*................. Gen 30:15
I have hired thee with my son's *m* ..... Gen 30:16
The *m* give a smell, and at our............ Song 7:13

**MANEH**
fifteen shekels, shall be your *m* ............ Eze 45:12

**MANGER**
clothes, and laid him in a *m*...................... Lk 2:7
swaddling clothes, lying in a *m* ................ Lk 2:12
Joseph, and the babe lying in a *m* .......... Lk 2:16

**MANIFEST**
of men, that God might *m* them ........... Eccl 3:18
secret, that shall not be made *m*............... Lk 8:17
he should be made *m* to Israel.................. Jn 1:31
that his deeds may be made *m*.................. Jn 3:21
of God should be made *m* in him ............... Jn 9:3
love him, and will *m* myself to him........ Jn 14:21
that thou wilt *m* thyself unto us.............. Jn 14:22
is *m* to all them that dwell in ................. Acts 4:16
may be known of God is *m* in them....... Rom 1:19
I was made *m* unto them that asked. Rom 10:20
But now is made *m*, and by the.......... Rom 16:26
Every man's work shall be made *m*...... 1Cor 3:13
will make *m* the counsels of the............. 1Cor 4:5
may be made *m* among you ............... 1Cor 11:19
the secrets of his heart made *m* ......... 1Cor 14:25
it is *m* that he is excepted,................. 1Cor 15:27
maketh *m* the savour of his.................. 2Cor 2:14
Jesus might be made *m* in our body.... 2Cor 4:10
be made *m* in our mortal flesh.............. 2Cor 4:11
but we are made *m* unto God................ 2Cor 5:11
are made *m* in your consciences .......... 2Cor 5:11
made *m* among you in all things........... 2Cor 11:6
Now the works of the flesh are *m*............ Gal 5:19
reproved are made *m* by the light ......... Eph 5:13
whatsoever doth make *m* is light .......... Eph 5:13
in Christ are *m* in all the palace............. Phil 1:13
but now is made *m* to his saints ............. Col 1:26
That I may make it *m*, as I ought............. Col 4:4
Which is a *m* token of the........................ 2Th 1:5
God was *m* in the flesh, justified............ 1Ti 3:16
works of some are *m* beforehand........... 1Ti 5:25
But is now made *m* by the...................... 2Ti 1:10
folly shall be *m* unto all men................... 2Ti 3:9
that is not *m* in his sight ........................ Heb 4:13
holiest of all was not yet made *m* ........... Heb 9:8
but was *m* in these last times for.......... 1Pet 1:20
that they might be made *m* that............ 1Jn 2:19
In this the children of God are *m*........... 1Jn 3:10
for thy judgments are made *m*.............. Rev 15:4

**MANIFESTATION**
for the *m* of the sons of God................. Rom 8:19
But the *m* of the Spirit is given ............ 1Cor 12:7
but by *m* of the truth commending ....... 2Cor 4:2

**MANIFESTED**
nothing hid, which shall not be *m*.......... Mk 4:22
of Galilee, and *m* forth his glory ............ Jn 2:11
I have *m* thy name unto the men ............ Jn 17:6
of God without the law is *m*................... Rom 3:21
But hath in due times *m* his word.......... Titus 1:3
(For the life was *m*, and we have ............ 1Jn 1:2
with the Father, and was *m* unto us......... 1Jn 1:2
ye know that he was *m* to take .............. 1Jn 3:5
this purpose the Son of God was *m* .......... 1Jn 3:8
In this was *m* the love of God................. 1Jn 4:9

**MANIFESTLY**
Forasmuch as ye are *m* declared to....... 2Cor 3:3

**MANIFOLD**
Yet thou in thy *m* mercies...................... Neh 9:19
according to thy *m* mercies thou............. Neh 9:27
O LORD, how *m* are thy works ............... Ps 104:24
For I know your *m* transgressions..... Amos 5:12
Who shall not receive *m* more in........... Lk 18:30
by the church the *m* wisdom of God.... Eph 3:10
heaviness through *m* temptations.......... 1Pet 1:6
stewards of the *m* grace of God........... 1Pet 4:10

**MANKIND**
Thou shalt not lie with *m* ..................... Lev 18:22
If a man also lie with *m*, as he ............ Lev 20:13
thing, and the breath of all *m*................ Job 12:10
nor abusers of themselves with *m* ......... 1Cor 6:9
that defile themselves with *m* ................ 1Ti 1:10
is tamed, and hath been tamed of *m*........ Jas 3:7

**MANNA**
they said one to another, It is *m*........... Ex 16:15
Israel called the name thereof *M* ........... Ex 16:31
and put an omer full of *m* therein ......... Ex 16:33
of Israel did eat *m* forty years ............... Ex 16:35
they did eat *m*, until they came............... Ex 16:35
is nothing at all, beside this *m*............... Num 11:6
the *m* was as coriander seed, and........ Num 11:7
in the night, the *m* fell upon it ............... Num 11:9
to hunger, and fed thee with *m*............... Deut 8:3
fed thee in the wilderness with *m*........ Deut 8:16
the *m* ceased on the morrow after.......... Josh 5:12
the children of Israel *m* any more.......... Josh 5:12
not thy *m* from their mouth .................. Neh 9:20
had rained down *m* upon them to........... Ps 78:24
fathers did eat *m* in the desert ................ Jn 6:31
did eat *m* in the wilderness ..................... Jn 6:49
not as your fathers did eat *m* ................. Jn 6:58
was the golden pot that had *m* .............. Heb 9:4

I give to eat of the hidden *m* Rev 2:17

**MANNER**

with Sarah after the *m* of women Gen 18:11
far from thee to do after this *m* Gen 18:25
us after the *m* of all the earth Gen 19:31
womb, and two *m* of people shall be Gen 25:23
On this *m* shall ye speak unto Gen 32:19
After this *m* did thy servant to Gen 39:19
after the former *m* when thou wast Gen 40:13
basket there was of all *m* of Gen 40:17
his father he sent after this *m* Gen 45:23
in all *m* of service in the field Ex 1:14
they also did in like *m* with Ex 7:11
no *m* of work shall be done in Ex 12:16
with her after the *m* of daughters Ex 21:9
For all *m* of trespass, whether it Ex 22:9
or for any *m* of lost thing, which Ex 22:9
In like *m* thou shalt deal with Ex 23:11
and in all *m* of workmanship, Ex 31:3
to work in all *m* of workmanship Ex 31:5
to bring for all *m* of work Ex 35:29
and in all *m* of workmanship Ex 35:31
to make any *m* of cunning work Ex 35:33
of heart, to work all *m* of work Ex 35:35
to know how to work all *m* of work Ex 36:1
offering, according to the *m* Lev 5:10
saying, Ye shall eat no *m* of fat Lev 7:23
ye shall eat no *m* of blood Lev 7:26
it be that eateth any *m* of blood Lev 7:27
and offered it according to the *m* Lev 9:16
among all *m* of beasts that go on Lev 11:27
ye defile yourselves with any *m* Lev 11:44
for all *m* of plague of leprosy Lev 14:54
you, that eateth any *m* of blood Lev 17:10
eat the blood of no *m* of flesh Lev 17:14
planted all *m* of trees for food Lev 19:23
or by any *m* of living thing that Lev 20:25
Ye shall do no *m* of work Lev 23:31
Ye shall have one *m* of law Lev 24:22
neither she be taken with the *m* Num 5:13
and according to the *m* thereof Num 9:14
do these things after this *m* Num 15:13
one *m* shall be for you, and for Num 15:16
offering, according to the *m* Num 15:24
ye shall do no *m* of servile work Num 28:18
After this *m* ye shall offer daily Num 28:24
offerings, according unto their *m* Num 29:6
to their number, after the *m* Num 29:18
to their number, after the *m* Num 29:21
to their number, after the *m* Num 29:24
to their number, after the *m* Num 29:27
to their number, after the *m* Num 29:30
to their number, after the *m* Num 29:33
to their number, after the *m* Num 29:37
of all *m* of beasts, and give them Num 31:30
for ye saw no *m* of similitude on Deut 4:15
this is the *m* of the release Deut 15:2
In like *m* shalt thou do with his Deut 22:3
he that lieth with any *m* of beast Deut 27:21
city after the same *m* seven times Josh 6:15
What *m* of men were they whom ye Judg 8:18
in like *m* they sent unto the king Judg 11:17
after the *m* of the Zidonians, Judg 18:7
Now this was the *m* in former time Ruth 4:7
shew them the *m* of the king that 1Sa 8:9
This will be the *m* of the king 1Sa 8:11
the people the *m* of the kingdom 1Sa 10:25
people answered him after this *m* 1Sa 17:27
and spake after the same *m* 1Sa 17:30
him again after the former *m* 1Sa 17:30
saying, On this *m* spake David 1Sa 18:24
before Samuel in like *m*, and lay 1Sa 19:24
and the bread is in a *m* common 1Sa 21:5
so will be his *m* all the while he 1Sa 27:11
played before the LORD on all *m* 2Sa 6:5
And is this the *m* of man, O Lord 2Sa 7:19
king, and speak on this *m* unto him 2Sa 14:3
on this *m* did Absalom to all 2Sa 15:6
hath spoken after this *m* 2Sa 17:6
work of the bases was on this *m* 1Kin 7:28
After this *m* he made the ten 1Kin 7:37
after their *m* with knives 1Kin 18:28
And one said on this *m* 1Kin 22:20
and another said on that *m* 1Kin 22:20
What *m* of man was he which came 2Kin 1:7
stood by a pillar, as the *m* was 2Kin 11:14
know not the *m* of the God of the 2Kin 17:26
not the *m* of the God of the land 2Kin 17:26
them the *m* of the God of the land 2Kin 17:27
after the *m* of the nations whom 2Kin 17:33
but they did after their former *m* 2Kin 17:40
*m* of service of the tabernacle of 1Chr 6:48
with all *m* of instruments of war 1Chr 12:37
with him all *m* of vessels of gold 1Chr 18:10
all *m* of cunning men for every 1Chr 22:15
cunning men for every *m* of work 1Chr 22:15
for all *m* of measure and size 1Chr 23:29
of the LORD, according to their *m* 1Chr 24:19
instruments of all *m* of service 1Chr 28:14
shall be with thee for all *m* of 1Chr 28:21
skilful man, for any *m* of service 1Chr 28:21
all *m* of precious stones, and 1Chr 29:2
for all *m* of work to be made by 1Chr 29:5
also to grave any *m* of graving 2Chr 2:14
after the *m* before the oracle 2Chr 4:20
*m* of the nations of other lands 2Chr 13:9
And one spake saying after this *m* 2Chr 18:19
and another saying after that *m* 2Chr 18:19
in their place after their *m* 2Chr 30:16
you, nor persuade you on this *m* 2Chr 32:15
for all *m* of pleasant jewels 2Chr 32:27
and stalls for all *m* of beasts 2Chr 32:28
the work in any *m* of service 2Chr 34:13
said we unto them after this *m* Ezr 5:4
I answered them after the same *m* Neh 6:4
*m* the fifth time with an open Neh 6:5
assembly, according unto the *m* Neh 8:18
and the fruit of all *m* of trees Neh 10:37
all *m* of burdens, which they Neh 13:15
all *m* of ware, and sold on the Neh 13:16
(for so was the king's *m* toward Est 1:13
according to the *m* of the women Est 2:12
soul abhorreth all *m* of meat Ps 107:18
be full, affording all *m* of store Ps 144:13
are all *m* of pleasant fruits Song 7:13
the lambs feed after their *m* Is 5:17
thee, after the *m* of Egypt Is 10:24
lift it up after the *m* of Egypt Is 10:26
dwell therein shall die in like *m* Is 51:6
After this *m* will I mar the pride Jer 13:9
hath been thy *m* from thy youth Jer 22:21
shall remain after the *m* thereof Jer 30:18
after the *m* of your fathers Eze 20:30
after the *m* of the Babylonians of Eze 23:15
them after the *m* of adulteresses Eze 23:45
after the *m* of women that shed Eze 23:45
no *m* of hurt was found upon him, Dan 6:23
pestilence after the *m* of Egypt Amos 4:10
The *m* of Beer-sheba liveth Amos 8:14
and healing all *m* of sickness Mt 4:23
all *m* of disease among the people Mt 4:23
shall say all *m* of evil against Mt 5:11
After this *m* therefore pray ye Mt 6:9
What *m* of man is this, that even Mt 8:27
out, and to heal all *m* of sickness Mt 10:1
of sickness and all *m* of disease Mt 10:1
All *m* of sin and blasphemy shall Mt 12:31
What *m* of man is this, that even Mk 4:41
see what *m* of stones and what Mk 13:1
So ye in like *m*, when ye shall Mk 13:29
cast in her mind what *m* of Lk 1:29
What *m* of child shall this be Lk 1:66
for in the like *m* did their Lk 6:23
what *m* of woman this is that Lk 7:39
to another, What *m* of man is this Lk 8:25
Ye know not what *m* of spirit ye Lk 9:55
all *m* of herbs, and pass over Lk 11:42
and in like *m* the seven also Lk 20:31
What *m* of communications are Lk 24:17
after the *m* of the purifying of Jn 2:6
What *m* of saying is this that he Jn 7:36
as the *m* of the Jews is to bury Jn 19:40
shall so come in like *m* as ye Acts 1:11
Wherein were all *m* of fourfooted Acts 10:12
circumcised after the *m* of Moses Acts 15:1
letters by them after this *m* Acts 15:23
And Paul, as his *m* was, went in Acts 17:2
after what *m* I have been with you Acts 20:18
*m* of the law of the fathers Acts 22:3
And he wrote a letter after this *m* Acts 23:25
It is not the *m* of the Romans to Acts 25:16
I doubted of such *m* of questions Acts 25:20
My *m* of life from my youth, which Acts 26:4
I speak after the *m* of men Rom 6:19
in me all *m* of concupiscence Rom 7:8
gift of God, one after this *m* 1Cor 7:7
After the same *m* also he took the 1Cor 11:25
If after the *m* of men I have 1Cor 15:32
were made sorry after a godly *m* 2Cor 7:9
livest after the *m* of Gentiles Gal 2:14
I speak after the *m* of men Gal 3:15
as ye know what *m* of men we were 1Th 1:5
*m* of entering in we had unto you 1Th 1:9
In like *m* also, that women adorn 1Ti 2:9
*m* of life, purpose, faith, 2Ti 3:10
together, as the *m* of some is Heb 10:25
forgetteth what *m* of man he was Jas 1:24
or what *m* of time the Spirit of 1Pet 1:11
ye holy in all *m* of conversation 1Pet 1:15
For after this *m* in the old time 1Pet 3:5
what *m* of persons ought ye to be 2Pet 3:11
what *m* of love the Father hath 1Jn 3:1
the cities about them in like *m* Jude 7
them, he must in this *m* be killed Rev 11:5
all *m* vessels of ivory Rev 18:12
all *m* vessels of most precious Rev 18:12
with all *m* of precious stones Rev 21:19
which bare twelve *m* of fruits Rev 22:2

**MANNERS**

not walk in the *m* of the nation Lev 20:23
day they do after the former *m* 2Kin 17:34
but have done after the *m* of the Eze 11:12
he their *m* in the wilderness Acts 13:18
communications corrupt good *m* 1Cor 15:33
in divers *m* spake in time past Heb 1:1

**MANOAH** (*ma-no'-ah*) *Father of Samson.*

of the Danites, whose name was *M* Judg 13:2
Then *M* intreated the LORD, and Judg 13:8
God hearkened to the voice of *M* Judg 13:9
but *M* her husband was not with Judg 13:9
*M* arose, and went after his wife, Judg 13:11
*M* said, Now let thy words come to Judg 13:12
the angel of the LORD said unto *M* Judg 13:13
*M* said unto the angel of the LORD Judg 13:15
the angel of the LORD said unto *M* Judg 13:16
For *M* knew not that he was an Judg 13:16
*M* said unto the angel of the LORD Judg 13:17
So *M* took a kid with a meat Judg 13:19
and *M* and his wife looked on Judg 13:19
*M* and his wife looked on it Judg 13:20
the LORD did no more appear to *M* Judg 13:21
Then *M* knew that he was an angel Judg 13:21
*M* said unto his wife, We shall Judg 13:22
the buryingplace of *M* his father Judg 16:31

**MAN'S**

the ground any more for *m* sake Gen 8:21
for the imagination of *m* heart is Gen 8:21
at the hand of every *m* brother Gen 9:5
Whoso sheddeth *m* blood, by man Gen 9:6
man, and every *m* hand against him Gen 16:12
for she is a *m* wife Gen 20:3
We are all one *m* sons Gen 42:11
to restore every *m* money into his Gen 42:25
every *m* bundle of money was in Gen 42:35
every *m* money was in the mouth of Gen 43:21
put every *m* money in his sack's Gen 44:1
for we may not see the *m* face Gen 44:26
unto him, Who hath made *m* mouth Ex 4:11
But every *m* servant that is Ex 12:44
if one *m* ox hurt another's, that Ex 21:35
and shall feed in another *m* field Ex 22:5
it be stolen out of the *m* house Ex 22:7
Upon *m* flesh shall it not be Ex 30:32
offereth any *m* burnt offering Lev 7:8
if any *m* seed of copulation go Lev 15:16
adultery with another *m* wife Lev 20:10
every *m* hallowed things shall be Num 5:10
If any *m* wife go aside, and commit Num 5:12
write thou every *m* name upon his Num 17:2
come to pass, that the *m* rod Num 17:5
every *m* inheritance shall be in Num 33:54
is *m* life) to employ them in the Deut 20:19
she may go and be another *m* wife Deut 24:2
for he taketh a *m* life to pledge Deut 24:6
he put a trumpet in every *m* hand Judg 7:16
the LORD set every *m* sword Judg 7:22
of the *m* house where her lord was Judg 19:26
The *m* name with whom I Ruth 2:19
thou taken ought of any *m* hand 1Sa 12:4
every *m* sword was against his 1Sa 14:20
Let no *m* heart fail because of 1Sa 17:32
but took the poor *m* lamb, and 2Sa 12:4
came to a *m* house in Bahurim, 2Sa 17:18
which Amasa was a *m* son, whose 2Sa 17:25
out of the sea, like a *m* hand 1Kin 18:44
*m* heart to bring into the house 2Kin 12:4
which were on a *m* left hand at 2Kin 23:8
every great *m* house burnt he with 2Kin 25:9
do according to every *m* pleasure Est 1:8
are thy years as *m* days, Job 10:5
I pray you, accept any *m* person Job 32:21
bread which strengtheneth *m* heart Ps 104:15
The rich *m* wealth is his strong Prov 10:15
the recompence of a *m* hands shall Prov 12:14
The ransom of a *m* life are his Prov 13:8
When a *m* ways please the LORD, he Prov 16:7
A *m* heart deviseth his way Prov 16:9
The words of a *m* mouth are as Prov 18:4
The rich *m* wealth is his strong Prov 18:11
A *m* gift maketh room for him, and Prov 18:16
A *m* belly shall be satisfied with Prov 18:20
are many devices in a *m* heart Prov 19:21
*M* goings are of the LORD Prov 20:24
of a *m* friend by hearty counsel Prov 27:9
A *m* pride shall bring him low Prov 29:23
but every *m* judgment cometh from Prov 29:26
The wise *m* eyes are in his head Eccl 2:14
a *m* wisdom maketh his face to Eccl 8:1
a wise *m* heart discerneth both Eccl 8:5
the poor *m* wisdom is despised Eccl 9:16
A wise *m* heart is at his right Eccl 10:2
of a wise *m* mouth are gracious Eccl 10:12
in it with a *m* pen concerning Is 8:1
and every *m* heart shall melt Is 13:7
go from him, and become another *m* Jer 3:1
for every *m* word shall be his Jer 23:36
given thee cow's dung for *m* dung Eze 4:15
of a *m* hand under their wings Eze 10:8
every *m* sword shall be against Eze 38:21
the land, when any seeth a *m* bone Eze 39:15
in the *m* hand a measuring reed of Eze 40:5
Let his heart be changed from *m* Dan 4:16
came forth fingers of a *m* hand Dan 5:5
a *m* heart was given to it Dan 7:4
I heard a *m* voice between the Dan 8:16
a *m* uncle shall take him up, and Amos 6:10
let us not perish for this *m* life Jonah 1:14
a *m* enemies are the men of his Mic 7:6
a *m* foes shall be they of his own Mt 10:36
receive a righteous *m* reward Mt 10:41
one enter into a strong *m* house Mt 12:29
can enter into a strong *m* house Mk 3:27
If a *m* brother die, and leave his Mk 12:19
as evil, for the Son of *m* sake Lk 6:22
for a *m* life consisteth not in Lk 12:15
in that which is another *m* Lk 16:12
which fell from the rich *m* table Lk 16:21
If any *m* brother die, having a Lk 20:28
thou also one of this *m* disciples Jn 18:17
to bring this *m* blood upon us Acts 5:28
their clothes at a young *m* feet Acts 7:58
and we entered into the *m* house Acts 11:12
Of this *m* seed hath God according Acts 13:23
stone, graven by art and *m* device Acts 17:29
and entered into a certain *m* house Acts 18:7
I have coveted no *m* silver Acts 20:33
no loss of any *m* life among you Acts 27:22
For if by one *m* offence death Rom 5:17
For as by one *m* disobedience many Rom 5:19

that judgest another *m* servant ... Rom 14:4
build upon another *m* foundation ... Rom 15:20
with enticing words of *m* wisdom ... 1Cor 2:4
the words which *m* wisdom teacheth.. 1Cor 2:13
Every *m* work shall be made ... 1Cor 3:13
every *m* work of what sort it is ... 1Cor 3:13
If any *m* work abide which he hath ... 1Cor 3:14
If any *m* work shall be burned, he ... 1Cor 3:15
judged of you, or of *m* judgment ... 1Cor 4:3
judged of another *m* conscience ... 1Cor 10:29
commending ourselves to every *m* ... 2Cor 4:2
not to boast in another *m* line of ... 2Cor 10:16
God accepteth no *m* person ... Gal 2:6
Though it be but a *m* covenant ... Gal 3:15
did we eat any *m* bread for nought ... 2Th 3:8
heart, this *m* religion is vain ... Jas 1:26
judgeth according to every *m* work ... 1Pet 1:17
the dumb ass speaking with *m* ... 2Pet 2:16

**MANSERVANT**
thy son, nor thy daughter, thy *m* ... Ex 20:10
thy neighbour's wife, nor his *m* ... Ex 20:17
shall push a *m* or a maidservant ... Ex 21:32
son, nor thy daughter, nor thy *m* ... Deut 5:14
that thy *m* and thy maidservant may. Deut 5:14
house, his field, or his *m* ... Deut 5:21
son, and thy daughter, and thy *m* ... Deut 12:18
son, and thy daughter, and thy *m* ... Deut 16:11
son, and thy daughter, and thy *m* ... Deut 16:14
of my *m* or of my maidservant ... Job 31:13
That every man should let his *m* ... Jer 34:9
that every one should let his *m* ... Jer 34:10

**MANSERVANT'S**
And if he smite out his *m* tooth ... Ex 21:27

**MANSERVANTS**
Beside their *m* and their ... Neh 7:67

**MANSIONS**
In my Father's house are many *m* ... Jn 14:2

**MANSLAYER**
which ye shall appoint for the *m* ... Num 35:6
that the *m* die not, until he ... Num 35:12

**MANSLAYERS**
and murderers of mothers, for *m* ... 1Ti 1:9

**MANTLE**
tent, she covered him with a *m* ... Judg 4:18
laid hold upon the skirt of his *m* ... 1Sa 15:27
and he is covered with a *m* ... 1Sa 28:14
that he wrapped his face in his *m* ... 1Kin 19:13
by him, and cast his *m* upon him ... 1Kin 19:19
And Elijah took his *m*, and wrapped ... 2Kin 2:8
He took up also the *m* of Elijah ... 2Kin 2:13
he took the *m* of Elijah that fell ... 2Kin 2:14
thing, I rent my garment and my *m* ... Ezr 9:3
and having rent my garment and my *m*. Ezr 9:5
Then Job arose, and rent his *m* ... Job 1:20
and they rent every one his *m* ... Job 2:12
their own confusion, as with a *m* ... Ps 109:29

**MANTLES**
suits of apparel, and the *m* ... Is 3:22

**MANY** See PREFACE.

**MAOCH** (*ma'-ok*) *Father of Achish.*
him unto Achish, the son of *M* ... 1Sa 27:2

**MAON** (*ma'-on*) See MAONITES.
*1. A city in Judah.*
*M*, Carmel, and Ziph, and Juttah, ... Josh 15:55
And there was a man in *M*, whose ... 1Sa 25:2
*2. A descendant of Caleb.*
And the son of Shammai was *M* ... 1Chr 2:45
*M* was the father of Beth-zur ... 1Chr 2:45
*3. A wilderness in Judah.*
men were in the wilderness of *M* ... 1Sa 23:24
and abode in the wilderness of *M* ... 1Sa 23:25
David in the wilderness of *M* ... 1Sa 23:25

**MAONITES** (*ma'-on-ites*) See MEHUNIM. *An enemy tribe of Israel.*
also, and the Amalekites, and the *M*. Judg 10:12

**MAR**
neither shalt thou *m* the corners ... Lev 19:27
lest I *m* mine own inheritance ... Ruth 4:6
of your mice that *m* the land ... 1Sa 6:5
*m* every good piece of land with ... 2Kin 3:19
They *m* my path, they set forward ... Job 30:13
will I *m* the pride of Judah ... Jer 13:9

**MARA** (*ma'-rah*) *Another name for Naomi.*
Call me not Naomi, call me *M* ... Ruth 1:20

**MARAH** (*ma'-rah*) *An Israelite encampment in the wilderness.*
And when they came to *M*, they ... Ex 15:23
not drink of the waters of *M* ... Ex 15:23
the name of it was called *M* ... Ex 15:23
of Etham, and pitched in *M* ... Num 33:8
And they removed from *M*, and came Num 33:9

**MARALAH** (*mar'-a-lah*) *A city in Zebulun.*
went up toward the sea, and *M* ... Josh 19:11

**MARANATHA**
Christ, let him be Anathema *M* ... 1Cor 16:22

**MARBLE**
stones, and *m* stones in abundance ... 1Chr 29:2
to silver rings and pillars of *m* ... Est 1:6
and blue, and white, and black, *m* ... Est 1:6
His legs are as pillars of *m* ... Song 5:15
wood, and of brass, and iron, and *m* ... Rev 18:12

**MARCH**
when thou didst *m* through the ... Ps 68:7
for they shall *m* with an army ... Jer 46:22
they shall *m* every one on his ... Joel 2:7
which shall *m* through the breadth ... Hab 1:6
Thou didst *m* through the land in ... Hab 3:12

**MARCHED**
the Egyptians *m* after them ... Ex 14:10

**MARCHEDST**
when thou *m* out of the field of ... Judg 5:4

**MARCUS** (*mar'-cus*) See MARK. *Latin form of Mark.*
fellowprisoner saluteth you, and *M* ... Col 4:10
*M*, Aristarchus, Demas, Lucas, my ... Philem 24
and so doth *M* my son ... 1Pet 5:13

**MARDUK** See MERODACH.

**MAREAL** See MARALAH.

**MARESHAH**
*1. A city in Judah.*
And Keilah, and Achzib, and *M* ... Josh 15:44
And Gath, and *M*, and Ziph, ... 2Chr 11:8
and came unto *M* ... 2Chr 14:9
in the valley of Zephathah at *M* ... 2Chr 14:10
Eliezer the son of Dodavah of *M* ... 2Chr 20:37
heir unto thee, O inhabitant of *M* ... Mic 1:15
*2. Father of Hebron.*
the sons of *M* the father of ... 1Chr 2:42
*3. A descendant of Shelah.*
Lecah, and Laadah the father of *M* ... 1Chr 4:21

**MARINERS**
of Zidon and Arvad were thy *m* ... Eze 27:8
*m* were in thee to occupy thy ... Eze 27:9
thy fairs, thy merchandise, thy *m* ... Eze 27:27
And all that handle the oar, the *m* ... Eze 27:29
Then the *m* were afraid, and cried ... Jonah 1:5

**MARISHES**
the *m* thereof shall not be healed ... Eze 47:11

**MARK** See MARCUS. *Missionary companion of Paul.*
And the LORD set a *m* upon Cain ... Gen 4:15
that thou shalt *m* the place where ... Ruth 3:4
thereof, as though I shot at a *m* ... 1Sa 20:20
*M* ye now when Amnon's heart is ... 2Sa 13:28
elders of the land, and said, *M* ... 1Kin 20:7
him, Go, strengthen thyself, and *m* ... 1Kin 20:22
thou set me as a *m* against thee ... Job 7:20
to pieces, and set me up for his *m* ... Job 16:12
*m*, and afterwards we will speak ... Job 18:2
*M* me, and be astonished, and lay ... Job 21:5
*M* well, O Job, hearken unto me ... Job 33:31
or canst thou *m* when the hinds do ... Job 39:1
*M* the perfect man, and behold the ... Ps 37:37
*M* ye well her bulwarks, consider ... Ps 48:13
they *m* my steps, when they wait ... Ps 56:6
shouldest *m* iniquities, O Lord, ... Ps 130:3
set me as a *m* for the arrow ... Lam 3:12
set a *m* upon the foreheads of the ... Eze 9:4
near any man upon whom is the *m* ... Eze 9:6
*m* well, and behold with thine eyes ... Eze 44:5
*m* well the entering in of the ... Eze 44:5
of John, whose surname was *M* ... Acts 12:12
them John, whose surname was *M* ... Acts 12:25
them John, whose surname was *M* ... Acts 15:37
and so Barnabas took *M*, and sailed ... Acts 15:39
*m* them which cause divisions and ... Rom 16:17
I press toward the *m* for the ... Phil 3:14
*m* them which walk so as ye have ... Phil 3:17
Take *M*, and bring him with thee ... 2Ti 4:11
to receive a *m* in their right ... Rev 13:16
or sell, save he that had the *m* ... Rev 13:17
receive his *m* in his forehead, or ... Rev 14:9
receiveth the *m* of his name ... Rev 14:11
and over his image, and over his *m* ... Rev 15:2
men which had the *m* of the beast ... Rev 16:2
had received the *m* of the beast ... Rev 19:20
his *m* upon their foreheads ... Rev 20:4

**MARKED**
the LORD, that Eli *m* her mouth ... 1Sa 1:12
Hast thou *m* the old way which ... Job 22:15
which they had *m* for themselves ... Job 24:16
yet thine iniquity is *m* before me ... Jer 2:22
who hath *m* his word, and heard it ... Jer 23:18
when he *m* how they chose out the ... Lk 14:7

**MARKEST**
If I sin, then thou *m* me, and thou ... Job 10:14

**MARKET**
men and vessels of brass in thy *m* ... Eze 27:13
traded in thy *m* wheat of Minnith ... Eze 27:17
cassia, and calamus, were in thy *m* ... Eze 27:19
did sing of thee in thy *m* ... Eze 27:25
And when they come from the *m* ... Mk 7:4
Jerusalem by the sheep *m* a pool ... Jn 5:2
in the *m* daily with them that met ... Acts 17:17

**MARKETH**
in the stocks, he *m* all my paths ... Job 33:11
he *m* it out with a line ... Is 44:13
he *m* it out with the compass, and ... Is 44:13

**MARKETPLACE**
saw others standing idle in the *m* ... Mt 20:3
unto children sitting in the *m* ... Lk 7:32
them into the *m* unto the rulers ... Acts 16:19

**MARKETPLACES**
and love salutations in the *m* ... Mk 12:38

**MARKETS**
unto children sitting in the *m* ... Mt 11:16
And greetings in the *m*, and to be ... Mt 23:7
synagogues, and greetings in the *m* ... Lk 11:43
robes, and love greetings in the *m* ... Lk 20:46

**MARKS**
dead, nor print any *m* upon you ... Lev 19:28
my body the *m* of the Lord Jesus ... Gal 6:17

**MAROTH** (*ma'-roth*) *A city in Judah.*
For the inhabitant of *M* waited ... Mic 1:12

**MARRED**
visage was so *m* more than any man ... Is 52:14
and, behold, the girdle was *m* ... Jer 13:7
was *m* in the hand of the potter ... Jer 18:4
out, and *m* their vine branches ... Nah 2:2
spilled, and the bottles will be *m* ... Mk 2:22

**MARRIAGE**
her raiment, and her duty of *m* ... Ex 21:10
their maidens were not given to *m* ... Ps 78:63
king, which made a *m* for his son ... Mt 22:2
are ready: come unto the *m* ... Mt 22:4
as ye shall find, bid to the *m* ... Mt 22:9
neither marry, nor are given in *m* ... Mt 22:30
drinking, marrying and giving in *m* ... Mt 24:38
ready went in with him to the *m* ... Mt 25:10
neither marry, nor are given in *m* ... Mk 12:25
wives, they were given in *m* ... Lk 17:27
world marry, and are given in *m* ... Lk 20:34
neither marry, nor are given in *m* ... Lk 20:35
there was a *m* in Cana of Galilee ... Jn 2:1
and his disciples, to the *m* ... Jn 2:2
that giveth her in *m* doeth well ... 1Cor 7:38
giveth her not in *m* doeth better ... 1Cor 7:38
*M* is honourable in all, and the ... Heb 13:4
for the *m* of the Lamb is come, and ... Rev 19:7
unto the *m* supper of the Lamb ... Rev 19:9

**MARRIAGES**
And make ye *m* with us, and give ... Gen 34:9
shalt thou make *m* with them ... Deut 7:3
you, and shall make *m* with them ... Josh 23:12

**MARRIED**
which *m* his daughters, and said, ... Gen 19:14
if he were *m*, then his wife shall ... Ex 21:3
also be *m* unto a stranger ... Lev 22:12
woman whom he had *m* ... Num 12:1
for he had *m* an Ethiopian woman ... Num 12:1
if they be *m* to any of the sons ... Num 36:3
were *m* unto their father's ... Num 36:11
they were *m* into the families of ... Num 36:12
with a woman *m* to an husband ... Deut 22:22
*m* her, and it come to pass that ... Deut 24:1
whom he *m* when he was threescore.. 1Chr 2:21
*m* fourteen wives, and begat twenty. 2Chr 13:21
I Jews that had *m* wives of Ashdod ... Neh 13:23
For an odious woman when she is *m* Prov 30:23
than the children of the *m* wife ... Is 54:1
in thee, and thy land shall be *m* ... Is 62:4
for I am *m* unto you ... Jer 3:14
hath *m* the daughter of a strange ... Mal 2:11
the first, when he had *m* a wife ... Mt 22:25
for he had *m* her ... Mk 6:17
be *m* to another, she committeth ... Mk 10:12
And another said, I have *m* a wife ... Lk 14:20
they *m* wives, they were given in ... Lk 17:27
she be *m* to another man, she ... Rom 7:3
though she be *m* to another man ... Rom 7:3
that ye should be *m* to another ... Rom 7:4
unto the *m* I command, yet not I, ... 1Cor 7:10
But he that is *m* careth for the ... 1Cor 7:33
but she that is *m* careth for the ... 1Cor 7:34
liberty to be *m* to whom she will ... 1Cor 7:39

**MARRIETH**
For as a young man *m* a virgin ... Is 62:5
whoso *m* her which is put away ... Mt 19:9
*m* another, committeth adultery ... Lk 16:18
whosoever *m* her that is put away ... Lk 16:18

**MARROW**
and his bones are moistened with *m* ... Job 21:24
soul shall be satisfied as with *m* ... Ps 63:5
to thy navel, and *m* to thy bones ... Prov 3:8
the lees, of fat things full of *m* ... Is 25:6
and spirit, and of the joints and *m* ... Heb 4:12

**MARRY**
*m* her, and raise up seed to thy ... Gen 38:8
Let them *m* to whom they think ... Num 36:6
of their father shall they *m* ... Num 36:6
not *m* without unto a stranger ... Deut 25:5
virgin, so shall thy sons *m* thee ... Is 62:5
whosoever shall *m* her that is ... Mt 5:32
shall *m* another, committeth ... Mt 19:9
his wife, it is not good to *m* ... Mt 19:10
his brother shall *m* his wife ... Mt 22:24
the resurrection they neither *m* ... Mt 22:30
*m* another, committeth adultery ... Mk 10:11
from the dead, they neither *m* ... Mk 12:25
The children of this world *m* ... Lk 20:34
from the dead, neither *m*, nor are ... Lk 20:35
they cannot contain, let them *m* ... 1Cor 7:9
it is better to *m* than to burn ... 1Cor 7:9
But and if thou *m*, thou hast not ... 1Cor 7:28
and if a virgin *m*, she hath not ... 1Cor 7:28
he sinneth not: let them *m* ... 1Cor 7:36
Forbidding to *m*, and commanding to ... 1Ti 4:3

against Christ, they will *m* 1Ti 5:11
that the younger women *m*, bear 1Ti 5:14

**MARRYING**
our God in *m* strange wives Neh 13:27
they were eating and drinking, *m* Mt 24:38

**MARS'** (*marz*) *Refers to a landmark in Athens.*
Paul stood in the midst of *M* hill Acts 17:22

**MARSENA** (*mar'-se-nah*) *A prince of Media and Persia.*
Admatha, Tarshish, Meres, *M* Est 1:14

**MART**
and she is a *m* of nations Is 23:3

**MARTHA** (*mar'-thah*) *Sister of Lazarus.*
a certain woman named *M* received Lk 10:38
But *M* was cumbered about much Lk 10:40
and said unto her, *M*, *M* Lk 10:41
the town of Mary and her sister *M* Jn 11:1
Now Jesus loved *M*, and her sister, Jn 11:5
And many of the Jews came to *M* Jn 11:19
Then *M*, as soon as she heard that Jn 11:20
Then said *M* unto Jesus, Lord, if Jn 11:21
*M* saith unto him, I know that he Jn 11:24
was in that place where *M* met him Jn 11:30
*M*, the sister of him that was Jn 11:39
a supper; and *M* served Jn 12:2

**MARTYR**
blood of thy *m* Stephen was shed Acts 22:20
wherein Antipas was my faithful *m* Rev 2:13

**MARTYRS**
with the blood of the *m* of Jesus Rev 17:6

**MARVEL**
a province, *m* not at the matter Eccl 5:8
and all men did *m* Mk 5:20
*M* not that I said unto thee, Ye Jn 3:7
works than these, that ye may *m* Jn 5:20
*M* not at this Jn 5:28
I have done one work, and ye all *m* Jn 7:21
men of Israel, why *m* ye at this Acts 3:12
And no *m*; for Satan himself 2Cor 11:14
I *m* that ye are so soon removed Gal 1:6
*M* not, my brethren, if the world 1Jn 3:13
unto me, Wherefore didst thou *m* Rev 17:7

**MARVELLED**
and the men *m* one at another Gen 43:33
They saw it, and so they *m* Ps 48:5
When Jesus heard it, he *m* Mt 8:10
But the men *m*, saying, What Mt 8:27
the multitudes saw it, they *m* Mt 9:8
and the multitudes *m*, saying, It Mt 9:33
when the disciples saw it, they *m* Mt 21:20
had heard these words, they *m* Mt 22:22
that the governor *m* greatly Mt 27:14
he *m* because of their unbelief Mk 6:6
And they *m* at him Mk 12:17
so that Pilate *m* Mk 15:5
Pilate *m* if he were already dead Mk 15:44
*m* that he tarried so long in the Lk 1:21
And they *m* all Lk 1:63
his mother *m* at those things Lk 2:33
he *m* at him, and turned him about, Lk 7:9
he *m* that he had not first washed Lk 11:38
they *m* at his answer, and held Lk 20:26
*m* that he talked with the woman Jn 4:27
And the Jews *m*, saying, How Jn 7:15
And they were all amazed and *m* Acts 2:7
unlearned and ignorant men, they *m* Acts 4:13

**MARVELLOUS**
Remember his *m* works that he hath 1Chr 16:12
his *m* works among all nations 1Chr 16:24
*m* things without number Job 5:9
thou shewest thyself *m* upon me Job 10:16
I will shew forth all thy *m* works Ps 9:1
Shew thy *m* lovingkindness, O thou Ps 17:7
his *m* kindness in a strong city Ps 31:21
*M* things did he in the sight of Ps 78:12
for he hath done *m* things Ps 98:1
Remember his *m* works that he hath Ps 105:5
it is *m* in our eyes Ps 118:23
*m* are thy works Ps 139:14
to do a *m* work among this people Is 29:14
among this people, even a *m* work Is 29:14
shall speak *m* things against the Dan 11:36
will I shew unto him *m* things Mic 7:15
If it be *m* in the eyes of the Zec 8:6
should it also be *m* in mine eyes Zec 8:6
doing, and it is *m* in our eyes Mt 21:42
doing, and it is *m* in our eyes Mk 12:11
them, Why herein is a *m* thing Jn 9:30
out of darkness into his *m* light 1Pet 2:9
sign in heaven, great and *m* Rev 15:1
*m* are thy works, Lord God Rev 15:3

**MARVELLOUSLY**
for he was *m* helped, till he was 2Chr 26:15
God thundereth *m* with his voice Job 37:5
heathen, and regard, and wonder *m* Hab 1:5

**MARVELS**
before all thy people I will do *m* Ex 34:10

**MARY** (*ma'-ry*)
*1. Mother of Jesus.*
begat Joseph the husband of *M* Mt 1:16
When as his mother *M* was espoused Mt 1:18
not to take unto thee *M* thy wife Mt 1:20
the young child with *M* his mother Mt 2:11
is not his mother called *M* Mt 13:55
this the carpenter, the son of *M* Mk 6:3
and the virgin's name was *M* Lk 1:27
angel said unto her, Fear not, *M* Lk 1:30
Then said *M* unto the angel, How Lk 1:34
*M* said, Behold the handmaid of Lk 1:38
*M* arose in those days, and went Lk 1:39
heard the salutation of *M* Lk 1:41
*M* said, My soul doth magnify the Lk 1:46
*M* abode with her about three Lk 1:56
To be taxed with *M* his espoused Lk 2:5
they came with haste, and found *M* Lk 2:16
But *M* kept all these things, and Lk 2:19
said unto *M* his mother, Behold, Lk 2:34
*M* the mother of Jesus, and with Acts 1:14
*2. A woman of Magdala.*
Among which was *M* Magdalene Mt 27:56
And there was *M* Magdalene, and the Mt 27:61
came *M* Magdalene and the other Mt 28:1
among whom was *M* Magdalene Mk 15:40
*M* Magdalene and Mary the mother of Mk 15:47
he appeared first to *M* Magdalene Mk 16:9
*M* called Magdalene, out of whom Lk 8:2
It was *M* Magdalene, and Joanna, and Lk 24:10
wife of Cleophas, and *M* Magdalene Jn 19:25
the week cometh *M* Magdalene early Jn 20:1
But *M* stood without at the Jn 20:11
Jesus saith unto her, *M* Jn 20:16
*M* Magdalene came and told the Jn 20:18
*3. Mother of James and Joses.*
*M* the mother of James and Joses, Mt 27:56
Mary Magdalene, and the other *M* Mt 27:61
the other *M* to see the sepulchre Mt 28:1
*M* the mother of James the less and Mk 15:40
*M* the mother of Joses beheld Mk 15:47
*M* Magdalene, and Mary the mother Mk 16:1
*M* the mother of James, and Salome, Mk 16:1
*M* the mother of James, and other Lk 24:10
*4. Wife of Cleophas.*
*M* the wife of Cleophas, and Mary Jn 19:25
*5. Sister of Lazarus.*
And she had a sister called *M* Lk 10:39
*M* hath chosen that good part, Lk 10:42
of Bethany, the town of *M* Jn 11:1
(It was that *M* which anointed the Jn 11:2
of the Jews came to Martha and *M* Jn 11:19
but *M* sat still in the house Jn 11:20
called *M* her sister secretly, Jn 11:28
and comforted her, when they saw *M* Jn 11:31
Then when *M* was come where Jesus Jn 11:32
many of the Jews which came to *M* Jn 11:45
Then took *M* a pound of ointment Jn 12:3
*6. Mother of John Mark.*
the house of *M* the mother of John Acts 12:12
*7. A Christian in Rome.*
Greet *M*, who bestowed much labour Rom 16:6

**MASCHIL** (*mas'-kil*) *A didactic poem.*
A Psalm of David, A *M* Ps 32:*t*
To the chief Musician, *M*, for the Ps 42:*t*
Musician for the sons of Korah, *M* Ps 44:*t*
for the sons of Korah, A *M* Ps 45:*t*
To the chief Musician, *M*, A Psalm Ps 52:*t*
chief Musician upon Mahalath, *M* Ps 53:*t*
the chief Musician on Neginoth, *M* Ps 54:*t*
the chief Musician on Neginoth, *M* Ps 55:*t*
*M* of Asaph Ps 74:*t*
*M* of Asaph Ps 78:*t*
Leannoth, *M* of Heman the Ezrahite Ps 88:*t*
*M* of Ethan the Ezrahite Ps 89:*t*
*M* of David Ps 142:*t*

**MASH** (*mash*) *A son of Aram.*
Uz, and Hul, and Gether, and *M* Gen 10:23

**MASHAL** (*ma'-shal*) *A Levitical city in Asher.*
*M* with her suburbs, and Abdon with 1Chr 6:74

**MASONS**
cedar trees, and carpenters, and *m* 2Sa 5:11
And to *m*, and hewers of stone, and 2Kin 12:12
carpenters, and builders, and *m* 2Kin 22:6
and timber of cedars, with *m* 1Chr 14:1
he set *m* to hew wrought stones to 1Chr 22:2
the house of the LORD, and hired *m* 2Chr 24:12
They gave money also unto the *m* Ezr 3:7

**MASREKAH** (*mas'-re-kah*) *A place in Edom.*
Samlah of *M* reigned in his stead Gen 36:36
Samlah of *M* reigned in his stead 1Chr 1:47

**MASSA** (*mas'-sah*) *A son of Ishmael.*
And Mishma, and Dumah, and *M* Gen 25:14
Mishma, and Dumah, *M*, Hadad, and 1Chr 1:30

**MASSAH** (*mas'-sah*) See MERIBAH. *A place in the wilderness where the Israelites murmured.*
he called the name of the place *M* Ex 17:7
your God, as ye tempted him in *M* Deut 6:16
And at Taberah, and at *M*, and at Deut 9:22
one, whom thou didst prove at *M* Deut 33:8

**MAST**
he that lieth upon the top of a *m* Prov 23:34
could not well strengthen their *m* Is 33:23

**MASTER**
under the thigh of Abraham his *m* Gen 24:9
ten camels of the camels of his *m* Gen 24:10
goods of his *m* were in his hand Gen 24:10
said, O LORD God of my *m* Abraham Gen 24:12
shew kindness unto my *m* Abraham Gen 24:12
hast shewed kindness unto my *m* Gen 24:14
be the LORD God of my *m* Abraham Gen 24:27
left destitute my *m* of his mercy Gen 24:27
LORD hath blessed my *m* greatly Gen 24:35
a son to my *m* when she was old Gen 24:36
my *m* made me swear, saying, Thou Gen 24:37
And I said unto my *m*, Peradventure Gen 24:39
said, O LORD God of my *m* Abraham Gen 24:42
the LORD God of my *m* Abraham Gen 24:48
deal kindly and truly with my *m* Gen 24:49
he said, Send me away unto my *m* Gen 24:54
me away that I may go to my *m* Gen 24:56
the servant had said, It is my *m* Gen 24:65
the house of his *m* the Egyptian Gen 39:2
his *m* saw that the LORD was with Gen 39:3
my *m* wotteth not what is with me Gen 39:8
when his *m* heard the words of his Gen 39:19
And Joseph's *m* took him, and put Gen 39:20
If his *m* have given him a wife, Ex 21:4
shall plainly say, I love my *m* Ex 21:5
Then his *m* shall bring him unto Ex 21:6
his *m* shall bore his ear through Ex 21:6
If she please not her *m*, who hath Ex 21:8
their *m* thirty shekels of silver Ex 21:32
then the *m* of the house shall be Ex 22:8
*m* the servant which is escaped Deut 23:15
is escaped from his *m* unto thee Deut 23:15
and the servant said unto his *m* Judg 19:11
his *m* said unto him, We will not Judg 19:12
and spake to the *m* of the house Judg 19:22
the *m* of the house, went out unto Judg 19:23
up the arrows, and came to his *m* 1Sa 20:38
I should do this thing unto my *m* 1Sa 24:6
break away every man from his *m* 1Sa 25:10
of the wilderness to salute our *m* 1Sa 25:14
evil is determined against our *m* 1Sa 25:17
because ye have not kept your *m* 1Sa 26:16
he reconcile himself unto his *m* 1Sa 29:4
my *m* left me, because three days 1Sa 30:13
deliver me into the hands of my *m* 1Sa 30:15
for your *m* Saul is dead, and also 2Sa 2:7
and the LORD said, These have no *m*. 1Kin 22:17
away thy *m* from thy head to day 2Kin 2:3
away thy *m* from thy head to day 2Kin 2:5
go, we pray thee, and seek thy *m* 2Kin 2:16
Syria, was a great man with his *m* 2Kin 5:1
that when my *m* goeth into the 2Kin 5:18
my *m* hath spared Naaman this 2Kin 5:20
My *m* hath sent me, saying, Behold 2Kin 5:22
he went in, and stood before his *m* 2Kin 5:25
and he cried, and said, Alas, *m* 2Kin 6:5
servant said unto him, Alas, my *m* 2Kin 6:15
eat and drink, and go to their *m* 2Kin 6:22
away, and they went to their *m* 2Kin 6:23
from Elisha, and came to his *m* 2Kin 8:14
smite the house of Ahab thy *m* 2Kin 9:7
Had Zimri peace, who slew his *m* 2Kin 9:31
behold, I conspired against my *m* 2Kin 10:9
Hath my *m* sent me to thy *m*, 2Kin 18:27
his *m* hath sent to reproach the 2Kin 19:4
them, Thus shall ye say to your *m* 2Kin 19:6
He will fall to his *m* Saul to the 1Chr 12:19
Chenaniah the *m* of the song with 1Chr 15:27
and the LORD said, These have no *m* 2Chr 18:16
and the servant is free from his *m* Job 3:19
on his *m* shall be honoured Prov 27:18
Accuse not a servant unto his *m* Prov 30:10
with the servant, so with his *m* Is 24:2
to my *m* the king of Assyria, and I Is 36:8
Hath my *m* sent me to thy *m* Is 36:12
his *m* hath sent to reproach the Is 37:4
Thus shall ye say unto your *m* Is 37:6
Ashpenaz the *m* of his eunuchs Dan 1:3
*m* of the magicians, because I Dan 4:9
father, made *m* of the magicians, Dan 5:11
his father, and a servant his *m* Mal 1:6
and if I be a *m*, where is my fear Mal 1:6
the man that doeth this, the *m* Mal 2:12
scribe came, and said unto him, *M* Mt 8:19
Why eateth your *M* with publicans Mt 9:11
The disciple is not above his *m* Mt 10:24
the disciple that he be as his *m* Mt 10:25
the *m* of the house Beelzebub Mt 10:25
the Pharisees answered, saying, *M* Mt 12:38
said, Doth not your *m* pay tribute Mt 17:24
one came and said unto him, Good *M* Mt 19:16
with the Herodians, saying, *M* Mt 22:16
Saying, *M*, Moses said, If a man Mt 22:24
*M*, which is the great commandment Mt 22:36
for one is your *M*, even Christ Mt 23:8
for one is your *M*, even Christ Mt 23:10
The *M* saith, My time is at hand Mt 26:18
betrayed him, answered and said, *M* Mt 26:25
came to Jesus, and said, Hail, *m* Mt 26:49
awake him, and say unto him, *M* Mk 4:38
troublest thou the *M* any further Mk 5:35
answered and said to Jesus, *M* Mk 9:5
the multitude answered and said, *M* Mk 9:17
And John answered him, saying, *M* Mk 9:38
to him, and asked him, Good *M* Mk 10:17
he answered and said unto him, *M* Mk 10:20
Zebedee, come unto him, saying, *M* Mk 10:35
to remembrance saith unto him, *M* Mk 11:21
were come, they say unto him, *M* Mk 12:14
*M*, Moses wrote unto us, If a Mk 12:19
the scribe said unto him, Well, *M* Mk 12:32
his disciples saith unto him, *M* Mk 13:1
when the *m* of the house cometh Mk 13:35
The *M* saith, Where is the Mk 14:14
to him, and saith, *M*, *m* Mk 14:45
be baptized, and said unto him, *M* Lk 3:12

Simon answering said unto him, *M* .......... Lk 5:5
The disciple is not above his *m* .......... Lk 6:40
that is perfect shall be as his *m* .......... Lk 6:40
And he saith, *M*, say on .......... Lk 7:40
and awoke him, saying, *M*, *m* .......... Lk 8:24
they that were with him said, *M* .......... Lk 8:45
trouble not the *M* .......... Lk 8:49
him, Peter said unto Jesus, *M* .......... Lk 9:33
the company cried out, saying, *M* .......... Lk 9:38
And John answered and said, *M* .......... Lk 9:49
up, and tempted him, saying, *M* .......... Lk 10:25
the lawyers, and said unto him, *M* .......... Lk 11:45
of the company said unto him, *M* .......... Lk 12:13
When once the *m* of the house is .......... Lk 13:25
Then the *m* of the house being .......... Lk 14:21
their voices, and said, Jesus, *M* .......... Lk 17:13
ruler asked him, saying, Good *M* .......... Lk 18:18
the multitude said unto him, *M* .......... Lk 19:39
And they asked him, saying, *M* .......... Lk 20:21
Saying, *M*, Moses wrote unto us .......... Lk 20:28
of the scribes answering said, *M* .......... Lk 20:39
And they asked him, saying, *M* .......... Lk 21:7
The *M* saith unto thee, Where is .......... Lk 22:11
is to say, being interpreted, *M* .......... Jn 1:38
unto him, Art thou a *m* of Israel .......... Jn 3:10
disciples prayed him, saying, *M* .......... Jn 4:31
They say unto him, *M*, this woman .......... Jn 8:4
disciples asked him, saying, *M* .......... Jn 9:2
His disciples say unto him, *M* .......... Jn 11:8
The *M* is come, and calleth for .......... Jn 11:28
Ye call me *M* and Lord .......... Jn 13:13
If I then, your Lord and *M* .......... Jn 13:14
which is to say, *M* .......... Jn 20:16
the centurion believed the *m* .......... Acts 27:11
to his own *m* he standeth or .......... Rom 14:4
that your *M* also is in heaven .......... Eph 6:9
that ye also have a *M* in heaven .......... Col 4:1

**MASTERBUILDER**
is given unto me, as a wise *m* .......... 1Cor 3:10

**MASTERIES**
And if a man also strive for *m* .......... 2Ti 2:5

**MASTER'S**
me to the house of my *m* brethren .......... Gen 24:27
Sarah my *m* wife bare a son to my .......... Gen 24:36
hath appointed out for my *m* son .......... Gen 24:44
me in the right way to take my *m* .......... Gen 24:48
and let her be thy *m* son's wife .......... Gen 24:51
that his *m* wife cast her eyes .......... Gen 39:7
refused, and said unto his *m* wife .......... Gen 39:8
and her children shall be her *m* .......... Ex 21:4
thy *m* servants that are come with .......... 1Sa 29:10
I have given unto thy *m* son all .......... 2Sa 9:9
that thy *m* son may have food to .......... 2Sa 9:10
but Mephibosheth thy *m* son shall .......... 2Sa 9:10
And I gave thee thy *m* house .......... 2Sa 12:8
thy *m* wives into thy bosom, and .......... 2Sa 12:8
king said, And where is thy *m* son .......... 2Sa 16:3
sound of his *m* feet behind him .......... 2Kin 6:32
seeing your *m* sons are with you .......... 2Kin 10:2
best and meetest of your *m* sons .......... 2Kin 10:3
throne, and fight for your *m* house .......... 2Kin 10:3
the heads of the men your *m* sons .......... 2Kin 10:6
of the least of my *m* servants .......... 2Kin 18:24
his owner, and the ass his *m* crib .......... Is 1:3
of the least of my *m* servants .......... Is 36:9
sanctified, and meet for the *m* use .......... 2Ti 2:21

**MASTERS**
look unto the hand of their *m* .......... Ps 123:2
he refresheth the soul of his *m* .......... Prov 25:13
fastened by the *m* of assemblies .......... Eccl 12:11
command them to say unto their *m* .......... Jer 27:4
Thus shall ye say unto your *m* .......... Jer 27:4
the needy, which say to their *m* .......... Amos 4:1
No man can serve two *m* .......... Mt 6:24
Neither be ye called *m* .......... Mt 23:10
No servant can serve two *m* .......... Lk 16:13
which brought her *m* much gain by .......... Acts 16:16
when her *m* saw that the hope of .......... Acts 16:19
are your *m* according to the flesh .......... Eph 6:5
And, ye *m*, do the same things unto .......... Eph 6:9
your *m* according to the flesh .......... Col 3:22
*M*, give unto your servants that .......... Col 4:1
their own *m* worthy of all honour .......... 1Ti 6:1
And they that have believing *m* .......... 1Ti 6:2
to be obedient unto their own *m* .......... Titus 2:9
My brethren, be not many *m* .......... Jas 3:1
subject to your *m* with all fear .......... 1Pet 2:18

**MASTERS'**
which fill their *m* houses with .......... Zeph 1:9
which fall from their *m* table .......... Mt 15:27

**MASTERY**
voice of them that shout for *m* .......... Ex 32:18
and the lions had the *m* of them .......... Dan 6:24
the *m* is temperate in all things .......... 1Cor 9:25

**MASTS**
from Lebanon to make *m* for thee .......... Eze 27:5

**MATE**
be gathered, every one with her *m* .......... Is 34:15
shall fail, none shall want her *m* .......... Is 34:16

**MATHUSALA** (*ma-thu'-sa-lah*) See METHUSALAH. *Son of Enoch; ancestor of Jesus.*
Which was the son of *M*, which was .......... Lk 3:37

**MATRED** (*ma'-tred*) *Mother of Mehetabel.*
was Mehetabel, the daughter of *M* .......... Gen 36:39
was Mehetabel, the daughter of *M* .......... 1Chr 1:50

**MATRI** (*ma'-tri*) *An ancestoral family of King Saul.*
the family of *M* was taken .......... 1Sa 10:21

**MATRITE** See MATRI.

**MATRIX**
the LORD all that openeth the *m* .......... Ex 13:12
the LORD all that openeth the *m* .......... Ex 13:15
All that openeth the *m* is mine .......... Ex 34:19
*m* among the children of Israel .......... Num 3:12
that openeth the *m* in all flesh .......... Num 18:15

**MATTAN** (*mat'-tan*)
*1. A priest of Baal.*
slew *M* the priest of Baal before .......... 2Kin 11:18
slew *M* the priest of Baal before .......... 2Chr 23:17
*2. Father of Shephatiah.*
Then Shephatiah the son of *M* .......... Jer 38:1

**MATTANAH** (*mat'-ta-nah*) *An encampment of Israel in the wilderness.*
the wilderness they went to *M* .......... Num 21:18
And from *M* to Nahaliel .......... Num 21:19

**MATTANIAH** (*mat-ta-ni'-ah*) See ZEDEKIAH.
*1. Same as Zedekiah, king of Judah.*
the king of Babylon made *M* his .......... 2Kin 24:17
*2. A family of exiles.*
*M* the son of Micah, the son of .......... 1Chr 9:15
the son of Jeiel, the son of *M* .......... 2Chr 20:14
*M* the son of Micha, the son of .......... Neh 11:17
son of Hashabiah, the son of *M* .......... Neh 11:22
Kadmiel, Sherebiah, Judah, and *M* .......... Neh 12:8
*M*, and Bakbukiah, Obadiah .......... Neh 12:25
the son of Shemaiah, the son of *M* .......... Neh 12:35
*3. A sanctuary servant.*
Bukkiah, *M*, Uzziel, Shebuel, and .......... 1Chr 25:4
The ninth to *M*, he, his sons, and .......... 1Chr 25:16
*4. A descendant of Asaph.*
Zechariah, and *M* .......... 2Chr 29:13
*5. A descendant of Elam.*
*M*, Zechariah, and Jehiel, and Abdi .......... Ezr 10:26
*6. A descendant of Zattu.*
Elioenai, Eliashib, *M*, and .......... Ezr 10:27
*7. A descendant of Pahath-Moab.*
and Chelal, Benaiah, Maaseiah, *M* .......... Ezr 10:30
*8. A descendant of Bani.*
*M*, Mattenai, and Jaasau .......... Ezr 10:37
*9. Father of Zaccur.*
the son of Zaccur, the son of *M* .......... Neh 13:13

**MATTATHA** (*mat'-ta-thah*) See MATTATHAH.
*A son of Nathan; ancestor of Jesus.*
of Menan, which was the son of *M* .......... Lk 3:31

**MATTATHAH** (*mat'-ta-thah*) See MATTATHA.
*Married a foreigner in exile.*
Mattenai, *M*, Zabad, Eliphelet .......... Ezr 10:33

**MATTATHIAH** See MATTATHIAS.

**MATTATHIAS** (*mat-ta-thi'-as*) See MATTITHIAH.
*1. A son of Amos; ancestor of Jesus.*
Which was the son of *M*, which was .......... Lk 3:25
*2. A son of Semei; ancestor of Jesus.*
of Maath, which was the son of *M* .......... Lk 3:26

**MATTATTAH** See MATTATHAH.

**MATTENAI** (*mat'-te-nahee*)
*1. A descendant of Hashum.*
*M*, Mattathah, Zabad, Eliphelet .......... Ezr 10:33
*2. A descendant of Bani.*
Mattaniah, *M*, and Jaasau .......... Ezr 10:37
*3. A priest.*
And of Joiarib, *M* .......... Neh 12:19

**MATTER**
and sware to him concerning that *m* .......... Gen 24:9
Is it a small *m* that thou hast .......... Gen 30:15
When they have a *m*, they come .......... Ex 18:16
that every great *m* they shall .......... Ex 18:22
but every small *m* they shall .......... Ex 18:22
but every small *m* they judged .......... Ex 18:26
Keep thee far from a false *m* .......... Ex 23:7
that died about the *m* of Korah .......... Num 16:49
beguiled you in the *m* of Peor .......... Num 25:18
in the *m* of Cozbi, the daughter .......... Num 25:18
against the LORD in the *m* of Peor .......... Num 31:16
speak no more unto me of this *m* .......... Deut 3:26
If there arise a *m* too hard for .......... Deut 17:8
shall the *m* be established .......... Deut 19:15
and slayeth him, even so is this *m* .......... Deut 22:26
thou know how the *m* will fall .......... Ruth 3:18
But of the *m* of the kingdom .......... 1Sa 10:16
And as touching the *m* which thou .......... 1Sa 20:23
only Jonathan and David knew the *m* .......... 1Sa 20:39
will hearken unto you in this *m* .......... 1Sa 30:24
said unto him, How went the *m* .......... 2Sa 1:4
for there is no *m* hid from the .......... 2Sa 18:13
then be ye angry for this *m* .......... 2Sa 19:42
and so they ended the *m* .......... 2Sa 20:18
The *m* is not so .......... 2Sa 20:21
all times, as the *m* shall require .......... 1Kin 8:59
save only in the *m* of Uriah the .......... 1Kin 15:5
for every *m* pertaining to God, and .......... 1Chr 26:32
the king in any *m* of the courses .......... 1Chr 27:1
and Levites concerning any *m* .......... 2Chr 8:15
year, and see that ye hasten the *m* .......... 2Chr 24:5
till the *m* came to Darius .......... Ezr 5:5
by letter concerning this *m* .......... Ezr 5:5
pleasure to us concerning this *m* .......... Ezr 5:17
for this *m* belongeth unto thee .......... Ezr 10:4
God, trembling because of this *m* .......... Ezr 10:9
God for this *m* be turned from us .......... Ezr 10:14
Tikvah were employed about this *m* .......... Ezr 10:15
the tenth month to examine the *m* .......... Ezr 10:16
might have *m* for an evil report .......... Neh 6:13
inquisition was made of the *m* .......... Est 2:23
they had seen concerning this *m* .......... Est 9:26
the root of the *m* is found in me .......... Job 19:28
For I am full of *m* .......... Job 32:18
My heart is inditing a good *m* .......... Ps 45:1
encourage themselves in an evil *m* .......... Ps 64:5
faithful spirit concealeth the *m* .......... Prov 11:13
He that handleth a *m* wisely shall .......... Prov 16:20
a *m* separateth very friends .......... Prov 17:9
He that answereth a *m* before he .......... Prov 18:13
of kings is to search out a *m* .......... Prov 25:2
a province, marvel not at the *m* .......... Eccl 5:8
which hath wings shall tell the *m* .......... Eccl 10:20
the conclusion of the whole *m* .......... Eccl 12:13
for the *m* was not perceived .......... Jer 38:27
by his side, reported the *m* .......... Eze 9:11
this of thy whoredoms a small *m* .......... Eze 16:20
So he consented to them in this *m* .......... Dan 1:14
earth that can shew the king's *m* .......... Dan 2:10
made known unto us the king's *m* .......... Dan 2:23
careful to answer thee in this *m* .......... Dan 3:16
This *m* is by the decree of the .......... Dan 4:17
Hitherto is the end of the *m* .......... Dan 7:28
but I kept the *m* in my heart .......... Dan 7:28
therefore understand the *m* .......... Dan 9:23
it much, and to blaze abroad the *m* .......... Mk 1:45
asked him again of the same *m* .......... Mk 10:10
neither part nor lot in this *m* .......... Acts 8:21
the *m* from the beginning, and .......... Acts 11:4
for to consider of this *m* .......... Acts 15:6
We will hear thee again of this *m* .......... Acts 17:32
If it were a *m* of wrong or wicked .......... Acts 18:14
have a *m* against any man, the law .......... Acts 19:38
will know the uttermost of your *m* .......... Acts 24:22
having a *m* against another, go to .......... 1Cor 6:1
yourselves to be clear in this *m* .......... 2Cor 7:11
as a *m* of bounty, and not as of .......... 2Cor 9:5
they were, it maketh no *m* to me .......... Gal 2:6
and defraud his brother in any *m* .......... 1Th 4:6
how great a *m* a little fire .......... Jas 3:5

**MATTERS**
if any man have any *m* to do .......... Ex 24:14
being *m* of controversy within thy .......... Deut 17:8
and a man of war, and prudent in *m* .......... 1Sa 16:18
the *m* of the war unto the king .......... 2Sa 11:19
him, See, thy *m* are good and right .......... 2Sa 15:3
speakest thou any more of thy *m* .......... 2Sa 19:29
is over you in all *m* of the LORD .......... 2Chr 19:11
of Judah, for all the king's *m* .......... 2Chr 19:11
in all *m* concerning the people .......... Neh 11:24
whether Mordecai's *m* would stand .......... Est 3:4
the *m* of the fastings and their .......... Est 9:31
Esther confirmed these *m* of Purim .......... Est 9:32
not account of any of his *m* .......... Job 33:13
but they devise deceitful *m* .......... Ps 35:20
do I exercise myself in great *m* .......... Ps 131:1
And in all *m* of wisdom and .......... Dan 1:20
dream, and told the sum of the *m* .......... Dan 7:1
the weightier *m* of the law .......... Mt 23:23
for I will be no judge of such *m* .......... Acts 18:15
any thing concerning other *m* .......... Acts 19:39
and there be judged of these *m* .......... Acts 25:20
unworthy to judge the smallest *m* .......... 1Cor 6:2
or as a busybody in other men's *m* .......... 1Pet 4:15

**MATTHAN** (*mat'-than*) *Son of Eleazar; ancestor of Jesus.*
and Eleazar begat *M* .......... Mt 1:15
and *M* begat Jacob .......... Mt 1:15

**MATTHAT** (*mat'-that*)
*1. Son of Levi; an ancestor of Jesus.*
Which was the son of *M*, which was .......... Lk 3:24
*2. Father of Jorim; an ancestor of Jesus.*
of Jorim, which was the son of *M* .......... Lk 3:29

**MATTHEW** (*math'-ew*) See LEVI. *A disciple of Jesus.*
thence, he saw a man, named *M* .......... Mt 9:9
Thomas, and *M* the publican .......... Mt 10:3
and Philip, and Bartholomew, and *M* .......... Mk 3:18
*M* and Thomas, James the son of .......... Lk 6:15
and Thomas, Bartholomew, and *M* .......... Acts 1:13

**MATTHIAS** (*mat'-thias*) *Successor to Judas Iscariot as apostle.*
who was surnamed Justus, and *M* .......... Acts 1:23
and the lot fell upon *M* .......... Acts 1:26

**MATTITHIAH** (*mat-tith-i'-ah*) See MATTATHIAS.
*1. A son of Shallum.*
And *M*, one of the Levites, who was .......... 1Chr 9:31
*2. A Levite gatekeeper.*
and Benaiah, and Maaseiah, and *M* .......... 1Chr 15:18
And *M*, and Elipheleh .......... 1Chr 15:21
and Shemiramoth, and Jehiel, and *M* .......... 1Chr 16:5
*3. Son of Jeduthun.*
and Jeshaiah, Hashabiah, and *M* .......... 1Chr 25:3
The fourteenth to *M*, he, his sons .......... 1Chr 25:21
*4. Married a foreigner in exile.*
Jeiel, *M*, Zabad, Zebina, Jadau .......... Ezr 10:43
*5. A priest who aided Ezra.*
and beside him stood *M*, and Shema .......... Neh 8:4

**MATTOCK**
- his coulter, and his ax, and his *m* 1Sa 13:20
- that shall be digged with the *m* Is 7:25

**MATTOCKS**
- Yet they had a file for the *m* 1Sa 13:21
- with their *m* round about 2Chr 34:6

**MAUL**
- against his neighbour is a *m* Prov 25:18

**MAW**
- and the two cheeks, and the *m* Deut 18:3

**MAY** See PREFACE.

**MAYEST**
- of the garden thou *m* freely eat Gen 2:16
- but that thou *m* bury thy dead Gen 23:6
- that thou *m* be a multitude of Gen 28:3
- that thou *m* inherit the land Gen 28:4
- that thou *m* come in unto me Gen 38:16
- that thou *m* bring forth my people Ex 3:10
- that thou *m* know that there is Ex 8:10
- to the end thou *m* know that I am Ex 8:22
- that thou *m* know that there is Ex 9:14
- that thou *m* know how that the Ex 9:29
- that thou *m* tell in the ears of Ex 10:2
- that thou *m* bring the causes unto Ex 18:19
- that thou *m* teach them Ex 24:12
- that thou *m* bring in thither Ex 26:33
- that *m* thou offer for a freewill Lev 22:23
- that thou *m* use them for the Num 10:2
- thou *m* be to us instead of eyes Num 10:31
- from whence thou *m* see them Num 23:13
- thou *m* curse me them from thence Num 23:27
- that thou *m* inherit his land Deut 2:31
- that thou *m* prolong thy days upon Deut 4:40
- with thee, and that thou *m* go in Deut 6:18
- thou *m* not consume them at once, Deut 7:22
- of whose hills thou *m* dig brass Deut 8:9
- that thou *m* gather in thy corn, Deut 11:14
- for thy cattle, that thou *m* eat Deut 11:15
- Notwithstanding thou *m* kill Deut 12:15
- Thou *m* not eat within thy gates Deut 12:17
- thou *m* eat flesh, whatsoever thy Deut 12:20
- thou *m* not eat the life with the Deut 12:23
- or thou *m* sell it unto an alien Deut 14:21
- that thou *m* learn to fear the Deut 14:23
- a foreigner thou *m* exact it again Deut 15:3
- that thou *m* remember the day when Deut 16:3
- Thou *m* not sacrifice the passover Deut 16:5
- thou follow, that thou *m* live Deut 16:20
- thou *m* not set a stranger over Deut 17:15
- for thou *m* eat of them, and thou Deut 20:19
- thou *m* not hide thyself Deut 22:3
- that thou *m* prolong thy days Deut 22:7
- a stranger thou *m* lend upon usury Deut 23:20
- then thou *m* eat grapes thy fill Deut 23:24
- then thou *m* pluck the ears with Deut 23:25
- that thou *m* be an holy people Deut 26:19
- that thou *m* go in unto the land Deut 27:3
- that thou *m* fear this glorious and Deut 28:58
- all thy soul, that thou *m* live Deut 30:6
- in thy heart, that thou *m* do it Deut 30:14
- his judgments, that thou *m* live Deut 30:16
- That thou *m* love the LORD thy God. Deut 30:20
- that thou *m* obey his voice, and Deut 30:20
- that thou *m* cleave unto him Deut 30:20
- that thou *m* dwell in the land Deut 30:20
- that thou *m* observe to do Josh 1:7
- that thou *m* prosper whithersoever Josh 1:7
- that thou *m* observe to do Josh 1:8
- then *m* thou do to them as thou Judg 9:33
- that thou *m* go with us, and fight Judg 11:8
- on your way, that thou *m* go home Judg 19:9
- away, that thou *m* go in peace 1Sa 20:13
- that thou *m* do to him as it shall 1Sa 24:4
- that thou *m* make known unto me 1Sa 28:15
- that thou *m* have strength, when 1Sa 28:22
- that thou *m* reign over all that 2Sa 3:21
- then *m* thou for me defeat the 2Sa 15:34
- that thou *m* bring them down 2Sa 22:28
- that thou *m* save thine own life, 1Kin 1:12
- that thou *m* prosper in all that 1Kin 2:3
- that thou *m* take away the 1Kin 2:31
- that thou *m* hearken unto the 1Kin 8:29
- that thou *m* recover him of his 2Kin 5:6
- him, Thou *m* certainly recover 2Kin 8:10
- that thou *m* keep the law of the 1Chr 22:12
- and thou *m* add thereto 1Chr 22:14
- that thou *m* judge my people, over 2Chr 1:11
- that thou *m* carry me out of the 2Chr 18:33
- That thou *m* buy speedily with Ezr 7:17
- That thou *m* hear the prayer of Neh 1:6
- that thou *m* be their king, Neh 6:6
- me, that thou *m* be righteous Job 40:8
- in a time when thou *m* be found Ps 32:6
- whom thou *m* make princes in all Ps 45:16
- That thou *m* give him rest from Ps 94:13
- that thou *m* give them their meat Ps 104:27
- with thee, that thou *m* be feared Ps 130:4
- That thou *m* walk in the way of Prov 2:20
- That thou *m* regard discretion, and Prov 5:2
- that thou *m* be wise in thy latter Prov 19:20
- that thou *m* be remembered Is 23:16
- thou, that thou *m* be justified Is 43:26
- that thou *m* know that I, the LORD Is 45:3
- profit, if so be thou *m* prevail Is 47:12
- that thou *m* be my salvation unto Is 49:6
- That thou *m* say to the prisoners, Is 49:9
- wickedness, that thou *m* be saved Jer 4:14
- among my people, that thou *m* know Jer 6:27
- cause, that thou *m* be bound up Jer 30:13
- That thou *m* bear thine own shame, Eze 16:54
- *m* be confounded in all that thou Eze 16:54
- That thou *m* remember, and be Eze 16:63
- that thou *m* look on their Hab 2:15
- that thou *m* eat the passover Mk 14:12
- that thou *m* be delivered from him Lk 12:58
- for thou *m* be no longer steward Lk 16:2
- with all thine heart, thou *m* Acts 8:37
- *m* take knowledge of all these Acts 24:8
- Because that thou *m* understand Acts 24:11
- but if thou *m* be made free, use 1Cor 7:21
- thou *m* live long on the earth Eph 6:3
- that thou *m* know how thou 1Ti 3:15
- all things that thou *m* prosper 3Jn 2
- in the fire, that thou *m* be rich Rev 3:18
- that thou *m* be clothed, and that Rev 3:18
- with eyesalve, that thou *m* see Rev 3:18

**MAZZAROTH** (*maz'-za-roth*) *The twelve signs of the Zodiac.*
- thou bring forth *M* in his season Job 38:32

**ME** See PREFACE.

**MEADOW**
- and they fed in a *m* Gen 41:2
- and they fed in a *m* Gen 41:18

**MEADOWS**
- even out of the *m* of Gibeah Judg 20:33

**MEAH** (*me'-ah*) *A tower on Jerusalem's wall.*
- the tower of *M* they sanctified it Neh 3:1
- of Hananeel, and the tower of *M* Neh 12:39

**MEAL**
- quickly three measures of fine *m* Gen 18:6
- part of an ephah of barley *m* Num 5:15
- and threescore measures of *m* 1Kin 4:22
- but an handful of *m* in a barrel 1Kin 17:12
- The barrel of *m* shall not waste, 1Kin 17:14
- And the barrel of *m* wasted not 1Kin 17:16
- But he said, Then bring *m* 2Kin 4:41
- on mules, and on oxen, and meat, *m* 1Chr 12:40
- Take the millstones, and grind *m* Is 47:2
- the bud shall yield no *m* Hos 8:7
- and hid in three measures of *m* Mt 13:33
- and hid in three measures of *m* Lk 13:21

**MEALTIME**
- At *m* come thou hither, and eat of Ruth 2:14

**MEAN**
- What *m* these seven ewe lambs Gen 21:29
- What *m* ye by this service Ex 12:26
- What *m* the testimonies, and the Deut 6:20
- What *m* ye by these stones Josh 4:6
- come, saying, What *m* these stones Josh 4:21
- And it came to pass in the *m* while 1Kin 18:45
- he shall not stand before *m* men Prov 22:29
- the *m* man boweth down, and the Is 2:9
- What *m* ye that ye beat my people Is 3:15
- the *m* man shall be brought down, Is 5:15
- and the sword, not of a *m* man Is 31:8
- Know ye not what these things *m* Eze 17:12
- What *m* ye, that ye use this Eze 18:2
- the rising from the dead should *m* Mk 9:10
- In the *m* time, when there were Lk 12:1
- In the *m* while his disciples Jn 4:31
- vision which he had seen should *m* Acts 10:17
- therefore what these things *m* Acts 17:20
- What *m* ye to weep and to break Acts 21:13
- Cilicia, a citizen of no *m* city Acts 21:39
- their thoughts the *m* while Rom 2:15
- For I *m* not that other men be 2Cor 8:13

**MEANEST**
- What *m* thou by all this drove Gen 33:8
- unto Ziba, What *m* thou by these 2Sa 16:2
- not shew us what thou *m* by these Eze 37:18
- and said unto him, What *m* thou Jonah 1:6

**MEANETH**
- what *m* the heat of this great Deut 29:24
- What *m* the noise of this great 1Sa 4:6
- What *m* the noise of this tumult 1Sa 4:14
- What *m* then this bleating of the 1Sa 15:14
- Howbeit he *m* not so, neither doth Is 10:7
- But go ye and learn what that *m* Mt 9:13
- But if ye had known what this *m* Mt 12:7
- one to another, What *m* this Acts 2:12

**MEANING**
- the vision, and sought for the *m* Dan 8:15
- *m* to sail by the coasts of Asia Acts 27:2
- if I know not the *m* of the voice 1Cor 14:11

**MEANS**
- that will by no *m* clear the Ex 34:7
- by no *m* clearing the guilty, Num 14:18
- broken by the *m* of the pransings Judg 5:22
- by what *m* we may prevail against Judg 16:5
- yet doth he devise *m*, that his 2Sa 14:14
- they bring them out by their *m* 1Kin 10:29
- if by any *m* he be missing, then 1Kin 20:39
- the kings of Syria, by their *m* 2Chr 1:17
- by this *m* thou shalt have no Ezr 4:16
- can by any *m* redeem his brother Ps 49:7
- For by *m* of a whorish woman a man. Prov 6:26
- the priests bear rule by their *m* Jer 5:31
- this hath been by your *m* Mal 1:9
- shalt by no *m* come out thence Mt 5:26
- they sought *m* to bring him in, and Lk 5:18
- *m* he that was possessed of the Lk 8:36
- nothing shall by any *m* hurt you Lk 10:19
- But by what *m* he now seeth, we Jn 9:21
- by what *m* he is made whole Acts 4:9
- I must by all *m* keep this feast Acts 18:21
- if by any *m* they might attain to Acts 27:12
- if by any *m* now at length I might Rom 1:10
- If by any *m* I may provoke to Rom 11:14
- But take heed lest by any *m* this 1Cor 8:9
- that I might by all *m* save some 1Cor 9:22
- lest that by any *m*, when I have 1Cor 9:27
- gift bestowed upon us by the *m* of 2Cor 1:11
- But I fear, lest by any *m* 2Cor 11:3
- lest by any *m* I should run, or Gal 2:2
- If by any *m* I might attain unto Phil 3:11
- lest by some *m* the tempter have 1Th 3:5
- Let no man deceive you by any *m* 2Th 2:3
- give you peace always by all *m* 2Th 3:16
- that by *m* of death, for the Heb 9:15
- *m* of those miracles which he had Rev 13:14

**MEANT**
- but God *m* it unto good, to bring Gen 50:20
- and asked what these things *m* Lk 15:26
- pass by, he asked what it *m* Lk 18:36

**MEARAH** (*me'-a-rah*) *A place near Sidon.*
- *M* that is beside the Sidonians, Josh 13:4

**MEASURE**
- of the curtains shall have one *m* Ex 26:2
- curtains shall be all of one *m* Ex 26:8
- in meteyard, in weight, or in *m* Lev 19:35
- ye shall *m* from without the city Num 35:5
- they shall *m* unto the cities Deut 21:2
- perfect and just *m* shalt thou have Deut 25:15
- about two thousand cubits by *m* Josh 3:4
- both the cherubims were of one *m* 1Kin 6:25
- of them had one casting, one *m* 1Kin 7:37
- a *m* of fine flour be sold for a 2Kin 7:1
- So a *m* of fine flour was sold for 2Kin 7:16
- a *m* of fine flour for a shekel, 2Kin 7:18
- is fried, and for all manner of *m* 1Chr 23:29
- the first *m* was threescore cubits 2Chr 3:3
- The *m* thereof is longer than the Job 11:9
- and he weigheth the waters by *m* Job 28:25
- the *m* of my days, what it is Ps 39:4
- them tears to drink in great *m* Ps 80:5
- and opened her mouth without *m* Is 5:14
- In *m*, when it shooteth forth, Is 27:8
- the dust of the earth in a *m* Is 40:12
- therefore will I *m* their former Is 65:7
- but I will correct thee in *m* Jer 30:11
- of thee, but correct thee in *m* Jer 46:28
- the *m* of thy covetousness Jer 51:13
- Thou shalt drink also water by *m* Eze 4:11
- and they shall drink water by *m* Eze 4:16
- they three were of one *m* Eze 40:10
- the posts had one *m* on this side Eze 40:10
- after the *m* of the first gate Eze 40:21
- were after the *m* of the gate that Eze 40:22
- about within and without, by *m* Eze 41:17
- and let them *m* the pattern Eze 43:10
- of this *m* shalt thou Eze 45:3
- shalt thou *m* the length of five Eze 45:3
- and the bath shall be of one *m* Eze 45:11
- the *m* thereof shall be after the Eze 45:11
- these four corners were of one *m* Eze 46:22
- east side ye shall *m* from Hauran Eze 47:18
- the scant *m* that is abominable Mic 6:10
- To *m* Jerusalem, to see what is Zec 2:2
- and with what *m* ye mete, it shall Mt 7:2
- ye up then the *m* of your fathers Mt 23:32
- with what *m* ye mete, it shall be Mk 4:24
- amazed in themselves beyond *m* Mk 6:51
- And were beyond *m* astonished Mk 7:37
- And they were astonished out of *m* Mk 10:26
- good *m*, pressed down, and shaken Lk 6:38
- For with the same *m* that ye mete Lk 6:38
- not the Spirit by *m* unto him Jn 3:34
- dealt to every man the *m* of faith Rom 12:3
- that we were pressed out of *m* 2Cor 1:8
- not boast of things without our *m* 2Cor 10:13
- but according to the *m* of the 2Cor 10:13
- a *m* to reach even unto you 2Cor 10:13
- not ourselves beyond our *m* 2Cor 10:14
- boasting of things without our *m* 2Cor 10:15
- more abundant, in stripes above *m* 2Cor 11:23
- *m* through the abundance of the 2Cor 12:7
- lest I should be exalted above *m* 2Cor 12:7
- how that beyond *m* I persecuted Gal 1:13
- to the *m* of the gift of Christ Eph 4:7
- unto the *m* of the stature of the Eph 4:13
- working in the *m* of every part Eph 4:16
- A *m* of wheat for a penny, and Rev 6:6
- *m* the temple of God, and the altar Rev 11:1
- the temple leave out, and *m* it not Rev 11:2
- had a golden reed to *m* the city Rev 21:15
- according to the *m* of a man Rev 21:17

**MEASURED**
- he *m* six measures of barley, and Ruth 3:15
- *m* them with a line, casting them 2Sa 8:2
- two lines *m* he to put to death 2Sa 8:2
- Who hath *m* the waters in the Is 40:12
- If heaven above can be *m*, and the Jer 31:37
- neither the sand of the sea *m* Jer 33:22
- so he *m* the breadth of the Eze 40:5
- *m* the threshold of the gate, Eze 40:6
- He *m* also the porch of the gate Eze 40:8
- Then *m* he the porch of the gate, Eze 40:9
- he *m* the breadth of the entry of Eze 40:11
- He *m* then the gate from the roof Eze 40:13
- Then he *m* the breadth from the Eze 40:19

he *m* the length thereof, and the.......... Eze 40:20
he *m* from gate to gate an hundred..... Eze 40:23
he *m* the posts thereof and the.......... Eze 40:24
he *m* from gate to gate toward the...... Eze 40:27
he *m* the south gate according to........ Eze 40:28
he *m* the gate according to these........ Eze 40:32
*m* it according to these measures......... Eze 40:35
So he *m* the court, an hundred.............. Eze 40:47
*m* each post of the porch, five.............. Eze 40:48
*m* the posts, six cubits broad on............ Eze 41:1
he *m* the length thereof, forty................ Eze 41:2
*m* the post of the door, two.................... Eze 41:3
So he *m* the length thereof,.................... Eze 41:4
After he *m* the wall of the house, .......... Eze 41:5
So he *m* the house, an hundred............ Eze 41:13
he *m* the length of the building............ Eze 41:15
the east, and *m* it round about............ Eze 42:15
He *m* the east side with the.................. Eze 42:16
He *m* the north side, five hundred........ Eze 42:17
He *m* the south side, five hundred....... Eze 42:18
*m* five hundred reeds with the............... Eze 42:19
He *m* it by the four sides...................... Eze 42:20
he *m* a thousand cubits, and he.............. Eze 47:3
Again he *m* a thousand, and brought.... Eze 47:4
Again he *m* a thousand, and brought.... Eze 47:4
Afterward he *m* a thousand.................... Eze 47:5
which cannot be *m* nor numbered......... Hos 1:10
He stood, and *m* the earth...................... Hab 3:6
it shall be *m* to you again........................... Mt 7:2
ye mete, it shall be *m* to you .................. Mk 4:24
withal it shall be *m* to you again ............. Lk 6:38
he *m* the city with the reed,................. Rev 21:16
he *m* the wall thereof, an hundred...... Rev 21:17

**MEASURES**

quickly three *m* of fine meal.................. Gen 18:6
not have in thine house divers *m*....... Deut 25:14
it, he measured six *m* of barley ........... Ruth 3:15
These six *m* of barley gave he me ....... Ruth 3:17
five *m* of parched corn, and an............. 1Sa 25:18
day was thirty *m* of fine flour ............. 1Kin 4:22
and threescore *m* of meal...................... 1Kin 4:22
*m* of wheat for food to his..................... 1Kin 5:11
and twenty *m* of pure oil........................ 1Kin 5:11
to the *m* of hewed stones, sawed .......... 1Kin 7:9
after the *m* of hewed stones, and......... 1Kin 7:11
as would contain two *m* of seed.......... 1Kin 18:32
two *m* of barley for a shekel, in.............. 2Kin 7:1
two *m* of barley for a shekel, ............... 2Kin 7:16
Two *m* of barley for a shekel, and ........ 2Kin 7:18
twenty thousand *m* of beaten wheat .. 2Chr 2:10
and twenty thousand *m* of barley....... 2Chr 2:10
and ten thousand *m* of wheat............... 2Chr 27:5
and to an hundred *m* of wheat................ Ezr 7:22
Who hath laid the *m* thereof.................... Job 38:5
Divers weights, and divers *m* ............... Prov 20:10
lot, the portion of thy *m* from me......... Jer 13:25
thereof according to these *m*............... Eze 40:24
south gate according to these *m*.......... Eze 40:28
thereof, according to these *m*.............. Eze 40:29
the gate according to these *m*............. Eze 40:32
were according to these *m*.................... Eze 40:33
measured it according to these *m*...... Eze 40:35
these are the *m* of the altar................ Eze 43:13
And these shall be the *m* thereof......... Eze 48:16
four thousand and five hundred *m* ...... Eze 48:30
four thousand and five hundred *m* ...... Eze 48:33
round about eighteen thousand *m*...... Eze 48:35
one came to an heap of twenty *m* ......... Hag 2:16
took, and hid in three *m* of meal........... Mt 13:33
took and hid in three *m* of meal........... Lk 13:21
And he said, An hundred *m* of oil............. Lk 16:6
And he said, An hundred *m* of wheat..... Lk 16:7
three *m* of barley for a penny................. Rev 6:6

**MEASURING**

the *m* line shall yet go forth.................. Jer 31:39
of flax in his hand, and a *m* reed........... Eze 40:3
in the man's hand a *m* reed of six.......... Eze 40:5
made an end of *m* the inner house...... Eze 42:15
the east side with the *m* reed ............ Eze 42:16
with the *m* reed round about ............. Eze 42:16
with the *m* reed round about ............. Eze 42:17
hundred reeds, with the *m* reed.......... Eze 42:18
hundred reeds with the *m* reed............ Eze 42:19
a man with a *m* line in his hand............... Zec 2:1
but they *m* themselves by................... 2Cor 10:12

**MEAT**

to you it shall be for *m* .......................... Gen 1:29
have given every green herb for *m*....... Gen 1:30
that liveth shall be *m* for you..................... Gen 9:3
there was set *m* before him to eat ...... Gen 24:33
And make me savoury *m*, such as I ..... Gen 27:4
me venison, and make me savoury *m*.. Gen 27:7
them savoury *m* for thy father ............... Gen 27:9
and his mother made savoury *m*......... Gen 27:14
And she gave the savoury *m*............... Gen 27:17
And he also had made savoury *m*....... Gen 27:31
*m* for his father by the way ................... Gen 45:23
to the *m* offering of the morning.......... Ex 29:41
burnt sacrifice, nor *m* offering ............... Ex 30:9
burnt offering and the *m* offering ........ Ex 40:29
when any will offer a *m* offering.............. Lev 2:1
the remnant of the *m* offerings.................. Lev 2:3
of a *m* offering baken in the oven............ Lev 2:4
if thy oblation be a *m* offering.................. Lev 2:5
it is a *m* offering....................................... Lev 2:6
if thy oblation be a *m* offering.................. Lev 2:7
thou shalt bring the *m* offering................ Lev 2:8
the *m* offering a memorial thereof............ Lev 2:9
the *m* offering shall be Aaron's............... Lev 2:10
No *m* offering, which ye shall ................ Lev 2:11
every oblation of thy *m* offering............. Lev 2:13
to be lacking from thy *m* offering........... Lev 2:13
if thou offer a *m* offering of thy ............ Lev 2:14
thou shalt offer for the *m*..................... Lev 2:14
it is a *m* offering ....................................... Lev 2:15
be the priest's, as a *m* offering ............. Lev 5:13
this is the law of the *m* offering ............ Lev 6:14
of the flour of the *m* offering ................. Lev 6:15
which is upon the *m* offering ................. Lev 6:15
flour for a *m* offering perpetual ............. Lev 6:20
the baken pieces of the *m*....................... Lev 6:21
For every *m* offering for the..................... Lev 6:23
all the *m* offering that is baken ............... Lev 7:9
every *m* offering, mingled with............... Lev 7:10
of the *m* offering, and of the sin............... Lev 7:37
a *m* offering mingled with oil..................... Lev 9:4
And he brought the *m* offering ............... Lev 9:17
left, Take the *m* offering that................. Lev 10:12
Of all *m* which may be eaten, that ...... Lev 11:34
of fine flour for a *m* offering.................. Lev 14:10
the *m* offering upon the altar.................. Lev 14:20
mingled with oil for a *m* offering ........ Lev 14:21
offering, with the *m* offering ................ Lev 14:31
they shall eat of his *m* ........................... Lev 22:11
she shall eat of her father's *m*.............. Lev 22:13
the *m* offering thereof shall be.............. Lev 23:13
ye shall offer a new *m* offering ............ Lev 23:16
the LORD, with their *m* offering ............ Lev 23:18
a *m* offering, a sacrifice, and ............... Lev 23:37
of the land shall be *m* for you................ Lev 25:6
all the increase thereof be *m*................. Lev 25:7
incense, and the daily *m* offering......... Num 4:16
their *m* offering, and their drink ......... Num 6:15
shall offer also his *m* offering............... Num 6:17
mingled with oil for a *m* offering.......... Num 7:13
mingled with oil for a *m* offering.......... Num 7:19
mingled with oil for a *m* offering.......... Num 7:25
mingled with oil for a *m* offering.......... Num 7:31
mingled with oil for a *m* offering.......... Num 7:37
mingled with oil for a *m* offering.......... Num 7:43
mingled with oil for a *m* offering.......... Num 7:49
mingled with oil for a *m* offering.......... Num 7:55
mingled with oil for a *m* offering.......... Num 7:61
mingled with oil for a *m* offering.......... Num 7:67
mingled with oil for a *m* offering.......... Num 7:73
mingled with oil for a *m* offering.......... Num 7:79
twelve, with their *m* offering ................ Num 7:87
young bullock with his *m* offering............ Num 8:8
a *m* offering of a tenth deal of.............. Num 15:4
thou shalt prepare for a *m*..................... Num 15:6
a *m* offering of three tenth deals.......... Num 15:9
the LORD, with his *m* offering ............. Num 15:24
every *m* offering of theirs, and ............. Num 18:9
ephah of flour for a *m* offering ............ Num 28:5
as the *m* offering of the morning,.......... Num 28:8
deals of flour for a *m* offering.............. Num 28:9
deals of flour for a *m* offering............ Num 28:12
deals of flour for a *m* offering............ Num 28:12
for a *m* offering unto one lamb .......... Num 28:13
their *m* offering shall be of................. Num 28:20
the *m* of the sacrifice made by ........... Num 28:24
when ye bring a new *m* offering ......... Num 28:26
their *m* offering of flour mingled......... Num 28:28
his *m* offering, (they shall be............... Num 28:31
their *m* offering shall be of................... Num 29:3
his *m* offering, and the daily ............... Num 29:6
his *m* offering, and their drink.............. Num 29:6
their *m* offering shall be of .................. Num 29:9
the *m* offering of it, and their ............. Num 29:11
their *m* offering shall be of................. Num 29:14
his *m* offering, and his drink............... Num 29:16
their *m* offering and their drink .......... Num 29:18
the *m* offering thereof, and their.......... Num 29:19
their *m* offering and their drink .......... Num 29:21
his *m* offering, and his drink............... Num 29:22
Their *m* offering and their drink.......... Num 29:24
his *m* offering, and his drink............... Num 29:25
their *m* offering and their drink .......... Num 29:27
his *m* offering, and his drink............... Num 29:28
their *m* offering and their drink .......... Num 29:30
his *m* offering, and his drink............... Num 29:31
their *m* offering and their drink .......... Num 29:33
his *m* offering, and his drink............... Num 29:34
Their *m* offering and their drink .......... Num 29:37
his *m* offering, and his drink............... Num 29:38
for your *m* offerings, and for your....... Num 29:39
Ye shall buy *m* of them for money,....... Deut 2:6
Thou shalt sell me *m* for money .......... Deut 2:28
that they be not trees for *m*................ Deut 20:20
thy carcase shall be *m* unto all.......... Deut 28:26
burnt offering or *m* offering .................. Josh 22:23
for *m* offerings, or for......................... Josh 22:29
gathered their *m* under my table.......... Judg 1:7
took a kid with a *m* offering .............. Judg 13:19
a *m* offering at our hands,.................... Judg 13:23
Out of the eater came forth *m* ............ Judg 14:14
fail to sit with the king at *m* ................. 1Sa 20:5
the king sat him down to eat *m* .......... 1Sa 20:24
cometh not the son of Jesse to *m* ....... 1Sa 20:27
did eat no *m* the second day of............. 1Sa 20:34
to eat *m* while it was yet day................. 2Sa 3:35
him a mess of *m* from the king............... 2Sa 11:8
it did eat of his own *m*, and drank......... 2Sa 12:3
sister Tamar come, and give me *m*......... 2Sa 13:5
dress the *m* in my sight, that I.............. 2Sa 13:5
Amnon's house, and dress him *m*............ 2Sa 13:7
Bring the *m* into the chamber,............. 2Sa 13:10
*m* offerings, and the fat of the.............. 1Kin 8:64
*m* offerings, and the fat of the .............. 1Kin 8:64
the *m* of his table, and the................... 1Kin 10:5
the strength of that *m* forty days......... 1Kin 19:8
when the *m* offering was offered,.......... 2Kin 3:20
his *m* offering, and poured his............ 2Kin 16:13
and the evening *m* offering ................. 2Kin 16:15
his *m* offering, with the burnt ............. 2Kin 16:15
their *m* offering, and their drink .......... 2Kin 16:15
and on mules, and on oxen, and *m*.... 1Chr 12:40
and the wheat for the *m* offering........ 1Chr 21:23
for the fine flour for *m* offering ........ 1Chr 23:29
the *m* offerings, and the fat..................... 2Chr 7:7
and the *m* of his table, and the.................. 2Chr 9:4
and *m*, and drink, and oil, unto them...... Ezr 3:7
lambs, with their *m* offerings.................... Ezr 7:17
and for the continual *m* offering .......... Neh 10:33
they laid the *m* offerings......................... Neh 13:5
house of God, with the *m* offering ......... Neh 13:9
to touch are as my sorrowful *m*............. Job 6:7
and the mouth taste his *m*.................... Job 12:11
Yet his *m* in his bowels is turned ......... Job 20:14
There shall none of his *m* be left.......... Job 20:21
and juniper roots for their *m*................ Job 30:4
bread, and his soul dainty *m*............... Job 33:20
words, as the mouth tasteth *m* ............ Job 34:3
he giveth *m* in abundance.................... Job 36:31
God, they wander for lack of *m*............ Job 38:41
My tears have been my *m* day.................... Ps 42:3
us like sheep appointed for *m*................ Ps 44:11
Let them wander up and down for *m*.... Ps 59:15
They gave me also gall for my *m* ........... Ps 69:21
gavest him to be *m* to the people ......... Ps 74:14
heart by asking *m* for their lust.............. Ps 78:18
he sent them *m* to the full....................... Ps 78:25
but while their *m* was yet in................... Ps 78:30
be *m* unto the fowls of the heaven .......... Ps 79:2
prey, and seek their *m* from God.......... Ps 104:21
give them their *m* in due season.......... Ps 104:27
soul abhorreth all manner of *m*............. Ps 107:18
He hath given *m* unto them that............. Ps 111:5
givest them their *m* in due season......... Ps 145:15
Provideth her *m* in the summer............... Prov 6:8
for they are deceitful *m*......................... Prov 23:3
a fool when he is filled with *m*............. Prov 30:22
prepare their *m* in the summer.............. Prov 30:25
giveth *m* to her household, and a....... Prov 31:15
thou hast offered a *m* offering................... Is 57:6
corn to be *m* for thine enemies................. Is 62:8
and dust shall be the serpent's *m* .......... Is 65:25
of this people shall be *m* for the ............ Jer 7:33
be *m* for the fowls of heaven................... Jer 16:4
*m* offerings, and incense, and.............. Jer 17:26
carcases will I give to be *m* for.............. Jer 19:7
to kindle *m* offerings .............................. Jer 33:18
*m* unto the fowls of the heaven............. Jer 34:20
things for *m* to relieve the soul............ Lam 1:11
their *m* to relieve their souls................. Lam 1:19
they were their *m* in the........................... Lam 4:10
thy *m* which thou shalt eat shall............ Eze 4:10
My *m* also which I gave thee, fine........ Eze 16:19
I have given thee for *m* to the................ Eze 29:5
they became *m* to all the beasts............. Eze 34:5
my flock became *m* to every beast ........ Eze 34:8
that they may not be *m* for them.......... Eze 34:10
the *m* offering, and the sin..................... Eze 42:13
They shall eat the *m* offering ............... Eze 44:29
for a *m* offering, and for a burnt .......... Eze 45:15
*m* offerings, and drink offerings,............ Eze 45:17
the *m* offering, and the burnt................. Eze 45:17
he shall prepare a *m* offering of............ Eze 45:24
and according to the *m* offering ........... Eze 45:25
the *m* offering shall be an ephah ............ Eze 46:5
the *m* offering for the lambs as................ Eze 46:5
And he shall prepare a *m* offering .......... Eze 46:7
in the solemnities the *m* offering.......... Eze 46:11
thou shalt prepare a *m* offering ........... Eze 46:14
a *m* offering continually by a................ Eze 46:14
the *m* offering, and the oil, every.......... Eze 46:15
they shall bake the *m* offering ............. Eze 46:20
side, shall grow all trees for *m*............. Eze 47:12
the fruit thereof shall be for *m* ............. Eze 47:12
a daily provision of the king's *m* ............. Dan 1:5
with the portion of the king's *m*............. Dan 1:8
king, who hath appointed your *m*.......... Dan 1:10
of the portion of the king's *m* ................ Dan 1:13
eat the portion of the king's *m* .............. Dan 1:15
took away the portion of their *m*............ Dan 1:16
much, and in it was *m* for all.................. Dan 4:12
much, and in it was *m* for all.................. Dan 4:21
of his *m* shall destroy him..................... Dan 11:26
their jaws, and I laid *m* unto them......... Hos 11:4
The *m* offering and the drink .................... Joel 1:9
for the *m* offering and the drink ............ Joel 1:13
Is not the *m* cut off before our.............. Joel 1:16
even a *m* offering and a drink ................. Joel 2:14
your *m* offerings, I will not................... Amos 5:22
is fat, and their *m* plenteous.................... Hab 1:16
and the fields shall yield no *m*............... Hab 3:17
or wine, or oil, or any *m*.......................... Hag 2:12
and the fruit thereof, even his *m* ............ Mal 1:12
that there may be *m* in mine house ......... Mal 3:10
his *m* was locusts and wild honey ............... Mt 3:4
Is not the life more than *m*........................ Mt 6:25
as Jesus sat at *m* in the house.................. Mt 9:10
the workman is worthy of his *m* .............. Mt 10:10
and them which sat with him at *m* ........... Mt 14:9
they took up of the broken *m* that ......... Mt 15:37
to give them *m* in due season................ Mt 24:45
I was an hungred, and ye gave me *m*... Mt 25:35
an hungred, and ye gave me no *m*........ Mt 25:42
it on his head, as he sat at *m*................... Mt 26:7

as Jesus sat at *m* in his house ................ Mk 2:15
they took up of the broken *m* that.......... Mk 8:8
Simon the leper, as he sat at *m* ............ Mk 14:3
unto the eleven as they sat at *m* .......... Mk 16:14
and he that hath *m*, let him do................ Lk 3:11
house, and sat down to *m*........................ Lk 7:36
sat at *m* in the Pharisee's house.............. Lk 7:37
they that sat at *m* with him began.......... Lk 7:49
and he commanded to give her *m* ............ Lk 8:55
buy *m* for all this people .......................... Lk 9:13
and he went in, and sat down to *m*....... Lk 11:37
The life is more than *m*, and the............ Lk 12:23
and make them to sit down to *m*............ Lk 12:37
their portion of *m* in due season ........... Lk 12:42
of them that sit at *m* with thee.............. Lk 14:10
at *m* with him heard these things............ Lk 14:15
the field, Go and sit down to *m*............... Lk 17:7
is greater, he that sitteth at *m*.............. Lk 22:27
is not he that sitteth at *m*...................... Lk 22:27
to pass, as he sat at *m* with them.......... Lk 24:30
unto them, Have ye here any *m*............... Lk 24:41
gone away unto the city to buy *m*.............. Jn 4:8
I have *m* to eat that ye know not ............ Jn 4:32
My *m* is to do the will of him.................... Jn 4:34
not for the *m* which perisheth................... Jn 6:27
but for that *m* which endureth ................. Jn 6:27
For my flesh is *m* indeed, and my ............ Jn 6:55
them, Children, have ye any *m* .................. Jn 21:5
did eat their *m* with gladness ................ Acts 2:46
And when he had received *m*.................. Acts 9:19
he set *m* before them, and rejoiced..... Acts 16:34
Paul besought them all to take *m* ...... Acts 27:33
I pray you to take some *m*................... Acts 27:34
cheer, and they also took some *m*...... Acts 27:36
thy brother be grieved with thy *m*...... Rom 14:15
Destroy not him with thy *m*................... Rom 14:15
For the kingdom of God is not *m*........ Rom 14:17
For *m* destroy not the work of God .. Rom 14:20
fed you with milk, and not with *m*....... 1Cor 3:2
But *m* commendeth us not to God ........ 1Cor 8:8
sit at *m* in the idol's temple................ 1Cor 8:10
if *m* make my brother to offend, I ....... 1Cor 8:13
did all eat the same spiritual *m*............ 1Cor 10:3
no man therefore judge you in *m*.......... Col 2:16
need of milk, and not of strong *m*........ Heb 5:12
But strong *m* belongeth to them........... Heb 5:14
morsel of *m* sold his birthright............. Heb 12:16

**MEATS**
neither desire thou his dainty *m*........... Prov 23:6
into the draught, purging all *m*.............. Mk 7:19
abstain from *m* offered to idols ........... Acts 15:29
*M* for the belly, and the belly for ......... 1Cor 6:13
for the belly, and the belly for *m*......... 1Cor 6:13
and commanding to abstain from *m* ....... 1Ti 4:3
Which stood only in *m* and drinks,....... Heb 9:10
not with *m*, which have not.................. Heb 13:9

**MEBUNNAI** (*me-bun'-nahee*) See SIBBECHAI. *A 'mighty man' of David.*
Anethothite, *M* the Hushathite,............. 2Sa 23:27

**MECHERATHITE** (*me-ker'-ath-ite*) *A family name of a "mighty man" of David.*
Hepher the *M*, Ahijah the Pelonite.... 1Chr 11:36

**MECONAH** See MEKONAH.

**MEDAD** (*me'-dad*) *An elder of Israel.*
Eldad, and the name of the other *M*. Num 11:26
*M* do prophesy in the camp.................. Num 11:27

**MEDAN** (*me'-dan*) *A son of Abraham.*
bare him Zimran, and Jokshan, and *M* Gen 25:2
she bare Zimran, and Jokshan, and *M* 1Chr 1:32

**MEDDLE**
*M* not with them.................................. Deut 2:5
them not, nor *m* with them.................. Deut 2:19
why shouldest thou *m* to thy hurt..... 2Kin 14:10
shouldest thou *m* to thine hurt.......... 2Chr 25:19
therefore *m* not with him that............ Prov 20:19
*m* not with them that are given to .... Prov 24:21

**MEDDLED**
contention, before it be *m* with ........... Prov 17:14

**MEDDLETH**
*m* with strife belonging not to ............ Prov 26:17

**MEDDLING**
forbear thee from *m* with God............ 2Chr 35:21
but every fool will be *m*....................... Prov 20:3

**MEDE** (*meed*) See MEDES, MEDIAN. *An inhabitant of Media.*
in the first year of Darius the *M*............ Dan 11:1

**MEDEBA** (*med'-e-bah*) *A city in Reuben.*
Nophah, which reacheth unto *M* ....... Num 21:30
and all the plain of *M* unto Dibon ........ Josh 13:9
the river, and all the plain by *M* ........ Josh 13:16
who came and pitched before *M*......... 1Chr 19:7
shall howl over Nebo, and over *M*............ Is 15:2

**MEDES** (*meeds*)
Gozan, and in the cities of the *M*......... 2Kin 17:6
Gozan, and in the cities of the *M*....... 2Kin 18:11
that is in the province of the *M*............. Ezr 6:2
the laws of the Persians and the *M*......... Est 1:19
I will stir up the *M* against them............ Is 13:17
Elam, and all the kings of the *M*............ Jer 25:25
the spirit of the kings of the *M*............. Jer 51:11
nations with the kings of the *M*............. Jer 51:28
is divided, and given to the *M*............... Dan 5:28
according to the law of the *M*................. Dan 6:8
according to the law of the *M*............... Dan 6:12
O king, that the law of the *M*............... Dan 6:15
Ahasuerus, of the seed of the *M*.............. Dan 9:1
Parthians, and *M*, and Elamites, and..... Acts 2:9

**MEDIA** (*me'-de-ah*) See MADAI, MEDE, MEDIAN. *A country north of Persia.*
the power of Persia and *M*, the ................ Est 1:3
the seven princes of Persia and *M* ........... Est 1:14
*M* say this day unto all the.................... Est 1:18
the chronicles of the kings of *M*.............. Est 10:2
besiege, O *M* ............................................. Is 21:2
two horns are the kings of *M*................ Dan 8:20

**MEDIAN** (*me'-de-an*) See MEDE. *A native of Media.*
Darius the *M* took the kingdom, .......... Dan 5:31

**MEDIATOR**
by angels in the hand of a *m*................... Gal 3:19
Now a *m* is not a..................................... Gal 3:20
is not a *m* of one..................................... Gal 3:20
one *m* between God and men, the man... 1Ti 2:5
he is the *m* of a better covenant............... Heb 8:6
he is the *m* of the new testament.......... Heb 9:15
to Jesus the *m* of the new.................... Heb 12:24

**MEDICINE**
A merry heart doeth good like a *m* ... Prov 17:22
meat, and the leaf thereof for *m*........... Eze 47:12

**MEDICINES**
thou hast no healing *m*.......................... Jer 30:13
in vain shalt thou use many *m* .............. Jer 46:11

**MEDITATE**
Isaac went out to *m* in the field .......... Gen 24:63
but thou shalt *m* therein day .................. Josh 1:8
and in his law doth he *m* day ..................... Ps 1:2
*m* on thee in the night watches................ Ps 63:6
I will *m* also of all thy work, and ........... Ps 77:12
I will *m* in thy precepts, and have.......... Ps 119:15
thy servant did *m* in thy statutes ......... Ps 119:23
and I will *m* in thy statutes.................. Ps 119:48
but I will *m* in thy precepts ................. Ps 119:78
that I might *m* in thy word................. Ps 119:148
I *m* on all thy works............................... Ps 143:5
Thine heart shall *m* terror....................... Is 33:18
not to *m* before what ye shall................ Lk 21:14
*M* upon these things............................... 1Ti 4:15

**MEDITATION**
consider my *m*............................................ Ps 5:1
the *m* of my heart, be acceptable ............ Ps 19:14
the *m* of my heart shall be of.................. Ps 49:3
My *m* of him shall be sweet................... Ps 104:34
it is my *m* all the day.......................... Ps 119:97
for thy testimonies are my *m* .............. Ps 119:99

**MEEK**
(Now the man Moses was very *m* ....... Num 12:3
The *m* shall eat and be satisfied.............. Ps 22:26
The *m* will he guide in judgment.............. Ps 25:9
the *m* will he teach his way..................... Ps 25:9
But the *m* shall inherit the earth ............. Ps 37:11
to save all the *m* of the earth .................. Ps 76:9
The LORD lifteth up the *m*....................... Ps 147:6
beautify the *m* with salvation.................. Ps 149:4
equity for the *m* of the earth.................... Is 11:4
The *m* also shall increase their................. Is 29:19
to preach good tidings unto the *m*............ Is 61:1
and turn aside the way of the *m* .......... Amos 2:7
all ye *m* of the earth, which have........... Zeph 2:3
Blessed are the *m*...................................... Mt 5:5
for I am *m* and lowly in heart................ Mt 11:29
thy King cometh unto thee, *m*................ Mt 21:5
even the ornament of a *m* ...................... 1Pet 3:4

**MEEKNESS**
because of truth and *m* and...................... Ps 45:4
seek righteousness, seek *m* ................... Zeph 2:3
or in love, and in the spirit of *m*........... 1Cor 4:21
Paul myself beseech you by the *m*...... 2Cor 10:1
*M*, temperance........................................ Gal 5:23
such an one in the spirit of *m* .................. Gal 6:1
With all lowliness and *m*, with................. Eph 4:2
kindness, humbleness of mind, *m* ......... Col 3:12
faith, love, patience, *m*............................ 1Ti 6:11
In *m* instructing those that ..................... 2Ti 2:25
shewing all *m* unto all men.................... Titus 3:2
receive with *m* the engrafted word......... Jas 1:21
his works with *m* of wisdom ................... Jas 3:13
of the hope that is in you with *m*.......... 1Pet 3:15

**MEET**
I will make him an help *m* for him....... Gen 2:18
was not found an help *m* for him......... Gen 2:20
*m* him after his return from the ......... Gen 14:17
he ran to *m* them from the tent ........... Gen 18:2
Lot seeing them rose up to *m* them....... Gen 19:1
And the servant ran to *m* her .............. Gen 24:17
that walketh in the field to *m* us.......... Gen 24:65
son, that he ran to *m* him ................... Gen 29:13
and Leah went out to *m* him............... Gen 30:16
Esau, and also he cometh to *m* thee..... Gen 32:6
Esau ran to *m* him ................................ Gen 33:4
went up to *m* Israel his father, ........... Gen 46:29
behold, he cometh forth to *m* thee .......... Ex 4:14
Go into the wilderness to *m* Moses ......... Ex 4:27
Moses said, It is not *m* so to do............. Ex 8:26
went out to *m* his father in law.............. Ex 18:7
out of the camp to *m* with God.............. Ex 19:17
If thou *m* thine enemy's ox or his ............ Ex 23:4
And there I will *m* with thee................. Ex 25:22
where I will *m* you, to speak................ Ex 29:42
there I will *m* with the children ............ Ex 29:43
where I will *m* with thee........................ Ex 30:6
where I will *m* with thee....................... Ex 30:36
where I will *m* with you....................... Num 17:4
he went out to *m* him unto a city ..... Num 22:36
the LORD will come to *m* me................ Num 23:3
while I *m* the LORD yonder.................. Num 23:15
went forth to *m* them without the.... Num 31:13
all that are *m* for the war .................... Deut 3:18
mountain, lest the pursuers *m* you....... Josh 2:16
for the journey, and go to *m* them......... Josh 9:11
And Jael went out to *m* Sisera.............. Judg 4:18
Sisera, Jael came out to *m* him............. Judg 4:22
*m* for the necks of them that take......... Judg 5:30
and they came up to *m* them................ Judg 6:35
of the doors of my house to *m* me..... Judg 11:31
came out to *m* him with timbrels...... Judg 11:34
saw him, he rejoiced to *m* him ............ Judg 19:3
that they *m* thee not in any other........ Ruth 2:22
there shall *m* thee three men ............... 1Sa 10:3
that thou shalt *m* a company of............ 1Sa 10:5
and Saul went out to *m* him.................. 1Sa 13:10
early to *m* Saul in the morning.............. 1Sa 15:12
and came and drew nigh to *m* David .. 1Sa 17:48
the army to *m* the Philistine................. 1Sa 17:48
to *m* king Saul, with tabrets,................. 1Sa 18:6
which sent thee this day to *m* me........ 1Sa 25:32
thou hadst hasted and come to *m* me. 1Sa 25:34
and they went forth to *m* David .......... 1Sa 30:21
to *m* the people that were with ............ 1Sa 30:21
of Saul came out to *m* David................. 2Sa 6:20
it unto David, he sent to *m* them.......... 2Sa 10:5
came to *m* him with his coat rent......... 2Sa 15:32
to Gilgal, to go to *m* the king............... 2Sa 19:15
the men of Judah to *m* king David...... 2Sa 19:16
to go down to *m* my lord the king....... 2Sa 19:20
of Saul came down to *m* the king........ 2Sa 19:24
come to Jerusalem to *m* the king......... 2Sa 19:25
he came down to *m* me at Jordan.......... 1Kin 2:8
And the king rose up to *m* her ............. 1Kin 2:19
So Obadiah went to *m* Ahab ................. 1Kin 18:16
and Ahab went to *m* Elijah.................. 1Kin 18:16
go down to *m* Ahab king of Israel,.... 1Kin 21:18
go up to *m* the messengers of the.......... 2Kin 1:3
him, There came a man up to *m* us........ 2Kin 1:6
man was he which came up to *m* you .. 2Kin 1:7
And they came to *m* him, and bowed. 2Kin 2:15
to *m* her, and say unto her, Is it........... 2Kin 4:26
if thou *m* any man, salute him not ....... 2Kin 4:29
Wherefore he went again to *m* him....... 2Kin 4:31
down from the chariot to *m* him........... 2Kin 5:21
again from his chariot to *m* thee.......... 2Kin 5:26
*m* the man of God, and enquire of.......... 2Kin 8:8
So Hazael went to *m* him, and took........ 2Kin 8:9
an horseman, and send to *m* them.......... 2Kin 9:17
went one on horseback to *m* him.......... 2Kin 9:18
the son of Rechab coming to *m* him. 2Kin 10:15
king Ahaz went to Damascus to *m* ... 2Kin 16:10
And David went out to *m* them .......... 1Chr 12:17
And he sent to *m* them......................... 1Chr 19:5
And he went out to *m* Asa, and said... 2Chr 15:2
Hanani the seer went out to *m* him ...... 2Chr 19:2
it was not *m* for us to see the................ Ezr 4:14
let us *m* together in some one of............ Neh 6:2
Let us *m* together in the house of........ Neh 6:10
which were *m* to be given her, out............ Est 2:9
They *m* with darkness in the.................. Job 5:14
Surely it is *m* to be said unto ............... Job 34:31
he goeth on to *m* the armed men............ Job 39:21
Therefore came I forth to *m* thee ........ Prov 7:15
that withholdeth more than is *m*.......... Prov 11:24
bear robbed of her whelps *m* a man .. Prov 17:12
The rich and poor *m* together ................ Prov 22:2
and the deceitful man *m* together...... Prov 29:13
Isaiah, Go forth now to *m* Ahaz................ Is 7:3
for thee to *m* thee at thy coming ............. Is 14:9
*m* with the wild beasts of the.................. Is 34:14
I will not *m* thee as a man ........................ Is 47:3
me as seemeth good and *m* unto you... Jer 26:14
it unto whom it seemed *m* unto me.......... Jer 27:5
went forth from Mizpah to *m* them........ Jer 41:6
One post shall run to *m* another.......... Jer 51:31
and one messenger to *m* another .......... Jer 51:31
Is it *m* for any work ................................ Eze 15:4
was whole, it was *m* for no work ........... Eze 15:5
shall it be *m* yet for any work................ Eze 15:5
I will *m* them as a bear that is ............. Hos 13:8
unto thee, prepare to *m* thy God......... Amos 4:12
another angel went out to *m* him ............ Zec 2:3
therefore fruits *m* for repentance ............. Mt 3:8
whole city came out to *m* Jesus............... Mt 8:34
and said, It is not *m* to take the ............ Mt 15:26
went forth to *m* the bridegroom ............... Mt 25:1
go ye out to *m* him .................................. Mt 25:6
for it is not *m* to take the........................ Mk 7:27
there shall *m* you a man bearing a......... Mk 14:13
to *m* him that cometh against him.......... Lk 14:31
It was *m* that we should make............... Lk 15:32
the city, there shall a man *m* you .......... Lk 22:10
trees, and went forth to *m* him............... Jn 12:13
do works *m* for repentance ................... Acts 26:20
they came to *m* us as far as Appii ...... Acts 28:15
of their error which was *m*..................... Rom 1:27
that am not *m* to be called an.............. 1Cor 15:9
if it be *m* that I go also, they .............. 1Cor 16:4
Even as it is *m* for me to think ................ Phil 1:7
which hath made us *m* to be ................... Col 1:12
clouds, to *m* the Lord in the air ............. 1Th 4:17
for you, brethren, as it is *m*..................... 2Th 1:3
*m* for the master's use, and .................... 2Ti 2:21

M

bringeth forth herbs *m* for them Heb 6:7
Yea, I think it *m*, as long as I 2Pet 1:13

**MEETEST**
*m* of your master's sons, and set 2Kin 10:3
Thou *m* him that rejoiceth and Is 64:5

**MEETETH**
When Esau my brother *m* thee Gen 32:17
when he *m* him, he shall slay him Num 35:19
slay the murderer, when he *m* him Num 35:21

**MEETING**
was afraid at the *m* of David 1Sa 21:1
it is iniquity, even the solemn *m* Is 1:13

**MEGIDDO** (*me-ghid'-do*) See MEGIDDON. *A city on the plain of Jezreel.*
the king of *M*, one Josh 12:21
towns, and the inhabitants of *M* Josh 17:11
towns, nor the inhabitants of *M* Judg 1:27
in Taanach by the waters of *M* Judg 5:19
to him pertained Taanach and *M* 1Kin 4:12
wall of Jerusalem, and Hazor, and *M* 1Kin 9:15
And he fled to *M*, and died there 2Kin 9:27
and he slew him at *M*, when he had 2Kin 23:29
him in a chariot dead from *M* 2Kin 23:30
towns, Taanach and her towns, *M* 1Chr 7:29
came to fight in the valley of *M* 2Chr 35:22

**MEGIDDON** (*me-ghid'-don*) See ARMAGEDDON, MEGIDDO. *Same as Megiddo.*
of Hadadrimmon in the valley of *M* Zec 12:11

**MEHETABEEL** (*me-het'-a-be-el*) See MEHETABEL. *Father of Delaiah.*
the son of Delaiah the son of *M* Neh 6:10

**MEHETABEL** (*me-het'-a-bel*) See MEHETABEEL. *Wife of Hadar.*
and his wife's name was *M*, the Gen 36:39
and his wife's name was *M*, the 1Chr 1:50

**MEHIDA** (*me-hi'-dah*) *A family of exiles.*
of Bazluth, the children of *M* Ezr 2:52
of Bazlith, the children of *M* Neh 7:54

**MEHIR** (*me'-hur*) *A son of Chelub.*
the brother of Shuah begat *M* 1Chr 4:11

**MEHOLATHITE** (*me-ho'-lath-ite*) *An inhabitant of a city in Issachar.*
given unto Adriel the *M* to wife 1Sa 18:19
Adriel the son of Barzillai the *M* 2Sa 21:8

**MEHUJAEL** (*me-hu'-ja-el*) *Son of Irad.*
and Irad begat *M* Gen 4:18
and *M* begat Methusael Gen 4:18

**MEHUMAN** (*me-hu'-man*) *A servant of King Ahasuerus.*
merry with wine, he commanded *M* Est 1:10

**MEHUNIM** (*me-hu'-nim*) See MAONITE, MEHUNIMS, MEUNIM. *A family of exiles.*
of Asnah, the children of *M* Ezr 2:50

**MEHUNIMS** (*me-hu'-nims*) See MEHUNIM. *A people who lived in Arabia.*
that dwelt in Gur-baal, and the *M* 2Chr 26:7

**ME-JARKON** (*me-jar'-kon*) *A city in Dan.*
And *M*, and Rakkon, with the border Josh 19:46

**MEKERATHITE** See MECHERATHITE.

**MEKONAH** (*me-ko'-nah*) *A city in Judah.*
And at Ziklag, and at *M*, and in the Neh 11:28

**MELATIAH** (*mel-a-ti'-ah*) *A repairer of Jerusalem's wall.*
them repaired *M* the Gibeonite Neh 3:7

**MELCHI** (*mel'-ki*) See MELCHI-SHUA, MELCHIZEDEK.
*1. Son of Janna; ancestor of Jesus.*
of Levi, which was the son of *M* Lk 3:24
*2. Son of Addi; ancestor of Jesus.*
Which was the son of *M*, which was Lk 3:28

**MELCHIAH** (*mel-ki'-ah*) See MALCHIAH. *Father of Pashur.*
sent unto him Pashur the son of *M* Jer 21:1

**MELCHISEDEC** (*mel-kis'-e-dek*) See MELCHIZEDEK. *Greek form of Melchizedek.*
for ever after the order of *M* Heb 5:6
high priest after the order of *M* Heb 5:10
for ever after the order of *M* Heb 6:20
For this *M*, king of Salem, priest Heb 7:1
of his father, when *M* met him Heb 7:10
should rise after the order of *M* Heb 7:11
of *M* there ariseth another priest Heb 7:15
for ever after the order of *M* Heb 7:17
for ever after the order of *M* Heb 7:21

**MELCHI-SHUA** (*mel'-ki-shu'-ah*) See MALCHISHUA. *A son of King Saul.*
were Jonathan, and Ishui, and *M* 1Sa 14:49
slew Jonathan, and Abinadab, and *M* 1Sa 31:2

**MELCHIZEDEK** (*mel-kiz'-e-dek*) See MELCHISEDEC. *King and priest of Salem.*
*M* king of Salem brought forth Gen 14:18
for ever after the order of *M* Ps 110:4

**MELEA** (*mel'-e-ah*) *Son of Menan; an ancestor of Jesus.*
Which was the son of *M*, which was Lk 3:31

**MELECH** (*me'-lek*) See EBED-MELECH, HAMMELECH, NATHAN-MELECH, REGEM-MELECH. *A son of Micah.*
sons of Micah were, Pithon, and *M* 1Chr 8:35
sons of Micah were, Pithon, and *M* 1Chr 9:41

**MELICHU** See MELICU.

**MELICU** (*mel'-i-cu*) See MALLUCH. *A priest.*
Of *M*, Jonathan Neh 12:14

**MELITA** (*mel'-i-tah*) *A Mediterranean island.*
knew that the island was called *M* Acts 28:1

**MELODY**
make sweet *m*, sing many songs, Is 23:16
thanksgiving, and the voice of *m* Is 51:3
will not hear the *m* of thy viols Amos 5:23
making *m* in your heart to the Eph 5:19

**MELONS**
the cucumbers, and the *m*, and the Num 11:5

**MELT**
of Canaan shall *m* away Ex 15:15
these things, our hearts did *m* Josh 2:11
me made the heart of the people *m* Josh 14:8
heart of a lion, shall utterly *m* 2Sa 17:10
Let them *m* away as waters which Ps 58:7
gnash with his teeth, and *m* away Ps 112:10
and every man's heart shall *m* Is 13:7
Egypt shall *m* in the midst of it Is 19:1
of hosts, Behold, I will *m* them Jer 9:7
and every heart shall *m*, and all Eze 21:7
to blow the fire upon it, to *m* it Eze 22:20
I will leave you there, and *m* you Eze 22:20
toucheth the land, and it shall *m* Amos 9:5
wine, and all the hills shall *m* Amos 9:13
quake at him, and the hills *m* Nah 1:5
shall *m* with fervent heat 2Pet 3:10
shall *m* with fervent heat 2Pet 3:12

**MELTED**
and when the sun waxed hot, it *m* Ex 16:21
passed over, that their heart *m* Josh 5:1
the hearts of the people *m* Josh 7:5
The mountains *m* from before the Judg 5:5
and, behold, the multitude *m* away 1Sa 14:16
it is *m* in the midst of my bowels Ps 22:14
he uttered his voice, the earth *m* Ps 46:6
The hills *m* like wax at the Ps 97:5
their soul is *m* because of Ps 107:26
shall be *m* with their blood Is 34:3
ye shall be *m* in the midst Eze 22:21
As silver is *m* in the midst of Eze 22:22
so shall ye be *m* in the midst Eze 22:22

**MELTETH**
As a snail which *m*, let every one Ps 58:8
as wax *m* before the fire, so let Ps 68:2
My soul *m* for heaviness Ps 119:28
sendeth out his word, and *m* them Ps 147:18
The workman *m* a graven image, and Is 40:19
the founder *m* in vain Jer 6:29
and the heart *m*, and the knees Nah 2:10

**MELTING**
As when the *m* fire burneth, the Is 64:2

**MELZAR** (*mel'-zar*) *Babylonian officer charged with Daniel and his companions.*
Then said Daniel to *M*, whom the Dan 1:11
Thus *M* took away the portion of Dan 1:16

**MEMBER**
or hath his privy *m* cut off Deut 23:1
For the body is not one *m* 1Cor 12:14
And if they were all one *m* 1Cor 12:19
And whether one *m* suffer, all the 1Cor 12:26
or one *m* be honoured, all the 1Cor 12:26
Even so the tongue is a little *m* Jas 3:5

**MEMBERS**
and all my *m* are as a shadow Job 17:7
in thy book all my *m* were written Ps 139:16
that one of thy *m* should perish Mt 5:29
that one of thy *m* should perish Mt 5:30
yield ye your *m* as instruments of Rom 6:13
dead, and your *m* as instruments of Rom 6:13
your *m* servants to uncleanness Rom 6:19
even so now yield your *m* servants Rom 6:19
did work in our *m* to bring forth Rom 7:5
But I see another law in my *m* Rom 7:23
the law of sin which is in my *m* Rom 7:23
For as we have many *m* in one body Rom 12:4
all *m* have not the same office Rom 12:4
every one *m* one of another Rom 12:5
your bodies are the *m* of Christ 1Cor 6:15
shall I then take the *m* of Christ 1Cor 6:15
and make them the *m* of an harlot 1Cor 6:15
the body is one, and hath many *m* 1Cor 12:12
all the *m* of that one body, being 1Cor 12:12
But now hath God set the *m* every 1Cor 12:18
But now are they many *m*, yet but 1Cor 12:20
much more those *m* of the body 1Cor 12:22
those *m* of the body, which we 1Cor 12:23
but that the *m* should have the 1Cor 12:25
suffer, all the *m* suffer with it 1Cor 12:26
all the *m* rejoice with it 1Cor 12:26
of Christ, and *m* in particular 1Cor 12:27
for we are *m* one of another Eph 4:25
For we are *m* of his body, of his Eph 5:30
Mortify therefore your *m* which Col 3:5
so is the tongue among our *m* Jas 3:6
of your lusts that war in your *m* Jas 4:1

**MEMORIAL**
this is my *m* unto all generations Ex 3:15
day shall be unto you for a *m* Ex 12:14
for a *m* between thine eyes, that Ex 13:9
Write this for a *m* in a book Ex 17:14
of the ephod for stones of *m* unto Ex 28:12
upon his two shoulders for a *m* Ex 28:12
place, for a *m* before the LORD Ex 28:29
that it may be a *m* unto the Ex 30:16
for a *m* to the children of Israel Ex 39:7
burn the *m* of it upon the altar Lev 2:2
the meat offering a *m* thereof Lev 2:9
the priest shall burn the *m* of it Lev 2:16
even a *m* thereof, and burn it on Lev 5:12
a sweet savour, even the *m* of it Lev 6:15
a *m* of blowing of trumpets, an Lev 23:24
it may be on the bread for a *m* Lev 24:7
of jealousy, an offering of *m* Num 5:15
the offering of *m* in her hands Num 5:18
the offering, even the *m* thereof Num 5:26
be to you for a *m* before your God Num 10:10
To be a *m* unto the children of Num 16:40
for a *m* for the children of Num 31:54
these stones shall be for a *m* Josh 4:7
have no portion, nor right, nor *m* Neh 2:20
nor the *m* of them perish from Est 9:28
their *m* is perished with them Ps 9:6
and thy *m*, O LORD, throughout all Ps 135:13
the LORD is his *m* Hos 12:5
for a *m* in the temple of the LORD Zec 6:14
hath done, be told for a *m* of her Mt 26:13
shall be spoken of for a *m* of her Mk 14:9
are come up for a *m* before God Acts 10:4

**MEMORY**
off the *m* of them from the earth Ps 109:15
utter the *m* of thy great goodness Ps 145:7
The *m* of the just is blessed Prov 10:7
for the *m* of them is forgotten Eccl 9:5
and made all their *m* to perish Is 26:14
if ye keep in *m* what I preached 1Cor 15:2

**MEMPHIS** (*mem'-fis*) See NOPH. *A city in Egypt.*
gather them up, *M* shall bury them Hos 9:6

**MEMUCAN** (*mem-u'-can*) *A prince of Media and Persia.*
Tarshish, Meres, Marsena, and *M* Est 1:14
*M* answered before the king and the Est 1:16
did according to the word of *M* Est 1:21

**MEN** See PREFACE.

**MENAHEM** (*men'-a-hem*) *Son of Gadi.*
For *M* the son of Gadi went up 2Kin 15:14
Then *M* smote Tiphsah, and all that 2Kin 15:16
*M* the son of Gadi to reign over 2Kin 15:17
*M* gave Pul a thousand talents of 2Kin 15:19
*M* exacted the money of Israel, 2Kin 15:20
And the rest of the acts of *M* 2Kin 15:21
And *M* slept with his fathers 2Kin 15:22
of Judah Pekahiah the son of *M* 2Kin 15:23

**MENAN** (*me'-nan*) *Father of Melea; ancestor of Jesus.*
of Melea, which was the son of *M* Lk 3:31

**MEND**
brass to *m* the house of the LORD 2Chr 24:12

**MENDING**
their father, *m* their nets Mt 4:21
were in the ship *m* their nets Mk 1:19

**MENE** (*me'-ne*) *Part of "the handwriting on the wall".*
writing that was written, *M*, *M* Dan 5:25
*M*; God hath numbered Dan 5:26

**MENI** See MENAN.

**MENNA** See MENAN.

**MENPLEASERS**
Not with eyeservice, as *m* Eph 6:6
not with eyeservice, as *m* Col 3:22

**MEN'S**
the *m* feet that were with him Gen 24:32
Fill the *m* sacks with food, as Gen 44:1
serve gods, the work of *m* hands Deut 4:28
Wherefore hearest thou *m* words 1Sa 24:9
forsook the old *m* counsel that 1Kin 12:13
*m* bones shall be burnt upon thee 1Kin 13:2
no gods, but the work of *m* hands 2Kin 19:18
burned *m* bones upon them, and 2Kin 23:20
and gold, the work of *m* hands Ps 115:4
and gold, the work of *m* hands Ps 135:15
no gods, but the work of *m* hands Is 37:19
the mighty *m* hearts in Moab at Jer 48:41
because of *m* blood, and for the Hab 2:8
them afraid, because of *m* blood Hab 2:17
borne, and lay them on *m* shoulders Mt 23:4
are within full of dead *m* bones Mt 23:27
is not come to destroy *m* lives Lk 9:56
*M* hearts failing them for fear, Lk 21:26
is worshipped with *m* hands Acts 17:25
that is, of other *m* labours 2Cor 10:15
be partaker of other *m* sins 1Ti 5:22
Some *m* sins are open beforehand, 1Ti 5:24
as a busybody in other *m* matters 1Pet 4:15
having *m* persons in admiration Jude 16

**MENSERVANTS**
sheep, and oxen, and he asses, and *m* Gen 12:16
took sheep, and oxen, and *m* Gen 20:14

herds, and silver, and gold, and *m* ........ Gen 24:35
cattle, and maidservants, and *m* ........ Gen 30:43
have oxen, and asses, flocks, and *m* ..... Gen 32:5
she shall not go out as the *m* do ........ Ex 21:7
and your daughters, and your *m* ........ Deut 12:12
And he will take your *m*, and your ........ 1Sa 8:16
and sheep, and oxen, and *m*, and ........ 2Kin 5:26
and shall begin to beat the *m* ........ Lk 12:45

**MENSTEALERS**
themselves with mankind, for *m* ........ 1Ti 1:10

**MENSTRUOUS**
shalt cast them away as a *m* cloth ........ Is 30:22
is as a *m* woman among them ........ Lam 1:17
hath come near to a *m* woman ........ Eze 18:6

**MENTION**
make *m* of me unto Pharaoh, and ........ Gen 40:14
make no *m* of the name of other ........ Ex 23:13
neither make *m* of the names of ........ Josh 23:7
when he made *m* of the ark of God, ........ 1Sa 4:18
No *m* shall be made of coral, or ........ Job 28:18
I will make *m* of thy ........ Ps 71:16
I will make *m* of Rahab and Babylon ..... Ps 87:4
make *m* that his name is exalted ........ Is 12:4
every one that maketh *m* thereof ........ Is 19:17
only will we make *m* of thy name ........ Is 26:13
make *m* of the God of Israel, but ........ Is 48:1
mother hath he made *m* of my name ....... Is 49:1
ye that make *m* of the LORD ........ Is 62:6
I will *m* the lovingkindnesses of ........ Is 63:7
Make ye *m* to the nations ........ Jer 4:16
I said, I will not make *m* of him ........ Jer 20:9
of the LORD shall ye *m* no more ........ Jer 23:36
for we may not make *m* of the name Amos 6:10
*m* of you always in my prayers ........ Rom 1:9
making *m* of you in my prayers ........ Eph 1:16
making *m* of you in our prayers ........ 1Th 1:2
making *m* of thee always in my ........ Philem 4
made *m* of the departing of the ........ Heb 11:22

**MENTIONED**
cities which are here *m* by name ........ Josh 21:9
These *m* by their names were ........ 1Chr 4:38
who is *m* in the book of the kings ..... 2Chr 20:34
For thy sister Sodom was not *m* by ..... Eze 16:56
they shall not be *m* unto him ........ Eze 18:22
that he hath done shall not be *m* ........ Eze 18:24
committed shall be *m* unto him ........ Eze 33:16

**MENUHOTH** See MANAHETHITES.

**MEONENIM** (*me-on'-e-nim*) *A place near Shechem.*
come along by the plain of *M* ........ Judg 9:37

**MEONOTHAI** (*me-on'-o-thahee*) *Descendant of Judah.*
And *M* begat Ophrah ........ 1Chr 4:14

**MEPHAATH** (*mef'-a-ath*) *A Levitical city in Reuben.*
And Jahaza, and Kedemoth, and *M* ... Josh 13:18
suburbs, and *M* with her suburbs ........ Josh 21:37
suburbs, and *M* with her suburbs ........ 1Chr 6:79
upon Jahazah, and upon *M* ........ Jer 48:21

**MEPHIBOSHETH** (*me-fib'-o-sheth*) See MERIBBAAL.
*1. Son of Jonathan.*
And his name was *M* ........ 2Sa 4:4
Now when *M*, the son of Jonathan, ........ 2Sa 9:6
And David said, *M* ........ 2Sa 9:6
but *M* thy master's son shall eat ........ 2Sa 9:10
As for *M*, said the king, he shall ........ 2Sa 9:11
*M* had a young son, whose name was ... 2Sa 9:12
of Ziba were servants unto *M* ........ 2Sa 9:12
So *M* dwelt in Jerusalem ........ 2Sa 9:13
Ziba the servant of *M* met him ........ 2Sa 16:1
are all that pertained unto *M* ........ 2Sa 16:4
*M* the son of Saul came down to ........ 2Sa 19:24
wentest not thou with me, *M* ........ 2Sa 19:25
*M* said unto the king, Yea, let ........ 2Sa 19:30
But the king spared *M*, the son of ........ 2Sa 21:7
*2. Son of Rizpah.*
she bare unto Saul, Armoni and *M* ........ 2Sa 21:8

**MERAB** (*me'-rab*) *Daughter of King Saul.*
the name of the firstborn *M* ........ 1Sa 14:49
David, Behold my elder daughter *M* .... 1Sa 18:17
*M* Saul's daughter should have ........ 1Sa 18:19

**MERAIAH** (*mer-a-i'-ah*) *A priest.*
fathers: of Seraiah, *M* ........ Neh 12:12

**MERAIOTH** (*me-rah'-yoth*) See MEREMOTH.
*1. An ancestor of Azariah.*
Zerahiah, and Zerahiah begat *M* ........ 1Chr 6:6
*M* begat Amariah, and Amariah begat .. 1Chr 6:7
*M* his son, Amariah his son, ........ 1Chr 6:52
the son of Azariah, the son of *M* ........ Ezr 7:3
*2. Another ancestor of Azariah.*
the son of Zadok, the son of *M* ........ 1Chr 9:11
the son of Zadok, the son of *M* ........ Neh 11:11
*3. A priest in exile.*
of *M*, Helkai ........ Neh 12:15

**MERARI** (*me-ra'-ri*) See MERARITES. *A son of Levi.*
Gershon, Kohath, and *M* ........ Gen 46:11
Gershon, and Kohath, and *M* ........ Ex 6:16
And the sons of *M* ........ Ex 6:19
Gershon, and Kohath, and *M* ........ Num 3:17
the sons of *M* by their families ........ Num 3:20
Of *M* was the family of the ........ Num 3:33
these are the families of *M* ........ Num 3:33
*M* was Zuriel the son of Abihail ........ Num 3:35
charge of the sons of *M* shall be ........ Num 3:36
As for the sons of *M*, thou shalt ........ Num 4:29
of the families of the sons of *M* ........ Num 4:33
of the families of the sons of *M* ........ Num 4:42
of the families of the sons of *M* ........ Num 4:45
oxen he gave unto the sons of *M* ........ Num 7:8
and the sons of *M* set forward ........ Num 10:17
of *M*, the family of the Merarites ...... Num 26:57
The children of *M* by their ........ Josh 21:7
the families of the children of *M* ........ Josh 21:34
children of *M* by their families ........ Josh 21:40
Gershon, Kohath, and *M* ........ 1Chr 6:1
Gershom, Kohath, and *M* ........ 1Chr 6:16
The sons of *M*; Mahli, and ........ 1Chr 6:19
The sons of *M*; Mahli, Libni ........ 1Chr 6:29
sons of *M* stood on the left hand ........ 1Chr 6:44
the son of Mushi, the son of *M* ........ 1Chr 6:47
Unto the sons of *M* were given by ........ 1Chr 6:63
the rest of the children of *M* ........ 1Chr 6:77
of Hashabiah, of the sons of *M* ........ 1Chr 9:14
Of the sons of *M* ........ 1Chr 15:6
of the sons of *M* their brethren ........ 1Chr 15:17
namely, Gershon, Kohath, and *M* ........ 1Chr 23:6
The sons of *M*; Mahli, and ........ 1Chr 23:21
sons of *M* were Mahli ........ 1Chr 24:26
The sons of *M* by Jaaziah ........ 1Chr 24:27
Also Hosah, of the children of *M* ....... 1Chr 26:10
of Kore, and among the sons of *M* .... 1Chr 26:19
and of the sons of *M*, Kish the son .... 2Chr 29:12
the Levites, of the sons of *M* ........ 2Chr 34:12
him Jeshaiah of the sons of *M* ........ Ezr 8:19

**MERARITES** (*me-ra'-rites*) *Descendants of Merari.*
of Merari, the family of the *M* ........ Num 26:57

**MERATHAIM** (*mer-a-tha'-im*) *A symbolic name for Babylon.*
Go up against the land of *M* ........ Jer 50:21

**MERCHANDISE**
thou shalt not make *m* of her ........ Deut 21:14
of Israel, and maketh *m* of him ........ Deut 24:7
For the *m* of it is better than ........ Prov 3:14
it is better than the *m* of silver ........ Prov 3:14
She perceiveth that her *m* is good ..... Prov 31:18
And her *m* and her hire shall be ........ Is 23:18
for her *m* shall be for them that ........ Is 23:18
*m* of Ethiopia and of the Sabeans, ........ Is 45:14
riches, and make a prey of thy *m* ........ Eze 26:12
were in thee to occupy thy *m* ........ Eze 27:9
isles were the *m* of thine hand ........ Eze 27:15
and made of cedar, among thy *m* ........ Eze 27:24
Thy riches, and thy fairs, thy *m* ........ Eze 27:27
and the occupiers of thy *m* ........ Eze 27:27
of thy riches and of thy *m* ........ Eze 27:33
in the depths of the waters thy *m* ........ Eze 27:34
By the multitude of thy *m* they ........ Eze 28:16
one to his farm, another to his *m* ........ Mt 22:5
my Father's house an house of *m* ........ Jn 2:16
with feigned words make *m* of you ........ 2Pet 2:3
no man buyeth their *m* any more ........ Rev 18:11
The *m* of gold, and silver, and ........ Rev 18:12

**MERCHANT**
silver, current money with the *m* ........ Gen 23:16
and delivereth girdles unto the *m* ...... Prov 31:24
with all powders of the *m* ........ Song 3:6
a commandment against the *m* city ...... Is 23:11
which art a *m* of the people for ........ Eze 27:3
Tarshish was thy *m* by reason of ........ Eze 27:12
Syria was thy *m* by reason of the ........ Eze 27:16
Damascus was thy *m* in the ........ Eze 27:18
Dedan was thy *m* in precious ........ Eze 27:20
He is a *m*, the balances of deceit ........ Hos 12:7
for all the *m* people are cut down ........ Zeph 1:11
of heaven is like unto a *m* man ........ Mt 13:45

**MERCHANTMEN**
Then there passed by Midianites *m* .... Gen 37:28
Beside that he had of the *m* ........ 1Kin 10:15

**MERCHANTS**
and of the traffick of the spice *m* ....... 1Kin 10:15
the king's *m* received the linen ........ 1Kin 10:28
the king's *m* received the linen ........ 2Chr 1:16
that which chapmen and *m* brought ... 2Chr 9:14
of the Nethinims, and of the *m* ........ Neh 3:31
repaired the goldsmiths and the *m* ........ Neh 3:32
So the *m* and sellers of all kind ........ Neh 13:20
shall they part him among the *m* ........ Job 41:6
thou whom the *m* of Zidon, that ........ Is 23:2
whose *m* are princes, whose ........ Is 23:8
thou hast laboured, even thy *m* ........ Is 47:15
he set it in a city of *m* ........ Eze 17:4
and Meshech, they were thy *m* ........ Eze 27:13
The men of Dedan were thy *m* ........ Eze 27:15
land of Israel, they were thy *m* ........ Eze 27:17
in these were they thy *m* ........ Eze 27:21
The *m* of Sheba and Raamah ........ Eze 27:22
Sheba and Raamah, they were thy *m*. Eze 27:22
the *m* of Sheba, Asshur, and ........ Eze 27:23
and Chilmad, were thy *m* ........ Eze 27:23
These were thy *m* in all sorts of ........ Eze 27:24
The *m* among the people shall hiss ........ Eze 27:36
the *m* of Tarshish, with all the ........ Eze 38:13
Thou hast multiplied thy *m* above ........ Nah 3:16
the *m* of the earth are waxed rich ........ Rev 18:3
the *m* of the earth shall weep and ........ Rev 18:11
The *m* of these things, which were .... Rev 18:15
for thy *m* were the great men of ........ Rev 18:23

**MERCHANTS'**
She is like the *m* ships ........ Prov 31:14

**MERCIES**
worthy of the least of all the *m* ........ Gen 32:10
for his *m* are great ........ 2Sa 24:14
for very great are his *m* ........ 1Chr 21:13
remember the *m* of David thy ........ 2Chr 6:42
Yet thou in thy manifold *m* ........ Neh 9:19
*m* thou gavest them saviours ........ Neh 9:27
deliver them according to thy *m* ........ Neh 9:28
Remember, O LORD, thy tender *m* ........ Ps 25:6
not thou thy tender *m* from me ........ Ps 40:11
*m* blot out my transgressions ........ Ps 51:1
to the multitude of thy tender *m* ........ Ps 69:16
he in anger shut up his tender *m* ........ Ps 77:9
let thy tender *m* speedily prevent ........ Ps 79:8
I will sing of the *m* of the LORD ........ Ps 89:1
with lovingkindness and tender *m* ........ Ps 103:4
not the multitude of thy *m* ........ Ps 106:7
to the multitude of his *m* ........ Ps 106:45
Let thy *m* come also unto me, O ........ Ps 119:41
Let thy tender *m* come unto me ........ Ps 119:77
Great are thy tender *m*, O LORD ........ Ps 119:156
his tender *m* are over all his ........ Ps 145:9
but the tender *m* of the wicked ........ Prov 12:10
but with great *m* will I gather ........ Is 54:7
you, even the sure *m* of David ........ Is 55:3
on them according to his *m* ........ Is 63:7
thy bowels and of thy *m* toward me ....... Is 63:15
LORD, even lovingkindness and *m* ........ Jer 16:5
And I will shew *m* unto you ........ Jer 42:12
It is of the LORD's *m* that we are ........ Lam 3:22
to the multitude of his *m* ........ Lam 3:32
That they would desire *m* of the ........ Dan 2:18
To the Lord our God belong *m* ........ Dan 9:9
but for thy great *m* ........ Dan 9:18
and in lovingkindness, and in *m* ........ Hos 2:19
I am returned to Jerusalem with *m* ........ Zec 1:16
will give you the sure *m* of David ...... Acts 13:34
brethren, by the *m* of God ........ Rom 12:1
Jesus Christ, the Father of *m* ........ 2Cor 1:3
of the Spirit, if any bowels and *m* ........ Phil 2:1
God, holy and beloved, bowels of *m* ...... Col 3:12

**MERCIES'**
Nevertheless for thy great *m* sake ........ Neh 9:31
oh save me for thy *m* sake ........ Ps 6:4
save me for thy *m* sake ........ Ps 31:16
help, and redeem us for thy *m* sake ...... Ps 44:26

**MERCIFUL**
the LORD being *m* unto him ........ Gen 19:16
The LORD, The LORD God, *m* ........ Ex 34:6
(For the LORD thy God is a *m* God ........ Deut 4:31
Be *m*, O LORD, unto thy people ........ Deut 21:8
will be *m* unto his land, and to ........ Deut 32:43
With the *m* thou wilt shew thyself ...... 2Sa 22:26
thou wilt shew thyself *m* ........ 2Sa 22:26
the house of Israel are *m* kings ........ 1Kin 20:31
LORD your God is gracious and *m* ........ 2Chr 30:9
ready to pardon, gracious and *m* ........ Neh 9:17
for thou art a gracious and *m* God ........ Neh 9:31
With the *m* thou wilt shew thyself ........ Ps 18:25
thou wilt shew thyself *m* ........ Ps 18:25
redeem me, and be *m* unto me ........ Ps 26:11
He is ever *m*, and lendeth ........ Ps 37:26
I said, LORD, be *m* unto me ........ Ps 41:4
be *m* unto me, and raise me up, ........ Ps 41:10
Be *m* unto me, O God ........ Ps 56:1
Be *m* unto me, O God, be *m* ........ Ps 57:1
be not *m* to any wicked ........ Ps 59:5
God be *m* unto us, and bless us ........ Ps 67:1
Be *m* unto me, O Lord ........ Ps 86:3
The LORD is *m* and gracious, slow ........ Ps 103:8
yea, our God is *m* ........ Ps 116:5
For his *m* kindness is great ........ Ps 117:2
be *m* unto me according to thy ........ Ps 119:58
thy *m* kindness be for my comfort, ...... Ps 119:76
be *m* unto me, as thou usest to do ..... Ps 119:132
The *m* man doeth good to his own .... Prov 11:17
*m* men are taken away, none ........ Is 57:1
for I am *m*, saith the LORD, and I ........ Jer 3:12
for he is gracious and *m*, slow to ........ Joel 2:13
thou art a gracious God, and *m* ........ Jonah 4:2
Blessed are the *m* ........ Mt 5:7
Be ye therefore *m*, as your Father ........ Lk 6:36
as your Father also is *m* ........ Lk 6:36
saying, God be *m* to me a sinner ........ Lk 18:13
brethren, that he might be a *m* ........ Heb 2:17
For I will be *m* to their ........ Heb 8:12

**MERCURIUS** (*mer-cu'-re-us*) *A Roman god.*
and Paul, *M*, because he was the ........ Acts 14:12

**MERCY**
and thou hast magnified thy *m* ........ Gen 19:19
left destitute my master of his *m* ........ Gen 24:27
was with Joseph, and shewed him *m*. Gen 39:21
give you *m* before the man ........ Gen 43:14
Thou in thy *m* hast led forth the ........ Ex 15:13
shewing *m* unto thousands of them ........ Ex 20:6
shalt make a *m* seat of pure gold ........ Ex 25:17
in the two ends of the *m* seat ........ Ex 25:18
even of the *m* seat shall ye make ........ Ex 25:19
covering the *m* seat with their ........ Ex 25:20
toward the *m* seat shall the faces ........ Ex 25:20
thou shalt put the *m* seat above ........ Ex 25:21
with thee from above the *m* seat ........ Ex 25:22
thou shalt put the *m* seat upon ........ Ex 26:34
before the *m* seat that is over ........ Ex 30:6
the *m* seat that is thereupon, and ........ Ex 31:7
shew *m* on whom I will shew *m* ........ Ex 33:19

Keeping *m* for thousands, Ex 34:7
staves thereof, with the *m* seat Ex 35:12
he made the *m* seat of pure gold Ex 37:6
on the two ends of the *m* seat Ex 37:7
out of the *m* seat made he the Ex 37:8
with their wings over the *m* seat Ex 37:9
even to the *m* seatward were the Ex 37:9
staves thereof, and the *m* seat, Ex 39:35
put the *m* seat above upon the ark Ex 40:20
within the vail before the *m* seat Lev 16:2
in the cloud upon the *m* seat Lev 16:2
of the incense may cover the *m* Lev 16:13
finger upon the *m* seat eastward Lev 16:14
before the *m* seat shall he Lev 16:14
and sprinkle it upon the *m* seat Lev 16:15
and before the *m* seat Lev 16:15
*m* seat that was upon the ark of Num 7:89
is longsuffering, and of great *m* Num 14:18
unto the greatness of thy *m* Num 14:19
shewing *m* unto thousands of them Deut 5:10
with them, nor shew *m* unto them Deut 7:2
*m* with them that love him and keep Deut 7:9
the *m* which he sware unto thy Deut 7:12
of his anger, and shew thee *m* Deut 13:17
the city, and we will shew thee *m* Judg 1:24
But my *m* shall not depart away 2Sa 7:15
*m* and truth be with thee 2Sa 15:20
sheweth *m* to his anointed, unto 2Sa 22:51
servant David my father great *m* 1Kin 3:6
*m* with thy servants that walk 1Kin 8:23
for his *m* endureth for ever 1Chr 16:34
because his *m* endureth for ever 1Chr 16:41
will not take my *m* away from him 1Chr 17:13
and of the place of the *m* seat 1Chr 28:11
great *m* unto David my father 2Chr 1:8
for his *m* endureth for ever 2Chr 5:13
shewest *m* unto thy servants, that 2Chr 6:14
for his *m* endureth for ever 2Chr 7:3
because his *m* endureth for ever, 2Chr 7:6
for his *m* endureth for ever 2Chr 20:21
for his *m* endureth for ever Ezr 3:11
hath extended *m* unto me before Ezr 7:28
but hath extended *m* unto us in Ezr 9:9
*m* for them that love him and Neh 1:5
grant him *m* in the sight of this Neh 1:11
God, who keepest covenant and *m* Neh 9:32
to the greatness of thy *m* Neh 13:22
or for his land, or for *m* Job 37:13
have *m* upon me, and hear my prayer Ps 4:1
house in the multitude of thy *m* Ps 5:7
Have *m* upon me, O LORD Ps 6:2
Have *m* upon me, O LORD Ps 9:13
But I have trusted in thy *m* Ps 13:5
sheweth *m* to his anointed, to Ps 18:50
through the *m* of the most High he Ps 21:7
*m* shall follow me all the days of Ps 23:6
according to thy *m* remember thou Ps 25:7
All the paths of the LORD are *m* Ps 25:10
thee unto me, and have *m* upon me Ps 25:16
have *m* also upon me, and answer me Ps 27:7
Hear, O LORD, and have *m* upon me Ps 30:10
will be glad and rejoice in thy *m* Ps 31:7
Have *m* upon me, O LORD, for I am Ps 31:9
*m* shall compass him about Ps 32:10
him, upon them that hope in his *m* Ps 33:18
Let thy *m*, O LORD, be upon us, Ps 33:22
Thy *m*, O LORD, is in the heavens Ps 36:5
but the righteous sheweth *m* Ps 37:21
Have *m* upon me, O God, according Ps 51:1
I trust in the *m* of God for ever Ps 52:8
God shall send forth his *m* Ps 57:3
For thy *m* is great unto the Ps 57:10
The God of my *m* shall prevent me Ps 59:10
aloud of thy *m* in the morning Ps 59:16
is my defence, and the God of my *m* Ps 59:17
O prepare *m* and truth, which may Ps 61:7
unto thee, O Lord, belongeth *m* Ps 62:12
away my prayer, nor his *m* from me Ps 66:20
in the multitude of thy *m* hear me Ps 69:13
Is his *m* clean gone for ever Ps 77:8
Shew us thy *m*, O LORD, and grant Ps 85:7
*M* and truth are met together Ps 85:10
plenteous in *m* unto all them that Ps 86:5
For great is thy *m* toward me Ps 86:13
longsuffering, and plenteous in *m* Ps 86:15
O turn unto me, and have *m* upon me Ps 86:16
*M* shall be built up for ever Ps 89:2
*m* and truth shall go before thy Ps 89:14
and my *m* shall be with him Ps 89:24
My *m* will I keep for him for Ps 89:28
O satisfy us early with thy *m* Ps 90:14
thy *m*, O LORD, held me up Ps 94:18
He hath remembered his *m* and his Ps 98:3
his *m* is everlasting Ps 100:5
I will sing of *m* and judgment Ps 101:1
shalt arise, and have *m* upon Zion Ps 102:13
slow to anger, and plenteous in *m* Ps 103:8
so great is his *m* toward them Ps 103:11
But the *m* of the LORD is from Ps 103:17
for his *m* endureth for ever Ps 106:1
for his *m* endureth for ever Ps 107:1
For thy *m* is great above the Ps 108:4
be none to extend *m* unto him Ps 109:12
that he remembered not to shew *m* Ps 109:16
because thy *m* is good, deliver Ps 109:21
O save me according to thy *m* Ps 109:26
thy name give glory, for thy *m* Ps 115:1
because his *m* endureth for ever Ps 118:1
that his *m* endureth for ever Ps 118:2
that his *m* endureth for ever Ps 118:3
that his *m* endureth for ever Ps 118:4
for his *m* endureth for ever Ps 118:29
earth, O LORD, is full of thy *m* Ps 119:64
thy servant according unto thy *m* Ps 119:124
God, until that he have *m* upon us Ps 123:2
Have *m* upon us, O LORD, have Ps 123:3
upon us, O LORD, have *m* upon us Ps 123:3
for with the LORD there is *m* Ps 130:7
for his *m* endureth for ever Ps 136:1
for his *m* endureth for ever Ps 136:2
for his *m* endureth for ever Ps 136:3
for his *m* endureth for ever Ps 136:4
for his *m* endureth for ever Ps 136:5
for his *m* endureth for ever Ps 136:6
for his *m* endureth for ever Ps 136:7
for his *m* endureth for ever Ps 136:8
for his *m* endureth for ever Ps 136:9
for his *m* endureth for ever Ps 136:10
for his *m* endureth for ever Ps 136:11
for his *m* endureth for ever Ps 136:12
for his *m* endureth for ever Ps 136:13
for his *m* endureth for ever Ps 136:14
for his *m* endureth for ever Ps 136:15
for his *m* endureth for ever Ps 136:16
for his *m* endureth for ever Ps 136:17
for his *m* endureth for ever Ps 136:18
for his *m* endureth for ever Ps 136:19
for his *m* endureth for ever Ps 136:20
for his *m* endureth for ever Ps 136:21
for his *m* endureth for ever Ps 136:22
for his *m* endureth for ever Ps 136:23
for his *m* endureth for ever Ps 136:24
for his *m* endureth for ever Ps 136:25
for his *m* endureth for ever Ps 136:26
thy *m*, O LORD, endureth for ever Ps 138:8
of thy *m* cut off mine enemies, and Ps 143:12
slow to anger, and of great *m* Ps 145:8
him, in those that hope in his *m* Ps 147:11
Let not *m* and truth forsake thee Prov 3:3
but he that hath *m* on the poor Prov 14:21
but *m* and truth shall be to them Prov 14:22
honoureth him hath *m* on the poor Prov 14:31
By *m* and truth iniquity is purged Prov 16:6
*M* and truth preserve the king Prov 20:28
and his throne is upholden by *m* Prov 20:28
*m* findeth life, righteousness, and Prov 21:21
and forsaketh them shall have *m* Prov 28:13
neither shall have *m* on their Is 9:17
For the LORD will have *m* on Jacob Is 14:1
And in *m* shall the throne be Is 16:5
made them will not have *m* on them Is 27:11
that he may have *m* upon you Is 30:18
thou didst shew them no *m* Is 47:6
for he that hath *m* on them shall Is 49:10
will have *m* upon his afflicted Is 49:13
kindness will I have *m* on thee Is 54:8
the LORD that hath *m* on thee Is 54:10
LORD, and he will have *m* upon him Is 55:7
in my favour have I had *m* on thee Is 60:10
they are cruel, and have no *m* Jer 6:23
not pity, nor spare, nor have *m* Jer 13:14
neither have pity, nor have *m* Jer 21:7
have *m* on his dwellingplaces Jer 30:18
I will surely have *m* upon him Jer 31:20
for his *m* endureth for ever Jer 33:11
to return, and have *m* on them Jer 33:26
you, that he may have *m* upon you Jer 42:12
are cruel, and will not shew *m* Jer 50:42
have *m* upon the whole house of Eze 39:25
by shewing *m* to the poor Dan 4:27
*m* to them that love him, and to Dan 9:4
for I will no more have *m* upon Hos 1:6
But I will have *m* upon the house Hos 1:7
I will not have *m* upon her Hos 2:4
I will have *m* upon her that had Hos 2:23
upon her that had not obtained *m* Hos 2:23
because there is no truth, nor *m* Hos 4:1
For I desired *m*, and not sacrifice Hos 6:6
in righteousness, reap in *m* Hos 10:12
keep *m* and judgment, and wait on Hos 12:6
in thee the fatherless findeth *m* Hos 14:3
vanities forsake their own *m* Jonah 2:8
but to do justly, and to love *m* Mic 6:8
ever, because he delighteth in *m* Mic 7:18
the *m* to Abraham, which thou hast Mic 7:20
in wrath remember *m* Hab 3:2
wilt thou not have *m* on Jerusalem Zec 1:12
Execute true judgment, and shew *m* Zec 7:9
for I have *m* upon them Zec 10:6
for they shall obtain *m* Mt 5:7
what that meaneth, I will have *m* Mt 9:13
Thou son of David, have *m* on us Mt 9:27
what this meaneth, I will have *m* Mt 12:7
Have *m* on me, O Lord, thou son of Mt 15:22
Lord, have *m* on my son Mt 17:15
Have *m* on us, O Lord, thou son of Mt 20:30
Have *m* on us, O Lord, thou son of Mt 20:31
matters of the law, judgment, *m* Mt 23:23
thou son of David, have *m* on me Mk 10:47
Thou son of David, have *m* on me Mk 10:48
his *m* is on them that fear him Lk 1:50
Israel, in remembrance of his *m* Lk 1:54
Lord had shewed great *m* upon her Lk 1:58
To perform the *m* promised to our Lk 1:72
Through the tender *m* of our God Lk 1:78
he said, He that shewed *m* on him Lk 10:37
have *m* on me, and send Lazarus, Lk 16:24
said, Jesus, Master, have *m* on us Lk 17:13
thou son of David, have *m* on me Lk 18:38
Thou son of David, have *m* on me Lk 18:39
I will have *m* on whom I will have Rom 9:15
have *m* on whom I will have *m* Rom 9:15
but of God that sheweth *m* Rom 9:16
Therefore hath he *m* on whom he Rom 9:18
on whom he will have *m* Rom 9:18
of his glory on the vessels of *m* Rom 9:23
yet have now obtained *m* through Rom 11:30
that through your *m* they also may Rom 11:31
they also may obtain *m* Rom 11:31
that he might have *m* upon all Rom 11:32
he that sheweth *m*, with Rom 12:8
might glorify God for his *m* Rom 15:9
as one that hath obtained *m* of 1Cor 7:25
ministry, as we have received *m* 2Cor 4:1
this rule, peace be on them, and *m* Gal 6:16
But God, who is rich in *m* Eph 2:4
but God had *m* on him Phil 2:27
Grace, *m*, and peace, from God our 1Ti 1:2
but I obtained *m*, because I did 1Ti 1:13
for this cause I obtained *m* 1Ti 1:16
Grace, *m*, and peace, from God the 2Ti 1:2
The Lord give *m* unto the house of 2Ti 1:16
find *m* of the Lord in that day 2Ti 1:18
Grace, *m*, and peace, from God the Titus 1:4
according to his *m* he saved us Titus 3:5
of grace, that we may obtain *m* Heb 4:16
Moses' law died without *m* under Heb 10:28
he shall have judgment without *m* Jas 2:13
that hath shewed no *m* Jas 2:13
*m* rejoiceth against judgment Jas 2:13
easy to be intreated, full of *m* Jas 3:17
is very pitiful, and of tender *m* Jas 5:11
*m* hath begotten us again unto a 1Pet 1:3
which had not obtained *m* 1Pet 2:10
but now have obtained *m* 1Pet 2:10
Grace be with you, *m*, and peace, 2Jn 3
*M* unto you, and peace, and love, be Jude 2
looking for the *m* of our Lord Jude 21

**MERCYSEAT**
of glory shadowing the *m* Heb 9:5

**MERED** (*me'-red*) *A descendant of Judah.*
sons of Ezra were, Jether, and *M* 1Chr 4:17
daughter of Pharaoh, which *M* took 1Chr 4:18

**MEREMOTH** (*mer'-e-moth*) See MERAIOTH.
*1. Son of Uriah the priest.*
of *M* the son of Uriah the priest Ezr 8:33
them repaired *M* the son of Urijah Neh 3:4
After him repaired *M* the son of Neh 3:21
*2. Married a foreigner in exile.*
Vaniah, *M*, Eliashib, Ezr 10:36
*3. A priest who renewed the covenant.*
Harim, *M*, Obadiah, Neh 10:5
Shechaniah, Rehum, *M*, Neh 12:3

**MERES** (*me'-res*) *A prince of Media and Persia.*
Shethar, Admatha, Tarshish, *M* Est 1:14

**MERIBAH** (*mer'-i-bah*) See MASSAH, MERIBAH-KADESH. *Same as Meribah-Kadesh.*
name of the place Massah, and *M* Ex 17:7
This is the water of *M* Num 20:13
against my word at the water of *M* Num 20:24
that is the water of *M* in Kadesh Num 27:14
didst strive at the waters of *M* Deut 33:8
I proved thee at the waters of *M* Ps 81:7

**MERIBAH-KADESH** (*mer'-i-bah-ka'-desh*) *A place between Zin and Sinai.*
of Israel at the waters of *M* Deut 32:51

**MERIBATH-KADESH** See MERIBAH-KADESH.

**MERIB-BAAL** (*me-rib'-ba-al*) See MEPHIBOSHETH. *Son of Jonathan.*
And the son of Jonathan was *M* 1Chr 8:34
and *M* begat Micah 1Chr 8:34
And the son of Jonathan was *M* 1Chr 9:40
and *M* begat Micah 1Chr 9:40

**MERODACH** (*mer'-o-dak*) See BERODACH, EVIL-MERODACH, MERODACH-BALADAN. *A Babylonian god of war.*
confounded, *M* is broken in pieces Jer 50:2

**MERODACH-BALADAN** (*mer'-o-dak-bal'-a-dan*) See BERODACH-BALADAN. *A king of Babylon.*
At that time *M*, the son of Is 39:1

**MEROM** (*me'-rom*) *A small lake north of the Sea of Chinneroth.*
together at the waters of *M* Josh 11:5
them by the waters of *M* suddenly Josh 11:7

**MERONOTHITE** (*me-ron'-o-thite*) *An inhabitant of a district of Zebulun.*
over the asses was Jehdeiah the *M* 1Chr 27:30
the Gibeonite, and Jadon the *M* Neh 3:7

**MEROZ** (*me'-roz*) *A place near Lake Merom.*
Curse ye *M*, said the angel of the Judg 5:23

**MERRILY**
then go thou in *m* with the king Est 5:14

**MERRY**
and were *m* with him Gen 43:34
and trode the grapes, and made *m* Judg 9:27
to pass, when their hearts were *m* Judg 16:25
night, and let thine heart be *m* Judg 19:6
here, that thine heart may be *m* Judg 19:9
they were making their hearts *m* Judg 19:22
and drunk, and his heart was *m* Ruth 3:7
Nabal's heart was *m* within him 1Sa 25:36

when Amnon's heart is *m* with wine ... 2Sa 13:28
eating and drinking, and making *m* ... 1Kin 4:20
bread, and let thine heart be *m* ... 1Kin 21:7
*m* in heart for the goodness that ... 2Chr 7:10
heart of the king was *m* with wine ... Est 1:10
A *m* heart maketh a cheerful ... Prov 15:13
but he that is of a *m* heart hath ... Prov 15:15
A *m* heart doeth good like a ... Prov 17:22
to eat, and to drink, and to be *m* ... Eccl 8:15
and drink thy wine with a *m* heart ... Eccl 9:7
for laughter, and wine maketh *m* ... Eccl 10:19
and the voice of them that make *m* ... Jer 30:19
in the dances of them that make *m* ... Jer 31:4
thine ease, eat, drink, and be *m* ... Lk 12:19
and let us eat, and be *m* ... Lk 15:23
And they began to be *m* ... Lk 15:24
I might make *m* with my friends ... Lk 15:29
It was meet that we should make *m* ... Lk 15:32
Is any *m*? ... Jas 5:13
rejoice over them, and make *m* ... Rev 11:10

**MERRYHEARTED**
languisheth, all the *m* do sigh ... Is 24:7

**MESECH** (*me'-sek*) See MESHECH. *A tribe joined to Kedar.*
Woe is me, that I sojourn in *M* ... Ps 120:5

**MESHA** (*me'-shah*)
*1. A place in southeastern Arabia.*
And their dwelling was from *M* ... Gen 10:30
*2. A king of Moab.*
*M* king of Moab was a sheepmaster, ... 2Kin 3:4
*3. A son of Caleb.*
*M* his firstborn, which was the ... 1Chr 2:42
*4. A son of Shaharaim.*
his wife, Jobab, and Zibia, and *M* ... 1Chr 8:9

**MESHACH** (*me'-shak*) *A companion of Daniel.*
and to Mishael, of *M* ... Dan 1:7
the king, and he set Shadrach, *M* ... Dan 2:49
province of Babylon, Shadrach, *M* ... Dan 3:12
commanded to bring Shadrach, *M* ... Dan 3:13
them, Is it true, O Shadrach, *M* ... Dan 3:14
Shadrach, *M*, and Abed-nego, ... Dan 3:16
was changed against Shadrach, *M* ... Dan 3:19
in his army to bind Shadrach, *M* ... Dan 3:20
men that took up Shadrach, *M* ... Dan 3:22
And these three men, Shadrach, *M* ... Dan 3:23
and spake, and said, Shadrach, *M* ... Dan 3:26
Then Shadrach, *M*, and Abed-nego, ... Dan 3:26
Blessed be the God of Shadrach, *M* ... Dan 3:28
against the God of Shadrach, *M* ... Dan 3:29
the king promoted Shadrach, *M* ... Dan 3:30

**MESHECH** (*me'-shek*) See MESECH.
*1. A son of Japheth.*
Madai, and Javan, and Tubal, and *M* ... Gen 10:2
Madai, and Javan, and Tubal, and *M* ... 1Chr 1:5
*2. A son of Shem.*
and Uz, and Hul, and Gether, and *M* .. 1Chr 1:17
*3. Descendants of Meschech 1.*
Javan, Tubal, and *M*, they were thy ... Eze 27:13
There is *M*, Tubal, and all her ... Eze 32:26
of Magog, the chief prince of *M* ... Eze 38:2
O Gog, the chief prince of *M* ... Eze 38:3
O Gog, the chief prince of *M* ... Eze 39:1

**MESHELEMIAH** (*me-shel-e-mi'-ah*) See MESHULLAM, SHELEMIAH, SHALLUM. *Father of Zechariah.*
Zechariah the son of *M* was porter ... 1Chr 9:21
Korhites was *M* the son of Kore ... 1Chr 26:1
And the sons of *M* were, Zechariah ... 1Chr 26:2
*M* had sons and brethren, strong ... 1Chr 26:9

**MESHEZABEEL** (*me-shez'-a-be-el*)
*1. Father of Berechiah.*
son of Berechiah, the son of *M* ... Neh 3:4
*2. An Israelite who renewed the covenant.*
*M*, Zadok, Jaddua, ... Neh 10:21
And Pethahiah the son of *M* ... Neh 11:24

**MESHEZABEL** See MESHEZABEEL.

**MESHILLEMITH** (*me-shil'-le-mith*) See MESHILLEMOTH. *A family of exiles.*
son of Meshullam, the son of *M* ... 1Chr 9:12

**MESHILLEMOTH** (*me-shil'-le-moth*) See MESHILLEMITH.
*1. Father of Berechiah.*
Johanan, Berechiah the son of *M* ... 2Chr 28:12
*2. A family of exiles.*
the son of Ahasai, the son of *M* ... Neh 11:13

**MESHOBAB** (*me-sho'-bab*) *A chief of Simeon.*
And *M*, and Jamlech, and Joshah the . 1Chr 4:34

**MESHULLAM** (*me-shul'-lam*) See MESHELLEMIAH.
*1. A scribe in Josiah's time.*
the son of Azaliah, the son of *M* ... 2Kin 22:3
*2. A descendant of Jeconiah.*
*M*, and Hananiah, and Shelomith ... 1Chr 3:19
*3. Head of a Gadite family.*
their fathers were, Michael, and *M* ... 1Chr 5:13
*4. A Benjamite of the Elpaal family.*
Zebadiah, and *M*, and Hezeki ... 1Chr 8:17
*5. Father of Sallu.*
Sallu the son of *M*, the son of ... 1Chr 9:7
*6. Son of Shephathiah.*
*M* the son of Shephatiah, the son ... 1Chr 9:8
*7. Father of Hilkiah.*
the son of Hilkiah, the son of *M* ... 1Chr 9:11
the son of Hilkiah, the son of *M* ... Neh 11:11
*8. Son of Meshillemith.*
the son of Jahzerah, the son of *M* ... 1Chr 9:12
*9. A Kohathite repairer of the wall.*
and Zechariah and *M*, of the sons of 2Chr 34:12
*10. A clan leader with Ezra.*
and for Zechariah, and for *M* ... Ezr 8:16
*11. A priest who accounted for the foreign wives.*
and *M* and Shabbethai the Levite ... Ezr 10:15
*12. A son of Bani.*
*M*, Malluch, and Adaiah, Jashub, and .. Ezr 10:29
*13. A son of Berechiah.*
repaired *M* the son of Berechiah ... Neh 3:4
After him repaired *M* the son of ... Neh 3:30
of *M* the son of Berechiah ... Neh 6:18
*14. A son of Besodeiah.*
Paseah, and *M* the son of Besodeiah ... Neh 3:6
*15. A Levite who aided Ezra.*
and Hashbadana, Zechariah, and *M* ... Neh 8:4
*16. A priest who renewed the covenant.*
*M*, Abijah, Mijamin, ... Neh 10:7
*17. A clan leader who renewed the covenant.*
Magpiash, *M*, Hezir, ... Neh 10:20
*18. A family of exiles.*
Sallu the son of *M*, the son of ... Neh 11:7
*19. A priest who dedicated the wall.*
Of Ezra, *M* ... Neh 12:13
And Azariah, Ezra, and *M*, ... Neh 12:33
*20. A descendant of Ginnethon.*
of Ginnethon, *M* ... Neh 12:16
*21. A Levite gatekeeper.*
and Bakbukiah, Obadiah, *M* ... Neh 12:25

**MESHULLEMETH** (*me-shul'-le-meth*) *Mother of King Amon.*
And his mother's name was *M* ... 2Kin 21:19

**MESOBAITE** (*me-so'-ba-ite*) *Family name of Jasiel.*
Eliel, and Obed, and Jasiel the *M* ... 1Chr 11:47

**MESOPOTAMIA** (*mes-o-po-ta'-me-ah*) See ARAM, NAHARAIM. *Land between the Tigris and Euphrates Rivers.*
and he arose, and went to *M* ... Gen 24:10
the son of Beor of Pethor of *M* ... Deut 23:4
of Chushan-rishathaim king of *M* ... Judg 3:8
king of *M* into his hand ... Judg 3:10
chariots and horsemen out of *M* ... 1Chr 19:6
and Elamites, and the dwellers in *M* ... Acts 2:9
father Abraham, when he was in *M* ... Acts 7:2

**MESS**
but Benjamin's *m* was five times ... Gen 43:34
there followed him a *m* of meat ... 2Sa 11:8

**MESSAGE**
I have a *m* from God unto thee ... Judg 3:20
pass, when Ben-hadad heard this *m* .. 1Kin 20:12
He that sendeth a *m* by the hand ... Prov 26:6
in the LORD's *m* unto the people ... Hag 1:13
sent a *m* after him, saying, We ... Lk 19:14
This then is the *m* which we have ... 1Jn 1:5
For this is the *m* that ye heard ... 1Jn 3:11

**MESSENGER**
And they sent a *m* unto Joseph ... Gen 50:16
the *m* answered and said, Israel is ... 1Sa 4:17
But there came a *m* unto Saul ... 1Sa 23:27
And charged the *m*, saying, When ... 2Sa 11:19
So the *m* went, and came and shewed 2Sa 11:22
the *m* said unto David, Surely the ... 2Sa 11:23
Then David said unto the *m* ... 2Sa 11:25
And there came a *m* to David ... 2Sa 15:13
Then Jezebel sent a *m* unto Elijah ... 1Kin 19:2
the *m* that was gone to call ... 1Kin 22:13
And Elisha sent a *m* unto him ... 2Kin 5:10
but ere the *m* came to him ... 2Kin 6:32
look, when the *m* cometh, shut the ... 2Kin 6:32
behold, the *m* came down unto him ... 2Kin 6:33
The *m* came to them, but he cometh .. 2Kin 9:18
And there came a *m*, and told him, ... 2Kin 10:8
the *m* that went to call Micaiah ... 2Chr 18:12
And there came a *m* unto Job ... Job 1:14
If there be a *m* with him, an ... Job 33:23
A wicked *m* falleth into mischief ... Prov 13:17
therefore a cruel *m* shall be sent ... Prov 17:11
so is a faithful *m* to them that ... Prov 25:13
or deaf, as my *m* that I sent ... Is 42:19
one *m* to meet another, to shew ... Jer 51:31
from far, unto whom a *m* was sent ... Eze 23:40
Then spake Haggai the LORD's *m* in ... Hag 1:13
for he is the *m* of the LORD of ... Mal 2:7
Behold, I will send my *m*, and he ... Mal 3:1
even the *m* of the covenant, whom ... Mal 3:1
I send my *m* before thy face, ... Mt 11:10
I send my *m* before thy face, ... Mk 1:2
I send my *m* before thy face, ... Lk 7:27
the *m* of Satan to buffet me, lest ... 2Cor 12:7
and fellow soldier, but your *m* ... Phil 2:25

**MESSENGERS**
Jacob sent *m* before him to Esau ... Gen 32:3
the *m* returned to Jacob, saying, ... Gen 32:6
Moses sent *m* from Kadesh unto the Num 20:14
Israel sent *m* unto Sihon king of ... Num 21:21
He sent *m* therefore unto Balaam ... Num 22:5
Spake I not also to thy *m* which ... Num 24:12
I sent *m* out of the wilderness of ... Deut 2:26
she hid the *m* that we sent ... Josh 6:17
because she hid the *m*, which ... Josh 6:25
So Joshua sent *m*, and they ran ... Josh 7:22
he sent *m* throughout all Manasseh ... Judg 6:35
he sent *m* unto Asher, and unto ... Judg 6:35
Gideon sent *m* throughout all ... Judg 7:24
he sent *m* unto Abimelech privily, ... Judg 9:31
Jephthah sent *m* unto the king of ... Judg 11:12
answered unto the *m* of Jephthah ... Judg 11:13
Jephthah sent *m* again unto the ... Judg 11:14
Then Israel sent *m* unto the king ... Judg 11:17
Israel sent *m* unto Sihon king of ... Judg 11:19
they sent *m* to the inhabitants of ... 1Sa 6:21
that we may send *m* unto all the ... 1Sa 11:3
Then came the *m* to Gibeah of Saul ... 1Sa 11:4
of Israel by the hands of *m* ... 1Sa 11:7
And they said unto the *m* that came ... 1Sa 11:9
the *m* came and shewed it to the ... 1Sa 11:9
Wherefore Saul sent *m* unto Jesse ... 1Sa 16:19
Saul also sent *m* unto David's ... 1Sa 19:11
And when Saul sent *m* to take David . 1Sa 19:14
Saul sent the *m* again to see ... 1Sa 19:15
when the *m* were come in, behold, ... 1Sa 19:16
Saul sent *m* to take David ... 1Sa 19:20
of God was upon the *m* of Saul ... 1Sa 19:20
it was told Saul, he sent other *m* ... 1Sa 19:21
Saul sent *m* again the third time, ... 1Sa 19:21
Behold, David sent *m* out of the ... 1Sa 25:14
and she went after the *m* of David ... 1Sa 25:42
David sent *m* unto the men of ... 2Sa 2:5
Abner sent *m* to David on his ... 2Sa 3:12
David sent *m* to Ish-bosheth ... 2Sa 3:14
he sent *m* after Abner, which ... 2Sa 3:26
king of Tyre sent *m* to David ... 2Sa 5:11
And David sent *m*, and took her ... 2Sa 11:4
And Joab sent *m* to David, and said, ... 2Sa 12:27
he sent *m* to Ahab king of Israel ... 1Kin 20:2
the *m* came again, and said, Thus ... 1Kin 20:5
he said unto the *m* of Ben-hadad ... 1Kin 20:9
the *m* departed, and brought him ... 1Kin 20:9
and he sent *m*, and said unto them, ... 2Kin 1:2
go up to meet the *m* of the king ... 2Kin 1:3
when the *m* turned back unto him, ... 2Kin 1:5
Forasmuch as thou hast sent *m* to ... 2Kin 1:16
the *m* returned, and told the king ... 2Kin 7:15
Then Amaziah sent *m* to Jehoash ... 2Kin 14:8
So Ahaz sent *m* to Tiglath-pileser ... 2Kin 16:7
for he had sent *m* to So king of ... 2Kin 17:4
he sent *m* again unto Hezekiah, ... 2Kin 19:9
the letter of the hand of the *m* ... 2Kin 19:14
By thy *m* thou hast reproached the ... 2Kin 19:23
king of Tyre sent *m* to David ... 1Chr 14:1
David sent *m* to comfort him ... 1Chr 19:2
worse before Israel, they sent *m* ... 1Chr 19:16
fathers sent to them by his *m* ... 2Chr 36:15
But they mocked the *m* of God ... 2Chr 36:16
I sent *m* unto them, saying, I am ... Neh 6:3
wrath of a king is as *m* of death ... Prov 16:14
then answer the *m* of the nation ... Is 14:32
waters, saying, Go, ye swift *m* ... Is 18:2
he sent *m* to Hezekiah, saying, ... Is 37:9
the letter from the hand of the *m* ... Is 37:14
performeth the counsel of his *m* ... Is 44:26
and didst send thy *m* far off ... Is 57:9
by the hand of the *m* which come ... Jer 27:3
sent *m* unto them into Chaldea ... Eze 23:16
In that day shall *m* go forth from ... Eze 30:9
the voice of thy *m* shall no more ... Nah 2:13
when the *m* of John were departed, ... Lk 7:24
And sent *m* before his face ... Lk 9:52
they are the *m* of the churches, ... 2Cor 8:23
when she had received the *m* ... Jas 2:25

**MESSES**
sent *m* unto them from before him ... Gen 43:34

**MESSIAH** (*mes-si'-ah*) See MESSIAS. *The great Deliverer of Israel.*
to build Jerusalem unto the *M* the ... Dan 9:25
and two weeks shall *M* be cut off ... Dan 9:26

**MESSIAS** (*mes-si'-as*) See MESSIAH. *Greek form of Messiah.*
unto him, We have found the *M* ... Jn 1:41
unto him, I know that *M* cometh ... Jn 4:25

**MET**
way, and the angels of God *m* him ... Gen 32:1
thou by all this drove which I *m* ... Gen 33:8
God of the Hebrews hath *m* with us ... Ex 3:18
in the inn, that the LORD *m* him ... Ex 4:24
*m* him in the mount of God, and ... Ex 4:27
God of the Hebrews hath *m* with us ... Ex 5:3
they *m* Moses and Aaron, who stood ... Ex 5:20
And God *m* Balaam ... Num 23:4
And the LORD *m* Balaam, and put a .. Num 23:16
Because they *m* you not with bread ... Deut 23:4
How he *m* thee by the way, and ... Deut 25:18
all these kings were *m* together ... Josh 11:5
they *m* together in Asher on the ... Josh 17:10
a company of prophets *m* him ... 1Sa 10:10
and she *m* them ... 1Sa 25:20
*m* together by the pool of Gibeon ... 2Sa 2:13
the servant of Mephibosheth *m* him ... 2Sa 16:1
Absalom *m* the servants of David ... 2Sa 18:9
a lion *m* him by the way, and slew ... 1Kin 13:24
in the way, behold, Elijah *m* him ... 1Kin 18:7
*m* him in the portion of Naboth ... 2Kin 9:21
Jehu *m* with the brethren of ... 2Kin 10:13
Because they *m* not the children ... Neh 13:2
Mercy and truth are *m* together ... Ps 85:10
there *m* him a woman with the ... Prov 7:10
and it came to pass, as he *m* them ... Jer 41:6
flee from a lion, and a bear *m* him ... Amos 5:19
there *m* him two possessed with ... Mt 8:28
disciples, behold, Jesus *m* them ... Mt 28:9

M

immediately there *m* him out of ... Mk 5:2
in a place where two ways *m* ... Mk 11:4
there *m* him out of the city a ... Lk 8:27
from the hill, much people *m* him ... Lk 9:37
there *m* him ten men that were ... Lk 17:12
going down, his servants *m* him ... Jn 4:51
Jesus was coming, went and *m* him ... Jn 11:20
in that place where Martha *m* him ... Jn 11:30
this cause the people also *m* him ... Jn 12:18
was coming in, Cornelius *m* him ... Acts 10:25
with a spirit of divination *m* us ... Acts 16:16
daily with them that *m* with him ... Acts 17:17
when he *m* with us at Assos, we ... Acts 20:14
into a place where two seas *m* ... Acts 27:41
who *m* Abraham returning from the ... Heb 7:1
father, when Melchisedec *m* him ... Heb 7:10

**METE**
when they did *m* it with an omer, ... Ex 16:18
*m* out the valley of Succoth ... Ps 60:6
*m* out the valley of Succoth ... Ps 108:7
and with what measure ye *m* ... Mt 7:2
with what measure ye *m*, it shall ... Mk 4:24
with the same measure that ye *m* ... Lk 6:38

**METED**
a nation *m* out and trodden down, ... Is 18:2
a nation *m* out and trodden under ... Is 18:7
*m* out heaven with the span, and ... Is 40:12

**METEYARD**
unrighteousness in judgment, in *m* ... Lev 19:35

**METHEG-AMMAH** (*me'-theg-am'-mah*) *A place in Philistia.*
David took *M* out of the hand of ... 2Sa 8:1

**METHUSAEL** (*me-thu'-sa-el*) *A descendant of Cain.*
and Mehujael begat *M* ... Gen 4:18
and *M* begat Lamech ... Gen 4:18

**METHUSELAH** (*me-thu'-se-lah*) See Methusala. *Son of Enoch.*
sixty and five years, and begat *M* ... Gen 5:21
he begat *M* three hundred years ... Gen 5:22
*M* lived an hundred eighty and ... Gen 5:25
*M* lived after he begat Lamech ... Gen 5:26
all the days of *M* were nine ... Gen 5:27
Henoch, *M*, Lamech, ... 1Chr 1:3

**METHUSHAEL** See Methusael.

**MEUNIM** (*me-u'-nim*) See Mehunim. *A family of exiles.*
of Besai, the children of *M* ... Neh 7:52

**MEUNITES** See Mehunims.

**MEZAHAB** (*mez'-a-hab*) *Grandmother of Mehetabel.*
of Matred, the daughter of *M* ... Gen 36:39
of Matred, the daughter of *M* ... 1Chr 1:50

**MEZOBAITE** See Mesobaite.

**MIAMIN** (*mi'-a-min*) See Mijamin, Miniamin.
*1. Married a foreigner in exile.*
and Jeziah, and Malchiah, and *M* ... Ezr 10:25
*2. A priest with Zerubbabel.*
*M*, Maadiah, Bilgah, ... Neh 12:5

**MIBHAR** (*mib'-har*) *A 'mighty man' of David.*
of Nathan, *M* the son of Haggeri, ... 1Chr 11:38

**MIBSAM** (*mib'-sam*)
*1. A son of Ishmael.*
and Kedar, and Adbeel, and *M* ... Gen 25:13
then Kedar, and Adbeel, and *M* ... 1Chr 1:29
*2. A son of Simeon.*
*M* his son, Mishma his son ... 1Chr 4:25

**MIBZAR** (*mib'-zar*) *A descendant of Esau.*
Duke Kenaz, duke Teman, duke *M* ... Gen 36:42
Duke Kenaz, duke Teman, duke *M* ... 1Chr 1:53

**MICA** See Micha.

**MICAH** (*mi'-cah*) See Micaiah, Micah's, Michah.
*1. An Ephraimite who set up idols.*
mount Ephraim, whose name was *M* .. Judg 17:1
and they were in the house of *M* ... Judg 17:4
the man *M* had an house of gods, ... Judg 17:5
mount Ephraim to the house of *M* ... Judg 17:8
*M* said unto him, Whence comest ... Judg 17:9
*M* said unto him, Dwell with me, ... Judg 17:10
And *M* consecrated the Levite ... Judg 17:12
priest, and was in the house of *M* ... Judg 17:12
Then said *M*, Now know I that the ... Judg 17:13
mount Ephraim, to the house of *M* ... Judg 18:2
When they were by the house of *M* ... Judg 18:3
Thus and thus dealeth *M* with me ... Judg 18:4
and came unto the house of *M* ... Judg 18:13
Levite, even unto the house of *M* ... Judg 18:15
a good way from the house of *M* ... Judg 18:22
their faces, and said unto *M* ... Judg 18:23
when *M* saw that they were too ... Judg 18:26
took the things which *M* had made... Judg 18:27
*2. Head of a Reubenite family.*
*M* his son, Reaia his son, Baal ... 1Chr 5:5
*3. Son of Merib-baal.*
and Merib-baal begat *M* ... 1Chr 8:34
And the sons of *M* were, Pithon, and.. 1Chr 8:35
and Merib-baal begat *M* ... 1Chr 9:40
And the sons of *M* were, Pithon, and.. 1Chr 9:41
*4. A family of exiles.*
Galal, and Mattaniah the son of *M* ... 1Chr 9:15
*5. A sanctuary servant.*
*M* the first, and Jesiah the second ... 1Chr 23:20
*6. Father of Abdon.*
and Abdon the son of *M* ... 2Chr 34:20
*7. A prophet.*
*M* the Morasthite prophesied in ... Jer 26:18
*M* the Morasthite in the days of ... Mic 1:1

**MICAH'S** (*mi'-cahs*) *Refers to Micah 1.*
And these went into *M* house ... Judg 18:18
to *M* house were gathered together... Judg 18:22
they set them up *M* graven image ... Judg 18:31

**MICAIAH** (*mi-ka-i'-ah*) See Micha, Michaiah.
*A prophet who foretold Ahab's fall.*
*M* the son of Imlah, by whom we ... 1Kin 22:8
Hasten hither *M* the son of Imlah ... 1Kin 22:9
was gone to call *M* spake unto him... 1Kin 22:13
*M* said, As the Lord liveth, what ... 1Kin 22:14
And the king said unto him, *M* ... 1Kin 22:15
smote *M* on the cheek, and said, ... 1Kin 22:24
*M* said, Behold, thou shalt see in ... 1Kin 22:25
the king of Israel said, Take *M* ... 1Kin 22:26
*M* said, If thou return at all in ... 1Kin 22:28
the same is *M* the son of Imla ... 2Chr 18:7
Fetch quickly *M* the son of Imla ... 2Chr 18:8
that went to call *M* spake to him ... 2Chr 18:12
*M* said, As the Lord liveth, even ... 2Chr 18:13
king, the king said unto him, *M* ... 2Chr 18:14
smote *M* upon the cheek, and said,... 2Chr 18:23
*M* said, Behold, thou shalt see on ... 2Chr 18:24
king of Israel said, Take ye *M* ... 2Chr 18:25
*M* said, If thou certainly return ... 2Chr 18:27

**MICE**
golden emerods, and five golden *m* ... 1Sa 6:4
images of your *m* that mar the ... 1Sa 6:5
and the coffer with the *m* of gold ... 1Sa 6:11
And the golden *m*, according to the ... 1Sa 6:18

**MICHA** (*mi'-cah*) See Micah, Micaiah.
*1. Son of Mephibosheth.*
had a young son, whose name was *M*... 2Sa 9:12
*2. A Levite who renewed the covenant.*
*M*, Rehob, Hashabiah, ... Neh 10:11
*3. A family of exiles.*
And Mattaniah the son of *M* ... Neh 11:17
son of Mattaniah, the son of *M* ... Neh 11:22

**MICHAEL** (*mi'-ka-el*)
*1. Father of Sethur.*
of Asher, Sethur the son of *M* ... Num 13:13
*2. A Gadite who settled in Bashan.*
house of their fathers were, *M* ... 1Chr 5:13
*3. Son of Jeshishai.*
the son of Gilead, the son of *M* ... 1Chr 5:14
*4. Son of Baaseiah.*
The son of *M*, the son of Baaseiah ... 1Chr 6:40
*5. A chief man of Issachar.*
*M*, and Obadiah, and Joel, Ishiah, ... 1Chr 7:3
*6. A Benjamite in Jerusalem.*
And *M*, and Ispah, and Joha, the sons 1Chr 8:16
*7. A warrior in David's army.*
and Jozabad, and Jediael, and *M* ... 1Chr 12:20
*8. Father of Omri.*
of Issachar, Omri the son of *M* ... 1Chr 27:18
*9. A son of Jehoshaphat.*
and Zechariah, and Azariah, and *M* ... 2Chr 21:2
*10. A family of exiles.*
Zebadiah the son of *M*, and with ... Ezr 8:8
*11. Angelic messenger who came to Daniel.*
but, lo, *M*, one of the chief ... Dan 10:13
these things, but *M* your prince ... Dan 10:21
And at that time shall *M* stand up ... Dan 12:1
Yet *M* the archangel, when ... Jude 9
*M* and his angels fought against ... Rev 12:7

**MICHAH** (*mi'-cah*) See Micah, Michaiah. *A sanctuary servant.*
sons of Uzziel; *M* ... 1Chr 24:24
of the sons of *M* ... 1Chr 24:24
The brother of *M* was Isshiah ... 1Chr 24:25

**MICHAIAH** (*mi-ka-i'-ah*) See Micah, Micaiah.
*1. Father of Achbor.*
Shaphan, and Achbor the son of *M*... 2Kin 22:12
*2. Wife of King Rehoboam.*
His mother's name also was *M* the ... 2Chr 13:2
*3. A prince of Judah.*
and to Nethaneel, and to *M* ... 2Chr 17:7
*4. A priest with Zerubbabel.*
son of Mattaniah, the son of *M* ... Neh 12:35
Eliakim, Maaseiah, Miniamin, *M* ... Neh 12:41
*5. Son of Gemariah.*
When *M* the son of Gemariah, the ... Jer 36:11
Then *M* declared unto them all the ... Jer 36:13

**MICHAL** (*mi'-kal*) See Eglah. *A wife of David.*
and the name of the younger *M* ... 1Sa 14:49
*M* Saul's daughter loved David ... 1Sa 18:20
Saul gave him *M* his daughter to ... 1Sa 18:27
that *M* Saul's daughter loved him ... 1Sa 18:28
*M* David's wife told him, saying, ... 1Sa 19:11
So *M* let David down through a ... 1Sa 19:12
*M* took an image, and laid it in ... 1Sa 19:13
And Saul said unto *M*, Why hast ... 1Sa 19:17
*M* answered Saul, He said unto me, ... 1Sa 19:17
But Saul had given *M* his daughter ... 1Sa 25:44
first bring *M* Saul's daughter ... 2Sa 3:13
son, saying, Deliver me my wife *M* ... 2Sa 3:14
*M* Saul's daughter looked through ... 2Sa 6:16
*M* the daughter of Saul came out ... 2Sa 6:20
And David said unto *M*, It was ... 2Sa 6:21
Therefore *M* the daughter of Saul ... 2Sa 6:23
the five sons of *M* the daughter ... 2Sa 21:8
that *M* the daughter of Saul ... 1Chr 15:29

**MICHMAS** (*mik'-mas*) See Michmash. *Home of some exiles.*
The men of *M*, an hundred twenty ... Ezr 2:27
The men of *M*, an hundred and ... Neh 7:31

**MICHMASH** (*mik'-mash*) See Michmas. *A city near Jerusalem.*
two thousand were with Saul in *M* ... 1Sa 13:2
and they came up, and pitched in *M* ... 1Sa 13:5
gathered themselves together at *M* ... 1Sa 13:11
but the Philistines encamped in *M* ... 1Sa 13:16
went out to the passage of *M* ... 1Sa 13:23
situate northward over against *M* ... 1Sa 14:5
that day from *M* to Aijalon ... 1Sa 14:31
of Benjamin from Geba dwelt at *M* ... Neh 11:31
at *M* he hath laid up his ... Is 10:28

**MICHMETHAH** (*mik'-me-thah*) *A city between Ephraim and Manasseh.*
the sea to *M* on the north side ... Josh 16:6
of Manasseh was from Asher to *M* ... Josh 17:7

**MICHMETHATH** See Michmethah.

**MICHRI** (*mik'-ri*) *Father of Uzzi.*
the son of Uzzi, the son of *M* ... 1Chr 9:8

**MICHTAM** (*mik'-tam*) *A type of psalm.*
*M* of David ... Ps 16:*t*
a *M* of David, when the ... Ps 56:*t*
*M* of David, when he fled from ... Ps 57:*t*
Musician, Altaschith, *M* of David ... Ps 58:*t*
Musician, Altaschith, *M* of David ... Ps 59:*t*
*M* of David, to teach ... Ps 60:*t*

**MICMASH** See Michmash.

**MICMETHAH** See Michmethah.

**MICRI** See Michri.

**MIDDAY**
to pass, when *m* was past, and they .. 1Kin 18:29
gate from the morning until *m* ... Neh 8:3
At *m*, O king, I saw in the way a ... Acts 26:13

**MIDDIN** (*mid'-din*) *A city in the wilderness south of Judah.*
In the wilderness, Beth-arabah, *M* ... Josh 15:61

**MIDDLE**
the *m* bar in the midst of the ... Ex 26:28
he made the *m* bar to shoot ... Ex 36:33
from the *m* of the river, and from ... Josh 12:2
in the beginning of the *m* watch ... Judg 7:19
people down by the *m* of the land ... Judg 9:37
Samson took hold of the two *m* ... Judg 16:29
out, as out of the *m* of a sling ... 1Sa 25:29
cut off their garments in the *m* ... 2Sa 10:4
the *m* was six cubits broad, and ... 1Kin 6:6
The door for the *m* chamber was in ... 1Kin 6:8
winding stairs into the *m* chamber ... 1Kin 6:8
out of the *m* into the third ... 1Kin 6:8
day did the king hallow the *m* of ... 1Kin 8:64
was gone out into the *m* court ... 2Kin 20:4
*m* of the court that was before ... 2Chr 7:7
came in, and sat in the *m* gate ... Jer 39:3
were a wheel in the *m* of a wheel ... Eze 1:16
hath broken down the *m* wall of ... Eph 2:14

**MIDDLEMOST**
than the *m* of the building ... Eze 42:5
lowest and the *m* from the ground ... Eze 42:6

**MIDIAN** (*mid'-e-an*) See Madian, Midianite.
*1. A son of Abraham.*
and Jokshan, and Medan, and *M* ... Gen 25:2
And the sons of *M* ... Gen 25:4
and Jokshan, and Medan, and *M* ... 1Chr 1:32
And the sons of *M* ... 1Chr 1:33
*2. A nation on the southern border of Israel.*
who smote *M* in the field of Moab, ... Gen 36:35
and dwelt in the land of *M* ... Ex 2:15
Now the priest of *M* had seven ... Ex 2:16
father in law, the priest of *M* ... Ex 3:1
And the Lord said unto Moses in *M* ... Ex 4:19
When Jethro, the priest of *M* ... Ex 18:1
And Moab said unto the elders of *M*... Num 22:4
the elders of *M* departed with the ... Num 22:7
people, and of a chief house in *M* ... Num 25:15
the daughter of a prince of *M* ... Num 25:18
and avenge the Lord of *M* ... Num 31:3
And they slew the kings of *M* ... Num 31:8
and Hur, and Reba, five kings of *M* ... Num 31:8
took all the women of *M* captives ... Num 31:9
Moses smote with the princes of *M* ... Josh 13:21
into the hand of *M* seven years ... Judg 6:1
the hand of *M* prevailed against ... Judg 6:2
the host of *M* was beneath him in ... Judg 7:8
bread tumbled into the host of *M* ... Judg 7:13
his hand hath God delivered *M* ... Judg 7:14
into your hand the host of *M* ... Judg 7:15
winepress of Zeeb, and pursued *M* ... Judg 7:25
into your hands the princes of *M* ... Judg 8:3
Zebah and Zalmunna, kings of *M* ... Judg 8:5
them, and took the two kings of *M* ... Judg 8:12
delivered us from the hand of *M* ... Judg 8:22
that was on the kings of *M* ... Judg 8:26
Thus was *M* subdued before the ... Judg 8:28
you out of the hand of *M* ... Judg 9:17
And they arose out of *M*, and came .. 1Kin 11:18
which smote *M* in the field of ... 1Chr 1:46
his oppressor, as in the day of *M* ... Is 9:4
of *M* at the rock of Oreb ... Is 10:26

cover thee, the dromedaries of *M* ............ Is 60:6
of the land of *M* did tremble ............ Hab 3:7

**MIDIANITE** (*mid'-e-an-ite*) See MIDIANITES, MIDIANITISH. *A descendant of Midian.*
Hobab, the son of Raguel the *M* ........ Num 10:29

**MIDIANITES** (*mid'-e-an-ites*) See KENITES.
there passed by *M* merchantmen ......... Gen 37:28
the *M* sold him into Egypt unto ........... Gen 37:36
Vex the *M*, and smite them ................ Num 25:17
the children of Israel of the *M* ............. Num 31:2
war, and let them go against the *M* .... Num 31:3
And they warred against the *M* ............ Num 31:7
because of the *M* the children of .......... Judg 6:2
had sown, that the *M* came up .............. Judg 6:3
impoverished because of the *M* ............ Judg 6:6
unto the LORD because of the *M* ........... Judg 6:7
winepress, to hide it from the *M* ........ Judg 6:11
us into the hands of the *M* .................. Judg 6:13
Israel from the hand of the *M* .............. Judg 6:14
thou shalt smite the *M* as one man ..... Judg 6:16
Then all the *M* and the Amalekites ..... Judg 6:33
so that the host of the *M* were on ......... Judg 7:1
me to give the *M* into their hands .......... Judg 7:2
deliver the *M* into thine hand ................ Judg 7:7
the *M* and the Amalekites ..................... Judg 7:12
Manasseh, and pursued after the *M* .... Judg 7:23
saying, Come down against the *M* ......... Judg 7:24
And they took two princes of the *M* ... Judg 7:25
thou wentest to fight with the *M* ........... Judg 8:1
Do unto them as unto the *M* ..................... Ps 83:9

**MIDIANITISH** (*mid'-e-an-i'-tish*) *Belonging to the land of Midian.*
a *M* woman in the sight of Moses ........ Num 25:6
that was slain with the *M* woman ..... Num 25:14
the name of the *M* woman that was. Num 25:15

**MIDNIGHT**
About *m* will I go out into the ................. Ex 11:4
that at *m* the LORD smote all the ........... Ex 12:29
lay till *m*, and arose at *m* ..................... Judg 16:3
And it came to pass at *m*, that the ........ Ruth 3:8
And she arose at *m*, and took my son 1Kin 3:20
the people shall be troubled at *m* ......... Job 34:20
At *m* I will rise to give thanks ............. Ps 119:62
at *m* there was a cry made, Behold .......... Mt 25:6
house cometh, at even, or at *m* ............. Mk 13:35
friend, and shall go unto him at *m* ......... Lk 11:5
at *m* Paul and Silas prayed, and ......... Acts 16:25
and continued his speech until *m* ......... Acts 20:7
about *m* the shipmen deemed that ..... Acts 27:27

**MIDST** See PREFACE.
firmament in the *m* of the waters ........... Gen 1:6
life also in the *m* of the garden ................ Gen 2:9
upon dry land in the *m* of the sea .......... Ex 14:29
on dry land in the *m* of the sea ............... Ex 15:19
God is in the *m* of her ............................... Ps 46:5
me not away in the *m* of my days ........ Ps 102:24
lieth down in the *m* of the sea .............. Prov 23:34
One of Israel in the *m* of thee ................... Is 12:6
walking in the *m* of the fire ................... Dan 3:25
the Holy One in the *m* of thee ................. Hos 11:9
forth as sheep in the *m* of wolves ........... Mt 10:16
him, and set him in the *m* of them ........... Mt 18:2
and set him in the *m* of them .................. Mk 9:36
himself stood in the *m* of them ............. Lk 24:36
came Jesus and stood in the *m* ............... Jn 20:19
being shut, and stood in the *m* ............... Jn 20:26

**MIDWIFE**
that the *m* said unto her, Fear ............ Gen 35:17
the *m* took and bound upon his hand Gen 38:28
office of a *m* to the Hebrew women ........ Ex 1:16

**MIDWIVES**
of Egypt spake to the Hebrew *m* ............ Ex 1:15
But the *m* feared God, and did not .......... Ex 1:17
king of Egypt called for the *m* ................. Ex 1:18
the *m* said unto Pharaoh, Because ........... Ex 1:19
ere the *m* come in unto them ................... Ex 1:19
God dealt well with the *m* ........................ Ex 1:20
to pass, because the *m* feared God .......... Ex 1:21

**MIGDAL EDER**

**MIGDAL-EL** (*mig'-dal-el*) *A city in Naphtali.*
And Iron, and *M*, Horem, and ............. Josh 19:38

**MIGDAL-GAD** (*mig'-dal-gad*) *A city in Judah.*
Zenan, and Hadashah, and *M*, ................ Josh 15:37

**MIGDOL** (*mig'-dol*)
*1. A place west of the Red Sea.*
before Pi-hahiroth, between *M* ................. Ex 14:2
and they pitched before *M* .................... Num 33:7
*2. A place in northern Egypt.*
land of Egypt, which dwell at *M* ............. Jer 44:1
ye in Egypt, and publish in *M* ............... Jer 46:14

**MIGHT** See PREFACE.
thy works, and according to thy *m* ..... Deut 3:24
all thy soul, and with all thy *m* ................. Deut 6:5
and in thine hand is power and *m* ..... 1Chr 29:12
that I *m* not sin against thee ............... Ps 119:11
of the *m* of thy terrible acts ................... Ps 145:6
findeth to do, do it with thy *m* ............... Eccl 9:10
let the mighty man glory in his *m* ......... Jer 9:23
unto Zerubbabel, saying, Not by *m* .......... Zec 4:6
all men through him *m* believe .................. Jn 1:7
the world through him *m* be saved ........... Jn 3:17
I am come that they *m* have life ............ Jn 10:10
life, and that they *m* have it more .......... Jn 10:10
to be strengthened with *m* by his ............ Eph 3:16
Strengthened with all *m*, ........................... Col 1:11
and honour, and power, and *m* .............. Rev 7:12

**MIGHTEST**
that thou *m* know that the LORD he ... Deut 4:35
That thou *m* fear the LORD thy God ....... Deut 6:2
wherewith thou *m* be bound to ............. Judg 16:6
thee, wherewith thou *m* be bound ..... Judg 16:10
tell me wherewith thou *m* be bound. Judg 16:13
down that thou *m* see the battle ......... 1Sa 17:28
that thou *m* bring them again unto ....... Neh 9:29
that thou *m* still the enemy and .................. Ps 8:2
that thou *m* be justified when ................. Ps 51:4
that thou *m* answer the words of ....... Prov 22:21
that thou *m* know the thoughts of ........ Dan 2:30
thou *m* be profited by me ........................ Mt 15:5
thou *m* be profited by me ......................... Mk 7:11
That thou *m* know the certainty of ........... Lk 1:4
that thou *m* receive thy sight, and ......... Acts 9:17
That thou *m* be justified in thy ............... Rom 3:4
*m* overcome when thou art judged ........ Rom 3:4
that thou *m* charge some that they ........ 1Ti 1:3
that thou by them *m* war a good ........... 1Ti 1:18

**MIGHTIER**
for thou art much *m* than we ............... Gen 26:16
of Israel are more and *m* than we ............ Ex 1:9
a greater nation and *m* than they ...... Num 14:12
*m* than thou art, to bring thee in ......... Deut 4:38
nations greater and *m* than thou ........... Deut 7:1
*m* than thyself, cities great and ............. Deut 9:1
and I will make of thee a nation *m* ...... Deut 9:14
nations and *m* than yourselves ............ Deut 11:23
The LORD on high is *m* than the ............. Ps 93:4
with him that is *m* than he .................... Eccl 6:10
that cometh after me is *m* than I ........... Mt 3:11
cometh one *m* than I after me ................. Mk 1:7
but one *m* than I cometh, the ................. Lk 3:16

**MIGHTIES**
who was one of the three *m* ............... 1Chr 11:12
the name among the three *m* ............. 1Chr 11:24

**MIGHTIEST**
These things did these three *m* ......... 1Chr 11:19

**MIGHTILY**
thee, and that ye may increase *m* .......... Deut 6:3
twenty years he *m* oppressed the .......... Judg 4:3
of the LORD came *m* upon him ............. Judg 14:6
of the LORD came *m* upon him ............ Judg 15:14
he shall *m* roar upon his ..................... Jer 25:30
with sackcloth, and cry *m* unto God ... Jonah 3:8
loins strong, fortify thy power *m* .............. Nah 2:1
For he *m* convinced the Jews, and ..... Acts 18:28
So *m* grew the word of God and .......... Acts 19:20
working, which worketh in me *m* ............ Col 1:29
he cried *m* with a strong voice, .............. Rev 18:2

**MIGHTY**
the same became *m* men which were .... Gen 6:4
began to be a *m* one in the earth ......... Gen 10:8
He was a *m* hunter before the LORD ....... Gen 10:9
Even as Nimrod the *m* hunter ............... Gen 10:9
*m* nation, and all the nations of ........... Gen 18:18
thou art a *m* prince among us .............. Gen 23:6
the hands of the *m* God of Jacob ....... Gen 49:24
multiplied, and waxed exceeding *m* ............ Ex 1:7
multiplied, and waxed very *m* .................. Ex 1:20
let you go, no, not by a *m* hand ............... Ex 3:19
there be no more *m* thunderings ............... Ex 9:28
LORD turned a *m* strong west wind ....... Ex 10:19
they sank as lead in the *m* waters ......... Ex 15:10
the *m* men of Moab, trembling .............. Ex 15:15
great power, and with a *m* hand ........... Lev 32:11
nor honour the person of the *m* ........... Lev 19:15
for they are too *m* for me .................... Num 22:6
thy greatness, and thy *m* hand ............... Deut 3:24
and by war, and by a *m* hand ............... Deut 4:34
with his *m* power out of Egypt .............. Deut 4:37
thee out thence through a *m* hand ...... Deut 5:15
us out of Egypt with a *m* hand ............ Deut 6:21
brought you out with a *m* hand .............. Deut 7:8
the *m* hand, and the stretched out ...... Deut 7:19
is among you, a *m* God and terrible ...... Deut 7:21
destroy them with a *m* destruction ....... Deut 7:23
forth out of Egypt with a *m* hand ....... Deut 9:26
broughtest out by thy *m* power ............. Deut 9:29
Lord of lords, a great God, a *m* .......... Deut 10:17
his *m* hand, and his stretched out ......... Deut 11:2
became there a nation, great, *m*, .......... Deut 26:5
forth out of Egypt with a *m* hand ......... Deut 26:8
And in all that *m* hand, and in all ...... Deut 34:12
all the *m* men of valour, and help ......... Josh 1:14
hand of the LORD, that it is *m* .............. Josh 4:24
thereof, and the *m* men of valour ........... Josh 6:2
thirty thousand *m* men of valour ........... Josh 8:3
Ai, and all the men thereof were *m* ...... Josh 10:2
him, and all the *m* men of valour .......... Josh 10:7
made me have dominion over the *m* ... Judg 5:13
the pransings of their *m* ones ................ Judg 5:22
help of the LORD against the *m* ............ Judg 5:23
with thee, thou *m* man of valour ........... Judg 6:12
Gileadite was a *m* man of valour ........... Judg 11:1
a *m* man of wealth, of the family ............. Ruth 2:1
The bows of the *m* men are broken ........... 1Sa 2:4
out of the hand of these *m* Gods .............. 1Sa 4:8
a Benjamite, a *m* man of power ................ 1Sa 9:1
a *m* valiant man, and a man of war, ...... 1Sa 16:18
how are the *m* fallen ............................... 2Sa 1:19
of the *m* is vilely cast away .................... 2Sa 1:21
the slain, from the fat of the *m* .............. 2Sa 1:22
How are the *m* fallen in the midst ......... 2Sa 1:25
How are the *m* fallen, and the ............... 2Sa 1:27
and all the host of the *m* men ............... 2Sa 10:7
all the *m* men were on his right ............. 2Sa 16:6
and his men, that they be *m* men ........... 2Sa 17:8
that thy father is a *m* man .................... 2Sa 17:10
the Pelethites, and all the *m* men ........... 2Sa 20:7
names of the *m* men whom David had. 2Sa 23:8
one of the three *m* men with David ......... 2Sa 23:9
the three *m* men brake through the .... 2Sa 23:16
things did these three *m* men ............... 2Sa 23:17
the name among three *m* men ............... 2Sa 23:22
the *m* men which belonged to David .... 1Kin 1:8
prophet, and Benaiah, and the *m* men 1Kin 1:10
Jeroboam was a *m* man of valour ...... 1Kin 11:28
he was also a *m* man in valour ............... 2Kin 5:1
even of all the *m* men of wealth ......... 2Kin 15:20
all the *m* men of valour, even ten ....... 2Kin 24:14
the *m* of the land, those carried ......... 2Kin 24:15
he began to be *m* upon the earth .......... 1Chr 1:10
*m* men of valour, famous men, and ..... 1Chr 5:24
of their fathers, *m* men of valour .......... 1Chr 7:7
*m* men of valour, was twenty ................. 1Chr 7:9
*m* men of valour, were seventeen ........ 1Chr 7:11
*m* men of valour, chief of the ............... 1Chr 7:40
sons of Ulam were *m* men of valour ... 1Chr 8:40
chief of the *m* men whom David had 1Chr 11:10
of the *m* men whom David had ........... 1Chr 11:11
and they were among the *m* men ............ 1Chr 12:1
a *m* man among the thirty, and over .. 1Chr 12:4
for they were all *m* men of valour ..... 1Chr 12:21
*m* men of valour for the war, ............... 1Chr 12:25
a young man *m* of valour ..................... 1Chr 12:28
hundred, *m* men of valour, famous .... 1Chr 12:30
and all the host of the *m* men ............... 1Chr 19:8
for they were men of valour ................. 1Chr 26:6
them *m* men of valour at Jazer of ..... 1Chr 26:31
who was *m* among the thirty, and ....... 1Chr 27:6
the officers, and with the *m* men ........... 1Chr 28:1
And all the princes, and the *m* men .. 1Chr 29:24
thy *m* hand, and thy stretched out ......... 2Chr 6:32
chosen men, being *m* men of valour ... 2Chr 13:3
But Abijah waxed *m*, and married ..... 2Chr 13:21
all these were *m* men of valour ............. 2Chr 14:8
of war, *m* men of valour, were in ....... 2Chr 17:13
with him *m* men of valour three ........ 2Chr 17:14
hundred thousand *m* men of valour .. 2Chr 17:16
Eliada a *m* man of valour, and with .. 2Chr 17:17
hired also an hundred thousand *m* ........ 2Chr 25:6
*m* men of valour were two thousand 2Chr 26:12
that made war with *m* power .............. 2Chr 26:13
So Jotham became *m*, because he ......... 2Chr 27:6
a *m* man of Ephraim, slew Maaseiah .. 2Chr 28:7
his *m* men to stop the waters of ........... 2Chr 32:3
cut off all the *m* men of valour ............ 2Chr 32:21
There have been *m* kings also over ......... Ezr 4:20
before all the king's *m* princes ............... Ezr 7:28
made, and unto the house of the *m* ........ Neh 3:16
as a stone into the *m* waters ................. Neh 9:11
our God, the great, the *m* ..................... Neh 9:32
*m* men of valour, an hundred ............... Neh 11:14
mouth, and from the hand of the *m* ...... Job 5:15
Redeem me from the hand of the *m* ...... Job 6:23
wise in heart, and *m* in strength .............. Job 9:4
spoiled, and overthroweth the *m* ........... Job 12:19
weakeneth the strength of the *m* ......... Job 12:21
become old, yea, are *m* in power ............ Job 21:7
But as for the *m* man, he had the ........... Job 22:8
draweth also the *m* with his power ...... Job 24:22
the *m* shall be taken away without ...... Job 34:20
in pieces *m* men without number .......... Job 34:24
out by reason of the arm of the *m* ......... Job 35:9
Behold, God is *m*, and despiseth ............. Job 36:5
he is *m* in strength and wisdom .............. Job 36:5
up himself, the *m* are afraid .................. Job 41:25
and *m*, the LORD *m* in battle ................... Ps 24:8
Give unto the LORD, O ye *m* ....................... Ps 29:1
a *m* man is not delivered by much ......... Ps 33:16
sword upon thy thigh, O most *m* ............ Ps 45:3
The *m* God, even the LORD, hath ............... Ps 50:1
thou thyself in mischief, O *m* man ........... Ps 52:1
the *m* are gathered against me ................. Ps 59:3
out his voice, and that a *m* voice ........... Ps 68:33
mine enemies wrongfully, are *m* ............... Ps 69:4
thou driedst up *m* rivers ......................... Ps 74:15
like a *m* man that shouteth by ................. Ps 78:65
in the congregation of the *m* ..................... Ps 82:1
who among the sons of the *m* can ............ Ps 89:6
Thou hast a *m* arm ................................. Ps 89:13
have laid help upon one that is *m* ........... Ps 89:19
the reproach of all the *m* people ............. Ps 89:50
than the *m* waves of the sea ...................... Ps 93:4
can utter the *m* acts of the LORD ............ Ps 106:2
make his *m* power to be known ............. Ps 106:8
His seed shall be *m* upon earth ............... Ps 112:2
Sharp arrows of the *m*, with coals .......... Ps 120:4
arrows are in the hand of a *m* man ......... Ps 127:4
and vowed unto the *m* God of Jacob ....... Ps 132:2
habitation for the *m* God of Jacob .......... Ps 132:5
great nations, and slew *m* kings ........... Ps 135:10
and shall declare thy *m* acts .................. Ps 145:4
to the sons of men his *m* acts ............... Ps 145:12
Praise him for his *m* acts ...................... Ps 150:2
to anger is better than the *m* ............... Prov 16:32
cease, and parteth between the *m* ....... Prov 18:18
man scaleth the city of the *m* ............... Prov 21:22
For their redeemer is *m* ....................... Prov 23:11
the wise more than ten *m* men ................. Eccl 7:19
bucklers, all shields of *m* men ................ Song 4:4
the *m* One of Israel, Ah, I will ................... Is 1:24
The *m* man, and the man of war, the ......... Is 3:2

by the sword, and thy *m* in the war Is 3:25
the *m* man shall be humbled, and Is 5:15
them that are *m* to drink wine Is 5:22
Wonderful, Counsellor, The *m* God Is 9:6
remnant of Jacob, unto the *m* God Is 10:21
and Lebanon shall fall by a *m* one Is 10:34
with his *m* wind shall he shake Is 11:15
called my *m* ones for mine anger Is 13:3
like the rushing of *m* waters Is 17:12
the *m* men of the children of Is 21:17
thee away with a *m* captivity Is 22:17
Behold, the Lord hath a *m* Is 28:2
storm, as a flood of *m* waters Is 28:2
the LORD, to the *m* One of Israel Is 30:29
with the sword, not of a *m* man Is 31:8
LORD shall go forth as a *m* man Is 42:13
sea, and a path in the *m* waters Is 43:16
the prey be taken from the *m* Is 49:24
of the *m* shall be taken away Is 49:25
thy Redeemer, the *m* One of Jacob Is 49:26
thy Redeemer, the *m* One of Jacob Is 60:16
speak in righteousness, *m* to save Is 63:1
it is a *m* nation, it is an Jer 5:15
sepulchre, they are all *m* men Jer 5:16
neither let the *m* man glory in Jer 9:23
as a *m* man that cannot save Jer 14:9
is with me as a *m* terrible one Jer 20:11
the king, with all his *m* men Jer 26:21
the Great, the *M* God, the LORD of Jer 32:18
Great in counsel, and *m* in work Jer 32:19
*m* things, which thou knowest not Jer 33:3
even *m* men of war, and the women, ... Jer 41:16
their *m* ones are beaten down, and Jer 46:5
flee away, nor the *m* man escape Jer 46:6
and let the *m* men come forth Jer 46:9
for the *m* man hath stumbled Jer 46:12
man hath stumbled against the *m* Jer 46:12
How say ye, We are *m* and strong Jer 48:14
the *m* men's hearts in Moab at Jer 48:41
*m* men of Edom be as the heart of Jer 49:22
shall be as of a *m* expert man Jer 50:9
a sword is upon her *m* men Jer 50:36
The *m* men of Babylon have forborn Jer 51:30
her *m* men are taken, every one of Jer 51:56
and her rulers, and her *m* men Jer 51:57
all my *m* men in the midst of me Lam 1:15
hath also taken the *m* of the land Eze 17:13
shall Pharaoh with his *m* army Eze 17:17
Lord GOD, surely with a *m* hand Eze 20:33
ye are scattered, with a *m* hand Eze 20:34
hand of the *m* one of the heathen Eze 31:11
By the swords of the *m* will I Eze 32:12
The strong among the *m* shall Eze 32:21
with the *m* that are fallen of the Eze 32:27
the *m* in the land of the living Eze 32:27
a great company, and a *m* army Eze 38:15
Ye shall eat the flesh of the *m* Eze 39:18
horses and chariots, with *m* men Eze 39:20
he commanded the most *m* men that .. Dan 3:20
and how *m* are his wonders Dan 4:3
And his power shall be *m*, but not Dan 8:24
practise, and shall destroy the *m* Dan 8:24
the land of Egypt with a *m* hand Dan 9:15
a *m* king shall stand up, that Dan 11:3
with a very great and *m* army Dan 11:25
in the multitude of thy *m* men Hos 10:13
They shall run like *m* men Joel 2:7
Prepare war, wake up the *m* men Joel 3:9
cause thy *m* ones to come down Joel 3:11
shall the *m* deliver himself Amos 2:14
*m* shall flee away naked in that Amos 2:16
transgressions and your *m* sins Amos 5:12
and righteousness as a *m* stream Amos 5:24
And thy *m* men, O Teman, shall be Obad 9
there was a *m* tempest in the sea, Jonah 1:4
shield of his *m* men is made red Nah 2:3
O *m* God, thou hast established Hab 1:12
the *m* man shall cry there Zeph 1:14
thy God in the midst of thee is *m* Zeph 3:17
made thee as the sword of a *m* man Zec 9:13
And they shall be as *m* men Zec 10:5
of Ephraim shall be like a *m* man Zec 10:7
because the *m* are spoiled Zec 11:2
most of his *m* works were done Mt 11:20
for if the *m* works, which were Mt 11:21
for if the *m* works, which have Mt 11:23
man this wisdom, and these *m* works .. Mt 13:54
he did not many *m* works there Mt 13:58
therefore *m* works do shew forth Mt 14:2
that even such *m* works are Mk 6:2
And he could there do no *m* work Mk 6:5
therefore *m* works do shew forth Mk 6:14
For he that is *m* hath done to me Lk 1:49
put down the *m* from their seats Lk 1:52
all amazed at the *m* power of God Lk 9:43
for if the *m* works had been done Lk 10:13
there arose a *m* famine in that Lk 15:14
the *m* works that they had seen Lk 19:37
which was a prophet *m* in deed Lk 24:19
heaven as of a rushing *m* wind Acts 2:2
was *m* in words and in deeds Acts 7:22
*m* in the scriptures, came to Acts 18:24
Through *m* signs and wonders, by Rom 15:19
men after the flesh, not many *m* 1Cor 1:26
confound the things which are *m* 1Cor 1:27
but *m* through God to the pulling 2Cor 10:4
in signs, and wonders, and *m* deeds .. 2Cor 12:12
is not weak, but is *m* in you 2Cor 13:3
the same was *m* in me toward the Gal 2:8
to the working of his *m* power Eph 1:19
from heaven with his *m* angels 2Th 1:7
therefore under the *m* hand of God 1Pet 5:6
when she is shaken of a *m* wind Rev 6:13
the chief captains, and the *m* men Rev 6:15
I saw another *m* angel come down Rev 10:1
so *m* an earthquake, and so great Rev 16:18
great city Babylon, that *m* city Rev 18:10
a *m* angel took up a stone like a Rev 18:21
and as the voice of *m* thunderings Rev 19:6
captains, and the flesh of *m* men Rev 19:18

**MIGRON** (*mi'-gron*) *A city in Benjamin.*
a pomegranate tree which is in *M* 1Sa 14:2
come to Aiath, he is passed to *M* Is 10:28

**MIJAMIN** (*mij'-a-min*) See MIAMIN.
*1. A priest in David's time.*
to Malchijah, the sixth to *M* 1Chr 24:9
*2. A priest who renewed the covenant.*
Meshullam, Abijah, *M*, Neh 10:7

**MIKLOTH** (*mik'-loth*)
*1. A Benjamite in Jerusalem.*
And *M* begat Shimeah 1Chr 8:32
and Ahio, and Zechariah, and *M* 1Chr 9:37
And *M* begat Shimeam 1Chr 9:38
*2. A ruler of David's guard.*
his course was *M* also the ruler 1Chr 27:4

**MIKNEIAH** (*mik-ne-i'-ah*) *A Levite musician.*
and Elipheleh, and *M* 1Chr 15:18
and Elipheleh, and *M* 1Chr 15:21

**MILALAI** (*mil'-a-lahee*) *A priest who purified the wall.*
brethren, Shemaiah, and Azarael, *M*.. Neh 12:36

**MILCAH** (*mil'-cah*)
*1. Daughter of Haran.*
and the name of Nahor's wife, *M* Gen 11:29
of Haran, the father of *M* Gen 11:29
told Abraham, saying, Behold, *M* Gen 22:20
these eight *M* did bear to Nahor, Gen 22:23
who was born to Bethuel, son of *M* Gen 24:15
daughter of Bethuel the son of *M* Gen 24:24
Nahor's son, whom *M* bare unto him. Gen 24:47
*2. A daughter of Zelophehad.*
were Mahlah, and Noah, Hoglah, *M*.. Num 26:33
Mahlah, Noah, and Hoglah, and *M*.. Num 27:1
Mahlah, Tirzah, and Hoglah, and *M*.. Num 36:11
Mahlah, and Noah, Hoglah, *M* Josh 17:3

**MILCH**
Thirty *m* camels with their colts, Gen 32:15
a new cart, and take two *m* kine 1Sa 6:7
and took two *m* kine, and tied them 1Sa 6:10

**MILCHAM**

**MILCOM** (*mil'-com*) See MALCHAM, MOLECH.
*Chief god of the Ammonites.*
after *M* the abomination of the 1Kin 11:5
*M* the god of the children of 1Kin 11:33
for *M* the abomination of the 2Kin 23:13

**MILDEW**
and with blasting, and with *m* Deut 28:22
there be pestilence, blasting, *m* 1Kin 8:37
if there be blasting, or *m* 2Chr 6:28
smitten you with blasting and *m* Amos 4:9
smote you with blasting and with *m* Hag 2:17

**MILE**
shall compel thee to go a *m* Mt 5:41

**MILETUM** (*mi-le'-tum*) See MILETUS. *A city in the Roman province of Caria.*
Trophimus have I left at *M* sick 2Ti 4:20

**MILETUS** (*mi-le-tus*) See MILETUM. *Same as Miletum.*
and the next day we came to *M* Acts 20:15
from *M* he sent to Ephesus, and Acts 20:17

**MILK**
And he took butter, and *m*, and the Gen 18:8
wine, and his teeth white with *m* Gen 49:12
large, unto a land flowing with *m* Ex 3:8
unto a land flowing with *m* Ex 3:17
give thee, a land flowing with *m* Ex 13:5
seethe a kid in his mother's *m* Ex 23:19
Unto a land flowing with *m* Ex 33:3
seethe a kid in his mother's *m* Ex 34:26
it, a land that floweth with *m* Lev 20:24
us, and surely it floweth with *m* Num 13:27
a land which floweth with *m* Num 14:8
out of a land that floweth with *m* Num 16:13
into a land that floweth with *m* Num 16:14
in the land that floweth with *m* Deut 6:3
seed, a land that floweth with *m* Deut 11:9
seethe a kid in his mother's *m* Deut 14:21
even a land that floweth with *m* Deut 26:9
a land that floweth with *m* Deut 26:15
thee, a land that floweth with *m* Deut 27:3
fathers, that floweth with *m* Deut 31:20
*m* of sheep, with fat of lambs, and Deut 32:14
us, a land that floweth with *m* Josh 5:6
And she opened a bottle of *m* Judg 4:19
He asked water, and she gave him *m*. Judg 5:25
Hast thou not poured me out as *m* Job 10:10
His breasts are full of *m* Job 21:24
have goats' *m* enough for thy food Prov 27:27
of *m* bringeth forth butter Prov 30:33
honey and *m* are under thy tongue Song 4:11
I have drunk my wine with my *m* Song 5:1
rivers of waters, washed with *m* Song 5:12
of *m* that they shall give Is 7:22
them that are weaned from the *m* Is 28:9
*m* without money and without price Is 55:1
also suck the *m* of the Gentiles Is 60:16
that ye may *m* out, and be Is 66:11
give them a land flowing with *m* Jer 11:5
give them, a land flowing with *m* Jer 32:22
snow, they were whiter than *m* Lam 4:7
espied for them, flowing with *m* Eze 20:6
I had given them, flowing with *m* Eze 20:15
fruit, and they shall drink thy *m* Eze 25:4
and the hills shall flow with *m* Joel 3:18
I have fed you with *m*, and not 1Cor 3:2
eateth not of the *m* of the flock 1Cor 9:7
are become such as have need of *m* Heb 5:12
For every one that useth *m* is Heb 5:13
desire the sincere *m* of the word 1Pet 2:2

**MILL**
maidservant that is behind the *m* Ex 11:5
women shall be grinding at the *m* Mt 24:41

**MILLET**
and beans, and lentiles, and *m* Eze 4:9

**MILLIONS**
thou the mother of thousands of *m* Gen 24:60

**MILLO** (*mil'-lo*)
*1. A fort near Shechem.*
together, and all the house of *M* Judg 9:6
men of Shechem, and the house of *M*. Judg 9:20
Shechem, and from the house of *M* Judg 9:20
*2. A fort near Jerusalem.*
And David built round about from *M* 2Sa 5:9
the LORD, and his own house, and *M*.. 1Kin 9:15
then did he build *M* 1Kin 9:24
Solomon built *M*, and repaired the 1Kin 11:27
and slew Joash in the house of *M* 2Kin 12:20
about, even from *M* round about 1Chr 11:8
repaired *M* in the city of David, 2Chr 32:5

**MILLS**
and gathered it, and ground it in *m* Num 11:8

**MILLSTONE**
nether or the upper *m* to pledge Deut 24:6
of a *m* upon Abimelech's head Judg 9:53
of a *m* upon him from the wall 2Sa 11:21
hard as a piece of the nether *m* Job 41:24
a *m* were hanged about his neck Mt 18:6
a *m* were hanged about his neck Mk 9:42
a *m* were hanged about his neck Lk 17:2
took up a stone like a great *m* Rev 18:21
the sound of a *m* shall be heard Rev 18:22

**MILLSTONES**
Take the *m*, and grind meal Is 47:2
of the bride, the sound of the *m* Jer 25:10

**MINCING**
*m* as they go, and making a Is 3:16

**MIND**
If it be your *m* that I should Gen 23:8
were a grief of *m* unto Isaac Gen 26:35
that the *m* of the LORD might be Lev 24:12
have not done them of mine own *m*. Num 16:28
either good or bad of mine own *m* Num 24:13
*m* unto the place which the LORD Deut 18:6
failing of eyes, and sorrow of *m* Deut 28:65
them to *m* among all the nations Deut 30:1
which is in mine heart and in my *m* 1Sa 2:35
days ago, set not thy *m* on them 1Sa 9:20
it was in my *m* to build an house 1Chr 22:7
perfect heart and with a willing *m* 1Chr 28:9
for the people had a *m* to work Neh 4:6
But he is in one *m*, and who can Job 23:13
Should it be according to thy *m* Job 34:33
forgotten as a dead man out of *m* Ps 31:12
he bringeth it with a wicked *m* Prov 21:27
A fool uttereth all his *m* Prov 29:11
whose *m* is stayed on thee Is 26:3
bring it again to *m*, O ye Is 46:8
be remembered, nor come into *m* Is 65:17
neither shall it come to *m* Jer 3:16
yet my *m* could not be toward this Jer 15:1
it, neither came it into my *m* Jer 19:5
not, neither came it into my *m* Jer 32:35
them, and came it not into his *m* Jer 44:21
and let Jerusalem come into your *m* Jer 51:50
This I recall to my *m*, therefore Lam 3:21
the things that come into your *m* Eze 11:5
into your *m* shall not be at all Eze 20:32
her *m* was alienated from them Eze 23:17
then my *m* was alienated from her, Eze 23:18
like as my *m* was alienated from Eze 23:18
from whom thy *m* is alienated Eze 23:22
them from whom thy *m* is alienated Eze 23:28
time shall things come into thy *m* Eze 38:10
came into thy *m* upon thy bed Dan 2:29
his *m* hardened in pride, he was Dan 5:20
Then shall his *m* change, and he Hab 1:11
all thy soul, and with all thy *m* Mt 22:37
and clothed, and in his right *m* Mk 5:15
all thy soul, and with all thy *m* Mk 12:30
Peter called to *m* the word that Mk 14:72
cast in her *m* what manner of Lk 1:29
Jesus, clothed, and in his right *m* Lk 8:35
thy strength, and with all thy *m* Lk 10:27
neither be ye of doubtful *m* Lk 12:29
the word with all readiness of *m* Acts 17:11
the Lord with all humility of *m* Acts 20:19
gave them over to a reprobate *m* Rom 1:28
warring against the law of my *m* Rom 7:23

So then with the *m* I myself serve ... Rom 7:25
do *m* the things of the flesh ... Rom 8:5
Because the carnal *m* is enmity ... Rom 8:7
what is the *m* of the Spirit ... Rom 8:27
who hath known the *m* of the Lord .. Rom 11:34
by the renewing of your *m* ... Rom 12:2
Be of the same *m* one toward ... Rom 12:16
*M* not high things, but condescend ... Rom 12:16
be fully persuaded in his own *m* ... Rom 14:5
That ye may with one *m* and one ... Rom 15:6
in some sort, as putting you in *m* ... Rom 15:15
joined together in the same *m* ... 1Cor 1:10
who hath known the *m* of the Lord ... 1Cor 2:16
But we have the *m* of Christ ... 1Cor 2:16
your fervent *m* toward me ... 2Cor 7:7
For if there be first a willing *m* ... 2Cor 8:12
and declaration of your ready *m* ... 2Cor 8:19
I know the forwardness of your *m* ... 2Cor 9:2
be of good comfort, be of one *m* ... 2Cor 13:11
desires of the flesh and of the *m* ... Eph 2:3
walk, in the vanity of their *m* ... Eph 4:17
renewed in the spirit of your *m* ... Eph 4:23
with one *m* striving together for ... Phil 1:27
being of one accord, of one *m* ... Phil 2:2
but in lowliness of *m* let each ... Phil 2:3
Let this *m* be in you, which was ... Phil 2:5
rule, let us *m* the same thing ... Phil 3:16
their shame, who *m* earthly things ... Phil 3:19
they be of the same *m* in the Lord ... Phil 4:2
enemies in your *m* by wicked works ... Col 1:21
vainly puffed up by his fleshly *m* ... Col 2:18
kindness, humbleness of *m* ... Col 3:12
That ye be not soon shaken in *m* ... 2Th 2:2
and of love, and of a sound *m* ... 2Ti 1:7
but even their *m* and conscience is ... Titus 1:15
Put them in *m* to be subject to ... Titus 3:1
But without thy *m* would I do ... Philem 14
I will put my laws into their *m* ... Heb 8:10
gird up the loins of your *m* ... 1Pet 1:13
Finally, be ye all of one *m* ... 1Pet 3:8
likewise with the same *m* ... 1Pet 4:1
filthy lucre, but of a ready *m* ... 1Pet 5:2
here is the *m* which hath wisdom ... Rev 17:9
These have one *m*, and shall give ... Rev 17:13

**MINDED**
was stedfastly *m* to go with her ... Ruth 1:18
that Joash was *m* to repair the ... 2Chr 24:4
which are *m* of their own freewill ... Ezr 7:13
was *m* to put her away privily ... Mt 1:19
shore, into the which they were *m* ... Acts 27:39
For to be carnally *m* is death ... Rom 8:6
but to be spiritually *m* is life ... Rom 8:6
I was *m* to come unto you before ... 2Cor 1:15
When I therefore was thus *m* ... 2Cor 1:17
that ye will be none otherwise *m* ... Gal 5:10
as many as be perfect, be thus *m* ... Phil 3:15
if in any thing ye be otherwise *m* ... Phil 3:15
men likewise exhort to be sober *m* ... Titus 2:6
A double *m* man is unstable in all ... Jas 1:8
purify your hearts, ye double *m* ... Jas 4:8

**MINDFUL**
Be ye *m* always of his covenant ... 1Chr 16:15
neither were *m* of thy wonders ... Neh 9:17
is man, that thou art *m* of him ... Ps 8:4
he will ever be *m* of his covenant ... Ps 111:5
The LORD hath been *m* of us ... Ps 115:12
hast not been *m* of the rock of ... Is 17:10
being *m* of thy tears, that I may ... 2Ti 1:4
is man, that thou art *m* of him ... Heb 2:6
if they had been *m* of that ... Heb 11:15
That ye may be *m* of the words ... 2Pet 3:2

**MINDING**
appointed, *m* himself to go afoot ... Acts 20:13

**MINDS**
it, take advice, and speak your *m* ... Judg 19:30
men, and they be chafed in their *m* ... 2Sa 17:8
And Jehu said, If it be your *m* ... 2Kin 9:15
that whereupon they set their *m* ... Eze 24:25
their heart, with despiteful *m* ... Eze 36:5
made their *m* evil affected ... Acts 14:2
come to him, they changed their *m* ... Acts 28:6
But their *m* were blinded ... 2Cor 3:14
the *m* of them which believe not ... 2Cor 4:4
so your *m* should be corrupted ... 2Cor 11:3
hearts and *m* through Christ Jesus ... Phil 4:7
disputings of men of corrupt *m* ... 1Ti 6:5
men of corrupt *m*, reprobate ... 2Ti 3:8
in their *m* will I write them ... Heb 10:16
ye be wearied and faint in your *m* ... Heb 12:3
your pure *m* by way of remembrance ... 2Pet 3:1

**MINE** See PREFACE.

**MINGLE**
men of strength to *m* strong drink ... Is 5:22
they shall *m* themselves with the ... Dan 2:43

**MINGLED**
fire *m* with the hail, very ... Ex 9:24
*m* with the fourth part of an hin ... Ex 29:40
cakes of fine flour *m* with oil ... Lev 2:4
fine flour unleavened, *m* with oil ... Lev 2:5
*m* with oil, and dry, shall all the ... Lev 7:10
unleavened cakes *m* with oil ... Lev 7:12
cakes *m* with oil, of fine flour ... Lev 7:12
and a meat offering *m* with oil ... Lev 9:4
*m* with oil, and one log of oil ... Lev 14:10
*m* with oil for a meat offering ... Lev 14:21
not sow thy field with *m* seed ... Lev 19:19
shall a garment *m* of linen ... Lev 19:19
deals of fine flour *m* with oil ... Lev 23:13
cakes of fine flour *m* with oil ... Num 6:15
*m* with oil for a meat offering ... Num 7:13
*m* with oil for a meat offering ... Num 7:19
*m* with oil for a meat offering ... Num 7:25
*m* with oil for a meat offering ... Num 7:31
*m* with oil for a meat offering ... Num 7:37
*m* with oil for a meat offering ... Num 7:43
*m* with oil for a meat offering ... Num 7:49
*m* with oil for a meat offering ... Num 7:55
*m* with oil for a meat offering ... Num 7:61
*m* with oil for a meat offering ... Num 7:67
*m* with oil for a meat offering ... Num 7:73
*m* with oil for a meat offering ... Num 7:79
even fine flour *m* with oil ... Num 8:8
of a tenth deal of flour *m* with ... Num 15:4
two tenth deals of flour *m* with ... Num 15:6
flour *m* with half an hin of oil ... Num 15:9
*m* with the fourth part of an hin ... Num 28:5
*m* with oil, and the drink offering ... Num 28:9
*m* with oil, for one bullock ... Num 28:12
offering, *m* with oil, for one ram ... Num 28:12
*m* with oil for a meat offering ... Num 28:13
shall be of flour *m* with oil ... Num 28:20
meat offering of flour *m* with oil ... Num 28:28
shall be of flour *m* with oil ... Num 29:3
shall be of flour *m* with oil ... Num 29:9
shall be of flour *m* with oil ... Num 29:14
so that the holy seed have *m* ... Ezr 9:2
and *m* my drink with weeping, ... Ps 102:9
But were *m* among the heathen, and .. Ps 106:35
she hath *m* her wine ... Prov 9:2
drink of the wine which I have *m* ... Prov 9:5
The LORD hath *m* a perverse spirit ... Is 19:14
And all the *m* people, and all the ... Jer 25:20
all the kings of the *m* people ... Jer 25:24
upon all the *m* people that are in ... Jer 50:37
and Lydia, and all the *m* people ... Eze 30:5
him vinegar to drink *m* with gall ... Mt 27:34
him to drink wine *m* with myrrh ... Mk 15:23
had *m* with their sacrifices ... Lk 13:1
fire *m* with blood, and they were ... Rev 8:7
were a sea of glass *m* with fire ... Rev 15:2

**MINIAMIN** (*min'-e-a-min*) See MIAMIN.
*1. A Levite.*
And next him were Eden, and *M* ... 2Chr 31:15
*2. A priest with Zerubbabel.*
of *M*, of Moadiah, Piltai ... Neh 12:17
Eliakim, Maaseiah, *M*, Michaiah, ... Neh 12:41

**MINISH**
Ye shall not *m* ought from your ... Ex 5:19

**MINISHED**
Again, they are *m* and brought low ... Ps 107:39

**MINISTER**
And Moses rose up, and his *m* Joshua .. Ex 24:13
that he may *m* unto me in the ... Ex 28:1
that he may *m* unto me in the ... Ex 28:3
that he may *m* unto me in the ... Ex 28:4
And it shall be upon Aaron to *m* ... Ex 28:35
that they may *m* unto me in the ... Ex 28:41
the altar to *m* in the holy place ... Ex 28:43
to *m* unto me in the priest's ... Ex 29:1
to *m* in the holy place ... Ex 29:30
to *m* to me in the priest's office ... Ex 29:44
they come near to the altar to *m* ... Ex 30:20
that they may *m* unto me in the ... Ex 30:30
to *m* in the priest's office, ... Ex 31:10
to *m* in the priest's office ... Ex 35:19
about the hem of the robe to *m* in ... Ex 39:26
to *m* in the priest's office ... Ex 39:41
that he may *m* unto me in the ... Ex 40:13
that they may *m* unto me in the ... Ex 40:15
*m* unto the LORD in the priest's ... Lev 7:35
whom he shall consecrate to *m* in ... Lev 16:32
and they shall *m* unto it, and shall ... Num 1:50
to *m* in the priest's office ... Num 3:3
priest, that they may *m* unto him ... Num 3:6
of the sanctuary wherewith they *m* ... Num 3:31
thereof, wherewith they *m* unto it ... Num 4:9
wherewith they *m* in the sanctuary ... Num 4:12
wherewith they *m* about it ... Num 4:14
But shall *m* with their brethren ... Num 8:26
the congregation to *m* unto them ... Num 16:9
joined unto thee, and *m* unto thee ... Num 18:2
shall *m* before the tabernacle of ... Num 18:2
before the LORD to *m* unto him ... Deut 10:8
the priest that standeth to *m* ... Deut 17:12
to stand to *m* in the name of the ... Deut 18:5
Then he shall *m* in the name of ... Deut 18:7
thy God hath chosen to *m* unto him ... Deut 21:5
Joshua the son of Nun, Moses' *m* ... Josh 1:1
the child did *m* unto the LORD ... 1Sa 2:11
stand to *m* because of the cloud ... 1Kin 8:11
of God, and to *m* unto him for ever ... 1Chr 15:2
certain of the Levites to *m* ... 1Chr 16:4
to *m* before the ark continually ... 1Chr 16:37
to *m* unto him, and to bless in his ... 1Chr 23:13
to *m* in the house of the LORD ... 1Chr 26:12
stand to *m* by reason of the cloud ... 2Chr 5:14
*m* before the priests, as the duty ... 2Chr 8:14
which *m* unto the LORD, are the ... 2Chr 13:10
they that *m* of the Levites ... 2Chr 23:6
of the LORD, even vessels to *m* ... 2Chr 24:14
him, and that ye should *m* unto him. 2Chr 29:11
and for peace offerings, to *m* ... 2Chr 31:2
unto the priests that *m* in the ... Neh 10:36
sanctuary, and the priests that *m* ... Neh 10:39
he shall *m* judgment to the people ... Ps 9:8
of Nebaioth shall *m* unto thee ... Is 60:7
and their kings shall *m* unto thee ... Is 60:10
and the Levites that *m* unto me ... Jer 33:22
near to the LORD to *m* unto him ... Eze 40:46
lay their garments wherein they *m* ... Eze 42:14
to *m* unto me, saith the Lord GOD, ... Eze 43:19
stand before them to *m* unto them ... Eze 44:11
come near to me to *m* unto me ... Eze 44:15
to *m* unto me, and they shall keep ... Eze 44:16
whiles they *m* in the gates of the ... Eze 44:17
to *m* in the sanctuary, he shall ... Eze 44:27
come near to *m* unto the LORD ... Eze 45:4
among you, let him be your *m* ... Mt 20:26
to be ministered unto, but to *m* ... Mt 20:28
in prison, and did not *m* unto thee ... Mt 25:44
great among you, shall be your *m* ... Mk 10:43
to be ministered unto, but to *m* ... Mk 10:45
and he gave it again to the *m* ... Lk 4:20
and they had also John to their *m* ... Acts 13:5
to *m* or come unto him ... Acts 24:23
this purpose, to make thee a *m* ... Acts 26:16
For he is the *m* of God to thee ... Rom 13:4
for he is the *m* of God, a ... Rom 13:4
a *m* of the circumcision for the ... Rom 15:8
That I should be the *m* of Jesus ... Rom 15:16
Jerusalem to *m* unto the saints ... Rom 15:25
their duty is also to *m* unto them ... Rom 15:27
*m* about holy things live of the ... 1Cor 9:13
sower both *m* bread for your food ... 2Cor 9:10
is therefore Christ the *m* of sin ... Gal 2:17
Whereof I was made a *m*, according ... Eph 3:7
that it may *m* grace unto the ... Eph 4:29
faithful *m* in the Lord, shall ... Eph 6:21
is for you a faithful *m* of Christ ... Col 1:7
whereof I Paul am made a *m* ... Col 1:23
Whereof I am made a *m*, according ... Col 1:25
beloved brother, and a faithful *m* ... Col 4:7
*m* of God, and our fellowlabourer ... 1Th 3:2
which *m* questions, rather than ... 1Ti 1:4
shalt be a good *m* of Jesus Christ ... 1Ti 4:6
sent forth to *m* for them who ... Heb 1:14
ministered to the saints, and do *m* ... Heb 6:10
A *m* of the sanctuary, and of the ... Heb 8:2
but unto us they did *m* the things ... 1Pet 1:12
even so *m* the same one to another ... 1Pet 4:10
if any man *m*, let him do it as of ... 1Pet 4:11

**MINISTERED**
Ithamar *m* in the priest's office ... Num 3:4
Eleazar his son *m* in the priest's ... Deut 10:6
But Samuel *m* before the LORD, ... 1Sa 2:18
the child Samuel *m* unto the LORD ... 1Sa 3:1
his servant that *m* unto him ... 2Sa 13:17
cherished the king, and *m* to him ... 1Kin 1:4
the Shunammite *m* unto the king ... 1Kin 1:15
went after Elijah, and *m* unto him ... 1Kin 19:21
vessels of brass wherewith they *m* ... 2Kin 25:14
they *m* before the dwelling place ... 1Chr 6:32
that *m* to the king by course ... 1Chr 28:1
that *m* to Ahaziah, he slew them ... 2Chr 22:8
king's servants that *m* unto him ... Est 2:2
king's servants that *m* unto him ... Est 6:3
vessels of brass wherewith they *m* ... Jer 52:18
Because they *m* unto them before ... Eze 44:12
off their garments wherein they *m* ... Eze 44:19
thousand thousands *m* unto him ... Dan 7:10
behold, angels came and *m* unto him ... Mt 4:11
and she arose, and *m* unto them ... Mt 8:15
Son of man came not to be *m* unto ... Mt 20:28
and the angels *m* unto him ... Mk 1:13
left her, and she *m* unto them ... Mk 1:31
Son of man came not to be *m* unto ... Mk 10:45
followed him, and *m* unto him ... Mk 15:41
she arose and *m* unto them ... Lk 4:39
which *m* unto him of their ... Lk 8:3
As they *m* to the Lord, and fasted, ... Acts 13:2
two of them that *m* unto him ... Acts 19:22
hands have *m* unto my necessities ... Acts 20:34
be the epistle of Christ *m* by us ... 2Cor 3:3
and he that *m* to my wants ... Phil 2:25
and bands having nourishment *m* ... Col 2:19
things he *m* unto me at Ephesus ... 2Ti 1:18
*m* unto me in the bonds of the ... Philem 13
in that ye have *m* to the saints ... Heb 6:10
For so an entrance shall be *m* ... 2Pet 1:11

**MINISTERETH**
Now he that *m* seed to the sower ... 2Cor 9:10
that *m* to you the Spirit, and ... Gal 3:5

**MINISTERING**
had the charge of the *m* vessels ... 1Chr 9:28
of the house, and *m* to the house ... Eze 44:11
Jesus from Galilee, *m* unto him ... Mt 27:55
Or ministry, let us wait on our *m* ... Rom 12:7
*m* the gospel of God, that the ... Rom 15:16
fellowship of the *m* to the saints ... 2Cor 8:4
as touching the *m* to the saints ... 2Cor 9:1
Are they not all *m* spirits ... Heb 1:14
And every priest standeth daily *m* ... Heb 10:11

**MINISTERS**
and the attendance of his *m* ... 1Kin 10:5
and the attendance of his *m* ... 2Chr 9:4
or *m* of this house of God, it ... Ezr 7:24
us *m* for the house of our God ... Ezr 8:17
ye *m* of his, that do his pleasure ... Ps 103:21
his *m* a flaming fire ... Ps 104:4
shall call you the *M* of our God ... Is 61:6
the Levites the priests, my *m* ... Jer 33:21
they shall be *m* in my sanctuary ... Eze 44:11

priests the *m* of the sanctuary ... Eze 45:4
the *m* of the house, have for ... Eze 45:5
where the *m* of the house shall ... Eze 46:24
the priests, the LORD's *m* ... Joel 1:9
howl, ye *m* of the altar ... Joel 1:13
in sackcloth, ye *m* of my God ... Joel 1:13
the *m* of the LORD, weep between ... Joel 2:17
eyewitnesses, and *m* of the word ... Lk 1:2
for they are God's *m*, attending ... Rom 13:6
but *m* by whom ye believed, even ... 1Cor 3:5
of us, as of the *m* of Christ ... 1Cor 4:1
us able *m* of the new testament ... 2Cor 3:6
ourselves as the *m* of God ... 2Cor 6:4
his *m* also be transformed as the ... 2Cor 11:15
as the *m* of righteousness ... 2Cor 11:15
Are they *m* of Christ? ... 2Cor 11:23
spirits, and his *m* a flame of fire ... Heb 1:7

**MINISTRATION**
days of his *m* were accomplished ... Lk 1:23
were neglected in the daily *m* ... Acts 6:1
But if the *m* of death, written and ... 2Cor 3:7
How shall not the *m* of the spirit ... 2Cor 3:8
For if the *m* of condemnation be ... 2Cor 3:9
be glory, much more doth the *m* of ... 2Cor 3:9
this *m* they glorify God for your ... 2Cor 9:13

**MINISTRY**
take all the instruments of *m* ... Num 4:12
came to do the service of the *m* ... Num 4:47
when David praised by their *m* ... 2Chr 7:6
by the *m* of the prophets ... Hos 12:10
and had obtained part of this *m* ... Acts 1:17
That he may take part of this *m* ... Acts 1:25
prayer, and to the *m* of the word ... Acts 6:4
when they had fulfilled their *m* ... Acts 12:25
my course with joy, and the *m* ... Acts 20:24
among the Gentiles by his *m* ... Acts 21:19
Or *m*, let us wait on our ... Rom 12:7
themselves to the *m* of the saints ... 1Cor 16:15
Therefore, seeing we have this *m* ... 2Cor 4:1
to us the *m* of reconciliation ... 2Cor 5:18
thing, that the *m* be not blamed ... 2Cor 6:3
the saints, for the work of the *m* ... Eph 4:12
Take heed to the *m* which thou ... Col 4:17
faithful, putting me into the *m* ... 1Ti 1:12
make full proof of thy *m* ... 2Ti 4:5
he is profitable to me for the *m* ... 2Ti 4:11
he obtained a more excellent *m* ... Heb 8:6
and all the vessels of the *m* ... Heb 9:21

**MINJAMIN** See MINIAMIN.

**MINNI** (*min'-ni*) *A district in Armenia.*
her the kingdoms of Ararat, *M* ... Jer 51:27

**MINNITH** (*min'-nith*) *An Ammonite city.*
Aroer, even till thou come to *M* ... Judg 11:33
traded in thy market wheat of *M* ... Eze 27:17

**MINSTREL**
But now bring me a *m* ... 2Kin 3:15
came to pass, when the *m* played ... 2Kin 3:15

**MINSTRELS**
the ruler's house, and saw the *m* ... Mt 9:23

**MINT**
for ye pay tithe of *m* and anise and ... Mt 23:23
for ye tithe *m* and rue and all ... Lk 11:42

**MIPHKAD** (*mif'-kad*) *A gate of Jerusalem.*
over against the gate *M*, and to ... Neh 3:31

**MIRACLE**
you, saying, Shew a *m* for you ... Ex 7:9
not the *m* of the loaves ... Mk 6:52
man which shall do a *m* in my name ... Mk 9:39
to have seen some *m* done by him ... Lk 23:8
again the second *m* that Jesus did ... Jn 4:54
had seen the *m* that Jesus did ... Jn 6:14
unto him, and said, John did no *m* ... Jn 10:41
heard that he had done this *m* ... Jn 12:18
*m* hath been done by them is ... Acts 4:16
on whom this *m* of healing was ... Acts 4:22

**MIRACLES**
my glory, and my *m* ... Num 14:22
And his *m*, and his acts, which he ... Deut 11:3
seen, the signs, and those great *m* ... Deut 29:3
where be all his *m* which our ... Judg 6:13
This beginning of *m* did Jesus in ... Jn 2:11
when they saw the *m* which he did ... Jn 2:23
can do these *m* that thou doest ... Jn 3:2
because they saw his *m* which he ... Jn 6:2
seek me, not because ye saw the *m* ... Jn 6:26
will he do more *m* than these ... Jn 7:31
a man that is a sinner do such *m* ... Jn 9:16
for this man doeth many *m* ... Jn 11:47
he had done so many *m* before them ... Jn 12:37
approved of God among you by *m* ... Acts 2:22
wonders and *m* among the people ... Acts 6:8
seeing the *m* which he did ... Acts 8:6
and wondered, beholding the *m* ... Acts 8:13
and Paul, declaring what *m* ... Acts 15:12
God wrought special *m* by the ... Acts 19:11
To another the working of *m* ... 1Cor 12:10
thirdly teachers, after that *m* ... 1Cor 12:28
are all workers of *m*? ... 1Cor 12:29
worketh *m* among you, doeth he it ... Gal 3:5
and wonders, and with divers *m* ... Heb 2:4
*m* which he had power to do in the ... Rev 13:14
the spirits of devils, working *m* ... Rev 16:14
prophet that wrought *m* before him ... Rev 19:20

**MIRE**
stamp them as the *m* of the street ... 2Sa 22:43
Can the rush grow up without *m* ... Job 8:11
He hath cast me into the *m* ... Job 30:19
sharp pointed things upon the *m* ... Job 41:30
I sink in deep *m*, where there is ... Ps 69:2
Deliver me out of the *m*, and let ... Ps 69:14
down like the *m* of the streets ... Is 10:6
rest, whose waters cast up *m* ... Is 57:20
dungeon there was no water, but *m* ... Jer 38:6
so Jeremiah sunk in the *m* ... Jer 38:6
thy feet are sunk in the *m* ... Jer 38:22
down as the *m* of the streets ... Mic 7:10
fine gold as the *m* of the streets ... Zec 9:3
*m* of the streets in the battle ... Zec 10:5
washed to her wallowing in the *m* ... 2Pet 2:22

**MIRIAM** (*mir'-e-am*) See MARY.
*1. Sister of Aaron.*
*M* the prophetess, the sister of ... Ex 15:20
*M* answered them, Sing ye to the ... Ex 15:21
*M* and Aaron spake against ... Num 12:1
Moses, and unto Aaron, and unto *M* ... Num 12:4
tabernacle, and called Aaron and *M* ... Num 12:5
*M* became leprous, white as snow ... Num 12:10
and Aaron looked upon *M*, and, ... Num 12:10
*M* was shut out from the camp ... Num 12:15
not till *M* was brought in again ... Num 12:15
*M* died there, and was buried there ... Num 20:1
Aaron and Moses, and *M* their sister Num 26:59
thy God did unto *M* by the way ... Deut 24:9
Aaron, and Moses, and *M* ... 1Chr 6:3
before thee Moses, Aaron, and *M* ... Mic 6:4
*2. A daughter of Ezra.*
and she bare *M*, and Shammai, and ... 1Chr 4:17

**MIRMA** (*mur'-mah*) *Son of Shaharaim.*
And Jeuz, and Shachia, and *M* ... 1Chr 8:10

**MIRMAH** See MIRMA.

**MIRTH**
might have sent thee away with *m* ... Gen 31:27
send portions, and to make great *m* ... Neh 8:12
that wasted us required of us *m* ... Ps 137:3
and the end of that *m* is heaviness ... Prov 14:13
to now, I will prove thee with *m* ... Eccl 2:1
and of *m*, What doeth it ... Eccl 2:2
of fools is in the house of *m* ... Eccl 7:4
Then I commended *m*, because a man Eccl 8:15
The *m* of tabrets ceaseth, the ... Is 24:8
the *m* of the land is gone ... Is 24:11
of Jerusalem, the voice of *m* ... Jer 7:34
and in your days, the voice of *m* ... Jer 16:9
take from them the voice of *m* ... Jer 25:10
should we then make *m*? ... Eze 21:10
also cause all her *m* to cease ... Hos 2:11

**MIRY**
horrible pit, out of the *m* clay ... Ps 40:2
But the *m* places thereof and the ... Eze 47:11
sawest the iron mixed with *m* clay ... Dan 2:41
sawest iron mixed with *m* clay ... Dan 2:43

**MISCARRYING**
give them a *m* womb and dry breasts ... Hos 9:14

**MISCHIEF**
Lest peradventure *m* befall him ... Gen 42:4
if *m* befall him by the way in the ... Gen 42:38
*m* befall him, ye shall bring down ... Gen 44:29
from her, and yet no *m* follow ... Ex 21:22
And if any *m* follow, then thou ... Ex 21:23
For *m* did he bring them out, to ... Ex 32:12
people, that they are set on *m* ... Ex 32:22
secretly practised *m* against him ... 1Sa 23:9
behold, thou art taken in thy *m* ... 2Sa 16:8
beside the *m* that Hadad did ... 1Kin 11:25
and see how this man seeketh *m* ... 1Kin 20:7
light, some *m* will come upon us ... 2Kin 7:9
But they thought to do me *m* ... Neh 6:2
away the *m* of Haman the Agagite ... Est 8:3
They conceive *m*, and bring forth ... Job 15:35
iniquity, and hath conceived *m* ... Ps 7:14
His *m* shall return upon his own ... Ps 7:16
under his tongue is *m* and vanity ... Ps 10:7
for thou beholdest *m* and spite, to ... Ps 10:14
In whose hands is *m*, and their ... Ps 26:10
but *m* is in their hearts ... Ps 28:3
He deviseth *m* upon his bed ... Ps 36:4
Why boastest thou thyself in *m* ... Ps 52:1
*m* also and sorrow are in the midst ... Ps 55:10
will ye imagine *m* against a man ... Ps 62:3
thee, which frameth *m* by a law ... Ps 94:20
draw nigh that follow after *m* ... Ps 119:150
let the *m* of their own lips cover ... Ps 140:9
not, except they have done *m* ... Prov 4:16
heart, he deviseth *m* continually ... Prov 6:14
that be swift in running to *m* ... Prov 6:18
It is as sport to a fool to do *m* ... Prov 10:23
but he that seeketh *m*, it shall ... Prov 11:27
the wicked shall be filled with *m* ... Prov 12:21
A wicked messenger falleth into *m* ... Prov 13:17
a perverse tongue falleth into *m* ... Prov 17:20
and their lips talk of *m* ... Prov 24:2
but the wicked shall fall into *m* ... Prov 24:16
his heart shall fall into *m* ... Prov 28:14
and *m* shall fall upon thee ... Is 47:11
they conceive *m*, and bring forth ... Is 59:4
*M* shall come upon *m* ... Eze 7:26
these are the men that devise *m* ... Eze 11:2
kings' hearts shall be to do *m* ... Dan 11:27
yet do they imagine *m* against me ... Hos 7:15
O full of all subtilty and all *m* ... Acts 13:10

**MISCHIEFS**
I will heap *m* upon them ... Deut 32:23
Thy tongue deviseth *m* ... Ps 52:2
Which imagine *m* in their heart ... Ps 140:2

**MISCHIEVOUS**
they imagined a *m* device, which ... Ps 21:11
that seek my hurt speak *m* things ... Ps 38:12
evil shall be called a *m* person ... Prov 24:8
the end of his talk is *m* madness ... Eccl 10:13
man, he uttereth his *m* desire ... Mic 7:3

**MISERABLE**
*m* comforters are ye all ... Job 16:2
Christ, we are of all men most *m* ... 1Cor 15:19
not that thou art wretched, and *m* ... Rev 3:17

**MISERABLY**
He will *m* destroy those wicked ... Mt 21:41

**MISERIES**
of her *m* all her pleasant things ... Lam 1:7
howl for your *m* that shall come ... Jas 5:1

**MISERY**
was grieved for the *m* of Israel ... Judg 10:16
light given to him that is in *m* ... Job 3:20
Because thou shalt forget thy *m* ... Job 11:16
and remember his *m* no more ... Prov 31:7
therefore the *m* of man is great ... Eccl 8:6
mine affliction and my *m*, the ... Lam 3:19
and *m* are in their ways ... Rom 3:16

**MISGAB** (*mis'-gab*) *The mountainous area in Moab.*
*M* is confounded and dismayed ... Jer 48:1

**MISHAEL** (*mish'-a-el*) See MISHAL.
*1. A son of Uzziel.*
*M*, and Elzaphan, and Zithri ... Ex 6:22
Moses called *M* and ... Lev 10:4
of Judah, Daniel, Hananiah, *M* ... Dan 1:6
and to *M*, of Meshach ... Dan 1:7
had set over Daniel, Hananiah, *M* ... Dan 1:11
none like Daniel, Hananiah, *M* ... Dan 1:19
the thing known to Hananiah, *M* ... Dan 2:17
*2. A priest who aided Ezra.*
on his left hand, Pedaiah, and *M* ... Neh 8:4

**MISHAL** (*mi'-shal*) See MISHAEL. *A Levitical city in Asher.*
*M* with her suburbs, Abdon with ... Josh 21:30

**MISHAM** (*mi'-sham*) *Son of Elpaal.*
Eber, and *M*, and Shamed, who built .. 1Chr 8:12

**MISHEAL** (*mish'-e-al*) *Same as Mishal.*
And Alammelech, and Amad, and *M*. Josh 19:26

**MISHMA** (*mish'-mah*) *A son of Ishmeal.*
And *M*, and Dumah, and Massa, ... Gen 25:14
*M*, and Dumah, Massa, Hadad, and ... 1Chr 1:30
son, Mibsam his son, *M* his son ... 1Chr 4:25
And the sons of *M* ... 1Chr 4:26

**MISHMANNAH** (*mish-man'-nah*) *A warrior in David's army.*
*M* the fourth, Jeremiah the fifth, ... 1Chr 12:10

**MISHRAITES** (*mish'-ra-ites*) *A family of Kirjath-jearim.*
and the Shumathites, and the *M* ... 1Chr 2:53

**MISPAR** See MIZPAR.

**MISPERETH** (*mis-pe'-reth*) See MIZPAR. *An exile with Ezra.*
Nahamani, Mordecai, Bilshan, *M* ... Neh 7:7

**MISREPHOTH-MAIM** *Same as Zarephath.*
them unto great Zidon, and unto *M* ... Josh 11:8
hill country from Lebanon unto *M* ... Josh 13:6

**MISS**
at an hair breadth, and not *m* ... Judg 20:16
If thy father at all *m* me ... 1Sa 20:6

**MISSED**
and thou shalt be *m*, because thy ... 1Sa 20:18
neither *m* we any thing, as long ... 1Sa 25:15
so that nothing was *m* of all that ... 1Sa 25:21

**MISSING**
was there ought *m* unto them ... 1Sa 25:7
if by any means he be *m*, then ... 1Kin 20:39

**MIST**
there went up a *m* from the earth ... Gen 2:6
immediately there fell on him a *m* ... Acts 13:11
to whom the *m* of darkness is ... 2Pet 2:17

**MISTRESS**
her *m* was despised in her eyes ... Gen 16:4
flee from the face of my *m* Sarai ... Gen 16:8
said unto her, Return to thy *m* ... Gen 16:9
the *m* of the house, fell sick ... 1Kin 17:17
And she said unto her *m*, Would God ... 2Kin 5:3
a maiden unto the hand of her *m* ... Ps 123:2
an handmaid that is heir to her *m* ... Prov 30:23
as with the maid, so with her *m* ... Is 24:2
the *m* of witchcrafts, that ... Nah 3:4

**MISUSED**
*m* his prophets, until the wrath ......... 2Chr 36:16

**MITE**
thou hast paid the very last *m*................ Lk 12:59

**MITES**
poor widow, and she threw in two *m*.. Mk 12:42
widow casting in thither two *m* .............. Lk 21:2

**MITHCAH** (*mith'-cah*) *An Israelite encampment in the wilderness.*
from Tarah, and pitched in *M*............ Num 33:28
And they went from *M*, and pitched. Num 33:29

**MITHCAK** See Mithcah.

**MITHKAH** See Mithcah.

**MITHNITE** (*mith'-nite*) *Family name of Joshaphat.*
of Maachah, and Joshaphat the *M*..... 1Chr 11:43

**MITHREDATH** (*mith'-re-dath*) *Treasurer for King Cyrus of Persia.*
by the hand of *M* the treasurer................ Ezr 1:8
of Artaxerxes wrote Bishlam, *M* .............. Ezr 4:7

**MITRE**
a robe, and a broidered coat, a *m*............ Ex 28:4
lace, that it may be upon the *m* ............ Ex 28:37
forefront of the *m* it shall be................. Ex 28:37
shalt make the *m* of fine linen................ Ex 28:39
shalt put the *m* upon his head.................. Ex 29:6
and put the holy crown upon the *m* ........ Ex 29:6
a *m* of fine linen, and goodly.................. Ex 39:28
to fasten it on high upon the *m* .............. Ex 39:31
he put the *m* upon his head...................... Lev 8:9
also upon the *m*, even upon his................ Lev 8:9
with the linen *m* shall he be.................... Lev 16:4
them set a fair *m* upon his head............... Zec 3:5
they set a fair *m* upon his head............... Zec 3:5

**MITYLENE** (*mit-i-le'-ne*) *Major city of the island of Lesbos.*
we took him in, and came to *M*......... Acts 20:14

**MIXED**
a *m* multitude went up also with.......... Ex 12:38
from Israel all the *m* multitude............. Neh 13:3
they that go to seek *m* wine............... Prov 23:30
dross, thy wine *m* with water.................... Is 1:22
sawest the iron *m* with miry clay......... Dan 2:41
thou sawest iron *m* with miry clay....... Dan 2:43
even as iron is not *m* with clay.......... Dan 2:43
he hath *m* himself among the.................. Hos 7:8
not being *m* with faith in them............. Heb 4:2

**MIXT**
the *m* multitude that was among......... Num 11:4

**MIXTURE**
it is full of *m* ........................................... Ps 75:8
by night, and brought a *m* of myrrh.... Jn 19:39
which is poured out without *m*........... Rev 14:10

**MIZAR** (*mi'-zar*) *A hill near Hermon.*
the Hermonites, from the hill *M* .............. Ps 42:6

**MIZPAH** (*miz'-pah*) See Mizpeh.
*1. A city in Gad.*
And *M*; for he said ................................ Gen 31:49
*2. A city in Benjamin.*
with them Geba of Benjamin, and *M* 1Kin 15:22
the men of Gibeon, and of *M* .................. Neh 3:7
*3. A city in Judah.*
there came to Gedaliah to *M*............. 2Kin 25:23
Chaldees that were with him at *M*..... 2Kin 25:25
and he built therewith Geba and *M*..... 2Chr 16:6
Gedaliah the son of Ahikam to *M*.......... Jer 40:6
Then they came to Gedaliah to *M*.......... Jer 40:8
I will dwell at *M* to serve the................. Jer 40:10
of Judah, to Gedaliah, unto *M*.............. Jer 40:12
the fields, came to Gedaliah to *M*......... Jer 40:13
spake to Gedaliah in *M* secretly............ Jer 40:15
Gedaliah the son of Ahikam to *M*.......... Jer 41:1
they did eat bread together in *M*........... Jer 41:1
him, even with Gedaliah, at *M*............... Jer 41:3
went forth from *M* to meet them ............ Jer 41:6
of the people that were in *M*................. Jer 41:10
all the people that remained in *M* ......... Jer 41:10
away captive from *M* cast about ............ Jer 41:14
the son of Nethaniah, from *M* ............... Jer 41:16
because ye have been a snare on *M*........ Hos 5:1
*4. A district ruled by Shallum.*
Colhozeh, the ruler of part of *M*........... Neh 3:15
*5. A place ruled by Ezer.*
the son of Jeshua, the ruler of *M* .......... Neh 3:19

**MIZPAR** (*miz'-par*) See Mispereth. *A clan leader with Zerubbabel.*
Reelaiah, Mordecai, Bilshan, *M* ............... Ezr 2:2

**MIZPEH** (*miz'-peh*) See Mizpah, Ramath-mizpeh.
*1. A valley near Mt. Hermon.*
under Hermon in the land of *M*............. Josh 11:3
and unto the valley of *M* eastward....... Josh 11:8
*2. A city in Judah.*
And Dilean, and *M*, and Joktheel, ...... Josh 15:38
of Gilead, unto the Lord in *M*.............. Judg 20:1
of Israel were gone up to *M* ................. Judg 20:3
the men of Israel had sworn in *M*......... Judg 21:1
that came not up to the Lord to *M*...... Judg 21:5
that came not up to *M* to the Lord..... Judg 21:8
said, Gather all Israel to *M* ..................... 1Sa 7:5
And they gathered together to *M*............ 1Sa 7:6
the children of Israel in *M*........................ 1Sa 7:6
were gathered together to *M*..................... 1Sa 7:7
the men of Israel went out of *M* ........... 1Sa 7:11
took a stone, and set it between *M*........ 1Sa 7:12
to Beth-el, and Gilgal, and *M*................. 1Sa 7:16
together unto the Lord to *M*................ 1Sa 10:17
*3. A city in Benjamin.*
And *M*, and Chephirah, and Mozah, .. Josh 18:26
*4. A city in Gad.*
together, and encamped in *M*............. Judg 10:17
his words before the Lord in *M* ........ Judg 11:11
and passed over *M* of Gilead ............... Judg 11:29
from *M* of Gilead he passed over........ Judg 11:29
Jephthah came to *M* unto his house. Judg 11:34
*5. A city in Moab.*
And David went thence to *M* of Moab.. 1Sa 22:3

**MIZRAIM** (*miz'-ra-im*) See Abel-mizraim. *Son of Ham.*
Cush, and *M*, and Phut, and Canaan.... Gen 10:6
*M* begat Ludim, and Anamim, and...... Gen 10:13
Cush, and *M*, Put, and Canaan.............. 1Chr 1:8
*M* begat Ludim, and Anamim, and...... 1Chr 1:11

**MIZZAH** (*miz'-zah*) *Son of Reuel.*
Zerah, Shammah, and *M* ...................... Gen 36:13
duke Zerah, duke Shammah, duke *M* Gen 36:17
Nahath, Zerah, Shammah, and *M*......... 1Chr 1:37

**MNASON** (*na'-son*) *A Christian in Jerusalem.*
brought with them one *M* of Cyprus. Acts 21:16

**MOAB** (*mo'-ab*)
*1. A nation east of Israel.*
smote Midian in the field of *M*............ Gen 36:35
the mighty men of *M*, trembling ............. Ex 15:15
the wilderness which is before *M*....... Num 21:11
is the border of *M*, between *M*........... Num 21:13
Ar, and lieth upon the border of *M*... Num 21:15
that is in the country of *M*................. Num 21:20
against the former king of *M*............. Num 21:26
it hath consumed Ar of *M*, and the... Num 21:28
Woe to thee, *M*..................................... Num 21:29
pitched in the plains of *M* on.............. Num 22:1
*M* was sore afraid of the people, ......... Num 22:3
*M* was distressed because of the......... Num 22:3
*M* said unto the elders of Midian, ....... Num 22:4
And the elders of *M* and the elders..... Num 22:7
the princes of *M* abode with................. Num 22:8
the son of Zippor, king of *M*.............. Num 22:10
And the princes of *M* rose up ............ Num 22:14
and went with the princes of *M*.......... Num 22:21
out to meet him unto a city of *M*...... Num 22:36
he, and all the princes of *M*................. Num 23:6
Balak the king of *M* hath brought....... Num 23:7
and the princes of *M* with him .......... Num 23:17
and shall smite the corners of *M*........ Num 24:17
whoredom with the daughters of *M*.... Num 25:1
of *M* by Jordan near Jericho ............... Num 26:3
of *M* by Jordan near Jericho .............. Num 26:63
unto the camp at the plains of *M* ...... Num 31:12
in Ije-abarim, in the border of *M* ..... Num 33:44
of *M* by Jordan near Jericho .............. Num 33:48
Abel-shittim in the plains of *M*........ Num 33:49
in the plains of *M* by Jordan ............ Num 33:50
of *M* by Jordan near Jericho ............... Num 35:1
of *M* by Jordan near Jericho .............. Num 36:13
side Jordan, in the land of *M* ................ Deut 1:5
by the way of the wilderness of *M* ....... Deut 2:8
over through Ar, the coast of *M* .......... Deut 2:18
of Israel in the land of *M*.................... Deut 29:1
Nebo, which is in the land of *M*........ Deut 32:49
of *M* unto the mountain of Nebo........ Deut 34:1
Lord died there in the land of *M*......... Deut 34:5
him in a valley in the land of *M*.......... Deut 34:6
in the plains of *M* thirty days ............. Deut 34:8
inheritance in the plains of *M*............. Josh 13:32
the son of Zippor, king of *M*................ Josh 24:9
the king of *M* against Israel ................ Judg 3:12
the king of *M* eighteen years ............... Judg 3:14
present unto Eglon the king of *M*......... Judg 3:15
the present unto Eglon king of *M*......... Judg 3:17
took the fords of Jordan toward *M*...... Judg 3:28
they slew of *M* at that time about ........ Judg 3:29
So *M* was subdued that day under........ Judg 3:30
gods of Zidon, and the gods of *M* ........ Judg 10:6
took not away the land of *M*................ Judg 11:15
they sent unto the king of *M*.............. Judg 11:17
land of Edom, and the land of *M*......... Judg 11:18
by the east side of the land of *M*......... Judg 11:18
came not within the border of *M* ......... Judg 11:18
for Arnon was the border of *M*........... Judg 11:18
the son of Zippor, king of *M* .............. Judg 11:25
to sojourn in the country of *M*................ Ruth 1:1
they came into the country of *M*............. Ruth 1:2
took them wives of the women of *M*..... Ruth 1:4
return from the country of *M*................ Ruth 1:6
*M* how that the Lord had visited ........... Ruth 1:6
returned out of the country of *M*........... Ruth 1:22
Naomi out of the country of *M*............. Ruth 2:6
again out of the country of *M*.............. Ruth 4:3
and into the hand of the king of *M* ....... 1Sa 12:9
enemies on every side, against *M*......... 1Sa 14:47
David went thence to Mizpeh of *M* ....... 1Sa 22:3
and he said unto the king of *M*.............. 1Sa 22:3
brought them before the king of *M* ........ 1Sa 22:4
And he smote *M*, and measured them..... 2Sa 8:2
Of Syria, and of *M*, and of the................. 2Sa 8:12
he slew two lionlike men of *M*............. 2Sa 23:20
for Chemosh, the abomination of *M*.... 1Kin 11:7
Then *M* rebelled against Israel............... 2Kin 1:1
Mesha king of *M* was a sheepmaster...... 2Kin 3:4
that the king of *M* rebelled..................... 2Kin 3:5
The king of *M* hath rebelled..................... 2Kin 3:7
go with me against *M* to battle.............. 2Kin 3:7
deliver them into the hand of *M*.......... 2Kin 3:10
deliver them into the hand of *M*.......... 2Kin 3:13
now therefore, *M*, to the spoil.............. 2Kin 3:23
when the king of *M* saw that the......... 2Kin 3:26
smote Midian in the field of *M*.............. 1Chr 1:46
Saraph, who had the dominion in *M*... 1Chr 4:22
children in the country of *M* ................. 1Chr 8:8
he slew two lionlike men of *M*........... 1Chr 11:22
And he smote *M*.................................... 1Chr 18:2
and from *M*, and from the ................... 1Chr 18:11
this also, that the children of *M* .......... 2Chr 20:1
the children of Ammon and *M*............. 2Chr 20:10
against the children of Ammon, *M*.... 2Chr 20:22
Ammon and *M* stood up against the. 2Chr 20:23
of Ashdod, of Ammon, and of *M* ........ Neh 13:23
*M* is my washpot........................................ Ps 60:8
of *M*, and the Hagarenes.......................... Ps 83:6
*M* is my washpot........................................ Ps 108:9
lay their hand upon Edom and *M*........... Is 11:14
The burden of *M*.......................................... Is 15:1
the night Ar of *M* is laid waste ................. Is 15:1
the night Kir of *M* is laid waste ................ Is 15:1
*M* shall howl over Nebo, and over............ Is 15:2
armed soldiers of *M* shall cry out ............ Is 15:4
My heart shall cry out for *M*..................... Is 15:5
gone round about the borders of *M* ........... Is 15:8
lions upon him that escapeth of *M*............ Is 15:9
so the daughters of *M* shall be at ............. Is 16:2
mine outcasts dwell with thee, *M*............. Is 16:4
We have heard of the pride of *M*............... Is 16:6
Therefore shall *M* howl for *M*.................. Is 16:7
Therefore shall *M* howl for *M*.................. Is 16:7
shall sound like an harp for *M* ............... Is 16:11
when it is seen that *M* is weary............... Is 16:12
concerning *M* since that time.................. Is 16:13
the glory of *M* shall be contemned........... Is 16:14
*M* shall be trodden down under him...... Is 25:10
and the children of Ammon, and *M*........ Jer 9:26
Edom, and *M*, and the children of......... Jer 25:21
king of Edom, and to the king of *M* ....... Jer 27:3
when all the Jews that were in *M*.......... Jer 40:11
Against *M* thus saith the Lord of.......... Jer 48:1
shall be no more praise of *M* ................. Jer 48:2
*M* is destroyed........................................ Jer 48:4
Give wings unto *M*, that it may............. Jer 48:9
*M* hath been at ease from his............... Jer 48:11
*M* shall be ashamed of Chemosh, as..... Jer 48:13
*M* is spoiled, and gone up out of.......... Jer 48:15
The calamity of *M* is near to come ...... Jer 48:16
for the spoiler of *M* shall come ............ Jer 48:18
*M* is confounded ................................... Jer 48:20
it in Arnon, that *M* is spoiled,............... Jer 48:20
all the cities of the land of *M* .............. Jer 48:24
The horn of *M* is cut off, and his.......... Jer 48:25
*M* also shall wallow in his vomit, .......... Jer 48:26
O ye that dwell in *M*, leave the............. Jer 48:28
We have heard the pride of *M* .............. Jer 48:29
Therefore will I howl for *M* ................. Jer 48:31
and I will cry out for all *M* ................. Jer 48:31
field, and from the land of *M*.............. Jer 48:33
I will cause to cease in *M*.................... Jer 48:35
shall sound for *M* like pipes ................ Jer 48:36
upon all the housetops of *M* ................ Jer 48:38
for I have broken *M* like a vessel ........ Jer 48:38
how hath *M* turned the back with ......... Jer 48:39
so shall *M* be a derision and a.............. Jer 48:39
and shall spread his wings over *M* ....... Jer 48:40
the mighty men's hearts in *M* at .......... Jer 48:41
*M* shall be destroyed from being a ........ Jer 48:42
be upon thee, O inhabitant of *M* ........... Jer 48:43
I will bring upon it, even upon *M* ........ Jer 48:44
and shall devour the corner of *M*......... Jer 48:45
Woe be unto thee, O *M*......................... Jer 48:46
captivity of *M* in the latter days............ Jer 48:47
Thus far is the judgment of *M* ............. Jer 48:47
Because that *M* and Seir do say, ........... Eze 25:8
the side of *M* from the cities.................. Eze 25:9
I will execute judgments upon *M*......... Eze 25:11
out of his hand, even Edom, and *M*.... Dan 11:41
For three transgressions of *M* .............. Amos 2:1
But I will send a fire upon *M*............... Amos 2:2
*M* shall die with tumult, with............... Amos 2:2
what Balak king of *M* consulted ............. Mic 6:5
I have heard the reproach of *M*............ Zeph 2:8
Surely *M* shall be as Sodom, and.......... Zeph 2:9
*2. Son of Lot.*
bare a son, and called his name *M*...... Gen 19:37

**MOABITE** (*mo'-ab-ite*) See Moabites, Moabitess, Moabitish. *An inhabitant of Moab.*
An Ammonite or *M* shall not enter ..... Deut 23:3
sons of Elnaam, and Ithmah the *M*... 1Chr 11:46
the *M* should not come into the .......... Neh 13:1

**MOABITES** (*mo'-ab-ites*)
the father of the *M* unto this day........ Gen 19:37
was king of the *M* at that time.......... Num 22:4
said unto me, Distress not the *M*........... Deut 2:9
but the *M* call them Emims................... Deut 2:11
the *M* which dwell in Ar, did unto........ Deut 2:29
your enemies the *M* into your hand.... Judg 3:28
so the *M* became David's servants,.......... 2Sa 8:2
of Pharaoh, women of the *M*................ 1Kin 11:1
Chemosh the god of the *M* ................. 1Kin 11:33
deliver the *M* also into your hand........ 2Kin 3:18
when all the *M* heard that the.............. 2Kin 3:21
the *M* saw the water on the other ....... 2Kin 3:22

Israelites rose up and smote the *M* 2Kin 3:24
they went forward smiting the *M* 2Kin 3:24
the bands of the *M* invaded the 2Kin 13:20
Chemosh the abomination of the *M* 2Kin 23:13
of the Syrians, and bands of the *M* 2Kin 24:2
the *M* became David's servants, and 1Chr 18:2
Jebusites, the Ammonites, the *M* Ezr 9:1

**MOABITESS** (*mo'-ab-i-tess*) *A female Moabite.*
So Naomi returned, and Ruth the *M* Ruth 1:22
Ruth the *M* said unto Naomi, Let Ruth 2:2
And Ruth the *M* said, He said unto Ruth 2:21
must buy it also of Ruth the *M* Ruth 4:5
Moreover Ruth the *M*, the wife of Ruth 4:10
Jehozabad the son of Shimrith a *M* 2Chr 24:26

**MOABITISH** (*mo'-ab-i-tish*) *Belonging to the Moabites.*
It is the *M* damsel that came back Ruth 2:6

**MOADIAH** (*mo-ad-i'-ah*) See MAADIAH. *A priest.*
of Miniamin, of *M*, Piltai Neh 12:17

**MOCK**
in an Hebrew unto us to *m* us Gen 39:14
unto us, came in unto me to *m* me Gen 39:17
mocketh another, do ye so *m* him Job 13:9
and after that I have spoken, *m* on Job 21:3
I will *m* when your fear cometh Prov 1:26
Fools make a *m* at sin Prov 14:9
me into their hand, and they *m* me Jer 38:19
saw her, and did *m* at her sabbaths Lam 1:7
be far from thee, shall *m* thee Eze 22:5
deliver him to the Gentiles to *m* Mt 20:19
And they shall *m* him, and shall Mk 10:34
all that behold it begin to *m* him Lk 14:29

**MOCKED**
one that *m* unto his sons in law Gen 19:14
the ass, Because thou hast *m* me Num 22:29
Samson, Behold, thou hast *m* me Judg 16:10
Samson, Hitherto thou hast *m* me Judg 16:13
thou hast *m* me these three times, Judg 16:15
pass at noon, that Elijah *m* them 1Kin 18:27
*m* him, and said unto him, Go up, 2Kin 2:23
laughed them to scorn, and *m* them 2Chr 30:10
But they *m* the messengers of God, 2Chr 36:16
great indignation, and *m* the Jews Neh 4:1
I am as one *m* of his neighbour, Job 12:4
saw that he was *m* of the wise men Mt 2:16
*m* him, saying, Hail, King of the Mt 27:29
And after that they had *m* him Mt 27:31
And when they had *m* him, they took Mk 15:20
unto the Gentiles, and shall be *m* Lk 18:32
And the men that held Jesus *m* him Lk 22:63
*m* him, and arrayed him in a Lk 23:11
And the soldiers also *m* him Lk 23:36
resurrection of the dead, some *m* Acts 17:32
God is not *m* Gal 6:7

**MOCKER**
Wine is a *m*, strong drink is Prov 20:1

**MOCKERS**
Are there not *m* with me Job 17:2
With hypocritical *m* in feasts Ps 35:16
Now therefore be ye not *m* Is 28:22
sat not in the assembly of the *m* Jer 15:17
should be *m* in the last time Jude 18

**MOCKEST**
and when thou *m*, shall no man make Job 11:3

**MOCKETH**
or as one man *m* another, do ye so Job 13:9
He *m* at fear, and is not Job 39:22
Whoso *m* the poor reproacheth his Prov 17:5
The eye that *m* at his father, and Prov 30:17
in derision daily, every one *m* me Jer 20:7

**MOCKING**
she had born unto Abraham, *m* Gen 21:9
heathen, and a *m* to all countries Eze 22:4
also the chief priests *m* him Mt 27:41
*m* said among themselves with the Mk 15:31
Others *m* said, These men are full Acts 2:13

**MOCKINGS**
And others had trial of cruel *m* Heb 11:36

**MODERATELY**
hath given you the former rain *m* Joel 2:23

**MODERATION**
Let your *m* be known unto all men Phil 4:5

**MODEST**
adorn themselves in *m* apparel 1Ti 2:9

**MOIST**
of grapes, nor eat *m* grapes Num 6:3

**MOISTENED**
and his bones are *m* with marrow Job 21:24

**MOISTURE**
my *m* is turned into the drought Ps 32:4
away, because it lacked *m* Lk 8:6

**MOLADAH** (*mo-la'-dah*) *A city in Judah.*
Amam, and Shema, and *M*, Josh 15:26
Beer-sheba, or Sheba, and *M* Josh 19:2
And they dwelt at Beer-sheba, and *M*. 1Chr 4:28
And at Jeshua, and at *M*, and at Neh 11:26

**MOLE**
lizard, and the snail, and the *m* Lev 11:30

**MOLECH** (*mo'-lek*) See MALCHAM, MOLOCH. *An Ammonite god.*
seed pass through the fire to *M* Lev 18:21
giveth any of his seed unto *M* Lev 20:2
he hath given of his seed unto *M* Lev 20:3
when he giveth of his seed unto *M* Lev 20:4
him, to commit whoredom with *M* Lev 20:5
is before Jerusalem, and for *M* 1Kin 11:7
to pass through the fire to *M* 2Kin 23:10
to pass through the fire unto *M* Jer 32:35

**MOLES**
for himself to worship, to the *m* Is 2:20

**MOLID** (*mo'-lid*) *A descendant of Jerahmeel.*
and she bare him Ahban, and *M* 1Chr 2:29

**MOLLIFIED**
bound up, neither *m* with ointment Is 1:6

**MOLOCH** (*mo'-loch*) See MILCHOM, MOLECH. *Same as Molech.*
borne the tabernacle of your *M* Amos 5:26
ye took up the tabernacle of *M* Acts 7:43

**MOLTEN**
after he had made it a *m* calf Ex 32:4
they have made them a *m* calf Ex 32:8
Thou shalt make thee no *m* gods Ex 34:17
nor make to yourselves *m* gods Lev 19:4
and destroy all their *m* images Num 33:52
they have made them a *m* image Deut 9:12
God, and had made you a *m* calf Deut 9:16
that maketh any graven or *m* image Deut 27:15
make a graven image and a *m* image Judg 17:3
a graven image and a *m* image Judg 17:4
and a graven image, and a *m* image Judg 18:14
and the teraphim, and the *m* image Judg 18:17
and the teraphim, and the *m* image Judg 18:18
he made two chapiters of *m* brass 1Kin 7:16
And he made a *m* sea, ten cubits 1Kin 7:23
the laver were undersetters *m* 1Kin 7:30
and their spokes, were all *m* 1Kin 7:33
*m* images, to provoke me to anger, 1Kin 14:9
their God, and made them *m* images 2Kin 17:16
Also he made a *m* sea of ten 2Chr 4:2
made also *m* images for Baalim 2Chr 28:2
carved images, and the *m* images 2Chr 34:3
the *m* images, he brake in pieces, 2Chr 34:4
when they had made them a *m* calf Neh 9:18
brass is *m* out of the stone Job 28:2
strong, and as a *m* looking glass Job 37:18
Horeb, and worshipped the *m* image Ps 106:19
ornament of thy *m* images of gold Is 30:22
their *m* images are wind and Is 41:29
images, that say to the *m* images Is 42:17
or *m* a graven image that is Is 44:10
my *m* image, hath commanded them Is 48:5
for his *m* image is falsehood, and Jer 10:14
for his *m* image is falsehood, and Jer 51:17
filthiness of it may be *m* in it Eze 24:11
have made them *m* images of their Hos 13:2
mountains shall be *m* under him Mic 1:4
the graven image and the *m* image Nah 1:14
the *m* image, and a teacher of lies Hab 2:18

**MOMENT**
up into the midst of thee in a *m* Ex 33:5
that I may consume them in a *m* Num 16:21
that I may consume them as in a *m*. Num 16:45
every morning, and try him every *m* Job 7:18
joy of the hypocrite but for a *m* Job 20:5
in a *m* go down to the grave Job 21:13
In a *m* shall they die, and the Job 34:20
For his anger endureth but a *m* Ps 30:5
into desolation, as in a *m* Ps 73:19
but a lying tongue is but for a *m* Prov 12:19
thyself as it were for a little *m* Is 26:20
I will water it every *m* Is 27:3
come to thee in a *m* in one day Is 47:9
For a small *m* have I forsaken Is 54:7
I hid my face from thee for a *m* Is 54:8
spoiled, and my curtains in a *m* Jer 4:20
that was overthrown as in a *m* Lam 4:6
and shall tremble at every *m* Eze 26:16
and they shall tremble at every *m* Eze 32:10
of the world in a *m* of time Lk 4:5
In a *m*, in the twinkling of an 1Cor 15:52
affliction, which is but for a *m* 2Cor 4:17

**MONEY**
or bought with *m* of any stranger, Gen 17:12
and he that is bought with thy *m* Gen 17:13
all that were bought with his *m* Gen 17:23
bought with *m* of the stranger, Gen 17:27
for as much *m* as it is worth he Gen 23:9
I will give thee *m* for the field Gen 23:13
current *m* with the merchant Gen 23:16
and hath quite devoured also our *m* Gen 31:15
for an hundred pieces of *m* Gen 33:19
every man's *m* into his sack Gen 42:25
in the inn, he espied his *m* Gen 42:27
his brethren, My *m* is restored Gen 42:28
man's bundle of *m* was in his sack Gen 42:35
their father saw the bundles of *m* Gen 42:35
take double *m* in your hand Gen 43:12
the *m* that was brought again in Gen 43:12
they took double *m* in their hand Gen 43:15
Because of the *m* that was Gen 43:18
every man's *m* was in the mouth of Gen 43:21
of his sack, our *m* in full weight Gen 43:21
other *m* have we brought down in Gen 43:22
tell who put our *m* in our sacks Gen 43:22
I had your *m* Gen 43:23
put every man's *m* in his sack's Gen 44:1
of the youngest, and his corn *m* Gen 44:2
Behold, the *m*, which we found in Gen 44:8
Joseph gathered up all the *m* that Gen 47:14
Joseph brought the *m* into Gen 47:14
when *m* failed in the land of Gen 47:15
for the *m* faileth Gen 47:15
you for your cattle, if *m* fail Gen 47:16
my lord, how that our *m* is spent Gen 47:18
servant that is bought for *m* Ex 12:44
shall she go out free without *m* Ex 21:11
for he is his *m* Ex 21:21
there be laid on him a sum of *m* Ex 21:30
give *m* unto the owner of them Ex 21:34
live ox, and divide the *m* of it Ex 21:35
his neighbour *m* or stuff to keep Ex 22:7
he shall pay *m* according to the Ex 22:17
If thou lend *m* to any of my Ex 22:25
*m* of the children of Israel Ex 30:16
priest buy any soul with his *m* Lev 22:11
not give him thy *m* upon usury Lev 25:37
of the *m* that he was bought for Lev 25:51
the *m* of thy estimation unto it Lev 27:15
shall reckon unto him the *m* Lev 27:18
the *m* of thy estimation unto it Lev 27:19
And thou shalt give the *m*, Num 3:48
*m* of them that were over and above Num 3:49
children of Israel took he the *m* Num 3:50
Moses gave the *m* of them that Num 3:51
for the *m* of five shekels, after Num 18:16
Ye shall buy meat of them for *m* Deut 2:6
also buy water of them for *m* Deut 2:6
Thou shalt sell me meat for *m* Deut 2:28
and give me water for *m*, that I Deut 2:28
Then shalt thou turn it into *m* Deut 14:25
bind up the *m* in thine hand, and Deut 14:25
thou shalt bestow that *m* for Deut 14:26
shalt not sell her at all for *m* Deut 21:14
usury of *m*, usury of victuals, Deut 23:19
they took no gain of *m* Judg 5:19
her, and brought *m* in their hand Judg 16:18
he restored the *m* unto his mother Judg 17:4
give thee the worth of it in *m* 1Kin 21:2
him, Give me thy vineyard for *m* 1Kin 21:6
he refused to give thee for *m* 1Kin 21:15
Is it a time to receive *m* 2Kin 5:26
All the *m* of the dedicated things 2Kin 12:4
even the *m* of every one that 2Kin 12:4
the *m* that every man is set at, 2Kin 12:4
all the *m* that cometh into any 2Kin 12:4
no more *m* of your acquaintance 2Kin 12:7
receive no more *m* of the people 2Kin 12:8
the door put therein all the *m* 2Kin 12:9
there was much *m* in the chest 2Kin 12:10
told the *m* that was found in the 2Kin 12:10
And they gave the *m*, being told, 2Kin 12:11
of the *m* that was brought into 2Kin 12:13
the *m* to be bestowed on workmen 2Kin 12:15
The trespass *m* and sin *m* was 2Kin 12:16
Menahem exacted the *m* of Israel 2Kin 15:20
*m* that was delivered into their 2Kin 22:7
the *m* that was found in the house 2Kin 22:9
he taxed the land to give the *m* 2Kin 23:35
gather of all Israel *m* to repair 2Chr 24:5
they saw that there was much *m* 2Chr 24:11
day, and gathered *m* in abundance 2Chr 24:11
the rest of the *m* before the king 2Chr 24:14
they delivered the *m* that was 2Chr 34:9
when they brought out the *m* that 2Chr 34:14
*m* that was found in the house of 2Chr 34:17
They gave *m* also unto the masons, Ezr 3:7
buy speedily with this *m* bullocks Ezr 7:17
We have borrowed *m* for the king's Neh 5:4
servants, might exact of them *m* Neh 5:10
also the hundredth part of the *m* Neh 5:11
of the sum of the *m* that Haman Est 4:7
the fruits thereof without *m* Job 31:39
man also gave him a piece of *m* Job 42:11
putteth not out his *m* to usury Ps 15:5
He hath taken a bag of *m* with him Prov 7:20
is a defence, and *m* is a defence Eccl 7:12
but *m* answereth all things Eccl 10:19
bought me no sweet cane with *m* Is 43:24
and ye shall be redeemed without *m* Is 52:3
the waters, and he that hath no *m* Is 55:1
come, buy wine and milk without *m* Is 55:1
Wherefore do ye spend *m* for that Is 55:2
in Anathoth, and weighed him the *m* Jer 32:9
weighed him the *m* in the balances Jer 32:10
GOD, Buy thee the field for *m* Jer 32:25
Men shall buy fields for *m* Jer 32:44
We have drunken our water for *m* Lam 5:4
the prophets thereof divine for *m* Mic 3:11
received tribute *m* came to Peter Mt 17:24
thou shalt find a piece of *m* Mt 17:27
Shew me the tribute *m* Mt 22:19
in the earth, and hid his lord's *m* Mt 25:18
have put my *m* to the exchangers Mt 25:27
they gave large *m* unto the Mt 28:12
So they took the *m*, and did as Mt 28:15
no bread, no *m* in their purse Mk 6:8
people cast *m* into the treasury Mk 12:41
glad, and promised to give him *m* Mk 14:11
scrip, neither bread, neither *m* Lk 9:3
him, to whom he had given the *m* Lk 19:15
not thou my *m* into the bank Lk 19:23
glad, and covenanted to give him *m* Lk 22:5

and the changers of *m* sitting Jn 2:14
and poured out the changers' *m* Jn 2:15
land, sold it, and brought the *m* Acts 4:37
Abraham bought for a sum of *m* of Acts 7:16
was given, he offered them *m* Acts 8:18
Thy *m* perish with thee, because Acts 8:20
of God may be purchased with *m* Acts 8:20
He hoped also that *m* should have Acts 24:26
For the love of *m* is the root of 1Ti 6:10

**MONEYCHANGERS**
and overthrew the tables of the *m* Mt 21:12
and overthrew the tables of the *m* Mk 11:15

**MONSTERS**
Even the sea *m* draw out the Lam 4:3

**MONTH**
of Noah's life, in the second *m* Gen 7:11
the seventeenth day of the *m* Gen 7:11
the ark rested in the seventh *m* Gen 8:4
on the seventeenth day of the *m* Gen 8:4
continually until the tenth *m* Gen 8:5
in the tenth *m*, on the first day Gen 8:5
on the first day of the *m* Gen 8:5
and first year, in the first *m* Gen 8:13
the first day of the *m* Gen 8:13
And in the second *m*, on the seven Gen 8:14
seven and twentieth day of the *m* Gen 8:14
abode with him the space of a *m* Gen 29:14
This *m* shall be unto you the Ex 12:2
be the first *m* of the year to you Ex 12:2
In the tenth day of this *m* they Ex 12:3
the fourteenth day of the same *m* Ex 12:6
In the first *m*, on the fourteenth Ex 12:18
fourteenth day of the *m* at even Ex 12:18
and twentieth day of the *m* at even Ex 12:18
day came ye out in the *m* Abib Ex 13:4
shalt keep this service in this *m* Ex 13:5
*m* after their departing out of Ex 16:1
In the third *m*, when the children Ex 19:1
the time appointed of the *m* Abib Ex 23:15
thee, in the time of the *m* Abib Ex 34:18
for in the *m* Abib thou camest out Ex 34:18
the first *m* shalt thou set up the Ex 40:2
in the first *m* in the second year Ex 40:17
on the first day of the *m* Ex 40:17
that in the seventh *m*, on the Lev 16:29
*m*, on the tenth day of the *m* Lev 16:29
*m* at even is the LORD's passover Lev 23:5
same *m* is the feast of unleavened Lev 23:6
Israel, saying, In the seventh *m* Lev 23:24
in the first day of the *m* Lev 23:24
seventh *m* there shall be a day of Lev 23:27
in the ninth day of the *m* at even Lev 23:32
seventh *m* shall be the feast of Lev 23:34
fifteenth day of the seventh *m* Lev 23:39
celebrate it in the seventh *m* Lev 23:41
on the tenth day of the seventh *m* Lev 25:9
if it be from a *m* old even unto Lev 27:6
on the first day of the second *m* Num 1:1
on the first day of the second *m* Num 1:18
every male from a *m* old and upward. Num 3:15
of all the males, from a *m* old Num 3:22
of all the males, from a *m* old Num 3:28
of all the males, from a *m* old Num 3:34
all the males from a *m* old Num 3:39
children of Israel from a *m* old Num 3:40
the number of names, from a *m* old Num 3:43
in the first *m* of the second year Num 9:1
In the fourteenth day of this *m* Num 9:3
*m* at even in the wilderness of Num 9:5
*m* at even they shall keep it Num 9:11
whether it were two days, or a *m* Num 9:22
the twentieth day of the second *m* Num 10:11
But even a whole *m*, until it come Num 11:20
that they may eat a whole *m* Num 11:21
from a *m* old shalt thou redeem Num 18:16
the desert of Zin in the first *m* Num 20:1
thousand, all males from a *m* old Num 26:62
*m* throughout the months of the Num 28:14
*m* is the passover of the LORD Num 28:16
day of this *m* is the feast Num 28:17
And in the seventh *m*, on the first Num 29:1
*m*, on the first day of the *m* Num 29:1
the burnt offering of the *m* Num 29:6
seventh *m* an holy convocation Num 29:7
seventh *m* ye shall have an holy Num 29:12
from Rameses in the first *m* Num 33:3
the fifteenth day of the first *m* Num 33:3
in the first day of the fifth *m* Num 33:38
fortieth year, in the eleventh *m* Deut 1:3
*m*, on the first day of the *m* Deut 1:3
Observe the *m* of Abib, and keep Deut 16:1
for in the *m* of Abib the LORD thy Deut 16:1
her father and her mother a full *m* Deut 21:13
on the tenth day of the first *m* Josh 4:19
of the *m* at even in the plains of Josh 5:10
which was the second day of the *m* 1Sa 20:27
no meat the second day of the *m* 1Sa 20:34
each man his *m* in a year made 1Kin 4:7
table, every man in his *m* 1Kin 4:27
ten thousand a *m* by courses 1Kin 5:14
a *m* they were in Lebanon, and two 1Kin 5:14
reign over Israel, in the *m* Zif 1Kin 6:1
*m* Zif, which is the second *m* 1Kin 6:1
of the LORD laid, in the *m* Zif 1Kin 6:37
the eleventh year, in the *m* Bul 1Kin 6:38
which is the eighth *m* 1Kin 6:38
at the feast in the *m* Ethanim 1Kin 8:2
which is the seventh *m* 1Kin 8:2
ordained a feast in the eighth *m* 1Kin 12:32
on the fifteenth day of the *m* 1Kin 12:32
the fifteenth day of the eighth *m* 1Kin 12:33
even in the *m* which he had 1Kin 12:33
and he reigned a full *m* in Samaria 2Kin 15:13
year of his reign, in the tenth *m* 2Kin 25:1
in the tenth day of the *m* 2Kin 25:1
*m* the famine prevailed in the 2Kin 25:3
And in the fifth *m*, on the seventh 2Kin 25:8
on the seventh day of the *m* 2Kin 25:8
it came to pass in the seventh *m* 2Kin 25:25
king of Judah, in the twelfth *m* 2Kin 25:27
seven and twentieth day of the *m* 2Kin 25:27
went over Jordan in the first *m* 1Chr 12:15
went out *m* by *m* throughout 1Chr 27:1
first *m* was Jashobeam the son of 1Chr 27:2
of the host for the first *m* 1Chr 27:3
the second *m* was Dodai an Ahohite 1Chr 27:4
of the host for the third *m* was 1Chr 27:5
fourth captain for the fourth *m* 1Chr 27:7
fifth *m* was Shamhuth the Izrahite 1Chr 27:8
*m* was Ira the son of Ikkesh the 1Chr 27:9
seventh *m* was Helez the Pelonite 1Chr 27:10
*m* was Sibbecai the Hushathite 1Chr 27:11
*m* was Abiezer the Anetothite 1Chr 27:12
*m* was Maharai the Netophathite 1Chr 27:13
captain for the eleventh *m* was 1Chr 27:14
*m* was Heldai the Netophathite 1Chr 27:15
in the second day of the second *m* 2Chr 3:2
feast which was in the seventh *m* 2Chr 5:3
*m* he sent the people away into 2Chr 7:10
at Jerusalem in the third *m* 2Chr 15:10
year of his reign, in the first *m* 2Chr 29:3
day of the first *m* to sanctify 2Chr 29:17
on the eighth day of the *m* came 2Chr 29:17
of the first *m* they made an end 2Chr 29:17
keep the passover in the second *m* 2Chr 30:2
unleavened bread in the second *m* 2Chr 30:13
fourteenth day of the second *m* 2Chr 30:15
In the third *m* they began to lay 2Chr 31:7
and finished them in the seventh *m* 2Chr 31:7
the fourteenth day of the first *m* 2Chr 35:1
And when the seventh *m* was come Ezr 3:1
*m* began they to offer burnt Ezr 3:6
God at Jerusalem, in the second *m* Ezr 3:8
on the third day of the *m* Adar Ezr 6:15
the fourteenth day of the first *m* Ezr 6:19
came to Jerusalem in the fifth *m* Ezr 7:8
*m* began he to go up from Babylon Ezr 7:9
the fifth *m* came he to Jerusalem Ezr 7:9
on the twelfth day of the first *m* Ezr 8:31
It was the ninth *m*, on the Ezr 10:9
on the twentieth day of the *m* Ezr 10:9
the tenth *m* to examine the matter Ezr 10:16
by the first day of the first *m* Ezr 10:17
it came to pass in the *m* Chisleu Neh 1:1
And it came to pass in the *m* Nisan Neh 2:1
twenty and fifth day of the *m* Elul Neh 6:15
and when the seventh *m* came Neh 7:73
the first day of the seventh *m* Neh 8:2
in the feast of the seventh *m* Neh 8:14
fourth day of this *m* the children Neh 9:1
his house royal in the tenth *m* Est 2:16
which is the *m* Tebeth Est 2:16
In the first *m*, that is Est 3:7
the *m* Nisan, in the twelfth year Est 3:7
*m* to *m*, to the twelfth *m* Est 3:7
that is, the *m* Adar Est 3:7
the thirteenth day of the first *m* Est 3:12
thirteenth day of the twelfth *m* Est 3:13
which is the *m* Adar Est 3:13
at that time in the third *m* Est 8:9
the *m* Sivan, on the three and Est 8:9
thirteenth day of the twelfth *m* Est 8:12
which is the *m* Adar Est 8:12
Now in the twelfth *m*, that is, Est 9:1
the *m* Adar, on the thirteenth day Est 9:1
fourteenth day also of the *m* Adar Est 9:15
the thirteenth day of the *m* Adar Est 9:17
of the *m* Adar a day of gladness Est 9:19
the fourteenth day of the *m* Adar Est 9:21
the *m* which was turned unto them Est 9:22
Jerusalem captive in the fifth *m* Jer 1:3
in her *m* they shall find her Jer 2:24
fourth year, and in the fifth *m* Jer 28:1
the same year in the seventh *m* Jer 28:17
king of Judah, in the ninth *m* Jer 36:9
in the winterhouse in the ninth *m* Jer 36:22
king of Judah, in the tenth *m* Jer 39:1
year of Zedekiah, in the fourth *m* Jer 39:2
the ninth day of the *m* Jer 39:2
it came to pass in the seventh *m* Jer 41:1
year of his reign, in the tenth *m* Jer 52:4
*m*, in the tenth day of the *m* Jer 52:4
And in the fourth *m*, in the ninth Jer 52:6
*m*, in the ninth day of the *m* Jer 52:6
Now in the fifth *m*, in the tenth Jer 52:12
*m*, in the tenth day of the *m* Jer 52:12
king of Judah, in the twelfth *m* Jer 52:31
five and twentieth day of the *m* Jer 52:31
thirtieth year, in the fourth *m* Eze 1:1
in the fifth day of the *m* Eze 1:1
In the fifth day of the *m* Eze 1:2
in the sixth year, in the sixth *m* Eze 8:1
in the fifth day of the *m* Eze 8:1
the seventh year, in the fifth *m* Eze 20:1
the tenth day of the *m* Eze 20:1
in the ninth year, in the tenth *m* Eze 24:1
in the tenth day of the *m* Eze 24:1
year, in the first day of the *m* Eze 26:1
In the tenth year, in the tenth *m* Eze 29:1
in the twelfth day of the *m* Eze 29:1
and twentieth year, in the first *m* Eze 29:17
in the first day of the *m* Eze 29:17
the eleventh year, in the first *m* Eze 30:20
in the seventh day of the *m* Eze 30:20
the eleventh year, in the third *m* Eze 31:1
in the first day of the *m* Eze 31:1
twelfth year, in the twelfth *m* Eze 32:1
in the first day of the *m* Eze 32:1
in the fifteenth day of the *m* Eze 32:17
of our captivity, in the tenth *m* Eze 33:21
in the fifth day of the *m* Eze 33:21
year, in the tenth day of the *m* Eze 40:1
In the first *m*, in the first day Eze 45:18
in the first day of the *m* Eze 45:18
the *m* for every one that erreth Eze 45:20
In the first *m*, in the fourteenth Eze 45:21
in the fourteenth day of the *m* Eze 45:21
In the seventh *m*, in the Eze 45:25
in the fifteenth day of the *m* Eze 45:25
and twentieth day of the first *m* Dan 10:4
now shall a *m* devour them with Hos 5:7
and the latter rain in the first *m* Joel 2:23
Darius the king, in the sixth *m* Hag 1:1
*m*, in the first day of the *m* Hag 1:1
and twentieth day of the sixth *m* Hag 1:15
In the seventh *m*, in the one and Hag 2:1
the one and twentieth day of the *m* Hag 2:1
and twentieth day of the ninth *m* Hag 2:10
and twentieth day of the ninth *m* Hag 2:18
four and twentieth day of the *m* Hag 2:20
In the eighth *m*, in the second Zec 1:1
twentieth day of the eleventh *m* Zec 1:7
which is the *m* Sebat Zec 1:7
in the fourth day of the ninth *m* Zec 7:1
Should I weep in the fifth *m* Zec 7:3
mourned in the fifth and seventh *m* Zec 7:5
The fast of the fourth *m*, and the Zec 8:19
shepherds also I cut off in one *m* Zec 11:8
in the sixth *m* the angel Gabriel Lk 1:26
and this is the sixth *m* with her Lk 1:36
for an hour, and a day, and a *m* Rev 9:15
and yielded her fruit every *m* Rev 22:2

**MONTHLY**
the *m* prognosticators, stand up, Is 47:13

**MONTHS**
came to pass about three *m* after Gen 38:24
goodly child, she hid him three *m* Ex 2:2
be unto you the beginning of *m* Ex 12:2
and in the beginnings of your *m* Num 10:10
in the beginnings of your *m* ye Num 28:11
throughout the *m* of the year Num 28:14
let me alone two *m*, that I may go Judg 11:37
And he sent her away for two *m* Judg 11:38
came to pass at the end of two *m* Judg 11:39
and was there four whole *m* Judg 19:2
abode in the rock Rimmon four *m* Judg 20:47
of the Philistines seven *m* 1Sa 6:1
was a full year and four *m* 1Sa 27:7
of Judah was seven years and six *m* 2Sa 2:11
over Judah seven years and six *m* 2Sa 5:5
of Obed-edom the Gittite three *m* 2Sa 6:11
to Jerusalem at the end of nine *m* 2Sa 24:8
flee three *m* before thine enemies 2Sa 24:13
were in Lebanon, and two *m* at home 1Kin 5:14
(For six *m* did Joab remain there 1Kin 11:16
over Israel in Samaria six *m* 2Kin 15:8
he reigned three *m* in Jerusalem 2Kin 23:31
he reigned in Jerusalem three *m* 2Kin 24:8
he reigned seven years and six *m* 1Chr 3:4
of Obed-edom in his house three *m* 1Chr 13:14
or three *m* to be destroyed before 1Chr 21:12
throughout all the *m* of the year 1Chr 27:1
he reigned three *m* in Jerusalem 2Chr 36:2
to reign, and he reigned three *m* 2Chr 36:9
after that she had been twelve *m* Est 2:12
six *m* with oil of myrrh, and six Est 2:12
six *m* with sweet odours, and with Est 2:12
not come into the number of the *m* Job 3:6
am I made to possess *m* of vanity Job 7:3
the number of his *m* are with thee Job 14:5
when the number of his *m* is cut Job 21:21
Oh that I were as in *m* past Job 29:2
number the *m* that they fulfil Job 39:2
seven *m* shall the house of Israel Eze 39:12
end of seven *m* shall they search Eze 39:14
new fruit according to his *m* Eze 47:12
At the end of twelve *m* he walked Dan 4:29
were yet three *m* to the harvest Amos 4:7
conceived, and hid herself five *m* Lk 1:24
Mary abode with her about three *m* Lk 1:56
was shut up three years and six *m* Lk 4:25
Say not ye, There are yet four *m* Jn 4:35
up in his father's house three *m* Acts 7:20
continued there a year and six *m* Acts 18:11
boldly for the space of three *m* Acts 19:8
And there abode three *m* Acts 20:3
after three *m* we departed in a Acts 28:11
Ye observe days, and *m*, and times, Gal 4:10
was hid three *m* of his parents, Heb 11:23
the space of three years and six *m* Jas 5:17
they should be tormented five *m* Rev 9:5
power was to hurt men five *m* Rev 9:10
tread under foot forty and two *m* Rev 11:2
him to continue forty and two *m* Rev 13:5

**MONUMENTS**
the graves, and lodge in the *m* Is 65:4

**MOON**
and, behold, the sun and the *m* Gen 37:9
when thou seest the sun, and the *m* Deut 4:19

them, either the sun, or *m* ... Deut 17:3
things put forth by the *m* ... Deut 33:14
and thou, *M*, in the valley of ... Josh 10:12
the *m* stayed, until the people ... Josh 10:13
Behold, to morrow is the new *m* ... 1Sa 20:5
to David, To morrow is the new *m* ... 1Sa 20:18
and when the new *m* was come ... 1Sa 20:24
it is neither new *m*, nor sabbath ... 2Kin 4:23
Baal, to the sun, and to the *m* ... 2Kin 23:5
Behold even to the *m*, and it ... Job 25:5
or the *m* walking in brightness ... Job 31:26
the work of thy fingers, the *m* ... Ps 8:3
sun and *m* endure, throughout all ... Ps 72:5
peace so long as the *m* endureth ... Ps 72:7
Blow up the trumpet in the new *m* ... Ps 81:3
be established for ever as the *m* ... Ps 89:37
He appointed the *m* for seasons ... Ps 104:19
thee by day, nor the *m* by night ... Ps 121:6
The *m* and stars to rule by night ... Ps 136:9
Praise ye him, sun and *m* ... Ps 148:3
the sun, or the light, or the *m* ... Eccl 12:2
as the morning, fair as the *m* ... Song 6:10
and their round tires like the *m* ... Is 3:18
the *m* shall not cause her light ... Is 13:10
Then the *m* shall be confounded, ... Is 24:23
Moreover the light of the *m* shall ... Is 30:26
shall the *m* give light unto thee ... Is 60:19
shall thy *m* withdraw itself ... Is 60:20
that from one new *m* to another ... Is 66:23
them before the sun, and the *m* ... Jer 8:2
day, and the ordinances of the *m* ... Jer 31:35
the *m* shall not give her light ... Eze 32:7
of the new *m* it shall be opened ... Eze 46:1
in the day of the new *m* it shall ... Eze 46:6
the *m* shall be dark, and the stars ... Joel 2:10
the *m* into blood, before the ... Joel 2:31
the *m* shall be darkened, and the ... Joel 3:15
When will the new *m* be gone ... Amos 8:5
*m* stood still in their habitation ... Hab 3:11
the *m* shall not give her light, ... Mt 24:29
the *m* shall not give her light, ... Mk 13:24
be signs in the sun, and in the *m* ... Lk 21:25
the *m* into blood, before that ... Acts 2:20
sun, and another glory of the *m* ... 1Cor 15:41
of an holyday, or of the new *m* ... Col 2:16
of hair, and the *m* became as blood ... Rev 6:12
and the third part of the *m* ... Rev 8:12
the *m* under her feet, and upon her ... Rev 12:1
need of the sun, neither of the *m* ... Rev 21:23

**MOONS**
in the sabbaths, in the new *m* ... 1Chr 23:31
on the sabbaths, and on the new *m* ... 2Chr 2:4
on the sabbaths, and on the new *m* ... 2Chr 8:13
the sabbaths, and for the new *m* ... 2Chr 31:3
burnt offering, both of the new *m* ... Ezr 3:5
of the sabbaths, of the new *m* ... Neh 10:33
the new *m* and sabbaths, the ... Is 1:13
Your new *m* and your appointed ... Is 1:14
in the feasts, and in the new *m* ... Eze 45:17
in the sabbaths and in the new *m* ... Eze 46:3
cease, her feast days, her new *m* ... Hos 2:11

**MORASTHITE** (*mo'-ras-thite*) *Family name of Micah the prophet.*
Micah the *M* prophesied in the ... Jer 26:18
Micah the *M* in the days of Jotham ... Mic 1:1

**MORDECAI** (*mor'-de-cahee*) See MORDECAI'S.
*1. A clan leader with Zerubbabel.*
Nehemiah, Seraiah, Reelaiah, *M* ... Ezr 2:2
Azariah, Raamiah, Nahamani, *M* ... Neh 7:7
*2. Cousin of Esther.*
a certain Jew, whose name was *M* ... Est 2:5
whom *M*, when her father and mother ... Est 2:7
for *M* had charged her that she ... Est 2:10
*M* walked every day before the ... Est 2:11
of Abihail the uncle of *M* ... Est 2:15
then *M* sat in the king's gate ... Est 2:19
as *M* had charged her ... Est 2:20
Esther did the commandment of *M* ... Est 2:20
while *M* sat in the king's gate, ... Est 2:21
And the thing was known to *M* ... Est 2:22
But *M* bowed not, nor did him ... Est 3:2
in the king's gate, said unto *M* ... Est 3:3
when Haman saw that *M* bowed not ... Est 3:5
scorn to lay hands on *M* alone ... Est 3:6
had shewed him the people of *M* ... Est 3:6
Ahasuerus, even the people of *M* ... Est 3:6
When *M* perceived all that was ... Est 4:1
*M* rent his clothes, and put on ... Est 4:1
and she sent raiment to clothe *M* ... Est 4:4
and gave him a commandment to *M* ... Est 4:5
So Hatach went forth to *M* unto ... Est 4:6
*M* told him of all that had ... Est 4:7
and told Esther the words of *M* ... Est 4:9
and gave him commandment unto *M* ... Est 4:10
they told to *M* Esther's words ... Est 4:12
Then *M* commanded to answer Esther .. Est 4:13
bade them return *M* this answer ... Est 4:15
So *M* went his way, and did ... Est 4:17
Haman saw *M* in the king's gate ... Est 5:9
was full of indignation against *M* ... Est 5:9
so long as I see *M* the Jew ... Est 5:13
king that *M* may be hanged thereon ... Est 5:14
that *M* had told of Bigthana and ... Est 6:2
hath been done to *M* for this ... Est 6:3
hang *M* on the gallows that he had ... Est 6:4
said, and do even so to *M* the Jew ... Est 6:10
and the horse, and arrayed *M* ... Est 6:11
*M* came again to the king's gate ... Est 6:12
If *M* be of the seed of the Jews, ... Est 6:13
high, which Haman had made for *M* ... Est 7:9
that he had prepared for *M* ... Est 7:10
And *M* came before the king ... Est 8:1
from Haman, and gave it unto *M* ... Est 8:2
Esther set *M* over the house of ... Est 8:2
to *M* the Jew, Behold, I have ... Est 8:7
that *M* commanded unto the Jews ... Est 8:9
*M* went out from the presence of ... Est 8:15
the fear of *M* fell upon them ... Est 9:3
For *M* was great in the king's ... Est 9:4
for this man *M* waxed greater and ... Est 9:4
*M* wrote these things, and sent ... Est 9:20
as *M* had written unto them ... Est 9:23
*M* the Jew, wrote with all ... Est 9:29
appointed, according as *M* the Jew ... Est 9:31
declaration of the greatness of *M* ... Est 10:2
For *M* the Jew was next unto king ... Est 10:3

**MORDECAI'S** (*mor'-de-cahees*) *Refers to Mordecai 2.*
the king thereof in *M* name ... Est 2:22
to see whether *M* matters would ... Est 3:4

**MORE** See PREFACE.

**MOREH** (*mo'-reh*)
*1. A place in Ephraim.*
of Sichem, unto the plain of *M* ... Gen 12:6
Gilgal, beside the plains of *M* ... Deut 11:30
*2. A place in Issachar.*
side of them, by the hill of *M* ... Judg 7:1

**MOREOVER**
She said *m* unto him, We have both .. Gen 24:25
And say ye *m*, Behold, thy servant ... Gen 32:20
*M* he kissed all his brethren, and ... Gen 45:15
They said *m* unto Pharaoh, For to ... Gen 47:4
*M* I have given to thee one ... Gen 48:22
*M* he said, I am the God of thy ... Ex 3:6
God said *m* unto Moses, Thus shalt ... Ex 3:15
*M* the man Moses was very great in ... Ex 11:3
*M* thou shalt provide out of all ... Ex 18:21
*M* thou shalt make the tabernacle ... Ex 26:1
*M* the LORD spake unto Moses, ... Ex 30:22
*M* the soul that shall touch any ... Lev 7:21
*M* ye shall eat no manner of blood ... Lev 7:26
*M* he that goeth into the house ... Lev 14:46
*M* thou shalt not lie carnally ... Lev 18:20
*M* of the children of the ... Lev 25:45
*m* we saw the children of Anak ... Num 13:28
*M* thou hast not brought us into a ... Num 16:14
*M* it shall come to pass, that I ... Num 33:56
*M* ye shall take no satisfaction ... Num 35:31
*m* we have seen the sons of the ... Deut 1:28
*M* your little ones, which ye said ... Deut 1:39
*M* the LORD thy God will send the ... Deut 7:20
*M* all these curses shall come ... Deut 28:45
*M* he will bring upon thee all the ... Deut 28:60
*M* the children of Ammon passed ... Judg 10:9
*M* Ruth the Moabitess, the wife of ... Ruth 4:10
*M* his mother made him a little ... 1Sa 2:19
*M* as for me, God forbid that I ... 1Sa 12:23
*M* the Hebrews that were with the ... 1Sa 14:21
David said *m*, The LORD that ... 1Sa 17:37
And David sware *m*, and said, Thy ... 1Sa 20:3
*M*, my father, see, yea, see the ... 1Sa 24:11
*M* the LORD will also deliver ... 1Sa 28:19
*M* I will appoint a place for my ... 2Sa 7:10
I would *m* have given unto thee ... 2Sa 12:8
Absalom said *m*, Oh that I were ... 2Sa 15:4
*M* Ahithophel said unto Absalom, ... 2Sa 17:1
*M*, if he be gotten into a city, ... 2Sa 17:13
*M* the Philistines had yet war ... 2Sa 21:15
*m* the king's servants came to ... 1Kin 1:47
*M* thou knowest also what Joab the ... 1Kin 2:5
He said *m*, I have somewhat to say ... 1Kin 2:14
The king said *m* to Shimei ... 1Kin 2:44
*M* concerning a stranger, that is ... 1Kin 8:41
*M* the king made a great throne of ... 1Kin 10:18
*M* the LORD shall raise him up a ... 1Kin 14:14
*M* they reckoned not with the men, .. 2Kin 12:15
*M* Manasseh shed innocent blood ... 2Kin 21:16
*M* the altar that was at Beth-el, ... 2Kin 23:15
*M* the workers with familiar ... 2Kin 23:24
*m* in time past, even when Saul ... 1Chr 11:2
*M* they that were nigh them, even ... 1Chr 12:40
*M* I will subdue all thine enemies ... 1Chr 17:10
*M*, Abishai the son Zeruiah slew ... 1Chr 18:12
*M* there are workmen with thee in ... 1Chr 22:15
*M* four thousand were porters ... 1Chr 23:5
*M* David and the captains of the ... 1Chr 25:1
*M* the sons of Obed-edom were, ... 1Chr 26:4
*M* I will establish his kingdom ... 1Chr 28:7
*M*, because I have set my ... 1Chr 29:3
*M* the brasen altar, that Bezaleel ... 2Chr 1:5
Huram said *m*, Blessed be the LORD ... 2Chr 2:12
*M* he made an altar of brass, ... 2Chr 4:1
*M* the candlesticks with their ... 2Chr 4:20
*M* concerning the stranger, which ... 2Chr 6:32
*M* Solomon hallowed the middle of ... 2Chr 7:7
*M* the king made a great throne of ... 2Chr 9:17
*m* he took away the high places and .. 2Chr 17:6
*M* in Jerusalem did Jehoshaphat ... 2Chr 19:8
*M* he made high places in the ... 2Chr 21:11
*M* the LORD stirred up against ... 2Chr 21:16
*M* Jehoiada the priest delivered ... 2Chr 23:9
*M* Amaziah gathered Judah together .. 2Chr 25:5
*M* Uzziah built towers in ... 2Chr 26:9
*M* Uzziah had an host of fighting ... 2Chr 26:11
*M* he built cities in the ... 2Chr 27:4
*M* he burnt incense in the valley ... 2Chr 28:3
*M* all the vessels, which king ... 2Chr 29:19
*M* Hezekiah the king and the ... 2Chr 29:30
*M* he commanded the people that ... 2Chr 31:4
*M* he provided him cities, and ... 2Chr 32:29
*M* Josiah kept a passover unto the ... 2Chr 35:1
*M* all the chief of the priests, ... 2Chr 36:14
*M* I make a decree what ye shall ... Ezr 6:8
*M* of Israel: of the sons ... Ezr 10:25
*M* I said unto the king, If it ... Neh 2:7
*M* the old gate repaired Jehoiada ... Neh 3:6
*M* the Nethinims dwelt in Ophel, ... Neh 3:26
*M* from the time that I was ... Neh 5:14
*M* there were at my table an ... Neh 5:17
*M* in those days the nobles of ... Neh 6:17
*M* thou leddest them in the day by ... Neh 9:12
*M* thou gavest them kingdoms and ... Neh 9:22
*M* the porters, Akkub, Talmon, and ... Neh 11:19
*M* the Levites: Jeshua ... Neh 12:8
Haman said *m*, Yea, Esther the ... Est 5:12
*M* Job continued his parable, and ... Job 27:1
*M* Job continued his parable, and ... Job 29:1
Elihu spake *m*, and said, ... Job 35:1
*M* the LORD answered Job, and said, ... Job 40:1
*M* by them is thy servant warned ... Ps 19:11
*M* he refused the tabernacle of ... Ps 78:67
*M* he called for a famine upon the ... Ps 105:16
*m* I saw under the sun the place ... Eccl 3:16
*M* the profit of the earth is for ... Eccl 5:9
*M* he hath not seen the sun, nor ... Eccl 6:5
And *m*, because the preacher was ... Eccl 12:9
*M* the LORD saith, Because the ... Is 3:16
*M* the LORD spake again unto Ahaz, ... Is 7:10
*M* the LORD said unto me, Take ... Is 8:1
*M* they that work in fine flax, and ... Is 19:9
*M* the multitude of thy strangers ... Is 29:5
*M* the light of the moon shall be ... Is 30:26
He said *m*, For there shall be ... Is 39:8
*M* the word of the LORD came unto ... Jer 1:11
*M* the word of the LORD came to me ... Jer 2:1
*M* thou shalt say unto them, Thus ... Jer 8:4
*M* I will deliver all the strength ... Jer 20:5
*M* I will take from them the voice ... Jer 25:10
*M* the word of the LORD came unto ... Jer 33:1
*M* the word of the LORD came to ... Jer 33:23
*M* Jeremiah said unto king ... Jer 37:18
*M* he put out Zedekiah's eyes, and ... Jer 39:7
*M* Johanan the son of Kareah, and ... Jer 40:13
*M* Jeremiah said unto all the ... Jer 44:24
*M* I will cause to cease in Moab, ... Jer 48:35
*M* he said unto me, Son of man, ... Eze 3:1
*M* he said unto me, Son of man, ... Eze 3:10
*M* take thou unto thee an iron pan ... Eze 4:3
*M* he said unto me, Son of man, ... Eze 4:16
*M* I will make thee waste, and a ... Eze 5:14
*M* the word of the LORD came unto ... Eze 7:1
*M* the spirit lifted me up, and ... Eze 11:1
*M* the word of the LORD came to me .. Eze 12:17
*M* thou hast taken thy sons and thy ... Eze 16:20
Thou hast *m* multiplied thy ... Eze 16:29
*M* the word of the LORD came unto ... Eze 17:11
*M* take thou up a lamentation for ... Eze 19:1
*M* also I gave them my sabbaths, ... Eze 20:12
*M* the word of the LORD came unto ... Eze 20:45
*M* the word of the LORD came unto ... Eze 22:1
The LORD said *m* unto me ... Eze 23:36
*M* this they have done unto me ... Eze 23:38
*M* the word of the LORD came unto ... Eze 28:11
*M* the word of the LORD came unto ... Eze 35:1
*M* the word of the LORD came unto ... Eze 36:16
*M*, thou son of man, take thee one ... Eze 37:16
*M* I will make a covenant of peace ... Eze 37:26
*M*, when ye shall divide by lot ... Eze 45:1
*M* the prince shall not take of ... Eze 46:18
*M* from the possession of the ... Eze 48:22
*M* the word of the LORD came unto ... Zec 4:8
He said *m*, This is their ... Zec 5:6
*M* when ye fast, be not, as the ... Mt 6:16
*M* if thy brother shall trespass ... Mt 18:15
*m* the dogs came and licked his ... Lk 16:21
*m* also my flesh shall rest in ... Acts 2:26
*M* these six brethren accompanied ... Acts 11:12
*M* ye see and hear, that not alone ... Acts 19:26
*M* the law entered, that the ... Rom 5:20
*M* whom he did predestinate, them ... Rom 8:30
*M* it is required in stewards, ... 1Cor 4:2
*M*, brethren, I would not that ye ... 1Cor 10:1
*M*, brethren, I declare unto you ... 1Cor 15:1
*M* I call God for a record upon my ... 2Cor 1:23
*M*, brethren, we do you to wit of ... 2Cor 8:1
*M* he must have a good report of ... 1Ti 3:7
*M* he sprinkled with blood both ... Heb 9:21
*m* of bonds and imprisonment ... Heb 11:36
*M* I will endeavour that ye may be ... 2Pet 1:15

**MORESHETH** See MORASTHITE.

**MORESHETH-GATH** (*mor'-e-sheth-gath*) See MORASTHITE. *A city in Judah.*
shalt thou give presents to *M* ... Mic 1:14

**MORIAH** (*mo-ri'-ah*) *The Temple Mount.*
and get thee into the land of *M* ... Gen 22:2
the LORD at Jerusalem in mount *M* ... 2Chr 3:1

**MORNING**
and the *m* were the first day ... Gen 1:5
the *m* were the second day ... Gen 1:8
and the *m* were the third day ... Gen 1:13
the *m* were the fourth day ... Gen 1:19
and the *m* were the fifth day ... Gen 1:23
and the *m* were the sixth day ... Gen 1:31
And when the *m* arose, then the ... Gen 19:15
the *m* to the place where he stood ... Gen 19:27

Abimelech rose early in the *m* ... Gen 20:8
And Abraham rose up early in the *m*. Gen 21:14
And Abraham rose up early in the *m*... Gen 22:3
and they rose up in the *m*, and he ... Gen 24:54
And they rose up betimes in the *m* ... Gen 26:31
And Jacob rose up early in the *m* ... Gen 28:18
And it came to pass, that in the *m* ... Gen 29:25
early in the *m* Laban rose up, and ... Gen 31:55
Joseph came in unto them in the *m* ... Gen 40:6
it came to pass in the *m* that his ... Gen 41:8
As soon as the *m* was light ... Gen 44:3
in the *m* he shall devour the prey ... Gen 49:27
Get thee unto Pharaoh in the *m* ... Ex 7:15
Moses, Rise up early in the *m* ... Ex 8:20
Moses, Rise up early in the *m* ... Ex 9:13
and when it was *m*, the east wind ... Ex 10:13
nothing of it remain until the *m* ... Ex 12:10
the *m* ye shall burn with fire ... Ex 12:10
the door of his house until the *m* ... Ex 12:22
that in the *m* watch the LORD ... Ex 14:24
his strength when the *m* appeared ... Ex 14:27
And in the *m*, then ye shall see ... Ex 16:7
in the *m* bread to the full ... Ex 16:8
in the *m* ye shall be filled with ... Ex 16:12
in the *m* the dew lay round about ... Ex 16:13
Let no man leave of it till the *m* ... Ex 16:19
of them left of it until the *m* ... Ex 16:20
And they gathered it every *m* ... Ex 16:21
up for you to be kept until the *m* ... Ex 16:23
And they laid it up till the *m* ... Ex 16:24
Moses from the *m* unto the evening ... Ex 18:13
stand by thee from *m* unto even ... Ex 18:14
to pass on the third day in the *m* ... Ex 19:16
my sacrifice remain until the *m* ... Ex 23:18
LORD, and rose up early in the *m* ... Ex 24:4
from evening to *m* before the LORD ... Ex 27:21
of the bread, remain unto the *m* ... Ex 29:34
lamb thou shalt offer in the *m* ... Ex 29:39
to the meat offering of the *m* ... Ex 29:41
thereon sweet incense every *m* ... Ex 30:7
And be ready in the *m*, and come up ... Ex 34:2
come up in the *m* unto mount Sinai ... Ex 34:2
and Moses rose up early in the *m* ... Ex 34:4
the passover be left unto the *m* ... Ex 34:25
unto him free offerings every *m* ... Ex 36:3
the altar all night unto the *m* ... Lev 6:9
shall burn wood on it every *m* ... Lev 6:12
perpetual, half of it in the *m* ... Lev 6:20
not leave any of it until the *m* ... Lev 7:15
the burnt sacrifice of the *m* ... Lev 9:17
with thee all night until the *m* ... Lev 19:13
the *m* before the LORD continually ... Lev 24:3
shall leave none of it unto the *m* ... Num 9:12
appearance of fire, until the *m* ... Num 9:15
cloud abode from even unto the *m* ... Num 9:21
the cloud was taken up in the *m* ... Num 9:21
And they rose up early in the *m* ... Num 14:40
And Balaam rose up in the *m* ... Num 22:13
And Balaam rose up in the *m* ... Num 22:21
lamb shalt thou offer in the *m* ... Num 28:4
as the meat offering of the *m* ... Num 28:8
the burnt offering in the *m* ... Num 28:23
remain all night until the *m* ... Deut 16:4
and thou shalt turn in the *m* ... Deut 16:7
In the *m* thou shalt say, Would ... Deut 28:67
shalt say, Would God it were *m* ... Deut 28:67
And Joshua rose early in the *m* ... Josh 3:1
And Joshua rose early in the *m* ... Josh 6:12
In the *m* therefore ye shall be ... Josh 7:14
So Joshua rose up early in the *m* ... Josh 7:16
And Joshua rose up early in the *m* ... Josh 8:10
of the city arose early in the *m* ... Judg 6:28
put to death whilst it is yet *m* ... Judg 6:31
And it shall be, that in the *m* ... Judg 9:33
all the night, saying, In the *m* ... Judg 16:2
when they arose early in the *m* ... Judg 19:5
he arose early in the *m* on the ... Judg 19:8
her all the night until the *m* ... Judg 19:25
And her lord rose up in the *m* ... Judg 19:27
of Israel rose up in the *m* ... Judg 20:19
even from the *m* until now ... Ruth 2:7
night, and it shall be in the *m* ... Ruth 3:13
lie down until the *m* ... Ruth 3:13
she lay at his feet until the *m* ... Ruth 3:14
And they rose up in the *m* early ... 1Sa 1:19
And Samuel lay until the *m* ... 1Sa 3:15
they arose early on the morrow *m* ... 1Sa 5:4
midst of the host in the *m* watch ... 1Sa 11:11
and spoil them until the *m* light ... 1Sa 14:36
rose early to meet Saul in the *m* ... 1Sa 15:12
And the Philistine drew near *m* ... 1Sa 17:16
And David rose up early in the *m* ... 1Sa 17:20
take heed to thyself until the *m* ... 1Sa 19:2
him, and to slay him in the *m* ... 1Sa 19:11
And it came to pass in the *m* ... 1Sa 20:35
*m* light any that pisseth against ... 1Sa 25:22
*m* light any that pisseth against ... 1Sa 25:34
less or more, until the *m* light ... 1Sa 25:36
But it came to pass in the *m* ... 1Sa 25:37
now rise up early in the *m* with ... 1Sa 29:10
soon as ye be up early in the *m* ... 1Sa 29:10
rose up early to depart in the *m* ... 1Sa 29:11
surely then in the *m* the people ... 2Sa 2:27
And it came to pass in the *m* ... 2Sa 11:14
by the *m* light there lacked not ... 2Sa 17:22
he shall be as the light of the *m* ... 2Sa 23:4
riseth, even a *m* without clouds ... 2Sa 23:4
For when David was up in the *m* ... 2Sa 24:11
the *m* even to the time appointed ... 2Sa 24:15
when I rose in the *m* to give my ... 1Kin 3:21
when I had considered it in the *m* ... 1Kin 3:21
him bread and flesh in the *m* ... 1Kin 17:6
of Baal from *m* even until noon ... 1Kin 18:26
And it came to pass in the *m* ... 2Kin 3:20
And they rose up early in the *m* ... 2Kin 3:22
if we tarry till the *m* light ... 2Kin 7:9
in of the gate until the *m* ... 2Kin 10:8
And it came to pass in the *m* ... 2Kin 10:9
altar burn the *m* burnt offering ... 2Kin 16:15
and when they arose early in the *m*.. 2Kin 19:35
thereof every *m* pertained to them ... 1Chr 9:27
the burnt offering continually *m* ... 1Chr 16:40
And to stand every *m* to thank ... 1Chr 23:30
and for the burnt offerings *m* ... 2Chr 2:4
they burn unto the LORD every *m* ... 2Chr 13:11
And they rose early in the *m* ... 2Chr 20:20
offerings, to wit, for the *m* ... 2Chr 31:3
the LORD, even burnt offerings *m* ... Ezr 3:3
of the *m* till the stars appeared ... Neh 4:21
gate from the *m* until midday ... Neh 8:3
them, and rose up early in the *m* ... Job 1:5
are destroyed from *m* to evening ... Job 4:20
thou shouldest visit him every *m* ... Job 7:18
and thou shalt seek me in the *m* ... Job 7:21
forth, thou shalt be as the *m* ... Job 11:17
For the *m* is to them even as the ... Job 24:17
When the *m* stars sang together, ... Job 38:7
commanded the *m* since thy days ... Job 38:12
are like the eyelids of the *m* ... Job 41:18
My voice shalt thou hear in the *m* ... Ps 5:3
in the *m* will I direct my prayer ... Ps 5:3
a night, but joy cometh in the *m* ... Ps 30:5
have dominion over them in the *m* ... Ps 49:14
Evening, and *m*, and at noon, will I ... Ps 55:17
sing aloud of thy mercy in the *m* ... Ps 59:16
makest the outgoings of the *m* ... Ps 65:8
plagued, and chastened every *m* ... Ps 73:14
in the *m* shall my prayer prevent ... Ps 88:13
in the *m* they are like grass ... Ps 90:5
In the *m* it flourisheth, and ... Ps 90:6
forth thy lovingkindness in the *m* ... Ps 92:2
holiness from the womb of the *m* ... Ps 110:3
I prevented the dawning of the *m* ... Ps 119:147
than they that watch for the *m* ... Ps 130:6
than they that watch for the *m* ... Ps 130:6
If I take the wings of the *m* ... Ps 139:9
hear thy lovingkindness in the *m* ... Ps 143:8
take our fill of love until the *m* ... Prov 7:18
loud voice, rising early in the *m* ... Prov 27:14
and thy princes eat in the *m* ... Eccl 10:16
In the *m* sow thy seed, and in the ... Eccl 11:6
she that looketh forth as the *m* ... Song 6:10
them that rise up early in the *m* ... Is 5:11
heaven, O Lucifer, son of the *m* ... Is 14:12
in the *m* shalt thou make thy seed ... Is 17:11
and before the *m* he is not ... Is 17:14
The *m* cometh, and also the night ... Is 21:12
for *m* by *m* shall it pass ... Is 28:19
be thou their arm every *m* ... Is 33:2
and when they arose early in the *m* ... Is 37:36
I reckoned till *m*, that, as a ... Is 38:13
he wakeneth *m* by *m*, he ... Is 50:4
thy light break forth as the *m* ... Is 58:8
They were as fed horses in the *m* ... Jer 5:8
and let him hear the cry in the *m* ... Jer 20:16
Execute judgment in the *m* ... Jer 21:12
They are new every *m* ... Lam 3:23
The *m* is come unto thee, O thou ... Eze 7:7
the *m* is gone forth ... Eze 7:10
in the *m* came the word of the ... Eze 12:8
I spake unto the people in the *m* ... Eze 24:18
I did in the *m* as I was commanded ... Eze 24:18
until he came to me in the *m* ... Eze 33:22
thou shalt prepare it every *m* ... Eze 46:13
a meat offering for it every *m* ... Eze 46:14
every *m* for a continual burnt ... Eze 46:15
king arose very early in the *m* ... Dan 6:19
the *m* which was told is true ... Dan 8:26
going forth is prepared as the *m* ... Hos 6:3
for your goodness is as a *m* cloud ... Hos 6:4
in the *m* it burneth as a flaming ... Hos 7:6
in a *m* shall the king of Israel ... Hos 10:15
they shall be as the *m* cloud ... Hos 13:3
as the *m* spread upon the ... Joel 2:2
and bring your sacrifices every *m* ... Amos 4:4
that maketh the *m* darkness ... Amos 4:13
the shadow of death into the *m* ... Amos 5:8
worm when the *m* rose the next day.. Jonah 4:7
when the *m* is light, they ... Mic 2:1
every *m* doth he bring his ... Zeph 3:5
And in the *m*, It will be foul ... Mt 16:3
the *m* to hire labourers into his ... Mt 20:1
Now in the *m* as he returned into ... Mt 21:18
When the *m* was come, all the ... Mt 27:1
And in the *m*, rising up a great ... Mk 1:35
And in the *m*, as they passed by, ... Mk 11:20
at the cockcrowing, or in the *m* ... Mk 13:35
straightway in the *m* the chief ... Mk 15:1
very early in the *m* the first day ... Mk 16:2
in the *m* to him in the temple ... Lk 21:38
of the week, very early in the *m* ... Lk 24:1
And And early in the *m* he came ... Jn 8:1
early in the *m* he came again into ... Jn 8:2
But when the *m* was now come ... Jn 21:4
into the temple early in the *m* ... Acts 5:21
the prophets, from *m* till evening ... Acts 28:23
And I will give him the *m* star ... Rev 2:28
of David, and the bright and *m* star.... Rev 22:16

**MORROW**
And it came to pass on the *m* ... Gen 19:34
And he said, To *m* ... Ex 8:10
to *m* shall this sign be ... Ex 8:23
and from his people, to *m* ... Ex 8:29
To *m* the LORD shall do this thing ... Ex 9:5
the LORD did that thing on the *m* ... Ex 9:6
to *m* about this time I will cause ... Ex 9:18
to *m* will I bring the locusts ... Ex 10:4
To *m* is the rest of the holy ... Ex 16:23
to *m* I will stand on the top of ... Ex 17:9
And it came to pass on the *m* ... Ex 18:13
and sanctify them to day and to *m* ... Ex 19:10
To *m* is a feast to the LORD ... Ex 32:5
And they rose up early on the *m* ... Ex 32:6
And it came to pass on the *m* ... Ex 32:30
on the *m* also the remainder of it ... Lev 7:16
same day ye offer it, and on the *m* ... Lev 19:6
leave none of it until the *m* ... Lev 22:30
on the *m* after the sabbath the ... Lev 23:11
you from the *m* after the sabbath ... Lev 23:15
Even unto the *m* after the seventh ... Lev 23:16
Sanctify yourselves against to *m* ... Num 11:18
To *m* turn you, and get you into ... Num 14:25
Even to *m* the LORD will shew who ... Num 16:5
in them before the LORD to *m* ... Num 16:7
thou, and they, and Aaron, to *m* ... Num 16:16
But on the *m* all the congregation ... Num 16:41
that on the *m* Moses went into the ... Num 17:8
And it came to pass on the *m* ... Num 22:41
on the *m* after the passover the ... Num 33:3
for to *m* the LORD will do wonders ... Josh 3:5
land on the *m* after the passover ... Josh 5:11
the manna ceased on the *m* after ... Josh 5:12
Sanctify yourselves against to *m* ... Josh 7:13
for to *m* about this time will I ... Josh 11:6
that to *m* he will be wroth with ... Josh 22:18
for he rose up early on the *m* ... Judg 6:38
And it came to pass on the *m* ... Judg 9:42
to *m* get you early on your way, ... Judg 19:9
for to *m* I will deliver them into ... Judg 20:28
And it came to pass on the *m* ... Judg 21:4
of Ashdod arose early on the *m* ... 1Sa 5:3
they arose early on the *m* morning ... 1Sa 5:4
To *m* about this time I will send ... 1Sa 9:16
to *m* I will let thee go, and will ... 1Sa 9:19
the men of Jabesh-gilead, To *m* ... 1Sa 11:9
To *m* we will come out unto you, ... 1Sa 11:10
And it was so on the *m*, that Saul ... 1Sa 11:11
And it came to pass on the *m* ... 1Sa 18:10
night, to *m* thou shalt be slain ... 1Sa 19:11
to *m* is the new moon, and I should ... 1Sa 20:5
my father about to *m* any time ... 1Sa 20:12
to David, To *m* is the new moon ... 1Sa 20:18
And it came to pass on the *m* ... 1Sa 20:27
to *m* shalt thou and thy sons be ... 1Sa 28:19
And it came to pass on the *m* ... 1Sa 31:8
to *m* I will let thee depart ... 2Sa 11:12
in Jerusalem that day, and the *m* ... 2Sa 11:12
of them by to *m* about this time ... 1Kin 19:2
unto thee to *m* about this time ... 1Kin 20:6
day, and we will eat my son to *m* ... 2Kin 6:28
To *m* about this time shall a ... 2Kin 7:1
shall be to *m* about this time in ... 2Kin 7:18
And it came to pass on the *m* ... 2Kin 8:15
me to Jezreel by to *m* this time ... 2Kin 10:6
And it came to pass on the *m* ... 1Chr 10:8
on the *m* after that day, even a ... 1Chr 29:21
To *m* go ye down against them ... 2Chr 20:16
to *m* go out against them ... 2Chr 20:17
on the *m* she returned into the ... Est 2:14
I will do to *m* as the king hath ... Est 5:8
to *m* am I invited unto her also ... Est 5:12
to *m* speak thou unto the king ... Est 5:14
which are in Shushan to do to *m* ... Est 9:13
come again, and to *m* I will give ... Prov 3:28
Boast not thyself of to *m* ... Prov 27:1
for to *m* we shall die ... Is 22:13
to *m* shall be as this day, and ... Is 56:12
And it came to pass on the *m* ... Jer 20:3
gnaw not the bones till the *m* ... Zeph 3:3
to *m* is cast into the oven, shall ... Mt 6:30
therefore no thought for the *m* ... Mt 6:34
for the *m* shall take thought for ... Mt 6:34
And on the *m*, when they were come.. Mk 11:12
on the *m* when he departed, he ... Lk 10:35
to *m* is cast into the oven ... Lk 12:28
and I do cures to day and to *m* ... Lk 13:32
I must walk to day, and to *m* ... Lk 13:33
And it came to pass on the *m* ... Acts 4:5
On the *m*, as they went on their ... Acts 10:9
on the *m* Peter went away with ... Acts 10:23
the *m* after they entered into ... Acts 10:24
them, ready to depart on the *m* ... Acts 20:7
On the *m*, because he would have ... Acts 22:30
he bring him down unto you to *m* ... Acts 23:15
down Paul to *m* into the council ... Acts 23:20
On the *m* they left the horsemen ... Acts 23:32
without any delay on the *m* I sat ... Acts 25:17
To *m*, said he, thou shalt hear ... Acts 25:22
And on the *m*, when Agrippa was ... Acts 25:23
for to *m* we die ... 1Cor 15:32
To day or to *m* we will go into ... Jas 4:13
know not what shall be on the *m* ... Jas 4:14

**MORSEL**
And I will fetch a *m* of bread ... Gen 18:5
thine heart with a *m* of bread ... Judg 19:5
and dip thy *m* in the vinegar ... Ruth 2:14
a *m* of bread, and shall say, Put ... 1Sa 2:36
let me set a *m* of bread before ... 1Sa 28:22

a *m* of bread in thine hand ... 1Kin 17:11
Or have eaten my *m* myself alone ... Job 31:17
Better is a dry *m*, and quietness ... Prov 17:1
The *m* which thou hast eaten shalt ... Prov 23:8
who for one *m* of meat sold his ... Heb 12:16

**MORSELS**
He casteth forth his ice like *m* ... Ps 147:17

**MORTAL**
Shall *m* man be more just than God ... Job 4:17
therefore reign in your *m* body ... Rom 6:12
your *m* bodies by his Spirit that ... Rom 8:11
this *m* must put on immortality ... 1Cor 15:53
and this *m* shall have put on ... 1Cor 15:54
be made manifest in our *m* flesh ... 2Cor 4:11

**MORTALITY**
that *m* might be swallowed up of ... 2Cor 5:4

**MORTALLY**
smite him *m* that he die, and ... Deut 19:11

**MORTAR**
it in mills, or beat it in a *m* ... Num 11:8
in a *m* among wheat with a pestle ... Prov 27:22

**MORTER**
stone, and slime had they for *m* ... Gen 11:3
bitter with hard bondage, in *m* ... Ex 1:14
and he shall take other *m*, and ... Lev 14:42
and all the *m* of the house ... Lev 14:45
shall come upon princes as upon *m* ... Is 41:25
daubed it with untempered *m* ... Eze 13:10
which daub it with untempered *m* ... Eze 13:11
ye have daubed with untempered *m* ... Eze 13:14
have daubed it with untempered *m* ... Eze 13:15
daubed them with untempered *m* ... Eze 22:28
go into clay, and tread the *m* ... Nah 3:14

**MORTGAGED**
We have *m* our lands, vineyards, ... Neh 5:3

**MORTIFY**
Spirit do *m* the deeds of the body ... Rom 8:13
*M* therefore your members which ... Col 3:5

**MOSERA** (*mo-se'-rah*) See MOSEROTH. *Where Aaron was buried.*
of the children of Jaakan to *M* ... Deut 10:6

**MOSERAH** See MOSERA.

**MOSEROTH** (*mo-se'-roth*) See MOSERA. *An Israelite encampment in the wilderness.*
and encamped at *M* ... Num 33:30
And they departed from *M*, and ... Num 33:31

**MOSES** (*mo'-zez*) See PREFACE. SEE ALSO MOSES'. *Led Israel out of Egypt.*
And she called his name *M* ... Ex 2:10
of the bush, and said, *M*, *M* ... Ex 3:4
And God said unto *M*, I AM THAT I ... Ex 3:14
*M* took his wife and his sons, and ... Ex 4:20
And *M* and Aaron went in unto ... Ex 7:10
*M* took the bones of Joseph with ... Ex 13:19
*M* stretched out his hand over the ... Ex 14:21
And the LORD said unto *M*, Stretch ... Ex 14:26
And the people murmured against *M* ... Ex 15:24
*M* went up unto God, and the LORD ... Ex 19:3
So *M* went down unto the people, ... Ex 19:25
And the LORD said unto *M*, Thus ... Ex 20:22
*M* wrote all the words of the LORD ... Ex 24:4
*M* went up into the mount of God ... Ex 24:13
*M* was in the mount forty days and ... Ex 24:18
when the people saw that *M* ... Ex 32:1
*M* said unto Aaron, What did this ... Ex 32:21
And the LORD said unto *M*, Hew thee ... Ex 34:1
And the LORD said unto *M*, Write ... Ex 34:27
when *M* came down from mount Sinai ... Ex 34:29
*M* brought Aaron and his sons, and ... Lev 8:6
as the LORD commanded *M* ... Lev 8:9
LORD spake unto *M* in mount Sinai ... Lev 25:1
And the LORD said unto *M*, Number ... Num 3:40
which *M* sent to spy out the land ... Num 13:16
*M* lifted up his hand, and with his ... Num 20:11
LORD spake unto *M* ... Num 20:12
And the LORD said unto *M*, Take ... Num 27:18
*M* called unto Joshua, and said ... Deut 31:7
So *M* the servant of the LORD died ... Deut 34:5
Now after the death of *M* the ... Josh 1:1
we hearkened unto *M* in all things ... Josh 1:17
be with thee, as he was with *M* ... Josh 1:17
the stones a copy of the law of *M* ... Josh 8:32
there appeared unto them *M* ... Mt 17:3
appeared unto them Elias with *M* ... Mk 9:4
with him two men, which were *M* ... Lk 9:30
In which time *M* was born, and was ... Acts 7:20
face of *M* for the glory of his ... 2Cor 3:7
as also *M* was faithful in all his ... Heb 3:2
By faith *M*, when he was born, was ... Heb 11:23
By faith *M*, when he was come to ... Heb 11:24
was the sight, that *M* said ... Heb 12:21
he disputed about the body of *M* ... Jude 9
the song of *M* the servant of God ... Rev 15:3

**MOSES'**
But *M* hands were heavy ... Ex 17:12
*M* father in law, heard of all ... Ex 18:1
*M* father in law, took Zipporah, ... Ex 18:2
*M* wife, after he had sent her ... Ex 18:2
*M* father in law, came with his ... Ex 18:5
*M* father in law, took a burnt ... Ex 18:12
to eat bread with *M* father in law ... Ex 18:12
when *M* father in law saw all that ... Ex 18:14
*M* father in law said unto him, ... Ex 18:17
*M* anger waxed hot, and he cast the ... Ex 32:19
two tables of testimony in *M* hand ... Ex 34:29
that the skin of *M* face shone ... Ex 34:35
ram of consecration it was *M* part ... Lev 8:29
*M* father in law, We are ... Num 10:29
son of Nun, *M* minister, saying, ... Josh 1:1
*M* father in law, went up out of ... Judg 1:16
and the Pharisees sit in *M* seat ... Mt 23:2
but we are *M* disciples ... Jn 9:28
He that despised *M* law died ... Heb 10:28

**MOST**
was the priest of the *m* high God ... Gen 14:18
be Abram of the *m* high God ... Gen 14:19
And blessed be the *m* high God ... Gen 14:20
the *m* high God, the possessor of ... Gen 14:22
the holy place and the *m* holy ... Ex 26:33
the testimony in the *m* holy place ... Ex 26:34
and it shall be an altar *m* holy ... Ex 29:37
it is *m* holy unto the LORD ... Ex 30:10
them, that they may be *m* holy ... Ex 30:29
it shall be unto you *m* holy ... Ex 30:36
and it shall be an altar *m* holy ... Ex 40:10
it is a thing *m* holy of the ... Lev 2:3
it is a thing *m* holy of the ... Lev 2:10
it is *m* holy, as is the sin ... Lev 6:17
it is *m* holy ... Lev 6:25
it is *m* holy ... Lev 6:29
it is *m* holy ... Lev 7:1
it is *m* holy ... Lev 7:6
for it is *m* holy ... Lev 10:12
holy place, seeing it is *m* holy ... Lev 10:17
it is *m* holy ... Lev 14:13
of his God, both of the *m* holy ... Lev 21:22
for it is *m* holy unto him of the ... Lev 24:9
thing is *m* holy unto the LORD ... Lev 27:28
about the *m* holy things ... Num 4:4
approach unto the *m* holy things ... Num 4:19
be thine of the *m* holy things ... Num 18:9
shall be *m* holy for thee and for ... Num 18:9
In the *m* holy place shalt thou ... Num 18:10
knew the knowledge of the *m* High ... Num 24:16
When the *M* High divided to the ... Deut 32:8
the *m* High uttered his voice ... 2Sa 22:14
Was he not *m* honourable of three ... 2Sa 23:19
oracle, even for the *m* holy place ... 1Kin 6:16
the *m* holy place, and for the ... 1Kin 7:50
to the *m* holy place, even under ... 1Kin 8:6
all the work of the place *m* holy ... 1Chr 6:49
should sanctify the *m* holy things ... 1Chr 23:13
And he made the *m* holy house ... 2Chr 3:8
in the *m* holy house he made two ... 2Chr 3:10
thereof for the *m* holy place ... 2Chr 4:22
into the *m* holy place, even under ... 2Chr 5:7
of the LORD, and the *m* holy things ... 2Chr 31:14
not eat of the *m* holy things ... Ezr 2:63
not eat of the *m* holy things ... Neh 7:65
one of the king's *m* noble princes ... Est 6:9
thou condemn him that is *m* just ... Job 34:17
to the name of the LORD *m* high ... Ps 7:17
praise to thy name, O thou *m* High ... Ps 9:2
hast made him *m* blessed for ever ... Ps 21:6
through the mercy of the *m* High ... Ps 21:7
O *m* mighty, with thy glory and thy ... Ps 45:3
of the tabernacles of the *m* High ... Ps 46:4
For the LORD *m* high is terrible ... Ps 47:2
and pay thy vows unto the *m* High ... Ps 50:14
fight against me, O thou *m* High ... Ps 56:2
I will cry unto God *m* high ... Ps 57:2
is there knowledge in the *m* High ... Ps 73:11
of the right hand of the *m* High ... Ps 77:10
the *m* High in the wilderness ... Ps 78:17
and provoked the *m* high God ... Ps 78:56
of you are children of the *m* High ... Ps 82:6
art the *m* high over all the earth ... Ps 83:18
the *m* High shall abide under the ... Ps 91:1
is my refuge, even the *m* High ... Ps 91:9
praises unto thy name, O *m* High ... Ps 92:1
LORD, art *m* high for evermore ... Ps 92:8
the counsel of the *m* High ... Ps 107:11
*M* men will proclaim every one his ... Prov 20:6
His head is as the *m* fine gold ... Song 5:11
His mouth is *m* sweet ... Song 5:16
which hath a *m* vehement flame ... Song 8:6
I will be like the *m* High ... Is 14:14
*m* upright, dost weigh the path of ... Is 26:7
an only son, *m* bitter lamentation ... Jer 6:26
I am against thee, O thou *m* proud ... Jer 50:31
the *m* proud shall stumble and fall ... Jer 50:32
man before the face of the *m* High ... Lam 3:35
Out of the mouth of the *m* High ... Lam 3:38
how is the *m* fine gold changed ... Lam 4:1
for they are *m* rebellious ... Eze 2:7
and rulers clothed *m* gorgeously ... Eze 23:12
I will lay the land *m* desolate ... Eze 33:28
when I have laid the land *m* ... Eze 33:29
and I will make thee *m* desolate ... Eze 35:3
will I make mount Seir *m* desolate ... Eze 35:7
unto me, This is the *m* holy place ... Eze 41:4
LORD shall eat the *m* holy things ... Eze 42:13
shall they lay the *m* holy things ... Eze 42:13
round about shall be *m* holy ... Eze 43:12
holy things, in the *m* holy place ... Eze 44:13
the sanctuary and the *m* holy place ... Eze 45:3
thing *m* holy by the border of the ... Eze 48:12
he commanded the *m* mighty men ... Dan 3:20
ye servants of the *m* high God ... Dan 3:26
the living may know that the *m* ... Dan 4:17
this is the decree of the *m* High ... Dan 4:24
till thou know that the *m* High ... Dan 4:25
until thou know that the *m* High ... Dan 4:32
unto me, and I blessed the *m* High ... Dan 4:34
O thou king, the *m* high God gave ... Dan 5:18
till he knew that the *m* high God ... Dan 5:21
But the saints of the *m* High ... Dan 7:18
given to the saints of the *m* High ... Dan 7:22
great words against the *m* High ... Dan 7:25
wear out the saints of the *m* High ... Dan 7:25
of the saints of the *m* High ... Dan 7:27
prophecy, and to anoint the *m* Holy ... Dan 9:24
and take the *m* fenced cities ... Dan 11:15
Thus shall he do in the *m* strong ... Dan 11:39
return, but not to the *m* High ... Hos 7:16
they called them to the *m* High ... Hos 11:7
provoked him to anger *m* bitterly ... Hos 12:14
the *m* upright is sharper than a ... Mic 7:4
*m* of his mighty works were done ... Mt 11:20
Jesus, thou Son of the *m* high God ... Mk 5:7
are *m* surely believed among us ... Lk 1:1
in order, *m* excellent Theophilus, ... Lk 1:3
which of them will love him *m* ... Lk 7:42
that he, to whom he forgave *m* ... Lk 7:43
Jesus, thou Son of God *m* high ... Lk 8:28
Howbeit the *m* High dwelleth not ... Acts 7:48
the servants of the *m* high God ... Acts 16:17
Sorrowing *m* of all for the words ... Acts 20:38
the *m* excellent governor Felix ... Acts 23:26
places, *m* noble Felix, with all ... Acts 24:3
that after the *m* straitest sect ... Acts 26:5
I am not mad, *m* noble Festus ... Acts 26:25
be by two, or at the *m* by three ... 1Cor 14:27
we are of all men *m* miserable ... 1Cor 15:19
*M* gladly therefore will I rather ... 2Cor 12:9
Salem, priest of the *m* high God ... Heb 7:1
yourselves on your *m* holy faith ... Jude 20
manner vessels of *m* precious wood ... Rev 18:12
was like unto a stone *m* precious ... Rev 21:11

**MOTE**
why beholdest thou the *m* that is ... Mt 7:3
pull out the *m* out of thine eye ... Mt 7:4
the *m* out of thy brother's eye ... Mt 7:5
why beholdest thou the *m* that is ... Lk 6:41
let me pull out the *m* that is in ... Lk 6:42
see clearly to pull out the *m* ... Lk 6:42

**MOTH**
which are crushed before the *m* ... Job 4:19
as a garment that is *m* eaten ... Job 13:28
He buildeth his house as a *m* ... Job 27:18
beauty to consume away like a *m* ... Ps 39:11
the *m* shall eat them up ... Is 50:9
For the *m* shall eat them up like ... Is 51:8
will I be unto Ephraim as a *m* ... Hos 5:12
treasures upon earth, where *m* ... Mt 6:19
where neither *m* nor rust doth ... Mt 6:20
approacheth, neither *m* corrupteth ... Lk 12:33

**MOTHEATEN**
corrupted, and your garments are *m* ... Jas 5:2

**MOTHER**
a man leave his father and his *m* ... Gen 2:24
she was the *m* of all living ... Gen 3:20
and she shall be a *m* of nations ... Gen 17:16
but not the daughter of my *m* ... Gen 20:12
his *m* took him a wife out of the ... Gen 21:21
and to her *m* precious things ... Gen 24:53
her *m* said, Let the damsel abide ... Gen 24:55
be thou the *m* of thousands of ... Gen 24:60
her into his *m* Sarah's tent ... Gen 24:67
And Jacob said to Rebekah his *m* ... Gen 27:11
his *m* said unto him, Upon me be ... Gen 27:13
fetched, and brought them to his *m* ... Gen 27:14
his *m* made savoury meat, such as ... Gen 27:14
of Rebekah, Jacob's and Esau's *m* ... Gen 28:5
Jacob obeyed his father and his *m* ... Gen 28:7
and brought them unto his *m* Leah ... Gen 30:14
me, and the *m* with the children ... Gen 32:11
Shall I and thy *m* and thy brethren ... Gen 37:10
and he alone is left of his *m* ... Gen 44:20
maid went and called the child's *m* ... Ex 2:8
Honour thy father and thy *m* ... Ex 20:12
that smiteth his father, or his *m* ... Ex 21:15
that curseth his father, or his *m* ... Ex 21:17
father, or the nakedness of thy *m* ... Lev 18:7
she is thy *m* ... Lev 18:7
thy father, or daughter of thy *m* ... Lev 18:9
Ye shall fear every man his *m* ... Lev 19:3
*m* shall be surely put to death ... Lev 20:9
hath cursed his father or his *m* ... Lev 20:9
And if a man take a wife and her *m* ... Lev 20:14
near unto him, that is, for his *m* ... Lev 21:2
for his father, or for his *m* ... Lev 21:11
for his father, or for his *m* ... Num 6:7
whom her *m* bare to Levi in Egypt ... Num 26:59
Honour thy father and thy *m* ... Deut 5:16
If thy brother, the son of thy *m* ... Deut 13:6
her father and her *m* a full month ... Deut 21:13
his father, or the voice of his *m* ... Deut 21:18
his *m* lay hold on him, and bring ... Deut 21:19
father of the damsel, and her *m* ... Deut 22:15
light by his father or his *m* ... Deut 27:16
father, or the daughter of his *m* ... Deut 27:22
he that lieth with his *m* in law ... Deut 27:23
said unto his father and to his *m* ... Deut 33:9
save alive my father, and my *m* ... Josh 2:13
shalt bring thy father, and thy *m* ... Josh 2:18
Rahab, and her father, and her *m* ... Josh 6:23
arose, that I arose a *m* in Israel ... Judg 5:7
The *m* of Sisera looked out at a ... Judg 5:28
brethren, even the sons of my *m* ... Judg 8:19
up, and told his father and his *m* ... Judg 14:2

his *m* said unto him, Is there Judg 14:3
his *m* knew not that it was of the Judg 14:4
down, and his father and his *m* Judg 14:5
father or his *m* what he had done Judg 14:6
and came to his father and *m* Judg 14:9
not told it my father nor my *m* Judg 14:16
And he said unto his *m*, The eleven Judg 17:2
his *m* said, Blessed be thou of Judg 17:2
shekels of silver to his *m* Judg 17:3
his *m* said, I had wholly Judg 17:3
he restored the money unto his *m* Judg 17:4
his *m* took two hundred shekels of Judg 17:4
and Orpah kissed her *m* in law Ruth 1:14
that thou hast done unto thy *m* in Ruth 2:11
hast left thy father and thy *m* Ruth 2:11
her *m* in law saw what she had Ruth 2:18
her *m* in law said unto her, Where Ruth 2:19
she shewed her *m* in law with whom Ruth 2:19
and dwelt with her *m* in law Ruth 2:23
Then Naomi her *m* in law said unto Ruth 3:1
to all that her *m* in law bade her Ruth 3:6
And when she came to her *m* in law Ruth 3:16
Go not empty unto thy *m* in law Ruth 3:17
Moreover his *m* made him a little 1Sa 2:19
so shall thy *m* be childless among 1Sa 15:33
of Moab, Let my father and my *m* 1Sa 22:3
sister to Zeruiah Joab's *m* 2Sa 17:25
the grave of my father and of my *m* 2Sa 19:37
destroy a city and a *m* in Israel 2Sa 20:19
his *m* bare him after Absalom 1Kin 1:6
unto Bath-sheba the *m* of Solomon 1Kin 1:11
to Bath-sheba the *m* of Solomon 1Kin 2:13
a seat to be set for the king's *m* 1Kin 2:19
king said unto her, Ask on, my *m* 1Kin 2:20
answered and said unto his *m* 1Kin 2:22
she is the *m* thereof 1Kin 3:27
And also Maachah his *m*, even her 1Kin 15:13
and delivered him unto his *m* 1Kin 17:23
pray thee, kiss my father and my *m* 1Kin 19:20
father, and in the way of his *m* 1Kin 22:52
like his father, and like his *m* 2Kin 3:2
and to the prophets of thy *m* 2Kin 3:13
said to a lad, Carry him to his *m* 2Kin 4:19
him, and brought him to his *m* 2Kin 4:20
the *m* of the child said, As the 2Kin 4:30
as the whoredoms of thy *m* Jezebel 2Kin 9:22
when Athaliah the *m* of Ahaziah 2Kin 11:1
the king of Babylon, he, and his *m* 2Kin 24:12
to Babylon, and the king's *m* 2Kin 24:15
she was the *m* of Onam 1Chr 2:26
his *m* called his name Jabez, 1Chr 4:9
Maachah the *m* of Asa the king 2Chr 15:16
for his *m* was his counsellor to 2Chr 22:3
But when Athaliah the *m* of 2Chr 22:10
for she had neither father nor *m* Est 2:7
*m* were dead, took for his own Est 2:7
to the worm, Thou art my *m* Job 17:14
my *m* forsake me, then the LORD Ps 27:10
as one that mourneth for his *m* Ps 35:14
and in sin did my *m* conceive me Ps 51:5
the sin of his *m* be blotted out Ps 109:14
and to be a joyful *m* of children Ps 113:9
a child that is weaned of his *m* Ps 131:2
and forsake not the law of thy *m* Prov 1:8
only beloved in the sight of my *m* Prov 4:3
and forsake not the law of thy *m* Prov 6:20
son is the heaviness of his *m* Prov 10:1
but a foolish man despiseth his *m* Prov 15:20
his father, and chaseth away his *m* Prov 19:26
Whoso curseth his father or his *m* Prov 20:20
despise not thy *m* when she is old Prov 23:22
thy *m* shall be glad, and she that Prov 23:25
Whoso robbeth his father or his *m* Prov 28:24
himself bringeth his *m* to shame Prov 29:15
father, and doth not bless their *m* Prov 30:11
and despiseth to obey his *m* Prov 30:17
prophecy that his *m* taught him Prov 31:1
with the crown wherewith his *m* Song 3:11
she is the only one of her *m* Song 6:9
that sucked the breasts of my *m* Song 8:1
there thy *m* brought thee forth Song 8:5
to cry, My father, and my *m* Is 8:4
from the bowels of my *m* hath he Is 49:1
transgressions is your *m* put away Is 50:1
As one whom his *m* comforteth Is 66:13
*m* of the young men a spoiler at Jer 15:8
Woe is me, my *m*, that thou hast Jer 15:10
for their father or for their *m* Jer 16:7
wherein my *m* bare me be blessed Jer 20:14
or that my *m* might have been my Jer 20:17
thy *m* that bare thee, into Jer 22:26
Your *m* shall be sore confounded Jer 50:12
an Amorite, and thy *m* an Hittite Eze 16:3
against thee, saying, As is the *m* Eze 16:44
your *m* was an Hittite, and your Eze 16:45
And say, What is thy *m* Eze 19:2
Thy *m* is like a vine in thy blood Eze 19:10
they set light by father and *m* Eze 22:7
two women, the daughters of one *m* Eze 23:2
but for father, or for *m*, or for Eze 44:25
Plead with your *m*, plead Hos 2:2
For their *m* hath played the Hos 2:5
night, and I will destroy thy *m* Hos 4:5
the *m* was dashed in pieces upon Hos 10:14
daughter riseth up against her *m* Mic 7:6
in law against her *m* in law Mic 7:6
his *m* that begat him shall say Zec 13:3
his *m* that begat him shall thrust Zec 13:3
When as his *m* Mary was espoused Mt 1:18
the young child with Mary his *m* Mt 2:11
and take the young child and his *m* Mt 2:13
his *m* by night, and departed into Mt 2:14
and take the young child and his *m* Mt 2:20
and took the young child and his *m* Mt 2:21
house, he saw his wife's *m* laid Mt 8:14
and the daughter against her *m* Mt 10:35
in law against her *m* in law Mt 10:35
He that loveth father or *m* more Mt 10:37
to the people, behold, his *m* Mt 12:46
one said unto him, Behold, thy *m* Mt 12:47
him that told him, Who is my *m* Mt 12:48
disciples, and said, Behold my *m* Mt 12:49
is my brother, and sister, and *m* Mt 12:50
is not his *m* called Mary Mt 13:55
being before instructed of her *m* Mt 14:8
and she brought it to her *m* Mt 14:11
saying, Honour thy father and *m* Mt 15:4
and, He that curseth father or *m* Mt 15:4
shall say to his father or his *m* Mt 15:5
And honour not his father or his *m* Mt 15:6
shall a man leave father and *m* Mt 19:5
Honour thy father and thy *m* Mt 19:19
or sisters, or father, or *m* Mt 19:29
Then came to him the *m* of Mt 20:20
Magdalene, and Mary the *m* of James Mt 27:56
the *m* of Zebedee's children Mt 27:56
But Simon's wife's *m* lay sick of Mk 1:30
came then his brethren and his *m* Mk 3:31
they said unto him, Behold, thy *m* Mk 3:32
them, saying, Who is my *m* Mk 3:33
about him, and said, Behold my *m* Mk 3:34
is my brother, and my sister, and *m* Mk 3:35
the *m* of the damsel, and them that Mk 5:40
went forth, and said unto her *m* Mk 6:24
and the damsel gave it to her *m* Mk 6:28
said, Honour thy father and thy *m* Mk 7:10
and, Whoso curseth father or *m* Mk 7:10
man shall say to his father or *m* Mk 7:11
do ought for his father or his *m* Mk 7:12
shall a man leave his father and *m* Mk 10:7
not, Honour thy father and *m* Mk 10:19
or sisters, or father, or *m* Mk 10:29
Mary the *m* of James the less and Mk 15:40
Mary the *m* of Joses beheld where Mk 15:47
Magdalene, and Mary the *m* of James Mk 16:1
that the *m* of my Lord should come Lk 1:43
his *m* answered and said, Not so Lk 1:60
his *m* marvelled at those things Lk 2:33
them, and said unto Mary his *m* Lk 2:34
and Joseph and his *m* knew not of it Lk 2:43
his *m* said unto him, Son, why Lk 2:48
but his *m* kept all these sayings Lk 2:51
Simon's wife's *m* was taken with a Lk 4:38
out, the only son of his *m* Lk 7:12
And he delivered him to his *m* Lk 7:15
Then came to him his *m* and his Lk 8:19
him by certain which said, Thy *m* Lk 8:20
answered and said unto them, My *m* Lk 8:21
the father and the *m* of the maiden Lk 8:51
the *m* against the daughter Lk 12:53
and the daughter against the *m* Lk 12:53
the *m* in law against her daughter Lk 12:53
in law against her *m* in law Lk 12:53
me, and hate not his father, and *m* Lk 14:26
Honour thy father and thy *m* Lk 18:20
and Joanna, and Mary the *m* of James Lk 24:10
and the *m* of Jesus was there Jn 2:1
the *m* of Jesus saith unto him, Jn 2:3
His *m* saith unto the servants, Jn 2:5
down to Capernaum, he, and his *m* Jn 2:12
Joseph, whose father and *m* we know Jn 6:42
stood by the cross of Jesus his *m* Jn 19:25
When Jesus therefore saw his *m* Jn 19:26
he loved, he saith unto his *m* Jn 19:26
he to the disciple, Behold thy *m* Jn 19:27
the women, and Mary the *m* of Jesus Acts 1:14
the house of Mary the *m* of John Acts 12:12
chosen in the Lord, and his *m* Rom 16:13
is free, which is the *m* of us all Gal 4:26
shall a man leave his father and *m* Eph 5:31
Honour thy father and *m* Eph 6:2
grandmother Lois, and thy *m* Eunice 2Ti 1:5
Without father, without *m* Heb 7:3
*M* OF HARLOTS AND Rev 17:5

## MOTHER'S

told them of her *m* house these Gen 24:28
was comforted after his *m* death Gen 24:67
let thy *m* sons bow down to thee Gen 27:29
the house of Bethuel thy *m* father Gen 28:2
daughters of Laban thy *m* brother Gen 28:2
daughter of Laban his *m* brother Gen 29:10
the sheep of Laban his *m* brother Gen 29:10
the flock of Laban his *m* brother Gen 29:10
his brother Benjamin, his *m* son Gen 43:29
not seethe a kid in his *m* milk Ex 23:19
not seethe a kid in his *m* milk Ex 34:26
the nakedness of thy *m* sister Lev 18:13
for she is thy *m* near kinswoman Lev 18:13
or his *m* daughter, and see her Lev 20:17
the nakedness of thy *m* sister Lev 20:19
his *m* name was Shelomith, the Lev 24:11
when he cometh out of his *m* womb Num 12:12
not seethe a kid in his *m* milk Deut 14:21
to Shechem unto his *m* brethren Judg 9:1
of the house of his *m* father Judg 9:1
his *m* brethren spake of him in Judg 9:3
unto God from my *m* womb Judg 16:17
Go, return each to her *m* house Ruth 1:8
the confusion of thy *m* nakedness 1Sa 20:30
*m* name was Zeruah 1Kin 11:26
And his *m* name was Naamah an 1Kin 14:21
And his *m* name was Naamah an 1Kin 14:31
his *m* name was Maachah, the 1Kin 15:2
his *m* name was Maachah, the 1Kin 15:10
his *m* name was Azubah the 1Kin 22:42
his *m* name was Athaliah, the 2Kin 8:26
And his *m* name was Zibiah of 2Kin 12:1
his *m* name was Jehoaddan of 2Kin 14:2
his *m* name was Jecholiah of 2Kin 15:2
his *m* name was Jerusha, the 2Kin 15:33
His *m* name also was Abi, the 2Kin 18:2
his *m* name was Hephzi-bah 2Kin 21:1
his *m* name was Meshullemeth, the 2Kin 21:19
his *m* name was Jedidah, the 2Kin 22:1
his *m* name was Hamutal, the 2Kin 23:31
his *m* name was Zebudah, the 2Kin 23:36
his *m* name was Nehushta, the 2Kin 24:8
his *m* name was Hamutal, the 2Kin 24:18
And his *m* name was Naamah an 2Chr 12:13
His *m* name also was Michaiah the 2Chr 13:2
his *m* name was Azubah the 2Chr 20:31
His *m* name also was Athaliah the 2Chr 22:2
His *m* name also was Zibiah of 2Chr 24:1
his *m* name was Jehoaddan of 2Chr 25:1
His *m* name also was Jecoliah of 2Chr 26:3
His *m* name also was Jerushah, the 2Chr 27:1
his *m* name was Abijah, the 2Chr 29:1
Naked came I out of my *m* womb Job 1:21
not up the doors of my *m* womb Job 3:10
I have guided her from my *m* womb Job 31:18
hope when I was upon my *m* breasts Ps 22:9
thou art my God from my *m* belly Ps 22:10
thou slanderest thine own *m* son Ps 50:20
and an alien unto my *m* children Ps 69:8
that took me out of my *m* bowels Ps 71:6
thou hast covered me in my *m* womb Ps 139:13
As he came forth of his *m* womb Eccl 5:15
my *m* children were angry with me Song 1:6
I had brought him into my *m* house Song 3:4
and bring thee into my *m* house Song 8:2
is the bill of your *m* divorcement Is 50:1
his *m* name was Hamutal the Jer 52:1
Thou art thy *m* daughter, that Eze 16:45
were so born from their *m* womb Mt 19:12
Holy Ghost, even from his *m* womb Lk 1:15
the second time into his *m* womb Jn 3:4
his *m* sister, Mary the wife of Jn 19:25
lame from his *m* womb was carried Acts 3:2
being a cripple from his *m* womb Acts 14:8
who separated me from my *m* womb Gal 1:15

## MOTHERS

and their queens thy nursing *m* Is 49:23
concerning their *m* that bare them Jer 16:3
They say to their *m*, Where is Lam 2:12
fatherless, our *m* are as widows Lam 5:3
and brethren, and sisters, and *m* Mk 10:30
of fathers and murderers of *m* 1Ti 1:9
The elder women as *m* 1Ti 5:2

## MOTHERS'

was poured out into their *m* bosom Lam 2:12

## MOTIONS

the *m* of sins, which were by the Rom 7:5

## MOULDY

of their provision was dry and *m* Josh 9:5
behold, it is dry, and it is *m* Josh 9:12

## MOUNT

goest unto Sephar a *m* of the east Gen 10:30
And the Horites in their *m* Seir Gen 14:6
In the *m* of the LORD it shall be Gen 22:14
set his face toward the *m* Gilead Gen 31:21
they overtook him in the *m* Gilead Gen 31:23
had pitched his tent in the *m* Gen 31:25
pitched in the *m* of Gilead Gen 31:25
offered sacrifice upon the *m* Gen 31:54
and tarried all night in the *m* Gen 31:54
Thus dwelt Esau in *m* Seir Gen 36:8
father of the Edomites in *m* Seir Gen 36:9
went, and met him in the *m* of God Ex 4:27
where he encamped at the *m* of God Ex 18:5
there Israel camped before the *m* Ex 19:2
of all the people upon *m* Sinai Ex 19:11
that ye go not up into the *m* Ex 19:12
whosoever toucheth the *m* shall be Ex 19:12
long, they shall come up to the *m* Ex 19:13
down from the *m* unto the people Ex 19:14
and a thick cloud upon the *m* Ex 19:16
stood at the nether part of the *m* Ex 19:17
*m* Sinai was altogether on a smoke Ex 19:18
the whole *m* quaked greatly Ex 19:18
*m* Sinai, on the top of the *m* Ex 19:20
Moses up to the top of the *m* Ex 19:20
people cannot come up to *m* Sinai Ex 19:23
saying, Set bounds about the *m* Ex 19:23
Moses, Come up to me into the *m* Ex 24:12
Moses went up into the *m* of God Ex 24:13
And Moses went up into the *m* Ex 24:15
and a cloud covered the *m* Ex 24:15
of the LORD abode upon *m* Sinai Ex 24:16
fire on the top of the *m* in the Ex 24:17
cloud, and gat him up into the *m* Ex 24:18
and Moses was in the *m* forty days Ex 24:18
which was shewed thee in the *m* Ex 25:40
which was shewed thee in the *m* Ex 26:30
as it was shewed thee in the *m* Ex 27:8
communing with him upon *m* Sinai Ex 31:18
delayed to come down out of the *m* Ex 32:1
turned, and went down from the *m* Ex 32:15
and brake them beneath the *m* Ex 32:19

M

of their ornaments by the *m* Horeb ... Ex 33:6
up in the morning unto *m* Sinai ... Ex 34:2
there to me in the top of the *m* ... Ex 34:2
man be seen throughout all the *m* ... Ex 34:3
nor herds feed before that *m* ... Ex 34:3
morning, and went up unto *m* Sinai ... Ex 34:4
when Moses came down from *m* Sinai . Ex 34:29
when he came down from the *m* ... Ex 34:29
had spoken with him in *m* Sinai ... Ex 34:32
LORD commanded Moses in *m* Sinai ... Lev 7:38
LORD spake unto Moses in *m* Sinai ... Lev 25:1
the children of Israel in *m* Sinai ... Lev 26:46
the children of Israel in *m* Sinai ... Lev 27:34
LORD spake with Moses in *m* Sinai ... Num 3:1
they departed from the *m* of the ... Num 10:33
from Kadesh, and came unto *m* Hor. Num 20:22
unto Moses and Aaron in *m* Hor ... Num 20:23
son, and bring them up unto *m* Hor . Num 20:25
they went up into *m* Hor in the ... Num 20:27
died there in the top of the *m* ... Num 20:28
and Eleazar came down from the *m* . Num 20:28
they journeyed from *m* Hor by the ... Num 21:4
Get thee up into this *m* Abarim ... Num 27:12
which was ordained in *m* Sinai for ... Num 28:6
and pitched in *m* Shapher ... Num 33:23
And they removed from *m* Shapher .. Num 33:24
from Kadesh, and pitched in *m* Hor .. Num 33:37
*m* Hor at the commandment of the ... Num 33:38
years old when he died in *m* Hor ... Num 33:39
And they departed from *m* Hor ... Num 33:41
ye shall point out for you *m* Hor ... Num 34:7
From *m* Hor ye shall point out ... Num 34:8
way of *m* Seir unto Kadesh-barnea ... Deut 1:2
have dwelt long enough in this *m* ... Deut 1:6
go to the *m* of the Amorites, and ... Deut 1:7
we compassed *m* Seir many days ... Deut 2:1
because I have given *m* Seir unto ... Deut 2:5
the river of Arnon unto *m* Hermon ... Deut 3:8
half *m* Gilead, and the cities ... Deut 3:12
even unto *m* Sion which is Hermon, ... Deut 4:48
*m* out of the midst of the fire ... Deut 5:4
fire, and went not up into the *m* ... Deut 5:5
*m* out of the midst of the fire ... Deut 5:22
When I was gone up into the *m* to ... Deut 9:9
then I abode in the *m* forty days ... Deut 9:9
the LORD spake with you in the *m* ... Deut 9:10
I turned and came down from the *m* .. Deut 9:15
and the *m* burned with fire ... Deut 9:15
brook that descended out of the *m* ... Deut 9:21
and come up unto me into the *m* ... Deut 10:1
the first, and went up into the *m* ... Deut 10:3
the LORD spake unto you in the *m* ... Deut 10:4
myself and came down from the *m* ... Deut 10:5
And I stayed in the *m*, according ... Deut 10:10
put the blessing upon *m* Gerizim ... Deut 11:29
and the curse upon *m* Ebal ... Deut 11:29
in *m* Ebal, and thou shalt plaister ... Deut 27:4
These shall stand upon *m* Gerizim ... Deut 27:12
shall stand upon *m* Ebal to curse ... Deut 27:13
this mountain Abarim, unto *m* Nebo Deut 32:49
die in the *m* whither thou goest ... Deut 32:50
Aaron thy brother died in *m* Hor ... Deut 32:50
he shined forth from *m* Paran ... Deut 33:2
the LORD God of Israel in *m* Ebal ... Josh 8:30
of them over against *m* Gerizim ... Josh 8:33
half of them over against *m* Ebal ... Josh 8:33
Even from the *m* Halak, that goeth ... Josh 11:17
valley of Lebanon under *m* Hermon .. Josh 11:17
the river Arnon unto *m* Hermon ... Josh 12:1
And reigned in *m* Hermon, and in ... Josh 12:5
of Lebanon even unto the *m* Halak ... Josh 12:7
from Baal-gad under *m* Hermon unto . Josh 13:5
all *m* Hermon, and all Bashan unto ... Josh 13:11
in the *m* of the valley, ... Josh 13:19
out to the cities of *m* Ephron ... Josh 15:9
from Baalah westward unto *m* Seir ... Josh 15:10
along unto the side of *m* Jearim ... Josh 15:10
and passed along to *m* Baalah ... Josh 15:11
from Jericho throughout *m* Beth-el ... Josh 16:1
if *m* Ephraim be too narrow for ... Josh 17:15
even Timnath-serah in *m* Ephraim ... Josh 19:50
Kedesh in Galilee in *m* Naphtali ... Josh 20:7
and Shechem in *m* Ephraim ... Josh 20:7
with her suburbs in *m* Ephraim ... Josh 21:21
and I gave unto Esau *m* Seir ... Josh 24:4
which is in *m* Ephraim, on the ... Josh 24:30
which was given him in *m* Ephraim .. Josh 24:33
would dwell in *m* Heres in Aijalon ... Judg 1:35
in the *m* of Ephraim, on the north ... Judg 2:9
Hivites that dwelt in *m* Lebanon ... Judg 3:3
from *m* Baal-hermon unto the ... Judg 3:3
went down with him from the *m* ... Judg 3:27
Ramah and Beth-el in *m* Ephraim ... Judg 4:5
saying, Go and draw toward *m* Tabor .. Judg 4:6
of Abinoam was gone up to *m* Tabor .. Judg 4:12
So Barak went down from *m* Tabor ... Judg 4:14
and depart early from *m* Gilead ... Judg 7:3
throughout all *m* Ephraim, saying, ... Judg 7:24
and stood in the top of *m* Gerizim ... Judg 9:7
Abimelech gat him up to *m* Zalmon ... Judg 9:48
he dwelt in Shamir in *m* Ephraim ... Judg 10:1
in the *m* of the Amalekites ... Judg 12:15
And there was a man of *m* Ephraim ... Judg 17:1
he came to *m* Ephraim to the house ... Judg 17:8
who when they came to *m* Ephraim ... Judg 18:2
they passed thence unto *m* Ephraim . Judg 18:13
on the side of *m* Ephraim, who ... Judg 19:1
even, which was also of *m* Ephraim .. Judg 19:16
toward the side of *m* Ephraim ... Judg 19:18
of *m* Ephraim, and his name was ... 1Sa 1:1

And he passed through *m* Ephraim ... 1Sa 9:4
in *m* Beth-el, and a thousand were ... 1Sa 13:2
had hid themselves in *m* Ephraim ... 1Sa 14:22
and fell down slain in *m* Gilboa ... 1Sa 31:1
his three sons fallen in *m* Gilboa ... 1Sa 31:8
happened by chance upon *m* Gilboa ... 2Sa 1:6
went up by the ascent of *m* Olivet ... 2Sa 15:30
was come to the top of the *m* ... 2Sa 15:32
but a man of *m* Ephraim, Sheba the ... 2Sa 20:21
The son of Hur, in *m* Ephraim ... 1Kin 4:8
built Shechem in *m* Ephraim ... 1Kin 12:25
to me all Israel unto *m* Carmel ... 1Kin 18:19
prophets together unto *m* Carmel ... 1Kin 18:20
nights unto Horeb the *m* of God ... 1Kin 19:8
stand upon the *m* before the LORD ... 1Kin 19:11
he went from thence to *m* Carmel ... 2Kin 2:25
unto the man of God to *m* Carmel ... 2Kin 4:25
*m* Ephraim two young men of the ... 2Kin 5:22
and they that escape out of *m* Zion .. 2Kin 19:31
right hand of the *m* of corruption ... 2Kin 23:13
that were there in the *m*, and sent ... 2Kin 23:16
five hundred men, went to *m* Seir ... 1Chr 4:42
and Senir, and unto *m* Hermon ... 1Chr 5:23
Shechem in *m* Ephraim with her ... 1Chr 6:67
and fell down slain in *m* Gilboa ... 1Chr 10:1
and his sons fallen in *m* Gilboa ... 1Chr 10:8
the LORD at Jerusalem in *m* Moriah ... 2Chr 3:1
Abijah stood up upon *m* Zemaraim ... 2Chr 13:4
Zemaraim, which is in *m* Ephraim ... 2Chr 13:4
which he had taken from *m* Ephraim . 2Chr 15:8
from Beer-sheba to *m* Ephraim ... 2Chr 19:4
*m* Seir, whom thou wouldest not ... 2Chr 20:10
*m* Seir, which were come against ... 2Chr 20:22
against the inhabitants of *m* Seir ... 2Chr 20:23
in the *m* of the house of the LORD ... 2Chr 33:15
saying, Go forth unto the *m* ... Neh 8:15
camest down also upon *m* Sinai ... Neh 9:13
excellency *m* up to the heavens ... Job 20:6
Doth the eagle *m* up at thy ... Job 39:27
is *m* Zion, on the sides of the ... Ps 48:2
Let *m* Zion rejoice, let the ... Ps 48:11
this *m* Zion, wherein thou hast ... Ps 74:2
the *m* Zion which he loved ... Ps 78:68
They *m* up to the heaven, they go ... Ps 107:26
in the LORD shall be as *m* Zion ... Ps 125:1
goats, that appear from *m* Gilead ... Song 4:1
every dwelling place of *m* Zion ... Is 4:5
hosts, which dwelleth in *m* Zion ... Is 8:18
they shall *m* up like the lifting ... Is 9:18
his whole work upon *m* Zion ... Is 10:12
the *m* of the daughter of Zion ... Is 10:32
upon the *m* of the congregation ... Is 14:13
unto the *m* of the daughter of ... Is 16:1
of the LORD of hosts, the *m* Zion ... Is 18:7
of hosts shall reign in *m* Zion ... Is 24:23
LORD in the holy *m* at Jerusalem ... Is 27:13
shall rise up as in *m* Perazim ... Is 28:21
lay siege against thee with a *m* ... Is 29:3
be, that fight against *m* Zion ... Is 29:8
come down to fight for *m* Zion ... Is 31:4
and they that escape out of *m* Zion ... Is 37:32
they shall *m* up with wings as ... Is 40:31
affliction from *m* Ephraim ... Jer 4:15
cast a *m* against Jerusalem ... Jer 6:6
upon the *m* Ephraim shall cry ... Jer 31:6
shall be satisfied upon *m* Ephraim ... Jer 50:19
Babylon should *m* up to heaven ... Jer 51:53
it, and cast a *m* against it ... Eze 4:2
wings to *m* up from the earth ... Eze 10:16
against the gates, to cast a *m* ... Eze 21:22
cast a *m* against thee, and lift up ... Eze 26:8
man, set thy face against *m* Seir ... Eze 35:2
O *m* Seir, I am against thee, and I ... Eze 35:3
Thus will I make *m* Seir most ... Eze 35:7
O *m* Seir, and all Idumea, even all ... Eze 35:15
north shall come, and cast up a *m* ... Dan 11:15
for in *m* Zion and in Jerusalem ... Joel 2:32
out of the *m* of Esau ... Obad 8
the *m* of Esau may be cut off by ... Obad 9
But upon *m* Zion shall be ... Obad 17
south shall possess the *m* of Esau ... Obad 19
*m* Zion to judge the *m* of Esau ... Obad 21
them in *m* Zion from henceforth ... Mic 4:7
and the Holy One from *m* Paran ... Hab 3:3
in that day upon the *m* of Olives ... Zec 14:4
the *m* of Olives shall cleave in ... Zec 14:4
unto the *m* of Olives, then sent ... Mt 21:1
And as he sat upon the *m* of Olives ... Mt 24:3
went out into the *m* of Olives ... Mt 26:30
at the *m* of Olives, he sendeth ... Mk 11:1
as he sat upon the *m* of Olives ... Mk 13:3
went out into the *m* of Olives ... Mk 14:26
at the *m* called the *m* of ... Lk 19:29
called the *m* of Olives ... Lk 19:29
at the descent of the *m* of Olives ... Lk 19:37
abode in the *m* that is called the ... Lk 21:37
that is called the *m* of Olives ... Lk 21:37
he was wont, to the *m* of Olives ... Lk 22:39
Jesus went unto the *m* of Olives ... Jn 8:1
from the *m* called Olivet, which ... Acts 1:12
to him in the wilderness of *m* ... Acts 7:30
which spake to him in the *m* Sina ... Acts 7:38
the one from the *m* Sinai, which ... Gal 4:24
this Agar is *m* Sinai in Arabia ... Gal 4:25
pattern shewed to thee in the *m* ... Heb 8:5
unto the *m* that might be touched ... Heb 12:18
But ye are come unto *m* Sion ... Heb 12:22
we were with him in the holy *m* ... 2Pet 1:18
lo, a Lamb stood on the *m* Sion ... Rev 14:1

**MOUNTAIN**

unto a *m* on the east of Beth-el ... Gen 12:8
they that remained fled to the *m* ... Gen 14:10
escape to the *m*, lest thou be ... Gen 19:17
and I cannot escape to the *m* ... Gen 19:19
up out of Zoar, and dwelt in the *m* ... Gen 19:30
desert, and came to the *m* of God ... Ex 3:1
ye shall serve God upon this *m* ... Ex 3:12
plant them in the *m* of thine ... Ex 15:17
LORD called unto him out of the *m* ... Ex 19:3
of the trumpet, and the *m* smoking ... Ex 20:18
southward, and go up into the *m* ... Num 13:17
gat them up into the top of the *m* ... Num 14:40
the way of the *m* of the Amorites ... Deut 1:19
come unto the *m* of the Amorites ... Deut 1:20
they turned and went up into the *m* ... Deut 1:24
Amorites, which dwelt in that *m* ... Deut 1:44
have compassed this *m* long enough ... Deut 2:3
is beyond Jordan, that goodly *m* ... Deut 3:25
ye came near and stood under the *m* . Deut 4:11
the *m* burned with fire unto the ... Deut 4:11
(for the *m* did burn with fire,) ... Deut 5:23
Get thee up into this *m* Abarim ... Deut 32:49
shall call the people unto the *m* ... Deut 33:19
plains of Moab unto the *m* of Nebo ... Deut 34:1
said unto them, Get you to the *m* ... Josh 2:16
And they went, and came unto the *m*. Josh 2:22
returned, and descended from the *m* ... Josh 2:23
the *m* of Israel, and the valley of ... Josh 11:16
Now therefore give me this *m* ... Josh 14:12
went up to the top of the *m* that ... Josh 15:8
But the *m* shall be thine ... Josh 17:18
came down to the end of the *m* ... Josh 18:16
is Hebron, in the *m* of Judah ... Josh 20:7
Canaanites, that dwelt in the *m* ... Judg 1:9
out the inhabitants of the *m* ... Judg 1:19
the children of Dan into the *m* ... Judg 1:34
a trumpet in the *m* of Ephraim ... Judg 3:27
stood on a *m* on the one side ... 1Sa 17:3
stood on a *m* on the other side ... 1Sa 17:3
remained in a *m* in the wilderness ... 1Sa 23:14
Saul went on this side of the *m* ... 1Sa 23:26
and his men on that side of the *m* ... 1Sa 23:26
him up, and cast him upon some *m* ... 2Kin 2:16
the *m* was full of horses and ... 2Kin 6:17
thousand to hew in the *m*, and ... 2Chr 2:2
thousand to be hewers in the *m* ... 2Chr 2:18
surely the *m* falling cometh to ... Job 14:18
my soul, Flee as a bird to your *m* ... Ps 11:1
hast made my *m* to stand strong ... Ps 30:7
our God, in the *m* of his holiness ... Ps 48:1
of his sanctuary, even to this *m* ... Ps 78:54
I will get me to the *m* of myrrh ... Song 4:6
that the *m* of the LORD's house ... Is 2:2
let us go up to the *m* of the LORD ... Is 2:3
hurt nor destroy in all my holy *m* ... Is 11:9
ye up a banner upon the high *m* ... Is 13:2
in this *m* shall the LORD of hosts ... Is 25:6
he will destroy in this *m* the ... Is 25:7
For in this *m* shall the hand of ... Is 25:10
as a beacon upon the top of a *m* ... Is 30:17
there shall be upon every high *m* ... Is 30:25
to come into the *m* of the LORD ... Is 30:29
shall be exalted, and every *m* ... Is 40:4
get thee up into the high *m* ... Is 40:9
them will I bring to my holy *m* ... Is 56:7
high *m* hast thou set thy bed ... Is 57:7
land, and shall inherit my holy *m* ... Is 57:13
the LORD, that forget my holy *m* ... Is 65:11
hurt nor destroy in all my holy *m* ... Is 65:25
beasts, to my holy *m* Jerusalem ... Is 66:20
she is gone up upon every high *m* ... Jer 3:6
they shall hunt them from every *m* ... Jer 16:16
O my *m* in the field, I will give ... Jer 17:3
the *m* of the house as the high ... Jer 26:18
of justice, and *m* of holiness ... Jer 31:23
they have gone from *m* to hill ... Jer 50:6
I am against thee, O destroying *m* ... Jer 51:25
and will make thee a burnt *m* ... Jer 51:25
Because of the *m* of Zion, which ... Lam 5:18
stood upon the *m* which is on the ... Eze 11:23
and will plant it upon an high *m* ... Eze 17:22
In the *m* of the height of Israel ... Eze 17:23
For in mine holy *m* ... Eze 20:40
in the *m* of the height of Israel, ... Eze 20:40
thou wast upon the holy *m* of God ... Eze 28:14
as profane out of the *m* of God ... Eze 28:16
and set me upon a very high *m* ... Eze 40:2
Upon the top of the *m* the whole ... Eze 43:12
smote the image became a great *m* ... Dan 2:35
cut out of the *m* without hands ... Dan 2:45
thy city Jerusalem, thy holy *m* ... Dan 9:16
my God for the holy *m* of my God ... Dan 9:20
the seas in the glorious holy *m* ... Dan 11:45
and sound an alarm in my holy *m* ... Joel 2:1
God dwelling in Zion, my holy *m* ... Joel 3:17
that are in the *m* of Samaria ... Amos 4:1
and trust in the *m* of Samaria ... Amos 6:1
as ye have drunk upon my holy *m* ... Obad 16
the *m* of the house as the high ... Mic 3:12
that the *m* of the house of the ... Mic 4:1
let us go up to the *m* of the LORD ... Mic 4:2
sea to sea, and from *m* to *m* ... Mic 7:12
be haughty because of my holy *m* ... Zeph 3:11
Go up to the *m*, and bring wood, and ... Hag 1:8
Who art thou, O great *m* ... Zec 4:7
the *m* of the LORD of hosts the ... Zec 8:3
of the LORD of hosts the holy *m* ... Zec 8:3
half of the *m* shall remove toward ... Zec 14:4
him up into an exceeding high *m* ... Mt 4:8

multitudes, he went up into a *m* Mt 5:1
When he was come down from the *m* Mt 8:1
he went up into a *m* apart to pray Mt 14:23
and went up into a *m*, and sat down Mt 15:29
them up into an high *m* apart Mt 17:1
And as they came down from the *m* Mt 17:9
seed, ye shall say unto this *m* Mt 17:20
also if ye shall say unto this *m* Mt 21:21
Galilee, into a *m* where Jesus had Mt 28:16
And he goeth up into a *m*, and Mk 3:13
he departed into a *m* to pray Mk 6:46
an high *m* apart by themselves Mk 9:2
And as they came down from the *m* Mk 9:9
whosoever shall say unto this *m* Mk 11:23
shall be filled, and every *m* Lk 3:5
taking him up into an high *m* Lk 4:5
that he went out into a *m* to pray Lk 6:12
of many swine feeding on the *m* Lk 8:32
and went up into a *m* to pray Lk 9:28
Our fathers worshipped in this *m* Jn 4:20
when ye shall neither in this *m* Jn 4:21
And Jesus went up into a *m* Jn 6:3
again into a *m* himself alone Jn 6:15
if so much as a beast touch the *m* Heb 12:20
and every *m* and island were moved Rev 6:14
as it were a great *m* burning with Rev 8:8
the spirit to a great and high *m* Rev 21:10

## MOUNTAINS

and the *m* were covered Gen 7:20
the month, upon the *m* of Ararat Gen 8:4
were the tops of the *m* seen Gen 8:5
the *m* which I will tell thee of Gen 22:2
them out, to slay them in the *m* Ex 32:12
and the Amorites, dwell in the *m* Num 13:29
out of the *m* of the east, saying, Num 23:7
and pitched in the *m* of Abarim Num 33:47
departed from the *m* of Abarim Num 33:48
nor unto the cities in the *m* Deut 2:37
their gods, upon the high *m* Deut 12:2
on fire the foundations of the *m* Deut 32:22
the chief things of the ancient *m* Deut 33:15
*m* are gathered together against Josh 10:6
that were on the north of the *m* Josh 11:2
and the Jebusite in the *m* Josh 11:3
and cut off the Anakims from the *m* Josh 11:21
Anab, and from all the *m* of Judah Josh 11:21
and from all the *m* of Israel Josh 11:21
In the *m*, and in the valleys, and Josh 12:8
And in the *m*, Shamir, and Jattir, Josh 15:48
up through the *m* westward Josh 18:12
The *m* melted from before the LORD Judg 5:5
them the dens which are in the *m* Judg 6:2
wait for him in the top of the *m* Judg 9:25
people down from the top of the *m* Judg 9:36
of the *m* as if they were men Judg 9:36
I may go up and down upon the *m* Judg 11:37
bewailed her virginity upon the *m* Judg 11:38
doth hunt a partridge in the *m* 1Sa 26:20
Ye *m* of Gilboa, let there be no 2Sa 1:21
thousand hewers in the *m* 1Kin 5:15
a great and strong wind rent the *m* 1Kin 19:11
am come up to the height of the *m* 2Kin 19:23
as swift as the roes upon the *m* 1Chr 12:8
all Israel scattered upon the *m* 2Chr 18:16
high places in the *m* of Judah 2Chr 21:11
also, and vine dressers in the *m* 2Chr 26:10
he built cities in the *m* of Judah 2Chr 27:4
Which removeth the *m*, and they Job 9:5
are wet with the showers of the *m* Job 24:8
he overturneth the *m* by the roots Job 28:9
The range of the *m* is his pasture Job 39:8
Surely the *m* bring him forth food Job 40:20
righteousness is like the great *m* Ps 36:6
though the *m* be carried into the Ps 46:2
though the *m* shake with the Ps 46:3
I know all the fowls of the *m* Ps 50:11
his strength setteth fast the *m* Ps 65:6
The *m* shall bring peace to the Ps 72:3
the earth upon the top of the *m* Ps 72:16
and excellent than the *m* of prey Ps 76:4
the flame setteth the *m* on fire Ps 83:14
His foundation is in the holy *m* Ps 87:1
Before the *m* were brought forth, Ps 90:2
the waters stood above the *m* Ps 104:6
They go up by the *m* Ps 104:8
The *m* skipped like rams, and the Ps 114:4
Ye *m*, that ye skipped like rams Ps 114:6
As the *m* are round about Ps 125:2
that descended upon the *m* of Zion Ps 133:3
touch the *m*, and they shall smoke Ps 144:5
maketh grass to grow upon the *m* Ps 147:8
*M*, and all hills Ps 148:9
Before the *m* were settled, before Prov 8:25
and herbs of the *m* are gathered Prov 27:25
he cometh leaping upon the *m* Song 2:8
a young hart upon the *m* of Bether Song 2:17
from the *m* of the leopards Song 4:8
a young hart upon the *m* of spices Song 8:14
established in the top of the *m* Is 2:2
And upon all the high *m*, and upon Is 2:14
The noise of a multitude in the *m* Is 13:4
upon my *m* tread him under foot Is 14:25
chaff of the *m* before the wind Is 17:13
he lifteth up an ensign on the *m* Is 18:3
together unto the fowls of the *m* Is 18:6
the walls, and of crying to the *m* Is 22:5
the *m* shall be melted with their Is 34:3
I come up to the height of the *m* Is 37:24
and weighed the *m* in scales Is 40:12
thou shalt thresh the *m*, and beat Is 41:15
them shout from the top of the *m* Is 42:11
I will make waste *m* and hills, and Is 42:15
break forth into singing, ye *m* Is 44:23
And I will make all my *m* a way Is 49:11
and break forth into singing, O *m* Is 49:13
How beautiful upon the *m* are the Is 52:7
For the *m* shall depart, and the Is 54:10
the *m* and the hills shall break Is 55:12
that the *m* might flow down at thy Is 64:1
the *m* flowed down at thy presence Is 64:3
have burned incense upon the *m* Is 65:7
out of Judah an inheritor of my *m* Is 65:9
hills, and from the multitude of *m* Jer 3:23
I beheld the *m*, and, lo, they Jer 4:24
For the *m* will I take up a Jer 9:10
your feet stumble upon the dark *m* Jer 13:16
and from the plain, and from the *m* Jer 17:26
plant vines upon the *m* of Samaria Jer 31:5
Judah, and in the cities of the *m* Jer 32:44
In the cities of the *m*, in the Jer 33:13
Surely as Tabor is among the *m* Jer 46:18
have turned them away on the *m* Jer 50:6
they pursued us upon the *m* Lam 4:19
thy face toward the *m* of Israel Eze 6:2
Ye *m* of Israel, hear the word of Eze 6:3
Thus saith the Lord GOD to the *m* Eze 6:3
hill, in all the tops of the *m* Eze 6:13
not the sounding again of the *m* Eze 7:7
shall be on the *m* like doves of Eze 7:16
And hath not eaten upon the *m* Eze 18:6
but even hath eaten upon the *m* Eze 18:11
That hath not eaten upon the *m* Eze 18:15
be heard upon the *m* of Israel Eze 19:9
and in thee they eat upon the *m* Eze 22:9
upon the *m* and in all the valleys Eze 31:12
I will lay thy flesh upon the *m* Eze 32:5
thou swimmest, even to the *m* Eze 32:6
the *m* of Israel shall be desolate Eze 33:28
sheep wandered through all the *m* Eze 34:6
feed them upon the *m* of Israel by Eze 34:13
upon the high *m* of Israel shall Eze 34:14
they feed upon the *m* of Israel Eze 34:14
I will fill his *m* with his slain Eze 35:8
spoken against the *m* of Israel Eze 35:12
prophesy unto the *m* of Israel Eze 36:1
Ye *m* of Israel, hear the word of Eze 36:1
ye *m* of Israel, hear the word of Eze 36:4
Thus saith the Lord GOD to the *m* Eze 36:4
land of Israel, and say unto the *m* Eze 36:6
O *m* of Israel, ye shall shoot Eze 36:8
in the land upon the *m* of Israel Eze 37:22
people, against the *m* of Israel Eze 38:8
the *m* shall be thrown down, and Eze 38:20
against him throughout all my *m* Eze 38:21
bring thee upon the *m* of Israel Eze 39:2
shalt fall upon the *m* of Israel Eze 39:4
sacrifice upon the *m* of Israel Eze 39:17
sacrifice upon the tops of the *m* Hos 4:13
and they shall say to the *m* Hos 10:8
as the morning spread upon the *m* Joel 2:2
on the tops of *m* shall they leap Joel 2:5
that the *m* shall drop down new Joel 3:18
yourselves upon the *m* of Samaria Amos 3:9
For, lo, he that formeth the *m* Amos 4:13
the *m* shall drop sweet wine, and Amos 9:13
went down to the bottoms of the *m* Jonah 2:6
the *m* shall be molten under him, Mic 1:4
established in the top of the *m* Mic 4:1
Arise, contend thou before the *m* Mic 6:1
Hear ye, O *m*, the LORD's Mic 6:2
The *m* quake at him, and the hills Nah 1:5
Behold upon the *m* the feet of him Nah 1:15
people is scattered upon the *m* Nah 3:18
the everlasting *m* were scattered Hab 3:6
The *m* saw thee, and they trembled Hab 3:10
upon the land, and upon the *m* Hag 1:11
chariots out from between two *m* Zec 6:1
and the *m* were *m* of brass Zec 6:1
shall flee to the valley of the *m* Zec 14:5
of the *m* shall reach unto Azal Zec 14:5
And I hated Esau, and laid his *m* Mal 1:3
and nine, and goeth into the *m* Mt 18:12
be in Judaea flee into the *m* Mt 24:16
night and day, he was in the *m* Mk 5:5
*m* a great herd of swine feeding Mk 5:11
that be in Judaea flee to the *m* Mk 13:14
which are in Judaea flee to the *m* Lk 21:21
shall they begin to say to the *m* Lk 23:30
faith, so that I could remove *m* 1Cor 13:2
they wandered in deserts, and in *m* Heb 11:38
the dens and in the rocks of the *m* Rev 6:15
And said to the *m* and rocks, Fall Rev 6:16
away, and the *m* were not found Rev 16:20
The seven heads are seven *m* Rev 17:9

## MOUNTED

*m* up from the earth in my sight Eze 10:19

## MOUNTING

for by the *m* up of Luhith with Is 15:5

## MOUNTS

Behold the *m*, they are come unto Jer 32:24
which are thrown down by the *m* Jer 33:4
him in the war, by casting up *m* Eze 17:17

## MOURN

and Abraham came to *m* for Sarah Gen 23:2
How long wilt thou *m* for Saul 1Sa 16:1
with sackcloth, and *m* before Abner 2Sa 3:31
prophet came to the city, to *m* 1Kin 13:29
And all Israel shall *m* for him 1Kin 14:13
*m* not, nor weep Neh 8:9
together to come to *m* with him Job 2:11
that those which *m* may be exalted Job 5:11
and his soul within him shall *m* Job 14:22
I *m* in my complaint, and make a Ps 55:2
thou *m* at the last, when thy Prov 5:11
wicked beareth rule, the people *m* Prov 29:2
a time to *m*, and a time to dance Eccl 3:4
And her gates shall lament and *m* Is 3:26
of Kir-hareseth shall ye *m* Is 16:7
The fishers also shall *m*, and all Is 19:8
I did *m* as a dove Is 38:14
like bears, and *m* sore like doves Is 59:11
to comfort all that *m* Is 61:2
appoint unto them that *m* in Zion Is 61:3
with her, all ye that *m* for her Is 66:10
For this shall the earth *m* Jer 4:28
How long shall the land *m* Jer 12:4
mine heart shall *m* for the men of Jer 48:31
The ways of Zion do *m*, because Lam 1:4
buyer rejoice, nor the seller *m* Eze 7:12
The king shall *m*, and the prince Eze 7:27
yet neither shalt thou *m* nor weep Eze 24:16
ye shall not *m* nor weep Eze 24:23
and *m* one toward another Eze 24:23
and I caused Lebanon to *m* for him Eze 31:15
Therefore shall the land *m* Hos 4:3
people thereof shall *m* over it Hos 10:5
priests, the LORD's ministers, *m* Joel 1:9
of the shepherds shall *m*, and the Amos 1:2
every one *m* that dwelleth therein Amos 8:8
and all that dwell therein shall *m* Amos 9:5
pierced, and they shall *m* for him Zec 12:10
And the land shall *m*, every family Zec 12:12
Blessed are they that *m* Mt 5:4
children of the bridechamber *m* Mt 9:15
all the tribes of the earth *m* Mt 24:30
for ye shall *m* and weep Lk 6:25
Be afflicted, and *m*, and weep Jas 4:9
earth shall weep and *m* over her Rev 18:11

## MOURNED

loins, and *m* for his son many days Gen 37:34
and the Egyptians *m* for him Gen 50:3
there they *m* with a great and very Gen 50:10
heard these evil tidings, they *m* Ex 33:4
and the people *m* greatly Num 14:39
they *m* for Aaron thirty days, Num 20:29
nevertheless Samuel *m* for Saul 1Sa 15:35
And they *m*, and wept, and fasted 2Sa 1:12
was dead, she *m* for her husband 2Sa 11:26
David *m* for his son every day 2Sa 13:37
had a long time *m* for the dead 2Sa 14:2
they *m* over him, saying, Alas, my 1Kin 13:30
and all Israel *m* for him, 1Kin 14:18
Ephraim their father *m* many days 1Chr 7:22
Judah and Jerusalem *m* for Josiah 2Chr 35:24
for he *m* because of the Ezr 10:6
*m* certain days, and fasted, and Neh 1:4
*m* in the fifth and seventh month, Zec 7:5
we have *m* unto you, and ye have Mt 11:17
that had been with him, as they *m* Mk 16:10
we have *m* to you, and ye have not Lk 7:32
puffed up, and have not rather *m* 1Cor 5:2

## MOURNER

thee, feign thyself to be a *m* 2Sa 14:2

## MOURNERS

as one that comforteth the *m* Job 29:25
the *m* go about the streets Eccl 12:5
comforts unto him and to his *m* Is 57:18
be unto them as the bread of *m* Hos 9:4

## MOURNETH

the king weepeth and *m* for Absalom 2Sa 19:1
as one that *m* for his mother Ps 35:14
Mine eye *m* by reason of Ps 88:9
The earth *m* and fadeth away, the Is 24:4
The new wine *m*, the vine Is 24:7
The earth *m* and languisheth Is 33:9
and being desolate it *m* unto me Jer 12:11
Judah *m*, and the gates thereof Jer 14:2
because of swearing the land *m* Jer 23:10
The field is wasted, the land *m* Joel 1:10
as one *m* for his only son, and Zec 12:10

## MOURNFULLY

that we have walked *m* before the Mal 3:14

## MOURNING

The days of *m* for my father are Gen 27:41
down into the grave unto my son *m* Gen 37:35
when the days of his *m* were past Gen 50:4
he made a *m* for his father seven Gen 50:10
saw the *m* in the floor of Atad, Gen 50:11
is a grievous *m* to the Egyptians Gen 50:11
I have not eaten thereof in my *m* Deut 26:14
weeping and *m* for Moses were ended Deut 34:8
And when the *m* was past, David 2Sa 11:27
mourner, and put on now *m* apparel 2Sa 14:2
turned into *m* unto all the people 2Sa 19:2
there was great *m* among the Jews Est 4:3
But Haman hasted to his house *m* Est 6:12
to joy, and from *m* into a good day Est 9:22
who are ready to raise up their *m* Job 3:8
I went *m* without the sun Job 30:28
My harp also is turned to *m* Job 30:31
turned for me my *m* into dancing Ps 30:11
I go *m* all the day long Ps 38:6
why go I *m* because of the Ps 42:9
Why go I *m* because of the Ps 43:2
is better to go to the house of *m* Eccl 7:2

of the wise is in the house of *m* Eccl 7:4
of hosts call to weeping, and to *m* Is 22:12
and sorrow and *m* shall flee away Is 51:11
the days of thy *m* shall be ended Is 60:20
for ashes, the oil of joy for *m* Is 61:3
make thee *m*, as for an only son, Jer 6:26
ye, and call for the *m* women Jer 9:17
Enter not into the house of *m* Jer 16:5
men tear themselves for them in *m* Jer 16:7
for I will turn their *m* into joy Jer 31:13
in the daughter of Judah *m* Lam 2:5
our dance is turned into *m* Lam 5:15
therein lamentations, and *m* Eze 2:10
of the valleys, all of them *m* Eze 7:16
make no *m* for the dead, bind the Eze 24:17
down to the grave I caused a *m* Eze 31:15
I Daniel was *m* three full weeks Dan 10:2
and with weeping, and with *m* Joel 2:12
shall call the husbandman to *m* Amos 5:16
And I will turn your feasts into *m* Amos 8:10
make it as the *m* of an only son Amos 8:10
the dragons, and *m* as the owls Mic 1:8
not forth in the *m* of Beth-ezel Mic 1:11
there be a great *m* in Jerusalem Zec 12:11
as the *m* of Hadadrimmon in the Zec 12:11
and weeping, and great *m*, Rachel Mt 2:18
us your earnest desire, your *m* 2Cor 7:7
let your laughter be turned to *m* Jas 4:9
come in one day, death, and *m* Rev 18:8

## MOUSE

the weasel, and the *m*, and the Lev 11:29
and the abomination, and the *m* Is 66:17

## MOUTH

which hath opened her *m* to Gen 4:11
in her *m* was an olive leaf pluckt Gen 8:11
the damsel, and enquire at her *m* Gen 24:57
great stone was upon the well's *m* Gen 29:2
the stone from the well's *m* Gen 29:3
upon the well's *m* in his place Gen 29:3
roll the stone from the well's *m* Gen 29:8
the stone from the well's *m* Gen 29:10
behold, it was in his sack's *m* Gen 42:27
again in the *m* of your sacks Gen 43:12
money was in the *m* of his sack Gen 43:21
every man's money in his sack's *m* Gen 44:1
in the sack's *m* of the youngest, Gen 44:2
that it is my *m* that speaketh Gen 45:12
unto him, Who hath made man's *m* Ex 4:11
go, and I will be with thy *m* Ex 4:12
unto him, and put words in his *m* Ex 4:15
be with thy *m*, and with his *m* Ex 4:15
shall be to thee instead of a *m* Ex 4:16
the LORD's law may be in thy *m* Ex 13:9
let it be heard out of thy *m* Ex 23:13
With him will I speak *m* to *m* Num 12:8
With him will I speak *m* to *m* Num 12:8
thing, and the earth open her *m* Num 16:30
And the earth opened her *m* Num 16:32
the LORD opened the *m* of the ass Num 22:28
the word that God putteth in my *m* Num 22:38
the LORD put a word in Balaam's *m* Num 23:5
which the LORD hath put in my *m* Num 23:12
Balaam, and put a word in his *m* Num 23:16
And the earth opened her *m* Num 26:10
all that proceedeth out of his *m* Num 30:2
hath proceeded out of your *m* Num 32:24
to death by the *m* of witnesses Num 35:30
the *m* of the LORD doth man live Deut 8:3
how the earth opened her *m* Deut 11:6
At the *m* of two witnesses, or Deut 17:6
but at the *m* of one witness he Deut 17:6
and will put my words in his *m* Deut 18:18
at the *m* of two witnesses Deut 19:15
or at the *m* of three witnesses, Deut 19:15
thou hast promised with thy *m* Deut 23:23
is very nigh unto thee, in thy *m* Deut 30:14
hear, O earth, the words of my *m* Deut 32:1
law shall not depart out of thy *m* Josh 1:8
any word proceed out of your *m* Josh 6:10
not counsel at the *m* of the LORD Josh 9:14
stones upon the *m* of the cave Josh 10:18
Open the *m* of the cave, and bring Josh 10:22
laid great stones in the cave's *m* Josh 10:27
putting their hand to their *m* Judg 7:6
unto him, Where is now thy *m* Judg 9:38
I have opened my *m* unto the LORD Judg 11:35
hast opened thy *m* unto the LORD Judg 11:36
which hath proceeded out of thy *m* Judg 11:36
peace, lay thine hand upon thy *m* Judg 18:19
the LORD, that Eli marked her *m* 1Sa 1:12
my *m* is enlarged over mine 1Sa 2:1
not arrogancy come out of your *m* 1Sa 2:3
but no man put his hand to his *m* 1Sa 14:26
and put his hand to his *m* 1Sa 14:27
him, and delivered it out of his *m* 1Sa 17:35
for thy *m* hath testified against 2Sa 1:16
So Joab put the words in her *m* 2Sa 14:3
words in the *m* of thine handmaid 2Sa 14:19
a covering over the well's *m* 2Sa 17:19
alone, there is tidings in his *m* 2Sa 18:25
and fire out of his *m* devoured 2Sa 22:9
the *m* of it within the chapiter 1Kin 7:31
but the *m* thereof was round after 1Kin 7:31
also upon the *m* of it were 1Kin 7:31
with his *m* unto David my father 1Kin 8:15
thou spakest also with thy *m* 1Kin 8:24
hast disobeyed the *m* of the LORD 1Kin 13:21
of the LORD in thy *m* is truth 1Kin 17:24
every *m* which hath not kissed him 1Kin 19:18
good unto the king with one *m* 1Kin 22:13
in the *m* of all his prophets 1Kin 22:22
the *m* of all these thy prophets 1Kin 22:23
and put his *m* upon his *m* 2Kin 4:34
and the judgments of his *m* 1Chr 16:12
with his *m* to my father David 2Chr 6:4
and spakest with thy *m*, and hast 2Chr 6:15
in the *m* of all his prophets 2Chr 18:21
in the *m* of these thy prophets 2Chr 18:22
words of Necho from the *m* of God 2Chr 35:22
speaking from the *m* of the LORD 2Chr 36:12
of the LORD by the *m* of Jeremiah 2Chr 36:21
by the *m* of Jeremiah might be 2Chr 36:22
the word of the LORD by the *m* of Ezr 1:1
not thy manna from their *m* Neh 9:20
the word went out of the king's *m* Est 7:8
After this opened Job his *m* Job 3:1
poor from the sword, from their *m* Job 5:15
hope, and iniquity stoppeth her *m* Job 5:16
Therefore I will not refrain my *m* Job 7:11
of thy *m* be like a strong wind Job 8:2
Till he fill thy *m* with laughing Job 8:21
mine own *m* shall condemn me Job 9:20
and the *m* taste his meat Job 12:11
For thy *m* uttereth thine iniquity Job 15:5
Thine own *m* condemneth thee, and Job 15:6
such words go out of thy *m* Job 15:13
breath of his *m* shall he go away Job 15:30
I would strengthen you with my *m* Job 16:5
have gaped upon me with their *m* Job 16:10
I intreated him with my *m* Job 19:16
wickedness be sweet in his *m* Job 20:12
but keep it still within his *m* Job 20:13
and lay your hand upon your *m* Job 21:5
I pray thee, the law from his *m* Job 22:22
him, and fill my *m* with arguments Job 23:4
his *m* more than my necessary food Job 23:12
and laid their hand on their *m* Job 29:9
cleaved to the roof of their *m* Job 29:10
they opened their *m* wide as for Job 29:23
or my *m* hath kissed my hand Job 31:27
(Neither have I suffered my *m* to Job 31:30
in the *m* of these three men Job 32:5
Behold, now I have opened my *m* Job 33:2
my tongue hath spoken in my *m* Job 33:2
words, as the *m* tasteth meat Job 34:3
doth Job open his *m* in vain Job 35:16
the sound that goeth out of his *m* Job 37:2
I will lay mine hand upon my *m* Job 40:4
he can draw up Jordan into his *m* Job 40:23
Out of his *m* go burning lamps, and Job 41:19
and a flame goeth out of his *m* Job 41:21
is no faithfulness in their *m* Ps 5:9
Out of the *m* of babes and Ps 8:2
His *m* is full of cursing and Ps 10:7
that my *m* shall not transgress Ps 17:3
with their *m* they speak proudly Ps 17:10
and fire out of his *m* devoured Ps 18:8
Let the words of my *m*, and the Ps 19:14
Save me from the lion's *m* Ps 22:21
whose *m* must be held in with bit Ps 32:9
of them by the breath of his *m* Ps 33:6
shall continually be in my *m* Ps 34:1
opened their *m* wide against me Ps 35:21
The words of his *m* are iniquity Ps 36:3
The *m* of the righteous speaketh Ps 37:30
a dumb man that openeth not his *m* Ps 38:13
in whose *m* are no reproofs Ps 38:14
I will keep my *m* with a bridle Ps 39:1
I was dumb, I opened not my *m* Ps 39:9
And he hath put a new song in my *m* Ps 40:3
My *m* shall speak of wisdom Ps 49:3
take my covenant in thy *m* Ps 50:16
Thou givest thy *m* to evil Ps 50:19
my *m* shall shew forth thy praise Ps 51:15
give ear to the words of my *m* Ps 54:2
The words of his *m* were smoother Ps 55:21
their teeth, O God, in their *m* Ps 58:6
they belch out with their *m* Ps 59:7
For the sin of their *m* and the Ps 59:12
they bless with their *m*, but they Ps 62:4
my *m* shall praise thee with Ps 63:5
but the *m* of them that speak lies Ps 63:11
my *m* hath spoken, when I was in Ps 66:14
I cried unto him with my *m* Ps 66:17
not the pit shut her *m* upon me Ps 69:15
Let my *m* be filled with thy Ps 71:8
My *m* shall shew forth thy Ps 71:15
They set their *m* against the Ps 73:9
your ears to the words of my *m* Ps 78:1
I will open my *m* in a parable Ps 78:2
they did flatter him with their *m* Ps 78:36
open thy *m* wide, and I will fill Ps 81:10
with my *m* will I make known thy Ps 89:1
satisfieth thy *m* with good things Ps 103:5
and the judgments of his *m* Ps 105:5
and all iniquity shall stop her *m* Ps 107:42
For the *m* of the wicked and the Ps 109:2
the *m* of the deceitful are opened Ps 109:2
greatly praise the LORD with my *m* Ps 109:30
all the judgments of thy *m* Ps 119:13
word of truth utterly out of my *m* Ps 119:43
The law of thy *m* is better unto Ps 119:72
I keep the testimony of thy *m* Ps 119:88
yea, sweeter than honey to my *m* Ps 119:103
the freewill offerings of my *m* Ps 119:108
I opened my *m*, and panted Ps 119:131
Then was our *m* filled with Ps 126:2
tongue cleave to the roof of my *m* Ps 137:6
when they hear the words of thy *m* Ps 138:4
Set a watch, O LORD, before my *m* Ps 141:3
are scattered at the grave's *m* Ps 141:7
Whose *m* speaketh vanity, and their Ps 144:8
whose *m* speaketh vanity, and their Ps 144:11
My *m* shall speak the praise of Ps 145:21
high praises of God be in their *m* Ps 149:6
out of his *m* cometh knowledge and Prov 2:6
decline from the words of my *m* Prov 4:5
Put away from thee a froward *m* Prov 4:24
her *m* is smoother than oil Prov 5:3
depart not from the words of my *m* Prov 5:7
snared with the words of thy *m* Prov 6:2
art taken with the words of thy *m* Prov 6:2
man, walketh with a froward *m* Prov 6:12
and attend to the words of my *m* Prov 7:24
For my *m* shall speak truth Prov 8:7
All the words of my *m* are in Prov 8:8
and the evil way, and the froward *m* Prov 8:13
covereth the *m* of the wicked Prov 10:6
The *m* of a righteous man is a Prov 10:11
covereth the *m* of the wicked Prov 10:11
but the *m* of the foolish is near Prov 10:14
The *m* of the just bringeth forth Prov 10:31
but the *m* of the wicked speaketh Prov 10:32
An hypocrite with his *m* Prov 11:9
overthrown by the *m* of the wicked Prov 11:11
but the *m* of the upright shall Prov 12:6
with good by the fruit of his *m* Prov 12:14
eat good by the fruit of his *m* Prov 13:2
keepeth his *m* keepeth his life Prov 13:3
In the *m* of the foolish is a rod Prov 14:3
but the *m* of fools poureth out Prov 15:2
but the *m* of fools feedeth on Prov 15:14
hath joy by the answer of his *m* Prov 15:23
but the *m* of the wicked poureth Prov 15:28
his *m* transgresseth not in Prov 16:10
heart of the wise teacheth his *m* Prov 16:23
for his *m* craveth it of him Prov 16:26
of a man's *m* are as deep waters Prov 18:4
his *m* calleth for strokes Prov 18:6
A fool's *m* is his destruction, and Prov 18:7
satisfied with the fruit of his *m* Prov 18:20
much as bring it to his *m* again Prov 19:24
the *m* of the wicked devoureth Prov 19:28
but afterwards his *m* shall be Prov 20:17
keepeth his *m* and his tongue Prov 21:23
The *m* of strange women is a deep Prov 22:14
he openeth not his *m* in the gate Prov 24:7
so is a parable in the *m* of fools Prov 26:7
so is a parable in the *m* of fools Prov 26:9
him to bring it again to his *m* Prov 26:15
and a flattering *m* worketh ruin Prov 26:28
praise thee, and not thine own *m* Prov 27:2
she eateth, and wipeth her *m* Prov 30:20
evil, lay thine hand upon thy *m* Prov 30:32
Open thy *m* for the dumb in the Prov 31:8
Open thy *m*, judge righteously, and Prov 31:9
She openeth her *m* with wisdom Prov 31:26
Be not rash with thy *m*, and let Eccl 5:2
Suffer not thy *m* to cause thy Eccl 5:6
the labour of man is for his *m* Eccl 6:7
of a wise man's *m* are gracious Eccl 10:12
the words of his *m* is foolishness Eccl 10:13
kiss me with the kisses of his *m* Song 1:2
His *m* is most sweet Song 5:16
the roof of thy *m* like the best Song 7:9
for the *m* of the LORD hath spoken Is 1:20
opened her *m* without measure Is 5:14
And he laid it upon my *m*, and said, Is 6:7
shall devour Israel with open *m* Is 9:12
and every *m* speaketh folly Is 9:17
moved the wing, or opened the *m* Is 10:14
the earth with the rod of his *m* Is 11:4
by the *m* of the brooks, and every Is 19:7
people draw near me with their *m* Is 29:13
Egypt, and have not asked at my *m* Is 30:2
for my *m* it hath commanded, and Is 34:16
for the *m* of the LORD hath spoken Is 40:5
gone out of my *m* in righteousness Is 45:23
and they went forth out of my *m* Is 48:3
he hath made my *m* like a sharp Is 49:2
And I have put my words in thy *m* Is 51:16
yet he opened not his *m* Is 53:7
is dumb, so he openeth not his *m* Is 53:7
neither was any deceit in his *m* Is 53:9
be that goeth forth out of my *m* Is 55:11
against whom make ye a wide *m* Is 57:4
for the *m* of the LORD hath spoken Is 58:14
words which I have put in thy *m* Is 59:21
shall not depart out of thy *m* Is 59:21
nor out of the *m* of thy seed Is 59:21
nor out of the *m* of thy seed's Is 59:21
which the *m* of the LORD shall Is 62:2
forth his hand, and touched my *m* Jer 1:9
I have put my words in thy *m* Jer 1:9
will make my words in thy *m* fire Jer 5:14
and is cut off from their *m* Jer 7:28
to his neighbour with his *m* Jer 9:8
who is he to whom the *m* of the Jer 9:12
ear receive the word of his *m* Jer 9:20
thou art near in their *m*, and far Jer 12:2
the vile, thou shalt be as my *m* Jer 15:19
and not out of the *m* of the LORD Jer 23:16
shall speak with him *m* to *m* Jer 32:4
shall speak with thee *m* to *m* Jer 34:3
Baruch wrote from the *m* of Jer 36:4
which thou hast written from my *m* Jer 36:6
write all these words at his *m* Jer 36:17
these words unto me with his *m* Jer 36:18
Baruch wrote at the *m* of Jeremiah Jer 36:27

who wrote therein from the *m* of ... Jer 36:32
goeth forth out of our own *m* ... Jer 44:17
shall no more be named in the *m* ... Jer 44:26
in a book at the *m* of Jeremiah ... Jer 45:1
nest in the sides of the hole's *m* ... Jer 48:28
I will bring forth out of his *m* ... Jer 51:44
have opened their *m* against thee ... Lam 2:16
He putteth his *m* in the dust ... Lam 3:29
Out of the *m* of the most High ... Lam 3:38
to the roof of his *m* for thirst ... Lam 4:4
open thy *m*, and eat that I give ... Eze 2:8
So I opened my *m*, and he caused me ... Eze 3:2
it was in my *m* as honey for ... Eze 3:3
therefore hear the word at my *m* ... Eze 3:17
cleave to the roof of thy *m* ... Eze 3:26
with thee, I will open thy *m* ... Eze 3:27
there abominable flesh into my *m* ... Eze 4:14
by thy *m* in the day of thy pride ... Eze 16:56
never open thy *m* any more because... Eze 16:63
to open the *m* in the slaughter, ... Eze 21:22
In that day shall thy *m* be opened ... Eze 24:27
of the *m* in the midst of them ... Eze 29:21
thou shalt hear the word at my *m* ... Eze 33:7
and had opened my *m*, until he came. Eze 33:22
my *m* was opened, and I was ... Eze 33:22
for with their *m* they shew much ... Eze 33:31
deliver my flock from their *m* ... Eze 34:10
Thus with your *m* ye have boasted ... Eze 35:13
*m* of the burning fiery furnace ... Dan 3:26
the word was in the king's *m* ... Dan 4:31
and laid upon the *m* of the den ... Dan 6:17
it had three ribs in the *m* of it ... Dan 7:5
a *m* speaking great things ... Dan 7:8
a *m* that spake very great things, ... Dan 7:20
came flesh nor wine in my *m* ... Dan 10:3
then I opened my *m*, and spake, and. Dan 10:16
the names of Baalim out of her *m* ... Hos 2:17
slain them by the words of my *m* ... Hos 6:5
Set the trumpet to thy *m* ... Hos 8:1
for it is cut off from your *m* ... Joel 1:5
out of the *m* of the lion two legs ... Amos 3:12
for the *m* of the LORD of hosts ... Mic 4:4
tongue is deceitful in their *m* ... Mic 6:12
keep the doors of thy *m* from her ... Mic 7:5
shall lay their hand upon their *m* ... Mic 7:16
even fall into the *m* of the eater ... Nah 3:12
tongue be found in their *m* ... Zeph 3:13
weight of lead upon the *m* thereof ... Zec 5:8
words by the *m* of the prophets ... Zec 8:9
take away his blood out of his *m* ... Zec 9:7
shall consume away in their *m* ... Zec 14:12
The law of truth was in his *m* ... Mal 2:6
they should seek the law at his *m* ... Mal 2:7
proceedeth out of the *m* of God ... Mt 4:4
And he opened his *m*, and taught ... Mt 5:2
of the heart the *m* speaketh ... Mt 12:34
I will open my *m* in parables ... Mt 13:35
draweth nigh unto me with their *m* ... Mt 15:8
goeth into the *m* defileth a man ... Mt 15:11
that which cometh out of the *m* ... Mt 15:11
in at the *m* goeth into the belly ... Mt 15:17
the *m* come forth from the heart ... Mt 15:18
and when thou hast opened his *m* ... Mt 17:27
that in the *m* of two or three ... Mt 18:16
never read, Out of the *m* of babes ... Mt 21:16
his *m* was opened immediately, and ... Lk 1:64
As he spake by the *m* of his holy ... Lk 1:70
which proceeded out of his *m* ... Lk 4:22
of the heart his *m* speaketh ... Lk 6:45
to catch something out of his *m* ... Lk 11:54
Out of thine own *m* will I judge ... Lk 19:22
For I will give you a *m* and wisdom ... Lk 21:15
ourselves have heard of his own *m* ... Lk 22:71
upon hyssop, and put it to his *m* ... Jn 19:29
by the *m* of David spake before ... Acts 1:16
by the *m* of all his prophets ... Acts 3:18
which God hath spoken by the *m* of ... Acts 3:21
Who by the *m* of thy servant David ... Acts 4:25
shearer, so opened he not his *m* ... Acts 8:32
Then Philip opened his *m*, and ... Acts 8:35
Then Peter opened his *m*, and said, ... Acts 10:34
at any time entered into my *m* ... Acts 11:8
that the Gentiles by my *m* should ... Acts 15:7
tell you the same things by *m* ... Acts 15:27
Paul was now about to open his *m* ... Acts 18:14
shouldest hear the voice of his *m* ... Acts 22:14
by him to smite him on the *m* ... Acts 23:2
Whose *m* is full of cursing and ... Rom 3:14
that every *m* may be stopped, and ... Rom 3:19
word is nigh thee, even in thy *m* ... Rom 10:8
confess with thy *m* the Lord Jesus ... Rom 10:9
with the *m* confession is made ... Rom 10:10
one *m* glorify God, even the ... Rom 15:6
Thou shalt not muzzle the *m* of ... 1Cor 9:9
our *m* is open unto you, our heart ... 2Cor 6:11
In the *m* of two or three ... 2Cor 13:1
proceed out of your *m*, but that ... Eph 4:29
me, that I may open my *m* boldly ... Eph 6:19
communication out of your *m* ... Col 3:8
consume with the spirit of his *m* ... 2Th 2:8
out of the *m* of the lion ... 2Ti 4:17
Out of the same *m* proceedeth ... Jas 3:10
neither was guile found in his *m* ... 1Pet 2:22
their *m* speaketh great swelling ... Jude 16
out of his *m* went a sharp ... Rev 1:16
them with the sword of my *m* ... Rev 2:16
hot, I will spue thee out of my *m* ... Rev 3:16
For their power is in their *m* ... Rev 9:19
shall be in thy *m* sweet as honey ... Rev 10:9
it was in my *m* sweet as honey ... Rev 10:10
fire proceedeth out of their *m* ... Rev 11:5
his *m* water as a flood after the ... Rev 12:15
woman, and the earth opened her *m* .. Rev 12:16
the dragon cast out of his *m* ... Rev 12:16
his *m* as the *m* of a lion ... Rev 13:2
and his *m* as the *m* of a lion ... Rev 13:2
him a *m* speaking great things ... Rev 13:5
he opened his *m* in blasphemy ... Rev 13:6
in their *m* was found no guile ... Rev 14:5
come out of the *m* of the dragon ... Rev 16:13
out of the *m* of the beast ... Rev 16:13
out of the *m* of the false prophet ... Rev 16:13
out of his *m* goeth a sharp sword, ... Rev 19:15
sword proceeded out of his *m* ... Rev 19:21

**MOUTHS**
which we found in our sacks' *m* ... Gen 44:8
put it in their *m*, that this song ... Deut 31:19
out of the *m* of their seed ... Deut 31:21
They gaped upon me with their *m* ... Ps 22:13
their meat was yet in their *m* ... Ps 78:30
They have *m*, but they speak not ... Ps 115:5
They have *m*, but they speak not ... Ps 135:16
is there any breath in their *m* ... Ps 135:17
kings shall shut their *m* at him ... Is 52:15
have both spoken with your *m* ... Jer 44:25
have opened their *m* against us ... Lam 3:46
angel, and hath shut the lions' *m* ... Dan 6:22
he that putteth not into their *m* ... Mic 3:5
Whose *m* must be stopped, who ... Titus 1:11
promises, stopped the *m* of lions ... Heb 11:33
we put bits in the horses' *m* ... Jas 3:3
and out of their *m* issued fire ... Rev 9:17
which issued out of their *m* ... Rev 9:18

**MOVE**
shall not a dog *m* his tongue ... Ex 11:7
of all that *m* in the waters, and ... Lev 11:10
but thou shalt not *m* a sickle ... Deut 23:25
I will *m* them to jealousy with ... Deut 32:21
*m* him at times in the camp of Dan... Judg 13:25
place of their own, and *m* no more ... 2Sa 7:10
*m* any more out of the land which ... 2Kin 21:8
let no man *m* his bones ... 2Kin 23:18
and with hammers, that it *m* not ... Jer 10:4
they shall *m* out of their holes ... Mic 7:17
but they themselves will not *m* ... Mt 23:4
For in him we live, and *m*, and have. Acts 17:28
But none of these things *m* me ... Acts 20:24

**MOVEABLE**
the path of life, her ways are *m* ... Prov 5:6

**MOVED**
the Spirit of God *m* upon the face ... Gen 1:2
flesh died that *m* upon the earth ... Gen 7:21
They have *m* me to jealousy with ... Deut 32:21
none *m* his tongue against any of ... Josh 10:21
that she *m* him to ask of her ... Josh 15:18
that she *m* him to ask of her ... Judg 1:14
all the city was *m* about them ... Ruth 1:19
only her lips *m*, but her voice ... 1Sa 1:13
And the king was much *m*, and went. 2Sa 18:33
the foundations of heaven *m* ... 2Sa 22:8
he *m* David against them to say, ... 2Sa 24:1
shall be stable, that it be not *m* ... 1Chr 16:30
place, and shall be *m* no more ... 1Chr 17:9
God *m* them to depart from him ... 2Chr 18:31
that they have *m* sedition within ... Ezr 4:15
nor *m* for him, he was full of ... Est 5:9
and is *m* out of his place ... Job 37:1
they cannot be *m* ... Job 41:23
in his heart, I shall not be *m* ... Ps 10:6
trouble me rejoice when I am *m* ... Ps 13:4
these things shall never be *m* ... Ps 15:5
my right hand, I shall not be *m* ... Ps 16:8
foundations also of the hills *m* ... Ps 18:7
the most High he shall not be *m* ... Ps 21:7
I said, I shall never be *m* ... Ps 30:6
she shall not be *m* ... Ps 46:5
raged, the kingdoms were *m* ... Ps 46:6
suffer the righteous to be *m* ... Ps 55:22
I shall not be greatly *m* ... Ps 62:2
I shall not be *m* ... Ps 62:6
and suffereth not our feet to be *m* ... Ps 66:9
even Sinai itself was *m* at the ... Ps 68:8
*m* him to jealousy with their ... Ps 78:58
stablished, that it cannot be *m* ... Ps 93:1
that it shall not be *m* ... Ps 96:10
let the earth be *m* ... Ps 99:1
Surely he shall not be *m* for ever ... Ps 112:6
will not suffer thy foot to be *m* ... Ps 121:3
of the righteous shall not be *m* ... Prov 12:3
door, and my bowels were *m* for him... Song 5:4
the posts of the door *m* at the ... Is 6:4
And his heart was *m*, and the heart ... Is 7:2
of the wood are *m* with the wind ... Is 7:2
and there was none that *m* the wing ... Is 10:14
Hell from beneath is *m* for thee ... Is 14:9
Egypt shall be *m* at his presence ... Is 19:1
the earth is *m* exceedingly ... Is 24:19
graven image, that shall not be *m* ... Is 40:20
nails, that it should not be *m* ... Is 41:7
and all the hills *m* lightly ... Jer 4:24
And they shall drink, and be *m* ... Jer 25:16
whose waters are *m* as the rivers ... Jer 46:7
his waters are *m* like the rivers ... Jer 46:8
The earth is *m* at the noise of ... Jer 49:21
taking of Babylon the earth is *m* ... Jer 50:46
he was *m* with choler against him, ... Dan 8:7
the south shall be *m* with choler ... Dan 11:11
he was *m* with compassion on them, ... Mt 9:36
was *m* with compassion toward them .. Mt 14:14
servant was *m* with compassion ... Mt 18:27
they were *m* with indignation ... Mt 20:24
Jerusalem, all the city was *m* ... Mt 21:10
*m* with compassion, put forth his ... Mk 1:41
was *m* with compassion toward them ... Mk 6:34
the chief priests *m* the people ... Mk 15:11
hand, that I should not be *m* ... Acts 2:25
*m* with envy, sold Joseph into ... Acts 7:9
*m* with envy, took unto them ... Acts 17:5
And all the city was *m*, and the ... Acts 21:30
be not *m* away from the hope of ... Col 1:23
should be *m* by these afflictions ... 1Th 3:3
*m* with fear, prepared an ark to ... Heb 11:7
a kingdom which cannot be *m* ... Heb 12:28
as they were *m* by the Holy Ghost ... 2Pet 1:21
island were *m* out of their places ... Rev 6:14

**MOVEDST**
although thou *m* me against him, ... Job 2:3

**MOVER**
a *m* of sedition among all the ... Acts 24:5

**MOVETH**
and every living creature that *m* ... Gen 1:21
thing that *m* upon the earth ... Gen 1:28
upon all that *m* upon the earth, ... Gen 9:2
creature that *m* in the waters ... Lev 11:46
He *m* his tail like a cedar ... Job 40:17
and every thing that *m* therein ... Ps 69:34
the cup, when it *m* itself aright ... Prov 23:31
every thing that liveth, which *m* ... Eze 47:9

**MOVING**
the *m* creature that hath life ... Gen 1:20
Every *m* thing that liveth shall ... Gen 9:3
the *m* of my lips should asswage ... Job 16:5
*m* his lips he bringeth evil to ... Prov 16:30
waiting for the *m* of the water ... Jn 5:3

**MOWER**
Wherewith the *m* filleth not his ... Ps 129:7

**MOWINGS**
latter growth after the king's *m* ... Amos 7:1

**MOWN**
down like rain upon the *m* grass ... Ps 72:6

**MOZA** (*mo'-zah*)
*1. A son of Caleb.*
concubine, bare Haran, and *M* ... 1Chr 2:46
*2. Descendant of King Saul.*
and Zimri begat *M*, ... 1Chr 8:36
And *M* begat Binea ... 1Chr 8:37
and Zimri begat *M* ... 1Chr 9:42
And *M* begat Binea ... 1Chr 9:43

**MOZAH** (*mo'-zah*) *A city in Benjamin.*
And Mizpeh, and Chephirah, and *M* .. Josh 18:26

**MUCH**
for as *m* money as it is worth he ... Gen 23:9
for thou art *m* mightier than we ... Gen 26:16
had *m* cattle, and maidservants, and .. Gen 30:43
Ask me never so *m* dowry and gift, ... Gen 34:12
as the sand of the sea, very *m* ... Gen 41:49
five times so *m* as any of theirs ... Gen 43:34
as *m* as they can carry, and put ... Gen 44:1
this day, to save *m* people alive ... Gen 50:20
and herds, even very *m* cattle ... Ex 12:38
It is a night to be *m* observed ... Ex 12:42
remained not so *m* as one of them ... Ex 14:28
twice as *m* as they gather daily ... Ex 16:5
that gathered *m* had nothing over ... Ex 16:18
they gathered twice as *m* bread ... Ex 16:22
and of sweet cinnamon half so *m* ... Ex 30:23
The people bring *m* more than ... Ex 36:5
all the work to make it, and too *m* ... Ex 36:7
Aaron have, one as *m* as another ... Lev 7:10
scab spread *m* abroad in the skin ... Lev 13:7
if it spread *m* abroad in the skin ... Lev 13:22
if it be spread *m* abroad in the ... Lev 13:27
But if the scall spread *m* in the ... Lev 13:35
if he be poor, and cannot get so *m* ... Lev 14:21
unto them, Ye take too *m* upon you... Num 16:3
ye take too *m* upon you, ye sons ... Num 16:7
out against him with *m* people ... Num 20:20
the soul of the people was *m* ... Num 21:4
and *m* people of Israel died ... Num 21:6
not so *m* as a footbreadth ... Deut 2:5
(for I know that ye have *m* cattle ... Deut 3:19
Thou shalt carry *m* seed out into ... Deut 28:38
how *m* more after my death ... Deut 31:27
*m* people, even as the sand that ... Josh 11:4
yet very *m* land to be possessed ... Josh 13:1
of Judah was too *m* for them ... Josh 19:9
Return with *m* riches unto your ... Josh 22:8
your tents, and with very *m* cattle ... Josh 22:8
with iron, and with very *m* raiment ... Josh 22:8
for it grieveth me *m* for your ... Ruth 1:13
then take as *m* as thy soul ... 1Sa 2:16
How *m* more, if haply the people ... 1Sa 14:30
a *m* greater slaughter among the ... 1Sa 14:30
so that his name was *m* set by ... 1Sa 18:30
Saul's son delighted *m* in David ... 1Sa 19:2
LORD do so and *m* more to Jonathan .. 1Sa 20:13
how *m* more then if we come to ... 1Sa 23:3
as thy life was *m* set by this day ... 1Sa 26:24
so let my life be *m* set by in the ... 1Sa 26:24
How *m* more, when wicked men have.. 2Sa 4:11
king David took exceeding *m* brass ... 2Sa 8:8
there came *m* people by the way of ... 2Sa 13:34
so *m* praised as Absalom for his ... 2Sa 14:25

how *m* more now may this Benjamite 2Sa 16:11
shall not be left so *m* as one 2Sa 17:12
And the king was *m* moved 2Sa 18:33
and understanding exceeding *m* 1Kin 4:29
how *m* less this house that I have 1Kin 8:27
that bare spices, and very *m* gold 1Kin 10:2
It is too *m* for you to go up to 1Kin 12:28
how *m* rather then, when he saith 2Kin 5:13
but Jehu shall serve him *m* 2Kin 10:18
there was *m* money in the chest 2Kin 12:10
he wrought *m* wickedness in the 2Kin 21:6
shed innocent blood very *m* 2Kin 21:16
brought David very *m* brass 1Chr 18:8
exceeding *m* spoil out of the city 1Chr 20:2
brought *m* cedar wood to David 1Chr 22:4
because thou hast shed *m* blood 1Chr 22:8
Lebanon, as *m* as thou shalt need 2Chr 2:16
how *m* less this house which I 2Chr 6:18
and they carried away very *m* spoil 2Chr 14:13
was exceeding *m* spoil in them 2Chr 14:14
he had *m* business in the cities 2Chr 17:13
of the spoil, it was so *m* 2Chr 20:25
they saw that there was *m* money 2Chr 24:11
to give thee *m* more than this 2Chr 25:9
thousand of them, and took *m* spoil 2Chr 25:13
for he had *m* cattle, both in the 2Chr 26:10
on the wall of Ophel he built *m* 2Chr 27:3
So *m* did the children of Ammon 2Chr 27:5
took also away *m* spoil from them, 2Chr 28:8
*m* people to keep the feast of 2Chr 30:13
was gathered *m* people together 2Chr 32:4
of Assyria come, and find *m* water 2Chr 32:4
how *m* less shall your God deliver 2Chr 32:15
Hezekiah had exceeding *m* riches 2Chr 32:27
had given him substance very *m* 2Chr 32:29
he wrought *m* evil in the sight of 2Chr 33:6
transgressed very *m* after all the 2Chr 36:14
and salt without prescribing how *m* Ezr 7:22
many, and it is a time of *m* rain Ezr 10:13
is decayed, and there is *m* rubbish Neh 4:10
they were *m* cast down in their Neh 6:16
it yieldeth *m* increase unto the Neh 9:37
shall there arise too *m* contempt Est 1:18
How *m* less in them that dwell in Job 4:19
How *m* less shall I answer him, and Job 9:14
aged men, *m* elder than thy father Job 15:10
How *m* more abominable and filthy Job 15:16
How *m* less man, that is a worm Job 25:6
and because mine hand had gotten *m*. Job 31:25
How *m* less to him that accepteth Job 34:19
Job twice as *m* as he had before Job 42:10
than gold, yea, than *m* fine gold Ps 19:10
is not delivered by *m* strength Ps 33:16
I will praise thee among *m* people Ps 35:18
as *m* as in all riches Ps 119:14
I am afflicted very *m* Ps 119:107
With her *m* fair speech she caused Prov 7:21
*m* more the wicked and the sinner Prov 11:31
*M* food is in the tillage of the Prov 13:23
but *m* increase is by the strength Prov 14:4
of the righteous is *m* treasure Prov 15:6
how *m* more then the hearts of the Prov 15:11
How *m* better is it to get wisdom Prov 16:16
*m* less do lying lips a prince Prov 17:7
how *m* more do his friends go far Prov 19:7
*m* less for a servant to have rule Prov 19:10
will not so *m* as bring it to his Prov 19:24
how *m* more, when he bringeth it Prov 21:27
eat so *m* as is sufficient for Prov 25:16
It is not good to eat *m* honey Prov 25:27
For in *m* wisdom is *m* grief Eccl 1:18
sweet, whether he eat little or *m* Eccl 5:12
in darkness, and he hath *m* sorrow Eccl 5:17
For he shall not *m* remember the Eccl 5:20
Be not righteous over *m* Eccl 7:16
Be not over *m* wicked, neither be Eccl 7:17
but one sinner destroyeth *m* good Eccl 9:18
By *m* slothfulness the building Eccl 10:18
*m* study is a weariness of the Eccl 12:12
how *m* better is thy love than Song 4:10
hearkened diligently with *m* heed Is 21:7
pile thereof is fire and *m* wood Is 30:33
as this day, and *m* more abundant Is 56:12
with nitre, and take thee *m* sope Jer 2:22
thou about so *m* to change thy way Jer 2:36
wine and summer fruits very *m* Jer 40:12
How *m* more when I send my four Eze 14:21
how *m* less shall it be meet yet Eze 15:5
might give him horses and *m* people Eze 17:15
which art infamous and *m* vexed Eze 22:5
it containeth *m* Eze 23:32
and companies, and *m* people Eze 26:7
with their mouth they shew *m* love Eze 33:31
were fair, and the fruit thereof *m* Dan 4:12
were fair, and the fruit thereof *m* Dan 4:21
unto it, Arise, devour *m* flesh Dan 7:5
my cogitations *m* troubled me Dan 7:28
a great army and with *m* riches Dan 11:13
face the people shall be *m* pained Joel 2:6
and also *m* cattle Jonah 4:11
*m* pain is in all loins, and the Nah 2:10
Ye have sown *m*, and bring in Hag 1:6
Ye looked for *m*, and, lo, it came Hag 1:9
have we spoken so *m* against thee Mal 3:13
be heard for their *m* speaking Mt 6:7
Are ye not *m* better than they Mt 6:26
shall he not *m* more clothe you, O Mt 6:30
how *m* more shall your Father Mt 7:11
how *m* more shall they call them Mt 10:25
How *m* then is a man better than a Mt 12:12
where they had not *m* earth Mt 13:5
have so *m* bread in the wilderness Mt 15:33
might have been sold for *m* Mt 26:9
out, and began to publish it *m* Mk 1:45
not so *m* as about the door Mk 2:2
they could not so *m* as eat bread Mk 3:20
ground, where it had not *m* earth Mk 4:5
he besought him *m* that he would Mk 5:10
*m* people gathered unto him Mk 5:21
*m* people followed him, and Mk 5:24
had no leisure so *m* as to eat Mk 6:31
saw *m* people, and was moved with Mk 6:34
so *m* the more a great deal they Mk 7:36
he was *m* displeased, and said unto Mk 10:14
they began to be *m* displeased Mk 10:41
and many that were rich cast in *m* Mk 12:41
But so *m* the more went there a Lk 5:15
Have ye not read so *m* as this Lk 6:3
to sinners, to receive as *m* again Lk 6:34
went with him, and *m* people Lk 7:11
*m* people of the city was with her Lk 7:12
you, and *m* more than a prophet Lk 7:26
for she loved *m* Lk 7:47
when *m* people were gathered Lk 8:4
from the hill, *m* people met him Lk 9:37
was cumbered about *m* serving Lk 10:40
how *m* more shall your heavenly Lk 11:13
thou hast *m* goods laid up for Lk 12:19
how *m* more are ye better than the Lk 12:24
how *m* more will he clothe you, O Lk 12:28
For unto whomsoever *m* is given Lk 12:48
of him shall be *m* required Lk 12:48
and to whom men have committed *m* Lk 12:48
How *m* owest thou unto my lord Lk 16:5
to another, And how *m* owest thou Lk 16:7
is least is faithful also in *m* Lk 16:10
in the least is unjust also in *m* Lk 16:10
would not lift up so *m* as his Lk 18:13
but he cried so *m* the more Lk 18:39
that he might know how *m* every Lk 19:15
to pass, as they were *m* perplexed Lk 24:4
because there was *m* water there Jn 3:23
Now there was *m* grass in the Jn 6:10
of the fishes as *m* as they would Jn 6:11
there was *m* murmuring among the Jn 7:12
*M* people of the Jews therefore Jn 12:9
On the next day *m* people that Jn 12:12
it die, it bringeth forth *m* fruit Jn 12:24
I will not talk *m* with you Jn 14:30
the same bringeth forth *m* fruit Jn 15:5
glorified, that ye bear *m* fruit Jn 15:8
whether ye sold the land for so *m* Acts 5:8
And she said, Yea, for so *m* Acts 5:8
drew away *m* people after him Acts 5:37
not so *m* as to set his foot on Acts 7:5
how *m* evil he hath done to thy Acts 9:13
which gave *m* alms to the people, Acts 10:2
*m* people was added unto the Lord Acts 11:24
the church, and taught *m* people Acts 11:26
faith, and that we must through *m* Acts 14:22
when there had been *m* disputing Acts 15:7
her masters *m* gain by soothsaying Acts 16:16
for I have *m* people in this city Acts 18:10
helped them *m* which had believed Acts 18:27
We have not so *m* as heard whether Acts 19:2
turned away *m* people Acts 19:26
and had given them *m* exhortation Acts 20:2
*m* learning doth make thee mad Acts 26:24
Now when *m* time was spent, and Acts 27:9
*m* damage, not only of the lading Acts 27:10
we had *m* work to come by the boat. Acts 27:16
as *m* as in me is, I am ready to Rom 1:15
*M* every way: chiefly Rom 3:2
*M* more then, being now justified Rom 5:9
*m* more, being reconciled, we Rom 5:10
*m* more the grace of God, and the Rom 5:15
*m* more they which receive Rom 5:17
abounded, grace did *m* more abound Rom 5:20
endured with *m* longsuffering the Rom 9:22
how *m* more their fulness Rom 11:12
how *m* more shall these, which be Rom 11:24
as *m* as lieth in you, live Rom 12:18
*m* hindered from coming to you Rom 15:22
Mary, who bestowed *m* labour on us Rom 16:6
which laboured *m* in the Lord Rom 16:12
and in fear, and in *m* trembling 1Cor 2:3
so *m* as named among the Gentiles 1Cor 5:1
how *m* more things that pertain to 1Cor 6:3
*m* more those members of the body, 1Cor 12:22
salute you *m* in the Lord, with 1Cor 16:19
For out of *m* affliction and 2Cor 2:4
*m* more doth the ministration of 2Cor 3:9
*m* more that which remaineth is 2Cor 3:11
in *m* patience, in afflictions, in 2Cor 6:4
Praying us with *m* intreaty that 2Cor 8:4
had gathered *m* had nothing over 2Cor 8:15
but now *m* more diligent, upon the 2Cor 8:22
are *m* more bold to speak the word Phil 1:14
but now *m* more in my absence, Phil 2:12
the Holy Ghost, and in *m* assurance 1Th 1:5
received the word in *m* affliction 1Th 1:6
gospel of God with *m* contention 1Th 2:2
not given to *m* wine, not greedy 1Ti 3:8
the coppersmith did me *m* evil 2Ti 4:14
accusers, not given to *m* wine Titus 2:3
though I might be *m* bold in Philem 8
but how *m* more unto thee, both in Philem 16
Being made so *m* better than the Heb 1:4
By so *m* was Jesus made a surety Heb 7:22
by how *m* also he is the mediator Heb 8:6
How *m* more shall the blood of Heb 9:14
so *m* the more, as ye see the day Heb 10:25
Of how *m* sorer punishment, Heb 10:29
shall we not *m* rather be in Heb 12:9
if so *m* as a beast touch the Heb 12:20
*m* more shall not we escape, if we Heb 12:25
of a righteous man availeth *m* Jas 5:16
being *m* more precious than of 1Pet 1:7
through *m* wantonness, those that 2Pet 2:18
And I wept *m*, because no man was Rev 5:4
was given unto him *m* incense Rev 8:3
How *m* she hath glorified herself, Rev 18:7
so *m* torment and sorrow give her Rev 18:7
great voice of *m* people in heaven Rev 19:1

### MUFFLERS
and the bracelets, and the *m* Is 3:19

### MULBERRY
them over against the *m* trees 2Sa 5:23
going in the tops of the *m* trees 2Sa 5:24
them over against the *m* trees 1Chr 14:14
going in the tops of the *m* trees 1Chr 14:15

### MULE
every man gat him up upon his *m* 2Sa 13:29
And Absalom rode upon a *m*, and the 2Sa 18:9
the *m* went under the thick boughs 2Sa 18:9
the *m* that was under him went 2Sa 18:9
my son to ride upon mine own *m* 1Kin 1:33
to ride upon king David's *m* 1Kin 1:38
him to ride upon the king's *m* 1Kin 1:44
ye not as the horse, or as the *m* Ps 32:9
the plague of the horse, of the *m* Zec 14:15

### MULES
found the *m* in the wilderness Gen 36:24
armour, and spices, horses, and *m* 1Kin 10:25
*m* alive, that we lose not all the 1Kin 18:5
on asses, and on camels, and on *m* 1Chr 12:40
harness, and spices, horses, and *m* 2Chr 9:24
their *m*, two hundred forty and Ezr 2:66
their *m*, two hundred forty and Neh 7:68
on horseback, and riders on *m* Est 8:10
So the posts that rode upon *m* Est 8:14
and in litters, and upon *m* Is 66:20
with horses and horsemen and *m* Eze 27:14

### MULES'
thy servant two *m* burden of earth 2Kin 5:17

### MULTIPLIED
and grew, and *m* exceedingly Gen 47:27
and increased abundantly, and *m* Ex 1:7
afflicted them, the more they *m* Ex 1:12
and the people *m*, and waxed very Ex 1:20
may be *m* in the land of Egypt Ex 11:9
The LORD your God hath *m* you Deut 1:10
and thy silver and thy gold is *m* Deut 8:13
and all that thou hast is *m* Deut 8:13
That your days may be *m*, and the Deut 11:21
*m* his seed, and gave him Isaac Josh 24:3
were *m* in the land of Gilead 1Chr 5:9
If his children be *m*, it is for Job 27:14
or if thy transgressions be *m* Job 35:6
Their sorrows shall be *m* that Ps 16:4
that hate me wrongfully are *m* Ps 38:19
also, so that they are *m* greatly Ps 107:38
For by me thy days shall be *m* Prov 9:11
When the wicked are *m*, Prov 29:16
Thou hast *m* the nation, and not Is 9:3
transgressions are *m* before thee Is 59:12
shall come to pass, when ye be *m* Jer 3:16
Because ye *m* more than the Eze 5:7
Ye have *m* your slain in this city Eze 11:6
passed by, and *m* thy whoredoms Eze 16:25
Thou hast moreover *m* thy Eze 16:29
but thou hast *m* thine Eze 16:51
may faint, and their ruins be *m* Eze 21:15
Yet she *m* her whoredoms, in Eze 23:19
the field, and his boughs were *m* Eze 31:5
have *m* your words against me Eze 35:13
Peace be *m* unto you Dan 4:1
Peace be *m* unto you Dan 6:25
*m* her silver and gold, which they Hos 2:8
Judah hath *m* fenced cities Hos 8:14
I have *m* visions, and used Hos 12:10
Thou hast *m* thy merchants above Nah 3:16
the number of the disciples was *m* Acts 6:1
disciples *m* in Jerusalem greatly Acts 6:7
the people grew and *m* in Egypt, Acts 7:17
comfort of the Holy Ghost, were *m* Acts 9:31
But the word of God grew and *m* Acts 12:24
Grace unto you, and peace, be *m* 1Pet 1:2
peace be *m* unto you through the 2Pet 1:2
unto you, and peace, and love, be *m* Jude 2

### MULTIPLIEDST
Their children also *m* thou as the Neh 9:23

### MULTIPLIETH
*m* my wounds without cause Job 9:17
us, and *m* his words against God Job 34:37
he *m* words without knowledge Job 35:16

### MULTIPLY
them, saying, Be fruitful, and *m* Gen 1:22
seas, and let fowl *m* in the earth Gen 1:22
said unto them, Be fruitful, and *m* Gen 1:28
said, I will greatly *m* thy sorrow Gen 3:16
when men began to *m* on the face Gen 6:1
be fruitful, and *m* upon the earth Gen 8:17
said unto them, Be fruitful, and *m* Gen 9:1
And you, be ye fruitful, and *m* Gen 9:7

in the earth, and *m* therein Gen 9:7
I will *m* thy seed exceedingly, Gen 16:10
thee, and will *m* thee exceedingly Gen 17:2
and will *m* him exceedingly Gen 17:20
in multiplying I will *m* thy seed Gen 22:17
seed to *m* as the stars of heaven Gen 26:4
*m* thy seed for my servant Gen 26:24
*m* thee, that thou mayest be a Gen 28:3
be fruitful and *m* Gen 35:11
*m* thee, and I will make of thee a Gen 48:4
lest they *m*, and it come to pass, Ex 1:10
*m* my signs and my wonders in the Ex 7:3
beast of the field *m* against thee Ex 23:29
I will *m* your seed as the stars Ex 32:13
*m* you, and establish my covenant Lev 26:9
thee, and bless thee, and *m* thee Deut 7:13
to do, that ye may live, and *m* Deut 8:1
thy herds and thy flocks *m* Deut 8:13
*m* thee, as he hath sworn unto thy ... Deut 13:17
But he shall not *m* horses to Deut 17:16
the end that he should *m* horses Deut 17:16
shall he *m* wives to himself Deut 17:17
he greatly *m* to himself silver Deut 17:17
you to do you good, and to *m* you .... Deut 28:63
good, and *m* thee above thy fathers Deut 30:5
that thou mayest live and *m* Deut 30:16
neither did all their family *m* 1Chr 4:27
I shall *m* my days as the sand Job 29:18
and I will *m* them, and they shall Jer 30:19
so will I *m* the seed of David my Jer 33:22
I have caused thee to *m* as the Eze 16:7
I will *m* men upon you, all the Eze 36:10
I will *m* upon you man and beast Eze 36:11
I will *m* the fruit of the tree, Eze 36:30
*m* them, and will set my sanctuary Eze 37:26
at Gilgal *m* transgression Amos 4:4
*m* your seed sown, and increase the 2Cor 9:10
and multiplying I will *m* thee Heb 6:14

**MULTIPLYING**
in *m* I will multiply thy seed as Gen 22:17
thee, and *m* I will multiply thee Heb 6:14

**MULTITUDE**
it shall not be numbered for *m* Gen 16:10
that thou mayest be a *m* of people Gen 28:3
and it is now increased unto a *m* Gen 30:30
which cannot be numbered for *m* Gen 32:12
I will make of thee a *m* of people Gen 48:4
let them grow into a *m* in the Gen 48:16
seed shall become a *m* of nations Gen 48:19
a mixed *m* went up also with them Ex 12:38
shalt not follow a *m* to do evil Ex 23:2
According to the *m* of years thou Lev 25:16
the mixt *m* that was among them Num 11:4
Gad had a very great *m* of cattle Num 32:1
day as the stars of heaven for *m* Deut 1:10
thee as the stars of heaven for *m* Deut 10:22
were as the stars of heaven for *m* Deut 28:62
that is upon the sea shore in *m* Josh 11:4
army, with his chariots and his *m* Judg 4:7
they came as grasshoppers for *m* Judg 6:5
valley like grasshoppers for *m* Judg 7:12
as the sand by the sea side for *m* Judg 7:12
which is on the sea shore in *m* 1Sa 13:5
the *m* melted away, and they went 1Sa 14:16
even among the whole *m* of Israel 2Sa 6:19
the sand that is by the sea for *m* 2Sa 17:11
be numbered nor counted for *m* 1Kin 3:8
the sand which is by the sea in *m* 1Kin 4:20
not be told nor numbered for *m* 1Kin 8:5
Hast thou seen all this great *m* 1Kin 20:13
all this great *m* into thine hand 1Kin 20:28
they are as all the *m* of Israel 2Kin 7:13
they are even as all the *m* of the 2Kin 7:13
With the *m* of my chariots I am 2Kin 19:23
with the remnant of the *m* 2Kin 25:11
like the dust of the earth in *m* 2Chr 1:9
not be told nor numbered for *m* 2Chr 5:6
and ye be a great *m*, and there are 2Chr 13:8
in thy name we go against this *m* 2Chr 14:11
There cometh a great *m* against 2Chr 20:2
by reason of this great *m* 2Chr 20:15
they looked unto the *m*, and, 2Chr 20:24
away a great *m* of them captives 2Chr 28:5
For a *m* of the people, even many 2Chr 30:18
nor for all the *m* that is with 2Chr 32:7
from Israel all the mixed *m* Neh 13:3
the *m* of his children, and all the Est 5:11
accepted of the *m* of his brethren Est 10:3
Should not the *m* of words be Job 11:2
Did I fear a great *m*, or did the Job 31:34
*m* of years should teach wisdom Job 32:7
the *m* of his bones with strong Job 33:19
By reason of the *m* of oppressions Job 35:9
He scorneth the *m* of the city Job 39:7
thy house in the *m* of thy mercy Ps 5:7
cast them out in the *m* of their Ps 5:10
no king saved by the *m* of an host Ps 33:16
for I had gone with the *m* Ps 42:4
with a *m* that kept holyday Ps 42:4
in the *m* of their riches Ps 49:6
according unto the *m* of thy Ps 51:1
the *m* of the bulls, with the Ps 68:30
in the *m* of thy mercy hear me, in Ps 69:13
to the *m* of thy tender mercies Ps 69:16
unto the *m* of the wicked Ps 74:19
In the *m* of my thoughts within me Ps 94:19
let the *m* of isles be glad Ps 97:1
not the *m* of thy mercies Ps 106:7
according to the *m* of his mercies Ps 106:45
I will praise him among the *m* Ps 109:30
In the *m* of words there wanteth Prov 10:19
but in the *m* of counsellors there Prov 11:14
In the *m* of people is the king's Prov 14:28
but in the *m* of counsellors they Prov 15:22
There is gold, and a *m* of rubies Prov 20:15
in *m* of counsellors there is Prov 24:6
cometh through the *m* of business Eccl 5:3
voice is known by *m* of words Eccl 5:3
For in the *m* of dreams and many Eccl 5:7
To what purpose is the *m* of your Is 1:11
their *m* dried up with thirst Is 5:13
and their glory, and their *m* Is 5:14
The noise of a *m* in the mountains Is 13:4
contemned, with all that great *m* Is 16:14
Woe to the *m* of many people, Is 17:12
Moreover the *m* of thy strangers Is 29:5
the *m* of the terrible ones shall Is 29:5
the *m* of all the nations that Is 29:7
so shall the *m* of all the nations Is 29:8
when a *m* of shepherds is called Is 31:4
the *m* of the city shall be left Is 32:14
By the *m* of my chariots am I come Is 37:24
for the *m* of thy sorceries Is 47:9
with the *m* of thy sorceries, Is 47:12
wearied in the *m* of thy counsels Is 47:13
The *m* of camels shall cover thee, Is 60:6
according to the *m* of his Is 63:7
hills, and from the *m* of mountains Jer 3:23
there is a *m* of waters in the Jer 10:13
they have called a *m* after thee Jer 12:6
for the *m* of thine iniquity Jer 30:14
for the *m* of thine iniquity Jer 30:15
women that stood by, a great *m* Jer 44:15
Behold, I will punish the *m* of No Jer 46:25
the *m* of their cattle a spoil Jer 49:32
there is a *m* of waters in the Jer 51:16
with the *m* of the waves thereof Jer 51:42
of Babylon, and the rest of the *m* Jer 52:15
for the *m* of her transgressions Lam 1:5
according to the *m* of his mercies Lam 3:32
them shall remain, nor of their *m* Eze 7:11
wrath is upon all the *m* thereof Eze 7:12
is touching the whole *m* thereof Eze 7:13
wrath is upon all the *m* thereof Eze 7:14
according to the *m* of his idols Eze 14:4
height with the *m* of her branches Eze 19:11
a voice of a *m* being at ease was Eze 23:42
of the *m* of all kind of riches Eze 27:12
the *m* of the wares of thy making Eze 27:16
was thy merchant in the *m* of the Eze 27:18
making, for the *m* of all riches Eze 27:18
earth with the *m* of thy riches Eze 27:33
By the *m* of thy merchandise they Eze 28:16
by the *m* of thine iniquities Eze 28:18
and he shall take her *m*, and take Eze 29:19
and they shall take away her *m* Eze 30:4
I will also make the *m* of Egypt Eze 30:10
and I will cut off the *m* of No Eze 30:15
king of Egypt, and to his *m* Eze 31:2
long because of the *m* of waters Eze 31:5
him fair by the *m* of his branches Eze 31:9
This is Pharaoh and all his *m* Eze 31:18
mighty will I cause thy *m* to fall Eze 32:12
all the *m* thereof shall be Eze 32:12
even for Egypt, and for all her *m* Eze 32:16
of man, wail for the *m* of Egypt Eze 32:18
all her *m* round about her grave, Eze 32:24
midst of the slain with all her *m* Eze 32:25
is Meshech, Tubal, and all her *m* Eze 32:26
shall be comforted over all his *m* Eze 32:31
sword, even Pharaoh and all his *m* Eze 32:32
shall they bury Gog and all his *m* Eze 39:11
shall be a very great *m* of fish Eze 47:9
his words like the voice of a *m* Dan 10:6
assemble a *m* of great forces Dan 11:10
and he shall set forth a great *m* Dan 11:11
but the *m* shall be given into his Dan 11:11
And when he hath taken away the *m* Dan 11:12
shall set forth a *m* greater than Dan 11:13
for the *m* of thine iniquity, and Hos 9:7
according to the *m* of his fruit Hos 10:1
in the *m* of thy mighty men Hos 10:13
noise by reason of the *m* of men Mic 2:12
and there is a *m* of slain, and a Nah 3:3
Because of the *m* of the whoredoms Nah 3:4
without walls for the *m* of men Zec 2:4
the whole *m* stood on the shore Mt 13:2
Jesus unto the *m* in parables Mt 13:34
Then Jesus sent the *m* away Mt 13:36
put him to death, he feared the *m* Mt 14:5
went forth, and saw a great *m* Mt 14:14
send the *m* away, that they may go Mt 14:15
he commanded the *m* to sit down on ... Mt 14:19
and the disciples to the *m* Mt 14:19
And he called the *m*, and said unto Mt 15:10
Insomuch that the *m* wondered Mt 15:31
said, I have compassion on the *m* Mt 15:32
as to fill so great a *m* Mt 15:33
he commanded the *m* to sit down on ... Mt 15:35
and the disciples to the *m* Mt 15:36
And he sent away the *m*, and took Mt 15:39
And when they were come to the *m* .... Mt 17:14
Jericho, a great *m* followed him Mt 20:29
the *m* rebuked them, because they Mt 20:31
a very great *m* spread their Mt 21:8
the *m* said, This is Jesus the Mt 21:11
hands on him, they feared the *m* Mt 21:46
when the *m* heard this, they were Mt 22:33
Then spake Jesus to the *m* Mt 23:1
and with him a great *m* with swords Mt 26:47
elders persuaded the *m* that they Mt 27:20
and washed his hands before the *m* Mt 27:24
all the *m* resorted unto him, and Mk 2:13
a great *m* from Galilee followed Mk 3:7
about Tyre and Sidon, a great *m* Mk 3:8
wait on him because of the *m* Mk 3:9
the *m* cometh together again, so Mk 3:20
the *m* sat about him, and they said Mk 3:32
was gathered unto him a great *m* Mk 4:1
the whole *m* was by the sea on the Mk 4:1
And when they had sent away the *m* Mk 4:36
Thou seest the *m* thronging thee Mk 5:31
And he took him aside from the *m* Mk 7:33
those days the *m* being very great Mk 8:1
I have compassion on the *m* Mk 8:2
he saw a great *m* about them Mk 9:14
And one of the *m* answered and said, Mk 9:17
and with him a great *m* with swords ... Mk 14:43
the *m* crying aloud began to Mk 15:8
the whole *m* of the people were Lk 1:10
there was with the angel a *m* of Lk 2:13
Then said he to the *m* that came Lk 3:7
they inclosed a great *m* of fishes Lk 5:6
bring him in because of the *m* Lk 5:19
a great *m* of people out of all Lk 6:17
the whole *m* sought to touch him Lk 6:19
Then the whole *m* of the country Lk 8:37
the *m* throng thee and press thee, Lk 8:45
and said unto him, Send the *m* away Lk 9:12
the disciples to set before the *m* Lk 9:16
an innumerable *m* of people Lk 12:1
And hearing the *m* pass by, he Lk 18:36
the whole *m* of the disciples Lk 19:37
from among the *m* said unto him Lk 19:39
unto them in the absence of the *m* Lk 22:6
And while he yet spake, behold a *m* Lk 22:47
the whole *m* of them arose, and led Lk 23:1
lay a great *m* of impotent folk Jn 5:3
away, a *m* being in that place Jn 5:13
a great *m* followed him, because Jn 6:2
to draw it for the *m* of fishes Jn 21:6
the *m* came together, and were Acts 2:6
the *m* of them that believed were Acts 4:32
There came also a *m* out of the Acts 5:16
the *m* of the disciples unto them Acts 6:2
And the saying pleased the whole *m* Acts 6:5
that a great *m* both of the Jews Acts 14:1
But the *m* of the city was divided Acts 14:4
Then all the *m* kept silence Acts 15:12
they had gathered the *m* together Acts 15:30
the *m* rose up together against Acts 16:22
and of the devout Greeks a great *m* Acts 17:4
evil of that way before the *m* Acts 19:9
they drew Alexander out of the *m* Acts 19:33
the *m* must needs come together Acts 21:22
thing, some another, among the *m* Acts 21:34
For the *m* of the people followed Acts 21:36
and the *m* was divided Acts 23:7
in the temple, neither with *m* Acts 24:18
about whom all the *m* of the Jews Acts 25:24
many as the stars of the sky in *m* Heb 11:12
death, and shall hide a *m* of sins Jas 5:20
charity shall cover the *m* of sins 1Pet 4:8
this I beheld, and, lo, a great *m* Rev 7:9
as it were the voice of a great *m* Rev 19:6

**MULTITUDES**
draw her and all her *m* Eze 32:20
*M*, *m* in the valley of Joel 3:14
great *m* of people from Galilee Mt 4:25
And seeing the *m*, he went up into Mt 5:1
mountain, great *m* followed him Mt 8:1
when Jesus saw great *m* about him Mt 8:18
But when the *m* saw it, they Mt 9:8
the *m* marvelled, saying, It was Mt 9:33
But when he saw the *m*, he was Mt 9:36
to say unto the *m* concerning John Mt 11:7
great *m* followed him, and he Mt 12:15
great *m* were gathered together Mt 13:2
side, while he sent the *m* away Mt 14:22
And when he had sent the *m* away Mt 14:23
great *m* came unto him, having Mt 15:30
And great *m* followed him Mt 19:2
the *m* that went before, and that Mt 21:9
same hour said Jesus to the *m* Mt 26:55
great *m* came together to hear, and Lk 5:15
And there went great *m* with him Lk 14:25
the Lord, *m* both of men and women .. Acts 5:14
But when the Jews saw the *m* Acts 13:45
whore sitteth, are peoples, and *m* Rev 17:15

**MUNITION**
that fight against her and her *m* Is 29:7
keep the *m*, watch the way, make Nah 2:1

**MUNITIONS**
defence shall be the *m* of rocks Is 33:16

**MUPPIM** (*mup'-pim*) See SHUPPIM. *A son of Benjamin.*
Gera, and Naaman, Ehi, and Rosh, *M* Gen 46:21

**MURDER**
places doth he *m* the innocent Ps 10:8
the stranger, and *m* the fatherless Ps 94:6
Will ye steal, *m*, and commit Jer 7:9
priests *m* in the way by consent Hos 6:9
Jesus said, Thou shalt do no *m* Mt 19:18
who had committed *m* in the Mk 15:7
made in the city, and for *m* Lk 23:19
*m* was cast into prison, whom they Lk 23:25
full of envy, *m*, debate, deceit, Rom 1:29

**MURDERER**
iron, so that he die, he is a *m* Num 35:16
the *m* shall surely be put to Num 35:16
he may die, and he die, he is a *m* Num 35:17
the *m* shall surely be put to Num 35:17
he may die, and he die, he is a *m* Num 35:18
the *m* shall surely be put to Num 35:18
of blood himself shall slay the *m* Num 35:19
for he is a *m* Num 35:21
of blood shall slay the *m* Num 35:21
the *m* shall be put to death by Num 35:30
satisfaction for the life of a *m* Num 35:31
See ye how this son of a *m* hath 2Kin 6:32
The *m* rising with the light Job 24:14
bring forth his children to the *m* Hos 9:13
He was a *m* from the beginning, and Jn 8:44
desired a *m* to be granted unto Acts 3:14
No doubt this man is a *m* Acts 28:4
But let none of you suffer as a *m* 1Pet 4:15
hateth his brother is a *m* 1Jn 3:15
ye know that no *m* hath eternal 1Jn 3:15

**MURDERERS**
the children of the *m* he slew not 2Kin 14:6
lodged in it; but now *m* Is 1:21
my soul is wearied because of *m* Jer 4:31
his armies, and destroyed those *m* Mt 22:7
have been now the betrayers and *m* Acts 7:52
four thousand men that were *m* Acts 21:38
for *m* of fathers and *m* of 1Ti 1:9
*m* of mothers, for manslayers, 1Ti 1:9
and the abominable, and *m*, and Rev 21:8
sorcerers, and whoremongers, and *m*. Rev 22:15

**MURDERS**
heart proceed evil thoughts, *m* Mt 15:19
adulteries, fornications, *m* Mk 7:21
Envyings, *m*, drunkenness, Gal 5:21
Neither repented they of their *m* Rev 9:21

**MURMUR**
what are we, that ye *m* against us Ex 16:7
murmurings which ye *m* against him Ex 16:8
congregation, which *m* against me Num 14:27
Israel, which they *m* against me Num 14:27
the congregation to *m* against him Num 14:36
is Aaron, that ye *m* against him Num 16:11
whereby they *m* against you Num 17:5
unto them, *M* not among yourselves Jn 6:43
Neither *m* ye, as some of them 1Cor 10:10

**MURMURED**
the people *m* against Moses, Ex 15:24
of Israel *m* against Moses Ex 16:2
the people *m* against Moses, and Ex 17:3
of Israel *m* against Moses Num 14:2
upward, which have *m* against me Num 14:29
of Israel *m* against Moses Num 16:41
ye *m* in your tents, and said, Deut 1:27
*m* against the princes Josh 9:18
But *m* in their tents, and Ps 106:25
they that *m* shall learn doctrine Is 29:24
they *m* against the goodman of the Mt 20:11
And they *m* against her Mk 14:5
Pharisees *m* against his disciples Lk 5:30
And the Pharisees and scribes *m* Lk 15:2
And when they saw it, they all *m* Lk 19:7
The Jews then *m* at him, because Jn 6:41
that his disciples *m* at it Jn 6:61
*m* such things concerning him Jn 7:32
murmur ye, as some of them also *m*. 1Cor 10:10

**MURMURERS**
These are *m*, complainers, walking Jude 16

**MURMURING**
there was much *m* among the people Jn 7:12
there arose a *m* of the Grecians Acts 6:1

**MURMURINGS**
heareth your *m* against the LORD Ex 16:7
*m* which ye murmur against him Ex 16:8
your *m* are not against us, but Ex 16:8
for he hath heard your *m* Ex 16:9
I have heard the *m* of the Ex 16:12
I have heard the *m* of the Num 14:27
the *m* of the children of Israel Num 17:5
quite take away their *m* from me Num 17:10
Do all things without *m* and Phil 2:14

**MURRAIN**
there shall be a very grievous *m* Ex 9:3

**MUSE**
I *m* on the work of thy hands Ps 143:5

**MUSED**
all men *m* in their hearts of John Lk 3:15

**MUSHI** (*mu'-shi*) See MUSHITES. *A son of Merari.*
of Merari; Mahali and *M* Ex 6:19
families; Mahli, and *M* Num 3:20
Merari; Mahli, and *M* 1Chr 6:19
The son of Mahli, the son of *M* 1Chr 6:47
Merari; Mahli, and *M* 1Chr 23:21
The sons of *M*; Mahli 1Chr 23:23
sons of Merari were Mahli and *M* 1Chr 24:26
The sons also of *M* 1Chr 24:30

**MUSHITES** (*mu'-shites*) *The family of Mushi.*
Mahlites, and the family of the *M* Num 3:33
the Mahlites, the family of the *M* Num 26:58

**MUSICAL**
with *m* instruments of God 1Chr 16:42
with the *m* instruments of David Neh 12:36
as *m* instruments, and that of all Eccl 2:8

**MUSICIAN**
To the chief *M* on Neginoth Ps 4:*t*
To the chief *M* upon Nehiloth, A Ps 5:*t*
To the chief *M* on Neginoth upon Ps 6:*t*
To the chief *M* upon Gittith Ps 8:*t*
To the chief *M* upon Muth-labben, Ps 9:*t*
To the chief *M*, A Psalm of David Ps 11:*t*
To the chief *M* upon Sheminith, A Ps 12:*t*
To the chief *M*, A Psalm of David Ps 13:*t*
To the chief *M*, A Psalm of David Ps 14:*t*
To the chief *M*, A Psalm of David, Ps 18:*t*
To the chief *M*, A Psalm of David Ps 19:*t*
To the chief *M*, A Psalm of David Ps 20:*t*
To the chief *M*, A Psalm of David Ps 21:*t*
To the chief *M* upon Aijeleth Ps 22:*t*
To the chief *M*, A Psalm of David Ps 31:*t*
To the chief *M*, A Psalm of David, Ps 36:*t*
To the chief *M*, even to Jeduthun, Ps 39:*t*
To the chief *M*, A Psalm of David Ps 40:*t*
To the chief *M*, A Psalm of David Ps 41:*t*
To the chief *M*, Maschil, for the Ps 42:*t*
To the chief *M* for the sons of Ps 44:*t*
To the chief *M* upon Shoshannim, Ps 45:*t*
To the chief *M* for the sons of Ps 46:*t*
To the chief *M*, A Psalm for the Ps 47:*t*
To the chief *M*, A Psalm for the Ps 49:*t*
To the chief *M*, A Psalm of David, Ps 51:*t*
To the chief *M*, Maschil, A Psalm Ps 52:*t*
To the chief *M* upon Mahalath, Ps 53:*t*
To the chief *M* on Neginoth Ps 54:*t*
To the chief *M* on Neginoth Ps 55:*t*
To the chief *M* upon Ps 56:*t*
To the chief *M*, Altaschith, Ps 57:*t*
To the chief *M*, Altaschith, Ps 58:*t*
To the chief *M*, Altaschith, Ps 59:*t*
To the chief *M* upon Shushan-eduth Ps 60:*t*
To the chief *M* upon Neginah Ps 61:*t*
To the chief *M*, to Jeduthun, A Ps 62:*t*
To the chief *M*, A Psalm of David Ps 64:*t*
To the chief *M*, A Psalm and Song Ps 65:*t*
To the chief *M*, A Song or Psalm Ps 66:*t*
To the chief *M* on Neginoth Ps 67:*t*
To the chief *M*, A Psalm or Song Ps 68:*t*
To the chief *M* upon Shoshannim, A Ps 69:*t*
To the chief *M*, A Psalm of David, Ps 70:*t*
To the chief *M*, Altaschith, A Ps 75:*t*
To the chief *M* on Neginoth Ps 76:*t*
To the chief *M*, to Jeduthun, A Ps 77:*t*
To the chief *M* upon Ps 80:*t*
To the chief *M* upon Gittith Ps 81:*t*
To the chief *M* upon Gittith Ps 84:*t*
To the chief *M*, A Psalm for the Ps 85:*t*
chief *M* upon Mahalath Leannoth Ps 88:*t*
To the chief *M*, A Psalm of David Ps 109:*t*
To the chief *M*, A Psalm of David Ps 139:*t*
To the chief *M*, A Psalm of David Ps 140:*t*

**MUSICIANS**
And the voice of harpers, and *m* Rev 18:22

**MUSICK**
joy, and with instruments of *m* 1Sa 18:6
the singers with instruments of *m* 1Chr 15:16
and cymbals and instruments of *m* 2Chr 5:13
with instruments of *m* of the LORD 2Chr 7:6
the singers with instruments of *m* 2Chr 23:13
could skill of instruments of *m* 2Chr 34:12
of *m* shall be brought low Eccl 12:4
I am their *m* Lam 3:63
gate, the young men from their *m* Lam 5:14
dulcimer, and all kinds of *m* Dan 3:5
psaltery, and all kinds of *m* Dan 3:7
and dulcimer, and all kinds of *m* Dan 3:10
and dulcimer, and all kinds of *m* Dan 3:15
of *m* brought before him Dan 6:18
to themselves instruments of *m* Amos 6:5
nigh to the house, he heard *m* Lk 15:25

**MUSING**
while I was *m* the fire burned Ps 39:3

**MUST**
thy money, *m* needs be circumcised Gen 17:13
*m* I needs bring thy son again Gen 24:5
It *m* not be so done in our Gen 29:26
and said, Thou *m* come in unto me Gen 30:16
If it *m* be so now, do this Gen 43:11
time drew nigh that Israel *m* die Gen 47:29
for we *m* hold a feast unto the Ex 10:9
Thou *m* give us also sacrifices and Ex 10:25
for thereof *m* we take to serve Ex 10:26
not with what we *m* serve the LORD Ex 10:26
save that which every man *m* eat Ex 12:16
them the way wherein they *m* walk Ex 18:20
walk, and the work that they *m* do Ex 18:20
it *m* be put into water, and it Lev 11:32
seven days ye *m* eat unleavened Lev 23:6
so he *m* do after the law of his Num 6:21
Neither *m* the children of Israel Num 18:22
*m* we fetch you water out of this Num 20:10
*M* I not take heed to speak that Num 23:12
the LORD speaketh, that I *m* do Num 23:26
word again by what way we *m* go up Deut 1:22
But I *m* die in this land, I *m* Deut 4:22
But thou *m* eat them before the Deut 12:18
for thou *m* go with this people Deut 31:7
thy days approach that thou *m* die Deut 31:14
may know the way by which ye *m* go Josh 3:4
But that ye *m* turn away this day Josh 22:18
thou *m* offer it unto the LORD Judg 13:16
There *m* be an inheritance for Judg 21:17
thou *m* buy it also of Ruth the Ruth 4:5
was in mine hand, and, lo, I *m* die 1Sa 14:43
For we *m* needs die, and are as 2Sa 14:14
He that ruleth over men *m* be just 2Sa 23:3
touch them *m* be fenced with iron 2Sa 23:7
he sleepeth, and *m* be awaked 1Kin 18:27
thou *m* go to be with thy fathers 1Chr 17:11
LORD *m* be exceeding magnifical 1Chr 22:5
As thou hast said, so *m* we do Ezr 10:12
whose mouth *m* be held in with bit Ps 32:9
friends *m* shew himself friendly Prov 18:24
him, yet thou *m* do it again Prov 19:19
then *m* he put to more strength Eccl 10:10
*m* have a thousand, and those that Song 8:12
For precept *m* be upon precept, Is 28:10
they *m* needs be borne, because Jer 10:5
this is a grief, and I *m* bear it Jer 10:19
but ye *m* tread down with your Eze 34:18
but ye *m* foul the residue with Eze 34:18
how that he *m* go unto Jerusalem, Mt 16:21
scribes that Elias *m* first come Mt 17:10
for it *m* needs be that offences Mt 18:7
all these things *m* come to pass Mt 24:6
be fulfilled, that thus it *m* be Mt 26:54
but new wine *m* be put into new Mk 2:22
Son of man *m* suffer many things Mk 8:31
scribes that Elias *m* first come Mk 9:11
that he *m* suffer many things, and Mk 9:12
for such things *m* needs be Mk 13:7
the gospel *m* first be published Mk 13:10
but the scriptures *m* be fulfilled Mk 14:49
wist ye not that I *m* be about my Lk 2:49
I *m* preach the kingdom of God to Lk 4:43
But new wine *m* be put into new Lk 5:38
The Son of man *m* suffer many Lk 9:22
Nevertheless I *m* walk to day Lk 13:33
ground, and I *m* needs go and see it Lk 14:18
But first *m* he suffer many things Lk 17:25
for to day I *m* abide at thy house Lk 19:5
for these things *m* first come to Lk 21:9
when the passover *m* be killed Lk 22:7
*m* yet be accomplished in me Lk 22:37
(For of necessity he *m* release Lk 23:17
The Son of man *m* be delivered Lk 24:7
that all things *m* be fulfilled Lk 24:44
unto thee, Ye *m* be born again Jn 3:7
even so *m* the Son of man be Jn 3:14
He *m* increase, but I Jn 3:30
increase, but I *m* decrease Jn 3:30
he *m* needs go through Samaria Jn 4:4
him *m* worship him in spirit Jn 4:24
I *m* work the works of him that Jn 9:4
them also I *m* bring, and they Jn 10:16
The Son of man *m* be lifted up Jn 12:34
that he *m* rise again from the Jn 20:9
this scripture *m* needs have been Acts 1:16
*m* one be ordained to be a witness Acts 1:22
Whom the heaven *m* receive until Acts 3:21
among men, whereby we *m* be saved Acts 4:12
shall be told thee what thou *m* do Acts 9:6
he *m* suffer for my name's sake Acts 9:16
faith, and that we *m* through much Acts 14:22
Ye *m* be circumcised, and keep the Acts 15:24
Sirs, what *m* I do to be saved Acts 16:30
that Christ *m* needs have suffered Acts 17:3
I *m* by all means keep this feast Acts 18:21
been there, I *m* also see Rome Acts 19:21
the multitude *m* needs come Acts 21:22
so *m* thou bear witness also at Acts 23:11
thou *m* be brought before Caesar Acts 27:24
Howbeit we *m* be cast upon a Acts 27:26
Wherefore ye *m* needs be subject, Rom 13:5
for then *m* ye needs go out of the 1Cor 5:10
For there *m* be also heresies 1Cor 11:19
For he *m* reign, till he hath put 1Cor 15:25
corruptible *m* put on incorruption 1Cor 15:53
this mortal *m* put on immortality 1Cor 15:53
For we *m* all appear before the 2Cor 5:10
If I *m* needs glory, I will glory 2Cor 11:30
A bishop then *m* be blameless 1Ti 3:2
Moreover he *m* have a good report 1Ti 3:7
Likewise *m* the deacons be grave, 1Ti 3:8
Even so *m* their wives be grave, 1Ti 3:11
The husbandman that laboureth *m* 2Ti 2:6
servant of the Lord *m* not strive 2Ti 2:24
For a bishop *m* be blameless Titus 1:7
Whose mouths *m* be stopped Titus 1:11
that some *m* enter therein Heb 4:6
there *m* also of necessity be the Heb 9:16
For then *m* he often have suffered Heb 9:26
to God *m* believe that he is Heb 11:6
as they that *m* give account Heb 13:17
*m* begin at the house of God 1Pet 4:17
Knowing that shortly I *m* put off 2Pet 1:14
which *m* shortly come to pass Rev 1:1
thee things which *m* be hereafter Rev 4:1
Thou *m* prophesy again before many. Rev 10:11
he *m* in this manner be killed Rev 11:5
sword *m* be killed with the sword Rev 13:10
he *m* continue a short space Rev 17:10
after that he *m* be loosed a Rev 20:3
things which *m* shortly be done Rev 22:6

**MUSTARD**
is like to a grain of *m* seed Mt 13:31
have faith as a grain of *m* seed Mt 17:20
It is like a grain of *m* seed Mk 4:31
It is like a grain of *m* seed Lk 13:19

ye had faith as a grain of *m* seed Lk 17:6

**MUSTERED**
which *m* the people of the land, 2Kin 25:19
who *m* the people of the land Jer 52:25

**MUSTERETH**
the LORD of hosts *m* the host of Is 13:4

**MUTH-LABBEN** (*muth-lab'-ben*) *A muscial notation.*
To the chief Musician upon *M* Ps 9:*t*

**MUTTER**
unto wizards that peep, and that *m* Is 8:19

**MUTTERED**
your tongue hath *m* perverseness Is 59:3

**MUTUAL**
you by the *m* faith both of you Rom 1:12

**MUZZLE**
Thou shalt not *m* the ox when he Deut 25:4
Thou shalt not *m* the mouth of the 1Cor 9:9
Thou shalt not *m* the ox that 1Ti 5:18

**MY** See PREFACE.

**MYRA** (*mi'-rah*) *A city in Lycia.*
and Pamphylia, we came to *M* Acts 27:5

**MYRRH**
bearing spicery and balm and *m* Gen 37:25
and a little honey, spices, and *m* Gen 43:11
of pure *m* five hundred shekels Ex 30:23
to wit, six months with oil of *m* Est 2:12
All thy garments smell of *m* Ps 45:8
I have perfumed my bed with *m* Prov 7:17
A bundle of *m* is my wellbeloved Song 1:13
pillars of smoke, perfumed with *m* Song 3:6
will get me to the mountain of *m* Song 4:6
*m* and aloes, with all the chief Song 4:14
have gathered my *m* with my spice Song 5:1
and my hands dropped with *m* Song 5:5
my fingers with sweet smelling *m* Song 5:5
lilies, dropping sweet smelling *m* Song 5:13
gold, and frankincense, and *m* Mt 2:11
him to drink wine mingled with *m* Mk 15:23
night, and brought a mixture of *m* Jn 19:39

**MYRTLE**
*m* branches, and palm branches, and Neh 8:15
cedar, the shittah tree, and the *m* Is 41:19
brier shall come up the *m* tree Is 55:13
he stood among the *m* trees that Zec 1:8
stood among the *m* trees answered Zec 1:10
LORD that stood among the *m* trees Zec 1:11

**MYSELF**
and I hid *m* Gen 3:10
By *m* have I sworn, saith the LORD Gen 22:16
wings, and brought you unto *m* Ex 19:4
of Egypt I sanctified them for *m* Num 8:17
I the LORD will make *m* known unto Num 12:6
I am not able to bear you *m* alone Deut 1:9
How can I *m* alone bear your Deut 1:12
And I turned *m* and came down from Deut 10:5
at other times before, and shake *m* Judg 16:20
said, I cannot redeem it for *m* Ruth 4:6
I forced *m* therefore, and offered 1Sa 13:12
that I may hide *m* in the field 1Sa 20:5
from avenging *m* with mine own 1Sa 25:33
surely go forth with you *m* also 2Sa 18:2
have kept *m* from mine iniquity 2Sa 22:24
surely shew *m* unto him to day 1Kin 18:15
Jehoshaphat, I will disguise *m* 1Kin 22:30
I bow *m* in the house of Rimmon 2Kin 5:18
when I bow down *m* in the house of 2Kin 5:18
to *m* for an house of sacrifice 2Chr 7:12
Jehoshaphat, I will disguise *m* 2Chr 18:29
Then I consulted with *m*, and I Neh 5:7
that she had prepared but *m* Est 5:12
to do honour more than to *m* Est 6:6
yea, I would harden *m* in sorrow Job 6:10
thee, so that I am a burden to *m* Job 7:20
If I justify *m*, mine own mouth Job 9:20
off my heaviness, and comfort *m* Job 9:27
If I wash *m* with snow water, and Job 9:30
I will leave my complaint upon *m* Job 10:1
then I will not hide *m* from thee Job 13:20
mine error remaineth with *m* Job 19:4
Whom I shall see for *m*, and mine Job 19:27
Or have eaten my morsel *m* alone Job 31:17
or lifted up *m* when evil found Job 31:29
Wherefore I abhor *m*, and repent in Job 42:6
I kept *m* from mine iniquity Ps 18:23
I behaved *m* as though he had been Ps 35:14
then I would have hid *m* from him Ps 55:12
I *m* will awake early Ps 57:8
I will behave *m* wisely in a Ps 101:2
I *m* will awake early Ps 108:2
but I give *m* unto prayer Ps 109:4
I will delight *m* in thy statutes Ps 119:16
And I will delight *m* in thy Ps 119:47
and have comforted *m* Ps 119:52
do I exercise *m* in great matters Ps 131:1
I have behaved and quieted *m* Ps 131:2
in mine heart to give *m* unto wine Eccl 2:3
I turned *m* to behold wisdom, and Eccl 2:12
I *m* perceived also that one event Eccl 2:14
have shewed *m* wise under the sun Eccl 2:19
now will I lift up *m* Is 33:10
I have been still, and refrained *m* Is 42:14
This people have I formed for *m* Is 43:21
spreadeth abroad the earth by *m* Is 44:24
I have sworn by *m*, the word is Is 45:23
I would comfort *m* against sorrow Jer 8:18
I *m* will fight against you with Jer 21:5
hear these words, I swear by *m* Jer 22:5
For I have sworn by *m*, saith the Jer 49:13
I the LORD will answer him by *m* Eze 14:7
made *m* known unto them in the Eze 20:5
sight I made *m* known unto them Eze 20:9
mine own, and I have made it for *m* Eze 29:3
I will make *m* known among them, Eze 35:11
I magnify *m*, and sanctify *m* Eze 38:23
neither did I anoint *m* at all Dan 10:3
bow *m* before the high God Mic 6:6
into my bones, and I trembled in *m* Hab 3:16
in the fifth month, separating *m* Zec 7:3
I *m* worthy to come unto thee Lk 7:7
hands and my feet, that it is I *m* Lk 24:39
If I bear witness of *m*, my Jn 5:31
of God, or whether I speak of *m* Jn 7:17
and I am not come of *m*, but he Jn 7:28
them, Though I bear record of *m* Jn 8:14
I am one that bear witness of *m* Jn 8:18
am he, and that I do nothing of *m* Jn 8:28
neither came I of *m*, but he sent Jn 8:42
Jesus answered, If I honour *m* Jn 8:54
from me, but I lay it down of *m* Jn 10:18
For I have not spoken of *m* Jn 12:49
come again, and receive you unto *m* Jn 14:3
I speak unto you I speak not of *m* Jn 14:10
him, and will manifest *m* to him Jn 14:21
And for their sakes I sanctify *m* Jn 17:19
I *m* also am a man Acts 10:26
count I my life dear unto *m* Acts 20:24
the more cheerfully answer for *m* Acts 24:10
And herein do I exercise *m* Acts 24:16
I would also hear the man *m* Acts 25:22
I think *m* happy, king Agrippa, Acts 26:2
because I shall answer for *m* this Acts 26:2
I verily thought with *m*, that I Acts 26:9
the mind I *m* serve the law of God Rom 7:25
For I could wish that *m* were Rom 9:3
reserved to *m* seven thousand men Rom 11:4
I *m* also am persuaded of you, my Rom 15:14
a succourer of many, and of *m* also Rom 16:2
For I know nothing by *m* 1Cor 4:4
have in a figure transferred to *m* 1Cor 4:6
that all men were even as I *m* 1Cor 7:7
yet have I made *m* servant unto 1Cor 9:19
others, I *m* should be a castaway 1Cor 9:27
But I determined this with *m* 2Cor 2:1
Now I Paul *m* beseech you by the 2Cor 10:1
*m* that ye might be exalted 2Cor 11:7
in all things I have kept *m* from 2Cor 11:9
unto you, and so will I keep *m* 2Cor 11:9
me, that I may boast *m* a little 2Cor 11:16
yet of *m* I will not glory, but in 2Cor 12:5
except it be that I *m* was not 2Cor 12:13
I make *m* a transgressor Gal 2:18
that I also *m* shall come shortly Phil 2:24
I count not *m* to have apprehended Phil 3:13
a partner, receive him as *m* Philem 17

**MYSIA** (*miz'-ye-ah*) *A Roman province in Asia Minor.*
After they were come to *M* Acts 16:7
they passing by *M* came down to Acts 16:8

**MYSTERIES**
the *m* of the kingdom of heaven Mt 13:11
know the *m* of the kingdom of God Lk 8:10
and stewards of the *m* of God 1Cor 4:1
of prophecy, and understand all *m* 1Cor 13:2
in the spirit he speaketh *m* 1Cor 14:2

**MYSTERY**
know the *m* of the kingdom of God Mk 4:11
ye should be ignorant of this *m* Rom 11:25
to the revelation of the *m* Rom 16:25
we speak the wisdom of God in a *m* 1Cor 2:7
Behold, I shew you a *m* 1Cor 15:51
known unto us the *m* of his will Eph 1:9
he made known unto me the *m* Eph 3:3
my knowledge in the *m* of Christ) Eph 3:4
what is the fellowship of the *m* Eph 3:9
This is a great *m* Eph 5:32
to make known the *m* of the gospel Eph 6:19
Even the *m* which hath been hid Col 1:26
of this *m* among the Gentiles Col 1:27
acknowledgement of the *m* of God Col 2:2
to speak the *m* of Christ Col 4:3
For the *m* of iniquity doth 2Th 2:7
Holding the *m* of the faith in a 1Ti 3:9
great is the *m* of godliness 1Ti 3:16
The *m* of the seven stars which Rev 1:20
the *m* of God should be finished, Rev 10:7
forehead was a name written, *M* Rev 17:5
will tell thee the *m* of the woman Rev 17:7

# N

**NAAM** (*na'-am*) *A son of Caleb.*
Iru, Elah, and *N* 1Chr 4:15

**NAAMAH** (*na'-a-mah*) See NAAMATHITE.
*1. Sister of Tubal-cain.*
and the sister of Tubal-cain was *N* Gen 4:22
*2. Mother of King Rehoboam.*
was *N* an Ammonitess 1Kin 14:21
was *N* an Ammonitess 1Kin 14:31
was *N* an Ammonitess 2Chr 12:13
*3. A city in Judah.*
And Gederoth, Beth-dagon, and *N* Josh 15:41

**NAAMAN** (*na'-a-man*) See NAAMAN'S, NAAMITES.
*1. A son of Benjamin.*
and Becher, and Ashbel, Gera, and *N*. Gen 46:21
*2. A son of Bela.*
of Bela were Ard and *N* Num 26:40
and of *N*, the family of the Num 26:40
And Abishua, and *N*, and Ahoah, 1Chr 8:4
*3. A son of Ehud.*
And *N*, and Ahiah, and Gera, he 1Chr 8:7
*4. A Syrian captain.*
Now *N*, captain of the host of the 2Kin 5:1
sent *N* my servant to thee 2Kin 5:6
So *N* came with his horses and with 2Kin 5:9
*N* was wroth, and went away 2Kin 5:11
*N* said, Shall there not then, I 2Kin 5:17
master hath spared *N* this Syrian 2Kin 5:20
So Gehazi followed after *N* 2Kin 5:21
when *N* saw him running after him, 2Kin 5:21
*N* said, Be content, take two 2Kin 5:23
of *N* shall cleave unto thee 2Kin 5:27
was cleansed, saving *N* the Syrian Lk 4:27

**NAAMAN'S** (*na'-a-mans*) *Refers fo Naaman 4.*
and she waited on *N* wife 2Kin 5:2

**NAAMATHITE** (*na'-a-math-ite*) *Family name of Zophar.*
the Shuhite, and Zophar the *N* Job 2:11
Then answered Zophar the *N* Job 11:1
Then answered Zophar the *N* Job 20:1
the Shuhite and Zophar the *N* went Job 42:9

**NAAMITES** (*na'-a-mites*) *Descendants of Naaman 3.*
and of Naaman, the family of the *N*. Num 26:40

**NAARAH** (*na'-a-rah*) See NAARAN, NAARATH. *A wife of Ashur.*
Tekoa had two wives, Helah and *N* 1Chr 4:5
*N* bare him Ahuzam, and Hepher, and. 1Chr 4:6
These were the sons of *N* 1Chr 4:6

**NAARAI** (*na'-a-rahee*) See PAARAI. *A 'mighty man' of David.*
Carmelite, *N* the son of Ezbai, 1Chr 11:37

**NAARAN** (*na'-a-ran*) *A city in Ephraim.*
the towns thereof, and eastward *N* 1Chr 7:28

**NAARATH** (*na'-a-rath*) See NAARAH, NAARAN. *Same as Naaran.*
from Janohah to Ataroth, and to *N* Josh 16:7

**NAASHON** (*na'-a-shon*) See NAHSHON. *Brother of Elisheba.*
of Amminadab, sister of *N* Ex 6:23

**NAASSON** (*na'-as-son*) See NAASHON. *Father of Salmon.*
and Aminadab begat *N* Mt 1:4
and *N* begat Salmon Mt 1:4
of Salmon, which was the son of *N* Lk 3:32

**NABAJOTH** See NABOTH.

**NABAL** (*na'-bal*) See NABAL'S. *A wife of David.*
Now the name of the man was *N* 1Sa 25:3
that *N* did shear his sheep 1Sa 25:4
Get you up to Carmel, and go to *N* 1Sa 25:5
they spake to *N* according to all 1Sa 25:9
*N* answered David's servants, and 1Sa 25:10
But she told not her husband *N* 1Sa 25:19
regard this man of Belial, even *N* 1Sa 25:25
*N* is his name, and folly is with 1Sa 25:25
seek evil to my lord, be as *N* 1Sa 25:26
there had not been left unto *N* by 1Sa 25:34
And Abigail came to *N* 1Sa 25:36
when the wine was gone out of *N* 1Sa 25:37
days after, that the LORD smote *N* 1Sa 25:38
when David heard that *N* was dead 1Sa 25:39
of my reproach from the hand of *N* 1Sa 25:39
wickedness of *N* upon his own head 1Sa 25:39
the wife of *N* the Carmelite 1Sa 30:5
the wife of *N* the Carmelite 2Sa 3:3

**NABAL'S** (*na'-balz*)
*N* wife, saying, Behold, David 1Sa 25:14
*N* heart was merry within him for 1Sa 25:36
Abigail the Carmelitess, *N* wife 1Sa 27:3
Abigail *N* wife the Carmelite 2Sa 2:2

**NABOTH** (*na'-both*) *A Jezreelite of Issachar.*
that *N* the Jezreelite had a 1Kin 21:1
And Ahab spake unto *N*, saying, 1Kin 21:2
*N* said to Ahab, The LORD forbid 1Kin 21:3
because of the word which *N* the 1Kin 21:4
I spake unto *N* the Jezreelite 1Kin 21:6
the vineyard of *N* the Jezreelite 1Kin 21:7
were in his city, dwelling with *N* 1Kin 21:8
set *N* on high among the people 1Kin 21:9
set *N* on high among the people 1Kin 21:12
against him, even against *N* 1Kin 21:13
*N* did blaspheme God and the king 1Kin 21:13
saying, *N* is stoned, and is dead 1Kin 21:14
Jezebel heard that *N* was stoned 1Kin 21:15
the vineyard of *N* the Jezreelite 1Kin 21:15
for *N* is not alive, but dead 1Kin 21:15
when Ahab heard that *N* was dead 1Kin 21:16
the vineyard of *N* the Jezreelite 1Kin 21:16
he is in the vineyard of *N* 1Kin 21:18

of *N* shall dogs lick thy blood ... 1Kin 21:19
the portion of *N* the Jezreelite ... 2Kin 9:21
of the field of *N* the Jezreelite ... 2Kin 9:25
seen yesterday the blood of *N* ... 2Kin 9:26

**NACHON** See NACHON'S.

**NACHON'S** (*na'-kons*)
they came to *N* threshingfloor ... 2Sa 6:6

**NACHOR** (*na'-kor*) See NAHOR.
*1. Brother of Abraham.*
of Abraham, and the father of *N* ... Josh 24:2
*2. Father of Thara; ancestor of Jesus.*
of Thara, which was the son of *N* ... Lk 3:34

**NACON** See NACHON'S.

**NADAB** (*na'-dab*)
*1. Son of Aaron.*
and she bare him *N*, and Abihu, ... Ex 6:23
unto the LORD, thou, and Aaron, *N* ... Ex 24:1
Then went up Moses, and Aaron, *N* ... Ex 24:9
priest's office, even Aaron, *N* ... Ex 28:1
And *N* and Abihu, the sons of Aaron, ... Lev 10:1
*N* the firstborn, and Abihu, ... Num 3:2
And *N* and Abihu died before the ... Num 3:4
And unto Aaron was born *N*, and ... Num 26:60
And *N* and Abihu died, when they ... Num 26:61
*N*, and Abihu, Eleazar, and Ithamar ... 1Chr 6:3
*N*, and Abihu, Eleazar, and Ithamar ... 1Chr 24:1
But *N* and Abihu died before their ... 1Chr 24:2
*2. Son of King Jeroboam I.*
*N* his son reigned in his stead ... 1Kin 14:20
*N* the son of Jeroboam began to ... 1Kin 15:25
for *N* and all Israel laid siege to ... 1Kin 15:27
Now the rest of the acts of *N* ... 1Kin 15:31
*3. Great-grandson of Jerahmeel.*
Shammai; *N*, and ... 1Chr 2:28
And the sons of *N* ... 1Chr 2:30
*4. A descendant of King Saul.*
and Zur, and Kish, and Baal, and *N* ... 1Chr 8:30
and Kish, and Baal, and Ner, and *N* ... 1Chr 9:36

**NAGGAI** See NAGGE.

**NAGGE** (*nag'-e*) See NEARIAH. *Father of Esli; ancestor of Jesus.*
of Esli, which was the son of *N* ... Lk 3:25

**NAHALAL** (*na'-ha-lal*) *A Levitical city in Zebulun.*
her suburbs, *N* with her suburbs ... Josh 21:35

**NAHALIEL** (*na-ha'-le-el*) *An Israelite encampment in the wilderness.*
And from Mattanah to *N* ... Num 21:19
and from *N* to Bamoth ... Num 21:19

**NAHALLAL** (*na'-hal-el*) See NAHALAL. *Same as Nahalal.*
and *N*, and Shimron ... Josh 19:15

**NAHALOL** (*na'-ha-lol*) *Same as Nahalal.*
Kitron, nor the inhabitants of *N* ... Judg 1:30

**NAHAM** (*na'-ham*) See ISHBAH. *A descendant of Caleb.*
his wife Hodiah the sister of *N* ... 1Chr 4:19

**NAHAMANI** (*na-ham'-a-ni*) *A clan chief with Zerubbabel.*
Nehemiah, Azariah, Raamiah, *N* ... Neh 7:7

**NAHARAI** (*na'-ha-rahee*) See NAHARI. *A 'mighty man' of David.*
*N* the Berothite, the armourbearer ... 1Chr 11:39

**NAHARI** (*na'-ha-ri*) See NAHARAI. *Same as Naharai.*
*N* the Beerothite, armourbearer to ... 2Sa 23:37

**NAHASH** (*na'-hash*) See IR-NAHASH.
*1. An Ammonite king.*
Then *N* the Ammonite came up, and ... 1Sa 11:1
all the men of Jabesh said unto *N* ... 1Sa 11:1
*N* the Ammonite answered them, On ... 1Sa 11:2
when ye saw that *N* the king of ... 1Sa 12:12
*2. Father of Shobi and Hanun.*
kindness unto Hanun the son of *N* ... 2Sa 10:2
that Shobi the son of *N* of Rabbah ... 2Sa 17:27
that *N* the king of the children ... 1Chr 19:1
kindness unto Hanun the son of *N* ... 1Chr 19:2
*3. Mother of Abigail.*
in to Abigail the daughter of *N* ... 2Sa 17:25

**NAHATH** (*na'-hath*) See TOHU.
*1. A son of Reuel.*
*N*, and Zerah, Shammah, and Mizzah Gen 36:13
duke *N*, duke Zerah, duke Shammah, Gen 36:17
*N*, Zerah, Shammah, and Mizzah ... 1Chr 1:37
*2. Son of Zophi.*
Zophai his son, and *N* his son, ... 1Chr 6:26
*3. A Temple servant.*
And Jehiel, and Azaziah, and *N* ... 2Chr 31:13

**NAHBI** (*nah'-bi*) *A spy sent to the Promised Land.*
of Naphtali, *N* the son of Vophsi ... Num 13:14

**NAHOR** (*na'-hor*) See NACHOR, NAHOR'S.
*1. Grandfather of Abraham.*
lived thirty years, and begat *N* ... Gen 11:22
he begat *N* two hundred years ... Gen 11:23
*N* lived nine and twenty years, and ... Gen 11:24
*N* lived after he begat Terah an ... Gen 11:25
Serug, *N*, Terah, ... 1Chr 1:26
*2. Son of Terah.*
seventy years, and begat Abram, *N* ... Gen 11:26
Terah begat Abram, *N*, and Haran ... Gen 11:27
And Abram and *N* took them wives ... Gen 11:29
born children unto thy brother *N* ... Gen 22:20
these eight Milcah did bear to *N* ... Gen 22:23
Mesopotamia, unto the city of *N* ... Gen 24:10
son of Milcah, the wife of *N* ... Gen 24:15
of Milcah, which she bare unto *N* ... Gen 24:24
them, Know ye Laban the son of *N* ... Gen 29:5
God of Abraham, and the God of *N* ... Gen 31:53

**NAHOR'S** (*na'-hors*) *Refers to Nahor 2.*
and the name of *N* wife, Milcah, ... Gen 11:29
*N* son, whom Milcah bare unto him ... Gen 24:47

**NAHSHON** (*nah'-shon*) See NAASHON, NAASSON. *Son of Amminadab.*
*N* the son of Amminadab ... Num 1:7
*N* the son of Amminadab shall be ... Num 2:3
day was *N* the son of Amminadab ... Num 7:12
of *N* the son of Amminadab ... Num 7:17
over his host was *N* the son of ... Num 10:14
And Amminadab begat *N*, and *N* ... Ruth 4:20
begat *N*, and *N* begat Salmon, ... Ruth 4:20
and Amminadab begat *N*, prince of ... 1Chr 2:10
*N* begat Salma, and Salma begat ... 1Chr 2:11

**NAHUM** (*na'-hum*) See NAUM. *A prophet who spoke against Nineveh.*
of the vision of *N* the Elkoshite ... Nah 1:1

**NAIL**
Heber's wife took a *n* of the tent ... Judg 4:21
smote the *n* into his temples, and ... Judg 4:21
dead, and the *n* was in his temples ... Judg 4:22
She put her hand to the *n* ... Judg 5:26
to give us a *n* in his holy place, ... Ezr 9:8
fasten him as a *n* in a sure place ... Is 22:23
shall the *n* that is fastened in ... Is 22:25
the corner, out of him the *n* ... Zec 10:4

**NAILING**
out of the way, *n* it to his cross ... Col 2:14

**NAILS**
shave her head, and pare her *n* ... Deut 21:12
iron in abundance for the *n* for ... 1Chr 22:3
the weight of the *n* was fifty ... 2Chr 3:9
as *n* fastened by the masters of ... Eccl 12:11
and he fastened it with *n*, that it ... Is 41:7
they fasten it with *n* and with ... Jer 10:4
and his *n* like birds' claws ... Dan 4:33
were of iron, and his *n* of brass ... Dan 7:19
in his hands the print of the *n* ... Jn 20:25
my finger into the print of the *n* ... Jn 20:25

**NAIN** (*nane*) *A city in Galilee.*
that he went into a city called *N* ... Lk 7:11

**NAIOTH** (*nay'-yoth*) *A place in Ramah.*
he and Samuel went and dwelt in *N* ... 1Sa 19:18
Behold, David is at *N* in Ramah ... 1Sa 19:19
Behold, they be at *N* in Ramah ... 1Sa 19:22
And he went thither to *N* in Ramah ... 1Sa 19:23
until he came to *N* in Ramah ... 1Sa 19:23
And David fled from *N* in Ramah ... 1Sa 20:1

**NAKED**
And they were both *n*, the man and ... Gen 2:25
and they knew that they were *n* ... Gen 3:7
and I was afraid, because I was *n* ... Gen 3:10
Who told thee that thou wast *n* ... Gen 3:11
Moses saw that the people were *n* ... Ex 32:25
(for Aaron had made them *n* unto ... Ex 32:25
lay down *n* all that day and all ... 1Sa 19:24
all that were *n* among them ... 2Chr 28:15
for he made Judah *n*, and ... 2Chr 28:19
*N* came I out of my mother's womb, ... Job 1:21
and *n* shall I return thither ... Job 1:21
stripped the *n* of their clothing ... Job 22:6
They cause the *n* to lodge without ... Job 24:7
him to go *n* without clothing ... Job 24:10
Hell is *n* before him, and ... Job 26:6
*n* shall he return to go as he ... Eccl 5:15
And he did so, walking *n* and ... Is 20:2
my servant Isaiah hath walked *n* ... Is 20:3
captives, young and old, *n* ... Is 20:4
when thou seest the *n*, that thou ... Is 58:7
drunken, and shalt make thyself *n* ... Lam 4:21
is grown, whereas thou wast *n* ... Eze 16:7
of thy youth, when thou wast *n* ... Eze 16:22
thy fair jewels, and leave thee *n* ... Eze 16:39
hath covered the *n* with a garment ... Eze 18:7
hath covered the *n* with a garment ... Eze 18:16
thy labour, and shall leave thee *n* ... Eze 23:29
Lest I strip her *n*, and set her as ... Hos 2:3
shall flee away *n* in that day ... Amos 2:16
and howl, I will go stripped and *n* ... Mic 1:8
of Saphir, having thy shame *n* ... Mic 1:11
Thy bow was made quite *n*, ... Hab 3:9
*N*, and ye clothed me ... Mt 25:36
or *n*, and clothed thee ... Mt 25:38
*n*, and ye clothed me not ... Mt 25:43
or athirst, or a stranger, or *n* ... Mt 25:44
linen cloth cast about his *n* body ... Mk 14:51
linen cloth, and fled from them *n* ... Mk 14:52
coat unto him, (for he was *n* ... Jn 21:7
they fled out of that house *n* ... Acts 19:16
both hunger, and thirst, and are *n* ... 1Cor 4:11
clothed we shall not be found *n* ... 2Cor 5:3
but all things are *n* and opened ... Heb 4:13
If a brother or sister be *n* ... Jas 2:15
and poor, and blind, and *n* ... Rev 3:17
his garments, lest he walk *n* ... Rev 16:15
and shall make her desolate and *n* ... Rev 17:16

**NAKEDNESS**
saw the *n* of his father, and told ... Gen 9:22
covered the *n* of their father ... Gen 9:23
and they saw not their father's *n* ... Gen 9:23
to see the *n* of the land ye are ... Gen 42:9
but to see the *n* of the land ye ... Gen 42:12
that thy *n* be not discovered ... Ex 20:26
linen breeches to cover their *n* ... Ex 28:42
of kin to him, to uncover their *n* ... Lev 18:6
The *n* of thy father ... Lev 18:7
or the *n* of thy mother, shalt ... Lev 18:7
thou shalt not uncover her *n* ... Lev 18:7
The *n* of thy father's wife shalt ... Lev 18:8
it is thy father's *n* ... Lev 18:8
The *n* of thy sister, the daughter ... Lev 18:9
even their *n* thou shalt not ... Lev 18:9
The *n* of thy son's daughter, or ... Lev 18:10
even their *n* thou shalt not ... Lev 18:10
for theirs is thine own *n* ... Lev 18:10
The *n* of thy father's wife's ... Lev 18:11
thou shalt not uncover her *n* ... Lev 18:11
the *n* of thy father's sister ... Lev 18:12
the *n* of thy mother's sister ... Lev 18:13
the *n* of thy father's brother ... Lev 18:14
the *n* of thy daughter in law ... Lev 18:15
thou shalt not uncover her *n* ... Lev 18:15
the *n* of thy brother's wife ... Lev 18:16
it is thy brother's *n* ... Lev 18:16
not uncover the *n* of a woman ... Lev 18:17
daughter, to uncover her *n* ... Lev 18:17
to vex her, to uncover her *n* ... Lev 18:18
unto a woman to uncover her *n* ... Lev 18:19
hath uncovered his father's *n* ... Lev 20:11
her *n*, and she see his *n* ... Lev 20:17
he hath uncovered his sister's *n* ... Lev 20:17
sickness, and shall uncover her *n* ... Lev 20:18
the *n* of thy mother's sister ... Lev 20:19
he hath uncovered his uncle's *n* ... Lev 20:20
he hath uncovered his brother's *n* ... Lev 20:21
in hunger, and in thirst, and in *n* ... Deut 28:48
the confusion of thy mother's *n* ... 1Sa 20:30
Thy *n* shall be uncovered, yea, ... Is 47:3
her, because they have seen her *n* ... Lam 1:8
skirt over thee, and covered thy *n* ... Eze 16:8
thy *n* discovered through thy ... Eze 16:36
and will discover thy *n* unto them ... Eze 16:37
that they may see all thy *n* ... Eze 16:37
they discovered their fathers' *n* ... Eze 22:10
These discovered her *n* ... Eze 23:10
whoredoms, and discovered her *n* ... Eze 23:18
the *n* of thy whoredoms shall be ... Eze 23:29
and my flax given to cover her *n* ... Hos 2:9
and I will shew the nations thy *n* ... Nah 3:5
that thou mayest look on their *n* ... Hab 2:15
or persecution, or famine, or *n* ... Rom 8:35
in fastings often, in cold and *n* ... 2Cor 11:27
the shame of thy *n* do not appear ... Rev 3:18

**NAME** See PREFACE.
bless thee, and make thy *n* great ... Gen 12:2
he said unto him, What is thy *n* ... Gen 32:27
God said unto him, Thy *n* is Jacob ... Gen 35:10
Jacob, but Israel shall be thy *n* ... Gen 35:10
and he called his *n* Israel ... Gen 35:10
shall say to me, What is his *n* ... Ex 3:13
this is my *n* for ever, and this is ... Ex 3:15
Thou shalt not take the *n* of the ... Ex 20:7
in my sight, and I know thee by *n* ... Ex 33:17
shall not swear by my *n* falsely ... Lev 19:12
thou profane the *n* of thy God ... Lev 19:12
they shall put my *n* upon the ... Num 6:27
Thou shalt not take the *n* of the ... Deut 5:11
his *n* shall be called in Israel, ... Deut 25:10
whose *n* is called by the *n* of ... 2Sa 6:2
and have made thee a great *n* ... 2Sa 7:9
He shall build an house for my *n* ... 2Sa 7:13
called the pillar after his own *n* ... 2Sa 18:18
he shall build an house unto my *n* ... 1Kin 5:5
the *n* of the LORD God of Israel ... 1Kin 8:17
And call ye on the *n* of your gods ... 1Kin 18:24
I will call on the *n* of the LORD ... 1Kin 18:24
Glory ye in his holy *n* ... 1Chr 16:10
people, which are called by my *n* ... 2Chr 7:14
blessed be the *n* of the LORD ... Job 1:21
to the *n* of the LORD most high ... Ps 7:17
Save me, O God, by thy *n*, and ... Ps 54:1
I will praise the *n* of God with a ... Ps 69:30
His *n* shall endure for ever ... Ps 72:17
is within me, bless his holy *n* ... Ps 103:1
that cometh in the *n* of the LORD ... Ps 118:26
Our help is in the *n* of the LORD ... Ps 124:8
take the *n* of my God in vain ... Prov 30:9
A good *n* is better than precious ... Eccl 7:1
my people shall know my *n* ... Is 52:6
thou shalt be called by a new *n* ... Is 62:2
they were not called by thy *n* ... Is 63:19
and thy people are called by thy *n* ... Dan 9:19
and thou shalt call his *n* JESUS ... Mt 1:21
and they shall call his *n* Emmanuel ... Mt 1:23
art in heaven, Hallowed be thy *n* ... Mt 6:9
are gathered together in my *n* ... Mt 18:20
For many shall come in my *n* ... Mt 24:5
that cometh in the *n* of the Lord ... Mk 11:9
For many shall come in my *n* ... Mk 13:6
and holy is his *n* ... Lk 1:49
whatsoever ye shall ask in my *n* ... Jn 14:13
If ye shall ask any thing in my *n* ... Jn 14:14
have ye asked nothing in my *n* ... Jn 16:24
At that day ye shall ask in my *n* ... Jn 16:26
keep through thine own *n* those ... Jn 17:11
in the *n* of Jesus Christ for the ... Acts 2:38

his *n* through faith in his *n* Acts 3:16
for there is none other *n* under Acts 4:12
calling on the *n* of the Lord Acts 22:16
him a *n* which is above every *n* Phil 2:9
That at the *n* of Jesus every knee Phil 2:10
do all in the *n* of the Lord Jesus Col 3:17
Let every one that nameth the *n* 2Ti 2:19
on the *n* of his Son Jesus Christ 1Jn 3:23
on the *n* of the Son of God 1Jn 5:13
and in the stone a new *n* written Rev 2:17
his *n* is called The Word of God Rev 19:13

**NAMED**
which he had *n* in the audience of Gen 23:16
said, Is not he rightly *n* Jacob Gen 27:36
and let my name be *n* on them Gen 48:16
house, *n* Rahab, and lodged there Josh 2:1
she *n* the child I-chabod, saying, 1Sa 4:21
*n* Goliath, of Gath, whose height 1Sa 17:4
*n* Abiathar, escaped, and fled 1Sa 22:20
of Jacob, whom he *n* Israel 2Kin 17:34
his sons were *n* of the tribe of 1Chr 23:14
That which hath been is *n* already Eccl 6:10
But ye shall be *n* the Priests of Is 61:6
be *n* in the mouth of any man of Jer 44:26
whom the king *n* Belteshazzar Dan 5:12
which are *n* chief of the nations, Amos 6:1
O thou that art *n* the house of Mic 2:7
*n* Matthew, sitting at the receipt Mt 9:9
*n* Joseph, who also himself was Mt 27:57
to a place which was *n* Gethsemane Mk 14:32
And there was one *n* Barabbas Mk 15:7
a certain priest *n* Zacharias Lk 1:5
a city of Galilee, *n* Nazareth, Lk 1:26
which was so *n* of the angel Lk 2:21
*n* Levi, sitting at the receipt of Lk 5:27
twelve, whom also he *n* apostles Lk 6:13
Simon, (whom he also *n* Peter Lk 6:14
behold, there came a man *n* Jairus Lk 8:41
a certain woman *n* Martha received Lk 10:38
was a certain beggar *n* Lazarus Lk 16:20
there was a man *n* Zacchaeus Lk 19:2
behold, there was a man *n* Joseph Lk 23:50
*n* Nicodemus, a ruler of the Jews Jn 3:1
*n* Lazarus, of Bethany, the town Jn 11:1
*n* Caiaphas, being the high priest Jn 11:49
But a certain man *n* Ananias Acts 5:1
*n* Gamaliel, a doctor of the law, Acts 5:34
disciple at Damascus, *n* Ananias Acts 9:10
vision a man *n* Ananias coming in Acts 9:12
he found a certain man *n* Aeneas Acts 9:33
a certain disciple *n* Tabitha Acts 9:36
stood up one of them *n* Agabus Acts 11:28
a damsel came to hearken, *n* Rhoda Acts 12:13
*n* Timotheus, the son of a certain Acts 16:1
And a certain woman *n* Lydia Acts 16:14
Areopagite, and a woman *n* Damaris. Acts 17:34
And found a certain Jew *n* Aquila Acts 18:2
*n* Justus, one that worshipped God Acts 18:7
And a certain Jew *n* Apollos Acts 18:24
For a certain man *n* Demetrius Acts 19:24
a certain young man *n* Eutychus Acts 20:9
a certain prophet, *n* Agabus Acts 21:10
with a certain orator *n* Tertullus Acts 24:1
other prisoners unto one *n* Julius Acts 27:1
gospel, not where Christ was *n* Rom 15:20
so much as *n* among the Gentiles 1Cor 5:1
dominion, and every name that is *n* Eph 1:21
family in heaven and earth is *n* Eph 3:15
let it not be once *n* among you Eph 5:3

**NAMELY**
his offering be of the flocks, *n* Lev 1:10
Of the children of Joseph, *n* Num 1:32
cloud covered the tabernacle, *n* Num 9:15
Of the tribe of Joseph, *n* Num 13:11
*n*, Evi, and Rekem, and Zur, and Hur, Num 31:8
*N*, Bezer in the wilderness, in Deut 4:43
*N*, of the gods of the people Deut 13:7
*n*, the Hittites, and the Amorites, Deut 20:17
*N*, five lords of the Philistines, Judg 3:3
to the house of Jerubbaal, *n* Judg 8:35
they gave the cities of Judah, *n* 1Chr 6:57
given out of the half tribe, *n* 1Chr 6:61
gates of the house of the LORD, *n* 1Chr 9:23
courses among the sons of Levi, *n* 1Chr 23:6
*n*, of the sons of Jeshua the son Ezr 10:18
*n*, Zechariah the son of Jonathan, Neh 12:35
provinces of king Ahasuerus, *n* Est 8:12
I have seen under the sun, *n* Eccl 5:13
with a razor that is hired, *n* Is 7:20
the king sent men into Egypt, *n* Jer 26:22
*n* this, Thou shalt love thy Mk 12:31
*n*, Judas surnamed Barsabas, and Acts 15:22
comprehended in this saying, *n* Rom 13:9

**NAME'S**
his people for his great *n* sake 1Sa 12:22
of a far country for thy *n* sake 1Kin 8:41
far country for thy great *n* sake 2Chr 6:32
of righteousness for his *n* sake Ps 23:3
For thy *n* sake, O LORD, pardon Ps 25:11
therefore for thy *n* sake lead me Ps 31:3
away our sins, for thy *n* sake Ps 79:9
he saved them for his *n* sake Ps 106:8
O GOD the Lord, for thy *n* sake Ps 109:21
me, O LORD, for thy *n* sake Ps 143:11
For my *n* sake will I defer mine Is 48:9
that cast you out for my *n* sake Is 66:5
us, do thou it for thy *n* sake Jer 14:7
Do not abhor us, for thy *n* sake Jer 14:21
But I wrought for my *n* sake Eze 20:9
But I wrought for my *n* sake Eze 20:14
hand, and wrought for my *n* sake Eze 20:22
wrought with you for my *n* sake Eze 20:44
Israel, but for mine holy *n* sake Eze 36:22
be hated of all men for my *n* sake Mt 10:22
children, or lands, for my *n* sake Mt 19:29
of all nations for my *n* sake Mt 24:9
be hated of all men for my *n* sake Mk 13:13
kings and rulers for my *n* sake Lk 21:12
be hated of all men for my *n* sake Lk 21:17
they do unto you for my *n* sake Jn 15:21
he must suffer for my *n* sake Acts 9:16
are forgiven you for his *n* sake 1Jn 2:12
for his *n* sake they went forth 3Jn 7
for my *n* sake hast laboured, and Rev 2:3

**NAMES**
Adam gave *n* to all cattle, and to Gen 2:20
these are the *n* of the sons of Gen 25:13
the sons of Ishmael, by their *n* Gen 25:13
of Ishmael, and these are their *n* Gen 25:16
he called their *n* after the *n* Gen 26:18
These are the *n* of Esau's sons Gen 36:10
these are the *n* of the dukes that Gen 36:40
after their places, by their *n* Gen 36:40
these are the *n* of the children Gen 46:8
Now these are the *n* of the Ex 1:1
these are the *n* of the sons of Ex 6:16
grave on them the *n* of the Ex 28:9
Six of their *n* on one stone Ex 28:10
the other six *n* of the rest on Ex 28:10
the *n* of the children of Israel Ex 28:11
Aaron shall bear their *n* before Ex 28:12
the *n* of the children of Israel Ex 28:21
twelve, according to their *n* Ex 28:21
Aaron shall bear the *n* of the Ex 28:29
with the *n* of the children of Ex 39:6
the *n* of the children of Israel Ex 39:14
twelve, according to their *n* Ex 39:14
with the number of their *n* Num 1:2
these are the *n* of the men that Num 1:5
which are expressed by their *n* Num 1:17
according to the number of the *n* Num 1:18
according to the number of the *n* Num 1:20
according to the number of the *n* Num 1:22
according to the number of the *n* Num 1:24
according to the number of the *n* Num 1:26
according to the number of the *n* Num 1:28
according to the number of the *n* Num 1:30
according to the number of the *n* Num 1:32
according to the number of the *n* Num 1:34
according to the number of the *n* Num 1:36
according to the number of the *n* Num 1:38
according to the number of the *n* Num 1:40
according to the number of the *n* Num 1:42
these are the *n* of the sons of Num 3:2
These are the *n* of the sons of Num 3:3
were the sons of Levi by their *n* Num 3:17
these are the *n* of the sons of Num 3:18
and take the number of their *n* Num 3:40
males by the number of *n*, from a Num 3:43
And these were their *n* Num 13:4
These are the *n* of the men which Num 13:16
the *n* of the daughters of Num 26:33
according to the number of *n* Num 26:53
according to the *n* of the tribes Num 26:55
these are the *n* of his daughters Num 27:1
(their *n* being changed,) and Num 32:38
gave other *n* unto the cities Num 32:38
These are the *n* of the men which Num 34:17
the *n* of the men are these Num 34:19
destroy the *n* of them out of that Deut 12:3
these are the *n* of his daughters, Josh 17:3
mention of the *n* of their gods Josh 23:7
the *n* of his two daughters were 1Sa 14:49
the *n* of his three sons that went 1Sa 17:13
these be the *n* of those that were 2Sa 5:14
These be the *n* of the mighty men 2Sa 23:8
And these are their *n* 1Kin 4:8
These mentioned by their *n* were 1Chr 4:38
these be the *n* of the sons of 1Chr 6:17
which are called by their *n* 1Chr 6:65
whose *n* are these, Azrikam, 1Chr 8:38
whose *n* are these, Azrikam, 1Chr 9:44
Now these are the *n* of his 1Chr 14:4
by number of *n* by their polls 1Chr 23:24
What are the *n* of the men that Ezr 5:4
We asked their *n* also, to certify Ezr 5:10
that we might write the *n* of the Ezr 5:10
whose *n* are these, Eliphelet, Ezr 8:13
and all of them by their *n* Ezr 10:16
nor take up their *n* into my lips Ps 16:4
their lands after their own *n* Ps 49:11
he calleth them all by their *n* Ps 147:4
he calleth them all by *n* by the Is 40:26
the *n* of them were Aholah the Eze 23:4
Thus were their *n* Eze 23:4
Now these are the *n* of the tribes Eze 48:1
the *n* of the tribes of Israel Eze 48:31
the prince of the eunuchs gave *n* Dan 1:7
For I will take away the *n* of Hos 2:17
that I will cut off the *n* of the Zec 13:2
Now the *n* of the twelve apostles Mt 10:2
because your *n* are written in Lk 10:20
(the number of *n* together were Acts 1:15
if it be a question of words and *n* Acts 18:15
whose *n* are in the book of life Phil 4:3
Thou hast a few *n* even in Sardis Rev 3:4
whose *n* are not written in the Rev 13:8
full of *n* of blasphemy, having Rev 17:3
whose *n* were not written in the Rev 17:8
*n* written thereon, which are the Rev 21:12
which are the *n* of the twelve Rev 21:12
in them the *n* of the twelve Rev 21:14

**NAMETH**
Let every one that *n* the name of 2Ti 2:19

**NAOMI** (*na'-o-mee*) See NAOMI'S. *Mother-in-law of Ruth.*
and the name of his wife *N* Ruth 1:2
*N* said unto her two daughters in Ruth 1:8
*N* said, Turn again, my daughters Ruth 1:11
them, and they said, Is this *N* Ruth 1:19
she said unto them, Call me not *N* Ruth 1:20
why then call ye me *N*, seeing the Ruth 1:21
So *N* returned, and Ruth the Ruth 1:22
*N* had a kinsman of her husband's, Ruth 2:1
And Ruth the Moabitess said unto *N* Ruth 2:2
with *N* out of the country of Moab Ruth 2:6
*N* said unto her daughter in law, Ruth 2:20
*N* said unto her, The man is near Ruth 2:20
*N* said unto Ruth her daughter in Ruth 2:22
Then *N* her mother in law said Ruth 3:1
And he said unto the kinsman, *N* Ruth 4:3
buyest the field of the hand of *N* Ruth 4:5
and Mahlon's, of the hand of *N* Ruth 4:9
And the women said unto *N*, Blessed. Ruth 4:14
*N* took the child, and laid it in Ruth 4:16
saying, There is a son born to *N* Ruth 4:17

**NAOMI'S** (*na'-o-meze*)
And Elimelech *N* husband died Ruth 1:3

**NAPHATH** See DOR.

**NAPHATH DOR** See DOR.

**NAPHETH** See DOR.

**NAPHISH** (*na'-fish*) See NEPHISH. *A son of Ishmael.*
Hadar, and Tema, Jetur, *N*, and Gen 25:15
Jetur, *N*, and Kedemah 1Chr 1:31

**NAPHTALI** (*naf'-ta-li*) See NEPHTHALIM.
*1. A son of Jacob.*
and she called his name *N* Gen 30:8
handmaid; Dan, and *N* Gen 35:25
And the sons of *N* Gen 46:24
*N* is a hind let loose Gen 49:21
Dan, and *N*, Gad, and Asher Ex 1:4
Dan, Joseph, and Benjamin, *N* 1Chr 2:2
The sons of *N* 1Chr 7:13
one gate of Asher, one gate of *N* Eze 48:34
*2. The tribe and land.*
Of *N*; Ahira the son Num 1:15
Of the children of *N*, throughout Num 1:42
of them, even of the tribe of *N* Num 1:43
Then the tribe of *N* Num 2:29
*N* shall be Ahira the son of Enan Num 2:29
Enan, prince of the children of *N* Num 7:78
of *N* was Ahira the son of Enan Num 10:27
Of the tribe of *N*, Nahbi the son Num 13:14
Of the sons of *N* after their Num 26:48
These are the families of *N* Num 26:50
of the tribe of the children of *N* Num 34:28
and Asher, and Zebulun, Dan, and *N* Deut 27:13
And of Naphtali he said, O *N* Deut 33:23
And all *N*, and the land of Ephraim, Deut 34:2
lot came out to the children of *N* Josh 19:32
even for the children of *N* Josh 19:32
of *N* according to their families Josh 19:39
Kedesh in Galilee in mount *N* Josh 20:7
Asher, and out of the tribe of *N* Josh 21:6
And out of the tribe of *N*, Kedesh Josh 21:32
Neither did *N* drive out the Judg 1:33
thousand men of the children of *N* Judg 4:6
called Zebulun and *N* to Kedesh Judg 4:10
*N* were a people that jeoparded Judg 5:18
Asher, and unto Zebulun, and unto *N* Judg 6:35
themselves together out of *N* Judg 7:23
Ahimaaz was in *N* 1Kin 4:15
a widow's son of the tribe of *N* 1Kin 7:14
Cinneroth, with all the land of *N* 1Kin 15:20
and Galilee, all the land of *N* 2Kin 15:29
Asher, and out of the tribe of *N* 1Chr 6:62
And out of the tribe of *N* 1Chr 6:76
of *N* a thousand captains, and with 1Chr 12:34
unto Issachar and Zebulun and *N* 1Chr 12:40
of *N*, Jerimoth the son of Azriel 1Chr 27:19
and all the store cities of *N* 2Chr 16:4
Ephraim, and Simeon, even unto *N* 2Chr 34:6
of Zebulun, and the princes of *N* Ps 68:27
land of Zebulun and the land of *N* Is 9:1
the west side, a portion for *N* Eze 48:3
And by the border of *N*, from the Eze 48:4

**NAPHTUHIM** (*naf'-too-him*) *Inhabitants of central Egypt.*
and Anamim, and Lehabim, and *N* Gen 10:13

**NAPKIN**
which I have kept laid up in a *n* Lk 19:20
his face was bound about with a *n* Jn 11:44
And the *n*, that was about his head Jn 20:7

**NAPTHTUHIM**
and Anamim, and Lehabim, and *N* 1Chr 1:11

**NARCISSUS** (*nar-sis'-sus*) *A Christian in Rome.*
that be of the household of *N* Rom 16:11

**NARROW**
further, and stood in a *n* place Num 22:26
mount Ephraim be too *n* for thee Josh 17:15

house he made windows of *n* lights .... 1Kin 6:4
and a strange woman is a *n* pit .... Prov 23:27
shall even now be too *n* by reason .... Is 49:19
there were *n* windows to the .... Eze 40:16
the *n* windows, and the galleries .... Eze 41:16
And there were *n* windows and palm .. Eze 41:26
*n* is the way, which leadeth unto .... Mt 7:14

**NARROWED**
house he made *n* rests round about .... 1Kin 6:6

**NARROWER**
the covering *n* than that he can .... Is 28:20

**NARROWLY**
lookest *n* unto all my paths .... Job 13:27
see thee shall *n* look upon thee .... Is 14:16

**NATHAN** (*na'-than*) See NATHAN-MELECH.
*1. A son of David.*
Shammuah, and Shobab, and *N* .... 2Sa 5:14
Shimea, and Shobab, and *N*, and .... 1Chr 3:5
and Shobab, *N*, and Solomon .... 1Chr 14:4
Mattatha, which was the son of *N* .... Lk 3:31
*2. A prophet in David's court.*
the king said unto *N* the prophet .... 2Sa 7:2
*N* said to the king, Go, do all .... 2Sa 7:3
the word of the LORD came unto *N* .... 2Sa 7:4
so did *N* speak unto David .... 2Sa 7:17
And the LORD sent *N* unto David .... 2Sa 12:1
and he said to *N*, As the LORD .... 2Sa 12:5
*N* said to David, Thou art the man .... 2Sa 12:7
And David said unto *N*, I have .... 2Sa 12:13
*N* said unto David, The LORD also .... 2Sa 12:13
*N* departed unto his house .... 2Sa 12:15
sent by the hand of *N* the prophet .... 2Sa 12:25
*N* the prophet, and Shimei, and Rei, .... 1Kin 1:8
But *N* the prophet, and Benaiah, and .. 1Kin 1:10
Wherefore *N* spake unto Bath-sheba .. 1Kin 1:11
*N* the prophet also came in .... 1Kin 1:22
saying, Behold *N* the prophet .... 1Kin 1:23
*N* said, My lord, O king, hast .... 1Kin 1:24
*N* the prophet, and Benaiah the son .... 1Kin 1:32
*N* the prophet anoint him there .... 1Kin 1:34
*N* the prophet, and Benaiah the son .... 1Kin 1:38
*N* the prophet, and Benaiah the son .... 1Kin 1:44
*N* the prophet have anointed him .... 1Kin 1:45
that David said to *N* the prophet .... 1Chr 17:1
Then *N* said unto David, Do all .... 1Chr 17:2
that the word of God came to *N* .... 1Chr 17:3
so did *N* speak unto David .... 1Chr 17:15
and in the book of *N* the prophet .... 1Chr 29:29
in the book of *N* the prophet .... 2Chr 9:29
the king's seer, and *N* the prophet .... 2Chr 29:25
when *N* the prophet came unto him, .... Ps 51:*t*
*3. Father of Igal.*
Igal the son of *N* of Zobah .... 2Sa 23:36
*4. Father of Azariah.*
Azariah the son of *N* was over the .... 1Kin 4:5
*5. Father of Zebud.*
Zabud the son of *N* was principal .... 1Kin 4:5
*6. Son of Attai.*
And Attai begat *N* .... 1Chr 2:36
and *N* begat Zabad .... 1Chr 2:36
*7. Brother of Joel.*
Joel the brother of *N*, Mibhar the .... 1Chr 11:38
*8. A clan leader with Ezra.*
Jarib, and for Elnathan, and for *N* .... Ezr 8:16
*9. Married a foreigner in exile.*
And Shelemiah, and *N*, and Adaiah, .... Ezr 10:39
*10. A family leader.*
family of the house of *N* apart .... Zec 12:12

**NATHANAEL** (*na-than'-a-el*) See BARTHOLOMEW. *A disciple of Jesus.*
Philip findeth *N*, and saith unto .... Jn 1:45
*N* said unto him, Can there any .... Jn 1:46
Jesus saw *N* coming to him, and .... Jn 1:47
*N* saith unto him, Whence knowest .... Jn 1:48
*N* answered and saith unto him, .... Jn 1:49
*N* of Cana in Galilee, and the sons .... Jn 21:2

**NATHAN-MELECH** (*na'-than-me'-lek*) *A servant of King Josiah.*
the chamber of *N* the chamberlain .... 2Kin 23:11

**NATION**
And I will make of thee a great *n* .... Gen 12:2
And also that *n*, whom they shall .... Gen 15:14
and I will make him a great *n* .... Gen 17:20
surely become a great and mighty *n* .. Gen 18:18
wilt thou slay also a righteous *n* .... Gen 20:4
of the bondwoman will I make a *n* .... Gen 21:13
for I will make him a great *n* .... Gen 21:18
a *n* and a company of nations shall .... Gen 35:11
will there make of thee a great *n* .... Gen 46:3
land of Egypt since it became a *n* .... Ex 9:24
kingdom of priests, and an holy *n* .... Ex 19:6
strange *n* he shall have no power .... Ex 21:8
and I will make of thee a great *n* .... Ex 32:10
that this *n* is thy people .... Ex 33:13
in all the earth, nor in any *n* .... Ex 34:10
neither any of your own *n* .... Lev 18:26
not walk in the manners of the *n* .... Lev 20:23
and will make of thee a greater *n* .... Num 14:12
Surely this great *n* is a wise .... Deut 4:6
For what *n* is there so great, who .... Deut 4:7
what *n* is there so great, that .... Deut 4:8
take him a *n* from the midst of .... Deut 4:34
from the midst of another *n* .... Deut 4:34
I will make of thee a *n* mightier .... Deut 9:14
with a few, and became there a *n* .... Deut 26:5
shall a *n* which thou knowest not .... Deut 28:33
unto a *n* which neither thou nor .... Deut 28:36
bring a *n* against thee from far .... Deut 28:49
a *n* whose tongue thou shalt not .... Deut 28:49
A *n* of fierce countenance, which .... Deut 28:50
them to anger with a foolish *n* .... Deut 32:21
For they are a *n* void of counsel, .... Deut 32:28
what one *n* in the earth is like .... 2Sa 7:23
liveth, there is no *n* or kingdom .... 1Kin 18:10
took an oath of the kingdom and *n* .. 1Kin 18:10
Howbeit every *n* made gods of .... 2Kin 17:29
every *n* in their cities wherein .... 2Kin 17:29
when they went from *n* to *n* .... 1Chr 16:20
what one *n* in the earth is like .... 1Chr 17:21
And *n* was destroyed of *n* .... 2Chr 15:6
for no god of any *n* or kingdom .... 2Chr 32:15
whether it be done against a *n* .... Job 34:29
Blessed is the *n* whose God is the .... Ps 33:12
my cause against an ungodly *n* .... Ps 43:1
us cut them off from being a *n* .... Ps 83:4
they went from one *n* to another .... Ps 105:13
rejoice in the gladness of thy *n* .... Ps 106:5
He hath not dealt so with any *n* .... Ps 147:20
Righteousness exalteth a *n* .... Prov 14:34
Ah sinful *n*, a people laden with .... Is 1:4
*n* shall not lift up sword against .... Is 2:4
shall not lift up sword against *n* .... Is 2:4
Thou hast multiplied the *n* .... Is 9:3
him against an hypocritical *n* .... Is 10:6
answer the messengers of the *n* .... Is 14:32
to a *n* scattered and peeled, to a .... Is 18:2
a *n* meted out and trodden down, .... Is 18:2
a *n* meted out and trodden under .... Is 18:7
that the righteous *n* which .... Is 26:2
Thou hast increased the *n* .... Is 26:15
O LORD, thou hast increased the *n* .... Is 26:15
to him whom the *n* abhorreth .... Is 49:7
and give ear unto me, O my *n* .... Is 51:4
thou shalt call a *n* that thou .... Is 55:5
as a *n* that did righteousness, and .... Is 58:2
For the *n* and kingdom that will .... Is 60:12
and a small one a strong *n* .... Is 60:22
unto a *n* that was not called by .... Is 65:1
or shall a *n* be born at once .... Is 66:8
Hath a *n* changed their gods, .... Jer 2:11
be avenged on such a *n* as this .... Jer 5:9
I will bring a *n* upon you from .... Jer 5:15
mighty *n*, it is an ancient *n* .... Jer 5:15
a *n* whose language thou knowest .... Jer 5:15
be avenged on such a *n* as this .... Jer 5:29
a great *n* shall be raised from .... Jer 6:22
This is a *n* that obeyeth not the .... Jer 7:28
be avenged on such a *n* as this .... Jer 9:9
pluck up and destroy that *n* .... Jer 12:17
I shall speak concerning a *n* .... Jer 18:7
If that *n*, against whom I have .... Jer 18:8
I shall speak concerning a *n* .... Jer 18:9
the king of Babylon, and that *n* .... Jer 25:12
shall go forth from *n* to *n* .... Jer 25:32
it shall come to pass, that the *n* .... Jer 27:8
that *n* will I punish, saith the .... Jer 27:8
LORD hath spoken against the *n* .... Jer 27:13
from being a *n* before me for ever .... Jer 31:36
should be no more a *n* before them .... Jer 33:24
let us cut it off from being a *n* .... Jer 48:2
get you up unto the wealthy *n* .... Jer 49:31
there shall be no *n* whither the .... Jer 49:36
there cometh up a *n* against her .... Jer 50:3
come from the north, and a great *n* .... Jer 50:41
for a *n* that could not save us .... Lam 4:17
to a rebellious *n* that hath .... Eze 2:3
I will make them one *n* in the .... Eze 37:22
a decree, That every people, *n* .... Dan 3:29
shall stand up out of the *n* .... Dan 8:22
was a *n* even to that same time .... Dan 12:1
For a *n* is come up upon my land, .... Joel 1:6
I will raise up against you a *n* .... Amos 6:14
*n* shall not lift up a sword .... Mic 4:3
not lift up a sword against *n* .... Mic 4:3
that was cast far off a strong *n* .... Mic 4:7
Chaldeans, that bitter and hasty *n* .... Hab 1:6
gather together, O *n* not desired .... Zeph 2:1
coast, the *n* of the Cherethites .... Zeph 2:5
people, and so is this *n* before me .... Hag 2:14
have robbed me, even this whole *n* .... Mal 3:9
given to a *n* bringing forth the .... Mt 21:43
For *n* shall rise against *n*, .... Mt 24:7
was a Greek, a Syrophenician by *n* .... Mk 7:26
For *n* shall rise against *n*, .... Mk 13:8
For he loveth our *n*, and he hath .... Lk 7:5
*N* shall rise against *n*, and .... Lk 21:10
this fellow perverting the *n* .... Lk 23:2
and take away both our place and *n* .... Jn 11:48
and that the whole *n* perish not .... Jn 11:50
that Jesus should die for that *n* .... Jn 11:51
And not for that *n* only, but that .... Jn 11:52
Thine own *n* and the chief priests .... Jn 18:35
men, out of every *n* under heaven .... Acts 2:5
the *n* to whom they shall be in .... Acts 7:7
among all the *n* of the Jews .... Acts 10:22
or come unto one of another *n* .... Acts 10:28
But in every *n* he that feareth .... Acts 10:35
unto this *n* by thy providence .... Acts 24:2
of many years a judge unto this *n* .... Acts 24:10
I came to bring alms to my *n* .... Acts 24:17
among mine own *n* at Jerusalem .... Acts 26:4
I had ought to accuse my *n* of .... Acts 28:19
by a foolish *n* I will anger you .... Rom 10:19
many my equals in mine own *n* .... Gal 1:14
midst of a crooked and perverse *n* .... Phil 2:15
a royal priesthood, an holy *n* .... 1Pet 2:9
and tongue, and people, and *n* .... Rev 5:9
dwell on the earth, and to every *n* .... Rev 14:6

**NATIONS**
after their families, in their *n* .... Gen 10:5
in their countries, and in their *n* .... Gen 10:20
in their lands, after their *n* .... Gen 10:31
their generations, in their *n* .... Gen 10:32
by these were the *n* divided in .... Gen 10:32
king of Elam, and Tidal king of *n* .... Gen 14:1
of Elam, and with Tidal king of *n* .... Gen 14:9
thou shalt be a father of many *n* .... Gen 17:4
father of many *n* have I made thee .... Gen 17:5
and I will make *n* of thee .... Gen 17:6
and she shall be a mother of *n* .... Gen 17:16
all the *n* of the earth shall be .... Gen 18:18
all the *n* of the earth be blessed .... Gen 22:18
princes according to their *n* .... Gen 25:16
Two *n* are in thy womb, and two .... Gen 25:23
all the *n* of the earth be blessed .... Gen 26:4
serve thee, and *n* bow down to thee .... Gen 27:29
a company of *n* shall be of thee, .... Gen 35:11
shall become a multitude of *n* .... Gen 48:19
I will cast out the *n* before thee .... Ex 34:24
for in all these the *n* are .... Lev 18:24
as it spued out the *n* that were .... Lev 18:28
then the *n* which have heard the .... Num 14:15
shall not be reckoned among the *n* .... Num 23:9
he shall eat up the *n* his enemies .... Num 24:8
Amalek was the first of the *n* .... Num 24:20
the fear of thee upon the *n* that .... Deut 2:25
in the sight of the *n*, which .... Deut 4:6
unto all *n* under the whole heaven .... Deut 4:19
shall scatter you among the *n* .... Deut 4:27
To drive out *n* from before thee .... Deut 4:38
hath cast out many *n* before thee .... Deut 7:1
seven *n* greater and mightier than .... Deut 7:1
heart, These *n* are more than I .... Deut 7:17
out those *n* before thee by little .... Deut 7:22
As the *n* which the LORD .... Deut 8:20
to go in to possess *n* greater .... Deut 9:1
*n* the LORD doth drive them out .... Deut 9:4
*n* the LORD thy God doth drive .... Deut 9:5
out all these *n* from before you .... Deut 11:23
and ye shall possess greater *n* .... Deut 11:23
wherein the *n* which ye shall .... Deut 12:2
cut off the *n* from before thee .... Deut 12:29
How did these *n* serve their gods .... Deut 12:30
above all the *n* that are upon the .... Deut 14:2
and thou shalt lend unto many *n* .... Deut 15:6
and thou shalt reign over many *n* .... Deut 15:6
like as all the *n* that are about .... Deut 17:14
after the abominations of those *n* .... Deut 18:9
For these *n*, which thou shalt .... Deut 18:14
LORD thy God hath cut off the *n* .... Deut 19:1
are not of the cities of these *n* .... Deut 20:15
above all *n* which he hath made .... Deut 26:19
on high above all *n* of the earth .... Deut 28:1
and thou shalt lend unto many *n* .... Deut 28:12
among all *n* whither the LORD .... Deut 28:37
among these *n* shalt thou find no .... Deut 28:65
through the *n* which ye passed by .... Deut 29:16
go and serve the gods of these *n* .... Deut 29:18
Even all *n* shall say, Wherefore .... Deut 29:24
call them to mind among all the *n* .... Deut 30:1
and gather thee from all the *n* .... Deut 30:3
destroy these *n* from before thee .... Deut 31:3
to the *n* their inheritance .... Deut 32:8
Rejoice, O ye *n*, with his people .... Deut 32:43
the king of the *n* of Gilgal .... Josh 12:23
unto all these *n* because of you .... Josh 23:3
you by lot these *n* that remain .... Josh 23:4
with all the *n* that I have cut .... Josh 23:4
That ye come not among these *n* .... Josh 23:7
out from before you great *n* .... Josh 23:9
unto the remnant of these *n* .... Josh 23:12
any of these *n* from before you .... Josh 23:13
*n* which Joshua left when he died .... Judg 2:21
Therefore the LORD left those *n* .... Judg 2:23
Now these are the *n* which the .... Judg 3:1
a king to judge us like all the *n* .... 1Sa 8:5
we also may be like all the *n* .... 1Sa 8:20
for those *n* were of old the .... 1Sa 27:8
to thee from Egypt, from the *n* .... 2Sa 7:23
of all *n* which he subdued .... 2Sa 8:11
his fame was in all *n* round about .... 1Kin 4:31
Of the *n* concerning which the .... 1Kin 11:2
*n* which the LORD cast out before .... 1Kin 14:24
The *n* which thou hast removed, and .... 2Kin 17:26
after the manner of the *n* whom .... 2Kin 17:33
So these *n* feared the LORD, and .... 2Kin 17:41
Hath any of the gods of the *n* .... 2Kin 18:33
Have the gods of the *n* delivered .... 2Kin 19:12
of Assyria have destroyed the *n* .... 2Kin 19:17
to do more evil than did the *n* .... 2Kin 21:9
the fear of him upon all *n* .... 1Chr 14:17
his marvellous works among all *n* .... 1Chr 16:24
and let men say among the *n* .... 1Chr 16:31
by driving out *n* from before thy .... 1Chr 17:21
that he brought from all these *n* .... 1Chr 18:11
a proverb and a byword among all *n* .. 2Chr 7:20
manner of the *n* of other lands .... 2Chr 13:9
were the gods of the *n* of those .... 2Chr 32:13
those *n* that my fathers utterly .... 2Chr 32:14
As the gods of the *n* of other .... 2Chr 32:17
sight of all *n* from thenceforth .... 2Chr 32:23
the rest of the *n* whom the great .... Ezr 4:10
scatter you abroad among the *n* .... Neh 1:8
thou gavest them kingdoms and *n* .... Neh 9:22
yet among many *n* was there no .... Neh 13:26
He increaseth the *n*, and .... Job 12:23

he enlargeth the *n*, and ... Job 12:23
all the *n* that forget God ... Ps 9:17
that the *n* may know themselves to ... Ps 9:20
all the kindreds of the *n* shall ... Ps 22:27
and he is the governor among the *n* ... Ps 22:28
under us, and the *n* under our feet ... Ps 47:3
I will sing unto thee among the *n* ... Ps 57:9
his eyes behold the *n* ... Ps 66:7
thy saving health among all *n* ... Ps 67:2
O let the *n* be glad and sing for ... Ps 67:4
and govern the *n* upon earth ... Ps 67:4
all *n* shall serve him ... Ps 72:11
all *n* shall call him blessed ... Ps 72:17
for thou shalt inherit all *n* ... Ps 82:8
All *n* whom thou hast made shall ... Ps 86:9
all the gods of the *n* are idols ... Ps 96:5
their seed also among the *n* ... Ps 106:27
They did not destroy the *n* ... Ps 106:34
praises unto thee among the *n* ... Ps 108:3
The LORD is high above all *n* ... Ps 113:4
O praise the LORD, all ye *n* ... Ps 117:1
All *n* compassed me about ... Ps 118:10
Who smote great *n*, and slew mighty .. Ps 135:10
people curse, *n* shall abhor him ... Prov 24:24
and all *n* shall flow unto it ... Is 2:2
And he shall judge among the *n* ... Is 2:4
up an ensign to the *n* from far ... Is 5:26
Jordan, in Galilee of the *n* ... Is 9:1
to destroy and cut off *n* not a few ... Is 10:7
shall set up an ensign for the *n* ... Is 11:12
kingdoms of *n* gathered together ... Is 13:4
he that ruled the *n* in anger ... Is 14:6
thrones all the kings of the *n* ... Is 14:9
ground, which didst weaken the *n* ... Is 14:12
All the kings of the *n*, even all ... Is 14:18
is stretched out upon all the *n* ... Is 14:26
and to the rushing of *n*, that make ... Is 17:12
The *n* shall rush like the rushing ... Is 17:13
and she is a mart of *n* ... Is 23:3
of the terrible *n* shall fear thee ... Is 25:3
vail that is spread over all *n* ... Is 25:7
the *n* that fight against Ariel ... Is 29:7
the multitude of all the *n* be ... Is 29:8
to sift the *n* with the sieve of ... Is 30:28
of thyself the *n* were scattered ... Is 33:3
Come near, ye *n*, to hear ... Is 34:1
of the LORD is upon all *n* ... Is 34:2
Hath any of the gods of the *n* ... Is 36:18
Have the gods of the *n* delivered ... Is 37:12
Assyria have laid waste all the *n* ... Is 37:18
the *n* are as a drop of a bucket, ... Is 40:15
All *n* before him are as nothing ... Is 40:17
gave the *n* before him, and made ... Is 41:2
Let all the *n* be gathered ... Is 43:9
holden, to subdue *n* before him ... Is 45:1
ye that are escaped of the *n* ... Is 45:20
holy arm in the eyes of all the *n* ... Is 52:10
So shall he sprinkle many *n* ... Is 52:15
*n* that knew not thee shall run ... Is 55:5
those *n* shall be utterly wasted ... Is 60:12
to spring forth before all the *n* ... Is 61:11
that the *n* may tremble at thy ... Is 64:2
come, that I will gather all *n* ... Is 66:18
that escape of them unto the *n* ... Is 66:19
the LORD out of all *n* upon horses ... Is 66:20
thee a prophet unto the *n* ... Jer 1:5
have this day set thee over the *n* ... Jer 1:10
all the *n* shall be gathered unto ... Jer 3:17
goodly heritage of the hosts of *n* ... Jer 3:19
the *n* shall bless themselves in ... Jer 4:2
Make ye mention to the *n* ... Jer 4:16
Therefore hear, ye *n*, and know, O ... Jer 6:18
for all these *n* are uncircumcised ... Jer 9:26
would not fear thee, O King of *n* ... Jer 10:7
among all the wise men of the *n* ... Jer 10:7
the *n* shall not be able to abide ... Jer 10:10
many *n* shall pass by this city, ... Jer 22:8
against all these *n* round about ... Jer 25:9
these *n* shall serve the king of ... Jer 25:11
hath prophesied against all the *n* ... Jer 25:13
For many *n* and great kings shall ... Jer 25:14
at my hand, and cause all the *n* ... Jer 25:15
hand, and made all the *n* to drink ... Jer 25:17
hath a controversy with the *n* ... Jer 25:31
a curse to all the *n* of the earth ... Jer 26:6
all *n* shall serve him, and his son ... Jer 27:7
and then many *n* and great kings ... Jer 27:7
But the *n* that bring their neck ... Jer 27:11
*n* within the space of two full ... Jer 28:11
iron upon the neck of all these *n* ... Jer 28:14
I will gather you from all the *n* ... Jer 29:14
among all the *n* whither I have ... Jer 29:18
*n* whither I have scattered thee ... Jer 30:11
and shout among the chief of the *n* ... Jer 31:7
Hear the word of the LORD, O ye *n* ... Jer 31:10
before all the *n* of the earth ... Jer 33:9
Judah, and against all the *n* ... Jer 36:2
that were returned from all *n* ... Jer 43:5
among all the *n* of the earth ... Jer 44:8
The *n* have heard of thy shame, and ... Jer 46:12
the *n* whither I have driven thee ... Jer 46:28
Declare ye among the *n*, and ... Jer 50:2
of great *n* from the north country ... Jer 50:9
of the *n* shall be a wilderness ... Jer 50:12
become a desolation among the *n* ... Jer 50:23
and the cry is heard among the *n* ... Jer 50:46
the *n* have drunken of her wine ... Jer 51:7
therefore the *n* are mad ... Jer 51:7
thee will I break in pieces the *n* ... Jer 51:20
blow the trumpet among the *n* ... Jer 51:27
prepare the *n* against her ... Jer 51:27
Prepare against her the *n* with ... Jer 51:28
an astonishment among the *n* ... Jer 51:41
the *n* shall not flow together any ... Jer 51:44
she that was great among the *n* ... Lam 1:1
have set it in the midst of the *n* ... Eze 5:5
into wickedness more than the *n* ... Eze 5:6
the *n* that are round about you ... Eze 5:7
to the judgments of the *n* that ... Eze 5:7
of thee in the sight of the *n* ... Eze 5:8
a reproach among the *n* that are ... Eze 5:14
an astonishment unto the *n* that ... Eze 5:15
escape the sword among the *n* ... Eze 6:8
*n* whither they shall be carried ... Eze 6:9
I shall scatter them among the *n* ... Eze 12:15
The *n* also heard of him ... Eze 19:4
Then the *n* set against him on ... Eze 19:8
may not be remembered among the *n* Eze 25:10
will cause many *n* to come up ... Eze 26:3
it shall become a spoil to the *n* ... Eze 26:5
upon thee, the terrible of the *n* ... Eze 28:7
scatter the Egyptians among the *n* ... Eze 29:12
exalt itself any more above the *n* ... Eze 29:15
shall no more rule over the *n* ... Eze 29:15
with him, the terrible of the *n* ... Eze 30:11
scatter the Egyptians among the *n* ... Eze 30:23
scatter the Egyptians among the *n* ... Eze 30:26
his shadow dwelt all great *n* ... Eze 31:6
strangers, the terrible of the *n* ... Eze 31:12
I made the *n* to shake at the ... Eze 31:16
art like a young lion of the *n* ... Eze 32:2
bring thy destruction among the *n* ... Eze 32:9
to fall, the terrible of the *n* ... Eze 32:12
of the *n* shall lament her ... Eze 32:16
and the daughters of the famous *n* ... Eze 32:18
thou hast said, These two *n* ... Eze 35:10
up men, and hast bereaved thy *n* ... Eze 36:13
neither bereave thy *n* any more ... Eze 36:14
thou cause thy *n* to fall any more ... Eze 36:15
and they shall be no more two *n* ... Eze 37:22
it is brought forth out of the *n* ... Eze 38:8
that are gathered out of the *n* ... Eze 38:12
be known in the eyes of many *n* ... Eze 38:23
in them in the sight of many *n* ... Eze 39:27
you it is commanded, O people, *n* ... Dan 3:4
of musick, all the people, the *n* ... Dan 3:7
the king, unto all people, *n* ... Dan 4:1
that he gave him, all people, *n* ... Dan 5:19
Darius wrote unto all people, *n* ... Dan 6:25
and a kingdom, that all people, *n* ... Dan 7:14
they have hired among the *n* ... Hos 8:10
shall be wanderers among the *n* ... Hos 9:17
I will also gather all *n*, and will ... Joel 3:2
they have scattered among the *n* ... Joel 3:2
which are named chief of the *n* ... Amos 6:1
the house of Israel among all *n* ... Amos 9:9
many *n* shall come, and say, Come, ... Mic 4:2
and rebuke strong *n* afar off ... Mic 4:3
Now also many *n* are gathered ... Mic 4:11
The *n* shall see and be confounded ... Mic 7:16
that selleth *n* through her ... Nah 3:4
I will shew the *n* thy nakedness ... Nah 3:5
spare continually to slay the *n* ... Hab 1:17
but gathereth unto him all *n* ... Hab 2:5
Because thou hast spoiled many *n* ... Hab 2:8
he beheld, and drove asunder the *n* ... Hab 3:6
of her, all the beasts of the *n* ... Zeph 2:14
I have cut off the *n* ... Zeph 3:6
determination is to gather the *n* ... Zeph 3:8
I will shake all *n* ... Hag 2:7
and the desire of all *n* shall come ... Hag 2:7
me unto the *n* which spoiled you ... Zec 2:8
many *n* shall be joined to the ... Zec 2:11
all the *n* whom they knew not ... Zec 7:14
strong *n* shall come to seek the ... Zec 8:22
out of all languages of the *n* ... Zec 8:23
the *n* that come against Jerusalem ... Zec 12:9
For I will gather all *n* against ... Zec 14:2
forth, and fight against those *n* ... Zec 14:3
one that is left of all the *n* ... Zec 14:16
the punishment of all *n* that come ... Zec 14:19
all *n* shall call you blessed ... Mal 3:12
hated of all *n* for my name's sake ... Mt 24:9
world for a witness unto all *n* ... Mt 24:14
him shall be gathered all *n* ... Mt 25:32
Go ye therefore, and teach all *n* ... Mt 28:19
of all *n* the house of prayer ... Mk 11:17
first be published among all *n* ... Mk 13:10
do the *n* of the world seek after ... Lk 12:30
be led away captive into all *n* ... Lk 21:24
and upon the earth distress of *n* ... Lk 21:25
preached in his name among all *n* ... Lk 24:47
seven *n* in the land of Chanaan ... Acts 13:19
all *n* to walk in their own ways ... Acts 14:16
hath made of one blood all *n* of ... Acts 17:26
to the faith among all *n*, for his ... Rom 1:5
have made thee a father of many *n* ... Rom 4:17
might become the father of many *n* ... Rom 4:18
made known to all *n* for the ... Rom 16:26
In thee shall all *n* be blessed ... Gal 3:8
him will I give power over the *n* ... Rev 2:26
no man could number, of all *n* ... Rev 7:9
again before many peoples, and *n* ... Rev 10:11
*n* shall see their dead bodies ... Rev 11:9
the *n* were angry, and thy wrath is ... Rev 11:18
to rule all *n* with a rod of iron ... Rev 12:5
all kindreds, and tongues, and *n* ... Rev 13:7
because she made all *n* drink of ... Rev 14:8
for all *n* shall come and worship ... Rev 15:4
and the cities of the *n* fell ... Rev 16:19
are peoples, and multitudes, and *n* ... Rev 17:15
For all *n* have drunk of the wine ... Rev 18:3
thy sorceries were all *n* deceived ... Rev 18:23
with it he should smite the *n* ... Rev 19:15
he should deceive the *n* no more ... Rev 20:3
shall go out to deceive the *n* ... Rev 20:8
the *n* of them which are saved ... Rev 21:24
glory and honour of the *n* into it ... Rev 21:26
were for the healing of the *n* ... Rev 22:2

**NATIVE**

no more, nor see his *n* country ... Jer 22:10

**NATIVITY**

father Terah in the land of his *n* ... Gen 11:28
thy mother, and the land of thy *n* ... Ruth 2:11
people, and to the land of our *n* ... Jer 46:16
thy *n* is of the land of Canaan ... Eze 16:3
And as for thy *n*, in the day thou ... Eze 16:4
created, in the land of thy *n* ... Eze 21:30
of Chaldea, the land of their *n* ... Eze 23:15

**NATURAL**

not dim, nor his *n* force abated ... Deut 34:7
*n* use into that which is against ... Rom 1:26
leaving the *n* use of the woman, ... Rom 1:27
without *n* affection, implacable, ... Rom 1:31
if God spared not the *n* branches ... Rom 11:21
these, which be the *n* branches ... Rom 11:24
But the *n* man receiveth not the ... 1Cor 2:14
It is sown a *n* body ... 1Cor 15:44
There is a *n* body, and there is a ... 1Cor 15:44
is spiritual, but that which is *n* ... 1Cor 15:46
Without *n* affection, ... 2Ti 3:3
beholding his *n* face in a glass ... Jas 1:23
as *n* brute beasts, made to be ... 2Pet 2:12

**NATURALLY**

who will *n* care for your state ... Phil 2:20
but what they know *n*, as brute ... Jude 10

**NATURE**

use into that which is against *n* ... Rom 1:26
do by *n* the things contained in ... Rom 2:14
not uncircumcision which is by *n* ... Rom 2:27
the olive tree which is wild by *n* ... Rom 11:24
to *n* into a good olive tree ... Rom 11:24
Doth not even *n* itself teach you, ... 1Cor 11:14
We who are Jews by *n*, and not ... Gal 2:15
unto them which by *n* are no gods ... Gal 4:8
were by *n* the children of wrath, ... Eph 2:3
took not on him the *n* of angels ... Heb 2:16
setteth on fire the course of *n* ... Jas 3:6
be partakers of the divine *n* ... 2Pet 1:4

**NAUGHT**

but the water is *n*, and the ground ... 2Kin 2:19
It is *n*, it is *n*, saith the ... Prov 20:14

**NAUGHTINESS**

pride, and the *n* of thine heart ... 1Sa 17:28
shall be taken in their own *n* ... Prov 11:6
filthiness and superfluity of *n* ... Jas 1:21

**NAUGHTY**

A *n* person, a wicked man, walketh ... Prov 6:12
a liar giveth ear to a *n* tongue ... Prov 17:4
the other basket had very *n* figs ... Jer 24:2

**NAUM** (*na'-um*) See NAHUM. *Father of Amos; ancestor of Jesus.*

of Amos, which was the son of *N* ... Lk 3:25

**NAVEL**

force is in the *n* of his belly ... Job 40:16
It shall be health to thy *n* ... Prov 3:8
Thy *n* is like a round goblet, ... Song 7:2
thou wast born thy *n* was not cut ... Eze 16:4

**NAVES**

their axletrees, and their *n* ... 1Kin 7:33

**NAVY**

king Solomon made a *n* of ships in ... 1Kin 9:26
Hiram sent in the *n* his servants ... 1Kin 9:27
the *n* also of Hiram, that brought ... 1Kin 10:11
For the king had at sea a *n* of ... 1Kin 10:22
of Tharshish with the *n* of Hiram ... 1Kin 10:22
years came the *n* of Tharshish ... 1Kin 10:22

**NAY**

And he said, *N*; but thou didst ... Gen 18:15
And they said, *N*; but we will ... Gen 19:2
*N*, my lord, hear me ... Gen 23:11
And Jacob said, *N*, I pray thee, if ... Gen 33:10
And they said unto him, *N*, my lord ... Gen 42:10
And he said unto them, *N*, but to ... Gen 42:12
And he said, *N*. ... Num 22:30
And he said, *N*; but as captain ... Josh 5:14
And the people said unto Joshua, *N* .. Josh 24:21
If he said, *N* ... Judg 12:5
unto them, and said unto them, *N* ... Judg 19:23
my brethren, *n*, I pray you ... Judg 19:23
*n*, my daughters; for it ... Ruth 1:13
then he would answer him, *N* ... 1Sa 2:16
*N*, my sons; for it is ... 1Sa 2:24
and they said, *N*; but we will ... 1Sa 8:19
and ye have said unto him, *N* ... 1Sa 10:19
against you, ye said unto me, *N* ... 1Sa 12:12
And she answered him, *N*, my ... 2Sa 13:12
And the king said to Absalom, *N* ... 2Sa 13:25
And Hushai said unto Absalom, *N* ... 2Sa 16:18
And the king said unto Araunah, *N* ... 2Sa 24:24
king, (for he will not say thee *n* ... 1Kin 2:17
I pray thee, say me not *n* ... 1Kin 2:20
for I will not say thee *n* ... 1Kin 2:20

And he said, N; but I 1Kin 2:30
And the other woman said, N 1Kin 3:22
and the other saith, N 1Kin 3:23
king of Israel said unto him, N 2Kin 3:13
And she said, N, my lord, thou man 2Kin 4:16
n, but let the shadow return 2Kin 20:10
And king David said to Ornan, N 1Chr 21:24
n, they were not at all ashamed, Jer 6:15
n, they were not at all ashamed, Jer 8:12
be, Yea, yea; N, n Mt 5:37
But he said, N; lest while Mt 13:29
I tell you, N; but rather Lk 12:51
I tell you, N: but, except Lk 13:3
I tell you, N: but, except Lk 13:5
And he said, N, father Abraham Lk 16:30
others said, N; but he Jn 7:12
n verily; but let them Acts 16:37
N: but by the law Rom 3:27
N, I had not known sin, but by Rom 7:7
N, in all these things we are Rom 8:37
N but, O man, who art thou that Rom 9:20
N, ye do wrong, and defraud, and 1Cor 6:8
N, much more those members of the 1Cor 12:22
there should be yea yea, and n n 2Cor 1:17
word toward you was not yea and n 2Cor 1:18
and Timotheus, was not yea and n 2Cor 1:19
be yea; and your n, n Jas 5:12

**NAZARENE** (*naz-a-reen'*) See NAZARENES. *Native to Nazareth.*
prophets, He shall be called a N Mt 2:23

**NAZARENES** (*naz-a-reens'*)
a ringleader of the sect of the N Acts 24:5

**NAZARETH** (*naz'-a-reth*) See NAZARENE. *A city in Galilee.*
came and dwelt in a city called N Mt 2:23
And leaving N, he came and dwelt in Mt 4:13
Jesus the prophet of N of Galilee Mt 21:11
fellow was also with Jesus of N Mt 26:71
that Jesus came from N of Galilee Mk 1:9
to do with thee, thou Jesus of N Mk 1:24
he heard that it was Jesus of N Mk 10:47
And thou also wast with Jesus of N Mk 14:67
Ye seek Jesus of N, which was Mk 16:6
unto a city of Galilee, named N Lk 1:26
Galilee, out of the city of N Lk 2:4
into Galilee, to their own city N Lk 2:39
went down with them, and came to N Lk 2:51
And he came to N, where he had Lk 4:16
to do with thee, thou Jesus of N Lk 4:34
him, that Jesus of N passeth by Lk 18:37
unto him, Concerning Jesus of N Lk 24:19
prophets, did write, Jesus of N Jn 1:45
any good thing come out of N Jn 1:46
They answered him, Jesus of N Jn 18:5
And they said, Jesus of N Jn 18:7
JESUS OF N THE Jn 19:19
Jesus of N, a man approved of God Acts 2:22
name of Jesus Christ of N rise up Acts 3:6
by the name of Jesus Christ of N Acts 4:10
that this Jesus of N shall Acts 6:14
Jesus of N with the Holy Ghost Acts 10:38
he said unto me, I am Jesus of N Acts 22:8
to the name of Jesus of N Acts 26:9

**NAZARITE** (*naz'-a-rite*) See NAZARITES. *Title applied to one making a special vow of abstention.*
themselves to vow a vow of a N Num 6:2
And this is the law of the N Num 6:13
the N shall shave the head of his Num 6:18
put them upon the hands of the N Num 6:19
after that the N may drink wine Num 6:20
the law of the N who hath vowed Num 6:21
be a N unto God from the womb Judg 13:5
for the child shall be a N to God Judg 13:7
for I have been a N unto God from Judg 16:17

**NAZARITES** (*naz'-a-rites*)
Her N were purer than snow, they Lam 4:7
and of your young men for N Amos 2:11
But ye gave the N wine to drink Amos 2:12

**NEAH** (*ne'-ah*) *A city in Zebulun.*
goeth out to Remmon-methoar to N. Josh 19:13

**NEAPOLIS** (*ne-ap'-o-lis*) *A Macedonian seaport.*
Samothracia, and the next day to N.. Acts 16:11

**NEAR**
when he was come n to enter into Gen 12:11
And Abraham drew n, and said, Wilt. Gen 18:23
Lot, and came n to break the door Gen 19:9
now, this city is n to flee unto Gen 19:20
But Abimelech had not come n her Gen 20:4
And Isaac said unto Jacob, Come n Gen 27:21
Jacob went n unto Isaac his Gen 27:22
And he said, Bring it n to me Gen 27:25
And he brought it n to him Gen 27:25
Isaac said unto him, Come n now Gen 27:26
And he came n, and kissed him Gen 27:27
brother, that Jacob went n Gen 29:10
until he came n to his brother Gen 33:3
Then the handmaidens came n Gen 33:6
also with her children came n Gen 33:7
and after came Joseph n and Rachel, Gen 33:7
even before he came n unto them Gen 37:18
they came n to the steward of Gen 43:19
Then Judah came n unto him Gen 44:18
Come n to me, I pray you Gen 45:4
And they came n Gen 45:4
and thou shalt be n unto me Gen 45:10
And he brought them n unto him Gen 48:10
hand, and brought them n unto him Gen 48:13
and then let him come n and keep Ex 12:48
Philistines, although that was n Ex 13:17
not n the other all the night Ex 14:20
of Israel, Come n before the LORD Ex 16:9
which come n to the LORD, Ex 19:22
Moses drew n unto the thick Ex 20:21
Moses alone shall come n the LORD Ex 24:2
or when they come n unto the Ex 28:43
or when they come n to the altar Ex 30:20
when they came n unto the altar Ex 40:32
and all the congregation drew n Lev 9:5
Aaron, and said unto them, Come n Lev 10:4
So they went n, and carried them Lev 10:5
to any that is n of kin to him Lev 18:6
she is thy father's n kinswoman Lev 18:12
she is thy mother's n kinswoman Lev 18:13
for they are her n kinswomen Lev 18:17
for he uncovereth his n kin Lev 20:19
that is n unto him, that is, for Lev 21:2
Bring the tribe of Levi n Num 3:6
And the priest shall bring her n Num 5:16
will cause him to come n unto him Num 16:5
will he cause to come n unto him Num 16:5
to bring you n to himself to do Num 16:9
And he hath brought thee n to him Num 16:10
come n to offer incense before Num 16:40
Whosoever cometh any thing n Num 17:13
of Moab by Jordan n Jericho Num 26:3
of Moab by Jordan n Jericho Num 26:63
which are by Jordan n Jericho Num 31:12
of hundreds, came n unto Moses Num 31:48
they came n unto him Num 32:16
of Moab by Jordan n Jericho Num 33:48
by Jordan, n Jericho, saying, Num 33:50
side Jordan n Jericho eastward Num 34:15
of Moab by Jordan n Jericho Num 35:1
of the sons of Joseph, came n Num 36:1
of Moab by Jordan n Jericho Num 36:13
ye came n unto me every one of Deut 1:22
And ye came n and stood under the Deut 4:11
fire,) that ye came n unto me Deut 5:23
Go thou n, and hear all that the Deut 5:27
n unto the altar of the LORD thy Deut 16:21
the sons of Levi shall come n Deut 21:5
the wife of the one draweth n for Deut 25:11
come not n unto it, that ye may Josh 3:4
war which went with him, Come n Josh 10:24
And they came n, and put their feet Josh 10:24
the sea, all that lay n Ashdod Josh 15:46
they came n before Eleazar the Josh 17:4
n the hill that lieth on the Josh 18:13
Then came n the heads of the Josh 21:1
n to Micah's house were gathered Judg 18:22
let us draw n to one of these Judg 19:13
came n against the children of Judg 20:24
knew not that evil was n them Judg 20:34
The man is n of kin unto us, one Ruth 2:20
for thou art a n kinsman Ruth 3:9
is true that I am thy n kinsman Ruth 3:12
was with child, n to be delivered 1Sa 4:19
the Philistines drew n to battle 1Sa 7:10
Then Saul drew n to Samuel in the 1Sa 9:18
the tribes of Israel to come n 1Sa 10:20
to come n by their families 1Sa 10:21
Let us draw n hither unto God 1Sa 14:36
And Saul said, Draw ye n hither 1Sa 14:38
And the Philistine drew n morning 1Sa 17:16
he drew n to the Philistine 1Sa 17:40
came on and drew n unto David 1Sa 17:41
when David came n to the people 1Sa 30:21
of the young men, and said, Go n 2Sa 1:15
See, Joab's field is n mine 2Sa 14:30
And he came apace, and drew n 2Sa 18:25
the king is n of kin to us 2Sa 19:42
Come n hither, that I may speak 2Sa 20:16
And when he was come n unto her 2Sa 20:17
the land of the enemy, far or n 1Kin 8:46
all the people, Come n unto me 1Kin 18:30
And all the people came n unto him. 1Kin 18:30
that Elijah the prophet came n 1Kin 18:36
because it is n unto my house 1Kin 21:2
the son of Chenaanah went n 1Kin 22:24
but Gehazi came n to thrust her 2Kin 4:27
And his servants came n, and spake 2Kin 5:13
captives unto a land far off or n 2Chr 6:36
the son of Chenaanah came n 2Chr 18:23
that were n the Ethiopians 2Chr 21:16
yourselves unto the LORD, come n 2Chr 29:31
So Esther drew n, and touched the Est 5:2
his decree drew n to be put in Est 9:1
as a prince would I go n unto him Job 31:37
his soul draweth n unto the grave Job 33:22
One is so n to another, that no Job 41:16
for trouble is n Ps 22:11
lest they come n unto thee Ps 32:9
is good for me to draw n to God Ps 73:28
for that thy name is n thy Ps 75:1
they draw n unto the gates of Ps 107:18
Thou art n, O LORD Ps 119:151
Let my cry come n before thee Ps 119:169
of Israel, a people n unto him Ps 148:14
through the street n her corner Prov 7:8
of the foolish is n destruction Prov 10:14
that is n than a brother far off Prov 27:10
and her time is n to come, and her Is 13:22
that draweth n the time of her Is 26:17
people draw n me with their mouth Is 29:13
and, ye that are n, acknowledge my Is 33:13
Come n, ye nations, to hear Is 34:1
let them come n Is 41:1
let us come n together to Is 41:1
of the earth were afraid, drew n Is 41:5
draw n together, ye that are Is 45:20
Tell ye, and bring them n Is 45:21
I bring n my righteousness Is 46:13
Come ye n unto me, hear ye this Is 48:16
He is n that justifieth me Is 50:8
let him come n to me Is 50:8
My righteousness is n Is 51:5
for it shall not come n thee Is 54:14
call ye upon him while he is n Is 55:6
for my salvation is n to come Is 56:1
But draw n hither, ye sons of the Is 57:3
is far off, and to him that is n Is 57:19
by thyself, come not n to me Is 65:5
thou art n in their mouth, and far Jer 12:2
the kings of the north, far and n Jer 25:26
and I will cause him to draw n Jer 30:21
even unto the greatest, came n Jer 42:1
and shield, and draw n to battle Jer 46:3
The calamity of Moab is n to come Jer 48:16
of the land of Moab, far or n Jer 48:24
that were n the king's person Jer 52:25
Thou drewest n in the day that I Lam 3:57
our end is n, our days are Lam 4:18
he that is n shall fall by the Eze 6:12
is come, the day of trouble is n Eze 7:7
time is come, the day draweth n Eze 7:12
charge over the city to draw n Eze 9:1
but come not n any man upon whom Eze 9:6
Which say, It is not n Eze 11:3
wife, neither hath come n to a Eze 18:6
hast caused thy days to draw n Eze 22:4
Those that be n, and those that be Eze 22:5
For the day is n, even the day of Eze 30:3
even the day of the LORD is n Eze 30:3
which come n to the LORD to Eze 40:46
And they shall not come n unto me Eze 44:13
nor to come n to any of my holy Eze 44:13
they shall come n to me to Eze 44:15
and they shall come n to my table Eze 44:16
which shall come n to minister Eze 45:4
time certain Chaldeans came n Dan 3:8
Then Nebuchadnezzar came n to the Dan 3:26
Then they came n, and spake before Dan 6:12
and they brought him n before him Dan 7:13
I came n unto one of them that Dan 7:16
So he came n where I stood Dan 8:17
and unto all Israel, that are n Dan 9:7
let all the men of war draw n Joel 3:9
is n in the valley of decision Joel 3:14
the seat of violence to come n Amos 6:3
LORD is n upon all the heathen Obad 15
The great day of the LORD is n Zeph 1:14
it is n, and hasteth greatly Zeph 1:14
she drew not n to her God Zeph 3:2
I will come n to you to judgment Mal 3:5
when the time of the fruit drew n Mt 21:34
these things, know that it is n Mt 24:33
leaves, ye know that summer is n Mk 13:28
Then drew n unto him all the Lk 15:1
and when he was come n, he asked Lk 18:40
And when he was come n, he beheld Lk 19:41
and the time draweth n Lk 21:8
drew n unto Jesus to kiss him Lk 22:47
and reasoned, Jesus himself drew n Lk 24:15
was baptizing in Aenon n to Salim Jn 3:23
n to the parcel of ground that Jn 4:5
a country n to the wilderness Jn 11:54
as he drew n to behold it, the Acts 7:31
the Spirit said unto Philip, Go n Acts 8:29
he journeyed, he came n Damascus Acts 9:3
together his kinsmen and n friends Acts 10:24
Then the chief captain came n Acts 21:33
and we, or ever he come n, are Acts 23:15
that they drew n to some country Acts 27:27
Let us draw n with a true heart Heb 10:22

**NEARER**
there is a kinsman n than I Ruth 3:12
salvation n than when we believed Rom 13:11

**NEARIAH** (*ne-a-ri'-ah*) See NAGGE.
*1. A son of Shemiah.*
and Igeal, and Bariah, and N 1Chr 3:22
And the sons of N 1Chr 3:23
*2. A son of Ishi.*
for their captains Pelatiah, and N 1Chr 4:42

**NEBAI** (*ne'-bahee*) *A renewer of the covenant.*
Hariph, Anathoth, N, Neh 10:19

**NEBAIOTH** (*ne-bah'-yoth*) See NEBAJOTH.
*1. A son of Ishmael.*
The firstborn of Ishmael, N 1Chr 1:29
*2. Descendants of Ishmael.*
the rams of N shall minister unto Is 60:7

**NEBAJOTH** (*ne-ba'-joth*) See NEBAIOTH. *Same as Nebaioth 1.*
the firstborn of Ishmael, N Gen 25:13
Abraham's son, the sister of N Gen 28:9
Ishmael's daughter, sister of N Gen 36:3

**NEBALLAT** (*ne-bal'-lat*) *A Benjamite city.*
Hadid, Zeboim, N, Neh 11:34

**NEBAT** (*ne'-bat*) *Father of King Jeroboam.*
And Jeroboam the son of N, an 1Kin 11:26
pass, when Jeroboam the son of N 1Kin 12:2

unto Jeroboam the son of *N* 1Kin 12:15
of *N* reigned Abijam over Judah 1Kin 15:1
house of Jeroboam the son of *N* 1Kin 16:3
the way of Jeroboam the son of *N* 1Kin 16:26
the sins of Jeroboam the son of *N* 1Kin 16:31
house of Jeroboam the son of *N* 1Kin 21:22
the way of Jeroboam the son of *N* 1Kin 22:52
the sins of Jeroboam the son of *N* 2Kin 3:3
house of Jeroboam the son of *N* 2Kin 9:9
the sins of Jeroboam the son of *N* 2Kin 10:29
the sins of Jeroboam the son of *N* 2Kin 13:2
the sins of Jeroboam the son of *N* 2Kin 13:11
the sins of Jeroboam the son of *N* 2Kin 14:24
the sins of Jeroboam the son of *N* 2Kin 15:9
the sins of Jeroboam the son of *N* 2Kin 15:18
the sins of Jeroboam the son of *N* 2Kin 15:24
the sins of Jeroboam the son of *N* 2Kin 15:28
made Jeroboam the son of *N* king 2Kin 17:21
place which Jeroboam the son of *N* 2Kin 23:15
against Jeroboam the son of *N* 2Chr 9:29
pass, when Jeroboam the son of *N* 2Chr 10:2
to Jeroboam the son of *N* 2Chr 10:15
Yet Jeroboam the son of *N* 2Chr 13:6

**NEBO** (*ne'-bo*) See PISGAH, SAMGAR-NEBO.
*1. A city in Reuben.*
and Elealeh, and Shebam, and *N* Num 32:3
And *N*, and Baal-meon, (their names Num 32:38
the mountains of Abarim, before *N* Num 33:47
who dwelt in Aroer, even unto *N* 1Chr 5:8
Moab shall howl over *N*, and over Is 15:2
Woe unto *N* Jer 48:1
upon Dibon, and upon *N* Jer 48:22
*2. A mountain east of the Jordan.*
mountain Abarim, unto mount *N* Deut 32:49
of Moab unto the mountain of *N* Deut 34:1
*3. A city in Judah.*
The children of *N*, fifty and two Ezr 2:29
The men of the other *N*, fifty and Neh 7:33
*4. A Chaldean idol.*
*N* stoopeth, their idols were upon Is 46:1
*5. Father of several who married foreigners.*
Of the sons of *N* Ezr 10:43

**NEBO-SARSEKIM** See SARSECHIM.

**NEBUCHADNEZZAR** (*neb-u-kad-nez'-zar*)
See NEBUCHADREZZAR. *King of Babylon.*
In his days *N* king of Babylon 2Kin 24:1
At that time the servants of *N* 2Kin 24:10
*N* king of Babylon came against 2Kin 24:11
that *N* king of Babylon came, he 2Kin 25:1
year of king *N* king of Babylon 2Kin 25:8
whom *N* king of Babylon had left 2Kin 25:22
and Jerusalem by the hand of *N* 1Chr 6:15
him came up *N* king of Babylon 2Chr 36:6
*N* also carried of the vessels of 2Chr 36:7
the year was expired, king *N* sent 2Chr 36:10
he also rebelled against king *N* 2Chr 36:13
which *N* had brought forth out of Ezr 1:7
whom *N* the king of Babylon had Ezr 2:1
the hand of *N* the king of Babylon Ezr 5:12
which *N* took out of the temple Ezr 5:14
which *N* took forth out of the Ezr 6:5
whom *N* the king of Babylon had Neh 7:6
whom *N* the king of Babylon had Est 2:6
the hand of *N* the king of Babylon Jer 27:6
the same *N* the king of Babylon Jer 27:8
Which *N* king of Babylon took not Jer 27:20
that *N* king of Babylon took away Jer 28:3
so will I break the yoke of *N* Jer 28:11
they may serve *N* king of Babylon Jer 28:14
to all the people whom *N* had Jer 29:1
to *N* king of Babylon) saying Jer 29:3
when *N* king of Babylon, and all Jer 34:1
they brought him up to *N* king of Jer 39:5
*N* king of Babylon unto Jerusalem Dan 1:1
eunuchs brought them in before *N* Dan 1:18
the second year of the reign of *N* Dan 2:1
*N* dreamed dreams, wherewith his Dan 2:1
maketh known to the king *N* what Dan 2:28
Then the king *N* fell upon his Dan 2:46
*N* the king made an image of gold Dan 3:1
Then *N* the king sent to gather Dan 3:2
image which *N* the king had set up Dan 3:2
image that *N* the king had set up Dan 3:3
the image that *N* had set up Dan 3:3
image that *N* the king hath set up Dan 3:5
image that *N* the king had set up Dan 3:7
They spake and said to the king *N* Dan 3:9
Then *N* in his rage and fury Dan 3:13
*N* spake and said unto them, Is it Dan 3:14
answered and said to the king, O *N* Dan 3:16
Then was *N* full of fury, and the Dan 3:19
Then *N* the king was astonied, and Dan 3:24
Then *N* came near to the mouth of Dan 3:26
Then *N* spake, and said, Blessed be Dan 3:28
*N* the king, unto all people Dan 4:1
I *N* was at rest in mine house, and Dan 4:4
This dream I king *N* have seen Dan 4:18
All this came upon the king *N* Dan 4:28
from heaven, saying, O king *N* Dan 4:31
was the thing fulfilled upon *N* Dan 4:33
at the end of the days I *N* lifted Dan 4:34
Now I *N* praise and extol and honour Dan 4:37
*N* had taken out of the temple Dan 5:2
whom the king *N* thy father Dan 5:11
God gave *N* thy father a kingdom Dan 5:18

**NEBUCHADREZZAR** (*neb-u-kad-rez'-zar*)
See NEBUCHADNEZZAR. *Same as Nebuchadnezzar.*
for *N* king of Babylon maketh war Jer 21:2
the hand of *N* king of Babylon Jer 21:7
the hand of *N* king of Babylon Jer 22:25
after that *N* king of Babylon had Jer 24:1
first year of *N* king of Babylon Jer 25:1
*N* the king of Babylon, my servant Jer 25:9
the hand of *N* king of Babylon Jer 29:21
was the eighteenth year of *N* Jer 32:1
the hand of *N* king of Babylon Jer 32:28
when *N* king of Babylon came up Jer 35:11
whom *N* king of Babylon made king Jer 37:1
came *N* king of Babylon and all his Jer 39:1
Now *N* king of Babylon gave charge Jer 39:11
take *N* the king of Babylon, my Jer 43:10
the hand of *N* king of Babylon Jer 44:30
which *N* king of Babylon smote in Jer 46:2
how *N* king of Babylon should come Jer 46:13
the hand of *N* king of Babylon Jer 46:26
which *N* king of Babylon shall Jer 49:28
for *N* king of Babylon hath taken Jer 49:30
last this *N* king of Babylon hath Jer 50:17
*N* the king of Babylon hath Jer 51:34
that *N* king of Babylon came, he Jer 52:4
year of *N* king of Babylon Jer 52:12
whom *N* carried away captive Jer 52:28
In the eighteenth year of *N* he Jer 52:29
twentieth year of *N* Nebuzar-adan Jer 52:30
upon Tyrus *N* king of Babylon Eze 26:7
*N* king of Babylon caused his army Eze 29:18
of Egypt unto *N* king of Babylon Eze 29:19
by the hand of *N* king of Babylon Eze 30:10

**NEBUSHASBAN** (*neb-u-shas'-ban*) *A Babylonian prince.*
captain of the guard sent, and *N* Jer 39:13

**NEBUSHAZBAN** See NEBUSHASBAN.

**NEBUZAR-ADAN** (*neb-u-zar'-a-dan*)
*Commander of Nebuchadnezzar's army.*
king of Babylon, came *N*, captain 2Kin 25:8
did *N* the captain of the guard 2Kin 25:11
*N* captain of the guard took these 2Kin 25:20
Then *N* the captain of the guard Jer 39:9
But *N* the captain of the guard Jer 39:10
to *N* the captain of the guard Jer 39:11
So *N* the captain of the guard Jer 39:13
after that *N* the captain of the Jer 40:1
whom *N* the captain of the guard Jer 41:10
every person that *N* the captain Jer 43:6
king of Babylon, came *N*, captain Jer 52:12
Then *N* the captain of the guard Jer 52:15
But *N* the captain of the guard Jer 52:16
So *N* the captain of the guard Jer 52:26
year of Nebuchadrezzar *N* the Jer 52:30

**NEBUZARADAN** See NEBUZAR-ADAN.

**NECESSARY**
of his mouth more than my *n* food Job 23:12
It was *n* that the word of God Acts 13:46
burden than these *n* things Acts 15:28
us with such things as were *n* Acts 28:10
seem to be more feeble, are *n* 1Cor 12:22
it *n* to exhort the brethren 2Cor 9:5
Yet I supposed it *n* to send to Phil 2:25
to maintain good works for *n* uses Titus 3:14
It was therefore *n* that the Heb 9:23

**NECESSITIES**
hands have ministered unto my *n* Acts 20:34
patience, in afflictions, in *n* 2Cor 6:4
infirmities, in reproaches, in *n* 2Cor 12:10

**NECESSITY**
(For of *n* he must release one Lk 23:17
Distributing to the *n* of saints Rom 12:13
in his heart, having no *n* 1Cor 7:37
for *n* is laid upon me 1Cor 9:16
not grudgingly, or of *n* 2Cor 9:7
ye sent once and again unto my *n* Phil 4:16
should not be as it were of *n* Philem 14
there is made of *n* a change also Heb 7:12
wherefore it is of *n* that this Heb 8:3
there must also of *n* be the death Heb 9:16

**NECHO** (*ne'-ko*) See PHARAOH-NECHOH. *A king of Egypt.*
*N* king of Egypt came up to fight 2Chr 35:20
words of *N* from the mouth of God 2Chr 35:22
*N* took Jehoahaz his brother, and 2Chr 36:4

**NECK**
and upon the smooth of his *n* Gen 27:16
break his yoke from off thy *n* Gen 27:40
and embraced him, and fell on his *n* Gen 33:4
and put a gold chain about his *n* Gen 41:42
upon his brother Benjamin's *n* Gen 45:14
and Benjamin wept upon his *n* Gen 45:14
and he fell on his *n*, and wept on Gen 46:29
wept on his *n* a good while Gen 46:29
be in the *n* of thine enemies Gen 49:8
it, then thou shalt break his *n* Ex 13:13
not, then shalt thou break his *n* Ex 34:20
and wring off his head from his *n* Lev 5:8
heifer's *n* there in the valley Deut 21:4
put a yoke of iron upon thy *n* Deut 28:48
thy rebellion, and thy stiff *n* Deut 31:27
gate, and his *n* brake, and he died 1Sa 4:18
like to the *n* of their fathers 2Kin 17:14
but he stiffened his *n*, and 2Chr 36:13
the shoulder, and hardened their *n* Neh 9:29
runneth upon him, even on his *n* Job 15:26
he hath also taken me by my *n* Job 16:12
thou clothed his *n* with thunder Job 39:19
In his *n* remaineth strength, and Job 41:22
speak not with a stiff *n* Ps 75:5
thy head, and chains about thy *n* Prov 1:9
bind them about thy *n* Prov 3:3
unto thy soul, and grace to thy *n* Prov 3:22
heart, and tie them about thy *n* Prov 6:21
often reproved hardeneth his *n* Prov 29:1
thy *n* with chains of gold Song 1:10
Thy *n* is like the tower of David Song 4:4
eyes, with one chain of thy *n* Song 4:9
Thy *n* is as a tower of ivory Song 7:4
he shall reach even to the *n* Is 8:8
and his yoke from off thy *n* Is 10:27
shall reach to the midst of the *n* Is 30:28
thy *n* is an iron sinew, and thy Is 48:4
thyself from the bands of thy *n* Is 52:2
lamb, as if he cut off a dog's *n* Is 66:3
their ear, but hardened their *n* Jer 7:26
their ear, but made their *n* stiff Jer 17:23
and yokes, and put them upon thy *n* Jer 27:2
that will not put their *n* under Jer 27:8
the nations that bring their *n* Jer 27:11
from off the prophet Jeremiah's *n* Jer 28:10
king of Babylon from the *n* of all Jer 28:11
off the *n* of the prophet Jeremiah Jer 28:12
upon the *n* of all these nations Jer 28:14
break his yoke from off thy *n* Jer 30:8
wreathed, and come up upon my *n* Lam 1:14
thy hands, and a chain on thy *n* Eze 16:11
have a chain of gold about his *n* Dan 5:7
have a chain of gold about thy *n* Dan 5:16
put a chain of gold about his *n* Dan 5:29
but I passed over upon her fair *n* Hos 10:11
the foundation unto the *n* Hab 3:13
millstone were hanged about his *n* Mt 18:6
millstone were hanged about his *n* Mk 9:42
and ran, and fell on his *n* Lk 15:20
millstone were hanged about his *n* Lk 17:2
yoke upon the *n* of the disciples Acts 15:10
wept sore, and fell on Paul's *n* Acts 20:37

**NECKS**
feet upon the *n* of these kings Josh 10:24
put their feet upon the *n* of them Josh 10:24
meet for the *n* of them that take Judg 5:30
that were on their camels' *n* Judg 8:21
that were about their camels' *n* Judg 8:26
given me the *n* of mine enemies 2Sa 22:41
not hear, but hardened their *n* 2Kin 17:14
their *n* to the work of their Lord Neh 3:5
proudly, and hardened their *n* Neh 9:16
but hardened their *n*, and in their Neh 9:17
given me the *n* of mine enemies Ps 18:40
and walk with stretched forth *n* Is 3:16
they have hardened their *n* Jer 19:15
Bring your *n* under the yoke of Jer 27:12
Our *n* are under persecution Lam 5:5
upon the *n* of them that are slain Eze 21:29
which ye shall not remove your *n* Mic 2:3
for my life laid down their own *n* Rom 16:4

**NECO** See NECHOH.

**NECROMANCER**
spirits, or a wizard, or a *n* Deut 18:11

**NEDABIAH** (*ned-a-bi'-ah*) *Son of Jeconiah.*
Shenazar, Jecamiah, Hoshama, and *N* 1Chr 3:18

**NEED**
lend him sufficient for his *n* Deut 15:8
Have I *n* of mad men, that ye have 1Sa 21:15
Lebanon, as much as thou shalt *n* 2Chr 2:16
Ye shall not *n* to fight in this 2Chr 20:17
And that which they have *n* of Ezr 6:9
that he shall have no *n* of spoil Prov 31:11
I have *n* to be baptized of thee Mt 3:14
knoweth what things ye have *n* of Mt 6:8
ye have *n* of all these things Mt 6:32
that be whole *n* not a physician Mt 9:12
said unto them, They *n* not depart Mt 14:16
say, The Lord hath *n* of them Mt 21:3
what further *n* have we of Mt 26:65
whole have no *n* of the physician Mk 2:17
what David did, when he had *n* Mk 2:25
ye that the Lord hath *n* of him Mk 11:3
What *n* we any further witnesses Mk 14:63
that are whole *n* not a physician Lk 5:31
healed them that had *n* of healing Lk 9:11
that ye have *n* of these things Lk 12:30
persons, which *n* no repentance Lk 15:7
Because the Lord hath *n* of him Lk 19:31
they said, The Lord hath *n* of him Lk 19:34
What *n* we any further witness Lk 22:71
we have *n* of against the feast Jn 13:29
to all men, as every man had *n* Acts 2:45
every man according as he had *n* Acts 4:35
business she hath *n* of you Rom 16:2
*n* so require, let him do what he 1Cor 7:36
the hand, I have no *n* of thee 1Cor 12:21
to the feet, I have no *n* of you 1Cor 12:21
For our comely parts have no *n* 1Cor 12:24
or *n* we, as some others, epistles 2Cor 3:1
both to abound and to suffer *n* Phil 4:12
your *n* according to his riches in Phil 4:19
so that we *n* not to speak any 1Th 1:8
ye *n* not that I write unto you 1Th 4:9
ye have no *n* that I write unto 1Th 5:1
find grace to help in time of *n* Heb 4:16
ye have *n* that one teach you Heb 5:12
are become such as have *n* of milk Heb 5:12
what further *n* was there that Heb 7:11

N

For ye have *n* of patience Heb 10:36
though now for a season, if *n* be 1Pet 1:6
ye *n* not that any man teach you 1Jn 2:27
good, and seeth his brother have *n* 1Jn 3:17
with goods, and have *n* of nothing Rev 3:17
And the city had no *n* of the sun Rev 21:23
they *n* no candle, neither light Rev 22:5

**NEEDED**
*n* not that any should testify of Jn 2:25
hands, as though he *n* any thing Acts 17:25

**NEEDEST**
*n* not that any man should ask Jn 16:30

**NEEDETH**
And he said, What *n* it Gen 33:15
rise and give him as many as he *n* Lk 11:8
He that is washed *n* not save to Jn 13:10
he may have to give to him that *n* Eph 4:28
a workman that *n* not to be 2Ti 2:15
Who *n* not daily, as those high Heb 7:27

**NEEDFUL**
be *n* for the house of thy God Ezr 7:20
But one thing is *n* Lk 10:42
That it was *n* to circumcise them, Acts 15:5
in the flesh is more *n* for you Phil 1:24
things which are *n* to the body Jas 2:16
it was *n* for me to write unto you Jude 3

**NEEDLE**
to go through the eye of a *n* Mt 19:24
to go through the eye of a *n* Mk 10:25

**NEEDLE'S**
for a camel to go through a *n* eye Lk 18:25

**NEEDLEWORK**
fine twined linen, wrought with *n* Ex 26:36
fine twined linen, wrought with *n* Ex 27:16
thou shalt make the girdle of *n* Ex 28:39
and fine twined linen, of *n* Ex 36:37
for the gate of the court was *n* Ex 38:18
blue, and purple, and scarlet, of *n* Ex 39:29
a prey of divers colours of *n* Judg 5:30
divers colours of *n* on both sides Judg 5:30
unto the king in raiment of *n* Ps 45:14

**NEEDS**
thy money, must *n* be circumcised Gen 17:13
sojourn, and he will *n* be a judge Gen 19:9
must I *n* bring thy son again unto Gen 24:5
though thou wouldest *n* be gone Gen 31:30
For we must *n* die, and are as 2Sa 14:14
they must *n* be borne, because Jer 10:5
for it must *n* be that offences Mt 18:7
for such things must *n* be Mk 13:7
a piece of ground, and I must *n* go Lk 14:18
he must *n* go through Samaria Jn 4:4
must *n* have been fulfilled Acts 1:16
that Christ must *n* have suffered Acts 17:3
multitude must *n* come together Acts 21:22
Wherefore ye must *n* be subject Rom 13:5
for then must ye *n* go out of the 1Cor 5:10
If I must *n* glory, I will glory 2Cor 11:30

**NEEDY**
brother, to thy poor, and to thy *n* Deut 15:11
hired servant that is poor and *n* Deut 24:14
They turn the *n* out of the way Job 24:4
the light killeth the poor and *n* Job 24:14
For the *n* shall not alway be Ps 9:18
poor, for the sighing of the *n* Ps 12:5
the *n* from him that spoileth him Ps 35:10
bow, to cast down the poor and *n* Ps 37:14
But I am poor and *n* Ps 40:17
But I am poor and *n* Ps 70:5
shall save the children of the *n* Ps 72:4
deliver the *n* when he crieth Ps 72:12
He shall spare the poor and *n* Ps 72:13
and shall save the souls of the *n* Ps 72:13
let the poor and *n* praise thy name Ps 74:21
do justice to the afflicted and *n* Ps 82:3
Deliver the poor and *n* Ps 82:4
for I am poor and *n* Ps 86:1
*n* man, that he might even slay Ps 109:16
For I am poor and *n*, and my heart Ps 109:22
lifteth the *n* out of the dunghill Ps 113:7
earth, and the *n* from among men Prov 30:14
plead the cause of the poor and *n* Prov 31:9
reacheth forth her hands to the *n* Prov 31:20
To turn aside the *n* from judgment Is 10:2
the *n* shall lie down in safety Is 14:30
strength to the *n* in his distress Is 25:4
the poor, and the steps of the *n* Is 26:6
even when the *n* speaketh right Is 32:7
*n* seek water, and there is none, Is 41:17
the right of the *n* do they not Jer 5:28
judged the cause of the poor and *n* Jer 22:16
the hand of the poor and *n* Eze 16:49
Hath oppressed the poor and *n* Eze 18:12
and have vexed the poor and *n* Eze 22:29
the poor, which crush the *n* Amos 4:1
this, O ye that swallow up the *n* Amos 8:4
the *n* for a pair of shoes Amos 8:6

**NEESINGS**
By his *n* a light doth shine, and Job 41:18

**NEGEV** See SOUTH.

**NEGINAH** (*neg'-i-nah*) See NEGINOTH. *A stringed instrument.*
To the chief Musician upon *N* Ps 61:*t*

**NEGINOTH** (*neg'-i-noth*) See NEGINAH. *Same as Neginah.*
To the chief Musician on *N* Ps 4:*t*
Musician on *N* upon Sheminith Ps 6:*t*
To the chief Musician on *N* Ps 54:*t*
To the chief Musician on *N* Ps 55:*t*
To the chief Musician on *N* Ps 67:*t*
To the chief Musician on *N* Ps 76:*t*

**NEGLECT**
if he shall *n* to hear them, tell Mt 18:17
but if he *n* to hear the church, Mt 18:17
*N* not the gift that is in thee, 1Ti 4:14
if we *n* so great salvation Heb 2:3

**NEGLECTED**
were *n* in the daily ministration Acts 6:1

**NEGLECTING**
and humility, and *n* of the body Col 2:23

**NEGLIGENT**
My sons, be not now *n* 2Chr 29:11
not be *n* to put you always in 2Pet 1:12

**NEHELAM** See NEHELAMITE.

**NEHELAMITE** (*ne-hel'-am-ite*) *Family name of Shemaiah.*
thou also speak to Shemaiah the *N* Jer 29:24
LORD concerning Shemaiah the *N* Jer 29:31
I will punish Shemaiah the *N* Jer 29:32

**NEHEMIAH** (*ne-he-mi'-ah*)
*1. A clan leader with Zerubbabel.*
Jeshua, *N*, Seraiah, Reelaiah, Ezr 2:2
came with Zerubbabel, Jeshua, *N* Neh 7:7
*2. Governor of Jerusalem.*
The words of *N* the son of Neh 1:1
And *N*, which is the Tirshatha, and Neh 8:9
Now those that sealed were, *N* Neh 10:1
and in the days of *N* the governor Neh 12:26
Zerubbabel, and in the days of *N* Neh 12:47
*3. A rebuilder of Jerusalem's wall.*
him repaired *N* the son of Azbuk Neh 3:16

**NEHILOTH** (*ne'-hi-loth*) *A musical choir or instrument.*
To the chief Musician upon *N* Ps 5:*t*

**NEHUM** (*ne'-hum*) See REHUM. *A clan leader with Zerubbabel.*
Bilshan, Mispereth, Bigvai, *N* Neh 7:7

**NEHUSHTA** (*ne-hush'-tah*) *Mother of King Jehoiachin.*
And his mother's name was *N* 2Kin 24:8

**NEHUSHTAN** (*ne-hush'-tan*) *Name given to the brazen serpents.*
and he called it *N* 2Kin 18:4

**NEIEL** (*ne-i'-el*) *A city in Asher.*
the north side of Beth-emek, and *N* Josh 19:27

**NEIGHBOUR**
every woman shall borrow of her *n* Ex 3:22
and let every man borrow of his *n* Ex 11:2
and every woman of her *n*, jewels Ex 11:2
his *n* next unto his house take it Ex 12:4
bear false witness against thy *n* Ex 20:16
come presumptuously upon his *n* Ex 21:14
unto his *n* money or stuff to keep Ex 22:7
he shall pay double unto his *n* Ex 22:9
a man deliver unto his *n* an ass Ex 22:10
And if a man borrow ought of his *n* Ex 22:14
his companion, and every man his *n* Ex 32:27
lie unto his *n* in that which was Lev 6:2
violence, or hath deceived his *n* Lev 6:2
Thou shalt not defraud thy *n* Lev 19:13
shalt thou judge thy *n* Lev 19:15
stand against the blood of thy *n* Lev 19:16
shalt in any wise rebuke thy *n* Lev 19:17
thou shalt love thy *n* as thyself Lev 19:18
if a man cause a blemish in his *n* Lev 24:19
And if thou sell ought unto thy *n* Lev 25:14
jubile thou shalt buy of thy *n* Lev 25:15
which should kill his *n* unawares Deut 4:42
bear false witness against thy *n* Deut 5:20
ought unto his *n* shall release it Deut 15:2
he shall not exact it of his *n* Deut 15:2
Whoso killeth his *n* ignorantly Deut 19:4
the wood with his *n* to hew wood Deut 19:5
the helve, and lighteth upon his *n* Deut 19:5
But if any man hate his *n* Deut 19:11
when a man riseth against his *n* Deut 22:26
into the standing corn of thy *n* Deut 23:25
be he that smiteth his *n* secretly Deut 27:24
he smote his *n* unwittingly Josh 20:5
off his shoe, and gave it to his *n* Ruth 4:7
and hath given it to a *n* of thine 1Sa 15:28
thine hand, and given it to thy *n* 1Sa 28:17
eyes, and give them unto thy *n* 2Sa 12:11
If any man trespass against his *n* 1Kin 8:31
his *n* in the word of the LORD 1Kin 20:35
If a man sin against his *n* 2Chr 6:22
I am as one mocked of his *n* Job 12:4
God, as a man pleadeth for his *n* Job 16:21
speak vanity every one with his *n* Ps 12:2
tongue, nor doeth evil to his *n* Ps 15:3
up a reproach against his *n* Ps 15:3
Whoso privily slandereth his *n* Ps 101:5
Say not unto thy *n*, Go, and come Prov 3:28
Devise not evil against thy *n* Prov 3:29
with his mouth destroyeth his *n* Prov 11:9
is void of wisdom despiseth his *n* Prov 11:12
is more excellent than his *n* Prov 12:26
poor is hated even of his own *n* Prov 14:20
He that despiseth his *n* sinneth Prov 14:21
A violent man enticeth his *n* Prov 16:29
but his *n* cometh and searcheth him. Prov 18:17
the poor is separated from his *n* Prov 19:4
his *n* findeth no favour in his Prov 21:10
against thy *n* without cause Prov 24:28
when thy *n* hath put thee to shame Prov 25:8
thy cause with thy *n* himself Prov 25:9
witness against his *n* is a maul Prov 25:18
is the man that deceiveth his *n* Prov 26:19
for better is a *n* that is near Prov 27:10
A man that flattereth his *n* Prov 29:5
for this a man is envied of his *n* Eccl 4:4
by another, and every one by his *n* Is 3:5
and every one against his *n* Is 19:2
They helped every one his *n* Is 41:6
the *n* and his friend shall perish Jer 6:21
judgment between a man and his *n* Jer 7:5
Take ye heed every one of his *n* Jer 9:4
every *n* will walk with slanders Jer 9:4
they will deceive every one his *n* Jer 9:5
peaceably to his *n* with his mouth Jer 9:8
and every one her *n* lamentation Jer 9:20
they shall say every man to his *n* Jer 22:8
they tell every man to his *n* Jer 23:27
my words every one from his *n* Jer 23:30
shall ye say every one to his *n* Jer 23:35
teach no more every man his *n* Jer 31:34
liberty every man to his *n* Jer 34:15
brother, and every man to his *n* Jer 34:17
the *n* cities thereof, saith the Jer 49:18
the *n* cities thereof, saith the Jer 50:40
unto him that giveth his *n* drink Hab 2:15
every man his *n* under the vine Zec 3:10
all men every one against his *n* Zec 8:10
ye every man the truth to his *n* Zec 8:16
evil in your hearts against his *n* Zec 8:17
every one on the hand of his *n* Zec 14:13
rise up against the hand of his *n* Zec 14:13
been said, Thou shalt love thy *n* Mt 5:43
Thou shalt love thy *n* as thyself Mt 19:19
Thou shalt love thy *n* as thyself Mt 22:39
Thou shalt love thy *n* as thyself Mk 12:31
and to love his *n* as himself Mk 12:33
and thy *n* as thyself Lk 10:27
said unto Jesus, And who is my *n* Lk 10:29
was *n* unto him that fell among Lk 10:36
But he that did his *n* wrong Acts 7:27
Thou shalt love thy *n* as thyself Rom 13:9
Love worketh no ill to his *n* Rom 13:10
his *n* for his good to edification Rom 15:2
Thou shalt love thy *n* as thyself Gal 5:14
speak every man truth with his *n* Eph 4:25
shall not teach every man his *n* Heb 8:11
Thou shalt love thy *n* as thyself Jas 2:8

**NEIGHBOUR'S**
Thou shalt not covet thy *n* house Ex 20:17
thou shalt not covet thy *n* wife Ex 20:17
ass, nor any thing that is thy *n* Ex 20:17
put his hand unto his *n* goods Ex 22:8
not put his hand unto his *n* goods Ex 22:11
all take thy *n* raiment to pledge Ex 22:26
not lie carnally with thy *n* wife Lev 18:20
adultery with his *n* wife, the Lev 20:10
or buyest ought of thy *n* hand Lev 25:14
shalt thou desire thy *n* wife Deut 5:21
shalt thou covet thy *n* house Deut 5:21
ass, or any thing that is thy *n* Deut 5:21
shalt not remove thy *n* landmark Deut 19:14
he hath humbled his *n* wife Deut 22:24
thou comest into thy *n* vineyard Deut 23:24
a sickle unto thy *n* standing corn Deut 23:25
he that removeth his *n* landmark Deut 27:17
if I have laid wait at my *n* door Job 31:9
So he that goeth in to his *n* wife Prov 6:29
thy foot from thy *n* house Prov 25:17
one neighed after his *n* wife Jer 5:8
that useth his *n* service without Jer 22:13
neither hath defiled his *n* wife Eze 18:6
mountains, and defiled his *n* wife Eze 18:11
hath not defiled his *n* wife Eze 18:15
abomination with his *n* wife Eze 22:11
and ye defile every one his *n* wife Eze 33:26
the men every one into his *n* hand Zec 11:6

**NEIGHBOURS**
they heard that they were their *n* Josh 9:16
the women her *n* gave it a name, Ruth 4:17
thee vessels abroad of all thy *n* 2Kin 4:3
which speak peace to their *n* Ps 28:3
but especially among my *n* Ps 31:11
makest us a reproach to our *n* Ps 44:13
We are become a reproach to our *n* Ps 79:4
render unto our *n* sevenfold into Ps 79:12
makest us a strife unto our *n* Ps 80:6
he is a reproach to his *n* Ps 89:41
the LORD against all mine evil *n* Jer 12:14
and his brethren, and his *n* Jer 49:10
with the Egyptians thy *n*, great Eze 16:26
gained of thy *n* by extortion Eze 22:12
lovers, on the Assyrians her *n* Eze 23:5
doted upon the Assyrians her *n* Eze 23:12
And her *n* and her cousins heard how Lk 1:58
thy kinsmen, nor thy rich *n* Lk 14:12
calleth together his friends and *n* Lk 15:6
her *n* together, saying, Rejoice Lk 15:9
The *n* therefore, and they which Jn 9:8

**NEIGHBOURS'**
adultery with their *n* wives.................... Jer 29:23

**NEIGHED**
every one *n* after his neighbour's............ Jer 5:8

**NEIGHING**
sound of the *n* of his strong ones........... Jer 8:16

**NEIGHINGS**
seen thine adulteries, and thy *n*............ Jer 13:27

**NEITHER** See PREFACE.

**NEKEB** (*ne'-keb*) *A city in Naphtali.*
Allon to Zaanannim, and Adami, *N*... Josh 19:33

**NEKODA** (*ne-ko'-dah*)
*1. A family of exiles.*
of Rezin, the children of *N*...................... Ezr 2:48
of Rezin, the children of *N*...................... Neh 7:50
*2. A family of uncertain origin.*
of Tobiah, the children of *N*.................... Ezr 2:60
of Tobiah, the children of *N*.................... Neh 7:62

**NEMUEL** (*ne-mu'-el*) See JEMUEL, NEMUELITES.
*1. Son of Eliab.*
*N*, and Dathan, and Abiram.................. Num 26:9
*2. A son of Simeon.*
of *N*, the family of the......................... Num 26:12
The sons of Simeon were, *N*................. 1Chr 4:24

**NEMUELITES** (*ne-mu'-el-ites*) *Descendants of Nemuel 2.*
of Nemuel, the family of the *N*.......... Num 26:12

**NEPHEG** (*ne'-feg*)
*1. A son of Izhar.*
Korah, and *N*, and Zichri.......................... Ex 6:21
*2. A son of David.*
Ibhar also, and Elishua, and *N*................ 2Sa 5:15
And Nogah, and *N*, and Japhia,............. 1Chr 3:7
And Nogah, and *N*, and Japhia,............ 1Chr 14:6

**NEPHEW**
have son nor *n* among his people......... Job 18:19
name, and remnant, and son, and *n*....... Is 14:22

**NEPHEWS**
And he had forty sons and thirty *n*... Judg 12:14
if any widow have children or *n*................ 1Ti 5:4

**NEPHILIM**

**NEPHISH** (*ne'-fish*) See NAPHISH. *Descendants of Naphish.*
the Hagarites, with Jetur, and *N*.......... 1Chr 5:19

**NEPHISHESIM** (*ne-fish'-e-sim*) See NEPHUSIM.
*A family of exiles.*
of Meunim, the children of *N*................ Neh 7:52

**NEPHISIM** See NEPHUSIM.

**NEPHTHALIM** (*nef'-tha-lim*) See NAPHTALI.
*Country and tribe of Naphtali.*
in the borders of Zabulon and *N*.............. Mt 4:13
land of Zabulon, and the land of *N*............ Mt 4:15

**NEPHTOAH** (*nef-to'-ah*) *A stream near Jerusalem.*
the fountain of the water of *N*............. Josh 15:9
out to the well of waters of *N*............ Josh 18:15

**NEPHUSHESIM** See NEPHISHESIM.

**NEPHUSIM** (*ne-fu'-sim*) See NEPHISHESIM. *A family of exiles.*
of Mehunim, the children of *N*................ Ezr 2:50

**NEPTHALIM**
Of the tribe of *N* were sealed.................... Rev 7:6

**NER** (*nur*) *Grandfather of King Saul.*
his host was Abner, the son of *N*......... 1Sa 14:50
*N* the father of Abner was the son...... 1Sa 14:51
Saul lay, and Abner the son of *N*......... 1Sa 26:5
people, and to Abner the son of *N*....... 1Sa 26:14
But Abner the son of *N*, captain............... 2Sa 2:8
And Abner the son of *N*, and the........... 2Sa 2:12
the son of *N* came to the king.................. 2Sa 3:23
Thou knowest Abner the son of *N*.......... 2Sa 3:25
the blood of Abner the son of *N*............ 2Sa 3:28
king to slay Abner the son of *N*............ 2Sa 3:37
Israel, unto Abner the son of *N*............ 1Kin 2:5
to wit, Abner the son of *N*.................... 1Kin 2:32
*N* begat Kish, and Kish begat Saul,..... 1Chr 8:33
then Zur, and Kish, and Baal, and *N*... 1Chr 9:36
And *N* begat Kish............................... 1Chr 9:39
of Kish, and Abner the son of *N*........ 1Chr 26:28

**NERAIAH** See NERIAH.

**NEREUS** (*ne'-re-us*) *A Christian acquaintance of Paul.*
Salute Philologus, and Julia, *N*........... Rom 16:15

**NERGAL** (*nur'-gal*) See NERGAL-SHAREZER. *War god of Cuth.*
and the men of Cuth made *N*.............. 2Kin 17:30

**NERGAL-SHAREZER** (*nur'-gal-sha-re'-zur*)
*1. A Babylonian prince.*
and sat in the middle gate, even *N*......... Jer 39:3
*2. Another Babylonian prince.*
Sarsechim, Rab-saris, *N*, Rab-mag.............. Jer 39:3
and Nebushasban, Rab-saris, and *N*...... Jer 39:13

**NERI** (*ne'-ri*) *Father of Salathiel; ancestor of Jesus.*
Salathiel, which was the son of *N*........... Lk 3:27

**NERIAH** (*ne-ri'-ah*) *Father of Baruch.*
purchase unto Baruch the son of *N*...... Jer 32:12
purchase unto Baruch the son of *N*...... Jer 32:16
called Baruch the son of *N*..................... Jer 36:4
Baruch the son of *N* did according......... Jer 36:8
So Baruch the son of *N* took the............ Jer 36:14
Baruch the scribe, the son of *N*............ Jer 36:32
But Baruch the son of *N* setteth.............. Jer 43:3
prophet, and Baruch the son of *N*.......... Jer 43:6
spake unto Baruch the son of *N*............. Jer 45:1
commanded Seraiah the son of *N*......... Jer 51:59

**NERO** (*ne'-ro*) *Emperor of Rome.*
brought before *N* the second time............. 2Ti s

**NEST**
and thou puttest thy *n* in a rock........ Num 24:21
If a bird's *n* chance to be before.......... Deut 22:6
As an eagle stirreth up her *n*............. Deut 32:11
Then I said, I shall die in my *n*............ Job 29:18
command, and make her *n* on high..... Job 39:27
and the swallow a *n* for herself................. Ps 84:3
a bird that wandereth from her *n*......... Prov 27:8
my hand hath found as a *n* the.............. Is 10:14
wandering bird cast out of the *n*............. Is 16:2
shall the great owl make her *n*.............. Is 34:15
that makest thy *n* in the cedars............ Jer 22:23
her *n* in the sides of the hole's............. Jer 48:28
make thy *n* as high as the eagle............ Jer 49:16
thou set thy *n* among the stars............... Obad 4
that he may set his *n* on high................... Hab 2:9

**NESTS**
Where the birds make their *n*............... Ps 104:17
heaven made their *n* in his boughs........ Eze 31:6
and the birds of the air have *n*.................. Mt 8:20
holes, and birds of the air have *n*............ Lk 9:58

**NET**
upon the *n* shalt thou make four............ Ex 27:4
that the *n* may be even to the................. Ex 27:5
is cast into a *n* by his own feet.............. Job 18:8
and hath compassed me with his *n*....... Job 19:6
in the *n* which they hid is their................. Ps 9:15
when he draweth him into his *n*............... Ps 10:9
shall pluck my feet out of the *n*.............. Ps 25:15
Pull me out of the *n* that they................. Ps 31:4
they hid for me their *n* in a pit................ Ps 35:7
let his *n* that he hath hid catch................ Ps 35:8
have prepared a *n* for my steps............... Ps 57:6
Thou broughtest us into the *n*.............. Ps 66:11
have spread a *n* by the wayside............. Ps 140:5
Surely in vain the *n* is spread in........... Prov 1:17
wicked desireth the *n* of evil men...... Prov 12:12
spreadeth a *n* for his feet..................... Prov 29:5
that are taken in an evil *n*..................... Eccl 9:12
streets, as a wild bull in a *n*................. Is 51:20
he hath spread a *n* for my feet............... Lam 1:13
My *n* also will I spread upon him,......... Eze 12:13
And I will spread my *n* upon him........ Eze 17:20
and spread their *n* over him.................. Eze 19:8
my *n* over thee with a company of......... Eze 32:3
they shall bring thee up in my *n*............ Eze 32:3
Mizpah, and a *n* spread upon Tabor......... Hos 5:1
go, I will spread my *n* upon them.......... Hos 7:12
every man his brother with a *n*............... Mic 7:2
angle, they catch them in their *n*............ Hab 1:15
they sacrifice unto their *n*..................... Hab 1:16
they therefore empty their *n*.................. Hab 1:17
brother, casting a *n* into the sea............... Mt 4:18
of heaven is like unto a *n*..................... Mt 13:47
brother casting a *n* into the sea................ Mk 1:16
at thy word I will let down the *n*.............. Lk 5:5
and their *n* brake...................................... Lk 5:6
Cast the *n* on the right side of................ Jn 21:6
dragging the *n* with fishes....................... Jn 21:8
drew the *n* to land full of great............... Jn 21:11
so many, yet was not the *n* broken......... Jn 21:11

**NETAIM** See PLANTS.

**NETHANEAL** See NETHANEEL.

**NETHANEEL** (*ne-than'-e-el*)
*1. A son of Zuar.*
*N* the son of Zuar.................................... Num 1:8
*N* the son of Zuar shall be..................... Num 2:5
the second day *N* the son of Zuar....... Num 7:18
the offering of *N* the son of Zuar......... Num 7:23
of Issachar was *N* the son of Zuar.... Num 10:15
*2. A brother of David.*
*N* the fourth, Raddai the fifth,.............. 1Chr 2:14
*3. A priest who relocated the Ark.*
Shebaniah, and Jehoshaphat, and *N*.. 1Chr 15:24
*4. A sanctuary servant.*
Shemaiah the son of *N* the scribe........ 1Chr 24:6
*5. A son of Obed-edom.*
Sacar the fourth, and *N* the fifth,........ 1Chr 26:4
*6. A prince of Judah.*
Obadiah, and to Zechariah, and to *N*.. 2Chr 17:7
*7. A chief Levite.*
Conaniah also, and Shemaiah and *N*.. 2Chr 35:9
*8. Married a foreigner in exile.*
Elioenai, Maaseiah, Ishmael, *N*............ Ezr 10:22
*9. A priest with Zerubbabel.*
of Jedaiah, *N*.......................................... Neh 12:21
*10. A priest who dedicated the wall.*
Milalai, Gilalai, Maai, *N*...................... Neh 12:36

**NETHANEL**

**NETHANIAH** (*neth-a-ni'-ah*)
*1. Father of Ishmael.*
Mizpah, even Ishmael the son of *N*... 2Kin 25:23
month, that Ishmael the son of *N*...... 2Kin 25:25
Mizpah, even Ishmael the son of *N*........ Jer 40:8
Ishmael the son of *N* to slay thee......... Jer 40:14
I will slay Ishmael the son of *N*............ Jer 40:15
the son of *N* the son of Elishama............ Jer 41:1
Then arose Ishmael the son of *N*............ Jer 41:2
Ishmael the son of *N* went forth............ Jer 41:6
Ishmael the son of *N* slew them............ Jer 41:7
Ishmael the son of *N* filled it................ Jer 41:9
Ishmael the son of *N* carried them....... Jer 41:10
Ishmael the son of *N* had done.............. Jer 41:11
fight with Ishmael the son of *N*............. Jer 41:12
But Ishmael the son of *N* escaped......... Jer 41:15
from Ishmael the son of *N*.................... Jer 41:16
because Ishmael the son of *N* had....... Jer 41:18
*2. A sanctuary servant.*
Zaccur, and Joseph, and *N*, and........... 1Chr 25:2
The fifth to *N*, he, his sons, and......... 1Chr 25:12
*3. A Levite.*
sent Levites, even Shemaiah, and *N*.... 2Chr 17:8
*4. Father of Jehudi.*
princes sent Jehudi the son of *N*........... Jer 36:14

**NETHER**
stood at the *n* part of the mount........ Ex 19:17
No man shall take the *n* or the........... Deut 24:6
upper springs, and the *n* springs......... Josh 15:19
the coast of Beth-horon the *n*.............. Josh 16:3
south side of the *n* Beth-horon............ Josh 18:13
upper springs and the *n* springs........... Judg 1:15
built Gezer, and Beth-horon the *n*....... 1Kin 9:17
who built Beth-horon the *n*................... 1Chr 7:24
the upper, and Beth-horon the *n*............ 2Chr 8:5
as a piece of the *n* millstone................. Job 41:24
to the *n* parts of the earth, in.............. Eze 31:14
in the *n* parts of the earth..................... Eze 31:16
unto the *n* parts of the earth.................. Eze 31:18
unto the *n* parts of the earth,................. Eze 32:18
into the *n* parts of the earth................... Eze 32:24

**NETHERMOST**
The *n* chamber was five cubits............... 1Kin 6:6

**NETHINIM** See NETHINIMS.

**NETHINIMS** (*neth'-in-ims*) *Assistants to the Levites.*
the priests, Levites, and the *N*............... 1Chr 9:2
The *N*: the children of Ziha..................... Ezr 2:43
All the *N*, and the children of................. Ezr 2:58
singers, and the porters, and the *N*......... Ezr 2:70
singers, and the porters, and the *N*.......... Ezr 7:7
and Levites, singers, porters, *N*............... Ezr 7:24
Iddo, and to his brethren the *N*............... Ezr 8:17
Also of the *N*, whom David and the...... Ezr 8:20
Levites, two hundred and twenty *N*........ Ezr 8:20
Moreover the *N* dwelt in Ophel,........... Neh 3:26
son unto the place of the *N*.................. Neh 3:31
The *N*: the children of Ziha.................. Neh 7:46
All the *N*, and the children of.............. Neh 7:60
and some of the people, and the *N*......... Neh 7:73
the porters, the singers, the *N*............. Neh 10:28
priests, and the Levites, and the *N*........ Neh 11:3
But the *N* dwelt in Ophel..................... Neh 11:21
and Ziha and Gispa were over the *N*.. Neh 11:21

**NETOPHAH** (*ne-to'-fah*) See NETOPHATHITE. *A city in Judah.*
The men of *N*, fifty and six...................... Ezr 2:22
The men of Beth-lehem and *N*................ Neh 7:26

**NETOPHATHI** (*ne-to'-fa-thi*) See NETOPHATHITE. *An inhabitant of Netophah.*
and from the villages of *N*.................... Neh 12:28

**NETOPHATHITE** (*ne-to'-fa-thite*) See NETOPHATHI, NETHOPHATHITES. *Same as Netophathi.*
Zalmon the Ahohite, Maharai the *N*... 2Sa 23:28
Heleb the son of Baanah, a *N*.............. 2Sa 23:29
the son of Tanhumeth the *N*............... 2Kin 25:23
Maharai the *N*, Heled the son of......... 1Chr 11:30
Heled the son of Baanah the *N*........... 1Chr 11:30
the tenth month was Maharai the *N*. 1Chr 27:13
twelfth month was Heldai the *N*......... 1Chr 27:15
and the sons of Ephai the *N*.................... Jer 40:8

**NETOPHATHITES** (*ne-to'-fa-thites*)
Beth-lehem, and the *N*, Ataroth,.......... 1Chr 2:54
dwelt in the villages of the *N*............... 1Chr 9:16

**NETS**
*n* of checker work, and wreaths of....... 1Kin 7:17
the wicked fall into their own *n*............ Ps 141:10
woman, whose heart is snares and *n*...... Eccl 7:26
they that spread *n* upon the..................... Is 19:8
of *n* in the midst of the sea.................... Eze 26:5
shalt be a place to spread *n* upon........ Eze 26:14
be a place to spread forth *n*................. Eze 47:10
And they straightway left their *n*........... Mt 4:20
their father, mending their *n*.................. Mt 4:21
straightway they forsook their *n*............ Mk 1:18
were in the ship mending their *n*........... Mk 1:19
of them, and were washing their *n*........... Lk 5:2
and let down your *n* for a draught............ Lk 5:4

**NETTLES**
under the *n* they were gathered............ Job 30:7
*n* had covered the face thereof,........... Prov 24:31
shall come up in her palaces, *n*.............. Is 34:13
silver, *n* shall possess them.................... Hos 9:6
Gomorrah, even the breeding of *n*.......... Zeph 2:9

**NETWORK**
make for it a grate of *n* of brass Ex 27:4
of *n* under the compass thereof Ex 38:4
rows round about upon the one *n* 1Kin 7:18
the belly which was by the *n* 1Kin 7:20
rows of pomegranates for one *n* 1Kin 7:42
chapiter was five cubits, with *n* Jer 52:22
the *n* were an hundred round about Jer 52:23

**NETWORKS**
and the two *n*, to cover the two 1Kin 7:41
pomegranates for the two *n* 1Kin 7:42
fine flax, and they that weave *n* Is 19:9

**NEVER**
Ask me *n* so much dowry and gift, Gen 34:12
such as I *n* saw in all the land Gen 41:19
it shall *n* go out Lev 6:13
and upon which *n* came yoke Num 19:2
For the poor shall *n* cease out of Deut 15:11
I will *n* break my covenant with Judg 2:1
Is there *n* a woman among the Judg 14:3
green withs that were *n* dried Judg 16:7
new ropes that *n* were occupied Judg 16:11
shall *n* depart from thine house 2Sa 12:10
for he *n* prophesied good unto me, 2Chr 18:7
that there was *n* a son left him 2Chr 21:17
as infants which *n* saw light Job 3:16
and make my hands *n* so clean Job 9:30
soul, and *n* eateth with pleasure Job 21:25
for I shall *n* be in adversity Ps 10:6
he will *n* see it Ps 10:11
these things shall *n* be moved Ps 15:5
I said, I shall *n* be moved Ps 30:6
let me *n* be ashamed Ps 31:1
they shall *n* see light Ps 49:19
he shall *n* suffer the righteous Ps 55:22
of charmers, charming *n* so wisely Ps 58:5
let me *n* be put to confusion Ps 71:1
I will *n* forget thy precepts Ps 119:93
The righteous shall *n* be removed Prov 10:30
Hell and destruction are *n* full Prov 27:20
the eyes of man are *n* satisfied Prov 27:20
three things that are *n* satisfied Prov 30:15
It shall *n* be inhabited, neither Is 13:20
of evildoers shall *n* be renowned Is 14:20
it shall *n* be built Is 25:2
dogs which can *n* have enough Is 56:11
which shall *n* hold their peace Is 62:6
thou *n* barest rule over them Is 63:19
confusion shall *n* be forgotten Jer 20:11
David shall *n* want a man to sit Jer 33:17
*n* open thy mouth any more because Eze 16:63
yet shalt thou *n* be found again Eze 26:21
a terror, and *n* shalt be any more Eze 27:36
and *n* shalt thou be any more Eze 28:19
which shall *n* be destroyed Dan 2:44
such as *n* was since there was a Dan 12:1
and my people shall *n* be ashamed Joel 2:26
and my people shall *n* be ashamed Joel 2:27
Surely I will *n* forget any of Amos 8:7
shall fall, and *n* rise up again Amos 8:14
and judgment doth *n* go forth Hab 1:4
I profess unto them, I *n* knew you Mt 7:23
It was *n* so seen in Israel Mt 9:33
have ye *n* read, Out of the mouth Mt 21:16
Did ye *n* read in the scriptures, Mt 21:42
of thee, yet will I *n* be offended Mt 26:33
And he answered him to *n* a word Mt 27:14
We *n* saw it on this fashion Mk 2:12
Have ye *n* read what David did, Mk 2:25
the Holy Ghost hath *n* forgiveness Mk 3:29
the fire that *n* shall be quenched Mk 9:43
the fire that *n* shall be quenched Mk 9:45
a colt tied, whereon *n* man sat Mk 11:2
that man if he had *n* been born Mk 14:21
yet thou *n* gavest me a kid, that Lk 15:29
colt tied, whereon yet *n* man sat Lk 19:30
barren, and the wombs that *n* bare Lk 23:29
and the paps which *n* gave suck Lk 23:29
wherein *n* man before was laid Lk 23:53
I shall give him shall *n* thirst Jn 4:14
that cometh to me shall *n* hunger Jn 6:35
believeth on me shall *n* thirst Jn 6:35
man letters, having *n* learned Jn 7:15
*N* man spake like this man Jn 7:46
were *n* in bondage to any man Jn 8:33
my saying, he shall *n* see death Jn 8:51
he shall *n* taste of death Jn 8:52
and they shall *n* perish, neither Jn 10:28
and believeth in me shall *n* die Jn 11:26
Thou shalt *n* wash my feet Jn 13:8
wherein was *n* man yet laid Jn 19:41
for I have *n* eaten any thing that Acts 10:14
mother's womb, who *n* had walked Acts 14:8
Charity *n* faileth 1Cor 13:8
*n* able to come to the knowledge 2Ti 3:7
can *n* with those sacrifices which Heb 10:1
which can *n* take away sins Heb 10:11
I will *n* leave thee, nor forsake Heb 13:5
do these things, ye shall *n* fall 2Pet 1:10

**NEVERTHELESS**
*n* in the day when I visit I will Ex 32:34
*N* these shall ye not eat of them Lev 11:4
*N* a fountain or pit, wherein Lev 11:36
*N* the people be strong that dwell Num 13:28
*n* the ark of the covenant of the Num 14:44
*n* the firstborn of man shalt thou Num 18:15
*N* the Kenite shall be wasted, Num 24:22
*n* it shall be purified with the Num 31:23
*N* these ye shall not eat of them Deut 14:7
*N* the LORD thy God would not Deut 23:5
*N* the children of Israel expelled Josh 13:13
*N* my brethren that went up with Josh 14:8
*n* the inhabitants of Beth-shemesh Judg 1:33
*N* the LORD raised up judges, Judg 2:16
*N* the people refused to obey the 1Sa 8:19
*n* Samuel mourned for Saul 1Sa 15:35
*N* Saul spake not any thing that 1Sa 20:26
*n* the lords favour thee not 1Sa 29:6
*N* David took the strong hold of 2Sa 5:7
*N* a lad saw them, and told Absalom 2Sa 17:18
*n* he would not drink thereof, but 2Sa 23:16
*N* thou shalt not build the house 1Kin 8:19
*N* for David's sake did the LORD 1Kin 15:4
*n* Asa's heart was perfect with 1Kin 15:14
*N* in the time of his old age he 1Kin 15:23
*n* the high places were not taken 1Kin 22:43
*n*, if thou see me when I am taken 2Kin 2:10
*N* he cleaved unto the sins of 2Kin 3:3
*N* they departed not from the sins 2Kin 13:6
*N* the priests of the high places 2Kin 23:9
*N* David took the castle of Zion, 1Chr 11:5
*N* the king's word prevailed 1Chr 21:4
*N* they shall be his servants 2Chr 12:8
*n* the heart of Asa was perfect 2Chr 15:17
*N* there are good things found in 2Chr 19:3
*N* divers of Asher and Manasseh and 2Chr 30:11
*N* the people did sacrifice still 2Chr 33:17
*N* Josiah would not turn his face 2Chr 35:22
*N* we made our prayer unto our God Neh 4:9
*N* they were disobedient, and Neh 9:26
*N* for thy great mercies' sake Neh 9:31
*n* even him did outlandish women Neh 13:26
*N* Haman refrained himself Est 5:10
*n* thou heardest the voice of my Ps 31:22
*N* man being in honour abideth not Ps 49:12
*N* I am continually with thee Ps 73:23
*N* they did flatter him with their Ps 78:36
*N* my lovingkindness will I not Ps 89:33
*N* he saved them for his name's Ps 106:8
*N* he regarded their affliction, Ps 106:44
*n* the counsel of the LORD, that Prov 19:21
*n* the poor man's wisdom is Eccl 9:16
*N* the dimness shall not be such Is 9:1
*N* in those days, saith the LORD, Jer 5:18
*N* the hand of Ahikam the son of Jer 26:24
*N* hear thou now this word that I Jer 28:7
*N* Elnathan and Delaiah Jer 36:25
*N* if thou warn the righteous man, Eze 3:21
*N* I will remember my covenant Eze 16:60
*N* mine eye spared them from Eze 20:17
*N* I withdrew mine hand, and Eze 20:22
*N*, if thou warn the wicked of his Eze 33:9
*N* leave the stump of his roots in Dan 4:15
*N* the men rowed hard to bring it Jonah 1:13
*n* for the oath's sake, and them Mt 14:9
*n* not as I will, but as thou wilt Mt 26:39
*n* I say unto you, Hereafter shall Mt 26:64
*n* not what I will, but what thou Mk 14:36
*n* at thy word I will let down the Lk 5:5
*N* I must walk to day, and to Lk 13:33
*N* when the Son of man cometh, Lk 18:8
*n* not my will, but thine, be done Lk 22:42
*n* let us go unto him Jn 11:15
*N* among the chief rulers also Jn 12:42
*N* I tell you the truth Jn 16:7
*N* he left not himself without Acts 14:17
*N* the centurion believed the Acts 27:11
*N* death reigned from Adam to Rom 5:14
*N*, brethren, I have written the Rom 15:15
*N*, to avoid fornication, let 1Cor 7:2
*N* such shall have trouble in the 1Cor 7:28
*N* he that standeth stedfast in 1Cor 7:37
*N* we have not used this power 1Cor 9:12
*N* neither is the man without the 1Cor 11:11
*N* when it shall turn to the Lord, 2Cor 3:16
*N* God, that comforteth those that 2Cor 7:6
*n*, being crafty, I caught you 2Cor 12:16
*n* I live; yet not I Gal 2:20
*N* what saith the scripture Gal 4:30
*N* let every one of you in Eph 5:33
*N* to abide in the flesh is more Phil 1:24
*N*, whereto we have already Phil 3:16
*n* I am not ashamed 2Ti 1:12
*N* the foundation of God standeth 2Ti 2:19
*n* afterward it yieldeth the Heb 12:11
*N* we, according to his promise, 2Pet 3:13
*N* I have somewhat against thee, Rev 2:4

**NEW**
arose up a *n* king over Egypt Ex 1:8
ye shall offer a *n* meat offering Lev 23:16
forth the old because of the *n* Lev 26:10
But if the LORD make a *n* thing Num 16:30
when ye bring a *n* meat offering Num 28:26
there that hath built a *n* house Deut 20:5
When thou buildest a *n* house Deut 22:8
When a man hath taken a *n* wife Deut 24:5
to *n* gods that came newly up, Deut 32:17
of wine, which we filled, were *n* Josh 9:13
They chose *n* gods Judg 5:8
they bound him with two *n* cords Judg 15:13
he found a *n* jawbone of an ass, Judg 15:15
If they bind me fast with *n* ropes Judg 16:11
Delilah therefore took *n* ropes Judg 16:12
Now therefore make a *n* cart 1Sa 6:7
Behold, to morrow is the *n* moon 1Sa 20:5
to David, To morrow is the *n* moon 1Sa 20:18
when the *n* moon was come, the 1Sa 20:24
set the ark of God upon a *n* cart 2Sa 6:3
of Abinadab, drave the *n* cart 2Sa 6:3
he being girded with a *n* sword 2Sa 21:16
had clad himself with a *n* garment 1Kin 11:29
Ahijah caught the *n* garment that 1Kin 11:30
And he said, Bring me a *n* cruse 2Kin 2:20
it is neither *n* moon, nor sabbath 2Kin 4:23
in a *n* cart out of the house of 1Chr 13:7
in the sabbaths, in the *n* moons 1Chr 23:31
the sabbaths, and on the *n* moons 2Chr 2:4
the sabbaths, and on the *n* moons 2Chr 8:13
of the LORD, before the *n* court 2Chr 20:5
the sabbaths, and for the *n* moons 2Chr 31:3
offering, both of the *n* moons Ezr 3:5
stones, and a row of *n* timber Ezr 6:4
of the sabbaths, of the *n* moons Neh 10:33
of the corn, of the *n* wine Neh 10:39
the *n* wine, and the oil, which was Neh 13:5
the *n* wine and the oil unto the Neh 13:12
is ready to burst like *n* bottles Job 32:19
Sing unto him a *n* song Ps 33:3
he hath put a *n* song in my mouth, Ps 40:3
Blow up the trumpet in the *n* moon Ps 81:3
O sing unto the LORD a *n* song Ps 96:1
O sing unto the LORD a *n* song Ps 98:1
I will sing a *n* song unto thee, O Ps 144:9
Sing unto the LORD a *n* song Ps 149:1
shall burst out with *n* wine Prov 3:10
there is no *n* thing under the sun Eccl 1:9
it may be said, See, this is *n* Eccl 1:10
all manner of pleasant fruits, *n* Song 7:13
the *n* moons and sabbaths, the Is 1:13
Your *n* moons and your appointed Is 1:14
The *n* wine mourneth, the vine Is 24:7
I will make thee a *n* sharp Is 41:15
to pass, and *n* things do I declare Is 42:9
Sing unto the LORD a *n* song Is 42:10
Behold, I will do a *n* thing Is 43:19
I have shewed thee *n* things from Is 48:6
thou shalt be called by a *n* name Is 62:2
As the *n* wine is found in the Is 65:8
I create *n* heavens and a *n* earth Is 65:17
For as the *n* heavens Is 66:22
the *n* earth, which I will make, Is 66:22
that from one *n* moon to another, Is 66:23
of the *n* gate of the LORD's house Jer 26:10
created a *n* thing in the earth Jer 31:22
that I will make a *n* covenant Jer 31:31
at the entry of the *n* gate of the Jer 36:10
They are *n* every morning Lam 3:23
I will put a *n* spirit within you Eze 11:19
you a *n* heart and a *n* spirit Eze 18:31
A *n* heart also will I give you, Eze 36:26
a *n* spirit will I put within you Eze 36:26
in the feasts, and in the *n* moons Eze 45:17
in the day of the *n* moon it shall Eze 46:1
in the sabbaths and in the *n* moons Eze 46:3
in the day of the *n* moon it shall Eze 46:6
it shall bring forth *n* fruit Eze 47:12
her *n* moons, and her sabbaths, and Hos 2:11
*n* wine take away the heart Hos 4:11
the *n* wine shall fail in her Hos 9:2
of wine, because of the *n* wine Joel 1:5
the *n* wine is dried up, the oil Joel 1:10
mountains shall drop down *n* wine Joel 3:18
When will the *n* moon be gone Amos 8:5
upon the corn, and upon the *n* wine Hag 1:11
men cheerful, and *n* wine the maids Zec 9:17
of *n* cloth unto an old garment Mt 9:16
Neither do men put *n* wine into Mt 9:17
but they put *n* wine into Mt 9:17
wine into *n* bottles Mt 9:17
out of his treasure things *n* Mt 13:52
is my blood of the *n* testament Mt 26:28
until that day when I drink it *n* Mt 26:29
And laid it in his own *n* tomb Mt 27:60
what *n* doctrine is this Mk 1:27
of *n* cloth on an old garment Mk 2:21
else the *n* piece that filled it Mk 2:21
no man putteth *n* wine into old Mk 2:22
else the *n* wine doth burst the Mk 2:22
but *n* wine must be put into Mk 2:22
wine must be put into *n* bottles Mk 2:22
is my blood of the *n* testament Mk 14:24
drink it *n* in the kingdom of God Mk 14:25
they shall speak with *n* tongues Mk 16:17
piece of a *n* garment upon an old Lk 5:36
then both the *n* maketh a rent Lk 5:36
of the *n* agreeth not with the old Lk 5:36
no man putteth *n* wine into old Lk 5:37
else the *n* wine will burst the Lk 5:37
But *n* wine must be put into Lk 5:38
wine must be put into *n* bottles Lk 5:38
old wine straightway desireth *n* Lk 5:39
This cup is the *n* testament in my Lk 22:20
A *n* commandment I give unto you, Jn 13:34
and in the garden a *n* sepulchre Jn 19:41
These men are full of *n* wine Acts 2:13
May we know what this *n* doctrine Acts 17:19
to tell, or to hear some *n* thing Acts 17:21
leaven, that ye may be a *n* lump 1Cor 5:7
This cup is the *n* testament in my 1Cor 11:25
able ministers of the *n* testament 2Cor 3:6
be in Christ, he is a *n* creature 2Cor 5:17
behold, all things are become *n* 2Cor 5:17
uncircumcision, but a *n* creature Gal 6:15
in himself of twain one *n* man Eph 2:15
And that ye put on the *n* man Eph 4:24
of an holyday, or of the *n* moon Col 2:16
And have put on the *n* man, which Col 3:10
when I will make a *n* covenant Heb 8:8
A *n* covenant, he hath made the Heb 8:13

the mediator of the *n* testament ... Heb 9:15
By a *n* and living way, which he ... Heb 10:20
the mediator of the *n* covenant ... Heb 12:24
his promise, look for *n* heavens ... 2Pet 3:13
a *n* earth, wherein dwelleth ... 2Pet 3:13
I write no *n* commandment unto you ... 1Jn 2:7
a *n* commandment I write unto you, ... 1Jn 2:8
I wrote a *n* commandment unto thee ... 2Jn 5
and in the stone a *n* name written ... Rev 2:17
which is *n* Jerusalem, which ... Rev 3:12
I will write upon him my *n* name ... Rev 3:12
And they sung a *n* song, saying, ... Rev 5:9
were a *n* song before the throne ... Rev 14:3
I saw a *n* heaven and a *n* earth ... Rev 21:1
*n* Jerusalem, coming down from God ... Rev 21:2
said, Behold, I make all things *n* ... Rev 21:5

**NEWBORN**
As *n* babes, desire the sincere ... 1Pet 2:2

**NEWLY**
not, to new gods that came *n* up ... Deut 32:17
they had but *n* set the watch ... Judg 7:19

**NEWNESS**
we also should walk in *n* of life ... Rom 6:4
we should serve in *n* of spirit ... Rom 7:6

**NEWS**
so is good *n* from a far country ... Prov 25:25

**NEXT**
at this set time in the *n* year ... Gen 17:21
his neighbour *n* unto his house ... Ex 12:4
those that do pitch *n* unto him ... Num 2:5
all that night, and all the *n* day ... Num 11:32
that is *n* to him of his family ... Num 27:11
which is *n* unto the slain man ... Deut 21:3
that are *n* unto the slain man, ... Deut 21:6
kin unto us, one of our *n* kinsmen ... Ruth 2:20
*n* unto him Abinadab, and the third ... 1Sa 17:13
Israel, and I shall be *n* unto thee ... 1Sa 23:17
unto the evening of the *n* day ... 1Sa 30:17
and I said unto her on the *n* day ... 2Kin 6:29
Joel the chief, and Shapham the *n* ... 1Chr 5:12
*n* to him Zechariah, Jeiel, and ... 1Chr 16:5
*n* to him was Jehohanan the ... 2Chr 17:15
*n* him was Amasiah the son of ... 2Chr 17:16
*n* him was Jehozabad, and with him . 2Chr 17:18
and Elkanah that was *n* to the king ... 2Chr 28:7
and Shimei his brother was the *n* ... 2Chr 31:12
*n* him were Eden ... 2Chr 31:15
*n* unto him builded the men of ... Neh 3:2
*n* to them builded Zaccur the son ... Neh 3:2
*n* unto them repaired Meremoth the ... Neh 3:4
*n* unto them repaired Meshullam ... Neh 3:4
*n* unto them repaired Zadok the ... Neh 3:4
*n* unto them the Tekoites repaired ... Neh 3:5
*n* unto them repaired Melatiah the ... Neh 3:7
*N* unto him repaired Uzziel the ... Neh 3:8
*N* unto him also repaired Hananiah ... Neh 3:8
*n* unto them repaired Rephaiah the ... Neh 3:9
*n* unto them repaired Jedaiah the ... Neh 3:10
*n* unto him repaired Hattush the ... Neh 3:10
*n* unto him repaired Shallum the ... Neh 3:12
*N* unto him repaired Hashabiah, ... Neh 3:17
*n* to him repaired Ezer the son of ... Neh 3:19
*n* to them was Hanan the son of ... Neh 13:13
the *n* unto him was Carshena, ... Est 1:14
the Jew was *n* unto king Ahasuerus ... Est 10:3
when the morning rose the *n* day ... Jonah 4:7
Now the *n* day, that followed the ... Mt 27:62
them, Let us go into the *n* towns ... Mk 1:38
came to pass, that on the *n* day ... Lk 9:37
The *n* day John seeth Jesus coming ... Jn 1:29
Again the *n* day after John stood, ... Jn 1:35
On the *n* day much people that ... Jn 12:12
put them in hold unto the *n* day ... Acts 4:3
the *n* day he shewed himself unto ... Acts 7:26
be preached to them the *n* sabbath ... Acts 13:42
the *n* sabbath day came almost the ... Acts 13:44
the *n* day he departed with ... Acts 14:20
and the *n* day to Neapolis ... Acts 16:11
came the *n* day over against Chios ... Acts 20:15
the *n* day we arrived at Samos, and ... Acts 20:15
the *n* day we came to Miletus ... Acts 20:15
the *n* day we that were of Paul's ... Acts 21:8
the *n* day purifying himself with ... Acts 21:26
the *n* day sitting on the judgment ... Acts 25:6
the *n* day we touched at Sidon ... Acts 27:3
the *n* day they lightened the ship ... Acts 27:18
we came the *n* day to Puteoli ... Acts 28:13

**NEZIAH** (*ne-zi'-ah*) *A family of exiles.*
The children of *N*, the children ... Ezr 2:54
The children of *N*, the children ... Neh 7:56

**NEZIB** (*ne'-zib*) *A city in Judah.*
And Jiphtah, and Ashnah, and *N* ... Josh 15:43

**NIBHAZ** (*nib'-haz*) *A god of the Avites.*
And the Avites made *N* and Tartak, .. 2Kin 17:31

**NIBSHAN** (*nib'-shan*) *A city in Judah.*
And *N*, and the city of Salt, and ... Josh 15:62

**NICANOR** (*ni-ca'-nor*) *A leader in the Jerusalem church.*
and Philip, and Prochorus, and *N* ... Acts 6:5

**NICODEMUS** (*nic-o-de'-mus*) *A Pharisee sympathetic to Jesus.*
a man of the Pharisees, named *N* ... Jn 3:1
*N* saith unto him, How can a man ... Jn 3:4
*N* answered and said unto him, How ... Jn 3:9
*N* saith unto them, (he that came ... Jn 7:50
And there came also *N*, which at ... Jn 19:39

**NICOLAITANES** (*nic-o-la'-i-tans*) *A group condemned in Revelation.*
thou hatest the deeds of the *N* ... Rev 2:6
that hold the doctrine of the *N* ... Rev 2:15

**NICOLAITANS** See NICOLAITANES.

**NICOLAS** (*nic'-o-las*) *A leader in the Jerusalem church.*
and *N* a proselyte of Antioch ... Acts 6:5

**NICOLAUS** See NICOLAS.

**NICOPOLIS** (*ni-cop'-o-lis*) *A city in Thrace.*
be diligent to come unto me to *N* ... Titus 3:12
the Cretians, from *N* of Macedonia ... Titus *s*

**NIGER** (*ni'-jur*) See SIMEON. *A Christian teacher and prophet at Antioch.*
and Simeon that was called *N* ... Acts 13:1

**NIGH**
the time drew *n* that Israel must ... Gen 47:29
And he said, Draw not *n* hither ... Ex 3:5
And when Pharaoh drew *n*, the ... Ex 14:10
but they shall not come *n* ... Ex 24:2
soon as he came *n* unto the camp ... Ex 32:19
and they were afraid to come *n* him ... Ex 34:30
all the children of Israel came *n* ... Ex 34:32
sanctified in them that come *n* me ... Lev 10:3
that is *n* unto him, which hath ... Lev 21:3
*n* to offer the offerings of the ... Lev 21:21
he shall not come *n* to offer the ... Lev 21:21
nor come *n* unto the altar, ... Lev 21:23
or any that is *n* of kin unto him ... Lev 25:49
cometh *n* shall be put to death ... Num 1:51
cometh *n* shall be put to death ... Num 3:10
cometh *n* shall be put to death ... Num 3:38
Israel come *n* unto the sanctuary ... Num 8:19
only they shall not come *n* the ... Num 18:3
shall not come *n* unto you ... Num 18:4
cometh *n* shall be put to death ... Num 18:7
come *n* the tabernacle of the ... Num 18:22
I shall behold him, but not *n* ... Num 24:17
unto all the places *n* thereunto ... Deut 1:7
when thou comest *n* over against ... Deut 2:19
who hath God so *n* unto them ... Deut 4:7
*n* unto thee, or far off from thee ... Deut 13:7
ye are come *n* unto the battle ... Deut 20:2
When thou comest *n* unto a city to .. Deut 20:10
if thy brother be not *n* unto thee ... Deut 22:2
But the word is very *n* unto thee ... Deut 30:14
were with him, went up, and drew *n* ... Josh 8:11
drew *n* to meet David, that David ... 1Sa 17:48
And Joab drew *n*, and the people ... 2Sa 10:13
Wherefore approached ye so *n* unto ... 2Sa 11:20
why went ye *n* the wall ... 2Sa 11:21
that when any man came *n* to him ... 2Sa 15:5
David drew *n* that he should die ... 1Kin 2:1
be *n* unto the LORD our God day and .. 1Kin 8:59
Moreover they that were *n* them ... 1Chr 12:40
*n* before the Syrians unto the ... 1Chr 19:14
of the king Ahasuerus, both *n* ... Est 9:20
they shall not come *n* unto him ... Ps 32:6
The LORD is *n* unto them that are ... Ps 34:18
Draw *n* unto my soul, and redeem it ... Ps 69:18
my steps had well *n* slipped ... Ps 73:2
salvation is *n* them that fear him ... Ps 85:9
my life draweth *n* unto the grave ... Ps 88:3
but it shall not come *n* thee ... Ps 91:7
any plague come *n* thy dwelling ... Ps 91:10
They draw *n* that follow after ... Ps 119:150
The LORD is *n* unto all them that ... Ps 145:18
come not *n* the door of her house ... Prov 5:8
come not, nor the years draw *n* ... Eccl 12:1
of the Holy One of Israel draw *n* ... Is 5:19
LORD cometh, for it is *n* at hand ... Joel 2:1
This people draweth *n* unto me ... Mt 15:8
came *n* unto the sea of Galilee ... Mt 15:29
when they drew *n* unto Jerusalem ... Mt 21:1
leaves, ye know that summer is *n* ... Mt 24:32
not come *n* unto him for the press ... Mk 2:4
Now there was there *n* unto the ... Mk 5:11
and he was *n* unto the sea ... Mk 5:21
And when they came *n* to Jerusalem ... Mk 11:1
come to pass, know that it is *n* ... Mk 13:29
Now when he came *n* to the gate of ... Lk 7:12
kingdom of God is come *n* unto you ... Lk 10:9
kingdom of God is come *n* unto you ... Lk 10:11
drew *n* to the house, he heard ... Lk 15:25
as he was come *n* unto Jericho ... Lk 18:35
because he was *n* to Jerusalem ... Lk 19:11
when he was come *n* to Bethphage ... Lk 19:29
And when he was come *n*, even now ... Lk 19:37
that the desolation thereof is *n* ... Lk 21:20
for your redemption draweth *n* ... Lk 21:28
that summer is now *n* at hand ... Lk 21:30
the kingdom of God is *n* at hand ... Lk 21:31
feast of unleavened bread drew *n* ... Lk 22:1
they drew *n* unto the village, ... Lk 24:28
a feast of the Jews, was *n* ... Jn 6:4
sea, and drawing *n* unto the ship ... Jn 6:19
*n* unto the place where they did ... Jn 6:23
Now Bethany was *n* unto Jerusalem ... Jn 11:18
the Jews' passover was *n* at hand ... Jn 11:55
was crucified was *n* to the city ... Jn 19:20
for the sepulchre was *n* at hand ... Jn 19:42
the time of the promise drew *n* ... Acts 7:17
forasmuch as Lydda was *n* to Joppa ... Acts 9:38
drew *n* unto the city, Peter went ... Acts 10:9
was come *n* unto Damascus about ... Acts 22:6
*n* whereunto was the city of Lasea ... Acts 27:8
The word is *n* thee, even in thy ... Rom 10:8
are made *n* by the blood of Christ ... Eph 2:13
afar off, and to them that were *n* ... Eph 2:17
indeed he was sick *n* unto death ... Phil 2:27
of Christ he was *n* unto death ... Phil 2:30
is rejected, and is *n* unto cursing ... Heb 6:8
by the which we draw *n* unto God ... Heb 7:19
Draw *n* to God, and he will draw ... Jas 4:8
to God, and he will draw *n* to you ... Jas 4:8
the coming of the Lord draweth *n* ... Jas 5:8

**NIGHT**
Day, and the darkness he called *N* ... Gen 1:5
to divide the day from the *n* ... Gen 1:14
and the lesser light to rule the *n* ... Gen 1:16
rule over the day and over the *n* ... Gen 1:18
and day and *n* shall not cease ... Gen 8:22
them, he and his servants, by *n* ... Gen 14:15
servant's house, and tarry all *n* ... Gen 19:2
we will abide in the street all *n* ... Gen 19:2
men which came in to thee this *n* ... Gen 19:5
their father drink wine that *n* ... Gen 19:33
make him drink wine this *n* also ... Gen 19:34
father drink wine that *n* also ... Gen 19:35
came to Abimelech in a dream by *n* ... Gen 20:3
were with him, and tarried all *n* ... Gen 24:54
LORD appeared unto him the same *n* .. Gen 26:24
place, and tarried there all *n* ... Gen 28:11
thee to *n* for thy son's mandrakes ... Gen 30:15
And he lay with her that *n* ... Gen 30:16
Laban the Syrian in a dream by *n* ... Gen 31:24
stolen by day, or stolen by *n* ... Gen 31:39
consumed me, and the frost by *n* ... Gen 31:40
tarried all *n* in the mount ... Gen 31:54
And he lodged there that same *n* ... Gen 32:13
lodged that *n* in the company ... Gen 32:21
And he rose up that *n*, and took his ... Gen 32:22
them, each man his dream in one *n* ... Gen 40:5
And we dreamed a dream in one *n* ... Gen 41:11
Israel in the visions of the *n* ... Gen 46:2
at *n* he shall divide the spoil ... Gen 49:27
land all that day, and all that *n* ... Ex 10:13
shall eat the flesh in that *n* ... Ex 12:8
through the land of Egypt this *n* ... Ex 12:12
And Pharaoh rose up in the *n* ... Ex 12:30
he called for Moses and Aaron by *n* ... Ex 12:31
It is a *n* to be much observed ... Ex 12:42
this is that *n* of the LORD to be ... Ex 12:42
by *n* in a pillar of fire, to give ... Ex 13:21
to go by day and *n* ... Ex 13:21
day, nor the pillar of fire by *n* ... Ex 13:22
but it gave light by *n* to these ... Ex 14:20
came not near the other all the *n* ... Ex 14:20
by a strong east wind all that *n* ... Ex 14:21
by day, and fire was on it by *n* ... Ex 40:38
the altar all *n* unto the morning ... Lev 6:9
the morning, and half thereof at *n* ... Lev 6:20
*n* seven days, and keep the charge ... Lev 8:35
the *n* hawk, and the cuckow, and the ... Lev 11:16
with thee all *n* until the morning ... Lev 19:13
and the appearance of fire by *n* ... Num 9:16
by *n* that the cloud was taken up ... Num 9:21
dew fell upon the camp in the *n* ... Num 11:9
up all that day, and all that *n* ... Num 11:32
and the people wept that *n* ... Num 14:1
and in a pillar of fire by *n* ... Num 14:14
said unto them, Lodge here this *n* ... Num 22:8
you, tarry ye also here this *n* ... Num 22:19
And God came unto Balaam at *n* ... Num 22:20
pitch your tents in, in fire by *n* ... Deut 1:33
*n* hawk, and the cuckow ... Deut 14:15
thee forth out of Egypt by *n* ... Deut 16:1
remain all *n* until the morning ... Deut 16:4
not remain all *n* upon the tree ... Deut 21:23
that chanceth him by *n*, then ... Deut 23:10
and thou shalt fear day and *n* ... Deut 28:66
shalt meditate therein day and *n* ... Josh 1:8
there came men in hither to *n* of ... Josh 2:2
where ye shall lodge this *n* ... Josh 4:3
of valour, and sent them away by *n* ... Josh 8:3
lodged that *n* among the people ... Josh 8:9
Joshua went that *n* into the midst ... Josh 8:13
and went up from Gilgal all *n* ... Josh 10:9
And it came to pass the same *n* ... Judg 6:25
do it by day, that he did it by *n* ... Judg 6:27
And God did so that *n* ... Judg 6:40
And it came to pass the same *n* ... Judg 7:9
Now therefore up by *n*, thou and ... Judg 9:32
people that were with him, by *n* ... Judg 9:34
laid wait for him all *n* in the ... Judg 16:2
the city, and were quiet all the *n* ... Judg 16:2
I pray thee, and tarry all *n* ... Judg 19:6
evening, I pray you tarry all *n* ... Judg 19:9
the man would not tarry that *n* ... Judg 19:10
of these places to lodge all *n* ... Judg 19:13
her all the *n* until the morning ... Judg 19:25
house round about upon me by *n* ... Judg 20:5
should have an husband also to *n* ... Ruth 1:12
barley to *n* in the threshingfloor ... Ruth 3:2
Tarry this *n*, and it shall be in ... Ruth 3:13
every man his ox with him that *n* ... 1Sa 14:34
down after the Philistines by *n* ... 1Sa 14:36
and he cried unto the LORD all *n* ... 1Sa 15:11
the LORD hath said to me this *n* ... 1Sa 15:16
and David fled, and escaped that *n* ... 1Sa 19:10
saying, If thou save not thy to *n* ... 1Sa 19:11
naked all that day and all that *n* ... 1Sa 19:24
were a wall unto us both by *n* ... 1Sa 25:16
Abishai came to the people by *n* ... 1Sa 26:7

and they came to the woman by *n* 1Sa 28:8
bread all the day, nor all the *n* 1Sa 28:20
they rose up, and went away that *n* 1Sa 28:25
valiant men arose, and went all *n* 1Sa 31:12
all that *n* through the plain 2Sa 2:29
And Joab and his men went all *n* 2Sa 2:32
them away through the plain all *n* 2Sa 4:7
And it came to pass that *n* 2Sa 7:4
in, and lay all *n* upon the earth 2Sa 12:16
and pursue after David this *n* 2Sa 17:1
Lodge not this *n* in the plains of 2Sa 17:16
not tarry one with thee this *n* 2Sa 19:7
nor the beasts of the field by *n* 2Sa 21:10
to Solomon in a dream by *n* 1Kin 3:5
this woman's child died in the *n* 1Kin 3:19
may be open toward this house *n* 1Kin 8:29
unto the LORD our God day and *n* 1Kin 8:59
and they came by *n*, and compassed 2Kin 6:14
And the king arose in the *n* 2Kin 7:12
and he rose by *n*, and smote the 2Kin 8:21
And it came to pass that *n* 2Kin 19:35
all the men of war fled by *n* by 2Kin 25:4
employed in that work day and *n* 1Chr 9:33
And it came to pass the same *n* 1Chr 17:3
In that *n* did God appear unto 2Chr 1:7
be open upon this house day and *n* 2Chr 6:20
the LORD appeared to Solomon by *n* 2Chr 7:12
and he rose up by *n*, and smote the 2Chr 21:9
offerings and the fat until *n* 2Chr 35:14
I pray before thee now, day and *n* Neh 1:6
And I arose in the *n*, I and some Neh 2:12
I went out by *n* by the gate of Neh 2:13
went I up in the *n* by the brook Neh 2:15
set a watch against them day and *n* Neh 4:9
that in the *n* they may be a guard Neh 4:22
in the *n* will they come to slay Neh 6:10
in the *n* by a pillar of fire, to Neh 9:12
neither the pillar of fire by *n* Neh 9:19
nor drink three days, *n* or day Est 4:16
On that *n* could not the king Est 6:1
the *n* in which it was said, There Job 3:3
As for that *n*, let darkness seize Job 3:6
Lo, let that *n* be solitary Job 3:7
from the visions of the *n* Job 4:13
grope in the noonday as in the *n* Job 5:14
shall I arise, and the *n* be gone Job 7:4
They change the *n* into day Job 17:12
chased away as a vision of the *n* Job 20:8
needy, and in the *n* is as a thief Job 24:14
until the day and *n* come to an end Job 26:10
stealeth him away in the *n* Job 27:20
the dew lay all *n* upon my branch Job 29:19
are pierced in me in the *n* season Job 30:17
In a dream, in a vision of the *n* Job 33:15
and he overturneth them in the *n* Job 34:25
maker, who giveth songs in the *n* Job 35:10
Desire not the *n*, when people are Job 36:20
his law doth he meditate day and *n* Ps 1:2
all the *n* make I my bed to swim Ps 6:6
also instruct me in the *n* seasons Ps 16:7
thou hast visited me in the *n* Ps 17:3
*n* unto *n* sheweth knowledge Ps 19:2
and in the *n* season, and am not Ps 22:2
weeping may endure for a *n* Ps 30:5
*n* thy hand was heavy upon me Ps 32:4
tears have been my meat day and *n* Ps 42:3
in the *n* his song shall be with Ps 42:8
*n* they go about it upon the walls Ps 55:10
meditate on thee in the *n* watches Ps 63:6
day is thine, the *n* also is thine Ps 74:16
my sore ran in the *n*, and ceased Ps 77:2
to remembrance my song in the *n* Ps 77:6
all the *n* with a light of fire Ps 78:14
I have cried day and *n* before thee Ps 88:1
is past, and as a watch in the *n* Ps 90:4
not be afraid for the terror by *n* Ps 91:5
and thy faithfulness every *n* Ps 92:2
Thou makest darkness, and it is *n* Ps 104:20
and fire to give light in the *n* Ps 105:39
thy name, O LORD, in the *n* Ps 119:55
Mine eyes prevent the *n* watches Ps 119:148
thee by day, nor the moon by *n* Ps 121:6
which by *n* stand in the house of Ps 134:1
The moon and stars to rule by *n* Ps 136:9
even the *n* shall be light about Ps 139:11
but the *n* shineth as the day Ps 139:12
evening, in the black and dark *n* Prov 7:9
She riseth also while it is yet *n* Prov 31:15
her candle goeth not out by *n* Prov 31:18
heart taketh not rest in the *n* Eccl 2:23
nor *n* seeth sleep with his eyes Eccl 8:16
he shall lie all *n* betwixt my Song 1:13
By *n* on my bed I sought him whom Song 3:1
thigh because of fear in the *n* Song 3:8
my locks with the drops of the *n* Song 5:2
shining of a flaming fire by *n* Is 4:5
that continue until *n*, till wine Is 5:11
Because in the *n* Ar of Moab is Is 15:1
because in the *n* Kir of Moab is Is 15:1
make thy shadow as the *n* in the Is 16:3
the *n* of my pleasure hath he Is 21:4
of Seir, Watchman, what of the *n* Is 21:11
Watchman, what of the *n* Is 21:11
The morning cometh, and also the *n* Is 21:12
soul have I desired thee in the *n* Is 26:9
any hurt it, I will keep it *n* Is 27:3
it pass over, by day and by *n* Is 28:19
shall be as a dream of a *n* vision Is 29:7
as in the *n* when a holy solemnity Is 30:29
shall not be quenched *n* nor day Is 34:10
from day even to *n* wilt thou make Is 38:12
from day even to *n* wilt thou make Is 38:13
we stumble at noonday as in the *n* Is 59:10
they shall not be shut day nor *n* Is 60:11
never hold their peace day nor *n* Is 62:6
Arise, and let us go by *n*, and let Jer 6:5
*n* for the slain of the daughter Jer 9:1
turneth aside to tarry for a *n* Jer 14:8
mine eyes run down with tears *n* Jer 14:17
ye serve other gods day and *n* Jer 16:13
and of the stars for a light by *n* Jer 31:35
the day, and my covenant of the *n* Jer 33:20
not be day and *n* in their season Jer 33:20
my covenant be not with day and *n* Jer 33:25
heat, and in the *n* to the frost Jer 36:30
went forth out of the city by *n* Jer 39:4
if thieves by *n*, they will Jer 49:9
went forth out of the city by *n* Jer 52:7
She weepeth sore in the *n* Lam 1:2
run down like a river day and *n* Lam 2:18
Arise, cry out in the *n* Lam 2:19
unto Daniel in a *n* vision Dan 2:19
In that *n* was Belshazzar the king Dan 5:30
palace, and passed the *n* fasting Dan 6:18
and said, I saw in my vision by *n* Dan 7:2
After this I saw in the *n* visions Dan 7:7
I saw in the *n* visions, and, Dan 7:13
shall fall with thee in the *n* Hos 4:5
their baker sleepeth all the *n* Hos 7:6
lie all *n* in sackcloth, ye Joel 1:13
and maketh the day dark with *n* Amos 5:8
came to thee, if robbers by *n* Obad 5
up in a *n*, and perished in a *n* Jonah 4:10
Therefore *n* shall be unto you, Mic 3:6
I saw by *n*, and behold a man Zec 1:8
known to the LORD, not day, nor *n* Zec 14:7
young child and his mother by *n* Mt 2:14
of the *n* Jesus went unto them Mt 14:25
be offended because of me this *n* Mt 26:31
I say unto thee, That this *n* Mt 26:34
day, lest his disciples come by *n* Mt 27:64
Say ye, His disciples came by *n* Mt 28:13
And should sleep, and rise *n* Mk 4:27
And always, *n* and day, he was in Mk 5:5
of the *n* he cometh unto them Mk 6:48
be offended because of me this *n* Mk 14:27
That this day, even in this *n* Mk 14:30
watch over their flock by *n* Lk 2:8
God with fastings and prayers *n* Lk 2:37
Master, we have toiled all the *n* Lk 5:5
continued all *n* in prayer to God Lk 6:12
this *n* thy soul shall be required Lk 12:20
in that *n* there shall be two men Lk 17:34
*n* unto him, though he bear long Lk 18:7
at *n* he went out, and abode in the Lk 21:37
The same came to Jesus by *n* Jn 3:2
them, (he that came to Jesus by *n* Jn 7:50
the *n* cometh, when no man can Jn 9:4
But if a man walk in the *n* Jn 11:10
and it was *n* Jn 13:30
at the first came to Jesus by *n* Jn 19:39
that *n* they caught nothing Jn 21:3
Lord by *n* opened the prison doors Acts 5:19
the gates day and *n* to kill him Acts 9:24
Then the disciples took him by *n* Acts 9:25
the same *n* Peter was sleeping Acts 12:6
vision appeared to Paul in the *n* Acts 16:9
took them the same hour of the *n* Acts 16:33
Paul and Silas by *n* unto Berea Acts 17:10
Lord to Paul in the *n* by a vision Acts 18:9
I ceased not to warn every one *n* Acts 20:31
the *n* following the Lord stood by Acts 23:11
at the third hour of the *n* Acts 23:23
and brought him by *n* to Antipatris Acts 23:31
instantly serving God day and *n* Acts 26:7
by me this *n* the angel of God Acts 27:23
when the fourteenth *n* was come Acts 27:27
The *n* is far spent, the day is at Rom 13:12
That the Lord Jesus the same *n* in 1Cor 11:23
thrice I suffered shipwreck, a *n* 2Cor 11:25
for labouring *n* and day, because 1Th 2:9
*N* and day praying exceedingly that 1Th 3:10
so cometh as a thief in the *n* 1Th 5:2
we are not of the *n*, nor of 1Th 5:5
they that sleep sleep in the *n* 1Th 5:7
be drunken are drunken in the *n* 1Th 5:7
wrought with labour and travail *n* 2Th 3:8
in supplications and prayers *n* 1Ti 5:5
of thee in my prayers *n* and day 2Ti 1:3
will come as a thief in the *n* 2Pet 3:10
and they rest not day and *n* Rev 4:8
serve him day and *n* in his temple Rev 7:15
part of it, and the *n* likewise Rev 8:12
them before our God day and *n* Rev 12:10
and they have no rest day nor *n* Rev 14:11
day and *n* for ever and ever Rev 20:10
for there shall be no *n* there Rev 21:25
And there shall be no *n* there Rev 22:5

**NIGHTS**

the earth forty days and forty *n* Gen 7:4
the earth forty days and forty *n* Gen 7:12
the mount forty days and forty *n* Ex 24:18
the LORD forty days and forty *n* Ex 34:28
the mount forty days and forty *n* Deut 9:9
the end of forty days and forty *n* Deut 9:11
the first, forty days and forty *n* Deut 9:18
the LORD forty days and forty *n* Deut 9:25
first time, forty days and forty *n* Deut 10:10
any water, three days and three *n* 1Sa 30:12
forty *n* unto Horeb the mount of 1Kin 19:8
the ground seven days and seven *n* Job 2:13
wearisome *n* are appointed to me Job 7:3
and I am set in my ward whole *n* Is 21:8
of the fish three days and three *n* Jonah 1:17
had fasted forty days and forty *n* Mt 4:2
three *n* in the whale's belly Mt 12:40
three *n* in the heart of the earth Mt 12:40

**NILE** See BROOKS, FLOOD, RIVER.

**NIMRAH** (*nim'-rah*) See BETH-NIMRAH. *A city in Gad.*
Ataroth, and Dibon, and Jazer, and *N* Num 32:3

**NIMRIM** (*nim'-rim*) *A body of water on the border of Gad.*
the waters of *N* shall be desolate Is 15:6
also of *N* shall be desolate Jer 48:34

**NIMROD** (*nim'-rod*) *Son of Cush.*
And Cush begat *N* Gen 10:8
Even as *N* the mighty hunter Gen 10:9
And Cush begat *N* 1Chr 1:10
the land of *N* in the entrances Mic 5:6

**NIMSHI** (*nim'-shi*) *Grandfather of Jehu.*
Jehu the son of *N* shalt thou 1Kin 19:16
son of Jehoshaphat the son of *N* 2Kin 9:2
son of *N* conspired against Joram 2Kin 9:14
the driving of Jehu the son of *N* 2Kin 9:20
Jehoram against Jehu the son of *N* 2Chr 22:7

**NINE**

that Adam lived were *n* hundred Gen 5:5
the days of Seth were *n* hundred Gen 5:8
the days of Enos were *n* hundred Gen 5:11
the days of Cainan were *n* hundred Gen 5:14
of Jared were *n* hundred sixty Gen 5:20
*n* hundred sixty and *n* years Gen 5:27
the days of Noah were *n* hundred Gen 9:29
*n* years, and begat sons and Gen 11:19
And Nahor lived *n* and twenty years, Gen 11:24
Abram was ninety years old and *n* Gen 17:1
Abraham was ninety years old and *n*. Gen 17:24
*n* talents, and seven hundred and Ex 38:24
be unto thee forty and *n* years Lev 25:8
*n* thousand and three hundred Num 1:23
*n* thousand and three hundred Num 2:13
And on the fifth day *n* bullocks Num 29:26
to give unto the *n* tribes Num 34:13
*n* cubits was the length thereof, Deut 3:11
an inheritance unto the *n* tribes Josh 13:7
hand of Moses, for the *n* tribes Josh 14:2
all the cities are twenty and *n* Josh 15:32
*n* cities with their villages Josh 15:44
*n* cities with their villages Josh 15:54
*n* cities out of those two tribes Josh 21:16
for he had *n* hundred chariots of Judg 4:3
even *n* hundred chariots of iron, Judg 4:13
Jerusalem at the end of *n* months 2Sa 24:8
twenty and *n* years in Jerusalem 2Kin 14:2
of Jabesh began to reign in the *n* 2Kin 15:13
In the *n* and thirtieth year of 2Kin 15:17
in Samaria over Israel *n* years 2Kin 17:1
twenty and *n* years in Jerusalem 2Kin 18:2
and Eliada, and Eliphelet, *n* 1Chr 3:8
*n* hundred and fifty and six 1Chr 9:9
twenty and *n* years in Jerusalem 2Chr 25:1
twenty years old, and he reigned *n* 2Chr 29:1
a thousand chargers of silver, *n* Ezr 1:9
of Zattu, *n* hundred forty and five Ezr 2:8
*n* hundred seventy and three Ezr 2:36
in all an hundred thirty and *n* Ezr 2:42
Senaah, three thousand *n* hundred Neh 7:38
*n* hundred seventy and three Neh 7:39
*n* parts to dwell in other cities Neh 11:1
*n* hundred twenty and eight Neh 11:8
doth he not leave the ninety and *n* Mt 18:12
ninety and *n* which went not astray Mt 18:13
*n* in the wilderness, and go after Lk 15:4
*n* just persons, which need no Lk 15:7
but where are the *n* Lk 17:17

**NINETEEN**

*n* years, and begat sons and Gen 11:25
*n* cities with their villages Josh 19:38
lacked of David's servants *n* men 2Sa 2:30

**NINETEENTH**

which is the *n* year of king 2Kin 25:8
The *n* to Pethahiah, the twentieth 1Chr 24:16
The *n* to Mallothi, he, his sons, 1Chr 25:26
month, which was the *n* year of Jer 52:12

**NINETY**

And Enos lived *n* years, and begat Gen 5:9
Mahalaleel were eight hundred *n* Gen 5:17
he begat Noah five hundred *n* Gen 5:30
And when Abram was *n* years old Gen 17:1
that is *n* years old, bear Gen 17:17
And Abraham was *n* years old Gen 17:24
Now Eli was *n* and eight years old 1Sa 4:15
their brethren, six hundred and *n* 1Chr 9:6
children of Ater of Hezekiah, *n* Ezr 2:16
The children of Gibbar, *n* Ezr 2:20
servants, were three hundred *n* Ezr 2:58
twelve bullocks for all Israel, *n* Ezr 8:35
children of Ater of Hezekiah, *n* Neh 7:21
The children of Gibeon, *n* Neh 7:25
servants, were three hundred *n* Neh 7:60
And there were *n* and six Jer 52:23
the days, three hundred and *n* days Eze 4:5
*n* days shalt thou eat thereof Eze 4:9
and the length thereof *n* cubits Eze 41:12

a thousand two hundred and *n* days.. Dan 12:11
astray, doth he not leave the *n* ........ Mt 18:12
more of that sheep, than of the *n*........ Mt 18:13
one of them, doth not leave the *n*........ Lk 15:4
that repenteth, more than over *n*........ Lk 15:7

**NINEVE** (*nen'-e-ve*) See NINEVEH, NINEVITES. *Same as Nineveh.*
The men of *N* shall rise up in the .......... Lk 11:32

**NINEVEH** (*nin'-e-veh*) See NINEVE. *Capital of Assyria.*
went forth Asshur, and builded *N*....... Gen 10:11
And Resen between *N* and Calah........ Gen 10:12
went and returned, and dwelt at *N*.... 2Kin 19:36
went and returned, and dwelt at *N*........ Is 37:37
Arise, go to *N*, that great city,............ Jonah 1:2
Arise, go unto *N*, that great city............ Jonah 3:2
So Jonah arose, and went unto *N*......... Jonah 3:3
Now *N* was an exceeding great city.... Jonah 3:3
days, and *N* shall be overthrown.......... Jonah 3:4
So the people of *N* believed God........... Jonah 3:5
For word came unto the king of *N*...... Jonah 3:6
published through *N* by the decree..... Jonah 3:7
And should not I spare *N*, that........... Jonah 4:11
The burden of *N*................................... Nah 1:1
But *N* is of old like a pool of................ Nah 2:8
thee, and say, *N* is laid waste............... Nah 3:7
will make *N* a desolation, and dry....... Zeph 2:13
The men of *N* shall rise in.................... Mt 12:41

**NINEVITES** (*nin'-e-vites*) *Inhabitants of Nineveh.*
as Jonas was a sign unto the *N*............. Lk 11:30

**NINTH**
in the *n* day of the month at even....... Lev 23:32
yet of old fruit until the *n* year.......... Lev 25:22
On the *n* day Abidan the son of........... Num 7:60
In the *n* year of Hoshea the king......... 2Kin 17:6
that is the *n* year of Hoshea king....... 2Kin 18:10
pass in the *n* year of his reign............. 2Kin 25:1
on the *n* day of the fourth month......... 2Kin 25:3
Johanan the eighth, Elzabad the *n*.... 1Chr 12:12
The *n* to Jeshua, the tenth to ............. 1Chr 24:11
The *n* to Mattaniah, he, his sons,....... 1Chr 25:16
The *n* captain for the *n* month .......... 1Chr 27:12
for the *n* month was Abiezer the....... 1Chr 27:12
*n* year of his reign was diseased......... 2Chr 16:12
It was the *n* month, on the.................... Ezr 10:9
king of Judah, in the *n* month ............. Jer 36:9
in the winterhouse in the *n* month....... Jer 36:22
In the *n* year of Zedekiah king of......... Jer 39:1
the *n* day of the month, the city ........... Jer 39:2
pass in the *n* year of his reign............... Jer 52:4
in the *n* day of the month, the............... Jer 52:6
Again in the *n* year, in the tenth.......... Eze 24:1
and twentieth day of the *n* month ........ Hag 2:10
and twentieth day of the *n* month ........ Hag 2:18
in the fourth day of the *n* month............ Zec 7:1
sixth and *n* hour, and did likewise.......... Mt 20:5
over all the land unto the *n* hour .......... Mt 27:45
about the *n* hour Jesus cried with........... Mt 27:46
the whole land until the *n* hour ........... Mk 15:33
at the *n* hour Jesus cried with a ........... Mk 15:34
all the earth until the *n* hour ............... Lk 23:44
hour of prayer, being the *n* hour ......... Acts 3:1
*n* hour of the day an angel of God....... Acts 10:3
at the *n* hour I prayed in my............... Acts 10:30
the *n*, a topaz........................................ Rev 21:20

**NISAN** (*ni'-san*) See ABIB. *First month of the Hebrew year.*
And it came to pass in the month *N*...... Neh 2:1
first month, that is, the month *N*............ Est 3:7

**NISROCH** (*nis'-rok*) *An Assyrian god.*
in the house of *N* his god.................... 2Kin 19:37
in the house of *N* his god........................ Is 37:38

**NITRE**
weather, and as vinegar upon *n* ......... Prov 25:20
For though thou wash thee with *n*......... Jer 2:22

**NO** See PREFACE.

**NOADIAH** (*no-a-di'-ah*)
*1. Son of Binnui.*
*N* the son of Binnui, Levites .................. Ezr 8:33
*2. An opponent of Nehemiah.*
works, and on the prophetess *N*............ Neh 6:14

**NOAH** (*no'-ah*) See NOAH's, NOE.
*1. Son of Lamech; built the ark.*
And he called his name *N*, saying,......... Gen 5:29
he begat *N* five hundred ninety............ Gen 5:30
*N* was five hundred years old................ Gen 5:32
*N* begat Shem, Ham, and Japheth.......... Gen 5:32
But *N* found grace in the eyes of ............ Gen 6:8
These are the generations of *N*.............. Gen 6:9
*N* was a just man and perfect in ............ Gen 6:9
generations, and *N* walked with God..... Gen 6:9
*N* begat three sons, Shem, Ham, and ... Gen 6:10
And God said unto *N*, The end of .......... Gen 6:13
Thus did *N*............................................. Gen 6:22
And the LORD said unto *N*, Come .......... Gen 7:1
*N* did according unto all that the............ Gen 7:5
*N* was six hundred years old when ........ Gen 7:6
*N* went in, and his sons, and his............ Gen 7:7
two unto *N* into the ark, the male ........... Gen 7:9
female, as God had commanded *N*.......... Gen 7:9
In the selfsame day entered *N*.............. Gen 7:13
and Ham, and Japheth, the sons of *N*.. Gen 7:13
they went in unto *N* into the ark ........... Gen 7:15
*N* only remained alive, and they............ Gen 7:23
And God remembered *N*, and every ....... Gen 8:1
that *N* opened the window of the .......... Gen 8:6
so *N* knew that the waters were ........... Gen 8:11
*N* removed the covering of the ark......... Gen 8:13
And God spake unto *N*, saying,.............. Gen 8:15
*N* went forth, and his sons, and his...... Gen 8:18
*N* builded an altar unto the LORD........... Gen 8:20
And God blessed *N* and his sons, and..... Gen 9:1
And God spake unto *N*, and to his......... Gen 9:8
And God said unto *N*, This is the .......... Gen 9:17
And the sons of *N*, that went forth....... Gen 9:18
These are the three sons of *N*.............. Gen 9:19
*N* began to be an husbandman, and..... Gen 9:20
*N* awoke from his wine, and knew ........ Gen 9:24
*N* lived after the flood three .................. Gen 9:28
all the days of *N* were nine.................... Gen 9:29
the generations of the sons of *N*........... Gen 10:1
are the families of the sons of *N*.......... Gen 10:32
*N*, Shem, Ham, and Japheth..................... 1Chr 1:4
is as the waters of *N* unto me ................ Is 54:9
of *N* should no more go over the............. Is 54:9
Though these three men, *N*.................. Eze 14:14
Though *N*, Daniel, and Job, were in..... Eze 14:20
By faith *N*, being warned of God........... Heb 11:7
of God waited in the days of *N* ............ 1Pet 3:20
but saved *N* the eighth person, a........... 2Pet 2:5
*2. A daughter of Zelophehad.*
of Zelophehad were Mahlah, and *N*.. Num 26:33
Mahlah, *N*, and Hoglah, and Milcah,.... Num 27:1
and Hoglah, and Milcah, and *N*.......... Num 36:11
of his daughters, Mahlah, and *N*........... Josh 17:3

**NOAH'S** (*no'-ahz*) *Refers to Noah 1.*
the six hundredth year of *N* life............. Gen 7:11
*N* wife, and the three wives of his ........ Gen 7:13

**NO-AMON** See No.

**NOB** (*nob*) *A Levitical city in Benjamin.*
Then came David to *N* to Ahimelech.... 1Sa 21:1
saw the son of Jesse coming to *N*......... 1Sa 22:9
house, the priests that were in *N* ......... 1Sa 22:11
And *N*, the city of the priests,.............. 1Sa 22:19
And at Anathoth, *N*, Ananiah,............. Neh 11:32
yet shall he remain at *N* that day........... Is 10:32

**NOBAH** (*no'-bah*) See KENAH, NOPHAH.
*1. A Manassite who captured an Amorite city.*
*N* went and took Kenath, and the..... Num 32:42
villages thereof, and called it *N*.......... Num 32:42
*2. A city in the Trachonitis.*
dwelt in tents on the east of *N*............. Judg 8:11

**NOBLE**
*n* Asnapper brought over, and set .......... Ezr 4:10
one of the king's most *n* princes .............. Est 6:9
Yet I had planted thee a *n* vine............... Jer 2:21
These were more *n* than those in....... Acts 17:11
places, most *n* Felix, with all ............... Acts 24:3
said, I am not mad, most *n* Festus..... Acts 26:25
not many mighty, not many *n*.............. 1Cor 1:26

**NOBLEMAN**
A certain *n* went into a far..................... Lk 19:12
And there was a certain *n*, whose.......... Jn 4:46
The *n* saith unto him, Sir, come.............. Jn 4:49

**NOBLES**
upon the *n* of the children of................ Ex 24:11
the *n* of the people digged it, by ........ Num 21:18
over the *n* among the people................. Judg 5:13
to the *n* that were in his city,............... 1Kin 21:8
the *n* who were the inhabitants in...... 1Kin 21:11
captains of hundreds, and the *n*......... 2Chr 23:20
nor to the priests, nor to the *n*............... Neh 2:16
but their *n* put not their necks ................ Neh 3:5
and rose up, and said unto the *n*........... Neh 4:14
And I said unto the *n*, and to the........... Neh 4:19
with myself, and I rebuked the *n*............ Neh 5:7
Moreover in those days the *n* of............ Neh 6:17
heart to gather together the *n* ................ Neh 7:5
clave to their brethren, their *n*............ Neh 10:29
I contended with the *n* of Judah ......... Neh 13:17
power of Persia and Media, the *n* ........... Est 1:3
The *n* held their peace, and their.......... Job 29:10
Make their *n* like Oreb, and like ............ Ps 83:11
their *n* with fetters of iron.................... Ps 149:8
By me princes rule, and *n*, even............ Prov 8:16
when thy king is the son of *n*............... Eccl 10:17
may go into the gates of the *n*................. Is 13:2
They shall call the *n* thereof to.............. Is 34:12
and have brought down all their *n*......... Is 43:14
their *n* have sent their little ................... Jer 14:3
all the *n* of Judah and Jerusalem.......... Jer 27:20
their *n* shall be of themselves,.............. Jer 30:21
Babylon slew all the *n* of Judah............ Jer 39:6
the decree of the king and his *n* .......... Jonah 3:7
thy *n* shall dwell in the dust................... Nah 3:18

**NOD** (*nod*) *A land east of Eden.*
LORD, and dwelt in the land of *N*.......... Gen 4:16

**NODAB** (*no'-dab*) *Name of tribe east of the Jordan.*
with Jetur, and Nephish, and *N*......... 1Chr 5:19

**NOE** (*no'-e*) See NOAH. *Greek form of Noah.*
But as the days of *N* were...................... Mt 24:37
until the day that *N* entered into........... Mt 24:38
of Sem, which was the son of *N*.............. Lk 3:36
And as it was in the days of *N*.............. Lk 17:26
until the day that *N* entered into........... Lk 17:27

**NOGAH** (*no'-gah*) *A son of David.*
And *N*, and Nepheg, and Japhia,........... 1Chr 3:7
And *N*, and Nepheg, and Japhia,......... 1Chr 14:6

**NOHAH** (*no'-hah*) *A son of Benjamin.*
*N* the fourth, and Rapha the fifth.......... 1Chr 8:2

**NOISE**
the *n* of the trumpet, and the ................. Ex 20:18
when Joshua heard the *n* of the.............. Ex 32:17
There is a *n* of war in the camp ............. Ex 32:17
but the *n* of them that sing do I ............. Ex 32:18
nor make any *n* with your voice,........... Josh 6:10
the *n* of archers in the places of........... Judg 5:11
heard the *n* of the shout, they ................. 1Sa 4:6
What meaneth the *n* of this great............ 1Sa 4:6
Eli heard the *n* of the crying ................. 1Sa 4:14
What meaneth the *n* of this tumult....... 1Sa 4:14
that the *n* that was in the host .............. 1Sa 14:19
Wherefore is this *n* of the city ............. 1Kin 1:41
This is the *n* that ye have heard........... 1Kin 1:45
Syrians to hear a *n* of chariots............... 2Kin 7:6
a *n* of horses, even the *n* of................... 2Kin 7:6
Athaliah heard the *n* of the guard..... 2Kin 11:13
making a *n* with psalteries and........... 1Chr 15:28
heard the *n* of the people running..... 2Chr 23:12
*n* of the shout of joy from the................ Ezr 3:13
*n* of the weeping of the people............... Ezr 3:13
and the *n* was heard afar off.................. Ezr 3:13
or the *n* of his tabernacle ..................... Job 36:29
The *n* thereof sheweth concerning........ Job 36:33
attentively the *n* of his voice................. Job 37:2
play skilfully with a loud *n*..................... Ps 33:3
deep at the *n* of thy waterspouts............. Ps 42:7
in my complaint, and make a *n*................ Ps 55:2
they make a *n* like a dog, and go ........... Ps 59:6
and let them make a *n* like a dog........... Ps 59:14
Which stilleth the *n* of the seas .............. Ps 65:7
the *n* of their waves, and the.................. Ps 65:7
Make a joyful *n* unto God, all ye........... Ps 66:1
make a joyful *n* unto the God of............. Ps 81:1
than the *n* of many waters..................... Ps 93:4
let us make a joyful *n* to the .................. Ps 95:1
make a joyful *n* unto him with ............... Ps 95:2
Make a joyful *n* unto the LORD.............. Ps 98:4
make a loud *n*, and rejoice, and............. Ps 98:4
make a joyful *n* before the LORD ............ Ps 98:6
Make a joyful *n* unto the LORD............. Ps 100:1
of the warrior is with confused *n*............ Is 9:5
The *n* of a multitude in the..................... Is 13:4
a tumultuous *n* of the kingdoms of .......... Is 13:4
the grave, and the *n* of thy viols ............ Is 14:11
a *n* like the *n* of the seas ...................... Is 17:12
the *n* of them that rejoice endeth ............ Is 24:8
that he who fleeth from the *n* of.............. Is 24:18
bring down the *n* of strangers.................. Is 25:5
and with earthquake, and great *n*............. Is 29:6
abase himself for the *n* of them ............... Is 31:4
At the *n* of the tumult the people ............ Is 33:3
A voice of *n* from the city, a................... Is 66:6
my heart maketh a *n* in me..................... Jer 4:19
flee for the *n* of the horsemen................ Jer 4:29
the *n* of the bruit is come, and a ........... Jer 10:22
with the *n* of a great tumult he.............. Jer 11:16
A *n* shall come even to the ends ............ Jer 25:31
Pharaoh king of Egypt is but a *n* .......... Jer 46:17
At the *n* of the stamping of the............... Jer 47:3
is moved at the *n* of their fall............... Jer 49:21
at the cry the *n* thereof was.................. Jer 49:21
At the *n* of the taking of Babylon .......... Jer 50:46
a *n* of their voice is uttered.................... Jer 51:55
they have made a *n* in the house............. Lam 2:7
I heard the *n* of their wings,.................. Eze 1:24
like the *n* of great waters, as.................. Eze 1:24
of speech, as the *n* of an host ................ Eze 1:24
I heard also the *n* of the wings................ Eze 3:13
the *n* of the wheels over against ............ Eze 3:13
them, and a *n* of a great rushing............ Eze 3:13
thereof, by the *n* of his roaring.............. Eze 19:7
shake at the *n* of the horsemen.............. Eze 26:10
I will cause the *n* of thy songs............... Eze 26:13
and as I prophesied, there was a *n* ........ Eze 37:7
voice was like a *n* of many waters.......... Eze 43:2
Like the *n* of chariots on the.................... Joel 2:5
like the *n* of a flame of fire..................... Joel 2:5
away from me the *n* of thy songs ...... Amos 5:23
they shall make great *n* by reason........ Mic 2:12
The *n* of a whip, and the *n* of................ Nah 3:2
that there shall be the *n* of a............... Zeph 1:10
and make a *n* as through wine.............. Zec 9:15
and the people making a *n*,...................... Mt 9:23
shall pass away with a great *n* ............. 2Pet 3:10
as it were the *n* of thunder.................... Rev 6:1

**NOISED**
his fame was *n* throughout all the ....... Josh 6:27
it was *n* that he was in the house .......... Mk 2:1
all these sayings were *n* abroad............. Lk 1:65
Now when this was *n* abroad ................. Acts 2:6

**NOISOME**
fowler, and from the *n* pestilence............ Ps 91:3
If I cause *n* beasts to pass.................... Eze 14:15
the *n* beast, and the pestilence,............ Eze 14:21
and there fell a *n* and grievous.............. Rev 16:2

**NON** (*non*) See NUN. *Son of Elishama.*
*N* his son, Jehoshuah his son ............... 1Chr 7:27

**NONE**
*n* of us shall withhold from thee........... Gen 23:6
this is *n* other but the house of.......... Gen 28:17
There is *n* greater in this house ........... Gen 39:9

N

there was *n* of the men of the Gen 39:11
but there was *n* that could Gen 41:8
there is *n* that can interpret it Gen 41:15
but there was *n* that could Gen 41:24
there is *n* so discreet and wise as Gen 41:39
is *n* like unto the LORD our God Ex 8:10
is *n* like me in all the earth Ex 9:14
such as there was *n* like it in Ex 9:24
such as there was *n* like it Ex 11:6
*n* of you shall go out at the door Ex 12:22
I will put *n* of these diseases Ex 15:26
sabbath, in it there shall be *n* Ex 16:26
for to gather, and they found *n* Ex 16:27
*n* shall appear before me empty Ex 23:15
*n* shall appear before me empty Ex 34:20
*N* of you shall approach to any Lev 18:6
There shall *n* be defiled for the Lev 21:1
ye shall leave *n* of it until the Lev 22:30
And if the man have *n* to redeem it Lev 25:26
down, and *n* shall make you afraid Lev 26:6
ye shall flee when *n* pursueth you Lev 26:17
they shall fall when *n* pursueth Lev 26:36
before a sword, when *n* pursueth Lev 26:37
*N* devoted, which shall be devoted Lev 27:29
unto the sons of Kohath he gave *n* Num 7:9
They shall leave *n* of it unto the Num 9:12
until there was *n* left him alive Num 21:35
she bound her soul, of *n* effect Num 30:8
Surely *n* of the men that came up Num 32:11
every city, we left *n* to remain Deut 2:34
we smote him until *n* was left to Deut 3:3
there is *n* else beside him Deut 4:35
there is *n* else Deut 4:39
Thou shalt have *n* other gods Deut 5:7
will put *n* of the evil diseases Deut 7:15
cried, and there was *n* to save her Deut 22:27
thou shalt have *n* to rescue them Deut 28:31
shalt have *n* assurance of thy Deut 28:66
is gone, and there is *n* shut up Deut 32:36
There is *n* like unto the God of Deut 33:26
*n* went out, and *n* came in Josh 6:1
so that they let *n* of them remain Josh 8:22
there shall *n* of you be freed Josh 9:23
*n* moved his tongue against any of Josh 10:21
he let *n* remain Josh 10:28
he let *n* remain in it Josh 10:30
until he had left him *n* remaining Josh 10:33
he left *n* remaining, according to Josh 10:37
he left *n* remaining Josh 10:39
he left *n* remaining, but utterly Josh 10:40
until they left them *n* remaining Josh 11:8
strength, Israel burned *n* of them Josh 11:13
There was *n* of the Anakims left Josh 11:22
of Levi he gave *n* inheritance Josh 13:14
he gave *n* inheritance among them Josh 14:3
But *n* answered Judg 19:28
there came *n* to the camp from Judg 21:8
there were *n* of the inhabitants Judg 21:9
for there is *n* to redeem it Ruth 4:4
There is *n* holy as the LORD 1Sa 2:2
for there is *n* beside thee 1Sa 2:2
did let *n* of his words fall to 1Sa 3:19
that there is *n* like him among 1Sa 10:24
So *n* of the people tasted any 1Sa 14:24
David said, There is *n* like that 1Sa 21:9
there is *n* that sheweth me that 1Sa 22:8
there is *n* of you that is sorry 1Sa 22:8
for there is *n* like thee, neither 2Sa 7:22
there was *n* to part them, but the 2Sa 14:6
*n* can turn to the right hand or 2Sa 14:19
was *n* to be so much praised as 2Sa 14:25
Beware that *n* touch the young man 2Sa 18:12
looked, but there was *n* to save 2Sa 22:42
so that there was *n* like thee 1Kin 3:12
is God, and that there is *n* else 1Kin 8:60
*n* were of silver 1Kin 10:21
there was *n* that followed the 1Kin 12:20
*n* was exempted 1Kin 15:22
But there was *n* like unto Ahab, 1Kin 21:25
whom I stand, I will receive *n* 2Kin 5:16
And one of his servants said, *N* 2Kin 6:12
and there shall be *n* to bury her 2Kin 9:10
then let *n* go forth nor escape 2Kin 9:15
until he left him *n* remaining 2Kin 10:11
let *n* be wanting 2Kin 10:19
you *n* of the servants of the LORD 2Kin 10:23
let *n* come forth 2Kin 10:25
there was *n* left but the tribe of 2Kin 17:18
so that after him was *n* like him 2Kin 18:5
*n* remained, save the poorest sort 2Kin 24:14
*N* ought to carry the ark of God 1Chr 15:2
there is *n* like thee, neither is 1Chr 17:20
And Eliezer had *n* other sons 1Chr 23:17
a shadow, and there is *n* abiding 1Chr 29:15
such as *n* of the kings have had 2Chr 1:12
there were *n* such seen before in 2Chr 9:11
*n* were of silver 2Chr 9:20
we have *n* inheritance in the son 2Chr 10:16
*n* go out or come in to Asa king 2Chr 16:1
so that *n* is able to withstand 2Chr 20:6
fallen to the earth, and *n* escaped 2Chr 20:24
But let *n* come into the house of 2Chr 23:6
that *n* which was unclean in any 2Chr 23:19
found there *n* of the sons of Levi Ezr 8:15
*n* of us put off our clothes, Neh 4:23
to the law; *n* did compel Est 1:8
for *n* might enter into the king's Est 4:2
that there is *n* like him in the Job 1:8
that there is *n* like him in the Job 2:3
and *n* spake a word unto him Job 2:13
let it look for light, but have *n* Job 3:9
there is *n* that can deliver out Job 10:7
down, and *n* shall make thee afraid Job 11:19
because it is *n* of his Job 18:15
There shall *n* of his meat be left Job 20:21
and him that had *n* to help him Job 29:12
there was *n* of you that convinced Job 32:12
But *n* saith, Where is God my Job 35:10
but *n* giveth answer, because of Job 35:12
*N* is so fierce that dare stir him Job 41:10
while there is *n* to deliver Ps 7:2
his wickedness till thou find *n* Ps 10:15
there is *n* that doeth good Ps 14:1
there is *n* that doeth good, no, Ps 14:3
but there was *n* to save them Ps 18:41
for there is *n* to help Ps 22:11
*n* can keep alive his own soul Ps 22:29
let *n* that wait on thee be Ps 25:3
devices of the people of *n* effect Ps 33:10
*n* of them that trust in him shall Ps 34:22
*n* of his steps shall slide Ps 37:31
*N* of them can by any means redeem Ps 49:7
pieces, and there be *n* to deliver Ps 50:22
there is *n* that doeth good Ps 53:1
there is *n* that doeth good, no, Ps 53:3
to take pity, but there was *n* Ps 69:20
and for comforters, but I found *n* Ps 69:20
let *n* dwell in their tents Ps 69:25
for there is *n* to deliver him Ps 71:11
there is *n* upon earth that I Ps 73:25
*n* of the men of might have found Ps 76:5
and there was *n* to bury them Ps 79:3
and Israel would *n* of me Ps 81:11
gods there is *n* like unto thee Ps 86:8
fell down, and there was *n* to help Ps 107:12
Let there be *n* to extend mercy Ps 109:12
when as yet there was *n* of them Ps 139:16
counsel, and would *n* of my reproof Prov 1:25
They would *n* of my counsel Prov 1:30
*N* that go unto her return again, Prov 2:19
and choose *n* of his ways Prov 3:31
twins, and *n* is barren among them Song 4:2
together, and *n* shall quench them Is 1:31
*N* shall be weary nor stumble Is 5:27
*n* shall slumber nor sleep Is 5:27
away safe, and *n* shall deliver it Is 5:29
there was *n* that moved the wing, Is 10:14
is persecuted, and *n* hindereth Is 14:6
*n* shall be alone in his appointed Is 14:31
down, and *n* shall make them afraid Is 17:2
so he shall open, and *n* shall shut Is 22:22
and he shall shut, and *n* shall open Is 22:22
*n* shall pass through it for ever Is 34:10
but *n* shall be there, and all her Is 34:12
shall fail, *n* shall want her mate Is 34:16
needy seek water, and there is *n* Is 41:17
there is *n* that sheweth, yea, Is 41:26
there is *n* that declareth, yea, Is 41:26
there is *n* that heareth your Is 41:26
are for a prey, and *n* delivereth Is 42:22
for a spoil, and *n* saith, Restore Is 42:22
there is *n* that can deliver out Is 43:13
*n* considereth in his heart, Is 44:19
I am the LORD, and there is *n* else Is 45:5
west, that there is *n* beside me Is 45:6
I am the LORD, and there is *n* else Is 45:6
and there is *n* else, there is no Is 45:14
and there is *n* else Is 45:18
there is *n* beside me Is 45:21
for I am God, and there is *n* else Is 45:22
for I am God, and there is *n* else Is 46:9
I am God, and there is *n* like me Is 46:9
heart, I am, and *n* else beside me Is 47:8
thou hast said, *N* seeth me Is 47:10
heart, I am, and *n* else beside me Is 47:10
*n* shall save thee Is 47:15
I called, was there *n* to answer Is 50:2
There is *n* to guide her among all Is 51:18
*n* considering that the righteous Is 57:1
*N* calleth for justice, nor any Is 59:4
look for judgment, but there is *n* Is 59:11
of the people there was *n* with me Is 63:3
I looked, and there was *n* to help Is 63:5
that there was *n* to uphold Is 63:5
there is *n* that calleth upon thy Is 64:7
when I called, *n* did answer Is 66:4
burn that *n* can quench it because Jer 4:4
they have *n* understanding Jer 4:22
and *n* shall fray them away Jer 7:33
so that *n* can pass through them Jer 9:10
that *n* passeth through Jer 9:12
and *n* shall gather them Jer 9:22
as there is *n* like unto thee Jer 10:6
there is *n* like unto thee Jer 10:7
there is *n* to stretch forth my Jer 10:20
be shut up, and *n* shall open them Jer 13:19
and they shall have *n* to bury them Jer 14:16
burn that *n* can quench it, Jer 21:12
that *n* doth return from his Jer 23:14
is great, so that *n* is like it Jer 30:7
quiet, and *n* shall make him afraid Jer 30:10
There is *n* to plead thy cause, Jer 30:13
that *n* should serve himself of Jer 34:9
that *n* should serve themselves of Jer 34:10
for unto this day they drink *n* Jer 35:14
He shall have *n* to sit upon the Jer 36:30
*n* of them shall remain or escape Jer 42:17
Judah, to leave you *n* to remain Jer 44:7
So that *n* of the remnant of Judah Jer 44:14
for *n* shall return but such as Jer 44:14
ease, and *n* shall make him afraid Jer 46:27
*n* shall tread with shouting Jer 48:33
*n* shall gather up him that Jer 49:5
and *n* shall dwell therein Jer 50:3
*n* shall return in vain Jer 50:9
sought for, and there shall be *n* Jer 50:20
let *n* thereof escape Jer 50:29
and fall, and *n* shall raise him up Jer 50:32
that *n* shall remain in it, Jer 51:62
lovers she hath *n* to comfort her Lam 1:2
because *n* come to the solemn Lam 1:4
of the enemy, and *n* did help her Lam 1:7
there is *n* to comfort her Lam 1:17
there is *n* to comfort me Lam 1:21
anger *n* escaped nor remained Lam 2:22
there is *n* that doth deliver us Lam 5:8
*n* of them shall remain, nor of Eze 7:11
but *n* goeth to the battle Eze 7:14
seek peace, and there shall be *n* Eze 7:25
There shall *n* of my words be Eze 12:28
*N* eye pitied thee, to do any of Eze 16:5
whereas *n* followeth thee to Eze 16:34
hath spoiled *n* by violence Eze 18:7
but I found *n* Eze 22:30
To the end that *n* of all the Eze 31:14
*N* of his sins that he hath Eze 33:16
that *n* shall pass through Eze 33:28
*n* did search or seek after them Eze 34:6
and *n* shall make them afraid Eze 34:28
their land, and *n* made them afraid Eze 39:26
have left *n* of them any more Eze 39:28
them all was found *n* like Daniel Dan 1:19
there is *n* other that can shew it Dan 2:11
*n* can stay his hand, or say unto Dan 4:35
could find *n* occasion nor fault Dan 6:4
there was *n* that could deliver Dan 8:7
the vision, but *n* understood it Dan 8:27
there is *n* that holdeth with me Dan 10:21
will, and *n* shall stand before him Dan 11:16
to his end, and *n* shall help him Dan 11:45
*n* of the wicked shall understand Dan 12:10
*n* shall deliver her out of mine Hos 2:10
take away, and *n* shall rescue him Hos 5:14
there is *n* among them that Hos 7:7
High, *n* at all would exalt him Hos 11:7
*n* iniquity in me that were sin Hos 12:8
I am the LORD your God, and *n* else Joel 2:27
there is *n* to raise her up Amos 5:2
there be *n* to quench it in Amos 5:6
there is *n* understanding in him Obad 7
Therefore thou shalt have *n* that Mic 2:5
*n* evil can come upon us Mic 3:11
and *n* shall make them afraid Mic 4:4
in pieces, and *n* can deliver Mic 5:8
there is *n* upright among men Mic 7:2
but *n* shall look back Nah 2:8
for there is *n* end of the store Nah 2:9
whelp, and *n* made them afraid Nah 2:11
there is *n* end of their corpses Nah 3:3
I am, and there is *n* beside me Zeph 2:15
streets waste, that *n* passeth by Zeph 3:6
man, that there is *n* inhabitant Zeph 3:6
down, and *n* shall make them afraid Zeph 3:13
clothe you, but there is *n* warm Hag 1:6
let *n* of you imagine evil against Zec 7:10
let *n* of you imagine evil in your Zec 8:17
let *n* deal treacherously against Mal 2:15
seeking rest, and findeth *n* Mt 12:43
God of *n* effect by your tradition Mt 15:6
there is *n* good but one, that is, Mt 19:17
But found *n*: yea, though Mt 26:60
witnesses came, yet found they *n* Mt 26:60
Making the word of God of *n* Mk 7:13
there is *n* good but one, that is, Mk 10:18
There is *n* other commandment Mk 12:31
and there is *n* other but he Mk 12:32
and found *n* Mk 14:55
There is *n* of thy kindred that is Lk 1:61
let him impart to him that hath *n* Lk 3:11
But unto *n* of them was Elias sent Lk 4:26
*n* of them was cleansed, saving Lk 4:27
and finding *n*, he saith, I will Lk 11:24
sought fruit thereon, and found *n* Lk 13:6
fruit on this fig tree, and find *n* Lk 13:7
That *n* of those men which were Lk 14:24
*n* is good, save one, that is, God Lk 18:19
they understood *n* of these things Lk 18:34
that there was *n* other boat there Jn 6:22
yet *n* of you keepeth the law Jn 7:19
saw *n* but the woman, he said unto Jn 8:10
the works which *n* other man did Jn 15:24
*n* of you asketh me, Whither goest Jn 16:5
*n* of them is lost, but the son of Jn 17:12
thou gavest me have I lost *n* Jn 18:9
*n* of the disciples durst ask him, Jn 21:12
said, Silver and gold have I *n* Acts 3:6
for there is *n* other name under Acts 4:12
he gave him *n* inheritance in it, Acts 7:5
yet he was fallen upon *n* of them Acts 8:16
that *n* of these things which ye Acts 8:24
preaching the word to *n* but unto Acts 11:19
cared for *n* of those things Acts 18:17
But *n* of these things move me, Acts 20:24
that he should forbid *n* of his Acts 24:23
but if there be *n* of these things Acts 25:11
they brought *n* accusation of such Acts 25:18
saying *n* other things than those Acts 26:22
for I am persuaded that *n* of Acts 26:26
There is *n* righteous, no, not one Rom 3:10
There is *n* that understandeth, Rom 3:11

there is *n* that seeketh after God — Rom 3:11
there is *n* that doeth good, no, — Rom 3:12
and the promise made of *n* effect — Rom 4:14
Spirit of Christ, he is *n* of his — Rom 8:9
word of God hath taken *n* effect — Rom 9:6
For *n* of us liveth to himself, and — Rom 14:7
God that I baptized *n* of you — 1Cor 1:14
Christ should be made of *n* effect — 1Cor 1:17
Which *n* of the princes of this — 1Cor 2:8
wives be as though they had *n* — 1Cor 7:29
that there is *n* other God but one — 1Cor 8:4
But I have used *n* of these things — 1Cor 9:15
Give *n* offence, neither to the — 1Cor 10:32
world, and *n* of them is without — 1Cor 14:10
For we write *n* other things unto — 2Cor 1:13
But other of the apostles saw I *n* — Gal 1:19
make the promise of *n* effect — Gal 3:17
that ye will be *n* otherwise — Gal 5:10
See that *n* render evil for evil — 1Th 5:15
give *n* occasion to the adversary — 1Ti 5:14
But let *n* of you suffer as a — 1Pet 4:15
there is *n* occasion of stumbling — 1Jn 2:10
Fear *n* of those things which thou — Rev 2:10
will put upon you *n* other burden — Rev 2:24

**NOON**
these men shall dine with me at *n* — Gen 43:16
present against Joseph came at *n* — Gen 43:25
who lay on a bed at *n* — 2Sa 4:5
of Baal from morning even until *n* — 1Kin 18:26
And it came to pass at *n*, that — 1Kin 18:27
And they went out at *n* — 1Kin 20:16
he sat on her knees till *n* — 2Kin 4:20
Evening, and morning, and at *n* — Ps 55:17
makest thy flock to rest at *n* — Song 1:7
arise, and let us go up at *n* — Jer 6:4
cause the sun to go down at *n* — Amos 8:9
come nigh unto Damascus about *n* — Acts 22:6

**NOONDAY**
And thou shalt grope at *n*, as the — Deut 28:29
grope in the *n* as in the night — Job 5:14
age shall be clearer than the *n* — Job 11:17
light, and thy judgment as the *n* — Ps 37:6
the destruction that wasteth at *n* — Ps 91:6
the night in the midst of the *n* — Is 16:3
and thy darkness be as the *n* — Is 58:10
we stumble at *n* as in the night — Is 59:10
of the young men a spoiler at *n* — Jer 15:8
shall drive out Ashdod at the *n* — Zeph 2:4

**NOONTIDE**
the morning, and the shouting at *n* — Jer 20:16

**NOPH** (*nof*) See MEMPHIS. *Same as Memphis.*
the princes of *N* are deceived — Is 19:13
Also the children of *N* and — Jer 2:16
Migdol, and at Tahpanhes, and at *N* — Jer 44:1
in Migdol, and publish in *N* — Jer 46:14
for *N* shall be waste and desolate — Jer 46:19
their images to cease out of *N* — Eze 30:13
*N* shall have distresses daily — Eze 30:16

**NOPHAH** (*no'-fah*) See NOBAH. *A city in Sihon.*
have laid them waste even unto *N* — Num 21:30

**NOR** See PREFACE.

**NORTH**
west, and to the east, and to the *n* — Gen 28:14
the *n* side there shall be twenty — Ex 26:20
shalt put the table on the *n* side — Ex 26:35
likewise for the *n* side in length — Ex 27:11
which is toward the *n* corner — Ex 36:25
for the *n* side the hangings were — Ex 38:11
be on the *n* side by their armies — Num 2:25
And this shall be your *n* border — Num 34:7
this shall be your *n* border — Num 34:9
on the *n* side two thousand cubits — Num 35:5
and pitched on the *n* side of Ai — Josh 8:11
that was on the *n* of the city — Josh 8:13
were on the *n* of the mountains — Josh 11:2
their border in the *n* quarter was — Josh 15:5
along by the *n* of Beth-arabah — Josh 15:6
which is Chesalon, on the *n* side — Josh 15:10
sea to Michmethah on the *n* side — Josh 16:6
was on the *n* side of the river — Josh 17:9
met together in Asher on the *n* — Josh 17:10
abide in their coasts on the *n* — Josh 18:5
their border on the *n* side was — Josh 18:12
the side of Jericho on the *n* side — Josh 18:12
the valley of the giants on the *n* — Josh 18:16
was drawn from the *n* — Josh 18:17
of the border were at the *n* bay — Josh 18:19
it on the *n* side to Hannathon — Josh 19:14
toward the *n* side of Beth-emek — Josh 19:27
on the *n* side of the hill of — Josh 24:30
on the *n* side of the hill Gaash — Judg 2:9
were on the *n* side of them — Judg 7:1
which is on the *n* side of Beth-el — Judg 21:19
oxen, three looking toward the *n* — 1Kin 7:25
put it on the *n* side of the altar — 2Kin 16:14
porters, toward the east, west, *n* — 1Chr 9:24
oxen, three looking toward the *n* — 2Chr 4:4
out the *n* over the empty place — Job 26:7
and cold out of the *n* — Job 37:9
Fair weather cometh out of the *n* — Job 37:22
mount Zion, on the sides of the *n* — Ps 48:2
The *n* and the south thou hast — Ps 89:12
and from the west, from the *n* — Ps 107:3
The *n* wind driveth away rain — Prov 25:23
and turneth about unto the *n* — Eccl 1:6
toward the south, or toward the *n* — Eccl 11:3
Awake, O *n* wind — Song 4:16
in the sides of the *n* — Is 14:13
shall come from the *n* a smoke — Is 14:31
I have raised up one from the *n* — Is 41:25
I will say to the *n*, Give up — Is 43:6
and, lo, these from the *n* and from — Is 49:12
the face thereof is toward the *n* — Jer 1:13
Out of the *n* an evil shall break — Jer 1:14
families of the kingdoms of the *n* — Jer 1:15
proclaim these words toward the *n* — Jer 3:12
*n* to the land that I have given — Jer 3:18
for I will bring evil from the *n* — Jer 4:6
for evil appeareth out of the *n* — Jer 6:1
people cometh from the *n* country — Jer 6:22
commotion out of the *n* country — Jer 10:22
behold them that come from the *n* — Jer 13:20
of Israel from the land of the *n* — Jer 16:15
of Israel out of the *n* country — Jer 23:8
and take all the families of the *n* — Jer 25:9
And all the kings of the *n* — Jer 25:26
bring them from the *n* country — Jer 31:8
fall toward the *n* by the river — Jer 46:6
hosts hath a sacrifice in the *n* — Jer 46:10
it cometh out of the *n* — Jer 46:20
the hand of the people of the *n* — Jer 46:24
waters rise up out of the *n* — Jer 47:2
For out of the *n* there cometh up — Jer 50:3
great nations from the *n* country — Jer 50:9
a people shall come from the *n* — Jer 50:41
shall come unto her from the *n* — Jer 51:48
a whirlwind came out of the *n* — Eze 1:4
gate, that looketh toward the *n* — Eze 8:3
eyes now the way toward the *n* — Eze 8:5
up mine eyes the way toward the *n* — Eze 8:5
house which was toward the *n* — Eze 8:14
gate, which lieth toward the *n* — Eze 9:2
to the *n* shall be burned therein — Eze 20:47
all flesh from the south to the *n* — Eze 21:4
a king of kings, from the *n* — Eze 26:7
There be the princes of the *n* — Eze 32:30
of Togarmah of the *n* quarters — Eze 38:6
from thy place out of the *n* parts — Eze 38:15
thee to come up from the *n* parts — Eze 39:2
court that looked toward the *n* — Eze 40:20
against the gate toward the *n* — Eze 40:23
And he brought me to the *n* gate — Eze 40:35
up to the entry of the *n* gate — Eze 40:40
was at the side of the *n* gate — Eze 40:44
having the prospect toward the *n* — Eze 40:44
toward the *n* is for the priests — Eze 40:46
was left, one door toward the *n* — Eze 41:11
utter court, the way toward the *n* — Eze 42:1
before the building toward the *n* — Eze 42:1
an hundred cubits was the *n* door — Eze 42:2
and their doors toward the *n* — Eze 42:4
chambers which were toward the *n* — Eze 42:11
The *n* chambers and the south — Eze 42:13
He measured the *n* side, five — Eze 42:17
of the *n* gate before the house — Eze 44:4
entereth in by the way of the *n* — Eze 46:9
go forth by the way of the *n* gate — Eze 46:9
which looked toward the *n* — Eze 46:19
of the land toward the *n* side — Eze 47:15
the *n* northward, and the border of — Eze 47:17
And this is the *n* side — Eze 47:17
From the *n* end to the coast of — Eze 48:1
toward the *n* five and twenty — Eze 48:10
the *n* side four thousand and five — Eze 48:16
shall be toward the *n* two hundred — Eze 48:17
out of the city on the *n* side — Eze 48:30
of the *n* to make an agreement — Dan 11:6
the fortress of the king of the *n* — Dan 11:7
more years than the king of the *n* — Dan 11:8
him, even with the king of the *n* — Dan 11:11
the king of the *n* shall return — Dan 11:13
So the king of the *n* shall come — Dan 11:15
the king of the *n* shall come — Dan 11:40
out of the *n* shall trouble him — Dan 11:44
from the *n* even to the east, they — Amos 8:12
out his hand against the *n* — Zeph 2:13
and flee from the land of the *n* — Zec 2:6
go forth into the *n* country — Zec 6:6
these that go toward the *n* — Zec 6:8
my spirit in the *n* country — Zec 6:8
shall remove toward the *n* — Zec 14:4
and from the west, and from the *n* — Lk 13:29
toward the south west and *n* west — Acts 27:12
on the *n* three gates — Rev 21:13

**NORTHERN**
Shall iron break the *n* iron — Jer 15:12
far off from you the *n* army — Joel 2:20

**NORTHWARD**
from the place where thou art *n* — Gen 13:14
upon the side of the tabernacle *n* — Ex 40:22
of the altar *n* before the LORD — Lev 1:11
on the side of the tabernacle *n* — Num 3:35
turn you *n* — Deut 2:3
lift up thine eyes westward, and *n* — Deut 3:27
even unto the borders of Ekron *n* — Josh 13:3
from the valley of Achor, and so *n* — Josh 15:7
end of the valley of the giants *n* — Josh 15:8
went out unto the side of Ekron *n* — Josh 15:11
*n* it was Manasseh's, and the sea — Josh 17:10
the side over against Arabah *n* — Josh 18:18
to the side of Beth-hoglah *n* — Josh 18:19
themselves together, and went *n* — Judg 12:1
situate *n* over against Michmash — 1Sa 14:5
and his lot came out *n* — 1Chr 26:14
*n* four a day, southward four a — 1Chr 26:17
behold *n* at the gate of the altar — Eze 8:5
an hundred cubits eastward and *n* — Eze 40:19
me out of the way of the gate *n* — Eze 47:2
of Damascus, and the north *n* — Eze 47:17
the border of Damascus *n* — Eze 48:1
three gates *n*; one gate — Eze 48:31
the ram pushing westward, and *n* — Dan 8:4

**NOSE**
a lame, or he that hath a flat *n* — Lev 21:18
I will put my hook in thy *n* — 2Kin 19:28
his *n* pierceth through snares — Job 40:24
Canst thou put an hook into his *n* — Job 41:2
the wringing of the *n* bringeth — Prov 30:33
thy *n* is as the tower of Lebanon — Song 7:4
and the smell of thy *n* like apples — Song 7:8
The rings, and *n* jewels, — Is 3:21
will I put my hook in thy *n* — Is 37:29
These are a smoke in my *n* — Is 65:5
they put the branch to their *n* — Eze 8:17
they shall take away thy *n* — Eze 23:25

**NOSES**
*n* have they, but they smell not — Ps 115:6
stop the *n* of the passengers — Eze 39:11

**NOSTRILS**
breathed into his *n* the breath of — Gen 2:7
All in whose *n* was the breath of — Gen 7:22
with the blast of thy *n* the — Ex 15:8
until it come out at your *n* — Num 11:20
went up a smoke out of his *n* — 2Sa 22:9
the blast of the breath of his *n* — 2Sa 22:16
breath of his *n* are they consumed — Job 4:9
and the spirit of God is in my *n* — Job 27:3
the glory of his *n* is terrible — Job 39:20
Out of his *n* goeth smoke, as out — Job 41:20
went up a smoke out of his *n* — Ps 18:8
the blast of the breath of thy *n* — Ps 18:15
man, whose breath is in his *n* — Is 2:22
The breath of our *n*, the anointed — Lam 4:20
your camps to come up unto your *n* — Amos 4:10

**NOT** See PREFACE.

**NOTABLE**
the goat had a *n* horn between his — Dan 8:5
for it came up four *n* ones toward — Dan 8:8
And they had then a *n* prisoner — Mt 27:16
great and *n* day of the Lord come — Acts 2:20
for that indeed a *n* miracle hath — Acts 4:16

**NOTE**
*n* it in a book, that it may be — Is 30:8
who are of *n* among the apostles, — Rom 16:7
*n* that man, and have no company — 2Th 3:14

**NOTED**
is *n* in the scripture of truth — Dan 10:21

**NOTHING**
now *n* will be restrained from — Gen 11:6
only unto these men do *n* — Gen 19:8
we have done unto thee *n* but good — Gen 26:29
here also have I done *n* that they — Gen 40:15
there shall *n* die of all that is — Ex 9:4
ye shall let *n* of it remain until — Ex 12:10
Ye shall eat *n* leavened — Ex 12:20
he that gathered much had *n* over — Ex 16:18
he shall go out free for *n* — Ex 21:2
if he have *n*, then he shall be — Ex 22:3
There shall *n* cast their young, — Ex 23:26
*n* that is made of the vine tree — Num 6:4
there is *n* at all, beside this — Num 11:6
touch *n* of theirs, lest ye be — Num 16:26
Balak the son of Zippor, Let *n* — Num 22:16
thou hast lacked *n* — Deut 2:7
shalt save alive *n* that breatheth — Deut 20:16
unto the damsel thou shalt do *n* — Deut 22:26
because he hath *n* left him in the — Deut 28:55
he left *n* undone of all that the — Josh 11:15
such as before knew *n* thereof — Judg 3:2
This is *n* else save the sword of — Judg 7:14
a kid, and he had *n* in his hand — Judg 14:6
him every whit, and hid *n* from him — 1Sa 3:18
my father will do *n* either great — 1Sa 20:2
thy servant knew *n* of all this — 1Sa 22:15
so that *n* was missed of all that — 1Sa 25:21
wherefore she told him *n*, less or — 1Sa 25:36
there is *n* better for me than — 1Sa 27:1
there was *n* lacking to them, — 1Sa 30:19
But the poor man had *n*, save one — 2Sa 12:3
God of that which doth cost me *n* — 2Sa 24:24
they lacked *n* — 1Kin 4:27
There was *n* in the ark save the — 1Kin 8:9
it was *n* accounted of in the days — 1Kin 10:21
And he answered, *N* — 1Kin 11:22
and looked, and said, There is *n* — 1Kin 18:43
*n* but that which is true in the — 1Kin 22:16
earth *n* of the word of the LORD — 2Kin 10:10
there was *n* in his house, nor in — 2Kin 20:13
there is *n* among my treasures — 2Kin 20:15
*n* shall be left, saith the LORD — 2Kin 20:17
There was *n* in the ark save the — 2Chr 5:10
there was *n* hid from Solomon — 2Chr 9:2
it is *n* with thee to help, — 2Chr 14:11
I adjure thee that thou say *n* but — 2Chr 18:15
Ye have *n* to do with us to build — Ezr 4:3
this is *n* else but sorrow of — Neh 2:2
their peace, and found *n* to answer — Neh 5:8
them, and will require *n* of them — Neh 5:12
unto them for whom *n* is prepared — Neh 8:10
wilderness, so that they lacked *n* — Neh 9:21
she required *n* but what Hegai the — Est 2:15

N

Yet all this availeth me n ... Est 5:13
unto him, There is n done for him ... Est 6:3
let n fail of all that thou hast ... Est 6:10
they go to n, and perish ... Job 6:18
are but of yesterday, and know n ... Job 8:9
a liar, and make my speech n worth ... Job 24:25
and hangeth the earth upon n ... Job 26:7
It profiteth a man n that he ... Job 34:9
hast tried me, and shalt find n ... Ps 17:3
there is n hid from the heat ... Ps 19:6
and mine age is as n before thee ... Ps 39:5
he dieth he shall carry n away ... Ps 49:17
and n shall offend them ... Ps 119:165
there is n froward or perverse in ... Prov 8:8
she is simple, and knoweth n ... Prov 9:13
Treasures of wickedness profit n ... Prov 10:2
the sluggard desireth, and hath n ... Prov 13:4
maketh himself rich, yet hath n ... Prov 13:7
he beg in harvest, and have n ... Prov 20:4
If thou hast n to pay, why should ... Prov 22:27
There is n better for a man, than ... Eccl 2:24
n can be put to it, nor any thing ... Eccl 3:14
I perceive that there is n better ... Eccl 3:22
a son, and there is n in his hand ... Eccl 5:14
shall take n of his labour, which ... Eccl 5:15
so that he wanteth n for his soul ... Eccl 6:2
that man should find n after him ... Eccl 7:14
and all her princes shall be n ... Is 34:12
there was n in his house, nor in ... Is 39:2
there is n among my treasures ... Is 39:4
n shall be left, saith the LORD ... Is 39:6
All nations before him are as n ... Is 40:17
are counted to him less than n ... Is 40:17
That bringeth the princes to n ... Is 40:23
they shall be as n ... Is 41:11
war against thee shall be as n ... Is 41:12
Behold, ye are of n, and your work ... Is 41:24
their works are n ... Is 41:29
image that is profitable for n ... Is 44:10
anger, lest thou bring me to n ... Jer 10:24
marred, it was profitable for n ... Jer 13:7
this girdle, which is good for n ... Jer 13:10
there is n too hard for thee ... Jer 32:17
they have done n of all that thou ... Jer 32:23
hide n from me ... Jer 38:14
poor of the people, which had n ... Jer 39:10
I will keep n back from you ... Jer 42:4
let n of her be left ... Jer 50:26
Is it n to you, all ye that pass ... Lam 1:12
their own spirit, and have seen n ... Eze 13:3
of the earth are reputed as n ... Dan 4:35
yea, and n shall escape them ... Joel 2:3
of his den, if he have taken n ... Amos 3:4
the earth, and have taken n at all ... Amos 3:5
Surely the Lord GOD will do n ... Amos 3:7
eyes in comparison of it as n ... Hag 2:3
it is thenceforth good for n ... Mt 5:13
for there is n covered, that ... Mt 10:26
now three days, and have n to eat ... Mt 15:32
n shall be impossible unto you ... Mt 17:20
found n thereon, but leaves only ... Mt 21:19
swear by the temple, it is n ... Mt 23:16
shall swear by the altar, it is n ... Mt 23:18
said unto him, Answerest thou n ... Mt 26:62
priests and elders, he answered n ... Mt 27:12
Have thou n to do with that just ... Mt 27:19
saw that he could prevail n ... Mt 27:24
him, See thou say n to any man ... Mk 1:44
For there is n hid, which shall ... Mk 4:22
was n bettered, but rather grew ... Mk 5:26
should take n for their journey ... Mk 6:8
for they have n to eat ... Mk 6:36
There is n from without a man ... Mk 7:15
very great, and having n to eat ... Mk 8:1
me three days, and have n to eat ... Mk 8:2
This kind can come forth by n ... Mk 9:29
came to it, he found n but leaves ... Mk 11:13
Jesus, saying, Answerest thou n ... Mk 14:60
he held his peace, and answered n ... Mk 14:61
but he answered n ... Mk 15:3
again, saying, Answerest thou n ... Mk 15:4
But Jesus yet answered n ... Mk 15:5
For with God n shall be ... Lk 1:37
And in those days he did eat n ... Lk 4:2
all the night, and have taken n ... Lk 5:5
good, and lend, hoping for n again ... Lk 6:35
And when they had n to pay ... Lk 7:42
For n is secret, that shall not ... Lk 8:17
Take n for your journey, neither ... Lk 9:3
n shall by any means hurt you ... Lk 10:19
I have n to set before him ... Lk 11:6
For there is n covered, that ... Lk 12:2
And they said, N ... Lk 22:35
but he answered him n ... Lk 23:9
n worthy of death is done unto ... Lk 23:15
but this man hath done n amiss ... Lk 23:41
and said, A man can receive n ... Jn 3:27
thou hast n to draw with, and the ... Jn 4:11
you, The Son can do n of himself ... Jn 5:19
I can of mine own self do n ... Jn 5:30
that remain, that n be lost ... Jn 6:12
he hath given me I should lose n ... Jn 6:39
the flesh profiteth n ... Jn 6:63
boldly, and they say n unto him ... Jn 7:26
I am he, and that I do n of myself ... Jn 8:28
I honour myself, my honour is n ... Jn 8:54
were not of God, he could do n ... Jn 9:33
said unto them, Ye know n at all ... Jn 11:49
Perceive ye how ye prevail n ... Jn 12:19
world cometh, and hath n in me ... Jn 14:30
for without me ye can do n ... Jn 15:5
And in that day ye shall ask me n ... Jn 16:23
have ye asked n in my name ... Jn 16:24
and in secret have I said n ... Jn 18:20
and that night they caught n ... Jn 21:3
them, they could say n against it ... Acts 4:14
finding n how they might punish ... Acts 4:21
down, and go with them, doubting n. ... Acts 10:20
for n common or unclean hath at ... Acts 11:8
bade me go with them, n doubting ... Acts 11:12
there spent their time in n else ... Acts 17:21
to be quiet, and to do n rashly ... Acts 19:36
how I kept back n that was ... Acts 20:20
informed concerning thee, are n ... Acts 21:24
that we will eat n until we have ... Acts 23:14
but to have n laid to his charge ... Acts 23:29
had committed n worthy of death ... Acts 25:25
This man doeth n worthy of death ... Acts 26:31
continued fasting, having taken n ... Acts 27:33
committed n against the people ... Acts 28:17
that there is n unclean of itself ... Rom 14:14
will bring to n the understanding ... 1Cor 1:19
For I know n by myself ... 1Cor 4:4
Therefore judge n before the time ... 1Cor 4:5
Circumcision is n, and ... 1Cor 7:19
and uncircumcision is n ... 1Cor 7:19
he knoweth n yet as he ought to ... 1Cor 8:2
that an idol is n in the world ... 1Cor 8:4
the gospel, I have n to glory of ... 1Cor 9:16
and have not charity, I am n ... 1Cor 13:2
not charity, it profiteth me n ... 1Cor 13:3
as having n, and yet possessing ... 2Cor 6:10
might receive damage by us in n ... 2Cor 7:9
that had gathered much had n over ... 2Cor 8:15
for in n am I behind the very ... 2Cor 12:11
chiefest apostles, though I be n ... 2Cor 12:11
For we can do n against the truth ... 2Cor 13:8
in conference added n to me ... Gal 2:6
differeth n from a servant ... Gal 4:1
Christ shall profit you n ... Gal 5:2
to be something, when he is n ... Gal 6:3
that in n I shall be ashamed, but ... Phil 1:20
And in n terrified by your ... Phil 1:28
Let n be done through strife or ... Phil 2:3
Be careful for n ... Phil 4:6
and that ye may have lack of n ... 1Th 4:12
n to be refused, if it be ... 1Ti 4:4
another, doing n by partiality ... 1Ti 5:21
He is proud, knowing n, but ... 1Ti 6:4
For we brought n into this world ... 1Ti 6:7
it is certain we can carry n out ... 1Ti 6:7
defiled and unbelieving is n pure ... Titus 1:15
that n be wanting unto them ... Titus 3:13
But without thy mind would I do n ... Philem 14
he left n that is not put under ... Heb 2:8
spake n concerning priesthood ... Heb 7:14
For the law made n perfect ... Heb 7:19
be perfect and entire, wanting n ... Jas 1:4
let him ask in faith, n wavering ... Jas 1:6
forth, taking n of the Gentiles ... 3Jn 7
with goods, and have need of n ... Rev 3:17

## NOTICE

And all the people took n of it ... 2Sa 3:36
bounty, whereof ye had n before ... 2Cor 9:5

## NOTWITHSTANDING

N they hearkened not unto Moses ... Ex 16:20
N, if he continue a day or two ... Ex 21:21
N the cities of the Levites, and ... Lev 25:32
N no devoted thing, that a man ... Lev 27:28
N the children of Korah died not ... Num 26:11
N the land shall be divided by ... Num 26:55
N ye would not go up, but ... Deut 1:26
N thou mayest kill and eat flesh ... Deut 12:15
N, if the land of your possession ... Josh 22:19
n the journey that thou takest ... Judg 4:9
n yet Jotham the youngest son of ... Judg 9:5
N they hearkened not unto the ... 1Sa 2:25
n, if there be in me iniquity ... 1Sa 20:8
n the princes of the Philistines ... 1Sa 29:9
N the king's word prevailed ... 2Sa 24:4
N in thy days I will not do it ... 1Kin 11:12
N they would not hear, but ... 2Kin 17:14
N the LORD turned not from the ... 2Kin 23:26
N thou shalt not build the house ... 2Chr 6:9
N Hezekiah humbled himself for ... 2Chr 32:26
n I have spoken unto you, rising ... Jer 35:14
N the children rebelled against ... Eze 20:21
N the land shall be desolate ... Mic 7:13
n, being warned of God in a dream ... Mt 2:22
n he that is least in the kingdom ... Mt 11:11
N, lest we should offend them, go ... Mt 17:27
n be ye sure of this, that the ... Lk 10:11
N in this rejoice not, that the ... Lk 10:20
N it pleased Silas to abide there ... Acts 15:34
N, that I be not further tedious ... Acts 24:4
n, every way, whether in pretence ... Phil 1:18
N ye have well done, that ye did ... Phil 4:14
N she shall be saved in ... 1Ti 2:15
N the Lord stood with me, and ... 2Ti 4:17
n ye give them not those things ... Jas 2:16
N I have a few things against ... Rev 2:20

## NOUGHT

thou therefore serve me for n ... Gen 29:15
there shall cleave n of the ... Deut 13:17
brother, and thou givest him n ... Deut 15:9
destroy you, and to bring you to n ... Deut 28:63
had brought their counsel to n ... Neh 4:15
and said, Doth Job fear God for n ... Job 1:9
of the wicked shall come to n ... Job 8:22
the mountain falling cometh to n ... Job 14:18
a pledge from thy brother for n ... Job 22:6
the counsel of the heathen to n ... Ps 33:10
Thou sellest thy people for n ... Ps 44:12
ye have set at n all my counsel ... Prov 1:25
together, and it shall come to n ... Is 8:10
the terrible one is brought to n ... Is 29:20
aside the just for a thing of n ... Is 29:21
be as nothing, and as a thing of n ... Is 41:12
are of nothing, and your work of n ... Is 41:24
I have spent my strength for n ... Is 49:4
Ye have sold yourselves for n ... Is 52:3
my people is taken away for n ... Is 52:5
and divination, and a thing of n ... Jer 14:14
and Beth-el shall come to n ... Amos 5:5
Ye which rejoice in a thing of n ... Amos 6:13
that would shut the doors for n ... Mal 1:10
kindle fire on mine altar for n ... Mal 1:10
many things, and be set at n ... Mk 9:12
with his men of war set him at n ... Lk 23:11
was set at n of you builders ... Acts 4:11
were scattered, and brought to n ... Acts 5:36
work be of men, it will come to n ... Acts 5:38
craft is in danger to be set at n ... Acts 19:27
dost thou set at n thy brother ... Rom 14:10
to bring to n things that are ... 1Cor 1:28
of this world, that come to n ... 1Cor 2:6
did we eat any man's bread for n ... 2Th 3:8
hour so great riches is come to n ... Rev 18:17

## NOURISH

And there will I n thee ... Gen 45:11
I will n you, and your little ones ... Gen 50:21
that a man shall n a young cow ... Is 7:21
neither do I n up young men ... Is 23:4
an ash, and the rain doth n it ... Is 44:14

## NOURISHED

Joseph n his father, and his ... Gen 47:12
lamb, which he had bought and n up ... 2Sa 12:3
the LORD hath spoken, I have n ... Is 1:2
she n her whelps among young ... Eze 19:2
n up in his father's house three ... Acts 7:20
him up, and n him for her own son ... Acts 7:21
was n by the king's country ... Acts 12:20
n up in the words of faith and of ... 1Ti 4:6
ye have n your hearts, as in a ... Jas 5:5
place, where she is n for a time ... Rev 12:14

## NOURISHER

thy life, and a n of thine old age ... Ruth 4:15

## NOURISHETH

but n and cherisheth it, even as ... Eph 5:29

## NOURISHING

so n them three years, that at ... Dan 1:5

## NOURISHMENT

and bands having n ministered ... Col 2:19

## NOVICE

Not a n, lest being lifted up ... 1Ti 3:6

**NOW** See PREFACE.

## NUMBER

so that if a man can n the dust ... Gen 13:16
stars, if thou be able to n them ... Gen 15:5
and I being few in n, they shall ... Gen 34:30
for it was without n ... Gen 41:49
according to the n of the souls ... Ex 12:4
to the n of your persons ... Ex 16:16
the n of thy days I will fulfil ... Ex 23:26
children of Israel after their n ... Ex 30:12
then he shall n to himself seven ... Lev 15:13
then she shall n to herself seven ... Lev 15:28
sabbath shall ye n fifty days ... Lev 23:16
thou shalt n seven sabbaths of ... Lev 25:8
According to the n of years after ... Lev 25:15
according unto the n of years of ... Lev 25:15
for according to the n of the ... Lev 25:16
be according unto the n of years ... Lev 25:50
your cattle, and make you few in n ... Lev 26:22
with the n of their names, every ... Num 1:2
Aaron shall n them by their ... Num 1:3
according to the n of the names ... Num 1:18
according to the n of the names ... Num 1:20
according to the n of the names ... Num 1:22
according to the n of the names ... Num 1:24
according to the n of the names ... Num 1:26
according to the n of the names ... Num 1:28
according to the n of the names ... Num 1:30
according to the n of the names ... Num 1:32
according to the n of the names ... Num 1:34
according to the n of the names ... Num 1:36
according to the n of the names ... Num 1:38
according to the n of the names ... Num 1:40
according to the n of the names ... Num 1:42
shalt not n the tribe of Levi ... Num 1:49
N the children of Levi after the ... Num 3:15
old and upward shalt thou n them ... Num 3:15
to the n of all the males ... Num 3:22
In the n of all the males, from a ... Num 3:28
to the n of all the males ... Num 3:34
N all the firstborn of the males ... Num 3:40
take the n of their names ... Num 3:40
firstborn males by the n of names ... Num 3:43
wherewith the odd n of them is to ... Num 3:48
fifty years old shalt thou n them ... Num 4:23
thou shalt n them after their ... Num 4:29
fifty years old shalt thou n them ... Num 4:30
Aaron did n according to the ... Num 4:37
Aaron did n according to the ... Num 4:41

of you, according to your whole *n* .... Num 14:29
After the *n* of the days in which .... Num 14:34
According to the *n* that ye shall .... Num 15:12
to every one according to their *n* .... Num 15:12
the *n* of the fourth part of .... Num 23:10
according to the *n* of names .... Num 26:53
shall be according to their *n* .... Num 29:18
shall be according to their *n* .... Num 29:21
shall be according to their *n* .... Num 29:24
shall be according to their *n* .... Num 29:27
shall be according to their *n* .... Num 29:30
shall be according to their *n* .... Num 29:33
shall be according to their *n* .... Num 29:37
was in *n* three hundred thousand .... Num 31:36
left few in *n* among the heathen .... Deut 4:27
ye were more in *n* than any people .... Deut 7:7
weeks shalt thou *n* unto thee .... Deut 16:9
begin to *n* the seven weeks from .... Deut 16:9
to his fault, by a certain *n* .... Deut 25:2
And ye shall be left few in *n* .... Deut 28:62
the *n* of the children of Israel .... Deut 32:8
according unto the *n* of the .... Josh 4:5
according to the *n* of the tribes .... Josh 4:8
and their camels were without *n* .... Judg 6:5
the *n* of them that lapped, .... Judg 7:6
and their camels were without *n* .... Judg 7:12
them wives, according to their *n* .... Judg 21:23
according to the *n* of the lords .... 1Sa 6:4
according to the *n* of all the .... 1Sa 6:18
*N* now, and see who is gone from us .. 1Sa 14:17
went over by *n* twelve of Benjamin .... 2Sa 2:15
six toes, four and twenty in *n* .... 2Sa 21:20
to say, Go, *n* Israel and Judah .... 2Sa 24:1
*n* ye the people, that I may know .... 2Sa 24:2
I may know the *n* of the people .... 2Sa 24:2
to *n* the people of Israel .... 2Sa 24:4
the *n* of the people unto the king .... 2Sa 24:9
according to the *n* of the tribes .... 1Kin 18:31
*n* thee an army, like the army .... 1Kin 20:25
whose *n* was in the days of David .... 1Chr 7:2
the *n* of them, after their .... 1Chr 7:9
the *n* throughout the genealogy of .... 1Chr 7:40
this is the *n* of the mighty men .... 1Chr 11:11
and provoked David to *n* Israel .... 1Chr 21:1
*n* Israel from Beer-sheba even to .... 1Chr 21:2
bring the *n* of them to me, that I .... 1Chr 21:2
of the *n* of the people unto David .... 1Chr 21:5
brass, and the iron, there is no *n* .... 1Chr 22:16
their *n* by their polls, man by .... 1Chr 23:3
by *n* of names by their polls .... 1Chr 23:24
moons, and on the set feasts, by *n* .... 1Chr 23:31
the *n* of the workmen according to .... 1Chr 25:1
So the *n* of them, with their .... 1Chr 25:7
children of Israel after their *n* .... 1Chr 27:1
But David took not the *n* of them .... 1Chr 27:23
the son of Zeruiah began to *n* .... 1Chr 27:24
neither was the *n* put in the .... 1Chr 27:24
the people were without *n* that .... 2Chr 12:3
according to the *n* of their .... 2Chr 26:11
The whole *n* of the chief of the .... 2Chr 26:12
the *n* of the burnt offerings, .... 2Chr 29:32
a great *n* of priests sanctified .... 2Chr 30:24
to the *n* of thirty thousand, and .... 2Chr 35:7
And this is the *n* of them .... Ezr 1:9
The *n* of the men of the people of .... Ezr 2:2
the daily burnt offerings by *n* .... Ezr 3:4
according to the *n* of the tribes .... Ezr 6:17
By *n* and by weight of every one .... Ezr 8:34
The *n*, I say, of the men of the .... Neh 7:7
On that day the *n* of those that .... Est 9:11
according to the *n* of them all .... Job 1:5
not come into the *n* of the months .... Job 3:6
marvellous things without *n* .... Job 5:9
yea, and wonders without *n* .... Job 9:10
the *n* of his months are with thee .... Job 14:5
the *n* of years is hidden to the .... Job 15:20
when the *n* of his months is cut .... Job 21:21
Is there any *n* of his armies .... Job 25:3
unto him the *n* of my steps .... Job 31:37
in pieces mighty men without *n* .... Job 34:24
neither can the *n* of his years be .... Job 36:26
or because the *n* of thy days is .... Job 38:21
Who can *n* the clouds in wisdom .... Job 38:37
Canst thou *n* the months that they .... Job 39:2
So teach us to *n* our days .... Ps 90:12
When they were but a few men in *n* .... Ps 105:12
caterpillers, and that without *n* .... Ps 105:34
they are more in *n* than the sand .... Ps 139:18
He telleth the *n* of the stars .... Ps 147:4
concubines, and virgins without *n* .... Song 6:8
the residue of the *n* of archers .... Is 21:17
that bringeth out their host by *n* .... Is 40:26
the drink offering unto that *n* .... Is 65:11
will I *n* you to the sword .... Is 65:12
for according to the *n* of thy .... Jer 2:28
have forgotten me days without *n* .... Jer 2:32
For according to the *n* of thy .... Jer 11:13
according to the *n* of the streets .... Jer 11:13
Yet a small *n* that escape the .... Jer 44:28
according to the *n* of the days .... Eze 4:4
according to the *n* of the days .... Eze 4:5
according to the *n* of the days .... Eze 4:9
also take thereof a few in *n* .... Eze 5:3
by books the *n* of the years .... Dan 9:2
Yet the *n* of the children of .... Hos 1:10
my land, strong, and without *n* .... Joel 1:6
slain, and a great *n* of carcases .... Nah 3:3
a great *n* of people, blind .... Mk 10:46
being of the *n* of the twelve .... Lk 22:3
down, in *n* about five thousand .... Jn 6:10
(the *n* of names together were .... Acts 1:15
the *n* of the men was about five .... Acts 4:4
to whom a *n* of men, about four .... Acts 5:36
when the *n* of the disciples was .... Acts 6:1
the *n* of the disciples multiplied .... Acts 6:7
a great *n* believed, and turned .... Acts 11:21
faith, and increased in *n* daily .... Acts 16:5
Though the *n* of the children of .... Rom 9:27
dare not make ourselves of the *n* .... 2Cor 10:12
the *n* under threescore years old .... 1Ti 5:9
the *n* of them was ten thousand .... Rev 5:11
I heard the *n* of them which were .... Rev 7:4
multitude, which no man could *n* .... Rev 7:9
the *n* of the army of the horsemen .... Rev 9:16
and I heard the *n* of them .... Rev 9:16
the beast, or the *n* of his name .... Rev 13:17
count the *n* of the beast .... Rev 13:18
for it is the *n* of a man .... Rev 13:18
his *n* is six hundred threescore .... Rev 13:18
over the *n* of his name, stand on .... Rev 15:2
the *n* of whom is as the sand of .... Rev 20:8

**NUMBERED**

then shall thy seed also be *n* .... Gen 13:16
it shall not be *n* for multitude .... Gen 16:10
which cannot be *n* for multitude .... Gen 32:12
passeth among them that are *n* .... Ex 30:13
passeth among them that are *n* .... Ex 30:14
were *n* of the congregation was an .... Ex 38:25
for every one that went to be *n* .... Ex 38:26
so he *n* them in the wilderness of .... Num 1:19
Those that were *n* of them .... Num 1:21
those that were *n* of them .... Num 1:22
Those that were *n* of them .... Num 1:23
Those that were *n* of them .... Num 1:25
Those that were *n* of them .... Num 1:27
Those that were *n* of them .... Num 1:29
Those that were *n* of them .... Num 1:31
Those that were *n* of them .... Num 1:33
Those that were *n* of them .... Num 1:35
Those that were *n* of them .... Num 1:37
Those that were *n* of them .... Num 1:39
Those that were *n* of them .... Num 1:41
Those that were *n* of them .... Num 1:43
*n*, which Moses and Aaron *n* .... Num 1:44
were *n* of the children of Israel .... Num 1:45
Even all they that were *n* were .... Num 1:46
fathers were not *n* among them .... Num 1:47
and those that were *n* of them .... Num 2:4
and those that were *n* thereof .... Num 2:6
and those that were *n* thereof .... Num 2:8
All that were *n* in the camp of .... Num 2:9
and those that were *n* thereof .... Num 2:11
and those that were *n* of them .... Num 2:13
and those that were *n* of them .... Num 2:15
All that were *n* in the camp of .... Num 2:16
and those that were *n* of them .... Num 2:19
and those that were *n* of them .... Num 2:21
and those that were *n* of them .... Num 2:23
All that were *n* of the camp of .... Num 2:24
and those that were *n* of them .... Num 2:26
and those that were *n* of them .... Num 2:28
and those that were *n* of them .... Num 2:30
All they that were *n* in the camp .... Num 2:31
These are those which were *n* of .... Num 2:32
all those that were *n* of the .... Num 2:32
But the Levites were not *n* among .... Num 2:33
Moses *n* them according to the .... Num 3:16
Those that were *n* of them .... Num 3:22
even those that were *n* of them .... Num 3:22
And those that were *n* of them .... Num 3:34
All that were *n* of the Levites, .... Num 3:39
Aaron *n* at the commandment of the . Num 3:39
Moses *n*, as the LORD .... Num 3:42
of those that were *n* of them .... Num 3:43
*n* the sons of the Kohathites .... Num 4:34
those that were *n* of them by .... Num 4:36
were *n* of the families of the .... Num 4:37
those that were *n* of the sons of .... Num 4:38
Even those that were *n* of them .... Num 4:40
These are they that were *n* of the .... Num 4:41
those that were *n* of the families .... Num 4:42
Even those that were *n* of them .... Num 4:44
These be those that were *n* of the .... Num 4:45
Aaron *n* according to the word of .... Num 4:45
those that were *n* of the Levites .... Num 4:46
and Aaron and the chief of Israel *n* .... Num 4:46
Even those that were *n* of them .... Num 4:48
they were *n* by the hand of Moses .... Num 4:49
thus were they *n* of him, as the .... Num 4:49
and were over them that were *n* .... Num 7:2
and all that were *n* of you .... Num 14:29
they that were *n* of them were .... Num 26:7
to those that were *n* of them .... Num 26:18
to those that were *n* of them .... Num 26:22
to those that were *n* of them .... Num 26:25
to those that were *n* of them .... Num 26:27
and those that were *n* of them .... Num 26:34
to those that were *n* of them .... Num 26:37
they that were *n* of them were .... Num 26:41
to those that were *n* of them .... Num 26:43
to those that were *n* of them .... Num 26:47
they that were *n* of them were .... Num 26:50
These were the *n* of the children .... Num 26:51
to those that were *n* of him .... Num 26:54
these are they that were *n* of the .... Num 26:57
those that were *n* of them were .... Num 26:62
for they were not *n* among the .... Num 26:62
are they that were *n* by Moses .... Num 26:63
who *n* the children of Israel in .... Num 26:63
whom Moses and Aaron the priest *n* Num 26:64
when they *n* the children of .... Num 26:64
*n* the people, and went up, he and .... Josh 8:10
the children of Benjamin were *n* .... Judg 20:15
which were *n* seven hundred chosen Judg 20:15
were *n* four hundred thousand men .. Judg 20:17
For the people were *n*, and, behold .... Judg 21:9
when he *n* them in Bezek, the .... 1Sa 11:8
Saul *n* the people that were .... 1Sa 13:15
And when they had *n*, behold, .... 1Sa 14:17
*n* them in Telaim, two hundred .... 1Sa 15:4
David *n* the people that were with .... 2Sa 18:1
after that he had *n* the people .... 2Sa 24:10
that cannot be *n* nor counted for .... 1Kin 3:8
not be told nor *n* for multitude .... 1Kin 8:5
Then he *n* the young men of the .... 1Kin 20:15
after them he *n* all the people, .... 1Kin 20:15
that Ben-hadad *n* the Syrians .... 1Kin 20:26
And the children of Israel were *n* .... 1Kin 20:27
the same time, and *n* all Israel .... 2Kin 3:6
that commanded the people to be *n* .. 1Chr 21:17
Now the Levites were *n* from the .... 1Chr 23:3
were *n* from twenty years old .... 1Chr 23:27
Solomon *n* all the strangers that .... 2Chr 2:17
David his father had *n* them .... 2Chr 2:17
not be told nor *n* for multitude .... 2Chr 5:6
he *n* them from twenty years old .... 2Chr 25:5
*n* them unto Sheshbazzar, the .... Ezr 1:8
them, they are more than can be *n* .... Ps 40:5
that which is wanting cannot be *n* .... Eccl 1:15
ye have *n* the houses of Jerusalem .... Is 22:10
he was *n* with the transgressors .... Is 53:12
As the host of heaven cannot be *n* .... Jer 33:22
God hath *n* thy kingdom, and .... Dan 5:26
which cannot be measured nor *n* .... Hos 1:10
very hairs of your head are all *n* .... Mt 10:30
he was *n* with the transgressors .... Mk 15:28
very hairs of your head are all *n* .... Lk 12:7
For he was *n* with us, and had .... Acts 1:17
he was *n* with the eleven apostles .... Acts 1:26

**NUMBEREST**

unto the LORD, when thou *n* them .... Ex 30:12
among them, when thou *n* them .... Ex 30:12
For now thou *n* my steps .... Job 14:16

**NUMBERING**

sea, very much, until he left *n* .... Gen 41:49
after the *n* wherewith David his .... 2Chr 2:17

**NUMBERS**

these are the *n* of the bands that .... 1Chr 12:23
these are the *n* of them according .... 2Chr 17:14
for I know not the *n* thereof .... Ps 71:15

**NUN** (*nun*) See NON. *Father of Joshua.*

his servant Joshua, the son of *N* .... Ex 33:11
And Joshua the son of *N*, the .... Num 11:28
of Ephraim, Oshea the son of *N* .... Num 13:8
Oshea the son of *N* Jehoshua .... Num 13:16
And Joshua the son of *N*, and Caleb... Num 14:6
Jephunneh, and Joshua the son of *N* Num 14:30
But Joshua the son of *N*, and Caleb.. Num 14:38
Jephunneh, and Joshua the son of *N* Num 26:65
Take thee Joshua the son of *N* .... Num 27:18
Kenezite, and Joshua the son of *N* .... Num 32:12
priest, and Joshua the son of *N* .... Num 32:28
priest, and Joshua the son of *N* .... Num 34:17
But Joshua the son of *N*, which .... Deut 1:38
gave Joshua the son of *N* a charge ... Deut 31:23
he, and Hoshea the son of *N* .... Deut 32:44
Joshua the son of *N* was full of .... Deut 34:9
spake unto Joshua the son of *N* .... Josh 1:1
Joshua the son of *N* sent out of .... Josh 2:1
and came to Joshua the son of *N* .... Josh 2:23
Joshua the son of *N* called the .... Josh 6:6
priest, and Joshua the son of *N* .... Josh 14:1
and before Joshua the son of *N* .... Josh 17:4
to Joshua the son of *N* among them .. Josh 19:49
priest, and Joshua the son of *N* .... Josh 19:51
and unto Joshua the son of *N* .... Josh 21:1
things, that Joshua the son of *N* .... Josh 24:29
And Joshua the son of *N*, the .... Judg 2:8
he spake by Joshua the son of *N* .... 1Kin 16:34
of *N* unto that day had not the .... Neh 8:17

**NURSE**

Rebekah their sister, and her *n* .... Gen 24:59
But Deborah Rebekah's *n* died .... Gen 35:8
call to thee a *n* of the Hebrew .... Ex 2:7
that she may *n* the child for thee .... Ex 2:7
*n* it for me, and I will give thee .... Ex 2:9
in her bosom, and became *n* unto it ... Ruth 4:16
his *n* took him up, and fled .... 2Sa 4:4
they hid him, even him and his *n* .... 2Kin 11:2
put him and his *n* in a bedchamber ... 2Chr 22:11
even as a *n* cherisheth her .... 1Th 2:7

**NURSED**

the woman took the child, and *n* it .... Ex 2:9
daughters shall be *n* at thy side .... Is 60:4

**NURSING**

as a *n* father beareth the sucking .... Num 11:12
And kings shall be thy *n* fathers .... Is 49:23
and their queens thy *n* mothers .... Is 49:23

**NURTURE**

but bring them up in the *n* .... Eph 6:4

**NUTS**

little honey, spices, and myrrh, *n* .... Gen 43:11
I went down into the garden of *n* .... Song 6:11

**NYMPHA** See NYMPHAS.

**NYMPHAS** (*nim'-fas*) *A Christian at Colosse.*
which are in Laodicea, and N Col 4:15

# O

**O** See PREFACE.

**OAK**
under the o which was by Shechem Gen 35:4
buried beneath Beth-el under an o Gen 35:8
and set it up there under an o Josh 24:26
sat under an o which was in Judg 6:11
it out unto him under the o Judg 6:19
the thick boughs of a great o 2Sa 18:9
and his head caught hold of the o 2Sa 18:9
I saw Absalom hanged in an o 2Sa 18:10
yet alive in the midst of the o 2Sa 18:14
and found him sitting under an o 1Kin 13:14
their bones under the o in Jabesh 1Chr 10:12
be as an o whose leaf fadeth Is 1:30
as a teil tree, and as an o Is 6:13
and taketh the cypress and the o Is 44:14
tree, and under every thick o Eze 6:13

**OAKS**
of the o which ye have desired Is 1:29
up, and upon all the o of Bashan Is 2:13
Of the o of Bashan have they made Eze 27:6
incense upon the hills, under o Hos 4:13
cedars, and he was strong as the o Amos 2:9
howl, O ye o of Bashan Zec 11:2

**OAR**
And all that handle the o, the Eze 27:29

**OARS**
wherein shall go no galley with o Is 33:21
of Bashan have they made thine o Eze 27:6

**OATH**
shalt be clear from this my o Gen 24:8
thou be clear from this my o Gen 24:41
thou shalt be clear from my o Gen 24:41
I will perform the o which I Gen 26:3
Let there be now an o betwixt us Gen 26:28
Joseph took an o of the children Gen 50:25
Then shall an o of the LORD be Ex 22:11
a man shall pronounce with an o Lev 5:4
priest shall charge her by an o Num 5:19
the woman with an o of cursing Num 5:21
an o among thy people, when the Num 5:21
or swear an o to bind his soul Num 30:2
her soul by a bond with an o Num 30:10
every binding o to afflict the Num 30:13
because he would keep the o which Deut 7:8
the LORD thy God, and into his o Deut 29:12
do I make this covenant and this o Deut 29:14
o which thou hast made us swear Josh 2:17
o which thou hast made us to Josh 2:20
because of the o which we sware Josh 9:20
For they had made a great o Judg 21:5
for the people feared the o 1Sa 14:26
charged the people with the o 1Sa 14:27
charged the people with an o 1Sa 14:28
LORD'S o that was between them 2Sa 21:7
thou not kept the o of the LORD 1Kin 2:43
an o be laid upon him to cause 1Kin 8:31
the o come before thine altar in 1Kin 8:31
he took an o of the kingdom and 1Kin 18:10
took an o of them in the house of 2Kin 11:4
Abraham, and of his o unto Isaac 1Chr 16:16
an o be laid upon him to make him 2Chr 6:22
the o come before thine altar in 2Chr 6:22
And all Judah rejoiced at the o 2Chr 15:15
the priests, and took an o of them Neh 5:12
into a curse, and into an o Neh 10:29
with Abraham, and his o unto Isaac Ps 105:9
and that in regard of the o of God Eccl 8:2
sweareth, as he that feareth an o Eccl 9:2
That I may perform the o which I Jer 11:5
which hast despised the o in Eze 16:59
him, and hath taken an o of him Eze 17:13
whose o he despised, and whose Eze 17:16
Seeing he despised the o by Eze 17:18
surely mine o that he hath Eze 17:19
the o that is written in the law Dan 9:11
and love no false o Zec 8:17
an o to give her whatsoever she Mt 14:7
And again he denied with an o Mt 26:72
The o which he sware to our Lk 1:73
God had sworn with an o to him Acts 2:30
have bound themselves with an o Acts 23:21
an o for confirmation is to them Heb 6:16
his counsel, confirmed it by an o Heb 6:17
without an o he was made priest Heb 7:20
priests were made without an o Heb 7:21
but this with an o by him that Heb 7:21
but the word of the o, which was Heb 7:28
the earth, neither by any other o Jas 5:12

**OATH'S**
nevertheless for the o sake Mt 14:9
yet for his o sake, and for their Mk 6:26

**OATHS**
sight, to them that have sworn o Eze 21:23
according to the o of the tribes Hab 3:9
perform unto the Lord thine o Mt 5:33

**OBADIAH** (*o-ba-di'-ah*)
*1. An officer in Ahab's court.*
And Ahab called O, which was the 1Kin 18:3
(Now O feared the LORD greatly 1Kin 18:3
that O took an hundred prophets, 1Kin 18:4
And Ahab said unto O, Go into the 1Kin 18:5
O went another way by himself 1Kin 18:6
as O was in the way, behold, 1Kin 18:7
So O went to meet Ahab, and told 1Kin 18:16
*2. A descendant of David.*
the sons of Arnan, the sons of O 1Chr 3:21
*3. A descendant of Tola.*
Michael, and O, and Joel, Ishiah, 1Chr 7:3
*4. Son of Azel.*
and Ishmael, and Sheariah, and O 1Chr 8:38
and Ishmael, and Sheariah, and O 1Chr 9:44
*5. Son of Shemaiah.*
O the son of Shemaiah, the son of 1Chr 9:16
*6. A warrior in David's army.*
O the second, Eliab the third, 1Chr 12:9
*7. A prince of Zebulun.*
Of Zebulun, Ishmaiah the son of O 1Chr 27:19
*8. A prince of Judah.*
even to Ben-hail, and to O 2Chr 17:7
*9. A Levite in Josiah's time.*
of them were Jahath and O, the 2Chr 34:12
*10. A clan leader with Ezra.*
O the son of Jehiel, and with him Ezr 8:9
*11. A priest who renewed the covenant.*
Harim, Meremoth, O, Neh 10:5
*12. A Temple gatekeeper.*
Mattaniah, and Bakbukiah, O Neh 12:25
*13. A prophet.*
The vision of O Obad 1

**OBAL** (*o'-bal*) *A son of Joktan.*
And O, and Abimael, and Sheba, Gen 10:28

**OBED** (*o'-bed*) See OBED-EDOM.
*1. Father of Jesse.*
and they called his name O Ruth 4:17
begat Boaz, and Boaz begat O Ruth 4:21
O begat Jesse, and Jesse begat Ruth 4:22
And Boaz begat O, and O begat 1Chr 2:12
and Booz begat O of Ruth Mt 1:5
and O begat Jesse Mt 1:5
of Jesse, which was the son of O Lk 3:32
*2. A descendant of Judah.*
begat Ephlal, and Ephlal begat O 1Chr 2:37
O begat Jehu, and Jehu begat 1Chr 2:38
*3. A 'mighty man' of David.*
Eliel, and O, and Jasiel the 1Chr 11:47
*4. A sanctuary servant.*
Othni, and Rephael, and O, Elzabad, 1Chr 26:7
*5. Father of Azariah.*
and Azariah the son of O, and 2Chr 23:1

**OBED-EDOM** (*o''-bed-e'-dom*)
*1. A Levite.*
into the house of O the Gittite 2Sa 6:10
of O the Gittite three months 2Sa 6:11
and the LORD blessed O, and all his 2Sa 6:11
LORD hath blessed the house of O 2Sa 6:12
of O into the city of David with 2Sa 6:12
into the house of O the Gittite 1Chr 13:13
of O in his house three months 1Chr 13:14
the LORD blessed the house of O 1Chr 13:14
and O and Jehiah were doorkeepers 1Chr 15:24
out of the house of O with joy 1Chr 15:25
*2. A priest who relocated the Ark.*
and Elipheleh, and Mikneiah, and O 1Chr 15:18
and Elipheleh, and Mikneiah, and O 1Chr 15:21
Moreover the sons of O were 1Chr 26:4
All these of the sons of O 1Chr 26:8
were threescore and two of O 1Chr 26:8
To O southward 1Chr 26:15
*3. Another priest who relocated the Ark.*
and Eliab, and Benaiah, and O 1Chr 16:5
O with their brethren, threescore 1Chr 16:38
*4. Son of Jeduthun.*
O also the son of Jeduthun and 1Chr 16:38
*5. A Temple servant.*
found in the house of God with O 2Chr 25:24

**OBEDIENCE**
for o to the faith among all Rom 1:5
so by the o of one shall many be Rom 5:19
or of o unto righteousness Rom 6:16
For your o is come abroad unto Rom 16:19
to all nations for the o of faith Rom 16:26
they are commanded to be under o 1Cor 14:34
he remembereth the o of you all 2Cor 7:15
every thought to the o of Christ 2Cor 10:5
when your o is fulfilled 2Cor 10:6
in thy o I wrote unto thee Philem 21
yet learned he o by the things Heb 5:8
of the Spirit, unto o and 1Pet 1:2

**OBEDIENT**
hath said will we do, and be o Ex 24:7
the children of Israel may be o Num 27:20
shalt be o unto his voice Deut 4:30
because ye would not be o unto Deut 8:20
hear, they shall be o unto me 2Sa 22:45
is a wise reprover upon an o ear Prov 25:12
If ye be willing and o, ye shall Is 1:19
neither were they o unto his law Is 42:24
the priests were o to the faith Acts 6:7
by me, to make the Gentiles o Rom 15:18
whether ye be o in all things 2Cor 2:9
be o to them that are your Eph 6:5
became o unto death, even the Phil 2:8
o to their own husbands, that the Titus 2:5
Exhort servants to be o unto Titus 2:9
As o children, not fashioning 1Pet 1:14

**OBEISANCE**
about, and made o to my sheaf Gen 37:7
and the eleven stars made o to me Gen 37:9
bowed down their heads, and made o Gen 43:28
meet his father in law, and did o Ex 18:7
he fell to the earth, and did o 2Sa 1:2
her face to the ground, and did o 2Sa 14:4
man came nigh to him to do him o 2Sa 15:5
bowed, and did o unto the king 1Kin 1:16
of Judah, and made o to the king 2Chr 24:17

**OBEY**
o my voice according to that Gen 27:8
only o my voice, and go fetch me Gen 27:13
Now therefore, my son, o my voice Gen 27:43
that I should o his voice to let Ex 5:2
if ye will o my voice indeed, and Ex 19:5
o his voice, provoke him not Ex 23:21
if thou shalt indeed o his voice Ex 23:22
if ye o the commandments of the Deut 11:27
if ye will not o the commandments Deut 11:28
o his voice, and ye shall serve Deut 13:4
which will not o the voice of his Deut 21:18
he will not o our voice Deut 21:20
Thou shalt therefore o the voice Deut 27:10
because thou wouldest not o the Deut 28:62
shalt o his voice according to Deut 30:2
o the voice of the LORD, and do Deut 30:8
and that thou mayest o his voice Deut 30:20
we serve, and his voice will we o Josh 24:24
refused to o the voice of Samuel 1Sa 8:19
o his voice, and not rebel against 1Sa 12:14
But if ye will not o the voice of 1Sa 12:15
thou not o the voice of the LORD 1Sa 15:19
to o is better than sacrifice, and 1Sa 15:22
And refused to o, neither were Neh 9:17
If they o and serve him, they Job 36:11
But if they o not, they shall Job 36:12
they hear of me, they shall o me Ps 18:44
and despiseth to o his mother Prov 30:17
children of Ammon shall o them Is 11:14
O my voice, and I will be your God Jer 7:23
O my voice, and do them, according Jer 11:4
and protesting, saying, O my voice Jer 11:7
But if they will not o, I will Jer 12:17
that it o not my voice, then I Jer 18:10
o the voice of the LORD your God Jer 26:13
but o their father's commandment Jer 35:14
O, I beseech thee, the voice of Jer 38:20
we will o the voice of the LORD Jer 42:6
when we o the voice of the LORD Jer 42:6
neither o the voice of the LORD Jer 42:13
dominions shall serve and o him Dan 7:27
that they might not o thy voice Dan 9:11
if ye will diligently o the voice Zec 6:15
even the winds and the sea o him Mt 8:27
unclean spirits, and they do o him Mk 1:27
even the wind and the sea o him Mk 4:41
the winds and water, and they o him Lk 8:25
and it should o you Lk 17:6
We ought to o God rather than men Acts 5:29
God hath given to them that o him Acts 5:32
To whom our fathers would not o Acts 7:39
do not o the truth Rom 2:8
but o unrighteousness Rom 2:8
that ye should o it in the lusts Rom 6:12
ye yield yourselves servants to o Rom 6:16
his servants ye are to whom ye o Rom 6:16
that ye should not o the truth Gal 3:1
that ye should not o the truth Gal 5:7
o your parents in the Lord Eph 6:1
o your parents in all things Col 3:20
o in all things your masters Col 3:22
that o not the gospel of our Lord 2Th 1:8
if any man o not our word by this 2Th 3:14
to o magistrates, to be ready to Titus 3:1
unto all them that o him Heb 5:9
O them that have the rule over Heb 13:17
mouths, that they may o us Jas 3:3
if any o not the word, they also 1Pet 3:1
them that o not the gospel of God 1Pet 4:17

**OBEYED**
because thou hast o my voice Gen 22:18
Because that Abraham o my voice Gen 26:5
And that Jacob o his father Gen 28:7
because they o not the voice of Josh 5:6
have o my voice in all that I Josh 22:2
but ye have not o my voice Judg 2:2
but ye have not o my voice Judg 6:10
I have o the voice of the LORD, 1Sa 15:20
the people, and o their voice 1Sa 15:24
thine handmaid hath o thy voice 1Sa 28:21
hast not o the voice of the LORD 1Kin 20:36
Because they o not the voice of 2Kin 18:12
and all Israel o him 1Chr 29:23
they o the words of the LORD, and 2Chr 11:4
have not o the voice of my Prov 5:13
tree, and ye have not o my voice Jer 3:13
have not o the voice of the LORD Jer 3:25
them, and have not o my voice Jer 9:13
Yet they o not, nor inclined Jer 11:8
But they o not, neither inclined Jer 17:23
but they o not thy voice, neither Jer 32:23
of them any more, then they o Jer 34:10
Thus have we o the voice of Jer 35:8
we have dwelt in tents, and have o Jer 35:10

Because ye have o the commandment. Jer 35:18
have not o his voice, therefore Jer 40:3
but ye have not o the voice of Jer 42:21
o not the voice of the LORD, to Jer 43:4
for they o not the voice of the Jer 43:7
have not o the voice of the LORD, Jer 44:23
Neither have we o the voice of Dan 9:10
for we o not his voice Dan 9:14
She o not the voice Zeph 3:2
o the voice of the LORD their God Hag 1:12
and all, as many as o him, were Acts 5:36
and all, even as many as o him Acts 5:37
but ye have o from the heart that Rom 6:17
they have not all o the gospel Rom 10:16
my beloved, as ye have always o Phil 2:12
receive for an inheritance, o Heb 11:8
Even as Sarah o Abraham, calling 1Pet 3:6

**OBEYEDST**
Because thou o not the voice of 1Sa 28:18
youth, that thou o not my voice Jer 22:21

**OBEYETH**
that o the voice of his servant, Is 50:10
This is a nation that o not the Jer 7:28
Cursed be the man that o not the Jer 11:3

**OBEYING**
o the commandments of the LORD Judg 2:17
as in o the voice of the LORD 1Sa 15:22
in o the truth through the Spirit 1Pet 1:22

**OBIL** (*o'-bil*) *An Ishmaelite camel driver.*
camels also was O the Ishmaelite 1Chr 27:30

**OBJECT**
have been here before thee, and o Acts 24:19

**OBLATION**
if thou bring an o of a meat Lev 2:4
if thy o be a meat offering baken Lev 2:5
if thy o be a meat offering baken Lev 2:7
As for the o of the firstfruits, Lev 2:12
every o of thy meat offering Lev 2:13
if his o be a sacrifice of peace Lev 3:1
offer one out of the whole o for Lev 7:14
unto the LORD shall bring his o Lev 7:29
will offer his o for all his vows Lev 22:18
every o of theirs, every meat Num 18:9
brought an o for the LORD Num 31:50
day, and shall do sacrifice and o Is 19:21
o chooseth a tree that will not Is 40:20
he that offereth an o, as if he Is 66:3
they offer burnt offering and an o Jer 14:12
every o of all, of every sort of Eze 44:30
ye shall offer an o unto the LORD Eze 45:1
over against the o of the holy Eze 45:6
side of the o of the holy portion Eze 45:7
before the o of the holy portion, Eze 45:7
This is the o that ye shall offer Eze 45:13
this o for the prince in Israel Eze 45:16
The o that ye shall offer unto Eze 48:9
the priests, shall be this holy o Eze 48:10
this o of the land that is Eze 48:12
in length over against the o of Eze 48:18
against the o of the holy portion Eze 48:18
All the o shall be five and twenty Eze 48:20
shall offer the holy o foursquare Eze 48:20
and on the other of the holy o Eze 48:21
of the o toward the east border Eze 48:21
and it shall be the holy o Eze 48:21
that they should offer an o Dan 2:46
about the time of the evening o Dan 9:21
the o to cease, and for the Dan 9:27

**OBLATIONS**
to offer their o unto the LORD Lev 7:38
to distribute the o of the LORD 2Chr 31:14
Bring no more vain o Is 1:13
and the firstfruits of your o Eze 20:40
of all, of every sort of your o Eze 44:30

**OBOTH** (*o'-both*) *An Israelite encampment in the wilderness.*
set forward, and pitched in O Num 21:10
And they journeyed from O, and Num 21:11
from Punon, and pitched in O Num 33:43
And they departed from O, and Num 33:44

**OBSCURE**
shall be put out in o darkness Prov 20:20

**OBSCURITY**
of the blind shall see out of o Is 29:18
then shall thy light rise in o Is 58:10
we wait for light, but behold o Is 59:9

**OBSERVATION**
kingdom of God cometh not with o Lk 17:20

**OBSERVE**
And ye shall o the feast of Ex 12:17
therefore shall ye o this day in Ex 12:17
ye shall o this thing for an Ex 12:24
to o the sabbath throughout their Ex 31:16
O thou that which I command thee Ex 34:11
thou shalt o the feast of weeks, Ex 34:22
ye use enchantment, nor o times Lev 19:26
shall ye o all my statutes Lev 19:37
shall ye o to offer unto me in Num 28:2
Ye shall o to do therefore as the Deut 5:32
O Israel, and o to do it Deut 6:3
if we o to do all these Deut 6:25
thee this day shall ye o to do Deut 8:1
ye shall o to do all the statutes Deut 11:32
which ye shall o to do in the Deut 12:1
O and hear all these words which I .. Deut 12:28
soever I command you, o to do it Deut 12:32
to o to do all these commandments Deut 15:5
O the month of Abib, and keep the Deut 16:1
and thou shalt o and do these Deut 16:12
Thou shalt o the feast of Deut 16:13
thou shalt o to do according to Deut 17:10
that thou o diligently, and do Deut 24:8
them, so ye shall o to do Deut 24:8
voice of the LORD thy God, to o Deut 28:1
I command thee this day, to o Deut 28:13
to o to do all his commandments Deut 28:15
If thou wilt not o to do all the Deut 28:58
o to do all the words of this law Deut 31:12
command your children to o to do Deut 32:46
that thou mayest o to do Josh 1:7
night, that thou mayest o to do Josh 1:8
that I commanded her let her o Judg 13:14
Now the men did diligently o 1Kin 20:33
ye shall o to do for evermore 2Kin 17:37
only if they will o to do 2Kin 21:8
shalt o my statutes and my 2Chr 7:17
love him and o his commandments Neh 1:5
Moses the servant of God, and to o Neh 10:29
That they might o his statutes Ps 105:45
will o these things, even they Ps 107:43
I shall o it with my whole heart Ps 119:34
and let thine eyes o my ways Prov 23:26
the swallow o the time of their Jer 8:7
neither o their judgments, nor Eze 20:18
o my statutes, and do them Eze 37:24
leopard by the way will I o them Hos 13:7
They that o lying vanities Jonah 2:8
they bid you o, that o Mt 23:3
Teaching them to o all things Mt 28:20
for us to receive, neither to o Acts 16:21
that they o no such thing Acts 21:25
Ye o days, and months, and times, Gal 4:10
that thou o these things without 1Ti 5:21

**OBSERVED**
but his father o the saying Gen 37:11
It is a night to be much o unto Ex 12:42
o of all the children of Israel Ex 12:42
not o all these commandments, Num 15:22
for they have o thy word, and kept Deut 33:9
to pass, when Joab o the city 2Sa 11:16
o times, and used enchantments, and . 2Kin 21:6
also he o times, and used 2Chr 33:6
I have heard him, and o him Hos 14:8
a just man and an holy, and o him Mk 6:20
all these have I o from my youth Mk 10:20

**OBSERVER**
or an o of times, or an enchanter Deut 18:10

**OBSERVERS**
hearkened unto o of times Deut 18:14

**OBSERVEST**
many things, but thou o not Is 42:20

**OBSERVETH**
He that o the wind shall not sow Eccl 11:4

**OBSTINATE**
his spirit, and made his heart o Deut 2:30
Because I knew that thou art o Is 48:4

**OBTAIN**
be that I may o children by her Gen 16:2
shall o favour of the LORD Prov 8:35
they shall o joy and gladness, and Is 35:10
they shall o gladness and joy Is 51:11
o the kingdom by flatteries Dan 11:21
for they shall o mercy Mt 5:7
accounted worthy to o that world Lk 20:35
your mercy they also may o mercy ... Rom 11:31
So run, that ye may o 1Cor 9:24
Now they do it to o a corruptible 1Cor 9:25
but to o salvation by our Lord 1Th 5:9
sakes, that they may also o the 2Ti 2:10
of grace, that we may o mercy Heb 4:16
that they might o a better Heb 11:35
and desire to have, and cannot o Jas 4:2

**OBTAINED**
after certain days o I leave of Neh 13:6
him, and she o kindness of him Est 2:9
Esther o favour in the sight of Est 2:15
she o grace and favour in his Est 2:17
that she o favour in his sight Est 5:2
upon her that had not o mercy Hos 2:23
had o part of this ministry Acts 1:17
With a great sum o I this freedom Acts 22:28
Having therefore o help of God Acts 26:22
that they had o their purpose Acts 27:13
Israel hath not o that which he Rom 11:7
but the election hath o it Rom 11:7
yet have now o mercy through Rom 11:30
as one that hath o mercy of the 1Cor 7:25
also we have o an inheritance Eph 1:11
but I o mercy, because I did it 1Ti 1:13
Howbeit for this cause I o mercy 1Ti 1:16
as he hath by inheritance o a Heb 1:4
endured, he o the promise Heb 6:15
But now hath he o a more Heb 8:6
having o eternal redemption for Heb 9:12
by it the elders o a good report Heb 11:2
by which he o witness that he was Heb 11:4
o promises, stopped the mouths of Heb 11:33
having o a good report through Heb 11:39
which had not o mercy 1Pet 2:10
but now have o mercy 1Pet 2:10
to them that have o like precious 2Pet 1:1

**OBTAINETH**
A good man o favour of the LORD Prov 12:2
thing, and o favour of the LORD Prov 18:22

**OBTAINING**
to the o of the glory of our Lord 2Th 2:14

**OCCASION**
that he may seek o against us Gen 43:18
do to them as thou shalt find o Judg 9:33
that he sought an o against the Judg 14:4
that thou do as o serve thee 1Sa 10:7
o to the enemies of the LORD to 2Sa 12:14
which thou shalt have o to bestow Ezr 7:20
in her o who can turn her away Jer 2:24
ye shall not have o any more to Eze 18:3
princes sought to find o against Dan 6:4
they could find none o nor fault Dan 6:4
find any o against this Daniel Dan 6:5
taking o by the commandment, Rom 7:8
taking o by the commandment, Rom 7:11
an o to fall in his brother's way Rom 14:13
but give you o to glory on our 2Cor 5:12
but by o of the forwardness of 2Cor 8:8
o from them which desire o 2Cor 11:12
not liberty for an o to the flesh Gal 5:13
give none o to the adversary to 1Ti 5:14
there is none o of stumbling in 1Jn 2:10

**OCCASIONED**
I have o the death of all the 1Sa 22:22

**OCCASIONS**
give o of speech against her, and Deut 22:14
he hath given o of speech against Deut 22:17
Behold, he findeth o against me Job 33:10

**OCCUPATION**
you, and shall say, What is your o Gen 46:33
unto his brethren, What is your o Gen 47:3
What is thine o Jonah 1:8
for by their o they were Acts 18:3
with the workmen of like o Acts 19:25

**OCCUPIED**
All the gold that was o for the Ex 38:24
with new ropes that never were o Judg 16:11
they o in thy fairs with emeralds Eze 27:16
going to and fro o in thy fairs Eze 27:19
they o with thee in lambs, and Eze 27:21
they o in thy fairs with chief of Eze 27:22
them that have been o therein Heb 13:9

**OCCUPIERS**
the o of thy merchandise, and all Eze 27:27

**OCCUPIETH**
how shall he that o the room of 1Cor 14:16

**OCCUPY**
were in thee to o thy merchandise Eze 27:9
and said unto them, O till I come Lk 19:13

**OCCURRENT**
is neither adversary nor evil o 1Kin 5:4

O

**OCHRAN** See OCRAN.

**OCRAN** (*o'-cran*) *An Asherite who counted the people.*
Pagiel the son of O Num 1:13
shall be Pagiel the son of O Num 2:27
eleventh day Pagiel the son of O Num 7:72
offering of Pagiel the son of O Num 7:77
of Asher was Pagiel the son of O Num 10:26

**ODD**
wherewith the o number of them is Num 3:48

**ODED** (*o'-ded*)
*1. Father of Azariah.*
came upon Azariah the son of O 2Chr 15:1
and the prophecy of O the prophet 2Chr 15:8
*2. A prophet of Samaria.*
LORD was there, whose name was O 2Chr 28:9

**ODIOUS**
had made themselves o to David 1Chr 19:6
For an o woman when she is Prov 30:23

**ODOUR**
filled with the o of the ointment Jn 12:3
you, an o of a sweet smell, a Phil 4:18

**ODOURS**
smell the savour of your sweet o Lev 26:31
bed which was filled with sweet o 2Chr 16:14
myrrh, and six months with sweet o Est 2:12
so shall they burn o for thee Jer 34:5
an oblation and sweet o unto him Dan 2:46
harps, and golden vials full of o Rev 5:8
And cinnamon, and o, and ointments, Rev 18:13

**OF** See PREFACE.

**OFF** See PREFACE.

**OFFENCE**
nor o of heart unto my lord, 1Sa 25:31
for a rock of o to both the Is 8:14
till they acknowledge their o Hos 5:15
thou art an o unto me Mt 16:23
to that man by whom the o cometh Mt 18:7
a conscience void of o toward God Acts 24:16
But not as the o, so also is the Rom 5:15
For if through the o of one many Rom 5:15
For if by one man's o death Rom 5:17
Therefore as by the o of one Rom 5:18

entered, that the o might abound ... Rom 5:20
a stumblingstone and rock of o ... Rom 9:33
for that man who eateth with o ... Rom 14:20
Give none o, neither to the Jews, ... 1Cor 10:32
Giving no o in any thing, that ... 2Cor 6:3
Have I committed an o in abasing ... 2Cor 11:7
then is the o of the cross ceased ... Gal 5:11
without o till the day of Christ ... Phil 1:10
of stumbling, and a rock of o ... 1Pet 2:8

### OFFENCES

for yielding pacifieth great o ... Eccl 10:4
Woe unto the world because of o ... Mt 18:7
for it must needs be that o come ... Mt 18:7
impossible but that o will come ... Lk 17:1
Who was delivered for our o ... Rom 4:25
is of many o unto justification ... Rom 5:16
o contrary to the doctrine which ... Rom 16:17

### OFFEND

I will not o any more ... Job 34:31
I should o against the generation ... Ps 73:15
and nothing shall o them ... Ps 119:165
all that devour him shall o ... Jer 2:3
We o not, because they have ... Jer 50:7
the harlot, yet let not Judah o ... Hos 4:15
and he shall pass over, and o ... Hab 1:11
And if thy right eye o thee ... Mt 5:29
And if thy right hand o thee ... Mt 5:30
of his kingdom all things that o ... Mt 13:41
lest we should o them, go thou ... Mt 17:27
But whoso shall o one of these ... Mt 18:6
if thy hand or thy foot o thee ... Mt 18:8
And if thine eye o thee, pluck it ... Mt 18:9
whosoever shall o one of these ... Mk 9:42
And if thy hand o thee, cut it off ... Mk 9:43
And if thy foot o thee, cut it off ... Mk 9:45
And if thine eye o thee, pluck it ... Mk 9:47
than that he should o one of ... Lk 17:2
said unto them, Doth this o you ... Jn 6:61
if meat make my brother to o ... 1Cor 8:13
lest I make my brother to o ... 1Cor 8:13
yet o in one point, he is guilty ... Jas 2:10
For in many things we o all ... Jas 3:2
If any man o not in word, the ... Jas 3:2

### OFFENDED

and what have I o thee, that thou ... Gen 20:9
his baker had o their lord the ... Gen 40:1
to Lachish, saying, I have o ... 2Kin 18:14
for whereas we have o against the ... 2Chr 28:13
A brother o is harder to be won ... Prov 18:19
What have I o against thee, or ... Jer 37:18
vengeance, and hath greatly o ... Eze 25:12
but when he o in Baal, he died ... Hos 13:1
whosoever shall not be o in me ... Mt 11:6
of the word, by and by he is o ... Mt 13:21
And they were o in him ... Mt 13:57
thou that the Pharisees were o ... Mt 15:12
And then shall many be o, and shall ... Mt 24:10
All ye shall be o because of me ... Mt 26:31
men shall be o because of thee ... Mt 26:33
yet will I never be o ... Mt 26:33
sake, immediately they are o ... Mk 4:17
And they were o at him ... Mk 6:3
All ye shall be o because of me ... Mk 14:27
unto him, Although all shall be o ... Mk 14:29
whosoever shall not be o in me ... Lk 7:23
unto you, that ye should not be o ... Jn 16:1
have I o any thing at all ... Acts 25:8
thy brother stumbleth, or is o ... Rom 14:21
who is o, and I burn not ... 2Cor 11:29

### OFFENDER

That make a man an o for a word ... Is 29:21
For if I be an o, or have ... Acts 25:11

### OFFENDERS

my son Solomon shall be counted o ... 1Kin 1:21

### OFFER

o him there for a burnt offering ... Gen 22:2
Thou shalt not delay to o the ... Ex 22:29
Thou shalt not o the blood of my ... Ex 23:18
thou shalt o every day a bullock ... Ex 29:36
which thou shalt o upon the altar ... Ex 29:38
lamb thou shalt o in the morning ... Ex 29:39
other lamb thou shalt o at even ... Ex 29:39
other lamb thou shalt o at even ... Ex 29:41
Ye shall o no strange incense ... Ex 30:9
Thou shalt not o the blood of my ... Ex 34:25
Every one that did o an offering ... Ex 35:24
let him o a male without blemish ... Lev 1:3
he shall o it of his own ... Lev 1:3
when any will o a meat offering ... Lev 2:1
ye shall o them unto the LORD ... Lev 2:12
thine offerings thou shalt o salt ... Lev 2:13
if thou o a meat offering of thy ... Lev 2:14
thou shalt o for the meat ... Lev 2:14
offering, if he o it of the herd ... Lev 3:1
he shall o it without blemish ... Lev 3:1
he shall o of the sacrifice of ... Lev 3:3
he shall o it without blemish ... Lev 3:6
If he o a lamb for his offering, ... Lev 3:7
then shall he o it before the ... Lev 3:7
he shall o of the sacrifice of ... Lev 3:9
then he shall o it before the ... Lev 3:12
he shall o thereof his offering, ... Lev 3:14
o a young bullock for the sin ... Lev 4:14
who shall o that which is for the ... Lev 5:8
he shall o the second for a burnt ... Lev 5:10
Aaron shall o it before the LORD ... Lev 6:14
which they shall o unto the LORD ... Lev 6:20
o for a sweet savour unto the ... Lev 6:21
anointed in his stead shall o it ... Lev 6:22
he shall o of it all the fat ... Lev 7:3
which he shall o unto the LORD ... Lev 7:11
If he o it for a thanksgiving, ... Lev 7:12
then he shall o with the ... Lev 7:12
he shall o for his offering ... Lev 7:13
of it he shall o one out of the ... Lev 7:14
of which men o an offering made ... Lev 7:25
the children of Israel to o their ... Lev 7:38
and o them before the LORD ... Lev 9:2
o thy sin offering, and thy burnt ... Lev 9:7
o the offering of the people, and ... Lev 9:7
Who shall o it before the LORD, ... Lev 12:7
o him for a trespass offering, and ... Lev 14:12
priest shall o the sin offering ... Lev 14:19
the priest shall o the burnt ... Lev 14:20
he shall o the one of the ... Lev 14:30
And the priest shall o them ... Lev 15:15
the priest shall o the one for a ... Lev 15:30
Aaron shall o his bullock of the ... Lev 16:6
fell, and o him for a sin offering ... Lev 16:9
o his burnt offering, and the ... Lev 16:24
to o an offering unto the LORD ... Lev 17:4
which they o in the open field, ... Lev 17:5
o them for peace offerings unto ... Lev 17:5
they shall no more o their ... Lev 17:7
to o it unto the LORD ... Lev 17:9
if ye o a sacrifice of peace ... Lev 19:5
ye shall o it at your own will ... Lev 19:5
be eaten the same day ye o it ... Lev 19:6
the bread of their God, they do o ... Lev 21:6
to o the bread of his God ... Lev 21:17
the priest shall come nigh to o ... Lev 21:21
nigh to o the bread of his God ... Lev 21:21
which they o unto the LORD ... Lev 22:15
that will o his oblation for all ... Lev 22:18
which they will o unto the LORD ... Lev 22:18
Ye shall o at your own will a ... Lev 22:19
a blemish, that shall ye not o ... Lev 22:20
ye shall not o these unto the ... Lev 22:22
that mayest thou o for a freewill ... Lev 22:23
Ye shall not o unto the LORD that ... Lev 22:24
o the bread of your God of any of ... Lev 22:25
when ye will o a sacrifice of ... Lev 22:29
the LORD, o it at your own will ... Lev 22:29
But ye shall o an offering made ... Lev 23:8
ye shall o that day when ye wave ... Lev 23:12
ye shall o a new meat offering ... Lev 23:16
ye shall o with the bread seven ... Lev 23:18
but ye shall o an offering made ... Lev 23:25
o an offering made by fire unto ... Lev 23:27
Seven days ye shall o an offering ... Lev 23:36
ye shall o an offering made by ... Lev 23:36
to o an offering made by fire ... Lev 23:37
beast, of which they do not o a ... Lev 27:11
the LORD, and o it upon the altar ... Num 5:25
the priest shall o the one for a ... Num 6:11
he shall o his offering unto the ... Num 6:14
shall o his sin offering, and his ... Num 6:16
And he shall o the ram for a ... Num 6:17
the priest shall o also his meat ... Num 6:17
They shall o their offering, each ... Num 7:11
Zuar, prince of Issachar, did o ... Num 7:18
of the children of Zebulun, did o ... Num 7:24
of the children of Reuben, did o ... Num 7:30
of the children of Simeon, did o ... Num 7:36
Aaron shall o the Levites before ... Num 8:11
thou shalt o the one for a sin ... Num 8:12
o them for an offering unto the ... Num 8:13
them, and o them for an offering ... Num 8:15
that we may not o an offering of ... Num 9:7
o the third part of an hin of ... Num 15:7
will o an offering made by fire, ... Num 15:14
ye shall o up an heave offering ... Num 15:19
Ye shall o up a cake of the first ... Num 15:20
o one young bullock for a burnt ... Num 15:24
come near to o incense before the ... Num 16:40
which they shall o unto the LORD ... Num 18:12
of Israel o unto the LORD ... Num 18:19
which they o as an heave offering ... Num 18:24
then ye shall o up an heave ... Num 18:26
Thus ye also shall o an heave ... Num 18:28
o every heave offering of the ... Num 18:29
shall ye observe to o unto me in ... Num 28:2
which ye shall o unto the LORD ... Num 28:3
lamb shalt thou o in the morning ... Num 28:4
other lamb shalt thou o at even ... Num 28:4
other lamb shalt thou o at even ... Num 28:8
offering thereof, thou shalt o it ... Num 28:8
of your months ye shall o a burnt ... Num 28:11
But ye shall o a sacrifice made ... Num 28:19
deals shall ye o for a bullock ... Num 28:20
deal shalt thou o for every lamb ... Num 28:21
Ye shall o these beside the burnt ... Num 28:23
this manner ye shall o daily ... Num 28:24
But ye shall o the burnt offering ... Num 28:27
Ye shall o them beside the ... Num 28:31
ye shall o a burnt offering for a ... Num 29:2
But ye shall o a burnt offering ... Num 29:8
ye shall o a burnt offering, a ... Num 29:13
ye shall o twelve young bullocks ... Num 29:17
But ye shall o a burnt offering, ... Num 29:36
thou o not thy burnt offerings in ... Deut 12:13
there thou shalt o thy burnt ... Deut 12:14
thou shalt o thy burnt offerings, ... Deut 12:27
from them that o a sacrifice ... Deut 18:3
thou shalt o burnt offerings ... Deut 27:6
thou shalt o peace offerings, and ... Deut 27:7
there they shall o sacrifices of ... Deut 33:19
or if to o thereon burnt offering ... Josh 22:23
or if to o peace offerings ... Josh 22:23
had made an end to o the present ... Judg 3:18
o a burnt sacrifice with the wood ... Judg 6:26
I will o it up for a burnt ... Judg 11:31
if thou wilt o a burnt offering, ... Judg 13:16
thou must o it unto the LORD ... Judg 13:16
to o a great sacrifice unto Dagon ... Judg 16:23
went up to o unto the LORD the ... 1Sa 1:21
husband to o the yearly sacrifice ... 1Sa 2:19
to o upon mine altar, to burn ... 1Sa 2:28
to o burnt offerings, and to ... 1Sa 10:8
the LORD, I o thee three things ... 2Sa 24:12
o up what seemeth good unto him ... 2Sa 24:22
neither will I o burnt offerings ... 2Sa 24:24
did Solomon o upon that altar ... 1Kin 3:4
did Solomon o burnt offerings ... 1Kin 9:25
upon thee shall he o the priests ... 1Kin 13:2
o neither burnt offering nor ... 2Kin 5:17
when they went in to o sacrifices ... 2Kin 10:24
To o burnt offerings unto the ... 1Chr 16:40
the LORD, I o thee three things ... 1Chr 21:10
nor o burnt offerings without ... 1Chr 21:24
to o all burnt sacrifices unto ... 1Chr 23:31
that we should be able to o so ... 1Chr 29:14
here, to o willingly unto thee ... 1Chr 29:17
to o the burnt offerings of the ... 2Chr 23:18
to o withal, and spoons, and ... 2Chr 24:14
priests the sons of Aaron to o ... 2Chr 29:21
Hezekiah commanded to o the burnt ... 2Chr 29:27
to o unto the LORD, as it is ... 2Chr 35:12
to o burnt offerings upon the ... 2Chr 35:16
to o burnt offerings thereon, as ... Ezr 3:2
o burnt offerings unto the LORD ... Ezr 3:6
That they may o sacrifices of ... Ezr 6:10
o them upon the altar of the ... Ezr 7:17
o up for yourselves a burnt ... Job 42:8
O the sacrifices of righteousness ... Ps 4:5
offerings of blood will I not o ... Ps 16:4
therefore will I o in his ... Ps 27:6
O unto God thanksgiving ... Ps 50:14
then shall they o bullocks upon ... Ps 51:19
I will o unto thee burnt ... Ps 66:15
I will o bullocks with goats ... Ps 66:15
of Sheba and Seba shall o gifts ... Ps 72:10
I will o to thee the sacrifice of ... Ps 116:17
wentest thou up to o sacrifice ... Is 57:7
the gods unto whom they o incense ... Jer 11:12
when they o burnt offering and an ... Jer 14:12
before me to o burnt offerings ... Jer 33:18
the place where they did o sweet ... Eze 6:13
For when ye o your gifts, when ye ... Eze 20:31
to o burnt offerings thereon, and ... Eze 43:18
o a kid of the goats without ... Eze 43:22
thou shalt o a young bullock ... Eze 43:23
thou shalt o them before the LORD ... Eze 43:24
they shall o them up for a burnt ... Eze 43:24
when ye o my bread, the fat and ... Eze 44:7
before me to o unto me the fat ... Eze 44:15
he shall o his sin offering, ... Eze 44:27
ye shall o an oblation unto the ... Eze 45:1
is the oblation that ye shall o ... Eze 45:13
ye shall o the tenth part of a ... Eze 45:14
o unto the LORD in the sabbath ... Eze 46:4
offering which ye shall o of five ... Eze 48:8
The oblation that ye shall o unto ... Eze 48:9
ye shall o the holy oblation ... Eze 48:20
that they should o an oblation ... Dan 2:46
They shall not o wine offerings ... Hos 9:4
o a sacrifice of thanksgiving ... Amos 4:5
Though ye o me burnt offerings and. Amos 5:22
that which they o there is ... Hag 2:14
Ye o polluted bread upon mine ... Mal 1:7
if ye o the blind for sacrifice, ... Mal 1:8
if ye o the lame and sick, is it ... Mal 1:8
o it now unto thy governor ... Mal 1:8
that they may o unto the LORD an ... Mal 3:3
and then come and o thy gift ... Mt 5:24
o the gift that Moses commanded, ... Mt 8:4
o for thy cleansing those things ... Mk 1:44
to o a sacrifice according to ... Lk 2:24
o for thy cleansing, according as ... Lk 5:14
on the one cheek o also the other ... Lk 6:29
an egg, will he o him a scorpion ... Lk 11:12
to God, that he may o both gifts ... Heb 5:1
also for himself, to o for sins ... Heb 5:3
to o up sacrifice, first for his ... Heb 7:27
priest is ordained to o gifts ... Heb 8:3
this man have somewhat also to o ... Heb 8:3
that o gifts according to the law ... Heb 8:4
that he should o himself often ... Heb 9:25
By him therefore let us o the ... Heb 13:15
to o up spiritual sacrifices, ... 1Pet 2:5
that he should o it with the ... Rev 8:3

### OFFERED

o burnt offerings on the altar ... Gen 8:20
o him up for a burnt offering in ... Gen 22:13
Then Jacob o sacrifice upon the ... Gen 31:54
o sacrifices unto the God of his ... Gen 46:1
which o burnt offerings, and ... Ex 24:5
o burnt offerings, and brought ... Ex 32:6
every man that o ... Ex 35:22
o an offering of gold ... Ex 35:22
o upon it the burnt offering and ... Ex 40:29
burnt offering which he hath o ... Lev 7:8
eaten the same day that it is o ... Lev 7:15
o it for sin, as the first ... Lev 9:15
o it according to the manner ... Lev 9:16
o strange fire before the LORD, ... Lev 10:1
have they o their sin offering ... Lev 10:19

when they o before the LORD, and Lev 16:1
when they o strange fire before Num 3:4
over them that were numbered, o Num 7:2
the princes o for dedicating of Num 7:10
even the princes o their offering Num 7:10
he that o his offering the first Num 7:12
He o for his offering one silver Num 7:19
prince of the children of Gad, o Num 7:42
of the children of Ephraim, o Num 7:48
On the eighth day o Gamaliel the Num 7:54
of the children of Benjamin, o Num 7:60
prince of the children of Dan, o Num 7:66
of the children of Asher, o Num 7:72
of the children of Naphtali, o Num 7:78
Aaron o them as an offering Num 8:21
and fifty men that o incense Num 16:35
for they o them before the LORD, Num 16:38
they that were burnt had o Num 16:39
Balak o oxen and sheep Num 22:40
Balaam o on every altar a bullock Num 23:2
I have o upon every altar a Num 23:4
o a bullock and a ram on every Num 23:14
o a bullock and a ram on every Num 23:30
when they o strange fire before Num 26:61
offering unto the LORD shall be o Num 28:15
it shall be o beside the Num 28:24
that they o up to the LORD Num 31:52
they o thereon burnt offerings Josh 8:31
the people willingly o themselves Judg 5:2
that o themselves willingly among Judg 5:9
the second bullock was o upon the Judg 6:28
o it upon a rock unto the LORD Judg 13:19
o burnt offerings and peace Judg 20:26
o burnt offerings and peace Judg 21:4
when the time was that Elkanah o 1Sa 1:4
that, when any man o sacrifice 1Sa 2:13
o the kine a burnt offering unto 1Sa 6:14
of Beth-shemesh o burnt offerings 1Sa 6:15
o it for a burnt offering wholly 1Sa 7:9
And he o the burnt offering 1Sa 13:9
therefore, and o a burnt offering 1Sa 13:12
David o burnt offerings and peace 2Sa 6:17
from Giloh, while he o sacrifices 2Sa 15:12
o burnt offerings and peace 2Sa 24:25
o up burnt offerings 1Kin 3:15
o peace offerings, and made a 1Kin 3:15
o sacrifice before the LORD 1Kin 8:62
Solomon o a sacrifice of peace 1Kin 8:63
which he o unto the LORD, two and 1Kin 8:63
for there he o burnt offerings, 1Kin 8:64
in Judah, and he o upon the altar 1Kin 12:32
So he o upon the altar which he 1Kin 12:33
he o upon the altar, and burnt 1Kin 12:33
for the people o and burnt incense 1Kin 22:43
when the meat offering was o 2Kin 3:20
o him for a burnt offering upon 2Kin 3:27
to the altar, and o thereon 2Kin 16:12
his sons o upon the altar of the 1Chr 6:49
that they o seven bullocks and 1Chr 15:26
they o burnt sacrifices and peace 1Chr 16:1
o burnt offerings and peace 1Chr 21:26
of the king's work, o willingly, 1Chr 29:6
for that they o willingly 1Chr 29:9
they o willingly to the LORD 1Chr 29:9
have willingly o all these things 1Chr 29:17
o burnt offerings unto the LORD, 1Chr 29:21
o a thousand burnt offerings upon 2Chr 1:6
such things as they o for the 2Chr 4:6
all the people o sacrifices 2Chr 7:4
king Solomon o a sacrifice of 2Chr 7:5
for there he o burnt offerings, 2Chr 7:7
Then Solomon o burnt offerings 2Chr 8:12
they o unto the LORD the same 2Chr 15:11
who willingly o himself unto the 2Chr 17:16
they o burnt offerings in the 2Chr 24:14
nor o burnt offerings in the holy 2Chr 29:7
beside all that was willingly o Ezr 1:6
o freely for the house of God to Ezr 2:68
they o burnt offerings thereon Ezr 3:3
o the daily burnt offerings by Ezr 3:4
afterward o the continual burnt Ezr 3:5
of every one that willingly o a Ezr 3:5
the place where they o sacrifices Ezr 6:3
o at the dedication of this house Ezr 6:17
freely o unto the God of Israel Ezr 7:15
all Israel there present, had o Ezr 8:25
o burnt offerings unto the God of Ezr 8:35
they o a ram of the flock for Ezr 10:19
that willingly o themselves to Neh 11:2
that day they o great sacrifices Neh 12:43
o burnt offerings according to Job 1:5
thou hast o a meat offering Is 57:6
as if he o swine's blood Is 66:3
they have o incense unto Baal Jer 32:29
they o there their sacrifices, and Eze 20:28
oblation of the land that is o Eze 48:12
the reproach o by him to cease Dan 11:18
Have ye o unto me sacrifices and Amos 5:25
o a sacrifice unto the LORD, and Jonah 1:16
incense shall be o unto my name Mal 1:11
o sacrifice unto the idol, and Acts 7:41
have ye o to me slain beasts and Acts 7:42
Ghost was given, he o them money, Acts 8:18
ye abstain from meats o to idols Acts 15:29
themselves from things o to idols Acts 21:25
should be o for every one of them Acts 21:26
as touching things o unto idols 1Cor 8:1
are o in sacrifice unto idols 1Cor 8:4
eat it as a thing o unto an idol 1Cor 8:7
those things which are o to idols 1Cor 8:10
or that which is o in sacrifice 1Cor 10:19
This is o in sacrifice unto idols 1Cor 10:28
if I be o upon the sacrifice and Phil 2:17
For I am now ready to be o 2Ti 4:6
flesh, when he had o up prayers Heb 5:7
he did once, when he o up himself Heb 7:27
which he o for himself, and for Heb 9:7
in which were o both gifts Heb 9:9
o himself without spot to God Heb 9:14
So Christ was once o to bear the Heb 9:28
those sacrifices which they o Heb 10:1
they not have ceased to be o Heb 10:2
which are o by the law Heb 10:8
after he had o one sacrifice for Heb 10:12
By faith Abel o unto God a more Heb 11:4
when he was tried, o up Isaac Heb 11:17
o up his only begotten son Heb 11:17
when he had o Isaac his son upon Jas 2:21

### OFFERETH

The priest that o it for sin Lev 6:26
the priest that o any man's burnt Lev 7:8
shall be the priest's that o it Lev 7:9
same day that he o his sacrifice Lev 7:16
it be imputed unto him that o it Lev 7:18
He that o the sacrifice of his Lev 7:29
that o the blood of the peace Lev 7:33
that o a burnt offering or Lev 17:8
for he o the bread of thy God Lev 21:8
whosoever o a sacrifice of peace Lev 22:21
Then shall he that o his offering Num 15:4
Whoso o praise glorifieth me Ps 50:23
he that o an oblation, as if he Is 66:3
him that o in the high places, and Jer 48:35
him that o an offering unto the Mal 2:12

### OFFERING

of the ground an o unto the LORD Gen 4:3
had respect unto Abel and to his o Gen 4:4
to his o he had not respect Gen 4:5
offer him there for a burnt o Gen 22:2
and clave the wood for the burnt o Gen 22:3
took the wood of the burnt o Gen 22:6
where is the lamb for a burnt o Gen 22:7
himself a lamb for a burnt o Gen 22:8
a burnt o in the stead of his son Gen 22:13
and he poured a drink o thereon Gen 35:14
father in law, took a burnt o Ex 18:12
Israel, that they bring me an o Ex 25:2
with his heart ye shall take my o Ex 25:2
this is the o which ye shall take Ex 25:3
it is a sin o Ex 29:14
it is a burnt o unto the LORD Ex 29:18
an o made by fire unto the LORD Ex 29:18
them for a wave o before the LORD Ex 29:24
them upon the altar for a burnt o Ex 29:25
it is an o made by fire unto the Ex 29:25
it for a wave o before the LORD Ex 29:26
sanctify the breast of the wave o Ex 29:27
and the shoulder of the heave o Ex 29:27
for it is an heave o Ex 29:28
it shall be an heave o from the Ex 29:28
even their heave o unto the LORD Ex 29:28
bullock for a sin o for atonement Ex 29:36
of an hin of wine for a drink o Ex 29:40
to the meat o of the morning Ex 29:41
according to the drink o thereof Ex 29:41
an o made by fire unto the LORD Ex 29:41
o throughout your generations at Ex 29:42
nor burnt sacrifice, nor meat o Ex 30:9
shall ye pour drink o thereon Ex 30:9
blood of the sin o of atonements Ex 30:10
shekel shall be the o of the LORD Ex 30:13
shall give an o unto the LORD Ex 30:14
when they give an o unto the LORD Ex 30:15
to burn o made by fire unto the Ex 30:20
the altar of burnt o with all his Ex 30:28
the altar of burnt o with all his Ex 31:9
from among you an o unto the LORD Ex 35:5
him bring it, an o of the LORD Ex 35:5
The altar of burnt o, with his Ex 35:16
they brought the LORD's o to the Ex 35:21
an o of gold unto the LORD Ex 35:22
one that did offer an o of silver Ex 35:24
and brass brought the LORD's o Ex 35:24
brought a willing o unto the LORD Ex 35:29
they received of Moses all the o Ex 36:3
work for the o of the sanctuary Ex 36:6
altar of burnt o of shittim wood Ex 38:1
place, even the gold of the o Ex 38:24
the brass of the o was seventy Ex 38:29
burnt o before the door of the Ex 40:6
anoint the altar of the burnt o Ex 40:10
he put the altar of burnt o by Ex 40:29
and offered upon it the burnt o Ex 40:29
and the meat o Ex 40:29
of you bring an o unto the LORD Lev 1:2
shall bring your o of the cattle Lev 1:2
If his o be a burnt sacrifice of Lev 1:3
hand upon the head of the burnt o Lev 1:4
And he shall flay the burnt o Lev 1:6
an o made by fire, of a sweet Lev 1:9
if his o be of the flocks, namely Lev 1:10
an o made by fire, of a sweet Lev 1:13
for his o to the LORD be of fowls Lev 1:14
shall bring his o of turtledoves Lev 1:14
an o made by fire, of a sweet Lev 1:17
will offer a meat o unto the LORD Lev 2:1
his o shall be of fine flour Lev 2:1
to be an o made by fire, of a Lev 2:2
of a meat o baken in the oven Lev 2:4
be a meat o baken in a pan Lev 2:5
it is a meat o Lev 2:6
a meat o baken in the frying pan Lev 2:7
thou shalt bring the meat o that Lev 2:8
the meat o a memorial thereof Lev 2:9
it is an o made by fire, of a Lev 2:9
of the meat o shall be Aaron's Lev 2:10
No meat o, which ye shall bring Lev 2:11
in any o of the LORD made by fire Lev 2:11
every oblation of thy meat o Lev 2:13
God to be lacking from thy meat o Lev 2:13
if thou offer a meat o of thy Lev 2:14
o of thy firstfruits green ears Lev 2:14
it is a meat o Lev 2:15
it is an o made by fire unto the Lev 2:16
be a sacrifice of peace o Lev 3:1
his hand upon the head of his o Lev 3:2
of the peace o an o made Lev 3:3
it is an o made by fire, of a Lev 3:5
if his o for a sacrifice of peace Lev 3:6
for a sacrifice of peace o unto Lev 3:6
If he offer a lamb for his o Lev 3:7
his hand upon the head of his o Lev 3:8
of the peace o an o made Lev 3:9
it is the food of the o made by Lev 3:11
if his o be a goat, then he shall Lev 3:12
And he shall offer thereof his o Lev 3:14
even an o made by fire unto the Lev 3:14
it is the food of the o made by Lev 3:16
blemish unto the LORD for a sin o Lev 4:3
of the altar of the burnt o Lev 4:7
fat of the bullock for the sin o Lev 4:8
upon the altar of the burnt o Lev 4:10
of the altar of the burnt o Lev 4:18
did with the bullock for a sin o Lev 4:20
it is a sin o for the Lev 4:21
he shall bring his o, a kid of Lev 4:23
kill the burnt o before the LORD Lev 4:24
it is a sin o Lev 4:24
of the sin o with his finger Lev 4:25
the horns of the altar of burnt o Lev 4:25
bottom of the altar of burnt o Lev 4:25
then he shall bring his o Lev 4:28
hand upon the head of the sin o Lev 4:29
slay the sin o in the place of Lev 4:29
in the place of the burnt o Lev 4:29
the horns of the altar of burnt o Lev 4:30
And if he bring a lamb for a sin o Lev 4:32
hand upon the head of the sin o Lev 4:33
slay it for a sin o in the place Lev 4:33
place where they kill the burnt o Lev 4:33
of the sin o with his finger Lev 4:34
the horns of the altar of burnt o Lev 4:34
he shall bring his trespass o Lev 5:6
a kid of the goats, for a sin o Lev 5:6
one for a sin o, and the other for Lev 5:7
and the other for a burnt o Lev 5:7
that which is for the sin o first Lev 5:8
of the blood of the sin o upon Lev 5:9
it is a sin o Lev 5:9
offer the second for a burnt o Lev 5:10
o the tenth part of an ephah of Lev 5:11
ephah of fine flour for a sin o Lev 5:11
for it is a sin o Lev 5:11
it is a sin o Lev 5:12
be the priest's, as a meat o Lev 5:13
the sanctuary, for a trespass o Lev 5:15
with the ram of the trespass o Lev 5:16
thy estimation, for a trespass o Lev 5:18
It is a trespass o Lev 5:19
in the day of his trespass o Lev 6:5
his trespass o unto the LORD Lev 6:6
thy estimation, for a trespass o Lev 6:6
This is the law of the burnt o Lev 6:9
It is the burnt o, because of the Lev 6:9
with the burnt o on the altar Lev 6:10
lay the burnt o in order upon it Lev 6:12
And this is the law of the meat o Lev 6:14
of the flour of the meat o Lev 6:15
which is upon the meat o, and Lev 6:15
it is most holy, as is the sin o Lev 6:17
and as the trespass o Lev 6:17
This is the o of Aaron and of his Lev 6:20
fine flour for a meat o perpetual Lev 6:20
o shalt thou offer for a sweet Lev 6:21
For every meat o for the priest Lev 6:23
This is the law of the sin o Lev 6:25
burnt o is killed shall the sin Lev 6:25
is killed shall the sin o be Lev 6:25
And no sin o, whereof any of the Lev 6:30
this is the law of the trespass o Lev 7:1
o shall they kill the trespass Lev 7:2
shall they kill the trespass o Lev 7:2
an o made by fire unto the LORD Lev 7:5
it is a trespass o Lev 7:5
o is, so is the trespass o Lev 7:7
that offereth any man's burnt o Lev 7:8
the burnt o which he hath offered Lev 7:8
all the meat o that is baken in Lev 7:9
And every meat o, mingled with oil Lev 7:10
he shall offer for his o leavened Lev 7:13
for an heave o unto the LORD Lev 7:14
the sacrifice of his o be a vow Lev 7:16
be a vow, or a voluntary o Lev 7:16
of which men offer an o made by Lev 7:25
for a wave o before the LORD Lev 7:30
unto the priest for an heave o of Lev 7:32
This is the law of the burnt o Lev 7:37
of the meat o Lev 7:37
o, and of the trespass o Lev 7:37

oil, and a bullock for the sin o Lev 8:2
brought the bullock for the sin o Lev 8:14
head of the bullock for the sin o Lev 8:14
brought the ram for the burnt o Lev 8:18
an o made by fire unto the LORD Lev 8:21
them for a wave o before the LORD Lev 8:27
on the altar upon the burnt o Lev 8:28
it is an o made by fire unto the Lev 8:28
it for a wave o before the LORD Lev 8:29
o, and a ram for a burnt o Lev 9:2
ye a kid of the goats for a sin o Lev 9:3
without blemish, for a burnt o Lev 9:3
a meat o mingled with oil Lev 9:4
the altar, and offer thy sin o Lev 9:7
and thy burnt o Lev 9:7
offer the o of the people, and Lev 9:7
and slew the calf of the sin o Lev 9:8
caul above the liver of the sin o Lev 9:10
And he slew the burnt o Lev 9:12
presented the burnt o unto him Lev 9:13
upon the burnt o on the altar Lev 9:14
And he brought the people's o Lev 9:15
was the sin o for the people Lev 9:15
And he brought the burnt o Lev 9:16
And he brought the meat o, and took Lev 9:17
for a wave o before the LORD Lev 9:21
came down from o of the sin Lev 9:22
the sin o, and the burnt o Lev 9:22
upon the altar the burnt o Lev 9:24
Take the meat o that remaineth of Lev 10:12
it for a wave o before the LORD Lev 10:15
sought the goat of the sin o Lev 10:16
eaten the sin o in the holy place Lev 10:17
day have they offered their sin o Lev 10:19
their burnt o before the LORD Lev 10:19
if I had eaten the sin o to day Lev 10:19
of the first year for a burnt o Lev 12:6
or a turtledove, for a sin o Lev 12:6
the one for the burnt o Lev 12:8
and the other for a sin o Lev 12:8
deals of fine flour for a meat o Lev 14:10
and offer him for a trespass o Lev 14:12
them for a wave o before the LORD Lev 14:12
the sin o and the burnt o Lev 14:13
for as the sin o is the priest's, Lev 14:13
so is the trespass o Lev 14:13
of the blood of the trespass o Lev 14:14
upon the blood of the trespass o Lev 14:17
the priest shall offer the sin o Lev 14:19
he shall kill the burnt o Lev 14:19
priest shall offer the burnt o Lev 14:20
the meat o upon the altar Lev 14:20
lamb for a trespass o to be waved Lev 14:21
mingled with oil for a meat o Lev 14:21
o, and the other a burnt o Lev 14:22
take the lamb of the trespass o Lev 14:24
them for a wave o before the LORD Lev 14:24
kill the lamb of the trespass o Lev 14:25
of the blood of the trespass o Lev 14:25
of the blood of the trespass o Lev 14:28
able to get, the one for a sin o Lev 14:31
and the other for a burnt o Lev 14:31
with the meat o Lev 14:31
offer them, the one for a sin o Lev 15:15
and the other for a burnt o Lev 15:15
shall offer the one for a sin o Lev 15:30
and the other for a burnt o Lev 15:30
o, and a ram for a burnt o Lev 16:3
two kids of the goats for a sin o Lev 16:5
and one ram for a burnt o Lev 16:5
offer his bullock of the sin o Lev 16:6
fell, and offer him for a sin o Lev 16:9
bring the bullock of the sin o Lev 16:11
of the sin o which is for himself Lev 16:11
he kill the goat of the sin o Lev 16:15
come forth, and offer his burnt o Lev 16:24
the burnt o of the people, and Lev 16:24
the fat of the sin o shall he Lev 16:25
And the bullock for the sin o Lev 16:27
and the goat for the sin o Lev 16:27
to offer an o unto the LORD Lev 17:4
offereth a burnt o or sacrifice Lev 17:8
his trespass o unto the LORD Lev 19:21
even a ram for a trespass o Lev 19:21
o before the LORD for his sin Lev 19:22
eat of an o of the holy things Lev 22:12
offer unto the LORD for a burnt o Lev 22:18
or a freewill o in beeves or Lev 22:21
nor make an o by fire of them Lev 22:22
thou offer for a freewill o Lev 22:23
make any o thereof in your land Lev 22:24
an o made by fire unto the LORD Lev 22:27
But ye shall offer an o made by Lev 23:8
year for a burnt o unto the LORD Lev 23:12
the meat o thereof shall be two Lev 23:13
an o made by fire unto the LORD Lev 23:13
the drink o thereof shall be of Lev 23:13
have brought an o unto your God Lev 23:14
brought the sheaf of the wave o Lev 23:15
offer a new meat o unto the LORD Lev 23:16
be for a burnt o unto the LORD Lev 23:18
unto the LORD, with their meat o Lev 23:18
even an o made by fire, of sweet Lev 23:18
one kid of the goats for a sin o Lev 23:19
for a wave o before the LORD Lev 23:20
but ye shall offer an o made by Lev 23:25
offer an o made by fire unto the Lev 23:27
an o made by fire unto the LORD Lev 23:36
ye shall offer an o made by fire Lev 23:36
to offer an o made by fire unto Lev 23:37
by fire unto the LORD, a burnt o Lev 23:37
and a meat o Lev 23:37
even an o made by fire unto the Lev 24:7
men bring an o unto the LORD Lev 27:9
incense, and the daily meat o Num 4:16
every o of all the holy things of Num 5:9
and he shall bring her o for her Num 5:15
for it is an o of jealousy Num 5:15
an o of memorial, bringing Num 5:15
put the o of memorial in her Num 5:18
hands, which is the jealousy o Num 5:18
o out of the woman's hand Num 5:25
shall wave the o before the LORD, Num 5:25
shall take an handful of the o Num 5:26
shall offer the one for a sin o Num 6:11
and the other for a burnt o Num 6:11
the first year for a trespass o Num 6:12
shall offer his o unto the LORD Num 6:14
without blemish for a burnt o Num 6:14
year without blemish for a sin o Num 6:14
with oil, and their meat o Num 6:15
his sin o, and his burnt o Num 6:16
shall offer also his meat o Num 6:17
and his drink o Num 6:17
them for a wave o before the LORD Num 6:20
of his o unto the LORD for his Num 6:21
brought their o before the LORD Num 7:3
offered their o before the altar Num 7:10
Moses, They shall offer their o Num 7:11
he that offered his o the first Num 7:12
his o was one silver charger, the Num 7:13
mingled with oil for a meat o Num 7:13
of the first year, for a burnt o Num 7:15
One kid of the goats for a sin o Num 7:16
this was the o of Nahshon the son Num 7:17
for his o one silver charger Num 7:19
mingled with oil for a meat o Num 7:19
of the first year, for a burnt o Num 7:21
One kid of the goats for a sin o Num 7:22
this was the o of Nethaneel the Num 7:23
His o was one silver charger, the Num 7:25
mingled with oil for a meat o Num 7:25
of the first year, for a burnt o Num 7:27
One kid of the goats for a sin o Num 7:28
this was the o of Eliab the son Num 7:29
His o was one silver charger of Num 7:31
mingled with oil for a meat o Num 7:31
of the first year, for a burnt o Num 7:33
One kid of the goats for a sin o Num 7:34
this was the o of Elizur the son Num 7:35
His o was one silver charger, the Num 7:37
mingled with oil for a meat o Num 7:37
of the first year, for a burnt o Num 7:39
One kid of the goats for a sin o Num 7:40
this was the o of Shelumiel the Num 7:41
His o was one silver charger of Num 7:43
mingled with oil for a meat o Num 7:43
of the first year, for a burnt o Num 7:45
One kid of the goats for a sin o Num 7:46
this was the o of Eliasaph the Num 7:47
His o was one silver charger, the Num 7:49
mingled with oil for a meat o Num 7:49
of the first year, for a burnt o Num 7:51
One kid of the goats for a sin o Num 7:52
this was the o of Elishama the Num 7:53
His o was one silver charger of Num 7:55
mingled with oil for a meat o Num 7:55
of the first year, for a burnt o Num 7:57
One kid of the goats for a sin o Num 7:58
this was the o of Gamaliel the Num 7:59
His o was one silver charger, the Num 7:61
mingled with oil for a meat o Num 7:61
of the first year, for a burnt o Num 7:63
One kid of the goats for a sin o Num 7:64
this was the o of Abidan the son Num 7:65
His o was one silver charger, the Num 7:67
mingled with oil for a meat o Num 7:67
of the first year, for a burnt o Num 7:69
One kid of the goats for a sin o Num 7:70
this was the o of Ahiezer the son Num 7:71
His o was one silver charger, the Num 7:73
mingled with oil for a meat o Num 7:73
of the first year, for a burnt o Num 7:75
One kid of the goats for a sin o Num 7:76
this was the o of Pagiel the son Num 7:77
His o was one silver charger, the Num 7:79
mingled with oil for a meat o Num 7:79
of the first year, for a burnt o Num 7:81
One kid of the goats for a sin o Num 7:82
this was the o of Ahira the son Num 7:83
the burnt o were twelve bullocks Num 7:87
year twelve, with their meat o Num 7:87
of the goats for sin o twelve Num 7:87
a young bullock with his meat o Num 8:8
shalt thou take for a sin o Num 8:8
an o of the children of Israel Num 8:11
shalt offer the one for a sin o Num 8:12
and the other for a burnt o Num 8:12
offer them for an o unto the LORD Num 8:13
them, and offer them for an o Num 8:15
them as an o before the LORD Num 8:21
that we may not offer an o of the Num 9:7
because he brought not the o of Num 9:13
will make an o by fire unto the Num 15:3
by fire unto the LORD, a burnt o Num 15:3
a vow, or in a freewill o Num 15:3
his o unto the LORD bring a meat Num 15:4
a meat o of a tenth deal of flour Num 15:4
o shalt thou prepare with the Num 15:5
with the burnt o or sacrifice Num 15:5
a meat o two tenth deals of flour Num 15:6
for a drink o thou shalt offer Num 15:7
preparest a bullock for a burnt o Num 15:8
o of three tenth deals of flour Num 15:9
for a drink o half an hin of wine Num 15:10
for an o made by fire, of a sweet Num 15:10
after this manner, in o Num 15:13
an o made by fire Num 15:13
and will offer an o made by fire Num 15:14
offer up an heave o unto the LORD Num 15:19
of your dough for an heave o Num 15:20
as ye do the heave o of the Num 15:20
an heave o in your generations Num 15:21
one young bullock for a burnt o Num 15:24
unto the LORD, with his meat o Num 15:24
and his drink o Num 15:24
one kid of the goats for a sin o Num 15:24
and they shall bring their o Num 15:25
their sin o before the LORD, for Num 15:25
of the first year for a sin o Num 15:27
LORD, Respect not thou their o Num 16:15
of theirs, every meat o of theirs Num 18:9
and every sin o of theirs Num 18:9
and every trespass o of theirs Num 18:9
the heave o of their gift, with Num 18:11
their fat for an o made by fire Num 18:17
offer as an heave o unto the LORD Num 18:24
up an heave o of it for the LORD Num 18:26
this your heave o shall be Num 18:27
heave o unto the LORD of all your Num 18:28
heave o to Aaron the priest Num 18:28
offer every heave o of the LORD Num 18:29
unto Balak, Stand by thy burnt o Num 23:3
Balak, Stand here by thy burnt o Num 23:15
behold, he stood by his burnt o Num 23:17
of Israel, and say unto them, My o Num 28:2
This is the o made by fire which Num 28:3
by day, for a continual burnt o Num 28:3
of an ephah of flour for a meat o Num 28:5
It is a continual burnt o Num 28:6
the drink o thereof shall be the Num 28:7
unto the LORD for a drink o Num 28:7
as the meat o of the morning, and Num 28:8
and as the drink o thereof Num 28:8
tenth deals of flour for a meat o Num 28:9
with oil, and the drink o thereof Num 28:9
is the burnt o of every sabbath Num 28:10
burnt o, and his drink o Num 28:10
offer a burnt o unto the LORD Num 28:11
tenth deals of flour for a meat o Num 28:12
tenth deals of flour for a meat o Num 28:12
oil for a meat o unto one lamb Num 28:13
for a burnt o of a sweet savour, Num 28:13
this is the burnt o of every Num 28:14
o unto the LORD shall be offered Num 28:15
burnt o, and his drink o Num 28:15
fire for a burnt o unto the LORD Num 28:19
their meat o shall be of flour Num 28:20
And one goat for a sin o, to make Num 28:22
beside the burnt o in the morning Num 28:23
which is for a continual burnt o Num 28:23
burnt o, and his drink o Num 28:24
bring a new meat o unto the LORD Num 28:26
o for a sweet savour unto the Num 28:27
their meat o of flour mingled Num 28:28
them beside the continual burnt o Num 28:31
and his meat o Num 28:31
ye shall offer a burnt o for a Num 29:2
their meat o shall be of flour Num 29:3
one kid of the goats for a sin o Num 29:5
Beside the burnt o of the month Num 29:6
of the month, and his meat o Num 29:6
and the daily burnt o Num 29:6
and his meat o Num 29:6
burnt o unto the LORD for a sweet Num 29:8
their meat o shall be of flour Num 29:9
One kid of the goats for a sin o Num 29:11
beside the sin o of atonement Num 29:11
and the continual burnt o Num 29:11
and the meat o of it Num 29:11
And ye shall offer a burnt o Num 29:13
their meat o shall be of flour Num 29:14
one kid of the goats for a sin o Num 29:16
beside the continual burnt o Num 29:16
his meat o Num 29:16
his meat o, and his drink o Num 29:16
And their meat o and their drink Num 29:18
one kid of the goats for a sin o Num 29:19
beside the continual burnt o Num 29:19
and the meat o thereof Num 29:19
And their meat o and their drink Num 29:21
And one goat for a sin o Num 29:22
beside the continual burnt o Num 29:22
and his meat o Num 29:22
and his drink o Num 29:22
Their meat o and their drink Num 29:24
one kid of the goats for a sin o Num 29:25
beside the continual burnt o Num 29:25
his meat o, and his drink Num 29:25
and his drink o Num 29:25
And their meat o and their drink Num 29:27
And one goat for a sin o Num 29:28
beside the continual burnt o Num 29:28
and his meat o Num 29:28
and his drink o Num 29:28
And their meat o and their drink Num 29:30
And one goat for a sin o Num 29:31
beside the continual burnt o Num 29:31
his meat o, and his drink Num 29:31
and his drink o Num 29:31

And their meat o and their drink Num 29:33
And one goat for a sin o Num 29:34
beside the continual burnt o Num 29:34
his meat o, and his drink Num 29:34
and his drink o Num 29:34
But ye shall offer a burnt o Num 29:36
Their meat o and their drink Num 29:37
And one goat for a sin o Num 29:38
beside the continual burnt o Num 29:38
and his meat o Num 29:38
and his drink o Num 29:38
for an heave o of the LORD Num 31:29
which was the LORD's heave o Num 31:41
all the gold of the o that they Num 31:52
the heave o of your hand, and all Deut 12:11
or heave o of thine hand Deut 12:17
of a freewill o of thine hand Deut 16:10
even a freewill o, according as Deut 23:23
thereon burnt o or meat Josh 22:23
or meat o, or if Josh 22:23
us an altar, not for burnt o Josh 22:26
I will offer it up for a burnt o Judg 11:31
and if thou wilt offer a burnt o Judg 13:16
Manoah took a kid with a meat o Judg 13:19
would not have received a burnt o Judg 13:23
a meat o at our hands, neither Judg 13:23
men abhorred the o of the LORD 1Sa 2:17
ye at my sacrifice and at mine o 1Sa 2:29
with sacrifice nor o for ever 1Sa 3:14
any wise return him a trespass o 1Sa 6:3
What shall be the trespass o 1Sa 6:4
ye return him for a trespass o 1Sa 6:8
the kine a burnt o unto the LORD 1Sa 6:14
for a trespass o unto the LORD 1Sa 6:17
a burnt o wholly unto the LORD 1Sa 7:9
as Samuel was o up the burnt 1Sa 7:10
up the burnt o 1Sa 7:10
Bring hither a burnt o to me 1Sa 13:9
And he offered the burnt o 1Sa 13:9
an end of o the burnt 1Sa 13:10
the burnt o, behold 1Sa 13:10
therefore, and offered a burnt o 1Sa 13:12
against me, let him accept an o 1Sa 26:19
made an end of o burnt offerings 2Sa 6:18
until the time of the o of the 1Kin 18:29
of the o of the evening sacrifice 1Kin 18:36
when the meat o was offered 2Kin 3:20
him for a burnt o upon the wall 2Kin 3:27
o nor sacrifice unto other gods 2Kin 5:17
an end of o the burnt 2Kin 10:25
the burnt o, that Jehu 2Kin 10:25
And he burnt his burnt o and his 2Kin 16:13
and his meat o 2Kin 16:13
and poured his drink o 2Kin 16:13
altar burn the morning burnt o 2Kin 16:15
and the evening meat o 2Kin 16:15
burnt sacrifice, and his meat o 2Kin 16:15
with the burnt o of all the 2Kin 16:15
of the land, and their meat o 2Kin 16:15
it all the blood of the burnt o 2Kin 16:15
upon the altar of the burnt o 1Chr 6:49
an end of o the burnt offerings 1Chr 16:2
bring an o, and come before him 1Chr 16:29
the burnt o continually morning 1Chr 16:40
wood, and the wheat for the meat o 1Chr 21:23
by fire upon the altar of burnt o 1Chr 21:26
and the altar of the burnt o 1Chr 21:29
altar of the burnt o for Israel 1Chr 22:1
and for the fine flour for meat o 1Chr 23:29
the burnt o they washed in them 2Chr 4:6
heaven, and consumed the burnt o 2Chr 7:1
o according to the commandment of 2Chr 8:13
the LORD, and the altar of burnt o 2Chr 29:18
for a sin o for the kingdom, and 2Chr 29:21
for the sin o before the king 2Chr 29:23
king commanded that the burnt o 2Chr 29:24
the sin o should be made for all 2Chr 29:24
offer the burnt o upon the altar 2Chr 29:27
And when the burnt o began 2Chr 29:27
until the burnt o was finished 2Chr 29:28
they had made an end of o 2Chr 29:29
were for a burnt o to the LORD 2Chr 29:32
drink offerings for every burnt o 2Chr 29:35
o peace offerings, and making 2Chr 30:22
busied in o of burnt offerings 2Chr 35:14
beside the freewill o for the Ezr 1:4
offered the continual burnt o Ezr 3:5
a freewill o unto the LORD Ezr 3:5
for a sin o for all Israel Ezr 6:17
with the freewill o of the people Ezr 7:16
o willingly for the house of Ezr 7:16
even the o of the house of our Ezr 8:25
the gold are a freewill o unto Ezr 8:28
twelve he goats for a sin o Ezr 8:35
this was a burnt o unto the LORD Ezr 8:35
and for the continual meat o Neh 10:33
and for the continual burnt o Neh 10:33
and the people, for the wood o Neh 10:34
shall bring the o of the corn Neh 10:39
the house of God, with the meat o Neh 13:9
And for the wood o, at times Neh 13:31
offer up for yourselves a burnt o Job 42:8
and o thou didst not desire Ps 40:6
burnt o and sin o hast thou Ps 40:6
thou delightest not in burnt o Ps 51:16
burnt o and whole burnt o Ps 51:19
bring an o, and come into his Ps 96:8
thereof sufficient for a burnt o Is 40:16
caused thee to serve with an o Is 43:23
shalt make his soul an o for sin Is 53:10
them hast thou poured a drink o Is 57:6
thou hast offered a meat o Is 57:6
I hate robbery for burnt o Is 61:8
the drink o unto that number Is 65:11
for an o unto the LORD out of all Is 66:20
an o in a clean vessel into the Is 66:20
to anger in o incense unto Baal Jer 11:17
and when they offer burnt o Jer 14:12
the provocation of their o Eze 20:28
where they washed the burnt o Eze 40:38
side, to slay thereon the burnt o Eze 40:39
sin o and the trespass o Eze 40:39
of hewn stone for the burnt o Eze 40:42
wherewith they slew the burnt o Eze 40:42
the tables was the flesh of the o Eze 40:43
most holy things, and the meat o Eze 42:13
sin o, and the trespass o Eze 42:13
GOD, a young bullock for a sin o Eze 43:19
the bullock also of the sin o Eze 43:21
goats without blemish for a sin o Eze 43:22
up for a burnt o unto the LORD Eze 43:24
every day a goat for a sin o Eze 43:25
they shall slay the burnt o Eze 44:11
he shall offer his sin o Eze 44:27
They shall eat the meat o Eze 44:29
sin o, and the trespass o Eze 44:29
for a meat o, and for a burnt Eze 45:15
and for a burnt o Eze 45:15
he shall prepare the sin o Eze 45:17
and the meat o Eze 45:17
and the burnt o Eze 45:17
take of the blood of the sin o Eze 45:19
of the land a bullock for a sin o Eze 45:22
prepare a burnt o to the LORD Eze 45:23
of the goats daily for a sin o Eze 45:23
he shall prepare a meat o of an Eze 45:24
days, according to the sin o Eze 45:25
according to the burnt o Eze 45:25
and according to the meat o Eze 45:25
priests shall prepare his burnt o Eze 46:2
the burnt o that the prince shall Eze 46:4
the meat o shall be an ephah for Eze 46:5
the meat o for the lambs as he Eze 46:5
And he shall prepare a meat o Eze 46:7
in the solemnities the meat o Eze 46:11
o or peace offerings voluntarily Eze 46:12
and he shall prepare his burnt o Eze 46:12
shalt daily prepare a burnt o Eze 46:13
a meat o for it every morning Eze 46:14
a meat o continually by a Eze 46:14
prepare the lamb, and the meat o Eze 46:15
morning for a continual burnt o Eze 46:15
trespass o and the sin o Eze 46:20
where they shall bake the meat o Eze 46:20
shall be the o which ye shall Eze 48:8
The meat o and the drink Joel 1:9
the drink o is cut off from the Joel 1:9
for the meat o and the drink Joel 1:13
the drink o is withholden from Joel 1:13
even a meat o and a drink Joel 2:14
a drink o unto the LORD your God Joel 2:14
my dispersed, shall bring mine o Zeph 3:10
will I accept an o at your hand Mal 1:10
offered unto my name, and a pure o Mal 1:11
thus ye brought an o Mal 1:13
him that offereth an o unto the Mal 2:12
he regardeth not the o any more Mal 2:13
the LORD an o in righteousness Mal 3:3
Then shall the o of Judah Mal 3:4
coming to him, and o him vinegar, Lk 23:36
until that an o should be offered Acts 21:26
that the o up of the Gentiles Rom 15:16
and hath given himself for us an o Eph 5:2
o thou wouldest not, but a body Heb 10:5
when he said, Sacrifice and o Heb 10:8
o for sin thou wouldest not, Heb 10:8
the o of the body of Jesus Christ Heb 10:10
o oftentimes the same sacrifices, Heb 10:11
For by one o he hath perfected Heb 10:14
is, there is no more o for sin Heb 10:18

**OFFERINGS**

and offered burnt o on the altar Gen 8:20
us also sacrifices and burnt o Ex 10:25
sacrifice thereon thy burnt o Ex 20:24
burnt o, and thy peace o Ex 20:24
of Israel, which offered burnt o Ex 24:5
sacrificed peace o of oxen unto Ex 24:5
of the sacrifice of their peace o Ex 29:28
on the morrow, and offered burnt o Ex 32:6
o, and brought peace o Ex 32:6
yet unto him free o every morning Ex 36:3
of the meat o shall be Aaron's Lev 2:3
of the o of the LORD made by fire Lev 2:3
of the o of the LORD made by fire Lev 2:10
with all thine o thou shalt offer Lev 2:13
of the sacrifice of peace o Lev 4:10
fat of the sacrifice of peace o Lev 4:26
from off the sacrifice of peace o Lev 4:31
from the sacrifice of the peace o Lev 4:35
according to the o made by fire Lev 4:35
according to the o made by fire Lev 5:12
thereon the fat of the peace o Lev 6:12
portion of my o made by fire Lev 6:17
the o of the LORD made by fire Lev 6:18
law of the sacrifice of peace o Lev 7:11
of thanksgiving of his peace o Lev 7:13
the blood of the peace o Lev 7:14
of the sacrifice of his peace o Lev 7:15
o be eaten at all on the third Lev 7:18
flesh of the sacrifice of peace o Lev 7:20
flesh of the sacrifice of peace o Lev 7:21
the sacrifice of his peace o unto Lev 7:29
of the sacrifice of his peace o Lev 7:29
the o of the LORD made by fire Lev 7:30
of the sacrifices of your peace o Lev 7:32
offereth the blood of the peace o Lev 7:33
the sacrifices of their peace o Lev 7:34
out of the o of the LORD made by Lev 7:35
of the sacrifice of the peace o Lev 7:37
a bullock and a ram for peace o Lev 9:4
ram for a sacrifice of peace o Lev 9:18
and the burnt offering, and peace o Lev 9:22
of the o of the LORD made by fire Lev 10:12
peace o of the children of Israel Lev 10:14
the o made by fire of the fat Lev 10:15
them for peace o unto the LORD Lev 17:5
of peace o unto the LORD, ye Lev 19:5
for the o of the LORD made by Lev 21:6
the o of the LORD made by fire Lev 21:21
vows, and for all his freewill o Lev 22:18
offereth a sacrifice of peace o Lev 22:21
meat offering, and their drink o Lev 23:18
year for a sacrifice of peace o Lev 23:19
offering, a sacrifice, and drink o Lev 23:37
and beside all your freewill o Lev 23:38
o of the LORD made by fire by a Lev 24:9
ram without blemish for peace o Num 6:14
meat offering, and their drink o Num 6:15
of peace o unto the LORD, with Num 6:17
the sacrifice of the peace o Num 6:18
And for a sacrifice of peace o Num 7:17
And for a sacrifice of peace o Num 7:23
And for a sacrifice of peace o Num 7:29
And for a sacrifice of peace o Num 7:35
And for a sacrifice of peace o Num 7:41
And for a sacrifice of peace o Num 7:47
And for a sacrifice of peace o Num 7:53
And for a sacrifice of peace o Num 7:59
And for a sacrifice of peace o Num 7:65
And for a sacrifice of peace o Num 7:71
And for a sacrifice of peace o Num 7:77
And for a sacrifice of peace o Num 7:83
of the peace o were twenty Num 7:88
the trumpets over your burnt o Num 10:10
the sacrifices of your peace o Num 10:10
a vow, or peace o unto the LORD Num 15:8
o of all the hallowed things of Num 18:8
with all the wave o of the Num 18:11
All the heave o of the holy Num 18:19
their drink o shall be half an Num 28:14
without blemish) and their drink o Num 28:31
meat offering, and their drink o Num 29:6
offering of it, and their drink o Num 29:11
their drink o for the bullocks, Num 29:18
thereof, and their drink o Num 29:19
their drink o for the bullocks, Num 29:21
their drink o for the bullocks, Num 29:24
their drink o for the bullocks, Num 29:27
their drink o for the bullocks, Num 29:30
their drink o for the bullocks, Num 29:33
their drink o for the bullock, Num 29:37
your vows, and your freewill o Num 29:39
for your burnt o Num 29:39
and for your meat o Num 29:39
and for your drink o Num 29:39
and for your peace o Num 29:39
ye shall bring your burnt o Deut 12:6
heave o of your hand, and your Deut 12:6
and your vows, and your freewill o Deut 12:6
your burnt o, and your sacrifices, Deut 12:11
that thou offer not thy burnt o Deut 12:13
thou shalt offer thy burnt o Deut 12:14
thou vowest, nor thy freewill o Deut 12:17
And thou shalt offer thy burnt o Deut 12:27
they shall eat the o of the LORD Deut 18:1
thou shalt offer burnt o thereon Deut 27:6
And thou shalt offer peace o Deut 27:7
drank the wine of their drink o Deut 32:38
thereon burnt o unto the LORD Josh 8:31
the LORD, and sacrificed peace o Josh 8:31
or if to offer peace o thereon Josh 22:23
LORD before him with our burnt o Josh 22:27
sacrifices, and with our peace o Josh 22:27
our fathers made, not for burnt o Josh 22:28
to build an altar for burnt o Josh 22:29
for burnt o, for meat o Josh 22:29
until even, and offered burnt o Judg 20:26
and peace o before the LORD Judg 20:26
burnt o and peace o Judg 21:4
o made by fire of the children of 1Sa 2:28
of all the o of Israel my people 1Sa 2:29
of Beth-shemesh offered burnt o 1Sa 6:15
down unto thee, to offer burnt o 1Sa 10:8
sacrifice sacrifices of peace o 1Sa 10:8
of peace o before the LORD 1Sa 11:15
burnt offering to me, and peace o 1Sa 13:9
LORD as great delight in burnt o 1Sa 15:22
rain, upon you, nor fields of o 2Sa 1:21
and David offered burnt o and peace 2Sa 6:17
and peace o before the LORD 2Sa 6:17
burnt o and peace o 2Sa 6:18
neither will I offer burnt o unto 2Sa 24:24
burnt o and peace o 2Sa 24:25
a thousand burnt o did Solomon 1Kin 3:4
the LORD, and offered up burnt o 1Kin 3:15
o, and offered peace o 1Kin 3:15
offered a sacrifice of peace o 1Kin 8:63
for there he offered burnt o 1Kin 8:64
and meat o 1Kin 8:64
and the fat of the peace o 1Kin 8:64

too little to receive the burnt o............ 1Kin 8:64
and meat o........................................ 1Kin 8:64
and the fat of the peace o ...................... 1Kin 8:64
a year did Solomon offer burnt o ......... 1Kin 9:25
peace o upon the altar which he ........ 1Kin 9:25
in to offer sacrifices and burnt o ........ 2Kin 10:24
the blood of his peace o, upon ........... 2Kin 16:13
meat offering, and their drink o.......... 2Kin 16:15
sacrifices and peace o before God........ 1Chr 16:1
burnt o and the peace o....................... 1Chr 16:2
To offer burnt o unto the LORD.......... 1Chr 16:40
thee the oxen also for burnt o ............. 1Chr 21:23
nor offer burnt o without cost............ 1Chr 21:24
burnt o and peace o.............................. 1Chr 21:26
and offered burnt o unto the LORD.... 1Chr 29:21
lambs, with their drink o..................... 1Chr 29:21
a thousand burnt o upon it.................... 2Chr 1:6
and for the burnt o morning .................. 2Chr 2:4
for there he offered burnt o................... 2Chr 7:7
and the fat of the peace o...................... 2Chr 7:7
not able to receive the burnt o............. 2Chr 7:7
and the meat o...................................... 2Chr 7:7
Then Solomon offered burnt o unto.... 2Chr 8:12
to offer the burnt o of the LORD......... 2Chr 23:18
they offered burnt o in the house ...... 2Chr 24:14
incense nor offered burnt o in.............. 2Chr 29:7
thank o into the house of the............ 2Chr 29:31
brought in sacrifices and thank o ...... 2Chr 29:31
as were of a free heart burnt o............ 2Chr 29:31
And the number of the burnt o .......... 2Chr 29:32
could not flay all the burnt o ............ 2Chr 29:34
And also the burnt o were in.............. 2Chr 29:35
with the fat of the peace o ................. 2Chr 29:35
the drink o for every burnt................. 2Chr 29:35
brought in the burnt o into the......... 2Chr 30:15
seven days, offering peace o............... 2Chr 30:22
priests and Levites for burnt o............ 2Chr 31:2
and for peace o .................................... 2Chr 31:2
of his substance for the burnt o ......... 2Chr 31:3
the morning and evening burnt o ........ 2Chr 31:3
the burnt o for the sabbaths, and......... 2Chr 31:3
the o into the house of the LORD........ 2Chr 31:10
And brought in the o and the tithes.. 2Chr 31:12
was over the freewill o of God............ 2Chr 31:14
and sacrificed thereon peace o............ 2Chr 33:16
and thank o, and commanded............. 2Chr 33:16
and kids, all for the passover o............ 2Chr 35:7
for the passover o two thousand.......... 2Chr 35:8
o five thousand small cattle................. 2Chr 35:9
And they removed the burnt o ........... 2Chr 35:12
the other holy o sod they in pots ....... 2Chr 35:13
busied in offering of burnt o.............. 2Chr 35:14
to offer burnt o upon the altar........... 2Chr 35:16
Israel, to offer burnt o thereon.................. Ezr 3:2
they offered burnt o thereon unto........... Ezr 3:3
the LORD, even burnt o morning............. Ezr 3:3
the daily burnt o by number.................... Ezr 3:4
to offer burnt o unto the LORD................ Ezr 3:6
for the burnt o of the God of.................... Ezr 6:9
rams, lambs, with their meat o............... Ezr 7:17
and their drink o ..................................... Ezr 7:17
offered burnt o unto the God of.............. Ezr 8:35
and for the sin o to make an.............. Neh 10:33
of our dough, and our o, and the.......... Neh 10:37
for the treasures, for the o .................. Neh 12:44
aforetime they laid the meat o ................ Neh 13:5
and the o of the priests.......................... Neh 13:5
offered burnt o according to the.................. Job 1:5
their drink o of blood will I not .................. Ps 16:4
Remember all thy o, and accept thy ........ Ps 20:3
for thy sacrifices or thy burnt o ................ Ps 50:8
go into thy house with burnt o.............. Ps 66:13
thee, the freewill o of my mouth ....... Ps 119:108
I have peace o with me.......................... Prov 7:14
I am full of the burnt o of rams................. Is 1:11
the small cattle of thy burnt o ............... Is 43:23
their burnt o and their sacrifices ............. Is 56:7
your burnt o are not acceptable,.............. Jer 6:20
pour out drink o unto other gods............. Jer 7:18
Put your burnt o unto your...................... Jer 7:21
concerning burnt o or sacrifices ............... Jer 7:22
from the south, bringing burnt o.......... Jer 17:26
and sacrifices, and meat o ..................... Jer 17:26
with fire for burnt o unto Baal ................. Jer 19:5
out drink o unto other gods................... Jer 19:13
out drink o unto other gods.................... Jer 32:29
a man before me to offer burnt o........... Jer 33:18
and to kindle meat o............................. Jer 33:18
and having cut themselves, with o............ Jer 41:5
and to pour out drink o unto her.......... Jer 44:17
and to pour out drink o unto her.......... Jer 44:18
and poured out drink o unto her........... Jer 44:19
and pour out drink o unto her............... Jer 44:19
and to pour out drink o unto her.......... Jer 44:25
and poured out there their drink o...... Eze 20:28
and there will I require your o............ Eze 20:40
make it, to offer burnt o thereon.......... Eze 43:18
make your burnt o upon the altar........ Eze 43:27
upon the altar, and your peace o.......... Eze 43:27
a burnt offering, and for peace o......... Eze 45:15
the prince's part to give burnt o.......... Eze 45:17
and meat o, and drink........................... Eze 45:17
and drink o, in the ............................... Eze 45:17
burnt offering, and the peace o ........... Eze 45:17
his burnt offering and his peace o.......... Eze 46:2
burnt offering or peace o...................... Eze 46:12
his burnt offering and his peace o........ Eze 46:12
of God more than burnt o........................ Hos 6:6
for the sacrifices of mine o .................... Hos 8:13
not offer wine o to the LORD.................. Hos 9:4
and proclaim and publish the free o .... Amos 4:5
Though ye offer me burnt o................ Amos 5:22
and your meat o................................... Amos 5:22
the peace o of your fat beasts ............ Amos 5:22
o in the wilderness forty years,........... Amos 5:25
I come before him with burnt o............... Mic 6:6
In tithes and o........................................ Mal 3:8
is more than all whole burnt o............ Mk 12:33
cast in unto the o of God......................... Lk 21:4
to bring alms to my nation, and o....... Acts 24:17
In burnt o and sacrifices for sin........... Heb 10:6
Sacrifice and offering and burnt o ....... Heb 10:8

### OFFICE

me he restored unto mine o.................. Gen 41:13
When ye do the o of a midwife to ........... Ex 1:16
unto me in the priest's o ........................... Ex 28:1
unto me in the priest's o ........................... Ex 28:3
unto me in the priest's o ........................... Ex 28:4
unto me in the priest's o ......................... Ex 28:41
unto me in the priest's o ........................... Ex 29:1
the priest's o shall be theirs...................... Ex 29:9
minister to me in the priest's o................ Ex 29:44
unto me in the priest's o ......................... Ex 30:30
to minister in the priest's o.................... Ex 31:10
to minister in the priest's o.................... Ex 35:19
to minister in the priest's o.................... Ex 39:41
unto me in the priest's o ......................... Ex 40:13
unto me in the priest's o ......................... Ex 40:15
unto the LORD in the priest's o ............... Lev 7:35
priest's o in his father's stead................ Lev 16:32
to minister in the priest's o...................... Num 3:3
ministered in the priest's o in................... Num 3:4
shall wait on their priest's o.................. Num 3:10
to the o of Eleazar the son of ................ Num 4:16
o for every thing of the altar ................... Num 18:7
I have given your priest's o unto......... Num 18:7
in the priest's o in his stead.................. Deut 10:6
o in the temple that Solomon ................. 1Chr 6:10
their o according to their order ............ 1Chr 6:32
seer did ordain in their set o ................ 1Chr 9:22
porters, were in their set o .................. 1Chr 9:26
had the set o over the things ................ 1Chr 9:31
Because their o was to wait on........... 1Chr 23:28
Ithamar executed the priest's o ............ 1Chr 24:2
the priest's o unto the LORD................. 2Chr 11:14
o by the hand of the Levites ................ 2Chr 24:11
of the priests, in their set o ............... 2Chr 31:15
for in their set o they......................... 2Chr 31:18
their o was to distribute unto............... Neh 13:13
and let another take his o.......................... Ps 109:8
to do the o of a priest unto me,............ Eze 44:13
o before God in the order of his................. Lk 1:8
to the custom of the priest's o................... Lk 1:9
of the Gentiles, I magnify mine o....... Rom 11:13
all members have not the same o.......... Rom 12:4
If a man desire the o of a bishop.............. 1Ti 3:1
let them use the o of a deacon............... 1Ti 3:10
For they that have used the o of............ 1Ti 3:13
of Levi, who receive the o of the............ Heb 7:5

### OFFICER

an o of Pharaoh's, and captain of......... Gen 37:36
an o of Pharaoh, captain of the ............ Gen 39:1
and Zebul his o ..................................... Judg 9:28
the son of Nathan was principal o .......... 1Kin 4:5
he was the only o which was in ........... 1Kin 4:19
the king of Israel called an o............... 1Kin 22:9
appointed unto her a certain o................ 2Kin 8:6
out of the city he took an o that........ 2Kin 25:19
and the high priest's o came .............. 2Chr 24:11
the judge deliver thee to the o ................ Mt 5:25
the judge deliver thee to the o .............. Lk 12:58
the o cast thee into prison ..................... Lk 12:58

### OFFICERS

was wroth against two of his o............... Gen 40:2
he asked Pharaoh's o that were.............. Gen 40:7
let him appoint o over the land........... Gen 41:34
of the people, and their o ............................ Ex 5:6
the people went out, and their o............. Ex 5:10
the o of the children of Israel,................ Ex 5:14
Then the o of the children of................... Ex 5:15
the o of the children of Israel .................. Ex 5:19
of the people, and o over them........... Num 11:16
was wroth with the o of the host ...... Num 31:14
the o which were over thousands......... Num 31:48
over tens, and o among your tribes...... Deut 1:15
o shalt thou make thee in all thy...... Deut 16:18
the o shall speak unto the people ........ Deut 20:5
the o shall speak further unto .............. Deut 20:8
when the o have made an end of............ Deut 20:9
tribes, your elders, and your o ........... Deut 29:10
elders of your tribes, and your o .......... Deut 31:28
commanded the o of the people............. Josh 1:10
that the o went through the host........... Josh 3:2
all Israel, and their elders, and o........... Josh 8:33
for their judges, and for their o ............ Josh 23:2
for their judges, and for their o ............ Josh 24:1
your vineyards, and give to his o ............ 1Sa 8:15
the son of Nathan was over the o........... 1Kin 4:5
had twelve o over all Israel................... 1Kin 4:7
those o provided victual for king........... 1Kin 4:27
unto the place where the o were........... 1Kin 4:28
o which were over the work.................. 1Kin 5:16
These were the chief of the o............... 1Kin 9:23
the o of the host, and said unto.......... 2Kin 11:15
the priest appointed o over the............ 2Kin 11:18
and his princes, and his o .................. 2Kin 24:12
and the king's wives, and his o........... 2Kin 24:15
and six thousand were o and judges.... 1Chr 23:4
business over Israel, for o ................... 1Chr 26:29
were o among them of Israel on ......... 1Chr 26:30
their o that served the king in........... 1Chr 27:1
king, and of his sons, with the o .......... 1Chr 28:1
the chief of king Solomon's o .............. 2Chr 8:10
of Israel called for one of his o ............ 2Chr 18:8
the Levites shall be o before you ....... 2Chr 19:11
Levites there were scribes, and o ....... 2Chr 34:13
to all the o of his house.............................. Est 1:8
let the king appoint o in all the.................. Est 2:3
o of the king, helped the Jews .................... Est 9:3
I will also make thy o peace.................... Is 60:17
that ye should be o in the house .......... Jer 29:26
chief priests sent o to take him................... Jn 7:32
Then came the o to the chief...................... Jn 7:45
The o answered, Never man spake............. Jn 7:46
o from the chief priests and........................ Jn 18:3
o of the Jews took Jesus, and................... Jn 18:12
o stood there, who had made a.................. Jn 18:18
one of the o which stood by ..................... Jn 18:22
o saw him, they cried out, saying............. Jn 19:6
But when the o came, and found........... Acts 5:22
Then went the captain with the o........ Acts 5:26

### OFFICES

thee, into one of the priests' o................ 1Sa 2:36
to their o in their service...................... 1Chr 24:3
And the priests waited on their o.............. 2Chr 7:6
Also Jehoiada appointed the o of....... 2Chr 23:18
of my God, and for the o thereof......... Neh 13:14

### OFFSCOURING

Thou hast made us as the o .................. Lam 3:45
are the o of all things unto this ........... 1Cor 4:13

### OFFSPRING

thine o as the grass of the earth ............ Job 5:25
their o before their eyes........................... Job 21:8
his o shall not be satisfied with............ Job 27:14
yea, let my o be rooted out .................... Job 31:8
of his father's house, the o....................... Is 22:24
seed, and my blessing upon thine o .......... Is 44:3
the o of thy bowels like the ..................... Is 48:19
and their o among the people.................... Is 61:9
of the LORD, and their o with them......... Is 65:23
have said, For we are also his o.......... Acts 17:28
then as we are the o of God.............. Acts 17:29
the o of David, and the bright and...... Rev 22:16

### OFT

that as o as he passed by, he................... 2Kin 4:8
How o is the candle of the wicked....... Job 21:17
how o cometh their destruction ............ Job 21:17
How o did they provoke him in the....... Ps 78:40
Why do we and the Pharisees fast o...... Mt 9:14
the fire, and o into the water............... Mt 17:15
how o shall my brother sin.................... Mt 18:21
except they wash their hands o.................. Mk 7:3
I punished them o in every .................. Acts 26:11
do ye, as o as ye drink it, in ............... 1Cor 11:25
more frequent, in deaths o.................. 2Cor 11:23
for he o refreshed me, and was not ........ 2Ti 1:16
in the rain that cometh o upon it............. Heb 6:7

### OFTEN

that being o reproved hardeneth .......... Prov 29:1
the LORD spake o one to another........... Mal 3:16
how o would I have gathered thy ......... Mt 23:37
he had been o bound with fetters.............. Mk 5:4
do the disciples of John fast o.................. Lk 5:33
how o would I have gathered thy ........... Lk 13:34
For as o as ye eat this bread, and ..... 1Cor 11:26
In journeyings o, in perils of .............. 2Cor 11:26
and painfulness, in watchings o........... 2Cor 11:27
hunger and thirst, in fastings o.......... 2Cor 11:27
walk, of whom I have told you o............ Phil 3:18
sake and thine o infirmities .................... 1Ti 5:23
that he should offer himself o................ Heb 9:25
For then must he o have suffered.......... Heb 9:26
all plagues, as o as they will................... Rev 11:6

### OFTENER

wherefore he sent for him the o ......... Acts 24:26

### OFTENTIMES

things worketh God o with man........... Job 33:29
For o also thine own heart................... Eccl 7:22
For o it had caught him ........................... Lk 8:29
that o I purposed to come unto............ Rom 1:13
whom we have o proved diligent in..... 2Cor 8:22
offering o the same sacrifices,............. Heb 10:11

### OFTTIMES

for o he falleth into the fire,................. Mt 17:15
o it hath cast him into the fire,............... Mk 9:22
for Jesus o resorted thither with.............. Jn 18:2

**OG** (og) *An Amorite king.*

O the king of Bashan went out .......... Num 21:33
the kingdom of O king of Bashan...... Num 32:33
O the king of Bashan, which dwelt ....... Deut 1:4
O the king of Bashan came out.............. Deut 3:1
delivered into our hands O also............ Deut 3:3
Argob, the kingdom of O in Bashan...... Deut 3:4
of the kingdom of O in Bashan ............ Deut 3:10
For only O king of Bashan .................. Deut 3:11
Bashan, being the kingdom of O........... Deut 3:13
the land of O king of Bashan, two....... Deut 4:47
O the king of Bashan, came out............ Deut 29:7
them as he did to Sihon and to O........ Deut 31:4
the other side Jordan, Sihon and O...... Josh 2:10
to O king of Bashan, which was at ....... Josh 9:10
the coast of O king of Bashan,.............. Josh 12:4
All the kingdom of O in Bashan.......... Josh 13:12
the kingdom of O king of Bashan....... Josh 13:30

of the kingdom of O in Bashan ... Josh 13:31
Amorites, and of O king of Bashan ... 1Kin 4:19
the land of O king of Bashan ... Neh 9:22
O king of Bashan, and all the ... Ps 135:11
And O the king of Bashan ... Ps 136:20

**OH**
O let not the LORD be angry, and I ... Gen 18:30
O let not the Lord be angry, and I ... Gen 18:32
And Lot said unto them, O, not so ... Gen 19:18
O, let me escape thither, (is it ... Gen 19:20
O my lord, let thy servant, I ... Gen 44:18
unto the LORD, and said, O ... Ex 32:31
O my Lord, if the LORD be with us ... Judg 6:13
O my Lord, wherewith shall I save ... Judg 6:15
O my lord, as thy soul liveth, my ... 1Sa 1:26
O that I were made judge in the ... 2Sa 15:4
O that one would give me drink of ... 2Sa 23:15
O that thou wouldest bless me ... 1Chr 4:10
O that one would give me drink of ... 1Chr 11:17
O that I might have my request ... Job 6:8
O that I had given up the ghost, ... Job 10:18
But o that God would speak, and ... Job 11:5
O that ye would altogether hold ... Job 13:5
O that thou wouldest hide me in ... Job 14:13
O that one might plead for a man ... Job 16:21
O that my words were now written ... Job 19:23
o that they were printed in a ... Job 19:23
O that I knew where I might find ... Job 23:3
O that I were as in months past, ... Job 29:2
O that we had of his flesh ... Job 31:31
O that one would hear me ... Job 31:35
o save me for thy mercies' sake ... Ps 6:4
O let the wickedness of the ... Ps 7:9
O that the salvation of Israel ... Ps 14:7
O how great is thy goodness ... Ps 31:19
O that the salvation of Israel ... Ps 53:6
O that I had wings like a dove ... Ps 55:6
O that my people had hearkened ... Ps 81:13
O that men would praise the LORD ... Ps 107:8
O that men would praise the LORD ... Ps 107:15
O that men would praise the LORD ... Ps 107:21
O that men would praise the LORD ... Ps 107:31
O that thou wouldest rend the ... Is 64:1
O that my head were waters, and ... Jer 9:1
O that I had in the wilderness a ... Jer 9:2
early and sending them, saying, O ... Jer 44:4

**OHAD** (*o'-had*) *A son of Simeon.*
Jamin, and O, and Jachin ... Gen 46:10
Jemuel, and Jamin, and O, and Jachin ... Ex 6:15

**OHEL** (*o'-hel*) *A son of Zerubbabel.*
and O, and Berechiah, ... 1Chr 3:20

**OHOLAH** See AHOLAH.

**OHOLIAB** See AHOLIAB.

**OHOLIBAH** See AHOLIBAH.

**OHOLIBAMAH** See AHOLIBAMAH.

**OIL**
poured o upon the top of it ... Gen 28:18
thereon, and he poured o thereon ... Gen 35:14
O for the light, spices for ... Ex 25:6
the light, spices for anointing o ... Ex 25:6
that they bring thee pure o olive ... Ex 27:20
cakes unleavened tempered with o ... Ex 29:2
wafers unleavened anointed with o ... Ex 29:2
shalt thou take the anointing o ... Ex 29:7
the altar, and of the anointing o ... Ex 29:21
fourth part of an hin of beaten o ... Ex 29:40
sanctuary, and of o olive an hin ... Ex 30:24
make it an o of holy ointment ... Ex 30:25
it shall be an holy anointing o ... Ex 30:25
o unto me throughout your ... Ex 30:31
And the anointing o, and sweet ... Ex 31:11
o for the light, and spices for ... Ex 35:8
light, and spices for anointing o ... Ex 35:8
with the o for the light, ... Ex 35:14
and his staves, and the anointing o ... Ex 35:15
o for the light, and for the ... Ex 35:28
the light, and for the anointing o ... Ex 35:28
And he made the holy anointing o ... Ex 37:29
thereof, and the o for light, ... Ex 39:37
golden altar, and the anointing o ... Ex 39:38
thou shalt take the anointing o ... Ex 40:9
and he shall pour o upon it ... Lev 2:1
of the o thereof, with all the ... Lev 2:2
of fine flour mingled with o ... Lev 2:4
unleavened wafers anointed with o ... Lev 2:4
flour unleavened, mingled with o ... Lev 2:5
it in pieces, and pour o thereon ... Lev 2:6
be made of fine flour with o ... Lev 2:7
And thou shalt put o upon it ... Lev 2:15
thereof, and part of the o thereof ... Lev 2:16
he shall put no o upon it ... Lev 5:11
of the o thereof, and all the ... Lev 6:15
In a pan it shall be made with o ... Lev 6:21
meat offering, mingled with o ... Lev 7:10
unleavened cakes mingled with o ... Lev 7:12
with o, and cakes mingled with o ... Lev 7:12
the garments, and the anointing o ... Lev 8:2
And Moses took the anointing o ... Lev 8:10
the anointing o upon Aaron's head ... Lev 8:12
And Moses took of the anointing o ... Lev 8:30
and a meat offering mingled with o ... Lev 9:4
for the anointing o of the LORD ... Lev 10:7
mingled with o, and one log of o ... Lev 14:10
offering, and the log of o ... Lev 14:12
shall take some of the log of o ... Lev 14:15
in the o that is in his left hand ... Lev 14:16
shall sprinkle of the o with his ... Lev 14:16
of the rest of the o that is in ... Lev 14:17
the remnant of the o that is in ... Lev 14:18
with o for a meat offering ... Lev 14:21
a meat offering, and a log of o ... Lev 14:21
offering, and the log of o ... Lev 14:24
the priest shall pour of the o ... Lev 14:26
his right finger some of the o ... Lev 14:27
the priest shall put of the o ... Lev 14:28
the rest of the o that is in the ... Lev 14:29
head the anointing o was poured ... Lev 21:10
o of his God is upon him ... Lev 21:12
of fine flour mingled with o ... Lev 23:13
pure o olive beaten for the light ... Lev 24:2
all the o vessels thereof, ... Num 4:9
pertaineth the o for the light ... Num 4:16
meat offering, and the anointing o ... Num 4:16
he shall pour no o upon it ... Num 5:15
of fine flour mingled with o ... Num 6:15
unleavened bread anointed with o ... Num 6:15
with o for a meat offering ... Num 7:13
with o for a meat offering ... Num 7:19
with o for a meat offering ... Num 7:25
with o for a meat offering ... Num 7:31
with o for a meat offering ... Num 7:37
with o for a meat offering ... Num 7:43
with o for a meat offering ... Num 7:49
with o for a meat offering ... Num 7:55
with o for a meat offering ... Num 7:61
with o for a meat offering ... Num 7:67
with o for a meat offering ... Num 7:73
with o for a meat offering ... Num 7:79
even fine flour mingled with o ... Num 8:8
of it was as the taste of fresh o ... Num 11:8
the fourth part of an hin of o ... Num 15:4
the third part of an hin of o ... Num 15:6
mingled with half an hin of o ... Num 15:9
All the best of the o, and all the ... Num 18:12
fourth part of an hin of beaten o ... Num 28:5
a meat offering, mingled with o ... Num 28:9
a meat offering, mingled with o ... Num 28:12
a meat offering, mingled with o ... Num 28:12
deal of flour mingled with o for ... Num 28:13
shall be of flour mingled with o ... Num 28:20
offering of flour mingled with o ... Num 28:28
shall be of flour mingled with o ... Num 29:3
shall be of flour mingled with o ... Num 29:9
shall be of flour mingled with o ... Num 29:14
was anointed with the holy o ... Num 35:25
thy corn, and thy wine, and thine o ... Deut 7:13
a land of o olive, and honey ... Deut 8:8
thy corn, and thy wine, and thine o ... Deut 11:14
corn, or of thy wine, or of thy o ... Deut 12:17
corn, of thy wine, and of thine o ... Deut 14:23
corn, of thy wine, and of thine o ... Deut 18:4
not anoint thyself with the o ... Deut 28:40
thee either corn, wine, or o ... Deut 28:51
rock, and o out of the flinty rock ... Deut 32:13
and let him dip his foot in o ... Deut 33:24
Then Samuel took a vial of o ... 1Sa 10:1
fill thine horn with o, and go, I ... 1Sa 16:1
Then Samuel took the horn of o ... 1Sa 16:13
he had not been anointed with o ... 2Sa 1:21
and anoint not thyself with o ... 2Sa 14:2
horn of o out of the tabernacle ... 1Kin 1:39
and twenty measures of pure o ... 1Kin 5:11
barrel, and a little o in a cruse ... 1Kin 17:12
neither shall the cruse of o fail ... 1Kin 17:14
neither did the cruse of o fail ... 1Kin 17:16
in the house, save a pot of o ... 2Kin 4:2
And the o stayed ... 2Kin 4:6
And he said, Go, sell the o ... 2Kin 4:7
take this box of o in thine hand ... 2Kin 9:1
Then take the box of o, and pour ... 2Kin 9:3
and he poured the o on his head ... 2Kin 9:6
and vineyards, a land of o olive ... 2Kin 18:32
fine flour, and the wine, and the o ... 1Chr 9:29
bunches of raisins, and wine, and o ... 1Chr 12:40
over the cellars of o was Joash ... 1Chr 27:28
and twenty thousand baths of o ... 2Chr 2:10
the wheat, and the barley, the o ... 2Chr 2:15
and store of victual, and of o ... 2Chr 11:11
firstfruits of corn, wine, and o ... 2Chr 31:5
increase of corn, and wine, and o ... 2Chr 32:28
and meat, and drink, and o, unto ... Ezr 3:7
heaven, wheat, salt, wine, and o ... Ezr 6:9
wine, and to an hundred baths of o ... Ezr 7:22
of the corn, the wine, and the o ... Neh 5:11
manner of trees, of wine and of o ... Neh 10:37
corn, of the new wine, and the o ... Neh 10:39
the corn, the new wine, and the o ... Neh 13:5
the o unto the treasuries ... Neh 13:12
wit, six months with o of myrrh ... Est 2:12
Which make o within their walls ... Job 24:11
rock poured me out rivers of o ... Job 29:6
thou anointest my head with o ... Ps 23:5
hath anointed thee with the o of ... Ps 45:7
his words were softer than o ... Ps 55:21
with my holy o have I anointed ... Ps 89:20
I shall be anointed with fresh o ... Ps 92:10
o to make his face to shine, and ... Ps 104:15
water, and like o into his bones ... Ps 109:18
it shall be an excellent o ... Ps 141:5
and her mouth is smoother than o ... Prov 5:3
wine and o shall not be rich ... Prov 21:17
o in the dwelling of the wise ... Prov 21:20
and the myrtle, and the o tree ... Is 41:19
the o of joy for mourning, the ... Is 61:3
for wheat, and for wine, and for o ... Jer 31:12
ye wine, and summer fruits, and o ... Jer 40:10
of wheat, and of barley, and of o ... Jer 41:8
thee, and I anointed thee with o ... Eze 16:9
eat fine flour, and honey, and o ... Eze 16:13
and thou hast set mine o and mine ... Eze 16:18
I gave thee, fine flour, and o ... Eze 16:19
hast set mine incense and mine o ... Eze 23:41
and Pannag, and honey, and o ... Eze 27:17
cause their rivers to run like o ... Eze 32:14
ordinance of o, the bath of o ... Eze 45:14
ram, and an hin of o for an ephah ... Eze 45:24
offering, and according to the o ... Eze 45:25
give, and an hin of o to an ephah ... Eze 46:5
unto, and an hin of o to an ephah ... Eze 46:7
give, and an hin of o to an ephah ... Eze 46:11
and the third part of an hin of o ... Eze 46:14
and the meat offering, and the o ... Eze 46:15
water, my wool and my flax, mine o ... Hos 2:5
I gave her corn, and wine, and o ... Hos 2:8
the corn, and the wine, and the o ... Hos 2:22
and o is carried into Egypt ... Hos 12:1
is dried up, the o languisheth ... Joel 1:10
will send you corn, and wine, and o ... Joel 2:19
shall overflow with wine and o ... Joel 2:24
with ten thousands of rivers of o ... Mic 6:7
thou shalt not anoint thee with o ... Mic 6:15
upon the new wine, and upon the o ... Hag 1:11
bread, or pottage, or wine, or o ... Hag 2:12
the golden o out of themselves ... Zec 4:12
lamps, and took no o with them ... Mt 25:3
But the wise took o in their ... Mt 25:4
unto the wise, Give us of your o ... Mt 25:8
anointed with o many that were ... Mk 6:13
My head with o thou didst not ... Lk 7:46
bound up his wounds, pouring in o ... Lk 10:34
he said, An hundred measures of o ... Lk 16:6
hath anointed thee with the o of ... Heb 1:9
anointing him with o in the name ... Jas 5:14
and see thou hurt not the o ... Rev 6:6
and frankincense, and wine, and o ... Rev 18:13

**OILED**
of bread, and one cake of o bread ... Ex 29:23
cake, and a cake of o bread ... Lev 8:26

**OINTMENT**
shalt make it an oil of holy o ... Ex 30:25
an o compound after the art of ... Ex 30:25
and the spices, and the precious o ... 2Kin 20:13
priests made the o of the spices ... 1Chr 9:30
he maketh the sea like a pot of o ... Job 41:31
like the precious o upon the head ... Ps 133:2
O and perfume rejoice the heart ... Prov 27:9
the o of his right hand, which ... Prov 27:16
name is better than precious o ... Eccl 7:1
and let thy head lack no o ... Eccl 9:8
Dead flies cause the o of the ... Eccl 10:1
thy name is as o poured forth ... Song 1:3
up, neither mollified with o ... Is 1:6
and the spices, and the precious o ... Is 39:2
thou wentest to the king with o ... Is 57:9
alabaster box of very precious o ... Mt 26:7
For this o might have been sold ... Mt 26:9
she hath poured this o on my body ... Mt 26:12
of o of spikenard very precious ... Mk 14:3
Why was this waste of the o made ... Mk 14:4
brought an alabaster box of o ... Lk 7:37
feet, and anointed them with the o ... Lk 7:38
hath anointed my feet with o ... Lk 7:46
which anointed the Lord with o ... Jn 11:2
Mary a pound of o of spikenard ... Jn 12:3
filled with the odour of the o ... Jn 12:3
Why was not this o sold for three ... Jn 12:5

**OINTMENTS**
of the savour of thy good o thy ... Song 1:3
smell of thine o than all spices ... Song 4:10
themselves with the chief o ... Amos 6:6
returned, and prepared spices and o ... Lk 23:56
And cinnamon, and odours, and o ... Rev 18:13

**OLD**
And Noah was five hundred years o ... Gen 5:32
became mighty men which were of o ... Gen 6:4
Noah was six hundred years o when ... Gen 7:6
Shem was an hundred years o ... Gen 11:10
five years o when he departed out ... Gen 12:4
me an heifer of three years o ... Gen 15:9
and a she goat of three years o ... Gen 15:9
and a ram of three years o ... Gen 15:9
shalt be buried in a good o age ... Gen 15:15
was fourscore and six years o ... Gen 16:16
And when Abram was ninety years o ... Gen 17:1
he that is eight days o shall be ... Gen 17:12
him that is an hundred years o ... Gen 17:17
Sarah, that is ninety years o ... Gen 17:17
And Abraham was ninety years o ... Gen 17:24
his son was thirteen years o ... Gen 17:25
Now Abraham and Sarah were o ... Gen 18:11
After I am waxed o shall I have ... Gen 18:12
pleasure, my lord being o also ... Gen 18:12
a surety bear a child, which am o ... Gen 18:13
compassed the house round, both o ... Gen 19:4
unto the younger, Our father is o ... Gen 19:31
bare Abraham a son in his o age ... Gen 21:2
his son Isaac being eight days o ... Gen 21:4
And Abraham was an hundred years o ... Gen 21:5
have born him a son in his o age ... Gen 21:7
and seven and twenty years o ... Gen 23:1
And Abraham was o, and well ... Gen 24:1
a son to my master when she was o ... Gen 24:36
ghost, and died in a good o age ... Gen 25:8
an o man, and full of years ... Gen 25:8

Isaac was forty years o when he ... Gen 25:20
years o when she bare them ... Gen 25:26
Esau was forty years o when he ... Gen 26:34
to pass, that when Isaac was o ... Gen 27:1
And he said, Behold now, I am o ... Gen 27:2
gathered unto his people, being o ... Gen 35:29
Joseph, being seventeen years o ... Gen 37:2
he was the son of his o age ... Gen 37:3
Joseph was thirty years o when he ... Gen 41:46
the o man of whom ye spake ... Gen 43:27
o man, and a child of his o age ... Gen 44:20
said unto Jacob, How o art thou ... Gen 47:8
as a lion, and as an o lion ... Gen 49:9
being an hundred and ten years o ... Gen 50:26
And Moses was fourscore years o ... Ex 7:7
Aaron fourscore and three years o ... Ex 7:7
go with our young and with our o ... Ex 10:9
are numbered, from twenty years o ... Ex 30:14
be numbered, from twenty years o ... Ex 38:26
It is an o leprosy in the skin of ... Lev 13:11
and honour the face of the o man ... Lev 19:32
eat yet of o fruit until the ... Lev 25:22
in ye shall eat of the o store ... Lev 25:22
And ye shall eat o store ... Lev 26:10
bring forth the o because of the ... Lev 26:10
years o even unto sixty years o ... Lev 27:3
o even unto twenty years o ... Lev 27:5
month o even unto five years o ... Lev 27:6
And if it be from sixty years o ... Lev 27:7
From twenty years o and upward, ... Num 1:3
of the names, from twenty years o ... Num 1:18
every male from twenty years o ... Num 1:20
every male from twenty years o ... Num 1:22
of the names, from twenty years o ... Num 1:24
of the names, from twenty years o ... Num 1:26
of the names, from twenty years o ... Num 1:28
of the names, from twenty years o ... Num 1:30
of the names, from twenty years o ... Num 1:32
of the names, from twenty years o ... Num 1:34
of the names, from twenty years o ... Num 1:36
of the names, from twenty years o ... Num 1:38
of the names, from twenty years o ... Num 1:40
of the names, from twenty years o ... Num 1:42
fathers, from twenty years o ... Num 1:45
every male from a month o ... Num 3:15
of all the males, from a month o ... Num 3:22
of all the males, from a month o ... Num 3:28
of all the males, from a month o ... Num 3:34
all the males from a month o ... Num 3:39
children of Israel from a month o ... Num 3:40
number of names, from a month o ... Num 3:43
From thirty years o and upward ... Num 4:3
upward even until fifty years o ... Num 4:3
From thirty years o and upward ... Num 4:23
years o shalt thou number them ... Num 4:23
From thirty years o and upward ... Num 4:30
years o shalt thou number them ... Num 4:30
From thirty years o and upward ... Num 4:35
and upward even unto fifty years o ... Num 4:35
From thirty years o and upward ... Num 4:39
and upward even unto fifty years o ... Num 4:39
From thirty years o and upward ... Num 4:43
and upward even unto fifty years o ... Num 4:43
From thirty years o and upward ... Num 4:47
and upward even unto fifty years o ... Num 4:47
from twenty and five years o ... Num 8:24
whole number, from twenty years o. Num 14:29
from a month o shalt thou redeem ... Num 18:16
of Israel, from twenty years o ... Num 26:2
the people, from twenty years o ... Num 26:4
all males from a month o ... Num 26:62
out of Egypt, from twenty years o ... Num 32:11
three years o when he died in ... Num 33:39
giants dwelt therein in o time ... Deut 2:20
Thy raiment waxed not o upon thee ... Deut 8:4
which they of o time have set in ... Deut 19:14
not regard the person of the o ... Deut 28:50
clothes are not waxen o upon you ... Deut 29:5
shoe is not waxen o upon thy foot ... Deut 29:5
and twenty years o this day ... Deut 31:2
Remember the days of o, consider ... Deut 32:7
and twenty years o when he died ... Deut 34:7
they did eat of the o corn of the ... Josh 5:11
eaten of the o corn of the land ... Josh 5:12
both man and woman, young and o ... Josh 6:21
took o sacks upon their asses, and ... Josh 9:4
their asses, and wine bottles, o ... Josh 9:4
o shoes and clouted upon their ... Josh 9:5
feet, and o garments upon them ... Josh 9:5
our shoes are become o by reason ... Josh 9:13
Now Joshua was o and stricken in ... Josh 13:1
LORD said unto him, Thou art o ... Josh 13:1
Forty years o was I when Moses ... Josh 14:7
day fourscore and five years o ... Josh 14:10
round about, that Joshua waxed o ... Josh 23:1
and said unto them, I am o ... Josh 23:2
other side of the flood in o time ... Josh 24:2
being an hundred and ten years o ... Josh 24:29
being an hundred and ten years o ... Judg 2:8
second bullock of seven years o ... Judg 6:25
son of Joash died in a good o age ... Judg 8:32
there came an o man from his work. Judg 19:16
the o man said, Whither goest ... Judg 19:17
the o man said, Peace be with ... Judg 19:20
master of the house, the o man ... Judg 19:22
for I am too o to have an husband ... Ruth 1:12
and a nourisher of thine o age ... Ruth 4:15
Now Eli was very o, and heard all ... 1Sa 2:22
not be an o man in thine house ... 1Sa 2:31
there shall not be an o man in ... 1Sa 2:32
Eli was ninety and eight years o ... 1Sa 4:15
for he was an o man, and heavy ... 1Sa 4:18
came to pass, when Samuel was o ... 1Sa 8:1
said unto him, Behold, thou art o ... 1Sa 8:5
and I am o and grayheaded ... 1Sa 12:2
for an o man in the days of Saul ... 1Sa 17:12
for those nations were of o the ... 1Sa 27:8
And she said, An o man cometh up ... 1Sa 28:14
Saul's son was forty years o when ... 2Sa 2:10
He was five years o when the ... 2Sa 4:4
years o when he began to reign ... 2Sa 5:4
aged man, even fourscore years o ... 2Sa 19:32
I am this day fourscore years o ... 2Sa 19:35
They were wont to speak in o time ... 2Sa 20:18
Now king David was o and stricken ... 1Kin 1:1
and the king was very o ... 1Kin 1:15
came to pass, when Solomon was o ... 1Kin 11:4
Rehoboam consulted with the o men .. 1Kin 12:6
forsook the counsel of the o men ... 1Kin 12:8
forsook the o men's counsel that ... 1Kin 12:13
dwelt an o prophet in Beth-el ... 1Kin 13:11
city where the o prophet dwelt ... 1Kin 13:25
the o prophet came to the city, ... 1Kin 13:29
one years o when he began to ... 1Kin 14:21
o age he was diseased in his feet ... 1Kin 15:23
five years o when he began to ... 1Kin 22:42
no child, and her husband is o ... 2Kin 4:14
two years o was he when he began ... 2Kin 8:17
twenty years o was Ahaziah when ... 2Kin 8:26
Seven years o was Jehoash when he. 2Kin 11:21
five years o when he began to ... 2Kin 14:2
which was sixteen years o ... 2Kin 14:21
Sixteen years o was he when he ... 2Kin 15:2
twenty years o was he when he ... 2Kin 15:33
Twenty years o was Ahaz when he ... 2Kin 16:2
five years o was he when he began ... 2Kin 18:2
years o when he began to reign ... 2Kin 21:1
two years o when he began to ... 2Kin 21:19
years o when he began to reign ... 2Kin 22:1
three years o when he began to ... 2Kin 23:31
five years o when he began to ... 2Kin 23:36
years o when he began to reign ... 2Kin 24:8
one years o when he began to ... 2Kin 24:18
when he was threescore years o ... 1Chr 2:21
they of Ham had dwelt there of o ... 1Chr 4:40
So when David was o and full of ... 1Chr 23:1
were numbered from twenty years o 1Chr 23:27
of them from twenty years o ... 1Chr 27:23
And he died in a good o age ... 1Chr 29:28
the o men that had stood before ... 2Chr 10:6
counsel which the o men gave him ... 2Chr 10:8
forsook the counsel of the o men ... 2Chr 10:13
forty years o when he began to ... 2Chr 12:13
five years o when he began to ... 2Chr 20:31
two years o when he began to ... 2Chr 21:5
two years o was he when he began ... 2Chr 21:20
two years o was Ahaziah when he ... 2Chr 22:2
Joash was seven years o when he ... 2Chr 24:1
But Jehoiada waxed o, and was full .. 2Chr 24:15
thirty years o was he when he ... 2Chr 24:15
five years o when he began to ... 2Chr 25:1
numbered them from twenty years o .. 2Chr 25:5
Uzziah, who was sixteen years o ... 2Chr 26:1
Sixteen years o was Uzziah when ... 2Chr 26:3
five years o when he began to ... 2Chr 27:1
twenty years o when he began to ... 2Chr 27:8
Ahaz was twenty years o when he ... 2Chr 28:1
he was five and twenty years o ... 2Chr 29:1
of males, from three years o ... 2Chr 31:16
the Levites from twenty years o ... 2Chr 31:17
years o when he began to reign ... 2Chr 33:1
twenty years o when he began to ... 2Chr 33:21
years o when he began to reign ... 2Chr 34:1
three years o when he began to ... 2Chr 36:2
five years o when he began to ... 2Chr 36:5
years o when he began to reign ... 2Chr 36:9
twenty years o when he began to ... 2Chr 36:11
o man, or him that stooped for ... 2Chr 36:17
the Levites, from twenty years o ... Ezr 3:8
within the same of o time ... Ezr 4:15
of o time hath made insurrection ... Ezr 4:19
Moreover the o gate repaired ... Neh 3:6
their clothes waxed not o ... Neh 9:21
of Ephraim, and above the o gate ... Neh 12:39
Asaph of o there were chief of ... Neh 12:46
perish, all Jews, both young and o ... Est 3:13
The o lion perisheth for lack of ... Job 4:11
root thereof wax o in the earth ... Job 14:8
Knowest thou not this of o ... Job 20:4
do the wicked live, become o ... Job 21:7
Hast thou marked the o way which ... Job 22:15
in whom o age was perished ... Job 30:2
I am young, and ye are very o ... Job 32:6
So Job died, being o and full of ... Job 42:17
it waxeth o because of all mine ... Ps 6:7
for they have been ever of o ... Ps 25:6
my bones waxed o through my ... Ps 32:3
I have been young, and now am o ... Ps 37:25
in their days, in the times of o ... Ps 44:1
them, even he that abideth of o ... Ps 55:19
of heavens, which were of o ... Ps 68:33
me not off in the time of o age ... Ps 71:9
Now also when I am o and ... Ps 71:18
which thou hast purchased of o ... Ps 74:2
For God is my King of o, working ... Ps 74:12
I have considered the days of o ... Ps 77:5
I will remember thy wonders of o ... Ps 77:11
I will utter dark sayings of o ... Ps 78:2
still bring forth fruit in o age ... Ps 92:14
Thy throne is established of o ... Ps 93:2
Of o hast thou laid the ... Ps 102:25
them shall wax o like a garment ... Ps 102:26
I remembered thy judgments of o ... Ps 119:52
I have known of o that thou hast ... Ps 119:152
I remember the days of o ... Ps 143:5
o men, and children ... Ps 148:12
of his way, before his works of o ... Prov 8:22
children are the crown of o men ... Prov 17:6
the beauty of o men is the grey ... Prov 20:29
and when he is o, he will not ... Prov 22:6
Remove not the o landmark ... Prov 23:10
not thy mother when she is o ... Prov 23:22
it hath been already of o time ... Eccl 1:10
a poor and a wise child than an o ... Eccl 4:13
of pleasant fruits, new and o ... Song 7:13
Zoar, an heifer of three years o ... Is 15:5
Ethiopians captives, young and o ... Is 20:4
walls for the water of the o pool ... Is 22:11
thy counsels of o are ... Is 25:1
o lion, the viper and fiery flying ... Is 30:6
For Tophet is ordained of o ... Is 30:33
neither consider the things of o ... Is 43:18
And even to your o age I am he ... Is 46:4
Remember the former things of o ... Is 46:9
they all shall wax o as a garment ... Is 50:9
earth shall wax o like a garment ... Is 51:6
days, in the generations of o ... Is 51:9
not I held my peace even of o ... Is 57:11
shall build the o waste places ... Is 58:12
And they shall build the o wastes ... Is 61:4
and carried them all the days of o ... Is 63:9
Then he remembered the days of o ... Is 63:11
nor an o man that hath not filled ... Is 65:20
shall die an hundred years o ... Is 65:20
hundred years o shall be accursed ... Is 65:20
For of o time I have broken thy ... Jer 2:20
and see, and ask for the o paths ... Jer 6:16
before thee of o prophesied both ... Jer 28:8
LORD hath appeared of o unto me ... Jer 31:3
both young men and o together ... Jer 31:13
and took thence o cast clouts ... Jer 38:11
o rotten rags, and let them down ... Jer 38:11
Put now these o cast clouts ... Jer 38:12
be inhabited, as in the days of o ... Jer 46:26
as an heifer of three years o ... Jer 48:34
thee will I break in pieces o ... Jer 51:22
twenty years o when he began to ... Jer 52:1
that she had in the days of o ... Lam 1:7
he had commanded in the days of o ... Lam 2:17
the o lie on the ground in the ... Lam 2:21
flesh and my skin hath he made o ... Lam 3:4
places, as they that be dead of o ... Lam 3:6
renew our days as of o ... Lam 5:21
Slay utterly o and young, both ... Eze 9:6
unto her that was o in adulteries ... Eze 23:43
to destroy it for the o hatred ... Eze 25:15
pit, with the people of o time ... Eze 26:20
earth, in places desolate of o ... Eze 26:20
settle you after your o estates ... Eze 36:11
in o time by my servants the ... Eze 38:17
about threescore and two years o ... Dan 5:31
ye o men, and give ear, all ye ... Joel 1:2
your o men shall dream dreams, ... Joel 2:28
will build it as in the days of o ... Amos 9:11
goings forth have been from of o ... Mic 5:2
with calves of a year o ... Mic 6:6
and Gilead, as in the days of o ... Mic 7:14
our fathers from the days of o ... Mic 7:20
But Nineveh is of o like a pool ... Nah 2:8
where the lion, even the o lion ... Nah 2:11
There shall yet o men ... Zec 8:4
o women dwell in the streets of ... Zec 8:4
the LORD, as in the days of o ... Mal 3:4
coasts thereof, from two years o ... Mt 2:16
it was said by them of o time ... Mt 5:21
it was said by them of o time ... Mt 5:27
hath been said by them of o time ... Mt 5:33
of new cloth unto an o garment ... Mt 9:16
men put new wine into o bottles ... Mt 9:17
of his treasure things new and o ... Mt 13:52
of new cloth on an o garment ... Mk 2:21
it up taketh away from the o ... Mk 2:21
putteth new wine into o bottles ... Mk 2:22
for I am an o man, and my wife ... Lk 1:18
also conceived a son in her o age ... Lk 1:36
And when he was twelve years o ... Lk 2:42
piece of a new garment upon an o ... Lk 5:36
of the new agreeth not with the o ... Lk 5:36
putteth new wine into o bottles ... Lk 5:37
No man also having drunk o wine ... Lk 5:39
for he saith, The o is better ... Lk 5:39
that one of the o prophets was ... Lk 9:8
that one of the o prophets is ... Lk 9:19
yourselves bags which wax not o ... Lk 12:33
can a man be born when he is o ... Jn 3:4
Thou art not yet fifty years o ... Jn 8:57
but when thou shalt be o, thou ... Jn 21:18
your o men shall dream dreams ... Acts 2:17
the man was above forty years o ... Acts 4:22
And when he was full forty years o ... Acts 7:23
For Moses of o time hath in every ... Acts 15:21
an o disciple, with whom we ... Acts 21:16
he was about an hundred years o ... Rom 4:19
that our o man is crucified with ... Rom 6:6
Purge out therefore the o leaven ... 1Cor 5:7
keep the feast, not with o leaven ... 1Cor 5:8
in the reading of the o testament ... 2Cor 3:14
o things are passed away ... 2Cor 5:17
the former conversation the o man ... Eph 4:22
put off the o man with his deeds ... Col 3:9

o wives' fables, and exercise ........ 1Ti 4:7
number under threescore years o........ 1Ti 5:9
all shall wax o as doth a garment........ Heb 1:11
he hath made the first o........ Heb 8:13
waxeth o is ready to vanish away........ Heb 8:13
in the o time the holy women also........ 1Pet 3:5
he was purged from his o sins........ 2Pet 1:9
not in o time by the will of man........ 2Pet 1:21
And spared not the o world........ 2Pet 2:5
word of God the heavens were of o........ 2Pet 3:5
but an o commandment which ye had.... 1Jn 2:7
The o commandment is the word........ 1Jn 2:7
who were before of o ordained to........ Jude 4
that o serpent, called the Devil,........ Rev 12:9
that o serpent, which is the........ Rev 20:2

**OLDNESS**
not in the o of the letter........ Rom 7:6

**OLIVE**
mouth was an o leaf pluckt off........ Gen 8:11
pure oil o beaten for the light........ Ex 27:20
the sanctuary, and of oil o an hin........ Ex 30:24
pure oil o beaten for the light........ Lev 24:2
o trees, which thou plantedst not........ Deut 6:11
a land of oil o, and honey........ Deut 8:8
When thou beatest thine o tree........ Deut 24:20
Thou shalt have o trees........ Deut 28:40
for thine o shall cast his fruit........ Deut 28:40
and they said unto the o tree........ Judg 9:8
But the o tree said unto them,........ Judg 9:9
he made two cherubims of o tree........ 1Kin 6:23
oracle he made doors of o tree........ 1Kin 6:31
The two doors also were of o tree........ 1Kin 6:32
of the temple posts of o tree........ 1Kin 6:33
and vineyards, a land of oil o........ 2Kin 18:32
And over the o trees and the........ 1Chr 27:28
fetch o branches, and pine........ Neh 8:15
cast off his flower as the o........ Job 15:33
But I am like a green o tree in........ Ps 52:8
thy children like o plants round........ Ps 128:3
it, as the shaking of an o tree........ Is 17:6
be as the shaking of an o tree........ Is 24:13
called thy name, A green o tree........ Jer 11:16
his beauty shall be as the o tree........ Hos 14:6
your o trees increased, the........ Amos 4:9
the labour of the o shall fail........ Hab 3:17
the o tree, hath not brought........ Hag 2:19
two o trees by it, one upon the........ Zec 4:3
What are these two o trees upon........ Zec 4:11
What be these two o branches........ Zec 4:12
off, and thou, being a wild o tree........ Rom 11:17
the root and fatness of the o tree........ Rom 11:17
o tree which is wild by nature........ Rom 11:24
to nature into a good o tree........ Rom 11:24
be graffed into their own o tree........ Rom 11:24
tree, my brethren, bear o berries........ Jas 3:12
These are the two o trees........ Rev 11:4

**OLIVES**
corn, with the vineyards and o........ Judg 15:5
thou shalt tread the o, but thou........ Mic 6:15
in that day upon the mount of O........ Zec 14:4
the mount of O shall cleave in........ Zec 14:4
to Bethphage, unto the mount of O........ Mt 21:1
And as he sat upon the mount of O........ Mt 24:3
they went out into the mount of O........ Mt 26:30
and Bethany, at the mount of O........ Mk 11:1
of O over against the temple........ Mk 13:3
they went out into the mount of O........ Mk 14:26
the mount called the mount of O........ Lk 19:29
at the descent of the mount of O........ Lk 19:37
that is called the mount of O........ Lk 21:37
as he was wont, to the mount of O........ Lk 22:39
Jesus went unto the mount of O........ Jn 8:1

**OLIVET** See MOUNT, OLIVES. *Hills east of Jerusalem.*
went up by the ascent of mount O........ 2Sa 15:30
Jerusalem from the mount called O........ Acts 1:12

**OLIVEYARD**
with thy vineyard, and with thy o........ Ex 23:11

**OLIVEYARDS**
o which ye planted not do ye eat........ Josh 24:13
and your vineyards, and your o........ 1Sa 8:14
and to receive garments, and o........ 2Kin 5:26
lands, their vineyards, their o........ Neh 5:11
wells digged, vineyards, and o........ Neh 9:25

**OLYMPAS** *(o-lim'-pas) A Christian acquaintance of Paul.*
Nereus, and his sister, and O........ Rom 16:15

**OMAR** *(o'-mar) A son of Eliphaz.*
the sons of Eliphaz were Teman, O........ Gen 36:11
duke Teman, duke O, duke Zepho,........ Gen 36:15
Teman, and O, Zephi, and Gatam,........ 1Chr 1:36

**OMEGA** *(o'-me-gah) Last letter of Greek alphabet; a title applied to Jesus.*
I am Alpha and O, the beginning and........ Rev 1:8
Saying, I am Alpha and O, the........ Rev 1:11
I am Alpha and O, the beginning and.. Rev 21:6
I am Alpha and O, the beginning and Rev 22:13

**OMER**
an o for every man, according to........ Ex 16:16
when they did mete it with an o........ Ex 16:18
Fill an o of it to be kept for........ Ex 16:32
put an o full of manna therein,........ Ex 16:33
Now an o is the tenth part of an........ Ex 16:36

**OMERS**
as much bread, two o for one man........ Ex 16:22

**OMITTED**
have o the weightier matters of........ Mt 23:23

**OMNIPOTENT**
for the Lord God o reigneth........ Rev 19:6

**OMRI** *(om'-ri)*
*1. A king of Israel.*
wherefore all Israel made O........ 1Kin 16:16
O went up from Gibbethon, and all... 1Kin 16:17
and half followed O........ 1Kin 16:21
O prevailed against the people........ 1Kin 16:22
so Tibni died, and O reigned........ 1Kin 16:22
began O to reign over Israel........ 1Kin 16:23
But O wrought evil in the eyes of........ 1Kin 16:25
of the acts of O which he did........ 1Kin 16:27
So O slept with his fathers, and........ 1Kin 16:28
the son of O to reign over Israel........ 1Kin 16:29
Ahab the son of O reigned over........ 1Kin 16:29
Ahab the son of O did evil in the........ 1Kin 16:30
the daughter of O king of Israel........ 2Kin 8:26
was Athaliah the daughter of O........ 2Chr 22:2
For the statutes of O are kept........ Mic 6:16
*2. Son of Becher.*
and Eliezer, and Elioenai, and O........ 1Chr 7:8
*3. A descendant of Pharez.*
the son of Ammihud, the son of O........ 1Chr 9:4
*4. A ruler of Issachar.*
of Issachar, O the son of Michael........ 1Chr 27:18

**ON** See PREFACE.

**ONAM** *(o'-nam)*
*1. A son of Shobal.*
Manahath, and Ebal, Shepho, and O.. Gen 36:23
Manahath, and Ebal, Shephi, and O.... 1Chr 1:40
*2. A son of Jerahmeel.*
she was the mother of O........ 1Chr 2:26
And the sons of O were, Shammai,........ 1Chr 2:28

**ONAN** *(o'-nan) A son of Judah.*
and she called his name O........ Gen 38:4
And Judah said unto O, Go in unto........ Gen 38:8
O knew that the seed should not........ Gen 38:9
Er, and O, and Shelah, and Pharez,........ Gen 46:12
O died in the land of Canaan........ Gen 46:12
The sons of Judah were Er and O........ Num 26:19
O died in the land of Canaan........ Num 26:19
Er, and O, and Shelah........ 1Chr 2:3

**ONCE**
and I will speak yet but this o........ Gen 18:32
I pray thee, my sin only this o........ Ex 10:17
atonement upon the horns of it o........ Ex 30:10
o in the year shall he make........ Ex 30:10
for all their sins o a year........ Lev 16:34
Moses, and said, Let us go up at o........ Num 13:30
thou mayest not consume them at o.. Deut 7:22
war, and go round about the city o........ Josh 6:3
the city, going about it o........ Josh 6:11
day they compassed the city o........ Josh 6:14
me, and I will speak but this o........ Judg 6:39
but this o with the fleece........ Judg 6:39
saying, Come up this o, for he........ Judg 16:18
me, I pray thee, only this o........ Judg 16:28
that I may be at o avenged of the........ Judg 16:28
the spear even to the earth at o........ 1Sa 26:8
o in three years came the navy of........ 1Kin 10:22
himself there, not o nor twice........ 2Kin 6:10
every three years o came the........ 2Chr 9:21
o in ten days store of all sorts........ Neh 5:18
without Jerusalem o or twice........ Neh 13:20
For God speaketh o, yea twice,........ Job 33:14
O have I spoken........ Job 40:5
God hath spoken o........ Ps 62:11
work thereof at o with axes........ Ps 74:6
thy sight when o thou art angry........ Ps 76:7
O have I sworn by my holiness........ Ps 89:35
in his ways shall fall at o........ Prov 28:18
I will destroy and devour at o........ Is 42:14
or shall a nation be born at o........ Is 66:8
inhabitants of the land at this o........ Jer 10:18
when shall it o be........ Jer 13:27
I will this o cause them to know,........ Jer 16:21
Yet o, it is a little while, and I........ Hag 2:6
When o the master of the house is........ Lk 13:25
And they cried out all at o........ Lk 23:18
that he died, he died unto sin o........ Rom 6:10
For I was alive without the law o........ Rom 7:9
above five hundred brethren at o........ 1Cor 15:6
o was I stoned, thrice I suffered........ 2Cor 11:25
the faith which o he destroyed........ Gal 1:23
let it not be o named among you,........ Eph 5:3
even in Thessalonica ye sent o........ Phil 4:16
come unto you, even I Paul, o........ 1Th 2:18
for those who were o enlightened........ Heb 6:4
for this he did o, when he........ Heb 7:27
high priest alone o every year........ Heb 9:7
entered in o into the holy place........ Heb 9:12
but now o in the end of the world........ Heb 9:26
it is appointed unto men o to die........ Heb 9:27
So Christ was o offered to bear........ Heb 9:28
because that the worshippers o........ Heb 10:2
body of Jesus Christ o for all........ Heb 10:10
Yet o more I shake not the earth........ Heb 12:26
Yet o more, signifieth the........ Heb 12:27
also hath o suffered for sins........ 1Pet 3:18
when o the longsuffering of God........ 1Pet 3:20
was o delivered unto the saints........ Jude 3
though ye o knew this, how that........ Jude 5

**ONE** See PREFACE.

**ONE'S**
of death than the day of o birth........ Eccl 7:1
every o bands were loosed........ Acts 16:26

**ONES** See PREFACE.

**ONESIMUS** *(o-nes'-i-mus) A Christian of Colosse.*
With O, a faithful and beloved........ Col 4:9
the Colossians by Tychicus and O........ Col *s*
I beseech thee for my son O........ Philem 10
from Rome to Philemon, by O........ Philem *s*

**ONESIPHORUS** *(o-ne-sif'-o-rus) A Christian of Ephesus.*
give mercy unto the house of O........ 2Ti 1:16
and Aquila, and the household of O........ 2Ti 4:19

**ONIONS**
melons, and the leeks, and the o........ Num 11:5

**ONLY**
his heart was o evil continually........ Gen 6:5
Noah o remained alive, and they........ Gen 7:23
Save o that which the young men........ Gen 14:24
o unto these men do nothing........ Gen 19:8
thine o son Isaac, whom thou........ Gen 22:2
thy son, thine o son from me........ Gen 22:12
not withheld thy son, thine o son........ Gen 22:16
o bring not my son thither again........ Gen 24:8
o obey my voice, and go fetch me........ Gen 27:13
O herein will the men consent........ Gen 34:22
o let us consent unto them, and........ Gen 34:23
o in the throne will I be greater........ Gen 41:40
O the land of the priests bought........ Gen 47:22
except the land of the priests o........ Gen 47:26
o their little ones, and their........ Gen 50:8
they may remain in the river o........ Ex 8:9
they shall remain in the river o........ Ex 8:11
o ye shall not go very far away........ Ex 8:28
O in the land of Goshen, where........ Ex 9:26
my sin o this once, and intreat........ Ex 10:17
take away from me this death o........ Ex 10:17
o let your flocks and your herds........ Ex 10:24
that o may be done of you........ Ex 12:16
o he shall pay for the loss of........ Ex 21:19
any god, save unto the LORD o........ Ex 22:20
For that is his covering o........ Ex 22:27
O he shall not go in unto the........ Lev 21:23
O the firstling of the beasts,........ Lev 27:26
O thou shalt not number the tribe........ Num 1:49
the LORD indeed spoken o by Moses... Num 12:2
O rebel not ye against the LORD,........ Num 14:9
o they shall not come nigh the........ Num 18:3
I will o, without doing any thing........ Num 20:19
but o the word that I shalt speak........ Num 22:35
O the gold, and the silver, the........ Num 31:22
o to the family of the tribe of........ Num 36:6
o I will pass through on my feet........ Deut 2:28
O the cattle we took for a prey........ Deut 2:35
O unto the land of the children........ Deut 2:37
For o Og king of Bashan remained........ Deut 3:11
O take heed to thyself, and keep........ Deut 4:9
o ye heard a voice........ Deut 4:12
that man doth not live by bread o........ Deut 8:3
O the LORD had a delight in thy........ Deut 10:15
O ye shall not eat the blood........ Deut 12:16
O be sure that thou eat not the........ Deut 12:23
O thy holy things which thou hast........ Deut 12:26
O if thou carefully hearken unto........ Deut 15:5
O thou shalt not eat the blood........ Deut 15:23
O the trees which thou knowest........ Deut 20:20
then the man o that lay with her........ Deut 22:25
and thou shalt be above o, and thou. Deut 28:13
and thou shalt be o oppressed........ Deut 28:29
and thou shalt be o oppressed........ Deut 28:33
Neither with you o do I make this........ Deut 29:14
O be thou strong and very........ Josh 1:7
o the LORD thy God be with thee,........ Josh 1:17
o be strong and of a good courage........ Josh 1:18
o on that day they compassed the........ Josh 6:15
o Rahab the harlot shall live,........ Josh 6:17
o the silver, and the gold, and the........ Josh 6:24
o the spoil thereof, and the........ Josh 8:2
O the cattle and the spoil of that........ Josh 8:27
burned none of them, save Hazor o... Josh 11:13
o in Gaza, in Gath, and in Ashdod,........ Josh 11:22
o divide thou it by lot unto the........ Josh 13:6
O unto the tribe of Levi he gave........ Josh 13:14
thou shalt not have one lot o........ Josh 17:17
O that the generations of the........ Judg 3:2
and if the dew be on the fleece o........ Judg 6:37
it now be dry o upon the fleece........ Judg 6:39
for it was dry upon the fleece o........ Judg 6:40
deliver us o, we pray thee, this........ Judg 10:15
and she was his o child........ Judg 11:34
o this once, O God, that I may be........ Judg 16:28
o lodge not in the street........ Judg 19:20
o her lips moved, but her voice........ 1Sa 1:13
o the LORD establish his word........ 1Sa 1:23
o the stump of Dagon was left to........ 1Sa 5:4
unto the LORD, and serve him o........ 1Sa 7:3
Ashtaroth, and served the LORD o........ 1Sa 7:4
O fear the LORD, and serve him in........ 1Sa 12:24
o be thou valiant for me, and........ 1Sa 18:17
thou shalt not o while yet I live........ 1Sa 20:14
o Jonathan and David knew the........ 1Sa 20:39
for Amnon o is dead........ 2Sa 13:32
for Amnon o is dead........ 2Sa 13:33
and I will smite the king o........ 2Sa 17:2
deliver him o, and I will depart........ 2Sa 20:21

O

returned after him *o* to spoil 2Sa 23:10
*O* the people sacrificed in high 1Kin 3:2
*o* he sacrificed and burnt incense 1Kin 3:3
he was the *o* officer which was in 1Kin 4:19
(for thou, even thou *o*, knowest 1Kin 8:39
David, but the tribe of Judah *o* 1Kin 12:20
to do that *o* which was right in 1Kin 14:8
for he *o* of Jeroboam shall come 1Kin 14:13
save *o* in the matter of Uriah the 1Kin 15:5
unto the people, I, even I *o* 1Kin 18:22
and I, even I *o*, am left 1Kin 19:10
and I, even I *o*, am left 1Kin 19:14
save *o* with the king of Israel 1Kin 22:31
*o* in Kir-haraseth left they the 2Kin 3:25
but the worshippers of Baal *o* 2Kin 10:23
left but the tribe of Judah *o* 2Kin 17:18
art the LORD God, even thou *o* 2Kin 19:19
*o* if they will observe to do 2Kin 21:8
*O* the LORD give thee wisdom and 1Chr 22:12
save *o* to burn sacrifice before 2Chr 2:6
(for thou *o* knowest the hearts of 2Chr 6:30
save *o* with the king of Israel 2Chr 18:30
yet unto the LORD their God *o* 2Chr 33:17
*O* Jonathan the son of Asahel and Ezr 10:15
hath not done wrong to the king *o* Est 1:16
*o* upon himself put not forth Job 1:12
I *o* am escaped alone to tell thee Job 1:15
I *o* am escaped alone to tell thee Job 1:16
I *o* am escaped alone to tell thee Job 1:17
I *o* am escaped alone to tell thee Job 1:19
*O* do not two things unto me Job 13:20
a nation, or against a man *o* Job 34:29
*o* makest me dwell in safety Ps 4:8
Against thee, thee *o*, have I Ps 51:4
He *o* is my rock and my salvation Ps 62:2
They *o* consult to cast him down Ps 62:4
My soul, wait thou *o* upon God Ps 62:5
He *o* is my rock and my salvation Ps 62:6
righteousness, even of thine *o* Ps 71:16
who *o* doeth wondrous things Ps 72:18
*O* with thine eyes shalt thou Ps 91:8
*o* beloved in the sight of my Prov 4:3
Let them be *o* thine own, and not Prov 5:17
desire of the righteous is *o* good Prov 11:23
*O* by pride cometh contention Prov 13:10
of the lips tendeth *o* to penury Prov 14:23
An evil man seeketh *o* rebellion Prov 17:11
diligent tend *o* to plenteousness Prov 21:5
every one that is hasty *o* to want Prov 21:5
this *o* have I found, that God Eccl 7:29
she is the *o* one of her mother, Song 6:9
*o* let us be called by thy name, Is 4:1
but by thee *o* will we make Is 26:13
it shall be a vexation *o* to Is 28:19
thou art the LORD, even thou *o* Is 37:20
*O* acknowledge thine iniquity, Jer 3:13
thee mourning, as for an *o* son Jer 6:26
the children of Judah have *o* done Jer 32:30
*o* provoked me to anger with the Jer 32:30
an *o* evil, behold, is come Eze 7:5
they *o* shall be delivered, but Eze 14:16
but they *o* shall be delivered Eze 14:18
they shall *o* poll their heads Eze 44:20
You *o* have I known of all the Amos 3:2
it as the mourning of an *o* son Amos 8:10
as one mourneth for his *o* son Zec 12:10
God, and him *o* shalt thou serve Mt 4:10
And if ye salute your brethren *o* Mt 5:47
but speak the word *o*, and my Mt 8:8
water *o* in the name of a disciple Mt 10:42
with him, but *o* for the priests Mt 12:4
*o* touch the hem of his garment Mt 14:36
they saw no man, save Jesus *o* Mt 17:8
nothing thereon, but leaves *o* Mt 21:19
ye shall not *o* do this which is Mt 21:21
angels of heaven, but my Father *o* Mt 24:36
who can forgive sins but God *o* Mk 2:7
Be not afraid, *o* believe Mk 5:36
for their journey, save a staff *o* Mk 6:8
save Jesus *o* with themselves Mk 9:8
God, and him *o* shalt thou serve Lk 4:8
the *o* son of his mother, and she Lk 7:12
For he had one *o* daughter Lk 8:42
believe *o*, and she shall be made Lk 8:50
for he is mine *o* child Lk 9:38
him, Art thou *o* a stranger in Lk 24:18
the glory as of the *o* begotten of Jn 1:14
the *o* begotten Son, which is in Jn 1:18
that he gave his *o* begotten Son Jn 3:16
name of the *o* begotten Son of God Jn 3:18
because he not *o* had broken the Jn 5:18
the honour that cometh from God *o* Jn 5:44
And not for that nation *o*, but Jn 11:52
they came not for Jesus' sake *o* Jn 12:9
unto him, Lord, not my feet *o* Jn 13:9
might know thee the *o* true God Jn 17:3
*o* they were baptized in the name Acts 8:16
word to none but unto the Jews *o* Acts 11:19
knowing *o* the baptism of John Acts 18:25
So that not *o* this our craft is Acts 19:27
for I am ready not to be bound *o* Acts 21:13
save *o* that they keep themselves Acts 21:25
I would to God, that not *o* thou Acts 26:29
not *o* of the lading and ship, but Acts 27:10
not *o* do the same, but have Rom 1:32
Is he the God of the Jews *o* Rom 3:29
then upon the circumcision *o* Rom 4:9
who are not of the circumcision *o* Rom 4:12
not to that *o* which is of the law Rom 4:16
And not *o* so, but we glory in Rom 5:3
And not *o* so, but we also joy in Rom 5:11
not *o* they, but ourselves also, Rom 8:23
And not *o* this Rom 9:10
he hath called, not of the Jews *o* Rom 9:24
not *o* for wrath, but also for Rom 13:5
unto whom not *o* I give thanks Rom 16:4
To God *o* wise, be glory through Rom 16:27
*o* in the Lord 1Cor 7:39
Or I *o* and Barnabas, have not we 1Cor 9:6
or came it unto you *o* 1Cor 14:36
If in this life *o* we have hope in 1Cor 15:19
And not by his coming *o*, but by 2Cor 7:7
not *o* to do, but also to be 2Cor 8:10
And not that *o*, but who was also 2Cor 8:19
not *o* in the sight of the Lord, 2Cor 8:21
of this service not *o* supplieth 2Cor 9:12
But they had heard *o*, That he Gal 1:23
*O* they would that we should Gal 2:10
This *o* would I learn of you, Gal 3:2
not *o* when I am present with you Gal 4:18
*o* use not liberty for an occasion Gal 5:13
*o* lest they should suffer Gal 6:12
not *o* in this world, but also in Eph 1:21
*O* let your conversation be as it Phil 1:27
not *o* to believe on him, but also Phil 1:29
obeyed, not as in my presence *o* Phil 2:12
and not on him *o*, but on me also, Phil 2:27
giving and receiving, but ye *o* Phil 4:15
These *o* are my fellow workers Col 4:11
came not unto you in word *o* 1Th 1:5
of the Lord not *o* in Macedonia 1Th 1:8
unto you, not the gospel of God *o* 1Th 2:8
*o* he who now letteth will let, 2Th 2:7
the *o* wise God, be honour and 1Ti 1:17
not *o* idle, but tattlers also and 1Ti 5:13
*o* Potentate, the King of kings, 1Ti 6:15
Who *o* hath immortality, dwelling 1Ti 6:16
there are not *o* vessels of gold 2Ti 2:20
and not to me *o*, but unto all them 2Ti 4:8
*O* Luke is with me 2Ti 4:11
Which stood *o* in meats and drinks, Heb 9:10
offered up his *o* begotten son Heb 11:17
once more I shake not the earth *o* Heb 12:26
of the word, and not hearers *o* Jas 1:22
is justified, and not by faith *o* Jas 2:24
not *o* to the good and gentle, but 1Pet 2:18
and not for ours *o*, but also for 1Jn 2:2
because that God sent his *o* 1Jn 4:9
not by water *o*, but by water and 1Jn 5:6
and not I *o*, but also all they 2Jn 1
and denying the *o* Lord God Jude 4
To the *o* wise God our Saviour, be Jude 25
but *o* those men which have not Rev 9:4
for thou *o* art holy Rev 15:4

## ONO (*o'-no*)

*1. A city in Benjamin.*
and Shamed, who built *O* 1Chr 8:12
The children of Lod, Hadid, and *O* Ezr 2:33
The children of Lod, Hadid, and *O* Neh 7:37
Lod, and *O*, the valley of Neh 11:35
*2. A valley near Jerusalem.*
of the villages in the plain of *O* Neh 6:2

## ONWARD

went *o* in all their journeys Ex 40:36

## ONYCHA

thee sweet spices, stacte, and *o* Ex 30:34

## ONYX

there is bdellium and the *o* stone Gen 2:12
*O* stones, and stones to be set in Ex 25:7
And thou shalt take two *o* stones Ex 28:9
the fourth row a beryl, and an *o* Ex 28:20
*o* stones, and stones to be set for Ex 35:9
And the rulers brought *o* stones Ex 35:27
they wrought *o* stones inclosed in Ex 39:6
And the fourth row, a beryl, an *o* Ex 39:13
*o* stones, and stones to be set, 1Chr 29:2
of Ophir, with the precious *o* Job 28:16
and the diamond, the beryl, the *o* Eze 28:13

## OPEN

in the *o* firmament of heaven Gen 1:20
herself, and sat in an *o* place Gen 38:14
And if a man shall *o* a pit Ex 21:33
bird loose into the *o* field Lev 14:7
out of the city into the *o* fields Lev 14:53
which they offer in the *o* field Lev 17:5
instead of such as *o* every womb Num 8:16
thing, and the earth *o* her mouth Num 16:30
every *o* vessel, which hath no Num 19:15
with a sword in the *o* fields Num 19:16
man whose eyes are *o* hath said Num 24:3
a trance, but having his eyes *o* Num 24:4
man whose eyes are *o* hath said Num 24:15
a trance, but having his eyes *o* Num 24:16
But thou shalt *o* thine hand wide Deut 15:8
Thou shalt *o* thine hand wide unto Deut 15:11
*o* unto thee, then it shall be, Deut 20:11
The LORD shall *o* unto thee his Deut 28:12
and they left the city *o*, and Josh 8:17
*O* the mouth of the cave, and bring Josh 10:22
there was no *o* vision 1Sa 3:1
are encamped in the *o* fields 2Sa 11:11
carved with knops and *o* flowers 1Kin 6:18
*o* flowers, within and without 1Kin 6:29
*o* flowers, and overlaid them with 1Kin 6:32
and palm trees and *o* flowers 1Kin 6:35
That thine eyes may be *o* toward 1Kin 8:29
That thine eyes may be *o* unto the 1Kin 8:52
*o* his eyes, that he may see 2Kin 6:17
*o* the eyes of these men, that 2Kin 6:20
Then *o* the door, and flee, and 2Kin 9:3
And he said, *O* the window eastward 2Kin 13:17
*o*, LORD, thine eyes, and see 2Kin 19:16
eyes may be *o* upon this house day 2Chr 6:20
I beseech thee, thine eyes be *o* 2Chr 6:40
Now mine eyes shall be *o*, and mine 2Chr 7:15
now be attentive, and thine eyes *o* Neh 1:6
time with an *o* letter in his hand Neh 6:5
speak, and *o* his lips against thee Job 11:5
dost thou *o* thine eyes upon such Job 14:3
I will *o* my lips and answer Job 32:20
men in the *o* sight of others Job 34:26
doth Job *o* his mouth in vain Job 35:16
Who can *o* the doors of his face Job 41:14
their throat is an *o* sepulchre Ps 5:9
his ears are *o* unto their cry Ps 34:15
I will *o* my dark saying upon the Ps 49:4
*O* Lord, *o* thou my lips Ps 51:15
I will *o* my mouth in a parable Ps 78:2
*o* thy mouth wide, and I will fill Ps 81:10
*O* to me the gates of Ps 118:19
*O* thou mine eyes, that I may Ps 119:18
but a fool layeth *o* his folly Prov 13:16
*o* thine eyes, and thou shalt be Prov 20:13
*O* rebuke is better than secret Prov 27:5
*O* thy mouth for the dumb in the Prov 31:8
*O* thy mouth, judge righteously, Prov 31:9
*O* to me, my sister, my love, my Song 5:2
I rose up to *o* to my beloved Song 5:5
shall devour Israel with *o* mouth Is 9:12
so he shall *o*, and none shall shut Is 22:22
and he shall shut, and none shall *o* Is 22:22
the windows from on high are *o* Is 24:18
*O* ye the gates, that the Is 26:2
doth he *o* and break the clods of Is 28:24
*o* thine eyes, O LORD, and see Is 37:17
I will *o* rivers in high places, Is 41:18
To *o* the blind eyes, to bring out Is 42:7
to *o* before him the two leaved Is 45:1
let the earth *o*, and let them Is 45:8
thy gates shall be *o* continually Is 60:11
Their quiver is as an *o* sepulchre Jer 5:16
fall as dung upon the *o* field Jer 9:22
be shut up, and none shall *o* them Jer 13:19
and custom, and that which was *o* Jer 32:11
and this evidence which is *o* Jer 32:14
for thine eyes are *o* upon all the Jer 32:19
utmost border, *o* her storehouses Jer 50:26
*o* thy mouth, and eat that I give Eze 2:8
I will *o* thy mouth, and thou shalt Eze 3:27
thou wast cast out in the *o* field Eze 16:5
never *o* thy mouth any more Eze 16:63
to *o* the mouth in the slaughter, Eze 21:22
I will *o* the side of Moab from Eze 25:9
thou shalt fall upon the *o* fields Eze 29:5
cast thee forth upon the *o* field Eze 32:4
him that is in the *o* field will I Eze 33:27
were very many in the *o* valley Eze 37:2
I will *o* your graves, and cause Eze 37:12
Thou shalt fall upon the *o* field Eze 39:5
one shall then *o* him the gate Eze 46:12
his windows being *o* in his Dan 6:10
*o* thine eyes, and behold our Dan 9:18
be set wide *o* unto thine enemies Nah 3:13
*O* thy doors, O Lebanon, that the Zec 11:1
I will *o* mine eyes upon the house Zec 12:4
if I will not *o* you the windows Mal 3:10
I will *o* my mouth in parables Mt 13:35
saying, Lord, Lord, *o* to us Mt 25:11
they may *o* unto him immediately Lk 12:36
saying, Lord, Lord, *o* unto us Lk 13:25
Hereafter ye shall see heaven *o* Jn 1:51
Can a devil *o* the eyes of the Jn 10:21
and seeing the prison doors *o* Acts 16:27
Paul was now about to *o* his mouth Acts 18:14
against any man, the law is *o* Acts 19:38
To *o* their eyes, and to turn them Acts 26:18
Their throat is an *o* sepulchre Rom 3:13
with *o* face beholding as in a 2Cor 3:18
our mouth is *o* unto you, our 2Cor 6:11
that I may *o* my mouth boldly, to Eph 6:19
that God would *o* unto us a door Col 4:3
Some men's sins are *o* beforehand 1Ti 5:24
afresh, and put him to an *o* shame Heb 6:6
his ears are *o* unto their prayers 1Pet 3:12
I have set before thee an *o* door Rev 3:8
*o* the door, I will come in to him Rev 3:20
Who is worthy to *o* the book Rev 5:2
the earth, was able to *o* the book Rev 5:3
no man was found worthy to *o* Rev 5:4
hath prevailed to *o* the book Rev 5:5
book, and to *o* the seals thereof Rev 5:9
had in his hand a little book *o* Rev 10:2
take the little book which is *o* Rev 10:8

## OPENED

then your eyes shall be *o* Gen 3:5
And the eyes of them both were *o* Gen 3:7
which hath *o* her mouth to receive Gen 4:11
and the windows of heaven were *o* Gen 7:11
that Noah *o* the window of the ark Gen 8:6
God *o* her eyes, and she saw a well Gen 21:19
Leah was hated, he *o* her womb Gen 29:31
hearkened to her, and *o* her womb Gen 30:22
Joseph *o* all the storehouses, and Gen 41:56
as one of them *o* his sack to give Gen 42:27
that we *o* our sacks, and, behold, Gen 43:21
ground, and *o* every man his sack Gen 44:11
And when she had *o* it, she saw the Ex 2:6
And the earth *o* her mouth, and Num 16:32

the LORD o the mouth of the ass, Num 22:28
Then the LORD o the eyes of Num 22:31
And the earth o her mouth, and Num 26:10
how the earth o her mouth Deut 11:6
he o not the doors of the parlour Judg 3:25
they took a key, and o them Judg 3:25
she o a bottle of milk, and gave Judg 4:19
for I have o my mouth unto the Judg 11:35
if thou hast o thy mouth unto the Judg 11:36
o the doors of the house, and went Judg 19:27
o the doors of the house of the 1Sa 3:15
times, and the child o his eyes 2Kin 4:35
the LORD o the eyes of the young 2Kin 6:17
the LORD o their eyes, and they 2Kin 6:20
And he o the door, and fled 2Kin 9:10
And he o it 2Kin 13:17
because they o not to him 2Kin 15:16
o the doors of the house of the 2Chr 29:3
be o until the sun be hot Neh 7:3
Ezra o the book in the sight of Neh 8:5
and when he o it, all the people Neh 8:5
not be o till after the sabbath Neh 13:19
After this o Job his mouth, and Job 3:1
they o their mouth wide as for Job 29:23
but I o my doors to the traveller Job 31:32
Behold, now I have o my mouth Job 33:2
gates of death been o unto thee Job 38:17
they o their mouth wide against Ps 35:21
I was dumb, I o not my mouth Ps 39:9
mine ears hast thou o Ps 40:6
above, and o the doors of heaven, Ps 78:23
He o the rock, and the waters Ps 105:41
The earth o and swallowed up Ps 106:17
of the deceitful are o against me Ps 109:2
I o my mouth, and panted Ps 119:131
I o to my beloved Song 5:6
o her mouth without measure Is 5:14
or o the mouth, or peeped Is 10:14
that o not the house of his Is 14:17
the eyes of the blind shall be o Is 35:5
time that thine ear was not o Is 48:8
The Lord GOD hath o mine ear Is 50:5
afflicted, yet he o not his mouth Is 53:7
for unto thee have I o my cause Jer 20:12
The LORD hath o his armoury Jer 50:25
All thine enemies have o their Lam 2:16
All our enemies have o their Lam 3:46
Chebar, that the heavens were o Eze 1:1
So I o my mouth, and he caused me Eze 3:2
hast o thy feet to every one that Eze 16:25
be o to him which is escaped Eze 24:27
had o my mouth, until he came to Eze 33:22
and my mouth was o, and I was no Eze 33:22
LORD, when I have o your graves Eze 37:13
shall be shut, it shall not be o Eze 44:2
but on the sabbath it shall be o Eze 46:1
day of the new moon it shall be o Eze 46:1
was set, and the books were o Dan 7:10
then I o my mouth, and spake, and Dan 10:16
gates of the rivers shall be o Nah 2:6
fountain o to the house of David Zec 13:1
when they had o their treasures, Mt 2:11
lo, the heavens were o unto him Mt 3:16
he o his mouth, and taught them, Mt 5:2
knock, and it shall be o unto you Mt 7:7
him that knocketh it shall be o Mt 7:8
And their eyes were o Mt 9:30
and when thou hast o his mouth Mt 17:27
him, Lord, that our eyes may be o Mt 20:33
And the graves were o Mt 27:52
the water, he saw the heavens o Mk 1:10
him, Ephphatha, that is, Be o Mk 7:34
And straightway his ears were o Mk 7:35
And his mouth was o immediately Lk 1:64
and praying, the heaven was o Lk 3:21
And when he had o the book Lk 4:17
knock, and it shall be o unto you Lk 11:9
him that knocketh it shall be o Lk 11:10
And their eyes were o, and they Lk 24:31
while he o to us the scriptures Lk 24:32
Then o he their understanding, Lk 24:45
unto him, How were thine eyes o Jn 9:10
made the clay, and o his eyes Jn 9:14
of him, that he hath o thine eyes Jn 9:17
or who hath o his eyes, we know Jn 9:21
how o he thine eyes Jn 9:26
he is, and yet he hath o mine eyes Jn 9:30
o the eyes of one that was born Jn 9:32
which o the eyes of the blind, Jn 11:37
Lord by night o the prison doors Acts 5:19
but when we had o, we found no Acts 5:23
said, Behold, I see the heavens o Acts 7:56
shearer, so o he not his mouth Acts 8:32
Then Philip o his mouth, and began Acts 8:35
and when his eyes were o, he saw Acts 9:8
And she o her eyes Acts 9:40
And saw heaven o, and a certain Acts 10:11
Then Peter o his mouth, and said, Acts 10:34
which o to them of his own accord Acts 12:10
she o not the gate for gladness, Acts 12:14
and when they had o the door Acts 12:16
how he had o the door of faith Acts 14:27
whose heart the Lord o, that she Acts 16:14
immediately all the doors were o Acts 16:26
door and effectual is o unto me 1Cor 16:9
a door was o unto me of the Lord, 2Cor 2:12
o unto the eyes of him with whom Heb 4:13
behold, a door was o in heaven Rev 4:1
when the Lamb o one of the seals Rev 6:1
when he had o the second seal, I Rev 6:3
when he had o the third seal, I Rev 6:5
when he had o the fourth seal, I Rev 6:7
when he had o the fifth seal, I Rev 6:9
when he had o the sixth seal Rev 6:12
when he had o the seventh seal, Rev 8:1
And he o the bottomless pit Rev 9:2
the temple of God was o in heaven Rev 11:19
woman, and the earth o her mouth Rev 12:16
he o his mouth in blasphemy Rev 13:6
of the testimony in heaven was o Rev 15:5
And I saw heaven o, and behold a Rev 19:11
and the books were o Rev 20:12
and another book was o, which is Rev 20:12

**OPENEST**
thou o thine hand, they are Ps 104:28
Thou o thine hand, and satisfiest Ps 145:16

**OPENETH**
whatsoever o the womb among the Ex 13:2
the LORD all that o the matrix Ex 13:12
to the LORD all that o the matrix Ex 13:15
All that o the matrix is mine Ex 34:19
of all the firstborn that o the Num 3:12
Every thing that o the matrix in Num 18:15
he o his eyes, and he is not Job 27:19
Then he o the ears of men, and Job 33:16
He o also their ear to discipline Job 36:10
o their ears in oppression Job 36:15
a dumb man that o not his mouth Ps 38:13
The LORD o the eyes of the blind Ps 146:8
but he that o wide his lips shall Prov 13:3
he o not his mouth in the gate Prov 24:7
She o her mouth with wisdom Prov 31:26
is dumb, so he o not his mouth Is 53:7
the fire all that o the womb Eze 20:26
Every male that o the womb shall Lk 2:23
To him the porter o Jn 10:3
hath the key of David, he that o Rev 3:7
and shutteth, and no man o Rev 3:7

**OPENING**
the o thereof every morning 1Chr 9:27
up a man, and there can be no o Job 12:14
the o of my lips shall be right Prov 8:6
o the ears, but he heareth not Is 42:20
the o of the prison to them that Is 61:1
I will give thee the o of the Eze 29:21
O and alleging, that Christ must Acts 17:3

**OPENINGS**
concourse, in the o of the gates Prov 1:21

**OPENLY**
that was o by the way side Gen 38:21
his righteousness hath he o Ps 98:2
himself shall reward thee o Mt 6:4
in secret shall reward thee o Mt 6:6
in secret, shall reward thee o Mt 6:18
no more o enter into the city Mk 1:45
And he spake that saying o Mk 8:32
he himself seeketh to be known o Jn 7:4
he also up unto the feast, not o Jn 7:10
Howbeit no man spake o of him for Jn 7:13
walked no more o among the Jews Jn 11:54
him, I spake o to the world Jn 18:20
up the third day, and shewed him o Acts 10:40
beaten us o uncondemned Acts 16:37
powers, he made a shew of them o Col 2:15

**OPERATION**
nor the o of his hands, he shall Ps 28:5
consider the o of his hands Is 5:12
through the faith of the o of God Col 2:12

**OPERATIONS**
And there are diversities of o 1Cor 12:6

**OPHEL** (*o'-fel*) *A fortified place near Jerusalem.*
and on the wall of O he built much 2Chr 27:3
fish gate, and compassed about O 2Chr 33:14
Moreover the Nethinims dwelt in O Neh 3:26
out, even unto the wall of O Neh 3:27
But the Nethinims dwelt in O Neh 11:21

**OPHIR** (*o'-fur*)
*1. A son of Joktan.*
And O, and Havilah, and Jobab Gen 10:29
And O, and Havilah, and Jobab 1Chr 1:23
*2. A place in southern Arabia.*
And they came to O, and fetched 1Kin 9:28
Hiram, that brought gold from O 1Kin 10:11
brought in from O great plenty of 1Kin 10:11
of Tharshish to go to O for gold 1Kin 22:48
talents of gold, of the gold of O 1Chr 29:4
with the servants of Solomon to O 2Chr 8:18
which brought gold from O 2Chr 9:10
the gold of O as the stones of Job 22:24
be valued with the gold of O Job 28:16
did stand the queen in gold of O Ps 45:9
a man than the golden wedge of O Is 13:12

**OPHNI** (*of'-ni*) *A place in Benjamin.*
And Chephar-haammonai, and O Josh 18:24

**OPHRAH** (*of'-rah*) See APHRAH.
*1. A city in Benjamin.*
And Avim, and Parah, and O, Josh 18:23
unto the way that leadeth to O 1Sa 13:17
*2. A city in Manasseh.*
sat under an oak which was in O Judg 6:11
it is yet in O of the Abi-ezrites Judg 6:24
and put it in his city, even in O Judg 8:27
father, in O of the Abi-ezrites Judg 8:32
went unto his father's house at O Judg 9:5
*3. Head of a family in Judah.*
And Meonothai begat O 1Chr 4:14

**OPINION**
and durst not shew you mine o Job 32:6
I also will shew mine o Job 32:10
my part, I also will shew mine o Job 32:17

**OPINIONS**
How long halt ye between two o 1Kin 18:21

**OPPORTUNITY**
time he sought o to betray him Mt 26:16
sought o to betray him unto them Lk 22:6
As we have therefore o, let us do Gal 6:10
also careful, but ye lacked o Phil 4:10
might have had o to have returned Heb 11:15

**OPPOSE**
those that o themselves 2Ti 2:25

**OPPOSED**
when they o themselves, and Acts 18:6

**OPPOSEST**
hand thou o thyself against me Job 30:21

**OPPOSETH**
Who o and exalteth himself above 2Th 2:4

**OPPOSITIONS**
o of science falsely so called 1Ti 6:20

**OPPRESS**
wherewith the Egyptians o them Ex 3:9
neither vex a stranger, nor o him Ex 22:21
Also thou shalt not o a stranger Ex 23:9
hand, ye shall not o one another Lev 25:14
shall not therefore o one another Lev 25:17
thou shalt not o him Deut 23:16
Thou shalt not o an hired servant Deut 24:14
and the Maonites, did o you Judg 10:12
unto thee that thou shouldest o Job 10:3
man of the earth may no more o Ps 10:18
From the wicked that o me Ps 17:9
let not the proud o me Ps 119:122
neither o the afflicted in the Prov 22:22
I will feed them that o thee with Is 49:26
If ye o not the stranger, the Jer 7:6
and I will punish all that o them Jer 30:20
princes shall no more o my people Eze 45:8
he loveth to o Hos 12:7
which o the poor, which crush the Amos 4:1
so they o a man and his house, Mic 2:2
And o not the widow, nor the Zec 7:10
against those that o the hireling Mal 3:5
Do not rich men o you, and draw Jas 2:6

**OPPRESSED**
and thou shalt be only o and Deut 28:29
and thou shalt be only o and Deut 28:33
by reason of them that o them Judg 2:18
mightily o the children of Israel Judg 4:3
out of the hand of all that o you Judg 6:9
vexed and o the children of Israel Judg 10:8
kingdoms, and of them that o you 1Sa 10:18
whom have I o 1Sa 12:3
hast not defrauded us, nor o us 1Sa 12:4
because the king of Syria o them 2Kin 13:4
But Hazael king of Syria o Israel 2Kin 13:22
Asa o some of the people the same 2Chr 16:10
Because he hath o and hath Job 20:19
they make the o to cry Job 35:9
also will be a refuge for the o Ps 9:9
To judge the fatherless and the o Ps 10:18
O let not the o return ashamed Ps 74:21
and judgment for all that are o Ps 103:6
Their enemies also o them Ps 106:42
executeth judgment for the o Ps 146:7
the tears of such as were o Eccl 4:1
seek judgment, relieve the o Is 1:17
And the people shall be o, every Is 3:5
no more rejoice, O thou o virgin Is 23:12
O LORD, I am o Is 38:14
the Assyrian o them without cause Is 52:4
He was o, and he was afflicted, Is 53:7
burdens, and to let the o go free Is 58:6
children of Judah were o together Jer 50:33
And hath not o any, but hath Eze 18:7
Hath o the poor and needy, hath Eze 18:12
Neither hath o any, hath not Eze 18:16
his father, because he cruelly o Eze 18:18
yea, they have o the stranger Eze 22:29
Ephraim is o and broken in Hos 5:11
the o in the midst thereof Amos 3:9
him, and avenged him that was o Acts 7:24
all that were o of the devil Acts 10:38

**OPPRESSETH**
land against the enemy that o you Num 10:9
he fighting daily o me Ps 56:1
He that o the poor reproacheth Prov 14:31
He that o the poor to increase Prov 22:16
A poor man that o the poor is Prov 28:3

**OPPRESSING**
of our nativity, from the o sword Jer 46:16
for fear of the o sword they Jer 50:16
filthy and polluted, to the o city Zeph 3:1

**OPPRESSION**
I have also seen the o wherewith Ex 3:9
and our labour, and our o Deut 26:7
for he saw the o of Israel 2Kin 13:4
and openeth their ears in o Job 36:15

For the o of the poor, for the ... Ps 12:5
because of the o of the enemy ... Ps 42:9
because of the o of the enemy ... Ps 43:2
our affliction and our o ... Ps 44:24
because of the o of the wicked ... Ps 55:3
Trust not in o, and become not ... Ps 62:10
and speak wickedly concerning o ... Ps 73:8
minished and brought low through o .. Ps 107:39
Deliver me from the o of man ... Ps 119:134
If thou seest the o of the poor ... Eccl 5:8
Surely o maketh a wise man mad ... Eccl 7:7
looked for judgment, but behold o ... Is 5:7
despise this word, and trust in o ... Is 30:12
thou shalt be far from o ... Is 54:14
away from our God, speaking o ... Is 59:13
she is wholly o in the midst of ... Jer 6:6
to shed innocent blood, and for o ... Jer 22:17
they dealt by o with the stranger ... Eze 22:7
people of the land have used o ... Eze 22:29
of the people's inheritance by o ... Eze 46:18

### OPPRESSIONS
By reason of the multitude of o ... Job 35:9
considered all the o that are ... Eccl 4:1
he that despiseth the gain of o ... Is 33:15

### OPPRESSOR
they hear not the voice of the o ... Job 3:18
of years is hidden to the o ... Job 15:20
and shall break in pieces the o ... Ps 72:4
Envy thou not the o, and choose ... Prov 3:31
understanding is also a great o ... Prov 28:16
of his shoulder, the rod of his o ... Is 9:4
and say, How hath the o ceased ... Is 14:4
day because of the fury of the o ... Is 51:13
and where is the fury of the o ... Is 51:13
spoiled out of the hand of the o ... Jer 21:12
spoiled out of the hand of the o ... Jer 22:3
of the fierceness of the o ... Jer 25:38
no o shall pass through them any ... Zec 9:8
bow, out of him every o together ... Zec 10:4

### OPPRESSORS
with God, and the heritage of o ... Job 27:13
me, and o seek after my soul ... Ps 54:3
leave me not to mine o ... Ps 119:121
side of their o there was power ... Eccl 4:1
my people, children are their o ... Is 3:12
and they shall rule over their o ... Is 14:2
the o are consumed out of the ... Is 16:4
unto the LORD because of the o ... Is 19:20

**OR** See PREFACE.

### ORACLE
man had enquired at the o of God ... 2Sa 16:23
both of the temple and of the o ... 1Kin 6:5
for it within, even for the o ... 1Kin 6:16
the o he prepared in the house ... 1Kin 6:19
the o in the forepart was twenty ... 1Kin 6:20
the chains of gold before the o ... 1Kin 6:21
by the o he overlaid with gold ... 1Kin 6:22
And within the o he made two ... 1Kin 6:23
for the entering of the o he made ... 1Kin 6:31
and five on the left, before the o ... 1Kin 7:49
into the o of the house, to the ... 1Kin 8:6
in the holy place before the o ... 1Kin 8:8
And he made chains, as in the o ... 2Chr 3:16
after the manner before the o ... 2Chr 4:20
to the o of the house, into the ... 2Chr 5:7
seen from the ark before the o ... 2Chr 5:9
up my hands toward thy holy o ... Ps 28:2

### ORACLES
the lively o to give unto us ... Acts 7:38
them were committed the o of God ... Rom 3:2
first principles of the o of God ... Heb 5:12
let him speak as the o of God ... 1Pet 4:11

### ORATION
throne, and made an o unto them ... Acts 12:21

### ORATOR
artificer, and the eloquent o ... Is 3:3
with a certain o named Tertullus, ... Acts 24:1

### ORCHARD
plants are an o of pomegranates ... Song 4:13

### ORCHARDS
I made me gardens and o, and I ... Eccl 2:5

### ORDAIN
seer did o in their set office ... 1Chr 9:22
Also I will o a place for my ... 1Chr 17:9
LORD, thou wilt o peace for us ... Is 26:12
And so o I in all churches ... 1Cor 7:17
o elders in every city, as I had ... Titus 1:5

### ORDAINED
which was o in mount Sinai for a ... Num 28:6
Jeroboam o a feast in the eighth ... 1Kin 12:32
o a feast unto the children of ... 1Kin 12:33
had o to burn incense in the high ... 2Kin 23:5
he o him priests for the high ... 2Chr 11:15
singing, as it was o by David ... 2Chr 23:18
with the instruments o by David ... 2Chr 29:27
The Jews o, and took upon them, and ... Est 9:27
sucklings hast thou o strength ... Ps 8:2
and the stars, which thou hast o ... Ps 8:3
This he o in Joseph for a ... Ps 81:5
I have o a lamp for mine anointed ... Ps 132:17
For Tophet is o of old ... Is 30:33
I o thee a prophet unto the ... Jer 1:5
whom the king had o to destroy ... Dan 2:24
thou hast o them for judgment ... Hab 1:12
he o twelve, that they should be ... Mk 3:14
o you, that ye should go and bring ... Jn 15:16
must one be o to be a witness ... Acts 1:22
o of God to be the Judge of quick ... Acts 10:42
as many as were o to eternal life ... Acts 13:48
when they had o them elders in ... Acts 14:23
that were o of the apostles and ... Acts 16:4
by that man whom he hath o ... Acts 17:31
commandment, which was o to life ... Rom 7:10
the powers that be are o of God ... Rom 13:1
which God o before the world unto ... 1Cor 2:7
Even so hath the Lord o that they ... 1Cor 9:14
it was o by angels in the hand of ... Gal 3:19
which God hath before o that we ... Eph 2:10
Whereunto I am o a preacher ... 1Ti 2:7
o the first bishop of the church ... 2Ti s
o the first bishop of the church ... Titus s
priest taken from among men is o ... Heb 5:1
high priest is o to offer gifts ... Heb 8:3
Now when these things were thus o ... Heb 9:6
of old o to this condemnation ... Jude 4

### ORDAINETH
he o his arrows against the ... Ps 7:13

### ORDER
there, and laid the wood in o ... Gen 22:9
set in o one against another ... Ex 26:17
his sons shall o it from evening ... Ex 27:21
with the lamps to be set in o ... Ex 39:37
set in o the things that are to ... Ex 40:4
that are to be set in o upon it ... Ex 40:4
he set the bread in o upon it ... Ex 40:23
lay the wood in o upon the fire ... Lev 1:7
in o upon the wood that is on the ... Lev 1:8
the priest shall lay them in o on ... Lev 1:12
the burnt offering in o upon it ... Lev 6:12
shall Aaron o it from the evening ... Lev 24:3
He shall o the lamps upon the ... Lev 24:4
sabbath he shall set it in o ... Lev 24:8
she had laid in o upon the roof ... Josh 2:6
How shall we o the child, and how ... Judg 13:12
city, and put his household in o ... 2Sa 17:23
And he put the wood in o, and cut ... 1Kin 18:33
he said, Who shall o the battle ... 1Kin 20:14
the LORD, Set thine house in o ... 2Kin 20:1
and the priests of the second o ... 2Kin 23:4
their office according to their o ... 1Chr 6:32
we sought him not after the due o ... 1Chr 15:13
according to the o commanded unto. 1Chr 23:31
according to the o of the king ... 1Chr 25:2
to the king's o to Asaph, ... 1Chr 25:6
according to the o of David his ... 2Chr 8:14
set they in o upon the pure table ... 2Chr 13:11
house of the LORD was set in o ... 2Chr 29:35
shadow of death, without any o ... Job 10:22
I would o my cause before him, and ... Job 23:4
me, set thy words in o before me ... Job 33:5
for we cannot o our speech by ... Job 37:19
be reckoned up in o unto thee ... Ps 40:5
set them in o before thine eyes ... Ps 50:21
ever after the o of Melchizedek ... Ps 110:4
O my steps in thy word ... Ps 119:133
out, and set in o many proverbs ... Eccl 12:9
and upon his kingdom, to o it ... Is 9:7
the LORD, Set thine house in o ... Is 38:1
declare it, and set it in o for me ... Is 44:7
O ye the buckler and shield, and ... Jer 46:3
one over another, and thirty in o ... Eze 41:6
o a declaration of those things ... Lk 1:1
first, to write unto thee in o ... Lk 1:3
before God in the o of his course ... Lk 1:8
and expounded it by o unto them ... Acts 11:4
of Galatia and Phrygia in o ... Acts 18:23
rest will I set in o when I come ... 1Cor 11:34
things be done decently and in o ... 1Cor 14:40
But every man in his own o ... 1Cor 15:23
as I have given o to the churches ... 1Cor 16:1
joying and beholding your o ... Col 2:5
that thou shouldest set in o the ... Titus 1:5
ever after the o of Melchisedec ... Heb 5:6
priest after the o of Melchisedec ... Heb 5:10
ever after the o of Melchisedec ... Heb 6:20
rise after the o of Melchisedec ... Heb 7:11
be called after the o of Aaron ... Heb 7:11
ever after the o of Melchisedec ... Heb 7:17
ever after the o of Melchisedec ... Heb 7:21

### ORDERED
top of this rock, in the o place ... Judg 6:26
o in all things, and sure ... 2Sa 23:5
Behold now, I have o my cause ... Job 13:18
of a good man are o by the LORD ... Ps 37:23

### ORDERETH
to him that o his conversation ... Ps 50:23

### ORDERINGS
These were the o of them in their ... 1Chr 24:19

### ORDERLY
that thou thyself also walkest o ... Acts 21:24

### ORDINANCE
keep it a feast by an o for ever ... Ex 12:14
your generations by an o for ever ... Ex 12:17
this thing for an o to thee ... Ex 12:24
This is the o of the passover ... Ex 12:43
Thou shalt therefore keep this o ... Ex 13:10
made for them a statute and an o ... Ex 15:25
Therefore shall ye keep mine o ... Lev 18:30
They shall therefore keep mine o ... Lev 22:9
to the o of the passover, and ... Num 9:14
ye shall have one o, both for the ... Num 9:14
for an o for ever throughout your ... Num 10:8
One o shall be both for you of ... Num 15:15
an o for ever in your generations ... Num 15:15
and to thy sons, by an o for ever ... Num 18:8
This is the o of the law which ... Num 19:2
This is the o of the law which ... Num 31:21
them a statute and an o in Shechem. Josh 24:25
an o for Israel unto this day ... 1Sa 30:25
This is an o for ever to Israel ... 2Chr 2:4
with fire according to the o ... 2Chr 35:13
day, and made them an o in Israel ... 2Chr 35:25
after the o of David king of ... Ezr 3:10
and the o that he gave them ... Ps 99:7
the laws, changed the o, broken ... Is 24:5
and forsook not the o of their God ... Is 58:2
Concerning the o of oil, the bath ... Eze 45:14
by a perpetual o unto the LORD ... Eze 46:14
is it that we have kept his o ... Mal 3:14
the power, resisteth the o of God ... Rom 13:2
o of man for the Lord's sake ... 1Pet 2:13

### ORDINANCES
And thou shalt teach them o ... Ex 18:20
neither shall ye walk in their o ... Lev 18:3
do my judgments, and keep mine o ... Lev 18:4
according to all the o of the ... Num 9:12
their statutes, or after their o ... 2Kin 17:34
And the statutes, and the o ... 2Kin 17:37
the o by the hand of Moses ... 2Chr 33:8
Also we made o for us, to charge ... Neh 10:32
Knowest thou the o of heaven ... Job 38:33
this day according to thine o ... Ps 119:91
they ask of me the o of justice ... Is 58:2
the o of the moon and of the stars ... Jer 31:35
If those o depart from before me, ... Jer 31:36
not appointed the o of heaven ... Jer 33:25
in my statutes, and keep mine o ... Eze 11:20
thereof, and all the o thereof ... Eze 43:11
thereof, and all the o thereof ... Eze 43:11
These are the o of the altar in ... Eze 43:18
the o of the house of the LORD ... Eze 44:5
ye are gone away from mine o ... Mal 3:7
and o of the Lord blameless ... Lk 1:6
me in all things, and keep the o ... 1Cor 11:2
of commandments contained in o ... Eph 2:15
of o that was against us, which ... Col 2:14
in the world, are ye subject to o ... Col 2:20
had also o of divine service ... Heb 9:1
and divers washings, and carnal o ... Heb 9:10

### ORDINARY
and have diminished thine o food ... Eze 16:27

### OREB (*o'-reb*)
*1. A prince of Midian.*
two princes of the Midianites, O ... Judg 7:25
they slew O upon the rock O, ... Judg 7:25
Midian, and brought the heads of O ... Judg 7:25
hands the princes of Midian, O ... Judg 8:3
Make their nobles like O, and like ... Ps 83:11
*2. A rock east of the Jordan.*
of Midian at the rock of O ... Is 10:26

### OREN (*o'-ren*) *A son of Jerahmeel.*
Ram the firstborn, and Bunah, and O. 1Chr 2:25

### ORGAN
all such as handle the harp and o ... Gen 4:21
and rejoice at the sound of the o ... Job 21:12
my o into the voice of them that ... Job 30:31

### ORGANS
with stringed instruments and o ... Ps 150:4

### ORION (*o'-ri'-on*) *A constellation of stars.*
Which maketh Arcturus, O, and ... Job 9:9
Pleiades, or loose the bands of O ... Job 38:31
that maketh the seven stars and O ... Amos 5:8

### ORNAMENT
For they shall be an o of grace ... Prov 1:9
give to thine head an o of grace ... Prov 4:9
an o of fine gold, so is a wise ... Prov 25:12
the o of thy molten images of ... Is 30:22
thee with them all, as with an o ... Is 49:18
As for the beauty of his o ... Eze 7:20
even the o of a meek and quiet ... 1Pet 3:4

### ORNAMENTS
and no man did put on him his o ... Ex 33:4
now put off thy o from thee ... Ex 33:5
of their o by the mount Horeb ... Ex 33:6
took away the o that were on ... Judg 8:21
beside o, and collars, and purple ... Judg 8:26
who put on o of gold upon your ... 2Sa 1:24
their tinkling o about their feet ... Is 3:18
the o of the legs, and the ... Is 3:20
bridegroom decketh himself with o ... Is 61:10
Can a maid forget her o, or a ... Jer 2:32
thou deckest thee with o of gold ... Jer 4:30
and thou art come to excellent o ... Eze 16:7
I decked thee also with o ... Eze 16:11
eyes, and deckedst thyself with o ... Eze 23:40

### ORNAN (*or'-nan*) See ARAUNAH. *A Jebusite prince.*
threshingfloor of O the Jebusite ... 1Chr 21:15
threshingfloor of O the Jebusite ... 1Chr 21:18
O turned back, and saw the angel ... 1Chr 21:20
Now O was threshing wheat ... 1Chr 21:20
And as David came to O, O ... 1Chr 21:21
Then David said to O, Grant me ... 1Chr 21:22
O said unto David, Take it to ... 1Chr 21:23
And king David said to O, Nay ... 1Chr 21:24

So David gave to O for the place 1Chr 21:25
threshingfloor of O the Jebusite 1Chr 21:28
threshingfloor of O the Jebusite 2Chr 3:1

**ORPAH** (*or'-pah*) *Daughter-in-law of Naomi.*
the name of the one was O Ruth 1:4
O kissed her mother in law Ruth 1:14

**ORPHANS**
We are o and fatherless, our Lam 5:3

**OSEE** (*o'-see*) See HOSEA, JOSHUA, OSHEA. *Greek form of Hoshea.*
As he saith also in O, I will Rom 9:25

**OSHEA** (*o-she'-ah*) See HOSHEA, OSEE. *Same as Joshua, son of Nun.*
of Ephraim, O the son of Nun Num 13:8
Moses called O the son of Nun Num 13:16

**OSNAPPAR** See ASNAPPER.

**OSPRAY**
eagle, and the ossifrage, and the o Lev 11:13
eagle, and the ossifrage, and the o Deut 14:12

**OSSIFRAGE**
the eagle, and the o, and the Lev 11:13
the eagle, and the o, and the Deut 14:12

**OSTRICH**
or wings and feathers unto the o Job 39:13

**OSTRICHES**
like the o in the wilderness Lam 4:3

**OTHER**
Adah, and the name of the o Zillah Gen 4:19
And he stayed yet o seven days Gen 8:10
And he stayed yet o seven days Gen 8:12
themselves the one from the o Gen 13:11
that are with thee, and with all o Gen 20:16
be stronger than the o people Gen 25:23
this is none o but the house of Gen 28:17
serve with me yet seven o years Gen 29:27
served with him yet seven o years Gen 29:30
or if thou shalt take o wives Gen 31:50
then the o company which is left Gen 32:8
seven o kine came up after them Gen 41:3
stood by the o kine upon the Gen 41:3
seven o kine came up after them, Gen 41:19
he may send away your o brother Gen 43:14
o money have we brought down in Gen 43:22
Egypt even to the o end thereof Gen 47:21
and the name of the o Puah Ex 1:15
was turned again as his o flesh Ex 4:7
came not near the o all the night Ex 14:20
side, and the o on the Ex 17:12
on the o side Ex 17:12
And the name of the o was Eliezer Ex 18:4
they asked each o of their Ex 18:7
shalt have no o gods before me Ex 20:3
no mention of the name of o gods Ex 23:13
and two rings in the o side of it Ex 25:12
the o cherub on the Ex 25:19
cherub on the o end Ex 25:19
the candlestick out of the o side Ex 25:32
made like almonds in the o branch Ex 25:33
o five curtains shall be coupled Ex 26:3
a cubit on the o side of that Ex 26:13
of the o side of the tabernacle Ex 26:27
on the o side shall be hangings Ex 27:15
the o six names of the rest on Ex 28:10
names of the rest on the o stone Ex 28:10
the o two ends of the two Ex 28:25
two o rings of gold thou shalt Ex 28:27
against the o coupling thereof Ex 28:27
And thou shalt take the o ram Ex 29:19
the o lamb thou shalt offer at Ex 29:39
the o lamb thou shalt offer at Ex 29:41
shall ye make any o like it Ex 30:32
on the o were they written Ex 32:15
For thou shalt worship no o god Ex 34:14
the o five curtains he coupled Ex 36:10
for the o side of the tabernacle, Ex 36:25
of the o side of the tabernacle Ex 36:32
boards from the one end to the o Ex 36:33
two rings upon the o side of it Ex 37:3
cherub on the o end on that side Ex 37:8
out of the o side thereof Ex 37:18
for the o side of the court gate, Ex 38:15
And they made two o golden rings Ex 39:20
against the o coupling thereof Ex 39:20
the o for a burnt offering Lev 5:7
put on o garments, and carry forth Lev 6:11
beasts, may be used in any o use Lev 7:24
And he brought the o ram, the ram Lev 8:22
But all o flying creeping things, Lev 11:23
and the o for a sin offering Lev 12:8
and it be no lower than the o skin Lev 13:26
and the o a burnt offering Lev 14:22
the o for a burnt offering, with Lev 14:31
And they shall take o stones Lev 14:42
and he shall take o morter Lev 14:42
the o for a burnt offering Lev 15:15
the o for a burnt offering Lev 15:30
the o lot for the scapegoat Lev 16:8
beside the o in her life time Lev 18:18
have separated you from o people Lev 20:24
and have severed you from o people Lev 20:26
the o shall not rule with rigour Lev 25:53
the o for a burnt offering, and Num 6:11
the o for a burnt offering, unto Num 8:12
the o did set up the tabernacle Num 10:21
Eldad, and the name of the o Medad Num 11:26
a day's journey on the o side Num 11:31
and pitched on the o side of Arnon Num 21:13
he went not, as at o times Num 24:1
the o lamb shalt thou offer at Num 28:4
the o lamb shalt thou offer at Num 28:8
gave o names unto the cities Num 32:38
the o tribes of the children of Num 36:3
the one side of heaven unto the o Deut 4:32
shalt have none o gods before me Deut 5:7
Ye shall not go after o gods Deut 6:14
me, that they may serve o gods Deut 7:4
thy God, and walk after o gods Deut 8:19
and ye turn aside, and serve o gods Deut 11:16
you this day, to go after o gods Deut 11:28
Are they not on the o side Jordan Deut 11:30
saying, Let us go after o gods Deut 13:2
saying, Let us go and serve o gods Deut 13:6
even unto the o end of the earth Deut 13:7
saying, Let us go and serve o gods Deut 13:13
And hath gone and served o gods Deut 17:3
shall speak in the name of o gods Deut 18:20
to go after o gods to serve them Deut 28:14
and there shalt thou serve o gods Deut 28:36
end of the earth even unto the o Deut 28:64
and there thou shalt serve o gods Deut 28:64
For they went and served o gods Deut 29:26
be drawn away, and worship o gods Deut 30:17
that they are turned unto o gods Deut 31:18
then will they turn unto o gods Deut 31:20
that were on the o side Jordan Josh 2:10
and dwelt on the o side Jordan Josh 7:7
the o issued out of the city Josh 8:22
all o they took in battle Josh 11:19
possessed their land on the o Josh 12:1
on the o side Jordan eastward Josh 13:27
on the o side Jordan, by Jericho, Josh 13:32
half tribe on the o side Jordan Josh 14:3
which were on the o side Jordan Josh 17:5
on the o side Jordan by Jericho Josh 20:8
out of the o half tribe of Josh 21:27
gave you on the o side Jordan Josh 22:4
but unto the o half thereof gave Josh 22:7
and have gone and served o gods Josh 23:16
Your fathers dwelt on the o side Josh 24:2
and they served o gods Josh 24:2
from the o side of the flood Josh 24:3
which dwelt on the o side Jordan Josh 24:8
served on the o side of the flood Josh 24:14
were on the o side of the flood Josh 24:15
forsake the LORD, to serve o gods Josh 24:16
land of Egypt, and followed o gods Judg 2:12
they went a whoring after o gods Judg 2:17
in following o gods to serve them Judg 2:19
let all the o people go every man Judg 7:7
to Gideon on the o side Jordan Judg 7:25
the two o companies ran upon all Judg 9:44
of Israel that were on the o side Judg 10:8
forsaken me, and served o gods Judg 10:13
and pitched on the o side of Arnon Judg 11:18
me, that came unto me the o day Judg 13:10
and be like any o man Judg 16:17
will go out as at o times before Judg 16:20
hand, and of the o with his left Judg 16:29
against Gibeah, as at o times Judg 20:30
people, and kill, as at o times Judg 20:31
the o to Gibeah in the field, Judg 20:31
Orpah, and the name of the o Ruth Ruth 1:4
they meet thee not in any o field Ruth 2:22
and the name of the o Peninnah 1Sa 1:2
and stood, and called as at o times 1Sa 3:10
forsaken me, and served o gods 1Sa 8:8
garrison, that is on the o side 1Sa 14:1
and a sharp rock on the o side 1Sa 14:4
Bozez, and the name of the o Seneh 1Sa 14:4
the o southward over against 1Sa 14:5
my son will be on the o side 1Sa 14:40
stood on a mountain on the o side 1Sa 17:3
with his hand, as at o times 1Sa 18:10
he sent o messengers, and they 1Sa 19:21
sat upon his seat, as at o times 1Sa 20:25
for there is no o save that here 1Sa 21:9
David went over to the o side 1Sa 26:13
LORD, saying, Go, serve o gods 1Sa 26:19
put on o raiment, and he went, and 1Sa 28:8
they drave before those o cattle 1Sa 30:20
were on the o side of the valley 1Sa 31:7
that were on the o side Jordan 1Sa 31:7
with o delights, who put on 2Sa 1:24
the o on the 2Sa 2:13
on the o side of the pool 2Sa 2:13
and the name of the o Rechab 2Sa 4:2
the one rich, and the o poor 2Sa 12:1
the o that thou didst unto me 2Sa 13:16
them, but the one smote the o 2Sa 14:6
in some pit, or in some o place 2Sa 17:9
o instruments of the oxen for 2Sa 24:22
And the o woman said, Nay 1Kin 3:22
and the o saith, Nay 1Kin 3:23
half to the one, and half to the o 1Kin 3:25
But the o said, Let it be neither 1Kin 3:26
five cubits the o wing of the 1Kin 6:24
part of the o were ten cubits 1Kin 6:24
the o cherub was ten cubits 1Kin 6:25
and so was it of the o cherub 1Kin 6:26
o cherub touched the o wall 1Kin 6:27
leaves of the o door were folding 1Kin 6:34
the o pillars and the thick beam 1Kin 7:6
one side of the floor to the o 1Kin 7:7
the height of the o chapiter was 1Kin 7:16
and seven for the o chapiter 1Kin 7:17
and so did he for the o chapiter 1Kin 7:18
round about upon the o chapiter 1Kin 7:20
cubits from the one brim to the o 1Kin 7:23
you, but go and serve o gods 1Kin 9:6
and have taken hold upon o gods 1Kin 9:9
on the o upon the six steps 1Kin 10:20
away his heart after o gods 1Kin 11:4
he should not go after o gods 1Kin 11:10
Beth-el, and the o put he in Dan 1Kin 12:29
hast gone and made thee o gods 1Kin 14:9
and I will dress the o bullock 1Kin 18:23
one over against the o seven days 1Kin 20:29
on the o side as red as blood 2Kin 3:22
nor sacrifice unto o gods 2Kin 5:17
the o priests, and said unto them, 2Kin 12:7
of Egypt, and had feared o gods 2Kin 17:7
saying, Ye shall not fear o gods 2Kin 17:35
and ye shall not fear o gods 2Kin 17:37
neither shall ye fear o gods 2Kin 17:38
have burned incense unto o gods 2Kin 22:17
on the o side Jordan by Jericho, 1Chr 6:78
o of their brethren, of the sons 1Chr 9:32
on the o side of Jordan, of the 1Chr 12:37
And Eliezer had none o sons 1Chr 23:17
the o wing was likewise five 2Chr 3:11
to the wing of the o cherub 2Chr 3:11
one wing of the o cherub was five 2Chr 3:12
the o wing was five cubits also, 2Chr 3:12
to the wing of the o cherub 2Chr 3:12
right hand, and the o on the left 2Chr 3:17
you, and shall go and serve o gods 2Chr 7:19
of Egypt, and laid hold on o gods 2Chr 7:22
on the o upon the six steps 2Chr 9:19
manner of the nations of o lands 2Chr 13:9
with them o beside the Ammonites, 2Chr 20:1
o ten thousand left alive did the 2Chr 25:12
to burn incense unto o gods 2Chr 28:25
ended, and until the o priests had 2Chr 29:34
took counsel to keep o seven days 2Chr 30:23
they kept o seven days with 2Chr 30:23
unto all the people of o lands 2Chr 32:13
As the gods of the nations of o 2Chr 32:17
and from the hand of all o 2Chr 32:22
o of the Levites, all that could 2Chr 34:12
have burned incense unto o gods 2Chr 34:25
but the o holy offerings sod they 2Chr 35:13
and ten, and o vessels a thousand Ezr 1:10
The children of the o Elam Ezr 2:31
Pahath-moab, repaired the o piece Neh 3:11
earnestly repaired the o piece Neh 3:20
the o half of them held both the Neh 4:16
with the o hand held a weapon Neh 4:17
for o men have our lands and Neh 5:5
The men of the o Nebo, fifty and Neh 7:33
The children of the o Elam Neh 7:34
nine parts to dwell in o cities Neh 11:1
the o company of them that gave Neh 12:38
with o things for the purifying Est 2:12
But the o Jews that were in the Est 9:16
it withereth before any o herb Job 8:12
are taken out of the way as all o Job 24:24
They are not in trouble as o men Ps 73:5
are they plagued like o men Ps 73:5
and peace have kissed each o Ps 85:10
as the one dieth, so dieth the o Eccl 3:19
this hath more rest than the o Eccl 6:5
set the one over against the o Eccl 7:14
o lords besides thee have had Is 26:13
have, after thou hast lost the o Is 49:20
have burned incense unto o gods Jer 1:16
walk after o gods to your hurt Jer 7:6
walk after o gods whom ye know Jer 7:9
out drink offerings unto o gods Jer 7:18
they went after o gods to serve Jer 11:10
even to the o end of the land Jer 12:12
their heart, and walk after o gods Jer 13:10
LORD, and have walked after o gods Jer 16:11
there shall ye serve o gods day Jer 16:13
burned incense in it unto o gods Jer 19:4
out drink offerings unto o gods Jer 19:13
their God, and worshipped o gods Jer 22:9
the o basket had very naughty Jer 24:2
go not after o gods to serve them Jer 25:6
even unto the o end of the earth Jer 25:33
day, and in Israel, and among o men Jer 32:20
out drink offerings unto o gods Jer 32:29
go not after o gods to serve them Jer 35:15
they were afraid both one and o Jer 36:16
burn incense, and to serve o gods Jer 44:3
to burn no incense unto o gods Jer 44:5
burning incense unto o gods in Jer 44:8
had burned incense unto o gods Jer 44:15
straight, the one toward the o Eze 1:23
from o women in thy whoredoms Eze 16:34
Go thee one way or o, either on Eze 21:16
the o threshold of the gate, Eze 40:6
and on the o side, which was at Eze 40:40
and six cubits broad on the o side Eze 41:1
and five cubits on the o side Eze 41:2
on the one side and on the o side Eze 41:15
the palm tree on the o side Eze 41:19
one as the appearance of the o Eze 41:21
and two leaves for the o door Eze 41:24
on the one side and on the o side Eze 41:26
and shall put on o garments Eze 42:14
and they shall put on o garments Eze 44:19
on the o side of the oblation of Eze 45:7
trees on the one side and on the o Eze 47:7
in length as one of the o parts Eze 48:8
on the o of the holy oblation, and Eze 48:21

there is none o that can shew it Dan 2:11
shall not be left to o people Dan 2:44
their o garments, and were cast Dan 3:21
because there is no o God that Dan 3:29
of the o which came up, and before Dan 7:20
but one was higher than the o Dan 8:3
and, behold, there stood o two Dan 12:5
the o on that side of the bank of Dan 12:5
of Israel, who look to o gods Hos 3:1
O Israel, for joy, as o people Hos 9:1
where is any o that may save thee Hos 13:10
that thou stoodest on the o side Obad 11
the o upon the left side thereof Zec 4:3
Beauty, and the o I called Bands Zec 11:7
Then I cut asunder mine o staff Zec 11:14
he saw o two brethren, James the Mt 4:21
cheek, turn to him the o also Mt 5:39
will hate the one, and love the o Mt 6:24
hold to the one, and despise the o Mt 6:24
to depart unto the o side Mt 8:18
when he was come to the o side Mt 8:28
was restored whole, like as the o Mt 12:13
seven o spirits more wicked than Mt 12:45
But o fell into good ground, and Mt 13:8
to go before him unto the o side Mt 14:22
disciples were come to the o side Mt 16:5
the o on the left, in thy kingdom Mt 20:21
he sent o servants more than the Mt 21:36
his vineyard unto o husbandmen Mt 21:41
Again, he sent forth o servants Mt 22:4
and not to leave the o undone Mt 23:23
from one end of heaven to the o Mt 24:31
one shall be taken, and the o left Mt 24:40
one shall be taken, and the o left Mt 24:41
Afterward came also the o virgins Mt 25:11
same, and made them o five talents Mt 25:16
two, he also gained o two Mt 25:17
brought o five talents, saying, Mt 25:20
I have gained two o talents Mt 25:22
the o Mary, sitting over against Mt 27:61
the o Mary to see the sepulchre Mt 28:1
hand was restored whole as the o Mk 3:5
o fell on good ground, and did Mk 4:8
the lusts of o things entering in Mk 4:19
Let us pass over unto the o side Mk 4:35
were also with him o little ships Mk 4:36
over unto the o side of the sea Mk 5:1
again by ship unto the o side Mk 5:21
to go to the o side before unto Mk 6:45
many o things there be, which Mk 7:4
many o such like things ye do Mk 7:8
ship again departed to the o side Mk 8:13
the o on thy left hand, in thy Mk 10:37
There is none o commandment Mk 12:31
and there is none o but he Mk 12:32
right hand, and the o on his left Mk 15:27
many o women which came up with Mk 15:41
many o things in his exhortation Lk 3:18
kingdom of God to o cities also Lk 4:43
which were in the o ship Lk 5:7
hand was restored whole as the o Lk 6:10
on the one cheek offer also the o Lk 6:29
hundred pence, and the o fifty Lk 7:41
o fell on good ground, and sprang Lk 8:8
over unto the o side of the lake Lk 8:22
the Lord appointed o seventy also Lk 10:1
him, he passed by on the o side Lk 10:31
him, and passed by on the o side Lk 10:32
taketh to him seven o spirits Lk 11:26
and not to leave the o undone Lk 11:42
while the o is yet a great way Lk 14:32
will hate the one, and love the o Lk 16:13
hold to the one, and despise the o Lk 16:13
shineth unto the o part under Lk 17:24
be taken, and the o shall be left Lk 17:34
one shall be taken, and the o left Lk 17:35
one shall be taken, and the o left Lk 17:36
a Pharisee, and the o a publican Lk 18:10
thee, that I am not as o men are Lk 18:11
house justified rather than the o Lk 18:14
many o things blasphemously spake Lk 22:65
right hand, and the o on the left Lk 23:33
But the o answering rebuked him, Lk 23:40
o women that were with them, Lk 24:10
o men laboured, and ye are entered Jn 4:38
the people which stood on the o Jn 6:22
that there was none o boat there Jn 6:22
(Howbeit there came o boats from Jn 6:23
him on the o side of the sea Jn 6:25
but climbeth up some o way Jn 10:1
o sheep I have, which are not of Jn 10:16
the works which none o man did Jn 15:24
Then went out that o disciple Jn 18:16
of the o which was crucified with Jn 19:32
to the o disciple, whom Jesus Jn 20:2
that o disciple, and came to the Jn 20:3
the o disciple did outrun Peter, Jn 20:4
Then went in also that o disciple Jn 20:8
the o at the feet, where the body Jn 20:12
The o disciples therefore said Jn 20:25
many o signs truly did Jesus in Jn 20:30
and two o of his disciples Jn 21:2
the o disciples came in a little Jn 21:8
there are also many o things Jn 21:25
and began to speak with o tongues Acts 2:4
with many o words did he testify Acts 2:40
is there salvation in any o Acts 4:12
for there is none o name under Acts 4:12
the o apostles answered and said, Acts 5:29
of himself, or of some o man Acts 8:34
and Barnabas, and certain o of them Acts 15:2
in asunder one from the o Acts 15:39
security of Jason, and of the o Acts 17:9
o some, He seemeth to be a setter Acts 17:18
any thing concerning o matters Acts 19:39
the o Pharisees, he cried out in Acts 23:6
saying none o things than those Acts 26:22
certain o prisoners unto one Acts 27:1
also, even as among o Gentiles Rom 1:13
nor any o creature, shall be able Rom 8:39
and if there be any o commandment Rom 13:9
know not whether I baptized any o 1Cor 1:16
For o foundation can no man lay 1Cor 3:11
Defraud ye not one the o, except 1Cor 7:5
that there is none o God but one 1Cor 8:4
a wife, as well as o apostles 1Cor 9:5
say, not thine own, but of the o 1Cor 10:29
taketh before o his own supper 1Cor 11:21
well, but the o is not edified 1Cor 14:17
is written, With men of o tongues 1Cor 14:21
o lips will I speak unto this 1Cor 14:21
two or three, and let the o judge 1Cor 14:29
of wheat, or of some o grain 1Cor 15:37
we write none o things unto you 2Cor 1:13
to the o the savour of life unto 2Cor 2:16
I mean not that o men be eased 2Cor 8:13
that is, of o men's labours 2Cor 10:15
I robbed o churches, taking wages 2Cor 11:8
ye were inferior to o churches 2Cor 12:13
have sinned, and to all o, that, 2Cor 13:2
preach any o gospel unto you than Gal 1:8
If any man preach any o gospel Gal 1:9
But o of the apostles saw I none, Gal 1:19
the o Jews dissembled likewise Gal 2:13
a bondmaid, the o by a freewoman Gal 4:22
are contrary the one to the o Gal 5:17
Which in o ages was not made Eph 3:5
walk not as o Gentiles walk Eph 4:17
the palace, and in all o places Phil 1:13
But the o of love, knowing that I Phil 1:17
esteem o better than themselves Phil 2:3
If any o man thinketh that he Phil 3:4
with o my fellowlabourers, whose Phil 4:3
you all toward each o aboundeth 2Th 1:3
that they teach no o doctrine 1Ti 1:3
if there be any o thing that is 1Ti 1:10
be partaker of o men's sins 1Ti 5:22
the earth, neither by any o oath Jas 5:12
as a busybody in o men's matters 1Pet 4:15
as they do also the o scriptures 2Pet 3:16
I will put upon you none o burden Rev 2:24
o voices of the trumpet of the Rev 8:13
one is, and the o is not yet come Rev 17:10

## OTHERS

and out of the earth shall o grow Job 8:19
and let o bow down upon her Job 31:10
number, and set o in their stead Job 34:24
wicked men in the open sight of o Job 34:26
and leave their wealth to o Ps 49:10
thou give thine honour unto o Prov 5:9
thyself likewise hast cursed o Eccl 7:22
saith, Yet will I gather o to him Is 56:8
houses shall be turned unto o Jer 6:12
will I give their wives unto o Jer 8:10
to the o he said in mine hearing, Eze 9:5
they have made o to hope that Eze 13:6
o daubed it with untempered Eze 13:10
which was diverse from all the o Dan 7:19
up, even for o beside those Dan 11:4
only, what do ye more than o Mt 5:47
blind, dumb, maimed, and many o Mt 15:30
and o, Jeremias, or one of the Mt 16:14
saw o standing idle in the Mt 20:3
found o standing idle, and saith Mt 20:6
o cut down branches from the Mt 21:8
o smote him with the palms of Mt 26:67
He saved o Mt 27:42
O said, That it is Elias Mk 6:15
o said, That it is a prophet, or Mk 6:15
and o, One of the prophets Mk 8:28
o cut down branches off the trees Mk 11:8
and him they killed, and many o Mk 12:5
and will give the vineyard unto o Mk 12:9
with the scribes, He saved o Mk 15:31
of o that sat down with them Lk 5:29
steward, and Susanna, and many o Lk 8:3
but to o in parables Lk 8:10
and of o, that one of the old Lk 9:8
o say, that one of the old Lk 9:19
And o, tempting him, sought of him Lk 11:16
were righteous, and despised o Lk 18:9
and shall give the vineyard to o Lk 20:16
And there were also two o, Lk 23:32
derided him, saying, He saved o Lk 23:35
prepared, and certain o with them Lk 24:1
o said, Nay Jn 7:12
O said, This is the Christ Jn 7:41
o said, He is like him Jn 9:9
O said, How can a man that is a Jn 9:16
O said, These are not the words Jn 10:21
o said, An angel spake to him Jn 12:29
or did o tell it thee of me Jn 18:34
two o with him, on either side Jn 19:18
O mocking said, These men are Acts 2:13
of the Lord, with many o also Acts 15:35
o said, We will hear thee again Acts 17:32
named Damaris, and o with them Acts 17:34
o also, which had diseases in the Acts 28:9
If I be not an apostle unto o 1Cor 9:2
If o be partakers of this power 1Cor 9:12
means, when I have preached to o 1Cor 9:27
by my voice I might teach o also 1Cor 14:19
or need we, as some o, epistles 2Cor 3:1
occasion of the forwardness of o 2Cor 8:8
the children of wrath, even as o Eph 2:3
every man also on the things of o Phil 2:4
neither of you, nor yet of o 1Th 2:6
even as o which have no hope 1Th 4:13
let us not sleep, as do o 1Th 5:6
before all, that o also may fear 1Ti 5:20
who shall be able to teach o also 2Ti 2:2
place every year with blood of o Heb 9:25
o were tortured, not accepting Heb 11:35
o had trial of cruel mockings and Heb 11:36
o save with fear, pulling them Jude 23

## OTHERWISE

O I should have wrought falsehood 2Sa 18:13
O it shall come to pass, when my 1Kin 1:21
passover o than it was written 2Chr 30:18
lest o they should rejoice over Ps 38:16
o ye have no reward of your Mt 6:1
if o, then both the new maketh a Lk 5:36
o grace is no more grace Rom 11:6
o work is no more work Rom 11:6
o thou also shalt be cut off Rom 11:22
if o, yet as a fool receive me, 2Cor 11:16
that ye will be none o minded Gal 5:10
and if in any thing ye be o minded Phil 3:15
and they that are o cannot be hid 1Ti 5:25
If any man teach o, and consent 1Ti 6:3
o it is of no strength at all Heb 9:17

**OTHNI** (*oth'-ni*) *A son of Shemiah.*
O, and Rephael, and Obed, Elzabad, 1Chr 26:7

**OTHNIEL** (*oth'-ne-el*)
*1. A brother of Caleb.*
O the son of Kenaz, the brother Josh 15:17
O the son of Kenaz, Caleb's Judg 1:13
even O the son of Kenaz, Caleb's Judg 3:9
And O the son of Kenaz died Judg 3:11
O, and Seraiah 1Chr 4:13
and the sons of O 1Chr 4:13
*2. Tribe or family of Othniel 1.*
was Heldai the Netophathite, of O 1Chr 27:15

## OUCHES

make them to be set in o of gold Ex 28:11
And thou shalt make o of gold Ex 28:13
the wreathen chains to the o Ex 28:14
thou shalt fasten in the two o Ex 28:25
onyx stones inclosed in o of gold Ex 39:6
they were inclosed in o of gold Ex 39:13
And they made two o of gold Ex 39:16
chains they fastened in the two o Ex 39:18

## OUGHT

unto me that o not to be done Gen 20:9
which thing o not to be done Gen 34:7
and he knew not o he had, save the Gen 39:6
there is not o left in the sight Gen 47:18
ye shall not diminish o thereof Ex 5:8
yet not o of your work shall be Ex 5:11
Ye shall not minish o from your Ex 5:19
thou shalt not carry forth o of Ex 12:46
And if a man borrow o of his Ex 22:14
And if o of the flesh of the Ex 29:34
things which o not to be done Lev 4:2
things which o not to be done Lev 4:27
whosoever beareth o of the Lev 11:25
if o remain until the third day, Lev 19:6
if thou sell o unto thy neighbour Lev 25:14
or buyest o of thy neighbour's Lev 25:14
if o be committed by ignorance Num 15:24
soul that doeth o presumptuously Num 15:30
or uttered o out of her lips, Num 30:6
shall ye diminish o from it Deut 4:2
o unto his neighbour shall Deut 15:2
neither have I taken away o Deut 26:14
nor given o thereof for the dead Deut 26:14
There failed not o of any good Josh 21:45
if o but death part thee and me Ruth 1:17
thou taken o of any man's hand 1Sa 12:4
ye have not found o in my hand 1Sa 12:5
was there o missing unto them 1Sa 25:7
we will not give them o of the 1Sa 30:22
or o else, till the sun be down 2Sa 3:35
for no such thing o to be done in 2Sa 13:12
said, Whosoever saith o unto thee 2Sa 14:10
from o that my lord the king hath 2Sa 14:19
to know what Israel o to do 1Chr 12:32
None o to carry the ark of God 1Chr 15:2
O ye not to know that the LORD 2Chr 13:5
o ye not to walk in the fear of Neh 5:9
unto him that o to be feared Ps 76:11
thy brother hath o against thee Mt 5:23
And if any man say o unto you Mt 21:3
these o ye to have done, and not Mt 23:23
ye suffer him no more to do o for Mk 7:12
him, he asked him if he saw o Mk 8:23
forgive, if ye have o against any Mk 11:25
prophet, standing where it o not Mk 13:14
these o ye to have done, and not Lk 11:42
in the same hour what ye o to say Lk 12:12
six days in which men o to work Lk 13:14
o not this woman, being a Lk 13:16
that men o always to pray, and not Lk 18:1
O not Christ to have suffered Lk 24:26
the place where men o to worship Jn 4:20
Hath any man brought him o to eat Jn 4:33
ye also o to wash one another's Jn 13:14
a law, and by our law he o to die Jn 19:7

that o of the things which he ... Acts 4:32
We o to obey God rather than men ... Acts 5:29
we o not to think that the ... Acts 17:29
ye o to be quiet, and to do ... Acts 19:36
ye o to support the weak, and to ... Acts 20:35
saying that they o not to ... Acts 21:21
Who o to have been here before ... Acts 24:19
object, if they had o against me ... Acts 24:19
seat, where I o to be judged ... Acts 25:10
crying that he o not to live any ... Acts 25:24
that I o to do many things ... Acts 26:9
not that I had o to accuse my ... Acts 28:19
what we should pray for as we o ... Rom 8:26
more highly than he o to think ... Rom 12:3
We then that are strong o to bear ... Rom 15:1
nothing yet as he o to know ... 1Cor 8:2
For a man indeed o not to cover ... 1Cor 11:7
For this cause o the woman to ... 1Cor 11:10
from them of whom I o to rejoice ... 2Cor 2:3
ye o rather to forgive him ... 2Cor 2:7
for I o to have been commended of ... 2Cor 12:11
for the children o not to lay up ... 2Cor 12:14
So o men to love their wives as ... Eph 5:28
may speak boldly, as I o to speak ... Eph 6:20
make it manifest, as I o to speak ... Col 4:4
know how ye o to answer every man ... Col 4:6
received of us how ye o to walk ... 1Th 4:1
know how ye o to follow us ... 2Th 3:7
speaking things which they o not ... 1Ti 5:13
teaching things which they o not ... Titus 1:11
wronged thee, or oweth thee o ... Philem 18
Therefore we o to give the more ... Heb 2:1
And by reason hereof he o, as for ... Heb 5:3
for the time ye o to be teachers ... Heb 5:12
these things o not so to be ... Jas 3:10
For that ye o to say, If the Lord ... Jas 4:15
of persons o ye to be in all holy ... 2Pet 3:11
in him o himself also so to walk ... 1Jn 2:6
we o to lay down our lives for ... 1Jn 3:16
we o also to love one another ... 1Jn 4:11
We therefore o to receive such, ... 3Jn 8

**OUGHTEST**
what thou o to do unto him ... 1Kin 2:9
Thou o therefore to have put my ... Mt 25:27
shall tell thee what thou o to do ... Acts 10:6
o to behave thyself in the house ... 1Ti 3:15

**OUR** See PREFACE.

**OURS**
herdmen, saying, The water is o ... Gen 26:20
taken from our father, that is o ... Gen 31:16
and every beast of theirs be o ... Gen 34:23
on this side Jordan may be o ... Num 32:32
ye that Ramoth in Gilead is o ... 1Kin 22:3
high places are o in possession ... Eze 36:2
and the inheritance shall be o ... Mk 12:7
that the inheritance may be o ... Lk 20:14
Christ our Lord, both theirs and o ... 1Cor 1:2
even as ye also are o in the day ... 2Cor 1:14
let o also learn to maintain good ... Titus 3:14
and not for o only, but also for ... 1Jn 2:2

**OURSELVES**
bow down o to thee to the earth ... Gen 37:10
or how shall we clear o ... Gen 44:16
But we o will go ready armed ... Num 32:17
cattle we took for a prey unto o ... Deut 2:35
cities, we took for a prey to o ... Deut 3:7
and we will discover o unto them ... 1Sa 14:8
let us behave o valiantly for our ... 1Chr 19:13
but we o together will build unto ... Ezr 4:3
we might afflict o before our God ... Ezr 8:21
to charge o yearly with the third ... Neh 10:32
let us know among o what is good ... Job 34:4
Let us take to o the houses of ... Ps 83:12
he that hath made us, and not we o ... Ps 100:3
let us solace o with loves ... Prov 7:18
and under falsehood have we hid o ... Is 28:15
we will fill o with strong drink ... Is 56:12
let us join o to the LORD in a ... Jer 50:5
for we o have heard of his own ... Lk 22:71
for we have heard him o, and know ... Jn 4:42
But we will give o continually to ... Acts 6:4
We have bound o under a great ... Acts 23:14
but o also, which have the ... Rom 8:23
even we o groan within ... Rom 8:23
groan within o, waiting for ... Rom 8:23
of the weak, and not to please o ... Rom 15:1
For if we would judge o, we ... 1Cor 11:31
we o are comforted of God ... 2Cor 1:4
we had the sentence of death in o ... 2Cor 1:9
that we should not trust in o ... 2Cor 1:9
Do we begin again to commend o ... 2Cor 3:1
of o to think any thing as of ... 2Cor 3:5
to think any thing as of o ... 2Cor 3:5
of the truth commending o to ... 2Cor 4:2
For we preach not o, but Christ ... 2Cor 4:5
o your servants for Jesus' sake ... 2Cor 4:5
we commend not o again unto you ... 2Cor 5:12
For whether we be beside o ... 2Cor 5:13
o as the ministers of God ... 2Cor 6:4
let us cleanse o from all ... 2Cor 7:1
we dare not make o of the number ... 2Cor 10:12
or compare o with some that ... 2Cor 10:12
stretch not o beyond our measure ... 2Cor 10:14
ye that we excuse o unto you ... 2Cor 12:19
we o also are found sinners, is ... Gal 2:17
behaved o among you that believe ... 1Th 2:10
So that we o glory in you in the ... 2Th 1:4
for we behaved not o disorderly ... 2Th 3:7
but to make o an ensample unto ... 2Th 3:9
For we o also were sometimes ... Titus 3:3
the assembling of o together ... Heb 10:25
that we have no sin, we deceive o ... 1Jn 1:8

**OUT** See PREFACE.

**OUTCAST**
because they called thee an O ... Jer 30:17

**OUTCASTS**
together the o of Israel ... Ps 147:2
and shall assemble the o of Israel ... Is 11:12
hide the o ... Is 16:3
Let mine o dwell with thee, Moab ... Is 16:4
the o in the land of Egypt, and ... Is 27:13
gathereth the o of Israel saith ... Is 56:8
the o of Elam shall not come ... Jer 49:36

**OUTER**
was heard even to the o court ... Eze 10:5
shall be cast out into o darkness ... Mt 8:12
away, and cast him into o darkness ... Mt 22:13
servant into o darkness ... Mt 25:30

**OUTGOINGS**
the o of it were at the sea ... Josh 17:9
the o of it shall be thine ... Josh 17:18
the o of the border were at the ... Josh 18:19
the o thereof are in the valley ... Josh 19:14
the o of their border were at ... Josh 19:22
the o thereof are at the sea from ... Josh 19:29
the o thereof were at Jordan ... Josh 19:33
thou makest the o of the morning ... Ps 65:8

**OUTLANDISH**
even him did o women cause to sin ... Neh 13:26

**OUTLIVED**
days of the elders that o Joshua ... Judg 2:7

**OUTMOST**
curtain that is o in the coupling ... Ex 26:10
o coast of the salt sea eastward ... Num 34:3
out unto the o parts of heaven ... Deut 30:4
four or five in the o fruitful ... Is 17:6

**OUTRAGEOUS**
Wrath is cruel, and anger is o ... Prov 27:4

**OUTRUN**
and the other disciple did o Peter ... Jn 20:4

**OUTSIDE**
Phurah his servant unto the o of ... Judg 7:11
when I come to the o of the camp ... Judg 7:17
came unto the o of the camp in ... Judg 7:19
so on the o toward the great ... 1Kin 7:9
behold a wall on the o of the ... Eze 40:5
ye make clean the o of the cup ... Mt 23:25
that the o of them may be clean ... Mt 23:26
make clean the o of the cup ... Lk 11:39

**OUTSTRETCHED**
a mighty hand, and with an o arm ... Deut 26:8
fight against you with an o hand ... Jer 21:5
by my great power and by my o arm ... Jer 27:5

**OUTWARD**
o a thousand cubits round about ... Num 35:4
man looketh on the o appearance ... 1Sa 16:7
for the o business over Israel ... 1Chr 26:29
had the oversight of the o ... Neh 11:16
the o court of the king's house ... Est 6:4
brought he me into the o court ... Eze 40:17
the gate of the o court that ... Eze 40:20
thereof were toward the o court ... Eze 40:34
o sanctuary which looketh toward ... Eze 44:1
which indeed appear beautiful o ... Mt 23:27
which is o in the flesh ... Rom 2:28
but though our o man perish ... 2Cor 4:16
on things after the o appearance ... 2Cor 10:7
adorning let it not be that o ... 1Pet 3:3

**OUTWARDLY**
Even so ye also o appear ... Mt 23:28
he is not a Jew, which is one o ... Rom 2:28

**OUTWENT**
o them, and came together unto him ... Mk 6:33

**OVEN**
of a meat offering baken in the o ... Lev 2:4
offering that is baken in the o ... Lev 7:9
whether it be o, or ranges for ... Lev 11:35
shall bake your bread in one o ... Lev 26:26
o in the time of thine anger ... Ps 21:9
Our skin was black like an o ... Lam 5:10
as an o heated by the baker, who ... Hos 7:4
made ready their heart like an o ... Hos 7:6
They are all hot as an o, and have ... Hos 7:7
cometh, that shall burn as an o ... Mal 4:1
and to morrow is cast into the o ... Mt 6:30
and to morrow is cast into the o ... Lk 12:28

**OVENS**
upon thy people, and into thine o ... Ex 8:3

**OVER** See PREFACE.

**OVERCAME**
o them, and prevailed against them ... Acts 19:16
me in my throne, even as I also o ... Rev 3:21
they o him by the blood of the ... Rev 12:11

**OVERCHARGE**
that I may not o you all ... 2Cor 2:5

**OVERCHARGED**
your hearts be o with surfeiting ... Lk 21:34

**OVERCOME**
Gad, a troop shall o him ... Gen 49:19
but he shall o at the last ... Gen 49:19
of them that cry for being o ... Ex 32:18
for we are well able to o it ... Num 13:30
I shall be able to o them ... Num 22:11
Ahaz, but could not o him ... 2Kin 16:5
eyes from me, for they have o me ... Song 6:5
of them that are o with wine ... Is 28:1
and like a man whom wine hath o ... Jer 23:9
o him, he taketh from him all his ... Lk 11:22
I have o the world ... Jn 16:33
mightest o when thou art judged ... Rom 3:4
Be not o of evil, but o ... Rom 12:21
for of whom a man is o, of the ... 2Pet 2:19
are again entangled therein, and o ... 2Pet 2:20
because ye have o the wicked one ... 1Jn 2:13
you, and ye have o the wicked one ... 1Jn 2:14
little children, and have o them ... 1Jn 4:4
war against them, and shall o them ... Rev 11:7
war with the saints, and to o them ... Rev 13:7
Lamb, and the Lamb shall o them ... Rev 17:14

**OVERCOMETH**
is born of God o the world ... 1Jn 5:4
is the victory that o the world ... 1Jn 5:4
Who is he that o the world ... 1Jn 5:5
To him that o will I give to eat ... Rev 2:7
He that o shall not be hurt of ... Rev 2:11
To him that o will I give to eat ... Rev 2:17
And he that o, and keepeth my works ... Rev 2:26
He that o, the same shall be ... Rev 3:5
Him that o will I make a pillar ... Rev 3:12
To him that o will I grant to sit ... Rev 3:21
He that o shall inherit all ... Rev 21:7

**OVERDRIVE**
and if men should o them one day ... Gen 33:13

**OVERFLOW**
the water of the Red sea to o ... Deut 11:4
waters, where the floods o me ... Ps 69:2
Let not the waterflood o me ... Ps 69:15
he shall o and go over, he shall ... Is 8:8
shall o with righteousness ... Is 10:22
waters shall o the hiding place ... Is 28:17
the rivers, they shall not o thee ... Is 43:2
shall o the land, and all that is ... Jer 47:2
and one shall certainly come, and o ... Dan 11:10
destroy him, and his army shall o ... Dan 11:26
into the countries, and shall o ... Dan 11:40
and the fats shall o with wine ... Joel 2:24
for the press is full, the fats o ... Joel 3:13

**OVERFLOWED**
gushed out, and the streams o ... Ps 78:20
being o with water, perished ... 2Pet 3:6

**OVERFLOWETH**
(for Jordan o all his banks all ... Josh 3:15

**OVERFLOWING**
He bindeth the floods from o ... Job 28:11
a watercourse for the o of waters ... Job 38:25
as a flood of mighty waters o ... Is 28:2
when the o scourge shall pass ... Is 28:15
when the o scourge shall pass ... Is 28:18
as an o stream, shall reach to ... Is 30:28
the north, and shall be an o flood ... Jer 47:2
there shall be an o shower ... Eze 13:11
there shall be an o shower in ... Eze 13:13
o rain, and great hailstones, fire ... Eze 38:22
the o of the water passed by ... Hab 3:10

**OVERFLOWN**
when it had o all his banks ... 1Chr 12:15
foundation was o with a flood ... Job 22:16
shall they be o from before him ... Dan 11:22

**OVERLAID**
of shittim wood o with gold ... Ex 26:32
he o the boards with gold, and ... Ex 36:34
the bars, and o the bars with gold ... Ex 36:34
shittim wood, and o them with gold ... Ex 36:36
he o their chapiters and their ... Ex 36:38
he o it with pure gold within and ... Ex 37:2
shittim wood, and o them with gold ... Ex 37:4
he o it with pure gold, and made ... Ex 37:11
o them with gold, to bear the ... Ex 37:15
he o it with pure gold, both the ... Ex 37:26
shittim wood, and o them with gold ... Ex 37:28
and he o it with brass ... Ex 38:2
wood, and o them with brass ... Ex 38:6
o their chapiters, and filleted ... Ex 38:28
because she o it ... 1Kin 3:19
and he o it with pure gold ... 1Kin 6:20
So Solomon o the house within ... 1Kin 6:21
and he o it with gold ... 1Kin 6:21
And the whole house he o with gold ... 1Kin 6:22
was by the oracle he o with gold ... 1Kin 6:22
he o the cherubims with gold ... 1Kin 6:28
floor of the house he o with gold ... 1Kin 6:30
o them with gold, and spread gold ... 1Kin 6:32
ivory, and o it with the best gold ... 1Kin 10:18
Hezekiah king of Judah had o ... 2Kin 18:16
he o it within with pure gold ... 2Chr 3:4
which he o with fine gold, and set ... 2Chr 3:5
He o also the house, the beams, ... 2Chr 3:7
he o it with fine gold, amounting ... 2Chr 3:8

O

he o the upper chambers with gold....... 2Chr 3:9
image work, and o them with gold...... 2Chr 3:10
o the doors of them with brass............... 2Chr 4:9
of ivory, and o it with pure gold......... 2Chr 9:17
as bright ivory o with sapphires............. Song 5:14
covenant o round about with gold.......... Heb 9:4

**OVERLAY**
thou shalt o it with pure gold,............... Ex 25:11
within and without shalt thou o it........... Ex 25:11
shittim wood, and o them with gold....... Ex 25:13
thou shalt o it with pure gold,............... Ex 25:24
o them with gold, that the table............. Ex 25:28
thou shalt o the boards with gold.......... Ex 26:29
thou shalt o the bars with gold.............. Ex 26:29
o them with gold, and their hooks......... Ex 26:37
thou shalt o it with brass........................ Ex 27:2
wood, and o them with brass.................... Ex 27:6
thou shalt o it with pure gold,............... Ex 30:3
shittim wood, and o them with gold....... Ex 30:5
to o the walls of the houses.................. 1Chr 29:4

**OVERLAYING**
the o of their chapiters of....................... Ex 38:17
the o of their chapiters and their........... Ex 38:19

**OVERLIVED**
days of the elders that o Joshua......... Josh 24:31

**OVERMUCH**
be swallowed up with o sorrow............. 2Cor 2:7

**OVERPASS**
they o the deeds of the wicked............... Jer 5:28

**OVERPAST**
until these calamities be o......................... Ps 57:1
until the indignation be o......................... Is 26:20

**OVERPLUS**
restore the o unto the man to................ Lev 25:27

**OVERRAN**
the way of the plain, and o Cushi ........ 2Sa 18:23

**OVERRUNNING**
But with an o flood he will make............ Nah 1:8

**OVERSEE**
were appointed to o the vessels........... 1Chr 9:29
thousand and six hundred to o them.... 2Chr 2:2

**OVERSEER**
he made him o over his house, and...... Gen 39:4
he had made him o in his house........... Gen 39:5
the son of Zichri was their o................ Neh 11:9
their o was Zabdiel, the son of............. Neh 11:14
The o also of the Levites at.................. Neh 11:22
sang loud, with Jezrahiah their o......... Neh 12:42
Which having no guide, o, or.................. Prov 6:7

**OVERSEERS**
six hundred o to set the people a......... 2Chr 2:18
were o under the hand of Cononiah.. 2Chr 31:13
the o of them were Jahath and........... 2Chr 34:12
were o of all that wrought the........... 2Chr 34:13
it into the hand of the o........................ 2Chr 34:17
the Holy Ghost hath made you o....... Acts 20:28

**OVERSHADOW**
power of the Highest shall o thee.......... Lk 1:35
passing by might o some of them.......... Acts 5:15

**OVERSHADOWED**
behold, a bright cloud o them................... Mt 17:5
And there was a cloud that o them......... Mk 9:7
there came a cloud, and o them.............. Lk 9:34

**OVERSIGHT**
peradventure it was an o....................... Gen 43:12
have the o of them that keep the........ Num 3:32
the o of all the tabernacle, and............ Num 4:16
that had the o of the house of............ 2Kin 12:11
that have the o of the house of............ 2Kin 22:5
that have the o of the house of............ 2Kin 22:9
their children had the o of the............ 1Chr 9:23
the o of the house of the LORD........... 2Chr 34:10
had the o of the outward business...... Neh 11:16
having the o of the chamber of........... Neh 13:4
among you, taking the o thereof............ 1Pet 5:2

**OVERSPREAD**
and of them was the whole earth o...... Gen 9:19

**OVERSPREADING**
for the o of abominations he................. Dan 9:27

**OVERTAKE**
and when thou dost o them, say........... Gen 44:4
said, I will pursue, I will o ..................... Ex 15:9
o him, because the way is long,............ Deut 19:6
o thee, if thou shalt hearken ............... Deut 28:2
shall come upon thee, and o thee...... Deut 28:15
o thee, till thou be destroyed ............. Deut 28:45
for ye shall o them ............................... Josh 2:5
shall I o them ....................................... 1Sa 30:8
for thou shalt surely o them ................ 1Sa 30:8
lest he o us suddenly, and bring......... 2Sa 15:14
us, neither doth justice o us.................... Is 59:9
shall o you there in the land of............ Jer 42:16
lovers, but she shall not o them ........... Hos 2:7
of iniquity did not o them..................... Hos 10:9
evil shall not o nor prevent us............ Amos 9:10
the plowman shall o the reaper............ Amos 9:13
that day should o you as a thief............. 1Th 5:4

**OVERTAKEN**
pursued mine enemies, and o them........ Ps 18:37
if a man be o in a fault........................... Gal 6:1

**OVERTAKETH**
the sword of thine enemies o thee..... 1Chr 21:12

**OVERTHREW**
he o those cities, and all the................. Gen 19:25
when he o the cities in the which ....... Gen 19:29
the LORD o the Egyptians in the............ Ex 14:27
which the LORD o in his anger........... Deut 29:23
But o Pharaoh and his host in the........ Ps 136:15
shall be as when God o Sodom ............... Is 13:19
be as the cities which the LORD o.......... Jer 20:16
God o Sodom and Gomorrah.................. Jer 50:40
some of you, as God o Sodom............... Amos 4:11
o the tables of the moneychangers.......... Mt 21:12
o the tables of the moneychangers....... Mk 11:15
changers' money, and o the tables .......... Jn 2:15

**OVERTHROW**
also, that I will not o this city............ Gen 19:21
Lot out of the midst of the o............... Gen 19:29
but thou shalt utterly o them................. Ex 23:24
ye shall o their altars, and break......... Deut 12:3
therein, like the o of Sodom............... Deut 29:23
and to spy it out, and to o it................... 2Sa 10:3
strong against the city, and o it........... 2Sa 11:25
unto thee for to search, and to o ........ 1Chr 19:3
to o them in the wilderness ................ Ps 106:26
To o their seed also among the............ Ps 106:27
who have purposed to o my goings........ Ps 140:4
hunt the violent man to o him ............ Ps 140:11
to o the righteous in judgment ............ Prov 18:5
As in the o of Sodom and Gomorrah.... Jer 49:18
I will o the throne of kingdoms,............ Hag 2:22
I will o the chariots, and those ............ Hag 2:22
if it be of God, ye cannot o it ............... Acts 5:39
and o the faith of some......................... 2Ti 2:18
ashes condemned them with an o.......... 2Pet 2:6

**OVERTHROWETH**
away spoiled, and o the mighty ........... Job 12:19
but wickedness o the sinner ................. Prov 13:6
but God o the wicked for their ............ Prov 21:12
and he o the words of the ................... Prov 22:12
but he that receiveth gifts o it ............. Prov 29:4

**OVERTHROWN**
of thine excellency thou hast o .............. Ex 15:7
fled before him, and many were o........ Judg 9:40
some of them be o at the first................. 2Sa 17:9
and the Ethiopians were o, that ......... 2Chr 14:13
Know now that God hath o me.............. Job 19:6
judges are o in stony places.................. Ps 141:6
but it is o by the mouth of the........... Prov 11:11
The wicked are o, and are not ............. Prov 12:7
house of the wicked shall be o............ Prov 14:11
it is desolate, as o by strangers .................... Is 1:7
but let them be o before thee............... Jer 18:23
that was o as in a moment, and no......... Lam 4:6
and many countries shall be o ............. Dan 11:41
I have o some of you, as God............... Amos 4:11
forty days, and Nineveh shall be o....... Jonah 3:4
for they were o in the wilderness......... 1Cor 10:5

**OVERTOOK**
they o him in the mount Gilead.......... Gen 31:23
Then Laban o Jacob.............................. Gen 31:25
he o them, and he spake unto them ..... Gen 44:6
o them encamping by the sea, ................. Ex 14:9
and o the children of Dan .................... Judg 18:22
but the battle o them ............................ Judg 20:42
o him in the plains of Jericho............... 2Kin 25:5
o Zedekiah in the plains of ..................... Jer 39:5
o Zedekiah in the plains of ..................... Jer 52:8
all her persecutors o her between........... Lam 1:3

**OVERTURN**
them out, and they o the earth............ Job 12:15
I will o, o, o.......................................... Eze 21:27

**OVERTURNED**
o it, that the tent lay along................. Judg 7:13

**OVERTURNETH**
which o them in his anger........................ Job 9:5
he o the mountains by the roots.......... Job 28:9
he o them in the night, so that ........... Job 34:25

**OVERWHELM**
ye o the fatherless, and ye dig a ............ Job 6:27

**OVERWHELMED**
come upon me, and horror hath o me..... Ps 55:5
cry unto thee, when my heart is o .......... Ps 61:2
I complained, and my spirit was o........... Ps 77:3
but the sea o their enemies .................... Ps 78:53
of the afflicted, when he is o ................ Ps 102:t
Then the waters had o us, the................ Ps 124:4
When my spirit was o within me............ Ps 142:3
is my spirit o within me ........................ Ps 143:4

**OWE**
O no man any thing, but to love......... Rom 13:8

**OWED**
which o him ten thousand talents......... Mt 18:24
which o him an hundred pence .............. Mt 18:28
the one o five hundred pence, and.......... Lk 7:41

**OWEST**
saying, Pay me that thou o ..................... Mt 18:28
How much o thou unto my lord................ Lk 16:5
he to another, And how much o thou ..... Lk 16:7
o unto me even thine own self.......... Philem 19

**OWETH**
or o thee ought, put that on mine........ Philem 18

**OWL**
And the o, and the night hawk, and.... Lev 11:16
And the little o, and the cormorant..... Lev 11:17
and the cormorant, and the great o...... Lev 11:17
And the o, and the night hawk, and . Deut 14:15
The little o, and the great .................. Deut 14:16
and the great o ..................................... Deut 14:16
I am like an o of the desert.................... Ps 102:6
the o also and the raven shall ................. Is 34:11
the screech o also shall rest .................. Is 34:14
shall the great o make her nest ............... Is 34:15

**OWLS**
to dragons, and a companion to o........ Job 30:29
o shall dwell there, and satyrs .............. Is 13:21
of dragons, and a court for o.................. Is 34:13
honour me, the dragons and the o ......... Is 43:20
the o shall dwell therein ....................... Jer 50:39
the dragons, and mourning as the o........ Mic 1:8

**OWN** See PREFACE.

**OWNER**
but the o of the ox shall be quit............ Ex 21:28
it hath been testified to his o .............. Ex 21:29
his o also shall be put to death ............ Ex 21:29
The o of the pit shall make it................. Ex 21:34
and give money unto the o of them...... Ex 21:34
his o hath not kept him in .................... Ex 21:36
the o of it shall accept thereof,............. Ex 22:11
restitution unto the o thereof............... Ex 22:12
the o thereof being not with it,............. Ex 22:14
But if the o thereof be with it,............... Ex 22:15
of Shemer, o of the hill, Samaria........ 1Kin 16:24
The ox knoweth his o, and the ass.............. Is 1:3
the o of the ship, more than ................. Acts 27:11

**OWNERS**
or have caused the o thereof to............ Job 31:39
away the life of the o thereof............... Prov 1:19
good is there to the o thereof................ Eccl 5:11
riches kept for the o thereof to............. Eccl 5:13
the o thereof said unto them, Why......... Lk 19:33

**OWNETH**
he that o the house shall come and..... Lev 14:35
bind the man that o this girdle........... Acts 21:11

**OX**
nor his maidservant, nor his o............... Ex 20:17
If an o gore a man or a woman,............ Ex 21:28
then the o shall be surely stoned ........... Ex 21:28
the owner of the o shall be quit ............ Ex 21:28
But if the o were wont to push.............. Ex 21:29
the o shall be stoned, and his................. Ex 21:29
If the o shall push a manservant............ Ex 21:32
silver, and the o shall be stoned ........... Ex 21:32
an o or an ass fall therein ..................... Ex 21:33
if one man's o hurt another's,................ Ex 21:35
then they shall sell the live o ................ Ex 21:35
the dead o also they shall divide ........... Ex 21:35
Or if it be known that the o hath .......... Ex 21:36
he shall surely pay o for o...................... Ex 21:36
If a man shall steal an o........................... Ex 22:1
shall restore five oxen for an o ............... Ex 22:1
his hand alive, whether it be o................. Ex 22:4
of trespass, whether it be for o................ Ex 22:9
his neighbour an ass, or an o ................. Ex 22:10
enemy's o or his ass going astray............ Ex 23:4
that thine o and thine ass may .............. Ex 23:12
whether o or sheep, that is male ........... Ex 34:19
shall eat no manner of fat, of o ............... Lev 7:23
of Israel, that killeth an o ...................... Lev 17:3
whether it be o, or sheep...................... Lev 27:26
the princes, and for each one an o ......... Num 7:3
as the o licketh up the grass of.............. Num 22:4
nor thy maidservant, nor thine o .......... Deut 5:14
or his maidservant, his o ....................... Deut 5:21
the o, the sheep, and the goat, ............... Deut 14:4
and the pygarg, and the wild o .............. Deut 14:5
whether it be o or sheep ........................ Deut 18:3
o or his sheep go astray, and hide ........ Deut 22:1
ass or his o fall down by the way ......... Deut 22:4
Thou shalt not plow with an o ........... Deut 22:10
Thou shalt not muzzle the o when........ Deut 25:4
Thine o shall be slain before................. Deut 28:31
young and old, and o ............................. Josh 6:21
six hundred men with an o goad........... Judg 3:31
for Israel, neither sheep, nor o................ Judg 6:4
whose o have I taken ............................... 1Sa 12:3
Bring me hither every man his o.......... 1Sa 14:34
man his o with him that night .............. 1Sa 14:34
and woman, infant and suckling, o.......... 1Sa 15:3
prepared for me daily was one o........... Neh 5:18
or loweth the o over his fodder................ Job 6:5
take the widow's o for a pledge ............. Job 24:3
he eateth grass as an o.......................... Job 40:15
an o or bullock that hath horns............. Ps 69:31
of an o that eateth grass ...................... Ps 106:20
as an o goeth to the slaughter,............. Prov 7:22
is by the strength of the o..................... Prov 14:4
where love is, than a stalled o............. Prov 15:17
The o knoweth his owner, and the .......... Is 1:3
lion shall eat straw like the o ................ Is 11:7
forth thither the feet of the o ............... Is 32:20
He that killeth an o is as if he............... Is 66:3
or an o that is brought to the................ Jer 11:19
the face of an o on the left side............. Eze 1:10
his o or his ass from the stall ............... Lk 13:15
an ass or an o fallen into a pit .............. Lk 14:5

the o that treadeth out the corn ... 1Cor 9:9
Thou shalt not muzzle the o that ... 1Ti 5:18

**OXEN**
and he had sheep, and o, and he ... Gen 12:16
And Abimelech took sheep, and o ... Gen 20:14
And Abraham took sheep and o ... Gen 21:27
And I have o, and asses, flocks, and ... Gen 32:5
They took their sheep, and their o ... Gen 34:28
upon the camels, upon the o ... Ex 9:3
offerings, thy sheep, and thine o ... Ex 20:24
he shall restore five o for an ox ... Ex 22:1
shalt thou do with thine o ... Ex 22:30
offerings of o unto the LORD ... Ex 24:5
six covered wagons, and twelve o ... Num 7:3
And Moses took the wagons and the o ... Num 7:6
four o he gave unto the sons of ... Num 7:7
eight o he gave unto the sons of ... Num 7:8
of peace offerings, two o ... Num 7:17
of peace offerings, two o ... Num 7:23
of peace offerings, two o ... Num 7:29
of peace offerings, two o ... Num 7:35
of peace offerings, two o ... Num 7:41
of peace offerings, two o ... Num 7:47
of peace offerings, two o ... Num 7:53
of peace offerings, two o ... Num 7:59
of peace offerings, two o ... Num 7:65
of peace offerings, two o ... Num 7:71
of peace offerings, two o ... Num 7:77
of peace offerings, two o ... Num 7:83
All the o for the burnt offering ... Num 7:87
all the o for the sacrifice of ... Num 7:88
And Balak offered o and sheep, and ... Num 22:40
and prepare me here seven o ... Num 23:1
thy soul lusteth after, for o ... Deut 14:26
sons, and his daughters, and his o ... Josh 7:24
And he took a yoke of o, and hewed ... 1Sa 11:7
so shall it be done unto his o ... 1Sa 11:7
which a yoke of o might plow ... 1Sa 14:14
the spoil, and took sheep, and o ... 1Sa 14:32
best of the sheep, and of the o ... 1Sa 15:9
the lowing of the o which I hear ... 1Sa 15:14
the best of the sheep and of the o ... 1Sa 15:15
took of the spoil, sheep and o ... 1Sa 15:21
children and sucklings, and o ... 1Sa 22:19
and took away the sheep, and the o ... 1Sa 27:9
for the o shook it ... 2Sa 6:6
gone six paces, he sacrificed o ... 2Sa 6:13
here be o for burnt sacrifice, and ... 2Sa 24:22
instruments of the o for wood ... 2Sa 24:22
the o for fifty shekels of silver ... 2Sa 24:24
And Adonijah slew sheep and o ... 1Kin 1:9
And he hath slain o and fat cattle ... 1Kin 1:19
down this day, and hath slain o ... 1Kin 1:25
Ten fat o, and twenty o out of ... 1Kin 4:23
It stood upon twelve o, three ... 1Kin 7:25
between the ledges were lions, o ... 1Kin 7:29
o were certain additions made of ... 1Kin 7:29
sea, and twelve o under the sea ... 1Kin 7:44
the ark, sacrificing sheep and o ... 1Kin 8:5
LORD, two and twenty thousand o ... 1Kin 8:63
with twelve yoke of o before him ... 1Kin 19:19
And he left the o, and ran after ... 1Kin 19:20
from him, and took a yoke of o ... 1Kin 19:21
with the instruments of the o ... 1Kin 19:21
and vineyards, and sheep, and o ... 2Kin 5:26
the brasen o that were under it ... 2Kin 16:17
on camels, and on mules, and on o ... 1Chr 12:40
of raisins, and wine, and oil, and o ... 1Chr 12:40
for the o stumbled ... 1Chr 13:9
I give thee the o also for burnt ... 1Chr 21:23
under it was the similitude of o ... 2Chr 4:3
Two rows of o were cast, when it ... 2Chr 4:3
It stood upon twelve o, three ... 2Chr 4:4
One sea, and twelve o under it ... 2Chr 4:15
the ark, sacrificed sheep and o ... 2Chr 5:6
of twenty and two thousand o ... 2Chr 7:5
they had brought, seven hundred o ... 2Chr 15:11
o for him in abundance, and for ... 2Chr 18:2
things were six hundred o ... 2Chr 29:33
also brought in the tithe of o ... 2Chr 31:6
small cattle, and three hundred o ... 2Chr 35:8
small cattle, and five hundred o ... 2Chr 35:9
And so did they with the o ... 2Chr 35:12
camels, and five hundred yoke of o ... Job 1:3
The o were plowing, and the asses ... Job 1:14
camels, and a thousand yoke of o ... Job 42:12
All sheep and o, yea, and the ... Ps 8:7
That our o may be strong to ... Ps 144:14
Where no o are, the crib is clean ... Prov 14:4
be for the sending forth of o ... Is 7:25
behold joy and gladness, slaying o ... Is 22:13
The o likewise and the young asses ... Is 30:24
the husbandman and his yoke of o ... Jer 51:23
shall make thee to eat grass as o ... Dan 4:25
shall make thee to eat grass as o ... Dan 4:32
from men, and did eat grass as o ... Dan 4:33
they fed him with grass like o ... Dan 5:21
will one plow there with o ... Amos 6:12
my o and my fatlings are killed, ... Mt 22:4
I have bought five yoke of o ... Lk 14:19
in the temple those that sold o ... Jn 2:14
temple, and the sheep, and the o ... Jn 2:15
was before their city, brought o ... Acts 14:13
Doth God take care for o ... 1Cor 9:9

**OZEM** (*o'-zem*)
*1. Son of Jesse.*
O the sixth, David the seventh ... 1Chr 2:15
*2. Son of Jerahmeel.*
and Bunah, and Oren, and O, and ... 1Chr 2:25

**OZIAS** (*o-zi'-as*) See UZZIAH. *Son of Joram; ancestor of Jesus.*
and Joram begat O ... Mt 1:8
And O begat Joatham ... Mt 1:9

**OZNI** (*oz'-ni*) See OZNITES. *A son of Gad.*
Of O, the family of the Oznites ... Num 26:16

**OZNITES** (*oz'-nites*) *Descendants of Ozni.*
Of Ozni, the family of the O ... Num 26:16

# P

**PAARAI** (*pa'-ar-ahee*) See NAARAI. *A 'mighty man' of David.*
the Carmelite, P the Arbite, ... 2Sa 23:35

**PACATIANA** (*pa-ca-she-a'-nah*) *A region of Phrygia in Asia Minor.*
is the chiefest city of Phrygia P ... 1Ti s

**PACES**
ark of the LORD had gone six p ... 2Sa 6:13

**PACIFIED**
Then was the king's wrath p ... Est 7:10
when I am p toward thee for all ... Eze 16:63

**PACIFIETH**
A gift in secret p anger ... Prov 21:14
for yielding p great offences ... Eccl 10:4

**PACIFY**
but a wise man will p it ... Prov 16:14

**PADAN** (*pa'-dan*) See PADAN-ARAM. *Same as Padan-aram.*
And as for me, when I came from P ... Gen 48:7

**PADAN-ARAM** (*pa''-dan-a'-ram*) *The plains of Mesopotamia.*
of Bethuel the Syrian of P ... Gen 25:20
Arise, go to P, to the house of ... Gen 28:2
and he went to P unto Laban ... Gen 28:5
Jacob, and sent him away to P ... Gen 28:6
and his mother, and was gone to P ... Gen 28:7
getting, which he had gotten in P ... Gen 31:18
of Canaan, when he came from P ... Gen 33:18
again, when he came out of P ... Gen 35:9
which were born to him in P ... Gen 35:26
which she bare unto Jacob in P ... Gen 46:15

**PADDLE**
shalt have a p upon thy weapon ... Deut 23:13

**PADON** (*pa'-don*) *A family of exiles.*
of Siaha, the children of P ... Ezr 2:44
of Sia, the children of P ... Neh 7:47

**PAGIEL** (*pa'-ghe-el*) *An Asherite who counted the people.*
P the son of Ocran ... Num 1:13
Asher shall be P the son of Ocran ... Num 2:27
eleventh day P the son of Ocran ... Num 7:72
offering of P the son of Ocran ... Num 7:77
of Asher was P the son of Ocran ... Num 10:26

**PAHATH-MOAB** (*pa''-hath-mo'-ab*)
*1. A family of exiles.*
The children of P, of the ... Ezr 2:6
And of the sons of P ... Ezr 10:30
of Harim, and Hashub the son of P ... Neh 3:11
The children of P, of the ... Neh 7:11
*2. Another family of exiles.*
Of the sons of P ... Ezr 8:4
*3. A family who renewed the covenant.*
Parosh, P, Elam, Zatthu, Bani, ... Neh 10:14

**PAI** (*pa'-i*) See PAU. *A city in Edom.*
and the name of his city was P ... 1Chr 1:50

**PAID**
and custom, was p unto them ... Ezr 4:20
so he p the fare thereof, and went ... Jonah 1:3
till thou hast p the uttermost ... Mt 5:26
till thou hast p the very last ... Lk 12:59

**PAIN**
his flesh upon him shall have p ... Job 14:22
travaileth with p all his days ... Job 15:20
also with p upon his bed, and the ... Job 33:19
of his bones with strong p ... Job 33:19
Look upon mine affliction and my p ... Ps 25:18
took hold upon them there, and p ... Ps 48:6
they shall be in p as a woman ... Is 13:8
are my loins filled with p ... Is 21:3
the time of her delivery, is in p ... Is 26:17
with child, we have been in p ... Is 26:18
before her p came, she was ... Is 66:7
hath taken hold of us, and p ... Jer 6:24
they have put themselves to p ... Jer 12:13
Why is my p perpetual, and my ... Jer 15:18
the p as of a woman in travail ... Jer 22:23
it shall fall with p upon the ... Jer 30:23
take balm for her p, if so be she ... Jer 51:8
great p shall be in Ethiopia, ... Eze 30:4
great p shall come upon them, as ... Eze 30:9
Sin shall have great p, and No ... Eze 30:16
Be in p, and labour to bring forth ... Mic 4:10
much p is in all loins, and the ... Nah 2:10
travaileth in p together until ... Rom 8:22
they gnawed their tongues for p ... Rev 16:10
neither shall there be any more p ... Rev 21:4

**PAINED**
My heart is sore p within me ... Ps 55:4
be sorely p at the report of Tyre ... Is 23:5
I am p at my very heart ... Jer 4:19
face the people shall be much p ... Joel 2:6
in birth, and p to be delivered ... Rev 12:2

**PAINFUL**
to know this, it was too p for me ... Ps 73:16

**PAINFULNESS**
In weariness and p, in watchings ... 2Cor 11:27

**PAINS**
for her p came upon her ... 1Sa 4:19
the p of hell gat hold upon me ... Ps 116:3
up, having loosed the p of death ... Acts 2:24
God of heaven because of their p ... Rev 16:11

**PAINTED**
she p her face, and tired her head ... 2Kin 9:30
with cedar, and p with vermilion ... Jer 22:14

**PAINTEDST**
p thy eyes, and deckedst thyself ... Eze 23:40

**PAINTING**
thou rentest thy face with p ... Jer 4:30

**PAIR**
and the poor for a p of shoes ... Amos 2:6
and the needy for a p of shoes ... Amos 8:6
A p of turtledoves, or two young ... Lk 2:24
had a p of balances in his hand ... Rev 6:5

**PALACE**
into the p of the king's house ... 1Kin 16:18
hard by the p of Ahab king of ... 1Kin 21:1
in the p of the king's house, ... 2Kin 15:25
in the p of the king of Babylon ... 2Kin 20:18
for the p is not for man, but for ... 1Chr 29:1
these things, and to build the p ... 1Chr 29:19
of the LORD, and to the king's p ... 2Chr 9:11
maintenance from the king's p ... Ezr 4:14
in the p that is in the province ... Ezr 6:2
year, as I was in Shushan the p ... Neh 1:1
p which appertained to the house ... Neh 2:8
and Hananiah the ruler of the p ... Neh 7:2
which was in Shushan the p ... Est 1:2
were present in Shushan the p ... Est 1:5
of the garden of the king's p ... Est 1:5
young virgins unto Shushan the p ... Est 2:3
Now in Shushan the p there was a ... Est 2:5
together unto Shushan the p ... Est 2:8
decree was given in Shushan the p ... Est 3:15
his wrath went into the p garden ... Est 7:7
p garden into the place of the ... Est 7:8
decree was given at Shushan the p ... Est 8:14
And in Shushan the p the Jews slew ... Est 9:6
the p was brought before the king ... Est 9:11
five hundred men in Shushan the p ... Est 9:12
shall enter into the king's p ... Ps 45:15
after the similitude of a p ... Ps 144:12
will build upon her a p of silver ... Song 8:9
a p of strangers to be no city ... Is 25:2
in the p of the king of Babylon ... Is 39:7
the p shall remain after the ... Jer 30:18
in them to stand in the king's p ... Dan 1:4
house, and flourishing in my p ... Dan 4:4
the p of the kingdom of Babylon ... Dan 4:29
of the wall of the king's p ... Dan 5:5
Then the king went to his p ... Dan 6:18
that I was at Shushan in the p ... Dan 8:2
of his p between the seas in the ... Dan 11:45
and ye shall cast them into the p ... Amos 4:3
and the p shall be dissolved ... Nah 2:6
unto the p of the high priest, ... Mt 26:3
afar off unto the high priest's p ... Mt 26:58
Now Peter sat without in the p ... Mt 26:69
even into the p of the high ... Mk 14:54
And as Peter was beneath in the p ... Mk 14:66
a strong man armed keepeth his p ... Lk 11:21
into the p of the high priest ... Jn 18:15
Christ are manifest in all the p ... Phil 1:13

**PALACES**
burnt all the p thereof with fire ... 2Chr 36:19
and cassia, out of the ivory p ... Ps 45:8
is known in her p for a refuge ... Ps 48:3
well her bulwarks, consider her p ... Ps 48:13
built his sanctuary like high p ... Ps 78:69
walls, and prosperity within thy p ... Ps 122:7
with her hands, and is in kings' p ... Prov 30:28
and dragons in their pleasant p ... Is 13:22
they raised up the p thereof ... Is 23:13
Because the p shall be forsaken ... Is 32:14
And thorns shall come up in her p ... Is 34:13
by night, and let us destroy her p ... Jer 6:5
windows, and is entered into our p ... Jer 9:21
shall devour the p of Jerusalem ... Jer 17:27
shall consume the p of Ben-hadad ... Jer 49:27
he hath swallowed up all her p ... Lam 2:5
of the enemy the walls of her p ... Lam 2:7
And he knew their desolate p ... Eze 19:7
and they shall set their p in thee ... Eze 25:4
and it shall devour the p thereof ... Hos 8:14
shall devour the p of Ben-hadad ... Amos 1:4
which shall devour the p thereof ... Amos 1:7
which shall devour the p thereof ... Amos 1:10
shall devour the p of Bozrah ... Amos 1:12
and it shall devour the p thereof ... Amos 1:14
it shall devour the p of Kirioth ... Amos 2:2
shall devour the p of Jerusalem ... Amos 2:5
Publish in the p at Ashdod ... Amos 3:9

P

in the *p* in the land of Egypt, and ........ Amos 3:9
up violence and robbery in their *p* ..... Amos 3:10
thee, and thy *p* shall be spoiled.......... Amos 3:11
of Jacob, and hate his *p* ..................... Amos 6:8
and when he shall tread in our *p* ............ Mic 5:5

**PALAL** (*pa'-lal*) *A rebuilder of Jerusalem's wall.*
*P* the son of Uzai, over against ............. Neh 3:25

**PALE**
neither shall his face now wax *p* ............ Is 29:22
And I looked, and behold a *p* horse ....... Rev 6:8

**PALENESS**
and all faces are turned into *p* ................ Jer 30:6

**PALESTINA** (*pal-es-ti'-nah*) See PALESTINE, PHILISTIA. *The west coast of Canaan.*
take hold on the inhabitants of *P* ......... Ex 15:14
Rejoice not thou, whole *P* ........................ Is 14:29
thou, whole *P*, art dissolved .................... Is 14:31

**PALESTINE** (*pal'-es-tine*) See PALESTINA. *Same as Palestina.*
and Zidon, and all the coasts of *P* .......... Joel 3:4

**PALLU** (*pal'-lu*) See PALLUITES, PHALLU. *A son of Reuben.*
Hanoch, and *P*, Hezron, and Carmi ......... Ex 6:14
of *P*, the family of the Palluites ........... Num 26:5
And the sons of *P* .................................. Num 26:8
of Israel were, Hanoch, and *P* ................ 1Chr 5:3

**PALLUITES** (*pal'-lu-ites*) *Descendants of Pallu.*
of Pallu, the family of the *P* ................. Num 26:5

**PALM**
and threescore and ten *p* trees .............. Ex 15:27
pour it into the *p* of his own ................ Lev 14:15
into the *p* of his own left hand ............ Lev 14:26
goodly trees, branches of *p* trees ........... Lev 23:40
and threescore and ten *p* trees ............ Num 33:9
of Jericho, the city of *p* trees .............. Deut 34:3
of *p* trees with the children of ............... Judg 1:16
and possessed the city of *p* trees .......... Judg 3:13
she dwelt under the *p* tree of ................. Judg 4:5
*p* trees and open flowers, within .......... 1Kin 6:29
*p* trees and open flowers, and ............... 1Kin 6:32
cherubims, and upon the *p* trees ........... 1Kin 6:32
and *p* trees and open flowers ................ 1Kin 6:35
*p* trees, according to the ...................... 1Kin 7:36
fine gold, and set thereon *p* trees ......... 2Chr 3:5
to Jericho, the city of *p* trees ............. 2Chr 28:15
*p* branches, and branches of thick ........ Neh 8:15
shall flourish like the *p* tree ................... Ps 92:12
thy stature is like to a *p* tree ................. Song 7:7
said, I will go up to the *p* tree ................ Song 7:8
They are upright as the *p* tree ................. Jer 10:5
and upon each post were *p* trees .......... Eze 40:16
and their arches, and their *p* trees ....... Eze 40:22
and it had *p* trees, one on this ............... Eze 40:26
*p* trees were upon the posts .................. Eze 40:31
*p* trees were upon the posts .................. Eze 40:34
*p* trees were upon the posts .................. Eze 40:37
toward the *p* tree on the one side ........ Eze 41:19
the *p* tree on the other side .................. Eze 41:19
*p* trees made, and on the wall of .......... Eze 41:20
*p* trees, like as were made upon ........... Eze 41:25
*p* trees on the one side and on the ....... Eze 41:26
the *p* tree also, and the apple ................ Joel 1:12
Took branches of *p* trees, and went ....... Jn 12:13
Jesus with the *p* of his hand ................. Jn 18:22

**PALMERWORM**
That which the *p* hath left hath ............. Joel 1:4
and the caterpiller, and the *p* ............... Joel 2:25
increased, the *p* devoured them ........... Amos 4:9

**PALMS**
both the *p* of his hands were cut ............ 1Sa 5:4
the feet, and the *p* of her hands ........... 2Kin 9:35
thee upon the *p* of my hands ................... Is 49:16
knees and upon the *p* of my hands ..... Dan 10:10
him with the *p* of their hands ................ Mt 26:67
him with the *p* of their hands ............... Mk 14:65
white robes, and *p* in their hands ........... Rev 7:9

**PALSIES**
and many taken with *p*, and that ........... Acts 8:7

**PALSY**
lunatick, and those that had the *p* .......... Mt 4:24
lieth at home sick of the *p* ..................... Mt 8:6
to him a man sick of the *p* ...................... Mt 9:2
faith said unto the sick of the *p* .............. Mt 9:2
saith he to the sick of the *p* ................... Mt 9:6
him, bringing one sick of the *p* ............... Mk 2:3
bed wherein the sick of the *p* lay ............ Mk 2:4
he said unto the sick of the *p* ................. Mk 2:5
to say to the sick of the *p* ...................... Mk 2:9
(he saith to the sick of the *p* ................. Mk 2:10
a man which was taken with a *p* ............. Lk 5:18
(he said unto the sick of the *p* ............... Lk 5:24
eight years, and was sick of the *p* ........ Acts 9:33

**PALTI** (*pal'-ti*) *A spy sent to the Promised Land.*
of Benjamin, *P* the son of Raphu ......... Num 13:9

**PALTIEL** (*pal'-te-el*) See PHALTIEL. *A chief of Issachar.*
of Issachar, *P* the son of Azzan ............ Num 34:26

**PALTITE** (*pal'-tite*) See PELONITE. *A resident of Beth-palet.*
Helez the *P*, Ira the son of .................... 2Sa 23:26

**PAMPHYLIA** (*pam-fil'-e-ah*) *A province of Asia Minor.*
Phrygia, and *P*, in Egypt, and in .......... Acts 2:10
Paphos, they came to Perga in *P* ........ Acts 13:13
Pisidia, they came to *P* ....................... Acts 14:24
who departed from them from *P* ........ Acts 15:38
over the sea of Cilicia and *P* ................. Acts 27:5

**PAN**
be a meat offering baken in a *p* ............... Lev 2:5
offering baken in the frying *p* ................ Lev 2:7
In a *p* it shall be made with oil ............ Lev 6:21
in the fryingpan, and in the *p* ................. Lev 7:9
And he struck it into the *p* ..................... 1Sa 2:14
And she took a *p*, and poured them ...... 2Sa 13:9
for that which is baked in the *p* ......... 1Chr 23:29
take thou unto thee an iron *p* ................. Eze 4:3

**PANGS**
*p* and sorrows shall take hold of ............... Is 13:8
*p* have taken hold upon me, as the .......... Is 21:3
upon me, as the *p* of a woman that ......... Is 21:3
in pain, and crieth out in her *p* .............. Is 26:17
thou be when *p* come upon thee .......... Jer 22:23
as the heart of a woman in her *p* ......... Jer 48:41
as the heart of a woman in her *p* ......... Jer 49:22
*p* as of a woman in travail ..................... Jer 50:43
for *p* have taken thee as a woman ......... Mic 4:9

**PANNAG** (*pan'-nag*) *A place on the Damascus-Baalbeck road.*
thy market wheat of Minnith, and *P* ... Eze 27:17

**PANS**
thou shalt make his *p* to receive ............ Ex 27:3
it in a mortar, and baked it in *p* ........... Num 11:8
things that were made in the *p* ............ 1Chr 9:31
in pots, and in caldrons, and in *p* ...... 2Chr 35:13

**PANT**
That *p* after the dust of the .................. Amos 2:7

**PANTED**
I opened my mouth, and *p* ................. Ps 119:131
My heart *p*, fearfulness ........................... Is 21:4

**PANTETH**
My heart *p*, my strength faileth ............. Ps 38:10
As the hart *p* after the water .................. Ps 42:1
so *p* my soul after thee, O God ................ Ps 42:1

**PAPER**
The *p* reeds by the brooks, by the ............ Is 19:7
you, I would not write with *p* ................... 2Jn 12

**PAPHOS** (*pa'-fos*) *Capital of Cyprus.*
had gone through the isle unto *P* ......... Acts 13:6
Paul and his company loosed from *P*. Acts 13:13

**PAPS**
Egyptians for the *p* of thy youth .......... Eze 23:21
the *p* which thou hast sucked ................... Lk 11:27
the *p* which never gave suck .................. Lk 23:29
girt about the *p* with a golden ............... Rev 1:13

**PARABLE**
And he took up his *p*, and said, ........... Num 23:7
And he took up his *p*, and said, .......... Num 23:18
And he took up his *p*, and said, ........... Num 24:3
And he took up his *p*, and said, .......... Num 24:15
on Amalek, he took up his *p* ................ Num 24:20
on the Kenites, and took up his *p* ....... Num 24:21
And he took up his *p*, and said, .......... Num 24:23
Moreover Job continued his *p* ................ Job 27:1
Moreover Job continued his *p* ................ Job 29:1
I will incline mine ear to a *p* .................. Ps 49:4
I will open my mouth in a *p* .................... Ps 78:2
so is a *p* in the mouth of fools ............. Prov 26:7
so is a *p* in the mouth of fools ............. Prov 26:9
speak a *p* unto the house of .................. Eze 17:2
utter a *p* unto the rebellious ................. Eze 24:3
shall one take up a *p* against you .......... Mic 2:4
all these take up a *p* against him ........... Hab 2:6
ye therefore the *p* of the sower .............. Mt 13:18
Another *p* put he forth unto them, ....... Mt 13:24
Another *p* put he forth unto them, ....... Mt 13:31
Another *p* spake he unto them .............. Mt 13:33
without a *p* spake he not unto ............. Mt 13:34
Declare unto us the *p* of the ................. Mt 13:36
unto him, Declare unto us this *p* ........... Mt 15:15
Hear another *p* ...................................... Mt 21:33
Now learn a *p* of the fig tree ................ Mt 24:32
the twelve asked of him the *p* ................ Mk 4:10
unto them, Know ye not this *p* ............... Mk 4:13
But without a *p* spake he not unto ......... Mk 4:34
asked him concerning the *p* .................... Mk 7:17
he had spoken the *p* against them ....... Mk 12:12
Now learn a *p* of the fig tree ................ Mk 13:28
And he spake also a *p* unto them ............ Lk 5:36
And he spake a *p* unto them ................... Lk 6:39
of every city, he spake by a *p* .................. Lk 8:4
him, saying, What might this *p* be ............ Lk 8:9
Now the *p* is this ..................................... Lk 8:11
And he spake a *p* unto them ................. Lk 12:16
speakest thou this *p* unto us ................. Lk 12:41
He spake also this *p* ............................... Lk 13:6
he put forth a *p* to those which ............. Lk 14:7
And he spake this *p* unto them .............. Lk 15:3
he spake a *p* unto them to this ............... Lk 18:1
he spake this *p* unto certain .................. Lk 18:9
things, he added and spake a *p* ............ Lk 19:11
he to speak to the people this *p* ............ Lk 20:9
he had spoken this *p* against them ....... Lk 20:19
And he spake to them a *p* ..................... Lk 21:29
This *p* spake Jesus unto them .................. Jn 10:6

**PARABLES**
say of me, Doth he not speak *p* ............ Eze 20:49
spake many things unto them in *p* .......... Mt 13:3
Why speakest thou unto them in *p* ....... Mt 13:10
Therefore speak I to them in *p* ............... Mt 13:13
Jesus unto the multitude in *p* ................. Mt 13:34
saying, I will open my mouth in *p* ......... Mt 13:35
when Jesus had finished these *p* ............ Mt 13:53
and Pharisees had heard his *p* ............... Mt 21:45
and spake unto them again by *p* ............. Mt 22:1
unto him, and said unto them in *p* .......... Mk 3:23
he taught them many things by *p* ............ Mk 4:2
all these things are done in *p* .................. Mk 4:11
and how then will ye know all *p* .............. Mk 4:13
with many such *p* spake he the ............... Mk 4:33
he began to speak unto them by *p* .......... Mk 12:1
but to others in *p* ..................................... Lk 8:10

**PARADISE**
To day shalt thou be with me in *p* ........ Lk 23:43
How that he was caught up into *p* ...... 2Cor 12:4
is in the midst of the *p* of God ................ Rev 2:7

**PARAH** (*pa'-rah*) *A city in Benjamin.*
And Avim, and *P*, and Ophrah, ........... Josh 18:23

**PARAMOURS**
For she doted upon their *p* .................. Eze 23:20

**PARAN** (*pa'-ran*) *A wilderness south of Canaan.*
he dwelt in the wilderness of *P* ............ Gen 21:21
rested in the wilderness of *P* ............... Num 10:12
and pitched in the wilderness of *P* ....... Num 12:16
them from the wilderness of *P* ............... Num 13:3
Israel, unto the wilderness of *P* ............ Num 13:26
against the Red sea, between *P* .............. Deut 1:1
he shined forth from mount *P* ............... Deut 33:2
went down to the wilderness of *P* .......... 1Sa 25:1
arose out of Midian, and came to *P* ... 1Kin 11:18
they took men with them out of *P* ... 1Kin 11:18
and the Holy One from mount *P* ............. Hab 3:3

**PARBAR** (*par'-bar*) *A place near the Temple in Jerusalem.*
At *P* westward, four at the ................. 1Chr 26:18
four at the causeway, and two at *P* .. 1Chr 26:18

**PARCEL**
And he bought a *p* of a field ................ Gen 33:19
in a *p* of ground which Jacob ............... Josh 24:32
of Moab, selleth a *p* of land ..................... Ruth 4:3
where was a *p* of ground full of ......... 1Chr 11:13
themselves in the midst of that *p* ...... 1Chr 11:14
near to the *p* of ground that .................... Jn 4:5

**PARCHED**
nor *p* corn, nor green ears, until ........... Lev 23:14
*p* corn in the selfsame day ................... Josh 5:11
and he reached her *p* corn, and she ..... Ruth 2:14
brethren an ephah of this *p* corn .......... 1Sa 17:17
and five measures of *p* corn ................. 1Sa 25:18
*p* corn, and beans, and lentiles, and ...... 2Sa 17:28
beans, and lentiles, and *p* pulse, .......... 2Sa 17:28
the *p* ground shall become a pool, ............ Is 35:7
but shall inhabit the *p* places in .............. Jer 17:6

**PARCHMENTS**
the books, but especially the *p* ............... 2Ti 4:13

**PARDON**
for he will not *p* your ............................ Ex 23:21
*p* our iniquity and our sin, and ................. Ex 34:9
*P*, I beseech thee, the iniquity ........... Num 14:19
*p* my sin, and turn again with me, ........ 1Sa 15:25
this thing the LORD *p* thy servant ....... 2Kin 5:18
the LORD *p* thy servant in this ............ 2Kin 5:18
which the LORD would not *p* ............... 2Kin 24:4
saying, The good LORD *p* every one .. 2Chr 30:18
but thou art a God ready to *p* ............... Neh 9:17
dost thou not *p* my transgression ........... Job 7:21
sake, O LORD, *p* mine iniquity ............... Ps 25:11
our God, for he will abundantly *p* ............ Is 55:7
and I will *p* it ............................................ Jer 5:1
How shall I *p* thee for this ....................... Jer 5:7
I will *p* all their iniquities, ................... Jer 33:8
for I will *p* them whom I reserve .......... Jer 50:20

**PARDONED**
I have *p* according to thy word ......... Num 14:20
that her iniquity is *p* ................................ Is 40:2
thou hast not *p* ........................................ Lam 3:42

**PARDONETH**
that *p* iniquity, and passeth by .............. Mic 7:18

**PARE**
shave her head, and *p* her nails ......... Deut 21:12

**PARENTS**
shall rise up against their *p* ................... Mt 10:21
shall rise up against their *p* ................. Mk 13:12
when the *p* brought in the child .............. Lk 2:27
Now his *p* went to Jerusalem every ........ Lk 2:41
And her *p* were astonished ..................... Lk 8:56
no man that hath left house, or *p* .......... Lk 18:29
And ye shall be betrayed both by *p* ....... Lk 21:16
who did sin, this man, or his *p* .................. Jn 9:2
hath this man sinned, nor his *p* ................. Jn 9:3
until they called the *p* of him ................. Jn 9:18
His *p* answered them and said, We .......... Jn 9:20
These words spake his *p*, because .......... Jn 9:22
Therefore said his *p*, He is of .................. Jn 9:23
of evil things, disobedient to *p* ............... Rom 1:30
ought not to lay up for the *p* ................. 2Cor 12:14
but the *p* for the children ...................... 2Cor 12:14

Children, obey your *p* in the Lord .......... Eph 6:1
obey your *p* in all things .......... Col 3:20
at home, and to requite their *p* .......... 1Ti 5:4
blasphemers, disobedient to *p* .......... 2Ti 3:2
was hid three months of his *p* .......... Heb 11:23

**PARLOUR**
and he was sitting in a summer *p* .......... Judg 3:20
shut the doors of the *p* upon him .......... Judg 3:23
the doors of the *p* were locked .......... Judg 3:24
he opened not the doors of the *p* .......... Judg 3:25
and brought them into the *p* .......... 1Sa 9:22

**PARLOURS**
and of the inner *p* thereof .......... 1Chr 28:11

**PARMASHTA** (*par-mash'-tah*) *A son of Haman.*
And *P*, and Arisai, and Aridai, and .......... Est 9:9

**PARMENAS** (*par'-me-nas*) *A leader in the Jerusalem church.*
and Nicanor, and Timon, and *P* .......... Acts 6:5

**PARNACH** (*par'-nak*) *A Zebulunite who apportioned the Promised Land.*
Zebulun, Elizaphan the son of *P* .......... Num 34:25

**PAROSH** (*pa'-rosh*) See PHAROSH.
*1. A family of exiles.*
The children of *P*, two thousand .......... Ezr 2:3
The children of *P*, two thousand .......... Neh 7:8
*2. Married a foreigner in exile.*
of the sons of *P* .......... Ezr 10:25
*3. Father of Pedaiah.*
After him Pedaiah the son of *P* .......... Neh 3:25
*4. A family who renewed the covenant.*
*P*, Pahath-moab, Elam, Zatthu, .......... Neh 10:14

**PARSHANDATHA** (*par-shan'-da-thah*) *A son of Haman.*
And *P*, and Dalphon, and Aspatha, .......... Est 9:7

**PART** See PREFACE.

**PARTAKER**
hast been *p* with adulterers .......... Ps 50:18
in hope should be *p* of his hope .......... 1Cor 9:10
that I might be *p* thereof with .......... 1Cor 9:23
For if I by grace be a *p*, why am .......... 1Cor 10:30
neither be *p* of other men's sins .......... 1Ti 5:22
but be thou *p* of the afflictions .......... 2Ti 1:8
must be first *p* of the fruits .......... 2Ti 2:6
also a *p* of the glory that shall .......... 1Pet 5:1
God speed is *p* of his evil deeds .......... 2Jn 11

**PARTAKERS**
we would not have been *p* with .......... Mt 23:30
made *p* of their spiritual things .......... Rom 15:27
If others be *p* of this power over .......... 1Cor 9:12
at the altar are *p* with the altar .......... 1Cor 9:13
for we are all *p* of that one .......... 1Cor 10:17
of the sacrifices *p* of the altar .......... 1Cor 10:18
ye cannot be *p* of the Lord's .......... 1Cor 10:21
knowing, that as ye are *p* of the .......... 2Cor 1:7
*p* of his promise in Christ by the .......... Eph 3:6
Be not ye therefore *p* with them .......... Eph 5:7
gospel, ye all are *p* of my grace .......... Phil 1:7
to be *p* of the inheritance of the .......... Col 1:12
and beloved, *p* of the benefit .......... 1Ti 6:2
as the children are *p* of flesh .......... Heb 2:14
*p* of the heavenly calling, .......... Heb 3:1
For we are made *p* of Christ .......... Heb 3:14
were made *p* of the Holy Ghost, .......... Heb 6:4
chastisement, whereof all are *p* .......... Heb 12:8
we might be *p* of his holiness .......... Heb 12:10
inasmuch as ye are *p* of Christ's .......... 1Pet 4:13
might be *p* of the divine nature .......... 2Pet 1:4
that ye be not *p* of her sins .......... Rev 18:4

**PARTAKEST**
with them *p* of the root and .......... Rom 11:17

**PARTED**
and from thence it was *p*, and .......... Gen 2:10
of fire, and *p* them both asunder .......... 2Kin 2:11
waters, they *p* hither and thither .......... 2Kin 2:14
By what way is the light *p* .......... Job 38:24
among the nations, and *p* my land .......... Joel 3:2
*p* his garments, casting lots .......... Mt 27:35
They *p* my garments among .......... Mt 27:35
they *p* his garments, casting lots .......... Mk 15:24
they *p* his raiment, and cast lots .......... Lk 23:34
he was *p* from them, and carried up .......... Lk 24:51
They *p* my raiment among them, and ... Jn 19:24
*p* them to all men, as every man .......... Acts 2:45

**PARTETH**
Whatsoever *p* the hoof, and is .......... Lev 11:3
And every beast that *p* the hoof .......... Deut 14:6
to cease, and *p* between the mighty .. Prov 18:18

**PARTHIANS** (*par-the'-uns*) *Inhabitants of Parthia, now Iran.*
*P*, and Medes, and Elamites, and the ..... Acts 2:9

**PARTIAL**
ways, but have been *p* in the law .......... Mal 2:9
Are ye not then *p* in yourselves .......... Jas 2:4

**PARTIALITY**
another, doing nothing by *p* .......... 1Ti 5:21
mercy and good fruits, without *p* .......... Jas 3:17

**PARTICULAR**
body of Christ, and members in *p* .......... 1Cor 12:27
let every one of you in *p* so love .......... Eph 5:33

**PARTICULARLY**
he declared *p* what things God had ... Acts 21:19
of which we cannot now speak *p* .......... Heb 9:5

**PARTIES**
the cause of both *p* shall come .......... Ex 22:9

**PARTING**
Babylon stood at the *p* of the way .......... Eze 21:21

**PARTITION**
he made a *p* by the chains of gold .......... 1Kin 6:21
the middle wall of *p* between us .......... Eph 2:14

**PARTLY**
be *p* strong, and *p* broken .......... Dan 2:42
and I *p* believe it .......... 1Cor 11:18
*P*, whilst ye were made a .......... Heb 10:33
and *p*, whilst ye became companions . Heb 10:33

**PARTNER**
Whoso is *p* with a thief hateth .......... Prov 29:24
do enquire of Titus, he is my *p* .......... 2Cor 8:23
If thou count me therefore a *p* .......... Philem 17

**PARTNERS**
And they beckoned unto their *p* .......... Lk 5:7
Zebedee, which were *p* with Simon .......... Lk 5:10

**PARTRIDGE**
doth hunt a *p* in the mountains .......... 1Sa 26:20
As the *p* sitteth on eggs, and .......... Jer 17:11

**PARTS** See PREFACE.

**PARUAH** (*par'-u-ah*) *Father of Jehoshaphat.*
Jehoshaphat the son of *P*, in .......... 1Kin 4:17

**PARVAIM** (*par-va'-im*) *A place rich in gold.*
and the gold was gold of *P* .......... 2Chr 3:6

**PARZITES** See PHARZITES.

**PASACH** (*pa'-sak*) *A son of Japhet.*
*P*, and Bimhal, and Ashvath .......... 1Chr 7:33

**PAS-DAMMIM** (*pas-dam'-mim*) *A place in Judah.*
He was with David at *P*, and there .... 1Chr 11:13

**PASEAH** (*pa-se'-ah*) See PHASEAH.
*1. A son of Eshton.*
And Eshton begat Beth-rapha, and *P* .. 1Chr 4:12
*2. A family of exiles.*
of Uzza, the children of *P* .......... Ezr 2:49
*3. Father of Jehoiada.*
repaired Jehoiada the son of *P* .......... Neh 3:6

**PASHUR** (*pash'-ur*)
*1. Head of a priestly family.*
the son of Jeroham, the son of *P* .......... 1Chr 9:12
The children of *P*, a thousand two .......... Ezr 2:38
And of the sons of *P* .......... Ezr 10:22
The children of *P*, a thousand two .......... Neh 7:41
son of Zechariah, the son of *P* .......... Neh 11:12
*2. A priest who renewed the covenant.*
*P*, Amariah, Malchijah, .......... Neh 10:3
*3. A son of Immer.*
Now *P* the son of Immer the priest .......... Jer 20:1
Then *P* smote Jeremiah the prophet .......... Jer 20:2
that *P* brought forth Jeremiah out .......... Jer 20:3
LORD hath not called thy name *P* .......... Jer 20:3
And thou, *P*, and all that dwell in .......... Jer 20:6
Mattan, and Gedaliah the son of *P* .......... Jer 38:1
*4. A son of Melchiah/Malchiah.*
unto him *P* the son of Melchiah .......... Jer 21:1
*P* the son of Malchiah, heard the .......... Jer 38:1

**PASS** See PREFACE.

**PASSAGE**
give Israel *p* through his border .......... Num 20:21
at the *p* of the children of .......... Josh 22:11
went out to the *p* of Michmash .......... 1Sa 13:23
They are gone over the *p* .......... Is 10:29

**PASSAGES**
took the *p* of Jordan before the .......... Judg 12:5
and slew him at the *p* of Jordan .......... Judg 12:6
And between the *p*, by which .......... 1Sa 14:4
in Bashan, and cry from the *p* .......... Jer 22:20
that the *p* are stopped, and the .......... Jer 51:32

**PASSED**
Abram *p* through the land unto the ..... Gen 12:6
a burning lamp that *p* between .......... Gen 15:17
*p* over the river, and set his face .......... Gen 31:21
my staff I *p* over this Jordan .......... Gen 32:10
sons, and *p* over the ford Jabbok .......... Gen 32:22
as he *p* over Penuel the sun rose .......... Gen 32:31
he *p* over before them, and bowed .......... Gen 33:3
Then there *p* by Midianites .......... Gen 37:28
who *p* over the houses of the .......... Ex 12:27
the LORD *p* by before him, and .......... Ex 34:6
which we *p* through to search it, .......... Num 14:7
left, until we have *p* thy borders .......... Num 20:17
*p* through the midst of the sea .......... Num 33:8
When ye are *p* over Jordan into .......... Num 33:51
when we *p* by from our brethren .......... Deut 2:8
*p* by the way of the wilderness of .......... Deut 2:8
of this law, when thou art *p* over .......... Deut 27:3
through the nations which ye *p* by ... Deut 29:16
*p* over, and came to Joshua the son .......... Josh 2:23
lodged there before they *p* over .......... Josh 3:1
for ye have not *p* this way .......... Josh 3:4
the people *p* over right against .......... Josh 3:16
Israelites *p* over on dry ground .......... Josh 3:17
people were *p* clean over Jordan .......... Josh 3:17
people were clean *p* over Jordan .......... Josh 4:1
when it *p* over Jordan, the waters .......... Josh 4:7
and the people hasted and *p* over .......... Josh 4:10
all the people were clean *p* over .......... Josh 4:11
that the ark of the LORD *p* over .......... Josh 4:11
*p* over armed before the children .......... Josh 4:12
war *p* over before the LORD unto .......... Josh 4:13
before you, until ye were *p* over .......... Josh 4:23
of Israel, until we were *p* over .......... Josh 5:1
rams' horns *p* on before the LORD .......... Josh 6:8
Then Joshua *p* from Makkedah, and . Josh 10:29
Joshua *p* from Libnah, and all .......... Josh 10:31
from Lachish Joshua *p* unto Eglon .... Josh 10:34
*p* along to Zin, and ascended up on .... Josh 15:3
*p* along to Hezron, and went up to ...... Josh 15:3
From thence it *p* toward Azmon .......... Josh 15:4
and *p* along by the north of .......... Josh 15:6
the border *p* toward the waters of .......... Josh 15:7
*p* along unto the side of mount .......... Josh 15:10
Beth-shemesh, and *p* on to Timnah .. Josh 15:10
*p* along to mount Baalah, and went ... Josh 15:11
*p* by it on the east to Janohah .......... Josh 16:6
*p* through the land, and described .......... Josh 18:9
*p* along toward the side over .......... Josh 18:18
the border *p* along to the side of .......... Josh 18:19
all the people through whom we *p* .......... Josh 24:17
*p* beyond the quarries, and escaped ..... Judg 3:26
*p* over, he, and the three hundred .......... Judg 8:4
Ammon *p* over Jordan to fight also ..... Judg 10:9
he *p* over Gilead, and Manasseh, and Judg 11:29
*p* over Mizpeh of Gilead, and from ... Judg 11:29
from Mizpeh of Gilead he *p* over ....... Judg 11:29
So Jephthah *p* over unto the .......... Judg 11:32
*p* over against the children of .......... Judg 12:3
they *p* thence unto mount Ephraim, . Judg 18:13
And they *p* on and went their way .... Judg 19:14
he *p* through mount Ephraim, and .......... 1Sa 9:4
*p* through the land of Shalisha, .......... 1Sa 9:4
then they *p* through the land of .......... 1Sa 9:4
he *p* through the land of the .......... 1Sa 9:4
pass on before us, (and he *p* on .......... 1Sa 9:27
the battle *p* over unto Beth-aven .......... 1Sa 14:23
*p* on, and gone down to Gilgal .......... 1Sa 15:12
he *p* over with the six hundred .......... 1Sa 27:2
the Philistines *p* on by hundreds .......... 1Sa 29:2
his men *p* on in the rereward with .......... 1Sa 29:2
*p* over Jordan, and went through .......... 2Sa 2:29
*p* over Jordan, and came to Helam ...... 2Sa 10:17
all his servants *p* on beside him .......... 2Sa 15:18
from Gath, *p* on before the king .......... 2Sa 15:18
And Ittai the Gittite *p* over .......... 2Sa 15:22
voice, and all the people *p* over .......... 2Sa 15:23
himself *p* over the brook Kidron .......... 2Sa 15:23
and all the people *p* over .......... 2Sa 15:23
with him, and they *p* over Jordan .......... 2Sa 17:22
Absalom *p* over Jordan, he and all .......... 2Sa 17:24
they *p* over Jordan, and pitched in .......... 2Sa 24:5
And, behold, men *p* by, and saw the . 1Kin 13:25
And, behold, the LORD *p* by .......... 1Kin 19:11
and Elijah *p* by him, and cast his ...... 1Kin 19:19
And as the king *p* by, he cried .......... 1Kin 20:39
on a day, that Elisha *p* to Shunem .......... 2Kin 4:8
so it was, that as oft as he *p* by .......... 2Kin 4:8
Gehazi *p* on before them, and laid .......... 2Kin 4:31
he *p* by upon the wall, and the .......... 2Kin 6:30
there *p* by a wild beast that was .......... 2Kin 14:9
*p* over Jordan, and came upon them, 1Chr 19:17
king Solomon *p* all the kings of .......... 2Chr 9:22
there *p* by a wild beast that was .......... 2Chr 25:18
So the posts *p* from city to city .......... 2Chr 30:10
Then a spirit *p* before my face .......... Job 4:15
They are *p* away as the swift .......... Job 9:26
and no stranger *p* among them .......... Job 15:19
it, nor the fierce lion *p* by it .......... Job 28:8
was before him his thick clouds *p* .......... Ps 18:12
Yet he *p* away, and, lo, he was not .......... Ps 37:36
assembled, they *p* by together .......... Ps 48:4
our days are *p* away in thy wrath .......... Ps 90:9
but a little that I *p* from them .......... Song 3:4
come to Aiath, he is *p* to Migron .......... Is 10:28
my judgment is *p* over from my God ..... Is 40:27
He pursued them, and *p* safely .......... Is 41:3
a land that no man *p* through .......... Jer 2:6
and the holy flesh is *p* from thee .......... Jer 11:15
*p* between the parts thereof, .......... Jer 34:18
which *p* between the parts of the .......... Jer 34:19
he hath *p* the time appointed .......... Jer 46:17
when I *p* by thee, and saw thee .......... Eze 16:6
Now when I *p* by thee, and looked .......... Eze 16:8
on every one that *p* by .......... Eze 16:15
thy feet to every one that *p* by .......... Eze 16:25
in the sight of all that *p* by .......... Eze 36:34
a river that could not be *p* over .......... Eze 47:5
the smell of fire had *p* on them .......... Dan 3:27
palace, and *p* the night fasting .......... Dan 6:18
but I *p* over upon her fair neck .......... Hos 10:11
billows and thy waves *p* over me .......... Jonah 2:3
have *p* through the gate, and are .......... Mic 2:13
not thy wickedness *p* continually .......... Nah 3:19
the overflowing of the water *p* by .......... Hab 3:10
that no man *p* through nor .......... Zec 7:14
*p* over, and came into his own city .......... Mt 9:1
as Jesus *p* forth from thence, he .......... Mt 9:9
when they heard that Jesus *p* by .......... Mt 20:30
they that *p* by reviled him, .......... Mt 27:39
And as he *p* by, he saw Levi the .......... Mk 2:14
when Jesus was *p* over again by .......... Mk 5:21
place, and now the time is far *p* .......... Mk 6:35
the sea, and would have *p* by them .......... Mk 6:48
And when they had *p* over, they .......... Mk 6:53
thence, and *p* through Galilee .......... Mk 9:30

P

And in the morning, as they *p* by Mk 11:20
one Simon a Cyrenian, who *p* by Mk 15:21
they that *p* by railed on him, Mk 15:29
he *p* by on the other side Lk 10:31
on him, and *p* by on the other side Lk 10:32
that he *p* through the midst of Lk 17:11
entered and *p* through Jericho Lk 19:1
but is *p* from death unto life Jn 5:24
the midst of them, and so *p* by Jn 8:59
And as Jesus *p* by, he saw a man Jn 9:1
as Peter *p* throughout all Acts 9:32
out, and *p* on through one street Acts 12:10
after they had *p* throughout Acts 14:24
they *p* through Phenice and Samaria Acts 15:3
Now when they had *p* through Acts 17:1
For as I *p* by, and beheld your Acts 17:23
Paul having *p* through the upper Acts 19:1
when he had *p* through Macedonia Acts 19:21
so death *p* upon all men, for that Rom 5:12
cloud, and all *p* through the sea 1Cor 10:1
old things are *p* away 2Cor 5:17
that is *p* into the heavens, Jesus Heb 4:14
By faith they *p* through the Red Heb 11:29
we have *p* from death unto life 1Jn 3:14
and the first earth were *p* away Rev 21:1
for the former things are *p* away Rev 21:4

**PASSEDST**
Wherefore *p* thou over to fight Judg 12:1

**PASSENGERS**
To call *p* who go right on their Prov 9:15
the valley of the *p* on the east Eze 39:11
it shall stop the noses of the *p* Eze 39:11
the land to bury with the *p* those Eze 39:14
the *p* that pass through the land, Eze 39:15

**PASSEST**
all the kingdoms whither thou *p* Deut 3:21
whither thou *p* over Jordan to go Deut 30:18
If thou *p* on with me, then thou 2Sa 15:33
*p* over the brook Kidron, thou 1Kin 2:37
When thou *p* through the waters, I Is 43:2

**PASSETH**
every one that *p* among them that Ex 30:13
Every one that *p* among them that Ex 30:14
come to pass, while my glory *p* by Ex 33:22
of whatsoever *p* under the rod Lev 27:32
*p* over before you into Jordan Josh 3:11
*p* along unto the borders of Archi Josh 16:2
from thence *p* on along on the Josh 19:13
every one that *p* by it shall be 1Kin 9:8
which *p* by us continually 2Kin 4:9
of every one that *p* the account 2Kin 12:4
to every one that *p* by it 2Chr 7:21
he *p* on also, but I perceive him Job 9:11
for ever against him, and he *p* Job 14:20
my welfare *p* away as a cloud Job 30:15
but the wind *p*, and cleanseth them Job 37:21
whatsoever *p* through the paths of Ps 8:8
a wind that *p* away, and cometh not Ps 78:39
For the wind *p* over it, and it is Ps 103:16
days are as a shadow that *p* away Ps 144:4
As the whirlwind *p*, so is the Prov 10:25
He that *p* by, and meddleth with Prov 26:17
One generation *p* away, and another Eccl 1:4
shall be as chaff that *p* away Is 29:5
a wilderness, that none *p* through Jer 9:12
that *p* away by the wind of the Jer 13:24
every one that *p* thereby shall be Jer 18:16
every one that *p* thereby shall be Jer 19:8
and cut off from it him that *p* out Eze 35:7
and as the early dew that *p* away Hos 13:3
*p* by the transgression of the Mic 7:18
every one that *p* by her shall Zeph 2:15
streets waste, that none *p* by Zeph 3:6
army, because of him that *p* by Zec 9:8
him, that Jesus of Nazareth *p* by Lk 18:37
the fashion of this world *p* away 1Cor 7:31
which *p* knowledge, that ye might Eph 3:19
which *p* all understanding, shall Phil 4:7
And the world *p* away, and the lust 1Jn 2:17

**PASSING**
We are *p* from Beth-lehem-judah Judg 19:18
wonderful, *p* the love of women 2Sa 1:26
people had done *p* out of the city 2Sa 15:24
of Israel was *p* by upon the wall 2Kin 6:26
Who *p* through the valley of Baca Ps 84:6
*P* through the street near her Prov 7:8
*p* over he will preserve it Is 31:5
*p* through the land to bury with Eze 39:14
But he *p* through the midst of Lk 4:30
*p* by might overshadow some of Acts 5:15
*p* through he preached in all the Acts 8:40
they *p* by Mysia came down to Acts 16:8
And, hardly *p* it, came unto a Acts 27:8

**PASSION**
his *p* by many infallible proofs Acts 1:3

**PASSIONS**
also are men of like *p* with you Acts 14:15
a man subject to like *p* as we are Jas 5:17

**PASSOVER**
it is the LORD's *p* Ex 12:11
to your families, and kill the *p* Ex 12:21
is the sacrifice of the LORD's *p* Ex 12:27
This is the ordinance of the *p* Ex 12:43
and will keep the *p* to the LORD Ex 12:48
of the *p* be left unto the morning Ex 34:25
month at even is the LORD's *p* Lev 23:5
the *p* at his appointed season Num 9:2
that they should keep the *p* Num 9:4
they kept the *p* on the fourteenth Num 9:5
could not keep the *p* on that day Num 9:6
he shall keep the *p* unto the LORD Num 9:10
of the *p* they shall keep it Num 9:12
and forbeareth to keep the *p* Num 9:13
and will keep the *p* unto the LORD Num 9:14
to the ordinance of the *p* Num 9:14
first month is the *p* of the LORD Num 28:16
on the morrow after the *p* the Num 33:3
keep the *p* unto the LORD thy God Deut 16:1
the *p* unto the LORD thy God Deut 16:2
the *p* within any of thy gates Deut 16:5
shalt sacrifice the *p* at even Deut 16:6
kept the *p* on the fourteenth day Josh 5:10
land on the morrow after the *p* Josh 5:11
Keep the *p* unto the LORD your God 2Kin 23:21
a *p* from the days of the judges 2Kin 23:22
wherein this *p* was holden to the 2Kin 23:23
to keep the *p* unto the LORD God 2Chr 30:1
to keep the *p* in the second month 2Chr 30:2
they should come to keep the *p* 2Chr 30:5
Then they killed the *p* on the 2Chr 30:15
yet did they eat the *p* otherwise 2Chr 30:18
Moreover Josiah kept a *p* unto the 2Chr 35:1
and they killed the *p* on the 2Chr 35:1
So kill the *p*, and sanctify 2Chr 35:6
and kids, all for the *p* offerings 2Chr 35:7
for the *p* offerings two thousand 2Chr 35:8
gave unto the Levites for *p* 2Chr 35:9
And they killed the *p*, and the 2Chr 35:11
they roasted the *p* with fire 2Chr 35:13
the same day, to keep the *p* 2Chr 35:16
present kept the *p* at that time 2Chr 35:17
there was no *p* like to that kept 2Chr 35:18
keep such a *p* as Josiah kept 2Chr 35:18
reign of Josiah was this *p* kept 2Chr 35:19
of the captivity kept the *p* upon Ezr 6:19
killed the *p* for all the children Ezr 6:20
of the month, ye shall have the *p* Eze 45:21
two days is the feast of the *p* Mt 26:2
we prepare for thee to eat the *p* Mt 26:17
I will keep the *p* at thy house Mt 26:18
and they made ready the *p* Mt 26:19
two days was the feast of the *p* Mk 14:1
bread, when they killed the *p* Mk 14:12
that thou mayest eat the *p* Mk 14:12
shall eat the *p* with my disciples Mk 14:14
and they made ready the *p* Mk 14:16
every year at the feast of the *p* Lk 2:41
drew nigh, which is called the *P* Lk 22:1
when the *p* must be killed Lk 22:7
saying, Go and prepare us the *p* Lk 22:8
shall eat the *p* with my disciples Lk 22:11
and they made ready the *p* Lk 22:13
this *p* with you before I suffer Lk 22:15
the Jews' *p* was at hand, and Jesus Jn 2:13
when he was in Jerusalem at the *p* Jn 2:23
And the *p*, a feast of the Jews, Jn 6:4
the Jews' *p* was nigh at hand Jn 11:55
up to Jerusalem before the *p* Jn 11:55
days before the *p* came to Bethany Jn 12:1
Now before the feast of the *p* Jn 13:1
but that they might eat the *p* Jn 18:28
release unto you one at the *p* Jn 18:39
it was the preparation of the *p* Jn 19:14
For even Christ our *p* is 1Cor 5:7
Through faith he kept the *p* Heb 11:28

**PASSOVERS**
the *p* for every one that was not 2Chr 30:17

**PAST**
the days of his mourning were *p* Gen 50:4
to push with his horn in time *p* Ex 21:29
ox hath used to push in time *p* Ex 21:36
way, until we be *p* thy borders Num 21:22
Emims dwelt therein in times *p* Deut 2:10
ask now of the days that are *p* Deut 4:32
and hated him not in times *p* Deut 4:42
whom he hated not in time *p* Deut 19:4
as he hated him not in time *p* Deut 19:6
the bitterness of death is *p* 1Sa 15:32
in his presence, as in times *p* 1Sa 19:7
in times *p* to be king over you 2Sa 3:17
Also in time *p*, when Saul was 2Sa 5:2
And when the mourning was *p* 2Sa 11:27
a little *p* the top of the hill 2Sa 16:1
came to pass, when midday was *p* 1Kin 18:29
was the ruler over them in time *p* 1Chr 9:20
And moreover in time *p*, even when 1Chr 11:2
doeth great things *p* finding out Job 9:10
me secret, until thy wrath be *p* Job 14:13
My days are *p*, my purposes are Job 17:11
Oh that I were as in months *p* Job 29:2
are but as yesterday when it is *p* Ps 90:4
and God requireth that which is *p* Eccl 3:15
For, lo, the winter is *p*, the Song 2:11
The harvest is *p*, the summer is Jer 8:20
place, and the time is now *p* Mt 14:15
And when the sabbath was *p* Mk 16:1
And when the voice was *p*, Jesus Lk 9:36
When they were *p* the first Acts 12:10
Who in times *p* suffered all Acts 14:16
the fast was now already *p* Acts 27:9
the remission of sins that are *p* Rom 3:25
For as ye in times *p* have not Rom 11:30
and his ways *p* finding out Rom 11:33
in time *p* in the Jews' religion Gal 1:13
*p* now preacheth the faith which Gal 1:23
as I have also told you in time *p* Gal 5:21
Wherein in time *p* ye walked Eph 2:2
times *p* in the lusts of our flesh Eph 2:3
in time *p* Gentiles in the flesh Eph 2:11
Who being *p* feeling have given Eph 4:19
the resurrection is *p* already 2Ti 2:18
Which in time *p* was to thee Philem 11
in time *p* unto the fathers by the Heb 1:1
of a child when she was *p* age Heb 11:11
Which in time *p* were not a people 1Pet 2:10
For the time *p* of our life may 1Pet 4:3
because the darkness is *p* 1Jn 2:8
One woe is *p* Rev 9:12
The second woe is *p* Rev 11:14

**PASTOR**
from being a *p* to follow thee Jer 17:16

**PASTORS**
the *p* also transgressed against Jer 2:8
I will give you *p* according to Jer 3:15
For the *p* are become brutish, and Jer 10:21
Many *p* have destroyed my vineyard Jer 12:10
The wind shall eat up all thy *p* Jer 22:22
Woe be unto the *p* that destroy Jer 23:1
against the *p* that feed my people Jer 23:2
and some, *p* and teachers Eph 4:11

**PASTURE**
have no *p* for their flocks Gen 47:4
to seek *p* for their flocks 1Chr 4:39
And they found fat *p* and good, and 1Chr 4:40
because there was *p* there for 1Chr 4:41
range of the mountains is his *p* Job 39:8
smoke against the sheep of thy *p* Ps 74:1
sheep of thy *p* will give thee Ps 79:13
and we are the people of his *p* Ps 95:7
his people, and the sheep of his *p* Ps 100:3
joy of wild asses, a *p* of flocks Is 32:14
and scatter the sheep of my *p* Jer 23:1
for the LORD hath spoiled their *p* Jer 25:36
become like harts that find no *p* Lam 1:6
I will feed them in a good *p* Eze 34:14
in a fat *p* shall they feed upon Eze 34:14
you to have eaten up the good *p* Eze 34:18
And ye my flock, the flock of my *p* Eze 34:31
According to their *p*, so were Hos 13:6
perplexed, because they have no *p* Joel 1:18
and shall go in and out, and find *p* Jn 10:9

**PASTURES**
oxen, and twenty oxen out of the *p* 1Kin 4:23
maketh me to lie down in green *p* Ps 23:2
drop upon the *p* of the wilderness Ps 65:12
The *p* are clothed with flocks Ps 65:13
shall thy cattle feed in large *p* Is 30:23
their *p* shall be in all high Is 49:9
your feet the residue of your *p* Eze 34:18
out of the fat *p* of Israel Eze 45:15
devoured the *p* of the wilderness Joel 1:19
devoured the *p* of the wilderness Joel 1:20
for the *p* of the wilderness do Joel 2:22

**PATARA** (*pat'-a-rah*) *A city in Lycia in Asia Minor.*
Rhodes, and from thence unto *P* Acts 21:1

**PATE**
shall come down upon his own *p* Ps 7:16

**PATH**
by the way, an adder in the *p* Gen 49:17
stood in a *p* of the vineyards Num 22:24
There is a *p* which no fowl Job 28:7
They mar my *p*, they set forward Job 30:13
He maketh a *p* to shine after him Job 41:32
Thou wilt shew me the *p* of life Ps 16:11
O LORD, and lead me in a plain *p* Ps 27:11
thy *p* in the great waters, and thy Ps 77:19
go in the *p* of thy commandments Ps 119:35
my feet, and a light unto my *p* Ps 119:105
Thou compassest my *p* and my lying Ps 139:3
within me, then thou knewest my *p* Ps 142:3
refrain thy foot from their *p* Prov 1:15
yea, every good *p* Prov 2:9
not into the *p* of the wicked Prov 4:14
But the *p* of the just is as the Prov 4:18
Ponder the *p* of thy feet, and let Prov 4:26
shouldest ponder the *p* of life Prov 5:6
dost weigh the *p* of the just Is 26:7
the way, turn aside out of the *p* Is 30:11
taught him in the *p* of judgment Is 40:14
sea, and a *p* in the mighty waters Is 43:16
shall walk every one in his *p* Joel 2:8

**PATHROS** (*path'-ros*) See PATHRUSIM. *A name for Upper Egypt.*
Assyria, and from Egypt, and from *P* Is 11:11
at Noph, and in the country of *P* Jer 44:1
dwell in the land of Egypt, in *P* Jer 44:15
them to return into the land of *P* Eze 29:14
And I will make *P* desolate Eze 30:14

**PATHRUS** See PATHROS.

**PATHRUSIM** (*path-ru'-sim*) *A descendant of Mizraim.*
And *P*, and Casluhim, (out of whom Gen 10:14
*P*, and Casluhim, (of whom 1Chr 1:12

**PATHS**
The *p* of their way are turned Job 6:18
So are the *p* of all that forget Job 8:13
and lookest narrowly unto all my *p* Job 13:27
and he hath set darkness in my *p* Job 19:8

nor abide in the p thereof ... Job 24:13
the stocks, he marketh all my p ... Job 33:11
know the p to the house thereof ... Job 38:20
passeth through the p of the seas ... Ps 8:8
me from the p of the destroyer ... Ps 17:4
Hold up my goings in thy p ... Ps 17:5
he leadeth me in the p of ... Ps 23:3
teach me thy p ... Ps 25:4
All the p of the LORD are mercy ... Ps 25:10
and thy p drop fatness ... Ps 65:11
He keepeth the p of judgment ... Prov 2:8
Who leave the p of uprightness, ... Prov 2:13
and they froward in their p ... Prov 2:15
death, and her p unto the dead ... Prov 2:18
take they hold of the p of life ... Prov 2:19
keep the p of the righteous ... Prov 2:20
him, and he shall direct thy p ... Prov 3:6
and all her p are peace ... Prov 3:17
I have led thee in right p ... Prov 4:11
her ways, go not astray in her p ... Prov 7:25
by the way in the places of the p ... Prov 8:2
in the midst of the p of judgment ... Prov 8:20
ways, and we will walk in his p ... Is 2:3
err, and destroy the way of thy p ... Is 3:12
I will lead them in p that they ... Is 42:16
The restorer of p to dwell in ... Is 58:12
and destruction are in their p ... Is 59:7
they have made them crooked p ... Is 59:8
and see, and ask for the old p ... Jer 6:16
in their ways from the ancient p ... Jer 18:15
the ancient p, to walk in p ... Jer 18:15
stone, he hath made my p crooked ... Lam 3:9
that she shall not find her p ... Hos 2:6
ways, and we will walk in his p ... Mic 4:2
of the Lord, make his p straight ... Mt 3:3
of the Lord, make his p straight ... Mk 1:3
of the Lord, make his p straight ... Lk 3:4
And make straight p for your feet ... Heb 12:13

**PATHWAY**
in the p thereof there is no ... Prov 12:28

**PATIENCE**
have p with me, and I will pay ... Mt 18:26
Have p with me, and I will pay ... Mt 18:29
it, and bring forth fruit with p ... Lk 8:15
In your p possess ye your souls ... Lk 21:19
that tribulation worketh p ... Rom 5:3
And p, experience ... Rom 5:4
then do we with p wait for it ... Rom 8:25
our learning, that we through p ... Rom 15:4
Now the God of p and consolation ... Rom 15:5
the ministers of God, in much p ... 2Cor 6:4
were wrought among you in all p ... 2Cor 12:12
to his glorious power, unto all p ... Col 1:11
p of hope in our Lord Jesus ... 1Th 1:3
in the churches of God for your p ... 2Th 1:4
godliness, faith, love, p ... 1Ti 6:11
faith, longsuffering, charity, p ... 2Ti 3:10
sound in faith, in charity, in p ... Titus 2:2
faith and p inherit the promises ... Heb 6:12
For ye have need of p, that ... Heb 10:36
let us run with p the race that ... Heb 12:1
trying of your faith worketh p ... Jas 1:3
But let p have her perfect work ... Jas 1:4
the earth, and hath long p for it ... Jas 5:7
of suffering affliction, and of p ... Jas 5:10
Ye have heard of the p of Job ... Jas 5:11
and to temperance p ... 2Pet 1:6
and to p godliness ... 2Pet 1:6
p of Jesus Christ, was in the ... Rev 1:9
works, and thy labour, and thy p ... Rev 2:2
And hast borne, and hast p, and for ... Rev 2:3
and service, and faith, and thy p ... Rev 2:19
thou hast kept the word of my p ... Rev 3:10
Here is the p and the faith of the ... Rev 13:10
Here is the p of the saints ... Rev 14:12

**PATIENT**
the p in spirit is better than ... Eccl 7:8
To them who by p continuance in ... Rom 2:7
p in tribulation ... Rom 12:12
the weak, be p toward all men ... 1Th 5:14
into the p waiting for Christ ... 2Th 3:5
but p, not a brawler, not ... 1Ti 3:3
unto all men, apt to teach, p ... 2Ti 2:24
Be p therefore, brethren, unto ... Jas 5:7
Be ye also p ... Jas 5:8

**PATIENTLY**
in the LORD, and wait p for him ... Ps 37:7
I waited p for the LORD ... Ps 40:1
I beseech thee to hear me p ... Acts 26:3
And so, after he had p endured ... Heb 6:15
your faults, ye shall take it p ... 1Pet 2:20
and suffer for it, ye take it p ... 1Pet 2:20

**PATMOS** (*pat'-mos*) *An island off the west coast of Asia Minor.*
was in the isle that is called P ... Rev 1:9

**PATRIARCH**
speak unto you of the p David ... Acts 2:29
unto whom even the p Abraham gave ... Heb 7:4

**PATRIARCHS**
and Jacob begat the twelve p ... Acts 7:8
And the p, moved with envy, sold ... Acts 7:9

**PATRIMONY**
which cometh of the sale of his p ... Deut 18:8

**PATROBAS** (*pat'-ro-bas*) *A Christian in Rome.*
Asyncritus, Phlegon, Hermas, P ... Rom 16:14

**PATTERN**
after the p of the tabernacle, and ... Ex 25:9
the p of all the instruments ... Ex 25:9
that thou make them after their p ... Ex 25:40
according unto the p which the ... Num 8:4
Behold the p of the altar of the ... Josh 22:28
the p of it, according to all the ... 2Kin 16:10
his son the p of the porch ... 1Chr 28:11
the p of all that he had by the ... 1Chr 28:12
gold for the p of the chariot of ... 1Chr 28:18
me, even all the works of this p ... 1Chr 28:19
and let them measure the p ... Eze 43:10
for a p to them which should ... 1Ti 1:16
shewing thyself a p of good works ... Titus 2:7
the p shewed to thee in the mount ... Heb 8:5

**PATTERNS**
therefore necessary that the p of ... Heb 9:23

**PAU** (*pa'-u*) See PAI. *City of King Hadar of Edom.*
and the name of his city was P ... Gen 36:39

**PAUL** (*pawl*) See PAUL'S, PAULUS, SAUL. *The apostle to the Gentiles.*
Then Saul, (who also is called P ... Acts 13:9
when P and his company ... Acts 13:13
Then P stood up, and beckoning ... Acts 13:16
religious proselytes followed P ... Acts 13:43
things which were spoken by P ... Acts 13:45
P and Barnabas waxed bold ... Acts 13:46
and raised persecution against P ... Acts 13:50
The same heard P speak ... Acts 14:9
the people saw what P had done ... Acts 14:11
and P, Mercurius, because he was ... Acts 14:12
when the apostles, Barnabas and P ... Acts 14:14
the people, and, having stoned P ... Acts 14:19
When therefore P and Barnabas had ... Acts 15:2
with them, they determined that P ... Acts 15:2
audience to Barnabas and P ... Acts 15:12
own company to Antioch with P ... Acts 15:22
with our beloved Barnabas and P ... Acts 15:25
P also and Barnabas continued in ... Acts 15:35
some days after P said unto ... Acts 15:36
But P thought not good to take ... Acts 15:38
P chose Silas, and departed, being ... Acts 15:40
Him would P have to go forth with ... Acts 16:3
vision appeared to P in the night ... Acts 16:9
the things which were spoken of P ... Acts 16:14
The same followed P and us, and ... Acts 16:17
But P, being grieved, turned and ... Acts 16:18
gains was gone, they caught P ... Acts 16:19
And at midnight P and Silas prayed ... Acts 16:25
But P cried with a loud voice ... Acts 16:28
trembling, and fell down before P ... Acts 16:29
the prison told this saying to P ... Acts 16:36
But P said unto them, They have ... Acts 16:37
And P, as his manner was, went in ... Acts 17:2
believed, and consorted with P ... Acts 17:4
brethren immediately sent away P ... Acts 17:10
of God was preached of P at Berea ... Acts 17:13
the brethren sent away P to go as ... Acts 17:14
they that conducted P brought him ... Acts 17:15
Now while P waited for them at ... Acts 17:16
Then P stood in the midst of ... Acts 17:22
So P departed from among them ... Acts 17:33
After these things P departed ... Acts 18:1
P was pressed in the spirit, and ... Acts 18:5
Then spake the Lord to P in the ... Acts 18:9
with one accord against P ... Acts 18:12
when P was now about to open his ... Acts 18:14
P after this tarried there yet a ... Acts 18:18
P having passed through the upper ... Acts 19:1
Then said P, John verily baptized ... Acts 19:4
when P had laid his hands upon ... Acts 19:6
miracles by the hands of P ... Acts 19:11
you by Jesus whom P preacheth ... Acts 19:13
said, Jesus I know, and P I know ... Acts 19:15
P purposed in the spirit, when he ... Acts 19:21
this P hath persuaded and turned ... Acts 19:26
when P would have entered in unto ... Acts 19:30
P called unto him the disciples ... Acts 20:1
P preached unto them, ready to ... Acts 20:7
as P was long preaching, he sunk ... Acts 20:9
P went down, and fell on him, and ... Acts 20:10
there intending to take in P ... Acts 20:13
For P had determined to sail by ... Acts 20:16
who said to P through the Spirit ... Acts 21:4
Then P answered, What mean ye to ... Acts 21:13
the day following P went in with ... Acts 21:18
Then P took the men, and the next ... Acts 21:26
whom they supposed that P had ... Acts 21:29
and they took P, and drew him out ... Acts 21:30
soldiers, they left beating of P ... Acts 21:32
as P was to be led into the ... Acts 21:37
But P said, I am a man which am a ... Acts 21:39
P stood on the stairs, and ... Acts 21:40
P said unto the centurion that ... Acts 22:25
P said, But I was free born ... Acts 22:28
to appear, and brought P down ... Acts 22:30
And P, earnestly beholding the ... Acts 23:1
Then said P unto him, God shall ... Acts 23:3
Then said P, I wist not, brethren ... Acts 23:5
But when P perceived that the one ... Acts 23:6
fearing lest P should have been ... Acts 23:10
him, and said, Be of good cheer, P ... Acts 23:11
nor drink till they had killed P ... Acts 23:12
eat nothing until we have slain P ... Acts 23:14
into the castle, and told P ... Acts 23:16
Then P called one of the ... Acts 23:17
P the prisoner called me unto him ... Acts 23:18
down P to morrow into the council ... Acts 23:20
beasts, that they may set P on ... Acts 23:24
as it was commanded them, took P ... Acts 23:31
presented P also before him ... Acts 23:33
informed the governor against P ... Acts 24:1
Then P, after that the governor ... Acts 24:10
commanded a centurion to keep P ... Acts 24:23
which was a Jewess, he sent for P ... Acts 24:24
should have been given him of P ... Acts 24:26
the Jews a pleasure, left P bound ... Acts 24:27
the Jews informed him against P ... Acts 25:2
that P should be kept at Caesarea ... Acts 25:4
seat commanded P to be brought ... Acts 25:6
and grievous complaints against P ... Acts 25:7
the Jews a pleasure, answered P ... Acts 25:9
Then said P, I stand at Caesar's ... Acts 25:10
whom P affirmed to be alive ... Acts 25:19
But when P had appealed to be ... Acts 25:21
commandment P was brought forth ... Acts 25:23
Then Agrippa said unto P, Thou ... Acts 26:1
Then P stretched forth the hand ... Acts 26:1
Festus said with a loud voice, P ... Acts 26:24
Then Agrippa said unto P, Almost ... Acts 26:28
P said, I would to God, that not ... Acts 26:29
sail into Italy, they delivered P ... Acts 27:1
And Julius courteously entreated P ... Acts 27:3
already past, P admonished them ... Acts 27:9
things which were spoken by P ... Acts 27:11
But after long abstinence P stood ... Acts 27:21
Saying, Fear not, P ... Acts 27:24
P said to the centurion and to the ... Acts 27:31
P besought them all to take meat ... Acts 27:33
the centurion, willing to save P ... Acts 27:43
when P had gathered a bundle of ... Acts 28:3
to whom P entered in, and prayed ... Acts 28:8
whom when P saw, he thanked God ... Acts 28:15
but P was suffered to dwell by ... Acts 28:16
that after three days P called ... Acts 28:17
after that P had spoken one word ... Acts 28:25
P dwelt two whole years in his ... Acts 28:30
P, a servant of Jesus Christ ... Rom 1:1
P, called to be an apostle of ... 1Cor 1:1
every one of you saith, I am of P ... 1Cor 1:12
was P crucified for you ... 1Cor 1:13
were ye baptized in the name of P ... 1Cor 1:13
For while one saith, I am of P ... 1Cor 3:4
Who then is P, and who is Apollos ... 1Cor 3:5
Whether P, or Apollos, or Cephas ... 1Cor 3:22
of me P with mine own hand ... 1Cor 16:21
P, an apostle of Jesus Christ by ... 2Cor 1:1
Now I P myself beseech you by the ... 2Cor 10:1
P, an apostle, (not of men ... Gal 1:1
I P say unto you, that if ye be ... Gal 5:2
P, an apostle of Jesus Christ by ... Eph 1:1
For this cause I P, the prisoner ... Eph 3:1
P and Timotheus, the servants of ... Phil 1:1
P, an apostle of Jesus Christ by ... Col 1:1
whereof I P am made a minister ... Col 1:23
salutation by the hand of me P ... Col 4:18
P, and Silvanus, and Timotheus ... 1Th 1:1
have come unto you, even I P ... 1Th 2:18
P, and Silvanus, and Timotheus ... 2Th 1:1
The salutation of P with mine own ... 2Th 3:17
P, an apostle of Jesus Christ by ... 1Ti 1:1
P, an apostle of Jesus Christ by ... 2Ti 1:1
when P was brought before Nero ... 2Ti s
P, a servant of God, and an ... Titus 1:1
P, a prisoner of Jesus Christ, and ... Philem 1
being such an one as P the aged ... Philem 9
I P have written it with mine own ... Philem 19
even as our beloved brother P ... 2Pet 3:15

**PAUL'S** (*pawls*)
P companions in travel, they ... Acts 19:29
all wept sore, and fell on P neck ... Acts 20:37
that were of P company departed ... Acts 21:8
come unto us, he took P girdle ... Acts 21:11
when P sister's son heard of ... Acts 23:16
Festus declared P cause unto the ... Acts 25:14

**PAULUS** See PAUL. *A Roman proconsul.*
deputy of the country, Sergius P ... Acts 13:7

**PAVED**
were a p work of a sapphire stone ... Ex 24:10
midst thereof being p with love ... Song 3:10

**PAVEMENT**
it, and put it upon a p of stones ... 2Kin 16:17
faces to the ground upon the p ... 2Chr 7:3
gold and silver, upon a p of red ... Est 1:6
a p made for the court round ... Eze 40:17
thirty chambers were upon the p ... Eze 40:17
the p by the side of the gates ... Eze 40:18
of the gates was the lower p ... Eze 40:18
over against the p which was for ... Eze 42:3
in a place that is called the P ... Jn 19:13

**PAVILION**
his p round about him were dark ... Ps 18:11
trouble he shall hide me in his p ... Ps 27:5
in a p from the strife of tongues ... Ps 31:20
spread his royal p over them ... Jer 43:10

**PAVILIONS**
made darkness p round about him ... 2Sa 22:12
he and the kings in the p ... 1Kin 20:12
drinking himself drunk in the p ... 1Kin 20:16

**PAW**
me out of the p of the lion ... 1Sa 17:37
out of the p of the bear, he will ... 1Sa 17:37

**PAWETH**
He p in the valley, and rejoiceth ... Job 39:21

**PAWS**
And whatsoever goeth upon his p ... Lev 11:27

**PAY**
only he shall p for the loss of ... Ex 21:19
and he shall p as the judges ... Ex 21:22

he shall surely p ox for ox ... Ex 21:36
thief be found, let him p double ... Ex 22:7
he shall p double unto his ... Ex 22:9
he shall p money according to the ... Ex 22:17
thy water, then I will p for it ... Num 20:19
God, thou shalt not slack to p it ... Deut 23:21
p my vow, which I have vowed unto ... 2Sa 15:7
thou shalt p a talent of silver ... 1Kin 20:39
p thy debt, and live thou and thy ... 2Kin 4:7
make to p tribute until this day ... 2Chr 8:8
the children of Ammon p unto him ... 2Chr 27:5
again, then will they not p toll ... Ezr 4:13
I will p ten thousand talents of ... Est 3:9
that Haman had promised to p to ... Est 4:7
thee, and thou shalt p thy vows ... Job 22:27
I will p my vows before them that ... Ps 22:25
p thy vows unto the most High ... Ps 50:14
I will p thee my vows, ... Ps 66:13
Vow, and p unto the LORD your God ... Ps 76:11
I will p my vows unto the LORD ... Ps 116:14
I will p my vows unto the LORD ... Ps 116:18
he hath given will he p him again ... Prov 19:17
If thou hast nothing to p ... Prov 22:27
a vow unto God, defer not to p it ... Eccl 5:4
p that which thou hast vowed ... Eccl 5:4
that thou shouldest vow and not p ... Eccl 5:5
I will p that that I have vowed ... Jonah 2:9
Doth not your master p tribute ... Mt 17:24
But forasmuch as he had not to p ... Mt 18:25
with me, and I will p thee all ... Mt 18:26
saying, P me that thou owest ... Mt 18:28
with me, and I will p thee all ... Mt 18:29
prison, till he should p the debt ... Mt 18:30
till he should p all that was due ... Mt 18:34
for ye p tithe of mint and anise ... Mt 23:23
And when they had nothing to p ... Lk 7:42
for this cause p ye tribute also ... Rom 13:6

**PAYED**

this day have I p my vows ... Prov 7:14
tithes, p tithes in Abraham ... Heb 7:9

**PAYETH**

wicked borroweth, and p not again ... Ps 37:21

**PAYMENT**

all that he had, and p to be made ... Mt 18:25

**PEACE**

thou shalt go to thy fathers in p ... Gen 15:15
man wondering at her held his p ... Gen 24:21
good, and have sent thee away in p ... Gen 26:29
and they departed from him in p ... Gen 26:31
again to my father's house in p ... Gen 28:21
Jacob held his p until they were ... Gen 34:5
shall give Pharaoh an answer of p ... Gen 41:16
And he said, P be to you, fear not ... Gen 43:23
get you up in p unto your father ... Gen 44:17
And Jethro said to Moses, Go in p ... Ex 4:18
for you, and ye shall hold your p ... Ex 14:14
shall also go to their place in p ... Ex 18:23
thy p offerings, thy sheep, and ... Ex 20:24
sacrificed p offerings of oxen ... Ex 24:5
sacrifice of their p offerings ... Ex 29:28
offerings, and brought p offerings ... Ex 32:6
be a sacrifice of p offering ... Lev 3:1
p offering an offering made by ... Lev 3:3
of p offering unto the LORD be of ... Lev 3:6
p offering an offering made by ... Lev 3:9
of the sacrifice of p offerings ... Lev 4:10
of the sacrifice of p offerings ... Lev 4:26
off the sacrifice of p offerings ... Lev 4:31
the sacrifice of the p offerings ... Lev 4:35
the fat of the p offerings ... Lev 6:12
of the sacrifice of p offerings ... Lev 7:11
thanksgiving of his p offerings ... Lev 7:13
the blood of the p offerings ... Lev 7:14
his p offerings for thanksgiving ... Lev 7:15
p offerings be eaten at all on ... Lev 7:18
of the sacrifice of p offerings ... Lev 7:20
of the sacrifice of p offerings ... Lev 7:21
p offerings unto the LORD shall ... Lev 7:29
the sacrifice of his p offerings ... Lev 7:29
sacrifices of your p offerings ... Lev 7:32
the blood of the p offerings ... Lev 7:33
sacrifices of their p offerings ... Lev 7:34
the sacrifice of the p offerings ... Lev 7:37
bullock and a ram for p offerings ... Lev 9:4
for a sacrifice of p offerings ... Lev 9:18
burnt offering, and p offerings ... Lev 9:22
And Aaron held his p ... Lev 10:3
of p offerings of the children of ... Lev 10:14
offer them for p offerings unto ... Lev 17:5
of p offerings unto the LORD ... Lev 19:5
offereth a sacrifice of p ... Lev 22:21
for a sacrifice of p offerings ... Lev 23:19
And I will give p in the land ... Lev 26:6
without blemish for p offerings ... Num 6:14
of p offerings unto the LORD ... Num 6:17
the sacrifice of the p offerings ... Num 6:18
upon thee, and give thee p ... Num 6:26
And for a sacrifice of p offerings ... Num 7:17
And for a sacrifice of p offerings ... Num 7:23
And for a sacrifice of p offerings ... Num 7:29
And for a sacrifice of p offerings ... Num 7:35
And for a sacrifice of p offerings ... Num 7:41
And for a sacrifice of p offerings ... Num 7:47
And for a sacrifice of p offerings ... Num 7:53
And for a sacrifice of p offerings ... Num 7:59
And for a sacrifice of p offerings ... Num 7:65
And for a sacrifice of p offerings ... Num 7:71
And for a sacrifice of p offerings ... Num 7:77
And for a sacrifice of p offerings ... Num 7:83
of the p offerings were twenty ... Num 7:88
sacrifices of your p offerings ... Num 10:10
or p offerings unto the LORD ... Num 15:8
I give unto him my covenant of p ... Num 25:12
and for your p offerings ... Num 29:39
father shall hold his p at her ... Num 30:4
held his p at her in the day that ... Num 30:7
heard it, and held his p at her ... Num 30:11
hold his p at her from day to day ... Num 30:14
because he held his p at her in ... Num 30:14
king of Heshbon with words of p ... Deut 2:26
it, then proclaim p unto it ... Deut 20:10
be, if it make thee answer of p ... Deut 20:11
And if it will make no p with thee ... Deut 20:12
Thou shalt not seek their p nor ... Deut 23:6
And thou shalt offer p offerings ... Deut 27:7
his heart, saying, I shall have p ... Deut 29:19
LORD, and sacrificed p offerings ... Josh 8:31
And Joshua made p with them ... Josh 9:15
of Gibeon had made p with Israel ... Josh 10:1
for it hath made p with Joshua ... Josh 10:4
camp to Joshua at Makkedah in p ... Josh 10:21
p with the children of Israel ... Josh 11:19
or if to offer p offerings ... Josh 22:23
and with our p offerings ... Josh 22:27
for there was p between Jabin the ... Judg 4:17
said unto him, P be unto thee ... Judg 6:23
saying, When I come again in p ... Judg 8:9
when I return in p from the ... Judg 11:31
priest said unto them, Go in p ... Judg 18:6
And they said unto him, Hold thy p ... Judg 18:19
the old man said, P be with thee ... Judg 19:20
p offerings before the LORD ... Judg 20:26
burnt offerings and p offerings ... Judg 21:4
Eli answered and said, Go in p ... 1Sa 1:17
there was p between Israel and the ... 1Sa 7:14
sacrifices of p offerings ... 1Sa 10:8
But he held his p ... 1Sa 10:27
of p offerings before the LORD ... 1Sa 11:15
offering to me, and p offerings ... 1Sa 13:9
thy servant shall have p ... 1Sa 20:7
away, that thou mayest go in p ... 1Sa 20:13
for there is p to thee, and no ... 1Sa 20:21
Jonathan said to David, Go in p ... 1Sa 20:42
P be both to thee ... 1Sa 25:6
p be to thine house ... 1Sa 25:6
p be unto all that thou hast ... 1Sa 25:6
Go up in p to thine house ... 1Sa 25:35
Wherefore now return, and go in p ... 1Sa 29:7
and he went in p ... 2Sa 3:21
him away, and he was gone in p ... 2Sa 3:22
sent him away, and he is gone in p ... 2Sa 3:23
p offerings before the LORD ... 2Sa 6:17
p offerings, he blessed the ... 2Sa 6:18
they made p with Israel, and ... 2Sa 10:19
but hold now thy p, my sister ... 2Sa 13:20
the king said unto him, Go in p ... 2Sa 15:9
return into the city in p ... 2Sa 15:27
so all the people shall be in p ... 2Sa 17:3
until the day he came again in p ... 2Sa 19:24
again in p unto his own house ... 2Sa 19:30
burnt offerings and p offerings ... 2Sa 24:25
and shed the blood of war in p ... 1Kin 2:5
head go down to the grave in p ... 1Kin 2:6
shall there be p for ever from ... 1Kin 2:33
offered p offerings, and made a ... 1Kin 3:15
he had p on all sides round about ... 1Kin 4:24
there was p between Hiram and ... 1Kin 5:12
a sacrifice of p offerings ... 1Kin 8:63
and the fat of the p offerings ... 1Kin 8:64
and the fat of the p offerings ... 1Kin 8:64
p offerings upon the altar which ... 1Kin 9:25
Whether they be come out for p ... 1Kin 20:18
every man to his house in p ... 1Kin 22:17
of affliction, until I come in p ... 1Kin 22:27
said, If thou return at all in p ... 1Kin 22:28
Jehoshaphat made p with the king ... 1Kin 22:44
hold ye your p ... 2Kin 2:3
hold ye your p ... 2Kin 2:5
And he said unto him, Go in p ... 2Kin 5:19
of good tidings, and we hold our p ... 2Kin 7:9
them, and let him say, Is it p ... 2Kin 9:17
Thus saith the king, Is it p ... 2Kin 9:18
said, What hast thou to do with p ... 2Kin 9:18
Thus saith the king, Is it p ... 2Kin 9:19
What hast thou to do with p ... 2Kin 9:19
saw Jehu, that he said, Is it p ... 2Kin 9:22
And he answered, What p, so long ... 2Kin 9:22
the gate, she said, Had Zimri p ... 2Kin 9:31
the blood of his p offerings ... 2Kin 16:13
But the people held their p ... 2Kin 18:36
And he said, Is it not good, if p ... 2Kin 20:19
be gathered into thy grave in p ... 2Kin 22:20
p, p be unto thee, and p ... 1Chr 12:18
thee, and p be to thine helpers ... 1Chr 12:18
and p offerings before God ... 1Chr 16:1
the p offerings, he blessed the ... 1Chr 16:2
they made p with David ... 1Chr 19:19
p offerings, and called upon the ... 1Chr 21:26
be Solomon, and I will give p ... 1Chr 22:9
and the fat of the p offerings ... 2Chr 7:7
was no p to him that went out ... 2Chr 15:5
every man to his house in p ... 2Chr 18:16
affliction, until I return in p ... 2Chr 18:26
If thou certainly return in p ... 2Chr 18:27
to his house in p to Jerusalem ... 2Chr 19:1
with the fat of the p offerings ... 2Chr 29:35
offering p offerings, and making ... 2Chr 30:22
for p offerings, to minister, and ... 2Chr 31:2
and sacrificed thereon p offerings ... 2Chr 33:16
be gathered to thy grave in p ... 2Chr 34:28
unto the rest beyond the river, P ... Ezr 4:17
Unto Darius the king, all p ... Ezr 5:7
of the God of heaven, perfect p ... Ezr 7:12
nor seek their p or their wealth ... Ezr 9:12
Then held they their p, and found ... Neh 5:8
the people, saying, Hold your p ... Neh 8:11
holdest thy p at this time ... Est 4:14
of Ahasuerus, with words of p ... Est 9:30
speaking p to all his seed ... Est 10:3
the field shall be at p with thee ... Job 5:23
that thy tabernacle shall be in p ... Job 5:24
thy lies make men hold their p ... Job 11:3
ye would altogether hold your p ... Job 13:5
Hold your p, let me alone, that I ... Job 13:13
now thyself with him, and be at p ... Job 22:21
he maketh p in his high places ... Job 25:2
The nobles held their p, and their ... Job 29:10
hold thy p, and I will speak ... Job 33:31
hold thy p, and I shall teach thee ... Job 33:33
I will both lay me down in p ... Ps 4:8
unto him that was at p with me ... Ps 7:4
which speak p to their neighbours ... Ps 28:3
LORD will bless his people with p ... Ps 29:11
seek p, and pursue it ... Ps 34:14
For they speak not p ... Ps 35:20
themselves in the abundance of p ... Ps 37:11
for the end of that man is p ... Ps 37:37
dumb with silence, I held my p ... Ps 39:2
hold not thy p at my tears ... Ps 39:12
in p from the battle that was ... Ps 55:18
against such as be at p with him ... Ps 55:20
shall bring p to the people ... Ps 72:3
abundance of p so long as the ... Ps 72:7
hold not thy p, and be not still, ... Ps 83:1
he will speak p unto his people ... Ps 85:8
and p have kissed each other ... Ps 85:10
Hold not thy p, O God of my ... Ps 109:1
Great p have they which love thy ... Ps 119:165
long dwelt with him that hateth p ... Ps 120:6
I am for p ... Ps 120:7
Pray for the p of Jerusalem ... Ps 122:6
P be within thy walls, and ... Ps 122:7
I will now say, P be within thee ... Ps 122:8
but p shall be upon Israel ... Ps 125:5
children, and p upon Israel ... Ps 128:6
He maketh p in thy borders, and ... Ps 147:14
of days, and long life, and p ... Prov 3:2
and all her paths are p ... Prov 3:17
I have p offerings with me ... Prov 7:14
of understanding holdeth his p ... Prov 11:12
to the counsellors of p is joy ... Prov 12:20
his enemies to be at p with him ... Prov 16:7
a fool, when he holdeth his p ... Prov 17:28
a time of war, and a time of p ... Eccl 3:8
Father, The Prince of P ... Is 9:6
p there shall be no end, upon the ... Is 9:7
Thou wilt keep him in perfect p ... Is 26:3
LORD, thou wilt ordain p for us ... Is 26:12
that he may make p with me ... Is 27:5
and he shall make p with me ... Is 27:5
work of righteousness shall be p ... Is 32:17
the ambassadors of p shall weep ... Is 33:7
But they held their p, and ... Is 36:21
for p I had great bitterness ... Is 38:17
moreover, For there shall be p ... Is 39:8
I have long time holden my p ... Is 42:14
I make p, and create evil ... Is 45:7
then had thy p been as a river, ... Is 48:18
There is no p, saith the LORD, ... Is 48:22
good tidings, that publisheth p ... Is 52:7
of our p was upon him ... Is 53:5
the covenant of my p be removed ... Is 54:10
shall be the p of thy children ... Is 54:13
with joy, and be led forth with p ... Is 55:12
He shall enter into p ... Is 57:2
have not I held my p even of old ... Is 57:11
P, p to him that is far off, ... Is 57:19
There is no p, saith my God, to ... Is 57:21
The way of p they know not ... Is 59:8
goeth therein shall not know p ... Is 59:8
I will also make thy officers p ... Is 60:17
Zion's sake will I not hold my p ... Is 62:1
never hold their p day nor night ... Is 62:6
wilt thou hold thy p, and afflict ... Is 64:12
I will extend p to her like a ... Is 66:12
saying, Ye shall have p ... Jer 4:10
I cannot hold my p, because thou ... Jer 4:19
people slightly, saying, P, p ... Jer 6:14
when there is no p ... Jer 6:14
people slightly, saying, P, p ... Jer 8:11
when there is no p ... Jer 8:11
We looked for p, but no good came ... Jer 8:15
and if in the land of p, wherein ... Jer 12:5
no flesh shall have p ... Jer 12:12
give you assured p in this place ... Jer 14:13
we looked for p, and there is no ... Jer 14:19
taken away my p from this people ... Jer 16:5
LORD hath said, Ye shall have p ... Jer 23:17
prophet which prophesieth of p ... Jer 28:9
seek the p of the city whither I ... Jer 29:7
the p thereof shall ye have p ... Jer 29:7
saith the LORD, thoughts of p ... Jer 29:11
trembling, of fear, and not of p ... Jer 30:5
unto them the abundance of p ... Jer 33:6
But thou shalt die in p ... Jer 34:5
shall go forth from thence in p ... Jer 43:12
removed my soul far off from p ... Lam 3:17
and they shall seek p, and there ... Eze 7:25

have seduced my people, saying, *P*...... Eze 13:10
and there was no *p*...... Eze 13:10
*p* for her, and there is no *p*...... Eze 13:16
make with them a covenant of *p*...... Eze 34:25
make a covenant of *p* with them...... Eze 37:26
the altar, and your *p* offerings...... Eze 43:27
and for *p* offerings, to make...... Eze 45:15
and the *p* offerings, to make...... Eze 45:17
his *p* offerings, and he shall...... Eze 46:2
a voluntary burnt offering or *p*...... Eze 46:12
his *p* offerings, as he did on the...... Eze 46:12
*P* be multiplied unto you...... Dan 4:1
*P* be multiplied unto you...... Dan 6:25
heart, and by *p* shall destroy many...... Dan 8:25
*p* be unto thee, be strong, yea,...... Dan 10:19
neither will I regard the *p*...... Amos 5:22
the men that were at *p* with thee...... Obad 7
bite with their teeth, and cry, *P*...... Mic 3:5
And this man shall be the *p*...... Mic 5:5
good tidings, that publisheth *p*...... Nah 1:15
Hold thy *p* at the presence of the...... Zeph 1:7
and in this place will I give *p*...... Hag 2:9
the counsel of *p* shall be between...... Zec 6:13
neither was there any *p* to him...... Zec 8:10
of truth and *p* in your gates...... Zec 8:16
therefore love the truth and *p*...... Zec 8:19
he shall speak *p* unto the heathen...... Zec 9:10
was with him of life and *p*...... Mal 2:5
he walked with me in *p* and equity,...... Mal 2:6
worthy, let your *p* come upon it...... Mt 10:13
worthy, let your *p* return to you...... Mt 10:13
that I am come to send *p* on earth...... Mt 10:34
I came not to send *p*, but a sword...... Mt 10:34
because they should hold their *p*...... Mt 20:31
But Jesus held his *p*...... Mt 26:63
rebuked him, saying, Hold thy *p*...... Mk 1:25
But they held their *p*...... Mk 3:4
the wind, and said unto the sea, *P*...... Mk 4:39
go in *p*, and be whole of thy...... Mk 5:34
But they held their *p*...... Mk 9:34
and have *p* one with another...... Mk 9:50
him that he should hold his *p*...... Mk 10:48
But he held his *p*, and answered...... Mk 14:61
guide our feet into the way of *p*...... Lk 1:79
God in the highest, and on earth *p*...... Lk 2:14
thou thy servant depart in *p*...... Lk 2:29
rebuked him, saying, Hold thy *p*...... Lk 4:35
go in *p*...... Lk 7:50
go in *p*...... Lk 8:48
first say, *P* be to this house...... Lk 10:5
And if the son of *p* be there...... Lk 10:6
your *p* shall rest upon it...... Lk 10:6
his palace, his goods are in *p*...... Lk 11:21
that I am come to give *p* on earth...... Lk 12:51
And they held their *p*...... Lk 14:4
and desireth conditions of *p*...... Lk 14:32
him, that he should hold his *p*...... Lk 18:39
*p* in heaven, and glory in the...... Lk 19:38
if these should hold their *p*...... Lk 19:40
things which belong unto thy *p*...... Lk 19:42
at his answer, and held their *p*...... Lk 20:26
and saith unto them, *P* be unto you...... Lk 24:36
*P* I leave with you, my *p* I...... Jn 14:27
you, that in me ye might have *p*...... Jn 16:33
and saith unto them, *P* be unto you...... Jn 20:19
to them again, *P* be unto you...... Jn 20:21
the midst, and said, *P* be unto you...... Jn 20:26
preaching *p* by Jesus Christ...... Acts 10:36
these things, they held their *p*...... Acts 11:18
with the hand to hold their *p*...... Acts 12:17
their friend, desired *p*...... Acts 12:20
And after they had held their *p*...... Acts 15:13
they were let go in *p* from the...... Acts 15:33
now therefore depart, and go in *p*...... Acts 16:36
but speak, and hold not thy *p*...... Acts 18:9
*p* from God our Father, and the...... Rom 1:7
But glory, honour, and *p*, to every...... Rom 2:10
the way of *p* have they not known...... Rom 3:17
we have *p* with God through our...... Rom 5:1
spiritually minded is life and *p*...... Rom 8:6
them that preach the gospel of *p*...... Rom 10:15
but righteousness, and *p*, and joy...... Rom 14:17
after the things which make for *p*...... Rom 14:19
*p* in believing, that ye may...... Rom 15:13
Now the God of *p* be with you all...... Rom 15:33
the God of *p* shall bruise Satan...... Rom 16:20
Grace be unto you, and *p*, from God...... 1Cor 1:3
but God hath called us to *p*...... 1Cor 7:15
by, let the first hold his *p*...... 1Cor 14:30
the author of confusion, but of *p*...... 1Cor 14:33
but conduct him forth in *p*...... 1Cor 16:11
*p* from God our Father, and from...... 2Cor 1:2
be of one mind, live in *p*...... 2Cor 13:11
of love and *p* shall be with you...... 2Cor 13:11
*p* from God the Father, and from...... Gal 1:3
of the Spirit is love, joy, *p*...... Gal 5:22
*p* be on them, and mercy, and upon...... Gal 6:16
Grace be to you, and *p*, from God...... Eph 1:2
For he is our *p*, who hath made...... Eph 2:14
of twain one new man, so making *p*...... Eph 2:15
preached *p* to you which were afar...... Eph 2:17
of the Spirit in the bond of *p*...... Eph 4:3
preparation of the gospel of *p*...... Eph 6:15
*P* be to the brethren, and love...... Eph 6:23
Grace be unto you, and *p*, from God...... Phil 1:2
the *p* of God, which passeth all...... Phil 4:7
the God of *p* shall be with you...... Phil 4:9
Grace be unto you, and *p*, from God...... Col 1:2
having made *p* through the blood...... Col 1:20
let the *p* of God rule in your...... Col 3:15
Grace be unto you, and *p*, from God...... 1Th 1:1
For when they shall say, *P*...... 1Th 5:3
And be at *p* among yourselves...... 1Th 5:13
the very God of *p* sanctify you...... 1Th 5:23
Grace unto you, and *p*, from God...... 2Th 1:2
Now the Lord of *p* himself give...... 2Th 3:16
give you *p* always by all means...... 2Th 3:16
Grace, mercy, and *p*, from God our...... 1Ti 1:2
Grace, mercy, and *p*, from God the...... 2Ti 1:2
righteousness, faith, charity, *p*...... 2Ti 2:22
Grace, mercy, and *p*, from God the...... Titus 1:4
Grace to you, and *p*, from God our...... Philem 3
of Salem, which is, King of *p*...... Heb 7:2
she had received the spies with *p*...... Heb 11:31
Follow *p* with all men, and...... Heb 12:14
Now the God of *p*, that brought...... Heb 13:20
of you say unto them, Depart in *p*...... Jas 2:16
sown in *p* of them that make *p*...... Jas 3:18
Grace unto you, and *p*, be...... 1Pet 1:2
let him seek *p*, and ensue it...... 1Pet 3:11
*P* be with you all that are in...... 1Pet 5:14
*p* be multiplied unto you through...... 2Pet 1:2
that ye may be found of him in *p*...... 2Pet 3:14
Grace be with you, mercy, and *p*...... 2Jn 3
*P* be to thee...... 3Jn 14
Mercy unto you, and *p*, and love, be...... Jude 2
Grace be unto you, and *p*, from him...... Rev 1:4
thereon to take *p* from the earth...... Rev 6:4

**PEACEABLE**
These men are *p* with us...... Gen 34:21
I am one of them that are *p*...... 2Sa 20:19
the land was wide, and quiet, and *p*...... 1Chr 4:40
shall dwell in a *p* habitation...... Is 32:18
the *p* habitations are cut down...... Jer 25:37
*p* life in all godliness and...... 1Ti 2:2
afterward it yieldeth the *p* fruit...... Heb 12:11
from above is first pure, then *p*...... Jas 3:17

**PEACEABLY**
and could not speak *p* unto him...... Gen 37:4
restore those lands again *p*...... Judg 11:13
Rimmon, and to call *p* unto them...... Judg 21:13
coming, and said, Comest thou *p*...... 1Sa 16:4
And he said, *P*...... 1Sa 16:5
And she said, Comest thou *p*...... 1Kin 2:13
And he said, *P*...... 1Kin 2:13
If ye be come *p* unto me to help...... 1Chr 12:17
one speaketh *p* to his neighbour...... Jer 9:8
but he shall come in *p*, and obtain...... Dan 11:21
He shall enter *p* even upon the...... Dan 11:24
lieth in you, live *p* with all men...... Rom 12:18

**PEACEMAKERS**
Blessed are the *p*...... Mt 5:9

**PEACOCKS**
and silver, ivory, and apes, and *p*...... 1Kin 10:22
and silver, ivory, and apes, and *p*...... 2Chr 9:21
thou the goodly wings unto the *p*...... Job 39:13

**PEARL**
he had found one *p* of great price...... Mt 13:46
every several gate was of one *p*...... Rev 21:21

**PEARLS**
shall be made of coral, or of *p*...... Job 28:18
cast ye your *p* before swine...... Mt 7:6
a merchant man, seeking goodly *p*...... Mt 13:45
with broided hair, or gold, or *p*...... 1Ti 2:9
with gold and precious stones and *p*...... Rev 17:4
and precious stones, and of *p*...... Rev 18:12
gold, and precious stones, and *p*...... Rev 18:16
And the twelve gates were twelve *p*...... Rev 21:21

**PECULIAR**
then ye shall be a *p* treasure...... Ex 19:5
to be a *p* people unto himself...... Deut 14:2
thee this day to be his *p* people...... Deut 26:18
and Israel for his *p* treasure...... Ps 135:4
the *p* treasure of kings and of the...... Eccl 2:8
and purify unto himself a *p* people...... Titus 2:14
an holy nation, a *p* people...... 1Pet 2:9

**PEDAHEL** (*ped'-a-hel*) *A Naphtalite who apportioned the Promised Land.*
of Naphtali, *P* the son of Ammihud...... Num 34:28

**PEDAHZUR** (*pe-dah'-zur*) *Father of Gamaliel.*
Gamaliel the son of *P*...... Num 1:10
shall be Gamaliel the son of *P*...... Num 2:20
day offered Gamaliel the son of *P*...... Num 7:54
offering of Gamaliel the son of *P*...... Num 7:59
was Gamaliel the son of *P*...... Num 10:23

**PEDAIAH** (*pe-dah'-yah*)
*1. Grandfather of King Josiah.*
the daughter of *P* of Rumah...... 2Kin 23:36
*2. Descendant of Jeconiah.*
Malchiram also, and *P*, and Shenazar...... 1Chr 3:18
And the sons of *P* were, Zerubbabel...... 1Chr 3:19
*3. Father of Joel.*
of Manasseh, Joel the son of *P*...... 1Chr 27:20
*4. Son of Parosh.*
After him *P* the son of Parosh...... Neh 3:25
*5. A priest who aided Ezra.*
and on his left hand, *P*, and...... Neh 8:4
the scribe, and of the Levites, *P*...... Neh 13:13
*6. A family of exiles.*
the son of Joed, the son of *P*...... Neh 11:7

**PEDIGREES**
they declared their *p* after their...... Num 1:18

**PEELED**
to a nation scattered and *p*...... Is 18:2
hosts of a people scattered and *p*...... Is 18:7
bald, and every shoulder was *p*...... Eze 29:18

**PEEP**
spirits, and unto wizards that *p*...... Is 8:19

**PEEPED**
wing, or opened the mouth, or *p*...... Is 10:14

**PEKAH** (*pe'-kah*) *A king of Israel.*
But *P* the son of Remaliah, a...... 2Kin 15:25
*P* the son of Remaliah began to...... 2Kin 15:27
In the days of *P* king of Israel...... 2Kin 15:29
against *P* the son of Remaliah...... 2Kin 15:30
And the rest of the acts of *P*...... 2Kin 15:31
In the second year of *P* the son...... 2Kin 15:32
Syria, and *P* the son of Remaliah...... 2Kin 15:37
In the seventeenth year of *P* the...... 2Kin 16:1
*P* son of Remaliah king of Israel...... 2Kin 16:5
For *P* the son of Remaliah slew in...... 2Chr 28:6
*P* the son of Remaliah, king of...... Is 7:1

**PEKAHIAH** (*pe-ka-hi'-ah*) *Son of King Menahem.*
*P* his son reigned in his stead...... 2Kin 15:22
*P* the son of Menahem began to...... 2Kin 15:23
And the rest of the acts of *P*...... 2Kin 15:26

**PEKOD** (*pe'-kod*) *Symbolic name for Chaldea.*
and against the inhabitants of *P*...... Jer 50:21
and all the Chaldeans, *P*, and Shoa...... Eze 23:23

**PELAIAH** (*pel-a-i'-ah*)
*1. A son of Elioenai.*
were, Hodaiah, and Eliashib, and *P*...... 1Chr 3:24
*2. A priest who aided Ezra.*
Azariah, Jozabad, Hanan, *P*...... Neh 8:7
*3. A Levite who renewed the covenant.*
Shebaniah, Hodijah, Kelita, *P*...... Neh 10:10

**PELALIAH** (*pel-a-li'-ah*) *A family of exiles.*
the son of Jeroham, the son of *P*...... Neh 11:12

**PELATIAH** (*pel-a-ti'-ah*)
*1. Son of Hananiah.*
of Hananiah; *P*, and Jesaiah...... 1Chr 3:21
*2. A Simeonite captain.*
Seir, having for their captains *P*...... 1Chr 4:42
*3. A family who renewed the covenant.*
*P*, Hanan, Anaiah,...... Neh 10:22
*4. Son of Benaiah.*
*P* the son of Benaiah, princes of...... Eze 11:1
that *P* the son of Benaiah died...... Eze 11:13

**PELEG** (*pe'-leg*) See PHALEG. *A son of Eber.*
the name of one was *P*...... Gen 10:25
four and thirty years, and begat *P*...... Gen 11:16
after he begat *P* four hundred...... Gen 11:17
*P* lived thirty years, and begat...... Gen 11:18
*P* lived after he begat Reu two...... Gen 11:19
the name of the one was *P*...... 1Chr 1:19
Eber, *P*, Reu,...... 1Chr 1:25

**PELET** (*pe'-let*) See BETH-PALET.
*1. A son of Jahdai.*
Jotham, and Gesham, and *P*...... 1Chr 2:47
*2. A captain in David's army.*
and Jeziel, and *P*, the sons of...... 1Chr 12:3

**PELETH** (*pe'-leth*)
*1. Father of On.*
of Eliab, and On, the son of *P*...... Num 16:1
of Jonathan; *P*, and Zaza...... 1Chr 2:33

**PELETHITES** (*pel'-e-thites*) *A company of David's bodyguards.*
both the Cherethites and the *P*...... 2Sa 8:18
all the Cherethites, and all the *P*...... 2Sa 15:18
men, and the Cherethites, and the *P*...... 2Sa 20:7
the Cherethites and over the *P*...... 2Sa 20:23
and the Cherethites, and the *P*...... 1Kin 1:38
and the Cherethites, and the *P*...... 1Kin 1:44
was over the Cherethites and the *P*...... 1Chr 18:17

**PELICAN**
And the swan, and the *p*, and the...... Lev 11:18
And the *p*, and the gier eagle, and...... Deut 14:17
I am like a *p* of the wilderness...... Ps 102:6

**PELONITE** (*pel'-o-nite*) See PALTITE.
*1. Family name of Helez.*
the Harorite, Helez the *P*...... 1Chr 11:27
the seventh month was Helez the *P*...... 1Chr 27:10
*2. Family name of Ahijah.*
the Mecherathite, Ahijah the *P*...... 1Chr 11:36

**PELUSIUM** See SIN.

**PEN**
that handle the *p* of the writer...... Judg 5:14
they were graven with an iron *p*...... Job 19:24
my tongue is the *p* of a ready...... Ps 45:1
in it with a man's *p* concerning...... Is 8:1
the *p* of the scribes is in vain...... Jer 8:8
Judah is written with a *p* of iron...... Jer 17:1
not with ink and *p* write unto thee...... 3Jn 13

**PENCE**
which owed him an hundred *p*...... Mt 18:28
for more than three hundred *p*...... Mk 14:5
the one owed five hundred *p*...... Lk 7:41
he departed, he took out two *p*...... Lk 10:35
ointment sold for three hundred *p*...... Jn 12:5

**PENIEL** (*pe-ni'-el*) See PENUEL. *Same as Penuel.*
called the name of the place *P*...... Gen 32:30

**PENINNAH** (*pe-nin'-nah*) *A wife of Elkanah.*
and the name of the other *P*...... 1Sa 1:2
*P* had children, but Hannah had no...... 1Sa 1:2

offered, he gave to *P* his wife ... 1Sa 1:4

**PENKNIFE**
four leaves, he cut it with the *p* ... Jer 36:23

**PENNY**
with the labourers for a *p* a day ... Mt 20:2
hour, they received every man a *p* ... Mt 20:9
likewise received every man a *p* ... Mt 20:10
not thou agree with me for a *p* ... Mt 20:13
And they brought unto him a *p* ... Mt 22:19
bring me a *p*, that I may see it ... Mk 12:15
Shew me a *p* ... Lk 20:24
say, A measure of wheat for a *p* ... Rev 6:6
three measures of barley for a *p* ... Rev 6:6

**PENNYWORTH**
go and buy two hundred *p* of bread ... Mk 6:37
Two hundred *p* of bread is not ... Jn 6:7

**PENTECOST** (*pen'-te-cost*) *Greek name for Feast of Weeks.*
when the day of *P* was fully come ... Acts 2:1
to be at Jerusalem the day of *P* ... Acts 20:16
I will tarry at Ephesus until *P* ... 1Cor 16:8

**PENUEL** (*pe-nu'-el*) See PENIEL.
*1. Where Jacob wrestled God.*
as he passed over *P* the sun rose ... Gen 32:31
And he went up thence to *P* ... Judg 8:8
the men of *P* answered him as the ... Judg 8:8
he spake also unto the men of *P* ... Judg 8:9
And he beat down the tower of *P* ... Judg 8:17
*2. Father of Gedor.*
*P* the father of Gedor, and Ezer ... 1Chr 4:4
*3. A son of Shashak.*
And Iphedeiah, and *P*, the sons of ... 1Chr 8:25

**PENURY**
of the lips tendeth only to *p* ... Prov 14:23
but she of her *p* hath cast in all ... Lk 21:4

**PEOPLE** See PREFACE.

**PEOPLE'S**
And he brought the *p* offering ... Lev 9:15
the *p* inheritance by oppression ... Eze 46:18
For this *p* heart is waxed gross ... Mt 13:15
his own sins, and then for the *p* ... Heb 7:27

**PEOPLES**
must prophesy again before many *p* ... Rev 10:11
where the whore sitteth, are *p* ... Rev 17:15

**PEOR** (*pe'-or*) See BAAL-PEOR, BETH-PEOR, PEOR'S.
*1. A Moabite god.*
beguiled you in the matter of *P* ... Num 25:18
the LORD in the matter of *P* ... Num 31:16
iniquity of *P* too little for us ... Josh 22:17
*2. A mountain.*
brought Balaam unto the top of *P* ... Num 23:28

**PEOR'S**
the day of the plague for *P* sake ... Num 25:18

**PERADVENTURE**
*P* there be fifty righteous within ... Gen 18:24
*P* there shall lack five of the ... Gen 18:28
*P* there shall be forty found ... Gen 18:29
*P* there shall thirty be found ... Gen 18:30
*P* there shall be twenty found ... Gen 18:31
*P* ten shall be found there ... Gen 18:32
*P* the woman will not be willing ... Gen 24:5
*P* the woman will not follow me ... Gen 24:39
My father *p* will feel me, and I ... Gen 27:12
*P* thou wouldest take by force thy ... Gen 31:31
*p* he will accept of me ... Gen 32:20
Lest *p* he die also, as his ... Gen 38:11
Lest *p* mischief befall him ... Gen 42:4
*p* it was an oversight ... Gen 43:12
lest *p* I see the evil that shall ... Gen 44:34
they said, Joseph will *p* hate us ... Gen 50:15
Lest *p* the people repent when ... Ex 13:17
*p* I shall make an atonement for ... Ex 32:30
*p* I shall prevail, that we may ... Num 22:6
*p* I shall be able to overcome ... Num 22:11
*p* the LORD will come to meet me ... Num 23:3
*p* it will please God that thou ... Num 23:27
the Hivites, *P* ye dwell among us ... Josh 9:7
*p* he will lighten his hand from ... 1Sa 6:5
*p* he can shew us our way that we ... 1Sa 9:6
*p* we may find grass to save the ... 1Kin 18:5
or *p* he sleepeth, and must be ... 1Kin 18:27
*p* he will save thy life ... 1Kin 20:31
lest *p* the Spirit of the LORD ... 2Kin 2:16
*P* he will be enticed, and we shall ... Jer 20:10
yet *p* for a good man some would ... Rom 5:7
if God *p* will give them ... 2Ti 2:25

**PERAZIM** (*per'-a-zim*) *Where David defeated the Philistines.*
LORD shall rise up as in mount *P* ... Is 28:21

**PERCEIVE**
hath not given you an heart to *p* ... Deut 29:4
This day we *p* that the LORD is ... Josh 22:31
that ye may *p* and see that your ... 1Sa 12:17
for this day I *p*, that if Absalom ... 2Sa 19:6
I *p* that this is an holy man of ... 2Kin 4:9
passeth on also, but I *p* him not ... Job 9:11
and backward, but I cannot *p* him ... Job 23:8
to *p* the words of understanding ... Prov 1:2
Wherefore I *p* that there is ... Eccl 3:22
and see ye indeed, but *p* not ... Is 6:9
a deeper speech than thou canst *p* ... Is 33:19
ye shall see, and shall not *p* ... Mt 13:14
seeing they may see, and not *p* ... Mk 4:12
Do ye not *p*, that whatsoever ... Mk 7:18
*p* ye not yet, neither understand ... Mk 8:17
for I *p* that virtue is gone out ... Lk 8:46
I *p* that thou art a prophet ... Jn 4:19
*P* ye how ye prevail nothing ... Jn 12:19
For I *p* that thou art in the gall ... Acts 8:23
Of a truth I *p* that God is no ... Acts 10:34
I *p* that in all things ye are too ... Acts 17:22
I *p* that this voyage will be with ... Acts 27:10
and seeing ye shall see, and not *p* ... Acts 28:26
for I *p* that the same epistle ... 2Cor 7:8
Hereby *p* we the love of God ... 1Jn 3:16

**PERCEIVED**
he *p* not when she lay down, nor ... Gen 19:33
he *p* not when she lay down, nor ... Gen 19:35
when Gideon *p* that he was an ... Judg 6:22
Eli *p* that the LORD had called ... 1Sa 3:8
Saul *p* that it was Samuel, and he ... 1Sa 28:14
David *p* that the LORD had ... 2Sa 5:12
David *p* that the child was dead ... 2Sa 12:19
*p* that the king's heart was ... 2Sa 14:1
*p* that it was not the king of ... 1Kin 22:33
David *p* that the LORD had ... 1Chr 14:2
*p* that it was not the king of ... 2Chr 18:32
I *p* that God had not sent him ... Neh 6:12
for they *p* that this work was ... Neh 6:16
I *p* that the portions of the ... Neh 13:10
When Mordecai *p* all that was done ... Est 4:1
Hast thou *p* the breadth of the ... Job 38:18
I *p* that this also is vexation of ... Eccl 1:17
I myself *p* also that one event ... Eccl 2:14
nor *p* by the ear, neither hath ... Is 64:4
counsel of the LORD, and hath *p* ... Jer 23:18
for the matter was not *p* ... Jer 38:27
Which when Jesus *p*, he said unto ... Mt 16:8
they *p* that he spake of them ... Mt 21:45
But Jesus *p* their wickedness, and ... Mt 22:18
immediately when Jesus *p* in his ... Mk 2:8
they *p* that he had seen a vision ... Lk 1:22
But when Jesus *p* their thoughts ... Lk 5:22
hid from them, that they *p* it not ... Lk 9:45
for they *p* that he had spoken ... Lk 20:19
But he *p* their craftiness, and ... Lk 20:23
therefore *p* that they would come ... Jn 6:15
*p* that they were unlearned and ... Acts 4:13
But when Paul *p* that the one part ... Acts 23:6
Whom I *p* to be accused of ... Acts 23:29
*p* the grace that was given unto ... Gal 2:9

**PERCEIVEST**
when thou *p* not in him the lips ... Prov 14:7
but *p* not the beam that is in ... Lk 6:41

**PERCEIVETH**
low, but he *p* it not of them ... Job 14:21
once, yea twice, yet man *p* it not ... Job 33:14
She *p* that her merchandise is ... Prov 31:18

**PERCEIVING**
*p* that he had answered them well ... Mk 12:28
*p* the thought of their heart ... Lk 9:47
*p* that he had faith to be healed ... Acts 14:9

**PERDITION**
of them is lost, but the son of *p* ... Jn 17:12
is to them an evident token of *p* ... Phil 1:28
of sin be revealed, the son of *p* ... 2Th 2:3
drown men in destruction and *p* ... 1Ti 6:9
not of them who draw back unto *p* ... Heb 10:39
of judgment and *p* of ungodly men ... 2Pet 3:7
the bottomless pit, and go into *p* ... Rev 17:8
is of the seven, and goeth into *p* ... Rev 17:11

**PERES** (*pe'-res*) *Portion of 'the handwriting on the wall.'*
*P*; Thy kingdom is ... Dan 5:28

**PERESH** (*pe'-resh*) *A son of Machir.*
a son, and she called his name *P* ... 1Chr 7:16

**PEREZ** (*pe'-rez*) See PEREZ-UZZAH, PHARES.
*1. An ancestor of Jashobeam.*
Of the children of *P* was the ... 1Chr 27:3
*2. A son of Judah; same as Pharez.*
Mahalaleel, of the children of *P* ... Neh 11:4
All the sons of *P* that dwelt at ... Neh 11:6

**PEREZITES** See PHARZITES.

**PEREZ-UZZA** (*pe''-rez-uz'-zah*) See PEREZ-UZZAH. *Where Uzza died.*
place is called *P* to this day ... 1Chr 13:11

**PEREZ-UZZAH** (*pe''-rez-uz'-zah*) See PEREZ-UZZA. *Same as Perez-uzza.*
name of the place *P* to this day ... 2Sa 6:8

**PERFECT**
*p* in his generations, and Noah ... Gen 6:9
walk before me, and be thou *p* ... Gen 17:1
it shall be *p* to be accepted ... Lev 22:21
Thou shalt be *p* with the LORD thy ... Deut 18:13
a *p* and just weight, a *p* ... Deut 25:15
He is the Rock, his work is *p* ... Deut 32:4
LORD God of Israel, Give a *p* lot ... 1Sa 14:41
As for God, his way is *p* ... 2Sa 22:31
and he maketh my way *p* ... 2Sa 22:33
be *p* with the LORD our God ... 1Kin 8:61
his heart was not *p* with the LORD ... 1Kin 11:4
his heart was not *p* with the LORD ... 1Kin 15:3
was *p* with the LORD all his days ... 1Kin 15:14
thee in truth and with a *p* heart ... 2Kin 20:3
came with a *p* heart to Hebron, to ... 1Chr 12:38
and serve him with a *p* heart ... 1Chr 28:9
because with *p* heart they offered ... 1Chr 29:9
unto Solomon my son a *p* heart ... 1Chr 29:19
made he of gold, and that *p* gold ... 2Chr 4:21
heart of Asa was *p* all his days ... 2Chr 15:17
them whose heart is *p* toward him ... 2Chr 16:9
faithfully, and with a *p* heart ... 2Chr 19:9
the LORD, but not with a *p* heart ... 2Chr 25:2
*p* peace, and at such a time ... Ezr 7:12
and that man was *p* and upright, and ... Job 1:1
none like him in the earth, a *p* ... Job 1:8
none like him in the earth, a *p* ... Job 2:3
God will not cast away a *p* man ... Job 8:20
if I say, I am *p*, it shall also ... Job 9:20
Though I were *p*, yet would I not ... Job 9:21
I said it, He destroyeth the *p* ... Job 9:22
him, that thou makest thy ways *p* ... Job 22:3
he that is *p* in knowledge is with ... Job 36:4
of him which is *p* in knowledge ... Job 37:16
As for God, his way is *p* ... Ps 18:30
with strength, and maketh my way *p* ... Ps 18:32
The law of the LORD is *p* ... Ps 19:7
Mark the *p* man, and behold the ... Ps 37:37
they may shoot in secret at the *p* ... Ps 64:4
behave myself wisely in a *p* way ... Ps 101:2
within my house with a *p* heart ... Ps 101:2
he that walketh in a *p* way ... Ps 101:6
The LORD will *p* that which ... Ps 138:8
I hate them with *p* hatred ... Ps 139:22
land, and the *p* shall remain in it ... Prov 2:21
more and more unto the *p* day ... Prov 4:18
of the *p* shall direct his way ... Prov 11:5
the harvest, when the bud is *p* ... Is 18:5
Thou wilt keep him in *p* peace ... Is 26:3
thee in truth and with a *p* heart ... Is 38:3
who is blind as he that is *p* ... Is 42:19
for it was *p* through my ... Eze 16:14
thou hast said, I am of *p* beauty ... Eze 27:3
they have made thy beauty *p* ... Eze 27:11
full of wisdom, and *p* in beauty ... Eze 28:12
Thou wast *p* in thy ways from the ... Eze 28:15
Be ye therefore *p*, even as your ... Mt 5:48
Father which is in heaven is *p* ... Mt 5:48
said unto him, If thou wilt be *p* ... Mt 19:21
having had *p* understanding of all ... Lk 1:3
but every one that is *p* shall be ... Lk 6:40
that they may be made *p* in one ... Jn 17:23
*p* soundness in the presence of ... Acts 3:16
taught according to the *p* manner ... Acts 22:3
having more *p* knowledge of that ... Acts 24:22
is that good, and acceptable, and *p* ... Rom 12:2
wisdom among them that are *p* ... 1Cor 2:6
But when that which is *p* is come ... 1Cor 13:10
my strength is made *p* in weakness ... 2Cor 12:9
Be *p*, be of good comfort, be of ... 2Cor 13:11
are ye now made *p* by the flesh ... Gal 3:3
of the Son of God, unto a *p* man ... Eph 4:13
attained, either were already *p* ... Phil 3:12
Let us therefore, as many as be *p* ... Phil 3:15
every man *p* in Christ Jesus ... Col 1:28
in prayers, that ye may stand *p* ... Col 4:12
might *p* that which is lacking in ... 1Th 3:10
That the man of God may be *p* ... 2Ti 3:17
salvation *p* through sufferings ... Heb 2:10
And being made *p*, he became the ... Heb 5:9
For the law made nothing *p* ... Heb 7:19
make him that did the service *p* ... Heb 9:9
more *p* tabernacle, not made with ... Heb 9:11
make the comers thereunto *p* ... Heb 10:1
without us should not be made *p* ... Heb 11:40
to the spirits of just men made *p* ... Heb 12:23
Make you *p* in every good work to ... Heb 13:21
But let patience have her *p* work ... Jas 1:4
that ye may be *p* ... Jas 1:4
every *p* gift is from above, and ... Jas 1:17
looketh into the *p* law of liberty ... Jas 1:25
and by works was faith made *p* ... Jas 2:22
not in word, the same is a *p* man ... Jas 3:2
have suffered a while, make you *p* ... 1Pet 5:10
Herein is our love made *p* ... 1Jn 4:17
but *p* love casteth out fear ... 1Jn 4:18
feareth is not made *p* in love ... 1Jn 4:18
not found thy works *p* before God ... Rev 3:2

**PERFECTED**
So the house of the LORD was *p* ... 2Chr 8:16
and the work was *p* by them ... 2Chr 24:13
thy builders have *p* thy beauty ... Eze 27:4
and sucklings thou hast *p* praise ... Mt 21:16
and the third day I shall be *p* ... Lk 13:32
he hath *p* for ever them that are ... Heb 10:14
him verily is the love of God *p* ... 1Jn 2:5
in us, and his love is *p* in us ... 1Jn 4:12

**PERFECTING**
*p* holiness in the fear of God ... 2Cor 7:1
For the *p* of the saints, for the ... Eph 4:12

**PERFECTION**
thou find out the Almighty unto *p* ... Job 11:7
the *p* thereof upon the earth ... Job 15:29
darkness, and searcheth out all *p* ... Job 28:3
the *p* of beauty, God hath shined ... Ps 50:2
I have seen an end of all *p* ... Ps 119:96
their *p* for the multitude of thy ... Is 47:9
that men call The *p* of beauty ... Lam 2:15
this life, and bring no fruit to *p* ... Lk 8:14
and this also we wish, even your *p* ... 2Cor 13:9
of Christ, let us go on unto *p* ... Heb 6:1
If therefore *p* were by the ... Heb 7:11

**PERFECTLY**
days ye shall consider it *p* ... Jer 23:20
many as touched were made *p* whole ... Mt 14:36

unto him the way of God more *p*...... Acts 18:26
something more *p* concerning him...... Acts 23:15
enquire somewhat of him more *p*...... Acts 23:20
but that ye be *p* joined together...... 1Cor 1:10
For yourselves know *p* that the...... 1Th 5:2

**PERFECTNESS**
charity, which is the bond of *p*...... Col 3:14

**PERFORM**
I will *p* the oath which I sware...... Gen 26:3
not able to *p* it thyself alone...... Ex 18:18
that enter in to *p* the service...... Num 4:23
which he commanded you to *p*...... Deut 4:13
that he may *p* the word which the...... Deut 9:5
of thy lips thou shalt keep and *p*...... Deut 23:23
*p* the duty of an husband's...... Deut 25:5
he will not *p* the duty of my...... Deut 25:7
that if he will *p* unto thee the...... Ruth 3:13
In that day I will *p* against Eli...... 1Sa 3:12
*p* the request of his handmaid...... 2Sa 14:15
then will I *p* my word with thee,...... 1Kin 6:12
LORD, that he might *p* his saying...... 1Kin 12:15
to *p* the words of this covenant...... 2Kin 23:3
that he might *p* the words of the...... 2Kin 23:24
that the LORD might *p* his word...... 2Chr 10:15
to *p* the words of the covenant...... 2Chr 34:31
to *p* my request, let the king and...... Est 5:8
hands cannot *p* their enterprise...... Job 5:12
which they are not able to *p*...... Ps 21:11
ever, that I may daily *p* my vows...... Ps 61:8
I have sworn, and I will *p* it...... Ps 119:106
heart to *p* thy statutes alway...... Ps 119:112
of the LORD of hosts will *p* this...... Is 9:7
vow a vow unto the LORD, and *p* it...... Is 19:21
and shall *p* all my pleasure...... Is 44:28
for I will hasten my word to *p* it...... Jer 1:12
That I may *p* the oath which I...... Jer 11:5
the LORD *p* thy words which thou...... Jer 28:6
*p* my good word toward you, in...... Jer 29:10
that I will *p* that good thing...... Jer 33:14
We will surely *p* our vows that we...... Jer 44:25
your vows, and surely *p* your vows...... Jer 44:25
will I say the word, and will *p* it...... Eze 12:25
Thou wilt *p* the truth to Jacob,...... Mic 7:20
thy solemn feasts, *p* thy vows...... Nah 1:15
but shalt *p* unto the Lord thine...... Mt 5:33
To *p* the mercy promised to our...... Lk 1:72
promised, he was able also to *p*...... Rom 4:21
but how to *p* that which is good I...... Rom 7:18
Now therefore *p* the doing of it...... 2Cor 8:11
will *p* it until the day of Jesus...... Phil 1:6

**PERFORMANCE**
for there shall be a *p* of those...... Lk 1:45
so there may be a *p* also out of...... 2Cor 8:11

**PERFORMED**
hath not *p* my commandments...... 1Sa 15:11
I have *p* the commandment of the...... 1Sa 15:13
and they *p* all that the king...... 2Sa 21:14
the LORD hath *p* his word that he...... 1Kin 8:20
The LORD therefore hath *p* his...... 2Chr 6:10
to his seed, and hast *p* thy words...... Neh 9:8
because she hath not *p* the...... Est 1:15
half of the kingdom it shall be *p*...... Est 5:6
and it shall be *p*, even to the...... Est 7:2
and unto thee shall the vow be *p*...... Ps 65:1
that when the Lord hath *p* his...... Is 10:12
till he have *p* the thoughts of...... Jer 23:20
until he have *p* the intents of...... Jer 30:24
which have not *p* the words of the...... Jer 34:18
his sons not to drink wine, are *p*...... Jer 35:14
Jonadab the son of Rechab have *p*...... Jer 35:16
LORD shall be *p* against Babylon...... Jer 51:29
it, and *p* it, saith the LORD...... Eze 37:14
day that these things shall be *p*...... Lk 1:20
when they had *p* all things...... Lk 2:39
When therefore I have *p* this...... Rom 15:28

**PERFORMETH**
that *p* not this promise, even...... Neh 5:13
For he *p* the thing that is...... Job 23:14
unto God that *p* all things for me...... Ps 57:2
*p* the counsel of his messengers...... Is 44:26

**PERFORMING**
or a sacrifice in *p* a vow...... Num 15:3
or for a sacrifice in *p* a vow...... Num 15:8

**PERFUME**
And thou shalt make it a *p*...... Ex 30:35
as for the *p* which thou shalt...... Ex 30:37
Ointment and *p* rejoice the heart...... Prov 27:9

**PERFUMED**
I have *p* my bed with myrrh, aloes...... Prov 7:17
*p* with myrrh and frankincense,...... Song 3:6

**PERFUMES**
ointment, and didst increase thy *p*...... Is 57:9

**PERGA** (*pur'-gah*) *Capital of Pamphylia.*
they came to *P* in Pamphylia...... Acts 13:13
But when they departed from *P*...... Acts 13:14
they had preached the word in *P*...... Acts 14:25

**PERGAMOS** (*pur'-ga-mos*) *A city in Mysia in Asia Minor.*
and unto Smyrna, and unto *P*...... Rev 1:11
angel of the church in *P* write...... Rev 2:12

**PERGAMUM** See PERGAMOS.

**PERHAPS**
if *p* the thought of thine heart...... Acts 8:22
lest *p* such a one should be...... 2Cor 2:7
For *p* he therefore departed for a...... Philem 15

**PERIDA** (*per-i'-dah*) *A family of exiles.*
of Sophereth, the children of *P*...... Neh 7:57

**PERIL**
We gat our bread with the *p* of...... Lam 5:9
or famine, or nakedness, or *p*...... Rom 8:35

**PERILOUS**
the last days *p* times shall come...... 2Ti 3:1

**PERILS**
in *p* of waters...... 2Cor 11:26
in *p* of robbers...... 2Cor 11:26
in *p* by mine own countrymen...... 2Cor 11:26
in *p* by the heathen...... 2Cor 11:26
in *p* in the city...... 2Cor 11:26
in *p* in the wilderness...... 2Cor 11:26
in *p* in the sea...... 2Cor 11:26
in *p* among false brethren...... 2Cor 11:26

**PERISH**
that the land *p* not through the...... Gen 41:36
LORD to gaze, and many of them *p*...... Ex 19:21
or the eye of his maid, that it *p*...... Ex 21:26
ye shall *p* among the heathen, and...... Lev 26:38
we die, we *p*, we all *p*...... Num 17:12
end shall be that he *p* for ever...... Num 24:20
Eber, and he also shall *p* for ever...... Num 24:24
that ye shall soon utterly *p* from...... Deut 4:26
this day that ye shall surely *p*...... Deut 8:19
before your face, so shall ye *p*...... Deut 8:20
lest ye *p* quickly from off the...... Deut 11:17
A Syrian ready to *p* was my father...... Deut 26:5
and until thou *p* quickly...... Deut 28:20
shall pursue thee until thou *p*...... Deut 28:22
this day, that ye shall surely *p*...... Deut 30:18
until ye *p* from off this good...... Josh 23:13
ye shall *p* quickly from off the...... Josh 23:16
So let all thine enemies *p*...... Judg 5:31
shall descend into battle, and *p*...... 1Sa 26:10
I shall now *p* one day by the hand...... 1Sa 27:1
the whole house of Ahab shall *p*...... 2Kin 9:8
to kill, and to cause to *p*...... Est 3:13
and if I *p*, I *p*...... Est 4:16
destroyed, to be slain, and to *p*...... Est 7:4
to slay, and to cause to *p*...... Est 8:11
of them *p* from their seed...... Est 9:28
Let the day *p* wherein I was born,...... Job 3:3
By the blast of God they *p*...... Job 4:9
they *p* for ever without any...... Job 4:20
they go to nothing, and *p*...... Job 6:18
and the hypocrite's hope shall *p*...... Job 8:13
shall *p* from the earth, and he...... Job 18:17
Yet he shall *p* for ever like his...... Job 20:7
that was ready to *p* came upon me...... Job 29:13
If I have seen any *p* for want of...... Job 31:19
All flesh shall *p* together...... Job 34:15
they shall *p* by the sword, and...... Job 36:12
the way of the ungodly shall *p*...... Ps 1:6
ye *p* from the way, when his wrath...... Ps 2:12
shall fall and *p* at thy presence...... Ps 9:3
of the poor shall not *p* for ever...... Ps 9:18
But the wicked shall *p*, and the...... Ps 37:20
When shall he die, and his name *p*...... Ps 41:5
the fool and the brutish person *p*...... Ps 49:10
he is like the beasts that *p*...... Ps 49:12
not, is like the beasts that *p*...... Ps 49:20
so let the wicked *p* at the...... Ps 68:2
that are far from thee shall *p*...... Ps 73:27
they *p* at the rebuke of thy...... Ps 80:16
let them be put to shame, and *p*...... Ps 83:17
for, lo, thine enemies shall *p*...... Ps 92:9
They shall *p*, but thou shalt...... Ps 102:26
the desire of the wicked shall *p*...... Ps 112:10
in that very day his thoughts *p*...... Ps 146:4
expectation of the wicked shall *p*...... Prov 10:28
dieth, his expectation shall *p*...... Prov 11:7
and when the wicked *p*, there is...... Prov 11:10
and he that speaketh lies shall *p*...... Prov 19:9
A false witness shall *p*...... Prov 21:28
but when they *p*, the righteous...... Prov 28:28
there is no vision, the people *p*...... Prov 29:18
drink unto him that is ready to *p*...... Prov 31:6
those riches *p* by evil travail...... Eccl 5:14
and made all their memory to *p*...... Is 26:14
ready to *p* in the land of Assyria...... Is 27:13
wisdom of their wise men shall *p*...... Is 29:14
that strive with thee shall *p*...... Is 41:11
that will not serve thee shall *p*...... Is 60:12
the heart of the king shall *p*...... Jer 4:9
neighbour and his friend shall *p*...... Jer 6:21
even they shall *p* from the earth...... Jer 10:11
of their visitation they shall *p*...... Jer 10:15
law shall not *p* from the priest...... Jer 18:18
drive you out, and ye should *p*...... Jer 27:10
drive you out, and that ye might *p*...... Jer 27:15
and the remnant in Judah *p*...... Jer 40:15
the valley also shall *p*, and the...... Jer 48:8
of their visitation they shall *p*...... Jer 51:18
the law shall *p* from the priest...... Eze 7:26
thee to *p* out of the countries...... Eze 25:7
his fellows should not *p* with the...... Dan 2:18
of the Philistines shall *p*...... Amos 1:8
the flight shall *p* from the swift...... Amos 2:14
and the houses of ivory shall *p*...... Amos 3:15
will think upon us, that we *p* not...... Jonah 1:6
let us not *p* for this man's life,...... Jonah 1:14
his fierce anger, that we *p* not...... Jonah 3:9
and the king shall *p* from Gaza...... Zec 9:5
that one of thy members should *p*...... Mt 5:29
that one of thy members should *p*...... Mt 5:30
Lord, save us: we *p*...... Mt 8:25
runneth out, and the bottles *p*...... Mt 9:17
one of these little ones should *p*...... Mt 18:14
the sword shall *p* with the sword...... Mt 26:52
Master, carest thou not that we *p*...... Mk 4:38
spilled, and the bottles shall *p*...... Lk 5:37
him, saying, Master, master, we *p*...... Lk 8:24
repent, ye shall all likewise *p*...... Lk 13:3
repent, ye shall all likewise *p*...... Lk 13:5
that a prophet *p* out of Jerusalem...... Lk 13:33
and to spare, and I *p* with hunger...... Lk 15:17
shall not an hair of your head *p*...... Lk 21:18
believeth in him should not *p*...... Jn 3:15
believeth in him should not *p*...... Jn 3:16
and they shall never *p*, neither...... Jn 10:28
and that the whole nation *p* not...... Jn 11:50
unto him, Thy money *p* with thee...... Acts 8:20
ye despisers, and wonder, and *p*...... Acts 13:41
law shall also *p* without law...... Rom 2:12
is to them that *p* foolishness...... 1Cor 1:18
shall the weak brother *p*, for...... 1Cor 8:11
that are saved, and in them that *p*...... 2Cor 2:15
but though our outward man *p*...... 2Cor 4:16
Which all are to *p* with the using...... Col 2:22
of unrighteousness in them that *p*...... 2Th 2:10
They shall *p*; but thou...... Heb 1:11
shall utterly *p* in their own...... 2Pet 2:12
not willing that any should *p*...... 2Pet 3:9

**PERISHED**
and they *p* from among the...... Num 16:33
Heshbon is *p* even unto Dibon, and...... Num 21:30
that man *p* not alone in his...... Josh 22:20
fallen, and the weapons of war *p*...... 2Sa 1:27
Remember, I pray thee, who ever *p*...... Job 4:7
profit me, in whom old age was *p*...... Job 30:2
their memorial is *p* with them...... Ps 9:6
the heathen are *p* out of his land...... Ps 10:16
Which *p* at En-dor...... Ps 83:10
then have *p* in mine affliction...... Ps 119:92
hatred, and their envy, is now *p*...... Eccl 9:6
truth is *p*, and is cut off from...... Jer 7:28
riches that he hath gotten are *p*...... Jer 48:36
is counsel *p* from the prudent...... Jer 49:7
my hope is *p* from the LORD...... Lam 3:18
the harvest of the field is *p*...... Joel 1:11
up in a night, and *p* in a night...... Jonah 4:10
is thy counsellor *p*...... Mic 4:9
The good man is *p* out of the...... Mic 7:2
into the sea, and *p* in the waters...... Mt 8:32
which *p* between the altar and the...... Lk 11:51
after him: he also *p*...... Acts 5:37
are fallen asleep in Christ are *p*...... 1Cor 15:18
By faith the harlot Rahab *p* not...... Heb 11:31
being overflowed with water, *p*...... 2Pet 3:6
*p* in the gainsaying of Core...... Jude 11

**PERISHETH**
The old lion *p* for lack of prey,...... Job 4:11
and the hope of unjust men *p*...... Prov 11:7
man that *p* in his righteousness...... Eccl 7:15
The righteous *p*, and no man layeth...... Is 57:1
declare it, for what the land *p*...... Jer 9:12
the people of Chemosh *p*...... Jer 48:46
Labour not for the meat which *p*...... Jn 6:27
the grace of the fashion of it *p*...... Jas 1:11
more precious than of gold that *p*...... 1Pet 1:7

**PERISHING**
and his life from *p* by the sword...... Job 33:18

**PERIZZITE** (*per'-iz-zite*) See PERIZZITES. *A tribe in Judah.*
the *P* dwelled then in the land...... Gen 13:7
Amorite, and the Hittite, and the *P*...... Ex 33:2
and the Hittite, and the *P*...... Ex 34:11
the Amorite, the Canaanite, the *P*...... Josh 9:1
Amorite, and the Hittite, and the *P*...... Josh 11:3

**PERIZZITES** (*per'-iz-zites*)
And the Hittites, and the *P*...... Gen 15:20
among the Canaanites and the *P*...... Gen 34:30
and the Amorites, and the *P*...... Ex 3:8
and the Amorites, and the *P*...... Ex 3:17
and the Hittites, and the *P*...... Ex 23:23
and the Canaanites, and the *P*...... Deut 7:1
the Canaanites, and the *P*...... Deut 20:17
and the Hivites, and the *P*...... Josh 3:10
and the Canaanites, the *P*...... Josh 12:8
there in the land of the *P*...... Josh 17:15
you, the Amorites, and the *P*...... Josh 24:11
and the *P* into their hand...... Judg 1:4
they slew the Canaanites and the *P*...... Judg 1:5
Hittites, and Amorites, and *P*...... Judg 3:5
left of the Amorites, Hittites, *P*...... 1Kin 9:20
and the Amorites, and the *P*...... 2Chr 8:7
Canaanites, the Hittites, the *P*...... Ezr 9:1
Hittites, the Amorites, and the *P*...... Neh 9:8

**PERJURED**
for *p* persons, and if there be any...... 1Ti 1:10

**PERMISSION**
But I speak this by *p*, and not of...... 1Cor 7:6

**PERMIT**
a while with you, if the Lord *p*...... 1Cor 16:7
And this will we do, if God *p*...... Heb 6:3

**PERMITTED**
Thou art *p* to speak for thyself...... Acts 26:1
for it is not *p* unto them to...... 1Cor 14:34

**PERNICIOUS**
And many shall follow their *p* ways...... 2Pet 2:2

**PERPETUAL**
is with you, for *p* generations...... Gen 9:12
shall be theirs for a *p* statute...... Ex 29:9

P

a *p* incense before the LORD ... Ex 30:8
generations, for a *p* covenant ... Ex 31:16
It shall be a *p* statute for your ... Lev 3:17
fine flour for a meat offering *p* ... Lev 6:20
LORD made by fire by a *p* statute ... Lev 24:9
for it is their *p* possession ... Lev 25:34
it shall be a *p* statute unto them ... Num 19:21
destructions are come to a *p* end ... Ps 9:6
thy feet unto the *p* desolations ... Ps 74:3
he put them to a *p* reproach ... Ps 78:66
bound of the sea by a *p* decree ... Jer 5:22
slidden back by a *p* backsliding ... Jer 8:5
Why is my pain *p*, and my wound ... Jer 15:18
land desolate, and a *p* hissing ... Jer 18:16
a *p* shame, which shall not be ... Jer 23:40
and an hissing, and *p* desolations ... Jer 25:9
and will make it *p* desolations ... Jer 25:12
cities thereof shall be *p* wastes ... Jer 49:13
in a *p* covenant that shall not be ... Jer 50:5
may rejoice, and sleep a *p* sleep ... Jer 51:39
and they shall sleep a *p* sleep ... Jer 51:57
Because thou hast had a *p* hatred ... Eze 35:5
I will make thee *p* desolations ... Eze 35:9
by a *p* ordinance unto the LORD ... Eze 46:14
scattered, the *p* hills did bow ... Hab 3:6
and saltpits, and a *p* desolation ... Zeph 2:9

**PERPETUALLY**
and mine heart shall be there *p* ... 1Kin 9:3
and mine heart shall be there *p* ... 2Chr 7:16
all pity, and his anger did tear *p* ... Amos 1:11

**PERPLEXED**
but the city Shushan was *p* ... Est 3:15
the herds of cattle are *p* ... Joel 1:18
and he was *p*, because that it was ... Lk 9:7
as they were much *p* thereabout ... Lk 24:4
we are *p*, but not in despair ... 2Cor 4:8

**PERPLEXITY**
of *p* by the Lord GOD of hosts in ... Is 22:5
now shall be their *p* ... Mic 7:4
earth distress of nations, with *p* ... Lk 21:25

**PERSECUTE**
Why do ye *p* me as God, and are not .. Job 19:22
Why *p* we him, seeing the root of ... Job 19:28
save me from all them that *p* me ... Ps 7:1
Let the enemy *p* my soul, and take ... Ps 7:5
in his pride doth *p* the poor ... Ps 10:2
enemies, and from them that *p* me ... Ps 31:15
the way against them that *p* me ... Ps 35:3
let the angel of the LORD *p* them ... Ps 35:6
For they *p* him whom thou hast ... Ps 69:26
*p* and take him ... Ps 71:11
So *p* them with thy tempest, and ... Ps 83:15
judgment on them that *p* me ... Ps 119:84
they *p* me wrongfully ... Ps 119:86
Let them be confounded that *p* me ... Jer 17:18
I will *p* them with the sword, ... Jer 29:18
*P* and destroy them in anger from ... Lam 3:66
*p* you, and shall say all manner of ... Mt 5:11
despitefully use you, and *p* you ... Mt 5:44
But when they *p* you in this city, ... Mt 10:23
and *p* them from city to city ... Mt 23:34
some of them they shall slay and *p* ... Lk 11:49
*p* you, delivering you up to the ... Lk 21:12
And therefore did the Jews *p* Jesus ... Jn 5:16
me, they will also *p* you ... Jn 15:20
Bless them which *p* you ... Rom 12:14

**PERSECUTED**
them that hate thee, which *p* thee ... Deut 30:7
but *p* the poor and needy man, that ... Ps 109:16
Princes have *p* me without a cause ... Ps 119:161
For the enemy hath *p* my soul ... Ps 143:3
ruled the nations in anger, is *p* ... Is 14:6
hast covered with anger, and *p* us ... Lam 3:43
are *p* for righteousness' sake ... Mt 5:10
for so *p* they the prophets which ... Mt 5:12
If they have *p* me, they will also ... Jn 15:20
prophets have not your fathers *p* ... Acts 7:52
I *p* this way unto the death, ... Acts 22:4
I *p* them even unto strange cities ... Acts 26:11
being *p*, we suffer it ... 1Cor 4:12
because I *p* the church of God ... 1Cor 15:9
*P*, but not forsaken ... 2Cor 4:9
measure I *p* the church of God ... Gal 1:13
That he which *p* us in times past ... Gal 1:23
*p* him that was born after the ... Gal 4:29
their own prophets, and have *p* us ... 1Th 2:15
he *p* the woman which brought ... Rev 12:13

**PERSECUTEST**
him, Saul, Saul, why *p* thou me ... Acts 9:4
Lord said, I am Jesus whom thou *p* ... Acts 9:5
me, Saul, Saul, why *p* thou me ... Acts 22:7
am Jesus of Nazareth, whom thou *p* ... Acts 22:8
tongue, Saul, Saul, why *p* thou me ... Acts 26:14
he said, I am Jesus whom thou *p* ... Acts 26:15

**PERSECUTING**
Concerning zeal, *p* the church ... Phil 3:6

**PERSECUTION**
Our necks are under *p* ... Lam 5:5
for when tribulation or *p* ariseth ... Mt 13:21
when affliction or *p* ariseth for ... Mk 4:17
at that time there was a great *p* ... Acts 8:1
the *p* that arose about Stephen ... Acts 11:19
raised *p* against Paul and Barnabas ... Acts 13:50
tribulation, or distress, or *p* ... Rom 8:35
why do I yet suffer *p* ... Gal 5:11
suffer *p* for the cross of Christ ... Gal 6:12
in Christ Jesus shall suffer *p* ... 2Ti 3:12

**PERSECUTIONS**
and children, and lands, with *p* ... Mk 10:30
reproaches, in necessities, in *p* ... 2Cor 12:10
patience and faith in all your *p* ... 2Th 1:4
*P*, afflictions, which came unto ... 2Ti 3:11
what *p* I endured ... 2Ti 3:11

**PERSECUTOR**
was before a blasphemer, and a *p* ... 1Ti 1:13

**PERSECUTORS**
their *p* thou threwest into the ... Neh 9:11
his arrows against the *p* ... Ps 7:13
Many are my *p* and mine enemies ... Ps 119:157
deliver me from my *p* ... Ps 142:6
visit me, and revenge me of my *p* ... Jer 15:15
therefore my *p* shall stumble, and ... Jer 20:11
all her *p* overtook her between ... Lam 1:3
Our *p* are swifter than the eagles ... Lam 4:19

**PERSEVERANCE**
and watching thereunto with all *p* ... Eph 6:18

**PERSIA** (*per'-she-ah*) See ELAM, PERSIAN. *An ancient world power located in present-day Iran.*
the reign of the kingdom of *P* ... 2Chr 36:20
the first year of Cyrus king of *P* ... 2Chr 36:22
up the spirit of Cyrus king of *P* ... 2Chr 36:22
Thus saith Cyrus king of *P* ... 2Chr 36:23
the first year of Cyrus king of *P* ... Ezr 1:1
up the spirit of Cyrus king of *P* ... Ezr 1:1
Thus saith Cyrus king of *P* ... Ezr 1:2
of *P* bring forth by the hand of ... Ezr 1:8
that they had of Cyrus king of *P* ... Ezr 3:7
the king of *P* hath commanded us ... Ezr 4:3
all the days of Cyrus king of *P* ... Ezr 4:5
the reign of Darius king of *P* ... Ezr 4:5
unto Artaxerxes king of *P* ... Ezr 4:7
of the reign of Darius king of *P* ... Ezr 4:24
Darius, and Artaxerxes king of *P* ... Ezr 6:14
the reign of Artaxerxes king of *P* ... Ezr 7:1
us in the sight of the kings of *P* ... Ezr 9:9
the power of *P* and Media, the ... Est 1:3
Memucan, the seven princes of *P* ... Est 1:14
Likewise shall the ladies of *P* ... Est 1:18
of the kings of Media and *P* ... Est 10:2
They of *P* and of Lud and of Phut ... Eze 27:10
*P*, Ethiopia, and Libya with them ... Eze 38:5
horns are the kings of Media and *P* ... Dan 8:20
of *P* a thing was revealed unto ... Dan 10:1
the kingdom of *P* withstood me one .. Dan 10:13
there with the kings of *P* ... Dan 10:13
to fight with the prince of *P* ... Dan 10:20
stand up yet three kings in *P* ... Dan 11:2

**PERSIAN** (*per'-she-un*) *A native of Persia.*
to the reign of Darius the *P* ... Neh 12:22
and in the reign of Cyrus the *P* ... Dan 6:28

**PERSIANS** (*per'-she-uns*) See ELAMITES.
written among the laws of the *P* ... Est 1:19
and given to the Medes and *P* ... Dan 5:28
to the law of the Medes and *P* ... Dan 6:8
to the law of the Medes and *P* ... Dan 6:12
*P* is, That no decree nor statute ... Dan 6:15

**PERSIS** (*pur'-sis*) *A Christian in Rome.*
Salute the beloved *P*, which ... Rom 16:12

**PERSON**
And Joseph was a goodly *p*, and well ... Gen 39:6
uncircumcised *p* shall eat thereof ... Ex 12:48
not respect the *p* of the poor ... Lev 19:15
nor honour the *p* of the mighty ... Lev 19:15
the LORD, and that *p* be guilty ... Num 5:6
for an unclean *p* they shall take ... Num 19:17
a clean *p* shall take hyssop, and ... Num 19:18
the clean *p* shall sprinkle upon ... Num 19:19
whatsoever the unclean *p* toucheth .. Num 19:22
whosoever hath killed any *p* ... Num 31:19
which killeth any *p* at unawares ... Num 35:11
any *p* unawares may flee thither ... Num 35:15
Whoso killeth any *p*, the murderer ... Num 35:30
against any *p* to cause him to die ... Num 35:30
the clean *p* shall eat it alike, ... Deut 15:22
reward to slay an innocent *p* ... Deut 27:25
shall not regard the *p* of the old ... Deut 28:50
that killeth any *p* unawares ... Josh 20:3
that whosoever killeth any *p* at ... Josh 20:9
of Israel a goodlier *p* than he ... 1Sa 9:2
prudent in matters, and a comely *p* ... 1Sa 16:18
thy voice, and have accepted thy *p* ... 1Sa 25:35
men have slain a righteous *p* in ... 2Sa 4:11
neither doth God respect any *p* ... 2Sa 14:14
thou go to battle in thine own *p* ... 2Sa 17:11
Will ye accept his *p* ... Job 13:8
and he shall save the humble *p* ... Job 22:29
I pray you, accept any man's *p* ... Job 32:21
whose eyes a vile *p* is contemned ... Ps 15:4
the fool and the brutish *p* perish ... Ps 49:10
I will not know a wicked *p* ... Ps 101:4
one feeble *p* among their tribes ... Ps 105:37
A naughty *p*, a wicked man, ... Prov 6:12
to accept the *p* of the wicked ... Prov 18:5
shall be called a mischievous *p* ... Prov 24:8
of any *p* shall flee to the pit ... Prov 28:17
The vile *p* shall be no more ... Is 32:5
For the vile *p* will speak villany ... Is 32:6
every *p* that Nebuzar-adan the ... Jer 43:6
them that were near the king's *p* ... Jer 52:25
field, to the lothing of thy *p* ... Eze 16:5
take any *p* from among them, he is ... Eze 33:6
at no dead *p* to defile themselves ... Eze 44:25
estate shall stand up a vile *p* ... Dan 11:21
with thee, or accept thy *p* ... Mal 1:8
thou regardest not the *p* of men ... Mt 22:16
of the blood of this just *p* ... Mt 27:24
thou regardest not the *p* of men ... Mk 12:14
acceptest thou the *p* of any ... Lk 20:21
among yourselves that wicked *p* ... 1Cor 5:13
forgave I it in the *p* of Christ ... 2Cor 2:10
God accepteth no man's *p* ... Gal 2:6
no whoremonger, nor unclean *p* ... Eph 5:5
and the express image of his *p* ... Heb 1:3
be any fornicator, or profane *p* ... Heb 12:16
but saved Noah the eighth *p* ... 2Pet 2:5

**PERSONS**
said unto Abram, Give me the *p* ... Gen 14:21
all the *p* of his house, and his ... Gen 36:6
according to the number of your *p* ... Ex 16:16
the *p* shall be for the LORD by ... Lev 27:2
upon the *p* that were there, and ... Num 19:18
of five hundred, both of the *p* ... Num 31:28
one portion of fifty, of the *p* ... Num 31:30
thirty and two thousand *p* in all ... Num 31:35
the *p* were sixteen thousand ... Num 31:40
tribute was thirty and two *p* ... Num 31:40
And sixteen thousand *p* ... Num 31:46
shall not respect *p* in judgment ... Deut 1:17
a terrible, which regardeth not *p* ... Deut 10:17
Egypt with threescore and ten *p* ... Deut 10:22
thou shalt not respect *p*, neither ... Deut 16:19
which are threescore and ten *p* ... Judg 9:2
Abimelech hired vain and light *p* ... Judg 9:4
being threescore and ten *p* ... Judg 9:5
his sons, threescore and ten *p* ... Judg 9:18
of the men of Israel about thirty *p* ... Judg 20:39
bidden, which were about thirty *p* ... 1Sa 9:22
five *p* that did wear a linen ... 1Sa 22:18
all the *p* of thy father's house ... 1Sa 22:22
the king's sons, being seventy *p* ... 2Kin 10:6
king's sons, and slew seventy *p* ... 2Kin 10:7
LORD our God, nor respect of *p* ... 2Chr 19:7
you, if ye do secretly accept *p* ... Job 13:10
accepteth not the *p* of princes ... Job 34:19
I have not sat with vain *p* ... Ps 26:4
accept the *p* of the wicked ... Ps 82:2
vain *p* is void of understanding ... Prov 12:11
to have respect of *p* in judgment ... Prov 24:23
vain *p* shall have poverty enough ... Prov 28:19
To have respect of *p* is not good ... Prov 28:21
eight hundred thirty and two *p* ... Jer 52:29
seven hundred forty and five *p* ... Jer 52:30
all the *p* were four thousand and ... Jer 52:30
not the *p* of the priests, they ... Lam 4:16
building forts, to cut off many *p* ... Eze 17:17
they traded the *p* of men and ... Eze 27:13
*p* that cannot discern between ... Jonah 4:11
are light and treacherous *p* ... Zeph 3:4
will he regard your *p* ... Mal 1:9
than over ninety and nine just *p* ... Lk 15:7
that God is no respecter of *p* ... Acts 10:34
the Jews, and with the devout *p* ... Acts 17:17
there is no respect of *p* with God ... Rom 2:11
upon us by the means of many *p* ... 2Cor 1:11
is there respect of *p* with him ... Eph 6:9
and there is no respect of *p* ... Col 3:25
for liars, for perjured *p* ... 1Ti 1:10
Lord of glory, with respect of *p* ... Jas 2:1
But if ye have respect to *p* ... Jas 2:9
who without respect of *p* judgeth ... 1Pet 1:17
what manner of *p* ought ye to be ... 2Pet 3:11
having men's *p* in admiration ... Jude 16

**PERSUADE**
the LORD said, Who shall *p* Ahab ... 1Kin 22:20
the LORD, and said, I will *p* him ... 1Kin 22:21
And he said, Thou shalt *p* him ... 1Kin 22:22
Doth not Hezekiah *p* you to give ... 2Chr 32:11
nor *p* you on this manner, neither ... 2Chr 32:15
Beware lest Hezekiah *p* you ... Is 36:18
governor's ears, we will *p* him ... Mt 28:14
the terror of the Lord, we *p* men ... 2Cor 5:11
For do I now *p* men, or God ... Gal 1:10

**PERSUADED**
*p* him to go up with him to ... 2Chr 18:2
By long forbearing is a prince *p* ... Prov 25:15
elders *p* the multitude that they ... Mt 27:20
prophets, neither will they be *p* ... Lk 16:31
for they be *p* that John was a ... Lk 20:6
*p* them to continue in the grace ... Acts 13:43
who *p* the people, and, having ... Acts 14:19
and *p* the Jews and the Greeks ... Acts 18:4
all Asia, this Paul hath *p* ... Acts 19:26
And when he would not be *p* ... Acts 21:14
for I am *p* that none of these ... Acts 26:26
And being fully *p* that, what he ... Rom 4:21
For I am *p*, that neither death, ... Rom 8:38
man be fully *p* in his own mind ... Rom 14:5
am *p* by the Lord Jesus, that ... Rom 14:14
And I myself also am *p* of you ... Rom 15:14
and I am *p* that in thee also ... 2Ti 1:5
am *p* that he is able to keep that ... 2Ti 1:12
we are *p* better things of you, and ... Heb 6:9
were *p* of them, and embraced them,. Heb 11:13

**PERSUADEST**
Paul, Almost thou *p* me to be a ... Acts 26:28

**PERSUADETH**
not unto Hezekiah, when he *p* you ... 2Kin 18:32
This fellow *p* men to worship God ... Acts 18:13

**PERSUADING**
*p* the things concerning the — Acts 19:8
*p* them concerning Jesus, both out — Acts 28:23

**PERSUASION**
This *p* cometh not of him that — Gal 5:8

**PERTAIN**
that *p* unto the LORD, having his — Lev 7:20
which *p* unto the LORD, even that — Lev 7:21
if I leave of all that *p* to him — 1Sa 25:22
in those things which *p* to God — Rom 15:17
more things that *p* to this life — 1Cor 6:3
us all things that *p* unto life — 2Pet 1:3

**PERTAINED**
(Now the half that *p* unto the — Num 31:43
a hill that *p* to Phinehas his son — Josh 24:33
that *p* unto Joash the Abi-ezrite — Judg 6:11
was missed of all that *p* unto him — 1Sa 25:21
which *p* to Ish-bosheth the son of — 2Sa 2:15
master's son all that *p* to Saul — 2Sa 9:9
are all that *p* unto Mephibosheth — 2Sa 16:4
to him *p* Sochoh, and all the land — 1Kin 4:10
to him *p* Taanach and Megiddo, and — 1Kin 4:12
to him *p* the towns of Jair the — 1Kin 4:13
to him also *p* the region of Argob — 1Kin 4:13
made all the vessels that *p* unto — 1Kin 7:48
all that *p* to the king of Egypt — 2Kin 24:7
thereof every morning *p* to them — 1Chr 9:27
that *p* to the children of — 1Chr 11:31
fenced cities which *p* to Judah — 2Chr 12:4
that *p* to the children of Israel — 2Chr 34:33

**PERTAINETH**
get that which *p* to his cleansing — Lev 14:32
priest *p* the oil for the light — Num 4:16
not wear that which *p* unto a man — Deut 22:5
wherefore Ziklag *p* unto the kings — 1Sa 27:6
Obed-edom, and all that *p* unto him — 2Sa 6:12
to whom *p* the adoption, and the — Rom 9:4
are spoken *p* to another tribe — Heb 7:13

**PERTAINING**
were *p* unto the children of — Josh 13:31
for every matter *p* to God — 1Chr 26:32
things *p* to the kingdom of God — Acts 1:3
as *p* to the flesh, hath found — Rom 4:1
of things *p* to this life, set — 1Cor 6:4
high priest in things *p* to God — Heb 2:17
for men in things *p* to God — Heb 5:1
perfect, as *p* to the conscience — Heb 9:9

**PERUDA** (*per'-u-dah*) See PERIDA. *A family of exiles.*
of Sophereth, the children of *P* — Ezr 2:55

**PERVERSE**
because thy way is *p* before me — Num 22:32
they are a *p* and crooked — Deut 32:5
Thou son of the *p* rebellious — 1Sa 20:30
cannot my taste discern *p* things — Job 6:30
perfect, it shall also prove me *p* — Job 9:20
and *p* lips put far from thee — Prov 4:24
is nothing froward or *p* in them — Prov 8:8
but he that is of a *p* heart shall — Prov 12:8
but he that is *p* in his ways — Prov 14:2
he that hath a *p* tongue falleth — Prov 17:20
than he that is *p* in his lips — Prov 19:1
thine heart shall utter *p* things — Prov 23:33
than he that is *p* in his ways — Prov 28:6
but he that is *p* in his ways — Prov 28:18
The LORD hath mingled a *p* spirit — Is 19:14
*p* generation, how long shall I be — Mt 17:17
*p* generation, how long shall I be — Lk 9:41
men arise, speaking *p* things — Acts 20:30
*p* nation, among whom ye shine as — Phil 2:15
*P* disputings of men of corrupt — 1Ti 6:5

**PERVERSELY**
that which thy servant did *p* the — 2Sa 19:19
We have sinned, and have done *p* — 1Kin 8:47
for they dealt *p* with me without — Ps 119:78

**PERVERSENESS**
neither hath he seen *p* in Israel — Num 23:21
but the *p* of transgressors shall — Prov 11:3
but *p* therein is a breach in the — Prov 15:4
word, and trust in oppression and *p* — Is 30:12
lies, your tongue hath muttered *p* — Is 59:3
of blood, and the city full of *p* — Eze 9:9

**PERVERT**
*p* the words of the righteous — Deut 16:19
Thou shalt not *p* the judgment of — Deut 24:17
Doth God *p* judgment — Job 8:3
or doth the Almighty *p* justice — Job 8:3
will the Almighty *p* judgment — Job 34:12
bosom to *p* the ways of judgment — Prov 17:23
*p* the judgment of any of the — Prov 31:5
abhor judgment, and *p* all equity — Mic 3:9
wilt thou not cease to *p* the — Acts 13:10
would *p* the gospel of Christ — Gal 1:7

**PERVERTED**
and took bribes, and *p* judgment — 1Sa 8:3
*p* that which was right, and it — Job 33:27
and thy knowledge, it hath *p* thee — Is 47:10
for they have *p* their way — Jer 3:21
for ye have *p* the words of the — Jer 23:36

**PERVERTETH**
*p* the words of the righteous — Ex 23:8
Cursed be he that *p* the judgment — Deut 27:19
but he that *p* his ways shall be — Prov 10:9
The foolishness of man *p* his way — Prov 19:3
unto me, as one that *p* the people — Lk 23:14

**PERVERTING**
violent *p* of judgment and justice — Eccl 5:8
We found this fellow *p* the nation — Lk 23:2

**PESTILENCE**
lest he fall upon us with *p* — Ex 5:3
smite thee and thy people with *p* — Ex 9:15
I will send the *p* among you — Lev 26:25
I will smite them with the *p* — Num 14:12
shall make the *p* cleave unto thee — Deut 28:21
be three days' *p* in thy land — 2Sa 24:13
So the LORD sent a *p* upon Israel — 2Sa 24:15
in the land famine, if there be *p* — 1Kin 8:37
the sword of the LORD, even the *p* — 1Chr 21:12
So the LORD sent *p* upon Israel — 1Chr 21:14
dearth in the land, if there be *p* — 2Chr 6:28
or if I send *p* among my people — 2Chr 7:13
us, as the sword, judgment, or *p* — 2Chr 20:9
but gave their life over to the *p* — Ps 78:50
the fowler, and from the noisome *p* — Ps 91:3
Nor for the *p* that walketh in — Ps 91:6
and by the famine, and by the *p* — Jer 14:12
they shall die of a great *p* — Jer 21:6
are left in this city from the *p* — Jer 21:7
and by the famine, and by the *p* — Jer 21:9
the sword, the famine, and the *p* — Jer 24:10
and with the famine, and with the *p* — Jer 27:8
sword, by the famine, and by the *p* — Jer 27:13
of war, and of evil, and of *p* — Jer 28:8
the sword, the famine, and the *p* — Jer 29:17
with the famine, and with the *p* — Jer 29:18
and of the famine, and of the *p* — Jer 32:24
and by the famine, and by the *p* — Jer 32:36
the LORD, to the sword, to the *p* — Jer 34:17
sword, by the famine, and by the *p* — Jer 38:2
sword, by the famine, and by the *p* — Jer 42:17
sword, by the famine, and by the *p* — Jer 42:22
sword, by the famine, and by the *p* — Jer 44:13
part of thee shall die with the *p* — Eze 5:12
and *p* and blood shall pass through — Eze 5:17
sword, by the famine, and by the *p* — Eze 6:11
is far off shall die of the *p* — Eze 6:12
The sword is without, and the *p* — Eze 7:15
famine and *p* shall devour him — Eze 7:15
from the famine, and from the *p* — Eze 12:16
Or if I send a *p* into that land — Eze 14:19
and the noisome beast, and the *p* — Eze 14:21
For I will send into her *p* — Eze 28:23
in the caves shall die of the *p* — Eze 33:27
I will plead against him with *p* — Eze 38:22
the *p* after the manner of Egypt — Amos 4:10
Before him went the *p*, and burning — Hab 3:5

**PESTILENCES**
and there shall be famines, and *p* — Mt 24:7
divers places, and famines, and *p* — Lk 21:11

**PESTILENT**
we have found this man a *p* fellow — Acts 24:5

**PESTLE**
in a mortar among wheat with a *p* — Prov 27:22

**PETER** (*pe'-tur*) See CEPHAS, PETER'S, SIMON. *A disciple of Jesus.*
saw two brethren, Simon called *P* — Mt 4:18
The first, Simon, who is called *P* — Mt 10:2
*P* answered him and said, Lord, if — Mt 14:28
when *P* was come down out of the — Mt 14:29
Then answered *P* and said unto him, — Mt 15:15
Simon *P* answered and said, Thou — Mt 16:16
also unto thee, That thou art *P* — Mt 16:18
Then *P* took him, and began to — Mt 16:22
But he turned, and said unto *P* — Mt 16:23
And after six days Jesus taketh *P* — Mt 17:1
Then answered *P*, and said unto — Mt 17:4
received tribute money came to *P* — Mt 17:24
*P* saith unto him, Of strangers — Mt 17:26
Then came *P* to him, and said, Lord — Mt 18:21
Then answered *P* and said unto him, — Mt 19:27
*P* answered and said unto him, — Mt 26:33
*P* said unto him, Though I should — Mt 26:35
And he took with him *P* and the two — Mt 26:37
them asleep, and saith unto *P* — Mt 26:40
But *P* followed him afar off unto — Mt 26:58
Now *P* sat without in the palace — Mt 26:69
they that stood by, and said to *P* — Mt 26:73
*P* remembered the word of Jesus, — Mt 26:75
And Simon he surnamed *P* — Mk 3:16
no man to follow him, save *P* — Mk 5:37
*P* answereth and saith unto him, — Mk 8:29
*P* took him, and began to rebuke — Mk 8:32
on his disciples, he rebuked *P* — Mk 8:33
six days Jesus taketh with him *P* — Mk 9:2
*P* answered and said to Jesus, — Mk 9:5
Then *P* began to say unto him, Lo, — Mk 10:28
*P* calling to remembrance saith — Mk 11:21
Olives over against the temple, *P* — Mk 13:3
But *P* said unto him, Although all — Mk 14:29
And he taketh with him *P* and James — Mk 14:33
them sleeping, and saith unto *P* — Mk 14:37
*P* followed him afar off, even — Mk 14:54
as *P* was beneath in the palace, — Mk 14:66
when she saw *P* warming himself, — Mk 14:67
that stood by said again to *P* — Mk 14:70
*P* called to mind the word that — Mk 14:72
*P* that he goeth before you into — Mk 16:7
When Simon *P* saw it, he fell down — Lk 5:8
Simon, (whom he also named *P* — Lk 6:14
When all denied, *P* and they that — Lk 8:45
suffered no man to go in, save *P* — Lk 8:51
*P* answering said, The Christ of — Lk 9:20
after these sayings, he took *P* — Lk 9:28
But *P* and they that were with him — Lk 9:32
*P* said unto Jesus, Master, it is — Lk 9:33
Then *P* said unto him, Lord, — Lk 12:41
Then *P* said, Lo, we have left all — Lk 18:28
And he sent *P* and John, saying, Go — Lk 22:8
And he said, I tell thee, *P* — Lk 22:34
And *P* followed afar off — Lk 22:54
together, *P* sat down among them — Lk 22:55
And *P* said, Man, I am not — Lk 22:58
*P* said, Man, I know not what thou — Lk 22:60
the Lord turned, and looked upon *P* — Lk 22:61
*P* remembered the word of the Lord — Lk 22:61
*P* went out, and wept bitterly — Lk 22:62
Then arose *P*, and ran unto the — Lk 24:12
the city of Andrew and *P* — Jn 1:44
Then Simon *P* answered him, Lord, — Jn 6:68
Then cometh he to Simon *P* — Jn 13:6
*P* saith unto him, Lord, dost thou — Jn 13:6
*P* saith unto him, Thou shalt — Jn 13:8
Simon *P* saith unto him, Lord, not — Jn 13:9
Simon *P* therefore beckoned to him — Jn 13:24
Simon *P* said unto him, Lord, — Jn 13:36
*P* said unto him, Lord, why cannot — Jn 13:37
Then Simon *P* having a sword drew — Jn 18:10
Then said Jesus unto *P*, Put up — Jn 18:11
Simon *P* followed Jesus, and so did — Jn 18:15
But *P* stood at the door without — Jn 18:16
kept the door, and brought in *P* — Jn 18:16
damsel that kept the door unto *P* — Jn 18:17
*P* stood with them, and warmed — Jn 18:18
And Simon *P* stood and warmed — Jn 18:25
his kinsman whose ear *P* cut off — Jn 18:26
*P* then denied again — Jn 18:27
she runneth, and cometh to Simon *P* — Jn 20:2
*P* therefore went forth, and that — Jn 20:3
the other disciple did outrun *P* — Jn 20:4
Then cometh Simon *P* following him — Jn 20:6
There were together Simon *P* — Jn 21:2
Simon *P* saith unto them, I go a — Jn 21:3
whom Jesus loved saith unto *P* — Jn 21:7
Now when Simon *P* heard that it — Jn 21:7
Simon *P* went up, and drew the net — Jn 21:11
had dined, Jesus saith to Simon *P* — Jn 21:15
*P* was grieved because he said — Jn 21:17
Then *P*, turning about, seeth the — Jn 21:20
*P* seeing him saith to Jesus, Lord — Jn 21:21
an upper room, where abode both *P* — Acts 1:13
in those days *P* stood up in the — Acts 1:15
But *P*, standing up with the — Acts 2:14
in their heart, and said unto *P* — Acts 2:37
Then *P* said unto them, Repent, and — Acts 2:38
Now *P* and John went up together — Acts 3:1
Who seeing *P* and John about to go — Acts 3:3
And *P*, fastening his eyes upon him — Acts 3:4
Then *P* said, Silver and gold have — Acts 3:6
lame man which was healed held *P* — Acts 3:11
when *P* saw it, he answered unto — Acts 3:12
Then *P*, filled with the Holy — Acts 4:8
when they saw the boldness of *P* — Acts 4:13
But *P* and John answered and said — Acts 4:19
But *P* said, Ananias, why hath — Acts 5:3
*P* answered unto her, Tell me — Acts 5:8
Then *P* said unto her, How is it — Acts 5:9
of *P* passing by might overshadow — Acts 5:15
Then *P* and the other apostles — Acts 5:29
of God, they sent unto them *P* — Acts 8:14
But *P* said unto him, Thy money — Acts 8:20
as *P* passed throughout all — Acts 9:32
*P* said unto him, Aeneas, Jesus — Acts 9:34
had heard that *P* was there — Acts 9:38
Then *P* arose and went with them — Acts 9:39
But *P* put them all forth, and — Acts 9:40
and when she saw *P*, she sat up — Acts 9:40
for one Simon, whose surname is *P* — Acts 10:5
*P* went up upon the housetop to — Acts 10:9
came a voice to him, Rise, *P* — Acts 10:13
But *P* said, Not so, Lord — Acts 10:14
Now while *P* doubted in himself — Acts 10:17
Simon, which was surnamed *P* — Acts 10:18
While *P* thought on the vision, — Acts 10:19
Then *P* went down to the — Acts 10:21
on the morrow *P* went away with — Acts 10:23
as *P* was coming in, Cornelius met — Acts 10:25
But *P* took him up, saying, Stand — Acts 10:26
hither Simon, whose surname is *P* — Acts 10:32
Then *P* opened his mouth, and said, — Acts 10:34
While *P* yet spake these words, — Acts 10:44
as many as came with *P*, because — Acts 10:45
Then answered *P*, — Acts 10:46
when *P* was come up to Jerusalem, — Acts 11:2
But *P* rehearsed the matter from — Acts 11:4
a voice saying unto me, Arise, *P* — Acts 11:7
for Simon, whose surname is *P* — Acts 11:13
proceeded further to take *P* also — Acts 12:3
*P* therefore was kept in prison — Acts 12:5
the same night *P* was sleeping — Acts 12:6
he smote *P* on the side, and raised — Acts 12:7
when *P* was come to himself, he — Acts 12:11
as *P* knocked at the door of the — Acts 12:13
told how *P* stood before the gate — Acts 12:14
But *P* continued knocking — Acts 12:16
soldiers, what was become of *P* — Acts 12:18
*P* rose up, and said unto them, Men — Acts 15:7
I went up to Jerusalem to see *P* — Gal 1:18
of the circumcision was unto *P* — Gal 2:7
in *P* to the apostleship of the — Gal 2:8
But when *P* was come to Antioch, I — Gal 2:11
I said unto *P* before them all, If — Gal 2:14

P, an apostle of Jesus Christ, to ... 1Pet 1:1
Simon P, a servant and an apostle ... 2Pet 1:1

**PETER'S** (*pe'-turz*)
when Jesus was come into P house ... Mt 8:14
him, was Andrew, Simon P brother ... Jn 1:40
Simon P brother, saith unto him, ... Jn 6:8
And when she knew P voice, she ... Acts 12:14

**PETHAHIAH** (*peth-a-hi'-ah*)
*1. A sanctuary servant.*
The nineteenth to P, the ... 1Chr 24:16
*2. Married a foreigner.*
Kelaiah, (the same is Kelita,) P ... Ezr 10:23
*3. A Levite who helped Ezra.*
Hodijah, Shebaniah, and P ... Neh 9:5
*4. An aide to Nehemiah.*
P the son of Meshezabeel, of the ... Neh 11:24

**PETHOR** (*pe'-thor*) *A city in Mesopotamia.*
unto Balaam the son of Beor to P ... Num 22:5
son of Beor of P of Mesopotamia ... Deut 23:4

**PETHUEL** *Father of Joel the prophet.*
that came to Joel the son of P ... Joel 1:1

**PETITION**
thy p that thou hast asked of him ... 1Sa 1:17
me my p which I asked of him ... 1Sa 1:27
And now I ask one p of thee ... 1Kin 2:16
I desire one small p of thee ... 1Kin 2:20
banquet of wine, What is thy p ... Est 5:6
answered Esther, and said, My p ... Est 5:7
it please the king to grant my p ... Est 5:8
banquet of wine, What is thy p ... Est 7:2
let my life be given me at my p ... Est 7:3
now what is thy p ... Est 9:12
that whosoever shall ask a p of ... Dan 6:7
p of any God or man within thirty ... Dan 6:12
but maketh his p three times a ... Dan 6:13

**PETITIONS**
the LORD fulfil all thy p ... Ps 20:5
have the p that we desired of him ... 1Jn 5:15

**PEULLETHAI** See PEULTHAI.

**PEULTHAI** (*pe-ul'-thahee*) *A sanctuary servant.*
the seventh, P the eighth ... 1Chr 26:5

**PHALEC** (*fa'-lek*) See PELEG. *Father of Ragau; ancestor of Jesus.*
of Ragau, which was the son of P ... Lk 3:35

**PHALLU** (*fal'-lu*) *Son of Reuben.*
Hanoch, and P, and Hezron ... Gen 46:9

**PHALTI** (*fal'-ti*) See PHALTIEL. *Son of Laish.*
to P the son of Laish, which was ... 1Sa 25:44

**PHALTIEL** (*fal'-te-el*) See PHALTI. *Same as Phalti.*
even from P the son of Laish ... 2Sa 3:15

**PHANUEL** (*fan-u'-el*) *Mother of Anna.*
a prophetess, the daughter of P ... Lk 2:36

**PHARAOH** (*fa'-ra-o*) See PHARAOH'S, PHARAOH-HOPHRA, PHARAOH-NECHO.
*1. Ruler of Egypt in Abraham's time.*
The princes also of P saw her ... Gen 12:15
and commended her before P ... Gen 12:15
And the LORD plagued P and his ... Gen 12:17
P called Abram, and said, What is ... Gen 12:18
P commanded his men concerning ... Gen 12:20
*2. Ruler of Egypt in Joseph's time.*
and Potiphar, an officer of P ... Gen 39:1
P was wroth against two of his ... Gen 40:2
days shall P lift up thine head ... Gen 40:13
me, and make mention of me unto P. Gen 40:14
of all manner of bakemeats for P ... Gen 40:17
Yet within three days shall P ... Gen 40:19
of two full years, that P dreamed ... Gen 41:1
So P awoke ... Gen 41:4
P awoke, and, behold, it was a ... Gen 41:7
and P told them his dream ... Gen 41:8
that could interpret them unto P ... Gen 41:8
spake the chief butler unto P ... Gen 41:9
P was wroth with his servants, and ... Gen 41:10
Then P sent and called Joseph, and ... Gen 41:14
his raiment, and came in unto P ... Gen 41:14
P said unto Joseph, I have ... Gen 41:15
And Joseph answered P, saying, It ... Gen 41:16
God shall give P an answer of ... Gen 41:16
P said unto Joseph, In my dream, ... Gen 41:17
And Joseph said unto P ... Gen 41:25
The dream of P is one ... Gen 41:25
God hath shewed P what he is ... Gen 41:25
thing which I have spoken unto P ... Gen 41:28
is about to do he sheweth unto P ... Gen 41:28
dream was doubled unto P twice ... Gen 41:32
Now therefore let P look out a ... Gen 41:33
Let P do this, and let him appoint ... Gen 41:34
lay up corn under the hand of P ... Gen 41:35
thing was good in the eyes of P ... Gen 41:37
P said unto his servants, Can we ... Gen 41:38
P said unto Joseph, Forasmuch as ... Gen 41:39
P said unto Joseph, See, I have ... Gen 41:41
P took off his ring from his hand ... Gen 41:42
P said unto Joseph, I am Pharaoh, ... Gen 41:44
And P called Joseph's name ... Gen 41:45
he stood before P king of Egypt ... Gen 41:46
went out from the presence of P ... Gen 41:46
the people cried to P for bread ... Gen 41:55
P said unto all the Egyptians, Go ... Gen 41:55
By the life of P ye shall not go ... Gen 42:15
the life of P surely ye are spies ... Gen 42:16
for thou art even as P ... Gen 44:18
Egyptians and the house of P heard ... Gen 45:2
and he hath made me a father to P ... Gen 45:8
and it pleased P well, and his ... Gen 45:16
P said unto Joseph, Say unto thy ... Gen 45:17
according to the commandment of P. Gen 45:21
in the wagons which P had sent to ... Gen 46:5
house, I will go up, and shew P ... Gen 46:31
when P shall call you, and shall ... Gen 46:33
Then Joseph came and told P ... Gen 47:1
men, and presented them unto P ... Gen 47:2
P said unto his brethren, What is ... Gen 47:3
And they said unto P, Thy servants ... Gen 47:3
They said moreover unto P ... Gen 47:4
P spake unto Joseph, saying, Thy ... Gen 47:5
his father, and set him before P ... Gen 47:7
and Jacob blessed P ... Gen 47:7
P said unto Jacob, How old art ... Gen 47:8
And Jacob said unto P, The days of ... Gen 47:9
And Jacob blessed P ... Gen 47:10
and went out from before P ... Gen 47:10
of Rameses, as P had commanded ... Gen 47:11
our land will be servants unto P ... Gen 47:19
all the land of Egypt for P ... Gen 47:20
had a portion assigned them of P ... Gen 47:22
their portion which P gave them ... Gen 47:22
you this day and your land for P ... Gen 47:23
shall give the fifth part unto P ... Gen 47:24
that P should have the fifth part ... Gen 47:26
Joseph spake unto the house of P ... Gen 50:4
I pray you, in the ears of P ... Gen 50:4
P said, Go up, and bury thy father ... Gen 50:6
him went up all the servants of P ... Gen 50:7
in the sight of P king of Egypt ... Acts 7:10
kindred was made known unto P ... Acts 7:13
*3. Ruler of Egypt during Moses' infancy.*
they built for P treasure cities, ... Ex 1:11
And the midwives said unto P ... Ex 1:19
P charged all his people, saying, ... Ex 1:22
the daughter of P came down to ... Ex 2:5
*4. Ruler of Egypt during Moses' adulthood.*
Now when P heard this thing, he ... Ex 2:15
But Moses fled from the face of P ... Ex 2:15
*5. Ruler of Egypt when Moses returned to Egypt.*
and I will send thee unto P ... Ex 3:10
Who am I, that I should go unto P ... Ex 3:11
do all those wonders before P ... Ex 4:21
And thou shalt say unto P, Thus ... Ex 4:22
Moses and Aaron went in, and told P ... Ex 5:1
P said, Who is the LORD, that I ... Ex 5:2
P said, Behold, the people of the ... Ex 5:5
P commanded the same day the ... Ex 5:6
the people, saying, Thus saith P ... Ex 5:10
of Israel came and cried unto P ... Ex 5:15
way, as they came forth from P ... Ex 5:20
to be abhorred in the eyes of P ... Ex 5:21
For since I came to P to speak in ... Ex 5:23
thou see what I will do to P ... Ex 6:1
speak unto P king of Egypt, that ... Ex 6:11
how then shall P hear me, who am ... Ex 6:12
unto P king of Egypt, to bring ... Ex 6:13
which spake to P king of Egypt ... Ex 6:27
speak thou unto P king of Egypt ... Ex 6:29
how shall P hearken unto me ... Ex 6:30
See, I have made thee a god to P ... Ex 7:1
thy brother shall speak unto P ... Ex 7:2
But P shall not hearken unto you, ... Ex 7:4
years old, when they spake unto P ... Ex 7:7
When P shall speak unto you, ... Ex 7:9
Take thy rod, and cast it before P ... Ex 7:9
And Moses and Aaron went in unto P ... Ex 7:10
Aaron cast down his rod before P ... Ex 7:10
Then P also called the wise men ... Ex 7:11
Get thee unto P in the morning ... Ex 7:15
in the river, in the sight of P ... Ex 7:20
P turned and went into his house, ... Ex 7:23
LORD spake unto Moses, Go unto P ... Ex 8:1
Then P called for Moses and Aaron, ... Ex 8:8
And Moses said unto P, Glory over ... Ex 8:9
And Moses and Aaron went out from P. Ex 8:12
which he had brought against P ... Ex 8:12
But when P saw that there was ... Ex 8:15
Then the magicians said unto P ... Ex 8:19
in the morning, and stand before P ... Ex 8:20
of flies into the house of P ... Ex 8:24
P called for Moses and for Aaron, ... Ex 8:25
P said, I will let you go, that ... Ex 8:28
swarms of flies may depart from P ... Ex 8:29
but let not P deal deceitfully ... Ex 8:29
And Moses went out from P, and ... Ex 8:30
the swarms of flies from P ... Ex 8:31
P hardened his heart at this time ... Ex 8:32
said unto Moses, Go in unto P ... Ex 9:1
P sent, and, behold, there was not ... Ex 9:7
And the heart of P was hardened ... Ex 9:7
the heaven in the sight of P ... Ex 9:8
of the furnace, and stood before P ... Ex 9:10
the LORD hardened the heart of P ... Ex 9:12
in the morning, and stand before P ... Ex 9:13
servants of P made his servants ... Ex 9:20
P sent, and called for Moses and ... Ex 9:27
Moses went out of the city from P ... Ex 9:33
when P saw that the rain and the ... Ex 9:34
And the heart of P was hardened ... Ex 9:35
said unto Moses, Go in unto P ... Ex 10:1
And Moses and Aaron came in unto P ... Ex 10:3
himself, and went out from P ... Ex 10:6
Aaron were brought again unto P ... Ex 10:8
Then P called for Moses and Aaron ... Ex 10:16
And he went out from P, and ... Ex 10:18
P called unto Moses, and said, Go ... Ex 10:24
P said unto him, Get thee from me ... Ex 10:28
I bring one plague more upon P ... Ex 11:1
from the firstborn of P that ... Ex 11:5
went out from P in a great anger ... Ex 11:8
P shall not hearken unto you ... Ex 11:9
did all these wonders before P ... Ex 11:10
from the firstborn of P that sat ... Ex 12:29
P rose up in the night, he, and ... Ex 12:30
when P would hardly let us go, ... Ex 13:15
when P had let the people go, ... Ex 13:17
For P will say of the children of ... Ex 14:3
and I will be honoured upon P ... Ex 14:4
and the heart of P and of his ... Ex 14:5
the heart of P king of Egypt ... Ex 14:8
all the horses and chariots of P ... Ex 14:9
when P drew nigh, the children of ... Ex 14:10
and I will get me honour upon P ... Ex 14:17
I have gotten me honour upon P ... Ex 14:18
all the host of P that came into ... Ex 14:28
For the horse of P went in with ... Ex 15:19
delivered me from the sword of P ... Ex 18:4
all that the LORD had done unto P ... Ex 18:8
and out of the hand of P, who ... Ex 18:10
great and sore, upon Egypt, upon P ... Deut 6:22
from the hand of P king of Egypt ... Deut 7:8
what the LORD thy God did unto P ... Deut 7:18
of Egypt unto P the king of Egypt ... Deut 11:3
eyes in the land of Egypt unto P ... Deut 29:2
to do in the land of Egypt to P ... Deut 34:11
and P hardened their hearts ... 1Sa 6:6
under the hand of P king of Egypt ... 2Kin 17:7
shewedst signs and wonders upon P ... Neh 9:10
midst of thee, O Egypt, upon P ... Ps 135:9
But overthrew P and his host in ... Ps 136:15
For the scripture saith unto P ... Rom 9:17
*6. Ruler of Egypt in Solomon's time.*
affinity with P king of Egypt ... 1Kin 3:1
For P king of Egypt had gone up, ... 1Kin 9:16
together with the daughter of P ... 1Kin 11:1
to Egypt, unto P king of Egypt ... 1Kin 11:18
great favour in the sight of P ... 1Kin 11:19
household among the sons of P ... 1Kin 11:20
host was dead, Hadad said to P ... 1Kin 11:21
Then P said unto him, But what ... 1Kin 11:22
brought up the daughter of P out ... 2Chr 8:11
*7. Ruler of Egypt in Isaiah's time.*
of P is become brutish ... Is 19:11
how say ye unto P, I am the son ... Is 19:11
themselves in the strength of P ... Is 30:2
the strength of P be your shame ... Is 30:3
so is P king of Egypt to all that ... Is 36:6
*8. Ruler of Egypt in Jeremiah's time.*
so is P king of Egypt unto all ... 2Kin 18:21
gave the silver and the gold to P ... 2Kin 23:35
according to the commandment of P 2Kin 23:35
sons of Bithiah the daughter of P ... 1Chr 4:18
P king of Egypt, and his servants, ... Jer 25:19
P king of Egypt is but a noise ... Jer 46:17
punish the multitude of No, and P ... Jer 46:25
even P, and all them that trust in ... Jer 46:25
before that P smote Gaza ... Jer 47:1
Neither shall P with his mighty ... Eze 17:17
thy face against P king of Egypt ... Eze 29:2
P king of Egypt, the great dragon ... Eze 29:3
broken the arm of P king of Egypt ... Eze 30:21
I am against P king of Egypt, and ... Eze 30:22
the arms of P shall fall down ... Eze 30:25
speak unto P king of Egypt, and to ... Eze 31:2
This is P and all his multitude, ... Eze 31:18
a lamentation for P king of Egypt ... Eze 32:2
P shall see them, and shall be ... Eze 32:31
over all his multitude, even P ... Eze 32:31
are slain with the sword, even P ... Eze 32:32

**PHARAOH-HOPHRA** (*fa''-ra-o-hof'-rah*) *Same as Pharaoh 8.*
I will give P king of Egypt into ... Jer 44:30

**PHARAOH-NECHO** (*fa''-ra-o-ne'-ko*) See PHARAOH-NECHOH. *Egyptian ruler during Josiah's time.*
the army of P king of Egypt ... Jer 46:2

**PHARAOH-NECHOH** (*fa''-ra-o-ne'-ko*) See PHARAOH-NECHO. *Same as Pharaoh-necho.*
In his days P king of Egypt went ... 2Kin 23:29
P put him in bands at Riblah in ... 2Kin 23:33
P made Eliakim the son of Josiah ... 2Kin 23:34
his taxation, to give it unto P ... 2Kin 23:35

**PHARAOH'S** (*fa'-ra-oze*)
the woman was taken into P house ... Gen 12:15
unto Potiphar, an officer of P ... Gen 37:36
he asked P officers that were ... Gen 40:7
And P cup was in my hand ... Gen 40:11
and pressed them into P cup ... Gen 40:11
and I gave the cup into P hand ... Gen 40:11
shalt deliver P cup into his hand ... Gen 40:13
third day, which was P birthday ... Gen 40:20
and he gave the cup into P hand ... Gen 40:21
fame thereof was heard in P house ... Gen 45:16
brought the money into P house ... Gen 47:14
so the land became P ... Gen 47:20
my lord, and we will be P servants ... Gen 47:25
priests only, which became not P ... Gen 47:26
said his sister to P daughter ... Ex 2:7
P daughter said to her, Go ... Ex 2:8
P daughter said unto her, Take ... Ex 2:9
she brought him unto P daughter ... Ex 2:10

which P taskmasters had set over ... Ex 5:14
And I will harden P heart, and ... Ex 7:3
And he hardened P heart, that he ... Ex 7:13
P heart is hardened, he refuseth ... Ex 7:14
P heart was hardened, neither did ... Ex 7:22
P heart was hardened, and he ... Ex 8:19
P servants said unto him, How ... Ex 10:7
were driven out from P presence ... Ex 10:11
But the LORD hardened P heart ... Ex 10:20
But the LORD hardened P heart ... Ex 10:27
Egypt, in the sight of P servants ... Ex 11:3
and the LORD hardened P heart ... Ex 11:10
And I will harden P heart, that he ... Ex 14:4
of the sea, even all P horses ... Ex 14:23
P chariots and his host hath he ... Ex 15:4
We were P bondmen in Egypt ... Deut 6:21
they were in Egypt in P house ... 1Sa 2:27
took P daughter, and brought her ... 1Kin 3:1
made also an house for P daughter ... 1Kin 7:8
But P daughter came up out of the ... 1Kin 9:24
whom Tahpenes weaned in P house.. 1Kin 11:20
was in P household among ... 1Kin 11:20
a company of horses in P chariots ... Song 1:9
Then P army was come forth out of ... Jer 37:5
P army, which is come forth to ... Jer 37:7
from Jerusalem for fear of P army ... Jer 37:11
the entry of P house in Tahpanhes ... Jer 43:9
but I will break P arms, and he ... Eze 30:24
P daughter took him up, and ... Acts 7:21
be called the son of P daughter ... Heb 11:24

**PHARES** (*fa'-rez*) See PHAREZ. *Same as Pharez.*
And Judas begat P and Zara of ... Mt 1:3
and P begat Esrom ... Mt 1:3
of Esrom, which was the son of P ... Lk 3:33

**PHAREZ** (*fa'-rez*) See PEREZ, PHARES, PHARZITES. *A son of Judah.*
therefore his name was called P ... Gen 38:29
Er, and Onan, and Shelah, and P ... Gen 46:12
And the sons of P were Hezron ... Gen 46:12
of P, the family of the Pharzites ... Num 26:20
And the sons of P were ... Num 26:21
thy house be like the house of P ... Ruth 4:12
these are the generations of P ... Ruth 4:18
P begat Hezron, ... Ruth 4:18
his daughter in law bare him P ... 1Chr 2:4
The sons of P ... 1Chr 2:5
P, Hezron, and Carmi, and Hur, and ... 1Chr 4:1
children of P the son of Judah ... 1Chr 9:4

**PHARISAIC** See PHARISEES.

**PHARISEE** (*far'-i-see*) See PHARISEE'S, PHARISEES. *A member of a Jewish sect.*
Thou blind P, cleanse first that ... Mt 23:26
Now when the P which had bidden ... Lk 7:39
a certain P besought him to dine ... Lk 11:37
And when the P saw it, he ... Lk 11:38
the one a P, and the other a ... Lk 18:10
The P stood and prayed thus with ... Lk 18:11
there up one in the council, a P ... Acts 5:34
I am a P, the son of a P ... Acts 23:6
sect of our religion I lived a P ... Acts 26:5
as touching the law, a P ... Phil 3:5

**PHARISEE'S** (*far'-i-seze*)
And he went into the P house ... Lk 7:36
Jesus sat at meat in the P house ... Lk 7:37

**PHARISEES** (*far'-i-seze*) See PHARISEES'. *A Jewish sect.*
But when he saw many of the P ... Mt 3:7
righteousness of the scribes and P ... Mt 5:20
And when the P saw it, they said ... Mt 9:11
the P fast oft, but thy disciples ... Mt 9:14
But the P said, He casteth out ... Mt 9:34
But when the P saw it, they said ... Mt 12:2
Then the P went out, and held a ... Mt 12:14
But when the P heard it, they ... Mt 12:24
of the P answered, saying, Master ... Mt 12:38
Then came to Jesus scribes and P ... Mt 15:1
thou that the P were offended ... Mt 15:12
The P also with the Sadducees ... Mt 16:1
and beware of the leaven of the P ... Mt 16:6
beware of the leaven of the P ... Mt 16:11
but of the doctrine of the P ... Mt 16:12
The P also came unto him, ... Mt 19:3
P had heard his parables, they ... Mt 21:45
Then went the P, and took counsel ... Mt 22:15
But when the P had heard that he ... Mt 22:34
While the P were gathered ... Mt 22:41
and the P sit in Moses' seat ... Mt 23:2
But woe unto you, scribes and P ... Mt 23:13
Woe unto you, scribes and P ... Mt 23:14
Woe unto you, scribes and P ... Mt 23:15
Woe unto you, scribes and P ... Mt 23:23
Woe unto you, scribes and P ... Mt 23:25
Woe unto you, scribes and P ... Mt 23:27
Woe unto you, scribes and P ... Mt 23:29
P came together unto Pilate, ... Mt 27:62
P saw him eat with publicans and ... Mk 2:16
of John and of the P used to fast ... Mk 2:18
of John and of the P fast, but thy ... Mk 2:18
the P said unto him, Behold, why ... Mk 2:24
the P went forth, and straightway ... Mk 3:6
Then came together unto him the P ... Mk 7:1
For the P, and all the Jews, ... Mk 7:3
Then the P and scribes asked him, ... Mk 7:5
the P came forth, and began to ... Mk 8:11
beware of the leaven of the P ... Mk 8:15
the P came to him, and asked him, ... Mk 10:2
send unto him certain of the P ... Mk 12:13
was teaching, that there were P ... Lk 5:17
the P began to reason, saying, ... Lk 5:21
P murmured against his disciples, ... Lk 5:30
likewise the disciples of the P ... Lk 5:33
certain of the P said unto them ... Lk 6:2
P watched him, whether he would ... Lk 6:7
But the P and lawyers rejected the ... Lk 7:30
one of the P desired him that he ... Lk 7:36
Now do ye P make clean the ... Lk 11:39
But woe unto you, P ... Lk 11:42
Woe unto you, P ... Lk 11:43
Woe unto you, scribes and P ... Lk 11:44
and the P began to urge him ... Lk 11:53
Beware ye of the leaven of the P ... Lk 12:1
day there came certain of the P ... Lk 13:31
the house of one of the chief P ... Lk 14:1
spake unto the lawyers and P ... Lk 14:3
And the P and scribes murmured, ... Lk 15:2
the P also, who were covetous, ... Lk 16:14
And when he was demanded of the P .. Lk 17:20
some of the P from among the ... Lk 19:39
which were sent were of the P ... Jn 1:24
There was a man of the P, named ... Jn 3:1
the P had heard that Jesus made ... Jn 4:1
The P heard that the people ... Jn 7:32
and the P and the chief priests ... Jn 7:32
to the chief priests and P ... Jn 7:45
Then answered them the P, Are ye ... Jn 7:47
or of the P believed on him ... Jn 7:48
P brought unto him a woman taken ... Jn 8:3
The P therefore said unto him, ... Jn 8:13
They brought to the P him that ... Jn 9:13
Then again the P also asked him ... Jn 9:15
Therefore said some of the P ... Jn 9:16
some of the P which were with him ... Jn 9:40
of them went their ways to the P ... Jn 11:46
the P a council, and said, What do ... Jn 11:47
the P had given a commandment, ... Jn 11:57
The P therefore said among ... Jn 12:19
but because of the P they did not ... Jn 12:42
from the chief priests and P ... Jn 18:3
the sect of the P which believed ... Acts 15:5
were Sadducees, and the other P ... Acts 23:6
arose a dissension between the P ... Acts 23:7
but the P confess both ... Acts 23:8

**PHARISEES'** (*far'-i-seez*)
that were of the P part arose ... Acts 23:9

**PHAROSH** (*fa'-rosh*) *A family of exiles.*
of Shechaniah, of the sons of P ... Ezr 8:3

**PHARPAR** (*far'-par*) *A river near Damascus.*
Are not Abana and P, rivers of ... 2Kin 5:12

**PHARZITES** (*far'-zites*) *Descendants of Pharez.*
of Pharez, the family of the P ... Num 26:20

**PHASEAH** (*fa-se'-ah*) See PASEAH. *A family of exiles.*
of Uzza, the children of P ... Neh 7:51

**PHEBE** (*fe'-be*) *A Christian acquaintance of Paul.*
I commend unto you P our sister ... Rom 16:1
sent by P servant of the church ... Rom *s*

**PHENICE** (*fe-ni'-se*) See PHENICIA.
*1. Same as Phenecia.*
Stephen travelled as far as P ... Acts 11:19
the church, they passed through P ... Acts 15:3
*2. A harbor on Crete.*
any means they might attain to P ... Acts 27:12

**PHENICIA** (*fe-nish'-e-ah*) See PHENICE. *Coastal region of northern Palestine.*
a ship sailing over unto P ... Acts 21:2

**PHICHOL** *The commander of Abimelech's army.*
P the chief captain of his host ... Gen 21:22
P the chief captain of his host, ... Gen 21:32
P the chief captain of his army ... Gen 26:26

**PHICOL** (*fi'-col*) See PHICHOL. *A Philistine commander.*

**PHILADELPHIA** (*fil-a-del'-fe-ah*) *A city in Lydia in Asia Minor.*
and unto Sardis, and unto P ... Rev 1:11
angel of the church in P write ... Rev 3:7

**PHILEMON** (*fi-le'-mon*) *A recipient of a New Testament epistle.*
unto P our dearly beloved, and ... Philem 1
Written from Rome to P, by ... Philem *s*

**PHILETUS** (*fi-le'tus*) *A false Christian teacher.*
of whom is Hymenaeus and P ... 2Ti 2:17

**PHILIP** (*fil'-ip*) See PHILIP'S.
*1. An apostle.*
P, and Bartholomew ... Mt 10:3
And Andrew, and P, and Bartholomew, ... Mk 3:18
his brother, James and John, P ... Lk 6:14
forth into Galilee, and findeth P ... Jn 1:43
Now P was of Bethsaida, the city ... Jn 1:44
P findeth Nathanael, and saith ... Jn 1:45
P saith unto him, Come and see ... Jn 1:46
him, Before that P called thee ... Jn 1:48
come unto him, he saith unto P ... Jn 6:5
P answered him, Two hundred ... Jn 6:7
The same came therefore to P ... Jn 12:21
P cometh and telleth Andrew ... Jn 12:22
and again Andrew and P tell Jesus ... Jn 12:22
P saith unto him, Lord, shew us ... Jn 14:8
and yet hast thou not known me, P ... Jn 14:9
and James, and John, and Andrew, P.. Acts 1:13
*2. A son of Herod the Great.*
his brother P tetrarch of Ituraea ... Lk 3:1
*3. The evangelist.*
faith and of the Holy Ghost, and P ... Acts 6:5
Then P went down to the city of ... Acts 8:5
unto those things which P spake ... Acts 8:6
But when they believed P ... Acts 8:12
was baptized, he continued with P ... Acts 8:13
angel of the Lord spake unto P ... Acts 8:26
Then the Spirit said unto P ... Acts 8:29
P ran thither to him, and heard ... Acts 8:30
he desired P that he would come ... Acts 8:31
And the eunuch answered P, and said Acts 8:34
Then P opened his mouth, and began . Acts 8:35
P said, If thou believest with ... Acts 8:37
down both into the water, both P ... Acts 8:38
Spirit of the Lord caught away P ... Acts 8:39
But P was found at Azotus ... Acts 8:40
the house of P the evangelist ... Acts 21:8

**PHILIPPI** (*fil-ip'-pi*) See PHILIPPIANS.
*1. A town in northern Palestine.*
into the coasts of Caesarea P ... Mt 16:13
into the towns of Caesarea P ... Mk 8:27
*2. A Macedonian city.*
And from thence to P, which is the... Acts 16:12
we sailed away from P after the ... Acts 20:6
was written from P by Stephanus ... 1Cor *s*
Corinthians was written from P ... 2Cor *s*
in Christ Jesus which are at P ... Phil 1:1
entreated, as ye know, at P ... 1Th 2:2

**PHILIPPIANS** (*fil-ip'-pe-uns*) *Residents of Philippi 2.*
Now ye P know also, that in the ... Phil 4:15
It was written to the P from Rome ... Phil *s*

**PHILIP'S** (*fil'-ips*) *Refers to Philip 2.*
sake, his brother P wife ... Mt 14:3
sake, his brother P wife ... Mk 6:17
for Herodias his brother P wife ... Lk 3:19

**PHILISTIA** (*fil-is'-te-ah*) See PALESTINE, PHILISTINE. *Land of the Philistines.*
P, triumph thou because of me ... Ps 60:8
behold P, and Tyre, with Ethiopia ... Ps 87:4
over P will I triumph ... Ps 108:9

**PHILISTIM** (*fil-is'-tim*) See PHILISTINES. *Descendents of Casluhim.*
and Casluhim, (out of whom came P . Gen 10:14

**PHILISTINE** (*fil-is'-tin*) See PHILISTINES. *An inhabitant of Philistia.*
am not I a P, and ye servants to ... 1Sa 17:8
the P said, I defy the armies of ... 1Sa 17:10
Israel heard those words of the P ... 1Sa 17:11
the P drew near morning and ... 1Sa 17:16
the P of Gath, Goliath by name, ... 1Sa 17:23
to the man that killeth this P ... 1Sa 17:26
for who is this uncircumcised P ... 1Sa 17:26
will go and fight with this P ... 1Sa 17:32
against this P to fight with him ... 1Sa 17:33
this uncircumcised P shall be as ... 1Sa 17:36
me out of the hand of this P ... 1Sa 17:37
and he drew near to the P ... 1Sa 17:40
the P came on and drew near unto ... 1Sa 17:41
when the P looked about, and saw ... 1Sa 17:42
the P said unto David, Am I a dog ... 1Sa 17:43
the P cursed David by his gods ... 1Sa 17:43
the P said to David, Come to me, ... 1Sa 17:44
Then said David to the P, Thou ... 1Sa 17:45
it came to pass, when the P arose ... 1Sa 17:48
ran toward the army to meet the P ... 1Sa 17:48
smote the P in his forehead, that ... 1Sa 17:49
prevailed over the P with a sling ... 1Sa 17:50
and with a stone, and smote the P ... 1Sa 17:50
David ran, and stood upon the P ... 1Sa 17:51
And David took the head of the P ... 1Sa 17:54
saw David go forth against the P ... 1Sa 17:55
from the slaughter of the P ... 1Sa 17:57
the head of the P in his hand ... 1Sa 17:57
from the slaughter of the P ... 1Sa 18:6
life in his hand, and slew the P ... 1Sa 19:5
said, The sword of Goliath the P ... 1Sa 21:9
him the sword of Goliath the P ... 1Sa 22:10
succoured him, and smote the P ... 2Sa 21:17

**PHILISTINES** (*fil-is'-tinz*) See PHILISTIM, PHILISTINES'.
returned into the land of the P ... Gen 21:32
king of the P unto Gerar ... Gen 26:1
of the P looked out at a window ... Gen 26:8
and the P envied him ... Gen 26:14
the P had stopped them, and filled ... Gen 26:15
for the P had stopped them after ... Gen 26:18
the way of the land of the P ... Ex 13:17
sea even unto the sea of the P ... Ex 23:31
all the borders of the P, and all ... Josh 13:2
five lords of the P ... Josh 13:3
Namely, five lords of the P ... Judg 3:3
which slew of the P six hundred ... Judg 3:31
of Ammon, and the gods of the P ... Judg 10:6
sold them into the hands of the P ... Judg 10:7
children of Ammon, and from the P.. Judg 10:11
the hand of the P forty years ... Judg 13:1
Israel out of the hand of the P ... Judg 13:5
Timnath of the daughters of the P ... Judg 14:1
Timnath of the daughters of the P ... Judg 14:2
a wife of the uncircumcised P ... Judg 14:3

P

sought an occasion against the *P* Judg 14:4
for at that time the *P* had Judg 14:4
I be more blameless than the *P* Judg 15:3
into the standing corn of the *P* Judg 15:5
Then the *P* said, Who hath done Judg 15:6
the *P* came up, and burnt her and Judg 15:6
Then the *P* went up, and pitched in Judg 15:9
not that the *P* are rulers over us Judg 15:11
thee into the hand of the *P* Judg 15:12
the *P* shouted against him Judg 15:14
in the days of the *P* twenty years Judg 15:20
lords of the *P* came up unto her Judg 16:5
Then the lords of the *P* brought Judg 16:8
The *P* be upon thee, Samson Judg 16:9
The *P* be upon thee, Samson Judg 16:12
The *P* be upon thee, Samson Judg 16:14
and called for the lords of the *P* Judg 16:18
lords of the *P* came up unto her Judg 16:18
The *P* be upon thee, Samson Judg 16:20
But the *P* took him, and put out Judg 16:21
Then the lords of the *P* gathered Judg 16:23
all the lords of the *P* were there Judg 16:27
avenged of the *P* for my two eyes Judg 16:28
said, Let me die with the *P* Judg 16:30
went out against the *P* to battle 1Sa 4:1
and the *P* pitched in Aphek 1Sa 4:1
the *P* put themselves in array 1Sa 4:2
Israel was smitten before the *P* 1Sa 4:2
smitten us to day before the *P* 1Sa 4:3
when the *P* heard the noise of the 1Sa 4:6
the *P* were afraid, for they said, 1Sa 4:7
quit yourselves like men, O ye *P* 1Sa 4:9
the *P* fought, and Israel was 1Sa 4:10
said, Israel is fled before the *P* 1Sa 4:17
the *P* took the ark of God, and 1Sa 5:1
When the *P* took the ark of God, 1Sa 5:2
all the lords of the *P* unto them 1Sa 5:8
together all the lords of the *P* 1Sa 5:11
the country of the *P* seven months 1Sa 6:1
the *P* called for the priests and 1Sa 6:2
the number of the lords of the *P* 1Sa 6:4
the lords of the *P* went after 1Sa 6:12
five lords of the *P* had seen it 1Sa 6:16
the *P* returned for a trespass 1Sa 6:17
the *P* belonging to the five lords 1Sa 6:18
The *P* have brought again the ark 1Sa 6:21
you out of the hand of the *P* 1Sa 7:3
when the *P* heard that the 1Sa 7:7
the lords of the *P* went up 1Sa 7:7
it, they were afraid of the *P* 1Sa 7:7
save us out of the hand of the *P* 1Sa 7:8
the *P* drew near to battle against 1Sa 7:10
thunder on that day upon the *P* 1Sa 7:10
out of Mizpeh, and pursued the *P* 1Sa 7:11
So the *P* were subdued, and they 1Sa 7:13
the *P* all the days of Samuel 1Sa 7:13
the cities which the *P* had taken 1Sa 7:14
deliver out of the hands of the *P* 1Sa 7:14
people out of the hand of the *P* 1Sa 9:16
where is the garrison of the *P* 1Sa 10:5
Hazor, and into the hand of the *P* 1Sa 12:9
of the *P* that was in Geba 1Sa 13:3
and the *P* heard of it 1Sa 13:3
had smitten a garrison of the *P* 1Sa 13:4
was had in abomination with the *P* 1Sa 13:4
the *P* gathered themselves 1Sa 13:5
that the *P* gathered themselves 1Sa 13:11
The *P* will come down now upon me 1Sa 13:12
but the *P* encamped in Michmash 1Sa 13:16
camp of the *P* in three companies 1Sa 13:17
for the *P* said, Lest the Hebrews 1Sa 13:19
the Israelites went down to the *P* 1Sa 13:20
the garrison of the *P* went out to 1Sa 13:23
unto the garrison of the *P* 1Sa 14:11
the *P* said, Behold, the Hebrews 1Sa 14:11
was in the host of the *P* went on 1Sa 14:19
were with the *P* before that time 1Sa 14:21
when they heard that the *P* fled 1Sa 14:22
greater slaughter among the *P* 1Sa 14:30
they smote the *P* that day from 1Sa 14:31
us go down after the *P* by night 1Sa 14:36
God, Shall I go down after the *P* 1Sa 14:37
Saul went up from following the *P* 1Sa 14:46
the *P* went to their own place 1Sa 14:46
kings of Zobah, and against the *P* 1Sa 14:47
the *P* all the days of Saul 1Sa 14:52
Now the *P* gathered together their 1Sa 17:1
the battle in array against the *P* 1Sa 17:2
the *P* stood on a mountain on the 1Sa 17:3
champion out of the camp of the *P* 1Sa 17:4
of Elah, fighting with the *P* 1Sa 17:19
the *P* had put the battle in array 1Sa 17:21
name, out of the armies of the *P* 1Sa 17:23
*P* this day unto the fowls of the 1Sa 17:46
when the *P* saw their champion was 1Sa 17:51
and shouted, and pursued the *P* 1Sa 17:52
the wounded of the *P* fell down by 1Sa 17:52
returned from chasing after the *P* 1Sa 17:53
let the hand of the *P* be upon him 1Sa 18:17
hand of the *P* may be against him 1Sa 18:21
but an hundred foreskins of the *P* 1Sa 18:25
David fall by the hand of the *P* 1Sa 18:25
slew of the *P* two hundred men 1Sa 18:27
the princes of the *P* went forth 1Sa 18:30
went out, and fought with the *P* 1Sa 19:8
the *P* fight against Keilah, and 1Sa 23:1
Shall I go and smite these *P* 1Sa 23:2
unto David, Go, and smite the *P* 1Sa 23:2
against the armies of the *P* 1Sa 23:3
deliver the *P* into thine hand 1Sa 23:4
to Keilah, and fought with the *P* 1Sa 23:5
for the *P* have invaded the land 1Sa 23:27
David, and went against the *P* 1Sa 23:28
was returned from following the *P* 1Sa 24:1
escape into the land of the *P* 1Sa 27:1
country of the *P* was a full year 1Sa 27:7
dwelleth in the country of the *P* 1Sa 27:11
that the *P* gathered their armies 1Sa 28:1
the *P* gathered themselves 1Sa 28:4
when Saul saw the host of the *P* 1Sa 28:5
for the *P* make war against me, and 1Sa 28:15
with thee into the hand of the *P* 1Sa 28:19
of Israel into the hand of the *P* 1Sa 28:19
Now the *P* gathered together all 1Sa 29:1
the lords of the *P* passed on by 1Sa 29:2
Then said the princes of the *P* 1Sa 29:3
said unto the princes of the *P* 1Sa 29:3
the princes of the *P* were wroth 1Sa 29:4
princes of the *P* said unto him 1Sa 29:4
displease not the lords of the *P* 1Sa 29:7
the princes of the *P* have said 1Sa 29:9
to return into the land of the *P* 1Sa 29:11
And the *P* went up to Jezreel 1Sa 29:11
taken out of the land of the *P* 1Sa 30:16
Now the *P* fought against Israel 1Sa 31:1
of Israel fled from before the *P* 1Sa 31:1
the *P* followed hard upon Saul and 1Sa 31:2
the *P* slew Jonathan, and Abinadab, 1Sa 31:2
the *P* came and dwelt in them 1Sa 31:7
when the *P* came to strip the 1Sa 31:8
the land of the *P* round about 1Sa 31:9
that which the *P* had done to Saul 1Sa 31:11
the daughters of the *P* rejoice 2Sa 1:20
for an hundred foreskins of the *P* 2Sa 3:14
Israel out of the hand of the *P* 2Sa 3:18
But when the *P* heard that they 2Sa 5:17
all the *P* came up to seek David 2Sa 5:17
The *P* also came and spread 2Sa 5:18
saying, Shall I go up to the *P* 2Sa 5:19
deliver the *P* into thine hand 2Sa 5:19
the *P* came up yet again, and 2Sa 5:22
thee, to smite the host of the *P* 2Sa 5:24
smote the *P* from Geba until thou 2Sa 5:25
to pass, that David smote the *P* 2Sa 8:1
out of the hand of the *P* 2Sa 8:1
children of Ammon, and of the *P* 2Sa 8:12
us out of the hand of the *P* 2Sa 19:9
where the *P* had hanged them 2Sa 21:12
when the *P* had slain Saul in 2Sa 21:12
Moreover the *P* had yet war again 2Sa 21:15
with him, and fought against the *P* 2Sa 21:15
again a battle with the *P* at Gob 2Sa 21:18
again a battle in Gob with the *P* 2Sa 21:19
when they defied the *P* that were 2Sa 23:9
smote the *P* until his hand was 2Sa 23:10
the *P* were gathered together into 2Sa 23:11
and the people fled from the *P* 2Sa 23:11
and defended it, and slew the *P* 2Sa 23:12
the troop of the *P* pitched in the 2Sa 23:13
the garrison of the *P* was then in 2Sa 23:14
brake through the host of the *P* 2Sa 23:16
the river unto the land of the *P* 1Kin 4:21
which belonged to the *P* 1Kin 15:27
which belonged to the *P* 1Kin 16:15
in the land of the *P* seven years 2Kin 8:2
returned out of the land of the *P* 2Kin 8:3
He smote the *P*, even unto Gaza, 2Kin 18:8
and Casluhim, (of whom came the *P* 1Chr 1:12
Now the *P* fought against Israel 1Chr 10:1
of Israel fled from before the *P* 1Chr 10:1
the *P* followed hard after Saul, 1Chr 10:2
the *P* slew Jonathan, and Abinadab, 1Chr 10:2
the *P* came and dwelt in them 1Chr 10:7
when the *P* came to strip the 1Chr 10:8
the land of the *P* round about 1Chr 10:9
all that the *P* had done to Saul 1Chr 10:11
there the *P* were gathered 1Chr 11:13
the people fled from before the *P* 1Chr 11:13
and delivered it, and slew the *P* 1Chr 11:14
the host of the *P* encamped in the 1Chr 11:15
brake through the host of the *P* 1Chr 11:18
when he came with the *P* against 1Chr 12:19
for the lords of the *P* upon 1Chr 12:19
when the *P* heard that David was 1Chr 14:8
all the *P* went up to seek David 1Chr 14:8
the *P* came and spread themselves 1Chr 14:9
Shall I go up against the *P* 1Chr 14:10
the *P* yet again spread themselves 1Chr 14:13
thee to smite the host of the *P* 1Chr 14:15
the *P* from Gibeon even to Gazer 1Chr 14:16
to pass, that David smote the *P* 1Chr 18:1
towns out of the hand of the *P* 1Chr 18:1
children of Ammon, and from the *P* 1Chr 18:11
arose war at Gezer with the *P* 1Chr 20:4
And there was war again with the *P* 1Chr 20:5
river even unto the land of the *P* 2Chr 9:26
Also some of the *P* brought 2Chr 17:11
Jehoram the spirit of the *P* 2Chr 21:16
forth and warred against the *P* 2Chr 26:6
about Ashdod, and among the *P* 2Chr 26:6
And God helped him against the *P* 2Chr 26:7
The *P* also had invaded the cities 2Chr 28:18
when the *P* took him in Gath Ps 56:t
the *P* with the inhabitants of Ps 83:7
and are soothsayers like the *P* Is 2:6
Syrians before, and the *P* behind Is 9:12
of the *P* toward the west Is 11:14
the kings of the land of the *P* Jer 25:20
the prophet against the *P* Jer 47:1
that cometh to spoil all the *P* Jer 47:4
for the LORD will spoil the *P* Jer 47:4
hate thee, the daughters of the *P* Eze 16:27
about her, the daughters of the *P* Eze 16:57
Because the *P* have dealt by Eze 25:15
stretch out mine hand upon the *P* Eze 25:16
the remnant of the *P* shall perish Amos 1:8
then go down to Gath of the *P* Amos 6:2
the *P* from Caphtor, and the Amos 9:7
and they of the plain the *P* Obad 19
O Canaan, the land of the *P* Zeph 2:5
I will cut off the pride of the *P* Zec 9:6

**PHILISTINES'** (*fil-is'-tinz*)
sojourned in the *P* land many days Gen 21:34
let us go over to the *P* garrison 1Sa 14:1
to go over unto the *P* garrison 1Sa 14:4
the *P* garrison was then at 1Chr 11:16

**PHILOLOGUS** (*fil-ol'-o-gus*) *A Christian in Rome.*
Salute P, and Julia, Nereus, and Rom 16:15

**PHILOSOPHERS**
Then certain *p* of the Epicureans, Acts 17:18

**PHILOSOPHY**
lest any man spoil you through *p* Col 2:8

**PHINEHAS** (*fin'-e-has*) See PHINEHAS'.
*1. A son of Eleazar.*
and she bare him *P* Ex 6:25
And when *P*, the son of Eleazar, Num 25:7
*P*, the son of Eleazar, the son of Num 25:11
*P* the son of Eleazar the priest, Num 31:6
*P* the son of Eleazar the priest, Josh 22:13
when *P* the priest, and the princes Josh 22:30
*P* the son of Eleazar the priest Josh 22:31
*P* the son of Eleazar the priest, Josh 22:32
hill that pertained to *P* his son Josh 24:33
And *P*, the son of Eleazar, the son Judg 20:28
Eleazar begat *P* 1Chr 6:4
*P* begat Abishua 1Chr 6:4
*P* his son, Abishua his son, 1Chr 6:50
*P* the son of Eleazar was the 1Chr 9:20
The son of Abishua, the son of *P* Ezr 7:5
Of the sons of *P* Ezr 8:2
Then stood up *P*, and executed Ps 106:30
*2. A son of Eli.*
the two sons of Eli, Hophni and *P* 1Sa 1:3
upon thy two sons, on Hophni and *P* 1Sa 2:34
the two sons of Eli, Hophni and *P* 1Sa 4:4
the two sons of Eli, Hophni and *P* 1Sa 4:11
and thy two sons also, Hophni and *P* 1Sa 4:17
I-chabod's brother, the son of *P* 1Sa 14:3
*3. Father of Eleazar.*
with him was Eleazar the son of *P* Ezr 8:33

**PHINEHAS'** (*fin'-e-has*) *Refers to Phinehas 2.*
*P* wife, was with child, near to 1Sa 4:19

**PHLEGON** (*fle'-gon*) *A Christian in Rome.*
Salute Asyncritus, *P*, Hermas, Rom 16:14

**PHOENIX** See PHENICE.

**PHRYGIA** (*frij'-e-ah*) *A Roman province in Asia Minor.*
*P*, and Pamphylia, in Egypt, and in Acts 2:10
when they had gone throughout *P* Acts 16:6
*P* in order, strengthening all the Acts 18:23
the chiefest city of *P* Pacatiana 1Ti *s*

**PHURAH** (*fu'-rah*) *A servant of Gideon.*
go thou with *P* thy servant down Judg 7:10
Then went he down with *P* his Judg 7:11

**PHUT** (*fut*) See PUT.
*1. A son of Ham.*
Cush, and Mizraim, and *P* Gen 10:6
*2. Land of Phut's descendants.*
of *P* were in thine army, thy men Eze 27:10

**PHUVAH** (*fu'-vah*) See PUAH. *A son of Issachar.*
Tola, and *P*, and Job, and Shimron Gen 46:13

**PHYGELLUS** (*fi-jel'-lus*) *An unfaithful Christian.*
of whom are *P* and Hermogenes 2Ti 1:15

**PHYGELUS** See PHYGELLUS.

**PHYLACTERIES**
they make broad their *p*, and Mt 23:5

**PHYSICIAN**
is there no *p* there Jer 8:22
They that be whole need not a *p* Mt 9:12
are whole have no need of the *p* Mk 2:17
say unto me this proverb, *P* Lk 4:23
They that are whole need not a *p* Lk 5:31
Luke, the beloved *p*, and Demas, Col 4:14

**PHYSICIANS**
the *p* to embalm his father Gen 50:2
and the *p* embalmed Israel Gen 50:2
not to the LORD, but to the *p* 2Chr 16:12
of lies, ye are all *p* of no value Job 13:4
suffered many things of many *p* Mk 5:26
had spent all her living upon *p* Lk 8:43

**PI-BESETH** *A city in Egypt.*
of P shall fall by the sword Eze 30:17

**PICK**
of the valley shall p it out Prov 30:17

**PICTURES**
you, and destroy all their p Num 33:52
apples of gold in p of silver Prov 25:11
Tarshish, and upon all pleasant p Is 2:16

**PIECE**
laid each p one against another Gen 15:10
beaten out of one p made he them Ex 37:7
of a whole p shalt thou make them Num 10:2
a certain woman cast a p of a Judg 9:53
crouch to him for a p of silver 1Sa 2:36
that I may eat a p of bread 1Sa 2:36
they gave him a p of a cake of 1Sa 30:12
a good p of flesh, and a flagon of 2Sa 6:19
did not a woman cast a p of a 2Sa 11:21
where was a p of ground full of 2Sa 23:11
mar every good p of land with 2Kin 3:19
on every good p of land cast 2Kin 3:25
a good p of flesh, and a flagon of 1Chr 16:3
Pahath-moab, repaired the other p Neh 3:11
another p over against the going Neh 3:19
earnestly repaired the other p Neh 3:20
Urijah the son of Koz another p Neh 3:21
the son of Henadad another p Neh 3:24
the Tekoites repaired another p Neh 3:27
sixth son of Zalaph, another p Neh 3:30
as hard as a p of the nether Job 41:24
man also gave him a p of money Job 42:11
a man is brought to a p of bread Prov 6:26
for for a p of bread that man Prov 28:21
thy temples are like a p of a Song 4:3
As a p of a pomegranate are thy Song 6:7
a p of bread out of the bakers' Jer 37:21
into it, even every good p Eze 24:4
bring it out p by p Eze 24:6
lion two legs, or a p of an ear Amos 3:12
one p was rained upon Amos 4:7
the p whereupon it rained not Amos 4:7
No man putteth a p of new cloth Mt 9:16
thou shalt find a p of money Mt 17:27
No man also seweth a p of new Mk 2:21
else the new p that filled it up Mk 2:21
No man putteth a p of a new Lk 5:36
the p that was taken out of the Lk 5:36
him, I have bought a p of ground Lk 14:18
of silver, if she lose one p Lk 15:8
have found the p which I had lost Lk 15:9
they gave him a p of a broiled Lk 24:42

**PIECES**
lamp that passed between those p Gen 15:17
brother a thousand p of silver Gen 20:16
father, for an hundred p of money Gen 33:19
for twenty p of silver Gen 37:28
Joseph is without doubt rent in p Gen 37:33
and I said, Surely he is torn in p Gen 44:28
he gave three hundred p of silver Gen 45:22
LORD, hath dashed in p the enemy Ex 15:6
If it be torn in p, then let him Ex 22:13
And thou shalt cut the ram in p Ex 29:17
his legs, and put them unto his p Ex 29:17
offering, and cut it into his p Lev 1:6
And he shall cut it into his p Lev 1:12
Thou shalt part it in p, and pour Lev 2:6
the baken p of the meat offering Lev 6:21
And he cut the ram into p Lev 8:20
and Moses burnt the head, and the p Lev 8:20
unto him, with the p thereof Lev 9:13
for an hundred p of silver Josh 24:32
ten p of silver out of the house Judg 9:4
of us eleven hundred p of silver Judg 16:5
with her bones, into twelve p Judg 19:29
my concubine, and cut her in p Judg 20:6
of the LORD shall be broken to p 1Sa 2:10
yoke of oxen, and hewed them in p 1Sa 11:7
Samuel hewed Agag in p before the 1Sa 15:33
on him, and rent it in twelve p 1Kin 11:30
said to Jeroboam, Take thee ten p 1Kin 11:31
for themselves, and cut it in p 1Kin 18:23
in order, and cut the bullock in p 1Kin 18:33
brake in p the rocks before the 1Kin 19:11
clothes, and rent them in two p 2Kin 2:12
silver, and six thousand p of gold 2Kin 5:5
sold for fourscore p of silver 2Kin 6:25
dove's dung for five p of silver 2Kin 6:25
images brake they in p thoroughly 2Kin 11:18
brake in p the brasen serpent 2Kin 18:4
And he brake in p the images 2Kin 23:14
cut in p all the vessels of gold 2Kin 24:13
LORD, did the Chaldees break in p 2Kin 25:13
his altars and his images in p 2Chr 23:17
that they all were broken in p 2Chr 25:12
cut in p the vessels of the house 2Chr 28:24
Judah, and brake the images in p 2Chr 31:1
the molten images, he brake in p 2Chr 34:4
me by my neck, and shaken me to p Job 16:12
soul, and break me in p with words Job 19:2
He shall break in p mighty men Job 34:24
bones are as strong p of brass Job 40:18
them in p like a potter's vessel Ps 2:9
soul like a lion, rending it in p Ps 7:2
forget God, lest I tear you in p Ps 50:22
arrows, let them be as cut in p Ps 58:7
submit himself with p of silver Ps 68:30
and shall break in p the oppressor Ps 72:4
the heads of leviathan in p Ps 74:14
Thou hast broken Rahab in p Ps 89:10
They break in p thy people Ps 94:5
to bring a thousand p of silver Song 8:11
ye that ye beat my people to p Is 3:15
and ye shall be broken in p Is 8:9
and ye shall be broken in p Is 8:9
and ye shall be broken in p Is 8:9
be dashed to p before their eyes Is 13:16
shall dash the young men to p Is 13:18
vessel that is broken in p Is 30:14
I will break in p the gates of Is 45:2
out thence shall be torn in p Jer 5:6
that breaketh the rock in p Jer 23:29
Merodach is broken in p Jer 50:2
her images are broken in p Jer 50:2
will I break in p the nations Jer 51:20
thee will I break in p the horse Jer 51:21
will I break in p the chariot Jer 51:21
thee also will I break in p man Jer 51:22
with thee will I break in p old Jer 51:22
will I break in p the young man Jer 51:22
I will also break in p with thee Jer 51:23
will I break in p the husbandman Jer 51:23
thee will I break in p captains Jer 51:23
aside my ways, and pulled me in p Lam 3:11
dieth of itself, or is torn in p Eze 4:14
for p of bread, to slay the souls Eze 13:19
Gather the p thereof into it Eze 24:4
thereof, ye shall be cut in p Dan 2:5
iron and clay, and brake them to p Dan 2:34
and the gold, broken to p together Dan 2:35
forasmuch as iron breaketh in p Dan 2:40
all these, shall it break in p Dan 2:40
people, but it shall break in p Dan 2:44
and that it brake in p the iron Dan 2:45
and Abed-nego, shall be cut in p Dan 3:29
brake all their bones in p or Dan 6:24
it devoured and brake in p Dan 7:7
which devoured, brake in p Dan 7:19
tread it down, and break it in p Dan 7:23
her to me for fifteen p of silver Hos 3:2
of Samaria shall be broken in p Hos 8:6
was dashed in p upon her children Hos 10:14
infants shall be dashed in p Hos 13:16
thereof shall be beaten to p Mic 1:7
their bones, and chop them in p Mic 3:3
thou shalt beat in p many people Mic 4:13
treadeth down, and teareth in p Mic 5:8
He that dasheth in p is come up Nah 2:1
The lion did tear in p enough for Nah 2:12
children also were dashed in p at Nah 3:10
for my price thirty p of silver Zec 11:12
And I took the thirty p of silver Zec 11:13
the fat, and tear their claws in p Zec 11:16
with it shall be cut in p Zec 12:3
with him for thirty p of silver Mt 26:15
brought again the thirty p of Mt 27:3
he cast down the p of silver in Mt 27:5
chief priests took the silver p Mt 27:6
they took the thirty p of silver Mt 27:9
him, and the fetters broken in p Mk 5:4
what woman having ten p of silver Lk 15:8
it fifty thousand p of silver Acts 19:19
have been pulled in p of them Acts 23:10
and some on broken p of the ship Acts 27:44

**PIERCE**
p them through with his arrows Num 24:8
it will go into his hand, and p it 2Kin 18:21
it will go into his hand, and p it Is 36:6
a sword shall p through thy own Lk 2:35

**PIERCED**
off his head, when she had p Judg 5:26
My bones are p in me in the night Job 30:17
they p my hands and my feet Ps 22:16
look upon me whom they have p Zec 12:10
soldiers with a spear p his side Jn 19:34
shall look on him whom they p Jn 19:37
p themselves through with many 1Ti 6:10
see him, and they also which p him Rev 1:7

**PIERCETH**
his nose p through snares Job 40:24

**PIERCING**
punish leviathan the p serpent Is 27:1
p even to the dividing asunder of Heb 4:12

**PIERCINGS**
speaketh like the p of a sword Prov 12:18

**PIETY**
learn first to shew p at home 1Ti 5:4

**PIGEON**
and a turtledove, and a young p Gen 15:9
a burnt offering, and a young p Lev 12:6

**PIGEONS**
of turtledoves, or of young p Lev 1:14
two turtledoves, or two young p Lev 5:7
two turtledoves, or two young p Lev 5:11
bring two turtles, or two young p Lev 12:8
two turtledoves, or two young p Lev 14:22
turtledoves, or of the young p Lev 14:30
two turtledoves, or two young p Lev 15:14
her two turtles, or two young p Lev 15:29
bring two turtles, or two young p Num 6:10
of turtledoves, or two young p Lk 2:24

**PI-HAHIROTH**
that they turn and encamp before P Ex 14:2
encamping by the sea, beside P Ex 14:9
Etham, and turned again unto P Num 33:7
And they departed from before P Num 33:8

**PILATE** (*pi'-lut*) *A Roman procurator of Judea.*
him to Pontius P the governor Mt 27:2
Then said P unto him, Hearest Mt 27:13
P said unto them, Whom will ye Mt 27:17
P saith unto them, What shall I Mt 27:22
When P saw that he could prevail Mt 27:24
He went to P, and begged the body Mt 27:58
Then P commanded the body to be Mt 27:58
and Pharisees came together unto P Mt 27:62
P said unto them, Ye have a watch Mt 27:65
him away, and delivered him to P Mk 15:1
P asked him, Art thou the King of Mk 15:2
P asked him again, saying, Mk 15:4
so that P marvelled Mk 15:5
But P answered them, saying, Will Mk 15:9
P answered and said again unto Mk 15:12
Then P said unto them, Why, what Mk 15:14
And so P, willing to content the Mk 15:15
came, and went in boldly unto P Mk 15:43
P marvelled if he were already Mk 15:44
Pontius P being governor of Lk 3:1
whose blood P had mingled with Lk 13:1
of them arose, and led him unto P Lk 23:1
P asked him, saying, Art thou the Lk 23:3
Then said P to the chief priests Lk 23:4
When P heard of Galilee, he asked Lk 23:6
robe, and sent him again to P Lk 23:11
And the same day P and Herod were Lk 23:12
And P, when he had called together Lk 23:13
P therefore, willing to release Lk 23:20
P gave sentence that it should be Lk 23:24
This man went unto P, and begged Lk 23:52
P then went out unto them, and Jn 18:29
Then said P unto them, Take ye Jn 18:31
Then P entered into the judgment Jn 18:33
P answered, Am I a Jew Jn 18:35
P therefore said unto him, Art Jn 18:37
P saith unto him, What is truth Jn 18:38
Then P therefore took Jesus, and Jn 19:1
P therefore went forth again, and Jn 19:4
P saith unto them, Behold the man Jn 19:5
P saith unto them, Take ye him, Jn 19:6
When P therefore heard that Jn 19:8
Then saith P unto him, Speakest Jn 19:10
from thenceforth P sought to Jn 19:12
When P therefore heard that Jn 19:13
P saith unto them, Shall I Jn 19:15
P wrote a title, and put it on the Jn 19:19
chief priests of the Jews to P Jn 19:21
P answered, What I have written I Jn 19:22
besought P that their legs might Jn 19:31
besought P that he might take Jn 19:38
and P gave him leave Jn 19:38
denied him in the presence of P Acts 3:13
both Herod, and Pontius P Acts 4:27
yet desired they P that he should Acts 13:28
who before Pontius P witnessed a 1Ti 6:13

**PILDASH** (*pil'-dash*) *A son of Nahor.*
And Chesed, and Hazo, and P, and Gen 22:22

**PILE**
the p thereof is fire and much Is 30:33
even make the p for fire great Eze 24:9

**PILEHA** (*pil'-e-hah*) *A renewer of the covenant.*
Hallohesh, P, Shobek, Neh 10:24

**PILGRIMAGE**
the years of my p are an hundred Gen 47:9
my fathers in the days of their p Gen 47:9
of Canaan, the land of their p Ex 6:4
my songs in the house of my p Ps 119:54

**PILGRIMS**
were strangers and p on the earth Heb 11:13
I beseech you as strangers and p 1Pet 2:11

**PILHA** See PILEHA.

**PILLAR**
him, and she became a p of salt Gen 19:26
his pillows, and set it up for a p Gen 28:18
stone, which I have set for a p Gen 28:22
where thou anointedst the p Gen 31:13
a stone, and set it up for a p Gen 31:45
this heap, and behold this p Gen 31:51
this p be witness, that I will Gen 31:52
heap and this p unto me, for harm Gen 31:52
Jacob set up a p in the place Gen 35:14
with him, even a p of stone Gen 35:14
Jacob set a p upon her grave Gen 35:20
that is the p of Rachel's grave Gen 35:20
them by day in a p of a cloud Ex 13:21
and by night in a p of fire Ex 13:21
away the p of the cloud by day Ex 13:22
nor the p of fire by night, from Ex 13:22
the p of the cloud went from Ex 14:19
Egyptians through the p of fire Ex 14:24
the cloudy p descended, and stood Ex 33:9
p stand at the tabernacle door Ex 33:10
came down in the p of the cloud Num 12:5
by daytime in a p of a cloud Num 14:14
and in a p of fire by night Num 14:14
the tabernacle in a p of a cloud Deut 31:15
the p of the cloud stood over the Deut 31:15
of the p that was in Shechem Judg 9:6
out of the city with a p of smoke Judg 20:40
and reared up for himself a p 2Sa 18:18
he called the p after his own 2Sa 18:18

P

and he set up the right *p*, and 1Kin 7:21
and he set up the left *p*, and 1Kin 7:21
behold, the king stood by a *p* 2Kin 11:14
And the king stood by a *p*, and made 2Kin 23:3
of the one *p* was eighteen cubits 2Kin 25:17
the second *p* with wreathen work 2Kin 25:17
stood at his *p* at the entering in 2Chr 23:13
them in the day by a cloudy *p* Neh 9:12
and in the night by a *p* of fire Neh 9:12
the *p* of the cloud departed not Neh 9:19
neither the *p* of fire by night, Neh 9:19
spake unto them in the cloudy *p* Ps 99:7
a *p* at the border thereof to the Is 19:19
day a defenced city, and an iron *p* Jer 1:18
the height of one *p* was eighteen Jer 52:21
The second *p* also and the Jer 52:22
church of the living God, the *p* 1Ti 3:15
make a *p* in the temple of my God Rev 3:12

**PILLARS**
altar under the hill, and twelve *p* Ex 24:4
thou shalt hang it upon four *p* of Ex 26:32
hanging five *p* of shittim wood Ex 26:37
And the twenty *p* thereof and their Ex 27:10
the hooks of the *p* and their Ex 27:10
cubits long, and his twenty *p* Ex 27:11
the hooks of the *p* and their Ex 27:11
their *p* ten, and their sockets ten Ex 27:12
their *p* three, and their sockets Ex 27:14
their *p* three, and their sockets Ex 27:15
their *p* shall be four, and their Ex 27:16
All the *p* round about the court Ex 27:17
and his boards, his bars, his *p* Ex 35:11
The hangings of the court, his *p* Ex 35:17
thereunto four *p* of shittim wood Ex 36:36
the five *p* of it with their hooks Ex 36:38
Their *p* were twenty, and their Ex 38:10
the hooks of the *p* and their Ex 38:10
their *p* were twenty, and their Ex 38:11
the hooks of the *p* and their Ex 38:11
of fifty cubits, their *p* ten Ex 38:12
the hooks of the *p* and their Ex 38:12
their *p* three, and their sockets Ex 38:14
their *p* three, and their sockets Ex 38:15
sockets for the *p* were of brass Ex 38:17
the hooks of the *p* and their Ex 38:17
all the *p* of the court were Ex 38:17
their *p* were four, and their Ex 38:19
shekels he made hooks for the *p* Ex 38:28
his boards, his bars, and his *p* Ex 39:33
The hangings of the court, his *p* Ex 39:40
bars thereof, and reared up his *p* Ex 40:18
the *p* thereof, and the sockets Num 3:36
the *p* of the court round about, Num 3:37
the *p* thereof, and sockets thereof Num 4:31
the *p* of the court round about, Num 4:32
their altars, and break their *p* Deut 12:3
and they set him between the *p* Judg 16:25
*p* whereupon the house standeth Judg 16:26
*p* upon which the house stood Judg 16:29
for the *p* of the earth are the 1Sa 2:8
cubits, upon four rows of cedar *p* 1Kin 7:2
with cedar beams upon the *p* 1Kin 7:2
beams, that lay on forty five *p* 1Kin 7:3
And he made a porch of *p* 1Kin 7:6
and the other *p* and the thick beam 1Kin 7:6
For he cast two *p* of brass 1Kin 7:15
to set upon the tops of the *p* 1Kin 7:16
which were upon the top of the *p* 1Kin 7:17
And he made the *p*, and two rows 1Kin 7:18
that were upon the top of the *p* 1Kin 7:19
the chapiters upon the two *p* had 1Kin 7:20
he set up the *p* in the porch of 1Kin 7:21
the top of the *p* was lily work 1Kin 7:22
so was the work of the *p* finished 1Kin 7:22
The two *p*, and the two bowls of 1Kin 7:41
that were on the top of the two *p* 1Kin 7:41
which were upon the top of the *p* 1Kin 7:41
chapiters that were upon the *p* 1Kin 7:42
trees *p* for the house of the LORD 1Kin 10:12
from the *p* which Hezekiah king of 2Kin 18:16
the *p* of brass that were in the 2Kin 25:13
The two *p*, one sea, and the bases 2Kin 25:16
made the brasen sea, and the *p* 1Chr 18:8
before the house two *p* of thirty 2Chr 3:15
and put them on the heads of the *p* 2Chr 3:16
he reared up the *p* before the 2Chr 3:17
To wit, the two *p*, and the pommels 2Chr 4:12
were on the top of the two *p* 2Chr 4:12
which were on the top of the *p* 2Chr 4:12
chapiters which were upon the *p* 2Chr 4:13
to silver rings and *p* of marble Est 1:6
place, and the *p* thereof tremble Job 9:6
The *p* of heaven tremble, and are Job 26:11
I bear up the *p* of it Ps 75:3
she hath hewn out her seven *p* Prov 9:1
of the wilderness like *p* of smoke Song 3:6
He made the *p* thereof of silver, Song 3:10
His legs are as *p* of marble Song 5:15
LORD of hosts concerning the *p* Jer 27:19
Also the *p* of brass that were in Jer 52:17
The two *p*, one sea, and twelve Jer 52:20
And concerning the *p*, the height Jer 52:21
there were *p* by the posts, one on Eze 40:49
*p* as the *p* of the courts Eze 42:6
blood, and fire, and *p* of smoke Joel 2:30
and John, who seemed to be *p* Gal 2:9
the sun, and his feet as *p* of fire Rev 10:1

**PILLED**
*p* white strakes in them, and made Gen 30:37
he had *p* before the flocks in the Gen 30:38

**PILLOW**
put a *p* of goats' hair for his 1Sa 19:13
with a *p* of goats' hair for his 1Sa 19:16
part of the ship, asleep on a *p* Mk 4:38

**PILLOWS**
that place, and put them for his *p* Gen 28:11
stone that he had put for his *p* Gen 28:18
women that sew *p* to all armholes Eze 13:18
Behold, I am against your *p* Eze 13:20

**PILOTS**
that were in thee, were thy *p* Eze 27:8
thy mariners, and thy *p*, thy Eze 27:27
at the sound of the cry of thy *p* Eze 27:28
all the *p* of the sea, shall come Eze 27:29

**PILTAI** (*pil'-tahee*) *A priest.*
of Miniamin, of Moadiah, *P* Neh 12:17

**PIN**
And she fastened it with the *p* Judg 16:14
went away with the *p* of the beam Judg 16:14
or will men take a *p* of it to Eze 15:3

**PINE**
*p* away in their iniquity in your Lev 26:39
shall they *p* away with them Lev 26:39
*p* branches, and myrtle branches, Neh 8:15
the desert the fir tree, and the *p* Is 41:19
the *p* tree, and the box together, Is 60:13
for these *p* away, stricken Lam 4:9
but ye shall *p* away for your Eze 24:23
we *p* away in them, how should we Eze 33:10

**PINETH**
with his teeth, and *p* away Mk 9:18

**PINING**
will cut me off with *p* sickness Is 38:12

**PINNACLE**
setteth him on a *p* of the temple Mt 4:5
set him on a *p* of the temple, and Lk 4:9

**PINON**
Aholibamah, duke Elah, duke *P* Gen 36:41
Aholibamah, duke Elah, duke *P* 1Chr 1:52

**PINS**
thereof, and all the *p* thereof Ex 27:19
all the *p* of the court, shall be Ex 27:19
The *p* of the tabernacle, and the Ex 35:18
the *p* of the court, and their Ex 35:18
all the *p* of the tabernacle, and Ex 38:20
all the *p* of the tabernacle, and Ex 38:31
all the *p* of the court round Ex 38:31
court gate, his cords, and his *p* Ex 39:40
and their sockets, and their *p* Num 3:37
and their sockets, and their *p* Num 4:32
and the wimples, and the crisping *p* Is 3:22

**PIPE**
a psaltery, and a tabret, and a *p* 1Sa 10:5
and the viol, the tabret, and *p* Is 5:12
as when one goeth with a *p* to Is 30:29
giving sound, whether *p* or harp 1Cor 14:7

**PIPED**
him, and the people *p* with pipes 1Kin 1:40
We have *p* unto you, and ye have Mt 11:17
We have *p* unto you, and ye have Lk 7:32
it be known what is *p* or harped 1Cor 14:7

**PIPERS**
of harpers, and musicians, and of *p* Rev 18:22

**PIPES**
him, and the people piped with *p* 1Kin 1:40
heart shall sound for Moab like *p* Jer 48:36
like *p* for the men of Kir-heres Jer 48:36
of thy *p* was prepared in thee in Eze 28:13
seven *p* to the seven lamps, which Zec 4:2
*p* empty the golden oil out of Zec 4:12

**PIRAM** (*pi'-ram*) *An Amorite king.*
unto *P* king of Jarmuth, and unto Josh 10:3

**PIRATHON** (*pir'-a-thon*) See PIRATHONITE. *A place in Ephraim.*
was buried in *P* in the land of Judg 12:15

**PIRATHONITE** (*pir'-a-thon-ite*) *An inhabitant of Pirathon.*
him Abdon the son of Hillel, a *P* Judg 12:13
the son of Hillel the *P* died Judg 12:15
Benaiah the *P*, Hiddai of the 2Sa 23:30
of Benjamin, Benaiah the *P* 1Chr 11:31
eleventh month was Benaiah the *P* 1Chr 27:14

**PISGAH** (*piz'-gah*) *A mountain peak in Moab.*
country of Moab, to the top of *P* Num 21:20
field of Zophim, to the top of *P* Num 23:14
Get thee up into the top of *P* Deut 3:27
the plain, under the springs of *P* Deut 4:49
mountain of Nebo, to the top of *P* Deut 34:1

**PISHON** See PISON.

**PISIDIA** (*pi-sid'-e-ah*) *A Roman province in Asia Minor.*
Perga, they came to Antioch in *P* Acts 13:14
they had passed throughout *P* Acts 14:24

**PISIDIAN ANTIOCH**

**PISON** (*pi'-son*) *A river of Eden.*
The name of the first is *P* Gen 2:11

**PISPA** See PISPAH.

**PISPAH** (*piz'-pah*) *A son of Jether.*
Jephunneh, and *P*, and Ara 1Chr 7:38

**PISS**
and drink their own *p* with you 2Kin 18:27
and drink their own *p* with you Is 36:12

**PISSETH**
light any that *p* against the wall 1Sa 25:22
light any that *p* against the wall 1Sa 25:34
him that *p* against the wall 1Kin 14:10
him not one that *p* against a wall 1Kin 16:11
Ahab him that *p* against the wall 1Kin 21:21
Ahab him that *p* against the wall 2Kin 9:8

**PIT**
slay him, and cast him into some *p* Gen 37:20
but cast him into this *p* that is Gen 37:22
took him, and cast him into a *p* Gen 37:24
the *p* was empty, there was no Gen 37:24
and lifted up Joseph out of the *p* Gen 37:28
And Reuben returned unto the *p* Gen 37:29
behold, Joseph was not in the *p* Gen 37:29
And if a man shall open a *p* Ex 21:33
or if a man shall dig a *p* Ex 21:33
The owner of the *p* shall make it Ex 21:34
Nevertheless a fountain or *p* Lev 11:36
and they go down quick into the *p* Num 16:30
them, went down alive into the *p* Num 16:33
Behold, he is hid now in some *p* 2Sa 17:9
him into a great *p* in the wood 2Sa 18:17
the midst of a *p* in time of snow 2Sa 23:20
slew them at the *p* of the 2Kin 10:14
slew a lion in a *p* in a snowy day 1Chr 11:22
ye dig a *p* for your friend Job 6:27
go down to the bars of the *p* Job 17:16
keepeth back his soul from the *p* Job 33:18
him from going down to the *p* Job 33:24
his soul from going into the *p* Job 33:28
To bring back his soul from the *p* Job 33:30
He made a *p*, and digged it, and is Ps 7:15
sunk down in the *p* that they made Ps 9:15
like them that go down into the *p* Ps 28:1
I should not go down to the *p* Ps 30:3
my blood, when I go down to the *p* Ps 30:9
they hid for me their net in a *p* Ps 35:7
me up also out of an horrible *p* Ps 40:2
down into the *p* of destruction Ps 55:23
they have digged a *p* before me Ps 57:6
let not the *p* shut her mouth upon Ps 69:15
with them that go down into the *p* Ps 88:4
Thou hast laid me in the lowest *p* Ps 88:6
until the *p* be digged for the Ps 94:13
unto them that go down into the *p* Ps 143:7
as those that go down into the *p* Prov 1:12
of strange women is a deep *p* Prov 22:14
and a strange woman is a narrow *p* Prov 23:27
Whoso diggeth a *p* shall fall Prov 26:27
shall fall himself into his own *p* Prov 28:10
of any person shall flee to the *p* Prov 28:17
He that diggeth a *p* shall fall Eccl 10:8
to hell, to the sides of the *p* Is 14:15
go down to the stones of the *p* Is 14:19
Fear, and the *p*, and the snare, are Is 24:17
of the fear shall fall into the *p* Is 24:18
up out of the midst of the *p* Is 24:18
prisoners are gathered in the *p* Is 24:22
to take water withal out of the *p* Is 30:14
it from the *p* of corruption Is 38:17
the *p* cannot hope for thy truth Is 38:18
to the hole of the *p* whence ye Is 51:1
that he should not die in the *p* Is 51:14
they have digged a *p* for my soul Jer 18:20
they have digged a *p* to take me Jer 18:22
cast them into the midst of the *p* Jer 41:7
Now the *p* wherein Ishmael had Jer 41:9
Fear, and the *p*, and the snare, Jer 48:43
the fear shall fall into the *p* Jer 48:44
the *p* shall be taken in the snare Jer 48:44
he was taken in their *p*, and they Eze 19:4
he was taken in their *p* Eze 19:8
with them that descend into the *p* Eze 26:20
with them that go down to the *p* Eze 26:20
shall bring thee down to the *p* Eze 28:8
with them that go down to the *p* Eze 31:14
with them that descend into the *p* Eze 31:16
with them that go down into the *p* Eze 32:18
are set in the sides of the *p* Eze 32:23
with them that go down to the *p* Eze 32:24
with them that go down to the *p* Eze 32:25
with them that go down to the *p* Eze 32:29
with them that go down to the *p* Eze 32:30
out of the *p* wherein is no water Zec 9:11
if it fall into a *p* on the Mt 12:11
an ass or an ox fallen into a *p* Lk 14:5
given the key of the bottomless *p* Rev 9:1
And he opened the bottomless *p* Rev 9:2
there arose a smoke out of the *p* Rev 9:2
by reason of the smoke of the *p* Rev 9:2
is the angel of the bottomless *p* Rev 9:11
*p* shall make war against them Rev 11:7
ascend out of the bottomless *p* Rev 17:8
the key of the bottomless *p* Rev 20:1
And cast him into the bottomless *p* Rev 20:3

**PITCH**
*p* it within and without with *p* Gen 6:14
and daubed it with slime and with *p* Ex 2:3
of Israel shall *p* their tents Num 1:52
But the Levites shall *p* round Num 1:53
shall *p* by his own standard Num 2:2
of the congregation shall they *p* Num 2:2
Judah *p* throughout their armies Num 2:3
those that do *p* next unto him Num 2:5
those which *p* by him shall be the Num 2:12
of the Gershonites shall *p* behind Num 3:23
of the sons of Kohath shall *p* on Num 3:29
these shall *p* on the side of the Num 3:35
out a place to *p* your tents in Deut 1:33

of Jordan, did Joshua *p* in Gilgal ... Josh 4:20
shall the Arabian *p* tent there ... Is 13:20
thereof shall be turned into *p* ... Is 34:9
thereof shall become burning *p* ... Is 34:9
they shall *p* their tents against ... Jer 6:3

### PITCHED
*p* his tent, having Beth-el on the ... Gen 12:8
plain, and *p* his tent toward Sodom ... Gen 13:12
*p* his tent in the valley of Gerar ... Gen 26:17
of the LORD, and *p* his tent there ... Gen 26:25
Now Jacob had *p* his tent in the ... Gen 31:25
brethren *p* in the mount of Gilead ... Gen 31:25
*p* his tent before the city ... Gen 33:18
of the LORD, and *p* in Rephidim ... Ex 17:1
Sinai, and had *p* in the wilderness ... Ex 19:2
*p* it without the camp, afar off ... Ex 33:7
and when the tabernacle is to be *p* ... Num 1:51
so they *p* by their standards, and ... Num 2:34
children of Israel *p* their tents ... Num 9:17
commandment of the LORD they *p* ... Num 9:18
*p* in the wilderness of Paran ... Num 12:16
Israel set forward, and *p* in Oboth ... Num 21:10
Oboth, and *p* at Ije-abarim, in the ... Num 21:11
and *p* in the valley of Zared ... Num 21:12
*p* on the other side of Arnon, ... Num 21:13
*p* in the plains of Moab on this ... Num 22:1
from Rameses, and *p* in Succoth ... Num 33:5
*p* in Etham, which is in the edge ... Num 33:6
and they *p* before Migdol ... Num 33:7
of Etham, and *p* in Marah ... Num 33:8
and they *p* there ... Num 33:9
*p* in the wilderness of Sinai ... Num 33:15
Sinai, and *p* at Kibroth-hattaavah ... Num 33:16
from Hazeroth, and *p* in Rithmah ... Num 33:18
Rithmah, and *p* at Rimmon-parez ... Num 33:19
and *p* in Libnah ... Num 33:20
from Libnah, and *p* at Rissah ... Num 33:21
from Rissah, and *p* in Kehelathah ... Num 33:22
and *p* in mount Shapher ... Num 33:23
from Haradah, and *p* in Makheloth ... Num 33:25
from Tahath, and *p* at Tarah ... Num 33:27
from Tarah, and *p* in Mithcah ... Num 33:28
from Mithcah, and *p* in Hashmonah ... Num 33:29
Moseroth, and *p* in Bene-jaakan ... Num 33:31
Hor-hagidgad, and *p* in Jotbathah ... Num 33:33
*p* in the wilderness of Zin, which ... Num 33:36
*p* in mount Hor, in the edge of ... Num 33:37
from mount Hor, and *p* in Zalmonah ... Num 33:41
from Zalmonah, and *p* in Punon ... Num 33:42
from Punon, and *p* in Oboth ... Num 33:43
*p* in Ije-abarim, in the border of ... Num 33:44
from Iim, and *p* in Dibon-gad ... Num 33:45
*p* in the mountains of Abarim, ... Num 33:47
*p* in the plains of Moab by Jordan ... Num 33:48
And they *p* by Jordan, from ... Num 33:49
*p* on the north side of Ai ... Josh 8:11
*p* together at the waters of Merom ... Josh 11:5
*p* his tent unto the plain of ... Judg 4:11
*p* in the valley of Jezreel ... Judg 6:33
*p* beside the well of Harod ... Judg 7:1
*p* on the other side of Arnon, but ... Judg 11:18
*p* in Jahaz, and fought against ... Judg 11:20
*p* in Judah, and spread themselves ... Judg 15:9
*p* in Kirjath-jearim, in Judah ... Judg 18:12
to battle, and *p* beside Eben-ezer ... 1Sa 4:1
and the Philistines *p* in Aphek ... 1Sa 4:1
*p* in Michmash, eastward from ... 1Sa 13:5
*p* between Shochoh and Azekah, in ... 1Sa 17:1
*p* by the valley of Elah, and set ... 1Sa 17:2
Saul *p* in the hill of Hachilah, ... 1Sa 26:3
to the place where Saul had *p* ... 1Sa 26:5
the people *p* round about him ... 1Sa 26:5
together, and came and *p* in Shunem ... 1Sa 28:4
together, and they *p* in Gilboa ... 1Sa 28:4
the Israelites *p* by a fountain ... 1Sa 29:1
that David had *p* for it ... 2Sa 6:17
Absalom *p* in the land of Gilead ... 2Sa 17:26
*p* in the valley of Rephaim ... 2Sa 23:13
*p* in Aroer, on the right side of ... 2Sa 24:5
the children of Israel *p* before ... 1Kin 20:27
they *p* one over against the other ... 1Kin 20:29
Jerusalem, and *p* against it ... 2Kin 25:1
ark of God, and *p* for it a tent ... 1Chr 15:1
the tent that David had *p* for it ... 1Chr 16:1
who came and *p* before Medeba ... 1Chr 19:7
for he had *p* a tent for it at ... 2Chr 1:4
*p* against it, and built forts ... Jer 52:4
true tabernacle, which the Lord *p* ... Heb 8:2

### PITCHER
whom I shall say, Let down thy *p* ... Gen 24:14
with her *p* upon her shoulder ... Gen 24:15
down to the well, and filled her *p* ... Gen 24:16
drink a little water of thy *p* ... Gen 24:17
let down her *p* upon her hand, and ... Gen 24:18
emptied her *p* into the trough, and ... Gen 24:20
a little water of thy *p* to drink ... Gen 24:43
forth with her *p* on her shoulder ... Gen 24:45
let down her *p* from her shoulder, ... Gen 24:46
or the *p* be broken at the ... Eccl 12:6
you a man bearing a *p* of water ... Mk 14:13
meet you, bearing a *p* of water ... Lk 22:10

### PITCHERS
in every man's hand, with empty *p* ... Judg 7:16
and lamps within the *p* ... Judg 7:16
brake the *p* that were in their ... Judg 7:19
blew the trumpets, and brake the *p* ... Judg 7:20
are they esteemed as earthen *p* ... Lam 4:2

### PITHOM (*pi'-thom*) *A city in Lower Egypt.*
for Pharaoh treasure cities, *P* ... Ex 1:11

### PITHON (*pi'-thon*) *A son of Micah.*
And the sons of Micah were, *P* ... 1Chr 8:35
And the sons of Micah were, *P* ... 1Chr 9:41

### PITIED
He made them also to be *p* of all ... Ps 106:46
of Jacob, and hath not *p* ... Lam 2:2
hath thrown down, and hath not *p* ... Lam 2:17
thou hast killed, and not *p* ... Lam 2:21
thou hast slain, thou hast not *p* ... Lam 3:43
None eye *p* thee, to do any of ... Eze 16:5

### PITIETH
Like as a father *p* his children ... Ps 103:13
so the LORD *p* them that fear him ... Ps 103:13
eyes, and that which your soul *p* ... Eze 24:21

### PITIFUL
The hands of the *p* women have ... Lam 4:10
that the Lord is very *p*, and of ... Jas 5:11
another, love as brethren, be *p* ... 1Pet 3:8

### PITS
rocks, and in high places, and in *p* ... 1Sa 13:6
The proud have digged *p* for me ... Ps 119:85
into deep *p*, that they rise not ... Ps 140:10
through a land of deserts and of *p* ... Jer 2:6
they came to the *p*, and found no ... Jer 14:3
of the LORD, was taken in their *p* ... Lam 4:20

### PITY
eye shall have no *p* upon them ... Deut 7:16
neither shall thine eye *p* him ... Deut 13:8
Thine eye shall not *p* him ... Deut 19:13
And thine eye shall not *p* ... Deut 19:21
hand, thine eye shall not *p* her ... Deut 25:12
thing, and because he had no *p* ... 2Sa 12:6
To him that is afflicted *p* should ... Job 6:14
Have *p* upon me, have *p* upon me ... Job 19:21
and I looked for some to take *p* ... Ps 69:20
He that hath *p* upon the poor ... Prov 19:17
it for him that will *p* the poor ... Prov 28:8
they shall have no *p* on the fruit ... Is 13:18
in his *p* he redeemed them ... Is 63:9
I will not *p*, nor spare, nor have ... Jer 13:14
For who shall have *p* upon thee ... Jer 15:5
not spare them, neither have *p* ... Jer 21:7
spare, neither will I have any *p* ... Eze 5:11
spare thee, neither will I have *p* ... Eze 7:4
not spare, neither will I have *p* ... Eze 7:9
not spare, neither will I have *p* ... Eze 8:18
your eye spare, neither have ye *p* ... Eze 9:5
not spare, neither will I have *p* ... Eze 9:10
But I had *p* for mine holy name, ... Eze 36:21
for his land, and *p* his people ... Joel 2:18
the sword, and did cast off all *p* ... Amos 1:11
Thou hast had *p* on the gourd ... Jonah 4:10
and their own shepherds *p* them not ... Zec 11:5
For I will no more *p* the ... Zec 11:6
even as I had *p* on thee ... Mt 18:33

### PLACE See PREFACE.

### PLACED
he *p* at the east of the garden of ... Gen 3:24
Joseph *p* his father and his ... Gen 47:11
he *p* in Beth-el the priests of ... 1Kin 12:32
*p* them in Halah and in Habor by ... 2Kin 17:6
*p* them in the cities of Samaria ... 2Kin 17:24
*p* in the cities of Samaria, know ... 2Kin 17:26
which he *p* in the chariot cities, ... 2Chr 1:14
*p* them in the temple, five on the ... 2Chr 4:8
he *p* forces in all the fenced ... 2Chr 17:2
old, since man was *p* upon earth ... Job 20:4
the tent which he *p* among men ... Ps 78:60
that they may be *p* alone in the ... Is 5:8
which have *p* the sand for the ... Jer 5:22
he *p* it by great waters, and set ... Eze 17:5

### PLACES See PREFACE.

### PLAGUE
I bring one *p* more upon Pharaoh ... Ex 11:1
the *p* shall not be upon you to ... Ex 12:13
that there be no *p* among them ... Ex 30:12
his flesh like the *p* of leprosy ... Lev 13:2
on the *p* in the skin of the flesh ... Lev 13:3
the hair in the *p* is turned white ... Lev 13:3
the *p* in sight be deeper than the ... Lev 13:3
his flesh, it is a *p* of leprosy ... Lev 13:3
up him that hath the *p* seven days ... Lev 13:4
if the *p* in his sight be at a ... Lev 13:5
the *p* spread not in the skin ... Lev 13:5
if the *p* be somewhat dark ... Lev 13:6
the *p* spread not in the skin ... Lev 13:6
When the *p* of leprosy is in a man ... Lev 13:9
the skin of him that hath the *p* ... Lev 13:12
him clean that hath the *p* ... Lev 13:13
if the *p* be turned into white ... Lev 13:17
him clean that hath the *p* ... Lev 13:17
it is a *p* of leprosy broken out ... Lev 13:20
it is a *p* ... Lev 13:22
it is the *p* of leprosy ... Lev 13:25
it is the *p* of leprosy ... Lev 13:27
If a man or woman have a *p* upon ... Lev 13:29
Then the priest shall see the *p* ... Lev 13:30
priest look on the *p* of the scall ... Lev 13:31
the *p* of the scall seven days ... Lev 13:31
the priest shall look on the *p* ... Lev 13:32
his *p* is in his head ... Lev 13:44
And the leper in whom the *p* is ... Lev 13:45
All the days wherein the *p* shall ... Lev 13:46
also that the *p* of leprosy is in ... Lev 13:47
if the *p* be greenish or reddish ... Lev 13:49
it is a *p* of leprosy, and shall be ... Lev 13:49
the priest shall look upon the *p* ... Lev 13:50
up it that hath the *p* seven days ... Lev 13:50
look on the *p* on the seventh day ... Lev 13:51
if the *p* be spread in the garment ... Lev 13:51
the *p* is a fretting leprosy ... Lev 13:51
thing of skin, wherein the *p* is ... Lev 13:52
the *p* be not spread in the ... Lev 13:53
wash the thing wherein the *p* is ... Lev 13:54
And the priest shall look on the *p* ... Lev 13:55
if the *p* have not changed his ... Lev 13:55
colour, and the *p* be not spread ... Lev 13:55
the *p* be somewhat dark after the ... Lev 13:56
it is a spreading *p* ... Lev 13:57
that wherein the *p* is with fire ... Lev 13:57
if the *p* be departed from them, ... Lev 13:58
This is the law of the *p* of ... Lev 13:59
if the *p* of leprosy be healed in ... Lev 14:3
him in whom is the *p* of leprosy ... Lev 14:32
I put the *p* of leprosy in a house ... Lev 14:34
is as it were a *p* in the house ... Lev 14:35
priest go into it to see the *p* ... Lev 14:36
And he shall look on the *p* ... Lev 14:37
if the *p* be in the walls of the ... Lev 14:37
if the *p* be spread in the walls ... Lev 14:39
away the stones in which the *p* is ... Lev 14:40
if the *p* come again, and break out ... Lev 14:43
if the *p* be spread in the house, ... Lev 14:44
the *p* hath not spread in the ... Lev 14:48
clean, because the *p* is healed ... Lev 14:48
for all manner of *p* of leprosy ... Lev 14:54
that there be no *p* among the ... Num 8:19
the people with a very great *p* ... Num 11:33
died by the *p* before the LORD ... Num 14:37
the *p* is begun ... Num 16:46
the *p* was begun among the people ... Num 16:47
and the *p* was stayed ... Num 16:48
in the *p* were fourteen thousand ... Num 16:49
and the *p* was stayed ... Num 16:50
So the *p* was stayed from the ... Num 25:8
that died in the *p* were twenty ... Num 25:9
the day of the *p* for Peor's sake ... Num 25:18
And it came to pass after the *p* ... Num 26:1
Peor, and there was a *p* among the ... Num 31:16
Take heed in the *p* of leprosy ... Deut 24:8
Also every sickness, and every *p* ... Deut 28:61
although there was a *p* in the ... Josh 22:17
for one *p* was on you all, and on ... 1Sa 6:4
that the *p* may be stayed from the ... 2Sa 24:21
the *p* was stayed from Israel ... 2Sa 24:25
whatsoever *p*, whatsoever sickness ... 1Kin 8:37
every man the *p* of his own heart ... 1Kin 8:38
that the *p* may be stayed from the ... 1Chr 21:22
with a great *p* will the LORD ... 2Chr 21:14
his face, and *p* them that hate him ... Ps 89:23
neither shall any *p* come nigh thy ... Ps 91:10
and the *p* brake in upon them ... Ps 106:29
and so the *p* was stayed ... Ps 106:30
this shall be the *p* wherewith the ... Zec 14:12
And so shall be the *p* of the horse ... Zec 14:15
be in these tents, as this *p* ... Zec 14:15
there shall be the *p*, wherewith ... Zec 14:18
that she was healed of that *p* ... Mk 5:29
go in peace, and be whole of thy *p* ... Mk 5:34
God because of the *p* of the hail ... Rev 16:21
for the *p* thereof was exceeding ... Rev 16:21

### PLAGUED
And the LORD *p* Pharaoh and his ... Gen 12:17
the LORD *p* the people, because ... Ex 32:35
I *p* Egypt, according to that ... Josh 24:5
thy people, that they should be *p* ... 1Chr 21:17
neither are they *p* like other men ... Ps 73:5
all the day long have I been *p* ... Ps 73:14

### PLAGUES
his house with great *p* because of ... Gen 12:17
send all my *p* upon thine heart ... Ex 9:14
I will bring seven times more *p* ... Lev 26:21
LORD will make thy *p* wonderful ... Deut 28:59
*p* of thy seed, even great *p* ... Deut 28:59
when they see the *p* of that land ... Deut 29:22
with all the *p* in the wilderness ... 1Sa 4:8
hiss because of all the *p* thereof ... Jer 19:8
shall hiss at all the *p* thereof ... Jer 49:17
astonished, and hiss at all her *p* ... Jer 50:13
O death, I will be thy *p* ... Hos 13:14
to touch him, as many as had *p* ... Mk 3:10
many of their infirmities and *p* ... Lk 7:21
*p* yet repented not of the works ... Rev 9:20
and to smite the earth with all *p* ... Rev 11:6
angels having the seven last *p* ... Rev 15:1
of the temple, having the seven *p* ... Rev 15:6
till the seven *p* of the seven ... Rev 15:8
which hath power over these *p* ... Rev 16:9
and that ye receive not of her *p* ... Rev 18:4
shall her *p* come in one day ... Rev 18:8
vials full of the seven last *p* ... Rev 21:9
God shall add unto him the *p* that ... Rev 22:18

### PLAIN
that they found a *p* in the land ... Gen 11:2
of Sichem, unto the *p* of Moreh ... Gen 12:6
and beheld all the *p* of Jordan ... Gen 13:10
Lot chose him all the *p* of Jordan ... Gen 13:11
dwelled in the cities of the *p* ... Gen 13:12
came and dwelt in the *p* of Mamre ... Gen 13:18
for he dwelt in the *p* of Mamre ... Gen 14:13
neither stay thou in all the *p* ... Gen 19:17
those cities, and all the *p* ... Gen 19:25

and toward all the land of the *p* ... Gen 19:28
God destroyed the cities of the *p* ... Gen 19:29
and Jacob was a *p* man, dwelling in ... Gen 25:27
in the *p* over against the Red sea ... Deut 1:1
places nigh thereunto, in the *p* ... Deut 1:7
the way of the *p* from Elath ... Deut 2:8
All the cities of the *p*, and all ... Deut 3:10
The *p* also, and Jordan, and the ... Deut 3:17
even unto the sea of the *p* ... Deut 3:17
in the *p* country, of the ... Deut 4:43
all the *p* on this side Jordan ... Deut 4:49
even unto the sea of the *p* ... Deut 4:49
the *p* of the valley of Jericho, ... Deut 34:3
came down toward the sea of the *p* ... Josh 3:16
at a time appointed, before the *p* ... Josh 8:14
Goshen, and the valley, and the *p* ... Josh 11:16
Hermon, and all the *p* on the east ... Josh 12:1
And from the *p* to the sea of ... Josh 12:3
east, and unto the sea of the *p* ... Josh 12:3
all the *p* of Medeba unto Dibon ... Josh 13:9
the river, and all the *p* by Medeba ... Josh 13:16
all her cities that are in the *p* ... Josh 13:17
And all the cities of the *p* ... Josh 13:21
the *p* out of the tribe of Reuben ... Josh 20:8
his tent unto the *p* of Zaanaim ... Judg 4:11
by the *p* of the pillar that was ... Judg 9:6
come along by the *p* of Meonenim ... Judg 9:37
unto the *p* of the vineyards, with ... Judg 11:33
thou shalt come to the *p* of Tabor ... 1Sa 10:3
in the *p* on the south of Jeshimon ... 1Sa 23:24
all that night through the *p* ... 2Sa 2:29
them away through the *p* all night ... 2Sa 4:7
tarry in the *p* of the wilderness ... 2Sa 15:28
Ahimaaz ran by the way of the *p* ... 2Sa 18:23
In the *p* of Jordan did the king ... 1Kin 7:46
us fight against them in the *p* ... 1Kin 20:23
will fight against them in the *p* ... 1Kin 20:25
of Hamath unto the sea of the *p* ... 2Kin 14:25
king went the way toward the *p* ... 2Kin 25:4
In the *p* of Jordan did the king ... 2Chr 4:17
the priests, the men of the *p* ... Neh 3:22
of the villages in the *p* of Ono ... Neh 6:2
both out of the *p* country round ... Neh 12:28
O LORD, and lead me in a *p* path ... Ps 27:11
They are all *p* to him that ... Prov 8:9
way of the righteous is made *p* ... Prov 15:19
he hath made *p* the face thereof ... Is 28:25
straight, and the rough places *p* ... Is 40:4
land of Benjamin, and from the *p* ... Jer 17:26
of the valley, and rock of the *p* ... Jer 21:13
and he went out the way of the *p* ... Jer 39:4
the *p* shall be destroyed, as the ... Jer 48:8
is come upon the *p* country ... Jer 48:21
and they went by the way of the *p* ... Jer 52:7
me, Arise, go forth into the *p* ... Eze 3:22
I arose, and went forth into the *p* ... Eze 3:23
to the vision that I saw in the *p* ... Eze 8:4
he set it up in the *p* of Dura ... Dan 3:1
the inhabitant from the *p* of Aven ... Amos 1:5
they of the *p* the Philistines ... Obad 19
make it *p* upon tables, that he ... Hab 2:2
Zerubbabel thou shalt become a *p* ... Zec 4:7
men inhabited the south and the *p* ... Zec 7:7
a *p* from Geba to Rimmon south of ... Zec 14:10
tongue was loosed, and he spake *p* ... Mk 7:35
down with them, and stood in the *p* ... Lk 6:17

**PLAINLY**

And if the servant shall *p* say ... Ex 21:5
all the words of this law very *p* ... Deut 27:8
Did I *p* appear unto the house of ... 1Sa 2:27
He told us *p* that the asses were ... 1Sa 10:16
us hath been *p* read before me ... Ezr 4:18
shall be ready to speak *p* ... Is 32:4
If thou be the Christ, tell us *p* ... Jn 10:24
Then said Jesus unto them *p* ... Jn 11:14
I shall shew you *p* of the Father ... Jn 16:25
unto him, Lo, now speakest thou *p* ... Jn 16:29
*p* that they seek a country ... Heb 11:14

**PLAINNESS**

hope, we use great *p* of speech ... 2Cor 3:12

**PLAINS**

unto him in the *p* of Mamre ... Gen 18:1
pitched in the *p* of Moab on this ... Num 22:1
priest spake with them in the *p* ... Num 26:3
the children of Israel in the *p* ... Num 26:63
unto the camp at the *p* of Moab ... Num 31:12
pitched in the *p* of Moab by ... Num 33:48
Abel-shittim in the *p* of Moab ... Num 33:49
Moses in the *p* of Moab by Jordan ... Num 33:50
LORD spake unto Moses in the *p* of ... Num 35:1
the children of Israel in the *p* ... Num 36:13
Gilgal, beside the *p* of Moreh ... Deut 11:30
Moses went up from the *p* of Moab ... Deut 34:1
in the *p* of Moab thirty days ... Deut 34:8
unto battle, to the *p* of Jericho ... Josh 4:13
month at even in the *p* of Jericho ... Josh 5:10
of the *p* south of Chinneroth, and ... Josh 11:2
and in the valleys, and in the *p* ... Josh 12:8
for inheritance in the *p* of Moab ... Josh 13:32
night in the *p* of the wilderness ... 2Sa 17:16
overtook him in the *p* of Jericho ... 2Kin 25:5
trees that were in the low *p* was ... 1Chr 27:28
are in the low *p* in abundance ... 2Chr 9:27
in the low country, and in the *p* ... 2Chr 26:10
Zedekiah in the *p* of Jericho ... Jer 39:5
Zedekiah in the *p* of Jericho ... Jer 52:8

**PLAISTER**

morter, and shall *p* the house ... Lev 14:42
stones, and *p* them with *p* ... Deut 27:2
thou shalt *p* them with *p* ... Deut 27:4
lay it for a *p* upon the boil, and ... Is 38:21
the candlestick upon the *p* of the ... Dan 5:5

**PLAISTERED**

the house, and after it is *p* ... Lev 14:43
the house, after the house was *p* ... Lev 14:48

**PLAITING**

outward adorning of *p* the hair ... 1Pet 3:3

**PLANES**

he fitteth it with *p*, and he ... Is 44:13

**PLANETS**

sun, and to the moon, and to the *p* ... 2Kin 23:5

**PLANKS**

floor of the house with *p* of fir ... 1Kin 6:15
there were thick *p* upon the face ... Eze 41:25
chambers of the house, and thick *p* ... Eze 41:26

**PLANT**

every *p* of the field before it ... Gen 2:5
*p* them in the mountain of thine ... Ex 15:17
Thou shalt not *p* thee a grove of ... Deut 16:21
thou shalt *p* a vineyard, and shalt ... Deut 28:30
Thou shalt *p* vineyards, and dress ... Deut 28:39
my people Israel, and will *p* them ... 2Sa 7:10
*p* vineyards, and eat the fruits ... 2Kin 19:29
my people Israel, and will *p* them ... 1Chr 17:9
and bring forth boughs like a *p* ... Job 14:9
*p* vineyards, which may yield ... Ps 107:37
a time to *p*, and a time to pluck ... Eccl 3:2
the men of Judah his pleasant *p* ... Is 5:7
shalt thou *p* pleasant plants ... Is 17:10
day shalt thou make thy *p* to grow ... Is 17:11
*p* vineyards, and eat the fruit ... Is 37:30
I will *p* in the wilderness the ... Is 41:19
that I may *p* the heavens, and lay ... Is 51:16
grow up before him as a tender *p* ... Is 53:2
and they shall *p* vineyards ... Is 65:21
they shall not *p*, and another eat ... Is 65:22
to throw down, to build, and to *p* ... Jer 1:10
*p* of a strange vine unto me ... Jer 2:21
a kingdom, to build and to *p* it ... Jer 18:9
and I will *p* them, and not pluck ... Jer 24:6
*p* gardens, and eat the fruit of ... Jer 29:5
*p* gardens, and eat the fruit of ... Jer 29:28
Thou shalt yet *p* vines upon the ... Jer 31:5
the planters shall *p*, and shall ... Jer 31:5
over them, to build, and to *p* ... Jer 31:28
I will *p* them in this land ... Jer 32:41
nor *p* vineyard, nor have any ... Jer 35:7
pull you down, and I will *p* you ... Jer 42:10
will *p* it upon an high mountain ... Eze 17:22
the height of Israel will I *p* it ... Eze 17:23
build houses, and *p* vineyards ... Eze 28:26
raise up for them a *p* of renown ... Eze 34:29
and *p* that that was desolate ... Eze 36:36
he shall *p* the tabernacles of his ... Dan 11:45
and they shall *p* vineyards ... Amos 9:14
I will *p* them upon their land, and ... Amos 9:15
and they shall *p* vineyards ... Zeph 1:13
But he answered and said, Every *p* ... Mt 15:13

**PLANTATION**

water it by the furrows of her *p* ... Eze 17:7

**PLANTED**

the LORD God *p* a garden eastward ... Gen 2:8
an husbandman, and he *p* a vineyard ... Gen 9:20
Abraham *p* a grove in Beer-sheba, ... Gen 21:33
shall have *p* all manner of trees ... Lev 19:23
lign aloes which the LORD hath *p* ... Num 24:6
man is he that hath *p* a vineyard ... Deut 20:6
which ye *p* not do ye eat ... Josh 24:13
a tree *p* by the rivers of water ... Ps 1:3
cast out the heathen, and *p* it ... Ps 80:8
which thy right hand hath *p* ... Ps 80:15
Those that be *p* in the house of ... Ps 92:13
He that *p* the ear, shall he not ... Ps 94:9
of Lebanon, which he hath *p* ... Ps 104:16
I *p* me vineyards ... Eccl 2:4
I *p* trees in them of all kind of ... Eccl 2:5
time to pluck up that which is *p* ... Eccl 3:2
*p* it with the choicest vine, and ... Is 5:2
Yea, they shall not be *p* ... Is 40:24
Yet I had *p* thee a noble vine, ... Jer 2:21
the LORD of hosts, that *p* thee ... Jer 11:17
Thou hast *p* them, yea, they have ... Jer 12:2
be as a tree *p* by the waters ... Jer 17:8
which I have *p* I will pluck up ... Jer 45:4
land, and *p* it in a fruitful field ... Eze 17:5
It was *p* in a good soil by great ... Eze 17:8
Yea, behold, being *p*, shall it ... Eze 17:10
in thy blood, *p* by the waters ... Eze 19:10
now she is *p* in the wilderness, ... Eze 19:13
Tyrus, is *p* in a pleasant place ... Hos 9:13
ye have *p* pleasant vineyards, but ... Amos 5:11
my heavenly Father hath not *p* ... Mt 15:13
which *p* a vineyard, and hedged it ... Mt 21:33
A certain man *p* a vineyard ... Mk 12:1
had a fig tree *p* in his vineyard ... Lk 13:6
the root, and be thou *p* in the sea ... Lk 17:6
they bought, they sold, they *p* ... Lk 17:28
A certain man *p* a vineyard ... Lk 20:9
For if we have been *p* together in ... Rom 6:5
I have *p*, Apollos watered ... 1Cor 3:6

**PLANTEDST**

and olive trees, which thou *p* not ... Deut 6:11
heathen with thy hand, and *p* them ... Ps 44:2

**PLANTERS**

the *p* shall plant, and shall eat ... Jer 31:5

**PLANTETH**

of her hands she *p* a vineyard ... Prov 31:16
he *p* an ash, and the rain doth ... Is 44:14
neither is he that *p* any thing ... 1Cor 3:7
Now he that *p* and he that watereth ... 1Cor 3:8
who *p* a vineyard, and eateth not ... 1Cor 9:7

**PLANTING**

land for ever, the branch of my *p* ... Is 60:21
the *p* of the LORD, that he might ... Is 61:3

**PLANTINGS**

the field, and as *p* of a vineyard ... Mic 1:6

**PLANTS**

and those that dwelt among *p* ... 1Chr 4:23
olive *p* round about thy table ... Ps 128:3
be as *p* grown up in their youth ... Ps 144:12
Thy *p* are an orchard of ... Song 4:13
down the principal *p* thereof ... Is 16:8
shalt thou plant pleasant *p* ... Is 17:10
thy *p* are gone over the sea, they ... Jer 48:32
rivers running round about his *p* ... Eze 31:4

**PLAT**

and I will requite thee in this *p* ... 2Kin 9:26
and cast him into the *p* of ground ... 2Kin 9:26

**PLATE**

thou shalt make a *p* of pure gold ... Ex 28:36
they made the *p* of the holy crown ... Ex 39:30
did he put the golden *p*, the ... Lev 8:9

**PLATES**

did beat the gold into thin *p* ... Ex 39:3
let them make them broad *p* for a ... Num 16:38
they were made broad *p* for a ... Num 16:39
four brasen wheels, and *p* of brass ... 1Kin 7:30
For on the *p* of the ledges ... 1Kin 7:36
Silver spread into *p* is brought ... Jer 10:9

**PLATTED**

when they had *p* a crown of thorns ... Mt 27:29
*p* a crown of thorns, and put it ... Mk 15:17
the soldiers *p* a crown of thorns, ... Jn 19:2

**PLATTER**

outside of the cup and of the *p* ... Mt 23:25
that which is within the cup and *p* ... Mt 23:26
the outside of the cup and the *p* ... Lk 11:39

**PLAY**

eat and to drink, and rose up to *p* ... Ex 32:6
to *p* the whore in her father's ... Deut 22:21
that he shall *p* with his hand ... 1Sa 16:16
me now a man that can *p* well ... 1Sa 16:17
to *p* the mad man in my presence ... 1Sa 21:15
men now arise, and *p* before us ... 2Sa 2:14
will I *p* before the LORD ... 2Sa 6:21
let us *p* the men for our people, ... 2Sa 10:12
all the beasts of the field *p* ... Job 40:20
Wilt thou *p* with him as with a ... Job 41:5
*p* skilfully with a loud noise ... Ps 33:3
whom thou hast made to *p* therein ... Ps 104:26
shall *p* on the hole of the asp ... Is 11:8
can *p* well on an instrument ... Eze 33:32
thou shalt not *p* the harlot ... Hos 3:3
*p* the harlot, yet let not Judah ... Hos 4:15
to eat and drink, and rose up to *p* ... 1Cor 10:7

**PLAYED**

daughter in law hath *p* the harlot ... Gen 38:24
his concubine *p* the whore against ... Judg 19:2
took an harp, and *p* with his hand ... 1Sa 16:23
answered one another as they *p* ... 1Sa 18:7
David *p* with his hand, as at ... 1Sa 18:10
and David *p* with his hand ... 1Sa 19:9
I have *p* the fool, and have erred ... 1Sa 26:21
all the house of Israel *p* before ... 2Sa 6:5
came to pass, when the minstrel *p* ... 2Kin 3:15
all Israel *p* before God with all ... 1Chr 13:8
but thou hast *p* the harlot with ... Jer 3:1
tree, and there hath *p* the harlot ... Jer 3:6
but went and *p* the harlot also ... Jer 3:8
Thou hast *p* the whore also with ... Eze 16:28
thou hast *p* the harlot with them ... Eze 16:28
Aholah *p* the harlot when she was ... Eze 23:5
wherein she had *p* the harlot in ... Eze 23:19
their mother hath *p* the harlot ... Hos 2:5

**PLAYEDST**

*p* the harlot because of thy ... Eze 16:15
and *p* the harlot thereupon ... Eze 16:16

**PLAYER**

who is a cunning *p* on an harp ... 1Sa 16:16

**PLAYERS**

the *p* on instruments followed ... Ps 68:25
As well the singers as the *p* on ... Ps 87:7

**PLAYETH**

in unto a woman that *p* the harlot ... Eze 23:44

**PLAYING**

profane herself by *p* the whore ... Lev 21:9
that is cunning in *p*, and a ... 1Sa 16:18
saw king David dancing and *p* ... 1Chr 15:29
were the damsels *p* with timbrels ... Ps 68:25
tree thou wanderest, *p* the harlot ... Jer 2:20
thee to cease from *p* the harlot ... Eze 16:41
girls *p* in the streets thereof ... Zec 8:5

### PLEA
blood and blood, between *p* and *p* ... Deut 17:8

### PLEAD
against him, Will ye *p* for Baal ... Judg 6:31
he that will *p* for him, let him ... Judg 6:31
let him *p* for himself, because ... Judg 6:31
Let Baal *p* against him, because ... Judg 6:32
*p* my cause, and deliver me out of ... 1Sa 24:15
who shall set me a time to *p* ... Job 9:19
Who is he that will *p* with me ... Job 13:19
Oh that one might *p* for a man ... Job 16:21
me, and *p* against me my reproach ... Job 19:5
Will he *p* against me with his ... Job 23:6
*P* my cause, O LORD, with them ... Ps 35:1
*p* my cause against an ungodly ... Ps 43:1
Arise, O God, *p* thine own cause ... Ps 74:22
*P* my cause, and deliver me ... Ps 119:154
For the LORD will *p* their cause ... Prov 22:23
he shall *p* their cause with thee ... Prov 23:11
*p* the cause of the poor and needy ... Prov 31:9
the fatherless, *p* for the widow ... Is 1:17
The LORD standeth up to *p* ... Is 3:13
let us *p* together ... Is 43:26
will the LORD *p* with all flesh ... Is 66:16
Wherefore I will yet *p* with you ... Jer 2:9
your children's children will I *p* ... Jer 2:9
Wherefore will ye *p* with me ... Jer 2:29
I will *p* with thee, because thou ... Jer 2:35
thou, O LORD, when I *p* with thee ... Jer 12:1
nations, he will *p* with all flesh ... Jer 25:31
There is none to *p* thy cause ... Jer 30:13
he shall throughly *p* their cause ... Jer 50:34
I will *p* thy cause, and take ... Jer 51:36
will *p* with him there for his ... Eze 17:20
there will I *p* with you face to ... Eze 20:35
of Egypt, so will I *p* with you ... Eze 20:36
I will *p* against him with ... Eze 38:22
*P* with your mother, *p* ... Hos 2:2
will *p* with them there for my ... Joel 3:2
people, and he will *p* with Israel ... Mic 6:2
against him, until he *p* my cause ... Mic 7:9

### PLEADED
that hath *p* the cause of my ... 1Sa 25:39
thou hast *p* the causes of my soul ... Lam 3:58
Like as I *p* with your fathers in ... Eze 20:36

### PLEADETH
as a man *p* for his neighbour ... Job 16:21
thy God that *p* the cause of his ... Is 51:22
for justice, nor any *p* for truth ... Is 59:4

### PLEADINGS
and hearken to the *p* of my lips ... Job 13:6

### PLEASANT
every tree that is *p* to the sight ... Gen 2:9
and that it was *p* to the eyes ... Gen 3:6
good, and the land that it was *p* ... Gen 49:15
*p* in their lives, and in their ... 2Sa 1:23
very *p* hast thou been unto me ... 2Sa 1:26
whatsoever is *p* in thine eyes ... 1Kin 20:6
the situation of this city is *p* ... 2Kin 2:19
and for all manner of *p* jewels ... 2Chr 32:27
are fallen unto me in *p* places ... Ps 16:6
the *p* harp with the psaltery ... Ps 81:2
Yea, they despised the *p* land ... Ps 106:24
how *p* it is for brethren to dwell ... Ps 133:1
for it is *p* ... Ps 135:3
knowledge is *p* unto thy soul ... Prov 2:10
be as the loving hind and *p* roe ... Prov 5:19
and bread eaten in secret is *p* ... Prov 9:17
the words of the pure are *p* words ... Prov 15:26
*P* words are as an honeycomb, ... Prov 16:24
For it is a *p* thing if thou keep ... Prov 22:18
with all precious and *p* riches ... Prov 24:4
a *p* thing it is for the eyes to ... Eccl 11:7
thou art fair, my beloved, yea, *p* ... Song 1:16
of pomegranates, with *p* fruits ... Song 4:13
his garden, and eat his *p* fruits ... Song 4:16
how *p* art thou, O love, for ... Song 7:6
gates are all manner of *p* fruits ... Song 7:13
Tarshish, and upon all *p* pictures ... Is 2:16
and the men of Judah his *p* plant ... Is 5:7
and dragons in their *p* palaces ... Is 13:22
shalt thou plant *p* plants ... Is 17:10
for the teats, for the *p* fields ... Is 32:12
and all thy borders of *p* stones ... Is 54:12
all our *p* things are laid waste ... Is 64:11
children, and give thee a *p* land ... Jer 3:19
they have made my *p* portion a ... Jer 12:10
the *p* places of the wilderness ... Jer 23:10
and ye shall fall like a *p* vessel ... Jer 25:34
is he a *p* child ... Jer 31:20
of her miseries all her *p* things ... Lam 1:7
his hand upon all her *p* things ... Lam 1:10
they have given their *p* things ... Lam 1:11
slew all that were *p* to the eye ... Lam 2:4
walls, and destroy thy *p* houses ... Eze 26:12
song of one that hath a *p* voice ... Eze 33:32
the east, and toward the *p* land ... Dan 8:9
I ate no *p* bread, neither came ... Dan 10:3
with precious stones, and *p* things ... Dan 11:38
the *p* places for their silver, ... Hos 9:6
Tyrus, is planted in a *p* place ... Hos 9:13
the treasure of all *p* vessels ... Hos 13:15
your temples my goodly *p* things ... Joel 3:5
ye have planted *p* vineyards ... Amos 5:11
ye cast out from their *p* houses ... Mic 2:9
glory out of all the *p* furniture ... Nah 2:9
for they laid the *p* land desolate ... Zec 7:14
Jerusalem be *p* unto the LORD, as ... Mal 3:4

### PLEASANTNESS
Her ways are ways of *p*, and all ... Prov 3:17

### PLEASE
If she *p* not her master, who hath ... Ex 21:8
peradventure it will *p* God that ... Num 23:27
but if it *p* my father to do thee ... 1Sa 20:13
Therefore now let it *p* thee to ... 2Sa 7:29
or else, if it *p* thee, I will ... 1Kin 21:6
Now therefore let it *p* thee to ... 1Chr 17:27
*p* them, and speak good words to ... 2Chr 10:7
If it *p* the king, and if thy ... Neh 2:5
If it *p* the king, let letters be ... Neh 2:7
If it *p* the king, let there go a ... Est 1:19
If it *p* the king, let it be ... Est 3:9
if it *p* the king to grant my ... Est 5:8
if it *p* the king, let my life be ... Est 7:3
If it *p* the king, and if I have ... Est 8:5
If it *p* the king, let it be ... Est 9:13
that it would *p* God to destroy me ... Job 6:9
children shall seek to *p* the poor ... Job 20:10
This also shall *p* the LORD better ... Ps 69:31
When a man's ways *p* the LORD ... Prov 16:7
up, nor awake my love, till he *p* ... Song 2:7
up, nor awake my love, till he *p* ... Song 3:5
up, nor awake my love, until he *p* ... Song 8:4
they *p* themselves in the children ... Is 2:6
shall accomplish that which I *p* ... Is 55:11
and choose the things that *p* me ... Is 56:4
do always those things that *p* him ... Jn 8:29
are in the flesh cannot *p* God ... Rom 8:8
the weak, and not to *p* ourselves ... Rom 15:1
Let every one of us *p* his ... Rom 15:2
the Lord, how he may *p* the Lord ... 1Cor 7:32
the world, how he may *p* his wife ... 1Cor 7:33
world, how she may *p* her husband ... 1Cor 7:34
Even as I *p* all men in all things ... 1Cor 10:33
or do I seek to *p* men ... Gal 1:10
they *p* not God, and are contrary ... 1Th 2:15
to *p* God, so ye would abound more ... 1Th 4:1
that he may *p* him who hath chosen ... 2Ti 2:4
to *p* them well in all things ... Titus 2:9
faith it is impossible to *p* him ... Heb 11:6

### PLEASED
of Canaan *p* not Isaac his father ... Gen 28:8
of God, and thou wast *p* with me ... Gen 33:10
And their words *p* Hamor, and ... Gen 34:18
it *p* Pharaoh well, and his ... Gen 45:16
when Balaam saw that it *p* the ... Num 24:1
And the saying *p* me well ... Deut 1:23
of Manasseh spake, it *p* them ... Josh 22:30
the thing *p* the children of ... Josh 22:33
If the LORD were *p* to kill us ... Judg 13:23
and she *p* Samson well ... Judg 14:7
because it hath *p* the LORD to ... 1Sa 12:22
told Saul, and the thing *p* him ... 1Sa 18:20
it *p* David well to be the king's ... 1Sa 18:26
took notice of it, and it *p* them ... 2Sa 3:36
the king did *p* all the people ... 2Sa 3:36
the saying *p* Absalom well, and all ... 2Sa 17:4
this day, then it had *p* thee well ... 2Sa 19:6
And the speech *p* the Lord, that ... 1Kin 3:10
desire which he was *p* to do ... 1Kin 9:1
and they *p* him not ... 1Kin 9:12
And the thing *p* the king and all ... 2Chr 30:4
So it *p* the king to send me ... Neh 2:6
And the saying *p* the king and the ... Est 1:21
And the thing *p* the king ... Est 2:4
And the maiden *p* him, and she ... Est 2:9
And the thing *p* Haman ... Est 5:14
Be *p*, O LORD, to deliver me ... Ps 40:13
Then shalt thou be *p* with the ... Ps 51:19
he hath done whatsoever he hath *p* ... Ps 115:3
Whatsoever the LORD *p*, that did ... Ps 135:6
The LORD is well *p* for his ... Is 42:21
Yet it *p* the LORD to bruise him ... Is 53:10
It *p* Darius to set over the ... Dan 6:1
O LORD, hast done as it *p* thee ... Jonah 1:14
Will the LORD be *p* with thousands ... Mic 6:7
will he be *p* with thee, or accept ... Mal 1:8
beloved Son, in whom I am well *p* ... Mt 3:17
in whom my soul is well *p* ... Mt 12:18
danced before them, and *p* Herod ... Mt 14:6
beloved Son, in whom I am well *p* ... Mt 17:5
beloved Son, in whom I am well *p* ... Mk 1:11
*p* Herod and them that sat with him ... Mk 6:22
in thee I am well *p* ... Lk 3:22
the saying *p* the whole multitude ... Acts 6:5
And because he saw it *p* the Jews ... Acts 12:3
Then *p* it the apostles and elders, ... Acts 15:22
Notwithstanding it *p* Silas to ... Acts 15:34
For even Christ *p* not himself ... Rom 15:3
For it hath *p* them of Macedonia ... Rom 15:26
It hath *p* them verily ... Rom 15:27
it *p* God by the foolishness of ... 1Cor 1:21
she be *p* to dwell with him, let ... 1Cor 7:12
if he be *p* to dwell with her, let ... 1Cor 7:13
many of them God was not well *p* ... 1Cor 10:5
in the body, as it hath *p* him ... 1Cor 12:18
giveth it a body as it hath *p* him ... 1Cor 15:38
for if I yet *p* men, I should not ... Gal 1:10
But when it *p* God, who separated ... Gal 1:15
For it *p* the Father that in him ... Col 1:19
had this testimony, that he *p* God ... Heb 11:5
such sacrifices God is well *p* ... Heb 13:16
beloved Son, in whom I am well *p* ... 2Pet 1:17

### PLEASETH
do to her as it *p* thee ... Gen 16:6
dwell where it *p* thee ... Gen 20:15
for she *p* me well ... Judg 14:3
let the maiden which *p* the king ... Est 2:4
whoso *p* God shall escape from her ... Eccl 7:26
for he doeth whatsoever *p* him ... Eccl 8:3

### PLEASING
I be *p* in his eyes, let it be ... Est 8:5
neither shall they be *p* unto him ... Hos 9:4
worthy of the Lord unto all *p* ... Col 1:10
for this is well *p* unto the Lord ... Col 3:20
not as *p* men, but God, which ... 1Th 2:4
things that are *p* in his sight ... 1Jn 3:22

### PLEASURE
I am waxed old shall I have *p* ... Gen 18:12
grapes thy fill at thine own *p* ... Deut 23:24
heart, and hast *p* in uprightness ... 1Chr 29:17
let the king send his *p* to us ... Ezr 5:17
God of your fathers, and do his *p* ... Ezr 10:11
and over our cattle, at their *p* ... Neh 9:37
do according to every man's *p* ... Est 1:8
For what *p* hath he in his house ... Job 21:21
his soul, and never eateth with *p* ... Job 21:25
Is it any *p* to the Almighty, that ... Job 22:3
a God that hath *p* in wickedness ... Ps 5:4
which hath *p* in the prosperity of ... Ps 35:27
Do good in thy good *p* unto Zion ... Ps 51:18
thy servants take *p* in her stones ... Ps 102:14
ministers of his, that do his *p* ... Ps 103:21
To bind his princes at his *p* ... Ps 105:22
of all them that have *p* therein ... Ps 111:2
he taketh not *p* in the legs of a ... Ps 147:10
The LORD taketh *p* in them that ... Ps 147:11
the LORD taketh *p* in his people ... Ps 149:4
He that loveth *p* shall be a poor ... Prov 21:17
with mirth, therefore enjoy *p* ... Eccl 2:1
for he hath no *p* in fools ... Eccl 5:4
shalt say, I have no *p* in them ... Eccl 12:1
the night of my *p* hath he turned ... Is 21:4
and shall perform all my *p* ... Is 44:28
stand, and I will do all my *p* ... Is 46:10
he will do his *p* on Babylon ... Is 48:14
the *p* of the LORD shall prosper ... Is 53:10
in the day of your fast ye find *p* ... Is 58:3
from doing thy *p* on my holy day ... Is 58:13
own ways, nor finding thine own *p* ... Is 58:13
snuffeth up the wind at her *p* ... Jer 2:24
is he a vessel wherein is no *p* ... Jer 22:28
he had set at liberty at their *p* ... Jer 34:16
like a vessel wherein is no *p* ... Jer 48:38
with whom thou hast taken *p* ... Eze 16:37
Have I any *p* at all that the ... Eze 18:23
For I have no *p* in the death of ... Eze 18:32
I have no *p* in the death of the ... Eze 33:11
as a vessel wherein is no *p* ... Hos 8:8
and I will take *p* in it, and I will ... Hag 1:8
I have no *p* in you, saith the ... Mal 1:10
good *p* to give you the kingdom ... Lk 12:32
willing to shew the Jews a *p* ... Acts 24:27
willing to do the Jews a *p* ... Acts 25:9
but have *p* in them that do them ... Rom 1:32
Therefore I take *p* in infirmities ... 2Cor 12:10
to the good *p* of his will ... Eph 1:5
according to his good *p* which he ... Eph 1:9
to will and to do of his good *p* ... Phil 2:13
all the good *p* of his goodness ... 2Th 1:11
but had *p* in unrighteousness ... 2Th 2:12
But she that liveth in *p* is dead ... 1Ti 5:6
for sin thou hast had no *p* ... Heb 10:6
not, neither hadst *p* therein ... Heb 10:8
my soul shall have no *p* in him ... Heb 10:38
chastened us after their own *p* ... Heb 12:10
Ye have lived in *p* on the earth ... Jas 5:5
as they that count it *p* to riot ... 2Pet 2:13
for thy *p* they are and were ... Rev 4:11

### PLEASURES
prosperity, and their years in *p* ... Job 36:11
hand there are *p* for evermore ... Ps 16:11
them drink of the river of thy *p* ... Ps 36:8
this, thou that art given to *p* ... Is 47:8
*p* of this life, and bring no fruit ... Lk 8:14
lovers of *p* more than lovers of ... 2Ti 3:4
serving divers lusts and *p* ... Titus 3:3
than to enjoy the *p* of sin for a ... Heb 11:25

### PLEDGE
she said, Wilt thou give me a *p* ... Gen 38:17
he said, What *p* shall I give thee ... Gen 38:18
to receive his *p* from the woman's ... Gen 38:20
take thy neighbour's raiment to *p* ... Ex 22:26
or the upper millstone to *p* ... Deut 24:6
for he taketh a man's life to *p* ... Deut 24:6
go into his house to fetch his *p* ... Deut 24:10
bring out the *p* abroad unto thee ... Deut 24:11
thou shalt not sleep with his *p* ... Deut 24:12
*p* again when the sun goeth down ... Deut 24:13
nor take a widow's raiment to *p* ... Deut 24:17
brethren fare, and take their *p* ... 1Sa 17:18
For thou hast taken a *p* from thy ... Job 22:6
they take the widow's ox for a *p* ... Job 24:3
breast, and take a *p* of the poor ... Job 24:9
take a *p* of him for a strange ... Prov 20:16
take a *p* of him for a strange ... Prov 27:13
hath restored to the debtor his *p* ... Eze 18:7
violence, hath not restored the *p* ... Eze 18:12
any, hath not withholden the *p* ... Eze 18:16
If the wicked restore the *p* ... Eze 33:15
clothes laid to *p* by every altar ... Amos 2:8

### PLEDGES
give *p* to my lord the king of ... 2Kin 18:23
Now therefore give *p*, I pray thee ... Is 36:8

**PLEIADES** (*ple'-ya-dez*) *A constellation of stars.*
maketh Arcturus, Orion, and *P* ........ Job 9:9
bind the sweet influences of *P* ........ Job 38:31

**PLENTEOUS**
of Egypt in the seven *p* years ........ Gen 41:34
in the seven *p* years the earth ........ Gen 41:47
LORD shall make thee *p* in goods ........ Deut 28:11
*p* in every work of thine hand ........ Deut 30:9
gold at Jerusalem as *p* as stones ........ 2Chr 1:15
*p* in mercy unto all them that ........ Ps 86:5
and *p* in mercy and truth ........ Ps 86:15
slow to anger, and *p* in mercy ........ Ps 103:8
and with him is *p* redemption ........ Ps 130:7
earth, and it shall be fat and *p* ........ Is 30:23
portion is fat, and their meat *p* ........ Hab 1:16
disciples, The harvest truly is *p* ........ Mt 9:37

**PLENTEOUSNESS**
And the seven years of *p*, that was ........ Gen 41:53
of the diligent tend only to *p* ........ Prov 21:5

**PLENTIFUL**
Thou, O God, didst send a *p* rain ........ Ps 68:9
away, and joy out of the *p* field ........ Is 16:10
And I brought you into a *p* country ........ Jer 2:7
is taken from the *p* field ........ Jer 48:33

**PLENTIFULLY**
how hast thou *p* declared the ........ Job 26:3
*p* rewardeth the proud doer ........ Ps 31:23
certain rich man brought forth *p* ........ Lk 12:16

**PLENTY**
the earth, and *p* of corn and wine ........ Gen 27:28
*p* throughout all the land of ........ Gen 41:29
all the *p* shall be forgotten in ........ Gen 41:30
the *p* shall not be known in the ........ Gen 41:31
pit, wherein there is *p* of water ........ Lev 11:36
from Ophir great *p* of almug trees ........ 1Kin 10:11
had enough to eat, and have left *p* ........ 2Chr 31:10
and thou shalt have *p* of silver ........ Job 22:25
in judgment, and in *p* of justice ........ Job 37:23
shall thy barns be filled with *p* ........ Prov 3:10
his land shall have *p* of bread ........ Prov 28:19
for then had we *p* of victuals ........ Jer 44:17
And ye shall eat in *p*, and be ........ Joel 2:26

**PLOTTETH**
The wicked *p* against the just, and ........ Ps 37:12

**PLOUGH**
man, having put his hand to the *p* ........ Lk 9:62

**PLOW**
Thou shalt not *p* with an ox ........ Deut 22:10
which a yoke of oxen might *p* ........ 1Sa 14:14
I have seen, they that *p* iniquity ........ Job 4:8
will not *p* by reason of the cold ........ Prov 20:4
Doth the plowman *p* all day to sow ........ Is 28:24
Judah shall *p*, and Jacob shall ........ Hos 10:11
will one *p* there with oxen ........ Amos 6:12
he that ploweth should *p* in hope ........ 1Cor 9:10

**PLOWED**
If ye had not *p* with my heifer, ........ Judg 14:18
The plowers *p* upon my back ........ Ps 129:3
Zion shall be *p* like a field ........ Jer 26:18
Ye have *p* wickedness, ye have ........ Hos 10:13
for your sake be *p* as a field ........ Mic 3:12

**PLOWERS**
The *p* plowed upon my back ........ Ps 129:3

**PLOWETH**
that he that *p* should plow in ........ 1Cor 9:10

**PLOWING**
who was *p* with twelve yoke of ........ 1Kin 19:19
Job, and said, The oxen were *p* ........ Job 1:14
the *p* of the wicked, is sin ........ Prov 21:4
having a servant *p* or feeding ........ Lk 17:7

**PLOWMAN**
Doth the *p* plow all day to sow ........ Is 28:24
that the *p* shall overtake the ........ Amos 9:13

**PLOWMEN**
sons of the alien shall be your *p* ........ Is 61:5
the *p* were ashamed, they covered ........ Jer 14:4

**PLOWSHARES**
shall beat their swords into *p* ........ Is 2:4
Beat your *p* into swords, and your ........ Joel 3:10
shall beat their swords into *p* ........ Mic 4:3

**PLUCK**
he shall *p* away his crop with his ........ Lev 1:16
quite *p* down all their high ........ Num 33:52
then thou mayest *p* the ears with ........ Deut 23:25
Then will I *p* them up by the ........ 2Chr 7:20
They *p* the fatherless from the ........ Job 24:9
for he shall *p* my feet out of the ........ Ps 25:15
*p* thee out of thy dwelling place, ........ Ps 52:5
*p* it out of thy bosom ........ Ps 74:11
which pass by the way do *p* her ........ Ps 80:12
a time to *p* up that which is ........ Eccl 3:2
I will *p* them out of their land, ........ Jer 12:14
*p* out the house of Judah from ........ Jer 12:14
not obey, I will utterly *p* up ........ Jer 12:17
and concerning a kingdom, to *p* up ........ Jer 18:7
hand, yet would I *p* thee thence ........ Jer 22:24
will plant them, and not *p* them up ........ Jer 24:6
I have watched over them, to *p* up ........ Jer 31:28
I will plant you, and not *p* you up ........ Jer 42:10
which I have planted I will *p* up ........ Jer 45:4
to *p* it up by the roots thereof ........ Eze 17:9
and *p* off thine own breasts ........ Eze 23:34
who *p* off their skin from off ........ Mic 3:2
I will *p* up thy groves out of the ........ Mic 5:14
*p* it out, and cast it from thee ........ Mt 5:29
began to *p* the ears of corn, and ........ Mt 12:1
*p* it out, and cast it from thee ........ Mt 18:9
they went, to *p* the ears of corn ........ Mk 2:23
thine eye offend thee, *p* it out ........ Mk 9:47
any man *p* them out of my hand ........ Jn 10:28
no man is able to *p* them out of ........ Jn 10:29

**PLUCKED**
*p* it out of his bosom, and, behold ........ Ex 4:7
ye shall be *p* from off the land ........ Deut 28:63
a man *p* off his shoe, and gave it ........ Ruth 4:7
*p* the spear out of the Egyptian's ........ 2Sa 23:21
*p* the spear out of the Egyptian's ........ 1Chr 11:23
*p* off the hair of my head and of ........ Ezr 9:3
*p* off their hair, and made them ........ Neh 13:25
*p* the spoil out of his teeth ........ Job 29:17
to them that *p* off the hair ........ Is 50:6
for the wicked are not *p* away ........ Jer 6:29
after that I have *p* them out I ........ Jer 12:15
it shall not be *p* up, nor thrown ........ Jer 31:40
But she was *p* up in fury, she was ........ Eze 19:12
till the wings thereof were *p* ........ Dan 7:4
the first horns *p* up by the roots ........ Dan 7:8
for his kingdom shall be *p* up ........ Dan 11:4
a firebrand *p* out of the burning ........ Amos 4:11
this a brand *p* out of the fire ........ Zec 3:2
chains had been *p* asunder by him ........ Mk 5:4
his disciples *p* the ears of corn, ........ Lk 6:1
Be thou *p* up by the root, and be ........ Lk 17:6
ye would have *p* out your own eyes ........ Gal 4:15
twice dead, *p* up by the roots ........ Jude 12

**PLUCKETH**
but the foolish *p* it down with ........ Prov 14:1

**PLUCKT**
her mouth was an olive leaf *p* off ........ Gen 8:11

**PLUMBLINE**
stood upon a wall made by a *p* ........ Amos 7:7
with a *p* in his hand ........ Amos 7:7
And I said, A *p* ........ Amos 7:8
I will set a *p* in the midst of my ........ Amos 7:8

**PLUMMET**
the *p* of the house of Ahab ........ 2Kin 21:13
line, and righteousness to the *p* ........ Is 28:17
shall see the *p* in the hand of ........ Zec 4:10

**PLUNGE**
Yet shalt thou *p* me in the ditch, ........ Job 9:31

**POCHERETH** (*po-ke'-reth*) *A family of exiles.*
the children of *P* of Zebaim ........ Ezr 2:57
the children of *P* of Zebaim ........ Neh 7:59

**POETS**
also of your own *p* have said ........ Acts 17:28

**POINT**
Behold, I am at the *p* to die ........ Gen 25:32
ye shall *p* out for you mount Hor ........ Num 34:7
From mount Hor ye shall *p* out ........ Num 34:8
ye shall *p* out your east border ........ Num 34:10
iron, and with the *p* of a diamond ........ Jer 17:1
I have set the *p* of the sword ........ Eze 21:15
daughter lieth at the *p* of death ........ Mk 5:23
for he was at the *p* of death ........ Jn 4:47
whole law, and yet offend in one *p* ........ Jas 2:10

**POINTED**
he spreadeth sharp *p* things upon ........ Job 41:30

**POINTS**
evil, that in all *p* as he came ........ Eccl 5:16
but was in all *p* tempted like as ........ Heb 4:15

**POISON**
with the *p* of serpents of the ........ Deut 32:24
Their wine is the *p* of dragons ........ Deut 32:33
the *p* whereof drinketh up my ........ Job 6:4
He shall suck the *p* of asps ........ Job 20:16
*p* is like the *p* of a serpent ........ Ps 58:4
adders' *p* is under their lips ........ Ps 140:3
the *p* of asps is under their lips ........ Rom 3:13
an unruly evil, full of deadly *p* ........ Jas 3:8

**POLE**
fiery serpent, and set it upon a *p* ........ Num 21:8
of brass, and put it upon a *p* ........ Num 21:9

**POLICY**
through his *p* also he shall cause ........ Dan 8:25

**POLISHED**
*p* after the similitude of a ........ Ps 144:12
he hid me, and made me a *p* shaft ........ Is 49:2
feet like in colour to *p* brass ........ Dan 10:6

**POLISHING**
rubies, their *p* was of sapphire ........ Lam 4:7

**POLL**
take five shekels apiece by the *p* ........ Num 3:47
they shall only *p* their heads ........ Eze 44:20
*p* thee for thy delicate children ........ Mic 1:16

**POLLED**
when he *p* his head, (for it was ........ 2Sa 14:26
at every year's end that he *p* it ........ 2Sa 14:26
heavy on him, therefore he *p* it ........ 2Sa 14:26

**POLLS**
names, every male by their *p* ........ Num 1:2
years old and upward, by their *p* ........ Num 1:18
number of the names, by their *p* ........ Num 1:20
number of the names, by their *p* ........ Num 1:22
and their number by their *p* ........ 1Chr 23:3
by number of names by their *p* ........ 1Chr 23:24

**POLLUTE**
neither shall ye *p* the holy ........ Num 18:32
So ye shall not *p* the land ........ Num 35:33
is called by my name, to *p* it ........ Jer 7:30
and they shall *p* it ........ Eze 7:21
they shall *p* my secret place ........ Eze 7:22
will ye *p* me among my people for ........ Eze 13:19
ye *p* yourselves with all your ........ Eze 20:31
but *p* ye my holy name no more ........ Eze 20:39
I will not let them *p* my holy ........ Eze 39:7
to be in my sanctuary, to *p* it ........ Eze 44:7
they shall *p* the sanctuary of ........ Dan 11:31

**POLLUTED**
thy tool upon it, thou hast *p* it ........ Ex 20:25
*p* it, according to the word of ........ 2Kin 23:16
*p* the house of the LORD which he ........ 2Chr 36:14
therefore were they, as *p* ........ Ezr 2:62
therefore were they, as *p* ........ Neh 7:64
and the land was *p* with blood ........ Ps 106:38
I have *p* mine inheritance, and ........ Is 47:6
for how should my name be *p* ........ Is 48:11
How canst thou say, I am not *p* ........ Jer 2:23
shall not that land be greatly *p* ........ Jer 3:1
thou hast *p* the land with thy ........ Jer 3:2
*p* my name, and caused every man ........ Jer 34:16
he hath *p* the kingdom and the ........ Lam 2:2
they have *p* themselves with blood ........ Lam 4:14
behold, my soul hath not been *p* ........ Eze 4:14
neither be *p* any more with all ........ Eze 14:11
saw thee *p* in thine own blood, I ........ Eze 16:6
and bare, and wast *p* in thy blood ........ Eze 16:22
not be *p* before the heathen ........ Eze 20:9
and my sabbaths they greatly *p* ........ Eze 20:13
not be *p* before the heathen ........ Eze 20:14
in my statutes, but *p* my sabbaths ........ Eze 20:16
they *p* my sabbaths ........ Eze 20:21
that it should not be *p* in the ........ Eze 20:22
had *p* my sabbaths, and their eyes ........ Eze 20:24
I *p* them in their own gifts, in ........ Eze 20:26
Are ye *p* after the manner of your ........ Eze 20:30
she was *p* with them, and her mind ........ Eze 23:17
thou art *p* with their idols ........ Eze 23:30
idols wherewith they had *p* it ........ Eze 36:18
work iniquity, and is *p* with blood ........ Hos 6:8
all that eat thereof shall be *p* ........ Hos 9:4
and thou shalt die in a *p* land ........ Amos 7:17
because it is *p*, it shall destroy ........ Mic 2:10
Woe to her that is filthy and *p* ........ Zeph 3:1
her priests have *p* the sanctuary ........ Zeph 3:4
Ye offer *p* bread upon mine altar ........ Mal 1:7
and ye say, Wherein have we *p* thee ........ Mal 1:7
say, The table of the LORD is *p* ........ Mal 1:12
temple, and hath *p* this holy place ........ Acts 21:28

**POLLUTING**
keepeth the sabbath from *p* it ........ Is 56:2
keepeth the sabbath from *p* it ........ Is 56:6

**POLLUTION**
her that was set apart for *p* ........ Eze 22:10

**POLLUTIONS**
that they abstain from *p* of idols ........ Acts 15:20
the *p* of the world through the ........ 2Pet 2:20

**POLLUX** *A Roman god.*
isle, whose sign was Castor and *P* ........ Acts 28:11

**POMEGRANATE**
A golden bell and a *p*, a golden ........ Ex 28:34
*p*, a golden bell and a *p* ........ Ex 28:34
A bell and a *p*, a bell and a ........ Ex 39:26
and a *p*, a bell and a *p* ........ Ex 39:26
part of Gibeah under a *p* tree ........ 1Sa 14:2
a piece of a *p* within thy locks ........ Song 4:3
As a piece of a *p* are thy temples ........ Song 6:7
spiced wine of the juice of my *p* ........ Song 8:2
the *p* tree, the palm tree also, ........ Joel 1:12
vine, and the fig tree, and the *p* ........ Hag 2:19

**POMEGRANATES**
of it thou shalt make *p* of blue ........ Ex 28:33
the hems of the robe *p* of blue ........ Ex 39:24
the *p* upon the hem of the robe ........ Ex 39:25
robe, round about between the *p* ........ Ex 39:25
and they brought of the *p*, and of ........ Num 13:23
or of figs, or of vines, or of *p* ........ Num 20:5
and vines, and fig trees, and *p* ........ Deut 8:8
that were upon the top, with *p* ........ 1Kin 7:18
the two pillars had *p* also above ........ 1Kin 7:20
the *p* were two hundred in rows ........ 1Kin 7:20
four hundred *p* for the two ........ 1Kin 7:42
two rows of *p* for one network ........ 1Kin 7:42
*p* upon the chapiter round about, ........ 2Kin 25:17
and made an hundred *p* ........ 2Chr 3:16
four hundred *p* on the two wreaths ........ 2Chr 4:13
two rows of *p* on each wreath, to ........ 2Chr 4:13
Thy plants are an orchard of *p* ........ Song 4:13
vine flourished, and the *p* budded ........ Song 6:11
grape appear, and the *p* bud forth ........ Song 7:12
*p* upon the chapiters round about, ........ Jer 52:22
the *p* were like unto these ........ Jer 52:22
were ninety and six *p* on a side ........ Jer 52:23
all the *p* upon the network were ........ Jer 52:23

### POMMELS
To wit, the two pillars, and the *p* 2Chr 4:12
two wreaths to cover the two *p* of 2Chr 4:12
to cover the two *p* of the 2Chr 4:13

### POMP
and their multitude, and their *p* Is 5:14
Thy *p* is brought down to the Is 14:11
I will also make the *p* of the Eze 7:24
the *p* of her strength shall cease Eze 30:18
they shall spoil the *p* of Egypt Eze 32:12
the *p* of her strength shall cease Eze 33:28
come, and Bernice, with great *p* Acts 25:23

### PONDER
*P* the path of thy feet, and let Prov 4:26
thou shouldest *p* the path of life Prov 5:6

### PONDERED
things, and *p* them in her heart Lk 2:19

### PONDERETH
the LORD, and he *p* all his goings Prov 5:21
but the LORD *p* the hearts Prov 21:2
doth not he that *p* the heart Prov 24:12

### PONDS
their rivers, and upon their *p* Ex 7:19
over the rivers, and over the *p* Ex 8:5
that make sluices and *p* for fish Is 19:10

### PONTIUS (*pon'-she-us*) *The family name of Pilate.*
delivered him to *P* Pilate the Mt 27:2
*P* Pilate being governor of Judaea Lk 3:1
*P* Pilate, with the Gentiles, and Acts 4:27
who before *P* Pilate witnessed a 1Ti 6:13

### PONTUS (*pon'-tus*) *A Roman province in Asia Minor.*
and in Judaea, and Cappadocia, in *P* Acts 2:9
Jew named Aquila, born in *P* Acts 18:2
strangers scattered throughout *P* 1Pet 1:1

### POOL
met together by the *p* of Gibeon 2Sa 2:13
the one on the one side of the *p* 2Sa 2:13
other on the other side of the *p* 2Sa 2:13
them up over the *p* in Hebron 2Sa 4:12
the chariot in the *p* of Samaria 1Kin 22:38
by the conduit of the upper *p* 2Kin 18:17
all his might, and how he made a *p* 2Kin 20:20
the fountain, and to the king's *p* Neh 2:14
the wall of the *p* of Siloah by Neh 3:15
to the *p* that was made, and unto Neh 3:16
*p* in the highway of the fuller's Is 7:3
the waters of the lower *p* Is 22:9
walls for the water of the old *p* Is 22:11
parched ground shall become a *p* Is 35:7
by the conduit of the upper *p* in Is 36:2
make the wilderness a *p* of water Is 41:18
is of old like a *p* of water Nah 2:8
Jerusalem by the sheep market a *p* Jn 5:2
at a certain season into the *p* Jn 5:4
is troubled, to put me into the *p* Jn 5:7
him, Go, wash in the *p* of Siloam Jn 9:7
unto me, Go to the *p* of Siloam Jn 9:11

### POOLS
and upon all their *p* of water Ex 7:19
the rain also filleth the *p* Ps 84:6
I made me *p* of water, to water Eccl 2:6
for the bittern, and *p* of water Is 14:23
islands, and I will dry up the *p* Is 42:15

### POOR
other kine came up after them, *p* Gen 41:19
of my people that is *p* by thee Ex 22:25
countenance a *p* man in his cause Ex 23:3
judgment of thy *p* in his cause Ex 23:6
that the *p* of thy people may eat Ex 23:11
the *p* shall not give less than Ex 30:15
And if he be *p*, and cannot get so Lev 14:21
thou shalt leave them for the *p* Lev 19:10
not respect the person of the *p* Lev 19:15
thou shalt leave them unto the *p* Lev 23:22
If thy brother be waxen *p* Lev 25:25
And if thy brother be waxen *p* Lev 25:35
that dwelleth by thee be waxen *p* Lev 25:39
that dwelleth by him wax *p* Lev 25:47
there shall be no *p* among you Deut 15:4
If there be among you a *p* man of Deut 15:7
thine hand from thy *p* brother Deut 15:7
eye be evil against thy *p* brother Deut 15:9
For the *p* shall never cease out Deut 15:11
wide unto thy brother, to thy *p* Deut 15:11
And if the man be *p*, thou shalt Deut 24:12
an hired servant that is *p* Deut 24:14
for he is *p*, and setteth his heart Deut 24:15
my family is *p* in Manasseh Judg 6:15
not young men, whether *p* or rich Ruth 3:10
The LORD maketh *p*, and maketh rich 1Sa 2:7
raiseth up the *p* out of the dust 1Sa 2:8
in law, seeing that I am a *p* man 1Sa 18:23
the one rich, and the other *p* 2Sa 12:1
But the *p* man had nothing, save 2Sa 12:3
but took the *p* man's lamb 2Sa 12:4
of the guard left of the *p* of the 2Kin 25:12
one to another, and gifts to the *p* Est 9:22
he saveth the *p* from the sword Job 5:15
So the *p* hath hope, and iniquity Job 5:16
shall seek to please the *p* Job 20:10
oppressed and hath forsaken the *p* Job 20:19
the *p* of the earth hide Job 24:4
breast, and take a pledge of the *p* Job 24:9
with the light killeth the *p* Job 24:14
I delivered the *p* that cried Job 29:12
I was a father to the *p* Job 29:16
was not my soul grieved for the *p* Job 30:25
withheld the *p* from their desire Job 31:16
or any *p* without covering Job 31:19
the rich more than the *p* Job 34:19
the cry of the *p* to come unto him Job 34:28
but giveth right to the *p* Job 36:6
the *p* in his affliction, and Job 36:15
the expectation of the *p* shall Ps 9:18
in his pride doth persecute the *p* Ps 10:2
are privily set against the *p* Ps 10:8
he lieth in wait to catch the *p* Ps 10:9
he doth catch the *p*, when he Ps 10:9
that the *p* may fall by his strong Ps 10:10
the *p* committeth himself unto Ps 10:14
For the oppression of the *p* Ps 12:5
have shamed the counsel of the *p* Ps 14:6
This *p* man cried, and the LORD Ps 34:6
which deliverest the *p* from him Ps 35:10
is too strong for him, yea, the *p* Ps 35:10
their bow, to cast down the *p* Ps 37:14
But I am *p* and needy Ps 40:17
is he that considereth the *p* Ps 41:1
Both low and high, rich and *p* Ps 49:2
of thy goodness for the *p* Ps 68:10
But I am *p* and sorrowful Ps 69:29
For the LORD heareth the *p* Ps 69:33
But I am *p* and needy Ps 70:5
and thy *p* with judgment Ps 72:2
shall judge the *p* of the people Ps 72:4
the *p* also, and him that hath no Ps 72:12
He shall spare the *p* and needy, and Ps 72:13
congregation of thy *p* for ever Ps 74:19
let the *p* and needy praise thy Ps 74:21
Defend the *p* and fatherless Ps 82:3
Deliver the *p* and needy Ps 82:4
for I am *p* and needy Ps 86:1
Yet setteth he the *p* on high from Ps 107:41
shew mercy, but persecuted the *p* Ps 109:16
For I am *p* and needy, and my heart Ps 109:22
stand at the right hand of the *p* Ps 109:31
dispersed, he hath given to the *p* Ps 112:9
raiseth up the *p* out of the dust Ps 113:7
I will satisfy her *p* with bread Ps 132:15
afflicted, and the right of the *p* Ps 140:12
He becometh *p* that dealeth with a Prov 10:4
of the *p* is their poverty Prov 10:15
there is that maketh himself *p* Prov 13:7
but the *p* heareth not rebuke Prov 13:8
food is in the tillage of the *p* Prov 13:23
The *p* is hated even of his own Prov 14:20
but he that hath mercy on the *p* Prov 14:21
the *p* reproacheth his Maker Prov 14:31
honoureth him hath mercy on the *p* Prov 14:31
Whoso mocketh the *p* reproacheth Prov 17:5
The *p* useth intreaties Prov 18:23
Better is the *p* that walketh in Prov 19:1
but the *p* is separated from his Prov 19:4
the brethren of the *p* do hate him Prov 19:7
upon the *p* lendeth unto the LORD Prov 19:17
a *p* man is better than a liar Prov 19:22
his ears at the cry of the *p* Prov 21:13
loveth pleasure shall be a *p* man Prov 21:17
The rich and *p* meet together Prov 22:2
The rich ruleth over the *p* Prov 22:7
he giveth of his bread to the *p* Prov 22:9
the *p* to increase his riches Prov 22:16
Rob not the *p*, because he is *p* Prov 22:22
A *p* man that oppresseth the Prov 28:3
*p* is like a sweeping rain which Prov 28:3
Better is the *p* that walketh in Prov 28:6
it for him that will pity the *p* Prov 28:8
but the *p* that hath understanding Prov 28:11
a wicked ruler over the *p* people Prov 28:15
giveth unto the *p* shall not lack Prov 28:27
considereth the cause of the *p* Prov 29:7
The *p* and the deceitful man meet Prov 29:13
that faithfully judgeth the *p* Prov 29:14
or lest I be *p*, and steal, and take Prov 30:9
to devour the *p* from off the Prov 30:14
and plead the cause of the *p* Prov 31:9
stretcheth out her hand to the *p* Prov 31:20
Better is a *p* and a wise child Eccl 4:13
is born in his kingdom becometh *p* Eccl 4:14
seest the oppression of the *p* Eccl 5:8
what hath the *p*, that knoweth to Eccl 6:8
was found in it a *p* wise man Eccl 9:15
no man remembered that same *p* man Eccl 9:15
nevertheless the *p* man's wisdom Eccl 9:16
the spoil of the *p* is in your Is 3:14
and grind the faces of the *p* Is 3:15
the right from the *p* of my people Is 10:2
be heard unto Laish, O *p* Anathoth Is 10:30
shall he judge the *p*, and reprove Is 11:4
the firstborn of the *p* shall feed Is 14:30
the *p* of his people shall trust Is 14:32
hast been a strength to the *p* Is 25:4
it down, even the feet of the *p* Is 26:6
the *p* among men shall rejoice in Is 29:19
to destroy the *p* with lying words Is 32:7
When the *p* and needy seek water, Is 41:17
that thou bring the *p* that are Is 58:7
I look, even to him that is *p* Is 66:2
of the souls of the *p* innocents Jer 2:34
I said, Surely these are *p* Jer 5:4
the *p* from the hand of evildoers Jer 20:13
He judged the cause of the *p* Jer 22:16
guard left of the *p* of the people Jer 39:10
of the *p* of the land, of them Jer 40:7
certain of the *p* of the people Jer 52:15
*p* of the land for vinedressers Jer 52:16
she strengthen the hand of the *p* Eze 16:49
Hath oppressed the *p* and needy, Eze 18:12
taken off his hand from the *p* Eze 18:17
robbery, and have vexed the *p* Eze 22:29
by shewing mercy to the *p* Dan 4:27
the *p* for a pair of shoes Amos 2:6
of the earth on the head of the *p* Amos 2:7
of Samaria, which oppress the *p* Amos 4:1
as your treading is upon the *p* Amos 5:11
they turn aside the *p* in the gate Amos 5:12
even to make the *p* of the land to Amos 8:4
That we may buy the *p* for silver Amos 8:6
was as to devour the *p* secretly Hab 3:14
*p* people, and they shall trust in Zeph 3:12
the stranger, nor the *p* Zec 7:10
even you, O *p* of the flock Zec 11:7
so the *p* of the flock that waited Zec 11:11
Blessed are the *p* in spirit Mt 5:3
the *p* have the gospel preached to Mt 11:5
that thou hast, and give to the *p* Mt 19:21
sold for much, and given to the *p* Mt 26:9
For ye have the *p* always with you Mt 26:11
thou hast, and give to the *p* Mk 10:21
And there came a certain *p* widow Mk 12:42
That this *p* widow hath cast more Mk 12:43
and have been given to the *p* Mk 14:5
For ye have the *p* with you always Mk 14:7
me to preach the gospel to the *p* Lk 4:18
and said, Blessed be ye *p* Lk 6:20
to the *p* the gospel is preached Lk 7:22
thou makest a feast, call the *p* Lk 14:13
city, and bring in hither the *p* Lk 14:21
hast, and distribute unto the *p* Lk 18:22
half of my goods I give to the *p* Lk 19:8
he saw also a certain *p* widow Lk 21:2
that this *p* widow hath cast in Lk 21:3
hundred pence, and given to the *p* Jn 12:5
said, not that he cared for the *p* Jn 12:6
For the *p* always ye have with you Jn 12:8
he should give something to the *p* Jn 13:29
*p* saints which are at Jerusalem Rom 15:26
bestow all my goods to feed the *p* 1Cor 13:3
as *p*, yet making many rich 2Cor 6:10
yet for your sakes he became *p* 2Cor 8:9
he hath given to the *p* 2Cor 9:9
that we should remember the *p* Gal 2:10
in also a *p* man in vile raiment Jas 2:2
and say to the *p*, Stand thou there Jas 2:3
Hath not God chosen the *p* of this Jas 2:5
But ye have despised the *p* Jas 2:6
art wretched, and miserable, and *p* Rev 3:17
both small and great, rich and *p* Rev 13:16

### POORER
But if he be *p* than thy Lev 27:8

### POOREST
save the *p* sort of the people of 2Kin 24:14

### POPLAR
And Jacob took him rods of green *p* Gen 30:37

### POPLARS
upon the hills, under oaks and *p* Hos 4:13

### POPULOUS
a nation, great, mighty, and *p* Deut 26:5
Art thou better than *p* No Nah 3:8

### PORATHA (*por'-a-thah*) *A son of Haman.*
And *P*, and Adalia, and Aridatha Est 9:8

### PORCH
Ehud went forth through the *p* Judg 3:23
the *p* before the temple of the 1Kin 6:3
And he made a *p* of pillars 1Kin 7:6
and the *p* was before them 1Kin 7:6
Then he made a *p* for the throne 1Kin 7:7
judge, even the *p* of judgment 1Kin 7:7
had another court within the *p* 1Kin 7:8
taken to wife, like unto this *p* 1Kin 7:8
LORD, and for the *p* of the house 1Kin 7:12
were of lily work in the *p* 1Kin 7:19
pillars in the *p* of the temple 1Kin 7:21
his son the pattern of the *p* 1Chr 28:11
the *p* that was in the front of 2Chr 3:4
which he had built before the *p* 2Chr 8:12
that was before the *p* of the LORD 2Chr 15:8
have shut up the doors of the *p* 2Chr 29:7
came they to the *p* of the LORD 2Chr 29:17
temple of the LORD, between the *p* Eze 8:16
threshold of the gate by the *p* of Eze 40:7
also the *p* of the gate within Eze 40:8
measured he the *p* of the gate Eze 40:9
the *p* of the gate was inward Eze 40:9
*p* of the inner gate were fifty Eze 40:15
in the *p* of the gate were two Eze 40:39
which was at the *p* of the gate Eze 40:40
brought me to the *p* of the house Eze 40:48
and measured each post of the *p* Eze 40:48
length of the *p* was twenty cubits Eze 40:49
upon the face of the *p* without Eze 41:25
other side, on the sides of the *p* Eze 41:26
by the way of the *p* of that gate Eze 44:3
way of the *p* of that gate without Eze 46:2
by the way of the *p* of that gate Eze 46:8
of the LORD, weep between the *p* Joel 2:17
when he was gone out into the *p* Mt 26:71
And he went out into the *p* Mk 14:68
in the temple in Solomon's *p* Jn 10:23

in the *p* that is called Solomon's .......... Acts 3:11
with one accord in Solomon's *p* .......... Acts 5:12

### ...RCHES
...emple, and the *p* of the court .......... Eze 41:15
tongue Bethesda, having five *p* .......... Jn 5:2

### PORCIUS (*por'-she-us*) *Family name of Festus.*
But after two years *P* Festus came .... Acts 24:27

### PORT
the dragon well, and to the dung *p* ....... Neh 2:13

### PORTER
and the watchman called unto the *p* ... 2Sa 18:26
and called unto the *p* of the city .......... 2Kin 7:10
the son of Meshelemiah was *p* of .......... 1Chr 9:21
the *p* toward the east, was over .......... 2Chr 31:14
work, and commanded the *p* to watch Mk 13:34
To him the *p* openeth .......... Jn 10:3

### PORTERS
And he called the *p* .......... 2Kin 7:11
the *p* were, Shallum, and Akkub, and. 1Chr 9:17
they were *p* in the companies of .......... 1Chr 9:18
*p* in the gates were two hundred .......... 1Chr 9:22
In four quarters were the *p* .......... 1Chr 9:24
these Levites, the four chief *p* .......... 1Chr 9:26
and Obed-edom, and Jeiel, the *p* ....... 1Chr 15:18
son of Jeduthun and Hosah to be *p* ... 1Chr 16:38
And the sons of Jeduthun were *p* ...... 1Chr 16:42
Moreover four thousand were *p* .......... 1Chr 23:5
Concerning the divisions of the *p* .......... 1Chr 26:1
these were the divisions of the *p* ........ 1Chr 26:12
of the *p* among the sons of Kore ....... 1Chr 26:19
the *p* also by their courses at .......... 2Chr 8:14
Levites, shall be *p* of the doors .......... 2Chr 23:4
he set the *p* at the gates of the .......... 2Chr 23:19
were scribes, and officers, and *p* .......... 2Chr 34:13
the *p* waited at every gate .......... 2Chr 35:15
The children of the *p* .......... Ezr 2:42
people, and the singers, and the *p* .......... Ezr 2:70
Levites, and the singers, and the *p* .......... Ezr 7:7
priests and Levites, singers, *p* .......... Ezr 7:24
the *p*; Shallum, and Telem .......... Ezr 10:24
I had set up the doors, and the *p* .......... Neh 7:1
The *p*: the children of Shallum .......... Neh 7:45
priests, and the Levites, and the *p* .......... Neh 7:73
the priests, the Levites, the *p* .......... Neh 10:28
priests that minister, and the *p* .......... Neh 10:39
Moreover the *p*, Akkub, Talmon, and Neh 11:19
were *p* keeping the ward at the .......... Neh 12:25
the *p* kept the ward of their God, ....... Neh 12:45
portions of the singers and the *p* .......... Neh 12:47
Levites, and the singers, and the *p* ....... Neh 13:5

### PORTION
the *p* of the men which went with ...... Gen 14:24
let them take their *p* .......... Gen 14:24
Is there yet any *p* or inheritance .......... Gen 31:14
for the priests had a *p* assigned .......... Gen 47:22
did eat their *p* which Pharaoh .......... Gen 47:22
to thee one *p* above thy brethren .......... Gen 48:22
*p* of my offerings made by fire .......... Lev 6:17
This is the *p* of the anointing of .......... Lev 7:35
thou shalt take one *p* of fifty .......... Num 31:30
which was the *p* of them that went .. Num 31:36
half, Moses took one *p* of fifty .......... Num 31:47
a double *p* of all that he hath .......... Deut 21:17
For the LORD's *p* is his people .......... Deut 32:9
in a *p* of the lawgiver, was he .......... Deut 33:21
one *p* to inherit, seeing I am a .......... Josh 17:14
Out of the *p* of the children of .......... Josh 19:9
unto Hannah he gave a worthy *p* .......... 1Sa 1:5
Bring the *p* which I gave thee, of .......... 1Sa 9:23
saying, What *p* have we in David ...... 1Kin 12:16
let a double *p* of thy spirit be .......... 2Kin 2:9
eat Jezebel in the *p* of Jezreel .......... 2Kin 9:10
met him in the *p* of Naboth the .......... 2Kin 9:21
cast him in the *p* of the field of .......... 2Kin 9:25
In the *p* of Jezreel shall dogs .......... 2Kin 9:36
of the field in the *p* of Jezreel .......... 2Kin 9:37
saying, What *p* have we in David ...... 2Chr 10:16
For Ahaz took away a *p* out of the ... 2Chr 28:21
He appointed also the king's *p* of .......... 2Chr 31:3
to give the *p* of the priests .......... 2Chr 31:4
his daily *p* for their service in .......... 2Chr 31:16
have no *p* on this side the river .......... Ezr 4:16
but ye have no *p*, nor right, nor .......... Neh 2:20
that a certain *p* should be for .......... Neh 11:23
and the porters, every day his *p* .......... Neh 12:47
This is the *p* of a wicked man .......... Job 20:29
their *p* is cursed in the earth .......... Job 24:18
how little a *p* is heard of him .......... Job 26:14
This is the *p* of a wicked man .......... Job 27:13
For what *p* of God is there from .......... Job 31:2
this shall be the *p* of their cup .......... Ps 11:6
The LORD is the *p* of mine .......... Ps 16:5
which have their *p* in this life .......... Ps 17:14
they shall be a *p* for foxes .......... Ps 63:10
of my heart, and my *p* for ever .......... Ps 73:26
Thou art my *p*, O LORD .......... Ps 119:57
my *p* in the land of the living .......... Ps 142:5
household, and a *p* to her maidens .... Prov 31:15
this was my *p* of all my labour .......... Eccl 2:10
shall he leave it for his *p* .......... Eccl 2:21
for that is his *p* .......... Eccl 3:22
for it is his *p* .......... Eccl 5:18
to eat thereof, and to take his *p* .......... Eccl 5:19
neither have they any more a *p* .......... Eccl 9:6
for that is thy *p* in this life .......... Eccl 9:9
Give a *p* to seven, and also to .......... Eccl 11:2
This is the *p* of them that spoil .......... Is 17:14
I divide him a *p* with the great .......... Is 53:12
stones of the stream is thy *p* .......... Is 57:6
they shall rejoice in their *p* .......... Is 61:7
The *p* of Jacob is not like them .......... Jer 10:16
they have trodden my *p* under foot ...... Jer 12:10
pleasant *p* a desolate wilderness .......... Jer 12:10
the *p* of thy measures from me, .......... Jer 13:25
The *p* of Jacob is not like them .......... Jer 51:19
every day a *p* until the day of .......... Jer 52:34
The LORD is my *p*, saith my soul .......... Lam 3:24
the LORD, an holy *p* of the land .......... Eze 45:1
The holy *p* of the land shall be .......... Eze 45:4
the oblation of the holy *p* .......... Eze 45:6
a *p* shall be for the prince on .......... Eze 45:7
of the oblation of the holy *p* .......... Eze 45:7
before the oblation of the holy *p* .......... Eze 45:7
a *p* for Dan .......... Eze 48:1
unto the west side, a *p* for Asher .......... Eze 48:2
the west side, a *p* for Naphtali .......... Eze 48:3
the west side, a *p* for Manasseh .......... Eze 48:4
the west side, a *p* for Ephraim .......... Eze 48:5
the west side, a *p* for Reuben .......... Eze 48:6
unto the west side, a *p* for Judah .......... Eze 48:7
the oblation of the holy *p* shall .......... Eze 48:18
the oblation of the holy *p* .......... Eze 48:18
side, Benjamin shall have a *p* .......... Eze 48:23
west side, Simeon shall have a *p* .......... Eze 48:24
unto the west side, Issachar a *p* .......... Eze 48:25
unto the west side, Zebulun a *p* .......... Eze 48:26
side unto the west side, Gad a *p* .......... Eze 48:27
with the *p* of the king's meat .......... Dan 1:8
eat of the *p* of the king's meat .......... Dan 1:13
did eat the *p* of the king's meat .......... Dan 1:15
took away the *p* of their meat .......... Dan 1:16
let his *p* be with the beasts in .......... Dan 4:15
let his *p* be with the beasts of .......... Dan 4:23
they that feed of the *p* of his .......... Dan 11:26
hath changed the *p* of my people .......... Mic 2:4
because by them their *p* is fat .......... Hab 1:16
Judah his *p* in the holy land .......... Zec 2:12
appoint him his *p* with the .......... Mt 24:51
to give them their *p* of meat in .......... Lk 12:42
him his *p* with the unbelievers .......... Lk 12:46
give me the *p* of goods that .......... Lk 15:12

### PORTIONS
They shall have like *p* to eat .......... Deut 18:8
And there fell ten *p* to Manasseh .......... Josh 17:5
all her sons and her daughters, *p* .......... 1Sa 1:4
to give *p* to all the males among .......... 2Chr 31:19
send *p* unto them for whom nothing .... Neh 8:10
to eat, and to drink, and to send *p* .... Neh 8:12
the *p* of the law for the priests .......... Neh 12:44
gave the *p* of the singers and the ....... Neh 12:47
I perceived that the *p* of the .......... Neh 13:10
of sending *p* one to another .......... Est 9:19
of sending *p* one to another, and .......... Est 9:22
be over against one of the *p* .......... Eze 45:7
Joseph shall have two *p* .......... Eze 47:13
over against the *p* for the prince .......... Eze 48:21
inheritance, and these are their *p* .......... Eze 48:29
a month devour them with their *p* .......... Hos 5:7

### POSSESS
thy seed shall *p* the gate of his .......... Gen 22:17
let thy seed *p* the gate of those .......... Gen 24:60
I will give it unto you to *p* it .......... Lev 20:24
Let us go up at once, and *p* it .......... Num 13:30
and his seed shall *p* it .......... Num 14:24
of his family, and he shall *p* it .......... Num 27:11
I have given you the land to *p* it .......... Num 33:53
*p* the land which the LORD sware .......... Deut 1:8
*p* it, as the LORD God of thy .......... Deut 1:21
I give it, and they shall *p* it .......... Deut 1:39
begin to *p* it, and contend with .......... Deut 2:24
begin to *p*, that thou mayest .......... Deut 2:31
hath given you this land to *p* it .......... Deut 3:18
until they also *p* the land which .......... Deut 3:20
*p* the land which the LORD God of .......... Deut 4:1
in the land whither ye go to *p* it .......... Deut 4:5
land whither ye go over to *p* it .......... Deut 4:14
go over, and *p* that good land .......... Deut 4:22
ye go over Jordan to *p* it .......... Deut 4:26
land which I give them to *p* it .......... Deut 5:31
days in the land which ye shall *p* .......... Deut 5:33
in the land whither ye go to *p* it .......... Deut 6:1
*p* the good land which the LORD .......... Deut 6:18
land whither thou goest to *p* it .......... Deut 7:1
*p* the land which the LORD sware .......... Deut 8:1
to go in to *p* nations greater and .......... Deut 9:1
hath brought me in to *p* this land .......... Deut 9:4
dost thou go to *p* their land .......... Deut 9:5
to *p* it for thy righteousness .......... Deut 9:6
*p* the land which I have given you ...... Deut 9:23
*p* the land, which I sware unto .......... Deut 10:11
*p* the land, whither ye go to .......... Deut 11:8
the land, whither ye go to *p* it .......... Deut 11:8
whither thou goest in to *p* it .......... Deut 11:10
the land, whither ye go to *p* it .......... Deut 11:11
ye shall *p* greater nations and .......... Deut 11:23
land whither thou goest to *p* it .......... Deut 11:29
to *p* the land which the LORD your ... Deut 11:31
God giveth you, and ye shall *p* it .......... Deut 11:31
thy fathers giveth thee to *p* it .......... Deut 12:1
ye shall *p* served their gods .......... Deut 12:2
whither thou goest to *p* them .......... Deut 12:29
thee for an inheritance to *p* it .......... Deut 15:4
God giveth thee, and shalt *p* it .......... Deut 17:14
these nations, which thou shalt *p* .......... Deut 18:14
LORD thy God giveth thee to *p* it .......... Deut 19:2
LORD thy God giveth thee to *p* it ....... Deut 19:14
LORD thy God giveth thee to *p* it .......... Deut 21:1
land whither thou goest to *p* it .......... Deut 23:20
thee for an inheritance to *p* it .......... Deut 25:19
land, whither thou goest to *p* it .......... Deut 28:21
land whither thou goest to *p* it .......... Deut 28:63
possessed, and thou shalt *p* it .......... Deut 30:5
land whither thou goest to *p* it .......... Deut 30:16
passest over Jordan to go to *p* it .......... Deut 30:18
before thee, and thou shalt *p* them ..... Deut 31:3
whither ye go over Jordan to *p* it ...... Deut 31:13
whither ye go over Jordan to *p* it ...... Deut 32:47
*p* thou the west and the south .......... Deut 33:23
Jordan, to go in to *p* the land .......... Josh 1:11
LORD your God giveth you to *p* it .......... Josh 1:11
are ye slack to go to *p* the land .......... Josh 18:3
ye shall *p* their land, as the .......... Josh 23:5
unto Esau mount Seir, to *p* it .......... Josh 24:4
hand, that ye might *p* their land .......... Josh 24:8
his inheritance to *p* the land .......... Judg 2:6
Israel, and shouldest thou *p* it .......... Judg 11:23
Wilt not thou *p* that which .......... Judg 11:24
Chemosh thy god giveth thee to *p* .... Judg 11:24
from before us, them will we *p* .......... Judg 11:24
to go, and to enter to *p* the land .......... Judg 18:9
whither he is gone down to *p* it .......... 1Kin 21:18
that ye may *p* this good land, and ....... 1Chr 28:8
land, unto which ye go to *p* it .......... Ezr 9:11
them that they should go in to *p* .......... Neh 9:15
that they should go in to *p* it .......... Neh 9:23
So am I made to *p* months of .......... Job 7:3
makest me to *p* the iniquities of .......... Job 13:26
the house of Israel shall *p* them .......... Is 14:2
nor *p* the land, nor fill the face .......... Is 14:21
and the bittern shall *p* it .......... Is 34:11
they shall *p* it for ever, from .......... Is 34:17
his trust in me shall *p* the land .......... Is 57:13
land they shall *p* the double .......... Is 61:7
their fathers, and they shall *p* it .......... Jer 30:3
they shall *p* their houses .......... Eze 7:24
and shall ye *p* the land .......... Eze 33:25
and shall ye *p* the land .......... Eze 33:26
shall be mine, and we will *p* it .......... Eze 35:10
and they shall *p* thee, and thou .......... Eze 36:12
*p* the kingdom for ever, even for .......... Dan 7:18
silver, nettles shall *p* them .......... Hos 9:6
to *p* the land of the Amorite .......... Amos 2:10
That they may *p* the remnant of .......... Amos 9:12
Jacob shall *p* their possessions .......... Obad 17
south shall *p* the mount of Esau .......... Obad 19
they shall *p* the fields of .......... Obad 19
and Benjamin shall *p* Gilead .......... Obad 19
shall *p* that of the Canaanites .......... Obad 20
shall *p* the cities of the south .......... Obad 20
to *p* the dwellingplaces that are .......... Hab 1:6
remnant of my people shall *p* them ...... Zeph 2:9
this people to *p* all these things .......... Zec 8:12
I give tithes of all that I *p* .......... Lk 18:12
In your patience *p* ye your souls .......... Lk 21:19
to *p* his vessel in sanctification .......... 1Th 4:4

### POSSESSED
*p* his land from Arnon unto Jabbok .. Num 21:24
and they *p* his land .......... Num 21:35
which we *p* at that time, from .......... Deut 3:12
they *p* his land, and the land of .......... Deut 4:47
into the land which thy fathers *p* .......... Deut 30:5
they also have *p* the land which .......... Josh 1:15
*p* their land on the other side .......... Josh 12:1
yet very much land to be *p* .......... Josh 13:1
*p* it, and dwelt therein, and called ...... Josh 19:47
and they *p* it, and dwelt therein .......... Josh 21:43
possession, whereof they were *p* .......... Josh 22:9
and *p* the city of palm trees .......... Judg 3:13
so Israel *p* all the land of the .......... Judg 11:21
they *p* all the coasts of the .......... Judg 11:22
they *p* Samaria, and dwelt in the .......... 2Kin 17:24
so they *p* the land of Sihon, and .......... Neh 9:22
*p* the land, and thou subduedst .......... Neh 9:24
*p* houses full of all goods, wells .......... Neh 9:25
For thou hast *p* my reins .......... Ps 139:13
The LORD *p* me in the beginning of ..... Prov 8:22
have *p* it but a little while .......... Is 63:18
shall be *p* again in this land .......... Jer 32:15
And they came in, and *p* it .......... Jer 32:23
that the saints *p* the kingdom .......... Dan 7:22
and those which were *p* with devils .......... Mt 4:24
him many that were *p* with devils .......... Mt 8:16
there met him two *p* with devils .......... Mt 8:28
befallen to the *p* of the devils .......... Mt 8:33
to him a dumb man *p* with a devil .......... Mt 9:32
unto him one *p* with a devil .......... Mt 12:22
and them that were *p* with devils .......... Mk 1:32
see him that was *p* with the devil .......... Mk 5:15
to him that was *p* with the devil .......... Mk 5:16
he that had been *p* with the devil .......... Mk 5:18
was *p* of the devils was healed .......... Lk 8:36
the things which he *p* was his own .......... Acts 4:32
out of many that were *p* with them .......... Acts 8:7
a certain damsel *p* with a spirit .......... Acts 16:16
that buy, as though they *p* not .......... 1Cor 7:30

### POSSESSEST
*p* it, and dwellest therein .......... Deut 26:1

### POSSESSETH
that *p* an inheritance in any .......... Num 36:8
of the things which he *p* .......... Lk 12:15

### POSSESSING
nothing, and yet *p* all things .......... 2Cor 6:10

### POSSESSION
of Canaan, for an everlasting *p* .......... Gen 17:8
give me a *p* of a buryingplace .......... Gen 23:4

a *p* of a buryingplace amongst you Gen 23:9
Unto Abraham for a *p* in the Gen 23:18
made sure unto Abraham for a *p* of Gen 23:20
For he had *p* of flocks, and Gen 26:14
*p* of herds, and great store of Gen 26:14
in the land of their *p* Gen 36:43
gave them a *p* in the land of Gen 47:11
after thee for an everlasting *p* Gen 48:4
Hittite for a *p* of a buryingplace Gen 49:30
bought with the field for a *p* of Gen 50:13
which I give to you for a *p* Lev 14:34
in a house of the land of your *p* Lev 14:34
shall return every man unto his *p* Lev 25:10
shall return every man unto his *p* Lev 25:13
in all the land of your *p* ye Lev 25:24
and hath sold away some of his *p* Lev 25:25
that he may return unto his *p* Lev 25:27
and he shall return unto his *p* Lev 25:28
houses of the cities of their *p* Lev 25:32
was sold, and the city of his *p* Lev 25:33
*p* among the children of Israel Lev 25:33
for it is their perpetual *p* Lev 25:34
unto the *p* of his fathers shall Lev 25:41
and they shall be your *p* Lev 25:45
you, to inherit them for a *p* Lev 25:46
some part of a field of his *p* Lev 27:16
the *p* thereof shall be the Lev 27:21
is not of the fields of his *p* Lev 27:22
whom the *p* of the land did belong Lev 27:24
beast, and of the field of his *p* Lev 27:28
And Edom shall be a *p* Num 24:18
also shall be a *p* for his enemies Num 24:18
According to the lot shall the *p* Num 26:56
Give unto us therefore a *p* among Num 27:4
a *p* of an inheritance among their Num 27:7
given unto thy servants for a *p* Num 32:5
shall be your *p* before the LORD Num 32:22
them the land of Gilead for a *p* Num 32:29
that the *p* of our inheritance on Num 32:32
of their *p* cities to dwell in Num 35:2
the *p* of the children of Israel Num 35:8
return into the land of his *p* Num 35:28
mount Seir unto Esau for a *p* Deut 2:5
give thee of their land for a *p* Deut 2:9
unto the children of Lot for a *p* Deut 2:9
Israel did unto the land of his *p* Deut 2:12
of the children of Ammon any *p* Deut 2:19
unto the children of Lot for a *p* Deut 2:19
ye return every man unto his *p* Deut 3:20
the substance that was in their *p* Deut 11:6
the children of Israel for a *p* Deut 32:49
return unto the land of your *p* Josh 1:15
it for a *p* unto the Reubenites Josh 12:6
a *p* according to their divisions Josh 12:7
this was the *p* of the half tribe Josh 13:29
the son of Jephunneh for his *p* Josh 21:12
of the Levites within the *p* of Josh 21:41
tents, and unto the land of your *p* Josh 22:4
Moses had given *p* in Bashan Josh 22:7
of Gilead, to the land of their *p* Josh 22:9
if the land of your *p* be unclean Josh 22:19
the land of the *p* of the LORD Josh 22:19
dwelleth, and take *p* among us Josh 22:19
take *p* of the vineyard of Naboth 1Kin 21:15
the Jezreelite, to take *p* of it 1Kin 21:16
Hast thou killed, and also taken *p* 1Kin 21:19
*p* of the king, and of his sons, 1Chr 28:1
left their suburbs and their *p* 2Chr 11:14
to come to cast us out of thy *p* 2Chr 20:11
returned, every man to his *p* 2Chr 31:1
one in his *p* in their cities Neh 11:3
parts of the earth for thy *p* Ps 2:8
the land in *p* by their own sword Ps 44:3
may dwell there, and have it in *p* Ps 69:35
ourselves the houses of God in *p* Ps 83:12
shall have good things in *p* Prov 28:10
also make it a *p* for the bittern Is 14:23
unto us is this land given in *p* Eze 11:15
to the men of the east for a *p* Eze 25:4
Ammonites, and will give them in *p* Eze 25:10
ancient high places are ours in *p* Eze 36:2
that ye might be a *p* unto the Eze 36:3
appointed my land into their *p* Eze 36:5
ye shall give them no *p* in Israel Eze 44:28
I am their *p* Eze 44:28
for a *p* for twenty chambers Eze 45:5
ye shall appoint the *p* of the Eze 45:6
of the *p* of the city, before the Eze 45:7
before the *p* of the city, from Eze 45:7
the land shall be his *p* in Israel Eze 45:8
shall be their *p* by inheritance Eze 46:16
to thrust them out of their *p* Eze 46:18
sons inheritance out of his own *p* Eze 46:18
scattered every man from his *p* Eze 46:18
with the *p* of the city Eze 48:20
of the *p* of the city, over Eze 48:21
from the *p* of the Levites Eze 48:22
from the *p* of the city, being in Eze 48:22
with Sapphira his wife, sold a *p* Acts 5:1
he would give it to him for a *p* Acts 7:5
Jesus into the *p* of the Gentiles Acts 7:45
the redemption of the purchased *p* Eph 1:14

**POSSESSIONS**
ye therein, and get you *p* therein Gen 34:10
and they had *p* therein, and grew, Gen 47:27
they shall have *p* among you in Num 32:30
in Maon, whose *p* were in Carmel 1Sa 25:2
And their *p* and habitations were, 1Chr 7:28
in their *p* in their cities were 1Chr 9:2
*p* of flocks and herds in abundance 2Chr 32:29
also I had great *p* of great Eccl 2:7
of Jacob shall possess their *p* Obad 17
for he had great *p* Mt 19:22
for he had great *p* Mk 10:22
And sold their *p* and goods, and Acts 2:45
In the same quarters were *p* of Acts 28:7

**POSSESSOR**
high God, *p* of heaven and earth Gen 14:19
the *p* of heaven and earth, Gen 14:22

**POSSESSORS**
Whose *p* slay them, and hold Zec 11:5
for as many as were *p* of lands or Acts 4:34

**POSSIBLE**
but with God all things are *p* Mt 19:26
insomuch that, if it were *p* Mt 24:24
saying, O my Father, if it be *p* Mt 26:39
all things are *p* to him that Mk 9:23
for with God all things are *p* Mk 10:27
wonders, to seduce, if it were *p* Mk 13:22
and prayed that, if it were *p* Mk 14:35
all things are *p* unto thee Mk 14:36
with men are *p* with God Lk 18:27
because it was not *p* that he Acts 2:24
he hasted, if it were *p* for him Acts 20:16
they were minded, if it were *p* Acts 27:39
If it be *p*, as much as lieth in Rom 12:18
record, that, if it had been *p* Gal 4:15
For it is not *p* that the blood of Heb 10:4

**POST**
on the upper door *p* of the houses Ex 12:7
to the door, or unto the door *p* Ex 21:6
by a *p* of the temple of the LORD 1Sa 1:9
Now my days are swifter than a *p* Job 9:25
One *p* shall run to meet another, Jer 51:31
even unto the *p* of the court Eze 40:14
upon each *p* were palm trees Eze 40:16
and measured each *p* of the porch Eze 40:48
and measured the *p* of the door Eze 41:3
their *p* by my posts, and the wall Eze 43:8
shall stand by the *p* of the gate Eze 46:2

**POSTERITY**
to preserve you a *p* in the earth Gen 45:7
If any man of you or of your *p* Num 9:10
I will take away the *p* of Baasha 1Kin 16:3
of Baasha, and the *p* of his house 1Kin 16:3
thee, and will take away thy *p* 1Kin 21:21
yet their *p* approve their sayings Ps 49:13
Let his *p* be cut off Ps 109:13
and not to his *p*, nor according to Dan 11:4
hooks, and your *p* with fishhooks Amos 4:2

**POSTS**
and strike it on the two side *p* Ex 12:7
the two side *p* with the blood Ex 12:22
the lintel, and on the two side *p* Ex 12:23
them upon the *p* of thy house Deut 6:9
upon the door *p* of thine house Deut 11:20
gate of the city, and the two *p* Judg 16:3
side *p* were a fifth part of the 1Kin 6:31
of the temple *p* of olive tree 1Kin 6:33
*p* were square, with the windows 1Kin 7:5
also the house, the beams, the *p* 2Chr 3:7
So the *p* went with the letters 2Chr 30:6
So the *p* passed from city to city 2Chr 30:10
the letters were sent by *p* into Est 3:13
The *p* went out, being hastened by Est 3:15
and sent letters by *p* on horseback Est 8:10
So the *p* that rode upon mules and Est 8:14
waiting at the *p* of my doors Prov 8:34
the *p* of the door moved at the Is 6:4
the *p* hast thou set up thy Is 57:8
the *p* thereof, two cubits Eze 40:9
the *p* had one measure on this Eze 40:10
He made also *p* of threescore Eze 40:14
to their *p* within the gate round Eze 40:16
the *p* thereof and the arches Eze 40:21
and he measured the *p* thereof Eze 40:24
on that side, upon the *p* thereof Eze 40:26
the *p* thereof, and the arches Eze 40:29
trees were upon the *p* thereof Eze 40:31
the *p* thereof, and the arches Eze 40:33
trees were upon the *p* thereof Eze 40:34
the *p* thereof, and the arches Eze 40:36
the *p* thereof were toward the Eze 40:37
trees were upon the *p* thereof Eze 40:37
were by the *p* of the gates Eze 40:38
and there were pillars by the *p* Eze 40:49
to the temple, and measured the *p* Eze 41:1
The door *p*, and the narrow windows Eze 41:16
The *p* of the temple were squared, Eze 41:21
thresholds, and their post by my *p* Eze 43:8
and put it upon the *p* of the house Eze 45:19
upon the *p* of the gate of the Eze 45:19
of the door, that the *p* may shake Amos 9:1

**POT**
Moses said unto Aaron, Take a *p* Ex 16:33
and if it be sodden in a brasen *p* Lev 6:28
and he put the broth in a *p* Judg 6:19
pan, or kettle, or caldron, or *p* 1Sa 2:14
in the house, save a *p* of oil 2Kin 4:2
his servant, Set on the great *p* 2Kin 4:38
shred them into the *p* of pottage 2Kin 4:39
of God, there is death in the *p* 2Kin 4:40
And he cast it into the *p* 2Kin 4:41
And there was no harm in the *p* 2Kin 4:41
as out of a seething *p* or caldron Job 41:20
maketh the deep to boil like a *p* Job 41:31
the sea like a *p* of ointment Job 41:31
The fining *p* is for silver, and Prov 17:3
As the fining *p* for silver Prov 27:21
the crackling of thorns under a *p* Eccl 7:6
and I said, I see a seething *p* Jer 1:13
Set on a *p*, set it on, and also Eze 24:3
to the *p* whose scum is therein, Eze 24:6
chop them in pieces, as for the *p* Mic 3:3
every *p* in Jerusalem and in Judah Zec 14:21
was the golden *p* that had manna Heb 9:4

**POTENTATE**
who is the blessed and only *P* 1Ti 6:15

**POTIPHAR** *(pot'i-far) A captain of Pharaoh's guard.*
sold him into Egypt unto *P* Gen 37:36
and *P*, an officer of Pharaoh, Gen 39:1

**POTI-PHERAH** *Priest of On.*
the daughter of *P* priest of On Gen 41:45
of *P* priest of On bare unto him Gen 41:50
of *P* priest of On bare unto him Gen 46:20

**POTS**
Egypt, when we sat by the flesh *p* Ex 16:3
the vessels of the altar, the *p* Ex 38:3
it be oven, or ranges for *p* Lev 11:35
And the *p*, and the shovels, and the 1Kin 7:45
And the *p*, and the shovels, and the 2Kin 25:14
And Huram made the *p*, and the 2Chr 4:11
The *p* also, and the shovels, and 2Chr 4:16
holy offerings sod they in *p* 2Chr 35:13
Before your *p* can feel the thorns Ps 58:9
Though ye have lien among the *p* Ps 68:13
hands were delivered from the *p* Ps 81:6
of the Rechabites *p* full of wine Jer 35:5
the *p* in the LORD's house shall Zec 14:20
as the washing of cups, and *p* Mk 7:4
of men, as the washing of *p* Mk 7:8

**POTSHERD**
he took him a *p* to scrape himself Job 2:8
My strength is dried up like a *p* Ps 22:15
a *p* covered with silver dross Prov 26:23
Let the *p* strive with the Is 45:9

**POTSHERDS**
strive with the *p* of the earth Is 45:9

**POTTAGE**
And Jacob sod *p* Gen 25:29
I pray thee, with that same red *p* Gen 25:30
gave Esau bread and *p* of lentiles Gen 25:34
seethe *p* for the sons of the 2Kin 4:38
and shred them into the pot of *p* 2Kin 4:39
as they were eating of the *p* 2Kin 4:40
his skirt do touch bread, or *p* Hag 2:12

**POTTER**
morter, and as the *p* treadeth clay Is 41:25
we are the clay, and thou our *p* Is 64:8
was marred in the hand of the *p* Jer 18:4
seemed good to the *p* to make it Jer 18:4
cannot I do with you as this *p* Jer 18:6
the work of the hands of the *p* Lam 4:2
said unto me, Cast it unto the *p* Zec 11:13
cast them to the *p* in the house Zec 11:13
Hath not the *p* power over the Rom 9:21
as the vessels of a *p* shall they Rev 2:27

**POTTER'S**
them in pieces like a *p* vessel Ps 2:9
shall be esteemed as the *p* clay Is 29:16
Arise, and go down to the *p* house Jer 18:2
Then I went down to the *p* house Jer 18:3
as the clay is in the *p* hand Jer 18:6
get a *p* earthen bottle, and take Jer 19:1
city, as one breaketh a *p* vessel Jer 19:11
and bought with them the *p* field Mt 27:7
And gave them for the *p* field Mt 27:10

**POTTERS**
These were the *p*, and those that 1Chr 4:23

**POTTERS'**
*p* vessel that is broken in pieces Is 30:14
the feet and toes, part of *p* clay Dan 2:41

**POUND**
three *p* of gold went to one 1Kin 10:17
and five thousand *p* of silver Ezr 2:69
thy *p* hath gained ten pounds Lk 19:16
thy *p* hath gained five pounds Lk 19:18
Lord, behold, here is thy *p* Lk 19:20
stood by, Take from him the *p* Lk 19:24
Then took Mary a *p* of ointment of Jn 12:3
aloes, about an hundred *p* weight Jn 19:39

**POUNDS**
and two hundred *p* of silver Neh 7:71
gold, and two thousand *p* of silver Neh 7:72
servants, and delivered them ten *p* Lk 19:13
Lord, thy pound hath gained ten *p* Lk 19:16
thy pound hath gained five *p* Lk 19:18
and give it to him that hath ten *p* Lk 19:24
unto him, Lord, he hath ten *p* Lk 19:25

**POUR**
river, and *p* it upon the dry land Ex 4:9
*p* it upon his head, and anoint him Ex 29:7
*p* all the blood beside the bottom Ex 29:12
neither shall ye *p* drink offering Ex 30:9
he shall *p* oil upon it, and put Lev 2:1
it in pieces, and *p* oil thereon Lev 2:6
shall *p* all the blood of the Lev 4:7
shall *p* out all the blood at the Lev 4:18

shall *p* out his blood at the ... Lev 4:25
shall *p* out all the blood thereof ... Lev 4:30
shall *p* out all the blood thereof ... Lev 4:34
*p* it into the palm of his own ... Lev 14:15
in the priest's hand he shall *p* ... Lev 14:18
the priest shall *p* of the oil ... Lev 14:26
they shall *p* out the dust that ... Lev 14:41
he shall even *p* out the blood ... Lev 17:13
he shall *p* no oil upon it, nor ... Num 5:15
He shall *p* the water out of his ... Num 24:7
ye shall *p* it upon the earth as ... Deut 12:16
thou shalt *p* it upon the earth as ... Deut 12:24
thou shalt *p* it upon the ground ... Deut 15:23
this rock, and *p* out the broth ... Judg 6:20
*p* it on the burnt sacrifice, and ... 1Kin 18:33
shalt *p* out into all those ... 2Kin 4:4
*P* out for the people, that they ... 2Kin 4:41
*p* it on his head, and say, Thus ... 2Kin 9:3
they *p* down rain according to the ... Job 36:27
things, I *p* out my soul in me ... Ps 42:4
*p* out your heart before him ... Ps 62:8
*P* out thine indignation upon them ... Ps 69:24
*P* out thy wrath upon the heathen ... Ps 79:6
I will *p* out my spirit unto you, ... Prov 1:23
For I will *p* water upon him that ... Is 44:3
I will *p* my spirit upon thy seed, ... Is 44:3
above, and let the skies *p* down ... Is 45:8
I will *p* it out upon the children ... Jer 6:11
to *p* out drink offerings unto ... Jer 7:18
*P* out thy fury upon the heathen ... Jer 10:25
for I will *p* their wickedness ... Jer 14:16
*p* out their blood by the force of ... Jer 18:21
to *p* out drink offerings unto her ... Jer 44:17
to *p* out drink offerings unto her ... Jer 44:18
*p* out drink offerings unto her, ... Jer 44:19
to *p* out drink offerings unto her ... Jer 44:25
*p* out thine heart like water ... Lam 2:19
Now will I shortly *p* out my fury ... Eze 7:8
*p* out my fury upon it in blood, ... Eze 14:19
I will *p* out my fury upon them, ... Eze 20:8
I would *p* out my fury upon them ... Eze 20:13
I would *p* out my fury upon them, ... Eze 20:21
I will *p* out mine indignation ... Eze 21:31
it on, and also *p* water into it ... Eze 24:3
I will *p* my fury upon Sin, the ... Eze 30:15
therefore I will *p* out my wrath ... Hos 5:10
that I will *p* out my spirit upon ... Joel 2:28
those days will I *p* out my spirit ... Joel 2:29
I will *p* down the stones thereof ... Mic 1:6
to *p* upon them mine indignation, ... Zeph 3:8
I will *p* upon the house of David, ... Zec 12:10
*p* you out a blessing, that there ... Mal 3:10
I will *p* out of my Spirit upon ... Acts 2:17
on my handmaidens I will *p* out in ... Acts 2:18
*p* out the vials of the wrath of ... Rev 16:1

## POURED

and *p* oil upon the top of it ... Gen 28:18
he *p* a drink offering thereon ... Gen 35:14
and he *p* oil thereon ... Gen 35:14
the rain was not *p* upon the earth ... Ex 9:33
man's flesh shall it not be *p* ... Ex 30:32
place, where the ashes are *p* out ... Lev 4:12
where the ashes are *p* out shall ... Lev 4:12
he *p* of the anointing oil upon ... Lev 8:12
*p* the blood at the bottom of the ... Lev 8:15
*p* out the blood at the bottom of ... Lev 9:9
head the anointing oil was *p* ... Lev 21:10
to be *p* unto the LORD for a drink ... Num 28:7
of thy sacrifices shall be *p* out ... Deut 12:27
but have *p* out my soul before the ... 1Sa 1:15
*p* it out before the LORD, and ... 1Sa 7:6
*p* it upon his head, and kissed him ... 1Sa 10:1
a pan, and *p* them out before him ... 2Sa 13:9
but *p* it out unto the LORD ... 2Sa 23:16
that are upon it shall be *p* out ... 1Kin 13:3
the ashes *p* out from the altar, ... 1Kin 13:5
which *p* water on the hands of ... 2Kin 3:11
and she *p* out ... 2Kin 4:5
So they *p* out for the men to eat ... 2Kin 4:40
he *p* the oil on his head, and said ... 2Kin 9:6
and *p* his drink offering, and ... 2Kin 16:13
but *p* it out to the LORD, ... 1Chr 11:18
my wrath shall not be *p* out upon ... 2Chr 12:7
of the LORD that is *p* out upon us ... 2Chr 34:21
shall be *p* out upon this place ... 2Chr 34:25
my roarings are *p* out like the ... Job 3:24
Hast thou not *p* me out as milk, ... Job 10:10
the rock *p* me out rivers of oil ... Job 29:6
And now my soul is *p* out upon me ... Job 30:16
I am *p* out like water, and all my ... Ps 22:14
grace is *p* into thy lips ... Ps 45:2
The clouds *p* out water ... Ps 77:17
I *p* out my complaint before him ... Ps 142:2
thy name is as ointment *p* forth ... Song 1:3
they *p* out a prayer when thy ... Is 26:16
For the LORD hath *p* out upon you ... Is 29:10
Until the spirit be *p* upon us ... Is 32:15
Therefore he hath *p* upon him the ... Is 42:25
because he hath *p* out his soul ... Is 53:12
them hast thou *p* a drink offering ... Is 57:6
my fury shall be *p* out upon this ... Jer 7:20
have *p* out drink offerings unto ... Jer 19:13
*p* out drink offerings unto other ... Jer 32:29
my fury hath been *p* forth upon ... Jer 42:18
shall my fury be *p* forth upon you ... Jer 42:18
my fury and mine anger was *p* forth ... Jer 44:6
*p* out drink offerings unto her, ... Jer 44:19
he *p* out his fury like fire ... Lam 2:4
my liver is *p* upon the earth, for ... Lam 2:11
when their soul was *p* out into ... Lam 2:12
*p* out in the top of every street ... Lam 4:1
he hath *p* out his fierce anger, ... Lam 4:11
Because thy filthiness was *p* out ... Eze 16:36
*p* out there their drink offerings ... Eze 20:28
out arm, and with fury *p* out ... Eze 20:33
out arm, and with fury *p* out ... Eze 20:34
LORD have *p* out my fury upon you ... Eze 22:22
Therefore have I *p* out mine ... Eze 22:31
*p* their whoredom upon her ... Eze 23:8
she *p* it not upon the ground, to ... Eze 24:7
Wherefore I *p* my fury upon them ... Eze 36:18
for I have *p* out my spirit upon ... Eze 39:29
therefore the curse is *p* upon us ... Dan 9:11
shall be *p* upon the desolate ... Dan 9:27
that are *p* down a steep place ... Mic 1:4
his fury is *p* out like fire, and ... Nah 1:6
blood shall be *p* out as dust ... Zeph 1:17
*p* it on his head, as he sat at ... Mt 26:7
For in that she hath *p* this ... Mt 26:12
the box, and *p* it on his head ... Mk 14:3
*p* out the changers' money, and ... Jn 2:15
that on the Gentiles also was *p* ... Acts 10:45
which is *p* out without mixture ... Rev 14:10
*p* out his vial upon the earth ... Rev 16:2
the second angel *p* out his vial ... Rev 16:3
the third angel *p* out his vial ... Rev 16:4
the fourth angel *p* out his vial ... Rev 16:8
the fifth angel *p* out his vial ... Rev 16:10
the sixth angel *p* out his vial ... Rev 16:12
the seventh angel *p* out his vial ... Rev 16:17

## POUREDST

*p* out thy fornications on every ... Eze 16:15

## POURETH

He *p* contempt upon princes, and ... Job 12:21
he *p* out my gall upon the ground ... Job 16:13
but mine eye *p* out tears unto God ... Job 16:20
and he *p* out of the same ... Ps 75:8
*p* out his complaint before the ... Ps 102:*t*
He *p* contempt upon princes, and ... Ps 107:40
mouth of fools *p* out foolishness ... Prov 15:2
of the wicked *p* out evil things ... Prov 15:28
*p* them out upon the face of the ... Amos 5:8
*p* them out upon the face of the ... Amos 9:6
After that he *p* water into a ... Jn 13:5

## POURING

the residue of Israel in thy *p* ... Eze 9:8
*p* in oil and wine, and set him on ... Lk 10:34

## POURTRAY

thee, and *p* upon it the city, even ... Eze 4:1

## POURTRAYED

*p* upon the wall round about ... Eze 8:10
when she saw men *p* upon the wall ... Eze 23:14
of the Chaldeans *p* with vermilion ... Eze 23:14

## POVERTY

and all that thou hast, come to *p* ... Gen 45:11
So shall thy *p* come as one that ... Prov 6:11
of the poor is their *p* ... Prov 10:15
than is meet, but it tendeth to *p* ... Prov 11:24
*P* and shame shall be to him that ... Prov 13:18
not sleep, lest thou come to *p* ... Prov 20:13
and the glutton shall come to *p* ... Prov 23:21
So shall thy *p* come as one that ... Prov 24:34
vain persons shall have *p* enough ... Prov 28:19
not that *p* shall come upon him ... Prov 28:22
give me neither *p* nor riches ... Prov 30:8
Let him drink, and forget his *p* ... Prov 31:7
their deep *p* abounded unto the ... 2Cor 8:2
ye through his *p* might be rich ... 2Cor 8:9
thy works, and tribulation, and *p* ... Rev 2:9

## POWDER

it in the fire, and ground it to *p* ... Ex 32:20
shall make the rain of thy land *p* ... Deut 28:24
Kidron, and stamped it small to *p* ... 2Kin 23:6
cast the *p* thereof upon the ... 2Kin 23:6
place, and stamped it small to *p* ... 2Kin 23:15
beaten the graven images into *p* ... 2Chr 34:7
fall, it will grind him to *p* ... Mt 21:44
fall, it will grind him to *p* ... Lk 20:18

## POWDERS

with all *p* of the merchant ... Song 3:6

## POWER

ye know that with all my *p* I have ... Gen 31:6
It is in the *p* of my hand to do ... Gen 31:29
as a prince hast thou *p* with God ... Gen 32:28
dignity, and the excellency of *p* ... Gen 49:3
thee up, for to shew in thee my *p* ... Ex 9:16
O LORD, is become glorious in *p* ... Ex 15:6
strange nation he shall have no *p* ... Ex 21:8
of the land of Egypt with great *p* ... Ex 32:11
I will break the pride of your *p* ... Lev 26:19
ye shall have no *p* to stand ... Lev 26:37
let the *p* of my LORD be great, ... Num 14:17
have I now any *p* at all to say ... Num 22:38
with his mighty *p* out of Egypt ... Deut 4:37
And thou say in thine heart, My *p* ... Deut 8:17
that giveth thee *p* to get wealth ... Deut 8:18
broughtest out by thy mighty *p* ... Deut 9:29
he seeth that their *p* is gone ... Deut 32:36
they had no *p* to flee this way or ... Josh 8:20
a great people, and hast great *p* ... Josh 17:17
a Benjamite, a mighty man of *p* ... 1Sa 9:1
until they had no more *p* to weep ... 1Sa 30:4
God is my strength and *p* ... 2Sa 22:33
of the land of Egypt with great *p* ... 2Kin 17:36
their inhabitants were of small *p* ... 2Kin 19:26
Joab led forth the *p* of the army ... 1Chr 20:1
LORD, is the greatness, and the *p* ... 1Chr 29:11
and in thine hand is *p* and might ... 1Chr 29:12
many, or with them that have no *p* ... 2Chr 14:11
and in thine hand is there not *p* ... 2Chr 20:6
no *p* to keep still the kingdom ... 2Chr 22:9
for God hath *p* to help, and to ... 2Chr 25:8
that made war with mighty *p* ... 2Chr 26:13
all his *p* with him,) unto ... 2Chr 32:9
made them to cease by force and *p* ... Ezr 4:23
but his *p* and his wrath is against ... Ezr 8:22
thou hast redeemed by thy great *p* ... Neh 1:10
is it in our *p* to redeem them ... Neh 5:5
the *p* of Persia and Media, the ... Est 1:3
all the *p* of the people and ... Est 8:11
Jews hoped to have *p* over them ... Est 9:1
And all the acts of his *p* and of ... Est 10:2
all that he hath is in thy *p* ... Job 1:12
and in war from the *p* of the sword ... Job 5:20
become old, yea, are mighty in *p* ... Job 21:7
plead against me with his great *p* ... Job 23:6
also the mighty with his *p* ... Job 24:22
thou helped him that is without *p* ... Job 26:2
He divideth the sea with his *p* ... Job 26:12
of his *p* who can understand ... Job 26:14
Behold, God exalteth by his *p* ... Job 36:22
he is excellent in *p*, and in ... Job 37:23
not conceal his parts, nor his *p* ... Job 41:12
so will we sing and praise thy *p* ... Ps 21:13
my darling from the *p* of the dog ... Ps 22:20
I have seen the wicked in great *p* ... Ps 37:35
my soul from the *p* of the grave ... Ps 49:15
scatter them by thy *p* ... Ps 59:11
But I will sing of thy *p* ... Ps 59:16
that *p* belongeth unto God ... Ps 62:11
To see thy *p* and thy glory, so as ... Ps 63:2
being girded with *p* ... Ps 65:6
thy *p* shall thine enemies submit ... Ps 66:3
He ruleth by his *p* for ever ... Ps 66:7
strength and *p* unto his people ... Ps 68:35
thy *p* to every one that is to ... Ps 71:18
by his *p* he brought in the south ... Ps 78:26
to the greatness of thy *p* ... Ps 79:11
Who knoweth the *p* of thine anger ... Ps 90:11
make his mighty *p* to be known ... Ps 106:8
be willing in the day of thy *p* ... Ps 110:3
his people the *p* of his works ... Ps 111:6
of thy kingdom, and talk of thy *p* ... Ps 145:11
Great is our Lord, and of great *p* ... Ps 147:5
him in the firmament of his *p* ... Ps 150:1
when it is in the *p* of thine hand ... Prov 3:27
life are in the *p* of the tongue ... Prov 18:21
of their oppressors there was *p* ... Eccl 4:1
hath given him *p* to eat thereof ... Eccl 5:19
giveth him not *p* to eat thereof ... Eccl 6:2
the word of a king is, there is *p* ... Eccl 8:4
There is no man that hath *p* over ... Eccl 8:8
neither hath he *p* in the day of ... Eccl 8:8
their inhabitants were of small *p* ... Is 37:27
might, for that he is strong in *p* ... Is 40:26
He giveth *p* to the faint ... Is 40:29
and horse, the army and the *p* ... Is 43:17
from the *p* of the flame ... Is 47:14
or have I no *p* to deliver ... Is 50:2
He hath made the earth by his *p* ... Jer 10:12
upon the ground, by my great *p* ... Jer 27:5
and the earth by thy great *p* ... Jer 32:17
He hath made the earth by his *p* ... Jer 51:15
even without great *p* or many ... Eze 17:9
in thee to their *p* to shed blood ... Eze 22:6
pride of her *p* shall come down ... Eze 30:6
hath given thee a kingdom, *p* ... Dan 2:37
whose bodies the fire had no *p* ... Dan 3:27
the kingdom by the might of my *p* ... Dan 4:30
Daniel from the *p* of the lions ... Dan 6:27
ran unto him in the fury of his *p* ... Dan 8:6
there was no *p* in the ram to ... Dan 8:7
of the nation, but not in his *p* ... Dan 8:22
his *p* shall be mighty ... Dan 8:24
but not by his own *p* ... Dan 8:24
shall not retain the *p* of the arm ... Dan 11:6
And he shall stir up his *p* ... Dan 11:25
But he shall have *p* over the ... Dan 11:43
scatter the *p* of the holy people ... Dan 12:7
by his strength he had *p* with God ... Hos 12:3
he had *p* over the angel, and ... Hos 12:4
them from the *p* of the grave ... Hos 13:14
it is in the *p* of their hand ... Mic 2:1
But truly I am full of *p* by the ... Mic 3:8
is slow to anger, and great in *p* ... Nah 1:3
strong, fortify thy *p* mightily ... Nah 2:1
imputing this his *p* unto his god ... Hab 1:11
be delivered from the *p* of evil ... Hab 2:9
and there was the hiding of his *p* ... Hab 3:4
saying, Not by might, nor by *p* ... Zec 4:6
and he will smite her *p* in the sea ... Zec 9:4
thine is the kingdom, and the *p* ... Mt 6:13
hath *p* on earth to forgive sins ... Mt 9:6
which had given such *p* unto men ... Mt 9:8
he gave them *p* against unclean ... Mt 10:1
the scriptures, nor the *p* of God ... Mt 22:29
in the clouds of heaven with *p* ... Mt 24:30
sitting on the right hand of *p* ... Mt 26:64
All *p* is given unto me in heaven ... Mt 28:18
hath *p* on earth to forgive sins ... Mk 2:10
to have *p* to heal sicknesses, and ... Mk 3:15
gave them *p* over unclean spirits ... Mk 6:7
the kingdom of God come with *p* ... Mk 9:1
scriptures, neither the *p* of God ... Mk 12:24
coming in the clouds with great *p* ... Mk 13:26

sitting on the right hand of p ... Mk 14:62
p of Elias, to turn the hearts of ... Lk 1:17
the p of the Highest shall ... Lk 1:35
All this p will I give thee, and ... Lk 4:6
Jesus returned in the p of the ... Lk 4:14
for his word was with p ... Lk 4:32
p he commandeth the unclean ... Lk 4:36
the p of the Lord was present to ... Lk 5:17
hath p upon earth to forgive sins ... Lk 5:24
together, and gave them p and ... Lk 9:1
all amazed at the mighty p of God ... Lk 9:43
I give unto you p to tread on ... Lk 10:19
and over all the p of the enemy ... Lk 10:19
killed hath p to cast into hell ... Lk 12:5
they might deliver him unto the p ... Lk 20:20
of man coming in a cloud with p ... Lk 21:27
your hour, and the p of darkness ... Lk 22:53
on the right hand of the p of God ... Lk 22:69
ye be endued with p from on high ... Lk 24:49
to them gave he p to become the ... Jn 1:12
I have p to lay it down, and I ... Jn 10:18
I have p to take it again ... Jn 10:18
hast given him p over all flesh ... Jn 17:2
not that I have p to crucify thee ... Jn 19:10
and have p to release thee ... Jn 19:10
have no p at all against me ... Jn 19:11
the Father hath put in his own p ... Acts 1:7
But ye shall receive p, after ... Acts 1:8
as though by our own p or ... Acts 3:12
the midst, they asked, By what p ... Acts 4:7
with great p gave the apostles ... Acts 4:33
sold, was it not in thine own p ... Acts 5:4
And Stephen, full of faith and p ... Acts 6:8
This man is the great p of God ... Acts 8:10
Saying, Give me also this p ... Acts 8:19
with the Holy Ghost and with p ... Acts 10:38
from the p of Satan unto God, ... Acts 26:18
to be the Son of God with p ... Rom 1:4
for it is the p of God unto ... Rom 1:16
that are made, even his eternal p ... Rom 1:20
that I might shew my p in thee ... Rom 9:17
not the potter p over the clay ... Rom 9:21
his wrath, and to make his p known ... Rom 9:22
For there is no p but of God ... Rom 13:1
therefore resisteth the p ... Rom 13:2
thou then not be afraid of the p ... Rom 13:3
through the p of the Holy Ghost ... Rom 15:13
by the p of the Spirit of God ... Rom 15:19
Now to him that is of p to ... Rom 16:25
are saved it is the p of God ... 1Cor 1:18
and Greeks, Christ the p of God ... 1Cor 1:24
of the Spirit and of p ... 1Cor 2:4
of men, but in the p of God ... 1Cor 2:5
which are puffed up, but the p ... 1Cor 4:19
of God is not in word, but in p ... 1Cor 4:20
with the p of our Lord Jesus ... 1Cor 5:4
not be brought under the p of any ... 1Cor 6:12
also raise up us by his own p ... 1Cor 6:14
wife hath not p of her own body ... 1Cor 7:4
hath not p of his own body ... 1Cor 7:4
but hath p over his own will, and ... 1Cor 7:37
Have we not p to eat and to drink ... 1Cor 9:4
Have we not p to lead about a ... 1Cor 9:5
have not we p to forbear working ... 1Cor 9:6
be partakers of this p over you ... 1Cor 9:12
we have not used this p ... 1Cor 9:12
I abuse not my p in the gospel ... 1Cor 9:18
have p on her head because of the ... 1Cor 11:10
all rule and all authority and p ... 1Cor 15:24
it is raised in p ... 1Cor 15:43
excellency of the p may be of God ... 2Cor 4:7
word of truth, by the p of God ... 2Cor 6:7
For to their p, I bear record, ... 2Cor 8:3
beyond their p they were willing ... 2Cor 8:3
that the p of Christ may rest ... 2Cor 12:9
yet he liveth by the p of God ... 2Cor 13:4
him by the p of God toward you ... 2Cor 13:4
according to the p which the Lord ... 2Cor 13:10
of his p to us-ward who believe ... Eph 1:19
to the working of his mighty p ... Eph 1:19
Far above all principality, and p ... Eph 1:21
to the prince of the p of the air ... Eph 2:2
by the effectual working of his p ... Eph 3:7
according to the p that worketh ... Eph 3:20
Lord, and in the p of his might ... Eph 6:10
the p of his resurrection, and the ... Phil 3:10
according to his glorious p ... Col 1:11
us from the p of darkness ... Col 1:13
the head of all principality and p ... Col 2:10
you in word only, but also in p ... 1Th 1:5
Lord, and from the glory of his p ... 2Th 1:9
and the work of faith with p ... 2Th 1:11
the working of Satan with all p ... 2Th 2:9
Not because we have not p ... 2Th 3:9
whom be honour and p everlasting ... 1Ti 6:16
but of p, and of love, and of a ... 2Ti 1:7
gospel according to the p of God ... 2Ti 1:8
but denying the p thereof ... 2Ti 3:5
all things by the word of his p ... Heb 1:3
him that had the p of death ... Heb 2:14
but after the p of an endless ... Heb 7:16
Who are kept by the p of God ... 1Pet 1:5
According as his divine p hath ... 2Pet 1:3
when we made known unto you the p ... 2Pet 1:16
angels, which are greater in p ... 2Pet 2:11
glory and majesty, dominion and p ... Jude 25
will I give p over the nations ... Rev 2:26
to receive glory and honour and p ... Rev 4:11
Lamb that was slain to receive p ... Rev 5:12
and honour, and glory, and p ... Rev 5:13
p was given to him that sat ... Rev 6:4
p was given unto them over the ... Rev 6:8
and thanksgiving, and honour, and p ... Rev 7:12
and unto them was given p, as the ... Rev 9:3
the scorpions of the earth have p ... Rev 9:3
their p was to hurt men five ... Rev 9:10
For their p is in their mouth, and ... Rev 9:19
I will give p unto my two ... Rev 11:3
These have p to shut heaven, that ... Rev 11:6
have p over waters to turn them ... Rev 11:6
hast taken to thee thy great p ... Rev 11:17
our God, and the p of his Christ ... Rev 12:10
and the dragon gave him his p ... Rev 13:2
which gave p unto the beast ... Rev 13:4
p was given unto him to continue ... Rev 13:5
p was given him over all kindreds ... Rev 13:7
he exerciseth all the p of the ... Rev 13:12
of those miracles which he had p ... Rev 13:14
he had p to give life unto the ... Rev 13:15
the altar, which had p over fire ... Rev 14:18
the glory of God, and from his p ... Rev 15:8
p was given unto him to scorch ... Rev 16:8
which hath p over these plagues ... Rev 16:9
but receive p as kings one hour ... Rev 17:12
one mind, and shall give their p ... Rev 17:13
down from heaven, having great p ... Rev 18:1
and glory, and honour, and p ... Rev 19:1
such the second death hath no p ... Rev 20:6

**POWERFUL**
The voice of the LORD is p ... Ps 29:4
say they, are weighty and p ... 2Cor 10:10
the word of God is quick, and p ... Heb 4:12

**POWERS**
the p of the heavens shall be ... Mt 24:29
the p that are in heaven shall be ... Mk 13:25
and unto magistrates, and p ... Lk 12:11
for the p of heaven shall be ... Lk 21:26
angels, nor principalities, nor p ... Rom 8:38
soul be subject unto the higher p ... Rom 13:1
the p that be are ordained of God ... Rom 13:1
p in heavenly places might be ... Eph 3:10
against principalities, against p ... Eph 6:12
or principalities, or p ... Col 1:16
spoiled principalities and p ... Col 2:15
be subject to principalities and p ... Titus 3:1
the p of the world to come, ... Heb 6:5
p being made subject unto him ... 1Pet 3:22

**PRACTICES**
have exercised with covetous p ... 2Pet 2:14

**PRACTISE**
to p wicked works with men that ... Ps 141:4
to p hypocrisy, and to utter error ... Is 32:6
and shall prosper, and p, and shall ... Dan 8:24
the morning is light, they p it ... Mic 2:1

**PRACTISED**
secretly p mischief against him ... 1Sa 23:9
and it p, and prospered ... Dan 8:12

**PRAETORIUM** *(pre-to'-re-um) Palace of the Roman procurator in Jerusalem.*
him away into the hall, called P ... Mk 15:16

**PRAISE**
she said, Now will I p the LORD ... Gen 29:35
art he whom thy brethren shall p ... Gen 49:8
be holy to p the LORD withal ... Lev 19:24
He is thy p, and he is thy God ... Deut 10:21
nations which he hath made, in p ... Deut 26:19
P ye the LORD for the avenging of ... Judg 5:2
I will sing p to the LORD God of ... Judg 5:3
thank and p the LORD God of Israel ... 1Chr 16:4
thy holy name, and glory in thy p ... 1Chr 16:35
made, said David, to p therewith ... 1Chr 23:5
p the LORD, and likewise at even ... 1Chr 23:30
to give thanks and to p the LORD ... 1Chr 25:3
thee, and p thy glorious name ... 1Chr 29:13
the king had made to p the LORD ... 2Chr 7:6
Levites to their charges, to p ... 2Chr 8:14
stood up to p the LORD God of ... 2Chr 20:19
that should p the beauty of ... 2Chr 20:21
the army, and to say, P the LORD ... 2Chr 20:21
when they began to sing and to p ... 2Chr 20:22
and such as taught to sing p ... 2Chr 23:13
commanded the Levites to sing p ... 2Chr 29:30
to p in the gates of the tents of ... 2Chr 31:2
cymbals, to p the LORD, after the ... Ezr 3:10
exalted above all blessing and p ... Neh 9:5
brethren over against them, to p ... Neh 12:24
of the singers, and songs of p ... Neh 12:46
I will p the LORD according to ... Ps 7:17
will sing p to the name of the ... Ps 7:17
I will p thee, O LORD, with my ... Ps 9:1
I will sing p to thy name ... Ps 9:2
That I may shew forth all thy p ... Ps 9:14
so will we sing and p thy power ... Ps 21:13
of the congregation will I p thee ... Ps 22:22
Ye that fear the LORD, p him ... Ps 22:23
My p shall be of thee in the ... Ps 22:25
they shall p the LORD that seek ... Ps 22:26
and with my song will I p him ... Ps 28:7
shall the dust p thee ... Ps 30:9
that my glory may sing p to thee ... Ps 30:12
for p is comely for the upright ... Ps 33:1
P the LORD with harp ... Ps 33:2
his p shall continually be in my ... Ps 34:1
I will p thee among much people ... Ps 35:18
of thy p all the day long ... Ps 35:28
in my mouth, even p unto our God ... Ps 40:3
God, with the voice of joy and p ... Ps 42:4
for I shall yet p him for the ... Ps 42:5
for I shall yet p him, who is the ... Ps 42:11
yea, upon the harp will I p thee ... Ps 43:4
for I shall yet p him, who is the ... Ps 43:5
day long, and p thy name for ever ... Ps 44:8
shall the people p thee for ever ... Ps 45:17
so is thy p unto the ends of the ... Ps 48:10
his soul, and men will p thee ... Ps 49:18
Whoso offereth p glorifieth me ... Ps 50:23
my mouth shall shew forth thy p ... Ps 51:15
I will p thee for ever, because ... Ps 52:9
I will p thy name, O LORD ... Ps 54:6
In God I will p his word, in God ... Ps 56:4
In God will I p his word ... Ps 56:10
in the LORD will I p his word ... Ps 56:10
I will sing and give p ... Ps 57:7
I will p thee, O Lord, among the ... Ps 57:9
So will I sing p unto thy name ... Ps 61:8
than life, my lips shall p thee ... Ps 63:3
my mouth shall p thee with joyful ... Ps 63:5
P waiteth for thee, O God in Sion ... Ps 65:1
make his p glorious ... Ps 66:2
the voice of his p to be heard ... Ps 66:8
Let the people p thee, O God ... Ps 67:3
let all the people p thee ... Ps 67:3
Let the people p thee, O God ... Ps 67:5
let all the people p thee ... Ps 67:5
I will p the name of God with a ... Ps 69:30
Let the heaven and earth p him ... Ps 69:34
my p shall be continually of thee ... Ps 71:6
Let my mouth be filled with thy p ... Ps 71:8
will yet p thee more and more ... Ps 71:14
I will also p thee with the ... Ps 71:22
let the poor and needy p thy name ... Ps 74:21
the wrath of man shall p thee ... Ps 76:10
forth thy p to all generations ... Ps 79:13
I will p thee, O Lord my God, ... Ps 86:12
shall the dead arise and p thee ... Ps 88:10
the heavens shall p thy wonders ... Ps 89:5
loud noise, and rejoice, and sing p ... Ps 98:4
Let them p thy great and terrible ... Ps 99:3
A Psalm of p ... Ps 100:*t*
and into his courts with p ... Ps 100:4
shall be created shall p the LORD ... Ps 102:18
in Zion, and his p in Jerusalem ... Ps 102:21
I will sing p to my God while I ... Ps 104:33
P ye the LORD ... Ps 104:35
P ye the LORD ... Ps 105:45
P ye the LORD ... Ps 106:1
who can shew forth all his p ... Ps 106:2
they sang his p ... Ps 106:12
holy name, and to triumph in thy p ... Ps 106:47
P ye the LORD ... Ps 106:48
Oh that men would p the LORD for ... Ps 107:8
Oh that men would p the LORD for ... Ps 107:15
Oh that men would p the LORD for ... Ps 107:21
Oh that men would p the LORD for ... Ps 107:31
p him in the assembly of the ... Ps 107:32
I will sing and give p, even with ... Ps 108:1
I will p thee, O LORD, among the ... Ps 108:3
Hold not thy peace, O God of my p ... Ps 109:1
I will greatly p the LORD with my ... Ps 109:30
I will p him among the multitude ... Ps 109:30
P ye the LORD ... Ps 111:1
I will p the LORD with my whole ... Ps 111:1
his p endureth for ever ... Ps 111:10
P ye the LORD ... Ps 112:1
P ye the LORD ... Ps 113:1
P, O ye servants of the LORD, ... Ps 113:1
p the name of the LORD ... Ps 113:1
P ye the LORD ... Ps 113:9
The dead p not the LORD, neither ... Ps 115:17
P the LORD ... Ps 115:18
P ye the LORD ... Ps 116:19
O p the LORD, all ye nations ... Ps 117:1
p him, all ye people ... Ps 117:1
P ye the LORD ... Ps 117:2
into them, and I will p the LORD ... Ps 118:19
I will p thee ... Ps 118:21
Thou art my God, and I will p thee ... Ps 118:28
I will p thee with uprightness of ... Ps 119:7
Seven times a day do I p thee ... Ps 119:164
My lips shall utter p, when thou ... Ps 119:171
my soul live, and it shall p thee ... Ps 119:175
P ye the LORD ... Ps 135:1
P ye the name of the LORD ... Ps 135:1
p him, O ye servants of the LORD ... Ps 135:1
P the LORD ... Ps 135:3
P ye the LORD ... Ps 135:21
I will p thee with my whole heart ... Ps 138:1
the gods will I sing p unto thee ... Ps 138:1
p thy name for thy lovingkindness ... Ps 138:2
kings of the earth shall p thee ... Ps 138:4
I will p thee ... Ps 139:14
of prison, that I may p thy name ... Ps 142:7
David's Psalm of p ... Ps 145:*t*
I will p thy name for ever and ... Ps 145:2
shall p thy works to another ... Ps 145:4
All thy works shall p thee ... Ps 145:10
shall speak the p of the LORD ... Ps 145:21
P ye the LORD ... Ps 146:1
P the LORD, O my soul ... Ps 146:1
While I live will I p the LORD ... Ps 146:2
P ye the LORD ... Ps 146:10
P ye the LORD ... Ps 147:1
and p is comely ... Ps 147:1
sing p upon the harp unto our God ... Ps 147:7
P the LORD, O Jerusalem ... Ps 147:12
p thy God, O Zion ... Ps 147:12

*P* ye the LORD ... Ps 147:20
*P* ye the LORD ... Ps 148:1
*P* ye the LORD from the heavens ... Ps 148:1
*p* him in the heights ... Ps 148:1
*P* ye him, all his angels ... Ps 148:2
*p* ye him, all his hosts ... Ps 148:2
*P* ye him, sun and moon ... Ps 148:3
*p* him, all ye stars of light ... Ps 148:3
*P* him, ye heavens of heavens, and ... Ps 148:4
Let them *p* the name of the LORD ... Ps 148:5
*P* the LORD from the earth, ye ... Ps 148:7
Let them *p* the name of the LORD ... Ps 148:13
people, the *p* of all his saints ... Ps 148:14
*P* ye the LORD ... Ps 148:14
*P* ye the LORD ... Ps 149:1
his *p* in the congregation of ... Ps 149:1
Let them *p* his name in the dance ... Ps 149:3
*P* ye the LORD ... Ps 149:9
*P* ye the LORD ... Ps 150:1
*P* God in his sanctuary ... Ps 150:1
*p* him in the firmament of his ... Ps 150:1
*P* him for his mighty acts ... Ps 150:2
*p* him according to his excellent ... Ps 150:2
*P* him with the sound of the ... Ps 150:3
*p* him with the psaltery and harp ... Ps 150:3
*P* him with the timbrel and dance ... Ps 150:4
*p* him with stringed instruments ... Ps 150:4
*P* him upon the loud cymbals ... Ps 150:5
*p* him upon the high sounding ... Ps 150:5
thing that hath breath *p* the LORD ... Ps 150:6
*P* ye the LORD ... Ps 150:6
Let another man *p* thee, and not ... Prov 27:2
so is a man to his *p* ... Prov 27:21
that forsake the law *p* the wicked ... Prov 28:4
her own works *p* her in the gates ... Prov 31:31
shalt say, O LORD, I will *p* thee ... Is 12:1
*P* the LORD, call upon his name, ... Is 12:4
exalt thee, I will *p* thy name ... Is 25:1
For the grave cannot *p* thee ... Is 38:18
the living, he shall *p* thee ... Is 38:19
neither my *p* to graven images ... Is 42:8
his *p* from the end of the earth, ... Is 42:10
declare his *p* in the islands ... Is 42:12
they shall shew forth my *p* ... Is 43:21
for my *p* will I refrain for thee, ... Is 48:9
walls Salvation, and thy gates *P* ... Is 60:18
the garment of *p* for the spirit ... Is 61:3
*p* to spring forth before all the ... Is 61:11
make Jerusalem a *p* in the earth ... Is 62:7
it shall eat it, and *p* the LORD ... Is 62:9
people, and for a name, and for a *p* ... Jer 13:11
for thou art my *p* ... Jer 17:14
and bringing sacrifices of *p* ... Jer 17:26
Sing unto the LORD, *p* ye the LORD ... Jer 20:13
*p* ye, and say, O LORD, save thy ... Jer 31:7
shall be to me a name of joy, a *p* ... Jer 33:9
shall say, *P* the LORD of hosts ... Jer 33:11
of *p* into the house of the LORD ... Jer 33:11
There shall be no more *p* of Moab ... Jer 48:2
How is the city of *p* not left ... Jer 49:25
how is the *p* of the whole earth ... Jer 51:41
*p* thee, O thou God of my fathers, ... Dan 2:23
Now I Nebuchadnezzar *p* and extol ... Dan 4:37
*p* the name of the LORD your God, ... Joel 2:26
and the earth was full of his *p* ... Hab 3:3
and I will get them *p* and fame in ... Zeph 3:19
a *p* among all people of the earth ... Zeph 3:20
sucklings thou hast perfected *p* ... Mt 21:16
when they saw it, gave *p* unto God ... Lk 18:43
*p* God with a loud voice for all ... Lk 19:37
and said unto him, Give God the *p* ... Jn 9:24
For they loved the *p* of men more ... Jn 12:43
of men more than the *p* of God ... Jn 12:43
whose *p* is not of men, but of God ... Rom 2:29
and thou shalt have *p* of the same ... Rom 13:3
*P* the Lord, all ye Gentiles ... Rom 15:11
shall every man have *p* of God ... 1Cor 4:5
Now I *p* you, brethren, that ye ... 1Cor 11:2
I declare unto you I *p* you not ... 1Cor 11:17
shall I *p* you in this ... 1Cor 11:22
I *p* you not ... 1Cor 11:22
brother, whose *p* is in the gospel ... 2Cor 8:18
To the *p* of the glory of his ... Eph 1:6
should be to the *p* of his glory ... Eph 1:12
unto the *p* of his glory ... Eph 1:14
unto the glory and *p* of God ... Phil 1:11
any virtue, and if there be any *p* ... Phil 4:8
church will I sing *p* unto thee ... Heb 2:12
sacrifice of *p* to God continually ... Heb 13:15
with fire, might be found unto *p* ... 1Pet 1:7
for the *p* of them that do well ... 1Pet 2:14
Jesus Christ, to whom be *p* ... 1Pet 4:11
*P* our God, all ye his servants, ... Rev 19:5

## PRAISED

people saw him, they *p* their god ... Judg 16:24
much *p* as Absalom for his beauty ... 2Sa 14:25
the LORD, who is worthy to be *p* ... 2Sa 22:4
is the LORD, and greatly to be *p* ... 1Chr 16:25
people said, Amen, and *p* the LORD ... 1Chr 16:36
four thousand *p* the LORD with the ... 1Chr 23:5
*p* the LORD, saying, For he is ... 2Chr 5:13
*p* the LORD, saying, For he is ... 2Chr 7:3
when David *p* by their ministry ... 2Chr 7:6
the priests *p* the LORD day by day ... 2Chr 30:21
great shout, when they *p* the LORD ... Ezr 3:11
said, Amen, and *p* the LORD ... Neh 5:13
the LORD, who is worthy to be *p* ... Ps 18:3
greatly to be *p* in the city of ... Ps 48:1
and daily shall he be *p* ... Ps 72:15
LORD is great, and greatly to be *p* ... Ps 96:4
same the LORD's name is to be *p* ... Ps 113:3
is the LORD, and greatly to be *p* ... Ps 145:3
feareth the LORD, she shall be *p* ... Prov 31:30
Wherefore I *p* the dead which are ... Eccl 4:2
and the concubines, and they *p* her ... Song 6:9
house, where our fathers *p* thee ... Is 64:11
I blessed the most High, and I *p* ... Dan 4:34
*p* the gods of gold, and of silver, ... Dan 5:4
thou hast *p* the gods of silver, ... Dan 5:23
loosed, and he spake, and *p* God ... Lk 1:64

## PRAISES

in holiness, fearful in *p* ... Ex 15:11
they sang *p* with gladness, and ... 2Chr 29:30
Sing *p* to the LORD, which ... Ps 9:11
heathen, and sing *p* unto thy name ... Ps 18:49
that inhabitest the *p* of Israel ... Ps 22:3
I will sing *p* unto the LORD ... Ps 27:6
Sing *p* to God, sing *p* ... Ps 47:6
*p* unto our King, sing *p* ... Ps 47:6
sing ye *p* with understanding ... Ps 47:7
I will render *p* unto thee ... Ps 56:12
Sing unto God, sing *p* to his name ... Ps 68:4
O sing *p* unto the Lord ... Ps 68:32
I will sing *p* to the God of Jacob ... Ps 75:9
to come the *p* of the LORD ... Ps 78:4
to sing *p* unto thy name, O most ... Ps 92:1
I will sing *p* unto thee among the ... Ps 108:3
sing *p* unto his name ... Ps 135:3
strings will I sing *p* unto thee ... Ps 144:9
I will sing *p* unto my God while I ... Ps 146:2
it is good to sing *p* unto our God ... Ps 147:1
let them sing *p* unto him with the ... Ps 149:3
Let the high *p* of God be in their ... Ps 149:6
shew forth the *p* of the LORD ... Is 60:6
the *p* of the LORD, according to ... Is 63:7
Silas prayed, and sang *p* unto God ... Acts 16:25
that ye should shew forth the *p* ... 1Pet 2:9

## PRAISETH

her husband also, and he *p* her ... Prov 31:28

## PRAISING

make one sound to be heard in *p* ... 2Chr 5:13
*p* the king, she came to the ... 2Chr 23:12
they sang together by course in *p* ... Ezr 3:11
they will be still *p* thee ... Ps 84:4
of the heavenly host *p* God ... Lk 2:13
*p* God for all the things that ... Lk 2:20
were continually in the temple, *p* ... Lk 24:53
*P* God, and having favour with all ... Acts 2:47
walking, and leaping, and *p* God ... Acts 3:8
people saw him walking and *p* God ... Acts 3:9

## PRANSING

of the wheels, and of the *p* horses ... Nah 3:2

## PRANSINGS

broken by the means of the *p* ... Judg 5:22
the *p* of their mighty ones ... Judg 5:22

## PRATING

but a *p* fool shall fall ... Prov 10:8
but a *p* fool shall fall ... Prov 10:10
*p* against us with malicious words ... 3Jn 10

## PRAY

I *p* thee, thou art my sister ... Gen 12:13
I *p* thee, between me and thee, and ... Gen 13:8
thyself, I *p* thee, from me ... Gen 13:9
I *p* thee, go in unto my maid ... Gen 16:2
I *p* thee, from thy servant ... Gen 18:3
I *p* you, be fetched, and wash your ... Gen 18:4
I *p* you, into your servant's ... Gen 19:2
I *p* you, brethren, do not so ... Gen 19:7
I *p* you, bring them out unto you, ... Gen 19:8
a prophet, and he shall *p* for thee ... Gen 20:7
wilt give it, I *p* thee, hear me ... Gen 23:13
I *p* thee, thy hand under my thigh ... Gen 24:2
I *p* thee, send me good speed this ... Gen 24:12
I *p* thee, that I may drink ... Gen 24:14
I *p* thee, drink a little water of ... Gen 24:17
tell me, I *p* thee ... Gen 24:23
I *p* thee, a little water of thy ... Gen 24:43
unto her, Let me drink, I *p* thee ... Gen 24:45
I *p* thee, with that same red ... Gen 25:30
I *p* thee, thy weapons, thy quiver ... Gen 27:3
I *p* thee, sit and eat of my ... Gen 27:19
I *p* thee, that I may feel thee, ... Gen 27:21
I *p* thee, of thy son's mandrakes ... Gen 30:14
I *p* thee, if I have found favour ... Gen 30:27
I *p* thee, from the hand of my ... Gen 32:11
said, Tell me, I *p* thee, thy name ... Gen 32:29
I *p* thee, if now I have found ... Gen 33:10
I *p* thee, my blessing that is ... Gen 33:11
I *p* thee, pass over before his ... Gen 33:14
I *p* you give her him to wife ... Gen 34:8
I *p* you, this dream which I have ... Gen 37:6
I *p* thee, see whether it be well ... Gen 37:14
I *p* thee, where they feed their ... Gen 37:16
I *p* thee, let me come in unto ... Gen 38:16
I *p* thee, whose are these, the ... Gen 38:25
tell me them, I *p* you ... Gen 40:8
I *p* thee, unto me, and make ... Gen 40:14
I *p* thee, speak a word in my ... Gen 44:18
I *p* thee, let thy servant abide ... Gen 44:33
Come near to me, I *p* you ... Gen 45:4
we *p* thee, let thy servants dwell ... Gen 47:4
I *p* thee, thy hand under my thigh ... Gen 47:29
bury me not, I *p* thee, in Egypt ... Gen 47:29
I *p* thee, unto me, and I will ... Gen 48:9
I *p* you, in the ears of Pharaoh, ... Gen 50:4
I *p* thee, and bury my father, and I ... Gen 50:5
I *p* thee now, the trespass of thy ... Gen 50:17
we *p* thee, forgive the trespass ... Gen 50:17
I *p* thee, by the hand of him whom ... Ex 4:13
I *p* thee, and return unto my ... Ex 4:18
we *p* thee, three days' journey ... Ex 5:3
I *p* thee, my sin only this once, ... Ex 10:17
I *p* thee, out of thy book which ... Ex 32:32
I *p* thee, if I have found grace ... Ex 33:13
my Lord, I *p* thee, go among us ... Ex 34:9
he said, Leave us not, I *p* thee ... Num 10:31
I *p* thee, out of hand, if I have ... Num 11:15
Hear, I *p* you, ye sons of Levi ... Num 16:8
I *p* you, from the tents of these ... Num 16:26
I *p* thee, through thy country ... Num 20:17
*p* unto the LORD, that he take ... Num 21:7
I *p* thee, curse me this people ... Num 22:6
I *p* thee, hinder thee from coming ... Num 22:16
I *p* thee, curse me this people ... Num 22:17
I *p* you, tarry ye also here this ... Num 22:19
I *p* thee, with me unto another ... Num 23:13
I *p* thee, I will bring thee unto ... Num 23:27
I *p* thee, let me go over, and see ... Deut 3:25
I *p* you, swear unto me by the ... Josh 2:12
I *p* thee, glory to the LORD God ... Josh 7:19
we *p* thee, the entrance into the ... Judg 1:24
I *p* thee, a little water to drink ... Judg 4:19
I *p* thee, until I come unto thee, ... Judg 6:18
I *p* thee, but this once with the ... Judg 6:39
I *p* you, loaves of bread unto the ... Judg 8:5
I *p* you, in the ears of all the ... Judg 9:2
I *p* now, and fight with them ... Judg 9:38
us only, we *p* thee, this day ... Judg 10:15
I *p* thee, pass through thy land ... Judg 11:17
we *p* thee, through thy land into ... Judg 11:19
I *p* thee, and drink not wine nor ... Judg 13:4
I *p* thee, let us detain thee, ... Judg 13:15
her, I *p* thee, instead of her ... Judg 15:2
I *p* thee, wherein thy great ... Judg 16:6
I *p* thee, wherewith thou mightest ... Judg 16:10
I *p* thee, and strengthen me ... Judg 16:28
I *p* thee, only this once, O God, ... Judg 16:28
we *p* thee, of God, that we may ... Judg 18:5
I *p* thee, and tarry all night, and ... Judg 19:6
Comfort thine heart, I *p* thee ... Judg 19:8
evening, I *p* you tarry all night ... Judg 19:9
I *p* thee, and let us turn in into ... Judg 19:11
I *p* you, do not so wickedly ... Judg 19:23
I *p* you, let me glean and gather ... Ruth 2:7
I *p* thee, into one of the ... 1Sa 2:36
I *p* thee hide it not from me ... 1Sa 3:17
I will *p* for you unto the LORD ... 1Sa 7:5
I *p* thee, where the seer's house ... 1Sa 9:18
I *p* thee, what Samuel said unto ... 1Sa 10:15
*P* for thy servants unto the LORD ... 1Sa 12:19
the LORD in ceasing to *p* for you ... 1Sa 12:23
I *p* you, how mine eyes have been ... 1Sa 14:29
I *p* thee, pardon my sin, and turn ... 1Sa 15:25
I *p* thee, before the elders of my ... 1Sa 15:30
I *p* thee, stand before me ... 1Sa 16:22
I *p* thee, take heed to thyself ... 1Sa 19:2
And he said, Let me go, I *p* thee ... 1Sa 20:29
I *p* thee, and see my brethren ... 1Sa 20:29
I *p* thee, come forth, and be with ... 1Sa 22:3
I *p* you, prepare yet, and know and ... 1Sa 23:22
I *p* thee, whatsoever cometh to ... 1Sa 25:8
I *p* thee, speak in thine audience ... 1Sa 25:24
I *p* thee, regard this man of ... 1Sa 25:25
I *p* thee, forgive the trespass of ... 1Sa 25:28
I *p* thee, with the spear even to ... 1Sa 26:8
I *p* thee, take thou now the spear ... 1Sa 26:11
I *p* thee, let my lord the king ... 1Sa 26:19
I *p* thee, divine unto me by the ... 1Sa 28:8
I *p* thee, hearken thou also unto ... 1Sa 28:22
I *p* thee, bring me hither the ... 1Sa 30:7
I *p* thee, tell me ... 2Sa 1:4
I *p* thee, upon me, and slay me ... 2Sa 1:9
heart to *p* this prayer unto thee ... 2Sa 7:27
I *p* thee, let my sister Tamar ... 2Sa 13:5
I *p* thee, let Tamar my sister ... 2Sa 13:6
I *p* thee, speak unto the king ... 2Sa 13:13
I *p* thee, let my brother Amnon go ... 2Sa 13:26
I *p* thee, feign thyself to be a ... 2Sa 14:2
I *p* thee, let the king remember ... 2Sa 14:11
I *p* thee, speak one word unto my ... 2Sa 14:12
I *p* thee, the thing that I shall ... 2Sa 14:18
I *p* thee, let me go and pay my vow ... 2Sa 15:7
I *p* thee, turn the counsel of ... 2Sa 15:31
I *p* thee, and take off his head ... 2Sa 16:9
I *p* thee, also run after Cushi ... 2Sa 18:22
I *p* thee, turn back again, that I ... 2Sa 19:37
I *p* you, unto Joab, Come near ... 2Sa 20:16
I *p* thee, be against me, and ... 2Sa 24:17
I *p* thee, give thee counsel, that ... 1Kin 1:12
I *p* thee, unto Solomon the king, ( ... 1Kin 2:17
I *p* thee, say me not nay ... 1Kin 2:20
I *p* thee, be verified, which thou ... 1Kin 8:26
when they shall *p* toward this ... 1Kin 8:30
thee, and confess thy name, and *p* ... 1Kin 8:33
if they *p* toward this place, and ... 1Kin 8:35
shall come and *p* toward this house ... 1Kin 8:42
shall *p* unto the LORD toward the ... 1Kin 8:44
*p* unto thee toward their land, ... 1Kin 8:48
*p* for me, that my hand may be ... 1Kin 13:6
I *p* thee, and disguise thyself, ... 1Kin 14:2
I *p* thee, a little water in a ... 1Kin 17:10
I *p* thee, a morsel of bread in ... 1Kin 17:11
I *p* thee, let this child's soul ... 1Kin 17:21
I *p* thee, kiss my father and my ... 1Kin 19:20
I *p* you, and see how this man ... 1Kin 20:7
I *p* thee, put sackcloth on our ... 1Kin 20:31

saith, I *p* thee, let me live 1Kin 20:32
of the LORD, Smite me, I *p* thee 1Kin 20:35
man, and said, Smite me, I *p* thee 1Kin 20:37
I *p* thee, at the word of the LORD 1Kin 22:5
I *p* thee, be like the word of one 1Kin 22:13
I *p* thee, let my life, and the 2Kin 1:13
unto Elisha, Tarry here, I *p* thee 2Kin 2:2
him, Elisha, tarry here, I *p* thee 2Kin 2:4
unto him, Tarry, I *p* thee, here 2Kin 2:6
I *p* thee, let a double portion of 2Kin 2:9
we *p* thee, and seek thy master 2Kin 2:16
I *p* thee, the situation of this 2Kin 2:19
chamber, I *p* thee, on the wall 2Kin 4:10
I *p* thee, one of the young men, 2Kin 4:22
I *p* thee, to meet her, and say 2Kin 4:26
I *p* you, and see how he seeketh a 2Kin 5:7
I *p* thee, take a blessing of thy 2Kin 5:15
I *p* thee, be given to thy servant 2Kin 5:17
I *p* thee, a talent of silver, and 2Kin 5:22
we *p* thee, unto Jordan, and take 2Kin 6:2
I *p* thee, and go with thy servants 2Kin 6:3
I *p* thee, open his eyes, that he 2Kin 6:17
people, I *p* thee, with blindness 2Kin 6:18
I *p* thee, five of the horses that 2Kin 7:13
I *p* thee, all the great things 2Kin 8:4
I *p* thee, give pledges to my lord 2Kin 18:23
I *p* thee, to thy servants in the 2Kin 18:26
in his heart to *p* before thee 1Chr 17:25
I *p* thee, O LORD my God, be on me 1Chr 21:17
return and confess thy name, and *p* 2Chr 6:24
yet if they *p* toward this place, 2Chr 6:26
if they come and *p* in this house 2Chr 6:32
they *p* unto thee toward this city 2Chr 6:34
*p* unto thee in the land of their 2Chr 6:37
*p* toward their land, which thou 2Chr 6:38
shall humble themselves, and *p* 2Chr 7:14
I *p* thee, at the word of the LORD 2Chr 18:4
I *p* thee, be like one of theirs, 2Chr 18:12
*p* for the life of the king, and of Ezr 6:10
which I *p* before thee now, day and Neh 1:6
I *p* thee, thy servant this day, Neh 1:11
I *p* you, let us leave off this Neh 5:10
I *p* you, to them, even this day, Neh 5:11
I *p* thee, who ever perished, Job 4:7
I *p* you, let it not be iniquity Job 6:29
I *p* thee, of the former age, and Job 8:8
should we have, if we *p* unto him Job 21:15
I *p* thee, the law from his mouth, Job 22:22
I *p* you, accept any man's person, Job 32:21
I *p* thee, hear my speeches, and Job 33:1
He shall *p* unto God, and he will Job 33:26
and my servant Job shall *p* for you Job 42:8
for unto thee will I *p* Ps 5:2
*p* unto thee in a time when thou Ps 32:6
and morning, and at noon, will I *p* Ps 55:17
I *p* thee, thy merciful kindness Ps 119:76
*P* for the peace of Jerusalem Ps 122:6
I *p* you, betwixt me and my Is 5:3
shall come to his sanctuary to *p* Is 16:12
saying, Read this, I *p* thee Is 29:11
saying, Read this, I *p* thee Is 29:12
I *p* thee, to my master the king Is 36:8
I *p* thee, unto thy servants in Is 36:11
*p* unto a god that cannot save Is 45:20
Therefore *p* not thou for this Jer 7:16
Therefore *p* not thou for this Jer 11:14
*P* not for this people for their Jer 14:11
I *p* thee, of the LORD for us Jer 21:2
and *p* unto the LORD for it Jer 29:7
*p* unto me, and I will hearken unto Jer 29:12
I *p* thee, that is in Anathoth, Jer 32:8
*P* now unto the LORD our God for Jer 37:3
I *p* thee, O my lord the king Jer 37:20
I *p* thee, be accepted before thee Jer 37:20
I *p* thee, and I will slay Ishmael Jer 40:15
*p* for us unto the LORD thy God, Jer 42:2
I will *p* unto the LORD your God Jer 42:4
*P* for us unto the LORD our God Jer 42:20
I *p* you, all people, and behold my Lam 1:18
I *p* you, and hear what is the word Eze 33:30
we *p* thee, for whose cause this Jonah 1:8
I *p* thee, O LORD, was not this my Jonah 4:2
I *p* you, O heads of Jacob, and ye Mic 3:1
I *p* you, ye heads of the house of Mic 3:9
I *p* you, consider from this day Hag 2:15
their men, to *p* before the LORD, Zec 7:2
go speedily to *p* before the LORD Zec 8:21
and to *p* before the LORD Zec 8:22
I *p* you, beseech God that he will Mal 1:9
*p* for them which despitefully use Mt 5:44
for they love to *p* standing in Mt 6:5
*p* to thy Father which is in Mt 6:6
But when ye *p*, use not vain Mt 6:7
After this manner therefore *p* ye Mt 6:9
*P* ye therefore the Lord of the Mt 9:38
up into a mountain apart to *p* Mt 14:23
put his hands on them, and *p* Mt 19:13
But *p* ye that your flight be not Mt 24:20
ye here, while I go and *p* yonder Mt 26:36
Watch and *p*, that ye enter not Mt 26:41
that I cannot now *p* to my Father Mt 26:53
they began to *p* him to depart out Mk 5:17
I *p* thee, come and lay thy hands Mk 5:23
he departed into a mountain to *p* Mk 6:46
soever ye desire, when ye *p* Mk 11:24
*p* ye that your flight be not in Mk 13:18
Take ye heed, watch and *p* Mk 13:33
Sit ye here, while I shall *p* Mk 14:32
Watch ye and *p*, lest ye enter into Mk 14:38
he went out into a mountain to *p* Lk 6:12
*p* for them which despitefully use Lk 6:28
and went up into a mountain to *p* Lk 9:28
*p* ye therefore the Lord of the Lk 10:2
unto him, Lord, teach us to *p* Lk 11:1
And he said unto them, When ye *p* Lk 11:2
I *p* thee have me excused Lk 14:18
I *p* thee have me excused Lk 14:19
I *p* thee therefore, father, that Lk 16:27
end, that men ought always to *p* Lk 18:1
men went up into the temple to *p* Lk 18:10
and *p* always, that ye may be Lk 21:36
them, *P* that ye enter not into Lk 22:40
rise and *p*, lest ye enter into Lk 22:46
I will *p* the Father, and he shall Jn 14:16
that I will *p* the Father for you Jn 16:26
I *p* for them Jn 17:9
I *p* not for the world, but for Jn 17:9
I *p* not that thou shouldest take Jn 17:15
Neither *p* I for these alone, but Jn 17:20
*p* God, if perhaps the thought of Acts 8:22
*P* ye to the Lord for me, that Acts 8:24
I *p* thee, of whom speaketh the Acts 8:34
to *p* about the sixth hour Acts 10:9
I *p* thee that thou wouldest hear Acts 24:4
Wherefore I *p* you to take some Acts 27:34
what we should *p* for as we ought Rom 8:26
*p* unto God uncovered 1Cor 11:13
tongue *p* that he may interpret 1Cor 14:13
For if I *p* in an unknown tongue, 1Cor 14:14
I will *p* with the spirit, and I 1Cor 14:15
I will *p* with the understanding 1Cor 14:15
we *p* you in Christ's stead, be ye 2Cor 5:20
Now I *p* to God that ye do no evil 2Cor 13:7
And this I *p*, that your love may Phil 1:9
it, do not cease to *p* for you Col 1:9
*P* without ceasing 1Th 5:17
I *p* God your whole spirit and soul 1Th 5:23
Brethren, *p* for us 1Th 5:25
also we *p* always for you, that 2Th 1:11
*p* for us, that the word of the 2Th 3:1
therefore that men *p* every where 1Ti 2:8
I *p* God that it may not be laid 2Ti 4:16
*P* for us Heb 13:18
let him *p* Jas 5:13
and let them *p* over him, anointing Jas 5:14
*p* one for another, that ye may be Jas 5:16
do not say that he shall *p* for it 1Jn 5:16

## PRAYED

So Abraham *p* unto God Gen 20:17
when Moses *p* unto the LORD, the Num 11:2
And Moses *p* for the people Num 21:7
I *p* for Aaron also the same time Deut 9:20
I *p* therefore unto the LORD, and Deut 9:26
*p* unto the LORD, and wept sore 1Sa 1:10
For this child I *p* 1Sa 1:27
And Hannah *p*, and said, My heart 1Sa 2:1
And Samuel *p* unto the LORD 1Sa 8:6
them twain, and *p* unto the LORD 2Kin 4:33
And Elisha *p*, and said, LORD, I 2Kin 6:17
Elisha *p* unto the LORD, and said, 2Kin 6:18
Hezekiah *p* before the LORD, and 2Kin 19:15
That which thou hast *p* to me 2Kin 19:20
wall, and *p* unto the LORD, saying, 2Kin 20:2
But Hezekiah *p* for them, saying, 2Chr 30:18
prophet Isaiah the son of Amoz, *p* 2Chr 32:20
to the death, and *p* unto the LORD 2Chr 32:24
And *p* unto him 2Chr 33:13
Now when Ezra had *p*, and when he Ezr 10:1
*p* before the God of heaven, Neh 1:4
So I *p* to the God of heaven Neh 2:4
when he *p* for his friends Job 42:10
Hezekiah *p* unto the LORD, saying, Is 37:15
Whereas thou hast *p* to me against Is 37:21
the wall, and *p* unto the LORD, Is 38:2
I *p* unto the LORD, saying, Jer 32:16
his knees three times a day, and *p* Dan 6:10
I *p* unto the LORD my God, and made Dan 9:4
Then Jonah *p* unto the LORD his Jonah 2:1
he *p* unto the LORD, and said, I Jonah 4:2
and fell on his face, and *p* Mt 26:39
away again the second time, and *p* Mt 26:42
*p* the third time, saying the same Mt 26:44
into a solitary place, and there *p* Mk 1:35
*p* him that he might be with him Mk 5:18
*p* that, if it were possible, the Mk 14:35
And again he went away, and *p* Mk 14:39
*p* him that he would thrust out a Lk 5:3
himself into the wilderness, and *p* Lk 5:16
And as he *p*, the fashion of his Lk 9:29
*p* thus with himself, God, I thank Lk 18:11
But I have *p* for thee, that thy Lk 22:32
cast, and kneeled down, and *p* Lk 22:41
in an agony he *p* more earnestly Lk 22:44
mean while his disciples *p* him Jn 4:31
And they *p*, and said, Thou, Lord, Acts 1:24
And when they had *p*, the place was Acts 4:31
and when they had *p*, they laid Acts 6:6
*p* for them, that they might Acts 8:15
all forth, and kneeled down, and *p* Acts 9:40
to the people, and *p* to God alway Acts 10:2
at the ninth hour I *p* in my house Acts 10:30
Then *p* they him to tarry certain Acts 10:48
And when they had fasted and *p* Acts 13:3
and had *p* with fasting, they Acts 14:23
*p* him, saying, Come over into Acts 16:9
And at midnight Paul and Silas *p* Acts 16:25
kneeled down, and *p* with them all Acts 20:36
kneeled down on the shore, and *p* Acts 21:5
even while I *p* in the temple, I Acts 22:17
*p* me to bring this young man unto Acts 23:18
to whom Paul entered in, and *p* Acts 28:8
he *p* earnestly that it might not Jas 5:17
he *p* again, and the heaven gave Jas 5:18

## PRAYER

heart to pray this *p* unto thee 2Sa 7:27
respect unto the *p* of thy servant 1Kin 8:28
herken unto the cry and to the *p* 1Kin 8:28
*p* which thy servant shall make 1Kin 8:29
What *p* and supplication soever be 1Kin 8:38
Then hear thou in heaven their *p* 1Kin 8:45
Then hear thou their *p* and their 1Kin 8:49
made an end of praying all this *p* 1Kin 8:54
said unto him, I have heard thy *p* 1Kin 9:3
wherefore lift up thy *p* for the 2Kin 19:4
thy father, I have heard thy *p* 2Kin 20:5
therefore to the *p* of thy servant 2Chr 6:19
the *p* which thy servant prayeth 2Chr 6:19
to hearken unto the *p* which thy 2Chr 6:20
Then what *p* or what supplication 2Chr 6:29
thou from the heavens their *p* 2Chr 6:35
from thy dwelling place, their *p* 2Chr 6:39
the *p* that is made in this place 2Chr 6:40
said unto him, I have heard thy *p* 2Chr 7:12
mine ears attent unto the *p* that 2Chr 7:15
their *p* came up to his holy 2Chr 30:27
his *p* unto his God, and the words 2Chr 33:18
His *p* also, and how God was 2Chr 33:19
mayest hear the *p* of thy servant Neh 1:6
attentive to the *p* of thy servant Neh 1:11
to the *p* of thy servants, who Neh 1:11
we made our *p* unto our God Neh 4:9
to begin the thanksgiving in *p* Neh 11:17
fear, and restrainest *p* before God Job 15:4
also my *p* is pure Job 16:17
Thou shalt make thy *p* unto him Job 22:27
have mercy upon me, and hear my *p* Ps 4:1
will I direct my *p* unto thee Ps 5:3
the LORD will receive my *p* Ps 6:9
A *P* of David Ps 17:*t*
unto my cry, give ear unto my *p* Ps 17:1
my *p* returned into mine own bosom Ps 35:13
Hear my *p*, O LORD, and give ear Ps 39:12
my *p* unto the God of my life Ps 42:8
Hear my *p*, O God Ps 54:2
Give ear to my *p*, O God Ps 55:1
attend unto my *p* Ps 61:1
Hear my voice, O God, in my *p* Ps 64:1
O thou that hearest *p*, unto thee Ps 65:2
attended to the voice of my *p* Ps 66:19
which hath not turned away my *p* Ps 66:20
my *p* is unto thee, O LORD, in an Ps 69:13
*p* also shall be made for him Ps 72:15
angry against the *p* of thy people Ps 80:4
O LORD God of hosts, hear my *p* Ps 84:8
A *P* of David Ps 86:*t*
Give ear, O LORD, unto my *p* Ps 86:6
Let my *p* come before thee Ps 88:2
morning shall my *p* prevent thee Ps 88:13
A *P* of Moses, the man of God Ps 90:*t*
A *P* of the afflicted, when he is Ps 102:*t*
Hear my *p*, O LORD, and let my cry Ps 102:1
regard the *p* of the destitute Ps 102:17
and not despise their *p* Ps 102:17
but I give myself unto *p* Ps 109:4
and let his *p* become sin Ps 109:7
Let my *p* be set forth before thee Ps 141:2
for yet my *p* also shall be in Ps 141:5
A *P* when he was in the cave Ps 142:*t*
Hear my *p*, O LORD, give ear to my Ps 143:1
but the *p* of the upright is his Prov 15:8
he heareth the *p* of the righteous Prov 15:29
even his *p* shall be abomination Prov 28:9
they poured out a *p* when thy Is 26:16
wherefore lift up thy *p* for the Is 37:4
thy father, I have heard thy *p* Is 38:5
make them joyful in my house of *p* Is 56:7
an house of *p* for all people Is 56:7
lift up cry nor *p* for them Jer 7:16
lift up a cry or *p* for them Jer 11:14
and shout, he shutteth out my *p* Lam 3:8
that our *p* should not pass Lam 3:44
unto the Lord God, to seek by *p* Dan 9:3
yet made we not our *p* before the Dan 9:13
hear the *p* of thy servant, and his Dan 9:17
Yea, whiles I was speaking in *p* Dan 9:21
my *p* came in unto thee, into Jonah 2:7
A *p* of Habakkuk the prophet upon Hab 3:1
this kind goeth not out but by *p* Mt 17:21
shall be called the house of *p* Mt 21:13
whatsoever ye shall ask in *p* Mt 21:22
and for a pretence make long *p* Mt 23:14
come forth by nothing, but by *p* Mk 9:29
of all nations the house of *p* Mk 11:17
for thy *p* is heard Lk 1:13
continued all night in *p* to God Lk 6:12
My house is the house of *p* Lk 19:46
And when he rose up from *p* Lk 22:45
continued with one accord in *p* Acts 1:14
into the temple at the hour of *p* Acts 3:1
give ourselves continually to *p* Acts 6:4
thy *p* is heard, and thine alms are Acts 10:31
but *p* was made without ceasing of Acts 12:5
where *p* was wont to be made Acts 16:13
it came to pass, as we went to *p* Acts 16:16
*p* to God for Israel is, that they Rom 10:1
continuing instant in *p* Rom 12:12
give yourselves to fasting and *p* 1Cor 7:5
also helping together by *p* for us 2Cor 1:11
And by their *p* for you, which long 2Cor 9:14
Praying always with all *p* Eph 6:18

P

Always in every *p* of mine for you ... Phil 1:4
to my salvation through your *p* ... Phil 1:19
but in every thing by *p* and ... Phil 4:6
Continue in *p*, and watch in the ... Col 4:2
by the word of God and *p* ... 1Ti 4:5
the *p* of faith shall save the ... Jas 5:15
The effectual fervent *p* of a ... Jas 5:16
therefore sober, and watch unto *p* ... 1Pet 4:7

**PRAYERS**
The *p* of David the son of Jesse ... Ps 72:20
yea, when ye make many *p*, I will ... Is 1:15
and for a pretence make long *p* ... Mk 12:40
with fastings and *p* night and day ... Lk 2:37
of John fast often, and make *p* ... Lk 5:33
houses, and for a shew make long *p* ... Lk 20:47
and in breaking of bread, and in *p* ... Acts 2:42
And he said unto him, Thy *p* ... Acts 10:4
mention of you always in my *p* ... Rom 1:9
with me in your *p* to God for me ... Rom 15:30
making mention of you in my *p* ... Eph 1:16
labouring fervently for you in *p* ... Col 4:12
making mention of you in our *p* ... 1Th 1:2
first of all, supplications, *p* ... 1Ti 2:1
supplications and *p* night and day ... 1Ti 5:5
remembrance of thee in my *p* night ... 2Ti 1:3
mention of thee always in my *p* ... Philem 4
your *p* I shall be given unto you ... Philem 22
flesh, when he had offered up *p* ... Heb 5:7
that your *p* be not hindered ... 1Pet 3:7
and his ears are open unto their *p* ... 1Pet 3:12
odours, which are the *p* of saints ... Rev 5:8
he should offer it with the *p* of ... Rev 8:3
came with the *p* of the saints ... Rev 8:4

**PRAYEST**
And when thou *p*, thou shalt not be ... Mt 6:5
But thou, when thou *p*, enter into ... Mt 6:6

**PRAYETH**
which thy servant *p* before thee ... 1Kin 8:28
which thy servant *p* before thee ... 2Chr 6:19
thy servant *p* toward this place ... 2Chr 6:20
*p* unto it, and saith, Deliver me ... Is 44:17
for, behold, he *p*, ... Acts 9:11
But every woman that *p* or ... 1Cor 11:5
in an unknown tongue, my spirit *p* ... 1Cor 14:14

**PRAYING**
she continued *p* before the LORD ... 1Sa 1:12
by thee here, *p* unto the LORD ... 1Sa 1:26
made an end of *p* all this prayer ... 1Kin 8:54
when Solomon had made an end of *p* ... 2Chr 7:1
men assembled, and found Daniel *p* ... Dan 6:11
And whiles I was speaking, and *p* ... Dan 9:20
And when ye stand *p*, forgive, if ... Mk 11:25
multitude of the people were *p* ... Lk 1:10
Jesus also being baptized, and *p* ... Lk 3:21
came to pass, as he was alone *p* ... Lk 9:18
as he was *p* in a certain place, ... Lk 11:1
I was in the city of Joppa *p* ... Acts 11:5
many were gathered together *p* ... Acts 12:12
Every man *p* or prophesying, ... 1Cor 11:4
*P* us with much intreaty that we ... 2Cor 8:4
*P* always with all prayer and ... Eph 6:18
Jesus Christ, *p* always for you, ... Col 1:3
Withal *p* also for us, that God ... Col 4:3
day *p* exceedingly that we might ... 1Th 3:10
holy faith, *p* in the Holy Ghost, ... Jude 20

**PREACH**
to *p* of thee at Jerusalem ... Neh 6:7
to *p* good tidings unto the meek ... Is 61:1
*p* unto it the preaching that I ... Jonah 3:2
From that time Jesus began to *p* ... Mt 4:17
And as ye go, *p*, saying, The ... Mt 10:7
that *p* ye upon the housetops ... Mt 10:27
to teach and to *p* in their cities ... Mt 11:1
*p* the baptism of repentance for ... Mk 1:4
towns, that I may *p* there also ... Mk 1:38
he might send them forth to *p* ... Mk 3:14
*p* the gospel to every creature ... Mk 16:15
me to *p* the gospel to the poor ... Lk 4:18
to *p* deliverance to the captives, ... Lk 4:18
To *p* the acceptable year of the ... Lk 4:19
I must *p* the kingdom of God to ... Lk 4:43
he sent them to *p* the kingdom of ... Lk 9:2
go thou and *p* the kingdom of God ... Lk 9:60
not to teach and *p* Jesus Christ ... Acts 5:42
commanded us to *p* unto the people ... Acts 10:42
*p* unto you that ye should turn ... Acts 14:15
in every city them that *p* him ... Acts 15:21
Holy Ghost to *p* the word in Asia ... Acts 16:6
us for to *p* the gospel unto them ... Acts 16:10
whom I *p* unto you, is Christ ... Acts 17:3
I am ready to *p* the gospel to you ... Rom 1:15
is, the word of faith, which we *p* ... Rom 10:8
And how shall they *p*, except they ... Rom 10:15
them that *p* the gospel of peace ... Rom 10:15
so have I strived to *p* the gospel ... Rom 15:20
to baptize, but to *p* the gospel ... 1Cor 1:17
But we *p* Christ crucified, unto ... 1Cor 1:23
*p* the gospel should live of the ... 1Cor 9:14
For though I *p* the gospel ... 1Cor 9:16
is unto me, if I *p* not the gospel ... 1Cor 9:16
when I *p* the gospel, I may make ... 1Cor 9:18
it were I or they, so we *p* ... 1Cor 15:11
to Troas to *p* Christ's gospel ... 2Cor 2:12
For we *p* not ourselves, but ... 2Cor 4:5
To *p* the gospel in the regions ... 2Cor 10:16
*p* any other gospel unto you than ... Gal 1:8
If any man *p* any other gospel ... Gal 1:9
that I might *p* him among the ... Gal 1:16
which I *p* among the Gentiles ... Gal 2:2
if I yet *p* circumcision, why do I ... Gal 5:11
that I should *p* among the ... Eph 3:8
Some indeed *p* Christ even of envy ... Phil 1:15
The one *p* Christ of contention, ... Phil 1:16
Whom we *p*, warning every man, and ... Col 1:28
*P* the word ... 2Ti 4:2
the everlasting gospel to *p* unto ... Rev 14:6

**PREACHED**
I have *p* righteousness in the ... Ps 40:9
poor have the gospel *p* to them ... Mt 11:5
*p* in all the world for a witness ... Mt 24:14
shall be *p* in the whole world ... Mt 26:13
And *p*, saying, There cometh one ... Mk 1:7
And he *p* in their synagogues ... Mk 1:39
and he *p* the word unto them ... Mk 2:2
out, and *p* that men should repent ... Mk 6:12
this gospel shall be *p* throughout ... Mk 14:9
*p* every where, the Lord working ... Mk 16:20
exhortation *p* he unto the people ... Lk 3:18
he *p* in the synagogues of Galilee ... Lk 4:44
to the poor the gospel is *p* ... Lk 7:22
that time the kingdom of God is *p* ... Lk 16:16
*p* the gospel, the chief priests ... Lk 20:1
remission of sins should be *p* in ... Lk 24:47
which before was *p* unto you ... Acts 3:20
*p* through Jesus the resurrection ... Acts 4:2
of Samaria, and *p* Christ unto them ... Acts 8:5
*p* the word of the Lord, returned ... Acts 8:25
*p* the gospel in many villages of ... Acts 8:25
scripture, and *p* unto him Jesus ... Acts 8:35
through he *p* in all the cities ... Acts 8:40
straightway he *p* Christ in the ... Acts 9:20
how he had *p* boldly at Damascus ... Acts 9:27
after the baptism which John *p* ... Acts 10:37
they *p* the word of God in the ... Acts 13:5
When John had first *p* before his ... Acts 13:24
that through this man is *p* unto ... Acts 13:38
be *p* to them the next sabbath ... Acts 13:42
And there they *p* the gospel ... Acts 14:7
when they had *p* the gospel to ... Acts 14:21
when they had *p* the word in Perga ... Acts 14:25
we have *p* the word of the Lord ... Acts 15:36
of God was *p* of Paul at Berea ... Acts 17:13
because he *p* unto them Jesus, and ... Acts 17:18
Paul *p* unto them, ready to depart ... Acts 20:7
I have fully *p* the gospel of ... Rom 15:19
means, when I have *p* to others ... 1Cor 9:27
you the gospel which I *p* unto you ... 1Cor 15:1
keep in memory what I *p* unto you ... 1Cor 15:2
Now if Christ be *p* that he rose ... 1Cor 15:12
who was *p* among you by us, even ... 2Cor 1:19
another Jesus, whom we have not *p* ... 2Cor 11:4
because I have *p* to you the ... 2Cor 11:7
that which we have *p* unto you ... Gal 1:8
was *p* of me is not after man ... Gal 1:11
*p* before the gospel unto Abraham, ... Gal 3:8
infirmity of the flesh I *p* the ... Gal 4:13
*p* peace to you which were afar ... Eph 2:17
or in truth, Christ is *p* ... Phil 1:18
which was *p* to every creature ... Col 1:23
we *p* unto you the gospel of God ... 1Th 2:9
*p* unto the Gentiles, believed on ... 1Ti 3:16
For unto us was the gospel *p* ... Heb 4:2
but the word *p* did not profit ... Heb 4:2
first *p* entered not in because of ... Heb 4:6
unto you by them that have *p* the ... 1Pet 1:12
which by the gospel is *p* unto you ... 1Pet 1:25
*p* unto the spirits in prison ... 1Pet 3:19
*p* also to them that are dead ... 1Pet 4:6

**PREACHER**
The words of the *P*, the son of ... Eccl 1:1
Vanity of vanities, saith the *P* ... Eccl 1:2
I the *P* was king over Israel in ... Eccl 1:12
this have I found, saith the *p* ... Eccl 7:27
Vanity of vanities, saith the *p* ... Eccl 12:8
moreover, because the *p* was wise ... Eccl 12:9
The *p* sought to find out ... Eccl 12:10
how shall they hear without a *p* ... Rom 10:14
Whereunto I am ordained a *p* ... 1Ti 2:7
Whereunto I am appointed a *p* ... 2Ti 1:11
a *p* of righteousness, bringing in ... 2Pet 2:5

**PREACHEST**
thou that *p* a man should not ... Rom 2:21

**PREACHETH**
adjure you by Jesus whom Paul *p* ... Acts 19:13
if he that cometh *p* another Jesus ... 2Cor 11:4
now *p* the faith which once he ... Gal 1:23

**PREACHING**
unto it the *p* that I bid thee ... Jonah 3:2
*p* in the wilderness of Judaea, ... Mt 3:1
*p* the gospel of the kingdom, and ... Mt 4:23
*p* the gospel of the kingdom, and ... Mt 9:35
they repented at the *p* of Jonas ... Mt 12:41
*p* the gospel of the kingdom of ... Mk 1:14
*p* the baptism of repentance for ... Lk 3:3
every city and village, *p* and ... Lk 8:1
*p* the gospel, and healing every ... Lk 9:6
they repented at the *p* of Jonas ... Lk 11:32
went every where *p* the word ... Acts 8:4
*p* the things concerning the ... Acts 8:12
Israel, *p* peace by Jesus Christ ... Acts 10:36
*p* the word to none but unto the ... Acts 11:19
the Grecians, *p* the Lord Jesus ... Acts 11:20
*p* the word of the Lord, with many ... Acts 15:35
and as Paul was long *p*, he sunk ... Acts 20:9
I have gone *p* the kingdom of God ... Acts 20:25
*P* the kingdom of God, and teaching ... Acts 28:31
the *p* of Jesus Christ, according ... Rom 16:25
For the *p* of the cross is to them ... 1Cor 1:18
of *p* to save them that believe ... 1Cor 1:21
my *p* was not with enticing words ... 1Cor 2:4
be not risen, then is our *p* vain ... 1Cor 15:14
also in *p* the gospel of Christ ... 2Cor 10:14
that by me the *p* might be fully ... 2Ti 4:17
manifested his word through *p* ... Titus 1:3

**PRECEPT**
For *p* must be upon *p*, ... Is 28:10
*p* upon *p*; line upon line ... Is 28:10
LORD was unto them *p* upon *p* ... Is 28:13
*p* upon *p*; line upon line ... Is 28:13
me is taught by the *p* of men ... Is 29:13
of your heart he wrote you this *p* ... Mk 10:5
*p* to all the people according to ... Heb 9:19

**PRECEPTS**
sabbath, and commandedst them *p* ... Neh 9:14
us to keep thy *p* diligently ... Ps 119:4
I will meditate in thy *p*, and have ... Ps 119:15
me to understand the way of thy *p* ... Ps 119:27
Behold, I have longed after thy *p* ... Ps 119:40
for I seek thy *p* ... Ps 119:45
This I had, because I kept thy *p* ... Ps 119:56
thee, and of them that keep thy *p* ... Ps 119:63
keep thy *p* with my whole heart ... Ps 119:69
but I will meditate in thy *p* ... Ps 119:78
but I forsook not thy *p* ... Ps 119:87
I will never forget thy *p* ... Ps 119:93
for I have sought thy *p* ... Ps 119:94
ancients, because I keep thy *p* ... Ps 119:100
Through thy *p* I get understanding ... Ps 119:104
yet I erred not from thy *p* ... Ps 119:110
Therefore I esteem all thy *p* ... Ps 119:128
so will I keep thy *p* ... Ps 119:134
yet do not I forget thy *p* ... Ps 119:141
Consider how I love thy *p* ... Ps 119:159
I have kept thy *p* and thy ... Ps 119:168
for I have chosen thy *p* ... Ps 119:173
your father, and kept all his *p* ... Jer 35:18
even by departing from thy *p* ... Dan 9:5

**PRECIOUS**
brother and to her mother *p* things ... Gen 24:53
for the *p* things of heaven, for ... Deut 33:13
for the *p* fruits brought forth by ... Deut 33:14
for the *p* things put forth by the ... Deut 33:14
for the *p* things of the lasting ... Deut 33:15
for the *p* things of the earth and ... Deut 33:16
of the LORD was *p* in those days ... 1Sa 3:1
because my soul was *p* in thine ... 1Sa 26:21
talent of gold with the *p* stones ... 2Sa 12:30
and very much gold, and *p* stones ... 1Kin 10:2
very great store, and *p* stones ... 1Kin 10:10
of almug trees, and *p* stones ... 1Kin 10:11
thy servants, be *p* in thy sight ... 2Kin 1:13
let my life now be *p* in thy sight ... 2Kin 1:14
all the house of his *p* things ... 2Kin 20:13
the *p* ointment, and all the house ... 2Kin 20:13
there were *p* stones in it ... 1Chr 20:2
and all manner of *p* stones ... 1Chr 29:2
they with whom *p* stones were ... 1Chr 29:8
house with *p* stones for beauty ... 2Chr 3:6
and gold in abundance, and *p* stones ... 2Chr 9:1
great abundance, and *p* stones ... 2Chr 9:9
brought algum trees and *p* stones ... 2Chr 9:10
*p* jewels, which they stripped off ... 2Chr 20:25
of *p* things, with fenced cities ... 2Chr 21:3
for *p* stones, and for spices, and ... 2Chr 32:27
with *p* things, beside all that ... Ezr 1:6
vessels of fine copper, *p* as gold ... Ezr 8:27
and his eye seeth every *p* thing ... Job 28:10
gold of Ophir, with the *p* onyx ... Job 28:16
the redemption of their soul is *p* ... Ps 49:8
*p* shall their blood be in his ... Ps 72:14
*P* in the sight of the LORD is the ... Ps 116:15
forth and weepeth, bearing *p* seed ... Ps 126:6
It is like the *p* ointment upon ... Ps 133:2
How *p* also are thy thoughts unto ... Ps 139:17
We shall find all *p* substance ... Prov 1:13
She is more *p* than rubies ... Prov 3:15
will hunt for the *p* life ... Prov 6:26
substance of a diligent man is *p* ... Prov 12:27
A gift is as a *p* stone in the ... Prov 17:8
lips of knowledge are a *p* jewel ... Prov 20:15
the chambers be filled with all *p* ... Prov 24:4
name is better than *p* ointment ... Eccl 7:1
make a man more *p* than fine gold ... Is 13:12
stone, a *p* corner stone, a sure ... Is 28:16
them the house of his *p* things ... Is 39:2
the *p* ointment, and all the house ... Is 39:2
Since thou wast *p* in my sight ... Is 43:4
take forth the *p* from the vile ... Jer 15:19
all the *p* things thereof, and all ... Jer 20:5
The *p* sons of Zion, comparable to ... Lam 4:2
taken the treasure and *p* things ... Eze 22:25
in *p* clothes for chariots ... Eze 27:20
all spices, and with all *p* stones ... Eze 27:22
every *p* stone was thy covering, ... Eze 28:13
with their *p* vessels of silver and ... Dan 11:8
with *p* stones, and pleasant things ... Dan 11:38
over all the *p* things of Egypt ... Dan 11:43
alabaster box of very *p* ointment ... Mt 26:7
of ointment of spikenard very *p* ... Mk 14:3
*p* stones, wood, hay, stubble ... 1Cor 3:12
for the *p* fruit of the earth ... Jas 5:7
being much more *p* than of gold ... 1Pet 1:7
But with the *p* blood of Christ, ... 1Pet 1:19
of men, but chosen of God, and *p* ... 1Pet 2:4
a chief corner stone, elect, *p* ... 1Pet 2:6

therefore which believe he is *p* ... 1Pet 2:7
like *p* faith with us through the ... 2Pet 1:1
us exceeding great and *p* promises ... 2Pet 1:4
*p* stones and pearls, having a ... Rev 17:4
*p* stones, and of pearls, and of fine ... Rev 18:12
all manner vessels of most *p* wood ... Rev 18:12
with gold, and *p* stones, and pearls ... Rev 18:16
was like unto a stone most *p* ... Rev 21:11
with all manner of *p* stones ... Rev 21:19

**PREDESTINATE**
he also did *p* to be conformed to ... Rom 8:29
Moreover whom he did *p*, them he ... Rom 8:30

**PREDESTINATED**
Having *p* us unto the adoption of ... Eph 1:5
being *p* according to the purpose ... Eph 1:11

**PREEMINENCE**
a man hath no *p* above a beast ... Eccl 3:19
in all things he might have the *p* ... Col 1:18
loveth to have the *p* among them ... 3Jn 9

**PREFER**
if I *p* not Jerusalem above my ... Ps 137:6

**PREFERRED**
he *p* her and her maids unto the ... Est 2:9
Daniel was *p* above the presidents ... Dan 6:3
cometh after me is *p* before me ... Jn 1:15
coming after me is *p* before me ... Jn 1:27
cometh a man which is *p* before me ... Jn 1:30

**PREFERRING**
in honour *p* one another ... Rom 12:10
without *p* one before another ... 1Ti 5:21

**PREMEDITATE**
ye shall speak, neither do ye *p* ... Mk 13:11

**PREPARATION**
will therefore now make *p* for it ... 1Chr 22:5
torches in the day of his *p* ... Nah 2:3
that followed the day of the *p* ... Mt 27:62
was come, because it was the *p* ... Mk 15:42
And that day was the *p*, and the ... Lk 23:54
it was the *p* of the passover, and ... Jn 19:14
therefore, because it was the *p* ... Jn 19:31
because of the Jews' *p* day ... Jn 19:42
with the *p* of the gospel of peace ... Eph 6:15

**PREPARATIONS**
The *p* of the heart in man, and the ... Prov 16:1

**PREPARE**
I will *p* him an habitation ... Ex 15:2
shall *p* that which they bring in ... Ex 16:5
thou *p* with the burnt offering or ... Num 15:5
thou shalt *p* for a meat offering ... Num 15:6
to the number that ye shall *p* ... Num 15:12
*p* me here seven oxen and seven ... Num 23:1
*p* me here seven bullocks and seven ... Num 23:29
Thou shalt *p* thee a way, and ... Deut 19:3
people, saying, *P* you victuals ... Josh 1:11
Let us now *p* to build us an altar ... Josh 22:26
*p* your hearts unto the LORD, and ... 1Sa 7:3
*p* yet, and know and see his place ... 1Sa 23:22
*P* thy chariot, and get thee down, ... 1Kin 18:44
shewbread, to *p* it every sabbath ... 1Chr 9:32
and *p* their heart unto thee ... 1Chr 29:18
Even to *p* me timber in abundance ... 2Chr 2:9
Then Hezekiah commanded to *p* ... 2Chr 31:11
*p* yourselves by the houses of ... 2Chr 35:4
*p* your brethren, that they may do ... 2Chr 35:6
banquet that I shall *p* for them ... Est 5:8
*p* thyself to the search of their ... Job 8:8
If thou *p* thine heart, and stretch ... Job 11:13
dust, and *p* raiment as the clay ... Job 27:16
He may *p* it, but the just shall ... Job 27:17
thou wilt *p* their heart, thou ... Ps 10:17
*p* themselves without my fault ... Ps 59:4
O *p* mercy and truth, which may ... Ps 61:7
that they may *p* a city for ... Ps 107:36
*P* thy work without, and make it ... Prov 24:27
yet they *p* their meat in the ... Prov 30:25
*P* slaughter for his children for ... Is 14:21
*P* the table, watch in the ... Is 21:5
*P* ye the way of the LORD, make ... Is 40:3
workman to *p* a graven image ... Is 40:20
ye up, *p* the way, take up the ... Is 57:14
*p* ye the way of the people ... Is 62:10
that *p* a table for that troop, and ... Is 65:11
*P* ye war against her ... Jer 6:4
*p* them for the day of slaughter ... Jer 12:3
I will *p* destroyers against thee, ... Jer 22:7
say ye, Stand fast, and *p* thee ... Jer 46:14
up the watchmen, *p* the ambushes ... Jer 51:12
*p* the nations against her, call ... Jer 51:27
*P* against her the nations with ... Jer 51:28
thou shalt *p* thy bread therewith ... Eze 4:15
*p* thee stuff for removing, and ... Eze 12:3
I will *p* thee unto blood, and ... Eze 35:6
*p* for thyself, thou, and all thy ... Eze 38:7
Seven days shalt thou *p* every day ... Eze 43:25
they shall also *p* a young bullock ... Eze 43:25
he shall *p* the sin offering, and ... Eze 45:17
shall the prince *p* for himself ... Eze 45:22
days of the feast he shall *p* a ... Eze 45:23
he shall *p* a meat offering of an ... Eze 45:24
the priests shall *p* his burnt ... Eze 46:2
he shall *p* a meat offering, an ... Eze 46:7
Now when the prince shall *p* a ... Eze 46:12
he shall *p* his burnt offering and ... Eze 46:12
Thou shalt daily *p* a burnt ... Eze 46:13
thou shalt *p* it every morning ... Eze 46:13
thou shalt *p* a meat offering for ... Eze 46:14
Thus shall they *p* the lamb ... Eze 46:15
*P* war, wake up the mighty men, ... Joel 3:9
*p* to meet thy God, O Israel ... Amos 4:12
they even *p* war against him ... Mic 3:5
he shall *p* the way before me ... Mal 3:1
*P* ye the way of the Lord, make ... Mt 3:3
which shall *p* thy way before thee ... Mt 11:10
Where wilt thou that we *p* for ... Mt 26:17
which shall *p* thy way before thee ... Mk 1:2
*P* ye the way of the Lord, make ... Mk 1:3
*p* that thou mayest eat the ... Mk 14:12
face of the Lord to *p* his ways ... Lk 1:76
*P* ye the way of the Lord, make ... Lk 3:4
which shall *p* thy way before thee ... Lk 7:27
*p* us the passover, that we may ... Lk 22:8
him, Where wilt thou that we *p* ... Lk 22:9
I go to *p* a place for you ... Jn 14:2
*p* a place for you, I will come ... Jn 14:3
who shall *p* himself to the battle ... 1Cor 14:8
But withal *p* me also a lodging ... Philem 22

**PREPARED**
for I have *p* the house, and room ... Gen 24:31
and the bread, which she had *p* ... Gen 27:17
neither had they *p* for themselves ... Ex 12:39
into the place which I have *p* ... Ex 23:20
the city of Sihon be built and *p* ... Num 21:27
I have *p* seven altars, and I have ... Num 23:4
whom he had *p* of the children of ... Josh 4:4
About forty thousand *p* for war ... Josh 4:13
this, that Absalom *p* him chariots ... 2Sa 15:1
he *p* him chariots and horsemen, and ... 1Kin 1:5
so they *p* timber and stones to ... 1Kin 5:18
the oracle he *p* in the house ... 1Kin 6:19
he *p* great provision for them ... 2Kin 6:23
for their brethren had *p* for them ... 1Chr 12:39
*p* a place for the ark of God, and ... 1Chr 15:1
his place, which he had *p* for it ... 1Chr 15:3
the place that I have *p* for it ... 1Chr 15:12
David *p* iron in abundance for the ... 1Chr 22:3
So David *p* abundantly before his ... 1Chr 22:5
in my trouble I have *p* for the ... 1Chr 22:14
timber also and stone have I *p* ... 1Chr 22:14
Now I have *p* with all my might ... 1Chr 29:2
that I have *p* for the holy house ... 1Chr 29:3
have *p* to build thee an house for ... 1Chr 29:16
place which David had *p* for it ... 2Chr 1:4
in the place that David had *p* in ... 2Chr 3:1
*p* unto the day of the foundation ... 2Chr 8:16
because he *p* not his heart to ... 2Chr 12:14
divers kinds of spices *p* by the ... 2Chr 16:14
thousand ready *p* for the war ... 2Chr 17:18
hast *p* thine heart to seek God ... 2Chr 19:3
*p* their hearts unto the God of ... 2Chr 20:33
Uzziah *p* for them throughout all ... 2Chr 26:14
because he *p* his ways before the ... 2Chr 27:6
in his transgression, have we *p* ... 2Chr 29:19
people, that God had *p* the people ... 2Chr 29:36
and they *p* them, ... 2Chr 31:11
So the service was *p*, and the ... 2Chr 35:10
the Levites *p* for themselves ... 2Chr 35:14
brethren the Levites *p* for them ... 2Chr 35:15
of the LORD was *p* the same day ... 2Chr 35:16
when Josiah had *p* the temple ... 2Chr 35:20
For Ezra had *p* his heart to seek ... Ezr 7:10
Now that which was *p* for me daily ... Neh 5:18
also fowls were *p* for me, and once ... Neh 5:18
unto them for whom nothing is *p* ... Neh 8:10
he had *p* for him a great chamber, ... Neh 13:5
the banquet that I have *p* for him ... Est 5:4
to the banquet that Esther had *p* ... Est 5:5
banquet that she had *p* but myself ... Est 5:12
the gallows that he had *p* for him ... Est 6:4
the banquet that Esther had *p* ... Est 6:14
that he had *p* for Mordecai ... Est 7:10
he *p* it, yea, and searched it out ... Job 28:27
when I *p* my seat in the street ... Job 29:7
He hath also *p* for him the ... Ps 7:13
he hath *p* his throne for judgment ... Ps 9:7
They have *p* a net for my steps ... Ps 57:6
hast *p* of thy goodness for the ... Ps 68:10
thou hast *p* the light and the sun ... Ps 74:16
The LORD hath *p* his throne in the ... Ps 103:19
When he *p* the heavens, I was ... Prov 8:27
Judgments are *p* for scorners ... Prov 19:29
The horse is *p* against the day of ... Prov 21:31
yea, for the king it is *p* ... Is 30:33
what he hath *p* for him that ... Is 64:4
a table *p* before it, whereupon ... Eze 23:41
of thy pipes was *p* in thee in the ... Eze 28:13
Be thou *p*, and prepare for thyself ... Eze 38:7
for ye have *p* lying and corrupt ... Dan 2:9
and gold, which they *p* for Baal ... Hos 2:8
going forth is *p* as the morning ... Hos 6:3
Now the LORD had *p* a great fish ... Jonah 1:17
And the LORD God *p* a gourd ... Jonah 4:6
But God *p* a worm when the morning ... Jonah 4:7
that God *p* a vehement east wind ... Jonah 4:8
and the defence shall be *p* ... Nah 2:5
for the LORD hath *p* a sacrifice ... Zeph 1:7
for whom it is *p* of my Father ... Mt 20:23
Behold, I have *p* my dinner ... Mt 22:4
inherit the kingdom *p* for you ... Mt 25:34
*p* for the devil and his angels ... Mt 25:41
be given to them for whom it is *p* ... Mk 10:40
a large upper room furnished and *p* ... Mk 14:15
ready a people *p* for the Lord ... Lk 1:17
Which thou hast *p* before the face ... Lk 2:31
*p* not himself, neither did ... Lk 12:47
and *p* spices and ointments ... Lk 23:56
the spices which they had *p* ... Lk 24:1
which he had afore *p* unto glory ... Rom 9:23
God hath *p* for them that love him ... 1Cor 2:9
use, and *p* unto every good work ... 2Ti 2:21
not, but a body hast thou *p* me ... Heb 10:5
*p* an ark to the saving of his ... Heb 11:7
for he hath *p* for them a city ... Heb 11:16
trumpets *p* themselves to sound ... Rev 8:6
like unto horses *p* unto battle ... Rev 9:7
which were *p* for an hour, and a ... Rev 9:15
where she hath a place *p* of God ... Rev 12:6
the kings of the east might be *p* ... Rev 16:12
*p* as a bride adorned for her ... Rev 21:2

**PREPAREDST**
Thou *p* room before it, and didst ... Ps 80:9

**PREPAREST**
when thou *p* a bullock for a burnt ... Num 15:8
Thou *p* a table before me in the ... Ps 23:5
thou *p* them corn, when thou hast ... Ps 65:9

**PREPARETH**
That *p* his heart to seek God, the ... 2Chr 30:19
vanity, and their belly *p* deceit ... Job 15:35
who *p* rain for the earth, who ... Ps 147:8

**PREPARING**
in *p* him a chamber in the courts ... Neh 13:7
of Noah, while the ark was a *p* ... 1Pet 3:20

**PRESBYTERY**
laying on of the hands of the *p* ... 1Ti 4:14

**PRESCRIBED**
grievousness which they have *p* ... Is 10:1

**PRESCRIBING**
oil, and salt without *p* how much ... Ezr 7:22

**PRESENCE**
the *p* of the LORD God amongst the ... Gen 3:8
went out from the *p* of the LORD ... Gen 4:16
in the *p* of all his brethren ... Gen 16:12
in the *p* of the sons of my people ... Gen 23:11
in the *p* of the children of Heth ... Gen 23:18
he died in the *p* of all his ... Gen 25:18
from the *p* of Isaac his father ... Gen 27:30
went out from the *p* of Pharaoh ... Gen 41:46
for they were troubled at his *p* ... Gen 45:3
for why should we die in thy *p* ... Gen 47:15
were driven out from Pharaoh's *p* ... Ex 10:11
My *p* shall go with thee, and I ... Ex 33:14
If thy *p* go not with me, carry us ... Ex 33:15
departed from the *p* of Moses ... Ex 35:20
soul shall be cut off from my *p* ... Lev 22:3
Aaron went from the *p* of the ... Num 20:6
unto him in the *p* of the elders ... Deut 25:9
priests, in the *p* of the people ... Josh 4:11
which he wrote in the *p* of twice ... Josh 8:32
David avoided out of his *p* twice ... 1Sa 18:11
David to Saul, and he was in his *p* ... 1Sa 19:7
he slipped away out of Saul's *p* ... 1Sa 19:10
to play the mad man in my *p* ... 1Sa 21:15
I not serve in the *p* of his son ... 2Sa 16:19
I have served in thy father's *p* ... 2Sa 16:19
so will I be in thy *p* ... 2Sa 16:19
went out from the *p* of the king ... 2Sa 24:4
And she came into the king's *p* ... 1Kin 1:28
the *p* of all the congregation of ... 1Kin 8:22
fled from the *p* of king Solomon ... 1Kin 12:2
in the *p* of the people, saying, ... 1Kin 21:13
the *p* of Jehoshaphat the king of ... 2Kin 3:14
he went out from his *p* a leper as ... 2Kin 5:27
cast he them from his *p* as yet ... 2Kin 13:23
he had cast them out from his *p* ... 2Kin 24:20
of them that were in the king's *p* ... 2Kin 25:19
Glory and honour are in his *p* ... 1Chr 16:27
sing out at the *p* of the LORD ... 1Chr 16:33
Aaron in the *p* of David the king ... 1Chr 24:31
the *p* of all the congregation of ... 2Chr 6:12
the earth sought the *p* of Solomon ... 2Chr 9:23
from the *p* of Solomon the king ... 2Chr 10:2
before this house, and in thy *p* ... 2Chr 20:9
the altars of Baalim in his *p* ... 2Chr 34:4
not been beforetime sad in his *p* ... Neh 2:1
in the *p* of Ahasuerus the king ... Est 1:10
Mordecai went out from the *p* of ... Est 8:15
went forth from the *p* of the LORD ... Job 1:12
forth from the *p* of the LORD ... Job 2:7
Therefore am I troubled at his *p* ... Job 23:15
shall fall and perish at thy *p* ... Ps 9:3
in thy *p* is fulness of joy ... Ps 16:11
my sentence come forth from thy *p* ... Ps 17:2
me in the *p* of mine enemies ... Ps 23:5
of thy *p* from the pride of man ... Ps 31:20
Cast me not away from thy *p* ... Ps 51:11
the wicked perish at the *p* of God ... Ps 68:2
also dropped at the *p* of God ... Ps 68:8
itself was moved at the *p* of God ... Ps 68:8
before his *p* with thanksgiving ... Ps 95:2
like wax at the *p* of the LORD ... Ps 97:5
at the *p* of the LORD of the whole ... Ps 97:5
come before his *p* with singing ... Ps 100:2
at the *p* of the Lord ... Ps 114:7
at the *p* of the God of Jacob ... Ps 114:7
now in the *p* of all his people ... Ps 116:14
now in the *p* of all his people ... Ps 116:18
whither shall I flee from thy *p* ... Ps 139:7
the upright shall dwell in thy *p* ... Ps 140:13
Go from the *p* of a foolish man, ... Prov 14:7
surety in the *p* of his friend ... Prov 17:18
thyself in the *p* of the king ... Prov 25:6
*p* of the prince whom thine eyes ... Prov 25:7

strangers devour it in your *p* ........ Is 1:7
of Egypt shall be moved at his *p* ........ Is 19:1
and the angel of his *p* saved them ........ Is 63:9
might flow down at thy *p*, ........ Is 64:1
the nations may tremble at thy *p* ........ Is 64:2
mountains flowed down at thy *p* ........ Is 64:3
broken down at the *p* of the LORD ........ Jer 4:26
will ye not tremble at my *p* ........ Jer 5:22
fathers, and cast you out of my *p* ........ Jer 23:39
in the *p* of the priests and of all ........ Jer 28:1
Hananiah in the *p* of the priests ........ Jer 28:5
in the *p* of all the people that ........ Jer 28:5
spake in the *p* of all the people ........ Jer 28:11
in the *p* of the witnesses that ........ Jer 32:12
he had cast them out from his *p* ........ Jer 52:3
of the earth, shall shake at my *p* ........ Eze 38:20
answered in the *p* of the king ........ Dan 2:27
Tarshish from the *p* of the LORD ........ Jonah 1:3
Tarshish from the *p* of the LORD ........ Jonah 1:3
he fled from the *p* of the LORD ........ Jonah 1:10
and the earth is burned at his *p* ........ Nah 1:5
peace at the *p* of the Lord GOD ........ Zeph 1:7
that stand in the *p* of God ........ Lk 1:19
We have eaten and drunk in thy *p* ........ Lk 13:26
*p* of them that sit at meat with ........ Lk 14:10
there is joy in the *p* of the ........ Lk 15:10
Jesus in the *p* of his disciples ........ Jn 20:30
and denied him in the *p* of Pilate ........ Acts 3:13
soundness in the *p* of you all ........ Acts 3:16
shall come from the *p* of the Lord ........ Acts 3:19
from the *p* of the council ........ Acts 5:41
thanks to God in *p* of them all ........ Acts 27:35
no flesh should glory in his *p* ........ 1Cor 1:29
who in *p* am base among you, but ........ 2Cor 10:1
but his bodily *p* is weak, and his ........ 2Cor 10:10
obeyed, not as in my *p* only ........ Phil 2:12
from you for a short time in *p* ........ 1Th 2:17
Are not even ye in the *p* of our ........ 1Th 2:19
from the *p* of the Lord, and from ........ 2Th 1:9
to appear in the *p* of God for us ........ Heb 9:24
you faultless before the *p* of his ........ Jude 24
brimstone in the *p* of the holy ........ Rev 14:10
angels, and in the *p* of the Lamb ........ Rev 14:10

**PRESENT**
his hand a *p* for Esau his brother ........ Gen 32:13
it is a *p* sent unto my lord Esau ........ Gen 32:18
with the *p* that goeth before me ........ Gen 32:20
So went the *p* over before him ........ Gen 32:21
then receive my *p* at my hand ........ Gen 33:10
and carry down the man a *p* ........ Gen 43:11
And the men took that *p*, and they ........ Gen 43:15
they made ready the *p* against ........ Gen 43:25
they brought him the *p* which was ........ Gen 43:26
*p* thyself there to me in the top ........ Ex 34:2
*p* the man that is to be made ........ Lev 14:11
*p* them before the LORD at the ........ Lev 16:7
then he shall *p* himself before ........ Lev 27:8
then he shall *p* the beast before ........ Lev 27:11
*p* them before Aaron the priest, ........ Num 3:6
*p* yourselves in the tabernacle of ........ Deut 31:14
a *p* unto Eglon the king of Moab ........ Judg 3:15
he brought the *p* unto Eglon king ........ Judg 3:17
he had made an end to offer the *p* ........ Judg 3:18
away the people that bare the *p* ........ Judg 3:18
unto thee, and bring forth my *p* ........ Judg 6:18
there is not a *p* to bring to the ........ 1Sa 9:7
Now therefore *p* yourselves before ........ 1Sa 10:19
the people that were *p* with him ........ 1Sa 13:15
the people that were *p* with them ........ 1Sa 13:16
in mine hand, or what there is *p* ........ 1Sa 21:3
Behold a *p* for you of the spoil ........ 1Sa 30:26
three days, and be thou here *p* ........ 2Sa 20:4
given it for a *p* unto his ........ 1Kin 9:16
And they brought every man his *p* ........ 1Kin 10:25
have sent unto thee a *p* of silver ........ 1Kin 15:19
were numbered, and were all *p* ........ 1Kin 20:27
Take a *p* in thine hand, and go, ........ 2Kin 8:8
took a *p* with him, even of every ........ 2Kin 8:9
sent it for a *p* to the king of ........ 2Kin 16:8
brought no *p* to the king of ........ 2Kin 17:4
Make an agreement with me by a *p* ........ 2Kin 18:31
sent letters and a *p* unto Hezekiah ........ 2Kin 20:12
joy thy people, which are *p* here ........ 1Chr 29:17
that were *p* were sanctified ........ 2Chr 5:11
And they brought every man his *p* ........ 2Chr 9:24
all that were *p* with him bowed ........ 2Chr 29:29
children of Israel that were *p* at ........ 2Chr 30:21
all Israel that were *p* went out ........ 2Chr 31:1
all that were *p* in Jerusalem ........ 2Chr 34:32
that were *p* in Israel to serve ........ 2Chr 34:33
offerings, for all that were *p* ........ 2Chr 35:7
children of Israel that were *p* ........ 2Chr 35:17
all Judah and Israel that were *p* ........ 2Chr 35:18
his lords, and all Israel there *p* ........ Ezr 8:25
that were *p* in Shushan the palace ........ Est 1:5
the Jews that are *p* in Shushan ........ Est 4:16
to *p* themselves before the LORD ........ Job 1:6
to *p* themselves before the LORD ........ Job 2:1
them to *p* himself before the LORD ........ Job 2:1
a very *p* help in trouble ........ Ps 46:1
In that time shall the *p* be ........ Is 18:7
Make an agreement with me by a *p* ........ Is 36:16
sent letters and a *p* to Hezekiah ........ Is 39:1
It may be they will *p* their ........ Jer 36:7
unto whom ye sent me to *p* your ........ Jer 42:9
thee for a *p* horns of ivory ........ Eze 27:15
for we do not *p* our supplications ........ Dan 9:18
Assyria for a *p* to king Jareb ........ Hos 10:6
Jerusalem, to *p* him to the Lord ........ Lk 2:22
of the Lord was *p* to heal them ........ Lk 5:17
There were *p* at that season some ........ Lk 13:1
manifold more in this *p* time ........ Lk 18:30
unto you, being yet *p* with you ........ Jn 14:25
are we all here *p* before God ........ Acts 10:33
and all the elders were *p* ........ Acts 21:18
all men which are here *p* with us ........ Acts 25:24
every one, because of the *p* rain ........ Acts 28:2
for to will is *p* with me ........ Rom 7:18
would do good, evil is *p* with me ........ Rom 7:21
this *p* time are not worthy to be ........ Rom 8:18
nor powers, nor things *p* ........ Rom 8:38
Even so then at this *p* time also ........ Rom 11:5
that ye *p* your bodies a living ........ Rom 12:1
or life, or death, or things *p* ........ 1Cor 3:22
Even unto this *p* hour we both ........ 1Cor 4:11
but *p* in spirit, have judged ........ 1Cor 5:3
already, as though I were *p* ........ 1Cor 5:3
this is good for the *p* distress ........ 1Cor 7:26
greater part remain unto this *p* ........ 1Cor 15:6
by Jesus, and shall *p* us with you ........ 2Cor 4:14
body, and to be *p* with the Lord ........ 2Cor 5:8
whether *p* or absent, we may be ........ 2Cor 5:9
when I am *p* with that confidence ........ 2Cor 10:2
we be also in deed when we are *p* ........ 2Cor 10:11
that I may *p* you as a chaste ........ 2Cor 11:2
And when I was *p* with you, and ........ 2Cor 11:9
and foretell you, as if I were *p* ........ 2Cor 13:2
lest being *p* I should use ........ 2Cor 13:10
deliver us from this *p* evil world ........ Gal 1:4
and not only when I am *p* with you ........ Gal 4:18
I desire to be *p* with you now ........ Gal 4:20
That he might *p* it to himself a ........ Eph 5:27
to *p* you holy and unblameable and ........ Col 1:22
that we may *p* every man perfect ........ Col 1:28
me, having loved this *p* world ........ 2Ti 4:10
and godly, in this *p* world ........ Titus 2:12
was a figure for the time then *p* ........ Heb 9:9
for the *p* seemeth to be joyous ........ Heb 12:11
and be established in the *p* truth ........ 2Pet 1:12
to *p* you faultless before the ........ Jude 24

**PRESENTED**
to Goshen, and *p* himself unto him ........ Gen 46:29
five men, and *p* them unto Pharaoh ........ Gen 47:2
when it is *p* unto the priest, he ........ Lev 2:8
in the day when he *p* them to ........ Lev 7:35
Aaron's sons *p* unto him the blood ........ Lev 9:12
they *p* the burnt offering unto ........ Lev 9:13
Aaron's sons *p* unto him the blood ........ Lev 9:18
shall be *p* alive before the LORD, ........ Lev 16:10
*p* themselves in the tabernacle of ........ Deut 31:14
they *p* themselves before God ........ Josh 24:1
unto him under the oak, and *p* it ........ Judg 6:19
*p* themselves in the assembly of ........ Judg 20:2
evening, and *p* himself forty days ........ 1Sa 17:16
I *p* my supplication before the ........ Jer 38:26
there they *p* the provocation of ........ Eze 20:28
treasures, they *p* unto him gifts ........ Mt 2:11
the saints and widows, *p* her alive ........ Acts 9:41
governor, *p* Paul also before him ........ Acts 23:33

**PRESENTING**
*p* my supplication before the LORD ........ Dan 9:20

**PRESENTLY**
them not fail to burn the fat *p* ........ 1Sa 2:16
A fool's wrath is *p* known ........ Prov 12:16
*p* the fig tree withered away ........ Mt 21:19
he shall *p* give me more than ........ Mt 26:53
Him therefore I hope to send *p* ........ Phil 2:23

**PRESENTS**
despised him, and brought him no *p* ........ 1Sa 10:27
they brought *p*, and served Solomon ........ 1Kin 4:21
became his servant, and gave him *p* ........ 2Kin 17:3
Judah brought to Jehoshaphat *p* ........ 2Chr 17:5
Philistines brought Jehoshaphat *p* ........ 2Chr 17:11
*p* to Hezekiah king of Judah ........ 2Chr 32:23
shall kings bring *p* unto thee ........ Ps 68:29
and of the isles shall bring *p* ........ Ps 72:10
bring *p* unto him that ought to be ........ Ps 76:11
thou give *p* to Moresheth-gath ........ Mic 1:14

**PRESERVE**
that we may *p* seed of our father ........ Gen 19:32
that we may *p* seed of our father ........ Gen 19:34
did send me before you to *p* life ........ Gen 45:5
God sent me before you to *p* you a ........ Gen 45:7
always, that he might *p* us alive ........ Deut 6:24
thou shalt *p* them from this ........ Ps 12:7
*P* me, O God ........ Ps 16:1
Let integrity and uprightness *p* me ........ Ps 25:21
thou shalt *p* me from trouble ........ Ps 32:7
and thy truth continually *p* me ........ Ps 40:11
The LORD will *p* him, and keep him ........ Ps 41:2
mercy and truth, which may *p* him ........ Ps 61:7
*p* my life from fear of the enemy ........ Ps 64:1
*p* thou those that are appointed ........ Ps 79:11
*P* my soul ........ Ps 86:2
The LORD shall *p* thee from all ........ Ps 121:7
he shall *p* thy soul ........ Ps 121:7
The LORD shall *p* thy going out ........ Ps 121:8
*p* me from the violent man ........ Ps 140:1
*p* me from the violent man ........ Ps 140:4
Discretion shall *p* thee, ........ Prov 2:11
her not, and she shall *p* thee ........ Prov 4:6
the lips of the wise shall *p* them ........ Prov 14:3
Mercy and truth *p* the king ........ Prov 20:28
The eyes of the LORD *p* knowledge ........ Prov 22:12
and passing over he will *p* it ........ Is 31:5
and I will *p* thee, and give thee ........ Is 49:8
children, I will *p* them alive ........ Jer 49:11
shall lose his life shall *p* it ........ Lk 17:33
will *p* me unto his heavenly ........ 2Ti 4:18

**PRESERVED**
God face to face, and my life is *p* ........ Gen 32:30
*p* us in all the way wherein we ........ Josh 24:17
LORD hath given us, who hath *p* us ........ 1Sa 30:23
the LORD *p* David whithersoever he ........ 2Sa 8:6
the LORD *p* David whithersoever he ........ 2Sa 8:14
Thus the LORD *p* David ........ 1Chr 18:6
Thus the LORD *p* David ........ 1Chr 18:13
thy visitation hath *p* my spirit ........ Job 10:12
as in the days when God *p* me ........ Job 29:2
they are *p* for ever ........ Ps 37:28
and to restore the *p* of Israel ........ Is 49:6
Egypt, and by a prophet was he *p* ........ Hos 12:13
into new bottles, and both are *p* ........ Mt 9:17
and both are *p* ........ Lk 5:38
body be *p* blameless unto the ........ 1Th 5:23
*p* in Jesus Christ, and called ........ Jude 1

**PRESERVER**
I do unto thee, O thou *p* of men ........ Job 7:20

**PRESERVEST**
is therein, and thou *p* them all ........ Neh 9:6
O LORD, thou *p* man and beast ........ Ps 36:6

**PRESERVETH**
He *p* not the life of the wicked ........ Job 36:6
for the LORD *p* the faithful ........ Ps 31:23
he *p* the souls of his saints ........ Ps 97:10
The LORD *p* the simple ........ Ps 116:6
The LORD *p* all them that love him ........ Ps 145:20
The LORD *p* the strangers ........ Ps 146:9
and *p* the way of his saints ........ Prov 2:8
that keepeth his way *p* his soul ........ Prov 16:17

**PRESIDENTS**
And over these three *p* ........ Dan 6:2
Daniel was preferred above the *p* ........ Dan 6:3
Then the *p* and princes sought to ........ Dan 6:4
Then these *p* and princes assembled ........ Dan 6:6
All the *p* of the kingdom, the ........ Dan 6:7

**PRESS**
for the *p* is full, the fats ........ Joel 3:13
out fifty vessels out of the *p* ........ Hag 2:16
not come nigh unto him for the *p* ........ Mk 2:4
of Jesus, came in the *p* behind ........ Mk 5:27
of him, turned him about in the *p* ........ Mk 5:30
could not come at him for the *p* ........ Lk 8:19
*p* thee, and sayest thou, Who ........ Lk 8:45
and could not for the *p*, because ........ Lk 19:3
I *p* toward the mark for the prize ........ Phil 3:14

**PRESSED**
And he *p* upon them greatly ........ Gen 19:3
they *p* sore upon the man, even ........ Gen 19:9
*p* them into Pharaoh's cup, and I ........ Gen 40:11
when she *p* him daily with her ........ Judg 16:16
And he *p* him ........ 2Sa 13:25
But Absalom *p* him, that he let ........ 2Sa 13:27
*p* on by the king's commandment ........ Est 8:14
there were their breasts *p* ........ Eze 23:3
I am *p* under you, as a cart is ........ Amos 2:13
as a cart is *p* that is full of ........ Amos 2:13
insomuch that they *p* upon him for ........ Mk 3:10
as the people *p* upon him to hear ........ Lk 5:1
*p* down, and shaken together, and ........ Lk 6:38
Paul was *p* in the spirit, and ........ Acts 18:5
that we were *p* out of measure, ........ 2Cor 1:8

**PRESSES**
thy *p* shall burst out with new ........ Prov 3:10
tread out no wine in their *p* ........ Is 16:10

**PRESSETH**
fast in me, and thy hand *p* me sore ........ Ps 38:2
preached, and every man *p* into it ........ Lk 16:16

**PRESSFAT**
when one came to the *p* for to ........ Hag 2:16

**PRESUME**
which shall *p* to speak a word in ........ Deut 18:20
that durst *p* in his heart to do ........ Est 7:5

**PRESUMED**
But they *p* to go up unto the hill ........ Num 14:44

**PRESUMPTUOUS**
back thy servant also from *p* sins ........ Ps 19:13
*P* are they, selfwilled, they are ........ 2Pet 2:10

**PRESUMPTUOUSLY**
But if a man come *p* upon his ........ Ex 21:14
But the soul that doeth ought *p* ........ Num 15:30
LORD, and went *p* up into the hill ........ Deut 1:43
And the man that will do *p* ........ Deut 17:12
hear, and fear, and do no more *p* ........ Deut 17:13
but the prophet hath spoken it *p* ........ Deut 18:22

**PRETENCE**
and for a *p* make long prayer ........ Mt 23:14
for a *p* make long prayers ........ Mk 12:40
every way, whether in *p*, or in ........ Phil 1:18

**PREVAIL**
cubits upward did the waters *p* ........ Gen 7:20
peradventure I shall *p*, that we ........ Num 22:6
what means we may *p* against him ........ Judg 16:5
for by strength shall no man *p* ........ 1Sa 2:9
but if I *p* against him, and kill ........ 1Sa 17:9
things, and also shalt still *p* ........ 1Sa 26:25
shalt persuade him, and *p* also ........ 1Kin 22:22
let not man *p* against thee ........ 2Chr 14:11
entice him, and thou shalt also *p* ........ 2Chr 18:21

thou shalt not p against him Est 6:13
they shall p against him, as a Job 15:24
and the robber shall p against him Job 18:9
let not man p Ps 9:19
said, With our tongue will we p Ps 12:4
Iniquities p against me Ps 65:3
if one p against him, two shall Eccl 4:12
it, but could not p against it Is 7:1
but he shall not p Is 16:12
he shall p against his enemies Is 42:13
to profit, if so be thou mayest p Is 47:12
but they shall not p against thee Jer 1:19
themselves, yet can they not p Jer 5:22
but they shall not p against thee Jer 15:20
we shall p against him, and we Jer 20:10
stumble, and they shall not p Jer 20:11
deal against them, and shall p Dan 11:7
of hell shall not p against it Mt 16:18
saw that he could p nothing Mt 27:24
Perceive ye how ye p nothing Jn 12:19

**PREVAILED**

And the waters p, and were Gen 7:18
the waters p exceedingly upon the Gen 7:19
the waters p upon the earth an Gen 7:24
with my sister, and I have p Gen 30:8
he saw that he p not against him Gen 32:25
with God and with men, and hast p Gen 32:28
because the famine p over them Gen 47:20
have p above the blessings of my Gen 49:26
held up his hand, that Israel p Ex 17:11
he let down his hand, Amalek p Ex 17:11
the hand of the house of Joseph p Judg 1:35
and his hand p against Judg 3:10
p against Jabin the king of Judg 4:24
hand of Midian p against Israel Judg 6:2
So David p over the Philistine 1Sa 17:50
Surely the men p against us 2Sa 11:23
the king's word p against Joab 2Sa 24:4
Omri p against the people that 1Kin 16:22
month the famine p in the city 2Kin 25:3
For Judah p above his brethren, 1Chr 5:2
the king's word p against Joab 1Chr 21:4
to Hamath-zobah, and p against it 2Chr 8:3
time, and the children of Judah p 2Chr 13:18
the Ammonites, and p against them 2Chr 27:5
enemy say, I have p against him Ps 13:4
yet they have not p against me Ps 129:2
art stronger than I, and hast p Jer 20:7
thee on, and have p against thee Jer 38:22
are desolate, because the enemy p Lam 1:16
the saints, and p against them Dan 7:21
he had power over the angel, and p Hos 12:4
deceived thee, and p against thee Obad 7
of them and of the chief priests p Lk 23:23
p against them, so that they fled Acts 19:16
grew the word of God and p Acts 19:20
hath p to open the book, and to Rev 5:5
And p not Rev 12:8

**PREVAILEST**

Thou p for ever against him, and Job 14:20

**PREVAILETH**

my bones, and it p against them Lam 1:13

**PREVENT**

Why did the knees p me Job 3:12
The God of my mercy shall p me Ps 59:10
thy tender mercies speedily p us Ps 79:8
morning shall my prayer p thee Ps 88:13
Mine eyes p the night watches, Ps 119:148
evil shall not overtake nor p us Amos 9:10
shall not p them which are asleep 1Th 4:15

**PREVENTED**

the snares of death p me 2Sa 22:6
They p me in the day of my 2Sa 22:19
the days of affliction p me Job 30:27
Who hath p me, that I should Job 41:11
the snares of death p me Ps 18:5
They p me in the day of my Ps 18:18
I p the dawning of the morning, Ps 119:147
they p with their bread him that Is 21:14
come into the house, Jesus p him Mt 17:25

**PREVENTEST**

For thou p him with the blessings Ps 21:3

**PREY**

from the p, my son, thou art gone Gen 49:9
the morning he shall devour the p Gen 49:27
and our children should be a p Num 14:3
ones, which ye said should be a p Num 14:31
lie down until he eat of the p Num 23:24
took all the spoil, and all the p Num 31:11
brought the captives, and the p Num 31:12
the sum of the p that was taken Num 31:26
divide the p into two parts Num 31:27
being the rest of the p which the Num 31:32
ones, which ye said should be a p Deut 1:39
we took for a p unto ourselves Deut 2:35
we took for a p to ourselves Deut 3:7
ye take for a p unto yourselves Josh 8:2
took for a p unto themselves Josh 8:27
took for a p unto themselves Josh 11:14
have they not divided the p Judg 5:30
to Sisera a p of divers colours, Judg 5:30
a p of divers colours of Judg 5:30
every man the earrings of his p Judg 8:24
every man the earrings of his p Judg 8:25
and they shall become a p and a 2Kin 21:14
give them for a p in the land of Neh 4:4
to take the spoil of them for a p Est 3:13
to take the spoil of them for a p Est 8:11
but on the p they laid not their Est 9:15
laid not their hands on the p Est 9:16
old lion perisheth for lack of p Job 4:11
the eagle that hasteth to the p Job 9:26
rising betimes for a p Job 24:5
Wilt thou hunt the p for the lion Job 38:39
From thence she seeketh the p Job 39:29
as a lion that is greedy of his p Ps 17:12
excellent than the mountains of p Ps 76:4
young lions roar after their p Ps 104:21
given us as a p to their teeth Ps 124:6
She also lieth in wait as for a p Prov 23:28
shall roar, and lay hold of the p Is 5:29
that widows may be their p Is 10:2
take the spoil, and to take the p Is 10:6
the young lion roaring on his p Is 31:4
then is the p of a great spoil Is 33:23
the lame take the p Is 33:23
they are for a p, and none Is 42:22
Shall the p be taken from the Is 49:24
the p of the terrible shall be Is 49:25
from evil maketh himself a p Is 59:15
life shall be unto him for a p Jer 21:9
all that p upon thee will I give Jer 30:16
upon thee will I give for a p Jer 30:16
he shall have his life for a p Jer 38:2
life shall be for a p unto thee Jer 39:18
a p in all places whither thou Jer 45:5
hands of the strangers for a p Eze 7:21
and it learned to catch the p Eze 19:3
lion, and learned to catch the p Eze 19:6
a roaring lion ravening the p Eze 22:25
are like wolves ravening the p Eze 22:27
make a p of thy merchandise Eze 26:12
and take her spoil, and take her p Eze 29:19
because my flock became a p Eze 34:8
and they shall no more be a p Eze 34:22
no more be a p to the heathen Eze 34:28
are forsaken, which became a p Eze 36:4
minds, to cast it out for a p Eze 36:5
To take a spoil, and to take a p Eze 38:12
gathered thy company to take a p Eze 38:13
he shall scatter among them the p Dan 11:24
in the forest, when he hath no p Amos 3:4
and filled his holes with p Nah 2:12
will cut off thy p from the earth Nah 2:13
the p departeth not Nah 3:1
the day that I rise up to the p Zeph 3:8

**PRICE**

thou shalt increase the p thereof Lev 25:16
thou shalt diminish the p of it Lev 25:16
the p of his sale shall be Lev 25:50
p of his redemption out of the Lev 25:51
him again the p of his redemption Lev 25:52
or the p of a dog, into the house Deut 23:18
will surely buy it of thee at a p 2Sa 24:24
received the linen yarn at a p 1Kin 10:28
shalt grant it me for the full p 1Chr 21:22
will verily buy it for the full p 1Chr 21:24
received the linen yarn at a p 2Chr 1:16
Man knoweth not the p thereof Job 28:13
be weighed for the p thereof Job 28:15
for the p of wisdom is above Job 28:18
increase thy wealth by their p Ps 44:12
Wherefore is there a p in the Prov 17:16
the goats are the p of the field Prov 27:26
for her p is far above rubies Prov 31:10
not for p nor reward, saith the Is 45:13
milk without money and without p Is 55:1
I give to the spoil without p Jer 15:13
If ye think good, give me my p Zec 11:12
So they weighed for my p thirty Zec 11:12
a goodly p that I was prised at Zec 11:13
he had found one pearl of great p Mt 13:46
because it is the p of blood Mt 27:6
the p of him that was valued, Mt 27:9
And kept back part of the p Acts 5:2
back part of the p of the land Acts 5:3
and they counted the p of them Acts 19:19
For ye are bought with a p 1Cor 6:20
Ye are bought with a p 1Cor 7:23
is in the sight of God of great p 1Pet 3:4

**PRICES**

brought the p of the things that Acts 4:34

**PRICKED**

grieved, and I was p in my reins Ps 73:21
they were p in their heart, and Acts 2:37

**PRICKING**

there shall be no more a p brier Eze 28:24

**PRICKS**

of them shall be p in your eyes Num 33:55
for thee to kick against the p Acts 9:5
for thee to kick against the p Acts 26:14

**PRIDE**

I will break the p of your power Lev 26:19
I know thy p, and the naughtiness 1Sa 17:28
himself for the p of his heart 2Chr 32:26
his purpose, and hide p from man Job 33:17
because of the p of evil men Job 35:12
His scales are his p, shut up Job 41:15
a king over all the children of p Job 41:34
The wicked in his p doth Ps 10:2
through the p of his countenance, Ps 10:4
of thy presence from the p of man Ps 31:20
not the foot of p come against me Ps 36:11
let them even be taken in their p Ps 59:12
Therefore p compasseth them about Ps 73:6
p, and arrogancy, and the evil way, Prov 8:13
When p cometh, then cometh shame Prov 11:2
Only by p cometh contention Prov 13:10
of the foolish is a rod of p Prov 14:3
P goeth before destruction, and an Prov 16:18
A man's p shall bring him low Prov 29:23
of Samaria, that say in the p Is 9:9
We have heard of the p of Moab Is 16:6
even of his haughtiness, and his p Is 16:6
it, to stain the p of all glory Is 23:9
he shall bring down their p Is 25:11
Woe to the crown of p, to the Is 28:1
The crown of p, the drunkards of Is 28:3
manner will I mar the p of Judah Jer 13:9
and the great p of Jerusalem Jer 13:9
weep in secret places for your p Jer 13:17
We have heard the p of Moab Jer 48:29
and his arrogancy, and his p Jer 48:29
the p of thine heart, O thou that Jer 49:16
rod hath blossomed, p hath budded Eze 7:10
iniquity of thy sister Sodom, p Eze 16:49
by thy mouth in the day of thy p Eze 16:56
the p of her power shall come Eze 30:6
those that walk in p he is able Dan 4:37
up, and his mind hardened in p Dan 5:20
the p of Israel doth testify to Hos 5:5
the p of Israel testifieth to his Hos 7:10
The p of thine heart hath Obad 3
This shall they have for their p Zeph 2:10
thee them that rejoice in thy p Zeph 3:11
cut off the p of the Philistines Zec 9:6
the p of Assyria shall be brought Zec 10:11
for the p of Jordan is spoiled Zec 11:3
an evil eye, blasphemy, p Mk 7:22
lest being lifted up with p he 1Ti 3:6
the p of life, is not of the 1Jn 2:16

**PRIEST**

he was the p of the most high God Gen 14:18
daughter of Poti-pherah p of On Gen 41:45
Poti-pherah p of On bare unto him Gen 41:50
Poti-pherah p of On bare unto him Gen 46:20
Now the p of Midian had seven Ex 2:16
father in law, the p of Midian Ex 3:1
the p of Midian, Moses' father in Ex 18:1
that son that is p in his stead Ex 29:30
the holy garments for Aaron the p Ex 31:10
the holy garments for Aaron the p Ex 35:19
of Ithamar, son to Aaron the p Ex 38:21
the holy garments for Aaron the p Ex 39:41
the sons of Aaron the p shall put Lev 1:7
the p shall burn all on the altar Lev 1:9
the p shall lay them in order on Lev 1:12
the p shall bring it all, and burn Lev 1:13
the p shall bring it unto the Lev 1:15
the p shall burn it upon the Lev 1:17
the p shall burn the memorial of Lev 2:2
when it is presented unto the p Lev 2:8
the p shall take from the meat Lev 2:9
the p shall burn the memorial of Lev 2:16
the p shall burn it upon the Lev 3:11
the p shall burn them upon the Lev 3:16
If the p that is anointed do sin Lev 4:3
the p that is anointed shall take Lev 4:5
the p shall dip his finger in the Lev 4:6
the p shall put some of the blood Lev 4:7
the p shall burn them upon the Lev 4:10
the p that is anointed shall Lev 4:16
the p shall dip his finger in Lev 4:17
the p shall make an atonement for Lev 4:20
the p shall take of the blood of Lev 4:25
the p shall make an atonement for Lev 4:26
the p shall take of the blood Lev 4:30
the p shall burn it upon the Lev 4:31
the p shall make an atonement for Lev 4:31
the p shall take of the blood of Lev 4:34
the p shall burn them upon the Lev 4:35
the p shall make an atonement for Lev 4:35
the p shall make an atonement for Lev 5:6
And he shall bring them unto the p Lev 5:8
the p shall make an atonement for Lev 5:10
Then shall he bring it to the p Lev 5:12
the p shall take his handful of Lev 5:12
the p shall make an atonement for Lev 5:13
thereto, and give it unto the p Lev 5:16
the p shall make an atonement for Lev 5:16
a trespass offering, unto the p Lev 5:18
the p shall make an atonement for Lev 5:18
a trespass offering, unto the p Lev 6:6
the p shall make an atonement for Lev 6:7
the p shall put on his linen Lev 6:10
the p shall burn wood on it every Lev 6:12
the p of his sons that is Lev 6:22
for the p shall be wholly burnt Lev 6:23
The p that offereth it for sin Lev 6:26
the p shall burn them upon the Lev 7:5
the p that maketh atonement Lev 7:7
the p that offereth any man's Lev 7:8
even the p shall have to himself Lev 7:8
the p shall burn the fat upon the Lev 7:31
p for an heave offering of the Lev 7:32
have given them unto Aaron the p Lev 7:34
of the congregation, unto the p Lev 12:6
the p shall make an atonement for Lev 12:8
shall be brought unto Aaron the p Lev 13:2
the p shall look on the plague in Lev 13:3
the p shall look on him, and Lev 13:3
then the p shall shut up him that Lev 13:4
the p shall look on him the Lev 13:5

P

then the *p* shall shut him up ... Lev 13:5
the *p* shall look on him again the ... Lev 13:6
the *p* shall pronounce him clean ... Lev 13:6
seen of the *p* for his cleansing ... Lev 13:7
he shall be seen of the *p* again ... Lev 13:7
if the *p* see that, behold, the ... Lev 13:8
then the *p* shall pronounce him ... Lev 13:8
he shall be brought unto the *p* ... Lev 13:9
And the *p* shall see him ... Lev 13:10
the *p* shall pronounce him unclean ... Lev 13:11
foot, wheresoever the *p* looketh ... Lev 13:12
Then the *p* shall consider ... Lev 13:13
the *p* shall see the raw flesh, and ... Lev 13:15
white, he shall come unto the *p* ... Lev 13:16
And the *p* shall see him ... Lev 13:17
then the *p* shall pronounce him ... Lev 13:17
reddish, and it be shewed to the *p* ... Lev 13:19
And if, when the *p* seeth it ... Lev 13:20
the *p* shall pronounce him unclean ... Lev 13:20
But if the *p* look on it, and, ... Lev 13:21
then the *p* shall shut him up ... Lev 13:21
then the *p* shall pronounce him ... Lev 13:22
the *p* shall pronounce him clean ... Lev 13:23
Then the *p* shall look upon it ... Lev 13:25
wherefore the *p* shall pronounce ... Lev 13:25
But if the *p* look on it, and, ... Lev 13:26
then the *p* shall shut him up ... Lev 13:26
the *p* shall look upon him the ... Lev 13:27
then the *p* shall pronounce him ... Lev 13:27
the *p* shall pronounce him clean ... Lev 13:28
Then the *p* shall see the plague ... Lev 13:30
then the *p* shall pronounce him ... Lev 13:30
if the *p* look on the plague of ... Lev 13:31
then the *p* shall shut up him that ... Lev 13:31
in the seventh day the *p* shall ... Lev 13:32
the *p* shall shut up him that hath ... Lev 13:33
in the seventh day the *p* shall ... Lev 13:34
then the *p* shall pronounce him ... Lev 13:34
Then the *p* shall look on him ... Lev 13:36
the *p* shall not seek for yellow ... Lev 13:36
the *p* shall pronounce him clean ... Lev 13:37
Then the *p* shall look ... Lev 13:39
Then the *p* shall look upon it ... Lev 13:43
the *p* shall pronounce him utterly ... Lev 13:44
and shall be shewed unto the *p* ... Lev 13:49
the *p* shall look upon the plague, ... Lev 13:50
if the *p* shall look, and, behold, ... Lev 13:53
Then the *p* shall command that ... Lev 13:54
the *p* shall look on the plague, ... Lev 13:55
And if the *p* look, and, behold, the ... Lev 13:56
He shall be brought unto the *p* ... Lev 14:2
the *p* shall go forth out of the ... Lev 14:3
the *p* shall look, and, behold, if ... Lev 14:3
Then shall the *p* command to take ... Lev 14:4
the *p* shall command that one of ... Lev 14:5
the *p* that maketh him clean shall ... Lev 14:11
the *p* shall take one he lamb, and ... Lev 14:12
the *p* shall take some of the ... Lev 14:14
the *p* shall put it upon the tip ... Lev 14:14
the *p* shall take some of the log ... Lev 14:15
the *p* shall dip his right finger ... Lev 14:16
*p* put upon the tip of the right ... Lev 14:17
the *p* shall make an atonement for ... Lev 14:18
the *p* shall offer the sin ... Lev 14:19
the *p* shall offer the burnt ... Lev 14:20
the *p* shall make an atonement for ... Lev 14:20
day for his cleansing unto the *p* ... Lev 14:23
the *p* shall take the lamb of the ... Lev 14:24
the *p* shall wave them for a wave ... Lev 14:24
the *p* shall take some of the ... Lev 14:25
the *p* shall pour of the oil into ... Lev 14:26
the *p* shall sprinkle with his ... Lev 14:27
the *p* shall put of the oil that ... Lev 14:28
the *p* shall make an atonement for ... Lev 14:31
house shall come and tell the *p* ... Lev 14:35
Then the *p* shall command that ... Lev 14:36
before the *p* go into it to see ... Lev 14:36
afterward the *p* shall go in to ... Lev 14:36
Then the *p* shall go out of the ... Lev 14:38
the *p* shall come again the ... Lev 14:39
Then the *p* shall command that ... Lev 14:40
Then the *p* shall come and look, and ... Lev 14:44
if the *p* shall come in, and look ... Lev 14:48
then the *p* shall pronounce the ... Lev 14:48
and give them unto the *p* ... Lev 15:14
the *p* shall offer them, the one ... Lev 15:15
the *p* shall make an atonement for ... Lev 15:15
pigeons, and bring them unto the *p* ... Lev 15:29
the *p* shall offer the one for a ... Lev 15:30
the *p* shall make an atonement for ... Lev 15:30
the *p* make an atonement for you ... Lev 16:30
And the *p*, whom he shall anoint, ... Lev 16:32
of the congregation, unto the *p* ... Lev 17:5
the *p* shall sprinkle the blood ... Lev 17:6
the *p* shall make an atonement for ... Lev 19:22
And the daughter of any *p*, if she ... Lev 21:9
is the high *p* among his brethren ... Lev 21:10
of the seed of Aaron the *p* shall ... Lev 21:21
a sojourner of the *p*, or an hired ... Lev 22:10
But if the *p* buy any soul with ... Lev 22:11
it unto the *p* with the holy thing ... Lev 22:14
of your harvest unto the *p* ... Lev 23:10
the sabbath the *p* shall wave it ... Lev 23:11
the *p* shall wave them with the ... Lev 23:20
be holy to the LORD for the *p* ... Lev 23:20
present himself before the *p* ... Lev 27:8
and the *p* shall value him ... Lev 27:8
that vowed shall the *p* value him ... Lev 27:8
present the beast before the *p* ... Lev 27:11
the *p* shall value it, whether it ... Lev 27:12
as thou valuest it, who art the *p* ... Lev 27:12
then the *p* shall estimate it, ... Lev 27:14
as the *p* shall estimate it, so ... Lev 27:14
then the *p* shall reckon unto him ... Lev 27:18
Then the *p* shall reckon unto him ... Lev 27:23
present them before Aaron the *p* ... Num 3:6
Eleazar the son of Aaron the *p* ... Num 3:32
the *p* pertaineth the oil for the ... Num 4:16
of Ithamar the son of Aaron the *p* ... Num 4:28
of Ithamar the son of Aaron the *p* ... Num 4:33
unto the LORD, even to the *p* ... Num 5:8
which they bring unto the *p* ... Num 5:9
whatsoever any man giveth the *p* ... Num 5:10
the man bring his wife unto the *p* ... Num 5:15
the *p* shall bring her near, and ... Num 5:16
the *p* shall take holy water in an ... Num 5:17
the tabernacle the *p* shall take ... Num 5:17
the *p* shall set the woman before ... Num 5:18
the *p* shall have in his hand the ... Num 5:18
the *p* shall charge her by an oath ... Num 5:19
Then the *p* shall charge the woman ... Num 5:21
the *p* shall say unto the woman, ... Num 5:21
the *p* shall write these curses in ... Num 5:23
Then the *p* shall take the ... Num 5:25
the *p* shall take an handful of ... Num 5:26
the *p* shall execute upon her all ... Num 5:30
or two young pigeons, to the *p* ... Num 6:10
the *p* shall offer the one for a ... Num 6:11
the *p* shall bring them before the ... Num 6:16
the *p* shall offer also his meat ... Num 6:17
the *p* shall take the sodden ... Num 6:19
the *p* shall wave them for a wave ... Num 6:20
this is holy for the *p*, with the ... Num 6:20
of Ithamar the son of Aaron the *p* ... Num 7:8
the *p* shall make an atonement for ... Num 15:25
the *p* shall make an atonement for ... Num 15:28
Eleazar the son of Aaron the *p* ... Num 16:37
Eleazar the *p* took the brasen ... Num 16:39
heave offering to Aaron the *p* ... Num 18:28
shall give her unto Eleazar the *p* ... Num 19:3
Eleazar the *p* shall take of her ... Num 19:4
the *p* shall take cedar wood, and ... Num 19:6
Then the *p* shall wash his clothes ... Num 19:7
the *p* shall be unclean until the ... Num 19:7
Eleazar, the son of Aaron the *p* ... Num 25:7
Eleazar, the son of Aaron the *p* ... Num 25:11
Eleazar the son of Aaron the *p* ... Num 26:1
Eleazar the *p* spake with them in ... Num 26:3
by Moses and Eleazar the *p* ... Num 26:63
Moses and Aaron the *p* numbered ... Num 26:64
Moses, and before Eleazar the *p* ... Num 27:2
And set him before Eleazar the *p* ... Num 27:19
shall stand before Eleazar the *p* ... Num 27:21
and set him before Eleazar the *p* ... Num 27:22
Phinehas the son of Eleazar the *p* ... Num 31:6
unto Moses, and Eleazar the *p* ... Num 31:12
And Moses, and Eleazar the *p* ... Num 31:13
Eleazar the *p* said unto the men ... Num 31:21
of beast, thou, and Eleazar the *p* ... Num 31:26
and give it unto Eleazar the *p* ... Num 31:29
Eleazar the *p* did as the LORD ... Num 31:31
offering, unto Eleazar the *p* ... Num 31:41
Eleazar the *p* took the gold of ... Num 31:51
Eleazar the *p* took the gold of ... Num 31:54
unto Moses, and to Eleazar the *p* ... Num 32:2
Moses commanded Eleazar the *p* ... Num 32:28
Aaron the *p* went up into mount ... Num 33:38
Eleazar the *p*, and Joshua the son ... Num 34:17
it unto the death of the high *p* ... Num 35:25
until the death of the high *p* ... Num 35:28
*p* the slayer shall return into ... Num 35:28
land, until the death of the *p* ... Num 35:32
will not hearken unto the *p* that ... Deut 17:12
give unto the *p* the shoulder ... Deut 18:3
that the *p* shall approach and ... Deut 20:2
thou shalt go unto the *p* that ... Deut 26:3
the *p* shall take the basket out ... Deut 26:4
of Canaan, which Eleazar the *p* ... Josh 14:1
came near before Eleazar the *p* ... Josh 17:4
inheritances, which Eleazar the *p* ... Josh 19:51
*p* that shall be in those days ... Josh 20:6
of the Levites unto Eleazar the *p* ... Josh 21:1
and the children of Aaron the *p* ... Josh 21:4
the *p* Hebron with her suburbs ... Josh 21:13
Phinehas the son of Eleazar the *p* ... Josh 22:13
And when Phinehas the *p*, and the ... Josh 22:30
the *p* said unto the children of ... Josh 22:31
Phinehas the son of Eleazar the *p* ... Josh 22:32
one of his sons, who became his *p* ... Judg 17:5
me, and be unto me a father and a *p* ... Judg 17:10
and the young man became his *p* ... Judg 17:12
seeing I have a Levite to my *p* ... Judg 17:13
and hath hired me, and I am his *p* ... Judg 18:4
the *p* said unto them, Go in peace ... Judg 18:6
the *p* stood in the entering of ... Judg 18:17
Then said the *p* unto them ... Judg 18:18
us, and be to us a father and a *p* ... Judg 18:19
be a *p* unto the house of one man ... Judg 18:19
or that thou be a *p* unto a tribe ... Judg 18:19
my gods which I made, and the *p* ... Judg 18:24
the *p* which he had, and came unto ... Judg 18:27
Now Eli the *p* sat upon a seat by ... 1Sa 1:9
unto the LORD before Eli the *p* ... 1Sa 2:11
brought up the *p* took for himself ... 1Sa 2:14
Give flesh to roast for the *p* ... 1Sa 2:15
the tribes of Israel to be my *p* ... 1Sa 2:28
I will raise me up a faithful *p* ... 1Sa 2:35
of Eli, the LORD's *p* in Shiloh ... 1Sa 14:3
while Saul talked unto the *p* ... 1Sa 14:19
and Saul said unto the *p*, Withdraw ... 1Sa 14:19
Then said the *p*, Let us draw near ... 1Sa 14:36
David to Nob to Ahimelech the *p* ... 1Sa 21:1
David said unto Ahimelech the *p* ... 1Sa 21:2
the *p* answered David, and said, ... 1Sa 21:4
And David answered the *p*, and said ... 1Sa 21:5
So the *p* gave him hallowed bread ... 1Sa 21:6
the *p* said, The sword of Goliath ... 1Sa 21:9
king sent to call Ahimelech the *p* ... 1Sa 22:11
and he said to Abiathar the *p* ... 1Sa 23:9
And David said to Abiathar the *p* ... 1Sa 30:7
king said also unto Zadok the *p* ... 2Sa 15:27
Zeruiah, and with Abiathar the *p* ... 1Kin 1:7
But Zadok the *p*, and Benaiah the ... 1Kin 1:8
of the king, and Abiathar the *p* ... 1Kin 1:19
of the host, and Abiathar the *p* ... 1Kin 1:25
me thy servant, and Zadok the *p* ... 1Kin 1:26
David said, Call me Zadok the *p* ... 1Kin 1:32
And let Zadok the *p* and Nathan the ... 1Kin 1:34
So Zadok the *p*, and Nathan the ... 1Kin 1:38
Zadok the *p* took an horn of oil ... 1Kin 1:39
the son of Abiathar the *p* came ... 1Kin 1:42
hath sent with him Zadok the *p* ... 1Kin 1:44
And Zadok the *p* and Nathan the ... 1Kin 1:45
for him, and for Abiathar the *p* ... 1Kin 2:22
unto Abiathar the *p* said the king ... 1Kin 2:26
from being *p* unto the LORD ... 1Kin 2:27
Zadok the *p* did the king put in ... 1Kin 2:35
Azariah the son of Zadok the *p* ... 1Kin 4:2
that Jehoiada the *p* commanded ... 2Kin 11:9
and came to Jehoiada the *p* ... 2Kin 11:9
the *p* give king David's spears ... 2Kin 11:10
But Jehoiada the *p* commanded the ... 2Kin 11:15
For the *p* had said, Let her not ... 2Kin 11:15
slew Mattan the *p* of Baal before ... 2Kin 11:18
the *p* appointed officers over the ... 2Kin 11:18
Jehoiada the *p* instructed him ... 2Kin 12:2
Jehoash called for Jehoiada the *p* ... 2Kin 12:7
But Jehoiada the *p* took a chest ... 2Kin 12:9
scribe and the high *p* came up ... 2Kin 12:10
the *p* the fashion of the altar ... 2Kin 16:10
Urijah the *p* built an altar ... 2Kin 16:11
so Urijah the *p* made it against ... 2Kin 16:11
king Ahaz commanded Urijah the *p* ... 2Kin 16:15
Thus did Urijah the *p*, according ... 2Kin 16:16
Go up to Hilkiah the high *p* ... 2Kin 22:4
Hilkiah the high *p* said unto ... 2Kin 22:8
Hilkiah the *p* hath delivered me a ... 2Kin 22:10
the king commanded Hilkiah the *p* ... 2Kin 22:12
So Hilkiah the *p*, and Ahikam, and ... 2Kin 22:14
king commanded Hilkiah the high *p* ... 2Kin 23:4
in the book that Hilkiah the *p* ... 2Kin 23:24
guard took Seraiah the chief *p* ... 2Kin 25:18
and Zephaniah the second *p* ... 2Kin 25:18
And Zadok the *p*, and his brethren ... 1Chr 16:39
and the princes, and Zadok the *p* ... 1Chr 24:6
the son of Jehoiada, a chief *p* ... 1Chr 27:5
chief governor, and Zadok to be *p* ... 1Chr 29:22
the same may be a *p* of them that ... 2Chr 13:9
true God, and without a teaching *p* ... 2Chr 15:3
Amariah the chief *p* is over you ... 2Chr 19:11
the wife of Jehoiada the *p* ... 2Chr 22:11
that Jehoiada the *p* had commanded ... 2Chr 23:8
for Jehoiada the *p* dismissed not ... 2Chr 23:8
Moreover Jehoiada the *p* delivered ... 2Chr 23:9
Then Jehoiada the *p* brought out ... 2Chr 23:14
For the *p* said, Slay her not in ... 2Chr 23:14
slew Mattan the *p* of Baal before ... 2Chr 23:17
all the days of Jehoiada the *p* ... 2Chr 24:2
the son of Jehoiada the *p* ... 2Chr 24:20
of the sons of Jehoiada the *p* ... 2Chr 24:25
Azariah the *p* went in after him, ... 2Chr 26:17
And Azariah the chief *p*, and all ... 2Chr 26:20
Azariah the chief *p* of the house ... 2Chr 31:10
they came to Hilkiah the high *p* ... 2Chr 34:9
Hilkiah the *p* found a book of the ... 2Chr 34:14
Hilkiah the *p* hath given me a ... 2Chr 34:18
till there stood up a *p* with Urim ... Ezr 2:63
the son of Aaron the chief *p* ... Ezr 7:5
Artaxerxes gave unto Ezra the *p* ... Ezr 7:11
king of kings, unto Ezra the *p* ... Ezr 7:12
river, that whatsoever Ezra the *p* ... Ezr 7:21
Meremoth the son of Uriah the *p* ... Ezr 8:33
And Ezra the *p* stood up, and said ... Ezr 10:10
And Ezra the *p*, with certain chief ... Ezr 10:16
Then Eliashib the high *p* rose up ... Neh 3:1
the house of Eliashib the high *p* ... Neh 3:20
till there stood up a *p* with Urim ... Neh 7:65
Ezra the *p* brought the law before ... Neh 8:2
Ezra the *p* the scribe, and the ... Neh 8:9
the *p* the son of Aaron shall be ... Neh 10:38
the governor, and of Ezra the *p* ... Neh 12:26
And before this, Eliashib the *p* ... Neh 13:4
the treasuries, Shelemiah the *p* ... Neh 13:13
the son of Eliashib the high *p* ... Neh 13:28
Thou art a *p* for ever after the ... Ps 110:4
witnesses to record, Uriah the *p* ... Is 8:2
as with the people, so with the *p* ... Is 24:2
the *p* and the prophet have erred ... Is 28:7
the *p* every one dealeth falsely ... Jer 6:13
the *p* every one dealeth falsely ... Jer 8:10
the *p* go about into a land that ... Jer 14:18
law shall not perish from the *p* ... Jer 18:18
Now Pashur the son of Immer the *p* ... Jer 20:1
the son of Maaseiah the *p* ... Jer 21:1
For both prophet and *p* are profane ... Jer 23:11
people, or the prophet, or a *p* ... Jer 23:33
And as for the prophet, and the *p* ... Jer 23:34
the son of Maaseiah the *p* ... Jer 29:25
The LORD hath made thee *p* in the ... Jer 29:26
in the stead of Jehoiada the *p* ... Jer 29:26

Zephaniah the *p* read this letter Jer 29:29
the *p* to the prophet Jeremiah Jer 37:3
guard took Seraiah the chief *p* Jer 52:24
and Zephaniah the second *p* Jer 52:24
of his anger the king and the *p* Lam 2:6
shall the *p* and the prophet be Lam 2:20
came expressly unto Ezekiel the *p* Eze 1:3
the law shall perish from the *p* Eze 7:26
to do the office of a *p* unto me Eze 44:13
Neither shall any *p* drink wine Eze 44:21
or a widow that had a *p* before Eze 44:22
the *p* the first of your dough Eze 44:30
the *p* shall take of the blood of Eze 45:19
as they that strive with the *p* Hos 4:4
that thou shalt be no *p* to me Hos 4:6
shall be, like people, like *p* Hos 4:9
Then Amaziah the *p* of Beth-el Amos 7:10
the son of Josedech, the high *p* Hag 1:1
the son of Josedech, the high *p* Hag 1:12
the son of Josedech, the high *p* Hag 1:14
the son of Josedech, the high *p* Hag 2:2
son of Josedech, the high *p* Hag 2:4
*p* standing before the angel of Zec 3:1
Hear now, O Joshua the high *p* Zec 3:8
the son of Josedech, the high *p* Zec 6:11
he shall be a *p* upon his throne Zec 6:13
go thy way, shew thyself to the *p* Mt 8:4
unto the palace of the high *p* Mt 26:3
him away to Caiaphas the high *p* Mt 26:57
And the high *p* arose, and said unto Mt 26:62
And the high *p* answered and said Mt 26:63
Then the high *p* rent his clothes, Mt 26:65
go thy way, shew thyself to the *p* Mk 1:44
the days of Abiathar the high *p* Mk 2:26
and staves, from the chief *p* Mk 14:43
and smote a servant of the high *p* Mk 14:47
they led Jesus away to the high *p* Mk 14:53
into the palace of the high *p* Mk 14:54
the high *p* stood up in the midst, Mk 14:60
Again the high *p* asked him Mk 14:61
Then the high *p* rent his clothes, Mk 14:63
one of the maids of the high *p* Mk 14:66
a certain *p* named Zacharias, of Lk 1:5
but go, and shew thyself to the *p* Lk 5:14
came down a certain *p* that way Lk 10:31
smote the servant of the high *p* Lk 22:50
being the high *p* that same year Jn 11:49
but being high *p* that year Jn 11:51
was the high *p* that same year Jn 18:13
was known unto the high *p* Jn 18:15
into the palace of the high *p* Jn 18:15
which was known unto the high *p* Jn 18:16
The high *p* then asked Jesus of Jn 18:19
Answerest thou the high *p* so Jn 18:22
bound unto Caiaphas the high *p* Jn 18:24
One of the servants of the high *p* Jn 18:26
And Annas the high *p*, and Caiaphas, Acts 4:6
were of the kindred of the high *p* Acts 4:6
Then the high *p* rose up, and all Acts 5:17
But the high *p* came, and they that Acts 5:21
Now when the high *p* and the Acts 5:24
and the high *p* asked them, Acts 5:27
Then said the high *p*, Are these Acts 7:1
of the Lord, went unto the high *p* Acts 9:1
Then the *p* of Jupiter, which was Acts 14:13
As also the high *p* doth bear me Acts 22:5
the high *p* Ananias commanded them. Acts 23:2
said, Revilest thou God's high *p* Acts 23:4
brethren, that he was the high *p* Acts 23:5
high *p* descended with the elders Acts 24:1
Then the high *p* and the chief of Acts 25:2
faithful high *p* in things Heb 2:17
High *P* of our profession, Christ Heb 3:1
then that we have a great high *p* Heb 4:14
For we have not an high *p* which Heb 4:15
For every high *p* taken from among Heb 5:1
not himself to be made an high *p* Heb 5:5
Thou art a *p* for ever after the Heb 5:6
Called of God an high *p* after the Heb 5:10
made an high *p* for ever after the Heb 6:20
*p* of the most high God, who met Heb 7:1
abideth a *p* continually Heb 7:3
need was there that another *p* Heb 7:11
there ariseth another *p*, Heb 7:15
Thou art a *p* for ever after the Heb 7:17
not without an oath he was made *p* Heb 7:20
Thou art a *p* for ever after the Heb 7:21
For such an high *p* became us Heb 7:26
We have such an high *p*, who is Heb 8:1
For every high *p* is ordained to Heb 8:3
on earth, he should not be a *p* Heb 8:4
the high *p* alone once every year Heb 9:7
an high *p* of good things to come Heb 9:11
as the high *p* entereth into the Heb 9:25
And every *p* standeth daily Heb 10:11
having an high *p* over the house Heb 10:21
sanctuary by the high *p* for sin Heb 13:11

## PRIESTHOOD

*p* throughout their generations Ex 40:15
and seek ye the *p* also Num 16:10
shall bear the iniquity of your *p* Num 18:1
the covenant of an everlasting *p* Num 25:13
for the *p* of the LORD is their Josh 18:7
they, as polluted, put from the *p* Ezr 2:62
they, as polluted, put from the *p* Neh 7:64
because they have defiled the *p* Neh 13:29
and the covenant of the *p* Neh 13:29
who receive the office of the *p* Heb 7:5
were by the Levitical *p*, (for Heb 7:11
For the *p* being changed, there is Heb 7:12
Moses spake nothing concerning *p* Heb 7:14
ever, hath an unchangeable *p* Heb 7:24
up a spiritual house, an holy *p* 1Pet 2:5
a chosen generation, a royal *p* 1Pet 2:9

## PRIEST'S

minister unto me in the *p* office Ex 28:1
minister unto me in the *p* office Ex 28:3
minister unto me in the *p* office Ex 28:4
minister unto me in the *p* office Ex 28:41
minister unto me in the *p* office Ex 29:1
the *p* office shall be theirs for Ex 29:9
to minister to me in the *p* office Ex 29:44
minister unto me in the *p* office Ex 30:30
sons, to minister in the *p* office Ex 31:10
sons, to minister in the *p* office Ex 35:19
to minister in the *p* office Ex 39:41
minister unto me in the *p* office Ex 40:13
minister unto me in the *p* office Ex 40:15
and the remnant shall be the *p* Lev 5:13
shall be the *p* that offereth it Lev 7:9
it shall be the *p* that sprinkleth Lev 7:14
unto the LORD in the *p* office Lev 7:35
for as the sin offering is the *p* Lev 14:13
of the oil that is in the *p* hand Lev 14:18
rest of the oil that is in the *p* Lev 14:29
*p* office in his father's stead Lev 16:32
If the *p* daughter also be married Lev 22:12
But if the *p* daughter be a widow, Lev 22:13
possession thereof shall be the *p* Lev 27:21
to minister in the *p* office Num 3:3
Ithamar ministered in the *p* Num 3:4
they shall wait on their *p* office Num 3:10
*p* office for every thing of the Num 18:7
I have given your *p* office unto Num 18:7
in the *p* office in his stead Deut 10:6
this shall be the *p* due from the Deut 18:3
the *p* heart was glad, and he took Judg 18:20
the *p* custom with the people was, 1Sa 2:13
the *p* servant came, while the 1Sa 2:13
the *p* servant came, and said to 1Sa 2:15
the *p* office in the temple that 1Chr 6:10
and Ithamar executed the *p* office 1Chr 24:2
the *p* office unto the LORD 2Chr 11:14
the high *p* officer came and 2Chr 24:11
of your oblations, shall be the *p* Eze 44:30
For the *p* lips should keep Mal 2:7
and struck a servant of the high *p* Mt 26:51
afar off unto the high *p* palace Mt 26:58
that while he executed the *p* Lk 1:8
to the custom of the *p* office Lk 1:9
brought him into the high *p* house Lk 22:54
it, and smote the high *p* servant Jn 18:10

## PRIESTS

the land of the *p* bought he not Gen 47:22
for the *p* had a portion assigned Gen 47:22
except the land of the *p* only Gen 47:26
shall be unto me a kingdom of *p* Ex 19:6
And let the *p* also, which come Ex 19:22
but let not the *p* and the people Ex 19:24
and the *p*, Aaron's sons, shall Lev 1:5
And the *p*, Aaron's sons, shall lay Lev 1:8
and the *p*, Aaron's sons, shall Lev 1:11
bring it to Aaron's sons the *p* Lev 2:2
Aaron's sons the *p* shall sprinkle Lev 3:2
among the *p* shall eat thereof Lev 6:29
among the *p* shall eat thereof Lev 7:6
or unto one of his sons the *p* Lev 13:2
shall make an atonement for the *p* Lev 16:33
Speak unto the *p* the sons of Lev 21:1
the *p* which were anointed, whom Num 3:3
And the sons of Aaron, the *p* Num 10:8
shalt come unto the *p* the Levites Deut 17:9
which is before the *p* the Levites Deut 17:18
The *p* the Levites, and all the Deut 18:1
before the LORD, before the *p* Deut 19:17
the *p* the sons of Levi shall come Deut 21:5
the *p* the Levites shall teach you Deut 24:8
the *p* the Levites spake unto all Deut 27:9
it unto the *p* the sons of Levi Deut 31:9
the *p* the Levites bearing it, Josh 3:3
And Joshua spake unto the *p* Josh 3:6
thou shalt command the *p* that Josh 3:8
*p* that bear the ark of the LORD Josh 3:13
the *p* bearing the ark of the Josh 3:14
the feet of the *p* that bare the Josh 3:15
the *p* that bare the ark of the Josh 3:17
the *p* which bare the ark of the Josh 4:9
For the *p* which bare the ark Josh 4:10
of the LORD passed over, and the *p* Josh 4:11
Command the *p* that bear the ark Josh 4:16
Joshua therefore commanded the *p* Josh 4:17
when the *p* that bare the ark of Josh 4:18
seven *p* shall bear before the ark Josh 6:4
the *p* shall blow with the Josh 6:4
the son of Nun called the *p* Josh 6:6
let seven *p* bear seven trumpets Josh 6:6
that the seven *p* bearing the Josh 6:8
the *p* that blew with the trumpets Josh 6:9
the *p* going on, and blowing with Josh 6:9
the *p* took up the ark of the LORD Josh 6:12
seven *p* bearing seven trumpets of Josh 6:13
the *p* going on, and blowing with Josh 6:13
when the *p* blew with the trumpets Josh 6:16
when the *p* blew with the trumpets Josh 6:20
side before the *p* the Levites Josh 8:33
of the children of Aaron, the *p* Josh 21:19
his sons were *p* to the tribe of Judg 18:30
the *p* of the LORD, were there 1Sa 1:3
Therefore neither the *p* of Dagon 1Sa 5:5
the Philistines called for the *p* 1Sa 6:2
house, the *p* that were in Nob 1Sa 22:11
Turn, and slay the *p* of the LORD 1Sa 22:17
to fall upon the *p* of the LORD 1Sa 22:17
Turn thou, and fall upon the *p* 1Sa 22:18
turned, and he fell upon the *p* 1Sa 22:18
And Nob, the city of the *p* 1Sa 22:19
that Saul had slain the LORD'S *p* 1Sa 22:21
the son of Abiathar, were the *p* 2Sa 8:17
with thee Zadok and Abiathar the *p* 2Sa 15:35
it to Zadok and Abiathar the *p* 2Sa 15:35
unto Zadok and to Abiathar the *p* 2Sa 17:15
to Zadok and to Abiathar the *p* 2Sa 19:11
and Zadok and Abiathar were the *p* 2Sa 20:25
and Zadok and Abiathar were the *p* 1Kin 4:4
came, and the *p* took up the ark 1Kin 8:3
tabernacle, even those did the *p* 1Kin 8:4
the *p* brought in the ark of the 1Kin 8:6
when the *p* were come out of the 1Kin 8:10
So that the *p* could not stand to 1Kin 8:11
made *p* of the lowest of the 1Kin 12:31
he placed in Beth-el the *p* of the 1Kin 12:32
*p* of the high places that burn 1Kin 13:2
the people *p* of the high places 1Kin 13:33
one of the *p* of the high places 1Kin 13:33
men, and his kinsfolks, and his *p* 2Kin 10:11
all his servants, and all his *p* 2Kin 10:19
And Jehoash said to the *p*, All the 2Kin 12:4
Let the *p* take it to them, every 2Kin 12:5
year of king Jehoash the *p* had 2Kin 12:6
the priest, and the other *p* 2Kin 12:7
the *p* consented to receive no 2Kin 12:8
the *p* that kept the door put 2Kin 12:9
Carry thither one of the *p* whom 2Kin 17:27
Then one of the *p* whom they had 2Kin 17:28
of them *p* of the high places 2Kin 17:32
scribe, and the elders of the *p* 2Kin 19:2
of Jerusalem with him, and the *p* 2Kin 23:2
the *p* of the second order, and the 2Kin 23:4
And he put down the idolatrous *p* 2Kin 23:5
he brought all the *p* out of the 2Kin 23:8
where the *p* had burned incense 2Kin 23:8
Nevertheless the *p* of the high 2Kin 23:9
he slew all the *p* of the high 2Kin 23:20
were, the Israelites, the *p* 1Chr 9:2
And of the *p*; Jedaiah 1Chr 9:10
some of the sons of the *p* made 1Chr 9:30
and with them also to the *p* 1Chr 13:2
for Zadok and Abiathar the *p* 1Chr 15:11
So the *p* and the Levites 1Chr 15:14
and Benaiah, and Eliezer, the *p* 1Chr 15:24
Jahaziel the *p* with trumpets 1Chr 16:6
the priest, and his brethren the *p* 1Chr 16:39
the son of Abiathar, were the *p* 1Chr 18:16
the princes of Israel, with the *p* 1Chr 23:2
the chief of the fathers of the *p* 1Chr 24:6
the chief of the fathers of the *p* 1Chr 24:31
Also for the courses of the *p* 1Chr 28:13
And, behold, the courses of the *p* 1Chr 28:21
the sea was for the *p* to wash in 2Chr 4:6
he made the court of the *p* 2Chr 4:9
the tabernacle, these did the *p* 2Chr 5:5
the *p* brought in the ark of the 2Chr 5:7
when the *p* were come out of the 2Chr 5:11
(for all the *p* that were present 2Chr 5:11
twenty *p* sounding with trumpets 2Chr 5:12
So that the *p* could not stand to 2Chr 5:14
let thy *p*, O LORD God, be clothed 2Chr 6:41
the *p* could not enter into the 2Chr 7:2
the *p* waited on their offices 2Chr 7:6
the *p* sounded trumpets before 2Chr 7:6
courses of the *p* to their service 2Chr 8:14
praise and minister before the *p* 2Chr 8:14
of the king unto the *p* and Levites 2Chr 8:15
And the *p* and the Levites that were 2Chr 11:13
he ordained him *p* for the high 2Chr 11:15
ye not cast out the *p* of the LORD 2Chr 13:9
have made you *p* after the manner 2Chr 13:9
and the *p*, which minister unto the 2Chr 13:10
his *p* with sounding trumpets to 2Chr 13:12
the *p* sounded with the trumpets 2Chr 13:14
with them Elishama and Jehoram, *p* 2Chr 17:8
set of the Levites, and of the *p* 2Chr 19:8
entering on the sabbath, of the *p* 2Chr 23:4
the house of the LORD, save the *p* 2Chr 23:6
by the hand of the *p* the Levites 2Chr 23:18
And he gathered together the *p* 2Chr 24:5
with him fourscore *p* of the LORD 2Chr 26:17
but to the *p* the sons of Aaron, 2Chr 26:18
and while he was wroth with the *p* 2Chr 26:19
the *p* in the house of the LORD 2Chr 26:19
the chief priest, and all the *p* 2Chr 26:20
And he brought in the *p* and the 2Chr 29:4
the *p* went into the inner part of 2Chr 29:16
he commanded the *p* the sons of 2Chr 29:21
the *p* received the blood, and 2Chr 29:22
the *p* killed them, and they made 2Chr 29:24
David, and the *p* with the trumpets 2Chr 29:26
But the *p* were too few, so that 2Chr 29:34
until the other *p* had sanctified 2Chr 29:34
to sanctify themselves than the *p* 2Chr 29:34
because the *p* had not sanctified 2Chr 30:3
and the *p* and the Levites were 2Chr 30:15
the *p* sprinkled the blood, which 2Chr 30:16
the *p* praised the LORD day by day 2Chr 30:21
a great number of *p* sanctified 2Chr 30:24
congregation of Judah, with the *p* 2Chr 30:25
Then the *p* the Levites arose and 2Chr 30:27
appointed the courses of the *p* 2Chr 31:2
according to his service, the *p* 2Chr 31:2

to give the portion of the p 2Chr 31:4
Hezekiah questioned with the p 2Chr 31:9
Shecaniah, in the cities of the p 2Chr 31:15
Both to the genealogy of the p by 2Chr 31:17
Also of the sons of Aaron the p 2Chr 31:19
to all the males among the p 2Chr 31:19
bones of the p upon their altars 2Chr 34:5
of Jerusalem, and the p, and the 2Chr 34:30
he set the p in their charges, and 2Chr 35:2
unto the people, to the p 2Chr 35:8
gave unto the p for the passover 2Chr 35:8
the p stood in their place, and 2Chr 35:10
the p sprinkled the blood from 2Chr 35:11
for themselves, and for the p 2Chr 35:14
because the p the sons of Aaron 2Chr 35:14
for the p the sons of Aaron 2Chr 35:14
passover as Josiah kept, and the p 2Chr 35:18
Moreover all the chief of the p 2Chr 36:14
of Judah and Benjamin, and the p Ezr 1:5
The p: the children of Ezr 2:36
And of the children of the p Ezr 2:61
So the p, and the Levites, and some Ezr 2:70
of Jozadak, and his brethren the p Ezr 3:2
remnant of their brethren the p Ezr 3:8
they set the p in their apparel Ezr 3:10
But many of the p and Levites and Ezr 3:12
of the p which are at Jerusalem Ezr 6:9
And the children of Israel, the p Ezr 6:16
they set the p in their divisions Ezr 6:18
For the p and the Levites were Ezr 6:20
and for their brethren the p Ezr 6:20
children of Israel, and of the p Ezr 7:7
the people of Israel, and of his p Ezr 7:13
of the people, and of the p Ezr 7:16
you, that touching any of the p Ezr 7:24
and I viewed the people, and the p Ezr 8:15
twelve of the chief of the p Ezr 8:24
them before the chief of the p Ezr 8:29
So took the p and the Levites the Ezr 8:30
The people of Israel, and the p Ezr 9:1
have we, our kings, and our p Ezr 9:7
arose Ezra, and made the chief p Ezr 10:5
among the sons of the p there Ezr 10:18
told it to the Jews, nor to the p Neh 2:16
rose up with his brethren the p Neh 3:1
And after him repaired the p Neh 3:22
the horse gate repaired the p Neh 3:28
Then I called the p, and took an Neh 5:12
The p: the children of Neh 7:39
And of the p: the children Neh 7:63
So the p, and the Levites, and the Neh 7:73
fathers of all the people, the p Neh 8:13
on our princes, and on our p Neh 9:32
our kings, our princes, our p Neh 9:34
and our princes, Levites, and p Neh 9:38
these were the p Neh 10:8
And the rest of the people, the p Neh 10:28
And we cast the lots among the p Neh 10:34
unto the p that minister in the Neh 10:36
of wine and of oil, unto the p Neh 10:37
the p that minister, and the Neh 10:39
cities, to wit, Israel, the p Neh 11:3
Of the p: Jedaiah Neh 11:10
the residue of Israel, of the p Neh 11:20
Now these are the p and the Neh 12:1
These were the chief of the p Neh 12:7
And in the days of Joiakim were p Neh 12:12
also the p, to the reign of Neh 12:22
And the p and the Levites purified Neh 12:30
And the p; Eliakim Neh 12:41
the portions of the law for the p Neh 12:44
for Judah rejoiced for the p Neh 12:44
and the offerings of the p Neh 13:5
and appointed the wards of the p Neh 13:30
Their p fell by the sword Ps 78:64
Moses and Aaron among his p Ps 99:6
Let thy p be clothed with Ps 132:9
also clothe her p with salvation Ps 132:16
the elders of the p covered with Is 37:2
shall be named the P of the LORD Is 61:6
And I will also take of them for p Is 66:21
of the p that were in Anathoth in Jer 1:1
thereof, against the p thereof Jer 1:18
The p said not, Where is the LORD Jer 2:8
kings, their princes, and their p Jer 2:26
the p shall be astonished, and the Jer 4:9
the p bear rule by their means Jer 5:31
princes, and the bones of the p Jer 8:1
sit upon David's throne, and the p Jer 13:13
and of the ancients of the p Jer 19:1
So the p and the prophets and all Jer 26:7
unto all the people, that the p Jer 26:8
Then spake the p and the prophets Jer 26:11
and all the people unto the p Jer 26:16
Also I spake to the p and to all Jer 27:16
LORD, in the presence of the p Jer 28:1
Hananiah in the presence of the p Jer 28:5
away captives, and to the p Jer 29:1
the priest, and to all the p Jer 29:25
the soul of the p with fatness Jer 31:14
kings, their princes, their p Jer 32:32
Neither shall the p the Levites Jer 33:18
and with the Levites the p Jer 33:21
Jerusalem, the eunuchs, and the p Jer 34:19
forth into captivity with his p Jer 48:7
shall go into captivity, and his p Jer 49:3
her p sigh, her virgins are Lam 1:4
my p and mine elders gave up the Lam 1:19
and the iniquities of her p Lam 4:13
not the persons of the p, they Lam 4:16
Her p have violated my law, and Eze 22:26
is toward the south, is for the p Eze 40:45
is toward the north is for the p Eze 40:46
where the p that approach unto Eze 42:13
When the p enter therein, then Eze 42:14
thou shalt give to the p the Eze 43:19
the p shall cast salt upon them, Eze 43:24
the p shall make your burnt Eze 43:27
But the p the Levites, the sons Eze 44:15
The p shall not eat of any thing Eze 44:31
of the land shall be for the p Eze 45:4
the p shall prepare his burnt Eze 46:2
into the holy chambers of the p Eze 46:19
the p shall boil the trespass Eze 46:20
And for them, even for the p Eze 48:10
It shall be for the p that are Eze 48:11
the p the Levites shall have five Eze 48:13
Hear ye this, O p Hos 5:1
so the company of p murder in the Hos 6:9
the p thereof that rejoiced on it Hos 10:5
the p, the LORD's ministers, Joel 1:9
Gird yourselves, and lament, ye p Joel 1:13
Let the p, the ministers of the Joel 2:17
the p thereof teach for hire, and Mic 3:11
name of the Chemarims with the p Zeph 1:4
her p have polluted the sanctuary Zeph 3:4
Ask now the p concerning the law, Hag 2:11
the p answered and said, No Hag 2:12
the p answered and said, It shall Hag 2:13
to speak unto the p which were in Zec 7:3
people of the land, and to the p Zec 7:5
the LORD of hosts unto you, O p Mal 1:6
And now, O ye p, this commandment Mal 2:1
he had gathered all the chief p Mt 2:4
were with him, but only for the p Mt 12:4
the p in the temple profane the Mt 12:5
things of the elders and chief p Mt 16:21
be betrayed unto the chief p Mt 20:18
And when the chief p and scribes Mt 21:15
come into the temple, the chief p Mt 21:23
And when the chief p and Pharisees Mt 21:45
assembled together the chief p Mt 26:3
Iscariot, went unto the chief p Mt 26:14
and staves, from the chief p Mt 26:47
Now the chief p, and elders, and Mt 26:59
morning was come, all the chief p Mt 27:1
pieces of silver to the chief p Mt 27:3
the chief p took the silver Mt 27:6
he was accused of the chief p Mt 27:12
But the chief p and elders Mt 27:20
also the chief p mocking him Mt 27:41
of the preparation, the chief p Mt 27:62
shewed unto the chief p all the Mt 28:11
not lawful to eat but for the p Mk 2:26
of the elders, and of the chief p Mk 8:31
be delivered unto the chief p Mk 10:33
chief p heard it, and sought how Mk 11:18
there come to him the chief p Mk 11:27
and the chief p and the scribes Mk 14:1
the twelve, went unto the chief p Mk 14:10
were assembled all the chief p Mk 14:53
And the chief p and all the council Mk 14:55
in the morning the chief p held a Mk 15:1
the chief p accused him of many Mk 15:3
p had delivered him for envy Mk 15:10
But the chief p moved the people, Mk 15:11
Likewise also the chief p mocking Mk 15:31
and Caiaphas being the high p Lk 3:2
lawful to eat but for the p alone Lk 6:4
rejected of the elders and chief p Lk 9:22
Go shew yourselves unto the p Lk 17:14
But the chief p and the scribes and Lk 19:47
preached the gospel, the chief p Lk 20:1
And the chief p and the scribes the Lk 20:19
And the chief p and scribes sought Lk 22:2
way, and communed with the chief p Lk 22:4
Then Jesus said unto the chief p Lk 22:52
of the people and the chief p Lk 22:66
Then said Pilate to the chief p Lk 23:4
And the chief p and scribes stood Lk 23:10
had called together the chief p Lk 23:13
them and of the chief p prevailed Lk 23:23
And how the chief p and our rulers Lk 24:20
of John, when the Jews sent p Jn 1:19
the chief p sent officers to take Jn 7:32
came the officers to the chief p Jn 7:45
Then gathered the chief p Jn 11:47
Now both the chief p and the Jn 11:57
But the chief p consulted that Jn 12:10
men and officers from the chief p Jn 18:3
the chief p have delivered thee Jn 18:35
When the chief p therefore Jn 19:6
The chief p answered, We have no Jn 19:15
Then said the chief p of the Jews Jn 19:21
they spake unto the people, the p Acts 4:1
and reported all that the chief p Acts 4:23
the chief p heard these things, Acts 5:24
a great company of the p were Acts 6:7
p to bind all that call on thy Acts 9:14
bring them bound unto the chief p Acts 9:21
Sceva, a Jew, and chief of the p Acts 19:14
bands, and commanded the chief p Acts 22:30
And they came to the chief p Acts 23:14
I was at Jerusalem, the chief p Acts 25:15
authority from the chief p Acts 26:10
and commission from the chief p Acts 26:12
(For those p were made without an Heb 7:21
And they truly were many p Heb 7:23
not daily, as those high p Heb 7:27
men high p which have infirmity Heb 7:28
seeing that there are p that Heb 8:4
the p went always into the first Heb 9:6
kings and p unto God and his Father Rev 1:6
made us unto our God kings and p Rev 5:10
power, but they shall be p of God Rev 20:6

## PRIESTS'

place where the p feet stood firm Josh 4:3
the soles of the p feet were Josh 4:18
thee, into one of the p offices 1Sa 2:36
it was the p 2Kin 12:16
silver, and one hundred p garments Ezr 2:69
five hundred and thirty p garments Neh 7:70
and threescore and seven p garments Neh 7:72
certain of the p sons with Neh 12:35

## PRINCE

thou art a mighty p among us Gen 23:6
for as a p hast thou power with Gen 32:28
p of the country, saw her, he Gen 34:2
And he said, Who made thee a p Ex 2:14
each p on his day, for the Num 7:11
of Zuar, p of Issachar, did offer Num 7:18
p of the children of Zebulun, did Num 7:24
p of the children of Reuben, did Num 7:30
p of the children of Simeon, did Num 7:36
p of the children of Gad, offered Num 7:42
p of the children of Ephraim, Num 7:48
p of the children of Manasseh Num 7:54
p of the children of Benjamin, Num 7:60
p of the children of Dan, offered Num 7:66
p of the children of Asher, Num 7:72
p of the children of Naphtali, Num 7:78
thyself altogether a p over us Num 16:13
him a rod apiece, for each p one Num 17:6
a p of a chief house among the Num 25:14
the daughter of a p of Midian Num 25:18
shall take one p of every tribe Num 34:18
the p of the tribe of the Num 34:22
The p of the children of Joseph, Num 34:23
the p of the tribe of the Num 34:24
the p of the tribe of the Num 34:25
the p of the tribe of the Num 34:26
the p of the tribe of the Num 34:27
the p of the tribe of the Num 34:28
princes, of each chief house a p Josh 22:14
Know ye not that there is a p 2Sa 3:38
but I will make him p all the 1Kin 11:34
made thee p over my people Israel 1Kin 14:7
made thee p over my people Israel 1Kin 16:2
p of the children of Judah 1Chr 2:10
he was p of the Reubenites 1Chr 5:6
unto Sheshbazzar, the p of Judah Ezr 1:8
say, Where is the house of the p Job 21:28
as a p would I go near unto him Job 31:37
is the destruction of the p Prov 14:28
much less do lying lips a p Prov 17:7
will intreat the favour of the p Prov 19:6
the p whom thine eyes have seen Prov 25:7
long forbearing is a p persuaded Prov 25:15
The p that wanteth understanding Prov 28:16
Father, The P of Peace Is 9:6
And this Seraiah was a quiet p Jer 51:59
the p shall be clothed with Eze 7:27
concerneth the p in Jerusalem Eze 12:10
the p that is among them shall Eze 12:12
thou, profane wicked p of Israel Eze 21:25
of man, say unto the p of Tyrus Eze 28:2
no more a p of the land of Egypt Eze 30:13
my servant David a p among them Eze 34:24
David shall be their p for ever Eze 37:25
the chief p of Meshech and Tubal, Eze 38:2
the chief p of Meshech and Tubal Eze 38:3
the chief p of Meshech and Tubal Eze 39:1
It is for the p Eze 44:3
the p, he shall sit in it to eat Eze 44:3
be for the p on the one side Eze 45:7
this oblation for the p in Israel Eze 45:16
shall the p prepare for himself Eze 45:22
the p shall enter by the way of Eze 46:2
the burnt offering that the p Eze 46:4
when the p shall enter, he shall Eze 46:8
the p in the midst of them, when Eze 46:10
Now when the p shall prepare a Eze 46:12
If the p give a gift unto any of Eze 46:16
after, it shall return to the p Eze 46:17
Moreover the p shall not take of Eze 46:18
And the residue shall be for the p Eze 48:21
against the portions for the p Eze 48:21
of Benjamin, shall be for the p Eze 48:22
Unto whom the p of the eunuchs Dan 1:7
p of the eunuchs that he might Dan 1:8
love with the p of the eunuchs Dan 1:9
the p of the eunuchs said unto Dan 1:10
whom the p of the eunuchs had set Dan 1:11
then the p of the eunuchs brought Dan 1:18
himself even to the p of the host Dan 8:11
stand up against the P of princes Dan 8:25
the P shall be seven weeks Dan 9:25
the people of the p that shall Dan 9:26
But the p of the kingdom of Persia Dan 10:13
to fight with the p of Persia Dan 10:20
the p of Grecia shall come Dan 10:20
these things, but Michael your p Dan 10:21
but a p for his own behalf shall Dan 11:18
also the p of the covenant Dan 11:22
the great p which standeth for Dan 12:1
without a king, and without a p Hos 3:4
the p asketh, and the judge asketh Mic 7:3
through the p of the devils Mt 9:34
by Beelzebub the p of the devils Mt 12:24

by the *p* of the devils casteth he ... Mk 3:22
now shall the *p* of this world be ... Jn 12:31
for the *p* of this world cometh, ... Jn 14:30
because the *p* of this world is ... Jn 16:11
And killed the *P* of life, whom God ... Acts 3:15
with his right hand to be a *P* ... Acts 5:31
according to the *p* of the power ... Eph 2:2
the *p* of the kings of the earth ... Rev 1:5

## PRINCE'S
thy feet with shoes, O *p* daughter ... Song 7:1
it shall be the *p* part to give ... Eze 45:17
the midst of that which is the *p* ... Eze 48:22

## PRINCES
The *p* also of Pharaoh saw her, and ... Gen 12:15
twelve *p* shall he beget, and I ... Gen 17:20
twelve *p* according to their ... Gen 25:16
*p* of the tribes of their fathers, ... Num 1:16
the *p* of Israel, being twelve men ... Num 1:44
That the *p* of Israel, heads of ... Num 7:2
who were the *p* of the tribes, and ... Num 7:2
a wagon for two of the *p*, and for ... Num 7:3
the *p* offered for dedicating of ... Num 7:10
even the *p* offered their offering ... Num 7:10
was anointed, by the *p* of Israel ... Num 7:84
but with one trumpet, then the *p* ... Num 10:4
fifty *p* of the assembly, famous ... Num 16:2
of all their *p* according to the ... Num 17:2
every one of their *p* gave him a ... Num 17:6
The *p* digged the well, the nobles ... Num 21:18
the *p* of Moab abode with Balaam ... Num 22:8
and said unto the *p* of Balak ... Num 22:13
the *p* of Moab rose up, and they ... Num 22:14
And Balak sent yet again *p* ... Num 22:15
ass, and went with the *p* of Moab ... Num 22:21
Balaam went with the *p* of Balak ... Num 22:35
to the *p* that were with him ... Num 22:40
he, and all the *p* of Moab ... Num 23:6
and the *p* of Moab with him ... Num 23:17
the priest, and before the *p* ... Num 27:2
all the *p* of the congregation, ... Num 31:13
unto the *p* of the congregation, ... Num 32:2
before Moses, and before the *p* ... Num 36:1
the *p* of the congregation sware ... Josh 9:15
because the *p* of the congregation ... Josh 9:18
murmured against the *p* ... Josh 9:18
But all the *p* said unto all the ... Josh 9:19
the *p* said unto them, Let them ... Josh 9:21
as the *p* had promised them ... Josh 9:21
Moses smote with the *p* of Midian ... Josh 13:21
the son of Nun, and before the *p* ... Josh 17:4
And with him ten *p*, of each chief ... Josh 22:14
the *p* of the congregation and ... Josh 22:30
of Eleazar the priest, and the *p* ... Josh 22:32
give ear, O ye *p* ... Judg 5:3
the *p* of Issachar were with ... Judg 5:15
they took two *p* of the Midianites ... Judg 7:25
into your hands the *p* of Midian ... Judg 8:3
the *p* of Succoth said, Are the ... Judg 8:6
unto him the *p* of Succoth ... Judg 8:14
*p* of Gilead said one to another, ... Judg 10:18
the dunghill, to set them among *p* ... 1Sa 2:8
Then the *p* of the Philistines ... 1Sa 18:30
Then said the *p* of the ... 1Sa 29:3
unto the *p* of the Philistines ... 1Sa 29:3
the *p* of the Philistines were ... 1Sa 29:4
the *p* of the Philistines said ... 1Sa 29:4
notwithstanding the *p* of the ... 1Sa 29:9
the *p* of the children of Ammon ... 2Sa 10:3
regardest neither *p* nor servants ... 2Sa 19:6
And these were the *p* which he had ... 1Kin 4:2
of war, and his servants, and his *p* ... 1Kin 9:22
men of the *p* of the provinces ... 1Kin 20:14
men of the *p* of the provinces ... 1Kin 20:15
the young men of the *p* of the ... 1Kin 20:17
So these young men of the *p* of ... 1Kin 20:19
as the manner was, and the *p* ... 2Kin 11:14
mother, and his servants, and his *p* ... 2Kin 24:12
away all Jerusalem, and all the *p* ... 2Kin 24:14
names were *p* in their families ... 1Chr 4:38
men of valour, chief of the *p* ... 1Chr 7:40
But the *p* of the children of ... 1Chr 19:3
David also commanded all the *p* of ... 1Chr 22:17
together all the *p* of Israel ... 1Chr 23:2
them before the king, and the *p* ... 1Chr 24:6
These were the *p* of the tribes of ... 1Chr 27:22
assembled all the *p* of Israel ... 1Chr 28:1
the *p* of the tribes, and the ... 1Chr 28:1
also the *p* and all the people will ... 1Chr 28:21
*p* of the tribes of Israel, and the ... 1Chr 29:6
And all the *p*, and the mighty men, ... 1Chr 29:24
to the *p* of Judah, that were ... 2Chr 12:5
Whereupon the *p* of Israel ... 2Chr 12:6
of his reign he sent to his *p* ... 2Chr 17:7
and divers also of the *p* of Israel ... 2Chr 21:4
Jehoram went forth with his *p* ... 2Chr 21:9
of Ahab, and found the *p* of Judah ... 2Chr 22:8
at the entering in, and the *p* ... 2Chr 23:13
And all the *p* and all the people ... 2Chr 24:10
of Jehoiada came the *p* of Judah ... 2Chr 24:17
destroyed all the *p* of the people ... 2Chr 24:23
and the spoil before the *p* ... 2Chr 28:14
house of the king, and of the *p* ... 2Chr 28:21
the *p* commanded the Levites to ... 2Chr 29:30
king had taken counsel, and his *p* ... 2Chr 30:2
his *p* throughout all Israel and ... 2Chr 30:6
of the king and of the *p*, by the ... 2Chr 30:12
the *p* gave to the congregation a ... 2Chr 30:24
the *p* came and saw the heaps, they ... 2Chr 31:8
He took counsel with his *p* ... 2Chr 32:3
ambassadors of the *p* of Babylon ... 2Chr 32:31
his *p* gave willingly unto the ... 2Chr 35:8
of the king, and of his *p* ... 2Chr 36:18
and before all the king's mighty *p* ... Ezr 7:28
the *p* had appointed for the ... Ezr 8:20
the *p* came to me, saying, The ... Ezr 9:1
yea, the hand of the *p* and rulers ... Ezr 9:2
according to the counsel of the *p* ... Ezr 10:8
upon us, on our kings, on our *p* ... Neh 9:32
Neither have our kings, our *p* ... Neh 9:34
and our *p*, Levites, and priests, ... Neh 9:38
Then I brought up the *p* of Judah ... Neh 12:31
and half of the *p* of Judah ... Neh 12:32
he made a feast unto all his *p* ... Est 1:3
*p* of the provinces, being before ... Est 1:3
the people and the *p* her beauty ... Est 1:11
and Memucan, the seven *p* of Persia ... Est 1:14
answered before the king and the *p* ... Est 1:16
king only, but also to all the *p* ... Est 1:16
this day unto all the king's *p* ... Est 1:18
saying pleased the king and the *p* ... Est 1:21
made a great feast unto all his *p* ... Est 2:18
all the *p* that were with him ... Est 3:1
he had advanced him above the *p* ... Est 5:11
of one of the king's most noble *p* ... Est 6:9
Or with *p* that had gold, who ... Job 3:15
He leadeth *p* away spoiled, and ... Job 12:19
He poureth contempt upon *p* ... Job 12:21
The *p* refrained talking, and laid ... Job 29:9
and to *p*, Ye are ungodly ... Job 34:18
accepteth not the persons of *p* ... Job 34:19
mayest make *p* in all the earth ... Ps 45:16
The *p* of the people are gathered ... Ps 47:9
the *p* of Judah and their council, ... Ps 68:27
the *p* of Zebulun ... Ps 68:27
and the *p* of Naphtali ... Ps 68:27
*P* shall come out of Egypt ... Ps 68:31
He shall cut off the spirit of *p* ... Ps 76:12
men, and fall like one of the *p* ... Ps 82:7
yea, all their *p* as Zebah ... Ps 83:11
To bind his *p* at his pleasure ... Ps 105:22
He poureth contempt upon *p* ... Ps 107:40
That he may set him with *p* ... Ps 113:8
even with the *p* of his people ... Ps 113:8
LORD than to put confidence in *p* ... Ps 118:9
*P* also did sit and speak against ... Ps 119:23
*P* have persecuted me without a ... Ps 119:161
Put not your trust in *p*, nor in ... Ps 146:3
*p*, and all judges of the earth ... Ps 148:11
kings reign, and *p* decree justice ... Prov 8:15
By me *p* rule, and nobles, even all ... Prov 8:16
good, nor to strike *p* for equity ... Prov 17:26
for a servant to have rule over *p* ... Prov 19:10
of a land many are the *p* thereof ... Prov 28:2
nor for *p* strong drink ... Prov 31:4
*p* walking as servants upon the ... Eccl 10:7
and thy *p* eat in the morning ... Eccl 10:16
thy *p* eat in due season, for ... Eccl 10:17
Thy *p* are rebellious, and ... Is 1:23
will give children to be their *p* ... Is 3:4
of his people, and the *p* thereof ... Is 3:14
Are not my *p* altogether kings ... Is 10:8
Surely the *p* of Zoan are fools, ... Is 19:11
The *p* of Zoan are become fools, ... Is 19:13
the *p* of Noph are deceived ... Is 19:13
arise, ye *p*, and anoint the shield ... Is 21:5
city, whose merchants are *p* ... Is 23:8
For his *p* were at Zoan, and his ... Is 30:4
his *p* shall be afraid of the ... Is 31:9
and *p* shall rule in judgment ... Is 32:1
all her *p* shall be nothing ... Is 34:12
That bringeth the *p* to nothing ... Is 40:23
shall come upon *p* as upon morter ... Is 41:25
profaned the *p* of the sanctuary ... Is 43:28
*p* also shall worship, because of ... Is 49:7
of Judah, against the *p* thereof ... Jer 1:18
they, their kings, their *p* ... Jer 2:26
perish, and the heart of the *p* ... Jer 4:9
of Judah, and the bones of his *p* ... Jer 8:1
*p* sitting upon the throne of ... Jer 17:25
and on horses, they, and their *p* ... Jer 17:25
and the *p* of Judah, with the ... Jer 24:1
the king of Judah, and his *p* ... Jer 24:8
the *p* thereof, to make them a ... Jer 25:18
Egypt, and his servants, and his *p* ... Jer 25:19
When the *p* of Judah heard these ... Jer 26:10
and the prophets unto the *p* ... Jer 26:11
spake Jeremiah unto all the *p* ... Jer 26:12
Then said the *p* and all the people ... Jer 26:16
all his mighty men, and all the *p* ... Jer 26:21
the *p* of Judah and Jerusalem, and ... Jer 29:2
anger, they, their kings, their *p* ... Jer 32:32
Now when all the *p*, and all the ... Jer 34:10
The *p* of Judah ... Jer 34:19
the *p* of Jerusalem, the eunuchs, ... Jer 34:19
his *p* will I give into the hand ... Jer 34:21
which was by the chamber of the *p* ... Jer 35:4
all the *p* sat there, even ... Jer 36:12
the son of Hananiah, and all the *p* ... Jer 36:12
Therefore all the *p* sent Jehudi ... Jer 36:14
Then said the *p* unto Baruch ... Jer 36:19
in the ears of all the *p* which ... Jer 36:21
Jeremiah, and brought him to the *p* ... Jer 37:14
Wherefore the *p* were wroth with ... Jer 37:15
Therefore the *p* said unto the ... Jer 38:4
unto the king of Babylon's *p* ... Jer 38:17
forth to the king of Babylon's *p* ... Jer 38:18
forth to the king of Babylon's *p* ... Jer 38:22
But if the *p* hear that I have ... Jer 38:25
Then came all the *p* unto Jeremiah ... Jer 38:27
all the *p* of the king of Babylon ... Jer 39:3
of the *p* of the king of Babylon ... Jer 39:3
and all the king of Babylon's *p* ... Jer 39:13
the *p* of the king, even ten men ... Jer 41:1
our fathers, our kings, and our *p* ... Jer 44:17
fathers, your kings, and your *p* ... Jer 44:21
his priests and his *p* together ... Jer 48:7
and his priests and his *p* together ... Jer 49:3
from thence the king and the *p* ... Jer 49:38
of Babylon, and upon her *p* ... Jer 50:35
And I will make drunk her *p* ... Jer 51:57
also all the *p* of Judah in Riblah ... Jer 52:10
her *p* are become like harts that ... Lam 1:6
the kingdom and the *p* thereof ... Lam 2:2
her *p* are among the Gentiles ... Lam 2:9
*P* are hanged up by their hand ... Lam 5:12
son of Benaiah, *p* of the people ... Eze 11:1
the *p* thereof, and led them with ... Eze 17:12
a lamentation for the *p* of Israel ... Eze 19:1
shall be upon all the *p* of Israel ... Eze 21:12
the *p* of Israel, every one were ... Eze 22:6
Her *p* in the midst thereof are ... Eze 22:27
heads, all of them *p* to look to ... Eze 23:15
Then all the *p* of the sea shall ... Eze 26:16
all the *p* of Kedar, they occupied ... Eze 27:21
is Edom, her kings, and all her *p* ... Eze 32:29
There be the *p* of the north ... Eze 32:30
the blood of the *p* of the earth ... Eze 39:18
my *p* shall no more oppress my ... Eze 45:8
Let it suffice you, O *p* of Israel ... Eze 45:9
of the king's seed, and of the *p* ... Dan 1:3
sent to gather together the *p* ... Dan 3:2
Then the *p*, the governors, and ... Dan 3:3
And the *p*, governors, and captains, ... Dan 3:27
that the king, and his *p*, his ... Dan 5:2
and the king, and his *p*, his wives, ... Dan 5:3
kingdom an hundred and twenty *p* ... Dan 6:1
that the *p* might give accounts ... Dan 6:2
above the presidents and *p* ... Dan 6:3
*p* sought to find occasion against ... Dan 6:4
*p* assembled together to the king, ... Dan 6:6
kingdom, the governors, and the *p* ... Dan 6:7
stand up against the Prince of *p* ... Dan 8:25
in thy name to our kings, our *p* ... Dan 9:6
of face, to our kings, to our *p* ... Dan 9:8
lo, Michael, one of the chief *p* ... Dan 10:13
shall be strong, and one of his *p* ... Dan 11:5
Egypt their gods, with their *p* ... Dan 11:8
The *p* of Judah were like them ... Hos 5:10
and the *p* with their lies ... Hos 7:3
In the day of our king the *p* have ... Hos 7:5
their *p* shall fall by the sword ... Hos 7:16
they have made *p*, and I knew it ... Hos 8:4
for the burden of the king of *p* ... Hos 8:10
all their *p* are revolters ... Hos 9:15
thou saidst, Give me a king and *p* ... Hos 13:10
his *p* together, saith the LORD ... Amos 1:15
slay all the *p* thereof with him ... Amos 2:3
ye *p* of the house of Israel ... Mic 3:1
*p* of the house of Israel, that ... Mic 3:9
the *p* shall be a scorn unto them ... Hab 1:10
that I will punish the *p* ... Zeph 1:8
Her *p* within her are roaring ... Zeph 3:3
not the least among the *p* of Juda ... Mt 2:6
Ye know that the *p* of the ... Mt 20:25
nor of the *p* of this world, that ... 1Cor 2:6
Which none of the *p* of this world ... 1Cor 2:8

## PRINCESS
*p* among the provinces, how is she ... Lam 1:1

## PRINCESSES
And he had seven hundred wives, *p* ... 1Kin 11:3

## PRINCIPAL
Take thou also unto thee *p* spices ... Ex 30:23
he shall even restore it in the *p* ... Lev 6:5
his trespass with the *p* thereof ... Num 5:7
the son of Nathan was *p* officer ... 1Kin 4:5
the *p* scribe of the host, which ... 2Kin 25:19
one *p* household being taken for ... 1Chr 24:6
even the *p* fathers over against ... 1Chr 24:31
of Asaph, was the *p* to begin the ... Neh 11:17
Wisdom is the *p* thing ... Prov 4:7
broken down the *p* plants thereof ... Is 16:8
cummin, and cast in the *p* wheat ... Is 28:25
in the ashes, ye *p* of the flock ... Jer 25:34
nor the *p* of the flock to escape ... Jer 25:35
an howling of the *p* of the flock ... Jer 25:36
the *p* scribe of the host, who ... Jer 52:25
seven shepherds, and eight *p* men ... Mic 5:5
*p* men of the city, at Festus' ... Acts 25:23

## PRINCIPALITIES
for your *p* shall come down, even ... Jer 13:18
nor life, nor angels, nor *p* ... Rom 8:38
To the intent that now unto the *p* ... Eph 3:10
flesh and blood, but against *p* ... Eph 6:12
be thrones, or dominions, or *p* ... Col 1:16
And having spoiled *p* and powers, he ... Col 2:15
them in mind to be subject to *p* ... Titus 3:1

## PRINCIPALITY
Far above all *p*, and power, and ... Eph 1:21
him, which is the head of all *p* ... Col 2:10

## PRINCIPLES
the first *p* of the oracles of God ... Heb 5:12
Therefore leaving the *p* of the ... Heb 6:1

## PRINT
dead, nor *p* any marks upon you ... Lev 19:28
thou settest a *p* upon the heels ... Job 13:27

in his hands the *p* of the nails .......... Jn 20:25
my finger into the *p* of the nails .......... Jn 20:25

**PRINTED**
oh that they were *p* in a book .......... Job 19:23

**PRISCA** (*pris'-cah*) See PRISCILLA. *Same as Priscilla.*
Salute *P* and Aquila, and the .......... 2Ti 4:19

**PRISCILLA** (*pris-sil'-lah*) See PRISCA. *Wife of Aquila and co-worker of Paul.*
come from Italy, with his wife *P* .......... Acts 18:2
thence into Syria, and with him *P* .......... Acts 18:18
*P* had heard, they took him unto .......... Acts 18:26
Greet *P* and Aquila my helpers in .......... Rom 16:3
*P* salute you much in the Lord, .......... 1Cor 16:19

**PRISED**
price that I was *p* at of them .......... Zec 11:13

**PRISON**
took him, and put him into the *p* .......... Gen 39:20
and he was there in the *p* .......... Gen 39:20
the sight of the keeper of the *p* .......... Gen 39:21
the keeper of the *p* committed to .......... Gen 39:22
the prisoners that were in the *p* .......... Gen 39:22
The keeper of the *p* looked not to .......... Gen 39:23
captain of the guard, into the *p* .......... Gen 40:3
Egypt, which were bound in the *p* .......... Gen 40:5
brother, and ye shall be kept in *p* .......... Gen 42:16
be bound in the house of your *p* .......... Gen 42:19
and he did grind in the *p* house .......... Judg 16:21
for Samson out of the *p* house .......... Judg 16:25
king, Put this fellow in the *p* .......... 1Kin 22:27
shut him up, and bound him in *p* .......... 2Kin 17:4
Jehoiachin king of Judah out of *p* .......... 2Kin 25:27
And changed his *p* garments .......... 2Kin 25:29
the seer, and put him in a *p* house .......... 2Chr 16:10
king, Put this fellow in the *p* .......... 2Chr 18:26
that was by the court of the *p* .......... Neh 3:25
and they stood still in the *p* gate .......... Neh 12:39
Bring my soul out of *p*, that I .......... Ps 142:7
For out of *p* he cometh to reign .......... Eccl 4:14
pit, and shall be shut up in the *p* .......... Is 24:22
out the prisoners from the *p* .......... Is 42:7
in darkness out of the *p* house .......... Is 42:7
and they are hid in *p* houses .......... Is 42:22
He was taken from *p* and from .......... Is 53:8
the opening of the *p* to them that .......... Is 61:1
that thou shouldest put him in *p* .......... Jer 29:26
was shut up in the court of the *p* .......... Jer 32:2
*p* according to the word of the .......... Jer 32:8
that sat in the court of the *p* .......... Jer 32:12
yet shut up in the court of the *p* .......... Jer 33:1
for they had not put him into *p* .......... Jer 37:4
put him in *p* in the house of .......... Jer 37:15
for they had made that the *p* .......... Jer 37:15
people, that ye have put me in *p* .......... Jer 37:18
Jeremiah into the court of the *p* .......... Jer 37:21
remained in the court of the *p* .......... Jer 37:21
that was in the court of the *p* .......... Jer 38:6
remained in the court of the *p* .......... Jer 38:13
abode in the court of the *p* until .......... Jer 38:28
out of the court of the *p* .......... Jer 39:14
was shut up in the court of the *p* .......... Jer 39:15
put him in *p* till the day of his .......... Jer 52:11
and brought him forth out of *p* .......... Jer 52:31
And changed his *p* garments .......... Jer 52:33
heard that John was cast into *p* .......... Mt 4:12
officer, and thou be cast into *p* .......... Mt 5:25
in the *p* the works of Christ .......... Mt 11:2
put him in *p* for Herodias' sake, .......... Mt 14:3
sent, and beheaded John in the *p* .......... Mt 14:10
but went and cast him into *p* .......... Mt 18:30
I was in *p*, and ye came unto me .......... Mt 25:36
Or when saw we thee sick, or in *p* .......... Mt 25:39
sick, and in *p*, and ye visited me .......... Mt 25:43
or naked, or sick, or in *p* .......... Mt 25:44
Now after that John was put in *p* .......... Mk 1:14
bound him in *p* for Herodias' sake .......... Mk 6:17
he went and beheaded him in the *p* .......... Mk 6:27
all, that he shut up John in *p* .......... Lk 3:20
and the officer cast thee into *p* .......... Lk 12:58
to go with thee, both into *p* .......... Lk 22:33
and for murder, was cast into *p* .......... Lk 23:19
and murder was cast into *p* .......... Lk 23:25
For John was not yet cast into *p* .......... Jn 3:24
and put them in the common *p* .......... Acts 5:18
Lord by night opened the *p* doors .......... Acts 5:19
sent to the *p* to have them .......... Acts 5:21
came, and found them not in the *p* .......... Acts 5:22
The *p* truly found we shut with .......... Acts 5:23
the men whom ye put in *p* are .......... Acts 5:25
men and women committed them to *p*. Acts 8:3
apprehended him, he put him in *p* .......... Acts 12:4
Peter therefore was kept in *p* .......... Acts 12:5
before the door kept the *p* .......... Acts 12:6
him, and a light shined in the *p* .......... Acts 12:7
Lord had brought him out of the *p* .......... Acts 12:17
upon them, they cast them into *p* .......... Acts 16:23
thrust them into the inner *p* .......... Acts 16:24
foundations of the *p* were shaken .......... Acts 16:26
the keeper of the *p* awaking out .......... Acts 16:27
sleep, and seeing the *p* doors open .......... Acts 16:27
the keeper of the *p* told this .......... Acts 16:36
Romans, and have cast us into *p* .......... Acts 16:37
And they went out of the *p* .......... Acts 16:40
of the saints did I shut up in *p* .......... Acts 26:10
and preached unto the spirits in *p* .......... 1Pet 3:19
shall cast some of you into *p* .......... Rev 2:10
shall be loosed out of his *p* .......... Rev 20:7

**PRISONER**
sighing of the *p* come before thee .......... Ps 79:11
To hear the groaning of the *p* .......... Ps 102:20
to release unto the people a *p* .......... Mt 27:15
And they had then a notable *p* .......... Mt 27:16
feast he released unto them one *p* .......... Mk 15:6
Paul the *p* called me unto him, and ... Acts 23:18
to me unreasonable to send a *p* .......... Acts 25:27
yet was I delivered *p* from .......... Acts 28:17
the *p* of Jesus Christ for you .......... Eph 3:1
the *p* of the Lord, beseech you .......... Eph 4:1
of our Lord, nor of me his *p* .......... 2Ti 1:8
a *p* of Jesus Christ, and Timothy .......... Philem 1
now also a *p* of Jesus Christ .......... Philem 9

**PRISONERS**
where the king's *p* were bound .......... Gen 39:20
all the *p* that were in the prison .......... Gen 39:22
Israel, and took some of them *p* .......... Num 21:1
There the *p* rest together .......... Job 3:18
the poor, and despiseth not his *p* .......... Ps 69:33
The LORD looseth the *p* .......... Ps 146:7
they shall bow down under the *p* .......... Is 10:4
opened not the house of his *p* .......... Is 14:17
Assyria lead away the Egyptians *p* .......... Is 20:4
as *p* are gathered in the pit, and .......... Is 24:22
bring out the *p* from the prison .......... Is 42:7
That thou mayest say to the *p* .......... Is 49:9
his feet all the *p* of the earth .......... Lam 3:34
*p* out of the pit wherein is no .......... Zec 9:11
to the strong hold, ye *p* of hope .......... Zec 9:12
and the *p* heard them .......... Acts 16:25
that the *p* had been fled .......... Acts 16:27
certain other *p* unto one named .......... Acts 27:1
counsel was to kill the *p* .......... Acts 27:42
the *p* to the captain of the guard .......... Acts 28:16

**PRISONS**
up to the synagogues, and into *p* .......... Lk 21:12
and delivering into *p* both men .......... Acts 22:4
in *p* more frequent, in deaths oft .......... 2Cor 11:23

**PRIVATE**
is of any *p* interpretation .......... 2Pet 1:20

**PRIVATELY**
the disciples came unto him *p* .......... Mt 24:3
into a desert place by ship *p* .......... Mk 6:32
house, his disciples asked him *p* .......... Mk 9:28
and John and Andrew asked him *p* .......... Mk 13:3
went aside *p* into a desert place .......... Lk 9:10
him unto his disciples, and said *p* .......... Lk 10:23
hand, and went with him aside *p* .......... Acts 23:19
but *p* to them which were of .......... Gal 2:2

**PRIVILY**
sent messengers unto Abimelech *p* .......... Judg 9:31
off the skirt of Saul's robe *p* .......... 1Sa 24:4
his eyes are *p* set against the .......... Ps 10:8
that they may *p* shoot at the .......... Ps 11:2
net that they have laid *p* for me .......... Ps 31:4
they commune of laying snares *p* .......... Ps 64:5
Whoso *p* slandereth his neighbour, .......... Ps 101:5
have they *p* laid a snare for me .......... Ps 142:3
let us lurk *p* for the innocent .......... Prov 1:11
they lurk *p* for their own lives .......... Prov 1:18
was minded to put her away *p* .......... Mt 1:19
when he had *p* called the wise men .......... Mt 2:7
and now do they thrust us out *p* .......... Acts 16:37
who came in *p* to spy out our .......... Gal 2:4
who *p* shall bring in damnable .......... 2Pet 2:1

**PRIVY**
or hath his *p* member cut off, .......... Deut 23:1
which thine heart is *p* to .......... 1Kin 2:44
entereth into their *p* chambers .......... Eze 21:14
his wife also being *p* to it .......... Acts 5:2

**PRIZE**
run all, but one receiveth the *p* .......... 1Cor 9:24
*p* of the high calling of God in .......... Phil 3:14

**PROCEED**
that *p* out of the candlestick .......... Ex 25:35
any word *p* out of your mouth .......... Josh 6:10
which shall *p* out of thy bowels, .......... 2Sa 7:12
but I will *p* no further .......... Job 40:5
I will *p* to do a marvellous work .......... Is 29:14
for a law shall *p* from me .......... Is 51:4
for they *p* from evil to evil, and .......... Jer 9:3
out of them shall *p* thanksgiving .......... Jer 30:19
their governor shall *p* from the .......... Jer 30:21
dignity shall *p* of themselves .......... Hab 1:7
But those things which *p* out of .......... Mt 15:18
out of the heart *p* evil thoughts .......... Mt 15:19
*p* evil thoughts, adulteries, .......... Mk 7:21
communication *p* out of your mouth .......... Eph 4:29
But they shall *p* no further .......... 2Ti 3:9

**PROCEEDED**
then whatsoever *p* out of her lips .......... Num 30:12
which hath *p* out of your mouth .......... Num 32:24
which hath *p* out of thy mouth .......... Judg 11:36
Elihu also *p*, and said, .......... Job 36:1
words which *p* out of his mouth .......... Lk 4:22
for I *p* forth and came from God .......... Jn 8:42
he *p* further to take Peter also .......... Acts 12:3
And out of the throne *p* lightnings .......... Rev 4:5
which sword *p* out of his mouth .......... Rev 19:21

**PROCEEDETH**
The thing *p* from the LORD .......... Gen 24:50
to all that *p* out of his mouth .......... Num 30:2
but by every word that *p* out of .......... Deut 8:3
Wickedness *p* from the wicked .......... 1Sa 24:13
an error which *p* from the ruler .......... Eccl 10:5
mouth of the most High *p* not evil .......... Lam 3:38
therefore wrong judgment *p* .......... Hab 1:4
but by every word that *p* out of .......... Mt 4:4
which *p* from the Father, he shall .......... Jn 15:26
Out of the same mouth *p* blessing .......... Jas 3:10
fire *p* out of their mouth, and .......... Rev 11:5

**PROCEEDING**
*p* out of the throne of God and of .......... Rev 22:1

**PROCESS**
in *p* of time it came to pass, .......... Gen 4:3
in *p* of time the daughter of .......... Gen 38:12
And it came to pass in *p* of time .......... Ex 2:23
And it came to pass in *p* of time .......... Judg 11:4
came to pass, that in *p* of time .......... 2Chr 21:19

**PROCHORUS** (*prok'-o-rus*) *A leader in the Jerusalem church.*
the Holy Ghost, and Philip, and *P* .......... Acts 6:5

**PROCLAIM**
I will *p* the name of the LORD .......... Ex 33:19
which ye shall *p* to be holy .......... Lev 23:2
which ye shall *p* in their seasons .......... Lev 23:4
ye shall *p* on the selfsame day, .......... Lev 23:21
which ye shall *p* to be holy .......... Lev 23:37
*p* liberty throughout all the land .......... Lev 25:10
against it, then *p* peace unto it .......... Deut 20:10
*p* in the ears of the people, .......... Judg 7:3
*P* a fast, and set Naboth on high .......... 1Kin 21:9
*P* a solemn assembly for Baal .......... 2Kin 10:20
*p* in all their cities, and in .......... Neh 8:15
*p* before him, Thus shall it be .......... Est 6:9
Most men will *p* every one his own .......... Prov 20:6
to *p* liberty to the captives, and .......... Is 61:1
To *p* the acceptable year of the .......... Is 61:2
*p* these words toward the north, .......... Jer 3:12
*p* there this word, and say, Hear .......... Jer 7:2
*P* all these words in the cities .......... Jer 11:6
*p* there the words that I shall .......... Jer 19:2
Jerusalem, to *p* liberty unto them .......... Jer 34:8
I *p* a liberty for you, saith the .......... Jer 34:17
*P* ye this among the Gentiles .......... Joel 3:9
of thanksgiving with leaven, and *p* .......... Amos 4:5

**PROCLAIMED**
there, and *p* the name of the LORD .......... Ex 34:5
LORD passed by before him, and *p* .......... Ex 34:6
it to be *p* throughout the camp .......... Ex 36:6
They *p* a fast, and set Naboth on .......... 1Kin 21:12
And they *p* it .......... 2Kin 10:20
God *p*, who *p* these words .......... 2Kin 23:16
*p* these things that thou hast .......... 2Kin 23:17
*p* a fast throughout all Judah .......... 2Chr 20:3
Then I *p* a fast there, at the .......... Ezr 8:21
*p* before him, Thus shall it be .......... Est 6:11
the LORD hath *p* unto the end of .......... Is 62:11
that they *p* a fast before the .......... Jer 36:9
*p* a fast, and put on sackcloth, .......... Jonah 3:5
And he caused it to be *p* and .......... Jonah 3:7
shall be *p* upon the housetops .......... Lk 12:3

**PROCLAIMETH**
the heart of fools *p* foolishness .......... Prov 12:23

**PROCLAIMING**
in *p* liberty every man to his .......... Jer 34:15
in *p* liberty, every one to his .......... Jer 34:17
strong angel *p* with a loud voice .......... Rev 5:2

**PROCLAMATION**
and Aaron made *p*, and said, To .......... Ex 32:5
Asa made a *p* throughout all Judah ... 1Kin 15:22
there went a *p* throughout the .......... 1Kin 22:36
they made a *p* through Judah and .......... 2Chr 24:9
to make *p* throughout all Israel .......... 2Chr 30:5
that he made a *p* throughout all .......... 2Chr 36:22
that he made a *p* throughout all .......... Ezr 1:1
they made *p* throughout Judah and .......... Ezr 10:7
made a *p* concerning him, that he .......... Dan 5:29

**PROCURE**
Thus might we *p* great evil .......... Jer 26:19
the prosperity that I *p* unto it .......... Jer 33:9

**PROCURED**
Hast thou not *p* this unto thyself .......... Jer 2:17
thy doings have *p* these things .......... Jer 4:18

**PROCURETH**
diligently seeketh good *p* favour .......... Prov 11:27

**PRODUCE**
*P* your cause, saith the LORD .......... Is 41:21

**PROFANE**
neither shalt thou *p* the name of .......... Lev 18:21
neither shalt thou *p* the name of .......... Lev 19:12
sanctuary, and to *p* my holy name .......... Lev 20:3
among his people, to *p* himself .......... Lev 21:4
not *p* the name of their God .......... Lev 21:6
take a wife that is a whore, or *p* .......... Lev 21:7
if she *p* herself by playing the .......... Lev 21:9
nor *p* the sanctuary of his God .......... Lev 21:12
widow, or a divorced woman, or *p* .......... Lev 21:14
Neither shall he *p* his seed among .......... Lev 21:15
that he *p* not my sanctuaries .......... Lev 21:23
that they *p* not my holy name in .......... Lev 22:2
and die therefore, if they *p* it .......... Lev 22:9
they shall not *p* the holy things .......... Lev 22:15
Neither shall ye *p* my holy name .......... Lev 22:32
that ye do, and *p* the sabbath day .......... Neh 13:17
For both prophet and priest are *p* .......... Jer 23:11
*p* wicked prince of Israel, whose .......... Eze 21:25

difference between the holy and p....... Eze 22:26
day into my sanctuary to p it............... Eze 23:39
I will p my sanctuary, the..................... Eze 24:21
as p out of the mountain of God.......... Eze 28:16
the sanctuary and the p place............... Eze 42:20
difference between the holy and p....... Eze 44:23
shall be a p place for the city,............ Eze 48:15
the same maid, to p my holy name...... Amos 2:7
in the temple p the sabbath ..................... Mt 12:5
hath gone about to p the temple .......... Acts 24:6
and for sinners, for unholy and p.............. 1Ti 1:9
But refuse p and old wives' fables............. 1Ti 4:7
to thy trust, avoiding p and vain.............. 1Ti 6:20
But shun p and vain babblings .................. 2Ti 2:16
or p person, as Esau, who for one....... Heb 12:16

## PROFANED

because he hath p the hallowed............ Lev 19:8
thou hast p his crown by casting ........... Ps 89:39
Therefore I have p the princes of........... Is 43:28
things, and hast p my sabbaths ............... Eze 22:8
law, and have p mine holy things........ Eze 22:26
my sabbaths, and I am p among them Eze 22:26
same day, and have p my sabbaths ..... Eze 23:38
my sanctuary, when it was p.................. Eze 25:3
they p my holy name, when they......... Eze 36:20
of Israel had p among the heathen...... Eze 36:21
which ye have p among the heathen.. Eze 36:22
which was p among the heathen,......... Eze 36:23
which ye have p in the midst of........... Eze 36:23
But ye have p it, in that ye say,............ Mal 1:12
for Judah hath p the holiness of............ Mal 2:11

## PROFANENESS

is p gone forth into all the land............ Jer 23:15

## PROFANETH

the whore, she p her father.................... Lev 21:9

## PROFANING

upon Israel by p the sabbath................ Neh 13:18
by p the covenant of our fathers .......... Mal 2:10

## PROFESS

I p this day unto the LORD thy............ Deut 26:3
And then will I p unto them..................... Mt 7:23
They p that they know God ................. Titus 1:16

## PROFESSED

they glorify God for your p.................. 2Cor 9:13
hast p a good profession before.............. 1Ti 6:12

## PROFESSING

P themselves to be wise, they ............. Rom 1:22
But (which becometh women p.................. 1Ti 2:10
Which some p have erred ........................ 1Ti 6:21

## PROFESSION

a good p before many witnesses.............. 1Ti 6:12
Apostle and High Priest of our p............... Heb 3:1
of God, let us hold fast our p................. Heb 4:14
Let us hold fast the p of our................ Heb 10:23

## PROFIT

what p shall this birthright do ............ Gen 25:32
What p is it if we slay our.................... Gen 37:26
which cannot p nor deliver.................... 1Sa 12:21
for the king's p to suffer them.................... Est 3:8
what p should we have, if we pray ...... Job 21:15
the strength of their hands p me............ Job 30:2
What p shall I have, if I be.................... Job 35:3
may p the son of man .............................. Job 35:8
What p is there in my blood, when.......... Ps 30:9
Treasures of wickedness p nothing........ Prov 10:2
Riches p not in the day of wrath........... Prov 11:4
In all labour there is p ........................ Prov 14:23
What p hath a man of all his .................. Eccl 1:3
there was no p under the sun ................ Eccl 2:11
What p hath he that worketh in.............. Eccl 3:9
Moreover the p of the earth is................. Eccl 5:9
what p hath he that hath laboured....... Eccl 5:16
by it there is p to them that see............ Eccl 7:11
of a people that could not p them............... Is 30:5
nor be an help nor p.................................. Is 30:5
to a people that shall not p them .............. Is 30:6
delectable things shall not p...................... Is 44:9
if so be thou shalt be able to p................. Is 47:12
thy God which teacheth thee to p............. Is 48:17
for they shall not p thee ........................... Is 57:12
walked after things that do not p............. Jer 2:8
glory for that which doth not p............... Jer 2:11
in lying words, that cannot p ................... Jer 7:8
to pain, but shall not p......................... Jer 12:13
and things wherein there is no p........... Jer 16:19
shall not p this people at all................. Jer 23:32
what p is it that we have kept............... Mal 3:14
For what shall it p a man ........................ Mk 8:36
or what p is there of............................... Rom 3:1
And this I speak for your own p .......... 1Cor 7:35
own p, but the p of many ................... 1Cor 10:33
is given to every man to p withal ........ 1Cor 12:7
with tongues, what shall I p you.......... 1Cor 14:6
Christ shall p you nothing........................ Gal 5:2
strive not about words to no p ............... 2Ti 2:14
the word preached did not p them........... Heb 4:2
but he for our p, that we might........... Heb 12:10
What doth it p, my brethren,................... Jas 2:14
what doth it p........................................ Jas 2:16

## PROFITABLE

Can a man be p unto God, as he........... Job 22:2
is wise may be p unto himself.................. Job 22:2
but wisdom is p to direct..................... Eccl 10:10
image that is p for nothing ..................... Is 44:10
was marred, it was p for nothing ........... Jer 13:7
for it is p for thee that one of.................. Mt 5:29
for it is p for thee that one of.................. Mt 5:30
back nothing that was p unto you..... Acts 20:20
godliness is p unto all things .................... 1Ti 4:8
is p for doctrine, for reproof,................... 2Ti 3:16
for he is p to me for the ........................ 2Ti 4:11
things are good and p unto men............ Titus 3:8
unprofitable, but now p to thee ........... Philem 11

## PROFITED

which was right, and it p me not ........ Job 33:27
thou mightest be p by me......................... Mt 15:5
For what is a man p, if he shall ............ Mt 16:26
thou mightest be p by me......................... Mk 7:11
p in the Jews' religion above .................. Gal 1:14
which have not p them that have........... Heb 13:9

## PROFITETH

It p a man nothing that he should......... Job 34:9
What p the graven image that the........ Hab 2:18
the flesh p nothing ................................... Jn 6:63
For circumcision verily p.......................... Rom 2:25
have not charity, it p me nothing ........ 1Cor 13:3
For bodily exercise p little........................ 1Ti 4:8

## PROFITING

that thy p may appear to all.................... 1Ti 4:15

## PROFOUND

revolters are p to make slaughter........... Hos 5:2

## PROGENITORS

above the blessings of my p unto........ Gen 49:26

## PROGNOSTICATORS

the stargazers, the monthly p.................. Is 47:13

## PROLONG

ye shall not p your days upon it, ........ Deut 4:26
that thou mayest p thy days upon ...... Deut 4:40
that ye may p your days in the ........... Deut 5:33
that ye may p your days in the ............ Deut 11:9
to the end that he may p his days........ Deut 17:20
and that thou mayest p thy days.......... Deut 22:7
that ye shall not p your days .............. Deut 30:18
ye shall p your days in the land ......... Deut 32:47
mine end, that I should p my life ........... Job 6:11
neither shall he p the perfection........... Job 15:29
Thou wilt p the king's life ........................ Ps 61:6
covetousness shall p his days .............. Prov 28:16
neither shall he p his days ................... Eccl 8:13
see his seed, he shall p his days ............ Is 53:10

## PROLONGED

that thy days may be p, and that......... Deut 5:16
and that thy days may be p .................. Deut 6:2
the state thereof shall be p .................. Prov 28:2
hundred times, and his days be p........... Eccl 8:12
come, and her days shall not be p............ Is 13:22
of Israel, saying, The days are p.......... Eze 12:22
it shall be no more p............................... Eze 12:25
none of my words be p any more.......... Eze 12:28
their lives were p for a season ............... Dan 7:12

## PROLONGETH

The fear of the LORD p days............... Prov 10:27
that p his life in his wickedness............ Eccl 7:15

## PROMISE

and ye shall know my breach of p .... Num 14:34
failed one word of all his good p.......... 1Kin 8:56
let thy p unto David my father be......... 2Chr 1:9
should do according to this p.................. Neh 5:12
that performeth not this p ..................... Neh 5:13
people did according to this p ............... Neh 5:13
doth his p fail for evermore...................... Ps 77:8
For he remembered his holy p............... Ps 105:42
I send the p of my Father upon ............ Lk 24:49
but wait for the p of the Father.............. Acts 1:4
Father the p of the Holy Ghost.............. Acts 2:33
For the p is unto you, and to your......... Acts 2:39
when the time of the p drew nigh .......... Acts 7:17
p raised unto Israel a Saviour............. Acts 13:23
how that the p which was made........... Acts 13:32
ready, looking for a p from thee .......... Acts 23:21
p made of God unto our fathers ........... Acts 26:6
Unto which p our twelve tribes, ........... Acts 26:7
For the p, that he should be the............ Rom 4:13
the p made of none effect ..................... Rom 4:14
to the end the p might be sure to........ Rom 4:16
at the p of God through unbelief ........ Rom 4:20
but the children of the p are ................... Rom 9:8
For this is the word of p......................... Rom 9:9
that we might receive the p of............... Gal 3:14
should make the p of none effect........... Gal 3:17
be of the law, it is no more of p............. Gal 3:18
but God gave it to Abraham by p .......... Gal 3:18
come to whom the p was made .............. Gal 3:19
that the p by faith of Jesus.................... Gal 3:22
seed, and heirs according to the p......... Gal 3:29
but he of the freewoman was by p ......... Gal 4:23
Isaac was, are the children of p.............. Gal 4:28
sealed with that holy Spirit of p ........... Eph 1:13
strangers from the covenants of p.......... Eph 2:12
partakers of his p in Christ by................ Eph 3:6
is the first commandment with p............. Eph 6:2
having p of the life that now is,............... 1Ti 4:8
according to the p of life which................ 2Ti 1:1
a p being left us of entering................... Heb 4:1
For when God made p to Abraham ...... Heb 6:13
endured, he obtained the p.................... Heb 6:15
to shew unto the heirs of p the............. Heb 6:17
the p of eternal inheritance................... Heb 9:15
of God, ye might receive the p............. Heb 10:36
he sojourned in the land of p ................ Heb 11:9
the heirs with him of the same p........... Heb 11:9
through faith, received not the p......... Heb 11:39
While they p them liberty, they ............ 2Pet 2:19
Where is the p of his coming .................. 2Pet 3:4
is not slack concerning his p.................... 2Pet 3:9
we, according to his p, look for............ 2Pet 3:13
this is the p that he hath ........................ 1Jn 2:25

## PROMISED

give you, according as he hath p ........... Ex 12:25
the place which the LORD hath p........ Num 14:40
and bless you, as he hath p you........... Deut 1:11
God of thy fathers hath p thee.............. Deut 6:3
into the land which he p them .............. Deut 9:28
as the LORD thy God p him .................. Deut 10:9
thy border, as he hath p thee............... Deut 12:20
God blesseth thee, as he p thee............ Deut 15:6
he p to give unto thy fathers ................ Deut 19:8
which thou hast p with thy mouth ... Deut 23:23
people, as he hath p thee..................... Deut 26:18
God of thy fathers hath p thee............. Deut 27:3
as the princes had p them ..................... Josh 9:21
unto your brethren, as he p them.......... Josh 22:4
the LORD your God hath p unto you ... Josh 23:5
for you, as he hath p you..................... Josh 23:10
which the LORD your God p you......... Josh 23:15
thou hast p this goodness unto ............... 2Sa 7:28
hath made me an house, as he p............ 1Kin 2:24
gave Solomon wisdom, as he p him..... 1Kin 5:12
throne of Israel, as the LORD p ........... 1Kin 8:20
according to all that he p........................ 1Kin 8:56
which he p by the hand of Moses ........ 1Kin 8:56
as I p to David thy father,...................... 1Kin 9:5
as he p him to give him alway a .......... 2Kin 8:19
hast p this goodness unto thy............. 1Chr 17:26
throne of Israel, as the LORD p............. 2Chr 6:10
father that which thou hast p him ...... 2Chr 6:15
father that which thou hast p him ...... 2Chr 6:16
as he p to give a light to him and......... 2Chr 21:7
thou hadst p to their fathers .................. Neh 9:23
p to pay to the king's treasuries................ Est 4:7
all the good that I have p them............ Jer 32:42
I have p unto the house of Israel.......... Jer 33:14
Whereupon he p with an oath to ........... Mt 14:7
were glad, and p to give him money.... Mk 14:11
the mercy p to our fathers......................... Lk 1:72
And he p, and sought opportunity to...... Lk 22:6
yet he p that he would give it to ........... Acts 7:5
(Which he had p afore by his................... Rom 1:2
persuaded that, what he had p ............. Rom 4:21
lie, p before the world began ................. Titus 1:2
(for he is faithful that p ....................... Heb 10:23
she judged him faithful who had p ....... Heb 11:11
but now he hath p, saying, Yet............. Heb 12:26
which the Lord hath p to them ............. Jas 1:12
he hath p to them that love him ............... Jas 2:5
is the promise that he hath p us............ 1Jn 2:25

## PROMISEDST

David my father that thou p him......... 1Kin 8:24
David my father that thou p him.......... 1Kin 8:25
p them that they should go in to........... Neh 9:15

## PROMISES

and the service of God, and the p.......... Rom 9:4
to confirm the p made unto the........... Rom 15:8
For all the p of God in him are........... 2Cor 1:20
therefore these p dearly beloved ........... 2Cor 7:1
and his seed were the p made .............. Gal 3:16
the law then against the p of God.......... Gal 3:21
faith and patience inherit the p............... Heb 6:12
and blessed him that had the p................ Heb 7:6
was established upon better p ............... Heb 8:6
faith, not having received the p............ Heb 11:13
he that had received the p .................... Heb 11:17
wrought righteousness, obtained p ..... Heb 11:33
us exceeding great and precious p.......... 2Pet 1:4

## PROMISING

his wicked way, by p him life............... Eze 13:22

## PROMOTE

For I will p thee unto very great ....... Num 22:17
able indeed to p thee to honour ......... Num 22:37
I thought to p thee unto great.............. Num 24:11
p Haman the son of Hammedatha the..... Est 3:1
Exalt her, and she shall p thee................. Prov 4:8

## PROMOTED

go to be p over the trees .......................... Judg 9:9
go to be p over the trees ......................... Judg 9:11
go to be p over the trees ......................... Judg 9:13
things wherein the king had p him ........ Est 5:11
Then the king p Shadrach, Meshach.... Dan 3:30

## PROMOTION

For p cometh neither from the.................. Ps 75:6
but shame shall be the p of fools.......... Prov 3:35

## PRONOUNCE

that a man shall p with an oath............. Lev 5:4
look on him, and p him unclean............. Lev 13:3
the priest shall p him clean................... Lev 13:6
the priest shall p him unclean.............. Lev 13:8
and the priest shall p him unclean....... Lev 13:11
he shall p him clean that hath .............. Lev 13:13
raw flesh, and p him to be unclean...... Lev 13:15
then the priest shall p him clean .......... Lev 13:17
the priest shall p him unclean............... Lev 13:20
the priest shall p him unclean.............. Lev 13:22
and the priest shall p him clean............ Lev 13:23
the priest shall p him unclean.............. Lev 13:25
the priest shall p him unclean.............. Lev 13:27
and the priest shall p him clean............ Lev 13:28

P

the priest shall *p* him unclean Lev 13:30
then the priest shall *p* him clean Lev 13:34
and the priest shall *p* him clean Lev 13:37
the priest shall *p* him utterly Lev 13:44
to *p* it clean, or to *p* it Lev 13:59
shall *p* him clean, and shall let Lev 14:7
priest shall *p* the house clean Lev 14:48
he could not frame to *p* it right Judg 12:6

### PRONOUNCED
but that he *p* this prophecy Neh 6:12
hath *p* evil against thee, for the Jer 11:17
Wherefore hath the LORD *p* all Jer 16:10
nation, against whom I have *p* Jer 18:8
the evil that I have *p* against it Jer 19:15
words which I have *p* against it Jer 25:13
evil that he hath *p* against you Jer 26:13
evil which he had *p* against them Jer 26:19
for I have *p* the word, saith the Jer 34:5
evil that I have *p* against them Jer 35:17
LORD hath *p* against this people Jer 36:7
He *p* all these words unto me with Jer 36:18
evil that I have *p* against them Jer 36:31
The LORD thy God hath *p* this evil Jer 40:2

### PRONOUNCING
*p* with his lips to do evil, or to Lev 5:4

### PROOF
that I might know the *p* of you 2Cor 2:9
the *p* of your love, and of our 2Cor 8:24
Since ye seek a *p* of Christ 2Cor 13:3
But ye know the *p* of him, that, Phil 2:22
make full *p* of thy ministry 2Ti 4:5

### PROOFS
his passion by many infallible *p* Acts 1:3

### PROPER
my God, I have of mine own *p* good 1Chr 29:3
field is called in their *p* tongue Acts 1:19
every man hath his *p* gift of God 1Cor 7:7
because they saw he was a *p* child Heb 11:23

### PROPHECIES
but whether there be *p*, they 1Cor 13:8
according to the *p* which went 1Ti 1:18

### PROPHECY
in the *p* of Ahijah the Shilonite, 2Chr 9:29
the *p* of Oded the prophet, he 2Chr 15:8
he pronounced this *p* against me Neh 6:12
Agur the son of Jakeh, even the *p* Prov 30:1
the *p* that his mother taught him Prov 31:1
and to seal up the vision and *p* Dan 9:24
them is fulfilled the *p* of Esaias Mt 13:14
that is given to us, whether *p* Rom 12:6
to another *p* 1Cor 12:10
And though I have the gift of *p* 1Cor 13:2
thee, which was given thee by *p* 1Ti 4:14
have also a more sure word of *p* 2Pet 1:19
that no *p* of the scripture is of 2Pet 1:20
For the *p* came not in old time by 2Pet 1:21
that hear the words of this *p* Rev 1:3
rain not in the days of their *p* Rev 11:6
of Jesus is the spirit of *p* Rev 19:10
the sayings of the *p* of this book Rev 22:7
the sayings of the *p* of this book Rev 22:10
the words of the *p* of this book Rev 22:18
the words of the book of this *p* Rev 22:19

### PROPHESIED
spirit rested upon them, they *p* Num 11:25
and they *p* in the camp Num 11:26
and he *p* among them 1Sa 10:10
he *p* among the prophets, then the 1Sa 10:11
he *p* in the midst of the house 1Sa 18:10
of Saul, and they also *p* 1Sa 19:20
messengers, and they *p* likewise 1Sa 19:21
the third time, and they *p* also 1Sa 19:21
him also, and he went on, and *p* 1Sa 19:23
*p* before Samuel in like manner, 1Sa 19:24
they *p* until the time of the 1Kin 18:29
and all the prophets *p* before them 1Kin 22:10
And all the prophets *p* so, saying, 1Kin 22:12
which *p* according to the order of 1Chr 25:2
who *p* with a harp, to give thanks 1Chr 25:3
for he never *p* good unto me 2Chr 18:7
and all the prophets *p* before them 2Chr 18:9
All the prophets *p* so, saying, 2Chr 18:11
of Mareshah *p* against Jehoshaphat 2Chr 20:37
*p* unto the Jews that were in Ezr 5:1
me, and the prophets *p* by Baal Jer 2:8
that Jeremiah *p* these things Jer 20:1
friends, to whom thou hast *p* lies Jer 20:6
they *p* in Baal, and caused my Jer 23:13
not spoken to them, yet they *p* Jer 23:21
which Jeremiah hath *p* against all Jer 25:13
Why hast thou *p* in the name of Jer 26:9
for he hath *p* against this city, Jer 26:11
Micah the Morasthite *p* in the Jer 26:18
that *p* in the name of the LORD Jer 26:20
who *p* against this city and Jer 26:20
thy words which thou hast *p* Jer 28:6
before thee of old *p* both against Jer 28:8
that Shemaiah hath *p* unto you Jer 29:31
your prophets which *p* unto you Jer 37:19
And it came to pass, when I *p* Eze 11:13
So I *p* as I was commanded Eze 37:7
and as I *p*, there was a noise, and Eze 37:7
So I *p* as he commanded me, and the Eze 37:10
which *p* in those days many years Eze 38:17
one of his vision, when he hath *p* Zec 13:4
Lord, have we not *p* in thy name Mt 7:22
prophets and the law *p* until John Mt 11:13
Well hath Esaias *p* of you Mk 7:6
filled with the Holy Ghost, and *p* Lk 1:67
he *p* that Jesus should die for Jn 11:51
and they spake with tongues, and *p* Acts 19:6
tongues, but rather that ye *p* 1Cor 14:5
who *p* of the grace that should 1Pet 1:10
*p* of these, saying, Behold, the Jude 14

### PROPHESIETH
The prophet which *p* of peace Jer 28:9
he *p* of the times that are far Eze 12:27
thrust him through when he *p* Zec 13:3
or *p* with her head uncovered 1Cor 11:5
But he that *p* speaketh unto men 1Cor 14:3
but he that *p* edifieth the church 1Cor 14:4
for greater is he that *p* than he 1Cor 14:5

### PROPHESY
Eldad and Medad do *p* in the camp Num 11:27
and they shall *p* 1Sa 10:5
thee, and thou shalt *p* with them 1Sa 10:6
for he doth not *p* good concerning 1Kin 22:8
he would *p* no good concerning me 1Kin 22:18
Jeduthun, who should *p* with harps 1Chr 25:1
that he would not *p* good unto me 2Chr 18:17
*P* not unto us right things, speak Is 30:10
unto us smooth things, *p* deceits Is 30:10
The prophets *p* falsely, and the Jer 5:31
*P* not in the name of the LORD, Jer 11:21
The prophets *p* lies in my name Jer 14:14
they *p* unto you a false vision and Jer 14:14
the prophets that *p* in my name Jer 14:15
the people to whom they *p* shall Jer 14:16
the LORD had sent him to *p* Jer 19:14
of the prophets that *p* unto you Jer 23:16
that *p* lies in my name, saying, I Jer 23:25
heart of the prophets that *p* lies Jer 23:26
against them that *p* false dreams Jer 23:32
Therefore *p* thou against them all Jer 25:30
sent me to *p* against this house Jer 26:12
For they *p* a lie unto you, to Jer 27:10
for they *p* a lie unto you Jer 27:14
yet they *p* a lie in my name Jer 27:15
and the prophets that *p* unto you Jer 27:15
of your prophets that *p* unto you Jer 27:16
for they *p* a lie unto you Jer 27:16
For they *p* falsely unto you in my Jer 29:9
which *p* a lie unto you in my name Jer 29:21
up, saying, Wherefore dost thou *p* Jer 32:3
and thou shalt *p* against it Eze 4:7
of Israel, and *p* against them, Eze 6:2
*p* against them, *p*, O son Eze 11:4
*p* against the prophets of Israel Eze 13:2
the prophets of Israel that *p* Eze 13:2
that *p* out of their own hearts Eze 13:2
which *p* concerning Jerusalem Eze 13:16
which *p* out of their own heart Eze 13:17
and *p* thou against them, Eze 13:17
*p* against the forest of the south Eze 20:46
*p* against the land of Israel, Eze 21:2
Son of man, *p*, and say, Thus saith Eze 21:9
Thou therefore, son of man, *p* Eze 21:14
And thou, son of man, *p* and say, Eze 21:28
the Ammonites, and *p* against them Eze 25:2
against Zidon, and *p* against it, Eze 28:21
*p* against him, and against all Eze 29:2
Son of man, *p* and say, Thus saith Eze 30:2
*p* against the shepherds of Israel Eze 34:2
the shepherds of Israel, *p* Eze 34:2
mount Seir, and *p* against it, Eze 35:2
*p* unto the mountains of Israel, Eze 36:1
Therefore *p* and say, Thus saith Eze 36:3
*P* therefore concerning the land Eze 36:6
*P* upon these bones, and say unto Eze 37:4
*P* unto the wind, *p*, son of Eze 37:9
Therefore *p* and say unto them, Eze 37:12
and Tubal, and *p* against him, Eze 38:2
Therefore, son of man, *p* and say Eze 38:14
*p* against Gog, and say, Thus saith Eze 39:1
sons and your daughters shall *p* Joel 2:28
the prophets, saying, *P* not Amos 2:12
GOD hath spoken, who can but *p* Amos 3:8
and there eat bread, and *p* there Amos 7:12
But *p* not again any more at Amos 7:13
me, Go, *p* unto my people Israel Amos 7:15
*P* not against Israel, and drop not Amos 7:16
*P* ye not, say they to them that Mic 2:6
ye not, say they to them that *p* Mic 2:6
they shall not *p* to them, that Mic 2:6
I will *p* unto thee of wine and of Mic 2:11
pass, that when any shall yet *p* Zec 13:3
well did Esaias *p* of you Mt 15:7
*P* unto us, thou Christ, Who is he Mt 26:68
buffet him, and to say unto him, *P* Mk 14:65
the face, and asked him, saying, *P* Lk 22:64
sons and your daughters shall *p* Acts 2:17
and they shall *p* Acts 2:18
daughters, virgins, which did *p* Acts 21:9
let us *p* according to the Rom 12:6
we know in part, and we *p* in part 1Cor 13:9
gifts, but rather that ye may *p* 1Cor 14:1
But if all *p*, and there come in 1Cor 14:24
For ye may all *p* one by one 1Cor 14:31
Wherefore, brethren, covet to *p* 1Cor 14:39
Thou must *p* again before many Rev 10:11
they shall *p* a thousand two Rev 11:3

### PROPHESYING
And when he had made an end of *p* 1Sa 10:13
saw the company of the prophets *p* 1Sa 19:20
the *p* of Haggai the prophet Ezr 6:14
Every man praying or *p*, having 1Cor 11:4
or by knowledge, or by *p* 1Cor 14:6
but *p* serveth not for them that 1Cor 14:22

### PROPHESYINGS
Despise not *p* 1Th 5:20

### PROPHET
for he is a *p*, and he shall pray Gen 20:7
Aaron thy brother shall be thy *p* Ex 7:1
If there be a *p* among you Num 12:6
If there arise among you a *p* Deut 13:1
hearken unto the words of that *p* Deut 13:3
And that *p*, or that dreamer of Deut 13:5
thee a *P* from the midst of thee Deut 18:15
I will raise them up a *P* from Deut 18:18
But the *p*, which shall presume to Deut 18:20
other gods, even that *p* shall die Deut 18:20
When a *p* speaketh in the name of Deut 18:22
spoken, but the *p* hath spoken it Deut 18:22
there arose not a *p* since in Deut 34:10
That the LORD sent a *p* unto the Judg 6:8
established to be a *p* of the LORD 1Sa 3:20
for he that is now called a *P* was 1Sa 9:9
the *p* Gad said unto David, Abide 1Sa 22:5
the king said unto Nathan the *p* 2Sa 7:2
sent by the hand of Nathan the *p* 2Sa 12:25
of the LORD came unto the *p* Gad 2Sa 24:11
son of Jehoiada, and Nathan the *p* 1Kin 1:8
But Nathan the *p*, and Benaiah, and 1Kin 1:10
Nathan the *p* also came in 1Kin 1:22
king, saying, Behold Nathan the *p* 1Kin 1:23
Zadok the priest, and Nathan the *p* 1Kin 1:32
Nathan the *p* anoint him there 1Kin 1:34
Zadok the priest, and Nathan the *p* 1Kin 1:38
Zadok the priest, and Nathan the *p* 1Kin 1:44
Nathan the *p* have anointed him 1Kin 1:45
that the *p* Ahijah the Shilonite 1Kin 11:29
there dwelt an old *p* in Beth-el 1Kin 13:11
I am a *p* also as thou art 1Kin 13:18
unto the *p* that brought him back 1Kin 13:20
for the *p* whom he had brought 1Kin 13:23
in the city where the old *p* dwelt 1Kin 13:25
when the *p* that brought him back 1Kin 13:26
the *p* took up the carcase of the 1Kin 13:29
the old *p* came to the city, to 1Kin 13:29
behold, there is Ahijah the *p* 1Kin 14:2
hand of his servant Ahijah the *p* 1Kin 14:18
also by the hand of the *p* Jehu 1Kin 16:7
against Baasha by Jehu the *p* 1Kin 16:12
I only, remain a *p* of the LORD 1Kin 18:22
that Elijah the *p* came near 1Kin 18:36
thou anoint to be *p* in thy room 1Kin 19:16
there came a *p* unto Ahab king of 1Kin 20:13
the *p* came to the king of Israel, 1Kin 20:22
So the *p* departed, and waited for 1Kin 20:38
not here a *p* of the LORD besides 1Kin 22:7
Is there not here a *p* of the LORD 2Kin 3:11
with the *p* that is in Samaria 2Kin 5:3
know that there is a *p* in Israel 2Kin 5:8
if the *p* had bid thee do some 2Kin 5:13
the *p* that is in Israel, telleth 2Kin 6:12
Elisha the *p* called one of the 2Kin 9:1
man, even the young man the *p* 2Kin 9:4
Jonah, the son of Amittai, the *p* 2Kin 14:25
to Isaiah the *p* the son of Amoz 2Kin 19:2
the *p* Isaiah the son of Amoz came 2Kin 20:1
Isaiah the *p* cried unto the LORD 2Kin 20:11
Isaiah the *p* unto king Hezekiah 2Kin 20:14
with the bones of the *p* that came 2Kin 23:18
that David said to Nathan the *p* 1Chr 17:1
and in the book of Nathan the *p* 1Chr 29:29
in the book of Nathan the *p* 2Chr 9:29
came Shemaiah the *p* to Rehoboam 2Chr 12:5
in the book of Shemaiah the *p* 2Chr 12:15
in the story of the *p* Iddo 2Chr 13:22
and the prophecy of Oded the *p* 2Chr 15:8
not here a *p* of the LORD besides 2Chr 18:6
writing to him from Elijah the *p* 2Chr 21:12
Amaziah, and he sent unto him a *p* 2Chr 25:15
Then the *p* forbare, and said, I 2Chr 25:16
first and last, did Isaiah the *p* 2Chr 26:22
But a *p* of the LORD was there, 2Chr 28:9
the king's seer, and Nathan the *p* 2Chr 29:25
the *p* Isaiah the son of Amoz, 2Chr 32:20
in the vision of Isaiah the *p* 2Chr 32:32
from the days of Samuel the *p* 2Chr 35:18
*p* speaking from the mouth of the 2Chr 36:12
Then the prophets, Haggai the *p* Ezr 5:1
the prophesying of Haggai the *p* Ezr 6:14
when Nathan the *p* came unto him Ps 51:*t*
there is no more any *p* Ps 74:9
man of war, the judge, and the *p* Is 3:2
the *p* that teacheth lies, he is Is 9:15
the *p* have erred through strong Is 28:7
unto Isaiah the *p* the son of Amoz Is 37:2
Isaiah the *p* the son of Amoz came Is 38:1
Isaiah the *p* unto king Hezekiah Is 39:3
thee a *p* unto the nations Jer 1:5
from the *p* even unto the priest Jer 6:13
from the *p* even unto the priest Jer 8:10
yea, both the *p* and the priest go Jer 14:18
the wise, nor the word from the *p* Jer 18:18
Then Pashur smote Jeremiah the *p* Jer 20:2
For both *p* and priest are profane Jer 23:11
The *p* that hath a dream, let him Jer 23:28
And when this people, or the *p* Jer 23:33
And as for the *p*, and the priest, Jer 23:34
Thus shalt thou say to the *p* Jer 23:37
The which Jeremiah the *p* spake Jer 25:2
Hananiah the son of Azur the *p* Jer 28:1

p Jeremiah said unto the p ... Jer 28:5
Even the p Jeremiah said, Amen ... Jer 28:6
The p which prophesieth of peace, ... Jer 28:9
word of the p shall come to pass ... Jer 28:9
then shall the p be known ... Jer 28:9
Then Hananiah the p took the yoke ... Jer 28:10
from off the p Jeremiah's neck ... Jer 28:10
the p Jeremiah went his way ... Jer 28:11
the LORD came unto Jeremiah the p ... Jer 28:12
after that Hananiah the p had ... Jer 28:12
off the neck of the p Jeremiah ... Jer 28:12
Then said the p Jeremiah unto ... Jer 28:15
Jeremiah unto Hananiah the p ... Jer 28:15
So Hananiah the p died the same ... Jer 28:17
p sent from Jerusalem unto the ... Jer 29:1
is mad, and maketh himself a p ... Jer 29:26
which maketh himself a p to you ... Jer 29:27
in the ears of Jeremiah the p ... Jer 29:29
Jeremiah the p was shut up in the ... Jer 32:2
Then Jeremiah the p spake all ... Jer 34:6
that Jeremiah the p commanded him ... Jer 36:8
the scribe and Jeremiah the p ... Jer 36:26
which he spake by the p Jeremiah ... Jer 37:2
the priest to the p Jeremiah ... Jer 37:3
of the LORD unto the p Jeremiah ... Jer 37:6
and he took Jeremiah the p ... Jer 37:13
they have done to Jeremiah the p ... Jer 38:9
Jeremiah the p out of the dungeon ... Jer 38:10
took Jeremiah the p unto him into ... Jer 38:14
And said unto Jeremiah the p ... Jer 42:2
Jeremiah the p said unto them ... Jer 42:4
son of Shaphan, and Jeremiah the p ... Jer 43:6
The word that Jeremiah the p ... Jer 45:1
the p against the Gentiles ... Jer 46:1
the LORD spake to Jeremiah the p ... Jer 46:13
the p against the Philistines ... Jer 47:1
p against Elam in the beginning ... Jer 49:34
the Chaldeans by Jeremiah the p ... Jer 50:1
The word which Jeremiah the p ... Jer 51:59
the p be slain in the sanctuary ... Lam 2:20
there hath been a p among them ... Eze 2:5
shall they seek a vision of the p ... Eze 7:26
his face, and cometh to the p ... Eze 14:4
cometh to a p to enquire of him ... Eze 14:7
if the p be deceived when he hath ... Eze 14:9
I the LORD have deceived that p ... Eze 14:9
the punishment of the p shall be ... Eze 14:10
that a p hath been among them ... Eze 33:33
the LORD came to Jeremiah the p ... Dan 9:2
the p also shall fall with thee ... Hos 4:5
the p is a fool, the spiritual ... Hos 9:7
but the p is a snare of a fowler ... Hos 9:8
by a p the LORD brought Israel ... Hos 12:13
Egypt, and by a p was he preserved ... Hos 12:13
and said to Amaziah, I was no p ... Amos 7:14
even be the p of this people ... Mic 2:11
which Habakkuk the p did see ... Hab 1:1
of Habakkuk the p upon Shigionoth ... Hab 3:1
the p unto Zerubbabel the son of ... Hag 1:1
word of the LORD by Haggai the p ... Hag 1:3
God, and the words of Haggai the p ... Hag 1:12
word of the LORD by the p Haggai ... Hag 2:1
word of the LORD by Haggai the p ... Hag 2:10
Berechiah, the son of Iddo the p ... Zec 1:1
Berechiah, the son of Iddo the p ... Zec 1:7
But he shall say, I am no p ... Zec 13:5
I will send you Elijah the p ... Mal 4:5
was spoken of the Lord by the p ... Mt 1:22
for thus it is written by the p ... Mt 2:5
was spoken of the Lord by the p ... Mt 2:15
which was spoken by Jeremy the p ... Mt 2:17
was spoken of by the p Esaias ... Mt 3:3
which was spoken by Esaias the p ... Mt 4:14
which was spoken by Esaias the p ... Mt 8:17
He that receiveth a p in the name ... Mt 10:41
of a p shall receive a prophet's ... Mt 10:41
for to see? A p? ... Mt 11:9
I say unto you, and more than a p ... Mt 11:9
which was spoken by Esaias the p ... Mt 12:17
it, but the sign of the p Jonas ... Mt 12:39
which was spoken by the p ... Mt 13:35
A p is not without honour, save ... Mt 13:57
because they counted him as a p ... Mt 14:5
it, but the sign of the p Jonas ... Mt 16:4
which was spoken by the p ... Mt 21:4
This is Jesus the p of Nazareth ... Mt 21:11
for all hold John as a p ... Mt 21:26
because they took him for a p ... Mt 21:46
spoken of by Daniel the p ... Mt 24:15
which was spoken by Jeremy the p ... Mt 27:9
which was spoken by the p ... Mt 27:35
A p is not without honour, but in ... Mk 6:4
And others said, That it is a p ... Mk 6:15
John, that he was a p indeed ... Mk 11:32
spoken of by Daniel the p ... Mk 13:14
be called the p of the Highest ... Lk 1:76
book of the words of Esaias the p ... Lk 3:4
unto him the book of the p Esaias ... Lk 4:17
No p is accepted in his own ... Lk 4:24
in the time of Eliseus the p ... Lk 4:27
That a great p is risen up among ... Lk 7:16
for to see? A p? ... Lk 7:26
unto you, and much more than a p ... Lk 7:26
a greater p than John the Baptist ... Lk 7:28
saying, This man, if he were a p ... Lk 7:39
it, but the sign of Jonas the p ... Lk 11:29
that a p perish out of Jerusalem ... Lk 13:33
be persuaded that John was a p ... Lk 20:6
which was a p mighty in deed and ... Lk 24:19
Art thou that p ... Jn 1:21
of the Lord, as said the p Esaias ... Jn 1:23
Christ, nor Elias, neither that p ... Jn 1:25
Sir, I perceive that thou art a p ... Jn 4:19
that a p hath no honour in his ... Jn 4:44
This is of a truth that p that ... Jn 6:14
said, Of a truth this is the P ... Jn 7:40
for out of Galilee ariseth no p ... Jn 7:52
He said, He is a p ... Jn 9:17
Esaias the p might be fulfilled ... Jn 12:38
which was spoken by the p Joel ... Acts 2:16
Therefore being a p, and knowing ... Acts 2:30
A p shall the Lord your God raise ... Acts 3:22
soul, which will not hear that p ... Acts 3:23
A p shall the Lord your God raise ... Acts 7:37
as saith the p, ... Acts 7:48
in his chariot read Esaias the p ... Acts 8:28
and heard him read the p Esaias ... Acts 8:30
thee, of whom speaketh the p this ... Acts 8:34
a certain sorcerer, a false p ... Acts 13:6
fifty years, until Samuel the p ... Acts 13:20
came down from Judaea a certain p ... Acts 21:10
by Esaias the p unto our fathers ... Acts 28:25
any man think himself to be a p ... 1Cor 14:37
even a p of their own, said, The ... Titus 1:12
voice forbad the madness of the p ... 2Pet 2:16
out of the mouth of the false p ... Rev 16:13
with him the false p that wrought ... Rev 19:20
the beast and the false p are ... Rev 20:10

## PROPHETESS

And Miriam the p, the sister of ... Ex 15:20
And Deborah, a p, the wife of ... Judg 4:4
Asahiah, went unto Huldah the p ... 2Kin 22:14
appointed, went to Huldah the p ... 2Chr 34:22
on the p Noadiah, and the rest of ... Neh 6:14
And I went unto the p ... Is 8:3
And there was one Anna, a p ... Lk 2:36
which calleth herself a p ... Rev 2:20

## PROPHET'S

prophet, neither was I an p son ... Amos 7:14
prophet shall receive a p reward ... Mt 10:41

## PROPHETS

that all the LORD's people were p ... Num 11:29
thou shalt meet a company of p ... 1Sa 10:5
behold, a company of p met him ... 1Sa 10:10
behold, he prophesied among the p ... 1Sa 10:11
Is Saul also among the p ... 1Sa 10:11
proverb, Is Saul also among the p ... 1Sa 10:12
the company of the p prophesying ... 1Sa 19:20
say, Is Saul also among the p ... 1Sa 19:24
by dreams, nor by Urim, nor by p ... 1Sa 28:6
me no more, neither by p, nor by ... 1Sa 28:15
Jezebel cut off the p of the LORD ... 1Kin 18:4
that Obadiah took an hundred p ... 1Kin 18:4
Jezebel slew the p of the LORD ... 1Kin 18:13
the LORD's p by fifty in a cave ... 1Kin 18:13
the p of Baal four hundred and ... 1Kin 18:19
the p of the groves four hundred, ... 1Kin 18:19
gathered the p together unto ... 1Kin 18:20
but Baal's p are four hundred and ... 1Kin 18:22
And Elijah said unto the p of Baal ... 1Kin 18:25
unto them, Take the p of Baal ... 1Kin 18:40
slain all the p with the sword ... 1Kin 19:1
slain thy p with the sword ... 1Kin 19:10
slain thy p with the sword ... 1Kin 19:14
p said unto his neighbour in the ... 1Kin 20:35
him that he was of the p ... 1Kin 20:41
of Israel gathered the p together ... 1Kin 22:6
all the p prophesied before them ... 1Kin 22:10
all the p prophesied so, saying, ... 1Kin 22:12
the words of the p declare good ... 1Kin 22:13
spirit in the mouth of all his p ... 1Kin 22:22
in the mouth of all these thy p ... 1Kin 22:23
the sons of the p that were at ... 2Kin 2:3
the sons of the p that were at ... 2Kin 2:5
men of the sons of the p went ... 2Kin 2:7
when the sons of the p which were ... 2Kin 2:15
get thee to the p of thy father ... 2Kin 3:13
and to the p of thy mother ... 2Kin 3:13
of the sons of the p unto Elisha ... 2Kin 4:1
the sons of the p were sitting ... 2Kin 4:38
pottage for the sons of the p ... 2Kin 4:38
young men of the sons of the p ... 2Kin 5:22
the sons of the p said unto ... 2Kin 6:1
one of the children of the p ... 2Kin 9:1
the blood of my servants the p ... 2Kin 9:7
call unto me all the p of Baal ... 2Kin 10:19
and against Judah, by all the p ... 2Kin 17:13
sent to you by my servants the p ... 2Kin 17:13
said by all his servants the p ... 2Kin 17:23
LORD spake by his servants the p ... 2Kin 21:10
him, and the priests, and the p ... 2Kin 23:2
he spake by his servants the p ... 2Kin 24:2
and do my p no harm ... 1Chr 16:22
together of p four hundred men ... 2Chr 18:5
all the p prophesied before them ... 2Chr 18:9
all the p prophesied so, saying, ... 2Chr 18:11
the words of the p declare good ... 2Chr 18:12
spirit in the mouth of all his p ... 2Chr 18:21
in the mouth of these thy p ... 2Chr 18:22
believe his p, so shall ye ... 2Chr 20:20
Yet he sent p to them, to bring ... 2Chr 24:19
commandment of the LORD by his p ... 2Chr 29:25
his words, and misused his p ... 2Chr 36:16
Then the p, Haggai the prophet, ... Ezr 5:1
with them were the p of God ... Ezr 5:2
commanded by thy servants the p ... Ezr 9:11
thou hast also appointed p to ... Neh 6:7
Noadiah, and the rest of the p ... Neh 6:14
slew thy p which testified ... Neh 9:26
them by thy spirit in thy p ... Neh 9:30
and on our priests, and on our p ... Neh 9:32
mine anointed, and do my p no harm ... Ps 105:15
the p and your rulers, the seers ... Is 29:10
and to the p, Prophesy not unto us ... Is 30:10
the p prophesied by Baal, and ... Jer 2:8
and their priests, and their p ... Jer 2:26
own sword hath devoured your p ... Jer 2:30
astonished, and the p shall wonder ... Jer 4:9
the p shall become wind, and the ... Jer 5:13
The p prophesy falsely, and the ... Jer 5:31
unto you all my servants the p ... Jer 7:25
priests, and the bones of the p ... Jer 8:1
throne, and the priests, and the p ... Jer 13:13
the p say unto them, Ye shall not ... Jer 14:13
The p prophesy lies in my name ... Jer 14:14
the p that prophesy in my name ... Jer 14:15
famine shall those p be consumed ... Jer 14:15
me is broken because of the p ... Jer 23:9
seen folly in the p of Samaria ... Jer 23:13
I have seen also in the p of ... Jer 23:14
LORD of hosts concerning the p ... Jer 23:15
for from the p of Jerusalem is ... Jer 23:15
of the p that prophesy unto you ... Jer 23:16
I have not sent these p, yet they ... Jer 23:21
I have heard what the p said ... Jer 23:25
heart of the p that prophesy lies ... Jer 23:26
they are p of the deceit of their ... Jer 23:26
behold, I am against the p ... Jer 23:30
Behold, I am against the p ... Jer 23:31
unto you all his servants the p ... Jer 25:4
to the words of my servants the p ... Jer 26:5
So the priests and the p and all ... Jer 26:7
people, that the priests and the p ... Jer 26:8
the p unto the princes and to all ... Jer 26:11
unto the priests and to the p ... Jer 26:16
hearken not ye to your p, nor to ... Jer 27:9
of the p that speak unto you ... Jer 27:14
the p that prophesy unto you ... Jer 27:15
of your p that prophesy unto you ... Jer 27:16
But if they be p, and if the word ... Jer 27:18
The p that have been before me and ... Jer 28:8
and to the priests, and to the p ... Jer 29:1
Let not your p and your diviners, ... Jer 29:8
hath raised us up p in Babylon ... Jer 29:15
unto them by my servants the p ... Jer 29:19
their priests, and their p ... Jer 32:32
unto you all my servants the p ... Jer 35:15
Where are now your p which ... Jer 37:19
unto you all my servants the p ... Jer 44:4
her p also find no vision from ... Lam 2:9
Thy p have seen vain and foolish ... Lam 2:14
For the sins of her p, and the ... Lam 4:13
prophesy against the p of Israel ... Eze 13:2
Woe unto the foolish p, that ... Eze 13:3
thy p are like the foxes in the ... Eze 13:4
be upon the p that see vanity ... Eze 13:9
the p of Israel which prophesy ... Eze 13:16
of her p in the midst thereof ... Eze 22:25
her p have daubed them with ... Eze 22:28
by my servants the p of Israel ... Eze 38:17
hearkened unto thy servants the p ... Dan 9:6
before us by his servants the p ... Dan 9:10
have I hewed them by the p ... Hos 6:5
I have also spoken by the p ... Hos 12:10
by the ministry of the p ... Hos 12:10
And I raised up of your sons for p ... Amos 2:11
and commanded the p, saying, ... Amos 2:12
secret unto his servants the p ... Amos 3:7
the p that make my people err ... Mic 3:5
the sun shall go down over the p ... Mic 3:6
the p thereof divine for money ... Mic 3:11
Her p are light and treacherous ... Zeph 3:4
unto whom the former p have cried ... Zec 1:4
and the p, do they live for ever ... Zec 1:5
I commanded my servants the p ... Zec 1:6
of the LORD of hosts, and to the p ... Zec 7:3
LORD hath cried by the former p ... Zec 7:7
in his spirit by the former p ... Zec 7:12
these words by the mouth of the p ... Zec 8:9
and also I will cause the p ... Zec 13:2
that the p shall be ashamed every ... Zec 13:4
which was spoken by the p ... Mt 2:23
they the p which were before you ... Mt 5:12
come to destroy the law, or the p ... Mt 5:17
for this is the law and the p ... Mt 7:12
Beware of false p, which come to ... Mt 7:15
For all the p and the law ... Mt 11:13
I say unto you, That many p ... Mt 13:17
others, Jeremias, or one of the p ... Mt 16:14
hang all the law and the p ... Mt 22:40
ye build the tombs of the p ... Mt 23:29
with them in the blood of the p ... Mt 23:30
of them which killed the p ... Mt 23:31
behold, I send unto you p ... Mt 23:34
thou that killest the p, and ... Mt 23:37
And many false p shall rise ... Mt 24:11
arise false Christs, and false p ... Mt 24:24
of the p might be fulfilled ... Mt 26:56
As it is written in the p ... Mk 1:2
is a prophet, or as one of the p ... Mk 6:15
and others, One of the p ... Mk 8:28
false p shall rise, and shall shew ... Mk 13:22
spake by the mouth of his holy p ... Lk 1:70
did their fathers unto the p ... Lk 6:23
did their fathers to the false p ... Lk 6:26
one of the old p was risen again ... Lk 9:8
one of the old p is risen again ... Lk 9:19
For I tell you, that many p ... Lk 10:24
ye build the sepulchres of the p ... Lk 11:47

P

wisdom of God, I will send them *p* Lk 11:49
That the blood of all the *p* Lk 11:50
and Isaac, and Jacob, and all the *p* Lk 13:28
Jerusalem, which killest the *p* Lk 13:34
The law and the *p* were until John Lk 16:16
him, They have Moses and the *p* Lk 16:29
If they hear not Moses and the *p* Lk 16:31
things that are written by the *p* Lk 18:31
all that the *p* have spoken Lk 24:25
beginning at Moses and all the *p* Lk 24:27
in the law of Moses, and in the *p* Lk 24:44
whom Moses in the law, and the *p* Jn 1:45
It is written in the *p*, And they Jn 6:45
Abraham is dead, and the *p* Jn 8:52
and the *p* are dead Jn 8:53
shewed by the mouth of all his *p* Acts 3:18
his holy *p* since the world began Acts 3:21
all the *p* from Samuel and those Acts 3:24
Ye are the children of the *p* Acts 3:25
is written in the book of the *p* Acts 7:42
Which of the *p* have not your Acts 7:52
To him give all the *p* witness Acts 10:43
in these days came *p* from Acts 11:27
that was at Antioch certain *p* Acts 13:1
the *p* the rulers of the synagogue Acts 13:15
nor yet the voices of the *p* which Acts 13:27
you, which is spoken of in the *p* Acts 13:40
to this agree the words of the *p* Acts 15:15
being *p* also themselves, exhorted Acts 15:32
written in the law and in the *p* Acts 24:14
things than those which the *p* Acts 26:22
Agrippa, believest thou the *p* Acts 26:27
the law of Moses, and out of the *p* Acts 28:23
by his *p* in the holy scriptures Rom 1:2
witnessed by the law and the *p* Rom 3:21
Lord, they have killed thy *p* Rom 11:3
and by the scriptures of the *p* Rom 16:26
first apostles, secondarily *p* 1Cor 12:28
are all *p*? 1Cor 12:29
Let the *p* speak two or three, and 1Cor 14:29
the *p* are subject to the *p* 1Cor 14:32
foundation of the apostles and *p* Eph 2:20
holy apostles and *p* by the Spirit Eph 3:5
and some, *p* Eph 4:11
the Lord Jesus, and their own *p* 1Th 2:15
past unto the fathers by the *p* Heb 1:1
also, and Samuel, and of the *p* Heb 11:32
Take, my brethren, the *p*, who Jas 5:10
salvation the *p* have enquired 1Pet 1:10
But there were false *p* also among 2Pet 2:1
were spoken before by the holy *p* 2Pet 3:2
because many false *p* are gone out 1Jn 4:1
declared to his servants the *p* Rev 10:7
because these two *p* tormented Rev 11:10
reward unto thy servants the *p* Rev 11:18
shed the blood of saints and *p* Rev 16:6
heaven, and ye holy apostles and *p* Rev 18:20
in her was found the blood of *p* Rev 18:24
the Lord God of the holy *p* sent Rev 22:6
and of thy brethren the *p* Rev 22:9

## PROPITIATION
be a *p* through faith in his blood Rom 3:25
And he is the *p* for our sins 1Jn 2:2
his Son to be the *p* for our sins 1Jn 4:10

## PROPORTION
according to the *p* of every one 1Kin 7:36
nor his power, nor his comely *p* Job 41:12
according to the *p* of faith Rom 12:6

## PROSELYTE
compass sea and land to make one *p* Mt 23:15
and Nicolas a *p* of Antioch Acts 6:5

## PROSELYTES
and strangers of Rome, Jews and *p* Acts 2:10
religious *p* followed Paul and Acts 13:43

## PROSPECT
their *p* was toward the south Eze 40:44
having the *p* toward the north Eze 40:44
whose *p* is toward the south, is Eze 40:45
the chamber whose *p* is toward the Eze 40:46
gate whose *p* is toward the east Eze 42:15
gate whose *p* is toward the east Eze 43:4

## PROSPER
his angel with thee, and *p* thy way Gen 24:40
if now thou do *p* my way which I Gen 24:42
all that he did to *p* in his hand Gen 39:3
he did, the LORD made it to *p* Gen 39:23
but it shall not *p* Num 14:41
and thou shalt not *p* in thy ways Deut 28:29
that ye may *p* in all that ye do Deut 29:9
that thou mayest *p* whithersoever Josh 1:7
that thou mayest *p* in all that 1Kin 2:3
Go up to Ramoth-gilead, and *p* 1Kin 22:12
And he answered him, Go, and *p* 1Kin 22:15
*p* thou, and build the house of the 1Chr 22:11
Then shalt thou *p*, if thou takest 1Chr 22:13
for ye shall not *p* 2Chr 13:12
Go up to Ramoth-gilead, and *p* 2Chr 18:11
And he said, Go ye up, and *p* 2Chr 18:14
his prophets, so shall ye *p* 2Chr 20:20
of the LORD, that ye cannot *p* 2Chr 24:20
the LORD, God made him to *p* 2Chr 26:5
and *p*, I pray thee, thy servant Neh 1:11
The God of heaven, he will *p* us Neh 2:20
The tabernacles of robbers *p* Job 12:6
and whatsoever he doeth shall *p* Ps 1:3
the ungodly, who *p* in the world Ps 73:12
they shall *p* that love thee Ps 122:6
covereth his sins shall not *p* Prov 28:13
thou knowest not whether shall *p* Eccl 11:6
of the LORD shall *p* in his hand Is 53:10
is formed against thee shall *p* Is 54:17
it shall *p* in the thing whereto I Is 55:11
and thou shalt not *p* in them Jer 2:37
of the fatherless, yet they *p* Jer 5:28
therefore they shall not *p* Jer 10:21
doth the way of the wicked *p* Jer 12:1
for they shall not *p* Jer 20:11
man that shall not *p* in his days Jer 22:30
for no man of his seed shall *p* Jer 22:30
and a King shall reign and *p* Jer 23:5
the Chaldeans, ye shall not *p* Jer 32:5
are the chief, her enemies *p* Lam 1:5
thou didst *p* into a kingdom Eze 16:13
Shall it *p*? Eze 17:9
behold, being planted, shall it *p* Eze 17:10
Shall he *p*? Eze 17:15
destroy wonderfully, and shall *p* Dan 8:24
cause craft to *p* in his hand Dan 8:25
but it shall not *p* Dan 11:27
shall *p* till the indignation be Dan 11:36
all things that thou mayest *p* 3Jn 2

## PROSPERED
seeing the LORD hath *p* my way Gen 24:56
hand of the children of Israel *p* Judg 4:24
the people did, and how the war *p* 2Sa 11:7
he *p* whithersoever he went forth 2Kin 18:7
instead of David his father, and *p* 1Chr 29:23
So they built and *p* 2Chr 14:7
did it with all his heart, and *p* 2Chr 31:21
Hezekiah *p* in all his works 2Chr 32:30
they *p* through the prophesying of Ezr 6:14
himself against him, and hath *p* Job 9:4
So this Daniel *p* in the reign of Dan 6:28
and it practised, and *p* Dan 8:12
him in store, as God hath *p* him 1Cor 16:2

## PROSPERETH
fast on, and *p* in their hands Ezr 5:8
because of him who *p* in his way Ps 37:7
whithersoever it turneth, it *p* Prov 17:8
be in health, even as thy soul *p* 3Jn 2

## PROSPERITY
nor their *p* all thy days for ever Deut 23:6
ye say to him that liveth in *p* 1Sa 25:6
*p* exceedeth the fame which I 1Kin 10:7
in *p* the destroyer shall come Job 15:21
they shall spend their days in *p* Job 36:11
in my *p* I said, I shall never be Ps 30:6
pleasure in the *p* of his servant Ps 35:27
when I saw the *p* of the wicked Ps 73:3
LORD, I beseech thee, send now *p* Ps 118:25
walls, and *p* within thy palaces Ps 122:7
the *p* of fools shall destroy them Prov 1:32
In the day of *p* be joyful Eccl 7:14
I spake unto thee in thy *p* Jer 22:21
for all the *p* that I procure unto Jer 33:9
I forgat *p* Lam 3:17
My cities through *p* shall yet be Zec 1:17
Jerusalem was inhabited and in *p* Zec 7:7

## PROSPEROUS
had made his journey *p* or not Gen 24:21
with Joseph, and he was a *p* man Gen 39:2
then thou shalt make thy way *p* Josh 1:8
our way which we go shall be *p* Judg 18:5
habitation of thy righteousness *p* Job 8:6
him, and he shall make his way *p* Is 48:15
For the seed shall be *p* Zec 8:12
now at length I might have a *p* Rom 1:10

## PROSPEROUSLY
in his own house, he *p* effected 2Chr 7:11
majesty ride *p* because of truth Ps 45:4

## PROSTITUTE
Do not *p* thy daughter, to cause Lev 19:29

## PROTECTION
rise up and help you, and be your *p* Deut 32:38

## PROTEST
The man did solemnly *p* unto us Gen 43:3
howbeit yet *p* solemnly unto them, 1Sa 8:9
I *p* by your rejoicing which I 1Cor 15:31

## PROTESTED
*p* unto thee, saying, Know for a 1Kin 2:42
For I earnestly *p* unto your Jer 11:7
angel of the LORD *p* unto Joshua Zec 3:6

## PROTESTING
unto this day, rising early and *p* Jer 11:7

## PROUD
the *p* helpers do stoop under him Job 9:13
he smiteth through the *p* Job 26:12
here shall thy *p* waves be stayed Job 38:11
and behold every one that is *p* Job 40:11
Look on every one that is *p* Job 40:12
the tongue that speaketh *p* things Ps 12:3
plentifully rewardeth the *p* doer Ps 31:23
trust, and respecteth not the *p* Ps 40:4
the *p* are risen against me, and Ps 86:14
render a reward to the *p* Ps 94:2
a *p* heart will not I suffer Ps 101:5
rebuked the *p* that are cursed Ps 119:21
The *p* have had me greatly in Ps 119:51
The *p* have forged a lie against Ps 119:69
Let the *p* be ashamed Ps 119:78
The *p* have digged pits for me, Ps 119:85
let not the *p* oppress me Ps 119:122
and with the contempt of the *p* Ps 123:4
Then the *p* waters had gone over Ps 124:5
but the *p* he knoweth afar off Ps 138:6
The *p* have hid a snare for me, and Ps 140:5
A *p* look, a lying tongue, and Prov 6:17
will destroy the house of the *p* Prov 15:25
Every one that is *p* in heart is Prov 16:5
to divide the spoil with the *p* Prov 16:19
a *p* heart, and the plowing of the Prov 21:4
*P* and haughty scorner is his name, Prov 21:24
who dealeth in *p* wrath Prov 21:24
He that is of a *p* heart stirreth Prov 28:25
is better than the *p* in spirit Eccl 7:8
shall be upon every one that is *p* Is 2:12
the arrogancy of the *p* to cease Is 13:11
he is very *p* Is 16:6
be not *p* Jer 13:15
son of Kareah, and all the *p* men Jer 43:2
(he is exceeding *p*) his loftiness Jer 48:29
she hath been *p* against the LORD Jer 50:29
I am against thee, O thou most *p* Jer 50:31
the most *p* shall stumble and fall, Jer 50:32
by wine, he is a *p* man, neither Hab 2:5
And now we call the *p* happy Mal 3:15
and all the *p*, yea, and all that do Mal 4:1
he hath scattered the *p* in the Lk 1:51
haters of God, despiteful, *p* Rom 1:30
He is *p*, knowing nothing, but 1Ti 6:4
own selves, covetous, boasters, *p* 2Ti 3:2
he saith, God resisteth the *p* Jas 4:6
for God resisteth the *p*, and 1Pet 5:5

## PROUDLY
they dealt *p* he was above them Ex 18:11
Talk no more so exceeding *p* 1Sa 2:3
that they dealt *p* against them Neh 9:10
But they and our fathers dealt *p* Neh 9:16
yet they dealt *p*, and hearkened Neh 9:29
with their mouth they speak *p* Ps 17:10
which speak grievous things *p* Ps 31:18
himself *p* against the ancient Is 3:5
spoken *p* in the day of distress Obad 12

## PROVE
rate every day, that I may *p* them Ex 16:4
for God is come to *p* you, and that Ex 20:20
to *p* thee, to know what was in Deut 8:2
thee, and that he might *p* thee Deut 8:16
one, whom thou didst *p* at Massah Deut 33:8
That through them I may *p* Israel Judg 2:22
to *p* Israel by them, even as many Judg 3:1
they were to *p* Israel by them, to Judg 3:4
let me *p*, I pray thee, but this Judg 6:39
she came to *p* him with hard 1Kin 10:1
she came to *p* Solomon with hard 2Chr 9:1
it shall also *p* me perverse Job 9:20
Examine me, O LORD, and *p* me Ps 26:2
I will *p* thee with mirth, Eccl 2:1
*P* thy servants, I beseech thee, Dan 1:12
*p* me now herewith, saith the LORD Mal 3:10
yoke of oxen, and I go to *p* them Lk 14:19
And this he said to *p* him Jn 6:6
Neither can they *p* the things Acts 24:13
Paul, which they could not *p* Acts 25:7
that ye may *p* what is that good, Rom 12:2
to *p* the sincerity of your love 2Cor 8:8
*p* your own selves 2Cor 13:5
But let every man *p* his own work Gal 6:4
*P* all things 1Th 5:21

## PROVED
Hereby ye shall be *p* Gen 42:15
prison, that your words may be *p* Gen 42:16
an ordinance, and there he *p* them Ex 15:25
for he had not *p* it 1Sa 17:39
for I have not *p* them 1Sa 17:39
Thou hast *p* mine heart Ps 17:3
For thou, O God, hast *p* us Ps 66:10
I *p* thee at the waters of Meribah Ps 81:7
tempted me, *p* me, and saw my work Ps 95:9
All this have I *p* by wisdom Eccl 7:23
this matter, and *p* them ten days Dan 1:14
for we have before *p* both Jews Rom 3:9
*p* diligent in many things 2Cor 8:22
And let these also first be *p* 1Ti 3:10
*p* me, and saw my works forty years Heb 3:9

## PROVENDER
*p* enough, and room to lodge in Gen 24:25
*p* for the camels, and water to Gen 24:32
sack to give his ass *p* in the inn Gen 42:27
and he gave their asses *p* Gen 43:24
is both straw and *p* for our asses Judg 19:19
house, and gave *p* unto the asses Judg 19:21
ear the ground shall eat clean *p* Is 30:24

## PROVERB
shalt become an astonishment, a *p* Deut 28:37
Therefore it became a *p*, Is Saul 1Sa 10:12
As saith the *p* of the ancients, 1Sa 24:13
and Israel shall be a *p* and a 1Kin 9:7
sight, and will make it to be a *p* 2Chr 7:20
and I became a *p* to them Ps 69:11
To understand a *p*, and the Prov 1:6
*p* against the king of Babylon Is 14:4
hurt, to be a reproach and a *p* Jer 24:9
what is that *p* that ye have in Eze 12:22
I will make this *p* to cease Eze 12:23
no more use it as a *p* in Israel Eze 12:23
and will make him a sign and a *p* Eze 14:8
shall use this *p* against thee Eze 16:44
that ye use this *p* concerning the Eze 18:2

any more to use this *p* in Israel ... Eze 18:3
a taunting *p* against him, and say, ... Hab 2:6
Ye will surely say unto me this *p* ... Lk 4:23
thou plainly, and speakest no *p* ... Jn 16:29
unto them according to the true *p* ... 2Pet 2:22

**PROVERBS**
they that speak in *p* say, Come ... Num 21:27
And he spake three thousand *p* ... 1Kin 4:32
The *P* of Solomon the son of David ... Prov 1:1
The *p* of Solomon ... Prov 10:1
These are also *p* of Solomon ... Prov 25:1
out, and set in order many *p* ... Eccl 12:9
every one that useth *p* shall use ... Eze 16:44
have I spoken unto you in *p* ... Jn 16:25
shall no more speak unto you in *p* ... Jn 16:25

**PROVETH**
for the LORD your God *p* you ... Deut 13:3

**PROVIDE**
God will *p* himself a lamb for a ... Gen 22:8
now when shall I *p* for mine own ... Gen 30:30
Moreover thou shalt *p* out of all ... Ex 18:21
*P* me now a man that can play well ... 1Sa 16:17
whom David my father did *p* ... 2Chr 2:7
can he *p* flesh for his people ... Ps 78:20
*P* neither gold, nor silver, nor ... Mt 10:9
*p* yourselves bags which wax not ... Lk 12:33
*p* them beasts, that they may set ... Acts 23:24
*P* things honest in the sight of ... Rom 12:17
But if any *p* not for his own, and ... 1Ti 5:8

**PROVIDED**
he *p* the first part for himself, ... Deut 33:21
for I have *p* me a king among his ... 1Sa 16:1
he had *p* the king of sustenance ... 2Sa 19:32
which *p* victuals for the king and ... 1Kin 4:7
those officers *p* victual for king ... 1Kin 4:27
Moreover he *p* him cities, and ... 2Chr 32:29
corn, when thou hast so *p* for it ... Ps 65:9
things be, which thou hast *p* ... Lk 12:20
God having *p* some better thing ... Heb 11:40

**PROVIDENCE**
done unto this nation by thy *p* ... Acts 24:2

**PROVIDETH**
Who *p* for the raven his food ... Job 38:41
*P* her meat in the summer, and ... Prov 6:8

**PROVIDING**
*P* for honest things, not only in ... 2Cor 8:21

**PROVINCE**
of the *p* that went up out of the ... Ezr 2:1
that we went into the *p* of Judea ... Ezr 5:8
that is in the *p* of the Medes ... Ezr 6:2
find in all the *p* of Babylon ... Ezr 7:16
in the *p* are in great affliction ... Neh 1:3
These are the children of the *p* ... Neh 7:6
of the *p* that dwelt in Jerusalem ... Neh 11:3
into every *p* according to the ... Est 1:22
governors that were over every *p* ... Est 3:12
every *p* according to the writing ... Est 3:12
to be given in every *p* was ... Est 3:14
And in every *p*, whithersoever the ... Est 4:3
unto every *p* according to the ... Est 8:9
*p* that would assault them, both ... Est 8:11
to be given in every *p* was ... Est 8:13
And in every *p*, and in every city, ... Est 8:17
generation, every family, every *p* ... Est 9:28
of judgment and justice in a *p* ... Eccl 5:8
ruler over the whole *p* of Babylon ... Dan 2:48
the affairs of the *p* of Babylon ... Dan 2:49
of Dura, in the *p* of Babylon ... Dan 3:1
the affairs of the *p* of Babylon ... Dan 3:12
and Abed-nego, in the *p* of Babylon ... Dan 3:30
palace, which is in the *p* of Elam ... Dan 8:2
upon the fattest places of the *p* ... Dan 11:24
letter, he asked of what *p* he was ... Acts 23:34
when Festus was come into the *p* ... Acts 25:1

**PROVINCES**
young men of the princes of the *p* ... 1Kin 20:14
young men of the princes of the *p* ... 1Kin 20:15
princes of the *p* went out first ... 1Kin 20:17
of the *p* came out of the city ... 1Kin 20:19
city, and hurtful unto kings and *p* ... Ezr 4:15
an hundred and seven and twenty *p* ... Est 1:1
the nobles and princes of the *p* ... Est 1:3
all the *p* of the king Ahasuerus ... Est 1:16
letters into all the king's *p* ... Est 1:22
in all the *p* of his kingdom ... Est 2:3
and he made a release to the *p* ... Est 2:18
in all the *p* of thy kingdom ... Est 3:8
by posts into all the king's *p* ... Est 3:13
and the people of the king's *p* ... Est 4:11
which are in all the king's *p* ... Est 8:5
rulers of the *p* which are from ... Est 8:9
an hundred twenty and seven *p* ... Est 8:9
in all the *p* of king Ahasuerus ... Est 8:12
all the *p* of the king Ahasuerus ... Est 9:2
And all the rulers of the *p* ... Est 9:3
went out throughout all the *p* ... Est 9:4
done in the rest of the king's *p* ... Est 9:12
*p* gathered themselves together ... Est 9:16
all the *p* of the king Ahasuerus ... Est 9:20
seven *p* of the kingdom of ... Est 9:30
treasure of kings and of the *p* ... Eccl 2:8
nations, and princess among the *p* ... Lam 1:1
him on every side from the *p* ... Eze 19:8
and all the rulers of the *p* ... Dan 3:2
and all the rulers of the *p* ... Dan 3:3

**PROVING**
*p* that this is very Christ ... Acts 9:22
*P* what is acceptable unto the ... Eph 5:10

**PROVISION**
and to give them *p* for the way ... Gen 42:25
and gave them *p* for the way ... Gen 45:21
all the bread of their *p* was dry ... Josh 9:5
our bread we took hot for our *p* ... Josh 9:12
man his month in a year made *p* ... 1Kin 4:7
Solomon's *p* for one day was ... 1Kin 4:22
And he prepared great *p* for them ... 2Kin 6:23
for the which I have made *p* ... 1Chr 29:19
I will abundantly bless her *p* ... Ps 132:15
them a daily *p* of the king's meat ... Dan 1:5
make not *p* for the flesh, to ... Rom 13:14

**PROVOCATION**
by his *p* wherewith he provoked ... 1Kin 15:30
for the *p* wherewith thou hast ... 1Kin 21:22
not mine eye continue in their *p* ... Job 17:2
not your heart, as in the *p* ... Ps 95:8
been to me as a *p* of mine anger ... Jer 32:31
presented the *p* of their offering ... Eze 20:28
not your hearts, as in the *p* ... Heb 3:8
not your hearts, as in the *p* ... Heb 3:15

**PROVOCATIONS**
because of all the *p* that ... 2Kin 23:26
of Egypt, and had wrought great *p* ... Neh 9:18
to thee, and they wrought great *p* ... Neh 9:26

**PROVOKE**
him, and obey his voice, *p* him not ... Ex 23:21
How long will this people *p* me ... Num 14:11
LORD thy God, to *p* him to anger ... Deut 4:25
of the LORD, to *p* him to anger ... Deut 9:18
*p* me, and break my covenant ... Deut 31:20
to *p* him to anger through the ... Deut 31:29
I will *p* them to anger with a ... Deut 32:21
to *p* me to anger, and hast cast me ... 1Kin 14:9
to *p* me to anger with their sins ... 1Kin 16:2
to *p* the LORD God of Israel to ... 1Kin 16:26
Ahab did more to *p* the LORD God ... 1Kin 16:33
things to *p* the LORD to anger ... 2Kin 17:11
of the LORD, to *p* him to anger ... 2Kin 17:17
of the LORD, to *p* him to anger ... 2Kin 21:6
that they might *p* me to anger ... 2Kin 22:17
had made to *p* the LORD to anger ... 2Kin 23:19
of the LORD, to *p* him to anger ... 2Chr 33:6
that they might *p* me to anger ... 2Chr 34:25
they that *p* God are secure ... Job 12:6
How oft did they *p* him in the ... Ps 78:40
to *p* the eyes of his glory ... Is 3:8
gods, that they may *p* me to anger ... Jer 7:18
Do they *p* me to anger ... Jer 7:19
do they not *p* themselves to the ... Jer 7:19
*p* me to anger in offering incense ... Jer 11:17
*p* me not to anger with the works ... Jer 25:6
that ye might *p* me to anger with ... Jer 25:7
unto other gods, to *p* me to anger ... Jer 32:29
they have done to *p* me to anger ... Jer 32:32
have committed to *p* me to anger ... Jer 44:3
In that ye *p* me unto wrath with ... Jer 44:8
and have returned to *p* me to anger ... Eze 8:17
thy whoredoms, to *p* me to anger ... Eze 16:26
to *p* him to speak of many things ... Lk 11:53
I will *p* you to jealousy by them ... Rom 10:19
for to *p* them to jealousy ... Rom 11:11
If by any means I may *p* to ... Rom 11:14
Do we *p* the Lord to jealousy ... 1Cor 10:22
*p* not your children to wrath ... Eph 6:4
*p* not your children to anger, ... Col 3:21
some, when they had heard, did *p* ... Heb 3:16
one another to *p* unto love ... Heb 10:24

**PROVOKED**
any of them that *p* me see it ... Num 14:23
that these men have *p* the LORD ... Num 16:30
Also in Horeb ye *p* the LORD to ... Deut 9:8
ye *p* the LORD to wrath ... Deut 9:22
They *p* him to jealousy with ... Deut 32:16
abominations *p* they him to anger ... Deut 32:16
they have *p* me to anger with ... Deut 32:21
unto them, and *p* the LORD to anger ... Judg 2:12
And her adversary also *p* her sore ... 1Sa 1:6
house of the LORD, so she *p* her ... 1Sa 1:7
they *p* him to jealousy with their ... 1Kin 14:22
*p* the LORD God of Israel to anger ... 1Kin 15:30
wherewith thou hast *p* me to anger ... 1Kin 21:22
*p* to anger the LORD God of Israel ... 1Kin 22:53
have *p* me to anger, since the day ... 2Kin 21:15
that Manasseh had *p* him withal ... 2Kin 23:26
and *p* David to number Israel ... 1Chr 21:1
*p* to anger the LORD God of his ... 2Chr 28:25
*p* the God of heaven unto wrath ... Ezr 5:12
for they have *p* thee to anger ... Neh 4:5
*p* the most high God, and kept not ... Ps 78:56
For they *p* him to anger with ... Ps 78:58
but *p* him at the sea, even at the ... Ps 106:7
Thus they *p* him to anger with ... Ps 106:29
Because they *p* his spirit ... Ps 106:33
but they *p* him with their counsel ... Ps 106:43
they have *p* the Holy One of ... Is 1:4
Why have they *p* me to anger with ... Jer 8:19
*p* me to anger with the work of ... Jer 32:30
Ephraim *p* him to anger most ... Hos 12:14
when your fathers *p* me to wrath ... Zec 8:14
not her own, is not easily *p* ... 1Cor 13:5
and your zeal hath *p* very many ... 2Cor 9:2

**PROVOKEDST**
how thou *p* the LORD thy God to ... Deut 9:7

**PROVOKETH**
whoso *p* him to anger sinneth ... Prov 20:2
A people that *p* me to anger ... Is 65:3
of jealousy, which *p* to jealousy ... Eze 8:3

**PROVOKING**
because of the *p* of his sons ... Deut 32:19
their groves, *p* the LORD to anger ... 1Kin 14:15
in *p* him to anger with the work ... 1Kin 16:7
in *p* the LORD God of Israel to ... 1Kin 16:13
sinned yet more against him by *p* ... Ps 78:17
*p* one another, envying one ... Gal 5:26

**PRUDENCE**
king a wise son, endued with *p* ... 2Chr 2:12
I wisdom dwell with *p*, and find ... Prov 8:12
toward us in all wisdom and *p* ... Eph 1:8

**PRUDENT**
*p* in matters, and a comely person, ... 1Sa 16:18
but a *p* man covereth shame ... Prov 12:16
A *p* man concealeth knowledge ... Prov 12:23
Every *p* man dealeth with ... Prov 13:16
The wisdom of the *p* is to ... Prov 14:8
but the *p* man looketh well to his ... Prov 14:15
but the *p* are crowned with ... Prov 14:18
he that regardeth reproof is *p* ... Prov 15:5
wise in heart shall be called *p* ... Prov 16:21
The heart of the *p* getteth ... Prov 18:15
a *p* wife is from the LORD ... Prov 19:14
A *p* man foreseeth the evil, and ... Prov 22:3
A *p* man foreseeth the evil, and ... Prov 27:12
judge, and the prophet, and the *p* ... Is 3:2
own eyes, and *p* in their own sight ... Is 5:21
for I am *p* ... Is 10:13
of their *p* men shall be hid ... Is 29:14
is counsel perished from the *p* ... Jer 49:7
*p*, and he shall know them ... Hos 14:9
Therefore the *p* shall keep ... Amos 5:13
these things from the wise and *p* ... Mt 11:25
these things from the wise and *p* ... Lk 10:21
country, Sergius Paulus, a *p* man ... Acts 13:7
the understanding of the *p* ... 1Cor 1:19

**PRUDENTLY**
Behold, my servant shall deal *p* ... Is 52:13

**PRUNE**
years thou shalt *p* thy vineyard ... Lev 25:3
sow thy field, nor *p* thy vineyard ... Lev 25:4

**PRUNED**
it shall not be *p*, nor digged ... Is 5:6

**PRUNINGHOOKS**
and their spears into *p* ... Is 2:4
both cut off the sprigs with *p* ... Is 18:5
swords, and your *p* into spears ... Joel 3:10
and their spears into *p* ... Mic 4:3

**PSALM**
day David delivered first this *p* ... 1Chr 16:7
A *P* of David, when he fled from ... Ps 3:*t*
on Neginoth, A *P* of David ... Ps 4:*t*
upon Nehiloth, A *P* of David ... Ps 5:*t*
upon Sheminith, A *P* of David ... Ps 6:*t*
upon Gittith, A *P* of David ... Ps 8:*t*
upon Muth-labben, A *P* of David ... Ps 9:*t*
the chief Musician, A *P* of David ... Ps 11:*t*
upon Sheminith, A *P* of David ... Ps 12:*t*
the chief Musician, A *P* of David ... Ps 13:*t*
the chief Musician, A *P* of David ... Ps 14:*t*
A *P* of David ... Ps 15:*t*
A *P* of David, the servant of the ... Ps 18:*t*
the chief Musician, A *P* of David ... Ps 19:*t*
the chief Musician, A *P* of David ... Ps 20:*t*
the chief Musician, A *P* of David ... Ps 21:*t*
Aijeleth Shahar, A *P* of David ... Ps 22:*t*
A *P* of David ... Ps 23:*t*
A *P* of David ... Ps 24:*t*
A *P* of David ... Ps 25:*t*
A *P* of David ... Ps 26:*t*
A *P* of David ... Ps 27:*t*
A *P* of David ... Ps 28:*t*
A *P* of David ... Ps 29:*t*
A *P* and Song at the dedication of ... Ps 30:*t*
the chief Musician, A *P* of David ... Ps 31:*t*
A *P* of David, A Maschil ... Ps 32:*t*
A *P* of David, when he changed his ... Ps 34:*t*
A *P* of David ... Ps 35:*t*
A *P* of David, the servant of the ... Ps 36:*t*
A *P* of David ... Ps 37:*t*
A *P* of David, to bring to ... Ps 38:*t*
even to Jeduthun, A *P* of David ... Ps 39:*t*
the chief Musician, A *P* of David ... Ps 40:*t*
the chief Musician, A *P* of David ... Ps 41:*t*
A *P* for the sons of Korah ... Ps 47:*t*
A Song and *P* for the sons of Korah ... Ps 48:*t*
A *P* for the sons of Korah ... Ps 49:*t*
A *P* of Asaph ... Ps 50:*t*
A *P* of David, when Nathan the ... Ps 51:*t*
A *P* of David, when Doeg the ... Ps 52:*t*
Mahalath, Maschil, A *P* of David ... Ps 53:*t*
A *P* of David, when the Ziphims ... Ps 54:*t*
Neginoth, Maschil, A *P* of David ... Ps 55:*t*
upon Neginah, A *P* of David ... Ps 61:*t*
to Jeduthun, A *P* of David ... Ps 62:*t*
A *P* of David, when he was in the ... Ps 63:*t*
the chief Musician, A *P* of David ... Ps 64:*t*
To the chief Musician, A *P* ... Ps 65:*t*
the chief Musician, A Song or *P* ... Ps 66:*t*

Musician on Neginoth, A P or Song Ps 67:t
Musician, A P or Song of David Ps 68:t
upon Shoshannim, A P of David Ps 69:t
A P of David, to bring to Ps 70:t
A P for Solomon Ps 72:t
A P of Asaph Ps 73:t
Altaschith, A P or Song of Asaph Ps 75:t
on Neginoth, A P or Song of Asaph Ps 76:t
to Jeduthun, A P of Asaph Ps 77:t
A P of Asaph Ps 79:t
Shoshannim-Eduth, A P of Asaph Ps 80:t
upon Gittith, A P of Asaph Ps 81:t
Take a p, and bring hither the Ps 81:2
A P of Asaph Ps 82:t
A Song or P of Asaph Ps 83:t
A P for the sons of Korah Ps 84:t
A P for the sons of Korah Ps 85:t
A P or Song for the sons of Korah Ps 87:t
A Song or P for the sons of Korah Ps 88:t
A P or Song for the sabbath day Ps 92:t
A P Ps 98:t
the harp, and the voice of a p Ps 98:5
A P of praise Ps 100:t
A P of David Ps 101:t
A P of David Ps 103:t
A Song or P of David Ps 108:t
the chief Musician, A P of David Ps 109:t
A P of David Ps 110:t
A P of David Ps 138:t
the chief Musician, A P of David Ps 139:t
the chief Musician, A P of David Ps 140:t
A P of David Ps 141:t
A P of David Ps 143:t
A P of David Ps 144:t
David's P of praise Ps 145:t
is also written in the second p Acts 13:33
he saith also in another p Acts 13:35
every one of you hath a p 1Cor 14:26

**PSALMIST**
Jacob, and the sweet p of Israel 2Sa 23:1

**PSALMS**
sing p unto him, talk ye of all 1Chr 16:9
a joyful noise unto him with p Ps 95:2
Sing unto him, sing p unto him Ps 105:2
himself saith in the book of P Lk 20:42
and in the prophets, and in the p Lk 24:44
it is written in the book of P Acts 1:20
Speaking to yourselves in p Eph 5:19
and admonishing one another in p Col 3:16
let him sing p Jas 5:13

**PSALTERIES**
fir wood, even on harps, and on p 2Sa 6:5
harps also and p for singers 1Kin 10:12
singing, and with harps, and with p 1Chr 13:8
with instruments of musick, p 1Chr 15:16
and Benaiah, with p on Alamoth 1Chr 15:20
cymbals, making a noise with p 1Chr 15:28
and Jeiel with p and with harps 1Chr 16:5
prophesy with harps, with p 1Chr 25:1
of the LORD, with cymbals, p 1Chr 25:6
white linen, having cymbals and p 2Chr 5:12
palace, and harps and p for singers 2Chr 9:11
And they came to Jerusalem with p 2Chr 20:28
of the LORD with cymbals, with p 2Chr 29:25
and with singing, with cymbals, p Neh 12:27

**PSALTERY**
down from the high place with a p 1Sa 10:5
sing unto him with the p and an Ps 33:2
awake, p and harp Ps 57:8
will also praise thee with the p Ps 71:22
the pleasant harp with the p Ps 81:2
of ten strings, and upon the p Ps 92:3
Awake, p and harp Ps 108:2
upon a p and an instrument of ten Ps 144:9
praise him with the p and harp Ps 150:3
cornet, flute, harp, sackbut, p Dan 3:5
cornet, flute, harp, sackbut, p Dan 3:7
cornet, flute, harp, sackbut, p Dan 3:10
cornet, flute, harp, sackbut, p Dan 3:15

**PTOLEMAIS** (tol-e-ma'-is) See ACCHO. *A seaport between Carmel and Tyre.*
course from Tyre, we came to P Acts 21:7

**PUA** (pu'ah) See PUAH. *A son of Issachar.*
of P, the family of the Punites Num 26:23

**PUAH** (pu'-ah) See PHUVAH, PUA, PUNITES.
*1. Same as Pua.*
sons of Issachar were, Tola, and P 1Chr 7:1
*2. Father of Tola.*
defend Israel Tola the son of P Judg 10:1
*3. A Hebrew midwife in Egypt.*
and the name of the other P Ex 1:15

**PUBLICAN**
Thomas, and Matthew the p Mt 10:3
thee as an heathen man and a p Mt 18:17
things he went forth, and saw a p Lk 5:27
one a Pharisee, and the other a p Lk 18:10
adulterers, or even as this p Lk 18:11
And the p, standing afar off, Lk 18:13

**PUBLICANS**
do not even the p the same Mt 5:46
do not even the p so Mt 5:47
meat in the house, behold, many p Mt 9:10
Why eateth your Master with p Mt 9:11
and a winebibber, a friend of p Mt 11:19
Verily I say unto you, That the p Mt 21:31
but the p and the harlots believed Mt 21:32
sat at meat in his house, many p Mk 2:15
and Pharisees saw him eat with p Mk 2:16
that he eateth and drinketh with p Mk 2:16
Then came also p to be baptized Lk 3:12
and there was a great company of p Lk 5:29
Why do ye eat and drink with p Lk 5:30
people that heard him, and the p Lk 7:29
and a winebibber, a friend of p Lk 7:34
Then drew near unto him all the p Lk 15:1
which was the chief among the p Lk 19:2

**PUBLICK**
willing to make her a p example Mt 1:19

**PUBLICKLY**
convinced the Jews, and that p Acts 18:28
shewed you, and have taught you p Acts 20:20

**PUBLISH**
Because I will p the name of the Deut 32:3
to p it in the house of their 1Sa 31:9
p it not in the streets of 2Sa 1:20
And that they should p and proclaim Neh 8:15
That I may p with the voice of Ps 26:7
ye in Judah, and p in Jerusalem Jer 4:5
p against Jerusalem, that Jer 4:16
Jacob, and p it in Judah, saying, Jer 5:20
p ye, praise ye, and say, O LORD, Jer 31:7
p in Migdol, and p in Noph Jer 46:14
ye among the nations, and p Jer 50:2
p, and conceal not Jer 50:2
P in the palaces at Ashdod, and in Amos 3:9
proclaim and p the free offerings Amos 4:5
went out, and began to p it much Mk 1:45
began to p in Decapolis how great Mk 5:20

**PUBLISHED**
be p throughout all his empire Est 1:20
that it should be p according to Est 1:22
province was p unto all people Est 3:14
province was p unto all people Est 8:13
the company of those that p it Ps 68:11
p through Nineveh by the decree Jonah 3:7
the more a great deal they p it Mk 7:36
must first be p among all nations Mk 13:10
p throughout the whole city how Lk 8:39
which was p throughout all Judaea Acts 10:37
the word of the Lord was p Acts 13:49

**PUBLISHETH**
good tidings, that p peace Is 52:7
tidings of good, that p salvation Is 52:7
p affliction from mount Ephraim Jer 4:15
good tidings, that p peace Nah 1:15

**PUBLIUS** (pub'-le-us) *A chief man on Melita.*
of the island, whose name was P Acts 28:7
that the father of P lay sick of Acts 28:8

**PUDENS** (pu'-denz) *A Christian in Rome.*
Eubulus greeteth thee, and P 2Ti 4:21

**PUFFED**
that no one of you be p up for 1Cor 4:6
Now some are p up, as though I 1Cor 4:18
the speech of them which are p up 1Cor 4:19
And ye are p up, and have not 1Cor 5:2
vaunteth not itself, is not p up 1Cor 13:4
vainly p up by his fleshly mind, Col 2:18

**PUFFETH**
for all his enemies, he p at them Ps 10:5
in safety from him that p at him Ps 12:5
Knowledge p up, but charity 1Cor 8:1

**PUHITES** (pu'-hites) *A family descended from Caleb.*
the Ithrites, and the P, and the 1Chr 2:53

**PUL** (pul)
*1. Same as Tiglath-pileser.*
P the king of Assyria came 2Kin 15:19
Menahem gave P a thousand talents. 2Kin 15:19
the spirit of P king of Assyria 1Chr 5:26
*2. A place near Libya.*
unto the nations, to Tarshish, P Is 66:19

**PULL**
he could not p it in again to him 1Kin 13:4
P me out of the net that they Ps 31:4
thy state shall he p thee down Is 22:19
to p down, and to destroy, and to Jer 1:10
p them out like sheep for the Jer 12:3
to p down, and to destroy it Jer 18:7
build them, and not p them down Jer 24:6
not p you down, and I will plant Jer 42:10
shall he not p up the roots Eze 17:9
ye p off the robe with the Mic 2:8
Let me p out the mote out of Mt 7:4
let me p out the mote that is in Lk 6:42
to p out the mote that is in thy Lk 6:42
I will p down my barns, and build Lk 12:18
will not straightway p him out on Lk 14:5

**PULLED**
p her in unto him into the ark Gen 8:9
p Lot into the house to them, and Gen 19:10
let timber be p down from his Ezr 6:11
aside my ways, and p me in pieces Lam 3:11
they shall no more be p up out of Amos 9:15
p away the shoulder, and stopped Zec 7:11
have been p in pieces of them Acts 23:10

**PULLING**
God to the p down of strong holds 2Cor 10:4
with fear, p them out of the fire Jude 23

**PULPIT**
the scribe stood upon a p of wood Neh 8:4

**PULSE**
beans, and lentiles, and parched p 2Sa 17:28
and let them give us p to eat Dan 1:12
and gave them p Dan 1:16

**PUNISH**
then I will p you seven times Lev 26:18
will p you yet seven times for Lev 26:24
Also to p the just is not good, Prov 17:26
I will p the fruit of the stout Is 10:12
I will p the world for their evil Is 13:11
that the LORD shall p the host of Is 24:21
to p the inhabitants of the earth Is 26:21
strong sword shall p leviathan Is 27:1
that I will p all them which are Jer 9:25
of hosts, Behold, I will p them Jer 11:22
thou say when he shall p thee Jer 13:21
But I will p you according to the Jer 21:14
the LORD, I will even p that man Jer 23:34
that I will p the king of Babylon Jer 25:12
of Babylon, that nation will I p Jer 27:8
I will p Shemaiah the Nehelamite, Jer 29:32
I will p all that oppress them Jer 30:20
And I will p him and his seed and Jer 36:31
For I will p them that dwell in Jer 44:13
that I will p you in this place, Jer 44:29
I will p the multitude of No, and Jer 46:25
I will p the king of Babylon and Jer 50:18
I will p Bel in Babylon, and I Jer 51:44
I will p them for their ways, and Hos 4:9
I will not p your daughters when Hos 4:14
will p Jacob according to his Hos 12:2
therefore I will p you for all Amos 3:2
that I will p the princes Zeph 1:8
I p all those that leap on the Zeph 1:9
p the men that are settled on Zeph 1:12
As I thought to p you, when your Zec 8:14
nothing how they might p them Acts 4:21

**PUNISHED**
he shall be surely p Ex 21:20
a day or two, he shall not be p Ex 21:21
he shall be surely p, according Ex 21:22
p us less than our iniquities Ezr 9:13
an iniquity to be p by the judges Job 31:11
an iniquity to be p by the judge Job 31:28
When the scorner is p, the simple Prov 21:11
but the simple pass on, and are p Prov 22:3
but the simple pass on, and are p Prov 27:12
of Egypt, as I have p Jerusalem Jer 44:13
as I have p the king of Assyria Jer 50:18
be cut off, howsoever I p them Zeph 3:7
the shepherds, and I p the goats Zec 10:3
bound unto Jerusalem, for to be p Acts 22:5
I p them oft in every synagogue, Acts 26:11
Who shall be p with everlasting 2Th 1:9
unto the day of judgment to be p 2Pet 2:9

**PUNISHMENT**
My p is greater than I can bear Gen 4:13
accept of the p of their iniquity Lev 26:41
accept of the p of their iniquity Lev 26:43
there shall no p happen to thee 1Sa 28:10
a strange p to the workers of Job 31:3
man of great wrath shall suffer p Prov 19:19
a man for the p of his sins Lam 3:39
For the p of the iniquity of the Lam 4:6
than the p of the sin of Sodom Lam 4:6
The p of thine iniquity is Lam 4:22
bear the p of their iniquity Eze 14:10
the p of the prophet shall be Eze 14:10
p of him that seeketh unto him Eze 14:10
will not turn away the p thereof Amos 1:3
will not turn away the p thereof Amos 1:6
will not turn away the p thereof Amos 1:9
will not turn away the p thereof Amos 1:11
will not turn away the p thereof Amos 1:13
will not turn away the p thereof Amos 2:1
will not turn away the p thereof Amos 2:4
will not turn away the p thereof Amos 2:6
This shall be the p of Egypt Zec 14:19
the p of all nations that come Zec 14:19
shall go away into everlasting p Mt 25:46
to such a man is this p, which 2Cor 2:6
Of how much sorer p, suppose ye, Heb 10:29
by him for the p of evildoers 1Pet 2:14

**PUNISHMENTS**
wrath bringeth the p of the sword Job 19:29
the heathen, and p upon the people Ps 149:7

**PUNITES** (pu'-nites) *Descendents of Pua.*
of Pua, the family of the P Num 26:23

**PUNON** (pu'-non) *An Edomite city.*
from Zalmonah, and pitched in P Num 33:42
And they departed from P, and Num 33:43

**PUR** (pur) See PURIM. *Same as Purim.*
of king Ahasuerus, they cast P Est 3:7
to destroy them, and had cast P Est 9:24
days Purim after the name of P Est 9:26

**PURAH** See PHURAH.

**PURCHASE**
The p of the field and of the cave Gen 49:32
if a man p of the Levites, then Lev 25:33
So I took the evidence of the p Jer 32:11
I gave the evidence of the p unto Jer 32:12
that subscribed the book of the p Jer 32:12
evidences, this evidence of the p Jer 32:14

*p* unto Baruch the son of Neriah Jer 32:16
*p* to themselves a good degree 1Ti 3:13

**PURCHASED**
Abraham *p* of the sons of Heth Gen 25:10
pass over, which thou hast *p* Ex 15:16
have I *p* to be my wife, to raise Ruth 4:10
which thou hast *p* of old Ps 74:2
which his right hand had *p* Ps 78:54
Now this man *p* a field with the Acts 1:18
gift of God may be *p* with money Acts 8:20
which he hath *p* with his own Acts 20:28
redemption of the *p* possession Eph 1:14

**PURE**
thou shalt overlay it with *p* gold Ex 25:11
shalt make a mercy seat of *p* gold Ex 25:17
thou shalt overlay it with *p* gold Ex 25:24
of *p* gold shalt thou make them Ex 25:29
make a candlestick of *p* gold Ex 25:31
be one beaten work of *p* gold Ex 25:36
thereof, shall be of *p* gold Ex 25:38
Of a talent of *p* gold shall he Ex 25:39
that they bring thee *p* oil olive Ex 27:20
two chains of *p* gold at the ends Ex 28:14
ends of wreathen work of *p* gold Ex 28:22
thou shalt make a plate of *p* gold Ex 28:36
thou shalt overlay it with *p* gold Ex 30:3
of *p* myrrh five hundred shekels Ex 30:23
sweet spices with *p* frankincense Ex 30:34
apothecary, tempered together, *p* Ex 30:35
the *p* candlestick with all his Ex 31:8
he overlaid it with *p* gold within Ex 37:2
he made the mercy seat of *p* gold Ex 37:6
And he overlaid it with *p* gold Ex 37:11
covers to cover withal, of *p* gold Ex 37:16
he made the candlestick of *p* gold Ex 37:17
it was one beaten work of *p* gold Ex 37:22
and his snuffdishes, of *p* gold Ex 37:23
Of a talent of *p* gold made he it, Ex 37:24
And he overlaid it with *p* gold Ex 37:26
the *p* incense of sweet spices, Ex 37:29
ends, of wreathen work of *p* gold Ex 39:15
And they made bells of *p* gold Ex 39:25
plate of the holy crown of *p* gold Ex 39:30
The *p* candlestick, with the lamps Ex 39:37
that they bring unto thee *p* oil Lev 24:2
the *p* candlestick before the LORD Lev 24:4
upon the *p* table before the LORD Lev 24:6
thou shalt put *p* frankincense Lev 24:7
drink the *p* blood of the grape Deut 32:14
With the *p* thou wilt shew thyself 2Sa 22:27
thou wilt shew thyself *p* 2Sa 22:27
and twenty measures of *p* oil 1Kin 5:11
and he overlaid it with *p* gold 1Kin 6:20
the house within with *p* gold 1Kin 6:21
And the candlesticks of *p* gold 1Kin 7:49
spoons, and the censers of *p* gold 1Kin 7:50
forest of Lebanon were of *p* gold 1Kin 10:21
Also *p* gold for the fleshhooks, 1Chr 28:17
he overlaid it within with *p* gold 2Chr 3:4
before the oracle, of *p* gold 2Chr 4:20
spoons, and the censers, of *p* gold 2Chr 4:22
ivory, and overlaid it with *p* gold 2Chr 9:17
forest of Lebanon were of *p* gold 2Chr 9:20
they in order upon the *p* table 2Chr 13:11
together, all of them were *p* Ezr 6:20
a man be more *p* than his maker Job 4:17
If thou wert *p* and upright Job 8:6
thou hast said, My doctrine is *p* Job 11:4
also my prayer is *p* Job 16:17
the stars are not *p* in his sight Job 25:5
shall it be valued with *p* gold Job 28:19
The words of the LORD are *p* words Ps 12:6
With the *p* thou wilt shew thyself Ps 18:26
thou wilt shew thyself *p* Ps 18:26
the commandment of the LORD is *p* Ps 19:8
a crown of *p* gold on his head Ps 21:3
hath clean hands, and a *p* heart Ps 24:4
Thy word is very *p* Ps 119:140
words of the *p* are pleasant words Prov 15:26
heart clean, I am *p* from my sin Prov 20:9
his doings, whether his work be *p* Prov 20:11
but as for the *p*, his work is Prov 21:8
Every word of God is *p* Prov 30:5
that are *p* in their own eyes Prov 30:12
hair of his head like the *p* wool Dan 7:9
Shall I count them *p* with the Mic 6:11
I turn to the people a *p* language Zeph 3:9
unto my name, and a *p* offering Mal 1:11
Blessed are the *p* in heart Mt 5:8
that I am *p* from the blood of all Acts 20:26
All things indeed are *p* Rom 14:20
are just, whatsoever things are *p* Phil 4:8
is charity out of a *p* heart 1Ti 1:5
of the faith in a *p* conscience 1Ti 3:9
keep thyself *p* 1Ti 5:22
my forefathers with *p* conscience 2Ti 1:3
call on the Lord out of a *p* heart 2Ti 2:22
Unto the *p* all things are *p* Titus 1:15
and unbelieving is nothing *p* Titus 1:15
and our bodies washed with *p* water Heb 10:22
*P* religion and undefiled before Jas 1:27
that is from above is first *p* Jas 3:17
another with a *p* heart fervently 1Pet 1:22
*p* minds by way of remembrance 2Pet 3:1
himself, even as he is *p* 1Jn 3:3
the seven plagues, clothed in *p* Rev 15:6
and the city was *p* gold, like unto Rev 21:18
the street of the city was *p* gold Rev 21:21
he shewed me a *p* river of water Rev 22:1

**PURELY**
*p* purge away thy dross, and take Is 1:25

**PURENESS**
delivered by the *p* of thine hands Job 22:30
He that loveth *p* of heart Prov 22:11
By *p*, by knowledge, by 2Cor 6:6

**PURER**
Her Nazarites were *p* than snow Lam 4:7
Thou art of *p* eyes than to behold Hab 1:13

**PURGE**
twelfth year he began to *p* Judah 2Chr 34:3
*P* me with hyssop, and I shall be Ps 51:7
thou shalt *p* them away Ps 65:3
*p* away our sins, for thy name's Ps 79:9
purely *p* away thy dross, and take Is 1:25
I will *p* out from among you the Eze 20:38
thus shalt thou cleanse and *p* it Eze 43:20
Seven days shall they *p* the altar Eze 43:26
shall fall, to try them, and to *p* Dan 11:35
*p* them as gold and silver, that Mal 3:3
and he will throughly *p* his floor Mt 3:12
and he will throughly *p* his floor Lk 3:17
*P* out therefore the old leaven, 1Cor 5:7
therefore *p* himself from these 2Ti 2:21
*p* your conscience from dead works Heb 9:14

**PURGED**
of Eli's house shall not be *p* 1Sa 3:14
his reign, when he had *p* the land 2Chr 34:8
By mercy and truth iniquity is *p* Prov 16:6
shall have *p* the blood of Is 4:4
is taken away, and thy sin *p* Is 6:7
not be *p* from you till ye die Is 22:14
shall the iniquity of Jacob be *p* Is 27:9
because I have *p* thee Eze 24:13
and thou wast not *p* Eze 24:13
thou shalt not be *p* from thy Eze 24:13
when he had by himself *p* our sins Heb 1:3
are by the law *p* with blood Heb 9:22
once *p* should have had no more Heb 10:2
that he was *p* from his old sins 2Pet 1:9

**PURGETH**
that beareth fruit, he *p* it Jn 15:2

**PURGING**
out into the draught, *p* all meats Mk 7:19

**PURIFICATION**
it is a *p* for sin Num 19:9
of the burnt heifer of *p* for sin Num 19:17
to the *p* of the sanctuary 2Chr 30:19
their God, and the ward of the *p* Neh 12:45
their things for *p* be given them Est 2:3
gave her her things for *p* Est 2:9
when the days of her *p* according Lk 2:22
accomplishment of the days of *p* Acts 21:26

**PURIFICATIONS**
the days of their *p* accomplished Est 2:12

**PURIFIED**
*p* the altar, and poured the blood Lev 8:15
And the Levites were *p*, and they Num 8:21
nevertheless it shall be *p* with Num 31:23
for she was *p* from her 2Sa 11:4
and the Levites were *p* together Ezr 6:20
and the Levites *p* themselves Neh 12:30
*p* the people, and the gates, and Neh 12:30
a furnace of earth, *p* seven times Ps 12:6
Many shall be *p*, and made white, Dan 12:10
Asia found me *p* in the temple Acts 24:18
heavens should be *p* with these Heb 9:23
Seeing ye have *p* your souls in 1Pet 1:22

**PURIFIER**
sit as a refiner and *p* of silver Mal 3:3

**PURIFIETH**
*p* not himself, defileth the Num 19:13
hath this hope in him *p* himself 1Jn 3:3

**PURIFY**
He shall *p* himself with it on the Num 19:12
but if he *p* not himself the third Num 19:12
seventh day he shall *p* himself Num 19:19
unclean, and shall not *p* himself Num 19:20
*p* both yourselves and your Num 31:19
*p* all your raiment, and all that Num 31:20
of breakings they *p* themselves Job 41:25
*p* themselves in the gardens Is 66:17
they purge the altar and *p* it Eze 43:26
he shall *p* the sons of Levi, and Mal 3:3
the passover, to *p* themselves Jn 11:55
*p* thyself with them, and be at Acts 21:24
*p* unto himself a peculiar people, Titus 2:14
*p* your hearts, ye double minded Jas 4:8

**PURIFYING**
in the blood of her *p* three Lev 12:4
the days of her *p* be fulfilled Lev 12:4
in the blood of her *p* threescore Lev 12:5
the days of her *p* are fulfilled Lev 12:6
Sprinkle water of *p* upon them Num 8:7
in the *p* of all holy things, and 1Chr 23:28
things for the *p* of the women Est 2:12
the manner of the *p* of the Jews Jn 2:6
disciples and the Jews about *p* Jn 3:25
and them, *p* their hearts by faith Acts 15:9
the next day *p* himself with them Acts 21:26
sanctifieth to the *p* of the flesh Heb 9:13

**PURIM** (*pu'-rim*) See PUR. *A Jewish festival celebrating the deliverance from Haman.*
days *P* after the name of Pur Est 9:26
that these days of *P* should not Est 9:28
confirm this second letter of *P* Est 9:29
of *P* in their times appointed Est 9:31
confirmed these matters of *P* Est 9:32

**PURITY**
in spirit, in faith, in *p* 1Ti 4:12
younger as sisters, with all *p* 1Ti 5:2

**PURLOINING**
Not *p*, but shewing all good Titus 2:10

**PURPLE**
And blue, and *p*, and scarlet, and Ex 25:4
fine twined linen, and blue, and *p* Ex 26:1
shalt make a vail of blue, and *p* Ex 26:31
door of the tent, of blue, and *p* Ex 26:36
of twenty cubits, of blue, and *p* Ex 27:16
shall take gold, and blue, and *p* Ex 28:5
ephod of gold, of blue, and of *p* Ex 28:6
even of gold, of blue, and *p* Ex 28:8
of gold, of blue, and of *p* Ex 28:15
pomegranates of blue, and of *p* Ex 28:33
And blue, and *p*, and scarlet, and Ex 35:6
with whom was found blue, and *p* Ex 35:23
had spun, both of blue, and of *p* Ex 35:25
the embroiderer, in blue, and in *p* Ex 35:35
fine twined linen, and blue, and *p* Ex 36:8
And he made a vail of blue, and *p* Ex 36:35
the tabernacle door of blue, and *p* Ex 36:37
was needlework, of blue, and *p* Ex 38:18
an embroiderer in blue, and in *p* Ex 38:23
And of the blue, and *p*, and scarlet, Ex 39:1
the ephod of gold, blue, and *p* Ex 39:2
work it in the blue, and in the *p* Ex 39:3
of gold, blue, and *p*, and scarlet, Ex 39:5
of gold, blue, and *p*, and scarlet, Ex 39:8
robe pomegranates of blue, and *p* Ex 39:24
fine twined linen, and blue, and *p* Ex 39:29
and spread a *p* cloth thereon Num 4:13
*p* raiment that was on the kings Judg 8:26
and in brass, and in iron, and in *p* 2Chr 2:7
in stone, and in timber, in *p* 2Chr 2:14
And he made the vail of blue, and *p* 2Chr 3:14
*p* to silver rings and pillars of Est 1:6
with a garment of fine linen and *p* Est 8:15
her clothing is silk and *p* Prov 31:22
of gold, the covering of it of *p* Song 3:10
and the hair of thine head like *p* Song 7:5
blue and *p* is their clothing Jer 10:9
*p* from the isles of Elishah was Eze 27:7
in thy fairs with emeralds, *p* Eze 27:16
And they clothed him with *p* Mk 15:17
him, they took off the *p* from him Mk 15:20
rich man, which was clothed in *p* Lk 16:19
head, and they put on him a *p* robe Jn 19:2
crown of thorns, and the *p* robe Jn 19:5
woman named Lydia, a seller of *p* Acts 16:14
And the woman was arrayed in *p* Rev 17:4
and of pearls, and fine linen, and *p* Rev 18:12
was clothed in fine linen, and *p* Rev 18:16

**PURPOSE**
some of the handfuls of *p* for her Ruth 2:16
I *p* to build an house unto the 1Kin 5:5
now ye *p* to keep under the 2Chr 28:10
them, to frustrate their *p* Ezr 4:5
which they had made for the *p* Neh 8:4
he may withdraw man from his *p* Job 33:17
Every *p* is established by counsel Prov 20:18
a time to every *p* under the Eccl 3:1
there is a time there for every *p* Eccl 3:17
Because to every *p* there is time Eccl 8:6
To what *p* is the multitude of Is 1:11
This is the *p* that is purposed Is 14:26
shall help in vain, and to no *p* Is 30:7
To what *p* cometh there to me Jer 6:20
which I *p* to do unto them because Jer 26:3
evil which I *p* to do unto them Jer 36:3
and hath conceived a *p* against you Jer 49:30
for every *p* of the LORD shall be Jer 51:29
that the *p* might not be changed Dan 6:17
saying, To what *p* is this waste Mt 26:8
that with *p* of heart they would Acts 11:23
appeared unto thee for this *p* Acts 26:16
that they had obtained their *p* Acts 27:13
save Paul, kept them from their *p* Acts 27:43
are the called according to his *p* Rom 8:28
that the *p* of God according to Rom 9:11
Even for this same *p* have I Rom 9:17
or the things that I *p* 2Cor 1:17
do I *p* according to the flesh, 2Cor 1:17
*p* of him who worketh all things Eph 1:11
According to the eternal *p* which Eph 3:11
have sent unto you for the same *p* Eph 6:22
have sent unto you for the same *p* Col 4:8
works, but according to his own *p* 2Ti 1:9
my doctrine, manner of life, *p* 2Ti 3:10
For this *p* the Son of God was 1Jn 3:8

**PURPOSED**
that he was *p* to fight against 2Chr 32:2
I am *p* that my mouth shall not Ps 17:3
who have *p* to overthrow my goings Ps 140:4
and as I have *p*, so shall it stand Is 14:24
that is *p* upon the whole earth Is 14:26
For the LORD of hosts hath *p* Is 14:27
LORD of hosts hath *p* upon Egypt Is 19:12
The LORD of hosts hath *p* it Is 23:9
I have *p* it, I will also do it Is 46:11

I have spoken it, I have *p* it ... Jer 4:28
that he hath *p* against the ... Jer 49:20
that he hath *p* against the land ... Jer 50:45
The LORD hath *p* to destroy the ... Lam 2:8
But Daniel *p* in his heart that he ... Dan 1:8
Paul *p* in the spirit, when he had ... Acts 19:21
he *p* to return through Macedonia ... Acts 20:3
oftentimes I *p* to come unto you ... Rom 1:13
which he hath *p* in himself ... Eph 1:9
he *p* in Christ Jesus our Lord ... Eph 3:11

**PURPOSES**
my *p* are broken off, even the ... Job 17:11
Without counsel *p* are ... Prov 15:22
shall be broken in the *p* thereof ... Is 19:10
and his *p*, that he hath purposed ... Jer 49:20
and his *p*, that he hath purposed ... Jer 50:45

**PURPOSETH**
according as he *p* in his heart ... 2Cor 9:7

**PURPOSING**
comfort himself, *p* to kill thee ... Gen 27:42

**PURSE**
let us all have one *p* ... Prov 1:14
no bread, no money in their *p* ... Mk 6:8
Carry neither *p*, nor scrip, nor ... Lk 10:4
them, When I sent you without *p* ... Lk 22:35
them, But now, he that hath a *p* ... Lk 22:36

**PURSES**
nor silver, nor brass in your *p* ... Mt 10:9

**PURSUE**
they did not *p* after the sons of ... Gen 35:5
The enemy said, I will *p*, I will ... Ex 15:9
avenger of the blood *p* the slayer ... Deut 19:6
they shall *p* thee until thou ... Deut 28:22
come upon thee, and shall *p* thee ... Deut 28:45
*p* after them quickly ... Josh 2:5
called together to *p* after them ... Josh 8:16
but *p* after your enemies, and ... Josh 10:19
the avenger of blood *p* after him ... Josh 20:5
after whom dost thou *p* ... 1Sa 24:14
Yet a man is risen to *p* thee ... 1Sa 25:29
my lord thus *p* after his servant ... 1Sa 26:18
Shall I *p* after this troop ... 1Sa 30:8
And he answered him, *P* ... 1Sa 30:8
arise and *p* after David this night ... 2Sa 17:1
*p* after him, lest he get him ... 2Sa 20:6
to *p* after Sheba the son of ... 2Sa 20:7
to *p* after Sheba the son of ... 2Sa 20:13
thine enemies, while they *p* thee ... 2Sa 24:13
wilt thou *p* the dry stubble ... Job 13:25
they *p* my soul as the wind ... Job 30:15
seek peace, and *p* it ... Ps 34:14
shall they that *p* you be swift ... Is 30:16
the sword shall *p* thee ... Jer 48:2
unto blood, and blood shall *p* thee ... Eze 35:6
blood, even blood shall *p* thee ... Eze 35:6
the enemy shall *p* him ... Hos 8:3
because he did *p* his brother with ... Amos 1:11
and darkness shall *p* his enemies ... Nah 1:8

**PURSUED**
and eighteen, and *p* them unto Dan ... Gen 14:14
*p* them unto Hobah, which is on ... Gen 14:15
*p* after him seven days' journey ... Gen 31:23
thou hast so hotly *p* after me ... Gen 31:36
he *p* after the children of Israel ... Ex 14:8
But the Egyptians *p* after them ... Ex 14:9
And the Egyptians *p*, and went in ... Ex 14:23
overflow them as they *p* after you ... Deut 11:4
the men *p* after them the way to ... Josh 2:7
as soon as they which *p* after ... Josh 2:7
they *p* after Joshua, and were ... Josh 8:16
the city open, and *p* after Israel ... Josh 8:17
the Egyptians *p* after your ... Josh 24:6
they *p* after him, and caught him, ... Judg 1:6
But Barak *p* after the chariots, ... Judg 4:16
And, behold, as Barak *p* Sisera ... Judg 4:22
and *p* after the Midianites ... Judg 7:23
*p* Midian, and brought the heads of ... Judg 7:25
he *p* after them, and took the two ... Judg 8:12
*p* hard after them unto Gidom, and ... Judg 20:45
*p* the Philistines, and smote them, ... 1Sa 7:11
*p* the Philistines, until thou ... 1Sa 17:52
that, he *p* after David in the ... 1Sa 23:25
But David *p*, he and four hundred ... 1Sa 30:10
And Asahel *p* after Abner ... 2Sa 2:19
also and Abishai *p* after Abner ... 2Sa 2:24
*p* after Israel no more, neither ... 2Sa 2:28
Abishai his brother *p* after Sheba ... 2Sa 20:10
I have *p* mine enemies, and ... 2Sa 22:38
and Israel *p* them ... 1Kin 20:20
of the Chaldees *p* after the king ... 2Kin 25:5
Abijah *p* after Jeroboam, and took ... 2Chr 13:19
were with him *p* them unto Gerar ... 2Chr 14:13
I have *p* mine enemies, and ... Ps 18:37
He *p* them, and passed safely ... Is 41:3
the Chaldeans' army *p* after them ... Jer 39:5
of the Chaldeans *p* after the king ... Jer 52:8
they *p* us upon the mountains, ... Lam 4:19

**PURSUER**
without strength before the *p* ... Lam 1:6

**PURSUERS**
the mountain, lest the *p* meet you ... Josh 2:16
days, until the *p* be returned ... Josh 2:16
until the *p* were returned ... Josh 2:22
the *p* sought them throughout all ... Josh 2:22
wilderness turned back upon the *p* ... Josh 8:20

**PURSUETH**
and ye shall flee when none *p* you ... Lev 26:17
and they shall fall when none *p* ... Lev 26:36
were before a sword, when none *p* ... Lev 26:37
so he that *p* evil *p* it to ... Prov 11:19
evil *p* it to his own death ... Prov 11:19
Evil *p* sinners ... Prov 13:21
he *p* them with words, yet they ... Prov 19:7
The wicked flee when no man *p* ... Prov 28:1

**PURSUING**
were with him, faint, yet *p* them ... Judg 8:4
I am *p* after Zebah and Zalmunna, ... Judg 8:5
Saul returned from *p* after David ... 1Sa 23:28
David and Joab came from *p* a troop ... 2Sa 3:22
returned from *p* after Israel ... 2Sa 18:16
either he is talking, or he is *p* ... 1Kin 18:27
that they turned back from *p* him ... 1Kin 22:33
they turned back again from *p* him ... 2Chr 18:32

**PURTENANCE**
his legs, and with the *p* thereof ... Ex 12:9

**PUSH**
to *p* with his horn in time past ... Ex 21:29
If the ox shall *p* a manservant or ... Ex 21:32
ox hath used to *p* in time past ... Ex 21:36
with them he shall *p* the people ... Deut 33:17
these shalt thou *p* the Syrians ... 1Kin 22:11
With these thou shalt *p* Syria ... 2Chr 18:10
they *p* away my feet, and they ... Job 30:12
thee will we *p* down our enemies ... Ps 44:5
the king of the south *p* at him ... Dan 11:40

**PUSHED**
*p* all the diseased with your ... Eze 34:21

**PUSHING**
I saw the ram *p* westward, and ... Dan 8:4

**PUT** See PREFACE.

**PUTEOLI** (*pu-te'-o-li*) *A seaport in Italy.*
and we came the next day to *P* ... Acts 28:13

**PUTHITES** See PUHITES.

**PUTIEL** (*pu'-te-el*) *Father-in-law of Eleazar.*
one of the daughters of *P* to wife ... Ex 6:25

**PUTRIFYING**
wounds, and bruises, and *p* sores ... Is 1:6

**PUTTEST**
thou *p* thy nest in a rock ... Num 24:21
all that thou *p* thine hands unto ... Deut 12:18
all that thou *p* thine hand unto ... Deut 15:10
that which thou *p* on me will I ... 2Kin 18:14
Thou *p* my feet also in the stocks ... Job 13:27
Thou *p* away all the wicked of the ... Ps 119:119
that *p* thy bottle to him, and ... Hab 2:15

**PUTTETH**
or whosoever *p* any of it upon a ... Ex 30:33
the word that God *p* in my mouth ... Num 22:38
*p* forth her hand, and taketh him ... Deut 25:11
and *p* it in a secret place ... Deut 27:15
boast himself as he that *p* it off ... 1Kin 20:11
he *p* no trust in his saints ... Job 15:15
He *p* forth his hand upon the rock ... Job 28:9
He *p* my feet in the stocks, he ... Job 33:11
He that *p* not out his money to ... Ps 15:5
he *p* down one, and setteth up ... Ps 75:7
but he that *p* his trust in the ... Prov 28:25
but whoso *p* his trust in the LORD ... Prov 29:25
The fig tree *p* forth her green ... Song 2:13
but he that *p* his trust in me ... Is 57:13
as a shepherd *p* on his garment ... Jer 43:12
He *p* his mouth in the dust ... Lam 3:29
*p* the stumblingblock of his ... Eze 14:4
*p* the stumblingblock of his ... Eze 14:7
he that *p* not into their mouths, ... Mic 3:5
No man *p* a piece of new cloth ... Mt 9:16
*p* forth leaves, ye know that ... Mt 24:32
no man *p* new wine into old ... Mk 2:22
immediately he *p* in the sickle ... Mk 4:29
*p* forth leaves, ye know that ... Mk 13:28
No man *p* a piece of a new garment ... Lk 5:36
no man *p* new wine into old ... Lk 5:37
a vessel, or *p* it under a bed ... Lk 8:16
*p* it in a secret place, neither ... Lk 11:33
Whosoever *p* away his wife, and ... Lk 16:18
when he *p* forth his own sheep, he ... Jn 10:4

**PUTTING**
*p* it on her shoulder, and the ... Gen 21:14
*p* them upon the head of the goat, ... Lev 16:21
*p* their hand to their mouth, were ... Judg 7:6
the *p* forth of the finger, and ... Is 58:9
saith that he hateth *p* away ... Mal 2:16
*p* his hand on him, that he might ... Acts 9:12
*p* his hands on him said, Brother ... Acts 9:17
multitude, the Jews *p* him forward ... Acts 19:33
as *p* you in mind, because of the ... Rom 15:15
Wherefore *p* away lying, speak ... Eph 4:25
in *p* off the body of the sins of ... Col 2:11
*p* on the breastplate of faith and ... 1Th 5:8
faithful, *p* me into the ministry ... 1Ti 1:12
in thee by the *p* on of my hands ... 2Ti 1:6
of gold, or of *p* on of apparel ... 1Pet 3:3
*p* away of the filth of the flesh ... 1Pet 3:21
to stir you up by *p* you in ... 2Pet 1:13

**PUVAH** See PUA.

**PUVVAH** See PHUVAH.

**PYGARG**
deer, and the wild goat, and the *p* ... Deut 14:5

**PYRRHUS** Not in KJV.

# Q

**QUAILS**
pass, that at even the *q* came up ... Ex 16:13
brought *q* from the sea, and let ... Num 11:31
next day, and they gathered the *q* ... Num 11:32
The people asked, and he brought *q* ... Ps 105:40

**QUAKE**
The earth shall *q* before them ... Joel 2:10
The mountains *q* at him, and the ... Nah 1:5
and the earth did *q*, and the rocks ... Mt 27:51
said, I exceedingly fear and *q* ... Heb 12:21

**QUAKED**
and the whole mount *q* greatly ... Ex 19:18
also trembled, and the earth *q* ... 1Sa 14:15

**QUAKING**
Son of man, eat thy bread with *q* ... Eze 12:18
but a great *q* fell upon them, so ... Dan 10:7

**QUANTITY**
the issue, all vessels of small *q* ... Is 22:24

**QUARREL**
shall avenge the *q* of my covenant ... Lev 26:25
see how he seeketh a *q* against me ... 2Kin 5:7
Herodias had a *q* against him ... Mk 6:19
if any man have a *q* against any ... Col 3:13

**QUARRIES**
from the *q* that were by Gilgal ... Judg 3:19
tarried, and passed beyond the *q* ... Judg 3:26

**QUARTER**
all the people from every *q* ... Gen 19:4
Then your south *q* shall be from ... Num 34:3
their border in the north *q* was ... Josh 15:5
this was the west *q* ... Josh 18:14
the south *q* was from the end of ... Josh 18:15
shall wander every one to his *q* ... Is 47:15
one for his gain, from his *q* ... Is 56:11
and they came to him from every *q* ... Mk 1:45

**QUARTERS**
seen with thee in all thy *q* ... Ex 13:7
upon the four *q* of thy vesture ... Deut 22:12
In four *q* were the porters, ... 1Chr 9:24
winds from the four *q* of heaven ... Jer 49:36
house of Togarmah of the north *q* ... Eze 38:6
as Peter passed throughout all *q* ... Acts 9:32
of the Jews which were in those *q* ... Acts 16:3
In the same *q* were possessions of ... Acts 28:7
are in the four *q* of the earth ... Rev 20:8

**QUARTUS** (*quar'-tus*) *A Christian in Rome.*
city saluteth you, and *Q* a brother ... Rom 16:23

**QUATERNIONS**
delivered him to four *q* of ... Acts 12:4

**QUEEN**
when the *q* of Sheba heard of the ... 1Kin 10:1
when the *q* of Sheba had seen all ... 1Kin 10:4
of spices as these which the *q* of ... 1Kin 10:10
the *q* of Sheba all her desire ... 1Kin 10:13
the sister of Tahpenes the *q* ... 1Kin 11:19
even her he removed from being *q* ... 1Kin 15:13
the king and the children of the *q* ... 2Kin 10:13
when the *q* of Sheba heard of the ... 2Chr 9:1
when the *q* of Sheba had seen the ... 2Chr 9:3
the *q* of Sheba gave king Solomon ... 2Chr 9:9
to the *q* of Sheba all her desire ... 2Chr 9:12
king, he removed her from being *q* ... 2Chr 15:16
(the *q* also sitting by him,) For ... Neh 2:6
Also Vashti the *q* made a feast ... Est 1:9
To bring Vashti the *q* before the ... Est 1:11
But the *q* Vashti refused to come ... Est 1:12
the *q* Vashti according to law ... Est 1:15
Vashti the *q* hath not done wrong ... Est 1:16
For this deed of the *q* shall come ... Est 1:17
the *q* to be brought in before him ... Est 1:17
have heard of the deed of the *q* ... Est 1:18
the king be *q* instead of Vashti ... Est 2:4
made her *q* instead of Vashti ... Est 2:17
who told it unto Esther the *q* ... Est 2:22
Then was the *q* exceedingly ... Est 4:4
the *q* standing in the court ... Est 5:2
her, What wilt thou, *q* Esther ... Est 5:3
Esther the *q* did let no man come ... Est 5:12
came to banquet with Esther the *q* ... Est 7:1
What is thy petition, *q* Esther ... Est 7:2
Then Esther the *q* answered ... Est 7:3
and said unto Esther the *q* ... Est 7:5
afraid before the king and the *q* ... Est 7:6
for his life to Esther the *q* ... Est 7:7
Will he force the *q* also before ... Est 7:8
the Jews' enemy unto Esther the *q* ... Est 8:1
Ahasuerus said unto Esther the *q* ... Est 8:7
the king said unto Esther the *q* ... Est 9:12
Then Esther the *q*, the daughter ... Est 9:29
Esther the *q* had enjoined them, ... Est 9:31

did stand the *q* in gold of Ophir ... Ps 45:9
to make cakes to the *q* of heaven ... Jer 7:18
Say unto the king and to the *q* ... Jer 13:18
that Jeconiah the king, and the *q* ... Jer 29:2
burn incense unto the *q* of heaven ... Jer 44:17
burn incense to the *q* of heaven ... Jer 44:18
burned incense to the *q* of heaven ... Jer 44:19
burn incense to the *q* of heaven ... Jer 44:25
Now the *q*, by reason of the words ... Dan 5:10
the *q* spake and said, O king, live ... Dan 5:10
The *q* of the south shall rise up ... Mt 12:42
The *q* of the south shall rise up ... Lk 11:31
under Candace *q* of the Ethiopians ... Acts 8:27
she saith in her heart, I sit a *q* ... Rev 18:7

**QUEENS**
There are threescore *q*, and ... Song 6:8
yea, the *q* and the concubines, and ... Song 6:9
their *q* thy nursing mothers ... Is 49:23

**QUENCH**
so they shall *q* my coal which is ... 2Sa 14:7
that thou *q* not the light of ... 2Sa 21:17
the wild asses *q* their thirst ... Ps 104:11
Many waters cannot *q* love ... Song 8:7
together, and none shall *q* them ... Is 1:31
the smoking flax shall he not *q* ... Is 42:3
burn that none can *q* it because ... Jer 4:4
fire, and burn that none can *q* it ... Jer 21:12
there be none to *q* it in Beth-el ... Amos 5:6
and smoking flax shall he not *q* ... Mt 12:20
to *q* all the fiery darts of the ... Eph 6:16
*Q* not the Spirit ... 1Th 5:19

**QUENCHED**
unto the LORD, the fire was *q* ... Num 11:2
this place, and shall not be *q* ... 2Kin 22:17
this place, and shall not be *q* ... 2Chr 34:25
they are *q* as the fire of thorns ... Ps 118:12
It shall not be *q* night nor day ... Is 34:10
are extinct, they are *q* as tow ... Is 43:17
neither shall their fire be *q* ... Is 66:24
it shall burn, and shall not be *q* ... Jer 7:20
Jerusalem, and it shall not be *q* ... Jer 17:27
the flaming flame shall not be *q* ... Eze 20:47
it shall not be *q* ... Eze 20:48
the fire that never shall be *q* ... Mk 9:43
dieth not, and the fire is not *q* ... Mk 9:44
the fire that never shall be *q* ... Mk 9:45
dieth not, and the fire is not *q* ... Mk 9:46
dieth not, and the fire is not *q* ... Mk 9:48
*Q* the violence of fire, escaped ... Heb 11:34

**QUESTION**
which was a lawyer, asked him a *q* ... Mt 22:35
forth, and began to *q* with him ... Mk 8:11
the scribes, What *q* ye with them ... Mk 9:16
I will also ask of you one *q* ... Mk 11:29
after that durst ask him any *q* ... Mk 12:34
durst not ask him any *q* at all ... Lk 20:40
Then there arose a *q* between some ... Jn 3:25
apostles and elders about this *q* ... Acts 15:2
But if it be a *q* of words ... Acts 18:15
called in *q* for this day's uproar ... Acts 19:40
of the dead I am called in *q* ... Acts 23:6
I am called in *q* by you this day ... Acts 24:21
asking no *q* for conscience sake ... 1Cor 10:25
asking no *q* for conscience sake ... 1Cor 10:27

**QUESTIONED**
Then Hezekiah *q* with the priests ... 2Chr 31:9
that they *q* among themselves ... Mk 1:27
Then he *q* with him in many words ... Lk 23:9

**QUESTIONING**
*q* one with another what the ... Mk 9:10
them, and the scribes *q* with them ... Mk 9:14

**QUESTIONS**
she came to prove him with hard *q* ... 1Kin 10:1
And Solomon told her all her *q* ... 1Kin 10:3
Solomon with hard *q* at Jerusalem ... 2Chr 9:1
And Solomon told her all her *q* ... 2Chr 9:2
that day forth ask him any more *q* ... Mt 22:46
hearing them, and asking them *q* ... Lk 2:46
to be accused of *q* of their law ... Acts 23:29
But had certain *q* against him of ... Acts 25:19
I doubted of such manner of *q* ... Acts 25:20
*q* which are among the Jews ... Acts 26:3
genealogies, which minister *q* ... 1Ti 1:4
nothing, but doting about *q* ... 1Ti 6:4
But foolish and unlearned *q* avoid ... 2Ti 2:23
But avoid foolish *q*, and ... Titus 3:9

**QUICK**
there be *q* raw flesh in the ... Lev 13:10
the *q* flesh that burneth have a ... Lev 13:24
and they go down *q* into the pit ... Num 16:30
and let them go down *q* into hell ... Ps 55:15
Then they had swallowed us up *q* ... Ps 124:3
shall make him of *q* understanding ... Is 11:3
of God to be the Judge of *q* ... Acts 10:42
Christ, who shall judge the *q* ... 2Ti 4:1
For the word of God is *q*, and ... Heb 4:12
him that is ready to judge the *q* ... 1Pet 4:5

**QUICKEN**
shalt *q* me again, and shalt bring ... Ps 71:20
*q* us, and we will call upon thy ... Ps 80:18
*q* thou me according to thy word ... Ps 119:25
and *q* thou me in thy way ... Ps 119:37
*q* me in thy righteousness ... Ps 119:40
*Q* me after thy lovingkindness ... Ps 119:88
*q* me, O LORD, according unto thy ... Ps 119:107
*q* me according to thy judgment ... Ps 119:149
*q* me according to thy word ... Ps 119:154
*q* me according to thy judgments ... Ps 119:156
*q* me, O LORD, according to thy ... Ps 119:159
*Q* me, O LORD, for thy name's sake ... Ps 143:11
also *q* your mortal bodies by his ... Rom 8:11

**QUICKENED**
for thy word hath *q* me ... Ps 119:50
for with them thou hast *q* me ... Ps 119:93
that which thou sowest is not *q* ... 1Cor 15:36
And you hath he *q*, who were dead ... Eph 2:1
hath *q* us together with Christ, ( ... Eph 2:5
hath he *q* together with him, ... Col 2:13
in the flesh, but *q* by the Spirit ... 1Pet 3:18

**QUICKENETH**
raiseth up the dead, and *q* them ... Jn 5:21
even so the Son *q* whom he will ... Jn 5:21
It is the spirit that *q* ... Jn 6:63
who *q* the dead, and calleth those ... Rom 4:17
who *q* all things, and before ... 1Ti 6:13

**QUICKENING**
the last Adam was made a *q* spirit ... 1Cor 15:45

**QUICKLY**
Make ready *q* three measures of ... Gen 18:6
it that thou hast found it so *q* ... Gen 27:20
aside *q* out of the way which I ... Ex 32:8
go *q* unto the congregation, and ... Num 16:46
drive them out, and destroy them *q* ... Deut 9:3
Arise, get thee down *q* from hence ... Deut 9:12
they are *q* turned aside out of ... Deut 9:12
ye had turned aside *q* out of the ... Deut 9:16
lest ye perish *q* from off the ... Deut 11:17
destroyed, and until thou perish *q* ... Deut 28:20
pursue after them *q* ... Josh 2:5
the ambush arose *q* out of their ... Josh 8:19
come up to us *q*, and save us, and ... Josh 10:6
ye shall perish *q* from off the ... Josh 23:16
they turned *q* out of the way ... Judg 2:17
days, then thou shalt go down *q* ... 1Sa 20:19
Now therefore send *q*, and tell ... 2Sa 17:16
but they went both of them away *q* ... 2Sa 17:18
Arise, and pass *q* over the water ... 2Sa 17:21
Come down *q* ... 2Kin 1:11
Fetch *q* Micaiah the son of Imla ... 2Chr 18:8
a threefold cord is not *q* broken ... Eccl 4:12
Agree with thine adversary *q* ... Mt 5:25
And go *q*, and tell his disciples ... Mt 28:7
And they departed *q* from the ... Mt 28:8
And they went out *q*, and fled from ... Mk 16:8
Go out *q* into the streets and ... Lk 14:21
him, Take thy bill, and sit down *q* ... Lk 16:6
as she heard that, she arose *q* ... Jn 11:29
unto him, That thou doest, do *q* ... Jn 13:27
raised him up, saying, Arise up *q* ... Acts 12:7
get thee *q* out of Jerusalem ... Acts 22:18
or else I will come unto thee *q* ... Rev 2:5
or else I will come unto thee *q* ... Rev 2:16
Behold, I come *q* ... Rev 3:11
behold, the third woe cometh *q* ... Rev 11:14
Behold, I come *q* ... Rev 22:7
And, behold, I come *q* ... Rev 22:12
things saith, Surely I come *q* ... Rev 22:20

**QUICKSANDS**
lest they should fall into the *q* ... Acts 27:17

**QUIET**
were *q* all the night, saying, In ... Judg 16:2
the manner of the Zidonians, *q* ... Judg 18:7
unto a people that were at *q* ... Judg 18:27
rejoiced, and the city was in *q* ... 2Kin 11:20
good, and the land was wide, and *q* ... 1Chr 4:40
his days the land was *q* ten years ... 2Chr 14:1
and the kingdom was *q* before him ... 2Chr 14:5
So the realm of Jehoshaphat was *q* ... 2Chr 20:30
and the city was *q*, after that ... 2Chr 23:21
I have lain still and been *q* ... Job 3:13
had I rest, neither was I *q* ... Job 3:26
being wholly at ease and *q* ... Job 21:23
them that are *q* in the land ... Ps 35:20
are they glad because they be *q* ... Ps 107:30
shall be *q* from fear of evil ... Prov 1:33
*q* more than the cry of him that ... Eccl 9:17
say unto him, Take heed, and be *q* ... Is 7:4
whole earth is at rest, and is *q* ... Is 14:7
dwellings, and in *q* resting places ... Is 32:18
see Jerusalem a *q* habitation ... Is 33:20
and shall be in rest, and be *q* ... Jer 30:10
how long will it be ere thou be *q* ... Jer 47:6
How can it be *q*, seeing the LORD ... Jer 47:7
it cannot be *q* ... Jer 49:23
And this Seraiah was a *q* prince ... Jer 51:59
depart from thee, and I will be *q* ... Eze 16:42
Though they be *q*, and likewise ... Nah 1:12
spoken against, ye ought to be *q* ... Acts 19:36
And that ye study to be *q*, and to ... 1Th 4:11
that we may lead a *q* and peaceable ... 1Ti 2:2
*q* spirit, which is in the sight ... 1Pet 3:4

**QUIETED**
*q* myself, as a child that is ... Ps 131:2
toward the north country have *q* ... Zec 6:8

**QUIETETH**
when he *q* the earth by the south ... Job 37:17

**QUIETLY**
in the gate to speak with him *q* ... 2Sa 3:27
*q* wait for the salvation of the ... Lam 3:26

**QUIETNESS**
the country was in *q* forty years ... Judg 8:28
*q* unto Israel in his days ... 1Chr 22:9
he shall not feel *q* in his belly ... Job 20:20
When he giveth *q*, who then can ... Job 34:29
*q* therewith, than an house full ... Prov 17:1
Better is an handful with *q* ... Eccl 4:6
in *q* and in confidence shall be ... Is 30:15
and the effect of righteousness *q* ... Is 32:17
that by thee we enjoy great *q* ... Acts 24:2
Christ, that with *q* they work ... 2Th 3:12

**QUIRINIUS** See CYRENIUS.

**QUIT**
then shall he that smote him be *q* ... Ex 21:19
the owner of the ox shall be *q* ... Ex 21:28
then we will be *q* of thine oath ... Josh 2:20
*q* yourselves like men, O ye ... 1Sa 4:9
*q* yourselves like men, and fight ... 1Sa 4:9
*q* you like men, be strong ... 1Cor 16:13

**QUITE**
hath *q* devoured also our money ... Gen 31:15
*q* break down their images ... Ex 23:24
thou shalt *q* take away their ... Num 17:10
*q* pluck down all their high ... Num 33:52
sent him away, and he is *q* gone ... 2Sa 3:24
and is wisdom driven *q* from me ... Job 6:13
Thy bow was made *q* naked, ... Hab 3:9

**QUIVER**
I pray thee, thy weapons, thy *q* ... Gen 27:3
The *q* rattleth against him, the ... Job 39:23
man that hath his *q* full of them ... Ps 127:5
Elam bare the *q* with chariots of ... Is 22:6
in his *q* hath he hid me ... Is 49:2
Their *q* is as an open sepulchre, ... Jer 5:16
of his *q* to enter into my reins ... Lam 3:13

**QUIVERED**
my lips *q* at the voice ... Hab 3:16

# R

**RAAMA** See RAAMAH.

**RAAMAH** (*ra'-a-mah*)
*1. A son of Cush.*
Seba, and Havilah, and Sabtah, and *R* ... Gen 10:7
and the sons of *R* ... Gen 10:7
Seba, and Havilah, and Sabta, and *R* ... 1Chr 1:9
And the sons of *R* ... 1Chr 1:9
*2. A place in Arabia.*
The merchants of Sheba and *R* ... Eze 27:22

**RAAMIAH** (*ra-a-mi'-ah*) *A clan leader in exile.*
Jeshua, Nehemiah, Azariah, *R* ... Neh 7:7

**RAAMSES** (*ra-am'-seze*) See RAMESES. *An Egyptian city.*
treasure cities, Pithom and *R* ... Ex 1:11

**RABBAH** (*rab'-bah*) See RABBATH.
*1. An Ammonite city.*
unto Aroer that is before *R* ... Josh 13:25
children of Ammon, and besieged *R* ... 2Sa 11:1
Joab fought against *R* of the ... 2Sa 12:26
and said, I have fought against *R* ... 2Sa 12:27
the people together, and went to *R* ... 2Sa 12:29
of *R* of the children of Ammon ... 2Sa 17:27
of Ammon, and came and besieged *R* ... 1Chr 20:1
And Joab smote *R*, and destroyed it ... 1Chr 20:1
to be heard in *R* of the Ammonites ... Jer 49:2
cry, ye daughters of *R*, gird you ... Jer 49:3
I will make *R* a stable for camels ... Eze 25:5
kindle a fire in the wall of *R* ... Amos 1:14
*2. A city in Judah.*
which is Kirjath-jearim, and *R* ... Josh 15:60

**RABBATH** (*rab'-bath*) See RABBAH. *Same as Rabbah 1.*
is it not in *R* of the children of ... Deut 3:11
may come to *R* of the Ammonites ... Eze 21:20

**RABBI** (*rab'-bi*) See RABBONI. *A Jewish title meaning 'teacher.'*
and to be called of men, *R*, *R* ... Mt 23:7
But be not ye called *R* ... Mt 23:8
They said unto him, *R*, (which is ... Jn 1:38
answered and saith unto him, *R* ... Jn 1:49
by night, and said unto him, *R* ... Jn 3:2
unto John, and said unto him, *R* ... Jn 3:26
of the sea, they said unto him, *R* ... Jn 6:25

**RABBITH** (*rab'-bith*) *A city in Issachar.*
And *R*, and Kishion, and Abez, ... Josh 19:20

**RABBONI** (*rab-bo'-ni*) See RABBI. *A Jewish title of respect.*
herself, and saith unto him, *R* ... Jn 20:16

**RAB-MAG** *A Babylonian prince.*
Rab-saris, Nergal-sharezer, *R* ... Jer 39:3
Rab-saris, and Nergal-sharezer, *R* ... Jer 39:13

**RAB-SARIS**
*1. A Babylonian prince.*
Samgar-nebo, Sarsechim, *R* ... Jer 39:3
the guard sent, and Nebushasban, *R* ... Jer 39:13
*2. An Assyrian officer.*
king of Assyria sent Tartan and *R* ... 2Kin 18:17

**RAB-SHAKEH** (*rab'-sha-keh*) See RABSHAKEH. *An Assyrian officer.*
*R* from Lachish to king Hezekiah ... 2Kin 18:17
*R* said unto them, Speak ye now to... 2Kin 18:19
and Shebna, and Joah, unto *R* ... 2Kin 18:26
But *R* said unto them, Hath my ... 2Kin 18:27
Then *R* stood and cried with a loud.. 2Kin 18:28
rent, and told him the words of *R*... 2Kin 18:37
God will hear all the words of *R* ... 2Kin 19:4
So *R* returned, and found the king ... 2Kin 19:8

**RABSHAKEH** (*rab'-sha-keh*) See RAB-SHAKEH. *Same as Rab-shakeh.*
the king of Assyria sent *R* from... Is 36:2
*R* said unto them, Say ye now to... Is 36:4
Eliakim and Shebna and Joah unto *R*.... Is 36:11
But *R* said, Hath my master sent... Is 36:12
Then *R* stood, and cried with a... Is 36:13
rent, and told him the words of *R*... Is 36:22
thy God will hear the words of *R*... Is 37:4
So *R* returned, and found the king ... Is 37:8

**RACA** (*ra'-cah*) *A Jewish term of disrespect.*
shall say to his brother, *R*... Mt 5:22

**RACAL** See RACHAL.

**RACE**
as a strong man to run a *r*... Ps 19:5
that the *r* is not to the swift,... Eccl 9:11
they which run in a *r* run all... 1Cor 9:24
the *r* that is set before us... Heb 12:1

**RACHAB** (*ra'kab*) See RAHAB. *Same as Rahab; ancestor of Jesus.*
And Salmon begat Booz of *R*... Mt 1:5

**RACHAL** (*ra'-kal*) *A city in Judah.*
And to them which were in *R*... 1Sa 30:29

**RACHEL** (*ra'-chel*) See RACHEL'S, RAHEL. *Wife of Jacob.*
*R* his daughter cometh with the... Gen 29:6
*R* came with her father's sheep ... Gen 29:9
when Jacob saw *R* the daughter of... Gen 29:10
And Jacob kissed *R*, and lifted up... Gen 29:11
Jacob told *R* that he was her... Gen 29:12
and the name of the younger was *R*.. Gen 29:16
but *R* was beautiful and well... Gen 29:17
And Jacob loved *R*... Gen 29:18
years for *R* thy younger daughter... Gen 29:18
And Jacob served seven years for *R*... Gen 29:20
did not I serve with thee for *R*... Gen 29:25
he gave him *R* his daughter to... Gen 29:28
Laban gave to *R* his daughter... Gen 29:29
And he went in also unto *R*... Gen 29:30
he loved also *R* more than Leah,... Gen 29:30
but *R* was barren... Gen 29:31
when *R* saw that she bare Jacob no... Gen 30:1
no children, *R* envied her sister... Gen 30:1
anger was kindled against *R*... Gen 30:2
*R* said, God hath judged me, and... Gen 30:6
*R* said, With great wrestlings... Gen 30:8
Then *R* said to Leah, Give me, I... Gen 30:14
*R* said, Therefore he shall lie... Gen 30:15
And God remembered *R*, and God... Gen 30:22
when *R* had born Joseph, that... Gen 30:25
And Jacob sent and called *R*... Gen 31:4
And *R* and Leah answered and said... Gen 31:14
*R* had stolen the images that were... Gen 31:19
knew not that *R* had stolen them... Gen 31:32
Now *R* had taken the images, and... Gen 31:34
the children unto Leah, and unto *R*... Gen 33:1
Leah and her children after, and *R*... Gen 33:2
and after came Joseph near and *R*... Gen 33:7
*R* travailed, and she had hard... Gen 35:16
*R* died, and was buried in the way... Gen 35:19
The sons of *R*... Gen 35:24
The sons of *R* Jacob's wife... Gen 46:19
These are the sons of *R*, which... Gen 46:22
Laban gave unto *R* his daughter... Gen 46:25
*R* died by me in the land of... Gen 48:7
is come into thine house like *R*... Ruth 4:11
*R* weeping for her children, and... Mt 2:18

**RACHEL'S** (*ra'-chelz*)
Bilhah *R* maid conceived again, and... Gen 30:7
tent, and entered into *R* tent... Gen 31:33
pillar of *R* grave unto this day... Gen 35:20
And the sons of Bilhah, *R* handmaid.. Gen 35:25
by *R* sepulchre in the border of... 1Sa 10:2

**RADDAI** (*rad'-dahee*) *Son of Jesse.*
the fourth, *R* the fifth,... 1Chr 2:14

**RAFTERS**
house are cedar, and our *r* of fir... Song 1:17

**RAGAU** (*ra'-gaw*) See REU. *Father of Saruch; ancestor of Jesus.*
of Saruch, which was the son of *R*... Lk 3:35

**RAGE**
So he turned and went away in a *r*... 2Kin 5:12
coming in, and thy *r* against me... 2Kin 19:27
Because thy *r* against me and thy... 2Kin 19:28
for he was in a *r* with him... 2Chr 16:10
ye have slain them in a *r* that... 2Chr 28:9
the ground with fierceness and *r*... Job 39:24
Cast abroad the *r* of thy wrath... Job 40:11
Why do the heathen *r*, and the... Ps 2:1
because of the *r* of mine enemies... Ps 7:6
For jealousy is the *r* of a man... Prov 6:34
man, whether he *r* or laugh... Prov 29:9
coming in, and thy *r* against me... Is 37:28
Because thy *r* against me, and thy... Is 37:29
and *r*, ye chariots... Jer 46:9
Then Nebuchadnezzar in his *r*... Dan 3:13
sword for the *r* of their tongue... Hos 7:16
chariots shall *r* in the streets... Nah 2:4
hast said, Why did the heathen *r*... Acts 4:25

**RAGED**
The heathen *r*, the kingdoms were... Ps 46:6

**RAGETH**
but the fool *r*, and is confident... Prov 14:16

**RAGGED**
and into the tops of the *r* rocks... Is 2:21

**RAGING**
Thou rulest the *r* of the sea... Ps 89:9
is a mocker, strong drink is *r*... Prov 20:1
and the sea ceased from her *r*... Jonah 1:15
the wind and the *r* of the water... Lk 8:24
*R* waves of the sea, foaming out... Jude 13

**RAGS**
shall clothe a man with *r*... Prov 23:21
righteousnesses are as filthy *r*... Is 64:6
old cast clouts and old rotten *r*... Jer 38:11
rotten *r* under thine armholes... Jer 38:12

**RAGUEL** (*ra-gu'-el*) *Father-in-law of Moses.*
the son of *R* the Midianite,... Num 10:29

**RAHAB** (*ra'-hab*) See RACHAB.
*1. A Jericho woman who befriended the spies.*
into an harlot's house, named *R*... Josh 2:1
the king of Jericho sent unto *R*... Josh 2:3
only *R* the harlot shall live, she... Josh 6:17
spies went in, and brought out *R*... Josh 6:23
Joshua saved *R* the harlot alive,... Josh 6:25
By faith the harlot *R* perished... Heb 11:31
Likewise also was not *R* the... Jas 2:25
*2. A symbolic name for Egypt.*
I will make mention of *R* and... Ps 87:4
Thou hast broken *R* in pieces... Ps 89:10
Art thou not it that hath cut *R*... Is 51:9

**RAHAM** (*ra'-ham*) *Son of Shema.*
And Shema begat *R*, the father of... 1Chr 2:44

**RAHEL** (*ra'-hel*) See RACHEL. *Same as Rachel.*
*R* weeping for her children... Jer 31:15

**RAIL**
He wrote also letters to *r* on the... 2Chr 32:17

**RAILED**
and he *r* on them... 1Sa 25:14
And they that passed by *r* on him... Mk 15:29
which were hanged *r* on him... Lk 23:39

**RAILER**
covetous, or an idolater, or a *r*... 1Cor 5:11

**RAILING**
evil for evil, or *r* for *r*... 1Pet 3:9
bring not *r* accusation against... 2Pet 2:11
bring against him a *r* accusation... Jude 9

**RAILINGS**
whereof cometh envy, strife, *r*... 1Ti 6:4

**RAIMENT**
silver, and jewels of gold, and *r*... Gen 24:53
Rebekah took goodly *r* of her... Gen 27:15
and he smelled the smell of his *r*... Gen 27:27
me bread to eat, and *r* to put on,... Gen 28:20
shaved himself, and changed his *r*... Gen 41:14
he gave each man changes of *r*... Gen 45:22
of silver, and five changes of *r*... Gen 45:22
silver, and jewels of gold, and *r*... Ex 3:22
silver, and jewels of gold, and *r*... Ex 12:35
her food, her *r*, and her duty of... Ex 21:10
for ox, for ass, for sheep, for *r*... Ex 22:9
take thy neighbour's *r* to pledge... Ex 22:26
only, it is his *r* for his skin... Ex 22:27
it be any vessel of wood, or *r*... Lev 11:32
And purify all your *r*, and all that... Num 31:20
Thy *r* waxed not old upon thee,... Deut 8:4
stranger, in giving him food and *r*... Deut 10:18
she shall put the *r* of her... Deut 21:13
and so shalt thou do with his *r*... Deut 22:3
that he may sleep in his own *r*... Deut 24:13
nor take a widow's *r* to pledge... Deut 24:17
and with iron, and with very much *r*... Josh 22:8
under his *r* upon his right thigh... Judg 3:16
purple *r* that was on the kings of... Judg 8:26
put thy *r* upon thee, and get thee... Ruth 3:3
himself, and put on other *r*... 1Sa 28:8
of gold, and ten changes of *r*... 2Kin 5:5
thence silver, and gold, and *r*... 2Kin 7:8
silver, and vessels of gold, and *r*... 2Chr 9:24
she sent *r* to clothe Mordecai, and... Est 4:4
dust, and prepare *r* as the clay... Job 27:16
unto the king in *r* of needlework... Ps 45:14
as the *r* of those that are slain,... Is 14:19
and I will stain all my *r*... Is 63:3
thy *r* was of fine linen, and silk,... Eze 16:13
will clothe thee with change of *r*... Zec 3:4
John had his *r* of camel's hair... Mt 3:4
than meat, and the body than *r*... Mt 6:25
And why take ye thought for *r*... Mt 6:28
A man clothed in soft *r*... Mt 11:8
his *r* was white as the light... Mt 17:2
from him, and put his own *r* on him... Mt 27:31
lightning, and his *r* white as snow... Mt 28:3
his *r* became shining, exceeding... Mk 9:3
A man clothed in soft *r*... Lk 7:25
his *r* was white and glistering... Lk 9:29
which stripped him of his *r*... Lk 10:30
meat, and the body is more than *r*... Lk 12:23
And they parted his *r*, and cast... Lk 23:34
They parted my *r* among them... Jn 19:24
and blasphemed, he shook his *r*... Acts 18:6
kept the *r* of them that slew him... Acts 22:20
*r* let us be therewith content... 1Ti 6:8
come in also a poor man in vile *r*... Jas 2:2
same shall be clothed in white *r*... Rev 3:5
and white *r*, that thou mayest be... Rev 3:18
sitting, clothed in white *r*... Rev 4:4

**RAIN**
not caused it to *r* upon the earth... Gen 2:5
I will cause it to *r* upon the... Gen 7:4
the *r* was upon the earth forty... Gen 7:12
the *r* from heaven was restrained... Gen 8:2
it to *r* a very grievous hail... Ex 9:18
the *r* was not poured upon the... Ex 9:33
And when Pharaoh saw that the *r*... Ex 9:34
I will *r* bread from heaven for... Ex 16:4
I will give you *r* in due season... Lev 26:4
drinketh water of the *r* of heaven... Deut 11:11
That I will give you the *r* of... Deut 11:14
in his due season, the first *r*... Deut 11:14
and the latter *r*... Deut 11:14
up the heaven, that there be no *r*... Deut 11:17
the heaven to give the *r* unto thy... Deut 28:12
make the *r* of thy land powder... Deut 28:24
My doctrine shall drop as the *r*... Deut 32:2
as the small *r* upon the tender... Deut 32:2
and he shall send thunder and *r*... 1Sa 12:17
LORD sent thunder and *r* that day... 1Sa 12:18
be no dew, neither let there be *r*... 2Sa 1:21
earth by clear shining after *r*... 2Sa 23:4
is shut up, and there is no *r*... 1Kin 8:35
give *r* upon thy land, which thou... 1Kin 8:36
not be dew nor *r* these years... 1Kin 17:1
there had been no *r* in the land... 1Kin 17:7
the LORD sendeth *r* upon the earth.... 1Kin 17:14
I will send *r* upon the earth... 1Kin 18:1
is a sound of abundance of *r*... 1Kin 18:41
down, that the *r* stop thee not... 1Kin 18:44
and wind, and there was a great *r*... 1Kin 18:45
see wind, neither shall ye see *r*... 2Kin 3:17
is shut up, and there is no *r*... 2Chr 6:26
send *r* upon thy land, which thou... 2Chr 6:27
shut up heaven that there be no *r*... 2Chr 7:13
this matter, and for the great *r*... Ezr 10:9
many, and it is a time of much *r*... Ezr 10:13
Who giveth *r* upon the earth, and... Job 5:10
shall *r* it upon him while he is... Job 20:23
When he made a decree for the *r*... Job 28:26
they waited for me as for the *r*... Job 29:23
mouth wide as for the latter *r*... Job 29:23
they pour down *r* according to the... Job 36:27
likewise to the small *r*, and to... Job 37:6
to the great *r* of his strength... Job 37:6
To cause it to *r* on the earth... Job 38:26
Hath the *r* a father... Job 38:28
Upon the wicked he shall *r* snares... Ps 11:6
O God, didst send a plentiful *r*... Ps 68:9
down like *r* upon the mown grass... Ps 72:6
the *r* also filleth the pools... Ps 84:6
He gave them hail for *r*, and... Ps 105:32
he maketh lightnings for the *r*... Ps 135:7
who prepareth *r* for the earth... Ps 147:8
is as a cloud of the latter *r*... Prov 16:15
is like clouds and wind without *r*... Prov 25:14
The north wind driveth away *r*... Prov 25:23
as *r* in harvest, so honour is not... Prov 26:1
sweeping *r* which leaveth no food... Prov 28:3
If the clouds be full of *r*... Eccl 11:3
nor the clouds return after the *r*... Eccl 12:2
is past, the *r* is over and gone... Song 2:11
for a covert from storm and from *r*... Is 4:6
that they *r* no *r* upon it... Is 5:6
that they *r* no *r* upon it... Is 5:6
shall he give the *r* of thy seed... Is 30:23
an ash, and the *r* doth nourish it... Is 44:14
For as the *r* cometh down, and the... Is 55:10
and there hath been no latter *r*... Jer 3:3
the LORD our God, that giveth *r*... Jer 5:24
he maketh lightnings with *r*... Jer 10:13
for there was no *r* in the earth... Jer 14:4
of the Gentiles that can cause *r*... Jer 14:22
he maketh lightnings with *r*... Jer 51:16
is in the cloud in the day of *r*... Eze 1:28
I will *r* upon him, and upon his... Eze 38:22
are with him, and overflowing *r*... Eze 38:22
and he shall come unto us as the *r*... Hos 6:3
latter and former *r* unto the earth... Hos 6:3
come and *r* righteousness upon you.... Hos 10:12
given you the former *r* moderately... Joel 2:23
cause to come down for you the *r*... Joel 2:23
the former *r*, and the latter... Joel 2:23
the latter *r* in the first month... Joel 2:23
I have withholden the *r* from you... Amos 4:7
and I caused it to *r* upon one city... Amos 4:7
caused it not to *r* upon another... Amos 4:7
Ask ye of the LORD *r* in the time... Zec 10:1
in the time of the latter *r*... Zec 10:1
clouds, and give them showers of *r*... Zec 10:1
even upon them shall be no *r*... Zec 14:17
up, and come not, that have no *r*... Zec 14:18
sendeth *r* on the just and on the... Mt 5:45
the *r* descended, and the floods... Mt 7:25
the *r* descended, and the floods... Mt 7:27
gave us *r* from heaven, and... Acts 14:17
one, because of the present *r*... Acts 28:2
in the *r* that cometh oft upon it... Heb 6:7

he receive the early and latter *r* ... Jas 5:7
earnestly that it might not *r* ... Jas 5:17
again, and the heaven gave *r* ... Jas 5:18
that it *r* not in the days of ... Rev 11:6

**RAINBOW**
there was a *r* round about the ... Rev 4:3
a *r* was upon his head, and his ... Rev 10:1

**RAINED**
Then the LORD *r* upon Sodom ... Gen 19:24
the LORD *r* hail upon the land of ... Ex 9:23
had *r* down manna upon them to eat ... Ps 78:24
He *r* flesh also upon them as dust ... Ps 78:27
nor *r* upon in the day of ... Eze 22:24
one piece was *r* upon, and the ... Amos 4:7
piece whereupon it *r* not withered ... Amos 4:7
Lot went out of Sodom it *r* fire ... Lk 17:29
it *r* not on the earth by the ... Jas 5:17

**RAINY**
dropping in a very *r* day and a ... Prov 27:15

**RAISE**
her, and *r* up seed to thy brother ... Gen 38:8
Thou shalt not *r* a false report ... Ex 23:1
The LORD thy God will *r* up unto ... Deut 18:15
I will *r* them up a Prophet from ... Deut 18:18
*r* up unto his brother a name in ... Deut 25:7
*r* thereon a great heap of stones, ... Josh 8:29
to *r* up the name of the dead upon ... Ruth 4:5
to *r* up the name of the dead upon ... Ruth 4:10
I will *r* me up a faithful priest, ... 1Sa 2:35
I will *r* up evil against thee out ... 2Sa 12:11
to *r* him up from the earth ... 2Sa 12:17
Moreover the LORD shall *r* him up ... 1Kin 14:14
that I will *r* up thy seed after ... 1Chr 17:11
who are ready to *r* up their ... Job 3:8
*r* up their way against me, and ... Job 19:12
they *r* up against me the ways of ... Job 30:12
*r* me up, that I may requite them ... Ps 41:10
shall *r* up a cry of destruction ... Is 15:5
I will *r* forts against thee ... Is 29:3
I will *r* up the decayed places ... Is 44:26
to *r* up the tribes of Jacob ... Is 49:6
thou shalt *r* up the foundations ... Is 58:12
they shall *r* up the former ... Is 61:4
that I will *r* unto David a ... Jer 23:5
whom I will *r* up unto them ... Jer 30:9
For, lo, I will *r* and cause to ... Jer 50:9
and fall, and none shall *r* him up ... Jer 50:32
I will *r* up against Babylon, and ... Jer 51:1
I will *r* up thy lovers against ... Eze 23:22
I will *r* up for them a plant of ... Eze 34:29
in the third day he will *r* us up ... Hos 6:2
I will *r* them out of the place ... Joel 3:7
there is none to *r* her up ... Amos 5:2
I will *r* up against you a nation, ... Amos 6:14
In that day will I *r* up the ... Amos 9:11
I will *r* up his ruins, and I will ... Amos 9:11
then shall we *r* against him seven ... Mic 5:5
and there are that *r* up strife ... Hab 1:3
I *r* up the Chaldeans, that bitter ... Hab 1:6
I will *r* up a shepherd in the ... Zec 11:16
to *r* up children unto Abraham ... Mt 3:9
*r* the dead, cast out devils ... Mt 10:8
*r* up seed unto his brother ... Mt 22:24
*r* up seed unto his brother ... Mk 12:19
to *r* up children unto Abraham ... Lk 3:8
*r* up seed unto his brother ... Lk 20:28
and in three days I will *r* it up ... Jn 2:19
but should *r* it up again at the ... Jn 6:39
I will *r* him up at the last day ... Jn 6:40
I will *r* him up at the last day ... Jn 6:44
I will *r* him up at the last day ... Jn 6:54
he would *r* up Christ to sit on ... Acts 2:30
*r* up unto you of your brethren ... Acts 3:22
*r* up unto you of your brethren ... Acts 7:37
you, that God should *r* the dead ... Acts 26:8
will also *r* up us by his own ... 1Cor 6:14
Jesus shall *r* up us also by Jesus ... 2Cor 4:14
that God was able to *r* him up ... Heb 11:19
sick, and the Lord shall *r* him up ... Jas 5:15

**RAISED**
for this cause have I *r* thee up ... Ex 9:16
whom he *r* up in their stead, them ... Josh 5:7
they *r* over him a great heap of ... Josh 7:26
Nevertheless the LORD *r* up judges ... Judg 2:16
when the LORD *r* them up judges ... Judg 2:18
the LORD *r* up a deliverer to the ... Judg 3:9
the LORD *r* them up a deliverer, ... Judg 3:15
and the man who was *r* up on high ... 2Sa 23:1
king Solomon *r* a levy out of all ... 1Kin 5:13
of the levy which king Solomon *r* ... 1Kin 9:15
*r* it up to the towers, and another ... 2Chr 32:5
*r* it up a very great height, and ... 2Chr 33:14
all them whose spirit God had *r* ... Ezr 1:5
nor be *r* out of their sleep ... Job 14:12
I *r* thee up under the apple tree ... Song 8:5
it hath *r* up from their thrones ... Is 14:9
they *r* up the palaces thereof ... Is 23:13
Who *r* up the righteous man from ... Is 41:2
I have *r* up one from the north, ... Is 41:25
I have *r* him up in righteousness, ... Is 45:13
a great nation shall be *r* from ... Jer 6:22
a great whirlwind shall be *r* up ... Jer 25:32
The LORD hath *r* us up prophets in ... Jer 29:15
many kings shall be *r* up from the ... Jer 50:41
the LORD hath *r* up the spirit of ... Jer 51:11
it *r* up itself on one side, and it ... Dan 7:5
I *r* up of your sons for prophets, ... Amos 2:11
for he is *r* up out of his holy ... Zec 2:13
*r* up thy sons, O Zion, against ... Zec 9:13
Then Joseph being *r* from sleep ... Mt 1:24
the deaf hear, the dead are *r* up ... Mt 11:5
and be *r* again the third day ... Mt 16:21
the third day he shall be *r* again ... Mt 17:23
hath *r* up an horn of salvation ... Lk 1:69
the deaf hear, the dead are *r* ... Lk 7:22
be slain, and be *r* the third day ... Lk 9:22
Now that the dead are *r*, even ... Lk 20:37
dead, whom he *r* from the dead ... Jn 12:1
whom he had *r* from the dead ... Jn 12:9
*r* him from the dead, bare record ... Jn 12:17
Whom God hath *r* up, having loosed ... Acts 2:24
This Jesus hath God *r* up, whereof ... Acts 2:32
whom God hath *r* from the dead ... Acts 3:15
having *r* up his Son Jesus, sent ... Acts 3:26
whom God *r* from the dead, even by ... Acts 4:10
The God of our fathers *r* up Jesus ... Acts 5:30
Him God *r* up the third day, and ... Acts 10:40
*r* him up, saying, Arise up ... Acts 12:7
he *r* up unto them David to be ... Acts 13:22
promise *r* unto Israel a Saviour ... Acts 13:23
But God *r* him from the dead ... Acts 13:30
in that he hath *r* up Jesus again ... Acts 13:33
that he *r* him up from the dead ... Acts 13:34
But he, whom God *r* again, saw no ... Acts 13:37
*r* persecution against Paul and ... Acts 13:50
in that he hath *r* him from the ... Acts 17:31
if we believe on him that *r* up ... Rom 4:24
was *r* again for our justification ... Rom 4:25
that like as Christ was *r* up from ... Rom 6:4
Knowing that Christ being *r* from ... Rom 6:9
to him who is *r* from the dead ... Rom 7:4
But if the Spirit of him that *r* ... Rom 8:11
he that *r* up Christ from the dead ... Rom 8:11
same purpose have I *r* thee up ... Rom 9:17
that God hath *r* him from the dead ... Rom 10:9
And God hath both *r* up the Lord ... 1Cor 6:14
of God that he *r* up Christ ... 1Cor 15:15
whom he *r* not up, if so be that ... 1Cor 15:15
rise not, then is not Christ *r* ... 1Cor 15:16
And if Christ be not *r*, your faith ... 1Cor 15:17
will say, How are the dead *r* up ... 1Cor 15:35
it is *r* in incorruption ... 1Cor 15:42
it is *r* in glory ... 1Cor 15:43
it is *r* in power ... 1Cor 15:43
it is *r* a spiritual body ... 1Cor 15:44
the dead shall be *r* incorruptible ... 1Cor 15:52
Knowing that he which *r* up the ... 2Cor 4:14
Father, who *r* him from the dead ... Gal 1:1
when he *r* him from the dead, and ... Eph 1:20
hath *r* us up together, and made us ... Eph 2:6
who hath *r* him from the dead ... Col 2:12
whom he *r* from the dead, even ... 1Th 1:10
*r* from the dead according to my ... 2Ti 2:8
their dead *r* to life again ... Heb 11:35
that *r* him up from the dead, and ... 1Pet 1:21

**RAISER**
a *r* of taxes in the glory of the ... Dan 11:20

**RAISETH**
He *r* up the poor out of the dust, ... 1Sa 2:8
When he *r* up himself, the mighty ... Job 41:25
*r* the stormy wind, which lifteth ... Ps 107:25
He *r* up the poor out of the dust, ... Ps 113:7
*r* up all those that be bowed down ... Ps 145:14
the LORD *r* them that are bowed ... Ps 146:8
For as the Father *r* up the dead ... Jn 5:21
but in God which *r* the dead ... 2Cor 1:9

**RAISING**
who ceaseth from *r* after he hath ... Hos 7:4
neither *r* up the people, neither ... Acts 24:12

**RAISINS**
corn, and an hundred clusters of *r* ... 1Sa 25:18
of figs, and two clusters of *r* ... 1Sa 30:12
bread, and an hundred bunches of *r* ... 2Sa 16:1
cakes of figs, and bunches of *r* ... 1Chr 12:40

**RAKEM** (*ra'-kem*) *Son of Sheresh.*
and his sons were Ulam and *R* ... 1Chr 7:16

**RAKKATH** (*rah'-kath*) *A city in Naphtali.*
are Ziddim, Zer, and Hammath, *R* ... Josh 19:35

**RAKKON** (*rak'-kon*) *A city in Dan.*
And Me-jarkon, and *R*, with the ... Josh 19:46

**RAM** (*ram*)
*1. Father of Aminadab.*
And Hezron begat *R* ... Ruth 4:19
and *R* begat Amminadab ... Ruth 4:19
Jerahmeel, and *R*, and Chelubai ... 1Chr 2:9
And *R* begat Amminadab ... 1Chr 2:10
*2. Son of Jerahmeel.*
*R* the firstborn, and Bunah, and ... 1Chr 2:25
the sons of *R* the firstborn of ... 1Chr 2:27
*3. Head of Elihu's family.*
the Buzite, of the kindred of *R* ... Job 32:2
*4. Male sheep.*
a *r* of three years old, and a ... Gen 15:9
behold behind him a *r* caught in a ... Gen 22:13
and Abraham went and took the *r* ... Gen 22:13
Thou shalt also take one *r* ... Ex 29:15
hands upon the head of the *r* ... Ex 29:15
And thou shalt slay the *r*, and thou ... Ex 29:16
And thou shalt cut the *r* in pieces ... Ex 29:17
burn the whole *r* upon the altar ... Ex 29:18
And thou shalt take the other *r* ... Ex 29:19
hands upon the head of the *r* ... Ex 29:19
Then shalt thou kill the *r* ... Ex 29:20
thou shalt take of the *r* the fat ... Ex 29:22
for it is a *r* of consecration ... Ex 29:22
of the *r* of Aaron's consecration ... Ex 29:26
of the *r* of the consecration, ... Ex 29:27
take the *r* of the consecration ... Ex 29:31
sons shall eat the flesh of the *r* ... Ex 29:32
a *r* without blemish out of the ... Lev 5:15
the *r* of the trespass offering ... Lev 5:16
he shall bring a *r* without ... Lev 5:18
a *r* without blemish out of the ... Lev 6:6
he brought the *r* for the burnt ... Lev 8:18
hands upon the head of the *r* ... Lev 8:18
And he cut the *r* into pieces ... Lev 8:20
burnt the whole *r* upon the altar ... Lev 8:21
other ram, the *r* of consecration ... Lev 8:22
hands upon the head of the *r* ... Lev 8:22
for of the *r* of consecration it ... Lev 8:29
a *r* for a burnt offering, without ... Lev 9:2
a *r* for peace offerings, to ... Lev 9:4
the *r* for a sacrifice of peace ... Lev 9:18
fat of the bullock and of the *r* ... Lev 9:19
and a *r* for a burnt offering ... Lev 16:3
one *r* for a burnt offering ... Lev 16:5
even a *r* for a trespass offering ... Lev 19:21
an atonement for him with the *r* ... Lev 19:22
beside the *r* of the atonement, ... Num 5:8
one *r* without blemish for peace ... Num 6:14
he shall offer the *r* for a ... Num 6:17
take the sodden shoulder of the *r* ... Num 6:19
One young bullock, one *r*, one ... Num 7:15
One young bullock, one *r*, one ... Num 7:21
One young bullock, one *r*, one ... Num 7:27
One young bullock, one *r*, one ... Num 7:33
One young bullock, one *r*, one ... Num 7:39
One young bullock, one *r*, one ... Num 7:45
One young bullock, one *r*, one ... Num 7:51
One young bullock, one *r*, one ... Num 7:57
One young bullock, one *r*, one ... Num 7:63
One young bullock, one *r*, one ... Num 7:69
One young bullock, one *r*, one ... Num 7:75
One young bullock, one *r*, one ... Num 7:81
Or for a *r*, thou shalt prepare ... Num 15:6
for one bullock, or for one *r* ... Num 15:11
on every altar a bullock and a *r* ... Num 23:2
upon every altar a bullock and a *r* ... Num 23:4
a bullock and a *r* on every altar ... Num 23:14
a bullock and a *r* on every altar ... Num 23:30
two young bullocks, and one *r* ... Num 28:11
mingled with oil, for one *r* ... Num 28:12
the third part of an hin unto a *r* ... Num 28:14
two young bullocks, and one *r* ... Num 28:19
and two tenth deals for a *r* ... Num 28:20
two young bullocks, one *r* ... Num 28:27
two tenth deals unto one *r* ... Num 28:28
one young bullock, one *r*, and ... Num 29:2
and two tenth deals for a *r* ... Num 29:3
one young bullock, one *r*, and ... Num 29:8
and two tenth deals to one *r* ... Num 29:9
deals to each *r* of the two rams ... Num 29:14
one bullock, one *r*, seven lambs ... Num 29:36
for the bullock, for the *r* ... Num 29:37
they offered a *r* of the flock for ... Ezr 10:19
a *r* out of the flock without ... Eze 43:23
a *r* out of the flock, without ... Eze 43:25
a bullock, and an ephah for a *r* ... Eze 45:24
blemish, and a *r* without blemish ... Eze 46:4
shall be an ephah for a *r* ... Eze 46:5
blemish, and six lambs, and a *r* ... Eze 46:6
a bullock, and an ephah for a *r* ... Eze 46:7
to a bullock, and an ephah to a *r* ... Eze 46:11
the river a *r* which had two horns ... Dan 8:3
I saw the *r* pushing westward, and ... Dan 8:4
he came to the *r* that had two ... Dan 8:6
I saw him come close unto the *r* ... Dan 8:7
against him, and smote the *r* ... Dan 8:7
in the *r* to stand before him ... Dan 8:7
deliver the *r* out of his hand ... Dan 8:7
The *r* which thou sawest having ... Dan 8:20

**RAMA** (*ra-mah*) See RAMAH. *Same as Ramah 1.*
In *R* was there a voice heard, ... Mt 2:18

**RAMAH** (*ra'-mah*) See RAMA, RAMATH.
*1. A city in Benjamin.*
Gibeon, and *R*, and Beeroth, ... Josh 18:25
palm tree of Deborah between *R* ... Judg 4:5
all night, in Gibeah, or in *R* ... Judg 19:13
went up against Judah, and built *R* ... 1Kin 15:17
that he left off building of *R* ... 1Kin 15:21
and they took away the stones of *R* ... 1Kin 15:22
came up against Judah, and built *R* ... 2Chr 16:1
that he left off building of *R* ... 2Chr 16:5
they carried away the stones of *R* ... 2Chr 16:6
The children of *R* and Gaba, six ... Ezr 2:26
The men of *R* and Gaba, six hundred ... Neh 7:30
Hazor, *R*, Gittaim, ... Neh 11:33
*R* is afraid ... Is 10:29
the guard had let him go from *R* ... Jer 40:1
in Gibeah, and the trumpet in *R* ... Hos 5:8
*2. A city in Naphtali.*
And then the coast turneth to *R* ... Josh 19:29
And Adamah, and *R*, and Hazor, ... Josh 19:36
*3. A city in Ephraim.*
and came to their house to *R* ... 1Sa 1:19
And Elkanah went to *R* to his house ... 1Sa 2:11
And his return was to *R* ... 1Sa 7:17
and came to Samuel unto *R* ... 1Sa 8:4
Then Samuel went to *R* ... 1Sa 15:34
So Samuel rose up, and went to *R* ... 1Sa 16:13
escaped, and came to Samuel to *R* ... 1Sa 19:18
Behold, David is at Naioth in *R* ... 1Sa 19:19
Then went he also to *R*, and came ... 1Sa 19:22

Behold, they be at Naioth in *R*. 1Sa 19:22
And he went thither to Naioth in *R*. 1Sa 19:23
until he came to Naioth in *R*. 1Sa 19:23
And David fled from Naioth in *R*. 1Sa 20:1
abode in Gibeah under a tree in *R*. 1Sa 22:6
and buried him in his house at *R*. 1Sa 25:1
lamented him, and buried him in *R*. 1Sa 28:3
A voice was heard in *R*,. Jer 31:15
*4. A short form of Ramoth-Gilead.*
the Syrians had given him at *R*. 2Kin 8:29
wounds which were given him at *R*. 2Chr 22:6

**RAMATH** (*ra-math*) *A city in Simeon.*
to Baalath-beer, *R* of the south. Josh 19:8

**RAMATHAIM-ZOPHIM** (*ram-a-tha''-im-zo'-fim*) *A city on Mt. Ephraim.*
Now there was a certain man of *R*. 1Sa 1:1

**RAMATHITE** (*ra'-math-ite*) *An inhabitant of Ramah 1.*
the vineyards was Shimei the *R*. 1Chr 27:27

**RAMATH-LEHI** (*ra''-math-le'-hi*) *A place in Judah.*
his hand, and called that place *R*. Judg 15:17

**RAMATH MIZPAH** See RAMATH-MIZPEH.

**RAMATH-MIZPEH** (*ra''-math-miz'-peh*) *A city in Gad.*
And from Heshbon unto *R*, and. Josh 13:26

**RAMESES** (*ram'-e-seze*) See RAAMSES. *A city in Goshen.*
of the land, in the land of *R*. Gen 47:11
journeyed from *R* to Succoth. Ex 12:37
from *R* in the first month. Num 33:3
children of Israel removed from *R*. Num 33:5

**RAMIAH** (*ra'-mi-ah*) *Married a foreigner while in exile.*
*R*, and Jeziah, and Malchiah, and. Ezr 10:25

**RAMOTH** (*ra'-moth*) See JARMUTH, RAMAH, RAMOTH-GILEAD, REMETH.
*1. A Levitical city in Gad.*
*R* in Gilead, of the Gadites. Deut 4:43
*R* in Gilead out of the tribe of. Josh 20:8
*R* in Gilead with her suburbs, to. Josh 21:38
*R* in Gilead with her suburbs, and. 1Chr 6:80
*2. A Levitical city in Issachar.*
*R* with her suburbs, and Anem with... 1Chr 6:73
*3. Married a foreigner in exile.*
and Adaiah, Jashub, and Sheal, and *R* Ezr 10:29
*4. A city in Simeon.*
and to them which were in south *R*. 1Sa 30:27
*5. Same as Ramoth-gilead.*
Know ye that *R* in Gilead is ours,. 1Kin 22:3

**RAMOTH-GILEAD** (*ra''-moth-ghil'-e-ad*) *A city in Gad.*
The son of Geber, in *R*. 1Kin 4:13
thou go with me to battle to *R*. 1Kin 22:4
Shall I go against *R* to battle. 1Kin 22:6
prophesied so, saying, Go up to *R*. 1Kin 22:12
shall we go against *R* to battle. 1Kin 22:15
that he may go up and fall at *R*. 1Kin 22:20
the king of Judah went up to *R*. 1Kin 22:29
against Hazael king of Syria in *R*. 2Kin 8:28
of oil in thine hand, and go to *R*. 2Kin 9:1
young man the prophet, went to *R*. 2Kin 9:4
(Now Joram had kept *R*, he and all. 2Kin 9:14
him to go up with him to *R*. 2Chr 18:2
Judah, Wilt thou go with me to *R*. 2Chr 18:3
them, Shall we go to *R* to battle. 2Chr 18:5
prophesied so, saying, Go up to *R*. 2Chr 18:11
shall we go to *R* to battle. 2Chr 18:14
that he may go up and fall at *R*. 2Chr 18:19
the king of Judah went up to *R*. 2Chr 18:28
against Hazael king of Syria at *R*. 2Chr 22:5

**RAMOTH NEGEV** See RAMOTH-GILEAD.

**RAMPART**
therefore he made the *r* and the. Lam 2:8
whose *r* was the sea, and her wall. Nah 3:8

**RAM'S**
make a long blast with the *r* horn. Josh 6:5

**RAMS**
the *r* which leaped upon the. Gen 31:10
all the *r* which leap upon the. Gen 31:12
the *r* of thy flock have I not. Gen 31:38
two hundred ewes, and twenty *r*. Gen 32:14
and two *r* without blemish,. Ex 29:1
with the bullock and the two *r*. Ex 29:3
and goats' hair, and red skins of *r*. Ex 35:23
for the sin offering, and two *r*. Lev 8:2
and one young bullock, and two *r*. Lev 23:18
peace offerings, two oxen, five *r*. Num 7:17
peace offerings, two oxen, five *r*. Num 7:23
peace offerings, two oxen, five *r*. Num 7:29
peace offerings, two oxen, five *r*. Num 7:35
peace offerings, two oxen, five *r*. Num 7:41
peace offerings, two oxen, five *r*. Num 7:47
peace offerings, two oxen, five *r*. Num 7:53
peace offerings, two oxen, five *r*. Num 7:59
peace offerings, two oxen, five *r*. Num 7:65
peace offerings, two oxen, five *r*. Num 7:71
peace offerings, two oxen, five *r*. Num 7:77
peace offerings, two oxen, five *r*. Num 7:83
the *r* twelve, the lambs of the. Num 7:87
the *r* sixty, the he goats sixty,. Num 7:88
me here seven oxen and seven *r*. Num 23:1
me here seven bullocks and seven *r*.. Num 23:29
thirteen young bullocks, two *r*. Num 29:13
deals to each ram of the two *r*. Num 29:14
twelve young bullocks, two *r*. Num 29:17
for the bullocks, for the *r*. Num 29:18
third day eleven bullocks, two *r*. Num 29:20
for the bullocks, for the *r*. Num 29:21
fourth day ten bullocks, two *r*. Num 29:23
for the bullocks, for the *r*. Num 29:24
fifth day nine bullocks, two *r*. Num 29:26
for the bullocks, for the *r*. Num 29:27
sixth day eight bullocks, two *r*. Num 29:29
for the bullocks, for the *r*. Num 29:30
seventh day seven bullocks, two *r*. Num 29:32
for the bullocks, for the *r*. Num 29:33
*r* of the breed of Bashan, and. Deut 32:14
and to hearken than the fat of *r*. 1Sa 15:22
lambs, and an hundred thousand *r*. 2Kin 3:4
offered seven bullocks and seven *r*. 1Chr 15:26
a thousand bullocks, a thousand *r*. 1Chr 29:21
with a young bullock and seven *r*. 2Chr 13:9
seven thousand and seven hundred *r* 2Chr 17:11
seven bullocks, and seven *r*. 2Chr 29:21
when they had killed the *r*. 2Chr 29:22
and ten bullocks, an hundred *r*. 2Chr 29:32
of, both young bullocks, and *r*. Ezr 6:9
hundred bullocks, two hundred *r*. Ezr 6:17
with this money bullocks, *r*. Ezr 7:17
for all Israel, ninety and six *r*. Ezr 8:35
you now seven bullocks and seven *r*. Job 42:8
fatlings, with the incense of *r*. Ps 66:15
The mountains skipped like *r*. Ps 114:4
mountains, that ye skipped like *r*. Ps 114:6
full of the burnt offerings of *r*. Is 1:11
with the fat of the kidneys of *r*. Is 34:6
the *r* of Nebaioth shall minister. Is 60:7
slaughter, like *r* with he goats. Jer 51:40
set battering *r* against it round. Eze 4:2
battering *r* against the gates. Eze 21:22
occupied with thee in lambs, and *r*. Eze 27:21
cattle and cattle, between the *r*. Eze 34:17
of the princes of the earth, of *r*. Eze 39:18
seven *r* without blemish daily the. Eze 45:23
be pleased with thousands of *r*. Mic 6:7

**RAMS'**
*r* skins dyed red, and badgers'. Ex 25:5
for the tent of *r* skins dyed red. Ex 26:14
*r* skins dyed red, and badgers'. Ex 35:7
for the tent of *r* skins dyed red. Ex 36:19
the covering of *r* skins dyed red. Ex 39:34
the ark seven trumpets of *r* horns. Josh 6:4
of *r* horns before the ark of the. Josh 6:6
bearing the seven trumpets of *r*. Josh 6:8
bearing seven trumpets of *r* horns. Josh 6:13

**RAN**
he *r* to meet them from the tent. Gen 18:2
Abraham *r* unto the herd, and. Gen 18:7
And the servant *r* to meet her. Gen 24:17
*r* again unto the well to draw. Gen 24:20
And the damsel *r*, and told them of. Gen 24:28
Laban *r* out unto the man, unto. Gen 24:29
and she *r* and told her father. Gen 29:12
that he *r* to meet him, and. Gen 29:13
Esau *r* to meet him, and embraced. Gen 33:4
the fire *r* along upon the ground. Ex 9:23
there *r* a young man, and told. Num 11:27
and *r* into the midst of the. Num 16:47
and they *r* unto the tent. Josh 7:22
and they *r* as soon as he had. Josh 8:19
and all the host *r*, and cried, and. Judg 7:21
And Jotham *r* away, and fled, and. Judg 9:21
the two other companies *r* upon. Judg 9:44
And the woman made haste, and *r*. Judg 13:10
he *r* unto Eli, and said, Here am I. 1Sa 3:5
there *r* a man of Benjamin out of. 1Sa 4:12
And they *r* and fetched him thence. 1Sa 10:23
*r* into the army, and came and. 1Sa 17:22
*r* toward the army to meet the. 1Sa 17:48
Therefore David *r*, and stood upon. 1Sa 17:51
And as the lad *r*, he shot an arrow. 1Sa 20:36
bowed himself unto Joab, and *r*. 2Sa 18:21
Then Ahimaaz *r* by the way of the. 2Sa 18:23
two of the servants of Shimei *r*. 1Kin 2:39
the water *r* round about the altar. 1Kin 18:35
*r* before Ahab to the entrance of. 1Kin 18:46
*r* after Elijah, and said, Let me,. 1Kin 19:20
the blood *r* out of the wound into. 1Kin 22:35
the brook that *r* through the. 2Chr 32:4
my sore *r* in the night, and ceased. Ps 77:2
they *r* in the dry places like a. Ps 105:41
that *r* down upon the beard, even. Ps 133:2
sent these prophets, yet they *r*. Jer 23:21
And the living creatures *r*. Eze 1:14
there *r* out waters on the right. Eze 47:2
*r* unto him in the fury of his. Dan 8:6
the whole herd of swine *r*. Mt 8:32
And straightway one of them *r*. Mt 27:48
when he saw Jesus afar off, he *r*. Mk 5:6
the herd *r* violently down a steep. Mk 5:13
*r* afoot thither out of all cities. Mk 6:33
*r* through that whole region round. Mk 6:55
And one *r* and filled a spunge full. Mk 15:36
the herd *r* violently down a steep. Lk 8:33
saw him, and had compassion, and *r*. Lk 15:20
he *r* before, and climbed up into a. Lk 19:4
Peter, and *r* unto the sepulchre. Lk 24:12
So they *r* both together. Jn 20:4
all the people *r* together unto. Acts 3:11
*r* upon him with one accord,. Acts 7:57
Philip *r* thither to him, and heard. Acts 8:30
the gate for gladness, but *r* in. Acts 12:14
*r* in among the people, crying out. Acts 14:14
moved, and the people *r* together. Acts 21:30
centurions, and *r* down unto them. Acts 21:32
seas met, they *r* the ship aground. Acts 27:41
*r* greedily after the error of. Jude 11

**RANG**
shout, so that the earth *r* again. 1Sa 4:5
so that the city *r* again. 1Kin 1:45

**RANGE**
The *r* of the mountains is his. Job 39:8

**RANGES**
or *r* for pots, they shall be. Lev 11:35
and he that cometh within the *r*. 2Kin 11:8
Have her forth without the *r*. 2Kin 11:15
them, Have her forth of the *r*. 2Chr 23:14

**RANGING**
As a roaring lion, and a *r* bear. Prov 28:15

**RANK**
of corn came up upon one stalk, *r*. Gen 41:5
thin ears devoured the seven *r*. Gen 41:7
shall set forth in the second *r*. Num 2:16
shall go forward in the third *r*. Num 2:24
thousand, which could keep *r*. 1Chr 12:33
men of war, that could keep *r*. 1Chr 12:38

**RANKS**
was against light in three *r*. 1Kin 7:4
was against light in three *r*. 1Kin 7:5
and they shall not break their *r*. Joel 2:7
And they sat down in *r*, by. Mk 6:40

**RANSOM**
then he shall give for the *r* of. Ex 21:30
a *r* for his soul unto the LORD. Ex 30:12
I have found a *r*. Job 33:24
then a great *r* cannot deliver. Job 36:18
nor give to God a *r* for him. Ps 49:7
He will not regard any *r*. Prov 6:35
The *r* of a man's life are his. Prov 13:8
shall be a *r* for the righteous. Prov 21:18
I gave Egypt for thy *r*, Ethiopia. Is 43:3
I will *r* them from the power of. Hos 13:14
and to give his life a *r* for many. Mt 20:28
and to give his life a *r* for many. Mk 10:45
Who gave himself a *r* for all. 1Ti 2:6

**RANSOMED**
the *r* of the LORD shall return,. Is 35:10
sea a way for the *r* to pass over. Is 51:10
*r* him from the hand of him that. Jer 31:11

**RAPHA** (*ra'-fah*) See BETH-RAPHA, REPHAIAH.
*1. Son of Benjamin.*
Nohah the fourth, and *R* the fifth. 1Chr 8:2
*2. A member of Saul's family.*
*R* was his son, Eleasah his son,. 1Chr 8:37

**RAPHAN** See RAPHA.

**RAPHU** (*ra'-fu*) *A Benjamite spy sent to the Promised Land.*
of Benjamin, Palti the son of *R*. Num 13:9

**RARE**
it is a *r* thing that the king. Dan 2:11

**RASE**
*R* it, *r* it, even to the. Ps 137:7

**RASH**
Be not *r* with thy mouth, and let. Eccl 5:2
The heart also of the *r* shall. Is 32:4

**RASHLY**
to be quiet, and to do nothing *r*. Acts 19:36

**RASOR**
like a sharp *r*, working. Ps 52:2

**RATE**
and gather a certain *r* every day. Ex 16:4
and mules, a *r* year by year. 1Kin 10:25
a daily *r* for every day, all the. 2Kin 25:30
Even after a certain *r* every day. 2Chr 8:13
and mules, a *r* year by year. 2Chr 9:24

**RATHER**
if we have not *r* done it for fear. Josh 22:24
hath not David *r* sent his. 2Sa 10:3
how much *r* then, when he saith to. 2Kin 5:13
and death *r* than my life. Job 7:15
he justified himself *r* than God. Job 32:2
thou chosen *r* than affliction. Job 36:21
and lying *r* than to speak. Ps 52:3
I had *r* be a doorkeeper in the. Ps 84:10
knowledge *r* than choice gold. Prov 8:10
to get understanding *r* to be. Prov 16:16
*r* than a fool in his folly. Prov 17:12
A good name is *r* to be chosen. Prov 22:1
and loving favour *r* than silver. Prov 22:1
death shall be chosen *r* than life. Jer 8:3
But go *r* to the lost sheep of the. Mt 10:6
but *r* fear him which is able to. Mt 10:28
*r* than having two hands or two. Mt 18:8
*r* than having two eyes to be cast. Mt 18:9
but go ye *r* to them that sell, and. Mt 25:9
but that *r* a tumult was made, he. Mt 27:24
bettered, but *r* grew worse,. Mk 5:26
that he should *r* release Barabbas. Mk 15:11
but *r* rejoice, because your names. Lk 10:20
But he said, Yea *r*, blessed are. Lk 11:28
But *r* give alms of such things as. Lk 11:41

But *r* seek ye the kingdom of God ... Lk 12:31
but *r* division ... Lk 12:51
will not *r* say unto him, Make ... Lk 17:8
house justified *r* than the other ... Lk 18:14
men loved darkness *r* than light ... Jn 3:19
We ought to obey God *r* than men ... Acts 5:29
And not *r*, (as we be slanderously ... Rom 3:8
It is Christ that died, yea *r* ... Rom 8:34
but *r* through their fall ... Rom 11:11
but *r* give place unto wrath ... Rom 12:19
but judge this *r*, that no man put ... Rom 14:13
puffed up, and have not *r* mourned ... 1Cor 5:2
Why do ye not *r* take wrong ... 1Cor 6:7
why do ye not *r* suffer yourselves ... 1Cor 6:7
mayest be made free, use it *r* ... 1Cor 7:21
this power over you, are not we *r* ... 1Cor 9:12
but *r* that ye may prophesy ... 1Cor 14:1
tongues, but *r* that ye prophesied ... 1Cor 14:5
Yet in the church I had *r* speak ... 1Cor 14:19
ye ought *r* to forgive him ... 2Cor 2:7
of the spirit be *r* glorious ... 2Cor 3:8
willing *r* to be absent from the ... 2Cor 5:8
will I *r* glory in my infirmities ... 2Cor 12:9
or *r* are known of God, how turn ... Gal 4:9
but *r* let him labour, working ... Eph 4:28
but *r* giving of thanks ... Eph 5:4
of darkness, but *r* reprove them ... Eph 5:11
unto me have fallen out *r* unto ... Phil 1:12
*r* than godly edifying which is in ... 1Ti 1:4
exercise thyself *r* unto godliness ... 1Ti 4:7
but *r* do them service, because ... 1Ti 6:2
for love's sake I *r* beseech thee ... Philem 9
Choosing *r* to suffer affliction ... Heb 11:25
shall we not much *r* be in ... Heb 12:9
but let it *r* be healed ... Heb 12:13
I beseech you the *r* to do this ... Heb 13:19
Wherefore the *r*, brethren, give ... 2Pet 1:10

**RATTLETH**
The quiver *r* against him, the ... Job 39:23

**RATTLING**
the noise of the *r* of the wheels ... Nah 3:2

**RAVEN**
And he sent forth a *r*, which went ... Gen 8:7
Every *r* after his kind ... Lev 11:15
And every *r* after his kind, ... Deut 14:14
Who provideth for the *r* his food ... Job 38:41
locks are bushy, and black as a *r* ... Song 5:11
also and the *r* shall dwell in it ... Is 34:11

**RAVENING**
upon me with their mouths, as a *r* ... Ps 22:13
like a roaring lion *r* the prey ... Eze 22:25
are like wolves *r* the prey ... Eze 22:27
but inwardly they are *r* wolves ... Mt 7:15
but your inward part is full of *r* ... Lk 11:39

**RAVENOUS**
nor any *r* beast shall go up ... Is 35:9
Calling a *r* bird from the east, ... Is 46:11
unto the *r* birds of every sort ... Eze 39:4

**RAVENS**
the *r* to feed thee there ... 1Kin 17:4
the *r* brought him bread and flesh ... 1Kin 17:6
food, and to the young *r* which cry ... Ps 147:9
the *r* of the valley shall pick it ... Prov 30:17
Consider the *r* ... Lk 12:24

**RAVIN**
Benjamin shall *r* as a wolf ... Gen 49:27
with prey, and his dens with *r* ... Nah 2:12

**RAVISHED**
be thou *r* always with her love ... Prov 5:19
be *r* with a strange woman, and ... Prov 5:20
Thou hast *r* my heart, my sister, ... Song 4:9
thou hast *r* my heart with one of ... Song 4:9
be spoiled, and their wives *r* ... Is 13:16
They *r* the women in Zion, and the ... Lam 5:11
the houses rifled, and the women *r* ... Zec 14:2

**RAW**
Eat not of it *r*, nor sodden at ... Ex 12:9
there be quick *r* flesh in the ... Lev 13:10
But when *r* flesh appeareth in him ... Lev 13:14
the priest shall see the *r* flesh ... Lev 13:15
for the *r* flesh is unclean ... Lev 13:15
Or if the *r* flesh turn again, and ... Lev 13:16
have sodden flesh of thee, but *r* ... 1Sa 2:15

**RAZOR**
shall no *r* come upon his head ... Num 6:5
no *r* shall come on his head ... Judg 13:5
hath not come a *r* upon mine head ... Judg 16:17
there shall no *r* come upon his ... 1Sa 1:11
Lord shave with a *r* that is hired ... Is 7:20
knife, take thee a barber's *r* ... Eze 5:1

**REACH**
whose top may *r* unto heaven ... Gen 11:4
boards shall *r* from end to end ... Ex 26:28
even unto the thighs they shall *r* ... Ex 28:42
shall *r* unto the vintage ... Lev 26:5
the vintage shall *r* unto the ... Lev 26:5
shall *r* unto the side of the sea ... Num 34:11
shall *r* from the wall of the city ... Num 35:4
his head *r* unto the clouds ... Job 20:6
he shall *r* even to the neck ... Is 8:8
shall *r* to the midst of the neck, ... Is 30:28
they *r* even to the sea of Jazer ... Jer 48:32
the mountains shall *r* unto Azal ... Zec 14:5
*R* hither thy finger, and behold my ... Jn 20:27
*r* hither thy hand, and thrust it ... Jn 20:27
a measure to *r* even unto you ... 2Cor 10:13

**REACHED**
and the top of it *r* to heaven ... Gen 28:12
*r* to Dabbasheth, and *r* to ... Josh 19:11
he *r* her parched corn, and she did ... Ruth 2:14
the height thereof *r* unto heaven ... Dan 4:11
whose height *r* unto the heaven, ... Dan 4:20
as though we *r* not unto you ... 2Cor 10:14
For her sins have *r* unto heaven ... Rev 18:5

**REACHETH**
unto Nophah, which *r* unto Medeba . Num 21:30
And the coast *r* to Tabor, and ... Josh 19:22
*r* to Carmel westward, and to ... Josh 19:26
*r* to Zebulun, and to the valley of ... Josh 19:27
*r* to Zebulun on the south side, ... Josh 19:34
*r* to Asher on the west side, and ... Josh 19:34
in a rage that *r* up unto heaven ... 2Chr 28:9
faithfulness *r* unto the clouds ... Ps 36:5
thy truth *r* unto the clouds ... Ps 108:4
she *r* forth her hands to the ... Prov 31:20
whereas the sword *r* unto the soul ... Jer 4:10
because it *r* unto thine heart ... Jer 4:18
for her judgment *r* unto heaven ... Jer 51:9
*r* unto heaven, and thy dominion to ... Dan 4:22

**REACHING**
*r* to the wall of the house ... 2Chr 3:11
*r* to the wing of the other cherub ... 2Chr 3:11
*r* to the wall of the house ... 2Chr 3:12
*r* forth unto those things which ... Phil 3:13

**READ**
*r* in the audience of the people ... Ex 24:7
he shall *r* therein all the days ... Deut 17:19
thou shalt *r* this law before all ... Deut 31:11
afterward he *r* all the words of ... Josh 8:34
which Joshua *r* not before all the ... Josh 8:35
king of Israel had *r* the letter ... 2Kin 5:7
hand of the messengers, and *r* it ... 2Kin 19:14
the book to Shaphan, and he *r* it ... 2Kin 22:8
Shaphan *r* it before the king ... 2Kin 22:10
which the king of Judah hath *r* ... 2Kin 22:16
he *r* in their ears all the words ... 2Kin 23:2
Shaphan *r* it before the king ... 2Chr 34:18
have *r* before the king of Judah ... 2Chr 34:24
he *r* in their ears all the words ... 2Chr 34:30
us hath been plainly *r* before me ... Ezr 4:18
letter was *r* before Rehum ... Ezr 4:23
he *r* therein before the street ... Neh 8:3
So they *r* in the book in the law ... Neh 8:8
he *r* in the book of the law of ... Neh 8:18
*r* in the book of the law of the ... Neh 9:3
On that day they *r* in the book of ... Neh 13:1
they were *r* before the king ... Est 6:1
saying, *R* this, I pray thee ... Is 29:11
saying, *R* this, I pray thee ... Is 29:12
out of the book of the LORD, and *r* ... Is 34:16
hand of the messengers, and *r* it ... Is 37:14
Zephaniah the priest *r* this ... Jer 29:29
*r* in the roll, which thou hast ... Jer 36:6
also thou shalt *r* them in the ... Jer 36:6
Then *r* Baruch in the book the ... Jer 36:10
when Baruch *r* the book in the ... Jer 36:13
hast *r* in the ears of the people ... Jer 36:14
Sit down now, and *r* it in our ears ... Jer 36:15
So Baruch *r* it in their ears ... Jer 36:15
Jehudi *r* it in the ears of the ... Jer 36:21
Jehudi had *r* three or four leaves ... Jer 36:23
see, and shalt *r* all these words ... Jer 51:61
Whosoever shall *r* this writing ... Dan 5:7
but they could not *r* the writing ... Dan 5:8
that they should *r* this writing ... Dan 5:15
now if thou canst *r* the writing ... Dan 5:16
yet I will *r* the writing unto the ... Dan 5:17
Have ye not *r* what David did, ... Mt 12:3
Or have ye not *r* in the law ... Mt 12:5
and said unto them, Have ye not *r* ... Mt 19:4
have ye never *r*, Out of the mouth ... Mt 21:16
Did ye never *r* in the scriptures, ... Mt 21:42
have ye not *r* that which was ... Mt 22:31
Have ye never *r* what David did, ... Mk 2:25
have ye not *r* this scripture ... Mk 12:10
have ye not *r* in the book of ... Mk 12:26
sabbath day, and stood up for to *r* ... Lk 4:16
Have ye not *r* so much as this, ... Lk 6:3
This title then *r* many of the ... Jn 19:20
his chariot *r* Esaias the prophet ... Acts 8:28
heard him *r* the prophet Esaias, ... Acts 8:30
the scripture which he *r* was this ... Acts 8:32
which are *r* every sabbath day ... Acts 13:27
being *r* in the synagogues every ... Acts 15:21
Which when they had *r*, they ... Acts 15:31
the governor had *r* the letter ... Acts 23:34
than what ye *r* or acknowledge ... 2Cor 1:13
our hearts, known and *r* of all men ... 2Cor 3:2
unto this day, when Moses is *r* ... 2Cor 3:15
Whereby, when ye *r*, ye may ... Eph 3:4
when this epistle is *r* among you ... Col 4:16
cause that it be *r* also in the ... Col 4:16
that ye likewise *r* the epistle ... Col 4:16
be *r* unto all the holy brethren ... 1Th 5:27
to *r* the book, neither to look ... Rev 5:4

**READEST**
how *r* thou ... Lk 10:26
Understandest thou what thou *r* ... Acts 8:30

**READETH**
tables, that he may run that *r* it ... Hab 2:2
stand in the holy place, (whoso *r* ... Mt 24:15
not, (let him that *r* understand ... Mk 13:14
Blessed is he that *r*, and they ... Rev 1:3

**READINESS**
the word with all *r* of mind ... Acts 17:11
that as there was a *r* to will ... 2Cor 8:11
having in a *r* to revenge all ... 2Cor 10:6

**READING**
caused them to understand the *r* ... Neh 8:8
*r* in the book the words of the ... Jer 36:8
hast made an end of *r* this book ... Jer 51:63
after the *r* of the law and the ... Acts 13:15
in the *r* of the old testament ... 2Cor 3:14
Till I come, give attendance to *r* ... 1Ti 4:13

**READY**
Make *r* quickly three measures of ... Gen 18:6
men home, and slay, and make *r* ... Gen 43:16
they made *r* the present against ... Gen 43:25
And Joseph made *r* his chariot ... Gen 46:29
he made *r* his chariot, and took ... Ex 14:6
they be almost *r* to stone me ... Ex 17:4
be *r* against the third day ... Ex 19:11
Be *r* against the third day ... Ex 19:15
be *r* in the morning, and come up ... Ex 34:2
But we ourselves will go *r* armed ... Num 32:17
ye were *r* to go up into the hill ... Deut 1:41
A Syrian *r* to perish was my ... Deut 26:5
from the city, but be ye all *r* ... Josh 8:4
made *r* a kid, and unleavened cakes ... Judg 6:19
shall have made *r* a kid for thee ... Judg 13:15
of wine, and five sheep *r* dressed ... 1Sa 25:18
Behold, thy servants are *r* to do ... 2Sa 15:15
that thou hast no tidings *r* ... 2Sa 18:22
was built of stone made *r* before ... 1Kin 6:7
And Joram said, Make *r* ... 2Kin 9:21
And his chariot was made *r* ... 2Kin 9:21
that were *r* armed to the war ... 1Chr 12:23
eight hundred, *r* armed to the war ... 1Chr 12:24
had made *r* for the building ... 1Chr 28:2
fourscore thousand *r* prepared for ... 2Chr 17:18
they made *r* for themselves ... 2Chr 35:14
he was a *r* scribe in the law of ... Ezr 7:6
but thou art a God *r* to pardon ... Neh 9:17
they should be *r* against that day ... Est 3:14
that the Jews should be *r* against ... Est 8:13
who are *r* to raise up their ... Job 3:8
He that is *r* to slip with his ... Job 12:5
day of darkness is *r* at his hand ... Job 15:23
as a king *r* to the battle ... Job 15:24
which are *r* to become heaps ... Job 15:28
extinct, the graves are *r* for me ... Job 17:1
shall be *r* at his side ... Job 18:12
that was *r* to perish came upon me ... Job 29:13
it is *r* to burst like new bottles ... Job 32:19
hath bent his bow, and made it *r* ... Ps 7:12
they make *r* their arrow upon the ... Ps 11:2
when thou shalt make *r* thine ... Ps 21:12
For I am *r* to halt, and my sorrow ... Ps 38:17
tongue is the pen of a *r* writer ... Ps 45:1
Lord, art good, and *r* to forgive ... Ps 86:5
*r* to die from my youth up ... Ps 88:15
and those that are *r* to be slain ... Prov 24:11
unto him that is *r* to perish ... Prov 31:6
of God, and be more *r* to hear ... Eccl 5:1
were *r* to perish in the land of ... Is 27:13
be to you as a breach *r* to fall ... Is 30:13
shall be *r* to speak plainly ... Is 32:4
The LORD was *r* to save me ... Is 38:20
saying, It is *r* for the sodering ... Is 41:7
as if he were *r* to destroy ... Is 51:13
the trumpet, even to make all *r* ... Eze 7:14
Now if ye be *r* that at what time ... Dan 3:15
For they have made *r* their heart ... Hos 7:6
are killed, and all things are *r* ... Mt 22:4
to his servants, The wedding is *r* ... Mt 22:8
Therefore be ye also *r* ... Mt 24:44
they that were *r* went in with him ... Mt 25:10
and they made *r* the passover ... Mt 26:19
there make *r* for us ... Mk 14:15
and they made *r* the passover ... Mk 14:16
The spirit truly is *r*, but the ... Mk 14:38
to make *r* a people prepared for ... Lk 1:17
unto him, was sick, and *r* to die ... Lk 7:2
the Samaritans, to make *r* for him ... Lk 9:52
Be ye therefore *r* also ... Lk 12:40
for all things are now *r* ... Lk 14:17
Make *r* wherewith I may sup, and ... Lk 17:8
there make *r* ... Lk 22:12
and they made *r* the passover ... Lk 22:13
I am *r* to go with thee, both into ... Lk 22:33
but your time is alway *r* ... Jn 7:6
but while they made *r*, he fell ... Acts 10:10
*r* to depart on the morrow ... Acts 20:7
for I am *r* not to be bound only, ... Acts 21:13
he come near, are *r* to kill him ... Acts 23:15
and now are they *r*, looking for a ... Acts 23:21
Make *r* two hundred soldiers to go ... Acts 23:23
I am *r* to preach the gospel to ... Rom 1:15
and declaration of your *r* mind ... 2Cor 8:19
that Achaia was *r* a year ago ... 2Cor 9:2
that, as I said, ye may be *r* ... 2Cor 9:3
before, that the same might be *r* ... 2Cor 9:5
line of things made *r* to our hand ... 2Cor 10:16
third time I am *r* to come to you ... 2Cor 12:14
*r* to distribute, willing to ... 1Ti 6:18
For I am now *r* to be offered, and ... 2Ti 4:6
to be *r* to every good work, ... Titus 3:1
waxeth old is *r* to vanish away ... Heb 8:13
through faith unto salvation *r* to ... 1Pet 1:5
be *r* always to give an answer to ... 1Pet 3:15

R

him that is *r* to judge the quick 1Pet 4:5
for filthy lucre, but of a *r* mind 1Pet 5:2
which remain, that are *r* to die Rev 3:2
woman which was *r* to be delivered Rev 12:4
and his wife hath made herself *r* Rev 19:7

**REAIA** (*re-ah'-yah*) *Grandfather of Beerah.*
his son, *R* his son, Baal his son, 1Chr 5:5

**REAIAH** (*re-ah'-yah*) See REAIA.
*1. Son of Shobal.*
*R* the son of Shobal begat Jahath 1Chr 4:2
*2. A family of exiles.*
of Gahar, the children of *R* Ezr 2:47
The children of *R*, the children Neh 7:50

**REALM**
So the *r* of Jehoshaphat was quiet 2Chr 20:30
his priests and Levites, in my *r* Ezr 7:13
wrath against the *r* of the king Ezr 7:23
that were in all his *r* Dan 1:20
to set him over the whole *r* Dan 6:3
king over the *r* of the Chaldeans Dan 9:1
up all against the *r* of Grecia Dan 11:2

**REAP**
when ye *r* the harvest of your Lev 19:9
thou shalt not wholly *r* the Lev 19:9
shall *r* the harvest thereof, then Lev 23:10
when ye *r* the harvest of your Lev 23:22
of thy harvest thou shalt not *r* Lev 25:5
neither *r* that which groweth of Lev 25:11
be on the field that they do *r* Ruth 2:9
to *r* his harvest, and to make his 1Sa 8:12
and in the third year sow ye, and *r* 2Kin 19:29
and sow wickedness, *r* the same Job 4:8
They *r* every one his corn in the Job 24:6
that sow in tears shall *r* in joy Ps 126:5
soweth iniquity shall *r* vanity Prov 22:8
regardeth the clouds shall not *r* Eccl 11:4
and in the third year sow ye, and *r* Is 37:30
sown wheat, but shall *r* thorns Jer 12:13
they shall *r* the whirlwind Hos 8:7
in righteousness, *r* in mercy Hos 10:12
shalt sow, but thou shalt not *r* Mic 6:15
they sow not, neither do they *r* Mt 6:26
that I *r* where I sowed not Mt 25:26
for they neither sow nor *r* Lk 12:24
I sent you to *r* that whereon ye Jn 4:38
if we shall *r* your carnal things 1Cor 9:11
sparingly shall *r* also sparingly 2Cor 9:6
shall *r* also bountifully 2Cor 9:6
man soweth, that shall he also *r* Gal 6:7
shall of the flesh *r* corruption Gal 6:8
of the Spirit *r* life everlasting Gal 6:8
for in due season we shall *r* Gal 6:9
cloud, Thrust in thy sickle, and *r* Rev 14:15
the time is come for thee to *r* Rev 14:15

**REAPED**
wickedness, ye have *r* iniquity Hos 10:13
who have *r* down your fields Jas 5:4
*r* are entered into the ears of Jas 5:4
and the earth was *r* Rev 14:16

**REAPER**
the plowman shall overtake the *r* Amos 9:13

**REAPERS**
gleaned in the field after the *r* Ruth 2:3
Beth-lehem, and said unto the *r* Ruth 2:4
servant that was set over the *r* Ruth 2:5
that was set over the *r* answered Ruth 2:6
gather after the *r* among the Ruth 2:7
And she sat beside the *r* Ruth 2:14
went out to his father to the *r* 2Kin 4:18
of harvest I will say to the *r* Mt 13:30
and the *r* are the angels Mt 13:39

**REAPEST**
corners of thy field when thou *r* Lev 23:22
*r* that thou didst not sow Lk 19:21

**REAPETH**
corn, and *r* the ears with his arm Is 17:5
he that *r* receiveth wages, and Jn 4:36
he that *r* may rejoice together Jn 4:36
true, One soweth, and another *r* Jn 4:37

**REAPING**
they of Beth-shemesh were *r* their 1Sa 6:13
*r* where thou hast not sown, and Mt 25:24
not down, and *r* that I did not sow Lk 19:22

**REAR**
thou shalt *r* up the tabernacle Ex 26:30
neither *r* you up a standing image Lev 26:1
*r* an altar unto the LORD in the 2Sa 24:18
wilt thou *r* it up in three days Jn 2:20

**REARED**
that the tabernacle was *r* up Ex 40:17
Moses *r* up the tabernacle, and Ex 40:18
bars thereof, and *r* up his pillars Ex 40:18
he *r* up the court round about the Ex 40:33
was *r* up the cloud covered the Num 9:15
*r* up for himself a pillar, which 2Sa 18:18
he *r* up an altar for Baal in the 1Kin 16:32
he *r* up altars for Baal, and made 2Kin 21:3
he *r* up the pillars before the 2Chr 3:17
he *r* up altars for Baalim, and 2Chr 33:3

**REASON**
by *r* of that famine following Gen 41:31
Canaan fainted by *r* of the famine Gen 47:13
Israel sighed by *r* of the bondage Ex 2:23
up unto God by *r* of the bondage Ex 2:23
cry by *r* of their taskmasters Ex 3:7
by *r* of the swarm of flies Ex 8:24
be unclean by *r* of a dead body Num 9:10
given them by *r* of the anointing Num 18:8
ye shall bear no sin by *r* of it Num 18:32
ye were afraid by *r* of the fire Deut 5:5
that is not clean by *r* of Deut 23:10
old by *r* of the very long journey Josh 9:13
by *r* of them that oppressed them Judg 2:18
that I may *r* with you before the 1Sa 12:7
this is the *r* of the levy which 1Kin 9:15
his eyes were set by *r* of his age 1Kin 14:4
to minister by *r* of the cloud 2Chr 5:14
by *r* of this great multitude 2Chr 20:15
by *r* of the sickness day by day 2Chr 21:15
fell out by *r* of his sickness 2Chr 21:19
are blackish by *r* of the ice Job 6:16
choose out my words to *r* with him Job 9:14
and I desire to *r* with God Job 13:3
Should he *r* with unprofitable Job 15:3
eye also is dim by *r* of sorrow Job 17:7
by *r* of his highness I could not Job 31:23
By *r* of the multitude of Job 35:9
they cry out by *r* of the arm of Job 35:9
order our speech by *r* of darkness Job 37:19
by *r* of breakings they purify Job 41:25
I have roared by *r* of the Ps 38:8
by *r* of the enemy and avenger Ps 44:16
man that shouteth by *r* of wine Ps 78:65
eye mourneth by *r* of affliction Ps 88:9
if by *r* of strength they be Ps 90:10
By *r* of the voice of my groaning Ps 102:5
will not plow by *r* of the cold Prov 20:4
seven men that can render a *r* Prov 26:16
the *r* of things, and to know the Eccl 7:25
let us *r* together, saith the LORD Is 1:18
narrow by *r* of the inhabitants Is 49:19
of branches by *r* of many waters Eze 19:10
terrors by *r* of the sword shall Eze 21:12
By *r* of the abundance of his Eze 26:10
Tarshish was thy merchant by *r* of Eze 27:12
Syria was thy merchant by *r* of Eze 27:16
thy wisdom by *r* of thy brightness Eze 28:17
same time my *r* returned unto me Dan 4:36
by *r* of the words of the king and Dan 5:10
sacrifice by *r* of transgression Dan 8:12
I cried by *r* of mine affliction Jonah 2:2
by *r* of the multitude of men Mic 2:12
why *r* ye among yourselves, Mt 16:8
Why *r* ye these things in your Mk 2:8
it, he saith unto them, Why *r* ye Mk 8:17
and the Pharisees began to *r* Lk 5:21
them, What *r* ye in your hearts Lk 5:22
the sea arose by *r* of a great Jn 6:18
Because that by *r* of him many of Jn 12:11
It is not *r* that we should leave Acts 6:2
*r* would that I should bear with Acts 18:14
but by *r* of him who hath Rom 8:20
by *r* of the glory that excelleth 2Cor 3:10
by *r* hereof he ought, as for the Heb 5:3
even those who by *r* of use have Heb 5:14
to continue by *r* of death Heb 7:23
to every man that asketh you a *r* 1Pet 3:15
by *r* of whom the way of truth 2Pet 2:2
by *r* of the other voices of the Rev 8:13
by *r* of the smoke of the pit Rev 9:2
in the sea by *r* of her costliness Rev 18:19

**REASONABLE**
unto God, which is your *r* service Rom 12:1

**REASONED**
they *r* among themselves, saying, Mt 16:7
they *r* with themselves, saying, Mt 21:25
that they so *r* within themselves Mk 2:8
they *r* among themselves, saying, Mk 8:16
they *r* with themselves, saying, Mk 11:31
they *r* with themselves, saying, Lk 20:5
they *r* among themselves, saying, Lk 20:14
while they communed together and *r* Lk 24:15
three sabbath days *r* with them Acts 17:2
he *r* in the synagogue every Acts 18:4
the synagogue, and *r* with the Jews Acts 18:19
as he *r* of righteousness, Acts 24:25

**REASONING**
Hear now my *r*, and hearken to the Job 13:6
there, and *r* in their hearts, Mk 2:6
and having heard them *r* together Mk 12:28
Then there arose a *r* among them Lk 9:46
had great *r* among themselves Acts 28:29

**REASONS**
I gave ear to your *r*, whilst ye Job 32:11
bring forth your strong *r* Is 41:21

**REBA** (*re'-bah*) *A king of Midian.*
and Rekem, and Zur, and Hur, and *R*. Num 31:8
and Zur, and Hur, and *R* Josh 13:21

**REBECCA** (*re-bek'-kah*) See REBEKAH. *Greek form of Rebekah.*
but when *R* also had conceived by Rom 9:10

**REBEKAH** (*re-bek'-kah*) See REBECCA, REBEKAH'S. *Wife of Isaac.*
And Bethuel begat *R* Gen 22:23
*R* came out, who was born to Gen 24:15
*R* had a brother, and his name was Gen 24:29
heard the words of *R* his sister Gen 24:30
*R* came forth with her pitcher on Gen 24:45
*R* is before thee, take her, and go Gen 24:51
and raiment, and gave them to *R* Gen 24:53
And they called *R*, and said unto Gen 24:58
And they sent away *R* their sister Gen 24:59
And they blessed *R*, and said unto Gen 24:60
*R* arose, and her damsels, and they Gen 24:61
and the servant took *R*, and went Gen 24:61
*R* lifted up her eyes, and when she Gen 24:64
mother Sarah's tent, and took *R* Gen 24:67
years old when he took *R* to wife Gen 25:20
of him, and *R* his wife conceived Gen 25:21
but *R* loved Jacob Gen 25:28
of the place should kill me for *R* Gen 26:7
was sporting with *R* his wife Gen 26:8
grief of mind unto Isaac and to *R* Gen 26:35
*R* heard when Isaac spake to Esau Gen 27:5
*R* spake unto Jacob her son Gen 27:6
And Jacob said to *R* his mother Gen 27:11
*R* took goodly raiment of her Gen 27:15
Esau her elder son were told to *R* Gen 27:42
*R* said to Isaac, I am weary of my Gen 27:46
the Syrian, the brother of *R* Gen 28:5
they buried Isaac and *R* his wife Gen 49:31

**REBEKAH'S** (*re-bek'-kahz*)
brother, and that he was *R* son Gen 29:12
But Deborah *R* nurse died, and she Gen 35:8

**REBEL**
Only *r* not ye against the LORD, Num 14:9
doth *r* against thy commandment Josh 1:18
that ye might *r* this day against Josh 22:16
seeing ye *r* to day against the Josh 22:18
but *r* not against the LORD Josh 22:19
nor *r* against us, in building you Josh 22:19
that we should *r* against the LORD Josh 22:29
not *r* against the commandment of 1Sa 12:14
but *r* against the commandment of 1Sa 12:15
will ye *r* against the king Neh 2:19
that thou and the Jews think to *r* Neh 6:6
of those that *r* against the light Job 24:13
But if ye refuse and *r*, ye shall Is 1:20
and wine, and they *r* against me Hos 7:14

**REBELLED**
and in the thirteenth year they *r* Gen 14:4
because ye *r* against my word at Num 20:24
For ye *r* against my commandment Num 27:14
but *r* against the commandment of Deut 1:26
but *r* against the commandment of Deut 1:43
then ye *r* against the commandment Deut 9:23
So Israel *r* against the house of 1Kin 12:19
Then Moab *r* against Israel after 2Kin 1:1
that the king of Moab *r* against 2Kin 3:5
king of Moab hath *r* against me 2Kin 3:7
he *r* against the king of Assyria, 2Kin 18:7
then he turned and *r* against him 2Kin 24:1
that Zedekiah *r* against the king 2Kin 24:20
Israel *r* against the house of 2Chr 10:19
up, and hath *r* against his lord 2Chr 13:6
And he also *r* against king 2Chr 36:13
*r* against thee, and cast thy law Neh 9:26
for they have *r* against thee Ps 5:10
they *r* not against his word Ps 105:28
Because they *r* against the words Ps 107:11
and they have *r* against me Is 1:2
But they *r*, and vexed his holy Is 63:10
that Zedekiah *r* against the king Jer 52:3
for I have *r* against his Lam 1:18
for I have grievously *r* Lam 1:20
We have transgressed and have *r* Lam 3:42
nation that hath *r* against me Eze 2:3
But he *r* against him in sending Eze 17:15
But they *r* against me, and would Eze 20:8
But the house of Israel *r* against Eze 20:13
the children *r* against me Eze 20:21
and have done wickedly, and have *r* Dan 9:5
though we have *r* against him Dan 9:9
for she hath *r* against her God Hos 13:16

**REBELLEST**
trust, that thou *r* against me 2Kin 18:20
trust, that thou *r* against me Is 36:5

**REBELLION**
For I know thy *r*, and thy stiff Deut 31:27
if it be in *r*, or if in Josh 22:22
For *r* is as the sin of witchcraft 1Sa 15:23
against kings, and that *r* and Ezr 4:19
in their *r* appointed a captain to Neh 9:17
For he addeth *r* unto his sin Job 34:37
An evil man seeketh only *r* Prov 17:11
hast taught *r* against the LORD Jer 28:16
he hath taught *r* against the LORD Jer 29:32

**REBELLIOUS**
ye have been *r* against the LORD Deut 9:7
Ye have been *r* against the LORD Deut 9:24
*r* son, which will not obey the Deut 21:18
This our son is stubborn and *r* Deut 21:20
ye have been *r* against the LORD Deut 31:27
Thou son of the perverse *r* woman 1Sa 20:30
unto Jerusalem, building the *r* Ezr 4:12
know that this city is a *r* city Ezr 4:15
let not the *r* exalt themselves Ps 66:7
but the *r* dwell in a dry land Ps 68:6
yea, for the *r* also, that the Ps 68:18
a stubborn and *r* generation Ps 78:8
Thy princes are *r*, and companions Is 1:23
Woe to the *r* children, saith the Is 30:1
That this is a *r* people, lying Is 30:9
opened mine ear, and I was not *r* Is 50:5
hands all the day unto a *r* people Is 65:2
she hath been *r* against me Jer 4:17

hath a revolting and a *r* heart Jer 5:23
to a *r* nation that hath rebelled Eze 2:3
forbear, (for they are a *r* house Eze 2:5
looks, though they be a *r* house Eze 2:6
for they are most *r* Eze 2:7
Be not thou *r* like that Eze 2:8
like that *r* house Eze 2:8
looks, though they be a *r* house Eze 3:9
for they are a *r* house Eze 3:26
for they are a *r* house Eze 3:27
in the midst of a *r* house Eze 12:2
for they are a *r* house Eze 12:2
though they be a *r* house Eze 12:3
the *r* house, said unto thee, What Eze 12:9
O *r* house, will I say the word, Eze 12:25
Say now to the *r* house, Know ye Eze 17:12
utter a parable unto the *r* house Eze 24:3
And thou shalt say to the *r* Eze 44:6

**REBELS**
be kept for a token against the *r* Num 17:10
he said unto them, Hear now, ye *r* Num 20:10
purge out from among you the *r* Eze 20:38

**REBUKE**
shalt in any wise *r* thy neighbour Lev 19:17
upon thee cursing, vexation, and *r* Deut 28:20
she may glean them, and *r* her not Ruth 2:16
day is a day of trouble, and of *r* 2Kin 19:3
our fathers look thereon, and *r* it 1Chr 12:17
*r* me not in thine anger, neither Ps 6:1
world were discovered at thy *r* Ps 18:15
O LORD, *r* me not in thy wrath Ps 38:1
*R* the company of spearmen, the Ps 68:30
At thy *r*, O God of Jacob, both Ps 76:6
at the *r* of thy countenance Ps 80:16
At thy *r* they fled Ps 104:7
*r* a wise man, and he will love Prov 9:8
but a scorner heareth not *r* Prov 13:1
but the poor heareth not *r* Prov 13:8
But to them that *r* him shall be Prov 24:25
Open *r* is better than secret love Prov 27:5
better to hear the *r* of the wise Eccl 7:5
nations, and shall *r* many people Is 2:4
but God shall *r* them, and they Is 17:13
the *r* of his people shall he take Is 25:8
shall flee at the *r* of one Is 30:17
at the *r* of five shall ye flee Is 30:17
day is a day of trouble, and of *r* Is 37:3
at my *r* I dry up the sea, I make Is 50:2
of the LORD, the *r* of thy God Is 51:20
be wroth with thee, nor *r* thee Is 54:9
his *r* with flames of fire Is 66:15
for thy sake I have suffered *r* Jer 15:15
shall be desolate in the day of *r* Hos 5:9
*r* strong nations afar off Mic 4:3
said unto Satan, The LORD *r* thee Zec 3:2
that hath chosen Jerusalem *r* thee Zec 3:2
I will *r* the devourer for your Mal 3:11
Peter took him, and began to *r* him Mt 16:22
Peter took him, and began to *r* him Mk 8:32
trespass against thee, *r* him Lk 17:3
unto him, Master, *r* thy disciples Lk 19:39
the sons of God, without *r* Phil 2:15
*R* not an elder, but intreat him 1Ti 5:1
Them that sin *r* before all 1Ti 5:20
reprove, *r*, exhort with all 2Ti 4:2
Wherefore *r* them sharply, that Titus 1:13
exhort, and *r* with all authority Titus 2:15
but said, The Lord *r* thee Jude 9
As many as I love, I *r* and chasten Rev 3:19

**REBUKED**
my hands, and *r* thee yesternight Gen 31:42
and his father *r* him, and said unto Gen 37:10
I *r* the nobles, and the rulers, and Neh 5:7
Thou hast *r* the heathen, thou Ps 9:5
He *r* the Red sea also, and it was Ps 106:9
Thou hast *r* the proud that are Ps 119:21
arose, and *r* the winds and the sea Mt 8:26
And Jesus *r* the devil Mt 17:18
and the disciples *r* them Mt 19:13
And the multitude *r* them, because Mt 20:31
And Jesus *r* him, saying, Hold thy Mk 1:25
*r* the wind, and said unto the sea, Mk 4:39
he *r* Peter, saying, Get thee Mk 8:33
he *r* the foul spirit, saying unto Mk 9:25
his disciples *r* those that Mk 10:13
And Jesus *r* him, saying, Hold thy Lk 4:35
he stood over her, and *r* the fever Lk 4:39
*r* the wind and the raging of the Lk 8:24
Jesus *r* the unclean spirit, and Lk 9:42
*r* them, and said, Ye know not what Lk 9:55
his disciples saw it, they *r* them Lk 18:15
And they which went before *r* him Lk 18:39
But the other answering *r* him Lk 23:40
nor faint when thou art *r* of him Heb 12:5
But was *r* for his iniquity 2Pet 2:16

**REBUKER**
I have been a *r* of them all Hos 5:2

**REBUKES**
When thou with *r* dost correct man Ps 39:11
anger and in fury and in furious *r* Eze 5:15
upon them with furious *r* Eze 25:17

**REBUKETH**
he that *r* a wicked man getteth Prov 9:7
He that *r* a man afterwards shall Prov 28:23
They hate him that *r* in the gate Amos 5:10
He *r* the sea, and maketh it dry, Nah 1:4

**REBUKING**
at the *r* of the LORD, at the 2Sa 22:16
he *r* them suffered them not to Lk 4:41

**RECALL**
This I *r* to my mind, therefore Lam 3:21

**RECEIPT**
sitting at the *r* of custom Mt 9:9
sitting at the *r* of custom Mk 2:14
Levi, sitting at the *r* of custom Lk 5:27

**RECEIVE**
to *r* thy brother's blood from thy Gen 4:11
then *r* my present at my hand Gen 33:10
to *r* his pledge from the woman's Gen 38:20
make his pans to *r* his ashes Ex 27:3
thou shalt *r* them of their hands, Ex 29:25
which ye *r* of the children of Num 18:28
mount to *r* the tables of stone Deut 9:9
every one shall *r* of thy words Deut 33:3
which thou shalt *r* of their hands 1Sa 10:4
Though I should *r* a thousand 2Sa 18:12
there, and thou shalt *r* them 1Kin 5:9
little to *r* the burnt offerings 1Kin 8:64
whom I stand, I will *r* none 2Kin 5:16
Is it a time to *r* money 2Kin 5:26
to *r* garments, and oliveyards, and 2Kin 5:26
now therefore *r* no more money of 2Kin 12:7
the priests consented to *r* no 2Kin 12:8
not able to *r* the burnt offerings 2Chr 7:7
shall we *r* good at the hand of Job 2:10
of God, and shall we not *r* evil Job 2:10
*R*, I pray thee, the law from his Job 22:22
they shall *r* of the Almighty Job 27:13
the LORD will *r* my prayer Ps 6:9
He shall *r* the blessing from the Ps 24:5
for he shall *r* me Ps 49:15
and afterward *r* me to glory Ps 73:24
When I shall *r* the congregation I Ps 75:2
To *r* the instruction of wisdom, Prov 1:3
My son, if thou wilt *r* my words Prov 2:1
Hear, O my son, and *r* my sayings Prov 4:10
*R* my instruction, and not silver Prov 8:10
wise in heart will *r* commandments Prov 10:8
*r* instruction, that thou mayest Prov 19:20
Should I *r* comfort in these Is 57:6
they have refused to *r* correction Jer 5:3
let your ear *r* the word of his Jer 9:20
might not hear, nor *r* instruction Jer 17:23
not hearkened to *r* instruction Jer 32:33
Will ye not *r* instruction to Jer 35:13
speak unto thee *r* in thine heart Eze 3:10
when thou shalt *r* thy sisters Eze 16:61
that ye shall *r* no more reproach Eze 36:30
ye shall *r* of me gifts and rewards Dan 2:6
Ephraim shall *r* shame, and Israel Hos 10:6
all iniquity, and *r* us graciously Hos 14:2
he shall *r* of you his standing Mic 1:11
fear me, thou wilt *r* instruction Zeph 3:7
shall not be room enough to *r* it Mal 3:10
And whosoever shall not *r* you Mt 10:14
shall *r* a prophet's reward Mt 10:41
shall *r* a righteous man's reward Mt 10:41
The blind *r* their sight, and the Mt 11:5
And if ye will *r* it, this is Elias Mt 11:14
whoso shall *r* one such little Mt 18:5
All men cannot *r* this saying Mt 19:11
He that is able to *r* it Mt 19:12
let him *r* it Mt 19:12
shall *r* an hundredfold, and shall Mt 19:29
is right, that shall ye *r* Mt 20:7
in prayer, believing, ye shall *r* Mt 21:22
that they might *r* the fruits of Mt 21:34
therefore ye shall *r* the greater Mt 23:14
that there was no room to *r* them Mk 2:2
immediately *r* it with gladness Mk 4:16
*r* it, and bring forth fruit, some Mk 4:20
And whosoever shall not *r* you Mk 6:11
Whosoever shall *r* one of such Mk 9:37
and whosoever shall *r* me Mk 9:37
Whosoever shall not *r* the kingdom Mk 10:15
But he shall *r* an hundredfold now Mk 10:30
Lord, that I might *r* my sight Mk 10:51
ye pray, believe that ye *r* them Mk 11:24
servant, that he might *r* from the Mk 12:2
these shall *r* greater damnation Mk 12:40
lend to them of whom ye hope to *r* Lk 6:34
to sinners, to *r* as much again Lk 6:34
they hear, *r* the word with joy Lk 8:13
And whosoever will not *r* you Lk 9:5
Whosoever shall *r* this child in Lk 9:48
whosoever shall *r* me receiveth Lk 9:48
And they did not *r* him, because Lk 9:53
city ye enter, and they *r* you Lk 10:8
they *r* you not, go your ways out Lk 10:10
they may *r* me into their houses Lk 16:4
they may *r* you into everlasting Lk 16:9
Whosoever shall not *r* the kingdom Lk 18:17
Who shall not *r* manifold more in Lk 18:30
said, Lord, that I may *r* my sight Lk 18:41
Jesus said unto him, *R* thy sight Lk 18:42
to *r* for himself a kingdom Lk 19:12
the same shall *r* greater Lk 20:47
for we *r* the due reward of our Lk 23:41
and ye *r* not our witness Jn 3:11
and said, A man can *r* nothing Jn 3:27
But I *r* not testimony from man Jn 5:34
I *r* not honour from men Jn 5:41
my Father's name, and ye *r* me not Jn 5:43
in his own name, him ye will *r* Jn 5:43
which *r* honour one of another, and Jn 5:44
on the sabbath day *r* circumcision Jn 7:23
they that believe on him should *r* Jn 7:39
come again, and *r* you unto myself Jn 14:3
whom the world cannot *r*, because Jn 14:17
for he shall *r* of mine, and shall Jn 16:14
ask, and ye shall *r*, that your joy Jn 16:24
unto them, *R* ye the Holy Ghost Jn 20:22
But ye shall *r* power, after that Acts 1:8
ye shall *r* the gift of the Holy Acts 2:38
expecting to *r* something of them Acts 3:5
Whom the heaven must *r* until the Acts 3:21
saying, Lord Jesus, *r* my spirit Acts 7:59
that they might *r* the Holy Ghost Acts 8:15
hands, he may *r* the Holy Ghost Acts 8:19
on him, that he might *r* his sight Acts 9:12
that thou mightest *r* thy sight Acts 9:17
in him shall *r* remission of sins Acts 10:43
which are not lawful for us to *r* Acts 16:21
exhorting the disciples to *r* him Acts 18:27
is more blessed to give than to *r* Acts 20:35
me, Brother Saul, *r* thy sight Acts 22:13
for they will not *r* thy testimony Acts 22:18
that they may *r* forgiveness of Acts 26:18
they which *r* abundance of grace Rom 5:17
they that resist shall *r* to Rom 13:2
that is weak in the faith *r* ye Rom 14:1
Wherefore *r* ye one another, as Rom 15:7
That ye *r* her in the Lord, as Rom 16:2
every man shall *r* his own reward 1Cor 3:8
thereupon, he shall *r* a reward 1Cor 3:14
hast thou that thou didst not *r* 1Cor 4:7
now if thou didst *r* it, why dost 1Cor 4:7
that the church may *r* edifying 1Cor 14:5
that every one may *r* the things 2Cor 5:10
beseech you also that ye *r* not 2Cor 6:1
and I will *r* you, 2Cor 6:17
*R* us; we have wronged 2Cor 7:2
that ye might *r* damage by us in 2Cor 7:9
intreaty that we would *r* the gift 2Cor 8:4
or if ye *r* another spirit, which 2Cor 11:4
if otherwise, yet as a fool *r* me 2Cor 11:16
that we might *r* the promise of Gal 3:14
that we might *r* the adoption of Gal 4:5
the same shall he *r* of the Lord Eph 6:8
*R* him therefore in the Lord with Phil 2:29
that of the Lord ye shall *r* the Col 3:24
*r* for the wrong which he hath Col 3:25
if he come unto you, *r* him Col 4:10
Against an elder *r* not an 1Ti 5:19
thou therefore *r* him, that is, Philem 12
thou shouldest *r* him for ever Philem 15
a partner, *r* him as myself Philem 17
of Levi, who *r* the office of the Heb 7:5
And here men that die *r* tithes Heb 7:8
might *r* the promise of eternal Heb 9:15
of God, ye might *r* the promise Heb 10:36
should after *r* for an inheritance Heb 11:8
he shall *r* any thing of the Lord Jas 1:7
he shall *r* the crown of life, Jas 1:12
*r* with meekness the engrafted Jas 1:21
knowing that we shall *r* the Jas 3:1
*r* not, because ye ask amiss, that Jas 4:3
until he *r* the early and latter Jas 5:7
ye shall *r* a crown of glory that 1Pet 5:4
And shall *r* the reward of 2Pet 2:13
we *r* of him, because we keep his 1Jn 3:22
If we *r* the witness of men, the 1Jn 5:9
but that we *r* a full reward 2Jn 8
*r* him not into your house, 2Jn 10
We therefore ought to *r* such 3Jn 8
doth he himself *r* the brethren 3Jn 10
to *r* glory and honour and power Rev 4:11
Lamb that was slain to *r* power Rev 5:12
to *r* a mark in their right hand, Rev 13:16
*r* his mark in his forehead, or in Rev 14:9
but *r* power as kings one hour Rev 17:12
that ye *r* not of her plagues Rev 18:4

**RECEIVED**
*r* in the same year an hundredfold Gen 26:12
he *r* them at their hand, and Ex 32:4
they *r* of Moses all the offering, Ex 36:3
after that let her be *r* in again Num 12:14
I have *r* commandment to bless Num 23:20
fathers, have *r* their inheritance Num 34:14
Manasseh have *r* their inheritance Num 34:14
the half tribe have *r* their Num 34:15
of the tribe whereunto they are *r* Num 36:3
of the tribe whereunto they are *r* Num 36:4
and the Gadites have *r* their Josh 13:8
had not yet *r* their inheritance Josh 18:2
have *r* their inheritance beyond Josh 18:7
would not have *r* a burnt offering Judg 13:23
or of whose hand have I *r* any 1Sa 12:3
So David *r* of her hand that which 1Sa 25:35
the king's merchants *r* the linen 1Kin 10:28
Hezekiah *r* the letter of the hand 2Kin 19:14
Then David *r* them, and made them 1Chr 12:18
the king's merchants *r* the linen 2Chr 1:16
and it *r* and held three thousand 2Chr 4:5
and the priests *r* the blood 2Chr 29:22
which they *r* of the hand of the 2Chr 30:16
but he *r* it not Est 4:4
mine ear *r* a little thereof Job 4:12
thou hast *r* gifts for men Ps 68:18
looked upon it, and *r* instruction Prov 24:32
Hezekiah *r* the letter from the Is 37:14
for she hath *r* of the LORD's hand Is 40:2
they *r* no correction Jer 2:30
that hath not *r* usury nor Eze 18:17
she *r* not correction Zeph 3:2

freely ye have *r*, freely give Mt 10:8
This is he which *r* seed by the Mt 13:19
But he that *r* the seed into stony Mt 13:20
He also that *r* seed among the Mt 13:22
But he that *r* seed into the good Mt 13:23
they that *r* tribute money came to Mt 17:24
hour, they *r* every man a penny Mt 20:9
that they should have *r* more Mt 20:10
they likewise *r* every man a penny Mt 20:10
And when they had *r* it, they Mt 20:11
and immediately their eyes *r* sight Mt 20:34
Then he that had *r* the five Mt 25:16
And likewise he that had *r* two Mt 25:17
But he that had *r* one went Mt 25:18
so he that had *r* five talents Mt 25:20
also that had *r* two talents came Mt 25:22
Then he which had *r* the one Mt 25:24
should have *r* mine own with usury Mt 25:27
be, which they have *r* to hold Mk 7:4
And immediately he *r* his sight Mk 10:52
but he *r* it not Mk 15:23
he was *r* up into heaven, and sat Mk 16:19
for ye have *r* your consolation Lk 6:24
returned, the people gladly *r* him Lk 8:40
he *r* them, and spake unto them of Lk 9:11
was come that he should be *r* up Lk 9:51
named Martha *r* him into her house Lk 10:38
calf, because he hath *r* him safe Lk 15:27
And immediately he *r* his sight Lk 18:43
and came down, and *r* him joyfully Lk 19:6
having *r* the kingdom, then he Lk 19:15
his own, and his own *r* him not Jn 1:11
But as many as *r* him, to them Jn 1:12
And of his fulness have all we *r* Jn 1:16
He that hath *r* his testimony hath Jn 3:33
Galilee, the Galilaeans *r* him Jn 4:45
willingly *r* him into the ship Jn 6:21
and I went and washed, and I *r* sight Jn 9:11
asked him how he had *r* his sight Jn 9:15
*r* his sight, until they called Jn 9:18
of him that had *r* his sight Jn 9:18
commandment have I *r* of my Father Jn 10:18
He then having *r* the sop went Jn 13:30
and they have *r* them, and have Jn 17:8
having *r* a band of men and Jn 18:3
Jesus therefore had *r* the vinegar Jn 19:30
a cloud *r* him out of their sight Acts 1:9
having *r* of the Father the Acts 2:33
Then they that gladly *r* his word Acts 2:41
feet and ancle bones *r* strength Acts 3:7
who *r* the lively oracles to give Acts 7:38
Who have *r* the law by the Acts 7:53
Samaria had *r* the word of God Acts 8:14
on them, and they *r* the Holy Ghost Acts 8:17
he *r* sight forthwith, and arose, Acts 9:18
And when he had *r* meat, he was Acts 9:19
the vessel was *r* up again into Acts 10:16
which have *r* the Holy Ghost as Acts 10:47
had also *r* the word of God Acts 11:1
they were *r* of the church, and of Acts 15:4
having *r* such a charge, thrust Acts 16:24
Whom Jason hath *r* Acts 17:7
in that they *r* the word with all Acts 17:11
Have ye *r* the Holy Ghost since ye Acts 19:2
which I have *r* of the Lord Jesus, Acts 20:24
the brethren *r* us gladly Acts 21:17
from whom also I *r* letters unto Acts 22:5
having *r* authority from the chief Acts 26:10
*r* us every one, because of the Acts 28:2
who *r* us, and lodged us three days Acts 28:7
We neither *r* letters out of Acts 28:21
*r* all that came in unto him, Acts 28:30
By whom we have *r* grace and Rom 1:5
he *r* the sign of circumcision, a Rom 4:11
whom we have now *r* the atonement Rom 5:11
For ye have not *r* the spirit of Rom 8:15
but ye have *r* the Spirit of Rom 8:15
for God hath *r* him Rom 14:3
as Christ also *r* us to the glory Rom 15:7
Now we have *r*, not the spirit of 1Cor 2:12
glory, as if thou hadst not *r* it 1Cor 4:7
For I have *r* of the Lord that 1Cor 11:23
unto you, which also ye have *r* 1Cor 15:1
first of all that which I also *r* 1Cor 15:3
this ministry, as we have *r* mercy 2Cor 4:1
with fear and trembling ye *r* him 2Cor 7:15
spirit, which ye have not *r* 2Cor 11:4
Of the Jews five times *r* I forty 2Cor 11:24
unto you than that ye have *r* Gal 1:9
For I neither *r* it of man Gal 1:12
*R* ye the Spirit by the works of Gal 3:2
but *r* me as an angel of God, even Gal 4:14
which ye have both learned, and *r* Phil 4:9
having *r* of Epaphroditus the Phil 4:18
As ye have therefore *r* Christ Col 2:6
(touching whom ye *r* commandments Col 4:10
which thou hast *r* in the Lord Col 4:17
having *r* the word in much 1Th 1:6
when ye *r* the word of God which 1Th 2:13
ye *r* it not as the word of men, 1Th 2:13
that as ye have *r* of us how ye 1Th 4:1
because they *r* not the love of 2Th 2:10
the tradition which he *r* of us 2Th 3:6
on in the world, *r* up into glory 1Ti 3:16
which God hath created to be *r* 1Ti 4:3
if it be *r* with thanksgiving 1Ti 4:4
disobedience *r* a just recompence Heb 2:2
from them *r* tithes of Abraham Heb 7:6
for under it the people *r* the law Heb 7:11
have *r* the knowledge of the truth Heb 10:26
*r* strength to conceive seed Heb 11:11
not having *r* the promises, but Heb 11:13
he that had *r* the promises Heb 11:17
whence also he *r* him in a figure Heb 11:19
when she had *r* the spies with Heb 11:31
Women *r* their dead raised to life Heb 11:35
through faith, *r* not the promise Heb 11:39
when she had *r* the messengers, and Jas 2:25
from your vain conversation *r* by 1Pet 1:18
As every man hath *r* the gift 1Pet 4:10
For he *r* from God the Father 2Pet 1:17
ye have *r* of him abideth in you 1Jn 2:27
as we have *r* a commandment from 2Jn 4
even as I *r* of my Father Rev 2:27
therefore how thou hast *r* Rev 3:3
which have *r* no kingdom as yet Rev 17:12
that had *r* the mark of the beast Rev 19:20
neither had *r* his mark upon their Rev 20:4

**RECEIVEDST**
in thy lifetime *r* thy good things Lk 16:25

**RECEIVER**
where is the *r* Is 33:18

**RECEIVETH**
is no man that *r* me to house Judg 19:18
or what *r* he of thine hand Job 35:7
is instructed, he *r* knowledge Prov 21:11
but he that *r* gifts overthroweth Prov 29:4
LORD their God, nor *r* correction Jer 7:28
or *r* it with good will at your Mal 2:13
For every one that asketh *r* Mt 7:8
He that *r* you *r* me, and he Mt 10:40
*r* me *r* him that sent me Mt 10:40
He that *r* a prophet in the name Mt 10:41
he that *r* a righteous man in the Mt 10:41
the word, and anon with joy *r* it Mt 13:20
such little child in my name *r* me Mt 18:5
of such children in my name, *r* me Mk 9:37
*r* not me, but him that sent me Mk 9:37
this child in my name *r* me Lk 9:48
receive me *r* him that sent me Lk 9:48
For every one that asketh *r* Lk 11:10
saying, This man *r* sinners Lk 15:2
and no man *r* his testimony Jn 3:32
And he that reapeth *r* wages Jn 4:36
*r* not my words, hath one that Jn 12:48
*r* whomsoever I send *r* me Jn 13:20
*r* me *r* him that sent me Jn 13:20
But the natural man *r* not the 1Cor 2:14
race run all, but one *r* the prize 1Cor 9:24
is dressed, *r* blessing from God Heb 6:7
but there he *r* them, of whom it Heb 7:8
who *r* tithes, payed tithes in Heb 7:9
and scourgeth every son whom he *r* Heb 12:6
preeminence among them, *r* us not 3Jn 9
man knoweth saving he that *r* it Rev 2:17
whosoever *r* the mark of his name Rev 14:11

**RECEIVING**
in not *r* at his hands that which 2Kin 5:20
*r* a commandment unto Silas and Acts 17:15
*r* in themselves that recompence Rom 1:27
what shall the *r* of them be Rom 11:15
with me as concerning giving and *r* Phil 4:15
Wherefore we *r* a kingdom which Heb 12:28
*R* the end of your faith, even the 1Pet 1:9

**RECHAB** (*re'-kab*) See RECHABITES.
*1. A son of Rimmon.*
and the name of the other *R* 2Sa 4:2
sons of Rimmon the Beerothite, *R* 2Sa 4:5
and *R* and Baanah his brother 2Sa 4:6
And David answered *R* and Baanah his 2Sa 4:9
*2. Founder of the Rechabites.*
the son of *R* coming to meet him 2Kin 10:15
went, and Jehonadab the son of *R* 2Kin 10:23
for Jonadab the son of *R* our Jer 35:6
*R* our father in all that he hath Jer 35:8
The words of Jonadab the son of *R* Jer 35:14
*R* have performed the commandment Jer 35:16
Jonadab the son of *R* shall not Jer 35:19
*3. A descendant of Hemath.*
the father of the house of *R* 1Chr 2:55
*4. Father of Malchiah.*
repaired Malchiah the son of *R* Neh 3:14

**RECHABITES** (*rek'-ab-ites*) *Descendants of Rechab 2.*
Go unto the house of the *R* Jer 35:2
sons, and the whole house of the *R* Jer 35:3
house of the *R* pots full of wine Jer 35:5
said unto the house of the *R* Jer 35:18

**RECHAH** *A family of Judah.*
These are the men of *R* 1Chr 4:12

**RECKON**
he shall *r* with him that bought Lev 25:50
then the priest shall *r* unto him Lev 27:18
Then the priest shall *r* unto him Lev 27:23
and by name ye shall *r* the Num 4:32
they shall *r* unto him seven days Eze 44:26
And when he had begun to *r* Mt 18:24
Likewise *r* ye also yourselves to Rom 6:11
For I *r* that the sufferings of Rom 8:18

**RECKONED**
offering shall be *r* unto you Num 18:27
shall not be *r* among the nations Num 23:9
Beeroth also was *r* to Benjamin 2Sa 4:2
Moreover they *r* not with the men, 2Kin 12:15
not to be *r* after the birthright 1Chr 5:1
of their generations was *r* 1Chr 5:7
All these were *r* by genealogies 1Chr 5:17
*r* in all by their genealogies 1Chr 7:5
were *r* by their genealogies 1Chr 7:7
all Israel were *r* by genealogies 1Chr 9:1
These were *r* by their genealogy 1Chr 9:22
to all that were *r* by genealogies 2Chr 31:19
those that were *r* by genealogy Ezr 2:62
with him were *r* by genealogy of Ezr 8:3
that they might be *r* by genealogy Neh 7:5
those that were *r* by genealogy Neh 7:64
they cannot be *r* up in order unto Ps 40:5
I *r* till morning, that, as a lion Is 38:13
he was *r* among the transgressors Lk 22:37
is the reward not *r* of grace Rom 4:4
for we say that faith was *r* to Rom 4:9
How was it then *r* Rom 4:10

**RECKONETH**
servants cometh, and *r* with them Mt 25:19

**RECKONING**
Howbeit there was no *r* made with 2Kin 22:7
therefore they were in one *r* 1Chr 23:11

**RECOMMENDED**
from whence they had been *r* to Acts 14:26
being *r* by the brethren unto the Acts 15:40

**RECOMPENCE**
To me belongeth vengeance, and *r* Deut 32:35
for vanity shall be his *r* Job 15:31
with vengeance, even God with a *r* Is 35:4
his adversaries, *r* to his enemies Is 59:18
to the islands he will repay *r* Is 59:18
that rendereth *r* to his enemies Is 66:6
he will render unto her a *r* Jer 51:6
Render unto them a *r*, O LORD, Lam 3:64
are come, the days of *r* are come Hos 9:7
will ye render me a *r* Joel 3:4
return your *r* upon your own head Joel 3:4
will return your *r* upon your own Joel 3:7
thee again, and a *r* be made thee Lk 14:12
receiving in themselves that *r* of Rom 1:27
stumblingblock, and a *r* unto them Rom 11:9
Now for a *r* in the same, (I speak 2Cor 6:13
received a just *r* of reward Heb 2:2
which hath great *r* of reward Heb 10:35
respect unto the *r* of the reward Heb 11:26

**RECOMPENCES**
the year of *r* for the controversy Is 34:8
for the LORD God of *r* shall Jer 51:56

**RECOMPENSE**
he shall *r* his trespass with the Num 5:7
no kinsman to *r* the trespass unto Num 5:8
The LORD *r* thy work, and a full Ruth 2:12
why should the king *r* it me with 2Sa 19:36
he will *r* it, whether thou refuse Job 34:33
the *r* of a man's hands shall be Prov 12:14
Say not thou, I will *r* evil Prov 20:22
will not keep silence, but will *r* Is 65:6
even *r* into their bosom, Is 65:6
first I will *r* their iniquity and Jer 16:18
I will *r* them according to their Jer 25:14
*r* her according to her work Jer 50:29
will *r* upon thee all thine Eze 7:3
but I will *r* thy ways upon thee, Eze 7:4
will *r* thee for all thine Eze 7:8
I will *r* thee according to thy Eze 7:9
but I will *r* their way upon their Eze 9:10
I will *r* their way upon their own Eze 11:21
therefore I also will *r* thy way Eze 16:43
even it will I *r* upon his own Eze 17:19
they shall *r* your lewdness upon Eze 23:49
to his doings will he *r* him Hos 12:2
and if ye *r* me, swiftly and Joel 3:4
for they cannot *r* thee Lk 14:14
*R* to no man evil for evil Rom 12:17
God to *r* tribulation to them that 2Th 1:6
belongeth unto me, I will *r* Heb 10:30

**RECOMPENSED**
the trespass be *r* unto the LORD Num 5:8
of my hands hath he *r* me 2Sa 22:21
LORD hath *r* me according to my 2Sa 22:25
of my hands hath he *r* me Ps 18:20
the LORD *r* me according to my Ps 18:24
righteous shall be *r* in the earth Prov 11:31
Shall evil be *r* for good Jer 18:20
own way have I *r* upon their heads Eze 22:31
for thou shalt be *r* at the Lk 14:14
it shall be *r* unto him again Rom 11:35

**RECOMPENSEST**
*r* the iniquity of the fathers Jer 32:18

**RECOMPENSING**
by *r* his way upon his own head 2Chr 6:23

**RECONCILE**
of the congregation to *r* withal Lev 6:30
he *r* himself unto his master 1Sa 29:4
so shall ye *r* the house Eze 45:20
that he might *r* both unto God in Eph 2:16
by him to *r* all things unto Col 1:20

**RECONCILED**
first be *r* to thy brother, and Mt 5:24
we were *r* to God by the death of Rom 5:10
of his Son, much more, being *r* Rom 5:10
unmarried, or be *r* to her husband 1Cor 7:11
who hath *r* us to himself by Jesus 2Cor 5:18
in Christ's stead, be ye *r* to God 2Cor 5:20

wicked works, yet now hath he *r* ... Col 1:21

**RECONCILIATION**
sanctified it, to make *r* upon it ... Lev 8:15
they made *r* with their blood upon ... 2Chr 29:24
to make *r* for them, saith the ... Eze 45:15
to make *r* for the house of Israel ... Eze 45:17
to make *r* for iniquity, and to ... Dan 9:24
given to us the ministry of *r* ... 2Cor 5:18
committed unto us the word of *r* ... 2Cor 5:19
to make *r* for the sins of the ... Heb 2:17

**RECONCILING**
made an end of *r* the holy place ... Lev 16:20
of them be the *r* of the world ... Rom 11:15
*r* the world unto himself, not ... 2Cor 5:19

**RECORD**
in all places where I *r* my name I ... Ex 20:24
earth to *r* this day against you, ... Deut 30:19
heaven and earth to *r* against them .. Deut 31:28
the ark of the LORD, and to *r* ... 1Chr 16:4
and therein was a *r* thus written ... Ezr 6:2
is in heaven, and my *r* is on high ... Job 16:19
unto me faithful witnesses to *r* ... Is 8:2
And this is the *r* of John, when ... Jn 1:19
And John bare *r*, saying, I saw the ... Jn 1:32
bare *r* that this is the Son of ... Jn 1:34
him, Thou bearest *r* of thyself ... Jn 8:13
thy *r* is not true ... Jn 8:13
them, Though I bear *r* of myself ... Jn 8:14
yet my *r* is true ... Jn 8:14
raised him from the dead, bare *r* ... Jn 12:17
And he that saw it bare *r*, and his ... Jn 19:35
and his *r* is true ... Jn 19:35
I take you to *r* this day, that I ... Acts 20:26
For I bear them *r* that they have ... Rom 10:2
I call God for a *r* upon my soul ... 2Cor 1:23
For to their power, I bear *r* ... 2Cor 8:3
for I bear you *r*, that, if it had ... Gal 4:15
For God is my *r*, how greatly I ... Phil 1:8
For I bear him *r*, that he hath a ... Col 4:13
are three that bear *r* in heaven ... 1Jn 5:7
the *r* that God gave of his Son ... 1Jn 5:10
And this is the *r*, that God hath ... 1Jn 5:11
yea, and we also bear *r* ... 3Jn 12
and ye know that our *r* is true ... 3Jn 12
Who bare *r* of the word of God, and ... Rev 1:2

**RECORDED**
were *r* chief of the fathers ... Neh 12:22

**RECORDER**
the son of Ahilud was *r* ... 2Sa 8:16
the son of Ahilud was *r* ... 2Sa 20:24
the son of Ahilud, the *r* ... 1Kin 4:3
and Joah the son of Asaph the *r* ... 2Kin 18:18
and Joah the son of Asaph the *r* ... 2Kin 18:37
Jehoshaphat the son of Ahilud, *r* ... 1Chr 18:15
and Joah the son of Joahaz the *r* ... 2Chr 34:8
and Joah, Asaph's son, the *r* ... Is 36:3
and Joah, the son of Asaph, the *r* ... Is 36:22

**RECORDS**
the book of the *r* of thy fathers ... Ezr 4:15
thou find in the book of the *r* ... Ezr 4:15
the book of *r* of the chronicles ... Est 6:1

**RECOUNT**
He shall *r* his worthies ... Nah 2:5

**RECOVER**
ye not *r* them within that time ... Judg 11:26
them, and without fail *r* all ... 1Sa 30:8
as he went to *r* his border at the ... 2Sa 8:3
whether I shall *r* of this disease ... 2Kin 1:2
for he would *r* him of his leprosy ... 2Kin 5:3
that thou mayest *r* him of his ... 2Kin 5:6
unto me to *r* a man of his leprosy ... 2Kin 5:7
over the place, and *r* the leper ... 2Kin 5:11
Shall I *r* of this disease ... 2Kin 8:8
Shall I *r* of this disease ... 2Kin 8:9
unto him, Thou mayest certainly *r* ... 2Kin 8:10
me that thou shouldest surely *r* ... 2Kin 8:14
Neither did Jeroboam *r* strength ... 2Chr 13:20
that they could not *r* themselves ... 2Chr 14:13
O spare me, that I may *r* strength ... Ps 39:13
to *r* the remnant of his people ... Is 11:11
so wilt thou *r* me, and make me to ... Is 38:16
upon the boil, and he shall *r* ... Is 38:21
will *r* my wool and my flax given ... Hos 2:9
on the sick, and they shall *r* ... Mk 16:18
that they may *r* themselves out of ... 2Ti 2:26

**RECOVERED**
David *r* all that the Amalekites ... 1Sa 30:18
David *r* all ... 1Sa 30:19
ought of the spoil that we have *r* ... 1Sa 30:22
him, and *r* the cities of Israel ... 2Kin 13:25
how he *r* Damascus, and Hamath, ... 2Kin 14:28
king of Syria *r* Elath to Syria ... 2Kin 16:6
and laid it on the boil, and he *r* ... 2Kin 20:7
sick, and was *r* of his sickness ... Is 38:9
that he had been sick, and was *r* ... Is 39:1
of the daughter of my people *r* ... Jer 8:22
he had *r* from Ishmael the son of ... Jer 41:16

**RECOVERING**
*r* of sight to the blind, to set ... Lk 4:18

**RED** *The sea dividing Egypt and Arabia.*
And the first came out *r*, all over ... Gen 25:25
thee, with that same *r* pottage ... Gen 25:30
His eyes shall be *r* with wine ... Gen 49:12
and cast them into the *R* sea ... Ex 10:19
of the wilderness of the *R* sea ... Ex 13:18
also are drowned in the *R* sea ... Ex 15:4
brought Israel from the *R* sea ... Ex 15:22
*R* sea even unto the sea of the ... Ex 23:31
And rams' skins dyed *r*, and ... Ex 25:5
the tent of rams' skins dyed *r* ... Ex 26:14
And rams' skins dyed *r*, and ... Ex 35:7
*r* skins of rams, and badgers' ... Ex 35:23
the tent of rams' skins dyed *r* ... Ex 36:19
covering of rams' skins dyed *r* ... Ex 39:34
by the way of the *R* sea ... Num 14:25
thee a *r* heifer without spot ... Num 19:2
mount Hor by the way of the *R* sea ... Num 21:4
LORD, What he did in the *R* sea ... Num 21:14
Elim, and encamped by the *R* sea ... Num 33:10
And they removed from the *R* sea ... Num 33:11
the plain over against the *R* sea ... Deut 1:1
by the way of the *R* sea ... Deut 1:40
by the way of the *R* sea, as the ... Deut 2:1
*R* sea to overflow them as they ... Deut 11:4
up the water of the *R* sea for you ... Josh 2:10
LORD your God did to the *R* sea ... Josh 4:23
and horsemen unto the *R* sea ... Josh 24:6
the wilderness unto the *R* sea ... Judg 11:16
Eloth, on the shore of the *R* sea ... 1Kin 9:26
on the other side as *r* as blood ... 2Kin 3:22
heardest their cry by the *R* sea ... Neh 9:9
and silver, upon a pavement of *r* ... Est 1:6
there is a cup, and the wine is *r* ... Ps 75:8
him at the sea, even at the *R* sea ... Ps 106:7
He rebuked the *R* sea also ... Ps 106:9
and terrible things by the *R* sea ... Ps 106:22
divided the *R* sea into parts ... Ps 136:13
Pharaoh and his host in the *R* sea ... Ps 136:15
thou upon the wine when it is *r* ... Prov 23:31
though they be *r* like crimson ... Is 1:18
ye unto her, A vineyard of *r* wine ... Is 27:2
art thou *r* in thine apparel ... Is 63:2
thereof was heard in the *R* sea ... Jer 49:21
of his mighty men is made *r* ... Nah 2:3
a man riding upon a *r* horse ... Zec 1:8
and behind him were there *r* horses ... Zec 1:8
the first chariot were *r* horses ... Zec 6:2
for the sky is *r* ... Mt 16:2
for the sky is *r* and lowring ... Mt 16:3
land of Egypt, and in the *R* sea ... Acts 7:36
through the *R* sea as by dry land ... Heb 11:29
went out another horse that was *r* ... Rev 6:4
and behold a great *r* dragon ... Rev 12:3

**REDDISH**
bright spot, white, and somewhat *r* ... Lev 13:19
a white bright spot, somewhat *r* ... Lev 13:24
or bald forehead, a white *r* sore ... Lev 13:42
sore be white *r* in his bald head ... Lev 13:43
be greenish or *r* in the garment ... Lev 13:49
hollow strakes, greenish or *r* ... Lev 14:37

**REDEEM**
I will *r* you with a stretched out ... Ex 6:6
an ass thou shalt *r* with a lamb ... Ex 13:13
and if thou wilt not *r* it, then ... Ex 13:13
among thy children shalt thou *r* ... Ex 13:13
the firstborn of my children I *r* ... Ex 13:15
an ass thou shalt *r* with a lamb ... Ex 34:20
and if thou *r* him not, then shalt ... Ex 34:20
of thy sons thou shalt *r* ... Ex 34:20
and if any of his kin come to *r* it ... Lev 25:25
then shall he *r* that which his ... Lev 25:25
And if the man have none to *r* it ... Lev 25:26
and himself be able to *r* it ... Lev 25:26
then he may *r* it within a whole ... Lev 25:29
within a full year may he *r* it ... Lev 25:29
may the Levites *r* at any time ... Lev 25:32
one of his brethren may *r* him ... Lev 25:48
or his uncle's son, may *r* him ... Lev 25:49
unto him of his family may *r* him ... Lev 25:49
if he be able, he may *r* himself ... Lev 25:49
But if he will at all *r* it ... Lev 27:13
sanctified it will *r* his house ... Lev 27:15
the field will in any wise *r* it ... Lev 27:19
And if he will not *r* the field ... Lev 27:20
then he shall *r* it according to ... Lev 27:27
will at all *r* ought of his tithes ... Lev 27:31
of man shalt thou surely *r* ... Num 18:15
of unclean beasts shalt thou *r* ... Num 18:15
from a month old shalt thou *r* ... Num 18:16
of a goat, thou shalt not *r* ... Num 18:17
If thou wilt *r* it ... Ruth 4:4
*r* it: but if thou wilt ... Ruth 4:4
but if thou wilt not *r* it ... Ruth 4:4
there is none to *r* it beside thee ... Ruth 4:4
And he said, I will *r* it ... Ruth 4:4
I cannot *r* it for myself, lest I ... Ruth 4:6
*r* thou my right to thyself ... Ruth 4:6
for I cannot *r* it ... Ruth 4:6
whom God went to *r* for a people ... 2Sa 7:23
whom God went to *r* to be his own .. 1Chr 17:21
is it in our power to *r* them ... Neh 5:5
famine he shall *r* thee from death ... Job 5:20
*R* me from the hand of the mighty ... Job 6:23
*R* Israel, O God, out of all his ... Ps 25:22
*r* me, and be merciful unto me ... Ps 26:11
*r* us for thy mercies' sake ... Ps 44:26
can by any means *r* his brother ... Ps 49:7
But God will *r* my soul from the ... Ps 49:15
Draw nigh unto my soul, and *r* it ... Ps 69:18
He shall *r* their soul from deceit ... Ps 72:14
he shall *r* Israel from all his ... Ps 130:8
at all, that it cannot *r* ... Is 50:2
I will *r* thee out of the hand of ... Jer 15:21
I will *r* them from death ... Hos 13:14
there the LORD shall *r* thee from ... Mic 4:10
To *r* them that were under the law ... Gal 4:5
that he might *r* us from all ... Titus 2:14

**REDEEMED**
The angel which *r* me from all ... Gen 48:16
the people which thou hast *r* ... Ex 15:13
then shall he let her be *r* ... Ex 21:8
to an husband, and not at all *r* ... Lev 19:20
if it be not *r* within the space ... Lev 25:30
they may be *r*, and they shall go ... Lev 25:31
that he is sold he may be *r* again ... Lev 25:48
if he be not *r* in these years, ... Lev 25:54
man, it shall not be *r* any more ... Lev 27:20
or if it be not *r*, then it shall ... Lev 27:27
possession, shall be sold or *r* ... Lev 27:28
be devoted of men, shall be *r* ... Lev 27:29
it shall not be *r* ... Lev 27:33
are to be *r* of the two hundred ... Num 3:46
the odd number of them is to be *r* ... Num 3:48
them that were *r* by the Levites ... Num 3:49
of them that were *r* unto Aaron ... Num 3:51
those that are to be *r* from a ... Num 18:16
*r* you out of the house of bondmen ... Deut 7:8
which thou hast *r* through thy ... Deut 9:26
*r* you out of the house of bondage ... Deut 13:5
Egypt, and the LORD thy God *r* thee. Deut 15:15
people Israel, whom thou hast *r* ... Deut 21:8
and the LORD thy God *r* thee thence Deut 24:18
who hath *r* my soul out of all ... 2Sa 4:9
that hath *r* my soul out of all ... 1Kin 1:29
whom thou hast *r* out of Egypt ... 1Chr 17:21
whom thou hast *r* by thy great ... Neh 1:10
have *r* our brethren the Jews ... Neh 5:8
thou hast *r* me, O LORD God of ... Ps 31:5
and my soul, which thou hast *r* ... Ps 71:23
inheritance, which thou hast *r* ... Ps 74:2
hast with thine arm *r* thy people ... Ps 77:15
*r* them from the hand of the enemy ... Ps 106:10
Let the *r* of the LORD say so, ... Ps 107:2
whom he hath *r* from the hand of ... Ps 107:2
hath *r* us from our enemies ... Ps 136:24
Zion shall be *r* with judgment ... Is 1:27
who *r* Abraham, concerning the ... Is 29:22
but the *r* shall walk there ... Is 35:9
for I have *r* thee, I have called ... Is 43:1
for I have *r* thee ... Is 44:22
for the LORD hath *r* Jacob ... Is 44:23
The LORD hath *r* his servant Jacob ... Is 48:20
Therefore the *r* of the LORD shall ... Is 51:11
ye shall be *r* without money ... Is 52:3
his people, he hath *r* Jerusalem ... Is 52:9
holy people, The *r* of the LORD ... Is 62:12
and the year of my *r* is come ... Is 63:4
his love and in his pity he *r* them ... Is 63:9
For the LORD hath *r* Jacob ... Jer 31:11
thou hast *r* my life ... Lam 3:58
though I have *r* them, yet they ... Hos 7:13
*r* thee out of the house of ... Mic 6:4
for I have *r* them ... Zec 10:8
he hath visited and *r* his people, ... Lk 1:68
he which should have *r* Israel ... Lk 24:21
Christ hath *r* us from the curse ... Gal 3:13
not *r* with corruptible things ... 1Pet 1:18
hast *r* us to God by thy blood out ... Rev 5:9
which were *r* from the earth ... Rev 14:3
These were *r* from among men, ... Rev 14:4

**REDEEMEDST**
which thou *r* to thee from Egypt, ... 2Sa 7:23

**REDEEMER**
For I know that my *r* liveth ... Job 19:25
O LORD, my strength, and my *r* ... Ps 19:14
rock, and the high God their *r* ... Ps 78:35
For their *r* is mighty ... Prov 23:11
thee, saith the LORD, and thy *r* ... Is 41:14
Thus saith the LORD, your *r* ... Is 43:14
and his *r* the LORD of hosts ... Is 44:6
Thus saith the LORD, thy *r* ... Is 44:24
As for our *r*, the LORD of hosts ... Is 47:4
Thus saith the LORD, thy *R* ... Is 48:17
the *R* of Israel, and his Holy One, ... Is 49:7
the LORD am thy Saviour and thy *R* ... Is 49:26
thy *R* the Holy One of Israel ... Is 54:5
on thee, saith the LORD thy *R* ... Is 54:8
the *R* shall come to Zion, and unto ... Is 59:20
the LORD am thy Saviour and thy *R* ... Is 60:16
O LORD, art our father, our *r* ... Is 63:16
Their *R* is strong ... Jer 50:34

**REDEEMETH**
The LORD *r* the soul of his ... Ps 34:22
Who *r* thy life from destruction ... Ps 103:4

**REDEEMING**
time in Israel concerning *r* ... Ruth 4:7
*R* the time, because the days are ... Eph 5:16
them that are without, *r* the time ... Col 4:5

**REDEMPTION**
ye shall grant a *r* for the land ... Lev 25:24
give again the price of his *r* out ... Lev 25:51
give him again the price of his *r* ... Lev 25:52
Moses took the *r* money of them ... Num 3:49
(For the *r* of their soul is ... Ps 49:8
He sent *r* unto his people ... Ps 111:9
mercy, and with him is plenteous *r* ... Ps 130:7
for the right of *r* is thine to ... Jer 32:7
is thine, and the *r* is thine ... Jer 32:8
that looked for *r* in Jerusalem ... Lk 2:38
for your *r* draweth nigh ... Lk 21:28

the r that is in Christ Jesus ... Rom 3:24
to wit, the r of our body ... Rom 8:23
and sanctification, and r ... 1Cor 1:30
In whom we have r through his ... Eph 1:7
the r of the purchased possession ... Eph 1:14
ye are sealed unto the day of r ... Eph 4:30
In whom we have r through his ... Col 1:14
having obtained eternal r for us ... Heb 9:12
for the r of the transgressions ... Heb 9:15

**REDNESS**
who hath r of eyes ... Prov 23:29

**REDOUND**
of many r to the glory of God ... 2Cor 4:15

**REED**
as a r is shaken in the water, and ... 1Kin 14:15
upon the staff of this bruised r ... 2Kin 18:21
trees, in the covert of the r ... Job 40:21
in the staff of this broken r ... Is 36:6
A bruised r shall he not break, ... Is 42:3
staff of r to the house of Israel ... Eze 29:6
in his hand, and a measuring r ... Eze 40:3
in the man's hand a measuring r ... Eze 40:5
breadth of the building, one r ... Eze 40:5
and the height, one r ... Eze 40:5
the gate, which was one r broad ... Eze 40:6
the gate, which was one r broad ... Eze 40:6
was one r long, and one r broad ... Eze 40:7
of the gate within was one r ... Eze 40:7
porch of the gate within, one r ... Eze 40:8
were a full r of six great cubits ... Eze 41:8
east side with the measuring r ... Eze 42:16
with the measuring r round about ... Eze 42:16
with the measuring r round about ... Eze 42:17
reeds, with the measuring r ... Eze 42:18
reeds with the measuring r ... Eze 42:19
A r shaken with the wind ... Mt 11:7
A bruised r shall he not break, ... Mt 12:20
head, and a r in his right hand ... Mt 27:29
they spit upon him, and took the r ... Mt 27:30
it with vinegar, and put it on a r ... Mt 27:48
smote him on the head with a r ... Mk 15:19
full of vinegar, and put it on a r ... Mk 15:36
A r shaken with the wind ... Lk 7:24
was given me a r like unto a rod ... Rev 11:1
a golden r to measure the city ... Rev 21:15
he measured the city with the r ... Rev 21:16

**REEDS**
the r and flags shall wither ... Is 19:6
The paper r by the brooks, by the ... Is 19:7
each lay, shall be grass with r ... Is 35:7
the r they have burned with fire, ... Jer 51:32
measuring reed, five hundred r ... Eze 42:16
the north side, five hundred r ... Eze 42:17
the south side, five hundred r ... Eze 42:18
measured five hundred r with the ... Eze 42:19
round about, five hundred r long ... Eze 42:20
of five and twenty thousand r ... Eze 45:1
and twenty thousand r in breadth ... Eze 48:8

**REEL**
They r to and fro, and stagger like ... Ps 107:27
The earth shall r to and fro like ... Is 24:20

**REELAIAH** *(re-el-ah'-yah) A clan leader with Zerubbabel.*
Jeshua, Nehemiah, Seraiah, R ... Ezr 2:2

**REFINE**
will r them as silver is refined, ... Zec 13:9

**REFINED**
altar of incense r gold by weight ... 1Chr 28:18
thousand talents of r silver ... 1Chr 29:4
of wines on the lees well r ... Is 25:6
Behold, I have r thee, but not ... Is 48:10
will refine them as silver is r ... Zec 13:9

**REFINER**
And he shall sit as a r and ... Mal 3:3

**REFINER'S**
for he is like a r fire, and like ... Mal 3:2

**REFORMATION**
on them until the time of r ... Heb 9:10

**REFORMED**
if ye will not be r by me by ... Lev 26:23

**REFRAIN**
Then Joseph could not r himself ... Gen 45:1
Therefore I will not r my mouth ... Job 7:11
r thy foot from their path ... Prov 1:15
a time to r from embracing ... Eccl 3:5
for my praise will I r for thee ... Is 48:9
Wilt thou r thyself for these ... Is 64:12
R thy voice from weeping, and ... Jer 31:16
R from these men, and let them ... Acts 5:38
let him r his tongue from evil, ... 1Pet 3:10

**REFRAINED**
r himself, and said, Set on bread ... Gen 43:31
Nevertheless Haman r himself ... Est 5:10
The princes r talking, and laid ... Job 29:9
lo, I have not r my lips, O LORD, ... Ps 40:9
I have r my feet from every evil ... Ps 119:101
I have been still, and r myself ... Is 42:14
they have not r their feet ... Jer 14:10

**REFRAINETH**
but he that r his lips is wise ... Prov 10:19

**REFRESH**
r thyself, and I will give thee a ... 1Kin 13:7
go unto his friends to r himself ... Acts 27:3
r my bowels in the Lord ... Philem 20

**REFRESHED**
and the stranger, may be r ... Ex 23:12
seventh day he rested, and was r ... Ex 31:17
so Saul was r, and was well, and ... 1Sa 16:23
came weary, and r themselves there ... 2Sa 16:14
I will speak, that I may be r ... Job 32:20
will of God, and may with you be r ... Rom 15:32
For they have r my spirit ... 1Cor 16:18
his spirit was r by you all ... 2Cor 7:13
for he oft r me, and was not ... 2Ti 1:16
of the saints are r by thee ... Philem 7

**REFRESHETH**
for he r the soul of his masters ... Prov 25:13

**REFRESHING**
and this is the r ... Is 28:12
when the times of r shall come ... Acts 3:19

**REFUGE**
there shall be six cities for r ... Num 35:6
cities to be cities of r for you ... Num 35:11
you cities for r from the avenger ... Num 35:12
six cities shall ye have for r ... Num 35:13
which shall be cities of r ... Num 35:14
These six cities shall be a r ... Num 35:15
restore him to the city of his r ... Num 35:25
the border of the city of his r ... Num 35:26
the borders of the city of his r ... Num 35:27
his r until the death of the high ... Num 35:28
that is fled to the city of his r ... Num 35:32
The eternal God is thy r, and ... Deut 33:27
Appoint out for you cities of r ... Josh 20:2
they shall be your r from the ... Josh 20:3
to be a city of r for the slayer ... Josh 21:13
to be a city of r for the slayer ... Josh 21:21
to be a city of r for the slayer ... Josh 21:27
to be a city of r for the slayer ... Josh 21:32
to be a city of r for the slayer ... Josh 21:38
salvation, my high tower, and my r ... 2Sa 22:3
namely, Hebron, the city of r ... 1Chr 6:57
unto them, of the cities of r ... 1Chr 6:67
will be a r for the oppressed ... Ps 9:9
a r in times of trouble ... Ps 9:9
poor, because the LORD is his r ... Ps 14:6
God is our r and strength, a very ... Ps 46:1
the God of Jacob is our r ... Ps 46:7
the God of Jacob is our r ... Ps 46:11
is known in her palaces for a r ... Ps 48:3
of thy wings will I make my r ... Ps 57:1
r in the day of my trouble ... Ps 59:16
the rock of my strength, and my r ... Ps 62:7
God is a r for us ... Ps 62:8
but thou art my strong r ... Ps 71:7
will say of the LORD, He is my r ... Ps 91:2
hast made the LORD, which is my r ... Ps 91:9
and my God is the rock of my r ... Ps 94:22
hills are a r for the wild goats ... Ps 104:18
r failed me ... Ps 142:4
I said, Thou art my r and my ... Ps 142:5
children shall have a place of r ... Prov 14:26
the heat, and for a place of r ... Is 4:6
a r from the storm, a shadow from ... Is 25:4
for we have made lies our r ... Is 28:15
shall sweep away the r of lies ... Is 28:17
my r in the day of affliction, ... Jer 16:19
who have fled for r to lay hold ... Heb 6:18

**REFUSE**
if thou r to let him go, behold, ... Ex 4:23
if thou r to let them go, behold, ... Ex 8:2
For if thou r to let them go, and ... Ex 9:2
How long wilt thou r to humble ... Ex 10:3
if thou r to let my people go, ... Ex 10:4
Moses, How long r ye to keep my ... Ex 16:28
utterly r to give her unto him ... Ex 22:17
every thing that was vile and r ... 1Sa 15:9
recompense it, whether thou r ... Job 34:33
and be wise, and r it not ... Prov 8:33
because they r to do judgment ... Prov 21:7
for his hands r to labour ... Prov 21:25
But if ye r and rebel, ye shall be ... Is 1:20
that he may know to r the evil ... Is 7:15
child shall know to r the evil ... Is 7:16
fast deceit, they r to return ... Jer 8:5
through deceit they r to know me ... Jer 9:6
which r to hear my words, which ... Jer 13:10
if they r to take the cup at ... Jer 25:28
But if thou r to go forth ... Jer 38:21
r in the midst of the people ... Lam 3:45
yea, and sell the r of the wheat ... Amos 8:6
worthy of death, I r not to die ... Acts 25:11
But r profane and old wives' ... 1Ti 4:7
But the younger widows r ... 1Ti 5:11
See that ye r not him that ... Heb 12:25

**REFUSED**
but he r to be comforted ... Gen 37:35
But he r, and said unto his ... Gen 39:8
And his father r, and said, I know ... Gen 48:19
Thus Edom r to give Israel ... Num 20:21
Nevertheless the people r to obey ... 1Sa 8:19
because I have r him ... 1Sa 16:7
But he r, and said, I will not eat ... 1Sa 28:23
Howbeit he r to turn aside ... 2Sa 2:23
but he r to eat ... 2Sa 13:9
And the man r to smite him ... 1Kin 20:35
which he r to give thee for money ... 1Kin 21:15
to take it; but he r ... 2Kin 5:16
r to obey, neither were mindful ... Neh 9:17
But the queen Vashti r to come at ... Est 1:12
The things that my soul r to ... Job 6:7
my soul r to be comforted ... Ps 77:2
of God, and r to walk in his law ... Ps 78:10
Moreover he r the tabernacle of ... Ps 78:67
The stone which the builders r is ... Ps 118:22
Because I have called, and ye r ... Prov 1:24
a wife of youth, when thou wast r ... Is 54:6
but they have r to receive ... Jer 5:3
they have r to return ... Jer 5:3
which r to hear my words ... Jer 11:10
r to be comforted for her ... Jer 31:15
they r to let them go ... Jer 50:33
for they have r my judgments ... Eze 5:6
king, because they r to return ... Hos 11:5
But they r to hearken, and pulled ... Zec 7:11
This Moses whom they r, saying, ... Acts 7:35
God is good, and nothing to be r ... 1Ti 4:4
r to be called the son of ... Heb 11:24
not who r him that spake on earth ... Heb 12:25

**REFUSEDST**
forehead, thou r to be ashamed ... Jer 3:3

**REFUSETH**
he r to let the people go ... Ex 7:14
for the LORD r to give me leave ... Num 22:13
and said, Balaam r to come with us ... Num 22:14
My husband's brother r to raise ... Deut 25:7
but he that r reproof erreth ... Prov 10:17
be to him that r instruction ... Prov 13:18
He that r instruction despiseth ... Prov 15:32
Forasmuch as this people r the ... Is 8:6
incurable, which r to be healed ... Jer 15:18

**REGARD**
Also r not your stuff ... Gen 45:20
and let them not r vain words ... Ex 5:9
R not them that have familiar ... Lev 19:31
which shall not r the person of ... Deut 28:50
not, neither did she r it ... 1Sa 4:20
r this man of Belial, even Nabal ... 1Sa 25:25
r not this thing ... 2Sa 13:20
were it not that I r the presence ... 2Kin 3:14
let not God r it from above, ... Job 3:4
neither will the Almighty r it ... Job 35:13
Take heed, r not iniquity ... Job 36:21
Because they r not the works of ... Ps 28:5
hated them that r lying vanities ... Ps 31:6
If I r iniquity in my heart, the ... Ps 66:18
shall the God of Jacob r it ... Ps 94:7
He will r the prayer of the ... Ps 102:17
That thou mayest r discretion ... Prov 5:2
He will not r any ransom ... Prov 6:35
that in r of the oath of God ... Eccl 8:2
but they r not the work of the ... Is 5:12
them, which shall not r silver ... Is 13:17
he will no more r them ... Lam 4:16
Neither shall he r the God of his ... Dan 11:37
desire of women, nor r any god ... Dan 11:37
neither will I r the peace ... Amos 5:22
Behold ye among the heathen, and r ... Hab 1:5
will he r your persons ... Mal 1:9
Though I fear not God, nor r man ... Lk 18:4
And to him they had r, because ... Acts 8:11
day, to the Lord he doth not r it ... Rom 14:6

**REGARDED**
he that r not the word of the ... Ex 9:21
nor any to answer, nor any that r ... 1Kin 18:29
hast r me according to the estate ... 1Chr 17:17
Nevertheless he r their ... Ps 106:44
out my hand, and no man r ... Prov 1:24
men, O king, have not r thee ... Dan 3:12
For he hath r the low estate of ... Lk 1:48
feared not God, neither r man ... Lk 18:2
I r them not, saith the Lord ... Heb 8:9

**REGARDEST**
that thou r neither princes nor ... 2Sa 19:6
I stand up, and thou r me not ... Job 30:20
for thou r not the person of men ... Mt 22:16
for thou r not the person of men, ... Mk 12:14

**REGARDETH**
which r not persons, nor taketh ... Deut 10:17
nor r the rich more than the poor ... Job 34:19
neither r he the crying of the ... Job 39:7
A righteous man r the life of his ... Prov 12:10
but he that r reproof shall be ... Prov 13:18
but he that r reproof is prudent ... Prov 15:5
but the wicked r not to know it ... Prov 29:7
that is higher than the highest r ... Eccl 5:8
he that r the clouds shall not ... Eccl 11:4
despised the cities, he r no man ... Is 33:8
r not thee, O king, nor the ... Dan 6:13
insomuch that he r not the ... Mal 2:13
He that r the day, r it ... Rom 14:6
he that r not the day, to the ... Rom 14:6

**REGARDING**
perish for ever without any r it ... Job 4:20
not r his life, to supply your ... Phil 2:30

**REGEM** *(re'-ghem) A son of Jahdai.*
R, and Jotham, and Gesham ... 1Chr 2:47

**REGEM-MELECH** *(re''-ghem-me'-lek) A messenger for Zechariah.*
the house of God Sherezer and R ... Zec 7:2

**REGENERATION**
in the *r* when the Son of man ... Mt 19:28
he saved us, by the washing of *r* ... Titus 3:5

**REGION**
all the *r* of Argob, the kingdom ... Deut 3:4
all the *r* of Argob, with all ... Deut 3:13
of Abinadab, in all the *r* of Dor ... 1Kin 4:11
him also pertained the *r* of Argob ... 1Kin 4:13
all the *r* on this side the river ... 1Kin 4:24
all the *r* round about Jordan, ... Mt 3:5
and to them which sat in the *r* ... Mt 4:16
all the *r* round about Galilee ... Mk 1:28
through that whole *r* round about ... Mk 6:55
of the *r* of Trachonitis, and ... Lk 3:1
him through all the *r* round about ... Lk 4:14
throughout all the *r* round about ... Lk 7:17
published throughout all the *r* ... Acts 13:49
unto the *r* that lieth round about ... Acts 14:6
the *r* of Galatia, and were ... Acts 16:6

**REGIONS**
abroad throughout the *r* of Judaea ... Acts 8:1
the gospel in the *r* beyond you ... 2Cor 10:16
this boasting in the *r* of Achaia ... 2Cor 11:10
I came into the *r* of Syria ... Gal 1:21

**REGISTER**
These sought their *r* among those ... Ezr 2:62
I found a *r* of the genealogy of ... Neh 7:5
These sought their *r* among those ... Neh 7:64

**REHABIAH** (*re-hab-i'-ah*) *A son of Eliezer.*
sons of Eliezer were, *R* the chief ... 1Chr 23:17
but the sons of *R* were very many ... 1Chr 23:17
Concerning *R* ... 1Chr 24:21
of the sons of *R*, the first was ... 1Chr 24:21
*R* his son, and Jeshaiah his son, ... 1Chr 26:25

**REHEARSE**
*r* it in the ears of Joshua ... Ex 17:14
there shall they *r* the righteous ... Judg 5:11

**REHEARSED**
he *r* them in the ears of the LORD ... 1Sa 8:21
spake, they *r* them before Saul ... 1Sa 17:31
But Peter *r* the matter from the ... Acts 11:4
they *r* all that God had done with ... Acts 14:27

**REHOB** (*re'-hob*)
*1. A Levitical city in Asher.*
from the wilderness of Zin unto *R* ... Num 13:21
and *R*, and Hammon ... Josh 19:28
Ummah also, and Aphek, and *R* ... Josh 19:30
suburbs, and *R* with her suburbs ... Josh 21:31
of Helbah, nor of Aphik, nor of *R* ... Judg 1:31
and the Syrians of Zoba, and of *R* ... 2Sa 10:8
suburbs, and *R* with her suburbs ... 1Chr 6:75
*2. Father of Hadadezer.*
also Hadadezer, the son of *R* ... 2Sa 8:3
the spoil of Hadadezer, son of *R* ... 2Sa 8:12
*3. A Levite.*
Micha, *R*, Hashabiah, ... Neh 10:11

**REHOBOAM** (*re-ho-bo'-am*) See ROBOAM. *A son of Solomon and king of Judah.*
*R* his son reigned in his stead ... 1Kin 11:43
And *R* went to Shechem ... 1Kin 12:1
of Israel came, and spake unto *R* ... 1Kin 12:3
king *R* consulted with the old men ... 1Kin 12:6
people came to *R* the third day ... 1Kin 12:12
of Judah, *R* reigned over them ... 1Kin 12:17
Then king *R* sent Adoram, who was ... 1Kin 12:18
Therefore king *R* made speed to ... 1Kin 12:18
when *R* was come to Jerusalem, he ... 1Kin 12:21
again to *R* the son of Solomon ... 1Kin 12:21
Speak unto *R*, the son of Solomon, ... 1Kin 12:23
even unto *R* king of Judah, and ... 1Kin 12:27
go again to *R* king of Judah ... 1Kin 12:27
*R* the son of Solomon reigned in ... 1Kin 14:21
*R* was forty and one years old when ... 1Kin 14:21
pass in the fifth year of king *R* ... 1Kin 14:25
king *R* made in their stead brasen ... 1Kin 14:27
Now the rest of the acts of *R* ... 1Kin 14:29
And there was war between *R* ... 1Kin 14:30
*R* slept with his fathers, and was ... 1Kin 14:31
And there was war between *R* ... 1Kin 15:6
And Solomon's son was *R*, Abia his ... 1Chr 3:10
*R* his son reigned in his stead ... 2Chr 9:31
And *R* went to Shechem ... 2Chr 10:1
and all Israel came and spake to *R* ... 2Chr 10:3
king *R* took counsel with the old ... 2Chr 10:6
people came to *R* on the third day ... 2Chr 10:12
king *R* forsook the counsel of the ... 2Chr 10:13
of Judah, *R* reigned over them ... 2Chr 10:17
Then king *R* sent Hadoram that was ... 2Chr 10:18
But king *R* made speed to get him ... 2Chr 10:18
when *R* was come to Jerusalem, he ... 2Chr 11:1
bring the kingdom again to *R* ... 2Chr 11:1
Speak unto *R* the son of Solomon, ... 2Chr 11:3
*R* dwelt in Jerusalem, and built ... 2Chr 11:5
made *R* the son of Solomon strong, ... 2Chr 11:17
*R* took him Mahalath the daughter ... 2Chr 11:18
*R* loved Maachah the daughter of ... 2Chr 11:21
*R* made Abijah the son of Maachah ... 2Chr 11:22
when *R* had established the ... 2Chr 12:1
*R* Shishak king of Egypt came up ... 2Chr 12:2
came Shemaiah the prophet to *R* ... 2Chr 12:5
king *R* made shields of brass ... 2Chr 12:10
So king *R* strengthened himself in ... 2Chr 12:13
for *R* was one and forty years old ... 2Chr 12:13
Now the acts of *R*, first and last, ... 2Chr 12:15
And there were wars between *R* ... 2Chr 12:15
*R* slept with his fathers, and was ... 2Chr 12:16
against *R* the son of Solomon ... 2Chr 13:7
when *R* was young and ... 2Chr 13:7

**REHOBOTH** (*re'-ho-both*)
*1. A city in Assyria.*
and builded Nineveh, and the city *R* ... Gen 10:11
Saul of *R* by the river reigned in ... Gen 36:37
Shaul of *R* by the river reigned ... 1Chr 1:48
*2. A well Isaac dug.*
And he called the name of it *R* ... Gen 26:22

**REHOBOTH-IR** See REHOBOTH.

**REHUM** (*re'-hum*) See NEHUM.
*1. A clan leader with Zerubbabel.*
Bilshan, Mizpar, Bigvai, *R* ... Ezr 2:2
Shechaniah, *R*, Meremoth, ... Neh 12:3
*2. An officer of King Artaxerxes.*
*R* the chancellor and Shimshai the ... Ezr 4:8
Then wrote *R* the chancellor, and ... Ezr 4:9
an answer unto *R* the chancellor ... Ezr 4:17
letter was read before *R*, and ... Ezr 4:23
*3. A Levite rebuilder of Jerusalem's wall.*
the Levites, *R* the son of Bani ... Neh 3:17
*4. A renewer of the covenant.*
*R*, Hashabnah, Maaseiah, ... Neh 10:25

**REI** (*re'-i*) *A friend of David.*
the prophet, and Shimei, and *R* ... 1Kin 1:8

**REIGN**
him, Shalt thou indeed *r* over us ... Gen 37:8
The LORD shall *r* for ever ... Ex 15:18
that hate you shall *r* over you ... Lev 26:17
thou shalt *r* over many nations, ... Deut 15:6
but they shall not *r* over thee ... Deut 15:6
*r* over you, or that one *r* ... Judg 9:2
the olive tree, *R* thou over us ... Judg 9:8
fig tree, Come thou, and *r* over us ... Judg 9:10
the vine, Come thou, and *r* over us ... Judg 9:12
bramble, Come thou, and *r* over us ... Judg 9:14
me, that I should not *r* over them ... 1Sa 8:7
the king that shall *r* over them ... 1Sa 8:9
of the king that shall *r* over you ... 1Sa 8:11
this same shall *r* over my people ... 1Sa 9:17
that said, Shall Saul *r* over us ... 1Sa 11:12
but a king shall *r* over us ... 1Sa 12:12
when he began to *r* over Israel ... 2Sa 2:10
that thou mayest *r* over all that ... 2Sa 3:21
years old when he began to *r* ... 2Sa 5:4
the son of Haggith doth *r* ... 1Kin 1:11
Solomon thy son shall *r* after me ... 1Kin 1:13
why then doth Adonijah *r* ... 1Kin 1:13
Solomon thy son shall *r* after me ... 1Kin 1:17
said, Adonijah shall *r* after me ... 1Kin 1:24
Solomon thy son shall *r* after me ... 1Kin 1:30
faces on me, that I should *r* ... 1Kin 2:15
year of Solomon's *r* over Israel ... 1Kin 6:1
thou shalt *r* according to all ... 1Kin 11:37
one years old when he began to *r* ... 1Kin 14:21
the son of Jeroboam began to *r* ... 1Kin 15:25
to *r* over all Israel in Tirzah ... 1Kin 15:33
Baasha to *r* over Israel in Tirzah ... 1Kin 16:8
came to pass, when he began to *r* ... 1Kin 16:11
did Zimri *r* seven days in Tirzah ... 1Kin 16:15
Judah began Omri to *r* over Israel ... 1Kin 16:23
the son of Omri to *r* over Israel ... 1Kin 16:29
the son of Asa began to *r* over ... 1Kin 22:41
five years old when he began to *r* ... 1Kin 22:42
the son of Ahab began to *r* over ... 1Kin 22:51
the son of Ahab began to *r* over ... 2Kin 3:1
king of Judah began to *r* ... 2Kin 8:16
old was he when he began to *r* ... 2Kin 8:17
Jehoram king of Judah begin to *r* ... 2Kin 8:25
was Ahaziah when he began to *r* ... 2Kin 8:26
began Ahaziah to *r* over Judah ... 2Kin 9:29
Athaliah did *r* over the land ... 2Kin 11:3
was Jehoash when he began to *r* ... 2Kin 11:21
year of Jehu Jehoash began to *r* ... 2Kin 12:1
began to *r* over Israel in Samaria ... 2Kin 13:1
to *r* over Israel in Samaria ... 2Kin 13:10
five years old when he began to *r* ... 2Kin 14:2
of Israel began to *r* in Samaria ... 2Kin 14:23
son of Amaziah king of Judah to *r* ... 2Kin 15:1
old was he when he began to *r* ... 2Kin 15:2
*r* over Israel in Samaria six ... 2Kin 15:8
of Jabesh began to *r* in the nine ... 2Kin 15:13
the son of Gadi to *r* over Israel ... 2Kin 15:17
began to *r* over Israel in Samaria ... 2Kin 15:23
began to *r* over Israel in Samaria ... 2Kin 15:27
son of Uzziah king of Judah to *r* ... 2Kin 15:32
old was he when he began to *r* ... 2Kin 15:33
Jotham king of Judah began to *r* ... 2Kin 16:1
old was Ahaz when he began to *r* ... 2Kin 16:2
to *r* in Samaria over Israel nine ... 2Kin 17:1
of Ahaz king of Judah began to *r* ... 2Kin 18:1
old was he when he began to *r* ... 2Kin 18:2
years old when he began to *r* ... 2Kin 21:1
two years old when he began to *r* ... 2Kin 21:19
years old when he began to *r* ... 2Kin 22:1
years old when he began to *r* ... 2Kin 23:31
that he might not *r* in Jerusalem ... 2Kin 23:33
five years old when he began to *r* ... 2Kin 23:36
years old when he began to *r* ... 2Kin 24:8
him in the eighth year of his *r* ... 2Kin 24:12
one years old when he began to *r* ... 2Kin 24:18
pass in the ninth year of his *r* ... 2Kin 25:1
to *r* did lift up the head of ... 2Kin 25:27
their cities unto the *r* of David ... 1Chr 4:31
In the fortieth year of the *r* of ... 1Chr 26:31
With all his *r* and his might, and ... 1Chr 29:30
and hast made me to *r* in his stead ... 2Chr 1:8
in the fourth year of his *r* ... 2Chr 3:2
years old when he began to *r* ... 2Chr 12:13
began Abijah to *r* over Judah ... 2Chr 13:1
fifteenth year of the *r* of Asa ... 2Chr 15:10
and thirtieth year of the *r* of Asa ... 2Chr 15:19
thirtieth year of the *r* of Asa ... 2Chr 16:1
ninth year of his *r* was diseased ... 2Chr 16:12
the one and fortieth year of his *r* ... 2Chr 16:13
of his *r* he sent to his princes ... 2Chr 17:7
five years old when he began to *r* ... 2Chr 20:31
two years old when he began to *r* ... 2Chr 21:5
old was he when he began to *r* ... 2Chr 21:20
was Ahaziah when he began to *r* ... 2Chr 22:2
Behold, the king's son shall *r* ... 2Chr 23:3
years old when he began to *r* ... 2Chr 24:1
five years old when he began to *r* ... 2Chr 25:1
old was Uzziah when he began to *r* ... 2Chr 26:3
five years old when he began to *r* ... 2Chr 27:1
years old when he began to *r* ... 2Chr 27:8
years old when he began to *r* ... 2Chr 28:1
began to *r* when he was five ... 2Chr 29:1
He in the first year of his *r* ... 2Chr 29:3
in his *r* did cast away in his ... 2Chr 29:19
years old when he began to *r* ... 2Chr 33:1
years old when he began to *r* ... 2Chr 33:21
years old when he began to *r* ... 2Chr 34:1
For in the eighth year of his *r* ... 2Chr 34:3
in the eighteenth year of his *r* ... 2Chr 34:8
the *r* of Josiah was this passover ... 2Chr 35:19
years old when he began to *r* ... 2Chr 36:2
five years old when he began to *r* ... 2Chr 36:5
years old when he began to *r* ... 2Chr 36:9
years old when he began to *r* ... 2Chr 36:11
his sons until the *r* of the ... 2Chr 36:20
even until the *r* of Darius king ... Ezr 4:5
in the *r* of Ahasuerus, in the ... Ezr 4:6
in the beginning of his *r* ... Ezr 4:6
of the *r* of Darius king of Persia ... Ezr 4:24
year of the *r* of Darius the king ... Ezr 6:15
in the *r* of Artaxerxes king of ... Ezr 7:1
in the *r* of Artaxerxes the king ... Ezr 8:1
to the *r* of Darius the Persian ... Neh 12:22
In the third year of his *r* ... Est 1:3
in the seventh year of his *r* ... Est 2:16
That the hypocrite *r* not, lest ... Job 34:30
The LORD shall *r* for ever ... Ps 146:10
By me kings *r*, and princes decree ... Prov 8:15
For out of prison he cometh to *r* ... Eccl 4:14
of hosts shall *r* in mount Zion ... Is 24:23
a king shall *r* in righteousness, ... Is 32:1
in the thirteenth year of his *r* ... Jer 1:2
Shalt thou *r*, because thou ... Jer 22:15
Branch, and a King shall *r* ... Jer 23:5
In the beginning of the *r* of ... Jer 26:1
In the beginning of the *r* of ... Jer 27:1
in the beginning of the *r* of ... Jer 28:1
have a son to *r* upon his throne ... Jer 33:21
the *r* of Zedekiah king of Judah ... Jer 49:34
in the fourth year of his *r* ... Jer 51:59
years old when he began to *r* ... Jer 52:1
pass in the ninth year of his *r* ... Jer 52:4
of his *r* lifted up the head of ... Jer 52:31
In the third year of the *r* of ... Dan 1:1
year of the *r* of Nebuchadnezzar ... Dan 2:1
prospered in the *r* of Darius ... Dan 6:28
in the *r* of Cyrus the Persian ... Dan 6:28
In the third year of the *r* of ... Dan 8:1
In the first year of his *r* I ... Dan 9:2
the LORD shall *r* over them in ... Mic 4:7
he heard that Archelaus did *r* in ... Mt 2:22
he shall *r* over the house of ... Lk 1:33
year of the *r* of Tiberius Caesar ... Lk 3:1
not have this man to *r* over us ... Lk 19:14
not that I should *r* over them ... Lk 19:27
shall *r* in life by one, Jesus ... Rom 5:17
even so might grace *r* through ... Rom 5:21
therefore *r* in your mortal body ... Rom 6:12
shall rise to *r* over the Gentiles ... Rom 15:12
and I would to God ye did *r* ... 1Cor 4:8
that we also might *r* with you ... 1Cor 4:8
For he must *r*, till he hath put ... 1Cor 15:25
suffer, we shall also *r* with him ... 2Ti 2:12
and we shall *r* on the earth ... Rev 5:10
and he shall *r* for ever and ever ... Rev 11:15
shall *r* with him a thousand years ... Rev 20:6
and they shall *r* for ever and ever ... Rev 22:5

**REIGNED**
kings that *r* in the land of Edom ... Gen 36:31
before there *r* any king over the ... Gen 36:31
And Bela the son of Beor *r* in Edom ... Gen 36:32
of Zerah of Bozrah *r* in his stead ... Gen 36:33
the land of Temani *r* in his stead ... Gen 36:34
the field of Moab, *r* in his stead ... Gen 36:35
Samlah of Masrekah *r* in his stead ... Gen 36:36
by the river *r* in his stead ... Gen 36:37
the son of Achbor *r* in his stead ... Gen 36:38
died, and Hadar *r* in his stead ... Gen 36:39
*r* in mount Hermon, and in Salcah, ... Josh 12:5
which *r* in Heshbon, unto the ... Josh 13:10
which *r* in Ashtaroth and in Edrei, ... Josh 13:12
which *r* in Heshbon, whom Moses ... Josh 13:21
king of Canaan, that *r* in Hazor ... Judg 4:2
When Abimelech had *r* three years ... Judg 9:22
Saul *r* one year ... 1Sa 13:1
when he had *r* two years over ... 1Sa 13:1
reign over Israel, and *r* two years ... 2Sa 2:10
to reign, and he *r* forty years ... 2Sa 5:4
In Hebron he *r* over Judah seven ... 2Sa 5:5
and in Jerusalem he *r* thirty ... 2Sa 5:5
And David *r* over all Israel ... 2Sa 8:15
and Hanun his son *r* in his stead ... 2Sa 10:1

Saul, in whose stead thou hast *r* ... 2Sa 16:8
the days that David *r* over Israel ... 1Kin 2:11
seven years *r* he in Hebron, and ... 1Kin 2:11
three years *r* he in Jerusalem ... 1Kin 2:11
Solomon *r* over all kingdoms from ... 1Kin 4:21
dwelt therein, and *r* in Damascus ... 1Kin 11:24
abhorred Israel, and *r* over Syria ... 1Kin 11:25
the time that Solomon *r* in ... 1Kin 11:42
Rehoboam his son *r* in his stead ... 1Kin 11:43
of Judah, Rehoboam *r* over them ... 1Kin 12:17
how he warred, and how he *r* ... 1Kin 14:19
days which Jeroboam *r* were two ... 1Kin 14:20
and Nadab his son *r* in his stead ... 1Kin 14:20
the son of Solomon *r* in Judah ... 1Kin 14:21
he *r* seventeen years in Jerusalem ... 1Kin 14:21
And Abijam his son *r* in his stead ... 1Kin 14:31
son of Nebat *r* Abijam over Judah ... 1Kin 15:1
Three years *r* he in Jerusalem ... 1Kin 15:2
Asa his son *r* in his stead ... 1Kin 15:8
king of Israel *r* Asa over Judah ... 1Kin 15:9
one years *r* he in Jerusalem ... 1Kin 15:10
his son *r* in his stead ... 1Kin 15:24
Judah, and *r* over Israel two years ... 1Kin 15:25
slay him, and *r* in his stead ... 1Kin 15:28
And it came to pass, when he *r* ... 1Kin 15:29
and Elah his son *r* in his stead ... 1Kin 16:6
king of Judah, and *r* in his stead ... 1Kin 16:10
so Tibni died, and Omri *r* ... 1Kin 16:22
six years *r* he in Tirzah ... 1Kin 16:23
and Ahab his son *r* in his stead ... 1Kin 16:28
Ahab the son of Omri *r* over ... 1Kin 16:29
and Ahaziah his son *r* in his stead ... 1Kin 22:40
he *r* twenty and five years in ... 1Kin 22:42
and Jehoram his son *r* in his stead ... 1Kin 22:50
Judah, and *r* two years over Israel ... 1Kin 22:51
Jehoram *r* in his stead in the ... 2Kin 1:17
king of Judah, and *r* twelve years ... 2Kin 3:1
that should have *r* in his stead ... 2Kin 3:27
and Hazael *r* in his stead ... 2Kin 8:15
he *r* eight years in Jerusalem ... 2Kin 8:17
and Ahaziah his son *r* in his stead ... 2Kin 8:24
he *r* one year in Jerusalem ... 2Kin 8:26
Jehoahaz his son *r* in his stead ... 2Kin 10:35
the time that Jehu *r* over Israel ... 2Kin 10:36
forty years *r* he in Jerusalem ... 2Kin 12:1
and Amaziah his son *r* in his stead ... 2Kin 12:21
in Samaria, and *r* seventeen years ... 2Kin 13:1
and Joash his son *r* in his stead ... 2Kin 13:9
in Samaria, and *r* sixteen years ... 2Kin 13:10
Ben-hadad his son *r* in his stead ... 2Kin 13:24
*r* Amaziah the son of Joash king ... 2Kin 14:1
*r* twenty and nine years in ... 2Kin 14:2
Jeroboam his son *r* in his stead ... 2Kin 14:16
Samaria, and *r* forty and one years ... 2Kin 14:23
Zachariah his son *r* in his stead ... 2Kin 14:29
he *r* two and fifty years in ... 2Kin 15:2
and Jotham his son *r* in his stead ... 2Kin 15:7
and slew him, and *r* in his stead ... 2Kin 15:10
he *r* a full month in Samaria ... 2Kin 15:13
and slew him, and *r* in his stead ... 2Kin 15:14
Israel, and *r* ten years in Samaria ... 2Kin 15:17
Pekahiah his son *r* in his stead ... 2Kin 15:22
Israel in Samaria, and *r* two years ... 2Kin 15:23
he killed him, and *r* in his room ... 2Kin 15:25
in Samaria, and *r* twenty years ... 2Kin 15:27
*r* in his stead, in the twentieth ... 2Kin 15:30
he *r* sixteen years in Jerusalem ... 2Kin 15:33
and Ahaz his son *r* in his stead ... 2Kin 15:38
*r* sixteen years in Jerusalem, and ... 2Kin 16:2
Hezekiah his son *r* in his stead ... 2Kin 16:20
he *r* twenty and nine years in ... 2Kin 18:2
his son *r* in his stead ... 2Kin 19:37
Manasseh his son *r* in his stead ... 2Kin 20:21
and *r* fifty and five years in ... 2Kin 21:1
and Amon his son *r* in his stead ... 2Kin 21:18
he *r* two years in Jerusalem ... 2Kin 21:19
and Josiah his son *r* in his stead ... 2Kin 21:26
he *r* thirty and one years in ... 2Kin 22:1
he *r* three months in Jerusalem ... 2Kin 23:31
he *r* eleven years in Jerusalem ... 2Kin 23:36
Jehoiachin his son *r* in his stead ... 2Kin 24:6
he *r* in Jerusalem three months ... 2Kin 24:8
he *r* eleven years in Jerusalem ... 2Kin 24:18
Now these are the kings that *r* in ... 1Chr 1:43
*r* over the children of Israel ... 1Chr 1:43
of Zerah of Bozrah *r* in his stead ... 1Chr 1:44
of the Temanites *r* in his stead ... 1Chr 1:45
the field of Moab, *r* in his stead ... 1Chr 1:46
Samlah of Masrekah *r* in his stead ... 1Chr 1:47
by the river *r* in his stead ... 1Chr 1:48
the son of Achbor *r* in his stead ... 1Chr 1:49
was dead, Hadad *r* in his stead ... 1Chr 1:50
there he *r* seven years and six ... 1Chr 3:4
and in Jerusalem he *r* thirty ... 1Chr 3:4
So David *r* over all Israel, and ... 1Chr 18:14
died, and his son *r* in his stead ... 1Chr 19:1
son of Jesse *r* over all Israel ... 1Chr 29:26
the time that he *r* over Israel ... 1Chr 29:27
seven years *r* he in Hebron, and ... 1Chr 29:27
three years *r* he in Jerusalem ... 1Chr 29:27
and Solomon his son *r* in his stead ... 1Chr 29:28
congregation, and *r* over Israel ... 2Chr 1:13
he *r* over all the kings from the ... 2Chr 9:26
Solomon *r* in Jerusalem over all ... 2Chr 9:30
Rehoboam his son *r* in his stead ... 2Chr 9:31
of Judah, Rehoboam *r* over them ... 2Chr 10:17
himself in Jerusalem, and *r* ... 2Chr 12:13
he *r* seventeen years in Jerusalem ... 2Chr 12:13
and Abijah his son *r* in his stead ... 2Chr 12:16
He *r* three years in Jerusalem ... 2Chr 13:2
Asa his son *r* in his stead ... 2Chr 14:1
his son *r* in his stead, and ... 2Chr 17:1
And Jehoshaphat *r* over Judah ... 2Chr 20:31
he *r* twenty and five years in ... 2Chr 20:31
And Jehoram his son *r* in his stead ... 2Chr 21:1
he *r* eight years in Jerusalem ... 2Chr 21:5
he *r* in Jerusalem eight years, and ... 2Chr 21:20
son of Jehoram king of Judah *r* ... 2Chr 22:1
he *r* one year in Jerusalem ... 2Chr 22:2
and Athaliah *r* over the land ... 2Chr 22:12
he *r* forty years in Jerusalem ... 2Chr 24:1
And Amaziah his son *r* in his stead ... 2Chr 24:27
he *r* twenty and nine years in ... 2Chr 25:1
he *r* fifty and two years in ... 2Chr 26:3
and Jotham his son *r* in his stead ... 2Chr 26:23
he *r* sixteen years in Jerusalem ... 2Chr 27:1
*r* sixteen years in Jerusalem ... 2Chr 27:8
and Ahaz his son *r* in his stead ... 2Chr 27:9
he *r* sixteen years in Jerusalem ... 2Chr 28:1
Hezekiah his son *r* in his stead ... 2Chr 28:27
he *r* nine and twenty years in ... 2Chr 29:1
Manasseh his son *r* in his stead ... 2Chr 32:33
he *r* fifty and five years in ... 2Chr 33:1
and Amon his son *r* in his stead ... 2Chr 33:20
and *r* two years in Jerusalem ... 2Chr 33:21
he *r* in Jerusalem one and thirty ... 2Chr 34:1
he *r* three months in Jerusalem ... 2Chr 36:2
he *r* eleven years in Jerusalem ... 2Chr 36:5
Jehoiachin his son *r* in his stead ... 2Chr 36:8
he *r* three months and ten days in ... 2Chr 36:9
*r* eleven years in Jerusalem ... 2Chr 36:11
(this is Ahasuerus which *r* from ... Est 1:1
his son *r* in his stead ... Is 37:38
which *r* instead of Josiah his ... Jer 22:11
*r* instead of Coniah the son of ... Jer 37:1
he *r* eleven years in Jerusalem ... Jer 52:1
death *r* from Adam to Moses ... Rom 5:14
one man's offence death *r* by one ... Rom 5:17
That as sin hath *r* unto death ... Rom 5:21
ye have *r* as kings without us ... 1Cor 4:8
thee thy great power, and hast *r* ... Rev 11:17
*r* with Christ a thousand years ... Rev 20:4

## REIGNEST

come of thee, and thou *r* over all ... 1Chr 29:12

## REIGNETH

also the king that *r* over you ... 1Sa 12:14
ye shall say, Absalom *r* in Hebron ... 2Sa 15:10
And now, behold, Adonijah *r* ... 1Kin 1:18
say among the nations, The LORD *r* ... 1Chr 16:31
God *r* over the heathen ... Ps 47:8
The LORD *r*, he is clothed with ... Ps 93:1
among the heathen that the LORD *r* ... Ps 96:10
The LORD *r* ... Ps 97:1
The LORD *r* ... Ps 99:1
For a servant when he *r* ... Prov 30:22
that saith unto Zion, Thy God *r* ... Is 52:7
which *r* over the kings of the ... Rev 17:18
for the Lord God omnipotent *r* ... Rev 19:6

## REIGNING

rejected him from *r* over Israel ... 1Sa 16:1

## REINS

about, he cleaveth my *r* asunder ... Job 16:13
though my *r* be consumed within me ... Job 19:27
God trieth the hearts and *r* ... Ps 7:9
my *r* also instruct me in the ... Ps 16:7
try my *r* and my heart ... Ps 26:2
grieved, and I was pricked in my *r* ... Ps 73:21
For thou hast possessed my *r* ... Ps 139:13
my *r* shall rejoice, when thy lips ... Prov 23:16
faithfulness the girdle of his *r* ... Is 11:5
righteously, that triest the *r* ... Jer 11:20
their mouth, and far from their *r* ... Jer 12:2
search the heart, I try the *r* ... Jer 17:10
the righteous, and seest the *r* ... Jer 20:12
of his quiver to enter into my *r* ... Lam 3:13
I am he which searcheth the *r* ... Rev 2:23

## REJECT

knowledge, I will also *r* thee ... Hos 4:6
sat with him, he would not *r* her ... Mk 6:26
Full well ye *r* the commandment of ... Mk 7:9
the first and second admonition *r* ... Titus 3:10

## REJECTED

*r* thee, but they have *r* me ... 1Sa 8:7
And ye have this day *r* your God ... 1Sa 10:19
Because thou hast *r* the word of ... 1Sa 15:23
he hath also *r* thee from being ... 1Sa 15:23
for thou hast *r* the word of the ... 1Sa 15:26
the LORD hath *r* thee from being ... 1Sa 15:26
seeing I have *r* him from reigning ... 1Sa 16:1
they *r* his statutes, and his ... 2Kin 17:15
the LORD *r* all the seed of Israel ... 2Kin 17:20
He is despised and *r* of men ... Is 53:3
the LORD hath *r* thy confidences ... Jer 2:37
my words, nor to my law, but *r* it ... Jer 6:19
because the LORD hath *r* them ... Jer 6:30
for the LORD hath *r* and forsaken ... Jer 7:29
they have *r* the word of the LORD ... Jer 8:9
Hast thou utterly *r* Judah ... Jer 14:19
But thou hast utterly *r* us ... Lam 5:22
because thou hast *r* knowledge ... Hos 4:6
The stone which the builders *r* ... Mt 21:42
be *r* of the elders, and of the ... Mk 8:31
*r* is become the head of the ... Mk 12:10
lawyers *r* the counsel of God ... Lk 7:30
be *r* of the elders and chief ... Lk 9:22
and be *r* of this generation ... Lk 17:25
The stone which the builders *r* ... Lk 20:17
my flesh ye despised not, nor *r* ... Gal 4:14
beareth thorns and briers is *r* ... Heb 6:8
inherited the blessing, he was *r* ... Heb 12:17

## REJECTETH

He that *r* me, and receiveth not my ... Jn 12:48

## REJOICE

ye shall *r* before the LORD your ... Lev 23:40
ye shall *r* in all that ye put ... Deut 12:7
ye shall *r* before the LORD your ... Deut 12:12
thou shalt *r* before the LORD thy ... Deut 12:18
the LORD thy God, and thou shalt *r* ... Deut 14:26
thou shalt *r* before the LORD thy ... Deut 16:11
thou shalt *r* in thy feast, thou, ... Deut 16:14
therefore thou shalt surely *r* ... Deut 16:15
thou shalt *r* in every good thing ... Deut 26:11
*r* before the LORD thy God ... Deut 27:7
so the LORD will *r* over you to ... Deut 28:63
will again *r* over thee for good ... Deut 30:9
*R*, O ye nations, with his people ... Deut 32:43
And of Zebulun he said, *R*, Zebulun ... Deut 33:18
then *r* ye in Abimelech ... Judg 9:19
and let him also *r* in you ... Judg 9:19
unto Dagon their god, and to *r* ... Judg 16:23
because I *r* in thy salvation ... 1Sa 2:1
thou sawest it, and didst *r* ... 1Sa 19:5
daughters of the Philistines *r* ... 2Sa 1:20
of them *r* that seek the LORD ... 1Chr 16:10
be glad, and let the earth *r* ... 1Chr 16:31
let the fields *r*, and all that is ... 1Chr 16:32
and let thy saints *r* in goodness ... 2Chr 6:41
made them to *r* over their enemies ... 2Chr 20:27
had made them *r* with great joy ... Neh 12:43
Which *r* exceedingly, and are glad, ... Job 3:22
be, and he shall not *r* therein ... Job 20:18
*r* at the sound of the organ ... Job 21:12
with fear, and *r* with trembling ... Ps 2:11
that put their trust in thee *r* ... Ps 5:11
I will be glad and *r* in thee ... Ps 9:2
I will *r* in thy salvation ... Ps 9:14
that trouble me *r* when I am moved ... Ps 13:4
my heart shall *r* in thy salvation ... Ps 13:5
of his people, Jacob shall *r* ... Ps 14:7
We will *r* in thy salvation, and in ... Ps 20:5
salvation how greatly shall he *r* ... Ps 21:1
not made my foes to *r* over me ... Ps 30:1
I will be glad and *r* in thy mercy ... Ps 31:7
Be glad in the LORD, and *r* ... Ps 32:11
*R* in the LORD, O ye righteous ... Ps 33:1
For our heart shall *r* in him ... Ps 33:21
it shall *r* in his salvation ... Ps 35:9
mine enemies wrongfully *r* over me ... Ps 35:19
and let them not *r* over me ... Ps 35:24
together that *r* at mine hurt ... Ps 35:26
otherwise they should *r* over me ... Ps 38:16
Let all those that seek thee *r* ... Ps 40:16
Let mount Zion *r*, let the ... Ps 48:11
which thou hast broken may *r* ... Ps 51:8
of his people, Jacob shall *r* ... Ps 53:6
The righteous shall *r* when he ... Ps 58:10
I will *r*, I will divide Shechem, ... Ps 60:6
the shadow of thy wings will I *r* ... Ps 63:7
But the king shall *r* in God ... Ps 63:11
of the morning and evening to *r* ... Ps 65:8
the little hills *r* on every side ... Ps 65:12
there did we *r* in him ... Ps 66:6
let them *r* before God ... Ps 68:3
yea, let them exceedingly *r* ... Ps 68:3
by his name JAH, and *r* before him ... Ps 68:4
Let all those that seek thee *r* ... Ps 70:4
greatly *r* when I sing unto thee ... Ps 71:23
that thy people may *r* in thee ... Ps 85:6
*R* the soul of thy servant ... Ps 86:4
and Hermon shall *r* in thy name ... Ps 89:12
thy name shall they *r* all the day ... Ps 89:16
hast made all his enemies to *r* ... Ps 89:42
that we may *r* and be glad all our ... Ps 90:14
Let the heavens *r*, and let the ... Ps 96:11
shall all the trees of the wood *r* ... Ps 96:12
let the earth *r* ... Ps 97:1
*R* in the LORD, ye righteous ... Ps 97:12
make a loud noise, and *r*, and sing ... Ps 98:4
the LORD shall *r* in his works ... Ps 104:31
of them *r* that seek the LORD ... Ps 105:3
that I may *r* in the gladness of ... Ps 106:5
The righteous shall see it, and *r* ... Ps 107:42
I will *r*, I will divide Shechem, ... Ps 108:7
but let thy servant *r* ... Ps 109:28
we will *r* and be glad in it ... Ps 118:24
I *r* at thy word, as one that ... Ps 119:162
Let Israel *r* in him that made him ... Ps 149:2
Who *r* to do evil, and delight in ... Prov 2:14
*r* with the wife of thy youth ... Prov 5:18
heart be wise, my heart shall *r* ... Prov 23:15
Yea, my reins shall *r*, when thy ... Prov 23:16
of the righteous shall greatly *r* ... Prov 23:24
and she that bare thee shall *r* ... Prov 23:25
*R* not when thine enemy falleth, ... Prov 24:17
Ointment and perfume *r* the heart ... Prov 27:9
When righteous men do *r*, there is ... Prov 28:12
are in authority, the people *r* ... Prov 29:2
but the righteous doth sing and *r* ... Prov 29:6
she shall *r* in time to come ... Prov 31:25
good in them, but for a man to *r* ... Eccl 3:12
a man should *r* in his own works ... Eccl 3:22
come after shall not *r* in him ... Eccl 4:16
portion, and to *r* in his labour ... Eccl 5:19
live many years, and *r* in them all ... Eccl 11:8
*R*, O young man, in thy youth ... Eccl 11:9
*r* in thee, we will remember thy ... Song 1:4

r in Rezin and Remaliah's son ... Is 8:6
as men r when they divide the ... Is 9:3
even them that r in my highness ... Is 13:3
Yea, the fir trees r at thee ... Is 14:8
R not thou, whole Palestina ... Is 14:29
And he said, Thou shalt no more r ... Is 23:12
the noise of them that r endeth ... Is 24:8
be glad and r in his salvation ... Is 25:9
the poor among men shall r in the ... Is 29:19
and the desert shall r, and blossom ... Is 35:1
r even with joy and singing ... Is 35:2
thou shalt r in the LORD, and ... Is 41:16
they shall r in their portion ... Is 61:7
I will greatly r in the LORD ... Is 61:10
so shall thy God r over thee ... Is 62:5
behold, my servants shall r ... Is 65:13
r for ever in that which I create ... Is 65:18
I will r in Jerusalem, and joy in ... Is 65:19
R ye with Jerusalem, and be glad ... Is 66:10
r for joy with her, all ye that ... Is 66:10
ye see this, your heart shall r ... Is 66:14
shall the virgin r in the dance ... Jer 31:13
make them r from their sorrow ... Jer 31:13
I will r over them to do them ... Jer 32:41
them drunken, that they may r ... Jer 51:39
caused thine enemy to r over thee ... Lam 2:17
R and be glad, O daughter of Edom, ... Lam 4:21
let not the buyer r, nor the ... Eze 7:12
As thou didst r at the ... Eze 35:15
R not, O Israel, for joy, as ... Hos 9:1
be glad and r ... Joel 2:21
Zion, and r in the LORD your God ... Joel 2:23
Ye which r in a thing of nought, ... Amos 6:13
R not against me, O mine enemy ... Mic 7:8
therefore they r and are glad ... Hab 1:15
Yet I will r in the LORD, I will ... Hab 3:18
of thee them that r in thy pride ... Zeph 3:11
r with all the heart, O daughter ... Zeph 3:14
he will r over thee with joy ... Zeph 3:17
Sing and r, O daughter of Zion ... Zec 2:10
for they shall r, and shall see ... Zec 4:10
R greatly, O daughter of Zion ... Zec 9:9
heart shall r as through wine ... Zec 10:7
their heart shall r in the LORD ... Zec 10:7
R, and be exceeding glad ... Mt 5:12
many shall r at his birth ... Lk 1:14
R ye in that day, and leap for joy ... Lk 6:23
Notwithstanding in this r not ... Lk 10:20
but rather r, because your names ... Lk 10:20
saying unto them, R with me ... Lk 15:6
together, saying, R with me ... Lk 15:9
of the disciples began to r ... Lk 19:37
and he that reapeth may r together ... Jn 4:36
for a season to r in his light ... Jn 5:35
If ye loved me, ye would r ... Jn 14:28
and lament, but the world shall r ... Jn 16:20
you again, and your heart shall r ... Jn 16:22
Therefore did my heart r, and my ... Acts 2:26
r in hope of the glory of God ... Rom 5:2
R with them that do r ... Rom 12:15
And again he saith, R, ye Gentiles ... Rom 15:10
and they that r, as though they ... 1Cor 7:30
all the members r with it ... 1Cor 12:26
from them of whom I ought to r ... 2Cor 2:3
Now I r, not that ye were made ... 2Cor 7:9
I r therefore that I have ... 2Cor 7:16
For it is written, R, thou barren ... Gal 4:27
do r, yea, and will r ... Phil 1:18
that I may r in the day of Christ ... Phil 2:16
faith, I joy, and r with you all ... Phil 2:17
also do ye joy, and r with me ... Phil 2:18
when ye see him again, ye may r ... Phil 2:28
my brethren, r in the Lord ... Phil 3:1
r in Christ Jesus, and have no ... Phil 3:3
R in the Lord alway ... Phil 4:4
and again I say, R ... Phil 4:4
Who now r in my sufferings for ... Col 1:24
R evermore ... 1Th 5:16
degree r in that he is exalted ... Jas 1:9
But now ye r in your boastings ... Jas 4:16
Wherein ye greatly r, though now ... 1Pet 1:6
ye r with joy unspeakable and full ... 1Pet 1:8
But r, inasmuch as ye are ... 1Pet 4:13
upon the earth shall r over them ... Rev 11:10
Therefore r, ye heavens, and ye ... Rev 12:12
R over her, thou heaven, and ye ... Rev 18:20
Let us be glad and r, and give ... Rev 19:7

## REJOICED
Jethro r for all the goodness ... Ex 18:9
that as the LORD r over you to do ... Deut 28:63
good, as he r over thy fathers ... Deut 30:9
damsel saw him, he r to meet him ... Judg 19:3
and saw the ark, and r to see it ... 1Sa 6:13
all the men of Israel r greatly ... 1Sa 11:15
r with great joy, so that the ... 1Kin 1:40
of Solomon, that he r greatly ... 1Kin 5:7
and all the people of the land r ... 2Kin 11:14
And all the people of the land r ... 2Kin 11:20
Then the people r, for that they ... 1Chr 29:9
the king also r with great joy ... 1Chr 29:9
And all Judah r at the oath ... 2Chr 15:15
and all the people of the land r ... 2Chr 23:13
And all the people of the land r ... 2Chr 23:21
the princes and all the people r ... 2Chr 24:10
And Hezekiah r, and all the people, .. 2Chr 29:36
Israel, and that dwelt in Judah, r ... 2Chr 30:25
offered great sacrifices, and r ... Neh 12:43
the wives also and the children r ... Neh 12:43
for Judah r for the priests and ... Neh 12:44
and the city of Shushan r and was ... Est 8:15
If I r because my wealth was ... Job 31:25
If I r at the destruction of him ... Job 31:29
But in mine adversity they r ... Ps 35:15
the daughters of Judah r because ... Ps 97:8
I have r in the way of thy ... Ps 119:14
for my heart r in all my labour ... Eccl 2:10
assembly of the mockers, nor r ... Jer 15:17
ye were glad, because ye r ... Jer 50:11
r in heart with all thy despite ... Eze 25:6
the priests thereof that r on it ... Hos 10:5
neither shouldest thou have r ... Obad 12
they r with exceeding great joy ... Mt 2:10
my spirit hath r in God my ... Lk 1:47
and they r with her ... Lk 1:58
In that hour Jesus r in spirit ... Lk 10:21
all the people r for all the ... Lk 13:17
father Abraham r to see my day ... Jn 8:56
r in the works of their own hands ... Acts 7:41
they r for the consolation ... Acts 15:31
he set meat before them, and r ... Acts 16:34
rejoice, as though they r not ... 1Cor 7:30
so that I r the more ... 2Cor 7:7
But I r in the Lord greatly, that ... Phil 4:10
I r greatly that I found of thy ... 2Jn 4
For I r greatly, when the ... 3Jn 3

## REJOICEST
when thou doest evil, then thou r ... Jer 11:15

## REJOICETH
My heart r in the LORD, mine horn ... 1Sa 2:1
the valley, and r in his strength ... Job 39:21
my heart is glad, and my glory r ... Ps 16:9
r as a strong man to run a race ... Ps 19:5
therefore my heart greatly r ... Ps 28:7
with the righteous, the city r ... Prov 11:10
The light of the righteous r ... Prov 13:9
The light of the eyes r the heart ... Prov 15:30
Whoso loveth wisdom r his father ... Prov 29:3
and their pomp, and he that r ... Is 5:14
the bridegroom r over the bride ... Is 62:5
Thou meetest him that r and ... Is 64:5
When the whole earth r, I will ... Eze 35:14
he r more of that sheep, than of ... Mt 18:13
him, r greatly because of the ... Jn 3:29
R not in iniquity ... 1Cor 13:6
but r in the truth ... 1Cor 13:6
and mercy r against judgment ... Jas 2:13

## REJOICING
and they are come up from thence r ... 1Kin 1:45
in the law of Moses, with r ... 2Chr 23:18
with laughing, and thy lips with r ... Job 8:21
the LORD are right, r the heart ... Ps 19:8
and r shall they be brought ... Ps 45:15
and declare his works with r ... Ps 107:22
The voice of r and salvation is in ... Ps 118:15
for they are the r of my heart ... Ps 119:111
shall doubtless come again with r ... Ps 126:6
his delight, r always before him ... Prov 8:30
R in the habitable part of his ... Prov 8:31
behold, I create Jerusalem a r ... Is 65:18
me the joy and r of mine heart ... Jer 15:16
their r was as to devour the poor ... Hab 3:14
This is the r city that dwelt ... Zeph 2:15
he layeth it on his shoulders, r ... Lk 15:5
r that they were counted worthy ... Acts 5:41
and he went on his way r ... Acts 8:39
R in hope ... Rom 12:12
I protest by your r which I have ... 1Cor 15:31
For our r is this, the testimony ... 2Cor 1:12
us in part, that we are your r ... 2Cor 1:14
As sorrowful, yet alway r ... 2Cor 6:10
shall he have r in himself alone ... Gal 6:4
That your r may be more abundant ... Phil 1:26
our hope, or joy, or crown of r ... 1Th 2:19
the r of the hope firm unto the ... Heb 3:6
all such r is evil ... Jas 4:16

## REKEM (re'-kem)
*1. A prince of Midian.*
namely, Evi, and R, and Zur, and Hur Num 31:8
the princes of Midian, Evi, and R ... Josh 13:21
*2. A son of Hebron.*
and Tappuah, and R ... 1Chr 2:43
and R begat Shammai ... 1Chr 2:44
*3. A city in Benjamin.*
And R, and Irpeel, and Taralah, ... Josh 18:27

## RELEASE
seven years thou shalt make a r ... Deut 15:1
And this is the manner of the r ... Deut 15:2
unto his neighbour shall r it ... Deut 15:2
because it is called the LORD's r ... Deut 15:2
thy brother thine hand shall r ... Deut 15:3
The seventh year, the year of r ... Deut 15:9
in the solemnity of the year of r ... Deut 31:10
he made a r to the provinces, and ... Est 2:18
to r unto the people a prisoner ... Mt 27:15
Whom will ye that I r unto you ... Mt 27:17
twain will ye that I r unto you ... Mt 27:21
Will ye that I r unto you the ... Mk 15:9
rather r Barabbas unto them ... Mk 15:11
therefore chastise him, and r him ... Lk 23:16
(For of necessity he must r one ... Lk 23:17
this man, and r unto us Barabbas ... Lk 23:18
therefore, willing to r Jesus ... Lk 23:20
that I should r unto you one at ... Jn 18:39
will ye therefore that I r unto ... Jn 18:39
thee, and have power to r thee ... Jn 19:10
Pilate sought to r him ... Jn 19:12

## RELEASED
Then r he Barabbas unto them ... Mt 27:26
Now at that feast he r unto them ... Mk 15:6
people, r Barabbas unto them, and ... Mk 15:15
he r unto them him that for ... Lk 23:25

## RELIED
because they r upon the LORD God ... 2Chr 13:18
Because thou hast r on the king ... 2Chr 16:7
not r on the LORD thy God, ... 2Chr 16:7

## RELIEF
determined to send r unto the ... Acts 11:29

## RELIEVE
then thou shalt r him ... Lev 25:35
r the oppressed, judge the ... Is 1:17
things for meat to r the soul ... Lam 1:11
should r my soul is far from me ... Lam 1:16
their meat to r their souls ... Lam 1:19
have widows, let them r them ... 1Ti 5:16
that it may r them that are ... 1Ti 5:16

## RELIEVED
if she have r the afflicted, if ... 1Ti 5:10

## RELIEVETH
he r the fatherless and widow ... Ps 146:9

## RELIGION
sect of our r I lived a Pharisee ... Acts 26:5
in time past in the Jews' r ... Gal 1:13
profited in the Jews' r above ... Gal 1:14
own heart, this man's r is vain ... Jas 1:26
Pure r and undefiled before God and ... Jas 1:27

## RELIGIOUS
r proselytes followed Paul and ... Acts 13:43
If any man among you seem to be r ... Jas 1:26

## RELY
because thou didst r on the LORD ... 2Chr 16:8

## REMAIN
R a widow at thy father's house, ... Gen 38:11
that they may r in the river only ... Ex 8:9
they shall r in the river only ... Ex 8:11
nothing of it r until the morning ... Ex 12:10
my sacrifice r until the morning ... Ex 23:18
r unto the morning, then thou ... Ex 29:34
if ought r until the third day, ... Lev 19:6
r in the hand of him that hath ... Lev 25:28
if there r but few years unto the ... Lev 25:52
according to the years that r ... Lev 27:18
that those which ye let r of them ... Num 33:55
of every city, we left none to r ... Deut 2:34
r all night until the morning ... Deut 16:4
And those which r shall hear ... Deut 19:20
shall r in thine house, and bewail ... Deut 21:13
His body shall not r all night ... Deut 21:23
shall r in the land which Moses ... Josh 1:14
neither did there r any more ... Josh 2:11
they let none of them r or escape ... Josh 8:22
which r until this very day ... Josh 10:27
he let none r ... Josh 10:28
he let none r in it ... Josh 10:30
you by lot these nations that r ... Josh 23:4
nations, these that r among you ... Josh 23:7
even these that r among you ... Josh 23:12
and why did Dan r in ships ... Judg 5:17
we do for wives for them that r ... Judg 21:7
we do for wives for them that r ... Judg 21:16
shalt r by the stone Ezel ... 1Sa 20:19
did Joab r there with all Israel ... 1Kin 11:16
I only, r a prophet of the LORD ... 1Kin 18:22
thee, five of the horses that r ... 2Kin 7:13
for we r yet escaped, as it is ... Ezr 9:15
the grave, and shall r in the tomb ... Job 21:32
Those that r of him shall be ... Job 27:15
into dens, and r in their places ... Job 37:8
far off, and r in the wilderness ... Ps 55:7
and the perfect shall r in it ... Prov 2:21
the way of understanding shall r ... Prov 21:16
As yet shall he r at Nob that day ... Is 10:32
righteousness r in the fruitful ... Is 32:16
that it may r in the house ... Is 44:13
Which r among the graves, and ... Is 65:4
shall r before me, saith the LORD ... Is 66:22
so shall your seed and your name r ... Is 66:22
them that r of this evil family ... Jer 8:3
which r in all the places whither ... Jer 8:3
and this city shall r for ever ... Jer 17:25
that r in this land, and them that ... Jer 24:8
those will I let r still in their ... Jer 27:11
the vessels that r in this city ... Jer 27:19
that r in the house of the LORD ... Jer 27:21
the palace shall r after the ... Jer 30:18
men of war that r in this city ... Jer 38:4
none of them shall r or escape ... Jer 42:17
of Judah, to leave you none to r ... Jer 44:7
sojourn there, shall escape or r ... Jer 44:14
it off, that none shall r in it ... Jer 51:62
none of them shall r, nor of ... Eze 7:11
they that r shall be scattered ... Eze 17:21
all the fowls of the heaven r ... Eze 31:13
of the heaven to r upon thee ... Eze 32:4
that r upon the face of the earth ... Eze 39:14
if there r ten men in one house, ... Amos 6:9
that did r in the day of distress ... Obad 14
it shall r in the midst of his ... Zec 5:4
All the families that r, every ... Zec 12:14
And in the same house r, eating and ... Lk 10:7
Gather up the fragments that r ... Jn 6:12
you, that my joy might r in you ... Jn 15:11

R

and that your fruit should *r* ... Jn 15:16
that the bodies should not *r* upon ... Jn 19:31
let her *r* unmarried, or be ... 1Cor 7:11
greater part *r* unto this present ... 1Cor 15:6
*r* unto the coming of the Lord ... 1Th 4:15
*r* shall be caught up together ... 1Th 4:17
which cannot be shaken may *r* ... Heb 12:27
from the beginning shall *r* in you ... 1Jn 2:24
and strengthen the things which *r* ... Rev 3:2

**REMAINDER**
thou shalt burn the *r* with fire ... Ex 29:34
the *r* thereof shall Aaron and his ... Lev 6:16
also the *r* of it shall be eaten ... Lev 7:16
But the *r* of the flesh of the ... Lev 7:17
neither name nor *r* upon the earth ... 2Sa 14:7
the *r* of wrath shalt thou ... Ps 76:10

**REMAINED**
and Noah only *r* alive, and they ... Gen 7:23
they that *r* fled to the mountain ... Gen 14:10
there *r* not one ... Ex 8:31
there *r* not any green thing in ... Ex 10:15
there *r* not one locust in all the ... Ex 10:19
there *r* not so much as one of ... Ex 14:28
But there *r* two of the men in the ... Num 11:26
Because he should have *r* in the ... Num 35:28
their inheritance *r* in the tribe ... Num 36:12
Bashan *r* of the remnant of giants ... Deut 3:11
ye shall have *r* long in the land, ... Deut 4:25
that the rest which *r* of them ... Josh 10:20
in Gath, and in Ashdod, there *r* ... Josh 11:22
who *r* of the remnant of the ... Josh 13:12
there *r* among the children of ... Josh 18:2
the Levites which *r* of the ... Josh 21:20
of the children of Kohath that *r* ... Josh 21:26
and there *r* ten thousand ... Judg 7:3
that they which *r* were scattered ... 1Sa 11:11
*r* in a mountain in the wilderness ... 1Sa 23:14
his men *r* in the sides of the ... 1Sa 24:3
So Tamar *r* desolate in her ... 2Sa 13:20
which *r* in the days of his father ... 1Kin 22:46
So Jehu slew all that *r* of the ... 2Kin 10:11
he slew all that *r* unto Ahab in ... 2Kin 10:17
there *r* the grove also in Samaria ... 2Kin 13:6
none *r*, save the poorest sort of ... 2Kin 24:14
that *r* in the land of Judah ... 2Kin 25:22
the ark of God *r* with the family ... 1Chr 13:14
also my wisdom *r* with me ... Eccl 2:9
cities *r* of the cities of Judah ... Jer 34:7
there *r* but wounded men among ... Jer 37:10
Jeremiah had *r* there many days ... Jer 37:16
Thus Jeremiah *r* in the court of ... Jer 37:21
Jeremiah *r* in the court of the ... Jer 38:13
of the people that *r* in the city ... Jer 39:9
the rest of the people that *r* ... Jer 39:9
all the people that *r* in Mizpah ... Jer 41:10
therefore his taste *r* in him ... Jer 48:11
they have *r* in their holds ... Jer 51:30
of the people that *r* in the city ... Jer 52:15
LORD's anger none escaped nor *r* ... Lam 2:22
*r* there astonished among them ... Eze 3:15
there *r* no strength in me ... Dan 10:8
I *r* there with the kings of ... Dan 10:13
there *r* no strength in me ... Dan 10:17
it would have *r* until this day ... Mt 11:23
that *r* twelve baskets full ... Mt 14:20
unto them, and *r* speechless ... Lk 1:22
that *r* to them twelve baskets ... Lk 9:17
five barley loaves, which *r* over ... Jn 6:13
Whiles it *r*, was it not thine own ... Acts 5:4
*r* unmoveable, but the hinder part ... Acts 27:41

**REMAINEST**
Thou, O LORD, *r* for ever ... Lam 5:19
but thou *r* ... Heb 1:11

**REMAINETH**
While the earth *r*, seedtime and ... Gen 8:22
which *r* unto you from the hail, ... Ex 10:5
that which *r* of it until the ... Ex 12:10
that which *r* over lay up for you ... Ex 16:23
the remnant that *r* of the ... Ex 26:12
the tent, the half curtain that *r* ... Ex 26:12
*r* in the length of the curtains ... Ex 26:13
that which *r* of the flesh and of ... Lev 8:32
Take the meat offering that *r* of ... Lev 10:12
that *r* among them in the midst of ... Lev 16:16
destroy him that *r* of the city ... Num 24:19
of stones, that *r* unto this day ... Josh 8:29
there *r* yet very much land to be ... Josh 13:1
This is the land that yet *r* ... Josh 13:2
Then he made him that *r* have ... Judg 5:13
which stone *r* unto this day in ... 1Sa 6:18
There *r* yet the youngest, and, ... 1Sa 16:11
of the LORD *r* under curtains ... 1Chr 17:1
whosoever *r* in any place where he ... Ezr 1:4
erred, mine error *r* with myself ... Job 19:4
in your answers there *r* falsehood ... Job 21:34
In his neck *r* strength, and sorrow ... Job 41:22
he that *r* in Jerusalem, shall be ... Is 4:3
He that *r* in this city shall die ... Jer 38:2
and Zidon every helper that *r* ... Jer 47:4
and he that *r* and is besieged shall ... Eze 6:12
Egypt, so my spirit *r* among you ... Hag 2:5
but he that *r*, even he, shall be ... Zec 9:7
therefore your sin *r* ... Jn 9:41
it *r*, that both they that have ... 1Cor 7:29
more that which *r* is glorious ... 2Cor 3:11
for until this day *r* the same ... 2Cor 3:14
his righteousness *r* for ever ... 2Cor 9:9
Seeing therefore it *r* that some ... Heb 4:6
There *r* therefore a rest to the ... Heb 4:9
there *r* no more sacrifice for ... Heb 10:26
for his seed *r* in him ... 1Jn 3:9

**REMAINING**
*r* thereon, the children of Israel ... Num 9:22
him until none was left to him *r* ... Deut 3:3
until he had left him none *r* ... Josh 10:33
he left none *r*, according to all ... Josh 10:37
he left none *r* ... Josh 10:39
he left none *r*, but utterly ... Josh 10:40
them, until they left them none *r* ... Josh 11:8
which were *r* of the families of ... Josh 21:40
we should be destroyed from *r* in ... 2Sa 21:5
priests, until he left him none *r* ... 2Kin 10:11
who *r* in the chambers were free ... 1Chr 9:33
nor any *r* in his dwellings ... Job 18:19
not be any *r* of the house of Esau ... Obad 18
*r* on him, the same is he which ... Jn 1:33

**REMALIAH** (*rem-a-li'-ah*) See REMALIAH'S.
*Father of Pekah.*
But Pekah the son of *R*, a captain ... 2Kin 15:25
*R* began to reign over Israel in ... 2Kin 15:27
against Pekah the son of *R* ... 2Kin 15:30
*R* king of Israel began Jotham the ... 2Kin 15:32
of Syria, and Pekah the son of *R* ... 2Kin 15:37
year of Pekah the son of *R* Ahaz ... 2Kin 16:1
Pekah son of *R* king of Israel ... 2Kin 16:5
For Pekah the son of *R* slew in ... 2Chr 28:6
of Syria, and Pekah the son of *R* ... Is 7:1
with Syria, and of the son of *R* ... Is 7:4
Syria, Ephraim, and the son of *R* ... Is 7:5

**REMALIAH'S** (*rem-a-li'-ahs*)
and the head of Samaria is *R* son ... Is 7:9
and rejoice in Rezin and *R* son ... Is 8:6

**REMEDY**
his people, till there was no *r* ... 2Chr 36:16
shall he be broken without *r* ... Prov 6:15
be destroyed, and that without *r* ... Prov 29:1

**REMEMBER**
I will *r* my covenant, which is ... Gen 9:15
that I may *r* the everlasting ... Gen 9:16
did not the chief butler *r* Joseph ... Gen 40:23
I do *r* my faults this day ... Gen 41:9
*R* this day, in which ye came out ... Ex 13:3
*R* the sabbath day, to keep it ... Ex 20:8
*R* Abraham, Isaac, and Israel, thy ... Ex 32:13
Then will I *r* my covenant with ... Lev 26:42
my covenant with Abraham will I *r* ... Lev 26:42
and I will *r* the land ... Lev 26:42
But I will for their sakes *r* the ... Lev 26:45
We *r* the fish, which we did eat ... Num 11:5
*r* all the commandments of the ... Num 15:39
That ye may *r*, and do all my ... Num 15:40
*r* that thou wast a servant in the ... Deut 5:15
but shalt well *r* what the LORD ... Deut 7:18
thou shalt *r* all the way which ... Deut 8:2
But thou shalt *r* the LORD thy God ... Deut 8:18
*R*, and forget not, how thou ... Deut 9:7
*R* thy servants, Abraham, Isaac, ... Deut 9:27
thou shalt *r* that thou wast a ... Deut 15:15
that thou mayest *r* the day when ... Deut 16:3
thou shalt *r* that thou wast a ... Deut 16:12
*R* what the LORD thy God did unto ... Deut 24:9
But thou shalt *r* that thou wast a ... Deut 24:18
thou shalt *r* that thou wast a ... Deut 24:22
*R* what Amalek did unto thee by ... Deut 25:17
*R* the days of old, consider the ... Deut 32:7
*R* the word which Moses the ... Josh 1:13
*r* also that I am your bone and ... Judg 9:2
*r* me, I pray thee, and strengthen ... Judg 16:28
*r* me, and not forget thine ... 1Sa 1:11
I *r* that which Amalek did to ... 1Sa 15:2
my lord, then *r* thine handmaid ... 1Sa 25:31
let the king *r* the LORD thy God, ... 2Sa 14:11
neither do thou *r* that which thy ... 2Sa 19:19
for *r* how that, when I and thou ... 2Kin 9:25
*r* now how I have walked before ... 2Kin 20:3
*R* his marvellous works that he ... 1Chr 16:12
*r* the mercies of David thy ... 2Chr 6:42
*R*, I beseech thee, the word that ... Neh 1:8
*r* the LORD, which is great and ... Neh 4:14
*R* me, O my God, concerning this, ... Neh 13:14
*R* me, O my God, concerning this ... Neh 13:22
*R* them, O my God, because they ... Neh 13:29
*R* me, O my God, for good ... Neh 13:31
*R*, I pray thee, who ever perished ... Job 4:7
O *r* that my life is wind ... Job 7:7
*R*, I beseech thee, that thou hast ... Job 10:9
*r* it as waters that pass away ... Job 11:16
appoint me a set time, and *r* me ... Job 14:13
Even when I *r* I am afraid ... Job 21:6
*R* that thou magnify his work, ... Job 36:24
him, *r* the battle, do no more ... Job 41:8
*R* all thy offerings, and accept ... Ps 20:3
but we will *r* the name of the ... Ps 20:7
All the ends of the world shall *r* ... Ps 22:27
*R*, O LORD, thy tender mercies and ... Ps 25:6
*R* not the sins of my youth, nor ... Ps 25:7
according to thy mercy *r* thou me ... Ps 25:7
When I *r* these things, I pour out ... Ps 42:4
therefore will I *r* thee from the ... Ps 42:6
When I *r* thee upon my bed, and ... Ps 63:6
*R* thy congregation, which thou ... Ps 74:2
*R* this, that the enemy hath ... Ps 74:18
*r* how the foolish man reproacheth ... Ps 74:22
but I will *r* the years of the ... Ps 77:10
I will *r* the works of the LORD ... Ps 77:11
surely I will *r* thy wonders of ... Ps 77:11
O *r* not against us former ... Ps 79:8
*R* how short my time is ... Ps 89:47
*R*, Lord, the reproach of thy ... Ps 89:50
to those that *r* his commandments ... Ps 103:18
*R* his marvellous works that he ... Ps 105:5
*R* me, O LORD, with the favour ... Ps 106:4
*R* the word unto thy servant, upon ... Ps 119:49
*r* David, and all his afflictions ... Ps 132:1
If I do not *r* thee, let my tongue ... Ps 137:6
*R*, O LORD, the children of Edom ... Ps 137:7
I *r* the days of old ... Ps 143:5
poverty, and *r* his misery no more ... Prov 31:7
not much *r* the days of his life ... Eccl 5:20
yet let him *r* the days of ... Eccl 11:8
*R* now thy Creator in the days of ... Eccl 12:1
we will *r* thy love more than wine ... Song 1:4
*R* now, O LORD, I beseech thee, ... Is 38:3
*R* ye not the former things, ... Is 43:18
own sake, and will not *r* thy sins ... Is 43:25
*R* these, O Jacob and Israel ... Is 44:21
*R* this, and shew yourselves men ... Is 46:8
*R* the former things of old ... Is 46:9
neither didst *r* the latter end of ... Is 47:7
shalt not *r* the reproach of thy ... Is 54:4
those that *r* thee in thy ways ... Is 64:5
neither *r* iniquity for ever ... Is 64:9
I *r* thee, the kindness of thy ... Jer 2:2
neither shall they *r* it ... Jer 3:16
he will now *r* their iniquity, and ... Jer 14:10
*r*, break not thy covenant with us ... Jer 14:21
*r* me, and visit me, and revenge me ... Jer 15:15
their children *r* their altars ... Jer 17:2
*R* that I stood before thee to ... Jer 18:20
him, I do earnestly *r* him still ... Jer 31:20
I will *r* their sin no more ... Jer 31:34
the land, did not the LORD *r* them ... Jer 44:21
*r* the LORD afar off, and let ... Jer 51:50
*R*, O LORD, what is come upon us ... Lam 5:1
*r* me among the nations whither ... Eze 6:9
Nevertheless I will *r* my covenant ... Eze 16:60
Then thou shalt *r* thy ways ... Eze 16:61
That thou mayest *r*, and be ... Eze 16:63
And there shall ye *r* your ways ... Eze 20:43
unto them, nor *r* Egypt any more ... Eze 23:27
Then shall ye *r* your own evil ... Eze 36:31
that I *r* all their wickedness ... Hos 7:2
now will he *r* their iniquity, and ... Hos 8:13
he will *r* their iniquity, he will ... Hos 9:9
*r* now what Balak king of Moab ... Mic 6:5
in wrath *r* mercy ... Hab 3:2
they shall *r* me in far countries ... Zec 10:9
*R* ye the law of Moses my servant, ... Mal 4:4
neither *r* the five loaves of the ... Mt 16:9
we *r* that that deceiver said, ... Mt 27:63
and do ye not *r* ... Mk 8:18
and to *r* his holy covenant ... Lk 1:72
*r* that thou in thy lifetime ... Lk 16:25
*R* Lot's wife ... Lk 17:32
*r* me when thou comest into thy ... Lk 23:42
*r* how he spake unto you when he ... Lk 24:6
*R* the word that I said unto you, ... Jn 15:20
ye may *r* that I told you of them ... Jn 16:4
Therefore watch, and *r*, that by ... Acts 20:31
to *r* the words of the Lord Jesus, ... Acts 20:35
that ye *r* me in all things, and ... 1Cor 11:2
would that we should *r* the poor ... Gal 2:10
Wherefore *r*, that ye being in ... Eph 2:11
*R* my bonds ... Col 4:18
For ye *r*, brethren, our labour and ... 1Th 2:9
*R* ye not, that, when I was yet ... 2Th 2:5
*R* that Jesus Christ of the seed ... 2Ti 2:8
their iniquities will I *r* no more ... Heb 8:12
and iniquities will I *r* no more ... Heb 10:17
*R* them that are in bonds, as ... Heb 13:3
*R* them which have the rule over ... Heb 13:7
I will *r* his deeds which he doeth ... 3Jn 10
*r* ye the words which were spoken ... Jude 17
*R* therefore from whence thou art ... Rev 2:5
*R* therefore how thou hast ... Rev 3:3

**REMEMBERED**
God *r* Noah, and every living thing ... Gen 8:1
of the plain, that God *r* Abraham ... Gen 19:29
God *r* Rachel, and God hearkened to ... Gen 30:22
Joseph *r* the dreams which he ... Gen 42:9
God *r* his covenant with Abraham, ... Ex 2:24
and I have *r* my covenant ... Ex 6:5
ye shall be *r* before the LORD ... Num 10:9
Israel *r* not the LORD their God ... Judg 8:34
and the LORD *r* her ... 1Sa 1:19
Thus Joash the king *r* not the ... 2Chr 24:22
he *r* Vashti, and what she had done ... Est 2:1
And that these days should be *r* ... Est 9:28
he shall be no more *r* ... Job 24:20
name to be *r* in all generations ... Ps 45:17
I *r* God, and was troubled ... Ps 77:3
they *r* that God was their rock, ... Ps 78:35
For he *r* that they were but flesh ... Ps 78:39
They *r* not his hand, nor the day ... Ps 78:42
He hath *r* his mercy and his truth ... Ps 98:3
He hath *r* his covenant for ever, ... Ps 105:8
For he *r* his holy promise, and ... Ps 105:42
they *r* not the multitude of thy ... Ps 106:7
he *r* for them his covenant, and ... Ps 106:45
of his fathers be *r* with the LORD ... Ps 109:14
Because that he *r* not to shew ... Ps 109:16
made his wonderful works to be *r* ... Ps 111:4
I *r* thy judgments of old, O LORD ... Ps 119:52
I have *r* thy name, O LORD, in the ... Ps 119:55
Who *r* us in our low estate ... Ps 136:23
yea, we wept, when we *r* Zion ... Ps 137:1

yet no man *r* that same poor man ... Eccl 9:15
many songs, that thou mayest be *r*... Is 23:16
thou hast lied, and hast not *r* me ... Is 57:11
Then he *r* the days of old, Moses,... Is 63:11
and the former shall not be *r*... Is 65:17
that his name may be no more *r*... Jer 11:19
Jerusalem *r* in the days of her... Lam 1:7
*r* not his footstool in the day of... Lam 2:1
which he hath done shall not be *r*... Eze 3:20
hast not *r* the days of thy youth ... Eze 16:22
hast not *r* the days of thy youth ... Eze 16:43
have made your iniquity to be *r*... Eze 21:24
thou shalt be no more *r*... Eze 21:32
may not be *r* among the nations ... Eze 25:10
righteousnesses shall not be *r*... Eze 33:13
shall no more be *r* by their name... Hos 2:17
*r* not the brotherly covenant ... Amos 1:9
fainted within me I *r* the LORD... Jonah 2:7
land, and they shall no more be *r*... Zec 13:2
Peter *r* the word of Jesus, which ... Mt 26:75
Peter *r* the word of the Lord, how... Lk 22:61
And they *r* his words,... Lk 24:8
his disciples *r* that it was... Jn 2:17
his disciples *r* that he had said ... Jn 2:22
then *r* they that these things... Jn 12:16
Then *r* I the word of the Lord,... Acts 11:16
God hath *r* her iniquities... Rev 18:5

**REMEMBEREST**
in the grave, whom thou *r* no more... Ps 88:5
there *r* that thy brother hath... Mt 5:23

**REMEMBERETH**
inquisition for blood, he *r* them... Ps 9:12
he *r* that we are dust... Ps 103:14
she *r* not her last end... Lam 1:9
she *r* no more the anguish, for... Jn 16:21
whilst he *r* the obedience of you... 2Cor 7:15

**REMEMBERING**
*R* mine affliction and my misery,... Lam 3:19
*R* without ceasing your work of ... 1Th 1:3

**REMEMBRANCE**
the *r* of Amalek from under heaven... Ex 17:14
memorial, bringing iniquity to *r*... Num 5:15
the *r* of Amalek from under heaven.. Deut 25:19
I would make the *r* of them to... Deut 32:26
have no son to keep my name in *r*... 2Sa 18:18
come unto me to call my sin to *r*... 1Kin 17:18
His *r* shall perish from the earth... Job 18:17
in death there is no *r* of thee... Ps 6:5
thanks at the *r* of his holiness... Ps 30:4
to cut off the *r* of them from the... Ps 34:16
A Psalm of David, to bring to *r*... Ps 38:*t*
A Psalm of David, to bring to *r*... Ps 70:*t*
I call to *r* my song in the night... Ps 77:6
of Israel may be no more in *r*... Ps 83:4
thanks at the *r* of his holiness... Ps 97:12
thy *r* unto all generations... Ps 102:12
shall be in everlasting *r*... Ps 112:6
There is no *r* of former things... Eccl 1:11
neither shall there be any *r* of... Eccl 1:11
For there is no *r* of the wise... Eccl 2:16
to thy name, and to the *r* of thee... Is 26:8
Put me in *r*... Is 43:26
the posts hast thou set up thy *r*... Is 57:8
My soul hath them still in *r*... Lam 3:20
he will call to *r* the iniquity... Eze 21:23
I say, that ye are come to *r*... Eze 21:24
in calling to *r* the days of her... Eze 23:19
Thus thou calledst to *r* the... Eze 23:21
bringeth their iniquity to *r*... Eze 29:16
a book of *r* was written before... Mal 3:16
Peter calling to *r* saith unto him... Mk 11:21
servant Israel, in *r* of his mercy ... Lk 1:54
this do in *r* of me... Lk 22:19
and bring all things to your *r*... Jn 14:26
are had in *r* in the sight of God... Acts 10:31
who shall bring you into *r* of my ... 1Cor 4:17
this do in *r* of me... 1Cor 11:24
as oft as ye drink it, in *r* of me... 1Cor 11:25
thank my God upon every *r* of you... Phil 1:3
that ye have good *r* of us always... 1Th 3:6
the brethren in *r* of these things ... 1Ti 4:6
*r* of thee in my prayers night... 2Ti 1:3
When I call to *r* the unfeigned... 2Ti 1:5
Wherefore I put thee in *r* that... 2Ti 1:6
Of these things put them in *r*... 2Ti 2:14
a *r* again made of sins every year... Heb 10:3
But call to *r* the former days, in... Heb 10:32
you always in *r* of these things... 2Pet 1:12
stir you up by putting you in *r*... 2Pet 1:13
to have these things always in *r*... 2Pet 1:15
up your pure minds by way of *r*... 2Pet 3:1
I will therefore put you in *r*... Jude 5
Babylon came in *r* before God... Rev 16:19

**REMEMBRANCES**
Your *r* are like unto ashes, your... Job 13:12

**REMETH** (*re'-meth*) See RAMOTH, JARMUTH. *A Levitical city in Issachar.*
*R*, and En-gannim, and En-haddah... Josh 19:21

**REMISSION**
shed for many for the *r* of sins... Mt 26:28
of repentance for the *r* of sins... Mk 1:4
his people by the *r* of their sins... Lk 1:77
of repentance for the *r* of sins... Lk 3:3
*r* of sins should be preached in... Lk 24:47
of Jesus Christ for the *r* of sins... Acts 2:38
in him shall receive *r* of sins... Acts 10:43
for the *r* of sins that are past... Rom 3:25
without shedding of blood is no *r*... Heb 9:22
Now where *r* of these is, there is... Heb 10:18

**REMIT**
Whose soever sins ye *r*, they are... Jn 20:23

**REMITTED**
ye remit, they are *r* unto them... Jn 20:23

**REMMON** (*rem'-mon*) See RIMMON. *A city in Judah.*
Ain, *R*, and Ether, and Ashan... Josh 19:7

**REMMON-METHOAR** (*rem''-mon-meth'-o-ar*) *A city in Zebulun.*
and goeth out to *R* to Neah... Josh 19:13

**REMNANT**
the *r* that remaineth of the... Ex 26:12
the *r* of the meat offerings shall... Lev 2:3
the *r* shall be the priest's, as a... Lev 5:13
the *r* of the oil that is in the... Lev 14:18
remained of the *r* of giants... Deut 3:11
toward the *r* of his children... Deut 28:54
which was of the *r* of the giants... Josh 12:4
remained of the *r* of the giants... Josh 13:12
cleave unto the *r* of these... Josh 23:12
but of the *r* of the Amorites... 2Sa 21:2
to the *r* of the people, saying,... 1Kin 12:23
will take away the *r* of the house ... 1Kin 14:10
the *r* of the sodomites, which... 1Kin 22:46
prayer for the *r* that are left... 2Kin 19:4
the *r* that is escaped of the... 2Kin 19:30
of Jerusalem shall go forth a *r*... 2Kin 19:31
I will forsake the *r* of mine... 2Kin 21:14
with the *r* of the multitude, did... 2Kin 25:11
of the *r* of the sons of Kohath... 1Chr 6:70
and he will return to the *r* of you... 2Chr 30:6
and of all the *r* of Israel... 2Chr 34:9
the *r* of their brethren the... Ezr 3:8
God, to leave us a *r* to escape... Ezr 9:8
there should be no *r* nor escaping... Ezr 9:14
The *r* that are left of the... Neh 1:3
but the *r* of them the fire... Job 22:20
had left unto us a very small *r*... Is 1:9
that the *r* of Israel, and such as... Is 10:20
The *r* shall return, even the... Is 10:21
shall return, even the *r* of Jacob... Is 10:21
yet a *r* of them shall return... Is 10:22
to recover the *r* of his people... Is 11:11
highway for the *r* of his people... Is 11:16
off from Babylon the name, and *r*... Is 14:22
famine, and he shall slay thy *r*... Is 14:30
Moab, and upon the *r* of the land... Is 15:9
the *r* shall be very small and... Is 16:14
from Damascus, and the *r* of Syria... Is 17:3
thy prayer for the *r* that is left... Is 37:4
the *r* that is escaped of the... Is 37:31
of Jerusalem shall go forth a *r*... Is 37:32
all the *r* of the house of Israel,... Is 46:3
glean the *r* of Israel as a vine... Jer 6:9
And there shall be no *r* of them... Jer 11:23
it shall be well with thy *r*... Jer 15:11
I will gather the *r* of my flock... Jer 23:3
and Ekron, and the *r* of Ashdod,... Jer 25:20
save thy people, the *r* of Israel... Jer 31:7
away captive into Babylon the *r*... Jer 39:9
of Babylon had left a *r* of Judah... Jer 40:11
and the *r* in Judah perish... Jer 40:15
all the *r* of the people whom he... Jer 41:16
LORD thy God, even for all this *r*... Jer 42:2
word of the LORD, ye *r* of Judah... Jer 42:15
concerning you, O ye *r* of Judah... Jer 42:19
forces, took all the *r* of Judah... Jer 43:5
And I will take the *r* of Judah... Jer 44:12
So that none of the *r* of Judah... Jer 44:14
all the *r* of Judah, that are gone... Jer 44:28
the *r* of the country of Caphtor... Jer 47:4
off with the *r* of their valley... Jer 47:5
the whole *r* of thee will I... Eze 5:10
Yet will I leave a *r*, that ye may... Eze 6:8
a full end of the *r* of Israel... Eze 11:13
therein shall be left a *r* that... Eze 14:22
thy *r* shall fall by the sword... Eze 23:25
destroy the *r* of the sea coast... Eze 25:16
in the *r* whom the LORD shall call... Joel 2:32
the *r* of the Philistines shall... Amos 1:8
be gracious unto the *r* of Joseph... Amos 5:15
they may possess the *r* of Edom... Amos 9:12
surely gather the *r* of Israel... Mic 2:12
I will make her that halted a *r*... Mic 4:7
then the *r* of his brethren shall... Mic 5:3
the *r* of Jacob shall be in the... Mic 5:7
the *r* of Jacob shall be among the... Mic 5:8
of the *r* of his heritage... Mic 7:18
all the *r* of the people shall... Hab 2:8
I will cut off the *r* of Baal from... Zeph 1:4
for the *r* of the house of Judah... Zeph 2:7
the *r* of my people shall possess... Zeph 2:9
The *r* of Israel shall not do... Zeph 3:13
with all the *r* of the people,... Hag 1:12
spirit of all the *r* of the people... Hag 1:14
*r* of this people in these days... Zec 8:6
I will cause the *r* of this people... Zec 8:12
the *r* took his servants, and... Mt 22:6
of the sea, a *r* shall be saved... Rom 9:27
a *r* according to the election of... Rom 11:5
the *r* were affrighted, and gave... Rev 11:13
make war with the *r* of her seed... Rev 12:17
the *r* were slain with the sword... Rev 19:21

**REMOVE**
to *r* it from Ephraim's head unto... Gen 48:17
of Israel *r* from tribe to tribe... Num 36:7
Neither shall the inheritance *r*... Num 36:9
Thou shalt not *r* thy neighbour's... Deut 19:14
then ye shall *r* from your place,... Josh 3:3
then would I *r* Abimelech... Judg 9:29
So David would not *r* the ark of... 2Sa 6:10
I will *r* Judah also out of my... 2Kin 23:27
to *r* them out of his sight, for... 2Kin 24:3
Neither will I any more *r* the... 2Chr 33:8
Some *r* the landmarks... Job 24:2
till I die I will not *r* mine... Job 27:5
not the hand of the wicked *r* me... Ps 36:11
*R* thy stroke away from me... Ps 39:10
*R* from me reproach and contempt... Ps 119:22
*R* from me the way of lying... Ps 119:29
*r* thy foot from evil... Prov 4:27
*R* thy way far from her, and come... Prov 5:8
*R* not the ancient landmark, which... Prov 22:28
*R* not the old landmark... Prov 23:10
*R* far from me vanity and lies... Prov 30:8
Therefore *r* sorrow from thy heart... Eccl 11:10
the earth shall *r* out of her... Is 13:13
from his place shall he not *r*... Is 46:7
my sight, then shalt thou not *r*... Jer 4:1
to *r* you far from your land... Jer 27:10
that I should *r* it from before my... Jer 32:31
they shall *r*, they shall depart,... Jer 50:3
*R* out of the midst of Babylon, and... Jer 50:8
and *r* by day in their sight... Eze 12:3
thou shalt *r* from thy place to... Eze 12:3
they shall *r* and go into captivity... Eze 12:11
*R* the diadem, and take off the... Eze 21:26
*r* violence and spoil, and execute... Eze 45:9
were like them that *r* the bound... Hos 5:10
But I will *r* far off from you the... Joel 2:20
that ye might *r* them far from... Joel 3:6
which ye shall not *r* your necks... Mic 2:3
I will *r* the iniquity of that... Zec 3:9
mountain shall *r* toward the north... Zec 14:4
mountain, *R* hence to yonder place... Mt 17:20
and it shall *r*... Mt 17:20
be willing, *r* this cup from me... Lk 22:42
so that I could *r* mountains... 1Cor 13:2
will *r* thy candlestick out of his... Rev 2:5

**REMOVED**
Noah *r* the covering of the ark,... Gen 8:13
he *r* from thence unto a mountain... Gen 12:8
Then Abram *r* his tent... Gen 13:18
he *r* from thence, and digged... Gen 26:22
he *r* that day the he goats that... Gen 30:35
he *r* them to cities from one end... Gen 47:21
he *r* the swarms of flies from... Ex 8:31
went before the camp of Israel, *r*... Ex 14:19
and when the people saw it, they *r*... Ex 20:18
the people *r* from Hazeroth... Num 12:16
From thence they *r*, and pitched in... Num 21:12
From thence they *r*, and pitched on.. Num 21:13
children of Israel *r* from Rameses... Num 33:5
they *r* from Etham, and turned... Num 33:7
they *r* from Marah, and came unto... Num 33:9
they *r* from Elim, and encamped by.. Num 33:10
they *r* from the Red sea, and... Num 33:11
they *r* from Alush, and encamped at. Num 33:14
they *r* from the desert of Sinai,... Num 33:16
they *r* from Libnah, and pitched at... Num 33:21
they *r* from mount Shapher, and... Num 33:24
they *r* from Haradah, and pitched... Num 33:25
they *r* from Makheloth, and... Num 33:26
they *r* from Tarah, and pitched in... Num 33:28
they *r* from Bene-jaakan, and... Num 33:32
they *r* from Jotbathah, and... Num 33:34
they *r* from Ezion-gaber, and... Num 33:36
they *r* from Kadesh, and pitched in... Num 33:37
they *r* from Dibon-gad, and... Num 33:46
they *r* from Almon-diblathaim, and... Num 33:47
shalt be *r* into all the kingdoms... Deut 28:25
they *r* from Shittim, and came to... Josh 3:1
when the people *r* from their... Josh 3:14
why his hand is not *r* from you... 1Sa 6:3
Therefore Saul *r* him from him... 1Sa 18:13
he *r* Amasa out of the highway... 2Sa 20:12
When he was *r* out of the highway,... 2Sa 20:13
*r* all the idols that his fathers... 1Kin 15:12
even her he *r* from being queen,... 1Kin 15:13
But the high places were not *r*... 1Kin 15:14
that the high places were not *r*... 2Kin 15:4
the high places were not *r*... 2Kin 15:35
*r* the laver from off them... 2Kin 16:17
and *r* them out of his sight... 2Kin 17:18
Until the LORD *r* Israel out of... 2Kin 17:23
The nations which thou hast *r*... 2Kin 17:26
He *r* the high places, and brake... 2Kin 18:4
of my sight, as I have *r* Israel... 2Kin 23:27
Geba, and they *r* them to Manahath... 1Chr 8:6
he *r* them, and begat Uzza, and... 1Chr 8:7
he *r* her from being queen,... 2Chr 15:16
they *r* the burnt offerings, that... 2Chr 35:12
the rock is *r* out of his place... Job 14:18
the rock be *r* out of his place... Job 18:4
mine hope hath he *r* like a tree... Job 19:10
Even so would he have *r* thee out... Job 36:16
we fear, though the earth be *r*... Ps 46:2
I *r* his shoulder from the burden... Ps 81:6
the west, so far hath he *r* our... Ps 103:12
that it should not be *r* for ever... Ps 104:5
as mount Zion, which cannot be *r*... Ps 125:1
The righteous shall never be *r*... Prov 10:30
And the LORD have *r* men far away... Is 6:12

I have *r* the bounds of the people ... Is 10:13
Madmenah is *r* ... Is 10:31
fastened in the sure place be *r* ... Is 22:25
shall be *r* like a cottage ... Is 24:20
thou hadst *r* it far unto all the ... Is 26:15
but have *r* their heart far from ... Is 29:13
be *r* into a corner any more ... Is 30:20
stakes thereof shall ever be *r* ... Is 33:20
is *r* from me as a shepherd's tent ... Is 38:12
shall depart, and the hills be *r* ... Is 54:10
the covenant of my peace be *r* ... Is 54:10
I will cause them to be *r* into ... Jer 15:4
I will deliver them to be *r* into ... Jer 24:9
will deliver them to be *r* to all ... Jer 29:18
I will make you to be *r* into all ... Jer 34:17
therefore she is *r* ... Lam 1:8
thou hast *r* my soul far off from ... Lam 3:17
streets, and their gold shall be *r* ... Eze 7:19
them, and will give them to be *r* ... Eze 23:46
as the uncleanness of a *r* woman ... Eze 36:17
stretched themselves shall be *r* ... Amos 6:7
how hath he *r* it from me ... Mic 2:4
day shall the decree be far *r* ... Mic 7:11
say unto this mountain, Be thou *r* ... Mt 21:21
say unto this mountain, Be thou *r* ... Mk 11:23
he *r* him into this land, wherein ... Acts 7:4
And when he had *r* him, he raised ... Acts 13:22
I marvel that ye are so soon *r* ... Gal 1:6

**REMOVETH**
Cursed be he that *r* his ... Deut 27:17
Which *r* the mountains, and they ... Job 9:5
He *r* away the speech of the ... Job 12:20
Whoso *r* stones shall be hurt ... Eccl 10:9
he *r* kings, and setteth up kings ... Dan 2:21

**REMOVING**
*r* from thence all the speckled and ... Gen 30:32
a captive, and *r* to and fro ... Is 49:21
of man, prepare thee stuff for *r* ... Eze 12:3
in their sight, as stuff for *r* ... Eze 12:4
signifieth the *r* of those things ... Heb 12:27

**REMPHAN** *(rem'-fan) An idol worshipped by Israel.*
Moloch, and the star of your god *R* ... Acts 7:43

**REND**
the hole, that it should not *r* ... Ex 39:23
heads, neither *r* your clothes ... Lev 10:6
then he shall *r* it out of the ... Lev 13:56
his head, nor *r* his clothes ... Lev 21:10
*R* your clothes, and gird you with ... 2Sa 3:31
I will surely *r* the kingdom from ... 1Kin 11:11
but I will *r* it out of the hand ... 1Kin 11:12
Howbeit I will not *r* away all the ... 1Kin 11:13
I will *r* the kingdom out of the ... 1Kin 11:31
didst *r* thy clothes, and weep ... 2Chr 34:27
A time to *r*, and a time to sew ... Eccl 3:7
that thou wouldest *r* the heavens ... Is 64:1
and a stormy wind shall *r* it ... Eze 13:11
I will even *r* it with a stormy ... Eze 13:13
break, and *r* all their shoulder ... Eze 29:7
will *r* the caul of their heart, ... Hos 13:8
*r* your heart, and not your ... Joel 2:13
feet, and turn again and *r* you ... Mt 7:6
among themselves, Let us not *r* it ... Jn 19:24

**RENDER**
which they shall *r* unto me ... Num 18:9
I will *r* vengeance to mine ... Deut 32:41
and will *r* vengeance to his ... Deut 32:43
did God *r* upon their heads ... Judg 9:57
The LORD *r* to every man his ... 1Sa 26:23
*r* unto every man according unto ... 2Chr 6:30
for he will *r* unto man his ... Job 33:26
work of a man shall he *r* unto him ... Job 34:11
*r* to them their desert ... Ps 28:4
They also that *r* evil for good ... Ps 38:20
I will *r* praises unto thee ... Ps 56:12
*r* unto our neighbours sevenfold ... Ps 79:12
*r* a reward to the proud ... Ps 94:2
What shall I *r* unto the LORD for ... Ps 116:12
shall not he *r* to every man ... Prov 24:12
I will *r* to the man according to ... Prov 24:29
seven men that can *r* a reason ... Prov 26:16
to *r* his anger with fury, and his ... Is 66:15
he will *r* unto her a recompence ... Jer 51:6
I will *r* unto Babylon and to all ... Jer 51:24
*R* unto them a recompence, O LORD, ... Lam 3:64
so will we *r* the calves of our ... Hos 14:2
will ye *r* me a recompence ... Joel 3:4
that I will *r* double unto thee ... Zec 9:12
which shall *r* him the fruits in ... Mt 21:41
*R* therefore unto Caesar the ... Mt 22:21
*R* to Caesar the things that are ... Mk 12:17
*R* therefore unto Caesar the ... Lk 20:25
Who will *r* to every man according ... Rom 2:6
*R* therefore to all their dues ... Rom 13:7
Let the husband *r* unto the wife ... 1Cor 7:3
can we *r* to God again for you ... 1Th 3:9
See that none *r* evil for evil ... 1Th 5:15

**RENDERED**
Thus God *r* the wickedness of ... Judg 9:56
*r* unto the king of Israel an ... 2Kin 3:4
But Hezekiah *r* not again ... 2Chr 32:25
a man's hands shall be *r* unto him ... Prov 12:14

**RENDEREST**
for thou *r* to every man according ... Ps 62:12

**RENDERETH**
a voice of the LORD that *r* ... Is 66:6

**RENDERING**
Not *r* evil for evil, or railing ... 1Pet 3:9

**RENDING**
*r* it in pieces, while there is ... Ps 7:2

**RENEW**
to Gilgal, and *r* the kingdom there ... 1Sa 11:14
*r* a right spirit within me ... Ps 51:10
the LORD shall *r* their strength ... Is 40:31
let the people *r* their strength ... Is 41:1
*r* our days as of old ... Lam 5:21
to *r* them again unto repentance ... Heb 6:6

**RENEWED**
*r* the altar of the LORD, that was ... 2Chr 15:8
in me, and my bow was *r* in my hand. Job 29:20
thy youth is *r* like the eagle's ... Ps 103:5
the inward man is *r* day by day ... 2Cor 4:16
be *r* in the spirit of your mind ... Eph 4:23
which is *r* in knowledge after the ... Col 3:10

**RENEWEST**
Thou *r* thy witnesses against me, ... Job 10:17
thou *r* the face of the earth ... Ps 104:30

**RENEWING**
transformed by the *r* of your mind ... Rom 12:2
and *r* of the Holy Ghost ... Titus 3:5

**RENOUNCED**
But have *r* the hidden things of ... 2Cor 4:2

**RENOWN**
men which were of old, men of *r* ... Gen 6:4
in the congregation, men of *r* ... Num 16:2
thy *r* went forth among the ... Eze 16:14
the harlot because of thy *r* ... Eze 16:15
raise up for them a plant of *r* ... Eze 34:29
it shall be to them a *r* the day ... Eze 39:13
hand, and hast gotten thee *r* ... Dan 9:15

**RENOWNED**
These were the *r* of the ... Num 1:16
of evildoers shall never be *r* ... Is 14:20
and rulers, great lords and *r* ... Eze 23:23
the *r* city, which wast strong in ... Eze 26:17

**RENT**
and he *r* his clothes ... Gen 37:29
is without doubt *r* in pieces ... Gen 37:33
Jacob *r* his clothes, and put ... Gen 37:34
Then they *r* their clothes, and ... Gen 44:13
of an habergeon, that it be not *r* ... Ex 28:32
plague is, his clothes shall be *r* ... Lev 13:45
the land, *r* their clothes ... Num 14:6
Joshua *r* his clothes, and fell to ... Josh 7:6
asses, and wine bottles, old, and *r* ... Josh 9:4
and, behold, they be *r* ... Josh 9:13
that he *r* his clothes, and said, ... Judg 11:35
he *r* him as he would have *r* a ... Judg 14:6
*r* him as he would have *r* a kid ... Judg 14:6
the same day with his clothes *r* ... 1Sa 4:12
the skirt of his mantle, and it *r* ... 1Sa 15:27
The LORD hath *r* the kingdom of ... 1Sa 15:28
for the LORD hath *r* the kingdom ... 1Sa 28:17
camp from Saul with his clothes *r* ... 2Sa 1:2
hold on his clothes, and *r* them ... 2Sa 1:11
*r* her garment of divers colours ... 2Sa 13:19
stood by with their clothes *r* ... 2Sa 13:31
came to meet him with his coat *r* ... 2Sa 15:32
so that the earth *r* with the ... 1Kin 1:40
on him, and *r* it in twelve pieces ... 1Kin 11:30
Behold, the altar shall be *r* ... 1Kin 13:3
The altar also was *r*, and the ... 1Kin 13:5
*r* the kingdom away from the house ... 1Kin 14:8
strong wind *r* the mountains, and ... 1Kin 19:11
that he *r* his clothes, and put ... 1Kin 21:27
clothes, and *r* them in two pieces ... 2Kin 2:12
that he *r* his clothes, and said, ... 2Kin 5:7
king of Israel had *r* his clothes ... 2Kin 5:8
Wherefore hast thou *r* thy clothes ... 2Kin 5:8
the woman, that he *r* his clothes ... 2Kin 6:30
Athaliah *r* her clothes, and cried, ... 2Kin 11:14
For he *r* Israel from the house of ... 2Kin 17:21
to Hezekiah with their clothes *r* ... 2Kin 18:37
that he *r* his clothes, and covered ... 2Kin 19:1
of the law, that he *r* his clothes ... 2Kin 22:11
hast *r* thy clothes, and wept ... 2Kin 22:19
Then Athaliah *r* her clothes ... 2Chr 23:13
of the law, that he *r* his clothes ... 2Chr 34:19
I *r* my garment and my mantle, and ... Ezr 9:3
having *r* my garment and my mantle, ... Ezr 9:5
Mordecai *r* his clothes, and put on ... Est 4:1
*r* his mantle, and shaved his head, ... Job 1:20
they *r* every one his mantle, and ... Job 2:12
and the cloud is not *r* under them ... Job 26:8
and instead of a girdle a *r* ... Is 3:24
to Hezekiah with their clothes *r* ... Is 36:22
that he *r* his clothes, and covered ... Is 37:1
nor *r* their garments, neither the ... Jer 36:24
beards shaven, and their clothes *r* ... Jer 41:5
pain, and No shall be *r* asunder ... Eze 30:16
garment, and the *r* is made worse ... Mt 9:16
the high priest *r* his clothes ... Mt 26:65
the veil of the temple was *r* in ... Mt 27:51
earth did quake, and the rocks *r* ... Mt 27:51
the old, and the *r* is made worse ... Mk 2:21
*r* him sore, and came out of him ... Mk 9:26
the high priest *r* his clothes ... Mk 14:63
the veil of the temple was *r* in ... Mk 15:38
then both the new maketh a *r* ... Lk 5:36
of the temple was *r* in the midst ... Lk 23:45
they *r* their clothes, and ran in ... Acts 14:14
the magistrates *r* off their ... Acts 16:22

**RENTEST**
though thou *r* thy face with ... Jer 4:30

**REPAID**
to the righteous good shall be *r* ... Prov 13:21

**REPAIR**
let them *r* the breaches of the ... 2Kin 12:5
Why *r* ye not the breaches of the ... 2Kin 12:7
neither to *r* the breaches of the ... 2Kin 12:8
hewed stone to *r* the breaches of ... 2Kin 12:12
laid out for the house to *r* it ... 2Kin 12:12
to *r* the breaches of the house, ... 2Kin 22:5
and hewn stone to *r* the house ... 2Kin 22:6
minded to *r* the house of the LORD ... 2Chr 24:4
gather of all Israel money to *r* ... 2Chr 24:5
carpenters to *r* the house of the ... 2Chr 24:12
to *r* the house of the LORD his ... 2Chr 34:8
in the house of the LORD, to *r* ... 2Chr 34:10
to *r* the desolations thereof, and ... Ezr 9:9
they shall *r* the waste cities, ... Is 61:4

**REPAIRED**
*r* the cities, and dwelt in them ... Judg 21:23
*r* the breaches of the city of ... 1Kin 11:27
he *r* the altar of the LORD that ... 1Kin 18:30
not *r* the breaches of the house ... 2Kin 12:6
*r* therewith the house of the LORD ... 2Kin 12:14
Joab *r* the rest of the city ... 1Chr 11:8
the house of the LORD, and *r* them ... 2Chr 29:3
*r* Millo in the city of David, and ... 2Chr 32:5
he *r* the altar of the LORD, and ... 2Chr 33:16
next unto them *r* Meremoth the son ... Neh 3:4
next unto them *r* Meshullam the ... Neh 3:4
next unto them *r* Zadok the son of ... Neh 3:4
And next unto them the Tekoites *r* ... Neh 3:5
Moreover the old gate *r* Jehoiada ... Neh 3:6
next unto them *r* Melatiah the ... Neh 3:7
Next unto him *r* Uzziel the son of ... Neh 3:8
Next unto him also *r* Hananiah the ... Neh 3:8
next unto them *r* Rephaiah the son ... Neh 3:9
next unto them *r* Jedaiah the son ... Neh 3:10
next unto him *r* Hattush the son ... Neh 3:10
*r* the other piece, and the tower ... Neh 3:11
next unto him *r* Shallum the son ... Neh 3:12
The valley gate *r* Hanun, and the ... Neh 3:13
But the dung gate *r* Malchiah the ... Neh 3:14
*r* Shallun the son of Colhozeh ... Neh 3:15
After him *r* Nehemiah the son of ... Neh 3:16
After him *r* the Levites, Rehum ... Neh 3:17
Next unto him *r* Hashabiah ... Neh 3:17
After him *r* their brethren, Bavai ... Neh 3:18
next to him *r* Ezer the son of ... Neh 3:19
earnestly *r* the other piece ... Neh 3:20
After him *r* Meremoth the son of ... Neh 3:21
after him *r* the priests, the men ... Neh 3:22
After him *r* Benjamin and Hashub ... Neh 3:23
After him *r* Azariah the son of ... Neh 3:23
After him *r* Binnui the son of ... Neh 3:24
them the Tekoites *r* another piece ... Neh 3:27
the horse gate *r* the priests ... Neh 3:28
After them *r* Zadok the son of ... Neh 3:29
After him *r* also Shemaiah the son ... Neh 3:29
After him *r* Hananiah the son of ... Neh 3:30
After him *r* Meshullam the son of ... Neh 3:30
After him *r* Malchiah the ... Neh 3:31
the sheep gate *r* the goldsmiths ... Neh 3:32

**REPAIRER**
The *r* of the breach, The restorer ... Is 58:12

**REPAIRING**
the *r* of the house of God, behold ... 2Chr 24:27

**REPAY**
he will *r* him to his face ... Deut 7:10
who shall *r* him what he hath done ... Job 21:31
prevented me, that I should *r* him ... Job 41:11
deeds, accordingly he will *r* ... Is 59:18
the islands he will *r* recompence ... Is 59:18
when I come again, I will *r* thee ... Lk 10:35
I will *r*, saith the Lord ... Rom 12:19
with mine own hand, I will *r* it ... Philem 19

**REPAYETH**
*r* them that hate him to their ... Deut 7:10

**REPEATETH**
but he that *r* a matter separateth ... Prov 17:9

**REPENT**
the people *r* when they see war ... Ex 13:17
*r* of this evil against thy people ... Ex 32:12
the son of man, that he should *r* ... Num 23:19
*r* himself for his servants, when ... Deut 32:36
of Israel will not lie nor *r* ... 1Sa 15:29
he is not a man, that he should *r* ... 1Sa 15:29
they were carried captives, and *r* ... 1Kin 8:47
myself, and *r* in dust and ashes ... Job 42:6
let it *r* thee concerning thy ... Ps 90:13
LORD hath sworn, and will not *r* ... Ps 110:4
he will *r* himself concerning his ... Ps 135:14
I have purposed it, and will not *r* ... Jer 4:28
I will *r* of the evil that I ... Jer 18:8
voice, then I will *r* of the good ... Jer 18:10
that I may *r* me of the evil, ... Jer 26:3

the LORD will *r* him of the evil ... Jer 26:13
for I *r* me of the evil that I ... Jer 42:10
*R*, and turn yourselves from your ... Eze 14:6
*R*, and turn yourselves from all ... Eze 18:30
will I spare, neither will I *r* ... Eze 24:14
knoweth if he will return and *r* ... Joel 2:14
can tell if God will turn and *r* ... Jonah 3:9
And saying, *R* ye ... Mt 3:2
began to preach, and to say, *R* ... Mt 4:17
*r* ye, and believe the gospel ... Mk 1:15
and preached that men should *r* ... Mk 6:12
but, except ye *r*, ye shall all ... Lk 13:3
but, except ye *r*, ye shall all ... Lk 13:5
them from the dead, they will *r* ... Lk 16:30
and if he *r*, forgive him ... Lk 17:3
turn again to thee, saying, I *r* ... Lk 17:4
Then Peter said unto them, *R* ... Acts 2:38
*R* ye therefore, and be converted, ... Acts 3:19
*R* therefore of this thy ... Acts 8:22
all men every where to *r* ... Acts 17:30
the Gentiles, that they should *r* ... Acts 26:20
I do not *r*, though I did *r* ... 2Cor 7:8
him, The Lord sware and will not *r* ... Heb 7:21
from whence thou art fallen, and *r* ... Rev 2:5
out of his place, except thou *r* ... Rev 2:5
*R*; or else I will ... Rev 2:16
her space to *r* of her fornication ... Rev 2:21
except they *r* of their deeds ... Rev 2:22
and heard, and hold fast, and *r* ... Rev 3:3
be zealous therefore, and *r* ... Rev 3:19

**REPENTANCE**
*r* shall be hid from mine eyes ... Hos 13:14
forth therefore fruits meet for *r* ... Mt 3:8
baptize you with water unto *r* ... Mt 3:11
the righteous, but sinners to *r* ... Mt 9:13
preach the baptism of *r* for the ... Mk 1:4
the righteous, but sinners to *r* ... Mk 2:17
preaching the baptism of *r* for ... Lk 3:3
therefore fruits worthy of *r* ... Lk 3:8
the righteous, but sinners to *r* ... Lk 5:32
just persons, which need no *r* ... Lk 15:7
And that *r* and remission of sins ... Lk 24:47
Saviour, for to give *r* to Israel ... Acts 5:31
the Gentiles granted *r* unto life ... Acts 11:18
his coming the baptism of *r* to ... Acts 13:24
baptized with the baptism of *r* ... Acts 19:4
*r* toward God, and faith toward our ... Acts 20:21
to God, and do works meet for *r* ... Acts 26:20
goodness of God leadeth thee to *r* ... Rom 2:4
and calling of God are without *r* ... Rom 11:29
sorry, but that ye sorrowed to *r* ... 2Cor 7:9
For godly sorrow worketh *r* to ... 2Cor 7:10
*r* to the acknowledging of the ... 2Ti 2:25
foundation of *r* from dead works ... Heb 6:1
away, to renew them again unto *r* ... Heb 6:6
for he found no place of *r* ... Heb 12:17
but that all should come to *r* ... 2Pet 3:9

**REPENTED**
it *r* the LORD that he had made ... Gen 6:6
the LORD *r* of the evil which he ... Ex 32:14
for it *r* the LORD because of ... Judg 2:18
the children of Israel *r* them for ... Judg 21:6
the people *r* them for Benjamin, ... Judg 21:15
the LORD *r* that he had made Saul ... 1Sa 15:35
the LORD *r* him of the evil, and ... 2Sa 24:16
he *r* him of the evil, and said to ... 1Chr 21:15
*r* according to the multitude of ... Ps 106:45
no man *r* him of his wickedness, ... Jer 8:6
the LORD overthrew, and *r* not ... Jer 20:16
the LORD *r* him of the evil which ... Jer 26:19
after that I was turned, I *r* ... Jer 31:19
The LORD *r* for this ... Amos 7:3
The LORD *r* for this ... Amos 7:6
God *r* of the evil, that he had ... Jonah 3:10
the LORD of hosts, and I *r* not ... Zec 8:14
were done, because they *r* not ... Mt 11:20
they would have *r* long ago in ... Mt 11:21
because they *r* at the preaching ... Mt 12:41
but afterward he *r*, and went ... Mt 21:29
*r* not afterward, that ye might ... Mt 21:32
*r* himself, and brought again the ... Mt 27:3
you, they had a great while ago *r* ... Lk 10:13
for they *r* at the preaching of ... Lk 11:32
to salvation not to be *r* of ... 2Cor 7:10
have not *r* of the uncleanness and ... 2Cor 12:21
and she *r* not ... Rev 2:21
*r* not of the works of their hands ... Rev 9:20
Neither *r* they of their murders, ... Rev 9:21
they *r* not to give him glory ... Rev 16:9
sores, and *r* not of their deeds ... Rev 16:11

**REPENTEST**
kindness, and *r* thee of the evil ... Jonah 4:2

**REPENTETH**
for it *r* me that I have made them ... Gen 6:7
It *r* me that I have set up Saul ... 1Sa 15:11
kindness, and *r* him of the evil ... Joel 2:13
in heaven over one sinner that *r* ... Lk 15:7
of God over one sinner that *r* ... Lk 15:10

**REPENTING**
I am weary with *r* ... Jer 15:6

**REPENTINGS**
my *r* are kindled together ... Hos 11:8

**REPETITIONS**
But when ye pray, use not vain *r* ... Mt 6:7

**REPHAEL** (*re'-fa-el*) *A sanctuary servant.*
Othni, and *R*, and Obed, Elzabad, ... 1Chr 26:7

**REPHAH** (*re'-fah*) *A grandson of Ephraim.*
*R* was his son, also Resheph, and ... 1Chr 7:25

**REPHAIAH** (*ref-a-i'-ah*) See RAPHA, RHESA.
*1. Head of a family.*
the sons of *R*, the sons of Arnan, ... 1Chr 3:21
*2. A captain of Simeon.*
Pelatiah, and Neariah, and *R* ... 1Chr 4:42
*3. A son of Tola.*
Uzzi, and *R*, and Jeriel, and Jahmai, ... 1Chr 7:2
*4. Son of Binea.*
*R* his son, Eleasah his son, Azel ... 1Chr 9:43
*5. A repairer of Jerusalem's wall.*
them repaired *R* the son of Hur ... Neh 3:9

**REPHAIM** (*re-fa'-im*) See REPHAIMS. *A valley near Jerusalem.*
themselves in the valley of *R* ... 2Sa 5:18
themselves in the valley of *R* ... 2Sa 5:22
pitched in the valley of *R* ... 2Sa 23:13
encamped in the valley of *R* ... 1Chr 11:15
themselves in the valley of *R* ... 1Chr 14:9
gathereth ears in the valley of *R* ... Is 17:5

**REPHAIMS** (*re-fa'-ims*) See REPHAIM. *A tribe of Canaanites.*
smote the *R* in Ashteroth Karnaim, ... Gen 14:5
and the Perizzites, and the *R* ... Gen 15:20

**REPHAN** See REMPHAN.

**REPHIDIM** (*ref'-i-dim*) *An Israelite encampment in the wilderness.*
of the LORD, and pitched in *R* ... Ex 17:1
and fought with Israel in *R* ... Ex 17:8
For they were departed from *R* ... Ex 19:2
from Alush, and encamped at *R* ... Num 33:14
And they departed from *R*, and ... Num 33:15

**REPLENISH**
*r* the earth, and subdue it ... Gen 1:28
and multiply, and *r* the earth ... Gen 9:1

**REPLENISHED**
because they be *r* from the east ... Is 2:6
that pass over the sea, have *r* ... Is 23:2
I have *r* every sorrowful soul ... Jer 31:25
I shall be *r*, now she is laid ... Eze 26:2
and thou wast *r*, and made very ... Eze 27:25

**REPLIEST**
who art thou that *r* against God ... Rom 9:20

**REPORT**
unto his father their evil *r* ... Gen 37:2
Thou shalt not raise a false *r* ... Ex 23:1
they brought up an evil *r* of the ... Num 13:32
bring up the evil *r* upon the land ... Num 14:37
heaven, who shall hear *r* of thee ... Deut 2:25
for it is no good *r* that I hear ... 1Sa 2:24
It was a true *r* that I heard in ... 1Kin 10:6
It was a true *r* which I heard in ... 2Chr 9:5
might have matter for an evil *r* ... Neh 6:13
a good *r* maketh the bones fat ... Prov 15:30
As at the *r* concerning Egypt, so ... Is 23:5
be sorely pained at the *r* of Tyre ... Is 23:5
vexation only to understand the *r* ... Is 28:19
Who hath believed our *r* ... Is 53:1
*R*, say they, and we will *r* it ... Jer 20:10
Babylon hath heard the *r* of them ... Jer 50:43
Lord, who hath believed our *r* ... Jn 12:38
among you seven men of honest *r* ... Acts 6:3
of good *r* among all the nation of ... Acts 10:22
having a good *r* of all the Jews ... Acts 22:12
Lord, who hath believed our *r* ... Rom 10:16
*r* that God is in you of a truth ... 1Cor 14:25
By honour and dishonour, by evil *r* ... 2Cor 6:8
and good *r*: as deceivers ... 2Cor 6:8
whatsoever things are of good *r* ... Phil 4:8
good *r* of them which are without ... 1Ti 3:7
it the elders obtained a good *r* ... Heb 11:2
obtained a good *r* through faith ... Heb 11:39
Demetrius hath good *r* of all men ... 3Jn 12

**REPORTED**
It is *r* among the heathen, and ... Neh 6:6
now shall it be *r* to the king ... Neh 6:7
Also they *r* his good deeds before ... Neh 6:19
in their eyes, when it shall be *r* ... Est 1:17
*r* the matter, saying, I have done ... Eze 9:11
this saying is commonly *r* among ... Mt 28:15
*r* all that the chief priests and ... Acts 4:23
Which was well *r* of by the ... Acts 16:2
rather, (as we be slanderously *r* ... Rom 3:8
It is *r* commonly that there is ... 1Cor 5:1
Well *r* of for good works ... 1Ti 5:10
which are now *r* unto you by them ... 1Pet 1:12

**REPROACH**
and said, God hath taken away my *r*. Gen 30:23
for that were a *r* unto us ... Gen 34:14
away the *r* of Egypt from off you ... Josh 5:9
among the sheaves, and *r* her not ... Ruth 2:15
lay it for a *r* upon all Israel ... 1Sa 11:2
and taketh away the *r* from Israel ... 1Sa 17:26
of my *r* from the hand of Nabal ... 1Sa 25:39
hath sent to *r* the living God ... 2Kin 19:4
hath sent him to *r* the living God ... 2Kin 19:16
are in great affliction and *r* ... Neh 1:3
Jerusalem, that we be no more a *r* ... Neh 2:17
turn their *r* upon their own head, ... Neh 4:4
the *r* of the heathen our enemies ... Neh 5:9
evil report, that they might *r* me ... Neh 6:13
me, and plead against me my *r* ... Job 19:5
I have heard the check of my *r* ... Job 20:3
my heart shall not *r* me so long ... Job 27:6
nor taketh up a *r* against his ... Ps 15:3
a *r* of men, and despised of the ... Ps 22:6
I was a *r* among all mine enemies, ... Ps 31:11
make me not the *r* of the foolish ... Ps 39:8
in my bones, mine enemies *r* me ... Ps 42:10
Thou makest us a *r* to our ... Ps 44:13
save me from the *r* of him that ... Ps 57:3
for thy sake I have borne *r* ... Ps 69:7
with fasting, that was to my *r* ... Ps 69:10
Thou hast known my *r*, and my shame ... Ps 69:19
*R* hath broken my heart ... Ps 69:20
let them be covered with *r* ... Ps 71:13
how long shall the adversary *r* ... Ps 74:10
he put them to a perpetual *r* ... Ps 78:66
We are become a *r* to our ... Ps 79:4
into their bosom their *r*, ... Ps 79:12
he is a *r* to his neighbours ... Ps 89:41
Lord, the *r* of thy servants ... Ps 89:50
the *r* of all the mighty people ... Ps 89:50
Mine enemies *r* me all the day ... Ps 102:8
I became also a *r* unto them ... Ps 109:25
Remove from me *r* and contempt ... Ps 119:22
Turn away my *r* which I fear ... Ps 119:39
his *r* shall not be wiped away ... Prov 6:33
but sin is a *r* to any people ... Prov 14:34
also contempt, and with ignominy *r* ... Prov 18:3
that causeth shame, and bringeth *r* ... Prov 19:26
yea, strife and *r* shall cease ... Prov 22:10
by thy name, to take away our *r* ... Is 4:1
profit, but a shame, and also a *r* ... Is 30:5
hath sent to *r* the living God ... Is 37:4
hath sent to *r* the living God ... Is 37:17
fear ye not the *r* of men, neither ... Is 51:7
shalt not remember the *r* of thy ... Is 54:4
word of the LORD is unto them a *r* ... Jer 6:10
of the LORD was made a *r* unto me ... Jer 20:8
bring an everlasting *r* upon you ... Jer 23:40
earth for their hurt, to be a *r* ... Jer 24:9
and an hissing, and a *r*, among all ... Jer 29:18
I did bear the *r* of my youth ... Jer 31:19
astonishment, and a curse, and a *r* ... Jer 42:18
a *r* among all the nations of the ... Jer 44:8
astonishment, and a curse, and a *r* ... Jer 44:12
shall become a desolation, a *r* ... Jer 49:13
because we have heard *r* ... Jer 51:51
he is filled full with *r* ... Lam 3:30
Thou hast heard their *r*, O LORD, ... Lam 3:61
consider, and behold our *r* ... Lam 5:1
a *r* among the nations that are ... Eze 5:14
So it shall be a *r* and a taunt, an ... Eze 5:15
as at the time of thy *r* of the ... Eze 16:57
Ammonites, and concerning their *r* ... Eze 21:28
I made thee a *r* unto the heathen ... Eze 22:4
bear the *r* of the people any more ... Eze 36:15
*r* of famine among the heathen ... Eze 36:30
thy people are become a *r* to all ... Dan 9:16
the *r* offered by him to cease ... Dan 11:18
without his own *r* he shall cause ... Dan 11:18
his *r* shall his Lord return unto ... Hos 12:14
and give not thine heritage to *r* ... Joel 2:17
make you a *r* among the heathen ... Joel 2:19
ye shall bear the *r* of my people ... Mic 6:16
I have heard the *r* of Moab ... Zeph 2:8
to whom the *r* of it was a burden ... Zeph 3:18
me, to take away my *r* among men ... Lk 1:25
their company, and shall *r* you ... Lk 6:22
I speak as concerning *r*, as ... 2Cor 11:21
lest he fall into *r* and the snare ... 1Ti 3:7
we both labour and suffer *r* ... 1Ti 4:10
Esteeming the *r* of Christ greater ... Heb 11:26
without the camp, bearing his *r* ... Heb 13:13

**REPROACHED**
Whom hast thou *r* and blasphemed ... 2Kin 19:22
messengers thou hast *r* the Lord ... 2Kin 19:23
These ten times have ye *r* me ... Job 19:3
For it was not an enemy that *r* me ... Ps 55:12
that *r* thee are fallen upon me ... Ps 69:9
this, that the enemy hath *r* ... Ps 74:18
wherewith they have *r* thee ... Ps 79:12
Wherewith thine enemies have *r* ... Ps 89:51
wherewith they have *r* the ... Ps 89:51
Whom hast thou *r* and blasphemed ... Is 37:23
thy servants hast thou *r* the Lord ... Is 37:24
whereby they have *r* my people ... Zeph 2:8
their pride, because they have *r* ... Zeph 2:10
of them that *r* thee fell on me ... Rom 15:3
If ye be *r* for the name of Christ ... 1Pet 4:14

**REPROACHES**
the *r* of them that reproached ... Ps 69:9
to the curse, and Israel to *r* ... Is 43:28
The *r* of them that reproached ... Rom 15:3
pleasure in infirmities, in *r* ... 2Cor 12:10
were made a gazingstock both by *r* ... Heb 10:33

**REPROACHEST**
thus saying thou *r* us also ... Lk 11:45

**REPROACHETH**
a stranger, the same *r* the LORD ... Num 15:30
For the voice of him that *r* ... Ps 44:16

how the foolish man *r* thee daily.......... Ps 74:22
wherewith to answer him that *r* me.... Ps 119:42
oppresseth the poor *r* his Maker......... Prov 14:31
mocketh the poor *r* his Maker............ Prov 17:5
that I may answer him that *r* me....... Prov 27:11

**REPROACHFULLY**
have smitten me upon the cheek *r*....... Job 16:10
to the adversary to speak *r*.................. 1Ti 5:14

**REPROBATE**
*R* silver shall men call them,.................. Jer 6:30
God gave them over to a *r* mind.......... Rom 1:28
minds, *r* concerning the faith.................. 2Ti 3:8
and unto every good work *r*................ Titus 1:16

**REPROBATES**
Christ is in you, except ye be *r*............ 2Cor 13:5
ye shall know that we are not *r*........... 2Cor 13:6
is honest, though we be as *r*............... 2Cor 13:7

**REPROOF**
and are astonished at his *r*.................. Job 26:11
Turn you at my *r*................................ Prov 1:23
my counsel, and would none of my *r*.. Prov 1:25
they despised all my *r*......................... Prov 1:30
and my heart despised *r*...................... Prov 5:12
but he that refuseth *r* erreth............. Prov 10:17
but he that hateth *r* is brutish............ Prov 12:1
regardeth *r* shall be honoured............ Prov 13:18
he that regardeth *r* is prudent............ Prov 15:5
and he that hateth *r* shall die............. Prov 15:10
The ear that heareth the *r* of............. Prov 15:31
but he that heareth *r* getteth............. Prov 15:32
A *r* entereth more into a wise man.... Prov 17:10
The rod and *r* give wisdom................ Prov 29:15
is profitable for doctrine, for *r*............. 2Ti 3:16

**REPROOFS**
not, and in whose mouth are no *r*.......... Ps 38:14
*r* of instruction are the way of............. Prov 6:23

**REPROVE**
will *r* the words which the LORD.......... 2Kin 19:4
but what doth your arguing *r*............... Job 6:25
Do ye imagine to *r* words, and the......... Job 6:26
He will surely *r* you, if ye do.............. Job 13:10
Will he *r* thee for fear of thee............... Job 22:4
I will not *r* thee for thy......................... Ps 50:8
but I will *r* thee, and set them in........... Ps 50:21
and let him *r* me................................. Ps 141:5
*R* not a scorner, lest he hate................ Prov 9:8
*r* one that hath understanding, and... Prov 19:25
unto his words, lest he *r* thee.............. Prov 30:6
neither *r* after the hearing of................. Is 11:3
*r* with equity for the meek of the............ Is 11:4
will *r* the words which the LORD............ Is 37:4
and thy backslidings shall *r* thee............ Jer 2:19
let no man strive, nor *r* another.............. Hos 4:4
he will *r* the world of sin, and of............. Jn 16:8
of darkness, but rather *r* them.............. Eph 5:11
*r*, rebuke, exhort with all........................ 2Ti 4:2

**REPROVED**
thus she was *r*.................................. Gen 20:16
Abraham *r* Abimelech because of a.... Gen 21:25
he *r* kings for their sakes,................... 1Chr 16:21
he *r* kings for their sakes................... Ps 105:14
that being often *r* hardeneth his............ Prov 29:1
thou not *r* Jeremiah of Anathoth.......... Jer 29:27
what I shall answer when I am *r*.............. Hab 2:1
being *r* by him for Herodias his................ Lk 3:19
light, lest his deeds should be *r*................ Jn 3:20
But all things that are *r* are.................. Eph 5:13

**REPROVER**
so is a wise *r* upon an obedient.......... Prov 25:12
dumb, and shalt not be to them a *r*....... Eze 3:26

**REPROVETH**
he that *r* God, let him answer it............ Job 40:2
He that *r* a scorner getteth to................ Prov 9:7
scorner loveth not one that *r* him...... Prov 15:12
snare for him that *r* in the gate............ Is 29:21

**REPUTATION**
folly him that is in *r* for wisdom........... Eccl 10:1
had in *r* among all the people, and....... Acts 5:34
privately to them which were of *r*.............. Gal 2:2
But made himself of no *r*, and took........ Phil 2:7
and hold such in *r*................................ Phil 2:29

**REPUTED**
beasts, and *r* vile in your sight.............. Job 18:3
of the earth are *r* as nothing................. Dan 4:35

**REQUEST**
them, I would desire a *r* of you............ Judg 8:24
perform the *r* of his handmaid............ 2Sa 14:15
fulfilled the *r* of his servant............... 2Sa 14:22
and the king granted him all his *r*............. Ezr 7:6
me, For what dost thou make *r*............... Neh 2:4
to make *r* before him for her.................... Est 4:8
and what is thy *r*...................................... Est 5:3
and what is thy *r*...................................... Est 5:6
and said, My petition and my *r* is............. Est 5:7
my petition, and to perform my *r*............ Est 5:8
and what is thy *r*...................................... Est 7:2
my petition, and my people at my *r*........ Est 7:3
Haman stood up to make *r* for his............ Est 7:7
or what is thy *r* further......................... Est 9:12
Oh that I might have my *r*....................... Job 6:8
not withholden the *r* of his lips............... Ps 21:2
And he gave them their *r*..................... Ps 106:15
Making *r*, if by any means now at....... Rom 1:10

for you all making *r* with joy.................. Phil 1:4

**REQUESTED**
earrings that he *r* was a thousand....... Judg 8:26
he *r* for himself that he might............ 1Kin 19:4
God granted him that which he *r*........ 1Chr 4:10
therefore he *r* of the prince of............... Dan 1:8
Then Daniel *r* of the king...................... Dan 2:49

**REQUESTS**
let your *r* be made known unto God....... Phil 4:6

**REQUIRE**
your blood of your lives will I *r*.............. Gen 9:5
hand of every beast will I *r* it................ Gen 9:5
brother will I *r* the life of man............... Gen 9:5
of my hand didst thou *r* it.................... Gen 31:39
of my hand shalt thou *r* him................. Gen 43:9
doth the LORD thy God *r* of thee....... Deut 10:12
in my name, I will *r* it of him.............. Deut 18:19
thy God will surely *r* it of thee.......... Deut 23:21
let the LORD himself *r* it..................... Josh 22:23
Let the LORD even *r* it at the............... 1Sa 20:16
but one thing I *r* of thee........................ 2Sa 3:13
now *r* his blood of your hand................. 2Sa 4:11
and whatsoever thou shalt *r* of me...... 2Sa 19:38
all times, as the matter shall *r*............... 1Kin 8:59
then doth my lord *r* this thing............... 1Chr 21:3
The LORD look upon it, and *r* it.......... 2Chr 24:22
shall *r* of you, it be done........................ Ezr 7:21
For I was ashamed to *r* of the................ Ezr 8:22
them, and will *r* nothing of them......... Neh 5:12
in his heart, Thou wilt not *r* it.............. Ps 10:13
his blood will I *r* at thine hand.............. Eze 3:18
his blood will I *r* at thine hand.............. Eze 3:20
there will I *r* your offerings, and.......... Eze 20:40
but his blood will I *r* at the.................... Eze 33:6
his blood will I *r* at thine hand.............. Eze 33:8
I will *r* my flock at their hand,............. Eze 34:10
and what doth the LORD *r* of thee.......... Mic 6:8
For the Jews *r* a sign, and the............. 1Cor 1:22
flower of her age, and need so *r*........... 1Cor 7:36

**REQUIRED**
behold, also his blood is *r*.................... Gen 42:22
unto them such things as they *r*............. Ex 12:36
the king's business *r* haste..................... 1Sa 21:8
and when he *r*, they set bread.............. 2Sa 12:20
as every day's work *r*........................... 1Chr 16:37
as the duty of every day *r*...................... 2Chr 8:14
Why hast thou not *r* of the.................. 2Chr 24:6
as the duty of every day *r*........................ Ezr 3:4
yet for all this *r* not I the....................... Neh 5:18
she *r* nothing but what Hegai the........... Est 2:15
and sin offering hast thou not *r*.............. Ps 40:6
us away captive *r* of us a song.............. Ps 137:3
they that wasted us *r* of us mirth.......... Ps 137:3
Two things have I *r* of thee................. Prov 30:7
who hath *r* this at your hand, to............... Is 1:12
may be *r* of this generation................... Lk 11:50
It shall be *r* of this generation.............. Lk 11:51
night thy soul shall be *r* of thee............ Lk 12:20
is given, of him shall be much *r*............. Lk 12:48
might have *r* mine own with usury....... Lk 19:23
that it should be as they *r*.................... Lk 23:24
Moreover it is *r* in stewards.................. 1Cor 4:2

**REQUIREST**
I will do to thee all that thou *r*............ Ruth 3:11

**REQUIRETH**
and God *r* that which is past................ Eccl 3:15
is a rare thing that the king *r*............... Dan 2:11

**REQUIRING**
*r* that he might be crucified.................. Lk 23:23

**REQUITE**
will certainly *r* us all the evil.............. Gen 50:15
Do ye thus *r* the LORD, O foolish.......... Deut 32:6
I also will *r* you this kindness,................. 2Sa 2:6
that the LORD will *r* me good for.......... 2Sa 16:12
I will *r* thee in this plat, saith............... 2Kin 9:26
and spite, to *r* it with thy hand.............. Ps 10:14
and raise me up, that I may *r* them....... Ps 41:10
God of recompences shall surely *r*........ Jer 51:56
at home, and to *r* their parents.................. 1Ti 5:4

**REQUITED**
as I have done, so God hath *r* me.......... Judg 1:7
he hath *r* me evil for good.................... 1Sa 25:21

**REQUITING**
by *r* the wicked, by recompensing....... 2Chr 6:23

**REREWARD**
which was the *r* of all the camps....... Num 10:25
the *r* came after the ark, the.................. Josh 6:9
but the *r* came after the ark of............. Josh 6:13
passed on in the *r* with Achish.............. 1Sa 29:2
the God of Israel will be your *r*.............. Is 52:12
glory of the LORD shall be thy *r*............... Is 58:8

**RESCUE**
and thou shalt have none to *r* them.. Deut 28:31
*r* my soul from their destructions........... Ps 35:17
take away, and none shall *r* him........... Hos 5:14

**RESCUED**
So the people *r* Jonathan, that he......... 1Sa 14:45
and David *r* his two wives.................... 1Sa 30:18
*r* him, having understood that he........ Acts 23:27

**RESCUETH**
He delivereth and *r*, and he worketh.... Dan 6:27

**RESEMBLANCE**
This is their *r* through all the.................... Zec 5:6

**RESEMBLE**
and whereunto shall I *r* it........................ Lk 13:18

**RESEMBLED**
each one *r* the children of a king......... Judg 8:18

**RESEN** (*re'-zen*) *A city between Nineveh and Calah.*
*R* between Nineveh and Calah............. Gen 10:12

**RESERVE**
Will he *r* his anger for ever....................... Jer 3:5
for I will pardon them whom I *r*........... Jer 50:20
to *r* the unjust unto the day of.............. 2Pet 2:9

**RESERVED**
Hast thou not *r* a blessing for me........ Gen 27:36
most holy things, *r* from the fire.......... Num 18:9
because we *r* not to each man his..... Judg 21:22
she had *r* after she was sufficed........... Ruth 2:18
but *r* of them for an hundred.................... 2Sa 8:4
but *r* of them an hundred chariots...... 1Chr 18:4
That the wicked is *r* to the day............. Job 21:30
Which I have *r* against the time............ Job 38:23
be *r* unto the hearing of Augustus..... Acts 25:21
I have *r* to myself seven thousand........ Rom 11:4
not away, *r* in heaven for you,.............. 1Pet 1:4
darkness, to be *r* unto judgment.............. 2Pet 2:4
mist of darkness is *r* for ever.............. 2Pet 2:17
*r* unto fire against the day of................ 2Pet 3:7
he hath *r* in everlasting chains................. Jude 6
to whom is *r* the blackness of.................. Jude 13

**RESERVETH**
he *r* unto us the appointed weeks........... Jer 5:24
he *r* wrath for his enemies...................... Nah 1:2

**RESHEPH** (*re'-shef*) *A son of Rephah.*
And Rephah was his son, also *R*.......... 1Chr 7:25

**RESIDUE**
they shall eat the *r* of that........................ Ex 10:5
the *r* of the families of the sons............ 1Chr 6:66
the *r* of Israel, of the priests,............... Neh 11:20
the *r* of the number of archers,.............. Is 21:17
unto the *r* of his people,........................... Is 28:5
am deprived of the *r* of my years............ Is 38:10
the *r* thereof he maketh a god,................ Is 44:17
shall I make the *r* thereof an................. Is 44:19
the *r* of them that remain of this............. Jer 8:3
the *r* of them will I deliver to.................. Jer 15:9
the *r* of Jerusalem, that remain.............. Jer 24:8
concerning the *r* of the vessels.............. Jer 27:19
the *r* of the elders which were................. Jer 29:1
with all the *r* of the princes of................ Jer 39:3
the *r* of the people that were in............. Jer 41:10
the *r* of the people that remained........... Jer 52:15
wilt thou destroy all the *r* of.................... Eze 9:8
thy *r* shall be devoured by the.............. Eze 23:25
your feet the *r* of your pastures............ Eze 34:18
ye must foul the *r* with your feet.......... Eze 34:18
unto the *r* of the heathen......................... Eze 36:3
derision to the *r* of the heathen............... Eze 36:4
against the *r* of the heathen.................... Eze 36:5
the *r* in length over against the............. Eze 48:18
the *r* shall be for the prince, on............. Eze 48:21
stamped the *r* with the feet of it.............. Dan 7:7
stamped the *r* with his feet..................... Dan 7:19
the *r* of my people shall spoil.................. Zeph 2:9
to the *r* of the people, saying,.................... Hag 2:2
But now I will not be unto the *r*............. Zec 8:11
the *r* of the people shall not be.............. Zec 14:2
Yet had he the *r* of the spirit................... Mal 2:15
they went and told it unto the *r*............ Mk 16:13
That the *r* of men might seek............. Acts 15:17

**RESIST**
at his right hand to *r* him......................... Zec 3:1
say unto you, That ye *r* not evil.............. Mt 5:39
not be able to gainsay nor *r*.................. Lk 21:15
were not able to *r* the wisdom............... Acts 6:10
ye do always *r* the Holy Ghost.............. Acts 7:51
they that *r* shall receive to.................... Rom 13:2
so do these also *r* the truth..................... 2Ti 3:8
*R* the devil, and he will flee from............. Jas 4:7
and he doth not *r* you............................... Jas 5:6
Whom *r* stedfast in the faith,................... 1Pet 5:9

**RESISTED**
For who hath *r* his will............................ Rom 9:19
Ye have not yet *r* unto blood................. Heb 12:4

**RESISTETH**
Whosoever therefore *r* the power......... Rom 13:2
the power, *r* the ordinance of God....... Rom 13:2
God *r* the proud, but giveth grace.......... Jas 4:6
for God *r* the proud, and giveth............ 1Pet 5:5

**RESOLVED**
I am *r* what to do, that, when I.............. Lk 16:4

**RESORT**
the trumpet, *r* ye thither unto us.......... Neh 4:20
whereunto I may continually *r*................. Ps 71:3
the people *r* unto him again..................... Mk 10:1
temple, whither the Jews always *r*......... Jn 18:20

**RESORTED**
*r* to him out of all their coasts............ 2Chr 11:13
and all the multitude *r* unto him.............. Mk 2:13
many *r* unto him, and said, John............ Jn 10:41

for Jesus ofttimes *r* thither with .............. Jn 18:2
unto the women which *r* thither......... Acts 16:13

**RESPECT**

And the LORD had *r* unto Abel.................. Gen 4:4
and to his offering he had not *r*................. Gen 4:5
of Israel, and God had *r* unto them......... Ex 2:25
thou shalt not *r* the person of.............. Lev 19:15
For I will have *r* unto you ....................... Lev 26:9
*R* not thou their offering...................... Num 16:15
Ye shall not *r* persons in ......................... Deut 1:17
thou shalt not *r* persons, neither......... Deut 16:19
neither doth God *r* any person.............. 2Sa 14:14
Yet have thou *r* unto the prayer ............ 1Kin 8:28
had *r* unto them, because of his........... 2Kin 13:23
Have *r* therefore to the prayer of.......... 2Chr 6:19
nor *r* of persons, nor taking of.............. 2Chr 19:7
Have *r* unto the covenant......................... Ps 74:20
when I have *r* unto all thy ........................ Ps 119:6
precepts, and have *r* unto thy ways..... Ps 119:15
I will have *r* unto thy statutes.............. Ps 119:117
yet hath he *r* unto the lowly...................... Ps 138:6
to have *r* of persons in judgment ....... Prov 24:23
To have *r* of persons is not good......... Prov 28:21
his eyes shall have *r* to the Holy ............... Is 17:7
neither shall *r* that which his .................. Is 17:8
neither had *r* unto him that........................ Is 22:11
For there is no *r* of persons with........... Rom 2:11
glorious had no glory in this *r* .............. 2Cor 3:10
neither is there *r* of persons..................... Eph 6:9
Not that I speak in *r* of want.................. Phil 4:11
or in *r* of an holyday, or of the................. Col 2:16
and there is no *r* of persons .................... Col 3:25
for he had *r* unto the recompence....... Heb 11:26
Lord of glory, with *r* of persons.................. Jas 2:1
ye have *r* to him that weareth the............ Jas 2:3
But if ye have *r* to persons ......................... Jas 2:9
who without *r* of persons judgeth ....... 1Pet 1:17

**RESPECTED**

they *r* not the persons of the.................. Lam 4:16

**RESPECTER**

that God is no *r* of persons..................... Acts 10:34

**RESPECTETH**

he *r* not any that are wise of................. Job 37:24
*r* not the proud, nor such as turn............. Ps 40:4

**RESPITE**

when Pharaoh saw that there was *r* ...... Ex 8:15
unto him, Give us seven days' *r*.............. 1Sa 11:3

**REST**

But the dove found no *r* for the................ Gen 8:9
*r* yourselves under the tree ...................... Gen 18:4
Jacob fed the *r* of Laban's flocks......... Gen 30:36
And he saw that *r* was good................... Gen 49:15
ye make them *r* from their burdens .......... Ex 5:5
To morrow is the *r* of the holy ............... Ex 16:23
seventh year thou shalt let it *r* ............... Ex 23:11
on the seventh day thou shalt *r* .............. Ex 23:12
that thine ox and thine ass may *r*........... Ex 23:12
names of the *r* on the other stone ......... Ex 28:10
the seventh is the sabbath of *r* ............... Ex 31:15
with thee, and I will give thee *r*............. Ex 33:14
on the seventh day thou shalt *r*............... Ex 34:21
time and in harvest thou shalt *r*............. Ex 34:21
day, a sabbath of *r* to the LORD................ Ex 35:2
the *r* of the blood shall be wrung.............. Lev 5:9
of the *r* of the oil that is in.................... Lev 14:17
the *r* of the oil that is in the..................... Lev 14:29
shall be a sabbath of *r* unto you.............. Lev 16:31
seventh day is the sabbath of *r*................ Lev 23:3
shall be unto you a sabbath of *r*............... Lev 23:32
be a sabbath of *r* unto the land .............. Lev 25:4
it is a year of *r* unto the land.................. Lev 25:5
even then shall the land *r*........................ Lev 26:34
as it lieth desolate it shall *r*................... Lev 26:35
it did not *r* in your sabbaths.................... Lev 26:35
beside the *r* of them that were............... Num 31:8
being the *r* of the prey which the...... Num 31:32
the *r* of Gilead, and all Bashan, .......... Deut 3:13
have given *r* unto your brethren............ Deut 3:20
maidservant may *r* as well as thou...... Deut 5:14
ye are not as yet come to the *r* .............. Deut 12:9
when he giveth you *r* from all.............. Deut 12:10
*r* from all thine enemies round........... Deut 25:19
shall the sole of thy foot have *r*.......... Deut 28:65
LORD your God hath given you *r*.............. Josh 1:13
LORD have given your brethren *r*............ Josh 1:15
shall *r* in the waters of Jordan, .............. Josh 3:13
that the *r* which remained of them.... Josh 10:20
the *r* of the kingdom of Sihon............ Josh 13:27
And the land had *r* from war.............. Josh 14:15
There was also a lot for the *r* of .......... Josh 17:2
the *r* of Manasseh's sons had the ......... Josh 17:6
the *r* of the children of Kohath........... Josh 21:5
the *r* of the Levites, out of the........... Josh 21:34
the LORD gave them *r* round about.... Josh 21:44
hath given *r* unto your brethren.......... Josh 22:4
*r* unto Israel from all their .................. Josh 23:1
And the land had *r* forty years ............ Judg 3:11
the land had *r* fourscore years............. Judg 3:30
And the land had *r* forty years ........... Judg 5:31
but all the *r* of the people bowed.......... Judg 7:6
he sent all the *r* of Israel every............ Judg 7:8
LORD grant you that ye may find *r*........ Ruth 1:9
shall I not seek *r* for thee ...................... Ruth 3:1
for the man will not be in *r*.................... Ruth 3:18
the *r* of the people he sent every.......... 1Sa 13:2
the *r* we have utterly destroyed............ 1Sa 15:15
Let it *r* on the head of Joab, and............ 2Sa 3:29
the LORD had given him *r* round ............. 2Sa 7:1
have caused thee to *r* from all ................ 2Sa 7:11
the *r* of the people he delivered............ 2Sa 10:10
the *r* of the people together................. 2Sa 12:28
of the air to *r* on them by day................ 2Sa 21:10
God hath given me *r* on every side........ 1Kin 5:4
that hath given *r* unto his people......... 1Kin 8:56
the *r* of the acts of Solomon, and......... 1Kin 11:41
the *r* of the acts of Jeroboam,.............. 1Kin 14:19
Now the *r* of the acts of Rehoboam .. 1Kin 14:29
Now the *r* of the acts of Abijam,........... 1Kin 15:7
The *r* of all the acts of Asa, and .......... 1Kin 15:23
Now the *r* of the acts of Nadab, ........ 1Kin 15:31
Now the *r* of the acts of Baasha,........... 1Kin 16:5
Now the *r* of the acts of Elah, and.... 1Kin 16:14
Now the *r* of the acts of Zimri,........... 1Kin 16:20
Now the *r* of the acts of Omri.............. 1Kin 16:27
But the *r* fled to Aphek, into the........ 1Kin 20:30
Now the *r* of the acts of Ahab, and... 1Kin 22:39
Now the *r* of the acts of...................... 1Kin 22:45
Now the *r* of the acts of Ahaziah......... 2Kin 1:18
spirit of Elijah doth *r* on Elisha.............. 2Kin 2:15
thou and thy children of the *r*................ 2Kin 4:7
the *r* of the acts of Joram, and ............. 2Kin 8:23
Now the *r* of the acts of Jehu, and.... 2Kin 10:34
the *r* of the acts of Joash, and ............ 2Kin 12:19
Now the *r* of the acts of Jehoahaz....... 2Kin 13:8
the *r* of the acts of Joash, and ............ 2Kin 13:12
Now the *r* of the acts of Jehoash ....... 2Kin 14:15
the *r* of the acts of Amaziah, are........ 2Kin 14:18
Now the *r* of the acts of Jeroboam .... 2Kin 14:28
the *r* of the acts of Azariah, and ......... 2Kin 15:6
the *r* of the acts of Zachariah,............ 2Kin 15:11
the *r* of the acts of Shallum, and......... 2Kin 15:15
the *r* of the acts of Menahem, and..... 2Kin 15:21
the *r* of the acts of Pekahiah, and...... 2Kin 15:26
the *r* of the acts of Pekah, and .......... 2Kin 15:31
Now the *r* of the acts of Jotham, ........ 2Kin 15:36
Now the *r* of the acts of Ahaz ............ 2Kin 16:19
the *r* of the acts of Hezekiah, and........ 2Kin 20:20
Now the *r* of the acts of Manasseh.... 2Kin 21:17
Now the *r* of the acts of Amon ........... 2Kin 21:25
Now the *r* of the acts of Josiah, ......... 2Kin 23:28
Now the *r* of the acts of ........................ 2Kin 24:5
Now the *r* of the people that were..... 2Kin 25:11
And they smote the *r* of the............... 1Chr 4:43
LORD, after that the ark had *r*.............. 1Chr 6:31
Unto the *r* of the children of............... 1Chr 6:77
Joab repaired the *r* of the city ............ 1Chr 11:8
all the *r* also of Israel were of............ 1Chr 12:38
the *r* that were chosen, who were ..... 1Chr 16:41
the *r* of the people he delivered.......... 1Chr 19:11
to thee, who shall be a man of *r* .......... 1Chr 22:9
I will give him *r* from all his ................ 1Chr 22:9
he not given you *r* on every side......... 1Chr 22:18
hath given *r* unto his people .............. 1Chr 23:25
the *r* of the sons of Levi were............. 1Chr 24:20
*r* for the ark of the covenant of .......... 1Chr 28:2
Now the *r* of the acts of Solomon,....... 2Chr 9:29
the *r* of the acts of Abijah, and ......... 2Chr 13:22
for the land had *r*, and he had no ........ 2Chr 14:6
because the LORD had given him *r* ....... 2Chr 14:6
he hath given us *r* on every side .......... 2Chr 14:7
for we *r* on thee, and in thy name..... 2Chr 14:11
the LORD gave them *r* round about... 2Chr 15:15
his God gave him *r* round about ........ 2Chr 20:30
Now the *r* of the acts of.................... 2Chr 20:34
they brought the *r* of the money ....... 2Chr 24:14
Now the *r* of the acts of Amaziah, .... 2Chr 25:26
Now the *r* of the acts of Uzziah,....... 2Chr 26:22
Now the *r* of the acts of Jotham,......... 2Chr 27:7
Now the *r* of his acts and of all ......... 2Chr 28:26
Now the *r* of the acts of Hezekiah..... 2Chr 32:32
Now the *r* of the acts of Manasseh ... 2Chr 33:18
Now the *r* of the acts of Josiah, ......... 2Chr 35:26
Now the *r* of the acts of.................... 2Chr 36:8
the *r* of the chief of the fathers................. Ezr 4:3
the *r* of their companions, unto ............... Ezr 4:7
the *r* of their companions ........................ Ezr 4:9
the *r* of the nations whom the .............. Ezr 4:10
the *r* that are on this side the................ Ezr 4:10
to the *r* of their companions that ........... Ezr 4:17
unto the *r* beyond the river,................... Ezr 4:17
the *r* of the children of the..................... Ezr 6:16
to do with the *r* of the silver.................. Ezr 7:18
nor to the *r* that did the work............... Neh 2:16
to the *r* of the people, Be not ye............ Neh 4:14
to the *r* of the people, The work.......... Neh 4:19
the *r* of our enemies, heard that.............. Neh 6:1
the *r* of the prophets, that would ........... Neh 6:14
that which the *r* of the people ............... Neh 7:72
But after they had *r*, they did................. Neh 9:28
the *r* of the people, the priests, ........... Neh 10:28
the *r* of the people also cast.................... Neh 11:1
in the *r* of the king's provinces.............. Est 9:12
had *r* from their enemies, and slew ....... Est 9:16
then had I been at *r*,............................... Job 3:13
and there the weary be at *r* .................... Job 3:17
There the prisoners *r* together............... Job 3:18
not in safety, neither had I *r* ................... Job 3:26
thou shalt take thy *r* in safety.............. Job 11:18
Turn from him, that he may *r*.................. Job 14:6
when our *r* together is in the................. Job 17:16
and my sinews take no *r*......................... Job 30:17
my flesh also shall *r* in hope ..................... Ps 16:9
leave the *r* of their substance to .......... Ps 17:14
*R* in the LORD, and wait patiently............. Ps 37:7
neither is there any *r* in my ...................... Ps 38:3
then would I fly away, and be at *r*............ Ps 55:6
That thou mayest give him *r* from......... Ps 94:13
they should not enter into my *r*.............. Ps 95:11
Return unto thy *r*, O my soul.................. Ps 116:7
*r* upon the lot of the righteous................. Ps 125:3
Arise, O LORD, into thy *r*........................... Ps 132:8
This is my *r* for ever ............................... Ps 132:14
neither will he *r* content........................ Prov 6:35
he rage or laugh, there is no *r*.............. Prov 29:9
thy son, and he shall give thee *r* ........ Prov 29:17
heart taketh not *r* in the night ............... Eccl 2:23
this hath more *r* than the other............... Eccl 6:5
makest thy flock to *r* at noon................. Song 1:7
shall *r* all of them in the ........................... Is 7:19
the *r* of the trees of his forest................. Is 10:19
of the LORD shall *r* upon him.................... Is 11:2
and his *r* shall be glorious ...................... Is 11:10
shall give thee *r* from thy sorrow ............ Is 14:3
The whole earth is at *r*, and is ................. Is 14:7
said unto me, I will take my *r*................... Is 18:4
there also shalt thou have no *r*................ Is 23:12
shall the hand of the LORD *r*.................... Is 25:10
This is the *r* wherewith ye may ............... Is 28:12
ye may cause the weary to *r* ................... Is 28:12
returning and *r* shall ye be saved ........... Is 30:15
screech owl also shall *r* there .................. Is 34:14
and find for herself a place of *r*.............. Is 34:14
to *r* for a light of the people ...................... Is 51:4
they shall *r* in their beds, each................... Is 57:2
troubled sea, when it cannot *r*................. Is 57:20
for Jerusalem's sake I will not *r*................. Is 62:1
And give him no *r*, till he ............................ Is 62:7
of the LORD caused him to *r* ..................... Is 63:14
and where is the place of my *r*................... Is 66:1
ye shall find *r* for your souls.................. Jer 6:16
shall return, and shall be in *r* ................ Jer 30:10
when I went to cause him to *r* ................ Jer 31:2
with the *r* of the people that ................. Jer 39:9
in my sighing, and I find no *r* ................ Jer 45:3
and Jacob shall return, and be in *r* ....... Jer 46:27
up thyself into thy scabbard, *r*............... Jer 47:6
that he may give *r* to the land .............. Jer 50:34
and the *r* of the multitude..................... Jer 52:15
the heathen, she findeth no *r*.................. Lam 1:3
give thyself no *r* ....................................... Lam 2:18
we labour, and have no *r*........................... Lam 5:5
will cause my fury to *r* upon them ........ Eze 5:13
I make my fury toward thee to *r* .......... Eze 16:42
and I will cause my fury to *r* ................ Eze 21:17
caused my fury to *r* upon thee................ Eze 24:13
I will go to them that are at *r*............... Eze 38:11
the blessing to *r* in thine house ........... Eze 44:30
the *r* of the land shall they give ............. Eze 45:8
As for the *r* of the tribes, from............. Eze 48:23
the *r* of the wise men of Babylon.............. Dan 2:18
was at *r* in mine house, and..................... Dan 4:4
As concerning the *r* of the beasts ......... Dan 7:12
for thou shalt *r*, and stand in thy......... Dan 12:13
for this is not your *r*.............................. Mic 2:10
that I might *r* in the day of..................... Hab 3:16
he will *r* in his love, he will.................. Zeph 3:17
earth sitteth still, and is at *r* .................. Zec 1:11
Damascus shall be the *r* thereof.............. Zec 9:1
let the *r* eat every one the flesh.............. Zec 11:9
heavy laden, and I will give you *r*.......... Mt 11:28
ye shall find *r* unto your souls............... Mt 11:29
through dry places, seeking *r* ................ Mt 12:43
Sleep on now, and take your *r*................ Mt 26:45
The *r* said, Let be, let us see ................ Mt 27:49
into a desert place, and *r* a while.......... Mk 6:31
Sleep on now, and take your *r*................ Mk 14:41
there, your peace shall *r* upon it ............ Lk 10:6
through dry places, seeking *r* ................. Lk 11:24
why take ye thought for the *r*.................. Lk 12:26
unto the eleven, and to all the *r*.............. Lk 24:9
spoken of taking of *r* in sleep ................ Jn 11:13
also my flesh shall *r* in hope ................. Acts 2:26
to the *r* of the apostles, Men and........ Acts 2:37
of the *r* durst no man join .................... Acts 5:13
or what is the place of my *r*.................. Acts 7:49
churches *r* throughout all Judaea......... Acts 9:31
the *r*, some on boards ......................... Acts 27:44
it, and the *r* were blinded....................... Rom 11:7
But to the *r* speak I, not the ................. 1Cor 7:12
the *r* will I set in order when I .......... 1Cor 11:34
I had no *r* in my spirit, because............. 2Cor 2:13
Macedonia, our flesh had no *r* .............. 2Cor 7:5
the power of Christ may *r* upon me .... 2Cor 12:9
to you who are troubled *r* with us........... 2Th 1:7
They shall not enter into my *r*............... Heb 3:11
they should not enter into his *r*............ Heb 3:18
left us of entering into his *r*.................... Heb 4:1
have believed do enter into *r*.................... Heb 4:3
if they shall enter into my *r*..................... Heb 4:3
God did *r* the seventh day from.............. Heb 4:4
If they shall enter into my *r* .................... Heb 4:5
For if Jesus had given them *r*................... Heb 4:8
a *r* to the people of God........................... Heb 4:9
For he that is entered into his *r* ............ Heb 4:10
therefore to enter into that *r*................... Heb 4:11
he no longer should live the *r* of.............. 1Pet 4:2
unto the *r* in Thyatira, as many ............. Rev 2:24
they *r* not day and night, saying,............. Rev 4:8
that they should *r* yet for a..................... Rev 6:11
the *r* of the men which were not........... Rev 9:20
they have no *r* day nor night, who...... Rev 14:11
that they may *r* from their ................... Rev 14:13
But the *r* of the dead lived not .............. Rev 20:5

**RESTED**

he *r* on the seventh day from all .............. Gen 2:2
because that in it he had *r* from ............. Gen 2:3
the ark *r* in the seventh month,.............. Gen 8:4

*r* in all the coasts of Egypt ... Ex 10:14
So the people *r* on the seventh ... Ex 16:30
in them is, and *r* the seventh day ... Ex 20:11
earth, and on the seventh day he *r* ... Ex 31:17
tabernacle they *r* in their tents ... Num 9:18
of the LORD they *r* in the tents ... Num 9:23
the cloud *r* in the wilderness of ... Num 10:12
And when it *r*, he said, Return, O ... Num 10:36
that, when the spirit *r* upon them ... Num 11:25
and the spirit *r* upon them ... Num 11:26
And the land *r* from war ... Josh 11:23
they *r* on the house with timber ... 1Kin 6:10
the people *r* themselves upon the ... 2Chr 32:8
fourteenth day of the same *r* they ... Est 9:17
fifteenth day of the same they *r* ... Est 9:18
the Jews *r* from their enemies ... Est 9:22
My bowels boiled, and *r* not ... Job 30:27
*r* the sabbath day according to ... Lk 23:56

**RESTEST**
*r* in the law, and makest thy boast ... Rom 2:17

**RESTETH**
him to be in safety, whereon he *r* ... Job 24:23
Wisdom *r* in the heart of him that ... Prov 14:33
for anger *r* in the bosom of fools ... Eccl 7:9
of glory and of God *r* upon you ... 1Pet 4:14

**RESTING**
to search out a *r* place for them ... Num 10:33
O LORD God, into thy *r* place ... 2Chr 6:41
spoil not his *r* place ... Prov 24:15
dwellings, and in quiet *r* places ... Is 32:18

**RESTINGPLACE**
hill, they have forgotten their *r* ... Jer 50:6

**RESTITUTION**
for he should make full *r* ... Ex 22:3
his own vineyard, shall he make *r* ... Ex 22:5
the fire shall surely make *r* ... Ex 22:6
he shall make *r* unto the owner ... Ex 22:12
to his substance shall the *r* be ... Job 20:18
the times of *r* of all things ... Acts 3:21

**RESTORE**
Now therefore *r* the man his wife ... Gen 20:7
and if thou *r* her not, know thou ... Gen 20:7
head, and *r* thee unto thy place ... Gen 40:13
to *r* every man's money into his ... Gen 42:25
he shall *r* five oxen for an ox, ... Ex 22:1
he shall *r* double ... Ex 22:4
that he shall *r* that which he ... Lev 6:4
he shall even *r* it in the ... Lev 6:5
killeth a beast, he shall *r* it ... Lev 24:21
*r* the overplus unto the man to ... Lev 25:27
if he be not able to *r* it to him ... Lev 25:28
the congregation shall *r* him to ... Num 35:25
thou shalt *r* it to him again ... Deut 22:2
now therefore *r* those lands again ... Judg 11:13
therefore I will *r* it unto thee ... Judg 17:3
and I will *r* it you ... 1Sa 12:3
will *r* thee all the land of Saul ... 2Sa 9:7
he shall *r* the lamb fourfold, ... 2Sa 12:6
*r* me the kingdom of my father ... 2Sa 16:3
took from thy father, I will *r* ... 1Kin 20:34
*R* all that was hers, and all the ... 2Kin 8:6
*R*, I pray you, to them, even this ... Neh 5:11
Then said they, We will *r* them ... Neh 5:12
and his hands shall *r* their goods ... Job 20:10
which he laboured for shall he *r* ... Job 20:18
*R* unto me the joy of thy ... Ps 51:12
he be found, he shall *r* sevenfold ... Prov 6:31
I will *r* thy judges as at the ... Is 1:26
for a spoil, and none saith, *R* ... Is 42:22
to *r* the preserved of Israel ... Is 49:6
*r* comforts unto him and to his ... Is 57:18
them up, and *r* them to this place ... Jer 27:22
For I will *r* health unto thee, and ... Jer 30:17
If the wicked *r* the pledge ... Eze 33:15
forth of the commandment to *r* ... Dan 9:25
I will *r* to you the years that ... Joel 2:25
shall first come, and *r* all things ... Mt 17:11
accusation, I *r* him fourfold ... Lk 19:8
wilt thou at this time *r* again ... Acts 1:6
*r* such an one in the spirit of ... Gal 6:1

**RESTORED**
Abraham, and *r* him Sarah his wife ... Gen 20:14
he *r* the chief butler unto his ... Gen 40:21
me he *r* unto mine office, and him ... Gen 41:13
unto his brethren, My money is *r* ... Gen 42:28
face, and shall not be *r* to thee ... Deut 28:31
when he had *r* the eleven hundred ... Judg 17:3
Yet he *r* the money unto his ... Judg 17:4
from Israel were *r* to Israel ... 1Sa 7:14
that my hand may be *r* me again ... 1Kin 13:6
the king's hand was *r* him again ... 1Kin 13:6
woman, whose son he had *r* to life ... 2Kin 8:1
how he had *r* a dead body to life ... 2Kin 8:5
woman, whose son he had *r* to life ... 2Kin 8:5
is her son, whom Elisha *r* to life ... 2Kin 8:5
*r* it to Judah, after that the ... 2Kin 14:22
He *r* the coast of Israel from the ... 2Kin 14:25
which Huram had *r* to Solomon ... 2Chr 8:2
*r* it to Judah, after that the ... 2Chr 26:2
and brought unto Babylon, be *r* ... Ezr 6:5
then I *r* that which I took not ... Ps 69:4
but hath *r* to the debtor his ... Eze 18:7
hath not *r* the pledge, and hath ... Eze 18:12
and it was *r* whole, like as the ... Mt 12:13
his hand was *r* whole as the other ... Mk 3:5
and he was *r*, and saw every man ... Mk 8:25
his hand was *r* whole as the other ... Lk 6:10
that I may be *r* to you the sooner ... Heb 13:19

**RESTORER**
be unto thee a *r* of thy life ... Ruth 4:15
The *r* of paths to dwell in ... Is 58:12

**RESTORETH**
He *r* my soul ... Ps 23:3
cometh first, and *r* all things ... Mk 9:12

**RESTRAIN**
dost thou *r* wisdom to thyself ... Job 15:8
remainder of wrath shalt thou *r* ... Ps 76:10

**RESTRAINED**
and the rain from heaven was *r* ... Gen 8:2
now nothing will be *r* from them ... Gen 11:6
the LORD hath *r* me from bearing ... Gen 16:2
the people were *r* from bringing ... Ex 36:6
themselves vile, and he *r* them not ... 1Sa 3:13
are they *r* ... Is 63:15
I *r* the floods thereof, and the ... Eze 31:15
sayings scarce *r* they the people ... Acts 14:18

**RESTRAINEST**
off fear, and *r* prayer before God ... Job 15:4

**RESTRAINT**
for there is no *r* to the LORD to ... 1Sa 14:6

**RESTS**
he made narrowed *r* round about ... 1Kin 6:6

**RESURRECTION**
which say that there is no *r* ... Mt 22:23
Therefore in the *r* whose wife ... Mt 22:28
For in the *r* they neither marry, ... Mt 22:30
But as touching the *r* of the dead ... Mt 22:31
out of the graves after his *r* ... Mt 27:53
which say there is no *r* ... Mk 12:18
In the *r* therefore, when they ... Mk 12:23
recompensed at the *r* of the just ... Lk 14:14
which deny that there is any *r* ... Lk 20:27
Therefore in the *r* whose wife of ... Lk 20:33
the *r* from the dead, neither ... Lk 20:35
God, being the children of the *r* ... Lk 20:36
done good, unto the *r* of life ... Jn 5:29
evil, unto the *r* of damnation ... Jn 5:29
again in the *r* at the last day ... Jn 11:24
Jesus said unto her, I am the *r* ... Jn 11:25
to be a witness with us of his *r* ... Acts 1:22
before spake of the *r* of Christ ... Acts 2:31
through Jesus the *r* from the dead ... Acts 4:2
of the *r* of the Lord Jesus ... Acts 4:33
unto them Jesus, and the *r* ... Acts 17:18
they heard of the *r* of the dead ... Acts 17:32
*r* of the dead I am called in ... Acts 23:6
Sadducees say that there is no *r* ... Acts 23:8
there shall be a *r* of the dead ... Acts 24:15
Touching the *r* of the dead I am ... Acts 24:21
holiness, by the *r* from the dead ... Rom 1:4
be also in the likeness of his *r* ... Rom 6:5
that there is no *r* of the dead ... 1Cor 15:12
But if there be no *r* of the dead ... 1Cor 15:13
man came also the *r* of the dead ... 1Cor 15:21
So also is the *r* of the dead ... 1Cor 15:42
know him, and the power of his *r* ... Phil 3:10
attain unto the *r* of the dead ... Phil 3:11
saying that the *r* is past already ... 2Ti 2:18
of *r* of the dead, and of eternal ... Heb 6:2
that they might obtain a better *r* ... Heb 11:35
*r* of Jesus Christ from the dead ... 1Pet 1:3
by the *r* of Jesus Christ ... 1Pet 3:21
This is the first *r* ... Rev 20:5
he that hath part in the first *r* ... Rev 20:6

**RETAIN**
Dost thou still *r* thine integrity ... Job 2:9
me, Let thine heart *r* my words ... Prov 4:4
and strong men *r* riches ... Prov 11:16
over the spirit to *r* the spirit ... Eccl 8:8
but she shall not *r* the power of ... Dan 11:6
and whose soever sins ye *r* ... Jn 20:23
like to *r* God in their knowledge ... Rom 1:28

**RETAINED**
*r* those three hundred men ... Judg 7:8
law, the damsel's father, *r* him ... Judg 19:4
corruption, and I *r* no strength ... Dan 10:8
upon me, and I have *r* no strength ... Dan 10:16
soever sins ye retain, they are *r* ... Jn 20:23
Whom I would have *r* with me ... Philem 13

**RETAINETH**
and happy is every one that *r* her ... Prov 3:18
A gracious woman *r* honour ... Prov 11:16
he *r* not his anger for ever, ... Mic 7:18

**RETIRE**
*r* ye from him, that he may be ... 2Sa 11:15
*r*, stay not ... Jer 4:6

**RETIRED**
the men of Israel *r* in the battle ... Judg 20:39
they *r* from the city, every man ... 2Sa 20:22

**RETURN**
till thou *r* unto the ground ... Gen 3:19
art, and unto dust shalt thou *r* ... Gen 3:19
after his *r* from the slaughter of ... Gen 14:17
*R* to thy mistress, and submit ... Gen 16:9
I will certainly *r* unto thee ... Gen 18:10
time appointed I will *r* unto thee ... Gen 18:14
*R* unto the land of thy fathers, ... Gen 31:3
*r* unto the land of thy kindred ... Gen 31:13
*R* unto thy country, and to thy ... Gen 32:9
*r* unto my brethren which are in ... Ex 4:18
Moses in Midian, Go, *r* into Egypt ... Ex 4:19
When thou goest to *r* into Egypt ... Ex 4:21
they see war, and they *r* to Egypt ... Ex 13:17
ye shall *r* every man unto his ... Lev 25:10
ye shall *r* every man unto his ... Lev 25:10
year of this jubile ye shall *r* ... Lev 25:13
that he may *r* unto his possession ... Lev 25:27
he shall *r* unto his possession ... Lev 25:28
shall *r* unto his own family, and ... Lev 25:41
of his fathers shall he *r* ... Lev 25:41
of the jubile the field shall *r* ... Lev 27:24
And when it rested, he said, *R* ... Num 10:36
not better for us to *r* into Egypt ... Num 14:3
a captain, and let us *r* into Egypt ... Num 14:4
*R* unto Balak, and thus thou shalt ... Num 23:5
We will not *r* unto our houses, ... Num 32:18
then afterward ye shall *r* ... Num 32:22
high priest the slayer shall *r* ... Num 35:28
then shall ye *r* every man unto ... Deut 3:20
cause the people to *r* to Egypt ... Deut 17:16
henceforth *r* no more that way ... Deut 17:16
*r* to his house, lest he die in ... Deut 20:5
*r* unto his house, lest he die in ... Deut 20:6
*r* unto his house, lest he die in ... Deut 20:7
*r* unto his house, lest his ... Deut 20:8
shalt *r* unto the LORD thy God, and ... Deut 30:2
compassion upon thee, and will *r* ... Deut 30:3
And thou shalt *r* and obey the voice ... Deut 30:8
then ye shall *r* unto the land of ... Josh 1:15
then shall the slayer *r*, and come ... Josh 20:6
therefore now *r* ye, and get you ... Josh 22:4
*R* with much riches unto your ... Josh 22:8
is fearful and afraid, let him *r* ... Judg 7:3
when I *r* in peace from the ... Judg 11:31
that she might *r* from the country ... Ruth 1:6
way to *r* unto the land of Judah ... Ruth 1:7
*r* each to her mother's house ... Ruth 1:8
Surely we will *r* with thee unto ... Ruth 1:10
*r* thou after thy sister in law ... Ruth 1:15
or to *r* from following after thee ... Ruth 1:16
but in any wise *r* him a trespass ... 1Sa 6:3
offering which we shall *r* to him ... 1Sa 6:4
which ye *r* him for a trespass ... 1Sa 6:8
If ye do *r* unto the LORD with all ... 1Sa 7:3
And his *r* was to Ramah ... 1Sa 7:17
was with him, Come, and let us *r* ... 1Sa 9:5
unto Saul, I will not *r* with thee ... 1Sa 15:26
*r*, my son David ... 1Sa 26:21
said unto him, Make this fellow *r* ... 1Sa 29:4
Wherefore now *r*, and go in peace, ... 1Sa 29:7
to *r* into the land of the ... 1Sa 29:11
ere thou bid the people *r* from ... 2Sa 2:26
Then said Abner unto him, Go, *r* ... 2Sa 3:16
your beards be grown, and then *r* ... 2Sa 10:5
to him, but he shall not *r* to me ... 2Sa 12:23
*r* to thy place, and abide with the ... 2Sa 15:19
*r* thou, and take back thy brethren ... 2Sa 15:20
*r* into the city in peace, and your ... 2Sa 15:27
But if thou *r* to the city ... 2Sa 15:34
*R* thou, and all thy servants ... 2Sa 19:14
I shall *r* to him that sent me ... 2Sa 24:13
the LORD shall *r* his blood upon ... 1Kin 2:32
therefore *r* upon the head of Joab ... 1Kin 2:33
therefore the LORD shall *r* thy ... 1Kin 2:44
so *r* unto thee with all their ... 1Kin 8:48
*r* every man to his house ... 1Kin 12:24
kingdom *r* to the house of David ... 1Kin 12:26
And he said, I may not *r* with thee ... 1Kin 13:16
*r* on thy way to the wilderness of ... 1Kin 19:15
for at the *r* of the year the king ... 1Kin 20:22
came to pass at the *r* of the year ... 1Kin 20:26
let them *r* every man to his house ... 1Kin 22:17
If thou *r* at all in peace, the ... 1Kin 22:28
*r* from me ... 2Kin 18:14
and shall *r* to his own land ... 2Kin 19:7
he came, by the same shall he *r* ... 2Kin 19:33
but let the shadow *r* backward ten ... 2Kin 20:10
your beards be grown, and then *r* ... 1Chr 19:5
and shall *r* and confess thy name, ... 2Chr 6:24
If they *r* to thee with all their ... 2Chr 6:38
ye me to *r* answer to this people ... 2Chr 10:6
we may *r* answer to this people ... 2Chr 10:9
*r* every man to his house ... 2Chr 11:4
let them *r* therefore every man to ... 2Chr 18:16
of affliction, until I *r* in peace ... 2Chr 18:26
If thou certainly *r* in peace ... 2Chr 18:27
he will *r* to the remnant of you, ... 2Chr 30:6
face from you, if ye *r* unto him ... 2Chr 30:9
and when wilt thou *r* ... Neh 2:6
*r* unto us they will be upon you ... Neh 4:12
a captain to *r* to their bondage ... Neh 9:17
bade them *r* Mordecai this answer ... Est 4:15
should *r* upon his own head, and ... Est 9:25
womb, and naked shall I *r* thither ... Job 1:21
*R*, I pray you, let it not be ... Job 6:29
*r* again, my righteousness is in ... Job 6:29
He shall *r* no more to his house, ... Job 7:10
Before I go whence I shall not *r* ... Job 10:21
that he shall *r* out of darkness ... Job 15:22
go the way whence I shall not *r* ... Job 16:22
But as for you all, do ye *r* ... Job 17:10
If thou *r* to the Almighty, thou ... Job 22:23
he shall *r* to the days of his ... Job 33:25
that they *r* from iniquity ... Job 36:10
they go forth, and *r* not unto them ... Job 39:4
*R*, O LORD, deliver my soul ... Ps 6:4
let them *r* and be ashamed suddenly ... Ps 6:10
sakes therefore *r* thou on high ... Ps 7:7
shall *r* upon his own head ... Ps 7:16

They *r* at evening ... Ps 59:6
And at evening let them *r* ... Ps 59:14
Therefore his people *r* hither ... Ps 73:10
O let not the oppressed *r* ashamed ... Ps 74:21
*R*, we beseech thee, O God of ... Ps 80:14
and sayest, *R*, ye children of men ... Ps 90:3
*R*, O LORD, how long ... Ps 90:13
shall *r* unto righteousness ... Ps 94:15
they die, and *r* to their dust ... Ps 104:29
*R* unto thy rest, O my soul ... Ps 116:7
None that go unto her *r* again ... Prov 2:19
a stone, it will *r* upon him ... Prov 26:27
rivers come, thither they *r* again ... Eccl 1:7
naked shall he *r* to go as he came ... Eccl 5:15
nor the clouds *r* after the rain ... Eccl 12:2
Then shall the dust *r* to the ... Eccl 12:7
the spirit shall *r* unto God who ... Eccl 12:7
*R*, *r*, O Shulamite ... Song 6:13
*r*, *r*, that we may look upon ... Song 6:13
shall be a tenth, and it shall *r* ... Is 6:13
The remnant shall *r*, even the ... Is 10:21
yet a remnant of them shall *r* ... Is 10:22
they shall *r* even to the LORD, and ... Is 19:22
enquire ye: *r*, come ... Is 21:12
the ransomed of the LORD shall *r* ... Is 35:10
a rumour, and *r* to his own land ... Is 37:7
he came, by the same shall he *r* ... Is 37:34
*r* unto me ... Is 44:22
in righteousness, and shall not *r* ... Is 45:23
the redeemed of the LORD shall *r* ... Is 51:11
let him *r* unto the LORD, and he ... Is 55:7
it shall not *r* unto me void ... Is 55:11
*R* for thy servants' sake, the ... Is 63:17
shall he *r* unto her again ... Jer 3:1
yet *r* again to me, saith the LORD ... Jer 3:1
words toward the north, and say, *R* ... Jer 3:12
*R*, ye backsliding children, and I ... Jer 3:22
If thou wilt *r*, O Israel, saith ... Jer 4:1
Israel, saith the LORD, *r* unto me ... Jer 4:1
they have refused to *r* ... Jer 5:3
shall he turn away, and not *r* ... Jer 8:4
fast deceit, they refuse to *r* ... Jer 8:5
I have plucked them out I will *r* ... Jer 12:15
since they *r* not from their ways ... Jer 15:7
thus saith the LORD, If thou *r* ... Jer 15:19
let them *r* unto thee ... Jer 15:19
but *r* not thou unto them ... Jer 15:19
*r* ye now every one from his evil ... Jer 18:11
for he shall *r* no more, nor see ... Jer 22:10
He shall not *r* thither any more ... Jer 22:11
land whereunto they desire to *r* ... Jer 22:27
thither shall they not *r* ... Jer 22:27
that none doth *r* from his ... Jer 23:14
The anger of the LORD shall not *r* ... Jer 23:20
for they shall *r* unto me with ... Jer 24:7
in causing you to *r* to this place ... Jer 29:10
I will cause them to *r* to the ... Jer 30:3
and Jacob shall *r*, and shall be in ... Jer 30:10
anger of the LORD shall not *r* ... Jer 30:24
a great company shall *r* thither ... Jer 31:8
I will cause their captivity to *r* ... Jer 32:44
and the captivity of Israel to *r* ... Jer 33:7
For I will cause to *r* the ... Jer 33:11
I will cause their captivity to *r* ... Jer 33:26
whom they had let go free, to *r* ... Jer 34:11
liberty at their pleasure, to *r* ... Jer 34:16
and cause them to *r* to this city ... Jer 34:22
*R* ye now every man from his evil ... Jer 35:15
that they may *r* every man from ... Jer 36:3
will *r* every one from his evil ... Jer 36:7
shall *r* to Egypt into their own ... Jer 37:7
that thou cause me not to *r* to ... Jer 37:20
cause me to *r* to Jonathan's house ... Jer 38:26
cause you to *r* to your own land ... Jer 42:12
that they should *r* into the land ... Jer 44:14
have a desire to *r* to dwell there ... Jer 44:14
for none shall *r* but such as ... Jer 44:14
that escape the sword shall *r* out ... Jer 44:28
and Jacob shall *r*, and be in rest ... Jer 46:27
none shall *r* in vain ... Jer 50:9
shall not *r* to that which is sold ... Eze 7:13
thereof, which shall not *r* ... Eze 7:13
that he should not *r* from his ... Eze 13:22
shall *r* to their former estate ... Eze 16:55
her daughters shall *r* to their ... Eze 16:55
thy daughters shall *r* to your ... Eze 16:55
that he should *r* from his ways ... Eze 18:23
it shall not *r* any more ... Eze 21:5
I cause it to *r* into his sheath ... Eze 21:30
will cause them to *r* into the ... Eze 29:14
and thy cities shall not *r* ... Eze 35:9
he shall not *r* by the way of the ... Eze 46:9
after, it shall *r* to the prince ... Eze 46:17
caused me to *r* to the brink of ... Eze 47:6
now will I *r* to fight with the ... Dan 10:20
shall *r* into his own land ... Dan 11:9
then shall he *r*, and be stirred up ... Dan 11:10
For the king of the north shall *r* ... Dan 11:13
Then shall he *r* into his land ... Dan 11:28
do exploits, and *r* to his own land ... Dan 11:28
At the time appointed he shall *r* ... Dan 11:29
he shall be grieved, and *r* ... Dan 11:30
he shall even *r*, and have ... Dan 11:30
will go and *r* to my first husband ... Hos 2:7
Therefore will I *r*, and take away ... Hos 2:9
shall the children of Israel *r* ... Hos 3:5
go and *r* to my place, till they ... Hos 5:15
Come, and let us *r* unto the LORD ... Hos 6:1
they do not *r* to the LORD their ... Hos 7:10
They *r*, but not to the most High ... Hos 7:16
they shall *r* to Egypt ... Hos 8:13
but Ephraim shall *r* to Egypt ... Hos 9:3
He shall not *r* into the land of ... Hos 11:5
king, because they refused to *r* ... Hos 11:5
I will not *r* to destroy Ephraim ... Hos 11:9
shall his Lord *r* unto him ... Hos 12:14
O Israel, *r* unto the LORD thy God ... Hos 14:1
dwell under his shadow shall *r* ... Hos 14:7
Who knoweth if he will *r* and ... Joel 2:14
speedily will I *r* your recompence ... Joel 3:4
will *r* your recompence upon your ... Joel 3:7
thy reward shall *r* upon thine own ... Obad 15
they shall *r* to the hire of an ... Mic 1:7
*r* unto the children of Israel ... Mic 5:3
are impoverished, but we will *r* ... Mal 1:4
*R* unto me, and I will *r* unto ... Mal 3:7
But ye said, Wherein shall we *r* ... Mal 3:7
Then shall ye *r*, and discern ... Mal 3:18
that they should not *r* to Herod ... Mt 2:12
worthy, let your peace *r* to you ... Mt 10:13
I will *r* into my house from ... Mt 12:44
field *r* back to take his clothes ... Mt 24:18
*R* to thine own house, and shew how ... Lk 8:39
I will *r* unto my house whence I ... Lk 11:24
when he will *r* from the wedding ... Lk 12:36
let him likewise not *r* back ... Lk 17:31
for himself a kingdom, and to *r* ... Lk 19:12
now no more to *r* to corruption ... Acts 13:34
After this I will *r*, and will ... Acts 15:16
but I will *r* again unto you, if ... Acts 18:21
Syria, he purposed to *r* through ... Acts 20:3

**RETURNED**

the waters *r* from off the earth ... Gen 8:3
she *r* unto him into the ark, for ... Gen 8:9
which *r* not again unto him any ... Gen 8:12
And they *r*, and came to En-mishpat ... Gen 14:7
and Abraham *r* unto his place ... Gen 18:33
they *r* into the land of the ... Gen 21:32
So Abraham *r* unto his young men ... Gen 22:19
departed, and *r* unto his place ... Gen 31:55
And the messengers *r* to Jacob ... Gen 32:6
So Esau *r* that day on his way ... Gen 33:16
And Reuben *r* unto the pit ... Gen 37:29
he *r* unto his brethren, and said ... Gen 37:30
he *r* to Judah, and said, I cannot ... Gen 38:22
*r* to them again, and communed with ... Gen 42:24
now we had *r* this second time ... Gen 43:10
Because of the money that was *r* ... Gen 43:18
man his ass, and *r* to the city ... Gen 44:13
Joseph *r* into Egypt, he, and his ... Gen 50:14
*r* to Jethro his father in law, and ... Ex 4:18
he *r* to the land of Egypt ... Ex 4:20
Moses *r* unto the LORD, and said ... Ex 5:22
the sea *r* to his strength when ... Ex 14:27
And the waters *r*, and covered the ... Ex 14:28
Moses *r* the words of the people ... Ex 19:8
Moses *r* unto the LORD, and said ... Ex 32:31
of the congregation *r* unto him ... Ex 34:31
is *r* unto her father's house, as ... Lev 22:13
they *r* from searching of the land ... Num 13:25
sent to search the land, who *r* ... Num 14:36
Aaron *r* unto Moses unto the door ... Num 16:50
he *r* unto him and, lo, he stood by ... Num 23:6
up, and went and *r* to his place ... Num 24:25
And ye *r* and wept before the LORD ... Deut 1:45
days, until the pursuers be *r* ... Josh 2:16
days, until the pursuers were *r* ... Josh 2:22
So the two men *r*, and descended ... Josh 2:23
of Jordan *r* unto their place ... Josh 4:18
the city once, and *r* into the camp ... Josh 6:14
they *r* to Joshua, and said unto ... Josh 7:3
that all the Israelites *r* unto Ai ... Josh 8:24
And Joshua *r*, and all Israel with ... Josh 10:15
all the people *r* to the camp to ... Josh 10:21
And Joshua *r*, and all Israel with ... Josh 10:38
And Joshua *r*, and all Israel with ... Josh 10:43
and the half tribe of Manasseh *r* ... Josh 22:9
*r* from the children of Reuben, and ... Josh 22:32
the judge was dead, that they *r* ... Judg 2:19
yea, she *r* answer to herself ... Judg 5:29
there *r* of the people twenty and ... Judg 7:3
*r* into the host of Israel, and ... Judg 7:15
Gideon the son of Joash *r* from ... Judg 8:13
that she *r* unto her father, who ... Judg 11:39
And after a time he *r* to take her ... Judg 14:8
*r* unto their inheritance, and ... Judg 21:23
So Naomi *r*, and Ruth the Moabitess ... Ruth 1:22
which *r* out of the country of ... Ruth 1:22
worshipped before the LORD, and *r* ... 1Sa 1:19
they *r* to Ekron the same day ... 1Sa 6:16
*r* for a trespass offering unto ... 1Sa 6:17
*r* from Saul to feed his father's ... 1Sa 17:15
Israel *r* from chasing after the ... 1Sa 17:53
as David *r* from the slaughter of ... 1Sa 17:57
when David was *r* from the ... 1Sa 18:6
Wherefore Saul *r* from pursuing ... 1Sa 23:28
when Saul was *r* from following ... 1Sa 24:1
for the LORD hath *r* the ... 1Sa 25:39
his way, and Saul *r* to his place ... 1Sa 26:25
the camels, and the apparel, and *r* ... 1Sa 27:9
when David was *r* from the ... 2Sa 1:1
and the sword of Saul *r* not empty ... 2Sa 1:22
Joab *r* from following Abner ... 2Sa 2:30
Go, return. And he *r* ... 2Sa 3:16
And when Abner was *r* to Hebron ... 2Sa 3:27
Then David *r* to bless his ... 2Sa 6:20
David gat him a name when he *r* ... 2Sa 8:13
So Joab *r* from the children of ... 2Sa 10:14
and she *r* unto her house ... 2Sa 11:4
all the people *r* unto Jerusalem ... 2Sa 12:31
So Absalom *r* to his own house, and ... 2Sa 14:24
The LORD hath *r* upon thee all the ... 2Sa 16:8
whom thou seekest is as if all *r* ... 2Sa 17:3
find them, they *r* to Jerusalem ... 2Sa 17:20
the people *r* from pursuing after ... 2Sa 18:16
So the king *r*, and came to Jordan ... 2Sa 19:15
and he *r* unto his own place ... 2Sa 19:39
Joab *r* to Jerusalem unto the king ... 2Sa 20:22
the people *r* after him only to ... 2Sa 23:10
*r* to depart, according to the ... 1Kin 12:24
*r* not by the way that he came to ... 1Kin 13:10
Jeroboam *r* not from his evil way ... 1Kin 13:33
he *r* back from him, and took a ... 1Kin 19:21
and from thence he *r* to Samaria ... 2Kin 2:25
from him, and *r* to their own land ... 2Kin 3:27
Then he *r*, and walked in the house ... 2Kin 4:35
he *r* to the man of God, he and all ... 2Kin 5:15
And the messengers *r*, and told the ... 2Kin 7:15
that the woman *r* out of the land ... 2Kin 8:3
But king Joram was *r* to be healed ... 2Kin 9:15
and hostages, and *r* to Samaria ... 2Kin 14:14
So Rab-shakeh *r*, and found the ... 2Kin 19:8
of Assyria departed, and went and *r* ... 2Kin 19:36
upon them, and *r* to Jerusalem ... 2Kin 23:20
David *r* to bless his house ... 1Chr 16:43
and all the people *r* to Jerusalem ... 1Chr 20:3
it, that Jeroboam *r* out of Egypt ... 2Chr 10:2
*r* from going against Jeroboam ... 2Chr 11:4
in abundance, and *r* to Jerusalem ... 2Chr 14:15
Judah *r* to his house in peace to ... 2Chr 19:1
when they *r* to Jerusalem ... 2Chr 19:8
Then they *r*, every man of Judah ... 2Chr 20:27
he *r* to be healed in Jezreel ... 2Chr 22:6
they *r* home in great anger ... 2Chr 25:10
hostages also, and *r* to Samaria ... 2Chr 25:24
then they *r* to Samaria ... 2Chr 28:15
Then all the children of Israel *r* ... 2Chr 31:1
So he *r* with shame of face to his ... 2Chr 32:21
land of Israel, he *r* to Jerusalem ... 2Chr 34:7
and they *r* to Jerusalem ... 2Chr 34:9
then they *r* answer by letter ... Ezr 5:5
And thus they *r* us answer, saying ... Ezr 5:11
the gate of the valley, and so *r* ... Neh 2:15
that we *r* all of us to the wall ... Neh 4:15
yet when they *r*, and cried unto ... Neh 9:28
on the morrow she *r* into the ... Est 2:14
Then the king *r* out of the palace ... Est 7:8
my prayer *r* into mine own bosom ... Ps 35:13
and with Aram-zobah, when Joab *r* ... Ps 60:t
and they *r* and enquired early after ... Ps 78:34
So I *r*, and considered all the ... Eccl 4:1
Then I *r*, and I saw vanity under ... Eccl 4:7
I *r*, and saw under the sun, that ... Eccl 9:11
So Rabshakeh *r*, and found the king ... Is 37:8
of Assyria departed, and went and *r* ... Is 37:37
So the sun *r* ten degrees, by ... Is 38:8
But she *r* not ... Jer 3:7
they *r* with their vessels empty ... Jer 14:3
Even all the Jews *r* out of all ... Jer 40:12
from Mizpah cast about and *r* ... Jer 41:14
that were *r* from all nations ... Jer 43:5
*r* as the appearance of a flash of ... Eze 1:14
have *r* to provoke me to anger ... Eze 8:17
Now when I had *r*, behold, at the ... Eze 47:7
and mine understanding *r* unto me ... Dan 4:34
the same time my reason *r* unto me ... Dan 4:36
honour and brightness *r* unto me ... Dan 4:36
when I *r* the captivity of my ... Hos 6:11
yet have ye not *r* unto me ... Amos 4:6
yet have ye not *r* unto me ... Amos 4:8
yet have ye not *r* unto me ... Amos 4:9
yet have ye not *r* unto me ... Amos 4:10
yet have ye not *r* unto me ... Amos 4:11
and they *r* and said, Like as the ... Zec 1:6
I am *r* to Jerusalem with mercies ... Zec 1:16
that no man passed through nor *r* ... Zec 7:14
I am *r* unto Zion, and will dwell ... Zec 8:3
the morning as he *r* into the city ... Mt 21:18
And when he *r*, he found them ... Mk 14:40
months, and *r* to her own house ... Lk 1:56
And the shepherds *r*, glorifying and ... Lk 2:20
they *r* into Galilee, to their own ... Lk 2:39
had fulfilled the days, as they *r* ... Lk 2:43
of the Holy Ghost *r* from Jordan ... Lk 4:1
Jesus *r* in the power of the ... Lk 4:14
up into the ship, and *r* back again ... Lk 8:37
to pass, that, when Jesus was *r* ... Lk 8:40
And the apostles, when they were *r* ... Lk 9:10
the seventy *r* again with joy ... Lk 10:17
found that *r* to give glory to God ... Lk 17:18
came to pass, that when he was *r* ... Lk 19:15
done, smote their breasts, and *r* ... Lk 23:48
And they *r*, and prepared spices and ... Lk 23:56
*r* from the sepulchre, and told all ... Lk 24:9
*r* to Jerusalem, and found the ... Lk 24:33
*r* to Jerusalem with great joy ... Lk 24:52
Then *r* they unto Jerusalem from ... Acts 1:12
them not in the prison, they *r* ... Acts 5:22
*r* to Jerusalem, and preached the ... Acts 8:25
Saul *r* from Jerusalem, when they ... Acts 12:25
from them *r* to Jerusalem ... Acts 13:13
they *r* again to Lystra, and to ... Acts 14:21
and they *r* home again ... Acts 21:6
go with him, and *r* to the castle ... Acts 23:32
Arabia, and *r* again unto Damascus ... Gal 1:17
have had opportunity to have *r* ... Heb 11:15
but are now *r* unto the Shepherd ... 1Pet 2:25

**RETURNETH**

goeth forth, he *r* to his earth ... Ps 146:4
As a dog *r* to his vomit ... Prov 26:11

so a fool r to his folly ... Prov 26:11
the wind r again according to his ... Eccl 1:6
r not thither, but watereth the ... Is 55:10
that passeth out and him that r ... Eze 35:7
by, and because of him that r ... Zec 9:8

**RETURNING**
In r and rest shall ye be saved ... Is 30:15
r to the house, found the servant ... Lk 7:10
Was r, and sitting in his chariot ... Acts 8:28
who met Abraham r from the ... Heb 7:1

**REU** (*re'-u*) See RAGAU. *Son of Peleg.*
lived thirty years, and begat R ... Gen 11:18
after he begat R two hundred ... Gen 11:19
R lived two and thirty years, and ... Gen 11:20
R lived after he begat Serug two ... Gen 11:21
Eber, Peleg, R, ... 1Chr 1:25

**REUBEN** (*ru'-ben*) See REUBENITE.
*1. A son of Jacob and Leah.*
a son, and she called his name R ... Gen 29:32
R went in the days of wheat ... Gen 30:14
dwelt in that land, that R went ... Gen 35:22
R, Jacob's firstborn, and Simeon, ... Gen 35:23
R heard it, and he delivered him ... Gen 37:21
R said unto them, Shed no blood, ... Gen 37:22
And R returned unto the pit ... Gen 37:29
R answered them, saying, Spake I ... Gen 42:22
R spake unto his father, saying, ... Gen 42:37
R, Jacob's firstborn ... Gen 46:8
And the sons of R ... Gen 46:9
as R and Simeon, they shall be ... Gen 48:5
R, thou art my firstborn, my ... Gen 49:3
R, Simeon, Levi, and Judah, ... Ex 1:2
The sons of R the firstborn of ... Ex 6:14
these be the families of R ... Ex 6:14
And the children of R, Israel's ... Num 1:20
On, the son of Peleth, sons of R ... Num 16:1
R, the eldest son of Israel ... Num 26:5
the children of R ... Num 26:5
the sons of Eliab, the son of R ... Deut 11:6
the stone of Bohan the son of R ... Josh 15:6
the stone of Bohan the son of R ... Josh 18:17
R, Simeon, Levi, and Judah, ... 1Chr 2:1
Now the sons of R the firstborn ... 1Chr 5:1
of R the firstborn of Israel were ... 1Chr 5:3
*2. Descendants of Reuben 1.*
of the tribe of R ... Num 1:5
of them, even of the tribe of R ... Num 1:21
of R according to their armies ... Num 2:10
of R shall be Elizur the son of ... Num 2:10
of R were an hundred thousand ... Num 2:16
prince of the children of R ... Num 7:30
the standard of the camp of R set ... Num 10:18
of the tribe of R, Shammua the ... Num 13:4
Now the children of R and the ... Num 32:1
of Gad and the children of R came ... Num 32:2
of Gad and to the children of R ... Num 32:6
the children of R spake unto ... Num 32:25
the children of R will pass with ... Num 32:29
Gad and the children of R answered. Num 32:31
of Gad, and to the children of R ... Num 32:33
the children of R built Heshbon ... Num 32:37
the tribe of the children of R ... Num 34:14
R, Gad, and Asher ... Deut 27:13
Let R live, and not die ... Deut 33:6
And the children of R, and the ... Josh 4:12
the tribe of the children of R ... Josh 13:15
of the children of R was Jordan ... Josh 13:23
of R after their families ... Josh 13:23
and Gad, and R, and half the tribe ... Josh 18:7
the plain out of the tribe of R ... Josh 20:8
had out of the tribe of R ... Josh 21:7
And out of the tribe of R, Bezer ... Josh 21:36
And the children of R and the ... Josh 22:9
land of Canaan, the children of R ... Josh 22:10
say, Behold, the children of R ... Josh 22:11
sent unto the children of R ... Josh 22:13
they came unto the children of R ... Josh 22:15
Then the children of R and the ... Josh 22:21
us and you, ye children of R ... Josh 22:25
the words that the children of R ... Josh 22:30
said unto the children of R ... Josh 22:31
returned from the children of R ... Josh 22:32
land wherein the children of R ... Josh 22:33
And the children of R and the ... Josh 22:34
For the divisions of R there were ... Judg 5:15
For the divisions of R there were ... Judg 5:16
The sons of R, and the Gadites, and ... 1Chr 5:18
families, out of the tribe of R ... 1Chr 6:63
given them out of the tribe of R ... 1Chr 6:78
the west side, a portion for R ... Eze 48:6
And by the border of R, from the ... Eze 48:7
one gate of R, one gate of Judah, ... Eze 48:31
Of the tribe of R were sealed ... Rev 7:5

**REUBENITE** (*ru'-ben-ite*) See REUBENITES. *A descendant of Reuben.*
Adina the son of Shiza the R ... 1Chr 11:42

**REUBENITES** (*ru'-ben-ites*)
These are the families of the R ... Num 26:7
cities thereof, gave I unto the R ... Deut 3:12
And unto the R and unto the Gadites Deut 3:16
in the plain country, of the R ... Deut 4:43
it for an inheritance unto the R ... Deut 29:8
And to the R, and to the Gadites, ... Josh 1:12
it for a possession unto the R ... Josh 12:6
With whom the R and the Gadites ... Josh 13:8
Then Joshua called the R, and the ... Josh 22:1
of Gilead, the Gadites, and the R ... 2Kin 10:33
he was prince of the R ... 1Chr 5:6
he carried them away, even the R ... 1Chr 5:26
the Reubenite, a captain of the R ... 1Chr 11:42
other side of Jordan, of the R ... 1Chr 12:37
king David made rulers over the R ... 1Chr 26:32
the ruler of the R was Eliezer ... 1Chr 27:16

**REUEL** (*re-u'-el*) See DEUEL, JETHRO, RAGUEL.
*1. A son of Esau.*
and Bashemath bare R ... Gen 36:4
R the son of Bashemath the wife ... Gen 36:10
And these are the sons of R ... Gen 36:13
are the sons of R Esau's son ... Gen 36:17
came of R in the land of Edom ... Gen 36:17
Eliphaz, R, and Jeush, and Jaalam, ... 1Chr 1:35
The sons of R ... 1Chr 1:37
*2. Same as Jethro.*
when they came to R their father ... Ex 2:18
*3. Father of Eliasaph.*
shall be Eliasaph the son of R ... Num 2:14
*4. A Benjamite.*
son of Shephatiah, the son of R ... 1Chr 9:8

**REUMAH** (*re-u'-mah*) *Concubine of Nahor.*
his concubine, whose name was R ... Gen 22:24

**REVEAL**
The heaven shall r his iniquity ... Job 20:27
will r unto them the abundance of ... Jer 33:6
seeing thou couldst r this secret ... Dan 2:47
to whomsoever the Son will r him ... Mt 11:27
and he to whom the Son will r him ... Lk 10:22
To r his Son in me, that I might ... Gal 1:16
God shall r even this unto you ... Phil 3:15

**REVEALED**
things which are r belong unto us ... Deut 29:29
word of the LORD yet r unto him ... 1Sa 3:7
for the LORD r himself to Samuel ... 1Sa 3:21
hast r to thy servant, saying, I ... 2Sa 7:27
it was r in mine ears by the LORD ... Is 22:14
land of Chittim it is r to them ... Is 23:1
the glory of the LORD shall be r ... Is 40:5
to whom is the arm of the LORD r ... Is 53:1
come, and my righteousness to be r ... Is 56:1
for unto thee have I r my cause ... Jer 11:20
Then was the secret r unto Daniel ... Dan 2:19
this secret is not r to me for ... Dan 2:30
Persia a thing was r unto Daniel ... Dan 10:1
covered, that shall not be r ... Mt 10:26
and hast r them unto babes ... Mt 11:25
and blood hath not r it unto thee ... Mt 16:17
it was r unto him by the Holy ... Lk 2:26
thoughts of many hearts may be r ... Lk 2:35
and hast r them unto babes ... Lk 10:21
covered, that shall not be r ... Lk 12:2
the day when the Son of man is r ... Lk 17:30
hath the arm of the Lord been r ... Jn 12:38
of God r from faith to faith ... Rom 1:17
God is r from heaven against all ... Rom 1:18
the glory which shall be r in us ... Rom 8:18
But God hath r them unto us by ... 1Cor 2:10
it, because it shall be r by fire ... 1Cor 3:13
If any thing be r to another that ... 1Cor 14:30
which should afterwards be r ... Gal 3:23
as it is now r unto his holy ... Eph 3:5
be r from heaven with his mighty ... 2Th 1:7
first, and that man of sin be r ... 2Th 2:3
that he might be r in his time ... 2Th 2:6
And then shall that Wicked be r ... 2Th 2:8
ready to be r in the last time ... 1Pet 1:5
Unto whom it was r, that not unto ... 1Pet 1:12
that, when his glory shall be r ... 1Pet 4:13
of the glory that shall be r ... 1Pet 5:1

**REVEALER**
a r of secrets, seeing thou ... Dan 2:47

**REVEALETH**
A talebearer r secrets ... Prov 11:13
about as a talebearer r secrets ... Prov 20:19
He r the deep and secret things ... Dan 2:22
is a God in heaven that r secrets ... Dan 2:28
he that r secrets maketh known to ... Dan 2:29
but he r his secret unto his ... Amos 3:7

**REVELATION**
r of the righteous judgment of ... Rom 2:5
according to the r of the mystery ... Rom 16:25
I shall speak to you either by r ... 1Cor 14:6
doctrine, hath a tongue, hath a r ... 1Cor 14:26
but by the r of Jesus Christ ... Gal 1:12
And I went up by r, and ... Gal 2:2
r in the knowledge of him ... Eph 1:17
How that by r he made known unto ... Eph 3:3
unto you at the r of Jesus Christ ... 1Pet 1:13
The R of Jesus Christ, which God ... Rev 1:1

**REVELATIONS**
come to visions and r of the Lord ... 2Cor 12:1
through the abundance of the r ... 2Cor 12:7

**REVELLINGS**
Envyings, murders, drunkenness, r ... Gal 5:21
lusts, excess of wine, r ... 1Pet 4:3

**REVENGE**
me, and r me of my persecutors ... Jer 15:15
and we shall take our r on him ... Jer 20:10
the Philistines have dealt by r ... Eze 25:15
yea, what zeal, yea, what r ... 2Cor 7:11
a readiness to r all disobedience ... 2Cor 10:6

**REVENGED**
offended, and r himself upon them ... Eze 25:12

**REVENGER**
The r of blood himself shall slay ... Num 35:19
the r of blood shall slay the ... Num 35:21
the r of blood according to these ... Num 35:24
out of the hand of the r of blood ... Num 35:25
the r of blood find him without ... Num 35:27
the r of blood kill the slayer ... Num 35:27
a r to execute wrath upon him ... Rom 13:4

**REVENGERS**
r of blood to destroy any more ... 2Sa 14:11

**REVENGES**
the beginning of r upon the enemy ... Deut 32:42

**REVENGETH**
God is jealous, and the LORD r ... Nah 1:2
the LORD r, and is furious ... Nah 1:2

**REVENGING**
r of the blood of thy servants ... Ps 79:10

**REVENUE**
shalt endamage the r of the kings ... Ezr 4:13
and my r than choice silver ... Prov 8:19
harvest of the river, is her r ... Is 23:3

**REVENUES**
but in the r of the wicked is ... Prov 15:6
than great r without right ... Prov 16:8
they shall be ashamed of your r ... Jer 12:13

**REVERENCE**
my sabbaths, and r my sanctuary ... Lev 19:30
my sabbaths, and r my sanctuary ... Lev 26:2
he fell on his face, and did r ... 2Sa 9:6
did r to the king, and said, Let ... 1Kin 1:31
Mordecai bowed not, nor did him r ... Est 3:2
Mordecai bowed not, nor did him r ... Est 3:5
to be had in r of all them that ... Ps 89:7
son, saying, They will r my son ... Mt 21:37
them, saying, They will r my son ... Mk 12:6
it may be they will r him when ... Lk 20:13
wife see that she r her husband ... Eph 5:33
corrected us, and we gave them r ... Heb 12:9
may serve God acceptably with r ... Heb 12:28

**REVERENCED**
king's gate, bowed, and r Haman ... Est 3:2

**REVEREND**
holy and r is his name ... Ps 111:9

**REVERSE**
and I cannot r it ... Num 23:20
let it be written to r the ... Est 8:5
the king's ring, may no man r ... Est 8:8

**REVILE**
Thou shalt not r the gods ... Ex 22:28
are ye, when men shall r you ... Mt 5:11

**REVILED**
And they that passed by r him ... Mt 27:39
were crucified with him r him ... Mk 15:32
Then they r him, and said, Thou ... Jn 9:28
being r, we bless ... 1Cor 4:12
when he was r, r not again ... 1Pet 2:23

**REVILERS**
covetous, nor drunkards, nor r ... 1Cor 6:10

**REVILEST**
by said, R thou God's high priest ... Acts 23:4

**REVILINGS**
neither be ye afraid of their r ... Is 51:7
the r of the children of Ammon, ... Zeph 2:8

**REVIVE**
will they r the stones out of the ... Neh 4:2
Wilt thou not r us again ... Ps 85:6
midst of trouble, thou wilt r me ... Ps 138:7
to r the spirit of the humble, and ... Is 57:15
to r the heart of the contrite ... Is 57:15
After two days will he r us ... Hos 6:2
they shall r as the corn, and grow ... Hos 14:7
r thy work in the midst of the ... Hab 3:2

**REVIVED**
spirit of Jacob their father r ... Gen 45:27
his spirit came again, and he r ... Judg 15:19
came into him again, and he r ... 1Kin 17:22
touched the bones of Elisha, he r ... 2Kin 13:21
when the commandment came, sin r ... Rom 7:9
Christ both died, and rose, and r ... Rom 14:9

**REVIVING**
give us a little r in our bondage ... Ezr 9:8
kings of Persia, to give us a r ... Ezr 9:9

**REVOLT**
did Libnah r from under his hand ... 2Chr 21:10
ye will r more and more ... Is 1:5
our God, speaking oppression and r ... Is 59:13

**REVOLTED**
In his days Edom r from under the ... 2Kin 8:20
Yet Edom r from under the hand of ... 2Kin 8:22
Then Libnah r at the same time ... 2Kin 8:22
In his days the Edomites r from ... 2Chr 21:8
So the Edomites r from under the ... 2Chr 21:10
children of Israel have deeply r ... Is 31:6
they are r and gone ... Jer 5:23

**REVOLTERS**
They are all grievous *r*, walking ... Jer 6:28
the *r* are profound to make ... Hos 5:2
all their princes are *r*. ... Hos 9:15

**REVOLTING**
But this people hath a *r* and a ... Jer 5:23

**REWARD**
shield, and thy exceeding great *r*. ... Gen 15:1
for it is your *r* for your service ... Num 18:31
not persons, nor taketh *r* ... Deut 10:17
Cursed be he that taketh *r* to ... Deut 27:25
and will *r* them that hate me ... Deut 32:41
a full *r* be given thee of the ... Ruth 2:12
wherefore the LORD *r* thee good ... 1Sa 24:19
the LORD shall *r* the doer of evil ... 2Sa 3:39
given him a *r* for his tidings ... 2Sa 4:10
recompense it me with such a *r*. ... 2Sa 19:36
thyself, and I will give thee a *r*. ... 1Kin 13:7
Behold, I say, how they *r* us ... 2Chr 20:11
Give a *r* for me of your substance ... Job 6:22
looketh for the *r* of his work ... Job 7:2
nor taketh *r* against the innocent ... Ps 15:5
keeping of them there is great *r* ... Ps 19:11
Let them be desolate for a *r* of ... Ps 40:15
He shall *r* evil unto mine enemies ... Ps 54:5
there is a *r* for the righteous ... Ps 58:11
for a *r* of their shame that say ... Ps 70:3
behold and see the *r* of the wicked ... Ps 91:8
render a *r* to the proud ... Ps 94:2
Let this be the *r* of mine ... Ps 109:20
and the fruit of the womb is his *r*. ... Ps 127:3
righteousness shall be a sure *r*. ... Prov 11:18
a *r* in the bosom strong wrath ... Prov 21:14
found it, then there shall be a *r*. ... Prov 24:14
shall be no *r* to the evil man ... Prov 24:20
head, and the LORD shall *r* thee ... Prov 25:22
have a good *r* for their labour ... Eccl 4:9
neither have they any more a *r*. ... Eccl 9:5
for the *r* of his hands shall be ... Is 3:11
Which justify the wicked for *r*. ... Is 5:23
his *r* is with him, and his work ... Is 40:10
my captives, not for price nor *r* ... Is 45:13
his *r* is with him, and his work ... Is 62:11
guard gave him victuals and a *r*. ... Jer 40:5
and in that thou givest a *r* ... Eze 16:34
and no *r* is given unto thee, ... Eze 16:34
ways, and *r* them their doings ... Hos 4:9
thou hast loved a *r* upon every ... Hos 9:1
thy *r* shall return upon thine own ... Obad 15
The heads thereof judge for *r* ... Mic 3:11
and the judge asketh for a *r*. ... Mic 7:3
for great is your *r* in heaven ... Mt 5:12
which love you, what *r* have ye ... Mt 5:46
otherwise ye have no *r* of your ... Mt 6:1
I say unto you, They have their *r*. ... Mt 6:2
himself shall *r* thee openly ... Mt 6:4
I say unto you, They have their *r*. ... Mt 6:5
in secret shall *r* thee openly ... Mt 6:6
I say unto you, They have their *r*. ... Mt 6:16
in secret, shall *r* thee openly ... Mt 6:18
shall receive a prophet's *r*. ... Mt 10:41
shall receive a righteous man's *r* ... Mt 10:41
he shall in no wise lose his *r*. ... Mt 10:42
then he shall *r* every man ... Mt 16:27
unto you, he shall not lose his *r*. ... Mk 9:41
your *r* is great in heaven ... Lk 6:23
your *r* shall be great, and ye ... Lk 6:35
we receive the due *r* of our deeds ... Lk 23:41
a field with the *r* of iniquity ... Acts 1:18
is the *r* not reckoned of grace ... Rom 4:4
own *r* according to his own labour ... 1Cor 3:8
thereupon, he shall receive a *r*. ... 1Cor 3:14
this thing willingly, I have a *r*. ... 1Cor 9:17
What is my *r* then ... 1Cor 9:18
of your *r* in a voluntary humility ... Col 2:18
receive the *r* of the inheritance ... Col 3:24
The labourer is worthy of his *r*. ... 1Ti 5:18
the Lord *r* him according to his ... 2Ti 4:14
received a just recompence of *r*. ... Heb 2:2
which hath great recompence of *r* ... Heb 10:35
unto the recompence of the *r*. ... Heb 11:26
And shall receive the *r* of ... 2Pet 2:13
but that we receive a full *r*. ... 2Jn 8
after the error of Balaam for *r* ... Jude 11
that thou shouldest give *r* unto ... Rev 11:18
*R* her even as she rewarded you, ... Rev 18:6
my *r* is with me, to give every ... Rev 22:12

**REWARDED**
Wherefore have ye *r* evil for good ... Gen 44:4
for thou hast *r* me good, whereas ... 1Sa 24:17
good, whereas I have *r* thee evil ... 1Sa 24:17
The LORD *r* me according to my ... 2Sa 22:21
for your work shall be *r*. ... 2Chr 15:7
If I have *r* evil unto him that ... Ps 7:4
The LORD *r* me according to my ... Ps 18:20
They *r* me evil for good to the ... Ps 35:12
nor *r* us according to our ... Ps 103:10
they have *r* me evil for good, and ... Ps 109:5
the commandment shall be *r*. ... Prov 13:13
for they have *r* evil unto ... Is 3:9
for thy work shall be *r*, saith ... Jer 31:16
Reward her even as she *r* you ... Rev 18:6

**REWARDER**
that he is a *r* of them that ... Heb 11:6

**REWARDETH**
he *r* him, and he shall know it ... Job 21:19
plentifully *r* the proud doer ... Ps 31:23
that *r* thee as thou hast served ... Ps 137:8
Whoso *r* evil for good, evil shall ... Prov 17:13
formed all things both *r* the fool ... Prov 26:10
and *r* transgressors ... Prov 26:10

**REWARDS**
the *r* of divination in their hand ... Num 22:7
gifts, and followeth after *r*. ... Is 1:23
ye shall receive of me gifts and *r* ... Dan 2:6
thyself, and give thy *r* to another ... Dan 5:17
These are my *r* that my lovers ... Hos 2:12

**REZEPH** (*re'-zef*) *A fortress near Haran.*
Gozan, and Haran, and *R*. ... 2Kin 19:12
as Gozan, and Haran, and *R* ... Is 37:12

**REZIA** (*re-zi'-ah*) *Son of Ulla.*
Arah, and Haniel, and *R* ... 1Chr 7:39

**REZIN** (*re'-zin*)
*1. A king of Syria.*
against Judah *R* the king of Syria ... 2Kin 15:37
Then *R* king of Syria and Pekah son ... 2Kin 16:5
At that time *R* king of Syria ... 2Kin 16:6
of it captive to Kir, and slew *R*. ... 2Kin 16:9
the fierce anger of *R* with Syria ... Is 7:4
and the head of Damascus is *R*. ... Is 7:8
that go softly, and rejoice in *R* ... Is 8:6
the adversaries of *R* against him ... Is 9:11
*2. A family of exiles.*
The children of *R*, the children ... Ezr 2:48
of Reaiah, the children of *R*. ... Neh 7:50

**REZON** (*re'-zon*) *An enemy of Solomon.*
*R* the son of Eliadah, which fled ... 1Kin 11:23

**RHEGIUM** (*re'-je-um*) *A port of southern Italy.*
fetched a compass, and came to *R* ... Acts 28:13

**RHESA** (*re'-sah*) *Son of Zorobabel; an ancestor of Jesus.*
of Joanna, which was the son of *R*. ... Lk 3:27

**RHODA** (*ro'-dah*) *A maiden in Mary's house.*
a damsel came to hearken, named *R*. ... Acts 12:13

**RHODES** (*rodes*) *A Mediterranean island.*
Coos, and the day following unto *R*. ... Acts 21:1

**RIB**
And the *r*, which the LORD God had ... Gen 2:22
spear smote him under the fifth *r* ... 2Sa 2:23
smote him there under the fifth *r* ... 2Sa 3:27
they smote him under the fifth *r*. ... 2Sa 4:6
him therewith in the fifth *r*. ... 2Sa 20:10

**RIBAI** (*rib'-ahee*) *Father of Ittai.*
Ittai the son of *R* out of Gibeah ... 2Sa 23:29
Ithai the son of *R* of Gibeah ... 1Chr 11:31

**RIBBAND**
fringe of the borders a *r* of blue ... Num 15:38

**RIBLAH** (*rib'-lah*) *A city on the Orontes River.*
shall go down from Shepham to *R* ... Num 34:11
put him in bands at *R* in the land ... 2Kin 23:33
up to the king of Babylon to *R* ... 2Kin 25:6
them to the king of Babylon to *R* ... 2Kin 25:20
slew them at *R* in the land of ... 2Kin 25:21
king of Babylon to *R* in the land ... Jer 39:5
of Zedekiah in *R* before his eyes ... Jer 39:6
to *R* in the land of Hamath ... Jer 52:9
all the princes of Judah in *R*. ... Jer 52:10
them to the king of Babylon to *R* ... Jer 52:26
put them to death in *R* in the ... Jer 52:27

**RIBS**
and he took one of his *r*, and ... Gen 2:21
it had three *r* in the mouth of it ... Dan 7:5

**RICH**
And Abram was very *r* in cattle ... Gen 13:2
say, I have made Abram *r* ... Gen 14:23
The *r* shall not give more, and the ... Ex 30:15
or stranger wax *r* by thee ... Lev 25:47
not young men, whether poor or *r*. ... Ruth 3:10
The LORD maketh poor, and maketh *r* ... 1Sa 2:7
the one *r*, and the other poor ... 2Sa 12:1
The *r* man had exceeding many ... 2Sa 12:2
came a traveller unto the *r* man ... 2Sa 12:4
He shall not be *r*, neither shall ... Job 15:29
The *r* man shall lie down, but he ... Job 27:19
nor regardeth the *r* more than the ... Job 34:19
even the *r* among the people shall ... Ps 45:12
Both low and high, *r* and poor, ... Ps 49:2
thou afraid when one is made *r* ... Ps 49:16
the hand of the diligent maketh *r* ... Prov 10:4
The *r* man's wealth is his strong ... Prov 10:15
blessing of the LORD, it maketh *r* ... Prov 10:22
There is that maketh himself *r* ... Prov 13:7
but the *r* hath many friends ... Prov 14:20
The *r* man's wealth is his strong ... Prov 18:11
but the *r* answereth roughly ... Prov 18:23
loveth wine and oil shall not be *r* ... Prov 21:17
The *r* and poor meet together ... Prov 22:2
The *r* ruleth over the poor, and ... Prov 22:7
and he that giveth to the *r* ... Prov 22:16
Labour not to be *r* ... Prov 23:4
in his ways, though he be *r* ... Prov 28:6
The *r* man is wise in his own ... Prov 28:11
to be *r* shall not be innocent ... Prov 28:20
hasteth to be *r* hath an evil eye ... Prov 28:22
but the abundance of the *r* will ... Eccl 5:12
and the *r* sit in low place ... Eccl 10:6
curse not the *r* in thy bedchamber ... Eccl 10:20
and with the *r* in his death ... Is 53:9
they are become great, and waxen *r* ... Jer 5:27
let not the *r* man glory in his ... Jer 9:23
work, and in chests of *r* apparel ... Eze 27:24
Ephraim said, Yet I am become *r* ... Hos 12:8
For the *r* men thereof are full of ... Mic 6:12
for I am *r* ... Zec 11:5
That a *r* man shall hardly enter ... Mt 19:23
than for a *r* man to enter into ... Mt 19:24
there came a *r* man of Arimathaea, ... Mt 27:57
than for a *r* man to enter into ... Mk 10:25
and many that were *r* cast in much ... Mk 12:41
the *r* he hath sent empty away ... Lk 1:53
But woe unto you that are *r* ... Lk 6:24
The ground of a certain *r* man ... Lk 12:16
himself, and is not *r* toward God ... Lk 12:21
thy kinsmen, nor thy *r* neighbours ... Lk 14:12
There was a certain *r* man ... Lk 16:1
There was a certain *r* man ... Lk 16:19
which fell from the *r* man's table ... Lk 16:21
the *r* man also died, and was ... Lk 16:22
for he was very *r* ... Lk 18:23
than for a *r* man to enter into ... Lk 18:25
among the publicans, and he was *r* ... Lk 19:2
saw the *r* men casting their gifts ... Lk 21:1
is *r* unto all that call upon him ... Rom 10:12
Now ye are full, now ye are *r* ... 1Cor 4:8
as poor, yet making many *r* ... 2Cor 6:10
Christ, that, though he was *r* ... 2Cor 8:9
ye through his poverty might be *r* ... 2Cor 8:9
who is *r* in mercy, for his great ... Eph 2:4
will be *r* fall into temptation ... 1Ti 6:9
them that are *r* in this world ... 1Ti 6:17
that they be *r* in good works, ... 1Ti 6:18
But the *r*, in that he is made low ... Jas 1:10
so also shall the *r* man fade away ... Jas 1:11
the poor of this world *r* in faith ... Jas 2:5
Do not *r* men oppress you, and draw ... Jas 2:6
ye *r* men, weep and howl for your ... Jas 5:1
and poverty, (but thou art *r*) ... Rev 2:9
Because thou sayest, I am *r* ... Rev 3:17
the fire, that thou mayest be *r* ... Rev 3:18
and the great men, and the *r* men ... Rev 6:15
all, both small and great, *r* ... Rev 13:16
of the earth are waxed *r* through ... Rev 18:3
things, which were made *r* by her ... Rev 18:15
wherein were made *r* all that had ... Rev 18:19

**RICHER**
shall be far *r* than they all ... Dan 11:2

**RICHES**
For all the *r* which God hath ... Gen 31:16
For their *r* were more than that ... Gen 36:7
with much *r* unto your tents ... Josh 22:8
king will enrich him with great *r* ... 1Sa 17:25
neither hast asked *r* for thyself ... 1Kin 3:11
which thou hast not asked, both *r* ... 1Kin 3:13
all the kings of the earth for *r* ... 1Kin 10:23
Both *r* and honour come ... 1Chr 29:12
a good old age, full of days, *r* ... 1Chr 29:28
heart, and thou hast not asked *r* ... 2Chr 1:11
and I will give thee *r*, and wealth, ... 2Chr 1:12
all the kings of the earth in *r* ... 2Chr 9:22
and he had *r* and honour in ... 2Chr 17:5
Now Jehoshaphat had *r* and honour ... 2Chr 18:1
both *r* with the dead bodies ... 2Chr 20:25
had exceeding much *r* ... 2Chr 32:27
When he shewed the *r* of his ... Est 1:4
told them of the glory of his *r* ... Est 5:11
He hath swallowed down *r*, and he ... Job 20:15
Will he esteem thy *r* ... Job 36:19
better than the *r* of many wicked ... Ps 37:16
he heapeth up *r*, and knoweth not ... Ps 39:6
in the multitude of their *r* ... Ps 49:6
trusted in the abundance of his *r* ... Ps 52:7
if *r* increase, set not your heart ... Ps 62:10
they increase in *r* ... Ps 73:12
the earth is full of thy *r* ... Ps 104:24
Wealth and *r* shall be in his house ... Ps 112:3
testimonies, as much as in all *r* ... Ps 119:14
and in her left hand *r* and honour ... Prov 3:16
*R* and honour are with me ... Prov 8:18
yea, durable *r* and righteousness ... Prov 8:18
*R* profit not in the day of wrath ... Prov 11:4
and strong men retain *r* ... Prov 11:16
that trusteth in his *r* shall fall ... Prov 11:28
himself poor, yet hath great *r* ... Prov 13:7
ransom of a man's life are his *r* ... Prov 13:8
The crown of the wise is their *r* ... Prov 14:24
*r* are the inheritance of fathers ... Prov 19:14
rather to be chosen than great *r* ... Prov 22:1
and the fear of the LORD are *r* ... Prov 22:4
the poor to increase his *r* ... Prov 22:16
for *r* certainly make themselves ... Prov 23:5
with all precious and pleasant *r* ... Prov 24:4
For *r* are not for ever ... Prov 27:24
give me neither poverty nor *r* ... Prov 30:8
is his eye satisfied with *r* ... Eccl 4:8
*r* kept for the owners thereof to ... Eccl 5:13
But those *r* perish by evil ... Eccl 5:14
man also to whom God hath given *r* ... Eccl 5:19
A man to whom God hath given *r* ... Eccl 6:2
nor yet *r* to men of understanding ... Eccl 9:11
the *r* of Damascus and the spoil of ... Is 8:4
as a nest the *r* of the people ... Is 10:14
they will carry their *r* upon the ... Is 30:6
hidden *r* of secret places, that ... Is 45:3
shall eat the *r* of the Gentiles ... Is 61:6
not the rich man glory in his *r* ... Jer 9:23
so he that getteth *r*, and not by ... Jer 17:11
because the *r* that he hath gotten ... Jer 48:36
they shall make a spoil of thy *r* ... Eze 26:12
of the multitude of all kind of *r* ... Eze 27:12

for the multitude of all *r* Eze 27:18
Thy *r*, and thy fairs, thy Eze 27:27
earth with the multitude of thy *r* Eze 27:33
thou hast gotten thee *r*, and hast Eze 28:4
hast thou increased thy *r* Eze 28:5
is lifted up because of thy *r* Eze 28:5
by his strength through his *r* he Dan 11:2
with a great army and with much *r* Dan 11:13
them the prey, and spoil, and *r* Dan 11:24
return into his land with great *r* Dan 11:28
world, and the deceitfulness of *r* Mt 13:22
world, and the deceitfulness of *r* Mk 4:19
*r* enter into the kingdom of God Mk 10:23
in *r* to enter into the kingdom of Mk 10:24
and are choked with cares and *r* Lk 8:14
commit to your trust the true *r* Lk 16:11
*r* enter into the kingdom of God Lk 18:24
thou the *r* of his goodness Rom 2:4
that he might make known the *r* of Rom 9:23
of them be the *r* of the world Rom 11:12
of them the *r* of the Gentiles Rom 11:12
depth of the *r* both of the wisdom Rom 11:33
unto the *r* of their liberality 2Cor 8:2
according to the *r* of his grace Eph 1:7
what the *r* of the glory of his Eph 1:18
he might shew the exceeding *r* of Eph 2:7
the unsearchable *r* of Christ Eph 3:8
according to the *r* of his glory Eph 3:16
to his *r* in glory by Christ Jesus Phil 4:19
*r* of the glory of this mystery Col 1:27
unto all *r* of the full assurance Col 2:2
nor trust in uncertain *r* 1Ti 6:17
*r* than the treasures in Egypt Heb 11:26
Your *r* are corrupted, and your Jas 5:2
was slain to receive power, and *r* Rev 5:12
hour so great *r* is come to nought Rev 18:17

**RICHLY**
dwell in you *r* in all wisdom Col 3:16
who giveth us *r* all things to 1Ti 6:17

**RID**
that he might *r* him out of their Gen 37:22
I will *r* you out of their bondage Ex 6:6
I will *r* evil beasts out of the Lev 26:6
*r* them out of the hand of the Ps 82:4
*r* me, and deliver me out of great Ps 144:7
*R* me, and deliver me from the hand Ps 144:11

**RIDDANCE**
thou shalt not make clean *r* of Lev 23:22
*r* of all them that dwell in the Zeph 1:18

**RIDDEN**
upon which thou hast *r* ever since Num 22:30

**RIDDLE**
I will now put forth a *r* unto you Judg 14:12
said unto him, Put forth thy *r* Judg 14:13
not in three days expound the *r* Judg 14:14
that he may declare unto us the *r* Judg 14:15
thou hast put forth a *r* unto the Judg 14:16
she told the *r* to the children of Judg 14:17
heifer, ye had not found out my *r* Judg 14:18
unto them which expounded the *r* Judg 14:19
Son of man, put forth a *r* Eze 17:2

**RIDE**
he made him to *r* in the second Gen 41:43
He made him *r* on the high places Deut 32:13
ye that *r* on white asses, ye that Judg 5:10
for the king's household to *r* on 2Sa 16:2
me an ass, that I may *r* thereon 2Sa 19:26
my son to *r* upon mine own mule 1Kin 1:33
caused Solomon to *r* upon king 1Kin 1:38
him to *r* upon the king's mule 1Kin 1:44
So they made him *r* in his chariot 2Kin 10:16
thou causest me to *r* upon it Job 30:22
in thy majesty *r* prosperously Ps 45:4
caused men to *r* over our heads Ps 66:12
and, We will *r* upon the swift Is 30:16
I will cause thee to *r* upon the Is 58:14
they *r* upon horses, set in array Jer 6:23
they shall *r* upon horses, every Jer 50:42
I will make Ephraim to *r* Hos 10:11
we will not *r* upon horses Hos 14:3
that thou didst *r* upon thine Hab 3:8
chariots, and those that *r* in them Hag 2:22

**RIDER**
so that his *r* shall fall backward Gen 49:17
his *r* hath he thrown into the sea Ex 15:1
his *r* hath he thrown into the sea Ex 15:21
she scorneth the horse and his *r* Job 39:18
in pieces the horse and his *r* Jer 51:21
in pieces the chariot and his *r* Jer 51:21
and his *r* with madness Zec 12:4

**RIDERS**
on thy part to set *r* upon them 2Kin 18:23
*r* on mules, camels, and young Est 8:10
on thy part to set *r* upon them Is 36:8
their *r* shall come down, every Hag 2:22
them, and the *r* on horses shall be Zec 10:5

**RIDETH**
what saddle soever he *r* upon that Lev 15:9
who *r* upon the heaven in thy help Deut 33:26
and the horse that the king *r* upon Est 6:8
extol him that *r* upon the heavens Ps 68:4
To him that *r* upon the heavens of Ps 68:33
the LORD *r* upon a swift cloud, and Is 19:1
neither shall he that *r* the horse Amos 2:15

**RIDGES**
Thou waterest the *r* thereof Ps 65:10

**RIDING**
Now he was *r* upon his ass, and his Num 22:22
slack not thy *r* for me, except I 2Kin 4:24
*r* in chariots and on horses, they Jer 17:25
*r* in chariots and on horses, he Jer 22:4
young men, horsemen *r* upon horses Eze 23:6
horsemen *r* upon horses, all of Eze 23:12
all of them *r* upon horses Eze 23:23
thee, all of them *r* upon horses Eze 38:15
behold a man *r* upon a red horse Zec 1:8
*r* upon an ass, and upon a colt the Zec 9:9

**RIE**
wheat and the *r* were not smitten Ex 9:32
barley and the *r* in their place Is 28:25

**RIFLED**
shall be taken, and the houses *r* Zec 14:2

**RIGHT**
hand, then I will go to the *r* Gen 13:9
or if thou depart to the *r* hand Gen 13:9
the Judge of all the earth do *r* Gen 18:25
in the *r* way to take my master's Gen 24:48
that I may turn to the *r* hand Gen 24:49
Ephraim in his *r* hand toward Gen 48:13
left hand toward Israel's *r* hand Gen 48:13
Israel stretched out his *r* hand Gen 48:14
saw that his father laid his *r* Gen 48:17
put thy *r* hand upon his head Gen 48:18
a wall unto them on their *r* hand Ex 14:22
a wall unto them on their *r* hand Ex 14:29
Thy *r* hand, O LORD, is become Ex 15:6
thy *r* hand, O LORD, hath dashed Ex 15:6
Thou stretchedst out thy *r* hand Ex 15:12
do that which is *r* in his sight Ex 15:26
the tip of the *r* ear of Aaron Ex 29:20
the tip of the *r* ear of his sons Ex 29:20
and upon the thumb of their *r* hand Ex 29:20
the great toe of their *r* foot Ex 29:20
is upon them, and the *r* shoulder Ex 29:22
the *r* shoulder shall ye give unto Lev 7:32
shall have the *r* shoulder for his Lev 7:33
it upon the tip of Aaron's *r* ear Lev 8:23
and upon the thumb of his *r* hand Lev 8:23
upon the great toe of his *r* foot Lev 8:23
blood upon the tip of their *r* ear Lev 8:24
upon the thumbs of their *r* hands Lev 8:24
the great toes of their *r* feet Lev 8:24
and their fat, and the *r* shoulder Lev 8:25
the fat, and upon the *r* shoulder Lev 8:26
the *r* shoulder Aaron waved for a Lev 9:21
of the *r* ear of him that is to be Lev 14:14
and upon the thumb of his *r* hand Lev 14:14
upon the great toe of his *r* foot Lev 14:14
the priest shall dip his *r* finger Lev 14:16
of the *r* ear of him that is to be Lev 14:17
and upon the thumb of his *r* hand Lev 14:17
upon the great toe of his *r* foot Lev 14:17
of the *r* ear of him that is to be Lev 14:25
and upon the thumb of his *r* hand Lev 14:25
upon the great toe of his *r* foot Lev 14:25
*r* finger some of the oil that is Lev 14:27
of the *r* ear of him that is to be Lev 14:28
and upon the thumb of his *r* hand Lev 14:28
upon the great toe of his *r* foot Lev 14:28
as the *r* shoulder are thine Num 18:18
to the *r* hand nor to the left Num 20:17
to the *r* hand or to the left Num 22:26
daughters of Zelophehad speak *r* Num 27:7
unto the *r* hand nor to the left Deut 2:27
to the *r* hand or to the left Deut 5:32
And thou shalt do that which is *r* Deut 6:18
whatsoever is *r* in his own eyes Deut 12:8
is *r* in the sight of the LORD Deut 12:25
*r* in the sight of the LORD thy Deut 12:28
to do that which is *r* in the eyes Deut 13:18
shall shew thee, to the *r* hand Deut 17:11
the commandment, to the *r* hand Deut 17:20
is *r* in the sight of the LORD Deut 21:9
the *r* of the firstborn is his Deut 21:17
thee this day, to the *r* hand Deut 28:14
without iniquity, just and *r* is he Deut 32:4
from his *r* hand went a fiery law Deut 33:2
it to the *r* hand or to the left Josh 1:7
passed over *r* against Jericho Josh 3:16
*r* unto thee to do unto us, do Josh 9:25
*r* hand unto the inhabitants of Josh 17:7
to the *r* hand or to the left Josh 23:6
his raiment upon his *r* thigh Judg 3:16
took the dagger from his *r* thigh Judg 3:21
her *r* hand to the workmen's Judg 5:26
in their *r* hands to blow withal Judg 7:20
could not frame to pronounce it *r* Judg 12:6
up, of the one with his *r* hand Judg 16:29
that which was *r* in his own eyes Judg 17:6
that which was *r* in his own eyes Judg 21:25
redeem thou my *r* to thyself Ruth 4:6
to the *r* hand or to the left 1Sa 6:12
I may thrust out all your *r* eyes 1Sa 11:2
teach you the good and the *r* way 1Sa 12:23
the *r* hand nor to the left from 2Sa 2:19
to thy *r* hand or to thy left 2Sa 2:21
none can turn to the *r* hand or to 2Sa 14:19
See, thy matters are good and *r* 2Sa 15:3
the mighty men were on his *r* hand 2Sa 16:6
What *r* therefore have I yet to 2Sa 19:28
have also more *r* in David than ye 2Sa 19:43
beard with the *r* hand to kiss him 2Sa 20:9
on the *r* side of the city that 2Sa 24:5
and she sat on his *r* hand 1Kin 2:19
was in the *r* side of the house 1Kin 6:8
and he set up the *r* pillar 1Kin 7:21
bases on the *r* side of the house 1Kin 7:39
he set the sea on the *r* side of 1Kin 7:39
of pure gold, five on the *r* side 1Kin 7:49
do that which is *r* in mine eyes 1Kin 11:33
do that is *r* in my sight, to keep 1Kin 11:38
only which was *r* in mine eyes 1Kin 14:8
was *r* in the eyes of the LORD 1Kin 15:5
Asa did that which was *r* in the 1Kin 15:11
standing by him on his *r* hand 1Kin 22:19
doing that which was *r* in the 1Kin 22:43
and said to him, Is thine heart *r* 2Kin 10:15
that which is *r* in mine eyes 2Kin 10:30
from the *r* corner of the temple 2Kin 11:11
Jehoash did that which was *r* in 2Kin 12:2
on the *r* side as one cometh into 2Kin 12:9
he did that which was *r* in the 2Kin 14:3
he did that which was *r* in the 2Kin 15:3
he did that which was *r* in the 2Kin 15:34
did not that which was *r* in the 2Kin 16:2
not *r* against the LORD their God 2Kin 17:9
he did that which was *r* in the 2Kin 18:3
he did that which was *r* in the 2Kin 22:2
to the *r* hand or to the left 2Kin 22:2
which were on the *r* hand of the 2Kin 23:13
Asaph, who stood on his *r* hand 1Chr 6:39
and could use both the *r* hand 1Chr 12:2
for the thing was *r* in the eyes 1Chr 13:4
the temple, one on the *r* hand 2Chr 3:17
name of that on the *r* hand Jachin 2Chr 3:17
lavers, and put five on the *r* hand 2Chr 4:6
in the temple, five on the *r* hand 2Chr 4:7
in the temple, five on the *r* side 2Chr 4:8
sea on the *r* side of the east end 2Chr 4:10
*r* in the eyes of the LORD his God 2Chr 14:2
of heaven standing on his *r* hand 2Chr 18:18
doing that which was *r* in the 2Chr 20:32
from the *r* side of the temple to 2Chr 23:10
Joash did that which was *r* in the 2Chr 24:2
he did that which was *r* in the 2Chr 25:2
he did that which was *r* in the 2Chr 26:4
he did that which was *r* in the 2Chr 27:2
was *r* in the sight of the LORD 2Chr 28:1
he did that which was *r* in the 2Chr 29:2
wrought that which was good and *r*. 2Chr 31:20
he did that which was *r* in the 2Chr 34:2
and declined neither to the *r* hand 2Chr 34:2
to seek of him a *r* way for us Ezr 8:21
but ye have no portion, nor *r* Neh 2:20
and Maaseiah, on his *r* hand Neh 8:4
and gavest them *r* judgments Neh 9:13
for thou hast done *r*, but we have Neh 9:33
whereof one went on the *r* hand Neh 12:31
the thing seem *r* before the king Est 8:5
How forcible are *r* words Job 6:25
he hideth himself on the *r* hand Job 23:9
Upon my *r* hand rise the youth Job 30:12
and perverted that which was *r* Job 33:27
Should I lie against my *r* Job 34:6
even he that hateth *r* govern Job 34:17
will not lay upon man more than *r* Job 34:23
Thinkest thou this to be *r* Job 35:2
but giveth *r* to the poor Job 36:6
thine own *r* hand can save thee Job 40:14
spoken of me the thing that is *r* Job 42:7
spoken of me the thing which is *r* Job 42:8
For thou hast maintained my *r* Ps 9:4
satest in the throne judging *r* Ps 9:4
because he is at my *r* hand Ps 16:8
at thy *r* hand there are pleasures Ps 16:11
Hear the *r*, O LORD, attend unto Ps 17:1
O thou that savest by thy *r* hand Ps 17:7
thy *r* hand hath holden me up, and Ps 18:35
The statutes of the LORD are *r* Ps 19:8
the saving strength of his *r* hand Ps 20:6
thy *r* hand shall find out those Ps 21:8
their *r* hand is full of bribes Ps 26:10
For the word of the LORD is *r* Ps 33:4
but thy *r* hand, and thine arm, and Ps 44:3
thy *r* hand shall teach thee Ps 45:4
of thy kingdom is a *r* sceptre Ps 45:6
upon thy *r* hand did stand the Ps 45:9
shall help her, and that *r* early Ps 46:5
thy *r* hand is full of Ps 48:10
renew a *r* spirit within me Ps 51:10
save with thy *r* hand, and hear me Ps 60:5
thy *r* hand upholdeth me Ps 63:8
thou hast holden me by my *r* hand Ps 73:23
thou thy hand, even thy *r* hand Ps 74:11
of the *r* hand of the most High Ps 77:10
their heart was not *r* with him Ps 78:37
which his *r* hand had purchased Ps 78:54
which thy *r* hand hath planted Ps 80:15
be upon the man of thy *r* hand Ps 80:17
thy hand, and high is thy *r* hand Ps 89:13
sea, and his *r* hand in the rivers Ps 89:25
Thou hast set up the *r* hand of Ps 89:42
and ten thousand at thy *r* hand Ps 91:7
his *r* hand, and his holy arm, hath Ps 98:1
And he led them forth by the *r* way Ps 107:7
save with thy *r* hand, and answer Ps 108:6
and let Satan stand at his *r* hand Ps 109:6
stand at the *r* hand of the poor Ps 109:31
my Lord, Sit thou at my *r* hand Ps 110:1
The LORD at thy *r* hand shall Ps 110:5
the *r* hand of the LORD doeth Ps 118:15
The *r* hand of the LORD is exalted Ps 118:16

the *r* hand of the LORD doeth Ps 118:16
O LORD, that thy judgments are *r* Ps 119:75
concerning all things to be *r* Ps 119:128
LORD is thy shade upon thy *r* hand Ps 121:5
let my *r* hand forget her cunning Ps 137:5
and thy *r* hand shall save me Ps 138:7
me, and thy *r* hand shall hold me Ps 139:10
and that my soul knoweth *r* well Ps 139:14
afflicted, and the *r* of the poor Ps 140:12
I looked on my *r* hand, and beheld, Ps 142:4
their *r* hand is a *r* hand of Ps 144:8
their *r* hand is a *r* hand of Ps 144:11
Length of days is in her *r* hand Prov 3:16
I have led thee in *r* paths Prov 4:11
Let thine eyes look *r* on, and let Prov 4:25
Turn not to the *r* hand nor to the Prov 4:27
of my lips shall be *r* things Prov 8:6
*r* to them that find knowledge Prov 8:9
passengers who go *r* on their ways Prov 9:15
thoughts of the righteous are *r* Prov 12:5
of a fool is *r* in his own eyes Prov 12:15
a way which seemeth *r* unto a man Prov 14:12
than great revenues without *r* Prov 16:8
and they love him that speaketh *r* Prov 16:13
a way that seemeth *r* unto a man Prov 16:25
work be pure, and whether it be *r* Prov 20:11
way of a man is *r* in his own eyes Prov 21:2
as for the pure, his work is *r* Prov 21:8
when thy lips speak *r* things Prov 23:16
his lips that giveth a *r* answer Prov 24:26
and the ointment of his *r* hand Prov 27:16
all travail, and every *r* work Eccl 4:4
wise man's heart is at his *r* hand Eccl 10:2
his *r* hand doth embrace me Song 2:6
his *r* hand should embrace me Song 8:3
And he shall snatch on the *r* hand Is 9:20
to take away the *r* from the poor Is 10:2
Prophesy not unto us *r* things Is 30:10
in it, when ye turn to the *r* hand Is 30:21
even when the needy speaketh *r* Is 32:7
the *r* hand of my righteousness Is 41:10
LORD thy God will hold thy *r* hand Is 41:13
Is there not a lie in my *r* hand Is 44:20
whose *r* hand I have holden, to Is 45:1
I declare things that are *r* Is 45:19
my *r* hand hath spanned the Is 48:13
shalt break forth on the *r* hand Is 54:3
The LORD hath sworn by his *r* hand Is 62:8
That led them by the *r* hand of Is 63:12
a noble vine, wholly a *r* seed Jer 2:21
the *r* of the needy do they not Jer 5:28
that getteth riches, and not by *r* Jer 17:11
out of my lips was *r* before thee Jer 17:16
were the signet upon my *r* hand Jer 22:24
is evil, and their force is not *r* Jer 23:10
for the *r* of redemption is thine Jer 32:7
for the *r* of inheritance is thine Jer 32:8
had done *r* in my sight, in Jer 34:15
be driven out every man *r* forth Jer 49:5
he hath drawn back his *r* hand Lam 2:3
he stood with his *r* hand as an Lam 2:4
To turn aside the *r* of a man Lam 3:35
the face of a lion, on the *r* side Eze 1:10
them, lie again on thy *r* side Eze 4:6
stood on the *r* side of the house Eze 10:3
that dwelleth at thy *r* hand Eze 16:46
and do that which is lawful and *r* Eze 18:5
done that which is lawful and *r* Eze 18:19
and do that which is lawful and *r* Eze 18:21
doeth that which is lawful and *r* Eze 18:27
or other, either on the *r* hand Eze 21:16
At his *r* hand was the divination Eze 21:22
more, until he come whose *r* it is Eze 21:27
and do that which is lawful and *r* Eze 33:14
done that which is lawful and *r* Eze 33:16
and do that which is lawful and *r* Eze 33:19
arrows to fall out of thy *r* hand Eze 39:3
from the *r* side of the house Eze 47:1
ran out waters on the *r* side Eze 47:2
river, when he held up his *r* hand Dan 12:7
for the ways of the LORD are *r* Hos 14:9
For they know not to do *r* Amos 3:10
the poor in the gate from their *r* Amos 5:12
discern between their *r* hand Jonah 4:11
the cup of the LORD's *r* hand Hab 2:16
at his *r* hand to resist him Zec 3:1
one upon the *r* side of the bowl, Zec 4:3
the *r* side of the candlestick Zec 4:11
upon his arm, and upon his *r* eye Zec 11:17
his *r* eye shall be utterly Zec 11:17
people round about, on the *r* hand Zec 12:6
aside the stranger from his *r* Mal 3:5
if thy *r* eye offend thee, pluck Mt 5:29
if thy *r* hand offend thee, cut it Mt 5:30
shall smite thee on thy *r* cheek Mt 5:39
hand know what thy *r* hand doeth Mt 6:3
whatsoever is *r* I will give you Mt 20:4
and whatsoever is *r*, that shall ye Mt 20:7
may sit, the one on thy *r* hand Mt 20:21
but to sit on my *r* hand, and on my Mt 20:23
my Lord, Sit thou on my *r* hand Mt 22:44
shall set the sheep on his *r* hand Mt 25:33
King say unto them on his *r* hand Mt 25:34
sitting on the *r* hand of power Mt 26:64
his head, and a reed in his *r* hand Mt 27:29
with him, one on the *r* hand Mt 27:38
and clothed, and in his *r* mind Mk 5:15
we may sit, one on thy *r* hand Mk 10:37
But to sit on my *r* hand and on my Mk 10:40
to my Lord, Sit thou on my *r* hand Mk 12:36
sitting on the *r* hand of power Mk 14:62
the one on his *r* hand, and the Mk 15:27
a young man sitting on the *r* side Mk 16:5
and sat on the *r* hand of God Mk 16:19
of the Lord standing on the *r* Lk 1:11
a man whose *r* hand was withered Lk 6:6
Jesus, clothed, and in his *r* mind Lk 8:35
unto him, Thou hast answered *r* Lk 10:28
yourselves judge ye not what is *r* Lk 12:57
my Lord, Sit thou on my *r* hand Lk 20:42
high priest, and cut off his *r* ear Lk 22:50
on the *r* hand of the power of God Lk 22:69
malefactors, one on the *r* hand Lk 23:33
servant, and cut off his *r* ear Jn 18:10
the net on the *r* side of the ship Jn 21:6
my face, for he is on my *r* hand Acts 2:25
by the *r* hand of God exalted Acts 2:33
my Lord, Sit thou on my *r* hand Acts 2:34
And he took him by the *r* hand Acts 3:7
Whether it be *r* in the sight of Acts 4:19
with his *r* hand to be a Prince Acts 5:31
standing on the *r* hand of God Acts 7:55
man standing on the *r* hand of God Acts 7:56
is not *r* in the sight of God Acts 8:21
to pervert the *r* ways of the Lord Acts 13:10
who is even at the *r* hand of God Rom 8:34
of righteousness on the *r* hand 2Cor 6:7
to me and Barnabas the *r* hands of Gal 2:9
set him at his own *r* hand in the Eph 1:20
for this is *r* Eph 6:1
sitteth on the *r* hand of God Col 3:1
sat down on the *r* hand of the Heb 1:3
he at any times, Sit on my *r* hand Heb 1:13
who is set on the *r* hand of the Heb 8:1
sat down on the *r* hand of God Heb 10:12
is set down at the *r* hand of the Heb 12:2
whereof they have no *r* to eat Heb 13:10
and is on the *r* hand of God 1Pet 3:22
Which have forsaken the *r* way 2Pet 2:15
he had in his *r* hand seven stars Rev 1:16
he laid his *r* hand upon me, Rev 1:17
which thou sawest in my *r* hand Rev 1:20
the seven stars in his *r* hand Rev 2:1
I saw in the *r* hand of him that Rev 5:1
took the book out of the *r* hand Rev 5:7
he set his *r* foot upon the sea, Rev 10:2
to receive a mark in their *r* hand Rev 13:16
that they may have *r* to the tree Rev 22:14

## RIGHTEOUS

for thee have I seen *r* before me Gen 7:1
destroy the *r* with the wicked Gen 18:23
there be fifty *r* within the city Gen 18:24
for the fifty *r* that are therein Gen 18:24
to slay the *r* with the wicked Gen 18:25
that the *r* should be as the Gen 18:25
in Sodom fifty *r* within the city Gen 18:26
shall lack five of the fifty *r* Gen 18:28
wilt thou slay also a *r* nation Gen 20:4
said, She hath been more *r* than I Gen 38:26
the LORD is *r*, and I and my people Ex 9:27
the innocent and *r* slay thou not Ex 23:7
and perverteth the words of the *r* Ex 23:8
Let me die the death of the *r* Num 23:10
judgments so *r* as all this law, Deut 4:8
and pervert the words of the *r* Deut 16:19
then they shall justify the *r* Deut 25:1
rehearse the *r* acts of the LORD Judg 5:11
even the *r* acts toward the Judg 5:11
of all the *r* acts of the LORD 1Sa 12:7
to David, Thou art more *r* than I 1Sa 24:17
a *r* person in his own house upon 2Sa 4:11
who fell upon two men more *r* 1Kin 2:32
and justifying the *r*, to give him 1Kin 8:32
said to all the people, Ye be *r* 2Kin 10:9
and by justifying the *r*, by giving 2Chr 6:23
and they said, The LORD is *r* 2Chr 12:6
O LORD God of Israel, thou art *r* Ezr 9:15
for thou art *r* Neh 9:8
or where were the *r* cut off Job 4:7
Whom, though I were *r*, yet would Job 9:15
and if I be *r*, yet will I not lift Job 10:15
of a woman, that he should be *r* Job 15:14
The *r* also shall hold on his way, Job 17:9
to the Almighty, that thou art *r* Job 22:3
The *r* see it, and are glad Job 22:19
There the *r* might dispute with Job 23:7
because he was *r* in his own eyes Job 32:1
For Job hath said, I am *r* Job 34:5
If thou be *r*, what givest thou Job 35:7
not his eyes from the *r* Job 36:7
condemn me, that thou mayest be *r* Job 40:8
in the congregation of the *r* Ps 1:5
the LORD knoweth the way of the *r* Ps 1:6
For thou, LORD, wilt bless the *r* Ps 5:12
for the *r* God trieth the hearts Ps 7:9
God judgeth the *r*, and God is Ps 7:11
be destroyed, what can the *r* do Ps 11:3
The LORD trieth the *r* Ps 11:5
For the *r* LORD loveth Ps 11:7
God is in the generation of the *r* Ps 14:5
the LORD are true and *r* altogether Ps 19:9
and contemptuously against the *r* Ps 31:18
in the LORD, and rejoice, ye *r* Ps 32:11
Rejoice in the LORD, O ye *r* Ps 33:1
eyes of the LORD are upon the *r* Ps 34:15
The *r* cry, and the LORD heareth, Ps 34:17
Many are the afflictions of the *r* Ps 34:19
that hate the *r* shall be desolate Ps 34:21
be glad, that favour my *r* cause Ps 35:27
A little that a *r* man hath is Ps 37:16
but the LORD upholdeth the *r* Ps 37:17
but the *r* sheweth mercy, and Ps 37:21
have I not seen the *r* forsaken Ps 37:25
The *r* shall inherit the land, and Ps 37:29
mouth of the *r* speaketh wisdom Ps 37:30
The wicked watcheth the *r* Ps 37:32
salvation of the *r* is of the LORD Ps 37:39
The *r* also shall see, and fear, and Ps 52:6
never suffer the *r* to be moved Ps 55:22
The *r* shall rejoice when he seeth Ps 58:10
there is a reward for the *r* Ps 58:11
The *r* shall be glad in the LORD, Ps 64:10
But let the *r* be glad Ps 68:3
and not be written with the *r* Ps 69:28
In his days shall the *r* flourish Ps 72:7
horns of the *r* shall be exalted Ps 75:10
The *r* shall flourish like the Ps 92:12
against the soul of the *r* Ps 94:21
Light is sown for the *r*, and Ps 97:11
Rejoice in the LORD, ye *r* Ps 97:12
The *r* shall see it, and rejoice Ps 107:42
and full of compassion, and *r* Ps 112:4
the *r* shall be in everlasting Ps 112:6
Gracious is the LORD, and *r* Ps 116:5
is in the tabernacles of the *r* Ps 118:15
into which the *r* shall enter Ps 118:20
have learned thy *r* judgments Ps 119:7
thee because of thy *r* judgments Ps 119:62
that I will keep thy *r* judgments Ps 119:106
*R* art thou, O LORD, and upright Ps 119:137
that thou hast commanded are *r* Ps 119:138
every one of thy *r* judgments Ps 119:160
thee because of thy *r* judgments Ps 119:164
not rest upon the lot of the *r* Ps 125:3
lest the *r* put forth their hands Ps 125:3
The LORD is *r* Ps 129:4
Surely the *r* shall give thanks Ps 140:13
Let the *r* smite me Ps 141:5
the *r* shall compass me about Ps 142:7
The LORD is *r* in all his ways, and Ps 145:17
the LORD loveth the *r* Ps 146:8
layeth up sound wisdom for the *r* Prov 2:7
men, and keep the paths of the *r* Prov 2:20
but his secret is with the *r* Prov 3:32
the soul of the *r* to famish Prov 10:3
The mouth of a *r* man is a well of Prov 10:11
labour of the *r* tendeth to life Prov 10:16
The lips of the *r* feed many Prov 10:21
desire of the *r* shall be granted Prov 10:24
but the *r* is an everlasting Prov 10:25
The hope of the *r* shall be Prov 10:28
The *r* shall never be removed Prov 10:30
The lips of the *r* know what is Prov 10:32
The *r* is delivered out of trouble Prov 11:8
When it goeth well with the *r* Prov 11:10
seed of the *r* shall be delivered Prov 11:21
The desire of the *r* is only good Prov 11:23
but the *r* shall flourish as a Prov 11:28
The fruit of the *r* is a tree of Prov 11:30
the *r* shall be recompensed in the Prov 11:31
root of the *r* shall not be moved Prov 12:3
The thoughts of the *r* are right Prov 12:5
the house of the *r* shall stand Prov 12:7
A *r* man regardeth the life of his Prov 12:10
the root of the *r* yieldeth fruit Prov 12:12
The *r* is more excellent than his Prov 12:26
A *r* man hateth lying Prov 13:5
The light of the *r* rejoiceth Prov 13:9
but to the *r* good shall be repaid Prov 13:21
The *r* eateth to the satisfying of Prov 13:25
but among the *r* there is favour Prov 14:9
the wicked at the gates of the *r* Prov 14:19
but the *r* hath hope in his death Prov 14:32
house of the *r* is much treasure Prov 15:6
the way of the *r* is made plain Prov 15:19
The heart of the *r* studieth to Prov 15:28
he heareth the prayer of the *r* Prov 15:29
*R* lips are the delight of kings Prov 16:13
to overthrow the *r* in judgment Prov 18:5
the *r* runneth into it, and is safe Prov 18:10
The *r* man wisely considereth the Prov 21:12
shall be a ransom for the *r* Prov 21:18
but the *r* giveth and spareth not Prov 21:26
The father of the *r* shall greatly Prov 23:24
against the dwelling of the *r* Prov 24:15
saith unto the wicked, Thou art *r* Prov 24:24
A *r* man falling down before the Prov 25:26
but the *r* are bold as a lion Prov 28:1
Whoso causeth the *r* to go astray Prov 28:10
When *r* men do rejoice, there is Prov 28:12
when they perish, the *r* increase Prov 28:28
When the *r* are in authority, the Prov 29:2
but the *r* doth sing and rejoice Prov 29:6
The *r* considereth the cause of Prov 29:7
but the *r* shall see their fall Prov 29:16
mine heart, God shall judge the *r* Eccl 3:17
Be not *r* over much Eccl 7:16
according to the work of the *r* Eccl 8:14
to declare all this, that the *r* Eccl 9:1
there is one event to the *r* Eccl 9:2
Say ye to the *r*, that it shall be Is 3:10
righteousness of the *r* from him Is 5:23
heard songs, even glory to the *r* Is 24:16
that the *r* nation which keepeth Is 26:2
raised up the *r* man from the east Is 41:2
that we may say, He is *r* Is 41:26
shall my *r* servant justify many Is 53:11
The *r* perisheth, and no man layeth Is 57:1
none considering that the *r* is Is 57:1
Thy people also shall be all *r* Is 60:21

*R* art thou, O LORD, when I plead ... Jer 12:1
LORD of hosts, that triest the *r* ... Jer 20:12
will raise unto David a *r* Branch ... Jer 23:5
The LORD is *r* ... Lam 1:18
When a *r* man doth turn from his ... Eze 3:20
if thou warn the *r* man ... Eze 3:21
that the *r* sin not ... Eze 3:21
have made the heart of the *r* sad ... Eze 13:22
they are more *r* than thou ... Eze 16:52
of the *r* shall be upon him ... Eze 18:20
But when the *r* turneth away from ... Eze 18:24
When a *r* man turneth away from ... Eze 18:26
and will cut off from thee the *r* ... Eze 21:3
I will cut off from thee the *r* ... Eze 21:4
And the *r* men, they shall judge ... Eze 23:45
The righteousness of the *r* shall ... Eze 33:12
neither shall the *r* be able to ... Eze 33:12
When I shall say to the *r* ... Eze 33:13
When the *r* turneth from his ... Eze 33:18
for the LORD our God is *r* in all ... Dan 9:14
they sold the *r* for silver ... Amos 2:6
wicked doth compass about the *r* ... Hab 1:4
the man that is more *r* than he ... Hab 1:13
return, and discern between the *r* ... Mal 3:18
for I am not come to call the *r* ... Mt 9:13
he that receiveth a *r* man in the ... Mt 10:41
a *r* man shall receive a *r* ... Mt 10:41
*r* men have desired to see those ... Mt 13:17
Then shall the *r* shine forth as ... Mt 13:43
also outwardly appear *r* unto men ... Mt 23:28
garnish the sepulchres of the *r* ... Mt 23:29
the *r* blood shed upon the earth ... Mt 23:35
from the blood of *r* Abel unto the ... Mt 23:35
Then shall the *r* answer him ... Mt 25:37
but the *r* into life eternal ... Mt 25:46
I came not to call the *r*, but ... Mk 2:17
And they were both *r* before God ... Lk 1:6
I came not to call the *r*, but ... Lk 5:32
in themselves that they were *r* ... Lk 18:9
Certainly this was a *r* man ... Lk 23:47
appearance, but judge *r* judgment ... Jn 7:24
O *r* Father, the world hath not ... Jn 17:25
of the *r* judgment of God ... Rom 2:5
As it is written, There is none *r* ... Rom 3:10
scarcely for a *r* man will one die ... Rom 5:7
of one shall many be made *r* ... Rom 5:19
token of the *r* judgment of God ... 2Th 1:5
Seeing it is a *r* thing with God ... 2Th 1:6
the law is not made for a *r* man ... 1Ti 1:9
the *r* judge, shall give me at ... 2Ti 4:8
he obtained witness that he was *r* ... Heb 11:4
prayer of a *r* man availeth much ... Jas 5:16
eyes of the Lord are over the *r* ... 1Pet 3:12
if the *r* scarcely be saved, where ... 1Pet 4:18
(For that *r* man dwelling among ... 2Pet 2:8
vexed his *r* soul from day to day ... 2Pet 2:8
the Father, Jesus Christ the *r* ... 1Jn 2:1
If ye know that he is *r*, ye know ... 1Jn 2:29
he that doeth righteousness is *r* ... 1Jn 3:7
even as he is *r* ... 1Jn 3:7
were evil, and his brother's *r* ... 1Jn 3:12
of the waters say, Thou art *r* ... Rev 16:5
true and *r* are thy judgments ... Rev 16:7
For true and *r* are his judgments ... Rev 19:2
is *r*, let him be *r* still ... Rev 22:11

## RIGHTEOUSLY

judge *r* between every man and his ... Deut 1:16
for thou shalt judge the people *r* ... Ps 67:4
he shall judge the people *r* ... Ps 96:10
Open thy mouth, judge *r*, and plead ... Prov 31:9
He that walketh *r*, and speaketh ... Is 33:15
O LORD of hosts, that judgest *r* ... Jer 11:20
lusts, we should live soberly, *r* ... Titus 2:12
himself to him that judgeth *r* ... 1Pet 2:23

## RIGHTEOUSNESS

and he counted it to him for *r* ... Gen 15:6
So shall my *r* answer for me in ... Gen 30:33
but in *r* shalt thou judge thy ... Lev 19:15
And it shall be our *r*, if we ... Deut 6:25
For my *r* the LORD hath brought me ... Deut 9:4
Not for thy *r*, or for the ... Deut 9:5
good land to possess it for thy *r* ... Deut 9:6
it shall be *r* unto thee before ... Deut 24:13
they shall offer sacrifices of *r* ... Deut 33:19
LORD render to every man his *r* ... 1Sa 26:23
rewarded me according to my *r* ... 2Sa 22:21
recompensed me according to my *r* ... 2Sa 22:25
before thee in truth, and in *r* ... 1Kin 3:6
to give him according to his *r* ... 1Kin 8:32
by giving him according to his *r* ... 2Chr 6:23
yea, return again, my *r* is in it ... Job 6:29
habitation of thy *r* prosperous ... Job 8:6
My *r* I hold fast, and will not let ... Job 27:6
I put on *r*, and it clothed me ... Job 29:14
for he will render unto man his *r* ... Job 33:26
saidst, My *r* is more than God's ... Job 35:2
thy *r* may profit the son of man ... Job 35:8
and will ascribe *r* to my Maker ... Job 36:3
me when I call, O God of my *r* ... Ps 4:1
Offer the sacrifices of *r* ... Ps 4:5
in thy *r* because of mine enemies ... Ps 5:8
me, O LORD, according to my *r* ... Ps 7:8
the LORD according to his *r* ... Ps 7:17
And he shall judge the world in *r* ... Ps 9:8
For the righteous LORD loveth *r* ... Ps 11:7
walketh uprightly, and worketh *r* ... Ps 15:2
me, I will behold thy face in *r* ... Ps 17:15
rewarded me according to my *r* ... Ps 18:20
recompensed me according to my *r* ... Ps 18:24
shall declare his *r* unto a people ... Ps 22:31
paths of *r* for his name's sake ... Ps 23:3
*r* from the God of his salvation ... Ps 24:5
deliver me in thy *r* ... Ps 31:1
He loveth *r* and judgment ... Ps 33:5
O LORD my God, according to thy *r* ... Ps 35:24
And my tongue shall speak of thy *r* ... Ps 35:28
Thy *r* is like the great mountains ... Ps 36:6
thy *r* to the upright in heart ... Ps 36:10
bring forth thy *r* as the light ... Ps 37:6
I have preached *r* in the great ... Ps 40:9
not hid thy *r* within my heart ... Ps 40:10
because of truth and meekness and *r* ... Ps 45:4
Thou lovest *r*, and hatest ... Ps 45:7
thy right hand is full of *r* ... Ps 48:10
the heavens shall declare his *r* ... Ps 50:6
tongue shall sing aloud of thy *r* ... Ps 51:14
pleased with the sacrifices of *r* ... Ps 51:19
and lying rather than to speak *r* ... Ps 52:3
Do ye indeed speak *r*, O ... Ps 58:1
things in *r* wilt thou answer us ... Ps 65:5
and let them not come into thy *r* ... Ps 69:27
Deliver me in thy *r*, and cause me ... Ps 71:2
My mouth shall shew forth thy *r* ... Ps 71:15
I will make mention of thy *r* ... Ps 71:16
Thy *r* also, O God, is very high, ... Ps 71:19
talk of thy *r* all the day long ... Ps 71:24
thy *r* unto the king's son ... Ps 72:1
He shall judge thy people with *r* ... Ps 72:2
people, and the little hills, by *r* ... Ps 72:3
*r* and peace have kissed each other ... Ps 85:10
*r* shall look down from heaven ... Ps 85:11
*R* shall go before him ... Ps 85:13
and thy *r* in the land of ... Ps 88:12
in thy *r* shall they be exalted ... Ps 89:16
But judgment shall return unto *r* ... Ps 94:15
he shall judge the world with *r* ... Ps 96:13
*r* and judgment are the habitation ... Ps 97:2
The heavens declare his *r* ... Ps 97:6
his *r* hath he openly shewed in ... Ps 98:2
with *r* shall he judge the world, ... Ps 98:9
executest judgment and *r* in Jacob ... Ps 99:4
The LORD executeth *r* and judgment ... Ps 103:6
his *r* unto children's children ... Ps 103:17
and he that doeth *r* at all times ... Ps 106:3
for *r* unto all generations for ... Ps 106:31
and his *r* endureth for ever ... Ps 111:3
and his *r* endureth for ever ... Ps 112:3
his *r* endureth for ever ... Ps 112:9
Open to me the gates of *r* ... Ps 118:19
quicken me in thy *r* ... Ps 119:40
and for the word of thy *r* ... Ps 119:123
Thy *r* is an everlasting ... Ps 119:142
*r* is an everlasting *r* ... Ps 119:142
The *r* of thy testimonies is ... Ps 119:144
for all thy commandments are *r* ... Ps 119:172
Let thy priests be clothed with *r* ... Ps 132:9
answer me, and in thy *r* ... Ps 143:1
goodness, and shall sing of thy *r* ... Ps 145:7
Then shalt thou understand *r* ... Prov 2:9
the words of my mouth are in *r* ... Prov 8:8
yea, durable riches and *r* ... Prov 8:18
I lead in the way of *r*, in the ... Prov 8:20
but *r* delivereth from death ... Prov 10:2
but *r* delivereth from death ... Prov 11:4
The *r* of the perfect shall direct ... Prov 11:5
The *r* of the upright shall ... Prov 11:6
soweth *r* shall be a sure reward ... Prov 11:18
As *r* tendeth to life ... Prov 11:19
speaketh truth sheweth forth *r* ... Prov 12:17
In the way of *r* is life ... Prov 12:28
*R* keepeth him that is upright in ... Prov 13:6
*R* exalteth a nation ... Prov 14:34
loveth him that followeth after *r* ... Prov 15:9
Better is a little with *r* than ... Prov 16:8
the throne is established by *r* ... Prov 16:12
if it be found in the way of *r* ... Prov 16:31
He that followeth after *r* ... Prov 21:21
and mercy findeth life, *r*, and ... Prov 21:21
throne shall be established in *r* ... Prov 25:5
and the place of *r*, that iniquity ... Eccl 3:16
just man that perisheth in his *r* ... Eccl 7:15
*r* lodged in it ... Is 1:21
shalt be called, The city of *r* ... Is 1:26
judgment, and her converts with *r* ... Is 1:27
for *r*, but behold a cry ... Is 5:7
is holy shall be sanctified in *r* ... Is 5:16
take away the *r* of the righteous ... Is 5:23
decreed shall overflow with *r* ... Is 10:22
But with *r* shall he judge the ... Is 11:4
*r* shall be the girdle of his ... Is 11:5
and seeking judgment, and hasting *r* ... Is 16:5
of the world will learn *r* ... Is 26:9
wicked, yet will he not learn *r* ... Is 26:10
to the line, and *r* to the plummet ... Is 28:17
Behold, a king shall reign in *r* ... Is 32:1
*r* remain in the fruitful field ... Is 32:16
the work of *r* shall be peace ... Is 32:17
and the effect of *r* quietness ... Is 32:17
filled Zion with judgment and *r* ... Is 33:5
thee with the right hand of my *r* ... Is 41:10
I the LORD have called thee in *r* ... Is 42:6
and let the skies pour down *r* ... Is 45:8
and let *r* spring up together ... Is 45:8
I have raised him up in *r* ... Is 45:13
I the LORD speak *r*, I declare ... Is 45:19
word is gone out of my mouth in *r* ... Is 45:23
one say, in the LORD have I *r* ... Is 45:24
stouthearted, that are far from *r* ... Is 46:12
I bring near my *r* ... Is 46:13
but not in truth, nor in *r* ... Is 48:1
thy *r* as the waves of the sea ... Is 48:18
to me, ye that follow after *r* ... Is 51:1
My *r* is near ... Is 51:5
my *r* shall not be abolished ... Is 51:6
Hearken unto me, ye that know *r* ... Is 51:7
but my *r* shall be for ever, and my ... Is 51:8
In *r* shalt thou be established ... Is 54:14
their *r* is of me, saith the LORD ... Is 54:17
to come, and my *r* to be revealed ... Is 56:1
I will declare thy *r*, and thy ... Is 57:12
my ways, as a nation that did *r* ... Is 58:2
thy *r* shall go before thee ... Is 58:8
and his *r*, it sustained him ... Is 59:16
For he put on *r* as a breastplate, ... Is 59:17
peace, and thine exactors *r* ... Is 60:17
they might be called trees of *r* ... Is 61:3
covered me with the robe of *r* ... Is 61:10
so the Lord GOD will cause *r* ... Is 61:11
until the *r* thereof go forth as ... Is 62:1
And the Gentiles shall see thy *r* ... Is 62:2
I that speak in *r*, mighty to save ... Is 63:1
him that rejoiceth and worketh *r* ... Is 64:5
in truth, in judgment, and in *r* ... Jer 4:2
lovingkindness, judgment, and *r* ... Jer 9:24
Execute ye judgment and *r*, and ... Jer 22:3
shall be called, THE LORD OUR *R* ... Jer 23:6
Branch of *r* to grow up unto David ... Jer 33:15
execute judgment and *r* in the land ... Jer 33:15
shall be called, The LORD our *r* ... Jer 33:16
The LORD hath brought forth our *r* ... Jer 51:10
man doth turn from his *r*, and ... Eze 3:20
his *r* which he hath done shall ... Eze 3:20
but their own souls by their *r* ... Eze 14:14
their own souls by their *r* ... Eze 14:20
the *r* of the righteous shall be ... Eze 18:20
in his *r* that he hath done he ... Eze 18:22
righteous turneth away from his *r* ... Eze 18:24
All his *r* that he hath done shall ... Eze 18:24
man turneth away from his *r* ... Eze 18:26
The *r* of the righteous shall not ... Eze 33:12
be able to live for his *r* in the ... Eze 33:12
if he trust to his own *r*, and ... Eze 33:13
the righteous turneth from his *r* ... Eze 33:18
thee, and break off thy sins by *r* ... Dan 4:27
*r* belongeth unto thee, but unto ... Dan 9:7
O Lord, according to all thy *r* ... Dan 9:16
and to bring in everlasting *r* ... Dan 9:24
many to *r* as the stars for ever ... Dan 12:3
I will betroth thee unto me in *r* ... Hos 2:19
Sow to yourselves in *r*, reap in ... Hos 10:12
till he come and rain *r* upon you ... Hos 10:12
leave off *r* in the earth, ... Amos 5:7
waters, and *r* as a mighty stream ... Amos 5:24
and the fruit of *r* into hemlock ... Amos 6:12
ye may know the *r* of the LORD ... Mic 6:5
light, and I shall behold his *r* ... Mic 7:9
seek *r*, seek meekness ... Zeph 2:3
be their God, in truth and in *r* ... Zec 8:8
unto the LORD an offering in *r* ... Mal 3:3
fear my name shall the Sun of *r* ... Mal 4:2
it becometh us to fulfil all *r* ... Mt 3:15
which do hunger and thirst after *r* ... Mt 5:6
That except your *r* shall exceed ... Mt 5:20
shall exceed the *r* of the scribes ... Mt 5:20
the kingdom of God, and his *r* ... Mt 6:33
came unto you in the way of *r* ... Mt 21:32
*r* before him, all the days of our ... Lk 1:75
reprove the world of sin, and of *r* ... Jn 16:8
Of *r*, because I go to my Father, ... Jn 16:10
he that feareth him, and worketh *r* ... Acts 10:35
of the devil, thou enemy of all *r* ... Acts 13:10
in *r* by that man whom he hath ... Acts 17:31
And as he reasoned of *r*, ... Acts 24:25
For therein is the *r* of God ... Rom 1:17
keep the *r* of the law, shall not ... Rom 2:26
commend the *r* of God, what shall ... Rom 3:5
But now the *r* of God without the ... Rom 3:21
Even the *r* of God which is by ... Rom 3:22
blood, to declare his *r* for the ... Rom 3:25
I say, at this time his *r* ... Rom 3:26
and it was counted unto him for *r* ... Rom 4:3
his faith is counted for *r* ... Rom 4:5
whom God imputeth *r* without works ... Rom 4:6
was reckoned to Abraham for *r* ... Rom 4:9
a seal of the *r* of the faith ... Rom 4:11
that *r* might be imputed unto them ... Rom 4:11
law, but through the *r* of faith ... Rom 4:13
it was imputed to him for *r* ... Rom 4:22
of the gift of *r* shall reign in ... Rom 5:17
even so by the *r* of one the free ... Rom 5:18
*r* unto eternal life by Jesus ... Rom 5:21
as instruments of *r* unto God ... Rom 6:13
death, or of obedience unto *r* ... Rom 6:16
sin, ye became the servants of *r* ... Rom 6:18
servants to *r* unto holiness ... Rom 6:19
of sin, ye were free from *r* ... Rom 6:20
That the *r* of the law might be ... Rom 8:4
the Spirit is life because of *r* ... Rom 8:10
the work, and cut it short in *r* ... Rom 9:28
which followed not after *r* ... Rom 9:30
have attained to *r* ... Rom 9:30
even the *r* which is of faith ... Rom 9:30
which followed after the law of *r* ... Rom 9:31
hath not attained to the law of *r* ... Rom 9:31
they being ignorant of God's *r* ... Rom 10:3
about to establish their own *r* ... Rom 10:3
themselves unto the *r* of God ... Rom 10:3
is the end of the law for *r* to ... Rom 10:4
the *r* which is of the law ... Rom 10:5

But the *r* which is of faith Rom 10:6
the heart man believeth unto *r* Rom 10:10
but *r*, and peace, and joy in the Rom 14:17
God is made unto us wisdom, and *r* 1Cor 1:30
Awake to *r*, and sin not 1Cor 15:34
ministration of *r* exceed in glory 2Cor 3:9
might be made the *r* of God in him 2Cor 5:21
by the armour of *r* on the right 2Cor 6:7
hath *r* with unrighteousness 2Cor 6:14
his *r* remaineth for ever 2Cor 9:9
and increase the fruits of your *r* 2Cor 9:10
transformed as the ministers of *r* 2Cor 11:15
for if *r* come by the law, then Gal 2:21
and it was accounted to him for *r* Gal 3:6
verily *r* should have been by the Gal 3:21
wait for the hope of *r* by faith Gal 5:5
which after God is created in *r* Eph 4:24
Spirit is in all goodness and *r* Eph 5:9
and having on the breastplate of *r* Eph 6:14
Being filled with the fruits of *r* Phil 1:11
touching the *r* which is in the Phil 3:6
in him, not having mine own *r* Phil 3:9
the *r* which is of God by faith Phil 3:9
and follow after *r*, godliness, 1Ti 6:11
but follow *r*, faith, charity, 2Ti 2:22
correction, for instruction in *r* 2Ti 3:16
is laid up for me a crown of *r* 2Ti 4:8
Not by works of *r* which we have Titus 3:5
a sceptre of *r* is the sceptre of Heb 1:8
Thou hast loved *r*, and hated Heb 1:9
is unskilful in the word of *r* Heb 5:13
being by interpretation King of *r* Heb 7:2
heir of the *r* which is by faith Heb 11:7
faith subdued kingdoms, wrought *r* Heb 11:33
*r* unto them which are exercised Heb 12:11
of man worketh not the *r* of God Jas 1:20
and it was imputed unto him for *r* Jas 2:23
the fruit of *r* is sown in peace Jas 3:18
dead to sins, should live unto *r* 1Pet 2:24
with us through the *r* of God 2Pet 1:1
eighth person, a preacher of *r* 2Pet 2:5
not to have known the way of *r* 2Pet 2:21
a new earth, wherein dwelleth *r* 2Pet 3:13
one that doeth *r* is born of him 1Jn 2:29
he that doeth *r* is righteous 1Jn 3:7
doeth not *r* is not of God 1Jn 3:10
the fine linen is the *r* of saints Rev 19:8
in *r* he doth judge and make war Rev 19:11

**RIGHTEOUSNESS'**
for thy *r* sake bring my soul out Ps 143:11
is well pleased for his *r* sake Is 42:21
which are persecuted for *r* sake Mt 5:10
But and if ye suffer for *r* sake 1Pet 3:14

**RIGHTEOUSNESSES**
all our *r* are as filthy rags Is 64:6
all his *r* shall not be remembered Eze 33:13
before thee for our *r*, but for Dan 9:18

**RIGHTLY**
he said, Is not he *r* named Jacob Gen 27:36
said unto him, Thou hast *r* judged Lk 7:43
that thou sayest and teachest *r* Lk 20:21
*r* dividing the word of truth 2Ti 2:15

**RIGOUR**
of Israel to serve with *r* Ex 1:13
they made them serve, was with *r* Ex 1:14
shalt not rule over him with *r* Lev 25:43
not rule one over another with *r* Lev 25:46
rule with *r* over him in thy sight Lev 25:53

**RIMMON** (*rim'-mon*)
*1. A city in Zebulun.*
Shilhim, and Ain, and *R* Josh 15:32
*R* with her suburbs, Tabor with 1Chr 6:77
from Geba to *R* south of Jerusalem Zec 14:10
*2. A rock near Gibeah.*
the wilderness unto the rock of *R* Judg 20:45
to the wilderness unto the rock *R* Judg 20:47
abode in the rock *R* four months Judg 20:47
Benjamin that were in the rock *R* Judg 21:13
*3. Father of Baanah and Rechab.*
the sons of *R* a Beerothite, of 2Sa 4:2
the sons of *R* the Beerothite, 2Sa 4:5
the sons of *R* the Beerothite, and 2Sa 4:9
*4. A Syrian god.*
the house of *R* to worship there 2Kin 5:18
and I bow myself in the house of *R* 2Kin 5:18
bow down myself in the house of *R* 2Kin 5:18
*5. A city in Simeon.*
villages were, Etam, and Ain, *R* 1Chr 4:32

**RIMMONO** See RIMMON.

**RIMMON-PAREZ** (*rim''-mon-pa'-rez*) *An Israelite encampment in the wilderness.*
from Rithmah, and pitched at *R* Num 33:19
And they departed from *R*, and Num 33:20

**RING**
took off his *r* from his hand Gen 41:42
above the head of it unto one *r* Ex 26:24
at the head thereof, to one *r* Ex 36:29
the king took his *r* from his hand Est 3:10
and sealed with the king's *r* Est 3:12
And the king took off his *r* Est 8:2
and seal it with the king's *r* Est 8:8
name, and sealed with the king's *r* Est 8:8
and sealed it with the king's *r* Est 8:10
put a *r* on his hand, and shoes on Lk 15:22
your assembly a man with a gold *r* Jas 2:2

**RINGLEADER**
a *r* of the sect of the Nazarenes Acts 24:5

**RINGS**
shalt cast four *r* of gold for it Ex 25:12
two *r* shall be in the one side of Ex 25:12
two *r* in the other side of it Ex 25:12
the *r* by the sides of the ark Ex 25:14
shall be in the *r* of the ark Ex 25:15
shalt make for it four *r* of gold Ex 25:26
put the *r* in the four corners Ex 25:26
against the border shall the *r* be Ex 25:27
make their *r* of gold for places Ex 26:29
*r* in the four corners thereof Ex 27:4
staves shall be put into the *r* Ex 27:7
the breastplate two *r* of gold Ex 28:23
shalt put the two *r* on the two Ex 28:23
chains of gold in the two *r* which Ex 28:24
And thou shalt make two *r* of gold Ex 28:26
two other *r* of gold thou shalt Ex 28:27
bind the breastplate by the *r* Ex 28:28
the *r* of the ephod with a lace of Ex 28:28
two golden *r* shalt thou make to Ex 30:4
bracelets, and earrings, and *r* Ex 35:22
made their *r* of gold to be places Ex 36:34
And he cast for it four *r* of gold Ex 37:3
even two *r* upon the one side of Ex 37:3
two *r* upon the other side of it Ex 37:3
the *r* by the sides of the ark Ex 37:5
And he cast for it four *r* of gold Ex 37:13
put the *r* upon the four corners Ex 37:13
against the border were the *r* Ex 37:14
he made two *r* of gold for it Ex 37:27
he cast four *r* for the four ends Ex 38:5
the *r* on the sides of the altar Ex 38:7
two ouches of gold, and two gold *r* Ex 39:16
put the two *r* in the two ends of Ex 39:16
chains of gold in the two *r* on Ex 39:17
And they made two *r* of gold Ex 39:19
And they made two other golden *r* Ex 39:20
his *r* unto the *r* of the ephod Ex 39:21
of gold, chains, and bracelets, *r* Num 31:50
fine linen and purple to silver *r* Est 1:6
are as gold *r* set with the beryl Song 5:14
The *r*, and nose jewels, Is 3:21
As for their *r*, they were so high Eze 1:18
their *r* were full of eyes round Eze 1:18

**RINGSTRAKED**
that day the he goats that were *r* Gen 30:35
rods, and brought forth cattle *r* Gen 30:39
faces of the flocks toward the *r* Gen 30:40
thus, The *r* shall be thy hire Gen 31:8
then bare all the cattle *r* Gen 31:8
leaped upon the cattle were *r* Gen 31:10
which leap upon the cattle are *r* Gen 31:12

**RINNAH** (*rin'-nah*) *A descendant of Caleb.*
sons of Shimon were, Amnon, and *R* 1Chr 4:20

**RINSED**
be both scoured, and *r* in water Lev 6:28
hath not *r* his hands in water, he Lev 15:11
of wood shall be *r* in water Lev 15:12

**RIOT**
not accused of *r* or unruly Titus 1:6
with them to the same excess of *r* 1Pet 4:4
it pleasure to *r* in the daytime 2Pet 2:13

**RIOTING**
not in *r* and drunkenness, not in Rom 13:13

**RIOTOUS**
among *r* eaters of flesh Prov 23:20
of *r* men shameth his father Prov 28:7
his substance with *r* living Lk 15:13

**RIP**
*r* up their women with child 2Kin 8:12

**RIPE**
thereof brought forth *r* grapes Gen 40:10
offer the first of thy *r* fruits Ex 22:29
whatsoever is first *r* in the land Num 18:13
like the figs that are first *r* Jer 24:2
the sickle, for the harvest is *r* Joel 3:13
for the harvest of the earth is *r* Rev 14:15
for her grapes are fully *r* Rev 14:18

**RIPENING**
the sour grape is *r* in the flower Is 18:5

**RIPHATH** (*ri'-fath*) *A son of Gomer.*
Ashkenaz, and *R*, and Togarmah Gen 10:3
Ashchenaz, and *R*, and Togarmah 1Chr 1:6

**RIPPED**
that were with child he *r* up 2Kin 15:16
women with child shall be *r* up Hos 13:16
because they have *r* up the women Amos 1:13

**RISE**
your feet, and ye shall *r* up early Gen 19:2
that I cannot *r* up before thee Gen 31:35
*R* up early in the morning, and Ex 8:20
*R* up early in the morning, and Ex 9:13
*R* up, and get you forth from among Ex 12:31
If he *r* again, and walk abroad Ex 21:19
Thou shalt *r* up before the hoary Lev 19:32
*R* up, LORD, and let thine enemies Num 10:35
call thee, *r* up, and go with them Num 22:20
and said, *R* up, Balak, and hear Num 23:18
the people shall *r* up as a great Num 23:24
a Sceptre shall *r* out of Israel Num 24:17
Now *r* up, said I, and get you over Deut 2:13
*R* ye up, take your journey, and Deut 2:24
*r* up against him, and smite him Deut 19:11
One witness shall not *r* up Deut 19:15
If a false witness *r* up against Deut 19:16
*r* up against thee to be smitten Deut 28:7
that shall *r* up after you Deut 29:22
and this people will *r* up, and go a Deut 31:16
Let them *r* up and help you, and be Deut 32:38
loins of them that *r* against him Deut 33:11
hate him, that they *r* not again Deut 33:11
Then ye shall *r* up from the Josh 8:7
I will send them, and they shall *r* Josh 18:4
said, *R* thou, and fall upon us Judg 8:21
the sun is up, thou shalt *r* early Judg 9:33
with smoke *r* up out of the city Judg 20:38
him, that he should *r* against me 1Sa 22:13
them not to *r* against Saul 1Sa 24:7
Wherefore now *r* up early in the 1Sa 29:10
the child was dead, thou didst *r* 2Sa 12:21
all that *r* against thee to do 2Sa 18:32
of Israel, which *r* up against me 2Kin 16:7
And they said, Let us *r* up Neh 2:18
the earth shall *r* up against him Job 20:27
Upon my right hand *r* the youth Job 30:12
are they that *r* up against me Ps 3:1
from those that *r* up against them Ps 17:7
them that they were not able to *r* Ps 18:38
above those that *r* up against me Ps 18:48
though war should *r* against me Ps 27:3
False witnesses did *r* up Ps 35:11
down, and shall not be able to *r* Ps 36:12
he lieth he shall *r* up no more Ps 41:8
them under that *r* up against us Ps 44:5
me from them that *r* up against me Ps 59:1
the tumult of those that *r* up Ps 74:23
the wicked that *r* up against me Ps 92:11
Who will *r* up for me against the Ps 94:16
At midnight I will *r* to give Ps 119:62
It is vain for you to *r* up early Ps 127:2
with those that *r* up against thee Ps 139:21
pits, that they *r* not up again Ps 140:10
their calamity shall *r* suddenly Prov 24:22
but when the wicked *r*, a man is Prov 28:12
When the wicked *r*, men hide Prov 28:28
of the ruler *r* up against thee Eccl 10:4
he shall *r* up at the voice of the Eccl 12:4
*R* up, my love, my fair one, and Song 2:10
I will *r* now, and go about the Song 3:2
Woe unto them that *r* up early in Is 5:11
that they do not *r*, nor possess Is 14:21
For I will *r* up against them, Is 14:22
and it shall fall, and not *r* again Is 24:20
are deceased, they shall not *r* Is 26:14
For the LORD shall *r* up as in Is 28:21
*R* up, ye women that are at ease Is 32:9
Now will I *r*, saith the LORD Is 33:10
down together, they shall not *r* Is 43:17
every tongue that shall *r* against Is 54:17
shall thy light *r* in obscurity Is 58:10
*r* no more, because of the sword Jer 25:27
yet should they *r* up every man in Jer 37:10
waters *r* up out of the north, and Jer 47:2
her, and *r* up to the battle Jer 49:14
of them that *r* up against me Jer 51:1
shall not *r* from the evil that I Jer 51:64
from whom I am not able to *r* up Lam 1:14
and another shall *r* after them Dan 7:24
she shall no more *r* Amos 5:2
I will *r* against the house of Amos 7:9
it shall *r* up wholly as a flood Amos 8:8
shall fall, and never *r* up again Amos 8:14
it shall *r* up wholly like a flood Amos 9:5
let us *r* up against her in battle Obad 1
shall not *r* up the second time Nah 1:9
Shall they not *r* up suddenly that Hab 2:7
the day that I *r* up to the prey Zeph 3:8
his hand shall *r* up against the Zec 14:13
maketh his sun to *r* on the evil Mt 5:45
the children shall *r* up against Mt 10:21
shall *r* in the judgment with this Mt 12:41
*r* up in the judgment with this Mt 12:42
and the third day he shall *r* again Mt 20:19
For nation shall *r* against nation Mt 24:7
And many false prophets shall *r* Mt 24:11
*R*, let us be going Mt 26:46
After three days I will *r* again Mt 27:63
if Satan *r* up against himself, and Mk 3:26
*r* night and day, and the seed Mk 4:27
and after three days *r* again Mk 8:31
killed, he shall *r* the third day Mk 9:31
and the third day he shall *r* again Mk 10:34
unto him, Be of good comfort, *r* Mk 10:49
therefore, when they shall *r* Mk 12:23
when they shall *r* from the dead Mk 12:25
as touching the dead, that they *r* Mk 12:26
For nation shall *r* against nation Mk 13:8
children shall *r* up against their Mk 13:12
Christs and false prophets shall *r* Mk 13:22
*R* up, let us go Mk 14:42
or to say, *R* up and walk Lk 5:23
*R* up, and stand forth in the midst Lk 6:8
I cannot *r* and give thee Lk 11:7
unto you, Though he will not *r* Lk 11:8
of his importunity he will *r* Lk 11:8
The queen of the south shall *r* up Lk 11:31
The men of Nineve shall *r* up in Lk 11:32
ye see a cloud *r* out of the west Lk 12:54
and the third day he shall *r* again Lk 18:33
Nation shall *r* against nation, and Lk 21:10
*r* and pray, lest ye enter into Lk 22:46

and the third day r again ... Lk 24:7
to r from the dead the third day ... Lk 24:46
Jesus saith unto him, R, take up ... Jn 5:8
her, Thy brother shall r again ... Jn 11:23
I know that he shall r again in ... Jn 11:24
that he must r again from the ... Jn 20:9
of Jesus Christ of Nazareth r up ... Acts 3:6
And there came a voice to him, R ... Acts 10:13
But r, and stand upon thy feet ... Acts 26:16
first that should r from the dead ... Acts 26:23
he that shall r to reign over the ... Rom 15:12
up, if so be that the dead r not ... 1Cor 15:15
For if the dead r not, then is ... 1Cor 15:16
dead, if the dead r not at all ... 1Cor 15:29
it me, if the dead r not ... 1Cor 15:32
the dead in Christ shall r first ... 1Th 4:16
that another priest should r ... Heb 7:11
and the angel stood, saying, R ... Rev 11:1
saw a beast r up out of the sea, ... Rev 13:1

**RISEN**
The sun was r upon the earth when ... Gen 19:23
If the sun be r upon him, there ... Ex 22:3
ye are r up in your fathers' ... Num 32:14
ye are r up against my father's ... Judg 9:18
And when she was r up to glean ... Ruth 2:15
Yet a man is r to pursue thee, and ... 1Sa 25:29
the whole family is r against ... 2Sa 14:7
I am r up in the room of David my ... 1Kin 8:20
of the man of God was r early ... 2Kin 6:15
for I am r up in the room of ... 2Chr 6:10
Solomon the son of David, is r up ... 2Chr 13:6
Now when Jehoram was r up to the ... 2Chr 21:4
but we are r, and stand upright ... Ps 20:8
witnesses are r up against me ... Ps 27:12
For strangers are r up against me ... Ps 54:3
O God, the proud are r against me ... Ps 86:14
glory of the LORD is r upon thee ... Is 60:1
Violence is r up into a rod of ... Eze 7:11
for the waters were r, waters to ... Eze 47:5
my people is r up as an enemy ... Mic 2:8
born of women there hath not r a ... Mt 11:11
he is r from the dead ... Mt 14:2
of man be r again from the dead ... Mt 17:9
But after I am r again, I will go ... Mt 26:32
the people, He is r from the dead ... Mt 27:64
for he is r, as he said ... Mt 28:6
that he is r from the dead ... Mt 28:7
the Baptist was r from the dead ... Mk 6:14
he is r from the dead ... Mk 6:16
Son of man were r from the dead ... Mk 9:9
But after that I am r, I will go ... Mk 14:28
he is r ... Mk 16:6
Now when Jesus was r early the ... Mk 16:9
which had seen him after he was r ... Mk 16:14
a great prophet is r up among us ... Lk 7:16
that John was r from the dead ... Lk 9:7
of the old prophets was r again ... Lk 9:8
of the old prophets is r again ... Lk 9:19
the master of the house is r up ... Lk 13:25
He is not here, but is r ... Lk 24:6
Saying, The Lord is r indeed ... Lk 24:34
therefore he was r from the dead ... Jn 2:22
after that he was r from the dead ... Jn 21:14
and r again from the dead ... Acts 17:3
died, yea rather, that is r again ... Rom 8:34
of the dead, then is Christ not r ... 1Cor 15:13
And if Christ be not r, then is ... 1Cor 15:14
But now is Christ r from the dead ... 1Cor 15:20
wherein also ye are r with him ... Col 2:12
If ye then be r with Christ ... Col 3:1
no sooner r with a burning heat ... Jas 1:11

**RISEST**
liest down, and when thou r up ... Deut 6:7
liest down, and when thou r up ... Deut 11:19

**RISETH**
for as when a man r against his ... Deut 22:26
man before the LORD, that r up ... Josh 6:26
of the morning, when the sun r ... 2Sa 23:4
commandeth the sun, and it r not ... Job 9:7
So man lieth down, and r not ... Job 14:12
he r up, and no man is sure of ... Job 24:22
he that r up against me as the ... Job 27:7
then shall I do when God r up ... Job 31:14
seven times, and r up again ... Prov 24:16
She r also while it is yet night, ... Prov 31:15
shalt not know from whence it r ... Is 47:11
Egypt r up like a flood, and his ... Jer 46:8
the daughter r up against her ... Mic 7:6
He r from supper, and laid aside ... Jn 13:4

**RISING**
have in the skin of his flesh a r ... Lev 13:2
if the r be white in the skin, and ... Lev 13:10
there be quick raw flesh in the r ... Lev 13:10
of the boil there be a white r ... Lev 13:19
it is a r of the burning, and the ... Lev 13:28
if the r of the sore be white ... Lev 13:43
And for a r, and for a scab, and for ... Lev 14:56
on the east side toward the r of ... Num 2:3
Jordan toward the r of the sun ... Josh 12:1
r up betimes, and sending ... 2Chr 36:15
r of the morning till the stars ... Neh 4:21
my leanness r up in me beareth ... Job 16:8
r betimes for a prey ... Job 24:5
The murderer r with the light ... Job 24:14
called the earth from the r of ... Ps 50:1
From the r of the sun unto the ... Ps 113:3
r early in the morning, it shall ... Prov 27:14
against whom there is no r up ... Prov 30:31
from the r of the sun shall he ... Is 41:25
may know from the r of the sun ... Is 45:6
his glory from the r of the sun ... Is 59:19
kings to the brightness of thy r ... Is 60:3
r up early and speaking, but ye ... Jer 7:13
daily r up early and sending them ... Jer 7:25
r early and protesting, saying, ... Jer 11:7
unto you, r early and speaking ... Jer 25:3
prophets, r early and sending them ... Jer 25:4
both r up early, and sending them, ... Jer 26:5
r up early and sending them ... Jer 29:19
r up early and teaching them, yet ... Jer 32:33
unto you, r early and speaking ... Jer 35:14
r up early and sending them, ... Jer 35:15
r early and sending them, saying, ... Jer 44:4
their sitting down, and their r up ... Lam 3:63
For from the r of the sun even ... Mal 1:11
r up a great while before day, he ... Mk 1:35
the r from the dead should mean ... Mk 9:10
the sepulchre at the r of the sun ... Mk 16:2
r again of many in Israel ... Lk 2:34

**RISSAH** (*ris'-sah*) *An Israelite encampment in the wilderness.*
from Libnah, and pitched at R ... Num 33:21
And they journeyed from R, and ... Num 33:22

**RITES**
according to all the r of it ... Num 9:3

**RITHMAH** (*rith'-mah*) *An Israelite encampment in the wilderness.*
from Hazeroth, and pitched in R ... Num 33:18
And they departed from R, and ... Num 33:19

**RIVER**
a r went out of Eden to water the ... Gen 2:10
the name of the second r is Gihon ... Gen 2:13
name of the third r is Hiddekel ... Gen 2:14
the fourth r is Euphrates ... Gen 2:14
from the r of Egypt unto the ... Gen 15:18
the great r, the r Euphrates ... Gen 15:18
he rose up, and passed over the r ... Gen 31:21
by the r reigned in his stead ... Gen 36:37
and, behold, he stood by the r ... Gen 41:1
of the r seven well favoured kine ... Gen 41:2
came up after them out of the r ... Gen 41:3
kine upon the brink of the r ... Gen 41:3
I stood upon the bank of the r ... Gen 41:17
came up out of the r seven kine ... Gen 41:18
is born ye shall cast into the r ... Ex 1:22
down to wash herself at the r ... Ex 2:5
shalt take of the water of the r ... Ex 4:9
which thou takest out of the r ... Ex 4:9
the waters which are in the r ... Ex 7:17
fish that is in the r shall die ... Ex 7:18
and the r shall stink ... Ex 7:18
to drink of the water of the r ... Ex 7:18
the waters that were in the r ... Ex 7:20
in the r were turned to blood ... Ex 7:20
the fish that was in the r died ... Ex 7:21
the r stank, and the Egyptians ... Ex 7:21
not drink of the water of the r ... Ex 7:21
about the r for water to drink ... Ex 7:24
not drink of the water of the r ... Ex 7:24
that the LORD had smitten the r ... Ex 7:25
the r shall bring forth frogs ... Ex 8:3
they may remain in the r only ... Ex 8:9
they shall remain in the r only ... Ex 8:11
rod, wherewith thou smotest the r ... Ex 17:5
and from the desert unto the r ... Ex 23:31
which is by the r of the land of ... Num 22:5
from Azmon unto the r of Egypt ... Num 34:5
and unto Lebanon, unto the great r ... Deut 1:7
the great r, the r Euphrates ... Deut 1:7
journey, and pass over the r Arnon ... Deut 2:24
is by the brink of the r of Arnon ... Deut 2:36
and from the city that is by the r ... Deut 2:36
unto any place of the r Jabbok ... Deut 2:37
from the r of Arnon unto mount ... Deut 3:8
Aroer, which is by the r Arnon ... Deut 3:12
unto the r Arnon half the valley ... Deut 3:16
the border even unto the r Jabbok ... Deut 3:16
is by the bank of the r Arnon ... Deut 4:48
wilderness and Lebanon, from the r ... Deut 11:24
the r Euphrates, even unto the ... Deut 11:24
Lebanon even unto the great r ... Josh 1:4
the r Euphrates, all the land of ... Josh 1:4
from the r Arnon unto mount ... Josh 12:1
is upon the bank of the r Arnon ... Josh 12:2
and from the middle of the r ... Josh 12:2
Gilead, even unto the r Jabbok ... Josh 12:2
is upon the bank of the r Arnon ... Josh 13:9
that is in the midst of the r ... Josh 13:9
is on the bank of the r Arnon ... Josh 13:16
that is in the midst of the r ... Josh 13:16
and went out unto the r of Egypt ... Josh 15:4
is on the south side of the r ... Josh 15:7
her villages, unto the r of Egypt ... Josh 15:47
Tappuah westward unto the r Kanah ... Josh 16:8
r Kanah, southward of the r ... Josh 17:9
was on the north side of the r ... Josh 17:9
reached to the r that is before ... Josh 19:11
draw unto thee to the r Kishon ... Judg 4:7
the Gentiles unto the r of Kishon ... Judg 4:13
The r of Kishon swept them away, ... Judg 5:21
that ancient r, the r Kishon ... Judg 5:21
his border at the r Euphrates ... 2Sa 8:3
Syrians that were beyond the r ... 2Sa 10:16
and we will draw it into the r ... 2Sa 17:13
in the midst of the r of Gad ... 2Sa 24:5
from the r unto the land of the ... 1Kin 4:21
all the region on this side the r ... 1Kin 4:24
all the kings on this side the r ... 1Kin 4:24
in of Hamath unto the r of Egypt ... 1Kin 8:65
shall scatter them beyond the r ... 1Kin 14:15
Aroer, which is by the r Arnon ... 2Kin 10:33
and in Habor by the r of Gozan ... 2Kin 17:6
and in Habor by the r of Gozan ... 2Kin 18:11
of Assyria to the r Euphrates ... 2Kin 23:29
the r of Egypt unto the r ... 2Kin 24:7
by the r reigned in his stead ... 1Chr 1:48
wilderness from the r Euphrates ... 1Chr 5:9
Habor, and Hara, and to the r Gozan ... 1Chr 5:26
his dominion by the r Euphrates ... 1Chr 18:3
Syrians that were beyond the r ... 1Chr 19:16
in of Hamath unto the r of Egypt ... 2Chr 7:8
the r even unto the land of the ... 2Chr 9:26
rest that are on this side the r ... Ezr 4:10
the men on this side the r ... Ezr 4:11
no portion on this side the r ... Ezr 4:16
and unto the rest beyond the r ... Ezr 4:17
over all countries beyond the r ... Ezr 4:20
governor on this side the r ... Ezr 5:3
governor on this side the r ... Ezr 5:6
which were on this side the r ... Ezr 5:6
Tatnai, governor beyond the r ... Ezr 6:6
which are beyond the r, be ye ... Ezr 6:6
even of the tribute beyond the r ... Ezr 6:8
governor on this side the r ... Ezr 6:13
treasurers which are beyond the r ... Ezr 7:21
the people that are beyond the r ... Ezr 7:25
to the r than runneth to Ahava ... Ezr 8:15
at the r of Ahava, that we might ... Ezr 8:21
Then we departed from the r of ... Ezr 8:31
the governors on this side the r ... Ezr 8:36
me to the governors beyond the r ... Neh 2:7
to the governors beyond the r ... Neh 2:9
the governor on this side the r ... Neh 3:7
Behold, he drinketh up a r ... Job 40:23
drink of the r of thy pleasures ... Ps 36:8
There is a r, the streams whereof ... Ps 46:4
enrichest it with the r of God ... Ps 65:9
from the r unto the ends of the ... Ps 72:8
sea, and her branches unto the r ... Ps 80:11
ran in the dry places like a r ... Ps 105:41
namely, by them beyond the r ... Is 7:20
up upon them the waters of the r ... Is 8:7
he shake his hand over the r ... Is 11:15
the r shall be wasted and dried up ... Is 19:5
of Sihor, the harvest of the r ... Is 23:3
Pass through thy land as a r ... Is 23:10
of the r unto the stream of Egypt ... Is 27:12
then had thy peace been as a r ... Is 48:18
will extend peace to her like a r ... Is 66:12
to drink the waters of the r ... Jer 2:18
spreadeth out her roots by the r ... Jer 17:8
which was by the r Euphrates in ... Jer 46:2
the north by the r Euphrates ... Jer 46:6
north country by the r Euphrates ... Jer 46:10
let tears run down like a r day ... Lam 2:18
the captives by the r of Chebar ... Eze 1:1
of the Chaldeans by the r Chebar ... Eze 1:3
that dwelt by the r of Chebar ... Eze 3:15
which I saw by the r of Chebar ... Eze 3:23
that I saw by the r of Chebar ... Eze 10:15
God of Israel by the r of Chebar ... Eze 10:20
which I saw by the r of Chebar ... Eze 10:22
My r is mine own, and I have made ... Eze 29:3
The r is mine, and I have made it ... Eze 29:9
vision that I saw by the r Chebar ... Eze 43:3
it was a r that I could not pass ... Eze 47:5
a r that could not be passed over ... Eze 47:5
to return to the brink of the r ... Eze 47:6
at the bank of the r were very ... Eze 47:7
shall live whither the r cometh ... Eze 47:9
by the r upon the bank thereof, ... Eze 47:12
in Kadesh, the r to the great sea ... Eze 47:19
to the r toward the great sea ... Eze 48:28
vision, and I was by the r of Ulai ... Dan 8:2
there stood before the r a ram ... Dan 8:3
I had seen standing before the r ... Dan 8:6
I was by the side of the great r ... Dan 10:4
on this side of the bank of the r ... Dan 12:5
on that side of the bank of the r ... Dan 12:5
was upon the waters of the r ... Dan 12:6
was upon the waters of the r ... Dan 12:7
unto the r of the wilderness ... Amos 6:14
from the fortress even to the r ... Mic 7:12
from the r even to the ends of ... Zec 9:10
the deeps of the r shall dry up ... Zec 10:11
of him in the r of Jordan ... Mk 1:5
went out of the city by a r side ... Acts 16:13
bound in the great r Euphrates ... Rev 9:14
vial upon the great r Euphrates ... Rev 16:12
me a pure r of water of life ... Rev 22:1
of it, and on either side of the r ... Rev 22:2

**RIVER'S**
it in the flags by the r brink ... Ex 2:3
walked along by the r side ... Ex 2:5
by the r brink against he come ... Ex 7:15
forth, as gardens by the r side ... Num 24:6

**RIVERS**
upon their streams, upon their r ... Ex 7:19
rod over the streams, over the r ... Ex 8:5
waters, in the seas, and in the r ... Lev 11:9
scales in the seas, and in the r ... Lev 11:10
to Jotbath, a land of r of waters ... Deut 10:7
r of Damascus, better than all ... 2Kin 5:12
up all the r of besieged places ... 2Kin 19:24
He shall not see the r, the ... Job 20:17

He cutteth out *r* among the rocks... Job 28:10
the rock poured me out *r* of oil... Job 29:6
a tree planted by the *r* of water... Ps 1:3
thou driedst up mighty *r*... Ps 74:15
caused waters to run down like *r*... Ps 78:16
And had turned their *r* into blood... Ps 78:44
sea, and his right hand in the *r*... Ps 89:25
He turneth *r* into a wilderness,... Ps 107:33
*R* of waters run down mine eyes,... Ps 119:136
By the *r* of Babylon, there we sat... Ps 137:1
*r* of waters in the streets... Prov 5:16
of the LORD, as the *r* of water... Prov 21:1
All the *r* run into the sea... Eccl 1:7
the place from whence the *r* come... Eccl 1:7
eyes of doves by the *r* of waters... Song 5:12
uttermost part of the *r* of Egypt... Is 7:18
which is beyond the *r* of Ethiopia... Is 18:1
whose land the *r* have spoiled... Is 18:2
whose land the *r* have spoiled... Is 18:7
And they shall turn the *r* far away... Is 19:6
and upon every high hill, *r*... Is 30:25
as *r* of water in a dry place, as... Is 32:2
be unto us a place of broad *r*... Is 33:21
all the *r* of the besieged places... Is 37:25
I will open *r* in high places, and... Is 41:18
and I will make the *r* islands... Is 42:15
and through the *r*, they shall not... Is 43:2
wilderness, and *r* in the desert... Is 43:19
*r* in the desert, to give drink to... Is 43:20
Be dry, and I will dry up thy *r*... Is 44:27
the thigh, pass over the *r*... Is 47:2
I make the *r* a wilderness... Is 50:2
the *r* of waters in a straight way... Jer 31:9
whose waters are moved as the *r*... Jer 46:7
his waters are moved like the *r*... Jer 46:8
Mine eye runneth down with *r* of... Lam 3:48
and to the hills, to the *r*... Eze 6:3
that lieth in the midst of his *r*... Eze 29:3
of thy *r* to stick unto thy scales... Eze 29:4
thee up out of the midst of thy *r*... Eze 29:4
all the fish of thy *r* shall stick... Eze 29:4
thee and all the fish of thy *r*... Eze 29:5
am against thee, and against thy *r*... Eze 29:10
And I will make the *r* dry, and sell... Eze 30:12
set him up on high with her *r*... Eze 31:4
sent out her little *r* unto all... Eze 31:4
broken by all the *r* of the land... Eze 31:12
and thou camest forth with thy *r*... Eze 32:2
thy feet, and fouledst their *r*... Eze 32:2
the *r* shall be full of thee... Eze 32:6
cause their *r* to run like oil,... Eze 32:14
the mountains of Israel by the *r*... Eze 34:13
in thy valleys, and in all thy *r*... Eze 35:8
and to the hills, to the *r*... Eze 36:4
and to the hills, to the *r*... Eze 36:6
whithersoever the *r* shall come... Eze 47:9
for the *r* of waters are dried up,... Joel 1:20
all the *r* of Judah shall flow... Joel 3:18
or with ten thousands of *r* of oil... Mic 6:7
it dry, and drieth up all the *r*... Nah 1:4
gates of the *r* shall be opened... Nah 2:6
No, that was situate among the *r*... Nah 3:8
the LORD displeased against the *r*... Hab 3:8
was thine anger against the *r*... Hab 3:8
didst cleave the earth with *r*... Hab 3:9
From beyond the *r* of Ethiopia my... Zeph 3:10
shall flow *r* of living water... Jn 7:38
fell upon the third part of the *r*... Rev 8:10
poured out his vial upon the *r*... Rev 16:4

**RIZIA** See REZIA.

**RIZPAH** (*riz'-pah*) *A concubine of Saul.*
had a concubine, whose name was *R*... 2Sa 3:7
sons of *R* the daughter of Aiah... 2Sa 21:8
*R* the daughter of Aiah took... 2Sa 21:10
David what *R* the daughter of Aiah... 2Sa 21:11

**ROAD**
Whither have ye made a *r* to day... 1Sa 27:10

**ROAR**
Let the sea *r*, and the fulness... 1Chr 16:32
Though the waters thereof *r*... Ps 46:3
Thine enemies *r* in the midst of... Ps 74:4
let the sea *r*, and the fulness... Ps 96:11
Let the sea *r*, and the fulness... Ps 98:7
The young lions *r* after their... Ps 104:21
they shall *r* like young lions... Is 5:29
yea, they shall *r*, and lay hold of... Is 5:29
in that day they shall *r* against... Is 5:30
he shall cry, yea, *r*... Is 42:13
We *r* all like bears, and mourn... Is 59:11
though they *r*, yet can they not... Jer 5:22
The LORD shall *r* from on high... Jer 25:30
he shall mightily *r* upon his... Jer 25:30
the sea when the waves thereof *r*... Jer 31:35
their voice shall *r* like the sea... Jer 50:42
They shall *r* together like lions... Jer 51:38
her waves do *r* like great waters... Jer 51:55
he shall *r* like a lion... Hos 11:10
when he shall *r*, then the... Hos 11:10
The LORD also shall *r* out of Zion... Joel 3:16
said, The LORD will *r* from Zion... Amos 1:2
Will a lion *r* in the forest, when... Amos 3:4

**ROARED**
a young lion *r* against him... Judg 14:5
I have *r* by reason of the... Ps 38:8
divided the sea, whose waves *r*... Is 51:15
The young lions *r* upon him... Jer 2:15
The lion hath *r*, who will not... Amos 3:8

**ROARETH**
After it a voice *r*... Job 37:4
their voice *r* like the sea... Jer 6:23
a loud voice, as when a lion *r*... Rev 10:3

**ROARING**
The *r* of the lion, and the voice... Job 4:10
me, and from the words of my *r*... Ps 22:1
mouths, as a ravening and a *r* lion... Ps 22:13
old through my *r* all the day long... Ps 32:3
wrath is as the *r* of a lion... Prov 19:12
of a king is as the *r* of a lion... Prov 20:2
As a *r* lion, and a ranging bear... Prov 28:15
Their *r* shall be like a lion,... Is 5:29
them like the *r* of the sea... Is 5:30
and the young lion *r* on his prey... Is 31:4
thereof, by the noise of his *r*... Eze 19:7
like a *r* lion ravening the prey... Eze 22:25
princes within her are *r* lions... Zeph 3:3
a voice of the *r* of young lions... Zec 11:3
the sea and the waves *r*... Lk 21:25
adversary the devil, as a *r* lion... 1Pet 5:8

**ROARINGS**
my *r* are poured out like the... Job 3:24

**ROAST**
*r* with fire, and unleavened bread... Ex 12:8
all with water, but *r* with fire... Ex 12:9
And thou shalt *r* and eat it in the... Deut 16:7
Give flesh to *r* for the priest... 1Sa 2:15
he roasteth *r*, and is satisfied... Is 44:16

**ROASTED**
they *r* the passover with fire... 2Chr 35:13
I have *r* flesh, and eaten it... Is 44:19
the king of Babylon *r* in the fire... Jer 29:22

**ROASTETH**
The slothful man *r* not that which... Prov 12:27
he *r* roast, and is satisfied... Is 44:16

**ROB**
thy neighbour, neither *r* him... Lev 19:13
which shall *r* you of your... Lev 26:22
they *r* the threshingfloors... 1Sa 23:1
*R* not the poor, because he is... Prov 22:22
that they may *r* the fatherless... Is 10:2
us, and the lot of them that *r* us... Is 17:14
*r* those that robbed them, saith... Eze 39:10
Will a man *r* God... Mal 3:8

**ROBBED**
they *r* all that came along that... Judg 9:25
as a bear *r* of her whelps in the... 2Sa 17:8
The bands of the wicked have *r* me... Ps 119:61
Let a bear *r* of her whelps meet a... Prov 17:12
have *r* their treasures, and I have... Is 10:13
But this is a people *r* and spoiled... Is 42:22
and they shall be *r*... Jer 50:37
pledge, give again that he had *r*... Eze 33:15
them, and rob those that *r* them... Eze 39:10
Yet ye have *r* me... Mal 3:8
ye say, Wherein have we *r* thee... Mal 3:8
for ye have *r* me, even this whole... Mal 3:9
I *r* other churches, taking wages... 2Cor 11:8

**ROBBER**
the *r* swalloweth up their... Job 5:5
the *r* shall prevail against him... Job 18:9
If he beget a son that is a *r*... Eze 18:10
way, the same is a thief and a *r*... Jn 10:1
Now Barabbas was a *r*... Jn 18:40

**ROBBERS**
The tabernacles of *r* prosper... Job 12:6
for a spoil, and Israel to the *r*... Is 42:24
become a den of *r* in your eyes... Jer 7:11
for the *r* shall enter into it, and... Eze 7:22
also the *r* of thy people shall... Dan 11:14
as troops of *r* wait for a man, so... Hos 6:9
the troop of *r* spoileth without... Hos 7:1
if *r* by night, (how art thou cut... Obad 5
came before me are thieves and *r*... Jn 10:8
which are neither *r* of churches... Acts 19:37
perils of waters, in perils of *r*... 2Cor 11:26

**ROBBERY**
and become not vain in *r*... Ps 62:10
The *r* of the wicked shall destroy... Prov 21:7
I hate *r* for burnt offering... Is 61:8
used oppression, and exercised *r*... Eze 22:29
up violence and *r* in their palaces... Amos 3:10
it is all full of lies and *r*... Nah 3:1
thought it not *r* to be equal with... Phil 2:6

**ROBBETH**
Whoso *r* his father or his mother,... Prov 28:24

**ROBE**
breastplate, and an ephod, and a *r*... Ex 28:4
thou shalt make the *r* of the... Ex 28:31
upon the hem of the *r* round about... Ex 28:34
the *r* of the ephod, and the ephod,... Ex 29:5
he made the *r* of the ephod of... Ex 39:22
was an hole in the midst of the *r*... Ex 39:23
of the *r* pomegranates of blue... Ex 39:24
upon the hem of the *r*, round... Ex 39:25
the hem of the *r* to minister in... Ex 39:26
girdle, and clothed him with the *r*... Lev 8:7
of the *r* that was upon him... 1Sa 18:4
off the skirt of Saul's *r* privily... 1Sa 24:4
see the skirt of thy *r* in my hand... 1Sa 24:11
that I cut off the skirt of thy *r*... 1Sa 24:11
clothed with a *r* of fine linen... 1Chr 15:27
my judgment was as a *r* and a... Job 29:14
And I will clothe him with thy *r*... Is 22:21
me with the *r* of righteousness... Is 61:10
throne, and he laid his *r* from him... Jonah 3:6
ye pull off the *r* with the... Mic 2:8
him, and put on him a scarlet *r*... Mt 27:28
him, they took the *r* off from him... Mt 27:31
servants, Bring forth the best *r*... Lk 15:22
and arrayed him in a gorgeous *r*... Lk 23:11
and they put on him a purple *r*... Jn 19:2
crown of thorns, and the purple *r*... Jn 19:5

**ROBES**
for with such *r* were the king's... 2Sa 13:18
his throne, having put on their *r*... 1Kin 22:10
but put thou on thy *r*... 1Kin 22:30
on his throne, clothed in their *r*... 2Chr 18:9
but put thou on thy *r*... 2Chr 18:29
thrones, and lay away their *r*... Eze 26:16
which desire to walk in long *r*... Lk 20:46
white *r* were given unto every one... Rev 6:11
the Lamb, clothed with white *r*... Rev 7:9
which are arrayed in white *r*... Rev 7:13
and have washed their *r*, and made... Rev 7:14

**ROBOAM** (*ro-bo'-am*) See REHOBOAM. *Same as Rehoboam; an ancestor of Jesus.*
And Solomon begat *R*... Mt 1:7
and *R* begat Abia... Mt 1:7

**ROCK**
thee there upon the *r* in Horeb... Ex 17:6
and thou shalt smite the *r*... Ex 17:6
me, and thou shalt stand upon a *r*... Ex 33:21
will put thee in a clift of the *r*... Ex 33:22
ye unto the *r* before their eyes... Num 20:8
forth to them water out of the *r*... Num 20:8
together before the *r*, and he said... Num 20:10
we fetch you water out of this *r*... Num 20:10
with his rod he smote the *r* twice... Num 20:11
and thou puttest thy nest in a *r*... Num 24:21
forth water out of the *r* of flint... Deut 8:15
He is the *R*, his work is perfect... Deut 32:4
him to suck honey out of the *r*... Deut 32:13
and oil out of the flinty *r*... Deut 32:13
esteemed the *R* of his salvation... Deut 32:15
Of the *R* that begat thee thou art... Deut 32:18
except their *R* had sold them, and... Deut 32:30
For their *r* is not as our *R*,... Deut 32:31
their *r* in whom they trusted,... Deut 32:37
going up to Akrabbim, from the *r*... Judg 1:36
cakes, and lay them upon this *r*... Judg 6:20
there rose up fire out of the *r*... Judg 6:21
thy God upon the top of this *r*... Judg 6:26
and they slew Oreb upon the *r* Oreb... Judg 7:25
offered it upon a *r* unto the LORD... Judg 13:19
and dwelt in the top of the *r* Etam... Judg 15:8
went to the top of the *r* Etam... Judg 15:11
and brought him up from the *r*... Judg 15:13
wilderness unto the *r* of Rimmon... Judg 20:45
the wilderness unto the *r* Rimmon... Judg 20:47
abode in the *r* Rimmon four months. Judg 20:47
that were in the *r* Rimmon... Judg 21:13
is there any *r* like our God... 1Sa 2:2
was a sharp *r* on the one side... 1Sa 14:4
a sharp *r* on the other side... 1Sa 14:4
wherefore he came down into a *r*... 1Sa 23:25
and spread it for her upon the *r*... 2Sa 21:10
And he said, The LORD is my *r*... 2Sa 22:2
The God of my *r*... 2Sa 22:3
and who is a *r*, save our God... 2Sa 22:32
and blessed be my *r*... 2Sa 22:47
the God of the *r* of my salvation... 2Sa 22:47
the *R* of Israel spake to me, He... 2Sa 23:3
went down to the *r* to David... 1Chr 11:15
them unto the top of the *r*... 2Chr 25:12
them down from the top of the *r*... 2Chr 25:12
out of the *r* for their thirst... Neh 9:15
the *r* is removed out of his place... Job 14:18
shall the *r* be removed out of his... Job 18:4
pen and lead in the *r* for ever... Job 19:24
embrace the *r* for want of a... Job 24:8
putteth forth his hand upon the *r*... Job 28:9
the *r* poured me out rivers of oil... Job 29:6
wild goats of the *r* bring forth... Job 39:1
She dwelleth and abideth on the *r*... Job 39:28
upon the crag of the *r*... Job 39:28
The LORD is my *r*, and my fortress,... Ps 18:2
or who is a *r* save our God... Ps 18:31
and blessed be my *r*... Ps 18:46
he shall set me up upon a *r*... Ps 27:5
Unto thee will I cry, O LORD my *r*... Ps 28:1
be thou my strong *r*, for an house... Ps 31:2
For thou art my *r* and my fortress... Ps 31:3
clay, and set my feet upon a *r*... Ps 40:2
I will say unto God my *r*, Why... Ps 42:9
lead me to the *r* that is higher... Ps 61:2
He only is my *r* and my salvation... Ps 62:2
He only is my *r* and my salvation... Ps 62:6
the *r* of my strength, and my... Ps 62:7
to save me, for thou art my *r*... Ps 71:3
brought streams also out of the *r*... Ps 78:16
Behold, he smote the *r*, that the... Ps 78:20
remembered that God was their *r*... Ps 78:35
with honey out of the *r* should I... Ps 81:16
my God, and the *r* of my salvation... Ps 89:26
he is my *r*, and there is no... Ps 92:15
and my God is the *r* of my refuge... Ps 94:22
noise to the *r* of our salvation... Ps 95:1
He opened the *r*, and the waters... Ps 105:41
Which turned the *r* into a... Ps 114:8
the way of a serpent upon a *r*... Prov 30:19
that art in the clefts of the *r*... Song 2:14

Enter into the *r*, and hide thee in ... Is 2:10
for a *r* of offence to both the ... Is 8:14
of Midian at the *r* of Oreb ... Is 10:26
mindful of the *r* of thy strength ... Is 17:10
an habitation for himself in a *r* ... Is 22:16
of a great *r* in a weary land ... Is 32:2
let the inhabitants of the *r* sing ... Is 42:11
to flow out of the *r* for them ... Is 48:21
he clave the *r* also, and the ... Is 48:21
look unto the *r* whence ye are ... Is 51:1
made their faces harder than a *r* ... Jer 5:3
hide it there in a hole of the *r* ... Jer 13:4
cometh from the *r* of the field ... Jer 18:14
*r* of the plain, saith the LORD ... Jer 21:13
that breaketh the *r* in pieces ... Jer 23:29
the cities, and dwell in the *r* ... Jer 48:28
dwellest in the clefts of the *r* ... Jer 49:16
she set it upon the top of a *r* ... Eze 24:7
set her blood upon the top of a *r* ... Eze 24:8
and make her like the top of a *r* ... Eze 26:4
make thee like the top of a *r* ... Eze 26:14
Shall horses run upon the *r* ... Amos 6:12
dwellest in the clefts of the *r* ... Obad 3
which built his house upon a *r* ... Mt 7:24
for it was founded upon a *r* ... Mt 7:25
upon this *r* I will build my ... Mt 16:18
which he had hewn out in the *r* ... Mt 27:60
which was hewn out of a *r* ... Mk 15:46
and laid the foundation on a *r* ... Lk 6:48
for it was founded upon a *r* ... Lk 6:48
And some fell upon a *r* ... Lk 8:6
They on the *r* are they, which, ... Lk 8:13
a stumblingstone and *r* of offence ... Rom 9:33
spiritual *R* that followed them ... 1Cor 10:4
and that *R* was Christ ... 1Cor 10:4
a *r* of offence, even to them ... 1Pet 2:8

**ROCKS**
from the top of the *r* I see him ... Num 23:9
in caves, and in thickets, and in *r* ... 1Sa 13:6
his men upon the *r* of the wild ... 1Sa 24:2
in pieces the *r* before the LORD ... 1Kin 19:11
He cutteth out rivers among the *r* ... Job 28:10
caves of the earth, and in the *r* ... Job 30:6
He clave the *r* in the wilderness, ... Ps 78:15
and the *r* for the conies ... Ps 104:18
make they their houses in the *r* ... Prov 30:26
shall go into the holes of the *r* ... Is 2:19
To go into the clefts of the *r* ... Is 2:21
and into the tops of the ragged *r* ... Is 2:21
valleys, and in the holes of the *r* ... Is 7:19
shall be the munitions of *r* ... Is 33:16
valleys under the clifts of the *r* ... Is 57:5
thickets, and climb up upon the *r* ... Jer 4:29
and out of the holes of the *r* ... Jer 16:16
and roll thee down from the *r* ... Jer 51:25
the *r* are thrown down by him ... Nah 1:6
earth did quake, and the *r* rent ... Mt 27:51
lest we should have fallen upon *r* ... Acts 27:29
in the *r* of the mountains ... Rev 6:15
And said to the mountains and *r* ... Rev 6:16

**ROD**
And he said, A *r* ... Ex 4:2
it, and it became a *r* in his hand ... Ex 4:4
shalt take this *r* in thine hand ... Ex 4:17
Moses took the *r* of God in his ... Ex 4:20
shalt say unto Aaron, Take thy *r* ... Ex 7:9
cast down his *r* before Pharaoh ... Ex 7:10
they cast down every man his *r* ... Ex 7:12
but Aaron's *r* swallowed up their ... Ex 7:12
the *r* which was turned to a ... Ex 7:15
I will smite with the *r* that is ... Ex 7:17
Moses, Say unto Aaron, Take thy *r* ... Ex 7:19
and he lifted up the *r*, and smote ... Ex 7:20
hand with thy *r* over the streams ... Ex 8:5
Say unto Aaron, Stretch out thy *r* ... Ex 8:16
stretched out his hand with his *r* ... Ex 8:17
forth his *r* toward heaven ... Ex 9:23
his *r* over the land of Egypt ... Ex 10:13
But lift thou up thy *r*, and ... Ex 14:16
and thy *r*, wherewith thou smotest ... Ex 17:5
with the *r* of God in mine hand ... Ex 17:9
servant, or his maid, with a *r* ... Ex 21:20
of whatsoever passeth under the *r* ... Lev 27:32
take of every one of them a *r* ... Num 17:2
thou every man's name upon his *r* ... Num 17:2
Aaron's name upon the *r* of Levi ... Num 17:3
for one *r* shall be for the head ... Num 17:3
come to pass, that the man's *r* ... Num 17:5
their princes gave him a *r* apiece ... Num 17:6
the *r* of Aaron was among their ... Num 17:6
the *r* of Aaron for the house of ... Num 17:8
looked, and took every man his *r* ... Num 17:9
Bring Aaron's *r* again before the ... Num 17:10
Take the *r*, and gather thou the ... Num 20:8
Moses took the *r* from before the ... Num 20:9
with his *r* he smote the rock ... Num 20:11
end of the *r* that was in his hand ... 1Sa 14:27
of the *r* that was in mine hand ... 1Sa 14:43
chasten him with the *r* of men ... 2Sa 7:14
Let him take his *r* away from me ... Job 9:34
neither is the *r* of God upon them ... Job 21:9
shalt break them with a *r* of iron ... Ps 2:9
thy *r* and thy staff they comfort ... Ps 23:4
the *r* of thine inheritance, which ... Ps 74:2
their transgression with the *r* ... Ps 89:32
The LORD shall send the *r* of thy ... Ps 110:2
For the *r* of the wicked shall not ... Ps 125:3
but a *r* is for the back of him ... Prov 10:13
that spareth his *r* hateth his son ... Prov 13:24
of the foolish is a *r* of pride ... Prov 14:3
the *r* of his anger shall fail ... Prov 22:8
but the *r* of correction shall ... Prov 22:15
if thou beatest him with the *r* ... Prov 23:13
Thou shalt beat him with the *r* ... Prov 23:14
ass, and a *r* for the fool's back ... Prov 26:3
The *r* and reproof give wisdom ... Prov 29:15
the *r* of his oppressor, as in the ... Is 9:4
the *r* of mine anger, and the staff ... Is 10:5
as if the *r* should shake itself ... Is 10:15
he shall smite thee with a *r* ... Is 10:24
as his *r* was upon the sea, so ... Is 10:26
a *r* out of the stem of Jesse ... Is 11:1
the earth with the *r* of his mouth ... Is 11:4
because the *r* of him that smote ... Is 14:29
a staff, and the cummin with a *r* ... Is 28:27
beaten down, which smote with a *r* ... Is 30:31
I see a *r* of an almond tree ... Jer 1:11
and Israel is the *r* of his ... Jer 10:16
staff broken, and the beautiful *r* ... Jer 48:17
and Israel is the *r* of his ... Jer 51:19
affliction by the *r* of his wrath ... Lam 3:1
the *r* hath blossomed, pride hath ... Eze 7:10
risen up into a *r* of wickedness ... Eze 7:11
gone out of a *r* of her branches ... Eze 19:14
strong *r* to be a sceptre to rule ... Eze 19:14
cause you to pass under the *r* ... Eze 20:37
it contemneth the *r* of my son ... Eze 21:10
if the sword contemn even the *r* ... Eze 21:13
of Israel with a *r* upon the cheek ... Mic 5:1
hear ye the *r*, and who hath ... Mic 6:9
Feed thy people with thy *r* ... Mic 7:14
shall I come unto you with a *r* ... 1Cor 4:21
Aaron's *r* that budded, and the ... Heb 9:4
shall rule them with a *r* of iron ... Rev 2:27
was given me a reed like unto a *r* ... Rev 11:1
rule all nations with a *r* of iron ... Rev 12:5
shall rule them with a *r* of iron ... Rev 19:15

**RODANIM** See DODANIM.

**RODE**
they *r* upon the camels, and ... Gen 24:61
sons that *r* on thirty ass colts ... Judg 10:4
that *r* on threescore and ten ass ... Judg 12:14
as she *r* on the ass, that she ... 1Sa 25:20
*r* upon an ass, with five damsels ... 1Sa 25:42
which *r* upon camels, and fled ... 1Sa 30:17
Absalom *r* upon a mule, and the ... 2Sa 18:9
he *r* upon a cherub, and did fly ... 2Sa 22:11
and he *r* thereon, ... 1Kin 13:13
And Ahab *r*, and went to Jezreel ... 1Kin 18:45
So Jehu *r* in a chariot, and went ... 2Kin 9:16
thou *r* together after Ahab his ... 2Kin 9:25
me, save the beast that I *r* upon ... Neh 2:12
So the posts that *r* upon mules ... Est 8:14
he *r* upon a cherub, and did fly ... Ps 18:10

**RODS**
Jacob took him *r* of green poplar, ... Gen 30:37
white appear which was in the *r* ... Gen 30:37
he set the *r* which he had pilled ... Gen 30:38
the flocks conceived before the *r* ... Gen 30:39
that Jacob laid the *r* before the ... Gen 30:41
they might conceive among the *r* ... Gen 30:41
Aaron's rod swallowed up their *r* ... Ex 7:12
house of their fathers twelve *r* ... Num 17:2
fathers' houses, even twelve *r* ... Num 17:6
rod of Aaron was among their *r* ... Num 17:6
Moses laid up the *r* before the ... Num 17:7
Moses brought out all the *r* from ... Num 17:9
she had strong *r* for the sceptres ... Eze 19:11
her strong *r* were broken and ... Eze 19:12
Thrice was I beaten with *r* ... 2Cor 11:25

**ROE**
was as light of foot as a wild *r* ... 2Sa 2:18
as the loving hind and pleasant *r* ... Prov 5:19
Deliver thyself as a *r* from the ... Prov 6:5
is like a *r* or a young hart ... Song 2:9
be thou like a *r* or a young hart ... Song 2:17
be thou like to a *r* or to a young ... Song 8:14
And it shall be as the chased *r* ... Is 13:14

**ROEBUCK**
may eat thereof, as of the *r* ... Deut 12:15
Even as the *r* and the hart is ... Deut 12:22
The hart, and the *r*, and the fallow ... Deut 14:5
shall eat it alike, as the *r* ... Deut 15:22

**ROEBUCKS**
hundred sheep, beside harts, and *r* ... 1Kin 4:23

**ROES**
swift as the *r* upon the mountains ... 1Chr 12:8
daughters of Jerusalem, by the *r* ... Song 2:7
daughters of Jerusalem, by the *r* ... Song 3:5
like two young *r* that are twins ... Song 4:5
like two young *r* that are twins ... Song 7:3

**ROGELIM** (*ro'-ghel-im*) *A city in Gilead.*
and Barzillai the Gileadite of *R* ... 2Sa 17:27
the Gileadite came down from *R* ... 2Sa 19:31

**ROHGAH** (*ro'-gah*) *A son of Shamer.*
Ahi, and *R*, Jehubbah, and Aram ... 1Chr 7:34

**ROLL**
till they *r* the stone from the ... Gen 29:8
*R* great stones upon the mouth of ... Josh 10:18
*r* a great stone unto me this day ... 1Sa 14:33
in the province of the Medes, a *r* ... Ezr 6:2
said unto me, Take thee a great *r* ... Is 8:1
Take thee a *r* of a book, and write ... Jer 36:2
unto him, upon a *r* of a book ... Jer 36:4
go thou, and read in the *r* ... Jer 36:6
Take in thine hand the *r* wherein ... Jer 36:14
of Neriah took the *r* in his hand ... Jer 36:14
but they laid up the *r* in the ... Jer 36:20
king sent Jehudi to fetch the *r* ... Jer 36:21
until all the *r* was consumed in ... Jer 36:23
king that he would not burn the *r* ... Jer 36:25
that the king had burned the *r* ... Jer 36:27
Take thee again another *r* ... Jer 36:28
words that were in the first *r* ... Jer 36:28
Thou hast burned this *r*, saying, ... Jer 36:29
Then took Jeremiah another *r* ... Jer 36:32
*r* thee down from the rocks, and ... Jer 51:25
a *r* of a book was therein ... Eze 2:9
eat this *r*, and go speak unto the ... Eze 3:1
and he caused me to eat that *r* ... Eze 3:2
with this *r* that I give thee ... Eze 3:3
of Aphrah *r* thyself in the dust ... Mic 1:10
and looked, and behold a flying *r* ... Zec 5:1
And I answered, I see a flying *r* ... Zec 5:2
Who shall *r* us away the stone ... Mk 16:3

**ROLLED**
they *r* the stone from the well's ... Gen 29:3
*r* the stone from the well's mouth ... Gen 29:10
This day have I *r* away the ... Josh 5:9
they *r* themselves upon me ... Job 30:14
noise, and garments *r* in blood ... Is 9:5
shall be *r* together as a scroll ... Is 34:4
he *r* a great stone to the door of ... Mt 27:60
*r* back the stone from the door, ... Mt 28:2
*r* a stone unto the door of the ... Mk 15:46
saw that the stone was *r* away ... Mk 16:4
they found the stone *r* away from ... Lk 24:2
as a scroll when it is *r* together ... Rev 6:14

**ROLLER**
to put a *r* to bind it, to make it ... Eze 30:21

**ROLLETH**
and he that *r* a stone, it will ... Prov 26:27

**ROLLING**
like a *r* thing before the ... Is 17:13

**ROLLS**
was made in the house of the *r* ... Ezr 6:1

**ROMAMTI-EZER** (*romam''-ti-e'-zur*) *A sanctuary servant.*
Hanani, Eliathah, Giddalti, and *R* ... 1Chr 25:4
The four and twentieth to *R* ... 1Chr 25:31

**ROMAN** (*ro'-mun*) See ROMANS. *A citizen of Rome.*
you to scourge a man that is a *R* ... Acts 22:25
for this man is a *R* ... Acts 22:26
unto him, Tell me, art thou a *R* ... Acts 22:27
after he knew that he was a *R* ... Acts 22:29
having understood that he was a *R* ... Acts 23:27

**ROMANS** (*ro'-muns*)
the *R* shall come and take away ... Jn 11:48
neither to observe, being *R* ... Acts 16:21
us openly uncondemned, being *R* ... Acts 16:37
when they heard that they were *R* ... Acts 16:38
the *R* to deliver any man to die ... Acts 25:16
Jerusalem into the hands of the *R* ... Acts 28:17
Written to the *R* from Corinthus ... Rom *s*

**ROME** (*rome*) See ROMAN. *Administrative center of the Roman Empire.*
about Cyrene, and strangers of *R* ... Acts 2:10
all Jews to depart from *R* ... Acts 18:2
been there, I must also see *R* ... Acts 19:21
must thou bear witness also at *R* ... Acts 23:11
and so we went toward *R* ... Acts 28:14
And when we came to *R*, the ... Acts 28:16
To all that be in *R*, beloved of ... Rom 1:7
gospel to you that are at *R* also ... Rom 1:15
Unto the Galatians written from *R* ... Gal *s*
Written from *R* unto the Ephesians ... Eph *s*
from *R* by Epaphroditus ... Phil *s*
Written from *R* to the Colossians ... Col *s*
But, when he was in *R*, he sought ... 2Ti 1:17
the Ephesians, was written from *R* ... 2Ti *s*
Written from *R* to Philemon ... Philem *s*

**ROMPHA** See REMPHAN.

**ROOF**
they under the shadow of my *r* ... Gen 19:8
shalt make a battlement for thy *r* ... Deut 22:8
them up to the *r* of the house ... Josh 2:6
she had laid in order upon the *r* ... Josh 2:6
she came up unto them upon the *r* ... Josh 2:8
there were upon the *r* about three ... Judg 16:27
walked upon the *r* of the king's ... 2Sa 11:2
from the *r* he saw a woman washing ... 2Sa 11:2
the *r* over the gate unto the wall ... 2Sa 18:24
every one upon the *r* of his house ... Neh 8:16
cleaved to the *r* of their mouth ... Job 29:10
cleave to the *r* of my mouth ... Ps 137:6
the *r* of thy mouth like the best ... Song 7:9
to the *r* of his mouth for thirst ... Lam 4:4
cleave to the *r* of thy mouth ... Eze 3:26
*r* of one little chamber to the ... Eze 40:13
chamber to the *r* of another ... Eze 40:13
thou shouldest come under my *r* ... Mt 8:8
they uncovered the *r* where he was ... Mk 2:4
thou shouldest enter under my *r* ... Lk 7:6

**ROOFS**
of all the houses upon whose *r* ... Jer 19:13
upon whose *r* they have offered ... Jer 32:29

**ROOM**
is there *r* in thy father's house ... Gen 24:23
enough, and *r* to lodge in ... Gen 24:25
the house, and *r* for the camels ... Gen 24:31
now the LORD hath made *r* for us ... Gen 26:22
me continually in the *r* of Joab ... 2Sa 19:13
Jehoiada in his *r* over the host ... 1Kin 2:35
the king put in the *r* of Abiathar ... 1Kin 2:35
him king in the *r* of his father ... 1Kin 5:1
will set upon thy throne in thy *r* ... 1Kin 5:5
up in the *r* of David my father ... 1Kin 8:20
anoint to be prophet in thy *r* ... 1Kin 19:16
killed him, and reigned in his *r* ... 2Kin 15:25
in the *r* of Josiah his father ... 2Kin 23:34
up in the *r* of David my father ... 2Chr 6:10
made him king in the *r* of his ... 2Chr 26:1
hast set my feet in a large *r* ... Ps 31:8
Thou preparedst *r* before it ... Ps 80:9
A man's gift maketh *r* for him ... Prov 18:16
not be *r* enough to receive it ... Mal 3:10
in the *r* of his father Herod ... Mt 2:22
there was no *r* to receive them ... Mk 2:2
you a large upper *r* furnished ... Mk 14:15
was no *r* for them in the inn ... Lk 2:7
because I have no *r* where to ... Lk 12:17
sit not down in the highest *r* ... Lk 14:8
with shame to take the lowest *r* ... Lk 14:9
go and sit down in the lowest *r* ... Lk 14:10
hast commanded, and yet there is *r* ... Lk 14:22
you a large upper *r* furnished ... Lk 22:12
in, they went up into an upper *r* ... Acts 1:13
Porcius Festus came into Felix' *r* ... Acts 24:27
*r* of the unlearned say Amen at ... 1Cor 14:16

**ROOMS**
*r* shalt thou make in the ark, and ... Gen 6:14
place, and put captains in their *r* ... 1Kin 20:24
this day, and dwelt in their *r* ... 1Chr 4:41
And love the uppermost *r* at feasts ... Mt 23:6
and the uppermost *r* at feasts ... Mk 12:39
how they chose out the chief *r* ... Lk 14:7
and the chief *r* at feasts ... Lk 20:46

**ROOT**
among you a *r* that beareth gall ... Deut 29:18
there a *r* of them against Amalek ... Judg 5:14
he shall *r* up Israel out of this ... 1Kin 14:15
shall yet again take *r* downward ... 2Kin 19:30
I have seen the foolish taking *r* ... Job 5:3
Though the *r* thereof wax old in ... Job 14:8
seeing the *r* of the matter is ... Job 19:28
My *r* was spread out by the waters ... Job 29:19
would *r* out all mine increase ... Job 31:12
*r* thee out of the land of the ... Ps 52:5
and didst cause it to take deep *r* ... Ps 80:9
but the *r* of the righteous shall ... Prov 12:3
but the *r* of the righteous ... Prov 12:12
so their *r* shall be as rottenness ... Is 5:24
day there shall be a *r* of Jesse ... Is 11:10
for out of the serpent's *r* shall ... Is 14:29
and I will kill thy *r* with famine ... Is 14:30
them that come of Jacob to take *r* ... Is 27:6
Judah shall again take *r* downward ... Is 37:31
shall not take *r* in the earth ... Is 40:24
as a *r* out of a dry ground ... Is 53:2
to *r* out, and to pull down, and to ... Jer 1:10
them, yea, they have taken *r* ... Jer 12:2
for his *r* was by great waters ... Eze 31:7
their *r* is dried up, they shall ... Hos 9:16
leave them neither *r* nor branch ... Mal 4:1
is laid unto the *r* of the trees ... Mt 3:10
and because they had no *r*, they ... Mt 13:6
Yet hath he not *r* in himself ... Mt 13:21
ye *r* up also the wheat with them ... Mt 13:29
and because it had no *r*, it ... Mk 4:6
have no *r* in themselves, and so ... Mk 4:17
is laid unto the *r* of the trees ... Lk 3:9
and these have no *r*, which for a ... Lk 8:13
tree, Be thou plucked up by the *r* ... Lk 17:6
if the *r* be holy, so are the ... Rom 11:16
and with them partakest of the *r* ... Rom 11:17
not the *r*, but the *r* thee ... Rom 11:18
There shall be a *r* of Jesse ... Rom 15:12
of money is the *r* of all evil ... 1Ti 6:10
lest any *r* of bitterness ... Heb 12:15
the *R* of David, hath prevailed to ... Rev 5:5
I am the *r* and the offspring of ... Rev 22:16

**ROOTED**
the LORD *r* them out of their land ... Deut 29:28
shall be *r* out of his tabernacle ... Job 18:14
yea, let my offspring be *r* out ... Job 31:8
shall be *r* out of it ... Prov 2:22
noonday, and Ekron shall be *r* up ... Zeph 2:4
hath not planted, shall be *r* up ... Mt 15:13
that ye, being *r* and grounded in ... Eph 3:17
*R* and built up in him, and ... Col 2:7

**ROOTS**
the *r* out of my land which I have ... 2Chr 7:20
His *r* are wrapped about the heap, ... Job 8:17
His *r* shall be dried up beneath, ... Job 18:16
the mountains by the *r* ... Job 28:9
and juniper *r* for their meat ... Job 30:4
a Branch shall grow out of his *r* ... Is 11:1
spreadeth out her *r* by the river ... Jer 17:8
the *r* thereof were under him ... Eze 17:6
vine did bend her *r* toward him ... Eze 17:7
he not pull up the *r* thereof ... Eze 17:9
to pluck it up by the *r* thereof ... Eze 17:9
the stump of his *r* in the earth ... Dan 4:15
of the *r* thereof in the earth ... Dan 4:23
to leave the stump of the tree *r* ... Dan 4:26
first horns plucked up by the *r* ... Dan 7:8
her *r* shall one stand up in his ... Dan 11:7
and cast forth his *r* as Lebanon ... Hos 14:5
from above, and his *r* from beneath ... Amos 2:9
the fig tree dried up from the *r* ... Mk 11:20
twice dead, plucked up by the *r* ... Jude 12

**ROPE**
and sin as it were with a cart *r* ... Is 5:18

**ROPES**
new *r* that never were occupied ... Judg 16:11
Delilah therefore took new *r* ... Judg 16:12
all Israel bring *r* to that city ... 2Sa 17:13
*r* upon our heads, and go out to ... 1Kin 20:31
put *r* on their heads, and came to ... 1Kin 20:32
cut off the *r* of the boat ... Acts 27:32

**ROSE**
that Cain *r* up against Abel his ... Gen 4:8
the men *r* up from thence, and ... Gen 18:16
Lot seeing them *r* up to meet them ... Gen 19:1
Therefore Abimelech *r* early in ... Gen 20:8
Abraham *r* up early in the morning ... Gen 21:14
then Abimelech *r* up, and Phichol ... Gen 21:32
Abraham *r* up early in the morning ... Gen 22:3
*r* up, and went unto the place of ... Gen 22:3
unto his young men, and they *r* up ... Gen 22:19
they *r* up in the morning, and he ... Gen 24:54
drink, and *r* up, and went his way ... Gen 25:34
they *r* up betimes in the morning, ... Gen 26:31
Jacob *r* up early in the morning, ... Gen 28:18
Then Jacob *r* up, and set his sons ... Gen 31:17
and he *r* up, and passed over the ... Gen 31:21
early in the morning Laban *r* up ... Gen 31:55
he *r* up that night, and took his ... Gen 32:22
over Penuel the sun *r* upon him ... Gen 32:31
his daughters *r* up to comfort him ... Gen 37:35
*r* up, and went down to Egypt, and ... Gen 43:15
Jacob *r* up from Beer-sheba ... Gen 46:5
neither *r* any from his place for ... Ex 10:23
Pharaoh *r* up in the night, he, and ... Ex 12:30
them that *r* up against thee ... Ex 15:7
*r* up early in the morning, and ... Ex 24:4
And Moses *r* up, and his minister ... Ex 24:13
they *r* up early on the morrow, and ... Ex 32:6
eat and to drink, and *r* up to play ... Ex 32:6
that all the people *r* up ... Ex 33:8
and all the people *r* up and ... Ex 33:10
Moses *r* up early in the morning, ... Ex 34:4
they *r* up early in the morning, ... Num 14:40
they *r* up before Moses, with ... Num 16:2
Moses *r* up and went unto ... Num 16:25
Balaam *r* up in the morning, and ... Num 22:13
And the princes of Moab *r* up ... Num 22:14
Balaam *r* up in the morning, and ... Num 22:21
And Balaam *r* up, and went and ... Num 24:25
saw it, he *r* up from among the ... Num 25:7
and *r* up from Seir unto them ... Deut 33:2
Joshua *r* early in the morning ... Josh 3:1
*r* up upon an heap very far from ... Josh 3:16
Joshua *r* early in the morning, and ... Josh 6:12
that they *r* early about the ... Josh 6:15
So Joshua *r* up early in the ... Josh 7:16
Joshua *r* up early in the morning, ... Josh 8:10
*r* up early, and the men of the ... Josh 8:14
there *r* up fire out of the rock, ... Judg 6:21
for he *r* up early on the morrow, ... Judg 6:38
*r* up early, and pitched beside the ... Judg 7:1
And Abimelech *r* up, and all the ... Judg 9:34
and Abimelech *r* up, and the people ... Judg 9:35
he *r* up against them, and smote ... Judg 9:43
morning, that he *r* up to depart ... Judg 19:5
And when the man *r* up to depart ... Judg 19:7
And when the man *r* up to depart ... Judg 19:9
not tarry that night, but he *r* up ... Judg 19:10
her lord *r* up in the morning, and ... Judg 19:27
up upon an ass, and the man *r* up ... Judg 19:28
And the men of Gibeah *r* against me ... Judg 20:5
of Israel *r* up in the morning ... Judg 20:19
of Israel *r* up out of their place ... Judg 20:33
morrow, that the people *r* early ... Judg 21:4
she *r* up before one could know ... Ruth 3:14
So Hannah *r* up after they had ... 1Sa 1:9
they *r* up in the morning early, ... 1Sa 1:19
when Samuel *r* early to meet Saul ... 1Sa 15:12
So Samuel *r* up, and went to Ramah ... 1Sa 16:13
David *r* up early in the morning, ... 1Sa 17:20
But Saul *r* up out of the cave, and ... 1Sa 24:7
Then they *r* up, and went away that ... 1Sa 28:25
his men *r* up early to depart in ... 1Sa 29:11
Absalom *r* up early, and stood ... 2Sa 15:2
all them that *r* up against thee ... 2Sa 18:31
them that *r* up against me hast ... 2Sa 22:40
above them that *r* up against me ... 2Sa 22:49
*r* up, and went every man his way ... 1Kin 1:49
the king *r* up to meet her, and ... 1Kin 2:19
when I *r* in the morning to give ... 1Kin 3:21
that Ahab *r* up to go down to the ... 1Kin 21:16
they *r* up early in the morning, ... 2Kin 3:22
of Israel, the Israelites *r* up ... 2Kin 3:24
they *r* up in the twilight, to go ... 2Kin 7:5
he *r* by night, and smote the ... 2Kin 8:21
they *r* early in the morning, and ... 2Chr 20:20
he *r* up by night, and smote the ... 2Chr 21:9
the leprosy even *r* up in his ... 2Chr 26:19
which were expressed by name *r* up ... 2Chr 28:15
Then Hezekiah the king *r* early ... 2Chr 29:20
Then *r* up the chief of the ... Ezr 1:5
Then *r* up Zerubbabel the son of ... Ezr 5:2
Then Ezra *r* up from before the ... Ezr 10:6
priest *r* up with his brethren the ... Neh 3:1
*r* up, and said unto the nobles, and ... Neh 4:14
*r* up early in the morning, and ... Job 1:5
me those that *r* up against me ... Ps 18:39
side, when men *r* up against us ... Ps 124:2
I am the *r* of Sharon, and the lily ... Song 2:1
I *r* up to open to my beloved ... Song 5:5
rejoice, and blossom as the *r* ... Is 35:1
Then *r* up certain of the elders ... Jer 26:17
of those that *r* up against me ... Lam 3:62
*r* up in haste, and spake, and said ... Dan 3:24
afterward I *r* up, and did the ... Dan 8:27
But Jonah *r* up to flee unto ... Jonah 1:3
when the morning *r* the next day ... Jonah 4:7
but they *r* early, and corrupted ... Zeph 3:7
he, casting away his garment, *r* ... Mk 10:50
*r* up, and thrust him out of the ... Lk 4:29
immediately he *r* up before them ... Lk 5:25
left all, *r* up, and followed him ... Lk 5:28
though one *r* from the dead ... Lk 16:31
when he *r* up from prayer, and was ... Lk 22:45
they *r* up the same hour, and ... Lk 24:33
that she *r* up hastily and went out ... Jn 11:31
Then the high priest *r* up ... Acts 5:17
before these days *r* up Theudas ... Acts 5:36
After this man *r* up Judas of ... Acts 5:37
with him after he *r* from the dead ... Acts 10:41
stood round about him, he *r* up ... Acts 14:20
But there *r* up certain of the ... Acts 15:5
been much disputing, Peter *r* up ... Acts 15:7
the multitude *r* up together ... Acts 16:22
he had thus spoken, the king *r* up ... Acts 26:30
this end Christ both died, and *r* ... Rom 14:9
to eat and drink, and *r* up to play ... 1Cor 10:7
that he *r* again the third day ... 1Cor 15:4
preached that he *r* from the dead ... 1Cor 15:12
which died for them, and *r* again ... 2Cor 5:15
*r* again, even so them also which ... 1Th 4:14
her smoke *r* up for ever and ever ... Rev 19:3

**ROSH** (*rosh*) *A son of Benjamin.*
Gera, and Naaman, Ehi, and *R* ... Gen 46:21

**ROT**
the LORD doth make thy thigh to *r* ... Num 5:21
belly to swell, and thy thigh to *r* ... Num 5:22
shall swell, and her thigh shall *r* ... Num 5:27
the name of the wicked shall *r* ... Prov 10:7
chooseth a tree that will not *r* ... Is 40:20

**ROTTEN**
as a *r* thing, consumeth, as a ... Job 13:28
iron as straw, and brass as *r* wood ... Job 41:27
old *r* rags, and let them down by ... Jer 38:11
*r* rags under thine armholes under ... Jer 38:12
The seed is *r* under their clods, ... Joel 1:17

**ROTTENNESS**
ashamed is as *r* in his bones ... Prov 12:4
but envy the *r* of the bones ... Prov 14:30
so their root shall be as *r* ... Is 5:24
and to the house of Judah as *r* ... Hos 5:12
*r* entered into my bones, and I ... Hab 3:16

**ROUGH**
down the heifer unto a *r* valley ... Deut 21:4
he stayeth his *r* wind in the day ... Is 27:8
straight, and the *r* places plain ... Is 40:4
to come up as the *r* caterpillers ... Jer 51:27
the *r* goat is the king of Grecia ... Dan 8:21
they wear a *r* garment to deceive ... Zec 13:4
the *r* ways shall be made smooth ... Lk 3:5

**ROUGHLY**
unto them, and spake *r* unto them ... Gen 42:7
lord of the land, spake *r* to us ... Gen 42:30
what if thy father answer thee *r* ... 1Sa 20:10
And the king answered the people *r* ... 1Kin 12:13
And the king answered them *r* ... 2Chr 10:13
but the rich answereth *r* ... Prov 18:23

**ROUND**
of Sodom, compassed the house *r* ... Gen 19:4
were in all the borders *r* about ... Gen 23:17
the cities that were *r* about them ... Gen 35:5
your sheaves stood *r* about ... Gen 37:7
which was *r* about every city, ... Gen 41:48
all the Egyptians digged *r* about ... Ex 7:24
the dew lay *r* about the host ... Ex 16:13
there lay a small *r* thing ... Ex 16:14
bounds unto the people *r* about ... Ex 19:12
upon it a crown of gold *r* about ... Ex 25:11
thereto a crown of gold *r* about ... Ex 25:24
border of an hand breadth *r* about ... Ex 25:25
to the border thereof *r* about ... Ex 25:25
All the pillars *r* about the court ... Ex 27:17
woven work *r* about the hole of it ... Ex 28:32
scarlet, *r* about the hem thereof ... Ex 28:33
of gold between them *r* about ... Ex 28:33
upon the hem of the robe *r* about ... Ex 28:34
sprinkle it *r* about upon the ... Ex 29:16
the blood upon the altar *r* about ... Ex 29:20
and the sides thereof *r* about ... Ex 30:3
unto it a crown of gold *r* about ... Ex 30:3
a crown of gold to it *r* about ... Ex 37:2
thereunto a crown of gold *r* about ... Ex 37:11
border of an handbreadth *r* about ... Ex 37:12
for the border thereof *r* about ... Ex 37:12
it, and the sides thereof *r* about ... Ex 37:26
unto it a crown of gold *r* about ... Ex 37:26
All the hangings of the court *r* ... Ex 38:16
and of the court *r* about, were of ... Ex 38:20
the sockets of the court *r* about ... Ex 38:31

R

all the pins of the court *r* about ... Ex 38:31
with a band *r* about the hole, ... Ex 39:23
*r* about between the pomegranates ... Ex 39:25
*r* about the hem of the robe to ... Ex 39:26
shalt set up the court *r* about ... Ex 40:8
the court *r* about the tabernacle ... Ex 40:33
sprinkle the blood *r* about upon ... Lev 1:5
his blood *r* about upon the altar ... Lev 1:11
the blood upon the altar *r* about ... Lev 3:2
thereof *r* about upon the altar ... Lev 3:8
thereof upon the altar *r* about ... Lev 3:13
sprinkle *r* about upon the altar ... Lev 7:2
the altar *r* about with his finger ... Lev 8:15
the blood upon the altar *r* about ... Lev 8:19
the blood upon the altar *r* about ... Lev 8:24
which he sprinkled *r* about upon ... Lev 9:12
sprinkled upon the altar *r* about ... Lev 9:18
to be scraped within *r* about ... Lev 14:41
the horns of the altar *r* about ... Lev 16:18
Ye shall not *r* the corners of ... Lev 19:27
*r* about them shall be counted as ... Lev 25:31
the heathen that are *r* about you ... Lev 25:44
it, and shall encamp *r* about the ... Num 1:50
pitch *r* about the tabernacle of ... Num 1:53
and by the altar *r* about, and the ... Num 3:26
the pillars of the court *r* about ... Num 3:37
and by the altar *r* about, and their ... Num 4:26
the pillars of the court *r* about ... Num 4:32
set them *r* about the tabernacle ... Num 11:24
*r* about the camp, and as it were ... Num 11:31
for themselves *r* about the camp ... Num 11:32
all Israel that were *r* about them ... Num 16:34
lick up all that are *r* about us ... Num 22:4
the cities of the country *r* about ... Num 32:33
with the coasts thereof *r* about ... Num 34:12
for the cities *r* about them ... Num 35:2
outward a thousand cubits *r* about ... Num 35:4
the people which are *r* about you ... Deut 6:14
from all your enemies *r* about ... Deut 12:10
the people which are *r* about you ... Deut 13:7
are *r* about him that is slain ... Deut 21:2
from all thine enemies *r* about ... Deut 25:19
war, and go *r* about the city once ... Josh 6:3
hear of it, and shall environ us *r* ... Josh 7:9
Judah *r* about according to their ... Josh 15:12
by the coasts thereof *r* about ... Josh 18:20
that were *r* about these cities to ... Josh 19:8
the suburbs thereof *r* about it ... Josh 21:11
with their suburbs *r* about them ... Josh 21:42
the LORD gave them rest *r* about ... Josh 21:44
from all their enemies *r* about ... Josh 23:1
the people that were *r* about them ... Judg 2:12
hands of their enemies *r* about ... Judg 2:14
man in his place *r* about the camp ... Judg 7:21
Belial, beset the house *r* about ... Judg 19:22
beset the house *r* about upon me ... Judg 20:5
set liers in wait *r* about Gibeah ... Judg 20:29
inclosed the Benjamites *r* about ... Judg 20:43
the camp from the country *r* about ... 1Sa 14:21
his men *r* about to take them ... 1Sa 23:26
and the people pitched *r* about him ... 1Sa 26:5
and the people lay *r* about him ... 1Sa 26:7
land of the Philistines *r* about ... 1Sa 31:9
David built *r* about from Millo and ... 2Sa 5:9
rest *r* about from all his enemies ... 2Sa 7:1
darkness pavilions *r* about him ... 2Sa 22:12
and the wall of Jerusalem *r* about ... 1Kin 3:1
peace on all sides *r* about him ... 1Kin 4:24
fame was in all nations *r* about ... 1Kin 4:31
house he built chambers *r* about ... 1Kin 6:5
the walls of the house *r* about ... 1Kin 6:5
and he made chambers *r* about ... 1Kin 6:5
he made narrowed rests *r* about ... 1Kin 6:6
all the walls of the house *r* ... 1Kin 6:29
the great court *r* about was with ... 1Kin 7:12
two rows *r* about upon the one ... 1Kin 7:18
were two hundred in rows *r* about ... 1Kin 7:20
it was *r* all about, and his height ... 1Kin 7:23
cubits did compass it *r* about ... 1Kin 7:23
under the brim of it *r* about ... 1Kin 7:24
cubit, compassing the sea *r* about ... 1Kin 7:24
but the mouth thereof was *r* after ... 1Kin 7:31
their borders, foursquare, not *r* ... 1Kin 7:31
a *r* compass of half a cubit high ... 1Kin 7:35
every one, and additions *r* about ... 1Kin 7:36
top of the throne was *r* behind ... 1Kin 10:19
the water ran *r* about the altar ... 1Kin 18:35
chariots of fire *r* about Elisha ... 2Kin 6:17
ye shall compass the king *r* about ... 2Kin 11:8
*r* about the king, from the right ... 2Kin 11:11
heathen that were *r* about them ... 2Kin 17:15
in the places *r* about Jerusalem ... 2Kin 23:5
built forts against it *r* about ... 2Kin 25:1
were against the city *r* about ... 2Kin 25:4
the walls of Jerusalem *r* about ... 2Kin 25:10
upon the chapiter *r* about ... 2Kin 25:17
that were *r* about the same cities ... 1Chr 4:33
and the suburbs thereof *r* about it ... 1Chr 6:55
they lodged *r* about the house of ... 1Chr 9:27
land of the Philistines *r* about ... 1Chr 10:9
And he built the city *r* about ... 1Chr 11:8
about, even from Millo *r* about ... 1Chr 11:8
rest from all his enemies *r* about ... 1Chr 22:9
and of all the chambers *r* about ... 1Chr 28:12
*r* in compass, and five cubits the ... 2Chr 4:2
cubits did compass it *r* about ... 2Chr 4:2
which did compass it *r* about ... 2Chr 4:3
cubit, compassing the sea *r* about ... 2Chr 4:3
all the cities *r* about Gerar ... 2Chr 14:14
the LORD gave them rest *r* about ... 2Chr 15:15
the lands that were *r* about Judah ... 2Chr 17:10
for his God gave him rest *r* about ... 2Chr 20:30
shall compass the king *r* about ... 2Chr 23:7
the temple, by the king *r* about ... 2Chr 23:10
with their mattocks *r* about ... 2Chr 34:6
plain country *r* about Jerusalem ... Neh 12:28
them villages *r* about Jerusalem ... Neh 12:29
and fashioned me together *r* about ... Job 10:8
His archers compass me *r* about ... Job 16:13
encamp *r* about my tabernacle ... Job 19:12
Therefore snares are *r* about thee ... Job 22:10
it is turned *r* about by his ... Job 37:12
his teeth are terrible *r* about ... Job 41:14
set themselves against me *r* about ... Ps 3:6
his pavilion *r* about him were ... Ps 18:11
bulls of Bashan have beset me *r* ... Ps 22:12
up above mine enemies *r* about me ... Ps 27:6
*r* about them that fear him ... Ps 34:7
to them that are *r* about us ... Ps 44:13
about Zion, and go *r* about her ... Ps 48:12
be very tempestuous *r* about him ... Ps 50:3
a dog, and go *r* about the city ... Ps 59:6
a dog, and go *r* about the city ... Ps 59:14
let all that be *r* about him bring ... Ps 76:11
*r* about their habitations ... Ps 78:28
shed like water *r* about Jerusalem ... Ps 79:3
to them that are *r* about us ... Ps 79:4
They came *r* about me daily like ... Ps 88:17
to thy faithfulness *r* about thee ... Ps 89:8
and darkness are *r* about him ... Ps 97:2
and burneth up his enemies *r* about ... Ps 97:3
mountains are *r* about Jerusalem ... Ps 125:2
so the LORD is *r* about his people ... Ps 125:2
olive plants *r* about thy table ... Ps 128:3
Thy navel is like a *r* goblet ... Song 7:2
their *r* tires like the moon, ... Is 3:18
For the cry is gone *r* about the ... Is 15:8
I will camp against thee *r* about ... Is 29:3
it hath set him on fire *r* about ... Is 42:25
Lift up thine eyes *r* about ... Is 49:18
Lift up thine eyes *r* about ... Is 60:4
all the walls thereof *r* about ... Jer 1:15
are they against her *r* about ... Jer 4:17
their tents against her *r* about ... Jer 6:3
the birds *r* about are against her ... Jer 12:9
devour all things *r* about it ... Jer 21:14
against all these nations *r* about ... Jer 25:9
for fear was *r* about, saith the ... Jer 46:5
sword shall devour *r* about thee ... Jer 46:14
in array against Babylon *r* about ... Jer 50:14
Shout against her *r* about ... Jer 50:15
the bow, camp against it *r* about ... Jer 50:29
it shall devour all *r* about him ... Jer 50:32
they shall be against her *r* about ... Jer 51:2
and built forts against it *r* about ... Jer 52:4
were by the city *r* about ... Jer 52:7
the walls of Jerusalem *r* about ... Jer 52:14
upon the chapiters *r* about ... Jer 52:22
network were an hundred *r* about ... Jer 52:23
adversaries should be *r* about him ... Lam 1:17
fire, which devoureth *r* about ... Lam 2:3
a solemn day my terrors *r* about ... Lam 2:22
full of eyes *r* about them four ... Eze 1:18
of fire *r* about within it ... Eze 1:27
and it had brightness *r* about ... Eze 1:27
of the brightness *r* about ... Eze 1:28
battering rams against it *r* about ... Eze 4:2
and countries that are *r* about her ... Eze 5:5
countries that are *r* about her ... Eze 5:6
the nations that are *r* about you ... Eze 5:7
the nations that are *r* about you ... Eze 5:7
fall by the sword *r* about thee ... Eze 5:12
the nations that are *r* about thee ... Eze 5:14
the nations that are *r* about thee ... Eze 5:15
your bones *r* about your altars ... Eze 6:5
their idols *r* about their altars ... Eze 6:13
pourtrayed upon the wall *r* about ... Eze 8:10
wheels, were full of eyes *r* about ... Eze 10:12
the heathen that are *r* about you ... Eze 11:12
gather them *r* about against thee ... Eze 16:37
and all that are *r* about her ... Eze 16:57
which despise thee *r* about ... Eze 16:57
and shield and helmet *r* about ... Eze 23:24
army were upon thy walls *r* about ... Eze 27:11
shields upon thy walls *r* about ... Eze 27:11
of all that are *r* about them ... Eze 28:24
that despise them *r* about them ... Eze 28:26
rivers running *r* about his plants ... Eze 31:4
her company is *r* about her grave ... Eze 32:23
her multitude *r* about her grave ... Eze 32:24
her graves are *r* about him ... Eze 32:25
her graves are *r* about him ... Eze 32:26
the places *r* about my hill a ... Eze 34:26
of the heathen that are *r* about ... Eze 36:4
Then the heathen that are left *r* ... Eze 36:36
caused me to pass by them *r* about ... Eze 37:2
the outside of the house *r* about ... Eze 40:5
of the court *r* about the gate ... Eze 40:14
posts within the gate *r* about ... Eze 40:16
and windows were *r* about inward ... Eze 40:16
made for the court *r* about ... Eze 40:17
and in the arches thereof *r* about ... Eze 40:25
and in the arches thereof *r* about ... Eze 40:29
the arches *r* about were five and ... Eze 40:30
and in the arches thereof *r* about ... Eze 40:33
and the windows to it *r* about ... Eze 40:36
an hand broad, fastened *r* about ... Eze 40:43
*r* about the house on every side ... Eze 41:5
for the side chambers *r* about ... Eze 41:6
still upward *r* about the house ... Eze 41:7
the height of the house *r* about ... Eze 41:8
*r* about the house on every side ... Eze 41:10
was left was five cubits *r* about ... Eze 41:11
was five cubits thick *r* about ... Eze 41:12
the galleries *r* about on their ... Eze 41:16
door, cieled with wood *r* about ... Eze 41:16
and by all the wall *r* about within ... Eze 41:17
through all the house *r* about ... Eze 41:19
the east, and measured it *r* about ... Eze 42:15
with the measuring reed *r* about ... Eze 42:16
with the measuring reed *r* about ... Eze 42:17
it had a wall *r* about, five ... Eze 42:20
the whole limit thereof *r* about ... Eze 43:12
thereof *r* about shall be a span ... Eze 43:13
and upon the border *r* about ... Eze 43:20
all the borders thereof *r* about ... Eze 45:1
in breadth, square *r* about ... Eze 45:2
fifty cubits *r* about for the ... Eze 45:2
a row of building *r* about in them ... Eze 46:23
*r* about them four, and it was made ... Eze 46:23
places under the rows *r* about ... Eze 46:23
It was *r* about eighteen thousand ... Eze 48:35
yourselves together *r* about ... Joel 3:11
to judge all the heathen *r* about ... Joel 3:12
shall be even *r* about the land ... Amos 3:11
the depth closed me *r* about ... Jonah 2:5
that had the waters *r* about it ... Nah 3:8
unto her a wall of fire *r* about ... Zec 2:5
and the cities thereof *r* about her ... Zec 7:7
unto all the people *r* about ... Zec 12:2
devour all the people *r* about ... Zec 12:6
heathen *r* about shall be gathered ... Zec 14:14
and all the region *r* about Jordan ... Mt 3:5
out into all that country *r* about ... Mt 14:35
a vineyard, and hedged it *r* about ... Mt 21:33
all the region *r* about Galilee ... Mk 1:28
when he had looked *r* about on ... Mk 3:5
he looked *r* about on them which ... Mk 3:34
he looked *r* about to see her that ... Mk 5:32
he went *r* about the villages, ... Mk 6:6
may go into the country *r* about ... Mk 6:36
through that whole region *r* about ... Mk 6:55
when they had looked *r* about ... Mk 9:8
And Jesus looked *r* about, and saith ... Mk 10:23
when he had looked *r* about upon ... Mk 11:11
on all that dwelt *r* about them ... Lk 1:65
of the Lord shone *r* about them ... Lk 2:9
through all the region *r* about ... Lk 4:14
place of the country *r* about ... Lk 4:37
looking *r* about upon them all, he ... Lk 6:10
throughout all the region *r* about ... Lk 7:17
*r* about besought him to depart ... Lk 8:37
into the towns and country *r* about ... Lk 9:12
about thee, and compass thee *r* ... Lk 19:43
Then came the Jews *r* about him ... Jn 10:24
the cities *r* about unto Jerusalem ... Acts 5:16
suddenly there shined *r* about him ... Acts 9:3
the region that lieth *r* about ... Acts 14:6
the disciples stood *r* about him ... Acts 14:20
heaven a great light *r* about me ... Acts 22:6
down from Jerusalem stood *r* about ... Acts 25:7
shining *r* about me and them which ... Acts 26:13
*r* about unto Illyricum, I have ... Rom 15:19
overlaid *r* about with gold ... Heb 9:4
was a rainbow *r* about the throne ... Rev 4:3
*r* about the throne were four and ... Rev 4:4
*r* about the throne, were four ... Rev 4:6
of many angels *r* about the throne ... Rev 5:11
angels stood *r* about the throne ... Rev 7:11

## ROUSE

who shall *r* him up ... Gen 49:9

## ROVERS

David against the band of the *r* ... 1Chr 12:21

## ROW

the first *r* shall be a sardius, a ... Ex 28:17
this shall be the first *r* ... Ex 28:17
the second *r* shall be an emerald, ... Ex 28:18
And the third *r* a ligure, an agate ... Ex 28:19
And the fourth *r* a beryl, and an ... Ex 28:20
the first *r* was a sardius, a ... Ex 39:10
this was the first *r* ... Ex 39:10
And the second *r*, an emerald, a ... Ex 39:11
And the third *r*, a ligure, an ... Ex 39:12
And the fourth *r*, a beryl, an onyx ... Ex 39:13
set them in two rows, six on a *r* ... Lev 24:6
put pure frankincense upon each *r* ... Lev 24:7
stone, and a *r* of cedar beams ... 1Kin 6:36
five pillars, fifteen in a *r* ... 1Kin 7:3
a *r* of cedar beams, both for the ... 1Kin 7:12
stones, and a *r* of new timber ... Ezr 6:4
there was a *r* of building round ... Eze 46:23

## ROWED

Nevertheless the men *r* hard to ... Jonah 1:13
So when they had *r* about five ... Jn 6:19

## ROWERS

Thy *r* have brought thee into ... Eze 27:26

## ROWING

And he saw them toiling in *r* ... Mk 6:48

## ROWS

of stones, even four *r* of stones ... Ex 28:17
they set in it four *r* of stones ... Ex 39:10
And thou shalt set them in two *r* ... Lev 24:6
court with three *r* of hewed stone ... 1Kin 6:36
upon four *r* of cedar pillars, ... 1Kin 7:2
And there were windows in three *r* ... 1Kin 7:4
was with three *r* of hewed stones ... 1Kin 7:12

two *r* round about upon the one 1Kin 7:18
were two hundred in *r* round about 1Kin 7:20
the knops were cast in two *r* 1Kin 7:24
even two *r* of pomegranates for 1Kin 7:42
Two *r* of oxen were cast, when it 2Chr 4:3
two *r* of pomegranates on each 2Chr 4:13
With three *r* of great stones, and Ezr 6:4
are comely with *r* of jewels Song 1:10
places under the *r* round about Eze 46:23

### ROYAL
fat, and he shall yield *r* dainties Gen 49:20
city, as one of the *r* cities Josh 10:2
dwell in the *r* city with thee 1Sa 27:5
of Ammon, and took the *r* city 2Sa 12:26
Solomon gave her of his *r* bounty 1Kin 10:13
arose and destroyed all the seed *r* 2Kin 11:1
son of Elishama, of the seed *r* 2Kin 25:25
bestowed upon him such *r* majesty 1Chr 29:25
the seed *r* of the house of Judah 2Chr 22:10
*r* wine in abundance, according to Est 1:7
*r* house which belonged to king Est 1:9
before the king with the crown *r* Est 1:11
let there go a *r* commandment from Est 1:19
let the king give her *r* estate Est 1:19
his house *r* in the tenth month Est 2:16
so that he set the *r* crown upon Est 2:17
that Esther put on her *r* apparel Est 5:1
his *r* throne in the *r* house Est 5:1
Let the *r* apparel be brought Est 6:8
the crown *r* which is set upon his Est 6:8
of the king in *r* apparel of blue Est 8:15
a *r* diadem in the hand of thy God Is 62:3
son of Elishama, of the seed *r* Jer 41:1
spread his *r* pavilion over them Jer 43:10
together to establish a *r* statute Dan 6:7
day Herod, arrayed in *r* apparel Acts 12:21
If ye fulfil the *r* law according Jas 2:8
a *r* priesthood, an holy nation, a 1Pet 2:9

### RUBBING
and did eat, *r* them in their hands Lk 6:1

### RUBBISH
heaps of the *r* which are burned Neh 4:2
is decayed, and there is much *r* Neh 4:10

### RUBIES
the price of wisdom is above *r* Job 28:18
She is more precious than *r* Prov 3:15
For wisdom is better than *r* Prov 8:11
is gold, and a multitude of *r* Prov 20:15
for her price is far above *r* Prov 31:10
were more ruddy in body than *r* Lam 4:7

### RUDDER
the sea, and loosed the *r* bands Acts 27:40

### RUDDY
Now he was *r*, and withal of a 1Sa 16:12
for he was but a youth, and *r* 1Sa 17:42
My beloved is white and *r*, the Song 5:10
they were more *r* in body than Lam 4:7

### RUDE
But though I be *r* in speech 2Cor 11:6

### RUDIMENTS
after the *r* of the world, and not Col 2:8
Christ from the *r* of the world Col 2:20

### RUE
for ye tithe mint and *r* and all Lk 11:42

### RUFUS (*ru'-fus*)
*1. Son of Simon the Cyrenian.*
the father of Alexander and *R* Mk 15:21
*2. A Christian in Rome.*
Salute *R* chosen in the Lord, and Rom 16:13

### RUHAMAH (*ru-ha'-mah*) *A symbolic name of Israel.*
and to your sisters, *R* Hos 2:1

### RUIN
But they were the *r* of him 2Chr 28:23
brought his strong holds to *r* Ps 89:40
who knoweth the *r* of Prov 24:22
and a flattering mouth worketh *r* Prov 26:28
let this *r* be under thy hand Is 3:6
and he brought it to *r* Is 23:13
of a defenced city a *r* Is 25:2
so iniquity shall not be your *r* Eze 18:30
of the seas in the day of thy *r* Eze 27:27
Upon his *r* shall all the fowls of Eze 31:13
the *r* of that house was great Lk 6:49

### RUINED
For Jerusalem is *r*, and Judah is Is 3:8
*r* cities are become fenced, and Eze 36:35
I the LORD build the *r* places Eze 36:36

### RUINOUS
waste fenced cities into *r* heaps 2Kin 19:25
a city, and it shall be a *r* heap Is 17:1
defenced cities into *r* heaps Is 37:26

### RUINS
faint, and their *r* be multiplied Eze 21:15
and I will raise up his *r*, and I Amos 9:11
I will build again the *r* thereof Acts 15:16

### RULE
the greater light to *r* the day Gen 1:16
the lesser light to *r* the night Gen 1:16
to *r* over the day and over the Gen 1:18
husband, and he shall *r* over thee Gen 3:16
desire, and thou shalt *r* over him Gen 4:7
Thou shalt not *r* over him with Lev 25:43
ye shall not *r* one over another Lev 25:46
the other shall not *r* with rigour Lev 25:53
*R* thou over us, both thou, and thy Judg 8:22
unto them, I will not *r* over you Judg 8:23
neither shall my son *r* over you Judg 8:23
the LORD shall *r* over you Judg 8:23
which bare *r* over the people that 1Kin 9:23
that had *r* over his chariots 1Kin 22:31
that bare *r* over the people 2Chr 8:10
servants bare *r* over the people Neh 5:15
should bear *r* in his own house Est 1:22
that the Jews had *r* over them Est 9:1
*r* thou in the midst of thine Ps 110:2
The sun to *r* by day Ps 136:8
The moon and stars to *r* by night Ps 136:9
By me princes *r*, and nobles, even Prov 8:16
hand of the diligent shall bear *r* Prov 12:24
A wise servant shall have *r* over Prov 17:2
a servant to have *r* over princes Prov 19:10
He that hath no *r* over his own Prov 25:28
but when the wicked beareth *r* Prov 29:2
yet shall he have *r* over all my Eccl 2:19
and babes shall *r* over them Is 3:4
oppressors, and women *r* over them Is 3:12
and they shall *r* over their Is 14:2
a fierce king shall *r* over them Is 19:4
that *r* this people which is in Is 28:14
and princes shall *r* in judgment Is 32:1
hand, and his arm shall *r* for him Is 40:10
him, and made him *r* over kings Is 41:2
carpenter stretcheth out his *r* Is 44:13
they that *r* over them make them Is 52:5
thou never barest *r* over them Is 63:19
the priests bear *r* by their means Jer 5:31
the sceptres of them that bare *r* Eze 19:11
strong rod to be a sceptre to *r* Eze 19:14
poured out, will I *r* over you Eze 20:33
shall no more *r* over the nations Eze 29:15
which shall bear *r* over all the Dan 2:39
have known that the heavens do *r* Dan 4:26
that shall *r* with great dominion Dan 11:3
shall cause them to *r* over many Dan 11:39
the heathen should *r* over them Joel 2:17
and shall sit and *r* upon his throne Zec 6:13
that shall *r* my people Israel Mt 2:6
to *r* over the Gentiles exercise Mk 10:42
when he shall have put down all *r* 1Cor 15:24
*r* which God hath distributed to 2Cor 10:13
you according to our *r* abundantly 2Cor 10:15
many as walk according to this *r* Gal 6:16
let us walk by the same *r* Phil 3:16
the peace of God *r* in your hearts Col 3:15
know not how to *r* his own house 1Ti 3:5
Let the elders that *r* well be 1Ti 5:17
them which have the *r* over you Heb 13:7
them that have the *r* over you Heb 13:17
all them that have the *r* over you Heb 13:24
he shall *r* them with a rod of Rev 2:27
who was to *r* all nations with a Rev 12:5
he shall *r* them with a rod of Rev 19:15

### RULED
that *r* over all that he had, Put Gen 24:2
thy word shall all my people be *r* Gen 41:40
*r* from Aroer, which is upon the Josh 12:2
in the days when the judges *r* Ruth 1:1
which *r* over the people that 1Kin 5:16
that *r* throughout the house of 1Chr 26:6
which have *r* over all countries Ezr 4:20
they that hated them *r* over them Ps 106:41
he that *r* the nations in anger Is 14:6
Servants have *r* over us Lam 5:8
and with cruelty have ye *r* them Eze 34:4
high God *r* in the kingdom of men Dan 5:21
to his dominion which he *r* Dan 11:4

### RULER
he made him *r* over all the land Gen 41:43
he said to the *r* of his house Gen 43:16
a *r* throughout all the land of Gen 45:8
nor curse the *r* of thy people Ex 22:28
When a *r* hath sinned, and done Lev 4:22
a man, every one a *r* among them Num 13:2
when Zebul the *r* of the city Judg 9:30
have appointed thee *r* over Israel 1Sa 25:30
to appoint me *r* over the people 2Sa 6:21
to be *r* over my people, over 2Sa 7:8
Jairite was a chief *r* about David 2Sa 20:26
appointed him to be *r* over Israel 1Kin 1:35
he made him *r* over all the charge 1Kin 11:28
of Ahikam, the son of Shaphan, *r* 2Kin 25:22
and of him came the chief *r* 1Chr 5:2
the *r* of the house of God 1Chr 9:11
was the *r* over them in time past 1Chr 9:20
thou shalt be *r* over my people 1Chr 11:2
be *r* over my people Israel 1Chr 17:7
of Moses, was *r* of the treasures 1Chr 26:24
his course was Mikloth also the *r* 1Chr 27:4
the *r* of the Reubenites was 1Chr 27:16
he hath chosen Judah to be the *r* 1Chr 28:4
to be a *r* over my people Israel 2Chr 6:5
fail thee a man to be *r* in Israel 2Chr 7:18
to be *r* among his brethren 2Chr 11:22
the *r* of the house of Judah, for 2Chr 19:11
the scribe and Maaseiah the *r* 2Chr 26:11
which Cononiah the Levite was *r* 2Chr 31:12
Azariah the *r* of the house of God 2Chr 31:13
the *r* of the half part of Neh 3:9
the *r* of the half part of Neh 3:12
the *r* of part of Beth-haccerem Neh 3:14
Colhozeh, the *r* of part of Mizpah Neh 3:15
the *r* of the half part of Neh 3:16
the *r* of the half part of Keilah, Neh 3:17
the *r* of the half part of Keilah Neh 3:18
the *r* of Mizpah, another piece Neh 3:19
Hananiah the *r* of the palace Neh 7:2
was the *r* of the house of God Neh 11:11
is little Benjamin with their *r* Ps 68:27
even the *r* of the people, and let Ps 105:20
house, and *r* of all his substance Ps 105:21
having no guide, overseer, or *r* Prov 6:7
When thou sittest to eat with a *r* Prov 23:1
so is a wicked *r* over the poor Prov 28:15
If a *r* hearken to lies, all his Prov 29:12
of the *r* rise up against thee Eccl 10:4
error which proceedeth from the *r* Eccl 10:5
Thou hast clothing, be thou our *r* Is 3:6
make me not a *r* of the people Is 3:7
Send ye the lamb to the *r* of the Is 16:1
in the land, *r* against *r* Jer 51:46
there is no king, lord, nor *r* Dan 2:10
and hath made thee *r* over them all Dan 2:38
made him *r* over the whole Dan 2:48
be the third *r* in the kingdom Dan 5:7
be the third *r* in the kingdom Dan 5:16
be the third *r* in the kingdom Dan 5:29
unto me that is to be *r* in Israel Mic 5:2
things, that have no *r* over them Hab 1:14
behold, there came a certain *r* Mt 9:18
hath made *r* over his household Mt 24:45
make him *r* over all his goods Mt 24:47
will make thee *r* over many things Mt 25:21
will make thee *r* over many things Mt 25:23
there came from the *r* of the Mk 5:35
saith unto the *r* of the synagogue Mk 5:36
house of the *r* of the synagogue Mk 5:38
he was a *r* of the synagogue Lk 8:41
the *r* of the synagogue's house Lk 8:49
shall make *r* over his household Lk 12:42
make him *r* over all that he hath Lk 12:44
the *r* of the synagogue answered Lk 13:14
And a certain *r* asked him, saying Lk 18:18
When the *r* of the feast had Jn 2:9
named Nicodemus, a *r* of the Jews Jn 3:1
away, saying, Who made thee a *r* Acts 7:27
saying, Who made thee a *r* Acts 7:35
the same did God send to be a *r* Acts 7:35
the chief *r* of the synagogue Acts 18:8
the chief *r* of the synagogue, and Acts 18:17
speak evil of the *r* of thy people Acts 23:5

### RULER'S
Many seek the *r* favour Prov 29:26
when Jesus came into the *r* house Mt 9:23

### RULERS
then make them *r* over my cattle Gen 47:6
all the *r* of the congregation Ex 16:22
to be *r* of thousands Ex 18:21
*r* of hundreds, *r* of fifties Ex 18:21
*r* of fifties, and *r* of tens Ex 18:21
*r* of thousands Ex 18:25
*r* of hundreds, *r* of fifties Ex 18:25
*r* of fifties, and *r* of tens Ex 18:25
all the *r* of the congregation Ex 34:31
the *r* brought onyx stones, and Ex 35:27
and I will make them *r* over you Deut 1:13
the Philistines are *r* over us Judg 15:11
and David's sons were chief *r* 2Sa 8:18
*r* of his chariots, and his 1Kin 9:22
unto the *r* of Jezreel, to the 2Kin 10:1
fetched the *r* over hundreds, with 2Kin 11:4
he took the *r* over hundreds, and 2Kin 11:19
to the *r* of the people, Go 1Chr 21:2
David made *r* over the Reubenites 1Chr 26:32
All these were the *r* of the 1Chr 27:31
with the *r* of the king's work 1Chr 29:6
and gathered the *r* of the city 2Chr 29:20
*r* of the house of God, gave unto 2Chr 35:8
*r* hath been chief in this Ezr 9:2
Let now our *r* of all the Ezr 10:14
the *r* knew not whither I went, or Neh 2:16
nor to the nobles, nor to the *r* Neh 2:16
said unto the nobles, and to the *r* Neh 4:14
the *r* were behind all the house Neh 4:16
said unto the nobles, and to the *r* Neh 4:19
and I rebuked the nobles, and the *r* Neh 5:7
hundred and fifty of the Jews and *r* Neh 5:17
together the nobles, and the *r* Neh 7:5
the *r* of the people dwelt at Neh 11:1
I, and the half of the *r* with me Neh 12:40
Then contended I with the *r* Neh 13:11
to the *r* of every people of every Est 3:12
*r* of the provinces which are from Est 8:9
all the *r* of the provinces, and Est 9:3
the *r* take counsel together Ps 2:2
word of the LORD, ye *r* of Sodom Is 1:10
wicked, and the sceptre of the *r* Is 14:5
All thy *r* are fled together, they Is 22:3
the prophets and your *r*, the seers Is 29:10
abhorreth, to a servant of *r* Is 49:7
to be *r* over the seed of Abraham Jer 33:26
I break in pieces captains and *r* Jer 51:23
thereof, and all the *r* thereof Jer 51:28
wise men, her captains, and her *r* Jer 51:57
clothed with blue, captains and *r* Eze 23:6
*r* clothed most gorgeously Eze 23:12
young men, captains and *r*, great Eze 23:23
all the *r* of the provinces, to Dan 3:2
all the *r* of the provinces, were Dan 3:3

her *r* with shame do love, Give ye Hos 4:18
one of the *r* of the synagogue Mk 5:22
and ye shall be brought before *r* Mk 13:9
kings and *r* for my name's sake Lk 21:12
the chief priests and the *r* Lk 23:13
the *r* also with them derided him, Lk 23:35
our *r* delivered him to be Lk 24:20
Do the *r* know indeed that this is Jn 7:26
Have any of the *r* or of the Jn 7:48
chief *r* also many believed on him Jn 12:42
ye did it, as did also your *r* Acts 3:17
pass on the morrow, that their *r* Acts 4:5
Ye *r* of the people, and elders of Acts 4:8
the *r* were gathered together Acts 4:26
the prophets the *r* of the Acts 13:15
dwell at Jerusalem, and their *r* Acts 13:27
and also of the Jews with their *r* Acts 14:5
into the marketplace unto the *r* Acts 16:19
brethren unto the *r* of the city Acts 17:6
the *r* of the city, when they Acts 17:8
For *r* are not a terror to good Rom 13:3
against the *r* of the darkness of Eph 6:12

**RULEST**
*r* not thou over all the kingdoms 2Chr 20:6
Thou *r* the raging of the sea Ps 89:9

**RULETH**
He that *r* over men must be just, 2Sa 23:3
let them know that God *r* in Jacob Ps 59:13
He *r* by his power for ever Ps 66:7
and his kingdom *r* over all Ps 103:19
he that *r* his spirit than he that Prov 16:32
The rich *r* over the poor, and the Prov 22:7
*r* over another to his own hurt Eccl 8:9
the cry of him that *r* among fools Eccl 9:17
most High *r* in the kingdom of men Dan 4:17
most High *r* in the kingdom of men Dan 4:25
most High *r* in the kingdom of men Dan 4:32
but Judah yet *r* with God, and is Hos 11:12
he that *r*, with diligence Rom 12:8
One that *r* well his own house, 1Ti 3:4

**RULING**
be just, *r* in the fear of God 2Sa 23:3
of David, and *r* any more in Judah Jer 22:30
*r* their children and their own 1Ti 3:12

**RUMAH** (*ru'-mah*) See ARUMAH. *Home of Jehoiakim's mother.*
the daughter of Pedaiah of *R* 2Kin 23:36

**RUMBLING**
at the *r* of his wheels, the Jer 47:3

**RUMOUR**
upon him, and he shall hear a *r* 2Kin 19:7
upon him, and he shall hear a *r* Is 37:7
I have heard a *r* from the LORD Jer 49:14
ye fear for the *r* that shall be Jer 51:46
a *r* shall both come one year, and Jer 51:46
in another year shall come a *r* Jer 51:46
and *r* shall be upon *r* Eze 7:26
We have heard a *r* from the LORD Obad 1
And this *r* of him went forth Lk 7:17

**RUMOURS**
shall hear of wars and *r* of wars Mt 24:6
*r* of wars, be ye not troubled Mk 13:7

**RUMP**
take of the ram the fat and the *r* Ex 29:22
the fat thereof, and the whole *r* Lev 3:9
the *r*, and the fat that covereth Lev 7:3
And he took the fat, and the *r* Lev 8:25
the bullock and of the ram, the *r* Lev 9:19

**RUN**
whose branches *r* over the wall Gen 49:22
his flesh *r* with his issue Lev 15:3
or if it *r* beyond the time of her Lev 15:25
lest angry fellows *r* upon thee Judg 18:25
some shall *r* before his chariots 1Sa 8:11
*r* to the camp to thy brethren 1Sa 17:17
he might *r* to Beth-lehem his city 1Sa 20:6
And he said unto his lad, *R* 1Sa 20:36
and fifty men to *r* before him 2Sa 15:1
the son of Zadok, Let me now *r* 2Sa 18:19
I pray thee, also *r* after Cushi 2Sa 18:22
Joab said, Wherefore wilt thou *r* 2Sa 18:22
But howsoever, said he, let me *r* 2Sa 18:23
And he said unto him, *R* 2Sa 18:23
by thee I have *r* through a troop 2Sa 22:30
and fifty men to *r* before him 1Kin 1:5
that I may *r* to the man of God, 2Kin 4:22
*R* now, I pray thee, to meet her, 2Kin 4:26
I will *r* after him, and take 2Kin 5:20
For the eyes of the LORD *r* to 2Chr 16:9
by thee I have *r* through a troop Ps 18:29
as a strong man to *r* a race Ps 19:5
as waters which *r* continually Ps 58:7
They *r* and prepare themselves Ps 59:4
waters to *r* down like rivers Ps 78:16
valleys, which *r* among the hills Ps 104:10
I will *r* the way of thy Ps 119:32
Rivers of waters *r* down mine eyes Ps 119:136
For their feet *r* to evil, and make Prov 1:16
All the rivers *r* into the sea Eccl 1:7
Draw me, we will *r* after thee Song 1:4
of locusts shall he *r* upon them Is 33:4
they shall *r*, and not be weary Is 40:31
that knew not thee shall *r* unto Is 55:5
Their feet *r* to evil, and they Is 59:7
*R* ye to and fro through the Jer 5:1
our eyes may *r* down with tears Jer 9:18
If thou hast *r* with the footmen, Jer 12:5
*r* down with tears, because the Jer 13:17
Let mine eyes *r* down with tears Jer 14:17
*r* to and fro by the hedges Jer 49:3
suddenly make him *r* away from her Jer 49:19
them suddenly *r* away from her Jer 50:44
One post shall *r* to meet another, Jer 51:31
let tears *r* down like a river day Lam 2:18
neither shall thy tears *r* down Eze 24:16
cause their rivers to *r* like oil Eze 32:14
many shall *r* to and fro, and Dan 12:4
and as horsemen, so shall they *r* Joel 2:4
They shall *r* like mighty men Joel 2:7
They shall *r* to and fro in the Joel 2:9
they shall *r* upon the wall, they Joel 2:9
But let judgment *r* down as waters Amos 5:24
Shall horses *r* upon the rock Amos 6:12
even to the east, they shall *r* to Amos 8:12
they shall *r* like the lightnings Nah 2:4
that he may *r* that readeth it Hab 2:2
ye *r* every man unto his own house Hag 1:9
And said unto him, *R*, speak to Zec 2:4
the eyes of the LORD, which *r* to Zec 4:10
did *r* to bring his disciples word Mt 28:8
they which *r* in a race *r* all 1Cor 9:24
So *r*, that ye may obtain 1Cor 9:24
I therefore so *r*, not as 1Cor 9:26
any means I should *r*, or had *r* Gal 2:2
Ye did *r* well Gal 5:7
Christ, that I have not *r* in vain Phil 2:16
let us *r* with patience the race Heb 12:1
ye *r* not with them to the same 1Pet 4:4

**RUNNEST**
and when thou *r*, thou shalt not Prov 4:12

**RUNNETH**
to the river than *r* to Ahava Ezr 8:15
He *r* upon him, even on his neck, Job 15:26
he *r* upon me like a giant Job 16:14
my cup *r* over Ps 23:5
his word *r* very swiftly Ps 147:15
the righteous *r* into it, and is Prov 18:10
mine eye *r* down with water, Lam 1:16
Mine eye *r* down with rivers of Lam 3:48
bottles break, and the wine *r* out Mt 9:17
Then she *r*, and cometh to Simon Jn 20:2
that willeth, nor of him that *r* Rom 9:16

**RUNNING**
in an earthen vessel over *r* water Lev 14:5
that was killed over the *r* water Lev 14:6
in an earthen vessel over *r* water Lev 14:50
the slain bird, and in the *r* water Lev 14:51
of the bird, and with the *r* water Lev 14:52
When any man hath a *r* issue out Lev 15:2
and bathe his flesh in *r* water Lev 15:13
is a leper, or hath a *r* issue Lev 22:4
*r* water shall be put thereto in a Num 19:17
looked, and behold a man *r* alone 2Sa 18:24
watchman saw another man *r* 2Sa 18:26
said, Behold another man *r* alone 2Sa 18:26
Me thinketh the *r* of the foremost 2Sa 18:27
the *r* of Ahimaaz the son of Zadok 2Sa 18:27
when Naaman saw him *r* after him 2Kin 5:21
heard the noise of the people *r* 2Chr 23:12
*r* waters out of thine own well Prov 5:15
that be swift in *r* to mischief Prov 6:18
as the *r* to and fro of locusts Is 33:4
rivers *r* round about his plants Eze 31:4
amazed, and *r* to him saluted him Mk 9:15
that the people came *r* together Mk 9:25
into the way, there came one *r* Mk 10:17
*r* over, shall men give into your Lk 6:38
*r* under a certain island which is Acts 27:16
of many horses *r* to battle Rev 9:9

**RUSH**
Can the *r* grow up without mire Job 8:11
Israel head and tail, branch and *r* Is 9:14
The nations shall *r* like the Is 17:13
the head or tail, branch or *r* Is 19:15

**RUSHED**
*r* forward, and stood in the Judg 9:44
in wait hasted, and *r* upon Gibeah Judg 20:37
they *r* with one accord into the Acts 19:29

**RUSHES**
shall be grass with reeds and *r* Is 35:7

**RUSHETH**
as the horse *r* into the battle Jer 8:6

**RUSHING**
to the *r* of nations Is 17:12
that make a *r* like the *r* of Is 17:12
rush like the *r* of many waters Is 17:13
at the *r* of his chariots, and at Jer 47:3
behind me a voice of a great *r* Eze 3:12
them, and a noise of a great *r* Eze 3:13
from heaven as of a *r* mighty wind Acts 2:2

**RUST**
*r* doth corrupt, and where thieves Mt 6:19
neither moth nor *r* doth corrupt Mt 6:20
the *r* of them shall be a witness Jas 5:3

**RUTH** (*rooth*) *Wife of Boaz; an ancestor of Jesus.*
Orpah, and the name of the other *R* Ruth 1:4
but *R* clave unto her Ruth 1:14
*R* said, Intreat me not to leave Ruth 1:16
*R* the Moabitess, her daughter in Ruth 1:22
*R* the Moabitess said unto Naomi, Ruth 2:2
Then said Boaz unto *R*, Hearest Ruth 2:8
*R* the Moabitess said, He said Ruth 2:21
Naomi said unto *R* her daughter in Ruth 2:22
answered, I am *R* thine handmaid Ruth 3:9
buy it also of *R* the Moabitess Ruth 4:5
Moreover *R* the Moabitess, the Ruth 4:10
So Boaz took *R*, and she was his Ruth 4:13
and Booz begat Obed of *R* Mt 1:5

# S

**SABACHTHANI**
voice, saying, Eli, Eli, lama *s* Mt 27:46
voice, saying, Eloi, Eloi, lama *s* Mk 15:34

**SABAOTH** (*sab'-a-oth*) *Title meaning "Lord of Hosts."*
the Lord of *S* had left us a seed Rom 9:29
into the ears of the Lord of *S* Jas 5:4

**SABBATH**
rest of the holy *s* unto the LORD Ex 16:23
for to day is a *s* unto the LORD Ex 16:25
the seventh day, which is the *s* Ex 16:26
the LORD hath given you the *s* Ex 16:29
Remember the *s* day, to keep it Ex 20:8
day is the *s* of the LORD thy God Ex 20:10
the LORD blessed the *s* day Ex 20:11
Ye shall keep the *s* therefore Ex 31:14
in the seventh is the *s* of rest Ex 31:15
doeth any work in the *s* day Ex 31:15
of Israel shall keep the *s* Ex 31:16
to observe the *s* throughout their Ex 31:16
holy day, a *s* of rest to the LORD Ex 35:2
your habitations upon the *s* day Ex 35:3
It shall be a *s* of rest unto you, Lev 16:31
the seventh day is the *s* of rest Lev 23:3
it is the *s* of the LORD in all Lev 23:3
on the morrow after the *s* the Lev 23:11
you from the morrow after the *s* Lev 23:15
*s* shall ye number fifty days Lev 23:16
of the month, shall ye have a *s* Lev 23:24
It shall be unto you a *s* of rest Lev 23:32
even, shall ye celebrate your *s* Lev 23:32
on the first day shall be a *s* Lev 23:39
and on the eighth day shall be a *s* Lev 23:39
Every *s* he shall set it in order Lev 24:8
the land keep a *s* unto the LORD Lev 25:2
be a *s* of rest unto the land Lev 25:4
unto the land, a *s* for the LORD Lev 25:4
the *s* of the land shall be meat Lev 25:6
gathered sticks upon the *s* day Num 15:32
on the *s* day two lambs of the Num 28:9
is the burnt offering of every *s* Num 28:10
Keep the *s* day to sanctify it, as Deut 5:12
day is the *s* of the LORD thy God Deut 5:14
commanded thee to keep the *s* day Deut 5:15
it is neither new moon, nor *s* 2Kin 4:23
of you that enter in on the *s* 2Kin 11:5
of all you that go forth on the *s* 2Kin 11:7
men that were to come in on the *s* 2Kin 11:9
them that should go out on the *s* 2Kin 11:9
the covert for the *s* that they 2Kin 16:18
shewbread, to prepare it every *s* 1Chr 9:32
part of you entering on the *s* 2Chr 23:4
men that were to come in on the *s* 2Chr 23:8
them that were to go out on the *s* 2Chr 23:8
as she lay desolate she kept *s* 2Chr 36:21
madest known unto them thy holy *s* Neh 9:14
any victuals on the *s* day to sell Neh 10:31
would not buy it of them on the *s* Neh 10:31
treading winepresses on the *s* Neh 13:15
into Jerusalem on the *s* day Neh 13:15
sold on the *s* unto the children Neh 13:16
that ye do, and profane the *s* day Neh 13:17
upon Israel by profaning the *s* Neh 13:18
began to be dark before the *s* Neh 13:19
not be opened till after the *s* Neh 13:19
burden be brought in on the *s* day Neh 13:19
forth came they no more on the *s* Neh 13:21
the gates, to sanctify the *s* day Neh 13:22
A Psalm or Song for the *s* day Ps 92:*t*
that keepeth the *s* from polluting Is 56:2
keepeth the *s* from polluting it Is 56:6
turn away thy foot from the *s* Is 58:13
call the *s* a delight, the holy of Is 58:13
from one *s* to another, shall all Is 66:23
and bear no burden on the *s* day Jer 17:21
out of your houses on the *s* day Jer 17:22
any work, but hallow ye the *s* day Jer 17:22
gates of this city on the *s* day Jer 17:24
but hallow the *s* day Jer 17:24
unto me to hallow the *s* day Jer 17:27
gates of Jerusalem on the *s* day Jer 17:27
but on the *s* it shall be opened, Eze 46:1
offer unto the LORD in the *s* day Eze 46:4
offerings, as he did on the *s* day Eze 46:12
and the *s*, that we may set forth Amos 8:5
on the *s* day through the corn Mt 12:1
not lawful to do upon the *s* day Mt 12:2
how that on the *s* days the Mt 12:5
in the temple profane the *s* Mt 12:5
of man is Lord even of the *s* day Mt 12:8
it lawful to heal on the *s* days Mt 12:10
it fall into a pit on the *s* day Mt 12:11
lawful to do well on the *s* days Mt 12:12

the winter, neither on the s day Mt 24:20
In the end of the s, as it began Mt 28:1
straightway on the s day he Mk 1:21
the corn fields on the s day Mk 2:23
why do they on the s day that Mk 2:24
The s was made for man Mk 2:27
and not man for the s Mk 2:27
Son of man is Lord also of the s Mk 2:28
he would heal him on the s day Mk 3:2
lawful to do good on the s days Mk 3:4
when the s day was come, he began Mk 6:2
that is, the day before the s Mk 15:42
And when the s was past, Mary Mk 16:1
into the synagogue on the s day Lk 4:16
and taught them on the s days Lk 4:31
on the second s after the first Lk 6:1
is not lawful to do on the s days Lk 6:2
Son of man is Lord also of the s Lk 6:5
it came to pass also on another s Lk 6:6
he would heal on the s day Lk 6:7
lawful on the s days to do good Lk 6:9
in one of the synagogues on the s Lk 13:10
Jesus had healed on the s day Lk 13:14
and be healed, and not on the s day Lk 13:14
s loose his ox or his ass from Lk 13:15
from this bond on the s day Lk 13:16
to eat bread on the s day Lk 14:1
Is it lawful to heal on the s day Lk 14:3
pull him out on the s day Lk 14:5
the preparation, and the s drew on Lk 23:54
rested the s day according to the Lk 23:56
and on the same day was the s Jn 5:9
that was cured, It is the s day Jn 5:10
done these things on the s day Jn 5:16
he not only had broken the s Jn 5:18
ye on the s day circumcise a man Jn 7:22
If a man on the s day receive Jn 7:23
man every whit whole on the s day Jn 7:23
it was the s day when Jesus made Jn 9:14
because he keepeth not the s day Jn 9:16
upon the cross on the s day Jn 19:31
(for that s day was an high day,) Jn 19:31
from Jerusalem a s day's journey Acts 1:12
into the synagogue on the s day Acts 13:14
which are read every s day Acts 13:27
be preached to them the next s Acts 13:42
the next s day came almost the Acts 13:44
in the synagogues every s day Acts 15:21
on the s we went out of the city Acts 16:13
three s days reasoned with them Acts 17:2
reasoned in the synagogue every s Acts 18:4
of the new moon, or of the s days Col 2:16

**SABBATHS**
Verily my s ye shall keep Ex 31:13
and his father, and keep my s Lev 19:3
Ye shall keep my s, and reverence Lev 19:30
seven s shall be complete Lev 23:15
Beside the s of the LORD, and Lev 23:38
number seven s of years unto thee Lev 25:8
the space of the seven s of years Lev 25:8
Ye shall keep my s, and reverence Lev 26:2
Then shall the land enjoy her s Lev 26:34
the land rest, and enjoy her s Lev 26:34
because it did not rest in your s Lev 26:35
of them, and shall enjoy her s Lev 26:43
sacrifices unto the LORD in the s 1Chr 23:31
morning and evening, on the s 2Chr 2:4
commandment of Moses, on the s 2Chr 8:13
and the burnt offerings for the s 2Chr 31:3
until the land had enjoyed her s 2Chr 36:21
burnt offering, of the s, of the Neh 10:33
the new moons and s, the calling Is 1:13
unto the eunuchs that keep my s Is 56:4
saw her, and did mock at her s Lam 1:7
s to be forgotten in Zion, and Lam 2:6
Moreover also I gave them my s Eze 20:12
my s they greatly polluted Eze 20:13
in my statutes, but polluted my s Eze 20:16
And hallow my s Eze 20:20
they polluted my s Eze 20:21
my statutes, and had polluted my s Eze 20:24
things, and hast profaned my s Eze 22:8
and have hid their eyes from my s Eze 22:26
same day, and have profaned my s Eze 23:38
and they shall hallow my s Eze 44:24
and in the new moons, and in the s Eze 45:17
gate before the LORD in the s Eze 46:3
days, her new moons, and her s Hos 2:11

**SABEANS** (*sab-e'-uns*)
*1. Descendants of Sheba.*
the *S* fell upon them, and took Job 1:15
and they shall sell them to the *S* Joel 3:8
*2. Descendants of Seba.*
of Ethiopia and of the *S*, men of Is 45:14
brought *S* from the wilderness Eze 23:42

**SABTA** (*sab'-tah*) See SABTAH. *A son of Cush.*
Seba, and Havilah, and S, and Raamah 1Chr 1:9

**SABTAH** (*sab'-tah*) See SABTA. *Same as Sabta.*
Seba, and Havilah, and *S* Gen 10:7

**SABTECA** See SABTECHAH.

**SABTECHA** (*sab'-te-kah*) See SABTECHAH. *A son of Cush.*
and Sabta, and Raamah, and *S* 1Chr 1:9

**SABTECHAH** (*sab'-te-kah*) See SABTECHA. *Same as Sabtecha.*
and Sabtah, and Raamah, and *S* Gen 10:7

**SACAR** (*sa'-kar*) See SHARAR.
*1. Father of Ahiham.*
Ahiam the son of *S* the Hararite 1Chr 11:35
*2. A sanctuary servant.*
*S* the fourth, and Nethaneel the 1Chr 26:4

**SACHIA** See SHACHIA.

**SACK**
every man's money into his s Gen 42:25
as one of them opened his s to Gen 42:27
and, lo, it is even in my s Gen 42:28
bundle of money was in his s Gen 42:35
money was in the mouth of his s Gen 43:21
every man his s to the ground Gen 44:11
and opened every man his s Gen 44:11
the cup was found in Benjamin's s Gen 44:12
wood, or raiment, or skin, or s Lev 11:32

**SACKBUT**
of the cornet, flute, harp, s Dan 3:5
of the cornet, flute, harp, s Dan 3:7
of the cornet, flute, harp, s Dan 3:10
of the cornet, flute, harp, s Dan 3:15

**SACKCLOTH**
put s upon his loins, and mourned Gen 37:34
your clothes, and gird you with s 2Sa 3:31
the daughter of Aiah took s 2Sa 21:10
put s on our loins, and ropes upon 1Kin 20:31
So they girded s on their loins 1Kin 20:32
put s upon his flesh, and fasted, 1Kin 21:27
his flesh, and fasted, and lay in s 1Kin 21:27
he had s within upon his flesh 2Kin 6:30
and covered himself with s 2Kin 19:1
of the priests, covered with s 2Kin 19:2
of Israel, who were clothed in s 1Chr 21:16
put on s with ashes, and went out Est 4:1
the king's gate clothed with s Est 4:2
and many lay in s and ashes Est 4:3
and to take away his s from him Est 4:4
I have sewed s upon my skin Job 16:15
thou hast put off my s, and girded Ps 30:11
they were sick, my clothing was s Ps 35:13
I made s also my garment Ps 69:11
of a stomacher a girding of s Is 3:24
they shall gird themselves with s Is 15:3
loose the s from off thy loins, Is 20:2
to baldness, and to girding with s Is 22:12
bare, and gird s upon your loins Is 32:11
and covered himself with s Is 37:1
of the priests covered with s Is 37:2
and I make s their covering Is 50:3
head as a bulrush, and to spread s Is 58:5
For this gird you with s, lament Jer 4:8
of my people, gird thee with s Jer 6:26
be cuttings, and upon the loins s Jer 48:37
of Rabbah, gird you with s Jer 49:3
have girded themselves with s Lam 2:10
shall also gird themselves with s Eze 7:18
for thee, and gird them with s Eze 27:31
supplications, with fasting, and s Dan 9:3
like a virgin girded with s for Joel 1:8
come, lie all night in s, ye Joel 1:13
I will bring up s upon all loins Amos 8:10
and proclaimed a fast, and put on s Jonah 3:5
from him, and covered him with s Jonah 3:6
man and beast be covered with s Jonah 3:8
would have repented long ago in s Mt 11:21
while ago repented, sitting in s Lk 10:13
the sun became black as s of hair Rev 6:12
and threescore days, clothed in s Rev 11:3

**SACKCLOTHES**
assembled with fasting, and with s Neh 9:1

**SACK'S**
behold, it was in his s mouth Gen 42:27
every man's money in his s mouth Gen 44:1
in the s mouth of the youngest, Gen 44:2

**SACKS**
to fill their s with corn Gen 42:25
to pass as they emptied their s Gen 42:35
again in the mouth of your s Gen 43:12
in our s at the first time are we Gen 43:18
to the inn, that we opened our s Gen 43:21
tell who put our money in our s Gen 43:22
hath given you treasure in your s Gen 43:23
Fill the men's s with food Gen 44:1
took old s upon their asses, and Josh 9:4

**SACKS'**
which we found in our s mouths Gen 44:8

**SACRIFICE**
Jacob offered s upon the mount Gen 31:54
that we may s to the LORD our God Ex 3:18
and s unto the LORD our God Ex 5:3
saying, Let us go and s to our God Ex 5:8
Let us go and do s to the LORD Ex 5:17
that they may do s unto the LORD Ex 8:8
s to your God in the land Ex 8:25
for we shall s the abomination of Ex 8:26
shall we s the abomination of the Ex 8:26
s to the LORD our God, as he Ex 8:27
that ye may s to the LORD your Ex 8:28
the people go to s to the LORD Ex 8:29
that we may s unto the LORD our Ex 10:25
It is the s of the LORD'S Ex 12:27
therefore I s to the LORD all Ex 13:15
shalt s thereon thy burnt Ex 20:24
blood of my s with leavened bread Ex 23:18
of my s remain until the morning Ex 23:18
of the s of their peace offerings Ex 29:28
incense thereon, nor burnt s Ex 30:9
do s unto their gods, and one call Ex 34:15
call thee, and thou eat of his s Ex 34:15
the blood of my s with leaven Ex 34:25
neither shall the s of the feast Ex 34:25
offering be a burnt s of the herd Lev 1:3
all on the altar, to be a burnt s Lev 1:9
or of the goats, for a burnt s Lev 1:10
it is a burnt s, an offering made Lev 1:13
if the burnt s for his offering Lev 1:14
it is a burnt s, an offering made Lev 1:17
oblation be a s of peace offering Lev 3:1
he shall offer of the s of the Lev 3:3
it on the altar upon the burnt s Lev 3:5
if his offering for a s of peace Lev 3:6
he shall offer of the s of the Lev 3:9
of the s of peace offerings Lev 4:10
as the fat of the s of peace Lev 4:26
from off the s of peace offerings Lev 4:31
from the s of the peace offerings Lev 4:35
law of the s of peace offerings Lev 7:11
the s of thanksgiving unleavened Lev 7:12
leavened bread with the s of Lev 7:13
the flesh of the s of his peace Lev 7:15
But if the s of his offering be a Lev 7:16
same day that he offereth his s Lev 7:16
remainder of the flesh of the s Lev 7:17
if any of the flesh of the s of Lev 7:18
flesh of the s of peace offerings Lev 7:20
flesh of the s of peace offerings Lev 7:21
He that offereth the s of his Lev 7:29
of the s of his peace offerings Lev 7:29
of the s of the peace offerings Lev 7:37
it was a burnt s for a sweet Lev 8:21
offerings, to s before the LORD Lev 9:4
beside the burnt s of the morning Lev 9:17
and the ram for a s of peace Lev 9:18
offereth a burnt offering or s Lev 17:8
And if ye offer a s of peace Lev 19:5
whosoever offereth a s of peace Lev 22:21
when ye will offer a s of Lev 22:29
Then ye shall s one kid of the Lev 23:19
year for a s of peace offerings Lev 23:19
offering, and a meat offering, a s Lev 23:37
do not offer a s unto the LORD Lev 27:11
a s of peace offerings unto the Num 6:17
the s of the peace offerings Num 6:18
for a s of peace offerings, two Num 7:17
for a s of peace offerings, two Num 7:23
for a s of peace offerings, two Num 7:29
for a s of peace offerings, two Num 7:35
for a s of peace offerings, two Num 7:41
for a s of peace offerings, two Num 7:47
for a s of peace offerings, two Num 7:53
for a s of peace offerings, two Num 7:59
for a s of peace offerings, two Num 7:65
for a s of peace offerings, two Num 7:71
for a s of peace offerings, two Num 7:77
for a s of peace offerings, two Num 7:83
all the oxen for the s of the Num 7:88
or a s in performing a vow, or in Num 15:3
with the burnt offering or s Num 15:5
or for a s in performing a vow, Num 15:8
a s made by fire unto the LORD, Num 15:25
and, lo, he stood by his burnt s Num 23:6
a s made by fire unto the LORD Num 28:6
a s made by fire, of a sweet Num 28:8
a s made by fire unto the LORD Num 28:13
But ye shall offer a s made by Num 28:19
the meat of the s made by fire Num 28:24
a s made by fire unto the LORD Num 29:6
a s made by fire, of a sweet Num 29:13
a s made by fire, of a sweet Num 29:36
thou shalt not s it unto the LORD Deut 15:21
Thou shalt therefore s the Deut 16:2
Thou mayest not s the passover Deut 16:5
there thou shalt s the passover Deut 16:6
Thou shalt not s unto the LORD Deut 17:1
people, from them that offer a s Deut 18:3
whole burnt s upon thine altar Deut 33:10
not for burnt offering, nor for s Josh 22:26
offer a burnt s with the wood of Judg 6:26
a great s unto Dagon their god Judg 16:23
to s unto the LORD of hosts in 1Sa 1:3
offer unto the LORD the yearly s 1Sa 1:21
was, that, when any man offered s 1Sa 2:13
her husband to offer the yearly s 1Sa 2:19
Wherefore kick ye at my s 1Sa 2:29
with s nor offering for ever 1Sa 3:14
for there is a s of the people to 1Sa 9:12
come, because he doth bless the s 1Sa 9:13
and to s sacrifices of peace 1Sa 10:8
to s unto the LORD thy God 1Sa 15:15
to s unto the LORD thy God in 1Sa 15:21
Behold, to obey is better than s 1Sa 15:22
say, I am come to s to the LORD 1Sa 16:2
And call Jesse to the s, and I will 1Sa 16:3
I am come to s unto the LORD 1Sa 16:5
and come with me to the s 1Sa 16:5
his sons, and called them to the s 1Sa 16:5
for there is a yearly s there for 1Sa 20:6
our family hath a s in the city 1Sa 20:29
behold, here be oxen for burnt s 2Sa 24:22
king went to Gibeon to s there 1Kin 3:4
offered s before the LORD 1Kin 8:62
Solomon offered a s of peace 1Kin 8:63
If this people go up to do s in 1Kin 12:27
of the offering of the evening s 1Kin 18:29
water, and pour it on the burnt s 1Kin 18:33

of the offering of the evening *s* ... 1Kin 18:36
fell, and consumed the burnt *s* ... 1Kin 18:38
offering nor *s* unto other gods ... 2Kin 5:17
I have a great *s* to do to Baal ... 2Kin 10:19
as yet the people did *s* and burnt ... 2Kin 14:4
offering, and the king's burnt *s* ... 2Kin 16:15
and all the blood of the *s* ... 2Kin 16:15
nor serve them, nor *s* to them ... 2Kin 17:35
worship, and to him shall ye do *s* ... 2Kin 17:36
save only to burn *s* before him ... 2Chr 2:6
Solomon offered a *s* of twenty ... 2Chr 7:5
place to myself for an house of *s* ... 2Chr 7:12
to *s* unto the LORD God of their ... 2Chr 11:16
them, therefore will I *s* to them ... 2Chr 28:23
did *s* still in the high places ... 2Chr 33:17
we do *s* unto him since the days ... Ezr 4:2
sat astonied until the evening *s* ... Ezr 9:4
at the evening *s* I arose up from ... Ezr 9:5
will they *s* ... Neh 4:2
offerings, and accept thy burnt *s* ... Ps 20:3
*S* and offering thou didst not ... Ps 40:6
have made a covenant with me by *s* ... Ps 50:5
For thou desirest not *s* ... Ps 51:16
I will freely *s* unto thee ... Ps 54:6
let them *s* the sacrifices of ... Ps 107:22
to thee the *s* of thanksgiving ... Ps 116:17
bind the *s* with cords, even unto ... Ps 118:27
up of my hands as the evening *s* ... Ps 141:2
The *s* of the wicked is an ... Prov 15:8
acceptable to the LORD than *s* ... Prov 21:3
The *s* of the wicked is ... Prov 21:27
hear, than to give the *s* of fools ... Eccl 5:1
LORD in that day, and shall do *s* ... Is 19:21
for the LORD hath a *s* in Bozrah ... Is 34:6
wentest thou up to offer *s* ... Is 57:7
of them that shall bring the *s* of ... Jer 33:11
offerings, and to do *s* continually ... Jer 33:18
a *s* in the north country by the ... Jer 46:10
every side to my *s* ... Eze 39:17
that I do *s* for you ... Eze 39:17
even a great *s* upon the mountains ... Eze 39:17
of my *s* which I have sacrificed ... Eze 39:19
slew the burnt offering and the *s* ... Eze 40:42
the *s* for the people, and they ... Eze 44:11
shall boil the *s* of the people ... Eze 46:24
by him the daily *s* was taken away ... Dan 8:11
*s* by reason of transgression ... Dan 8:12
the vision concerning the daily *s* ... Dan 8:13
of the week he shall cause the *s* ... Dan 9:27
and shall take away the daily *s* ... Dan 11:31
the daily *s* shall be taken away ... Dan 12:11
without a prince, and without a *s* ... Hos 3:4
They *s* upon the tops of the ... Hos 4:13
whores, and they *s* with harlots ... Hos 4:14
For I desired mercy, and not *s* ... Hos 6:6
They *s* flesh for the sacrifices ... Hos 8:13
they *s* bullocks in Gilgal ... Hos 12:11
the men that *s* kiss the calves ... Hos 13:2
offer a *s* of thanksgiving with ... Amos 4:5
offered a *s* unto the LORD, and ... Jonah 1:16
But I will *s* unto thee with the ... Jonah 2:9
Therefore they *s* unto their net ... Hab 1:16
for the LORD hath prepared a *s* ... Zeph 1:7
pass in the day of the LORD's *s* ... Zeph 1:8
and all they that *s* shall come ... Zec 14:21
And if ye offer the blind for *s* ... Mal 1:8
I will have mercy, and not *s* ... Mt 9:13
I will have mercy, and not *s* ... Mt 12:7
every *s* shall be salted with salt ... Mk 9:49
to offer a *s* according to that ... Lk 2:24
offered *s* unto the idol, and ... Acts 7:41
would have done *s* with the people ... Acts 14:13
they had not done *s* unto them ... Acts 14:18
ye present your bodies a living *s* ... Rom 12:1
that are offered in *s* unto idols ... 1Cor 8:4
in *s* to idols is any thing ... 1Cor 10:19
the things which the Gentiles *s* ... 1Cor 10:20
they *s* to devils, and not to God ... 1Cor 10:20
This is offered in *s* unto idols ... 1Cor 10:28
a *s* to God for a sweetsmelling ... Eph 5:2
and if I be offered upon the *s* ... Phil 2:17
a *s* acceptable, wellpleasing to ... Phil 4:18
those high priests, to offer up *s* ... Heb 7:27
put away sin by the *s* of himself ... Heb 9:26
into the world, he saith, *S* ... Heb 10:5
Above when he said, *S* and offering ... Heb 10:8
offered one *s* for sins for ever ... Heb 10:12
remaineth no more *s* for sins ... Heb 10:26
God a more excellent *s* than Cain ... Heb 11:4
*s* of praise to God continually ... Heb 13:15

## SACRIFICED

*s* peace offerings of oxen unto ... Ex 24:5
have *s* thereunto, and said, These ... Ex 32:8
They *s* unto devils, not to God ... Deut 32:17
the LORD, and *s* peace offerings ... Josh 8:31
they *s* there unto the LORD ... Judg 2:5
came, and said to the man that *s* ... 1Sa 2:15
*s* sacrifices the same day unto ... 1Sa 6:15
there they *s* sacrifices of peace ... 1Sa 11:15
six paces, he *s* oxen and fatlings ... 2Sa 6:13
Only the people *s* in high places ... 1Kin 3:2
only he *s* and burnt incense in ... 1Kin 3:3
incense and *s* unto their gods ... 1Kin 11:8
the people still *s* and burnt ... 2Kin 12:3
the people *s* and burnt incense ... 2Kin 15:4
the people *s* and burned incense ... 2Kin 15:35
And he *s* and burnt incense in the ... 2Kin 16:4
which *s* for them in the houses of ... 2Kin 17:32
the Jebusite, then he *s* there ... 1Chr 21:28
they *s* sacrifices unto the LORD, ... 1Chr 29:21
*s* sheep and oxen, which could not ... 2Chr 5:6
He *s* also and burnt incense in the ... 2Chr 28:4
For he *s* unto the gods of ... 2Chr 28:23
*s* thereon peace offerings and ... 2Chr 33:16
for Amon *s* unto all the carved ... 2Chr 33:22
of them that had *s* unto them ... 2Chr 34:4
they *s* their sons and their ... Ps 106:37
whom they *s* unto the idols of ... Ps 106:38
these hast thou *s* unto them to be ... Eze 16:20
sacrifice which I have *s* for you ... Eze 39:19
they *s* unto Baalim, and burned ... Hos 11:2
Christ our passover is *s* for us ... 1Cor 5:7
to eat things *s* unto idols ... Rev 2:14
and to eat things *s* unto idols ... Rev 2:20

## SACRIFICEDST

which thou *s* the first day at ... Deut 16:4

## SACRIFICES

offered *s* unto the God of his ... Gen 46:1
said, Thou must give us also *s* ... Ex 10:25
a burnt offering and *s* for God ... Ex 18:12
of the *s* of your peace offerings ... Lev 7:32
the *s* of their peace offerings ... Lev 7:34
of the *s* of the LORD made by fire ... Lev 10:13
the *s* of peace offerings of the ... Lev 10:14
of Israel may bring their *s* ... Lev 17:5
no more offer their *s* unto devils ... Lev 17:7
and over the *s* of your peace ... Num 10:10
people unto the *s* of their gods ... Num 25:2
and my bread for my *s* made by fire ... Num 28:2
your burnt offerings, and your *s* ... Deut 12:6
your burnt offerings, and your *s* ... Deut 12:11
the blood of thy *s* shall be ... Deut 12:27
Which did eat the fat of their *s* ... Deut 32:38
shall offer *s* of righteousness ... Deut 33:19
the *s* of the LORD God of Israel ... Josh 13:14
burnt offerings, and with our *s* ... Josh 22:27
for burnt offerings, nor for *s* ... Josh 22:28
for meat offerings, or for *s* ... Josh 22:29
sacrificed *s* the same day unto ... 1Sa 6:15
to sacrifice *s* of peace offerings ... 1Sa 10:8
there they sacrificed *s* of peace ... 1Sa 11:15
delight in burnt offerings and *s* ... 1Sa 15:22
from Giloh, while he offered *s* ... 2Sa 15:12
And when they went in to offer *s* ... 2Kin 10:24
and they offered burnt *s* and peace ... 1Chr 16:1
to offer all burnt *s* unto the ... 1Chr 23:31
they sacrificed *s* unto the LORD ... 1Chr 29:21
*s* in abundance for all Israel ... 1Chr 29:21
the burnt offering and the *s* ... 2Chr 7:1
people offered *s* before the LORD ... 2Chr 7:4
morning and every evening burnt *s* .. 2Chr 13:11
the LORD, come near and bring *s* .. 2Chr 29:31
And the congregation brought in *s* ... 2Chr 29:31
the place where they offered *s* ... Ezr 6:3
That they may offer *s* of sweet ... Ezr 6:10
that day they offered great *s* ... Neh 12:43
Offer the *s* of righteousness, and ... Ps 4:5
offer in his tabernacle *s* of joy ... Ps 27:6
for thy *s* or thy burnt offerings ... Ps 50:8
The *s* of God are a broken spirit ... Ps 51:17
with the *s* of righteousness ... Ps 51:19
unto thee burnt *s* of fatlings ... Ps 66:15
and ate the *s* of the dead ... Ps 106:28
sacrifice the *s* of thanksgiving ... Ps 107:22
an house full of *s* with strife ... Prov 17:1
the multitude of your *s* unto me ... Is 1:11
let them kill *s* ... Is 29:1
hast thou honoured me with thy *s* ... Is 43:23
filled me with the fat of thy *s* ... Is 43:24
their *s* shall be accepted upon ... Is 56:7
nor your *s* sweet unto me ... Jer 6:20
your burnt offerings unto your *s* ... Jer 7:21
concerning burnt offerings or *s* ... Jer 7:22
bringing burnt offerings, and *s* ... Jer 17:26
bringing *s* of praise, unto the ... Jer 17:26
and they offered there their *s* ... Eze 20:28
whereupon they slew their *s* ... Eze 40:41
be ashamed because of their *s* ... Hos 4:19
flesh for the *s* of mine offerings ... Hos 8:13
their *s* shall be unto them as the ... Hos 9:4
bring your *s* every morning, and ... Amos 4:4
Have ye offered unto me *s* ... Amos 5:25
all whole burnt offerings and *s* ... Mk 12:33
Pilate had mingled with their *s* ... Lk 13:1
*s* by the space of forty years in ... Acts 7:42
of the *s* partakers of the altar ... 1Cor 10:18
offer both gifts and *s* for sins ... Heb 5:1
is ordained to offer gifts and *s* ... Heb 8:3
were offered both gifts and *s* ... Heb 9:9
with better *s* than these ... Heb 9:23
can never with those *s* which they ... Heb 10:1
But in those *s* there is a ... Heb 10:3
*s* for sin thou hast had no ... Heb 10:6
and offering oftentimes the same *s* ... Heb 10:11
for with such *s* God is well ... Heb 13:16
to offer up spiritual *s*, ... 1Pet 2:5

## SACRIFICETH

He that *s* unto any god, save unto ... Ex 22:20
to him that *s*, and to him that ... Eccl 9:2
*s*, and to him that *s* not ... Eccl 9:2
that *s* in gardens, and burneth ... Is 65:3
he that *s* a lamb, as if he cut ... Is 66:3
*s* unto the Lord a corrupt thing ... Mal 1:14

## SACRIFICING

*s* sheep and oxen, that could not ... 1Kin 8:5
*s* unto the calves that he had ... 1Kin 12:32

## SACRILEGE

idols, dost thou commit *s* ... Rom 2:22

## SAD

them, and, behold, they were *s* ... Gen 40:6
and her countenance was no more *s* ... 1Sa 1:18
unto him, Why is thy spirit so *s* ... 1Kin 21:5
been beforetime *s* in his presence ... Neh 2:1
unto me, Why is thy countenance *s* ... Neh 2:2
should not my countenance be *s* ... Neh 2:3
made the heart of the righteous *s* ... Eze 13:22
*s*, whom I have not made *s* ... Eze 13:22
hypocrites, of a *s* countenance ... Mt 6:16
he was *s* at that saying, and went ... Mk 10:22
to another, as ye walk, and are *s* ... Lk 24:17

## SADDLE

what *s* soever he rideth upon that ... Lev 15:9
I will *s* me an ass, that I may ... 2Sa 19:26
said unto his sons, *S* me the ass ... 1Kin 13:13
to his sons, saying, *S* me the ass ... 1Kin 13:27

## SADDLED

*s* his ass, and took two of his ... Gen 22:3
*s* his ass, and went with the ... Num 22:21
there were with him two asses *s* ... Judg 19:10
met him, with a couple of asses *s* ... 2Sa 16:1
he *s* his ass, and arose, and gat ... 2Sa 17:23
*s* his ass, and went to Gath to ... 1Kin 2:40
So they *s* him the ass ... 1Kin 13:13
that he *s* for him the ass, to wit ... 1Kin 13:23
And they *s* him ... 1Kin 13:27
Then she *s* an ass, and said to her ... 2Kin 4:24

## SADDUCEES (*sad'-du-sees*) *Members of a Jewish sect.*

*S* come to his baptism, he said ... Mt 3:7
Pharisees also with the *S* came ... Mt 16:1
of the Pharisees and of the *S* ... Mt 16:6
of the Pharisees and of the *S* ... Mt 16:11
of the Pharisees and of the *S* ... Mt 16:12
The same day came to him the *S* ... Mt 22:23
that he had put the *S* to silence ... Mt 22:34
Then come unto him the *S*, which ... Mk 12:18
Then came to him certain of the *S* ... Lk 20:27
captain of the temple, and the *S* ... Acts 4:1
him, (which is the sect of the *S* ... Acts 5:17
that the one part were *S*, and the ... Acts 23.6
between the Pharisees and the *S* ... Acts 23:7
For the *S* say that there is no ... Acts 23:8

## SADLY

Wherefore look ye so *s* to day ... Gen 40:7

## SADNESS

for by the *s* of the countenance ... Eccl 7:3

## SADOC (*sa'-dok*) *Father of Achim; an ancestor of Jesus.*

And Azor begat *S* ... Mt 1:14
and *S* begat Achim ... Mt 1:14

## SAFE

on every side, and ye dwelled *s* ... 1Sa 12:11
said, Is the young man Absalom *s* ... 2Sa 18:29
Cushi, Is the young man Absalom *s* ... 2Sa 18:32
Their houses are *s* from fear ... Job 21:9
Hold thou me up, and I shall be *s* ... Ps 119:117
runneth into it, and is *s* ... Prov 18:10
his trust in the LORD shall be *s* ... Prov 29:25
prey, and shall carry it away *s* ... Is 5:29
and they shall be *s* in their land ... Eze 34:27
because he hath received him *s* ... Lk 15:27
bring him *s* unto Felix the ... Acts 23:24
that they escaped all *s* to land ... Acts 27:44
not grievous, but for you it is *s* ... Phil 3:1

## SAFEGUARD

but with me thou shalt be in *s* ... 1Sa 22:23

## SAFELY

the full, and dwell in your land *s* ... Lev 26:5
And Judah and Israel dwelt *s* ... 1Kin 4:25
And he led them on *s*, so that they ... Ps 78:53
hearkeneth unto me shall dwell *s* ... Prov 1:33
Then shalt thou walk in thy way *s* ... Prov 3:23
her husband doth *s* trust in her ... Prov 31:11
He pursued them, and passed *s* ... Is 41:3
be saved, and Israel shall dwell *s* ... Jer 23:6
and I will cause them to dwell *s* ... Jer 32:37
saved, and Jerusalem shall dwell *s* ... Jer 33:16
And they shall dwell *s* therein ... Eze 28:26
they shall dwell *s* in the ... Eze 34:25
but they shall dwell *s*, and none ... Eze 34:28
and they shall dwell *s* all of them ... Eze 38:8
that are at rest, that dwell *s* ... Eze 38:11
my people of Israel dwelleth *s* ... Eze 38:14
when they dwelt *s* in their land ... Eze 39:26
and will make them to lie down *s* ... Hos 2:18
Jerusalem shall be *s* inhabited ... Zec 14:11
take him, and lead him away *s* ... Mk 14:44
the jailer to keep them *s* ... Acts 16:23

## SAFETY

ye shall dwell in the land in *s* ... Lev 25:18
your fill, and dwell therein in *s* ... Lev 25:19
about, so that ye dwell in *s* ... Deut 12:10
the LORD shall dwell in *s* by him ... Deut 33:12
then shall dwell in *s* alone ... Deut 33:28
I was not in *s*, neither had I ... Job 3:26
His children are far from *s* ... Job 5:4
which mourn may be exalted to *s* ... Job 5:11
and thou shalt take thy rest in *s* ... Job 11:18
Though it be given him to be in *s* ... Job 24:23
LORD, only makest me dwell in *s* ... Ps 4:8

I will set him in s from him that ... Ps 12:5
An horse is a vain thing for s ... Ps 33:17
of counsellors there is s ... Prov 11:14
but s is of the LORD ... Prov 21:31
of counsellors there is s ... Prov 24:6
and the needy shall lie down in s ... Is 14:30
truly found we shut with all s ... Acts 5:23
when they shall say, Peace and s ... 1Th 5:3

**SAFFRON**
Spikenard and s ... Song 4:14

**SAID** See PREFACE.

**SAIDST**
Why s thou, She is my sister ... Gen 12:19
how s thou, She is my sister ... Gen 26:9
Isaac, the LORD which s unto me ... Gen 32:9
And thou s, I will surely do thee ... Gen 32:12
thou s unto thy servants, Bring ... Gen 44:21
thou s unto thy servants, Except ... Gen 44:23
s unto them, I will multiply your ... Ex 32:13
now thy mouth, wherewith thou s ... Judg 9:38
thou s unto me, The word that I ... 1Kin 2:42
this to be right, that thou s ... Job 35:2
For thou s, What advantage will ... Job 35:3
When thou s, Seek ye my face ... Ps 27:8
in vision to thy holy one, and s ... Ps 89:19
And thou s, I shall be a lady for ... Is 47:7
yet s thou not, There is no hope ... Is 57:10
and thou s, I will not transgress ... Jer 2:20
but thou s, There is no hope ... Jer 2:25
but thou s, I will not hear ... Jer 22:21
thou s, Fear not ... Lam 3:57
Because thou s, Aha, against my ... Eze 25:3
and thy judges of whom thou s ... Hos 13:10
in that s thou truly ... Jn 4:18

**SAIL**
mast, they could not spread the s ... Is 33:23
thou spreadest forth to be thy s ... Eze 27:7
as he was about to s into Syria ... Acts 20:3
had determined to s by Ephesus ... Acts 20:16
that we should s into Italy ... Acts 27:1
meaning to s by the coasts of ... Acts 27:2
into the quicksands, strake s ... Acts 27:17
thee all them that s with thee ... Acts 27:24

**SAILED**
But as they s he fell asleep ... Lk 8:23
and from thence they s to Cyprus ... Acts 13:4
thence s to Antioch, from whence ... Acts 14:26
took Mark, and s unto Cyprus ... Acts 15:39
s thence into Syria, and with him ... Acts 18:18
And he s from Ephesus ... Acts 18:21
we s away from Philippi after the ... Acts 20:6
s unto Assos, there intending to ... Acts 20:13
we s thence, and came the next day ... Acts 20:15
s into Syria, and landed at Tyre ... Acts 21:3
we s under Cyprus, because the ... Acts 27:4
when we had s over the sea of ... Acts 27:5
when we had s slowly many days, ... Acts 27:7
we s under Crete, over against ... Acts 27:7
thence, they s close by Crete ... Acts 27:13

**SAILING**
finding a ship s over unto ... Acts 21:2
a ship of Alexandria s into Italy ... Acts 27:6
when s was now dangerous, because ... Acts 27:9

**SAILORS**
and all the company in ships, and s ... Rev 18:17

**SAINT**
camp, and Aaron the s of the LORD ... Ps 106:16
Then I heard one s speaking ... Dan 8:13
another s said unto that certain ... Dan 8:13
unto that certain s which spake ... Dan 8:13
Salute every s in Christ Jesus ... Phil 4:21

**SAINTS**
he came with ten thousands of s ... Deut 33:2
all his s are in thy hand ... Deut 33:3
He will keep the feet of his s ... 1Sa 2:9
let thy s rejoice in goodness ... 2Chr 6:41
to which of the s wilt thou turn ... Job 5:1
he putteth no trust in his s ... Job 15:15
But to the s that are in the ... Ps 16:3
O ye s of his, and give thanks at ... Ps 30:4
O love the LORD, all ye his s ... Ps 31:23
O fear the LORD, ye his s ... Ps 34:9
judgment, and forsaketh not his s ... Ps 37:28
Gather my s together unto me ... Ps 50:5
for it is good before thy s ... Ps 52:9
the flesh of thy s unto the ... Ps 79:2
unto his people, and to his s ... Ps 85:8
also in the congregation of the s ... Ps 89:5
feared in the assembly of the s ... Ps 89:7
he preserveth the souls of his s ... Ps 97:10
of the LORD is the death of his s ... Ps 116:15
and let thy s shout for joy ... Ps 132:9
her s shall shout aloud for joy ... Ps 132:16
and thy s shall bless thee ... Ps 145:10
people, the praise of all his s ... Ps 148:14
praise in the congregation of s ... Ps 149:1
Let the s be joyful in glory ... Ps 149:5
this honour have all his s ... Ps 149:9
and preserveth the way of his s ... Prov 2:8
But the s of the most High shall ... Dan 7:18
the same horn made war with the s ... Dan 7:21
given to the s of the most High ... Dan 7:22
that the s possessed the kingdom ... Dan 7:22
wear out the s of the most High ... Dan 7:25
people of the s of the most High ... Dan 7:27
God, and is faithful with the s ... Hos 11:12
come, and all the s with thee ... Zec 14:5
bodies of the s which slept arose ... Mt 27:52
hath done to thy s at Jerusalem ... Acts 9:13
to the s which dwelt at Lydda ... Acts 9:32
up, and when he had called the s ... Acts 9:41
many of the s did I shut up in ... Acts 26:10
beloved of God, called to be s ... Rom 1:7
s according to the will of God ... Rom 8:27
to the necessity of s ... Rom 12:13
Jerusalem to minister unto the s ... Rom 15:25
the poor s which are at Jerusalem ... Rom 15:26
may be accepted of the s ... Rom 15:31
her in the Lord, as becometh s ... Rom 16:2
all the s which are with them ... Rom 16:15
in Christ Jesus, called to be s ... 1Cor 1:2
the unjust, and not before the s ... 1Cor 6:1
that the s shall judge the world ... 1Cor 6:2
as in all churches of the s ... 1Cor 14:33
the collection for the s, as I ... 1Cor 16:1
to the ministry of the s,) ... 1Cor 16:15
with all the s which are in all ... 2Cor 1:1
of the ministering to the s ... 2Cor 8:4
touching the ministering to the s ... 2Cor 9:1
only supplieth the want of the s ... 2Cor 9:12
All the s salute you ... 2Cor 13:13
to the s which are at Ephesus, and ... Eph 1:1
Jesus, and love unto all the s ... Eph 1:15
glory of his inheritance in the s ... Eph 1:18
but fellowcitizens with the s ... Eph 2:19
am less than the least of all s ... Eph 3:8
with all s what is the breadth ... Eph 3:18
For the perfecting of the s ... Eph 4:12
named among you, as becometh s ... Eph 5:3
and supplication for all s ... Eph 6:18
to all the s in Christ Jesus ... Phil 1:1
All the s salute you, chiefly ... Phil 4:22
To the s and faithful brethren in ... Col 1:2
love which ye have to all the s ... Col 1:4
the inheritance of the s in light ... Col 1:12
but now is made manifest to his s ... Col 1:26
Lord Jesus Christ with all his s ... 1Th 3:13
come to be glorified in his s ... 2Th 1:10
the Lord Jesus, and toward all s ... Philem 5
of the s are refreshed by thee ... Philem 7
that ye have ministered to the s ... Heb 6:10
the rule over you, and all the s ... Heb 13:24
was once delivered unto the s ... Jude 3
with ten thousands of his s ... Jude 14
which are the prayers of s ... Rev 5:8
it with the prayers of all s upon ... Rev 8:3
came with the prayers of the s ... Rev 8:4
the prophets, and to the s ... Rev 11:18
unto him to make war with the s ... Rev 13:7
patience and the faith of the s ... Rev 13:10
Here is the patience of the s ... Rev 14:12
true are thy ways, thou King of s ... Rev 15:3
For they have shed the blood of s ... Rev 16:6
drunken with the blood of the s ... Rev 17:6
the blood of prophets, and of s ... Rev 18:24
linen is the righteousness of s ... Rev 19:8
compassed the camp of the s about ... Rev 20:9

**SAINTS'**
if she have washed the s feet ... 1Ti 5:10

**SAITH** See PREFACE.

**SAKE**
cursed is the ground for thy s ... Gen 3:17
the ground any more for man's s ... Gen 8:21
it may be well with me for thy s ... Gen 12:13
he entreated Abram well for her s ... Gen 12:16
I will not do it for forty's s ... Gen 18:29
not destroy it for twenty's s ... Gen 18:31
I will not destroy it for ten's s ... Gen 18:32
they will slay me for my wife's s ... Gen 20:11
seed for my servant Abraham's s ... Gen 26:24
LORD hath blessed me for thy s ... Gen 30:27
Egyptian's house for Joseph's s ... Gen 39:5
to the Egyptians for Israel's s ... Ex 18:8
let him go free for his eye's s ... Ex 21:26
let him go free for his tooth's s ... Ex 21:27
unto him, Enviest thou for my s ... Num 11:29
was zealous for my s among them ... Num 25:11
day of the plague for Peor's s ... Num 25:18
his people for his great name's s ... 1Sa 12:22
to destroy the city for my s ... 1Sa 23:10
kingdom for his people Israel's s ... 2Sa 5:12
For thy word's s, and according to ... 2Sa 7:21
him kindness for Jonathan's s ... 2Sa 9:1
for Jonathan thy father's s ... 2Sa 9:7
for my s with the young man ... 2Sa 18:5
of a far country for thy name's s ... 1Kin 8:41
do it for David thy father's s ... 1Kin 11:12
thy son for David my servant's s ... 1Kin 11:13
for Jerusalem's s which I have ... 1Kin 11:13
tribe for my servant David's s ... 1Kin 11:32
and for Jerusalem's s ... 1Kin 11:32
his life for David my servant's s ... 1Kin 11:34
Nevertheless for David's s did ... 1Kin 15:4
Judah for David his servant's s ... 2Kin 8:19
city, to save it, for mine own s ... 2Kin 19:34
s, and for my servant David's s ... 2Kin 19:34
defend this city for mine own s ... 2Kin 20:6
and for my servant David's s ... 2Kin 20:6
O LORD, for thy servant's s ... 1Chr 17:19
country for thy great name's s ... 2Chr 6:32
for thy great mercies' s thou ... Neh 9:31
the children's s of mine own body ... Job 19:17
oh save me for thy mercies' s ... Ps 6:4
of righteousness for his name's s ... Ps 23:3
thou me for thy goodness' s ... Ps 25:7
For thy name's s, O LORD, pardon ... Ps 25:11
for thy name's s lead me, and ... Ps 31:3
save me for thy mercies' s ... Ps 31:16
for thy s are we killed all the ... Ps 44:22
and redeem us for thy mercies' s ... Ps 44:26
GOD of hosts, be ashamed for my s ... Ps 69:6
seek thee be confounded for my s ... Ps 69:6
Because for thy s I have borne ... Ps 69:7
away our sins, for thy name's s ... Ps 79:9
he saved them for his name's s ... Ps 106:8
O GOD the Lord, for thy name's s ... Ps 109:21
thy mercy, and for thy truth's s ... Ps 115:1
For thy servant David's s turn ... Ps 132:10
me, O LORD, for thy name's s ... Ps 143:11
for thy righteousness' s bring my ... Ps 143:11
city to save it for mine own s ... Is 37:35
and for my servant David's s ... Is 37:35
pleased for his righteousness' s ... Is 42:21
For your s I have sent to Babylon ... Is 43:14
thy transgressions for mine own s ... Is 43:25
For Jacob my servant's s, and ... Is 45:4
For my name's s will I defer mine ... Is 48:9
own s, even for mine own s ... Is 48:11
against thee shall fall for thy s ... Is 54:15
For Zion's s will I not hold my ... Is 62:1
for Jerusalem's s I will not rest ... Is 62:1
Return for thy servants' s ... Is 63:17
that cast you out for my name's s ... Is 66:5
us, do thou it for thy name's s ... Jer 14:7
Do not abhor us, for thy name's s ... Jer 14:21
know that for thy s I have ... Jer 15:15
But I wrought for my name's s ... Eze 20:9
But I wrought for my name's s ... Eze 20:14
hand, and wrought for my name's s ... Eze 20:22
wrought with you for my name's s ... Eze 20:44
but for mine holy name's s ... Eze 36:22
is desolate, for the Lord's s ... Dan 9:17
defer not, for thine own s ... Dan 9:19
for I know that for my s this ... Jonah 1:12
for your s be plowed as a field ... Mic 3:12
persecuted for righteousness' s ... Mt 5:10
against you falsely, for my s ... Mt 5:11
governors and kings for my s ... Mt 10:18
hated of all men for my name's s ... Mt 10:22
his life for my s shall find it ... Mt 10:39
put him in prison for Herodias' s ... Mt 14:3
nevertheless for the oath's s ... Mt 14:9
his life for my s shall find it ... Mt 16:25
for the kingdom of heaven's s ... Mt 19:12
or lands, for my name's s ... Mt 19:29
of all nations for my name's s ... Mt 24:9
but for the elect's s those days ... Mt 24:22
ariseth for the word's s ... Mk 4:17
him in prison for Herodias' s ... Mk 6:17
yet for his oath's s, and for ... Mk 6:26
shall lose his life for my s ... Mk 8:35
or children, or lands, for my s ... Mk 10:29
before rulers and kings for my s ... Mk 13:9
hated of all men for my name's s ... Mk 13:13
but for the elect's s, whom he ... Mk 13:20
as evil, for the Son of man's s ... Lk 6:22
will lose his life for my s ... Lk 9:24
for the kingdom of God's s ... Lk 18:29
kings and rulers for my name's s ... Lk 21:12
hated of all men for my name's s ... Lk 21:17
they came not for Jesus' s only ... Jn 12:9
I will lay down my life for thy s ... Jn 13:37
thou lay down thy life for my s ... Jn 13:38
believe me for the very works' s ... Jn 14:11
they do unto you for my name's s ... Jn 15:21
he must suffer for my name's s ... Acts 9:16
For which hope's s, king Agrippa, ... Acts 26:7
was not written for his s alone ... Rom 4:23
For thy s we are killed all the ... Rom 8:36
wrath, but also for conscience s ... Rom 13:5
for the Lord Jesus Christ's s ... Rom 15:30
We are fools for Christ's s ... 1Cor 4:10
And this I do for the gospel's s ... 1Cor 9:23
no question for conscience s ... 1Cor 10:25
no question for conscience s ... 1Cor 10:27
eat not for his s that shewed it ... 1Cor 10:28
shewed it, and for conscience s ... 1Cor 10:28
your servants for Jesus' s ... 2Cor 4:5
delivered unto death for Jesus' s ... 2Cor 4:11
in distresses for Christ's s ... 2Cor 12:10
for Christ's s hath forgiven you ... Eph 4:32
him, but also to suffer for his s ... Phil 1:29
in my flesh for his body's s ... Col 1:24
For which things' s the wrath of ... Col 3:6
men we were among you for your s ... 1Th 1:5
highly in love for their work's s ... 1Th 5:13
a little wine for thy stomach's s ... 1Ti 5:23
ought not, for filthy lucre's s ... Titus 1:11
Yet for love's s I rather beseech ... Philem 9
ordinance of man for the Lord's s ... 1Pet 2:13
if ye suffer for righteousness' s ... 1Pet 3:14
are forgiven you for his name's s ... 1Jn 2:12
For the truth's s, which dwelleth ... 2Jn 2
for his name's s they went forth ... 3Jn 7
and for my name's s hast laboured ... Rev 2:3

**SAKES**
spare all the place for their s ... Gen 18:26
But I will for their s remember ... Lev 26:45
LORD was angry with me for your s ... Deut 1:37
LORD was wroth with me for your s ... Deut 3:26
LORD was angry with me for your s ... Deut 4:21
Be favourable unto them for our s ... Judg 21:22
s that the hand of the LORD is ... Ruth 1:13
he reproved kings for their s ... 1Chr 16:21

for their *s* therefore return thou ... Ps 7:7
he reproved kings for their *s* ... Ps 105:14
went ill with Moses for their *s* ... Ps 106:32
For my brethren and companions' *s* ... Ps 122:8
so will I do for my servants' *s* ... Is 65:8
I do not this for your *s*, O house ... Eze 36:22
Not for your *s* do I this, saith ... Eze 36:32
but for their *s* that shall make ... Dan 2:30
rebuke the devourer for your *s* ... Mal 3:11
for their *s* which sat with him, ... Mk 6:26
I am glad for your *s* that I was ... Jn 11:15
not because of me, but for your *s* ... Jn 12:30
for their *s* I sanctify myself, ... Jn 17:19
they are enemies for your *s* ... Rom 11:28
are beloved for the fathers' *s* ... Rom 11:28
myself and to Apollos for your *s* ... 1Cor 4:6
saith he it altogether for our *s* ... 1Cor 9:10
For our *s*, no doubt, this is ... 1Cor 9:10
for your *s* forgave I it in the ... 2Cor 2:10
For all things are for your *s* ... 2Cor 4:15
yet for your *s* he became poor, ... 2Cor 8:9
we joy for your *s* before our God ... 1Th 3:9
all things for the elect's *s* ... 2Ti 2:10

**SAKIA** See SHACHIA.

**SALA** (*sa'-lah*) See SALAH. *Father of Heber; an ancestor of Jesus.*
of Heber, which was the son of *S* ... Lk 3:35

**SALAH** (*sa'-lah*) See SALA. *Son of Arphaxad.*
And Arphaxad begat *S* ... Gen 10:24
and *S* begat Eber ... Gen 10:24
five and thirty years, and begat *S* ... Gen 11:12
after he begat *S* four hundred ... Gen 11:13
*S* lived thirty years, and begat ... Gen 11:14
*S* lived after he begat Eber four ... Gen 11:15

**SALAMIS** (*sal'-a-mis*) *A city on Cyprus.*
And when they were at *S*, they ... Acts 13:5

**SALATHIEL** (*sa-la'-the-el*) See SHEALTIEL. *Descendant of Jehoiakim; an ancestor of Jesus.*
Assir, *S* his son, ... 1Chr 3:17
to Babylon, Jechonias begat *S* ... Mt 1:12
and *S* begat Zorobabel ... Mt 1:12
Zorobabel, which was the son of *S* ... Lk 3:27

**SALCAH** (*sal'-kah*) See SALCHAH. *A city in Gad.*
reigned in mount Hermon, and in *S* ... Josh 12:5
Hermon, and all Bashan unto *S* ... Josh 13:11

**SALCHAH** (*sal'-kah*) See SALCAH. *Same as Salcah.*
all Gilead, and all Bashan, unto *S* ... Deut 3:10
in the land of Bashan unto *S* ... 1Chr 5:11

**SALE**
count the years of the *s* thereof ... Lev 25:27
the price of his *s* shall be ... Lev 25:50
cometh of the *s* of his patrimony ... Deut 18:8

**SALECAH** See SALCHAH.

**SALEM** (*sa'-lem*) See JERUSALEM. *The city of Melchizedek.*
king of *S* brought forth bread ... Gen 14:18
In *S* also is his tabernacle, and ... Ps 76:2
For this Melchisedec, king of *S* ... Heb 7:1
and after that also King of *S* ... Heb 7:2

**SALIM** (*sa'-lim*) *A city near Aenon.*
was baptizing in Aenon near to *S* ... Jn 3:23

**SALLAI** (*sal'-lahee*) See SALLU.
*1. An exile.*
And after him Gabbai, *S*, nine ... Neh 11:8
*2. A priest with Zerubbabel.*
Of *S*, Kallai ... Neh 12:20

**SALLU** (*sal'-lu*) See SALLAI. *A priest with Zerubbabel.*
*S*, Amok, Hilkiah, Jedaiah ... Neh 12:7
*S* the son of Meshullam, the son ... 1Chr 9:7
*S* the son of Meshullam, the son ... Neh 11:7

**SALMA** (*sal'-mah*) See SALMON, ZALMA.
*1. Father of Boaz.*
And Nahshon begat *S*, and *S* ... 1Chr 2:11
*2. A son of Caleb.*
begat Salma, and *S* begat Boaz, ... 1Chr 2:11
*S* the father of Beth-lehem, ... 1Chr 2:51
The sons of *S* ... 1Chr 2:54

**SALMI** See SALMA.

**SALMON** (*sal'-mon*) See SALMA.
*1. Father of Boaz.*
begat Nahshon, and Nahshon begat *S* Ruth 4:20
*S* begat Boaz, and Boaz begat Obed, ... Ruth 4:21
and Naasson begat *S* ... Mt 1:4
And *S* begat Booz of Rachab ... Mt 1:5
of Booz, which was the son of *S* ... Lk 3:32
*2. A mountain near Shechem.*
in it, it was white as snow in *S* ... Ps 68:14

**SALMONE** (*sal-mo'-ne*) *A promontory on Crete.*
under Crete, over against *S* ... Acts 27:7

**SALOME** (*sa-lo'-me*) *A woman follower of Jesus.*
James the less and of Joses, and *S* ... Mk 15:40
and Mary the mother of James, and *S* .. Mk 16:1

**SALT**
of Siddim, which is the *S* Sea ... Gen 14:3
him, and she became a pillar of *s* ... Gen 19:26
offering shalt thou season with *s* ... Lev 2:13
*s* of the covenant of thy God to ... Lev 2:13
offerings thou shalt offer *s* ... Lev 2:13
it is a covenant of *s* for ever ... Num 18:19
coast of the *s* sea eastward ... Num 34:3
out of it shall be at the *s* sea ... Num 34:12
sea of the plain, even the *s* sea ... Deut 3:17
land thereof is brimstone, and *s* ... Deut 29:23
sea of the plain, even the *s* sea ... Josh 3:16
even the *s* sea on the east, the ... Josh 12:3
was from the shore of the *s* sea ... Josh 15:2
And the east border was the *s* sea ... Josh 15:5
And Nibshan, and the city of *S* ... Josh 15:62
were at the north bay of the *s* ... Josh 18:19
down the city, and sowed it with *s* ... Judg 9:45
of the Syrians in the valley of *s* ... 2Sa 8:13
me a new cruse, and put *s* therein ... 2Kin 2:20
waters, and cast the *s* in there ... 2Kin 2:21
in the valley of *s* ten thousand ... 2Kin 14:7
the valley of *s* eighteen thousand ... 1Chr 18:12
and to his sons by a covenant of *s* ... 2Chr 13:5
and went to the valley of *s* ... 2Chr 25:11
of the God of heaven, wheat, *s* ... Ezr 6:9
*s* without prescribing how much ... Ezr 7:22
is unsavoury be eaten without *s* ... Job 6:6
the valley of *s* twelve thousand ... Ps 60:*t*
in the wilderness, in a *s* land ... Jer 17:6
priests shall cast *s* upon them ... Eze 43:24
they shall be given to *s* ... Eze 47:11
Ye are the *s* of the earth ... Mt 5:13
but if the *s* have lost his savour ... Mt 5:13
sacrifice shall be salted with *s* ... Mk 9:49
*S* is good ... Mk 9:50
but if the *s* have lost his ... Mk 9:50
Have *s* in yourselves, and have ... Mk 9:50
*S* is good ... Lk 14:34
but if the *s* have lost his savour ... Lk 14:34
alway with grace, seasoned with *s* ... Col 4:6
no fountain both yield *s* water ... Jas 3:12

**SALTED**
thou wast not *s* at all, nor ... Eze 16:4
savour, wherewith shall it be *s* ... Mt 5:13
every one shall be *s* with fire ... Mk 9:49
sacrifice shall be *s* with salt ... Mk 9:49

**SALTNESS**
but if the salt have lost his *s* ... Mk 9:50

**SALTPITS**
the breeding of nettles, and *s* ... Zeph 2:9

**SALU** (*sa'-lu*) *Father of Zimri.*
woman, was Zimri, the son of *S* ... Num 25:14

**SALUTATION**
what manner of *s* this should be ... Lk 1:29
Elisabeth heard the *s* of Mary ... Lk 1:41
of thy *s* sounded in mine ears ... Lk 1:44
The *s* of me Paul with mine own ... 1Cor 16:21
The *s* by the hand of me Paul ... Col 4:18
The *s* of Paul with mine own hand, ... 2Th 3:17

**SALUTATIONS**
love *s* in the marketplaces, ... Mk 12:38

**SALUTE**
And they will *s* thee, and give thee ... 1Sa 10:4
to meet him, that he might *s* him ... 1Sa 13:10
of the wilderness to *s* our master ... 1Sa 25:14
to *s* him, and to bless him, ... 2Sa 8:10
if thou meet any man, *s* him not ... 2Kin 4:29
and if any *s* thee, answer him not ... 2Kin 4:29
we go down to *s* the children of ... 2Kin 10:13
if ye *s* your brethren only, what ... Mt 5:47
when ye come into an house, *s* it ... Mt 10:12
And began to *s* him, Hail, King of ... Mk 15:18
and *s* no man by the way ... Lk 10:4
came unto Caesarea to *s* Festus ... Acts 25:13
*S* my wellbeloved Epaenetus, who ... Rom 16:5
*S* Andronicus and Junia, my kinsmen. Rom 16:7
*S* Urbane, our helper in Christ, ... Rom 16:9
*S* Apelles approved in Christ ... Rom 16:10
*S* them which are of Aristobulus' ... Rom 16:10
*S* Herodion my kinsman ... Rom 16:11
*S* Tryphena and Tryphosa, who ... Rom 16:12
*S* the beloved Persis, which ... Rom 16:12
*S* Rufus chosen in the Lord, and ... Rom 16:13
*S* Asyncritus, Phlegon, Hermas, ... Rom 16:14
*S* Philologus, and Julia, Nereus, ... Rom 16:15
*S* one another with an holy kiss ... Rom 16:16
The churches of Christ *s* you ... Rom 16:16
and Sosipater, my kinsmen, *s* you ... Rom 16:21
this epistle, *s* you in the Lord ... Rom 16:22
The churches of Asia *s* you ... 1Cor 16:19
Priscilla *s* you much in the Lord, ... 1Cor 16:19
All the saints *s* you ... 2Cor 13:13
*S* every saint in Christ Jesus ... Phil 4:21
All the saints *s* you, chiefly ... Phil 4:22
*S* the brethren which are in ... Col 4:15
*S* Prisca and Aquila, and the ... 2Ti 4:19
All that are with me *s* thee ... Titus 3:15
There *s* thee Epaphras, my ... Philem 23
*S* all them that have the rule ... Heb 13:24
They of Italy *s* you ... Heb 13:24
Our friends *s* thee ... 3Jn 14

**SALUTED**
unto the house of Micah, and *s* him .. Judg 18:15
army, and came and *s* his brethren ... 1Sa 17:22
near to the people, he *s* them ... 1Sa 30:21
he *s* him, and said to him, Is ... 2Kin 10:15
amazed, and running to him *s* him ... Mk 9:15
of Zacharias, and *s* Elisabeth ... Lk 1:40
*s* the church, he went down to ... Acts 18:22
*s* the brethren, and abode with ... Acts 21:7
And when he had *s* them, he ... Acts 21:19

**SALUTETH**
and of the whole church, *s* you ... Rom 16:23
the chamberlain of the city *s* you ... Rom 16:23
my fellowprisoner *s* you, and ... Col 4:10
*s* you, always labouring fervently ... Col 4:12
elected together with you, *s* you ... 1Pet 5:13

**SALVATION**
I have waited for thy *s*, O LORD ... Gen 49:18
see the *s* of the LORD, which he ... Ex 14:13
and song, and he is become my *s* ... Ex 15:2
esteemed the Rock of his *s* ... Deut 32:15
because I rejoice in thy *s* ... 1Sa 2:1
the LORD hath wrought *s* in Israel ... 1Sa 11:13
wrought this great *s* in Israel ... 1Sa 14:45
wrought a great *s* for all Israel ... 1Sa 19:5
is my shield, and the horn of my *s* ... 2Sa 22:3
also given me the shield of thy *s* ... 2Sa 22:36
be the God of the rock of my *s* ... 2Sa 22:47
He is the tower of *s* for his king ... 2Sa 22:51
for this is all my *s*, and all my ... 2Sa 23:5
shew forth from day to day his *s* ... 1Chr 16:23
say ye, Save us, O God of our *s* ... 1Chr 16:35
O LORD God, be clothed with *s* ... 2Chr 6:41
see the *s* of the LORD with you, O ... 2Chr 20:17
He also shall be my *s* ... Job 13:16
*S* belongeth unto the LORD ... Ps 3:8
I will rejoice in thy *s* ... Ps 9:14
my heart shall rejoice in thy *s* ... Ps 13:5
Oh that the *s* of Israel were come ... Ps 14:7
my buckler, and the horn of my *s* ... Ps 18:2
also given me the shield of thy *s* ... Ps 18:35
and let the God of my *s* be exalted ... Ps 18:46
We will rejoice in thy *s*, and in ... Ps 20:5
in thy *s* how greatly shall he ... Ps 21:1
His glory is great in thy *s* ... Ps 21:5
from the God of his *s* ... Ps 24:5
for thou art the God of my *s* ... Ps 25:5
The LORD is my light and my *s* ... Ps 27:1
neither forsake me, O God of my *s* ... Ps 27:9
say unto my soul, I am thy *s* ... Ps 35:3
it shall rejoice in his *s* ... Ps 35:9
But the *s* of the righteous is of ... Ps 37:39
haste to help me, O Lord my *s* ... Ps 38:22
thy faithfulness and thy *s* ... Ps 40:10
as love thy *s* say continually ... Ps 40:16
aright will I shew the *s* of God ... Ps 50:23
Restore unto me the joy of thy *s* ... Ps 51:12
O God, thou God of my *s* ... Ps 51:14
Oh that the *s* of Israel were come ... Ps 53:6
from him cometh my *s* ... Ps 62:1
He only is my rock and my *s* ... Ps 62:2
He only is my rock and my *s* ... Ps 62:6
In God is my *s* and my glory ... Ps 62:7
thou answer us, O God of our *s* ... Ps 65:5
benefits, even the God of our *s* ... Ps 68:19
that is our God is the God of *s* ... Ps 68:20
hear me, in the truth of thy *s* ... Ps 69:13
let thy *s*, O God, set me up on ... Ps 69:29
as love thy *s* say continually ... Ps 70:4
and thy *s* all the day ... Ps 71:15
working *s* in the midst of the ... Ps 74:12
in God, and trusted not in his *s* ... Ps 78:22
Help us, O God of our *s*, for the ... Ps 79:9
Turn us, O God of our *s*, and cause ... Ps 85:4
mercy, O LORD, and grant us thy *s* ... Ps 85:7
Surely his *s* is nigh them that ... Ps 85:9
O lord God of my *s*, I have cried ... Ps 88:1
my God, and the rock of my *s* ... Ps 89:26
I satisfy him, and shew him my *s* ... Ps 91:16
joyful noise to the rock of our *s* ... Ps 95:1
shew forth his *s* from day to day ... Ps 96:2
The LORD hath made known his *s* ... Ps 98:2
earth have seen the *s* of our God ... Ps 98:3
O visit me with thy *s* ... Ps 106:4
I will take the cup of *s*, and call ... Ps 116:13
and song, and is become my *s* ... Ps 118:14
*s* is in the tabernacles of the ... Ps 118:15
hast heard me, and art become my *s* ... Ps 118:21
also unto me, O LORD, even thy *s* ... Ps 119:41
My soul fainteth for thy *s* ... Ps 119:81
Mine eyes fail for thy *s*, and for ... Ps 119:123
*S* is far from the wicked ... Ps 119:155
LORD, I have hoped for thy *s* ... Ps 119:166
I have longed for thy *s*, O LORD ... Ps 119:174
also clothe her priests with *s* ... Ps 132:16
the Lord, the strength of my *s* ... Ps 140:7
It is he that giveth *s* unto kings ... Ps 144:10
he will beautify the meek with *s* ... Ps 149:4
Behold, God is my *s* ... Is 12:2
he also is become my *s* ... Is 12:2
draw water out of the wells of *s* ... Is 12:3
hast forgotten the God of thy *s* ... Is 17:10
will be glad and rejoice in his *s* ... Is 25:9
*s* will God appoint for walls and ... Is 26:1
our *s* also in the time of trouble ... Is 33:2
of thy times, and strength of *s* ... Is 33:6
open, and let them bring forth *s* ... Is 45:8
in the LORD with an everlasting *s* ... Is 45:17
far off, and my *s* shall not tarry ... Is 46:13
I will place *s* in Zion for Israel ... Is 46:13
that thou mayest be my *s* unto the ... Is 49:6
in a day of *s* have I helped thee ... Is 49:8
my *s* is gone forth, and mine arms ... Is 51:5

but my s shall be for ever, and my Is 51:6
ever, and my s from generation to Is 51:8
of good, that publisheth s Is 52:7
earth shall see the s of our God Is 52:10
for my s is near to come, and my Is 56:1
for s, but it is far off from us Is 59:11
his arm brought s unto him Is 59:16
an helmet of s upon his head Is 59:17
but thou shalt call thy walls S Is 60:18
clothed me with the garments of s Is 61:10
the s thereof as a lamp that Is 62:1
of Zion, Behold, thy s cometh Is 62:11
mine own arm brought s unto me Is 63:5
Truly in vain is s hoped for from Jer 3:23
LORD our God is the s of Israel Jer 3:23
wait for the s of the LORD Lam 3:26
S is of the LORD Jonah 2:9
I will wait for the God of my s Mic 7:7
thine horses and thy chariots of s Hab 3:8
forth for the s of thy people Hab 3:13
even for s with thine anointed Hab 3:13
I will joy in the God of my s Hab 3:18
he is just, and having s Zec 9:9
hath raised up an horn of s for Lk 1:69
To give knowledge of s unto his Lk 1:77
For mine eyes have seen thy s Lk 2:30
all flesh shall see the s of God Lk 3:6
This day is s come to this house, Lk 19:9
for s is of the Jews Jn 4:22
Neither is there s in any other Acts 4:12
to you is the word of this s sent Acts 13:26
for s unto the ends of the earth Acts 13:47
which shew unto us the way of s Acts 16:17
that the s of God is sent unto Acts 28:28
s to every one that believeth Rom 1:16
mouth confession is made unto s Rom 10:10
fall s is come unto the Gentiles Rom 11:11
for now is our s nearer than when Rom 13:11
it is for your consolation and s 2Cor 1:6
it is for your consolation and s 2Cor 1:6
in the day of s have I succoured 2Cor 6:2
behold, now is the day of s 2Cor 6:2
to s not to be repented of 2Cor 7:10
of truth, the gospel of your s Eph 1:13
And take the helmet of s, and the Eph 6:17
turn to my s through your prayer Phil 1:19
of perdition, but to you of s Phil 1:28
work out your own s with fear Phil 2:12
and for an helmet, the hope of s 1Th 5:8
but to obtain s by our Lord Jesus 1Th 5:9
the beginning chosen you to s 2Th 2:13
s which is in Christ Jesus with 2Ti 2:10
unto s through faith which is in 2Ti 3:15
s hath appeared to all men Titus 2:11
for them who shall be heirs of s Heb 1:14
escape, if we neglect so great s Heb 2:3
s perfect through sufferings Heb 2:10
s unto all them that obey him Heb 5:9
you, and things that accompany s Heb 6:9
second time without sin unto s Heb 9:28
s ready to be revealed in the 1Pet 1:5
faith, even the s of your souls 1Pet 1:9
Of which s the prophets have 1Pet 1:10
longsuffering of our Lord is s 2Pet 3:15
to write unto you of the common s Jude 3
S to our God which sitteth upon Rev 7:10
saying in heaven, Now is come s Rev 12:10
S, and glory, and honour, and power, Rev 19:1

**SAMARIA** (*sa-ma'-re-ah*) See SAMARITAN.
*1. A city in Ephraim.*
he bought the hill S of Shemer 1Kin 16:24
of Shemer, owner of the hill, S 1Kin 16:24
his fathers, and was buried in S 1Kin 16:28
reigned over Israel in S twenty 1Kin 16:29
of Baal, which he had built in S 1Kin 16:32
And there was a sore famine in S 1Kin 18:2
and he went up and besieged S 1Kin 20:1
if the dust of S shall suffice 1Kin 20:10
There are men come out of S 1Kin 20:17
Damascus, as my father made in S 1Kin 20:34
heavy and displeased, and came to S 1Kin 20:43
king of Israel, which is in S 1Kin 21:18
in the entrance of the gate of S 1Kin 22:10
king died, and was brought to S 1Kin 22:37
and they buried the king in S 1Kin 22:37
the chariot in the pool of S 1Kin 22:38
in S the seventeenth year of 1Kin 22:51
his upper chamber that was in S 2Kin 1:2
and from thence he returned to S 2Kin 2:25
in S the eighteenth year of 2Kin 3:1
went out of S the same time 2Kin 3:6
with the prophet that is in S 2Kin 5:3
But he led them to S 2Kin 6:19
pass, when they were come into S 2Kin 6:20
they were in the midst of S 2Kin 6:20
host, and went up, and besieged S 2Kin 6:24
And there was a great famine in S 2Kin 6:25
for a shekel, in the gate of S 2Kin 7:1
about this time in the gate of S 2Kin 7:18
And Ahab had seventy sons in S 2Kin 10:1
Jehu wrote letters, and sent to S 2Kin 10:1
arose and departed, and came to S 2Kin 10:12
And when he came to S, he slew all 2Kin 10:17
all that remained unto Ahab in S 2Kin 10:17
and they buried him in S 2Kin 10:35
over Israel in S was twenty 2Kin 10:36
began to reign over Israel in S 2Kin 13:1
remained the grove also in S 2Kin 13:6
and they buried him in S 2Kin 13:9
to reign over Israel in S 2Kin 13:10
Joash was buried in S with the 2Kin 13:13
and hostages, and returned to S 2Kin 14:14
was buried in S with the kings of 2Kin 14:16
of Israel began to reign in S 2Kin 14:23
reign over Israel in S six months 2Kin 15:8
and he reigned a full month in S 2Kin 15:13
went up from Tirzah, and came to S. 2Kin 15:14
Shallum the son of Jabesh in S 2Kin 15:14
Israel, and reigned ten years in S 2Kin 15:17
began to reign over Israel in S 2Kin 15:23
against him, and smote him in S 2Kin 15:25
began to reign over Israel in S 2Kin 15:27
reign in S over Israel nine years 2Kin 17:1
all the land, and went up to S 2Kin 17:5
Hoshea the king of Assyria took S 2Kin 17:6
king of Assyria came up against S 2Kin 18:9
king of Israel, S was taken 2Kin 18:10
they delivered S out of mine hand 2Kin 18:34
over Jerusalem the line of S 2Kin 21:13
the entering in of the gate of S 2Chr 18:9
caught him, (for he was hid in S 2Chr 22:9
from S even unto Beth-horon, and 2Chr 25:13
hostages also, and returned to S 2Chr 25:24
them, and brought the spoil to S 2Chr 28:8
before the host that came to S 2Chr 28:9
then they returned to S 2Chr 28:15
And the head of Ephraim is S Is 7:9
the head of S is Remaliah's son Is 7:9
the spoil of S shall be taken Is 8:4
Ephraim and the inhabitant of S Is 9:9
is not S as Damascus Is 10:9
excel them of Jerusalem and of S Is 10:10
I not, as I have done unto S Is 10:11
And thine elder sister is S Eze 16:46
Neither hath S committed half of Eze 16:51
daughters, and the captivity of S Eze 16:53
to their former estate, and S Eze 16:55
S is Aholah, and Jerusalem Eze 23:4
with the cup of thy sister S Eze 23:33
S shall become desolate Hos 13:16
dwell in S in the corner of a bed Amos 3:12
Judah, which he saw concerning S Mic 1:1
is it not S Mic 1:5
Therefore I will make S as an Mic 1:6
Philip went down to the city of S Acts 8:5
and bewitched the people of S Acts 8:9
S had received the word of God Acts 8:14
*2. Territory of the northern tribes.*
which are in the cities of S 1Kin 13:32
by the palace of Ahab king of S 1Kin 21:1
the messengers of the king of S 2Kin 1:3
of S instead of the children of 2Kin 17:24
and they possessed S, and dwelt in 2Kin 17:24
and placed in the cities of S 2Kin 17:26
they had carried away from S came 2Kin 17:28
of the prophet that came out of S 2Kin 23:18
that were in the cities of S 2Kin 23:19
years he went down to Ahab to S 2Chr 18:2
over, and set in the cities of S Ezr 4:10
their companions that dwell in S Ezr 4:17
his brethren and the army of S Neh 4:2
they delivered S out of my hand Is 36:19
seen folly in the prophets of S Jer 23:13
vines upon the mountains of S Jer 31:5
Shechem, from Shiloh, and from S Jer 41:5
and the wickedness of S Hos 7:1
Thy calf, O S, hath cast thee off Hos 8:5
but the calf of S shall be broken Hos 8:6
The inhabitants of S shall fear Hos 10:5
As for S, her king is cut off as Hos 10:7
upon the mountains of S, and Amos 3:9
that are in the mountain of S Amos 4:1
and trust in the mountain of S Amos 6:1
They that swear by the sin of S Amos 8:14
of Ephraim, and the fields of S Obad 19
*3. District north of Judah.*
he passed through the midst of S Lk 17:11
And he must needs go through S Jn 4:4
Then cometh he to a city of S Jn 4:5
cometh a woman of S to draw water Jn 4:7
saith the woman of S unto him Jn 4:9
of me, which am a woman of S Jn 4:9
and in all Judaea, and in S Acts 1:8
the regions of Judaea and S Acts 8:1
all Judaea and Galilee and S Acts 9:31
they passed through Phenice and S Acts 15:3

**SAMARITAN** (*sa-mar'-i-tun*) See SAMARITANS.
*An inhabitant of Samaria.*
But a certain S, as he journeyed, Lk 10:33
and he was a S Lk 17:16
Say we not well that thou art a S Jn 8:48

**SAMARITANS** (*sa-mar'-i-tuns*)
high places which the S had made 2Kin 17:29
any city of the S enter ye not Mt 10:5
entered into a village of the S Lk 9:52
Jews have no dealings with the S Jn 4:9
many of the S of that city Jn 4:39
So when the S were come unto him, Jn 4:40
gospel in many villages of the S Acts 8:25

**SAME** See PREFACE.

**SAMGAR-NEBO** (*sam''-gar-ne'-bo*) *A prince of Babylon.*
gate, even Nergal-sharezer, S Jer 39:3

**SAMLAH** (*sam'-lah*) *A king of Edom.*
S of Masrekah reigned in his Gen 36:36
S died, and Saul of Rehoboth by Gen 36:37
S of Masrekah reigned in his 1Chr 1:47
when S was dead, Shaul of 1Chr 1:48

**SAMOS** (*sa'-mos*) *An island in the Aegean Sea.*
and the next day we arrived at S Acts 20:15

**SAMOTHRACE** See SAMOTHRACIA.

**SAMOTHRACIA** (*sam-o-thra'-she-ah*) *An island in the Aegean Sea.*
came with a straight course to S Acts 16:11

**SAMSON** (*sam'-sun*) See SAMSON'S. *A judge of Israel.*
bare a son, and called his name S Judg 13:24
S went down to Timnath, and saw a Judg 14:1
S said unto his father, Get her Judg 14:3
Then went S down, and his father Judg 14:5
and she pleased S well Judg 14:7
and S made there a feast Judg 14:10
S said unto them, I will now put Judg 14:12
that S visited his wife with a Judg 15:1
S said concerning them, Now shall Judg 15:3
S went and caught three hundred Judg 15:4
And they answered, S, the son in Judg 15:6
S said unto them, Though ye have Judg 15:7
To bind S are we come up, to do Judg 15:10
of the rock Etam, and said to S Judg 15:11
S said unto them, Swear unto me, Judg 15:12
S said, With the jawbone of an Judg 15:16
Then went S to Gaza, and saw there Judg 16:1
Gazites, saying, S is come hither Judg 16:2
S lay till midnight, and arose at Judg 16:3
And Delilah said to S, Tell me, I Judg 16:6
S said unto her, If they bind me Judg 16:7
The Philistines be upon thee, S Judg 16:9
And Delilah said unto S, Behold, Judg 16:10
The Philistines be upon thee, S Judg 16:12
And Delilah said unto S, Hitherto Judg 16:13
The Philistines be upon thee, S Judg 16:14
The Philistines be upon thee, S Judg 16:20
Our god hath delivered S our Judg 16:23
merry, that they said, Call for S Judg 16:25
they called for S out of the Judg 16:25
S said unto the lad that held him Judg 16:26
that beheld while S made sport Judg 16:27
S called unto the LORD, and said, Judg 16:28
S took hold of the two middle Judg 16:29
S said, Let me die with the Judg 16:30
of Gedeon, and of Barak, and of S Heb 11:32

**SAMSON'S** (*sam'-suns*)
day, that they said unto S wife Judg 14:15
S wife wept before him, and said, Judg 14:16
But S wife was given to his Judg 14:20

**SAMUEL** (*sam'-u-el*) See SHEMUEL. *A priest and judge of Israel.*
bare a son, and called his name S 1Sa 1:20
But S ministered before the LORD, 1Sa 2:18
the child S grew before the LORD 1Sa 2:21
And the child S grew on, and was in 1Sa 2:26
the child S ministered unto the 1Sa 3:1
was, and S was laid down to sleep 1Sa 3:3
That the LORD called S 1Sa 3:4
And the LORD called yet again, S 1Sa 3:6
S arose and went to Eli, and said, 1Sa 3:6
Now S did not yet know the LORD, 1Sa 3:7
the LORD called S again the third 1Sa 3:8
Therefore Eli said unto S 1Sa 3:9
So S went and lay down in his 1Sa 3:9
as at other times, S, S 1Sa 3:10
Then S answered, Speak 1Sa 3:10
And the LORD said to S, Behold, I 1Sa 3:11
S lay until the morning, and 1Sa 3:15
S feared to shew Eli the vision 1Sa 3:15
Eli called S, and said, S 1Sa 3:16
S told him every whit, and hid 1Sa 3:18
S grew, and the LORD was with him, 1Sa 3:19
even to Beer-sheba knew that S 1Sa 3:20
to S in Shiloh by the word of the 1Sa 3:21
the word of S came to all Israel 1Sa 4:1
S spake unto all the house of 1Sa 7:3
S said, Gather all Israel to 1Sa 7:5
S judged the children of Israel 1Sa 7:6
the children of Israel said to S 1Sa 7:8
S took a sucking lamb, and offered 1Sa 7:9
S cried unto the LORD for Israel 1Sa 7:9
as S was offering up the burnt 1Sa 7:10
Then S took a stone, and set it 1Sa 7:12
the Philistines all the days of S 1Sa 7:13
S judged Israel all the days of 1Sa 7:15
when S was old, that he made his 1Sa 8:1
and came to S unto Ramah, 1Sa 8:4
But the thing displeased S 1Sa 8:6
And S prayed unto the LORD 1Sa 8:6
And the LORD said unto S, Hearken 1Sa 8:7
S told all the words of the LORD 1Sa 8:10
refused to obey the voice of S 1Sa 8:19
S heard all the words of the 1Sa 8:21
And the LORD said to S, Hearken 1Sa 8:22
S said unto the men of Israel, Go 1Sa 8:22
S came out against them, for to 1Sa 9:14
Now the LORD had told S in his 1Sa 9:15
when S saw Saul, the LORD said 1Sa 9:17
Saul drew near to S in the gate 1Sa 9:18
S answered Saul, and said, I am 1Sa 9:19
S took Saul and his servant, and 1Sa 9:22
S said unto the cook, Bring the 1Sa 9:23
S said, Behold that which is left 1Sa 9:24
So Saul did eat with S that day 1Sa 9:24
S communed with Saul upon the top 1Sa 9:25
that S called Saul to the top of 1Sa 9:26
went out both of them, he and S 1Sa 9:26
S said to Saul, Bid the servant 1Sa 9:27
Then S took a vial of oil, and 1Sa 10:1

had turned his back to go from *S* 1Sa 10:9
they were no where, we came to *S* 1Sa 10:14
I pray thee, what *S* said unto you 1Sa 10:15
of the kingdom, whereof *S* spake 1Sa 10:16
*S* called the people together unto 1Sa 10:17
when *S* had caused all the tribes 1Sa 10:20
*S* said to all the people, See ye 1Sa 10:24
Then *S* told the people the manner 1Sa 10:25
*S* sent all the people away, every 1Sa 10:25
not forth after Saul and after *S* 1Sa 11:7
And the people said unto *S* 1Sa 11:12
Then said *S* to the people, Come, 1Sa 11:14
*S* said unto all Israel, Behold, I 1Sa 12:1
*S* said unto the people, It is the 1Sa 12:6
and Bedan, and Jephthah, and *S* 1Sa 12:11
So *S* called unto the LORD 1Sa 12:18
greatly feared the LORD and *S* 1Sa 12:18
And all the people said unto *S* 1Sa 12:19
*S* said unto the people, Fear not 1Sa 12:20
the set time that *S* had appointed 1Sa 13:8
but *S* came not to Gilgal 1Sa 13:8
burnt offering, behold, *S* came 1Sa 13:10
*S* said, What hast thou done 1Sa 13:11
*S* said to Saul, Thou hast done 1Sa 13:13
*S* arose, and gat him up from 1Sa 13:15
*S* also said unto Saul, The LORD 1Sa 15:1
came the word of the LORD unto *S* 1Sa 15:10
And it grieved *S* 1Sa 15:11
when *S* rose early to meet Saul in 1Sa 15:12
in the morning, it was told *S* 1Sa 15:12
And *S* came to Saul 1Sa 15:13
*S* said, What meaneth then this 1Sa 15:14
Then *S* said unto Saul, Stay, and I 1Sa 15:16
*S* said, When thou wast little in 1Sa 15:17
And Saul said unto *S*, Yea, I have 1Sa 15:20
*S* said, Hath the LORD as great 1Sa 15:22
And Saul said unto *S*, I have 1Sa 15:24
*S* said unto Saul, I will not 1Sa 15:26
as *S* turned about to go away, he 1Sa 15:27
*S* said unto him, The LORD hath 1Sa 15:28
So *S* turned again after Saul 1Sa 15:31
Then said *S*, Bring ye hither to 1Sa 15:32
*S* said, As thy sword hath made 1Sa 15:33
*S* hewed Agag in pieces before the 1Sa 15:33
Then *S* went to Ramah 1Sa 15:34
*S* came no more to see Saul until 1Sa 15:35
nevertheless *S* mourned for Saul 1Sa 15:35
And the LORD said unto *S*, How long 1Sa 16:1
And *S* said, How can I go 1Sa 16:2
*S* did that which the LORD spake, 1Sa 16:4
But the LORD said unto *S*, Look 1Sa 16:7
and made him pass before *S* 1Sa 16:8
of his sons to pass before *S* 1Sa 16:10
*S* said unto Jesse, The LORD hath 1Sa 16:10
*S* said unto Jesse, Are here all 1Sa 16:11
*S* said unto Jesse, Send and fetch 1Sa 16:11
Then *S* took the horn of oil, and 1Sa 16:13
So *S* rose up, and went to Ramah 1Sa 16:13
came to *S* to Ramah, and told him 1Sa 19:18
*S* went and dwelt in Naioth 1Sa 19:18
*S* standing as appointed over them 1Sa 19:20
and he asked and said, Where are *S* 1Sa 19:22
before *S* in like manner, and lay 1Sa 19:24
And *S* died 1Sa 25:1
Now *S* was dead, and all Israel had 1Sa 28:3
And he said, Bring me up *S* 1Sa 28:11
And when the woman saw *S*, she 1Sa 28:12
And Saul perceived that it was *S* 1Sa 28:14
*S* said to Saul, Why hast thou 1Sa 28:15
Then said *S*, Wherefore then dost 1Sa 28:16
afraid, because of the words of *S* 1Sa 28:20
And the sons of *S* 1Chr 6:28
*S* the seer did ordain in their 1Chr 9:22
to the word of the LORD by *S* 1Chr 11:3
And all that *S* the seer, and Saul 1Chr 26:28
written in the book of *S* the seer 1Chr 29:29
from the days of *S* the prophet 2Chr 35:18
*S* among them that call upon his Ps 99:6
*S* stood before me, yet my mind Jer 15:1
Yea, and all the prophets from *S* Acts 3:24
fifty years, until *S* the prophet Acts 13:20
of David also, and *S*, and of the Heb 11:32

**SANBALLAT** (*san-bal'-lat*) *An opponent of Nehemiah.*
When *S* the Horonite, and Tobiah Neh 2:10
But when *S* the Horonite, and Neh 2:19
that when *S* heard that we builded Neh 4:1
But it came to pass, that when *S* Neh 4:7
Now it came to pass, when *S* Neh 6:1
That *S* and Geshem sent unto me, Neh 6:2
Then sent *S* his servant unto me Neh 6:5
for Tobiah and *S* had hired him Neh 6:12
*S* according to these their works, Neh 6:14
was son in law to *S* the Horonite Neh 13:28

**SANCTIFICATION**
us wisdom, and righteousness, and *s* 1Cor 1:30
is the will of God, even your *s* 1Th 4:3
how to possess his vessel in *s* 1Th 4:4
salvation through *s* of the Spirit 2Th 2:13
through *s* of the Spirit, unto 1Pet 1:2

**SANCTIFIED**
blessed the seventh day, and *s* it Gen 2:3
unto the people, and *s* the people Ex 19:14
tabernacle shall be *s* by my glory Ex 29:43
all that was therein, and *s* them Lev 8:10
*s* it, to make reconciliation upon Lev 8:15
*s* Aaron, and his garments, and his Lev 8:30
I will be *s* in them that come Lev 10:3
if he that *s* it will redeem his Lev 27:15
if he that *s* the field will in Lev 27:19
*s* it, and all the instruments Num 7:1
and had anointed them, and *s* them Num 7:1
land of Egypt I *s* them for myself Num 8:17
the LORD, and he was *s* in them Num 20:13
because ye *s* me not in the midst Deut 32:51
*s* Eleazar his son to keep the ark 1Sa 7:1
he *s* Jesse and his sons, and called 1Sa 16:5
though it were *s* this day in the 1Sa 21:5
the Levites *s* themselves to bring 1Chr 15:14
priests that were present were *s* 2Chr 5:11
*s* this house, that my name may be 2Chr 7:16
house, which I have *s* for my name 2Chr 7:20
*s* themselves, and came, according 2Chr 29:15
so they *s* the house of the LORD 2Chr 29:17
have we prepared and *s*, and, 2Chr 29:19
other priests had *s* themselves 2Chr 29:34
had not *s* themselves sufficiently 2Chr 30:3
which he hath *s* for ever 2Chr 30:8
*s* themselves, and brought in the 2Chr 30:15
the congregation that were not *s* 2Chr 30:17
number of priests *s* themselves 2Chr 30:24
they *s* themselves in holiness 2Chr 31:18
they *s* it, and set up the doors of Neh 3:1
unto the tower of Meah they *s* it Neh 3:1
they *s* holy things unto the Neh 12:47
the Levites *s* them unto the Neh 12:47
*s* them, and rose up early in the Job 1:5
holy shall be *s* in righteousness Is 5:16
I have commanded my *s* ones Is 13:3
forth out of the womb I *s* thee Jer 1:5
I will be *s* in you before the Eze 20:41
in her, and shall be *s* in her Eze 28:22
shall be *s* in them in the sight Eze 28:25
when I shall be *s* in you before Eze 36:23
me, when I shall be *s* in thee Eze 38:16
am *s* in them in the sight of many Eze 39:27
that are *s* of the sons of Zadok Eze 48:11
ye of him, whom the Father hath *s* Jn 10:36
also might be *s* through the truth Jn 17:19
among all them which are *s* Acts 20:32
among them which are *s* by faith Acts 26:18
being *s* by the Holy Ghost Rom 15:16
them that are *s* in Christ Jesus 1Cor 1:2
but ye are washed, but ye are *s* 1Cor 6:11
husband is *s* by the wife, and the 1Cor 7:14
wife is *s* by the husband 1Cor 7:14
For it is *s* by the word of God and 1Ti 4:5
shall be a vessel unto honour, *s* 2Ti 2:21
they who are *s* are all of one Heb 2:11
By the which will we are *s* Heb 10:10
for ever them that are *s* Heb 10:14
the covenant, wherewith he was *s* Heb 10:29
to them that are *s* by God the Jude 1

**SANCTIFIETH**
or the temple that *s* the gold Mt 23:17
or the altar that *s* the gift Mt 23:19
For both he that *s* and they who Heb 2:11
*s* to the purifying of the flesh Heb 9:13

**SANCTIFY**
*S* unto me all the firstborn, Ex 13:2
*s* them to day and to morrow, and Ex 19:10
*s* themselves, lest the LORD break Ex 19:22
bounds about the mount, and *s* it Ex 19:23
*s* them, that they may minister Ex 28:41
thou shalt *s* the breast of the Ex 29:27
made, to consecrate and to *s* them Ex 29:33
and thou shalt anoint it, to *s* it Ex 29:36
atonement for the altar, and *s* it Ex 29:37
I will *s* the tabernacle of the Ex 29:44
I will *s* also both Aaron and his Ex 29:44
And thou shalt *s* them, that they Ex 30:29
I am the LORD that doth *s* you Ex 31:13
all his vessels, and *s* the altar Ex 40:10
the laver and his foot, and *s* it Ex 40:11
garments, and anoint him, and *s* him Ex 40:13
the laver and his foot, to *s* them Lev 8:11
head, and anointed him, to *s* him Lev 8:12
ye shall therefore *s* yourselves Lev 11:44
*S* yourselves therefore, and be ye Lev 20:7
I am the LORD which *s* you Lev 20:8
Thou shalt *s* him therefore Lev 21:8
for I the LORD, which *s* you Lev 21:8
for I the LORD do *s* him Lev 21:15
for I the LORD do *s* them Lev 21:23
I the LORD do *s* them Lev 22:9
for I the LORD do *s* them Lev 22:16
when a man shall *s* his house to Lev 27:14
if a man shall *s* unto the LORD Lev 27:16
If he *s* his field from the year Lev 27:17
But if he *s* his field after the Lev 27:18
if a man *s* unto the LORD a field Lev 27:22
firstling, no man shall *s* it Lev 27:26
*S* yourselves against to morrow, Num 11:18
to *s* me in the eyes of the Num 20:12
to *s* me at the water before their Num 27:14
Keep the sabbath day to *s* it Deut 5:12
shalt *s* unto the LORD thy God Deut 15:19
unto the people, *S* yourselves Josh 3:5
*s* the people, and say, *S* Josh 7:13
*s* yourselves, and come with me to 1Sa 16:5
*s* yourselves, both ye and your 1Chr 15:12
that he should *s* the most holy 1Chr 23:13
*s* now yourselves 2Chr 29:5
*s* the house of the LORD God of 2Chr 29:5
first day of the first month to *s* 2Chr 29:17
to *s* themselves than the priests 2Chr 29:34
clean, to *s* them unto the LORD 2Chr 30:17
*s* yourselves, and prepare your 2Chr 35:6
the gates, to *s* the sabbath day Neh 13:22
*S* the LORD of hosts himself Is 8:13
of him, they shall *s* my name Is 29:23
*s* the Holy One of Jacob, and shall Is 29:23
They that *s* themselves, and purify Is 66:17
that I am the LORD that *s* them Eze 20:12
I will *s* my great name, which was Eze 36:23
know that I the LORD do *s* Israel Eze 37:28
I magnify myself, and *s* myself Eze 38:23
they shall not *s* the people with Eze 44:19
the utter court, to *s* the people Eze 46:20
*S* ye a fast, call a solemn Joel 1:14
*s* a fast, call a solemn assembly Joel 2:15
*s* the congregation, assemble the Joel 2:16
*S* them through thy truth Jn 17:17
And for their sakes I *s* myself Jn 17:19
That he might *s* and cleanse it Eph 5:26
very God of peace *s* you wholly 1Th 5:23
that he might *s* the people with Heb 13:12
But *s* the Lord God in your hearts 1Pet 3:15

**SANCTUARIES**
that he profane not my *s* Lev 21:23
bring your *s* unto desolation, and Lev 26:31
into the *s* of the LORD's house Jer 51:51
Thou hast defiled thy *s* by the Eze 28:18
the *s* of Israel shall be laid Amos 7:9

**SANCTUARY**
for thee to dwell in, in the *S* Ex 15:17
And let them make me a *s* Ex 25:8
shekel after the shekel of the *s* Ex 30:13
after the shekel of the *s* Ex 30:24
of work for the service of the *s* Ex 36:1
the work of the service of the *s* Ex 36:3
wrought all the work of the *s* Ex 36:4
work for the offering of the *s* Ex 36:6
after the shekel of the *s* Ex 38:24
after the shekel of the *s* Ex 38:25
shekel, after the shekel of the *s* Ex 38:26
were cast the sockets of the *s* Ex 38:27
LORD, before the vail of the *s* Lev 4:6
silver, after the shekel of the *s* Lev 5:15
from before the *s* out of the camp Lev 10:4
thing, nor come into the *s* Lev 12:4
make an atonement for the holy *s* Lev 16:33
my sabbaths, and reverence my *s* Lev 19:30
seed unto Molech, to defile my *s* Lev 20:3
Neither shall he go out of the *s* Lev 21:12
nor profane the *s* of his God Lev 21:12
my sabbaths, and reverence my *s* Lev 26:2
silver, after the shekel of the *s* Lev 27:3
according to the shekel of the *s* Lev 27:25
keeping the charge of the *s* Num 3:28
the vessels of the *s* wherewith Num 3:31
that keep the charge of the *s* Num 3:32
keeping the charge of the *s* for Num 3:38
of the *s* shalt thou take them Num 3:47
after the shekel of the *s* Num 3:50
wherewith they minister in the *s* Num 4:12
made an end of covering the *s* Num 4:15
and all the vessels of the *s* Num 4:15
of all that therein is, in the *s* Num 4:16
because the service of the *s* Num 7:9
after the shekel of the *s* Num 7:13
after the shekel of the *s* Num 7:19
after the shekel of the *s* Num 7:25
after the shekel of the *s* Num 7:31
after the shekel of the *s* Num 7:37
after the shekel of the *s* Num 7:43
after the shekel of the *s* Num 7:49
after the shekel of the *s* Num 7:55
after the shekel of the *s* Num 7:61
after the shekel of the *s* Num 7:67
after the shekel of the *s* Num 7:73
after the shekel of the *s* Num 7:79
after the shekel of the *s* Num 7:85
apiece, after the shekel of the *s* Num 7:86
of Israel come nigh unto the *s* Num 8:19
set forward, bearing the *s* Num 10:21
shall bear the iniquity of the *s* Num 18:1
come nigh the vessels of the *s* Num 18:3
ye shall keep the charge of the *s* Num 18:5
after the shekel of the *s* Num 18:16
he hath defiled the *s* of the LORD Num 19:20
that was by the *s* of the LORD Josh 24:26
and all the instruments of the *s* 1Chr 9:29
build ye the *s* of the LORD God, 1Chr 22:19
for the governors of the *s* 1Chr 24:5
thee to build an house for the *s* 1Chr 28:10
have built thee a *s* therein for 2Chr 20:8
go out of the *s* 2Chr 26:18
for the kingdom, and for the *s* 2Chr 29:21
the LORD, and enter into his *s* 2Chr 30:8
to the purification of the *s* 2Chr 30:19
the sword in the house of their *s* 2Chr 36:17
where are the vessels of the *s* Neh 10:39
Send thee help from the *s* Ps 20:2
so as I have seen thee in the *s* Ps 63:2
of my God, my King, in the *s* Ps 68:24
Until I went into the *s* of God Ps 73:17
enemy hath done wickedly in the *s* Ps 74:3
They have cast fire into thy *s* Ps 74:7
Thy way, O God, is in the *s* Ps 77:13
them to the border of his *s* Ps 78:54
he built his *s* like high palaces, Ps 78:69
strength and beauty are in his *s* Ps 96:6
down from the height of his *s* Ps 102:19

Judah was his *s*, and Israel his ... Ps 114:2
Lift up your hands in the *s* ... Ps 134:2
Praise God in his *s* ... Ps 150:1
And he shall be for a *s* ... Is 8:14
he shall come to his *s* to pray ... Is 16:12
profaned the princes of the *s* ... Is 43:28
to beautify the place of my *s* ... Is 60:13
have trodden down thy *s* ... Is 63:18
beginning is the place of our *s* ... Jer 17:12
the heathen entered into her *s* ... Lam 1:10
his altar, he hath abhorred his *s* ... Lam 2:7
be slain in the *s* of the Lord ... Lam 2:20
the stones of the *s* are poured ... Lam 4:1
because thou hast defiled my *s* ... Eze 5:11
I should go far off from my *s* ... Eze 8:6
and begin at my *s* ... Eze 9:6
*s* in the countries where they ... Eze 11:16
have defiled my *s* in the same day ... Eze 23:38
same day into my *s* to profane it ... Eze 23:39
Behold, I will profane my *s* ... Eze 24:21
thou saidst, Aha, against my *s* ... Eze 25:3
will set my *s* in the midst of ... Eze 37:26
when my *s* shall be in the midst ... Eze 37:28
squared, and the face of the *s* ... Eze 41:21
the temple and the *s* had two doors ... Eze 41:23
make a separation between the *s* ... Eze 42:20
place of the house, without the *s* ... Eze 43:21
*s* which looketh toward the east ... Eze 44:1
with every going forth of the *s* ... Eze 44:5
have brought into my *s* strangers ... Eze 44:7
in flesh, to be in my *s*, to ... Eze 44:7
my charge in my *s* for yourselves ... Eze 44:8
in flesh, shall enter into my *s* ... Eze 44:9
they shall be ministers in my *s* ... Eze 44:11
that kept the charge of my *s* when ... Eze 44:15
They shall enter into my *s* ... Eze 44:16
the day that he goeth into the *s* ... Eze 44:27
inner court, to minister in the *s* ... Eze 44:27
for the *s* five hundred in length ... Eze 45:2
and in it shall be the *s* and the ... Eze 45:3
priests the ministers of the *s* ... Eze 45:4
and an holy place for the *s* ... Eze 45:4
without blemish, and cleanse the *s* ... Eze 45:18
they they issued out of the *s* ... Eze 47:12
the *s* shall be in the midst of it ... Eze 48:8
the *s* of the LORD shall be in the ... Eze 48:10
the *s* of the house shall be in ... Eze 48:21
the place of his *s* was cast down ... Dan 8:11
of desolation, to give both the *s* ... Dan 8:13
then shall the *s* be cleansed ... Dan 8:14
shine upon thy *s* that is desolate ... Dan 9:17
shall destroy the city and the *s* ... Dan 9:26
shall pollute the *s* of strength ... Dan 11:31
her priests have polluted the *s* ... Zeph 3:4
A minister of the *s*, and of the ... Heb 8:2
of divine service, and a worldly *s* ... Heb 9:1
which is called the *s* ... Heb 9:2
the *s* by the high priest for sin ... Heb 13:11

**SAND**
as the *s* which is upon the sea ... Gen 22:17
make thy seed as the *s* of the sea ... Gen 32:12
gathered corn as the *s* of the sea ... Gen 41:49
the Egyptian, and hid him in the *s* ... Ex 2:12
and of treasures hid in the *s* ... Deut 33:19
even as the *s* that is upon the ... Josh 11:4
as the *s* by the sea side for ... Judg 7:12
people as the *s* which is on the ... 1Sa 13:5
as the *s* that is by the sea for ... 2Sa 17:11
as the *s* which is by the sea in ... 1Kin 4:20
even as the *s* that is on the sea ... 1Kin 4:29
be heavier than the *s* of the sea ... Job 6:3
I shall multiply my days as the *s* ... Job 29:18
fowls like as the *s* of the sea ... Ps 78:27
are more in number than the *s* ... Ps 139:18
stone is heavy, and the *s* weighty ... Prov 27:3
Israel be as the *s* of the sea ... Is 10:22
Thy seed also had been as the *s* ... Is 48:19
which have placed the *s* for the ... Jer 5:22
to me above the *s* of the seas ... Jer 15:8
neither the *s* of the sea measured ... Jer 33:22
shall be as the *s* of the sea ... Hos 1:10
gather the captivity as the *s* ... Hab 1:9
which built his house upon the *s* ... Mt 7:26
of Israel be as the *s* of the sea ... Rom 9:27
as the *s* which is by the sea ... Heb 11:12
And I stood upon the *s* of the sea ... Rev 13:1
of whom is as the *s* of the sea ... Rev 20:8

**SANDALS**
But be shod with *s* ... Mk 6:9
Gird thyself, and bind on thy *s* ... Acts 12:8

**SANG**
Then *s* Moses and the children of ... Ex 15:1
Then Israel *s* this song, Spring ... Num 21:17
Then *s* Deborah and Barak the son ... Judg 5:1
of whom they *s* one to another in ... 1Sa 29:5
worshipped, and the singers *s* ... 2Chr 29:28
they *s* praises with gladness, and ... 2Chr 29:30
they *s* together by course in ... Ezr 3:11
And the singers *s* loud, with ... Neh 12:42
When the morning stars *s* together ... Job 38:7
which he *s* unto the LORD, ... Ps 7:t
they *s* his praise ... Ps 106:12
prayed, and *s* praises unto God ... Acts 16:25

**SANK**
they *s* into the bottom as a stone ... Ex 15:5
they *s* as lead in the mighty ... Ex 15:10

**SANSANNAH** (*san-san'-nah*) *A city in Judah.*
And Ziklag, and Madmannah, and *S* . Josh 15:31

**SAP**
trees of the LORD are full of *s* ... Ps 104:16

**SAPH** (*saf*) See SIPHAI. *A descendant of Rapha.*
Sibbechai the Hushathite slew *S* ... 2Sa 21:18

**SAPHIR** (*sa'-fur*) *A city in Ephraim.*
ye away, thou inhabitant of *S* ... Mic 1:11

**SAPPHIRA** (*saf-fi'-rah*) *Wife of Ananias.*
Ananias, with *S* his wife, sold a ... Acts 5:1

**SAPPHIRE**
it were a paved work of a *s* stone ... Ex 24:10
row shall be an emerald, a *s* ... Ex 28:18
the second row, an emerald, a *s* ... Ex 39:11
with the precious onyx, or the *s* ... Job 28:16
rubies, their polishing was of *s* ... Lam 4:7
as the appearance of a *s* stone ... Eze 1:26
over them as it were a *s* stone ... Eze 10:1
the onyx, and the jasper, the *s* ... Eze 28:13
the second, *s* ... Rev 21:19

**SAPPHIRES**
stones of it are the place of *s* ... Job 28:6
as bright ivory overlaid with *s* ... Song 5:14
and lay thy foundations with *s* ... Is 54:11

**SARA** (*sa'-rah*) See SARAH. *Greek form of Sarah 1.*
Through faith also *S* herself ... Heb 11:11

**SARAH** (*sa'-rah*) See SARA, SARAH'S, SARAI, SERAH.
*1. Wife of Abraham.*
Sarai, but *S* shall her name be ... Gen 17:15
and shall *S*, that is ninety years ... Gen 17:17
*S* thy wife shall bear thee a son ... Gen 17:19
which *S* shall bear unto thee at ... Gen 17:21
hastened into the tent unto *S* ... Gen 18:6
unto him, Where is *S* thy wife ... Gen 18:9
*S* thy wife shall have a son ... Gen 18:10
*S* heard it in the tent door, ... Gen 18:10
*S* were old and well stricken in ... Gen 18:11
it ceased to be with *S* after the ... Gen 18:11
Therefore *S* laughed within ... Gen 18:12
Abraham, Wherefore did *S* laugh ... Gen 18:13
of life, and *S* shall have a son ... Gen 18:14
Then *S* denied, saying, I laughed ... Gen 18:15
And Abraham said of *S* his wife ... Gen 20:2
king of Gerar sent, and took *S* ... Gen 20:2
and restored him *S* his wife ... Gen 20:14
unto *S* he said, Behold, I have ... Gen 20:16
because of *S* Abraham's wife ... Gen 20:18
the LORD visited *S* as he had said ... Gen 21:1
LORD did unto *S* as he had spoken ... Gen 21:1
For *S* conceived, and bare Abraham ... Gen 21:2
whom *S* bare to him, Isaac ... Gen 21:3
*S* said, God hath made me to laugh ... Gen 21:6
that *S* should have given children ... Gen 21:7
*S* saw the son of Hagar the ... Gen 21:9
in all that *S* hath said unto thee ... Gen 21:12
*S* was an hundred and seven and ... Gen 23:1
were the years of the life of *S* ... Gen 23:1
And *S* died in Kirjath-arba ... Gen 23:2
and Abraham came to mourn for *S* ... Gen 23:2
Abraham buried *S* his wife in the ... Gen 23:19
*S* my master's wife bare a son to ... Gen 24:36
was Abraham buried, and *S* his wife ... Gen 25:10
they buried Abraham and *S* his wife .. Gen 49:31
father, and unto *S* that bare you ... Is 51:2
I come, and *S* shall have a son ... Rom 9:9
Even as *S* obeyed Abraham, calling ... 1Pet 3:6
*2. A daughter of Asher.*
of the daughter of Asher was *S* ... Num 26:46

**SARAH'S** (*sa'-rahs*)
her into his mother *S* tent ... Gen 24:67
*S* handmaid, bare unto Abraham ... Gen 25:12
yet the deadness of *S* womb ... Rom 4:19

**SARAI** (*sa'-rahee*) See SARAH, SARAI'S. *The original name of Sarah.*
the name of Abram's wife was *S* ... Gen 11:29
But *S* was barren ... Gen 11:30
*S* his daughter in law, his son ... Gen 11:31
And Abram took *S* his wife, and Lot ... Gen 12:5
that he said unto *S* his wife ... Gen 12:11
plagues because of *S* Abram's wife ... Gen 12:17
Now *S* Abram's wife bare him no ... Gen 16:1
*S* said unto Abram, Behold now, ... Gen 16:2
Abram hearkened to the voice of *S* ... Gen 16:2
*S* Abram's wife took Hagar her ... Gen 16:3
*S* said unto Abram, My wrong be ... Gen 16:5
But Abram said unto *S*, Behold, ... Gen 16:6
when *S* dealt hardly with her, she ... Gen 16:6
from the face of my mistress *S* ... Gen 16:8
As for *S* thy wife, thou shalt not ... Gen 17:15
thou shalt not call her name *S* ... Gen 17:15

**SARAI'S** (*sa'-rahees*)
*S* maid, whence camest thou ... Gen 16:8

**SARAPH** (*sa'-raf*) *A descendant of Shelah.*
men of Chozeba, and Joash, and *S* ... 1Chr 4:22

**SARDINE**
upon like a jasper and a *s* stone ... Rev 4:3

**SARDIS** (*sar'-dis*) *A city in Lydia in Asia Minor.*
and unto Thyatira, and unto *S* ... Rev 1:11
angel of the church in *S* write ... Rev 3:1
in *S* which have not defiled their ... Rev 3:4

**SARDITES** (*sar'-dites*) *Descendants of Sered.*
of Sered, the family of the *S* ... Num 26:26

**SARDIUS**
the first row shall be a *s* ... Ex 28:17
the first row was a *s*, a topaz, ... Ex 39:10
stone was thy covering, the *s* ... Eze 28:13
the sixth, *s* ... Rev 21:20

**SARDONYX**
The fifth, *s* ... Rev 21:20

**SAREPTA** (*sa-rep'-tah*) See ZAREPHATH. *A city near Sidon.*
them was Elias sent, save unto *S* ... Lk 4:26

**SARGON** (*sar'-gon*) *An Assyrian king.*
(when *S* the king of Assyria sent ... Is 20:1

**SARID** (*sa'-rid*) *A city in Zebulun.*
of their inheritance was unto *S* ... Josh 19:10
turned from *S* eastward toward the ... Josh 19:12

**SARON** (*sa'-ron*) See SHARON. *The area between Joppa and Caesarea.*
*S* saw him, and turned to the Lord ... Acts 9:35

**SARSECHIM** (*sar'-se-kim*) *A prince of Babylon.*
Nergal-sharezer, Samgar-nebo, *S* ... Jer 39:3

**SAR-SEKIM** See SARSECHIM.

**SARUCH** (*sa'-ruk*) See SERUG. *Father of Nahor; an ancestor of Jesus.*
Which was the son of *S*, which was ... Lk 3:35

**SAT**
he *s* in the tent door in the heat ... Gen 18:1
Lot *s* in the gate of Sodom ... Gen 19:1
*s* her down over against him a ... Gen 21:16
she *s* over against him, and lift ... Gen 21:16
camel's furniture, and *s* upon them ... Gen 31:34
And they *s* down to eat bread ... Gen 37:25
*s* in an open place, which is by ... Gen 38:14
they *s* before him, the firstborn ... Gen 43:33
himself, and *s* upon the bed ... Gen 48:2
and he *s* down by a well ... Ex 2:15
that *s* on his throne unto the ... Ex 12:29
when we *s* by the flesh pots, and ... Ex 16:3
put it under him, and he *s* thereon ... Ex 17:12
that Moses *s* to judge the people ... Ex 18:13
the people *s* down to eat and to ... Ex 32:6
*s* that hath the issue shall wash ... Lev 15:6
she *s* upon shall wash his clothes ... Lev 15:22
and they *s* down at thy feet ... Deut 33:3
*s* under an oak which was in ... Judg 6:11
the woman as she *s* in the field ... Judg 13:9
And they *s* down, and did eat and ... Judg 19:6
he *s* him down in a street of the ... Judg 19:15
*s* there before the LORD, and ... Judg 20:26
And she *s* beside the reapers ... Ruth 2:14
to the gate, and *s* him down there ... Ruth 4:1
And he turned aside, and *s* down ... Ruth 4:1
And they *s* down ... Ruth 4:2
Now Eli the priest *s* upon a seat ... 1Sa 1:9
Eli *s* upon a seat by the wayside ... 1Sa 4:13
as he *s* in his house with his ... 1Sa 19:9
the king *s* him down to eat meat ... 1Sa 20:24
the king *s* upon his seat, as at ... 1Sa 20:25
Abner *s* by Saul's side, and ... 1Sa 20:25
from the earth, and *s* upon the bed ... 1Sa 28:23
and they *s* down, the one on the ... 2Sa 2:13
when the king *s* in his house ... 2Sa 7:1
*s* before the LORD, and he said, ... 2Sa 7:18
David *s* between the two gates ... 2Sa 18:24
the king arose, and *s* in the gate ... 2Sa 19:8
The Tachmonite that *s* in the seat ... 2Sa 23:8
Then *s* Solomon upon the throne of ... 1Kin 2:12
*s* down on his throne, and caused a ... 1Kin 2:19
and she *s* on his right hand ... 1Kin 2:19
as they *s* at the table, that the ... 1Kin 13:20
as soon as he *s* on his throne ... 1Kin 16:11
*s* down under a juniper tree ... 1Kin 19:4
of Belial, and *s* before him ... 1Kin 21:13
of Judah *s* each on his throne ... 1Kin 22:10
he *s* on the top of an hill ... 2Kin 1:9
he *s* on her knees till noon, and ... 2Kin 4:20
But Elisha *s* in his house, and the ... 2Kin 6:32
house, and the elders *s* with him ... 2Kin 6:32
he *s* on the throne of the kings ... 2Kin 11:19
Jeroboam *s* upon his throne ... 2Kin 13:13
as David *s* in his house, that ... 1Chr 17:1
*s* before the LORD, and said, Who ... 1Chr 17:16
Then Solomon *s* on the throne of ... 1Chr 29:23
Jehoshaphat king of Judah *s* ... 2Chr 18:9
they *s* in a void place at the ... 2Chr 18:9
of my beard, and *s* down astonied ... Ezr 9:3
I *s* astonied until the evening ... Ezr 9:4
all the people *s* in the street of ... Ezr 10:9
*s* down in the first day of the ... Ezr 10:16
heard these words, that I *s* down ... Neh 1:4
booths, and *s* under the booths ... Neh 8:17
when the king Ahasuerus *s* on the ... Est 1:2
which *s* the first in the kingdom ... Est 1:14
then Mordecai *s* in the king's ... Est 2:19
while Mordecai *s* in the king's ... Est 2:21
the king and Haman *s* down to drink ... Est 3:15
the king *s* upon his royal throne ... Est 5:1
he *s* down among the ashes ... Job 2:8
So they *s* down with him upon the ... Job 2:13
*s* chief, and dwelt as a king in ... Job 29:25
I have not *s* with vain persons, ... Ps 26:4
of Babylon, there we *s* down ... Ps 137:1
I *s* down under his shadow with ... Song 2:3

S

In the ways hast thou *s* for them Jer 3:2
I *s* not in the assembly of the Jer 15:17
I *s* alone because of thy hand Jer 15:17
*s* down in the entry of the new Jer 26:10
before all the Jews that *s* in the Jer 32:12
and, lo, all the princes *s* there Jer 36:12
Now the king *s* in the winterhouse Jer 36:22
*s* in the middle gate, even Jer 39:3
I *s* where they *s*, and remained Eze 3:15
of Chebar, and I *s* where they *s* Eze 3:15
as I *s* in mine house, and the Eze 8:1
the elders of Judah *s* before me Eze 8:1
there *s* women weeping for Tammuz Eze 8:14
of Israel unto me, and *s* before me Eze 14:1
of the LORD, and *s* before me Eze 20:1
but Daniel *s* in the gate of the Dan 2:49
him with sackcloth, and *s* in ashes Jonah 3:6
*s* on the east side of the city, Jonah 4:5
*s* under it in the shadow, till he Jonah 4:5
The people which *s* in darkness Mt 4:16
and to them which *s* in the region Mt 4:16
as Jesus *s* at meat in the house, Mt 9:10
*s* down with him and his disciples Mt 9:10
the house, and *s* by the sea side Mt 13:1
so that he went into a ship, and *s* Mt 13:2
*s* down, and gathered the good into Mt 13:48
them which *s* with him at meat, he Mt 14:9
into a mountain, and *s* down there Mt 15:29
as he *s* upon the mount of Olives Mt 24:3
it on his head, as he *s* at meat Mt 26:7
he *s* down with the twelve Mt 26:20
I *s* daily with you teaching in Mt 26:55
*s* with the servants, to see the Mt 26:58
Now Peter *s* without in the palace Mt 26:69
stone from the door, and *s* upon it Mt 28:2
as Jesus *s* at meat in his house, Mk 2:15
sinners *s* also together with Mk 2:15
And the multitude *s* about him Mk 3:32
about on them which *s* about him Mk 3:34
into a ship, and *s* in the sea Mk 4:1
Herod and them that *s* with him Mk 6:22
for their sakes which *s* with him Mk 6:26
they *s* down in ranks, by hundreds Mk 6:40
he *s* down, and called the twelve, Mk 9:35
*s* by the highway side begging Mk 10:46
a colt tied, whereon never man *s* Mk 11:2
and he *s* upon him Mk 11:7
Jesus *s* over against the treasury Mk 12:41
as he *s* upon the mount of Olives Mk 13:3
as he *s* at meat, there came a Mk 14:3
And as they *s* and did eat, Jesus Mk 14:18
he *s* with the servants, and warmed Mk 14:54
unto the eleven as they *s* at meat Mk 16:14
*s* on the right hand of God Mk 16:19
again to the minister, and *s* down Lk 4:20
he *s* down, and taught the people Lk 5:3
of others that *s* down with them Lk 5:29
And he that was dead *s* up, and Lk 7:15
house, and *s* down to meat Lk 7:36
when she knew that Jesus *s* at Lk 7:37
they that *s* at meat with him Lk 7:49
which also *s* at Jesus' feet, and Lk 10:39
and he went in, and *s* down to meat Lk 11:37
when one of them that *s* at meat Lk 14:15
a certain blind man *s* by the way Lk 18:35
tied, whereon yet never man *s* Lk 19:30
he *s* down, and the twelve apostles Lk 22:14
together, Peter *s* down among them Lk 22:55
beheld him as he *s* by the fire Lk 22:56
as he *s* at meat with them, he Lk 24:30
his journey, *s* thus on the well Jn 4:6
there he *s* with his disciples Jn 6:3
So the men *s* down, in number Jn 6:10
he *s* down, and taught them Jn 8:2
said, Is not this he that *s* Jn 9:8
but Mary *s* still in the house Jn 11:20
them that *s* at the table with him Jn 12:2
had found a young ass, *s* thereon Jn 12:14
*s* down in the judgment seat in a Jn 19:13
fire, and it *s* upon each of them Acts 2:3
*s* for alms at the Beautiful gate Acts 3:10
all that *s* in the council, Acts 6:15
and when she saw Peter, she *s* up Acts 9:40
*s* upon his throne, and made an Acts 12:21
on the sabbath day, and *s* down Acts 13:14
there *s* a certain man at Lystra, Acts 14:8
we *s* down, and spake unto the Acts 16:13
there *s* in a window a certain Acts 20:9
morrow I *s* on the judgment seat Acts 25:17
Bernice, and they that *s* with them Acts 26:30
The people *s* down to eat and drink 1Cor 10:7
*s* down on the right hand of the Heb 1:3
*s* down on the right hand of God Heb 10:12
in heaven, and one *s* on the throne Rev 4:2
he that *s* was to look upon like a Rev 4:3
to him that *s* on the throne Rev 4:9
before him that *s* on the throne Rev 4:10
*s* on the throne a book written Rev 5:1
of him that *s* upon the throne Rev 5:7
he that *s* on him had a bow Rev 6:2
power was given to him that *s* Rev 6:4
he that *s* on him had a pair of Rev 6:5
his name that *s* on him was Death, Rev 6:8
vision, and them that *s* on them Rev 9:17
which *s* before God on their seats Rev 11:16
upon the cloud one *s* like unto Rev 14:14
voice to him that *s* on the cloud Rev 14:15
he that *s* on the cloud thrust in Rev 14:16
God that *s* on the throne, saying, Rev 19:4
he that *s* upon him was called Rev 19:11
against him that *s* on the horse Rev 19:19
of him that *s* upon the horse Rev 19:21
they *s* upon them, and judgment was Rev 20:4
white throne, and him that *s* on it Rev 20:11
he that *s* upon the throne said, Rev 21:5

**SATAN** (*sa'-tun*) *The adversary.*
*S* stood up against Israel, and 1Chr 21:1
LORD, and *S* came also among them Job 1:6
And the LORD said unto *S*, Whence Job 1:7
Then *S* answered the LORD, and said Job 1:7
And the LORD said unto *S*, Hast Job 1:8
Then *S* answered the LORD, and said Job 1:9
And the LORD said unto *S*, Behold, Job 1:12
So *S* went forth from the presence Job 1:12
*S* came also among them to present Job 2:1
And the LORD said unto *S*, From Job 2:2
*S* answered the LORD, and said, Job 2:2
And the LORD said unto *S*, Hast Job 2:3
*S* answered the LORD, and said, Job 2:4
And the LORD said unto *S*, Behold, Job 2:6
So went *S* forth from the presence Job 2:7
let *S* stand at his right hand Ps 109:6
*S* standing at his right hand to Zec 3:1
*S*, The LORD rebuke thee, O *S* Zec 3:2
Jesus unto him, Get thee hence, *S* Mt 4:10
And if *S* cast out *S*, he is Mt 12:26
unto Peter, Get thee behind me, *S* Mt 16:23
forty days, tempted of *S* Mk 1:13
How can *S* cast out *S* Mk 3:23
if *S* rise up against himself, and Mk 3:26
*S* cometh immediately, and taketh Mk 4:15
saying, Get thee behind me, *S* Mk 8:33
unto him, Get thee behind me, *S* Lk 4:8
I beheld *S* as lightning fall from Lk 10:18
If *S* also be divided against Lk 11:18
whom *S* hath bound, lo, these Lk 13:16
Then entered *S* into Judas Lk 22:3
*S* hath desired to have you, that Lk 22:31
after the sop *S* entered into him Jn 13:27
why hath *S* filled thine heart to Acts 5:3
and from the power of *S* unto God Acts 26:18
bruise *S* under your feet shortly Rom 16:20
unto *S* for the destruction of the 1Cor 5:5
that *S* tempt you not for your 1Cor 7:5
Lest *S* should get an advantage of 2Cor 2:11
for *S* himself is transformed into 2Cor 11:14
the messenger of *S* to buffet me 2Cor 12:7
but *S* hindered us 1Th 2:18
the working of *S* with all power 2Th 2:9
whom I have delivered unto *S* 1Ti 1:20
are already turned aside after *S* 1Ti 5:15
not, but are the synagogue of *S* Rev 2:9
slain among you, where *S* dwelleth Rev 2:13
have not known the depths of *S* Rev 2:24
make them of the synagogue of *S* Rev 3:9
serpent, called the Devil, and *S* Rev 12:9
serpent, which is the Devil, and *S* Rev 20:2
*S* shall be loosed out of his Rev 20:7

**SATAN'S** (*sa'-tuns*)
dwellest, even where *S* seat is Rev 2:13

**SATEST**
thou *s* in the throne judging Ps 9:4
*s* upon a stately bed, and a table Eze 23:41

**SATIATE**
I will *s* the soul of the priests Jer 31:14
shall devour, and it shall be *s* Jer 46:10

**SATIATED**
For I have *s* the weary soul, and I Jer 31:25

**SATISFACTION**
Moreover ye shall take no *s* for Num 35:31
ye shall take no *s* for him that Num 35:32

**SATISFIED**
my lust shall be *s* upon them Ex 15:9
and ye shall eat, and not be *s* Lev 26:26
shall come, and shall eat and be *s* Deut 14:29
*s* with favour, and full with the Deut 33:23
God, and are not *s* with my flesh Job 19:22
shall not be *s* with bread Job 27:14
we cannot be *s* Job 31:31
I shall be *s*, when I awake, with Ps 17:15
The meek shall eat and be *s* Ps 22:26
They shall be abundantly *s* with Ps 36:8
days of famine they shall be *s* Ps 37:19
meat, and grudge if they be not *s* Ps 59:15
My soul shall be *s* as with marrow Ps 63:5
we shall be *s* with the goodness Ps 65:4
of the rock should I have *s* thee Ps 81:16
the earth is *s* with the fruit of Ps 104:13
*s* them with the bread of heaven Ps 105:40
his land shall be *s* with bread Prov 12:11
A man shall be *s* with good by the Prov 12:14
good man shall be *s* from himself Prov 14:14
A man's belly shall be *s* with the Prov 18:20
and he that hath it shall abide *s* Prov 19:23
and thou shalt be *s* with bread Prov 20:13
so the eyes of man are never *s* Prov 27:20
are three things that are never *s* Prov 30:15
the eye is not *s* with seeing Eccl 1:8
neither is his eye *s* with riches Eccl 4:8
silver shall not be *s* with silver Eccl 5:10
left hand, and they shall not be *s* Is 9:20
he roasteth roast, and is *s* Is 44:16
of his soul, and shall be *s* Is 53:11
be *s* with the breasts of her Is 66:11
shall be *s* with my goodness Jer 31:14
all that spoil her shall be *s* Jer 50:10
his soul shall be *s* upon mount Jer 50:19
the Assyrians, to be *s* with bread Lam 5:6
them, and yet couldest not be *s* Eze 16:28
and yet thou wast not *s* herewith Eze 16:29
oil, and ye shall be *s* therewith Joel 2:19
ye shall eat in plenty, and be *s* Joel 2:26
but they were not *s* Amos 4:8
Thou shalt eat, but not be *s* Mic 6:14
and is as death, and cannot be *s* Hab 2:5

**SATISFIEST**
*s* the desire of every living Ps 145:16

**SATISFIETH**
Who *s* thy mouth with good things Ps 103:5
For he *s* the longing soul, and Ps 107:9
your labour for that which *s* not Is 55:2

**SATISFY**
To *s* the desolate and waste ground Job 38:27
O *s* us early with thy mercy Ps 90:14
With long life will I *s* him Ps 91:16
I will *s* her poor with bread Ps 132:15
let her breasts *s* thee at all Prov 5:19
if he steal to *s* his soul when he Prov 6:30
hungry, and *s* the afflicted soul Is 58:10
*s* thy soul in drought, and make Is 58:11
they shall not *s* their souls Eze 7:19
From whence can a man *s* these men Mk 8:4

**SATISFYING**
eateth to the *s* of his soul Prov 13:25
any honour to the *s* of the flesh Col 2:23

**SATYR**
the *s* shall cry to his fellow Is 34:14

**SATYRS**
there, and *s* shall dance there Is 13:21

**SAUL** (*sawl*) See PAUL, SAUL'S, SHAUL.
*1. The first king of Israel.*
And he had a son, whose name was *S* 1Sa 9:2
And Kish said to *S* his son 1Sa 9:3
*S* said to his servant that was 1Sa 9:5
Then said *S* to his servant, But, 1Sa 9:7
And the servant answered *S* again 1Sa 9:8
Then said *S* to his servant, Well 1Sa 9:10
in his ear a day before *S* came 1Sa 9:15
And when Samuel saw *S*, the LORD 1Sa 9:17
Then *S* drew near to Samuel in the 1Sa 9:18
And Samuel answered *S*, and said, I 1Sa 9:19
*S* answered and said, Am not I a 1Sa 9:21
And Samuel took *S* and his servant, 1Sa 9:22
was upon it, and set it before *S* 1Sa 9:24
So *S* did eat with Samuel that day 1Sa 9:24
Samuel communed with *S* upon the 1Sa 9:25
that Samuel called *S* to the top 1Sa 9:26
*S* arose, and they went out both of 1Sa 9:26
end of the city, Samuel said to *S* 1Sa 9:27
Is *S* also among the prophets 1Sa 10:11
Is *S* also among the prophets 1Sa 10:12
*S* said unto his uncle, He told us 1Sa 10:16
*S* the son of Kish was taken 1Sa 10:21
*S* also went home to Gibeah 1Sa 10:26
the messengers to Gibeah of *S* 1Sa 11:4
*S* came after the herd out of the 1Sa 11:5
*S* said, What aileth the people 1Sa 11:5
*S* when he heard those tidings 1Sa 11:6
cometh not forth after *S* and after 1Sa 11:7
that *S* put the people in three 1Sa 11:11
that said, Shall *S* reign over us 1Sa 11:12
*S* said, There shall not a man be 1Sa 11:13
there they made *S* king before the 1Sa 11:15
and there *S* and all the men of 1Sa 11:15
*S* reigned one year 1Sa 13:1
*S* chose him three thousand men of 1Sa 13:2
thousand were with *S* in Michmash 1Sa 13:2
*S* blew the trumpet throughout all 1Sa 13:3
all Israel heard say that *S* had 1Sa 13:4
called together after *S* to Gilgal 1Sa 13:4
As for *S*, he was yet in Gilgal 1Sa 13:7
*S* said, Bring hither a burnt 1Sa 13:9
*S* went out to meet him, that he 1Sa 13:10
*S* said, Because I saw that the 1Sa 13:11
And Samuel said to *S*, Thou hast 1Sa 13:13
*S* numbered the people that were 1Sa 13:15
And *S*, and Jonathan his son, and the 1Sa 13:16
of the people that were with *S* 1Sa 13:22
but with *S* and with Jonathan his 1Sa 13:22
that Jonathan the son of *S* said 1Sa 14:1
*S* tarried in the uttermost part 1Sa 14:2
the watchmen of *S* in Gibeah of 1Sa 14:16
Then said *S* unto the people that 1Sa 14:17
*S* said unto Ahiah, Bring hither 1Sa 14:18
while *S* talked unto the priest, 1Sa 14:19
*S* said unto the priest, Withdraw 1Sa 14:19
And *S* and all the people that were 1Sa 14:20
the Israelites that were with *S* 1Sa 14:21
for *S* had adjured the people, 1Sa 14:24
Then they told *S*, saying, Behold, 1Sa 14:33
*S* said, Disperse yourselves among 1Sa 14:34
*S* built an altar unto the LORD 1Sa 14:35
*S* said, Let us go down after the 1Sa 14:36
*S* asked counsel of God, Shall I 1Sa 14:37
*S* said, Draw ye near hither, all 1Sa 14:38
And the people said unto *S* 1Sa 14:40
Therefore *S* said unto the LORD 1Sa 14:41
And *S* and Jonathan were taken 1Sa 14:41
*S* said, Cast lots between me and 1Sa 14:42
Then *S* said to Jonathan, Tell me 1Sa 14:43
*S* answered, God do so and more 1Sa 14:44

And the people said unto *S* 1Sa 14:45
Then *S* went up from following the 1Sa 14:46
So *S* took the kingdom over Israel 1Sa 14:47
Now the sons of *S* were Jonathan 1Sa 14:49
And Kish was the father of *S* 1Sa 14:51
the Philistines all the days of *S* 1Sa 14:52
when *S* saw any strong man, or any 1Sa 14:52
Samuel also said unto *S*, The LORD 1Sa 15:1
*S* gathered the people together, 1Sa 15:4
*S* came to a city of Amalek, and 1Sa 15:5
*S* said unto the Kenites, Go, 1Sa 15:6
*S* smote the Amalekites from 1Sa 15:7
But *S* and the people spared Agag, 1Sa 15:9
that I have set up *S* to be king 1Sa 15:11
early to meet *S* in the morning 1Sa 15:12
*S* came to Carmel, and, behold, he 1Sa 15:12
And Samuel came to *S* 1Sa 15:13
*S* said unto him, Blessed be thou 1Sa 15:13
*S* said, They have brought them 1Sa 15:15
Then Samuel said unto *S*, Stay, and 1Sa 15:16
*S* said unto Samuel, Yea, I have 1Sa 15:20
*S* said unto Samuel, I have sinned 1Sa 15:24
And Samuel said unto *S*, I will not 1Sa 15:26
So Samuel turned again after *S* 1Sa 15:31
and *S* worshipped the LORD 1Sa 15:31
*S* went up to his house to Gibeah 1Sa 15:34
up to his house to Gibeah of *S* 1Sa 15:34
see *S* until the day of his death 1Sa 15:35
nevertheless Samuel mourned for *S* 1Sa 15:35
he had made *S* king over Israel 1Sa 15:35
How long wilt thou mourn for *S* 1Sa 16:1
if *S* hear it, he will kill me 1Sa 16:2
of the LORD departed from *S* 1Sa 16:14
*S* said unto his servants, Provide 1Sa 16:17
Wherefore *S* sent messengers unto 1Sa 16:19
sent them by David his son unto *S* 1Sa 16:20
And David came to *S*, and stood 1Sa 16:21
*S* sent to Jesse, saying, Let 1Sa 16:22
evil spirit from God was upon *S* 1Sa 16:23
so *S* was refreshed, and was well, 1Sa 16:23
And *S* and the men of Israel were 1Sa 17:2
a Philistine, and ye servants to *S* 1Sa 17:8
When *S* and all Israel heard those 1Sa 17:11
for an old man in the days of *S* 1Sa 17:12
went and followed *S* to the battle 1Sa 17:13
and the three eldest followed *S* 1Sa 17:14
returned from *S* to feed his 1Sa 17:15
Now *S*, and they, and all the men of 1Sa 17:19
they rehearsed them before *S* 1Sa 17:31
And David said to *S*, Let no man's 1Sa 17:32
*S* said to David, Thou art not 1Sa 17:33
And David said unto *S*, Thy servant 1Sa 17:34
*S* said unto David, Go, and the 1Sa 17:37
*S* armed David with his armour, and 1Sa 17:38
And David said unto *S*, I cannot go 1Sa 17:39
when *S* saw David go forth against 1Sa 17:55
brought him before *S* with the 1Sa 17:57
*S* said to him, Whose son art thou 1Sa 17:58
made an end of speaking unto *S* 1Sa 18:1
*S* took him that day, and would let 1Sa 18:2
went out whithersoever *S* sent him 1Sa 18:5
*S* set him over the men of war, and 1Sa 18:5
and dancing, to meet king *S* 1Sa 18:6
*S* hath slain his thousands, and 1Sa 18:7
*S* was very wroth, and the saying 1Sa 18:8
*S* eyed David from that day and 1Sa 18:9
evil spirit from God came upon *S* 1Sa 18:10
And *S* cast the javelin 1Sa 18:11
*S* was afraid of David, because 1Sa 18:12
with him, and was departed from *S* 1Sa 18:12
Therefore *S* removed him from him, 1Sa 18:13
Wherefore when *S* saw that he 1Sa 18:15
*S* said to David, Behold my elder 1Sa 18:17
For *S* said, Let not mine hand be 1Sa 18:17
And David said unto *S*, Who am I 1Sa 18:18
and they told *S*, and the thing 1Sa 18:20
*S* said, I will give him her, that 1Sa 18:21
Wherefore *S* said to David, Thou 1Sa 18:21
*S* commanded his servants, saying, 1Sa 18:22
And the servants of *S* told him 1Sa 18:24
*S* said, Thus shall ye say to 1Sa 18:25
But *S* thought to make David fall 1Sa 18:25
*S* gave him Michal his daughter to 1Sa 18:27
*S* saw and knew that the LORD was 1Sa 18:28
*S* was yet the more afraid of 1Sa 18:29
and *S* became David's enemy 1Sa 18:29
wisely than all the servants of *S* 1Sa 18:30
*S* spake to Jonathan his son, and 1Sa 19:1
*S* my father seeketh to kill thee 1Sa 19:2
good of David unto *S* his father 1Sa 19:4
*S* hearkened unto the voice of 1Sa 19:6
*S* sware, As the LORD liveth, he 1Sa 19:6
And Jonathan brought David to *S* 1Sa 19:7
spirit from the LORD was upon *S* 1Sa 19:9
*S* sought to smite David even to 1Sa 19:10
*S* also sent messengers unto 1Sa 19:11
when *S* sent messengers to take 1Sa 19:14
*S* sent the messengers again to 1Sa 19:15
*S* said unto Michal, Why hast thou 1Sa 19:17
And Michal answered *S*, He said 1Sa 19:17
him all that *S* had done to him 1Sa 19:18
And it was told *S*, saying, Behold, 1Sa 19:19
*S* sent messengers to take David 1Sa 19:20
God was upon the messengers of *S* 1Sa 19:20
And when it was told *S*, he sent 1Sa 19:21
*S* sent messengers again the third 1Sa 19:21
Is *S* also among the prophets 1Sa 19:24
Nevertheless *S* spake not any 1Sa 20:26
*S* said unto Jonathan his son, 1Sa 20:27
And Jonathan answered *S*, David 1Sa 20:28
And Jonathan answered *S* his father 1Sa 20:32
*S* cast a javelin at him to smite 1Sa 20:33
servants of *S* was there that day 1Sa 21:7
of the herdmen that belonged to *S* 1Sa 21:7
and fled that day for fear of *S* 1Sa 21:10
*S* hath slain his thousands, and 1Sa 21:11
When *S* heard that David was 1Sa 22:6
(now *S* abode in Gibeah under a 1Sa 22:6
Then *S* said unto his servants 1Sa 22:7
was set over the servants of *S* 1Sa 22:9
*S* said, Hear now, thou son of 1Sa 22:12
*S* said unto him, Why have ye 1Sa 22:13
Abiathar shewed David that *S* had 1Sa 22:21
that he would surely tell *S* 1Sa 22:22
it was told *S* that David was come 1Sa 23:7
*S* said, God hath delivered him 1Sa 23:7
*S* called all the people together 1Sa 23:8
David knew that *S* secretly 1Sa 23:9
that *S* seeketh to come to Keilah 1Sa 23:10
will *S* come down, as thy servant 1Sa 23:11
me and my men into the hand of *S* 1Sa 23:12
it was told *S* that David was 1Sa 23:13
*S* sought him every day, but God 1Sa 23:14
David saw that *S* was come out to 1Sa 23:15
for the hand of *S* my father shall 1Sa 23:17
that also *S* my father knoweth 1Sa 23:17
up the Ziphites to *S* to Gibeah 1Sa 23:19
*S* said, Blessed be ye of the LORD 1Sa 23:21
arose, and went to Ziph before *S* 1Sa 23:24
*S* also and his men went to seek 1Sa 23:25
when *S* heard that, he pursued 1Sa 23:25
*S* went on this side of the 1Sa 23:26
haste to get away for fear of *S* 1Sa 23:26
for *S* and his men compassed David 1Sa 23:26
But there came a messenger unto *S* 1Sa 23:27
Wherefore *S* returned from 1Sa 23:28
to pass, when *S* was returned from 1Sa 24:1
Then *S* took three thousand chosen 1Sa 24:2
*S* went in to cover his feet 1Sa 24:3
them not to rise against *S* 1Sa 24:7
But *S* rose up out of the cave, and 1Sa 24:7
out of the cave, and cried after *S* 1Sa 24:8
when *S* looked behind him, David 1Sa 24:8
And David said to *S*, Wherefore 1Sa 24:9
words unto *S*, that *S* said 1Sa 24:16
*S* lifted up his voice, and wept 1Sa 24:16
And David sware unto *S* 1Sa 24:22
And *S* went home 1Sa 24:22
But *S* had given Michal his 1Sa 25:44
Ziphites came unto *S* to Gibeah 1Sa 26:1
Then *S* arose, and went down to the 1Sa 26:2
*S* pitched in the hill of Hachilah 1Sa 26:3
he saw that *S* came after him into 1Sa 26:3
understood that *S* was come in 1Sa 26:4
to the place where *S* had pitched 1Sa 26:5
beheld the place where *S* lay 1Sa 26:5
*S* lay in the trench, and the 1Sa 26:5
go down with me to *S* to the camp 1Sa 26:6
*S* lay sleeping within the trench, 1Sa 26:7
*S* knew David's voice, and said, Is 1Sa 26:17
Then said *S*, I have sinned 1Sa 26:21
Then *S* said to David, Blessed be 1Sa 26:25
way, and *S* returned to his place 1Sa 26:25
perish one day by the hand of *S* 1Sa 27:1
*S* shall despair of me, to seek me 1Sa 27:1
it was told *S* that David was fled 1Sa 27:4
*S* had put away those that had 1Sa 28:3
*S* gathered all Israel together, 1Sa 28:4
when *S* saw the host of the 1Sa 28:5
when *S* enquired of the LORD, the 1Sa 28:6
Then said *S* unto his servants, 1Sa 28:7
*S* disguised himself, and put on 1Sa 28:8
thou knowest what *S* hath done 1Sa 28:9
*S* sware to her by the LORD, 1Sa 28:10
and the woman spake to *S*, saying, 1Sa 28:12
for thou art *S* 1Sa 28:12
And the woman said unto *S*, I saw 1Sa 28:13
*S* perceived that it was Samuel, 1Sa 28:14
And Samuel said to *S*, Why hast 1Sa 28:15
*S* answered, I am sore distressed 1Sa 28:15
Then *S* fell straightway all along 1Sa 28:20
the woman came unto *S* 1Sa 28:21
And she brought it before *S* 1Sa 28:25
the servant of *S* the king of 1Sa 29:3
*S* slew his thousands, and David 1Sa 29:5
Philistines followed hard upon *S* 1Sa 31:2
And the battle went sore against *S* 1Sa 31:3
Then said *S* unto his armourbearer 1Sa 31:4
Therefore *S* took a sword, and fell 1Sa 31:4
armourbearer saw that *S* was dead 1Sa 31:5
So *S* died, and his three sons, and 1Sa 31:6
the men of Israel fled, and that *S* 1Sa 31:7
the slain, that they found *S* 1Sa 31:8
the Philistines had done to *S* 1Sa 31:11
all night, and took the body of *S* 1Sa 31:12
came to pass after the death of *S* 2Sa 1:1
camp from *S* with his clothes rent 2Sa 1:2
and *S* and Jonathan his son are dead 2Sa 1:4
told him, How knowest thou that *S* 2Sa 1:5
behold, *S* leaned upon his spear 2Sa 1:6
wept, and fasted until even, for *S* 2Sa 1:12
with this lamentation over *S* 2Sa 1:17
vilely cast away, the shield of *S* 2Sa 1:21
the sword of *S* returned not empty 2Sa 1:22
*S* and Jonathan were lovely and 2Sa 1:23
daughters of Israel, weep over *S* 2Sa 1:24
were they that buried *S* 2Sa 2:4
unto your lord, even unto *S* 2Sa 2:5
for your master *S* is dead 2Sa 2:7
took Ish-bosheth the son of *S* 2Sa 2:8
of Ish-bosheth the son of *S* 2Sa 2:12
to Ish-bosheth the son of *S* 2Sa 2:15
long war between the house of *S* 2Sa 3:1
and the house of *S* waxed weaker 2Sa 3:1
was war between the house of *S* 2Sa 3:6
himself strong for the house of *S* 2Sa 3:6
*S* had a concubine, whose name was 2Sa 3:7
unto the house of *S* thy father 2Sa 3:8
the kingdom from the house of *S* 2Sa 3:10
old when the tidings came of *S* 2Sa 4:4
the son of *S* thine enemy, which 2Sa 4:8
my lord the king this day of *S* 2Sa 4:8
*S* is dead, thinking to have 2Sa 4:10
when *S* was king over us, thou 2Sa 5:2
of *S* came out to meet David 2Sa 6:20
Michal the daughter of *S* had no 2Sa 6:23
from him, as I took it from *S* 2Sa 7:15
that is left of the house of *S* 2Sa 9:1
there was of the house of *S* a 2Sa 9:2
not yet any of the house of *S* 2Sa 9:3
the son of Jonathan, the son of *S* 2Sa 9:6
thee all the land of *S* thy father 2Sa 9:7
son all that pertained to *S* 2Sa 9:9
thee out of the hand of *S* 2Sa 12:7
of the family of the house of *S* 2Sa 16:5
all the blood of the house of *S* 2Sa 16:8
the servant of the house of *S* 2Sa 19:17
Mephibosheth the son of *S* came 2Sa 19:24
And the LORD answered, It is for *S* 2Sa 21:1
*S* sought to slay them in his zeal 2Sa 21:2
will have no silver nor gold of *S* 2Sa 21:4
up unto the LORD in Gibeah of *S* 2Sa 21:6
the son of Jonathan the son of *S* 2Sa 21:7
David and Jonathan the son of *S* 2Sa 21:7
of Aiah, whom she bare unto *S* 2Sa 21:8
sons of Michal the daughter of *S* 2Sa 21:8
of Aiah, the concubine of *S* 2Sa 21:11
David went and took the bones of *S* 2Sa 21:12
Philistines had slain *S* in Gilboa 2Sa 21:12
up from thence the bones of *S* 2Sa 21:13
And the bones of *S* and Jonathan his 2Sa 21:14
enemies, and out of the hand of *S* 2Sa 22:1
in the days of *S* they made war 1Chr 5:10
Ner begat Kish, and Kish begat *S* 1Chr 8:33
*S* begat Jonathan, and Malchi-shua, 1Chr 8:33
and Kish begat *S* 1Chr 9:39
*S* begat Jonathan, and Malchi-shua, 1Chr 9:39
Philistines followed hard after *S* 1Chr 10:2
and Malchi-shua, the sons of *S* 1Chr 10:2
And the battle went sore against *S* 1Chr 10:3
Then said *S* to his armourbearer, 1Chr 10:4
So *S* took a sword, and fell upon 1Chr 10:4
armourbearer saw that *S* was dead 1Chr 10:5
So *S* died, and his three sons, and 1Chr 10:6
saw that they fled, and that *S* 1Chr 10:7
the slain, that they found *S* 1Chr 10:8
the Philistines had done to *S* 1Chr 10:11
men, and took away the body of *S* 1Chr 10:12
So *S* died for his transgression 1Chr 10:13
time past, even when *S* was king 1Chr 11:2
because of *S* the son of Kish 1Chr 12:1
Philistines against *S* to battle 1Chr 12:19
He will fall to his master *S* to 1Chr 12:19
to turn the kingdom of *S* to him 1Chr 12:23
of Benjamin, the kindred of *S* 1Chr 12:29
kept the ward of the house of *S* 1Chr 12:29
not at it in the days of *S* 1Chr 13:3
of *S* looking out at a window saw 1Chr 15:29
*S* the son of Kish, and Abner the 1Chr 26:28
enemies, and from the hand of *S* Ps 18:*t*
Doeg the Edomite came and told *S* Ps 52:*t*
the Ziphims came and said to *S* Ps 54:*t*
when he fled from *S* in the cave Ps 57:*t*
when *S* sent, and they watched the Ps 59:*t*
Gibeah of *S* is fled Is 10:29
gave unto them *S* the son of Cis Acts 13:21

2. *An Edomite king.*

*S* of Rehoboth by the river Gen 36:37
*S* died, and Baal-hanan the son of Gen 36:38

3. *Original name of Paul.*

man's feet, whose name was *S* Acts 7:58
*S* was consenting unto his death Acts 8:1
As for *S*, he made havock of the Acts 8:3
And *S*, yet breathing out Acts 9:1
a voice saying unto him, Saul, *S* Acts 9:4
And *S* arose from the earth Acts 9:8
house of Judas for one called *S* Acts 9:11
his hands on him said, Brother *S* Acts 9:17
Then was *S* certain days with the Acts 9:19
But *S* increased the more in Acts 9:22
their laying await was known of *S* Acts 9:24
when *S* was come to Jerusalem, he Acts 9:26
Barnabas to Tarsus, for to seek *S* Acts 11:25
by the hands of Barnabas and *S* Acts 11:30
*S* returned from Jerusalem, when Acts 12:25
up with Herod the tetrarch, and *S* Acts 13:1
*S* for the work whereunto I have Acts 13:2
who called for Barnabas and *S* Acts 13:7
Then *S*, (who also is called Paul, Acts 13:9
a voice saying unto me, Saul, *S* Acts 22:7
stood, and said unto me, Brother *S* Acts 22:13
in the Hebrew tongue, Saul, *S* Acts 26:14

**SAUL'S**

asses of Kish *S* father were lost 1Sa 9:3
*S* uncle said unto him and to his 1Sa 10:14
*S* uncle said, Tell me, I pray 1Sa 10:15
the name of *S* wife was Ahinoam, 1Sa 14:50
Abner, the son of Ner, *S* uncle 1Sa 14:50
*S* servants said unto him, Behold 1Sa 16:15
also in the sight of *S* servants 1Sa 18:5

and there was a javelin in *S* hand ... 1Sa 18:10
to pass at the time when Merab *S* ... 1Sa 18:19
Michal *S* daughter loved David ... 1Sa 18:20
*S* servants spake those words in ... 1Sa 18:23
that Michal *S* daughter loved him ... 1Sa 18:28
But Jonathan *S* son delighted much ... 1Sa 19:2
he slipped away out of *S* presence ... 1Sa 19:10
arose, and Abner sat by *S* side ... 1Sa 20:25
Then *S* anger was kindled against ... 1Sa 20:30
Jonathan *S* son arose, and went to ... 1Sa 23:16
off the skirt of *S* robe privily ... 1Sa 24:4
because he had cut off *S* skirt ... 1Sa 24:5
the cruse of water from *S* bolster ... 1Sa 26:12
Abinadab, and Melchi-shua, *S* sons ... 1Sa 31:2
the son of Ner, captain of *S* host ... 2Sa 2:8
Ish-bosheth *S* son was forty years ... 2Sa 2:10
first bring Michal *S* daughter ... 2Sa 3:13
messengers to Ish-bosheth *S* son ... 2Sa 3:14
when *S* son heard that Abner was ... 2Sa 4:1
*S* son had two men that were ... 2Sa 4:2
*S* son, had a son that was lame of ... 2Sa 4:4
Michal *S* daughter looked through ... 2Sa 6:16
*S* servant, and said unto him, I ... 2Sa 9:9
even of *S* brethren of Benjamin ... 1Chr 12:2

### SAVE

me, but they will *s* thee alive ... Gen 12:12
*S* only that which the young men ... Gen 14:24
*s* the bread which he did eat ... Gen 39:6
to *s* your lives by a great ... Gen 45:7
this day, to *s* much people alive ... Gen 50:20
every daughter ye shall *s* alive ... Ex 1:22
*s* that which every man must eat, ... Ex 12:16
*s* unto the LORD only, he shall be ... Ex 22:20
*s* Caleb the son of Jephunneh, and ... Num 14:30
*s* Caleb the son of Jephunneh, and ... Num 26:65
*S* Caleb the son of Jephunneh the ... Num 32:12
*S* Caleb the son of Jephunneh ... Deut 1:36
*S* when there shall be no poor ... Deut 15:4
against your enemies, to *s* you ... Deut 20:4
thou shalt *s* alive nothing that ... Deut 20:16
cried, and there was none to *s* her ... Deut 22:27
evermore, and no man shall *s* thee ... Deut 28:29
that ye will *s* alive my father, ... Josh 2:13
us quickly, and *s* us, and help us ... Josh 10:6
burned none of them, *s* Hazor only ... Josh 11:13
*s* the Hivites the inhabitants of ... Josh 11:19
*s* cities to dwell in, with their ... Josh 14:4
the LORD, (*s* us not this day,) ... Josh 22:22
thou shalt *s* Israel from the hand ... Judg 6:14
Lord, wherewith shall I *s* Israel ... Judg 6:15
will ye *s* him ... Judg 6:31
If thou wilt *s* Israel by mine ... Judg 6:36
thou wilt *s* Israel by mine hand ... Judg 6:37
men that lapped will I *s* you ... Judg 7:7
This is nothing else *s* the sword ... Judg 7:14
it may *s* us out of the hand of ... 1Sa 4:3
that he will *s* us out of the hand ... 1Sa 7:8
that he may *s* my people out of ... 1Sa 9:16
shouted, and said, God *s* the king ... 1Sa 10:24
said, How shall this man *s* us ... 1Sa 10:27
then, if there be no man to *s* us ... 1Sa 11:3
the LORD to *s* by many or by few ... 1Sa 14:6
If thou *s* not thy to night, to ... 1Sa 19:11
for there is no other *s* that here ... 1Sa 21:9
the Philistines, and *s* Keilah ... 1Sa 23:2
*s* four hundred young men, which ... 1Sa 30:17
*s* to every man his wife and his ... 1Sa 30:22
*s* my people Israel out of the ... 2Sa 3:18
*s* one little ewe lamb, which he ... 2Sa 12:3
God *s* the king, God *s* the king ... 2Sa 16:16
God *s* the king, God *s* the king ... 2Sa 16:16
the afflicted people thou wilt *s* ... 2Sa 22:28
For who is God, *s* the LORD ... 2Sa 22:32
and who is a rock, *s* our God ... 2Sa 22:32
looked, but there was none to *s* ... 2Sa 22:42
that thou mayest *s* thine own life ... 1Kin 1:12
him, and say, God *s* king Adonijah ... 1Kin 1:25
and say, God *s* king Solomon ... 1Kin 1:34
people said, God *s* king Solomon ... 1Kin 1:39
the house, *s* we two in the house ... 1Kin 3:18
the ark *s* the two tables of stone ... 1Kin 8:9
*s* only in the matter of Uriah the ... 1Kin 15:5
we may find grass to *s* the horses ... 1Kin 18:5
peradventure he will *s* thy life ... 1Kin 20:31
*s* only with the king of Israel ... 1Kin 22:31
in the house, *s* a pot of oil ... 2Kin 4:2
if they *s* us alive, we shall live ... 2Kin 7:4
hands, and said, God *s* the king ... 2Kin 11:12
*S* that the high places were not ... 2Kin 15:4
*s* me out of the hand of the king ... 2Kin 16:7
*s* thou us out of his hand, that ... 2Kin 19:19
I will defend this city, to *s* it ... 2Kin 19:34
*s* the poorest sort of the people ... 2Kin 24:14
*S* us, O God of our salvation, and ... 1Chr 16:35
*s* only to burn sacrifice before ... 2Chr 2:6
There was nothing in the ark *s* ... 2Chr 5:10
*s* only with the king of Israel ... 2Chr 18:30
*s* Jehoahaz, the youngest of his ... 2Chr 21:17
*s* the priests, and they that ... 2Chr 23:6
him, and said, God *s* the king ... 2Chr 23:11
*s* the beast that I rode upon ... Neh 2:12
go into the temple to *s* his life ... Neh 6:11
but *s* his life ... Job 2:6
he shall not *s* of that which he ... Job 20:20
he shall *s* the humble person ... Job 22:29
thine own right hand can *s* thee ... Job 40:14
*s* me, O my God ... Ps 3:7
oh *s* me for thy mercies' sake ... Ps 6:4
*s* me from all them that persecute ... Ps 7:1
For thou wilt *s* the afflicted ... Ps 18:27
For who is God *s* the LORD ... Ps 18:31
or who is a rock *s* our God ... Ps 18:31
but there was none to *s* them ... Ps 18:41
*S*, LORD ... Ps 20:9
*S* me from the lion's mouth ... Ps 22:21
*S* thy people, and bless thine ... Ps 28:9
for an house of defence to *s* me ... Ps 31:2
*s* me for thy mercies' sake ... Ps 31:16
*s* them, because they trust in him ... Ps 37:40
neither did their own arm *s* them ... Ps 44:3
bow, neither shall my sword *s* me ... Ps 44:6
*S* me, O God, by thy name, and ... Ps 54:1
and the LORD shall *s* me ... Ps 55:16
*s* me from the reproach of him ... Ps 57:3
iniquity, and *s* me from bloody men ... Ps 59:2
*s* with thy right hand, and hear me ... Ps 60:5
*S* me, O God ... Ps 69:1
For God will *s* Zion, and will ... Ps 69:35
thine ear unto me, and *s* me ... Ps 71:2
hast given commandment to *s* me ... Ps 71:3
he shall *s* the children of the ... Ps 72:4
shall *s* the souls of the needy ... Ps 72:13
to *s* all the meek of the earth ... Ps 76:9
up thy strength, and come and *s* us ... Ps 80:2
*s* thy servant that trusteth in ... Ps 86:2
*s* the son of thine handmaid ... Ps 86:16
*S* us, O LORD our God, and gather ... Ps 106:47
*s* with thy right hand, and answer ... Ps 108:6
O *s* me according to thy mercy ... Ps 109:26
to *s* him from those that condemn ... Ps 109:31
*S* now, I beseech thee, O LORD ... Ps 118:25
I am thine, *s* me ... Ps 119:94
*s* me, and I shall keep thy ... Ps 119:146
and thy right hand shall *s* me ... Ps 138:7
hear their cry, and will *s* them ... Ps 145:19
on the LORD, and he shall *s* thee ... Prov 20:22
waited for him, and he will *s* us ... Is 25:9
he will *s* us ... Is 33:22
he will come and *s* you ... Is 35:4
*s* us from his hand, that all the ... Is 37:20
city to *s* it for mine own sake ... Is 37:35
The LORD was ready to *s* me ... Is 38:20
and pray unto a god that cannot *s* ... Is 45:20
nor *s* him out of his trouble ... Is 46:7
*s* thee from these things that ... Is 47:13
none shall *s* thee ... Is 47:15
thee, and I will *s* thy children ... Is 49:25
not shortened, that it cannot *s* ... Is 59:1
in righteousness, mighty to *s* ... Is 63:1
they will say, Arise, and *s* us ... Jer 2:27
if they can *s* thee in the time of ... Jer 2:28
but they shall not *s* them at all ... Jer 11:12
as a mighty man that cannot *s* ... Jer 14:9
for I am with thee to *s* thee ... Jer 15:20
*s* me, and I shall be saved ... Jer 17:14
I will *s* thee from afar, and thy ... Jer 30:10
thee, saith the LORD, to *s* thee ... Jer 30:11
*s* thy people, the remnant of ... Jer 31:7
for I am with you to *s* you ... Jer 42:11
I will *s* thee from afar off, and ... Jer 46:27
*s* your lives, and be like the ... Jer 48:6
for a nation that could not *s* us ... Lam 4:17
his wicked way, to *s* his life ... Eze 3:18
will ye *s* the souls alive that ... Eze 13:18
to *s* the souls alive that should ... Eze 13:19
he shall *s* his soul alive ... Eze 18:27
Therefore will I *s* my flock ... Eze 34:22
I will also *s* you from all your ... Eze 36:29
but I will *s* them out of all ... Eze 37:23
*s* of thee, O king, he shall be ... Dan 6:7
*s* of thee, O king, shall be cast ... Dan 6:12
will *s* them by the LORD their God ... Hos 1:7
will not *s* them by bow, nor by ... Hos 1:7
that may *s* thee in all thy cities ... Hos 13:10
Asshur shall not *s* us ... Hos 14:3
of violence, and thou wilt not *s* ... Hab 1:2
he will *s*, he will rejoice over ... Zeph 3:17
I will *s* her that halteth, and ... Zeph 3:19
I will *s* my people from the east ... Zec 8:7
so will I *s* you, and ye shall be a ... Zec 8:13
the LORD their God shall *s* them ... Zec 9:16
I will *s* the house of Joseph, and ... Zec 10:6
The LORD also shall *s* the tents ... Zec 12:7
for he shall *s* his people from ... Mt 1:21
and awoke him, saying, Lord, *s* us ... Mt 8:25
*s* the Son, and he to whomsoever ... Mt 11:27
*s* in his own country, and in his ... Mt 13:57
he cried, saying, Lord, *s* me ... Mt 14:30
For whosoever will *s* his life ... Mt 16:25
they saw no man, *s* Jesus only ... Mt 17:8
is come to *s* that which was lost ... Mt 18:11
*s* they to whom it is given ... Mt 19:11
it in three days, *s* thyself ... Mt 27:40
himself he cannot *s* ... Mt 27:42
whether Elias will come to *s* him ... Mt 27:49
to *s* life, or to kill ... Mk 3:4
*s* Peter, and James, and John the ... Mk 5:37
*s* that he laid his hands upon a ... Mk 6:5
for their journey, *s* a staff only ... Mk 6:8
For whosoever will *s* his life ... Mk 8:35
the gospel's, the same shall *s* it ... Mk 8:35
*S* Jesus only with themselves ... Mk 9:8
*S* thyself, and come down from the ... Mk 15:30
himself he cannot *s* ... Mk 15:31
*s* unto Sarepta, a city of Sidon, ... Lk 4:26
to *s* life, or to destroy it ... Lk 6:9
*s* Peter, and James, and John, and ... Lk 8:51
For whosoever will *s* his life ... Lk 9:24
for my sake, the same shall *s* it ... Lk 9:24
men's lives, but to *s* them ... Lk 9:56
glory to God, *s* this stranger ... Lk 17:18
seek to *s* his life shall lose it ... Lk 17:33
none is good, *s* one, that is, God ... Lk 18:19
seek and to *s* that which was lost ... Lk 19:10
let him *s* himself, if he be ... Lk 23:35
the king of the Jews, *s* thyself ... Lk 23:37
thou be Christ, *s* thyself and us ... Lk 23:39
there, *s* that one whereinto his ... Jn 6:22
*s* he which is of God, he hath ... Jn 6:46
Father, *s* me from this hour ... Jn 12:27
the world, but to *s* the world ... Jn 12:47
needeth not *s* to wash his feet ... Jn 13:10
*S* yourselves from this untoward ... Acts 2:40
*S* that the Holy Ghost witnesseth ... Acts 20:23
*s* only that they keep themselves ... Acts 21:25
the centurion, willing to *s* Paul ... Acts 27:43
my flesh, and might *s* some of them ... Rom 11:14
preaching to *s* them that believe ... 1Cor 1:21
*s* Jesus Christ, and him crucified ... 1Cor 2:2
*s* the spirit of man which is in ... 1Cor 2:11
whether thou shalt *s* thy husband ... 1Cor 7:16
whether thou shalt *s* thy wife ... 1Cor 7:16
that I might by all means *s* some ... 1Cor 9:22
received I forty stripes *s* one ... 2Cor 11:24
*s* James the Lord's brother ... Gal 1:19
*s* in the cross of our Lord Jesus ... Gal 6:14
came into the world to *s* sinners ... 1Ti 1:15
this thou shalt both *s* thyself ... 1Ti 4:16
that was able to *s* him from death ... Heb 5:7
Wherefore he is able also to *s* ... Heb 7:25
which is able to *s* your souls ... Jas 1:21
can faith *s* him ... Jas 2:14
is one lawgiver, who is able to *s* ... Jas 4:12
prayer of faith shall *s* the sick ... Jas 5:15
his way shall *s* a soul from death ... Jas 5:20
even baptism doth also now *s* us ( ... 1Pet 3:21
others *s* with fear, pulling them ... Jude 23
*s* he that had the mark, or the ... Rev 13:17

### SAVED

they said, Thou hast *s* our lives ... Gen 47:25
but *s* the men children alive ... Ex 1:17
have *s* the men children alive ... Ex 1:18
Thus the LORD *s* Israel that day ... Ex 14:30
ye shall be *s* from your enemies ... Num 10:9
I had slain thee, and *s* her alive ... Num 22:33
Have ye *s* all the women alive ... Num 31:15
O people *s* by the LORD, the ... Deut 33:29
Joshua *s* Rahab the harlot alive, ... Josh 6:25
saying, Mine own hand hath *s* me ... Judg 7:2
if ye had *s* them alive, I would ... Judg 8:19
they had *s* alive of the women of ... Judg 21:14
who himself *s* you out of all your ... 1Sa 10:19
So the LORD *s* Israel that day ... 1Sa 14:23
So David *s* the inhabitants of ... 1Sa 23:5
David *s* neither man nor woman ... 1Sa 27:11
which this day have *s* thy life ... 2Sa 19:5
The king *s* us out of the hand of ... 2Sa 19:9
so shall I be *s* from mine enemies ... 2Sa 22:4
*s* himself there, not once nor ... 2Kin 6:10
but he *s* them by the hand of ... 2Kin 14:27
the LORD *s* them by a great ... 1Chr 11:14
Thus the LORD *s* Hezekiah and the ... 2Chr 32:22
who *s* them out of the hand of ... Neh 9:27
so shall I be *s* from mine enemies ... Ps 18:3
There is no king *s* by the ... Ps 33:16
*s* him out of all his troubles ... Ps 34:6
But thou hast *s* us from our ... Ps 44:7
and we shall be *s* ... Ps 80:3
and we shall be *s* ... Ps 80:7
and we shall be *s* ... Ps 80:19
Nevertheless he *s* them for his ... Ps 106:8
he *s* them from the hand of him ... Ps 106:10
he *s* them out of their distresses ... Ps 107:13
walketh uprightly shall be *s* ... Prov 28:18
returning and rest shall ye be *s* ... Is 30:15
I have declared, and have *s* ... Is 43:12
But Israel shall be *s* in the LORD ... Is 45:17
Look unto me, and be ye *s*, all the ... Is 45:22
the angel of his presence *s* them ... Is 63:9
is continuance, and we shall be *s* ... Is 64:5
wickedness, that thou mayest be *s* ... Jer 4:14
summer is ended, and we are not *s* ... Jer 8:20
save me, and I shall be *s* ... Jer 17:14
In his days Judah shall be *s* ... Jer 23:6
but he shall be *s* out of it ... Jer 30:7
In those days shall Judah be *s* ... Jer 33:16
endureth to the end shall be *s* ... Mt 10:22
amazed, saying, Who then can be *s* ... Mt 19:25
unto the end, the same shall be *s* ... Mt 24:13
there should no flesh be *s* ... Mt 24:22
He *s* others; himself he ... Mt 27:42
themselves, Who then can be *s* ... Mk 10:26
unto the end, the same shall be *s* ... Mk 13:13
those days, no flesh should be *s* ... Mk 13:20
with the scribes, He *s* others ... Mk 15:31
and is baptized shall be *s* ... Mk 16:16
we should be *s* from our enemies ... Lk 1:71
the woman, Thy faith hath *s* thee ... Lk 7:50
lest they should believe and be *s* ... Lk 8:12
Lord, are there few that be *s* ... Lk 13:23
heard it said, Who then can be *s* ... Lk 18:26
thy faith hath *s* thee ... Lk 18:42
derided him, saying, He *s* others ... Lk 23:35
the world through him might be *s* ... Jn 3:17
things I say, that ye might be *s* ... Jn 5:34
any man enter in, he shall be *s* ... Jn 10:9
the name of the Lord shall be *s* ... Acts 2:21
church daily such as should be *s* ... Acts 2:47
among men, whereby we must be *s* ... Acts 4:12
thou and all thy house shall be *s* ... Acts 11:14

manner of Moses, ye cannot be s ........ Acts 15:1
Lord Jesus Christ we shall be s ........ Acts 15:11
Sirs, what must I do to be s ........ Acts 16:30
Jesus Christ, and thou shalt be s ........ Acts 16:31
should be s was then taken away ........ Acts 27:20
abide in the ship, ye cannot be s ........ Acts 27:31
we shall be s from wrath through ........ Rom 5:9
we shall be s by his life ........ Rom 5:10
For we are s by hope ........ Rom 8:24
of the sea, a remnant shall be s ........ Rom 9:27
Israel is, that they might be s ........ Rom 10:1
from the dead, thou shalt be s ........ Rom 10:9
the name of the Lord shall be s ........ Rom 10:13
And so all Israel shall be s ........ Rom 11:26
but unto us which are s it is the ........ 1Cor 1:18
but he himself shall be s ........ 1Cor 3:15
that the spirit may be s in the ........ 1Cor 5:5
of many, that they may be s ........ 1Cor 10:33
By which also ye are s, if ye ........ 1Cor 15:2
of Christ, in them that are s ........ 2Cor 2:15
with Christ, (by grace ye are s ........ Eph 2:5
by grace are ye s through faith ........ Eph 2:8
the Gentiles that they might be s ........ 1Th 2:16
the truth, that they might be s ........ 2Th 2:10
Who will have all men to be s ........ 1Ti 2:4
she shall be s in childbearing ........ 1Ti 2:15
Who hath s us, and called us with ........ 2Ti 1:9
according to his mercy he s us ........ Titus 3:5
is, eight souls were s by water ........ 1Pet 3:20
And if the righteous scarcely be s ........ 1Pet 4:18
but s Noah the eighth person, a ........ 2Pet 2:5
having s the people out of the ........ Jude 5
s shall walk in the light of it ........ Rev 21:24

**SAVEST**
thou s me from violence ........ 2Sa 22:3
how s thou the arm that hath no ........ Job 26:2
O thou that s by thy right hand ........ Ps 17:7

**SAVETH**
which s Israel, though it be in ........ 1Sa 14:39
that the LORD s not with sword ........ 1Sa 17:47
But he s the poor from the sword, ........ Job 5:15
which s the upright in heart ........ Ps 7:10
I that the LORD s his anointed ........ Ps 20:6
s such as be of a contrite spirit ........ Ps 34:18
he s them out of their distresses ........ Ps 107:19

**SAVING**
hast shewed unto me in s my life ........ Gen 19:19
s that every one put them off for ........ Neh 4:23
the s strength of his right hand ........ Ps 20:6
he is the s strength of his ........ Ps 28:8
thy s health among all nations ........ Ps 67:2
s the beholding of them with ........ Eccl 5:11
s that I will not utterly destroy ........ Amos 9:8
s for the cause of fornication, ........ Mt 5:32
was cleansed, s Naaman the Syrian ........ Lk 4:27
that believe to the s of the soul ........ Heb 10:39
an ark to the s of his house ........ Heb 11:7
knoweth s he that receiveth it ........ Rev 2:17

**SAVIOUR**
my high tower, and my refuge, my s ........ 2Sa 22:3
(And the LORD gave Israel a s ........ 2Kin 13:5
They forgat God their s, which ........ Ps 106:21
and he shall send them a s ........ Is 19:20
the Holy One of Israel, thy S ........ Is 43:3
and beside me there is no s ........ Is 43:11
thyself, O God of Israel, the S ........ Is 45:15
a just God and a S ........ Is 45:21
know that I the LORD am thy S ........ Is 49:26
know that I the LORD am thy S ........ Is 60:16
so he was their S ........ Is 63:8
the s thereof in time of trouble, ........ Jer 14:8
for there is no s beside me ........ Hos 13:4
spirit hath rejoiced in God my S ........ Lk 1:47
this day in the city of David a S ........ Lk 2:11
the Christ, the S of the world ........ Jn 4:42
right hand to be a Prince and a S ........ Acts 5:31
promise raised unto Israel a S ........ Acts 13:23
and he is the s of the body ........ Eph 5:23
whence also we look for the S ........ Phil 3:20
by the commandment of God our S ........ 1Ti 1:1
in the sight of God our S ........ 1Ti 2:3
God, who is the S of all men ........ 1Ti 4:10
appearing of our S Jesus Christ ........ 2Ti 1:10
to the commandment of God our S ........ Titus 1:3
and the Lord Jesus Christ our S ........ Titus 1:4
of God our S in all things ........ Titus 2:10
great God and our S Jesus Christ ........ Titus 2:13
love of God our S toward man ........ Titus 3:4
through Jesus Christ our S ........ Titus 3:6
of God and our S Jesus Christ ........ 2Pet 1:1
of our Lord and S Jesus Christ ........ 2Pet 1:11
S Jesus Christ, they are again ........ 2Pet 2:20
us the apostles of the Lord and S ........ 2Pet 3:2
of our Lord and S Jesus Christ ........ 2Pet 3:18
the Son to be the S of the world ........ 1Jn 4:14
To the only wise God our S ........ Jude 25

**SAVIOURS**
mercies thou gavest them s ........ Neh 9:27
s shall come up on mount Zion to ........ Obad 21

**SAVOUR**
And the LORD smelled a sweet s ........ Gen 8:21
because ye have made our s to be ........ Ex 5:21
it is a sweet s, an offering made ........ Ex 29:18
for a sweet s before the LORD ........ Ex 29:25
offering thereof, for a sweet s ........ Ex 29:41
of a sweet s unto the LORD ........ Lev 1:9
of a sweet s unto the LORD ........ Lev 1:13
of a sweet s unto the LORD ........ Lev 1:17
of a sweet s unto the LORD ........ Lev 2:2
of a sweet s unto the LORD ........ Lev 2:9
burnt on the altar for a sweet s ........ Lev 2:12
of a sweet s unto the LORD ........ Lev 3:5
made by fire for a sweet s ........ Lev 3:16
altar for a sweet s unto the LORD ........ Lev 4:31
it upon the altar for a sweet s ........ Lev 6:15
offer for a sweet s unto the LORD ........ Lev 6:21
a burnt sacrifice for a sweet s ........ Lev 8:21
were consecrations for a sweet s ........ Lev 8:28
fat for a sweet s unto the LORD ........ Lev 17:6
fire unto the LORD for a sweet s ........ Lev 23:13
by fire, of sweet s unto the LORD ........ Lev 23:18
smell the s of your sweet odours ........ Lev 26:31
to make a sweet s unto the LORD ........ Num 15:3
for a sweet s unto the LORD ........ Num 15:7
of a sweet s unto the LORD ........ Num 15:10
of a sweet s unto the LORD ........ Num 15:13
of a sweet s unto the LORD ........ Num 15:14
for a sweet s unto the LORD, with ........ Num 15:24
for a sweet s unto the LORD ........ Num 18:17
by fire, for a sweet s unto me ........ Num 28:2
in mount Sinai for a sweet s ........ Num 28:6
of a sweet s unto the LORD ........ Num 28:8
for a burnt offering of a sweet s ........ Num 28:13
of a sweet s unto the LORD ........ Num 28:24
for a sweet s unto the LORD ........ Num 28:27
for a sweet s unto the LORD ........ Num 29:2
unto their manner, for a sweet s ........ Num 29:6
unto the LORD for a sweet s ........ Num 29:8
of a sweet s unto the LORD ........ Num 29:13
of a sweet s unto the LORD ........ Num 29:36
to send forth a stinking s ........ Eccl 10:1
Because of the s of thy good ........ Song 1:3
offer sweet s to all their idols ........ Eze 6:13
set it before them for a sweet s ........ Eze 16:19
also they made their sweet s ........ Eze 20:28
will accept you with your sweet s ........ Eze 20:41
his ill s shall come up, because ........ Joel 2:20
but if the salt have lost his s ........ Mt 5:13
but if the salt have lost his s ........ Lk 14:34
maketh manifest the s of his ........ 2Cor 2:14
are unto God a sweet s of Christ ........ 2Cor 2:15
we are the s of death unto death ........ 2Cor 2:16
to the other the s of life unto ........ 2Cor 2:16
to God for a sweetsmelling s ........ Eph 5:2

**SAVOUREST**
for thou s not the things that be ........ Mt 16:23
for thou s not the things that be ........ Mk 8:33

**SAVOURS**
of sweet s unto the God of heaven ........ Ezr 6:10

**SAVOURY**
And make me s meat, such as I love ........ Gen 27:4
me venison, and make me s meat ........ Gen 27:7
I will make them s meat for thy ........ Gen 27:9
and his mother made s meat ........ Gen 27:14
And she gave the s meat and the ........ Gen 27:17
And he also had made s meat ........ Gen 27:31

**SAW** See PREFACE.

**SAWED**
s with saws, within and without, ........ 1Kin 7:9

**SAWEST**
said unto Abraham, What s thou ........ Gen 20:10
thou s it, and didst rejoice ........ 1Sa 19:5
for what s thou ........ 1Sa 28:13
told him, And, behold, thou s him ........ 2Sa 18:11
When thou s a thief, then thou ........ Ps 50:18
lovedst their bed where thou s it ........ Is 57:8
Thou, O king, s, and behold a ........ Dan 2:31
Thou s till that a stone was cut ........ Dan 2:34
And whereas thou s the feet ........ Dan 2:41
forasmuch as thou s the iron ........ Dan 2:41
whereas thou s iron mixed with ........ Dan 2:43
Forasmuch as thou s that the ........ Dan 2:45
The tree that thou s, which grew, ........ Dan 4:20
The ram which thou s having two ........ Dan 8:20
which thou s in my right hand ........ Rev 1:20
thou s are the seven churches ........ Rev 1:20
The beast that thou s was ........ Rev 17:8
horns which thou s are ten kings ........ Rev 17:12
unto me, The waters which thou s ........ Rev 17:15
horns which thou s upon the beast ........ Rev 17:16
which thou s is that great city ........ Rev 17:18

**SAWN**
were stoned, they were s asunder ........ Heb 11:37

**SAWS**
were therein, and put them under s ........ 2Sa 12:31
of hewed stones, sawed with s ........ 1Kin 7:9
were in it, and cut them with s ........ 1Chr 20:3

**SAY** See PREFACE.

**SAYEST**
thou s unto me, Bring up this ........ Ex 33:12
will do whatsoever thou s unto me ........ Num 22:17
All that thou s unto me I will do ........ Ruth 3:5
And now thou s, Go, tell thy lord, ........ 1Kin 18:11
And now thou s, Go, tell thy lord, ........ 1Kin 18:14
Thou s, (but they are but vain ........ 2Kin 18:20
Thou s, Lo, thou hast smitten the ........ 2Chr 25:19
so will we do as thou s ........ Neh 5:12
are no such things done as thou s ........ Neh 6:8
And thou s, How doth God know ........ Job 22:13
Although thou s thou shalt not ........ Job 35:14
and s, Return, ye children of men ........ Ps 90:3
If thou s, Behold, we knew it not ........ Prov 24:12
s thou, (but they are but vain ........ Is 36:5
Why s thou, O Jacob, and speakest, ........ Is 40:27
that s in thine heart, I am, and ........ Is 47:8
Yet thou s, Because I am innocent ........ Jer 2:35
plead with thee, because thou s ........ Jer 2:35
Thou s, Prophesy not against ........ Amos 7:16
saying, I know not what thou s ........ Mt 26:70
And Jesus said unto him, Thou s ........ Mt 27:11
thee, and s thou, Who touched me ........ Mk 5:31
neither understand I what thou s ........ Mk 14:68
said unto him, Thou s it ........ Mk 15:2
thee, and s thou, Who touched me ........ Lk 8:45
Master, we know that thou s ........ Lk 20:21
said, Man, I know not what thou s ........ Lk 22:60
answered him and said, Thou s it ........ Lk 23:3
What s thou of thyself ........ Jn 1:22
but what s thou ........ Jn 8:5
how s thou, Ye shall be made free ........ Jn 8:33
and thou s, If a man keep my ........ Jn 8:52
What s thou of him, that he hath ........ Jn 9:17
how s thou, The Son of man must ........ Jn 12:34
how s thou then, Shew us the ........ Jn 14:9
S thou this thing of thyself, or ........ Jn 18:34
answered, Thou s that I am a king ........ Jn 18:37
Thou that s a man should not ........ Rom 2:22
he understandeth not what thou s ........ 1Cor 14:16
Because thou s, I am rich, and ........ Rev 3:17

**SAYING** See PREFACE.

**SAYINGS**
Moses told these s unto all the ........ Num 14:39
that when thy s come to pass we ........ Judg 13:17
and came and told him all those s ........ 1Sa 25:12
of Abijah, and his ways, and his s ........ 2Chr 13:22
written among the s of the seers ........ 2Chr 33:19
their posterity approve their s ........ Ps 49:13
I will utter dark s of old ........ Ps 78:2
of the wise, and their dark s ........ Prov 1:6
Hear, O my son, and receive my s ........ Prov 4:10
incline thine ear unto my s ........ Prov 4:20
whosoever heareth these s of mine ........ Mt 7:24
one that heareth these s of mine ........ Mt 7:26
when Jesus had ended these s ........ Mt 7:28
when Jesus had finished these s ........ Mt 19:1
Jesus had finished all these s ........ Mt 26:1
all these s were noised abroad ........ Lk 1:65
kept all these s in her heart ........ Lk 2:51
cometh to me, and heareth my s ........ Lk 6:47
s in the audience of the people ........ Lk 7:1
about an eight days after these s ........ Lk 9:28
Let these s sink down into your ........ Lk 9:44
again among the Jews for these s ........ Jn 10:19
loveth me not keepeth not my s ........ Jn 14:24
with these s scarce restrained ........ Acts 14:18
And when they heard these s ........ Acts 19:28
mightest be justified in thy s ........ Rom 3:4
me, These are the true s of God ........ Rev 19:9
These s are faithful and true ........ Rev 22:6
s of the prophecy of this book ........ Rev 22:7
which keep the s of this book ........ Rev 22:9
Seal not the s of the prophecy of ........ Rev 22:10

**SCAB**
skin of his flesh a rising, a s ........ Lev 13:2
it is but a s ........ Lev 13:6
But if the s spread much abroad ........ Lev 13:7
the s spreadeth in the skin, then ........ Lev 13:8
And for a rising, and for a s ........ Lev 14:56
with the emerods, and with the s ........ Deut 28:27
the Lord will smite with a s the ........ Is 3:17

**SCABBARD**
put up thyself into thy s ........ Jer 47:6

**SCABBED**
in his eye, or be scurvy, or s ........ Lev 21:20
or having a wen, or scurvy, or s ........ Lev 22:22

**SCAFFOLD**
For Solomon had made a brasen s ........ 2Chr 6:13

**SCALES**
s in the waters, in the seas, and ........ Lev 11:9
s in the seas, and in the rivers, ........ Lev 11:10
hath no fins nor s in the waters ........ Lev 11:12
that have fins and s shall ye eat ........ Deut 14:9
hath not fins and s ye may not eat ........ Deut 14:10
His s are his pride, shut up ........ Job 41:15
and weighed the mountains in s ........ Is 40:12
of thy rivers to stick unto thy s ........ Eze 29:4
thy rivers shall stick unto thy s ........ Eze 29:4
from his eyes as it had been s ........ Acts 9:18

**SCALETH**
A wise man s the city of the ........ Prov 21:22

**SCALL**
it is a dry s, even a leprosy ........ Lev 13:30
look on the plague of the s ........ Lev 13:31
the plague of the s seven days ........ Lev 13:31
if the s spread not, and there be ........ Lev 13:32
the s be not in sight deeper than ........ Lev 13:32
but the s shall he not shave ........ Lev 13:33
that hath the s seven days more ........ Lev 13:33
the priest shall look on the s ........ Lev 13:34
if the s be not spread in the ........ Lev 13:34
But if the s spread much in the ........ Lev 13:35
if the s be spread in the skin, ........ Lev 13:36
But if the s be in his sight at a ........ Lev 13:37
the s is healed, he is clean ........ Lev 13:37
manner of plague of leprosy, and s ........ Lev 14:54

**SCALP**
the hairy *s* of such an one as ... Ps 68:21

**SCANT**
the *s* measure that is abominable ... Mic 6:10

**SCAPEGOAT**
LORD, and the other lot for the *s* ... Lev 16:8
on which the lot fell to be the *s* ... Lev 16:10
go for a *s* into the wilderness ... Lev 16:10
for the *s* shall wash his clothes ... Lev 16:26

**SCARCE**
Jacob was yet *s* gone out from the ... Gen 27:30
with these sayings *s* restrained ... Acts 14:18
*s* were come over against Cnidus, ... Acts 27:7

**SCARCELY**
For *s* for a righteous man will ... Rom 5:7
And if the righteous *s* be saved ... 1Pet 4:18

**SCARCENESS**
thou shalt eat bread without *s* ... Deut 8:9

**SCAREST**
Then thou *s* me with dreams, and ... Job 7:14

**SCARLET**
and bound upon his hand a *s* thread .. Gen 38:28
that had the *s* thread upon his ... Gen 38:30
And blue, and purple, and *s*, and fine ... Ex 25:4
linen, and blue, and purple, and *s* ... Ex 26:1
a vail of blue, and purple, and *s* ... Ex 26:31
tent, of blue, and purple, and *s* ... Ex 26:36
cubits, of blue, and purple, and *s* ... Ex 27:16
gold, and blue, and purple, and *s* ... Ex 28:5
gold, of blue, and of purple, of *s* ... Ex 28:6
of gold, of blue, and purple, and *s* ... Ex 28:8
of blue, and of purple, and of *s* ... Ex 28:15
of blue, and of purple, and of *s* ... Ex 28:33
And blue, and purple, and *s*, and fine ... Ex 35:6
was found blue, and purple, and *s* ... Ex 35:23
of blue, and of purple, and of *s* ... Ex 35:25
in blue, and in purple, in *s* ... Ex 35:35
linen, and blue, and purple, and *s* ... Ex 36:8
a vail of blue, and purple, and *s* ... Ex 36:35
door of blue, and purple, and *s* ... Ex 36:37
of blue, and purple, and *s* ... Ex 38:18
in blue, and in purple, and in *s* ... Ex 38:23
And of the blue, and purple, and *s* ... Ex 39:1
of gold, blue, and purple, and *s* ... Ex 39:2
and in the purple, and in the *s* ... Ex 39:3
of gold, blue, and purple, and *s* ... Ex 39:5
of gold, blue, and purple, and *s* ... Ex 39:8
of blue, and purple, and *s*, and ... Ex 39:24
linen, and blue, and purple, and *s* ... Ex 39:29
and clean, and cedar wood, and *s* ... Lev 14:4
it, and the cedar wood, and the *s* ... Lev 14:6
two birds, and cedar wood, and *s* ... Lev 14:49
wood, and the hyssop, and the *s* ... Lev 14:51
and with the hyssop, and with the *s* ... Lev 14:52
spread upon them a cloth of *s* ... Num 4:8
take cedar wood, and hyssop, and *s* ... Num 19:6
thou shalt bind this line of *s* ... Josh 2:18
she bound the *s* line in the ... Josh 2:21
over Saul, who clothed you in *s* ... 2Sa 1:24
her household are clothed with *s* ... Prov 31:21
Thy lips are like a thread of *s* ... Song 4:3
though your sins be as *s*, they ... Is 1:18
brought up in *s* embrace dunghills ... Lam 4:5
thereof, shall be clothed with *s* ... Dan 5:7
thou shalt be clothed with *s* ... Dan 5:16
and they clothed Daniel with *s* ... Dan 5:29
red, the valiant men are in *s* ... Nah 2:3
him, and put on him a *s* robe ... Mt 27:28
*s* wool, and hyssop, and sprinkled ... Heb 9:19
woman sit upon a *s* coloured beast ... Rev 17:3
*s* colour, and decked with gold and ... Rev 17:4
linen, and purple, and silk, and *s* ... Rev 18:12
in fine linen, and purple, and *s* ... Rev 18:16

**SCATTER**
from thence did the LORD *s* them ... Gen 11:9
in Jacob, and *s* them in Israel ... Gen 49:7
I will *s* you among the heathen, ... Lev 26:33
and *s* thou the fire yonder ... Num 16:37
the LORD shall *s* you among the ... Deut 4:27
the LORD shall *s* thee among all ... Deut 28:64
I would *s* them into corners, I ... Deut 32:26
shall *s* them beyond the river, ... 1Kin 14:15
I will *s* you abroad among the ... Neh 1:8
*s* them by thy power ... Ps 59:11
*s* thou the people that delight in ... Ps 68:30
and to *s* them in the lands ... Ps 106:27
Cast forth lightning, and *s* them ... Ps 144:6
*s* the cummin, and cast in the ... Is 28:25
and the whirlwind shall *s* them ... Is 41:16
I will *s* them also among the ... Jer 9:16
Therefore will I *s* them as the ... Jer 13:24
I will *s* them as with an east ... Jer 18:17
*s* the sheep of my pasture ... Jer 23:1
I will *s* into all winds them that ... Jer 49:32
will *s* them toward all those ... Jer 49:36
part thou shalt *s* in the wind ... Eze 5:2
thee will I *s* into all the winds ... Eze 5:10
I will *s* a third part into all ... Eze 5:12
I will *s* your bones round about ... Eze 6:5
and *s* them over the city ... Eze 10:2
I will *s* toward every wind all ... Eze 12:14
when I shall *s* them among the ... Eze 12:15
that I would *s* them among the ... Eze 20:23
I will *s* thee among the heathen, ... Eze 22:15
I will *s* the Egyptians among the ... Eze 29:12
I will *s* the Egyptians among the ... Eze 30:23
I will *s* the Egyptians among the ... Eze 30:26
off his leaves, and *s* his fruit ... Dan 4:14
he shall *s* among them the prey, ... Dan 11:24
to *s* the power of the holy people ... Dan 12:7
came out as a whirlwind to *s* me ... Hab 3:14
over the land of Judah to *s* it ... Zec 1:21

**SCATTERED**
lest we be *s* abroad upon the face ... Gen 11:4
So the LORD *s* them abroad from ... Gen 11:8
So the people were *s* abroad ... Ex 5:12
LORD, and let thine enemies be *s* ... Num 10:35
the LORD thy God hath *s* thee ... Deut 30:3
that they which remained were *s* ... 1Sa 11:11
and the people were *s* from him ... 1Sa 13:8
that the people were *s* from me ... 1Sa 13:11
there *s* over the face of all the ... 2Sa 18:8
And he sent out arrows, and *s* them ... 2Sa 22:15
I saw all Israel *s* upon the hills ... 1Kin 22:17
and all his army were *s* from him ... 2Kin 25:5
all Israel *s* upon the mountains ... 2Chr 18:16
is a certain people *s* abroad ... Est 3:8
stout lion's whelps are *s* abroad ... Job 4:11
brimstone shall be *s* upon his ... Job 18:15
he sent out his arrows, and *s* them ... Ps 18:14
hast *s* us among the heathen ... Ps 44:11
for God hath *s* the bones of him ... Ps 53:5
hast cast us off, thou hast *s* us ... Ps 60:1
God arise, let his enemies be *s* ... Ps 68:1
When the Almighty *s* kings in it ... Ps 68:14
thou hast *s* thine enemies with ... Ps 89:10
workers of iniquity shall be *s* ... Ps 92:9
Our bones are *s* at the grave's ... Ps 141:7
swift messengers, to a nation *s* ... Is 18:2
the LORD of hosts of a people *s* ... Is 18:7
up of thyself the nations were *s* ... Is 33:3
hast *s* thy ways to the strangers ... Jer 3:13
and all their flocks shall be *s* ... Jer 10:21
Ye have *s* my flock, and driven ... Jer 23:2
all nations whither I have *s* thee ... Jer 30:11
He that *s* Israel will gather him, ... Jer 31:10
gathered unto thee should be *s* ... Jer 40:15
Israel is a *s* sheep ... Jer 50:17
and all his army was *s* from him ... Jer 52:8
when ye shall be *s* through the ... Eze 6:8
although I have *s* them among the ... Eze 11:16
countries where ye have been *s* ... Eze 11:17
shall be *s* toward all winds ... Eze 17:21
of the countries wherein ye are *s* ... Eze 20:34
countries wherein ye have been *s* ... Eze 20:41
the people among whom they are *s* ... Eze 28:25
the people whither they were *s* ... Eze 29:13
And they were *s*, because there is ... Eze 34:5
of the field, when they were *s* ... Eze 34:5
my flock was *s* upon all the face ... Eze 34:6
he is among his sheep that are *s* ... Eze 34:12
they have been *s* in the cloudy ... Eze 34:12
horns, till ye have *s* them abroad ... Eze 34:21
I *s* them among the heathen, and ... Eze 36:19
that my people be not *s* every man ... Eze 46:18
whom they have *s* among the ... Joel 3:2
thy people is *s* upon the ... Nah 3:18
the everlasting mountains were *s* ... Hab 3:6
are the horns which have *s* Judah ... Zec 1:19
are the horns which have *s* Judah ... Zec 1:21
But I *s* them with a whirlwind ... Zec 7:14
shepherd, and the sheep shall be *s* ... Zec 13:7
were *s* abroad, as sheep having no ... Mt 9:36
of the flock shall be *s* abroad ... Mt 26:31
shepherd, and the sheep shall be *s* ... Mk 14:27
he hath *s* the proud in the ... Lk 1:51
of God that were *s* abroad ... Jn 11:52
is now come, that ye shall be *s* ... Jn 16:32
as many as obeyed him, were *s* ... Acts 5:36
they were all *s* abroad throughout ... Acts 8:1
were *s* abroad went every where ... Acts 8:4
Now they which were *s* abroad upon Acts 11:19
twelve tribes which are *s* abroad ... Jas 1:1
to the strangers *s* throughout ... 1Pet 1:1

**SCATTERETH**
he *s* his bright cloud ... Job 37:11
which *s* the east wind upon the ... Job 38:24
he *s* the hoar frost like ashes ... Ps 147:16
There is that *s*, and yet ... Prov 11:24
in the throne of judgment *s* away ... Prov 20:8
A wise king *s* the wicked, and ... Prov 20:26
*s* abroad the inhabitants thereof ... Is 24:1
gathereth not with me *s* abroad ... Mt 12:30
he that gathereth not with me *s* ... Lk 11:23
catcheth them, and *s* the sheep ... Jn 10:12

**SCATTERING**
flame of a devouring fire, with *s* ... Is 30:30

**SCENT**
Yet through the *s* of water it ... Job 14:9
in him, and his *s* is not changed ... Jer 48:11
the *s* thereof shall be as the ... Hos 14:7

**SCEPTRE**
The *s* shall not depart from Judah ... Gen 49:10
a *S* shall rise out of Israel, and ... Num 24:17
king shall hold out the golden *s* ... Est 4:11
the golden *s* that was in his hand ... Est 5:2
near, and touched the top of the *s* ... Est 5:2
out the golden *s* toward Esther ... Est 8:4
the *s* of thy kingdom is a right ... Ps 45:6
of thy kingdom is a right *s* ... Ps 45:6
wicked, and the *s* of the rulers ... Is 14:5
no strong rod to be a *s* to rule ... Eze 19:14
him that holdeth the *s* from the ... Amos 1:5
that holdeth the *s* from Ashkelon ... Amos 1:8
the *s* of Egypt shall depart away ... Zec 10:11
a *s* of righteousness is the ... Heb 1:8
is the *s* of thy kingdom ... Heb 1:8

**SCEPTRES**
for the *s* of them that bare rule ... Eze 19:11

**SCEVA** (*see'-vah*) *A Jewish priest at Ephesus.*
And there were seven sons of one *S*.. Acts 19:14

**SCHISM**
there should be no *s* in the body ... 1Cor 12:25

**SCHOLAR**
the great, the teacher as the *s* ... 1Chr 25:8
doeth this, the master and the *s* ... Mal 2:12

**SCHOOL**
daily in the *s* of one Tyrannus ... Acts 19:9

**SCHOOLMASTER**
was our *s* to bring us unto Christ ... Gal 3:24
come, we are no longer under a *s* ... Gal 3:25

**SCIENCE**
in knowledge, and understanding *s* ... Dan 1:4
oppositions of *s* falsely so ... 1Ti 6:20

**SCOFF**
they shall *s* at the kings, and the ... Hab 1:10

**SCOFFERS**
shall come in the last days *s* ... 2Pet 3:3

**SCORCH**
given unto him to *s* men with fire ... Rev 16:8

**SCORCHED**
when the sun was up, they were *s* ... Mt 13:6
But when the sun was up, it was *s* ... Mk 4:6
men were *s* with great heat, and ... Rev 16:9

**SCORN**
thee, and laughed thee to *s* ... 2Kin 19:21
but they laughed them to *s* ... 2Chr 30:10
heard it, they laughed us to *s* ... Neh 2:19
he thought *s* to lay hands on ... Est 3:6
just upright man is laughed to *s* ... Job 12:4
My friends *s* me ... Job 16:20
and the innocent laugh them to *s* ... Job 22:19
they that see me laugh me to *s* ... Ps 22:7
a reproach to our neighbours, a *s* ... Ps 44:13
a reproach to our neighbours, a *s* ... Ps 79:4
thee, and laughed thee to *s* ... Is 37:22
thou shalt be laughed to *s* ... Eze 23:32
princes shall be a *s* unto them ... Hab 1:10
And they laughed him to *s* ... Mt 9:24
And they laughed him to *s* ... Mk 5:40
And they laughed him to *s*, knowing ... Lk 8:53

**SCORNER**
He that reproveth a *s* getteth to ... Prov 9:7
Reprove not a *s*, lest he hate ... Prov 9:8
but a *s* heareth not rebuke ... Prov 13:1
A *s* seeketh wisdom, and findeth it ... Prov 14:6
A *s* loveth not one that reproveth ... Prov 15:12
Smite a *s*, and the simple will ... Prov 19:25
When the *s* is punished, the ... Prov 21:11
haughty *s* is his name, who ... Prov 21:24
Cast out the *s*, and contention ... Prov 22:10
the *s* is an abomination to men ... Prov 24:9
the *s* is consumed, and all that ... Is 29:20

**SCORNERS**
the *s* delight in their scorning, ... Prov 1:22
Surely he scorneth the *s* ... Prov 3:34
Judgments are prepared for *s* ... Prov 19:29
he stretched out his hand with *s* ... Hos 7:5

**SCORNEST**
but if thou *s*, thou alone shalt ... Prov 9:12
as an harlot, in that thou *s* hire ... Eze 16:31

**SCORNETH**
He *s* the multitude of the city, ... Job 39:7
she *s* the horse and his rider ... Job 39:18
Surely he *s* the scorners ... Prov 3:34
An ungodly witness *s* judgment ... Prov 19:28

**SCORNFUL**
nor sitteth in the seat of the *s* ... Ps 1:1
*S* men bring a city into a snare ... Prov 29:8
ye *s* men, that rule this people ... Is 28:14

**SCORNING**
Job, who drinketh up *s* like water ... Job 34:7
the *s* of those that are at ease ... Ps 123:4
the scorners delight in their *s* ... Prov 1:22

**SCORPION**
ask an egg, will he offer him a *s* ... Lk 11:12
torment was as the torment of a *s* ... Rev 9:5

**SCORPION PASS** See MAALEH-ACRABBIM.

**SCORPIONS**
wherein were fiery serpents, and *s* ... Deut 8:15
but I will chastise you with *s* ... 1Kin 12:11
but I will chastise you with *s* ... 1Kin 12:14
but I will chastise you with *s* ... 2Chr 10:11
but I will chastise you with *s* ... 2Chr 10:14
thee, and thou dost dwell among *s* ... Eze 2:6
power to tread on serpents and *s* ... Lk 10:19
as the *s* of the earth have power ... Rev 9:3
And they had tails like unto *s* ... Rev 9:10

**SCOURED**
a brasen pot, it shall be both *s* ... Lev 6:28

**SCOURGE**
be hid from the *s* of the tongue ... Job 5:21
If the *s* slay suddenly, he will ... Job 9:23
up a *s* for him according to the ... Is 10:26
overflowing *s* shall pass through ... Is 28:15
overflowing *s* shall pass through ... Is 28:18
and they will *s* you in their ... Mt 10:17
to the Gentiles to mock, and to *s* ... Mt 20:19
shall ye *s* in your synagogues ... Mt 23:34
shall mock him, and shall *s* him ... Mk 10:34
And they shall *s* him, and put him ... Lk 18:33
he had made a *s* of small cords ... Jn 2:15
you to *s* a man that is a Roman ... Acts 22:25

**SCOURGED**
she shall be *s* ... Lev 19:20
and when he had *s* Jesus, he ... Mt 27:26
Jesus, when he had *s* him, to be ... Mk 15:15
therefore took Jesus, and *s* him ... Jn 19:1

**SCOURGES**
*s* in your sides, and thorns in ... Josh 23:13

**SCOURGETH**
*s* every son whom he receiveth ... Heb 12:6

**SCOURGING**
that he should be examined by *s* ... Acts 22:24

**SCOURGINGS**
had trial of cruel mockings and *s* ... Heb 11:36

**SCRABBLED**
*s* on the doors of the gate, and ... 1Sa 21:13

**SCRAPE**
pour out the dust that they *s* off ... Lev 14:41
a potsherd to *s* himself withal ... Job 2:8
I will also *s* her dust from her, ... Eze 26:4

**SCRAPED**
house to be *s* within round about ... Lev 14:41
and after he hath *s* the house ... Lev 14:43

**SCREECH**
the *s* owl also shall rest there, ... Is 34:14

**SCRIBE**
and Seraiah was the *s* ... 2Sa 8:17
And Sheva was *s* ... 2Sa 20:25
in the chest, that the king's *s* ... 2Kin 12:10
the household, and Shebna the *s* ... 2Kin 18:18
the household, and Shebna the *s* ... 2Kin 18:37
the household, and Shebna the *s* ... 2Kin 19:2
the son of Meshullam, the *s* ... 2Kin 22:3
priest said unto Shaphan the *s* ... 2Kin 22:8
Shaphan the *s* came to the king, ... 2Kin 22:9
Shaphan the *s* shewed the king, ... 2Kin 22:10
son of Michaiah, and Shaphan the *s* . 2Kin 22:12
and the principal *s* of the host ... 2Kin 25:19
and Shavsha was *s* ... 1Chr 18:16
the son of Nethaneel the *s* ... 1Chr 24:6
a counsellor, a wise man, and a *s* ... 1Chr 27:32
was much money, the king's *s* ... 2Chr 24:11
by the hand of Jeiel the *s* ... 2Chr 26:11
answered and said to Shaphan the *s*. 2Chr 34:15
Then Shaphan the *s* told the king ... 2Chr 34:18
son of Micah, and Shaphan the *s* ... 2Chr 34:20
Shimshai the *s* wrote a letter ... Ezr 4:8
the chancellor, and Shimshai the *s* ... Ezr 4:9
chancellor, and to Shimshai the *s* ... Ezr 4:17
before Rehum, and Shimshai the *s* ... Ezr 4:23
he was a ready *s* in the law of ... Ezr 7:6
gave unto Ezra the priest, the *s* ... Ezr 7:11
even a *s* of the words of the ... Ezr 7:11
a *s* of the law of the God of ... Ezr 7:12
the *s* of the law of the God of ... Ezr 7:21
they spake unto Ezra the *s* to ... Neh 8:1
Ezra the *s* stood upon a pulpit of ... Neh 8:4
and Ezra the priest the *s* ... Neh 8:9
and the Levites, unto Ezra the *s* ... Neh 8:13
and of Ezra the priest, the *s* ... Neh 12:26
of God, and Ezra the *s* before them ... Neh 12:36
the priest, and Zadok the *s* ... Neh 13:13
Where is the *s* ... Is 33:18
over the house, and Shebna the *s* ... Is 36:3
the household, and Shebna the *s* ... Is 36:22
the household, and Shebna the *s* ... Is 37:2
Gemariah the son of Shaphan the *s* ... Jer 36:10
sat there, even Elishama the *s* ... Jer 36:12
in the chamber of Elishama the *s* ... Jer 36:20
of Abdeel, to take Baruch the *s* ... Jer 36:26
roll, and gave it to Baruch the *s* ... Jer 36:32
in the house of Jonathan the *s* ... Jer 37:15
to the house of Jonathan the *s* ... Jer 37:20
and the principal *s* of the host ... Jer 52:25
And a certain *s* came, and said unto ... Mt 8:19
Therefore every *s* which is ... Mt 13:52
the *s* said unto him, Well, Master ... Mk 12:32
where is the *s* ... 1Cor 1:20

**SCRIBE'S**
king's house, into the *s* chamber ... Jer 36:12
it out of Elishama the *s* chamber ... Jer 36:21

**SCRIBES**
and Ahiah, the sons of Shisha, *s* ... 1Kin 4:3
the families of the *s* which dwelt ... 1Chr 2:55
and of the Levites there were *s* ... 2Chr 34:13
Then were the king's *s* called on ... Est 3:12
Then were the king's *s* called at ... Est 8:9
the pen of the *s* is in vain ... Jer 8:8
*s* of the people together, he ... Mt 2:4
exceed the righteousness of the *s* ... Mt 5:20
having authority, and not as the *s* ... Mt 7:29
certain of the *s* said within ... Mt 9:3
Then certain of the *s* and of the ... Mt 12:38
Then came to Jesus *s* and Pharisees ... Mt 15:1
the elders and chief priests and *s* ... Mt 16:21
Why then say the *s* that Elias ... Mt 17:10
the chief priests and unto the *s* ... Mt 20:18
*s* saw the wonderful things that ... Mt 21:15
Saying, The *s* and the Pharisees ... Mt 23:2
But woe unto you, *s* and Pharisees, ... Mt 23:13
Woe unto you, *s* and Pharisees, ... Mt 23:14
Woe unto you, *s* and Pharisees, ... Mt 23:15
Woe unto you, *s* and Pharisees, ... Mt 23:23
Woe unto you, *s* and Pharisees, ... Mt 23:25
Woe unto you, *s* and Pharisees, ... Mt 23:27
Woe unto you, *s* and Pharisees, ... Mt 23:29
you prophets, and wise men, and *s* ... Mt 23:34
the chief priests, and the *s* ... Mt 26:3
the high priest, where the *s* ... Mt 26:57
priests mocking him, with the *s* ... Mt 27:41
had authority, and not as the *s* ... Mk 1:22
certain of the *s* sitting there ... Mk 2:6
And when the *s* and Pharisees saw ... Mk 2:16
the *s* which came down from ... Mk 3:22
Pharisees, and certain of the *s* ... Mk 7:1
*s* asked him, Why walk not thy ... Mk 7:5
and of the chief priests, and *s* ... Mk 8:31
Why say the *s* that Elias must ... Mk 9:11
the *s* questioning with them ... Mk 9:14
And he asked the *s*, What question ... Mk 9:16
the chief priests, and unto the *s* ... Mk 10:33
And the *s* and chief priests heard ... Mk 11:18
him the chief priests, and the *s* ... Mk 11:27
And one of the *s* came, and having ... Mk 12:28
How say the *s* that Christ is the ... Mk 12:35
in his doctrine, Beware of the *s* ... Mk 12:38
the *s* sought how they might take ... Mk 14:1
from the chief priest and the *s* ... Mk 14:43
priests and the elders and the *s* ... Mk 14:53
consultation with the elders and *s* ... Mk 15:1
said among themselves with the *s* ... Mk 15:31
And the *s* and the Pharisees began ... Lk 5:21
But their *s* and Pharisees murmured ... Lk 5:30
And the *s* and Pharisees watched him ... Lk 6:7
the elders and chief priests and *s* ... Lk 9:22
Woe unto you, *s* and Pharisees, ... Lk 11:44
these things unto them, the *s* ... Lk 11:53
*s* murmured, saying, This man ... Lk 15:2
But the chief priests and the *s* ... Lk 19:47
the *s* came upon him with the ... Lk 20:1
the *s* the same hour sought to lay ... Lk 20:19
certain of the *s* answering said ... Lk 20:39
Beware of the *s*, which desire to ... Lk 20:46
*s* sought how they might kill him ... Lk 22:2
the *s* came together, and led him ... Lk 22:66
*s* stood and vehemently accused him ... Lk 23:10
And the *s* and Pharisees brought ... Jn 8:3
their rulers, and elders, and *s* ... Acts 4:5
people, and the elders, and the *s* ... Acts 6:12
the *s* that were of the Pharisees' ... Acts 23:9

**SCRIP**
bag which he had, even in a *s* ... 1Sa 17:40
Nor *s* for your journey, neither ... Mt 10:10
no *s*, no bread, no money in their ... Mk 6:8
journey, neither staves, nor *s* ... Lk 9:3
Carry neither purse, nor *s* ... Lk 10:4
I sent you without purse, and *s* ... Lk 22:35
him take it, and likewise his *s* ... Lk 22:36

**SCRIPTURE**
which is noted in the *s* of truth ... Dan 10:21
And have ye not read this *s* ... Mk 12:10
the *s* was fulfilled, which saith, ... Mk 15:28
This day is this *s* fulfilled in ... Lk 4:21
and they believed the *s*, and the ... Jn 2:22
as the *s* hath said, out of his ... Jn 7:38
Hath not the *s* said, That Christ ... Jn 7:42
came, and the *s* cannot be broken ... Jn 10:35
but that the *s* may be fulfilled, ... Jn 13:18
that the *s* might be fulfilled, ... Jn 17:12
that the *s* might be fulfilled, ... Jn 19:24
that the *s* might be fulfilled, ... Jn 19:28
that the *s* should be fulfilled, A ... Jn 19:36
And again another *s* saith, They ... Jn 19:37
For as yet they knew not the *s* ... Jn 20:9
this *s* must needs have been ... Acts 1:16
The place of the *s* which he read ... Acts 8:32
his mouth, and began at the same *s* ... Acts 8:35
For what saith the *s* ... Rom 4:3
For the *s* saith unto Pharaoh, ... Rom 9:17
For the *s* saith, Whosoever ... Rom 10:11
ye not what the *s* saith of Elias ... Rom 11:2
And the *s*, foreseeing that God ... Gal 3:8
But the *s* hath concluded all ... Gal 3:22
Nevertheless what saith the *s* ... Gal 4:30
For the *s* saith, Thou shalt not ... 1Ti 5:18
All *s* is given by inspiration of ... 2Ti 3:16
the royal law according to the *s* ... Jas 2:8
the *s* was fulfilled which saith, ... Jas 2:23
ye think that the *s* saith in vain ... Jas 4:5
also it is contained in the *s* ... 1Pet 2:6
of the *s* is of any private ... 2Pet 1:20

**SCRIPTURES**
them, Did ye never read in the *s* ... Mt 21:42
Ye do err, not knowing the *s* ... Mt 22:29
how then shall the *s* be fulfilled ... Mt 26:54
that the *s* of the prophets might ... Mt 26:56
err, because ye know not the *s* ... Mk 12:24
but the *s* must be fulfilled ... Mk 14:49
*s* the things concerning himself ... Lk 24:27
and while he opened to us the *s* ... Lk 24:32
that they might understand the *s* ... Lk 24:45
Search the *s* ... Jn 5:39
reasoned with them out of the *s* ... Acts 17:2
of mind, and searched the *s* daily ... Acts 17:11
eloquent man, and mighty in the *s* ... Acts 18:24
shewing by the *s* that Jesus was ... Acts 18:28
by his prophets in the holy *s* ... Rom 1:2
comfort of the *s* might have hope ... Rom 15:4
by the *s* of the prophets, ... Rom 16:26
for our sins according to the *s* ... 1Cor 15:3
the third day according to the *s* ... 1Cor 15:4
child thou hast known the holy *s* ... 2Ti 3:15
as they do also the other *s* ... 2Pet 3:16

**SCROLL**
shall be rolled together as a *s* ... Is 34:4
the heaven departed as a *s* when ... Rev 6:14

**SCUM**
to the pot whose *s* is therein ... Eze 24:6
whose *s* is not gone out of it ... Eze 24:6
that the *s* of it may be consumed ... Eze 24:11
her great *s* went not forth out of ... Eze 24:12
her *s* shall be in the fire ... Eze 24:12

**SCURVY**
a blemish in his eye, or be *s* ... Lev 21:20
or maimed, or having a wen, or *s* ... Lev 22:22

**SCYTHIAN** *(sith'-e-un) A barbarous people north of the Black Sea.*
nor uncircumcision, Barbarian, *S* ... Col 3:11

**SEA**
dominion over the fish of the *s* ... Gen 1:26
dominion over the fish of the *s* ... Gen 1:28
and upon all the fishes of the *s* ... Gen 9:2
of Siddim, which is the Salt *S* ... Gen 14:3
sand which is upon the *s* shore ... Gen 22:17
thy seed as the sand of the *s* ... Gen 32:12
corn as the sand of the *s* ... Gen 41:49
shall dwell at the haven of the *s* ... Gen 49:13
and cast them into the Red *s* ... Ex 10:19
of the wilderness of the Red *s* ... Ex 13:18
between Migdol and the *s*, over ... Ex 14:2
it shall ye encamp by the *s* ... Ex 14:2
overtook them encamping by the *s* ... Ex 14:9
stretch out thine hand over the *s* ... Ex 14:16
ground through the midst of the *s* ... Ex 14:16
stretched out his hand over the *s* ... Ex 14:21
the LORD caused the *s* to go back ... Ex 14:21
night, and made the *s* dry land ... Ex 14:21
of the *s* upon the dry ground ... Ex 14:22
after them to the midst of the *s* ... Ex 14:23
Stretch out thine hand over the *s* ... Ex 14:26
forth his hand over the *s* ... Ex 14:27
the *s* returned to his strength ... Ex 14:27
Egyptians in the midst of the *s* ... Ex 14:27
that came into the *s* after them ... Ex 14:28
dry land in the midst of the *s* ... Ex 14:29
Egyptians dead upon the *s* shore ... Ex 14:30
rider hath he thrown into the *s* ... Ex 15:1
his host hath he cast into the *s* ... Ex 15:4
also are drowned in the Red *s* ... Ex 15:4
congealed in the heart of the *s* ... Ex 15:8
with thy wind, the *s* covered them ... Ex 15:10
and with his horsemen into the *s* ... Ex 15:19
the waters of the *s* upon them ... Ex 15:19
on dry land in the midst of the *s* ... Ex 15:19
rider hath he thrown into the *s* ... Ex 15:21
brought Israel from the Red *s* ... Ex 15:22
LORD made heaven and earth, the *s* ... Ex 20:11
Red *s* even unto the *s* of the ... Ex 23:31
or shall all the fish of the *s* be ... Num 11:22
and brought quails from the *s* ... Num 11:31
and the Canaanites dwell by the *s* ... Num 13:29
by the way of the Red *s* ... Num 14:25
mount Hor by the way of the Red *s* ... Num 21:4
LORD, What he did in the Red *s* ... Num 21:14
of the *s* into the wilderness ... Num 33:8
Elim, and encamped by the Red *s* ... Num 33:10
And they removed from the Red *s* ... Num 33:11
coast of the salt *s* eastward ... Num 34:3
out of it shall be at the *s* ... Num 34:5
have the great *s* for a border ... Num 34:6
from the great *s* ye shall point ... Num 34:7
of the *s* of Chinnereth eastward ... Num 34:11
out of it shall be at the salt *s* ... Num 34:12
the plain over against the Red *s* ... Deut 1:1
and in the south, and by the *s* side ... Deut 1:7
by the way of the Red *s* ... Deut 1:40
by the way of the Red *s*, as the ... Deut 2:1
*s* of the plain, even the salt *s* ... Deut 3:17
even unto the *s* of the plain ... Deut 4:49
Red *s* to overflow them as they ... Deut 11:4
uttermost *s* shall your coast be ... Deut 11:24
Neither is it beyond the *s* ... Deut 30:13
Who shall go over the *s* for us ... Deut 30:13
land of Judah, unto the utmost *s* ... Deut 34:2
unto the great *s* toward the going ... Josh 1:4
up the water of the Red *s* for you ... Josh 2:10
*s* of the plain, even the salt *s* ... Josh 3:16
LORD your God did to the Red *s* ... Josh 4:23
Canaanites, which were by the *s* ... Josh 5:1
the great *s* over against Lebanon ... Josh 9:1
is upon the *s* shore in multitude ... Josh 11:4
from the plain to the *s* of ... Josh 12:3
unto the *s* of the plain ... Josh 12:3
even the salt *s* on the east ... Josh 12:3

even unto the edge of the s of ... Josh 13:27
was from the shore of the salt s ... Josh 15:2
out of that coast were at the s ... Josh 15:4
And the east border was the salt s ... Josh 15:5
s at the uttermost part of Jordan ... Josh 15:5
out of the border were at the s ... Josh 15:11
west border was to the great s ... Josh 15:12
From Ekron even unto the s ... Josh 15:46
river of Egypt, and the great s ... Josh 15:47
goings out thereof are at the s ... Josh 16:3
the border went out toward the s ... Josh 16:6
goings out thereof were at the s ... Josh 16:8
the outgoings of it were at the s ... Josh 17:9
and the s is his border ... Josh 17:10
the corner of the s southward ... Josh 18:14
salt s at the south end of Jordan ... Josh 18:19
their border went up toward the s ... Josh 19:11
at the s from the coast to Achzib ... Josh 19:29
even unto the great s westward ... Josh 23:4
and ye came unto the s ... Josh 24:6
and horsemen unto the Red s ... Josh 24:6
and brought the s upon them ... Josh 24:7
Asher continued on the s shore ... Judg 5:17
sand by the s side for multitude ... Judg 7:12
the wilderness unto the Red s ... Judg 11:16
is on the s shore in multitude ... 1Sa 13:5
that is by the s for multitude ... 2Sa 17:11
And the channels of the s appeared ... 2Sa 22:16
which is by the s in multitude ... 1Kin 4:20
the sand that is on the s shore ... 1Kin 4:29
them down from Lebanon unto the s ... 1Kin 5:9
I will convey them by s in floats ... 1Kin 5:9
And he made a molten s, ten cubits ... 1Kin 7:23
compassing the s round about ... 1Kin 7:24
the s was set above upon them, and ... 1Kin 7:25
he set the s on the right side of ... 1Kin 7:39
And one s, and twelve oxen under ... 1Kin 7:44
s, and twelve oxen under the s ... 1Kin 7:44
Eloth, on the shore of the Red s ... 1Kin 9:26
that had knowledge of the s ... 1Kin 9:27
For the king had at s a navy of ... 1Kin 10:22
Go up now, look toward the s ... 1Kin 18:43
a little cloud out of the s ... 1Kin 18:44
of Hamath unto the s of the plain ... 2Kin 14:25
took down the s from off the ... 2Kin 16:17
the brasen s that was in the ... 2Kin 25:13
The two pillars, one s, and the ... 2Kin 25:16
Let the s roar, and the fulness ... 1Chr 16:32
Solomon made the brasen s ... 1Chr 18:8
to thee in flotes by s to Joppa ... 2Chr 2:16
Also he made a molten s of ten ... 2Chr 4:2
compassing the s round about ... 2Chr 4:3
the s was set above upon them, and ... 2Chr 4:4
but the s was for the priests to ... 2Chr 4:6
he set the s on the right side of ... 2Chr 4:10
One s, and twelve oxen under it ... 2Chr 4:15
at the s side in the land of Edom ... 2Chr 8:17
that had knowledge of the s ... 2Chr 8:18
beyond the s on this side Syria ... 2Chr 20:2
from Lebanon to the s of Joppa ... Ezr 3:7
heardest their cry by the Red s ... Neh 9:9
didst divide the s before them ... Neh 9:11
midst of the s on the dry land ... Neh 9:11
land, and upon the isles of the s ... Est 10:1
be heavier than the sand of the s ... Job 6:3
Am I a s, or a whale, that thou ... Job 7:12
treadeth upon the waves of the s ... Job 9:8
the earth, and broader than the s ... Job 11:9
the fishes of the s shall declare ... Job 12:8
As the waters fail from the s ... Job 14:11
He divideth the s with his power ... Job 26:12
the s saith, It is not with me ... Job 28:14
and covereth the bottom of the s ... Job 36:30
Or who shut up the s with doors ... Job 38:8
entered into the springs of the s ... Job 38:16
he maketh the s like a pot of ... Job 41:31
of the air, and the fish of the s ... Ps 8:8
of the s together as an heap ... Ps 33:7
carried into the midst of the s ... Ps 46:2
them that are afar off upon the s ... Ps 65:5
He turned the s into dry land ... Ps 66:6
again from the depths of the s ... Ps 68:22
have dominion also from s to s ... Ps 72:8
divide the s by thy strength ... Ps 74:13
Thy way is in the s, and thy path ... Ps 77:19
He divided the s, and caused them ... Ps 78:13
fowls like as the sand of the s ... Ps 78:27
but the s overwhelmed their ... Ps 78:53
sent out her boughs unto the s ... Ps 80:11
Thou rulest the raging of the s ... Ps 89:9
I will set his hand also in the s ... Ps 89:25
than the mighty waves of the s ... Ps 93:4
The s is his, and he made it ... Ps 95:5
let the s roar, and the fulness ... Ps 96:11
Let the s roar, and the fulness ... Ps 98:7
So is this great and wide s ... Ps 104:25
him at the s, even at the Red s ... Ps 106:7
He rebuked the Red s also ... Ps 106:9
and terrible things by the Red s ... Ps 106:22
that go down to the s in ships ... Ps 107:23
The s saw it, and fled ... Ps 114:3
What ailed thee, O thou s ... Ps 114:5
divided the Red s into parts ... Ps 136:13
Pharaoh and his host in the Red s ... Ps 136:15
in the uttermost parts of the s ... Ps 139:9
made heaven, and earth, the s ... Ps 146:6
When he gave to the s his decree ... Prov 8:29
lieth down in the midst of the s ... Prov 23:34
of a ship in the midst of the s ... Prov 30:19
All the rivers run into the s ... Eccl 1:7
yet the s is not full ... Eccl 1:7
them like the roaring of the s ... Is 5:30
afflict her by the way of the s ... Is 9:1
Israel be as the sand of the s ... Is 10:22
and as his rod was upon the s ... Is 10:26
LORD, as the waters cover the s ... Is 11:9
and from the islands of the s ... Is 11:11
the tongue of the Egyptian s ... Is 11:15
out, they are gone over the s ... Is 16:8
That sendeth ambassadors by the s ... Is 18:2
the waters shall fail from the s ... Is 19:5
The burden of the desert of the s ... Is 21:1
of Zidon, that pass over the s ... Is 23:2
for the s hath spoken, even the ... Is 23:4
even the strength of the s ... Is 23:4
stretched out his hand over the s ... Is 23:11
they shall cry aloud from the s ... Is 24:14
of Israel in the isles of the s ... Is 24:15
slay the dragon that is in the s ... Is 27:1
earth, ye that go down to the s ... Is 42:10
LORD, which maketh a way in the s ... Is 43:16
as the waves of the s ... Is 48:18
at my rebuke I dry up the s ... Is 50:2
not it which hath dried the s ... Is 51:10
hath made the depths of the s a ... Is 51:10
LORD thy God, that divided the s ... Is 51:15
wicked are like the troubled s ... Is 57:20
s shall be converted unto thee ... Is 60:5
s with the shepherd of his flock ... Is 63:11
of the s by a perpetual decree ... Jer 5:22
their voice roareth like the s ... Jer 6:23
the isles which are beyond the s ... Jer 25:22
the pillars, and concerning the s ... Jer 27:19
which divideth the s when the ... Jer 31:35
the sand of the s measured ... Jer 33:22
mountains, and as Carmel by the s ... Jer 46:18
Ashkelon, and against the s shore ... Jer 47:7
thy plants are gone over the s ... Jer 48:32
they reach even to the s of Jazer ... Jer 48:32
thereof was heard in the Red s ... Jer 49:21
there is sorrow on the s ... Jer 49:23
their voice shall roar like the s ... Jer 50:42
and I will dry up her s, and make ... Jer 51:36
The s is come up upon Babylon ... Jer 51:42
the brasen s that was in the ... Jer 52:17
The two pillars, one s, and twelve ... Jer 52:20
thy breach is great like the s ... Lam 2:13
Even the s monsters draw out the ... Lam 4:3
the remnant of the s coast ... Eze 25:16
as the s causeth his waves to ... Eze 26:3
of nets in the midst of the s ... Eze 26:5
the s shall come down from their ... Eze 26:16
city, which wast strong in the s ... Eze 26:17
in the s shall be troubled at thy ... Eze 26:18
art situate at the entry of the s ... Eze 27:3
all the ships of the s with their ... Eze 27:9
and all the pilots of the s ... Eze 27:29
destroyed in the midst of the s ... Eze 27:32
So that the fishes of the s ... Eze 38:20
passengers on the east of the s ... Eze 39:11
into the desert, and go into the s ... Eze 47:8
being brought forth into the s ... Eze 47:8
kinds, as the fish of the great s ... Eze 47:10
the north side, from the great s ... Eze 47:15
from the s shall be Hazar-enan ... Eze 47:17
from the border unto the east s ... Eze 47:18
Kadesh, the river to the great s ... Eze 47:19
be the great s from the border ... Eze 47:20
to the river toward the great s ... Eze 48:28
heaven strove upon the great s ... Dan 7:2
great beasts came up from the s ... Dan 7:3
shall be as the sand of the s ... Hos 1:10
the fishes of the s also shall be ... Hos 4:3
with his face toward the east s ... Joel 2:20
hinder part toward the utmost s ... Joel 2:20
calleth for the waters of the s ... Amos 5:8
they shall wander from s to s ... Amos 8:12
my sight in the bottom of the s ... Amos 9:3
calleth for the waters of the s ... Amos 9:6
sent out a great wind into the s ... Jonah 1:4
was a mighty tempest in the s ... Jonah 1:4
that were in the ship into the s ... Jonah 1:5
of heaven, which hath made the s ... Jonah 1:9
that the s may be calm unto us ... Jonah 1:11
for the s wrought, and was ... Jonah 1:11
up, and cast me forth into the s ... Jonah 1:12
so shall the s be calm unto you ... Jonah 1:12
for the s wrought, and was ... Jonah 1:13
and cast him forth into the s ... Jonah 1:15
the s ceased from her raging ... Jonah 1:15
from s to s, and from mountain ... Mic 7:12
sins into the depths of the s ... Mic 7:19
He rebuketh the s, and maketh it ... Nah 1:4
about it, whose rampart was the s ... Nah 3:8
and her wall was from the s ... Nah 3:8
makest men as the fishes of the s ... Hab 1:14
LORD, as the waters cover the s ... Hab 2:14
was thy wrath against the s ... Hab 3:8
through the s with thine horses ... Hab 3:15
heaven, and the fishes of the s ... Zeph 1:3
the inhabitants of the s coast ... Zeph 2:5
the s coast shall be dwellings and ... Zeph 2:6
heavens, and the earth, and the s ... Hag 2:6
he will smite her power in the s ... Zec 9:4
shall be from s even to s ... Zec 9:10
through the s with affliction ... Zec 10:11
and shall smite the waves in the s ... Zec 10:11
half of them toward the former s ... Zec 14:8
half of them toward the hinder s ... Zec 14:8
which is upon the s coast ... Mt 4:13
Nephthalim, by the way of the s ... Mt 4:15
walking by the s of Galilee ... Mt 4:18
brother, casting a net into the s ... Mt 4:18
arose a great tempest in the s ... Mt 8:24
and rebuked the winds and the s ... Mt 8:26
even the winds and the s obey him ... Mt 8:27
down a steep place into the s ... Mt 8:32
the house, and sat by the s side ... Mt 13:1
a net, that was cast into the s ... Mt 13:47
was now in the midst of the s ... Mt 14:24
went unto them, walking on the s ... Mt 14:25
saw him walking on the s, they ... Mt 14:26
came nigh unto the s of Galilee ... Mt 15:29
offend them, go thou to the s ... Mt 17:27
drowned in the depth of the s ... Mt 18:6
and be thou cast into the s ... Mt 21:21
for ye compass s and land to make ... Mt 23:15
as he walked by the s of Galilee ... Mk 1:16
brother casting a net into the s ... Mk 1:16
he went forth again by the s side ... Mk 2:13
with his disciples to the s ... Mk 3:7
again to teach by the s side ... Mk 4:1
into a ship, and sat in the s ... Mk 4:1
was by the s on the land ... Mk 4:1
the wind, and said unto the s ... Mk 4:39
even the wind and the s obey him ... Mk 4:41
over unto the other side of the s ... Mk 5:1
down a steep place into the s ... Mk 5:13
and were choked in the s ... Mk 5:13
and he was nigh unto the s ... Mk 5:21
ship was in the midst of the s ... Mk 6:47
unto them, walking upon the s ... Mk 6:48
they saw him walking upon the s ... Mk 6:49
he came unto the s of Galilee ... Mk 7:31
neck, and he were cast into the s ... Mk 9:42
and be thou cast into the s ... Mk 11:23
from the s coast of Tyre and Sidon ... Lk 6:17
his neck, and he cast into the s ... Lk 17:2
root, and be thou planted in the s ... Lk 17:6
the s and the waves roaring ... Lk 21:25
Jesus went over the s of Galilee ... Jn 6:1
which is the s of Tiberias ... Jn 6:1
disciples went down unto the s ... Jn 6:16
went over the s toward Capernaum ... Jn 6:17
the s arose by reason of a great ... Jn 6:18
they see Jesus walking on the s ... Jn 6:19
s saw that there was none other ... Jn 6:22
him on the other side of the s ... Jn 6:25
disciples at the s of Tiberias ... Jn 21:1
and did cast himself into the s ... Jn 21:7
made heaven, and earth, and the s ... Acts 4:24
land of Egypt, and in the Red s ... Acts 7:36
whose house is by the s side ... Acts 10:6
one Simon a tanner by the s side ... Acts 10:32
made heaven, and earth, and the s ... Acts 14:15
Paul to go as it were to the s ... Acts 17:14
had sailed over the s of Cilicia ... Acts 27:5
had let down the boat into the s ... Acts 27:30
and cast out the wheat into the s ... Acts 27:38
committed themselves unto the s ... Acts 27:40
cast themselves first into the s ... Acts 27:43
though he hath escaped the s ... Acts 28:4
of Israel be as the sand of the s ... Rom 9:27
and all passed through the s ... 1Cor 10:1
Moses in the cloud and in the s ... 1Cor 10:2
wilderness, in perils in the s ... 2Cor 11:26
is by the s shore innumerable ... Heb 11:12
through the Red s as by dry land ... Heb 11:29
of the s driven with the wind ... Jas 1:6
serpents, and of things in the s ... Jas 3:7
Raging waves of the s, foaming ... Jude 13
a s of glass like unto crystal ... Rev 4:6
earth, and such as are in the s ... Rev 5:13
blow on the earth, nor on the s ... Rev 7:1
given to hurt the earth and the s ... Rev 7:2
Hurt not the earth, neither the s ... Rev 7:3
with fire was cast into the s ... Rev 8:8
third part of the s became blood ... Rev 8:8
the creatures which were in the s ... Rev 8:9
he set his right foot upon the s ... Rev 10:2
which I saw stand upon the s ... Rev 10:5
things that therein are, and the s ... Rev 10:6
angel which standeth upon the s ... Rev 10:8
of the earth and of the s ... Rev 12:12
And I stood upon the sand of the s ... Rev 13:1
saw a beast rise up out of the s ... Rev 13:1
made heaven, and earth, and the s ... Rev 14:7
I saw as it were a s of glass ... Rev 15:2
his name, stand on the s of glass ... Rev 15:2
poured out his vial upon the s ... Rev 16:3
every living soul died in the s ... Rev 16:3
sailors, and as many as trade by s ... Rev 18:17
the s by reason of her costliness ... Rev 18:19
millstone, and cast it into the s ... Rev 18:21
of whom is as the sand of the s ... Rev 20:8
the s gave up the dead which were ... Rev 20:13
and there was no more s ... Rev 21:1

**SEAFARING**

that wast inhabited of s men ... Eze 26:17

**SEAL**

name, and sealed them with his s ... 1Kin 21:8
Levites, and priests, s unto it ... Neh 9:38
s it with the king's ring ... Est 8:8
It is turned as clay to the s ... Job 38:14
up together as with a close s ... Job 41:15
Set me as a s upon thine heart, ... Song 8:6
heart, as a s upon thine arm ... Song 8:6
s the law among my disciples ... Is 8:16
s them, and take witnesses in the ... Jer 32:44

to s up the vision and prophecy, ... Dan 9:24
s the book, even to the time of ... Dan 12:4
set to his s that God is true ... Jn 3:33
a s of the righteousness of the ... Rom 4:11
for the s of mine apostleship are ... 1Cor 9:2
God standeth sure, having this s ... 2Ti 2:19
when he had opened the second s ... Rev 6:3
And when he had opened the third s ... Rev 6:5
when he had opened the fourth s ... Rev 6:7
And when he had opened the fifth s ... Rev 6:9
when he had opened the sixth s ... Rev 6:12
having the s of the living God ... Rev 7:2
when he had opened the seventh s ... Rev 8:1
the s of God in their foreheads ... Rev 9:4
S up those things which the seven ... Rev 10:4
set a s upon him, that he should ... Rev 20:3
S not the sayings of the prophecy ... Rev 22:10

## SEALED
me, and s up among my treasures ... Deut 32:34
s them with his seal, and sent the ... 1Kin 21:8
Now those that s were, Nehemiah, ... Neh 10:1
and s with the king's ring ... Est 3:12
s with the king's ring, may no ... Est 8:8
s it with the king's ring, and ... Est 8:10
My transgression is s up in a bag ... Job 14:17
a spring shut up, a fountain s ... Song 4:12
as the words of a book that is s ... Is 29:11
for it is s ... Is 29:11
s it, and took witnesses, and ... Jer 32:10
both that which was s according ... Jer 32:11
of the purchase, both which is s ... Jer 32:14
the king s it with his own signet ... Dan 6:17
s till the time of the end ... Dan 12:9
for him hath God the Father s ... Jn 6:27
have s to them this fruit, I will ... Rom 15:28
Who hath also s us, and given the ... 2Cor 1:22
ye were s with that holy Spirit ... Eph 1:13
whereby ye are s unto the day of ... Eph 4:30
the backside, s with seven seals ... Rev 5:1
till we have s the servants of ... Rev 7:3
the number of them which were s ... Rev 7:4
and there were s an hundred ... Rev 7:4
of Juda were s twelve thousand ... Rev 7:5
of Reuben were s twelve thousand ... Rev 7:5
of Gad were s twelve thousand ... Rev 7:5
of Aser were s twelve thousand ... Rev 7:6
Nepthalim were s twelve thousand ... Rev 7:6
Manasses were s twelve thousand ... Rev 7:6
of Simeon were s twelve thousand ... Rev 7:7
of Levi were s twelve thousand ... Rev 7:7
Issachar were s twelve thousand ... Rev 7:7
of Zabulon were s twelve thousand ... Rev 7:8
of Joseph were s twelve thousand ... Rev 7:8
Benjamin were s twelve thousand ... Rev 7:8

## SEALEST
Thou s up the sum, full of wisdom ... Eze 28:12

## SEALETH
and s up the stars ... Job 9:7
of men, and s their instruction, ... Job 33:16
He s up the hand of every man ... Job 37:7

## SEALING
s the stone, and setting a watch ... Mt 27:66

## SEALS
the backside, sealed with seven s ... Rev 5:1
book, and to loose the s thereof ... Rev 5:2
and to loose the seven s thereof ... Rev 5:5
book, and to open the s thereof ... Rev 5:9
when the Lamb opened one of the s ... Rev 6:1

## SEAM
now the coat was without s ... Jn 19:23

## SEARCH
He shall not s whether it be good ... Lev 27:33
to s out a resting place for them ... Num 10:33
that they may s the land of ... Num 13:2
which we have gone to s it ... Num 13:32
which we passed through to s it ... Num 14:7
which Moses sent to s the land ... Num 14:36
the men that went to s the land ... Num 14:38
they shall s us out the land, and ... Deut 1:22
to s you out a place to pitch ... Deut 1:33
shalt thou enquire, and make s ... Deut 13:14
of Israel to s out the country ... Josh 2:2
be come to s out all the country ... Josh 2:3
to spy out the land, and to s it ... Judg 18:2
said unto them, Go, s the land ... Judg 18:2
that I will s him out throughout ... 1Sa 23:23
to s the city, and to spy it out, ... 2Sa 10:3
they shall s thine house, and the ... 1Kin 20:6
unto the worshippers of Baal, S ... 2Kin 10:23
servants come unto thee for to s ... 1Chr 19:3
That s may be made in the book of ... Ezr 4:15
s hath been made, and it is found ... Ezr 4:19
let there be s made in the king's ... Ezr 5:17
s was made in the house of the ... Ezr 6:1
thyself to the s of their fathers ... Job 8:8
it good that he should s you out ... Job 13:9
thou walked in the s of the depth ... Job 38:16
Shall not God s this out ... Ps 44:21
They s out iniquities ... Ps 64:6
they accomplish a diligent s ... Ps 64:6
and my spirit made diligent s ... Ps 77:6
S me, O God, and know my heart ... Ps 139:23
of kings is to s out a matter ... Prov 25:2
so for men to s their own glory ... Prov 25:27
s out by wisdom concerning all ... Eccl 1:13
mine heart to know, and to s ... Eccl 7:25
I have not found it by secret s ... Jer 2:34
I the LORD s the heart, I try the ... Jer 17:10
when ye shall s for me with all ... Jer 29:13
Let us s and try our ways, and turn ... Lam 3:40
none did s or seek after them ... Eze 34:6
did my shepherds s for my flock ... Eze 34:8
I, even I, will both s my sheep ... Eze 34:11
end of seven months shall they s ... Eze 39:14
in the top of Carmel, I will s ... Amos 9:3
that I will s Jerusalem with ... Zeph 1:12
s diligently for the young child ... Mt 2:8
S the scriptures ... Jn 5:39
S, and look ... Jn 7:52

## SEARCHED
Laban s all the tent, but found ... Gen 31:34
And he s, but found not the images ... Gen 31:35
Whereas thou hast s all my stuff ... Gen 31:37
And he s, and began at the eldest, ... Gen 44:12
s the land from the wilderness of ... Num 13:21
of the land which they had s unto ... Num 13:32
were of them that s the land ... Num 14:6
the days in which ye s the land ... Num 14:34
the valley of Eshcol, and s it out ... Deut 1:24
Lo this, we have s it, so it is ... Job 5:27
he prepared it, yea, and s it out ... Job 28:27
cause which I knew not I s out ... Job 29:16
whilst ye s out what to say ... Job 32:11
the number of his years be s out ... Job 36:26
O lord, thou hast s me, and known ... Ps 139:1
of the earth s out beneath ... Jer 31:37
the LORD, though it cannot be s ... Jer 46:23
How are the things of Esau s out ... Obad 6
s the scriptures daily, whether ... Acts 17:11
s diligently, who prophesied of ... 1Pet 1:10

## SEARCHEST
mine iniquity, and s after my sin ... Job 10:6
s for her as for hid treasures ... Prov 2:4

## SEARCHETH
for the LORD s all hearts ... 1Chr 28:9
darkness, and s out all perfection ... Job 28:3
he s after every green thing ... Job 39:8
but his neighbour cometh and s him. ... Prov 18:17
that hath understanding s him out ... Prov 28:11
he that s the hearts knoweth what ... Rom 8:27
for the Spirit s all things ... 1Cor 2:10
that I am he which s the reins ... Rev 2:23

## SEARCHING
they returned from s of the land ... Num 13:25
Canst thou by s find out God ... Job 11:7
s all the inward parts of the ... Prov 20:27
there is no s of his ... Is 40:28
S what, or what manner of time ... 1Pet 1:11

## SEARCHINGS
there were great s of heart ... Judg 5:16

## SEARED
conscience s with a hot iron ... 1Ti 4:2

## SEAS
of the waters called he S ... Gen 1:10
and fill the waters in the s ... Gen 1:22
and scales in the waters, in the s ... Lev 11:9
have not fins and scales in the s ... Lev 11:10
suck of the abundance of the s ... Deut 33:19
things that are therein, the s ... Neh 9:6
through the paths of the s ... Ps 8:8
For he hath founded it upon the s ... Ps 24:2
Which stilleth the noise of the s ... Ps 65:7
heaven and earth praise him, the s ... Ps 69:34
in heaven, and in earth, in the s ... Ps 135:6
a noise like the noise of the s ... Is 17:12
to me above the sand of the s ... Jer 15:8
borders are in the midst of the s ... Eze 27:4
glorious in the midst of the s ... Eze 27:25
broken thee in the midst of the s ... Eze 27:26
of the s in the day of thy ruin ... Eze 27:27
thy wares went forth out of the s ... Eze 27:33
thou shalt be broken by the s in ... Eze 27:34
of God, in the midst of the s ... Eze 28:2
are slain in the midst of the s ... Eze 28:8
and thou art as a whale in the s ... Eze 32:2
of his palace between the s in ... Dan 11:45
the deep, in the midst of the s ... Jonah 2:3
into a place where two s met ... Acts 27:41

## SEASON
and they continued a s in ward ... Gen 40:4
in his s from year to year ... Ex 13:10
offering shalt thou s with salt ... Lev 2:13
I will give you rain in due s ... Lev 26:4
the passover at his appointed s ... Num 9:2
shall keep it in his appointed s ... Num 9:3
s among the children of Israel ... Num 9:7
of the LORD in his appointed s ... Num 9:13
to offer unto me in their due s ... Num 28:2
rain of your land in his due s ... Deut 11:14
at the s that thou camest forth ... Deut 16:6
the rain unto thy land in his s ... Deut 28:12
dwelt in the wilderness a long s ... Josh 24:7
And he said, About this s, ... 2Kin 4:16
bare a son at that s that Elisha ... 2Kin 4:17
were at that s in the high place ... 1Chr 21:29
Now for a long s Israel hath been ... 2Chr 15:3
shock of corn cometh in in his s ... Job 5:26
are pierced in me in the night s ... Job 30:17
bring forth Mazzaroth in his s ... Job 38:32
bringeth forth his fruit in his s ... Ps 1:3
and in the night s, and am not ... Ps 22:2
give them their meat in due s ... Ps 104:27
givest them their meat in due s ... Ps 145:15
and a word spoken in due s ... Prov 15:23
To every thing there is a s ... Eccl 3:1
and thy princes eat in due s ... Eccl 10:17
a word in s to him that is weary ... Is 50:4
former and the latter, in his s ... Jer 5:24
not be day and night in their s ... Jer 33:20
the shower to come down in his s ... Eze 34:26
lives were prolonged for a s ... Dan 7:12
and my wine in the s thereof ... Hos 2:9
to give them meat in due s ... Mt 24:45
saltness, wherewith will ye s it ... Mk 9:50
And at the s he sent to the ... Mk 12:2
shall be fulfilled in their s ... Lk 1:20
he departed from him for a s ... Lk 4:13
their portion of meat in due s ... Lk 12:42
that s some that told him of the ... Lk 13:1
at the s he sent a servant to the ... Lk 20:10
desirous to see him of a long s ... Lk 23:8
down at a certain s into the pool ... Jn 5:4
ye were willing for a s to ... Jn 5:35
blind, not seeing the sun for a s ... Acts 13:11
he himself stayed in Asia for a s ... Acts 19:22
when I have a convenient s ... Acts 24:25
sorry, though it were but for a s ... 2Cor 7:8
for in due s we shall reap, if we ... Gal 6:9
be instant in s ... 2Ti 4:2
out of s; reprove ... 2Ti 4:2
he therefore departed for a s ... Philem 15
the pleasures of sin for a s ... Heb 11:25
rejoice, though now for a s ... 1Pet 1:6
should rest yet for a little s ... Rev 6:11
that he must be loosed a little s ... Rev 20:3

## SEASONED
savour, wherewith shall it be s ... Lk 14:34
s with salt, that ye may know how ... Col 4:6

## SEASONS
let them be for signs, and for s ... Gen 1:14
them judge the people at all s ... Ex 18:22
they judged the people at all s ... Ex 18:26
ye shall proclaim in their s ... Lev 23:4
also instruct me in the night s ... Ps 16:7
He appointed the moon for s ... Ps 104:19
And he changeth the times and the s ... Dan 2:21
render him the fruits in their s ... Mt 21:41
you to know the times or the s ... Acts 1:7
rain from heaven, and fruitful s ... Acts 14:17
I have been with you at all s ... Acts 20:18
But of the times and the s ... 1Th 5:1

## SEAT
shalt make a mercy s of pure gold ... Ex 25:17
in the two ends of the mercy s ... Ex 25:18
even of the mercy s shall ye make ... Ex 25:19
the mercy s with their wings ... Ex 25:20
toward the mercy s shall the ... Ex 25:20
the mercy s above upon the ark ... Ex 25:21
with thee from above the mercy s ... Ex 25:22
thou shalt put the mercy s upon ... Ex 26:34
before the mercy s that is over ... Ex 30:6
the mercy s that is thereupon, and ... Ex 31:7
staves thereof, with the mercy s ... Ex 35:12
he made the mercy s of pure gold ... Ex 37:6
on the two ends of the mercy s ... Ex 37:7
out of the mercy s made he the ... Ex 37:8
with their wings over the mercy s ... Ex 37:9
staves thereof, and the mercy s ... Ex 39:35
put the mercy s above upon the ... Ex 40:20
the vail before the mercy s ... Lev 16:2
in the cloud upon the mercy s ... Lev 16:2
s that is upon the testimony ... Lev 16:13
finger upon the mercy s eastward ... Lev 16:14
before the mercy s shall he ... Lev 16:14
and sprinkle it upon the mercy s ... Lev 16:15
and before the mercy s ... Lev 16:15
mercy s that was upon the ark of ... Num 7:89
And he arose out of his s ... Judg 3:20
Now Eli the priest sat upon a s ... 1Sa 1:9
Eli sat upon a s by the wayside ... 1Sa 4:13
that he fell from off the s ... 1Sa 4:18
because thy s will be empty ... 1Sa 20:18
And the king sat upon his s ... 1Sa 20:25
times, even upon a s by the wall ... 1Sa 20:25
The Tachmonite that sat in the s ... 2Sa 23:8
caused a s to be set for the ... 1Kin 2:19
either side on the place of the s ... 1Kin 10:19
and of the place of the mercy s ... 1Chr 28:11
set his s above all the princes ... Est 3:1
that I might come even to his s ... Job 23:3
I prepared my s in the street ... Job 29:7
sitteth in the s of the scornful ... Ps 1:1
on a s in the high places of the ... Prov 9:14
where was the s of the image of ... Eze 8:3
I am a God, I sit in the s of God ... Eze 28:2
cause the s of violence to come ... Amos 6:3
and the Pharisees sit in Moses' s ... Mt 23:2
he was set down on the judgment s ... Mt 27:19
sat down in the judgment s in a ... Jn 19:13
and brought him to the judgment s ... Acts 18:12
he drave them from the judgment s ... Acts 18:16
and beat him before the judgment s ... Acts 18:17
day sitting on the judgment s ... Acts 25:6
I stand at Caesar's judgment s ... Acts 25:10
morrow I sat on the judgment s ... Acts 25:17
before the judgment s of Christ ... Rom 14:10
before the judgment s of Christ ... 2Cor 5:10
dwellest, even where Satan's s is ... Rev 2:13
gave him his power, and his s ... Rev 13:2
his vial upon the s of the beast ... Rev 16:10

**SEATED**
portion of the lawgiver, was he s Deut 33:21

**SEATS**
the s of them that sold doves, Mt 21:12
the chief s in the synagogues, Mt 23:6
the s of them that sold doves Mk 11:15
the chief s in the synagogues, and Mk 12:39
put down the mighty from their s Lk 1:52
the uppermost s in the synagogues Lk 11:43
the highest s in the synagogues, Lk 20:46
and draw you before the judgment s Jas 2:6
the throne were four and twenty s Rev 4:4
upon the s I saw four and twenty Rev 4:4
which sat before God on their s Rev 11:16

**SEATWARD**
even to the mercy s were the Ex 37:9

**SEBA** (*se'-bah*) See SABEANS, SHEBA.
*1. A son of Cush.*
S, and Havilah, and Sabtah, and Gen 10:7
S, and Havilah, and Sabta, and 1Chr 1:9
*2. The land.*
of Sheba and S shall offer gifts Ps 72:10
ransom, Ethiopia and S for thee Is 43:3

**SEBAM** See SHEBAM.

**SEBAT** (*se'-bat*) *The eleventh month of the Hebrew year.*
month, which is the month S Zec 1:7

**SECACAH** (*se-ca'-cah*) *A village in Judah.*
Beth-arabah, Middin, and S Josh 15:61

**SECHU** (*se'-ku*) *A city in Benjamin.*
came to a great well that is in S 1Sa 19:22

**SECOND**
and the morning were the s day Gen 1:8
the name of the s river is Gihon Gen 2:13
with lower, s, and third stories Gen 6:16
of Noah's life, in the s month Gen 7:11
And in the s month, on the seven Gen 8:14
Abraham out of heaven the s time Gen 22:15
again, and bare Jacob a s son Gen 30:7
Leah's maid bare Jacob a s son Gen 30:12
And so commanded he the s, and the Gen 32:19
And he slept and dreamed the s time Gen 41:5
in the s chariot which he had Gen 41:43
the name of the s called he Gen 41:52
now we had returned this s time Gen 43:10
they came unto him the s year Gen 47:18
And when he went out the s day Ex 2:13
on the fifteenth day of the s Ex 16:1
curtain, in the coupling of the s Ex 26:4
that is in the coupling of the s Ex 26:5
the curtain which coupleth the s Ex 26:10
for the s side of the tabernacle Ex 26:20
the s row shall be an emerald, a Ex 28:18
curtain, in the coupling of the s Ex 36:11
was in the coupling of the s Ex 36:12
the curtain which coupleth the s Ex 36:17
And the s row, an emerald, a Ex 39:11
in the first month in the s year Ex 40:17
he shall offer the s for a burnt Lev 5:10
it shall be washed the s time Lev 13:58
on the first day of the s month Num 1:1
in the s year after they were Num 1:1
on the first day of the s month Num 1:18
shall set forth in the s rank Num 2:16
On the s day Nethaneel the son of Num 7:18
in the first month of the s year Num 9:1
The fourteenth day of the s month Num 9:11
When ye blow an alarm the s time Num 10:6
the s month, in the s year Num 10:11
on the s day ye shall offer Num 29:17
the children of Israel the s time Josh 5:2
the s day they compassed the city Josh 6:14
which took it on the s day Josh 10:32
the s lot came forth to Simeon, Josh 19:1
even the s bullock of seven years Judg 6:25
place, and take the s bullock Judg 6:26
the s bullock was offered upon Judg 6:28
children of Benjamin the s day Judg 20:24
them out of Gibeah the s day Judg 20:25
and the name of his s, Abiah 1Sa 8:2
which was the s day of the month, 1Sa 20:27
no meat the s day of the month 1Sa 20:34
I will not smite him the s time 1Sa 26:8
And his s, Chileab, of Abigail the 2Sa 3:3
and when he sent again the s time 2Sa 14:29
month Zif, which is the s month 1Kin 6:1
appeared to Solomon the s time 1Kin 9:2
the s year of Asa king of Judah 1Kin 15:25
And he said, Do it the s time 1Kin 18:34
And they did it the s time 1Kin 18:34
of the LORD came again the s time 1Kin 19:7
the s year of Jehoram the son of 2Kin 1:17
Then he sent out a s on horseback 2Kin 9:19
wrote a letter the s time to them 2Kin 10:6
In the s year of Joash son of 2Kin 14:1
In the s year of Pekah the son of 2Kin 15:32
and in the s year that which 2Kin 19:29
and the priests of the s order 2Kin 23:4
like unto these had the s pillar 2Kin 25:17
priest, and Zephaniah the s priest 2Kin 25:18
Eliab, and Abinadab the s, and 1Chr 2:13
the s Daniel, of Abigail the 1Chr 3:1
the s Jehoiakim, the third 1Chr 3:15
the name of the s was Zelophehad 1Chr 7:15
Bela his firstborn, Ashbel the s 1Chr 8:1
Ulam his firstborn, Jehush the s 1Chr 8:39
Ezer the first, Obadiah the s 1Chr 12:9
their brethren of the s degree 1Chr 15:18
was the chief, and Zizah the s 1Chr 23:11
Jeriah the first, Amariah the s 1Chr 23:19
Micah the first, and Jesiah the s 1Chr 23:20
to Jehoiarib, the s to Jedaiah, 1Chr 24:7
Jeriah the first, Amariah the s 1Chr 24:23
the s to Gedaliah, who with his 1Chr 25:9
the firstborn, Jediael the s 1Chr 26:2
the firstborn, Jehozabad the s 1Chr 26:4
Hilkiah the s, Tebaliah the third 1Chr 26:11
over the course of the s month 1Chr 27:4
the son of David king the s time 1Chr 29:22
in the s day of the s month 2Chr 3:2
pay unto him, both the s year 2Chr 27:5
keep the passover in the s month 2Chr 30:2
unleavened bread in the s month 2Chr 30:13
the fourteenth day of the s month 2Chr 30:15
put him in the s chariot that he 2Chr 35:24
basons of a s sort four hundred Ezr 1:10
Now in the s year of their coming Ezr 3:8
God at Jerusalem, in the s month Ezr 3:8
So it ceased unto the s year of Ezr 4:24
on the s day were gathered Neh 8:13
son of Senuah was s over the city Neh 11:9
Bakbukiah the s among his Neh 11:17
into the s house of the women Est 2:14
were gathered together the s time Est 2:19
the s day at the banquet of wine Est 7:2
to confirm this s letter of Purim Est 9:29
and the name of the s, Kezia Job 42:14
is one alone, and there is not a s Eccl 4:8
with the s child that shall stand Eccl 4:15
shall set his hand again the s Is 11:11
the s year that which springeth Is 37:30
the LORD came unto me the s time Jer 1:13
the LORD came unto me the s time Jer 13:3
came unto Jeremiah the s time Jer 33:1
it came to pass the s day after Jer 41:4
The s pillar also and the Jer 52:22
priest, and Zephaniah the s priest Jer 52:24
the s face was the face of a man, Eze 10:14
on the s day thou shalt offer a Eze 43:22
in the s year of the reign of Dan 2:1
And behold another beast, a s Dan 7:5
LORD came unto Jonah the s time Jonah 3:1
shall not rise up the s time Nah 1:9
gate, and an howling from the s Zeph 1:10
In the s year of Darius the king, Hag 1:1
in the s year of Darius the king Hag 1:15
in the s year of Darius, came the Hag 2:10
in the s year of Darius, came the Zec 1:1
in the s year of Darius, came the Zec 1:7
in the s chariot black horses Zec 6:2
And he came to the s, and said Mt 21:30
Likewise the s also, and the third Mt 22:26
the s is like unto it, Thou shalt Mt 22:39
He went away again the s time Mt 26:42
the s took her, and died, neither Mk 12:21
the s is like, namely this, Thou Mk 12:31
And the s time the cock crew Mk 14:72
it came to pass on the s sabbath Lk 6:1
if he shall come in the s watch Lk 12:38
the s came, saying, Lord, thy Lk 19:18
the s took her to wife, and he Lk 20:30
can he enter the s time into his Jn 3:4
This is again the s miracle that Jn 4:54
He saith to him again the s time Jn 21:16
at the s time Joseph was made Acts 7:13
spake unto him again the s time Acts 10:15
the s ward, they came unto the Acts 12:10
it is also written in the s psalm Acts 13:33
the s man is the Lord from heaven 1Cor 15:47
that ye might have a s benefit 2Cor 1:15
as if I were present, the s time 2Cor 13:2
The s epistle to the Corinthians 2Cor s
The s epistle to the 2Th s
The s epistle unto Timotheus, 2Ti s
brought before Nero the s time 2Ti s
the first and s admonition reject Titus 3:10
place have been sought for the s Heb 8:7
And after the s veil, the Heb 9:3
But into the s went the high Heb 9:7
for him shall he appear the s Heb 9:28
that he may establish the s Heb 10:9
This s epistle, beloved, I now 2Pet 3:1
shall not be hurt of the s death Rev 2:11
the s beast like a calf, and the Rev 4:7
And when he had opened the s seal Rev 6:3
I heard the s beast say Rev 6:3
the s angel sounded, and as it Rev 8:8
The s woe is past Rev 11:14
the s angel poured out his vial Rev 16:3
on such the s death hath no power Rev 20:6
This is the s death Rev 20:14
which is the s death Rev 21:8
the s, sapphire Rev 21:19

**SECONDARILY**
s prophets, thirdly teachers, 1Cor 12:28

**SECRET**
soul, come not thou into their s Gen 49:6
and putteth it in a s place Deut 27:15
The s things belong unto the LORD Deut 29:29
I have a s errand unto thee, O Judg 3:19
after my name, seeing it is s Judg 13:18
they had emerods in their s parts 1Sa 5:9
morning, and abide in a s place 1Sa 19:2
that thou wouldest keep me s Job 14:13
Hast thou heard the s of God Job 15:8
is there any s thing with thee Job 15:11
shall be hid in his s places Job 20:26
when the s of God was upon my Job 29:4
and bind their faces in s Job 40:13
in the s places doth he murder Ps 10:8
a young lion lurking in s places Ps 17:12
He made darkness his s place Ps 18:11
cleanse thou me from s faults Ps 19:12
The s of the LORD is with them Ps 25:14
in the s of his tabernacle shall Ps 27:5
Thou shalt hide them in the s of Ps 31:20
Hide me from the s counsel of the Ps 64:2
may shoot in s at the perfect Ps 64:4
thee in the s place of thunder Ps 81:7
our s sins in the light of thy Ps 90:8
He that dwelleth in the s place Ps 91:1
from thee, when I was made in s Ps 139:15
but his s is with the righteous Prov 3:32
and bread eaten in s is pleasant Prov 9:17
A gift in s pacifieth anger Prov 21:14
and discover not a s to another Prov 25:9
Open rebuke is better than s love Prov 27:5
into judgment, with every s thing Eccl 12:14
in the s places of the stairs, Song 2:14
LORD will discover their s parts Is 3:17
and hidden riches of s places Is 45:3
I have not spoken in s, in a dark Is 45:19
spoken in s from the beginning Is 48:16
I have not found it by s search Jer 2:34
weep in s places for your pride Jer 13:17
Can any hide himself in s places Jer 23:24
I have uncovered his s places Jer 49:10
in wait, and as a lion in s places Lam 3:10
and they shall pollute my s place Eze 7:22
there is no s that they can hide Eze 28:3
God of heaven concerning this s Dan 2:18
Then was the s revealed unto Dan 2:19
He revealeth the deep and s things Dan 2:22
The s which the king hath Dan 2:27
this s is not revealed to me for Dan 2:30
seeing thou couldst reveal this s Dan 2:47
no s troubleth thee, tell me the Dan 4:9
but he revealeth his s unto his Amos 3:7
That thine alms may be in s Mt 6:4
in s himself shall reward thee Mt 6:4
pray to thy Father which is in s Mt 6:6
in s shall reward thee openly Mt 6:6
but unto thy Father which is in s Mt 6:18
and thy Father, which seeth in s Mt 6:18
kept s from the foundation of the Mt 13:35
behold, he is in the s chambers Mt 24:26
neither was any thing kept s Mk 4:22
For nothing is s, that shall not Lk 8:17
a candle, putteth it in a s place Lk 11:33
no man that doeth any thing in s Jn 7:4
not openly, but as it were in s Jn 7:10
and in s have I said nothing Jn 18:20
which was kept s since the world Rom 16:25
which are done of them in s Eph 5:12

**SECRETLY**
Wherefore didst thou flee away s Gen 31:27
as thine own soul, entice thee s Deut 13:6
he that smiteth his neighbour s Deut 27:24
want of all things s in the siege Deut 28:57
out of Shittim two men to spy s Josh 2:1
saying, Commune with David s 1Sa 18:22
David knew that Saul s practised 1Sa 23:9
For thou didst it s 2Sa 12:12
did s those things that were not 2Kin 17:9
Now a thing was s brought to me Job 4:12
if ye do s accept persons Job 13:10
And my heart hath been s enticed Job 31:27
He lieth in wait s as a lion in Ps 10:9
thou shalt keep them s in a Ps 31:20
the king asked him s in his house Jer 37:17
the king sware s unto Jeremiah Jer 38:16
spake to Gedaliah in Mizpah s Jer 40:15
was as to devour the poor s Hab 3:14
way, and called Mary her sister s Jn 11:28
but s for fear of the Jews, Jn 19:38

**SECRETS**
her hand, and taketh him by the s Deut 25:11
would shew thee the s of wisdom Job 11:6
for he knoweth the s of the heart Ps 44:21
A talebearer revealeth s Prov 11:13
about as a talebearer revealeth s Prov 20:19
a God in heaven that revealeth s Dan 2:28
he that revealeth s maketh known Dan 2:29
LORD of kings, and a revealer of s Dan 2:47
the s of men by Jesus Christ Rom 2:16
thus are the s of his heart made 1Cor 14:25

**SECT**
(which is the s of the Sadducees, Acts 5:17
there rose up certain of the s of Acts 15:5
of the s of the Nazarenes Acts 24:5
s of our religion I lived a Acts 26:5
for as concerning this s, we know Acts 28:22

**SECU** See SECHU.

**SECUNDUS** (*se-cun'-dus*) *A Christian in Thessalonica.*
Thessalonians, Aristarchus and S Acts 20:4

**SECURE**
for the host was s Judg 8:11
of the Zidonians, quiet and s Judg 18:7
go, ye shall come unto a people s Judg 18:10
a people that were at quiet and s Judg 18:27
And thou shalt be s, because there Job 11:18

and they that provoke God are *s* ... Job 12:6
we will persuade him, and *s* you ... Mt 28:14

**SECURELY**
seeing he dwelleth *s* by thee ... Prov 3:29
pass by *s* as men averse from war ... Mic 2:8

**SECURITY**
And when they had taken *s* of Jason .. Acts 17:9

**SEDITION**
that they have moved *s* within the ... Ezr 4:15
and *s* have been made therein ... Ezr 4:19
for a certain *s* made in the city ... Lk 23:19
released unto them him that for *s* ... Lk 23:25
a mover of *s* among all the Jews ... Acts 24:5

**SEDITIONS**
emulations, wrath, strife, *s* ... Gal 5:20

**SEDUCE**
shall shew signs and wonders, to *s* ... Mk 13:22
you concerning them that *s* you ... 1Jn 2:26
to *s* my servants to commit ... Rev 2:20

**SEDUCED**
Manasseh *s* them to do more evil ... 2Kin 21:9
they have also *s* Egypt, even they ... Is 19:13
because they have *s* my people ... Eze 13:10

**SEDUCERS**
*s* shall wax worse and worse, ... 2Ti 3:13

**SEDUCETH**
but the way of the wicked *s* them ... Prov 12:26

**SEDUCING**
faith, giving heed to *s* spirits ... 1Ti 4:1

**SEE** See PREFACE.

**SEED**
forth grass, the herb yielding *s* ... Gen 1:11
whose *s* is in itself, upon the ... Gen 1:11
herb yielding *s* after his kind, ... Gen 1:12
whose *s* was in itself, after his ... Gen 1:12
given you every herb bearing *s* ... Gen 1:29
is the fruit of a tree yielding *s* ... Gen 1:29
and between thy *s* and her *s* ... Gen 3:15
me another *s* instead of Abel ... Gen 4:25
to keep *s* alive upon the face of ... Gen 7:3
you, and with your *s* after you ... Gen 9:9
Unto thy *s* will I give this land ... Gen 12:7
I give it, and to thy *s* for ever ... Gen 13:15
I will make thy *s* as the dust of ... Gen 13:16
then shall thy *s* also be numbered ... Gen 13:16
to me thou hast given no *s* ... Gen 15:3
said unto him, So shall thy *s* be ... Gen 15:5
Know of a surety that thy *s* shall ... Gen 15:13
Unto thy *s* have I given this land ... Gen 15:18
I will multiply thy *s* exceedingly ... Gen 16:10
thy *s* after thee in their ... Gen 17:7
unto thee, and to thy *s* after thee ... Gen 17:7
to thy *s* after thee, the land ... Gen 17:8
thy *s* after thee in their ... Gen 17:9
me and you and thy *s* after thee ... Gen 17:10
stranger, which is not of thy *s* ... Gen 17:12
covenant, and with his *s* after him ... Gen 17:19
we may preserve *s* of our father ... Gen 19:32
we may preserve *s* of our father ... Gen 19:34
in Isaac shall thy *s* be called ... Gen 21:12
a nation, because he is thy *s* ... Gen 21:13
thy *s* as the stars of the heaven ... Gen 22:17
thy *s* shall possess the gate of ... Gen 22:17
in thy *s* shall all the nations of ... Gen 22:18
Unto thy *s* will I give this land ... Gen 24:7
let thy *s* possess the gate of ... Gen 24:60
for unto thee, and unto thy *s* ... Gen 26:3
I will make thy *s* to multiply as ... Gen 26:4
will give unto thy *s* all these ... Gen 26:4
in thy *s* shall all the nations of ... Gen 26:4
multiply thy *s* for my servant ... Gen 26:24
to thee, and to thy *s* with thee ... Gen 28:4
thee will I give it, and to thy *s* ... Gen 28:13
thy *s* shall be as the dust of the ... Gen 28:14
in thy *s* shall all the families ... Gen 28:14
make thy *s* as the sand of the sea ... Gen 32:12
to thy *s* after thee will I give ... Gen 35:12
raise up *s* to thy brother ... Gen 38:8
knew that the *s* should not be his ... Gen 38:9
he should give *s* to his brother ... Gen 38:9
Jacob, and all his *s* with him ... Gen 46:6
all his *s* brought he with him ... Gen 46:7
and give us *s*, that we may live, ... Gen 47:19
lo, here is *s* for you, and ye ... Gen 47:23
for *s* of the field, and for your ... Gen 47:24
will give this land to thy *s* ... Gen 48:4
lo, God hath shewed me also thy *s* ... Gen 48:11
his *s* shall become a multitude of ... Gen 48:19
and it was like coriander *s* ... Ex 16:31
ever unto him and his *s* after him ... Ex 28:43
to his *s* throughout their ... Ex 30:21
I will multiply your *s* as the ... Ex 32:13
spoken of will I give unto your *s* ... Ex 32:13
Unto thy *s* will I give it ... Ex 33:1
any sowing *s* which is to be sown ... Lev 11:37
if any water be put upon the *s* ... Lev 11:38
If a woman have conceived *s* ... Lev 12:2
if any man's *s* of copulation go ... Lev 15:16
whereon is the *s* of copulation ... Lev 15:17
shall lie with *s* of copulation ... Lev 15:18
of him whose *s* goeth from him, and ... Lev 15:32
thou shalt not let any of thy *s* ... Lev 18:21
not sow thy field with mingled *s* ... Lev 19:19
giveth any of his *s* unto Molech ... Lev 20:2
hath given of his *s* unto Molech ... Lev 20:3
he giveth of his *s* unto Molech ... Lev 20:4
he profane his *s* among his people ... Lev 21:15
Whosoever he be of thy *s* in their ... Lev 21:17
*s* of Aaron the priest shall come ... Lev 21:21
all your *s* among your generations ... Lev 22:3
of the *s* of Aaron is a leper ... Lev 22:4
or a man whose *s* goeth from him ... Lev 22:4
and ye shall sow your *s* in vain ... Lev 26:16
be according to the *s* thereof ... Lev 27:16
a homer of barley *s* shall be ... Lev 27:16
whether of the *s* of the land ... Lev 27:30
be free, and shall conceive *s* ... Num 5:28
And the manna was as coriander *s* ... Num 11:7
and his *s* shall possess it ... Num 14:24
which is not of the *s* of Aaron ... Num 16:40
unto thee and to thy *s* with thee ... Num 18:19
it is no place of *s*, or of figs, ... Num 20:5
his *s* shall be in many waters, and ... Num 24:7
his *s* after him, even the ... Num 25:13
them and to their *s* after them ... Deut 1:8
he chose their *s* after them ... Deut 4:37
and he chose their *s* after them ... Deut 10:15
to give unto them and to their *s* ... Deut 11:9
out, where thou sowedst thy *s* ... Deut 11:10
tithe all the increase of thy *s* ... Deut 14:22
of thy *s* which thou hast sown ... Deut 22:9
carry much *s* out into the field ... Deut 28:38
a wonder, and upon thy *s* for ever ... Deut 28:46
and the plagues of thy *s*, even ... Deut 28:59
heart, and the heart of thy *s* ... Deut 30:6
that both thou and thy *s* may live ... Deut 30:19
out of the mouths of their *s* ... Deut 31:21
saying, I will give it unto thy *s* ... Deut 34:4
of Canaan, and multiplied his *s* ... Josh 24:3
of the *s* which the LORD shall ... Ruth 4:12
The LORD give thee *s* of this ... 1Sa 2:20
he will take the tenth of your *s* ... 1Sa 8:15
between my *s* and thy *s* for ever ... 1Sa 20:42
wilt not cut off my *s* after me ... 1Sa 24:21
this day of Saul, and of his *s* ... 2Sa 4:8
I will set up thy *s* after thee ... 2Sa 7:12
David, and to his *s* for evermore ... 2Sa 22:51
upon the head of his *s* for ever ... 1Kin 2:33
but upon David, and upon his *s* ... 1Kin 2:33
he was of the king's *s* in Edom ... 1Kin 11:14
for this afflict the *s* of David ... 1Kin 11:39
would contain two measures of *s* ... 1Kin 18:32
unto thee, and unto thy *s* for ever ... 2Kin 5:27
and destroyed all the *s* royal ... 2Kin 11:1
LORD rejected all the *s* of Israel ... 2Kin 17:20
son of Elishama, of the *s* royal ... 2Kin 25:25
O ye *s* of Israel his servant, ye ... 1Chr 16:13
I will raise up thy *s* after thee ... 1Chr 17:11
gavest it to the *s* of Abraham thy ... 2Chr 20:7
destroyed all the *s* royal of the ... 2Chr 22:10
their father's house, and their *s* ... Ezr 2:59
so that the holy *s* have mingled ... Ezr 9:2
their father's house, nor their *s* ... Neh 7:61
the *s* of Israel separated ... Neh 9:2
to give it, I say, to his *s* ... Neh 9:8
Mordecai be of the *s* of the Jews ... Est 6:13
took upon them, and upon their *s* ... Est 9:27
of them perish from their *s* ... Est 9:28
for themselves and for their *s* ... Est 9:31
and speaking peace to all his *s* ... Est 10:3
also that thy *s* shall be great ... Job 5:25
Their *s* is established in their ... Job 21:8
that he will bring home thy *s* ... Job 39:12
David, and to his *s* for evermore ... Ps 18:50
their *s* from among the children ... Ps 21:10
all ye the *s* of Jacob, glorify ... Ps 22:23
fear him, all ye the *s* of Israel ... Ps 22:23
A *s* shall serve him ... Ps 22:30
his *s* shall inherit the earth ... Ps 25:13
forsaken, nor his *s* begging bread ... Ps 37:25
and his *s* is blessed ... Ps 37:26
but the *s* of the wicked shall be ... Ps 37:28
The *s* also of his servants shall ... Ps 69:36
Thy *s* will I establish for ever, ... Ps 89:4
His *s* also will I make to endure ... Ps 89:29
His *s* shall endure for ever, and ... Ps 89:36
their *s* shall be established ... Ps 102:28
O ye *s* of Abraham his servant, ye ... Ps 105:6
To overthrow their *s* also among ... Ps 106:27
His *s* shall be mighty upon earth ... Ps 112:2
and weepeth, bearing precious *s* ... Ps 126:6
but the *s* of the righteous shall ... Prov 11:21
In the morning sow thy *s*, and in ... Eccl 11:6
a *s* of evildoers, children that ... Is 1:4
the *s* of an homer shall yield an ... Is 5:10
so the holy *s* shall be the ... Is 6:13
the *s* of evildoers shall never be ... Is 14:20
shalt thou make thy *s* to flourish ... Is 17:11
And by great waters the *s* of Sihor ... Is 23:3
shall he give the rain of thy *s* ... Is 30:23
the *s* of Abraham my friend ... Is 41:8
I will bring thy *s* from the east ... Is 43:5
I will pour my spirit upon thy *s* ... Is 44:3
I said not unto the *s* of Jacob ... Is 45:19
all the *s* of Israel be justified ... Is 45:25
Thy *s* also had been as the sand, ... Is 48:19
for sin, he shall see his *s* ... Is 53:10
thy *s* shall inherit the Gentiles, ... Is 54:3
that it may give *s* to the sower ... Is 55:10
the *s* of the adulterer and the ... Is 57:3
transgression, a *s* of falsehood, ... Is 57:4
nor out of the mouth of thy *s* ... Is 59:21
out of the mouth of thy seed's *s* ... Is 59:21
their *s* shall be known among the ... Is 61:9
that they are the *s* which the ... Is 61:9
will bring forth a *s* out of Jacob ... Is 65:9
for they are the *s* of the blessed ... Is 65:23
saith the LORD, so shall your *s* ... Is 66:22
a noble vine, wholly a right *s* ... Jer 2:21
even the whole *s* of Ephraim ... Jer 7:15
are they cast out, he and his *s* ... Jer 22:28
for no man of his *s* shall prosper ... Jer 22:30
which led the *s* of the house of ... Jer 23:8
Shemaiah the Nehelamite, and his *s* ... Jer 29:32
thy *s* from the land of their ... Jer 30:10
house of Judah with the *s* of man ... Jer 31:27
of man, and with the *s* of beast ... Jer 31:27
then the *s* of Israel also shall ... Jer 31:36
the *s* of Israel for all that they ... Jer 31:37
the *s* of David my servant ... Jer 33:22
will I cast away the *s* of Jacob ... Jer 33:26
*s* to be rulers over the *s* of ... Jer 33:26
be rulers over the *s* of Abraham ... Jer 33:26
shall ye build house, nor sow *s* ... Jer 35:7
we vineyard, nor field, nor *s* ... Jer 35:9
And I will punish him and his *s* ... Jer 36:31
son of Elishama, of the *s* royal ... Jer 41:1
thy *s* from the land of their ... Jer 46:27
his *s* is spoiled, and his brethren ... Jer 49:10
He took also of the *s* of the land ... Eze 17:5
And hath taken of the king's *s* ... Eze 17:13
unto the *s* of the house of Jacob ... Eze 20:5
Levites that be of the *s* of Zadok ... Eze 43:19
of the *s* of the house of Israel ... Eze 44:22
of Israel, and of the king's *s* ... Dan 1:3
themselves with the *s* of men ... Dan 2:43
of the *s* of the Medes, which was ... Dan 9:1
The *s* is rotten under their clods ... Joel 1:17
of grapes him that soweth *s* ... Amos 9:13
Is the *s* yet in the barn ... Hag 2:19
For the *s* shall be prosperous ... Zec 8:12
Behold, I will corrupt your *s* ... Mal 2:3
That he might seek a godly *s* ... Mal 2:15
which received *s* by the way side ... Mt 13:19
received the *s* into stony places ... Mt 13:20
He also that received *s* among the ... Mt 13:22
But he that received *s* into the ... Mt 13:23
which sowed good *s* in his field ... Mt 13:24
not thou sow good *s* in thy field ... Mt 13:27
is like to a grain of mustard *s* ... Mt 13:31
the good *s* is the Son of man ... Mt 13:37
the good *s* are the children of ... Mt 13:38
faith as a grain of mustard *s* ... Mt 17:20
raise up *s* unto his brother ... Mt 22:24
man should cast *s* into the ground ... Mk 4:26
the *s* should spring and grow up, ... Mk 4:27
It is like a grain of mustard *s* ... Mk 4:31
raise up *s* unto his brother ... Mk 12:19
took a wife, and dying left no *s* ... Mk 12:20
and died, neither left he any *s* ... Mk 12:21
the seven had her, and left no *s* ... Mk 12:22
to Abraham, and to his *s* for ever ... Lk 1:55
A sower went out to sow his *s* ... Lk 8:5
The *s* is the word of God ... Lk 8:11
It is like a grain of mustard *s* ... Lk 13:19
had faith as a grain of mustard *s* ... Lk 17:6
raise up *s* unto his brother ... Lk 20:28
Christ cometh of the *s* of David ... Jn 7:42
answered him, We be Abraham's *s* ... Jn 8:33
I know that ye are Abraham's *s* ... Jn 8:37
in thy *s* shall all the kindreds ... Acts 3:25
to his *s* after him, when as yet ... Acts 7:5
That his *s* should sojourn in a ... Acts 7:6
Of this man's *s* hath God ... Acts 13:23
which was made of the *s* of David ... Rom 1:3
was not to Abraham, or to his *s* ... Rom 4:13
might be sure to all the *s* ... Rom 4:16
was spoken, So shall thy *s* be ... Rom 4:18
because they are the *s* of Abraham ... Rom 9:7
In Isaac shall thy *s* be called ... Rom 9:7
the promise are counted for the *s* ... Rom 9:8
Lord of Sabaoth had left us a *s* ... Rom 9:29
of the *s* of Abraham, of the tribe ... Rom 11:1
him, and to every *s* his own body ... 1Cor 15:38
Now he that ministereth *s* to the ... 2Cor 9:10
food, and multiply your *s* sown ... 2Cor 9:10
Are they the *s* of Abraham ... 2Cor 11:22
his *s* were the promises made ... Gal 3:16
but as of one, And to thy *s* ... Gal 3:16
till the *s* should come to whom ... Gal 3:19
Christ's, then are ye Abraham's *s* ... Gal 3:29
that Jesus Christ of the *s* of ... 2Ti 2:8
he took on him the *s* of Abraham ... Heb 2:16
received strength to conceive *s* ... Heb 11:11
in Isaac shall thy *s* be called ... Heb 11:18
born again, not of corruptible *s* ... 1Pet 1:23
for his *s* remaineth in him ... 1Jn 3:9
war with the remnant of her *s* ... Rev 12:17

**SEED'S**
out of the mouth of thy *s* seed ... Is 59:21

**SEEDS**
sow thy vineyard with divers *s* ... Deut 22:9
some *s* fell by the way side, and ... Mt 13:4
indeed is the least of all *s* ... Mt 13:32
all the *s* that be in the earth ... Mk 4:31
He saith not, And to *s*, as of many ... Gal 3:16

**SEEDTIME**
While the earth remaineth, *s* ... Gen 8:22

**SEEING**
*s* I go childless, and the steward ... Gen 15:2
*S* that Abraham shall surely ... Gen 18:18
Lot *s* them rose up to meet them ... Gen 19:1

*s* thou hast not withheld thy son, Gen 22:12
*s* the LORD hath prospered my way Gen 24:56
*s* ye hate me, and have sent me Gen 26:27
Esau *s* that the daughters of Gen 28:8
*s* that his life is bound up in Gen 44:30
the dumb, or deaf, or the *s* Ex 4:11
*s* he hath dealt deceitfully with Ex 21:8
hurt, or driven away, no man *s* it Ex 22:10
*s* ye were strangers in the land Ex 23:9
*s* it is most holy, and God hath Lev 10:17
*s* all the people were in Num 15:26
*s* all the congregation are holy, Num 16:3
*s* him not, and cast it upon him, Num 35:23
*s* I am a great people, forasmuch Josh 17:14
*s* ye rebel to day against the Josh 22:18
after my name, *s* it is secret Judg 13:18
*s* I have a Levite to my priest Judg 17:13
*s* that this man is come into mine Judg 19:23
*s* we have sworn by the LORD that Judg 21:7
*s* the women are destroyed out of Judg 21:16
*s* the LORD hath testified against Ruth 1:21
of me, *s* I am a stranger Ruth 2:10
*s* I have rejected him from 1Sa 16:1
*s* he hath defied the armies of 1Sa 17:36
*s* that I am a poor man, and 1Sa 18:23
*s* he is the anointed of the LORD 1Sa 24:6
*s* the LORD hath withholden thee 1Sa 25:26
*s* the LORD is departed from thee, 1Sa 28:16
concerning Amnon, *s* he was dead 2Sa 13:39
*s* I go whither I may, return thou 2Sa 15:20
*s* that thou hast no tidings ready 2Sa 18:22
*s* the speech of all Israel is 2Sa 19:11
this day, mine eyes even *s* it 1Kin 1:48
Solomon *s* the young man that he 1Kin 11:28
*s* your master's sons are with you 2Kin 10:2
*s* there is no wrong in mine hands 1Chr 12:17
*s* the heaven and heaven of heavens 2Chr 2:6
*s* that thou our God hast punished Ezr 9:13
sad, *s* thou art not sick Neh 2:2
*S* his days are determined, the Job 14:5
*s* the root of the matter is found Job 19:28
*s* he judgeth those that are high Job 21:22
*s* in your answers there remaineth Job 21:34
*s* times are not hidden from the Job 24:1
*S* it is hid from the eyes of all Job 28:21
him, *s* he delighted in him Ps 22:8
*S* thou hatest instruction, and Ps 50:17
*s* he dwelleth securely by thee Prov 3:29
wisdom, *s* he hath no heart to it Prov 17:16
The hearing ear, and the *s* eye Prov 20:12
the eye is not satisfied with *s* Eccl 1:8
*s* that which now is in the days Eccl 2:16
*S* there be many things that Eccl 6:11
I was dismayed at the *s* of it Is 21:3
and shutteth his eyes from *s* evil Is 33:15
*S* many things, but thou observest Is 42:20
*s* I have lost my children, and am Is 49:21
*s* she hath wrought lewdness with Jer 11:15
*s* the LORD hath given it a charge Jer 47:7
*s* thou doest all these things, Eze 16:30
*S* he despised the oath by Eze 17:18
*S* then that I will cut off from Eze 21:4
*s* vanity, and divining lies unto Eze 22:28
*s* thou couldst reveal this secret Dan 2:47
*s* thou hast forgotten the law of Hos 4:6
*s* the multitudes, he went up into Mt 5:1
Jesus *s* their faith said unto the Mt 9:2
because they *s* see not Mt 13:13
*s* ye shall see, and shall not Mt 13:14
That *s* they may see, and not Mk 4:12
*s* a fig tree afar off having Mk 11:13
shall this be, *s* I know not a man Lk 1:34
who *s* Jesus fell on his face, and Lk 5:12
that *s* they might not see, and Lk 8:10
fear God, *s* thou art in the same Lk 23:40
*s* that thou doest these things Jn 2:18
therefore, and washed, and came *s* Jn 9:7
Peter *s* him saith to Jesus, Lord, Jn 21:21
*s* it is but the third hour of the Acts 2:15
He *s* this before spake of the Acts 2:31
Who *s* Peter and John about to go Acts 3:3
*s* one of them suffer wrong, he Acts 7:24
*s* the miracles which he did Acts 8:6
hearing a voice, but *s* no man Acts 9:7
not *s* the sun for a season Acts 13:11
but *s* ye put it from you, and Acts 13:46
*s* the prison doors open, he drew Acts 16:27
*s* that he is Lord of heaven and Acts 17:24
*s* he giveth to all life, and Acts 17:25
*S* then that these things cannot Acts 19:36
*S* that by thee we enjoy great Acts 24:2
*s* ye shall see, and not perceive Acts 28:26
*S* it is one God, which shall Rom 3:30
*s* he understandeth not what thou 1Cor 14:16
*S* then that we have such hope, we 2Cor 3:12
*s* we have this ministry, as we 2Cor 4:1
*S* that many glory after the flesh 2Cor 11:18
gladly, *s* ye yourselves are wise 2Cor 11:19
*s* that ye have put off the old Col 3:9
*S* it is a righteous thing with 2Th 1:6
*S* therefore it remaineth that Heb 4:6
*S* then that we have a great high Heb 4:14
uttered, *s* ye are dull of hearing Heb 5:11
*s* they crucify to themselves the Heb 6:6
by him, *s* he ever liveth to make Heb 7:25
*s* that there are priests that Heb 8:4
as *s* him who is invisible Heb 11:27
Wherefore *s* we also are compassed Heb 12:1
*S* ye have purified your souls in 1Pet 1:22
man dwelling among them, in *s* 2Pet 2:8
*S* then that all these things 2Pet 3:11
*s* that ye look for such things, 2Pet 3:14
*s* ye know these things before, 2Pet 3:17

**SEEK**

And he said, I *s* my brethren Gen 37:16
that he may *s* occasion against us Gen 43:18
shall not *s* for yellow hair Lev 13:36
neither *s* after wizards, to be Lev 19:31
that ye *s* not after your own Num 15:39
and *s* ye the priesthood also Num 16:10
to *s* for enchantments, but he set Num 24:1
thou shalt *s* the LORD thy God Deut 4:29
if thou *s* him with all thy heart Deut 4:29
unto his habitation shall ye *s* Deut 12:5
thee until thy brother *s* after it Deut 22:2
Thou shalt not *s* their peace nor Deut 23:6
shall I not *s* rest for thee, that Ruth 3:1
thee, and arise, go *s* the asses 1Sa 9:3
which thou wentest to *s* are found 1Sa 10:2
And he said, To *s* the asses 1Sa 10:14
to *s* out a man, who is a cunning 1Sa 16:16
Saul was come out to *s* his life 1Sa 23:15
also and his men went to *s* him 1Sa 23:25
of all Israel, and went to *s* David 1Sa 24:2
they that *s* evil to my lord, be 1Sa 25:26
to pursue thee, and to *s* thy soul 1Sa 25:29
to *s* David in the wilderness of 1Sa 26:2
of Israel is come out to *s* a flea 1Sa 26:20
to *s* me any more in any coast of 1Sa 27:1
*S* me a woman that hath a familiar 1Sa 28:7
Philistines came up to *s* David 2Sa 5:17
Gath to Achish to *s* his servants 1Kin 2:40
my lord hath not sent to *s* thee 1Kin 18:10
they *s* my life, to take it away 1Kin 19:10
they *s* my life, to take it away 1Kin 19:14
go, we pray thee, and *s* thy master 2Kin 2:16
bring you to the man whom ye *s* 2Kin 6:19
to *s* pasture for their flocks 1Chr 4:39
Philistines went up to *s* David 1Chr 14:8
of them rejoice that *s* the LORD 1Chr 16:10
*S* the LORD and his strength 1Chr 16:11
*s* his face continually 1Chr 16:11
your soul to *s* the LORD your God 1Chr 22:19
*s* for all the commandments of the 1Chr 28:8
if thou *s* him, he will be found 1Chr 28:9
*s* my face, and turn from their 2Chr 7:14
such as set their hearts to *s* the 2Chr 11:16
not his heart to *s* the LORD 2Chr 12:14
commanded Judah to *s* the LORD God 2Chr 14:4
and if ye *s* him, he will be found 2Chr 15:2
*s* the LORD God of their fathers 2Chr 15:12
That whosoever would not *s* the 2Chr 15:13
prepared thine heart to *s* God 2Chr 19:3
and set himself to *s* the LORD 2Chr 20:3
of Judah they came to *s* the LORD 2Chr 20:4
That prepareth his heart to *s* God 2Chr 30:19
to *s* his God, he did it with all 2Chr 31:21
he began to *s* after the God of 2Chr 34:3
for we *s* your God, as ye do Ezr 4:2
to *s* the LORD God of Israel, did Ezr 6:21
heart to *s* the law of the LORD Ezr 7:10
to *s* of him a right way for us, Ezr 8:21
upon all them for good that *s* him Ezr 8:22
nor *s* their peace or their wealth Ezr 9:12
that there was come a man to *s* Neh 2:10
I would *s* unto God, and unto God Job 5:8
thou shalt *s* me in the morning, Job 7:21
thou wouldest *s* unto God betimes Job 8:5
shall *s* to please the poor Job 20:10
love vanity, and *s* after leasing Ps 4:2
not forsaken them that *s* thee Ps 9:10
countenance, will not *s* after God Ps 10:4
*s* out his wickedness till thou Ps 10:15
any that did understand, and *s* God Ps 14:2
shall praise the LORD that *s* him Ps 22:26
the generation of them that *s* him Ps 24:6
him, that *s* thy face, O Jacob Ps 24:6
of the LORD, that will I *s* after Ps 27:4
When thou saidst, *S* ye my face Ps 27:8
thee, Thy face, LORD, will I *s* Ps 27:8
but they that *s* the LORD shall Ps 34:10
*s* peace, and pursue it Ps 34:14
put to shame that *s* after my soul Ps 35:4
They also that *s* after my life Ps 38:12
they that *s* my hurt speak Ps 38:12
confounded together that *s* after Ps 40:14
Let all those that *s* thee rejoice Ps 40:16
did understand, that did *s* God Ps 53:2
oppressors *s* after my soul Ps 54:3
early will I *s* thee Ps 63:1
But those that *s* my soul, to Ps 63:9
let not those that *s* thee be Ps 69:6
your heart shall live that *s* God Ps 69:32
confounded that *s* after my soul Ps 70:2
Let all those that *s* thee rejoice Ps 70:4
and dishonour that *s* my hurt Ps 71:13
unto shame, that *s* my hurt Ps 71:24
that they may *s* thy name, O LORD Ps 83:16
prey, and *s* their meat from God Ps 104:21
of them rejoice that *s* the LORD Ps 105:3
*S* the LORD, and his strength Ps 105:4
*s* his face evermore Ps 105:4
let them *s* their bread also out Ps 109:10
that *s* him with the whole heart Ps 119:2
for I *s* thy precepts Ps 119:45
for they *s* not thy statutes Ps 119:155
*s* thy servant Ps 119:176
LORD our God I will *s* thy good Ps 122:9
they shall *s* me early, but they Prov 1:28
thee, diligently to *s* thy face Prov 7:15
those that *s* me early shall find Prov 8:17
to and fro of them that *s* death Prov 21:6
they that go to *s* mixed wine Prov 23:30
I will *s* it yet again Prov 23:35
but they that *s* the LORD Prov 28:5
but the just *s* his soul Prov 29:10
Many *s* the ruler's favour Prov 29:26
And I gave my heart to *s* and search Eccl 1:13
to *s* out wisdom, and the reason of Eccl 7:25
though a man labour to *s* it out Eccl 8:17
I will *s* him whom my soul loveth Song 3:2
that we may *s* him with thee Song 6:1
*s* judgment, relieve the oppressed Is 1:17
*S* unto them that have familiar Is 8:19
not a people *s* unto their God Is 8:19
neither do they *s* the LORD of Is 9:13
to it shall the Gentiles *s* Is 11:10
they shall *s* to the idols, and to Is 19:3
within me will I *s* thee early Is 26:9
Woe unto them that *s* deep to hide Is 29:15
One of Israel, neither *s* the LORD Is 31:1
*S* ye out of the book of the LORD, Is 34:16
Thou shalt *s* them, and shalt not Is 41:12
When the poor and needy *s* water Is 41:17
seed of Jacob, *S* ye me in vain Is 45:19
righteousness, ye that *s* the LORD Is 51:1
*S* ye the LORD while he may be Is 55:6
Yet they *s* me daily, and delight Is 58:2
all they that *s* her will not Jer 2:24
trimmest thou thy way to *s* love Jer 2:33
thee, they will *s* thy life Jer 4:30
*s* in the broad places thereof, if Jer 5:1
that *s* thy life, saying, Prophesy Jer 11:21
hands of them that *s* their lives Jer 19:7
they that *s* their lives, shall Jer 19:9
hand of those that *s* their life Jer 21:7
the hand of them that *s* thy life Jer 22:25
*s* the peace of the city whither I Jer 29:7
And ye shall *s* me, and find me, Jer 29:13
they *s* thee not Jer 30:14
hand of them that *s* their life Jer 34:20
hand of them that *s* their life Jer 34:21
hand of these men that *s* thy life Jer 38:16
the hand of them that *s* his life Jer 44:30
*s* them not Jer 45:5
hand of those that *s* their lives Jer 46:26
and before them that *s* their life Jer 49:37
shall go, and *s* the LORD their God Jer 50:4
All her people sigh, they *s* bread Lam 1:11
and they shall *s* peace, and there Eze 7:25
then shall they *s* a vision of the Eze 7:26
none did search or *s* after them Eze 34:6
search my sheep, and *s* them out Eze 34:11
so will I *s* out my sheep, and will Eze 34:12
I will *s* that which was lost, and Eze 34:16
to *s* by prayer and supplications, Dan 9:3
and she shall *s* them, but shall Hos 2:7
*s* the LORD their God, and David Hos 3:5
and with their herds to *s* the LORD Hos 5:6
their offence, and *s* my face Hos 5:15
affliction they will *s* me early Hos 5:15
their God, nor *s* him for all this Hos 7:10
for it is time to *s* the LORD Hos 10:12
*S* ye me, and ye shall live Amos 5:4
But *s* not Beth-el, nor enter into Amos 5:5
*S* the LORD, and ye shall live Amos 5:6
*S* him that maketh the seven stars Amos 5:8
*S* good, and not evil, that ye may Amos 5:14
fro to *s* the word of the LORD, and Amos 8:12
whence shall I *s* comforters for Nah 3:7
thou also shalt *s* strength Nah 3:11
*S* ye the LORD, all ye meek of the Zeph 2:3
*s* righteousness, *s* meekness Zeph 2:3
LORD, and to *s* the LORD of hosts Zec 8:21
strong nations shall come to *s* Zec 8:22
neither shall *s* the young one Zec 11:16
that I will *s* to destroy all the Zec 12:9
they should *s* the law at his Mal 2:7
That he might *s* a godly seed Mal 2:15
and the Lord, whom ye *s*, shall Mal 3:1
for Herod will *s* the young child Mt 2:13
these things do the Gentiles *s* Mt 6:32
But *s* ye first the kingdom of God Mt 6:33
*s*, and ye shall find Mt 7:7
for I know that ye *s* Jesus Mt 28:5
said unto him, All men *s* for thee Mk 1:37
thy brethren without *s* for thee Mk 3:32
this generation *s* after a sign Mk 8:12
Ye *s* Jesus of Nazareth, which was Mk 16:6
*s*, and ye shall find Lk 11:9
they *s* a sign Lk 11:29
*s* not ye what ye shall eat, or Lk 12:29
the nations of the world *s* after Lk 12:30
But rather *s* ye the kingdom of Lk 12:31
will *s* to enter in, and shall not Lk 13:24
*s* diligently till she find it Lk 15:8
Whosoever shall *s* to save his Lk 17:33
For the Son of man is come to *s* Lk 19:10
Why *s* ye the living among the Lk 24:5
and saith unto them, What *s* ye Jn 1:38
because I *s* not mine own will, Jn 5:30
*s* not the honour that cometh from Jn 5:44
verily, I say unto you, Ye *s* me Jn 6:26
not this he, whom they *s* to kill Jn 7:25
Ye shall *s* me, and shall not find Jn 7:34
this that he said, Ye shall *s* me Jn 7:36
I go my way, and ye shall *s* me Jn 8:21
but ye *s* to kill me, because my Jn 8:37
But now ye *s* to kill me, a man Jn 8:40
And I *s* not mine own glory Jn 8:50

Ye shall s me Jn 13:33
and said unto them, Whom s ye Jn 18:4
asked he them again, Whom s ye Jn 18:7
if therefore ye s me, let these Jn 18:8
him, Behold, three men s thee Acts 10:19
said, Behold, I am he whom ye s Acts 10:21
Barnabas to Tarsus, for to s Saul Acts 11:25
of men might s after the Lord Acts 15:17
That they should s the Lord Acts 17:27
in well doing s for glory Rom 2:7
am left alone, and they s my life Rom 11:3
the Greeks s after wisdom 1Cor 1:22
s not to be loosed 1Cor 7:27
s not a wife 1Cor 7:27
Let no man s his own, but every 1Cor 10:24
s that ye may excel to the 1Cor 14:12
for I s not yours, but you 2Cor 12:14
Since ye s a proof of Christ 2Cor 13:3
or do I s to please men Gal 1:10
while we s to be justified by Gal 2:17
For all s their own, not the Phil 2:21
s those things which are above, Col 3:1
of them that diligently s him Heb 11:6
plainly that they s a country Heb 11:14
city, but we s one to come Heb 13:14
let him s peace, and ensue it 1Pet 3:11
in those days shall men s death Rev 9:6

## SEEKEST

asked him, saying, What s thou Gen 37:15
shew thee the man whom thou s Judg 4:22
the man whom thou s is as if all 2Sa 17:3
thou s to destroy a city and a 2Sa 20:19
thou s to go to thine own country 1Kin 11:22
If thou s her as silver, and Prov 2:4
s thou great things for thyself Jer 45:5
yet no man said, What s thou Jn 4:27
whom s thou Jn 20:15

## SEEKETH

Saul my father s to kill thee 1Sa 19:2
thy father, that he s my life 1Sa 20:1
for he that s my life s thy 1Sa 22:23
that s my life s thy life 1Sa 22:23
that Saul s to come to Keilah 1Sa 23:10
saying, Behold, David s thy hurt 1Sa 24:9
forth of my bowels, s my life 2Sa 16:11
and see how this man s mischief 1Kin 20:7
see how he s a quarrel against me 2Kin 5:7
From thence she s the prey Job 39:29
the righteous, and s to slay him Ps 37:32
He that diligently s good Prov 11:27
but he that s mischief, it shall Prov 11:27
A scorner s wisdom, and findeth it Prov 14:6
hath understanding s knowledge Prov 15:14
covereth a transgression s love Prov 17:9
An evil man s only rebellion Prov 17:11
exalteth his gate s destruction Prov 17:19
man, having separated himself, s Prov 18:1
the ear of the wise s knowledge Prov 18:15
She s wool, and flax, and worketh Prov 31:13
Which yet my soul s, but I find Eccl 7:28
he s unto him a cunning workman Is 40:20
judgment, that s the truth Jer 5:1
This is Zion, whom no man s after Jer 30:17
for this man s not the welfare of Jer 38:4
for him, to the soul that s him Lam 3:25
punishment of him that s unto him Eze 14:10
As a shepherd s out his flock in Eze 34:12
and he that s findeth Mt 7:8
generation s after a sign Mt 12:39
generation s after a sign Mt 16:4
s that which is gone astray Mt 18:12
and he that s findeth Lk 11:10
for the Father s such to worship Jn 4:23
he himself s to be known openly Jn 7:4
of himself s his own glory Jn 7:18
but he that s his glory that sent Jn 7:18
there is one that s and judgeth Jn 8:50
there is none that s after God Rom 3:11
not obtained that which he s for Rom 11:7
s not her own, is not easily 1Cor 13:5

## SEEKING

s the wealth of his people, and Est 10:3
and s judgment, and hasting Is 16:5
places, s rest, and findeth none Mt 12:43
a merchant man, s goodly pearls Mt 13:45
s of him a sign from heaven, Mk 8:11
back again to Jerusalem, s him Lk 2:45
through dry places, s rest Lk 11:24
s to catch something out of his Lk 11:54
I come s fruit on this fig tree Lk 13:7
and came to Capernaum, s for Jesus Jn 6:24
s to turn away the deputy from Acts 13:8
he went about s some to lead him Acts 13:11
not s mine own profit, but the 1Cor 10:33
about, s whom he may devour 1Pet 5:8

## SEEM

I shall s to him as a deceiver Gen 27:12
It shall not s hard unto thee, Deut 15:18
brother should s vile unto thee Deut 25:3
if it s evil unto you to serve Josh 24:15
him as it shall s good unto thee 1Sa 24:4
him what shall s good unto thee 2Sa 19:37
that which shall s good unto thee 2Sa 19:38
if it s good to thee, I will give 1Kin 21:2
If it s good unto you, and that it 1Chr 13:2
if it s good to the king, let Ezr 5:17
whatsoever shall s good to thee Ezr 7:18
the trouble s little before thee Neh 9:32
If it s good unto the king, let Est 5:4
the thing s right before the king Est 8:5
If it s good unto thee to come Jer 40:4
but if it s ill unto thee to come Jer 40:4
they shall s like torches, they Nah 2:4
But if any man s to be 1Cor 11:16
which s to be more feeble, are 1Cor 12:22
That I may not s as if I would 2Cor 10:9
any of you should s to come short Heb 4:1
man among you s to be religious Jas 1:26

## SEEMED

But he s as one that mocked unto Gen 19:14
they s unto him but a few days, Gen 29:20
Hebron all that s good to Israel 2Sa 3:19
that s good to the whole house of 2Sa 3:19
the sun, and it s great unto me Eccl 9:13
as s good to the potter to make Jer 18:4
it unto whom it s meet unto me Jer 27:5
for so it s good in thy sight Mt 11:26
It s good to me also, having had Lk 1:3
for so it s good in thy sight Lk 10:21
their words s to them as idle Lk 24:11
It s good unto us, being Acts 15:25
For it s good to the Holy Ghost, Acts 15:28
But of these who s to be somewhat Gal 2:6
for they who s to be somewhat in Gal 2:6
who s to be pillars, perceived Gal 2:9

## SEEMETH

It s to me there is as it were a Lev 14:35
S it but a small thing unto you, Num 16:9
as it s good and right unto thee Josh 9:25
us whatsoever s good unto thee Judg 10:15
do with them what s good unto you Judg 19:24
unto her, Do what s thee good 1Sa 1:23
let him do what s him good 1Sa 3:18
with us all that s good unto you 1Sa 11:10
Do whatsoever s good unto thee 1Sa 14:36
Saul, Do what s good unto thee 1Sa 14:40
S it to you a light thing to be a 1Sa 18:23
the LORD do that which s him good 2Sa 10:12
him do to me as s good unto him 2Sa 15:26
What s you best I will do 2Sa 18:4
and offer up what s good unto him 2Sa 24:22
do with them as it s good to thee Est 3:11
is a way which s right unto a man Prov 14:12
is a way that s right unto a man Prov 16:25
is first in his own cause s just Prov 18:17
do with me as s good and meet unto Jer 26:14
whither it s good and convenient Jer 40:4
or go wheresoever it s convenient Jer 40:5
S it a small thing unto you to Eze 34:18
even that which he s to have Lk 8:18
He s to be a setter forth of Acts 17:18
For it s to me unreasonable to Acts 25:27
If any man among you s to be wise 1Cor 3:18
for the present s to be joyous Heb 12:11

## SEEMLY

Delight is not s for a fool Prov 19:10
so honour is not s for a fool Prov 26:1

## SEEN

for thee have I s righteous Gen 7:1
were the tops of the mountains s Gen 8:5
the bow shall be s in the cloud Gen 9:14
mount of the LORD it shall be s Gen 22:14
for I have s all that Laban doeth Gen 31:12
God hath s mine affliction and the Gen 31:42
for I have s God face to face, and Gen 32:30
for therefore I have s thy face Gen 33:10
as though I had s the face of God Gen 33:10
Egypt, and of all that ye have s Gen 45:13
me die, since I have s thy face Gen 46:30
I have surely s the affliction of Ex 3:7
I have also s the oppression Ex 3:9
s that which is done to you in Ex 3:16
nor thy fathers' fathers have s Ex 10:6
no leavened bread be s with thee Ex 13:7
s with thee in all thy quarters Ex 13:7
Egyptians whom ye have s to day Ex 14:13
Ye have s what I did unto the Ex 19:4
Ye have s that I have talked with Ex 20:22
I have s this people, and, behold, Ex 32:9
but my face shall not be s Ex 33:23
thee, neither let any man be s Ex 34:3
whether he hath s or known of it Lev 5:1
after that he hath been s of the Lev 13:7
he shall be s of the priest again Lev 13:7
that thou LORD art s face to face Num 14:14
those men which have s my glory Num 14:22
neither hath he s perverseness in Num 23:21
And when thou hast s it, thou also Num 27:13
moreover we have s the sons of Deut 1:28
where thou hast s how that the Deut 1:31
Thine eyes have s all that the Deut 3:21
Your eyes have s what the LORD Deut 4:3
things which thine eyes have s Deut 4:9
we have s this day that God doth Deut 5:24
I have s this people, and, behold, Deut 9:13
things, which thine eyes have s Deut 10:21
which have not s the chastisement Deut 11:2
But your eyes have s all the Deut 11:7
s with thee in all thy coast Deut 16:4
blood, neither have our eyes s it Deut 21:7
Ye have s all that the LORD did Deut 29:2
which thine eyes have s, the Deut 29:3
ye have s their abominations, and Deut 29:17
to his mother, I have not s him Deut 33:9
ye have s all that the LORD your Josh 23:3
your eyes have s what I have done Josh 24:7
who had s all the great works of Judg 2:7
was there a shield or spear s Judg 5:8
for because I have s an angel of Judg 6:22
with him, What ye have s me do Judg 9:48
surely die, because we have s God Judg 13:22
I have s a woman in Timnath of Judg 14:2
for we have s the land, and, Judg 18:9
s from the day that the children Judg 19:30
lords of the Philistines had s it 1Sa 6:16
I have s a son of Jesse the 1Sa 16:18
Have ye s this man that is come 1Sa 17:25
haunt is, and who hath s him there 1Sa 23:22
this day thine eyes have s how 1Sa 24:10
not be s to come into the city 2Sa 17:17
Go tell the king what thou hast s 2Sa 18:21
he was s upon the wings of the 2Sa 22:11
there was no stone s 1Kin 6:18
the ends of the staves were s out 1Kin 8:8
and they were not s without 1Kin 8:8
Sheba had s all Solomon's wisdom 1Kin 10:4
I came, and mine eyes had s it 1Kin 10:7
trees, nor were s unto this day 1Kin 10:12
For his sons had s what way the 1Kin 13:12
Hast thou s all this great 1Kin 20:13
Surely I have s yesterday the 2Kin 9:26
thy prayer, I have s thy tears 2Kin 20:5
What have they s in thine house 2Kin 20:15
are in mine house have they s 2Kin 20:15
him at Megiddo, when he had s him 2Kin 23:29
now have I s with joy thy people, 1Chr 29:17
the ends of the staves were s 2Chr 5:9
but they were not s without 2Chr 5:9
Sheba had s the wisdom of Solomon 2Chr 9:3
I came, and mine eyes had s it 2Chr 9:6
there were none such s before in 2Chr 9:11
that had s the first house, when Ezr 3:12
they had s concerning this matter Est 9:26
Even as I have s, they that plow Job 4:8
I have s the foolish taking root Job 5:3
hath s me shall see me no more Job 7:8
him, saying, I have not s thee Job 8:18
up the ghost, and no eye had s me Job 10:18
Lo, mine eye hath s all this Job 13:1
which I have s I will declare Job 15:17
they which have s him shall say Job 20:7
all ye yourselves have s it Job 27:12
the vulture's eye hath not s Job 28:7
If I have s any perish for want Job 31:19
away, that it cannot be s Job 33:21
bones that were not s stick out Job 33:21
or hast thou s the doors of the Job 38:17
or hast thou s the treasures of Job 38:22
Thou hast s it Ps 10:14
the channels of waters were s Ps 18:15
said, Aha, aha, our eye hath s it Ps 35:21
This thou hast s, O LORD Ps 35:22
yet have I not s the righteous Ps 37:25
I have s the wicked in great Ps 37:35
so have we s in the city of the Ps 48:8
mine eye hath s his desire upon Ps 54:7
for I have s violence and strife Ps 55:9
so as I have s thee in the Ps 63:2
They have s thy goings, O God Ps 68:24
the years wherein we have s evil Ps 90:15
have s the salvation of our God Ps 98:3
I have s an end of all perfection Ps 119:96
the prince whom thine eyes have s Prov 25:7
I have s all the works that are Eccl 1:14
I have s the travail, which God Eccl 3:10
who hath not s the evil work that Eccl 4:3
evil which I have s under the sun Eccl 5:13
Behold that which I have s Eccl 5:18
evil which I have s under the sun Eccl 6:1
Moreover he hath not s the sun Eccl 6:5
twice told, yet hath he s no good Eccl 6:6
All things have I s in the days Eccl 7:15
All this have I s, and applied my Eccl 8:9
have I s also under the sun Eccl 9:13
evil which I have s under the sun Eccl 10:5
I have s servants upon horses, and Eccl 10:7
for mine eyes have s the King Is 6:5
in darkness have s a great light Is 9:2
when it is s that Moab is weary Is 16:12
Ye have s also the breaches of Is 22:9
thy prayer, I have s thy tears Is 38:5
What have they s in thine house Is 39:4
that is in mine house have they s Is 39:4
Aha, I am warm, I have s the fire Is 44:16
yea, thy shame shall be s Is 47:3
I have s his ways, and will heal Is 57:18
and his glory shall be s upon thee Is 60:2
the ear, neither hath the eye s Is 64:4
who hath s such things Is 66:8
my fame, neither have s my glory Is 66:19
LORD unto me, Thou hast well s Jer 1:12
the king, Hast thou s that which Jer 3:6
Behold, even I have s it, saith Jer 7:11
thou hast s me, and tried mine Jer 12:3
I have s thine adulteries, and thy Jer 13:27
I have s folly in the prophets of Jer 23:13
I have s also in the prophets of Jer 23:14
Ye have s all the evil that I Jer 44:2
Wherefore have I s them dismayed Jer 46:5
because they have s her nakedness Lam 1:8
for she hath s that the heathen Lam 1:10
Thy prophets have s vain and Lam 2:14
but have s for thee false burdens Lam 2:14
we have found, we have s it Lam 2:16
I am the man that hath s Lam 3:1
O LORD, thou hast s my wrong Lam 3:59

S

Thou hast *s* all their vengeance Lam 3:60
hast thou *s* what the ancients of Eze 8:12
said he unto me, Hast thou *s* this Eze 8:15
he said unto me, Hast thou *s* this Eze 8:17
that I had *s* went up from me Eze 11:24
own spirit, and have *s* nothing Eze 13:3
They have *s* vanity and lying Eze 13:6
Have ye not *s* a vain vision, and Eze 13:7
*s* lies, therefore, behold, I am Eze 13:8
me, Son of man, hast thou *s* this Eze 47:6
unto me the dream which I have *s* Dan 2:26
visions of my dream that I have *s* Dan 4:9
I king Nebuchadnezzar have *s* Dan 4:18
which I had *s* standing before the Dan 8:6
had *s* the vision, and sought for Dan 8:15
whom I had *s* in the vision at the Dan 9:21
I have *s* an horrible thing in the Hos 6:10
for now have I *s* with mine eyes Zec 9:8
And the LORD shall be *s* over them Zec 9:14
and the diviners have *s* a lie Zec 10:2
for we have *s* his star in the Mt 2:2
alms before men, to be *s* of them Mt 6:1
that they may be *s* of men Mt 6:5
It was never so *s* in Israel Mt 9:33
which ye see, and have not *s* them Mt 13:17
and ye, when ye had *s* it, repented Mt 21:32
works they do for to be *s* of men Mt 23:5
till they have *s* the kingdom of Mk 9:1
no man what things they had *s* Mk 9:9
was alive, and had been *s* of her Mk 16:11
had *s* him after he was risen Mk 16:14
he had *s* a vision in the temple Lk 1:22
And when they had *s* it, they made Lk 2:17
things that they had heard and *s* Lk 2:20
before he had *s* the Lord's Christ Lk 2:26
mine eyes have *s* thy salvation Lk 2:30
We have *s* strange things to day Lk 5:26
tell John what things ye have *s* Lk 7:22
of those things which they had *s* Lk 9:36
which ye see, and have not *s* them Lk 10:24
the mighty works that they had *s* Lk 19:37
he hoped to have *s* some miracle Lk 23:8
had also *s* a vision of angels Lk 24:23
supposed that they had *s* a spirit Lk 24:37
No man hath *s* God at any time Jn 1:18
know, and testify that we have *s* Jn 3:11
And what he hath *s* and heard, that Jn 3:32
having *s* all the things that he Jn 4:45
at any time, nor *s* his shape Jn 5:37
when they had *s* the miracle that Jn 6:14
unto you, That ye also have *s* me Jn 6:36
that any man hath *s* the Father Jn 6:46
is of God, he hath *s* the Father Jn 6:46
which I have *s* with my Father Jn 8:38
which ye have *s* with your father Jn 8:38
years old, and hast thou *s* Abraham Jn 8:57
had *s* him that he was blind Jn 9:8
unto him, Thou hast both *s* him Jn 9:37
had *s* the things which Jesus did, Jn 11:45
ye know him, and have *s* him Jn 14:7
hath *s* me hath *s* the Father Jn 14:9
but now have they both *s* and hated Jn 15:24
disciples that she had *s* the Lord Jn 20:18
said unto him, We have *s* the Lord Jn 20:25
Thomas, because thou hast *s* me Jn 20:29
blessed are they that have not *s* Jn 20:29
being *s* of them forty days, and Acts 1:3
as ye have *s* him go into heaven Acts 1:11
speak the things which we have *s* Acts 4:20
I have *s*, I have *s* the Acts 7:34
to the fashion that he had *s* Acts 7:44
hath *s* in a vision a man named Acts 9:12
how he had *s* the Lord in the way Acts 9:27
vision which he had *s* should mean Acts 10:17
he had *s* an angel in his house Acts 11:13
had *s* the grace of God, was glad, Acts 11:23
he was *s* many days of them which Acts 13:31
And after he had *s* the vision Acts 16:10
and when they had *s* the brethren Acts 16:40
(For they had *s* before with him Acts 21:29
unto all men of what thou hast *s* Acts 22:15
of these things which thou hast *s* Acts 26:16
of the world are clearly *s* Rom 1:20
but hope that is *s* is not hope Rom 8:24
as it is written, Eye hath not *s* 1Cor 2:9
have I not *s* Jesus Christ our 1Cor 9:1
And that he was *s* of Cephas 1Cor 15:5
he was *s* of above five hundred 1Cor 15:6
After that, he was *s* of James 1Cor 15:7
last of all he was *s* of me also 1Cor 15:8
not at the things which are *s* 2Cor 4:18
but at the things which are not *s* 2Cor 4:18
things which are *s* are temporal 2Cor 4:18
which are not *s* are eternal 2Cor 4:18
and heard, and *s* in me, do Phil 4:9
have not *s* my face in the flesh Col 2:1
those things which he hath not *s* Col 2:18
*s* of angels, preached unto the 1Ti 3:16
whom no man hath *s*, nor can see 1Ti 6:16
for, the evidence of things not *s* Heb 11:1
so that things which are *s* were Heb 11:3
of God of things not *s* as yet Heb 11:7
but having *s* them afar off, and Heb 11:13
have *s* the end of the Lord Jas 5:11
Whom having not *s*, ye love 1Pet 1:8
which we have *s* with our eyes 1Jn 1:1
was manifested, and we have *s* it 1Jn 1:2
That which we have *s* and heard 1Jn 1:3
whosoever sinneth hath not *s* him 1Jn 3:6
No man hath *s* God at any time 1Jn 4:12
And we have *s* and do testify that 1Jn 4:14
not his brother whom he hath *s* 1Jn 4:20
he love God whom he hath not *s* 1Jn 4:20
he that doeth evil hath not *s* God 3Jn 11
the things which thou hast *s* Rev 1:19
there was *s* in his temple the ark Rev 11:19
And when I had heard and *s*, I fell Rev 22:8

**SEER**
Come, and let us go to the *s* 1Sa 9:9
Prophet was beforetime called a *S* 1Sa 9:9
and said unto them, Is the *s* here 1Sa 9:11
Saul, and said, I am the *s* 1Sa 9:19
the priest, Art not thou a *s* 2Sa 15:27
unto the prophet Gad, David's *s* 2Sa 24:11
Samuel the *s* did ordain in their 1Chr 9:22
LORD spake unto Gad, David's *s* 1Chr 21:9
the king's *s* in the words of God 1Chr 25:5
And all that Samuel the *s*, and Saul 1Chr 26:28
in the book of Samuel the *s* 1Chr 29:29
and in the book of Gad the *s* 1Chr 29:29
in the visions of Iddo the *s* 2Chr 9:29
and of Iddo the *s* concerning 2Chr 12:15
at that time Hanani the *s* came to 2Chr 16:7
Then Asa was wroth with the *s* 2Chr 16:10
Hanani the *s* went out to meet him 2Chr 19:2
of David, and of Gad the king's *s* 2Chr 29:25
words of David, and of Asaph the *s* 2Chr 29:30
Heman, and Jeduthun the king's *s* 2Chr 35:15
Amaziah said unto Amos, O thou *s* Amos 7:12

**SEER'S**
I pray thee, where the *s* house is 1Sa 9:18

**SEERS**
all the prophets, and by all the *s* 2Kin 17:13
the words of the *s* that spake to 2Chr 33:18
among the sayings of the *s* 2Chr 33:19
rulers, the *s* hath he covered Is 29:10
Which say to the *s*, See not Is 30:10
Then shall the *s* be ashamed Mic 3:7

**SEEST**
For all the land which thou *s* Gen 13:15
spake unto her, Thou God *s* me Gen 16:13
and all that thou *s* is mine Gen 31:43
for in that day thou *s* my face Ex 10:28
heaven, and when thou *s* the sun Deut 4:19
in every place that thou *s* Deut 12:13
*s* horses, and chariots, and a Deut 20:1
*s* among the captives a beautiful Deut 21:11
him, Thou *s* the shadow of the Judg 9:36
*S* thou how Ahab humbleth himself 1Kin 21:29
or *s* thou as man seeth Job 10:4
*S* thou a man diligent in his Prov 22:29
*S* thou a man wise in his own Prov 26:12
*S* thou a man that is hasty in his Prov 29:20
If thou *s* the oppression of the Eccl 5:8
fasted, say they, and thou *s* not Is 58:3
when thou *s* the naked, that thou Is 58:7
me, saying, Jeremiah, what *s* thou Jer 1:11
second time, saying, What *s* thou Jer 1:13
*S* thou not what they do in the Jer 7:17
*s* the reins and the heart, let me Jer 20:12
the LORD unto me, What *s* thou Jer 24:3
and, behold, thou *s* it Jer 32:24
Son of man, *s* thou what they do Eze 8:6
declare all that thou *s* to the Eze 40:4
and as thou *s*, deal with thy Dan 1:13
said unto me, Amos, what *s* thou Amos 7:8
And he said, Amos, what *s* thou Amos 8:2
And said unto me, What *s* thou Zec 4:2
And he said unto me, What *s* thou Zec 5:2
Thou *s* the multitude thronging Mk 5:31
*S* thou these great buildings Mk 13:2
unto Simon, *S* thou this woman Lk 7:44
Lord, and said unto him, Thou *s* Acts 21:20
*S* thou how faith wrought with his Jas 2:22
and, What thou *s*, write in a book, Rev 1:11

**SEETH**
here looked after him that *s* me Gen 16:13
when he *s* that the lad is not Gen 44:31
and when he *s* thee, he will be Ex 4:14
when he *s* the blood upon the Ex 12:23
And if, when the priest *s* it Lev 13:20
when he *s* that their power is Deut 32:36
for the LORD *s* not as man *s* 1Sa 16:7
city is pleasant, as my lord *s* 2Kin 2:19
heap, and *s* the place of stones Job 8:17
or seest thou as man *s* Job 10:4
he *s* wickedness also Job 11:11
a covering to him, that he *s* not Job 22:14
his eye *s* every precious thing Job 28:10
and *s* under the whole heaven Job 28:24
of man, and he *s* all his goings Job 34:21
but now mine eye *s* thee Job 42:5
for he *s* that his day is coming Ps 37:13
For he *s* that wise men die, Ps 49:10
rejoice when he *s* the vengeance Ps 58:10
nor night *s* sleep with his eyes Eccl 8:16
let him declare what he *s* Is 21:6
when he that looketh upon it *s* Is 28:4
the dark, and they say, Who *s* us Is 29:15
But when he *s* his children, the Is 29:23
thou hast said, None *s* me Is 47:10
for they say, The LORD *s* us not Eze 8:12
the earth, and the LORD *s* not Eze 9:9
The vision that he *s* is for many Eze 12:27
that *s* all his father's sins Eze 18:14
If when he *s* the sword come upon Eze 33:3
when any *s* a man's bone, then Eze 39:15
thy Father which *s* in secret Mt 6:4
thy Father which *s* in secret Mt 6:6
which *s* in secret, shall reward Mt 6:18
*s* the tumult, and them that wept Mk 5:38
*s* Abraham afar off, and Lazarus in Lk 16:23
The next day John *s* Jesus coming Jn 1:29
but what he *s* the Father do Jn 5:19
that every one which *s* the Son Jn 6:40
But by what means he now *s* Jn 9:21
*s* the wolf coming, and leaveth the Jn 10:12
because he *s* the light of this Jn 11:9
that *s* me *s* him that sent me Jn 12:45
receive, because it *s* him not Jn 14:17
while, and the world *s* me no more Jn 14:19
*s* the stone taken away from the Jn 20:1
and *s* the linen clothes lie, Jn 20:6
*s* two angels in white sitting, Jn 20:12
*s* the disciple whom Jesus loved Jn 21:20
for what a man *s*, why doth he yet Rom 8:24
me above that which he *s* me to be 2Cor 12:6
*s* his brother have need, and 1Jn 3:17

**SEETHE**
to day, and *s* that ye will *s* Ex 16:23
Thou shalt not *s* a kid in his Ex 23:19
*s* his flesh in the holy place Ex 29:31
Thou shalt not *s* a kid in his Ex 34:26
Thou shalt not *s* a kid in his Deut 14:21
*s* pottage for the sons of the 2Kin 4:38
let them *s* the bones of it Eze 24:5
and take of them, and *s* therein Zec 14:21

**SEETHING**
came, while the flesh was in *s* 1Sa 2:13
as out of a *s* pot or caldron Job 41:20
and I said, I see a *s* pot Jer 1:13

**SEGUB** (*se'-gub*)
*1. A son of Hiel.*
thereof in his youngest son *S* 1Kin 16:34
*2. A son of Hezron.*
and she bare him *S* 1Chr 2:21
*S* begat Jair, who had three and 1Chr 2:22

**SEIR** (*se'-ur*)
*1. A region south of the Dead Sea.*
And the Horites in their mount *S* Gen 14:6
his brother unto the land of *S* Gen 32:3
until I come unto my lord unto *S* Gen 33:14
that day on his way unto *S* Gen 33:16
Thus dwelt Esau in mount *S* Gen 36:8
father of the Edomites in mount *S* Gen 36:9
the children of *S* in the land of Gen 36:21
their dukes in the land of *S* Gen 36:30
*S* also shall be a possession for Num 24:18
way of mount *S* unto Kadesh-barnea Deut 1:2
as bees do, and destroyed you in *S* Deut 1:44
and we compassed mount *S* Deut 2:1
of Esau, which dwell in *S* Deut 2:4
*S* unto Esau for a possession Deut 2:5
of Esau, which dwelt in *S* Deut 2:8
Horims also dwelt in *S* beforetime Deut 2:12
of Esau, which dwelt in *S* Deut 2:22
children of Esau which dwell in *S* Deut 2:29
and rose up from *S* unto them Deut 33:2
mount Halak, that goeth up to *S* Josh 11:17
mount Halak, that goeth up to *S* Josh 12:7
from Baalah westward unto mount *S* Josh 15:10
and I gave unto Esau mount *S* Josh 24:4
LORD, when thou wentest out of *S* Judg 5:4
five hundred men, went to mount *S* 1Chr 4:42
of Ammon and Moab and mount *S* 2Chr 20:10
of Ammon, Moab, and mount *S* 2Chr 20:22
the inhabitants of mount *S* 2Chr 20:23
an end of the inhabitants of *S* 2Chr 20:23
of the children of *S* ten thousand 2Chr 25:11
the gods of the children of *S* 2Chr 25:14
He calleth to me out of *S* Is 21:11
*S* do say, Behold, the house of Eze 25:8
man, set thy face against mount *S* Eze 35:2
Behold, O mount *S*, I am against Eze 35:3
will I make mount *S* most desolate Eze 35:7
thou shalt be desolate, O mount *S* Eze 35:15
*2. Grandfather of Hori.*
are the sons of *S* the Horite Gen 36:20
And the sons of *S* 1Chr 1:38

**SEIRAH** See SEIRATH.

**SEIRATH** (*se'-ur-ath*) *A city in Ephraim.*
the quarries, and escaped unto *S* Judg 3:26

**SEIZE**
the ambush, and *s* upon the city Josh 8:7
night, let darkness *s* upon it Job 3:6
Let death *s* upon them, and let Ps 55:15
let us *s* on his inheritance Mt 21:38

**SEIZED**
to flee, and fear hath *s* on her Jer 49:24

**SELA** (*se'-lah*) See SELAH. *Same as Selah 1.*
the land from *S* to the wilderness Is 16:1

**SELAH** (*se'-lah*) See JOKTHEEL, SELA.
*1. Capital of Edom.*
took *S* by war, and called the name 2Kin 14:7
*2. A musical notation.*
no help for him in God. *S* Ps 3:2
me out of his holy hill. *S* Ps 3:4
blessing is upon thy people. *S* Ps 3:8
vanity, and seek after leasing? *S* Ps 4:2
your bed, and be still. *S* Ps 4:4
mine honour in the dust. *S* Ps 7:5
his own hands. Higgaion. *S* Ps 9:16
themselves to be but men. *S* Ps 9:20

accept thy burnt sacrifice; S — Ps 20:3
the request of his lips. S — Ps 21:2
thy face, O Jacob. S — Ps 24:6
he is the King of glory. S — Ps 24:10
the drought of summer. S — Ps 32:4
the iniquity of my sin. S — Ps 32:5
songs of deliverance. S — Ps 32:7
state is altogether vanity. S — Ps 39:5
every man is vanity. S — Ps 39:11
thy name for ever. S — Ps 44:8
with the swelling thereof. S — Ps 46:3
Jacob is our refuge. S — Ps 46:7
Jacob is our refuge. S — Ps 46:11
Jacob whom he loved. S — Ps 47:4
establish it for ever. S — Ps 48:8
approve their sayings. S — Ps 49:13
he shall receive me. S — Ps 49:15
God is judge himself. S — Ps 50:6
to speak righteousness. S — Ps 52:3
land of the living. S — Ps 52:5
set God before them. S — Ps 54:3
remain in the wilderness. S — Ps 55:7
that abideth of old. S — Ps 55:19
swallow me up. S — Ps 57:3
are fallen themselves. S — Ps 57:6
wicked transgressors. S — Ps 59:5
ends of the earth. S — Ps 59:13
because of the truth. S — Ps 60:4
the covert of thy wings. S — Ps 61:4
but they curse inwardly. S — Ps 62:4
is a refuge for us. S — Ps 62:8
sing to thy name. S — Ps 66:4
exalt themselves. S — Ps 66:7
offer bullocks with goats. S — Ps 66:15
face to shine upon us; S — Ps 67:1
the nations upon earth. S — Ps 67:4
through the wilderness; S — Ps 68:7
the God of our salvation. S — Ps 68:19
praises unto the Lord. S — Ps 68:32
up the pillars of it. S — Ps 75:3
sword, and the battle. S — Ps 76:3
the meek of the earth. S — Ps 76:9
was overwhelmed. S — Ps 77:3
up his tender mercies? S — Ps 77:9
of Jacob and Joseph. S — Ps 77:15
the waters of Meribah. S — Ps 81:7
persons of the wicked? S — Ps 82:2
the children of Lot. S — Ps 83:8
be still praising thee. S — Ps 84:4
O God of Jacob. S — Ps 84:8
covered all their sin. S — Ps 85:2
O city of God. S — Ps 87:3
man was born there. S — Ps 87:6
me with all thy waves. S — Ps 88:7
dead arise and praise thee? S — Ps 88:10
throne to all generations. S — Ps 89:4
witness in heaven. S — Ps 89:37
him with shame. S — Ps 89:45
hand of the grave? S — Ps 89:48
is under their lips. S — Ps 140:3
have set gins for me. S — Ps 140:5
they exalt themselves. S — Ps 140:8
as a thirsty land. S — Ps 143:6
from mount Paran. S — Hab 3:3
even thy word. S — Hab 3:9
foundation unto the neck. S — Hab 3:13

**SELA-HAMMAHLEKOTH** (*se''-lah-ham-mah'-le-koth*) *A hill in the wilderness of Maon.*
they called that place S — 1Sa 23:28

**SELED** (*se'-led*) *A descendant of Jerahmeel.*
S, and Appaim: but S died — 1Chr 2:30

**SELEUCIA** (*sel-u-si'-ah*) *A city in Syria.*
the Holy Ghost, departed unto S — Acts 13:4

**SELF**
whom thou swarest by thine own s — Ex 32:13
I can of mine own s do nothing — Jn 5:30
glorify thou me with thine own s — Jn 17:5
yea, I judge not mine own s — 1Cor 4:3
unto me even thine own s besides — Philem 19
Who his own s bare our sins in — 1Pet 2:24

**SELFSAME**
In the s day entered Noah, and — Gen 7:13
of their foreskin in the s day — Gen 17:23
In the s day was Abraham — Gen 17:26
for in this s day have I brought — Ex 12:17
even the s day it came to pass, — Ex 12:41
And it came to pass the s day — Ex 12:51
until the s day that ye have — Lev 23:14
And ye shall proclaim on the s day — Lev 23:21
LORD spake unto Moses that s day — Deut 32:48
and parched corn in the s day — Josh 5:11
in the s day the hand of the LORD — Eze 40:1
servant was healed in the s hour — Mt 8:13
the s Spirit, dividing to every — 1Cor 12:11
wrought us for the s thing is God — 2Cor 5:5
For behold this s thing, that ye — 2Cor 7:11

**SELFWILL**
in their s they digged down a — Gen 49:6

**SELFWILLED**
not s, not soon angry, not given — Titus 1:7
Presumptuous are they, s, they — 2Pet 2:10

**SELL**
S me this day thy birthright — Gen 25:31
let us s him to the Ishmeelites, — Gen 37:27
if a man s his daughter to be a — Ex 21:7
to s her unto a strange nation he — Ex 21:8
then they shall s the live ox — Ex 21:35
or a sheep, and kill it, or s it — Ex 22:1
And if thou s ought unto thy — Lev 25:14
the fruits he shall s unto thee — Lev 25:15
of the fruits doth he s unto thee — Lev 25:16
if a man s a dwelling house in a — Lev 25:29
s himself unto the stranger or — Lev 25:47
Thou shalt s me meat for money, — Deut 2:28
or thou mayest s it unto an alien — Deut 14:21
but thou shalt not s her at all — Deut 21:14
for the LORD shall s Sisera into — Judg 4:9
which did s himself to work — 1Kin 21:25
s the oil, and pay thy debt, and — 2Kin 4:7
will ye even s your brethren — Neh 5:8
victuals on the sabbath day to s — Neh 10:31
Buy the truth, and s it not — Prov 23:23
s the land into the hand of the — Eze 30:12
And they shall not s of it — Eze 48:14
I will s your sons and your — Joel 3:8
they shall s them to the Sabeans, — Joel 3:8
moon be gone, that we may s corn — Amos 8:5
s the refuse of the wheat — Amos 8:6
and they that s them say, Blessed — Zec 11:5
s that thou hast, and give to the — Mt 19:21
but go ye rather to them that s — Mt 25:9
s whatsoever thou hast, and give — Mk 10:21
S that ye have, and give alms — Lk 12:33
s all that thou hast, and — Lk 18:22
let him s his garment, and buy one — Lk 22:36
there a year, and buy and s — Jas 4:13
And that no man might buy or s — Rev 13:17

**SELLER**
as with the buyer, so with the s — Is 24:2
buyer rejoice, nor the s mourn — Eze 7:12
For the s shall not return to — Eze 7:13
a s of purple, of the city of — Acts 16:14

**SELLERS**
s of all kind of ware lodged — Neh 13:20

**SELLEST**
Thou s thy people for nought, and — Ps 44:12

**SELLETH**
s him, or if he be found in his — Ex 21:16
merchandise of him, or s him — Deut 24:7
s a parcel of land, which was our — Ruth 4:3
be upon the head of him that s it — Prov 11:26
She maketh fine linen, and s it — Prov 31:24
that s nations through her — Nah 3:4
s all that he hath, and buyeth — Mt 13:44

**SELVEDGE**
from the s in the coupling — Ex 26:4
from the s in the coupling — Ex 36:11

**SELVES**
know of your own s that summer is — Lk 21:30
of your own s shall men arise — Acts 20:30
gave their own s to the Lord — 2Cor 8:5
prove your own s — 2Cor 13:5
Know ye not your own s, how that — 2Cor 13:5
shall be lovers of their own s — 2Ti 3:2
only, deceiving your own s — Jas 1:22

**SEM** (*sem*) See SHEM. *Greek form of Shem.*
Arphaxad, which was the son of S — Lk 3:36

**SEMACHIAH** (*sem-a-ki'-ah*) *A sanctuary servant.*
were strong men, Elihu, and S — 1Chr 26:7

**SEMEI** (*sem'-e-i*) See SHEMAIAH. *A son of Joseph; an ancestor of Jesus.*
which was the son of S, which — Lk 3:26

**SEMEIN** See SEMEI.

**SENAAH** (*sen'-a-ah*) See HASSENAAH. *A city in Judah.*
The children of S, three thousand — Ezr 2:35
The children of S, three thousand — Neh 7:38

**SENATE**
all the s of the children of — Acts 5:21

**SENATORS**
and teach his s wisdom — Ps 105:22

**SEND**
he shall s his angel before thee, — Gen 24:7
s me good speed this day, and shew — Gen 24:12
will s his angel with thee, and — Gen 24:40
he said, S me away unto my master — Gen 24:54
s me away that I may go to my — Gen 24:56
then I will s, and fetch thee from — Gen 27:45
S me away, that I may go unto — Gen 30:25
come, and I will s thee unto them — Gen 37:13
I will s thee a kid from the — Gen 38:17
give me a pledge, till thou s it — Gen 38:17
S one of you, and let him fetch — Gen 42:16
If thou wilt s our brother with — Gen 43:4
But if thou wilt not s him — Gen 43:5
S the lad with me, and we will — Gen 43:8
that he may s away your other — Gen 43:14
for God did s me before you to — Gen 45:5
I will s thee unto Pharaoh, that — Ex 3:10
And he said, O my Lord, s, I pray — Ex 4:13
the hand of him whom thou wilt s — Ex 4:13
that he s the children of Israel — Ex 7:2
I will s swarms of flies upon — Ex 8:21
For I will at this time s all my — Ex 9:14
S therefore now, and gather thy — Ex 9:19
that they might s them out of the — Ex 12:33
I s an Angel before thee, to keep — Ex 23:20
I will s my fear before thee, and — Ex 23:27
I will s hornets before thee, — Ex 23:28
I will s an angel before thee — Ex 33:2
me know whom thou wilt s with me — Ex 33:12
shall s him away by the hand of a — Lev 16:21
I will also s wild beasts among — Lev 26:22
I will s the pestilence among you — Lev 26:25
are left alive of you I will s a — Lev 26:36
S thou men, that they may search — Num 13:2
of their fathers shall ye s a man — Num 13:2
Did I not earnestly s unto thee — Num 22:37
of Israel, shall ye s to the war — Num 31:4
We will s men before us, and they — Deut 1:22
God will s the hornet among them — Deut 7:20
I will s grass in thy fields for — Deut 11:15
the elders of his city shall s — Deut 19:12
hand, and s her out of his house — Deut 24:1
The LORD shall s upon thee — Deut 28:20
the LORD shall s against thee — Deut 28:48
I will also s the teeth of beasts — Deut 32:24
and I will s them, and they shall — Josh 18:4
thou didst s come again unto us — Judg 13:8
S away the ark of the God of — 1Sa 5:11
we shall s it to his place — 1Sa 6:2
If ye s away the ark of the God — 1Sa 6:3
the God of Israel, s it not empty — 1Sa 6:3
s it away, that it may go — 1Sa 6:8
s thee a man out of the land of — 1Sa 9:16
Up, that I may s thee away — 1Sa 9:26
that we may s messengers unto all — 1Sa 11:3
the LORD, and he shall s thunder — 1Sa 12:17
I will s thee to Jesse the — 1Sa 16:1
And Samuel said unto Jesse, S — 1Sa 16:11
S me David thy son, which is with — 1Sa 16:19
I then s not unto thee, and shew — 1Sa 20:12
s thee away, that thou mayest go — 1Sa 20:13
And, behold, I will s a lad — 1Sa 20:21
Wherefore now s and fetch him unto — 1Sa 20:31
the business whereabout I s thee — 1Sa 21:2
men of my lord, whom thou didst s — 1Sa 25:25
saying, S me Uriah the Hittite — 2Sa 11:6
that I may s thee to the king, to — 2Sa 14:32
by them ye shall s unto me every — 2Sa 15:36
Now therefore s quickly, and tell — 2Sa 17:16
whithersoever thou shalt s them — 1Kin 8:44
I will s rain upon the earth — 1Kin 18:1
Now therefore s, and gather to me — 1Kin 18:19
Yet I will s my servants unto — 1Kin 20:6
All that thou didst s for to thy — 1Kin 20:9
I will s thee away with this — 1Kin 20:34
And he said, Ye shall not s — 2Kin 2:16
till he was ashamed, he said, S — 2Kin 2:17
S me, I pray thee, one of the — 2Kin 4:22
I will s a letter unto the king — 2Kin 5:5
that this man doth s unto me to — 2Kin 5:7
and spy where he is, that I may s — 2Kin 6:13
and let us s and see — 2Kin 7:13
s to meet them, and let him say, — 2Kin 9:17
s against Judah Rezin the king of — 2Kin 15:37
I will s a blast upon him, and he — 2Kin 19:7
let us s abroad unto our brethren — 1Chr 13:2
didst s him cedars to build him — 2Chr 2:3
S me now therefore a man cunning — 2Chr 2:7
S me also cedar trees, fir trees, — 2Chr 2:8
let him s unto his servants — 2Chr 2:15
s rain upon thy land, which thou — 2Chr 6:27
by the way that thou shalt s them — 2Chr 6:34
or if I s pestilence among my — 2Chr 7:13
At that time did king Ahaz s unto — 2Chr 28:16
s his servants to Jerusalem — 2Chr 32:9
let the king s his pleasure to us — Ezr 5:17
thou wouldest s me unto Judah — Neh 2:5
So it pleased the king to s me — Neh 2:6
s portions unto them for whom — Neh 8:10
to s portions, and to make great — Neh 8:12
They s forth their little ones — Job 21:11
Canst thou s lightnings, that — Job 38:35
S thee help from the sanctuary, — Ps 20:2
O s out thy light and thy truth — Ps 43:3
He shall s from heaven, and save — Ps 57:3
God shall s forth his mercy and — Ps 57:3
didst s a plentiful rain, whereby — Ps 68:9
he doth s out his voice, and that — Ps 68:33
The LORD shall s the rod of thy — Ps 110:2
I beseech thee, s now prosperity — Ps 118:25
S thine hand from above — Ps 144:7
the sluggard to them that s him — Prov 10:26
of truth to them that s unto thee — Prov 22:21
messenger to them that s him — Prov 25:13
to s forth a stinking savour — Eccl 10:1
the Lord, saying, Whom shall I s — Is 6:8
Here am I; s me — Is 6:8
I will s him against an — Is 10:6
s among his fat ones leanness — Is 10:16
S ye the lamb to the ruler of the — Is 16:1
he shall s them a saviour, and a — Is 19:20
that s forth thither the feet of — Is 32:20
I will s a blast upon him, and he — Is 37:7
didst s thy messengers far off, — Is 57:9
I will s those that escape of — Is 66:19
go to all that I shall s thee — Jer 1:7
s unto Kedar, and consider — Jer 2:10
I will s serpents, cockatrices, — Jer 8:17
I will s a sword after them, till — Jer 9:16
s for cunning women, that they — Jer 9:17
I will s for many fishers, saith — Jer 16:16
after will I s for many hunters, — Jer 16:16
I will s the sword, the famine, — Jer 24:10
Behold, I will s and take all the — Jer 25:9
all the nations, to whom I s thee — Jer 25:15

sword that I will s among them Jer 25:16
sword which I will s among you Jer 25:27
s them to the king of Edom, and to Jer 27:3
I will s upon them the sword, the Jer 29:17
S to all them of the captivity, Jer 29:31
LORD thy God shall s thee to us Jer 42:5
LORD our God, to whom we s thee Jer 42:6
Behold, I will s and take Jer 43:10
that I will s unto him wanderers, Jer 48:12
I will s the sword after them, Jer 49:37
will s unto Babylon fanners, that Jer 51:2
I s thee to the children of Eze 2:3
I do s thee unto them Eze 2:4
When I shall s upon them the evil Eze 5:16
which I will s to destroy you Eze 5:16
So will I s upon you famine and Eze 5:17
I will s mine anger upon thee, and Eze 7:3
will s famine upon it, and will Eze 14:13
Or if I s a pestilence into that Eze 14:19
How much more when I s my four Eze 14:21
For I will s into her pestilence, Eze 28:23
I will s a fire on Magog, and Eze 39:6
but I will s a fire upon his Hos 8:14
I will s you corn, and wine, and Joel 2:19
But I will s a fire into the Amos 1:4
But I will s a fire on the wall Amos 1:7
But I will s a fire on the wall Amos 1:10
But I will s a fire upon Teman, Amos 1:12
But I will s a fire upon Moab, and Amos 2:2
But I will s a fire upon Judah, Amos 2:5
that I will s a famine in the Amos 8:11
I will even s a curse upon you, Mal 2:2
I will s my messenger, and he Mal 3:1
I will s you Elijah the prophet Mal 4:5
that he will s forth labourers Mt 9:38
I s you forth as sheep in the Mt 10:16
I am come to s peace on earth Mt 10:34
I came not to s peace, but a Mt 10:34
I s my messenger before thy face, Mt 11:10
till he s forth judgment unto Mt 12:20
of man shall s forth his angels Mt 13:41
s the multitude away, that they Mt 14:15
besought him, saying, S her away Mt 15:23
I will not s them away fasting, Mt 15:32
and straightway he will s them Mt 21:3
I s unto you prophets, and wise Mt 23:34
he shall s his angels with a Mt 24:31
I s my messenger before thy face, Mk 1:2
that he might s them forth to Mk 3:14
him much that he would not s them Mk 5:10
S us into the swine, that we may Mk 5:12
began to s them forth by two and Mk 6:7
S them away, that they may go Mk 6:36
if I s them away fasting to their Mk 8:3
straightway he will s him hither Mk 11:3
they s unto him certain of the Mk 12:13
And then shall he s his angels Mk 13:27
I s my messenger before thy face, Lk 7:27
S the multitude away, that they Lk 9:12
that he would s forth labourers Lk 10:2
I s you forth as lambs among Lk 10:3
I will s them prophets and Lk 11:49
I am come to s fire on the earth Lk 12:49
s Lazarus, that he may dip the Lk 16:24
that thou wouldest s him to my Lk 16:27
I will s my beloved son Lk 20:13
I s the promise of my Father upon Lk 24:49
whomsoever I s receiveth me Jn 13:20
whom the Father will s in my name Jn 14:26
whom I will s unto you from the Jn 15:26
I depart, I will s him unto you Jn 16:7
believed that thou didst s me Jn 17:8
hath sent me, even so s I you Jn 20:21
he shall s Jesus Christ, which Acts 3:20
come, I will s thee into Egypt Acts 7:34
the same did God s to be a ruler Acts 7:35
now s men to Joppa, and call for Acts 10:5
to s for thee into his house Acts 10:22
S therefore to Joppa, and call Acts 10:32
S men to Joppa, and call for Simon Acts 11:13
determined to s relief unto the Acts 11:29
to s chosen men of their own Acts 15:22
brethren s greeting unto the Acts 15:23
to s chosen men unto you with our Acts 15:25
for I will s thee far hence unto Acts 22:21
that he would s for him to Acts 25:3
kept till I might s him to Caesar Acts 25:21
I have determined to s him Acts 25:25
me unreasonable to s a prisoner Acts 25:27
Gentiles, unto whom now I s thee Acts 26:17
them will I s to bring your 1Cor 16:3
to s Timotheus shortly unto you Phil 2:19
therefore I hope to s presently Phil 2:23
to s to you Epaphroditus, my Phil 2:25
God shall s them strong delusion 2Th 2:11
When I shall s Artemas unto thee, Titus 3:12
Doth a fountain s forth at the Jas 3:11
s it unto the seven churches Rev 1:11
shall s gifts one to another Rev 11:10

**SENDEST**
when thou s him out free from Deut 15:13
when thou s him away free from Deut 15:18
do, and whithersoever thou s us Josh 1:16
that thou s to enquire of 2Kin 1:6
his countenance, and s him away Job 14:20
Thou s forth thy spirit, they are Ps 104:30

**SENDETH**
hand, and s her out of his house Deut 24:3
the LORD s rain upon the earth 1Kin 17:14
and s waters upon the fields Job 5:10
also he s them out, and they Job 12:15
He s the springs into the valleys Ps 104:10
He s forth his commandment upon Ps 147:15
He s out his word, and melteth Ps 147:18
He that s a message by the hand Prov 26:6
my spikenard s forth the smell Song 1:12
That s ambassadors by the sea, Is 18:2
s rain on the just and on the Mt 5:45
he s forth two of his disciples, Mk 11:1
he s forth two of his disciples, Mk 14:13
he s an ambassage, and desireth Lk 14:32
governor Felix s greeting Acts 23:26

**SENDING**
this evil in s me away is greater 2Sa 13:16
rising up betimes, and s 2Chr 36:15
of s portions one to another Est 9:19
of s portions one to another, and Est 9:22
by s evil angels among them Ps 78:49
shall be for the s forth of oxen Is 7:25
daily rising up early and s them Jer 7:25
prophets, rising early and s them Jer 25:4
s them, but ye have not hearkened Jer 26:5
rising up early and s them Jer 29:19
s them, saying, Return ye now Jer 35:15
s them, saying, Oh, do not this Jer 44:4
in s his ambassadors into Egypt Eze 17:15
God s his own Son in the likeness Rom 8:3

**SENEH** (*se'-neh*) *A rock in Benjamin.*
Bozez, and the name of the other S 1Sa 14:4

**SENIR** (*se'-nur*) See SHENIR. *A mountain between Amana and Hermon.*
from Bashan unto Baal-hermon and S 1Chr 5:23
thy ship boards of fir trees of S Eze 27:5

**SENNACHERIB** (*sen-nak'-er-ib*) *An Assyrian king.*
year of king Hezekiah did S king 2Kin 18:13
and hear the words of S, which 2Kin 19:16
S king of Assyria I have heard 2Kin 19:20
So S king of Assyria departed, and 2Kin 19:36
S king of Assyria came, and 2Chr 32:1
when Hezekiah saw that S was come. 2Chr 32:2
After this did S king of Assyria 2Chr 32:9
Thus saith S king of Assyria, 2Chr 32:10
the hand of S the king of Assyria 2Chr 32:22
that S king of Assyria came up Is 36:1
and hear all the words of S Is 37:17
to me against S king of Assyria Is 37:21
So S king of Assyria departed, and Is 37:37

**SENSE**
of God distinctly, and gave the s Neh 8:8

**SENSES**
s exercised to discern both good Heb 5:14

**SENSUAL**
not from above, but is earthly, s Jas 3:15
they who separate themselves, s Jude 19

**SENT** See PREFACE.

**SENTENCE**
shall shew thee the s of judgment Deut 17:9
thou shalt do according to the s Deut 17:10
According to the s of the law Deut 17:11
the s which they shall shew thee Deut 17:11
Let my s come forth from thy Ps 17:2
A divine s is in the lips of the Prov 16:10
Because s against an evil work is Eccl 8:11
also will I give s against them Jer 4:12
Pilate gave s that it should be Lk 23:24
Wherefore my s is, that we Acts 15:19
But we had the s of death in 2Cor 1:9

**SENTENCES**
of dreams, and shewing of hard s Dan 5:12
and understanding dark s, shall Dan 8:23

**SENTEST**
thou s forth thy wrath, which Ex 15:7
unto the land whither thou s us Num 13:27
messengers which thou s unto me Num 24:12
the things which thou s to me for 1Kin 5:8

**SENUAH** (*sen'-u-ah*) See HASSENUAH. *Father of Judah.*
Judah the son of S was second Neh 11:9

**SEORIM** (*se-o'-rim*) *A sanctuary servant.*
third to Harim, the fourth to S 1Chr 24:8

**SEPARATE**
s thyself, I pray thee, from me Gen 13:9
And Jacob did s the lambs, and set Gen 30:40
him that was s from his brethren Gen 49:26
Thus shall ye s the children of Lev 15:31
that they s themselves from the Lev 22:2
s themselves to vow a vow of a Num 6:2
to s themselves unto the LORD Num 6:2
He shall s himself from wine and Num 6:3
Thus shalt thou s the Levites Num 8:14
S yourselves from among this Num 16:21
Thou shalt s three cities for Deut 19:2
Thou shalt s three cities for Deut 19:7
the LORD shall s him unto evil Deut 29:21
the s cities for the children of Josh 16:9
For thou didst s them from among 1Kin 8:53
s yourselves from the people of Ezr 10:11
to s himself thence in the midst Jer 37:12
the s place at the end toward the Eze 41:12
the s place, and the building, Eze 41:13
of the s place toward the east, Eze 41:14
the s place which was behind it Eze 41:15
that was over against the s place Eze 42:1
east, over against the s place Eze 42:10
which are before the s place Eze 42:13
he shall s them one from another, Mt 25:32
when they shall s you from their Lk 6:22
S me Barnabas and Saul for the Acts 13:2
Who shall s us from the love of Rom 8:35
shall be able to s us from the Rom 8:39
out from among them, and be ye s 2Cor 6:17
s from sinners, and made higher Heb 7:26
These be they who s themselves Jude 19

**SEPARATED**
they s themselves the one from Gen 13:11
after that Lot was s from him Gen 13:14
people shall be s from thy bowels Gen 25:23
so shall we be s, I and thy people Ex 33:16
which have s you from other Lev 20:24
which I have s from you as Lev 20:25
that the God of Israel hath s you Num 16:9
time the LORD s the tribe of Levi Deut 10:8
when he s the sons of Adam, he Deut 32:8
him that was s from his brethren Deut 33:16
of the Gadites there s themselves 1Chr 12:8
and Aaron was s, that he should 1Chr 23:13
the captains of the host s to the 1Chr 25:1
Then Amaziah s them, to wit, the 2Chr 25:10
all such as had s themselves unto Ezr 6:21
Then I s twelve of the chief of Ezr 8:24
have not s themselves from the Ezr 9:1
himself s from the congregation Ezr 10:8
of them by their names, were s Ezr 10:16
we are s upon the wall, one far Neh 4:19
the seed of Israel s themselves Neh 9:2
all they that had s themselves Neh 10:28
that they s from Israel all the Neh 13:3
having s himself, seeketh and Prov 18:1
but the poor is s from his Prov 19:4
hath utterly s me from his people Is 56:3
iniquities have s between you Is 59:2
for themselves are s with whores Hos 4:14
s themselves unto that shame Hos 9:10
s the disciples, disputing daily Acts 19:9
s unto the gospel of God, Rom 1:1
who s me from my mother's womb, Gal 1:15
s himself, fearing them which Gal 2:12

**SEPARATETH**
in the which he s himself unto Num 6:5
All the days that he s himself Num 6:6
a whisperer s chief friends Prov 16:28
repeateth a matter s very friends Prov 17:9
which s himself from me, and Eze 14:7

**SEPARATING**
s myself, as I have done these so Zec 7:3

**SEPARATION**
according to the days of the s Lev 12:2
be unclean two weeks, as in her s Lev 12:5
upon in her s shall be unclean Lev 15:20
days out of the time of her s Lev 15:25
it run beyond the time of her s Lev 15:25
shall be as the days of her s Lev 15:25
be unto her as the bed of her s Lev 15:26
as the uncleanness of her s Lev 15:26
All the days of his s shall he Num 6:4
s there shall no razor come upon Num 6:5
All the days of his s he is holy Num 6:8
unto the LORD the days of his s Num 6:12
lost, because his s was defiled Num 6:12
the days of his s are fulfilled Num 6:13
shall shave the head of his s at Num 6:18
the hair of the head of his s Num 6:18
after the hair of his s is shaven Num 6:19
offering unto the LORD for his s Num 6:21
he must do after the law of his s Num 6:21
of Israel for a water of s Num 19:9
because the water of s was not Num 19:13
the water of s hath not been Num 19:20
water of s shall wash his clothes Num 19:21
of s shall be unclean until even Num 19:21
be purified with the water of s Num 31:23
to make a s between the sanctuary Eze 42:20

**SEPHAR** (*se'-far*) *A mountain in Arabia.*
as thou goest unto S a mount of Gen 10:30

**SEPHARAD** (*sef'-a-rad*) *A city in Media.*
of Jerusalem, which is in S Obad 20

**SEPHARVAIM** (*sef-ar-va'-im*) See SEPHARVITES. *A city in Mesopotamia.*
Ava, and from Hamath, and from S 2Kin 17:24
and Anammelech, the gods of S 2Kin 17:31
where are the gods of S, Hena, and 2Kin 18:34
and the king of the city of S 2Kin 19:13
where are the gods of S Is 36:19
and the king of the city of S Is 37:13

**SEPHARVITES** (*sef'-ar-vites*) *Inhabitants of Sepharvaim.*
the S burnt their children in 2Kin 17:31

**SEPULCHRE**
us shall withhold from thee his s Gen 23:6
knoweth of his s unto this day Deut 34:6
was buried in the s of Joash his Judg 8:32
s in the border of Benjamin at 1Sa 10:2
buried him in the s of his father 2Sa 2:32
buried it in the s of Abner in 2Sa 4:12
was buried in the s of his father 2Sa 17:23
in the s of Kish his father 2Sa 21:14

come unto the s of thy fathers 1Kin 13:22
then bury me in the s wherein the 1Kin 13:31
buried him in his s with his 2Kin 9:28
cast the man into the s of Elisha 2Kin 13:21
he was buried in his s in the 2Kin 21:26
It is the s of the man of God, 2Kin 23:17
and buried him in his own s 2Kin 23:30
their throat is an open s Ps 5:9
thou hast hewed thee out a s here Is 22:16
that heweth him out an s on high Is 22:16
Their quiver is as an open s Jer 5:16
great stone to the door of the s Mt 27:60
Mary, sitting over against the s Mt 27:61
Command therefore that the s be Mt 27:64
So they went, and made the s sure Mt 27:66
and the other Mary to see the s Mt 28:1
quickly from the s with fear Mt 28:8
laid him in a s which was hewn Mk 15:46
a stone unto the door of the s Mk 15:46
they came unto the s at the Mk 16:2
the stone from the door of the s Mk 16:3
And entering into the s, they saw Mk 16:5
out quickly, and fled from the s Mk 16:8
laid it in a s that was hewn in Lk 23:53
followed after, and beheld the s Lk 23:55
the morning, they came unto the s Lk 24:1
the stone rolled away from the s Lk 24:2
And returned from the s, and told Lk 24:9
arose Peter, and ran unto the s Lk 24:12
which were early at the s Lk 24:22
which were with us went to the s Lk 24:24
and in the garden a new s, wherein Jn 19:41
for the s was nigh at hand Jn 19:42
when it was yet dark, unto the s Jn 20:1
the stone taken away from the s Jn 20:1
taken away the Lord out of the s Jn 20:2
other disciple, and came to the s Jn 20:3
Peter, and came first to the s Jn 20:4
following him, and went into the s Jn 20:6
which came first to the s Jn 20:8
stood without at the s weeping Jn 20:11
down, and looked into the s Jn 20:11
his s is with us unto this day Acts 2:29
laid in the s that Abraham bought Acts 7:16
from the tree, and laid him in a s Acts 13:29
Their throat is an open s Rom 3:13

**SEPULCHRES**
the choice of our s bury thy dead Gen 23:6
he spied the s that were there in 2Kin 23:16
and took the bones out of the s 2Kin 23:16
And they buried him in his own s 2Chr 16:14
but not in the s of the kings 2Chr 21:20
him not in the s of the kings 2Chr 24:25
into the s of the kings of Israel 2Chr 28:27
of the s of the sons of David 2Chr 32:33
in one of the s of his fathers 2Chr 35:24
city, the place of my fathers' s Neh 2:3
unto the city of my fathers' s Neh 2:5
place over against the s of David Neh 3:16
for ye are like unto whited s Mt 23:27
garnish the s of the righteous, Mt 23:29
ye build the s of the prophets Lk 11:47
killed them, and ye build their s Lk 11:48

**SERAH** (*se'-rah*) See SARAH. *A daughter of Asher.*
and Beriah, and S their sister Gen 46:17
and Beriah, and S their sister 1Chr 7:30

**SERAIAH** (*se-ra-i'-ah*) See SHAVSHA.
*1. David's scribe.*
and S was the scribe 2Sa 8:17
*2. High priest in Zedekiah's time.*
the guard took S the chief priest 2Kin 25:18
And Azariah begat S, and Seraiah 1Chr 6:14
Seraiah, and S begat Jehozadak, 1Chr 6:14
king of Persia, Ezra the son of S Ezr 7:1
the guard took S the chief priest Jer 52:24
*3. Son of Tanhumeth.*
S the son of Tanhumeth the 2Kin 25:23
S the son of Tanhumeth, and the Jer 40:8
*4. A son of Kenaz.*
Othniel, and S 1Chr 4:13
S begat Joab, the father of the 1Chr 4:14
*5. Son of Asiel.*
the son of Josibiah, the son of S 1Chr 4:35
*6. A priest with Zerubbabel.*
Jeshua, Nehemiah, S, Reelaiah, Ezr 2:2
S, Azariah, Jeremiah, Neh 10:2
S, Jeremiah, Ezra, Neh 12:1
of S, Meraiah Neh 12:12
*7. An exile.*
S the son of Hilkiah, the son of Neh 11:11
*8. Son of Azriel.*
S the son of Azriel, and Shelemiah Jer 36:26
*9. Son of Neriah.*
commanded S the son of Neriah Jer 51:59
this S was a quiet prince Jer 51:59
And Jeremiah said to S, When thou Jer 51:61

**SERAPHIMS**
Above it stood the s Is 6:2
Then flew one of the s unto me Is 6:6

**SERED** (*se'-red*) See SARDITES. *A son of Zebulun.*
S, and Elon, and Jahleel Gen 46:14
of S, the family of the Sardites Num 26:26

**SEREDITES** See SARDITES.

**SERGIUS** (*sur'-je-us*) *Roman governor of Cyprus.*
country, S Paulus, a prudent man Acts 13:7

**SERJEANTS**
day, the magistrates sent the s Acts 16:35
the s told these words unto the Acts 16:38

**SERPENT**
Now the s was more subtil than Gen 3:1
And the woman said unto the s Gen 3:2
the s said unto the woman, Ye Gen 3:4
The s beguiled me, and I did eat Gen 3:13
And the LORD God said unto the s Gen 3:14
Dan shall be a s by the way Gen 49:17
on the ground, and it became a s Ex 4:3
Pharaoh, and it shall become a s Ex 7:9
his servants, and it became a s Ex 7:10
a s shalt thou take in thine hand Ex 7:15
unto Moses, Make thee a fiery s Num 21:8
And Moses made a s of brass Num 21:9
that if a s had bitten any man, Num 21:9
when he beheld the s of brass Num 21:9
the brasen s that Moses had made 2Kin 18:4
hand hath formed the crooked s Job 26:13
poison is like the poison of a s Ps 58:4
sharpened their tongues like a s Ps 140:3
At the last it biteth like a s Prov 23:32
the way of a s upon a rock Prov 30:19
an hedge, a s shall bite him Eccl 10:8
Surely the s will bite without Eccl 10:11
fruit shall be a fiery flying s Is 14:29
punish leviathan the piercing s Is 27:1
even leviathan that crooked s Is 27:1
lion, the viper and fiery flying s Is 30:6
voice thereof shall go like a s Jer 46:22
hand on the wall, and a s bit him Amos 5:19
sea, thence will I command the s Amos 9:3
They shall lick the dust like a s Mic 7:17
ask a fish, will he give him a s Mt 7:10
will he for a fish give him a s Lk 11:11
lifted up the s in the wilderness Jn 3:14
as the s beguiled Eve through his 2Cor 11:3
dragon was cast out, that old s Rev 12:9
a time, from the face of the s Rev 12:14
the s cast out of his mouth water Rev 12:15
hold on the dragon, that old s Rev 20:2

**SERPENT'S**
for out of the s root shall come Is 14:29
and dust shall be the s meat Is 65:25

**SERPENTS**
man his rod, and they became s Ex 7:12
sent fiery s among the people Num 21:6
that he take away the s from us Num 21:7
wilderness, wherein were fiery s Deut 8:15
with the poison of s of the dust Deut 32:24
For, behold, I will send s Jer 8:17
be ye therefore wise as s Mt 10:16
Ye s, ye generation of vipers, Mt 23:33
They shall take up s Mk 16:18
give unto you power to tread on s Lk 10:19
tempted, and were destroyed of s 1Cor 10:9
of beasts, and of birds, and of s Jas 3:7
for their tails were like unto s Rev 9:19

**SERUG** (*se'-rug*) See SARUCH. *Father of Nahor.*
two and thirty years, and begat S Gen 11:20
after he begat S two hundred Gen 11:21
S lived thirty years, and begat Gen 11:22
S lived after he begat Nahor two Gen 11:23
S, Nahor, Terah, 1Chr 1:26

**SERVANT** See PREFACE.
for thy s heareth 1Sa 3:9
Give therefore thy s an 1Kin 3:9
O ye seed of Israel his s 1Chr 16:13
I called my s, and he gave me no Job 19:16
put not thy s away in anger Ps 27:9
O LORD, truly I am thy s Ps 116:16
I am thy s, and the son of thine Ps 116:16
Deal bountifully with thy s Ps 119:17
the borrower is s to the lender Prov 22:7
as with the s, so with his master Is 24:2
and said unto thee, Thou art my s Is 41:9
shall my righteous s justify many Is 53:11
Is Israel a s Jer 2:14
his s was healed in the selfsame Mt 8:13
master, nor the s above his lord Mt 10:24
his master, and the s as his lord Mt 10:25
Who then is a faithful and wise s Mt 24:45
done, thou good and faithful s Mt 25:21
shall be last of all, and s of all Mk 9:35
the chiefest, shall be s of all Mk 10:44
And that s, which knew his lord's Lk 12:47
No s can serve two masters Lk 16:13
The s is not greater than his Jn 13:16
for the s knoweth not what his Jn 15:15
The s is not greater than his Jn 15:20
Art thou called being a s 1Cor 7:21
and took upon him the form of a s Phil 2:7

**SERVANT'S**
in, I pray you, into your s house Gen 19:2
thou hast spoken also of thy s 2Sa 7:19
to thy son for David my s sake 1Kin 11:13
of his life for David my s sake 1Kin 11:34
Judah for David his s sake 2Kin 8:19
thou hast also spoken of thy s 1Chr 17:17
O LORD, for thy s sake, and 1Chr 17:19
For Jacob my s sake, and Israel Is 45:4
The s name was Malchus Jn 18:10

**SERVANTS** See PREFACE.
my s shall be with thy s, 2Chr 2:8
LORD redeemeth the soul of his s Ps 34:22
it, and my s shall dwell there Is 65:9
unto you all my s the prophets Jer 35:15
How many hired s of my father's Lk 15:17
Henceforth I call you not s Jn 15:15
ye yield yourselves s to obey Rom 6:16
his s ye are to whom ye obey Rom 6:16
be not ye the s of men 1Cor 7:23
but as the s of God 1Pet 2:16
Praise our God, all ye his s Rev 19:5

**SERVANTS'**
Thy s trade hath been about Gen 46:34
of Pharaoh, and into his s houses Ex 8:24
Return for thy s sake, the tribes Is 63:17
so will I do for my s sakes Is 65:8

**SERVE**
is not theirs, and shall s them Gen 15:13
that nation, whom they shall s Gen 15:14
and the elder shall s the younger Gen 25:23
Let people s thee, and nations bow Gen 27:29
thou live, and shalt s thy brother Gen 27:40
thou therefore s me for nought Gen 29:15
I will s thee seven years for Gen 29:18
did not I s with thee for Rachel Gen 29:25
the service which thou shalt s Gen 29:27
of Israel to s with rigour Ex 1:13
service, wherein they made them s Ex 1:14
ye shall s God upon this mountain Ex 3:12
Let my son go, that he may s me Ex 4:23
that they may s me in the Ex 7:16
my people go, that they may s me Ex 8:1
my people go, that they may s me Ex 8:20
my people go, that they may s me Ex 9:1
my people go, that they may s me Ex 9:13
my people go, that they may s me Ex 10:3
that they may s the LORD their Ex 10:7
them, Go, s the LORD your God Ex 10:8
ye that are men, and s the LORD Ex 10:11
Moses, and said, Go ye, s the LORD Ex 10:24
we take to s the LORD our God Ex 10:26
not with what we must s the LORD Ex 10:26
s the LORD, as ye have said Ex 12:31
that we may s the Egyptians Ex 14:12
better for us to s the Egyptians Ex 14:12
down thyself to them, nor s them Ex 20:5
servant, six years he shall s Ex 21:2
and he shall s him for ever Ex 21:6
nor s them, nor do after their Ex 23:24
ye shall s the LORD your God, and Ex 23:25
for if thou s their gods, it will Ex 23:33
compel him to s as a bondservant Lev 25:39
shall s thee unto the year of Lev 25:40
families of the Gershonites, to s Num 4:24
so shall they s Num 4:26
thereof, and shall s no more Num 8:25
and ye shall s Num 18:7
for their service which they s Num 18:21
s them, which the LORD thy God Deut 4:19
And there ye shall s gods, the Deut 4:28
thyself unto them, nor s them Deut 5:9
s him, and shalt swear by his name Deut 6:13
me, that they may s other gods Deut 7:4
neither shalt thou s their gods Deut 7:16
s them, and worship them, I Deut 8:19
to s the LORD thy God with all Deut 10:12
him shalt thou s, and to him shalt Deut 10:20
to s him with all your heart and Deut 11:13
s other gods, and worship them Deut 11:16
did these nations s their gods Deut 12:30
hast not known, and let us s them Deut 13:2
obey his voice, and ye shall s him Deut 13:4
s other gods, which thou hast not Deut 13:6
s other gods, which ye have not Deut 13:13
unto thee, and s thee six years Deut 15:12
unto thee, and they shall s thee Deut 20:11
to go after other gods to s them Deut 28:14
and there shalt thou s other gods Deut 28:36
Therefore shalt thou s thine Deut 28:48
and there thou shalt s other gods Deut 28:64
s the gods of these nations Deut 29:18
and worship other gods, and s them Deut 30:17
s them, and provoke me, and break Deut 31:20
unto this day, and s under tribute Josh 16:10
to s him with all your heart and Josh 22:5
to swear by them, neither s them Josh 23:7
s him in sincerity and in truth Josh 24:14
and s ye the LORD Josh 24:14
seem evil unto you to s the LORD Josh 24:15
you this day whom ye will s Josh 24:15
and my house, we will s the LORD Josh 24:15
forsake the LORD, to s other gods Josh 24:16
therefore will we also s the LORD Josh 24:18
the people, Ye cannot s the LORD Josh 24:19
s strange gods, then he will turn Josh 24:20
but we will s the LORD Josh 24:21
chosen you the LORD, to s him Josh 24:22
The LORD our God will we s Josh 24:24
in following other gods to s them Judg 2:19
is Shechem, that we should s him Judg 9:28
s the men of Hamor the father of Judg 9:28
for why should we s him Judg 9:28
Abimelech, that we should s him Judg 9:38
unto the LORD, and s him only 1Sa 7:3
that thou do as occasion s thee 1Sa 10:7
with us, and we will s thee 1Sa 11:1
of our enemies, and we will s thee 1Sa 12:10
s him, and obey his voice, and not 1Sa 12:14
but s the LORD with all your 1Sa 12:20
s him in truth with all your 1Sa 12:24
shall ye be our servants, and s us 1Sa 17:9
LORD, saying, Go, s other gods 1Sa 26:19
Jerusalem, then I will s the LORD 2Sa 15:8

S

And again, whom should I *s* 2Sa 16:19
should I not *s* in the presence of 2Sa 16:19
which I knew not shall *s* me 2Sa 22:44
*s* other gods, and worship them 1Kin 9:6
us, lighter, and we will *s* thee 1Kin 12:4
people this day, and wilt *s* them 1Kin 12:7
but Jehu shall *s* him much 2Kin 10:18
nor *s* them, nor sacrifice to them 2Kin 17:35
land, and *s* the king of Babylon 2Kin 25:24
*s* him with a perfect heart and 1Chr 28:9
*s* other gods, and worship them 2Chr 7:19
he put upon us, and we will *s* thee 2Chr 10:4
to *s* him, and that ye should 2Chr 29:11
*s* the LORD your God, that the 2Chr 30:8
commanded Judah to *s* the 2Chr 33:16
that were present in Israel to *s* 2Chr 34:33
even to *s* the LORD their God 2Chr 34:33
*s* now the LORD your God, and his 2Chr 35:3
Almighty, that we should *s* him Job 21:15
*s* him, they shall spend their Job 36:11
the unicorn be willing to *s* thee Job 39:9
*S* the LORD with fear, and rejoice Ps 2:11
whom I have not known shall *s* me Ps 18:43
A seed shall *s* him Ps 22:30
all nations shall *s* him Ps 72:11
be all they that *s* graven images Ps 97:7
*S* the LORD with gladness Ps 100:2
in a perfect way, he shall *s* me Ps 101:6
and the kingdoms, to *s* the LORD Ps 102:22
wherein thou wast made to *s* Is 14:3
shall *s* with the Assyrians Is 19:23
caused thee to *s* with an offering Is 43:23
hast made me to *s* with thy sins Is 43:24
to *s* him, and to love the name of Is 56:6
that will not *s* thee shall perish Is 60:12
so shall ye *s* strangers in a land Jer 5:19
went after other gods to *s* them Jer 11:10
to *s* them, and to worship them, Jer 13:10
there shall ye *s* other gods day Jer 16:13
I will cause thee to *s* thine Jer 17:4
go not after other gods to *s* them Jer 25:6
these nations shall *s* the king of Jer 25:11
great kings shall *s* themselves of Jer 25:14
field have I given also to *s* him Jer 27:6
And all nations shall *s* him Jer 27:7
kings shall *s* themselves of him Jer 27:7
kingdom which will not *s* the same Jer 27:8
Ye shall not *s* the king of Jer 27:9
*s* him, those will I let remain Jer 27:11
*s* him and his people, and live Jer 27:12
will not *s* the king of Babylon Jer 27:13
Ye shall not *s* the king of Jer 27:14
*s* the king of Babylon, and live Jer 27:17
that they may *s* Nebuchadnezzar Jer 28:14
and they shall *s* him Jer 28:14
shall no more *s* themselves of him Jer 30:8
But they shall *s* the LORD their Jer 30:9
none should *s* himself of them Jer 34:9
that none should *s* themselves of Jer 34:10
go not after other gods to *s* them Jer 35:15
Fear not to *s* the Chaldeans Jer 40:9
*s* the king of Babylon, and it Jer 40:9
at Mizpah to *s* the Chaldeans Jer 40:10
to *s* other gods, whom they knew Jer 44:3
the countries, to *s* wood and stone Eze 20:32
*s* ye every one his idols, and Eze 20:39
all of them in the land, *s* me Eze 20:40
*s* a great service against Tyrus Eze 29:18
food unto them that *s* the city Eze 48:18
they that *s* the city shall *s* Eze 48:19
they *s* not thy gods, nor worship Dan 3:12
and Abed-nego, do not ye *s* my gods Dan 3:14
our God whom we *s* is able to Dan 3:17
king, that we will not *s* thy gods Dan 3:18
might not *s* nor worship any god Dan 3:28
and languages, should *s* him Dan 7:14
kingdom, and all dominions shall *s* Dan 7:27
to *s* him with one consent Zeph 3:9
Ye have said, It is vain to *s* God Mal 3:14
thy God, and him only shalt thou *s* Mt 4:10
No man can *s* two masters Mt 6:24
Ye cannot *s* God and mammon Mt 6:24
enemies might *s* him without fear Lk 1:74
thy God, and him only shalt thou *s* Lk 4:8
my sister hath left me to *s* alone Lk 10:40
and will come forth and *s* them Lk 12:37
Lo, these many years do I *s* thee Lk 15:29
No servant can *s* two masters Lk 16:13
Ye cannot *s* God and mammon Lk 16:13
*s* me, till I have eaten and Lk 17:8
that is chief, as he that doth *s* Lk 22:26
If any man *s* me, let him follow Jn 12:26
if any man *s* me, him will my Jn 12:26
the word of God, and *s* tables Acts 6:2
come forth, and *s* me in this place Acts 7:7
of God, whose I am, and whom I *s* Acts 27:23
whom I *s* with my spirit in the Rom 1:9
henceforth we should not *s* sin Rom 6:6
that we should *s* in newness of Rom 7:6
mind I myself *s* the law of God Rom 7:25
The elder shall *s* the younger Rom 9:12
For they that are such *s* not our Rom 16:18
flesh, but by love *s* one another Gal 5:13
for ye *s* the Lord Christ Col 3:24
to God from idols to *s* the living 1Th 1:9
whom I *s* from my forefathers with 2Ti 1:3
Who *s* unto the example and shadow Heb 8:5
dead works to *s* the living God Heb 9:14
whereby we may *s* God acceptably Heb 12:28
to eat which *s* the tabernacle Heb 13:10
*s* him day and night in his temple Rev 7:15
and his servants shall *s* him Rev 22:3

**SERVED**

Twelve years they *s* Chedorlaomer Gen 14:4
Jacob *s* seven years for Rachel Gen 29:20
*s* with him yet seven other years Gen 29:30
children, for whom I have *s* thee Gen 30:26
Thou knowest how I have *s* thee Gen 30:29
all my power I have *s* your father Gen 31:6
I *s* thee fourteen years for thy Gen 31:41
grace in his sight, and he *s* him Gen 39:4
Joseph with them, and he *s* them Gen 40:4
ye shall possess *s* their gods Deut 12:2
*s* other gods, and worshipped them, Deut 17:3
*s* other gods, and worshipped them, Deut 29:26
*s* other gods, and bowed yourselves Josh 23:16
and they *s* other gods Josh 24:2
the gods which your fathers *s* on Josh 24:14
the gods which your fathers *s* Josh 24:15
Israel *s* the LORD all the days of Josh 24:31
the people *s* the LORD all the Judg 2:7
sight of the LORD, and *s* Baalim Judg 2:11
the LORD, and *s* Baal and Ashtaroth Judg 2:13
to their sons, and *s* their gods Judg 3:6
God, and *s* Baalim and the groves Judg 3:7
and the children of Israel *s* Judg 3:8
So the children of Israel *s* Eglon Judg 3:14
unto him, Why hast thou *s* us thus Judg 8:1
*s* Baalim, and Ashtaroth, and the Judg 10:6
and forsook the LORD, and *s* not him Judg 10:6
our God, and also *s* Baalim Judg 10:10
have forsaken me, and *s* other gods Judg 10:13
from among them, and *s* the LORD Judg 10:16
and Ashtaroth, and *s* the LORD only 1Sa 7:4
*s* other gods, so do they also 1Sa 8:8
have *s* Baalim and Ashtaroth 1Sa 12:10
made peace with Israel, and *s* them 2Sa 10:19
as I have *s* in thy father's 2Sa 16:19
*s* Solomon all the days of his 1Kin 4:21
have worshipped them, and *s* them 1Kin 9:9
*s* Baal, and worshipped him 1Kin 16:31
For he *s* Baal, and worshipped him, 1Kin 22:53
unto them, Ahab *s* Baal a little 2Kin 10:18
For they *s* idols, whereof the 2Kin 17:12
all the host of heaven, and *s* Baal 2Kin 17:16
*s* their own gods, after the 2Kin 17:33
*s* their graven images, both their 2Kin 17:41
the king of Assyria, and *s* him not 2Kin 18:7
all the host of heaven, and *s* them 2Kin 21:3
*s* the idols that his father 2Kin 21:21
the idols that his father *s* 2Kin 21:21
and told David how the men were *s* 1Chr 19:5
their officers that *s* the king in 1Chr 27:1
and worshipped them, and *s* them 2Chr 7:22
fathers, and *s* groves and idols 2Chr 24:18
all the host of heaven, and *s* them 2Chr 33:3
his father had made, and *s* them 2Chr 33:22
For they have not *s* thee in their Neh 9:35
the seven chamberlains that *s* in Est 1:10
And they *s* their idols Ps 106:36
rewardeth thee as thou hast *s* us Ps 137:8
king himself is *s* by the field Eccl 5:9
*s* strange gods in your land, so Jer 5:19
have loved, and whom they have *s* Jer 8:2
after other gods, and have *s* them Jer 16:11
worshipped other gods, and *s* them Jer 22:9
when he hath *s* thee six years, Jer 34:14
which *s* the king of Babylon, into Jer 52:12
service that he had *s* against it Eze 29:18
labour wherewith he *s* against it Eze 29:20
those that *s* themselves of them Eze 34:27
Israel *s* for a wife, and for a Hos 12:12
but *s* God with fastings and Lk 2:37
and Martha *s* Jn 12:2
after he had *s* his own generation Acts 13:36
*s* the creature more than the Rom 1:25
he hath *s* with me in the gospel Phil 2:22

**SERVEDST**

Because thou *s* not the LORD thy Deut 28:47

**SERVEST**

Thy God whom thou *s* continually Dan 6:16
whom thou *s* continually, able to Dan 6:20

**SERVETH**

thereof, and all that *s* thereto Num 3:36
spareth his own son that *s* him Mal 3:17
*s* God and him that *s* him not Mal 3:18
sitteth at meat, or he that *s* Lk 22:27
but I am among you as he that *s* Lk 22:27
*s* Christ is acceptable to God Rom 14:18
but prophesying *s* not for them 1Cor 14:22
Wherefore then *s* the law Gal 3:19

**SERVICE**

give thee this also for the *s* Gen 29:27
for thou knowest my *s* which I Gen 30:26
in all manner of *s* in the field Ex 1:14
all their *s*, wherein they made Ex 1:14
that ye shall keep this *s* Ex 12:25
unto you, What mean ye by this *s* Ex 12:26
shalt keep this *s* in this month Ex 13:5
tabernacle in all the *s* thereof Ex 27:19
the *s* of the tabernacle of the Ex 30:16
And the cloths of *s*, and the holy Ex 31:10
The cloths of *s*, to do *s* in Ex 35:19
to do *s* in the holy place, the Ex 35:19
congregation, and for all his *s* Ex 35:21
wood for any work of the *s* Ex 35:24
work for the *s* of the sanctuary Ex 36:1
work of the *s* of the sanctuary Ex 36:3
than enough for the *s* of the work Ex 36:5
for the *s* of the Levites, by the Ex 38:21
and scarlet, they made cloths of *s* Ex 39:1
to do *s* in the holy place, and Ex 39:1
of the *s* of the tabernacle Ex 39:40
The cloths of *s* to do Ex 39:41
to do *s* in the holy place Ex 39:41
to do the *s* of the tabernacle Num 3:7
to do the *s* of the tabernacle Num 3:8
cords of it for all the *s* thereof Num 3:26
the hanging, and all the *s* thereof Num 3:31
This shall be the *s* of the sons Num 4:4
appoint them every one to his *s* Num 4:19
that enter in to perform the *s* Num 4:23
This is the *s* of the families of Num 4:24
and all the instruments of their *s* Num 4:26
his sons shall be all the *s* of Num 4:27
their burdens, and in all their *s* Num 4:27
This is the *s* of the families of Num 4:28
one that entereth into the *s* Num 4:30
according to all their *s* in the Num 4:31
instruments, and with all their *s* Num 4:32
This is the *s* of the families of Num 4:33
Merari, according to all their *s* Num 4:33
one that entereth into the *s* Num 4:35
all that might do *s* in the Num 4:37
one that entereth into the *s* Num 4:39
of all that might do *s* in the Num 4:41
one that entereth into the *s* Num 4:43
came to do the *s* of the ministry Num 4:47
the *s* of the burden in the Num 4:47
every one according to his *s* Num 4:49
do the *s* of the tabernacle of the Num 7:5
to every man according to his *s* Num 7:5
of Gershon, according to their *s* Num 7:7
of Merari, according unto their *s* Num 7:8
because the *s* of the sanctuary Num 7:9
may execute the *s* of the LORD Num 8:11
do the *s* of the tabernacle of the Num 8:15
to do the *s* of the children of Num 8:19
their *s* in the tabernacle of the Num 8:22
the *s* of the tabernacle of the Num 8:24
cease waiting upon the *s* thereof Num 8:25
keep the charge, and shall do no *s* Num 8:26
*s* of the tabernacle of the LORD Num 16:9
for all the *s* of the tabernacle Num 18:4
to do the *s* of the tabernacle of Num 18:6
office unto you as a *s* of gift Num 18:7
for their *s* which they serve, Num 18:21
even the *s* of the tabernacle of Num 18:21
do the *s* of the tabernacle of the Num 18:23
your *s* in the tabernacle of the Num 18:31
that we might do the *s* of the Josh 22:27
thou the grievous *s* of thy father 1Kin 12:4
the *s* of song in the house of the 1Chr 6:31
appointed unto all manner of *s* of 1Chr 6:48
work of the *s* of the house of God 1Chr 9:13
were over the work of the *s* 1Chr 9:19
the *s* of the house of the LORD 1Chr 23:24
vessels of it for the *s* thereof 1Chr 23:26
the *s* of the house of the LORD 1Chr 23:28
the work of the *s* of the house of 1Chr 23:28
in the *s* of the house of the LORD 1Chr 23:32
to their offices in their *s* 1Chr 24:3
*s* to come into the house of the 1Chr 24:19
to the *s* of the sons of Asaph 1Chr 25:1
workmen according to their *s* was 1Chr 25:1
for the *s* of the house of God, 1Chr 25:6
able men for strength for the *s* 1Chr 26:8
the LORD, and in the *s* of the king 1Chr 26:30
for all the work of the *s* of the 1Chr 28:13
for all the vessels of *s* in the 1Chr 28:13
instruments of all manner of *s* 1Chr 28:14
instruments of every kind of *s* 1Chr 28:14
the *s* of the house of the LORD 1Chr 28:20
for all the *s* of the house of God 1Chr 28:21
skilful man, for any manner of *s* 1Chr 28:21
his *s* this day unto the LORD 1Chr 29:5
gave for the *s* of the house of 1Chr 29:7
courses of the priests to their *s* 2Chr 8:14
that they may know my *s*, and the 2Chr 12:8
the *s* of the kingdoms of the 2Chr 12:8
of the *s* of the house of the LORD 2Chr 24:12
So the *s* of the house of the LORD 2Chr 29:35
every man according to his *s* 2Chr 31:2
his daily portion for their *s* in 2Chr 31:16
in the *s* of the house of God 2Chr 31:21
the work in any manner of *s* 2Chr 34:13
encouraged them to the *s* of the 2Chr 35:2
So the *s* was prepared, and the 2Chr 35:10
might not depart from their *s* 2Chr 35:15
So all the *s* of the LORD was 2Chr 35:16
their courses, for the *s* of God Ezr 6:18
for the *s* of the house of thy God Ezr 7:19
for the *s* of the Levites, two Ezr 8:20
for the *s* of the house of our God Neh 10:32
cattle, and herb for the *s* of man Ps 104:14
his neighbour's *s* without wages Jer 22:13
to serve a great *s* against Tyrus Eze 29:18
for the *s* that he had served Eze 29:18
the house, for all the *s* thereof Eze 44:14
will think that he doeth God *s* Jn 16:2
the *s* of God, and the promises Rom 9:4
God, which is your reasonable *s* Rom 12:1
that my *s* which I have for Rom 15:31
*s* not only supplieth the want of 2Cor 9:12
taking wages of them, to do you *s* 2Cor 11:8
ye did *s* unto them which by Gal 4:8
With good will doing *s*, as to the Eph 6:7
*s* of your faith, I joy, and Phil 2:17

supply your lack of *s* toward me — Phil 2:30
but rather do them *s*, because — 1Ti 6:2
had also ordinances of divine *s* — Heb 9:1
accomplishing the *s* of God — Heb 9:6
make him that did the *s* perfect — Heb 9:9
know thy works, and charity, and *s* — Rev 2:19

**SERVILE**
ye shall do no *s* work therein — Lev 23:7
ye shall do no *s* work therein — Lev 23:8
ye shall do no *s* work therein — Lev 23:21
Ye shall do no *s* work therein — Lev 23:25
ye shall do no *s* work therein — Lev 23:35
and ye shall do no *s* work therein — Lev 23:36
do no manner of *s* work therein — Num 28:18
ye shall do no *s* work — Num 28:25
ye shall do no *s* work — Num 28:26
ye shall do no *s* work — Num 29:1
ye shall do no *s* work, and ye — Num 29:12
ye shall do no *s* work therein — Num 29:35

**SERVING**
we have let Israel go from *s* us — Ex 14:5
to thee, in *s* thee six years — Deut 15:18
Martha was cumbered about much *s* — Lk 10:40
*S* the Lord with all humility of — Acts 20:19
tribes, instantly *s* God day — Acts 26:7
fervent in spirit; *s* the Lord — Rom 12:11
*s* divers lusts and pleasures, — Titus 3:3

**SERVITOR**
his *s* said, What, should I set — 2Kin 4:43

**SERVITUDE**
the grievous *s* of thy father — 2Chr 10:4
affliction, and because of great *s* — Lam 1:3

**SET** See PREFACE.

**SETH** (*seth*) See SHETH. *A son of Adam and Eve.*
bare a son, and called his name *S* — Gen 4:25
And to *S*, to him also there was — Gen 4:26
and called his name *S* — Gen 5:3
*S* were eight hundred years — Gen 5:4
*S* lived an hundred and five years, — Gen 5:6
*S* lived after he begat Enos eight — Gen 5:7
all the days of *S* were nine — Gen 5:8
of Enos, which was the son of *S* — Lk 3:38

**SETHUR** (*se'-thur*) *A spy sent to the Promised Land.*
of Asher, *S* the son of Michael — Num 13:13

**SETTER**
He seemeth to be a *s* forth of — Acts 17:18

**SETTEST**
thou *s* thine hand to in the land — Deut 23:20
all that thou *s* thine hand unto — Deut 28:8
in all that thou *s* thine hand — Deut 28:20
that thou *s* a watch over me — Job 7:12
thou *s* a print upon the heels of — Job 13:27
thou *s* a crown of pure gold on — Ps 21:3
*s* me before thy face for ever — Ps 41:12

**SETTETH**
And when the tabernacle *s* forward — Num 1:51
And when the camp *s* forward — Num 4:5
is poor, and *s* his heart upon it — Deut 24:15
Cursed be he that *s* light by his — Deut 27:16
and *s* me upon my high places — 2Sa 22:34
He *s* an end to darkness, and — Job 28:3
feet, and *s* me upon my high places — Ps 18:33
he *s* himself in a way that is not — Ps 36:4
his strength *s* fast the mountains — Ps 65:6
God *s* the solitary in families — Ps 68:6
putteth down one, and *s* up another — Ps 75:7
as the flame *s* the mountains on — Ps 83:14
Yet *s* he the poor on high from — Ps 107:41
lay wait, as he that *s* snares — Jer 5:26
of Neriah *s* thee on against us — Jer 43:3
that *s* up his idols in his heart — Eze 14:4
*s* up his idols in his heart, and — Eze 14:7
he removeth kings, and *s* up kings — Dan 2:21
*s* up over it the basest of men — Dan 4:17
*s* him on a pinnacle of the temple — Mt 4:5
but *s* it on a candlestick, that — Lk 8:16
*s* on fire the course of nature — Jas 3:6

**SETTING**
In their *s* of their threshold by — Eze 43:8
sealing the stone, and *s* a watch — Mt 27:66
Now when the sun was *s*, all they — Lk 4:40

**SETTINGS**
thou shalt set in it *s* of stones — Ex 28:17

**SETTLE**
But I will *s* him in mine house and — 1Chr 17:14
I will *s* you after your old — Eze 36:11
the lower *s* shall be two cubits — Eze 43:14
from the lesser *s* even to the — Eze 43:14
greater *s* shall be four cubits — Eze 43:14
the *s* shall be fourteen cubits — Eze 43:17
and on the four corners of the *s* — Eze 43:20
corners of the *s* of the altar — Eze 45:19
*S* it therefore in your hearts, — Lk 21:14
stablish, strengthen, *s* you — 1Pet 5:10

**SETTLED**
a *s* place for thee to abide in — 1Kin 8:13
he *s* his countenance stedfastly, — 2Kin 8:11
O LORD, thy word is *s* in heaven — Ps 119:89
Before the mountains were *s* — Prov 8:25
he hath *s* on his lees, and hath — Jer 48:11
the men that are *s* on their lees — Zeph 1:12
in the faith grounded and *s* — Col 1:23

**SETTLEST**
thou *s* the furrows thereof — Ps 65:10

**SEVEN**
*s* years, and begat sons and — Gen 5:7
and *s* years, and begat Lamech — Gen 5:25
he begat Lamech *s* hundred eighty — Gen 5:26
*s* hundred seventy and *s* years — Gen 5:31
For yet *s* days, and I will cause — Gen 7:4
And it came to pass after *s* days — Gen 7:10
And he stayed yet other *s* days — Gen 8:10
And he stayed yet other *s* days — Gen 8:12
And in the second month, on the *s* — Gen 8:14
*s* years, and begat sons and — Gen 11:21
Abraham set *s* ewe lambs of the — Gen 21:28
What mean these *s* ewe lambs which — Gen 21:29
For these *s* ewe lambs shalt thou — Gen 21:30
And Sarah was an hundred and *s* — Gen 23:1
an hundred and thirty and *s* years — Gen 25:17
I will serve thee *s* years for — Gen 29:18
Jacob served *s* years for Rachel — Gen 29:20
serve with me yet *s* other years — Gen 29:27
served with him yet *s* other years — Gen 29:30
pursued after him *s* days' journey — Gen 31:23
himself to the ground *s* times — Gen 33:3
of the river *s* well favoured kine — Gen 41:2
*s* other kine came up after them — Gen 41:3
did eat up the *s* well favoured — Gen 41:4
*s* ears of corn came up upon one — Gen 41:5
*s* thin ears and blasted with the — Gen 41:6
the *s* thin ears devoured the — Gen 41:7
thin ears devoured the *s* rank — Gen 41:7
came up out of the river *s* kine — Gen 41:18
*s* other kine came up after them, — Gen 41:19
did eat up the first *s* fat kine — Gen 41:20
*s* ears came up in one stalk, full — Gen 41:22
*s* ears, withered, thin, and — Gen 41:23
ears devoured the *s* good ears — Gen 41:24
The *s* good kine are *s* years — Gen 41:26
the *s* good ears are *s* years — Gen 41:26
the *s* thin and ill favoured kine — Gen 41:27
came up after them are *s* years — Gen 41:27
the *s* empty ears blasted with the — Gen 41:27
wind shall be *s* years of famine — Gen 41:27
there come *s* years of great — Gen 41:29
after them *s* years of famine — Gen 41:30
of Egypt in the *s* plenteous years — Gen 41:34
against the *s* years of famine — Gen 41:36
in the *s* plenteous years the — Gen 41:47
up all the food of the *s* years — Gen 41:48
the *s* years of plenteousness, — Gen 41:53
the *s* years of dearth began to — Gen 41:54
all the souls were *s* — Gen 46:25
was an hundred forty and *s* years — Gen 47:28
a mourning for his father *s* days — Gen 50:10
priest of Midian had *s* daughters — Ex 2:16
were an hundred thirty and *s* years — Ex 6:16
an hundred and thirty and *s* years — Ex 6:20
*s* days were fulfilled, after that — Ex 7:25
*S* days shall ye eat unleavened — Ex 12:15
*S* days shall there be no leaven — Ex 12:19
*S* days thou shalt eat unleavened — Ex 13:6
bread shall be eaten *s* days — Ex 13:7
*s* days it shall be with his dam — Ex 22:30
shalt eat unleavened bread *s* days — Ex 23:15
shalt make the *s* lamps thereof — Ex 25:37
stead shall put them on *s* days — Ex 29:30
*s* days shalt thou consecrate them — Ex 29:35
*S* days thou shalt make an — Ex 29:37
*S* days thou shalt eat unleavened — Ex 34:18
And he made his *s* lamps, and his — Ex 37:23
*s* hundred and thirty shekels, — Ex 38:24
talents, and a thousand *s* hundred — Ex 38:25
of the thousand *s* hundred seventy — Ex 38:28
the blood *s* times before the LORD — Lev 4:6
sprinkle it *s* times before the — Lev 4:17
thereof upon the altar *s* times — Lev 8:11
of the congregation in *s* days — Lev 8:33
for *s* days shall he consecrate — Lev 8:33
congregation day and night *s* days — Lev 8:35
then she shall be unclean *s* days — Lev 12:2
him that hath the plague *s* days — Lev 13:4
shall shut him up *s* days more — Lev 13:5
priest shall shut him up *s* days — Lev 13:21
priest shall shut him up *s* days — Lev 13:26
the plague of the scall *s* days — Lev 13:31
that hath the scall *s* days more — Lev 13:33
up it that hath the plague *s* days — Lev 13:50
he shall shut it up *s* days more — Lev 13:54
cleansed from the leprosy *s* times — Lev 14:7
abroad out of his tent *s* days — Lev 14:8
finger *s* times before the LORD — Lev 14:16
left hand *s* times before the LORD — Lev 14:27
and shut up the house *s* days — Lev 14:38
and sprinkle the house *s* times — Lev 14:51
himself *s* days for his cleansing — Lev 15:13
she shall be put apart *s* days — Lev 15:19
him, he shall be unclean *s* days — Lev 15:24
shall number to herself *s* days — Lev 15:28
the blood with his finger *s* times — Lev 16:14
upon it with his finger *s* times — Lev 16:19
then it shall be *s* days under the — Lev 22:27
*s* days ye must eat unleavened — Lev 23:6
made by fire unto the LORD *s* days — Lev 23:8
*s* sabbaths shall be complete — Lev 23:15
*s* lambs without blemish of the — Lev 23:18
for *s* days unto the LORD — Lev 23:34
*S* days ye shall offer an offering — Lev 23:36
keep a feast unto the LORD *s* days — Lev 23:39
before the LORD your God *s* days — Lev 23:40
unto the LORD *s* days in the year — Lev 23:41
Ye shall dwell in booths *s* days — Lev 23:42
thou shalt number *s* sabbaths of — Lev 25:8
unto thee, *s* times *s* years — Lev 25:8
the space of the *s* sabbaths of — Lev 25:8
then I will punish you *s* times — Lev 26:18
I will bring *s* times more plagues — Lev 26:21
you yet *s* times for your sins — Lev 26:24
will chastise you *s* times for — Lev 26:28
*s* thousand and four hundred — Num 1:31
and two thousand and *s* hundred — Num 1:39
*s* thousand and four hundred — Num 2:8
and two thousand and *s* hundred — Num 2:26
*s* thousand and six hundred — Num 2:31
numbered of them were *s* thousand — Num 3:22
were two thousand *s* hundred — Num 4:36
the *s* lamps shall give light over — Num 8:2
should she not be ashamed *s* days — Num 12:14
be shut out from the camp *s* days — Num 12:14
was shut out from the camp *s* days — Num 12:15
(Now Hebron was built *s* years — Num 13:22
*s* hundred, beside them that died — Num 16:49
of the congregation *s* times — Num 19:4
any man shall be unclean *s* days — Num 19:11
the tent, shall be unclean *s* days — Num 19:14
a grave, shall be unclean *s* days — Num 19:16
Balak, Build me here *s* altars — Num 23:1
me here *s* oxen and *s* rams — Num 23:1
him, I have prepared *s* altars — Num 23:4
built *s* altars, and offered a — Num 23:14
Balak, Build me here *s* altars — Num 23:29
me here *s* bullocks and *s* rams — Num 23:29
thousand and *s* hundred and thirty — Num 26:7
and two thousand and *s* hundred — Num 26:34
thousand and a thousand *s* hundred. — Num 26:51
*s* lambs of the first year without — Num 28:11
*s* days shall unleavened bread be — Num 28:17
*s* lambs of the first year — Num 28:19
lamb, throughout the *s* lambs — Num 28:21
daily, throughout the *s* days — Num 28:24
*s* lambs of the first year — Num 28:27
one lamb, throughout the *s* lambs — Num 28:29
*s* lambs of the first year without — Num 29:2
one lamb, throughout the *s* lambs — Num 29:4
*s* lambs of the first year — Num 29:8
one lamb, throughout the *s* lambs — Num 29:10
keep a feast unto the LORD *s* days — Num 29:12
And on the seventh day *s* bullocks — Num 29:32
*s* lambs of the first year without — Num 29:36
ye abide without the camp *s* days — Num 31:19
three hundred thousand and *s* — Num 31:36
*s* thousand and five hundred sheep, — Num 31:43
was sixteen thousand *s* hundred — Num 31:52
*s* nations greater and mightier — Deut 7:1
At the end of every *s* years thou — Deut 15:1
*s* days shalt thou eat unleavened — Deut 16:3
with thee in all thy coast *s* days — Deut 16:4
*S* weeks shalt thou number unto — Deut 16:9
begin to number the *s* weeks from — Deut 16:9
the feast of tabernacles *s* days — Deut 16:13
*S* days shalt thou keep a solemn — Deut 16:15
way, and flee before thee *s* ways — Deut 28:7
them, and flee *s* ways before them — Deut 28:25
At the end of every *s* years — Deut 31:10
*s* priests shall bear before the — Josh 6:4
the ark *s* trumpets of rams' horns — Josh 6:4
ye shall compass the city *s* times — Josh 6:4
let *s* priests bear *s* trumpets — Josh 6:6
the *s* priests bearing the *s* — Josh 6:8
*s* priests bearing *s* trumpets — Josh 6:13
after the same manner *s* times — Josh 6:15
they compassed the city *s* times — Josh 6:15
the children of Israel *s* tribes — Josh 18:2
they shall divide it into *s* parts — Josh 18:5
describe the land into *s* parts — Josh 18:6
by cities into *s* parts in a book — Josh 18:9
into the hand of Midian *s* years — Judg 6:1
the second bullock of *s* years old — Judg 6:25
*s* hundred shekels of gold — Judg 8:26
And he judged Israel *s* years — Judg 12:9
me within the *s* days of the feast — Judg 14:12
And she wept before him the *s* days. — Judg 14:17
If they bind me with *s* green — Judg 16:7
Philistines brought up to her *s* — Judg 16:8
If thou weavest the *s* locks of my — Judg 16:13
shave off the *s* locks of his head — Judg 16:19
numbered *s* hundred chosen men — Judg 20:15
all this people there were *s* — Judg 20:16
is better to thee than *s* sons — Ruth 4:15
so that the barren hath born *s* — 1Sa 2:5
of the Philistines *s* months — 1Sa 6:1
*s* days shalt thou tarry, till I — 1Sa 10:8
Give us *s* days' respite, that we — 1Sa 11:3
And he tarried *s* days, according — 1Sa 13:8
Jesse made *s* of his sons to pass — 1Sa 16:10
tree at Jabesh, and fasted *s* days — 1Sa 31:13
the house of Judah was *s* years — 2Sa 2:11
he reigned over Judah *s* years — 2Sa 5:5
*s* hundred horsemen, and twenty — 2Sa 8:4
David slew the men of *s* hundred — 2Sa 10:18
Let *s* men of his sons be — 2Sa 21:6
and they fell all *s* together — 2Sa 21:9
thirty and *s* in all — 2Sa 23:39
Shall *s* years of famine come unto — 2Sa 24:13
*s* years reigned he in Hebron, and — 1Kin 2:11
and the third was *s* cubits broad — 1Kin 6:6
So was he *s* years in building it — 1Kin 6:38
*s* for the one chapiter — 1Kin 7:17
and *s* for the other chapiter — 1Kin 7:17

S

*s* days and *s* days, even ........ 1Kin 8:65
And he had *s* hundred wives, ........ 1Kin 11:3
did Zimri reign *s* days in Tirzah ........ 1Kin 16:15
And he said, Go again *s* times ........ 1Kin 18:43
have left me *s* thousand in Israel ........ 1Kin 19:18
of Israel, being *s* thousand ........ 1Kin 20:15
one over against the other *s* days ........ 1Kin 20:29
*s* thousand of the men that were ........ 1Kin 20:30
a compass of *s* days' journey ........ 2Kin 3:9
he took with him *s* hundred men ........ 2Kin 3:26
and the child sneezed *s* times ........ 2Kin 4:35
Go and wash in Jordan *s* times ........ 2Kin 5:10
dipped himself *s* times in Jordan, ........ 2Kin 5:14
also come upon the land *s* years ........ 2Kin 8:1
land of the Philistines *s* years ........ 2Kin 8:2
came to pass at the *s* years' end ........ 2Kin 8:3
*S* years old was Jehoash when he ........ 2Kin 11:21
even *s* thousand, and craftsmen and . 2Kin 24:16
And it came to pass in the *s* ........ 2Kin 25:27
in the twelfth month, on the *s* ........ 2Kin 25:27
and there he reigned *s* years ........ 1Chr 3:4
Johanan, and Dalaiah, and Anani, *s* .... 1Chr 3:24
and Jachan, and Zia, and Heber, *s* ........ 1Chr 5:13
four and forty thousand *s* hundred ........ 1Chr 5:18
fourscore and *s* thousand ........ 1Chr 7:5
and *s* hundred and threescore ........ 1Chr 9:13
were to come after *s* days from ........ 1Chr 9:25
oak in Jabesh, and fasted *s* days ........ 1Chr 10:12
*s* thousand and one hundred ........ 1Chr 12:25
were three thousand and *s* hundred.. 1Chr 12:27
and spear thirty and *s* thousand ........ 1Chr 12:34
offered *s* bullocks and *s* rams ........ 1Chr 15:26
*s* thousand horsemen, and twenty ........ 1Chr 18:4
David slew of the Syrians *s* ........ 1Chr 19:18
*s* hundred, were officers among ........ 1Chr 26:30
*s* hundred chief fathers, whom ........ 1Chr 26:32
*s* thousand talents of refined ........ 1Chr 29:4
*s* years reigned he in Hebron, and ........ 1Chr 29:27
Solomon kept the feast *s* days ........ 2Chr 7:8
dedication of the altar *s* days ........ 2Chr 7:9
*s* days, and the feast *s* days ........ 2Chr 7:9
*s* rams, the same may be a priest ........ 2Chr 13:9
*s* hundred oxen and *s* thousand ........ 2Chr 15:11
*s* thousand and *s* hundred rams, ........ 2Chr 17:11
*s* thousand and *s* hundred he ........ 2Chr 17:11
Joash was *s* years old when he ........ 2Chr 24:1
*s* thousand and five hundred, that ........ 2Chr 26:13
And they brought *s* bullocks ........ 2Chr 29:21
*s* rams, and *s* lambs ........ 2Chr 29:21
*s* he goats, for a sin offering ........ 2Chr 29:21
bread *s* days with great gladness ........ 2Chr 30:21
eat throughout the feast *s* days ........ 2Chr 30:22
took counsel to keep other *s* days ........ 2Chr 30:23
they kept other *s* days with ........ 2Chr 30:23
bullocks and *s* thousand sheep ........ 2Chr 30:24
feast of unleavened bread *s* days ........ 2Chr 35:17
*s* hundred seventy and five ........ Ezr 2:5
Zaccai, *s* hundred and threescore ........ Ezr 2:9
*s* hundred and forty and three ........ Ezr 2:25
and Ono, *s* hundred twenty and five ........ Ezr 2:33
a thousand two hundred forty and *s* ........ Ezr 2:38
of whom there were *s* thousand ........ Ezr 2:65
three hundred thirty and *s* ........ Ezr 2:65
horses were *s* hundred thirty ........ Ezr 2:66
asses, six thousand *s* hundred ........ Ezr 2:67
unleavened bread *s* days with joy ........ Ezr 6:22
of his *s* counsellors, to enquire ........ Ezr 7:14
*s* lambs, twelve he goats for a ........ Ezr 8:35
Zaccai, *s* hundred and threescore ........ Neh 7:14
six hundred threescore and *s* ........ Neh 7:18
two thousand threescore and *s* ........ Neh 7:19
Beeroth, *s* hundred forty and three ........ Neh 7:29
and Ono, *s* hundred twenty and one ........ Neh 7:37
a thousand two hundred forty and *s* ........ Neh 7:41
of whom there were *s* thousand ........ Neh 7:67
three hundred thirty and *s* ........ Neh 7:67
horses, *s* hundred thirty and six ........ Neh 7:68
six thousand *s* hundred and twenty ........ Neh 7:69
threescore and *s* priests' garments ........ Neh 7:72
And they kept the feast *s* days ........ Neh 8:18
Ethiopia, over an hundred and *s* ........ Est 1:1
*s* days, in the court of the ........ Est 1:5
the *s* chamberlains that served in ........ Est 1:10
the *s* princes of Persia and Media, ........ Est 1:14
*s* maidens, which were meet to be ........ Est 2:9
*s* provinces, unto every province ........ Est 8:9
*s* provinces of the kingdom of ........ Est 9:30
there were born unto him *s* sons ........ Job 1:2
also was *s* thousand sheep ........ Job 1:3
with him upon the ground *s* days ........ Job 2:13
*s* nights, and none spake a word ........ Job 2:13
in *s* there shall no evil touch ........ Job 5:19
take unto you now *s* bullocks ........ Job 42:8
*s* rams, and go to my servant Job, ........ Job 42:8
He had also *s* sons and three ........ Job 42:13
of earth, purified *s* times ........ Ps 12:6
*S* times a day do I praise thee ........ Ps 119:164
*s* are an abomination unto him ........ Prov 6:16
she hath hewn out her *s* pillars ........ Prov 9:1
For a just man falleth *s* times ........ Prov 24:16
*s* men that can render a reason ........ Prov 26:16
for there are *s* abominations in ........ Prov 26:25
Give a portion to *s*, and also to ........ Eccl 11:2
in that day *s* women shall take ........ Is 4:1
shall smite it in the *s* streams ........ Is 11:15
sevenfold, as the light of *s* days ........ Is 30:26
She that hath borne *s* languisheth ........ Jer 15:9
At the end of *s* years let ye go ........ Jer 34:14
*s* men of them that were near the ........ Jer 52:25
of the Jews *s* hundred forty ........ Jer 52:30
And it came to pass in the *s* ........ Jer 52:31
astonished among them *s* days ........ Eze 3:15
came to pass at the end of *s* days ........ Eze 3:16
And it came to pass in the *s* ........ Eze 29:17
shall burn them with fire *s* years ........ Eze 39:9
*s* months shall the house of ........ Eze 39:12
after the end of *s* months shall ........ Eze 39:14
they went up unto it by *s* steps ........ Eze 40:22
there were *s* steps to go up to it ........ Eze 40:26
the breadth of the door, *s* cubits ........ Eze 41:3
*S* days shalt thou prepare every ........ Eze 43:25
*S* days shall they purge the altar ........ Eze 43:26
they shall reckon unto him *s* days ........ Eze 44:26
the passover, a feast of *s* days ........ Eze 45:21
*s* days of the feast he shall ........ Eze 45:23
*s* bullocks and *s* rams without ........ Eze 45:23
*s* rams without blemish daily the ........ Eze 45:23
without blemish daily the *s* days ........ Eze 45:23
like in the feast of the *s* days ........ Eze 45:25
should heat the furnace one *s* ........ Dan 3:19
let *s* times pass over him ........ Dan 4:16
till *s* times pass over him ........ Dan 4:23
*s* times shall pass over thee, ........ Dan 4:25
*s* times shall pass over thee, ........ Dan 4:32
the Prince shall be *s* weeks ........ Dan 9:25
Seek him that maketh the *s* stars ........ Amos 5:8
we raise against him *s* shepherds ........ Mic 5:5
upon one stone shall be *s* eyes ........ Zec 3:9
his *s* lamps thereon ........ Zec 4:2
and *s* pipes to the *s* lamps ........ Zec 4:2
hand of Zerubbabel with those *s* ........ Zec 4:10
taketh with himself *s* other ........ Mt 12:45
And they said, *S*, and a few little ........ Mt 15:34
And he took the *s* loaves and the ........ Mt 15:36
meat that was left *s* baskets full ........ Mt 15:37
Neither the *s* loaves of the four ........ Mt 16:10
till *s* times ........ Mt 18:21
say not unto thee, Until *s* times ........ Mt 18:22
but, Until seventy times *s* ........ Mt 18:22
Now there were with us *s* brethren ........ Mt 22:25
whose wife shall she be of the *s* ........ Mt 22:28
And they said, *S* ........ Mk 8:5
and he took the *s* loaves, and gave ........ Mk 8:6
meat that was left *s* baskets ........ Mk 8:8
when the *s* among four thousand, ........ Mk 8:20
And they said, *S* ........ Mk 8:20
Now there were *s* brethren ........ Mk 12:20
the *s* had her, and left no seed ........ Mk 12:22
for the *s* had her to wife ........ Mk 12:23
out of whom he had cast *s* devils ........ Mk 16:9
*s* years from her virginity ........ Lk 2:36
out of whom went *s* devils ........ Lk 8:2
taketh to him *s* other spirits ........ Lk 11:26
against thee *s* times in a day ........ Lk 17:4
*s* times in a day turn again to ........ Lk 17:4
There were therefore *s* brethren ........ Lk 20:29
and in like manner the *s* also ........ Lk 20:31
for *s* had her to wife ........ Lk 20:33
among you *s* men of honest report ........ Acts 6:3
when he had destroyed *s* nations ........ Acts 13:19
there were *s* sons of one Sceva, a ........ Acts 19:14
where we abode *s* days ........ Acts 20:6
we tarried there *s* days ........ Acts 21:4
which was one of the *s* ........ Acts 21:8
when the *s* days were almost ended.. Acts 21:27
desired to tarry with them *s* days ........ Acts 28:14
reserved to myself *s* thousand men ........ Rom 11:4
they were compassed about *s* days ........ Heb 11:30
John to the *s* churches which are ........ Rev 1:4
from the *s* Spirits which are ........ Rev 1:4
send it unto the *s* churches which ........ Rev 1:11
I saw *s* golden candlesticks ........ Rev 1:12
And in the midst of the *s* ........ Rev 1:13
he had in his right hand *s* stars ........ Rev 1:16
The mystery of the *s* stars which ........ Rev 1:20
the *s* golden candlesticks ........ Rev 1:20
The *s* stars are the angels of the ........ Rev 1:20
are the angels of the *s* churches ........ Rev 1:20
the *s* candlesticks which thou ........ Rev 1:20
thou sawest are the *s* churches ........ Rev 1:20
the *s* stars in his right hand ........ Rev 2:1
of the *s* golden candlesticks ........ Rev 2:1
he that hath the *s* Spirits of God ........ Rev 3:1
Spirits of God, and the *s* stars ........ Rev 3:1
there were *s* lamps of fire ........ Rev 4:5
which are the *s* Spirits of God ........ Rev 4:5
the backside, sealed with *s* seals ........ Rev 5:1
to loose the *s* seals thereof ........ Rev 5:5
it had been slain, having *s* horns ........ Rev 5:6
horns and *s* eyes, which are ........ Rev 5:6
which are the *s* Spirits of God ........ Rev 5:6
I saw the *s* angels which stood ........ Rev 8:2
and to them were given *s* trumpets ........ Rev 8:2
the *s* angels which had the *s* ........ Rev 8:6
*s* thunders uttered their voices ........ Rev 10:3
when the *s* thunders had uttered ........ Rev 10:4
which the *s* thunders uttered ........ Rev 10:4
were slain of men *s* thousand ........ Rev 11:13
great red dragon, having *s* heads ........ Rev 12:3
horns, and *s* crowns upon his heads ........ Rev 12:3
up out of the sea, having *s* heads ........ Rev 13:1
*s* angels having the *s* last ........ Rev 15:1
the *s* angels came out of the ........ Rev 15:6
the temple, having the *s* plagues ........ Rev 15:6
gave unto the *s* angels *s* ........ Rev 15:7
till the *s* plagues of the *s* ........ Rev 15:8
the temple saying to the *s* angels ........ Rev 16:1
there came one of the *s* angels ........ Rev 17:1
angels which had the *s* vials ........ Rev 17:1
of blasphemy, having *s* heads ........ Rev 17:3
her, which hath the *s* heads ........ Rev 17:7
The *s* heads are *s* mountains, ........ Rev 17:9
And there are *s* kings ........ Rev 17:10
he is the eighth, and is of the *s* ........ Rev 17:11
the *s* angels which had the ........ Rev 21:9
*s* vials full of the *s* last ........ Rev 21:9

## SEVENFOLD

vengeance shall be taken on him *s* ........ Gen 4:15
If Cain shall be avenged *s* ........ Gen 4:24
truly Lamech seventy and *s* ........ Gen 4:24
render unto our neighbours *s* into ........ Ps 79:12
he be found, he shall restore *s* ........ Prov 6:31
the light of the sun shall be *s* ........ Is 30:26

## SEVENS

thou shalt take to thee by *s* ........ Gen 7:2
Of fowls also of the air by *s* ........ Gen 7:3

## SEVENTEEN

being *s* years old, was feeding ........ Gen 37:2
in the land of Egypt *s* years ........ Gen 47:28
thereof, even threescore and *s* men ........ Judg 8:14
he reigned *s* years in Jerusalem, ........ 1Kin 14:21
in Samaria, and reigned *s* years ........ 2Kin 13:1
were *s* thousand and two hundred ........ 1Chr 7:11
he reigned *s* years in Jerusalem, ........ 2Chr 12:13
of Harim, a thousand and *s* ........ Ezr 2:39
of Harim, a thousand and *s* ........ Neh 7:42
money, even *s* shekels of silver ........ Jer 32:9

## SEVENTEENTH

the *s* day of the month, the same ........ Gen 7:11
on the *s* day of the month, upon ........ Gen 8:4
over Israel in Samaria the *s* year ........ 1Kin 22:51
In the *s* year of Pekah the son of ........ 2Kin 16:1
The *s* to Hezir, the eighteenth to ........ 1Chr 24:15
The *s* to Joshbekashah, he, his ........ 1Chr 25:24

## SEVENTH

on the *s* day God ended his work ........ Gen 2:2
he rested on the *s* day from all ........ Gen 2:2
And God blessed the *s* day, and ........ Gen 2:3
And the ark rested in the *s* month ........ Gen 8:4
the first day until the *s* day ........ Ex 12:15
in the *s* day there shall be an ........ Ex 12:16
in the *s* day shall be a feast to ........ Ex 13:6
but on the *s* day, which is the ........ Ex 16:26
people on the *s* day for to gather ........ Ex 16:27
go out of his place on the *s* day ........ Ex 16:29
So the people rested on the *s* day ........ Ex 16:30
But the *s* day is the sabbath of ........ Ex 20:10
in them is, and rested the *s* day ........ Ex 20:11
in the *s* he shall go out free for ........ Ex 21:2
But the *s* year thou shalt let it ........ Ex 23:11
on the *s* day thou shalt rest ........ Ex 23:12
the *s* day he called unto Moses ........ Ex 24:16
but in the *s* is the sabbath of ........ Ex 31:15
on the *s* day he rested, and was ........ Ex 31:17
but on the *s* day thou shalt rest ........ Ex 34:21
but on the *s* day there shall be ........ Ex 35:2
shall look on him the *s* day ........ Lev 13:5
shall look on him again the *s* day ........ Lev 13:6
shall look upon him the *s* day ........ Lev 13:27
in the *s* day the priest shall ........ Lev 13:32
in the *s* day the priest shall ........ Lev 13:34
look on the plague on the *s* day ........ Lev 13:51
But it shall be on the *s* day ........ Lev 14:9
priest shall come again the *s* day ........ Lev 14:39
that in the *s* month, on the tenth ........ Lev 16:29
but the *s* day is the sabbath of ........ Lev 23:3
in the *s* day is an holy ........ Lev 23:8
*s* sabbath shall ye number fifty ........ Lev 23:16
of Israel, saying, In the *s* month ........ Lev 23:24
*s* month there shall be a day of ........ Lev 23:27
The fifteenth day of this *s* month ........ Lev 23:34
the fifteenth day of the *s* month ........ Lev 23:39
shall celebrate it in the *s* month ........ Lev 23:41
But in the *s* year shall be a ........ Lev 25:4
on the tenth day of the *s* month ........ Lev 25:9
say, What shall we eat the *s* year ........ Lev 25:20
on the *s* day shall he shave it ........ Num 6:9
On the *s* day Elishama the son of ........ Num 7:48
on the *s* day he shall be clean ........ Num 19:12
then the *s* day he shall not be ........ Num 19:12
on the third day, and on the *s* day ........ Num 19:19
on the *s* day he shall purify ........ Num 19:19
on the *s* day ye shall have an ........ Num 28:25
And in the *s* month, on the first ........ Num 29:1
this *s* month an holy convocation ........ Num 29:7
the *s* month ye shall have an holy ........ Num 29:12
on the *s* day seven bullocks, two ........ Num 29:32
on the third day, and on the *s* day ........ Num 31:19
wash your clothes on the *s* day ........ Num 31:24
But the *s* day is the sabbath of ........ Deut 5:14
The *s* year, the year of release, ........ Deut 15:9
then in the *s* year thou shalt let ........ Deut 15:12
on the *s* day shall be a solemn ........ Deut 16:8
the *s* day ye shall compass the ........ Josh 6:4
And it came to pass on the *s* day ........ Josh 6:15
And it came to pass at the *s* time ........ Josh 6:16
the *s* lot came out for the tribe ........ Josh 19:40
And it came to pass on the *s* day ........ Judg 14:15
and it came to pass on the *s* day ........ Judg 14:17
*s* day before the sun went down ........ Judg 14:18
And it came to pass on the *s* day ........ 2Sa 12:18
Ethanim, which is the *s* month ........ 1Kin 8:2
*s* year of Asa king of Judah, and ........ 1Kin 16:10
*s* year of Asa king of Judah did ........ 1Kin 16:15
And it came to pass at the *s* time ........ 1Kin 18:44
that in the *s* day the battle was ........ 1Kin 20:29
the *s* year Jehoiada sent and ........ 2Kin 11:4

In the *s* year of Jehu Jehoash ............ 2Kin 12:1
*s* year of Joash king of Judah ............ 2Kin 13:10
*s* year of Jeroboam king of Israel ............ 2Kin 15:1
which was the *s* year of Hoshea ............ 2Kin 18:9
on the *s* day of the month, which ............ 2Kin 25:8
it came to pass in the *s* month ............ 2Kin 25:25
Ozem the sixth, David the *s* ............ 1Chr 2:15
Attai the sixth, Eliel the *s* ............ 1Chr 12:11
The *s* to Hakkoz, the eighth to ............ 1Chr 24:10
The *s* to Jesharelah, he, his sons ............ 1Chr 25:14
the sixth, Elioenai the *s* ............ 1Chr 26:3
Ammiel the sixth, Issachar the *s* ............ 1Chr 26:5
The *s* captain for the *s* ............ 1Chr 27:10
feast which was in the *s* month ............ 2Chr 5:3
twentieth day of the *s* month he ............ 2Chr 7:10
And in the *s* year Jehoiada ............ 2Chr 23:1
and finished them in the *s* month ............ 2Chr 31:7
when the *s* month was come, and the ............ Ezr 3:1
From the first day of the *s* month ............ Ezr 3:6
in the *s* year of Artaxerxes the ............ Ezr 7:7
was in the *s* year of the king ............ Ezr 7:8
when the *s* month came, the ............ Neh 7:73
upon the first day of the *s* month ............ Neh 8:2
in the feast of the *s* month ............ Neh 8:14
and that we would leave the *s* year ............ Neh 10:31
On the *s* day, when the heart of ............ Est 1:10
in the *s* year of his reign ............ Est 2:16
died the same year in the *s* month ............ Jer 28:17
it came to pass in the *s* month ............ Jer 41:1
in the *s* year three thousand Jews ............ Jer 52:28
And it came to pass in the *s* year ............ Eze 20:1
in the *s* day of the month, that ............ Eze 30:20
so thou shalt do the *s* day of the ............ Eze 45:20
In the *s* month, in the fifteenth ............ Eze 45:25
In the *s* month, in the one and ............ Hag 2:1
*s* month, even those seventy years ............ Zec 7:5
the fifth, and the fast of the *s* ............ Zec 8:19
also, and the third, unto the *s* ............ Mt 22:26
Yesterday at the *s* hour the fever ............ Jn 4:52
place of the *s* day on this wise ............ Heb 4:4
God did rest the *s* day from all ............ Heb 4:4
the *s* from Adam, prophesied of ............ Jude 14
And when he had opened the *s* seal ............ Rev 8:1
days of the voice of the *s* angel ............ Rev 10:7
And the *s* angel sounded ............ Rev 11:15
the *s* angel poured out his vial ............ Rev 16:17
the *s*, chrysolite ............ Rev 21:20

**SEVENTY**
avenged sevenfold, truly Lamech *s* ............ Gen 4:24
And Cainan lived *s* years, and begat ............ Gen 5:12
of Lamech were seven hundred *s* ............ Gen 5:31
And Terah lived *s* years, and begat ............ Gen 11:26
and Abram was *s* and five years old ............ Gen 12:4
the loins of Jacob were *s* souls ............ Ex 1:5
*s* of the elders of Israel ............ Ex 24:1
*s* of the elders of Israel ............ Ex 24:9
of the thousand seven hundred *s* ............ Ex 38:28
of the offering was *s* talents ............ Ex 38:29
one silver bowl of *s* shekels ............ Num 7:13
one silver bowl of *s* shekels ............ Num 7:19
one silver bowl of *s* shekels ............ Num 7:25
one silver bowl of *s* shekels ............ Num 7:31
one silver bowl of *s* shekels ............ Num 7:37
a silver bowl of *s* shekels ............ Num 7:43
one silver bowl of *s* shekels ............ Num 7:49
one silver bowl of *s* shekels ............ Num 7:55
one silver bowl of *s* shekels ............ Num 7:61
one silver bowl of *s* shekels ............ Num 7:67
one silver bowl of *s* shekels ............ Num 7:73
one silver bowl of *s* shekels ............ Num 7:79
and thirty shekels, each bowl *s* ............ Num 7:85
Gather unto me *s* men of the ............ Num 11:16
gathered the *s* men of the elders ............ Num 11:24
him, and gave it unto the *s* elders ............ Num 11:25
*s* thousand and five thousand sheep ............ Num 31:32
father, in slaying his *s* brethren ............ Judg 9:56
even to Beer-sheba *s* thousand men ............ 2Sa 24:15
Ahab had *s* sons in Samaria ............ 2Kin 10:1
being *s* persons, were with the ............ 2Kin 10:6
slew *s* persons, and put their ............ 2Kin 10:7
fell of Israel *s* thousand men ............ 1Chr 21:14
Parosh, two thousand an hundred *s* ............ Ezr 2:3
of Shephatiah, three hundred *s* ............ Ezr 2:4
children of Arah, seven hundred *s* ............ Ezr 2:5
house of Jeshua, nine hundred *s* ............ Ezr 2:36
of the children of Hodaviah, *s* ............ Ezr 2:40
of Athaliah, and with him *s* males ............ Ezr 8:7
and Zabbud, and with them *s* males ............ Ezr 8:14
all Israel, ninety and six rams, *s* ............ Ezr 8:35
Parosh, two thousand an hundred *s* ............ Neh 7:8
of Shephatiah, three hundred *s* ............ Neh 7:9
house of Jeshua, nine hundred *s* ............ Neh 7:39
and of the children of Hodevah, *s* ............ Neh 7:43
kept the gates, were an hundred *s* ............ Neh 11:19
enemies, and slew of their foes *s* ............ Est 9:16
Tyre shall be forgotten *s* years ............ Is 23:15
after the end of *s* years shall ............ Is 23:15
to pass after the end of *s* years ............ Is 23:17
serve the king of Babylon *s* years ............ Jer 25:11
when *s* years are accomplished ............ Jer 25:12
the LORD, That after *s* years be ............ Jer 29:10
there stood before them *s* men of ............ Eze 8:11
the west was *s* cubits broad ............ Eze 41:12
that he would accomplish *s* years ............ Dan 9:2
*S* weeks are determined upon thy ............ Dan 9:24
seventh month, even those *s* years ............ Zec 7:5
but, Until *s* times seven ............ Mt 18:22
the Lord appointed other *s* also ............ Lk 10:1
the *s* returned again with joy, ............ Lk 10:17

**SEVER**
I will *s* in that day the land of ............ Ex 8:22
the LORD shall *s* between the ............ Ex 9:4
they shall *s* out men of continual ............ Eze 39:14
*s* the wicked from among the just, ............ Mt 13:49

**SEVERAL**
a *s* tenth deal of flour mingled ............ Num 28:13
A *s* tenth deal shalt thou offer ............ Num 28:21
A *s* tenth deal unto one lamb, ............ Num 28:29
A *s* tenth deal for one lamb, ............ Num 29:10
a *s* tenth deal to each lamb of ............ Num 29:15
his death, and dwelt in a *s* house ............ 2Kin 15:5
in every *s* city he put shields and ............ 2Chr 11:12
his death, and dwelt in a *s* house ............ 2Chr 26:21
in every *s* city of Judah he made ............ 2Chr 28:25
of their cities, in every *s* city ............ 2Chr 31:19
man according to his *s* ability ............ Mt 25:15
every *s* gate was of one pearl ............ Rev 21:21

**SEVERALLY**
to every man *s* as he will ............ 1Cor 12:11

**SEVERED**
have *s* you from other people, ............ Lev 20:26
Then Moses *s* three cities on this ............ Deut 4:41
had *s* himself from the Kenites, ............ Judg 4:11

**SEVERITY**
the goodness and *s* of God ............ Rom 11:22
on them which fell, *s* ............ Rom 11:22

**SEW**
A time to rend, and a time to *s* ............ Eccl 3:7
Woe to the women that *s* pillows ............ Eze 13:18

**SEWED**
they *s* fig leaves together, and ............ Gen 3:7
I have *s* sackcloth upon my skin, ............ Job 16:15

**SEWEST**
a bag, and thou *s* up mine iniquity ............ Job 14:17

**SEWETH**
No man also *s* a piece of new ............ Mk 2:21

**SHAALABBIN** (*sha-al-ab'-bin*) See SHAALBIM. *A city in Dan.*
And *S*, and Ajalon, and Jethlah, ............ Josh 19:42

**SHAALBIM** (*sha-al'-bim*) See SHAALABBIN, SHAALBONITE. *Same as Shaalabbin.*
mount Heres in Aijalon, and in *S* ............ Judg 1:35
son of Dekar, and in Makaz, and in *S* ............ 1Kin 4:9

**SHAALBON** See SHAALBONITE.

**SHAALBONITE** (*sha-al'-bo-nite*) *A native of Shaalabbin.*
Eliahba the *S*, of the sons of ............ 2Sa 23:32
the Baharumite, Eliahba the *S* ............ 1Chr 11:33

**SHAALIM** See SHALIM.

**SHAAPH** (*sha'-af*) *A son of Jahdai.*
Gesham, and Pelet, and Ephah, and *S* ............ 1Chr 2:47
*S*he bare also *S* the father of ............ 1Chr 2:49

**SHAARAIM** (*sha-a-ra'-im*) See SHARAIM, SHARUHEN. *A city in Judah.*
fell down by the way to *S* ............ 1Sa 17:52
and at Beth-birei, and at *S* ............ 1Chr 4:31

**SHAASHGAZ** (*sha-ash'-gaz*) *A servant of King Ahasuerus.*
of the women, to the custody of *S* ............ Est 2:14

**SHABBETHAI** (*shab'-be-thahee*)
*1. A Levite who dealt with the foreign wife problem.*
and *S* the Levite helped them ............ Ezr 10:15
*2. A Levite who aided Ezra.*
and Sherebiah, Jamin, Akkub, *S* ............ Neh 8:7
*3. A family of exiles.*
And *S* and Jozabad, of the chief of ............ Neh 11:16

**SHACHIA** (*sha-ki'-ah*) *A son of Shaharaim.*
And Jeuz, and *S*, and Mirma ............ 1Chr 8:10

**SHADE**
the LORD is thy *s* upon thy right ............ Ps 121:5

**SHADOW**
came they under the *s* of my roof ............ Gen 19:8
come and put your trust in my *s* ............ Judg 9:15
Thou seest the *s* of the mountains ............ Judg 9:36
shall the *s* go forward ten ............ 2Kin 20:9
for the *s* to go down ten degrees ............ 2Kin 20:10
but let the *s* return backward ten ............ 2Kin 20:10
he brought the *s* ten degrees ............ 2Kin 20:11
our days on the earth are as a *s* ............ 1Chr 29:15
and the *s* of death stain it ............ Job 3:5
servant earnestly desireth the *s* ............ Job 7:2
our days upon earth are a *s* ............ Job 8:9
of darkness and the *s* of death ............ Job 10:21
of the *s* of death, without any ............ Job 10:22
out to light the *s* of death ............ Job 12:22
he fleeth also as a *s*, and ............ Job 14:2
on my eyelids is the *s* of death ............ Job 16:16
and all my members are as a *s* ............ Job 17:7
is to them even as the *s* of death ............ Job 24:17
in the terrors of the *s* of death ............ Job 24:17
of darkness, and the *s* of death ............ Job 28:3
nor *s* of death, where the workers ............ Job 34:22
seen the doors of the *s* of death ............ Job 38:17
trees cover him with their *s* ............ Job 40:22
hide me under the *s* of thy wings ............ Ps 17:8
the valley of the *s* of death ............ Ps 23:4
trust under the *s* of thy wings ............ Ps 36:7
and covered us with the *s* of death ............ Ps 44:19
in the *s* of thy wings will I make ............ Ps 57:1
therefore in the *s* of thy wings ............ Ps 63:7
were covered with the *s* of it ............ Ps 80:10
abide under the *s* of the Almighty ............ Ps 91:1
days are like a *s* that declineth ............ Ps 102:11
in the *s* of death, being bound in ............ Ps 107:10
the *s* of death, and brake their ............ Ps 107:14
gone like the *s* when it declineth ............ Ps 109:23
days are as a *s* that passeth away ............ Ps 144:4
life which he spendeth as a *s* ............ Eccl 6:12
his days, which are as a *s* ............ Eccl 8:13
under his *s* with great delight ............ Song 2:3
shall be a tabernacle for a *s* in ............ Is 4:6
in the land of the *s* of death ............ Is 9:2
make thy *s* as the night in the ............ Is 16:3
a *s* from the heat, when the blast ............ Is 25:4
the heat with the *s* of a cloud ............ Is 25:5
and to trust in the *s* of Egypt ............ Is 30:2
the trust in the *s* of Egypt your ............ Is 30:3
as the *s* of a great rock in a ............ Is 32:2
and hatch, and gather under her *s* ............ Is 34:15
bring again the *s* of the degrees ............ Is 38:8
in the *s* of his hand hath he hid ............ Is 49:2
thee in the *s* of mine hand ............ Is 51:16
of the *s* of death, through a land ............ Jer 2:6
he turn it into the *s* of death ............ Jer 13:16
They that fled stood under the *s* ............ Jer 48:45
Under his *s* we shall live among ............ Lam 4:20
in the *s* of the branches thereof ............ Eze 17:23
under his *s* dwelt all great ............ Eze 31:6
earth are gone down from his *s* ............ Eze 31:12
that dwelt under his *s* in the ............ Eze 31:17
of the field had *s* under it ............ Dan 4:12
because the *s* thereof is good ............ Hos 4:13
dwell under his *s* shall return ............ Hos 14:7
turneth the *s* of death into the ............ Amos 5:8
a booth, and sat under it in the *s* ............ Jonah 4:5
it might be a *s* over his head ............ Jonah 4:6
*s* of death light is sprung up ............ Mt 4:16
air may lodge under the *s* of it ............ Mk 4:32
in the *s* of death, to guide our ............ Lk 1:79
that at the least the *s* of Peter ............ Acts 5:15
Which are a *s* of things to come ............ Col 2:17
*s* of heavenly things, as Moses ............ Heb 8:5
For the law having a *s* of good ............ Heb 10:1
neither *s* of turning ............ Jas 1:17

**SHADOWING**
Woe to the land *s* with wings ............ Is 18:1
fair branches, and with a *s* shroud ............ Eze 31:3
of glory *s* the mercyseat ............ Heb 9:5

**SHADOWS**
the *s* flee away, turn, my beloved ............ Song 2:17
the *s* flee away, I will get me to ............ Song 4:6
for the *s* of the evening are ............ Jer 6:4

**SHADRACH** (*sha'-drak*) See HANANIAH. *A companion of Daniel.*
and to Hananiah, of *S* ............ Dan 1:7
of the king, and he set *S*, Meshach ............ Dan 2:49
of the province of Babylon, *S* ............ Dan 3:12
rage and fury commanded to bring *S* ............ Dan 3:13
said unto them, Is it true, O *S* ............ Dan 3:14
*S*, Meshach, and Abed-nego, ............ Dan 3:16
his visage was changed against *S* ............ Dan 3:19
that were in his army to bind *S* ............ Dan 3:20
slew those men that took up *S* ............ Dan 3:22
And these three men, *S*, Meshach, ............ Dan 3:23
furnace, and spake, and said, *S* ............ Dan 3:26
Then *S*, Meshach, and Abed-nego, ............ Dan 3:26
and said, Blessed be the God of *S* ............ Dan 3:28
thing amiss against the God of *S* ............ Dan 3:29
Then the king promoted *S*, Meshach ............ Dan 3:30

**SHADY**
He lieth under the *s* trees ............ Job 40:21
The *s* trees cover him with their ............ Job 40:22

**SHAFT**
his *s*, and his branches, his bowls ............ Ex 25:31
his *s*, and his branch, his bowls, ............ Ex 37:17
beaten gold, unto the *s* thereof ............ Num 8:4
hid me, and made me a polished *s* ............ Is 49:2

**SHAGE** (*sha'-ghe*) *A 'mighty man' of David.*
the son of *S* the Hararite ............ 1Chr 11:34

**SHAGEE** See SHAGE.

**SHAGEH** See SHAGE.

**SHAHAR** (*sha'-har*) *A musical notation.*
chief Musician upon Aijeleth *S* ............ Ps 22:t

**SHAHARAIM** (*sha-ha-ra'-im*) *A Benjamite from Moab.*
*S* begat children in the country ............ 1Chr 8:8

**SHAHAZIMAH** (*sha-haz'-i-mah*) *A city in Issachar.*
the coast reacheth to Tabor, and *S* ............ Josh 19:22

**SHAHAZUMAH** See SHAHAZIMAH.

**SHAKE**
other times before, and *s* myself ............ Judg 16:20
So God *s* out every man from his ............ Neh 5:13
which made all my bones to *s* ............ Job 4:14
He shall *s* off his unripe grape ............ Job 15:33
you, and *s* mine head at you ............ Job 16:4
the lip, they *s* the head, saying, ............ Ps 22:7
though the mountains *s* with the ............ Ps 46:3
make their loins continually to *s* ............ Ps 69:23
thereof shall *s* like Lebanon ............ Ps 72:16

ariseth to s terribly the earth ... Is 2:19
ariseth to s terribly the earth ... Is 2:21
as if the rod should s itself ... Is 10:15
he shall s his hand against the ... Is 10:32
he s his hand over the river ... Is 11:15
s the hand, that they may go into ... Is 13:2
Therefore I will s the heavens ... Is 13:13
to tremble, that did s kingdoms ... Is 14:16
the foundations of the earth do s ... Is 24:18
Carmel s off their fruits ... Is 33:9
S thyself from the dust ... Is 52:2
all my bones s ... Jer 23:9
thy walls shall s at the noise of ... Eze 26:10
Shall not the isles s at the ... Eze 26:15
The suburbs shall s at the sound ... Eze 27:28
I made the nations to s at the ... Eze 31:16
shall s at my presence, and the ... Eze 38:20
s off his leaves, and scatter his ... Dan 4:14
the heavens and the earth shall s ... Joel 3:16
of the door, that the posts may s ... Amos 9:1
I will s the heavens, and the ... Hag 2:6
I will s all nations, and the ... Hag 2:7
I will s the heavens and the earth ... Hag 2:21
I will s mine hand upon them, and ... Zec 2:9
s off the dust of your feet ... Mt 10:14
for fear of him the keepers did s ... Mt 28:4
s off the dust under your feet ... Mk 6:11
that house, and could not s it ... Lk 6:48
s off the very dust from your ... Lk 9:5
Yet once more I s not the earth ... Heb 12:26

**SHAKED**
looked upon me they s their heads ... Ps 109:25

**SHAKEN**
the sound of a s leaf shall chase ... Lev 26:36
as a reed is s in the water ... 1Kin 14:15
Jerusalem hath s her head at thee ... 2Kin 19:21
promise, even thus be he s out ... Neh 5:13
s me to pieces, and set me up for ... Job 16:12
the wicked might be s out of it ... Job 38:13
also of the hills moved and were s ... Ps 18:7
Jerusalem hath s her head at thee ... Is 37:22
the fir trees shall be terribly s ... Nah 2:3
if they be s, they shall even ... Nah 3:12
A reed s with the wind ... Mt 11:7
powers of the heavens shall be s ... Mt 24:29
that are in heaven shall be s ... Mk 13:25
s together, and running over, ... Lk 6:38
A reed s with the wind ... Lk 7:24
the powers of heaven shall be s ... Lk 21:26
the place was s where they were ... Acts 4:31
foundations of the prison were s ... Acts 16:26
That ye be not soon s in mind ... 2Th 2:2
of those things that are s ... Heb 12:27
which cannot be s may remain ... Heb 12:27
when she is s of a mighty wind ... Rev 6:13

**SHAKETH**
Which s the earth out of her ... Job 9:6
of the LORD s the wilderness ... Ps 29:8
the LORD s the wilderness of ... Ps 29:8
thereof; for it s ... Ps 60:2
itself against him that s it ... Is 10:15
LORD of hosts, which he s over it ... Is 19:16
that s his hands from holding of ... Is 33:15

**SHAKING**
he laugheth at the s of a spear ... Job 41:29
a s of the head among the people ... Ps 44:14
as the s of an olive tree, two or ... Is 17:6
fear because of the s of the hand ... Is 19:16
be as the s of an olive tree ... Is 24:13
in battles of s will he fight ... Is 30:32
there was a noise, and behold a s ... Eze 37:7
a great s in the land of Israel ... Eze 38:19

**SHALEM** (sha'-lem) *A city in Ephraim.*
And Jacob came to S, a city of ... Gen 33:18

**SHALIM** (sha'-lim) *A district in Dan.*
they passed through the land of S ... 1Sa 9:4

**SHALISHA** (shal'-i-shah) *A district in Ephraim.*
and passed through the land of S ... 1Sa 9:4

**SHALISHAH** See SHALISHA.

**SHALL** See PREFACE.

**SHALLECHETH** (shal'-le-keth) *A gate of the First Temple.*
forth westward, with the gate S ... 1Chr 26:16

**SHALLIM** See SHALIM.

**SHALLUM** (shal'-lum) See JEHOAHAZ, MESHELEMIAH, SHILLEM.
*1. A king of Israel.*
S the son of Jabesh conspired ... 2Kin 15:10
S the son of Jabesh began to ... 2Kin 15:13
smote S the son of Jabesh in ... 2Kin 15:14
And the rest of the acts of S ... 2Kin 15:15
*2. Husband of Huldah.*
the wife of S the son of Tikvah, ... 2Kin 22:14
the wife of S the son of Tikvath, ... 2Chr 34:22
*3. A descendant of Jerahmeel.*
begat Sisamai, and Sisamai begat S ... 1Chr 2:40
S begat Jekamiah, and Jekamiah ... 1Chr 2:41
*4. A son of King Josiah.*
the third Zedekiah, the fourth S ... 1Chr 3:15
thus saith the LORD touching S ... Jer 22:11
*5. Grandson of Simeon.*
S his son, Mibsam his son, Mishma ... 1Chr 4:25
*6. Father of Hilkiah.*
begat Zadok, and Zadok begat S ... 1Chr 6:12
S begat Hilkiah, and Hilkiah begat ... 1Chr 6:13
The son of S, the son of Zadok, ... Ezr 7:2
*7. Son of Naphtali.*
Jahziel, and Guni, and Jezer, and S ... 1Chr 7:13
*8. A family of exiles.*
And the porters were, S, and Akkub, ... 1Chr 9:17
S was the chief ... 1Chr 9:17
S the son of Kore, the son of ... 1Chr 9:19
the firstborn of S the Korahite ... 1Chr 9:31
the children of S, the children ... Ezr 2:42
the children of S, the children ... Neh 7:45
*9. Father of Jehizkiah.*
and Jehizkiah the son of S ... 2Chr 28:12
*10. A gatekeeper who married a foreigner.*
S, and Telem, and Uri ... Ezr 10:24
*11. A son of Bani who married a foreigner.*
S, Amariah, and Joseph ... Ezr 10:42
*12. A rebuilder of Jerusalem's wall.*
repaired S the son of Halohesh ... Neh 3:12
*13. Father of Hanameel.*
Hanameel the son of S thine uncle ... Jer 32:7
*14. Father of Maaseiah.*
chamber of Maaseiah the son of S ... Jer 35:4

**SHALLUN** (shal'-lun) *A rebuilder of Jerusalem's wall.*
repaired S the son of Colhozeh ... Neh 3:15

**SHALMAI** (shal'-mahee) *A family of exiles.*
of Hagab, the children of S ... Ezr 2:46
of Hagaba, the children of S ... Neh 7:48

**SHALMAN** (shal'-man) See SHALMANESER. *A king of Assyria.*
as S spoiled Beth-arbel in the ... Hos 10:14

**SHALMANESER** (shal-man-e'-zer) See SHALMAN. *A king of Assyria.*
him came up S king of Assyria ... 2Kin 17:3
that S king of Assyria came up ... 2Kin 18:9

**SHALT** See PREFACE.

**SHAMA** (sha'-mah) *A "mighty man" of David.*
Uzzia the Ashterathite, S ... 1Chr 11:44

**SHAMARIAH** *Son of Rehoboam.*
Jeush, and S, and Zaham ... 2Chr 11:19

**SHAMBLES**
Whatsoever is sold in the s ... 1Cor 10:25

**SHAME**
unto their s among their enemies ... Ex 32:25
might put them to s in any thing ... Judg 18:7
because his father had done him s ... 1Sa 20:34
whither shall I cause my s to go ... 2Sa 13:13
So he returned with s of face to ... 2Chr 32:21
hate thee shall be clothed with s ... Job 8:22
long will ye turn my glory into s ... Ps 4:2
put to s that seek after my soul ... Ps 35:4
let them be clothed with s ... Ps 35:26
put to s that wish me evil ... Ps 40:14
of their s that say unto me ... Ps 40:15
hast put them to s that hated us ... Ps 44:7
hast cast off, and put us to s ... Ps 44:9
the s of my face hath covered me, ... Ps 44:15
thou hast put them to s, because ... Ps 53:5
s hath covered my face ... Ps 69:7
hast known my reproach, and my s ... Ps 69:19
for a reward of their s that say ... Ps 70:3
for they are brought unto s ... Ps 71:24
Fill their faces with s ... Ps 83:16
yea, let them be put to s ... Ps 83:17
thou hast covered him with s ... Ps 89:45
adversaries be clothed with s ... Ps 109:29
O LORD, put me not to s ... Ps 119:31
His enemies will I clothe with s ... Ps 132:18
but s shall be the promotion of ... Prov 3:35
a scorner getteth to himself s ... Prov 9:7
harvest is a son that causeth s ... Prov 10:5
When pride cometh, then cometh s ... Prov 11:2
but a prudent man covereth s ... Prov 12:16
man is loathsome, and cometh to s ... Prov 13:5
s shall be to him that refuseth ... Prov 13:18
is against him that causeth s ... Prov 14:35
rule over a son that causeth s ... Prov 17:2
it, it is folly and s unto him ... Prov 18:13
mother, is a son that causeth s ... Prov 19:26
thy neighbour hath put thee to s ... Prov 25:8
he that heareth it put thee to s ... Prov 25:10
himself bringeth his mother to s ... Prov 29:15
uncovered, to the s of Egypt ... Is 20:4
be the s of thy lord's house ... Is 22:18
the strength of Pharaoh be your s ... Is 30:3
be an help nor profit, but a s ... Is 30:5
yea, thy s shall be seen ... Is 47:3
I hid not my face from s and ... Is 50:6
for thou shalt not be put to s ... Is 54:4
shalt forget the s of thy youth ... Is 54:4
For your s ye shall have double ... Is 61:7
For s hath devoured the labour of ... Jer 3:24
We lie down in our s, and our ... Jer 3:25
thy face, that thy s may appear ... Jer 13:26
my days should be consumed with s ... Jer 20:18
upon you, and a perpetual s ... Jer 23:40
The nations have heard of thy s ... Jer 46:12
hath Moab turned the back with s ... Jer 48:39
s hath covered our faces ... Jer 51:51
s shall be upon all faces, and ... Eze 7:18
bear thine own s for thy sins ... Eze 16:52
confounded also, and bear thy s ... Eze 16:52
That thou mayest bear thine own s ... Eze 16:54
mouth any more because of thy s ... Eze 16:63
yet have they borne their s with ... Eze 32:24
yet have they borne their s with ... Eze 32:25
bear their s with them that go ... Eze 32:30
neither bear the s of the heathen ... Eze 34:29
have borne the s of the heathen ... Eze 36:6
you, they shall bear their s ... Eze 36:7
the s of the heathen any more ... Eze 36:15
that they have borne their s ... Eze 39:26
but they shall bear their s ... Eze 44:13
to everlasting life, and some to s ... Dan 12:2
will I change their glory into s ... Hos 4:7
her rulers with s do love ... Hos 4:18
separated themselves unto that s ... Hos 9:10
Ephraim shall receive s, and ... Hos 10:6
brother Jacob s shall cover thee ... Obad 10
of Saphir, having thy s naked ... Mic 1:11
them, that they shall not take s ... Mic 2:6
s shall cover her which said unto ... Mic 7:10
nakedness, and the kingdoms thy s ... Nah 3:5
Thou hast consulted s to thy ... Hab 2:10
Thou art filled with s for glory ... Hab 2:16
but the unjust knoweth no s ... Zeph 3:5
where they have been put to s ... Zeph 3:19
thou begin with s to take the ... Lk 14:9
worthy to suffer s for his name ... Acts 5:41
I write not these things to s you ... 1Cor 4:14
I speak to your s ... 1Cor 6:5
but if it be a s for a woman to ... 1Cor 11:6
long hair, it is a s unto him ... 1Cor 11:14
of God, and s them that have not ... 1Cor 11:22
for it is a s for women to speak ... 1Cor 14:35
I speak this to your s ... 1Cor 15:34
For it is a s even to speak of ... Eph 5:12
and whose glory is in their s ... Phil 3:19
afresh, and put him to an open s ... Heb 6:6
the cross, despising the s ... Heb 12:2
the sea, foaming out their own s ... Jude 13
that the s of thy nakedness do ... Rev 3:18
he walk naked, and they see his s ... Rev 16:15

**SHAMED** (sha'-med) *A son of Elpaal.*
her take it to her, lest we be s ... Gen 38:23
said Thou hast s this day the ... 2Sa 19:5
Eber, and Misham, and S, who built ... 1Chr 8:12
Ye have s the counsel of the poor ... Ps 14:6

**SHAMEFACEDNESS**
in modest apparel, with s ... 1Ti 2:9

**SHAMEFUL**
ye set up altars to that s thing ... Jer 11:13
s spewing shall be on thy glory ... Hab 2:16

**SHAMEFULLY**
that conceived them hath done s ... Hos 2:5
head, and sent him away s handled ... Mk 12:4
beat him also, and entreated him s ... Lk 20:11
were s entreated, as ye know, at ... 1Th 2:2

**SHAMELESSLY**
vain fellows s uncovereth himself ... 2Sa 6:20

**SHAMER** (sha'-mur) See SHOMER.
*1. Son of Mahli.*
the son of Bani, the son of S ... 1Chr 6:46
*2. Son of Heber.*
And the sons of S ... 1Chr 7:34

**SHAMETH**
of riotous men s his father ... Prov 28:7

**SHAMGAR** (sham'-gar) *A judge of Israel.*
after him was S the son of Anath, ... Judg 3:31
In the days of S the son of Anath ... Judg 5:6

**SHAMHUTH** (sham'-huth) See SHAMMOTH. *A captain in David's army.*
fifth month was S the Izrahite ... 1Chr 27:8

**SHAMIR** (sha'-mur)
*1. A city in Judah.*
And in the mountains, S, and Jattir ... Josh 15:48
*2. A city near Mt. Ephraim.*
he dwelt in S in mount Ephraim ... Judg 10:1
and died, and was buried in S ... Judg 10:2
*3. Son of Micah the Levite.*
the sons of Michah; S ... 1Chr 24:24

**SHAMLAI** See SAMLAH.

**SHAMMA** (sham'-mah) See SHAMMAH. *A son of Zophah.*
Bezer, and Hod, and S, and Shilshah, ... 1Chr 7:37

**SHAMMAH** (sham'-mah) See SHAMMA, SHAMMOTH, SHIMEA, SHIMMA.
*1. A son of Reuel.*
Nahath, and Zerah, S, and Mizzah ... Gen 36:13
duke Nahath, duke Zerah, duke S ... Gen 36:17
Nahath, Zerah, S, and Mizzah ... 1Chr 1:37
*2. A son of Jesse.*
Then Jesse made S to pass by ... 1Sa 16:9
unto him Abinadab, and the third S ... 1Sa 17:13
*3. A "mighty man" of David.*
after him was S the son of Agee ... 2Sa 23:11
*4. A Hararite "mighty man" of David.*
S the Hararite, Ahiam the son of ... 2Sa 23:33
*5. A Harodite "mighty man" of David.*
S the Harodite, Elika the ... 2Sa 23:25

**SHAMMAI** (sham'-mahee)
*1. A son of Onan.*
And the sons of Onam were, S ... 1Chr 2:28
And the sons of S ... 1Chr 2:28
the sons of Jada the brother of S ... 1Chr 2:32
*2. Father of Maon.*
and Rekem begat S ... 1Chr 2:44

And the son of *S* was Maon .................. 1Chr 2:45
*3. A descendant of Caleb.*
and she bare Miriam, and *S*, and.......... 1Chr 4:17

**SHAMMOTH** (*sham'-moth*) See SHAMMAH, SHAMHUTH. *A "mighty man" of David.*
*S* the Harorite, Helez the .................... 1Chr 11:27

**SHAMMUA** (*sham-mu'-ah*) See SHAMMUAH, SHEMAIH, SHIMEA.
*1. A spy sent to the Promised Land.*
of Reuben, *S* the son of Zaccur........... Num 13:4
*2. A son of David.*
*S*, and Shobab, Nathan, and Solomon, 1Chr 14:4
*3. A family of exiles.*
brethren, and Abda the son of *S*......... Neh 11:17
*4. A priest with Zerubbabel.*
Of Bilgah, *S*.......................................... Neh 12:18

**SHAMMUAH** (*sham-mu'-ah*) See SHAMMUA. *Same as Shammua 2.*
*S*, and Shobab, and Nathan, and ............ 2Sa 5:14

**SHAMSHERAI** (*sham'-she-rahee*) *A son of Jeroham.*
And *S*, and Sheheriah, and Athaliah,.. 1Chr 8:26

**SHAPE**
a bodily *s* like a dove upon him............... Lk 3:22
voice at any time, nor seen his *s* ............ Jn 5:37

**SHAPEN**
Behold, I was *s* in iniquity........................ Ps 51:5

**SHAPES**
the *s* of the locusts were like.................. Rev 9:7

**SHAPHAM** (*sha'-fam*) *A Gadite chief.*
*S* the next, and Jaanai, and Shaphat... 1Chr 5:12

**SHAPHAN** (*sha'-fan*)
*1. A scribe in Josiah's time.*
king sent *S* the son of Azaliah............ 2Kin 22:3
priest said unto *S* the scribe ................ 2Kin 22:8
And Hilkiah gave the book to *S*.......... 2Kin 22:8
*S* the scribe came to the king, and ....... 2Kin 22:9
*S* the scribe shewed the king, ............ 2Kin 22:10
*S* read it before the king..................... 2Kin 22:10
*S* the scribe, and Asahiah a ................ 2Kin 22:12
and Ahikam, and Achbor, and *S* .......... 2Kin 22:14
he sent *S* the son of Azaliah, and ....... 2Chr 34:8
said to *S* the scribe, I have.................. 2Chr 34:15
Hilkiah delivered the book to *S*............ 2Chr 34:15
*S* carried the book to the king,............ 2Chr 34:16
Then *S* the scribe told the king,.......... 2Chr 34:18
*S* read it before the king .................... 2Chr 34:18
*S* the scribe, and Asaiah a servant..... 2Chr 34:20
Gemariah the son of *S* the scribe......... Jer 36:10
the son of Gemariah, the son of *S*......... Jer 36:11
Achbor, and Gemariah the son of *S* ..... Jer 36:12
*2. Father of Ahikam.*
priest, and Ahikam the son of *S*......... 2Kin 22:12
the son of Ahikam, the son of *S*......... 2Kin 25:22
Hilkiah, and Ahikam the son of *S*...... 2Chr 34:20
the son of *S* was with Jeremiah........... Jer 26:24
the son of Ahikam the son of *S*............ Jer 39:14
the son of Ahikam the son of *S*............ Jer 40:5
the son of *S* sware unto them............... Jer 40:9
the son of Ahikam the son of *S*............ Jer 40:11
the son of *S* with the sword .................. Jer 41:2
the son of Ahikam the son of *S*............ Jer 43:6
*3. Messenger for Jeremiah.*
the hand of Elasah the son of *S*............. Jer 29:3
*4. Father of Jaazaniah.*
them stood Jaazaniah the son of *S*........ Eze 8:11

**SHAPHAT** (*sha'-fat*)
*1. A spy sent to the Promised Land.*
of Simeon, *S* the son of Hori............... Num 13:5
*2. Father of Elisha the prophet.*
and Elisha the son of *S* of.................. 1Kin 19:16
and found Elisha the son of *S*............ 1Kin 19:19
said, Here is Elisha the son of *S* .......... 2Kin 3:11
of *S* shall stand on him this day ............ 2Kin 6:31
*3. A grandson of Shechaniah.*
and Bariah, and Neariah, and *S*............. 1Chr 3:22
*4. A chief Gadite.*
next, and Jaanai, and *S* in Bashan....... 1Chr 5:12
*5. A shepherd of David's herds.*
valleys was *S* the son of Adlai ............. 1Chr 27:29

**SHAPHER** (*sha'-fur*) *An Israelite encampment in the wilderness.*
Kehelathah, and pitched in mount *S* Num 33:23
And they removed from mount *S*...... Num 33:24

**SHAPHIR** See SHAPHER.

**SHARAI** (*sha'-rahee*) *Married a foreigner in exile.*
Machnadebai, Shashai, *S*,....................... Ezr 10:40

**SHARAIM** (*sha-ra'-im*) See SHAARAIM. *Same as Shaaraim.*
*S*, and Adithaim, and Gederah ............ Josh 15:36

**SHARAR** (*sha'-rar*) See SARAR. *A "mighty man" of David.*
Ahiam the son of *S* the Hararite .......... 2Sa 23:33

**SHARE**
to sharpen every man his *s*.................... 1Sa 13:20

**SHAREZER** (*sha-re'-zur*) See SHEREZER. *Son of Sennacherib.*
*S* his sons smote him with the........... 2Kin 19:37
*S* his sons smote him with the.................... Is 37:38

**SHARON** (*sha'-run*) See SARON, SHARONITE.
*1. A plain of Ephraim.*
in *S* was Shitrai the Sharonite........... 1Chr 27:29
I am the rose of *S*, and the lily ............. Song 2:1
*S* is like a wilderness ................................ Is 33:9
it, the excellency of Carmel and *S* ........... Is 35:2
*S* shall be a fold of flocks, and ................. Is 65:10
*2. A plain or city in Gad.*
towns, and in all the suburbs of *S*....... 1Chr 5:16

**SHARONITE** (*sha'-run-ite*) *An inhabitant of Sharon 1.*
fed in Sharon was Shitrai the *S*......... 1Chr 27:29

**SHARP**
Then Zipporah took a *s* stone............... Ex 4:25
unto Joshua, Make thee *s* knives........... Josh 5:2
And Joshua made him *s* knives.............. Josh 5:3
there was a *s* rock on the one.............. 1Sa 14:4
a *s* rock on the other side .................... 1Sa 14:4
*S* stones are under him ......................... Job 41:30
he spreadeth *s* pointed things.............. Job 41:30
Thine arrows are *s* in the heart............. Ps 45:5
like a *s* rasor, working............................ Ps 52:2
arrows, and their tongue a *s* sword......... Ps 57:4
*S* arrows of the mighty, with................. Ps 120:4
wormwood, *s* as a twoedged sword ....... Prov 5:4
a maul, and a sword, and a *s* arrow... Prov 25:18
Whose arrows are *s*, and all their.............. Is 5:28
Behold, I will make thee a new *s* ........... Is 41:15
hath made my mouth like a *s* sword ....... Is 49:2
son of man, take thee a *s* knife ............... Eze 5:1
contention was so *s* between them .... Acts 15:39
his mouth went a *s* twoedged sword .... Rev 1:16
hath the *s* sword with two edges........... Rev 2:12
crown, and in his hand a *s* sickle......... Rev 14:14
heaven, he also having a *s* sickle.......... Rev 14:17
cry to him that had the *s* sickle........... Rev 14:18
saying, Thrust in thy *s* sickle.............. Rev 14:18
out of his mouth goeth a *s* sword......... Rev 19:15

**SHARPEN**
to *s* every man his share, and his......... 1Sa 13:20
for the axes, and to *s* the goads.......... 1Sa 13:21

**SHARPENED**
They have *s* their tongues like a............ Ps 140:3
Say, A sword, a sword is *s* ..................... Eze 21:9
It is *s* to make a sore slaughter.......... Eze 21:10
this sword is *s*, and it is ...................... Eze 21:11

**SHARPENETH**
mine enemy *s* his eyes upon me ............ Job 16:9
Iron *s* iron ........................................... Prov 27:17
so a man *s* the countenance of his..... Prov 27:17

**SHARPER**
upright is *s* than a thorn hedge............. Mic 7:4
*s* than any twoedged sword,................... Heb 4:12

**SHARPLY**
And they did chide with him *s*............... Judg 8:1
Wherefore rebuke them *s*, that........... Titus 1:13

**SHARPNESS**
lest being present I should use *s* ....... 2Cor 13:10

**SHARUHEN** (*sha-ru'-hen*) See SHAARAIM, SHILHIM. *A city in Simeon.*
And Beth-lebaoth, and *S*......................... Josh 19:6

**SHASHAI** (*sha'-shahee*) *Married a foreigner in exile.*
Machnadebai, *S*, Sharai,......................... Ezr 10:40

**SHASHAK** (*sha'-shak*) *A son of Elpaal.*
And Ahio, *S*, and Jeremoth, ................ 1Chr 8:14
and Penuel, the sons of *S*.................... 1Chr 8:25

**SHAUL** (*sha'-ul*) See SAUL, SHAULITES.
*1. A son of Simeon.*
*S* the son of a Canaanitish woman..... Gen 46:10
*S* the son of a Canaanitish woman......... Ex 6:15
of *S*, the family of the Shaulites......... Num 26:13
and Jamin, Jarib, Zerah, and *S* ............ 1Chr 4:24
*2. A king of Edom.*
*S* of Rehoboth by the river ................... 1Chr 1:48
when *S* was dead, Baal-hanan the........ 1Chr 1:49
*3. Son of Kohath.*
son, Uzziah his son, and *S* his son......... 1Chr 6:24

**SHAULITES** (*sha'-ul-ites*) *Decendants of Shaul 1.*
of Shaul, the family of the *S*............... Num 26:13

**SHAVE**
but the scall shall he not *s*..................... Lev 13:33
*s* off all his hair, and wash .................... Lev 14:8
that he shall *s* all his hair off.................. Lev 14:9
even all his hair he shall *s* off ................ Lev 14:9
neither shall they *s* off the...................... Lev 21:5
then he shall *s* his head in the............... Num 6:9
on the seventh day shall he *s* it............... Num 6:9
the Nazarite shall *s* the head of ........... Num 6:18
let them *s* all their flesh, and ................ Num 8:7
and she shall *s* her head, and pare....... Deut 21:12
she caused him to *s* off the seven ...... Judg 16:19
Lord *s* with a razor that is hired............... Is 7:20
Neither shall they *s* their heads .......... Eze 44:20
them, that they may *s* their heads ........ Acts 21:24

**SHAVED**
he *s* himself, and changed his............... Gen 41:14
*s* off the one half of their........................ 2Sa 10:4
*s* them, and cut off their garments ....... 1Chr 19:4
*s* his head, and fell down upon the ........ Job 1:20

**SHAVEH** (*sha'-veh*) *A valley near Aenon.*
Ham, and the Emims in *S* Kiriathaim .. Gen 14:5
were with him, at the valley of *S*........ Gen 14:17

**SHAVEN**
He shall be *s*, but the scall .................. Lev 13:33
the hair of his separation is *s*.............. Num 6:19
if I be *s*, then my strength will ........... Judg 16:17
to grow again after he was *s*................ Judg 16:22
men, having their beards *s*...................... Jer 41:5
is even all one as if she were *s*............... 1Cor 11:5
for a woman to be shorn or *s*................ 1Cor 11:6

**SHAVSHA** (*shav'-shah*) See SERAIAH, SHEVA, SHISHA. *David's scribe.*
and *S* was scribe.................................. 1Chr 18:16

**SHE** See PREFACE.

**SHEAF**
my *s* arose, and also stood upright ....... Gen 37:7
about, and made obeisance to my *s*....... Gen 37:7
then ye shall bring a *s* of the ............... Lev 23:10
shall wave the *s* before the LORD ......... Lev 23:11
*s* an he lamb without blemish of........... Lev 23:12
the *s* of the wave offering ..................... Lev 23:15
and hast forgot a *s* in the field ........... Deut 24:19
take away the *s* from the hungry.......... Job 24:10
and like a torch of fire in a *s*.................. Zec 12:6

**SHEAL** (*she'-al*) *Married a foreigner in exile.*
Malluch, and Adaiah, Jashub, and *S*.... Ezr 10:29

**SHEALTIEL** (*she-al'-te-el*) See SALATHIEL. *Father of Zerubbabel.*
and Zerubbabel the son of *S*....................... Ezr 3:2
began Zerubbabel the son of *S*.................. Ezr 3:8
rose up Zerubbabel the son of *S*............... Ezr 5:2
up with Zerubbabel the son of *S*........... Neh 12:1
unto Zerubbabel the son of *S*.................... Hag 1:1
Then Zerubbabel the son of *S*................ Hag 1:12
spirit of Zerubbabel the son of *S*........... Hag 1:14
now to Zerubbabel the son of *S* ............... Hag 2:2
my servant, the son of *S*.......................... Hag 2:23

**SHEAR**
And Laban went to *s* his sheep............ Gen 31:19
up to Timnath to *s* his sheep............... Gen 38:13
nor *s* the firstling of thy sheep .......... Deut 15:19
that Nabal did *s* his sheep .................... 1Sa 25:4

**SHEARER**
and like a lamb dumb before his *s*........ Acts 8:32

**SHEARERS**
now I have heard that thou hast *s* ........ 1Sa 25:7
flesh that I have killed for my *s* ........... 1Sa 25:11
as a sheep before her *s* is dumb.................. Is 53:7

**SHEARIAH** (*she-a-ri'-ah*) *Son of Azel.*
Bocheru, and Ishmael, and *S* ............... 1Chr 8:38
Bocheru, and Ishmael, and *S* ............... 1Chr 9:44

**SHEARING**
he was *s* his sheep in Carmel ................. 1Sa 25:2
he was at the *s* house in the way....... 2Kin 10:12
them at the pit of the *s* house............ 2Kin 10:14

**SHEAR-JASHUB** (*she'-ar-ja'-shub*) *Symbolic name of a son of Isaiah.*
*S* thy son, at the end of the........................... Is 7:3

**SHEATH**
and drew it out of the *s* thereof............ 1Sa 17:51
upon his loins in the *s* thereof.............. 2Sa 20:8
sword again into the *s* thereof............. 1Chr 21:27
draw forth my sword out of his *s*........... Eze 21:3
his *s* against all flesh from the............... Eze 21:4
drawn forth my sword out of his *s* ........ Eze 21:5
I cause it to return into his *s* ............... Eze 21:30
Put up thy sword into the *s* ..................... Jn 18:11

**SHEAVES**
we were binding *s* in the field............... Gen 37:7
your *s* stood round about, and made.... Gen 37:7
after the reapers among the *s*.................. Ruth 2:7
Let her glean even among the *s*............ Ruth 2:15
on the sabbath, and bringing in *s*.......... Neh 13:15
bringing his *s* with him.......................... Ps 126:6
nor he that bindeth *s* his bosom ........... Ps 129:7
cart is pressed that is full of *s* ............. Amos 2:13
them as the *s* into the floor ..................... Mic 4:12

**SHEBA** (*she'-bah*) See BATH-SHEBA, BEERSHEBA, SHEBAH.
*1. Son of Raamah.*
Raamah; *S*, and Dedan............................ Gen 10:7
Raamah; *S*, and Dedan............................. 1Chr 1:9
*2. Son of Yoktan.*
And Obal, and Abimael, and *S*............ Gen 10:28
And Ebal, and Abimael, and *S* ............ 1Chr 1:22
*3. Son of Yokshan.*
And Jokshan begat *S*, and Dedan ........... Gen 25:3
Jokshan; *S*, and Dedan .......................... 1Chr 1:32
*4. A region in southwestern Arabia.*
when the queen of *S* heard of the........ 1Kin 10:1
when the queen of *S* had seen all ........ 1Kin 10:4
queen of *S* gave to king Solomon ...... 1Kin 10:10
the queen of *S* all her desire .............. 1Kin 10:13
when the queen of *S* heard of the .......... 2Chr 9:1
when the queen of *S* had seen the ........ 2Chr 9:3
the queen of *S* gave king Solomon........ 2Chr 9:9
to the queen of *S* all her desire ........... 2Chr 9:12
companies of *S* waited for them ............ Job 6:19
the kings of *S* and Seba shall ................. Ps 72:10
shall be given of the gold of *S*................ Ps 72:15
all they from *S* shall come ........................ Is 60:6

cometh there to me incense from *S* ... Jer 6:20
The merchants of *S* and Raamah, ... Eze 27:22
and Eden, the merchants of *S* ... Eze 27:23
*S*, and Dedan, and the merchants of ... Eze 38:13
*5. A city in Simeon.*
inheritance Beer-sheba, or *S* ... Josh 19:2
*6. A son of Bichri.*
a man of Belial, whose name was *S* ... 2Sa 20:1
followed *S* the son of Bichri ... 2Sa 20:2
Now shall *S* the son of Bichri do ... 2Sa 20:6
to pursue after *S* the son of ... 2Sa 20:7
pursued after *S* the son of Bichri ... 2Sa 20:10
to pursue after *S* the son of ... 2Sa 20:13
*S* the son of Bichri by name, hath ... 2Sa 20:21
the head of *S* the son of Bichri ... 2Sa 20:22
*7. A chief Gadite.*
were, Michael, and Meshullam, and *S*. 1Chr 5:13

**SHEBAH** (*she'-bah*) See SHEBA. *A well at Beersheba.*
And he called it *S* ... Gen 26:33

**SHEBAM** (*she'-bam*) See SHIBMAH. *A city in Reuben.*
and Heshbon, and Elealeh, and *S* ... Num 32:3

**SHEBANIAH** (*sheb-a-ni'-ah*) See SHECHANIAH.
*1. A priest who moved the Ark.*
And *S*, and Jehoshaphat, and ... 1Chr 15:24
*2. A Levite who aided Ezra.*
Jeshua, and Bani, Kadmiel, *S* ... Neh 9:4
Hashabniah, Sherebiah, Hodijah, *S* ... Neh 9:5
And their brethren, *S*, Hodijah, ... Neh 10:10
*3. A priest who renewed the covenant.*
Hattush, *S*, Malluch, ... Neh 10:4
of *S*, Joseph ... Neh 12:14
*4. A Levite who renewed the covenant.*
Zaccur, Sherebiah, *S*, ... Neh 10:12

**SHEBARIM** (*sheb'-a-rim*) *A place near Jericho.*
from before the gate even unto *S* ... Josh 7:5

**SHEBAT** See SEBAT.

**SHEBER** (*she'-bur*) *A son of Caleb.*
Caleb's concubine, bare *S* ... 1Chr 2:48

**SHEBNA** (*sheb'-nah*)
*1. King Hezekiah's scribe.*
*S* the scribe, and Joah the son of ... 2Kin 18:18
Eliakim the son of Hilkiah, and *S* ... 2Kin 18:26
*S* the scribe, and Joah the son of ... 2Kin 18:37
*S* the scribe, and the elders of ... 2Kin 19:2
*S* the scribe, and Joah, Asaph's ... Is 36:3
Then said Eliakim and *S* and Joah ... Is 36:11
*S* the scribe, and Joah, the son of ... Is 36:22
*S* the scribe, and the elders of ... Is 37:2
*2. An unspecified treasurer.*
unto this treasurer, even unto *S* ... Is 22:15

**SHEBNAH** See SHEBNA.

**SHEBUEL** (*she-bu'-el*) See SHUBAEL.
*1. A son of Gershom.*
sons of Gershom, *S* was the chief ... 1Chr 23:16
*S* the son of Gershom, the son of ... 1Chr 26:24
*2. A son of Haman.*
Bukkiah, Mattaniah, Uzziel, *S* ... 1Chr 25:4

**SHECANIAH** (*shek-a-ni'-ah*) See SHEBANIAH, SHECHANIAH.
*1. A priest in David's time.*
ninth to Jeshua, the tenth to *S* ... 1Chr 24:11
*2. A priest in Hezekiah's time.*
and Shemaiah, Amariah, and *S* ... 2Chr 31:15

**SHECHANIAH** (*shek-a-ni'-ah*) See SHEBANIAH, SHECANIAH.
*1. Head of a Davidic family.*
sons of Obadiah, the sons of *S* ... 1Chr 3:21
And the sons of *S* ... 1Chr 3:22
*2. A family of exiles.*
Of the sons of *S*, of the sons of ... Ezr 8:3
*3. Another family of exiles.*
Of the sons of *S* ... Ezr 8:5
*4. Married a foreigner in exile.*
*S* the son of Jehiel, one of the ... Ezr 10:2
*5. Father of Shemaiah.*
also Shemaiah the son of *S* ... Neh 3:29
*6. Son of Arah.*
son in law of *S* the son of Arah ... Neh 6:18
*7. A priest with Zerubbabel.*
*S*, Rehum, Meremoth, ... Neh 12:3

**SHECHEM** (*she'-kem*) See SHECHEMITES, SHECHEM'S, SICHEM, SYCHEM.
*1. A Levitical city near Mt. Ephraim.*
Jacob came to Shalem, a city of *S* ... Gen 33:18
them under the oak which was by *S* ... Gen 35:4
to feed their father's flock in *S* ... Gen 37:12
thy brethren feed the flock in *S* ... Gen 37:13
vale of Hebron, and he came to *S* ... Gen 37:14
Michmethah, that lieth before *S* ... Josh 17:7
and *S* in mount Ephraim, and ... Josh 20:7
For they gave them *S* with her ... Josh 21:21
all the tribes of Israel to *S* ... Josh 24:1
a statute and an ordinance in *S* ... Josh 24:25
And his concubine that was in *S* ... Judg 8:31
to *S* unto his mother's brethren ... Judg 9:1
in the ears of all the men of *S* ... Judg 9:2
all the men of *S* all these words ... Judg 9:3
all the men of *S* gathered ... Judg 9:6
plain of the pillar that was in *S* ... Judg 9:6
Hearken unto me, ye men of *S* ... Judg 9:7
king over the men of *S*, because ... Judg 9:18
Abimelech, and devour the men of *S* .. Judg 9:20
fire come out from the men of *S* ... Judg 9:20
between Abimelech and the men of *S* Judg 9:23
the men of *S* dealt treacherously ... Judg 9:23
and upon the men of *S*, which aided ... Judg 9:24
the men of *S* set liers in wait ... Judg 9:25
his brethren, and went over to *S* ... Judg 9:26
the men of *S* put their confidence ... Judg 9:26
Ebed and his brethren be come to *S* ... Judg 9:31
wait against *S* in four companies ... Judg 9:34
Gaal went out before the men of *S* ... Judg 9:39
that they should not dwell in *S* ... Judg 9:41
men of the tower of *S* heard that ... Judg 9:46
tower of *S* were gathered together ... Judg 9:47
men of the tower of *S* died also ... Judg 9:49
all the evil of the men of *S* did ... Judg 9:57
that goeth up from Beth-el to *S* ... Judg 21:19
And Rehoboam went to *S* ... 1Kin 12:1
were come to *S* to make him king ... 1Kin 12:1
Jeroboam built *S* in mount Ephraim . 1Kin 12:25
*S* in mount Ephraim with her ... 1Chr 6:67
*S* also and the towns thereof, unto ... 1Chr 7:28
And Rehoboam went to *S* ... 2Chr 10:1
for to *S* were all Israel come to ... 2Chr 10:1
I will rejoice, I will divide *S* ... Ps 60:6
I will rejoice, I will divide *S* ... Ps 108:7
That there came certain from *S* ... Jer 41:5
*2. Son of Hamor.*
when *S* the son of Hamor the ... Gen 34:2
*S* spake unto his father Hamor, ... Gen 34:4
Hamor the father of *S* went out ... Gen 34:6
The soul of my son *S* longeth for ... Gen 34:8
*S* said unto her father and unto ... Gen 34:11
And the sons of Jacob answered *S* ... Gen 34:13
pleased Hamor, and *S* Hamor's son ... Gen 34:18
*S* his son came unto the gate of ... Gen 34:20
unto *S* his son hearkened all that ... Gen 34:24
*S* his son with the edge of the ... Gen 34:26
up out of Egypt, buried they in *S* ... Josh 24:32
*S* for an hundred pieces of silver ... Josh 24:32
Who is Abimelech, and who is *S* ... Judg 9:28
the men of Hamor the father of *S* ... Judg 9:28
*3. Son of Gilead.*
and of *S*, the family of the ... Num 26:31
Asriel, and for the children of *S* ... Josh 17:2
*4. A son of Shemidah.*
of Shemidah were, Ahian, and *S* ... 1Chr 7:19

**SHECHEMITES** (*she'-kem-ites*) *Descendants of Shechem.*
of Shechem, the family of the *S* ... Num 26:31

**SHECHEM'S** (*she'-kems*) *Refers to Shechem 2.*
*S* father, for an hundred pieces ... Gen 33:19
and took Dinah out of *S* house ... Gen 34:26

**SHED**
by man shall his blood be *s* ... Gen 9:6
*S* no blood, but cast him into ... Gen 37:22
there shall no blood be *s* for him ... Ex 22:2
there shall be blood *s* for him ... Ex 22:3
he hath *s* blood ... Lev 17:4
of the blood that is *s* therein ... Num 35:33
but by the blood of him that *s* it ... Num 35:33
blood be not *s* in thy land ... Deut 19:10
Our hands have not *s* this blood ... Deut 21:7
thee from coming to *s* blood ... 1Sa 25:26
that thou hast *s* blood causeless ... 1Sa 25:31
this day from coming to *s* blood ... 1Sa 25:33
*s* out his bowels to the ground, ... 2Sa 20:10
*s* the blood of war in peace, and ... 1Kin 2:5
the innocent blood, which Joab *s* ... 1Kin 2:31
Moreover Manasseh *s* innocent ... 2Kin 21:16
for the innocent blood that he *s* ... 2Kin 24:4
Thou hast *s* blood abundantly, and ... 1Chr 22:8
because thou hast *s* much blood ... 1Chr 22:8
a man of war, and hast *s* blood ... 1Chr 28:3
Their blood have they *s* like ... Ps 79:3
blood of thy servants which is *s* ... Ps 79:10
*s* innocent blood, even the blood ... Ps 106:38
to evil, and make haste to *s* blood ... Prov 1:16
hands that *s* innocent blood, ... Prov 6:17
make haste to *s* innocent blood ... Is 59:7
*s* not innocent blood in this ... Jer 7:6
neither *s* innocent blood in this ... Jer 22:3
for to *s* innocent blood, and for ... Jer 22:17
that have *s* the blood of the just ... Lam 4:13
wedlock and *s* blood are judged ... Eze 16:38
in thy blood that thou hast *s* ... Eze 22:4
in thee to their power to *s* blood ... Eze 22:6
men that carry tales to *s* blood ... Eze 22:9
have they taken gifts to *s* blood ... Eze 22:12
to *s* blood, and to destroy souls, ... Eze 22:27
the manner of women that *s* blood ... Eze 23:45
toward your idols, and *s* blood ... Eze 33:25
hast *s* the blood of the children ... Eze 35:5
that they had *s* upon the land ... Eze 36:18
because they have *s* innocent ... Joel 3:19
righteous blood *s* upon the earth ... Mt 23:35
which is *s* for many for the ... Mt 26:28
testament, which is *s* for many ... Mk 14:24
which was *s* from the foundation ... Lk 11:50
in my blood, which is *s* for you ... Lk 22:20
he hath *s* forth this, which ye ... Acts 2:33
blood of thy martyr Stephen was *s* ... Acts 22:20
Their feet are swift to *s* blood ... Rom 3:15
because the love of God is *s* ... Rom 5:5
Which he *s* on us abundantly ... Titus 3:6
For they have *s* the blood of ... Rev 16:6

**SHEDDER**
a *s* of blood, and that doeth the ... Eze 18:10

**SHEDDETH**
Whoso *s* man's blood, by man shall ... Gen 9:6
The city *s* blood in the midst of ... Eze 22:3

**SHEDDING**
and without *s* of blood is no ... Heb 9:22

**SHEDEUR** (*shed'-e-ur*) *A Reubenite who counted the people.*
Elizur the son of *S* ... Num 1:5
shall be Elizur the son of *S* ... Num 2:10
fourth day Elizur the son of *S* ... Num 7:30
offering of Elizur the son of *S* ... Num 7:35
his host was Elizur the son of *S* ... Num 10:18

**SHEEP**
And Abel was a keeper of *s* ... Gen 4:2
and he had *s*, and oxen, and he asses. Gen 12:16
And Abimelech took *s*, and oxen, and Gen 20:14
And Abraham took *s* and oxen, and ... Gen 21:27
three flocks of *s* lying by it ... Gen 29:2
well's mouth, and watered the *s* ... Gen 29:3
his daughter cometh with the *s* ... Gen 29:6
water ye the *s*, and go and feed ... Gen 29:7
then we water the *s* ... Gen 29:8
Rachel came with her father's *s* ... Gen 29:9
the *s* of Laban his mother's ... Gen 29:10
all the brown cattle among the *s* ... Gen 30:32
the goats, and brown among the *s* ... Gen 30:33
it, and all the brown among the *s* ... Gen 30:35
And Laban went to shear his *s* ... Gen 31:19
They took their *s*, and their oxen, ... Gen 34:28
up to Timnath to shear his *s* ... Gen 38:13
upon the oxen, and upon the *s* ... Ex 9:3
ye shall take it out from the *s* ... Ex 12:5
and thy peace offerings, thy *s* ... Ex 20:24
a man shall steal an ox, or a *s* ... Ex 22:1
for an ox, and four *s* for a *s* ... Ex 22:1
whether it be ox, or ass, or *s* ... Ex 22:4
it be for ox, for ass, for *s* ... Ex 22:9
an ass, or an ox, or a *s*, or any ... Ex 22:10
do with thine oxen, and with thy *s* ... Ex 22:30
among thy cattle, whether ox or *s* ... Ex 34:19
of the flocks, namely, of the *s* ... Lev 1:10
no manner of fat, of ox, or of *s* ... Lev 7:23
blemish, of the beeves, of the *s* ... Lev 22:19
freewill offering in beeves or *s* ... Lev 22:21
When a bullock, or a *s*, or a goat ... Lev 22:27
whether it be ox, or *s* ... Lev 27:26
of a cow, or the firstling of a *s* ... Num 18:17
And Balak offered oxen and *s* ... Num 22:40
of the LORD be not as *s* which ... Num 27:17
and of the asses, and of the *s* ... Num 31:28
thousand and five thousand *s* ... Num 31:32
thirty thousand and five hundred *s* ... Num 31:36
tribute of the *s* was six hundred ... Num 31:37
seven thousand and five hundred *s* ... Num 31:43
little ones, and folds for your *s* ... Num 32:24
and folds of *s* ... Num 32:36
thy kine, and the flocks of thy *s* ... Deut 7:13
the ox, the *s*, and the goat, ... Deut 14:4
lusteth after, for oxen, or for *s* ... Deut 14:26
nor shear the firstling of thy *s* ... Deut 15:19
LORD thy God any bullock, or *s* ... Deut 17:1
sacrifice, whether it be ox or *s* ... Deut 18:3
the first of the fleece of thy *s* ... Deut 18:4
brother's ox or his *s* go astray ... Deut 22:1
thy kine, and the flocks of thy *s* ... Deut 28:4
thy kine, and the flocks of thy *s* ... Deut 28:18
thy *s* shall be given unto thine ... Deut 28:31
of thy kine, or flocks of thy *s* ... Deut 28:51
Butter of kine, and milk of *s* ... Deut 32:14
woman, young and old, and ox, and *s*. Josh 6:21
his oxen, and his asses, and his *s* ... Josh 7:24
sustenance for Israel, neither *s* ... Judg 6:4
He will take the tenth of your *s* ... 1Sa 8:17
flew upon the spoil, and took *s* ... 1Sa 14:32
man his ox, and every man his *s* ... 1Sa 14:34
infant and suckling, ox and *s* ... 1Sa 15:3
spared Agag, and the best of the *s* ... 1Sa 15:9
bleating of the *s* in mine ears ... 1Sa 15:14
people spared the best of the *s* ... 1Sa 15:15
the people took of the spoil, *s* ... 1Sa 15:21
and, behold, he keepeth the *s* ... 1Sa 16:11
thy son, which is with the *s* ... 1Sa 16:19
feed his father's *s* at Beth-lehem ... 1Sa 17:15
left the *s* with a keeper, and took ... 1Sa 17:20
those few *s* in the wilderness ... 1Sa 17:28
Thy servant kept his father's *s* ... 1Sa 17:34
and oxen, and asses, and *s*, with ... 1Sa 22:19
great, and he had three thousand *s* ... 1Sa 25:2
he was shearing his *s* in Carmel ... 1Sa 25:2
that Nabal did shear his *s* ... 1Sa 25:4
we were with them keeping the *s* ... 1Sa 25:16
five *s* ready dressed, and five ... 1Sa 25:18
woman alive, and took away the *s* ... 1Sa 27:9
sheepcote, from following the *s* ... 2Sa 7:8
And honey, and butter, and *s* ... 2Sa 17:29
but these *s*, what have they done ... 2Sa 24:17
And Adonijah slew *s* and oxen and fat. 1Kin 1:9
*s* in abundance, and hath called ... 1Kin 1:19
*s* in abundance, and hath called ... 1Kin 1:25
of the pastures, and an hundred *s* ... 1Kin 4:23
him before the ark, sacrificing *s* ... 1Kin 8:5
an hundred and twenty thousand *s* ... 1Kin 8:63
as *s* that have not a shepherd ... 1Kin 22:17
and oliveyards, and vineyards, and *s* ... 2Kin 5:26

of s two hundred and fifty ... 1Chr 5:21
and oil, and oxen, and s abundantly.. 1Chr 12:40
even from following the s ... 1Chr 17:7
but as for these s, what have ... 1Chr 21:17
him before the ark, sacrificed s ... 2Chr 5:6
an hundred and twenty thousand s ... 2Chr 7:5
of cattle, and carried away s ... 2Chr 14:15
hundred oxen and seven thousand s. 2Chr 15:11
And Ahab killed s and oxen for him ... 2Chr 18:2
as s that have no shepherd ... 2Chr 18:16
hundred oxen and three thousand s.. 2Chr 29:33
bullocks and seven thousand s ... 2Chr 30:24
bullocks and ten thousand s ... 2Chr 30:24
brought in the tithe of oxen and s ... 2Chr 31:6
and they builded the s gate ... Neh 3:1
s gate repaired the goldsmiths ... Neh 3:32
daily was one ox and six choice s ... Neh 5:18
of Meah, even unto the s gate ... Neh 12:39
also was seven thousand s ... Job 1:3
heaven, and hath burned up the s ... Job 1:16
warmed with the fleece of my s ... Job 31:20
for he had fourteen thousand s ... Job 42:12
All s and oxen, yea, and the beasts ... Ps 8:7
us like s appointed for meat ... Ps 44:11
counted as s for the slaughter ... Ps 44:22
Like s they are laid in the grave ... Ps 49:14
against the s of thy pasture ... Ps 74:1
his own people to go forth like s ... Ps 78:52
s of thy pasture will give thee ... Ps 79:13
his pasture, and the s of his hand ... Ps 95:7
people, and the s of his pasture ... Ps 100:3
I have gone astray like a lost s ... Ps 119:176
that our s may bring forth ... Ps 144:13
a flock of s that are even shorn ... Song 4:2
Thy teeth are as a flock of s ... Song 6:6
nourish a young cow, and two s ... Is 7:21
as a s that no man taketh up ... Is 13:14
slaying oxen, and killing s ... Is 22:13
All we like s have gone astray ... Is 53:6
as a s before her shearers is ... Is 53:7
them out like s for the slaughter ... Jer 12:3
scatter the s of my pasture ... Jer 23:1
My people hath been lost s ... Jer 50:6
Israel is a scattered s ... Jer 50:17
My s wandered through all the ... Eze 34:6
I, even I, will both search my s ... Eze 34:11
is among his s that are scattered ... Eze 34:12
so will I seek out my s, and will ... Eze 34:12
a wife, and for a wife he kept s ... Hos 12:12
the flocks of s are made desolate ... Joel 1:18
them together as the s of Bozrah ... Mic 2:12
young lion among the flocks of s ... Mic 5:8
and the s shall be scattered ... Zec 13:7
abroad, as s having no shepherd ... Mt 9:36
the lost s of the house of Israel ... Mt 10:6
I send you forth as s in the ... Mt 10:16
among you, that shall have one s ... Mt 12:11
then is a man better than a s ... Mt 12:12
the lost s of the house of Israel ... Mt 15:24
if a man have an hundred s ... Mt 18:12
you, he rejoiceth more of that s ... Mt 18:13
divideth his s from the goats ... Mt 25:32
he shall set the s on his right ... Mt 25:33
the s of the flock shall be ... Mt 26:31
because they were as s not having ... Mk 6:34
and the s shall be scattered ... Mk 14:27
man of you, having an hundred s ... Lk 15:4
I have found my s which was lost ... Lk 15:6
temple those that sold oxen and s ... Jn 2:14
all out of the temple, and the s ... Jn 2:15
Jerusalem by the s market a pool ... Jn 5:2
the door is the shepherd of the s ... Jn 10:2
and the s hear his voice ... Jn 10:3
and he calleth his own s by name ... Jn 10:3
when he putteth forth his own s ... Jn 10:4
before them, and the s follow him ... Jn 10:4
unto you, I am the door of the s ... Jn 10:7
but the s did not hear them ... Jn 10:8
giveth his life for the s ... Jn 10:11
shepherd, whose own the s are not ... Jn 10:12
the wolf coming, and leaveth the s ... Jn 10:12
them, and scattereth the s ... Jn 10:12
hireling, and careth not for the s ... Jn 10:13
the good shepherd, and know my s ... Jn 10:14
and I lay down my life for the s ... Jn 10:15
other s I have, which are not of ... Jn 10:16
not, because ye are not of my s ... Jn 10:26
My s hear my voice, and I know ... Jn 10:27
He saith unto him, Feed my s ... Jn 21:16
Jesus saith unto him, Feed my s ... Jn 21:17
this, He was led as a s to the ... Acts 8:32
accounted as s for the slaughter ... Rom 8:36
that great shepherd of the s ... Heb 13:20
For ye were as s going astray ... 1Pet 2:25
flour, and wheat, and beasts, and s ... Rev 18:13

**SHEEPCOTE**
of hosts, I took thee from the s ... 2Sa 7:8
of hosts, I took thee from the s ... 1Chr 17:7

**SHEEPCOTES**
And he came to the s by the way ... 1Sa 24:3

**SHEEPFOLD**
not by the door into the s ... Jn 10:1

**SHEEPFOLDS**
We will build s here for our ... Num 32:16
Why abodest thou among the s ... Judg 5:16
servant, and took him from the s ... Ps 78:70

**SHEEPMASTER**
And Mesha king of Moab was a s ... 2Kin 3:4

**SHEEP'S**
which come to you in s clothing ... Mt 7:15

**SHEEPSHEARERS**
and went up unto his s to Timnath ... Gen 38:12
that Absalom had s in Baal-hazor ... 2Sa 13:23
Behold now, thy servant hath s ... 2Sa 13:24

**SHEEPSKINS**
they wandered about in s and ... Heb 11:37

**SHEERAH** See SHERAH.

**SHEET**
as it had been a great s knit at ... Acts 10:11
descend, as it had been a great s ... Acts 11:5

**SHEETS**
then I will give you thirty s ... Judg 14:12
then shall ye give me thirty s ... Judg 14:13

**SHEHARIAH** (*she-ha-ri'-ah*) *A son of Jeroham.*
and S, and Athaliah ... 1Chr 8:26

**SHEKEL**
golden earring of half a s weight ... Gen 24:22
half a s after the s of the ... Ex 30:13
(a s is twenty gerahs ... Ex 30:13
an half s shall be the offering ... Ex 30:13
shall not give less than half a s ... Ex 30:15
after the s of the sanctuary, and ... Ex 30:24
after the s of the sanctuary ... Ex 38:24
after the s of the sanctuary ... Ex 38:25
for every man, that is, half a s ... Ex 38:26
after the s of the sanctuary, for ... Ex 38:26
after the s of the sanctuary, for ... Lev 5:15
after the s of the sanctuary ... Lev 27:3
to the s of the sanctuary ... Lev 27:25
twenty gerahs shall be the s ... Lev 27:25
after the s of the sanctuary ... Num 3:47
(the s is twenty gerahs ... Num 3:47
after the s of the sanctuary ... Num 3:50
after the s of the sanctuary ... Num 7:13
after the s of the sanctuary ... Num 7:19
after the s of the sanctuary ... Num 7:25
after the s of the sanctuary ... Num 7:31
after the s of the sanctuary ... Num 7:37
after the s of the sanctuary ... Num 7:43
after the s of the sanctuary ... Num 7:49
after the s of the sanctuary ... Num 7:55
after the s of the sanctuary ... Num 7:61
after the s of the sanctuary ... Num 7:67
after the s of the sanctuary ... Num 7:73
after the s of the sanctuary ... Num 7:79
after the s of the sanctuary ... Num 7:85
after the s of the sanctuary ... Num 7:86
after the s of the sanctuary, ... Num 18:16
the fourth part of a s of silver ... 1Sa 9:8
of fine flour be sold for a s ... 2Kin 7:1
and two measures of barley for a s ... 2Kin 7:1
of fine flour was sold for a s ... 2Kin 7:16
and two measures of barley for a s ... 2Kin 7:16
Two measures of barley for a s ... 2Kin 7:18
a measure of fine flour for a s ... 2Kin 7:18
s for the service of the house of ... Neh 10:32
the s shall be twenty gerahs ... Eze 45:12
the s great, and falsifying the ... Amos 8:5

**SHEKELS**
is worth four hundred s of silver ... Gen 23:15
of Heth, four hundred s of silver ... Gen 23:16
her hands of ten s weight of gold ... Gen 24:22
their master thirty s of silver ... Ex 21:32
of pure myrrh five hundred s ... Ex 30:23
much, even two hundred and fifty s ... Ex 30:23
calamus two hundred and fifty s ... Ex 30:23
And of cassia five hundred s ... Ex 30:24
and seven hundred and thirty s ... Ex 38:24
and threescore and fifteen s ... Ex 38:25
five s he made hooks for the ... Ex 38:28
and two thousand and four hundred s.. Ex 38:29
thy estimation by s of silver ... Lev 5:15
shall be fifty s of silver ... Lev 27:3
thy estimation shall be thirty s ... Lev 27:4
shall be of the male twenty s ... Lev 27:5
and for the female ten s ... Lev 27:5
be of the male five s of silver ... Lev 27:6
shall be three s of silver ... Lev 27:6
thy estimation shall be fifteen s ... Lev 27:7
and for the female ten s ... Lev 27:7
be valued at fifty s of silver ... Lev 27:16
take five s apiece by the poll ... Num 3:47
hundred and threescore and five s ... Num 3:50
was an hundred and thirty s ... Num 7:13
one silver bowl of seventy s ... Num 7:13
One spoon of ten s of gold ... Num 7:14
was an hundred and thirty s ... Num 7:19
one silver bowl of seventy s ... Num 7:19
One spoon of gold of ten s ... Num 7:20
was an hundred and thirty s ... Num 7:25
one silver bowl of seventy s ... Num 7:25
One golden spoon of ten s ... Num 7:26
weight of an hundred and thirty s ... Num 7:31
one silver bowl of seventy s ... Num 7:31
One golden spoon of ten s ... Num 7:32
was an hundred and thirty s ... Num 7:37
one silver bowl of seventy s ... Num 7:37
One golden spoon of ten s ... Num 7:38
weight of an hundred and thirty s ... Num 7:43
a silver bowl of seventy s ... Num 7:43
One golden spoon of ten s ... Num 7:44
was an hundred and thirty s ... Num 7:49
one silver bowl of seventy s ... Num 7:49
One golden spoon of ten s ... Num 7:50
weight of an hundred and thirty s ... Num 7:55
one silver bowl of seventy s ... Num 7:55
One golden spoon of ten s ... Num 7:56
was an hundred and thirty s ... Num 7:61
one silver bowl of seventy s ... Num 7:61
One golden spoon of ten s ... Num 7:62
was an hundred and thirty s ... Num 7:67
one silver bowl of seventy s ... Num 7:67
One golden spoon of ten s ... Num 7:68
was an hundred and thirty s ... Num 7:73
one silver bowl of seventy s ... Num 7:73
One golden spoon of ten s ... Num 7:74
was an hundred and thirty s ... Num 7:79
one silver bowl of seventy s ... Num 7:79
One golden spoon of ten s ... Num 7:80
weighing an hundred and thirty s ... Num 7:85
two thousand and four hundred s ... Num 7:85
of incense, weighing ten s apiece ... Num 7:86
spoons was an hundred and twenty s. Num 7:86
for the money of five s, after ... Num 18:16
thousand seven hundred and fifty s .. Num 31:52
him in an hundred s of silver ... Deut 22:19
damsel's father fifty s of silver ... Deut 22:29
and two hundred s of silver ... Josh 7:21
a wedge of gold of fifty s weight ... Josh 7:21
and seven hundred s of gold ... Judg 8:26
The eleven hundred s of silver ... Judg 17:2
hundred s of silver to his mother ... Judg 17:3
took two hundred s of silver ... Judg 17:4
I will give thee ten s of silver ... Judg 17:10
coat was five thousand s of brass ... 1Sa 17:5
weighed six hundred s of iron ... 1Sa 17:7
hundred s after the king's weight ... 2Sa 14:26
have given thee ten s of silver ... 2Sa 18:11
thousand s of silver in mine hand ... 2Sa 18:12
hundred s of brass in weight ... 2Sa 21:16
and the oxen for fifty s of silver ... 2Sa 24:24
six hundred s of gold went to one ... 1Kin 10:16
Egypt for six hundred s of silver ... 1Kin 10:29
of each man fifty s of silver ... 2Kin 15:20
six hundred s of gold by weight ... 1Chr 21:25
for six hundred s of silver ... 2Chr 1:17
of the nails was fifty s of gold ... 2Chr 3:9
six hundred s of beaten gold went ... 2Chr 9:15
three hundred s of gold went to ... 2Chr 9:16
and wine, beside forty s of silver ... Neh 5:15
money, even seventeen s of silver ... Jer 32:9
be by weight, twenty s a day ... Eze 4:10
twenty s, five and twenty ... Eze 45:12
five and twenty s, fifteen s ... Eze 45:12

**SHELAH** (*she'-lah*) See SALAH, SHELANITES.
*1. Son of Judah.*
and called his name S ... Gen 38:5
house, till S my son be grown ... Gen 38:11
for she saw that S was grown ... Gen 38:14
that I gave her not to S my son ... Gen 38:26
and Onan, and S, and Pharez ... Gen 46:12
of S, the family of the ... Num 26:20
Er, and Onan, and S ... 1Chr 2:3
The sons of S the son of Judah ... 1Chr 4:21
*2. Son of Arphaxad.*
And Arphaxad begat S, and Shelah ... 1Chr 1:18
begat Shelah, and S begat Eber ... 1Chr 1:18
Shem, Arphaxad, S, ... 1Chr 1:24

**SHELANITE** See SHELANITES.

**SHELANITES** (*she'-lan-ites*) *Descendants of Shelah.*
of Shelah, the family of the S ... Num 26:20

**SHELEMIAH** (*shel-e-mi'-ah*) See MESHELEMIAH, SHALLUM.
*1. A sanctuary servant.*
And the lot eastward fell to S ... 1Chr 26:14
*2. A son of Bani who married a foreigner.*
And S, and Nathan, and Adaiah, ... Ezr 10:39
*3. Another son of Bani.*
Azareel, and S, Shemariah, ... Ezr 10:41
*4. Father of Hananiah.*
repaired Hananiah the son of S ... Neh 3:30
*5. A treasury sevant.*
S the priest, and Zadok the scribe ... Neh 13:13
*6. Son of Cushi.*
son of Nethaniah, the son of S ... Jer 36:14
*7. Son of Abdeel.*
S the son of Abdeel, to take ... Jer 36:26
*8. Father of Jehucal.*
king sent Jehucal the son of S ... Jer 37:3
of Pashur, and Jucal the son of S ... Jer 38:1
*9. Father of Irijah.*
name was Irijah, the son of S ... Jer 37:13

**SHELEPH** (*she'-lef*) *A son of Joktan.*
And Joktan begat Almodad, and S ... Gen 10:26
And Joktan begat Almodad, and S ... 1Chr 1:20

**SHELESH** (*she'-lesh*) *A son of Helem.*
Zophah, and Imna, and S, and Amal .. 1Chr 7:35

**SHELOMI** (*shel'-o-mi*) *Father of Ahihud.*
of Asher, Ahihud the son of S ... Num 34:27

**SHELOMITH** (*shel'-o-mith*)
*1. Daughter of Debri.*
(and his mother's name was S ... Lev 24:11
*2. Daughter of Zerubbabel.*
and Hananiah, and S their sister ... 1Chr 3:19
*3. A son of Shimei.*
S, and Haziel, and Haran, three ... 1Chr 23:9

S

*4. A son of Izhar.*
*S* the chief ... 1Chr 23:18
*5. A descendant of Eliezer.*
and Zichri his son, and *S* his son ... 1Chr 26:25
Which *S* and his brethren were over 1Chr 26:26
thing, it was under the hand of *S* ... 1Chr 26:28
*6. A child of King Rehoboam.*
Abijah, and Attai, and Ziza, and *S* ... 2Chr 11:20
*7. A family of exiles.*
And of the sons of *S* ... Ezr 8:10

**SHELOMOTH** (*shel'-o-moth*) See SHELOMITH.
*A descendant of Izhar.*
*S*: of the sons of *S* ... 1Chr 24:22

**SHELTER**
embrace the rock for want of a *s* ... Job 24:8
For thou hast been a *s* for me ... Ps 61:3

**SHELUMIEL**
*S* the son of Zurishaddai ... Num 1:6
shall be *S* the son of Zurishaddai ... Num 2:12
On the fifth day *S* the son of ... Num 7:36
of *S* the son of Zurishaddai ... Num 7:41
was *S* the son of Zurishaddai ... Num 10:19

**SHEM** (*shem*) See SEM. *A son of Noah.*
and Noah begat *S*, Ham, and Japheth .. Gen 5:32
And Noah begat three sons, *S* ... Gen 6:10
selfsame day entered Noah, and *S* ... Gen 7:13
went forth of the ark, were *S* ... Gen 9:18
And *S* and Japheth took a garment, ... Gen 9:23
Blessed be the LORD God of *S* ... Gen 9:26
he shall dwell in the tents of *S* ... Gen 9:27
of the sons of Noah, *S*, Ham, and ... Gen 10:1
Unto *S* also, the father of all ... Gen 10:21
The children of *S* ... Gen 10:22
These are the sons of *S*, after ... Gen 10:31
These are the generations of *S* ... Gen 11:10
*S* was an hundred years old, and ... Gen 11:10
*S* lived after he begat Arphaxad ... Gen 11:11
Noah, *S*, Ham, and Japheth ... 1Chr 1:4
The sons of *S* ... 1Chr 1:17
*S*, Arphaxad, Shelah, ... 1Chr 1:24

**SHEMA** (*she'-mah*) See SHEMAIAH, SHIMHI.
*1. A city in Judah.*
Amam, and *S*, and Moladah, ... Josh 15:26
*2. A son of Hebron.*
Tappuah, and Rekem, and *S* ... 1Chr 2:43
*S* begat Raham, the father of ... 1Chr 2:44
*3. Father of Azaz.*
the son of Azaz, the son of *S* ... 1Chr 5:8
*4. A Benjamite Chief.*
Beriah also, and *S*, who were heads ... 1Chr 8:13
*5. A priest who aided Ezra.*
beside him stood Mattithiah, and *S* ... Neh 8:4

**SHEMAAH** (*shem'-a-ah*) *Father of two warriors in David's army.*
the sons of *S* the Gibeathite ... 1Chr 12:3

**SHEMAIAH** (*shem-a-i'-ah*) See SHAMMUA, SHEMA, SHIMEI, SIMEI.
*1. A prophet in King Rehoboam's time.*
of God came unto *S* the man of God 1Kin 12:22
the LORD came to *S* the man of God ... 2Chr 11:2
Then came *S* the prophet to ... 2Chr 12:5
the word of the LORD came to *S* ... 2Chr 12:7
in the book of *S* the prophet ... 2Chr 12:15
*2. Son of Shechaniah.*
*S*: and the sons of Shemaiah ... 1Chr 3:22
*3. Father of Shimri.*
the son of Shimri, the son of *S* ... 1Chr 4:37
*4. Son of Joel.*
*S* his son, Gog his son, Shimei ... 1Chr 5:4
*5. Son of Hasshub.*
*S* the son of Hasshub, the son of ... 1Chr 9:14
*S* the son of Hashub, the son of ... Neh 11:15
*6. Father of Obadiah.*
And Obadiah the son of *S*, the son ... 1Chr 9:16
*7. A priest who moved the Ark.*
*S* the chief, and his brethren two ... 1Chr 15:8
for Uriel, Asaiah, and Joel, *S* ... 1Chr 15:11
*8. Son of Nathaneel.*
*S* the son of Nethaneel the scribe ... 1Chr 24:6
*9. A sanctuary servant.*
*S* the firstborn, Jehozabad the ... 1Chr 26:4
Also unto *S* his son were sons ... 1Chr 26:6
The sons of *S* ... 1Chr 26:7
*10. A Levite teacher of the people.*
with them he sent Levites, even *S* ... 2Chr 17:8
*11. A Levite who cleansed the temple.*
*S*, and Uzziel ... 2Chr 29:14
*12. A Levite in Hezekiah's time.*
and Miniamin, and Jeshua, and *S* ... 2Chr 31:15
*13. A Levite in Josiah's time.*
Conaniah also, and *S* and Nethaneel, . 2Chr 35:9
*14. A family of exiles.*
are these, Eliphelet, Jeiel, and *S* ... Ezr 8:13
*15. A messenger of Ezra.*
I for Eliezer, for Ariel, for *S* ... Ezr 8:16
*16. A priest who married a foreigner.*
Maaseiah, and Elijah, and *S* ... Ezr 10:21
*17. A son of Harim.*
Eliezer, Ishijah, Malchiah, *S* ... Ezr 10:31
*18. A rebuilder of Jerusalem's wall.*
also *S* the son of Shechaniah ... Neh 3:29
*19. Son of Delaiah.*
I came unto the house of *S* the ... Neh 6:10
*20. A priest who renewed the covenant.*
Maaziah, Bilgai, *S* ... Neh 10:8
*S*, and Joiarib, Jedaiah, ... Neh 12:6
of *S*, Jehonathan ... Neh 12:18
Judah, and Benjamin, and *S*, and ... Neh 12:34
the son of Jonathan, the son of *S* ... Neh 12:35
*21. A priest who dedicated the wall.*
And his brethren, *S*, and Azarael, ... Neh 12:36
*22. A priest who gave thanks at the wall.*
Maaseiah, and *S*, and Eleazar ... Neh 12:42
*23. Father of Urijah.*
the son of *S* of Kirjath-jearim ... Jer 26:20
*24. A false prophet.*
also speak to *S* the Nehelamite ... Jer 29:24
LORD concerning *S* the Nehelamite ... Jer 29:31
Because that *S* hath prophesied ... Jer 29:31
I will punish *S* the Nehelamite, ... Jer 29:32
*25. Father of Delaiah.*
scribe, and Delaiah the son of *S* ... Jer 36:12

**SHEMARIAH** (*shem-a-ri'-ah*)
*1. A warrior in David's army.*
and Jerimoth, and Bealiah, and *S* ... 1Chr 12:5
*2. Married a foreigner in exile.*
Benjamin, Malluch, and *S* ... Ezr 10:32
*3. Married a foreigner in exile.*
Azareel, and Shelemiah, *S*, ... Ezr 10:41

**SHEMEBER** (*shem-e'-ber*) *King of Zeboim.*
*S* king of Zeboiim, and the king of ... Gen 14:2

**SHEMED** See SHAMED.

**SHEMER** (*she'-mur*) *Owner of a hill, later the site of Samaria.*
of *S* for two talents of silver ... 1Kin 16:24
he built, after the name of *S* ... 1Kin 16:24

**SHEMIDA** (*shem-i'-dah*) See SHEMIDAH. *Son of Gilead.*
And of *S*, the family of the ... Num 26:32
Hepher, and for the children of *S* ... Josh 17:2

**SHEMIDAH** (*shem-i'-dah*) See SHEMIDA, SHEMIDAITES. *Same as Shemida.*
And the sons of *S* were, Ahian, and ... 1Chr 7:19

**SHEMIDAITES** (*shem'-i-dah-ites*)
*Descendants of Shemida.*
of Shemida, the family of the *S* ... Num 26:32

**SHEMINITH** (*shem'-i-nith*) *A musical notation.*
with harps on the *S* to excel ... 1Chr 15:21
chief Musician on Neginoth upon *S* ... Ps 6:*t*
To the chief Musician upon *S* ... Ps 12:*t*

**SHEMIRAMOTH** (*she-mir'-a-moth*)
*1. A priest who moved the Ark.*
Zechariah, Ben, and Jaaziel, and *S* ... 1Chr 15:18
And Zechariah, and Aziel, and *S* ... 1Chr 15:20
to him Zechariah, Jeiel, and *S* ... 1Chr 16:5
*2. A Levite in Jehoshaphat's time.*
and Zebadiah, and Asahel, and *S* ... 2Chr 17:8

**SHEMUEL** (*shem-u-'el*) See SAMUEL.
*1. A Simeonite prince.*
of Simeon, *S* the son of Ammihud ... Num 34:20
*2. Another name for Samuel the prophet.*
the son of Joel, the son of *S* ... 1Chr 6:33
*3. Head of a family in Issachar.*
and Jahmai, and Jibsam, and *S* ... 1Chr 7:2

**SHEN** (*shen*) *A place in Benjamin.*
and set it between Mizpeh and *S* ... 1Sa 7:12

**SHENAZAR** (*she-na'-zar*) *Descendant of King Jehoiakim.*
Malchiram also, and Pedaiah, and *S* ... 1Chr 3:18

**SHENAZZAR** See SHENAZAR.

**SHENIR** (*she'-nur*) See SENIR, SION. *A mountain between Amana and Hermon.*
and the Amorites call it *S* ... Deut 3:9
top of Amana, from the top of *S* ... Song 4:8

**SHEOL** See HELL.

**SHEPHAM** (*she'-fam*) See SHIPMITE. *A place east of the Sea of Cinneroth.*
east border from Hazar-enan to *S* ... Num 34:10
shall go down from *S* to Riblah ... Num 34:11

**SHEPHATIAH** (*shef-a-ti'-ah*)
*1. A son of David.*
and the fifth, *S* the son of Abital ... 2Sa 3:4
The fifth, *S* of Abital ... 1Chr 3:3
*2. A son of Ruel.*
Michri, and Meshullam the son of *S* ... 1Chr 9:8
*3. A warrior in David's army.*
and Shemariah, and *S* the Haruphite, . 1Chr 12:5
*4. A Simeonite prince.*
Simeonites, *S* the son of Maachah ... 1Chr 27:16
*5. A son of King Jehoshaphat.*
and Azariah, and Michael, and *S* ... 2Chr 21:2
*6. A family of exiles with Zerubbabel.*
The children of *S*, three hundred ... Ezr 2:4
The children of *S*, three hundred ... Neh 7:9
*7. Descendants of a servant of Solomon.*
The children of *S*, the children ... Ezr 2:57
The children of *S*, the children ... Neh 7:59
*8. A family of exiles with Ezra.*
And of the sons of *S* ... Ezr 8:8
*9. A family of exiles who resettled in Jerusalem.*
the son of Amariah, the son of *S* ... Neh 11:4
*10. A prince of Judah.*
Then *S* the son of Mattan, and ... Jer 38:1

**SHEPHELAH** See PLAIN.

**SHEPHER** See SHAPHER.

**SHEPHERD**
for every *s* is an abomination ... Gen 46:34
(from thence is the *s*, the stone ... Gen 49:24
be not as sheep which have no *s* ... Num 27:17
hills, as sheep that have not a *s* ... 1Kin 22:17
as sheep that have no *s* ... 2Chr 18:16
The LORD is my *s* ... Ps 23:1
O *S* of Israel, thou that leadest ... Ps 80:1
which are given from one *s* ... Eccl 12:11
He shall feed his flock like a *s* ... Is 40:11
That saith of Cyrus, He is my *s* ... Is 44:28
the sea with the *s* of his flock ... Is 63:11
keep him, as a *s* doth his flock ... Jer 31:10
as a *s* putteth on his garment ... Jer 43:12
who is that *s* that will stand ... Jer 49:19
who is that *s* that will stand ... Jer 50:44
break in pieces with thee the *s* ... Jer 51:23
scattered, because there is no *s* ... Eze 34:5
the field, because there was no *s* ... Eze 34:8
As a *s* seeketh out his flock in ... Eze 34:12
And I will set up one *s* over them ... Eze 34:23
feed them, and he shall be their *s* ... Eze 34:23
and they all shall have one *s* ... Eze 37:24
As the *s* taketh out of the mouth ... Amos 3:12
troubled, because there was no *s* ... Zec 10:2
the instruments of a foolish *s* ... Zec 11:15
I will raise up a *s* in the land ... Zec 11:16
Woe to the idol *s* that leaveth ... Zec 11:17
Awake, O sword, against my *s* ... Zec 13:7
smite the *s*, and the sheep shall ... Zec 13:7
abroad, as sheep having no *s* ... Mt 9:36
as a *s* divideth his sheep from ... Mt 25:32
it is written, I will smite the *s* ... Mt 26:31
they were as sheep not having a *s* ... Mk 6:34
it is written, I will smite the *s* ... Mk 14:27
by the door is the *s* of the sheep ... Jn 10:2
I am the good *s* ... Jn 10:11
the good *s* giveth his life for ... Jn 10:11
that is an hireling, and not the *s* ... Jn 10:12
I am the good *s*, and know my sheep ... Jn 10:14
there shall be one fold, and one *s* ... Jn 10:16
that great *s* of the sheep, ... Heb 13:20
but are now returned unto the *S* ... 1Pet 2:25
And when the chief *S* shall appear ... 1Pet 5:4

**SHEPHERD'S**
put them in a *s* bag which he had, ... 1Sa 17:40
and is removed from me as a *s* tent ... Is 38:12

**SHEPHERDS**
And the men are *s*, for their trade ... Gen 46:32
unto Pharaoh, Thy servants are *s* ... Gen 47:3
the *s* came and drove them away ... Ex 2:17
us out of the hand of the *s* ... Ex 2:19
now thy *s* which were with us, we ... 1Sa 25:7
neither shall the *s* make their ... Is 13:20
when a multitude of *s* is called ... Is 31:4
they are *s* that cannot understand ... Is 56:11
The *s* with their flocks shall ... Jer 6:3
I will set up *s* over them which ... Jer 23:4
Howl, ye *s*, and cry ... Jer 25:34
the *s* shall have no way to flee, ... Jer 25:35
A voice of the cry of the *s* ... Jer 25:36
shall be an habitation of *s* ... Jer 33:12
their *s* have caused them to go ... Jer 50:6
prophesy against the *s* of Israel ... Eze 34:2
saith the Lord GOD unto the *s* ... Eze 34:2
Woe be to the *s* of Israel that do ... Eze 34:2
should not the *s* feed the flocks ... Eze 34:2
Therefore, ye *s*, hear the word of ... Eze 34:7
neither did my *s* search for my ... Eze 34:8
but the *s* fed themselves, and fed ... Eze 34:8
Therefore, O ye *s*, hear the word ... Eze 34:9
Behold, I am against the *s* ... Eze 34:10
neither shall the *s* feed ... Eze 34:10
habitations of the *s* shall mourn ... Amos 1:2
we raise against him seven *s* ... Mic 5:5
Thy *s* slumber, O king of Assyria ... Nah 3:18
be dwellings and cottages for *s* ... Zeph 2:6
anger was kindled against the *s* ... Zec 10:3
a voice of the howling of the *s* ... Zec 11:3
their own *s* pity them not ... Zec 11:5
Three *s* also I cut off in one ... Zec 11:8
country *s* abiding in the field ... Lk 2:8
the *s* said one to another, Let us ... Lk 2:15
which were told them by the *s* ... Lk 2:18
the *s* returned, glorifying and ... Lk 2:20

**SHEPHERDS'**
feed thy kids beside the *s* tents ... Song 1:8

**SHEPHI** (*she'-fi*) See SHEPHO. *A son of Shobal.*
Alian, and Manahath, and Ebal, *S* ... 1Chr 1:40

**SHEPHO** (*she'-fo*) See SHEPHI. *Same as Shephi.*
Alvan, and Manahath, and Ebal, *S* ... Gen 36:23

**SHEPHUPHAM** See SHUPHAM.

**SHEPHUPHAN** (*shef'-u-fan*) See SHUPHAM, SHUPPIM. *A son of Bela.*
And Gera, and *S*, and Huram ... 1Chr 8:5

**SHERAH** (*she'-rah*) *Daughter of Beriah.*
(And his daughter was *S*, who built ... 1Chr 7:24

**SHERD**
a *s* to take fire from the hearth ... Is 30:14

**SHERDS**
and thou shalt break the *s* thereof ... Eze 23:34

**SHEREBIAH** (*sher-e-bi'-ah*)
*1. A family of exiles.*
and *S*, with his sons and his ... Ezr 8:18

of the chief of the priests, *S*. Ezr 8:24
Also Jeshua, and Bani, and *S* Neh 8:7
Kadmiel, Shebaniah, Bunni, *S* Neh 9:4
and Kadmiel, Bani, Hashabniah, *S* Neh 9:5
*2. A Levite who renewed the covenant.*
Zaccur, *S*, Shebaniah, Neh 10:12
Jeshua, Binnui, Kadmiel, *S* Neh 12:8
Hashabiah, *S*, and Jeshua the son Neh 12:24

**SHERESH** (*she'-resh*) *Son of Machir.*
and the name of his brother was *S* 1Chr 7:16

**SHEREZER** (*she-re'-zur*) See SHAREZER. *A messenger in Zechariah's time.*
had sent unto the house of God *S* Zec 7:2

**SHERIFFS**
the counsellors, the *s*, and all Dan 3:2
the counsellors, the *s*, and all Dan 3:3

**SHESHACH** (*she'-shak*) See BABYLON. *Another name for Babylon.*
the king of *S* shall drink after Jer 25:26
How is *S* taken Jer 51:41

**SHESHAI** (*she'-shahee*) *A son of Anak.*
where Ahiman, *S*, and Talmai, the Num 13:22
thence the three sons of Anak, *S* Josh 15:14
and they slew *S*, and Ahiman, and Judg 1:10

**SHESHAK** See SHESHACH.

**SHESHAN** (*she'-shan*) *A descendant of Jerahmeel.*
*S*. And the children of *S* 1Chr 2:31
Now *S* had no sons, but daughters 1Chr 2:34
*S* had a servant, an Egyptian, 1Chr 2:34
*S* gave his daughter to Jarha his 1Chr 2:35

**SHESHBAZZAR** (*shesh-baz'-zur*) See ZERUBBABEL. *Same as Zerubbabel.*
and numbered them unto *S*, the Ezr 1:8
All these did *S* bring up with Ezr 1:11
unto one, whose name was *S* Ezr 5:14
Then came the same *S*, and laid the Ezr 5:16

**SHETH** (*sheth*) See SETH.
*1. A Moabite chief.*
and destroy all the children of *S* Num 24:17
*2. Same as Seth.*
Adam, *S*, Enosh, 1Chr 1:1

**SHETHAR** (*she'-thar*) *A prince of Media and Persia.*
the next unto him was Carshena, *S* Est 1:14

**SHETHAR-BOZENAI** See SHETHAR-BOZNAI.

**SHETHAR-BOZNAI** (*she''-thar-boz'-nahee*) *A Persian official.*
on this side the river, and *S* Ezr 5:3
on this side the river, and *S* Ezr 5:6
governor beyond the river, *S* Ezr 6:6
on this side the river, *S* Ezr 6:13

**SHETHER BAZNAI** See SHETHAR BOZNAI.

**SHEVA** (*she'-vah*) See SHAVSHA.
*1. David's scribe.*
And *S* was scribe 2Sa 20:25
*2. Son of Maachah.*
*S* the father of Machbenah, and the 1Chr 2:49

**SHEW**
unto a land that I will *s* thee Gen 12:1
which thou shalt *s* unto me Gen 20:13
*s* kindness unto my master Abraham. Gen 24:12
*s* kindness, I pray thee, unto me, Gen 40:14
*s* Pharaoh, and say unto him, My Gen 46:31
you, saying, *S* a miracle for you Ex 7:9
for to *s* in thee my power Ex 9:16
that I might *s* these my signs Ex 10:1
thou shalt *s* thy son in that day, Ex 13:8
which he will *s* to you to day Ex 14:13
shalt *s* them the way wherein they Ex 18:20
According to all that I *s* thee Ex 25:9
*s* me now thy way, that I may know Ex 33:13
I beseech thee, *s* me thy glory Ex 33:18
*s* mercy on whom I will *s* mercy Ex 33:19
the LORD will *s* who are his Num 16:5
to *s* you by what way ye should go Deut 1:33
thou hast begun to *s* thy servant Deut 3:24
to *s* you the word of the LORD Deut 5:5
with them, nor *s* mercy unto them Deut 7:2
*s* thee mercy, and have compassion Deut 13:17
they shall *s* thee the sentence of Deut 17:9
LORD shall choose shall *s* thee Deut 17:10
sentence which they shall *s* thee Deut 17:11
nor *s* favour to the young Deut 28:50
ask thy father, and he will *s* thee Deut 32:7
that ye will also *s* kindness unto Josh 2:12
that he would not *s* them the land Josh 5:6
*S* us, we pray thee, the entrance Judg 1:24
the city, and we will *s* thee mercy Judg 1:24
I will *s* thee the man whom thou Judg 4:22
then *s* me a sign that thou Judg 6:17
Samuel feared to *s* Eli the vision 1Sa 3:15
*s* them the manner of the king 1Sa 8:9
peradventure he can *s* us our way 1Sa 9:6
that I may *s* thee the word of God 1Sa 9:27
*s* thee what thou shalt do 1Sa 10:8
to us, and we will *s* you a thing 1Sa 14:12
I will *s* thee what thou shalt do 1Sa 16:3
small, but that he will *s* it me 1Sa 20:2
send not unto thee, and *s* it thee 1Sa 20:12
thee evil, then I will *s* it thee 1Sa 20:13
*s* me the kindness of the LORD 1Sa 20:14
he fled, and did not *s* it to me 1Sa 22:17
young men, and they will *s* thee 1Sa 25:8
And now the LORD *s* kindness 2Sa 2:6
which against Judah do *s* kindness 2Sa 3:8
that I may *s* him kindness for 2Sa 9:1
that I may *s* the kindness of God 2Sa 9:3
for I will surely *s* thee kindness 2Sa 9:7
I will *s* kindness unto Hanun the 2Sa 10:2
*s* me both it, and his habitation 2Sa 15:25
thou wilt *s* thyself merciful 2Sa 22:26
man thou wilt *s* thyself upright 2Sa 22:26
the pure thou wilt *s* thyself pure 2Sa 22:27
thou wilt *s* thyself unsavoury 2Sa 22:27
If he will *s* himself a worthy man 1Kin 1:52
therefore, and *s* thyself a man 1Kin 2:2
But *s* kindness unto the sons of 1Kin 2:7
saying, Go, *s* thyself unto Ahab 1Kin 18:1
Elijah went to *s* himself unto 1Kin 18:2
I will surely *s* myself unto him 1Kin 18:15
Will ye not *s* me which of us is 2Kin 6:11
I will now *s* you what the Syrians 2Kin 7:12
*s* forth from day to day his 1Chr 16:23
I will *s* kindness unto Hanun the 1Chr 19:2
to *s* himself strong in the behalf 2Chr 16:9
but they could not *s* their Ezr 2:59
but they could not *s* their Neh 7:61
to *s* them light, and the way Neh 9:19
to *s* the people and the princes Est 1:11
her that she should not *s* it Est 2:10
to *s* it unto Esther, and to Est 4:8
*s* me wherefore thou contendest Job 10:2
that he would *s* thee the secrets Job 11:6
I will *s* thee, hear me Job 15:17
durst not *s* you mine opinion Job 32:6
I also will *s* mine opinion Job 32:10
I also will *s* mine opinion Job 32:17
to *s* unto man his uprightness Job 33:23
I will *s* thee that I have yet to Job 36:2
that say, Who will *s* us any good Ps 4:6
I will *s* forth all thy marvellous Ps 9:1
That I may *s* forth all thy praise Ps 9:14
Thou wilt *s* me the path of life Ps 16:11
*S* thy marvellous lovingkindness, Ps 17:7
thou wilt *s* thyself merciful Ps 18:25
man thou wilt *s* thyself upright Ps 18:25
the pure thou wilt *s* thyself pure Ps 18:26
thou wilt *s* thyself froward Ps 18:26
*S* me thy ways, O LORD Ps 25:4
he will *s* them his covenant Ps 25:14
every man walketh in a vain *s* Ps 39:6
will I *s* the salvation of God Ps 50:23
my mouth shall *s* forth thy praise Ps 51:15
My mouth shall *s* forth thy Ps 71:15
we will *s* forth thy praise to all Ps 79:13
*S* us thy mercy, O LORD, and grant Ps 85:7
*S* me a token for good Ps 86:17
Wilt thou *s* wonders to the dead Ps 88:10
him, and *s* him my salvation Ps 91:16
To *s* forth thy lovingkindness in Ps 92:2
To *s* that the LORD is upright Ps 92:15
vengeance belongeth, *s* thyself Ps 94:1
*s* forth his salvation from day to Ps 96:2
who can *s* forth all his praise Ps 106:2
that he remembered not to *s* mercy Ps 109:16
friends must *s* himself friendly Prov 18:24
The *s* of their countenance doth Is 3:9
formed them will *s* them no favour Is 27:11
shall *s* the lighting down of his Is 30:30
forth, and *s* us what shall happen Is 41:22
let them *s* the former things, Is 41:22
*S* the things that are to come Is 41:23
this, and *s* us former things Is 43:9
they shall *s* forth my praise Is 43:21
shall come, let them *s* unto them Is 44:7
this, and *s* yourselves men Is 46:8
thou didst *s* them no mercy Is 47:6
are in darkness, *S* yourselves Is 49:9
*s* my people their transgression, Is 58:1
they shall *s* forth the praises of Is 60:6
when thou shalt *s* this people all Jer 16:10
where I will not *s* you favour Jer 16:13
I will *s* them the back, and not Jer 18:17
*s* thee great and mighty things, Jer 33:3
That the LORD thy God may *s* us Jer 42:3
I will *s* mercies unto you, that Jer 42:12
are cruel, and will not *s* mercy Jer 50:42
to *s* the king of Babylon that his Jer 51:31
yea, thou shalt *s* her all her Eze 22:2
with their mouth they *s* much love Eze 33:31
Wilt thou not *s* us what thou Eze 37:18
upon all that I shall *s* thee Eze 40:4
for to the intent that I might *s* Eze 40:4
*s* the house to the house of Eze 43:10
*s* them the form of the house, and Eze 43:11
for to *s* the king his dreams Dan 2:2
we will *s* the interpretation Dan 2:4
But if ye *s* the dream, and the Dan 2:6
therefore *s* me the dream, and the Dan 2:6
we will *s* the interpretation of Dan 2:7
I shall know that ye can *s* me the Dan 2:9
that can *s* the king's matter Dan 2:10
that can *s* it before the king Dan 2:11
that he would *s* the king the Dan 2:16
I will *s* unto the king the Dan 2:24
the soothsayers, *s* unto the king Dan 2:27
I thought it good to *s* the signs Dan 4:2
*s* me the interpretation thereof, Dan 5:7
he will *s* the interpretation Dan 5:12
but they could not *s* the Dan 5:15
forth, and I am come to *s* thee Dan 9:23
But I will *s* thee that which is Dan 10:21
now will I *s* thee the truth Dan 11:2
I will *s* wonders in the heavens Joel 2:30
I *s* unto him marvellous things Mic 7:15
face, and I will *s* the nations thy Nah 3:5
Why dost thou *s* me iniquity Hab 1:3
I will *s* thee what these be Zec 1:9
*s* mercy and compassions every man Zec 7:9
*s* thyself to the priest, and offer Mt 8:4
*s* John again those things which Mt 11:4
he shall *s* judgment to the Mt 12:18
do *s* forth themselves in him Mt 14:2
would *s* them a sign from heaven Mt 16:1
Jesus to *s* unto his disciples Mt 16:21
*S* me the tribute money Mt 22:19
disciples came to him for to *s* Mt 24:1
shall *s* great signs and wonders Mt 24:24
*s* thyself to the priest, and offer Mk 1:44
do *s* forth themselves in him Mk 6:14
shall rise, and shall *s* signs Mk 13:22
he will *s* you a large upper room Mk 14:15
to *s* thee these glad tidings Lk 1:19
*s* thyself to the priest, and offer Lk 5:14
I will *s* you to whom he is like Lk 6:47
*s* how great things God hath done Lk 8:39
Go *s* yourselves unto the priests Lk 17:14
*S* me a penny Lk 20:24
for a *s* make long prayers Lk 20:47
he shall *s* you a large upper room Lk 22:12
he will *s* him greater works than Jn 5:20
things, *s* thyself to the world Jn 7:4
where he were, he should *s* it Jn 11:57
*s* us the Father, and it sufficeth Jn 14:8
sayest thou then, *S* us the Father Jn 14:9
he will *s* you things to come Jn 16:13
of mine, and shall *s* it unto you Jn 16:14
of mine, and shall *s* it unto you Jn 16:15
but I shall *s* you plainly of the Jn 16:25
*s* whether of these two thou hast Acts 1:24
I will *s* wonders in heaven above, Acts 2:19
the land which I shall *s* thee Acts 7:3
For I will *s* him how great things Acts 9:16
Go *s* these things unto James, and Acts 12:17
which *s* unto us the way of Acts 16:17
willing to *s* the Jews a pleasure, Acts 24:27
should *s* light unto the people, Acts 26:23
Which *s* the work of the law Rom 2:15
that I might *s* my power in thee, Rom 9:17
if God, willing to *s* his wrath Rom 9:22
ye do *s* the Lord's death till he 1Cor 11:26
yet *s* I unto you a more excellent 1Cor 12:31
Behold, I *s* you a mystery 1Cor 15:51
Wherefore *s* ye to them, and before 2Cor 8:24
to make a fair *s* in the flesh Gal 6:12
*s* the exceeding riches of his Eph 2:7
he made a *s* of them openly, Col 2:15
a *s* of wisdom in will worship Col 2:23
For they themselves *s* of us what 1Th 1:9
might *s* forth all longsuffering 1Ti 1:16
learn first to *s* piety at home 1Ti 5:4
Which in his times he shall *s* 1Ti 6:15
Study to *s* thyself approved unto 2Ti 2:15
*s* the same diligence to the full Heb 6:11
willing more abundantly to *s* unto Heb 6:17
*s* me thy faith without thy works, Jas 2:18
I will *s* thee my faith by my Jas 2:18
let him *s* out of a good Jas 3:13
that ye should *s* forth the 1Pet 2:9
*s* unto you that eternal life, 1Jn 1:2
to *s* unto his servants things Rev 1:1
I will *s* thee things which must Rev 4:1
I will *s* unto thee the judgment Rev 17:1
I will *s* thee the bride, the Rev 21:9
to *s* unto his servants the things Rev 22:6

**SHEWBREAD**
upon the table *s* before me alway Ex 25:30
and all his vessels, and the *s* Ex 35:13
all the vessels thereof, and the *s* Ex 39:36
upon the table of *s* they shall Num 4:7
was no bread there but the *s* 1Sa 21:6
of gold, whereupon the *s* was 1Kin 7:48
the Kohathites, were over the *s* 1Chr 9:32
Both for the *s*, and for the fine 1Chr 23:29
he gave gold for the tables of *s* 1Chr 28:16
incense, and for the continual *s* 2Chr 2:4
the tables whereon the *s* was set 2Chr 4:19
the *s* also set they in order upon 2Chr 13:11
the *s* table, with all the vessels 2Chr 29:18
For the *s*, and for the continual Neh 10:33
house of God, and did eat the *s* Mt 12:4
the high priest, and did eat the *s* Mk 2:26
of God, and did take and eat the *s* Lk 6:4
and the table, and the *s* Heb 9:2

**SHEWED**
which thou hast *s* unto me in Gen 19:19
hast *s* kindness unto my master Gen 24:14
which thou hast *s* unto thy Gen 32:10
*s* him mercy, and gave him favour Gen 39:21
God hath *s* Pharaoh what he is Gen 41:25
as God hath *s* thee all this Gen 41:39
God hath *s* me also thy seed Gen 48:11
the LORD *s* him a tree, which when Ex 15:25
which was *s* thee in the mount Ex 25:40
which was *s* thee in the mount Ex 26:30
as it was *s* thee in the mount, so Ex 27:8
reddish, and it be *s* to the priest Lev 13:19
shall be *s* unto the priest Lev 13:49
mind of the LORD might be *s* them Lev 24:12
which the LORD had *s* Moses Num 8:4
*s* them the fruit of the land Num 13:26

signs which I have *s* among them ... Num 14:11
Unto thee it was *s*, that thou ... Deut 4:35
upon earth he *s* thee his great ... Deut 4:36
LORD our God hath *s* us his glory ... Deut 5:24
And the LORD *s* signs and wonders, ... Deut 6:22
the LORD *s* him all the land of ... Deut 34:1
*s* in the sight of all Israel ... Deut 34:12
LORD, since I have *s* you kindness ... Josh 2:12
when he *s* them the entrance into ... Judg 1:25
they *s* Sisera that Barak the son ... Judg 4:12
Neither *s* they kindness to the ... Judg 8:35
which he had *s* unto Israel ... Judg 8:35
*s* her husband, and said unto him, ... Judg 13:10
he have *s* us all these things ... Judg 13:23
for he hath *s* me all his heart ... Judg 16:18
unto her, It hath fully been *s* me ... Ruth 2:11
she *s* her mother in law with whom ... Ruth 2:19
for thou hast *s* more kindness in ... Ruth 3:10
*s* it to the men of Jabesh ... 1Sa 11:9
for ye *s* kindness to all the ... 1Sa 15:6
Jonathan *s* him all those things ... 1Sa 19:7
Abiathar *s* David that Saul had ... 1Sa 22:21
thou hast *s* this day how that ... 1Sa 24:18
that ye have *s* this kindness unto ... 2Sa 2:5
as his father *s* kindness unto me ... 2Sa 10:2
*s* David all that Joab had sent ... 2Sa 11:22
thou hast not *s* it unto thy ... 1Kin 1:27
Thou hast *s* unto thy servant ... 1Kin 3:6
he did, and his might that he *s* ... 1Kin 16:27
and his might that he *s*, and how ... 1Kin 22:45
And he *s* him the place ... 2Kin 6:6
howbeit the LORD hath *s* me that ... 2Kin 8:10
The LORD hath *s* me that thou ... 2Kin 8:13
LORD, and *s* them the king's son ... 2Kin 11:4
*s* them all the house of his ... 2Kin 20:13
that Hezekiah *s* them not ... 2Kin 20:13
treasures that I have not *s* them ... 2Kin 20:15
And Shaphan the scribe *s* the king ... 2Kin 22:10
his father *s* kindness to me ... 1Chr 19:2
Thou hast *s* great mercy unto ... 2Chr 1:8
that the LORD had *s* unto David ... 2Chr 7:10
hath been *s* from the LORD our God ... Ezr 9:8
When he *s* the riches of his ... Est 1:4
Esther had not *s* her people nor ... Est 2:10
Esther had not yet *s* her kindred ... Est 2:20
for they had *s* him the people of ... Est 3:6
pity should be *s* from his friend ... Job 6:14
for he hath *s* me his marvellous ... Ps 31:21
Thou hast *s* thy people hard ... Ps 60:3
until I have *s* thy strength unto ... Ps 71:18
Thou, which hast *s* me great ... Ps 71:20
and his wonders that he had *s* them ... Ps 78:11
*s* in the sight of the heathen ... Ps 98:2
They *s* his signs among them, and ... Ps 105:27
He hath *s* his people the power of ... Ps 111:6
the LORD, which hath *s* us light ... Ps 118:27
I *s* before him my trouble ... Ps 142:2
his wickedness shall be *s* before ... Prov 26:26
wherein I have *s* myself wise ... Eccl 2:19
Let favour be *s* to the wicked ... Is 26:10
*s* them the house of his precious ... Is 39:2
that Hezekiah *s* them not ... Is 39:2
treasures that I have not *s* them ... Is 39:4
*s* to him the way of understanding ... Is 40:14
and have saved, and I have *s* ... Is 43:12
out of my mouth, and I *s* them ... Is 48:3
it came to pass I *s* it thee ... Is 48:5
I have *s* thee new things from ... Is 48:6
The LORD *s* me, and, behold, two ... Jer 24:1
the word that the LORD hath *s* me ... Jer 38:21
the things that the LORD had *s* me ... Eze 11:25
*s* them my judgments, which if a ... Eze 20:11
neither have they *s* difference ... Eze 22:26
Thus hath the Lord GOD *s* unto me ... Amos 7:1
Thus hath the Lord GOD *s* unto me ... Amos 7:4
Thus he *s* me ... Amos 7:7
Thus hath the Lord GOD *s* unto me ... Amos 8:1
He hath *s* thee, O man, what is ... Mic 6:8
the LORD *s* me four carpenters ... Zec 1:20
he *s* me Joshua the high priest ... Zec 3:1
*s* unto the chief priests all the ... Mt 28:11
He hath *s* strength with his arm ... Lk 1:51
Lord had *s* great mercy upon her ... Lk 1:58
*s* unto him all the kingdoms of ... Lk 4:5
the disciples of John *s* him of ... Lk 7:18
he said, He that *s* mercy on him ... Lk 10:37
came, and *s* his lord these things ... Lk 14:21
even Moses *s* at the bush, when he ... Lk 20:37
he *s* them his hands and his feet ... Lk 24:40
works have I *s* you from my Father ... Jn 10:32
he *s* unto them his hands and his ... Jn 20:20
After these things Jesus *s* ... Jn 21:1
and on this wise *s* he himself ... Jn 21:1
Jesus *s* himself to his disciples ... Jn 21:14
To whom also he *s* himself alive ... Acts 1:3
which God before had *s* by the ... Acts 3:18
this miracle of healing was *s* ... Acts 4:22
the next day he *s* himself unto ... Acts 7:26
out, after that he had *s* wonders ... Acts 7:36
they have slain them which *s* ... Acts 7:52
but God hath *s* me that I should ... Acts 10:28
up the third day, and *s* him openly ... Acts 10:40
he *s* us how he had seen an angel ... Acts 11:13
and confessed, and *s* their deeds ... Acts 19:18
unto you, but have *s* you, and have ... Acts 20:20
I have *s* you all things, how that ... Acts 20:35
thou hast *s* these things to me ... Acts 23:22
But *s* first unto them of Damascus ... Acts 26:20
the barbarous people *s* us no ... Acts 28:2
came *s* or spake any harm of thee ... Acts 28:21
for God hath *s* it unto them ... Rom 1:19
eat not for his sake that *s* it ... 1Cor 10:28
which ye have *s* toward his name, ... Heb 6:10
pattern *s* to thee in the mount ... Heb 8:5
mercy, that hath *s* no mercy ... Jas 2:13
our Lord Jesus Christ hath *s* me ... 2Pet 1:14
*s* me that great city, the holy ... Rev 21:10
he *s* me a pure river of water of ... Rev 22:1
the angel which *s* me these things ... Rev 22:8

## SHEWEDST

*s* signs and wonders upon Pharaoh, ... Neh 9:10
then thou *s* me their doings ... Jer 11:18

## SHEWEST

*s* mercy unto thy servants, that ... 2Chr 6:14
again thou *s* thyself marvellous ... Job 10:16
Thou *s* lovingkindness unto ... Jer 32:18
What sign *s* thou unto us, seeing ... Jn 2:18
unto him, What sign *s* thou then ... Jn 6:30

## SHEWETH

is about to do he *s* unto Pharaoh ... Gen 41:28
whatsoever he *s* me I will tell ... Num 23:3
there is none that *s* me that my ... 1Sa 22:8
or *s* unto me that my son hath ... 1Sa 22:8
*s* mercy to his anointed, unto ... 2Sa 22:51
Then he *s* them their work, and ... Job 36:9
The noise thereof *s* concerning it ... Job 36:33
*s* mercy to his anointed, to David ... Ps 18:50
and the firmament *s* his handywork ... Ps 19:1
and night unto night *s* knowledge ... Ps 19:2
but the righteous *s* mercy ... Ps 37:21
A good man *s* favour, and lendeth ... Ps 112:5
He *s* his word unto Jacob, his ... Ps 147:19
truth *s* forth righteousness ... Prov 12:17
and the tender grass *s* itself ... Prov 27:25
yea, there is none that *s* ... Is 41:26
*s* him all the kingdoms of the ... Mt 4:8
*s* him all things that himself ... Jn 5:20
runneth, but of God that *s* mercy ... Rom 9:16
he that *s* mercy, with ... Rom 12:8

## SHEWING

*s* mercy unto thousands of them ... Ex 20:6
*s* mercy unto thousands of them ... Deut 5:10
*s* to the generation to come the ... Ps 78:4
*s* himself through the lattice ... Song 2:9
iniquities by *s* mercy to the poor ... Dan 4:27
and *s* of hard sentences, and ... Dan 5:12
till the day of his *s* unto Israel ... Lk 1:80
*s* the glad tidings of the kingdom ... Lk 8:1
*s* the coats and garments which ... Acts 9:39
*s* by the scriptures that Jesus ... Acts 18:28
of God, *s* himself that he is God ... 2Th 2:4
In all things *s* thyself a pattern ... Titus 2:7
in doctrine *s* uncorruptness, ... Titus 2:7
but *s* all good fidelity ... Titus 2:10
*s* all meekness unto all men ... Titus 3:2

**SHIBAH** See SHEBAH.

**SHIBBOLETH** (*shib'-bo-leth*) See SIBBOLETH. *Password that distinguished Gileadites from Ephraimites.*
said they unto him, Say now *S* ... Judg 12:6

**SHIBMAH** (*shib'-mah*) See SHEBAM, SIBMAH. *A city in Reuben.*
(their names being changed,) and *S* .. Num 32:38

**SHICRON** (*shi'-cron*) *A city in Judah.*
and the border was drawn to *S* ... Josh 15:11

## SHIELD

I am thy *s*, and thy exceeding ... Gen 15:1
the *s* of thy help, and who is the ... Deut 33:29
was there a *s* or spear seen among ... Judg 5:8
one bearing a *s* went before him ... 1Sa 17:7
that bare the *s* went before him ... 1Sa 17:41
and with a spear, and with a *s* ... 1Sa 17:45
for there the *s* of the mighty is ... 2Sa 1:21
the *s* of Saul, as though he had ... 2Sa 1:21
he is my *s*, and the horn of my ... 2Sa 22:3
given me the *s* of thy salvation ... 2Sa 22:36
three pound of gold went to one *s* ... 1Kin 10:17
there, nor come before it with *s* ... 2Kin 19:32
the battle, that could handle *s* ... 1Chr 12:8
The children of Judah that bare *s* ... 1Chr 12:24
captains, and with them with *s* ... 1Chr 12:34
shekels of gold went to one *s* ... 2Chr 9:16
bow and *s* two hundred thousand ... 2Chr 17:17
war, that could handle spear and *s* ... 2Chr 25:5
the glittering spear and the *s* ... Job 39:23
But thou, O LORD, art a *s* for me ... Ps 3:3
wilt thou compass him as with a *s* ... Ps 5:12
given me the *s* of thy salvation ... Ps 18:35
The LORD is my strength and my *s* ... Ps 28:7
he is our help and our *s* ... Ps 33:20
Take hold of *s* and buckler, and ... Ps 35:2
and bring them down, O Lord our *s* ... Ps 59:11
he the arrows of the bow, the *s* ... Ps 76:3
Behold, O God our *s*, and look upon ... Ps 84:9
For the LORD God is a sun and *s* ... Ps 84:11
his truth shall be thy *s* and ... Ps 91:4
he is their help and their *s* ... Ps 115:9
he is their help and their *s* ... Ps 115:10
he is their help and their *s* ... Ps 115:11
Thou art my hiding place and my *s* ... Ps 119:114
my *s*, and he in whom I trust ... Ps 144:2
he is a *s* unto them that put ... Prov 30:5
ye princes, and anoint the *s* ... Is 21:5
horsemen, and Kir uncovered the *s* ... Is 22:6
Order ye the buckler and *s* ... Jer 46:3
and the Libyans, that handle the *s* ... Jer 46:9
set against thee buckler and *s* ... Eze 23:24
they hanged the *s* and helmet in ... Eze 27:10
all of them with *s* and helmet ... Eze 38:5
The *s* of his mighty men is made ... Nah 2:3
Above all, taking the *s* of faith ... Eph 6:16

## SHIELDS

David took the *s* of gold that ... 2Sa 8:7
three hundred *s* of beaten gold ... 1Kin 10:17
he took away all the *s* of gold ... 1Kin 14:26
made in their stead brasen *s* ... 1Kin 14:27
give king David's spears and *s* ... 2Kin 11:10
David took the *s* of gold that ... 1Chr 18:7
three hundred *s* made he of beaten ... 2Chr 9:16
And in every several city he put *s* ... 2Chr 11:12
he carried away also the *s* of ... 2Chr 12:9
king Rehoboam made *s* of brass ... 2Chr 12:10
and out of Benjamin, that bare *s* ... 2Chr 14:8
spears, and bucklers, and *s* ... 2Chr 23:9
them throughout all the host *s* ... 2Chr 26:14
and made darts and *s* in abundance ... 2Chr 32:5
stones, and for spices, and for *s* ... 2Chr 32:27
them held both the spears, the *s* ... Neh 4:16
for the *s* of the earth belong ... Ps 47:9
bucklers, all *s* of mighty men ... Song 4:4
there, nor come before it with *s* ... Is 37:33
gather the *s* ... Jer 51:11
they hanged their *s* upon thy ... Eze 27:11
great company with bucklers and *s* ... Eze 38:4
and burn the weapons, both the *s* ... Eze 39:9

**SHIGGAION** (*shig-gah'-yon*) See SHIGIONOTH. *A musical notation.*
*S* of David, which he sang unto ... Ps 7:t

**SHIGIONOTH** (*shig-i'-o-noth*) See SHIGGAION. *A musical notation.*
of Habakkuk the prophet upon *S* ... Hab 3:1

**SHIHON** (*shi'-hon*) *A city in Issachar.*
and *S*, and Anaharath ... Josh 19:19

**SHIHOR** (*shi'-hor*) See SHIHOR-LIBNATH. *Same as Sihor.*
from *S* of Egypt even unto the ... 1Chr 13:5

**SHIHOR-LIBNATH** (*shi''-hor-lib'-nath*) *A small river in Asher.*
to Carmel westward, and to *S* ... Josh 19:26

**SHIKKERON** See SHICRON.

**SHILHI** (*shil'-hi*) *Father of Azubah.*
name was Azubah the daughter of *S* 1Kin 22:42
name was Azubah the daughter of *S* 2Chr 20:31

**SHILHIM** (*shil'-him*) See SHAARAIM, SHARUHEN. *A city in Judah.*
And Lebaoth, and *S*, and Ain, and ... Josh 15:32

**SHILLEM** (*shil'-lem*) See SHALLUM, SHILLEMITES. *A son of Naphtali.*
Jahzeel, and Guni, and Jezer, and *S* ... Gen 46:24
of *S*, the family of the ... Num 26:49

**SHILLEMITES** (*shil'-lem-ites*) *Descendants of Shillem.*
of Shillem, the family of the *S* ... Num 26:49

**SHILOAH** (*shi-lo'-ah*) See SILOAH, SILOAM. *A fountain in Jerusalem.*
the waters of *S* that go softly ... Is 8:6

**SHILOH** (*shi'-loh*) See SHILONITE.
*1. Symbolic name for the Ruler from Judah.*
between his feet, until *S* come ... Gen 49:10
*2. A city in Ephraim.*
of Israel assembled together at *S* ... Josh 18:1
lots for you before the LORD in *S* ... Josh 18:8
again to Joshua to the host at *S* ... Josh 18:9
for them in *S* before the LORD ... Josh 18:10
by lot in *S* before the LORD ... Josh 19:51
them at *S* in the land of Canaan ... Josh 21:2
the children of Israel out of *S* ... Josh 22:9
gathered themselves together at *S* ... Josh 22:12
that the house of God was in *S* ... Judg 18:31
brought them unto the camp to *S* ... Judg 21:12
*S* yearly in a place which is on ... Judg 21:19
if the daughters of *S* come out to ... Judg 21:21
his wife of the daughters of *S* ... Judg 21:21
unto the LORD of hosts in *S* ... 1Sa 1:3
rose up after they had eaten in *S* ... 1Sa 1:9
unto the house of the LORD in *S* ... 1Sa 1:24
So they did in *S* unto all the ... 1Sa 2:14
And the LORD appeared again in *S* ... 1Sa 3:21
in *S* by the word of the LORD ... 1Sa 3:21
of the LORD out of *S* unto us ... 1Sa 4:3
So the people sent to *S*, that ... 1Sa 4:4
came to *S* the same day with his ... 1Sa 4:12
of Eli, the LORD's priest in *S* ... 1Sa 14:3
concerning the house of Eli in *S* ... 1Kin 2:27
and get thee to *S* ... 1Kin 14:2
did so, and arose, and went to *S* ... 1Kin 14:4
he forsook the tabernacle of *S* ... Ps 78:60
now unto my place which was in *S* ... Jer 7:12
your fathers, as I have done to *S* ... Jer 7:14
will I make this house like *S* ... Jer 26:6
This house shall be like *S* ... Jer 26:9
came certain from Shechem, from *S* ... Jer 41:5

**SHILONI** (*shi-lo'-ni*) See SHILONITE. *Father of Zechariah.*
son of Zechariah, the son of *S* ... Neh 11:5

**SHILONITE** (*shi'-lon-ite*) See SHILONI, SHILONITES. *An inhabitant of Shiloh.*
Ahijah the *S* found him in the way ... 1Kin 11:29
the LORD spake by Ahijah the *S* ... 1Kin 12:15
spake by his servant Ahijah the *S* ... 1Kin 15:29
in the prophecy of Ahijah the *S* ... 2Chr 9:29
*S* to Jeroboam the son of Nebat ... 2Chr 10:15

**SHILONITES** (*shi'-lon-ites*)
And of the *S* ... 1Chr 9:5

**SHILSHAH** (*shil'-shah*) *Son of Zophah.*
Bezer, and Hod, and Shamma, and *S* .. 1Chr 7:37

**SHIMEA** (*shim'-e-ah*) See SHAMMAH, SHAMMUA, SHAMMUAH, SHIMEAH, SHIMEATHITES, SHIMMA.
*1. David's brother.*
Jonathan the son of *S* David's ... 1Chr 20:7
*2. A son of David.*
*S*, and Shobab, and Nathan, and ... 1Chr 3:5
*3. Father of Haggiah.*
*S* his son, Haggiah his son, ... 1Chr 6:30
*4. Father of Berachiah.*
son of Berachiah, the son of *S* ... 1Chr 6:39

**SHIMEAH** (*shim'-e-ah*) See SHIMEA, SHIMEAM.
*1. Same as Shimea 1.*
the son of *S* David's brother ... 2Sa 13:3
the son of *S* David's brother, ... 2Sa 13:32
Jonathan the son of *S* the brother ... 2Sa 21:21
*2. A relative of King Saul.*
And Mikloth begat *S* ... 1Chr 8:32

**SHIMEAM** (*shim'-e-am*) See SHIMEA. *Son of Mikloth.*
And Mikloth begat *S* ... 1Chr 9:38

**SHIMEATH** (*shim'-e-ath*) *Mother of Jozachar.*
For Jozachar the son of *S* ... 2Kin 12:21
Zabad the son of *S* an Ammonitess... 2Chr 24:26

**SHIMEATHITES** (*shim'-e-ath-ites*) *A family of scribes.*
the Tirathites, the *S*, and ... 1Chr 2:55

**SHIMEI** (*shim'-e-i*) See SHEMAIAH, SHIMHI, SHIMI, SHIMITES.
*1. A son of Gershon.*
families; Libni, and *S* ... Num 3:18
Gershom; Libni, and *S* ... 1Chr 6:17
the son of Zimmah, the son of *S* ... 1Chr 6:42
Gershonites were, Laadan, and *S* ... 1Chr 23:7
And the sons of *S* were, Jahath, ... 1Chr 23:10
These four were the sons of *S* ... 1Chr 23:10
*2. A son of Gera.*
house of Saul, whose name was *S* ... 2Sa 16:5
thus said *S* when he cursed, Come ... 2Sa 16:7
*S* went along on the hill's side ... 2Sa 16:13
*S* the son of Gera, a Benjamite, ... 2Sa 19:16
*S* the son of Gera fell down ... 2Sa 19:18
Shall not *S* be put to death for ... 2Sa 19:21
Therefore the king said unto *S* ... 2Sa 19:23
hast with thee *S* the son of Gera ... 1Kin 2:8
And the king sent and called for *S* ... 1Kin 2:36
*S* said unto the king, The saying ... 1Kin 2:38
*S* dwelt in Jerusalem many days ... 1Kin 2:38
of *S* ran away unto Achish son of ... 1Kin 2:39
And they told *S*, saying, Behold, ... 1Kin 2:39
*S* arose, and saddled his ass, and ... 1Kin 2:40
*S* went, and brought his servants ... 1Kin 2:40
it was told Solomon that *S* had ... 1Kin 2:41
And the king sent and called for *S* ... 1Kin 2:42
The king said moreover to *S* ... 1Kin 2:44
*3. An officer of David.*
and Nathan the prophet, and *S* ... 1Kin 1:8
*4. An officer of Solomon.*
*S* the son of Elah, in Benjamin ... 1Kin 4:18
*5. A descendant of King Jehoiakim.*
of Pedaiah were, Zerubbabel, and *S* ... 1Chr 3:19
*6. Son of Zacchur.*
son, Zacchur his son, *S* his son ... 1Chr 4:26
*S* had sixteen sons and six ... 1Chr 4:27
*7. Son of Gog.*
his son, Gog his son, *S* his son, ... 1Chr 5:4
*8. Son of Libni.*
his son, *S* his son, Uzza his son, ... 1Chr 6:29
*9. A Levite of the Laadan family.*
The sons of *S* ... 1Chr 23:9
*10. A sanctuary servant.*
The tenth to *S*, he, his sons, and ... 1Chr 25:17
*11. A vineyard keeper.*
the vineyards was *S* the Ramathite... 1Chr 27:27
*12. A Levite who cleansed the Temple.*
Jehiel, and *S* ... 2Chr 29:14
*13. A Temple servant in Hezekiah's time.*
*S* his brother was the next ... 2Chr 31:12
*S* his brother, at the commandment.. 2Chr 31:13
*14. A Levite who married a foreigner.*
Jozabad, and *S*, and Kelaiah, (the ... Ezr 10:23
*15. A Hashumite who married a foreigner.*
Jeremai, Manasseh, and *S* ... Ezr 10:33
*16. A Banite who married a foreigner.*
And Bani, and Binnui, *S*, ... Ezr 10:38
*17. Grandfather of Mordecai.*
the son of Jair, the son of *S* ... Est 2:5
*18. A representative of the Gershonites.*
the family of *S* apart, and their ... Zec 12:13

**SHIMEITES** See SHIMITES.

**SHIMEON** (*shim'-e-on*) See SIMEON. *A member of the Harim family.*
Ishijah, Malchiah, Shemaiah, *S* ... Ezr 10:31

**SHIMHI** (*shim'-hi*) See SHEMA, SHIMEI. *Father of a chief family in Judah.*
and Shimrath, the sons of *S* ... 1Chr 8:21

**SHIMI** (*shi'-mi*) See SHIMEI, SHIMITES. *Same as Shimei 1.*
Libni, and *S*, according to their ... Ex 6:17

**SHIMITES** (*shi'-mites*) *Descendants of Shimei 1.*
Libnites, and the family of the *S* ... Num 3:21

**SHIMMA** (*shim'-mah*) See SHAMMAH. *Same as Shamma.*
the second, and *S* the third, ... 1Chr 2:13

**SHIMON** (*shi'-mon*) *A descendant of Caleb.*
And the sons of *S* were, Amnon, and . 1Chr 4:20

**SHIMRATH** (*shim'-rath*) *A son of Shimri.*
And Adaiah, and Beraiah, and *S* ... 1Chr 8:21

**SHIMRI** (*shim'-ri*) See SIMRI.
*1. Head of a family in Simeon.*
the son of Jedaiah, the son of *S* ... 1Chr 4:37
*2. Father of Jedaiah.*
Jediael the son of *S*, and Joha his ... 1Chr 11:45
*3. A Levite who cleansed the Temple.*
*S*, and Jeiel ... 2Chr 29:13

**SHIMRITH** (*shim'-rith*) See SHOMER. *Mother of Jehozabad.*
the son of *S* a Moabitess ... 2Chr 24:26

**SHIMROM** (*shim'-rom*) See SHIMRON. *A son of Issachar.*
were, Tola, and Puah, Jashub, and *S* ... 1Chr 7:1

**SHIMRON** (*shim'-ron*) See SHIMROM, SHIMRONITES. *Same as Shimron.*
Tola, and Phuvah, and Job, and *S* ... Gen 46:13
of *S*, the family of the ... Num 26:24
of Madon, and to the king of *S* ... Josh 11:1
And Kattath, and Nahallal, and *S* ... Josh 19:15

**SHIMRONITE** See SHIMRONITES.

**SHIMRONITES** (*shim'-ron-ites*) *Descendants of Shimrom.*
of Shimron, the family of the *S* ... Num 26:24

**SHIMRON-MERON** (*shim''-ron-me'-ron*) *A city in Galilee.*
The king of *S*, one ... Josh 12:20

**SHIMSHAI** (*shim'-shahee*) *An opponent of Nehemiah.*
*S* the scribe wrote a letter ... Ezr 4:8
*S* the scribe, and the rest of ... Ezr 4:9
to *S* the scribe, and to the rest ... Ezr 4:17
*S* the scribe, and their companions ... Ezr 4:23

**SHINAB** (*shi'-nab*) *King of Admah.*
*S* king of Admah, and Shemeber king . Gen 14:2

**SHINAR** (*shi'-nar*) *A nation in Babylonia.*
and Calneh, in the land of *S* ... Gen 10:10
found a plain in the land of *S* ... Gen 11:2
in the days of Amraphel king of *S* ... Gen 14:1
of nations, and Amraphel king of *S* ... Gen 14:9
Cush, and from Elam, and from *S* ... Is 11:11
land of *S* to the house of his god ... Dan 1:2
it an house in the land of *S* ... Zec 5:11

**SHINE**
LORD make his face *s* upon thee ... Num 6:25
neither let the light *s* upon it ... Job 3:4
*s* upon the counsel of the wicked ... Job 10:3
thou shalt *s* forth, thou shalt be ... Job 11:17
the spark of his fire shall not *s* ... Job 18:5
the light shall *s* upon thy ways ... Job 22:28
commandeth it not to *s* by the ... Job 36:32
the light of his cloud to *s* ... Job 37:15
By his neesings a light doth *s* ... Job 41:18
He maketh a path to *s* after him ... Job 41:32
thy face to *s* upon thy servant ... Ps 31:16
and cause his face to *s* upon us ... Ps 67:1
between the cherubims, *s* forth ... Ps 80:1
O God, and cause thy face to *s* ... Ps 80:3
of hosts, and cause thy face to *s* ... Ps 80:7
God of hosts, cause thy face to *s* ... Ps 80:19
man, and oil to make his face to *s* ... Ps 104:15
thy face to *s* upon thy servant ... Ps 119:135
man's wisdom maketh his face to *s* ... Eccl 8:1
shall not cause her light to *s* ... Is 13:10
Arise, *s*; for thy light ... Is 60:1
They are waxen fat, they *s* ... Jer 5:28
cause thy face to *s* upon thy ... Dan 9:17
they that be wise shall *s* as the ... Dan 12:3
Let your light so *s* before men ... Mt 5:16
Then shall the righteous *s* forth ... Mt 13:43
and his face did *s* as the sun ... Mt 17:2
image of God, should *s* unto them ... 2Cor 4:4
the light to *s* out of darkness ... 2Cor 4:6
among whom ye *s* as lights in the ... Phil 2:15
shall *s* no more at all in thee ... Rev 18:23
neither of the moon, to *s* in it ... Rev 21:23

**SHINED**
he *s* forth from mount Paran, and ... Deut 33:2
When his candle *s* upon my head ... Job 29:3
If I beheld the sun when it *s* ... Job 31:26
perfection of beauty, God hath *s* ... Ps 50:2
death, upon them hath the light *s* ... Is 9:2
the earth *s* with his glory ... Eze 43:2
suddenly there *s* round about him ... Acts 9:3
him, and a light *s* in the prison ... Acts 12:7
hath *s* in our hearts, to give the ... 2Cor 4:6

**SHINETH**
even to the moon, and it *s* not ... Job 25:5
but the night *s* as the day ... Ps 139:12
as the shining light, that *s* more ... Prov 4:18
the east, and *s* even unto the west ... Mt 24:27
*s* unto the other part under ... Lk 17:24
And the light *s* in darkness ... Jn 1:5
a light that *s* in a dark place ... 2Pet 1:19
is past, and the true light now *s* ... 1Jn 2:8
was as the sun *s* in his strength ... Rev 1:16

**SHINING**
the earth by clear *s* after rain ... 2Sa 23:4
of the just is as the *s* light ... Prov 4:18
the *s* of a flaming fire by night ... Is 4:5
the stars shall withdraw their *s* ... Joel 2:10
the stars shall withdraw their *s* ... Joel 3:15
at the *s* of thy glittering spear ... Hab 3:11
And his raiment became *s*, ... Mk 9:3
as when the bright *s* of a candle ... Lk 11:36
men stood by them in *s* garments ... Lk 24:4
He was a burning and a *s* light ... Jn 5:35
*s* round about me and them which ... Acts 26:13

**SHION** See SHIHON.

**SHIP**
the way of a *s* in the midst of ... Prov 30:19
shall gallant *s* pass thereby ... Is 33:21
They have made all thy *s* boards ... Eze 27:5
he found a *s* going to Tarshish ... Jonah 1:3
so that the *s* was like to be ... Jonah 1:4
that were in the *s* into the sea ... Jonah 1:5
gone down into the sides of the *s* ... Jonah 1:5
in a *s* with Zebedee their father, ... Mt 4:21
And they immediately left the *s* ... Mt 4:22
And when he was entered into a *s* ... Mt 8:23
insomuch that the *s* was covered ... Mt 8:24
And he entered into a *s*, and passed ... Mt 9:1
him, so that he went into a *s* ... Mt 13:2
he departed thence by *s* into a ... Mt 14:13
his disciples to get into a *s* ... Mt 14:22
But the *s* was now in the midst of ... Mt 14:24
Peter was come down out of the *s* ... Mt 14:29
And when they were come into the *s* ... Mt 14:32
Then they that were in the *s* came ... Mt 14:33
away the multitude, and took *s* ... Mt 15:39
were in the *s* mending their nets ... Mk 1:19
in the *s* with the hired servants ... Mk 1:20
that a small *s* should wait on him ... Mk 3:9
so that he entered into a *s* ... Mk 4:1
took him even as he was in the *s* ... Mk 4:36
and the waves beat into the *s* ... Mk 4:37
was in the hinder part of the *s* ... Mk 4:38
And when he was come out of the *s* ... Mk 5:2
And when he was come into the *s* ... Mk 5:18
again by *s* unto the other side ... Mk 5:21
a desert place by *s* privately ... Mk 6:32
his disciples to get into the *s* ... Mk 6:45
the *s* was in the midst of the sea ... Mk 6:47
he went up unto them into the *s* ... Mk 6:51
when they were come out of the *s* ... Mk 6:54
into a *s* with his disciples ... Mk 8:10
entering into the *s* again ... Mk 8:13
neither had they in the *s* with ... Mk 8:14
and taught the people out of the *s* ... Lk 5:3
which were in the other *s* ... Lk 5:7
went into a *s* with his disciples ... Lk 8:22
and he went up into the *s*, and ... Lk 8:37
And entered into a *s*, and went over ... Jn 6:17
sea, and drawing nigh unto the *s* ... Jn 6:19
willingly received him into the *s* ... Jn 6:21
immediately the *s* was at the land ... Jn 6:21
and entered into a *s* immediately ... Jn 21:3
net on the right side of the *s* ... Jn 21:6
disciples came in a little *s* ... Jn 21:8
And we went before to *s*, and sailed.. Acts 20:13
they accompanied him unto the *s* ... Acts 20:38
finding a *s* sailing over unto ... Acts 21:2
for there the *s* was to unlade her ... Acts 21:3
leave one of another, we took *s* ... Acts 21:6
entering into a *s* of Adramyttium ... Acts 27:2
a *s* of Alexandria sailing into ... Acts 27:6
not only of the lading and *s* ... Acts 27:10
the master and the owner of the *s* ... Acts 27:11
when the *s* was caught, and could ... Acts 27:15
used helps, undergirding the *s* ... Acts 27:17
the next day they lightened the *s* ... Acts 27:18
own hands the tackling of the *s* ... Acts 27:19
life among you, but of the *s* ... Acts 27:22
were about to flee out of the *s* ... Acts 27:30
Except these abide in the *s* ... Acts 27:31
we were in all in the *s* two ... Acts 27:37
enough, they lightened the *s* ... Acts 27:38
were possible, to thrust in the *s* ... Acts 27:39
seas met, they ran the *s* aground ... Acts 27:41
and some on broken pieces of the *s* ... Acts 27:44
we departed in a *s* of Alexandria ... Acts 28:11

**SHIPHI** (*shi'-fi*) *Father of Ziza.*
And Ziza the son of *S*, the son of ... 1Chr 4:37

**SHIPHMITE** (*shif'-mite*) *Family name of Zabdi.*
the wine cellars was Zabdi the *S* ... 1Chr 27:27

**SHIPHRAH** (*shif'-rah*) *A Hebrew midwife in Egypt.*
which the name of the one was *S* ... Ex 1:15

**SHIPHTAN** (*shif'-tan*) *Father of Kemuel.*
of Ephraim, Kemuel the son of *S* ... Num 34:24

**SHIPMASTER**
So the *s* came to him, and said ... Jonah 1:6
And every *s*, and all the company in .. Rev 18:17

**SHIPMEN**
s that had knowledge of the sea,.......... 1Kin 9:27
about midnight the s deemed that ..... Acts 27:27
as the s were about to flee out........... Acts 27:30

**SHIPPING**
his disciples, they also took s..................... Jn 6:24

**SHIPS**
and he shall be for an haven of s........ Gen 49:13
s shall come come from the coast....... Num 24:24
thee into Egypt again with s............... Deut 28:68
and why did Dan remain in s.............. Judg 5:17
made a navy of s in Ezion-geber.......... 1Kin 9:26
Jehoshaphat made s of Tharshish...... 1Kin 22:48
for the s were broken at..................... 1Kin 22:48
go with thy servants in the s.............. 1Kin 22:49
by the hands of his servants s ............ 2Chr 8:18
For the king's s went to Tarshish........ 2Chr 9:21
the s of Tarshish bringing gold............ 2Chr 9:21
him to make s to go to Tarshish......... 2Chr 20:36
they made the s in Ezion-gaber.......... 2Chr 20:36
the s were broken, that they were..... 2Chr 20:37
are passed away as the swift s ............. Job 9:26
Thou breakest the s of Tarshish .............. Ps 48:7
There go the s ...................................... Ps 104:26
They that go down to the sea in s......... Ps 107:23
She is like the merchants' s................. Prov 31:14
And upon all the s of Tarshish.................. Is 2:16
Howl, ye s of Tarshish................................ Is 23:1
Howl, ye s of Tarshish............................ Is 23:14
Chaldeans, whose cry is in the s........... Is 43:14
the s of Tarshish first, to bring.................. Is 60:9
all the s of the sea with their .................. Eze 27:9
The s of Tarshish did sing of................. Eze 27:25
sea, shall come down from their s........ Eze 27:29
messengers go forth from me in s......... Eze 30:9
For the s of Chittim shall come........... Dan 11:30
and with horsemen, and with many s Dan 11:40
were also with him other little s ........... Mk 4:36
saw two s standing by the lake.................. Lk 5:2
And he entered into one of the s ............ Lk 5:3
they came, and filled both the s ............... Lk 5:7
they had brought their s to land............. Lk 5:11
Behold also the s, which though .............. Jas 3:4
part of the s were destroyed .................... Rev 8:9
and all the company in s, and.............. Rev 18:17
had s in the sea by reason of her....... Rev 18:19

**SHIPWRECK**
was I stoned, thrice I suffered s......... 2Cor 11:25
away concerning faith have made s...... 1Ti 1:19

**SHISHA** (*shi'-shah*) See SHAVSHA. *Father of Elihoreph and Ahiah.*
Elihoreph and Ahiah, the sons of S....... 1Kin 4:3

**SHISHAK** (*shi'-shak*) *A king of Egypt.*
unto S king of Egypt, and was in....... 1Kin 11:40
that S king of Egypt came up............. 1Kin 14:25
S king of Egypt came up against......... 2Chr 12:2
to Jerusalem because of S..................... 2Chr 12:5
I also left you in the hand of S.............. 2Chr 12:5
upon Jerusalem by the hand of S ......... 2Chr 12:7
So S king of Egypt came up.................. 2Chr 12:9

**SHITRAI** (*shit'-ra-i*) *A herdsman in David's court.*
fed in Sharon was S the Sharonite.... 1Chr 27:29

**SHITTAH**
the s tree, and the myrtle, and the.......... Is 41:19

**SHITTIM** (*shit'-tim*) *A place in Moab.*
and badgers' skins, and s wood,............ Ex 25:5
they shall make an ark of s wood.......... Ex 25:10
thou shalt make staves of s wood.......... Ex 25:13
shalt also make a table of s wood.......... Ex 25:23
shalt make the staves of s wood........... Ex 25:28
tabernacle of s wood standing up.......... Ex 26:15
And thou shalt make bars of s wood.... Ex 26:26
of s wood overlaid with gold................. Ex 26:32
hanging five pillars of s wood............... Ex 26:37
shalt make an altar of s wood .................. Ex 27:1
for the altar, staves of s wood ................ Ex 27:6
of s wood shalt thou make it .................. Ex 30:1
shalt make the staves of s wood............. Ex 30:5
and badgers' skins, and s wood,............. Ex 35:7
with whom was found s wood for......... Ex 35:24
for the tabernacle of s wood ................. Ex 36:20
And he made bars of s wood................... Ex 36:31
thereunto four pillars of s wood............ Ex 36:36
Bezaleel made the ark of s wood ............. Ex 37:1
And he made staves of s wood................ Ex 37:4
And he made the table of s wood.......... Ex 37:10
And he made the staves of s wood......... Ex 37:15
made the incense altar of s wood .......... Ex 37:25
And he made the staves of s wood......... Ex 37:28
altar of burnt offering of s wood ............. Ex 38:1
And he made the staves of s wood.......... Ex 38:6
And Israel abode in S, and the.............. Num 25:1
And I made an ark of s wood............... Deut 10:3
out of S two men to spy secretly............ Josh 2:1
and they removed from S, and came..... Josh 3:1
and shall water the valley of S.............. Joel 3:18
answered him from S unto Gilgal............ Mic 6:5

**SHIVERS**
potter shall they be broken to s............. Rev 2:27

**SHIZA** (*shi'-zah*) *A 'mighty man' of David.*
Adina the son of S the Reubenite...... 1Chr 11:42

**SHOA** (*sho'-ah*) *A tribal enemy of Israel.*
and all the Chaldeans, Pekod, and S... Eze 23:23

**SHOBAB** (*sho'-bab*)
*1. A son of David.*
Shammuah, and S, and Nathan, and..... 2Sa 5:14
Shimea, and S, and Nathan, and............ 1Chr 3:5
and S, Nathan, and Solomon.................. 1Chr 14:4
*2. A son of Caleb.*
Jesher, and S, and Ardon ..................... 1Chr 2:18

**SHOBACH** (*sho'-bak*) See SHOPHACH. *A Syrian defeated by David.*
S the captain of the host of.................... 2Sa 10:16
smote S the captain of their host......... 2Sa 10:18

**SHOBAI** (*sho'-bahee*) *A family of exiles.*
of Hatita, the children of S........................ Ezr 2:42
of Hatita, the children of S ...................... Neh 7:45

**SHOBAL** (*sho'-bal*)
*1. A son of Seir.*
Lotan, and S, and Zibeon, and Anah,. Gen 36:20
And the children of S were these....... Gen 36:23
duke Lotan, duke S, duke Zibeon, ...... Gen 36:29
Lotan, and S, and Zibeon, and Anah,.. 1Chr 1:38
The sons of S ......................................... 1Chr 1:40
*2. A son of Caleb.*
S the father of Kirjath-jearim,.............. 1Chr 2:50
S the father of Kirjath-jearim................ 1Chr 2:52
*3. A son of Judah.*
Hezron, and Carmi, and Hur, and S...... 1Chr 4:1
Reaiah the son of S begat Jahath .......... 1Chr 4:2

**SHOBEK** (*sho'-bek*) *A clan leader who renewed the covenant.*
Hallohesh, Pileha, S,.............................. Neh 10:24

**SHOBI** (*sho'-bi*) *A son of Nahash.*
that S the son of Nahash of.................... 2Sa 17:27

**SHOCHO** (*sho'-ko*) See CHOCHO. *A city in Judah.*
S with the villages thereof, and.......... 2Chr 28:18

**SHOCHOH** (*sho'-ko*) See SHOCHO, SHOCO, SOCHOH, SOCO, SOCOH. *Same as Shocho.*
and were gathered together at S............. 1Sa 17:1
to Judah, and pitched between S ........... 1Sa 17:1

**SHOCK**
like as a s of corn cometh in in............... Job 5:26

**SHOCKS**
and burnt up both the s, and also.......... Judg 15:5

**SHOCO** (*sho'-ko*) See SHOCHOH. *Same as Shocho.*
And Beth-zur, and S, and Adullam,..... 2Chr 11:7

**SHOD**
s them, and gave them to eat and to 2Chr 28:15
s thee with badgers' skin, and I............ Eze 16:10
But be s with sandals................................. Mk 6:9
your feet s with the preparation ............ Eph 6:15

**SHOE**
loose his s from off his foot, and........... Deut 25:9
of him that hath his s loosed .............. Deut 25:10
thy s is not waxen old upon thy .......... Deut 29:5
Loose thy s from off thy foot.................. Josh 5:15
a man plucked off his s, and gave ........... Ruth 4:7
So he drew off his s................................. Ruth 4:8
over Edom will I cast out my s .................. Ps 60:8
over Edom will I cast out my s ................ Ps 108:9
put off thy s from thy foot......................... Is 20:2

**SHOELATCHET**
take from a thread even to a s............. Gen 14:23

**SHOE'S**
whose s latchet I am not worthy.............. Jn 1:27

**SHOES**
put off thy s from off thy feet,................... Ex 3:5
your s on your feet, and your ................. Ex 12:11
Thy s shall be iron and brass .............. Deut 33:25
And old s and clouted upon their ........... Josh 9:5
our s are become old by reason of ....... Josh 9:13
in his s that were on his feet................... 1Kin 2:5
How beautiful are thy feet with s.......... Song 7:1
the latchet of their s be broken ................. Is 5:27
put on thy s upon thy feet, and............ Eze 24:17
heads, and your s upon your feet.......... Eze 24:23
and the poor for a pair of s.................. Amos 2:6
and the needy for a pair of s ............... Amos 8:6
whose s I am not worthy to bear .............. Mt 3:11
neither two coats, neither s.................... Mt 10:10
the latchet of whose s I am not................. Mk 1:7
the latchet of whose s I am not ............... Lk 3:16
neither purse, nor scrip, nor s ................. Lk 10:4
on his hand, and s on his feet................ Lk 15:22
you without purse, and scrip, and s ...... Lk 22:35
Put off thy s from thy feet .................... Acts 7:33
whose s of his feet I am not ............... Acts 13:25

**SHOHAM** (*sho'-ham*) *A Merarite.*
Beno, and S, and Zaccur, and Ibri ..... 1Chr 24:27

**SHOMER** (*sho'-mur*) See SHAMER, SHIMRITH. *Same as Shimrith.*
and Jehozabad the son of S................. 2Kin 12:21
*Son of Heber.*
And Heber begat Japhlet, and S............ 1Chr 7:32

**SHONE**
face s while he talked with him ............. Ex 34:29
behold, the skin of his face s.................. Ex 34:30
that the skin of Moses' face s ............... Ex 34:35
the sun s upon the water, and the....... 2Kin 3:22
of the Lord s round about them................. Lk 2:9
suddenly there s from heaven a.......... Acts 22:6
the day s not for a third part of............ Rev 8:12

**SHOOK**
for the oxen s it ....................................... 2Sa 6:6
Then the earth s and trembled................ 2Sa 22:8
foundations of heaven moved and s ...... 2Sa 22:8
Also I s my lap, and said, So God ......... Neh 5:13
Then the earth s and trembled.................... Ps 18:7
The earth s, the heavens also .................... Ps 68:8
the earth trembled and s......................... Ps 77:18
over the sea, he s the kingdoms .............. Is 23:11
But they s off the dust of their........... Acts 13:51
he s his raiment, and said unto............. Acts 18:6
he s off the beast into the fire,............. Acts 28:5
Whose voice then s the earth............... Heb 12:26

**SHOOT**
he made the middle bar to s.................. Ex 36:33
I will s three arrows on the side.......... 1Sa 20:20
find out now the arrows which I s....... 1Sa 20:36
that they would s from the wall ........... 2Sa 11:20
Then Elisha said, S............................. 2Kin 13:17
nor s an arrow there, nor come .......... 2Kin 19:32
to s with bow, and skilful in war, ........ 1Chr 5:18
to s arrows and great stones ............. 2Chr 26:15
that they may privily s at the.................... Ps 11:2
they s out the lip, they shake ................... Ps 22:7
bendeth his bow to s his arrows.............. Ps 58:7
bend their bows to s their arrows............ Ps 64:3
That they may s in secret at the.............. Ps 64:4
suddenly do they s at him ........................ Ps 64:4
But God shall s at them with an.............. Ps 64:7
s out thine arrows, and destroy ............. Ps 144:6
nor s an arrow there, nor come ............. Is 37:33
s at her, spare no arrows..................... Jer 50:14
neither s up their top among the ......... Eze 31:14
ye shall s forth your branches,.............. Eze 36:8
When they now s forth, ye see and....... Lk 21:30

**SHOOTERS**
the s shot from off the wall upon......... 2Sa 11:24

**SHOOTETH**
his branch s forth in his garden............ Job 8:16
In measure, when it s forth ..................... Is 27:8
herbs, and s out great branches ............. Mk 4:32

**SHOOTING**
s arrows out of a bow, even of............ 1Chr 12:2
of the s up of the latter growth............ Amos 7:1

**SHOPHACH** (*sho'-fak*) See SHOBACH. *Same as Shoback.*
S the captain of the host of................ 1Chr 19:16
killed S the captain of the host .......... 1Chr 19:18

**SHOPHAN** (*sho'-fan*) See ZAPHON. *A city in Gad.*
And Atroth, S, and Jaazer, and.......... Num 32:35

**SHORE**
the sand which is upon the sea s......... Gen 22:17
the Egyptians dead upon the sea s ....... Ex 14:30
is upon the sea s in multitude ............... Josh 11:4
was from the s of the salt sea.............. Josh 15:2
Asher continued on the sea s ............... Judg 5:17
is on the sea s in multitude..................... 1Sa 13:5
as the sand that is on the sea s ............ 1Kin 4:29
on the s of the Red sea, in the.............. 1Kin 9:26
Ashkelon, and against the sea s .............. Jer 47:7
whole multitude stood on the s................ Mt 13:2
when it was full, they drew to s ............ Mt 13:48
of Gennesaret, and drew to the s............ Mk 6:53
now come, Jesus stood on the s................ Jn 21:4
and we kneeled down on the s............. Acts 21:5
a certain creek with a s, into............... Acts 27:39
to the wind, and made toward s .......... Acts 27:40
which is by the sea s innumerable ...... Heb 11:12

**SHORN**
a flock of sheep that are even s ............. Song 4:2
having s his head in Cenchrea ........... Acts 18:18
be not covered, let her also be s........... 1Cor 11:6
for a woman to be s or shaven ............. 1Cor 11:6

**SHORT**
Moses, Is the LORD's hand waxed s... Num 11:23
the LORD began to cut Israel s ............ 2Kin 10:32
the light is s because of ........................ Job 17:12
the triumphing of the wicked is s............ Job 20:5
Remember how s my time is ................. Ps 89:47
come s of the glory of God .................... Rom 3:23
cut it s in righteousness........................ Rom 9:28
because a s work will the Lord ............. Rom 9:28
I say, brethren, the time is s................. 1Cor 7:29
from you for a s time in presence.......... 1Th 2:17
you should seem to come s of it............... Heb 4:1
knoweth that he hath but a s time ..... Rev 12:12
he must continue a s space.................. Rev 17:10

**SHORTENED**
The days of his youth hast thou s.......... Ps 89:45
he s my days.......................................... Ps 102:23
years of the wicked shall be s ............. Prov 10:27
Is my hand s at all, that it........................ Is 50:2
Behold, the LORD's hand is not s ............. Is 59:1
And except those days should be s ....... Mt 24:22
sake those days shall be s...................... Mt 24:22
that the Lord had s those days............. Mk 13:20
hath chosen, he hath s the days ........... Mk 13:20

**SHORTER**
For the bed is s than that a man............ Is 28:20
Now the upper chambers were s............ Eze 42:5

**SHORTLY**
God will s bring it to pass .................... Gen 41:32
s be brought again from Babylon .......... Jer 27:16
Now will I s pour out my fury ................. Eze 7:8
he himself would depart s thither......... Acts 25:4
bruise Satan under your feet s........... Rom 16:20
But I will come to you s, if the............ 1Cor 4:19

to send Timotheus *s* unto you ... Phil 2:19
that I also myself shall come *s* ... Phil 2:24
thee, hoping to come unto thee *s* ... 1Ti 3:14
thy diligence to come *s* unto me ... 2Ti 4:9
with whom, if he come *s*, I will ... Heb 13:23
Knowing that *s* I must put off ... 2Pet 1:14
But I trust I shall *s* see thee ... 3Jn 14
things which must *s* come to pass ... Rev 1:1
the things which must *s* be done ... Rev 22:6

**SHOSHANNIM** (*sho-shan'-nim*) *A musical notation.*
To the chief Musician upon *S* ... Ps 45:*t*
To the chief Musician upon *S* ... Ps 69:*t*

**SHOSHANNIM-EDUTH** (*sho-shan''-nim-e'-duth*) *A musical notation.*
To the chief Musician upon *S* ... Ps 80:*t*

**SHOT**
budded, and her blossoms *s* forth ... Gen 40:10
him, and *s* at him, and hated him ... Gen 49:23
surely be stoned, or *s* through ... Ex 19:13
We have *s* at them ... Num 21:30
thereof, as though I *s* at a mark ... 1Sa 20:20
lad ran, he *s* an arrow beyond him ... 1Sa 20:36
of the arrow which Jonathan had *s* ... 1Sa 20:37
the shooters *s* from off the wall ... 2Sa 11:24
said, Shoot. And he *s* ... 2Kin 13:17
the archers *s* at king Josiah ... 2Chr 35:23
and he *s* out lightnings, and ... Ps 18:14
Their tongue is as an arrow *s* out ... Jer 9:8
forth branches, and *s* forth sprigs ... Eze 17:6
*s* forth her branches toward him, ... Eze 17:7
of waters, when he *s* forth ... Eze 31:5
he hath *s* up his top among the ... Eze 31:10

**SHOULD** See PREFACE.

**SHOULDER**
unto Hagar, putting it on her *s* ... Gen 21:14
with her pitcher upon her *s* ... Gen 24:15
forth with her pitcher on her *s* ... Gen 24:45
let down her pitcher from her *s* ... Gen 24:46
and bowed his *s* to bear, and became. Gen 49:15
that is upon them, and the right *s* ... Ex 29:22
the *s* of the heave offering, ... Ex 29:27
the right *s* shall ye give unto ... Lev 7:32
have the right *s* for his part ... Lev 7:33
the heave *s* have I taken of the ... Lev 7:34
and their fat, and the right *s* ... Lev 8:25
on the fat, and upon the right *s* ... Lev 8:26
the right *s* Aaron waved for a ... Lev 9:21
heave *s* shall ye eat in a clean ... Lev 10:14
The heave *s* and the wave breast ... Lev 10:15
take the sodden *s* of the ram ... Num 6:19
with the wave breast and heave *s* ... Num 6:20
and as the right *s* are thine ... Num 18:18
shall give unto the priest the *s* ... Deut 18:3
man of you a stone upon his *s* ... Josh 4:5
and took it, and laid it on his *s* ... Judg 9:48
And the cook took up the *s* ... 1Sa 9:24
and withdrew the *s*, and hardened ... Neh 9:29
let mine arm fall from my *s* blade ... Job 31:22
Surely I would take it upon my *s* ... Job 31:36
I removed his *s* from the burden ... Ps 81:6
his burden, and the staff of his *s* ... Is 9:4
government shall be upon his *s* ... Is 9:6
be taken away from off thy *s* ... Is 10:27
of David will I lay upon his *s* ... Is 22:22
They bear him upon the *s*, they ... Is 46:7
bare it upon my *s* in their sight ... Eze 12:7
bear upon his *s* in the twilight ... Eze 12:12
good piece, the thigh, and the *s* ... Eze 24:4
didst break, and rend all their *s* ... Eze 29:7
made bald, and every *s* was peeled ... Eze 29:18
have thrust with side and with *s* ... Eze 34:21
to hearken, and pulled away the *s* ... Zec 7:11

**SHOULDERPIECES**
It shall have the two *s* thereof ... Ex 28:7
put them on the *s* of the ephod ... Ex 28:25
They made *s* for it, to couple it ... Ex 39:4
and put them on the *s* of the ephod ... Ex 39:18

**SHOULDERS**
and laid it upon both their *s* ... Gen 9:23
up in their clothes upon their *s* ... Ex 12:34
the *s* of the ephod for stones of ... Ex 28:12
upon his two *s* for a memorial ... Ex 28:12
he put them on the *s* of the ephod ... Ex 39:7
they should bear upon their *s* ... Num 7:9
and he shall dwell between his *s* ... Deut 33:12
and all, and put them upon his *s* ... Judg 16:3
from his *s* and upward he was ... 1Sa 9:2
than any of the people from his *s* ... 1Sa 10:23
a target of brass between his *s* ... 1Sa 17:6
their *s* with the staves thereon ... 1Chr 15:15
shall not be a burden upon your *s* ... 2Chr 35:3
But they shall fly upon the *s* of ... Is 11:14
burden depart from off their *s* ... Is 14:25
riches upon the *s* of young asses ... Is 30:6
shall be carried upon their *s* ... Is 49:22
shalt thou bear it upon thy *s* ... Eze 12:6
be borne, and lay them on men's *s* ... Mt 23:4
found it, he layeth it on his *s* ... Lk 15:5

**SHOULDEST**
thee that thou *s* not eat ... Gen 3:11
that is thine, lest thou *s* say ... Gen 14:23
thou *s* have brought guiltiness ... Gen 26:10
*s* thou therefore serve me for ... Gen 29:15
that thou *s* say unto me, Carry ... Num 11:12
*s* be driven to worship them, and ... Deut 4:19
thee, and that thou *s* keep all his ... Deut 26:18
That thou *s* enter into covenant ... Deut 29:12
is not in heaven, that thou *s* say ... Deut 30:12
beyond the sea, that thou *s* say ... Deut 30:13
Israel, and *s* thou possess it ... Judg 11:23
that thou *s* take knowledge of me, ... Ruth 2:10
for why *s* thou bring me to thy ... 1Sa 20:8
that thou *s* look upon such a dead ... 2Sa 9:8
that thou *s* tell them who shall ... 1Kin 1:20
me that thou *s* surely recover ... 2Kin 8:14
Thou *s* have smitten five or six ... 2Kin 13:19
for why *s* thou meddle to thy hurt ... 2Kin 14:10
to thy hurt, that thou *s* fall ... 2Kin 14:10
that thou *s* be to lay waste ... 2Kin 19:25
that thou *s* be ruler over my ... 1Chr 17:7
*S* thou help the ungodly, and love ... 2Chr 19:2
why *s* thou be smitten ... 2Chr 25:16
why *s* thou meddle to thine hurt, ... 2Chr 25:19
to thine hurt, that thou *s* fall ... 2Chr 25:19
is man, that thou *s* magnify him ... Job 7:17
that thou *s* set thine heart upon ... Job 7:17
that thou *s* visit him every ... Job 7:18
unto thee that thou *s* oppress ... Job 10:3
that thou *s* despise the work of ... Job 10:3
That thou *s* take it to the bound ... Job 38:20
that thou *s* know the paths to the ... Job 38:20
or that thou *s* take my covenant ... Ps 50:16
*s* mark iniquities, O Lord, who ... Ps 130:3
Lest thou *s* ponder the path of ... Prov 5:6
than that thou *s* be put lower in ... Prov 25:7
Though thou *s* bray a fool in a ... Prov 27:22
Better is it that thou *s* not vow ... Eccl 5:5
than that thou *s* vow ... Eccl 5:5
why *s* thou destroy thyself ... Eccl 7:16
why *s* thou die before thy time ... Eccl 7:17
that thou *s* take hold of this ... Eccl 7:18
that thou *s* be to lay waste ... Is 37:26
lest thou *s* say, Mine idol hath ... Is 48:5
lest thou *s* say, Behold, I knew ... Is 48:7
thee by the way that thou *s* go ... Is 48:17
*s* be my servant to raise up the ... Is 49:6
that thou *s* be afraid of a man ... Is 51:12
why *s* thou be as a stranger in ... Jer 14:8
Why *s* thou be as a man astonied, ... Jer 14:9
that thou *s* put him in prison, and ... Jer 29:26
though thou *s* make thy nest as ... Jer 49:16
But thou *s* not have looked on the ... Obad 12
neither *s* thou have rejoiced over ... Obad 12
neither *s* thou have spoken ... Obad 12
Thou *s* not have entered into the ... Obad 13
thou *s* not have looked on their ... Obad 13
Neither *s* thou have stood in the ... Obad 14
neither *s* thou have delivered up ... Obad 14
that thou *s* come under my roof ... Mt 8:8
*S* not thou also have had ... Mt 18:33
we would that thou *s* do for us ... Mk 10:35
that thou *s* enter under my roof ... Lk 7:6
thou *s* see the glory of God ... Jn 11:40
I pray not that thou *s* take them ... Jn 17:15
but that thou *s* keep them from ... Jn 17:15
that thou *s* be for salvation unto ... Acts 13:47
that thou *s* know his will, and see ... Acts 22:14
*s* hear the voice of his mouth ... Acts 22:14
that thou *s* set in order the ... Titus 1:5
that thou *s* receive him for ever ... Philem 15
that thou *s* give reward unto thy ... Rev 11:18
*s* destroy them which destroy the ... Rev 11:18

**SHOUT**
voice of them that *s* for mastery ... Ex 32:18
the *s* of a king is among them ... Num 23:21
people shall *s* with a great *s* ... Josh 6:5
people shall *s* with a great *s* ... Josh 6:5
people, saying, Ye shall not *s* ... Josh 6:10
mouth, until the day I bid you *s* ... Josh 6:10
then shall ye *s* ... Josh 6:10
Joshua said unto the people, *S* ... Josh 6:16
the people shouted with a great *s* ... Josh 6:20
all Israel shouted with a great *s* ... 1Sa 4:5
heard the noise of the *s*, they ... 1Sa 4:6
*s* in the camp of the Hebrews ... 1Sa 4:6
Then the men of Judah gave a *s* ... 2Chr 13:15
the people shouted with a great *s* ... Ezr 3:11
*s* of joy from the noise of the ... Ezr 3:13
the people shouted with a loud *s* ... Ezr 3:13
let them ever *s* for joy, because ... Ps 5:11
*s* for joy, all ye that are ... Ps 32:11
Let them *s* for joy, and be glad, ... Ps 35:27
*s* unto God with the voice of ... Ps 47:1
God is gone up with a *s*, the LORD ... Ps 47:5
they *s* for joy, they also sing ... Ps 65:13
and let thy saints *s* for joy ... Ps 132:9
her saints shall *s* aloud for joy ... Ps 132:16
Cry out and *s*, thou inhabitant of ... Is 12:6
let them *s* from the top of the ... Is 42:11
*s*, ye lower parts of the earth ... Is 44:23
he shall give a *s*, as they that ... Jer 25:30
*s* among the chief of the nations ... Jer 31:7
*S* against her round about ... Jer 50:15
shall lift up a *s* against thee ... Jer 51:14
Also when I cry and *s*, he shutteth ... Lam 3:8
*s*, O Israel ... Zeph 3:14
*s*, O daughter of Jerusalem ... Zec 9:9
And the people gave a *s*, saying, ... Acts 12:22
descend from heaven with a *s* ... 1Th 4:16

**SHOUTED**
the noise of the people as they *s* ... Ex 32:17
when all the people saw, they *s* ... Lev 9:24
So the people *s* when the priests ... Josh 6:20
the people *s* with a great shout, ... Josh 6:20
the Philistines *s* against him ... Judg 15:14
all Israel *s* with a great shout, ... 1Sa 4:5
And all the people *s*, and said, God ... 1Sa 10:24
to the fight, and *s* for the battle ... 1Sa 17:20
of Israel and of Judah arose, and *s* ... 1Sa 17:52
and as the men of Judah *s*, it came ... 2Chr 13:15
all the people *s* with a great ... Ezr 3:11
and many *s* aloud for joy ... Ezr 3:12
for the people *s* with a loud ... Ezr 3:13
and all the sons of God *s* for joy ... Job 38:7

**SHOUTETH**
man that *s* by reason of wine ... Ps 78:65

**SHOUTING**
up the ark of the LORD with *s* ... 2Sa 6:15
the covenant of the LORD with *s* ... 1Chr 15:28
LORD with a loud voice, and with *s* ... 2Chr 15:14
thunder of the captains, and the *s* ... Job 39:25
the wicked perish, there is *s* ... Prov 11:10
for the *s* for thy summer fruits ... Is 16:9
singing, neither shall there be *s* ... Is 16:10
made their vintage *s* to cease ... Is 16:10
the morning, and the *s* at noontide ... Jer 20:16
none shall tread with *s* ... Jer 48:33
their *s* shall be no *s* ... Jer 48:33
to lift up the voice with *s* ... Eze 21:22
with *s* in the day of battle, with ... Amos 1:14
shall die with tumult, with *s* ... Amos 2:2

**SHOUTINGS**
the headstone thereof with *s* ... Zec 4:7

**SHOVEL**
hath been winnowed with the *s* ... Is 30:24

**SHOVELS**
to receive his ashes, and his *s* ... Ex 27:3
of the altar, the pots, and the *s* ... Ex 38:3
censers, the fleshhooks, and the *s* ... Num 4:14
Hiram made the lavers, and the *s* ... 1Kin 7:40
And the pots, and the *s*, and the ... 1Kin 7:45
And the pots, and the *s*, and the ... 2Kin 25:14
And Huram made the pots, and the *s*. 2Chr 4:11
The pots also, and the *s*, and the ... 2Chr 4:16
The caldrons also, and the *s* ... Jer 52:18

**SHOWER**
there shall be an overflowing *s* ... Eze 13:11
be an overflowing *s* in mine anger ... Eze 13:13
I will cause the *s* to come down ... Eze 34:26
ye say, There cometh a *s* ... Lk 12:54

**SHOWERS**
herb, and as the *s* upon the grass ... Deut 32:2
wet with the *s* of the mountains ... Job 24:8
thou makest it soft with *s* ... Ps 65:10
as *s* that water the earth ... Ps 72:6
Therefore the *s* have been ... Jer 3:3
or can the heavens give *s* ... Jer 14:22
there shall be *s* of blessing ... Eze 34:26
as the *s* upon the grass, that ... Mic 5:7
clouds, and give them *s* of rain ... Zec 10:1

**SHRANK**
eat not of the sinew which *s* ... Gen 32:32
Jacob's thigh in the sinew that *s* ... Gen 32:32

**SHRED**
*s* them into the pot of pottage ... 2Kin 4:39

**SHRINES**
which made silver *s* for Diana ... Acts 19:24

**SHROUD**
branches, and with a shadowing *s* ... Eze 31:3

**SHRUBS**
cast the child under one of the *s* ... Gen 21:15

**SHUA** (*shu'-ah*) See SHUAH.
*1. Daughter of Judah.*
the daughter of *S* the Canaanitess ... 1Chr 2:3
*2. Daughter of Heber.*
and Hotham, and *S* their sister ... 1Chr 7:32

**SHUAH** (*shu'-ah*)
*1. A son of Abraham.*
Medan, and Midian, and Ishbak, and *S* Gen 25:2
and Midian, and Ishbak, and *S* ... 1Chr 1:32
*2. Same as Shua 1.*
Canaanite, whose name was *S* ... Gen 38:2
daughter of *S* Judah's wife died ... Gen 38:12
*3. A descendant of Caleb.*
the brother of *S* begat Mehir ... 1Chr 4:11

**SHUAL** (*shu'-al*)
*1. A district in Benjamin.*
to Ophrah, unto the land of *S* ... 1Sa 13:17
*2. Son of Zophah.*
Suah, and Harnepher, and *S*, and Beri 1Chr 7:36

**SHUBAEL** (*shu'-ba-el*) See SHEBUEL.
*1. Son of Amram.*
sons of Amram; *S* ... 1Chr 24:20
of the sons of *S* ... 1Chr 24:20
*2. A sanctuary servant.*
The thirteenth to *S*, he, his sons ... 1Chr 25:20

**SHUHAH** See SHUAH.

**SHUHAM** (*shu'-ham*) See HUSHIM, SHUHAMITES. *A son of Dan.*
of *S*, the family of the ... Num 26:42

**SHUHAMITES** (*shu'-ham-ites*) *Descendants of Shuham.*
of Shuham, the family of the *S* ... Num 26:42
All the families of the *S* ... Num 26:43

**SHUHITE** (*shu'-hite*) *A descendant of Shuah.*
the Temanite, and Bildad the *S* ... Job 2:11
Then answered Bildad the *S* ... Job 8:1

S

Then answered Bildad the *S* ... Job 18:1
Then answered Bildad the *S* ... Job 25:1
the Temanite and Bildad the *S* ... Job 42:9

**SHULAMITE** (*shu'-lam-ite*) *An inhabitant of Shulam.*
Return, return, O *S* ... Song 6:13
What will ye see in the *S* ... Song 6:13

**SHULAMMITE** See SHULAMITE.

**SHUMATHITES** (*shu'-math-ites*) *Descendants of Shobal.*
and the Puhites, and the *S* ... 1Chr 2:53

**SHUN**
But *s* profane and vain babblings ... 2Ti 2:16

**SHUNAMMITE** (*shu'-nam-mite*) *An inhabitant of Shunem.*
of Israel, and found Abishag a *S* ... 1Kin 1:3
Abishag the *S* ministered unto the ... 1Kin 1:15
he give me Abishag the *S* to wife ... 1Kin 2:17
Let Abishag the *S* be given to ... 1Kin 2:21
ask Abishag the *S* for Adonijah ... 1Kin 2:22
Gehazi his servant, Call this *S* ... 2Kin 4:12
servant, Behold, yonder is that *S* ... 2Kin 4:25
Gehazi, and said, Call this *S* ... 2Kin 4:36

**SHUNEM** (*shu'-nem*) See SHUNAMMITE. *A city in Issachar.*
Jezreel, and Chesulloth, and *S* ... Josh 19:18
together, and came and pitched in *S* ... 1Sa 28:4
on a day, that Elisha passed to *S* ... 2Kin 4:8

**SHUNI** (*shu'-ni*) See SHUNITES. *A son of Gad.*
Ziphion, and Haggi, *S*, and Ezbon, ... Gen 46:16
of *S*, the family of the Shunites ... Num 26:15

**SHUNITES** (*shu'-nites*) *Descendants of Shuni.*
of Shuni, the family of the *S* ... Num 26:15

**SHUNNED**
For I have not *s* to declare unto ... Acts 20:27

**SHUPHAM** (*shu'-fam*) See SHEPHUPHAN, SHUPHAMITES. *A son of Benjamin.*
Of *S*, the family of the ... Num 26:39

**SHUPHAMITES** (*shu'-fam-ites*) *Descendants of Shupham.*
Of Shupham, the family of the *S* ... Num 26:39

**SHUPPIM** (*shup'-pim*) See MUPPIM, SHEPHUPHAN.
*1. A Benjamite.*
*S* also, and Huppim, the children ... 1Chr 7:12
to wife the sister of Huppim and *S* ... 1Chr 7:15
*2. A Levite gatekeeper.*
To *S* and Hosah the lot came forth ... 1Chr 26:16

**SHUR** (*shur*) *A wilderness east of Egypt.*
by the fountain in the way to *S* ... Gen 16:7
and dwelled between Kadesh and *S* ... Gen 20:1
And they dwelt from Havilah unto *S* ... Gen 25:18
went out into the wilderness of *S* ... Ex 15:22
Havilah until thou comest to *S* ... 1Sa 15:7
of the land, as thou goest to *S* ... 1Sa 27:8

**SHUSHAN** (*shu'-shan*) See SHOSHANNIM. *Capital of Persia.*
year, as I was in *S* the palace ... Neh 1:1
which was in *S* the palace ... Est 1:2
that were present in *S* the palace ... Est 1:5
young virgins unto *S* the palace ... Est 2:3
Now in *S* the palace there was a ... Est 2:5
together unto *S* the palace ... Est 2:8
decree was given in *S* the palace ... Est 3:15
but the city *S* was perplexed ... Est 3:15
was given at *S* to destroy them ... Est 4:8
the Jews that are present in *S* ... Est 4:16
decree was given at *S* the palace ... Est 8:14
and the city of *S* rejoiced ... Est 8:15
in *S* the palace the Jews slew and ... Est 9:6
of those that were slain in *S* the ... Est 9:11
five hundred men in *S* the palace ... Est 9:12
to the Jews which are in *S* to do ... Est 9:13
and the decree was given at *S* ... Est 9:14
For the Jews that were in *S* ... Est 9:15
and slew three hundred men at *S* ... Est 9:15
at *S* assembled together on the ... Est 9:18
that I was at *S* in the palace ... Dan 8:2

**SHUSHAN-EDUTH** (*shu'-shan-e'-duth*) *shu"-shan-e'-duth*
To the chief Musician upon *S* ... Ps 60:*t*

**SHUT**
and the LORD *s* him in ... Gen 7:16
them, and *s* the door after him, ... Gen 19:6
house to them, and *s* to the door ... Gen 19:10
the wilderness hath *s* them in ... Ex 14:3
then the priest shall *s* up him ... Lev 13:4
then the priest shall *s* him up ... Lev 13:5
unclean, and shall not *s* him up ... Lev 13:11
priest shall *s* him up seven days ... Lev 13:21
priest shall *s* him up seven days ... Lev 13:26
then the priest shall *s* up him ... Lev 13:31
the priest shall *s* up him that ... Lev 13:33
*s* up it that hath the plague ... Lev 13:50
he shall *s* it up seven days more ... Lev 13:54
*s* up the house seven days ... Lev 14:38
*s* up shall be unclean until the ... Lev 14:46
let her be *s* out from the camp ... Num 12:14
Miriam was *s* out from the camp ... Num 12:15
he *s* up the heaven, that there be ... Deut 11:17
nor *s* thine hand from thy poor ... Deut 15:7
them, and the LORD had *s* them up ... Deut 32:30
is gone, and there is none *s* up ... Deut 32:36
were gone out, they *s* the gate ... Josh 2:7
Now Jericho was straitly *s* up ... Josh 6:1
*s* the doors of the parlour upon ... Judg 3:23
*s* it to them, and gat them up to ... Judg 9:51
but the LORD had *s* up her womb ... 1Sa 1:5
the LORD had *s* up her womb ... 1Sa 1:6
*s* up their calves at home ... 1Sa 6:10
for he is *s* in, by entering into ... 1Sa 23:7
So they were *s* up unto the day of ... 2Sa 20:3
When heaven is *s* up, and there is ... 1Kin 8:35
the wall, and him that is *s* up ... 1Kin 14:10
the wall, and him that is *s* up ... 1Kin 21:21
thou shalt *s* the door upon thee ... 2Kin 4:4
*s* the door upon her and upon her ... 2Kin 4:5
*s* the door upon him, and went out ... 2Kin 4:21
*s* the door upon them twain, and ... 2Kin 4:33
*s* the door, and hold him fast at ... 2Kin 6:32
the wall, and him that is *s* up ... 2Kin 9:8
for there was not any *s* up ... 2Kin 14:26
the king of Assyria *s* him up ... 2Kin 17:4
When the heaven is *s* up, and there ... 2Chr 6:26
If I *s* up heaven that there be no ... 2Chr 7:13
*s* up the doors of the house of ... 2Chr 28:24
Also they have *s* up the doors of ... 2Chr 29:7
son of Mehetabeel, who was *s* up ... Neh 6:10
let us *s* the doors of the temple ... Neh 6:10
let them *s* the doors, and bar them ... Neh 7:3
that the gates should be *s* ... Neh 13:19
Because it *s* not up the doors of ... Job 3:10
*s* up, or gather together, then ... Job 11:10
Or who *s* up the sea with doors, ... Job 38:8
*s* up together as with a close ... Job 41:15
hast not *s* me up into the hand of ... Ps 31:8
let not the pit *s* her mouth upon ... Ps 69:15
hath he in anger *s* up his tender ... Ps 77:9
I am *s* up, and I cannot come forth ... Ps 88:8
doors shall be *s* in the streets ... Eccl 12:4
a spring *s* up, a fountain sealed ... Song 4:12
their ears heavy, and *s* their eyes ... Is 6:10
so he shall open, and none shall *s* ... Is 22:22
and he shall *s*, and none shall open ... Is 22:22
every house is *s* up, that no man ... Is 24:10
shall be *s* up in the prison, and ... Is 24:22
and *s* thy doors about thee ... Is 26:20
for he hath *s* their eyes, that ... Is 44:18
and the gates shall not be *s* ... Is 45:1
the kings shall *s* their mouths at ... Is 52:15
they shall not be *s* day nor night ... Is 60:11
to bring forth, and *s* the womb ... Is 66:9
cities of the south shall be *s* up ... Jer 13:19
a burning fire *s* up in my bones ... Jer 20:9
Jeremiah the prophet was *s* up in ... Jer 32:2
king of Judah had *s* him up ... Jer 32:3
while he was yet *s* up in the ... Jer 33:1
Baruch, saying, I am *s* up ... Jer 36:5
while he was *s* up in the court of ... Jer 39:15
*s* thyself within thine house ... Eze 3:24
and it was *s* ... Eze 44:1
This gate shall be *s*, it shall ... Eze 44:2
in by it, therefore it shall be *s* ... Eze 44:2
shall be *s* the six working days ... Eze 46:1
shall not be *s* until the evening ... Eze 46:2
going forth one shall *s* the gate ... Eze 46:12
hath *s* the lions' mouths, that ... Dan 6:22
wherefore *s* thou up the vision ... Dan 8:26
*s* up the words, and seal the book, ... Dan 12:4
that would *s* the doors for nought ... Mal 1:10
and when thou hast *s* thy door ... Mt 6:6
for ye *s* up the kingdom of heaven ... Mt 23:13
and the door was *s* ... Mt 25:10
that he *s* up John in prison ... Lk 3:20
the heaven was *s* up three years ... Lk 4:25
the door is now *s*, and my children ... Lk 11:7
hath *s* to the door, and ye begin ... Lk 13:25
when the doors were *s* where the ... Jn 20:19
came Jesus, the doors being *s* ... Jn 20:26
truly found we *s* with all safety ... Acts 5:23
and forthwith the doors were *s* ... Acts 21:30
the saints did I *s* up in prison ... Acts 26:10
*s* up unto the faith which should ... Gal 3:23
an open door, and no man can *s* it ... Rev 3:8
These have power to *s* heaven ... Rev 11:6
*s* him up, and set a seal upon him, ... Rev 20:3
it shall not be *s* at all by day ... Rev 21:25

**SHUTHALHITES** (*shu'-thal-hites*) *Descendants of Shuthelah.*
of Shuthelah, the family of the *S* ... Num 26:35

**SHUTHELAH** (*shu'-the-lah*) See SHUTHALHITES.
*1. A son of Ephraim.*
of *S*, the family of the ... Num 26:35
And these are the sons of *S* ... Num 26:36
*S*, and Bered his son, and Tahath ... 1Chr 7:20
*2. Son of Zabad.*
*S* his son, and Ezer, and Elead, ... 1Chr 7:21

**SHUTHELAHITES** See SHUTHALHITES.

**SHUTTETH**
he *s* up a man, and there can be no ... Job 12:14
He *s* his eyes to devise froward ... Prov 16:30
he that *s* his lips is esteemed a ... Prov 17:28
*s* his eyes from seeing evil ... Is 33:15
cry and shout, he *s* out my prayer ... Lam 3:8
*s* up his bowels of compassion ... 1Jn 3:17
he that openeth, and no man *s* ... Rev 3:7
and *s*, and no man openeth ... Rev 3:7

**SHUTTING**
about the time of *s* of the gate ... Josh 2:5

**SHUTTLE**
are swifter than a weaver's *s* ... Job 7:6

**SIA** (*si'-ah*) See SIAHA. *A family of exiles.*
of Keros, the children of *S* ... Neh 7:47

**SIAHA** (*si'-a-hah*) See SIA. *Same as Sia.*
of Keros, the children of *S* ... Ezr 2:44

**SIBBECAI** (*sib'-be-cahee*) See SIBBECHAI. *A "mighty man" of David.*
*S* the Hushathite, Ilai the ... 1Chr 11:29
eighth month was *S* the Hushathite ... 1Chr 27:11

**SIBBECHAI** (*sib'-be-kahee*) See SIBBECAI. *Same as Sibbecai.*
then *S* the Hushathite slew Saph, ... 2Sa 21:18
at which time *S* the Hushathite ... 1Chr 20:4

**SIBBOLETH** (*sib'-bo-leth*) See SHIBBOLETH. *The Ephraimite pronunciation of Shibboleth.*
and he said *S* ... Judg 12:6

**SIBMAH** (*sib'-mah*) *A city in Reuben.*
And Kirjathaim, and *S*, and ... Josh 13:19
languish, and the vine of *S* ... Is 16:8
weeping of Jazer the vine of *S* ... Is 16:9
O vine of *S*, I will weep for thee ... Jer 48:32

**SIBRAIM** (*sib'-ra-im*) *A city in Syria between Damascus and Hamath.*
Hamath, Berothah, *S*, which is ... Eze 47:16

**SICHEM** (*si'-kem*) See SHECHEM, SYCHEM. *A place on the plain of Moreh.*
the land unto the place of *S* ... Gen 12:6

**SICK**
Joseph, Behold, thy father is *s* ... Gen 48:1
of her that is *s* of her flowers ... Lev 15:33
to take David, she said, He is *s* ... 1Sa 19:14
because three days agone I fell *s* ... 1Sa 30:13
bare unto David, and it was very *s* ... 2Sa 12:15
that he fell *s* for his sister ... 2Sa 13:2
on thy bed, and make thyself *s* ... 2Sa 13:5
Amnon lay down, and made himself *s* ... 2Sa 13:6
Abijah the son of Jeroboam fell *s* ... 1Kin 14:1
for he is *s* ... 1Kin 14:5
the mistress of the house, fell *s* ... 1Kin 17:17
that was in Samaria, and was *s* ... 2Kin 1:2
Ben-hadad the king of Syria was *s* ... 2Kin 8:7
Ahab in Jezreel, because he was *s* ... 2Kin 8:29
Now Elisha was fallen *s* of his ... 2Kin 13:14
days was Hezekiah *s* unto death ... 2Kin 20:1
heard that Hezekiah had been *s* ... 2Kin 20:12
Ahab at Jezreel, because he was *s* ... 2Chr 22:6
days Hezekiah was *s* to the death ... 2Chr 32:24
sad, seeing thou art not *s* ... Neh 2:2
But as for me, when they were *s* ... Ps 35:13
Hope deferred maketh the heart *s* ... Prov 13:12
shalt thou say, and I was not *s* ... Prov 23:35
for I am *s* of love ... Song 2:5
ye tell him, that I am *s* of love ... Song 5:8
the whole head is *s*, and the whole ... Is 1:5
inhabitant shall not say, I am *s* ... Is 33:24
days was Hezekiah *s* unto death ... Is 38:1
king of Judah, when he had been *s* ... Is 38:9
he had heard that he had been *s* ... Is 39:1
them that are *s* with famine ... Jer 14:18
have ye healed that which was *s* ... Eze 34:4
will strengthen that which was *s* ... Eze 34:16
fainted, and was *s* certain days ... Dan 8:27
made him *s* with bottles of wine ... Hos 7:5
I make thee *s* in smiting thee ... Mic 6:13
and if ye offer the lame and *s* ... Mal 1:8
was torn, and the lame, and the *s* ... Mal 1:13
they brought unto him all *s* ... Mt 4:24
lieth at home *s* of the palsy ... Mt 8:6
mother laid, and *s* of a fever ... Mt 8:14
word, and healed all that were *s* ... Mt 8:16
to him a man *s* of the palsy ... Mt 9:2
said unto the *s* of the palsy ... Mt 9:2
saith he to the *s* of the palsy ... Mt 9:6
a physician, but they that are *s* ... Mt 9:12
Heal the *s*, cleanse the lepers ... Mt 10:8
toward them, and he healed their *s* ... Mt 14:14
I was *s*, and ye visited me ... Mt 25:36
Or when saw we thee *s*, or in ... Mt 25:39
*s*, and in prison, and ye visited me ... Mt 25:43
or a stranger, or naked, or *s* ... Mt 25:44
wife's mother lay *s* of a fever ... Mk 1:30
that were *s* of divers diseases ... Mk 1:34
him, bringing one *s* of the palsy ... Mk 2:3
wherein the *s* of the palsy lay ... Mk 2:4
he said unto the *s* of the palsy ... Mk 2:5
to say to the *s* of the palsy ... Mk 2:9
(he saith to the *s* of the palsy ... Mk 2:10
physician, but they that are *s* ... Mk 2:17
laid his hands upon a few *s* folk ... Mk 6:5
with oil many that were *s* ... Mk 6:13
about in beds those that were *s* ... Mk 6:55
they laid the *s* in the streets, ... Mk 6:56
they shall lay hands on the *s* ... Mk 16:18
all they that had any *s* with ... Lk 4:40
(he said unto the *s* of the palsy ... Lk 5:24
but they that are *s* ... Lk 5:31
who was dear unto him, was *s* ... Lk 7:2
the servant whole that had been *s* ... Lk 7:10
kingdom of God, and to heal the *s* ... Lk 9:2
heal the *s* that are therein, and ... Lk 10:9
whose son was *s* at Capernaum ... Jn 4:46
Now a certain man was *s*, named ... Jn 11:1

hair, whose brother Lazarus was *s* ... Jn 11:2
behold, he whom thou lovest is *s* ... Jn 11:3
had heard therefore that he was *s* ... Jn 11:6
forth the *s* into the streets ... Acts 5:15
unto Jerusalem, bringing *s* folks ... Acts 5:16
years, and was *s* of the palsy ... Acts 9:33
in those days, that she was *s* ... Acts 9:37
the *s* handkerchiefs or aprons ... Acts 19:12
of Publius lay *s* of a fever ... Acts 28:8
ye had heard that he had been *s* ... Phil 2:26
indeed he was *s* nigh unto death ... Phil 2:27
have I left at Miletum *s* ... 2Ti 4:20
Is any *s* among you ... Jas 5:14
prayer of faith shall save the *s* ... Jas 5:15

**SICKLE**
to put the *s* to the corn ... Deut 16:9
but thou shalt not move a *s* unto ... Deut 23:25
him that handleth the *s* in the ... Jer 50:16
Put ye in the *s*, for the harvest ... Joel 3:13
immediately he putteth in the *s* ... Mk 4:29
crown, and in his hand a sharp *s* ... Rev 14:14
sat on the cloud, Thrust in thy *s* ... Rev 14:15
thrust in his *s* on the earth ... Rev 14:16
heaven, he also having a sharp *s* ... Rev 14:17
cry to him that had the sharp *s* ... Rev 14:18
saying, Thrust in thy sharp *s* ... Rev 14:18
thrust in his *s* into the earth ... Rev 14:19

**SICKLY**
*s* among you, and many sleep ... 1Cor 11:30

**SICKNESS**
I will take *s* away from the midst ... Ex 23:25
lie with a woman having her *s* ... Lev 20:18
will take away from thee all *s* ... Deut 7:15
Also every *s*, and every plague, ... Deut 28:61
plague, whatsoever *s* there be ... 1Kin 8:37
his *s* was so sore, that there was ... 1Kin 17:17
sick of his *s* whereof he died ... 2Kin 13:14
sore or whatsoever *s* there be ... 2Chr 6:28
thou shalt have great *s* by ... 2Chr 21:15
out by reason of the *s* day by day ... 2Chr 21:15
fell out by reason of his *s* ... 2Chr 21:19
wilt make all his bed in his *s* ... Ps 41:3
much sorrow and wrath with his *s* ... Eccl 5:17
sick, and was recovered of his *s* ... Is 38:9
he will cut me off with pining *s* ... Is 38:12
When Ephraim saw his *s*, and Judah ... Hos 5:13
and healing all manner of *s* ... Mt 4:23
the kingdom, and healing every *s* ... Mt 9:35
out, and to heal all manner of *s* ... Mt 10:1
This *s* is not unto death, but for ... Jn 11:4

**SICKNESSES**
and of long continuance, and sore *s*.. Deut 28:59
the *s* which the LORD hath laid ... Deut 29:22
our infirmities, and bare our *s* ... Mt 8:17
And to have power to heal *s* ... Mk 3:15

**SIDDIM** *(sid'-dim) Area of Sodom and Gomorrah.*
joined together in the vale of *S* ... Gen 14:3
battle with them in the vale of *S* ... Gen 14:8
the vale of *S* was full of ... Gen 14:10

**SIDE**
shalt thou set in the *s* thereof ... Gen 6:16
that was openly by the way *s* ... Gen 38:21
walked along by the river's *s* ... Ex 2:5
and strike it on the two *s* posts ... Ex 12:7
the two *s* posts with the blood ... Ex 12:22
the lintel, and on the two *s* posts ... Ex 12:23
his hands, the one on the one *s* ... Ex 17:12
and the other on the other *s* ... Ex 17:12
rings shall be in the one *s* of it ... Ex 25:12
and two rings in the other *s* of it ... Ex 25:12
the candlestick out of the one *s* ... Ex 25:32
candlestick out of the other *s* ... Ex 25:32
And a cubit on the one *s* ... Ex 26:13
a cubit on the other *s* of that ... Ex 26:13
on this *s* and on that *s* ... Ex 26:13
boards on the south *s* southward ... Ex 26:18
And for the second *s* of the ... Ex 26:20
*s* there shall be twenty boards ... Ex 26:20
of the one *s* of the tabernacle ... Ex 26:26
of the other *s* of the tabernacle ... Ex 26:27
boards of the *s* of the tabernacle ... Ex 26:27
*s* of the tabernacle toward the ... Ex 26:35
put the table on the north *s* ... Ex 26:35
for the south *s* southward there ... Ex 27:9
an hundred cubits long for one *s* ... Ex 27:9
likewise for the north *s* in ... Ex 27:11
of the court on the west *s* shall ... Ex 27:12
of the court on the east *s* ... Ex 27:13
The hangings of one *s* of the gate ... Ex 27:14
on the other *s* shall be hangings ... Ex 27:15
which is in the *s* of the ephod ... Ex 28:26
on the one *s* and on the other were ... Ex 32:15
and said, Who is on the LORD's *s* ... Ex 32:26
Put every man his sword by his *s* ... Ex 32:27
uttermost *s* of another curtain ... Ex 36:11
boards for the south *s* southward ... Ex 36:23
for the other *s* of the tabernacle ... Ex 36:25
of the one *s* of the tabernacle ... Ex 36:31
of the other *s* of the tabernacle ... Ex 36:32
two rings upon the one *s* of it ... Ex 37:3
two rings upon the other *s* of it ... Ex 37:3
One cherub on the end on this *s* ... Ex 37:8
cherub on the other end on that *s* ... Ex 37:8
out of the one *s* thereof, and ... Ex 37:18
out of the other *s* thereof ... Ex 37:18
on the south *s* southward the ... Ex 38:9
for the north *s* the hangings were ... Ex 38:11
for the west *s* were hangings of ... Ex 38:12
for the east *s* eastward fifty ... Ex 38:13
The hangings of the one *s* of the ... Ex 38:14
for the other *s* of the court gate ... Ex 38:15
which was on the *s* of the ephod ... Ex 39:19
upon the *s* of the tabernacle ... Ex 40:22
on the *s* of the tabernacle ... Ex 40:24
he shall kill it on the *s* of the ... Lev 1:11
wrung out at the *s* of the altar ... Lev 1:15
offering upon the *s* of the altar ... Lev 5:9
on the east *s* toward the rising ... Num 2:3
On the south *s* shall be the ... Num 2:10
On the west *s* shall be the ... Num 2:18
be on the north *s* by their armies ... Num 2:25
the *s* of the tabernacle southward ... Num 3:29
these shall pitch on the *s* of the ... Num 3:35
south *s* shall take their journey ... Num 10:6
it were a day's journey on this *s* ... Num 11:31
a day's journey on the other *s* ... Num 11:31
Dathan, and Abiram, on every *s* ... Num 16:27
pitched on the other *s* of Arnon ... Num 21:13
Moab on this *s* Jordan by Jericho ... Num 22:1
on this *s*, and a wall on that *s* ... Num 22:24
as gardens by the river's *s* ... Num 24:6
with them on yonder *s* Jordan ... Num 32:19
to us on this *s* Jordan eastward ... Num 32:19
on this *s* Jordan may be ours ... Num 32:32
to Riblah, on the east *s* of Ain ... Num 34:11
shall reach unto the *s* of the sea ... Num 34:11
their inheritance on this *s* ... Num 34:15
on the east *s* two thousand cubits ... Num 35:5
on the south *s* two thousand ... Num 35:5
on the west *s* two thousand cubits ... Num 35:5
on the north *s* two thousand ... Num 35:5
three cities on this *s* Jordan ... Num 35:14
this *s* Jordan in the wilderness ... Deut 1:1
On this *s* Jordan, in the land of ... Deut 1:5
and in the south, and by the sea *s* ... Deut 1:7
land that was on this *s* Jordan ... Deut 3:8
ask from the one *s* of heaven unto ... Deut 4:32
*s* Jordan toward the sunrising ... Deut 4:41
On this *s* Jordan, in the valley ... Deut 4:46
which were on this *s* Jordan ... Deut 4:47
plain on this *s* Jordan eastward ... Deut 4:49
they not on the other *s* Jordan ... Deut 11:30
put it in the *s* of the ark of the ... Deut 31:26
Moses gave you on this *s* Jordan ... Josh 1:14
*s* Jordan toward the sunrising ... Josh 1:15
that were on the other *s* Jordan ... Josh 2:10
which were on the *s* of Jordan ... Josh 5:1
on the east *s* of Beth-el ... Josh 7:2
and dwelt on the other *s* Jordan ... Josh 7:7
and Ai, on the west *s* of Ai ... Josh 8:9
and pitched on the north *s* of Ai ... Josh 8:11
and Ai, on the west *s* of the city ... Josh 8:12
on this *s*, and some on that *s* ... Josh 8:22
judges, stood on this *s* the ark ... Josh 8:33
on that *s* before the priests the ... Josh 8:33
kings which were on this *s* Jordan ... Josh 9:1
their land on the other *s* Jordan ... Josh 12:1
on this *s* Jordan on the west ... Josh 12:7
on the other *s* Jordan eastward ... Josh 13:27
of Moab, on the other *s* Jordan ... Josh 13:32
half tribe on the other *s* Jordan ... Josh 14:3
to the south *s* to Maaleh-acrabbim ... Josh 15:3
on the south *s* unto Kadesh-barnea ... Josh 15:3
is on the south *s* of the river ... Josh 15:7
unto the south *s* of the Jebusite ... Josh 15:8
along unto the *s* of mount Jearim ... Josh 15:10
which is Chesalon, on the north *s* ... Josh 15:10
out unto the *s* of Ekron northward ... Josh 15:11
on the east *s* was Ataroth-addar ... Josh 16:5
sea to Michmethah on the north *s* ... Josh 16:6
which were on the other *s* Jordan ... Josh 17:5
was on the north *s* of the river ... Josh 17:9
on the north *s* was from Jordan ... Josh 18:12
the border went up to the *s* of ... Josh 18:12
of Jericho on the north *s* ... Josh 18:12
toward Luz, to the *s* of Luz ... Josh 18:13
south *s* of the nether Beth-horon ... Josh 18:13
to the *s* of Jebusi on the south, ... Josh 18:16
passed along toward the *s* over ... Josh 18:18
to the *s* of Beth-hoglah northward ... Josh 18:19
the border of it on the east *s* ... Josh 18:20
it on the north *s* to Hannathon ... Josh 19:14
toward the north *s* of Beth-emek ... Josh 19:27
to Zebulun on the south *s* ... Josh 19:34
reacheth to Asher on the west *s* ... Josh 19:34
on the other *s* Jordan by Jericho ... Josh 20:8
gave you on the other *s* Jordan ... Josh 22:4
on this *s* Jordan westward ... Josh 22:7
other *s* of the flood in old time ... Josh 24:2
from the other *s* of the flood ... Josh 24:3
which dwelt on the other *s* Jordan ... Josh 24:8
on the other *s* of the flood ... Josh 24:14
were on the other *s* of the flood ... Josh 24:15
on the north *s* of the hill of ... Josh 24:30
on the north *s* of the hill Gaash ... Judg 2:9
were on the north *s* of them ... Judg 7:1
sand by the sea *s* for multitude ... Judg 7:12
also on every *s* of all the camp ... Judg 7:18
to Gideon on the other *s* Jordan ... Judg 7:25
of all their enemies on every *s* ... Judg 8:34
other *s* Jordan in the land of the ... Judg 10:8
came by the east *s* of the land of ... Judg 11:18
pitched on the other *s* of Arnon ... Judg 11:18
on the *s* of mount Ephraim ... Judg 19:1
toward the *s* of mount Ephraim ... Judg 19:18
is on the north *s* of Beth-el ... Judg 21:19
on the east *s* of the highway that ... Judg 21:19
backward by the *s* of the gate ... 1Sa 4:18
in a coffer by the *s* thereof ... 1Sa 6:8
hand of your enemies on every *s* ... 1Sa 12:11
garrison, that is on the other *s* ... 1Sa 14:1
was a sharp rock on the one *s* ... 1Sa 14:4
and a sharp rock on the other *s* ... 1Sa 14:4
unto all Israel, Be ye on one *s* ... 1Sa 14:40
my son will be on the other *s* ... 1Sa 14:40
all his enemies on every *s* ... 1Sa 14:47
stood on a mountain on the one *s* ... 1Sa 17:3
on a mountain on the other *s* ... 1Sa 17:3
three arrows on the *s* thereof ... 1Sa 20:20
the arrows are on this *s* of thee ... 1Sa 20:21
arose, and Abner sat by Saul's *s* ... 1Sa 20:25
went on this *s* of the mountain ... 1Sa 23:26
his men on that *s* of the mountain ... 1Sa 23:26
David went over to the other *s* ... 1Sa 26:13
were on the other *s* of the valley ... 1Sa 31:7
that were on the other *s* Jordan ... 1Sa 31:7
the one on the one *s* of the pool ... 2Sa 2:13
other on the other *s* of the pool ... 2Sa 2:13
his sword in his fellow's *s* ... 2Sa 2:16
the way of the hill *s* behind him ... 2Sa 13:34
on the hill's *s* over against him ... 2Sa 16:13
And the king stood by the gate *s* ... 2Sa 18:4
on the right *s* of the city that ... 2Sa 24:5
the region on this *s* the river ... 1Kin 4:24
all the kings on this *s* the river ... 1Kin 4:24
which were about him on every *s* ... 1Kin 5:3
God hath given me rest on every *s* ... 1Kin 5:4
was in the right *s* of the house ... 1Kin 6:8
*s* posts were a fifth part of the ... 1Kin 6:31
one *s* of the floor to the other ... 1Kin 7:7
at the *s* of every addition ... 1Kin 7:30
bases on the right *s* of the house ... 1Kin 7:39
five on the left *s* of the house ... 1Kin 7:39
*s* of the house eastward over ... 1Kin 7:39
of pure gold, five on the right *s* ... 1Kin 7:49
either *s* on the place of the seat ... 1Kin 10:19
lions stood there on the one *s* ... 1Kin 10:20
on the other *s* as red as blood ... 2Kin 3:22
window, and said, Who is on my *s* ... 2Kin 9:32
on the right *s* as one cometh into ... 2Kin 12:9
it on the north *s* of the altar ... 2Kin 16:14
unto the east *s* of the valley ... 1Chr 4:39
on the other *s* Jordan by Jericho, ... 1Chr 6:78
on the east *s* of Jordan ... 1Chr 6:78
Thine are we, David, and on thy *s* ... 1Chr 12:18
And on the other *s* of Jordan ... 1Chr 12:37
he not given you rest on every *s* ... 1Chr 22:18
this *s* Jordan westward in all the ... 1Chr 26:30
the temple, five on the right *s* ... 2Chr 4:8
on the right *s* of the east end ... 2Chr 4:10
at the sea *s* in the land of Edom ... 2Chr 8:17
stays on each *s* of the sitting ... 2Chr 9:18
lions stood there on the one *s* ... 2Chr 9:19
having Judah and Benjamin on his *s* 2Chr 11:12
he hath given us rest on every *s* ... 2Chr 14:7
beyond the sea on this *s* Syria ... 2Chr 20:2
from the right *s* of the temple to ... 2Chr 23:10
to the left *s* of the temple ... 2Chr 23:10
other, and guided them on every *s* ... 2Chr 32:22
the west *s* of the city of David ... 2Chr 32:30
of David, on the west *s* of Gihon ... 2Chr 33:14
rest that are on this *s* the river ... Ezr 4:10
the men on this *s* the river ... Ezr 4:11
no portion on this *s* the river ... Ezr 4:16
governor on this *s* the river ... Ezr 5:3
governor on this *s* the river ... Ezr 5:6
which were on this *s* the river ... Ezr 5:6
governor on this *s* the river ... Ezr 6:13
the governors on this *s* the river ... Ezr 8:36
the governor on this *s* the river ... Neh 3:7
one had his sword girded by his *s* ... Neh 4:18
about all that he hath on every *s* ... Job 1:10
shall make him afraid on every *s* ... Job 18:11
shall be ready at his *s* ... Job 18:12
He hath destroyed me on every *s* ... Job 19:10
The wicked walk on every *s* ... Ps 12:8
fear was on every *s* ... Ps 31:13
little hills rejoice on every *s* ... Ps 65:12
and comfort me on every *s* ... Ps 71:21
A thousand shall fall at thy *s* ... Ps 91:7
The LORD is on my *s* ... Ps 118:6
been the LORD who was on our *s* ... Ps 124:1
been the LORD who was on our *s* ... Ps 124:2
on the *s* of their oppressors ... Eccl 4:1
shall be nursed at thy *s* ... Is 60:4
the enemy and fear is on every *s* ... Jer 6:25
defaming of many, fear on every *s* ... Jer 20:10
cry unto them, Fear is on every *s* ... Jer 49:29
ninety and six pomegranates on a *s* ... Jer 52:23
face of a lion, on the right *s* ... Eze 1:10
the face of an ox on the left *s* ... Eze 1:10
had two, which covered on this *s* ... Eze 1:23
had two, which covered on that *s* ... Eze 1:23
Lie thou also upon thy left *s* ... Eze 4:4
them, lie again on thy right *s* ... Eze 4:6
turn thee from one *s* to another ... Eze 4:8
that thou shalt lie upon thy *s* ... Eze 4:9
with a writer's inkhorn by his *s* ... Eze 9:2
had the writer's inkhorn by his *s* ... Eze 9:3
which had the inkhorn by his *s* ... Eze 9:11
stood on the right *s* of the house ... Eze 10:3
is on the east *s* for the city ... Eze 11:23
thee on every *s* for thy whoredom ... Eze 16:33
him on every *s* from the provinces ... Eze 19:8
them against thee on every *s* ... Eze 23:22
I will open the *s* of Moab from ... Eze 25:9

by the sword upon her on every s Eze 28:23
Because ye have thrust with s Eze 34:21
and swallowed you up on every s Eze 36:3
and will gather them on every s Eze 37:21
every s to my sacrifice that I do Eze 39:17
on this s, and three on that s Eze 40:10
measure on this s and on that s Eze 40:10
chambers was one cubit on this s Eze 40:12
the space was one cubit on that s Eze 40:12
were six cubits on this s Eze 40:12
and six cubits on that s Eze 40:12
the pavement by the s of the Eze 40:18
on this s and three on that s Eze 40:21
this s, and another on that s Eze 40:26
on this s, and on that s Eze 40:34
on this s, and on that s Eze 40:37
gate were two tables on this s Eze 40:39
and two tables on that s Eze 40:39
at the s without, as one goeth up Eze 40:40
and on the other s, which was at Eze 40:40
Four tables were on this s Eze 40:41
that s, by the s of the gate Eze 40:41
which was at the s of the north Eze 40:44
one at the s of the east gate Eze 40:44
the porch, five cubits on this s Eze 40:48
and five cubits on that s Eze 40:48
gate was three cubits on this s Eze 40:48
and three cubits on that s Eze 40:48
this s, and another on that s Eze 40:49
six cubits broad on the one s Eze 41:1
six cubits broad on the other s Eze 41:1
were five cubits on the one s Eze 41:2
and five cubits on the other s Eze 41:2
and the breadth of every s chamber Eze 41:5
round about the house on every s Eze 41:5
the s chambers were three, one Eze 41:6
for the s chambers round about Eze 41:6
still upward to the s chambers Eze 41:7
the foundations of the s chambers Eze 41:8
was for the s chamber without Eze 41:9
the s chambers that were within Eze 41:9
round about the house on every s Eze 41:10
the doors of the s chambers were Eze 41:11
on the one s and on the other s Eze 41:15
toward the palm tree on the one s Eze 41:19
the palm tree on the other s Eze 41:19
on the one s and on the other s Eze 41:26
upon the s chambers of the house, Eze 41:26
was the entry on the east s Eze 42:9
He measured the east s with the Eze 42:16
He measured the north s, five Eze 42:17
He measured the south s, five Eze 42:18
He turned about to the west s Eze 42:19
be for the prince on the one s Eze 45:7
on the other s of the oblation of Eze 45:7
city, from the west s westward Eze 45:7
and from the east s eastward Eze 45:7
which was at the s of the gate Eze 46:19
from the right s of the house Eze 47:1
at the south s of the altar Eze 47:1
ran out waters on the right s Eze 47:2
were very many trees on the one s Eze 47:7
on this s and on that s Eze 47:12
of the land toward the north s Eze 47:15
And this is the north s Eze 47:17
the east s ye shall measure from Eze 47:18
And this is the east s Eze 47:18
And the south s southward, from Eze 47:19
And this is the south s southward Eze 47:19
The west s also shall be the Eze 47:20
This is the west s Eze 47:20
the east s unto the west s Eze 48:2
east s even unto the west s Eze 48:3
the east s unto the west s Eze 48:4
the east s unto the west s Eze 48:5
east s even unto the west s Eze 48:6
the east s unto the west s Eze 48:7
the east s unto the west s Eze 48:8
the east s unto the west s Eze 48:8
the north s four thousand and five Eze 48:16
the south s four thousand and five Eze 48:16
on the east s four thousand and Eze 48:16
the west s four thousand and five Eze 48:16
be for the prince, on the one s Eze 48:21
the east s unto the west s Eze 48:23
the east s unto the west s Eze 48:24
the east s unto the west s Eze 48:25
the east s unto the west s Eze 48:26
the east s unto the west s Eze 48:27
of Gad, at the south s southward Eze 48:28
out of the city on the north s Eze 48:30
at the east s four thousand and Eze 48:32
at the south s four thousand and Eze 48:33
At the west s four thousand and Eze 48:34
and it raised up itself on one s Dan 7:5
as I was by the s of the great Dan 10:4
but she shall not stand on his s Dan 11:17
the one on this s of the bank of Dan 12:5
the other on that s of the bank Dan 12:5
that thou stoodest on the other s Obad 11
and sat on the east s of the city Jonah 4:5
one upon the right s of the bowl Zec 4:3
the other upon the left s thereof Zec 4:3
the right s of the candlestick Zec 4:11
and upon the left s thereof Zec 4:11
off as on this s according to it Zec 5:3
off as on that s according to it Zec 5:3
to depart unto the other s Mt 8:18
other s into the country of the Mt 8:28
of the house, and sat by the sea s Mt 13:1
some seeds fell by the way s Mt 13:4
which received seed by the way s Mt 13:19
to go before him unto the other s Mt 14:22
were come to the other s, they Mt 16:5
blind men sitting by the way s Mt 20:30
he went forth again by the sea s Mk 2:13
began again to teach by the sea s Mk 4:1
he sowed, some fell by the way s Mk 4:4
And these are they by the way s Mk 4:15
Let us pass over unto the other s Mk 4:35
over unto the other s of the sea Mk 5:1
again by ship unto the other s Mk 5:21
to go to the other s before unto Mk 6:45
again departed to the other s Mk 8:13
Judaea by the farther s of Jordan Mk 10:1
sat by the highway s begging Mk 10:46
young man sitting on the right s Mk 16:5
right s of the altar of incense Lk 1:11
he sowed, some fell by the way s Lk 8:5
Those by the way s are they that Lk 8:12
over unto the other s of the lake Lk 8:22
him, he passed by on the other s Lk 10:31
him, and passed by on the other s Lk 10:32
man sat by the way s begging Lk 18:35
round, and keep thee in on every s Lk 19:43
s of the sea saw that there was Jn 6:22
him on the other s of the sea Jn 6:25
others with him, on either s one Jn 19:18
with a spear pierced his s Jn 19:34
unto them his hands and his s Jn 20:20
and thrust my hand into his s Jn 20:25
thy hand, and thrust it into my s Jn 20:27
net on the right s of the ship Jn 21:6
whose house is by the sea s Acts 10:6
one Simon a tanner by the sea s Acts 10:32
and he smote Peter on the s Acts 12:7
went out of the city by a river s Acts 16:13
We are troubled on every s 2Cor 4:8
but we were troubled on every s 2Cor 7:5
on either s of the river, was Rev 22:2

### SIDES

the rings by the s of the ark Ex 25:14
shall come out of the s of it Ex 25:32
it shall hang over the s of the Ex 26:13
for the s of the tabernacle Ex 26:22
of the tabernacle in the two s Ex 26:23
for the two s westward Ex 26:27
be upon the two s of the altar Ex 27:7
the two s of the ephod underneath Ex 28:27
the s thereof round about, and the Ex 30:3
upon the two s of it shalt thou Ex 30:4
were written on both their s Ex 32:15
for the s of the tabernacle Ex 36:27
of the tabernacle in the two s Ex 36:28
the tabernacle for the s westward Ex 36:32
the rings by the s of the ark Ex 37:5
going out of the s thereof Ex 37:18
the s thereof round about, and the Ex 37:26
of it, upon the two s thereof Ex 37:27
the rings on the s of the altar Ex 38:7
put them on the two s of the Ex 39:20
in your eyes, and thorns in your s Num 33:55
unto you, and scourges in your s Josh 23:13
they shall be as thorns in your s Judg 2:3
colours of needlework on both s Judg 5:30
men remained in the s of the cave 1Sa 24:3
peace on all s round about him 1Kin 4:24
cubits on the s of the house 1Kin 6:16
to the s of Lebanon, and will cut 2Kin 19:23
on the s of the north, the city Ps 48:2
vine by the s of thine house Ps 128:3
in the s of the north Is 14:13
down to hell, to the s of the pit Is 14:15
mountains, to the s of Lebanon Is 37:24
ye shall be borne upon her s Is 66:12
be raised from the s of the earth Jer 6:22
nest in the s of the hole's mouth Jer 48:28
their calamity from all s thereof Jer 49:32
under their wings on their four s Eze 1:8
went, they went upon their four s Eze 1:17
went, they went upon their four s Eze 10:11
are set in the s of the pit Eze 32:23
the s of the door were five Eze 41:2
on the s of the porch, and upon Eze 41:26
He measured it by the four s Eze 42:20
was a place on the two s westward Eze 46:19
for these are his s east and west Eze 48:1
him that is by the s of the house Amos 6:10
gone down into the s of the ship Jonah 1:5

### SIDON (*si'-don*) See SIDONIANS, ZIDON.

*1. Son of Canaan.*
Canaan begat *S* his firstborn, and Gen 10:15
*2. Phoenician city north of Tyre.*
of the Canaanites was from *S* Gen 10:19
you, had been done in Tyre and *S* Mt 11:21
*S* at the day of judgment, than Mt 11:22
into the coasts of Tyre and *S* Mt 15:21
and they about Tyre and *S*, a great Mk 3:8
into the borders of Tyre and *S* Mk 7:24
from the coasts of Tyre and *S* Mk 7:31
save unto Sarepta, a city of *S* Lk 4:26
from the sea coast of Tyre and *S* Lk 6:17
works had been done in Tyre and *S* Lk 10:13
*S* at the judgment, than for you Lk 10:14
displeased with them of Tyre and *S* Acts 12:20
And the next day we touched at *S* Acts 27:3

### SIDONIANS (*si-do'-ne-uns*) See ZIDONIANS.

*Inhabitants of Sidon.*
(Which Hermon the *S* call Sirion Deut 3:9
and Mearah that is beside the *S* Josh 13:4
Misrephoth-maim, and all the *S* Josh 13:6
and all the Canaanites, and the *S* Judg 3:3
to hew timber like unto the *S* 1Kin 5:6

### SIEGE

life) to employ them in the s Deut 20:19
thy God hath given thee, in the s Deut 28:53
he hath nothing left him in the s Deut 28:55
of all things secretly in the s Deut 28:57
and all Israel laid s to Gibbethon 1Kin 15:27
he himself laid s against Lachish 2Chr 32:9
ye abide in the s in Jerusalem 2Chr 32:10
will lay s against thee with a Is 29:3
the flesh of his friend in the s Jer 19:9
lay s against it, and build a fort Eze 4:2
and thou shalt lay s against it Eze 4:3
face toward the s of Jerusalem Eze 4:7
thou hast ended the days of thy s Eze 4:8
the days of the s are fulfilled Eze 5:2
he hath laid s against us Mic 5:1
Draw thee waters for the s Nah 3:14
be in the s both against Judah Zec 12:2

### SIEVE

the nations with the s of vanity Is 30:28
like as corn is sifted in a s Amos 9:9

### SIFT

to s the nations with the sieve Is 30:28
I will s the house of Israel Amos 9:9
that he may s you as wheat Lk 22:31

### SIFTED

like as corn is s in a sieve Amos 9:9

### SIGH

all the merryhearted do s Is 24:7
her priests s, her virgins are Lam 1:4
All her people s, they seek bread Lam 1:11
They have heard that I s Lam 1:21
the foreheads of the men that s Eze 9:4
*S* therefore, thou son of man, Eze 21:6
with bitterness s before their Eze 21:6

### SIGHED

the children of Israel s by Ex 2:23
And looking up to heaven, he s Mk 7:34
he s deeply in his spirit, and Mk 8:12

### SIGHEST

say unto thee, Wherefore s thou Eze 21:7

### SIGHETH

yea, she s, and turneth backward Lam 1:8

### SIGHING

For my s cometh before I eat, and Job 3:24
for the s of the needy, now will Ps 12:5
with grief, and my years with s Ps 31:10
Let the s of the prisoner come Ps 79:11
all the s thereof have I made to Is 21:2
and sorrow and s shall flee away Is 35:10
I fainted in my s, and I find no Jer 45:3

### SIGHS

for my s are many, and my heart is Lam 1:22

### SIGHT

tree that is pleasant to the s Gen 2:9
now I have found favour in thy s Gen 18:3
servant hath found grace in thy s Gen 19:19
in Abraham's s because of his son Gen 21:11
in thy s because of the lad Gen 21:12
I may bury my dead out of my s Gen 23:4
I should bury my dead out of my s Gen 23:8
that I may find grace in thy s Gen 32:5
to find grace in the s of my lord Gen 33:8
now I have found grace in thy s Gen 33:10
me find grace in the s of my lord Gen 33:15
was wicked in the s of the LORD Gen 38:7
And Joseph found grace in his s Gen 39:4
gave him favour in the s of the Gen 39:21
ought left in the s of my lord Gen 47:18
us find grace in the s of my lord Gen 47:25
now I have found grace in thy s Gen 47:29
turn aside, and see this great s Ex 3:3
favour in the s of the Egyptians Ex 3:21
the signs in the s of the people Ex 4:30
in the s of Pharaoh, and in the Ex 7:20
and in the s of his servants Ex 7:20
the heaven in the s of Pharaoh Ex 9:8
favour in the s of the Egyptians Ex 11:3
in the s of Pharaoh's servants, Ex 11:3
and in the s of the people Ex 11:3
favour in the s of the Egyptians Ex 12:36
do that which is right in his s Ex 15:26
Moses did so in the s of the Ex 17:6
s of all the people upon mount Ex 19:11
the s of the glory of the LORD Ex 24:17
hast also found grace in my s Ex 33:12
if I have found grace in thy s Ex 33:13
that I may find grace in thy s Ex 33:13
people have found grace in thy s Ex 33:16
for thou hast found grace in my s Ex 33:17
now I have found grace in thy s Ex 34:9
in the s of all the house of Ex 40:38
accepted in the s of the LORD Lev 10:19
the plague in s be deeper than Lev 13:3
in s be not deeper than the skin, Lev 13:4
the plague in his s be at a stay Lev 13:5
it be in s lower than the skin, Lev 13:20
it be in s deeper than the skin Lev 13:25
if it be in s deeper than the Lev 13:30
it be not in s deeper than the Lev 13:31

the scall be not in s deeper than Lev 13:32
nor be in s deeper than the skin Lev 13:34
the scall be in his s at a stay Lev 13:37
which in s are lower than the Lev 14:37
cut off in the s of their people Lev 20:17
with rigour over him in thy s Lev 25:53
of Egypt in the s of the heathen Lev 26:45
in the s of Aaron their father Num 3:4
have I not found favour in thy s Num 11:11
if I have found favour in thy s Num 11:15
were in our own s as grasshoppers Num 13:33
and so we were in their s Num 13:33
shall burn the heifer in his s Num 19:5
in the s of all the congregation Num 20:27
woman in the s of Moses, and in Num 25:6
in the s of all the congregation Num 25:6
and give him a charge in their s Num 27:19
if we have found grace in thy s Num 32:5
done evil in the s of the LORD Num 32:13
in the s of all the Egyptians Num 33:3
in the s of the nations, which Deut 4:6
evil in the s of the LORD thy God Deut 4:25
brought thee out in his s with Deut 4:37
and good in the s of the LORD Deut 6:18
wickedly in the s of the LORD Deut 9:18
is right in the s of the LORD Deut 12:25
right in the s of the LORD thy Deut 12:28
in the s of the LORD thy God Deut 17:2
is right in the s of the LORD Deut 21:9
s of thine eyes which thou shalt Deut 28:34
for the s of thine eyes which Deut 28:67
unto him in the s of all Israel Deut 31:7
will do evil in the s of the LORD Deut 31:29
shewed in the s of all Israel Deut 34:12
in the s of all Israel Josh 3:7
Joshua in the s of all Israel Josh 4:14
and he said in the s of Israel Josh 10:12
and drive them from out of your s Josh 23:5
did those great signs in our s Josh 24:17
did evil in the s of the LORD Judg 2:11
did evil in the s of the LORD Judg 3:7
evil again in the s of the LORD Judg 3:12
done evil in the s of the LORD Judg 3:12
did evil in the s of the LORD Judg 4:1
did evil in the s of the LORD Judg 6:1
now I have found grace in thy s Judg 6:17
of the LORD departed out of his s Judg 6:21
evil again in the s of the LORD Judg 10:6
evil again in the s of the LORD Judg 13:1
him in whose s I shall find grace Ruth 2:2
said, Let me find favour in thy s Ruth 2:13
handmaid find grace in thy s 1Sa 1:18
ye have done in the s of the LORD 1Sa 12:17
thou wast little in thine own s 1Sa 15:17
didst evil in the s of the LORD 1Sa 15:19
for he hath found favour in my s 1Sa 16:22
in the s of all the people 1Sa 18:5
also in the s of Saul's servants 1Sa 18:5
me in the host is good in my s 1Sa 29:6
I know that thou art good in my s 1Sa 29:9
and will be base in mine own s 2Sa 6:22
all thine enemies out of thy s 2Sa 7:9
was yet a small thing in thy s 2Sa 7:19
of the LORD, to do evil in his s 2Sa 12:9
thy wives in the s of this sun 2Sa 12:11
meat, and dress the meat in my s 2Sa 13:5
make me a couple of cakes in my s 2Sa 13:6
it, and made cakes in his s 2Sa 13:8
that I have found grace in thy s 2Sa 14:22
that I may find grace in thy s 2Sa 16:4
concubines in the s of all Israel 2Sa 16:22
to my cleanness in his eye s 2Sa 22:25
s to sit on the throne of Israel 1Kin 8:25
my name, will I cast out of my s 1Kin 9:7
did evil in the s of the LORD 1Kin 11:6
great favour in the s of Pharaoh 1Kin 11:19
ways, and do that is right in my s 1Kin 11:38
did evil in the s of the LORD 1Kin 14:22
he did evil in the s of the LORD 1Kin 15:26
he did evil in the s of the LORD 1Kin 15:34
that he did in the s of the LORD 1Kin 16:7
doing evil in the s of the LORD 1Kin 16:19
s of the LORD above all that were 1Kin 16:30
to work evil in the s of the LORD 1Kin 21:20
wickedness in the s of the LORD 1Kin 21:25
he did evil in the s of the LORD 1Kin 22:52
servants, be precious in thy s 2Kin 1:13
my life now be precious in thy s 2Kin 1:14
wrought evil in the s of the LORD 2Kin 3:2
light thing in the s of the LORD 2Kin 3:18
he did evil in the s of the LORD 2Kin 8:18
and did evil in the s of the LORD 2Kin 8:27
in the s of the LORD all his days 2Kin 12:2
was evil in the s of the LORD 2Kin 13:2
was evil in the s of the LORD 2Kin 13:11
was right in the s of the LORD 2Kin 14:3
was evil in the s of the LORD 2Kin 14:24
was right in the s of the LORD 2Kin 15:3
was evil in the s of the LORD 2Kin 15:9
was evil in the s of the LORD 2Kin 15:18
was evil in the s of the LORD 2Kin 15:24
was evil in the s of the LORD 2Kin 15:28
was right in the s of the LORD 2Kin 15:34
in the s of the LORD his God 2Kin 16:2
was evil in the s of the LORD 2Kin 17:2
to do evil in the s of the LORD 2Kin 17:17
and removed them out of his s 2Kin 17:18
he had cast them out of his s 2Kin 17:20
LORD removed Israel out of his s 2Kin 17:23
was right in the s of the LORD 2Kin 18:3
done that which is good in thy s 2Kin 20:3
was evil in the s of the LORD 2Kin 21:2
wickedness in the s of the LORD 2Kin 21:6
done that which was evil in my s 2Kin 21:15
was evil in the s of the LORD 2Kin 21:16
was evil in the s of the LORD 2Kin 21:20
was right in the s of the LORD 2Kin 22:2
remove Judah also out of my s 2Kin 23:27
was evil in the s of the LORD 2Kin 23:32
was evil in the s of the LORD 2Kin 23:37
to remove them out of his s 2Kin 24:3
was evil in the s of the LORD 2Kin 24:9
was evil in the s of the LORD 2Kin 24:19
was evil in the s of the LORD 1Chr 2:3
do that which is good in his s 1Chr 19:13
much blood upon the earth in my s 1Chr 22:8
in the s of all Israel the 1Chr 28:8
in the s of all Israel, and 1Chr 29:25
in my s to sit upon the throne of 2Chr 6:16
my name, will I cast out of my s 2Chr 7:20
was right in the s of the LORD 2Chr 20:32
Wherefore he did evil in the s of 2Chr 22:4
the s of the LORD all the days of 2Chr 24:2
was right in the s of the LORD 2Chr 25:2
was right in the s of the LORD 2Chr 26:4
was right in the s of the LORD 2Chr 27:2
was right in the s of the LORD 2Chr 28:1
was right in the s of the LORD 2Chr 29:2
s of all nations from thenceforth 2Chr 32:23
was evil in the s of the LORD 2Chr 33:2
much evil in the s of the LORD 2Chr 33:6
was evil in the s of the LORD 2Chr 33:22
was right in the s of the LORD 2Chr 34:2
evil in the s of the LORD his God 2Chr 36:5
was evil in the s of the LORD 2Chr 36:9
evil in the s of the LORD his God 2Chr 36:12
in the s of the kings of Persia Ezr 9:9
him mercy in the s of this man Neh 1:11
have found favour in thy s Neh 2:5
the book in the s of all people Neh 8:5
s of all them that looked upon Est 2:15
favour in his s more than all the Est 2:17
that she obtained favour in his s Est 5:2
found favour in the s of the king Est 5:8
If I have found favour in thy s Est 7:3
if I have found favour in his s Est 8:5
heavens are not clean in his s Job 15:15
beasts, and reputed vile in your s Job 18:3
I am an alien in their s Job 19:15
established in their s with them Job 21:8
the stars are not pure in his s Job 25:5
men in the open s of others Job 34:26
be cast down even at the s of him Job 41:9
foolish shall not stand in thy s Ps 5:5
the heathen be judged in thy s Ps 9:19
are far above out of his s Ps 10:5
my heart, be acceptable in thy s Ps 19:14
and done this evil in thy s Ps 51:4
shall their blood be in his s Ps 72:14
who may stand in thy s when once Ps 76:7
did he in the s of their fathers Ps 78:12
s by the revenging of the blood Ps 79:10
For a thousand years in thy s are Ps 90:4
shewed in the s of the heathen Ps 98:2
lies shall not tarry in my s Ps 101:7
Precious in the s of the LORD is Ps 116:15
for in thy s shall no man living Ps 143:2
is spread in the s of any bird Prov 1:17
understanding in the s of God Prov 3:4
beloved in the s of my mother Prov 4:3
man that is good in his s wisdom Eccl 2:26
Better is the s of the eyes than Eccl 6:9
Be not hasty to go out of his s Eccl 8:3
heart, and in the s of thine eyes Eccl 11:9
eyes, and prudent in their own s Is 5:21
not judge after the s of his eyes Is 11:3
so have we been in thy s, O LORD Is 26:17
done that which is good in thy s Is 38:3
Since thou wast precious in my s Is 43:4
thine abominations out of my s Jer 4:1
And I will cast you out of my s Jer 7:15
of Judah have done evil in my s Jer 7:30
cast them out of my s, and let Jer 15:1
If it do evil in my s, that it Jer 18:10
blot out their sin from thy s Jer 18:23
s of the men that go with thee Jer 19:10
in the s of Hanameel mine uncle's Jer 32:12
turned, and had done right in my s Jer 34:15
in the s of the men of Judah Jer 43:9
they have done in Zion in your s Jer 51:24
cometh out of man, in their s Eze 4:12
of thee in the s of the nations Eze 5:8
in the s of all that pass by Eze 5:14
And he went in in my s Eze 10:2
mounted up from the earth in my s Eze 10:19
and remove by day in their s Eze 12:3
place to another place in their s Eze 12:3
forth thy stuff by day in their s Eze 12:4
shalt go forth at even in their s Eze 12:4
thou through the wall in their s Eze 12:5
In their s shalt thou bear it Eze 12:6
it upon my shoulder in their s Eze 12:7
upon thee in the s of many women Eze 16:41
in whose s I made myself known Eze 20:9
in whose s I brought them out Eze 20:14
polluted in the s of the heathen Eze 20:22
in whose s I brought them forth Eze 20:22
lothe yourselves in your own s Eze 20:43
as a false divination in their s Eze 21:23
thyself in the s of the heathen Eze 22:16
s of all them that behold thee Eze 28:18
in them in the s of the heathen Eze 28:25
in your own s for your iniquities Eze 36:31
in the s of all that passed by Eze 36:34
in them in the s of many nations Eze 39:27
and write it in their s, that they Eze 43:11
the s thereof to the end of all Dan 4:11
the s thereof to all the earth Dan 4:20
away her whoredoms out of her s Hos 2:2
lewdness in the s of her lovers Hos 2:10
us up, and we shall live in his s Hos 6:2
my s in the bottom of the sea Amos 9:3
I said, I am cast out of thy s Jonah 2:4
evil is good in the s of the LORD Mal 2:17
The blind receive their s Mt 11:5
for so it seemed good in thy s Mt 11:26
immediately their eyes received s Mt 20:34
Lord, that I might receive my s Mk 10:51
And immediately he received his s Mk 10:52
be great in the s of the Lord Lk 1:15
and recovering of s to the blind Lk 4:18
many that were blind he gave s Lk 7:21
for so it seemed good in thy s Lk 10:21
against heaven, and in thy s Lk 15:21
is abomination in the s of God Lk 16:15
Lord, that I may receive my s Lk 18:41
said unto him, Receive thy s Lk 18:42
And immediately he received his s Lk 18:43
that came together to that s Lk 23:48
and he vanished out of their s Lk 24:31
I went and washed, and I received s Jn 9:11
him how he had received his s Jn 9:15
had been blind, and received his s Jn 9:18
of him that had received his s Jn 9:18
cloud received him out of their s Acts 1:9
Whether it be right in the s of Acts 4:19
wisdom in the s of Pharaoh king Acts 7:10
saw it, he wondered at the s Acts 7:31
is not right in the s of God Acts 8:21
And he was three days without s Acts 9:9
him, that he might receive his s Acts 9:12
that thou mightest receive thy s Acts 9:17
and he received s forthwith Acts 9:18
in remembrance in the s of God Acts 10:31
me, Brother Saul, receive thy s Acts 22:13
no flesh be justified in his s Rom 3:20
things honest in the s of all men Rom 12:17
in the s of God speak we in 2Cor 2:17
man's conscience in the s of God 2Cor 4:2
(For we walk by faith, not by s 2Cor 5:7
s of God might appear unto you 2Cor 7:12
not only in the s of the Lord 2Cor 8:21
but also in the s of men 2Cor 8:21
by the law in the s of God Gal 3:11
and unreproveable in his s Col 1:22
Jesus Christ, in the s of God 1Th 1:3
acceptable in the s of God our 1Ti 2:3
give thee charge in the s of God 1Ti 6:13
that is not manifest in his s Heb 4:13
And so terrible was the s, that Heb 12:21
which is wellpleasing in his s Heb 13:21
yourselves in the s of the Lord Jas 4:10
which is in the s of God of great 1Pet 3:4
things that are pleasing in his s 1Jn 3:22
in s like unto an emerald Rev 4:3
on the earth in the s of men Rev 13:13
power to do in the s of the beast Rev 13:14

## SIGHTS

and fearful s and great signs shall Lk 21:11

## SIGN

to the voice of the first s Ex 4:8
believe the voice of the latter s Ex 4:8
to morrow shall this s be Ex 8:23
it shall be for a s unto thee Ex 13:9
for it is a s between me and you Ex 31:13
It is a s between me and the Ex 31:17
they shall be a s unto the Num 16:38
and they became a s Num 26:10
bind them for a s upon thine hand Deut 6:8
bind them for a s upon your hand Deut 11:18
and giveth thee a s or a wonder Deut 13:1
the s or the wonder come to pass, Deut 13:2
they shall be upon thee for a s Deut 28:46
That this may be a s among you Josh 4:6
then shew me a s that thou Judg 6:17
s between the men of Israel Judg 20:38
And this shall be a s unto thee 1Sa 2:34
and this shall be a s unto us 1Sa 14:10
he gave a s the same day, saying, 1Kin 13:3
This is the s which the LORD hath 1Kin 13:3
according to the s which the man 1Kin 13:5
And this shall be a s unto thee 2Kin 19:29
What shall be the s that the LORD 2Kin 20:8
This s shalt thou have of the 2Kin 20:9
unto him, and he gave him a s 2Chr 32:24
Ask thee a s of the LORD thy God Is 7:11
Lord himself shall give you a s Is 7:14
And it shall be for a s and for a Is 19:20
and barefoot three years for a s Is 20:3
And this shall be a s unto thee Is 37:30
this shall be a s unto thee from Is 38:7
What is the s that I shall go up Is 38:22
for an everlasting s that shall Is 55:13
And I will set a s among them Is 66:19
Tekoa, and set up a s of fire in Jer 6:1
And this shall be a s unto you Jer 44:29
This shall be a s to the house of Eze 4:3
for a s unto the house of Israel Eze 12:6
Say, I am your s Eze 12:11

that man, and will make him a *s*............ Eze 14:8
to be a *s* between me and them,........... Eze 20:12
and they shall be a *s* between me........ Eze 20:20
Thus Ezekiel is unto you a *s*................. Eze 24:24
and thou shalt be a *s* unto them.......... Eze 24:27
then shall he set up a *s* by it................ Eze 39:15
*s* the writing, that it be not...................... Dan 6:8
we would see a *s* from thee.................... Mt 12:38
generation seeketh after a *s*................... Mt 12:39
there shall no *s* be given to it................ Mt 12:39
but the *s* of the prophet Jonas.............. Mt 12:39
would shew them a *s* from heaven......... Mt 16:1
generation seeketh after a *s*................... Mt 16:4
there shall no *s* be given unto it............ Mt 16:4
but the *s* of the prophet Jonas.............. Mt 16:4
what shall be the *s* of thy coming........... Mt 24:3
then shall appear the *s* of the................ Mt 24:30
that betrayed him gave them a *s*............ Mt 26:48
seeking of him a *s* from heaven.............. Mk 8:11
this generation seek after a *s*................ Mk 8:12
There shall no *s* be given unto............... Mk 8:12
what shall be the *s* when all.................. Mk 13:4
And this shall be a *s* unto you................ Lk 2:12
for a *s* which shall be spoken.................. Lk 2:34
sought of him a *s* from heaven................ Lk 11:16
they seek a *s*.............................................. Lk 11:29
and there shall no *s* be given it.............. Lk 11:29
but the *s* of Jonas the prophet............... Lk 11:29
Jonas was a *s* unto the Ninevites............ Lk 11:30
what *s* will there be when these.............. Lk 21:7
What *s* shewest thou unto us,.................. Jn 2:18
What *s* shewest thou then, that we......... Jn 6:30
whose *s* was Castor and Pollux............ Acts 28:11
he received the *s* of circumcision............ Rom 4:11
For the Jews require a *s*, and the......... 1Cor 1:22
Wherefore tongues are for a *s*............ 1Cor 14:22
And I saw another *s* in heaven.............. Rev 15:1

**SIGNED**
king Darius *s* the writing.......................... Dan 6:9
knew that the writing was *s*.................... Dan 6:10
Hast thou not *s* a decree, that................ Dan 6:12
nor the decree that thou hast *s*.............. Dan 6:13

**SIGNET**
And she said, Thy *s*, and thy................ Gen 38:18
pray thee, whose are these, the *s*........ Gen 38:25
stone, like the engravings of a *s*............ Ex 28:11
names, like the engravings of a *s*.......... Ex 28:21
it, like the engravings of a *s*.................. Ex 28:36
names, like the engravings of a *s*.......... Ex 39:14
like to the engravings of a *s*.................. Ex 39:30
were the *s* upon my right hand............... Jer 22:24
the king sealed it with his own *s*............ Dan 6:17
and with the *s* of his lords...................... Dan 6:17
LORD, and will make thee as a *s*............. Hag 2:23

**SIGNETS**
as *s* are graven, with the names............... Ex 39:6

**SIGNIFICATION**
and none of them is without *s*............ 1Cor 14:10

**SIGNIFIED**
*s* by the Spirit that there should......... Acts 11:28
*s* it by his angel unto his........................... Rev 1:1

**SIGNIFIETH**
*s* the removing of those things............. Heb 12:27

**SIGNIFY**
to *s* the accomplishment of the........... Acts 21:26
*s* to the chief captain that he............... Acts 23:15
not withal to *s* the crimes laid.............. Acts 25:27
of Christ which was in them did *s*........ 1Pet 1:11

**SIGNIFYING**
*s* what death he should die...................... Jn 12:33
*s* what death he should die...................... Jn 18:32
*s* by what death he should glorify............ Jn 21:19
The Holy Ghost this *s*, that the................ Heb 9:8

**SIGNS**
and let them be for *s*, and for............... Gen 1:14
will not believe also these two *s*................. Ex 4:9
hand, wherewith thou shalt do *s*.............. Ex 4:17
all the *s* which he had commanded.......... Ex 4:28
did the *s* in the sight of the..................... Ex 4:30
Pharaoh's heart, and multiply my *s*........... Ex 7:3
might shew these my *s* before him........... Ex 10:1
my *s* which I have done among them..... Ex 10:2
for all the *s* which I have shewed...... Num 14:11
nation, by temptations, by *s*.................. Deut 4:34
And the LORD shewed *s* and wonders, Deut 6:22
which thine eyes saw, and the *s*........... Deut 7:19
great terribleness, and with *s*............... Deut 26:8
which thine eyes have seen, the *s*....... Deut 29:3
In all the *s* and the wonders,............. Deut 34:11
did those great *s* in our sight............. Josh 24:17
when these *s* are come unto thee,.......... 1Sa 10:7
all those *s* came to pass that day.......... 1Sa 10:9
And shewedst *s* and wonders upon....... Neh 9:10
they set up their ensigns for *s*................ Ps 74:4
We see not our *s*........................................ Ps 74:9
How he had wrought his *s* in Egypt....... Ps 78:43
They shewed his *s* among them.......... Ps 105:27
the LORD hath given me are for *s*............ Is 8:18
not dismayed at the *s* of heaven............ Jer 10:2
Which hast set *s* and wonders in.......... Jer 32:20
out of the land of Egypt with *s*............ Jer 32:21
I thought it good to shew the *s*.............. Dan 4:2
How great are his *s*.................................. Dan 4:3
and rescueth, and he worketh *s*............ Dan 6:27
ye not discern the *s* of the times............ Mt 16:3
prophets, and shall shew great *s*........... Mt 24:24
shall rise, and shall shew *s*.................... Mk 13:22
these *s* shall follow them that............... Mk 16:17
the word with *s* following........................ Mk 16:20
they made *s* to his father, how he........... Lk 1:62
great *s* shall there be from..................... Lk 21:11
And there shall be *s* in the sun............... Lk 21:25
Jesus unto him, Except ye see *s*............... Jn 4:48
many other *s* truly did Jesus in.............. Jn 20:30
above, and *s* in the earth beneath........ Acts 2:19
you by miracles and wonders and *s*..... Acts 2:22
*s* were done by the apostles.................... Acts 2:43
and that *s* and wonders may be done.. Acts 4:30
hands of the apostles were many *s*...... Acts 5:12
*s* in the land of Egypt, and in the........ Acts 7:36
the miracles and *s* which were done.... Acts 8:13
word of his grace, and granted *s*.......... Acts 14:3
Through mighty *s* and wonders, by... Rom 15:19
Truly the *s* of an apostle were......... 2Cor 12:12
among you in all patience, in *s*......... 2Cor 12:12
of Satan with all power and *s*.................. 2Th 2:9
bearing them witness, both with *s*.......... Heb 2:4

**SIHON** (*si'-hon*) *An Amorite king.*
unto *S* king of the Amorites.............. Num 21:21
*S* would not suffer Israel to pass........ Num 21:23
but *S* gathered all his people.............. Num 21:23
of *S* the king of the Amorites.............. Num 21:26
let the city of *S* be built....................... Num 21:27
a flame from the city of *S*.................. Num 21:28
into captivity unto *S* king of the........ Num 21:29
didst unto *S* king of the Amorites...... Num 21:34
the kingdom of *S* king of the.............. Num 32:33
After he had slain *S* the king of.......... Deut 1:4
into thine hand *S* the Amorite.............. Deut 2:24
*S* king of Heshbon with words of......... Deut 2:26
But *S* king of Heshbon would not........ Deut 2:30
Behold, I have begun to give *S*............ Deut 2:31
Then *S* came out against us, he and... Deut 2:32
didst unto *S* king of the Amorites......... Deut 3:2
as we did unto *S* king of Heshbon,......... Deut 3:6
in the land of *S* king of the.................. Deut 4:46
*S* the king of Heshbon, and Og the..... Deut 29:7
shall do unto them as he did to *S*....... Deut 31:4
were on the other side Jordan, *S*.......... Josh 2:10
to *S* king of Heshbon, and to Og........... Josh 9:10
*S* king of the Amorites, who dwelt....... Josh 12:2
the border of *S* king of Heshbon.......... Josh 12:5
all the cities of *S* king of the.............. Josh 13:10
all the kingdom of *S* king of the.......... Josh 13:21
and Reba, which were dukes of *S*......... Josh 13:21
the kingdom of *S* king of Heshbon....... Josh 13:27
unto *S* king of the Amorites.................. Judg 11:19
But *S* trusted not Israel to pass........... Judg 11:20
but *S* gathered all his people................ Judg 11:20
LORD God of Israel delivered *S*........... Judg 11:21
in the country of *S* king of the............. 1Kin 4:19
so they possessed the land of *S*.............. Neh 9:22
*S* king of the Amorites, and Og............ Ps 135:11
*S* king of the Amorites......................... Ps 136:19
and a flame from the midst of *S*........... Jer 48:45

**SIHOR** (*si'-hor*) See SHIHOR. *A river in southern Canaan.*
From *S*, which is before Egypt,.............. Josh 13:3
And by great waters the seed of *S*........... Is 23:3
Egypt, to drink the waters of *S*................ Jer 2:18

**SIKKUTH** See MOLOCH.

**SILAS** (*si'-las*) See SILVANUS. *A co-worker with Paul.*
Judas surnamed Barsabas, and *S*.......... Acts 15:22
We have sent therefore Judas and *S*. Acts 15:27
And Judas and *S*, being prophets....... Acts 15:32
it pleased *S* to abide there still............. Acts 15:34
And Paul chose *S*, and departed,......... Acts 15:40
was gone, they caught Paul and *S*..... Acts 16:19
*S* prayed, and sang praises unto......... Acts 16:25
and fell down before Paul and *S*......... Acts 16:29
and consorted with Paul and *S*............. Acts 17:4
Paul and *S* by night unto Berea............ Acts 17:10
but *S* and Timotheus abode there...... Acts 17:14
a commandment unto *S*........................ Acts 17:15
*S* and Timotheus were come................... Acts 18:5

**SILENCE**
who said, Keep *s*..................................... Judg 3:19
was before mine eyes, there was *s*......... Job 4:16
waited, and kept *s* at my counsel.......... Job 29:21
terrify me, that I kept *s*........................ Job 31:34
Let the lying lips be put to *s*................... Ps 31:18
When I kept *s*, my bones waxed old......... Ps 32:3
keep not *s*................................................ Ps 35:22
I was dumb with *s*, I held my.................... Ps 39:2
shall come, and shall not keep *s*............. Ps 50:3
hast thou done, and I kept *s*.................... Ps 50:21
Keep not thou *s*, O God............................ Ps 83:1
my soul had almost dwelt in *s*................. Ps 94:17
neither any that go down into *s*............ Ps 115:17
a time to keep *s*, and a time to.............. Eccl 3:7
*s* is laid waste, and brought to *s*............... Is 15:1
is laid waste, and brought to *s*............... Is 15:1
Keep *s* before me, O islands..................... Is 41:1
mention of the LORD, keep not *s*.............. Is 62:6
I will not keep *s*, but will......................... Is 65:6
the LORD our God hath put us to *s*.......... Jer 8:14
sit upon the ground, and keep *s*........... Lam 2:10
He sitteth alone and keepeth *s*............. Lam 3:28
prudent shall keep *s* in that time........ Amos 5:13
they shall cast them forth with *s*........... Amos 8:3
all the earth keep *s* before him............. Hab 2:20
he had put the Sadducees to *s*.............. Mt 22:34
Then all the multitude kept *s*............. Acts 15:12
And when there was made a great *s*. Acts 21:40
to them, they kept the more *s*............. Acts 22:2
let him keep *s* in the church.............. 1Cor 14:28
your women keep *s* in the churches.. 1Cor 14:34
learn in *s* with all subjection................... 1Ti 2:11
over the man, but to be in *s*..................... 1Ti 2:12
to *s* the ignorance of foolish men......... 1Pet 2:15
there was *s* in heaven about the............. Rev 8:1

**SILENT**
the wicked shall be *s* in darkness.............. 1Sa 2:9
in the night season, and am not *s*............ Ps 22:2
be not *s* to me.............................................. Ps 28:1
lest, if thou be *s* to me, I.......................... Ps 28:1
sing praise to thee, and not be *s*............ Ps 30:12
let them be *s* in the grave...................... Ps 31:17
Sit thou *s*, and get thee into....................... Is 47:5
cities, and let us be *s* there...................... Jer 8:14
Be *s*, O all flesh, before the...................... Zec 2:13

**SILK**
her clothing is *s* and purple.................. Prov 31:22
linen, and I covered thee with *s*........... Eze 16:10
raiment was of fine linen, and *s*.......... Eze 16:13
and fine linen, and purple, and *s*......... Rev 18:12

**SILLA** (*sil'-lah*) *A place near Jerusalem.*
of Millo, which goeth down to *S*....... 2Kin 12:20

**SILLY**
man, and envy slayeth the *s* one............. Job 5:2
is like a *s* dove without heart.................. Hos 7:11
lead captive *s* women laden with.............. 2Ti 3:6

**SILOAH** (*si-lo'-ah*) See SHILOAH, SILOAM. *Same as Siloam.*
pool of *S* by the king's garden............... Neh 3:15

**SILOAM** (*si'-lo-am*) See SILOAH. *A pool south of Jerusalem.*
upon whom the tower in *S* fell................ Lk 13:4
him, Go, wash in the pool of *S*................. Jn 9:7
said unto me, Go to the pool of *S*........... Jn 9:11

**SILVANUS** (*sil-va'-nus*) See SILAS.
*1. A co-worker with Paul.*
among you by us, even by me and *S*.. 2Cor 1:19
Paul, and *S*, and Timotheus, unto............ 1Th 1:1
Paul, and *S*, and Timotheus, unto............ 2Th 1:1
*2. A messenger for Peter.*
By *S*, a faithful brother unto you.......... 1Pet 5:12

**SILVER**
was very rich in cattle, in *s*.................... Gen 13:2
brother a thousand pieces of *s*.............. Gen 20:16
worth four hundred shekels of *s*........... Gen 23:15
Abraham weighed to Ephron the *s*..... Gen 23:16
Heth, four hundred shekels of *s*........... Gen 23:16
given him flocks, and herds, and *s*...... Gen 24:35
servant brought forth jewels of *s*........ Gen 24:53
for twenty pieces of *s*............................ Gen 37:28
And put my cup, the *s* cup, in the........ Gen 44:2
out of thy lord's house *s* or gold............ Gen 44:8
he gave three hundred pieces of *s*....... Gen 45:22
in her house, jewels of *s*........................... Ex 3:22
of her neighbour, jewels of *s*..................... Ex 11:2
of the Egyptians jewels of *s*.................... Ex 12:35
shall not make with me gods of *s*........... Ex 20:23
their master thirty shekels of *s*............. Ex 21:32
gold, and *s*, and brass,.............................. Ex 25:3
of *s* under the twenty boards................. Ex 26:19
And their forty sockets of *s*.................... Ex 26:21
boards, and their sockets of *s*................ Ex 26:25
gold, upon the four sockets of *s*............ Ex 26:32
and their fillets shall be of *s*.................. Ex 27:10
the pillars and their fillets of *s*.............. Ex 27:11
court shall be filleted with *s*.................. Ex 27:17
their hooks shall be of *s*......................... Ex 27:17
works, to work in gold, and in *s*.............. Ex 31:4
gold, and *s*, and brass,.............................. Ex 35:5
that did offer an offering of *s*................. Ex 35:24
works, to work in gold, and in *s*............. Ex 35:32
forty sockets of *s* he made under........... Ex 36:24
And their forty sockets of *s*..................... Ex 36:26
sockets were sixteen sockets of *s*.......... Ex 36:30
cast for them four sockets of *s*............... Ex 36:36
and their fillets were of *s*........................ Ex 38:10
the pillars and their fillets of *s*.............. Ex 38:11
the pillars and their fillets of *s*.............. Ex 38:12
the pillars and their fillets of *s*.............. Ex 38:17
of their chapiters of *s*............................. Ex 38:17
of the court were filleted with *s*............ Ex 38:17
their hooks of *s*, and the.......................... Ex 38:19
chapiters and their fillets of *s*................ Ex 38:19
the *s* of them that were numbered.......... Ex 38:25
of the hundred talents of *s* were........... Ex 38:27
thy estimation by shekels of *s*.................. Lev 5:15
shall be fifty shekels of *s*........................ Lev 27:3
be of the male five shekels of *s*................ Lev 27:6
shall be three shekels of *s*........................ Lev 27:6
be valued at fifty shekels of *s*.............. Lev 27:16
And his offering was one *s* charger..... Num 7:13
one *s* bowl of seventy shekels,.............. Num 7:13
for his offering one *s* charger................ Num 7:19
one *s* bowl of seventy shekels,............... Num 7:19
His offering was one *s* charger............. Num 7:25
one *s* bowl of seventy shekels,............... Num 7:25
His offering was one *s* charger of......... Num 7:31
one *s* bowl of seventy shekels,............... Num 7:31
His offering was one *s* charger............. Num 7:37
one *s* bowl of seventy shekels,............... Num 7:37
His offering was one *s* charger of......... Num 7:43
a *s* bowl of seventy shekels,................... Num 7:43

His offering was one s charger Num 7:49
one s bowl of seventy shekels, Num 7:49
His offering was one s charger of Num 7:55
one s bowl of seventy shekels, Num 7:55
His offering was one s charger Num 7:61
one s bowl of seventy shekels, Num 7:61
His offering was one s charger Num 7:67
one s bowl of seventy shekels, Num 7:67
His offering was one s charger Num 7:73
one s bowl of seventy shekels, Num 7:73
His offering was one s charger Num 7:79
one s bowl of seventy shekels, Num 7:79
of s, twelve s bowls Num 7:84
Each charger of s weighing an Num 7:85
all the s vessels weighed two Num 7:85
Make thee two trumpets of s Num 10:2
would give me his house full of s Num 22:18
would give me his house full of s Num 24:13
Only the gold, and the s, the Num 31:22
the s or gold that is on them Deut 7:25
and thy flocks multiply, and thy s Deut 8:13
he greatly multiply to himself s Deut 17:17
him in an hundred shekels of s Deut 22:19
father fifty shekels of s Deut 22:29
and their idols, wood and stone, s Deut 29:17
But all the s, and gold, and Josh 6:19
only the s, and the gold, and the Josh 6:24
and two hundred shekels of s Josh 7:21
of my tent, and the s under it Josh 7:21
in his tent, and the s under it Josh 7:22
Achan the son of Zerah, and the s Josh 7:24
and with very much cattle, with s Josh 22:8
for an hundred pieces of s Josh 24:32
ten pieces of s out of the house Judg 9:4
of us eleven hundred pieces of s Judg 16:5
of s that were taken from thee Judg 17:2
ears, behold, the s is with me Judg 17:2
shekels of s to his mother Judg 17:3
I had wholly dedicated the s unto Judg 17:3
took two hundred shekels of s Judg 17:4
thee ten shekels of s by the year Judg 17:10
and crouch to him for a piece of s 1Sa 2:36
the fourth part of a shekel of s 1Sa 9:8
brought with him vessels of s 2Sa 8:10
unto the LORD, with the s 2Sa 8:11
have given thee ten shekels of s 2Sa 18:11
shekels of s in mine hand 2Sa 18:12
We will have no s nor gold of 2Sa 21:4
the oxen for fifty shekels of s 2Sa 24:24
even the s, and the gold, and the 1Kin 7:51
none were of s 1Kin 10:21
of Tharshish, bringing gold, and s 1Kin 10:22
man his present, vessels of s 1Kin 10:25
And the king made s to be in 1Kin 10:27
for six hundred shekels of s 1Kin 10:29
into the house of the LORD, s 1Kin 15:15
Then Asa took all the s and the 1Kin 15:18
sent unto thee a present of s 1Kin 15:19
of Shemer for two talents of s 1Kin 16:24
Thy s and thy gold is mine 1Kin 20:3
Thou shalt deliver me thy s 1Kin 20:5
and for my children, and for my s 1Kin 20:7
else thou shalt pay a talent of s 1Kin 20:39
and took with him ten talents of s 2Kin 5:5
them, I pray thee, a talent of s 2Kin 5:22
two talents of s in two bags 2Kin 5:23
sold for fourscore pieces of s 2Kin 6:25
dove's dung for five pieces of s 2Kin 6:25
eat and drink, and carried thence s 2Kin 7:8
the house of the LORD bowls of s 2Kin 12:13
vessels of gold, or vessels of s 2Kin 12:13
And he took all the gold and s 2Kin 14:14
gave Pul a thousand talents of s 2Kin 15:19
of each man fifty shekels of s 2Kin 15:20
And Ahaz took the s and gold that 2Kin 16:8
Judah three hundred talents of s 2Kin 18:14
Hezekiah gave him all the s that 2Kin 18:15
of his precious things, the s 2Kin 20:13
that he may sum the s which is 2Kin 22:4
of an hundred talents of s 2Kin 23:33
And Jehoiakim gave the s and the 2Kin 23:35
he exacted the s and the gold of 2Kin 23:35
gold, in gold, and of s, in s 2Kin 25:15
manner of vessels of gold and s 1Chr 18:10
unto the LORD, with the s 1Chr 18:11
of s to hire them chariots 1Chr 19:6
a thousand thousand talents of s 1Chr 22:14
Of the gold, the s, and the brass, 1Chr 22:16
s also for all instruments of 1Chr 28:14
all instruments of s by weight 1Chr 28:14
the candlesticks of s by weight 1Chr 28:15
s for the tables of s 1Chr 28:16
likewise s by weight for every 1Chr 28:17
by weight for every bason of s 1Chr 28:17
the s for things of s, and 1Chr 29:2
own proper good, of gold and s 1Chr 29:3
thousand talents of refined s 1Chr 29:4
and the s for things of s 1Chr 29:5
of s ten thousand talents, and of 1Chr 29:7
And the king made s and gold at 2Chr 1:15
for six hundred shekels of s 2Chr 1:17
cunning to work in gold, and in s 2Chr 2:7
skilful to work in gold, and in s 2Chr 2:14
and the s, and the gold, and all the 2Chr 5:1
brought gold and s to Solomon 2Chr 9:14
none were of s 2Chr 9:20
of Tarshish bringing gold, and s 2Chr 9:21
man his present, vessels of s 2Chr 9:24
the king made s in Jerusalem as 2Chr 9:27
that he himself had dedicated, s 2Chr 15:18
Then Asa brought out s and gold 2Chr 16:2
behold, I have sent thee s 2Chr 16:3
presents, and tribute s 2Chr 17:11
father gave them great gifts of s 2Chr 21:3
spoons, and vessels of gold and s 2Chr 24:14
for an hundred talents of s 2Chr 25:6
same year an hundred talents of s 2Chr 27:5
he made himself treasuries for s 2Chr 32:27
land in an hundred talents of s 2Chr 36:3
men of his place help him with s Ezr 1:4
their hands with vessels of s Ezr 1:6
of gold, a thousand chargers of s Ezr 1:9
s basons of a second sort four Ezr 1:10
of s were five thousand and four Ezr 1:11
gold, and five thousand pound of s Ezr 2:69
s of the house of God, which Ezr 5:14
s vessels of the house of God, Ezr 6:5
And to carry the s and gold, which Ezr 7:15
And all the s and gold that thou Ezr 7:16
to do with the rest of the s Ezr 7:18
Unto an hundred talents of s Ezr 7:22
And weighed unto them the s Ezr 8:25
six hundred and fifty talents of s Ezr 8:26
s vessels an hundred talents, and Ezr 8:26
and the s and the gold are a Ezr 8:28
the Levites the weight of the s Ezr 8:30
Now on the fourth day was the s Ezr 8:33
wine, beside forty shekels of s Neh 5:15
and two hundred pounds of s Neh 7:71
gold, and two thousand pounds of s Neh 7:72
fine linen and purple to s rings Est 1:6
the beds were of gold and s Est 1:6
pay ten thousand talents of s to Est 3:9
The s is given to thee, the Est 3:11
who filled their houses with s Job 3:15
and thou shalt have plenty of s Job 22:25
Though he heap up s as the dust Job 27:16
the innocent shall divide the s Job 27:17
Surely there is a vein for the s Job 28:1
neither shall s be weighed for Job 28:15
as s tried in a furnace of earth, Ps 12:6
thou hast tried us, as s is tried Ps 66:10
wings of a dove covered with s Ps 68:13
submit himself with pieces of s Ps 68:30
He brought them forth also with s Ps 105:37
Their idols are s and gold, the Ps 115:4
me than thousands of gold and s Ps 119:72
The idols of the heathen are s Ps 135:15
If thou seekest her as s, and Prov 2:4
better than the merchandise of s Prov 3:14
Receive my instruction, and not s Prov 8:10
and my revenue than choice s Prov 8:19
tongue of the just is as choice s Prov 10:20
rather to be chosen than s Prov 16:16
The fining pot is for s, and the Prov 17:3
and loving favour rather than s Prov 22:1
Take away the dross from the s Prov 25:4
apples of gold in pictures of s Prov 25:11
a potsherd covered with s dross Prov 26:23
As the fining pot for s, and the Prov 27:21
I gathered me also s and gold, and Eccl 2:8
He that loveth s shall not be Eccl 5:10
shall not be satisfied with s Eccl 5:10
Or ever the s cord be loosed, or Eccl 12:6
borders of gold with studs of s Song 1:11
He made the pillars thereof of s Song 3:10
will build upon her a palace of s Song 8:9
to bring a thousand pieces of s Song 8:11
Thy s is become dross, thy wine Is 1:22
Their land also is full of s Is 2:7
a man shall cast his idols of s Is 2:20
them, which shall not regard s Is 13:17
of thy graven images of s Is 30:22
shall cast away his idols of s Is 31:7
of his precious things, the s Is 39:2
with gold, and casteth s chains Is 40:19
weigh s in the balance, and hire a Is 46:6
have refined thee, but not with s Is 48:10
bring thy sons from far, their s Is 60:9
gold, and for iron I will bring s Is 60:17
Reprobate s shall men call them, Jer 6:30
They deck it with s and with gold Jer 10:4
S spread into plates is brought Jer 10:9
even seventeen shekels of s Jer 32:9
and that which was of s in s Jer 52:19
shall cast their s in the streets Eze 7:19
their s and their gold shall not Eze 7:19
wast thou decked with gold and s Eze 16:13
fair jewels of my gold and of my s Eze 16:17
they are even the dross of s Eze 22:18
As they gather s, and brass, and Eze 22:20
As s is melted in the midst of Eze 22:22
with s, iron, tin, and lead, they Eze 27:12
gold and s into thy treasures Eze 28:4
to carry away s and gold, to take Eze 38:13
gold, his breast and his arms of s Dan 2:32
iron, the clay, the brass, the s Dan 2:35
iron, the brass, the clay, the s Dan 2:45
s vessels which his father Dan 5:2
praised the gods of gold, and of s Dan 5:4
thou hast praised the gods of s Dan 5:23
with their precious vessels of s Dan 11:8
shall he honour with gold, and s Dan 11:38
the treasures of gold and of s Dan 11:43
wine, and oil, and multiplied her s Hos 2:8
her to me for fifteen pieces of s Hos 3:2
of their s and their gold have Hos 8:4
the pleasant places for their s Hos 9:6
them molten images of their s Hos 13:2
Because ye have taken my s Joel 3:5
they sold the righteous for s Amos 2:6
That we may buy the poor for s Amos 8:6
Take ye the spoil of s, take the Nah 2:9
it is laid over with gold and s Hab 2:19
all they that bear s are cut off Zeph 1:11
Neither their s nor their gold Zeph 1:18
The s is mine, and the gold is Hag 2:8
Then take s and gold, and make Zec 6:11
heaped up s as the dust, and fine Zec 9:3
for my price thirty pieces of s Zec 11:12
And I took the thirty pieces of s Zec 11:13
will refine them as s is refined Zec 13:9
be gathered together, gold, and s Zec 14:14
sit as a refiner and purifier of s Mal 3:3
Levi, and purge them as gold and s Mal 3:3
Provide neither gold, nor s Mt 10:9
with him for thirty pieces of s Mt 26:15
pieces of s to the chief priests Mt 27:3
the pieces of s in the temple Mt 27:5
chief priests took the s pieces Mt 27:6
they took the thirty pieces of s Mt 27:9
what woman having ten pieces of s Lk 15:8
Then Peter said, S and gold have I Acts 3:6
Godhead is like unto gold, or s Acts 17:29
it fifty thousand pieces of s Acts 19:19
which made s shrines for Diana, Acts 19:24
I have coveted no man's s Acts 20:33
upon this foundation gold, s 1Cor 3:12
not only vessels of gold and of s 2Ti 2:20
Your gold and s is cankered Jas 5:3
with corruptible things, as s 1Pet 1:18
devils, and idols of gold, and s Rev 9:20
The merchandise of gold, and s Rev 18:12

**SILVERLINGS**
a thousand vines at a thousand s Is 7:23

**SILVERSMITH**
certain man named Demetrius, a s Acts 19:24

**SIMEON** (*sim'-e-un*) See SHIMEON, SIMEONITES, SIMON.
*1. A son of Jacob.*
and she called his name S Gen 29:33
that two of the sons of Jacob, S Gen 34:25
And Jacob said to S and Levi, Ye Gen 34:30
Reuben, Jacob's firstborn, and S Gen 35:23
with them, and took from them S Gen 42:24
S is not, and ye will take Gen 42:36
he brought S out unto them Gen 43:23
And the sons of S Gen 46:10
as Reuben and S, they shall be Gen 48:5
S and Levi are brethren Gen 49:5
Reuben, S, Levi, and Judah, Ex 1:2
And the sons of S Ex 6:15
these are the families of S Ex 6:15
*2. Descendants of Simeon 1 and their land.*
Of S Num 1:6
Of the children of S, by their Num 1:22
of them, even of the tribe of S Num 1:23
by him shall be the tribe of S Num 2:12
S shall be Shelumiel the son of Num 2:12
prince of the children of S Num 7:36
of S was Shelumiel the son of Num 10:19
Of the tribe of S, Shaphat the Num 13:5
The sons of S after their Num 26:12
of the tribe of the children of S Num 34:20
S, and Levi, and Judah, and Issachar Deut 27:12
And the second lot came forth to S Josh 19:1
of S according to their families Josh 19:1
of S according to their families Josh 19:8
inheritance of the children of S Josh 19:9
therefore the children of S had Josh 19:9
Judah, and out of the tribe of S Josh 21:4
of the tribe of the children of S Josh 21:9
And Judah said unto S his brother Judg 1:3
So S went with him Judg 1:3
And Judah went with S his brother Judg 1:17
Reuben, S, Levi, and Judah, 1Chr 2:1
The sons of S were, Nemuel, and 1Chr 4:24
of them, even of the sons of S 1Chr 4:42
of the tribe of the children of S 1Chr 6:65
Of the children of S, mighty men 1Chr 12:25
Ephraim and Manasseh, and out of S 2Chr 15:9
of Manasseh, and Ephraim, and S 2Chr 34:6
west side, S shall have a portion Eze 48:24
And by the border of S, from the Eze 48:25
one gate of S, one gate of Eze 48:33
Of the tribe of S were sealed Rev 7:7
*3. A devout man who blessed Jesus.*
in Jerusalem, whose name was S Lk 2:25
S blessed them, and said unto Mary Lk 2:34
*4. Father of Levi; an ancestor of Jesus.*
Which was the son of S, which was Lk 3:30
*5. A prophet of Antioch.*
S that was called Niger, and Acts 13:1
*6. Same as Simon Peter.*
S hath declared how God at the Acts 15:14

**SIMEONITES** (*sim'-e-un-ites*) *Descendants of Simeon 1.*
of a chief house among the S Num 25:14
These are the families of the S Num 26:14
of the S, Shephatiah the son of 1Chr 27:16

**SIMILITUDE**
the s of the LORD shall he behold Num 12:8
voice of the words, but saw no s Deut 4:12
for ye saw no manner of s on the Deut 4:15
the s of any figure, the likeness Deut 4:16
And under it was the s of oxen 2Chr 4:3
the s of an ox that eateth grass Ps 106:20
polished after the s of a palace Ps 144:12

one like the *s* of the sons of men — Dan 10:16
the *s* of Adam's transgression — Rom 5:14
for that after the *s* of — Heb 7:15
which are made after the *s* of God — Jas 3:9

**SIMILITUDES**
multiplied visions, and used *s* — Hos 12:10

**SIMON** (*si'mun*) See BAR-JONA, NIGER, PETER, SIMEON, SIMON'S, ZELOTES.
*1. Same as Peter.*
*S* called Peter, and Andrew his — Mt 4:18
The first, *S*, who is called Peter — Mt 10:2
*S* Peter answered and said, Thou — Mt 16:16
him, Blessed art thou, *S* Bar-jona — Mt 16:17
saying, What thinkest thou, *S* — Mt 17:25
by the sea of Galilee, he saw *S* — Mk 1:16
they entered into the house of *S* — Mk 1:29
And *S* and they that were with him — Mk 1:36
And *S* he surnamed Peter — Mk 3:16
sleeping, and saith unto Peter, *S* — Mk 14:37
had left speaking, he said unto *S* — Lk 5:4
*S* answering said unto him, Master — Lk 5:5
When *S* Peter saw it, he fell down — Lk 5:8
which were partners with *S* — Lk 5:10
And Jesus said unto *S*, Fear not — Lk 5:10
*S*, (whom he also named Peter,) and — Lk 6:14
And the Lord said, *S*, *S*, — Lk 22:31
indeed, and hath appeared to *S* — Lk 24:34
was Andrew, *S* Peter's brother — Jn 1:40
first findeth his own brother *S* — Jn 1:41
Thou art *S* the son of Jona — Jn 1:42
*S* Peter's brother, saith unto him — Jn 6:8
Then *S* Peter answered him, Lord, — Jn 6:68
Then cometh he to *S* Peter — Jn 13:6
*S* Peter saith unto him, Lord, not — Jn 13:9
*S* Peter therefore beckoned to him — Jn 13:24
*S* Peter said unto him, Lord, — Jn 13:36
Then *S* Peter having a sword drew — Jn 18:10
*S* Peter followed Jesus, and so did — Jn 18:15
*S* Peter stood and warmed himself — Jn 18:25
she runneth, and cometh to *S* Peter — Jn 20:2
Then cometh *S* Peter following him — Jn 20:6
There were together *S* Peter — Jn 21:2
*S* Peter saith unto them, I go a — Jn 21:3
Now when *S* Peter heard that it — Jn 21:7
*S* Peter went up, and drew the net — Jn 21:11
Jesus saith to *S* Peter, *S* — Jn 21:15
to him again the second time, *S* — Jn 21:16
saith unto him the third time, *S* — Jn 21:17
men to Joppa, and call for one *S* — Acts 10:5
And called, and asked whether *S* — Acts 10:18
to Joppa, and call hither *S* — Acts 10:32
Send men to Joppa, and call for *S* — Acts 11:13
*S* Peter, a servant and an apostle — 2Pet 1:1
*2. A Canaanite disciple of Jesus.*
*S* the Canaanite, and Judas — Mt 10:4
and Thaddaeus, and *S* the Canaanite, — Mk 3:18
of Alphaeus, and *S* called Zelotes, — Lk 6:15
*S* Zelotes, and Judas the brother — Acts 1:13
*3. A brother of Jesus.*
brethren, James, and Joses, and *S* — Mt 13:55
James, and Joses, and of Juda, and *S* — Mk 6:3
*4. A leper in Bethany.*
in the house of *S* the leper — Mt 26:6
in the house of *S* the leper — Mk 14:3
*5. A Cyrenian who bore Jesus' cross.*
found a man of Cyrene, *S* by name — Mt 27:32
And they compel one *S* a Cyrenian — Mk 15:21
away, they laid hold upon one *S* — Lk 23:26
*6. A Pharisee.*
Jesus answering said unto him, *S* — Lk 7:40
*S* answered and said, I suppose — Lk 7:43
to the woman, and said unto *S* — Lk 7:44
*7. Father of Judas Iscariot.*
of Judas Iscariot the son of *S* — Jn 6:71
to Judas Iscariot, the son of *S* — Jn 13:26
*8. A Samaritan sorcerer.*
there was a certain man, called *S* — Acts 8:9
Then *S* himself believed also — Acts 8:13
when *S* saw that through laying on — Acts 8:18
Then answered *S*, and said, Pray ye — Acts 8:24
*9. A tanner at Joppa.*
days in Joppa with one *S* a tanner — Acts 9:43
He lodgeth with one *S* a tanner — Acts 10:6
of one *S* a tanner by the sea side — Acts 10:32

**SIMON'S** (*si'-muns*)
*1. Refers to Simon 1.*
But *S* wife's mother lay sick of a — Mk 1:30
and entered into *S* house — Lk 4:38
*S* wife's mother was taken with a — Lk 4:38
one of the ships, which was *S* — Lk 5:3
*2. Refers to Simon 7.*
*S* son, which should betray him, — Jn 12:4
Iscariot, *S* son, to betray him — Jn 13:2
*3. Refers to Simon 9.*
had made enquiry for *S* house — Acts 10:17

**SIMPLE**
LORD is sure, making wise the *s* — Ps 19:7
The LORD preserveth the *s* — Ps 116:6
giveth understanding unto the *s* — Ps 119:130
To give subtilty to the *s* — Prov 1:4
How long, ye *s* ones, will ye love — Prov 1:22
away of the *s* shall slay them — Prov 1:32
And beheld among the *s* ones — Prov 7:7
O ye *s*, understand wisdom — Prov 8:5
Whoso is *s*, let him turn in — Prov 9:4
she is *s*, and knoweth nothing — Prov 9:13
Whoso is *s*, let him turn in — Prov 9:16
The *s* believeth every word — Prov 14:15
The *s* inherit folly — Prov 14:18
a scorner, and the *s* will beware — Prov 19:25
is punished, the *s* is made wise — Prov 21:11
but the *s* pass on, and are — Prov 22:3
but the *s* pass on, and are — Prov 27:12
that erreth, and for him that is *s* — Eze 45:20
deceive the hearts of the *s* — Rom 16:18
is good, and *s* concerning evil — Rom 16:19

**SIMPLICITY**
and they went in their *s*, and they — 2Sa 15:11
ye simple ones, will ye love *s* — Prov 1:22
that giveth, let him do it with *s* — Rom 12:8
of our conscience, that in *s* — 2Cor 1:12
from the *s* that is in Christ — 2Cor 11:3

**SIMRI** (*sim'-ri*) See SHIMRI. *A sanctuary servant.*
*S* the chief, (for though he was — 1Chr 26:10

**SIN** (*sin*)
*1. A transgression.*
not well, *s* lieth at the door — Gen 4:7
because their *s* is very grievous — Gen 18:20
on me and on my kingdom a great *s* — Gen 20:9
what is my *s*, that thou hast so — Gen 31:36
wickedness, and *s* against God — Gen 39:9
Do not *s* against the child — Gen 42:22
of thy brethren, and their *s* — Gen 50:17
my *s* only this once, and intreat — Ex 10:17
before your faces, that ye *s* not — Ex 20:20
lest they make thee *s* against me — Ex 23:33
it is a *s* offering — Ex 29:14
for a *s* offering for atonement — Ex 29:36
of the *s* offering of atonements — Ex 30:10
brought so great a *s* upon them — Ex 32:21
people, Ye have sinned a great *s* — Ex 32:30
make an atonement for your *s* — Ex 32:30
this people have sinned a great *s* — Ex 32:31
now, if thou wilt forgive their *s* — Ex 32:32
I will visit their *s* upon them — Ex 32:34
iniquity and transgression and *s* — Ex 34:7
and pardon our iniquity and our *s* — Ex 34:9
If a soul shall *s* through — Lev 4:2
do *s* according to the — Lev 4:3
according to the *s* of the people — Lev 4:3
then let him bring for his *s* — Lev 4:3
unto the LORD for a *s* offering — Lev 4:3
of the bullock for the *s* offering — Lev 4:8
of Israel *s* through ignorance — Lev 4:13
When the *s*, which they have — Lev 4:14
offer a young bullock for the *s* — Lev 4:14
with the bullock for a *s* offering — Lev 4:20
it is a *s* offering for the — Lev 4:21
Or if his *s*, wherein he hath — Lev 4:23
it is a *s* offering — Lev 4:24
of the *s* offering with his finger — Lev 4:25
for him as concerning his *s* — Lev 4:26
common people *s* through ignorance — Lev 4:27
Or if his *s*, which he hath sinned — Lev 4:28
for his *s* which he hath sinned — Lev 4:28
upon the head of the *s* offering — Lev 4:29
slay the *s* offering in the place — Lev 4:29
he bring a lamb for a *s* offering — Lev 4:32
upon the head of the *s* offering — Lev 4:33
slay it for a *s* offering in the — Lev 4:33
of the *s* offering with his finger — Lev 4:34
for his *s* that he hath committed — Lev 4:35
And if a soul *s*, and hear the voice — Lev 5:1
for his *s* which he hath sinned — Lev 5:6
of the goats, for a *s* offering — Lev 5:6
for him concerning his *s* — Lev 5:6
one for a *s* offering, and the — Lev 5:7
which is for the *s* offering first — Lev 5:8
sprinkle of the blood of the *s* — Lev 5:9
it is a *s* offering — Lev 5:9
for his *s* which he hath sinned — Lev 5:10
of fine flour for a *s* offering — Lev 5:11
for it is a *s* offering — Lev 5:11
it is a *s* offering — Lev 5:12
for him as touching his *s* that he — Lev 5:13
*s* through ignorance, in the holy — Lev 5:15
And if a soul *s*, and commit any of — Lev 5:17
If a soul *s*, and commit a trespass — Lev 6:2
most holy, as is the *s* offering — Lev 6:17
This is the law of the *s* offering — Lev 6:25
offering is killed shall the *s* — Lev 6:25
offereth it for *s* shall eat it — Lev 6:26
no *s* offering, whereof any of the — Lev 6:30
As the *s* offering is, so is the — Lev 7:7
of the *s* offering, and of the — Lev 7:37
and a bullock for the *s* offering — Lev 8:2
the bullock for the *s* offering — Lev 8:14
of the bullock for the *s* offering — Lev 8:14
a young calf for a *s* offering — Lev 9:2
kid of the goats for a *s* offering — Lev 9:3
altar, and offer thy *s* offering — Lev 9:7
slew the calf of the *s* offering — Lev 9:8
above the liver of the *s* offering — Lev 9:10
which was the *s* offering for the — Lev 9:15
and slew it, and offered it for *s* — Lev 9:15
from offering of the *s* offering — Lev 9:22
sought the goat of the *s* offering — Lev 10:16
the *s* offering in the holy place — Lev 10:17
they offered their *s* offering — Lev 10:19
I had eaten the *s* offering to day — Lev 10:19
for a *s* offering, unto the door — Lev 12:6
and the other for a *s* offering — Lev 12:8
he shall kill the *s* offering — Lev 14:13
for as the *s* offering is the — Lev 14:13
priest shall offer the *s* offering — Lev 14:19
and the one shall be a *s* offering — Lev 14:22
to get, the one for a *s* offering — Lev 14:31
them, the one for a *s* offering — Lev 15:15
offer the one for a *s* offering — Lev 15:30
a young bullock for a *s* offering — Lev 16:3
of the goats for a *s* offering — Lev 16:5
his bullock of the *s* offering — Lev 16:6
and offer him for a *s* offering — Lev 16:9
the bullock of the *s* offering — Lev 16:11
*s* offering which is for himself — Lev 16:11
kill the goat of the *s* offering — Lev 16:15
the fat of the *s* offering shall — Lev 16:25
And the bullock for the *s* offering — Lev 16:27
and the goat for the *s* offering — Lev 16:27
and not suffer *s* upon him — Lev 19:17
LORD for his *s* which he hath done — Lev 19:22
the *s* which he hath done shall be — Lev 19:22
they shall bear their *s* — Lev 20:20
lest they bear *s* for it, and die — Lev 22:9
kid of the goats for a *s* offering — Lev 23:19
curseth his God shall bear his *s* — Lev 24:15
commit any *s* that men commit — Num 5:6
their *s* which they have done — Num 5:7
offer the one for a *s* offering — Num 6:11
without blemish for a *s* offering — Num 6:14
and shall offer his *s* offering — Num 6:16
kid of the goats for a *s* offering — Num 7:16
kid of the goats for a *s* offering — Num 7:22
kid of the goats for a *s* offering — Num 7:28
kid of the goats for a *s* offering — Num 7:34
kid of the goats for a *s* offering — Num 7:40
kid of the goats for a *s* offering — Num 7:46
kid of the goats for a *s* offering — Num 7:52
kid of the goats for a *s* offering — Num 7:58
kid of the goats for a *s* offering — Num 7:64
kid of the goats for a *s* offering — Num 7:70
kid of the goats for a *s* offering — Num 7:76
kid of the goats for a *s* offering — Num 7:82
the goats for *s* offering twelve — Num 7:87
shalt thou take for a *s* offering — Num 8:8
offer the one for a *s* offering — Num 8:12
season, that man shall bear his *s* — Num 9:13
thee, lay not the *s* upon us — Num 12:11
kid of the goats for a *s* offering — Num 15:24
their *s* offering before the LORD, — Num 15:25
if any soul *s* through ignorance, — Num 15:27
the first year for a *s* offering — Num 15:27
of all flesh, shall one man *s* — Num 16:22
every *s* offering of theirs, and — Num 18:9
congregation, lest they bear *s* — Num 18:22
shall bear no *s* by reason of it — Num 18:32
it is a purification for *s* — Num 19:9
heifer of purification for *s* — Num 19:17
but died in his own *s*, and had no — Num 27:3
one kid of the goats for a *s* — Num 28:15
And one goat for a *s* offering — Num 28:22
kid of the goats for a *s* offering — Num 29:5
kid of the goats for a *s* offering — Num 29:11
beside the *s* offering of — Num 29:11
kid of the goats for a *s* offering — Num 29:16
kid of the goats for a *s* offering — Num 29:19
And one goat for a *s* offering — Num 29:22
kid of the goats for a *s* offering — Num 29:25
And one goat for a *s* offering — Num 29:28
And one goat for a *s* offering — Num 29:31
And one goat for a *s* offering — Num 29:34
And one goat for a *s* offering — Num 29:38
be sure your *s* will find you out — Num 32:23
And I took your *s*, the calf which — Deut 9:21
their wickedness, nor to their *s* — Deut 9:27
thee, and it be *s* unto thee — Deut 15:9
for any iniquity, or for any *s* — Deut 19:15
in any *s* that he sinneth — Deut 19:15
so should ye *s* against the LORD — Deut 20:18
committed a *s* worthy of death — Deut 21:22
the damsel no *s* worthy of death — Deut 22:26
and it would be *s* in thee — Deut 23:21
to vow, it shall be no *s* in thee — Deut 23:22
shalt not cause the land to *s* — Deut 24:4
the LORD, and it be *s* unto thee — Deut 24:15
be put to death for his own *s* — Deut 24:16
Wherefore the *s* of the young men — 1Sa 2:17
If one man *s* against another, the — 1Sa 2:25
but if a man *s* against the LORD, — 1Sa 2:25
God forbid that I should *s* — 1Sa 12:23
the people *s* against the LORD, in — 1Sa 14:33
*s* not against the LORD in eating — 1Sa 14:34
see wherein this *s* hath been this — 1Sa 14:38
is as the *s* of witchcraft — 1Sa 15:23
I pray thee, pardon my *s* — 1Sa 15:25
Let not the king *s* against his — 1Sa 19:4
thou *s* against innocent blood — 1Sa 19:5
what is my *s* before thy father, — 1Sa 20:1
The LORD also hath put away thy *s* — 2Sa 12:13
forgive the *s* of thy people — 1Kin 8:34
thy name, and turn from their *s* — 1Kin 8:35
forgive the *s* of thy servants, and — 1Kin 8:36
If they *s* against thee, (for — 1Kin 8:46
And this thing became a *s* — 1Kin 12:30
this thing became *s* unto the — 1Kin 13:34
the sins of Jeroboam, who did *s* — 1Kin 14:16
and who made Israel to *s* — 1Kin 14:16
in his *s* wherewith he made Israel — 1Kin 15:26
wherewith he made Israel to *s* — 1Kin 15:26
sinned, and which he made Israel *s* — 1Kin 15:30
in his *s* wherewith he made Israel — 1Kin 15:34
wherewith he made Israel to *s* — 1Kin 15:34
hast made my people Israel to *s* — 1Kin 16:2
and by which they made Israel to *s* — 1Kin 16:13
in his *s* which he did, to make — 1Kin 16:19
which he did, to make Israel to *s* — 1Kin 16:19

in his s wherewith he made Israel 1Kin 16:26
wherewith he made Israel to s 1Kin 16:26
me to call my s to remembrance 1Kin 17:18
me to anger, and made Israel to s 1Kin 21:22
of Nebat, who made Israel to s 1Kin 22:52
of Nebat, which made Israel to s 2Kin 3:3
of Nebat, who made Israel to s 2Kin 10:29
Jeroboam, which made Israel to s 2Kin 10:31
s money was not brought into the 2Kin 12:16
of Nebat, which made Israel to s 2Kin 13:2
of Jeroboam, who made Israel s 2Kin 13:6
son of Nebat, who made Israel s 2Kin 13:11
be put to death for his own s 2Kin 14:6
of Nebat, who made Israel to s 2Kin 14:24
of Nebat, who made Israel to s 2Kin 15:9
of Nebat, who made Israel to s 2Kin 15:18
of Nebat, who made Israel to s 2Kin 15:24
of Nebat, who made Israel to s 2Kin 15:28
LORD, and made them s 2Kin 17:21
a great s 2Kin 17:21
Judah also to s with his idols 2Kin 21:11
beside his s wherewith he made 2Kin 21:16
wherewith he made Judah to s 2Kin 21:16
his s that he sinned, are they 2Kin 21:17
of Nebat, who made Israel to s 2Kin 23:15
If a man s against his neighbour, 2Chr 6:22
forgive the s of thy people 2Chr 6:25
thy name, and turn from their s 2Chr 6:26
forgive the s of thy servants, and 2Chr 6:27
If they s against thee, (for 2Chr 6:36
heaven, and will forgive their s 2Chr 7:14
every man shall die for his own s 2Chr 25:4
for a s offering for the kingdom, 2Chr 29:21
the s offering before the king 2Chr 29:23
the s offering should be made for 2Chr 29:24
intreated of him, and all his s 2Chr 33:19
for a s offering for all Israel, Ezr 6:17
twelve he goats for a s offering Ezr 8:35
let not their s be blotted out Neh 4:5
should be afraid, and do so, and s Neh 6:13
for the s offerings to make an Neh 10:33
king of Israel s by these things Neh 13:26
did outlandish women cause to s Neh 13:26
this did not Job s with his lips Job 2:10
thy habitation, and shalt not s Job 5:24
iniquity, and searchest after my s Job 10:6
If I s, then thou markest me, and Job 10:14
to know my transgression and my s Job 13:23
dost thou not watch over my s Job 14:16
are full of the s of his youth Job 20:11
have I suffered my mouth to s by Job 31:30
he addeth rebellion unto his s Job 34:37
have, if I be cleansed from my s Job 35:3
Stand in awe, and s not Ps 4:4
is forgiven, whose s is covered Ps 32:1
I acknowledged my s unto thee Ps 32:5
forgavest the iniquity of my s Ps 32:5
rest in my bones because of my s Ps 38:3
I will be sorry for my s Ps 38:18
that I s not with my tongue Ps 39:1
s offering hast thou not required Ps 40:6
iniquity, and cleanse me from my s Ps 51:2
and my s is ever before me Ps 51:3
in s did my mother conceive me Ps 51:5
my transgression, nor for my s Ps 59:3
For the s of their mouth and the Ps 59:12
thou hast covered all their s Ps 85:2
and let his prayer become s Ps 109:7
let not the s of his mother be Ps 109:14
that I might not s against thee Ps 119:11
the fruit of the wicked to s Prov 10:16
of words there wanteth not s Prov 10:19
Fools make a mock at s Prov 14:9
but s is a reproach to any people Prov 14:34
heart clean, I am pure from my s Prov 20:9
the plowing of the wicked, is s Prov 21:4
The thought of foolishness is s Prov 24:9
thy mouth to cause thy flesh to s Eccl 5:6
and they declare their s as Sodom Is 3:9
s as it were with a cart rope Is 5:18
is taken away, and thy s purged Is 6:7
all the fruit to take away his s Is 27:9
that they may add s to s Is 30:1
hands have made unto you for a s Is 31:7
make his soul an offering for s Is 53:10
and he bare the s of many, and made Is 53:12
or what is our s that we have Jer 16:10
their iniquity and their s double Jer 16:18
The s of Judah is written with a Jer 17:1
spoil, and thy high places for s Jer 17:3
blot out their s from thy sight Jer 18:23
I will remember their s no more Jer 31:34
abomination, to cause Judah to s Jer 32:35
forgive their iniquity and their s Jer 36:3
their land was filled with s Jer 51:5
the punishment of the s of Sodom Lam 4:6
warning, he shall die in his s Eze 3:20
s not, and he doth not s Eze 3:21
in his s that he hath sinned, in Eze 18:24
if he turn from his s, and do that Eze 33:14
the s offering and the trespass Eze 40:39
the s offering, and the trespass Eze 42:13
a young bullock for a s offering Eze 43:19
bullock also of the s offering Eze 43:21
without blemish for a s offering Eze 43:22
every day a goat for a s offering Eze 43:25
he shall offer his s offering Eze 44:27
the s offering, and the trespass Eze 44:29
he shall prepare the s offering Eze 45:17
of the blood of the s offering Eze 45:19
land a bullock for a s offering Eze 45:22
the goats daily for a s offering Eze 45:23
days, according to the s offering Eze 45:25
the s offering, where they shall Eze 46:20
and praying, and confessing my s Dan 9:20
the s of my people Israel, and Dan 9:20
They eat up the s of my people Hos 4:8
hath made many altars to s Hos 8:11
altars shall be unto him to s Hos 8:11
the s of Israel, shall be Hos 10:8
none iniquity in me that were s Hos 12:8
And now they s more and more, and Hos 13:2
his s is hid Hos 13:12
that swear by the s of Samaria Amos 8:14
of the s to the daughter of Zion Mic 1:13
transgression, and to Israel his s Mic 3:8
of my body for the s of my soul Mic 6:7
inhabitants of Jerusalem for s Zec 13:1
I say unto you, All manner of s Mt 12:31
oft shall my brother s against me Mt 18:21
taketh away the s of the world Jn 1:29
s no more, lest a worse thing Jn 5:14
He that is without s among you Jn 8:7
go, and s no more Jn 8:11
Whosoever committeth s is the Jn 8:34
is the servant of s Jn 8:34
Which of you convinceth me of s Jn 8:46
him, saying, Master, who did s Jn 9:2
were blind, ye should have no s Jn 9:41
therefore your s remaineth Jn 9:41
unto them, they had not had s Jn 15:22
they have no cloke for their s Jn 15:22
other man did, they had not had s Jn 15:24
he will reprove the world of s Jn 16:8
Of s, because they believe not on Jn 16:9
me unto thee hath the greater s Jn 19:11
lay not this s to their charge Acts 7:60
that they are all under s Rom 3:9
by the law is the knowledge of s Rom 3:20
whom the Lord will not impute s Rom 4:8
as by one man s entered into the Rom 5:12
into the world, and death by s Rom 5:12
until the law s was in the world Rom 5:13
but s is not imputed when there Rom 5:13
But where s abounded, grace did Rom 5:20
That as s hath reigned unto death Rom 5:21
Shall we continue in s, that Rom 6:1
How shall we, that are dead to s Rom 6:2
that the body of s might be Rom 6:6
henceforth we should not serve s Rom 6:6
he that is dead is freed from s Rom 6:7
that he died, he died unto s once Rom 6:10
to be dead indeed unto s, but Rom 6:11
Let not s therefore reign in your Rom 6:12
of unrighteousness unto s Rom 6:13
For s shall not have dominion Rom 6:14
shall we s, because we are not Rom 6:15
whether of s unto death, or of Rom 6:16
that ye were the servants of s Rom 6:17
Being then made free from s Rom 6:18
when ye were the servants of s Rom 6:20
But now being made free from s Rom 6:22
For the wages of s is death Rom 6:23
Is the law s Rom 7:7
Nay, I had not known s, but by Rom 7:7
But s, taking occasion by the Rom 7:8
For without the law s was dead Rom 7:8
came, s revived, and I died Rom 7:9
For s, taking occasion by the Rom 7:11
But s, that it might appear s, Rom 7:13
that s by the commandment might Rom 7:13
but I am carnal, sold under s Rom 7:14
but s that dwelleth in me Rom 7:17
but s that dwelleth in me Rom 7:20
law of s which is in my members Rom 7:23
but with the flesh the law of s Rom 7:25
made me free from the law of s Rom 8:2
for s, condemned s in the flesh Rom 8:3
the body is dead because of s Rom 8:10
whatsoever is not of faith is s Rom 14:23
Every s that a man doeth is 1Cor 6:18
But when ye s so against the 1Cor 8:12
conscience, ye s against Christ 1Cor 8:12
Awake to righteousness, and s not 1Cor 15:34
The sting of death is s 1Cor 15:56
and the strength of s is the law 1Cor 15:56
to be s for us, who knew no s 2Cor 5:21
Christ the minister of s Gal 2:17
hath concluded all under s Gal 3:22
Be ye angry, and s not Eph 4:26
and that man of s be revealed 2Th 2:3
Them that s rebuke before all, 1Ti 5:20
through the deceitfulness of s Heb 3:13
like as we are, yet without s Heb 4:15
s by the sacrifice of himself Heb 9:26
time without s unto salvation Heb 9:28
sacrifices for s thou hast had no Heb 10:6
offering for s thou wouldest not, Heb 10:8
there is no more offering for s Heb 10:18
For if we s wilfully after that Heb 10:26
the pleasures of s for a season Heb 11:25
the s which doth so easily beset Heb 12:1
unto blood, striving against s Heb 12:4
by the high priest for s, are Heb 13:11
conceived, it bringeth forth s Jas 1:15
and s, when it is finished, Jas 1:15
respect to persons, ye commit s Jas 2:9
and doeth it not, to him it is s Jas 4:17
Who did no s, neither was guile 1Pet 2:22
in the flesh hath ceased from s 1Pet 4:1
and that cannot cease from s 2Pet 2:14
his Son cleanseth us from all s 1Jn 1:7
If we say that we have no s 1Jn 1:8
write I unto you, that ye s not 1Jn 2:1
And if any man s, we have an 1Jn 2:1
Whosoever committeth s 1Jn 3:4
for s is the transgression of the 1Jn 3:4
and in him is no s 1Jn 3:5
that committeth s is of the devil 1Jn 3:8
is born of God doth not commit s 1Jn 3:9
and he cannot s, because he is 1Jn 3:9
s a s which is not unto death 1Jn 5:16
for them that s not unto death 1Jn 5:16
There is a s unto death 1Jn 5:16
All unrighteousness is s 1Jn 5:17
there is a s not unto death 1Jn 5:17

*2. Eastern border of Egypt.*

And I will pour my fury upon S Eze 30:15
S shall have great pain, and No Eze 30:16

*3. Desert between Elim and Sinai.*

came unto the wilderness of S Ex 16:1
from the wilderness of S, after Ex 17:1
encamped in the wilderness of S Num 33:11
out of the wilderness of S Num 33:12

**SINA** (*si'-nah*) See SINAI. *Greek form of Sinai.*

him in the wilderness of mount S Acts 7:30
which spake to him in the mount S Acts 7:38

**SINAI** (*si'-nahee*) See HOREB, SINA.
*Mountainous district in the southern Sinai peninsula.*

Sin, which is between Elim and S Ex 16:1
they into the wilderness of S Ex 19:1
and were come to the desert of S Ex 19:2
of all the people upon mount S Ex 19:11
mount S was altogether on a smoke Ex 19:18
the LORD came down upon mount S Ex 19:20
people cannot come up to mount S Ex 19:23
of the LORD abode upon mount S Ex 24:16
communing with him upon mount S Ex 31:18
up in the morning unto mount S Ex 34:2
morning, and went up unto mount S Ex 34:4
mount S with the two tables of Ex 34:29
had spoken with him in mount S Ex 34:32
LORD commanded Moses in mount S Lev 7:38
the LORD, in the wilderness of S Lev 7:38
LORD spake unto Moses in mount S Lev 25:1
in mount S by the hand of Moses Lev 26:46
the children of Israel in mount S Lev 27:34
unto Moses in the wilderness of S Num 1:1
them in the wilderness of S Num 1:19
LORD spake with Moses in mount S Num 3:1
the LORD, in the wilderness of S Num 3:4
unto Moses in the wilderness of S Num 3:14
unto Moses in the wilderness of S Num 9:1
at even in the wilderness of S Num 9:5
out of the wilderness of S Num 10:12
of Israel in the wilderness of S Num 26:64
in mount S for a sweet savour Num 28:6
and pitched in the wilderness of S Num 33:15
they removed from the desert of S Num 33:16
And he said, The LORD came from S Deut 33:2
even that S from before the LORD Judg 5:5
camest down also upon mount S Neh 9:13
even S itself was moved at the Ps 68:8
the Lord is among them, as in S Ps 68:17
the one from the mount S, which Gal 4:24
this Agar is mount S in Arabia Gal 4:25

**SINCE**

hath blessed thee s my coming Gen 30:30
and I saw him not s Gen 44:28
s I have seen thy face, because Gen 46:30
nor s thou hast spoken unto thy Ex 4:10
For s I came to Pharaoh to speak Ex 5:23
s the foundation thereof even Ex 9:18
of Egypt s it became a nation Ex 9:24
s the day that they were upon the Ex 10:6
ever s I was thine unto this day Num 22:30
s the day that God created man Deut 4:32
s in Israel like unto Moses Deut 34:10
s I have shewed you kindness, Josh 2:12
even s the LORD spake this word Josh 14:10
law s the death of thine husband Ruth 2:11
s the day that I brought them up 1Sa 8:8
it been kept for thee s I said 1Sa 9:24
s I came out, and the vessels of 1Sa 21:5
I have found no fault in him s he 1Sa 29:3
s the day of thy coming unto me 1Sa 29:6
I have not dwelt in any house s 2Sa 7:6
as s the time that I commanded 2Sa 7:11
S the day that I brought forth my 1Kin 8:16
all the fruits of the field s the 2Kin 8:6
s the day their fathers came 2Kin 21:15
house s the day that I brought up 1Chr 17:5
s the time that I commanded 1Chr 17:10
S the day that I brought forth my 2Chr 6:5
for s the time of Solomon the son 2Chr 30:26
S the people began to bring the 2Chr 31:10
we do sacrifice unto him s the Ezr 4:2
s that time even until now hath Ezr 5:16
S the days of our fathers have we Ezr 9:7
for s the days of Jeshua the son Neh 8:17
s the time of the kings of Neh 9:32
s man was placed upon earth, Job 20:4
commanded the morning s thy days Job 38:12
S thou art laid down, no feller Is 14:8
concerning Moab s that time Is 16:13
S thou wast precious in my sight, Is 43:4
s I appointed the ancient people Is 44:7
For s the beginning of the world Is 64:4

S

*S* the day that your fathers came... Jer 7:25
*s* they return not from their ways... Jer 15:7
For *s* I spake, I cried out, I... Jer 20:8
But *s* ye say, The burden of the... Jer 23:38
for *s* I spake against him, I do... Jer 31:20
But *s* we left off to burn incense... Jer 44:18
for *s* thou spakest of him, thou... Jer 48:27
such as never was *s* there was a... Dan 12:1
*S* those days were, when one came... Hag 2:16
such as was not *s* the beginning... Mt 24:21
is it ago *s* this came unto him... Mk 9:21
which have been *s* the world began... Lk 1:70
but this woman *s* the time I came... Lk 7:45
*s* that time the kingdom of God is... Lk 16:16
day *s* these things were done... Lk 24:21
*S* the world began was it not... Jn 9:32
holy prophets *s* the world began... Acts 3:21
the Holy Ghost *s* ye believed... Acts 19:2
*s* I went up to Jerusalem for to... Acts 24:11
was kept secret *s* the world began... Rom 16:25
For *s* by man came death, by man... 1Cor 15:21
*S* ye seek a proof of Christ... 2Cor 13:3
*S* we heard of your faith in... Col 1:4
*s* the day ye heard of it, and knew... Col 1:6
*s* the day we heard it, do not... Col 1:9
of the oath, which was *s* the law... Heb 7:28
*s* the foundation of the world... Heb 9:26
for *s* the fathers fell asleep,... 2Pet 3:4
such as was not *s* men were upon... Rev 16:18

**SINCERE**
that ye may be *s* and without... Phil 1:10
desire the *s* milk of the word,... 1Pet 2:2

**SINCERELY**
if ye have done truly and *s*... Judg 9:16
*s* with Jerubbaal and with his... Judg 9:19
Christ of contention, not *s*... Phil 1:16

**SINCERITY**
fear the LORD, and serve him in *s*... Josh 24:14
with the unleavened bread of *s*... 1Cor 5:8
that in simplicity and godly *s*... 2Cor 1:12
but as of *s*, but as of God, in... 2Cor 2:17
and to prove the *s* of your love... 2Cor 8:8
love our Lord Jesus Christ in *s*... Eph 6:24
shewing uncorruptness, gravity, *s*... Titus 2:7

**SINEW**
eat not of the *s* which shrank... Gen 32:32
thigh in the *s* that shrank... Gen 32:32
and thy neck is an iron *s*... Is 48:4

**SINEWS**
and hast fenced me with bones and *s*. Job 10:11
and my *s* take no rest... Job 30:17
the *s* of his stones are wrapped... Job 40:17
And I will lay *s* upon you, and will... Eze 37:6
And when I beheld, lo, the *s*... Eze 37:8

**SINFUL**
stead, an increase of *s* men... Num 32:14
Ah *s* nation, a people laden with... Is 1:4
Lord GOD are upon the *s* kingdom... Amos 9:8
this adulterous and *s* generation... Mk 8:38
for I am a *s* man, O Lord... Lk 5:8
delivered into the hands of *s* men... Lk 24:7
might become exceeding *s*... Rom 7:13
Son in the likeness of *s* flesh... Rom 8:3

**SING**
I will *s* unto the LORD, for he... Ex 15:1
*S* ye to the LORD, for he hath... Ex 15:21
noise of them that *s* do I hear... Ex 32:18
*s* ye unto it... Num 21:17
I, even I, will *s* unto the LORD... Judg 5:3
I will *s* praise to the LORD God... Judg 5:3
did they not *s* one to another of... 1Sa 21:11
*S* unto him, *s* psalms unto him,... 1Chr 16:9
*S* unto the LORD, all the earth... 1Chr 16:23
shall the trees of the wood *s* out... 1Chr 16:33
And when they began to *s* and to... 2Chr 20:22
and such as taught to *s* praise... 2Chr 23:13
commanded the Levites to *s* praise... 2Chr 29:30
the widow's heart to *s* for joy... Job 29:13
will *s* praise to the name of the... Ps 7:17
I will *s* praise to thy name, O... Ps 9:2
*S* praises to the LORD, which... Ps 9:11
I will *s* unto the LORD, because... Ps 13:6
and *s* praises unto thy name... Ps 18:49
so will we *s* and praise thy power... Ps 21:13
I will *s*, yea... Ps 27:6
I will *s* praises unto the LORD... Ps 27:6
*S* unto the LORD, O ye saints of... Ps 30:4
my glory may *s* praise to thee... Ps 30:12
*s* unto him with the psaltery and... Ps 33:2
*S* unto him a new song... Ps 33:3
*S* praises to God, *s* praises... Ps 47:6
*s* praises unto our King, *s*... Ps 47:6
*s* ye praises with understanding... Ps 47:7
my tongue shall *s* aloud of thy... Ps 51:14
I will *s* and give praise... Ps 57:7
I will *s* unto thee among the... Ps 57:9
But I will *s* of thy power... Ps 59:16
I will *s* aloud of thy mercy in... Ps 59:16
thee, O my strength, will I *s*... Ps 59:17
So will I *s* praise unto thy name... Ps 61:8
they shout for joy, they also *s*... Ps 65:13
*S* forth the honour of his name... Ps 66:2
thee, and shall *s* unto thee... Ps 66:4
they shall *s* to thy name... Ps 66:4
the nations be glad and *s* for joy... Ps 67:4
*S* unto God... Ps 68:4
*s* praises to his name... Ps 68:4
*S* unto God, ye kingdoms of the... Ps 68:32
O *s* praises unto the Lord... Ps 68:32
unto thee will I *s* with the harp... Ps 71:22
rejoice when I *s* unto thee... Ps 71:23
I will *s* praises to the God of... Ps 75:9
*S* aloud unto God our strength... Ps 81:1
I will *s* of the mercies of the... Ps 89:1
to *s* praises unto thy name, O... Ps 92:1
O come, let us *s* unto the LORD... Ps 95:1
O *s* unto the LORD a new song... Ps 96:1
*s* unto the LORD, all the earth... Ps 96:1
*S* unto the LORD, bless his name... Ps 96:2
O *s* unto the LORD a new song... Ps 98:1
noise, and rejoice, and *s* praise... Ps 98:4
*S* unto the LORD with the harp... Ps 98:5
I will *s* of mercy and judgment... Ps 101:1
unto thee, O LORD, will I *s*... Ps 101:1
which *s* among the branches... Ps 104:12
I will *s* unto the LORD as long as... Ps 104:33
I will *s* praise to my God while I... Ps 104:33
*S* unto him... Ps 105:2
*s* psalms unto him... Ps 105:2
I will *s* and give praise, even... Ps 108:1
I will *s* praises unto thee among... Ps 108:3
*s* praises unto his name... Ps 135:3
*S* us one of the songs of Zion... Ps 137:3
How shall we *s* the LORD's song in... Ps 137:4
gods will I *s* praise unto thee... Ps 138:1
they shall *s* in the ways of the... Ps 138:5
I will *s* a new song unto thee, O... Ps 144:9
will I *s* praises unto thee... Ps 144:9
shall *s* of thy righteousness... Ps 145:7
I will *s* praises unto my God... Ps 146:2
for it is good to *s* praises unto... Ps 147:1
*S* unto the LORD with thanksgiving... Ps 147:7
*s* praise upon the harp unto our... Ps 147:7
*S* unto the LORD a new song, and... Ps 149:1
let them *s* praises unto him with... Ps 149:3
let them *s* aloud upon their beds... Ps 149:5
but the righteous doth *s* and... Prov 29:6
Now will I *s* to my wellbeloved a... Is 5:1
*S* unto the LORD... Is 12:5
years shall Tyre *s* as an harlot... Is 23:15
*s* many songs, that thou mayest be... Is 23:16
they shall *s* for the majesty of... Is 24:14
Awake and *s*, ye that dwell in dust... Is 26:19
In that day *s* ye unto her... Is 27:2
hart, and the tongue of the dumb *s*... Is 35:6
therefore we will *s* my songs to... Is 38:20
*S* unto the LORD a new song, and... Is 42:10
let the inhabitants of the rock *s*... Is 42:11
*S*, O ye heavens... Is 44:23
*S*, O heavens... Is 49:13
the voice together shall they *s*... Is 52:8
*s* together, ye waste places of... Is 52:9
*S*, O barren, thou that didst not... Is 54:1
servants shall *s* for joy of heart... Is 65:14
*S* unto the LORD, praise ye the... Jer 20:13
*S* with gladness for Jacob, and... Jer 31:7
*s* in the height of Zion, and shall... Jer 31:12
is therein, shall *s* for Babylon... Jer 51:48
did *s* of thee in thy market... Eze 27:25
and she shall *s* there, as in the... Hos 2:15
voice shall *s* in the windows... Zeph 2:14
*S*, O daughter of Zion... Zeph 3:14
*S* and rejoice, O daughter of Zion... Zec 2:10
the Gentiles, and *s* unto thy name... Rom 15:9
I will *s* with the spirit... 1Cor 14:15
I will *s* with the understanding... 1Cor 14:15
church will I *s* praise unto thee... Heb 2:12
let him *s* psalms... Jas 5:13
they *s* the song of Moses the... Rev 15:3

**SINGED**
nor was an hair of their head *s*... Dan 3:27

**SINGER**
Heman a *s*, the son of Joel, the... 1Chr 6:33
To the chief *s* on my stringed... Hab 3:19

**SINGERS**
harps also and psalteries for *s*... 1Kin 10:12
And these are the *s*, chief of the... 1Chr 9:33
their brethren to be the *s* with... 1Chr 15:16
So the *s*, Heman, Asaph, and Ethan,. 1Chr 15:19
that bare the ark, and the *s*... 1Chr 15:27
the master of the song with the *s*... 1Chr 15:27
Also the Levites which were the *s*... 2Chr 5:12
*s* were as one, to make one sound... 2Chr 5:13
and harps and psalteries for *s*... 2Chr 9:11
he appointed *s* unto the LORD, and... 2Chr 20:21
also the *s* with instruments of... 2Chr 23:13
the *s* sang, and the trumpeters... 2Chr 29:28
the *s* the sons of Asaph were in... 2Chr 35:15
The *s*: the children of Asaph... Ezr 2:41
and some of the people, and the *s*... Ezr 2:70
priests, and the Levites, and the *s*... Ezr 7:7
any of the priests and Levites, *s*... Ezr 7:24
Of the *s* also... Ezr 10:24
doors, and the porters and the *s*... Neh 7:1
The *s*: the children of Asaph... Neh 7:44
Levites, and the porters, and the *s*... Neh 7:73
the Levites, the porters, the *s*... Neh 10:28
and the porters, and the *s*... Neh 10:39
the *s* were over the business of... Neh 11:22
portion should be for the *s*... Neh 11:23
the sons of the *s* gathered... Neh 12:28
for the *s* had builded them... Neh 12:29
the *s* sang loud, with Jezrahiah... Neh 12:42
And both the *s* and the porters kept.. Neh 12:45
of old there were chief of the *s*... Neh 12:46
gave the portions of the *s*... Neh 12:47
be given to the Levites, and the *s*... Neh 13:5
for the Levites and the *s*, that... Neh 13:10
The *s* went before, the players on... Ps 68:25
As well the *s* as the players on... Ps 87:7
I gat me men *s* and women *s*... Eccl 2:8
of the *s* in the inner court... Eze 40:44

**SINGETH**
so is he that *s* songs to an heavy... Prov 25:20

**SINGING**
out of all cities of Israel, *s*... 1Sa 18:6
voice of *s* men and *s* women... 2Sa 19:35
of the congregation with *s*... 1Chr 6:32
with all their might, and with *s*... 1Chr 13:8
Moses, with rejoicing and with *s*... 2Chr 23:18
*s* with loud instruments unto the... 2Chr 30:21
and all the *s* men and the *s*... 2Chr 35:25
hundred *s* men and *s* women... Ezr 2:65
and five *s* men and *s* women... Neh 7:67
with thanksgivings, and with *s*... Neh 12:27
come before his presence with *s*... Ps 100:2
laughter, and our tongue with *s*... Ps 126:2
the time of the *s* of birds is... Song 2:12
they break forth into *s*... Is 14:7
the vineyards there shall be no *s*... Is 16:10
and rejoice even with joy and *s*... Is 35:2
break forth into *s*, ye mountains,... Is 44:23
with a voice of *s* declare ye... Is 48:20
and break forth into *s*, O... Is 49:13
return, and come with *s* unto Zion... Is 51:11
break forth into *s*, and cry aloud,... Is 54:1
break forth before you into *s*... Is 55:12
he will joy over thee with *s*... Zeph 3:17
and hymns and spiritual songs, *s*... Eph 5:19
*s* with grace in your hearts to... Col 3:16

**SINGLE**
if therefore thine eye be *s*... Mt 6:22
therefore when thine eye is *s*... Lk 11:34

**SINGLENESS**
meat with gladness and *s* of heart,... Acts 2:46
in *s* of your heart, as unto... Eph 6:5
but in *s* of heart, fearing God... Col 3:22

**SINGULAR**
When a man shall make a *s* vow... Lev 27:2

**SINIM** (*si'-nim*) *An unspecified people.*
and these from the land of *S*... Is 49:12

**SINITE** (*si'-nite*) *A tribe of Canaanites.*
Hivite, and the Arkite, and the *S*... Gen 10:17
Hivite, and the Arkite, and the *S*... 1Chr 1:15

**SINK**
I *s* in deep mire, where there is... Ps 69:2
out of the mire, and let me not *s*... Ps 69:14
shalt say, Thus shall Babylon *s*... Jer 51:64
and beginning to *s*, he cried,... Mt 14:30
ships, so that they began to *s*... Lk 5:7
Let these sayings *s* down into... Lk 9:44

**SINNED**
unto them, I have *s* this time... Ex 9:27
he *s* yet more, and hardened his... Ex 9:34
I have *s* against the LORD your... Ex 10:16
the people, Ye have *s* a great sin... Ex 32:30
this people have *s* a great sin... Ex 32:31
Whosoever hath *s* against me... Ex 32:33
for his sin, which he hath *s*... Lev 4:3
sin, which they have *s* against it... Lev 4:14
When a ruler hath *s*, and done... Lev 4:22
Or if his sin, wherein he hath *s*... Lev 4:23
Or if his sin, which he hath *s*... Lev 4:28
for his sin which he hath *s*... Lev 4:28
that he hath *s* in that thing... Lev 5:5
LORD for his sin which he hath *s*... Lev 5:6
him for his sin which he hath *s*... Lev 5:10
then he that *s* shall bring for... Lev 5:11
that he hath *s* in one of these... Lev 5:13
it shall be, because he hath *s*... Lev 6:4
him, for that he *s* by the dead... Num 6:11
foolishly, and wherein we have *s*... Num 12:11
for we have *s*... Num 14:40
came to Moses, and said, We have *s*... Num 21:7
the angel of the LORD, I have *s*... Num 22:34
ye have *s* against the LORD... Num 32:23
We have *s* against the LORD, we... Deut 1:41
ye had *s* against the LORD your... Deut 9:16
of all your sins which ye *s*... Deut 9:18
Israel hath *s*, and they have also... Josh 7:11
Indeed I have *s* against the LORD... Josh 7:20
We have *s* against thee, both... Judg 10:10
said unto the LORD, We have *s*... Judg 10:15
I have not *s* against thee... Judg 11:27
We have *s* against the LORD... 1Sa 7:6
unto the LORD, and said, We have *s*... 1Sa 12:10
Saul said unto Samuel, I have *s*... 1Sa 15:24
Then he said, I have *s*... 1Sa 15:30
he hath not *s* against thee... 1Sa 19:4
I have not *s* against thee... 1Sa 24:11
Then said Saul, I have *s*... 1Sa 26:21
I have *s* against the LORD... 2Sa 12:13
servant doth know that I have *s*... 2Sa 19:20
I have *s* greatly in that I have... 2Sa 24:10
the people, and said, Lo, I have *s*... 2Sa 24:17
because they have *s* against thee... 1Kin 8:33
because they have *s* against thee... 1Kin 8:35
them captives, saying, We have *s*... 1Kin 8:47
people that have *s* against thee... 1Kin 8:50
the sins of Jeroboam which he *s*... 1Kin 15:30

of Elah his son, by which they s......... 1Kin 16:13
For his sins which he s in doing......... 1Kin 16:19
And he said, What have I s......... 1Kin 18:9
had s against the LORD their God......... 2Kin 17:7
that he did, and his sin that he s......... 2Kin 21:17
I have s greatly, because I have......... 1Chr 21:8
even I it is that have s and done......... 1Chr 21:17
because they have s against thee......... 2Chr 6:24
because they have s against thee......... 2Chr 6:26
captivity, saying, We have s......... 2Chr 6:37
people which have s against thee......... 2Chr 6:39
which we have s against thee......... Neh 1:6
I and my father's house have s......... Neh 1:6
but s against thy judgments, (......... Neh 9:29
It may be that my sons have s......... Job 1:5
In all this Job s not, nor......... Job 1:22
I have s......... Job 7:20
thy children have s against him......... Job 8:4
doth the grave those which have s......... Job 24:19
upon men, and if any say, I have s......... Job 33:27
for I have s against thee......... Ps 41:4
Against thee, thee only, have I s......... Ps 51:4
they s yet more against him by......... Ps 78:17
For all this they s still......... Ps 78:32
We have s with our fathers, we......... Ps 106:6
LORD, he against whom we have s......... Is 42:24
Thy first father hath s, and thy......... Is 43:27
for we have s......... Is 64:5
because thou sayest, I have not s......... Jer 2:35
for we have s against the LORD......... Jer 3:25
because we have s against the......... Jer 8:14
we have s against thee......... Jer 14:7
for we have s against thee......... Jer 14:20
whereby they have s against me......... Jer 33:8
iniquities, whereby they have s......... Jer 33:8
because ye have s against the......... Jer 40:3
because ye have s against the......... Jer 44:23
they have s against the LORD......... Jer 50:7
for she hath s against the LORD......... Jer 50:14
Jerusalem hath grievously s......... Lam 1:8
Our fathers have s, and are not......... Lam 5:7
woe unto us, that we have s......... Lam 5:16
and in his sin that he hath s......... Eze 18:24
with violence, and thou hast s......... Eze 28:16
wherein they have s, and will......... Eze 37:23
We have s, and have committed......... Dan 9:5
because we have s against thee......... Dan 9:8
because we have s against him......... Dan 9:11
we have s, we have done wickedly......... Dan 9:15
increased, so they s against me......... Hos 4:7
thou hast s from the days of......... Hos 10:9
because I have s against him......... Mic 7:9
and hast s against thy soul......... Hab 2:10
they have s against the LORD......... Zeph 1:17
I have s in that I have betrayed......... Mt 27:4
I have s against heaven, and......... Lk 15:18
I have s against heaven, and in......... Lk 15:21
answered, Neither hath this man s......... Jn 9:3
For as many as have s without law......... Rom 2:12
as many as have s in the law......... Rom 2:12
For all have s, and come short of......... Rom 3:23
upon all men, for that all have s......... Rom 5:12
even over them that had not s......... Rom 5:14
And not as it was by one that s......... Rom 5:16
and if thou marry, thou hast not s......... 1Cor 7:28
if a virgin marry, she hath not s......... 1Cor 7:28
bewail many which have s already......... 2Cor 12:21
to them which heretofore have s......... 2Cor 13:2
was it not with them that had s......... Heb 3:17
God spared not the angels that s......... 2Pet 2:4
If we say that we have not s......... 1Jn 1:10

## SINNER

much more the wicked and the s......... Prov 11:31
but wickedness overthroweth the s......... Prov 13:6
the wealth of the s is laid up......... Prov 13:22
but to the s he giveth travail,......... Eccl 2:26
but the s shall be taken by her......... Eccl 7:26
Though a s do evil an hundred......... Eccl 8:12
as is the good, so is the s......... Eccl 9:2
but one s destroyeth much good......... Eccl 9:18
but the s being an hundred years......... Is 65:20
woman in the city, which was a s......... Lk 7:37
for she is a s......... Lk 7:39
heaven over one s that repenteth......... Lk 15:7
of God over one s that repenteth......... Lk 15:10
saying, God be merciful to me a s......... Lk 18:13
be guest with a man that is a s......... Lk 19:7
man that is a s do such miracles......... Jn 9:16
we know that this man is a s......... Jn 9:24
and said, Whether he be a s or no......... Jn 9:25
why yet am I also judged as a s......... Rom 3:7
that he which converteth the s......... Jas 5:20
shall the ungodly and the s appear......... 1Pet 4:18

## SINNERS

s before the LORD exceedingly......... Gen 13:13
The censers of these s against......... Num 16:38
destroy the s the Amalekites......... 1Sa 15:18
nor standeth in the way of s......... Ps 1:1
nor s in the congregation of the......... Ps 1:5
will he teach s in the way......... Ps 25:8
Gather not my soul with s......... Ps 26:9
s shall be converted unto thee......... Ps 51:13
Let the s be consumed out of the......... Ps 104:35
if s entice thee, consent thou......... Prov 1:10
Evil pursueth s......... Prov 13:21
Let not thine heart envy s......... Prov 23:17
of the s shall be together, and......... Is 1:28
destroy the s thereof out of it......... Is 13:9
The s in Zion are afraid......... Is 33:14
All the s of my people shall die......... Amos 9:10
s came and sat down with him and......... Mt 9:10
your Master with publicans and s......... Mt 9:11
righteous, but s to repentance......... Mt 9:13
a friend of publicans and s......... Mt 11:19
is betrayed into the hands of s......... Mt 26:45
s sat also together with Jesus and......... Mk 2:15
saw him eat with publicans and s......... Mk 2:16
and drinketh with publicans and s......... Mk 2:16
righteous, but s to repentance......... Mk 2:17
is betrayed into the hands of s......... Mk 14:41
eat and drink with publicans and s......... Lk 5:30
righteous, but s to repentance......... Lk 5:32
for s also love those that love......... Lk 6:32
for s also do even the same......... Lk 6:33
for s also lend to s......... Lk 6:34
a friend of publicans and s......... Lk 7:34
were s above all the Galilaeans......... Lk 13:2
think ye that they were s above......... Lk 13:4
publicans and s for to hear him......... Lk 15:1
saying, This man receiveth s......... Lk 15:2
we know that God heareth not s......... Jn 9:31
us, in that, while we were yet s......... Rom 5:8
disobedience many were made s......... Rom 5:19
nature, and not s of the Gentiles,......... Gal 2:15
we ourselves also are found s......... Gal 2:17
for the ungodly and for s......... 1Ti 1:9
came into the world to save s......... 1Ti 1:15
undefiled, separate from s......... Heb 7:26
of s against himself, lest ye be......... Heb 12:3
Cleanse your hands, ye s......... Jas 4:8
ungodly s have spoken against him......... Jude 15

## SINNEST

If thou s, what doest thou......... Job 35:6

## SINNETH

for the soul that s ignorantly......... Num 15:28
when he s by ignorance before the......... Num 15:28
for him that s through ignorance......... Num 15:29
for any sin, in any sin that he s......... Deut 19:15
(for there is no man that s not......... 1Kin 8:46
(for there is no man which s not......... 2Chr 6:36
But he that s against me wrongeth......... Prov 8:36
He that despiseth his neighbour s......... Prov 14:21
he that hasteth with his feet s......... Prov 19:2
to anger s against his own soul......... Prov 20:2
earth, that doeth good, and s not......... Eccl 7:20
when the land s against me by......... Eze 14:13
the soul that s, it shall die......... Eze 18:4
The soul that s, it shall die......... Eze 18:20
in the day that he s......... Eze 33:12
s against his own body......... 1Cor 6:18
let him do what he will, he s not......... 1Cor 7:36
that is such is subverted, and s......... Titus 3:11
Whosoever abideth in him s not......... 1Jn 3:6
whosoever s hath not seen him,......... 1Jn 3:6
for the devil s from the......... 1Jn 3:8
whosoever is born of God s not......... 1Jn 5:18

## SINNING

withheld thee from s against me......... Gen 20:6
these that a man doeth, s therein......... Lev 6:3

## SINS

transgressions in all their s......... Lev 16:16
transgressions in all their s......... Lev 16:21
from all your s before the LORD......... Lev 16:30
for all their s once a year......... Lev 16:34
you seven times more for your s......... Lev 26:18
upon you according to your s......... Lev 26:21
you yet seven times for your s......... Lev 26:24
you seven times for your s......... Lev 26:28
ye be consumed in all their s......... Num 16:26
of all your s which ye sinned......... Deut 9:18
your transgressions nor your s......... Josh 24:19
added unto all our s this evil......... 1Sa 12:19
up because of the s of Jeroboam......... 1Kin 14:16
their s which they had committed......... 1Kin 14:22
walked in all the s of his father......... 1Kin 15:3
Because of the s of Jeroboam......... 1Kin 15:30
provoke me to anger with their s......... 1Kin 16:2
For all the s of Baasha, and the......... 1Kin 16:13
the s of Elah his son, by which......... 1Kin 16:13
For his s which he sinned in......... 1Kin 16:19
s of Jeroboam the son of Nebat......... 1Kin 16:31
he cleaved unto the s of Jeroboam......... 2Kin 3:3
Howbeit from the s of Jeroboam......... 2Kin 10:29
not from the s of Jeroboam......... 2Kin 10:31
followed the s of Jeroboam the......... 2Kin 13:2
the s of the house of Jeroboam......... 2Kin 13:6
s of Jeroboam the son of Nebat......... 2Kin 13:11
s of Jeroboam the son of Nebat......... 2Kin 14:24
he departed not from the s of......... 2Kin 15:9
not all his days from the s of......... 2Kin 15:18
he departed not from the s of......... 2Kin 15:24
he departed not from the s of......... 2Kin 15:28
the s of Jeroboam which he did......... 2Kin 17:22
for the s of Manasseh, according......... 2Kin 24:3
s against the LORD your God......... 2Chr 28:10
ye intend to add more to our s......... 2Chr 28:13
confess the s of the children of......... Neh 1:6
and stood and confessed their s......... Neh 9:2
hast set over us because of our s......... Neh 9:37
How many are mine iniquities and s......... Job 13:23
servant also from presumptuous s......... Ps 19:13
Remember not the s of my youth......... Ps 25:7
and forgive all my s......... Ps 25:18
Hide thy face from my s, and blot......... Ps 51:9
my s are not hid from thee......... Ps 69:5
deliver us, and purge away our s......... Ps 79:9
our secret s in the light of thy......... Ps 90:8
not dealt with us after our s......... Ps 103:10
be holden with the cords of his s......... Prov 5:22
but love covereth all s......... Prov 10:12
covereth his s shall not prosper......... Prov 28:13
though your s be as scarlet, they......... Is 1:18
cast all my s behind thy back......... Is 38:17
LORD's hand double for all her s......... Is 40:2
hast made me to serve with thy s......... Is 43:24
sake, and will not remember thy s......... Is 43:25
and, as a cloud, thy s......... Is 44:22
and the house of Jacob their s......... Is 58:1
your s have hid his face from you......... Is 59:2
thee, and our s testify against us......... Is 59:12
your s have withholden good......... Jer 5:25
their iniquity, and visit their s......... Jer 14:10
price, and that for all thy s......... Jer 15:13
because thy s were increased......... Jer 30:14
because thy s were increased, I......... Jer 30:15
the s of Judah, and they shall not......... Jer 50:20
a man for the punishment of his s......... Lam 3:39
For the s of her prophets, and the......... Lam 4:13
he will discover thy s......... Lam 4:22
Samaria committed half of thy s......... Eze 16:51
bear thine own shame for thy s......... Eze 16:52
his father's s which he hath done......... Eze 18:14
all his s that he hath committed......... Eze 18:21
all your doings your s do appear......... Eze 21:24
ye shall bear the s of your idols......... Eze 23:49
our s be upon us, and we pine away......... Eze 33:10
None of his s that he hath......... Eze 33:16
break off thy s by righteousness,......... Dan 4:27
because for our s, and for the......... Dan 9:16
and to make an end of s, and to......... Dan 9:24
their iniquity, and visit their s......... Hos 8:13
iniquity, he will visit their s......... Hos 9:9
transgressions and your mighty s......... Amos 5:12
for the s of the house of Israel......... Mic 1:5
thee desolate because of thy s......... Mic 6:13
thou wilt cast all their s into......... Mic 7:19
save his people from their s......... Mt 1:21
him in Jordan, confessing their s......... Mt 3:6
thy s be forgiven thee......... Mt 9:2
to say, Thy s be forgiven thee......... Mt 9:5
hath power on earth to forgive s......... Mt 9:6
for many for the remission of s......... Mt 26:28
repentance for the remission of s......... Mk 1:4
of Jordan, confessing their s......... Mk 1:5
Son, thy s be forgiven thee......... Mk 2:5
who can forgive s but God only......... Mk 2:7
the palsy, Thy s be forgiven thee......... Mk 2:9
hath power on earth to forgive s......... Mk 2:10
All s shall be forgiven unto the......... Mk 3:28
their s should be forgiven them......... Mk 4:12
by the remission of their s......... Lk 1:77
repentance for the remission of s......... Lk 3:3
him, Man, thy s are forgiven thee......... Lk 5:20
Who can forgive s, but God alone......... Lk 5:21
to say, Thy s be forgiven thee......... Lk 5:23
power upon earth to forgive s......... Lk 5:24
Wherefore I say unto thee, Her s......... Lk 7:47
said unto her, Thy s are forgiven......... Lk 7:48
Who is this that forgiveth s also......... Lk 7:49
And forgive us our s......... Lk 11:4
remission of s should be preached......... Lk 24:47
seek me, and shall die in your s......... Jn 8:21
you, that ye shall die in your s......... Jn 8:24
I am he, ye shall die in your s......... Jn 8:24
Thou wast altogether born in s......... Jn 9:34
Whose soever s ye remit, they are......... Jn 20:23
and whose soever s ye retain......... Jn 20:23
Christ for the remission of s......... Acts 2:38
that your s may be blotted out,......... Acts 3:19
to Israel, and forgiveness of s......... Acts 5:31
him shall receive remission of s......... Acts 10:43
unto you the forgiveness of s......... Acts 13:38
be baptized, and wash away thy s......... Acts 22:16
they may receive forgiveness of s......... Acts 26:18
the remission of s that are past......... Rom 3:25
forgiven, and whose s are covered......... Rom 4:7
in the flesh, the motions of s......... Rom 7:5
when I shall take away their s......... Rom 11:27
our s according to the scriptures......... 1Cor 15:3
ye are yet in your s......... 1Cor 15:17
Who gave himself for our s......... Gal 1:4
his blood, the forgiveness of s......... Eph 1:7
who were dead in trespasses and s......... Eph 2:1
Even when we were dead in s......... Eph 2:5
blood, even the forgiveness of s......... Col 1:14
body of the s of the flesh by the......... Col 2:11
And you, being dead in your s......... Col 2:13
saved, to fill up their s alway......... 1Th 2:16
be partaker of other men's s......... 1Ti 5:22
Some men's s are open beforehand,......... 1Ti 5:24
captive silly women laden with s......... 2Ti 3:6
he had by himself purged our s......... Heb 1:3
for the s of the people......... Heb 2:17
both gifts and sacrifices for s......... Heb 5:1
also for himself, to offer for s......... Heb 5:3
up sacrifice, first for his own s......... Heb 7:27
their unrighteousness, and their s......... Heb 8:12
offered to bear the s of many......... Heb 9:28
have had no more conscience of s......... Heb 10:2
again made of s every year......... Heb 10:3
and of goats should take away s......... Heb 10:4
which can never take away s......... Heb 10:11
one sacrifice for s for ever......... Heb 10:12
And their s and iniquities will I......... Heb 10:17
remaineth no more sacrifice for s......... Heb 10:26
and if he have committed s......... Jas 5:15
and shall hide a multitude of s......... Jas 5:20

Who his own self bare our *s* in ... 1Pet 2:24
tree, that we, being dead to *s* ... 1Pet 2:24
also hath once suffered for *s* ... 1Pet 3:18
shall cover the multitude of *s* ... 1Pet 4:8
that he was purged from his old *s* ... 2Pet 1:9
If we confess our *s*, he is ... 1Jn 1:9
and just to forgive us our *s* ... 1Jn 1:9
he is the propitiation for our *s* ... 1Jn 2:2
but also for the *s* of the whole ... 1Jn 2:2
because your *s* are forgiven you ... 1Jn 2:12
was manifested to take away our *s* ... 1Jn 3:5
to be the propitiation for our *s* ... 1Jn 4:10
us from our *s* in his own blood ... Rev 1:5
that ye be not partakers of her *s* ... Rev 18:4
For her *s* have reached unto ... Rev 18:5

**SION** (*si'-on*) See SHENIR, SIRION, ZION.
*1. The peak of Mount Hermon.*
even unto mount *S* which is Hermon. Deut 4:48
*2. A district of Jerusalem.*
waiteth for thee, O God in *S* ... Ps 65:1
Tell ye the daughter of *S* ... Mt 21:5
Fear not, daughter of *S* ... Jn 12:15
I lay in *S* a stumblingstone and ... Rom 9:33
shall come out of *S* the Deliverer ... Rom 11:26
But ye are come unto mount *S* ... Heb 12:22
I lay in *S* a chief corner stone, ... 1Pet 2:6
lo, a Lamb stood on the mount *S* ... Rev 14:1

**SIPHMOTH** (*sif'-moth*) *A city in Judah.*
Aroer, and to them which were in *S* ... 1Sa 30:28

**SIPPAI** (*sip'-pahee*) See SAPH. *Son of Rapha.*
Sibbechai the Hushathite slew *S* ... 1Chr 20:4

**SIR**
And said, O *s*, we came indeed down. Gen 43:20
came and said unto him, *S*, didst ... Mt 13:27
And he answered and said, I go *s* ... Mt 21:30
Saying, *S*, we remember that that ... Mt 27:63
The woman saith unto him, *S* ... Jn 4:11
The woman saith unto him, *S* ... Jn 4:15
The woman saith unto him, *S* ... Jn 4:19
The nobleman saith unto him, *S* ... Jn 4:49
The impotent man answered him, *S* ... Jn 5:7
and desired him, saying, *S* ... Jn 12:21
the gardener, saith unto him, *S* ... Jn 20:15
And I said unto him, *S*, thou ... Rev 7:14

**SIRAH** (*si'-rah*) *A well near Hebron.*
him again from the well of *S* ... 2Sa 3:26

**SIRION** (*sir'-e-on*) See HERMON. *A Sidonian name for Mount Hermon.*
Which Hermon the Sidonians call *S* ... Deut 3:9
Lebanon and *S* like a young unicorn ... Ps 29:6

**SIRS**
set them at one again, saying, *S* ... Acts 7:26
And saying, *S*, why do ye these ... Acts 14:15
And brought them out, and said, *S* ... Acts 16:30
of like occupation, and said, *S* ... Acts 19:25
And said unto them, *S*, I perceive ... Acts 27:10
in the midst of them, and said, *S* ... Acts 27:21
Wherefore, *s*, be of good cheer ... Acts 27:25

**SISAMAI** (*sis'-a-mahee*) *Son of Eleasah.*
And Eleasah begat *S* ... 1Chr 2:40
and *S* begat Shallum ... 1Chr 2:40

**SISERA** (*sis'-e-rah*)
*1. A captain in the Canaanite army.*
the captain of whose host was *S* ... Judg 4:2
unto thee to the river Kishon, *S* ... Judg 4:7
for the LORD shall sell *S* into ... Judg 4:9
they shewed *S* that Barak the son ... Judg 4:12
*S* gathered together all his ... Judg 4:13
hath delivered *S* into thine hand ... Judg 4:14
And the LORD discomfited *S* ... Judg 4:15
so that *S* lighted down off his ... Judg 4:15
all the host of *S* fell upon the ... Judg 4:16
Howbeit *S* fled away on his feet ... Judg 4:17
And Jael went out to meet *S* ... Judg 4:18
And, behold, as Barak pursued *S* ... Judg 4:22
*S* lay dead, and the nail was in ... Judg 4:22
in their courses fought against *S* ... Judg 5:20
and with the hammer she smote *S* ... Judg 5:26
The mother of *S* looked out at a ... Judg 5:28
to *S* a prey of divers colours, a ... Judg 5:30
he sold them into the hand of *S* ... 1Sa 12:9
as to *S*, as to Jabin, at the ... Ps 83:9
*2. A family of exiles.*
of Barkos, the children of *S* ... Ezr 2:53
of Barkos, the children of *S* ... Neh 7:55

**SISMAI** See SISAMAI.

**SISTER**
the *s* of Tubal-cain was Naamah ... Gen 4:22
Say, I pray thee, thou art my *s* ... Gen 12:13
Why saidst thou, She is my *s* ... Gen 12:19
of Sarah his wife, She is my *s* ... Gen 20:2
Said he not unto me, She is my *s* ... Gen 20:5
And yet indeed she is my *s* ... Gen 20:12
heard the words of Rebekah his *s* ... Gen 24:30
And they sent away Rebekah their *s*. Gen 24:59
and said unto her, Thou art our *s* ... Gen 24:60
the *s* to Laban the Syrian ... Gen 25:20
and he said, She is my *s* ... Gen 26:7
and how saidst thou, She is my *s* ... Gen 26:9
the *s* of Nebajoth, to be his wife ... Gen 28:9
no children, Rachel envied her *s* ... Gen 30:1
have I wrestled with my *s* ... Gen 30:8
he had defiled Dinah their *s* ... Gen 34:13
to give our *s* to one that is ... Gen 34:14
because they had defiled their *s* ... Gen 34:27
deal with our *s* as with an harlot ... Gen 34:31
Ishmael's daughter, *s* of Nebajoth ... Gen 36:3
and Lotan's *s* was Timna ... Gen 36:22
Isui, and Beriah, and Serah their *s* ... Gen 46:17
his *s* stood afar off, to wit what ... Ex 2:4
Then said his *s* to Pharaoh's ... Ex 2:7
Jochebed his father's *s* to wife ... Ex 6:20
Amminadab, *s* of Naashon, to wife ... Ex 6:23
the *s* of Aaron, took a timbrel in ... Ex 15:20
The nakedness of thy *s*, the ... Lev 18:9
of thy father, she is thy *s* ... Lev 18:11
the nakedness of thy father's *s* ... Lev 18:12
the nakedness of thy mother's *s* ... Lev 18:13
shalt thou take a wife to her *s* ... Lev 18:18
And if a man shall take his *s* ... Lev 20:17
the nakedness of thy mother's *s* ... Lev 20:19
nor of thy father's *s* ... Lev 20:19
for his *s* a virgin, that is nigh ... Lev 21:3
for his brother, or for his *s* ... Num 6:7
of a prince of Midian, their *s* ... Num 25:18
and Miriam their *s* ... Num 26:59
be he that lieth with his *s* ... Deut 27:22
not her younger *s* fairer than she ... Judg 15:2
thy *s* in law is gone back unto ... Ruth 1:15
return thou after thy *s* in law ... Ruth 1:15
the son of David had a fair *s* ... 2Sa 13:1
that he fell sick for his *s* Tamar ... 2Sa 13:2
Tamar, my brother Absalom's *s* ... 2Sa 13:4
let my *s* Tamar come, and give me ... 2Sa 13:5
I pray thee, let Tamar my *s* come ... 2Sa 13:6
unto her, Come lie with me, my *s* ... 2Sa 13:11
but hold now thy peace, my *s* ... 2Sa 13:20
because he had forced his *s* Tamar ... 2Sa 13:22
day that he forced his *s* Tamar ... 2Sa 13:32
*s* to Zeruiah Joab's mother ... 2Sa 17:25
him to wife the *s* of his own wife ... 1Kin 11:19
the *s* of Tahpenes the queen ... 1Kin 11:19
the *s* of Tahpenes bare him ... 1Kin 11:20
*s* of Ahaziah, took Joash the son ... 2Kin 11:2
and Timna was Lotan's *s* ... 1Chr 1:39
the concubines, and Tamar their *s* ... 1Chr 3:9
and Hananiah, and Shelomith their *s*.. 1Chr 3:19
name of their *s* was Hazelelponi ... 1Chr 4:3
of his wife Hodiah the *s* of Naham ... 1Chr 4:19
took to wife the *s* of Huppim ... 1Chr 7:15
his *s* Hammoleketh bare Ishod, and ... 1Chr 7:18
and Beriah, and Serah their *s* ... 1Chr 7:30
and Hotham, and Shua their *s* ... 1Chr 7:32
(for she was the *s* of Ahaziah ... 2Chr 22:11
worm, Thou art my mother, and my *s* Job 17:14
Say unto wisdom, Thou art my *s* ... Prov 7:4
Thou hast ravished my heart, my *s* ... Song 4:9
How fair is thy love, my *s* ... Song 4:10
A garden inclosed is my *s* ... Song 4:12
I am come into my garden, my *s* ... Song 5:1
saying, Open to me, my *s* ... Song 5:2
We have a little *s*, and she hath ... Song 8:8
what shall we do for our *s* in the ... Song 8:8
And her treacherous *s* Judah saw it ... Jer 3:7
treacherous *s* Judah feared not ... Jer 3:8
for all this her treacherous *s* ... Jer 3:10
my brother! or, Ah *s*! ... Jer 22:18
thou art the *s* of thy sisters, ... Eze 16:45
And thine elder *s* is Samaria ... Eze 16:46
and thy younger *s*, that dwelleth ... Eze 16:46
Sodom thy *s* hath not done, she ... Eze 16:48
was the iniquity of thy *s* Sodom ... Eze 16:49
For thy *s* Sodom was not mentioned .. Eze 16:56
in thee hath humbled his *s* ... Eze 22:11
the elder, and Aholibah her *s* ... Eze 23:4
when her *s* Aholibah saw this, she ... Eze 23:11
more than her *s* in her whoredoms ... Eze 23:11
my mind was alienated from her *s* ... Eze 23:18
hast walked in the way of thy *s* ... Eze 23:31
with the cup of thy *s* Samaria ... Eze 23:33
or for *s* that hath had no husband ... Eze 44:25
the same is my brother, and *s* ... Mt 12:50
the same is my brother, and my *s* ... Mk 3:35
she had a *s* called Mary, which ... Lk 10:39
dost thou not care that my *s* hath ... Lk 10:40
the town of Mary and her *s* Martha ... Jn 11:1
Now Jesus loved Martha, and her *s* ... Jn 11:5
and called Mary her *s* secretly ... Jn 11:28
the *s* of him that was dead, saith ... Jn 11:39
his mother, and his mother's *s* ... Jn 19:25
I commend unto you Phebe our *s* ... Rom 16:1
and Julia, Nereus, and his *s* ... Rom 16:15
A brother or a *s* is not under ... 1Cor 7:15
we not power to lead about a *s* ... 1Cor 9:5
If a brother or *s* be naked ... Jas 2:15
of thy elect *s* greet thee ... 2Jn 13

**SISTER'S**
and bracelets upon his *s* hands ... Gen 24:30
the tidings of Jacob his *s* son ... Gen 29:13
he hath uncovered his *s* nakedness ... Lev 20:17
Shuppim, whose *s* name ... 1Chr 7:15
shalt drink of thy *s* cup deep ... Eze 23:32
when Paul's *s* son heard of their ... Acts 23:16
*s* son to Barnabas, (touching whom ... Col 4:10

**SISTERS**
mother, and my brethren, and my *s* ... Josh 2:13
Whose *s* were Zeruiah, and Abigail ... 1Chr 2:16
called for their three *s* to eat ... Job 1:4
all his brethren, and all his *s* ... Job 42:11
and thou art the sister of thy *s* ... Eze 16:45
hast justified thy *s* in all thine ... Eze 16:51
also, which hast judged thy *s* ... Eze 16:52
in that thou hast justified thy *s* ... Eze 16:52
When thy *s*, Sodom and her ... Eze 16:55
when thou shalt receive thy *s* ... Eze 16:61
and to your *s*, Ruhamah ... Hos 2:1
And his *s*, are they not all with ... Mt 13:56
houses, or brethren, or *s* ... Mt 19:29
are not his *s* here with us ... Mk 6:3
left house, or brethren, or *s* ... Mk 10:29
time, houses, and brethren, and *s* ... Mk 10:30
and children, and brethren, and *s* ... Lk 14:26
Therefore his *s* sent unto him ... Jn 11:3
the younger as *s*, with all purity ... 1Ti 5:2

**SIT**
arise, I pray thee, *s* and eat of ... Gen 27:19
go to war, and shall ye *s* here ... Num 32:6
ye that *s* in judgment, and walk by ... Judg 5:10
*S* still, my daughter, until thou ... Ruth 3:18
turn aside, *s* down here ... Ruth 4:1
the city, and said, *S* ye down here ... Ruth 4:2
made them *s* in the chiefest place ... 1Sa 9:22
for we will not *s* down till he ... 1Sa 16:11
I should not fail to *s* with the ... 1Sa 20:5
the king doth *s* in the gate ... 2Sa 19:8
he shall *s* upon my throne ... 1Kin 1:13
he shall *s* upon my throne ... 1Kin 1:17
*s* on the throne of my lord the ... 1Kin 1:20
he shall *s* upon my throne ... 1Kin 1:24
who should *s* on the throne of my ... 1Kin 1:27
he shall *s* upon my throne in my ... 1Kin 1:30
he may come and *s* upon my throne ... 1Kin 1:35
one to *s* on my throne this day ... 1Kin 1:48
him a son to *s* on his throne ... 1Kin 3:6
*s* on the throne of Israel, as the ... 1Kin 8:20
to *s* on the throne of Israel ... 1Kin 8:25
Why *s* we here until we die ... 2Kin 7:3
if we *s* still here, we die also ... 2Kin 7:4
shall *s* on the throne of Israel ... 2Kin 10:30
Thy sons shall *s* on the throne of ... 2Kin 15:12
me to the men which *s* on the wall ... 2Kin 18:27
hath chosen Solomon my son to *s* ... 1Chr 28:5
to *s* upon the throne of Israel ... 2Chr 6:16
will not *s* with the wicked ... Ps 26:5
They that *s* in the gate speak ... Ps 69:12
Such as *s* in darkness and in the ... Ps 107:10
*S* thou at my right hand, until I ... Ps 110:1
Princes also did *s* and speak ... Ps 119:23
to *s* up late, to eat the bread of ... Ps 127:2
their children shall also *s* upon ... Ps 132:12
and the rich *s* in low place ... Eccl 10:6
desolate shall *s* upon the ground ... Is 3:26
I will *s* also upon the mount of ... Is 14:13
he shall *s* upon it in truth in ... Is 16:5
Their strength is to *s* still ... Is 30:7
to the men that *s* upon the wall ... Is 36:12
them that *s* in darkness out of ... Is 42:7
*s* in the dust, O virgin daughter ... Is 47:1
of Babylon, *s* on the ground ... Is 47:1
*S* thou silent, and get thee into ... Is 47:5
I shall not *s* as a widow, neither ... Is 47:8
warm at, nor fire to *s* before it ... Is 47:14
arise, and *s* down, O Jerusalem ... Is 52:2
Why do we *s* still ... Jer 8:14
kings that *s* upon David's throne ... Jer 13:13
queen, Humble yourselves, *s* down ... Jer 13:18
to *s* with them to eat and to drink ... Jer 16:8
*s* upon the throne of the house of ... Jer 33:17
*S* down now, and read it in our ... Jer 36:15
He shall have none to *s* upon the ... Jer 36:30
from thy glory, and *s* in thirst ... Jer 48:18
How doth the city *s* solitary ... Lam 1:1
of Zion *s* upon the ground ... Lam 2:10
they shall *s* upon the ground, and ... Eze 26:16
I *s* in the seat of God, in the ... Eze 28:2
they *s* before thee as my people, ... Eze 33:31
he shall *s* in it to eat bread ... Eze 44:3
and the Ancient of days did *s* ... Dan 7:9
But the judgment shall *s*, and they ... Dan 7:26
for there will I *s* to judge all ... Joel 3:12
But they shall *s* every man under ... Mic 4:4
when I *s* in darkness, the LORD ... Mic 7:8
and thy fellows that *s* before thee ... Zec 3:8
shall bear the glory, and shall *s* ... Zec 6:13
he shall *s* as a refiner and ... Mal 3:3
shall *s* down with Abraham, and ... Mt 8:11
multitude to *s* down on the grass ... Mt 14:19
multitude to *s* down on the ground ... Mt 15:35
when the Son of man shall *s* in ... Mt 19:28
ye also shall *s* upon twelve ... Mt 19:28
that these my two sons may *s* ... Mt 20:21
but to *s* on my right hand, and on ... Mt 20:23
*S* thou on my right hand, till I ... Mt 22:44
the Pharisees *s* in Moses' seat ... Mt 23:2
then shall he *s* upon the throne ... Mt 25:31
*S* ye here, while I go and pray ... Mt 26:36
all *s* down by companies upon the ... Mk 6:39
people to *s* down on the ground ... Mk 8:6
him, Grant unto us that we may *s* ... Mk 10:37
But to *s* on my right hand and on ... Mk 10:40
*S* thou on my right hand, till I ... Mk 12:36
*S* ye here, while I shall pray ... Mk 14:32
light to them that *s* in darkness ... Lk 1:79
Make them *s* down by fifties in a ... Lk 9:14
did so, and made them all *s* down ... Lk 9:15
and make them to *s* down to meat ... Lk 12:37
shall *s* down in the kingdom of ... Lk 13:29
*s* not down in the highest room ... Lk 14:8
*s* down in the lowest room ... Lk 14:10
of them that *s* at meat with thee ... Lk 14:10
*s* down quickly, and write fifty ... Lk 16:6
the field, Go and *s* down to meat ... Lk 17:7
my Lord, *S* thou on my right hand, ... Lk 20:42

s on thrones judging the twelve Lk 22:30
s on the right hand of the power Lk 22:69
Jesus said, Make the men s down Jn 6:10
up Christ to s on his throne Acts 2:30
my Lord, *S* thou on my right hand, Acts 2:34
he would come up and s with him Acts 8:31
s at meat in the idol's temple 1Cor 8:10
made us s together in heavenly Eph 2:6
*S* on my right hand, until I make Heb 1:13
*S* thou here in a good place Jas 2:3
or s here under my footstool Jas 2:3
I grant to s with me in my throne Rev 3:21
I saw a woman s upon a scarlet Rev 17:3
I s a queen, and am no widow, and Rev 18:7
horses, and of them that s on them Rev 19:18

**SITH**
s thou hast not hated blood, even Eze 35:6

**SITHRI** See ZITHRI.

**SITNAH** (*sit'-nah*) *A well near Gerar.*
and he called the name of it *S* Gen 26:21

**SITTEST**
why s thou thyself alone, and all Ex 18:14
them when thou s in thine house Deut 6:7
them when thou s in thine house Deut 11:19
Thou s and speakest against thy Ps 50:20
When thou s to eat with a ruler, Prov 23:1
that s upon the throne of David, Jer 22:2
for s thou to judge me after the Acts 23:3

**SITTETH**
of Pharaoh that s upon his throne Ex 11:5
and every thing, whereon he s Lev 15:4
he that s on any thing whereon he Lev 15:6
that she s upon shall be unclean Lev 15:20
or on any thing whereon she s Lev 15:23
whatsoever she s upon shall be Lev 15:26
when he s upon the throne of his Deut 17:18
also Solomon s on the throne of 1Kin 1:46
that s at the king's gate Est 6:10
nor s in the seat of the scornful Ps 1:1
He that s in the heavens shall Ps 2:4
He s in the lurking places of the Ps 10:8
The LORD s upon the flood Ps 29:10
yea, the LORD s King for ever Ps 29:10
God s upon the throne of his Ps 47:8
he s between the cherubims Ps 99:1
For she s at the door of her Prov 9:14
A king that s in the throne of Prov 20:8
when he s among the elders of the Prov 31:23
While the king s at his table Song 1:12
to him that s in judgment Is 28:6
It is he that s upon the circle Is 40:22
As the partridge s on eggs Jer 17:11
that s upon the throne of David Jer 29:16
He s alone and keepeth silence, Lam 3:28
and, behold, all the earth s still Zec 1:11
this is a woman that s in the Zec 5:7
of God, and by him that s thereon Mt 23:22
s not down first, and counteth the Lk 14:28
s not down first, and consulteth Lk 14:31
is greater, he that s at meat Lk 22:27
is not he that s at meat Lk 22:27
be revealed to another that s by 1Cor 14:30
where Christ s on the right hand Col 3:1
so that he as God s in the temple 2Th 2:4
unto him that s upon the throne Rev 5:13
face of him that s on the throne Rev 6:16
our God which s upon the throne Rev 7:10
he that s on the throne shall Rev 7:15
whore that s upon many waters Rev 17:1
mountains, on which the woman s Rev 17:9
thou sawest, where the whore s Rev 17:15

**SITTING**
the dam s upon the young, or upon Deut 22:6
he was s in a summer parlour, Judg 3:20
the s of his servants, and the 1Kin 10:5
God, and found him s under an oak 1Kin 13:14
I saw the LORD s on his throne 1Kin 22:19
of the prophets were s before him 2Kin 4:38
the captains of the host were s 2Kin 9:5
the s of his servants, and the 2Chr 9:4
stays on each side of the s place 2Chr 9:18
I saw the LORD s upon his throne, 2Chr 18:18
unto me, (the queen also s by him Neh 2:6
the Jew s at the king's gate Est 5:13
saw also the Lord s upon a throne Is 6:1
princes s upon the throne of Jer 17:25
kings s upon the throne of David Jer 22:4
s upon the throne of David, and Jer 22:30
the king then s in the gate of Jer 38:7
Behold their s down, and their Lam 3:63
s at the receipt of custom Mt 9:9
unto children s in the markets Mt 11:16
two blind men s by the way side, Mt 20:30
s upon an ass, and a colt the foal Mt 21:5
man s on the right hand of power Mt 26:64
s down they watched him there Mt 27:36
s over against the sepulchre Mt 27:61
certain of the scribes s there Mk 2:6
s at the receipt of custom Mk 2:14
the devil, and had the legion, s Mk 5:15
man s on the right hand of power Mk 14:62
a young man s on the right side Mk 16:5
s in the midst of the doctors, Lk 2:46
and doctors of the law s by Lk 5:17
s at the receipt of custom Lk 5:27
children s in the marketplace Lk 7:32
s at the feet of Jesus, clothed, Lk 8:35
repented, s in sackcloth and ashes Lk 10:13
doves, and the changers of money s Jn 2:14
King cometh, s on an ass's colt Jn 12:15
And seeth two angels in white s Jn 20:12
all the house where they were s Acts 2:2
s in his chariot read Esaias the Acts 8:28
the next day s on the judgment Acts 25:6
I saw four and twenty elders s Rev 4:4

**SITUATE**
The forefront of the one was s 1Sa 14:5
O thou that art s at the entry of Eze 27:3
that was s among the rivers, that Nah 3:8

**SITUATION**
the s of this city is pleasant, 2Kin 2:19
Beautiful for s, the joy of the Ps 48:2

**SIVAN** (*si'-van*) *Third month of the Hebrew year.*
third month, that is, the month *S* Est 8:9

**SIX**
Noah was s hundred years old when Gen 7:6
In the s hundredth year of Noah's Gen 7:11
came to pass in the s hundredth Gen 8:13
s years old, when Hagar bare Gen 16:16
because I have born him s sons Gen 30:20
and s years for thy cattle Gen 31:41
the souls were threescore and s Gen 46:26
about s hundred thousand on foot Ex 12:37
he took s hundred chosen chariots Ex 14:7
*S* days ye shall gather it Ex 16:26
*S* days shalt thou labour, and do Ex 20:9
For in s days the LORD made Ex 20:11
servant, s years he shall serve Ex 21:2
s years thou shalt sow thy land, Ex 23:10
*S* days thou shalt do thy work, and Ex 23:12
and the cloud covered it s days Ex 24:16
s branches shall come out of the Ex 25:32
so in the s branches that come Ex 25:33
according to the s branches that Ex 25:35
s curtains by themselves, and Ex 26:9
westward thou shalt make s boards Ex 26:22
*S* of their names on one stone, and Ex 28:10
the other s names of the rest on Ex 28:10
*S* days may work be done Ex 31:15
for in s days the LORD made Ex 31:17
*S* days thou shalt work, but on Ex 34:21
*S* days shall work be done, but on Ex 35:2
and s curtains by themselves Ex 36:16
westward he made s boards Ex 36:27
s branches going out of the sides Ex 37:18
so throughout the s branches Ex 37:19
according to the s branches going Ex 37:21
for s hundred thousand and three Ex 38:26
purifying threescore and s days Lev 12:5
*S* days shall work be done Lev 23:3
s on a row, upon the pure table Lev 24:6
*S* years thou shalt sow thy field, Lev 25:3
s years thou shalt prune thy Lev 25:3
s thousand and five hundred Num 1:21
forty and five thousand s hundred Num 1:25
and fourteen thousand and s hundred Num 1:27
numbered were s hundred thousand Num 1:46
and fourteen thousand and s hundred Num 2:4
s thousand and four hundred, Num 2:9
s thousand and five hundred Num 2:11
thousand and s hundred and fifty Num 2:15
and seven thousand and s hundred Num 2:31
hosts were s hundred thousand Num 2:32
s hundred, keeping the charge of Num 3:28
were s thousand and two hundred Num 3:34
thousand and s hundred and thirty Num 4:40
s covered wagons, and twelve oxen Num 7:3
are s hundred thousand footmen Num 11:21
and five thousand and s hundred Num 26:41
s hundred thousand and a thousand Num 26:51
was s hundred thousand Num 31:32
of the sheep was s hundred Num 31:37
beeves were thirty and s thousand Num 31:38
And thirty and s thousand beeves, Num 31:44
shall be s cities for refuge Num 35:6
cities which ye shall give s Num 35:13
These s cities shall be a refuge, Num 35:15
*S* days thou shalt labour, and do Deut 5:13
unto thee, and serve thee s years Deut 15:12
to thee, in serving thee s years Deut 15:18
*S* days thou shalt eat unleavened Deut 16:8
Thus shalt thou do s days Josh 6:3
so they did s days Josh 6:14
of them about thirty and s men Josh 7:5
s cities with their villages Josh 15:59
s cities with their villages Josh 15:62
s hundred men with an ox goad Judg 3:31
And Jephthah judged Israel s years Judg 12:7
s hundred men appointed with Judg 18:11
the s hundred men appointed with Judg 18:16
entering of the gate with the s Judg 18:17
s thousand men that drew sword, Judg 20:15
But s hundred men turned and fled Judg 20:47
he measured s measures of barley, Ruth 3:15
These s measures of barley gave Ruth 3:17
s thousand horsemen, and people as 1Sa 13:5
with him, about s hundred men 1Sa 13:15
with him were about s hundred men 1Sa 14:2
Gath, whose height was s cubits 1Sa 17:4
weighed s hundred shekels of iron 1Sa 17:7
men, which were about s hundred 1Sa 23:13
he passed over with the s hundred 1Sa 27:2
the s hundred men that were with 1Sa 30:9
Judah was seven years and s months 2Sa 2:11
Judah seven years and s months 2Sa 5:5
ark of the LORD had gone s paces 2Sa 6:13
s hundred men which came after 2Sa 15:18
that had on every hand s fingers 2Sa 21:20
fingers, and on every foot s toes 2Sa 21:20
and the middle was s cubits broad 1Kin 6:6
one year was s hundred threescore 1Kin 10:14
threescore and s talents of gold, 1Kin 10:14
s hundred shekels of gold went to 1Kin 10:16
The throne had s steps, and the 1Kin 10:19
and on the other upon the s steps 1Kin 10:20
went out of Egypt for s hundred 1Kin 10:29
(For s months did Joab remain 1Kin 11:16
s years reigned he in Tirzah 1Kin 16:23
s thousand pieces of gold, and ten 2Kin 5:5
in the house of the LORD s years 2Kin 11:3
have smitten five or s times 2Kin 13:19
over Israel in Samaria s months 2Kin 15:8
These s were born unto him in 1Chr 3:4
reigned seven years and s months 1Chr 3:4
Bariah, and Neariah, and Shaphat, s 1Chr 3:22
had sixteen sons and s daughters 1Chr 4:27
and twenty thousand and s hundred 1Chr 7:2
were bands of soldiers for war, s 1Chr 7:4
was twenty and s thousand men 1Chr 7:40
And Azel had s sons, whose names 1Chr 8:38
brethren, s hundred and ninety 1Chr 9:6
nine hundred and fifty and s 1Chr 9:9
And Azel had s sons, whose names 1Chr 9:44
shield and spear were s thousand 1Chr 12:24
Levi four thousand and s hundred 1Chr 12:26
and eight thousand and s hundred 1Chr 12:35
s on each hand, and s on each 1Chr 20:6
s hundred shekels of gold by 1Chr 21:25
s thousand were officers and 1Chr 23:4
Hashabiah, and Mattithiah, s 1Chr 25:3
Eastward were s Levites, 1Chr 26:17
for s hundred shekels of silver 2Chr 1:17
s hundred to oversee them 2Chr 2:2
and three thousand and s hundred 2Chr 2:17
s hundred overseers to set the 2Chr 2:18
amounting to s hundred talents 2Chr 3:8
Solomon in one year was s hundred 2Chr 9:13
threescore and s talents of gold 2Chr 9:13
s hundred shekels of beaten gold 2Chr 9:15
there were s steps to the throne, 2Chr 9:18
and on the other upon the s steps 2Chr 9:19
In the s and thirtieth year of the 2Chr 16:1
hid in the house of God s years 2Chr 22:12
were two thousand and s hundred 2Chr 26:12
things were s hundred oxen 2Chr 29:33
s hundred small cattle, and three 2Chr 35:8
of Bani, s hundred forty and two Ezr 2:10
s hundred twenty and three Ezr 2:11
Adonikam, s hundred sixty and s Ezr 2:13
Bigvai, two thousand fifty and s Ezr 2:14
The men of Netophah, fifty and s Ezr 2:22
and Gaba, s hundred twenty and one Ezr 2:26
of Magbish, an hundred fifty and s Ezr 2:30
thousand and s hundred and thirty Ezr 2:35
of Nekoda, s hundred fifty and two Ezr 2:60
were seven hundred thirty and s Ezr 2:66
s thousand seven hundred and Ezr 2:67
weighed unto their hand s hundred Ezr 8:26
s rams, seventy and seven lambs, Ezr 8:35
was one ox and s choice sheep Neh 5:18
of Arah, s hundred fifty and two Neh 7:10
Binnui, s hundred forty and eight Neh 7:15
s hundred twenty and eight Neh 7:16
s hundred threescore and seven Neh 7:18
of Adin, s hundred fifty and five Neh 7:20
and Gaba, s hundred twenty and one Neh 7:30
of Nekoda, s hundred forty and two Neh 7:62
horses, seven hundred thirty and s Neh 7:68
s thousand seven hundred and Neh 7:69
s months with oil of myrrh, and Est 2:12
s months with sweet odours, and Est 2:12
shall deliver thee in s troubles Job 5:19
s thousand camels, and a thousand Job 42:12
These s things doth the LORD hate Prov 6:16
each one had s wings Is 6:2
when he hath served thee s years Jer 34:14
and s pomegranates on a side Jer 52:23
were four thousand and s hundred Jer 52:30
s men came from the way of the Eze 9:2
of s cubits long by the cubit Eze 40:5
were s cubits on this side Eze 40:12
and s cubits on that side Eze 40:12
s cubits broad on the one side, Eze 41:1
s cubits broad on the other side, Eze 41:1
and the door, s cubits Eze 41:3
the wall of the house, s cubits Eze 41:5
a full reed of s great cubits Eze 41:8
shall be shut the s working days Eze 46:1
shall be s lambs without blemish Eze 46:4
blemish, and s lambs, and a ram Eze 46:6
and the breadth thereof s cubits Dan 3:1
after s days Jesus taketh Peter, Mt 17:1
after s days Jesus taketh with Mk 9:2
s months, when great famine was Lk 4:25
There are s days in which men Lk 13:14
set there s waterpots of stone Jn 2:6
s years was this temple in Jn 2:20
Then Jesus s days before the Jn 12:1
Moreover these s brethren Acts 11:12
s months, teaching the word of Acts 18:11
space of three years and s months Jas 5:17
each of them s wings about him Rev 4:8
is s hundred threescore and s Rev 13:18
a thousand and s hundred furlongs Rev 14:20

**SIXSCORE**
to the king s talents of gold 1Kin 9:14
wherein are more than s thousand Jonah 4:11

**SIXTEEN**
she bare unto Jacob, even s souls Gen 46:18
sockets of silver, s sockets Ex 26:25
sockets were s sockets of silver Ex 36:30
s thousand and five hundred Num 26:22
And the persons were s thousand Num 31:40
And s thousand persons Num 31:46
was s thousand seven hundred and... Num 31:52
s cities with their villages Josh 15:41
s cities with their villages Josh 19:22
in Samaria, and reigned s years 2Kin 13:10
Azariah, which was s years old 2Kin 14:21
S years old was he when he began 2Kin 15:2
he reigned s years in Jerusalem 2Kin 15:33
reigned s years in Jerusalem, and 2Kin 16:2
And Shimei had s sons and six 1Chr 4:27
the sons of Eleazar there were s 1Chr 24:4
and two sons, and s daughters 2Chr 13:21
who was s years old, and made him 2Chr 26:1
S years old was Uzziah when he 2Chr 26:3
he reigned s years in Jerusalem 2Chr 27:1
reigned s years in Jerusalem 2Chr 27:8
he reigned s years in Jerusalem 2Chr 28:1
two hundred threescore and s souls... Acts 27:37

**SIXTEENTH**
to Bilgah, the s to Immer, 1Chr 24:14
The s to Hananiah, he, his sons, 1Chr 25:23
in the s day of the first month 2Chr 29:17

**SIXTH**
and the morning were the s day Gen 1:31
again, and bare Jacob the s son Gen 30:19
that on the s day they shall Ex 16:5
that on the s day they gathered Ex 16:22
the s day the bread of two days Ex 16:29
shalt double the s curtain in the Ex 26:9
blessing upon you in the s year Lev 25:21
On the s day Eliasaph the son of Num 7:42
on the s day eight bullocks, two Num 29:29
The s lot came out to the Josh 19:32
And the s, Ithream, by Eglah 2Sa 3:5
s year of Asa king of Judah began 1Kin 16:8
even in the s year of Hezekiah, 2Kin 18:10
Ozem the s, David the seventh 1Chr 2:15
the s, Ithream by Eglah his wife 1Chr 3:3
Attai the s, Eliel the seventh, 1Chr 12:11
to Malchijah, the s to Mijamin, 1Chr 24:9
The s to Bukkiah, he, his sons, 1Chr 25:13
Elam the fifth, Jehohanan the s 1Chr 26:3
Ammiel the s, Issachar the 1Chr 26:5
The s captain for the s month 1Chr 27:9
which was in the s year of the Ezr 6:15
Hanun the s son of Zalaph, Neh 3:30
by measure, the s part of an hin Eze 4:11
in the s year, in the s month Eze 8:1
and leave but the s part of thee Eze 39:2
the s part of an ephah of an Eze 45:13
ye shall give the s part of an Eze 45:13
the s part of an ephah, and the Eze 46:14
Darius the king, in the s month Hag 1:1
and twentieth day of the s month Hag 1:15
Again he went out about the s Mt 20:5
Now from the s hour there was Mt 27:45
when the s hour was come, there Mk 15:33
in the s month the angel Gabriel Lk 1:26
this is the s month with her, who Lk 1:36
And it was about the s hour Lk 23:44
and it was about the s hour Jn 4:6
the passover, and about the s hour Jn 19:14
housetop to pray about the s hour Acts 10:9
when he had opened the s seal Rev 6:12
the s angel sounded, and I heard a Rev 9:13
Saying to the s angel which had Rev 9:14
the s angel poured out his vial Rev 16:12
the s, sardius Rev 21:20

**SIXTY**
And Mahalaleel lived s and five Gen 5:15
And Jared lived an hundred s Gen 5:18
days of Jared were nine hundred s Gen 5:20
And Enoch lived s and five years, Gen 5:21
of Enoch were three hundred s Gen 5:23
of Methuselah were nine hundred s Gen 5:27
years old even unto s years old Lev 27:3
And if it be from s years old Lev 27:7
the rams s, the he goats s Num 7:88
the lambs of the first year s Num 7:88
of Adonikam, six hundred s Ezr 2:13
some an hundredfold, some s Mt 13:23
forth, some thirty, and some s Mk 4:8
fruit, some thirtyfold, some s Mk 4:20

**SIXTYFOLD**
some an hundredfold, some s Mt 13:8

**SIYON** See SION.

**SIZE**
the curtains were all of one s Ex 36:9
the eleven curtains were of one s Ex 36:15
were of one measure and one s 1Kin 6:25
casting, one measure, and one s 1Kin 7:37
and for all manner of measure and s 1Chr 23:29

**SKIES**
waters, and thick clouds of the s 2Sa 22:12
waters and thick clouds of the s Ps 18:11
the s sent out a sound Ps 77:17
let the s pour down righteousness Is 45:8

and is lifted up even to the s Jer 51:9

**SKILFUL**
s in war, were four and forty 1Chr 5:18
about the song, because he was s 1Chr 15:22
workmanship every willing s man 1Chr 28:21
s to work in gold, and in silver, 2Chr 2:14
of brutish men, and s to destroy Eze 21:31
s in all wisdom, and cunning in Dan 1:4
such as are s of lamentation to Amos 5:16

**SKILFULLY**
play s with a loud noise Ps 33:3

**SKILFULNESS**
guided them by the s of his hands Ps 78:72

**SKILL**
can s to hew timber like unto the 1Kin 5:6
that can s to grave with the 2Chr 2:7
can s to cut timber in Lebanon 2Chr 2:8
all that could s of instruments 2Chr 34:12
nor yet favour to men of s Eccl 9:11
s in all learning and wisdom Dan 1:17
am now come forth to give thee s Dan 9:22

**SKIN**
only, it is his raiment for his s Ex 22:27
flesh of the bullock, and his s Ex 29:14
the s of his face shone while he Ex 34:29
behold, the s of his face shone Ex 34:30
that the s of Moses' face shone Ex 34:35
the s of the bullock, and all his Lev 4:11
shall have to himself the s of Lev 7:8
vessel of wood, or raiment, or s Lev 11:32
in the s of his flesh a rising Lev 13:2
it be in the s of his flesh like Lev 13:2
the plague in the s of the flesh Lev 13:3
be deeper than the s of his flesh Lev 13:3
be white in the s of his flesh Lev 13:4
in sight be not deeper than the s Lev 13:4
and the plague spread not in the s Lev 13:5
and the plague spread not in the s Lev 13:6
scab spread much abroad in the s Lev 13:7
the scab spreadeth in the s Lev 13:8
if the rising be white in the s Lev 13:10
old leprosy in the s of his flesh Lev 13:11
leprosy break out abroad in the s Lev 13:12
the leprosy cover all the s of Lev 13:12
in which, even in the s thereof Lev 13:18
it be in sight lower than the s Lev 13:20
and if it be not lower than the s Lev 13:21
if it spread much abroad in the s Lev 13:22
in the s whereof there is a hot Lev 13:24
it be in sight deeper than the s Lev 13:25
it be no lower than the other s Lev 13:26
it be spread much abroad in the s Lev 13:27
his place, and spread not in the s Lev 13:28
it be in sight deeper than the s Lev 13:30
be not in sight deeper than the s Lev 13:31
be not in sight deeper than the s Lev 13:32
the scall be not spread in the s Lev 13:34
nor be in sight deeper than the s Lev 13:34
much in the s after his cleansing Lev 13:35
if the scall be spread in the s Lev 13:36
the s of their flesh bright spots Lev 13:38
if the bright spots in the s of Lev 13:39
spot that groweth in the s Lev 13:39
appeareth in the s of the flesh Lev 13:43
a s, or in any thing made of s Lev 13:48
in the garment, or in the s Lev 13:49
in the woof, or in any thing of s Lev 13:49
warp, or in the woof, or in a s Lev 13:51
or in any work that is made of s Lev 13:51
or in linen, or any thing of s Lev 13:52
in the woof, or in any thing of s Lev 13:53
of the garment, or out of the s Lev 13:56
in the woof, or in any thing of s Lev 13:57
or whatsoever thing of s it be Lev 13:58
And every garment, and every s Lev 15:17
her s, and her flesh, and her blood Num 19:5
S for s, yea, all that a man Job 2:4
my s is broken, and become Job 7:5
Thou hast clothed me with s Job 10:11
I have sewed sackcloth upon my s Job 16:15
devour the strength of his s Job 18:13
My bone cleaveth to my s and to my.. Job 19:20
am escaped with the s of my teeth Job 19:20
though after my s worms destroy Job 19:26
My s is black upon me, and my Job 30:30
thou fill his s with barbed irons Job 41:7
groaning my bones cleave to my s Ps 102:5
Can the Ethiopian change his s Jer 13:23
My flesh and my s hath he made old Lam 3:4
their s cleaveth to their bones Lam 4:8
Our s was black like an oven Lam 5:10
and shod thee with badgers' s Eze 16:10
upon you, and cover you with s Eze 37:6
them, and the s covered them above Eze 37:8
pluck off their s from off them Mic 3:2
flay their s from off them Mic 3:3
a girdle of a s about his loins Mk 1:6

**SKINS**
did the LORD God make coats of s Gen 3:21
she put the s of the kids of the Gen 27:16
s dyed red, and badgers' s Ex 25:5
for the tent of rams' s dyed red Ex 26:14
and a covering above of badgers' s Ex 26:14
s dyed red, and badgers' s Ex 35:7
red s of rams, and badgers' s Ex 35:23
for the tent of rams' s dyed red Ex 36:19
covering of badgers' s above that Ex 36:19

the covering of rams' s dyed red Ex 39:34
and the covering of badgers' s Ex 39:34
warp, or woof, or any thing of s Lev 13:59
shall burn in the fire their s Lev 16:27
the covering of badgers' s Num 4:6
with a covering of badgers' s Num 4:8
within a covering of badgers' s Num 4:10
it with a covering of badgers' s Num 4:11
with a covering of badgers' s Num 4:12
upon it a covering of badgers' s Num 4:14
badgers' s that is above upon it Num 4:25
raiment, and all that is made of s Num 31:20

**SKIP**
maketh them also to s like a calf Ps 29:6

**SKIPPED**
The mountains s like rams Ps 114:4
Ye mountains, that ye s like rams Ps 114:6

**SKIPPEDST**
spakest of him, thou s for joy Jer 48:27

**SKIPPING**
the mountains, s upon the hills Song 2:8

**SKIRT**
wife, nor discover his father's s Deut 22:30
he uncovereth his father's s Deut 27:20
thy s over thine handmaid Ruth 3:9
hold upon the s of his mantle 1Sa 15:27
cut off the s of Saul's robe 1Sa 24:4
because he had cut off Saul's s 1Sa 24:5
see the s of thy robe in my hand 1Sa 24:11
that I cut off the s of thy robe 1Sa 24:11
and I spread my s over thee Eze 16:8
flesh in the s of his garment Hag 2:12
with his s do touch bread, or Hag 2:12
of the s of him that is a Jew Zec 8:23

**SKIRTS**
down to the s of his garments Ps 133:2
Also in thy s is found the blood Jer 2:34
iniquity are thy s discovered Jer 13:22
I discover thy s upon thy face Jer 13:26
Her filthiness is in her s Lam 1:9
in number, and bind them in thy s Eze 5:3
will discover thy s upon thy face Nah 3:5

**SKULL**
head, and all to brake his s Judg 9:53
found no more of her than the s 2Kin 9:35
that is to say, a place of a s Mt 27:33
interpreted, The place of a s Mk 15:22
a place called the place of a s Jn 19:17

**SKY**
and in his excellency on the s Deut 33:26
thou with him spread out the s Job 37:18
for the s is red Mt 16:2
for the s is red and lowring Mt 16:3
ye can discern the face of the s Mt 16:3
ye can discern the face of the s Lk 12:56
the stars of the s in multitude Heb 11:12

**SLACK**
he will not be s to him that Deut 7:10
God, thou shalt not s to pay it Deut 23:21
S not thy hand from thy servants Josh 10:6
How long are ye s to go to Josh 18:3
s not thy riding for me, except I 2Kin 4:24
poor that dealeth with a s hand Prov 10:4
to Zion, Let not thine hands be s Zeph 3:16
The Lord is not s concerning his 2Pet 3:9

**SLACKED**
Therefore the law is s, and Hab 1:4

**SLACKNESS**
his promise, as some men count s 2Pet 3:9

**SLAIN**
for I have s a man to my wounding Gen 4:23
The sons of Jacob came upon the s Gen 34:27
them in the blood of the s bird Lev 14:51
ye shall be s before your enemies Lev 26:17
flocks and the herds be s for them Num 11:22
therefore he hath s them in the Num 14:16
whosoever toucheth one that is s Num 19:16
him that touched a bone, or one s Num 19:18
me, surely now also I had s thee Num 22:33
prey, and drink the blood of the s Num 23:24
name of the Israelite that was s Num 25:14
even that was s with the Num 25:14
woman that was s was Cozbi Num 25:15
which was s in the day of the Num 25:18
the rest of them that were s Num 31:8
and whosoever hath touched any s Num 31:19
After he had s Sihon the king of Deut 1:4
If one be found s in the land Deut 21:1
and it be not known who hath s him Deut 21:1
are round about him that is s Deut 21:2
city which is next unto the s man Deut 21:3
that are next unto the s man Deut 21:6
ox shall be s before thine eyes Deut 28:31
and that with the blood of the s Deut 32:42
them up all s before Israel Josh 11:6
among them that were s by them Josh 13:22
have s his sons, threescore and Judg 9:18
of an ass have I s a thousand men Judg 15:16
husband of the woman that was s Judg 20:4
by night, and thought to have s me Judg 20:5
Eli, Hophni and Phinehas, were s 1Sa 4:11
Saul hath s his thousands, and 1Sa 18:7
LORD liveth, he shall not be s 1Sa 19:6
night, to morrow thou shalt be s 1Sa 19:11

unto him, Wherefore shall he be *s* ... 1Sa 20:32
Saul hath *s* his thousands, and ... 1Sa 21:11
Saul had *s* the LORD'S priests ... 1Sa 22:21
fell down *s* in mount Gilboa ... 1Sa 31:1
Philistines came to strip the *s* ... 1Sa 31:8
I have *s* the LORD'S anointed ... 2Sa 1:16
Israel is *s* upon thy high places ... 2Sa 1:19
From the blood of the *s*, from the ... 2Sa 1:22
thou wast *s* in thine high places ... 2Sa 1:25
because he had *s* their brother ... 2Sa 3:30
more, when wicked men have *s* a ... 2Sa 4:11
hast *s* him with the sword of the ... 2Sa 12:9
Absalom hath *s* all the king's ... 2Sa 13:30
*s* all the young men the king's ... 2Sa 13:32
*s* before the servants of David ... 2Sa 18:7
Philistines had *s* Saul in Gilboa ... 2Sa 21:12
sword, thought to have *s* David ... 2Sa 21:16
And he hath *s* oxen and fat cattle ... 1Kin 1:19
down this day, and hath *s* oxen ... 1Kin 1:25
*s* the Canaanites that dwelt in ... 1Kin 9:16
host was gone up to bury the *s* ... 1Kin 11:15
*s* him, according to the word of ... 1Kin 13:26
and hath also *s* the king ... 1Kin 16:16
withal how he had *s* all the ... 1Kin 19:1
*s* thy prophets with the sword ... 1Kin 19:10
*s* thy prophets with the sword ... 1Kin 19:14
the kings are surely *s*, and they ... 2Kin 3:23
the king's sons which were *s* ... 2Kin 11:2
Athaliah, so that he was not *s* ... 2Kin 11:2
within the ranges, let him be *s* ... 2Kin 11:8
Let her not be *s* in the house of ... 2Kin 11:15
and there was she *s* ... 2Kin 11:16
which had *s* the king his father ... 2Kin 14:5
For there fell down many *s* ... 1Chr 5:22
fell down *s* in mount Gilboa ... 1Chr 10:1
Philistines came to strip the *s* ... 1Chr 10:8
hundred *s* by him at one time ... 1Chr 11:11
so there fell down *s* of Israel ... 2Chr 13:17
also hast *s* thy brethren of thy ... 2Chr 21:13
to the camp had *s* all the eldest ... 2Chr 22:1
and when they had *s* him, they ... 2Chr 22:9
among the king's sons that were *s* ... 2Chr 22:11
let him be *s* with the sword ... 2Chr 23:14
after that they had *s* Athaliah ... 2Chr 23:21
ye have *s* them in a rage that ... 2Chr 28:9
people, to be destroyed, to be *s* ... Est 7:4
were *s* in Shushan the palace was ... Est 9:11
Esther the queen, The Jews have *s* ... Est 9:12
they have *s* the servants with the ... Job 1:15
*s* the servants with the edge of ... Job 1:17
and where the *s* are, there is she ... Job 39:30
ye shall be *s* all of you ... Ps 62:3
like the *s* that lie in the grave, ... Ps 88:5
Rahab in pieces, as one that is *s* ... Ps 89:10
strong men have been *s* by her ... Prov 7:26
I shall be *s* in the streets ... Prov 22:13
and those that are ready to be *s* ... Prov 24:11
and they shall fall under the *s* ... Is 10:4
the raiment of those that are *s* ... Is 14:19
thy land, and *s* thy people ... Is 14:20
thy *s* men are not *s* with the ... Is 22:2
and shall no more cover her *s* ... Is 26:21
or is he *s* according to the ... Is 27:7
of them that are *s* by him ... Is 27:7
Their *s* also shall be cast out, ... Is 34:3
the *s* of the LORD shall be many ... Is 66:16
night for the *s* of the daughter ... Jer 9:1
then behold the *s* with the sword ... Jer 14:18
men be *s* by the sword in battle ... Jer 18:21
the *s* of the LORD shall be at ... Jer 25:33
whom I have *s* in mine anger and in ... Jer 33:5
day after he had *s* Gedaliah ... Jer 41:4
whom he had *s* because of Gedaliah ... Jer 41:9
filled it with them that were *s* ... Jer 41:9
after that he had *s* Gedaliah the ... Jer 41:16
the son of Nethaniah had *s* ... Jer 41:18
Thus the *s* shall fall in the land ... Jer 51:4
all her *s* shall fall in the midst ... Jer 51:47
caused the *s* of Israel to fall ... Jer 51:49
shall fall the *s* of all the earth ... Jer 51:49
the prophet be *s* in the sanctuary ... Lam 2:20
thou hast *s* them in the day of ... Lam 2:21
thou hast *s*, thou hast not pitied ... Lam 3:43
They that be *s* with the sword are ... Lam 4:9
than they that be *s* with hunger ... Lam 4:9
down your *s* men before your idols ... Eze 6:4
the *s* shall fall in the midst of ... Eze 6:7
when their *s* men shall be among ... Eze 6:13
and fill the courts with the *s* ... Eze 9:7
multiplied your *s* in this city ... Eze 11:6
the streets thereof with the *s* ... Eze 11:6
Your *s* whom ye have laid in the ... Eze 11:7
That thou hast *s* my children ... Eze 16:21
third time, the sword of the *s* ... Eze 21:14
sword of the great men that are *s* ... Eze 21:14
upon the necks of them that are *s* ... Eze 21:29
For when they had *s* their ... Eze 23:39
the field shall be *s* by the sword ... Eze 26:6
are *s* in the midst of the seas ... Eze 28:8
when the *s* shall fall in Egypt, ... Eze 30:4
and fill the land with the *s* ... Eze 30:11
them that be *s* with the sword ... Eze 31:17
with them that be *s* by the sword ... Eze 31:18
of them that are *s* by the sword ... Eze 32:20
lie uncircumcised, *s* by the sword ... Eze 32:21
all of them *s*, fallen by the ... Eze 32:22
all of them *s*, fallen by the ... Eze 32:23
about her grave, all of them *s* ... Eze 32:24
of the *s* with all her multitude ... Eze 32:25
uncircumcised, *s* by the sword ... Eze 32:25
in the midst of them that be *s* ... Eze 32:25
*s* by the sword, though they ... Eze 32:26
them that are *s* with the sword ... Eze 32:28
by them that were *s* by the sword ... Eze 32:29
which are gone down with the *s* ... Eze 32:30
with them that be *s* by the sword ... Eze 32:30
and all his army *s* by the sword ... Eze 32:31
them that are *s* with the sword ... Eze 32:32
fill his mountains with his *s* men ... Eze 35:8
fall that are *s* with the sword ... Eze 35:8
O breath, and breathe upon these *s* ... Eze 37:9
that the wise men should be *s* ... Dan 2:13
Daniel and his fellows to be *s* ... Dan 2:13
the king of the Chaldeans *s* ... Dan 5:30
beheld even till the beast was *s* ... Dan 7:11
and many shall fall down *s* ... Dan 11:26
I have *s* them by the words of my ... Hos 6:5
young men have I *s* with the sword.. Amos 4:10
and there is a multitude of *s* ... Nah 3:3
also, ye shall be *s* by my sword ... Zeph 2:12
chief priests and scribes, and be *s* ... Lk 9:22
wicked hands have crucified and *s* ... Acts 2:23
who was *s*; and all ... Acts 5:36
have ye offered to me *s* beasts ... Acts 7:42
they have *s* them which shewed ... Acts 7:52
they Pilate that he should be *s* ... Acts 13:28
eat nothing until we have *s* Paul ... Acts 23:14
having *s* the enmity thereby ... Eph 2:16
tempted, were *s* with the sword ... Heb 11:37
who was *s* among you, where Satan ... Rev 2:13
stood a Lamb as it had been *s* ... Rev 5:6
for thou wast *s*, and hast redeemed ... Rev 5:9
Lamb that was *s* to receive power ... Rev 5:12
that were *s* for the word of God ... Rev 6:9
were *s* of men seven thousand ... Rev 11:13
Lamb *s* from the foundation of the ... Rev 13:8
of all that were *s* upon the earth ... Rev 18:24
the remnant were *s* with the sword ... Rev 19:21

**SLANDER**
by bringing up a *s* upon the land ... Num 14:36
For I have heard the *s* of many ... Ps 31:13
lips, and he that uttereth a *s* ... Prov 10:18

**SLANDERED**
he hath *s* thy servant unto my ... 2Sa 19:27

**SLANDERERS**
must their wives be grave, not *s* ... 1Ti 3:11

**SLANDEREST**
thou *s* thine own mother's son ... Ps 50:20

**SLANDERETH**
Whoso privily *s* his neighbour ... Ps 101:5

**SLANDEROUSLY**
not rather, (as we be *s* reported ... Rom 3:8

**SLANDERS**
revolters, walking with *s* ... Jer 6:28
every neighbour will walk with *s* ... Jer 9:4

**SLANG**
*s* it, and smote the Philistine in ... 1Sa 17:49

**SLAUGHTER**
return from the *s* of Chedorlaomer ... Gen 14:17
them with a great *s* at Gibeon ... Josh 10:10
slaying them with a very great *s* ... Josh 10:20
vineyards, with a very great *s* ... Judg 11:33
them hip and thigh with a great *s* ... Judg 15:8
and there was a very great *s* ... 1Sa 4:10
also a great *s* among the people ... 1Sa 4:17
many of the people with a great *s* ... 1Sa 6:19
And that first *s*, which Jonathan ... 1Sa 14:14
greater *s* among the Philistines ... 1Sa 14:30
from the *s* of the Philistine ... 1Sa 17:57
from the *s* of the Philistine ... 1Sa 18:6
and slew them with a great *s* ... 1Sa 19:8
and smote them with a great *s* ... 1Sa 23:5
from the *s* of the Amalekites ... 2Sa 1:1
There is a *s* among the people ... 2Sa 17:9
there was there a great *s* that ... 2Sa 18:7
slew the Syrians with a great *s* ... 1Kin 20:21
people slew them with a great *s* ... 2Chr 13:17
come from the *s* of the Edomites ... 2Chr 25:14
who smote him with a great *s* ... 2Chr 28:5
the stroke of the sword, and *s* ... Est 9:5
we are counted as sheep for the *s* ... Ps 44:22
as an ox goeth to the *s*, or as a ... Prov 7:22
for him according to the *s* of ... Is 10:26
Prepare *s* for his children for ... Is 14:21
*s* of them that are slain by him ... Is 27:7
waters in the day of the great *s* ... Is 30:25
he hath delivered them to the *s* ... Is 34:2
a great *s* in the land of Idumea ... Is 34:6
he is brought as a lamb to the *s* ... Is 53:7
and ye shall all bow down to the *s* ... Is 65:12
of Hinnom, but the valley of *s* ... Jer 7:32
or an ox that is brought to the *s* ... Jer 11:19
them out like sheep for the *s* ... Jer 12:3
and prepare them for the day of *s* ... Jer 12:3
of Hinnom, but The valley of *s* ... Jer 19:6
for the days of your *s* and of your ... Jer 25:34
young men are gone down to the *s* ... Jer 48:15
let them go down to the *s* ... Jer 50:27
them down like lambs to the *s* ... Jer 51:40
every man a *s* weapon in his hand ... Eze 9:2
It is sharpened to make a sore *s* ... Eze 21:10
it is wrapped up for the *s* ... Eze 21:15
to open the mouth in the *s* ... Eze 21:22
for the *s* it is furbished, to ... Eze 21:28
when the *s* is made in the midst ... Eze 26:15
revolters are profound to make *s* ... Hos 5:2
mount of Esau may be cut off by *s* ... Obad 9
Feed the flock of the *s* ... Zec 11:4
And I will feed the flock of *s* ... Zec 11:7
He was led as a sheep to the *s* ... Acts 8:32
*s* against the disciples of the ... Acts 9:1
are accounted as sheep for the *s* ... Rom 8:36
returning from the *s* of the kings ... Heb 7:1
your hearts, as in a day of *s* ... Jas 5:5

**SLAVE**
is he a homeborn *s* ... Jer 2:14

**SLAVES**
and horses, and chariots, and *s* ... Rev 18:13

**SLAY**
one that findeth me shall *s* me ... Gen 4:14
to *s* the righteous with the ... Gen 18:25
wilt thou *s* also a righteous ... Gen 20:4
they will *s* me for my wife's sake ... Gen 20:11
and took the knife to *s* his son ... Gen 22:10
then will I *s* my brother Jacob ... Gen 27:41
together against me, and *s* me ... Gen 34:30
conspired against him to *s* him ... Gen 37:18
now therefore, and let us *s* him ... Gen 37:20
profit is it if we *s* our brother ... Gen 37:26
*S* my two sons, if I bring him not ... Gen 42:37
house, Bring these men home, and *s*.. Gen 43:16
this thing, he sought to *s* Moses ... Ex 2:15
I will *s* thy son, even thy ... Ex 4:23
put a sword in their hand to *s* us ... Ex 5:21
neighbour, to *s* him with guile ... Ex 21:14
innocent and righteous *s* thou not ... Ex 23:7
And thou shalt *s* the ram, and thou ... Ex 29:16
to *s* them in the mountains, and to ... Ex 32:12
*s* every man his brother, and every ... Ex 32:27
*s* the sin offering in the place ... Lev 4:29
*s* it for a sin offering in the ... Lev 4:33
he shall *s* the lamb in the place ... Lev 14:13
and ye shall *s* the beast ... Lev 20:15
one shall *s* her before his face ... Num 19:3
*S* ye every one his men that were ... Num 25:5
himself shall *s* the murderer ... Num 35:19
he meeteth him, he shall *s* him ... Num 35:19
of blood shall *s* the murderer ... Num 35:21
out to *s* them in the wilderness ... Deut 9:28
because the way is long, and *s* him ... Deut 19:6
reward to *s* an innocent person ... Deut 27:25
did the children of Israel *s* with ... Josh 13:22
them alive, I would not *s* you ... Judg 8:19
his firstborn, Up, and *s* them ... Judg 8:20
*s* me, that men say not of me, A ... Judg 9:54
because the LORD would *s* them ... 1Sa 2:25
the God of Israel to us, to *s* us ... 1Sa 5:10
his own place, that it *s* us not ... 1Sa 5:11
his sheep, and *s* them here, and eat ... 1Sa 14:34
but *s* both man and woman, infant ... 1Sa 15:3
to *s* David without a cause ... 1Sa 19:5
him, and to *s* him in the morning ... 1Sa 19:11
me in the bed, that I may *s* him ... 1Sa 19:15
be in me iniquity, *s* me thyself ... 1Sa 20:8
of his father to *s* David ... 1Sa 20:33
*s* the priests of the LORD ... 1Sa 22:17
I pray thee, upon me, and *s* me ... 2Sa 1:9
king to *s* Abner the son of Ner ... 2Sa 3:37
Saul sought to *s* them in his zeal ... 2Sa 21:2
not *s* his servant with the sword ... 1Kin 1:51
living child, and in no wise *s* it ... 1Kin 3:26
living child, and in no wise *s* it ... 1Kin 3:27
king of Judah did Baasha *s* him ... 1Kin 15:28
to remembrance, and to *s* my son ... 1Kin 17:18
into the hand of Ahab, to *s* me ... 1Kin 18:9
cannot find thee, he shall *s* me ... 1Kin 18:12
and he shall *s* me ... 1Kin 18:14
the sword of Hazael shall Jehu *s* ... 1Kin 19:17
the sword of Jehu shall Elisha *s* ... 1Kin 19:17
from me, a lion shall *s* thee ... 1Kin 20:36
men wilt thou *s* with the sword ... 2Kin 8:12
to the captains, Go in, and *s* them ... 2Kin 10:25
them, and, behold, they *s* them ... 2Kin 17:26
of mount Seir, utterly to *s* ... 2Chr 20:23
*S* her not in the house of the ... 2Chr 23:14
*s* them, and cause the work to ... Neh 4:11
for they will come to *s* thee ... Neh 6:10
night will they come to *s* thee ... Neh 6:10
for their life, to destroy, to *s* ... Est 8:11
If the scourge *s* suddenly ... Job 9:23
Though he *s* me, yet will I trust ... Job 13:15
the viper's tongue shall *s* him ... Job 20:16
Evil shall *s* the wicked ... Ps 34:21
to *s* such as be of upright ... Ps 37:14
righteous, and seeketh to *s* him ... Ps 37:32
*S* them not, lest my people forget ... Ps 59:11
They *s* the widow and the stranger, ... Ps 94:6
that he might even *s* the broken ... Ps 109:16
Surely thou wilt *s* the wicked ... Ps 139:19
away of the simple shall *s* them ... Prov 1:32
of his lips shall he *s* the wicked ... Is 11:4
famine, and he shall *s* thy remnant ... Is 14:30
he shall *s* the dragon that is in ... Is 27:1
for the Lord GOD shall *s* thee ... Is 65:15
out of the forest shall *s* them ... Jer 5:6
the sword to *s*, and the dogs to ... Jer 15:3
their counsel against me to *s* me ... Jer 18:23
shall *s* them with the sword ... Jer 20:4
he shall *s* them before your eyes ... Jer 29:21
the son of Nethaniah to *s* thee ... Jer 40:14
I will *s* Ishmael the son of ... Jer 40:15
wherefore should he *s* thee ... Jer 40:15
that said unto Ishmael, *S* us not ... Jer 41:8
*S* all her bullocks ... Jer 50:27

*S* utterly old and young, both ... Eze 9:6
to *s* the souls that should not ... Eze 13:19
they shall *s* their sons and their ... Eze 23:47
He shall *s* with the sword thy ... Eze 26:8
he shall *s* thy people by the ... Eze 26:11
to *s* thereon the burnt offering ... Eze 40:39
they shall *s* the burnt offering ... Eze 44:11
to *s* the wise men of Babylon ... Dan 2:14
a dry land, and *s* her with thirst ... Hos 2:3
yet will I *s* even the beloved ... Hos 9:16
will *s* all the princes thereof ... Amos 2:3
I will *s* the last of them with ... Amos 9:1
the sword, and it shall *s* them ... Amos 9:4
continually to *s* the nations ... Hab 1:17
Whose possessors *s* them, and hold ... Zec 11:5
and some of them they shall *s* ... Lk 11:49
bring hither, and *s* them before me ... Lk 19:27
Jesus, and sought to *s* him ... Jn 5:16
heart, and took counsel to *s* them ... Acts 5:33
but they went about to *s* him ... Acts 9:29
*s* and eat ... Acts 11:7
for to *s* the third part of men ... Rev 9:15

**SLAYER**
that the *s* may flee thither, ... Num 35:11
shall judge between the *s* ... Num 35:24
congregation shall deliver the *s* ... Num 35:25
But if the *s* shall at any time ... Num 35:26
the revenger of blood kill the *s* ... Num 35:27
death of the high priest the *s* ... Num 35:28
That the *s* might flee thither, ... Deut 4:42
that every *s* may flee thither ... Deut 19:3
And this is the case of the *s* ... Deut 19:4
avenger of the blood pursue the *s* ... Deut 19:6
That the *s* that killeth any ... Josh 20:3
deliver the *s* up into his hand ... Josh 20:5
then shall the *s* return, and come ... Josh 20:6
to be a city of refuge for the *s* ... Josh 21:13
to be a city of refuge for the *s* ... Josh 21:21
to be a city of refuge for the *s* ... Josh 21:27
to be a city of refuge for the *s* ... Josh 21:32
to be a city of refuge for the *s* ... Josh 21:38
to give it into the hand of the *s* ... Eze 21:11

**SLAYETH**
him, Therefore whosoever *s* Cain ... Gen 4:15
*s* him, even so is this matter ... Deut 22:26
man, and envy *s* the silly one ... Job 5:2
yet say before him that *s* thee ... Eze 28:9
in the hand of him that *s* thee ... Eze 28:9

**SLAYING**
of *s* all the inhabitants of Ai in ... Josh 8:24
end of *s* them with a very great ... Josh 10:20
in *s* his seventy brethren ... Judg 9:56
with whom I sojourn, by *s* her son ... 1Kin 17:20
*s* oxen, and killing sheep, eating ... Is 22:13
*s* the children in the valleys ... Is 57:5
to pass, while they were *s* them ... Eze 9:8

**SLEEP**
caused a deep *s* to fall upon Adam ... Gen 2:21
down, a deep *s* fell upon Abram ... Gen 15:12
and lay down in that place to *s* ... Gen 28:11
And Jacob awaked out of his *s* ... Gen 28:16
my *s* departed from mine eyes ... Gen 31:40
wherein shall he *s* ... Ex 22:27
thou shalt not *s* with his pledge ... Deut 24:12
that he may *s* in his own raiment, ... Deut 24:13
thou shalt *s* with thy fathers ... Deut 31:16
And he awaked out of his *s* ... Judg 16:14
she made him *s* upon her knees ... Judg 16:19
And he awoke out of his *s*, and said. ... Judg 16:20
was, and Samuel was laid down to *s* ... 1Sa 3:3
because a deep *s* from the LORD ... 1Sa 26:12
thou shalt *s* with thy fathers, I ... 2Sa 7:12
the king shall *s* with his fathers ... 1Kin 1:21
that night could not the king *s* ... Est 6:1
when deep *s* falleth on men, ... Job 4:13
for now shall I *s* in the dust ... Job 7:21
nor be raised out of their *s* ... Job 14:12
when deep *s* falleth upon men, in ... Job 33:15
both lay me down in peace, and *s* ... Ps 4:8
lest I *s* the *s* of death ... Ps 13:3
spoiled, they have slept their *s* ... Ps 76:5
and horse are cast into a dead *s* ... Ps 76:6
the Lord awaked as one out of *s* ... Ps 78:65
they are as a *s* ... Ps 90:5
shall neither slumber nor *s* ... Ps 121:4
for so he giveth his beloved *s* ... Ps 127:2
I will not give *s* to mine eyes ... Ps 132:4
lie down, and thy *s* shall be sweet ... Prov 3:24
For they *s* not, except they have ... Prov 4:16
their *s* is taken away, unless ... Prov 4:16
Give not *s* to thine eyes, nor ... Prov 6:4
How long wilt thou *s*, O sluggard ... Prov 6:9
when wilt thou arise out of thy *s* ... Prov 6:9
Yet a little *s*, a little slumber, ... Prov 6:10
little folding of the hands to *s* ... Prov 6:10
casteth into a deep *s* ... Prov 19:15
Love not *s*, lest thou come to ... Prov 20:13
Yet a little *s*, a little slumber, ... Prov 24:33
little folding of the hands to *s* ... Prov 24:33
The *s* of a labouring man is sweet ... Eccl 5:12
the rich will not suffer him to *s* ... Eccl 5:12
nor night seeth *s* with his eyes ... Eccl 8:16
I *s*, but my heart waketh ... Song 5:2
none shall slumber nor *s* ... Is 5:27
out upon you the spirit of deep *s* ... Is 29:10
and my *s* was sweet unto me ... Jer 31:26
they may rejoice, and *s* ... Jer 51:39
a perpetual *s*, and not wake ... Jer 51:39
they shall *s* a perpetual *s*, ... Jer 51:57
and they shall *s* a perpetual *s* ... Jer 51:57
the wilderness, and *s* in the woods ... Eze 34:25
troubled, and his *s* brake from him ... Dan 2:1
and his *s* went from him ... Dan 6:18
I was in a deep *s* on my face ... Dan 8:18
then was I in a deep *s* on my face ... Dan 10:9
many of them that *s* in the dust ... Dan 12:2
man that is wakened out of his *s* ... Zec 4:1
*s* did as the angel of the Lord ... Mt 1:24
*S* on now, and take your rest ... Mt 26:45
And should *s*, and rise night and day ... Mk 4:27
*S* on now, and take your rest ... Mk 14:41
were with him were heavy with *s* ... Lk 9:32
And said unto them, Why *s* ye ... Lk 22:46
go, that I may awake him out of *s* ... Jn 11:11
said his disciples, Lord, if he *s* ... Jn 11:12
had spoken of taking of rest in *s* ... Jn 11:13
by the will of God, fell on *s* ... Acts 13:36
the prison awaking out of his *s* ... Acts 16:27
being fallen into a deep *s* ... Acts 20:9
preaching, he sunk down with *s* ... Acts 20:9
it is high time to awake out of *s* ... Rom 13:11
and sickly among you, and many *s* ... 1Cor 11:30
We shall not all *s*, but we shall ... 1Cor 15:51
even so them also which *s* in ... 1Th 4:14
Therefore let us not *s*, as do ... 1Th 5:6
they that *s* *s* in the night ... 1Th 5:7
us, that, whether we wake or *s* ... 1Th 5:10

**SLEEPER**
unto him, What meanest thou, O *s* ... Jonah 1:6

**SLEEPEST**
Awake, why *s* thou, O Lord ... Ps 44:23
when thou *s*, it shall keep thee ... Prov 6:22
saith unto Peter, Simon, *s* thou ... Mk 14:37
he saith, Awake thou that *s* ... Eph 5:14

**SLEEPETH**
a journey, or peradventure he *s* ... 1Kin 18:27
but he that *s* in harvest is a son ... Prov 10:5
their baker *s* all the night ... Hos 7:6
for the maid is not dead, but *s* ... Mt 9:24
the damsel is not dead, but *s* ... Mk 5:39
she is not dead, but *s* ... Lk 8:52
unto them, Our friend Lazarus *s* ... Jn 11:11

**SLEEPING**
Saul lay *s* within the trench, and ... 1Sa 26:7
*s*, lying down, loving to slumber ... Is 56:10
coming suddenly he find you *s* ... Mk 13:36
And he cometh, and findeth them *s* ... Mk 14:37
he found them *s* for sorrow ... Lk 22:45
Peter was *s* between two soldiers ... Acts 12:6

**SLEIGHT**
wind of doctrine, by the *s* of men ... Eph 4:14

**SLEPT**
sleep to fall upon Adam, and he *s* ... Gen 2:21
And he *s* and dreamed the second ... Gen 41:5
But Uriah *s* at the door of the ... 2Sa 11:9
So David *s* with his fathers, and ... 1Kin 2:10
beside me, while thine handmaid *s* ... 1Kin 3:20
that David *s* with his fathers ... 1Kin 11:21
Solomon *s* with his fathers, and ... 1Kin 11:43
he *s* with his fathers, and Nadab ... 1Kin 14:20
Rehoboam *s* with his fathers, and ... 1Kin 14:31
Abijam *s* with his fathers ... 1Kin 15:8
Asa *s* with his fathers, and was ... 1Kin 15:24
So Baasha *s* with his fathers, and ... 1Kin 16:6
So Omri *s* with his fathers, and ... 1Kin 16:28
*s* under a juniper tree, behold, ... 1Kin 19:5
So Ahab *s* with his fathers ... 1Kin 22:40
Jehoshaphat *s* with his fathers ... 1Kin 22:50
Joram *s* with his fathers, and was ... 2Kin 8:24
And Jehu *s* with his fathers ... 2Kin 10:35
Jehoahaz *s* with his fathers ... 2Kin 13:9
And Joash *s* with his fathers ... 2Kin 13:13
Jehoash *s* with his fathers, and ... 2Kin 14:16
that the king *s* with his fathers ... 2Kin 14:22
Jeroboam *s* with his fathers, even ... 2Kin 14:29
So Azariah *s* with his fathers ... 2Kin 15:7
Menahem *s* with his fathers ... 2Kin 15:22
Jotham *s* with his fathers, and was ... 2Kin 15:38
Ahaz *s* with his fathers, and was ... 2Kin 16:20
Hezekiah *s* with his fathers ... 2Kin 20:21
Manasseh *s* with his fathers, and ... 2Kin 21:18
So Jehoiakim *s* with his fathers ... 2Kin 24:6
Solomon *s* with his fathers, and he ... 2Chr 9:31
Rehoboam *s* with his fathers, and ... 2Chr 12:16
So Abijah *s* with his fathers, and ... 2Chr 14:1
Asa *s* with his fathers, and died ... 2Chr 16:13
Now Jehoshaphat *s* with his ... 2Chr 21:1
that the king *s* with his fathers ... 2Chr 26:2
So Uzziah *s* with his fathers, and ... 2Chr 26:23
Jotham *s* with his fathers, and ... 2Chr 27:9
Ahaz *s* with his fathers, and they ... 2Chr 28:27
Hezekiah *s* with his fathers, and ... 2Chr 32:33
So Manasseh *s* with his fathers, ... 2Chr 33:20
and been quiet, I should have *s* ... Job 3:13
I laid me down and *s* ... Ps 3:5
spoiled, they have *s* their sleep ... Ps 76:5
But while men *s*, his enemy came ... Mt 13:25
tarried, they all slumbered and *s* ... Mt 25:5
of the saints which *s* arose ... Mt 27:52
and stole him away while we *s* ... Mt 28:13
the firstfruits of them that *s* ... 1Cor 15:20

**SLEW**
Abel his brother, and *s* him ... Gen 4:8
seed instead of Abel, whom Cain *s* ... Gen 4:25
city boldly, and *s* all the males ... Gen 34:25
they *s* Hamor and Shechem his son ... Gen 34:26
and the LORD *s* him ... Gen 38:7
wherefore he *s* him also ... Gen 38:10
for in their anger they *s* a man ... Gen 49:6
he *s* the Egyptian, and hid him in ... Ex 2:12
that the LORD *s* all the firstborn ... Ex 13:15
And he *s* it ... Lev 8:15
And he *s* it ... Lev 8:23
*s* the calf of the sin offering, ... Lev 9:8
And he *s* the burnt offering ... Lev 9:12
*s* it, and offered it for sin, as ... Lev 9:15
He *s* also the bullock and the ram ... Lev 9:18
and they *s* all the males ... Num 31:7
they *s* the kings of Midian, ... Num 31:8
son of Beor they *s* with the sword ... Num 31:8
turned again, and *s* the men of Ai ... Josh 8:21
of Israel, that they *s* them not ... Josh 9:26
*s* them with a great slaughter at ... Josh 10:10
of Israel *s* with the sword ... Josh 10:11
*s* them, and hanged them on five ... Josh 10:26
smote them, and *s* them ... Josh 11:17
they *s* of them in Bezek ten ... Judg 1:4
they *s* the Canaanites and the ... Judg 1:5
they *s* Sheshai, and Ahiman, and ... Judg 1:10
they *s* the Canaanites that ... Judg 1:17
they *s* of Moab at that time about ... Judg 3:29
which *s* of the Philistines six ... Judg 3:31
they *s* Oreb upon the rock Oreb, ... Judg 7:25
Zeeb they *s* at the winepress of ... Judg 7:25
Penuel, and *s* the men of the city ... Judg 8:17
men were they whom ye *s* at Tabor ... Judg 8:18
*s* Zebah and Zalmunna ... Judg 8:21
*s* his brethren the sons of ... Judg 9:5
their brother, which *s* them ... Judg 9:24
were in the fields, and *s* them ... Judg 9:44
*s* the people that was therein, and ... Judg 9:45
men say not of me, A woman *s* him ... Judg 9:54
*s* him at the passages of Jordan ... Judg 12:6
*s* thirty men of them, and took ... Judg 14:19
*s* a thousand men therewith ... Judg 15:15
our country, which *s* many of us ... Judg 16:24
So the dead which he *s* at his ... Judg 16:30
than they which he *s* in his life ... Judg 16:30
*s* two thousand men of them ... Judg 20:45
they *s* a bullock, and brought the ... 1Sa 1:25
they *s* of the army in the field ... 1Sa 4:2
*s* the Ammonites until the heat of ... 1Sa 11:11
and his armourbearer *s* after him ... 1Sa 14:13
calves, and *s* them on the ground ... 1Sa 14:32
him that night, and *s* them there ... 1Sa 14:34
his beard, and smote him, and *s* him ... 1Sa 17:35
Thy servant *s* both the lion and ... 1Sa 17:36
and smote the Philistine, and *s* him ... 1Sa 17:50
*s* him, and cut off his head ... 1Sa 17:51
*s* of the Philistines two hundred ... 1Sa 18:27
*s* the Philistine, and the LORD ... 1Sa 19:5
*s* them with a great slaughter ... 1Sa 19:8
*s* on that day fourscore and five ... 1Sa 22:18
Saul *s* his thousands, and David ... 1Sa 29:5
they *s* not any, either great or ... 1Sa 30:2
and the Philistines *s* Jonathan ... 1Sa 31:2
*s* him, because I was sure that he ... 2Sa 1:10
and Abishai his brother *s* Abner ... 2Sa 3:30
*s* him, and beheaded him, and took ... 2Sa 4:7
*s* him in Ziklag, who thought that ... 2Sa 4:10
his young men, and they *s* them ... 2Sa 4:12
David *s* of the Syrians two and ... 2Sa 8:5
David *s* the men of seven hundred ... 2Sa 10:18
the one smote the other, and *s* him ... 2Sa 14:6
the life of his brother whom he *s* ... 2Sa 14:7
about and smote Absalom, and *s* him. ... 2Sa 18:15
because he *s* the Gibeonites ... 2Sa 21:1
Sibbechai the Hushathite *s* Saph ... 2Sa 21:18
*s* the brother of Goliath the ... 2Sa 21:19
the brother of David *s* him ... 2Sa 21:21
hundred, whom he *s* at one time ... 2Sa 23:8
defended it, and *s* the Philistines ... 2Sa 23:12
*s* them, and had the name among ... 2Sa 23:18
he *s* two lionlike men of Moab ... 2Sa 23:20
*s* a lion in the midst of a pit in ... 2Sa 23:20
he *s* an Egyptian, a goodly man ... 2Sa 23:21
hand, and *s* him with his own spear ... 2Sa 23:21
And Adonijah *s* sheep and oxen and ... 1Kin 1:9
the son of Jether, whom he *s* ... 1Kin 2:5
*s* them with the sword, my father ... 1Kin 2:32
up, and fell upon him, and *s* him ... 1Kin 2:34
when David *s* them of Zobah ... 1Kin 11:24
lion met him by the way, and *s* him ... 1Kin 13:24
that he *s* all the house of Baasha ... 1Kin 16:11
*s* the prophets of the LORD ... 1Kin 18:13
the brook Kishon, and *s* them there ... 1Kin 18:40
*s* them, and boiled their flesh ... 1Kin 19:21
And they *s* every one his man ... 1Kin 20:20
*s* the Syrians with a great ... 1Kin 20:21
the children of Israel *s* of the ... 1Kin 20:29
him, a lion found him, and *s* him ... 1Kin 20:36
Had Zimri peace, who *s* his master ... 2Kin 9:31
*s* seventy persons, and put their ... 2Kin 10:7
against my master, and *s* him ... 2Kin 10:9
but who *s* all these ... 2Kin 10:9
So Jehu *s* all that remained of ... 2Kin 10:11
*s* them at the pit of the shearing ... 2Kin 10:14
he *s* all that remained unto Ahab ... 2Kin 10:17
*s* Mattan the priest of Baal ... 2Kin 11:18
they *s* Athaliah with the sword ... 2Kin 11:20
*s* Joash in the house of Millo ... 2Kin 12:20
that he *s* his servants which had ... 2Kin 14:5
of the murderers he *s* not ... 2Kin 14:6
He *s* of Edom in the valley of ... 2Kin 14:7

him to Lachish, and *s* him there … 2Kin 14:19
*s* him, and reigned in his stead … 2Kin 15:10
*s* him, and reigned in his stead … 2Kin 15:14
*s* him, and reigned in his stead, … 2Kin 15:30
of it captive to Kir, and *s* Rezin … 2Kin 16:9
among them, which *s* some of them .. 2Kin 17:25
*s* the king in his own house … 2Kin 21:23
the people of the land *s* all them … 2Kin 21:24
he *s* all the priests of the high … 2Kin 23:20
he *s* him at Megiddo, when he had … 2Kin 23:29
they *s* the sons of Zedekiah … 2Kin 25:7
*s* them at Riblah in the land of … 2Kin 25:21
and he *s* him … 1Chr 2:3
that were born in that land *s* … 1Chr 7:21
and the Philistines *s* Jonathan … 1Chr 10:2
therefore he *s* him, and turned the … 1Chr 10:14
it, and *s* the Philistines … 1Chr 11:14
he *s* them, and had a name among … 1Chr 11:20
he *s* two lionlike men of Moab … 1Chr 11:22
*s* a lion in a pit in a snowy day … 1Chr 11:22
he *s* an Egyptian, a man of great … 1Chr 11:23
hand, and *s* him with his own spear .. 1Chr 11:23
David *s* of the Syrians two and … 1Chr 18:5
Abishai the son Zeruiah *s* of the … 1Chr 18:12
David *s* of the Syrians seven … 1Chr 19:18
Sibbechai the Hushathite *s* Sippai … 1Chr 20:4
Elhanan the son of Jair *s* Lahmi … 1Chr 20:5
of Shimea David's brother *s* him … 1Chr 20:7
his people *s* them with a great … 2Chr 13:17
*s* all his brethren with the sword … 2Chr 21:4
ministered to Ahaziah, he *s* them … 2Chr 22:8
Athaliah, so that she *s* him not … 2Chr 22:11
king's house, they *s* her there … 2Chr 23:15
*s* Mattan the priest of Baal … 2Chr 23:17
had done to him, but *s* his son … 2Chr 24:22
*s* him on his bed, and he died … 2Chr 24:25
that he *s* his servants that had … 2Chr 25:3
But he *s* not their children, but … 2Chr 25:4
Lachish after him, and *s* him there … 2Chr 25:27
of Remaliah *s* in Judah an hundred … 2Chr 28:6
*s* Maaseiah the king's son, and … 2Chr 28:7
bowels *s* him there with the sword … 2Chr 32:21
him, and *s* him in his own house … 2Chr 33:24
But the people of the land *s* all … 2Chr 33:25
who *s* their young men with the … 2Chr 36:17
*s* thy prophets which testified … Neh 9:26
in Shushan the palace the Jews *s* … Est 9:6
the enemy of the Jews, *s* they … Est 9:10
*s* three hundred men at Shushan … Est 9:15
*s* of their foes seventy and five … Est 9:16
*s* the fattest of them, and smote … Ps 78:31
When he *s* them, then they sought … Ps 78:34
into blood, and *s* their fish … Ps 105:29
great nations, and *s* mighty kings … Ps 135:10
And *s* famous kings … Ps 136:18
killeth an ox is as if he *s* a man … Is 66:3
Because he *s* me not from the womb … Jer 20:17
who *s* him with the sword, and cast … Jer 26:23
Then the king of Babylon *s* the … Jer 39:6
Babylon *s* all the nobles of Judah … Jer 39:6
*s* him, whom the king of Babylon … Jer 41:2
Ishmael also *s* all the Jews that … Jer 41:3
the son of Nethaniah *s* them … Jer 41:7
*s* them not among their brethren … Jer 41:8
the king of Babylon *s* the sons of … Jer 52:10
he *s* also all the princes of … Jer 52:10
*s* all that were pleasant to the … Lam 2:4
they went forth, and *s* in the city … Eze 9:7
and *s* her with the sword … Eze 23:10
whereupon they *s* their sacrifices … Eze 40:41
they *s* the burnt offering … Eze 40:42
the flame of the fire *s* those men … Dan 3:22
whom he would he *s* … Dan 5:19
*s* all the children that were in … Mt 2:16
him out of the vineyard, and *s* him … Mt 21:39
them spitefully, and *s* them … Mt 22:6
whom ye *s* between the temple and … Mt 23:35
*s* them, think ye that they were … Lk 13:4
raised up Jesus, whom ye *s* … Acts 5:30
whom they *s* and hanged on a tree … Acts 10:39
the raiment of them that *s* him … Acts 22:20
deceived me, and by it *s* me … Rom 7:11
that wicked one, and *s* his brother … 1Jn 3:12
And wherefore *s* he him … 1Jn 3:12

**SLEWEST**
whom thou *s* in the valley of Elah … 1Sa 21:9

**SLIDDEN**
is this people of Jerusalem *s* … Jer 8:5

**SLIDE**
their foot shall *s* in due time … Deut 32:35
therefore I shall not *s* … Ps 26:1
none of his steps shall *s* … Ps 37:31

**SLIDETH**
For Israel *s* back as a … Hos 4:16

**SLIGHTLY**
of the daughter of my people *s* … Jer 6:14
of the daughter of my people *s* … Jer 8:11

**SLIME**
stone, and *s* had they for morter … Gen 11:3
of bulrushes, and daubed it with *s* … Ex 2:3

**SLIMEPITS**
the vale of Siddim was full of *s* … Gen 14:10

**SLING**
every one could *s* stones at an … Judg 20:16
and his *s* was in his hand … 1Sa 17:40
over the Philistine with a *s* … 1Sa 17:50
enemies, them shall he *s* out … 1Sa 25:29
as out of the middle of a *s* … 1Sa 25:29
As he that bindeth a stone in a *s* … Prov 26:8
I will *s* out the inhabitants of … Jer 10:18
devour, and subdue with *s* stones … Zec 9:15

**SLINGERS**
howbeit the *s* went about it, and … 2Kin 3:25

**SLINGS**
and bows, and *s* to cast stones … 2Chr 26:14

**SLINGSTONES**
*s* are turned with him into … Job 41:28

**SLIP**
so that my feet did not *s* … 2Sa 22:37
He that is ready to *s* with his … Job 12:5
paths, that my footsteps *s* not … Ps 17:5
under me, that my feet did not *s* … Ps 18:36
at any time we should let them *s* … Heb 2:1

**SLIPPED**
but he *s* away out of Saul's … 1Sa 19:10
my steps had well nigh *s* … Ps 73:2

**SLIPPERY**
Let their way be dark and *s* … Ps 35:6
thou didst set them in *s* places … Ps 73:18
them as *s* ways in the darkness … Jer 23:12

**SLIPPETH**
the head *s* from the helve, and … Deut 19:5
when my foot *s*, they magnify … Ps 38:16
When I said, My foot *s* … Ps 94:18

**SLIPS**
and shalt set it with strange *s* … Is 17:10

**SLOTHFUL**
be not *s* to go, and to enter to … Judg 18:9
but the *s* shall be under tribute … Prov 12:24
The *s* man roasteth not that which … Prov 12:27
The way of the *s* man is as an … Prov 15:19
He also that is *s* in his work is … Prov 18:9
A *s* man hideth his hand in his … Prov 19:24
The desire of the *s* killeth him … Prov 21:25
The *s* man saith, There is a lion … Prov 22:13
I went by the field of the *s* … Prov 24:30
The *s* man saith, There is a lion … Prov 26:13
so doth the *s* upon his bed … Prov 26:14
The *s* hideth his hand in his … Prov 26:15
*s* servant, thou knewest that I … Mt 25:26
Not *s* in business … Rom 12:11
That ye be not *s*, but followers … Heb 6:12

**SLOTHFULNESS**
*S* casteth into a deep sleep … Prov 19:15
By much *s* the building decayeth … Eccl 10:18

**SLOW**
but I am *s* of speech … Ex 4:10
and of a *s* tongue … Ex 4:10
*s* to anger, and of great kindness, … Neh 9:17
*s* to anger, and plenteous in mercy … Ps 103:8
*s* to anger, and of great mercy … Ps 145:8
He that is *s* to wrath is of great … Prov 14:29
but he that is *s* to anger … Prov 15:18
He that is *s* to anger is better … Prov 16:32
*s* to anger, and of great kindness, … Joel 2:13
*s* to anger, and of great kindness, … Jonah 4:2
The LORD is *s* to anger, and great … Nah 1:3
*s* of heart to believe all that … Lk 24:25
liars, evil beasts, *s* bellies … Titus 1:12
*s* to speak, *s* to wrath … Jas 1:19

**SLOWLY**
And when we had sailed *s* many days. Acts 27:7

**SLUGGARD**
Go to the ant, thou *s* … Prov 6:6
How long wilt thou sleep, O *s* … Prov 6:9
so is the *s* to them that send him … Prov 10:26
The soul of the *s* desireth … Prov 13:4
The *s* will not plow by reason of … Prov 20:4
The *s* is wiser in his own conceit … Prov 26:16

**SLUICES**
purposes thereof, all that make *s* … Is 19:10

**SLUMBER**
he that keepeth thee will not *s* … Ps 121:3
Israel shall neither *s* nor sleep … Ps 121:4
mine eyes, or *s* to mine eyelids, … Ps 132:4
eyes, nor *s* to thine eyelids … Prov 6:4
Yet a little sleep, a little *s* … Prov 6:10
Yet a little sleep, a little *s* … Prov 24:33
none shall *s* nor sleep … Is 5:27
sleeping, lying down, loving to *s* … Is 56:10
Thy shepherds *s*, O king of … Nah 3:18
hath given them the spirit of *s* … Rom 11:8

**SLUMBERED**
bridegroom tarried, they all *s* … Mt 25:5

**SLUMBERETH**
not, and their damnation *s* not … 2Pet 2:3

**SLUMBERINGS**
upon men, in *s* upon the bed … Job 33:15

**SMALL**
the house with blindness, both *s* … Gen 19:11
Is it a *s* matter that thou hast … Gen 30:15
it shall become *s* dust in all the … Ex 9:9
there lay a *s* round thing … Ex 16:14
as *s* as the hoar frost on the … Ex 16:14
but every *s* matter they shall … Ex 18:22
but every *s* matter they judged … Ex 18:26
thou shalt beat some of it very *s* … Ex 30:36
full of sweet incense beaten *s* … Lev 16:12
Seemeth it but a *s* thing unto you … Num 16:9
Is it a *s* thing that thou hast … Num 16:13
took the *s* towns thereof, and … Num 32:41
hear the *s* as well as the great … Deut 1:17
stamped it, and ground it very *s* … Deut 9:21
even until it was as *s* as dust … Deut 9:21
divers weights, a great and a *s* … Deut 25:13
divers measures, a great and a *s* … Deut 25:14
as the *s* rain upon the tender … Deut 32:2
smote the men of the city, both *s* … 1Sa 5:9
will do nothing either great or *s* … 1Sa 20:2
slew not any, either great or *s* … 1Sa 30:2
neither *s* nor great, neither sons … 1Sa 30:19
this was yet a *s* thing in thy … 2Sa 7:19
be not one *s* stone found there … 2Sa 17:13
Then did I beat them as *s* as the … 2Sa 22:43
I desire one *s* petition of thee … 1Kin 2:20
and after the fire a still *s* voice … 1Kin 19:12
Fight neither with *s* nor great … 1Kin 22:31
their inhabitants were of *s* power … 2Kin 19:26
and all the people, both *s* … 2Kin 23:2
Kidron, and stamped it *s* to powder … 2Kin 23:6
place, and stamped it *s* to powder … 2Kin 23:15
And all the people, both *s* … 2Kin 25:26
yet this was a *s* thing in thine … 1Chr 17:17
as well the *s* as the great, the … 1Chr 25:8
as well the *s* as the great, … 1Chr 26:13
whether *s* or great, whether man … 2Chr 15:13
Fight ye not with *s* or great … 2Chr 18:30
came with a *s* company of men … 2Chr 24:24
as well to the great as to the *s* … 2Chr 31:15
and all the people, great and *s* … 2Chr 34:30
thousand and six hundred *s* cattle … 2Chr 35:8
offerings five thousand *s* cattle … 2Chr 35:9
of the house of God, great and *s* … 2Chr 36:18
the palace, both unto great and *s* … Est 1:5
honour, both to great and *s* … Est 1:20
The *s* and great are there … Job 3:19
Though thy beginning was *s* … Job 8:7
consolations of God *s* with thee … Job 15:11
For he maketh *s* the drops of … Job 36:27
likewise to the *s* rain, and to the … Job 37:6
Then did I beat them *s* as the … Ps 18:42
creeping innumerable, both *s* … Ps 104:25
them that fear the LORD, both *s* … Ps 115:13
I am *s* and despised … Ps 119:141
of adversity, thy strength is *s* … Prov 24:10
*s* cattle above all that were in … Eccl 2:7
had left unto us a very *s* remnant … Is 1:9
Is it a *s* thing for you to weary … Is 7:13
and the remnant shall be very *s* … Is 16:14
issue, all vessels of *s* quantity … Is 22:24
strangers shall be like *s* dust … Is 29:5
their inhabitants were of *s* power … Is 37:27
are counted as the *s* dust of the … Is 40:15
the mountains, and beat them *s* … Is 41:15
Thou hast not brought me the *s* … Is 43:23
For a *s* moment have I forsaken … Is 54:7
and a *s* one a strong nation … Is 60:22
the *s* shall die in this land … Jer 16:6
them, and they shall not be *s* … Jer 30:19
Yet a *s* number that escape the … Jer 44:28
I will make thee *s* among the … Jer 49:15
this of thy whoredoms a *s* matter … Eze 16:20
Seemeth it a *s* thing unto you to … Eze 34:18
become strong with a *s* people … Dan 11:23
for he is *s* … Amos 7:2
for he is *s* … Amos 7:5
forth wheat, making the ephah *s* … Amos 8:5
I have made thee *s* among the … Obad 2
hath despised the day of *s* things … Zec 4:10
that a *s* ship should wait on him … Mk 3:9
And they had a few *s* fishes … Mk 8:7
he had made a scourge of *s* cords … Jn 2:15
barley loaves, and two *s* fishes … Jn 6:9
there was no *s* stir among the … Acts 12:18
and Barnabas had no *s* dissension … Acts 15:2
arose no *s* stir about that way … Acts 19:23
brought no *s* gain unto the … Acts 19:24
this day, witnessing both to *s* … Acts 26:22
no *s* tempest lay on us, all hope … Acts 27:20
But with me it is a very *s* thing … 1Cor 4:3
turned about with a very *s* helm … Jas 3:4
and them that fear thy name, *s* … Rev 11:18
And he causeth all, both *s* … Rev 13:16
and ye that fear him, both *s* … Rev 19:5
men, both free and bond, both *s* … Rev 19:18
And I saw the dead, *s* and great, … Rev 20:12

**SMALLEST**
of the *s* of the tribes of Israel … 1Sa 9:21
unworthy to judge the *s* matters … 1Cor 6:2

**SMART**
for a stranger shall *s* for it … Prov 11:15

**SMELL**
he smelled the *s* of his raiment … Gen 27:27
the *s* of my son is as the *s* … Gen 27:27
to *s* thereto, shall even be cut … Ex 30:38
I will not *s* the savour of your … Lev 26:31
see, nor hear, nor eat, nor *s* … Deut 4:28
All thy garments *s* of myrrh … Ps 45:8
noses have they, but they *s* not … Ps 115:6
sendeth forth the *s* thereof … Song 1:12
the tender grape give a good *s* … Song 2:13
the *s* of thine ointments than all … Song 4:10

S

the s of thy garments is like the Song 4:11
garments is like the s of Lebanon Song 4:11
the s of thy nose like apples Song 7:8
The mandrakes give a s, and at our Song 7:13
of sweet s there shall be stink Is 3:24
nor the s of fire had passed on Dan 3:27
olive tree, and his s as Lebanon Hos 14:6
I will not s in your solemn Amos 5:21
from you, an odour of a sweet s Phil 4:18

**SMELLED**

the LORD s a sweet savour Gen 8:21
he s the smell of his raiment, and Gen 27:27

**SMELLETH**

he s the battle afar off, the Job 39:25

**SMELLING**

and my fingers with sweet s myrrh Song 5:5
lilies, dropping sweet s myrrh Song 5:13
were hearing, where were the s 1Cor 12:17

**SMITE**

neither will I again s any more Gen 8:21
s it, then the other company Gen 32:8
s me, and the mother with the Gen 32:11
s Egypt with all my wonders which Ex 3:20
I will s with the rod that is in Ex 7:17
I will s all thy borders with Ex 8:2
s the dust of the land, that it Ex 8:16
out my hand, that I may s thee Ex 9:15
will s all the firstborn in the Ex 12:12
when I s the land of Egypt Ex 12:13
pass through to s the Egyptians Ex 12:23
come in unto your houses to s you Ex 12:23
and thou shalt s the rock, and Ex 17:6
one s another with a stone, or Ex 21:18
if a man s his servant, or his Ex 21:20
if a man s the eye of his servant Ex 21:26
if he s out his manservant's Ex 21:27
I will s them with the pestilence Num 14:12
shall prevail, that we may s them Num 22:6
shall s the corners of Moab, and Num 24:17
Vex the Midianites, and s them Num 25:17
if he s him with an instrument of Num 35:16
if he s him with throwing a stone Num 35:17
Or if he s him with an hand Num 35:18
Or in enmity s him with his hand, Num 35:21
thou shalt s them, and utterly Deut 7:2
Thou shalt surely s the Deut 13:15
s him mortally that he die, and Deut 19:11
thou shalt s every male thereof Deut 20:13
The LORD shall s thee with a Deut 28:22
The LORD will s thee with the Deut 28:27
The LORD shall s thee with Deut 28:28
The LORD shall s thee in the Deut 28:35
s through the loins of them that Deut 33:11
three thousand men go up and s Ai Josh 7:3
and help me, that we may s Gibeon Josh 10:4
and s the hindmost of them Josh 10:19
LORD and the children of Israel s Josh 12:6
for these did Moses s, and cast Josh 13:12
thou shalt s the Midianites as Judg 6:16
and they began to s of the people Judg 20:31
the battle, Benjamin began to s Judg 20:39
Go and s the inhabitants of Judg 21:10
s Amalek, and utterly destroy all 1Sa 15:3
and I will s thee, and take thine 1Sa 17:46
I will s David even to the wall 1Sa 18:11
Saul sought to s David even to 1Sa 19:10
cast a javelin at him to s him 1Sa 20:33
Shall I go and s these Philistines 1Sa 23:2
s the Philistines, and save Keilah 1Sa 23:2
now therefore let me s him 1Sa 26:8
I will not s him the second time 1Sa 26:8
LORD liveth, the LORD shall s him 1Sa 26:10
should I s thee to the ground 2Sa 2:22
to s the host of the Philistines 2Sa 5:24
and when I say unto you, S Amnon 2Sa 13:28
s the city with the edge of the 2Sa 15:14
and I will s the king only 2Sa 17:2
why didst thou not s him there to 2Sa 18:11
For the LORD shall s Israel 1Kin 14:15
of the LORD, S me, I pray thee 1Kin 20:35
And the man refused to s him 1Kin 20:35
man, and said, S me, I pray thee 1Kin 20:37
ye shall s every fenced city, and 2Kin 3:19
S this people, I pray thee, with 2Kin 6:18
them, My father, shall I s them 2Kin 6:21
shall I s them 2Kin 6:21
answered, Thou shalt not s them 2Kin 6:22
wouldest thou s those whom thou 2Kin 6:22
thou shalt s the house of Ahab 2Kin 9:7
S him also in the chariot 2Kin 9:27
for thou shalt s the Syrians in 2Kin 13:17
king of Israel, S upon the ground 2Kin 13:18
now thou shalt s Syria but thrice 2Kin 13:19
to s the host of the Philistines 1Chr 14:15
plague will the LORD s thy people 2Chr 21:14
The sun shall not s thee by day Ps 121:6
Let the righteous s me Ps 141:5
S a scorner, and the simple will Prov 19:25
Therefore the Lord will s with a Is 3:17
he shall s thee with a rod, and Is 10:24
he shall s the earth with the rod Is 11:4
shall s it in the seven streams, Is 11:15
And the LORD shall s Egypt Is 19:22
he shall s and heal it Is 19:22
shall the heat nor sun s them Is 49:10
to s with the fist of wickedness Is 58:4
let us s him with the tongue, and Jer 18:18
I will s the inhabitants of this Jer 21:6
he shall s them with the edge of Jer 21:7
he shall s the land of Egypt, and Jer 43:11
come and s the land of Egypt Jer 46:13
king of Babylon shall s, thus Jer 49:28
part, and s about it with a knife Eze 5:2
S with thine hand, and stamp with Eze 6:11
after him through the city, and s Eze 9:5
s therefore upon thy thigh Eze 21:12
s thine hands together, and let Eze 21:14
I will also s mine hands together Eze 21:17
when I shall s all them that Eze 32:15
I will s thy bow out of thy left Eze 39:3
I will s the winter house with Amos 3:15
he will s the great house with Amos 6:11
S the lintel of the door, that Amos 9:1
they shall s the judge of Israel Mic 5:1
melteth, and the knees s together Nah 2:10
he will s her power in the sea Zec 9:4
shall s the waves in the sea, and Zec 10:11
and they shall s the land, and out Zec 11:6
I will s every horse with Zec 12:4
will s every horse of the people Zec 12:4
s the shepherd, and the sheep Zec 13:7
plague wherewith the LORD will s Zec 14:12
wherewith the LORD will s the Zec 14:18
come and s the earth with a curse Mal 4:6
but whosoever shall s thee on thy Mt 5:39
And shall begin to s his Mt 24:49
I will s the shepherd, and the Mt 26:31
I will s the shepherd, and the Mk 14:27
shall we s with the sword Lk 22:49
by him to s him on the mouth Acts 23:2
Paul unto him, God shall s thee Acts 23:3
if a man s you on the face 2Cor 11:20
to s the earth with all plagues, Rev 11:6
with it he should s the nations Rev 19:15

**SMITERS**

I gave my back to the s, and my Is 50:6

**SMITEST**

Wherefore s thou thy fellow Ex 2:13
but if well, why s thou me Jn 18:23

**SMITETH**

He that s a man, so that he die, Ex 21:12
he that s his father, or his Ex 21:15
out of the hand of him that s him Deut 25:11
Cursed be he that s his neighbour Deut 27:24
He that s Kirjath-sepher, and Josh 15:16
He that s Kirjath-sepher, and Judg 1:12
s the Jebusites, and the lame and 2Sa 5:8
Whosoever s the Jebusites first 1Chr 11:6
he s through the proud Job 26:12
turneth not unto him that s them Is 9:13
his cheek to him that s him Lam 3:30
know that I am the LORD that s Eze 7:9
unto him that s thee on the one Lk 6:29

**SMITH**

Now there was no s found 1Sa 13:19
The s with the tongs both worketh Is 44:12
I have created the s that bloweth Is 54:16

**SMITHS**

and all the craftsmen and s 2Kin 24:14
s a thousand, all that were 2Kin 24:16
Judah, with the carpenters and s Jer 24:1
and the carpenters, and the s Jer 29:2

**SMITING**

he spied an Egyptian s an Hebrew Ex 2:11
a name when he returned from s of 2Sa 8:13
so that in s he wounded him 1Kin 20:37
they went forward s the Moabites 2Kin 3:24
will I make thee sick in s thee Mic 6:13

**SMITTEN**

that the LORD had s the river Ex 7:25
And the flax and the barley was s Ex 9:31
the wheat and the rie were not s Ex 9:32
be s that he die, there shall no Ex 22:2
that ye be not s before your Num 14:42
that thou hast s me these three Num 22:28
Wherefore hast thou s thine ass Num 22:32
which the LORD had s among them Num 33:4
lest ye be s before your enemies Deut 1:42
thee to be s before thy face Deut 28:7
thee to be s before thine enemies Deut 28:25
s it with the edge of the sword, Judg 1:8
They are s down before us, as at Judg 20:32
of Benjamin saw that they were s Judg 20:36
Surely they are s down before us Judg 20:39
battle, Israel was s before the 1Sa 4:2
the LORD s us to day before the 1Sa 4:3
fought, and Israel was s, and they 1Sa 4:10
died not were s with the emerods 1Sa 5:12
because the LORD had s many of 1Sa 6:19
they were s before Israel 1Sa 7:10
s a garrison of the Philistines 1Sa 13:4
s Ziklag, and burned it with fire 1Sa 30:1
of David had s of Benjamin 2Sa 2:31
had s all the host of Hadadezer 2Sa 8:9
against Hadadezer, and s him 2Sa 8:10
that they were s before Israel 2Sa 10:15
that they were s before Israel 2Sa 10:19
ye from him, that he may be s 2Sa 11:15
Israel be s down before the enemy 1Kin 8:33
after he had s every male in Edom 1Kin 11:15
and when he also had s the waters 2Kin 2:14
slain, and they have s one another 2Kin 3:23
have s five or six times 2Kin 13:19
then hadst thou s Syria till thou 2Kin 13:19
Thou hast indeed s Edom, and thine 2Kin 14:10
of Hamath heard how David had s 1Chr 18:9
against Hadarezer, and s him 1Chr 18:10
and they were s 2Chr 20:22
why shouldest thou be s 2Chr 25:16
Lo, thou hast s the Edomites 2Chr 25:19
out, because the LORD had s him 2Chr 26:20
s Judah, and carried away captives 2Chr 28:17
they have s me upon the cheek Job 16:10
for thou hast s all mine enemies Ps 3:7
persecute him whom thou hast s Ps 69:26
My heart is s, and withered like Ps 102:4
he hath s my life down to the Ps 143:3
hand against them, and hath s them Is 5:25
the gate is s with destruction Is 24:12
Hath he s him, as he smote those Is 27:7
stricken, s of God, and afflicted Is 53:4
In vain have I s your children Jer 2:30
why hast thou s us, and there is Jer 14:19
For though ye had s the whole Jer 37:10
therefore I have s mine hand at Eze 22:13
unto me, saying, The city is s Eze 33:21
year after that the city was s Eze 40:1
he hath s, and he will bind us up Hos 6:1
Ephraim is s, their root is dried Hos 9:16
I have s you with blasting and Amos 4:9
me to be s contrary to the law Acts 23:3
the third part of the sun was s Rev 8:12

**SMOKE**

the s of the country went up as Gen 19:28
went up as the s of a furnace Gen 19:28
mount Sinai was altogether on a s Ex 19:18
the s thereof ascended as the Ex 19:18
ascended as the s of a furnace Ex 19:18
jealousy shall s against that man Deut 29:20
the s of the city ascended up to Josh 8:20
that the s of the city ascended, Josh 8:21
with s rise up out of the city Judg 20:38
of the city with a pillar of s Judg 20:40
There went up a s out of his 2Sa 22:9
Out of his nostrils goeth s Job 41:20
There went up a s out of his Ps 18:8
into s shall they consume away Ps 37:20
As s is driven away, so drive Ps 68:2
why doth thine anger s against Ps 74:1
For my days are consumed like s Ps 102:3
he toucheth the hills, and they s Ps 104:32
am become like a bottle in the s Ps 119:83
the mountains, and they shall s Ps 144:5
as s to the eyes, so is the Prov 10:26
the wilderness like pillars of s Song 3:6
s by day, and the shining of a Is 4:5
and the house was filled with s Is 6:4
mount up like the lifting up of s Is 9:18
shall come from the north a s Is 14:31
the s thereof shall go up for Is 34:10
heavens shall vanish away like s Is 51:6
These are a s in my nose, a fire Is 65:5
as the s out of the chimney Hos 13:3
blood, and fire, and pillars of s Joel 2:30
I will burn her chariots in the s Nah 2:13
blood, and fire, and vapour of s Acts 2:19
the s of the incense, which came Rev 8:4
there arose a s out of the pit, Rev 9:2
as the s of a great furnace Rev 9:2
by reason of the s of the pit Rev 9:2
there came out of the s locusts Rev 9:3
of their mouths issued fire and s Rev 9:17
killed, by the fire, and by the s Rev 9:18
the s of their torment ascendeth Rev 14:11
with s from the glory of God Rev 15:8
shall see the s of her burning Rev 18:9
they saw the s of her burning Rev 18:18
her s rose up for ever and ever Rev 19:3

**SMOKING**

it was dark, behold a s furnace Gen 15:17
of the trumpet, and the mountain s Ex 20:18
two tails of these s firebrands Is 7:4
the s flax shall he not quench Is 42:3
s flax shall he not quench, till Mt 12:20

**SMOOTH**

is a hairy man, and I am a s man Gen 27:11
hands, and upon the s of his neck Gen 27:16
chose him five s stones out of 1Sa 17:40
things, speak unto us s things Is 30:10
Among the s stones of the stream Is 57:6
and the rough ways shall be made s Lk 3:5

**SMOOTHER**

of his mouth were s than butter Ps 55:21
and her mouth is s than oil Prov 5:3

**SMOOTHETH**

he that s with the hammer him Is 41:7

**SMOTE**

s the Rephaims in Ashteroth Gen 14:5
and s all the country of the Gen 14:7
s them, and pursued them unto Gen 14:15
they s the men that were at the Gen 19:11
who s Midian in the field of Moab Gen 36:35
s the waters that were in the Ex 7:20
s the dust of the earth, and it Ex 8:17
the hail s throughout all the Ex 9:25
the hail s every herb of the Ex 9:25
when he s the Egyptians, and Ex 12:27
that at midnight the LORD s all Ex 12:29
then shall he that s him be quit Ex 21:19

for on the day that I *s* all the Num 3:13
on the day that I *s* every Num 8:17
the LORD *s* the people with a very Num 11:33
*s* them, and discomfited them, even Num 14:45
with his rod he *s* the rock twice Num 20:11
Israel *s* him with the edge of the Num 21:24
So they *s* him, and his sons, and Num 21:35
Balaam *s* the ass, to turn her Num 22:23
and he *s* her again Num 22:25
he *s* the ass with a staff Num 22:27
and he *s* his hands together Num 24:10
LORD *s* before the congregation of Num 32:4
he that *s* him shall surely be put Num 35:21
we *s* him, and his sons, and all his Deut 2:33
we *s* him until none was left to Deut 3:3
Moses and the children of Israel *s* Deut 4:46
*s* the hindmost of thee, even all Deut 25:18
us unto battle, and we *s* them Deut 29:7
the men of Ai *s* of them about Josh 7:5
and *s* them in the going down Josh 7:5
and they *s* them, so that they let Josh 8:22
*s* it with the edge of the sword Josh 8:24
the children of Israel *s* them not Josh 9:18
*s* them to Azekah, and unto Josh 10:10
And afterward Joshua *s* them Josh 10:26
*s* it with the edge of the sword, Josh 10:28
he *s* it with the edge of the Josh 10:30
*s* it with the edge of the sword, Josh 10:32
and Joshua *s* him and his people, Josh 10:33
*s* it with the edge of the sword, Josh 10:35
*s* it with the edge of the sword, Josh 10:37
they *s* them with the edge of the Josh 10:39
So Joshua *s* all the country of Josh 10:40
Joshua *s* them from Kadesh-barnea Josh 10:41
who *s* them, and chased them unto Josh 11:8
and they *s* them, until they left Josh 11:8
*s* the king thereof with the sword Josh 11:10
they *s* all the souls that were Josh 11:11
*s* them with the edge of the sword Josh 11:12
but every man they *s* with the Josh 11:14
he took, and *s* them, and slew them Josh 11:17
which the children of Israel *s* Josh 12:1
the children of Israel *s* on this Josh 12:7
whom Moses *s* with the princes of Josh 13:21
*s* it with the edge of the sword, Josh 19:47
because he *s* his neighbour Josh 20:5
they *s* the city with the edge of Judg 1:25
*s* Israel, and possessed the city Judg 3:13
*s* the nail into his temples, and Judg 4:21
and with the hammer she *s* Sisera Judg 5:26
she *s* off his head, when she had Judg 5:26
*s* it that it fell, and overturned Judg 7:13
Nobah and Jogbehah, and *s* the host Judg 8:11
rose up against them, and *s* them Judg 9:43
hand of Israel, and they *s* them Judg 11:21
he *s* them from Aroer, even till Judg 11:33
and the men of Gilead *s* Ephraim Judg 12:4
he *s* them hip and thigh with a Judg 15:8
they *s* them with the edge of the Judg 18:27
the LORD *s* Benjamin before Israel Judg 20:35
*s* all the city with the edge of Judg 20:37
*s* them with the edge of the sword Judg 20:48
these are the Gods that *s* the 1Sa 4:8
*s* them with emerods, even Ashdod 1Sa 5:6
he *s* the men of the city, both 1Sa 5:9
that it is not his hand that *s* us 1Sa 6:9
he *s* the men of Beth-shemesh, 1Sa 6:19
even he *s* of the people fifty 1Sa 6:19
*s* them, until they came under 1Sa 7:11
Jonathan *s* the garrison of the 1Sa 13:3
they *s* the Philistines that day 1Sa 14:31
*s* the Amalekites, and delivered 1Sa 14:48
Saul *s* the Amalekites from 1Sa 15:7
*s* him, and delivered it out of his 1Sa 17:35
his beard, and *s* him, and slew him 1Sa 17:35
*s* the Philistine in his forehead, 1Sa 17:49
*s* the Philistine, and slew him 1Sa 17:50
he *s* the javelin into the wall 1Sa 19:10
*s* he with the edge of the sword, 1Sa 22:19
*s* them with a great slaughter 1Sa 23:5
that David's heart *s* him 1Sa 24:5
days after, that the LORD *s* Nabal 1Sa 25:38
David *s* the land, and left neither 1Sa 27:9
David *s* them from the twilight 1Sa 30:17
And he *s* him that he died 2Sa 1:15
spear *s* him under the fifth rib 2Sa 2:23
*s* him there under the fifth rib, 2Sa 3:27
they *s* him under the fifth rib 2Sa 4:6
in his bedchamber, and they *s* him 2Sa 4:7
David *s* them there, and said, The 2Sa 5:20
*s* the Philistines from Geba until 2Sa 5:25
God *s* him there for his error 2Sa 6:7
that David *s* the Philistines, and 2Sa 8:1
he *s* Moab, and measured them with 2Sa 8:2
David *s* also Hadadezer, the son 2Sa 8:3
*s* Shobach the captain of their 2Sa 10:18
Who *s* Abimelech the son of 2Sa 11:21
them, but the one *s* the other 2Sa 14:6
Deliver him that *s* his brother 2Sa 14:7
about and *s* Absalom, and slew him 2Sa 18:15
so he *s* him therewith in the 2Sa 20:10
*s* the Philistine, and killed him 2Sa 21:17
*s* the Philistines until his hand 2Sa 23:10
David's heart *s* him after that he 2Sa 24:10
saw the angel that *s* the people 2Sa 24:17
of Israel, and *s* Ijon, and Dan, and 1Kin 15:20
Baasha *s* him at Gibbethon, which 1Kin 15:27
that he *s* all the house of 1Kin 15:29
*s* him, and killed him, in the 1Kin 16:10
*s* the horses and chariots, and slew 1Kin 20:21
And the man *s* him, so that in 1Kin 20:37
*s* Micaiah on the cheek, and said, 1Kin 22:24
*s* the king of Israel between the 1Kin 22:34
*s* the waters, and they were 2Kin 2:8
*s* the waters, and said, Where is 2Kin 2:14
*s* the Moabites, so that they fled 2Kin 3:24
slingers went about it, and *s* it 2Kin 3:25
And he *s* them with blindness 2Kin 6:18
*s* the Edomites which compassed 2Kin 8:21
*s* Jehoram between his arms, and 2Kin 9:24
they *s* them with the edge of the 2Kin 10:25
Hazael *s* them in all the coasts 2Kin 10:32
his servants, *s* him, and he died 2Kin 12:21
And he *s* thrice, and stayed 2Kin 13:18
And the LORD *s* the king, so that 2Kin 15:5
*s* him before the people, and slew 2Kin 15:10
*s* Shallum the son of Jabesh in 2Kin 15:14
Then Menahem *s* Tiphsah, and all 2Kin 15:16
not to him, therefore he *s* it 2Kin 15:16
*s* him in Samaria, in the palace 2Kin 15:25
*s* him, and slew him, and reigned in 2Kin 15:30
He *s* the Philistines, even unto 2Kin 18:8
*s* in the camp of the Assyrians an 2Kin 19:35
Sharezer his sons *s* him with the 2Kin 19:37
And the king of Babylon *s* them 2Kin 25:21
*s* Gedaliah, that he died, and the 2Kin 25:25
which *s* Midian in the field of 1Chr 1:46
*s* their tents, and the habitations 1Chr 4:41
they *s* the rest of the Amalekites 1Chr 4:43
he *s* him, because he put his hand 1Chr 13:10
and David *s* them there 1Chr 14:11
and they *s* the host of the 1Chr 14:16
that David *s* the Philistines, and 1Chr 18:1
And he *s* Moab 1Chr 18:2
David *s* Hadarezer king of Zobah 1Chr 18:3
Joab *s* Rabbah, and destroyed it 1Chr 20:1
therefore he *s* Israel 1Chr 21:7
came to pass, that God *s* Jeroboam 2Chr 13:15
So the LORD *s* the Ethiopians 2Chr 14:12
they *s* all the cities round about 2Chr 14:14
They *s* also the tents of cattle, 2Chr 14:15
and they *s* Ijon, and Dan, and 2Chr 16:4
*s* Micaiah upon the cheek, and said 2Chr 18:23
*s* the king of Israel between the 2Chr 18:33
*s* the Edomites which compassed 2Chr 21:9
after all this the LORD *s* him in 2Chr 21:18
and the Syrians *s* Joram 2Chr 22:5
*s* of the children of Seir ten 2Chr 25:11
*s* three thousand of them, and took 2Chr 25:13
and they *s* him, and carried away a 2Chr 28:5
who *s* him with a great slaughter 2Chr 28:5
the gods of Damascus, which *s* him 2Chr 28:23
*s* certain of them, and plucked off Neh 13:25
Thus the Jews *s* all their enemies Est 9:5
*s* the four corners of the house, Job 1:19
*s* Job with sore boils from the Job 2:7
*s* of Edom in the valley of salt Ps 60:t
he *s* the rock, that the waters Ps 78:20
*s* down the chosen men of Israel Ps 78:31
*s* all the firstborn in Egypt Ps 78:51
he *s* his enemies in the hinder Ps 78:66
He *s* their vines also and their Ps 105:33
He *s* also all the firstborn in Ps 105:36
Who *s* the firstborn of Egypt, Ps 135:8
Who *s* great nations, and slew Ps 135:10
To him that *s* Egypt in their Ps 136:10
To him which *s* great kings Ps 136:17
the city found me, they *s* me Song 5:7
again stay upon him that *s* them Is 10:20
He who *s* the people in wrath with Is 14:6
rod of him that *s* thee is broken Is 14:29
as he *s* those that Is 27:7
those that *s* him Is 27:7
beaten down, which *s* with a rod Is 30:31
*s* in the camp of the Assyrians an Is 37:36
Sharezer his sons *s* him with the Is 37:38
the hammer him that *s* the anvil Is 41:7
was I wroth, and *s* him Is 57:17
for in my wrath I *s* thee, but in Is 60:10
Then Pashur *s* Jeremiah the Jer 20:2
was instructed, I *s* upon my thigh Jer 31:19
*s* him, and put him in prison in Jer 37:15
*s* Gedaliah the son of Ahikam the Jer 41:2
Nebuchadrezzar king of Babylon *s* Jer 46:2
before that Pharaoh *s* Gaza Jer 47:1
And the king of Babylon *s* them Jer 52:27
which *s* the image upon his feet Dan 2:34
the stone that *s* the image became Dan 2:35
his knees *s* one against another Dan 5:6
*s* the ram, and brake his two horns Dan 8:7
it *s* the gourd that it withered Jonah 4:7
I *s* you with blasting and with Hag 2:17
high priest's, and *s* off his ear Mt 26:51
others *s* him with the palms of Mt 26:67
Christ, Who is he that *s* thee Mt 26:68
the reed, and *s* him on the head Mt 27:30
*s* a servant of the high priest, Mk 14:47
they *s* him on the head with a Mk 15:19
but *s* upon his breast, saying, Lk 18:13
one of them *s* the servant of the Lk 22:50
held Jesus mocked him, and *s* him Lk 22:63
Prophesy, who is it that *s* thee Lk 22:64
*s* their breasts, and returned Lk 23:48
*s* the high priest's servant, and Jn 18:10
they *s* him with their hands Jn 19:3
was oppressed, and *s* the Egyptian Acts 7:24
he *s* Peter on the side, and raised Acts 12:7
the angel of the Lord *s* him Acts 12:23

**SMOTEST**
rod, wherewith thou *s* the river Ex 17:5

**SMYRNA** *(smir'-na) A city of Ionia in Asia Minor.*
unto Ephesus, and unto *S*, and unto Rev 1:11
angel of the church in *S* write Rev 2:8

**SNAIL**
and the lizard, and the *s*, and the Lev 11:30
As a *s* which melteth, let every Ps 58:8

**SNARE**
shall this man be a *s* unto us Ex 10:7
it will surely be a *s* unto thee Ex 23:33
lest it be for a *s* in the midst Ex 34:12
for that will be a *s* unto thee Deut 7:16
their gods shall be a *s* unto you Judg 2:3
thing became a *s* unto Gideon Judg 8:27
her, that she may be a *s* to him 1Sa 18:21
then layest thou a *s* for my life 1Sa 28:9
own feet, and he walketh upon a *s* Job 18:8
The *s* is laid for him in the Job 18:10
table become a *s* before them Ps 69:22
thee from the *s* of the fowler Ps 91:3
which were a *s* unto them Ps 106:36
The wicked have laid a *s* for me Ps 119:110
bird out of the *s* of the fowlers Ps 124:7
the *s* is broken, and we are Ps 124:7
The proud have hid a *s* for me Ps 140:5
have they privily laid a *s* for me Ps 142:3
as a bird hasteth to the *s* Prov 7:23
and his lips are the *s* of his soul Prov 18:7
It is a *s* to the man who Prov 20:25
his ways, and get a *s* to thy soul Prov 22:25
of an evil man there is a *s* Prov 29:6
men bring a city into a *s* Prov 29:8
The fear of man bringeth a *s* Prov 29:25
birds that are caught in the *s* Eccl 9:12
for a *s* to the inhabitants of Is 8:14
Fear, and the pit, and the *s* Is 24:17
the pit shall be taken in the *s* Is 24:18
lay a *s* for him that reproveth in Is 29:21
Fear, and the pit, and the *s* Jer 48:43
the pit shall be taken in the *s* Jer 48:44
I have laid a *s* for thee, and thou Jer 50:24
a *s* is come upon us, desolation Lam 3:47
him, and he shall be taken in my *s* Eze 12:13
him, and he shall be taken in my *s* Eze 17:20
ye have been a *s* on Mizpah Hos 5:1
but the prophet is a *s* of a Hos 9:8
a bird fall in a *s* upon the earth Amos 3:5
one take up a *s* from the earth Amos 3:5
For as a *s* shall it come on all Lk 21:35
Let their table be made a *s* Rom 11:9
not that I may cast a *s* upon you 1Cor 7:35
reproach and the *s* of the devil 1Ti 3:7
rich fall into temptation and a *s* 1Ti 6:9
out of the *s* of the devil 2Ti 2:26

**SNARED**
unto thee, lest thou be *s* therein Deut 7:25
thou be not *s* by following them Deut 12:30
the wicked is *s* in the work of Ps 9:16
Thou art *s* with the words of thy Prov 6:2
The wicked is *s* by the Prov 12:13
the sons of men *s* in an evil time Eccl 9:12
and fall, and be broken, and be *s* Is 8:15
fall backward, and be broken, and *s* Is 28:13
they are all of them *s* in holes Is 42:22

**SNARES**
but they shall be *s* and traps unto Josh 23:13
the *s* of death prevented me 2Sa 22:6
Therefore *s* are round about thee, Job 22:10
his nose pierceth through *s* Job 40:24
Upon the wicked he shall rain *s* Ps 11:6
the *s* of death prevented me Ps 18:5
seek after my life lay *s* for me Ps 38:12
they commune of laying *s* privily Ps 64:5
Keep me from the *s* which they Ps 141:9
to depart from the *s* of death Prov 13:14
to depart from the *s* of death Prov 14:27
*s* are in the way of the froward Prov 22:5
death the woman, whose heart is *s* Eccl 7:26
lay wait, as he that setteth *s* Jer 5:26
to take me, and hid *s* for my feet Jer 18:22

**SNATCH**
he shall *s* on the right hand, and Is 9:20

**SNEEZED**
the child *s* seven times, and the 2Kin 4:35

**SNORTING**
The *s* of his horses was heard Jer 8:16

**SNOUT**
As a jewel of gold in a swine's *s* Prov 11:22

**SNOW**
behold, his hand was leprous as *s* Ex 4:6
Miriam became leprous, white as *s* Num 12:10
the midst of a pit in time of *s* 2Sa 23:20
presence a leper as white as *s* 2Kin 5:27
the ice, and wherein the *s* is hid Job 6:16
If I wash myself with *s* water Job 9:30
and heat consume the *s* waters Job 24:19
For he saith to the *s*, Be thou on Job 37:6
into the treasures of the *s* Job 38:22
me, and I shall be whiter than *s* Ps 51:7
it was white as *s* in Salmon Ps 68:14
He giveth *s* like wool Ps 147:16
Fire, and hail; *s*, and vapours Ps 148:8
As the cold of *s* in the time of Prov 25:13

As s in summer, and as rain in ............ Prov 26:1
afraid of the s for her household........ Prov 31:21
they shall be as white as s.......................... Is 1:18
the s from heaven, and returneth.......... Is 55:10
Will a man leave the s of Lebanon ......... Jer 18:14
Her Nazarites were purer than s............ Lam 4:7
sit, whose garment was white as s.......... Dan 7:9
and his raiment white as s ....................... Mt 28:3
shining, exceeding white as s.................... Mk 9:3
white like wool, as white as s................. Rev 1:14

**SNOWY**
slew a lion in a pit in a s day............. 1Chr 11:22

**SNUFFDISHES**
the s thereof, shall be of pure ................. Ex 25:38
lamps, and his snuffers, and his s............ Ex 37:23
his lamps, and his tongs, and his s ........ Num 4:9

**SNUFFED**
they s up the wind like dragons ............. Jer 14:6
and ye have s at it, saith the.................. Mal 1:13

**SNUFFERS**
he made his seven lamps, and his s....... Ex 37:23
And the bowls, and the s, and the ....... 1Kin 7:50
of the LORD bowls of silver, s............. 2Kin 12:13
pots, and the shovels, and the s.......... 2Kin 25:14
And the s, and the basons, and the..... 2Chr 4:22
also, and the shovels, and the s ............ Jer 52:18

**SNUFFETH**
that s up the wind at her......................... Jer 2:24

**SO** See PREFACE.

**SOAKED**
their land shall be s with blood................ Is 34:7

**SOBER**
or whether we be s, it is for ................ 2Cor 5:13
but let us watch and be s.......................... 1Th 5:6
let us, who are of the day, be s ............... 1Th 5:8
husband of one wife, vigilant, s.............. 1Ti 3:2
wives be grave, not slanderers, s............ 1Ti 3:11
a lover of good men, s, just,..................... Titus 1:8
That the aged men be s, grave,.................. Titus 2:2
may teach the young women to be s ... Titus 2:4
likewise exhort to be s minded.............. Titus 2:6
up the loins of your mind, be s............. 1Pet 1:13
be ye therefore s, and watch unto........... 1Pet 4:7
Be s, be vigilant........................................ 1Pet 5:8

**SOBERLY**
but to think s, according as God.......... Rom 12:3
worldly lusts, we should live s............. Titus 2:12

**SOBERNESS**
forth the words of truth and s.......... Acts 26:25

**SOBRIETY**
apparel, with shamefacedness and s......... 1Ti 2:9
and charity and holiness with s............... 1Ti 2:15

**SOCHO** (*so'-ko*) See SOCHOH. *A son of Heber.*
Gedor, and Heber the father of S........... 1Chr 4:18

**SOCHOH** (*so'-ko*) See SHOCHOH, SOCHO, SOCOH. *A city in Judah near Adullam.*
to him pertained S, and all the ............ 1Kin 4:10

**SOCKET**
hundred talents, a talent for a s ............ Ex 38:27

**SOCKETS**
thou shalt make forty s of silver............ Ex 26:19
two s under one board for his two ......... Ex 26:19
two s under another board for his......... Ex 26:19
And their forty s of silver........................ Ex 26:21
two s under one board............................. Ex 26:21
two s under another board ...................... Ex 26:21
s of silver, sixteen s ................................ Ex 26:25
two s under one board.............................. Ex 26:25
two s under another board ...................... Ex 26:25
gold, upon the four s of silver................. Ex 26:32
cast five s of brass for them ................... Ex 26:37
their twenty s shall be of brass............... Ex 27:10
and their twenty s of brass....................... Ex 27:11
their pillars ten, and their s ten............ Ex 27:12
pillars three, and their s three................ Ex 27:14
pillars three, and their s three................ Ex 27:15
shall be four, and their s four................. Ex 27:16
be of silver, and their s of brass ............ Ex 27:17
twined linen, and their s of brass........... Ex 27:18
his bars, his pillars, and his s................. Ex 35:11
court, his pillars, and their s.................. Ex 35:17
forty s of silver he made under............... Ex 36:24
two s under one board for his two ......... Ex 36:24
two s under another board for his.......... Ex 36:24
And their forty s of silver....................... Ex 36:26
two s under one board............................. Ex 36:26
two s under another board ...................... Ex 36:26
s were sixteen s of silver......................... Ex 36:30
under every board two s........................... Ex 36:30
he cast for them four s of silver............. Ex 36:36
but their five s were of brass.................. Ex 36:38
twenty, and their brasen s twenty.......... Ex 38:10
and their s of brass twenty...................... Ex 38:11
their pillars ten, and their s ten............ Ex 38:12
pillars three, and their s three.............. Ex 38:14
pillars three, and their s three............... Ex 38:15
the s for the pillars were of.................... Ex 38:17
four, and their s of brass four ................ Ex 38:19
were cast the s of the sanctuary ............ Ex 38:27
and the s of the vail ................................. Ex 38:27
an hundred s of the hundred................... Ex 38:27
therewith he made the s to the ............. Ex 38:30
the s of the court round about, ............. Ex 38:31
the s of the court gate, and all .............. Ex 38:31
bars, and his pillars, and his s ............... Ex 39:33
the court, his pillars, and his s.............. Ex 39:40
the tabernacle, and fastened his s......... Ex 40:18
the s thereof, and all the vessels.......... Num 3:36
the court round about, and their s ....... Num 3:37
pillars thereof, and s thereof,................ Num 4:31
the court round about, and their s ...... Num 4:32
marble, set upon s of fine gold ............ Song 5:15

**SOCOH** (*so'-ko*) See SOCHOH.
*1. Same as Sochoh.*
Jarmuth, and Adullam, S....................... Josh 15:35
*2. A city in the hill country of Judah.*
Shamir, and Jattir, and S,...................... Josh 15:48

**SOD**
And Jacob s pottage.............................. Gen 25:29
holy offerings s they in pots.................. 2Chr 35:13

**SODDEN**
nor s at all with water, but..................... Ex 12:9
wherein it is s shall be broken ............... Lev 6:28
if it be s in a brasen pot, it..................... Lev 6:28
take the s shoulder of the ram ............ Num 6:19
he will not have s flesh of thee............... 1Sa 2:15
women have s their own children ........ Lam 4:10

**SODERING**
saying, It is ready for the s........................ Is 41:7

**SODI** (*so'-di*) *A spy sent to the Promised Land.*
of Zebulun, Gaddiel the son of S ...... Num 13:10

**SODOM** (*sod'-om*) See SODOMA, SODOMITE. *A city on the Salt Sea.*
as thou goest, unto S, and ................... Gen 10:19
before the LORD destroyed S ................. Gen 13:10
and pitched his tent toward S............... Gen 13:12
But the men of S were wicked.............. Gen 13:13
made war with Bera king of S ............... Gen 14:2
And there went out the king of S......... Gen 14:8
and the kings of S and Gomorrah....... Gen 14:10
And they took all the goods of S......... Gen 14:11
brother's son, who dwelt in S............... Gen 14:12
the king of S went out to meet ........... Gen 14:17
the king of S said unto Abram,............ Gen 14:21
And Abram said to the king of S ....... Gen 14:22
from thence, and looked toward S...... Gen 18:16
LORD said, Because the cry of S........... Gen 18:20
from thence, and went toward S.......... Gen 18:22
If I find in S fifty righteous ................ Gen 18:26
came two angels to S at even ............... Gen 19:1
and Lot sat in the gate of S................. Gen 19:1
of the city, even the men of S.............. Gen 19:4
Then the LORD rained upon S............. Gen 19:24
toward S and Gomorrah....................... Gen 19:28
therein, like the overthrow of S ......... Deut 29:23
their vine is of the vine of S.............. Deut 32:32
remnant, we should have been as S.......... Is 1:9
word of the LORD, ye rulers of S............. Is 1:10
and they declare their sin as S................. Is 3:9
shall be as when God overthrew S......... Is 13:19
they are all of them unto me as S......... Jer 23:14
As in the overthrow of S and............... Jer 49:18
overthrew S and Gomorrah.................. Jer 50:40
the punishment of the sin of S.............. Lam 4:6
dwelleth at thy right hand, is S........... Eze 16:46
S thy sister hath not done, she........... Eze 16:48
was the iniquity of thy sister S........... Eze 16:49
captivity, the captivity of S ................ Eze 16:53
When thy sisters, S and her ............... Eze 16:55
For thy sister S was not ..................... Eze 16:56
some of you, as God overthrew S ...... Amos 4:11
Israel, Surely Moab shall be as S.......... Zeph 2:9
more tolerable for the land of S .......... Mt 10:15
done in thee, had been done in S ......... Mt 11:23
land of S in the day of judgment.......... Mt 11:24
It shall be more tolerable for S ............ Mk 6:11
more tolerable in that day for S............ Lk 10:12
Lot went out of S it rained fire.............. Lk 17:29
And turning the cities of S ................... 2Pet 2:6
Even as S and Gomorrha, and the ........... Jude 7
which spiritually is called S................... Rev 11:8

**SODOMA** (*sod'-o-mah*) See SODOM. *Greek form of Sodom.*
left us a seed, we had been as S.......... Rom 9:29

**SODOMITE**
nor a s of the sons of Israel................. Deut 23:17

**SODOMITES**
And there were also s in the land ...... 1Kin 14:24
took away the s out of the land .......... 1Kin 15:12
And the remnant of the s, which ....... 1Kin 22:46

**SOEVER**
what saddle s he rideth upon that ........ Lev 15:9
What man s there be of the house ........ Lev 17:3
What man s of the seed of Aaron.......... Lev 22:4
What thing s I command you,............. Deut 12:32
that what thing s thou shalt hear ........ 2Sa 15:35
the people, how many s they be............ 2Sa 24:3
supplication s be made by any man..... 1Kin 8:38
s shall be made of any man................. 2Chr 6:29
what cause s shall come to you of..... 2Chr 19:10
wherewith s they shall blaspheme.......... Mk 3:28
In what place s ye enter into a .............. Mk 6:10
unto you, What things s ye desire........ Mk 11:24
for what things s he doeth ....................... Jn 5:19
Whose s sins ye remit, they are............. Jn 20:23
whose s sins ye retain, they are ............ Jn 20:23
that what things s the law saith........... Rom 3:19

**SOFT**
For God maketh my heart s .................. Job 23:16
will he speak s words unto thee ........... Job 41:3
thou makest it s with showers................. Ps 65:10
A s answer turneth away wrath .......... Prov 15:1
a s tongue breaketh the bone............. Prov 25:15
A man clothed in s raiment.................... Mt 11:8
they that wear s clothing are in............. Mt 11:8
A man clothed in s raiment...................... Lk 7:25

**SOFTER**
his words were s than oil.......................... Ps 55:21

**SOFTLY**
and I will lead on s, according as........... Gen 33:14
went s unto him, and smote the........... Judg 4:21
and she came s, and uncovered his....... Ruth 3:7
and lay in sackcloth, and went s........ 1Kin 21:27
the waters of Shiloah that go s .................. Is 8:6
I shall go s all my years in the................ Is 38:15
And when the south wind blew s...... Acts 27:13

**SOIL**
in a good s by great waters .................... Eze 17:8

**SOJOURN**
went down into Egypt to s there......... Gen 12:10
This one fellow came in to s.................... Gen 19:9
S in this land, and I will be with ........... Gen 26:3
For to s in the land are we come ........... Gen 47:4
when a stranger shall s with thee.......... Ex 12:48
the strangers which s among you .......... Lev 17:8
of the strangers that s among you......... Lev 17:10
of the strangers that s among you....... Lev 17:13
if a stranger s with thee in your.......... Lev 19:33
of the strangers that s in Israel ............ Lev 20:2
the strangers that do s among you...... Lev 25:45
if a stranger shall s among you ........... Num 9:14
And if a stranger s with you ............. Num 15:14
to s where he could find a place.......... Judg 17:8
I go to s where I may find a................. Judg 17:9
went to s in the country of Moab........... Ruth 1:1
evil upon the widow with whom I s.. 1Kin 17:20
s wheresoever thou canst s...................... 2Kin 8:1
that I s in Mesech, that I dwell............. Ps 120:5
shall carry her afar off to s .................... Is 23:7
aforetime into Egypt to s there.................. Is 52:4
into Egypt, and go to s there................. Jer 42:15
faces to go into Egypt to s there .......... Jer 42:17
whither ye desire to go and to s ........... Jer 42:22
say, Go not into Egypt to s there............ Jer 43:2
into the land of Egypt to s there .......... Jer 44:12
into the land of Egypt to s there .......... Jer 44:14
into the land of Egypt to s there .......... Jer 44:28
They shall no more s there.................... Lam 4:15
out of the country where they s........... Eze 20:38
to the strangers that s among you....... Eze 47:22
seed should s in a strange land .............. Acts 7:6

**SOJOURNED**
Kadesh and Shur, and s in Gerar .......... Gen 20:1
to the land wherein thou hast s........... Gen 21:23
Abraham s in the Philistines'............... Gen 21:34
I have s with Laban, and stayed............ Gen 32:4
Hebron, where Abraham and Isaac s . Gen 35:27
out of all Israel, where he s................... Deut 18:6
s there with a few, and became............ Deut 26:5
who was a Levite, and he s there......... Judg 17:7
and he s in Gibeah.............................. Judg 19:16
s in the land of the Philistines................ 2Kin 8:2
Jacob s in the land of Ham ................... Ps 105:23
By faith he s in the land of .................... Heb 11:9

**SOJOURNER**
I am a stranger and a s with you.......... Gen 23:4
a s of the priest, or an hired ................ Lev 22:10
though he be a stranger, or a s.............. Lev 25:35
as an hired servant, and as a s.............. Lev 25:40
if a s or stranger wax rich by................ Lev 25:47
unto the stranger or s by thee .............. Lev 25:47
stranger, and for the s among them.. Num 35:15
I am a stranger with thee, and a s ........ Ps 39:12

**SOJOURNERS**
for ye are strangers and s with me...... Lev 25:23
were s there until this day .......................... 2Sa 4:3
are strangers before thee, and s ......... 1Chr 29:15

**SOJOURNETH**
of her that s in her house, ........................ Ex 3:22
the stranger that s among you ............... Ex 12:49
or a stranger that s among you ............ Lev 16:29
that s among you eat blood..................... Lev 17:12
nor any stranger that s among you....... Lev 18:26
for thy stranger that s with thee............. Lev 25:6
for the stranger that s with you.......... Num 15:15
for the stranger that s with you.......... Num 15:16
and the stranger that s among them Num 15:26
the stranger that s among them........ Num 15:29
the stranger that s among them........ Num 19:10
the stranger that s among them .......... Josh 20:9
remaineth in any place where he s .......... Ezr 1:4
of the stranger that s in Israel ............ Eze 14:7
that in what tribe the stranger s .......... Eze 47:23

**SOJOURNING**
Now the s of the children of ................. Ex 12:40
s on the side of mount Ephraim .......... Judg 19:1
the time of your s here in fear............. 1Pet 1:17

**SOLACE**
let us s ourselves with loves .................. Prov 7:18

**SOLD**
he s his birthright unto Jacob............ Gen 25:33
for he hath s us, and hath quite .......... Gen 31:15

*s* Joseph to the Ishmeelites for ... Gen 37:28
the Midianites *s* him into Egypt ... Gen 37:36
and *s* unto the Egyptians ... Gen 41:56
he it was that *s* to all the ... Gen 42:6
brother, whom ye *s* into Egypt ... Gen 45:4
yourselves, that ye *s* me hither ... Gen 45:5
for the Egyptians *s* every man his ... Gen 47:20
wherefore they *s* not their lands ... Gen 47:22
then he shall be *s* for his theft ... Ex 22:3
The land shall not be *s* for ever ... Lev 25:23
poor, and hath *s* away some of his ... Lev 25:25
redeem that which his brother *s* ... Lev 25:25
unto the man to whom he *s* it ... Lev 25:27
then that which is *s* shall remain ... Lev 25:28
within a whole year after it is *s* ... Lev 25:29
then the house that was *s* ... Lev 25:33
of their cities may not be *s* ... Lev 25:34
be waxen poor, and be *s* unto thee ... Lev 25:39
they shall not be *s* as bondmen ... Lev 25:42
After that he is *s* he may be ... Lev 25:48
him from the year that he was *s* ... Lev 25:50
or if he have *s* the field to ... Lev 27:20
then it shall be *s* according to ... Lev 27:27
shall be *s* or redeemed ... Lev 27:28
be *s* unto thee, and serve thee six ... Deut 15:12
there ye shall be *s* unto your ... Deut 28:68
except their Rock had *s* them ... Deut 32:30
he *s* them into the hands of their ... Judg 2:14
he *s* them into the hand of ... Judg 3:8
the LORD *s* them into the hand of ... Judg 4:2
he *s* them into the hands of the ... Judg 10:7
he *s* them into the hand of Sisera ... 1Sa 12:9
because thou hast *s* thyself to ... 1Kin 21:20
until an ass's head was *s* for ... 2Kin 6:25
of fine flour be *s* for a shekel ... 2Kin 7:1
of fine flour was *s* for a shekel ... 2Kin 7:16
*s* themselves to do evil in the ... 2Kin 17:17
which were *s* unto the heathen ... Neh 5:8
or shall they be *s* unto us ... Neh 5:8
the day wherein they *s* victuals ... Neh 13:15
*s* on the sabbath unto the ... Neh 13:16
For we are *s*, I and my people, to ... Est 7:4
But if we had been *s* for bondmen ... Est 7:4
Joseph, who was *s* for a servant ... Ps 105:17
is it to whom I have *s* you ... Is 50:1
iniquities have ye *s* yourselves ... Is 50:1
Ye have *s* yourselves for nought ... Is 52:3
which hath been *s* unto thee ... Jer 34:14
our wood is *s* unto us ... Lam 5:4
not return to that which is *s* ... Eze 7:13
*s* a girl for wine, that they ... Joel 3:3
have ye *s* unto the Grecians ... Joel 3:6
the place whither ye have *s* them ... Joel 3:7
because they *s* the righteous for ... Amos 2:6
not two sparrows *s* for a farthing ... Mt 10:29
*s* all that he had, and bought it ... Mt 13:46
his lord commanded him to be *s* ... Mt 18:25
God, and cast out all them that *s* ... Mt 21:12
and the seats of them that *s* doves ... Mt 21:12
might have been *s* for much ... Mt 26:9
and began to cast out them that *s* ... Mk 11:15
and the seats of them that *s* doves ... Mk 11:15
For it might have been *s* for more ... Mk 14:5
five sparrows *s* for two farthings ... Lk 12:6
they drank, they bought, they *s* ... Lk 17:28
to cast out them that *s* therein ... Lk 19:45
in the temple those that *s* oxen ... Jn 2:14
And said unto them that *s* doves ... Jn 2:16
*s* for three hundred pence ... Jn 12:5
*s* their possessions and goods, and ... Acts 2:45
of lands or houses *s* them ... Acts 4:34
prices of the things that were *s* ... Acts 4:34
*s* it, and brought the money, and ... Acts 4:37
his wife, *s* a possession, ... Acts 5:1
and after it was *s*, was it not in ... Acts 5:4
Tell me whether ye *s* the land for ... Acts 5:8
with envy, *s* Joseph into Egypt ... Acts 7:9
but I am carnal, *s* under sin ... Rom 7:14
Whatsoever is *s* in the shambles, ... 1Cor 10:25
morsel of meat *s* his birthright ... Heb 12:16

**SOLDIER**

four parts, to every *s* a part ... Jn 19:23
a devout *s* of them that waited on ... Acts 10:7
by himself with a *s* that kept him ... Acts 28:16
companion in labour, and fellow *s* ... Phil 2:25
as a good *s* of Jesus Christ ... 2Ti 2:3
him who hath chosen him to be a *s* ... 2Ti 2:4

**SOLDIERS**

fathers, were bands of *s* for war ... 1Chr 7:4
thousand and two hundred *s* ... 1Chr 7:11
But the *s* of the army which ... 2Chr 25:13
require of the king a band of *s* ... Ezr 8:22
therefore the armed *s* of Moab ... Is 15:4
authority, having *s* under me ... Mt 8:9
Then the *s* of the governor took ... Mt 27:27
unto him the whole band of *s* ... Mt 27:27
they gave large money unto the *s* ... Mt 28:12
the *s* led him away into the hall, ... Mk 15:16
the *s* likewise demanded of him, ... Lk 3:14
authority, having under me *s* ... Lk 7:8
the *s* also mocked him, coming to ... Lk 23:36
the *s* platted a crown of thorns, ... Jn 19:2
Then the *s*, when they had ... Jn 19:23
These things therefore the *s* did ... Jn 19:24
Then came the *s*, and brake the ... Jn 19:32
But one of the *s* with a spear ... Jn 19:34
four quaternions of *s* to keep him ... Acts 12:4
Peter was sleeping between two *s* ... Acts 12:6
was no small stir among the *s* ... Acts 12:18
Who immediately took *s* and ... Acts 21:32
saw the chief captain and the *s* ... Acts 21:32
that he was borne of the *s* for ... Acts 21:35
them, commanded the *s* to go down ... Acts 23:10
two hundred *s* to go to Caesarea ... Acts 23:23
Then the *s*, as it was commanded ... Acts 23:31
said to the centurion and to the *s* ... Acts 27:31
Then the *s* cut off the ropes of ... Acts 27:32

**SOLDIERS'**

the *s* counsel was to kill the ... Acts 27:42

**SOLE**

no rest for the *s* of her foot ... Gen 8:9
from the *s* of thy foot unto the ... Deut 28:35
would not adventure to set the *s* ... Deut 28:56
neither shall the *s* of thy foot ... Deut 28:65
Every place that the *s* of your ... Josh 1:3
from the *s* of his foot even to ... 2Sa 14:25
with the *s* of my feet have I ... 2Kin 19:24
the *s* of his foot unto his crown ... Job 2:7
From the *s* of the foot even unto ... Is 1:6
with the *s* of my feet have I ... Is 37:25
the *s* of their feet was like the ... Eze 1:7
was like the *s* of a calf's foot ... Eze 1:7

**SOLEMN**

it is a *s* assembly ... Lev 23:36
your gladness, and in your *s* days ... Num 10:10
offering, or in your *s* feasts ... Num 15:3
day ye shall have a *s* assembly ... Num 29:35
a *s* assembly to the LORD thy God ... Deut 16:8
Seven days shalt thou keep a *s* ... Deut 16:15
Proclaim a *s* assembly for Baal ... 2Kin 10:20
on the *s* feasts of the LORD our ... 2Chr 2:4
eighth day they made a *s* assembly ... 2Chr 7:9
the new moons, and on the *s* feasts ... 2Chr 8:13
the eighth day was a *s* assembly ... Neh 8:18
appointed, on our *s* feast day ... Ps 81:3
upon the harp with a *s* sound ... Ps 92:3
is iniquity, even the *s* meeting ... Is 1:13
because none come to the *s* feasts ... Lam 1:4
the LORD hath caused the *s* feasts ... Lam 2:6
LORD, as in the day of a *s* feast ... Lam 2:7
Thou hast called as in a *s* day my ... Lam 2:22
of Jerusalem in her *s* feasts ... Eze 36:38
before the LORD in the *s* feasts ... Eze 46:9
her sabbaths, and all her *s* feasts ... Hos 2:11
What will ye do in the *s* day ... Hos 9:5
as in the days of the *s* feast ... Hos 12:9
call a *s* assembly, gather the ... Joel 1:14
a fast, call a *s* assembly ... Joel 2:15
not smell in your *s* assemblies ... Amos 5:21
O Judah, keep thy *s* feasts ... Nah 1:15
are sorrowful for the *s* assembly ... Zeph 3:18
even the dung of your *s* feasts ... Mal 2:3

**SOLEMNITIES**

Look upon Zion, the city of our *s* ... Is 33:20
in all *s* of the house of Israel ... Eze 45:17
in the *s* the meat offering shall ... Eze 46:11

**SOLEMNITY**

in the *s* of the year of release, ... Deut 31:10
the night when a holy *s* is kept ... Is 30:29

**SOLEMNLY**

The man did *s* protest unto us, ... Gen 43:3
howbeit yet protest *s* unto them ... 1Sa 8:9

**SOLES**

Every place whereon the *s* of your ... Deut 11:24
as soon as the *s* of the feet of ... Josh 3:13
the *s* of the priests' feet were ... Josh 4:18
put them under the *s* of his feet ... 1Kin 5:3
down at the *s* of thy feet ... Is 60:14
and the place of the *s* of my feet ... Eze 43:7
they shall be ashes under the *s* ... Mal 4:3

**SOLITARILY**

which dwell *s* in the wood ... Mic 7:14

**SOLITARY**

Lo, let that night be *s* ... Job 3:7
For want and famine they were *s* ... Job 30:3
God setteth the *s* in families ... Ps 68:6
in the wilderness in a *s* way ... Ps 107:4
the *s* place shall be glad for ... Is 35:1
How doth the city sit *s*, that was ... Lam 1:1
out, and departed into a *s* place ... Mk 1:35

**SOLOMON** (*sol'-o-mun*) See JEDIDIAH, SOLOMON'S. *Son of David; king of Israel.*

and Shobab, and Nathan, and *S* ... 2Sa 5:14
a son, and he called his name *S* ... 2Sa 12:24
*S* his brother, he called not ... 1Kin 1:10
unto Bath-sheba the mother of *S* ... 1Kin 1:11
life, and the life of thy son *S* ... 1Kin 1:12
Assuredly *S* thy son shall reign ... 1Kin 1:13
Assuredly *S* thy son shall reign ... 1Kin 1:17
but *S* thy servant hath he not ... 1Kin 1:19
my son *S* shall be counted ... 1Kin 1:21
son of Jehoiada, and thy servant *S* ... 1Kin 1:26
Assuredly *S* thy son shall reign ... 1Kin 1:30
cause *S* my son to ride upon mine ... 1Kin 1:33
trumpet, and say, God save king *S* ... 1Kin 1:34
the king, even so be he with *S* ... 1Kin 1:37
caused *S* to ride upon king ... 1Kin 1:38
of the tabernacle, and anointed *S* ... 1Kin 1:39
the people said, God save king *S* ... 1Kin 1:39
lord king David hath made *S* king ... 1Kin 1:43
also *S* sitteth on the throne of ... 1Kin 1:46
name of *S* better than thy name ... 1Kin 1:47
And Adonijah feared because of *S* ... 1Kin 1:50
And it was told *S*, saying, Behold, ... 1Kin 1:51
Behold, Adonijah feareth king *S* ... 1Kin 1:51
Let king *S* swear unto me to day ... 1Kin 1:51
*S* said, If he will shew himself a ... 1Kin 1:52
So king *S* sent, and they brought ... 1Kin 1:53
came and bowed himself to king *S* ... 1Kin 1:53
*S* said unto him, Go to thine ... 1Kin 1:53
and he charged *S* his son, saying, ... 1Kin 2:1
Then sat *S* upon the throne of ... 1Kin 2:12
to Bath-sheba the mother of *S* ... 1Kin 2:13
unto *S* the king, (for he will not ... 1Kin 2:17
therefore went unto king *S* ... 1Kin 2:19
king *S* answered and said unto his ... 1Kin 2:22
Then king *S* sware by the LORD, ... 1Kin 2:23
king *S* sent by the hand of ... 1Kin 2:25
So *S* thrust out Abiathar from ... 1Kin 2:27
it was told king *S* that Joab was ... 1Kin 2:29
Then *S* sent Benaiah the son of ... 1Kin 2:29
it was told *S* that Shimei had ... 1Kin 2:41
king *S* shall be blessed, and the ... 1Kin 2:45
was established in the hand of *S* ... 1Kin 2:46
*S* made affinity with Pharaoh king ... 1Kin 3:1
*S* loved the LORD, walking in the ... 1Kin 3:3
did *S* offer upon that altar ... 1Kin 3:4
appeared to *S* in a dream by night ... 1Kin 3:5
*S* said, Thou hast shewed unto thy ... 1Kin 3:6
that *S* had asked this thing ... 1Kin 3:10
And *S* awoke ... 1Kin 3:15
So king *S* was king over all ... 1Kin 4:1
*S* had twelve officers over all ... 1Kin 4:7
Taphath the daughter of *S* to wife ... 1Kin 4:11
Basmath the daughter of *S* to wife ... 1Kin 4:15
*S* reigned over all kingdoms from ... 1Kin 4:21
served *S* all the days of his life ... 1Kin 4:21
to Beer-sheba, all the days of *S* ... 1Kin 4:25
*S* had forty thousand stalls of ... 1Kin 4:26
provided victual for king *S* ... 1Kin 4:27
And God gave *S* wisdom and ... 1Kin 4:29
people to hear the wisdom of *S* ... 1Kin 4:34
of Tyre sent his servants unto *S* ... 1Kin 5:1
And *S* sent to Hiram, saying, ... 1Kin 5:2
when Hiram heard the words of *S* ... 1Kin 5:7
And Hiram sent to *S*, saying, I ... 1Kin 5:8
So Hiram gave *S* cedar trees ... 1Kin 5:10
*S* gave Hiram twenty thousand ... 1Kin 5:11
thus gave *S* to Hiram year by year ... 1Kin 5:11
And the LORD gave *S* wisdom ... 1Kin 5:12
was peace between Hiram and *S* ... 1Kin 5:12
king *S* raised a levy out of all ... 1Kin 5:13
*S* had threescore and ten thousand ... 1Kin 5:15
which king *S* built for the LORD ... 1Kin 6:2
And the word of the LORD came to *S* . 1Kin 6:11
So *S* built the house, and finished ... 1Kin 6:14
So *S* overlaid the house within ... 1Kin 6:21
But *S* was building his own house ... 1Kin 7:1
*S* made also an house for ... 1Kin 7:8
And king *S* sent and fetched Hiram ... 1Kin 7:13
And he came to king *S*, and wrought . 1Kin 7:14
king *S* for the house of the LORD ... 1Kin 7:40
which Hiram made to king *S* for ... 1Kin 7:45
*S* left all the vessels unweighed, ... 1Kin 7:47
*S* made all the vessels that ... 1Kin 7:48
ended all the work that king *S* ... 1Kin 7:51
*S* brought in the things which ... 1Kin 7:51
Then *S* assembled the elders of ... 1Kin 8:1
unto king *S* in Jerusalem, that ... 1Kin 8:1
king *S* at the feast in the month ... 1Kin 8:2
And king *S*, and all the ... 1Kin 8:5
Then spake *S*, The LORD said that ... 1Kin 8:12
*S* stood before the altar of the ... 1Kin 8:22
that when *S* had made an end of ... 1Kin 8:54
*S* offered a sacrifice of peace ... 1Kin 8:63
And at that time *S* held a feast ... 1Kin 8:65
when *S* had finished the building ... 1Kin 9:1
appeared to *S* the second time ... 1Kin 9:2
when *S* had built the two houses, ... 1Kin 9:10
had furnished *S* with cedar trees ... 1Kin 9:11
that then king *S* gave Hiram ... 1Kin 9:11
the cities which *S* had given him ... 1Kin 9:12
of the levy which king *S* raised ... 1Kin 9:15
*S* built Gezer, and Beth-horon the ... 1Kin 9:17
the cities of store that *S* had ... 1Kin 9:19
that which *S* desired to build in ... 1Kin 9:19
upon those did *S* levy a tribute ... 1Kin 9:21
of Israel did *S* make no bondmen ... 1Kin 9:22
house which *S* had built for her ... 1Kin 9:24
year did *S* offer burnt offerings ... 1Kin 9:25
king *S* made a navy of ships in ... 1Kin 9:26
the sea, with the servants of *S* ... 1Kin 9:27
talents, and brought it to king *S* ... 1Kin 9:28
of Sheba heard of the fame of *S* ... 1Kin 10:1
and when she was come to *S* ... 1Kin 10:2
*S* told her all her questions ... 1Kin 10:3
the queen of Sheba gave to king *S* ... 1Kin 10:10
king *S* gave unto the queen of ... 1Kin 10:13
beside that which *S* gave her of ... 1Kin 10:13
to *S* in one year was six hundred ... 1Kin 10:14
king *S* made two hundred targets ... 1Kin 10:16
accounted of in the days of *S* ... 1Kin 10:21
So king *S* exceeded all the kings ... 1Kin 10:23
And all the earth sought to *S* ... 1Kin 10:24
*S* gathered together chariots and ... 1Kin 10:26
*S* had horses brought out of Egypt ... 1Kin 10:28
But king *S* loved many strange ... 1Kin 11:1
*S* clave unto these in love ... 1Kin 11:2
when *S* was old, that his wives ... 1Kin 11:4
For *S* went after Ashtoreth the ... 1Kin 11:5
*S* did evil in the sight of the ... 1Kin 11:6
Then did *S* build an high place ... 1Kin 11:7
And the LORD was angry with *S* ... 1Kin 11:9
Wherefore the LORD said unto *S* ... 1Kin 11:11
stirred up an adversary unto *S* ... 1Kin 11:14
to Israel all the days of *S* ... 1Kin 11:25

S

*S* built Millo, and repaired the 1Kin 11:27
*S* seeing the young man that he 1Kin 11:28
the kingdom out of the hand of *S* 1Kin 11:31
*S* sought therefore to kill 1Kin 11:40
was in Egypt until the death of *S* 1Kin 11:40
And the rest of the acts of *S* 1Kin 11:41
in the book of the acts of *S* 1Kin 11:41
the time that *S* reigned in 1Kin 11:42
*S* slept with his fathers, and was 1Kin 11:43
fled from the presence of king *S* 1Kin 12:2
that stood before *S* his father 1Kin 12:6
again to Rehoboam the son of *S* 1Kin 12:21
Speak unto Rehoboam, the son of *S* 1Kin 12:23
the son of *S* reigned in Judah 1Kin 14:21
shields of gold which *S* had made 1Kin 14:26
to *S* his son, In this house, and 2Kin 21:7
which *S* the king of Israel had 2Kin 23:13
all the vessels of gold which *S* 2Kin 24:13
the bases which *S* had made for 2Kin 25:16
and Shobab, and Nathan, and *S* 1Chr 3:5
temple that *S* built in Jerusalem 1Chr 6:10
until *S* had built the house of 1Chr 6:32
and Shobab, Nathan, and *S* 1Chr 14:4
wherewith *S* made the brasen sea, 1Chr 18:8
*S* my son is young and tender, and 1Chr 22:5
Then he called for *S* his son 1Chr 22:6
And David said to *S*, My son, as 1Chr 22:7
for his name shall be *S*, and I 1Chr 22:9
of Israel to help *S* his son 1Chr 22:17
he made *S* his son king over 1Chr 23:1
he hath chosen *S* my son to sit 1Chr 28:5
*S* thy son, he shall build my 1Chr 28:6
*S* my son, know thou the God of 1Chr 28:9
Then David gave to *S* his son the 1Chr 28:11
And David said to *S* his son 1Chr 28:20
*S* my son, whom alone God hath 1Chr 29:1
give unto *S* my son a perfect 1Chr 29:19
they made *S* the son of David king 1Chr 29:22
Then *S* sat on the throne of the 1Chr 29:23
themselves unto *S* the king 1Chr 29:24
the LORD magnified *S* exceedingly 1Chr 29:25
*S* his son reigned in his stead 1Chr 29:28
And *S* the son of David was 2Chr 1:1
Then *S* spake unto all Israel, to 2Chr 1:2
So *S*, and all the congregation 2Chr 1:3
and *S* and the congregation sought 2Chr 1:5
*S* went up thither to the brasen 2Chr 1:6
that night did God appear unto *S* 2Chr 1:7
*S* said unto God, Thou hast shewed 2Chr 1:8
And God said to *S*, Because this 2Chr 1:11
Then *S* came from his journey to 2Chr 1:13
*S* gathered chariots and horsemen 2Chr 1:14
*S* had horses brought out of Egypt 2Chr 1:16
*S* determined to build an house 2Chr 2:1
*S* told out threescore and ten 2Chr 2:2
*S* sent to Huram the king of Tyre, 2Chr 2:3
in writing, which he sent to *S* 2Chr 2:11
*S* numbered all the strangers that 2Chr 2:17
Then *S* began to build the house 2Chr 3:1
these are the things wherein *S* 2Chr 3:3
for king *S* for the house of God 2Chr 4:11
*S* for the house of the LORD of 2Chr 4:16
Thus *S* made all these vessels in 2Chr 4:18
*S* made all the vessels that were 2Chr 4:19
Thus all the work that *S* made for 2Chr 5:1
*S* brought in all the things that 2Chr 5:1
Then *S* assembled the elders of 2Chr 5:2
Also king *S*, and all the 2Chr 5:6
Then said *S*, The LORD hath said 2Chr 6:1
For *S* had made a brasen scaffold, 2Chr 6:13
Now when *S* had made an end of 2Chr 7:1
king *S* offered a sacrifice of 2Chr 7:5
Moreover *S* hallowed the middle of 2Chr 7:7
which *S* had made was not able to 2Chr 7:7
Also at the same time *S* kept the 2Chr 7:8
had shewed unto David, and to *S* 2Chr 7:10
Thus *S* finished the house of the 2Chr 7:11
the LORD appeared to *S* by night 2Chr 7:12
wherein *S* had built the house of 2Chr 8:1
which Huram had restored to *S* 2Chr 8:2
*S* built them, and caused the 2Chr 8:2
*S* went to Hamath-zobah, and 2Chr 8:3
all the store cities that *S* had 2Chr 8:6
all that *S* desired to build in 2Chr 8:6
them did *S* make to pay tribute 2Chr 8:8
*S* make no servants for his work 2Chr 8:9
*S* brought up the daughter of 2Chr 8:11
Then *S* offered burnt offerings 2Chr 8:12
Now all the work of *S* was 2Chr 8:16
Then went *S* to Ezion-geber, and to 2Chr 8:17
with the servants of *S* to Ophir 2Chr 8:18
gold, and brought them to king *S* 2Chr 8:18
of Sheba heard of the fame of *S* 2Chr 9:1
she came to prove *S* with hard 2Chr 9:1
and when she was come to *S* 2Chr 9:1
*S* told her all her questions 2Chr 9:2
hid from *S* which he told her not 2Chr 9:2
of Sheba had seen the wisdom of *S* 2Chr 9:3
as the queen of Sheba gave king *S* 2Chr 9:9
of Huram, and the servants of *S* 2Chr 9:10
king *S* gave to the queen of Sheba 2Chr 9:12
to *S* in one year was six hundred 2Chr 9:13
brought gold and silver to *S* 2Chr 9:14
king *S* made two hundred targets 2Chr 9:15
vessels of king *S* were of gold 2Chr 9:20
accounted of in the days of *S* 2Chr 9:20
king *S* passed all the kings of 2Chr 9:22
earth sought the presence of *S* 2Chr 9:23
*S* had four thousand stalls for 2Chr 9:25
they brought unto *S* horses out of 2Chr 9:28
Now the rest of the acts of *S* 2Chr 9:29
*S* reigned in Jerusalem over all 2Chr 9:30
*S* slept with his fathers, and 2Chr 9:31
from the presence of *S* the king 2Chr 10:2
*S* his father while he yet lived 2Chr 10:6
Speak unto Rehoboam the son of *S* 2Chr 11:3
made Rehoboam the son of *S* strong 2Chr 11:17
walked in the way of David and *S* 2Chr 11:17
shields of gold which *S* had made 2Chr 12:9
the servant of *S* the son of David 2Chr 13:6
against Rehoboam the son of *S* 2Chr 13:7
for since the time of *S* the son 2Chr 30:26
to *S* his son, In this house, and 2Chr 33:7
*S* the son of David king of Israel 2Chr 35:3
to the writing of *S* his son 2Chr 35:4
of David, and of *S* his son Neh 12:45
Did not *S* king of Israel sin by Neh 13:26
A Psalm for *S* Ps 72:*t*
A Song of degrees for *S* Ps 127:*t*
The Proverbs of *S* the son of Prov 1:1
The proverbs of *S* Prov 10:1
These are also proverbs of *S* Prov 25:1
of Kedar, as the curtains of *S* Song 1:5
King *S* made himself a chariot of Song 3:9
behold king *S* with the crown Song 3:11
*S* had a vineyard at Baal-hamon Song 8:11
thou, O *S*, must have a thousand, Song 8:12
which king *S* had made in the Jer 52:20
David the king begat *S* of her Mt 1:6
And *S* begat Roboam Mt 1:7
That even *S* in all his glory was Mt 6:29
the earth to hear the wisdom of *S* Mt 12:42
behold, a greater than *S* is here Mt 12:42
the earth to hear the wisdom of *S* Lk 11:31
behold, a greater than *S* is here Lk 11:31
that *S* in all his glory was not Lk 12:27
But *S* built him an house Acts 7:47

**SOLOMON'S** (*sol'-o-muns*)

*S* provision for one day was 1Kin 4:22
all that came unto king *S* table 1Kin 4:27
*S* wisdom excelled the wisdom of 1Kin 4:30
Beside the chief of *S* officers 1Kin 5:16
*S* builders and Hiram's builders 1Kin 5:18
year of *S* reign over Israel 1Kin 6:1
all *S* desire which he was pleased 1Kin 9:1
present unto his daughter, *S* wife 1Kin 9:16
officers that were over *S* work 1Kin 9:23
of Sheba had seen all *S* wisdom 1Kin 10:4
all king *S* drinking vessels were 1Kin 10:21
*S* servant, whose mother's name 1Kin 11:26
*S* son was Rehoboam, Abia his son, 1Chr 3:10
all that came into *S* heart to 2Chr 7:11
were the chief of king *S* officers 2Chr 8:10
The children of *S* servants Ezr 2:55
and the children of *S* servants Ezr 2:58
The children of *S* servants Neh 7:57
and the children of *S* servants Neh 7:60
and the children of *S* servants Neh 11:3
The song of songs, which is *S* Song 1:1
Behold his bed, which is *S* Song 3:7
walked in the temple in *S* porch Jn 10:23
in the porch that is called *S* Acts 3:11
all with one accord in *S* porch Acts 5:12

**SOME**

lest *s* evil take me, and I die Gen 19:19
the field, and take me *s* venison Gen 27:3
every one that had *s* white in it Gen 30:35
Let me now leave with thee *s* of Gen 33:15
slay him, and cast him into *s* pit Gen 37:20
*S* evil beast hath devoured him Gen 37:20
he took *s* of his brethren, even Gen 47:2
and gathered, *s* more, *s* less Ex 16:17
but *s* of them left of it until Ex 16:20
that there went out *s* of the Ex 16:27
thou shalt beat *s* of it very Ex 30:36
the priest shall put *s* of the Lev 4:7
dip his finger in *s* of the blood Lev 4:17
he shall put *s* of the blood upon Lev 4:18
the priest shall take *s* of the Lev 14:14
shall take *s* of the log of oil Lev 14:15
the priest shall take *s* of the Lev 14:25
*s* of the oil that is in his left Lev 14:27
poor, and hath sold away *s* of his Lev 25:25
the LORD *s* part of a field of his Lev 27:16
*s* man have lain with thee beside Num 5:20
and took *s* of them prisoners Num 21:1
thou shalt put *s* of thine honour Num 27:20
Arm *s* of yourselves unto the war, Num 31:3
hath found *s* uncleanness in her Deut 24:1
*s* on this side, and *s* on that Josh 8:22
*s* to speak to the children of Judg 21:13
let fall also *s* of the handfuls Ruth 2:16
*s* shall run before his chariots 1Sa 8:11
*s* of the Hebrews went over Jordan 1Sa 13:7
and *s* bade me kill thee 1Sa 24:10
a place in *s* town in the country 1Sa 27:5
there fell *s* of the people of the 2Sa 11:17
*s* of the king's servants be dead, 2Sa 11:24
in *s* pit, or in *s* other place 2Sa 17:9
when *s* of them be overthrown at 2Sa 17:9
So shall we come upon him in *s* 2Sa 17:12
because in him there is found *s* 1Kin 14:13
up, and cast him upon *s* mountain 2Kin 2:16
*s* mountain, or into *s* valley 2Kin 2:16
had bid thee do *s* great thing 2Kin 5:13
*s* mischief will come upon us 2Kin 7:9
Let *s* take, I pray thee, five of 2Kin 7:13
*s* of her blood was sprinkled on 2Kin 9:33
among them, which slew *s* of them 2Kin 17:25
*s* of them, even of the sons of 1Chr 4:42
*S* of them also were appointed to 1Chr 9:29
*s* of the sons of the priests made 1Chr 9:30
there fell *s* of Manasseh to David 1Chr 12:19
I will grant them *s* deliverance 2Chr 12:7
Asa oppressed *s* of the people the 2Chr 16:10
Also *s* of the Philistines brought 2Chr 17:11
Then there came *s* that told 2Chr 20:2
*s* of the chief of the fathers, Ezr 2:68
*s* of the people, and the singers, Ezr 2:70
there went up *s* of the children Ezr 7:7
*s* of them had wives by whom they Ezr 10:44
the night, I and *s* few men with me Neh 2:12
*S* also there were that said, We Neh 5:3
*s* of our daughters are brought Neh 5:5
let us meet together in *s* one of Neh 6:2
*s* of the chief of the fathers Neh 7:70
*s* of the chief of the fathers Neh 7:71
*s* of the people, and the Nethinims Neh 7:73
*s* of the children of Judah dwelt Neh 11:25
at that time were *s* appointed Neh 12:44
*s* treading winepresses on the Neh 13:15
*s* of my servants set I at the Neh 13:19
*S* remove the landmarks Job 24:2
*S* trust in chariots, and *s* in Ps 20:7
and I looked for *s* to take pity Ps 69:20
away, unless they cause *s* to fall Prov 4:16
they not leave *s* gleaning grapes Jer 49:9
that ye may have *s* that shall Eze 6:8
and it cast down *s* of the host Dan 8:10
*s* of them of understanding shall Dan 11:35
*s* to everlasting life, and *s* to Dan 12:2
I have overthrown *s* of you Amos 4:11
would they not leave *s* grapes Obad 5
*s* seeds fell by the way side, and Mt 13:4
*S* fell upon stony places, where Mt 13:5
And *s* fell among thorns Mt 13:7
*s* an hundredfold, *s* sixtyfold, Mt 13:8
*s* sixtyfold, *s* thirtyfold Mt 13:8
*s* an hundredfold, *s* sixty, Mt 13:23
*s* sixty, *s* thirty Mt 13:23
*S* say that thou art John the Mt 16:14
*s*, Elias Mt 16:14
There be *s* standing here, which Mt 16:28
For there are *s* eunuchs, which Mt 19:12
and there are *s* eunuchs, which Mt 19:12
*s* of them ye shall kill and Mt 23:34
*s* of them shall ye scourge in Mt 23:34
*S* of them that stood there, when Mt 27:47
*s* of the watch came into the city Mt 28:11
but *s* doubted Mt 28:17
into Capernaum after *s* days Mk 2:1
*s* fell by the way side, and the Mk 4:4
*s* fell on stony ground, where it Mk 4:5
*s* fell among thorns, and the Mk 4:7
*s* thirty, and *s* sixty, and *s* Mk 4:8
*s* thirtyfold, *s* sixty, and *s* Mk 4:20
when they saw *s* of his disciples Mk 7:2
but *s* say, Elias Mk 8:28
That there be *s* of them that Mk 9:1
beating *s*, and killing *s* Mk 12:5
there were *s* that had indignation Mk 14:4
*s* began to spit on him, and to Mk 14:65
*s* of them that stood by, when Mk 15:35
he sowed, *s* fell by the way side Lk 8:5
And *s* fell upon a rock Lk 8:6
And *s* fell among thorns Lk 8:7
because that it was said of *s* Lk 9:7
And of *s*, that Elias had appeared Lk 9:8
but *s* say Elias Lk 9:19
there be *s* standing here, which Lk 9:27
But *s* of them said, He casteth Lk 11:15
*s* of them they shall slay and Lk 11:49
were present at that season *s* Lk 13:1
*s* of the Pharisees from among the Lk 19:39
as *s* spake of the temple, how it Lk 21:5
*s* of you shall they cause to be Lk 21:16
have seen *s* miracle done by him Lk 23:8
between *s* of John's disciples Jn 3:25
But there are *s* of you that Jn 6:64
for *s* said, He is a good man Jn 7:12
Then said *s* of them of Jerusalem, Jn 7:25
But *s* said, Shall Christ come out Jn 7:41
*s* of them would have taken him Jn 7:44
*S* said, This is he Jn 9:9
Therefore said *s* of the Pharisees Jn 9:16
*s* of the Pharisees which were Jn 9:40
but climbeth up *s* other way Jn 10:1
*s* of them said, Could not this Jn 11:37
But *s* of them went their ways to Jn 11:46
For *s* of them thought, because Jn 13:29
Then said *s* of his disciples Jn 16:17
by might overshadow *s* of them Acts 5:15
out that himself was *s* great one Acts 8:9
except *s* man should guide me Acts 8:31
of himself, or of *s* other man Acts 8:34
*s* of them were men of Cyprus and Acts 11:20
he went about seeking *s* to lead Acts 13:11
*s* days after Paul said unto Acts 15:36
*s* of them believed, and consorted Acts 17:4
*s* said, What will this babbler Acts 17:18
other *s*, He seemeth to be a Acts 17:18
to tell, or to hear *s* new thing Acts 17:21
of the dead, *s* mocked Acts 17:32
after he had spent *s* time there Acts 18:23
*S* therefore cried one thing, and Acts 19:32
cried one thing, and *s* another Acts 19:32
*s* cried one thing, *s* another, Acts 21:34
that they drew near to *s* country Acts 27:27
I pray you to take *s* meat Acts 27:34

cheer, and they also took s meat Acts 27:36
s on boards, and s on broken Acts 27:44
s believed the things which were Acts 28:24
were spoken, and s believed not Acts 28:24
impart unto you s spiritual gift Rom 1:11
that I might have s fruit among Rom 1:13
For what if s did not believe Rom 3:3
as s affirm that we say,) Let us Rom 3:8
good man s would even dare to die Rom 5:7
my flesh, and might save s of them Rom 11:14
if s of the branches be broken Rom 11:17
more boldly unto you in s sort Rom 15:15
Now s are puffed up, as though I 1Cor 4:18
And such were s of you 1Cor 6:11
for s with conscience of the idol 1Cor 8:7
that I might by all means save s 1Cor 9:22
ye idolaters, as were s of them 1Cor 10:7
as s of them committed, and fell 1Cor 10:8
as s of them also tempted, and 1Cor 10:9
as s of them also murmured, and 1Cor 10:10
God hath set s in the church, 1Cor 12:28
present, but s are fallen asleep 1Cor 15:6
how say s among you that there is 1Cor 15:12
for s have not the knowledge of 1Cor 15:34
But s man will say, How are the 1Cor 15:35
of wheat, or of s other grain 1Cor 15:37
need we, as s others, epistles of 2Cor 3:1
I think to be bold against s 2Cor 10:2
with s that commend themselves 2Cor 10:12
but there be s that trouble you, Gal 1:7
And he gave s, apostles Eph 4:11
and s, prophets Eph 4:11
and s, evangelists Eph 4:11
and s, pastors and teachers Eph 4:11
S indeed preach Christ even of Phil 1:15
and s also of good will Phil 1:15
the which ye also walked s time Col 3:7
lest by s means the tempter have 1Th 3:5
For we hear that there are s 2Th 3:11
charge s that they teach no other 1Ti 1:3
From which s having swerved have 1Ti 1:6
which s having put away 1Ti 1:19
that in the latter times s shall 1Ti 4:1
For s are already turned aside 1Ti 5:15
S men's sins are open beforehand, 1Ti 5:24
and s men they follow after 1Ti 5:24
of s are manifest beforehand 1Ti 5:25
which while s coveted after, they 1Ti 6:10
Which s professing have erred 1Ti 6:21
and overthrow the faith of s 2Ti 2:18
s to honour, and s to dishonour 2Ti 2:20
every house is builded by s man Heb 3:4
For s, when they had heard, did Heb 3:16
that s must enter therein Heb 4:6
together, as the manner of s is Heb 10:25
provided s better thing for us Heb 11:40
for thereby s have entertained Heb 13:2
as though s strange thing 1Pet 4:12
promise, as s men count slackness 2Pet 3:9
in which are s things hard to be 2Pet 3:16
of s have compassion, making a Jude 22
shall cast s of you into prison Rev 2:10

## SOMEBODY
And Jesus said, S hath touched me Lk 8:46
Theudas, boasting himself to be s Acts 5:36

## SOMETHING
S hath befallen him, he is not 1Sa 20:26
commanded that s should be given Mk 5:43
to catch s out of his mouth Lk 11:54
that he should give s to the poor Jn 13:29
expecting to receive s of them Acts 3:5
as though ye would enquire s more Acts 23:15
who hath s to say unto thee Acts 23:18
if a man think himself to be s Gal 6:3

## SOMETIME
And you, that were s alienated Col 1:21
Which s were disobedient, when 1Pet 3:20

## SOMETIMES
s were far off are made nigh by Eph 2:13
For ye were s darkness, but now Eph 5:8
we ourselves also were s foolish Titus 3:3

## SOMEWHAT
they have done s against any of Lev 4:13
done s through ignorance against Lev 4:22
while he doeth s against any of Lev 4:27
behold, if the plague be s dark Lev 13:6
s reddish, and it be shewed to the Lev 13:19
than the skin, but be s dark Lev 13:21
bright spot, s reddish, or white Lev 13:24
the other skin, but be s dark Lev 13:26
not in the skin, but it be s dark Lev 13:28
the plague be s dark after the Lev 13:56
I have s to say unto thee 1Kin 2:14
run after him, and take s of him 2Kin 5:20
now therefore ease thou s the 2Chr 10:4
Ease s the yoke that thy father 2Chr 10:9
but make thou it s lighter for us 2Chr 10:10
I have s to say unto thee Lk 7:40
enquire s of him more perfectly Acts 23:20
had, I might have s to write Acts 25:26
if first I be s filled with your Rom 15:24
that ye may have s to answer them 2Cor 5:12
boast s more of our authority 2Cor 10:8
But of these who seemed to be s Gal 2:6
for they who seemed to be s in Gal 2:6
this man have s also to offer Heb 8:3
I have s against thee, because Rev 2:4

## SON See PREFACE.
bare Abraham a s in his old age Gen 21:2
of his s that was born unto him Gen 21:3
in order, and bound Isaac his s Gen 22:9
he answered, I called not, my s 1Sa 3:6
O Absalom, my s, my s 2Sa 19:4
So we boiled my s, and did eat him 2Kin 6:29
her on the next day, Give thy s 2Kin 6:29
And he said unto me, Solomon thy s 1Chr 28:6
for I have chosen him to be my s 1Chr 28:6
hath said unto me, Thou art my S Ps 2:7
the s of man, that thou visitest Ps 8:4
or the s of man, that thou makest Ps 144:3
My s, forget not my law Prov 3:1
A wise s maketh a glad father Prov 15:20
Chasten thy s while there is hope Prov 19:18
shall conceive, and bear a s Is 7:14
is born, unto us a s is given Is 9:6
of the s of man which shall be Is 51:12
doth not the s bear the iniquity Eze 18:19
the fourth is like the S of God Dan 3:25
him, and called my s out of Egypt Hos 11:1
his own s that serveth him Mal 3:17
saying, This is my beloved S Mt 3:17
and no man knoweth the S, but the Mt 11:27
any man the Father, save the S Mt 11:27
whomsoever the S will reveal him Mt 11:27
Of a truth thou art the S of God Mt 14:33
which said, This is my beloved S Mt 17:5
For the S of man is come to save Mt 18:11
whose s is he Mt 22:42
the coming of the S of man be Mt 24:37
If thou be the S of God, come Mt 27:40
for he said, I am the S of God Mt 27:43
Truly this was the S of God Mt 27:54
Truly this man was the S of God Mk 15:39
thee shall be called the S of God Lk 1:35
of Adam, which was the s of God Lk 3:38
Thou art Christ the S of God Lk 4:41
Jesus, thou S of God most high Lk 8:28
saying, This is my beloved S Lk 9:35
For the S of man is come to seek Lk 19:10
then shall they see the S of man Lk 21:27
all, Art thou then the S of God Lk 22:70
record that this is the S of God Jn 1:34
him, Rabbi, thou art the S of God Jn 1:49
that he gave his only begotten S Jn 3:16
of the only begotten S of God Jn 3:18
The S can do nothing of himself, Jn 5:19
That all men should honour the S Jn 5:23
Christ, the S of the living God Jn 6:69
If the S therefore shall make you Jn 8:36
his mother, Woman, behold thy s Jn 19:26
Jesus is the Christ, the S of God Jn 20:31
that Jesus Christ is the S of God Acts 8:37
that he is the S of God Acts 9:20
to be the S of God with power Rom 1:4
God sending his own S in the Rom 8:3
was come, God sent forth his S Gal 4:4
art no more a servant, but a s Gal 4:7
and if a s, then an heir of God Gal 4:7
as a s with the father, he hath Phil 2:22
offered up his only begotten s Heb 11:17
for what s is he whom the father Heb 12:7
He that hath the S hath life 1Jn 5:12
not the S of God hath not life 1Jn 5:12

## SONG
of Israel this s unto the LORD Ex 15:1
The LORD is my strength and s Ex 15:2
Then Israel sang this s, Spring Num 21:17
therefore write ye this s for you Deut 31:19
that this s may be a witness for Deut 31:19
that this s shall testify against Deut 31:21
wrote this s the same day Deut 31:22
of Israel the words of this s Deut 31:30
this s in the ears of the people Deut 32:44
awake, awake, utter a s Judg 5:12
unto the LORD the words of this s 2Sa 22:1
of s in the house of the LORD 1Chr 6:31
chief of the Levites, was for s 1Chr 15:22
he instructed about the s 1Chr 15:22
master of the s with the singers 1Chr 15:27
for s in the house of the LORD 1Chr 25:6
the s of the LORD began also with 2Chr 29:27
And now am I their s, yea, I am Job 30:9
this s in the day that the LORD Ps 18:t
with my s will I praise him Ps 28:7
S at the dedication of the house Ps 30:t
Sing unto him a new s Ps 33:3
he hath put a new s in my mouth Ps 40:3
the night his s shall be with me Ps 42:8
of Korah, A Maschil, A S of loves Ps 45:t
sons of Korah, A S upon Alamoth Ps 46:t
A S and Psalm for the sons of Ps 48:t
Musician, A Psalm and S of David Ps 65:t
the chief Musician, A S or Psalm Ps 66:t
on Neginoth, A Psalm or S Ps 67:t
Musician, A Psalm or S of David Ps 68:t
I was the s of the drunkards Ps 69:12
praise the name of God with a s Ps 69:30
Altaschith, A Psalm or S of Asaph Ps 75:t
Neginoth, A Psalm or S of Asaph Ps 76:t
to remembrance my s in the night Ps 77:6
A S or Psalm of Asaph Ps 83:t
A Psalm or S for the sons of Ps 87:t
A S or Psalm for the sons of Ps 88:t
A Psalm or S for the sabbath day Ps 92:t
O sing unto the LORD a new s Ps 96:1
O sing unto the LORD a new s Ps 98:1
A S or Psalm of David Ps 108:t
The LORD is my strength and s Ps 118:14
A S of degrees Ps 120:t
A S of degrees Ps 121:t
A S of degrees of David Ps 122:t
A S of degrees Ps 123:t
A S of degrees of David Ps 124:t
A S of degrees Ps 125:t
A S of degrees Ps 126:t
A S of degrees for Solomon Ps 127:t
A S of degrees Ps 128:t
A S of degrees Ps 129:t
A S of degrees Ps 130:t
A S of degrees of David Ps 131:t
A S of degrees Ps 132:t
A S of degrees of David Ps 133:t
A S of degrees Ps 134:t
away captive required of us a s Ps 137:3
the LORD's s in a strange land Ps 137:4
I will sing a new s unto thee Ps 144:9
Sing unto the LORD a new s Ps 149:1
for a man to hear the s of fools Eccl 7:5
The s of songs, which is Song 1:1
a s of my beloved touching his Is 5:1
JEHOVAH is my strength and my s Is 12:2
shall not drink wine with a s Is 24:9
In that day shall this s be sung Is 26:1
Ye shall have a s, as in the Is 30:29
Sing unto the LORD a new s Is 42:10
and their s all the day Lam 3:14
s of one that hath a pleasant Eze 33:32
And they sung a new s, saying, Rev 5:9
it were a new s before the throne Rev 14:3
learn that s but the hundred Rev 14:3
they sing the s of Moses the Rev 15:3
the s of the Lamb, saying, Great Rev 15:3

## SONGS
thee away with mirth, and with s Gen 31:27
his s were a thousand and five 1Kin 4:32
instructed in the s of the LORD 1Chr 25:7
s of praise and thanksgiving unto Neh 12:46
who giveth s in the night Job 35:10
me about with s of deliverance Ps 32:7
Thy statutes have been my s in Ps 119:54
Sing us one of the s of Zion Ps 137:3
that singeth s to an heavy heart Prov 25:20
The song of s, which is Solomon's Song 1:1
make sweet melody, sing many s Is 23:16
part of the earth have we heard s Is 24:16
return, and come to Zion with s Is 35:10
therefore we will sing my s to Is 38:20
cause the noise of thy s to cease Eze 26:13
away from me the noise of thy s Amos 5:23
the s of the temple shall be Amos 8:3
all your s into lamentation Amos 8:10
in psalms and hymns and spiritual s Eph 5:19
in psalms and hymns and spiritual s Col 3:16

## SON'S
and Lot the son of Haran his s son Gen 11:31
and Abram called his s name Gen 16:15
with my son, nor with my s son Gen 21:23
and let her be thy master's s wife Gen 24:51
me, and I will eat of my s venison Gen 27:25
arise, and eat of his s venison Gen 27:31
I pray thee, of thy s mandrakes Gen 30:14
take away my s mandrakes also Gen 30:15
thee to night for thy s mandrakes Gen 30:15
hired thee with my s mandrakes Gen 30:16
whether it be thy s coat or no Gen 37:32
knew it, and said, It is my s coat Gen 37:33
ears of thy son, and of thy s son Ex 10:2
The nakedness of thy s daughter Lev 18:10
she is thy s wife Lev 18:15
shalt thou take her s daughter Lev 18:17
thou, and thy son, and thy s son Deut 6:2
and thy son, and thy s son also Judg 8:22
the kingdom out of his s hand 1Kin 11:35
but in his s days will I bring 1Kin 21:29
his name, and what is his s name Prov 30:4
him, and his son, and his s son Jer 27:7

## SONS See PREFACE.

## SONS'
wife, and thy s wives with thee Gen 6:18
his s wives with him, into the Gen 7:7
sons, and thy s wives with thee Gen 8:16
his wife, and his s wives with him Gen 8:18
sons, and his s sons with him, his Gen 46:7
his s daughters, and all his seed Gen 46:7
loins, besides Jacob's s wives Gen 46:26
sons, and his s garments with him Ex 29:21
his s by a statute for ever from Ex 29:28
of Aaron shall be his s after him Ex 29:29
his s garments, to minister in Ex 39:41
shall be Aaron's and his s Lev 2:3
shall be Aaron's and his s Lev 2:10
breast shall be Aaron's and his s Lev 7:31
hands, and upon his s hands Lev 8:27
upon his s garments with him Lev 8:30
sons, and his s garments with him Lev 8:30
it is thy due, and thy s due Lev 10:13
for they be thy due, and thy s due Lev 10:14
thy s with thee, by a statute for Lev 10:15
And it shall be Aaron's and his s Lev 24:9
them thy sons, and thy s sons Deut 4:9
s sons, an hundred and fifty 1Chr 8:40
his s sons, even four generations Job 42:16
thereof shall be his s Eze 46:16
shall be his s for them Eze 46:17

**SOON**
- as *s* as he had left communing ... Gen 18:33
- as *s* as Isaac had made an end of ... Gen 27:30
- As *s* as the morning was light, ... Gen 44:3
- it that ye are come so *s* to day ... Ex 2:18
- As *s* as I am gone out of the city ... Ex 9:29
- as *s* as he came nigh unto the ... Ex 32:19
- that ye shall *s* utterly perish ... Deut 4:26
- as *s* as they which pursued after ... Josh 2:7
- as *s* as we had heard these things ... Josh 2:11
- as *s* as the soles of the feet of ... Josh 3:13
- they ran as *s* as he had stretched ... Josh 8:19
- as *s* as the sun was down, Joshua ... Josh 8:29
- as *s* as Gideon was dead, that the ... Judg 8:33
- as *s* as the sun is up, thou shalt ... Judg 9:33
- As *s* as ye be come into the city, ... 1Sa 9:13
- that as *s* as he had made an end ... 1Sa 13:10
- as *s* as the lad was gone, David ... 1Sa 20:41
- as *s* as ye be up early in the ... 1Sa 29:10
- as *s* as David had made an end of ... 2Sa 6:18
- as *s* as he had made an end of ... 2Sa 13:36
- As *s* as ye hear the sound of the ... 2Sa 15:10
- as *s* as they hear, they shall be ... 2Sa 22:45
- as *s* as he sat on his throne, ... 1Kin 16:11
- as *s* as I am gone from thee, that ... 1Kin 18:12
- as *s* as thou art departed from me ... 1Kin 20:36
- as *s* as he was departed from him, ... 1Kin 20:36
- Now as *s* as this letter cometh to ... 2Kin 10:2
- as *s* as he had made an end of ... 2Kin 10:25
- as *s* as the kingdom was confirmed ... 2Kin 14:5
- as *s* as the commandment came ... 2Chr 31:5
- my maker would *s* take me away ... Job 32:22
- As *s* as they hear of me, they ... Ps 18:44
- For they shall *s* be cut down like ... Ps 37:2
- go astray as *s* as they be born ... Ps 58:3
- Ethiopia shall *s* stretch out her ... Ps 68:31
- I should *s* have subdued their ... Ps 81:14
- for it is *s* cut off, and we fly ... Ps 90:10
- They *s* forgat his works ... Ps 106:13
- He that is *s* angry dealeth ... Prov 14:17
- for as *s* as Zion travailed, she ... Is 66:8
- as *s* as she saw them with her ... Eze 23:16
- How *s* is the fig tree withered ... Mt 21:20
- And as *s* as he had spoken, ... Mk 1:42
- As *s* as Jesus heard the word that ... Mk 5:36
- as *s* as ye be entered into it, ye ... Mk 11:2
- as *s* as he was come, he goeth ... Mk 14:45
- that, as *s* as the days of his ... Lk 1:23
- For, lo, as *s* as the voice of thy ... Lk 1:44
- as *s* as it was sprung up, it ... Lk 8:6
- But as *s* as this thy son was come ... Lk 15:30
- as *s* as it was day, the elders of ... Lk 22:66
- as *s* as he knew that he belonged ... Lk 23:7
- as *s* as she heard that Jesus was ... Jn 11:20
- As *s* as she heard that, she arose ... Jn 11:29
- but as *s* as she is delivered of ... Jn 16:21
- As *s* then as he had said unto ... Jn 18:6
- As *s* then as they were come to ... Jn 21:9
- as *s* as I was sent for ... Acts 10:29
- Now as *s* as it was day, there was ... Acts 12:18
- I marvel that ye are so *s* removed ... Gal 1:6
- so *s* as I shall see how it will ... Phil 2:23
- That ye be not *s* shaken in mind ... 2Th 2:2
- not *s* angry, not given to wine, ... Titus 1:7
- as *s* as I had eaten it, my belly ... Rev 10:10
- her child as *s* as it was born ... Rev 12:4

**SOONER**
- I may be restored to you the *s* ... Heb 13:19
- For the sun is no *s* risen with a ... Jas 1:11

**SOOTHSAYER**
- also the son of Beor, the *s* ... Josh 13:22

**SOOTHSAYERS**
- are *s* like the Philistines, and ... Is 2:6
- astrologers, the magicians, the *s* ... Dan 2:27
- the Chaldeans, and the *s* ... Dan 4:7
- the Chaldeans, and the *s* ... Dan 5:7
- astrologers, Chaldeans, and *s* ... Dan 5:11
- and thou shalt have no more *s* ... Mic 5:12

**SOOTHSAYING**
- her masters much gain by *s* ... Acts 16:16

**SOP**
- it is, to whom I shall give a *s* ... Jn 13:26
- And when he had dipped the *s* ... Jn 13:26
- after the *s* Satan entered into ... Jn 13:27
- the *s* went immediately out ... Jn 13:30

**SOPATER** (*so'-pa-ter*) See SOSIPATER. *A Christian from Berea.*
- him into Asia *S* of Berea ... Acts 20:4

**SOPE**
- with nitre, and take thee much *s* ... Jer 2:22
- fire, and like fullers' *s* ... Mal 3:2

**SOPHERETH** (*so-fe'-reth*) *A family of exiles.*
- of Sotai, the children of *S* ... Ezr 2:55
- of Sotai, the children of *S* ... Neh 7:57

**SORCERER**
- Paphos, they found a certain *s* ... Acts 13:6
- But Elymas the *s* (for so is his ... Acts 13:8

**SORCERERS**
- also called the wise men and the *s* ... Ex 7:11
- to your enchanters, nor to your *s* ... Jer 27:9
- and the astrologers, and the *s* ... Dan 2:2
- be a swift witness against the *s* ... Mal 3:5
- murderers, and whoremongers, and *s* ... Rev 21:8
- For without are dogs, and *s* ... Rev 22:15

**SORCERESS**
- near hither, ye sons of the *s* ... Is 57:3

**SORCERIES**
- for the multitude of thy *s* ... Is 47:9
- and with the multitude of thy *s* ... Is 47:12
- time he had bewitched them with *s* ... Acts 8:11
- of their murders, nor of their *s* ... Rev 9:21
- for by thy *s* were all nations ... Rev 18:23

**SORCERY**
- in the same city used *s*, and ... Acts 8:9

**SORE**
- And they pressed *s* upon the man ... Gen 19:9
- and the men were *s* afraid ... Gen 20:8
- because thou *s* longedst after thy ... Gen 31:30
- the third day, when they were *s* ... Gen 34:25
- the famine waxed *s* in the land of ... Gen 41:56
- the famine was so *s* in all lands ... Gen 41:57
- And the famine was *s* in the land ... Gen 43:1
- for the famine is *s* in the land ... Gen 47:4
- for the famine was very *s* ... Gen 47:13
- a great and very *s* lamentation ... Gen 50:10
- and they were *s* afraid ... Ex 14:10
- bald forehead, a white reddish *s* ... Lev 13:42
- if the rising of the *s* be white ... Lev 13:43
- Moab was *s* afraid of the people, ... Num 22:3
- signs and wonders, great and *s* ... Deut 6:22
- with a *s* botch that cannot be ... Deut 28:35
- and *s* sicknesses, and of long ... Deut 28:59
- therefore we were *s* afraid of our ... Josh 9:24
- so that Israel was *s* distressed ... Judg 10:9
- her, because she lay *s* upon him ... Judg 14:17
- he was *s* athirst, and called on ... Judg 15:18
- all Israel, and the battle was *s* ... Judg 20:34
- lifted up their voices, and wept *s* ... Judg 21:2
- her adversary also provoked her *s* ... 1Sa 1:6
- prayed unto the LORD, and wept *s* ... 1Sa 1:10
- for his hand is *s* upon us ... 1Sa 5:7
- there was *s* war against the ... 1Sa 14:52
- fled from him, and were *s* afraid ... 1Sa 17:24
- was *s* afraid of Achish the king ... 1Sa 21:12
- Saul answered, I am *s* distressed ... 1Sa 28:15
- was *s* afraid, because of the ... 1Sa 28:20
- and saw that he was *s* troubled ... 1Sa 28:21
- And the battle went *s* against Saul ... 1Sa 31:3
- he was *s* wounded of the archers ... 1Sa 31:3
- for he was *s* afraid ... 1Sa 31:4
- was a very *s* battle that day ... 2Sa 2:17
- and all his servants wept very *s* ... 2Sa 13:36
- and his sickness was so *s*, that ... 1Kin 17:17
- there was a *s* famine in Samaria ... 1Kin 18:2
- that the battle was too *s* for him ... 2Kin 3:26
- was *s* troubled for this thing ... 2Kin 6:11
- And Hezekiah wept *s* ... 2Kin 20:3
- And the battle went *s* against Saul ... 1Chr 10:3
- for he was *s* afraid ... 1Chr 10:4
- whatsoever *s* or whatsoever ... 2Chr 6:28
- every one shall know his own *s* ... 2Chr 6:29
- so he died of *s* diseases ... 2Chr 21:19
- transgressed *s* against the LORD ... 2Chr 28:19
- for I am *s* wounded ... 2Chr 35:23
- for the people wept very *s* ... Ezr 10:1
- Then I was very *s* afraid, ... Neh 2:2
- And it grieved me *s* ... Neh 13:8
- smote Job with *s* boils from the ... Job 2:7
- For he maketh *s*, and bindeth up ... Job 5:18
- and vex them in his *s* displeasure ... Ps 2:5
- My soul is also *s* vexed ... Ps 6:3
- enemies be ashamed and *s* vexed ... Ps 6:10
- in me, and thy hand presseth me *s* ... Ps 38:2
- I am feeble and *s* broken ... Ps 38:8
- my friends stand aloof from my *s* ... Ps 38:11
- Though thou hast *s* broken us in ... Ps 44:19
- My heart is *s* pained within me ... Ps 55:4
- *s* troubles, shalt quicken me ... Ps 71:20
- my *s* ran in the night, and ceased ... Ps 77:2
- Thou hast thrust *s* at me that I ... Ps 118:13
- The LORD hath chastened me *s* ... Ps 118:18
- this *s* travail hath God given to ... Eccl 1:13
- vanity, yea, it is a *s* travail ... Eccl 4:8
- There is a *s* evil which I have ... Eccl 5:13
- And this also is a *s* evil, that in ... Eccl 5:16
- In that day the LORD with his *s* ... Is 27:1
- And Hezekiah wept *s* ... Is 38:3
- like bears, and mourn *s* like doves ... Is 59:11
- Be not wroth very *s*, O LORD, ... Is 64:9
- thy peace, and afflict us very *s* ... Is 64:12
- and mine eye shall weep *s*, and run ... Jer 13:17
- but weep *s* for him that goeth ... Jer 22:10
- Your mother shall be *s* confounded ... Jer 50:12
- the famine was *s* in the city ... Jer 52:6
- She weepeth *s* in the night, and ... Lam 1:2
- Mine enemies chased me *s*, like a ... Lam 3:52
- four *s* judgments upon Jerusalem ... Eze 14:21
- sharpened to make a *s* slaughter ... Eze 21:10
- and their kings shall be *s* afraid ... Eze 27:35
- was *s* displeased with himself, and ... Dan 6:14
- you, even with a *s* destruction ... Mic 2:10
- The LORD hath been *s* displeased ... Zec 1:2
- I am very *s* displeased with the ... Zec 1:15
- on their face, and were *s* afraid ... Mt 17:6
- for he is lunatick, and *s* vexed ... Mt 17:15
- they were *s* displeased, ... Mt 21:15
- they were *s* amazed in themselves ... Mk 6:51
- for they were *s* afraid ... Mk 9:6
- the spirit cried, and rent him *s* ... Mk 9:26
- and John, and began to be *s* amazed ... Mk 14:33
- and they were *s* afraid ... Lk 2:9
- And they all wept *s*, and fell on ... Acts 20:37
- grievous *s* upon the men which had ... Rev 16:2

**SOREK** (*so'-rek*) *A valley between Ashkelon and Gaza.*
- loved a woman in the valley of *S* ... Judg 16:4

**SORELY**
- The archers have *s* grieved him ... Gen 49:23
- so shall they be *s* pained at the ... Is 23:5

**SORER**
- Of how much *s* punishment, suppose. Heb 10:29

**SORES**
- and bruises, and putrifying *s* ... Is 1:6
- was laid at his gate, full of *s* ... Lk 16:20
- the dogs came and licked his *s* ... Lk 16:21
- because of their pains and their *s* ... Rev 16:11

**SORROW**
- I will greatly multiply thy *s* ... Gen 3:16
- in *s* thou shalt bring forth ... Gen 3:16
- in *s* shalt thou eat of it all the ... Gen 3:17
- my gray hairs with *s* to the grave ... Gen 42:38
- my gray hairs with *s* to the grave ... Gen 44:29
- our father with *s* to the grave ... Gen 44:31
- *s* shall take hold on the ... Ex 15:14
- the eyes, and cause *s* of heart ... Lev 26:16
- and failing of eyes, and *s* of mind ... Deut 28:65
- saying, Because I bare him with *s* ... 1Chr 4:9
- is nothing else but *s* of heart ... Neh 2:2
- turned unto them from *s* to joy ... Est 9:22
- womb, nor hid *s* from mine eyes ... Job 3:10
- yea, I would harden myself in *s* ... Job 6:10
- eye also is dim by reason of *s* ... Job 17:7
- *s* is turned into joy before him ... Job 41:22
- having *s* in my heart daily ... Ps 13:2
- my *s* is continually before me ... Ps 38:17
- and my *s* was stirred ... Ps 39:2
- also and *s* are in the midst of it ... Ps 55:10
- yet is their strength labour and *s* ... Ps 90:10
- oppression, affliction, and *s* ... Ps 107:39
- I found trouble and *s* ... Ps 116:3
- winketh with the eye causeth *s* ... Prov 10:10
- rich, and he addeth no *s* with it ... Prov 10:22
- but by *s* of the heart the spirit ... Prov 15:13
- a fool doeth it to his *s* ... Prov 17:21
- who hath *s* ... Prov 23:29
- increaseth knowledge increaseth *s* ... Eccl 1:18
- in darkness, and he hath much *s* ... Eccl 5:17
- *S* is better than laughter ... Eccl 7:3
- Therefore remove *s* from thy heart ... Eccl 11:10
- the land, behold darkness and *s* ... Is 5:30
- shall give thee rest from thy *s* ... Is 14:3
- day of grief and of desperate *s* ... Is 17:11
- and there shall be heaviness and *s* ... Is 29:2
- obtain joy and gladness, and *s* ... Is 35:10
- ye shall lie down in *s* ... Is 50:11
- and *s* and mourning shall flee away ... Is 51:11
- but ye shall cry for *s* of heart ... Is 65:14
- I would comfort myself against *s* ... Jer 8:18
- of the womb to see labour and *s* ... Jer 20:18
- thy *s* is incurable for the ... Jer 30:15
- they shall not *s* any more at all ... Jer 31:12
- and make them rejoice from their *s* ... Jer 31:13
- the LORD hath added grief to my *s* ... Jer 45:3
- there is *s* on the sea ... Jer 49:23
- And the land shall tremble and *s* ... Jer 51:29
- be any *s* like unto my *s* ... Lam 1:12
- you, all people, and behold my *s* ... Lam 1:18
- Give them *s* of heart, thy curse ... Lam 3:65
- be filled with drunkenness and *s* ... Eze 23:33
- they shall *s* a little for the ... Hos 8:10
- he found them sleeping for *s* ... Lk 22:45
- you, *s* hath filled your heart ... Jn 16:6
- but your *s* shall be turned into ... Jn 16:20
- when she is in travail hath *s* ... Jn 16:21
- And ye now therefore have *s* ... Jn 16:22
- and continual *s* in my heart ... Rom 9:2
- I should have *s* from them of whom ... 2Cor 2:3
- be swallowed up with overmuch *s* ... 2Cor 2:7
- For godly *s* worketh repentance to ... 2Cor 7:10
- but the *s* of the world worketh ... 2Cor 7:10
- lest I should have *s* upon *s* ... Phil 2:27
- which are asleep, that ye *s* not ... 1Th 4:13
- so much torment and *s* give her ... Rev 18:7
- and am no widow, and shall see no *s* ... Rev 18:7
- shall be no more death, neither *s* ... Rev 21:4

**SORROWED**
- but that ye *s* to repentance ... 2Cor 7:9
- that ye *s* after a godly sort, ... 2Cor 7:11

**SORROWETH**
- *s* for you, saying, What shall I ... 1Sa 10:2

**SORROWFUL**
- lord, I am a woman of a *s* spirit ... 1Sa 1:15
- refused to touch are as my *s* meat ... Job 6:7
- But I am poor and *s* ... Ps 69:29
- Even in laughter the heart is *s* ... Prov 14:13
- I have replenished every *s* soul ... Jer 31:25
- are *s* for the solemn assembly ... Zeph 3:18
- also shall see it, and be very *s* ... Zec 9:5
- heard that saying, he went away *s* ... Mt 19:22
- And they were exceeding *s*, and ... Mt 26:22
- sons of Zebedee, and began to be *s* ... Mt 26:37
- unto them, My soul is exceeding *s* ... Mt 26:38
- And they began to be *s*, and to say ... Mk 14:19
- My soul is exceeding *s* unto death ... Mk 14:34
- when he heard this, he was very *s* ... Lk 18:23
- when Jesus saw that he was very *s* ... Lk 18:24
- and ye shall be *s*, but your sorrow ... Jn 16:20
- As *s*, yet alway rejoicing ... 2Cor 6:10
- and that I may be the less *s* ... Phil 2:28

**SORROWING**
father and I have sought thee s ... Lk 2:48
*S* most of all for the words which ... Acts 20:38

**SORROWS**
for I know their s ... Ex 3:7
The s of hell compassed me about ... 2Sa 22:6
I am afraid of all my s, I know ... Job 9:28
God distributeth s in his anger ... Job 21:17
young ones, they cast out their s ... Job 39:3
Their s shall be multiplied that ... Ps 16:4
The s of death compassed me, and ... Ps 18:4
The s of hell compassed me about ... Ps 18:5
Many s shall be to the wicked ... Ps 32:10
The s of death compassed me, and ... Ps 116:3
up late, to eat the bread of s ... Ps 127:2
For all his days are s, and his ... Eccl 2:23
s shall take hold of them ... Is 13:8
a man of s, and acquainted with ... Is 53:3
our griefs, and carried our s ... Is 53:4
shall not s take thee, as a woman ... Jer 13:21
s have taken her, as a woman in ... Jer 49:24
by the vision my s are turned ... Dan 10:16
The s of a travailing woman shall ... Hos 13:13
All these are the beginning of s ... Mt 24:8
these are the beginnings of s ... Mk 13:8
themselves through with many s ... 1Ti 6:10

**SORRY**
is none of you that is s for me ... 1Sa 22:8
neither be ye s ... Neh 8:10
I will be s for my sin ... Ps 38:18
who shall be s for thee ... Is 51:19
And the king was s ... Mt 14:9
And they were exceeding s ... Mt 17:23
what was done, they were very s ... Mt 18:31
And the king was exceeding s ... Mk 6:26
For if I make you s, who is he ... 2Cor 2:2
the same which is made s by me ... 2Cor 2:2
though I made you s with a letter ... 2Cor 7:8
the same epistle hath made you s ... 2Cor 7:8
rejoice, not that ye were made s ... 2Cor 7:9
for ye were made s after a godly ... 2Cor 7:9

**SORT**
two of every s shalt thou bring ... Gen 6:19
two of every s shall come unto ... Gen 6:20
his kind, every bird of every s ... Gen 7:14
save the poorest s of the people ... 2Kin 24:14
by lot, one s with another ... 1Chr 24:5
offer so willingly after this s ... 1Chr 29:14
time in such s as it was written ... 2Chr 30:5
basons of a second s four hundred ... Ezr 1:10
to Artaxerxes the king in this s ... Ezr 4:8
unto me four times after this s ... Neh 6:4
with the men of the common s were .. Eze 23:42
the ravenous birds of every s ... Eze 39:4
of every s of your oblations ... Eze 44:30
the children which are of your s ... Dan 1:10
God that can deliver after this s ... Dan 3:29
lewd fellows of the baser s ... Acts 17:5
more boldly unto you in some s ... Rom 15:15
every man's work of what s it is ... 1Cor 3:13
that ye sorrowed after a godly s ... 2Cor 7:11
For of this s are they which ... 2Ti 3:6
on their journey after a godly s ... 3Jn 6

**SORTS**
not wear a garment of divers s ... Deut 22:11
ten days store of all s of wine ... Neh 5:18
He sent divers s of flies among ... Ps 78:45
and there came divers s of flies ... Ps 105:31
instruments, and that of all s ... Eccl 2:8
thy merchants in all s of things ... Eze 27:24
them clothed with all s of armour ... Eze 38:4

**SOSIPATER** (*so-sip'-a-tur*) See SOPATER. *A relative of Paul.*
and Lucius, and Jason, and *S* ... Rom 16:21

**SOSTHENES** (*sos'-the-neze*)
*1. Chief ruler of a synagogue in Corinth.*
Then all the Greeks took *S* ... Acts 18:17
*2. A co-worker with Paul.*
will of God, and *S* our brother, ... 1Cor 1:1

**SOTAI** (*so'-tahee*) *A family of Temple servants.*
the children of *S*, the children ... Ezr 2:55
the children of *S*, the children ... Neh 7:57

**SOTTISH**
they are s children, and they have ... Jer 4:22

**SOUGHT** See PREFACE.

**SOUL**
and man became a living s ... Gen 2:7
my s shall live because of thee ... Gen 12:13
that s shall be cut off from his ... Gen 17:14
and my s shall live ... Gen 19:20
that my s may bless thee before I ... Gen 27:4
venison, that thy s may bless me ... Gen 27:19
venison, that thy s may bless thee ... Gen 27:25
venison, that thy s may bless me ... Gen 27:31
his s clave unto Dinah the ... Gen 34:3
The s of my son Shechem longeth ... Gen 34:8
as her s was in departing, (for ... Gen 35:18
that we saw the anguish of his s ... Gen 42:21
O my s, come not thou into their ... Gen 49:6
that s shall be cut off from ... Ex 12:15
even that s shall be cut off from ... Ex 12:19
a ransom for his s unto the LORD ... Ex 30:12
that s shall be cut off from ... Ex 31:14
saying, If a s shall sin through ... Lev 4:2
And if a s sin, and hear the voice ... Lev 5:1
Or if a s touch any unclean thing ... Lev 5:2
Or if a s swear, pronouncing with ... Lev 5:4
If a s commit a trespass, and sin ... Lev 5:15
And if a s sin, and commit any of ... Lev 5:17
If a s sin, and commit a trespass ... Lev 6:2
the s that eateth of it shall ... Lev 7:18
But the s that eateth of the ... Lev 7:20
even that s shall be cut off from ... Lev 7:20
Moreover the s that shall touch ... Lev 7:21
even that s shall be cut off from ... Lev 7:21
even the s that eateth it shall ... Lev 7:25
Whatsoever s it be that eateth ... Lev 7:27
even that s shall be cut off from ... Lev 7:27
against that s that eateth blood ... Lev 17:10
maketh an atonement for the s ... Lev 17:11
No s of you shall eat blood, ... Lev 17:12
every s that eateth that which ... Lev 17:15
that s shall be cut off from ... Lev 19:8
the s that turneth after such as ... Lev 20:6
even set my face against that s ... Lev 20:6
that s shall be cut off from my ... Lev 22:3
The s which hath touched any such ... Lev 22:6
priest buy any s with his money ... Lev 22:11
For whatsoever s it be that shall ... Lev 23:29
whatsoever s it be that doeth any ... Lev 23:30
the same s will I destroy from ... Lev 23:30
and my s shall not abhor you ... Lev 26:11
or if your s abhor my judgments, ... Lev 26:15
idols, and my s shall abhor you ... Lev 26:30
because their s abhorred my ... Lev 26:43
even the same s shall be cut off ... Num 9:13
But now our s is dried away ... Num 11:6
if any s sin through ignorance, ... Num 15:27
for the s that sinneth ignorantly ... Num 15:28
But the s that doeth ought ... Num 15:30
that s shall be cut off from ... Num 15:30
that s shall utterly be cut off ... Num 15:31
that s shall be cut off from ... Num 19:13
that s shall be cut off from ... Num 19:20
the s that toucheth it shall be ... Num 19:22
the s of the people was much ... Num 21:4
our s loatheth this light bread ... Num 21:5
an oath to bind his s with a bond ... Num 30:2
wherewith she hath bound her s ... Num 30:4
she hath bound her s shall stand ... Num 30:4
wherewith she hath bound her s ... Num 30:5
lips, wherewith she bound her s ... Num 30:6
she bound her s shall stand ... Num 30:7
lips, wherewith she bound her s ... Num 30:8
or bound her s by a bond with an ... Num 30:10
she bound her s shall stand ... Num 30:11
or concerning the bond of her s ... Num 30:12
binding oath to afflict the s ... Num 30:13
one s of five hundred, both of ... Num 31:28
keep thy s diligently, lest thou ... Deut 4:9
all thy heart and with all thy s ... Deut 4:29
thine heart, and with all thy s ... Deut 6:5
all thy heart and with all thy s ... Deut 10:12
all your heart and with all your s ... Deut 11:13
words in your heart and in your s ... Deut 11:18
whatsoever thy s lusteth after ... Deut 12:15
because thy s longeth to eat ... Deut 12:20
whatsoever thy s lusteth after ... Deut 12:20
whatsoever thy s lusteth after ... Deut 12:21
all your heart and with all your s ... Deut 13:3
friend, which is as thine own s ... Deut 13:6
whatsoever thy s lusteth after ... Deut 14:26
or for whatsoever thy s desireth ... Deut 14:26
thine heart, and with all thy s ... Deut 26:16
thine heart, and with all thy s ... Deut 30:2
thine heart, and with all thy s ... Deut 30:6
thine heart, and with all thy s ... Deut 30:10
all your heart and with all your s ... Josh 22:5
O my s, thou hast trodden down ... Judg 5:21
his s was grieved for the misery ... Judg 10:16
so that his s was vexed unto ... Judg 16:16
And she was in bitterness of s ... 1Sa 1:10
poured out my s before the LORD ... 1Sa 1:15
said, Oh my lord, as thy s liveth ... 1Sa 1:26
take as much as thy s desireth ... 1Sa 2:16
And Abner said, As thy s liveth ... 1Sa 17:55
that the s of Jonathan was knit ... 1Sa 18:1
was knit with the s of David ... 1Sa 18:1
Jonathan loved him as his own s ... 1Sa 18:1
because he loved him as his own s ... 1Sa 18:3
LORD liveth, and as thy s liveth ... 1Sa 20:3
David, Whatsoever thy s desireth ... 1Sa 20:4
loved him as he loved his own s ... 1Sa 20:17
the desire of thy s to come down ... 1Sa 23:20
yet thou huntest my s to take it ... 1Sa 24:11
LORD liveth, and as thy s liveth ... 1Sa 25:26
to pursue thee, and to seek thy s ... 1Sa 25:29
but the s of my lord shall be ... 1Sa 25:29
because my s was precious in ... 1Sa 26:21
because the s of all the people ... 1Sa 30:6
my s out of all adversity ... 2Sa 4:9
that are hated of David's s ... 2Sa 5:8
thou livest, and as thy s liveth ... 2Sa 11:11
the s of king David longed to go ... 2Sa 13:39
answered and said, As thy s liveth ... 2Sa 14:19
redeemed my s out of all distress ... 1Kin 1:29
their heart and with all their s ... 1Kin 2:4
their heart, and with all their s ... 1Kin 8:48
to all that thy s desireth ... 1Kin 11:37
let this child's s come into him ... 1Kin 17:21
the s of the child came into him ... 1Kin 17:22
LORD liveth, and as thy s liveth ... 2Kin 2:2
LORD liveth, and as thy s liveth ... 2Kin 2:4
LORD liveth, and as thy s liveth ... 2Kin 2:6
for her s is vexed within her ... 2Kin 4:27
LORD liveth, and as thy s liveth ... 2Kin 4:30
all their heart and all their s ... 2Kin 23:3
all his heart, and with all his s ... 2Kin 23:25
your s to seek the LORD your God ... 1Chr 22:19
with all their s in the land of ... 2Chr 6:38
their heart and with all their s ... 2Chr 15:12
all his heart, and with all his s ... 2Chr 34:31
and life unto the bitter in s ... Job 3:20
The things that my s refused to ... Job 6:7
in the bitterness of my s ... Job 7:11
So that my s chooseth strangling, ... Job 7:15
yet would I not know my s ... Job 9:21
My s is weary of my life ... Job 10:1
speak in the bitterness of my s ... Job 10:1
In whose hand is the s of every ... Job 12:10
his s within him shall mourn ... Job 14:22
if your s were in my soul's stead ... Job 16:4
How long will ye vex my s ... Job 19:2
dieth in the bitterness of his s ... Job 21:25
And what his s desireth, even that ... Job 23:13
the s of the wounded crieth out ... Job 24:12
the Almighty, who hath vexed my s ... Job 27:2
when God taketh away his s ... Job 27:8
they pursue my s as the wind ... Job 30:15
now my s is poured out upon me ... Job 30:16
was not my s grieved for the poor ... Job 30:25
sin by wishing a curse to his s ... Job 31:30
keepeth back his s from the pit ... Job 33:18
bread, and his s dainty meat ... Job 33:20
his s draweth near unto the grave ... Job 33:22
He will deliver his s from going ... Job 33:28
To bring back his s from the pit ... Job 33:30
Many there be which say of my s ... Ps 3:2
My s is also sore vexed ... Ps 6:3
Return, O LORD, deliver my s ... Ps 6:4
Lest he tear my s like a lion ... Ps 7:2
Let the enemy persecute my s ... Ps 7:5
how say ye to my s, Flee as a ... Ps 11:1
that loveth violence his s hateth ... Ps 11:5
long shall I take counsel in my s ... Ps 13:2
O my s, thou hast said unto the ... Ps 16:2
thou wilt not leave my s in hell ... Ps 16:10
deliver my s from the wicked, ... Ps 17:13
LORD is perfect, converting the s ... Ps 19:7
Deliver my s from the sword ... Ps 22:20
and none can keep alive his own s ... Ps 22:29
He restoreth my s ... Ps 23:3
not lifted up his s unto vanity ... Ps 24:4
thee, O LORD, do I lift up my s ... Ps 25:1
His s shall dwell at ease ... Ps 25:13
O keep my s, and deliver me ... Ps 25:20
Gather not my s with sinners ... Ps 26:9
brought up my s from the grave ... Ps 30:3
hast known my s in adversities ... Ps 31:7
is consumed with grief, yea, my s ... Ps 31:9
To deliver their s from death ... Ps 33:19
Our s waiteth for the LORD ... Ps 33:20
My s shall make her boast in the ... Ps 34:2
redeemeth the s of his servants ... Ps 34:22
say unto my s, I am thy salvation ... Ps 35:3
put to shame that seek after my s ... Ps 35:4
cause they have digged for my s ... Ps 35:7
my s shall be joyful in the LORD ... Ps 35:9
for good to the spoiling of my s ... Ps 35:12
I humbled my s with fasting ... Ps 35:13
rescue my s from their ... Ps 35:17
seek after my s to destroy it ... Ps 40:14
heal my s ... Ps 41:4
so panteth my s after thee ... Ps 42:1
My s thirsteth for God, for the ... Ps 42:2
things, I pour out my s in me ... Ps 42:4
Why art thou cast down, O my s ... Ps 42:5
my s is cast down within me ... Ps 42:6
Why art thou cast down, O my s ... Ps 42:11
Why art thou cast down, O my s ... Ps 43:5
For our s is bowed down to the ... Ps 44:25
redemption of their s is precious ... Ps 49:8
But God will redeem my s from the ... Ps 49:15
while he lived he blessed his s ... Ps 49:18
me, and oppressors seek after my s ... Ps 54:3
is with them that uphold my s ... Ps 54:4
He hath delivered my s in peace ... Ps 55:18
my steps, when they wait for my s ... Ps 56:6
hast delivered my s from death ... Ps 56:13
for my s trusteth in thee ... Ps 57:1
My s is among lions ... Ps 57:4
my s is bowed down ... Ps 57:6
lo, they lie in wait for my s ... Ps 59:3
Truly my s waiteth upon God ... Ps 62:1
My s, wait thou only upon God ... Ps 62:5
my s thirsteth for thee, my flesh ... Ps 63:1
My s shall be satisfied as with ... Ps 63:5
My s followeth hard after thee ... Ps 63:8
But those that seek my s, to ... Ps 63:9
Which holdeth our s in life ... Ps 66:9
what he hath done for my s ... Ps 66:16
the waters are come in unto my s ... Ps 69:1
and chastened my s with fasting ... Ps 69:10
Draw nigh unto my s, and redeem it ... Ps 69:18
confounded that seek after my s ... Ps 70:2
for my s take counsel together ... Ps 71:10
that are adversaries to my s ... Ps 71:13
and my s, which thou hast redeemed ... Ps 71:23
shall redeem their s from deceit ... Ps 72:14
O deliver not the s of thy ... Ps 74:19
my s refused to be comforted ... Ps 77:2
he spared not their s from death ... Ps 78:50
My s longeth, yea, even fainteth ... Ps 84:2
Preserve my s ... Ps 86:2
Rejoice the s of thy servant ... Ps 86:4

thee, O Lord, do I lift up my s ... Ps 86:4
my s from the lowest hell ... Ps 86:13
men have sought after my s ... Ps 86:14
For my s is full of troubles ... Ps 88:3
LORD, why castest thou off my s ... Ps 88:14
shall he deliver his s from the ... Ps 89:48
my s had almost dwelt in silence ... Ps 94:17
me thy comforts delight my s ... Ps 94:19
against the s of the righteous ... Ps 94:21
Bless the LORD, O my s ... Ps 103:1
Bless the LORD, O my s, and forget ... Ps 103:2
bless the LORD, O my s ... Ps 103:22
Bless the LORD, O my s ... Ps 104:1
Bless thou the LORD, O my s ... Ps 104:35
but sent leanness into their s ... Ps 106:15
thirsty, their s fainted in them ... Ps 107:5
For he satisfieth the longing s ... Ps 107:9
the hungry s with goodness ... Ps 107:9
Their s abhorreth all manner of ... Ps 107:18
their s is melted because of ... Ps 107:26
them that speak evil against my s ... Ps 109:20
him from those that condemn his s ... Ps 109:31
I beseech thee, deliver my s ... Ps 116:4
Return unto thy rest, O my s ... Ps 116:7
hast delivered my s from death ... Ps 116:8
My s breaketh for the longing ... Ps 119:20
My s cleaveth unto the dust ... Ps 119:25
My s melteth for heaviness ... Ps 119:28
My s fainteth for thy salvation ... Ps 119:81
My s is continually in my hand ... Ps 119:109
therefore doth my s keep them ... Ps 119:129
My s hath kept thy testimonies ... Ps 119:167
Let my s live, and it shall praise ... Ps 119:175
Deliver my s, O LORD, from lying ... Ps 120:2
My s hath long dwelt with him ... Ps 120:6
he shall preserve thy s ... Ps 121:7
Our s is exceedingly filled with ... Ps 123:4
the stream had gone over our s ... Ps 124:4
proud waters had gone over our s ... Ps 124:5
Our s is escaped as a bird out of ... Ps 124:7
my s doth wait, and in his word do ... Ps 130:5
My s waiteth for the Lord more ... Ps 130:6
my s is even as a weaned child ... Ps 131:2
me with strength in my s ... Ps 138:3
that my s knoweth right well ... Ps 139:14
leave not my s destitute ... Ps 141:8
no man cared for my s ... Ps 142:4
Bring my s out of prison, that I ... Ps 142:7
the enemy hath persecuted my s ... Ps 143:3
my s thirsteth after thee, as a ... Ps 143:6
for I lift up my s unto thee ... Ps 143:8
sake bring my s out of trouble ... Ps 143:11
all them that afflict my s ... Ps 143:12
Praise the LORD, O my s ... Ps 146:1
knowledge is pleasant unto thy s ... Prov 2:10
So shall they be life unto thy s ... Prov 3:22
satisfy his s when he is hungry ... Prov 6:30
doeth it destroyeth his own s ... Prov 6:32
against me wrongeth his own s ... Prov 8:36
the s of the righteous to famish ... Prov 10:3
man doeth good to his own s ... Prov 11:17
The liberal s shall be made fat ... Prov 11:25
but the s of the transgressors ... Prov 13:2
The s of the sluggard desireth ... Prov 13:4
but the s of the diligent shall ... Prov 13:4
accomplished is sweet to the s ... Prov 13:19
eateth to the satisfying of his s ... Prov 13:25
instruction despiseth his own s ... Prov 15:32
keepeth his way preserveth his s ... Prov 16:17
as an honeycomb, sweet to the s ... Prov 16:24
his lips are the snare of his s ... Prov 18:7
that the s be without knowledge ... Prov 19:2
getteth wisdom loveth his own s ... Prov 19:8
an idle s shall suffer hunger ... Prov 19:15
keepeth his own s ... Prov 19:16
let not thy s spare for his ... Prov 19:18
anger sinneth against his own s ... Prov 20:2
The s of the wicked desireth evil ... Prov 21:10
keepeth his s from troubles ... Prov 21:23
he that doth keep his s shall be ... Prov 22:5
spoil the s of those that spoiled ... Prov 22:23
his ways, and get a snare to thy s ... Prov 22:25
and shalt deliver his s from hell ... Prov 23:14
and he that keepeth thy s, doth ... Prov 24:12
knowledge of wisdom be unto thy s .. Prov 24:14
refresheth the s of his masters ... Prov 25:13
As cold waters to a thirsty s ... Prov 25:25
The full s loatheth an honeycomb ... Prov 27:7
but to the hungry s every bitter ... Prov 27:7
but the just seek his s ... Prov 29:10
he shall give delight unto thy s ... Prov 29:17
with a thief hateth his own s ... Prov 29:24
that he should make his s enjoy ... Eccl 2:24
I labour, and bereave my s of good ... Eccl 4:8
for his s of all that he desireth ... Eccl 6:2
his s be not filled with good, and ... Eccl 6:3
Which yet my s seeketh, but I ... Eccl 7:28
Tell me, O thou whom my s loveth ... Song 1:7
bed I sought him whom my s loveth ... Song 3:1
I will seek him whom my s loveth ... Song 3:2
said, Saw ye him whom my s loveth ... Song 3:3
but I found him whom my s loveth ... Song 3:4
my s failed when he spake ... Song 5:6
my s made me like the chariots of ... Song 6:12
your appointed feasts my s hateth ... Is 1:14
Woe unto their s ... Is 3:9
and of his fruitful field, both s ... Is 10:18
desire of our s is to thy name ... Is 26:8
With my s have I desired thee in ... Is 26:9
but he awaketh, and his s is empty ... Is 29:8
is faint, and his s hath appetite ... Is 29:8
to make empty the s of the hungry ... Is 32:6
years in the bitterness of my s ... Is 38:15
but thou hast in love to my s ... Is 38:17
elect, in whom my s delighteth ... Is 42:1
that he cannot deliver his s ... Is 44:20
which have said to thy s, Bow ... Is 51:23
make his s an offering for sin ... Is 53:10
shall see of the travail of his s ... Is 53:11
hath poured out his s unto death ... Is 53:12
let your s delight itself in ... Is 55:2
hear, and your s shall live ... Is 55:3
wherefore have we afflicted our s ... Is 58:3
a day for a man to afflict his s ... Is 58:5
thou draw out thy s to the hungry ... Is 58:10
and satisfy the afflicted s ... Is 58:10
and satisfy thy s in drought ... Is 58:11
my s shall be joyful in my God ... Is 61:10
their s delighteth in their ... Is 66:3
the sword reacheth unto the s ... Jer 4:10
because thou hast heard, O my s ... Jer 4:19
for my s is wearied because of ... Jer 4:31
shall not my s be avenged on such ... Jer 5:9
shall not my s be avenged on such ... Jer 5:29
lest my s depart from thee ... Jer 6:8
shall not my s be avenged on such ... Jer 9:9
my s into the hand of her enemies ... Jer 12:7
my s shall weep in secret places ... Jer 13:17
hath thy s lothed Zion ... Jer 14:19
they have digged a pit for my s ... Jer 18:20
for he hath delivered the s of ... Jer 20:13
their s shall be as a watered ... Jer 31:12
I will satiate the s of the ... Jer 31:14
For I have satiated the weary s ... Jer 31:25
replenished every sorrowful s ... Jer 31:25
my whole heart and with my whole s .. Jer 32:41
LORD liveth, that made us this s ... Jer 38:16
then thy s shall live, and this ... Jer 38:17
unto thee, and thy s shall live ... Jer 38:20
his s shall be satisfied upon ... Jer 50:19
and deliver ye every man his s ... Jer 51:6
deliver ye every man his s from ... Jer 51:45
things for meat to relieve the s ... Lam 1:11
relieve my s is far from me ... Lam 1:16
when their s was poured out into ... Lam 2:12
removed my s far off from peace ... Lam 3:17
My s hath them still in ... Lam 3:20
LORD is my portion, saith my s ... Lam 3:24
to the s that seeketh him ... Lam 3:25
hast pleaded the causes of my s ... Lam 3:58
but thou hast delivered thy s ... Eze 3:19
also thou hast delivered thy s ... Eze 3:21
my s hath not been polluted ... Eze 4:14
as the s of the father, so also ... Eze 18:4
so also the s of the son is mine ... Eze 18:4
the s that sinneth, it shall die ... Eze 18:4
The s that sinneth, it shall die ... Eze 18:20
right, he shall save his s alive ... Eze 18:27
and that which your s pitieth ... Eze 24:21
warning shall deliver his s ... Eze 33:5
but thou hast delivered thy s ... Eze 33:9
for their bread for their s shall ... Hos 9:4
compassed me about, even to the s ... Jonah 2:5
When my s fainted within me I ... Jonah 2:7
of my body for the sin of my s ... Mic 6:7
my s desired the firstripe fruit ... Mic 7:1
his s which is lifted up is not ... Hab 2:4
and hast sinned against thy s ... Hab 2:10
my s lothed them ... Zec 11:8
and their s also abhorred me ... Zec 11:8
but are not able to kill the s ... Mt 10:28
which is able to destroy both s ... Mt 10:28
in whom my s is well pleased ... Mt 12:18
whole world, and lose his own s ... Mt 16:26
a man give in exchange for his s ... Mt 16:26
all thy heart, and with all thy s ... Mt 22:37
My s is exceeding sorrowful, even ... Mt 26:38
whole world, and lose his own s ... Mk 8:36
a man give in exchange for his s ... Mk 8:37
all thy heart, and with all thy s ... Mk 12:30
understanding, and with all the s ... Mk 12:33
My s is exceeding sorrowful unto ... Mk 14:34
My s doth magnify the Lord ... Lk 1:46
pierce through thy own s also ... Lk 2:35
all thy heart, and with all thy s ... Lk 10:27
And I will say to my s, S, thou ... Lk 12:19
And I will say to my s, S ... Lk 12:19
this night thy s shall be ... Lk 12:20
Now is my s troubled ... Jn 12:27
thou wilt not leave my s in hell ... Acts 2:27
that his s was not left in hell ... Acts 2:31
And fear came upon every s ... Acts 2:43
shall come to pass, that every s ... Acts 3:23
were of one heart and of one s ... Acts 4:32
upon every s of man that doeth ... Rom 2:9
Let every s be subject unto the ... Rom 13:1
man Adam was made a living s ... 1Cor 15:45
I call God for a record upon my s ... 2Cor 1:23
I pray God your whole spirit and s ... 1Th 5:23
even to the dividing asunder of s ... Heb 4:12
we have as an anchor of the s ... Heb 6:19
my s shall have no pleasure in ... Heb 10:38
believe to the saving of the s ... Heb 10:39
his way shall save a s from death ... Jas 5:20
lusts, which war against the s ... 1Pet 2:11
vexed his righteous s from day to ... 2Pet 2:8
health, even as thy s prospereth ... 3Jn 2
every living s died in the sea ... Rev 16:3
the fruits that thy s lusted ... Rev 18:14

## SOUL'S

if your soul were in my s stead ... Job 16:4

## SOULS

the s that they had gotten in ... Gen 12:5
all the s of his sons and his ... Gen 46:15
bare unto Jacob, even sixteen s ... Gen 46:18
all the s were fourteen ... Gen 46:22
all the s were seven ... Gen 46:25
All the s that came with Jacob ... Gen 46:26
all the s were threescore and six ... Gen 46:26
born him in Egypt, were two s ... Gen 46:27
all the s of the house of Jacob ... Gen 46:27
all the s that came out of the ... Ex 1:5
the loins of Jacob were seventy s ... Ex 1:5
according to the number of the s ... Ex 12:4
to make an atonement for your s ... Ex 30:15
to make an atonement for your s ... Ex 30:16
month, ye shall afflict your s ... Lev 16:29
you, and ye shall afflict your s ... Lev 16:31
to make an atonement for your s ... Lev 17:11
even the s that commit them shall ... Lev 18:29
make your s abominable by beast ... Lev 20:25
and ye shall afflict your s ... Lev 23:27
rest, and ye shall afflict your s ... Lev 23:32
these sinners against their own s ... Num 16:38
and ye shall afflict your s ... Num 29:7
wherewith they have bound their s ... Num 30:9
for our s before the LORD ... Num 31:50
all the s that were therein ... Josh 10:28
all the s that were therein ... Josh 10:30
all the s that were therein ... Josh 10:32
all the s that were therein he ... Josh 10:35
all the s that were therein ... Josh 10:37
all the s that were therein ... Josh 10:37
all the s that were therein ... Josh 10:39
they smote all the s that were ... Josh 11:11
all your hearts and in all your s ... Josh 23:14
the s of thine enemies, them ... 1Sa 25:29
and shall save the s of the needy ... Ps 72:13
he preserveth the s of his saints ... Ps 97:10
and he that winneth s is wise ... Prov 11:30
A true witness delivereth s ... Prov 14:25
me, and the s which I have made ... Is 57:16
of the s of the poor innocents ... Jer 2:34
and ye shall find rest for your s ... Jer 6:16
procure great evil against our s ... Jer 26:19
ye this great evil against your s ... Jer 44:7
their meat to relieve their s ... Lam 1:19
they shall not satisfy their s ... Eze 7:19
head of every stature to hunt s ... Eze 13:18
Will ye hunt the s of my people ... Eze 13:18
will ye save the s alive that ... Eze 13:18
to slay the s that should not die ... Eze 13:19
to save the s alive that should ... Eze 13:19
there hunt the s to make them fly ... Eze 13:20
your arms, and will let the s go ... Eze 13:20
even the s that ye hunt to make ... Eze 13:20
own s by their righteousness ... Eze 14:14
own s by their righteousness ... Eze 14:20
Behold, all s are mine ... Eze 18:4
they have devoured s ... Eze 22:25
to shed blood, and to destroy s ... Eze 22:27
and ye shall find rest unto your s ... Mt 11:29
your patience possess ye your s ... Lk 21:19
unto them about three thousand s ... Acts 2:41
kindred, threescore and fifteen s ... Acts 7:14
Confirming the s of the disciples ... Acts 14:22
you with words, subverting your s ... Acts 15:24
hundred threescore and sixteen s ... Acts 27:37
of God only, but also our own s ... 1Th 2:8
for they watch for your s ... Heb 13:17
which is able to save your s ... Jas 1:21
even the salvation of your s ... 1Pet 1:9
s in obeying the truth through ... 1Pet 1:22
the Shepherd and Bishop of your s ... 1Pet 2:25
eight s were saved by water ... 1Pet 3:20
of their s to him in well doing ... 1Pet 4:19
beguiling unstable s ... 2Pet 2:14
I saw under the altar the s of ... Rev 6:9
chariots, and slaves, and s of men ... Rev 18:13
I saw the s of them that were ... Rev 20:4

## SOUND

his s shall be heard when he ... Ex 28:35
the trumpet of the jubile to s on ... Lev 25:9
s throughout all your land ... Lev 25:9
the s of a shaken leaf shall ... Lev 26:36
blow, but ye shall not s an alarm ... Num 10:7
when ye hear the s of the trumpet ... Josh 6:5
people heard the s of the trumpet ... Josh 6:20
when thou hearest the s of a ... 2Sa 5:24
with the s of the trumpet ... 2Sa 6:15
as ye hear the s of the trumpet ... 2Sa 15:10
the earth rent with the s of them ... 1Kin 1:40
Joab heard the s of the trumpet ... 1Kin 1:41
Ahijah heard the s of her feet ... 1Kin 14:6
for there is a s of abundance of ... 1Kin 18:41
is not the s of his master's feet ... 2Kin 6:32
when thou shalt hear a s of going ... 1Chr 14:15
were appointed to s with cymbals ... 1Chr 15:19
with s of the cornet, and with ... 1Chr 15:28
but Asaph made a s with cymbals ... 1Chr 16:5
for those that should make a s ... 1Chr 16:42
to make one s to be heard in ... 2Chr 5:13
ye hear the s of the trumpet ... Neh 4:20
A dreadful s is in his ears ... Job 15:21
and rejoice at the s of the organ ... Job 21:12
the s that goeth out of his mouth ... Job 37:2
that it is the s of the trumpet ... Job 39:24
the LORD with the s of a trumpet ... Ps 47:5

the skies sent out a *s* ... Ps 77:17
the people that know the joyful *s* ... Ps 89:15
upon the harp with a solemn *s* ... Ps 92:3
*s* of cornet make a joyful noise ... Ps 98:6
Let my heart be *s* in thy statutes ... Ps 119:80
him with the *s* of the trumpet ... Ps 150:3
He layeth up *s* wisdom for the ... Prov 2:7
keep *s* wisdom and discretion ... Prov 3:21
Counsel is mine, and *s* wisdom ... Prov 8:14
A *s* heart is the life of the ... Prov 14:30
when the *s* of the grinding is low ... Eccl 12:4
shall *s* like an harp for Moab ... Is 16:11
the *s* of the trumpet, the alarm ... Jer 4:19
hear the *s* of the trumpet ... Jer 4:21
Hearken to the *s* of the trumpet ... Jer 6:17
*s* of the neighing of his strong ... Jer 8:16
the *s* of the millstones, and the ... Jer 25:10
nor hear the *s* of the trumpet, ... Jer 42:14
heart shall *s* for Moab like pipes ... Jer 48:36
mine heart shall *s* like pipes for ... Jer 48:36
A *s* of battle is in the land, and ... Jer 50:22
A *s* of a cry cometh from Babylon, ... Jer 51:54
the *s* of the cherubims' wings was ... Eze 10:5
the *s* of thy harps shall be no ... Eze 26:13
isles shake at the *s* of thy fall ... Eze 26:15
at the *s* of the cry of thy pilots ... Eze 27:28
to shake at the *s* of his fall ... Eze 31:16
heareth the *s* of the trumpet ... Eze 33:4
He heard the *s* of the trumpet, and ... Eze 33:5
time ye hear the *s* of the cornet ... Dan 3:5
people heard the *s* of the cornet ... Dan 3:7
shall hear the *s* of the cornet ... Dan 3:10
time ye hear the *s* of the cornet ... Dan 3:15
*s* an alarm in my holy mountain ... Joel 2:1
with the *s* of the trumpet ... Amos 2:2
That chant to the *s* of the viol ... Amos 6:5
do not *s* a trumpet before thee, ... Mt 6:2
with a great *s* of a trumpet ... Mt 24:31
he hath received him safe and *s* ... Lk 15:27
and thou hearest the *s* thereof ... Jn 3:8
suddenly there came a *s* from ... Acts 2:2
their *s* went into all the earth, ... Rom 10:18
even things without life giving *s* ... 1Cor 14:7
the trumpet give an uncertain *s* ... 1Cor 14:8
for the trumpet shall *s*, and the ... 1Cor 15:52
that is contrary to *s* doctrine ... 1Ti 1:10
power, and of love, and of a *s* mind ... 2Ti 1:7
Hold fast the form of *s* words ... 2Ti 1:13
they will not endure *s* doctrine ... 2Ti 4:3
that he may be able by *s* doctrine ... Titus 1:9
that they may be *s* in the faith ... Titus 1:13
things which become *s* doctrine ... Titus 2:1
*s* in faith, in charity, in ... Titus 2:2
*S* speech, that cannot be ... Titus 2:8
the *s* of a trumpet, and the voice ... Heb 12:19
his voice as the *s* of many waters ... Rev 1:15
trumpets prepared themselves to *s* ... Rev 8:6
three angels, which are yet to *s* ... Rev 8:13
the *s* of their wings was as the ... Rev 9:9
the *s* of chariots of many horses ... Rev 9:9
angel, when he shall begin to *s* ... Rev 10:7
the *s* of a millstone shall be ... Rev 18:22

## SOUNDED
the voice of the trumpet *s* long ... Ex 19:19
when I have *s* my father about to ... 1Sa 20:12
the priests *s* trumpets before ... 2Chr 7:6
the priests *s* with the trumpets ... 2Chr 13:14
*s* with trumpets, also the singers ... 2Chr 23:13
singers sang, and the trumpeters *s* ... 2Chr 29:28
he that *s* the trumpet was by me ... Neh 4:18
of thy salutation *s* in mine ears ... Lk 1:44
And *s*, and found it twenty fathoms .. Acts 27:28
they *s* again, and found it fifteen ... Acts 27:28
For from you *s* out the word of ... 1Th 1:8
The first angel *s*, and there ... Rev 8:7
And the second angel *s*, and as it ... Rev 8:8
And the third angel *s*, and there ... Rev 8:10
And the fourth angel *s*, and the ... Rev 8:12
And the fifth angel *s*, and I saw a ... Rev 9:1
And the sixth angel *s*, and I heard ... Rev 9:13
And the seventh angel *s* ... Rev 11:15

## SOUNDETH
when the trumpet *s* long, they ... Ex 19:13

## SOUNDING
psalteries and harps and cymbals, *s* ... 1Chr 15:16
and twenty priests *s* with trumpets ... 2Chr 5:12
his priests with *s* trumpets to ... 2Chr 13:12
him upon the high *s* cymbals ... Ps 150:5
the *s* of thy bowels and of thy ... Is 63:15
not the *s* again of the mountains ... Eze 7:7
charity, I am become as *s* brass ... 1Cor 13:1

## SOUNDNESS
There is no *s* in my flesh because ... Ps 38:3
and there is no *s* in my flesh ... Ps 38:7
unto the head there is no *s* in it ... Is 1:6
*s* in the presence of you all ... Acts 3:16

## SOUNDS
they give a distinction in the *s* ... 1Cor 14:7

## SOUR
the *s* grape is ripening in the ... Is 18:5
The fathers have eaten a *s* grape ... Jer 31:29
every man that eateth the *s* grape ... Jer 31:30
The fathers have eaten *s* grapes ... Eze 18:2
Their drink is *s* ... Hos 4:18

## SOUTH
going on still toward the *s* ... Gen 12:9
had, and Lot with him, into the *s* ... Gen 13:1
from the *s* even to Beth-el ... Gen 13:3
from thence toward the *s* country ... Gen 20:1
for he dwelt in the *s* country ... Gen 24:62
and to the north, and to the *s* ... Gen 28:14
boards on the *s* side southward ... Ex 26:18
of the tabernacle toward the *s* ... Ex 26:35
for the *s* side southward there ... Ex 27:9
boards for the *s* side southward ... Ex 36:23
on the *s* side southward the ... Ex 38:9
On the *s* side shall be the ... Num 2:10
*s* side shall take their journey ... Num 10:6
And they ascended by the *s* ... Num 13:22
dwell in the land of the *s* ... Num 13:29
Canaanite, which dwelt in the *s* ... Num 21:1
which dwelt in the *s* in the land ... Num 33:40
Then your *s* quarter shall be from ... Num 34:3
your *s* border shall be the ... Num 34:3
the *s* to the ascent of Akrabbim ... Num 34:4
be from the *s* to Kadesh-barnea ... Num 34:4
on the *s* side two thousand cubits ... Num 35:5
and in the vale, and in the *s* ... Deut 1:7
possess thou the west and the *s* ... Deut 33:23
And the *s*, and the plain of the ... Deut 34:3
country of the hills, and of the *s* ... Josh 10:40
and of the plains *s* of Chinneroth ... Josh 11:2
the hills, and all the *s* country ... Josh 11:16
and from the *s*, under ... Josh 12:3
wilderness, and in the *s* country ... Josh 12:8
From the *s*, all the land of the ... Josh 13:4
the uttermost part of the *s* coast ... Josh 15:1
their *s* border was from the shore ... Josh 15:2
it went out to the *s* side to ... Josh 15:3
ascended up on the *s* side unto ... Josh 15:3
this shall be your *s* coast ... Josh 15:4
which is on the *s* side of the ... Josh 15:7
unto the *s* side of the Jebusite ... Josh 15:8
for thou hast given me a *s* land ... Josh 15:19
abide in their coast on the *s* ... Josh 18:5
*s* side of the nether Beth-horon ... Josh 18:13
the *s* quarter was from the end of ... Josh 18:15
to the side of Jebusi on the *s* ... Josh 18:16
salt sea at the *s* end of Jordan ... Josh 18:19
this was the *s* coast ... Josh 18:19
to Baalath-beer, Ramath of the *s* ... Josh 19:8
reacheth to Zebulun on the *s* side ... Josh 19:34
in the mountain, and in the *s* ... Judg 1:9
for thou hast given me a *s* land ... Judg 1:15
which lieth in the *s* of Arad ... Judg 1:16
Shechem, and on the *s* of Lebonah ... Judg 21:19
arose out of a place toward the *s* ... 1Sa 20:41
which is on the *s* of Jeshimon ... 1Sa 23:19
in the plain on the *s* of Jeshimon ... 1Sa 23:24
said, Against the *s* of Judah ... 1Sa 27:10
of Judah, and against the *s* of the ... 1Sa 27:10
against the *s* of the Kenites ... 1Sa 27:10
the Amalekites had invaded the *s* ... 1Sa 30:1
upon the *s* of the Cherethites ... 1Sa 30:14
to Judah, and upon the *s* of Caleb ... 1Sa 30:14
and to them which were in *s* Ramoth. 1Sa 30:27
they went out to the *s* of Judah ... 2Sa 24:7
and three looking toward the *s* ... 1Kin 7:25
house eastward over against the *s* ... 1Kin 7:39
the east, west, north, and *s* ... 1Chr 9:24
and three looking toward the *s* ... 2Chr 4:4
the east end, over against the *s* ... 2Chr 4:10
of the *s* of Judah, and had taken ... 2Chr 28:18
and the chambers of the *s* ... Job 9:9
Out of the *s* cometh the whirlwind ... Job 37:9
quieteth the earth by the *s* wind ... Job 37:17
and stretch her wings toward the *s* ... Job 39:26
nor from the west, nor from the *s* ... Ps 75:6
power he brought in the *s* wind ... Ps 78:26
the *s* thou hast created them ... Ps 89:12
from the north, and from the *s* ... Ps 107:3
O LORD, as the streams in the *s* ... Ps 126:4
The wind goeth toward the *s* ... Eccl 1:6
and if the tree fall toward the *s* ... Eccl 11:3
and come, thou *s* ... Song 4:16
whirlwinds in the *s* pass through ... Is 21:1
The burden of the beasts of the *s* ... Is 30:6
and to the *s*, Keep not back ... Is 43:6
cities of the *s* shall be shut up ... Jer 13:19
from the mountains, and from the *s* ... Jer 17:26
valley, and in the cities of the *s* ... Jer 32:44
vale, and in the cities of the *s* ... Jer 33:13
of man, set thy face toward the *s* ... Eze 20:46
and drop thy word toward the *s* ... Eze 20:46
against the forest of the *s* field ... Eze 20:46
And say to the forest of the *s* ... Eze 20:47
all faces from the *s* to the north ... Eze 20:47
all flesh from the *s* to the north ... Eze 21:4
as the frame of a city on the *s* ... Eze 40:2
that he brought me toward the *s* ... Eze 40:24
and behold a gate toward the *s* ... Eze 40:24
in the inner court toward the *s* ... Eze 40:27
toward the *s* an hundred cubits ... Eze 40:27
to the inner court by the *s* gate ... Eze 40:28
he measured the *s* gate according ... Eze 40:28
their prospect was toward the *s* ... Eze 40:44
whose prospect is toward the *s* ... Eze 40:45
and another door toward the *s* ... Eze 41:11
*s* was a door in the head of the ... Eze 42:12
the *s* chambers, which are before ... Eze 42:13
He measured the *s* side, five ... Eze 42:18
go out by the way of the *s* gate ... Eze 46:9
*s* gate shall go forth by the way ... Eze 46:9
at the *s* side of the altar ... Eze 47:1
the *s* side southward, from Tamar ... Eze 47:19
this is the *s* side southward ... Eze 47:19
in breadth, and toward the *s* five ... Eze 48:10
the *s* side four thousand and five ... Eze 48:16
toward the *s* two hundred and fifty ... Eze 48:17
at the *s* side southward, the ... Eze 48:28
at the *s* side four thousand and ... Eze 48:33
exceeding great, toward the *s* ... Dan 8:9
the king of the *s* shall be strong ... Dan 11:5
*s* shall come to the king of the ... Dan 11:6
So the king of the *s* shall come ... Dan 11:9
the king of the *s* shall be moved ... Dan 11:11
up against the king of the *s* ... Dan 11:14
the arms of the *s* shall not ... Dan 11:15
king of the *s* with a great army ... Dan 11:25
the king of the *s* shall be ... Dan 11:25
return, and come toward the *s* ... Dan 11:29
the king of the *s* push at him ... Dan 11:40
they of the *s* shall possess the ... Obad 19
shall possess the cities of the *s* ... Obad 20
go forth toward the *s* country ... Zec 6:6
her, when men inhabited the *s* ... Zec 7:7
shall go with whirlwinds of the *s* ... Zec 9:14
north, and half of it toward the *s* ... Zec 14:4
Geba to Rimmon *s* of Jerusalem ... Zec 14:10
The queen of the *s* shall rise up ... Mt 12:42
The queen of the *s* shall rise up ... Lk 11:31
And when ye see the *s* wind blow ... Lk 12:55
and from the north, and from the *s* ... Lk 13:29
go toward the *s* unto the way that ... Acts 8:26
Crete, and lieth toward the *s* west ... Acts 27:12
when the *s* wind blew softly, ... Acts 27:13
and after one day the *s* wind blew ... Acts 28:13
on the *s* three gates ... Rev 21:13

## SOUTHWARD
where thou art northward, and *s* ... Gen 13:14
twenty boards on the south side *s* ... Ex 26:18
for the south side *s* there shall ... Ex 27:9
boards for the south side *s* ... Ex 36:23
on the south side *s* the hangings ... Ex 38:9
on the side of the tabernacle *s* ... Ex 40:24
on the side of the tabernacle *s* ... Num 3:29
unto them, Get you up this way *s* ... Num 13:17
eyes westward, and northward, and *s*. Deut 3:27
*s* was the uttermost part of the ... Josh 15:1
sea, from the bay that looketh *s* ... Josh 15:2
the coast of Edom *s* were Kabzeel ... Josh 15:21
the river Kanah, *s* of the river ... Josh 17:9
*S* it was Ephraim's, and northward ... Josh 17:10
side of Luz, which is Beth-el, *s* ... Josh 18:13
compassed the corner of the sea *s* ... Josh 18:14
that lieth before Beth-horon *s* ... Josh 18:14
the other *s* over against Gibeah ... 1Sa 14:5
To Obed-edom *s* ... 1Chr 26:15
*s* four a day, and toward Asuppim ... 1Chr 26:17
And the south side *s*, from Tamar ... Eze 47:19
And this is the south side *s* ... Eze 47:19
of Gad, at the south side *s* ... Eze 48:28
westward, and northward, and *s* ... Dan 8:4

## SOW
for you, and ye shall *s* the land ... Gen 47:23
six years thou shalt *s* thy land ... Ex 23:10
thou shalt not *s* thy field with ... Lev 19:19
Six years thou shalt *s* thy field ... Lev 25:3
thou shalt neither *s* thy field ... Lev 25:4
ye shall not *s*, neither reap that ... Lev 25:11
behold, we shall not *s*, nor ... Lev 25:20
ye shall *s* the eighth year, and ... Lev 25:22
ye shall *s* your seed in vain, for ... Lev 26:16
Thou shalt not *s* thy vineyard ... Deut 22:9
and in the third year *s* ye ... 2Kin 19:29
*s* wickedness, reap the same ... Job 4:8
Then let me *s*, and let another eat ... Job 31:8
*s* the fields, and plant vineyards, ... Ps 107:37
They that *s* in tears shall reap ... Ps 126:5
observeth the wind shall not *s* ... Eccl 11:4
In the morning *s* thy seed ... Eccl 11:6
the plowman plow all day to *s* ... Is 28:24
that thou shalt *s* the ground ... Is 30:23
are ye that *s* beside all waters ... Is 32:20
and in the third year *s* ye ... Is 37:30
ground, and *s* not among thorns ... Jer 4:3
that I will *s* the house of Israel ... Jer 31:27
nor *s* seed, nor plant vineyard, ... Jer 35:7
I will *s* her unto me in the earth ... Hos 2:23
*S* to yourselves in righteousness, ... Hos 10:12
Thou shalt *s*, but thou shalt not ... Mic 6:15
I will *s* them among the people ... Zec 10:9
for they *s* not, neither do they ... Mt 6:26
Behold, a sower went forth to *s* ... Mt 13:3
didst not thou *s* good seed in thy ... Mt 13:27
there went out a sower to *s* ... Mk 4:3
A sower went out to *s* his seed ... Lk 8:5
for they neither *s* nor reap ... Lk 12:24
and reapest that thou didst not *s* ... Lk 19:21
down, and reaping that I did not *s* ... Lk 19:22
the *s* that was washed to her ... 2Pet 2:22

## SOWED
Then Isaac *s* in that land, and ... Gen 26:12
down the city, and *s* it with salt ... Judg 9:45
And when he *s*, some seeds fell by ... Mt 13:4
which *s* good seed in his field ... Mt 13:24
*s* tares among the wheat, and went ... Mt 13:25
a man took, and *s* in his field ... Mt 13:31
The enemy that *s* them is the ... Mt 13:39
knewest that I reap where I *s* not ... Mt 25:26
And it came to pass, as he *s* ... Mk 4:4
and as he *s*, some fell by the way ... Lk 8:5

S

**SOWEDST**
came out, where thou *s* thy seed....... Deut 11:10

**SOWER**
that it may give seed to the *s*.................. Is 55:10
Cut off the *s* from Babylon, and........... Jer 50:16
Behold, a *s* went forth to sow................ Mt 13:3
ye therefore the parable of the *s*............. Mt 13:18
Behold, there went out a *s* to sow........... Mk 4:3
The *s* soweth the word.......................... Mk 4:14
A *s* went out to sow his seed.................. Lk 8:5
*s* both minister bread for your............. 2Cor 9:10

**SOWEST**
fool, that which thou *s* is not.............. 1Cor 15:36
And that which thou *s*........................ 1Cor 15:37
thou *s* not that body that shall.......... 1Cor 15:37

**SOWETH**
he *s* discord............................................ Prov 6:14
he that *s* discord among brethren........ Prov 6:19
but to him that *s* righteousness......... Prov 11:18
A froward man *s* strife......................... Prov 16:28
He that *s* iniquity shall reap................ Prov 22:8
treader of grapes him that *s* seed...... Amos 9:13
He that *s* the good seed is the............... Mt 13:37
The sower *s* the word........................... Mk 4:14
that both he that *s* and he that.............. Jn 4:36
herein is that saying true, One *s*........... Jn 4:37
He which *s* sparingly shall reap............ 2Cor 9:6
he which *s* bountifully shall reap.......... 2Cor 9:6
for whatsoever a man *s*, that.................. Gal 6:7
For he that *s* to his flesh shall............... Gal 6:8
but he that *s* to the Spirit shall............. Gal 6:8

**SOWING**
any *s* seed which is to be sown........... Lev 11:37
shall reach unto the *s* time................... Lev 26:5

**SOWN**
which thou hast *s* in the field............... Ex 23:16
any sowing seed which is to be *s*......... Lev 11:37
which is neither eared nor *s*................. Deut 21:4
of thy seed which thou hast *s*................ Deut 22:9
and burning, that it is not *s*................ Deut 29:23
And so it was, when Israel had *s*........... Judg 6:3
Light is *s* for the righteous, and............. Ps 97:11
every thing *s* by the brooks,...................... Is 19:7
yea, they shall not be *s*............................ Is 40:24
that are *s* in it to spring forth................ Is 61:11
in a land that was not *s*............................. Jer 2:2
They have *s* wheat, but shall reap......... Jer 12:13
you, and ye shall be tilled and *s*............. Eze 36:9
For they have *s* the wind, and they........ Hos 8:7
that no more of thy name be *s*.............. Nah 1:14
Ye have *s* much, and bring in................. Hag 1:6
that which was *s* in his heart................ Mt 13:19
reaping where thou hast not *s*.............. Mt 25:24
the way side, where the word is *s*......... Mk 4:15
word that was *s* in their hearts............. Mk 4:15
which are *s* on stony ground................... Mk 4:16
are they which are *s* among thorns........ Mk 4:18
they which are *s* on good ground............ Mk 4:20
when it is *s* in the earth, is................... Mk 4:31
But when it is *s*, it groweth up,.............. Mk 4:32
If we have *s* unto you spiritual........... 1Cor 9:11
It is *s* in corruption............................ 1Cor 15:42
It is *s* in dishonour............................. 1Cor 15:43
it is *s* in weakness.............................. 1Cor 15:43
It is *s* a natural body........................... 1Cor 15:44
food, and multiply your seed *s*.............. 2Cor 9:10
is *s* in peace of them that make............. Jas 3:18

**SPACE**
abode with him the *s* of a month........ Gen 29:14
put a *s* betwixt drove and drove.......... Gen 32:16
the *s* of the seven sabbaths of................ Lev 25:8
within the *s* of a full year................... Lev 25:30
the *s* in which we came from................ Deut 2:14
there shall be a *s* between you................. Josh 3:4
a great *s* being between them............ 1Sa 26:13
now for a little *s* grace hath..................... Ezr 9:8
within the *s* of two full years.............. Jer 28:11
The *s* also before the little................... Eze 40:12
the *s* was one cubit on that side........... Eze 40:12
about the *s* of one hour after................ Lk 22:59
it was about the *s* of three hours........... Acts 5:7
put the apostles forth a little *s*............ Acts 5:34
sacrifices by the *s* of forty.................... Acts 7:42
about the *s* of four hundred................. Acts 13:20
Benjamin, by the *s* of forty years....... Acts 13:21
after they had tarried there a *s*.......... Acts 15:33
boldly for the *s* of three months.......... Acts 19:8
continued by the *s* of two years........... Acts 19:10
the *s* of two hours cried out................. Acts 19:34
that by the *s* of three years I............... Acts 20:31
the earth by the *s* of three years............ Jas 5:17
I gave her *s* to repent of her................... Rev 2:21
about the *s* of half an hour...................... Rev 8:1
by the *s* of a thousand and six............. Rev 14:20
he must continue a short *s*.................. Rev 17:10

**SPAIN** (*spane*) *Land at the western extremity of the Mediterranean Sea.*
I take my journey into *S*, I will.......... Rom 15:24
fruit, I will come by you into *S*.......... Rom 15:28

**SPAKE** See PREFACE.

**SPAKEST**
the man that *s* unto the woman......... Judg 13:11
*s* of also in mine ears, behold,............... Judg 17:2
thy words which thou *s* unto me......... 1Sa 28:21
thou *s* also with thy mouth, and.......... 1Kin 8:24
which thou *s* unto thy servant............. 1Kin 8:26
as thou *s* by the hand of Moses............ 1Kin 8:53
*s* with thy mouth, and hast.................. 2Chr 6:15
*s* with them from heaven, and.............. Neh 9:13
Then thou *s* in vision to thy holy.......... Ps 89:19
for since thou *s* of him, thou................. Jer 48:27

**SPAN**
a *s* shall be the length thereof,.............. Ex 28:16
a *s* shall be the breadth thereof............. Ex 28:16
a *s* was the length thereof, and a............. Ex 39:9
a *s* the breadth thereof, being................. Ex 39:9
height was six cubits and a *s*................. 1Sa 17:4
and meted out heaven with the *s*............. Is 40:12
fruit, and children of a *s* long............... Lam 2:20
thereof round about shall be a *s*........... Eze 43:13

**SPANNED**
my right hand hath *s* the heavens.......... Is 48:13

**SPARE**
not *s* the place for the fifty.................. Gen 18:24
then I will *s* all the place for................ Gen 18:26
pity him, neither shalt thou *s*............... Deut 13:8
The LORD will not *s* him, but then..... Deut 29:20
all that they have, and *s* them not......... 1Sa 15:3
*s* me according to the greatness.......... Neh 13:22
let him not *s*............................................ Job 6:10
my reins asunder, and doth not *s*......... Job 16:13
Though he *s* it, and forsake it not........ Job 20:13
God shall cast upon him, and not *s*....... Job 27:22
me, and *s* not to spit in my face........... Job 30:10
O *s* me, that I may recover................... Ps 39:13
He shall *s* the poor and needy, and....... Ps 72:13
therefore he will not *s* in the................. Prov 6:34
let not thy soul *s* for his crying.......... Prov 19:18
no man shall *s* his brother....................... Is 9:19
their eye shall not *s* children................. Is 13:18
he shall not *s*.......................................... Is 30:14
*s* not, lengthen thy cords, and.................. Is 54:2
*s* not, lift up thy voice like a.................... Is 58:1
I will not pity, nor *s*, nor have.............. Jer 13:14
he shall not *s* them, neither have........... Jer 21:7
bow, shoot at her, *s* no arrows.............. Jer 50:14
and *s* ye not her young men.................... Jer 51:3
neither shall mine eye *s*, neither............. Eze 5:11
And mine eye shall not *s* thee................. Eze 7:4
And mine eye shall not *s*, neither............ Eze 7:9
mine eye shall not *s*, neither.................. Eze 8:18
let not your eye *s*, neither have............... Eze 9:5
for me also, mine eye shall not *s*........... Eze 9:10
not go back, neither will I *s*................. Eze 24:14
*S* thy people, O LORD, and give not....... Joel 2:17
And should not I *s* Nineveh................. Jonah 4:11
not *s* continually to slay the................... Hab 1:17
and I will *s* them, as a man.................... Mal 3:17
have bread enough and to *s*.................... Lk 15:17
take heed lest he also *s* not thee........ Rom 11:21
but I *s* you............................................ 1Cor 7:28
that to *s* you I came not as yet............ 2Cor 1:23
if I come again, I will not *s*............... 2Cor 13:2

**SPARED**
But Saul and the people *s* Agag............ 1Sa 15:9
for the people *s* the best of the............. 1Sa 15:15
but mine eye *s* thee.............................. 1Sa 24:10
he *s* to take of his own flock and.......... 2Sa 12:4
But the king *s* Mephibosheth............... 2Sa 21:7
my master hath *s* Naaman this............ 2Kin 5:20
he *s* not their soul from death,............. Ps 78:50
Nevertheless mine eye *s* them from..... Eze 20:17
He that *s* not his own Son, but............. Rom 8:32
For if God *s* not the natural............... Rom 11:21
For if God *s* not the angels that............ 2Pet 2:4
*s* not the old world, but saved.............. 2Pet 2:5

**SPARETH**
He that *s* his rod hateth his son......... Prov 13:24
that hath knowledge *s* his words....... Prov 17:27
but the righteous giveth and *s* not...... Prov 21:26
as a man *s* his own son that................ Mal 3:17

**SPARING**
in among you, not *s* the flock............. Acts 20:29

**SPARINGLY**
He which soweth *s* shall reap also......... 2Cor 9:6
shall reap also *s*..................................... 2Cor 9:6

**SPARK**
the *s* of his fire shall not shine............... Job 18:5
as tow, and the maker of it as a *s*............. Is 1:31

**SPARKLED**
they *s* like the colour of.............................. Eze 1:7

**SPARKS**
unto trouble, as the *s* fly upward............. Job 5:7
lamps, and *s* of fire leap out................. Job 41:19
compass yourselves about with *s*........... Is 50:11
in the *s* that ye have kindled................ Is 50:11

**SPARROW**
the *s* hath found an house, and the......... Ps 84:3
am as a *s* alone upon the house............ Ps 102:7

**SPARROWS**
Are not two *s* sold for a farthing........... Mt 10:29
ye are of more value than many *s*......... Mt 10:31
Are not five *s* sold for two....................... Lk 12:6
ye are of more value than many *s*........... Lk 12:7

**SPAT**
he *s* on the ground, and made clay........... Jn 9:6

**SPEAK** See PREFACE.

**SPEAKER**
Let not an evil *s* be established........... Ps 140:11
because he was the chief *s*.................. Acts 14:12

**SPEAKEST**
wherefore then *s* thou so to me.............. 1Sa 9:21
Why *s* thou any more of thy................ 2Sa 19:29
that thou *s* in thy bedchamber............ 2Kin 6:12
Thou *s* as one of the foolish.................... Job 2:10
sittest and *s* against thy brother............ Ps 50:20
mightest be justified when thou *s*............ Ps 51:4
Why sayest thou, O Jacob, and *s*............. Is 40:27
for thou *s* falsely of Ishmael.................. Jer 40:16
unto Jeremiah, Thou *s* falsely.................. Jer 43:2
nor *s* to warn the wicked from his......... Eze 3:18
for thou *s* lies in the name of................ Zec 13:3
Why *s* thou unto them in parables........ Mt 13:10
*s* thou this parable unto us, or............. Lk 12:41
now *s* thou plainly.................................. Jn 16:29
thou plainly, and *s* no proverb.............. Jn 16:29
unto him, *S* thou not unto me................ Jn 19:10
this new doctrine, whereof thou *s*...... Acts 17:19

**SPEAKETH**
it is my mouth that *s* unto you........... Gen 45:12
as a man *s* unto his friend...................... Ex 33:11
thee, saying, All that the LORD *s*......... Num 23:26
When a prophet *s* in the name of...... Deut 18:22
Thus *s* Ben-hadad, saying,.................... 1Kin 20:5
as one of the foolish women *s*................ Job 2:10
He that *s* flattery to his friends.............. Job 17:5
For God *s* once, yea twice, yet............ Job 33:14
and the tongue that *s* proud things......... Ps 12:3
and *s* the truth in his heart...................... Ps 15:2
mouth of the righteous *s* wisdom........... Ps 37:30
if he come to see me, he *s* vanity............ Ps 41:6
Whose mouth *s* vanity, and their.......... Ps 144:8
children, whose mouth *s* vanity........... Ps 144:11
the man that *s* froward things............... Prov 2:12
he *s* with his feet, he teacheth............ Prov 6:13
A false witness that *s* lies..................... Prov 6:19
mouth of the wicked *s* frowardness... Prov 10:32
He that *s* truth sheweth forth............ Prov 12:17
There is that *s* like the......................... Prov 12:18
but a deceitful witness *s* lies................ Prov 14:25
and they love him that *s* right............. Prov 16:13
he that *s* lies shall not escape................ Prov 19:5
he that *s* lies shall perish..................... Prov 19:9
the man that heareth *s* constantly..... Prov 21:28
When he *s* fair, believe him not......... Prov 26:25
evildoer, and every mouth *s* folly............. Is 9:17
even when the needy *s* right.................... Is 32:7
righteously, and *s* uprightly................... Is 33:15
it *s* deceit................................................ Jer 9:8
one *s* peaceably to his neighbour.............. Jer 9:8
word which the LORD *s* unto you............ Jer 10:1
Thus *s* the LORD of hosts, the God.......... Jer 28:2
Thus *s* the LORD of hosts, the God....... Jer 29:25
Thus *s* the LORD God of Israel,.............. Jer 30:2
of the Almighty God when he *s*............. Eze 10:5
they abhor him that *s* uprightly.......... Amos 5:10
Thus *s* the LORD of hosts, saying,........... Hag 1:2
Thus *s* the LORD of hosts, saying,.......... Zec 6:12
Thus *s* the LORD of hosts, saying,............ Zec 7:9
of your Father which *s* in you............. Mt 10:20
whosoever *s* a word against the............ Mt 12:32
but whosoever *s* against the Holy......... Mt 12:32
of the heart the mouth *s*...................... Mt 12:34
Who is this which *s* blasphemies.......... Lk 5:21
of the heart his mouth *s*......................... Lk 6:45
is earthly, and *s* of the earth................. Jn 3:31
God hath sent *s* the words of God.......... Jn 3:34
He that *s* of himself seeketh his.............. Jn 7:18
he *s* boldly, and they say nothing........... Jn 7:26
*s* a lie, he *s* of his own.......................... Jn 8:44
himself a king *s* against Caesar............ Jn 19:12
For David *s* concerning him, I.............. Acts 2:25
of whom *s* the prophet this.................. Acts 8:34
which is of faith *s* on this wise............. Rom 10:6
For he that *s* in an unknown............... 1Cor 14:2
an unknown tongue *s* not unto men... 1Cor 14:2
in the spirit he *s* mysteries................... 1Cor 14:2
*s* unto men to edification...................... 1Cor 14:3
He that *s* in an unknown tongue.......... 1Cor 14:4
than he that *s* with tongues................. 1Cor 14:5
be unto him that *s* a barbarian.......... 1Cor 14:11
he that *s* shall be a barbarian............ 1Cor 14:11
Wherefore let him that *s* in an.......... 1Cor 14:13
Now the Spirit *s* expressly........................ 1Ti 4:1
and by it he being dead yet *s*................ Heb 11:4
which *s* unto you as unto children........ Heb 12:5
that *s* better things than that of.......... Heb 12:24
See that ye refuse not him that *s*......... Heb 12:25
away from him that *s* from heaven..... Heb 12:25
He that *s* evil of his brother, and......... Jas 4:11
*s* evil of the law, and judgeth the.......... Jas 4:11
their mouth *s* great swelling................... Jude 16

**SPEAKING**
to pass, before he had done *s*.............. Gen 24:15
before I had done *s* in mine heart....... Gen 24:45
till Moses had done *s* with them.......... Ex 34:33
one *s* unto him from off the mercy..... Num 7:89
made an end of *s* all these words...... Num 16:31
*s* out of the midst of the fire................. Deut 4:33
the voice of the living God *s* out........ Deut 5:26
*s* of them when thou sittest in............ Deut 11:19
made an end of *s* unto the people....... Deut 20:9

Moses made an end of s all these ...... Deut 32:45
when he had made an end of s ........... Judg 15:17
her, then she left s unto her.................. Ruth 1:18
he had made an end of s unto Saul ....... 1Sa 18:1
an end of s these words unto Saul....... 1Sa 24:16
soon as he had made an end of s ......... 2Sa 13:36
s from the mouth of the LORD ........... 2Chr 36:12
and s peace to all his seed ...................... Est 10:3
While he was yet s, there came ............. Job 1:16
While he was yet s, there came ............. Job 1:17
While he was yet s, there came ............. Job 1:18
who can withhold himself from s........... Job 4:2
they left off s ........................................... Job 32:15
evil, and thy lips from s guile ............... Ps 34:13
as soon as they be born, s lies................. Ps 58:3
forth of the finger, and s vanity................. Is 58:9
pleasure, nor s thine own words............. Is 58:13
our God, s oppression and revolt,........... Is 59:13
and while they are yet s, I will............... Is 65:24
unto you, rising up early and s ............... Jer 7:13
unto you, rising early and s ................... Jer 25:3
all the people heard Jeremiah s ............... Jer 26:7
Jeremiah had made an end of s all......... Jer 26:8
unto you, rising early and s.................. Jer 35:14
in s such words unto them..................... Jer 38:4
So they left off s with him ..................... Jer 38:27
of s unto all the people all the ............... Jer 43:1
I heard him s unto me out of the............. Eze 43:6
of man, and a mouth s great things ....... Dan 7:8
Then I heard one saint s, and ................ Dan 8:13
Now as he was s with me, I was in ...... Dan 8:18
And whiles I was s, and praying, and .. Dan 9:20
Yea, whiles I was s in prayer ................ Dan 9:21
shall be heard for their much s ................ Mt 6:7
Now when he had left s, he said ................ Lk 5:4
s of the things pertaining to the ............ Acts 1:3
s unto Moses, that he should make...... Acts 7:44
s to them, persuaded them to............. Acts 13:43
abode they s boldly in the Lord ........... Acts 14:3
s perverse things, to draw away ......... Acts 20:30
earth, I heard a voice s unto me......... Acts 26:14
that no man s by the Spirit of.............. 1Cor 12:3
if I come unto you s with tongues........ 1Cor 14:6
ye seek a proof of Christ s in me........ 2Cor 13:3
But s the truth in love, may grow......... Eph 4:15
and anger, and clamour, and evil s ...... Eph 4:31
S to yourselves in psalms and ............... Eph 5:19
S lies in hypocrisy......................................... 1Ti 4:2
s things which they ought not................... 1Ti 5:13
excess of riot, s evil of you...................... 1Pet 4:4
the dumb ass s with man's voice .......... 2Pet 2:16
s in them of these things ...................... 2Pet 3:16
unto him a mouth s great things.......... Rev 13:5

**SPEAKINGS**
and envies, and all evil s ........................... 1Pet 2:1

**SPEAR**
Stretch out the s that is in thy.............. Josh 8:18
Joshua stretched out the s that............. Josh 8:18
wherewith he stretched out the s......... Josh 8:26
was there a shield or s seen.................. Judg 5:8
there was neither sword nor s............... 1Sa 13:22
the staff of his s was like a .................... 1Sa 17:7
to me with a sword, and with a s......... 1Sa 17:45
LORD saveth not with sword and s....... 1Sa 17:47
here under thine hand s or sword .......... 1Sa 21:8
having his s in his hand, and all .......... 1Sa 22:6
his s stuck in the ground at his ............ 1Sa 26:7
with the s even to the earth at ............. 1Sa 26:8
take thou now the s that is at............... 1Sa 26:11
So David took the s and the cruse........ 1Sa 26:12
And now see where the king's s is........ 1Sa 26:16
and said, Behold the king's s ............... 1Sa 26:22
behold, Saul leaned upon his s .................. 2Sa 1:6
with the hinder end of the s .................... 2Sa 2:23
that the s came out behind him.............. 2Sa 2:23
the weight of whose s weighed.............. 2Sa 21:16
the staff of whose s was like a............. 2Sa 21:19
with iron and the staff of a s.................. 2Sa 23:7
he lift up his s against eight ................... 2Sa 23:8
he lifted up his s against three.............. 2Sa 23:18
the Egyptian had a s in his hand........... 2Sa 23:21
and plucked the s out of the.................... 2Sa 23:21
hand, and slew him with his own s........ 2Sa 23:21
he lifted up his s against three ........... 1Chr 11:11
for lifting up his s against.................. 1Chr 11:20
hand was a s like a weaver's beam..... 1Chr 11:23
and plucked the s out of the ............... 1Chr 11:23
hand, and slew him with his own s... 1Chr 11:23
s were six thousand and eight ............ 1Chr 12:24
s thirty and seven thousand................. 1Chr 12:34
whose s staff was like a weaver's........ 1Chr 20:5
forth to war, that could handle s ......... 2Chr 25:5
against him, the glittering s .................. Job 39:23
the s, the dart, nor the ........................... Job 41:26
he laugheth at the shaking of a s......... Job 41:29
Draw out also the s, and stop the............ Ps 35:3
bow, and cutteth the s in sunder............ Ps 46:9
They shall lay hold on bow and s........... Jer 6:23
bright sword and the glittering s............ Nah 3:3
the shining of thy glittering s................. Hab 3:11
with a s pierced his side........................ Jn 19:34

**SPEARMEN**
Rebuke the company of s, the................. Ps 68:30
s two hundred, at the third hour ........ Acts 23:23

**SPEAR'S**
his s head weighed six hundred............. 1Sa 17:7

**SPEARS**
the Hebrews make them swords or s .. 1Sa 13:19
the priest give king David's s ............. 2Kin 11:10
several city he put shields and s......... 2Chr 11:12
of men that bare targets and s ............ 2Chr 14:8
to the captains of hundreds s............... 2Chr 23:9
all the host shields, and s.................. 2Chr 26:14
with their swords, their s ....................... Neh 4:13
half of them held both the s ................... Neh 4:16
half of them held the s from the............ Neh 4:21
or his head with fish s ........................... Job 41:7
sons of men, whose teeth are s ............... Ps 57:4
their s into pruninghooks........................... Is 2:4
furbish the s, and put on the .................. Jer 46:4
and the handstaves, and the s................ Eze 39:9
and your pruninghooks into s ................. Joel 3:10
their s into pruninghooks........................ Mic 4:3

**SPECIAL**
to be a s people unto himself................ Deut 7:6
God wrought s miracles by the .......... Acts 19:11

**SPECIALLY**
S the day that thou stoodest................ Deut 4:10
s before thee, O king Agrippa,............ Acts 25:26
all men, s of those that believe ............... 1Ti 4:10
s for those of his own house, he................ 1Ti 5:8
s they of the circumcision ..................... Titus 1:10
s to me, but how much more unto ..... Philem 16

**SPECKLED**
removing from thence all the s........... Gen 30:32
the spotted and s among the goats..... Gen 30:32
every one that is not s and.................. Gen 30:33
and all the she goats that were s........ Gen 30:35
forth cattle ringstraked, s..................... Gen 30:39
thus, The s shall be thy wages .............. Gen 31:8
then all the cattle bare s......................... Gen 31:8
the cattle were ringstraked, s............... Gen 31:10
the cattle are ringstraked, s................ Gen 31:12
heritage is unto me as a s bird.............. Jer 12:9
him were there red horses, s .................. Zec 1:8

**SPECTACLE**
we are made a s unto the world............ 1Cor 4:9

**SPED**
Have they not s ...................................... Judg 5:30

**SPEECH**
of Lamech, hearken unto my s ............. Gen 4:23
was of one language, and of one s ....... Gen 11:1
not understand one another's s............. Gen 11:7
but I am slow of s, and of a slow............ Ex 4:10
give occasions of s against her............ Deut 22:14
given occasions of s against her......... Deut 22:17
my s shall distil as the dew, as ............ Deut 32:2
To fetch about this form of s ............... 2Sa 14:20
seeing the s of all Israel is................... 2Sa 19:11
the s pleased the Lord, that ................. 1Kin 3:10
s unto the people of Jerusalem.......... 2Chr 32:18
spake half in the s of Ashdod.............. Neh 13:24
removeth away the s of the trusty....... Job 12:20
Hear diligently my s, and my................ Job 13:17
Hear diligently my s, and let this.......... Job 21:2
liar, and make my s nothing worth....... Job 24:25
and my s dropped upon them................ Job 29:22
order our s by reason of darkness ........ Job 37:19
thine ear unto me, and hear my s ........... Ps 17:6
Day unto day uttereth s, and night........... Ps 19:2
There is no s nor language, where .......... Ps 19:3
With her much fair s she caused........... Prov 7:21
Excellent s becometh not a fool ............ Prov 17:7
of scarlet, and thy s is comely.............. Song 4:3
hearken, and hear my s ........................... Is 28:23
thy s shall be low out of the...................... Is 29:4
thy s shall whisper out of the.................... Is 29:4
give ear unto my s .................................... Is 32:9
a people of a deeper s than thou ............ Is 33:19
use this s in the land of Judah ............. Jer 31:23
of the Almighty, the voice of s ............. Eze 1:24
sent to a people of a strange s ............... Eze 3:5
Not to many people of a strange s........... Eze 3:6
O LORD, I have heard thy s.................... Hab 3:2
for thy s bewrayeth thee.......................... Mt 26:73
and had an impediment in his s ............. Mk 7:32
and thy s agreeth thereto ....................... Mk 14:70
Why do ye not understand my s.............. Jn 8:43
saying in the s of Lycaonia ................. Acts 14:11
continued his s until midnight............... Acts 20:7
with excellency of s or of wisdom......... 1Cor 2:1
And my s and my preaching was not.... 1Cor 2:4
not the s of them which are.................. 1Cor 4:19
hope, we use great plainness of s........ 2Cor 3:12
is my boldness of s toward you ............ 2Cor 7:4
is weak, and his s contemptible.......... 2Cor 10:10
But though I be rude in s.................... 2Cor 11:6
Let your s be alway with grace,............... Col 4:6
Sound s, that cannot be condemned..... Titus 2:8

**SPEECHES**
even apparently, and not in dark s...... Num 12:8
the s of one that is desperate, ............... Job 6:26
or with s wherewith he can do no ........ Job 15:3
will I answer him with your s .............. Job 32:14
Job, I pray thee, hear my s .................... Job 33:1
fair s deceive the hearts of the .......... Rom 16:18
of all their hard s which ungodly ........... Jude 15

**SPEECHLESS**
And he was s ........................................ Mt 22:12
beckoned unto them, and remained s..... Lk 1:22
which journeyed with him stood s.......... Acts 9:7

**SPEED**
thee, send me good s this day .............. Gen 24:12
cried after the lad, Make s .................. 1Sa 20:38
make s to depart, lest he ..................... 2Sa 15:14
s to get him up to his chariot............. 1Kin 12:18
But king Rehoboam made s to get .... 2Chr 10:18
let it be done with s ................................... Ezr 6:12
That say, Let him make s, and.................. Is 5:19
they shall come with s swiftly.................. Is 5:26
for to come to him with all s.............. Acts 17:15
your house, neither bid him God s ........... 2Jn 10
For he that biddeth him God s is.............. 2Jn 11

**SPEEDILY**
Then they s took down every man..... Gen 44:11
for me than that I should s....................... 1Sa 27:1
the wilderness, but s pass over ............ 2Sa 17:16
divided them s among all the............. 2Chr 35:13
the king had sent, so they did s ............... Ezr 6:13
That thou mayest buy s with this ........... Ezr 7:17
require of you, it be done s ..................... Ezr 7:21
judgment be executed s upon him ......... Ezr 7:26
he s gave her her things for ..................... Est 2:9
deliver me s.................................................. Ps 31:2
hear me s ..................................................... Ps 69:17
thy tender mercies s prevent us................. Ps 79:8
the day when I call answer me s ............ Ps 102:2
Hear me s, O LORD ................................. Ps 143:7
an evil work is not executed s ............... Eccl 8:11
thine health shall spring forth s................ Is 58:8
s will I return your recompence............. Joel 3:4
Let us go s to pray before the................ Zec 8:21
you that he will avenge them s ................. Lk 18:8

**SPEEDY**
for he shall make even a s .................... Zeph 1:18

**SPEND**
I will s mine arrows upon them ......... Deut 32:23
They s their days in wealth, and........... Job 21:13
they shall s their days in..................... Job 36:11
we s our years as a tale that is................ Ps 90:9
Wherefore do ye s money for that .......... Is 55:2
he would not s the time in Asia .......... Acts 20:16
And I will very gladly s and be.......... 2Cor 12:15

**SPENDEST**
and whatsoever thou s more................... Lk 10:35

**SPENDETH**
but a foolish man s it up ...................... Prov 21:20
with harlots s his substance.................. Prov 29:3
vain life which he s as a shadow........... Eccl 6:12

**SPENT**
And the water was s in the bottle...... Gen 21:15
my lord, how that our money is s ...... Gen 47:18
your strength shall be s in vain .......... Lev 26:20
were by Jebus, the day was far s ....... Judg 19:11
for the bread is s in our vessels ............... 1Sa 9:7
shuttle, and are s without hope .............. Job 7:6
For my life is s with grief ...................... Ps 31:10
I have s my strength for nought, ............. Is 49:4
all the bread in the city were s ............. Jer 37:21
had s all that she had, and was............... Mk 5:26
And when the day was now far s............ Mk 6:35
which had s all her living upon ............... Lk 8:43
And when he had s all, there arose....... Lk 15:14
evening, and the day is far s .................. Lk 24:29
s their time in nothing else .............. Acts 17:21
after he had s some time there,........... Acts 18:23
Now when much time was s.................... Acts 27:9
The night is far s, the day is at......... Rom 13:12
very gladly spend and be s for you..... 2Cor 12:15

**SPEWING**
shameful s shall be on thy glory............ Hab 2:16

**SPICE**
And s, and oil for the light, and ............ Ex 35:28
the traffick of the s merchants......... 1Kin 10:15
neither was there any such s as............. 2Chr 9:9
have gathered my myrrh with my s......... Song 5:1
s it well, and let the bones be.............. Eze 24:10

**SPICED**
of s wine of the juice of my................... Song 8:2

**SPICERY**
with their camels bearing s.................. Gen 37:25

**SPICES**
little balm, and a little honey, s ........... Gen 43:11
s for anointing oil, and for sweet ............. Ex 25:6
s of pure myrrh five hundred.................. Ex 30:23
Moses, Take unto thee sweet s................ Ex 30:34
these sweet s with pure........................... Ex 30:34
s for anointing oil, and for the................... Ex 35:8
and the pure incense of sweet s ............. Ex 37:29
train, with camels that bare s ............... 1Kin 10:2
of s very great store, and ..................... 1Kin 10:10
of s as these which the queen of........ 1Kin 10:10
and garments, and armour, and s........ 1Kin 10:25
the silver, and the gold, and the s...... 2Kin 20:13
and the frankincense, and the s .......... 1Chr 9:29
made the ointment of the s ................... 1Chr 9:30
company, and camels that bare s ........... 2Chr 9:1
of s great abundance, and precious....... 2Chr 9:9
gold, and raiment, harness, and s ......... 2Chr 9:24
divers kinds of s prepared by the...... 2Chr 16:14
and for precious stones, and for s ...... 2Chr 32:27
of thine ointments than all s................. Song 4:10
and aloes, with all the chief s .............. Song 4:14
that the s thereof may flow out ........... Song 4:16
His cheeks are as a bed of s................. Song 5:13
into his garden, to the beds of s............... Song 6:2
hart upon the mountains of s................ Song 8:14
the silver, and the gold, and the s ............. Is 39:2
in thy fairs with chief of all s............. Eze 27:22
and Salome, had bought sweet s.............. Mk 16:1

S

And they returned, and prepared *s* ........ Lk 23:56
bringing the *s* which they had ........ Lk 24:1
it in linen clothes with the *s* ........ Jn 19:40

**SPIDER**
The *s* taketh hold with her hands, .... Prov 30:28

**SPIDER'S**
and whose trust shall be a *s* web ........ Job 8:14
eggs, and weave the *s* web ........ Is 59:5

**SPIED**
he *s* an Egyptian smiting an ........ Ex 2:11
men that had *s* out the country ........ Josh 6:22
he *s* the company of Jehu as he ........ 2Kin 9:17
behold, they *s* a band of men ........ 2Kin 13:21
he *s* the sepulchres that were ........ 2Kin 23:16
that were *s* in the land of Judah ........ 2Kin 23:24

**SPIES**
them, and said unto them, Ye are *s* ...... Gen 42:9
true men, thy servants are no *s* ........ Gen 42:11
spake unto you, saying, Ye are *s* ........ Gen 42:14
life of Pharaoh surely ye are *s* ........ Gen 42:16
took us for *s* of the country ........ Gen 42:30
we are no *s* ........ Gen 42:31
shall I know that ye are no *s* ........ Gen 42:34
Israel came by the way of the *s* ........ Num 21:1
the young men that were *s* went in ..... Josh 6:23
the *s* saw a man come forth out of ........ Judg 1:24
David therefore sent out *s* ........ 1Sa 26:4
But Absalom sent *s* throughout all ...... 2Sa 15:10
they watched him, and sent forth *s* ...... Lk 20:20
she had received the *s* with peace ...... Heb 11:31

**SPIKENARD**
my *s* sendeth forth the smell ........ Song 1:12
camphire, with *s*, ........ Song 4:13
*S* and saffron ........ Song 4:14
of ointment of *s* very precious ........ Mk 14:3
Mary a pound of ointment of *s* ........ Jn 12:3

**SPILLED**
that he *s* it on the ground, lest ........ Gen 38:9
the bottles, and the wine is *s* ........ Mk 2:22
will burst the bottles, and be *s* ........ Lk 5:37

**SPILT**
are as water *s* on the ground, ........ 2Sa 14:14

**SPIN**
hearted did *s* with their hands ........ Ex 35:25
they toil not, neither do they *s* ........ Mt 6:28
they toil not, they *s* not ........ Lk 12:27

**SPINDLE**
She layeth her hands to the *s* ........ Prov 31:19

**SPIRIT**
the *S* of God moved upon the face ........ Gen 1:2
My *s* shall not always strive with ........ Gen 6:3
morning that his *s* was troubled ........ Gen 41:8
is, a man in whom the *S* of God is ...... Gen 41:38
the *s* of Jacob their father ........ Gen 45:27
not unto Moses for anguish of *s* ........ Ex 6:9
have filled with the *s* of wisdom ........ Ex 28:3
have filled him with the *s* of God ........ Ex 31:3
every one whom his *s* made willing ...... Ex 35:21
hath filled him with the *s* of God ........ Ex 35:31
or woman that hath a familiar *s* ........ Lev 20:27
the *s* of jealousy come upon him, ........ Num 5:14
or if the *s* of jealousy come upon ........ Num 5:14
Or when the *s* of jealousy cometh ........ Num 5:30
take of the *s* which is upon thee ........ Num 11:17
took of the *s* that was upon him, ........ Num 11:25
when the *s* rested upon them, they ... Num 11:25
and the *s* rested upon them ........ Num 11:26
LORD would put his *s* upon them ........ Num 11:29
because he had another *s* with him ... Num 14:24
the *s* of God came upon him ........ Num 24:2
of Nun, a man in whom is the *s* ........ Num 27:18
the LORD thy God hardened his *s* ........ Deut 2:30
Nun was full of the *s* of wisdom ........ Deut 34:9
was there *s* in them any more ........ Josh 5:1
the *s* of the LORD came upon him, ........ Judg 3:10
But the *S* of the LORD came upon ........ Judg 6:34
sent an evil *s* between Abimelech ........ Judg 9:23
Then the *S* of the LORD came upon ... Judg 11:29
the *S* of the LORD began to move ........ Judg 13:25
the *S* of the LORD came mightily ........ Judg 14:6
the *S* of the LORD came upon him, .... Judg 14:19
the *S* of the LORD came mightily ........ Judg 15:14
his *s* came again, and he revived ........ Judg 15:19
I am a woman of a sorrowful *s* ........ 1Sa 1:15
the *S* of the LORD will come upon ........ 1Sa 10:6
the *S* of God came upon him, and he .. 1Sa 10:10
the *S* of God came upon Saul when ...... 1Sa 11:6
the *S* of the LORD came upon David .... 1Sa 16:13
But the *S* of the LORD departed ........ 1Sa 16:14
an evil *s* from the LORD troubled ........ 1Sa 16:14
an evil *s* from God troubleth thee ........ 1Sa 16:15
when the evil *s* from God is upon ........ 1Sa 16:16
when the evil *s* from God was upon ...... 1Sa 16:23
the evil *s* departed from him ........ 1Sa 16:23
that the evil *s* from God came ........ 1Sa 18:10
the evil *s* from the LORD was upon ........ 1Sa 19:9
the *S* of God was upon the ........ 1Sa 19:20
the *S* of God was upon him also, ........ 1Sa 19:23
me a woman that hath a familiar *s* ........ 1Sa 28:7
that hath a familiar *s* at En-dor ........ 1Sa 28:7
divine unto me by the familiar *s* ........ 1Sa 28:8
eaten, his *s* came again to him ........ 1Sa 30:12
The *S* of the LORD spake by me, and .... 2Sa 23:2
there was no more *s* in her ........ 1Kin 10:5
that the *S* of the LORD shall ........ 1Kin 18:12
unto him, Why is thy *s* so sad ........ 1Kin 21:5
And there came forth a *s*, and stood . 1Kin 22:21
I will be a lying *s* in the mouth ........ 1Kin 22:22
the LORD hath put a lying *s* in ........ 1Kin 22:23
Which way went the *S* of the LORD .. 1Kin 22:24
portion of thy *s* be upon me ........ 2Kin 2:9
The *s* of Elijah doth rest on ........ 2Kin 2:15
lest peradventure the *S* of the ........ 2Kin 2:16
up the *s* of Pul king of Assyria ........ 1Chr 5:26
the *s* of Tilgath-pilneser king of ........ 1Chr 5:26
of one that had a familiar *s* ........ 1Chr 10:13
Then the *s* came upon Amasai, who . 1Chr 12:18
of all that he had by the *s* ........ 1Chr 28:12
there was no more *s* in her ........ 2Chr 9:4
the *S* of God came upon Azariah ........ 2Chr 15:1
Then there came out a *s*, and stood .. 2Chr 18:20
be a lying *s* in the mouth of all ........ 2Chr 18:21
lying *s* in the mouth of these thy ........ 2Chr 18:22
Which way went the *S* of the LORD .. 2Chr 18:23
came the *S* of the LORD in the ........ 2Chr 20:14
Jehoram the *s* of the Philistines ........ 2Chr 21:16
the *S* of God came upon Zechariah ... 2Chr 24:20
and dealt with a familiar *s* ........ 2Chr 33:6
up the *s* of Cyrus king of Persia ........ 2Chr 36:22
up the *s* of Cyrus king of Persia ........ Ezr 1:1
all them whose *s* God had raised ........ Ezr 1:5
also thy good *s* to instruct them ........ Neh 9:20
them by thy *s* in thy prophets ........ Neh 9:30
Then a *s* passed before my face ........ Job 4:15
poison whereof drinketh up my *s* ........ Job 6:4
will speak in the anguish of my *s* ........ Job 7:11
visitation hath preserved my *s* ........ Job 10:12
thou turnest thy *s* against God ........ Job 15:13
the *s* of my understanding causeth ........ Job 20:3
why should not my *s* be troubled ........ Job 21:4
and whose *s* came from thee ........ Job 26:4
By his *s* he hath garnished the ........ Job 26:13
the *s* of God is in my nostrils ........ Job 27:3
But there is a *s* in man ........ Job 32:8
the *s* within me constraineth me ........ Job 32:18
The *s* of God hath made me, and the .... Job 33:4
if he gather unto himself his *s* ........ Job 34:14
Into thine hand I commit my *s* ........ Ps 31:5
in whose *s* there is no guile ........ Ps 32:2
saveth such as be of a contrite *s* ........ Ps 34:18
and renew a right *s* within me ........ Ps 51:10
and take not thy holy *s* from me ........ Ps 51:11
and uphold me with thy free *s* ........ Ps 51:12
sacrifices of God are a broken *s* ........ Ps 51:17
He shall cut off the *s* of princes ........ Ps 76:12
and my *s* was overwhelmed ........ Ps 77:3
my *s* made diligent search ........ Ps 77:6
whose *s* was not stedfast with God ........ Ps 78:8
Thou sendest forth thy *s*, they ........ Ps 104:30
Because they provoked his *s* ........ Ps 106:33
Whither shall I go from thy *s* ........ Ps 139:7
When my *s* was overwhelmed within .... Ps 142:3
Therefore is my *s* overwhelmed ........ Ps 143:4
my *s* faileth ........ Ps 143:7
thy *s* is good ........ Ps 143:10
I will pour out my *s* unto you ........ Prov 1:23
faithful *s* concealeth the matter ........ Prov 11:13
that is hasty of *s* exalteth folly ........ Prov 14:29
therein is a breach in the *s* ........ Prov 15:4
of the heart the *s* is broken ........ Prov 15:13
an haughty *s* before a fall ........ Prov 16:18
be of an humble *s* with the lowly ........ Prov 16:19
he that ruleth his *s* than he that ........ Prov 16:32
but a broken *s* drieth the bones ........ Prov 17:22
is of an excellent *s* ........ Prov 17:27
The *s* of a man will sustain his ........ Prov 18:14
but a wounded *s* who can bear ........ Prov 18:14
The *s* of man is the candle of the ........ Prov 20:27
*s* is like a city that is broken ........ Prov 25:28
shall uphold the humble in *s* ........ Prov 29:23
all is vanity and vexation of *s* ........ Eccl 1:14
that this also is vexation of *s* ........ Eccl 1:17
all was vanity and vexation of *s* ........ Eccl 2:11
all is vanity and vexation of *s* ........ Eccl 2:17
also is vanity and vexation of *s* ........ Eccl 2:26
Who knoweth the *s* of man that ........ Eccl 3:21
the *s* of the beast that goeth ........ Eccl 3:21
is also vanity and vexation of *s* ........ Eccl 4:4
with travail and vexation of *s* ........ Eccl 4:6
also is vanity and vexation of *s* ........ Eccl 4:16
is also vanity and vexation of *s* ........ Eccl 6:9
the patient in *s* is better than ........ Eccl 7:8
is better than the proud in *s* ........ Eccl 7:8
Be not hasty in thy *s* to be angry ........ Eccl 7:9
over the *s* to retain the *s* ........ Eccl 8:8
If the *s* of the ruler rise up ........ Eccl 10:4
not what is the way of the *s* ........ Eccl 11:5
the *s* shall return unto God who ........ Eccl 12:7
thereof by the *s* of judgment ........ Is 4:4
and by the *s* of burning ........ Is 4:4
the *s* of the LORD shall rest upon ........ Is 11:2
the *s* of wisdom and understanding, ........ Is 11:2
the *s* of counsel and might ........ Is 11:2
the *s* of knowledge and of the fear ........ Is 11:2
the *s* of Egypt shall fail in the ........ Is 19:3
a perverse *s* in the midst thereof ........ Is 19:14
with my *s* within me will I seek ........ Is 26:9
for a *s* of judgment to him that ........ Is 28:6
as of one that hath a familiar *s* ........ Is 29:4
out upon you the *s* of deep sleep ........ Is 29:10
They also that erred in *s* shall ........ Is 29:24
with a covering, but not of my *s* ........ Is 30:1
and their horses flesh, and not *s* ........ Is 31:3
Until the *s* be poured upon us ........ Is 32:15
his *s* it hath gathered them ........ Is 34:16
these things is the life of my *s* ........ Is 38:16
because the *s* of the LORD bloweth ........ Is 40:7
hath directed the *S* of the LORD ........ Is 40:13
I have put my *s* upon him ........ Is 42:1
*s* to them that walk therein ........ Is 42:5
I will pour my *s* upon thy seed ........ Is 44:3
and now the Lord GOD, and his *S* ........ Is 48:16
a woman forsaken and grieved in *s* ........ Is 54:6
that is of a contrite and humble *s* ........ Is 57:15
to revive the *s* of the humble ........ Is 57:15
for the *s* should fail before me, ........ Is 57:16
the *S* of the LORD shall lift up a ........ Is 59:19
My *s* that is upon thee, and my ........ Is 59:21
The *S* of the Lord GOD is upon me ........ Is 61:1
of praise for the *s* of heaviness ........ Is 61:3
rebelled, and vexed his holy *S* ........ Is 63:10
he that put his holy *S* within him ........ Is 63:11
the *S* of the LORD caused him to ........ Is 63:14
and shall howl for vexation of *s* ........ Is 65:14
that is poor and of a contrite *s* ........ Is 66:2
the *s* of the kings of the Medes ........ Jer 51:11
whither the *s* was to go, they ........ Eze 1:12
Whithersoever the *s* was to go ........ Eze 1:20
went, thither was their *s* to go ........ Eze 1:20
for the *s* of the living creature ........ Eze 1:20
for the *s* of the living creature ........ Eze 1:21
the *s* entered into me when he ........ Eze 2:2
Then the *s* took me up, and I heard ...... Eze 3:12
So the *s* lifted me up, and took me ........ Eze 3:14
bitterness, in the heat of my *s* ........ Eze 3:14
Then the *s* entered into me, and ........ Eze 3:24
the *s* lifted me up between the ........ Eze 8:3
for the *s* of the living creature ........ Eze 10:17
Moreover the *s* lifted me up ........ Eze 11:1
the *S* of the LORD fell upon me, ........ Eze 11:5
and I will put a new *s* within you ........ Eze 11:19
Afterwards the *s* took me up ........ Eze 11:24
by the *S* of God into Chaldea ........ Eze 11:24
prophets, that follow their own *s* ........ Eze 13:3
make you a new heart and a new *s* .... Eze 18:31
every *s* shall faint, and all knees ........ Eze 21:7
a new *s* will I put within you ........ Eze 36:26
And I will put my *s* within you ........ Eze 36:27
me out in the *s* of the LORD ........ Eze 37:1
And shall put my *s* in you, and ye ........ Eze 37:14
out my *s* upon the house of Israel ........ Eze 39:29
So the *s* took me up, and brought ........ Eze 43:5
wherewith his *s* was troubled ........ Dan 2:1
my *s* was troubled to know the ........ Dan 2:3
in whom is the *s* of the holy gods ........ Dan 4:8
because I know that the *s* of the ........ Dan 4:9
for the *s* of the holy gods is in ........ Dan 4:18
in whom is the *s* of the holy gods ........ Dan 5:11
Forasmuch as an excellent *s* ........ Dan 5:12
that the *s* of the gods is in thee ........ Dan 5:14
because an excellent *s* was in him ........ Dan 6:3
in my *s* in the midst of my body ........ Dan 7:15
for the *s* of whoredoms hath ........ Hos 4:12
for the *s* of whoredoms is in the ........ Hos 5:4
will pour out my *s* upon all flesh ........ Joel 2:28
those days will I pour out my *s* ........ Joel 2:29
is the *s* of the LORD straitened ........ Mic 2:7
If a man walking in the *s* ........ Mic 2:11
of power by the *s* of the LORD ........ Mic 3:8
the LORD stirred up the *s* of ........ Hag 1:14
the *s* of Joshua the son of ........ Hag 1:14
the *s* of all the remnant of the ........ Hag 1:14
so my *s* remaineth among you ........ Hag 2:5
might, nor by power, but by my *s* ........ Zec 4:6
quieted my *s* in the north country ........ Zec 6:8
in his *s* by the former prophets ........ Zec 7:12
formeth the *s* of man within him ........ Zec 12:1
Jerusalem, the *s* of grace and of ........ Zec 12:10
the unclean *s* to pass out of the ........ Zec 13:2
Yet had he the residue of the *s* ........ Mal 2:15
Therefore take heed to your *s* ........ Mal 2:15
therefore take heed to your *s* ........ Mal 2:16
he saw the *S* of God descending ........ Mt 3:16
the *s* into the wilderness to be ........ Mt 4:1
Blessed are the poor in *s* ........ Mt 5:3
but the *S* of your Father which ........ Mt 10:20
I will put my *S* upon him, and he ........ Mt 12:18
I cast out devils by the *S* of God ........ Mt 12:28
When the unclean *s* is gone out of ....... Mt 12:43
were troubled, saying, It is a *s* ........ Mt 14:26
doth David in *s* call him Lord ........ Mt 22:43
the *s* indeed is willing, but the ........ Mt 26:41
the *S* like a dove descending upon ........ Mk 1:10
immediately the *s* driveth him ........ Mk 1:12
synagogue a man with an unclean *s* ...... Mk 1:23
when the unclean *s* had torn him ........ Mk 1:26
when Jesus perceived in his *s* ........ Mk 2:8
they said, He hath an unclean *s* ........ Mk 3:30
the tombs a man with an unclean *s* ........ Mk 5:2
out of the man, thou unclean *s* ........ Mk 5:8
they supposed it had been a *s* ........ Mk 6:49
young daughter had an unclean *s* ........ Mk 7:25
And he sighed deeply in his *s* ........ Mk 8:12
thee my son, which hath a dumb *s* ........ Mk 9:17
him, straightway the *s* tare him ........ Mk 9:20
together, he rebuked the foul *s* ........ Mk 9:25
unto him, Thou dumb and deaf *s* ........ Mk 9:25
the *s* cried, and rent him sore, and ........ Mk 9:26
The *s* truly is ready, but the ........ Mk 14:38
he shall go before him in the *s* ........ Lk 1:17
my *s* hath rejoiced in God my ........ Lk 1:47
child grew, and waxed strong in *s* ........ Lk 1:80
he came by the *S* into the temple ........ Lk 2:27
child grew, and waxed strong in *s* ........ Lk 2:40
was led by the *S* into the ........ Lk 4:1

the power of the S into Galilee ... Lk 4:14
The S of the Lord is upon me, ... Lk 4:18
which had a s of an unclean devil ... Lk 4:33
unclean s to come out of the man ... Lk 8:29
her s came again, and she arose ... Lk 8:55
a s taketh him, and he suddenly ... Lk 9:39
And Jesus rebuked the unclean s ... Lk 9:42
not what manner of s ye are of ... Lk 9:55
In that hour Jesus rejoiced in s ... Lk 10:21
the Holy S to them that ask him ... Lk 11:13
When the unclean s is gone out of ... Lk 11:24
a s of infirmity eighteen years ... Lk 13:11
into thy hands I commend my s ... Lk 23:46
supposed that they had seen a s ... Lk 24:37
for a s hath not flesh and bones, ... Lk 24:39
I saw the S descending from ... Jn 1:32
thou shalt see the S descending ... Jn 1:33
man be born of water and of the S ... Jn 3:5
which is born of the S is s ... Jn 3:6
every one that is born of the S ... Jn 3:8
not the S by measure unto him ... Jn 3:34
shall worship the Father in s ... Jn 4:23
God is a S ... Jn 4:24
worship him must worship him in s ... Jn 4:24
It is the s that quickeneth ... Jn 6:63
that I speak unto you, they are s ... Jn 6:63
(But this spake he of the S ... Jn 7:39
with her, he groaned in the s ... Jn 11:33
thus said, he was troubled in s ... Jn 13:21
Even the S of truth ... Jn 14:17
the Father, even the S of truth ... Jn 15:26
the S of truth, is come, he will ... Jn 16:13
as the S gave them utterance ... Acts 2:4
pour out of my S upon all flesh ... Acts 2:17
pour out in those days of my S ... Acts 2:18
to tempt the S of the Lord ... Acts 5:9
wisdom and the s by which he spake .. Acts 6:10
saying, Lord Jesus, receive my s ... Acts 7:59
Then the S said unto Philip, Go ... Acts 8:29
the S of the Lord caught away ... Acts 8:39
the S said unto him, Behold, ... Acts 10:19
the S bade me go with them, ... Acts 11:12
signified by the S that there ... Acts 11:28
but the S suffered them not ... Acts 16:7
with a s of divination met us ... Acts 16:16
grieved, turned and said to the s ... Acts 16:18
his s was stirred in him, when he ... Acts 17:16
Paul was pressed in the s ... Acts 18:5
and being fervent in the s ... Acts 18:25
And the evil s answered and said, ... Acts 19:15
the evil s was leaped on them ... Acts 19:16
ended, Paul purposed in the s ... Acts 19:21
go bound in the s unto Jerusalem ... Acts 20:22
who said to Paul through the S ... Acts 21:4
neither angel, nor s ... Acts 23:8
but if a s or an angel hath ... Acts 23:9
according to the s of holiness ... Rom 1:4
whom I serve with my s in the ... Rom 1:9
is that of the heart, in the s ... Rom 2:29
we should serve in newness of s ... Rom 7:6
after the flesh, but after the S ... Rom 8:1
For the law of the the S of life ... Rom 8:2
after the flesh, but after the S ... Rom 8:4
the S the things of the S ... Rom 8:5
not in the flesh, but in the S ... Rom 8:9
if so be that the S of God dwell ... Rom 8:9
any man have not the S of Christ ... Rom 8:9
but the S is life because of ... Rom 8:10
But if the S of him that raised ... Rom 8:11
by his S that dwelleth in you ... Rom 8:11
but if ye through the S do ... Rom 8:13
many as are led by the S of God ... Rom 8:14
the s of bondage again to fear ... Rom 8:15
have received the S of adoption ... Rom 8:15
The S itself beareth witness with ... Rom 8:16
itself beareth witness with our s ... Rom 8:16
have the firstfruits of the S ... Rom 8:23
Likewise the S also helpeth our ... Rom 8:26
but the S itself maketh ... Rom 8:26
knoweth what is the mind of the S ... Rom 8:27
hath given them the s of slumber ... Rom 11:8
fervent in s ... Rom 12:11
by the power of the S of God ... Rom 15:19
sake, and for the love of the S ... Rom 15:30
but in demonstration of the S ... 1Cor 2:4
revealed them unto us by his S ... 1Cor 2:10
for the S searcheth all things, ... 1Cor 2:10
save the s of man which is in him ... 1Cor 2:11
knoweth no man, but the S of God ... 1Cor 2:11
not the s of the world ... 1Cor 2:12
but the s which is of God ... 1Cor 2:12
not the things of the S of God ... 1Cor 2:14
that the S of God dwelleth in you ... 1Cor 3:16
in love, and in the s of meekness ... 1Cor 4:21
absent in body, but present in s ... 1Cor 5:3
ye are gathered together, and my s ... 1Cor 5:4
that the s may be saved in the ... 1Cor 5:5
Jesus, and by the S of our God ... 1Cor 6:11
is joined unto the Lord is one s ... 1Cor 6:17
God in your body, and in your s ... 1Cor 6:20
may be holy both in body and in s ... 1Cor 7:34
also that I have the S of God ... 1Cor 7:40
that no man speaking by the S of ... 1Cor 12:3
of gifts, but the same S ... 1Cor 12:4
But the manifestation of the S is ... 1Cor 12:7
given by the S the word of wisdom ... 1Cor 12:8
word of knowledge by the same S ... 1Cor 12:8
To another faith by the same S ... 1Cor 12:9
gifts of healing by the same S ... 1Cor 12:9
that one and the selfsame S ... 1Cor 12:11
For by one S are we all baptized ... 1Cor 12:13
been all made to drink into one S ... 1Cor 12:13
howbeit in the s he speaketh ... 1Cor 14:2
tongue, my s prayeth, but my ... 1Cor 14:14
I will pray with the s, and I will ... 1Cor 14:15
I will sing with the s, and I will ... 1Cor 14:15
when thou shalt bless with the s ... 1Cor 14:16
last Adam was made a quickening s . 1Cor 15:45
For they have refreshed my s ... 1Cor 16:18
earnest of the S in our hearts ... 2Cor 1:22
I had no rest in my s, because I ... 2Cor 2:13
but with the S of the living God ... 2Cor 3:3
not of the letter, but of the s ... 2Cor 3:6
killeth, but the s giveth life ... 2Cor 3:6
of the s be rather glorious ... 2Cor 3:8
Now the Lord is that S ... 2Cor 3:17
where the S of the Lord is, there ... 2Cor 3:17
even as by the S of the Lord ... 2Cor 3:18
We having the same s of faith ... 2Cor 4:13
unto us the earnest of the S ... 2Cor 5:5
all filthiness of the flesh and s ... 2Cor 7:1
because his s was refreshed by ... 2Cor 7:13
or if ye receive another s ... 2Cor 11:4
walked we not in the same s ... 2Cor 12:18
Received ye the S by the works of ... Gal 3:2
having begun in the S, are ye now ... Gal 3:3
that ministereth to you the S ... Gal 3:5
promise of the S through faith ... Gal 3:14
God hath sent forth the S of his ... Gal 4:6
him that was born after the S ... Gal 4:29
For we through the S wait for the ... Gal 5:5
This I say then, Walk in the S ... Gal 5:16
the flesh lusteth against the S ... Gal 5:17
and the S against the flesh ... Gal 5:17
But if ye be led of the S ... Gal 5:18
But the fruit of the S is love ... Gal 5:22
If we live in the S, let us also ... Gal 5:25
let us also walk in the S ... Gal 5:25
such an one in the s of meekness ... Gal 6:1
but he that soweth to the S shall ... Gal 6:8
of the S reap life everlasting ... Gal 6:8
Lord Jesus Christ be with your s ... Gal 6:18
with that holy S of promise ... Eph 1:13
may give unto you the s of wisdom ... Eph 1:17
the s that now worketh in the ... Eph 2:2
access by one S unto the Father ... Eph 2:18
habitation of God through the S ... Eph 2:22
apostles and prophets by the S ... Eph 3:5
might by his S in the inner man ... Eph 3:16
of the S in the bond of peace ... Eph 4:3
There is one body, and one S ... Eph 4:4
be renewed in the s of your mind ... Eph 4:23
And grieve not the holy S of God ... Eph 4:30
fruit of the S is in all goodness ... Eph 5:9
but be filled with the S ... Eph 5:18
salvation, and the sword of the S ... Eph 6:17
prayer and supplication in the S ... Eph 6:18
supply of the S of Jesus Christ ... Phil 1:19
that ye stand fast in one s ... Phil 1:27
love, if any fellowship of the S ... Phil 2:1
which worship God in the s ... Phil 3:3
unto us your love in the S ... Col 1:8
flesh, yet am I with you in the s ... Col 2:5
also given unto us his holy S ... 1Th 4:8
Quench not the S ... 1Th 5:19
and I pray God your whole s ... 1Th 5:23
or be troubled, neither by s ... 2Th 2:2
consume with the s of his mouth ... 2Th 2:8
through sanctification of the S ... 2Th 2:13
in the flesh, justified in the S ... 1Ti 3:16
Now the S speaketh expressly, ... 1Ti 4:1
in conversation, in charity, in s ... 1Ti 4:12
hath not given us the s of fear ... 2Ti 1:7
Lord Jesus Christ be with thy s ... 2Ti 4:22
Lord Jesus Christ be with your s ... Philem 25
the dividing asunder of soul and s ... Heb 4:12
who through the eternal S offered ... Heb 9:14
done despite unto the S of grace ... Heb 10:29
as the body without the s is dead ... Jas 2:26
The s that dwelleth in us lusteth ... Jas 4:5
through sanctification of the S ... 1Pet 1:2
or what manner of time the S of ... 1Pet 1:11
the S unto unfeigned love of the ... 1Pet 1:22
the ornament of a meek and quiet s ... 1Pet 3:4
the flesh, but quickened by the S ... 1Pet 3:18
live according to God in the s ... 1Pet 4:6
for the s of glory and of God ... 1Pet 4:14
by the S which he hath given us ... 1Jn 3:24
Beloved, believe not every s ... 1Jn 4:1
Hereby know ye the S of God ... 1Jn 4:2
Every s that confesseth that ... 1Jn 4:2
every s that confesseth not that ... 1Jn 4:3
this is that s of antichrist, ... 1Jn 4:3
Hereby know we the s of truth ... 1Jn 4:6
of truth, and the s of error ... 1Jn 4:6
because he hath given us of his S ... 1Jn 4:13
it is the S that beareth witness, ... 1Jn 5:6
witness, because the S is truth ... 1Jn 5:6
that bear witness in earth, the s ... 1Jn 5:8
sensual, having not the S ... Jude 19
I was in the S on the Lord's day, ... Rev 1:10
let him hear what the S saith ... Rev 2:7
let him hear what the S saith ... Rev 2:11
let him hear what the S saith ... Rev 2:17
let him hear what the S saith ... Rev 2:29
let him hear what the S saith ... Rev 3:6
let him hear what the S saith ... Rev 3:13
let him hear what the S saith ... Rev 3:22
And immediately I was in the s ... Rev 4:2
an half the S of life from God ... Rev 11:11
Yea, saith the S, that they may ... Rev 14:13
away in the s into the wilderness ... Rev 17:3
and the hold of every foul s ... Rev 18:2
of Jesus is the s of prophecy ... Rev 19:10
me away in the s to a great ... Rev 21:10
And the S and the bride say, Come ... Rev 22:17

## SPIRITS

not them that have familiar s ... Lev 19:31
after such as have familiar s ... Lev 20:6
the God of the s of all flesh ... Num 16:22
the God of the s of all flesh ... Num 27:16
or a consulter with familiar s ... Deut 18:11
away those that had familiar s ... 1Sa 28:3
off those that have familiar s ... 1Sa 28:9
and dealt with familiar s ... 2Kin 21:6
the workers with familiar s ... 2Kin 23:24
Who maketh his angels s ... Ps 104:4
but the LORD weigheth the s ... Prov 16:2
unto them that have familiar s ... Is 8:19
and to them that have familiar s ... Is 19:3
are the four s of the heavens ... Zec 6:5
he cast out the s with his word ... Mt 8:16
gave them power against unclean s ... Mt 10:1
other s more wicked than himself ... Mt 12:45
commandeth he even the unclean s ... Mk 1:27
And unclean s, when they saw him, ... Mk 3:11
And the unclean s went out ... Mk 5:13
and gave them power over unclean s ... Mk 6:7
power he commandeth the unclean s ... Lk 4:36
that were vexed with unclean s ... Lk 6:18
and plagues, and of evil s ... Lk 7:21
which had been healed of evil s ... Lk 8:2
that the s are subject unto you ... Lk 10:20
other s more wicked than himself ... Lk 11:26
which were vexed with unclean s ... Acts 5:16
For unclean s, crying with loud ... Acts 8:7
the evil s went out of them ... Acts 19:12
evil s the name of the Lord Jesus ... Acts 19:13
to another discerning of s ... 1Cor 12:10
the s of the prophets are subject ... 1Cor 14:32
faith, giving heed to seducing s ... 1Ti 4:1
he saith, Who maketh his angels s ... Heb 1:7
Are they not all ministering s ... Heb 1:14
subjection unto the Father of s ... Heb 12:9
to the s of just men made perfect ... Heb 12:23
and preached unto the s in prison ... 1Pet 3:19
but try the s whether they are of ... 1Jn 4:1
from the seven S which are before ... Rev 1:4
he that hath the seven S of God ... Rev 3:1
which are the seven S of God ... Rev 4:5
which are the seven S of God sent ... Rev 5:6
I saw three unclean s like frogs ... Rev 16:13
For they are the s of devils ... Rev 16:14

## SPIRITUAL

the s man is mad, for the ... Hos 9:7
I may impart unto you some s gift ... Rom 1:11
For we know that the law is s ... Rom 7:14
made partakers of their s things ... Rom 15:27
comparing s things with s ... 1Cor 2:13
But he that is s judgeth all ... 1Cor 2:15
not speak unto you as unto s ... 1Cor 3:1
If we have sown unto you s things ... 1Cor 9:11
And did all eat the same s meat ... 1Cor 10:3
And did all drink the same s drink ... 1Cor 10:4
for they drank of that s Rock ... 1Cor 10:4
Now concerning s gifts, brethren, ... 1Cor 12:1
after charity, and desire s gifts ... 1Cor 14:1
as ye are zealous of s gifts ... 1Cor 14:12
himself to be a prophet, or s ... 1Cor 14:37
it is raised a s body ... 1Cor 15:44
body, and there is a s body ... 1Cor 15:44
that was not first which is s ... 1Cor 15:46
and afterward that which is s ... 1Cor 15:46
in a fault, ye which are s ... Gal 6:1
who hath blessed us with all s ... Eph 1:3
s songs, singing and making melody ... Eph 5:19
against s wickedness in high ... Eph 6:12
in all wisdom and s understanding ... Col 1:9
s songs, singing with grace in ... Col 3:16
stones, are built up a s house ... 1Pet 2:5
to offer up s sacrifices ... 1Pet 2:5

## SPIRITUALLY

but to be s minded is life and ... Rom 8:6
because they are s discerned ... 1Cor 2:14
which s is called Sodom and Egypt, ... Rev 11:8

## SPIT

issue s upon him that is clean ... Lev 15:8
her father had but s in her face ... Num 12:14
s in his face, and shall answer and ... Deut 25:9
me, and spare not to s in my face ... Job 30:10
Then did they s in his face ... Mt 26:67
they s upon him, and took the reed ... Mt 27:30
fingers into his ears, and he s ... Mk 7:33
and when he had s on his eyes ... Mk 8:23
shall s upon him, and shall kill ... Mk 10:34
And some began to s on him ... Mk 14:65
did s upon him, and bowing their ... Mk 15:19

## SPITE

for thou beholdest mischief and s ... Ps 10:14

## SPITEFULLY

his servants, and entreated them s ... Mt 22:6
s entreated, and spitted on ... Lk 18:32

### SPITTED
and spitefully entreated, and *s* on ... Lk 18:32

### SPITTING
I hid not my face from shame and *s* ... Is 50:6

### SPITTLE
let his *s* fall down upon his ... 1Sa 21:13
me alone till I swallow down my *s* ... Job 7:19
the ground, and made clay of the *s* ... Jn 9:6

### SPOIL
and at night he shall divide the *s* ... Gen 49:27
and ye shall *s* the Egyptians ... Ex 3:22
overtake, I will divide the *s* ... Ex 15:9
took the *s* of all their cattle ... Num 31:9
And they took all the *s*, and all ... Num 31:11
captives, and the prey, and the *s* ... Num 31:12
(For the men of war had taken *s* ... Num 31:53
the *s* of the cities which we took ... Deut 2:35
the *s* of the cities, we took for ... Deut 3:7
thou shalt gather all the *s* of it ... Deut 13:16
all the *s* thereof every whit, for ... Deut 13:16
the city, even all the *s* thereof ... Deut 20:14
shalt eat the *s* of thine enemies ... Deut 20:14
only the *s* thereof, and the cattle ... Josh 8:2
the *s* of that city Israel took ... Josh 8:27
all the *s* of these cities, and the ... Josh 11:14
divide the *s* of your enemies with ... Josh 22:8
the necks of them that take the *s* ... Judg 5:30
men of them, and took their *s* ... Judg 14:19
the *s* of their enemies which they ... 1Sa 14:30
And the people flew upon the *s* ... 1Sa 14:32
*s* them until the morning light, ... 1Sa 14:36
LORD, but didst fly upon the *s* ... 1Sa 15:19
But the people took of the *s* ... 1Sa 15:21
because of all the great *s* that ... 1Sa 30:16
sons nor daughters, neither *s* ... 1Sa 30:19
and said, This is David's *s* ... 1Sa 30:20
of the *s* that we have recovered ... 1Sa 30:22
he sent of the *s* unto the elders ... 1Sa 30:26
the *s* of the enemies of the LORD ... 1Sa 30:26
and brought in a *s* with them ... 2Sa 3:22
of the *s* of Hadadezer, son of ... 2Sa 8:12
he brought forth the *s* of the ... 2Sa 12:30
returned after him only to *s* ... 2Sa 23:10
now therefore, Moab, to the *s* ... 2Kin 3:23
prey and a *s* to all their enemies ... 2Kin 21:14
exceeding much *s* out of the city ... 1Chr 20:2
and they carried away very much *s* .. 2Chr 14:13
was exceeding much *s* in them ... 2Chr 14:14
of the *s* which they had brought, ... 2Chr 15:11
came to take away the *s* of them ... 2Chr 20:25
three days in gathering of the *s* ... 2Chr 20:25
sent all the *s* of them unto the ... 2Chr 24:23
thousand of them, and took much *s*. 2Chr 25:13
took also away much *s* from them ... 2Chr 28:8
and brought the *s* to Samaria ... 2Chr 28:8
the *s* before the princes and all ... 2Chr 28:14
with the *s* clothed all that were ... 2Chr 28:15
sword, to captivity, and to a *s* ... Ezr 9:7
to take the *s* of them for a prey ... Est 3:13
to take the *s* of them for a prey, ... Est 8:11
but on the *s* laid they not their ... Est 9:10
plucked the *s* out of his teeth ... Job 29:17
which hate us *s* for themselves ... Ps 44:10
tarried at home divided the *s* ... Ps 68:12
All that pass by the way *s* him ... Ps 89:41
and let the strangers *s* his labour ... Ps 109:11
word, as one that findeth great *s* ... Ps 119:162
we shall fill our houses with *s* ... Prov 1:13
to divide the *s* with the proud ... Prov 16:19
*s* the soul of those that spoiled ... Prov 22:23
*s* not his resting place ... Prov 24:15
that he shall have no need of *s* ... Prov 31:11
little foxes, that *s* the vines ... Song 2:15
the *s* of the poor is in your ... Is 3:14
the *s* of Samaria shall be taken ... Is 8:4
rejoice when they divide the *s* ... Is 9:3
give him a charge, to take the *s* ... Is 10:6
they shall *s* them of the east ... Is 11:14
is the portion of them that *s* us ... Is 17:14
when thou shalt cease to *s* ... Is 33:1
your *s* shall be gathered like the ... Is 33:4
is the prey of a great *s* divided ... Is 33:23
for a *s*, and none saith, Restore ... Is 42:22
Who gave Jacob for a *s*, and Israel ... Is 42:24
divide the *s* with the strong ... Is 53:12
wolf of the evenings shall *s* them ... Jer 5:6
violence and *s* is heard in her ... Jer 6:7
I give to the *s* without price ... Jer 15:13
and all thy treasures to the *s* ... Jer 17:3
their enemies, which shall *s* them ... Jer 20:5
cried out, I cried violence and *s* ... Jer 20:8
they that *s* thee shall be a ... Jer 30:16
thee shall be a *s* ... Jer 30:16
cometh to *s* all the Philistines ... Jer 47:4
the LORD will *s* the Philistines ... Jer 47:4
Kedar, and *s* the men of the east ... Jer 49:28
the multitude of their cattle a *s* ... Jer 49:32
And Chaldea shall be a *s* ... Jer 50:10
all that *s* her shall be satisfied ... Jer 50:10
the wicked of the earth for a *s* ... Eze 7:21
through the land, and they *s* it ... Eze 14:15
thee for a *s* to the heathen ... Eze 25:7
shall become a *s* to the nations ... Eze 26:5
they shall make a *s* of thy riches ... Eze 26:12
take her multitude, and take her *s* ... Eze 29:19
they shall *s* the pomp of Egypt, ... Eze 32:12
To take a *s*, and to take a prey ... Eze 38:12
thee, Art thou come to take a *s* ... Eze 38:13
and goods, to take a great *s* ... Eze 38:13
they shall *s* those that spoiled ... Eze 39:10
remove violence and *s*, and execute ... Eze 45:9
scatter among them the prey, and *s* ... Dan 11:24
by flame, by captivity, and by *s* ... Dan 11:33
altars, he shall *s* their images ... Hos 10:2
he shall *s* the treasure of all ... Hos 13:15
Take ye the *s* of silver, take the ... Nah 2:9
of silver, take the *s* of gold ... Nah 2:9
of the people shall *s* thee ... Hab 2:8
the *s* of beasts, which made them ... Hab 2:17
residue of my people shall *s* them ... Zeph 2:9
they shall be a *s* to their ... Zec 2:9
thy *s* shall be divided in the ... Zec 14:1
*s* his goods, except he first bind ... Mt 12:29
and then he will *s* his house ... Mt 12:29
*s* his goods, except he will first ... Mk 3:27
and then he will *s* his house ... Mk 3:27
Beware lest any man *s* you through ... Col 2:8

### SPOILED
*s* the city, because they had ... Gen 34:27
*s* even all that was in the house ... Gen 34:29
And they *s* the Egyptians ... Ex 12:36
*s* evermore, and no man shall save ... Deut 28:29
the hands of spoilers that *s* them ... Judg 2:14
of the hand of those that *s* them ... Judg 2:16
of the hands of them that *s* them ... 1Sa 14:48
and they *s* their tents ... 1Sa 17:53
*s* the tents of the Syrians ... 2Kin 7:16
and they *s* all the cities ... 2Chr 14:14
He leadeth counsellors away *s* ... Job 12:17
He leadeth princes away *s* ... Job 12:19
The stouthearted are *s*, they have ... Ps 76:5
the soul of those that *s* them ... Prov 22:23
their houses shall be *s*, and their ... Is 13:16
whose land the rivers have *s* ... Is 18:2
whose land the rivers have *s* ... Is 18:7
be utterly emptied, and utterly *s* ... Is 24:3
that spoilest, and thou wast not *s* ... Is 33:1
cease to spoil, thou shalt be *s* ... Is 33:1
But this is a people robbed and *s* ... Is 42:22
why is he *s* ... Jer 2:14
for we are *s* ... Jer 4:13
for the whole land is *s* ... Jer 4:20
suddenly are my tents *s*, and my ... Jer 4:20
And when thou art *s*, what wilt ... Jer 4:30
heard out of Zion, How are we *s* ... Jer 9:19
My tabernacle is *s*, and all my ... Jer 10:20
deliver him that is *s* out of the ... Jer 21:12
deliver the *s* out of the hand of ... Jer 22:3
for the LORD hath *s* their pasture ... Jer 25:36
for it is *s* ... Jer 48:1
Moab is *s*, and gone up out of her ... Jer 48:15
ye it in Arnon, that Moab is *s* ... Jer 48:20
Howl, O Heshbon, for Ai is *s* ... Jer 49:3
his seed is *s*, and his brethren, ... Jer 49:10
Because the LORD hath *s* Babylon ... Jer 51:55
hath *s* none by violence, hath ... Eze 18:7
hath *s* by violence, hath not ... Eze 18:12
neither hath *s* by violence ... Eze 18:16
*s* his brother by violence, and did ... Eze 18:18
will give them to be removed and *s* ... Eze 23:46
shall spoil those that *s* them ... Eze 39:10
and all thy fortresses shall be *s* ... Hos 10:14
as Shalman *s* Beth-arbel in the ... Hos 10:14
thee, and thy palaces shall be *s* ... Amos 3:11
the *s* against the strong, so that ... Amos 5:9
so that the *s* shall come against ... Amos 5:9
and say, We be utterly *s* ... Mic 2:4
Because thou hast *s* many nations ... Hab 2:8
me unto the nations which *s* you ... Zec 2:8
because the mighty are *s* ... Zec 11:2
for their glory is *s* ... Zec 11:3
for the pride of Jordan is *s* ... Zec 11:3
having *s* principalities and powers ... Col 2:15

### SPOILER
to them from the face of the *s* ... Is 16:4
the *s* ceaseth, the oppressors are ... Is 16:4
treacherously, and the *s* spoileth ... Is 21:2
for the *s* shall suddenly come ... Jer 6:26
of the young men a *s* at noonday ... Jer 15:8
the *s* shall come upon every city, ... Jer 48:8
for the *s* of Moab shall come upon ... Jer 48:18
the *s* is fallen upon thy summer ... Jer 48:32
Because the *s* is come upon her, ... Jer 51:56

### SPOILERS
the hands of *s* that spoiled them ... Judg 2:14
the *s* came out of the camp of the ... 1Sa 13:17
the garrison, and the *s*, they also ... 1Sa 14:15
delivered them into the hand of *s* ... 2Kin 17:20
The *s* are come upon all high ... Jer 12:12
for the *s* shall come unto her ... Jer 51:48
yet from me shall *s* come unto her ... Jer 51:53

### SPOILEST
Woe to thee that *s*, and thou wast ... Is 33:1

### SPOILETH
and the needy from him that *s* him ... Ps 35:10
treacherously, and the spoiler *s* ... Is 21:2
and the troop of robbers *s* without ... Hos 7:1
the cankerworm *s*, and fleeth away ... Nah 3:16

### SPOILING
evil for good to the *s* of my soul ... Ps 35:12
because of the *s* of the daughter ... Is 22:4
crying shall be from Horonaim, *s* ... Jer 48:3
for *s* and violence are before me ... Hab 1:3
took joyfully the *s* of your goods ... Heb 10:34

### SPOILS
When I saw among the *s* a goodly ... Josh 7:21
Out of the *s* won in battles did ... 1Chr 26:27
with the *s* of their hands ... Is 25:11
he trusted, and divideth his *s* ... Lk 11:22
Abraham gave the tenth of the *s* ... Heb 7:4

### SPOKEN
as the LORD had *s* unto him ... Gen 12:4
that which he hath *s* of him ... Gen 18:19
city, for the which thou hast *s* ... Gen 19:21
LORD did unto Sarah as he had *s* ... Gen 21:1
time of which God had *s* to him ... Gen 21:2
son's wife, as the LORD hath *s* ... Gen 24:51
that which I have *s* to thee of ... Gen 28:15
thing which I have *s* unto Pharaoh ... Gen 41:28
to the word that Joseph had *s* ... Gen 44:2
thou hast *s* unto thy servant ... Ex 4:10
which the LORD had *s* unto Moses ... Ex 4:30
as the LORD had *s* unto Moses ... Ex 9:12
as the LORD had *s* by Moses ... Ex 9:35
And Moses said, Thou hast *s* well ... Ex 10:29
that the LORD hath *s* we will do ... Ex 19:8
all this land that I have *s* of ... Ex 32:13
place of which I have *s* unto thee ... Ex 32:34
this thing also that thou hast *s* ... Ex 33:17
all that the LORD had *s* with him ... Ex 34:32
statutes which the LORD hath *s* ... Lev 10:11
For the LORD had *s* unto Moses ... Num 1:48
for the LORD hath *s* good ... Num 10:29
the LORD indeed *s* only by Moses ... Num 12:2
hath he not *s* also by us ... Num 12:2
great, according as thou hast *s* ... Num 14:17
as ye have *s* in mine ears, so ... Num 14:28
which the LORD hath *s* unto Moses ... Num 15:22
for we have *s* against the LORD, ... Num 21:7
And Balak did as Balaam had *s* ... Num 23:2
unto him, What hath the LORD *s* ... Num 23:17
thou hast *s* is good for us to do ... Deut 1:14
which they have *s* unto thee ... Deut 5:28
well said all that they have *s* ... Deut 5:28
before thee, as the LORD hath *s* ... Deut 6:19
because he hath *s* to turn you ... Deut 13:5
They have well *s* that which they ... Deut 18:17
that which they have *s* ... Deut 18:17
word which the LORD hath not *s* ... Deut 18:21
thing which the LORD hath not *s* ... Deut 18:22
prophet hath *s* it presumptuously ... Deut 18:22
the LORD thy God, as he hath *s* ... Deut 26:19
when Joshua had *s* unto the people ... Josh 6:8
had *s* unto the house of Israel ... Josh 21:45
for that thou hast *s* friendly ... Ruth 2:13
and grief have I *s* hitherto ... 1Sa 1:16
I have *s* concerning his house ... 1Sa 3:12
matter which thou and I have *s* of ... 1Sa 20:23
that he hath *s* concerning thee ... 1Sa 25:30
God liveth, unless thou hadst *s* ... 2Sa 2:27
for the LORD hath *s* of David ... 2Sa 3:18
maidservants which thou hast *s* of ... 2Sa 6:22
but thou hast *s* also of thy ... 2Sa 7:19
hast *s* concerning thy servant ... 2Sa 7:25
for thou, O Lord GOD, hast *s* it ... 2Sa 7:29
that my lord the king hath *s* ... 2Sa 14:19
Ahithophel hath *s* after this ... 2Sa 17:6
if Adonijah have not *s* this word ... 1Kin 2:23
this people, who have *s* to me ... 1Kin 12:9
is the sign which the LORD hath *s* ... 1Kin 13:3
which he had *s* unto the king ... 1Kin 13:11
for the LORD hath *s* it ... 1Kin 14:11
answered and said, It is well *s* ... 1Kin 18:24
the Jezreelite had *s* to him ... 1Kin 21:4
the LORD hath *s* evil concerning ... 1Kin 22:23
peace, the LORD hath not *s* by me ... 1Kin 22:28
of the LORD which Elijah had *s* ... 2Kin 1:17
thou be *s* for to the king ... 2Kin 4:13
the man of God had *s* to the king ... 2Kin 7:18
the LORD hath *s* concerning him ... 2Kin 19:21
will do the thing that he hath *s* ... 2Kin 20:9
of the LORD which thou hast *s* ... 2Kin 20:19
for thou hast also *s* of thy ... 1Chr 17:17
hast *s* concerning thy servant ... 1Chr 17:23
the wine, which my lord hath *s* of ... 2Chr 2:15
performed his word that he hath *s* ... 2Chr 6:10
which thou hast *s* unto thy ... 2Chr 6:17
this people, which have *s* to me ... 2Chr 10:9
the LORD hath *s* evil against thee ... 2Chr 18:22
then hath not the LORD *s* by me ... 2Chr 18:27
that the word of the LORD *s* by ... 2Chr 36:22
because we had *s* unto the king ... Ezr 8:22
words that he had *s* unto me ... Neh 2:18
fail of all that thou hast *s* ... Est 6:10
who had *s* good for the king, ... Est 7:9
and after that I have *s*, mock on ... Job 21:3
Elihu had waited till Job had *s* ... Job 32:4
my tongue hath *s* in my mouth ... Job 33:2
thou hast *s* in mine hearing ... Job 33:8
Job hath *s* without knowledge, and ... Job 34:35
Once have I *s* ... Job 40:5
LORD had *s* these words unto Job ... Job 42:7
for ye have not *s* of me the thing ... Job 42:7
in that ye have not *s* of me the ... Job 42:8
mighty God, even the LORD, hath *s* ... Ps 50:1
God hath *s* in his holiness ... Ps 60:6
God hath *s* once ... Ps 62:11
have uttered, and my mouth hath *s* ... Ps 66:14
Glorious things are *s* of thee ... Ps 87:3
God hath *s* in his holiness ... Ps 108:7
they have *s* against me with a ... Ps 109:2
I believed, therefore have I *s* ... Ps 116:10
a word *s* in due season, how good ... Prov 15:23
A word fitly *s* is like apples of ... Prov 25:11

no heed unto all words that are *s* ... Eccl 7:21
the day when she shall be *s* for ... Song 8:8
for the LORD hath *s*, I have ... Is 1:2
the mouth of the LORD hath *s* it ... Is 1:20
is the word that the LORD hath *s* ... Is 16:13
But now the LORD hath *s*, saying, ... Is 16:14
the LORD God of Israel hath *s* it ... Is 21:17
for the LORD hath *s* it ... Is 22:25
for the sea hath *s*, even the ... Is 23:4
for the LORD hath *s* this word ... Is 24:3
for the LORD hath *s* it ... Is 25:8
For thus hath the LORD *s* unto me ... Is 31:4
the LORD hath *s* concerning him ... Is 37:22
will do this thing that he hath *s* ... Is 38:7
He hath both *s* unto me, and ... Is 38:15
of the LORD which thou hast *s* ... Is 39:8
the mouth of the LORD hath *s* it ... Is 40:5
I have not *s* in secret, in a dark ... Is 45:19
yea, I have *s* it, I will also ... Is 46:11
I, even I, have *s* ... Is 48:15
I have not *s* in secret from the ... Is 48:16
the mouth of the LORD hath *s* it ... Is 58:14
your lips have *s* lies, your ... Is 59:3
Behold, thou hast *s* and done evil ... Jer 3:5
because I have *s* it, I have ... Jer 4:28
whom the mouth of the LORD hath *s* ... Jer 9:12
for the LORD hath *s* ... Jer 13:15
I have not *s* to them, yet they ... Jer 23:21
and, What hath the LORD *s* ... Jer 23:35
and, What hath the LORD *s* ... Jer 23:37
I have *s* unto you, rising early ... Jer 25:3
for he hath *s* to us in the name ... Jer 26:16
as the LORD hath *s* against the ... Jer 27:13
have *s* lying words in my name, ... Jer 29:23
that I have *s* unto thee in a book ... Jer 30:2
what thou hast *s* is come to pass ... Jer 32:24
thou not what this people have *s* ... Jer 33:24
notwithstanding I have *s* unto you ... Jer 35:14
because I have *s* unto them ... Jer 35:17
I have *s* unto thee against Israel ... Jer 36:2
the LORD, which he had *s* unto him ... Jer 36:4
had *s* unto all the people ... Jer 38:1
As for the word that thou hast *s* ... Jer 44:16
have both *s* with your mouths ... Jer 44:25
be destroyed, as the LORD hath *s* ... Jer 48:8
thou hast *s* against this place, ... Jer 51:62
I the LORD have *s* it in my zeal ... Eze 5:13
I the LORD have *s* it ... Eze 5:15
I the LORD have *s* it ... Eze 5:17
word which I have *s* shall be done ... Eze 12:28
have ye not *s* a lying divination, ... Eze 13:7
albeit I have not *s* ... Eze 13:7
Because ye have *s* vanity, and seen ... Eze 13:8
deceived when he hath *s* a thing ... Eze 14:9
know that I the LORD have *s* it ... Eze 17:21
I the LORD have *s* and have done it ... Eze 17:24
for I the LORD have *s* it ... Eze 21:32
I the LORD have *s* it, and will do ... Eze 22:14
GOD, when the LORD hath not *s* ... Eze 22:28
for I have *s* it, saith the Lord ... Eze 23:34
I the LORD have *s* it ... Eze 24:14
for I have *s* it, saith the Lord ... Eze 26:5
for I the LORD have *s* it, saith ... Eze 26:14
for I have *s* it, saith the Lord ... Eze 28:10
I the LORD have *s* it ... Eze 30:12
I the LORD have *s* it ... Eze 34:24
*s* against the mountains of Israel ... Eze 35:12
I *s* against the residue of the ... Eze 36:5
I have *s* in my jealousy and in my ... Eze 36:6
I the LORD have *s* it, and I will ... Eze 36:36
ye know that I the LORD have *s* it ... Eze 37:14
Art thou he of whom I have *s* in ... Eze 38:17
in the fire of my wrath have I *s* ... Eze 38:19
for I have *s* it, saith the Lord ... Eze 39:5
this is the day whereof I have *s* ... Eze 39:8
Nebuchadnezzar, to thee it is *s* ... Dan 4:31
when he had *s* this word unto me, ... Dan 10:11
when he had *s* such words unto me, .. Dan 10:15
And when he had *s* unto me, I was ... Dan 10:19
yet they have *s* lies against me ... Hos 7:13
They have *s* words, swearing ... Hos 10:4
I have also *s* by the prophets, and ... Hos 12:10
for the LORD hath *s* it ... Joel 3:8
that the LORD hath *s* against you ... Amos 3:1
the Lord GOD hath *s*, who can but ... Amos 3:8
shall be with you, as ye have *s* ... Amos 5:14
neither shouldest thou have *s* ... Obad 12
for the LORD hath *s* it ... Obad 18
of the LORD of hosts hath *s* it ... Mic 4:4
inhabitants thereof have *s* lies ... Mic 6:12
For the idols have *s* vanity ... Zec 10:2
What have we *s* so much against ... Mal 3:13
was *s* of the Lord by the prophet ... Mt 1:22
was *s* of the Lord by the prophet ... Mt 2:15
which was *s* by Jeremy the prophet ... Mt 2:17
which was *s* by the prophets ... Mt 2:23
For this is he that was *s* of by ... Mt 3:3
which was *s* by Esaias the prophet ... Mt 4:14
which was *s* by Esaias the prophet ... Mt 8:17
which was *s* by Esaias the prophet ... Mt 12:17
which was *s* by the prophet ... Mt 13:35
which was *s* by the prophet ... Mt 21:4
that which was *s* unto you by God ... Mt 22:31
*s* of by Daniel the prophet, stand ... Mt 24:15
saying, He hath *s* blasphemy ... Mt 26:65
which was *s* by Jeremy the prophet ... Mt 27:9
which was *s* by the prophet ... Mt 27:35
And as soon as he had *s*, ... Mk 1:42
Jesus heard the word that was *s* ... Mk 5:36
he had *s* the parable against them ... Mk 12:12
*s* of by Daniel the prophet, ... Mk 13:14
be *s* of for a memorial of her ... Mk 14:9
after the Lord had *s* unto them ... Mk 16:19
those things which were *s* of him ... Lk 2:33
a sign which shall be *s* against ... Lk 2:34
Therefore whatsoever ye have *s* in ... Lk 12:3
that which ye have *s* in the ear ... Lk 12:3
knew they the things which were *s* ... Lk 18:34
And when he had thus *s*, he went ... Lk 19:28
had *s* this parable against them ... Lk 20:19
all that the prophets have *s* ... Lk 24:25
And when he had thus *s*, he shewed ... Lk 24:40
word that Jesus had *s* unto him ... Jn 4:50
When he had thus *s*, he spat on ... Jn 9:6
had *s* of taking of rest in sleep ... Jn 11:13
And when he thus had *s*, he cried ... Jn 11:43
the word that I have *s*, the same ... Jn 12:48
For I have not *s* of myself ... Jn 12:49
These things have I *s* unto you ... Jn 14:25
the word which I have *s* unto you ... Jn 15:3
These things have I *s* unto you ... Jn 15:11
*s* unto them, they had not had sin ... Jn 15:22
These things have I *s* unto you ... Jn 16:1
These things have I *s* unto you in ... Jn 16:25
These things I have *s* unto you ... Jn 16:33
When Jesus had *s* these words ... Jn 18:1
And when he had thus *s*, one of the ... Jn 18:22
answered him, If I have *s* evil ... Jn 18:23
that he had *s* these things unto ... Jn 20:18
And when he had *s* this, he saith ... Jn 21:19
when he had *s* these things, while ... Acts 1:9
which was *s* by the prophet Joel ... Acts 2:16
which God hath *s* by the mouth of ... Acts 3:21
follow after, as many as have *s* ... Acts 3:24
which ye have *s* come upon me ... Acts 8:24
the way, and that he had *s* to him ... Acts 9:27
which is *s* of in the prophets ... Acts 13:40
those things which were *s* by Paul ... Acts 13:45
should first have been *s* to you ... Acts 13:46
the things which were *s* of Paul ... Acts 16:14
these things cannot be *s* against ... Acts 19:36
And when he had thus *s*, he ... Acts 19:41
And when he had thus *s*, he kneeled. Acts 20:36
spirit or an angel hath *s* to him ... Acts 23:9
And when he had thus *s*, the king ... Acts 26:30
those things which were *s* by Paul ... Acts 27:11
And when he had thus *s*, he took ... Acts 27:35
that every where it is *s* against ... Acts 28:22
believed the things which were *s* ... Acts 28:24
after that Paul had *s* one word ... Acts 28:25
you all, that your faith is *s* of ... Rom 1:8
according to that which was *s* ... Rom 4:18
not then your good be evil *s* of ... Rom 14:16
written, To whom he was not *s* of ... Rom 15:21
why am I evil *s* of for that for ... 1Cor 10:30
how shall it be known what is *s* ... 1Cor 14:9
I believed, and therefore have I *s* ... 2Cor 4:13
last days *s* unto us by his Son ... Heb 1:2
For if the word *s* by angels was ... Heb 2:2
first began to be *s* by the Lord ... Heb 2:3
things which were to be *s* after ... Heb 3:5
afterward have *s* of another day ... Heb 4:8
are *s* pertaineth to another tribe ... Heb 7:13
which we have *s* this is the sum ... Heb 8:1
For when Moses had *s* every ... Heb 9:19
should not be *s* to them any more ... Heb 12:19
who have *s* unto you the word of ... Heb 13:7
who have *s* in the name of the ... Jas 5:10
on their part he is evil *s* of ... 1Pet 4:14
way of truth shall be evil *s* of ... 2Pet 2:2
*s* before by the holy prophets ... 2Pet 3:2
sinners have *s* against him ... Jude 15
ye the words which were *s* before ... Jude 17

**SPOKES**

and their felloes, and their *s* ... 1Kin 7:33

**SPOKESMAN**

he shall be thy *s* unto the people ... Ex 4:16

**SPOON**

One *s* of ten shekels of gold, ... Num 7:14
One *s* of gold of ten shekels, ... Num 7:20
One golden *s* of ten shekels, full ... Num 7:26
One golden *s* of ten shekels, full ... Num 7:32
One golden *s* of ten shekels, full ... Num 7:38
One golden *s* of ten shekels, full ... Num 7:44
One golden *s* of ten shekels, full ... Num 7:50
One golden *s* of ten shekels, full ... Num 7:56
One golden *s* of ten shekels, full ... Num 7:62
One golden *s* of ten shekels, full ... Num 7:68
One golden *s* of ten shekels, full ... Num 7:74
One golden *s* of ten shekels, full ... Num 7:80

**SPOONS**

*s* thereof, and covers thereof, and ... Ex 25:29
the table, his dishes, and his *s* ... Ex 37:16
put thereon the dishes, and the *s* ... Num 4:7
silver bowls, twelve *s* of gold ... Num 7:84
The golden *s* were twelve, full of ... Num 7:86
the gold of the *s* was an hundred ... Num 7:86
snuffers, and the basons, and the *s* ... 1Kin 7:50
and the snuffers, and the *s* ... 2Kin 25:14
snuffers, and the basons, and the *s* ... 2Chr 4:22
and to offer withal, and *s* ... 2Chr 24:14
snuffers, and the bowls, and the *s* ... Jer 52:18
and the candlesticks, and the *s* ... Jer 52:19

**SPORT**

for Samson, that he may make us *s* .. Judg 16:25
and he made them *s* ... Judg 16:25
that beheld while Samson made *s* ... Judg 16:27
It is as *s* to a fool to do ... Prov 10:23
and saith, Am not I in *s* ... Prov 26:19
Against whom do ye *s* yourselves ... Is 57:4

**SPORTING**

Isaac was *s* with Rebekah his wife ... Gen 26:8
*s* themselves with their own ... 2Pet 2:13

**SPOT**

a rising, a scab, or bright *s* ... Lev 13:2
If the bright *s* be white in the ... Lev 13:4
be a white rising, or a bright *s* ... Lev 13:19
if the bright *s* stay in his place ... Lev 13:23
burneth have a white bright *s* ... Lev 13:24
in the bright *s* be turned white ... Lev 13:25
be no white hair in the bright *s* ... Lev 13:26
if the bright *s* stay in his place ... Lev 13:28
it is a freckled *s* that groweth ... Lev 13:39
and for a scab, and for a bright *s* ... Lev 14:56
bring thee a red heifer without *s* ... Num 19:2
first year without *s* day by day ... Num 28:3
lambs of the first year without *s* ... Num 28:9
lambs of the first year without *s* ... Num 28:11
lambs of the first year without *s* ... Num 29:17
lambs of the first year without *s* ... Num 29:26
their *s* is not the *s* of his ... Deut 32:5
is not the *s* of his children ... Deut 32:5
thou lift up thy face without *s* ... Job 11:15
there is no *s* in thee ... Song 4:7
a glorious church, not having *s* ... Eph 5:27
keep this commandment without *s* ... 1Ti 6:14
offered himself without *s* to God ... Heb 9:14
lamb without blemish and without *s* ... 1Pet 1:19
found of him in peace, without *s* ... 2Pet 3:14

**SPOTS**

bright *s*, even white bright *s* ... Lev 13:38
if the bright *s* in the skin of ... Lev 13:39
his skin, or the leopard his *s* ... Jer 13:23
*S* they are and blemishes, sporting ... 2Pet 2:13
These are *s* in your feasts of ... Jude 12

**SPOTTED**

*s* cattle, and all the brown cattle ... Gen 30:32
cattle among the sheep, and the *s* ... Gen 30:32
*s* among the goats ... Gen 30:33
goats that were ringstraked and *s* ... Gen 30:35
she goats that were speckled and *s* ... Gen 30:35
ringstraked, speckled, and *s* ... Gen 30:39
even the garment *s* by the flesh ... Jude 23

**SPOUSE**

Come with me from Lebanon, my *s* ... Song 4:8
my heart, my sister, my *s* ... Song 4:9
fair is thy love, my sister, my *s* ... Song 4:10
Thy lips, O my *s*, drop as the ... Song 4:11
inclosed is my sister, my *s* ... Song 4:12
into my garden, my sister, my *s* ... Song 5:1

**SPOUSES**

your *s* shall commit adultery ... Hos 4:13
nor your *s* when they commit ... Hos 4:14

**SPRANG**

and immediately it *s* up, because ... Mk 4:5
and did yield fruit that *s* up ... Mk 4:8
and the thorns *s* up with it ... Lk 8:7
ground, and *s* up, and bare fruit an ... Lk 8:8
*s* in, and came trembling, and fell ... Acts 16:29
that our Lord *s* out of Juda ... Heb 7:14
Therefore *s* there even of one, and ... Heb 11:12

**SPREAD**

of the Canaanites *s* abroad ... Gen 10:18
thou shalt *s* abroad to the west, ... Gen 28:14
a field, where he had *s* his tent ... Gen 33:19
*s* his tent beyond the tower of ... Gen 35:21
I will *s* abroad my hands unto the ... Ex 9:29
*s* abroad his hands unto the LORD ... Ex 9:33
the cherubims *s* out their wings ... Ex 37:9
he *s* abroad the tent over the ... Ex 40:19
the plague *s* not in the skin ... Lev 13:5
the plague *s* not in the skin, the ... Lev 13:6
But if the scab *s* much abroad in ... Lev 13:7
if it *s* much abroad in the skin, ... Lev 13:22
*s* not, it is a burning boil ... Lev 13:23
if it be *s* much abroad in the ... Lev 13:27
*s* not in the skin, but it be ... Lev 13:28
and, behold, if the scall *s* not ... Lev 13:32
if the scall be not *s* in the skin ... Lev 13:34
But if the scall *s* much in the ... Lev 13:35
if the scall be *s* in the skin ... Lev 13:36
if the plague be *s* in the garment ... Lev 13:51
plague be not *s* in the garment ... Lev 13:53
colour, and the plague be not *s* ... Lev 13:55
if the plague be *s* in the walls ... Lev 14:39
if the plague be *s* in the house ... Lev 14:44
plague hath not *s* in the house ... Lev 14:48
shall *s* over it a cloth wholly of ... Num 4:6
they shall *s* a cloth of blue ... Num 4:7
they shall *s* upon them a cloth of ... Num 4:8
they shall *s* a cloth of blue ... Num 4:11
and *s* a purple cloth thereon ... Num 4:13
they shall *s* upon it a covering ... Num 4:14
they *s* them all abroad for ... Num 11:32
As the valleys are they *s* forth ... Num 24:6
they shall *s* the cloth before the ... Deut 22:17
they *s* a garment, and did cast ... Judg 8:25
in Judah, and *s* themselves in Lehi ... Judg 15:9
*s* therefore thy skirt over thine ... Ruth 3:9
they were *s* abroad upon all the ... 1Sa 30:16
*s* themselves in the valley of ... 2Sa 5:18
*s* themselves in the valley of ... 2Sa 5:22
So they *s* Absalom a tent upon the ... 2Sa 16:22
*s* a covering over the well's ... 2Sa 17:19

S

mouth, and *s* ground corn thereon ...... 2Sa 17:19
*s* it for her upon the rock, from ...... 2Sa 21:10
the street, and did *s* them abroad ...... 2Sa 22:43
*s* gold upon the cherubims, and ...... 1Kin 6:32
For the cherubims *s* forth their ...... 1Kin 8:7
*s* forth his hands toward heaven ...... 1Kin 8:22
*s* forth his hands toward this ...... 1Kin 8:38
with his hands *s* up to heaven ...... 1Kin 8:54
*s* it on his face, so that he died ...... 2Kin 8:15
the LORD, and *s* it before the LORD .... 2Kin 19:14
*s* themselves in the valley of ...... 1Chr 14:9
the Philistines yet again *s* ...... 1Chr 14:13
that *s* out their wings, and ...... 1Chr 28:18
The wings of these cherubims *s* ...... 2Chr 3:13
For the cherubims *s* forth their ...... 2Chr 5:8
of Israel, and *s* forth his hands ...... 2Chr 6:12
*s* forth his hands toward heaven, ...... 2Chr 6:13
shall *s* forth his hands in this ...... 2Chr 6:29
his name *s* abroad even to the ...... 2Chr 26:8
And his name *s* far abroad ...... 2Chr 26:15
*s* out my hands unto the LORD my ...... Ezr 9:5
My root was *s* out by the waters, ...... Job 29:19
Hast thou with him *s* out the sky ...... Job 37:18
He *s* a cloud for a covering ...... Ps 105:39
they have *s* a net by the wayside ...... Ps 140:5
net is *s* in the sight of any bird ...... Prov 1:17
when ye *s* forth your hands, I ...... Is 1:15
the worm is *s* under thee, and the ...... Is 14:11
they that *s* nets upon the waters ...... Is 19:8
vail that is *s* over all nations ...... Is 25:7
he shall *s* forth his hands in the ...... Is 25:11
mast, they could not *s* the sail ...... Is 33:23
the LORD, and *s* it before the LORD ...... Is 37:14
he that *s* forth the earth, and ...... Is 42:5
to *s* sackcloth and ashes under him ...... Is 58:5
I have *s* out my hands all the day ...... Is 65:2
they shall *s* them before the sun, ...... Jer 8:2
Silver *s* into plates is brought ...... Jer 10:9
he shall *s* his royal pavilion ...... Jer 43:10
shall *s* his wings over Moab ...... Jer 48:40
eagle, and *s* his wings over Bozrah ...... Jer 49:22
The adversary hath *s* out his hand ...... Lam 1:10
he hath *s* a net for my feet, he ...... Lam 1:13
And he *s* it before me ...... Eze 2:10
My net also will I *s* upon him ...... Eze 12:13
I *s* my skirt over thee, and ...... Eze 16:8
I will *s* my net upon him, and he ...... Eze 17:20
and *s* their net over him ...... Eze 19:8
shalt be a place to *s* nets upon ...... Eze 26:14
I will therefore *s* out my net ...... Eze 32:3
shall be a place to *s* forth nets ...... Eze 47:10
on Mizpah, and a net *s* upon Tabor ...... Hos 5:1
I will *s* my net upon them ...... Hos 7:12
His branches shall *s*, and his ...... Hos 14:6
as the morning *s* upon the ...... Joel 2:2
their horsemen shall *s* themselves ...... Hab 1:8
prosperity shall yet be *s* abroad ...... Zec 1:17
for I have *s* you abroad as the ...... Zec 2:6
*s* dung upon your faces, even the ...... Mal 2:3
*s* abroad his fame in all that ...... Mt 9:31
a very great multitude *s* their ...... Mt 21:8
immediately his fame *s* abroad ...... Mk 1:28
(for his name was *s* abroad ...... Mk 6:14
many *s* their garments in the way ...... Mk 11:8
they *s* their clothes in the way ...... Lk 19:36
But that it *s* no further among ...... Acts 4:17
faith to God-ward is *s* abroad ...... 1Th 1:8

**SPREADEST**
which thou *s* forth to be thy sail ...... Eze 27:7

**SPREADETH**
the scab *s* in the skin, then the ...... Lev 13:8
*s* abroad her wings, taketh them, ...... Deut 32:11
Which alone *s* out the heavens, and ...... Job 9:8
throne, and *s* his cloud upon it ...... Job 26:9
he *s* his light upon it, and ...... Job 36:30
he *s* sharp pointed things upon ...... Job 41:30
neighbour *s* a net for his feet ...... Prov 29:5
as he that swimmeth *s* forth his ...... Is 25:11
the goldsmith *s* it over with gold ...... Is 40:19
*s* them out as a tent to dwell in ...... Is 40:22
that *s* abroad the earth by myself ...... Is 44:24
that *s* her hands, saying, Woe is ...... Jer 4:31
that *s* out her roots by the river ...... Jer 17:8
Zion *s* forth her hands, and there ...... Lam 1:17

**SPREADING**
it is a *s* plague ...... Lev 13:57
*s* himself like a green bay tree ...... Ps 37:35
became a *s* vine of low stature, ...... Eze 17:6
It shall be a place for the *s* of ...... Eze 26:5

**SPREADINGS**
understand the *s* of the clouds ...... Job 36:29

**SPRIGS**
cut off the *s* with pruninghooks ...... Is 18:5
forth branches, and shot forth *s* ...... Eze 17:6

**SPRING**
sang this song, *S* up, O well ...... Num 21:17
depths that *s* out of valleys and ...... Deut 8:7
and when the day began to *s* ...... Judg 19:25
to pass about the *s* of the day ...... 1Sa 9:26
forth unto the *s* of the waters ...... 2Kin 2:21
doth trouble *s* out of the ground ...... Job 5:6
bud of the tender herb to *s* forth ...... Job 38:27
Truth shall *s* out of the earth ...... Ps 85:11
When the wicked *s* as the grass ...... Ps 92:7
troubled fountain, and a corrupt *s* ..... Prov 25:26
a *s* shut up, a fountain sealed ...... Song 4:12
before they *s* forth I tell you of ...... Is 42:9
now it shall *s* forth ...... Is 43:19
they shall *s* up as among the ...... Is 44:4
let righteousness *s* up together ...... Is 45:8
health shall *s* forth speedily ...... Is 58:8
like a *s* of water, whose waters ...... Is 58:11
that are sown in it to *s* forth ...... Is 61:11
praise to *s* forth before all the ...... Is 61:11
wither in all the leaves of her *s* ...... Eze 17:9
his *s* shall become dry, and his ...... Hos 13:15
pastures of the wilderness do *s* ...... Joel 2:22
and day, and the seed should *s* ...... Mk 4:27

**SPRINGETH**
the hyssop that *s* out of the wall ...... 1Kin 4:33
year that which *s* of the same ...... 2Kin 19:29
year that which *s* of the same ...... Is 37:30
thus judgment *s* up as hemlock in ...... Hos 10:4

**SPRINGING**
and found there a well of *s* water ...... Gen 26:19
as the tender grass *s* out of the ...... 2Sa 23:4
thou blessest the *s* thereof ...... Ps 65:10
water *s* up into everlasting life ...... Jn 4:14
of bitterness *s* up trouble you ...... Heb 12:15

**SPRINGS**
the plain, under the *s* of Pisgah ...... Deut 4:49
and of the vale, and of the *s* ...... Josh 10:40
and in the plains, and in the *s* ...... Josh 12:8
give me also *s* of water ...... Josh 15:19
upper *s*, and the nether *s* ...... Josh 15:19
give me also *s* of water ...... Judg 1:15
the upper *s* and the nether *s* ...... Judg 1:15
entered into the *s* of the sea ...... Job 38:16
all my *s* are in thee ...... Ps 87:7
He sendeth the *s* into the valleys ...... Ps 104:10
and the thirsty land *s* of water ...... Is 35:7
water, and the dry land *s* of water ...... Is 41:18
even by the *s* of water shall he ...... Is 49:10
dry up her sea, and make her *s* dry ...... Jer 51:36

**SPRINKLE**
let Moses *s* it toward the heaven ...... Ex 9:8
*s* it round about upon the altar ...... Ex 29:16
*s* the blood upon the altar round ...... Ex 29:20
*s* it upon Aaron, and upon his ...... Ex 29:21
*s* the blood round about upon the ...... Lev 1:5
shall *s* his blood round about ...... Lev 1:11
*s* the blood upon the altar round ...... Lev 3:2
Aaron's sons shall *s* the blood ...... Lev 3:8
the sons of Aaron shall *s* the ...... Lev 3:13
*s* of the blood seven times before ...... Lev 4:6
*s* it seven times before the LORD, ...... Lev 4:17
he shall *s* of the blood of the ...... Lev 5:9
he *s* round about upon the altar ...... Lev 7:2
he shall *s* upon him that is to be ...... Lev 14:7
shall *s* of the oil with his ...... Lev 14:16
the priest shall *s* with his right ...... Lev 14:27
water, and *s* the house seven times ..... Lev 14:51
*s* it with his finger upon the ...... Lev 16:14
he *s* of the blood with his finger ...... Lev 16:14
*s* it upon the mercy seat, and ...... Lev 16:15
he shall *s* of the blood upon it ...... Lev 16:19
the priest shall *s* the blood upon ...... Lev 17:6
*S* water of purifying upon them, ...... Num 8:7
thou shalt *s* their blood upon the ...... Num 18:17
*s* of her blood directly before ...... Num 19:4
*s* it upon the tent, and upon all ...... Num 19:18
the clean person shall *s* upon the ...... Num 19:19
*s* upon it all the blood of the ...... 2Kin 16:15
So shall he *s* many nations ...... Is 52:15
Then will I *s* clean water upon ...... Eze 36:25
thereon, and to *s* blood thereon ...... Eze 43:18

**SPRINKLED**
Moses *s* it up toward heaven ...... Ex 9:10
of the blood he *s* on the altar ...... Ex 24:6
*s* it on the people, and said, ...... Ex 24:8
when there is *s* of the blood ...... Lev 6:27
it was *s* in the holy place ...... Lev 6:27
he *s* thereof upon the altar seven ...... Lev 8:11
Moses *s* the blood upon the altar ...... Lev 8:19
Moses *s* the blood upon the altar ...... Lev 8:24
*s* it upon Aaron, and upon his ...... Lev 8:30
which he *s* round about upon the ...... Lev 9:12
which he *s* upon the altar round ...... Lev 9:18
of separation was not *s* upon him ...... Num 19:13
hath not been *s* upon him ...... Num 19:20
of her blood was *s* on the wall ...... 2Kin 9:33
and *s* the blood of his peace ...... 2Kin 16:13
the blood, and *s* it on the altar ...... 2Chr 29:22
they *s* the blood upon the altar ...... 2Chr 29:22
they *s* the blood upon the altar ...... 2Chr 29:22
the priests *s* the blood, which ...... 2Chr 30:16
the priests *s* the blood from ...... 2Chr 35:11
*s* dust upon their heads toward ...... Job 2:12
blood shall be *s* upon my garments ...... Is 63:3
*s* both the book, and all the ...... Heb 9:19
Moreover he *s* with blood both the ...... Heb 9:21
having our hearts *s* from an evil ...... Heb 10:22

**SPRINKLETH**
that *s* the blood of the peace ...... Lev 7:14
that he that *s* the water of ...... Num 19:21

**SPRINKLING**
ashes of an heifer *s* the unclean ...... Heb 9:13
the *s* of blood, lest he that ...... Heb 11:28
covenant, and to the blood of *s* ...... Heb 12:24
*s* of the blood of Jesus Christ ...... 1Pet 1:2

**SPROUT**
be cut down, that it will *s* again ...... Job 14:7

**SPRUNG**
the east wind *s* up after them ...... Gen 41:6
the east wind, *s* up after them ...... Gen 41:23
it is a leprosy *s* up in his bald ...... Lev 13:42
and shadow of death light is *s* up ...... Mt 4:16
and forthwith they *s* up, because ...... Mt 13:5
and the thorns *s* up, and choked ...... Mt 13:7
But when the blade was *s* up ...... Mt 13:26
and as soon as it was *s* up ...... Lk 8:6

**SPUE**
That the land *s* not you out also, ...... Lev 18:28
to dwell therein, *s* you not out ...... Lev 20:22
Drink ye, and be drunken, and *s* ...... Jer 25:27
I will *s* thee out of my mouth ...... Rev 3:16

**SPUED**
as it *s* out the nations that were ...... Lev 18:28

**SPUN**
and brought that which they had *s* ...... Ex 35:25
them up in wisdom *s* goats' hair ...... Ex 35:26

**SPUNGE**
one of them ran, and took a *s* ...... Mt 27:48
filled a *s* full of vinegar, and ...... Mk 15:36
and they filled a *s* with vinegar ...... Jn 19:29

**SPY**
Moses sent to *s* out the land ...... Num 13:16
Moses sent them to *s* out the land .... Num 13:17
And Moses sent to *s* out Jaazer ...... Num 21:32
of Shittim two men to *s* secretly ...... Josh 2:1
Joshua sent to *s* out Jericho ...... Josh 6:25
to *s* out the land, and to search ...... Judg 18:2
to *s* out the country of Laish ...... Judg 18:14
went to *s* out the land went up ...... Judg 18:17
to *s* it out, and to overthrow it ...... 2Sa 10:3
*s* where he is, that I may send and ...... 2Kin 6:13
overthrow, and to *s* out the land ...... 1Chr 19:3
who came in privily to *s* out our ...... Gal 2:4

**SQUARE**
And all the doors and posts were *s* ...... 1Kin 7:5
*s* in the four squares thereof ...... Eze 43:16
hundred in breadth, *s* round about ...... Eze 45:2

**SQUARED**
The posts of the temple were *s* ...... Eze 41:21

**SQUARES**
square in the four *s* thereof ...... Eze 43:16
broad in the four *s* thereof ...... Eze 43:17

**STABILITY**
shall be the *s* of thy times ...... Is 33:6

**STABLE**
the world also shall be *s* ...... 1Chr 16:30
I will make Rabbah a *s* for camels ...... Eze 25:5

**STABLISH**
I will *s* the throne of his ...... 2Sa 7:13
I will *s* his throne for ever ...... 1Chr 17:12
as he went to *s* his dominion by ...... 1Chr 18:3
Then will I *s* the throne of thy ...... 2Chr 7:18
To *s* this among them, that they ...... Est 9:21
*S* thy word unto thy servant, who ...... Ps 119:38
to *s* you according to my gospel ...... Rom 16:25
To the end he may *s* your hearts ...... 1Th 3:13
*s* you in every good word and work ...... 2Th 2:17
Lord is faithful, who shall *s* you ...... 2Th 3:3
*s* your hearts ...... Jas 5:8
a while, make you perfect, *s* ...... 1Pet 5:10

**STABLISHED**
Therefore the LORD *s* the kingdom ...... 2Chr 17:5
the world also is *s*, that it ...... Ps 93:1
He hath also *s* them for ever and ...... Ps 148:6
*s* in the faith, as ye have been ...... Col 2:7

**STABLISHETH**
blood, and *s* a city by iniquity ...... Hab 2:12
Now he which *s* us with you in ...... 2Cor 1:21

**STACHYS** (*sta'-kis*) *A Christian in Rome.*
helper in Christ, and *S* my beloved ...... Rom 16:9

**STACKS**
in thorns, so that the *s* of corn ...... Ex 22:6

**STACTE**
Take unto thee sweet spices, *s* ...... Ex 30:34

**STAFF**
for with my *s* I passed over this ...... Gen 32:10
thy *s* that is in thine hand ...... Gen 38:18
the signet, and bracelets, and *s* ...... Gen 38:25
your feet, and your *s* in your hand ...... Ex 12:11
again, and walk abroad upon his *s* ...... Ex 21:19
I have broken the *s* of your bread ...... Lev 26:26
they bare it between two upon a *s* .... Num 13:23
and he smote the ass with a *s* ...... Num 22:27
end of the *s* that was in his hand ...... Judg 6:21
the *s* of his spear was like a ...... 1Sa 17:7
And he took his *s* in his hand ...... 1Sa 17:40
a leper, or that leaneth on a *s* ...... 2Sa 3:29
the *s* of whose spear was like a ...... 2Sa 21:19
with iron and the *s* of a spear ...... 2Sa 23:7
but he went down to him with a *s* ...... 2Sa 23:21
take my *s* in thine hand, and go ...... 2Kin 4:29
lay my *s* upon the face of the ...... 2Kin 4:29
laid the *s* upon the face of the ...... 2Kin 4:31
upon the *s* of this bruised reed ...... 2Kin 18:21
and he went down to him with a *s* .... 1Chr 11:23
whose spear *s* was like a weaver's ...... 1Chr 20:5
thy rod and thy *s* they comfort me ...... Ps 23:4
he brake the whole *s* of bread ...... Ps 105:16
and from Judah the stay and the *s* ...... Is 3:1
the *s* of his shoulder, the rod of ...... Is 9:4
the *s* in their hand is mine ...... Is 10:5
or as if the *s* should lift up ...... Is 10:15

shall lift up his *s* against thee ... Is 10:24
hath broken the *s* of the wicked ... Is 14:5
fitches are beaten out with a *s* ... Is 28:27
where the grounded *s* shall pass ... Is 30:32
in the *s* of this broken reed ... Is 36:6
say, How is the strong *s* broken ... Jer 48:17
I will break the *s* of bread in ... Eze 4:16
and will break your *s* of bread ... Eze 5:16
will break the *s* of the bread ... Eze 14:13
because they have been a *s* of ... Eze 29:6
their *s* declareth unto them ... Hos 4:12
every man with his *s* in his hand ... Zec 8:4
And I took my *s*, even Beauty, and ... Zec 11:10
Then I cut asunder mine other *s* ... Zec 11:14
for their journey, save a *s* only ... Mk 6:8
leaning upon the top of his *s* ... Heb 11:21

**STAGGER**
he maketh them to *s* like a ... Job 12:25
*s* like a drunken man, and are at ... Ps 107:27
they *s*, but not with strong drink ... Is 29:9

**STAGGERED**
He *s* not at the promise of God ... Rom 4:20

**STAGGERETH**
as a drunken man *s* in his vomit ... Is 19:14

**STAIN**
and the shadow of death *s* it ... Job 3:5
to *s* the pride of all glory, and ... Is 23:9
and I will *s* all my raiment ... Is 63:3

**STAIRS**
winding *s* into the middle chamber ... 1Kin 6:8
it under him on the top of the *s* ... 2Kin 9:13
unto the *s* that go down from the ... Neh 3:15
Then stood up upon the *s*, of the ... Neh 9:4
they went up by the *s* of the city ... Neh 12:37
in the secret places of the *s* ... Song 2:14
east, and went up the *s* thereof ... Eze 40:6
his *s* shall look toward the east ... Eze 43:17
And when he came upon the *s* ... Acts 21:35
him licence, Paul stood on the *s* ... Acts 21:40

**STAKES**
not one of the *s* thereof shall ... Is 33:20
thy cords, and strengthen thy *s* ... Is 54:2

**STALK**
ears of corn came up upon one *s* ... Gen 41:5
seven ears came up in one *s* ... Gen 41:22
it hath no *s* ... Hos 8:7

**STALKS**
and hid them with the *s* of flax ... Josh 2:6

**STALL**
calves out of the midst of the *s* ... Amos 6:4
and grow up as calves of the *s* ... Mal 4:2
his ox or his ass from the *s* ... Lk 13:15

**STALLED**
herbs where love is, than a *s* ox ... Prov 15:17

**STALLS**
*s* of horses for his chariots ... 1Kin 4:26
had four thousand *s* for horses ... 2Chr 9:25
*s* for all manner of beasts, and ... 2Chr 32:28
there shall be no herd in the *s* ... Hab 3:17

**STAMMERERS**
the tongue of the *s* shall be ... Is 32:4

**STAMMERING**
For with *s* lips and another tongue ... Is 28:11
of a *s* tongue, that thou canst ... Is 33:19

**STAMP**
I did *s* them as the mire of the ... 2Sa 22:43
*s* with thy foot, and say, Alas for ... Eze 6:11

**STAMPED**
*s* it, and ground it very small, ... Deut 9:21
*s* it small to powder, and cast the ... 2Kin 23:6
*s* it small to powder, and burned ... 2Kin 23:15
*s* it, and burnt it at the brook ... 2Chr 15:16
*s* with the feet, and rejoiced in ... Eze 25:6
*s* the residue with the feet of it ... Dan 7:7
*s* the residue with his feet ... Dan 7:19
down to the ground, and *s* upon him ... Dan 8:7
to the ground, and *s* upon them ... Dan 8:10

**STAMPING**
At the noise of the *s* of the ... Jer 47:3

**STANCHED**
immediately her issue of blood *s* ... Lk 8:44

**STAND**
And they said, *S* back ... Gen 19:9
I *s* here by the well of water ... Gen 24:13
Behold, I *s* by the well of water ... Gen 24:43
thou shalt *s* by the river's brink ... Ex 7:15
the morning, and *s* before Pharaoh ... Ex 8:20
the magicians could not *s* before ... Ex 9:11
*s* before Pharaoh, and say unto him ... Ex 9:13
*s* still, and see the salvation of ... Ex 14:13
I will *s* before thee there upon ... Ex 17:6
to morrow I will *s* on the top of ... Ex 17:9
all the people *s* by thee from ... Ex 18:14
pillar *s* at the tabernacle door ... Ex 33:10
me, and thou shalt *s* upon a rock ... Ex 33:21
neither shall any woman *s* before ... Lev 18:23
neither shalt thou *s* against the ... Lev 19:16
no power to *s* before your enemies ... Lev 26:37
shall estimate it, so shall it *s* ... Lev 27:14
to thy estimation it shall *s* ... Lev 27:17
of the men that shall *s* with you ... Num 1:5
*S* still, and I will hear what the ... Num 9:8
that they may *s* there with thee ... Num 11:16
to *s* before the congregation to ... Num 16:9
*S* by thy burnt offering, and I ... Num 23:3
*S* here by thy burnt offering, ... Num 23:15
he shall *s* before Eleazar the ... Num 27:21
then all her vows shall *s* ... Num 30:4
she hath bound her soul shall *s* ... Num 30:4
she hath bound her soul, shall *s* ... Num 30:5
then her vows shall *s*, and her ... Num 30:7
she bound her soul shall *s* ... Num 30:7
their souls, shall *s* against her ... Num 30:9
then all her vows shall *s* ... Num 30:11
she bound her soul shall *s* ... Num 30:11
the bond of her soul, shall not *s* ... Num 30:12
die not, until he *s* before the ... Num 35:12
*s* thou here by me, and I will ... Deut 5:31
no man be able to *s* before thee ... Deut 7:24
Who can *s* before the children of ... Deut 9:2
to *s* before the LORD to minister ... Deut 10:8
no man be able to *s* before you ... Deut 11:25
to *s* to minister in the name of ... Deut 18:5
which *s* there before the LORD ... Deut 18:7
shall *s* before the LORD, before ... Deut 19:17
Thou shalt *s* abroad, and the man ... Deut 24:11
and if he *s* to it, and say, I like ... Deut 25:8
These shall *s* upon mount Gerizim ... Deut 27:12
these shall *s* upon mount Ebal to ... Deut 27:13
Ye *s* this day all of you before ... Deut 29:10
shall not any man be able to *s* ... Josh 1:5
ye shall *s* still in Jordan ... Josh 3:8
they shall *s* upon an heap ... Josh 3:13
could not *s* before their enemies ... Josh 7:12
thou canst not *s* before thine ... Josh 7:13
not a man of them *s* before thee ... Josh 10:8
Sun, *s* thou still upon Gibeon ... Josh 10:12
*s* at the entering of the gate of ... Josh 20:4
that city, until he *s* before the ... Josh 20:6
to *s* before you unto this day ... Josh 23:9
any longer *s* before their enemies ... Judg 2:14
*S* in the door of the tent, and it ... Judg 4:20
Who is able to *s* before this holy ... 1Sa 6:20
but *s* thou still a while, that I ... 1Sa 9:27
Now therefore *s* still, that I may ... 1Sa 12:7
Now therefore *s* and see this great ... 1Sa 12:16
then we will *s* still in our place ... 1Sa 14:9
David, I pray thee, *s* before me ... 1Sa 16:22
*s* beside my father in the field ... 1Sa 19:3
He said unto me again, *S*, I pray ... 2Sa 1:9
unto him, Turn aside, and *s* here ... 2Sa 18:30
let her *s* before the king, and let ... 1Kin 1:2
not *s* to minister because of the ... 1Kin 8:11
which *s* continually before thee, ... 1Kin 10:8
of Israel liveth, before whom I *s* ... 1Kin 17:1
of hosts liveth, before whom I *s* ... 1Kin 18:15
*s* upon the mount before the LORD ... 1Kin 19:11
of hosts liveth, before whom I *s* ... 2Kin 3:14
will surely come out to me, and *s* ... 2Kin 5:11
the LORD liveth, before whom I *s* ... 2Kin 5:16
Shaphat shall *s* on him this day ... 2Kin 6:31
how then shall we *s* ... 2Kin 10:4
of the LORD *s* between the earth ... 1Chr 21:16
to *s* every morning to thank and ... 1Chr 23:30
*s* to minister by reason of the ... 2Chr 5:14
which *s* continually before thee, ... 2Chr 9:7
we *s* before this house, and in thy ... 2Chr 20:9
*s* ye still, and see the salvation ... 2Chr 20:17
hath chosen you to *s* before him ... 2Chr 29:11
Jerusalem and Benjamin to *s* to it ... 2Chr 34:32
*s* in the holy place according to ... 2Chr 35:5
for we cannot *s* before thee ... Ezr 9:15
and we are not able to *s* without ... Ezr 10:13
rulers of all the congregation *s* ... Ezr 10:14
and while they *s* by, let them shut ... Neh 7:3
*S* up and bless the LORD your God ... Neh 9:5
Mordecai's matters would *s* ... Est 3:4
to *s* for their life, to destroy, ... Est 8:11
his house, but it shall not *s* ... Job 8:15
that he shall *s* at the latter day ... Job 19:25
I *s* up, and thou regardest me not ... Job 30:20
words in order before me, *s* up ... Job 33:5
*s* still, and consider the wondrous ... Job 37:14
and they *s* as a garment ... Job 38:14
who then is able to *s* before me ... Job 41:10
shall not *s* in the judgment ... Ps 1:5
*S* in awe, and sin not ... Ps 4:4
foolish shall not *s* in thy sight ... Ps 5:5
but we are risen, and *s* upright ... Ps 20:8
or who shall *s* in his holy place ... Ps 24:3
hast made my mountain to *s* strong ... Ps 30:7
of the world *s* in awe of him ... Ps 33:8
and buckler, and *s* up for mine help ... Ps 35:2
my friends *s* aloof from my sore ... Ps 38:11
and my kinsmen *s* afar off ... Ps 38:11
upon thy right hand did *s* the ... Ps 45:9
Their eyes *s* out with fatness ... Ps 73:7
who may *s* in thy sight when once ... Ps 76:7
made the waters to *s* as an heap ... Ps 78:13
my covenant shall *s* fast with him ... Ps 89:28
not made him to *s* in the battle ... Ps 89:43
or who will *s* up for me against ... Ps 94:16
let Satan *s* at his right hand ... Ps 109:6
For he shall *s* at the right hand ... Ps 109:31
They *s* fast for ever and ever, and ... Ps 111:8
Our feet shall *s* within thy gates ... Ps 122:2
iniquities, O Lord, who shall *s* ... Ps 130:3
which by night *s* in the house of ... Ps 134:1
Ye that *s* in the house of the ... Ps 135:2
who can *s* before his cold ... Ps 147:17
house of the righteous shall *s* ... Prov 12:7
counsel of the LORD, that shall *s* ... Prov 19:21
he shall *s* before kings ... Prov 22:29
he shall not *s* before mean men ... Prov 22:29
*s* not in the place of great men ... Prov 25:6
but who is able to *s* before envy ... Prov 27:4
that shall *s* up in his stead ... Eccl 4:15
*s* not in an evil thing ... Eccl 8:3
the Lord GOD, It shall not *s* ... Is 7:7
speak the word, and it shall not *s* ... Is 8:10
which shall *s* for an ensign of ... Is 11:10
as I have purposed, so shall it *s* ... Is 14:24
My lord, I *s* continually upon the ... Is 21:8
groves and images shall not *s* up ... Is 27:9
agreement with hell shall not *s* ... Is 28:18
and by liberal things shall he *s* ... Is 32:8
word of our God shall *s* for ever ... Is 40:8
gathered together, let them *s* up ... Is 44:11
done, saying, My counsel shall *s* ... Is 46:10
*S* now with thine enchantments, and ... Is 47:12
*s* up, and save thee from these ... Is 47:13
unto them, they *s* up together ... Is 48:13
let us *s* together ... Is 50:8
*s* up, O Jerusalem, which hast ... Is 51:17
And strangers shall *s* and feed your ... Is 61:5
*S* by thyself, come not near to me ... Is 65:5
*S* ye in the ways, and see, and ask ... Jer 6:16
*S* in the gate of the LORD's house ... Jer 7:2
*s* before me in this house, which ... Jer 7:10
asses did *s* in the high places ... Jer 14:6
again, and thou shalt *s* before me ... Jer 15:19
*s* in the gate of the children of ... Jer 17:19
*S* in the court of the LORD's ... Jer 26:2
a man to *s* before me for ever ... Jer 35:19
shall know whose words shall *s* ... Jer 44:28
surely *s* against you for evil ... Jer 44:29
*s* forth with your helmets ... Jer 46:4
say ye, *S* fast, and prepare thee ... Jer 46:14
they did not *s*, because the day ... Jer 46:21
of Aroer, *s* by the way, and espy ... Jer 48:19
shepherd that will *s* before me ... Jer 49:19
shepherd that will *s* before me ... Jer 50:44
the sword, go away, *s* not still ... Jer 51:50
*s* upon thy feet, and I will speak ... Eze 2:1
for the house of Israel to *s* in ... Eze 13:5
of his covenant it might *s* ... Eze 17:14
*s* in the gap before me for the ... Eze 22:30
they shall *s* upon the land ... Eze 27:29
all their loins to be at a *s* ... Eze 29:7
their trees *s* up in their height ... Eze 31:14
Ye *s* upon your sword, ye work ... Eze 33:26
they shall *s* before them to ... Eze 44:11
they shall *s* before me to offer ... Eze 44:15
they shall *s* in judgment ... Eze 44:24
shall *s* by the post of the gate, ... Eze 46:2
that the fishers shall *s* upon it ... Eze 47:10
in them to *s* in the king's palace ... Dan 1:4
they might *s* before the king ... Dan 1:5
kingdoms, and it shall *s* for ever ... Dan 2:44
made *s* upon the feet as a man, and ... Dan 7:4
that no beasts might *s* before him ... Dan 8:4
power in the ram to *s* before him ... Dan 8:7
four kingdoms shall *s* up out of ... Dan 8:22
dark sentences, shall *s* up ... Dan 8:23
he shall also *s* up against the ... Dan 8:25
I speak unto thee, and *s* upright ... Dan 10:11
there shall *s* up yet three kings ... Dan 11:2
And a mighty king shall *s* up ... Dan 11:3
And when he shall *s* up, his ... Dan 11:4
neither shall he *s*, nor his arm ... Dan 11:6
shall one *s* up in his estate ... Dan 11:7
many *s* up against the king of the ... Dan 11:14
will, and none shall *s* before him ... Dan 11:16
he shall *s* in the glorious land, ... Dan 11:16
but she shall not *s* on his side ... Dan 11:17
Then shall *s* up in his estate a ... Dan 11:20
estate shall *s* up a vile person ... Dan 11:21
but he shall not *s* ... Dan 11:25
arms shall *s* on his part, and they ... Dan 11:31
at that time shall Michael *s* up ... Dan 12:1
*s* in thy lot at the end of the ... Dan 12:13
Neither shall he *s* that handleth ... Amos 2:15
And he shall *s* and feed in the ... Mic 5:4
Who can *s* before his indignation ... Nah 1:6
*S*, *s*, shall they cry ... Nah 2:8
I will *s* upon my watch, and set me ... Hab 2:1
to walk among these that *s* by ... Zec 3:7
that *s* by the Lord of the whole ... Zec 4:14
his feet shall *s* in that day upon ... Zec 14:4
away while they *s* upon their feet ... Zec 14:12
who shall *s* when he appeareth ... Mal 3:2
against itself shall not *s* ... Mt 12:25
how shall then his kingdom *s* ... Mt 12:26
mother and thy brethren *s* without ... Mt 12:47
Why *s* ye here all the day idle ... Mt 20:6
*s* in the holy place, (whoso ... Mt 24:15
had the withered hand, *S* forth ... Mk 3:3
itself, that kingdom cannot *s* ... Mk 3:24
itself, that house cannot *s* ... Mk 3:25
and be divided, he cannot *s* ... Mk 3:26
there be some of them that *s* here ... Mk 9:1
And when ye *s* praying, forgive, if ... Mk 11:25
that *s* in the presence of God ... Lk 1:19
Rise up, and *s* forth in the midst ... Lk 6:8
mother and thy brethren *s* without ... Lk 8:20
himself, how shall his kingdom *s* ... Lk 11:18
door, and ye begin to *s* without ... Lk 13:25
to *s* before the Son of man ... Lk 21:36
the people which *s* by I said it ... Jn 11:42
why *s* ye gazing up into heaven ... Acts 1:11
this man *s* here before you whole ... Acts 4:10

S

Go, *s* and speak in the temple to .......... Acts 5:20
commanded the chariot to *s* still .......... Acts 8:38
Peter took him up, saying, *S* up.......... Acts 10:26
loud voice, *S* upright on thy feet........ Acts 14:10
I *s* at Caesar's judgment seat, ............ Acts 25:10
And now I *s* and am judged for the..... Acts 26:6
But rise, and *s* upon thy feet .............. Acts 26:16
into this grace wherein we *s* .................. Rom 5:2
God according to election might *s* ....... Rom 9:11
for God is able to make him *s*.............. Rom 14:4
for we shall all *s* before the ................ Rom 14:10
should not *s* in the wisdom of men ....... 1Cor 2:5
ye have received, and wherein ye *s*..... 1Cor 15:1
why *s* we in jeopardy every hour....... 1Cor 15:30
*s* fast in the faith, quit you ................. 1Cor 16:13
for by faith ye *s* ..................................... 2Cor 1:24
for I *s* in doubt of you............................ Gal 4:20
*S* fast therefore in the liberty ................... Gal 5:1
that ye may be able to *s* against........... Eph 6:11
day, and having done all, to *s*.............. Eph 6:13
*S* therefore, having your loins ............... Eph 6:14
that ye *s* fast in one spirit..................... Phil 1:27
so *s* fast in the Lord, my dearly.............. Phil 4:1
in prayers, that ye may *s* perfect ........... Col 4:12
we live, if ye *s* fast in the Lord............... 1Th 3:8
*s* fast, and hold the traditions ............... 2Th 2:15
*S* thou there, or sit here under ............... Jas 2:3
true grace of God wherein ye *s*............ 1Pet 5:12
I *s* at the door, and knock..................... Rev 3:20
and who shall be able to *s*..................... Rev 6:17
angel which I saw *s* upon the sea.......... Rev 10:5
*s* on the sea of glass, having the........... Rev 15:2
shall *s* afar off for the fear of.............. Rev 18:15
small and great, *s* before God............... Rev 20:12

## STANDARD

camp, and every man by his own *s*..... Num 1:52
Israel shall pitch by his own *s*............... Num 2:2
the *s* of the camp of Judah pitch ........... Num 2:3
On the south side shall be the *s* ........... Num 2:10
be the *s* of the camp of Ephraim........... Num 2:18
The *s* of the camp of Dan shall be....... Num 2:25
In the first place went the *s* of.......... Num 10:14
the *s* of the camp of Reuben set ....... Num 10:18
the *s* of the camp of the children...... Num 10:22
the *s* of the camp of the children....... Num 10:25
set up my *s* to the people ..................... Is 49:22
shall lift up a *s* against him.................. Is 59:19
lift up a *s* for the people ........................ Is 62:10
Set up the *s* toward Zion.......................... Jer 4:6
How long shall I see the *s*...................... Jer 4:21
and publish, and set up a *s*..................... Jer 50:2
Set up the *s* upon the walls of .............. Jer 51:12
Set ye up a *s* in the land.......................... Jer 51:27

## STANDARD-BEARER

shall be as when a *s* fainteth .................... Is 10:18

## STANDARDS

every man in his place by their *s*......... Num 2:17
shall go hindmost with their *s*.............. Num 2:31
so they pitched by their *s* ..................... Num 2:34

## STANDEST

wherefore *s* thou without..................... Gen 24:31
whereon thou *s* is holy ground................. Ex 3:5
the place whereon thou *s* is holy.......... Josh 5:15
Why *s* thou afar off, O LORD..................... Ps 10:1
place where thou *s* is holy ground ....... Acts 7:33
broken off, and thou *s* by faith ........... Rom 11:20

## STANDETH

and that thy cloud *s* over them.......... Num 14:14
which *s* before thee, he shall go.......... Deut 1:38
*s* to minister there before the ............ Deut 17:12
But with him that *s* here with us....... Deut 29:15
the pillars whereupon the house *s*..... Judg 16:26
him, Behold, Haman *s* in the court.......... Est 6:5
the king, *s* in the house of Haman ........... Est 7:9
nor *s* in the way of sinners, nor ................ Ps 1:1
My foot *s* in an even place..................... Ps 26:12
counsel of the LORD *s* for ever ............... Ps 33:11
God *s* in the congregation of the............. Ps 82:1
but my heart *s* in awe of thy word .... Ps 119:161
She *s* in the top of high places,............... Prov 8:2
he *s* behind our wall, he looketh.............. Song 2:9
The LORD *s* up to plead ............................. Is 3:13
and *s* to judge the people ......................... Is 3:13
and set him in his place, and he *s* ........... Is 46:7
backward, and justice *s* afar off............... Is 59:14
the great prince which *s* for the............ Dan 12:1
nor feed that that *s* still...................... Zec 11:16
but there *s* one among you, whom .......... Jn 1:26
friend of the bridegroom, which *s* ............ Jn 3:29
to his own master he *s* or falleth.......... Rom 14:4
Nevertheless he that *s* stedfast ............. 1Cor 7:37
eat no flesh while the world *s* ............. 1Cor 8:13
he *s* take heed lest he fall ................... 1Cor 10:12
the foundation of God *s* sure ................ 2Ti 2:19
every priest *s* daily ministering ........... Heb 10:11
the judge *s* before the door ...................... Jas 5:9
of the angel which *s* upon the sea........ Rev 10:8

## STANDING

the stacks of corn, or the *s* corn ............ Ex 22:6
tabernacle of shittim wood *s* up........... Ex 26:15
tabernacle of shittim wood, *s* up........... Ex 36:20
neither rear you up a *s* image............... Lev 26:1
angel of the LORD *s* in the way ........ Num 22:23
angel of the LORD *s* in the way ......... Num 22:31
into the *s* corn of thy neighbour........ Deut 23:25
unto thy neighbour's *s* corn.............. Deut 23:25
the *s* corn of the Philistines.................. Judg 15:5
the shocks, and also the *s* corn............ Judg 15:5
Samuel *s* as appointed over them,........ 1Sa 19:20
all his servants were *s* about him........... 1Sa 22:6
the lion *s* by the carcase...................... 1Kin 13:25
the lion *s* by the carcase...................... 1Kin 13:28
all the host of heaven *s* by him .......... 1Kin 22:19
and two lions *s* by the stays................. 2Chr 9:18
of heaven *s* on his right hand ............ 2Chr 18:18
Esther the queen *s* in the court................. Est 5:2
in deep mire, where there is no *s*............. Ps 69:2
the wilderness into a *s* water............. Ps 107:35
turned the rock into a *s* water ............... Ps 114:8
I had seen *s* before the river.................... Dan 8:6
I saw the Lord *s* upon the altar ............ Amos 9:1
he shall receive of you his *s* ................... Mic 1:11
thy *s* images out of the midst of .......... Mic 5:13
me Joshua the high priest *s*...................... Zec 3:1
Satan *s* at his right hand to...................... Zec 3:1
which go forth from *s* before the.......... Zec 6:5
love to pray *s* in the synagogues ............. Mt 6:5
unto you, There be some *s* here............ Mt 16:28
hour, and saw others *s* idle in the ........... Mt 20:3
went out, and found others *s* idle.......... Mt 20:6
*s* without, sent unto him, calling ............ Mk 3:31
*s* where it ought not, (let him.............. Mk 13:14
unto him an angel of the Lord *s* ............. Lk 1:11
And saw two ships *s* by the lake............... Lk 5:2
of a truth, there be some *s* here............. Lk 9:27
*s* afar off, would not lift up so ............... Lk 18:13
and the woman *s* in the midst..................... Jn 8:9
his mother, and the disciple *s* by ........... Jn 19:26
herself back, and saw Jesus *s* ................. Jn 20:14
*s* up with the eleven, lifted up............... Acts 2:14
man which was healed *s* with them..... Acts 4:14
the keepers *s* without before the.......... Acts 5:23
put in prison are *s* in the temple............ Acts 5:25
Jesus *s* on the right hand of God,......... Acts 7:55
the Son of man *s* on the right ............... Acts 7:56
Stephen was shed, I also was *s* by ..... Acts 22:20
voice, that I cried *s* among them........ Acts 24:21
as the first tabernacle was yet *s* ............. Heb 9:8
the earth *s* out of the water and............ 2Pet 3:5
*s* on the four corners of the ..................... Rev 7:1
the two candlesticks *s* before the......... Rev 11:4
*S* afar off for the fear of her................ Rev 18:10
And I saw an angel *s* in the sun .......... Rev 19:17

## STANK

and the river *s*, and the Egyptians........... Ex 7:21
and the land *s* ........................................... Ex 8:14
morning, and it bred worms, and *s*........ Ex 16:20
saw that they *s* before David................ 2Sa 10:6

## STAR

there shall come a *S* out of Jacob...... Num 24:17
the *s* of your god, which ye made...... Amos 5:26
we have seen his *s* in the east ................... Mt 2:2
what time the *s* appeared .......................... Mt 2:7
and, lo, the *s*, which they saw in ............... Mt 2:9
When they saw the *s*, they...................... Mt 2:10
the *s* of your god Remphan,................ Acts 7:43
for one *s* differeth from another........ 1Cor 15:41
differeth from another *s* in glory....... 1Cor 15:41
the day *s* arise in your hearts ............... 2Pet 1:19
And I will give him the morning *s* ........ Rev 2:28
there fell a great *s* from heaven........... Rev 8:10
the name of the *s* is called.................... Rev 8:11
I saw a *s* fall from heaven unto ................ Rev 9:1
David, and the bright and morning *s*.. Rev 22:16

## STARE

they look and *s* upon me ........................ Ps 22:17

## STARGAZERS

Let now the astrologers, the *s*................. Is 47:13

## STARS

he made the *s* also ................................ Gen 1:16
now toward heaven, and tell the *s*........ Gen 15:5
thy seed as the *s* of the heaven ........... Gen 22:17
to multiply as the *s* of heaven.............. Gen 26:4
the eleven *s* made obeisance to me........ Gen 37:9
your seed as the *s* of heaven................ Ex 32:13
ye are this day as the *s* of.................... Deut 1:10
the sun, and the moon, and the *s* ........ Deut 4:19
as the *s* of heaven for multitude ........ Deut 10:22
whereas ye were as the *s* of ................ Deut 28:62
the *s* in their courses fought ................. Judg 5:20
like to the *s* of the heavens................. 1Chr 27:23
the morning till the *s* appeared............. Neh 4:21
thou as the *s* of heaven, and ................. Neh 9:23
Let the *s* of the twilight thereof.............. Job 3:9
and sealeth up the *s*................................... Job 9:7
and behold the height of the *s* ............. Job 22:12
the *s* are not pure in his sight ................. Job 25:5
When the morning *s* sang together ........ Job 38:7
of thy fingers, the moon and the *s* .......... Ps 8:3
The moon and *s* to rule by night........... Ps 136:9
He telleth the number of the *s* ............. Ps 147:4
praise him, all ye *s* of light................... Ps 148:3
the light, or the moon, or the *s*............. Eccl 12:2
For the *s* of heaven and the.................... Is 13:10
my throne above the *s* of God.................. Is 14:13
of the *s* for a light by night,................. Jer 31:35
and make the *s* thereof dark ................. Eze 32:7
of the *s* to the ground, and..................... Dan 8:10
righteousness as the *s* for ever............... Dan 12:3
the *s* shall withdraw their....................... Joel 2:10
the *s* shall withdraw their....................... Joel 3:15
Seek him that maketh the seven *s*....... Amos 5:8
thou set thy nest among the *s* .................. Obad 4
merchants above the *s* of heaven.......... Nah 3:16
the *s* shall fall from heaven, and........... Mt 24:29
the *s* of heaven shall fall, and................ Mk 13:25
sun, and in the moon, and in the *s*........ Lk 21:25
when neither sun nor *s* in many......... Acts 27:20
moon, and another glory of the *s*...... 1Cor 15:41
so many as the *s* of the sky in ............. Heb 11:12
wandering *s*, to whom is reserved........... Jude 13
he had in his right hand seven *s*........... Rev 1:16
The mystery of the seven *s* which.......... Rev 1:20
The seven *s* are the angels of the.......... Rev 1:20
the seven *s* in his right hand.................. Rev 2:1
Spirits of God, and the seven *s*.............. Rev 3:1
the *s* of heaven fell unto the................... Rev 6:13
moon, and the third part of the *s* .......... Rev 8:12
upon her head a crown of twelve *s*........ Rev 12:1
the third part of the *s* of heaven........... Rev 12:4

## STATE

man asked us straitly of our *s*................ Gen 43:7
set the house of God in his *s*.............. 2Chr 24:13
according to the *s* of the king.................... Est 1:7
according to the *s* of the king.................. Est 2:18
his best *s* is altogether vanity................... Ps 39:5
to know the *s* of thy flocks................. Prov 27:23
knowledge the *s* thereof shall be.......... Prov 28:2
from thy *s* shall he pull thee.................... Is 22:19
the last *s* of that man is worse.............. Mt 12:45
the last *s* of that man is worse.............. Lk 11:26
good comfort, when I know your *s*....... Phil 2:19
will naturally care for your *s* ............... Phil 2:20
learned, in whatsoever *s* I am................. Phil 4:11
All my *s* shall Tychicus declare................ Col 4:7

## STATELY

And satest upon a *s* bed, and a............ Eze 23:41

## STATION

And I will drive thee from thy *s* ............. Is 22:19

## STATURE

we saw in it are men of a great *s* ...... Num 13:32
or on the height of his *s* ........................ 1Sa 16:7
Gath, where was a man of great *s* ....... 2Sa 21:20
an Egyptian, a man of great *s*............ 1Chr 11:23
Gath, where was a man of great *s*...... 1Chr 20:6
This thy *s* is like to a palm tree ............ Song 7:7
the high ones of *s* shall be hewn ............ Is 10:33
and of the Sabeans, men of *s*.................. Is 45:14
the head of every *s* to hunt souls......... Eze 13:18
became a spreading vine of low *s*.......... Eze 17:6
her *s* was exalted among the thick...... Eze 19:11
shadowing shroud, and of an high *s*...... Eze 31:3
can add one cubit unto his *s*..................... Mt 6:27
And Jesus increased in wisdom and *s*.... Lk 2:52
can add to his *s* one cubit...................... Lk 12:25
press, because he was little of *s*............... Lk 19:3
unto the measure of the *s* of the .......... Eph 4:13

## STATUTE

there he made for them a *s* .................... Ex 15:25
it shall be a *s* for ever unto ................... Ex 27:21
it shall be a *s* for ever unto him............. Ex 28:43
shall be theirs for a perpetual *s* ................ Ex 29:9
his sons' by a *s* for ever from.................. Ex 29:28
it shall be a *s* for ever to them,............... Ex 30:21
It shall be a perpetual *s* for.................... Lev 3:17
It shall be a *s* for ever in your ................ Lev 6:18
it is a *s* for ever unto the LORD............... Lev 6:22
unto his sons by a *s* for ever.................... Lev 7:34
by a *s* for ever throughout their.............. Lev 7:36
it shall be a *s* for ever ............................ Lev 10:9
sons' with thee, by a *s* for ever............ Lev 10:15
this shall be a *s* for ever unto ................ Lev 16:29
your souls, by a *s* for ever.................... Lev 16:31
be an everlasting *s* unto you ................. Lev 16:34
This shall be a *s* for ever unto ................ Lev 17:7
it shall be a *s* for ever ........................... Lev 23:14
it shall be a *s* for ever in all.................. Lev 23:21
it shall be a *s* for ever ........................... Lev 23:31
It shall be a *s* for ever in your ............... Lev 23:41
it shall be a *s* for ever in your.................. Lev 24:3
made by fire by a perpetual *s*.................... Lev 24:9
with thee, by a *s* for ever...................... Num 18:11
with thee, by a *s* for ever...................... Num 18:19
it shall be a *s* for ever .......................... Num 18:23
among them, for a *s* for ever ................. Num 19:10
shall be a perpetual *s* unto them........ Num 19:21
of Israel a *s* of judgment...................... Num 27:11
So these things shall be for a *s*............ Num 35:29
people that day, and set them a *s*...... Josh 24:25
day forward, that he made it a *s* .......... 1Sa 30:25
For this was a *s* for Israel......................... Ps 81:4
together to establish a royal *s*................... Dan 6:7
That no decree nor *s* which the............ Dan 6:15

## STATUTES

my charge, my commandments, my *s*.. Gen 26:5
commandments, and keep all his *s* ......... Ex 15:26
I do make them know the *s* of God ...... Ex 18:16
the children of Israel all the *s*............... Lev 10:11
Ye shall therefore keep my *s*................... Lev 18:5
Ye shall therefore keep my *s*................. Lev 18:26
Ye shall keep my *s*................................. Lev 19:19
shall ye observe all my *s* ......................... Lev 19:37
And ye shall keep my *s*, and do them... Lev 20:8
Ye shall therefore keep all my *s* .......... Lev 20:22
Wherefore ye shall do my *s* ................... Lev 25:18
If ye walk in my *s*, and keep my............ Lev 26:3
And if ye shall despise my *s* .................. Lev 26:15
because their soul abhorred my *s*........... Lev 26:43
These are the *s* and judgments and..... Lev 26:46
These are the *s*, which the LORD........ Num 30:16
hearken, O Israel, unto the *s* ................. Deut 4:1
Behold, I have taught you *s*.................... Deut 4:5

which shall hear all these *s* Deut 4:6
is there so great, that hath *s* Deut 4:8
me at that time to teach you *s* Deut 4:14
Thou shalt keep therefore his *s* Deut 4:40
are the testimonies, and the *s* Deut 4:45
unto them, Hear, O Israel, the *s* Deut 5:1
all the commandments, and the *s* Deut 5:31
these are the commandments, the *s* Deut 6:1
LORD thy God, to keep all his *s* Deut 6:2
God, and his testimonies, and his *s* Deut 6:17
mean the testimonies, and the *s* Deut 6:20
commanded us to do all these *s* Deut 6:24
keep the commandments, and the *s* Deut 7:11
and his judgments, and his *s* Deut 8:11
of the LORD, and his *s*, which I Deut 10:13
God, and keep his charge, and his *s* Deut 11:1
ye shall observe to do all the *s* Deut 11:32
These are the *s* and judgments, Deut 12:1
thou shalt observe and do these *s* Deut 16:12
the words of this law and these *s* Deut 17:19
hath commanded thee to do these *s*. Deut 26:16
in his ways, and to keep his *s* Deut 26:17
and do his commandments and his *s* Deut 27:10
his *s* which I command thee this Deut 28:15
his *s* which he commanded thee Deut 28:45
his *s* which are written in this Deut 30:10
commandments and his *s* Deut 30:16
and as for his *s*, I did not depart 2Sa 22:23
walk in his ways, to keep his *s* 1Kin 2:3
walking in the *s* of David his 1Kin 3:3
walk in my ways, to keep my *s* 1Kin 3:14
if thou wilt walk in my *s* 1Kin 6:12
keep his commandments, and his *s* 1Kin 8:58
LORD our God, to walk in his *s* 1Kin 8:61
commanded thee, and wilt keep my *s* 1Kin 9:4
my *s* which I have set before you, 1Kin 9:6
hast not kept my covenant and my *s* 1Kin 11:11
in mine eyes, and to keep my *s* 1Kin 11:33
my commandments and my *s* 1Kin 11:34
right in my sight, to keep my *s* 1Kin 11:38
walked in the *s* of the heathen, 2Kin 17:8
my commandments and my *s* 2Kin 17:13
And they rejected his *s*, and his 2Kin 17:15
but walked in the *s* of Israel 2Kin 17:19
neither do they after their *s* 2Kin 17:34
And the *s*, and the ordinances, and 2Kin 17:37
his *s* with all their heart and all 2Kin 23:3
thou takest heed to fulfil the *s* 1Chr 22:13
thy testimonies, and thy *s* 1Chr 29:19
thee, and shalt observe my *s* 2Chr 7:17
if ye turn away, and forsake my *s* 2Chr 7:19
between law and commandment, *s* 2Chr 19:10
to the whole law and the *s* 2Chr 33:8
and his testimonies, and his *s* 2Chr 34:31
to do it, and to teach in Israel *s* Ezr 7:10
the LORD, and of his *s* to Israel Ezr 7:11
kept the commandments, nor the *s* Neh 1:7
judgments, and true laws, good *s* Neh 9:13
and commandedst them precepts, *s* Neh 9:14
Lord, and his judgments and his *s* Neh 10:29
I did not put away his *s* from me Ps 18:22
The *s* of the LORD are right, Ps 19:8
hast thou to do to declare my *s* Ps 50:16
If they break my *s*, and keep not Ps 89:31
That they might observe his *s* Ps 105:45
ways were directed to keep thy *s* Ps 119:5
I will keep thy *s* Ps 119:8
teach me thy *s* Ps 119:12
I will delight myself in thy *s* Ps 119:16
thy servant did meditate in thy *s* Ps 119:23
teach me thy *s* Ps 119:26
me, O LORD, the way of thy *s* Ps 119:33
and I will meditate in thy *s* Ps 119:48
Thy *s* have been my songs in the Ps 119:54
teach me thy *s* Ps 119:64
teach me thy *s* Ps 119:68
that I might learn thy *s* Ps 119:71
Let my heart be sound in thy *s* Ps 119:80
yet do I not forget thy *s* Ps 119:83
mine heart to perform thy *s* alway Ps 119:112
respect unto thy *s* continually Ps 119:117
down all them that err from thy *s* Ps 119:118
unto thy mercy, and teach me thy *s* Ps 119:124
and teach me thy *s* Ps 119:135
I will keep thy *s* Ps 119:145
for they seek not thy *s* Ps 119:155
when thou hast taught me thy *s* Ps 119:171
his word unto Jacob, his *s* Ps 147:19
nor walked in my law, nor in my *s* Jer 44:10
walked in his law, nor in his *s* Jer 44:23
my *s* more than the countries that Eze 5:6
have refused my judgments and my *s* Eze 5:6
you, and have not walked in my *s* Eze 5:7
for ye have not walked in my *s* Eze 11:12
That they may walk in my *s* Eze 11:20
Hath walked in my *s*, and hath kept Eze 18:9
my judgments, hath walked in my *s* Eze 18:17
and right, and hath kept all my *s* Eze 18:19
hath committed, and keep all my *s* Eze 18:21
And I gave them my *s*, and shewed Eze 20:11
they walked not in my *s*, and they Eze 20:13
judgments, and walked not in my *s* Eze 20:16
ye not in the *s* of your fathers Eze 20:18
walk in my *s*, and keep my Eze 20:19
they walked not in my *s*, neither Eze 20:21
judgments, but had despised my *s* Eze 20:24
them also *s* that were not good Eze 20:25
had robbed, walk in the *s* of life Eze 33:15
you, and cause you to walk in my *s* Eze 36:27
in my judgments, and observe my *s* Eze 37:24
my *s* in all mine assemblies Eze 44:24
For the *s* of Omri are kept, and Mic 6:16
But my words and my *s*, which I Zec 1:6
Horeb for all Israel, with the *s* Mal 4:4

## STAVES

thou shalt make *s* of shittim wood Ex 25:13
thou shalt put the *s* into the Ex 25:14
The *s* shall be in the rings of Ex 25:15
places of the *s* to bear the table Ex 25:27
shalt make the *s* of shittim wood Ex 25:28
thou shalt make *s* for the altar Ex 27:6
*s* of shittim wood, and overlay Ex 27:6
the *s* shall be put into the rings Ex 27:7
the *s* shall be upon the two sides Ex 27:7
for the *s* to bear it withal Ex 30:4
shalt make the *s* of shittim wood Ex 30:5
the *s* thereof, with the mercy Ex 35:12
The table, and his *s*, and all his Ex 35:13
And the incense altar, and his *s* Ex 35:15
with his brasen grate, his *s* Ex 35:16
he made *s* of shittim wood, and Ex 37:4
he put the *s* into the rings by Ex 37:5
for the *s* to bear the table Ex 37:14
he made the *s* of shittim wood, and Ex 37:15
for the *s* to bear it withal Ex 37:27
he made the *s* of shittim wood, and Ex 37:28
of brass, to be places for the *s* Ex 38:5
he made the *s* of shittim wood, and Ex 38:6
he put the *s* into the rings on Ex 38:7
the *s* thereof, and the mercy seat, Ex 39:35
and his grate of brass, his *s* Ex 39:39
set the *s* on the ark, and put the Ex 40:20
and shall put in the *s* thereof Num 4:6
and shall put in the *s* thereof Num 4:8
and shall put to the *s* thereof Num 4:11
skins, and put to the *s* of it Num 4:14
of the lawgiver, with their *s* Num 21:18
that thou comest to me with *s* 1Sa 17:43
the ark and the *s* thereof above 1Kin 8:7
And they drew out the *s*, that the 1Kin 8:8
that the ends of the *s* were seen 1Kin 8:8
shoulders with the *s* thereon 1Chr 15:15
the ark and the *s* thereof above 2Chr 5:8
And they drew out the *s* of the ark 2Chr 5:9
that the ends of the *s* were seen 2Chr 5:9
his *s* the head of his villages Hab 3:14
And I took unto me two *s* Zec 11:7
coats, neither shoes, nor yet *s* Mt 10:10
great multitude with swords and *s* Mt 26:47
with swords and *s* for to take me Mt 26:55
great multitude with swords and *s* Mk 14:43
with swords and with *s* to take me Mk 14:48
for your journey, neither *s* Lk 9:3
against a thief, with swords and *s* Lk 22:52

## STAY

neither *s* thou in all the plain Gen 19:17
you go, and ye shall *s* no longer Ex 9:28
the plague in his sight be at a *s* Lev 13:5
if the bright spot *s* in his place Lev 13:23
if the bright spot *s* in his place Lev 13:28
the scall be in his sight at a *s* Lev 13:37
*s* ye not, but pursue after your Josh 10:19
would ye *s* for them from having Ruth 1:13
Then Samuel said unto Saul, *S* 1Sa 15:16
the lad, Make speed, haste, *s* not 1Sa 20:38
but the LORD was my *s* 2Sa 22:19
*s* now thine hand 2Sa 24:16
It is enough, *s* now thine hand 1Chr 21:15
he will not *s* them when his voice Job 37:4
or who can *s* the bottles of Job 38:37
but the LORD was my *s* Ps 18:18
let no man *s* him Prov 28:17
*S* me with flagons, comfort me Song 2:5
Jerusalem and from Judah the *s* Is 3:1
the staff, the whole *s* of bread Is 3:1
of bread, and the whole *s* of water Is 3:1
shall no more again *s* upon him Is 10:20
but shall *s* upon the LORD, the Is 10:20
are the *s* of the tribes thereof Is 19:13
*S* yourselves, and wonder Is 29:9
and perverseness, and *s* thereon Is 30:12
*s* on horses, and trust in chariots Is 31:1
*s* themselves upon the God of Is 48:2
of the LORD, and *s* upon his God Is 50:10
retire, *s* not Jer 4:6
with forbearing, and I could not *s* Jer 20:9
and none can *s* his hand, or say Dan 4:35
for he should not *s* long in the Hos 13:13

## STAYED

he *s* yet other seven days Gen 8:10
he *s* yet other seven days Gen 8:12
with Laban, and *s* there until now Gen 32:4
your flocks and your herds be *s* Ex 10:24
Hur *s* up his hands, the one on Ex 17:12
and the plague was *s* Num 16:48
and the plague was *s* Num 16:50
So the plague was *s* from the Num 25:8
I *s* in the mount, according to Deut 10:10
sun stood still, and the moon *s* Josh 10:13
And when thou hast *s* three days 1Sa 20:19
So David *s* his servants with 1Sa 24:7
those that were left behind *s* 1Sa 30:9
Jonathan and Ahimaaz *s* by En-rogel 2Sa 17:17
plague may be *s* from the people 2Sa 24:21
and the plague was *s* from Israel 2Sa 24:25
the king was *s* up in his chariot 1Kin 22:35
And the oil *s* 2Kin 4:6
And he smote thrice, and *s* 2Kin 13:18
back, and *s* not there in the land 2Kin 15:20
plague may be *s* from the people 1Chr 21:22
*s* himself up in his chariot 2Chr 18:34
here shall thy proud waves be *s* Job 38:11
and so the plague was *s* Ps 106:30
peace, whose mind is *s* on thee Is 26:3
in a moment, and no hands *s* on her Lam 4:6
and the great waters were *s* Eze 31:15
the heaven over you is *s* from dew Hag 1:10
the earth is *s* from her fruit Hag 1:10
*s* him, that he should not depart Lk 4:42
but he himself *s* in Asia for a Acts 19:22

## STAYETH

he *s* his rough wind in the day of Is 27:8

## STAYS

there were *s* on either side on 1Kin 10:19
and two lions stood beside the *s* 1Kin 10:19
*s* on each side of the sitting 2Chr 9:18
and two lions standing by the *s* 2Chr 9:18

## STEAD

offering in the *s* of his son Gen 22:13
and he said, Am I in God's *s* Gen 30:2
Zerah of Bozrah reigned in his *s* Gen 36:33
land of Temani reigned in his *s* Gen 36:34
field of Moab, reigned in his *s* Gen 36:35
of Masrekah reigned in his *s* Gen 36:36
by the river reigned in his *s* Gen 36:37
son of Achbor reigned in his *s* Gen 36:38
died, and Hadar reigned in his *s* Gen 36:39
*s* shall put them on seven days Ex 29:30
anointed in his *s* shall offer it Lev 6:22
priest's office in his father's *s* Lev 16:32
are risen up in your fathers' *s* Num 32:14
before them, and dwelt in their *s* Deut 2:12
them, and dwelt in their *s* Deut 2:21
dwelt in their *s* even unto this Deut 2:22
them, and dwelt in their *s* Deut 2:23
in the priest's office in his *s* Deut 10:6
whom he raised up in their *s* Josh 5:7
and Hanun his son reigned in his *s* 2Sa 10:1
in whose *s* thou hast reigned 2Sa 16:8
shall sit upon my throne in my *s* 1Kin 1:30
for he shall be king in my *s* 1Kin 1:35
Rehoboam his son reigned in his *s* 1Kin 11:43
and Nadab his son reigned in his *s* 1Kin 14:20
made in their *s* brasen shields 1Kin 14:27
Abijam his son reigned in his *s* 1Kin 14:31
and Asa his son reigned in his *s* 1Kin 15:8
his son reigned in his *s* 1Kin 15:24
slay him, and reigned in his *s* 1Kin 15:28
and Elah his son reigned in his *s* 1Kin 16:6
of Judah, and reigned in his *s* 1Kin 16:10
and Ahab his son reigned in his *s* 1Kin 16:28
Ahaziah his son reigned in his *s* 1Kin 22:40
Jehoram his son reigned in his *s* 1Kin 22:50
Jehoram reigned in his *s* in the 2Kin 1:17
that should have reigned in his *s* 2Kin 3:27
and Hazael reigned in his *s* 2Kin 8:15
Ahaziah his son reigned in his *s* 2Kin 8:24
Jehoahaz his son reigned in his *s* 2Kin 10:35
Amaziah his son reigned in his *s* 2Kin 12:21
and Joash his son reigned in his *s* 2Kin 13:9
his son reigned in his *s* 2Kin 13:24
Jeroboam his son reigned in his *s* 2Kin 14:16
his son reigned in his *s* 2Kin 14:29
Jotham his son reigned in his *s* 2Kin 15:7
and slew him, and reigned in his *s* 2Kin 15:10
and slew him, and reigned in his *s* 2Kin 15:14
Pekahiah his son reigned in his *s* 2Kin 15:22
and slew him, and reigned in his *s* 2Kin 15:30
and Ahaz his son reigned in his *s* 2Kin 15:38
Hezekiah his son reigned in his *s* 2Kin 16:20
his son reigned in his *s* 2Kin 19:37
Manasseh his son reigned in his *s* 2Kin 20:21
and Amon his son reigned in his *s* 2Kin 21:18
made Josiah his son king in his *s* 2Kin 21:24
Josiah his son reigned in his *s* 2Kin 21:26
made him king in his father's *s* 2Kin 23:30
his son reigned in his *s* 2Kin 24:6
father's brother king in his *s* 2Kin 24:17
Zerah of Bozrah reigned in his *s* 1Chr 1:44
of the Temanites reigned in his *s* 1Chr 1:45
field of Moab, reigned in his *s* 1Chr 1:46
of Masrekah reigned in his *s* 1Chr 1:47
by the river reigned in his *s* 1Chr 1:48
son of Achbor reigned in his *s* 1Chr 1:49
was dead, Hadad reigned in his *s* 1Chr 1:50
died, and his son reigned in his *s* 1Chr 19:1
Solomon his son reigned in his *s* 1Chr 29:28
and hast made me to reign in his *s* 2Chr 1:8
Rehoboam his son reigned in his *s* 2Chr 9:31
Abijah his son reigned in his *s* 2Chr 12:16
and Asa his son reigned in his *s* 2Chr 14:1
his son reigned in his *s*, and 2Chr 17:1
Jehoram his son reigned in his *s* 2Chr 21:1
his youngest son king in his *s* 2Chr 22:1
Amaziah his son reigned in his *s* 2Chr 24:27
Jotham his son reigned in his *s* 2Chr 26:23
and Ahaz his son reigned in his *s* 2Chr 27:9
Hezekiah his son reigned in his *s* 2Chr 28:27
Manasseh his son reigned in his *s* 2Chr 32:33
and Amon his son reigned in his *s* 2Chr 33:20
made Josiah his son king in his *s* 2Chr 33:25
in his father's *s* in Jerusalem 2Chr 36:1
his son reigned in his *s* 2Chr 36:8
if your soul were in my soul's *s* Job 16:4
according to thy wish in God's *s* Job 33:6
number, and set others in their *s* Job 34:24
and the wicked cometh in his *s* Prov 11:8
that shall stand up in his *s* Eccl 4:15

S

his son reigned in his *s* Is 37:38
in the *s* of Jehoiada the priest Jer 29:26
we pray you in Christ's *s* 2Cor 5:20
that in thy *s* he might have Philem 13

### STEADS
in their *s* until the captivity 1Chr 5:22

### STEADY
his hands were *s* until the going Ex 17:12

### STEAL
away secretly, and *s* away from me Gen 31:27
how then should we *s* out of thy Gen 44:8
Thou shalt not *s* Ex 20:15
If a man shall *s* an ox, or a Ex 22:1
Ye shall not *s*, neither deal Lev 19:11
Neither shalt thou *s* Deut 5:19
as people being ashamed *s* away 2Sa 19:3
if he *s* to satisfy his soul when Prov 6:30
or lest I be poor, and *s*, and take Prov 30:9
Will ye *s*, murder, and commit Jer 7:9
that *s* my words every one from Jer 23:30
where thieves break through and *s* Mt 6:19
do not break through nor *s* Mt 6:20
commit adultery, Thou shalt not *s* Mt 19:18
*s* him away, and say unto the Mt 27:64
adultery, Do not kill, Do not *s* Mk 10:19
adultery, Do not kill, Do not *s* Lk 18:20
thief cometh not, but for to *s* Jn 10:10
man should not *s*, dost thou *s* Rom 2:21
shalt not kill, Thou shalt not *s* Rom 13:9
Let him that stole *s* no more Eph 4:28

### STEALETH
And he that *s* a man, and selleth Ex 21:16
a tempest *s* him away in the night Job 27:20
for every one that *s* shall be cut Zec 5:3

### STEALING
If a man be found *s* any of his Deut 24:7
and lying, and killing, and *s* Hos 4:2

### STEALTH
them by *s* that day into the city 2Sa 19:3

### STEDFAST
yea, thou shalt be *s*, and shalt Job 11:15
whose spirit was not *s* with God Ps 78:8
were they *s* in his covenant Ps 78:37
*s* for ever, and his kingdom that Dan 6:26
he that standeth *s* in his heart 1Cor 7:37
my beloved brethren, be ye *s* 1Cor 15:58
And our hope of you is *s*, knowing, 2Cor 1:7
the word spoken by angels was *s* Heb 2:2
of our confidence *s* unto the end Heb 3:14
of the soul, both sure and *s* Heb 6:19
Whom resist *s* in the faith, 1Pet 5:9

### STEDFASTLY
she was *s* minded to go with her Ruth 1:18
And he settled his countenance *s* 2Kin 8:11
he *s* set his face to go to Lk 9:51
while they looked *s* toward heaven Acts 1:10
they continued *s* in the apostles' Acts 2:42
in the council, looking *s* on him Acts 6:15
looked up *s* into heaven, and saw Acts 7:55
who *s* beholding him, and Acts 14:9
*s* behold the face of Moses for 2Cor 3:7
children of Israel could not *s* 2Cor 3:13

### STEDFASTNESS
the *s* of your faith in Christ Col 2:5
the wicked, fall from your own *s* 2Pet 3:17

### STEEL
so that a bow of *s* is broken by 2Sa 22:35
the bow of *s* shall strike him Job 20:24
so that a bow of *s* is broken by Ps 18:34
break the northern iron and the *s* Jer 15:12

### STEEP
the *s* places shall fall, and every Eze 38:20
that are poured down a *s* place Mic 1:4
down a *s* place into the sea Mt 8:32
down a *s* place into the sea Mk 5:13
down a *s* place into the lake Lk 8:33

### STEM
forth a rod out of the *s* of Jesse Is 11:1

### STEP
there is but a *s* between me 1Sa 20:3
If my *s* hath turned out of the Job 31:7

### STEPHANAS (*stef'-a-nas*) *A convert of Paul from Achaia.*
baptized also the household of *S* 1Cor 1:16
brethren, (ye know the house of *S* 1Cor 16:15
I am glad of the coming of *S* 1Cor 16:17

### STEPHANUS
was written from Philippi by *S* 1Cor *s*

### STEPHEN (*ste'-ven*) *A leader of the Jerusalem church.*
and they chose *S*, a man full of Acts 6:5
And *S*, full of faith and power, did Acts 6:8
and of Asia, disputing with *S* Acts 6:9
And they stoned *S*, calling upon Acts 7:59
men carried *S* to his burial Acts 8:2
*S* travelled as far as Phenice Acts 11:19
blood of thy martyr *S* was shed Acts 22:20

### STEPPED
the troubling of the water *s* in Jn 5:4

### STEPPETH
coming, another *s* down before me Jn 5:7

### STEPS
thou go up by *s* unto mine altar Ex 20:26
Thou hast enlarged my *s* under me 2Sa 22:37
The throne had six *s*, and the top 1Kin 10:19
and on the other upon the six *s* 1Kin 10:20
And there were six *s* to the throne 2Chr 9:18
and on the other upon the six *s* 2Chr 9:19
For now thou numberest my *s* Job 14:16
The *s* of his strength shall be Job 18:7
My foot hath held his *s*, his way Job 23:11
When I washed my *s* with butter Job 29:6
he see my ways, and count all my *s* Job 31:4
unto him the number of my *s* Job 31:37
have now compassed us in our *s* Ps 17:11
Thou hast enlarged my *s* under me Ps 18:36
The *s* of a good man are ordered Ps 37:23
none of his *s* shall slide Ps 37:31
neither have our *s* declined from Ps 44:18
hide themselves, they mark my *s* Ps 56:6
They have prepared a net for my *s* Ps 57:6
my *s* had well nigh slipped Ps 73:2
shall set us in the way of his *s* Ps 85:13
Order my *s* in thy word Ps 119:133
thy *s* shall not be straitened Prov 4:12
her *s* take hold on hell Prov 5:5
but the LORD directeth his *s* Prov 16:9
the poor, and the *s* of the needy Is 26:6
man that walketh to direct his *s* Jer 10:23
They hunt our *s*, that we cannot Lam 4:18
they went up unto it by seven *s* Eze 40:22
there were seven *s* to go up to it Eze 40:26
and the going up to it had eight *s* Eze 40:31
and the going up to it had eight *s* Eze 40:34
and the going up to it had eight *s* Eze 40:37
he brought me by the *s* whereby Eze 40:49
the Ethiopians shall be at his *s* Dan 11:43
but who also walk in the *s* of Rom 4:12
walked we not in the same *s* 2Cor 12:18
that ye should follow his *s* 1Pet 2:21

### STERN
cast four anchors out of the *s* Acts 27:29

### STEWARD
the *s* of my house is this Eliezer Gen 15:2
near to the *s* of Joseph's house Gen 43:19
he commanded the *s* of his house Gen 44:1
far off, Joseph said unto his *s* Gen 44:4
of Arza *s* of his house in Tirzah 1Kin 16:9
of the vineyard saith unto his *s* Mt 20:8
the wife of Chuza Herod's *s* Lk 8:3
then is that faithful and wise *s* Lk 12:42
a certain rich man, which had a *s* Lk 16:1
for thou mayest be no longer *s* Lk 16:2
Then the *s* said within himself, Lk 16:3
the lord commended the unjust *s* Lk 16:8
be blameless, as the *s* of God Titus 1:7

### STEWARDS
the *s* over all the substance and 1Chr 28:1
*s* of the mysteries of God 1Cor 4:1
Moreover it is required in *s* 1Cor 4:2
as good *s* of the manifold grace 1Pet 4:10

### STEWARDSHIP
give an account of thy *s* Lk 16:2
my lord taketh away from me the *s* Lk 16:3
that, when I am put out of the *s* Lk 16:4

### STICK
And he cut down a *s*, and cast it in 2Kin 6:6
bones that were not seen *s* out Job 33:21
they *s* together, that they cannot Job 41:17
For thine arrows *s* fast in me Ps 38:2
withered, it is become like a *s* Lam 4:8
thy rivers to *s* unto thy scales Eze 29:4
rivers shall *s* unto thy scales Eze 29:4
thou son of man, take thee one *s* Eze 37:16
then take another *s*, and write Eze 37:16
the *s* of Ephraim, and for all the Eze 37:16
them one to another into one *s* Eze 37:17
I will take the *s* of Joseph Eze 37:19
him, even with the *s* of Judah Eze 37:19
of Judah, and make them one *s* Eze 37:19

### STICKETH
that *s* closer than a brother Prov 18:24

### STICKS
gathered *s* upon the sabbath day Num 15:32
*s* brought him unto Moses Num 15:33
woman was there gathering of *s* 1Kin 17:10
and, behold, I am gathering two *s* 1Kin 17:12
the *s* whereon thou writest shall Eze 37:20
Paul had gathered a bundle of *s* Acts 28:3

### STIFF
know thy rebellion, and thy *s* neck Deut 31:27
speak not with a *s* neck Ps 75:5
their ear, but made their neck *s* Jer 17:23

### STIFFENED
but he *s* his neck, and hardened 2Chr 36:13

### STIFFHEARTED
they are impudent children and *s* Eze 2:4

### STIFFNECKED
and, behold, it is a *s* people Ex 32:9
for thou art a *s* people Ex 33:3
of Israel, Ye are a *s* people Ex 33:5
for it is a *s* people Ex 34:9
for thou art a *s* people Deut 9:6
and, behold, it is a *s* people Deut 9:13
of your heart, and be no more *s* Deut 10:16
Now be ye not *s*, as your fathers 2Chr 30:8
Ye *s* and uncircumcised in heart and Acts 7:51

### STILL
going on *s* toward the south Gen 12:9
but they were *s* ill favoured Gen 41:21
let them go, and wilt hold them *s* Ex 9:2
the people, Fear ye not, stand *s* Ex 14:13
arm they shall be as *s* as a stone Ex 15:16
thou shalt let it rest and lie *s* Ex 23:11
if it appear *s* in the garment, Lev 13:57
And Moses said unto them, Stand *s* Num 9:8
went to search the land, lived *s* Num 14:38
ye shall stand *s* in Jordan Josh 3:8
Sun, stand thou *s* upon Gibeon Josh 10:12
And the sun stood *s*, and the moon Josh 10:13
So the sun stood *s* in the midst Josh 10:13
that stood *s* in their strength Josh 11:13
therefore he blessed you *s* Josh 24:10
and are ye *s* Judg 18:9
Then said she, Sit *s*, my daughter Ruth 3:18
on,) but stand thou *s* a while 1Sa 9:27
Now therefore stand *s*, that I may 1Sa 12:7
But if ye shall *s* do wickedly 1Sa 12:25
then we will stand *s* in our place 1Sa 14:9
things, and also shalt *s* prevail 1Sa 26:25
Asahel fell down and died stood *s* 2Sa 2:23
and all the people stood *s* 2Sa 2:28
But David tarried *s* at Jerusalem 2Sa 11:1
good for me to have been there *s* 2Sa 14:32
forth, and cursed *s* as he came 2Sa 16:5
And he turned aside, and stood *s* 2Sa 18:30
saw that all the people stood *s* 2Sa 20:12
one that came by him stood *s* 2Sa 20:12
and after the fire a *s* small voice 1Kin 19:12
in Gilead is ours, and we be *s* 1Kin 22:3
came to pass, as they *s* went on 2Kin 2:11
and if we sit *s* here, we die also 2Kin 7:4
the people *s* sacrificed and burnt 2Kin 12:3
burnt incense *s* on the high 2Kin 15:4
burned incense *s* in the high 2Kin 15:35
set yourselves, stand ye *s* 2Chr 20:17
no power to keep *s* the kingdom 2Chr 22:9
sacrifice *s* in the high places 2Chr 33:17
they stood *s* in the prison gate Neh 12:39
*s* he holdeth fast his integrity, Job 2:3
him, Dost thou *s* retain thine Job 2:9
For now should I have lain *s* Job 3:13
It stood *s*, but I could not Job 4:16
but keep it *s* within his mouth Job 20:13
(for they spake not, but stood *s* Job 32:16
stand *s*, and consider the wondrous Job 37:14
own heart upon your bed, and be *s* Ps 4:4
that thou mightest *s* the enemy Ps 8:2
he leadeth me beside the *s* waters Ps 23:2
Be *s*, and know that I am God Ps 46:10
That he should *s* live for ever Ps 49:9
as goeth on *s* in his trespasses Ps 68:21
the earth feared, and was *s* Ps 76:8
For all this they sinned *s* Ps 78:32
hold not thy peace, and be not *s* Ps 83:1
they will be *s* praising thee Ps 84:4
They shall *s* bring forth fruit in Ps 92:14
so that the waves thereof are *s* Ps 107:29
when I awake, I am *s* with thee Ps 139:18
he *s* taught the people knowledge Eccl 12:9
but his hand is stretched out *s* Is 5:25
but his hand is stretched out *s* Is 9:12
but his hand is stretched out *s* Is 9:17
but his hand is stretched out *s* Is 9:21
but his hand is stretched out *s* Is 10:4
Be *s*, ye inhabitants of the isle Is 23:2
this, Their strength is to sit *s* Is 30:7
I have been *s*, and refrained Is 42:14
Why do we sit *s* Jer 8:14
They say *s* unto them that despise Jer 23:17
I let remain *s* in their own land Jer 27:11
I do earnestly remember him *s* Jer 31:20
If ye will *s* abide in this land, Jer 42:10
into thy scabbard, rest, and be *s* Jer 47:6
the sword, go away, stand not *s* Jer 51:50
soul hath them *s* in remembrance Lam 3:20
the children of thy people *s* are Eze 33:30
a winding about *s* upward to the Eze 41:7
*s* upward round about the house Eze 41:7
breadth of the house was *s* upward Eze 41:7
moon stood *s* in their habitation Hab 3:11
behold, all the earth sitteth *s* Zec 1:11
nor feed that that standeth *s* Zec 11:16
And Jesus stood *s*, and called them, Mt 20:32
and said unto the sea, Peace, be *s* Mk 4:39
And Jesus stood *s*, and commanded Mk 10:49
and they that bare him stood *s* Lk 7:14
unto them, he abode *s* in Galilee Jn 7:9
he abode two days *s* in the same Jn 11:6
but Mary sat *s* in the house Jn 11:20
commanded the chariot to stand *s* Acts 8:38
it pleased Silas to abide there *s* Acts 15:34
Silas and Timotheus abode there *s* Acts 17:14
if they abide not *s* in unbelief Rom 11:23
thee to abide *s* at Ephesus 1Ti 1:3
is unjust, let him be unjust *s* Rev 22:11
is filthy, let him be filthy *s* Rev 22:11
righteous, let him be righteous *s* Rev 22:11
that is holy, let him be holy *s* Rev 22:11

**STILLED**
Caleb *s* the people before Moses, ... Num 13:30
So the Levites *s* all the people ... Neh 8:11

**STILLEST**
waves thereof arise, thou *s* them ... Ps 89:9

**STILLETH**
Which *s* the noise of the seas, ... Ps 65:7

**STING**
O death, where is thy *s* ... 1Cor 15:55
The *s* of death is sin ... 1Cor 15:56

**STINGETH**
a serpent, and *s* like an adder ... Prov 23:32

**STINGS**
there were *s* in their tails ... Rev 9:10

**STINK**
to *s* among the inhabitants of the ... Gen 34:30
shall die, and the river shall *s* ... Ex 7:18
and it did not *s*, neither was ... Ex 16:24
My wounds *s* and are corrupt ... Ps 38:5
of sweet smell there shall be *s* ... Is 3:24
their *s* shall come up out of ... Is 34:3
his *s* shall come up, and his ill ... Joel 2:20
I have made the *s* of your camps ... Amos 4:10

**STINKETH**
their fish *s*, because there is no ... Is 50:2
unto him, Lord, by this time he *s* ... Jn 11:39

**STINKING**
to send forth a *s* savour ... Eccl 10:1

**STIR**
who shall *s* him up ... Num 24:9
the innocent shall *s* up himself ... Job 17:8
is so fierce that dare *s* him up ... Job 41:10
*S* up thyself, and awake to my ... Ps 35:23
did not *s* up all his wrath ... Ps 78:38
Manasseh *s* up thy strength, and ... Ps 80:2
but grievous words *s* up anger ... Prov 15:1
of the field, that ye *s* not up ... Song 2:7
of the field, that ye *s* not up ... Song 3:5
of Jerusalem, that ye *s* not up ... Song 8:4
the LORD of hosts shall *s* up a ... Is 10:26
I will *s* up the Medes against ... Is 13:17
he shall *s* up jealousy like a man ... Is 42:13
*s* up all against the realm of ... Dan 11:2
he shall *s* up his power and his ... Dan 11:25
was no small *s* among the soldiers ... Acts 12:18
arose no small *s* about that way ... Acts 19:23
that thou *s* up the gift of God ... 2Ti 1:6
to *s* you up by putting you in ... 2Pet 1:13
in both which I *s* up your pure ... 2Pet 3:1

**STIRRED**
every one whose heart *s* him up ... Ex 35:21
all the women whose heart *s* them ... Ex 35:26
even every one whose heart *s* him ... Ex 36:2
hath *s* up my servant against me ... 1Sa 22:8
If the LORD have *s* thee up ... 1Sa 26:19
the LORD *s* up an adversary unto ... 1Kin 11:14
God *s* him up another adversary, ... 1Kin 11:23
LORD, whom Jezebel his wife *s* up ... 1Kin 21:25
the God of Israel *s* up the spirit ... 1Chr 5:26
Moreover the LORD *s* up against ... 2Chr 21:16
the LORD *s* up the spirit of Cyrus ... 2Chr 36:22
the LORD *s* up the spirit of Cyrus ... Ezr 1:1
and my sorrow was *s* ... Ps 39:2
But his sons shall be *s* up ... Dan 11:10
then shall he return, and be *s* up ... Dan 11:10
*s* up to battle with a very great ... Dan 11:25
the LORD *s* up the spirit of ... Hag 1:14
they *s* up the people, and the ... Acts 6:12
But the Jews *s* up the devout and ... Acts 13:50
Jews *s* up the Gentiles, and made ... Acts 14:2
thither also, and *s* up the people ... Acts 17:13
Athens, his spirit was *s* in him ... Acts 17:16
*s* up all the people, and laid ... Acts 21:27

**STIRRETH**
As an eagle *s* up her nest ... Deut 32:11
Hatred *s* up strifes ... Prov 10:12
A wrathful man *s* up strife ... Prov 15:18
is of a proud heart *s* up strife ... Prov 28:25
An angry man *s* up strife, and a ... Prov 29:22
it *s* up the dead for thee, even ... Is 14:9
that *s* up himself to take hold of ... Is 64:7
He *s* up the people, teaching ... Lk 23:5

**STIRS**
Thou that art full of *s*, a ... Is 22:2

**STOCK**
or to the *s* of the stranger's ... Lev 25:47
the *s* thereof die in the ground ... Job 14:8
their *s* shall not take root in ... Is 40:24
I fall down to the *s* of a tree ... Is 44:19
Saying to a *s*, Thou art my father ... Jer 2:27
the *s* is a doctrine of vanities ... Jer 10:8
children of the *s* of Abraham ... Acts 13:26
of the *s* of Israel, of the tribe ... Phil 3:5

**STOCKS**
puttest my feet also in the *s* ... Job 13:27
He putteth my feet in the *s* ... Job 33:11
a fool to the correction of the *s* ... Prov 7:22
adultery with stones and with *s* ... Jer 3:9
put him in the *s* that were in the ... Jer 20:2
forth Jeremiah out of the *s* ... Jer 20:3
put him in prison, and in the *s* ... Jer 29:26
My people ask counsel at their *s* ... Hos 4:12
and made their feet fast in the *s* ... Acts 16:24

**STOIC** See STOICKS.

**STOICKS** (*sto'-ics*) *A sect of Greek philosophers.*
of the Epicureans, and of the *S* ... Acts 17:18

**STOLE**
Jacob *s* away unawares to Laban ... Gen 31:20
so Absalom *s* the hearts of the ... 2Sa 15:6
*s* him from among the king's sons ... 2Kin 11:2
*s* him from among the king's sons ... 2Chr 22:11
*s* him away while we slept ... Mt 28:13
Let him that *s* steal no more ... Eph 4:28

**STOLEN**
that shall be counted *s* with me ... Gen 30:33
Rachel had *s* the images that were ... Gen 31:19
that thou hast *s* away unawares to ... Gen 31:26
yet wherefore hast thou *s* my gods ... Gen 31:30
knew not that Rachel had *s* them ... Gen 31:32
*s* by day, or *s* by night ... Gen 31:39
For indeed I was *s* away out of ... Gen 40:15
it be *s* out of the man's house ... Ex 22:7
And if it be *s* from him, he shall ... Ex 22:12
accursed thing, and have also *s* ... Josh 7:11
the men of Judah *s* thee away ... 2Sa 19:41
which had *s* them from the street ... 2Sa 21:12
*S* waters are sweet, and bread ... Prov 9:17
not have *s* till they had enough ... Obad 5

**STOMACHER**
instead of a *s* a girding of ... Is 3:24

**STOMACH'S**
use a little wine for thy *s* sake ... 1Ti 5:23

**STONE**
there is bdellium and the onyx *s* ... Gen 2:12
And they had brick for *s*, and slime ... Gen 11:3
took the *s* that he had put for ... Gen 28:18
And this *s*, which I have set for a ... Gen 28:22
a great *s* was upon the well's ... Gen 29:2
they rolled the *s* from the well's ... Gen 29:3
put the *s* again upon the well's ... Gen 29:3
till they roll the *s* from the ... Gen 29:8
rolled the *s* from the well's ... Gen 29:10
And Jacob took a *s*, and set it up ... Gen 31:45
with him, even a pillar of *s* ... Gen 35:14
is the shepherd, the *s* of Israel ... Gen 49:24
Then Zipporah took a sharp *s* ... Ex 4:25
of wood, and in vessels of *s* ... Ex 7:19
their eyes, and will they not *s* us ... Ex 8:26
they sank into the bottom as a *s* ... Ex 15:5
arm they shall be as still as a *s* ... Ex 15:16
they be almost ready to *s* me ... Ex 17:4
and they took a *s*, and put it under ... Ex 17:12
thou wilt make me an altar of *s* ... Ex 20:25
thou shalt not build it of hewn *s* ... Ex 20:25
and one smite another with a *s* ... Ex 21:18
were a paved work of a sapphire *s* ... Ex 24:10
and I will give thee tables of *s* ... Ex 24:12
Six of their names on one *s* ... Ex 28:10
names of the rest on the other *s* ... Ex 28:10
With the work of an engraver in *s* ... Ex 28:11
tables of testimony, tables of *s* ... Ex 31:18
tables of *s* like unto the first ... Ex 34:1
tables of *s* like unto the first ... Ex 34:4
in his hand the two tables of *s* ... Ex 34:4
the land shall *s* him with stones ... Lev 20:2
they shall *s* them with stones ... Lev 20:27
and let all the congregation *s* him ... Lev 24:14
shall certainly *s* him ... Lev 24:16
of the camp, and *s* him with stones ... Lev 24:23
up any image of *s* in your land ... Lev 26:1
bade *s* them with stones ... Num 14:10
all the congregation shall *s* him ... Num 15:35
if he smite him with throwing a *s* ... Num 35:17
Or with any *s*, wherewith a man ... Num 35:23
wrote them upon two tables of *s* ... Deut 4:13
work of men's hands, wood and *s* ... Deut 4:28
he wrote them in two tables of *s* ... Deut 5:22
mount to receive the tables of *s* ... Deut 9:9
*s* written with the finger of God ... Deut 9:10
LORD gave me the two tables of *s* ... Deut 9:11
tables of *s* like unto the first ... Deut 10:1
tables of *s* like unto the first ... Deut 10:3
thou shalt *s* him with stones, ... Deut 13:10
shalt *s* them with stones, till ... Deut 17:5
his city shall *s* him with stones ... Deut 21:21
the men of her city shall *s* her ... Deut 22:21
ye shall *s* them with stones that ... Deut 22:24
thou serve other gods, wood and *s* ... Deut 28:36
have known, even wood and *s* ... Deut 28:64
and their idols, wood and *s* ... Deut 29:17
man of you a *s* upon his shoulder ... Josh 4:5
the border went up to the *s* of ... Josh 15:6
descended to the *s* of Bohan the ... Josh 18:17
the law of God, and took a great *s* ... Josh 24:26
this *s* shall be a witness unto us ... Josh 24:27
and ten persons, upon one *s* ... Judg 9:5
and ten persons, upon one *s* ... Judg 9:18
there, where there was a great *s* ... 1Sa 6:14
were, and put them on the great *s* ... 1Sa 6:15
even unto the great *s* of Abel ... 1Sa 6:18
which *s* remaineth unto this day ... 1Sa 6:18
Then Samuel took a *s*, and set it ... 1Sa 7:12
roll a great *s* unto me this day ... 1Sa 14:33
in his bag, and took thence a *s* ... 1Sa 17:49
that the *s* sunk into his forehead ... 1Sa 17:49
with a sling and with a *s*, and ... 1Sa 17:50
and shalt remain by the *s* Ezel ... 1Sa 20:19
within him, and he became as a *s* ... 1Sa 25:37
be not one small *s* found there ... 2Sa 17:13
at the great *s* which is in Gibeon ... 2Sa 20:8
fat cattle by the *s* of Zoheleth ... 1Kin 1:9
was built of *s* made ready before ... 1Kin 6:7
there was no *s* seen ... 1Kin 6:18
court with three rows of hewed *s* ... 1Kin 6:36
the ark save the two tables of *s* ... 1Kin 8:9
out, and *s* him, that he may die ... 1Kin 21:10
of land cast every man his *s* ... 2Kin 3:25
And to masons, and hewers of *s* ... 2Kin 12:12
hewed *s* to repair the breaches of ... 2Kin 12:12
work of men's hands, wood and *s* ... 2Kin 19:18
hewn *s* to repair the house ... 2Kin 22:6
timber also and *s* have I prepared ... 1Chr 22:14
abundance, hewers and workers of *s* ... 1Chr 22:15
silver, in brass, in iron, in *s* ... 2Chr 2:14
gave they it, to buy hewn *s* ... 2Chr 34:11
even break down their *s* wall ... Neh 4:3
as a *s* into the mighty waters ... Neh 9:11
and brass is molten out of the *s* ... Job 28:2
or who laid the corner *s* thereof ... Job 38:6
The waters are hid as with a *s* ... Job 38:30
His heart is as firm as a *s* ... Job 41:24
thou dash thy foot against a *s* ... Ps 91:12
The *s* which the builders refused ... Ps 118:22
become the head *s* of the corner ... Ps 118:22
A gift is as a precious *s* in the ... Prov 17:8
the *s* wall thereof was broken ... Prov 24:31
As he that bindeth a *s* in a sling ... Prov 26:8
and he that rolleth a *s*, it will ... Prov 26:27
A *s* is heavy, and the sand weighty ... Prov 27:3
but for a *s* of stumbling and for a ... Is 8:14
a foundation a *s*, a tried *s* ... Is 28:16
a precious corner *s* ... Is 28:16
work of men's hands, wood and *s* ... Is 37:19
and to a *s*, Thou hast brought me ... Jer 2:27
not take of thee a *s* for a corner ... Jer 51:26
a corner, nor a *s* for foundations ... Jer 51:26
that thou shalt bind a *s* to it ... Jer 51:63
hath inclosed my ways with hewn *s* ... Lam 3:9
the dungeon, and cast a *s* upon me ... Lam 3:53
as the appearance of a sapphire *s* ... Eze 1:26
over them as it were a sapphire *s* ... Eze 10:1
was as the colour of a beryl *s* ... Eze 10:9
they shall *s* thee with stones, and ... Eze 16:40
the countries, to serve wood and *s* ... Eze 20:32
company shall *s* them with stones ... Eze 23:47
every precious *s* was thy covering ... Eze 28:13
of hewn *s* for the burnt offering ... Eze 40:42
Thou sawest till that a *s* was cut ... Dan 2:34
the *s* that smote the image became ... Dan 2:35
as thou sawest that the *s* was cut ... Dan 2:45
brass, of iron, of wood, and of *s* ... Dan 5:4
gold, of brass, iron, wood, and *s* ... Dan 5:23
a *s* was brought, and laid upon the ... Dan 6:17
ye have built houses of hewn *s* ... Amos 5:11
For the *s* shall cry out of the ... Hab 2:11
to the dumb *s*, Arise, it shall ... Hab 2:19
from before a *s* was laid upon a ... Hag 2:15
a *s* in the temple of the LORD ... Hag 2:15
For behold the *s* that I have laid ... Zec 3:9
upon one *s* shall be seven eyes ... Zec 3:9
made their hearts as an adamant *s* ... Zec 7:12
a burdensome *s* for all people ... Zec 12:3
thou dash thy foot against a *s* ... Mt 4:6
ask bread, will he give him a *s* ... Mt 7:9
The *s* which the builders rejected ... Mt 21:42
fall on this *s* shall be broken ... Mt 21:44
be left here one *s* upon another ... Mt 24:2
he rolled a great *s* to the door ... Mt 27:60
the sepulchre sure, sealing the *s* ... Mt 27:66
rolled back the *s* from the door ... Mt 28:2
The *s* which the builders rejected ... Mk 12:10
not be left one *s* upon another ... Mk 13:2
rolled a *s* unto the door of the ... Mk 15:46
Who shall roll us away the *s* from ... Mk 16:3
saw that the *s* was rolled away ... Mk 16:4
command this *s* that it be made ... Lk 4:3
thou dash thy foot against a *s* ... Lk 4:11
is a father, will he give him a *s* ... Lk 11:11
leave in thee one *s* upon another ... Lk 19:44
all the people will *s* us ... Lk 20:6
The *s* which the builders rejected ... Lk 20:17
fall upon that *s* shall be broken ... Lk 20:18
not be left one *s* upon another ... Lk 21:6
in a sepulchre that was hewn in *s* ... Lk 23:53
they found the *s* rolled away from ... Lk 24:2
which is by interpretation, A *s* ... Jn 1:42
were set there six waterpots of *s* ... Jn 2:6
let him first cast a *s* at her ... Jn 8:7
took up stones again to *s* him ... Jn 10:31
which of those works do ye *s* me ... Jn 10:32
For a good work we *s* thee not ... Jn 10:33
the Jews of late sought to *s* thee ... Jn 11:8
It was a cave, and a *s* lay upon it ... Jn 11:38
Jesus said, Take ye away the *s* ... Jn 11:39
Then they took away the *s* from ... Jn 11:41
seeth the *s* taken away from the ... Jn 20:1
This is the *s* which was set at ... Acts 4:11
them despitefully, and to *s* them, ... Acts 14:5
like unto gold, or silver, or *s* ... Acts 17:29
not in tables of *s*, but in ... 2Cor 3:3
himself being the chief corner *s* ... Eph 2:20
whom coming, as unto a living *s* ... 1Pet 2:4
I lay in Sion a chief corner *s* ... 1Pet 2:6
the *s* which the builders ... 1Pet 2:7
a *s* of stumbling, and a rock of ... 1Pet 2:8
manna, and will give him a white *s* ... Rev 2:17
in the *s* a new name written, ... Rev 2:17
upon like a jasper and a sardine *s* ... Rev 4:3
gold, and silver, and brass, and *s* ... Rev 9:20

every *s* about the weight of a Rev 16:21
up a *s* like a great millstone Rev 18:21
was like unto a *s* most precious Rev 21:11
precious, even like a jasper *s* Rev 21:11

## STONED
it, but he shall surely be *s* Ex 19:13
then the ox shall be surely *s* Ex 21:28
the ox shall be *s*, and his owner Ex 21:29
of silver, and the ox shall be *s* Ex 21:32
*s* him with stones, and he died Num 15:36
all Israel *s* him with stones, and Josh 7:25
after they had *s* them with stones Josh 7:25
all Israel *s* him with stones, 1Kin 12:18
*s* him with stones, that he died 1Kin 21:13
to Jezebel, saying, Naboth is *s* 1Kin 21:14
Jezebel heard that Naboth was *s* 1Kin 21:15
of Israel *s* him with stones 2Chr 10:18
him, and *s* him with stones at the 2Chr 24:21
and killed another, and *s* another Mt 21:35
us, that such should be *s* Jn 8:5
lest they should have been *s* Acts 5:26
him out of the city, and *s* him Acts 7:58
they *s* Stephen, calling upon God, Acts 7:59
the people, and, having *s* Paul Acts 14:19
I beaten with rods, once was I *s* 2Cor 11:25
They were *s*, they were sawn Heb 11:37
touch the mountain, it shall be *s* Heb 12:20

## STONE'S
from them about a *s* cast, and Lk 22:41

## STONES
and he took of the *s* of that place Gen 28:11
said unto his brethren, Gather *s* Gen 31:46
and they took *s*, and made an heap Gen 31:46
Onyx *s*, and *s* to be set in Ex 25:7
And thou shalt take two onyx *s* Ex 28:9
shalt thou engrave the two *s* with Ex 28:11
thou shalt put the two *s* upon the Ex 28:12
*s* of memorial unto the children Ex 28:12
shalt set in it settings of *s* Ex 28:17
even four rows of *s* Ex 28:17
the *s* shall be with the names of Ex 28:21
And in cutting of *s*, to set them, Ex 31:5
And onyx *s*, and *s* to be set Ex 35:9
And the rulers brought onyx *s* Ex 35:27
*s* to be set, for the ephod, and Ex 35:27
And in the cutting of *s*, to set Ex 35:33
they wrought onyx *s* inclosed in Ex 39:6
that they should be *s* for a Ex 39:7
And they set in it four rows of *s* Ex 39:10
the *s* were according to the names Ex 39:14
away the *s* in which the plague is Lev 14:40
And they shall take other *s* Lev 14:42
put them in the place of those *s* Lev 14:42
that he hath taken away the *s* Lev 14:43
the *s* of it, and the timber Lev 14:45
the land shall stone him with *s* Lev 20:2
they shall stone them with *s* Lev 20:27
or scabbed, or hath his *s* broken Lev 21:20
of the camp, and stone him with *s* Lev 24:23
bade stone them with *s* Num 14:10
stone him with *s* without the camp Num 15:35
the camp, and stoned him with *s* Num 15:36
a land whose *s* are iron, and out Deut 8:9
And thou shalt stone him with *s* Deut 13:10
woman, and shalt stone them with *s* Deut 17:5
his city shall stone him with *s* Deut 21:21
stone her with *s* that she die Deut 22:21
stone them with *s* that they die Deut 22:24
He that is wounded in the *s* Deut 23:1
thou shalt set thee up great *s* Deut 27:2
that ye shall set up these *s* Deut 27:4
the LORD thy God, an altar of *s* Deut 27:5
of the LORD thy God of whole *s* Deut 27:6
thou shalt write upon the *s* all Deut 27:8
feet stood firm, twelve *s* Josh 4:3
saying, What mean ye by these *s* Josh 4:6
these *s* shall be for a memorial Josh 4:7
took up twelve *s* out of the midst Josh 4:8
Joshua set up twelve *s* in the Josh 4:9
And those twelve *s*, which they Josh 4:20
come, saying, What mean these *s* Josh 4:21
And all Israel stoned him with *s* Josh 7:25
after they had stoned them with *s* Josh 7:25
a great heap of *s* unto this day Josh 7:26
raise thereon a great heap of *s* Josh 8:29
law of Moses, an altar of whole *s* Josh 8:31
he wrote there upon the *s* a copy Josh 8:32
*s* from heaven upon them unto Josh 10:11
Roll great *s* upon the mouth of Josh 10:18
laid great *s* in the cave's mouth, Josh 10:27
could sling *s* at an hair breadth Judg 20:16
five smooth *s* out of the brook 1Sa 17:40
of gold with the precious *s* 2Sa 12:30
he cast *s* at David, and at all the 2Sa 16:6
threw *s* at him, and cast dust 2Sa 16:13
a very great heap of *s* upon him 2Sa 18:17
*s*, costly *s*, and hewed *s* 1Kin 5:17
timber and *s* to build the house 1Kin 5:18
All these were of costly *s* 1Kin 7:9
to the measures of hewed *s* 1Kin 7:9
of costly *s*, even great *s* 1Kin 7:10
*s* of ten cubits, and *s* of 1Kin 7:10
And above were costly *s*, after the 1Kin 7:11
after the measures of hewed *s* 1Kin 7:11
was with three rows of hewed *s* 1Kin 7:12
and very much gold, and precious *s* 1Kin 10:2
very great store, and precious *s* 1Kin 10:10
of almug trees, and precious *s* 1Kin 10:11
silver to be in Jerusalem as *s* 1Kin 10:27
and all Israel stoned him with *s* 1Kin 12:18
and they took away the *s* of Ramah 1Kin 15:22
And Elijah took twelve *s*, 1Kin 18:31
with the *s* he built an altar in 1Kin 18:32
sacrifice, and the wood, and the *s* 1Kin 18:38
of the city, and stoned him with *s* 1Kin 21:13
every good piece of land with *s* 2Kin 3:19
left they the *s* thereof 2Kin 3:25
and put it upon a pavement of *s* 2Kin 16:17
hand and the left in hurling *s* 1Chr 12:2
and there were precious *s* in it 1Chr 20:2
*s* to build the house of God 1Chr 22:2
onyx *s*, and *s* to be set, 1Chr 29:2
to be set, glistering *s* 1Chr 29:2
and all manner of precious *s* 1Chr 29:2
*s*, and marble *s* in abundance 1Chr 29:2
they with whom precious *s* were 1Chr 29:8
at Jerusalem as plenteous as *s* 2Chr 1:15
house with precious *s* for beauty 2Chr 3:6
gold in abundance, and precious *s* 2Chr 9:1
great abundance, and precious *s* 2Chr 9:9
brought algum trees and precious *s* 2Chr 9:10
made silver in Jerusalem as *s* 2Chr 9:27
of Israel stoned him with *s* 2Chr 10:18
they carried away the *s* of Ramah 2Chr 16:6
him, and stoned him with *s* at the 2Chr 24:21
and bows, and slings to cast *s* 2Chr 26:14
to shoot arrows and great *s* withal 2Chr 26:15
and for gold, and for precious *s* 2Chr 32:27
which is builded with great *s* Ezr 5:8
With three rows of great *s* Ezr 6:4
will they revive the *s* out of the Neh 4:2
in league with the *s* of the field Job 5:23
Is my strength the strength of *s* Job 6:12
the heap, and seeth the place of *s* Job 8:17
The waters wear the *s* Job 14:19
of Ophir as the *s* of the brooks Job 22:24
the *s* of darkness, and the shadow Job 28:3
The *s* of it are the place of Job 28:6
the sinews of his *s* are wrapped Job 40:17
Sharp *s* are under him Job 41:30
his thick clouds passed, hail *s* Ps 18:12
hail *s* and coals of fire Ps 18:13
servants take pleasure in her *s* Ps 102:14
thy little ones against the *s* Ps 137:9
our daughters may be as corner *s* Ps 144:12
A time to cast away *s*, and a time Eccl 3:5
and a time to gather *s* together Eccl 3:5
Whoso removeth *s* shall be hurt Eccl 10:9
it, and gathered out the *s* thereof Is 5:2
but we will build with hewn *s* Is 9:10
that go down to the *s* of the pit Is 14:19
when he maketh all the *s* of the Is 27:9
confusion, and the *s* of emptiness Is 34:11
I will lay thy *s* with fair colors Is 54:11
and all thy borders of pleasant *s* Is 54:12
Among the smooth *s* of the stream Is 57:6
and for wood brass, and for *s* iron Is 60:17
gather out the *s* Is 62:10
and committed adultery with *s* Jer 3:9
Take great *s* in thine hand, and Jer 43:9
upon these *s* that I have hid Jer 43:10
broken my teeth with gravel *s* Lam 3:16
the *s* of the sanctuary are poured Lam 4:1
and they shall stone thee with *s* Eze 16:40
company shall stone them with *s* Eze 23:47
and they shall lay thy *s* and thy Eze 26:12
spices, and with all precious *s* Eze 27:22
in the midst of the *s* of fire Eze 28:14
from the midst of the *s* of fire Eze 28:16
and silver, and with precious *s* Dan 11:38
I will pour down the *s* thereof Mic 1:6
timber thereof and the *s* thereof Zec 5:4
devour, and subdue with sling *s* Zec 9:15
they shall be as the *s* of a crown Zec 9:16
these *s* to raise up children unto Mt 3:9
that these *s* be made bread Mt 4:3
crying, and cutting himself with *s* Mk 5:5
and at him they cast *s*, and wounded Mk 12:4
him, Master, see what manner of *s* Mk 13:1
these *s* to raise up children unto Lk 3:8
the *s* would immediately cry out Lk 19:40
how it was adorned with goodly *s* Lk 21:5
took they up *s* to cast at him Jn 8:59
Jews took up *s* again to stone him Jn 10:31
gold, silver, precious *s*, wood, 1Cor 3:12
death, written and engraven in *s* 2Cor 3:7
Ye also, as lively *s*, are built 1Pet 2:5
and decked with gold and precious *s* Rev 17:4
of gold, and silver, and precious *s* Rev 18:12
decked with gold, and precious *s* Rev 18:16
with all manner of precious *s* Rev 21:19

## STONESQUARERS
builders did hew them, and the *s* 1Kin 5:18

## STONEST
*s* them which are sent unto thee, Mt 23:37
*s* them that are sent unto thee Lk 13:34

## STONING
for the people spake of *s* him 1Sa 30:6

## STONY
judges are overthrown in *s* places Ps 141:6
I will take the *s* heart out of Eze 11:19
I will take away the *s* heart out Eze 36:26
Some fell upon *s* places, where Mt 13:5
received the seed into *s* places Mt 13:20
And some fell on *s* ground, where Mk 4:5
which are sown on *s* ground Mk 4:16

## STOOD
and, lo, three men *s* by him Gen 18:2
he *s* by them under the tree, and Gen 18:8
but Abraham *s* yet before the LORD Gen 18:22
place where he *s* before the LORD Gen 19:27
Abraham *s* up from before his dead Gen 23:3
Abraham *s* up, and bowed Gen 23:7
he *s* by the camels at the well Gen 24:30
And, behold, the LORD *s* above it Gen 28:13
my sheaf arose, and also *s* upright Gen 37:7
your sheaves *s* round about Gen 37:7
and, behold, he *s* by the river Gen 41:1
*s* by the other kine upon the Gen 41:3
I *s* upon the bank of the river Gen 41:17
he *s* before Pharaoh king of Egypt Gen 41:46
down to Egypt, and *s* before Joseph Gen 43:15
before all them that *s* by him Gen 45:1
there *s* no man with him, while Gen 45:1
And his sister *s* afar off, to wit Ex 2:4
but Moses *s* up and helped them, and Ex 2:17
who *s* in the way, as they came Ex 5:20
the furnace, and *s* before Pharaoh Ex 9:10
their face, and *s* behind them Ex 14:19
the floods *s* upright as an heap, Ex 15:8
the people *s* by Moses from the Ex 18:13
they *s* at the nether part of the Ex 19:17
it, they removed, and *s* afar off Ex 20:18
And the people *s* afar off, and Ex 20:21
Then Moses *s* in the gate of the Ex 32:26
*s* every man at his tent door, and Ex 33:8
*s* at the door of the tabernacle, Ex 33:9
*s* with him there, and proclaimed Ex 34:5
drew near and *s* before the LORD Lev 9:5
the people *s* up all that day, and Num 11:32
*s* in the door of the tabernacle, Num 12:5
*s* in the door of the tabernacle Num 16:18
*s* in the door of their tents, and Num 16:27
he *s* between the dead and the Num 16:48
the angel of the LORD *s* in the Num 22:22
But the angel of the LORD *s* in a Num 22:24
*s* in a narrow place, where was no Num 22:26
he *s* by his burnt sacrifice, he, Num 23:6
he *s* by his burnt offering, and Num 23:17
they *s* before Moses, and before Num 27:2
came near and *s* under the mountain Deut 4:11
(I *s* between the LORD and you at Deut 5:5
the pillar of the cloud *s* over Deut 31:15
which came down from above *s* Josh 3:16
*s* firm on dry ground in the midst Josh 3:17
where the priests' feet *s* firm Josh 4:3
bare the ark of the covenant *s* Josh 4:9
the ark *s* in the midst of Jordan Josh 4:10
there *s* a man over against him Josh 5:13
*s* on this side the ark and on that Josh 8:33
And the sun *s* still, and the moon Josh 10:13
So the sun *s* still in the midst Josh 10:13
that *s* still in their strength Josh 11:13
of blood, until he *s* before the Josh 20:9
there *s* not a man of all their Josh 21:44
all that *s* by him went out from Judg 3:19
said unto all that *s* against him Judg 6:31
they *s* every man in his place Judg 7:21
*s* in the top of mount Gerizim, and Judg 9:7
*s* in the entering of the gate of Judg 9:35
*s* in the entering of the gate of Judg 9:44
pillars upon which the house *s* Judg 16:29
*s* by the entering of the gate Judg 18:16
the priest *s* in the entering of Judg 18:17
*s* before it in those days,) Judg 20:28
am the woman that *s* by thee here 1Sa 1:26
And the LORD came, and *s*, and called 1Sa 3:10
women that *s* by her said unto her 1Sa 4:20
*s* there, where there was a great 1Sa 6:14
when he *s* among the people, he 1Sa 10:23
came to Saul, and *s* before him 1Sa 16:21
the Philistines *s* on a mountain 1Sa 17:3
Israel *s* on a mountain on the 1Sa 17:3
And he *s* and cried unto the armies 1Sa 17:8
spake to the men that *s* by him 1Sa 17:26
*s* upon the Philistine, and took 1Sa 17:51
his servants that *s* about him 1Sa 22:7
unto the footmen that *s* about him 1Sa 22:17
*s* on the top of an hill afar off 1Sa 26:13
So I *s* upon him, and slew him, 2Sa 1:10
Asahel fell down and died *s* still 2Sa 2:23
troop, and *s* on the top of an hill 2Sa 2:25
and all the people *s* still 2Sa 2:28
all his servants *s* by with their 2Sa 13:31
*s* beside the way of the gate 2Sa 15:2
the king *s* by the gate side, and 2Sa 18:4
And he turned aside, and *s* still 2Sa 18:30
And one of Joab's men *s* by him 2Sa 20:11
saw that all the people *s* still 2Sa 20:12
one that came by him *s* still 2Sa 20:12
the city, and it *s* in the trench 2Sa 20:15
But he *s* in the midst of the 2Sa 23:12
presence, and *s* before the king 1Kin 1:28
*s* before the ark of the covenant 1Kin 3:15
unto the king, and *s* before him 1Kin 3:16
It *s* upon twelve oxen, three 1Kin 7:25
all the congregation of Israel *s* 1Kin 8:14
Solomon *s* before the altar of the 1Kin 8:22
And he *s*, and blessed all the 1Kin 8:55
two lions *s* beside the stays 1Kin 10:19
twelve lions *s* there on the one 1Kin 10:20
that *s* before Solomon his father 1Kin 12:6
with him, and which *s* before him 1Kin 12:8
Jeroboam *s* by the altar to burn 1Kin 13:1
in the way, and the ass *s* by it 1Kin 13:24
the lion also *s* by the carcase 1Kin 13:24

s in the entering in of the cave 1Kin 19:13
s before the LORD, and said, I 1Kin 22:21
went, and s to view afar off 2Kin 2:7
and they two s by Jordan 2Kin 2:7
back, and s by the bank of Jordan 2Kin 2:13
and upward, and s in the border 2Kin 3:21
had called her, she s before him 2Kin 4:12
had called her, she s in the door 2Kin 4:15
s at the door of the house of 2Kin 5:9
company, and came, and s before him 2Kin 5:15
went in, and s before his master 2Kin 5:25
s before him, and said, Thy son 2Kin 8:9
there s a watchman on the tower 2Kin 9:17
two kings s not before him 2Kin 10:4
morning, that he went out, and s 2Kin 10:9
And the guard s, every man with 2Kin 11:11
the king s by a pillar, as the 2Kin 11:14
he revived, and s up on his feet 2Kin 13:21
s by the conduit of the upper 2Kin 18:17
Then Rab-shakeh s and cried with a. 2Kin 18:28
the king s by a pillar, and made a 2Kin 23:3
all the people s to the covenant 2Kin 23:3
who s on his right hand, even 1Chr 6:39
sons of Merari s on the left hand 1Chr 6:44
Satan s up against Israel, and 1Chr 21:1
the angel of the LORD s by the 1Chr 21:15
David the king s up upon his feet 1Chr 28:2
they s on their feet, and their 2Chr 3:13
It s upon twelve oxen, three 2Chr 4:4
s at the east end of the altar, 2Chr 5:12
all the congregation of Israel s 2Chr 6:3
he s before the altar of the LORD 2Chr 6:12
and upon it he s, and kneeled down 2Chr 6:13
before them, and all Israel s 2Chr 7:6
twelve lions s there on the one 2Chr 9:19
with the old men that had s 2Chr 10:6
up with him, that s before him 2Chr 10:8
Abijah s up upon mount Zemaraim, 2Chr 13:4
s before the LORD, and said, I 2Chr 18:20
Jehoshaphat s in the congregation 2Chr 20:5
all Judah s before the LORD, with 2Chr 20:13
s up to praise the LORD God of 2Chr 20:19
as they went forth, Jehoshaphat s 2Chr 20:20
Moab s up against the inhabitants 2Chr 20:23
the king s at his pillar at the 2Chr 23:13
which s above the people, and said 2Chr 24:20
s up against them that came from 2Chr 28:12
And the Levites s with the 2Chr 29:26
they s in their place after their 2Chr 30:16
the king s in his place, and made 2Chr 34:31
the priests s in their place, and 2Chr 35:10
till there s up a priest with Ezr 2:63
Then s up Jeshua the son of Ezr 3:2
Then s Jeshua with his sons and Ezr 3:9
And Ezra the priest s up, and said Ezr 10:10
till there s up a priest with Neh 7:65
Ezra the scribe s upon a pulpit Neh 8:4
and beside him s Mattithiah Neh 8:4
he opened it, all the people s up Neh 8:5
the people s in their place Neh 8:7
from all strangers, and s and Neh 9:2
they s up in their place, and read Neh 9:3
Then s up upon the stairs, of the Neh 9:4
they s still in the prison gate Neh 12:39
So s the two companies of them Neh 12:40
s in the inner court of the Est 5:1
the king's gate, that he s not up Est 5:9
Haman s up to make request for Est 7:7
arose, and s before the king, Est 8:4
s for their lives, and had rest Est 9:16
the hair of my flesh s up Job 4:15
It s still, but I could not Job 4:16
and the aged arose, and s up Job 29:8
I s up, and I cried in the Job 30:28
but s still, and answered no more Job 32:16
he commanded, and it s fast Ps 33:9
the waters s above the mountains Ps 104:6
chosen s before him in the breach Ps 106:23
Then s up Phinehas, and executed Ps 106:30
Above it s the seraphims Is 6:2
he s by the conduit of the upper Is 36:2
Then Rabshakeh s, and cried with a Is 36:13
Samuel s before me, yet my mind Jer 15:1
Remember that I s before thee to Jer 18:20
he s in the court of the LORD'S Jer 19:14
For who hath s in the counsel of Jer 23:18
But if they had s in my counsel Jer 23:22
that s in the house of the LORD Jer 28:5
princes which s beside the king Jer 36:21
gods, and all the women that s by Jer 44:15
they s not, because the LORD did Jer 46:15
They that fled s under the shadow Jer 48:45
he s with his right hand as an Lam 2:4
and when those s, these s Eze 1:21
when they s, they let down their Eze 1:24
was over their heads, when they s Eze 1:25
the glory of the LORD s there Eze 3:23
there s before them seventy men Eze 8:11
in the midst of them s Jaazaniah Eze 8:11
s beside the brasen altar Eze 9:2
Now the cherubims s on the right Eze 10:3
s over the threshold of the house Eze 10:4
went in, and s beside the wheels Eze 10:6
When they s, these s Eze 10:17
house, and s over the cherubims Eze 10:18
every one s at the door of the Eze 10:19
s upon the mountain which is on Eze 11:23
For the king of Babylon s at the Eze 21:21
and s up upon their feet, an Eze 37:10
and he s in the gate Eze 40:3
and the man s by me Eze 43:6
of the house s toward the east Eze 47:1
therefore s they before the king Dan 1:19
So they came and s before the king Dan 2:2
was excellent, s before thee Dan 2:31
they s before the image that Dan 3:3
times ten thousand s before him Dan 7:10
near unto one of them that s by Dan 7:16
there s before the river a ram Dan 8:3
behold, there s before me as the Dan 8:15
So he came near where I s Dan 8:17
broken, whereas four s up for it Dan 8:22
this word unto me, I s trembling Dan 10:11
and said unto him that s before me Dan 10:16
s to confirm and to strengthen him Dan 11:1
there s other two, the one on Dan 12:5
there they s Hos 10:9
the Lord s upon a wall made by a Amos 7:7
thou have s in the crossway Obad 14
He s, and measured the earth Hab 3:6
moon s still in their habitation Hab 3:11
he s among the myrtle trees that Zec 1:8
the man that s among the myrtle Zec 1:10
that s among the myrtle trees Zec 1:11
garments, and s before the angel Zec 3:3
unto those that s before him Zec 3:4
And the angel of the LORD s by Zec 3:5
s over where the young child was Mt 2:9
mother and his brethren s without Mt 12:46
whole multitude s on the shore Mt 13:2
And Jesus s still, and called them, Mt 20:32
came unto him they that s by Mt 26:73
Jesus s before the governor Mt 27:11
Some of them that s there Mt 27:47
And Jesus s still, and commanded Mk 10:49
them that s there said unto them Mk 11:5
of them that s by drew a sword Mk 14:47
the high priest s up in the midst Mk 14:60
and began to say to them that s by Mk 14:69
they that s by said again to Mk 14:70
And some of them that s by Mk 15:35
which s over against him, saw Mk 15:39
sabbath day, and s up for to read Lk 4:16
he s over her, and rebuked the Lk 4:39
he s by the lake of Gennesaret, Lk 5:1
And he arose and s forth Lk 6:8
s in the plain, and the company of Lk 6:17
and they that bare him s still Lk 7:14
s at his feet behind him weeping, Lk 7:38
and the two men that s with him Lk 9:32
And, behold, a certain lawyer s up Lk 10:25
were lepers, which s afar off Lk 17:12
The Pharisee s and prayed thus Lk 18:11
And Jesus s, and commanded him to Lk 18:40
And Zacchaeus s, and said unto the Lk 19:8
And he said unto them that s by Lk 19:24
And the chief priests and scribes s Lk 23:10
And the people s beholding Lk 23:35
s afar off, beholding these Lk 23:49
two men s by them in shining Lk 24:4
Jesus himself s in the midst of Lk 24:36
Again the next day after John s Jn 1:35
when the people which s on the Jn 6:22
great day of the feast, Jesus s Jn 7:37
as they s in the temple, What Jn 11:56
The people therefore, that s by Jn 12:29
which betrayed him, s with them Jn 18:5
But Peter s at the door without Jn 18:16
the servants and officers s there Jn 18:18
Peter s with them, and warmed Jn 18:18
one of the officers which s by Jn 18:22
And Simon Peter s and warmed Jn 18:25
Now there s by the cross of Jesus Jn 19:25
But Mary s without at the Jn 20:11
s in the midst, and saith unto Jn 20:19
s in the midst, and said, Peace be Jn 20:26
now come, Jesus s on the shore Jn 21:4
two men s by them in white Acts 1:10
in those days Peter s up in the Acts 1:15
And he leaping up s, and walked, and Acts 3:8
The kings of the earth s up Acts 4:26
Then s there up one in the Acts 5:34
journeyed with him s speechless Acts 9:7
all the widows s by him weeping Acts 9:39
house, and s before the gate, Acts 10:17
a man s before me in bright Acts 10:30
an angel in his house, which s Acts 11:13
there s up one of them named Acts 11:28
told how Peter s before the gate Acts 12:14
Then Paul s up, and beckoning with . Acts 13:16
the disciples s round about him Acts 14:20
There s a man of Macedonia, and Acts 16:9
Then Paul s in the midst of Mars' Acts 17:22
Paul s on the stairs, and beckoned Acts 21:40
Came unto me, and s, and said unto . Acts 22:13
said unto the centurion that s by Acts 22:25
that s by him to smite him on the Acts 23:2
And they that s by said, Revilest Acts 23:4
night following the Lord s by him Acts 23:11
while I s before the council, Acts 24:20
down from Jerusalem s round about Acts 25:7
whom when the accusers s up Acts 25:18
Paul s forth in the midst of them Acts 27:21
For there s by me this night the Acts 27:23
my first answer no man s with me 2Ti 4:16
the Lord s with me, and 2Ti 4:17
Which s only in meats and drinks, Heb 9:10
s a Lamb as it had been slain, Rev 5:6
s before the throne, and before Rev 7:9
all the angels s round about the Rev 7:11
seven angels which s before God Rev 8:2
s at the altar, having a golden Rev 8:3
and the angel s, saying, Rise, and Rev 11:1
them, and they s upon their feet Rev 11:11
the dragon s before the woman Rev 12:4
I s upon the sand of the sea, and Rev 13:1
a Lamb s on the mount Sion, and Rev 14:1
many as trade by sea, s afar off, Rev 18:17

**STOODEST**
that thou s in the way against me Num 22:34
thou s before the LORD thy God in Deut 4:10
day that thou s on the other side Obad 11

**STOOL**
there a bed, and a table, and a s 2Kin 4:10

**STOOLS**
women, and see them upon the s Ex 1:16

**STOOP**
the proud helpers do s under him Job 9:13
in the heart of man maketh it s Prov 12:25
They s, they bow down together Is 46:2
shoes I am not worthy to s down Mk 1:7

**STOOPED**
he s down, he couched as a lion, Gen 49:9
David s with his face to the 1Sa 24:8
he s with his face to the ground, 1Sa 28:14
old man, or him that s for age 2Chr 36:17
But Jesus s down, and with his Jn 8:6
And again he s down, and wrote on Jn 8:8
she s down, and looked into the Jn 20:11

**STOOPETH**
Bel boweth down, Nebo s, their Is 46:1

**STOOPING**
s down, he beheld the linen Lk 24:12
he s down, and looking in, saw the Jn 20:5

**STOP**
down, that the rain s thee not 1Kin 18:44
s all wells of water, and mar 2Kin 3:19
his mighty men to s the waters of 2Chr 32:3
s the way against them that Ps 35:3
and all iniquity shall s her mouth Ps 107:42
it shall s the noses of the Eze 39:11
no man shall s me of this 2Cor 11:10

**STOPPED**
and the windows of heaven were s Gen 8:2
the Philistines had s them Gen 26:15
for the Philistines had s them Gen 26:18
or his flesh be s from his issue Lev 15:3
they s all the wells of water, and 2Kin 3:25
who s all the fountains, and the 2Chr 32:4
This same Hezekiah also s the 2Chr 32:30
that the breaches began to be s Neh 4:7
them that speak lies shall be s Ps 63:11
And that the passages are s Jer 51:32
s their ears, that they should Zec 7:11
s their ears, and ran upon him Acts 7:57
that every mouth may be s Rom 3:19
Whose mouths must be s, who Titus 1:11
promises, s the mouths of lions, Heb 11:33

**STOPPETH**
hope, and iniquity s her mouth Job 5:16
the deaf adder that s her ear Ps 58:4
Whoso s his ears at the cry of Prov 21:13
that s his ears from hearing of Is 33:15

**STORE**
of herds, and great s of servants Gen 26:14
that food shall be for s to the Gen 41:36
come in ye shall eat of the old s Lev 25:22
And ye shall eat old s, and bring Lev 26:10
shall be thy basket and thy s Deut 28:5
shall be thy basket and thy s Deut 28:17
Is not this laid up in s with me Deut 32:34
the cities of s that Solomon had 1Kin 9:19
gold, and of spices very great s 1Kin 10:10
have laid up in s unto this day 2Kin 20:17
all this s that we have prepared 1Chr 29:16
wilderness, and all the s cities 2Chr 8:4
all the s cities that Solomon had 2Chr 8:6
s of victual, and of oil and wine 2Chr 11:11
all the s cities of Naphtali 2Chr 16:4
in Judah castles, and cities of s 2Chr 17:12
which is left is this great s 2Chr 31:10
once in ten days s of all sorts Neh 5:18
full, affording all manner of s Ps 144:13
have laid up in s until this day Is 39:6
who s up violence and robbery in Amos 3:10
for there is none end of the s Nah 2:9
every one of you lay by him in s 1Cor 16:2
Laying up in s for themselves a 1Ti 6:19
by the same word are kept in s 2Pet 3:7

**STOREHOUSE**
ye all the tithes into the s Mal 3:10
which neither have s nor barn Lk 12:24

**STOREHOUSES**
And Joseph opened all the s Gen 41:56
the blessing upon thee in thy s Deut 28:8
over the s in the fields, in the 1Chr 27:25
S also for the increase of corn, 2Chr 32:28
he layeth up the depth in s Ps 33:7
the utmost border, open her s Jer 50:26

**STORIES**
third s shalt thou make it Gen 6:16
round about on their three s Eze 41:16
against gallery in three s Eze 42:3

For they were in three *s*, but had ... Eze 42:6
that buildeth his *s* in the heaven ... Amos 9:6

**STORK**
And the *s*, the heron after her ... Lev 11:19
And the *s*, and the heron after her ... Deut 14:18
as for the *s*, the fir trees are ... Ps 104:17
the *s* in the heaven knoweth her ... Jer 8:7
had wings like the wings of a *s* ... Zec 5:9

**STORM**
as chaff that the *s* carrieth away ... Job 21:18
as a *s* hurleth him out of his ... Job 27:21
hasten my escape from the windy *s* ... Ps 55:8
and make them afraid with thy *s* ... Ps 83:15
He maketh the *s* a calm, so that ... Ps 107:29
of refuge, and for a covert from *s* ... Is 4:6
his distress, a refuge from the *s* ... Is 25:4
ones is as a *s* against the wall ... Is 25:4
tempest of hail and a destroying *s* ... Is 28:2
and great noise, with *s* and ... Is 29:6
shalt ascend and come like a *s* ... Eze 38:9
way in the whirlwind and in the *s* ... Nah 1:3
And there arose a great *s* of wind ... Mk 4:37
there came down a *s* of wind on ... Lk 8:23

**STORMY**
commandeth, and raiseth the *s* wind ... Ps 107:25
*s* wind fulfilling his word ... Ps 148:8
and a *s* wind shall rend it ... Eze 13:11
rend it with a *s* wind in my fury ... Eze 13:13

**STORY**
are written in the *s* of the ... 2Chr 13:22
they are written in the *s* of the ... 2Chr 24:27

**STOUT**
the *s* lion's whelps are scattered ... Job 4:11
*s* heart of the king of Assyria ... Is 10:12
look was more *s* than his fellows ... Dan 7:20
Your words have been *s* against me ... Mal 3:13

**STOUTHEARTED**
The *s* are spoiled, they have ... Ps 76:5
Hearken unto me, ye *s*, that are ... Is 46:12

**STOUTNESS**
say in the pride and *s* of heart, ... Is 9:9

**STRAIGHT**
ascend up every man *s* before him ... Josh 6:5
every man *s* before him, and they ... Josh 6:20
the kine took the *s* way to the ... 1Sa 6:12
brought it *s* down to the west ... 2Chr 32:30
make thy way *s* before my face ... Ps 5:8
thine eyelids look *s* before thee ... Prov 4:25
which is crooked cannot be made *s* ... Eccl 1:15
for who can make that *s*, which he ... Eccl 7:13
make *s* in the desert a highway ... Is 40:3
and the crooked shall be made *s* ... Is 40:4
before them, and crooked things *s* ... Is 42:16
and make the crooked places *s* ... Is 45:2
the rivers of waters in a *s* way ... Jer 31:9
And their feet were *s* feet ... Eze 1:7
they went every one *s* forward ... Eze 1:9
And they went every one *s* forward ... Eze 1:12
the firmament were their wings *s* ... Eze 1:23
they went every one *s* forward ... Eze 10:22
way of the Lord, make his paths *s* ... Mt 3:3
way of the Lord, make his paths *s* ... Mk 1:3
way of the Lord, make his paths *s* ... Lk 3:4
and the crooked shall be made *s* ... Lk 3:5
and immediately she was made *s* ... Lk 13:13
Make *s* the way of the Lord, as ... Jn 1:23
into the street which is called *S* ... Acts 9:11
we came with a *s* course to ... Acts 16:11
we came with a *s* course unto Coos ... Acts 21:1
make *s* paths for your feet, lest ... Heb 12:13

**STRAIGHTWAY**
the city, ye shall *s* find him ... 1Sa 9:13
Then Saul fell *s* all along on the ... 1Sa 28:20
He goeth after her *s*, as an ox ... Prov 7:22
*s* there remained no strength in ... Dan 10:17
went up *s* out of the water ... Mt 3:16
they *s* left their nets, and ... Mt 4:20
And *s* Jesus constrained his ... Mt 14:22
But *s* Jesus spake unto them, ... Mt 14:27
*s* ye shall find an ass tied, and a ... Mt 21:2
and *s* he will send them ... Mt 21:3
and *s* took his journey ... Mt 25:15
*s* one of them ran, and took a ... Mt 27:48
*s* coming up out of the water, he ... Mk 1:10
*s* they forsook their nets, and ... Mk 1:18
And *s* he called them ... Mk 1:20
*s* on the sabbath day he entered ... Mk 1:21
*s* many were gathered together, ... Mk 2:2
*s* took counsel with the Herodians ... Mk 3:6
*s* the fountain of her blood was ... Mk 5:29
*s* the damsel arose, and walked ... Mk 5:42
she came in *s* with haste unto the ... Mk 6:25
*s* he constrained his disciples to ... Mk 6:45
out of the ship, *s* they knew him, ... Mk 6:54
*s* his ears were opened, and the ... Mk 7:35
*s* he entered into a ship with his ... Mk 8:10
*s* all the people, when they ... Mk 9:15
he saw him, *s* the spirit tare him ... Mk 9:20
*s* the father of the child cried ... Mk 9:24
*s* he will send him hither ... Mk 11:3
as he was come, he goeth *s* to him ... Mk 14:45
*s* in the morning the chief ... Mk 15:1
drunk old wine *s* desireth new ... Lk 5:39
spirit came again, and she arose *s* ... Lk 8:55
*s* ye say, There cometh a shower ... Lk 12:54
will not *s* pull him out on the ... Lk 14:5
himself, and shall *s* glorify him ... Jn 13:32
Then fell she down *s* at his feet ... Acts 5:10
*s* he preached Christ in the ... Acts 9:20
and was baptized, he and all his, *s* ... Acts 16:33
Then *s* they departed from him ... Acts 22:29
I sent *s* to thee, and gave ... Acts 23:30
*s* forgetteth what manner of man ... Jas 1:24

**STRAIN**
which *s* at a gnat, and swallow a ... Mt 23:24

**STRAIT**
Israel saw that they were in a *s* ... 1Sa 13:6
said unto Gad, I am in a great *s* ... 2Sa 24:14
dwell with thee is too *s* for us ... 2Kin 6:1
said unto Gad, I am in a great *s* ... 1Chr 21:13
out of the *s* into a broad place ... Job 36:16
ears, The place is too *s* for me ... Is 49:20
Enter ye in at the *s* gate ... Mt 7:13
Because *s* is the gate, and narrow ... Mt 7:14
Strive to enter in at the *s* gate ... Lk 13:24
For I am in a *s* betwixt two ... Phil 1:23

**STRAITEN**
seek their lives, shall *s* them ... Jer 19:9

**STRAITENED**
steps of his strength shall be *s* ... Job 18:7
and the breadth of the waters is *s* ... Job 37:10
goest, thy steps shall not be *s* ... Prov 4:12
was *s* more than the lowest ... Eze 42:6
is the spirit of the LORD *s* ... Mic 2:7
and how am I *s* till it be ... Lk 12:50
Ye are not *s* in us, but ye are ... 2Cor 6:12
but ye are *s* in your own bowels ... 2Cor 6:12

**STRAITENETH**
the nations, and *s* them again ... Job 12:23

**STRAITEST**
that after the most *s* sect of our ... Acts 26:5

**STRAITLY**
The man asked us *s* of our state ... Gen 43:7
for he had *s* sworn the children ... Ex 13:19
Now Jericho was *s* shut up because ... Josh 6:1
Thy father *s* charged the people ... 1Sa 14:28
Jesus *s* charged them, saying, See ... Mt 9:30
he *s* charged him, and forthwith ... Mk 1:43
he *s* charged them that they ... Mk 3:12
he charged them *s* that no man ... Mk 5:43
he *s* charged them, and commanded ... Lk 9:21
let us *s* threaten them, that they ... Acts 4:17
Did not we *s* command you that ye ... Acts 5:28

**STRAITNESS**
thee, in the siege, and in the *s* ... Deut 28:53
him in the siege, and in the *s* ... Deut 28:55
things secretly in the siege and *s* ... Deut 28:57
broad place, where there is no *s* ... Job 36:16
of his friend in the siege and *s* ... Jer 19:9

**STRAITS**
his sufficiency he shall be in *s* ... Job 20:22
overtook her between the *s* ... Lam 1:3

**STRAKE**
*s* sail, and so were driven ... Acts 27:17

**STRAKES**
and pilled white *s* in them ... Gen 30:37
walls of the house with hollow *s* ... Lev 14:37

**STRANGE**
Put away the *s* gods that are ... Gen 35:2
they gave unto Jacob all the *s* ... Gen 35:4
but made himself *s* unto them ... Gen 42:7
have been a stranger in a *s* land ... Ex 2:22
I have been an alien in a *s* land ... Ex 18:3
to sell her unto a *s* nation he ... Ex 21:8
shall offer no *s* incense thereon ... Ex 30:9
offered *s* fire before the LORD, ... Lev 10:1
when they offered *s* fire before ... Num 3:4
when they offered *s* fire before ... Num 26:61
and there was no *s* god with him ... Deut 32:12
him to jealousy with *s* gods ... Deut 32:16
forsake the LORD, and serve *s* gods ... Josh 24:20
the *s* gods which are among you, ... Josh 24:23
they put away the *s* gods from ... Judg 10:16
for thou art the son of a *s* woman ... Judg 11:2
hearts, then put away the *s* gods ... 1Sa 7:3
king Solomon loved many *s* women ... 1Kin 11:1
did he for all his *s* wives ... 1Kin 11:8
drunk *s* waters, and with the sole ... 2Kin 19:24
away the altars of the *s* gods ... 2Chr 14:3
And he took away the *s* gods ... 2Chr 33:15
have taken *s* wives of the people ... Ezr 10:2
and have taken *s* wives, to ... Ezr 10:10
of the land, and from the *s* wives ... Ezr 10:11
*s* wives in our cities come at ... Ezr 10:14
*s* wives by the first day of the ... Ezr 10:17
were found that had taken *s* wives ... Ezr 10:18
All these had taken *s* wives ... Ezr 10:44
our God in marrying *s* wives ... Neh 13:27
that ye make yourselves *s* to me ... Job 19:3
My breath is *s* to my wife ... Job 19:17
a *s* punishment to the workers of ... Job 31:3
out our hands to a *s* god ... Ps 44:20
There shall no *s* god be in thee ... Ps 81:9
shalt thou worship any *s* god ... Ps 81:9
Jacob from a people of *s* language ... Ps 114:1
sing the LORD's song in a *s* land ... Ps 137:4
from the hand of *s* children ... Ps 144:7
me from the hand of *s* children ... Ps 144:11
To deliver thee from the *s* woman ... Prov 2:16
For the lips of a *s* woman drop as ... Prov 5:3
son, be ravished with a *s* woman ... Prov 5:20
of the tongue of a *s* woman ... Prov 6:24
may keep thee from the *s* woman ... Prov 7:5
a pledge of him for a *s* woman ... Prov 20:16
The way of man is froward and *s* ... Prov 21:8
The mouth of *s* women is a deep ... Prov 22:14
a *s* woman is a narrow pit ... Prov 23:27
Thine eyes shall behold *s* women ... Prov 23:33
a pledge of him for a *s* woman ... Prov 27:13
and shalt set it with *s* slips ... Is 17:10
he may do his work, his *s* work ... Is 28:21
bring to pass his act, his *s* act ... Is 28:21
when there was no *s* god among you ... Is 43:12
plant of a *s* vine unto me ... Jer 2:21
served *s* gods in your land, so ... Jer 5:19
graven images, and with *s* vanities ... Jer 8:19
sent to a people of a *s* speech ... Eze 3:5
Not to many people of a *s* speech ... Eze 3:6
most strong holds with a *s* god ... Dan 11:39
for they have begotten *s* children ... Hos 5:7
they were counted as a *s* thing ... Hos 8:12
as are clothed with *s* apparel ... Zeph 1:8
married the daughter of a *s* god ... Mal 2:11
We have seen *s* things to day ... Lk 5:26
seed should sojourn in a *s* land ... Acts 7:6
to be a setter forth of *s* gods ... Acts 17:18
certain *s* things to our ears ... Acts 17:20
them even unto *s* cities ... Acts 26:11
of promise, as in a *s* country ... Heb 11:9
about with divers and *s* doctrines ... Heb 13:9
Wherein they think it *s* that ye ... 1Pet 4:4
think it not *s* concerning the ... 1Pet 4:12
as though some *s* thing happened ... 1Pet 4:12
and going after *s* flesh, are set ... Jude 7

**STRANGELY**
should behave themselves *s* ... Deut 32:27

**STRANGER**
a *s* in a land that is not theirs ... Gen 15:13
the land wherein thou art a *s* ... Gen 17:8
or bought with money of any *s* ... Gen 17:12
and bought with money of the *s* ... Gen 17:27
I am a *s* and a sojourner with you ... Gen 23:4
the land wherein thou art a *s* ... Gen 28:4
land wherein his father was a *s* ... Gen 37:1
I have been a *s* in a strange land ... Ex 2:22
of Israel, whether he be a *s* ... Ex 12:19
There shall no *s* eat thereof ... Ex 12:43
when a *s* shall sojourn with thee, ... Ex 12:48
unto the *s* that sojourneth among ... Ex 12:49
nor thy *s* that is within thy ... Ex 20:10
Thou shalt neither vex a *s* ... Ex 22:21
Also thou shalt not oppress a *s* ... Ex 23:9
for ye know the heart of a *s* ... Ex 23:9
the son of thy handmaid, and the *s* ... Ex 23:12
but a *s* shall not eat thereof, ... Ex 29:33
putteth any of it upon a *s* ... Ex 30:33
or a *s* that sojourneth among you ... Lev 16:29
blood, neither shall any *s* that ... Lev 17:12
one of your own country, or a *s* ... Lev 17:15
nor any *s* that sojourneth among ... Lev 18:26
leave them for the poor and *s* ... Lev 19:10
if a *s* sojourn with thee in your ... Lev 19:33
But the *s* that dwelleth with you ... Lev 19:34
There shall no *s* eat of the holy ... Lev 22:10
daughter also be married unto a *s* ... Lev 22:12
but there shall no *s* eat thereof ... Lev 22:13
them unto the poor, and to the *s* ... Lev 23:22
as well the *s*, as he that is born ... Lev 24:16
manner of law, as well for the *s* ... Lev 24:22
for thy *s* that sojourneth with ... Lev 25:6
yea, though he be a *s*, or a ... Lev 25:35
a sojourner or *s* wax rich by thee ... Lev 25:47
unto the *s* or sojourner by thee ... Lev 25:47
the *s* that cometh nigh shall be ... Num 1:51
the *s* that cometh nigh shall be ... Num 3:10
the *s* that cometh nigh shall be ... Num 3:38
if a *s* shall sojourn among you, ... Num 9:14
one ordinance, both for the *s* ... Num 9:14
if a *s* sojourn with you, or ... Num 15:14
also for the *s* that sojourneth ... Num 15:15
so shall the *s* be before the LORD ... Num 15:15
for the *s* that sojourneth with ... Num 15:16
the *s* that sojourneth among them ... Num 15:26
for the *s* that sojourneth among ... Num 15:29
he be born in the land, or a *s* ... Num 15:30
the children of Israel, that no *s* ... Num 16:40
a *s* shall not come nigh unto you ... Num 18:4
the *s* that cometh nigh shall be ... Num 18:7
unto the *s* that sojourneth among ... Num 19:10
children of Israel, and for the *s* ... Num 35:15
and the *s* that is with him ... Deut 1:16
nor thy *s* that is within thy ... Deut 5:14
and widow, and loveth the *s* ... Deut 10:18
Love ye therefore the *s* ... Deut 10:19
unto the *s* that is in thy gates ... Deut 14:21
inheritance with thee,) and the *s* ... Deut 14:29
is within thy gates, and the *s* ... Deut 16:11
maidservant, and the Levite, the *s* ... Deut 16:14
thou mayest not set a *s* over thee ... Deut 17:15
because thou wast a *s* in his land ... Deut 23:7
Unto a *s* thou mayest lend upon ... Deut 23:20
not pervert the judgment of the *s* ... Deut 24:17
it shall be for the *s*, for the ... Deut 24:19
it shall be for the *s*, for the ... Deut 24:20
it shall be for the *s*, for the ... Deut 24:21
shall not marry without unto a *s* ... Deut 25:5
and the *s* that is among you ... Deut 26:11
given it unto the Levite, the *s* ... Deut 26:12

unto the Levite, and unto the *s* Deut 26:13
perverteth the judgment of the *s* Deut 27:19
The *s* that is within thee shall Deut 28:43
thy *s* that is in thy camp, from Deut 29:11
the *s* that shall come from a far Deut 29:22
thy *s* that is within thy gates, Deut 31:12
of the LORD, as well the *s* Josh 8:33
for the *s* that sojourneth among Josh 20:9
aside hither into the city of a *s* Judg 19:12
knowledge of me, seeing I am a *s* Ruth 2:10
he answered, I am the son of a *s* 2Sa 1:13
for thou art a *s*, and also an 2Sa 15:19
there was no *s* with us in the 1Kin 3:18
Moreover concerning a *s*, that is 1Kin 8:41
that the *s* calleth to thee for 1Kin 8:43
Moreover concerning the *s* 2Chr 6:32
that the *s* calleth to thee for 2Chr 6:33
given, and no *s* passed among them Job 15:19
and my maids, count me for a *s* Job 19:15
The *s* did not lodge in the street Job 31:32
for I am a *s* with thee, and a Ps 39:12
I am become a *s* unto my brethren, Ps 69:8
They slay the widow and the *s* Ps 94:6
I am a *s* in the earth Ps 119:19
even from the *s* which flattereth Prov 2:16
labours be in the house of a *s* Prov 5:10
and embrace the bosom of a *s* Prov 5:20
hast stricken thy hand with a *s* Prov 6:1
from the *s* which flattereth with Prov 7:5
surety for a *s* shall smart for it Prov 11:15
a *s* doth not intermeddle with his Prov 14:10
garment that is surety for a *s* Prov 20:16
a *s*, and not thine own lips Prov 27:2
garment that is surety for a *s* Prov 27:13
to eat thereof, but a *s* eateth it Eccl 6:2
Neither let the son of the *s* Is 56:3
Also the sons of the *s*, that join Is 56:6
the sons of the *s* shall not drink Is 62:8
If ye oppress not the *s*, the Jer 7:6
thou be as a *s* in the land Jer 14:8
no wrong, do no violence to the *s* Jer 22:3
or of the *s* that sojourneth in Eze 14:7
dealt by oppression with the *s* Eze 22:7
have oppressed the *s* wrongfully Eze 22:29
No *s*, uncircumcised in heart, nor Eze 44:9
of any *s* that is among the Eze 44:9
in what tribe the *s* sojourneth Eze 47:23
in the day that he became a *s* Obad 12
widow, nor the fatherless, the *s* Zec 7:10
turn aside the *s* from his right Mal 3:5
I was a *s*, and ye took me in Mt 25:35
When saw we thee a *s*, and took Mt 25:38
I was a *s*, and ye took me not in Mt 25:43
an hungred, or athirst, or a *s* Mt 25:44
to give glory to God, save this *s* Lk 17:18
Art thou only a *s* in Jerusalem Lk 24:18
a *s* will they not follow, but Jn 10:5
was a *s* in the land of Madian, Acts 7:29

**STRANGER'S**
Neither from a *s* hand shall ye Lev 22:25
or to the stock of the *s* family Lev 25:47

**STRANGERS**
Are we not counted of him *s* Gen 31:15
the land wherein they were *s* Gen 36:7
pilgrimage, wherein they were *s* Ex 6:4
for ye were *s* in the land of Ex 22:21
seeing ye were *s* in the land of Ex 23:9
or of the *s* which sojourn among Lev 17:8
or of the *s* that sojourn among Lev 17:10
or of the *s* that sojourn among Lev 17:13
for ye were *s* in the land of Lev 19:34
or of the *s* that sojourn in Lev 20:2
of Israel, or of the *s* in Israel Lev 22:18
for ye are *s* and sojourners with Lev 25:23
the *s* that do sojourn among you Lev 25:45
for ye were *s* in the land of Deut 10:19
or of thy *s* that are in thy land Deut 24:14
the gods of the *s* of the land Deut 31:16
the *s* that were conversant among Josh 8:35
*S* shall submit themselves unto me 2Sa 22:45
*S* shall fade away, and they shall 2Sa 22:46
but few, even a few, and *s* in it 1Chr 16:19
to gather together the *s* that 1Chr 22:2
For we are *s* before thee, and 1Chr 29:15
Solomon numbered all the *s* that 2Chr 2:17
the *s* with them out of Ephraim and 2Chr 15:9
the *s* that came out of the land 2Chr 30:25
separated themselves from all *s* Neh 9:2
Thus cleansed I them from all *s* Neh 13:30
the *s* shall submit themselves Ps 18:44
The *s* shall fade away, and be Ps 18:45
For *s* are risen up against me, and Ps 54:3
yea, very few, and *s* in it Ps 105:12
let the *s* spoil his labour Ps 109:11
The LORD preserveth the *s* Ps 146:9
Lest *s* be filled with thy wealth Prov 5:10
*s* devour it in your presence, and Is 1:7
is desolate, as overthrown by *s* Is 1:7
themselves in the children of *s* Is 2:6
of the fat ones shall *s* eat Is 5:17
the *s* shall be joined with them, Is 14:1
a palace of *s* to be no city Is 25:2
shalt bring down the noise of *s* Is 25:5
of thy *s* shall be like small dust Is 29:5
the sons of *s* shall build up thy Is 60:10
*s* shall stand and feed your flocks Is 61:5
for I have loved *s*, and after them Jer 2:25
to the *s* under every green tree Jer 3:13
so shall ye serve *s* in a land Jer 5:19
*s* shall no more serve themselves Jer 30:8
days in the land where ye be *s* Jer 35:7
for *s* are come into the Jer 51:51
Our inheritance is turned to *s* Lam 5:2
the hands of the *s* for a prey Eze 7:21
deliver you into the hands of *s* Eze 11:9
which taketh *s* instead of her Eze 16:32
I will bring *s* upon thee, the Eze 28:7
uncircumcised by the hand of *s* Eze 28:10
that is therein, by the hand of *s* Eze 30:12
And *s*, the terrible of the nations Eze 31:12
have brought into my sanctuary *s* Eze 44:7
to the *s* that sojourn among you, Eze 47:22
*S* have devoured his strength, and Hos 7:9
the *s* shall swallow it up Hos 8:7
there shall no *s* pass through her Joel 3:17
in the day that the *s* carried Obad 11
of their own children, or of *s* Mt 17:25
Peter saith unto him, Of *s* Mt 17:26
the potter's field, to bury *s* in Mt 27:7
for they know not the voice of *s* Jn 10:5
*s* of Rome, Jews and proselytes, Acts 2:10
dwelt as *s* in the land of Egypt Acts 13:17
*s* which were there spent their Acts 17:21
*s* from the covenants of promise, Eph 2:12
Now therefore ye are no more *s* Eph 2:19
up children, if she have lodged *s* 1Ti 5:10
and confessed that they were *s* Heb 11:13
Be not forgetful to entertain *s* Heb 13:2
to the *s* scattered throughout 1Pet 1:1
beloved, I beseech you as *s* 1Pet 2:11
doest to the brethren, and to *s* 3Jn 5

**STRANGERS'**
thine own, and not *s* with thee Prov 5:17

**STRANGLED**
*s* for his lionesses, and filled Nah 2:12
fornication, and from things *s* Acts 15:20
and from blood, and from things *s* Acts 15:29
idols, and from blood, and from *s* Acts 21:25

**STRANGLING**
So that my soul chooseth *s* Job 7:15

**STRAW**
moreover unto him, We have both *s* Gen 24:25
he ungirded his camels, and gave *s* Gen 24:32
give the people *s* to make brick Ex 5:7
go and gather *s* for themselves Ex 5:7
Pharaoh, I will not give you *s* Ex 5:10
get you *s* where ye can find it Ex 5:11
to gather stubble instead of *s* Ex 5:12
daily tasks, as when there was *s* Ex 5:13
There is no *s* given unto thy Ex 5:16
for there shall no *s* be given you Ex 5:18
Yet there is both *s* and provender Judg 19:19
*s* for the horses and dromedaries 1Kin 4:28
He esteemeth iron as *s*, and brass Job 41:27
the lion shall eat *s* like the ox Is 11:7
even as *s* is trodden down for the Is 25:10
lion shall eat *s* like the bullock Is 65:25

**STRAWED**
*s* it upon the water, and made the Ex 32:20
the trees, and *s* them in the way Mt 21:8
gathering where thou hast not *s* Mt 25:24
not, and gather where I have not *s* Mt 25:26
the trees, and *s* them in the way Mk 11:8

**STREAM**
at the *s* of the brooks that goeth Num 21:15
as the *s* of brooks they pass away Job 6:15
the *s* had gone over our soul Ps 124:4
of the river unto the *s* of Egypt Is 27:12
his breath, as an overflowing *s* Is 30:28
like a *s* of brimstone, doth Is 30:33
stones of the *s* is thy portion Is 57:6
of the Gentiles like a flowing *s* Is 66:12
A fiery *s* issued and came forth Dan 7:10
and righteousness as a mighty *s* Amos 5:24
the *s* beat vehemently upon that Lk 6:48
against which the *s* did beat Lk 6:49

**STREAMS**
the waters of Egypt, upon their *s* Ex 7:19
hand with thy rod over the *s* Ex 8:5
the *s* whereof shall make glad the Ps 46:4
He brought *s* also out of the rock Ps 78:16
gushed out, and the *s* overflowed Ps 78:20
O LORD, as the *s* in the south Ps 126:4
living waters, and *s* from Lebanon Song 4:15
and shall smite it in the seven *s* Is 11:15
*s* of waters in the day of the Is 30:25
us a place of broad rivers and *s* Is 33:21
the *s* thereof shall be turned Is 34:9
break out, and *s* in the desert Is 35:6

**STREET**
we will abide in the *s* all night Gen 19:2
into the midst of the *s* thereof Deut 13:16
the doors of thy house into the *s* Josh 2:19
sat him down in a *s* of the city Judg 19:15
man in the *s* of the city Judg 19:17
only lodge not in the *s* Judg 19:20
them from the *s* of Beth-shan 2Sa 21:12
stamp them as the mire of the *s* 2Sa 22:43
them together into the east *s* 2Chr 29:4
in the *s* of the gate of the city 2Chr 32:6
sat in the *s* of the house of God Ezr 10:9
together as one man into the *s* Neh 8:1
he read therein before the *s* that Neh 8:3
in the *s* of the water gate, and in Neh 8:16
in the *s* of the gate of Ephraim Neh 8:16
Mordecai unto the *s* of the city Est 4:6
through the *s* of the city Est 6:9
through the *s* of the city Est 6:11
and he shall have no name in the *s* Job 18:17
when I prepared my seat in the *s* Job 29:7
stranger did not lodge in the *s* Job 31:32
through the *s* near her corner Prov 7:8
his voice to be heard in the *s* Is 42:2
body as the ground, and as the *s* Is 51:23
for truth is fallen in the *s* Is 59:14
of bread out of the bakers' *s* Jer 37:21
for hunger in the top of every *s* Lam 2:19
poured out in the top of every *s* Lam 4:1
thee an high place in every *s* Eze 16:24
thine high place in every *s* Eze 16:31
pestilence, and blood into her *s* Eze 28:23
the *s* shall be built again, and Dan 9:25
go into the *s* which is called Acts 9:11
out, and passed on through one *s* Acts 12:10
lie in the *s* of the great city Rev 11:8
the *s* of the city was pure gold, Rev 21:21
In the midst of the *s* of it Rev 22:2

**STREETS**
it not in the *s* of Askelon 2Sa 1:20
thou shalt make *s* for thee in 1Kin 20:34
them out as the dirt in the *s* Ps 18:42
and guile depart not from her *s* Ps 55:11
and ten thousands in our *s* Ps 144:13
there be no complaining in our *s* Ps 144:14
she uttereth her voice in the *s* Prov 1:20
and rivers of waters in the *s* Prov 5:16
Now is she without, now in the *s* Prov 7:12
I shall be slain in the *s* Prov 22:13
a lion is in the *s* Prov 26:13
the doors shall be shut in the *s* Eccl 12:4
and the mourners go about the *s* Eccl 12:5
and go about the city in the *s* Song 3:2
were torn in the midst of the *s* Is 5:25
them down like the mire of the *s* Is 10:6
In their *s* they shall gird Is 15:3
of their houses, and in their *s* Is 15:3
is a crying for wine in the *s* Is 24:11
they lie at the head of all the *s* Is 51:20
and fro through the *s* of Jerusalem Jer 5:1
of Judah and in the *s* of Jerusalem Jer 7:17
from the *s* of Jerusalem, the Jer 7:34
and the young men from the *s* Jer 9:21
in the *s* of Jerusalem, saying, Jer 11:6
the *s* of Jerusalem have ye set up Jer 11:13
shall be cast out in the *s* of Jer 14:16
in the *s* of Jerusalem, that are Jer 33:10
of Judah and in the *s* of Jerusalem Jer 44:6
Judah, and in the *s* of Jerusalem Jer 44:9
Judah, and in the *s* of Jerusalem Jer 44:17
in the *s* of Jerusalem, ye, and Jer 44:21
of Moab, and in the *s* thereof Jer 48:38
her young men shall fall in her *s* Jer 49:26
shall her young men fall in the *s* Jer 50:30
that are thrust through in her *s* Jer 51:4
swoon in the *s* of the city Lam 2:11
the wounded in the *s* of the city Lam 2:12
old lie on the ground in the *s* Lam 2:21
delicately are desolate in the *s* Lam 4:5
they are not known in the *s* Lam 4:8
wandered as blind men in the *s* Lam 4:14
steps, that we cannot go in our *s* Lam 4:18
shall cast their silver in the *s* Eze 7:19
ye have filled the *s* thereof with Eze 11:6
shall he tread down all thy *s* Eze 26:11
Wailing shall be in all *s* Amos 5:16
trodden down as the mire of the *s* Mic 7:10
The chariots shall rage in the *s* Nah 2:4
in pieces at the top of all the *s* Nah 3:10
I made their *s* waste, that none Zeph 3:6
women dwell in the *s* of Jerusalem Zec 8:4
the *s* of the city shall be full Zec 8:5
and girls playing in the *s* thereof Zec 8:5
and fine gold as the mire of the *s* Zec 9:3
the mire of the *s* in the battle Zec 10:5
do in the synagogues and in the *s* Mt 6:2
and in the corners of the *s* Mt 6:5
any man hear his voice in the *s* Mt 12:19
they laid the sick in the *s* Mk 6:56
ways out into the *s* of the same Lk 10:10
and thou hast taught in our *s* Lk 13:26
Go out quickly into the *s* Lk 14:21
brought forth the sick into the *s* Acts 5:15

**STRENGTH**
henceforth yield unto thee her *s* Gen 4:12
might, and the beginning of my *s* Gen 49:3
But his bow abode in *s*, and the Gen 49:24
for by *s* of hand the LORD brought Ex 13:3
By *s* of hand the LORD brought us Ex 13:14
for by *s* of hand the LORD brought Ex 13:16
the sea returned to his *s* when Ex 14:27
The LORD is my *s* and song, and he Ex 15:2
in thy *s* unto thy holy habitation Ex 15:13
your *s* shall be spent in vain Lev 26:20
as it were the *s* of a unicorn Num 23:22
as it were the *s* of a unicorn Num 24:8
for he is the beginning of his *s* Deut 21:17
and as thy days, so shall thy *s* be Deut 33:25
that stood still in their *s* Josh 11:13
as my *s* was then, even so is my Josh 14:11
was then, even so is my *s* now Josh 14:11
my soul, thou hast trodden down *s* Judg 5:21
for as the man is, so is his *s* Judg 8:21
and see wherein his great *s* lieth Judg 16:5
thee, wherein thy great *s* lieth Judg 16:6

So his s was not known Judg 16:9
told me wherein thy great s lieth Judg 16:15
then my s will go from me, and I Judg 16:17
him, and his s went from him Judg 16:19
that stumbled are girded with s 1Sa 2:4
for by s shall no man prevail 1Sa 2:9
and he shall give s unto his king 1Sa 2:10
also the S of Israel will not lie 1Sa 15:29
and there was no s in him 1Sa 28:20
and eat, that thou mayest have s 1Sa 28:22
God is my s and power 2Sa 22:33
hast girded me with s to battle 2Sa 22:40
went in the s of that meat forty 1Kin 19:8
Jehu drew a bow with his full s 2Kin 9:24
I have counsel and s for the war 2Kin 18:20
there is not s to bring forth 2Kin 19:3
Seek the LORD and his s, seek his 1Chr 16:11
s and gladness are in his place 1Chr 16:27
give unto the LORD glory and s 1Chr 16:28
able men for s for the service, 1Chr 26:8
make great, and to give s unto all 1Chr 29:12
place, thou, and the ark of thy s 2Chr 6:41
s again in the days of Abijah 2Chr 13:20
The s of the bearers of burdens Neh 4:10
for the joy of the LORD is your s Neh 8:10
What is my s, that I should hope Job 6:11
Is my s the s of stones Job 6:12
is wise in heart, and mighty in s Job 9:4
If I speak of s, lo, he is strong Job 9:19
With him is wisdom and s, he hath Job 12:13
With him is s and wisdom Job 12:16
and weakeneth the s of the mighty Job 12:21
The steps of his s shall be Job 18:7
His s shall be hungerbitten, and Job 18:12
It shall devour the s of his skin Job 18:13
of death shall devour his s Job 18:13
One dieth in his full s, being Job 21:23
but he would put s in me Job 23:6
thou the arm that hath no s Job 26:2
whereto might the s of their Job 30:2
he is mighty in s and wisdom Job 36:5
not gold, nor all the forces of s Job 36:19
and to the great rain of his s Job 37:6
trust him, because his s is great Job 39:11
Hath thou given the horse s Job 39:19
the valley, and rejoiceth in his s Job 39:21
his s is in his loins, and his Job 40:16
In his neck remaineth s, and Job 41:22
s because of thine enemies Ps 8:2
I will love thee, O LORD, my s Ps 18:1
my God, my s, in whom I will Ps 18:2
It is God that girdeth me with s Ps 18:32
girded me with s unto the battle Ps 18:39
in thy sight, O LORD, my s Ps 19:14
the saving s of his right hand Ps 20:6
The king shall joy in thy s Ps 21:1
exalted, LORD, in thine own s Ps 21:13
My s is dried up like a potsherd Ps 22:15
O my s, haste thee to help me Ps 22:19
the LORD is the s of my life Ps 27:1
The LORD is my s and my shield Ps 28:7
The LORD is their s, and he is the Ps 28:8
is the saving s of his anointed Ps 28:8
give unto the LORD glory and s Ps 29:1
LORD will give s unto his people Ps 29:11
for thou art my s Ps 31:4
my s faileth because of mine Ps 31:10
man is not delivered by much s Ps 33:16
he deliver any by his great s Ps 33:17
he is their s in the time of Ps 37:39
My heart panteth, my s faileth me Ps 38:10
O spare me, that I may recover s Ps 39:13
For thou art the God of my s Ps 43:2
God is our refuge and s, a very Ps 46:1
the man that made not God his s Ps 52:7
by thy name, and judge me by thy s Ps 54:1
Because of his s will I wait upon Ps 59:9
Unto thee, O my s, will I sing Ps 59:17
also is the s of mine head Ps 60:7
the rock of my s, and my refuge, Ps 62:7
Which by his s setteth fast the Ps 65:6
Thy God hath commanded thy s Ps 68:28
Ascribe ye s unto God Ps 68:34
Israel, and his s is in the clouds Ps 68:34
God of Israel is he that giveth s Ps 68:35
forsake me not when my s faileth Ps 71:9
will go in the s of the Lord GOD Ps 71:16
shewed thy s unto this generation Ps 71:18
but their s is firm Ps 73:4
but God is the s of my heart Ps 73:26
didst divide the sea by thy s Ps 74:13
declared thy s among the people Ps 77:14
the praises of the LORD, and his s Ps 78:4
the chief of their s in the Ps 78:51
delivered his s into captivity, Ps 78:61
and Manasseh stir up thy s Ps 80:2
Sing aloud unto God our s Ps 81:1
is the man whose s is in thee Ps 84:5
They go from s to s Ps 84:7
give thy s unto thy servant, and Ps 86:16
I am as a man that hath no s Ps 88:4
For thou art the glory of their s Ps 89:17
if by reason of s they be Ps 90:10
years, yet is their s labour Ps 90:10
the LORD is clothed with s Ps 93:1
the s of the hills is his also Ps 95:4
s and beauty are in his sanctuary Ps 96:6
give unto the LORD glory and s Ps 96:7
The king's s also loveth judgment Ps 99:4
He weakened my s in the way Ps 102:23
ye his angels, that excel in s Ps 103:20
Seek the LORD, and his s Ps 105:4
land, the chief of all their s Ps 105:36
also is the s of mine head Ps 108:8
send the rod of thy s out of Zion Ps 110:2
The LORD is my s and song, and is Ps 118:14
thou, and the ark of thy s Ps 132:8
me with s in my soul Ps 138:3
the s of my salvation, thou hast Ps 140:7
Blessed be the LORD my s, which Ps 144:1
not in the s of the horse Ps 147:10
I have s Prov 8:14
of the LORD is s to the upright Prov 10:29
increase is by the s of the ox Prov 14:4
The glory of young men is their s Prov 20:29
casteth down the s of the Prov 21:22
a man of knowledge increaseth s Prov 24:5
day of adversity, thy s is small Prov 24:10
Give not thy s unto women Prov 31:3
She girdeth her loins with s Prov 31:17
S and honour are her clothing Prov 31:25
said I, Wisdom is better than s Eccl 9:16
edge, then must he put to more s Eccl 10:10
princes eat in due season, for s Eccl 10:17
men of s to mingle strong drink Is 5:22
By the s of my hand I have done Is 10:13
for the LORD JEHOVAH is my s Is 12:2
been mindful of the rock of thy s Is 17:10
even the s of the sea, saying, I Is 23:4
there is no more s Is 23:10
for your s is laid waste Is 23:14
thou hast been a s to the poor Is 25:4
a s to the needy in his distress, Is 25:4
the LORD JEHOVAH is everlasting s Is 26:4
Or let him take hold of my s Is 27:5
for s to them that turn the Is 28:6
themselves in the s of Pharaoh Is 30:2
Therefore shall the s of Pharaoh Is 30:3
this, Their s is to sit still Is 30:7
and in confidence shall be your s Is 30:15
of thy times, and s of salvation Is 33:6
I have counsel and s for war Is 36:5
there is not s to bring forth Is 37:3
tidings, lift up thy voice with s Is 40:9
have no might he increaseth s Is 40:29
upon the LORD shall renew their s Is 40:31
and let the people renew their s Is 41:1
of his anger, and the s of battle Is 42:25
worketh it with the s of his arms Is 44:12
he is hungry, and his s faileth Is 44:12
LORD have I righteousness and s Is 45:24
I have spent my s for nought Is 49:4
the LORD, and my God shall be my s Is 49:5
Awake, awake, put on s, O arm of Is 51:9
put on thy s, O Zion Is 52:1
hand, and by the arm of his s Is 62:8
in the greatness of his s Is 63:1
bring down their s to the earth Is 63:6
where is thy zeal and thy s Is 63:15
O LORD, my s, and my fortress, and Jer 16:19
deliver all the s of this city Jer 20:5
fortify the height of her s Jer 51:53
gone without s before the pursuer Lam 1:6
he hath made my s to fall Lam 1:14
And I said, My s and my hope is Lam 3:18
the excellency of your s Eze 24:21
day when I take from them their s Eze 24:25
my fury upon Sin, the s of Egypt Eze 30:15
the pomp of her s shall cease in Eze 30:18
and the pomp of her s shall cease Eze 33:28
given thee a kingdom, power, and s Dan 2:37
be in it of the s of the iron Dan 2:41
and there remained no s in me Dan 10:8
corruption, and I retained no s Dan 10:8
upon me, and I have retained no s Dan 10:16
there remained no s in me Dan 10:17
by his s through his riches he Dan 11:2
shall there be any s to withstand Dan 11:15
with the s of his whole kingdom Dan 11:17
shall pollute the sanctuary of s Dan 11:31
Strangers have devoured his s Hos 7:9
by his s he had power with God Hos 12:3
tree and the vine do yield their s Joel 2:22
the s of the children of Israel Joel 3:16
shall bring down thy s from thee Amos 3:11
taken to us horns by our own s Amos 6:13
and feed in the s of the LORD Mic 5:4
Ethiopia and Egypt were her s Nah 3:9
shalt seek s because of the enemy Nah 3:11
The LORD God is my s, and he will Hab 3:19
I will destroy the s of the Hag 2:22
of Jerusalem shall be my s in the Zec 12:5
all thy mind, and with all thy s Mk 12:30
all the soul, and with all the s Mk 12:33
He hath shewed s with his arm Lk 1:51
all thy soul, and with all thy s Lk 10:27
feet and ancle bones received s Acts 3:7
But Saul increased the more in s Acts 9:22
For when we were yet without s Rom 5:6
and the s of sin is the law 1Cor 15:56
pressed out of measure, above s 2Cor 1:8
for my s is made perfect in 2Cor 12:9
otherwise it is of no s at all Heb 9:17
received s to conceive seed Heb 11:11
was as the sun shineth in his s Rev 1:16
for thou hast a little s, and hast Rev 3:8
power, and riches, and wisdom, and s Rev 5:12
Now is come salvation, and s Rev 12:10
their power and s unto the beast Rev 17:13

## STRENGTHEN

and encourage him, and s him Deut 3:28
s me, I pray thee, only this once Judg 16:28
s thyself, and mark, and see what 1Kin 20:22
to s their hands in the work of Ezr 6:22
Now therefore, O God, s my hands Neh 6:9
But I would s you with my mouth, Job 16:5
sanctuary, and s thee out of Zion Ps 20:2
and he shall s thine heart Ps 27:14
he shall s your heart, all ye Ps 31:24
The LORD will s him upon the bed Ps 41:3
s, O God, that which thou hast Ps 68:28
mine arm also shall s him Ps 89:21
s thou me according unto thy word Ps 119:28
s him with thy girdle, and I will Is 22:21
to s themselves in the strength Is 30:2
they could not well s their mast Is 33:23
S ye the weak hands, and confirm Is 35:3
I will s thee Is 41:10
thy cords, and s thy stakes Is 54:2
they s also the hands of Jer 23:14
neither shall any s himself in Eze 7:13
neither did she s the hand of the Eze 16:49
I will s the arms of the king of Eze 30:24
But I will s the arms of the king Eze 30:25
will s that which was sick Eze 34:16
I, stood to confirm and to s him Dan 11:1
the strong shall not s his force Amos 2:14
I will s the house of Judah, and I Zec 10:6
I will s them in the LORD Zec 10:12
art converted, s thy brethren Lk 22:32
make you perfect, stablish, s 1Pet 5:10
s the things which remain, that Rev 3:2

## STRENGTHENED

Israel s himself, and sat upon the Gen 48:2
the LORD s Eglon the king of Moab Judg 3:12
be s to go down unto the host Judg 7:11
the wood, and s his hand in God 1Sa 23:16
Therefore now let your hands be s 2Sa 2:7
who s themselves with him in his 1Chr 11:10
son of David was s in his kingdom 2Chr 1:1
So they s the kingdom of Judah, 2Chr 11:17
had s himself, he forsook the law 2Chr 12:1
So king Rehoboam s himself in 2Chr 12:13
have s themselves against 2Chr 13:7
and s himself against Israel 2Chr 17:1
he s himself, and slew all his 2Chr 21:4
seventh year Jehoiada s himself 2Chr 23:1
of God in his state, and s it 2Chr 24:13
And Amaziah s himself, and led 2Chr 25:11
for he s himself exceedingly 2Chr 26:8
and distressed him, but s him not 2Chr 28:20
Also he s himself, and built up 2Chr 32:5
s their hands with vessels of Ezr 1:6
I was s as the hand of the LORD Ezr 7:28
So they s their hands for this Neh 2:18
thou hast s the weak hands Job 4:3
thou hast s the feeble knees Job 4:4
s himself in his wickedness Ps 52:7
For he hath s the bars of thy Ps 147:13
when he s the fountains of the Prov 8:28
s the hands of the wicked, that Eze 13:22
The diseased have ye not s Eze 34:4
appearance of a man, and he s me Dan 10:18
he had spoken unto me, I was s Dan 10:19
for thou hast s me Dan 10:19
he that s her in these times Dan 11:6
but he shall not be s by it Dan 11:12
s their arms, yet do they imagine Hos 7:15
he had received meat, he was s Acts 9:19
to be s with might by his Spirit Eph 3:16
S with all might, according to Col 1:11
the Lord stood with me, and s me 2Ti 4:17

## STRENGTHENEDST

s me with strength in my soul Ps 138:3

## STRENGTHENETH

s himself against the Almighty Job 15:25
and bread which s man's heart Ps 104:15
with strength, and s her arms Prov 31:17
Wisdom s the wise more than ten Eccl 7:19
which he s for himself among the Is 44:14
That s the spoiled against the Amos 5:9
things through Christ which s me Phil 4:13

## STRENGTHENING

angel unto him from heaven, s him Lk 22:43
in order, s all the disciples Acts 18:23

## STRETCH

I will s out my hand, and smite Ex 3:20
when I s forth mine hand upon Ex 7:5
s out thine hand upon the waters Ex 7:19
S forth thine hand with thy rod Ex 8:5
S out thy rod, and smite the dust Ex 8:16
For now I will s out my hand Ex 9:15
S forth thine hand toward heaven, Ex 9:22
S out thine hand over the land of Ex 10:12
S out thine hand toward heaven, Ex 10:21
s out thine hand over the sea, and Ex 14:16
S out thine hand over the sea, Ex 14:26
the cherubim shall s forth their Ex 25:20
S out the spear that is in thy Josh 8:18
to s forth mine hand against him, 1Sa 24:6
for who can s forth his hand 1Sa 26:9
s forth mine hand against the 1Sa 26:11
but I would not s forth mine hand 1Sa 26:23
How wast thou not afraid to s 2Sa 1:14
I will s over Jerusalem the line 2Kin 21:13
s out thine hands toward him Job 11:13
Howbeit he will not s out his Job 30:24

*s* her wings toward the south ... Job 39:26
Ethiopia shall soon *s* out her ... Ps 68:31
thou shalt *s* forth thine hand ... Ps 138:7
I *s* forth my hands unto thee ... Ps 143:6
that a man can *s* himself on it ... Is 28:20
the LORD shall *s* out his hand ... Is 31:3
he shall *s* out upon it the line ... Is 34:11
let them *s* forth the curtains of ... Is 54:2
for I will *s* out my hand upon the ... Jer 6:12
there is none to *s* forth my tent ... Jer 10:20
therefore will I *s* out my hand ... Jer 15:6
I will *s* out mine hand upon thee, ... Jer 51:25
So will I *s* out my hand upon them ... Eze 6:14
I will *s* out my hand upon him, and ... Eze 14:9
then will I *s* out mine hand upon ... Eze 14:13
therefore I will *s* out mine hand ... Eze 25:7
I will also *s* out mine hand upon ... Eze 25:13
I will *s* out mine hand upon the ... Eze 25:16
he shall *s* it out upon the land ... Eze 30:25
I will *s* out mine hand against ... Eze 35:3
He shall *s* forth his hand also ... Dan 11:42
*s* themselves upon their couches, ... Amos 6:4
I will also *s* out mine hand upon ... Zeph 1:4
he will *s* out his hand against ... Zeph 2:13
he to the man, *S* forth thine hand ... Mt 12:13
unto the man, *S* forth thine hand ... Mk 3:5
unto the man, *S* forth thy hand ... Lk 6:10
thou shalt *s* forth thy hands, and ... Jn 21:18
For we *s* not ourselves beyond our ... 2Cor 10:14

**STRETCHED**
Abraham *s* forth his hand, and took ... Gen 22:10
Israel *s* out his right hand, and ... Gen 48:14
will redeem you with a *s* out arm ... Ex 6:6
Aaron *s* out his hand over the ... Ex 8:6
for Aaron *s* out his hand with his ... Ex 8:17
Moses *s* forth his rod toward ... Ex 9:23
Moses *s* forth his rod over the ... Ex 10:13
Moses *s* forth his hand toward ... Ex 10:22
Moses *s* out his hand over the sea ... Ex 14:21
Moses *s* forth his hand over the ... Ex 14:27
by a *s* out arm, and by great ... Deut 4:34
a mighty hand and by a *s* out arm ... Deut 5:15
the *s* out arm, whereby the LORD ... Deut 7:19
mighty power and by thy *s* out arm ... Deut 9:29
mighty hand, and his *s* out arm, ... Deut 11:2
Joshua *s* out the spear that he ... Josh 8:18
as soon as he had *s* out his hand ... Josh 8:19
wherewith he *s* out the spear, ... Josh 8:26
when the angel *s* out his hand ... 2Sa 24:16
they *s* forth the wings of the ... 1Kin 6:27
strong hand, and of thy *s* out arm ... 1Kin 8:42
he *s* himself upon the child three ... 1Kin 17:21
he *s* himself upon the child ... 2Kin 4:34
and went up, and *s* himself upon him. 2Kin 4:35
a *s* out arm, him shall ye fear, ... 2Kin 17:36
in his hand *s* out over Jerusalem ... 1Chr 21:16
thy mighty hand, and thy *s* out arm ... 2Chr 6:32
or who hath *s* the line upon it ... Job 38:5
or *s* out our hands to a strange ... Ps 44:20
I have *s* out my hands unto thee ... Ps 88:9
To him that *s* out the earth above ... Ps 136:6
strong hand, and with a *s* out arm ... Ps 136:12
I have *s* out my hand, and no man ... Prov 1:24
walk with *s* forth necks and wanton ... Is 3:16
he hath *s* forth his hand against ... Is 5:25
away, but his hand is *s* out still ... Is 5:25
away, but his hand is *s* out still ... Is 9:12
away, but his hand is *s* out still ... Is 9:17
away, but his hand is *s* out still ... Is 9:21
away, but his hand is *s* out still ... Is 10:4
is *s* out upon all the nations ... Is 14:26
and his hand is *s* out, and who ... Is 14:27
her branches are *s* out, they are ... Is 16:8
He *s* out his hand over the sea, ... Is 23:11
the heavens, and *s* them out ... Is 42:5
have *s* out the heavens, and all ... Is 45:12
that hath *s* forth the heavens, and ... Is 51:13
shadows of the evening are *s* out ... Jer 6:4
hath *s* out the heavens by his ... Jer 10:12
*s* out arm, and there is nothing ... Jer 32:17
with a *s* out arm, and with great ... Jer 32:21
hath *s* out the heaven by his ... Jer 51:15
he hath *s* out a line, he hath not ... Lam 2:8
and their wings were *s* upward ... Eze 1:11
*s* forth over their heads above ... Eze 1:22
one cherub *s* forth his hand from ... Eze 10:7
therefore I have *s* out my hand ... Eze 16:27
with a *s* out arm, and with fury ... Eze 20:33
with a *s* out arm, and with fury ... Eze 20:34
he *s* out his hand with scorners ... Hos 7:5
the banquet of them that *s* ... Amos 6:7
a line shall be *s* forth upon ... Zec 1:16
And he *s* it forth ... Mt 12:13
he *s* forth his hand toward his ... Mt 12:49
Jesus *s* forth his hand, and caught ... Mt 14:31
were with Jesus *s* out his hand ... Mt 26:51
And he *s* it out ... Mk 3:5
ye *s* forth no hands against me ... Lk 22:53
*s* forth his hands to vex certain ... Acts 12:1
Then Paul *s* forth the hand, and ... Acts 26:1
All day long I have *s* forth my ... Rom 10:21

**STRETCHEDST**
Thou *s* out thy right hand, the ... Ex 15:12

**STRETCHEST**
who *s* out the heavens like a ... Ps 104:2

**STRETCHETH**
For he *s* out his hand against God ... Job 15:25
He *s* out the north over the empty ... Job 26:7
She *s* out her hand to the poor ... Prov 31:20
that *s* out the heavens as a ... Is 40:22
The carpenter *s* out his rule ... Is 44:13
that *s* forth the heavens alone ... Is 44:24
which *s* forth the heavens, and ... Zec 12:1

**STRETCHING**
the *s* out of his wings shall fill ... Is 8:8
By *s* forth thine hand to heal ... Acts 4:30

**STRICKEN**
Sarah were old and well *s* in age ... Gen 18:11
Abraham was old, and well *s* in age ... Gen 24:1
Now Joshua was old and *s* in years ... Josh 13:1
*s* in years, and there remaineth ... Josh 13:1
that Joshua waxed old and *s* in age ... Josh 23:1
unto them, I am old and *s* in age ... Josh 23:2
pierced and *s* through his temples ... Judg 5:26
king David was old and *s* in years ... 1Kin 1:1
if thou hast *s* thy hand with a ... Prov 6:1
They have *s* me, shalt thou say, ... Prov 23:35
Why should ye be *s* any more ... Is 1:5
surely they are *s* ... Is 16:7
yet we did esteem him *s*, smitten ... Is 53:4
of my people was he *s* ... Is 53:8
thou hast *s* them, but they have ... Jer 5:3
*s* through for want of the fruits ... Lam 4:9
both were now well *s* in years ... Lk 1:7
man, and my wife well *s* in years ... Lk 1:18

**STRIFE**
there was a *s* between the herdmen ... Gen 13:7
said unto Lot, Let there be no *s* ... Gen 13:8
in the *s* of the congregation, to ... Num 27:14
and your burden, and your *s* ... Deut 1:12
my people were at great *s* with ... Judg 12:2
And all the people were at *s* ... 2Sa 19:9
a pavilion from the *s* of tongues ... Ps 31:20
seen violence and *s* in the city ... Ps 55:9
Thou makest us a *s* unto our ... Ps 80:6
him also at the waters of *s* ... Ps 106:32
A wrathful man stirreth up *s* ... Prov 15:18
that is slow to anger appeaseth *s* ... Prov 15:18
A froward man soweth *s* ... Prov 16:28
house full of sacrifices with *s* ... Prov 17:1
The beginning of *s* is as when one ... Prov 17:14
transgression that loveth *s* ... Prov 17:19
honour for a man to cease from *s* ... Prov 20:3
yea, *s* and reproach shall cease ... Prov 22:10
meddleth with *s* belonging not to ... Prov 26:17
is no talebearer, the *s* ceaseth ... Prov 26:20
is a contentious man to kindle *s* ... Prov 26:21
is of a proud heart stirreth up *s* ... Prov 28:25
An angry man stirreth up *s* ... Prov 29:22
forcing of wrath bringeth forth *s* ... Prov 30:33
Behold, ye fast for *s* and debate, ... Is 58:4
thou hast borne me a man of *s* ... Jer 15:10
even to the waters of *s* in Kadesh ... Eze 47:19
unto the waters of *s* in Kadesh ... Eze 48:28
and there are that raise up *s* ... Hab 1:3
And there was also a *s* among them ... Lk 22:24
and wantonness, not in *s* and ... Rom 13:13
there is among you envying, and *s* ... 1Cor 3:3
variance, emulations, wrath, *s* ... Gal 5:20
preach Christ even of envy and *s* ... Phil 1:15
be done through *s* or vainglory ... Phil 2:3
of words, whereof cometh envy, *s* ... 1Ti 6:4
is to them an end of all *s* ... Heb 6:16
*s* in your hearts, glory not, and ... Jas 3:14
*s* is, there is confusion and every ... Jas 3:16

**STRIFES**
Hatred stirreth up *s* ... Prov 10:12
be debates, envyings, wraths, *s* ... 2Cor 12:20
*s* of words, whereof cometh envy, ... 1Ti 6:4
knowing that they do gender *s* ... 2Ti 2:23

**STRIKE**
*s* it on the two side posts and on ... Ex 12:7
*s* the lintel and the two side ... Ex 12:22
shall *s* off the heifer's neck ... Deut 21:4
*s* his hand over the place, and ... 2Kin 5:11
is he that will *s* hands with me ... Job 17:3
bow of steel shall *s* him through ... Job 20:24
LORD at thy right hand shall *s* ... Ps 110:5
Till a dart *s* through his liver ... Prov 7:23
nor to *s* princes for equity ... Prov 17:26
not thou one of them that *s* hands ... Prov 22:26
Thou didst *s* through with his ... Hab 3:14
the servants did *s* him with the ... Mk 14:65

**STRIKER**
Not given to wine, no *s*, not ... 1Ti 3:3
angry, not given to wine, no *s* ... Titus 1:7

**STRIKETH**
He *s* them as wicked men in the ... Job 34:26
man void of understanding *s* hands ... Prov 17:18
of a scorpion, when he *s* a man ... Rev 9:5

**STRING**
make ready their arrow upon the *s* ... Ps 11:2
the *s* of his tongue was loosed, ... Mk 7:35

**STRINGED**
praise him with *s* instruments ... Ps 150:4
we will sing my songs to the *s* ... Is 38:20
chief singer on my *s* instruments ... Hab 3:19

**STRINGS**
thy *s* against the face of them ... Ps 21:12
and an instrument of ten *s* ... Ps 33:2
Upon an instrument of ten *s* ... Ps 92:3
an instrument of ten *s* will I ... Ps 144:9

**STRIP**
*s* Aaron of his garments, and put ... Num 20:26
Philistines came to *s* the slain ... 1Sa 31:8
Philistines came to *s* the slain ... 1Chr 10:8
*s* you, and make you bare, and gird ... Is 32:11
they shall *s* thee also of thy ... Eze 16:39
They shall also *s* thee out of thy ... Eze 23:26
Lest I *s* her naked, and set her as ... Hos 2:3

**STRIPE**
wound for wound, *s* for *s* ... Ex 21:25

**STRIPES**
Forty *s* he may give him, and not ... Deut 25:3
beat him above these with many *s* ... Deut 25:3
with the *s* of the children of men ... 2Sa 7:14
the rod, and their iniquity with *s* ... Ps 89:32
man than an hundred *s* into a fool ... Prov 17:10
and *s* for the back of fools ... Prov 19:29
so do *s* the inward parts of the ... Prov 20:30
and with his *s* we are healed ... Is 53:5
will, shall be beaten with many *s* ... Lk 12:47
and did commit things worthy of *s* ... Lk 12:48
shall be beaten with few *s* ... Lk 12:48
they had laid many *s* upon them ... Acts 16:23
of the night, and washed their *s* ... Acts 16:33
In *s*, in imprisonments, in ... 2Cor 6:5
in *s* above measure, in prisons ... 2Cor 11:23
times received I forty *s* save one ... 2Cor 11:24
by whose *s* ye were healed ... 1Pet 2:24

**STRIPLING**
Enquire thou whose son the *s* is ... 1Sa 17:56

**STRIPPED**
And the children of Israel *s* ... Ex 33:6
Moses *s* Aaron of his garments, and. Num 20:28
Jonathan *s* himself of the robe ... 1Sa 18:4
*s* off his armour, and sent into ... 1Sa 31:9
And when they had *s* him, they took. 1Chr 10:9
which they *s* off for themselves, ... 2Chr 20:25
He hath *s* me of my glory, and ... Job 19:9
*s* the naked of their clothing ... Job 22:6
I will wail and howl, I will go *s* ... Mic 1:8
And they *s* him, and put on him a ... Mt 27:28
which *s* him of his raiment, and ... Lk 10:30

**STRIPT**
that they *s* Joseph out of his ... Gen 37:23
he *s* off his clothes also, and ... 1Sa 19:24

**STRIVE**
shall not always *s* with man ... Gen 6:3
Gerar did *s* with Isaac's herdmen ... Gen 26:20
if men *s* together, and one smite ... Ex 21:18
If men *s*, and hurt a woman with ... Ex 21:22
When men *s* together one with ... Deut 25:11
with whom thou didst *s* at the ... Deut 33:8
did he ever *s* against Israel, or ... Judg 11:25
Why dost thou *s* against him ... Job 33:13
O LORD, with them that *s* with me ... Ps 35:1
*S* not with a man without cause, ... Prov 3:30
Go not forth hastily to *s* ... Prov 25:8
they that *s* with thee shall ... Is 41:11
Let the potsherd *s* with the ... Is 45:9
Yet let no man *s*, nor reprove ... Hos 4:4
as they that *s* with the priest ... Hos 4:4
He shall not *s*, nor cry ... Mt 12:19
*S* to enter in at the strait gate ... Lk 13:24
that ye *s* together with me in ... Rom 15:30
And if a man also *s* for masteries ... 2Ti 2:5
not crowned, except he *s* lawfully ... 2Ti 2:5
*s* not about words to no profit ... 2Ti 2:14
servant of the Lord must not *s* ... 2Ti 2:24

**STRIVED**
so have I *s* to preach the gospel, ... Rom 15:20

**STRIVEN**
thou hast *s* against the LORD ... Jer 50:24

**STRIVETH**
unto him that *s* with his Maker ... Is 45:9
every man that *s* for the mastery ... 1Cor 9:25

**STRIVING**
with one mind *s* together for the ... Phil 1:27
*s* according to his working, which ... Col 1:29
unto blood, *s* against sin ... Heb 12:4

**STRIVINGS**
me from the *s* of my people ... 2Sa 22:44
me from the *s* of the people ... Ps 18:43
contentions, and *s* about the law ... Titus 3:9

**STROKE**
and plea, and between *s* and *s* ... Deut 17:8
his hand fetcheth a *s* with the ... Deut 19:5
controversy and every *s* be tried ... Deut 21:5
enemies with the *s* of the sword ... Est 9:5
my *s* is heavier than my groaning ... Job 23:2
lest he take thee away with his *s* ... Job 36:18
Remove thy *s* away from me ... Ps 39:10
in wrath with a continual *s* ... Is 14:6
healeth the *s* of their wound ... Is 30:26
the desire of thine eyes with a *s* ... Eze 24:16

**STROKES**
and his mouth calleth for *s* ... Prov 18:6

**STRONG**
Issachar is a *s* ass couching down ... Gen 49:14
*s* by the hands of the mighty God ... Gen 49:24
for with a *s* hand shall he let ... Ex 6:1
with a *s* hand shall he drive them ... Ex 6:1
LORD turned a mighty *s* west wind ... Ex 10:19
for with a *s* hand hath the LORD ... Ex 13:9

by a *s* east wind all that night ... Ex 14:21
Do not drink wine nor *s* drink ... Lev 10:9
*s* drink, and shall drink no ... Num 6:3
of wine, or vinegar of *s* drink ... Num 6:3
whether they be *s* or weak ... Num 13:18
whether in tents, or in *s* holds ... Num 13:19
be *s* that dwell in the land ... Num 13:28
much people, and with a *s* hand ... Num 20:20
of the children of Ammon was *s* ... Num 21:24
*S* is thy dwellingplace, and thou ... Num 24:21
*s* wine to be poured unto the LORD ... Num 28:7
was not one city too *s* for us ... Deut 2:36
you this day, that ye may be *s* ... Deut 11:8
or for wine, or for *s* drink ... Deut 14:26
have ye drunk wine or *s* drink ... Deut 29:6
Be *s* and of a good courage, fear ... Deut 31:6
in the sight of all Israel, Be *s* ... Deut 31:7
of Nun a charge, and said, Be *s* ... Deut 31:23
Be *s* and of a good courage ... Josh 1:6
Only be thou *s* and very courageous ... Josh 1:7
Be *s* and of a good courage ... Josh 1:9
only be *s* and of a good courage ... Josh 1:18
Fear not, nor be dismayed, be *s* ... Josh 10:25
As yet I am as *s* this day as I ... Josh 14:11
children of Israel were waxen *s* ... Josh 17:13
chariots, and though they be *s* ... Josh 17:18
to Ramah, and to the *s* city Tyre ... Josh 19:29
before you great nations and *s* ... Josh 23:9
came to pass, when Israel was *s* ... Judg 1:28
mountains, and caves, and *s* holds ... Judg 6:2
But there was a *s* tower within ... Judg 9:51
and drink not wine nor *s* drink ... Judg 13:4
and now drink no wine nor *s* drink ... Judg 13:7
let her drink wine or *s* drink ... Judg 13:14
out of the *s* came forth sweetness ... Judg 14:14
saw that they were too *s* for him ... Judg 18:26
drunken neither wine nor *s* drink ... 1Sa 1:15
Be *s*, and quit yourselves like men ... 1Sa 4:9
and when Saul saw any *s* man ... 1Sa 14:52
in the wilderness in *s* holds ... 1Sa 23:14
with us in *s* holds in the wood ... 1Sa 23:19
dwelt in *s* holds at En-gedi ... 1Sa 23:29
himself *s* for the house of Saul ... 2Sa 3:6
David took the *s* hold of Zion ... 2Sa 5:7
If the Syrians be too *s* for me ... 2Sa 10:11
of Ammon be too *s* for thee ... 2Sa 10:11
battle more *s* against the city ... 2Sa 11:25
And the conspiracy was *s* ... 2Sa 15:12
of all that are with thee be *s* ... 2Sa 16:21
He delivered me from my *s* enemy ... 2Sa 22:18
for they were too *s* for me ... 2Sa 22:18
came to the *s* hold of Tyre, and to ... 2Sa 24:7
be thou *s* therefore, and shew ... 1Kin 2:2
thy great name, and of thy *s* hand ... 1Kin 8:42
*s* wind rent the mountains, and ... 1Kin 19:11
be with thy servants fifty *s* men ... 2Kin 2:16
their *s* holds wilt thou set on ... 2Kin 8:12
a thousand, all that were *s* ... 2Kin 24:16
If the Syrians be too *s* for me ... 1Chr 19:12
of Ammon be too *s* for thee ... 1Chr 19:12
be *s*, and of good courage ... 1Chr 22:13
whose brethren were *s* men ... 1Chr 26:7
sons and brethren, *s* men, eighteen ... 1Chr 26:9
be *s*, and do it ... 1Chr 28:10
said to Solomon his son, Be *s* ... 1Chr 28:20
And he fortified the *s* holds ... 2Chr 11:11
spears, and made them exceeding *s* ... 2Chr 11:12
Rehoboam the son of Solomon *s* ... 2Chr 11:17
Be ye *s* therefore, and let not ... 2Chr 15:7
to shew himself *s* in the behalf ... 2Chr 16:9
go, do it, be *s* for the battle ... 2Chr 25:8
helped, till he was *s* ... 2Chr 26:15
But when he was *s*, his heart was ... 2Chr 26:16
Be *s* and courageous, be not afraid ... 2Chr 32:7
that ye may be *s*, and eat the good ... Ezr 9:12
thy great power, and by thy *s* hand ... Neh 1:10
And they took *s* cities, and a fat ... Neh 9:25
of thy mouth be like a *s* wind ... Job 8:2
I speak of strength, lo, he is *s* ... Job 9:19
with thy *s* hand thou opposest ... Job 30:21
of his bones with *s* pain ... Job 33:19
spread out the sky, which is *s* ... Job 37:18
crag of the rock, and the *s* place ... Job 39:28
bones are as *s* pieces of brass ... Job 40:18
the poor may fall by his *s* ones ... Ps 10:10
He delivered me from my *s* enemy ... Ps 18:17
for they were too *s* for me ... Ps 18:17
rejoiceth as a *s* man to run a ... Ps 19:5
*s* bulls of Bashan have beset me ... Ps 22:12
The LORD *s* and mighty, the LORD ... Ps 24:8
hast made my mountain to stand *s* ... Ps 30:7
be thou my *s* rock, for an house ... Ps 31:2
marvellous kindness in a *s* city ... Ps 31:21
from him that is too *s* for him ... Ps 35:10
enemies are lively, and they are *s* ... Ps 38:19
Who will bring me into the *s* city ... Ps 60:9
me, and a *s* tower from the enemy ... Ps 61:3
Be thou my *s* habitation ... Ps 71:3
but thou art my *s* refuge ... Ps 71:7
that thou madest *s* for thyself ... Ps 80:15
whom thou madest *s* for thyself ... Ps 80:17
who is a *s* LORD like unto thee ... Ps 89:8
thine enemies with thy *s* arm ... Ps 89:10
*s* is thy hand, and high is thy ... Ps 89:13
hast brought his *s* holds to ruin ... Ps 89:40
Who will bring me into the *s* city ... Ps 108:10
With a *s* hand, and with a ... Ps 136:12
That our oxen may be *s* to labour ... Ps 144:14
many *s* men have been slain by her ... Prov 7:26
rich man's wealth is his *s* city ... Prov 10:15
and *s* men retain riches ... Prov 11:16
fear of the LORD is *s* confidence ... Prov 14:26
The name of the LORD is a *s* tower ... Prov 18:10
rich man's wealth is his *s* city ... Prov 18:11
is harder to be won than a *s* city ... Prov 18:19
is a mocker, *s* drink is raging ... Prov 20:1
and a reward in the bosom *s* wrath ... Prov 21:14
A wise man is *s* ... Prov 24:5
The ants are a people not *s* ... Prov 30:25
nor for princes *s* drink ... Prov 31:4
Give *s* drink unto him that is ... Prov 31:6
swift, nor the battle to the *s* ... Eccl 9:11
the *s* men shall bow themselves ... Eccl 12:3
for love is *s* as death ... Song 8:6
the *s* shall be as tow, and the ... Is 1:31
that they may follow *s* drink ... Is 5:11
men of strength to mingle *s* drink ... Is 5:22
them the waters of the river, *s* ... Is 8:7
spake thus to me with a *s* hand ... Is 8:11
In that day shall his *s* cities be ... Is 17:9
to destroy the *s* holds thereof ... Is 23:11
*s* drink shall be bitter to them ... Is 24:9
shall the *s* people glorify thee ... Is 25:3
We have a *s* city ... Is 26:1
*s* sword shall punish leviathan ... Is 27:1
*s* one, which as a tempest of hail ... Is 28:2
through *s* drink are out of the ... Is 28:7
have erred through *s* drink ... Is 28:7
out of the way through *s* drink ... Is 28:7
lest your bands be made *s* ... Is 28:22
stagger, but not with *s* drink ... Is 29:9
horsemen, because they are very *s* ... Is 31:1
pass over to his *s* hold for fear ... Is 31:9
that are of a fearful heart, Be *s* ... Is 35:4
Lord GOD will come with *s* hand ... Is 40:10
might, for that he is *s* in power ... Is 40:26
bring forth your *s* reasons ... Is 41:21
shall divide the spoil with the *s* ... Is 53:12
will fill ourselves with *s* drink ... Is 56:12
and a small one a *s* nation ... Is 60:22
of the neighing of his *s* ones ... Jer 8:16
outstretched hand and with a *s* arm ... Jer 21:5
and with wonders, and with a *s* hand ... Jer 32:21
of the hoofs of his *s* horses ... Jer 47:3
are mighty and *s* men for the war ... Jer 48:14
How is the *s* staff broken, and the ... Jer 48:17
and he shall destroy thy *s* holds ... Jer 48:18
the *s* holds are surprised, and the ... Jer 48:41
against the habitation of the *s* ... Jer 49:19
Their Redeemer is *s* ... Jer 50:34
unto the habitation of the *s* ... Jer 50:44
of Babylon, make the watch *s* ... Jer 51:12
thrown down in his wrath the *s* ... Lam 2:2
he hath destroyed his *s* holds ... Lam 2:5
thy face *s* against their faces ... Eze 3:8
thy forehead *s* against their ... Eze 3:8
hand of the LORD was *s* upon me ... Eze 3:14
make the pomp of the *s* to cease ... Eze 7:24
she had *s* rods for the sceptres ... Eze 19:11
her *s* rods were broken and ... Eze 19:12
so that she hath no *s* rod to be a ... Eze 19:14
endure, or can thine hands be *s* ... Eze 22:14
thy *s* garrisons shall go down to ... Eze 26:11
city, which wast *s* in the sea ... Eze 26:17
to make it *s* to hold the sword ... Eze 30:21
and will break his arms, the *s* ... Eze 30:22
The *s* among the mighty shall ... Eze 32:21
I will destroy the fat and the *s* ... Eze 34:16
fourth kingdom shall be *s* as iron ... Dan 2:40
so the kingdom shall be partly *s* ... Dan 2:42
The tree grew, and was *s*, and the ... Dan 4:11
thou sawest, which grew, and was *s* ... Dan 4:20
king, that art grown and become *s* ... Dan 4:22
and terrible, and *s* exceedingly ... Dan 7:7
and when he was *s*, the great horn ... Dan 8:8
unto thee, be *s*, yea, be *s* ... Dan 10:19
the king of the south shall be *s* ... Dan 11:5
and he shall be *s* above him ... Dan 11:5
shall become *s* with a small ... Dan 11:23
his devices against the *s* holds ... Dan 11:24
that do know their God shall be *s* ... Dan 11:32
most *s* holds with a strange god ... Dan 11:39
nation is come up upon my land, *s* ... Joel 1:6
a great people and a *s* ... Joel 2:2
as a *s* people set in battle array ... Joel 2:5
for he is *s* that executeth his ... Joel 2:11
let the weak say, I am *s* ... Joel 3:10
cedars, and he was *s* as the oaks ... Amos 2:9
the *s* shall not strengthen his ... Amos 2:14
the spoiled against the *s* ... Amos 5:9
unto thee of wine and of *s* drink ... Mic 2:11
rebuke *s* nations afar off ... Mic 4:3
that was cast far off a *s* nation ... Mic 4:7
the *s* hold of the daughter of ... Mic 4:8
and throw down all thy *s* holds ... Mic 5:11
ye *s* foundations of the earth ... Mic 6:2
a *s* hold in the day of trouble ... Nah 1:7
watch the way, make thy loins *s* ... Nah 2:1
All thy *s* holds shall be like fig ... Nah 3:12
the siege, fortify thy *s* holds ... Nah 3:14
the morter, make *s* the brickkiln ... Nah 3:14
they shall deride every *s* hold ... Hab 1:10
Yet now be *s*, O Zerubbabel, saith ... Hag 2:4
and be *s*, O Joshua, son of ... Hag 2:4
and be *s*, all ye people of the ... Hag 2:4
Let your hands be *s*, ye that hear ... Zec 8:9
fear not, but let your hands be *s* ... Zec 8:13
*s* nations shall come to seek the ... Zec 8:22
Tyrus did build herself a *s* hold ... Zec 9:3
Turn you to the *s* hold, ye ... Zec 9:12
one enter into a *s* man's house ... Mt 12:29
except he first bind the *s* man ... Mt 12:29
can enter into a *s* man's house ... Mk 3:27
he will first bind the *s* man ... Mk 3:27
drink neither wine nor *s* drink ... Lk 1:15
waxed *s* in spirit, and was in the ... Lk 1:80
waxed *s* in spirit, filled with ... Lk 2:40
When a *s* man armed keepeth his ... Lk 11:21
in his name hath made this man *s* ... Acts 3:16
but was *s* in faith, giving glory ... Rom 4:20
We then that are *s* ought to bear ... Rom 15:1
we are weak, but ye are *s* ... 1Cor 4:10
faith, quit you like men, be *s* ... 1Cor 16:13
to the pulling down of *s* holds ... 2Cor 10:4
for when I am weak, then am I *s* ... 2Cor 12:10
when we are weak, and ye are *s* ... 2Cor 13:9
be *s* in the Lord, and in the power ... Eph 6:10
God shall send them *s* delusion ... 2Th 2:11
be *s* in the grace that is in ... 2Ti 2:1
and supplications with *s* crying ... Heb 5:7
need of milk, and not of *s* meat ... Heb 5:12
But *s* meat belongeth to them that ... Heb 5:14
we might have a *s* consolation ... Heb 6:18
out of weakness were made *s* ... Heb 11:34
you, young men, because ye are *s* ... 1Jn 2:14
I saw a *s* angel proclaiming with ... Rev 5:2
he cried mightily with a *s* voice ... Rev 18:2
for *s* is the Lord God who judgeth ... Rev 18:8

**STRONGER**
shall be *s* than the other people ... Gen 25:23
whensoever the *s* cattle did ... Gen 30:41
were Laban's, and the *s* Jacob's ... Gen 30:42
for they are *s* than we ... Num 13:31
And what is *s* than a lion ... Judg 14:18
eagles, they were *s* than lions ... 2Sa 1:23
but David waxed *s* and *s*, and ... 2Sa 3:1
being *s* than she, forced her, and ... 2Sa 13:14
therefore they were *s* than we ... 1Kin 20:23
and surely we shall be *s* than they ... 1Kin 20:23
and surely we shall be *s* than they ... 1Kin 20:25
hands shall be *s* and *s* ... Job 17:9
made them *s* than their enemies ... Ps 105:24
for they are *s* than I ... Ps 142:6
thou art *s* than I, and hast ... Jer 20:7
hand of him that was *s* than he ... Jer 31:11
But when a *s* than he shall come ... Lk 11:22
the weakness of God is *s* than men ... 1Cor 1:25
are we *s* than he ... 1Cor 10:22

**STRONGEST**
A lion which is *s* among beasts ... Prov 30:30

**STRONGLY**
the foundations thereof be *s* laid ... Ezr 6:3

**STROVE**
because they *s* with him ... Gen 26:20
another well, and *s* for that also ... Gen 26:21
and for that they *s* not ... Gen 26:22
two men of the Hebrews *s* together ... Ex 2:13
a man of Israel *s* together in the ... Lev 24:10
of Israel *s* with the LORD ... Num 20:13
who *s* against Moses and against ... Num 26:9
when they *s* against the LORD ... Num 26:9
they two *s* together in the field ... 2Sa 14:6
when he *s* with Aram-naharaim and ... Ps 60:t
the heaven *s* upon the great sea ... Dan 7:2
Jews therefore *s* among themselves ... Jn 6:52
himself unto them as they *s* ... Acts 7:26
the Pharisees' part arose, and *s* ... Acts 23:9

**STROWED**
*s* it upon the graves of them that ... 2Chr 34:4

**STRUCK**
he *s* it into the pan, or kettle ... 1Sa 2:14
the LORD *s* the child that Uriah's ... 2Sa 12:15
to the ground, and *s* him not again ... 2Sa 20:10
and the LORD *s* him, and he died ... 2Chr 13:20
*s* a servant of the high priest's ... Mt 26:51
they *s* him on the face, and asked ... Lk 22:64
of the officers which stood by *s* ... Jn 18:22

**STRUGGLED**
the children *s* together within ... Gen 25:22

**STUBBLE**
to gather *s* instead of straw ... Ex 5:12
wrath, which consumed them as *s* ... Ex 15:7
and wilt thou pursue the dry *s* ... Job 13:25
They are as *s* before the wind, and ... Job 21:18
are turned with him into *s* ... Job 41:28
Darts are counted as *s* ... Job 41:29
as the *s* before the wind ... Ps 83:13
as the fire devoureth the *s* ... Is 5:24
chaff, ye shall bring forth *s* ... Is 33:11
shall take them away as *s* ... Is 40:24
sword, and as driven *s* to his bow ... Is 41:2
Behold, they shall be as *s* ... Is 47:14
will I scatter them as the *s* that ... Jer 13:24
of fire that devoureth the *s* ... Joel 2:5
flame, and the house of Esau for *s* ... Obad 18
shall be devoured as *s* fully dry ... Nah 1:10
all that do wickedly, shall be *s* ... Mal 4:1
precious stones, wood, hay, *s* ... 1Cor 3:12

**STUBBORN**
If a man have a *s* and rebellious ... Deut 21:18
of his city, This our son is *s* ... Deut 21:20
own doings, nor from their *s* way ... Judg 2:19
not be as their fathers, a *s* ... Ps 78:8
(She is loud and *s* ... Prov 7:11

**STUBBORNNESS**
not unto the *s* of this people ........ Deut 9:27
*s* is as iniquity and idolatry ........ 1Sa 15:23

**STUCK**
his spear *s* in the ground at his ........ 1Sa 26:7
I have *s* unto thy testimonies ........ Ps 119:31
and the forepart *s* fast, and ........ Acts 27:41

**STUDIETH**
of the righteous *s* to answer ........ Prov 15:28
For their heart *s* destruction ........ Prov 24:2

**STUDS**
borders of gold with *s* of silver ........ Song 1:11

**STUDY**
much *s* is a weariness of the ........ Eccl 12:12
that ye *s* to be quiet, and to do ........ 1Th 4:11
*S* to shew thyself approved unto ........ 2Ti 2:15

**STUFF**
thou hast searched all my *s* ........ Gen 31:37
thou found of all thy household *s* ........ Gen 31:37
Also regard not your *s* ........ Gen 45:20
his neighbour money or *s* to keep ........ Ex 22:7
For the *s* they had was sufficient ........ Ex 36:7
put it even among their own *s* ........ Josh 7:11
he hath hid himself among the *s* ........ 1Sa 10:22
and two hundred abode by the *s* ........ 1Sa 25:13
part be that tarrieth by the *s* ........ 1Sa 30:24
*s* of Tobiah out of the chamber ........ Neh 13:8
man, prepare thee *s* for removing ........ Eze 12:3
forth thy *s* by day in their sight ........ Eze 12:4
in their sight, as *s* for removing ........ Eze 12:4
I brought forth my *s* by day ........ Eze 12:7
as *s* for captivity, and in the ........ Eze 12:7
his *s* in the house, let him not ........ Lk 17:31

**STUMBLE**
safely, and thy foot shall not *s* ........ Prov 3:23
thou runnest, thou shalt not *s* ........ Prov 4:12
they know not at what they *s* ........ Prov 4:19
shall be weary nor *s* among them ........ Is 5:27
And many among them shall *s* ........ Is 8:15
err in vision, they *s* in judgment ........ Is 28:7
we *s* at noonday as in the night ........ Is 59:10
that they should not *s* ........ Is 63:13
before your feet *s* upon the dark ........ Jer 13:16
they have caused them to *s* in ........ Jer 18:15
therefore my persecutors shall *s* ........ Jer 20:11
way, wherein they shall not *s* ........ Jer 31:9
they shall *s*, and fall toward the ........ Jer 46:6
And the most proud shall *s* ........ Jer 50:32
but he shall *s* and fall, and not be ........ Dan 11:19
they shall *s* in their walk ........ Nah 2:5
they *s* upon their corpses ........ Nah 3:3
have caused many to *s* at the law ........ Mal 2:8
even to them which *s* at the word ........ 1Pet 2:8

**STUMBLED**
they that *s* are girded with ........ 1Sa 2:4
for the oxen *s* ........ 1Chr 13:9
me to eat up my flesh, they *s* ........ Ps 27:2
man hath *s* against the mighty ........ Jer 46:12
For they *s* at that stumblingstone ........ Rom 9:32
Have they *s* that they should fall ........ Rom 11:11

**STUMBLETH**
not thine heart be glad when he *s* ........ Prov 24:17
he *s* not, because he seeth the ........ Jn 11:9
if a man walk in the night, he *s* ........ Jn 11:10
any thing whereby thy brother *s* ........ Rom 14:21

**STUMBLING**
but for a stone of *s* and for a ........ Is 8:14
And a stone of *s*, and a rock of ........ 1Pet 2:8
is none occasion of *s* in him ........ 1Jn 2:10

**STUMBLINGBLOCK**
nor put a *s* before the blind, but ........ Lev 19:14
take up the *s* out of the way of ........ Is 57:14
I lay a *s* before him, he shall ........ Eze 3:20
it is the *s* of their iniquity ........ Eze 7:19
put the *s* of their iniquity ........ Eze 14:3
putteth the *s* of his iniquity ........ Eze 14:4
putteth the *s* of his iniquity ........ Eze 14:7
made a snare, and a trap, and a *s* ........ Rom 11:9
that no man put a *s* or an ........ Rom 14:13
crucified, unto the Jews a *s* ........ 1Cor 1:23
become a *s* to them that are weak ........ 1Cor 8:9
who taught Balac to cast a *s* ........ Rev 2:14

**STUMBLINGBLOCKS**
I will lay *s* before this people, ........ Jer 6:21
the sea, and the *s* with the wicked ........ Zeph 1:3

**STUMBLINGSTONE**
For they stumbled at that *s* ........ Rom 9:32
Behold, I lay in Sion a *s* ........ Rom 9:33

**STUMP**
only the *s* of Dagon was left to ........ 1Sa 5:4
Nevertheless leave the *s* of his ........ Dan 4:15
yet leave the *s* of the roots ........ Dan 4:23
to leave the *s* of the tree roots ........ Dan 4:26

**SUAH** (*su'-ah*) *Son of Zophah.*
*S*, and Harnepher, and Shual, and ........ 1Chr 7:36

**SUBDUE**
and replenish the earth, and *s* it ........ Gen 1:28
Moreover I will *s* all thine ........ 1Chr 17:10
He shall *s* the people under us, ........ Ps 47:3
holden, to *s* nations before him ........ Is 45:1
first, and he shall *s* three kings ........ Dan 7:24
he will *s* our iniquities ........ Mic 7:19
devour, and *s* with sling stones ........ Zec 9:15
even to *s* all things unto himself ........ Phil 3:21

**SUBDUED**
the land be *s* before the LORD ........ Num 32:22
and the land shall be *s* before you ........ Num 32:29
war with thee, until it be *s* ........ Deut 20:20
And the land was *s* before them ........ Josh 18:1
So Moab was *s* that day under the ........ Judg 3:30
So God *s* on that day Jabin the ........ Judg 4:23
Thus was Midian *s* before the ........ Judg 8:28
*s* before the children of Israel ........ Judg 11:33
So the Philistines were *s* ........ 1Sa 7:13
smote the Philistines, and *s* them ........ 2Sa 8:1
of all nations which he *s* ........ 2Sa 8:11
against me hast thou *s* under me ........ 2Sa 22:40
*s* them, and took Gath and her towns 1Chr 18:1
and they were *s* ........ 1Chr 20:4
the land is *s* before the LORD, and ........ 1Chr 22:18
thou hast *s* under me those that ........ Ps 18:39
should soon have *s* their enemies ........ Ps 81:14
all things shall be *s* unto him ........ 1Cor 15:28
Who through faith *s* kingdoms ........ Heb 11:33

**SUBDUEDST**
land, and thou *s* before them the ........ Neh 9:24

**SUBDUETH**
me, and *s* the people under me ........ Ps 18:47
who *s* my people under me ........ Ps 144:2
in pieces and *s* all things ........ Dan 2:40

**SUBJECT**
to Nazareth, and was *s* unto them ........ Lk 2:51
even the devils are *s* unto us ........ Lk 10:17
that the spirits are *s* unto you ........ Lk 10:20
for it is not *s* to the law of God ........ Rom 8:7
the creature was made *s* to vanity ........ Rom 8:20
Let every soul be *s* unto the ........ Rom 13:1
Wherefore ye must needs be *s* ........ Rom 13:5
prophets are *s* to the prophets ........ 1Cor 14:32
be *s* unto him that put all things ........ 1Cor 15:28
as the church is *s* unto Christ ........ Eph 5:24
world, are ye *s* to ordinances, ........ Col 2:20
in mind to be *s* to principalities ........ Titus 3:1
all their lifetime *s* to bondage ........ Heb 2:15
Elias was a man *s* to like ........ Jas 5:17
be *s* to your masters with all ........ 1Pet 2:18
and powers being made *s* unto him ........ 1Pet 3:22
all of you be *s* one to another, ........ 1Pet 5:5

**SUBJECTED**
him who hath *s* the same in hope ........ Rom 8:20

**SUBJECTION**
brought into *s* under their hand ........ Ps 106:42
brought them into *s* for servants ........ Jer 34:11
to return, and brought them into *s* ........ Jer 34:16
under my body, and bring it into *s* ........ 1Cor 9:27
*s* into the gospel of Christ ........ 2Cor 9:13
To whom we gave place by *s* ........ Gal 2:5
woman learn in silence with all *s* ........ 1Ti 2:11
children in *s* with all gravity ........ 1Ti 3:4
he not put in *s* the world to come ........ Heb 2:5
all things in *s* under his feet ........ Heb 2:8
in that he put all in *s* under him ........ Heb 2:8
in *s* unto the Father of spirits ........ Heb 12:9
be in *s* to your own husbands ........ 1Pet 3:1
being in *s* unto their own ........ 1Pet 3:5

**SUBMIT**
*s* thyself under her hands ........ Gen 16:9
Strangers shall *s* themselves unto ........ 2Sa 22:45
shall *s* themselves unto me ........ Ps 18:44
enemies *s* themselves unto thee ........ Ps 66:3
till every one *s* himself with ........ Ps 68:30
That ye *s* yourselves unto such, ........ 1Cor 16:16
*s* yourselves unto your own ........ Eph 5:22
*s* yourselves unto your own ........ Col 3:18
rule over you, and *s* yourselves ........ Heb 13:17
*S* yourselves therefore to God ........ Jas 4:7
*S* yourselves to every ordinance ........ 1Pet 2:13
*s* yourselves unto the elder ........ 1Pet 5:5

**SUBMITTED**
*s* themselves unto Solomon the ........ 1Chr 29:24
should have *s* themselves unto him ........ Ps 81:15
have not *s* themselves unto the ........ Rom 10:3

**SUBMITTING**
*S* yourselves one to another in ........ Eph 5:21

**SUBORNED**
Then they *s* men, which said, We ........ Acts 6:11

**SUBSCRIBE**
another shall *s* with his hand ........ Is 44:5
*s* evidences, and seal them, and ........ Jer 32:44

**SUBSCRIBED**
I *s* the evidence, and sealed it, ........ Jer 32:10
that *s* the book of the purchase ........ Jer 32:12

**SUBSTANCE**
every living *s* that I have made ........ Gen 7:4
every living *s* was destroyed ........ Gen 7:23
all their *s* that they had ........ Gen 12:5
for their *s* was great, so that ........ Gen 13:6
shall they come out with great *s* ........ Gen 15:14
Shall not their cattle and their *s* ........ Gen 34:23
and all his beasts, and all his *s* ........ Gen 36:6
all the *s* that was in their ........ Deut 11:6
Bless, LORD, his *s*, and accept the ........ Deut 33:11
for their cattle and for their *s* ........ Josh 14:4
of the *s* which was king David's ........ 1Chr 27:31
and the stewards over all the *s* ........ 1Chr 28:1
carried away all the *s* that was ........ 2Chr 21:17
of his *s* for the burnt offerings ........ 2Chr 31:3
for God had given him *s* very much.. 2Chr 32:29
these were of the king's *s* ........ 2Chr 35:7
our little ones, and for all our *s* ........ Ezr 8:21
all his *s* should be forfeited, and ........ Ezr 10:8
His *s* also was seven thousand ........ Job 1:3
his *s* is increased in the land ........ Job 1:10
the robber swalloweth up their *s* ........ Job 5:5
Give a reward for me of your *s* ........ Job 6:22
neither shall his *s* continue ........ Job 15:29
according to his *s* shall the ........ Job 20:18
Whereas our *s* is not cut down, ........ Job 22:20
ride upon it, and dissolvest my *s* ........ Job 30:22
rest of their *s* to their babes ........ Ps 17:14
his house, and ruler of all his *s* ........ Ps 105:21
My *s* was not hid from thee, when ........ Ps 139:15
Thine eyes did see my *s*, yet ........ Ps 139:16
We shall find all precious *s* ........ Prov 1:13
Honour the LORD with thy *s* ........ Prov 3:9
shall give all the *s* of his house ........ Prov 6:31
those that love me to inherit *s* ........ Prov 8:21
casteth away the *s* of the wicked ........ Prov 10:3
but the *s* of a diligent man is ........ Prov 12:27
and unjust gain increaseth his *s* ........ Prov 28:8
with harlots spendeth his *s* ........ Prov 29:3
all the *s* of his house for love ........ Song 8:7
whose *s* is in them, when they ........ Is 6:13
holy seed shall be the *s* thereof ........ Is 6:13
Thy *s* and thy treasures will I ........ Jer 15:13
in the field, I will give thy *s* ........ Jer 17:3
rich, I have found me out *s* ........ Hos 12:8
*s* in the day of their calamity ........ Obad 13
their *s* unto the Lord of the ........ Mic 4:13
ministered unto him of their *s* ........ Lk 8:3
there wasted his *s* with riotous ........ Lk 15:13
heaven a better and an enduring *s* ........ Heb 10:34
Now faith is the *s* of things ........ Heb 11:1

**SUBTIL**
Now the serpent was more *s* than ........ Gen 3:1
and Jonadab was a very *s* man ........ 2Sa 13:3
of an harlot, and *s* of heart ........ Prov 7:10

**SUBTILLY**
is told me that he dealeth very *s* ........ 1Sa 23:22
to deal *s* with his servants ........ Ps 105:25
The same dealt *s* with our kindred ........ Acts 7:19

**SUBTILTY**
he said, Thy brother came with *s* ........ Gen 27:35
But Jehu did it in *s*, to the ........ 2Kin 10:19
To give *s* to the simple, to the ........ Prov 1:4
that they might take Jesus by *s* ........ Mt 26:4
And said, O full of all *s* and all ........ Acts 13:10
beguiled Eve through his *s* ........ 2Cor 11:3

**SUBURBS**
But the field of the *s* of their ........ Lev 25:34
give also unto the Levites *s* for ........ Num 35:2
the *s* of them shall be for their ........ Num 35:3
the *s* of the cities, which ye ........ Num 35:4
be to them the *s* of the cities ........ Num 35:5
them shall ye give with their *s* ........ Num 35:7
with their *s* for their cattle and ........ Josh 14:4
with the *s* thereof for our cattle ........ Josh 21:2
the LORD, these cities and their *s* ........ Josh 21:3
Levites these cities with their *s* ........ Josh 21:8
with the *s* thereof round about it ........ Josh 21:11
the priest Hebron with her *s* ........ Josh 21:13
and Libnah with her *s* ........ Josh 21:13
And Jattir with her *s*, and Eshtemoa. Josh 21:14
and Eshtemoa with her *s* ........ Josh 21:14
And Holon with her *s*, and Debir ........ Josh 21:15
and Debir with her *s* ........ Josh 21:15
And Ain with her *s*, and Juttah with. Josh 21:16
and Juttah with her *s* ........ Josh 21:16
and Beth-shemesh with her *s* ........ Josh 21:16
of Benjamin, Gibeon with her *s* ........ Josh 21:17
Geba with her *s* ........ Josh 21:17
Anathoth with her *s*, and Almon ........ Josh 21:18
and Almon with her *s* ........ Josh 21:18
were thirteen cities with their *s* ........ Josh 21:19
with her *s* in mount Ephraim ........ Josh 21:21
and Gezer with her *s*, ........ Josh 21:21
And Kibzaim with her *s*, and ........ Josh 21:22
and Beth-horon with her *s* ........ Josh 21:22
tribe of Dan, Eltekeh with her *s* ........ Josh 21:23
Gibbethon with her *s* ........ Josh 21:23
Aijalon with her *s*, Gath-rimmon ........ Josh 21:24
Gath-rimmon with her *s* ........ Josh 21:24
of Manasseh, Tanach with her *s* ........ Josh 21:25
and Gath-rimmon with her *s* ........ Josh 21:25
their *s* for the families of the ........ Josh 21:26
gave Golan in Bashan with her *s* ........ Josh 21:27
and Beesh-terah with her *s* ........ Josh 21:27
of Issachar, Kishon with her *s* ........ Josh 21:28
Dabareh with her *s* ........ Josh 21:28
Jarmuth with her *s*, En-gannim ........ Josh 21:29
En-gannim with her *s* ........ Josh 21:29
tribe of Asher, Mishal with her *s* ........ Josh 21:30
Abdon with her *s* ........ Josh 21:30
Helkath with her *s*, and Rehob with.. Josh 21:31
Rehob with her *s* ........ Josh 21:31
Kedesh in Galilee with her *s* ........ Josh 21:32
and Hammoth-dor with her *s* ........ Josh 21:32
and Kartan with her *s* ........ Josh 21:32
were thirteen cities with their *s* ........ Josh 21:33
of Zebulun, Jokneam with her *s* ........ Josh 21:34
and Kartah with her *s* ........ Josh 21:34
Dimnah with her *s*, Nahalal with ........ Josh 21:35
her *s*, Nahalal with her *s* ........ Josh 21:35

tribe of Reuben, Bezer with her *s* ...... Josh 21:36
and Jahazah with her *s* ...... Josh 21:36
Kedemoth with her *s*, and Mephaath Josh 21:37
and Mephaath with her *s* ...... Josh 21:37
Gad, Ramoth in Gilead with her *s* ...... Josh 21:38
and Mahanaim with her *s*, ...... Josh 21:38
Heshbon with her *s*, Jazer with ...... Josh 21:39
Jazer with her *s* ...... Josh 21:39
and eight cities with their *s* ...... Josh 21:41
one with their *s* round about them .... Josh 21:42
chamberlain, which was in the *s* ...... 2Kin 23:11
towns, and in all the *s* of Sharon ...... 1Chr 5:16
the *s* thereof round about it ...... 1Chr 6:55
of refuge, and Libnah with her *s* ...... 1Chr 6:57
Jattir, and Eshtemoa, with their *s* ...... 1Chr 6:57
And Hilen with her *s*, Debir with ...... 1Chr 6:58
Debir with her *s* ...... 1Chr 6:58
And Ashan with her *s*, and ...... 1Chr 6:59
and Beth-shemesh with her *s* ...... 1Chr 6:59
Geba with her *s* ...... 1Chr 6:60
and Alemeth with her *s* ...... 1Chr 6:60
and Anathoth with her *s* ...... 1Chr 6:60
Levites these cities with their *s* ...... 1Chr 6:64
in mount Ephraim with her *s* ...... 1Chr 6:67
they gave also Gezer with her *s* ...... 1Chr 6:67
And Jokmeam with her *s*, and ...... 1Chr 6:68
and Beth-horon with her *s* ...... 1Chr 6:68
And Aijalon with her *s*, and ...... 1Chr 6:69
and Gath-rimmon with her *s* ...... 1Chr 6:69
Aner with her *s*, and Bileam with ...... 1Chr 6:70
and Bileam with her *s* ...... 1Chr 6:70
Golan in Bashan with her *s* ...... 1Chr 6:71
and Ashtaroth with her *s* ...... 1Chr 6:71
Kedesh with her *s* ...... 1Chr 6:72
Daberath with her *s* ...... 1Chr 6:72
And Ramoth with her *s* ...... 1Chr 6:73
and Anem with her *s* ...... 1Chr 6:73
Mashal with her *s* ...... 1Chr 6:74
and Abdon with her *s* ...... 1Chr 6:74
And Hukok with her *s* ...... 1Chr 6:75
and Rehob with her *s* ...... 1Chr 6:75
Kedesh in Galilee with her *s* ...... 1Chr 6:76
and Hammon with her *s* ...... 1Chr 6:76
and Kirjathaim with her *s* ...... 1Chr 6:76
of Zebulun, Rimmon with her *s* ...... 1Chr 6:77
Tabor with her *s* ...... 1Chr 6:77
in the wilderness with her *s* ...... 1Chr 6:78
and Jahzah with her *s* ...... 1Chr 6:78
Kedemoth also with her *s*, and ...... 1Chr 6:79
and Mephaath with her *s* ...... 1Chr 6:79
Ramoth in Gilead with her *s* ...... 1Chr 6:80
and Mahanaim with her *s* ...... 1Chr 6:80
And Heshbon with her *s*, and Jazer .... 1Chr 6:81
and Jazer with her *s* ...... 1Chr 6:81
which are in their cities and *s* ...... 1Chr 13:2
For the Levites left their *s* ...... 2Chr 11:14
fields of the *s* of their cities ...... 2Chr 31:19
The *s* shall shake at the sound of ...... Eze 27:28
round about for the *s* thereof ...... Eze 45:2
the city, for dwelling, and for *s* ...... Eze 48:15
the *s* of the city shall be toward ...... Eze 48:17

**SUBVERT**
To *s* a man in his cause, the Lord ...... Lam 3:36
who *s* whole houses, teaching ...... Titus 1:11

**SUBVERTED**
Knowing that he that is such is *s* ...... Titus 3:11

**SUBVERTING**
*s* your souls, saying, Ye must be ...... Acts 15:24
but to the *s* of the hearers ...... 2Ti 2:14

**SUCATHITES** See SUCHATHITES.

**SUCCEED**
which she beareth shall *s* in the ...... Deut 25:6

**SUCCEEDED**
but the children of Esau *s* them ...... Deut 2:12
and they *s* them, and dwelt in their .... Deut 2:21
and they *s* them, and dwelt in their .... Deut 2:22

**SUCCEEDEST**
to possess them, and thou *s* them ...... Deut 12:29
God giveth thee, and thou *s* them ...... Deut 19:1

**SUCCESS**
and then thou shalt have good *s* ...... Josh 1:8

**SUCCOTH** (*suc'-coth*)
*1. A place east of the Jordan.*
And Jacob journeyed to *S*, and built .. Gen 33:17
the name of the place is called *S* ...... Gen 33:17
*2. An Israelite encampment in the wilderness.*
journeyed from Rameses to *S* ...... Ex 12:37
And they took their journey from *S* ..... Ex 13:20
from Rameses, and pitched in *S* ...... Num 33:5
And they departed from *S*, and ...... Num 33:6
*3. A place in Gad.*
Beth-aram, and Beth-nimrah, and *S* ... Josh 13:27
And he said unto the men of *S* ...... Judg 8:5
And the princes of *S* said, Are the ...... Judg 8:6
as the men of *S* had answered him ...... Judg 8:8
a young man of the men of *S* ...... Judg 8:14
unto him the princes of *S* ...... Judg 8:14
And he came unto the men of *S* ...... Judg 8:15
with them he taught the men of *S* ..... Judg 8:16
*4. A city in Ephraim.*
in the clay ground between *S* ...... 1Kin 7:46
in the clay ground between *S* ...... 2Chr 4:17
and mete out the valley of *S* ...... Ps 60:6
and mete out the valley of *S* ...... Ps 108:7

**SUCCOTH-BENOTH** (*suc''-coth-be'-noth*) *A Babylonian god.*
And the men of Babylon made *S* ...... 2Kin 17:30

**SUCCOUR**
came to *s* Hadadezer king of Zobah ...... 2Sa 8:5
that thou *s* us out of the city ...... 2Sa 18:3
he is able to *s* them that are ...... Heb 2:18

**SUCCOURED**
Abishai the son of Zeruiah *s* him ...... 2Sa 21:17
day of salvation have I *s* thee ...... 2Cor 6:2

**SUCCOURER**
for she hath been a *s* of many ...... Rom 16:2

**SUCH**
the father of *s* as dwell in tents ...... Gen 4:20
in tents, and of *s* as have cattle ...... Gen 4:20
of all *s* as handle the harp ...... Gen 4:21
*s* as I love, and bring it to me, ...... Gen 27:4
for thy father, *s* as he loveth ...... Gen 27:9
meat, *s* as his father loved ...... Gen 27:14
*s* as these which are of the ...... Gen 27:46
and of *s* shall be my hire ...... Gen 30:32
*s* as I never saw in all the land ...... Gen 41:19
Can we find *s* a one as this is, a ...... Gen 41:38
wot ye not that *s* a man as I can ...... Gen 44:15
*s* as hath not been in Egypt since ...... Ex 9:18
*s* as there was none like it in ...... Ex 9:24
there were no *s* locusts as they ...... Ex 10:14
neither after them shall be *s* ...... Ex 10:14
*s* as there was none like it, nor ...... Ex 11:6
them *s* things as they required ...... Ex 12:36
*s* as fear God, men of truth, ...... Ex 18:21
place *s* over them, to be rulers ...... Ex 18:21
*s* as have not been done in all ...... Ex 34:10
*s* things have befallen me ...... Lev 10:19
that on which *s* water cometh ...... Lev 11:34
every *s* vessel shall be unclean ...... Lev 11:34
pigeons, *s* as he is able to get ...... Lev 14:22
young pigeons, *s* as he can get ...... Lev 14:30
Even *s* as he is able to get, the ...... Lev 14:31
after *s* as have familiar spirits ...... Lev 20:6
any *s* shall be unclean until even ...... Lev 22:6
all that any man giveth of *s* unto ...... Lev 27:9
instead of *s* as open every womb, ...... Num 8:16
whether there hath been any *s* ...... Deut 4:32
there were *s* an heart in them ...... Deut 5:29
shall do no more any *s* wickedness ... Deut 13:11
that *s* abomination is wrought ...... Deut 13:14
*s* time as thou beginnest to put ...... Deut 16:9
that *s* abomination is wrought in ...... Deut 17:4
no more any *s* evil among you ...... Deut 19:20
For all that do *s* things, and all ...... Deut 25:16
at the least *s* as before knew ...... Judg 3:2
have told us *s* things as these ...... Judg 13:23
that thou comest with *s* a company .. Judg 18:23
There was no *s* deed done nor seen .. Judg 19:30
unto whom he said, Ho, *s* a one ...... Ruth 4:1
unto them, Why do ye *s* things ...... 1Sa 2:23
not been *s* a thing heretofore ...... 1Sa 4:7
I have appointed my servants to *s* ...... 1Sa 21:2
and *s* a place ...... 1Sa 21:2
for he is *s* a son of Belial, that ...... 1Sa 25:17
look upon *s* a dead dog as I am ...... 2Sa 9:8
given unto thee *s* and *s* things ...... 2Sa 12:8
for no *s* thing ought to be done ...... 2Sa 13:12
for with *s* robes were the king's ...... 2Sa 13:18
then hast thou thought *s* a thing ...... 2Sa 14:13
that *s* as be faint in the ...... 2Sa 16:2
recompense it me with *s* a reward ...... 2Sa 19:36
there came no more *s* abundance of . 1Kin 10:10
there came no *s* almug trees ...... 1Kin 10:12
with his servants, saying, In *s* ...... 2Kin 6:8
*s* a place shall be my camp ...... 2Kin 6:8
that thou pass not *s* a place ...... 2Kin 6:9
in heaven, might *s* a thing be ...... 2Kin 7:19
Ye shall eat this year *s* things ...... 2Kin 19:29
I am bringing *s* evil upon ...... 2Kin 21:12
Surely there was not holden *s* a ...... 2Kin 23:22
*s* things as were of gold, in gold ...... 2Kin 25:15
*s* as went forth to battle, expert ...... 1Chr 12:33
*s* as went forth to battle, expert ...... 1Chr 12:36
bestowed upon him *s* royal majesty .. 1Chr 29:25
*s* as none of the kings have had ...... 2Chr 1:12
*s* things as they offered for the ...... 2Chr 4:6
neither was there any *s* spice as ...... 2Chr 9:9
there were none *s* seen before in ...... 2Chr 9:11
*s* as set their hearts to seek the ...... 2Chr 11:16
*s* as taught to sing praise ...... 2Chr 23:13
Jehoiada gave it to *s* as did the ...... 2Chr 24:12
also *s* as wrought iron and brass ...... 2Chr 24:12
time in *s* sort as it was written ...... 2Chr 30:5
keep *s* a passover as Josiah kept ...... 2Chr 35:18
side the river, and at *s* a time ...... Ezr 4:10
side the river, and at *s* a time ...... Ezr 4:11
the river, Peace, and at *s* a time ...... Ezr 4:17
all *s* as had separated themselves ...... Ezr 6:21
perfect peace, and at *s* a time ...... Ezr 7:12
all *s* as know the laws of thy God ...... Ezr 7:25
which hath put *s* a thing as this ...... Ezr 7:27
of *s* as lay in wait by the way ...... Ezr 8:31
hast given us *s* deliverance as ...... Ezr 9:13
*s* as are born of them, according ...... Ezr 10:3
There are no *s* things done as ...... Neh 6:8
I said, Should *s* a man as I flee ...... Neh 6:11
with *s* things as belonged to her, ...... Est 2:9
except *s* to whom the king shall ...... Est 4:11
the kingdom for *s* a time as this ...... Est 4:14
to lay hand on *s* as sought their ...... Est 9:2
upon all *s* as joined themselves ...... Est 9:27
who knoweth not *s* things as these ...... Job 12:3
open thine eyes upon *s* an one ...... Job 14:3
lettest *s* words go out of thy ...... Job 15:13
I have heard many *s* things ...... Job 16:2
Surely *s* are the dwellings of the ...... Job 18:21
many *s* things are with him ...... Job 23:14
truth unto *s* as keep his covenant ...... Ps 25:10
me, and *s* as breathe out cruelty ...... Ps 27:12
saveth *s* as be of a contrite ...... Ps 34:18
to slay *s* as be of upright ...... Ps 37:14
For *s* as be blessed of him shall ...... Ps 37:22
nor *s* as turn aside to lies ...... Ps 40:4
let *s* as love thy salvation say ...... Ps 40:16
altogether *s* an one as thyself ...... Ps 50:21
against *s* as be at peace with him ...... Ps 55:20
the hairy scalp of *s* an one as ...... Ps 68:21
let *s* as love thy salvation say ...... Ps 70:4
even to *s* as are of a clean heart ...... Ps 73:1
To *s* as keep his covenant, and to ...... Ps 103:18
*S* as sit in darkness and in the ...... Ps 107:10
As for *s* as turn aside unto their ...... Ps 125:5
*S* knowledge is too wonderful for ...... Ps 139:6
that people, that is in *s* a case ...... Ps 144:15
but *s* as are upright in their way ...... Prov 11:20
but *s* as keep the law contend ...... Prov 28:4
*S* is the way of an adulterous ...... Prov 30:20
the dumb in the cause of all *s* as ...... Prov 31:8
the tears of *s* as were oppressed ...... Eccl 4:1
not be *s* as was in her vexation ...... Is 9:1
*s* as are escaped of the house of ...... Is 10:20
*s* is our expectation, whither we ...... Is 20:6
this year *s* as groweth of itself ...... Is 37:30
Is it *s* a fast that I have chosen ...... Is 58:5
Who hath heard *s* a thing ...... Is 66:8
who hath seen *s* things ...... Is 66:8
and see if there be *s* a thing ...... Jer 2:10
be avenged on *s* a nation as this ...... Jer 5:9
be avenged on *s* a nation as this ...... Jer 5:29
be avenged on *s* a nation as this ...... Jer 9:9
*S* as are for death, to death ...... Jer 15:2
*s* as are for the sword, to the ...... Jer 15:2
*s* as are for the famine, to the ...... Jer 15:2
*s* as are for the captivity, to ...... Jer 15:2
heathen, who hath heard *s* things ...... Jer 18:13
*s* as are left in this city from ...... Jer 21:7
in speaking *s* words unto them ...... Jer 38:4
deliver *s* as are for death to ...... Jer 43:11
*s* as are for captivity to ...... Jer 43:11
*s* as are for the sword to the ...... Jer 43:11
return but *s* as shall escape ...... Jer 44:14
he escape that doeth *s* things ...... Eze 17:15
considereth, and doeth not *s* like ...... Eze 18:14
*s* as had ability in them to stand ...... Dan 1:4
that asked *s* things at any ...... Dan 2:10
he had spoken *s* words unto me ...... Dan 10:15
*s* as do wickedly against the ...... Dan 11:32
*s* as never was since there was a ...... Dan 12:1
*s* as are skilful of lamentation ...... Amos 5:16
heathen, *s* as they have not heard ...... Mic 5:15
all *s* as are clothed with strange ...... Zeph 1:8
which had given *s* power unto men ...... Mt 9:8
one *s* little child in my name ...... Mt 18:5
for of *s* is the kingdom of heaven ...... Mt 19:14
*s* as was not since the beginning ...... Mt 24:21
for in *s* an hour as ye think not ...... Mt 24:44
said, Go into the city to *s* a man ...... Mt 26:18
*s* as hear the word, ...... Mk 4:18
*s* as hear the word, and receive it ...... Mk 4:20
with many *s* parables spake he the ...... Mk 4:33
that even *s* mighty works are ...... Mk 6:2
many other *s* like things ye do ...... Mk 7:8
and many *s* like things do ye ...... Mk 7:13
one of *s* children in my name ...... Mk 9:37
for of *s* is the kingdom of God ...... Mk 10:14
for *s* things must needs be ...... Mk 13:7
*s* as was not from the beginning ...... Mk 13:19
is this, of whom I hear *s* things ...... Lk 9:9
drinking *s* things as they give ...... Lk 10:7
eat *s* things as are set before ...... Lk 10:8
give alms of *s* things as ye have ...... Lk 11:41
because they suffered *s* things ...... Lk 13:2
for of *s* is the kingdom of God ...... Lk 18:16
Father seeketh *s* to worship him ...... Jn 4:23
murmured *s* things concerning him ...... Jn 7:32
us, that *s* should be stoned ...... Jn 8:5
that is a sinner do *s* miracles ...... Jn 9:16
church daily *s* as should be saved ...... Acts 2:47
but *s* as I have give I thee ...... Acts 3:6
gave no *s* commandment ...... Acts 15:24
Who, having received *s* a charge ...... Acts 16:24
I will be no judge of *s* matters ...... Acts 18:15
that they observe no *s* thing ...... Acts 21:25
Away with *s* a fellow from the ...... Acts 22:22
of *s* things as I supposed ...... Acts 25:18
doubted of *s* manner of questions ...... Acts 25:20
almost, and altogether *s* as I am ...... Acts 26:29
they laded us with *s* things as ...... Acts 28:10
that they which commit *s* things ...... Rom 1:32
them which commit *s* things ...... Rom 2:2
judgest them which do *s* things ...... Rom 2:3
For they that are *s* serve not our ...... Rom 16:18
*s* fornication as is not so much ...... 1Cor 5:1
To deliver *s* a one unto Satan for ...... 1Cor 5:5
with *s* an one, no not to eat ...... 1Cor 5:11
And *s* were some of you ...... 1Cor 6:11
is not under bondage in *s* cases ...... 1Cor 7:15
Nevertheless *s* shall have trouble ...... 1Cor 7:28
you but *s* as is common to man ...... 1Cor 10:13
contentious, we have no *s* custom ...... 1Cor 11:16
*s* are they also that are earthy ...... 1Cor 15:48

s are they also that are heavenly....... 1Cor 15:48
That ye submit yourselves unto s...... 1Cor 16:16
acknowledge ye them that are s....... 1Cor 16:18
Sufficient to s a man is this.................. 2Cor 2:6
lest perhaps s a one should be................ 2Cor 2:7
s trust have we through Christ to.......... 2Cor 3:4
Seeing then that we have s hope......... 2Cor 3:12
Let s an one think this, that,............... 2Cor 10:11
s as we are in word by letters............ 2Cor 10:11
s will we be also in deed when we..... 2Cor 10:11
For s are false apostles,........................ 2Cor 11:13
s an one caught up to the third............ 2Cor 12:2
And I knew s a man, (whether in........ 2Cor 12:3
Of s an one will I glory......................... 2Cor 12:5
I shall not find you s as I would........ 2Cor 12:20
found unto you s as ye would not..... 2Cor 12:20
revellings, and s like.................................. Gal 5:21
that they which do s things shall........... Gal 5:21
against s there is no law........................ Gal 5:23
restore s an one in the spirit of................ Gal 6:1
spot, or wrinkle, or any s thing............. Eph 5:27
and hold s in reputation.......................... Phil 2:29
the Lord is the avenger of all s................ 1Th 4:6
Now them that are s we command....... 2Th 3:12
from s withdraw thyself............................ 1Ti 6:5
from s turn away........................................... 2Ti 3:5
that he that is s is subverted............... Titus 3:11
being s an one as Paul the aged,.......... Philem 9
are become s as have need of milk....... Heb 5:12
For s an high priest became us,............. Heb 7:26
We have s an high priest, who is............ Heb 8:1
For they that say s things.................... Heb 11:14
s contradiction of sinners...................... Heb 12:3
be content with s things as ye............... Heb 13:5
for with s sacrifices God is well.......... Heb 13:16
morrow we will go into s a city.............. Jas 4:13
all s rejoicing is evil.................................. Jas 4:16
when there came s a voice to him....... 2Pet 1:17
seeing that ye look for s things........... 2Pet 3:14
We therefore ought to receive s.................. 3Jn 8
s as are in the sea, and all that................ Rev 5:13
s as was not since men were upon...... Rev 16:18
on s the second death hath no.............. Rev 20:6

**SUCHATHITES** (*soo'-kath-ites*) *A family of scribes.*
the Shimeathites, and *S*........................ 1Chr 2:55

**SUCK**
should have given children s................. Gen 21:7
he made him to s honey out of the... Deut 32:13
for they shall s of the abundance...... Deut 33:19
gave her son s until she weaned............ 1Sa 1:23
in the morning to give my child s........ 1Kin 3:21
why the breasts that I should s............... Job 3:12
He shall s the poison of asps................ Job 20:16
Her young ones also s up blood........... Job 39:30
Thou shalt also s the milk of the............ Is 60:16
shalt s the breast of kings.......................... Is 60:16
That ye may s, and be satisfied.............. Is 66:11
then shall ye s, ye shall be....................... Is 66:12
they give s to their young ones............... Lam 4:3
s it out, and thou shalt break the......... Eze 23:34
and those that s the breasts.................... Joel 2:16
to them that give s in those days.......... Mt 24:19
to them that give s in those days......... Mk 13:17
child, and to them that give s................ Lk 21:23
and the paps which never gave s.......... Lk 23:29

**SUCKED**
that s the breasts of my mother............ Song 8:1
and the paps which thou hast s.............. Lk 11:27

**SUCKING**
father beareth the s child...................... Num 11:12
And Samuel took a s lamb, and................ 1Sa 7:9
the s child shall play on the........................ Is 11:8
Can a woman forget her s child............ Is 49:15
The tongue of the s child.......................... Lam 4:4

**SUCKLING**
the s also with the man of gray......... Deut 32:25
both man and woman, infant and s....... 1Sa 15:3
from you man and woman, child and s. Jer 44:7

**SUCKLINGS**
both men and women, children and s. 1Sa 22:19
s hast thou ordained strength.......................... Ps 8:2
the s swoon in the streets of the............ Lam 2:11
s thou hast perfected praise................... Mt 21:16

**SUDDEN**
thee, and s fear troubleth thee............. Job 22:10
Be not afraid of s fear, neither.............. Prov 3:25
then s destruction cometh upon.............. 1Th 5:3

**SUDDENLY**
And if any man die very s by him......... Num 6:9
And the LORD spake s unto Moses...... Num 12:4
if he thrust him s without enmity...... Num 35:22
against you, and destroy thee s.............. Deut 7:4
Joshua therefore came unto them s..... Josh 10:9
them by the waters of Merom s............ Josh 11:7
to depart, lest he overtake us s............ 2Sa 15:14
for the thing was done s.................... 2Chr 29:36
but s I cursed his habitation...................... Job 5:3
If the scourge slay s, he will.................... Job 9:23
let them return and be ashamed s............ Ps 6:10
s do they shoot at him, and fear............ Ps 64:4
s shall they be wounded............................. Ps 64:7
shall his calamity come s....................... Prov 6:15
s shall he be broken without................. Prov 6:15
For their calamity shall rise s.............. Prov 24:22
shall s be destroyed, and that............... Prov 29:1

time, when it falleth s upon them......... Eccl 9:12
yea, it shall be at an instant s.................... Is 29:5
breaking cometh s at an instant.............. Is 30:13
desolation shall come upon thee s.......... Is 47:11
I did them s, and they came to................. Is 48:3
s are my tents spoiled, and my.............. Jer 4:20
the spoiler shall s come upon us............ Jer 6:26
have caused him to fall upon it s............ Jer 15:8
shalt bring a troop s upon them........... Jer 18:22
but I will s make him run away........... Jer 49:19
make them s run away from her.......... Jer 50:44
Babylon is s fallen and destroyed........... Jer 51:8
rise up s that shall bite thee.................... Hab 2:7
shall s come to his temple, even................ Mal 3:1
And s, when they had looked round........ Mk 9:8
Lest coming s he find you..................... Mk 13:36
s there was with the angel a.................... Lk 2:13
taketh him, and he s crieth out................ Lk 9:39
s there came a sound from heaven........ Acts 2:2
s there shined round about him a......... Acts 9:3
s there was a great earthquake,.......... Acts 16:26
s there shone from heaven a great....... Acts 22:6
swollen, or fallen down dead s............. Acts 28:6
Lay hands s on no man, neither be........ 1Ti 5:22

**SUE**
if any man will s thee at the law............ Mt 5:40

**SUFFER**
will not s the destroyer to come............ Ex 12:23
Thou shalt not s a witch to live............ Ex 22:18
neither shalt thou s the salt of.............. Lev 2:13
neighbour, and not s sin upon him...... Lev 19:17
Or s them to bear the iniquity of......... Lev 22:16
Sihon would not s Israel to pass........ Num 21:23
s them not to enter into their.............. Josh 10:19
for they would not s them to come..... Judg 1:34
father would not s him to go in........... Judg 15:1
*S* me that I may feel the pillars.......... Judg 16:26
that thou wouldest not s the.................. 2Sa 14:11
that he might not s any to go out...... 1Kin 15:17
for the king's profit to s them.................... Est 3:8
He will not s me to take my................... Job 9:18
*S* me that I may speak............................ Job 21:3
their winepresses, and s thirst.............. Job 24:11
*S* me a little, and I will shew.................. Job 36:2
which I s of them that hate me.................. Ps 9:13
neither wilt thou s thine Holy............... Ps 16:10
young lions do lack, and s hunger........... Ps 34:10
he shall never s the righteous to............ Ps 55:22
while I s thy terrors I am........................ Ps 88:15
nor s my faithfulness to fail..................... Ps 89:33
and a proud heart will not I s.................. Ps 101:5
He will not s thy foot to be.................... Ps 121:3
The LORD will not s the soul of.............. Prov 10:3
and an idle soul shall s hunger............ Prov 19:15
of great wrath shall s punishment..... Prov 19:19
*S* not thy mouth to cause thy................... Eccl 5:6
the rich will not s him to sleep.............. Eccl 5:12
nor s their locks to grow long.............. Eze 44:20
said unto him, *S* it to be so now............ Mt 3:15
s me first to go and bury my..................... Mt 8:21
s us to go away into the herd of.............. Mt 8:31
s many things of the elders and........... Mt 16:21
also the Son of man s of them.............. Mt 17:12
how long shall I s you.............................. Mt 17:17
*S* little children, and forbid them........... Mt 19:14
neither s ye them that are....................... Mt 23:13
ye s him no more to do ought for.......... Mk 7:12
the Son of man must s many things...... Mk 8:31
man, that he must s many things........... Mk 9:12
how long shall I s you................................ Mk 9:19
*S* the little children to come................. Mk 10:14
would not s that any man should.......... Mk 11:16
would s them to enter into them.............. Lk 8:32
The Son of man must s many things...... Lk 9:22
shall I be with you, and s you................... Lk 9:41
s me first to go and bury my.................... Lk 9:59
But first must he s many things............ Lk 17:25
*S* little children to come unto me........... Lk 18:16
this passover with you before I s........... Lk 22:15
answered and said, *S* ye thus far........... Lk 22:51
and thus it behoved Christ to s.............. Lk 24:46
neither wilt thou s thine Holy............... Acts 2:27
prophets, that Christ should s............... Acts 3:18
worthy to s shame for his name........... Acts 5:41
And seeing one of them s wrong............ Acts 7:24
he must s for my name's sake............... Acts 9:16
Thou shalt not s thine Holy One........ Acts 13:35
s me to speak unto the people............ Acts 21:39
That Christ should s, and that he....... Acts 26:23
if so be that we s with him.................... Rom 8:17
shall be burned, he shall s loss............ 1Cor 3:15
being persecuted, we s it......................... 1Cor 4:12
why do ye not rather s yourselves......... 1Cor 6:7
but s all things, lest we should............ 1Cor 9:12
who will not s you to be tempted........ 1Cor 10:13
And whether one member s, all the.. 1Cor 12:26
s, all the members s with it.................. 1Cor 12:26
same sufferings which we also s.............. 2Cor 1:6
For ye s fools gladly, seeing ye........... 2Cor 11:19
For ye s, if a man bring you into....... 2Cor 11:20
why do I yet s persecution...................... Gal 5:11
only lest they should s............................... Gal 6:12
but also to s for his sake....................... Phil 1:29
both to abound and to s need............... Phil 4:12
that we should s tribulation...................... 1Th 3:4
of God, for which ye also s........................ 2Th 1:5
But I s not a woman to teach, nor......... 1Ti 2:12
s reproach, because we trust in............. 1Ti 4:10
which cause I also s these things........... 2Ti 1:12

Wherein I s trouble, as an evil..................... 2Ti 2:9
If we s, we shall also reign with.............. 2Ti 2:12
Christ Jesus shall s persecution............... 2Ti 3:12
Choosing rather to s affliction............. Heb 11:25
and them which s adversity..................... Heb 13:3
s the word of exhortation....................... Heb 13:22
s for it, ye take it patiently,..................... 1Pet 2:20
if ye s for righteousness' sake,.................. 1Pet 3:14
that ye s for well doing, than.................. 1Pet 3:17
let none of you s as a murderer............. 1Pet 4:15
Yet if any man s as a Christian.............. 1Pet 4:16
Wherefore let them that s....................... 1Pet 4:19
those things which thou shalt s................ Rev 2:10
shall not s their dead bodies to............... Rev 11:9

**SUFFERED**
therefore s I thee not to touch.............. Gen 20:6
but God s him not to hurt me................. Gen 31:7
hast not s me to kiss my sons and...... Gen 31:28
s thee to hunger, and fed thee.............. Deut 8:3
thy God hath not s thee so to do....... Deut 18:14
Moab, and s not a man to pass over... Judg 3:28
s them not to rise against Saul............ 1Sa 24:7
s neither the birds of the air to............ 2Sa 21:10
He s no man to do them wrong......... 1Chr 16:21
(Neither have I s my mouth to sin....... Job 31:30
He s no man to do them wrong........... Ps 105:14
that for thy sake I have s rebuke.......... Jer 15:15
Then he s him.............................................. Mt 3:15
s you to put away your wives.................. Mt 19:8
would not have s his house to be........... Mt 24:43
for I have s many things this day.......... Mt 27:19
s not the devils to speak,.......................... Mk 1:34
Howbeit Jesus s him not, but................... Mk 5:19
had s many things of many....................... Mk 5:26
he s no man to follow him, save............ Mk 5:37
Moses s to write a bill of......................... Mk 10:4
he rebuking them s them not to.............. Lk 4:41
And he s them.............................................. Lk 8:32
he s no man to go in, save Peter,........... Lk 8:51
not have s his house to be broken......... Lk 12:39
because they s such things........................ Lk 13:2
not Christ to have s these things........... Lk 24:26
years s he their manners in the.......... Acts 13:18
Who in times past s all nations.......... Acts 14:16
but the Spirit s them not........................ Acts 16:7
that Christ must needs have s................. Acts 17:3
people, the disciples s him not............ Acts 19:30
but Paul was s to dwell by.................... Acts 28:16
nor for his cause that s wrong.............. 2Cor 7:12
thrice I s shipwreck, a night and........ 2Cor 11:25
Have ye s so many things in vain............ Gal 3:4
for whom I have s the loss of all.......... Phil 3:8
even after that we had s before............... 1Th 2:2
for ye also have s like things of............ 1Th 2:14
he himself hath s being tempted........... Heb 2:18
by the things which he s........................... Heb 5:8
because they were not s to..................... Heb 7:23
s since the foundation of the................. Heb 9:26
his own blood, s without the gate........ Heb 13:12
because Christ also s for us.................... 1Pet 2:21
when he s, he threatened not................. 1Pet 2:23
Christ also hath once s for sins............. 1Pet 3:18
Christ hath s for us in the flesh............. 1Pet 4:1
for he that hath s in the flesh................ 1Pet 4:1
after that ye have s a while.................. 1Pet 5:10

**SUFFEREST**
because thou s that woman Jezebel...... Rev 2:20

**SUFFERETH**
s not our feet to be moved......................... Ps 66:9
s not their cattle to decrease................. Ps 107:38
the kingdom of heaven s violence......... Mt 11:12
sea, yet vengeance s not to live............ Acts 28:4
Charity s long, and is kind.................... 1Cor 13:4

**SUFFERING**
against Cnidus, the wind not s us........ Acts 27:7
the angels for the s of death.................... Heb 2:9
for an example of s affliction.................. Jas 5:10
God endure grief, s wrongfully.............. 1Pet 2:19
s the vengeance of eternal fire.................. Jude 7

**SUFFERINGS**
For I reckon that the s of this............... Rom 8:18
For as the s of Christ abound in............ 2Cor 1:5
the same s which we also suffer............ 2Cor 1:6
that as ye are partakers of the s............ 2Cor 1:7
and the fellowship of his s...................... Phil 3:10
Who now rejoice in my s for you.......... Col 1:24
their salvation perfect through s........... Heb 2:10
beforehand the s of Christ...................... 1Pet 1:11
as ye are partakers of Christ's s............. 1Pet 4:13
and a witness of the s of Christ............. 1Pet 5:1

**SUFFICE**
be slain for them, to s them................ Num 11:22
together for them, to s them................ Num 11:22
LORD said unto me, Let it s thee.......... Deut 3:26
if the dust of Samaria shall s.............. 1Kin 20:10
Israel, let it s you of all your.................. Eze 44:6
Let it s you, O princes of Israel............ Eze 45:9
the time past of our life may s................ 1Pet 4:3

**SUFFICED**
and yet so they s them not................. Judg 21:14
corn, and she did eat, and was s.......... Ruth 2:14
she had reserved after she was s......... Ruth 2:18

**SUFFICETH**
shew us the Father, and it s us................ Jn 14:8

**SUFFICIENCY**
In the fulness of his s he shall............. Job 20:22
but our s is of God.................................... 2Cor 3:5

always having all s in all things 2Cor 9:8

**SUFFICIENT**
For the stuff they had was s for Ex 36:7
surely lend him s for his need Deut 15:8
let his hands be s for him Deut 33:7
eat so much as is s for thee Prov 25:16
And Lebanon is not s to burn Is 40:16
thereof s for a burnt offering Is 40:16
S unto the day is the evil Mt 6:34
whether he have s to finish it Lk 14:28
of bread is not s for them Jn 6:7
S to such a man is this 2Cor 2:6
who is s for these things 2Cor 2:16
Not that we are s of ourselves to 2Cor 3:5
unto me, My grace is s for thee 2Cor 12:9

**SUFFICIENTLY**
had not sanctified themselves s 2Chr 30:3
dwell before the LORD, to eat s Is 23:18

**SUIT**
a s of apparel, and thy victuals Judg 17:10
any s or cause might come unto me 2Sa 15:4
yea, many shall make s unto thee Job 11:19

**SUITS**
The changeable s of apparel Is 3:22

**SUKKIIMS** *(suk'-ke-ims) An Egyptian tribe.*
the Lubim, the S, and the 2Chr 12:3

**SUM**
there be laid on him a s of money Ex 21:30
When thou takest the s of the Ex 30:12
This is the s of the tabernacle, Ex 38:21
Take ye the s of all the Num 1:2
neither take the s of them among Num 1:49
Take the s of the sons of Kohath Num 4:2
Take also the s of the sons of Num 4:22
Take the s of all the Num 26:2
Take the s of the people, from Num 26:4
Take the s of the prey that was Num 31:26
the s of the men of war which are Num 31:49
Joab gave up the s of the number 2Sa 24:9
that he may s the silver which is 2Kin 22:4
Joab gave the s of the number of 1Chr 21:5
of the s of the money that Haman Est 4:7
How great is the s of them Ps 139:17
Thou sealest up the s, full of Eze 28:12
told the s of the matters Dan 7:1
that Abraham bought for a s of Acts 7:16
With a great s obtained I this Acts 22:28
we have spoken this is the s Heb 8:1

**SUMMER**
and harvest, and cold and heat, and s Gen 8:22
and he was sitting in a s parlour Judg 3:20
his feet in his s chamber Judg 3:24
and an hundred of s fruits 2Sa 16:1
s fruit for the young men to eat 2Sa 16:2
is turned into the drought of s Ps 32:4
thou hast made s and winter Ps 74:17
Provideth her meat in the s Prov 6:8
that gathereth in s is a wise son Prov 10:5
As snow in s, and as rain in Prov 26:1
they prepare their meat in the s Prov 30:25
for the shouting for thy s fruits Is 16:9
and the fowls shall s upon them Is 18:6
as the hasty fruit before the s Is 28:4
the s is ended, and we are not Jer 8:20
s fruits, and oil, and put them in Jer 40:10
wine and s fruits very much Jer 40:12
is fallen upon thy s fruits Jer 48:32
chaff of the s threshingfloors Dan 2:35
the winter house with the s house Amos 3:15
and behold a basket of s fruit Amos 8:1
And I said, A basket of s fruit Amos 8:2
they have gathered the s fruits Mic 7:1
in s and in winter shall it be Zec 14:8
leaves, ye know that s is nigh Mt 24:32
leaves, ye know that s is near Mk 13:28
selves that s is now nigh at hand Lk 21:30

**SUMPTUOUSLY**
fine linen, and fared s every day Lk 16:19

**SUN**
when the s was going down, a deep Gen 15:12
when the s went down, and it was Gen 15:17
The s was risen upon the earth Gen 19:23
all night, because the s was set Gen 28:11
over Penuel the s rose upon him Gen 32:31
and, behold, the s and the moon and Gen 37:9
when the s waxed hot, it melted Ex 16:21
until the going down of the s Ex 17:12
If the s be risen upon him, there Ex 22:3
unto him by that the s goeth down Ex 22:26
And when the s is down, he shall Lev 22:7
s shall they of the standard of Num 2:3
up before the LORD against the s Num 25:4
heaven, and when thou seest the s Deut 4:19
by the way where the s goeth down Deut 11:30
even, at the going down of the s Deut 16:6
and worshipped them, either the s Deut 17:3
and when the s is down, he shall Deut 23:11
again when the s goeth down Deut 24:13
shall the s go down upon it Deut 24:15
fruits brought forth by the s Deut 33:14
toward the going down of the s Josh 1:4
and as soon as the s was down Josh 8:29
he said in the sight of Israel, S Josh 10:12
the s stood still, and the moon Josh 10:13
So the s stood still in the midst Josh 10:13
time of the going down of the s Josh 10:27
Jordan toward the rising of the s Josh 12:1
the s when he goeth forth in his Judg 5:31
from battle before the s was up Judg 8:13
morning, as soon as the s is up Judg 9:33
day before the s went down Judg 14:18
the s went down upon them when Judg 19:14
morrow, by that time the s be hot 1Sa 11:9
the s went down when they were 2Sa 2:24
or ought else, till the s be down 2Sa 3:35
thy wives in the sight of this s 2Sa 12:11
all Israel, and before the s 2Sa 12:12
of the morning, when the s riseth 2Sa 23:4
about the going down of the s 1Kin 22:36
the s shone upon the water, and 2Kin 3:22
incense unto Baal, to the s 2Kin 23:5
kings of Judah had given to the s 2Kin 23:11
the chariots of the s with fire 2Kin 23:11
time of the s going down he died 2Chr 18:34
be opened until the s be hot Neh 7:3
He is green before the s, and his Job 8:16
Which commandeth the s, and it Job 9:7
I went mourning without the s Job 30:28
If I beheld the s when it shined Job 31:26
he set a tabernacle for the s Ps 19:4
the s unto the going down thereof Ps 50:1
that they may not see the s Ps 58:8
shall fear thee as long as the s Ps 72:5
be continued as long as the s Ps 72:17
hast prepared the light and the s Ps 74:16
For the LORD God is a s and shield Ps 84:11
and his throne as the s before me Ps 89:36
the s knoweth his going down Ps 104:19
The s ariseth, they gather Ps 104:22
From the rising of the s unto the Ps 113:3
The s shall not smite thee by day Ps 121:6
The s to rule by day Ps 136:8
Praise ye him, s and moon Ps 148:3
which he taketh under the s Eccl 1:3
The s also ariseth Eccl 1:5
the s goeth down, and hasteth to Eccl 1:5
there is no new thing under the s Eccl 1:9
works that are done under the s Eccl 1:14
there was no profit under the s Eccl 2:11
under the s is grievous unto me Eccl 2:17
which I had taken under the s Eccl 2:18
shewed myself wise under the s Eccl 2:19
labour which I took under the s Eccl 2:20
he hath laboured under the s Eccl 2:22
under the s the place of judgment Eccl 3:16
that are done under the s Eccl 4:1
work that is done under the s Eccl 4:3
and I saw vanity under the s Eccl 4:7
the living which walk under the s Eccl 4:15
which I have seen under the s Eccl 5:13
the s all the days of his life Eccl 5:18
which I have seen under the s Eccl 6:1
Moreover he hath not seen the s Eccl 6:5
shall be after him under the s Eccl 6:12
is profit to them that see the s Eccl 7:11
work that is done under the s Eccl 8:9
hath no better thing under the s Eccl 8:15
which God giveth him under the s Eccl 8:15
the work that is done under the s Eccl 8:17
things that are done under the s Eccl 9:3
thing that is done under the s Eccl 9:6
he hath given thee under the s Eccl 9:9
which thou takest under the s Eccl 9:9
I returned, and saw under the s Eccl 9:11
have I seen also under the s Eccl 9:13
which I have seen under the s Eccl 10:5
is for the eyes to behold the s Eccl 11:7
While the s, or the light, or the Eccl 12:2
because the s hath looked upon me Song 1:6
fair as the moon, clear as the s Song 6:10
the s shall be darkened in his Is 13:10
the s ashamed, when the LORD of Is 24:23
shall be as the light of the s Is 30:26
the light of the s shall be Is 30:26
gone down in the s dial of Ahaz Is 38:8
So the s returned ten degrees, by Is 38:8
from the rising of the s shall he Is 41:25
may know from the rising of the s Is 45:6
shall the heat nor s smite them Is 49:10
glory from the rising of the s Is 59:19
The s shall be no more thy light Is 60:19
Thy s shall no more go down Is 60:20
shall spread them before the s Jer 8:2
her s is gone down while it was Jer 15:9
which giveth the s for a light by Jer 31:35
worshipped the s toward the east Eze 8:16
I will cover the s with a cloud Eze 32:7
down of the s to deliver him Dan 6:14
the s and the moon shall be dark, Joel 2:10
The s shall be turned into Joel 2:31
The s and the moon shall be Joel 3:15
cause the s to go down at noon Amos 8:9
when the s did arise, that God Jonah 4:8
the s beat upon the head of Jonah Jonah 4:8
the s shall go down over the Mic 3:6
but when the s ariseth they flee Nah 3:17
The s and moon stood still in Hab 3:11
For from the rising of the s even Mal 1:11
the S of righteousness arise with Mal 4:2
for he maketh his s to rise on Mt 5:45
And when the s was up, they were Mt 13:6
righteous shine forth as the s in Mt 13:43
and his face did shine as the s Mt 17:2
days shall the s be darkened Mt 24:29
And at even, when the s did set Mk 1:32
But when the s was up, it was Mk 4:6
the s shall be darkened, and the Mk 13:24
sepulchre at the rising of the s Mk 16:2
Now when the s was setting Lk 4:40
And there shall be signs in the s Lk 21:25
the s was darkened, and the veil Lk 23:45
The s shall be turned into Acts 2:20
not seeing the s for a season Acts 13:11
above the brightness of the s Acts 26:13
when neither s nor stars in many Acts 27:20
There is one glory of the s 1Cor 15:41
let not the s go down upon your Eph 4:26
For the s is no sooner risen with Jas 1:11
as the s shineth in his strength Rev 1:16
the s became black as sackcloth Rev 6:12
neither shall the s light on them Rev 7:16
third part of the s was smitten Rev 8:12
and the s and the air were darkened Rev 9:2
and his face was as it were the s Rev 10:1
a woman clothed with the s Rev 12:1
poured out his vial upon the s Rev 16:8
I saw an angel standing in the s Rev 19:17
And the city had no need of the s Rev 21:23
no candle, neither light of the s Rev 22:5

**SUNDER**
bow, and cutteth the spear in s Ps 46:9
death, and brake their bands in s Ps 107:14
and cut the bars of iron in s Ps 107:16
chalkstones that are beaten in s Is 27:9
cut in s the bars of iron Is 45:2
and will burst thy bonds in s Nah 1:13
not aware, and will cut him in s Lk 12:46

**SUNDERED**
together, that they cannot be s Job 41:17

**SUNDRY**
God, who at s times and in divers Heb 1:1

**SUNG**
song be s in the land of Judah Is 26:1
And when they had s an hymn Mt 26:30
And when they had s an hymn Mk 14:26
they s a new song, saying, Thou Rev 5:9
they s as it were a new song Rev 14:3

**SUNK**
that the stone s into his 1Sa 17:49
and he s down in his chariot 2Kin 9:24
The heathen are s down in the pit Ps 9:15
so Jeremiah s in the mire Jer 38:6
thy feet are s in the mire Jer 38:22
Her gates are s into the ground Lam 2:9
he s down with sleep, and fell Acts 20:9

**SUNRISING**
is before Moab, toward the s Num 21:11
Jericho eastward, toward the s Num 34:15
on this side Jordan toward the s Deut 4:41
on this side Jordan toward the s Deut 4:47
on this side Jordan toward the s Josh 1:15
and all Lebanon, toward the s Josh 13:5
toward the s unto the border of Josh 19:12
toward the s to Beth-dagon Josh 19:27
to Judah upon Jordan toward the s Josh 19:34
over against Gibeah toward the s Judg 20:43

**SUP**
their faces shall s up as the Hab 1:9
him, Make ready wherewith I may s Lk 17:8
will s with him, and he with me Rev 3:20

**SUPERFLUITY**
s of naughtiness, and receive with Jas 1:21

**SUPERFLUOUS**
hath a flat nose, or any thing s Lev 21:18
thing s or lacking in his parts Lev 22:23
it is s for me to write to you 2Cor 9:1

**SUPERSCRIPTION**
them, Whose is this image and s Mt 22:20
them, Whose is this image and s Mk 12:16
the s of his accusation was Mk 15:26
Whose image and s hath it Lk 20:24
a s also was written over him in Lk 23:38

**SUPERSTITION**
against him of their own s Acts 25:19

**SUPERSTITIOUS**
that in all things ye are too s Acts 17:22

**SUPPED**
he took the cup, when he had s 1Cor 11:25

**SUPPER**
birthday made a s to his lords Mk 6:21
When thou makest a dinner or a s Lk 14:12
him, A certain man made a great s Lk 14:16
sent his servant at s time to say Lk 14:17
were bidden shall taste of my s Lk 14:24
Likewise also the cup after s Lk 22:20
There they made him a s Jn 12:2
s being ended, the devil having Jn 13:2
He riseth from s, and laid aside Jn 13:4
also leaned on his breast at s Jn 21:20
this is not to eat the Lord's s 1Cor 11:20
one taketh before other his own s 1Cor 11:21
unto the marriage s of the Lamb Rev 19:9
unto the s of the great God Rev 19:17

**SUPPLANT**
for every brother will utterly *s* ... Jer 9:4

**SUPPLANTED**
for he hath *s* me these two times ... Gen 27:36

**SUPPLE**
thou washed in water to *s* thee ... Eze 16:4

**SUPPLIANTS**
the rivers of Ethiopia my *s* ... Zeph 3:10

**SUPPLICATION**
I have not made *s* unto the LORD ... 1Sa 13:12
of thy servant, and to his *s* ... 1Kin 8:28
thou to the *s* of thy servant ... 1Kin 8:30
make *s* unto thee in this house ... 1Kin 8:33
*s* soever be made by any man, or ... 1Kin 8:38
in heaven their prayer and their *s* ... 1Kin 8:45
make *s* unto thee in the land of ... 1Kin 8:47
their *s* in heaven thy dwelling ... 1Kin 8:49
be open unto the *s* of thy servant ... 1Kin 8:52
unto the *s* of thy people Israel, ... 1Kin 8:52
*s* unto the LORD, he arose from ... 1Kin 8:54
I have made *s* before the LORD ... 1Kin 8:59
I have heard thy prayer and thy *s* ... 1Kin 9:3
of thy servant, and to his *s* ... 2Chr 6:19
make *s* before thee in this house ... 2Chr 6:24
Then what prayer or what *s* soever ... 2Chr 6:29
heavens their prayer and their *s* ... 2Chr 6:35
intreated of him, and heard his *s* ... 2Chr 33:13
to make *s* unto him, and to make ... Est 4:8
make thy *s* to the Almighty ... Job 8:5
but I would make *s* to my judge ... Job 9:15
The LORD hath heard my *s* ... Ps 6:9
and unto the LORD I made *s* ... Ps 30:8
and hide not thyself from my *s* ... Ps 55:1
Let my *s* come before thee ... Ps 119:170
unto the LORD did I make my *s* ... Ps 142:1
thee, they shall make *s* unto thee ... Is 45:14
present their *s* before the LORD ... Jer 36:7
let my *s*, I pray thee, be ... Jer 37:20
I presented my *s* before the king, ... Jer 38:26
our *s* be accepted before thee, and ... Jer 42:2
me to present your *s* before him ... Jer 42:9
and making *s* before his God ... Dan 6:11
presenting my *s* before the LORD ... Dan 9:20
he wept, and made *s* unto him ... Hos 12:4
with one accord in prayer and *s* ... Acts 1:14
*s* in the Spirit, and watching ... Eph 6:18
perseverance and *s* for all saints ... Eph 6:18
*s* with thanksgiving let your ... Phil 4:6

**SUPPLICATIONS**
unto the *s* of thy servant ... 2Chr 6:21
place, their prayer and their *s* ... 2Chr 6:39
Will he make many *s* unto thee ... Job 41:3
Hear the voice of my *s*, when I ... Ps 28:2
he hath heard the voice of my *s* ... Ps 28:6
of my *s* when I cried unto thee ... Ps 31:22
and attend to the voice of my *s* ... Ps 86:6
he hath heard my voice and my *s* ... Ps 116:1
be attentive to the voice of my *s* ... Ps 130:2
hear the voice of my *s*, O LORD ... Ps 140:6
prayer, O LORD, give ear to my *s* ... Ps 143:1
*s* of the children of Israel ... Jer 3:21
and with *s* will I lead them ... Jer 31:9
Lord God, to seek by prayer and *s* ... Dan 9:3
prayer of thy servant, and his *s* ... Dan 9:17
present our *s* before thee for our ... Dan 9:18
At the beginning of thy *s* the ... Dan 9:23
the spirit of grace and of *s* ... Zec 12:10
therefore, that, first of all, *s* ... 1Ti 2:1
in God, and continueth in *s* ... 1Ti 5:5
*s* with strong crying and tears ... Heb 5:7

**SUPPLIED**
lacking on your part they have *s* ... 1Cor 16:17
which came from Macedonia *s* ... 2Cor 11:9

**SUPPLIETH**
not only *s* the want of the saints ... 2Cor 9:12
by that which every joint *s* ... Eph 4:16

**SUPPLY**
may be a *s* for their want ... 2Cor 8:14
also may be a *s* for your want ... 2Cor 8:14
the *s* of the Spirit of Jesus ... Phil 1:19
to *s* your lack of service toward ... Phil 2:30
But my God shall *s* all your need ... Phil 4:19

**SUPPORT**
labouring ye ought to *s* the weak ... Acts 20:35
*s* the weak, be patient toward all ... 1Th 5:14

**SUPPOSE**
Let not my lord *s* that they have ... 2Sa 13:32
I *s* that he, to whom he forgave ... Lk 7:43
*S* ye that I am come to give peace ... Lk 12:51
*S* ye that these Galilaeans were ... Lk 13:2
I *s* that even the world itself ... Jn 21:25
these are not drunken, as ye *s* ... Acts 2:15
I *s* therefore that this is good ... 1Cor 7:26
For I *s* I was not a whit behind ... 2Cor 11:5
*s* ye, shall he be thought worthy, ... Heb 10:29
faithful brother unto you, as I *s* ... 1Pet 5:12

**SUPPOSED**
they *s* that they should have ... Mt 20:10
they *s* it had been a spirit, and ... Mk 6:49
being (as was *s*) the son of ... Lk 3:23
*s* that they had seen a spirit ... Lk 24:37
For he *s* his brethren would have ... Acts 7:25
whom they *s* that Paul had brought ... Acts 21:29
accusation of such things as I *s* ... Acts 25:18
Yet I *s* it necessary to send to ... Phil 2:25

**SUPPOSING**
*s* him to have been in the company ... Lk 2:44
*s* him to be the gardener, saith ... Jn 20:15
of the city, *s* he had been dead ... Acts 14:19
*s* that the prisoners had been ... Acts 16:27
*s* that they had obtained their ... Acts 27:13
*s* to add affliction to my bonds ... Phil 1:16
truth, *s* that gain is godliness ... 1Ti 6:5

**SUPREME**
whether it be to the king, as *s* ... 1Pet 2:13

**SUR** (*sur*) *A gate of the Temple.*
part shall be at the gate of *S* ... 2Kin 11:6

**SURE**
borders round about, were made *s* ... Gen 23:17
were made *s* unto Abraham for a ... Gen 23:20
I am *s* that the king of Egypt ... Ex 3:19
be *s* your sin will find you out ... Num 32:23
Only be *s* that thou eat not the ... Deut 12:23
and I will build him a *s* house ... 1Sa 2:35
then be *s* that evil is determined ... 1Sa 20:7
certainly make my lord a *s* house ... 1Sa 25:28
because I was *s* that he could not ... 2Sa 1:10
ordered in all things, and *s* ... 2Sa 23:5
thee, and build thee a *s* house ... 1Kin 11:38
of all this we make a *s* covenant ... Neh 9:38
riseth up, and no man is *s* of life ... Job 24:22
the testimony of the LORD is *s* ... Ps 19:7
Thy testimonies are very *s* ... Ps 93:5
all his commandments are *s* ... Ps 111:7
thyself, and make *s* thy friend ... Prov 6:3
and he that hateth suretiship is *s* ... Prov 11:15
righteousness shall be a *s* reward ... Prov 11:18
fasten him as a nail in a *s* place ... Is 22:23
in the *s* place be removed ... Is 22:25
corner stone, a *s* foundation ... Is 28:16
in *s* dwellings, and in quiet ... Is 32:18
his waters shall be *s* ... Is 33:16
even the *s* mercies of David ... Is 55:3
and the interpretation thereof *s* ... Dan 2:45
thy kingdom shall be *s* unto thee ... Dan 4:26
be made *s* until the third day ... Mt 27:64
your way, make it as *s* as ye can ... Mt 27:65
went, and made the sepulchre *s* ... Mt 27:66
notwithstanding be ye *s* of this ... Lk 10:11
are *s* that thou art that Christ, ... Jn 6:69
Now are we *s* that thou knowest ... Jn 16:30
give you the *s* mercies of David ... Acts 13:34
But we are *s* that the judgment of ... Rom 2:2
might be *s* to all the seed ... Rom 4:16
And I am *s* that, when I come unto .. Rom 15:29
the foundation of God standeth *s* ... 2Ti 2:19
as an anchor of the soul, both *s* ... Heb 6:19
make your calling and election *s* ... 2Pet 1:10
also a more *s* word of prophecy ... 2Pet 1:19

**SURELY**
eatest thereof thou shalt *s* die ... Gen 2:17
the woman, Ye shall not *s* die ... Gen 3:4
*s* your blood of your lives will I ... Gen 9:5
Abraham shall *s* become a great ... Gen 18:18
know thou that thou shalt *s* die ... Gen 20:7
*S* the fear of God is not in this ... Gen 20:11
his wife shall *s* be put to death ... Gen 26:11
*S* the LORD is in this place ... Gen 28:16
I will *s* give the tenth unto thee ... Gen 28:22
*S* thou art my bone and my flesh ... Gen 29:14
*S* the LORD hath looked upon my ... Gen 29:32
for *s* I have hired thee with my ... Gen 30:16
*s* thou hadst sent me away now ... Gen 31:42
I will *s* do thee good, and make ... Gen 32:12
life of Pharaoh *s* ye are spies ... Gen 42:16
*s* now we had returned this second ... Gen 43:10
and I said, *S* he is torn in pieces ... Gen 44:28
I will also *s* bring thee up again ... Gen 46:4
God will *s* visit you, and bring ... Gen 50:24
God will *s* visit you, and ye shall ... Gen 50:25
and said, *S* this thing is known ... Ex 2:14
I have *s* seen the affliction of ... Ex 3:7
I have *s* visited you, and seen ... Ex 3:16
*S* a bloody husband art thou to me ... Ex 4:25
he shall *s* thrust you out hence ... Ex 11:1
saying, God will *s* visit you ... Ex 13:19
Thou wilt *s* wear away, both thou, ... Ex 18:18
the mount shall be *s* put to death ... Ex 19:12
it, but he shall *s* be stoned ... Ex 19:13
he die, shall be *s* put to death ... Ex 21:12
mother, shall be *s* put to death ... Ex 21:15
he shall *s* be put to death ... Ex 21:16
mother, shall *s* be put to death ... Ex 21:17
he shall be *s* punished ... Ex 21:20
he shall be *s* punished, according ... Ex 21:22
then the ox shall be *s* stoned ... Ex 21:28
he shall *s* pay ox for ox ... Ex 21:36
the fire shall *s* make restitution ... Ex 22:6
with it, he shall *s* make it good ... Ex 22:14
he shall *s* endow her to be his ... Ex 22:16
a beast shall *s* be put to death ... Ex 22:19
unto me, I will *s* hear their cry ... Ex 22:23
thou shalt *s* bring it back to him ... Ex 23:4
thou shalt *s* help with him ... Ex 23:5
it will *s* be a snare unto thee ... Ex 23:33
it shall *s* be put to death ... Ex 31:14
he shall *s* be put to death ... Ex 31:15
for their anointing shall *s* be an ... Ex 40:15
he shall *s* be put to death ... Lev 20:2
mother shall be *s* put to death ... Lev 20:9
shall *s* be put to death ... Lev 20:10
of them shall *s* be put to death ... Lev 20:11
of them shall *s* be put to death ... Lev 20:12
they shall *s* be put to death ... Lev 20:13
he shall *s* be put to death ... Lev 20:15
they shall *s* be put to death ... Lev 20:16
a wizard, shall *s* be put to death ... Lev 20:27
he shall *s* be put to death, and ... Lev 24:16
any man shall *s* be put to death ... Lev 24:17
but shall *s* be put to death ... Lev 27:29
*s* it floweth with milk and honey ... Num 13:27
*S* they shall not see the land ... Num 14:23
I will *s* do it unto all this evil ... Num 14:35
The man shall be *s* put to death ... Num 15:35
of man shalt thou *s* redeem ... Num 18:15
*s* now also I had slain thee, and ... Num 22:33
*S* there is no enchantment against ... Num 23:23
of them, They shall *s* die in the ... Num 26:65
thou shalt *s* give them a ... Num 27:7
*S* none of the men that came up ... Num 32:11
murderer shall *s* be put to death ... Num 35:16
murderer shall *s* be put to death ... Num 35:17
murderer shall *s* be put to death ... Num 35:18
smote him shall *s* be put to death ... Num 35:21
but he shall be *s* put to death ... Num 35:31
*S* there shall not one of these ... Deut 1:35
*S* this great nation is a wise and ... Deut 4:6
this day that ye shall *s* perish ... Deut 8:19
But thou shalt *s* kill him ... Deut 13:9
Thou shalt *s* smite the ... Deut 13:15
shalt *s* lend him sufficient for ... Deut 15:8
Thou shalt *s* give him, and thine ... Deut 15:10
therefore thou shalt *s* rejoice ... Deut 16:15
thou shalt *s* help him to lift ... Deut 22:4
thy God will *s* require it of thee ... Deut 23:21
this day, that ye shall *s* perish ... Deut 30:18
I will *s* hide my face in that day ... Deut 31:18
*S* the land whereon thy feet have ... Josh 14:9
*S* he covereth his feet in his ... Judg 3:24
she said, I will *s* go with thee ... Judg 4:9
*S* I will be with thee, and thou ... Judg 6:16
shall *s* be the LORD's, and I will ... Judg 11:31
unto his wife, We shall *s* die ... Judg 13:22
but *s* we will not kill thee ... Judg 15:13
*S* they are smitten down before us ... Judg 20:39
He shall *s* be put to death ... Judg 21:5
*S* we will return with thee unto ... Ruth 1:10
that he saith cometh *s* to pass ... 1Sa 9:6
Jonathan my son, he shall *s* die ... 1Sa 14:39
for thou shalt *s* die, Jonathan ... 1Sa 14:44
*S* the bitterness of death is past ... 1Sa 15:32
*S* the LORD's anointed is before ... 1Sa 16:6
*s* to defy Israel is he come up ... 1Sa 17:25
*s* he is not clean ... 1Sa 20:26
him unto me, for he shall *s* die ... 1Sa 20:31
the king said, Thou shalt *s* die ... 1Sa 22:16
there, that he would *s* tell Saul ... 1Sa 22:22
well that thou shalt *s* be king ... 1Sa 24:20
*S* in vain have I kept all that ... 1Sa 25:21
*s* there had not been left unto ... 1Sa 25:34
*S* thou shalt know what thy ... 1Sa 28:2
called David, and said unto him, *S* ... 1Sa 29:6
for thou shalt *s* overtake them ... 1Sa 30:8
*s* then in the morning the people ... 2Sa 2:27
for I will *s* shew thee kindness ... 2Sa 9:7
*S* the men prevailed against us, ... 2Sa 11:23
hath done this thing shall *s* die, ... 2Sa 12:5
is born unto thee shall *s* die ... 2Sa 12:14
*s* in what place my lord the king ... 2Sa 15:21
I will *s* go forth with you myself ... 2Sa 18:2
They shall *s* ask counsel at Abel ... 2Sa 20:18
but I will *s* buy it of thee at a ... 2Sa 24:24
for certain that thou shalt *s* die ... 1Kin 2:37
whither, that thou shalt *s* die ... 1Kin 2:42
I have *s* built thee an house to ... 1Kin 8:13
for *s* they will turn away your ... 1Kin 11:2
I will *s* rend the kingdom from ... 1Kin 11:11
of Samaria, shall *s* come to pass ... 1Kin 13:32
I will *s* shew myself unto him to ... 1Kin 18:15
*s* we shall be stronger than they ... 1Kin 20:23
*s* we shall be stronger than they ... 1Kin 20:25
*S* it is the king of Israel ... 1Kin 22:32
thou art gone up, but shalt *s* die ... 2Kin 1:4
thou art gone up, but shalt *s* die ... 2Kin 1:6
thou art gone up, but shalt *s* die ... 2Kin 1:16
liveth, before whom I stand, *s* ... 2Kin 3:14
the kings are *s* slain, and they ... 2Kin 3:23
He will *s* come out to me, and ... 2Kin 5:11
shewed me that he shall *s* die ... 2Kin 8:10
me that thou shouldest *s* recover ... 2Kin 8:14
*S* I have seen yesterday the blood ... 2Kin 9:26
The LORD will *s* deliver us ... 2Kin 18:30
*S* there was not holden such a ... 2Kin 23:22
*S* at the commandment of the LORD ... 2Kin 24:3
but shalt *s* fall before him ... Est 6:13
*s* now he would awake for thee, and ... Job 8:6
*S* I would speak to the Almighty, ... Job 13:3
He will *s* reprove you, if ye do ... Job 13:10
*s* the mountain falling cometh to ... Job 14:18
*S* such are the dwellings of the ... Job 18:21
*S* he shall not feel quietness in ... Job 20:20
*S* there is a vein for the silver, ... Job 28:1
*S* I would take it upon my ... Job 31:36
*S* thou hast spoken in mine ... Job 33:8
*s* God will not do wickedly, ... Job 34:12
*S* it is meet to be said unto God, ... Job 34:31
*S* God will not hear vanity, ... Job 35:13
*s* he shall be swallowed up ... Job 37:20
*S* the mountains bring him forth ... Job 40:20
*S* goodness and mercy shall follow ... Ps 23:6
*s* in the floods of great waters ... Ps 32:6
*S* every man walketh in a vain ... Ps 39:6

S

*s* they are disquieted in vain ... Ps 39:6
*s* every man is vanity ... Ps 39:11
*S* men of low degree are vanity, ... Ps 62:9
*S* thou didst set them in slippery ... Ps 73:18
*S* the wrath of man shall praise ... Ps 76:10
*s* I will remember thy wonders of ... Ps 77:11
*S* his salvation is nigh them that ... Ps 85:9
*S* he shall deliver thee from the ... Ps 91:3
*S* he shall not be moved for ever ... Ps 112:6
*S* I have behaved and quieted ... Ps 131:2
*S* I will not come into the ... Ps 132:3
*S* the darkness shall cover me ... Ps 139:11
*S* thou wilt slay the wicked, O ... Ps 139:19
*S* the righteous shall give thanks ... Ps 140:13
*S* in vain the net is spread in ... Prov 1:17
*S* he scorneth the scorners ... Prov 3:34
that walketh uprightly walketh *s* ... Prov 10:9
to the rich, shall *s* come to want ... Prov 22:16
For *s* there is an end ... Prov 23:18
*S* I am more brutish than any man, ... Prov 30:2
*S* the churning of milk bringeth ... Prov 30:33
*S* this also is vanity and vexation ... Eccl 4:16
*S* oppression maketh a wise man ... Eccl 7:7
yet *s* I know that it shall be ... Eccl 8:12
*S* the serpent will bite without ... Eccl 10:11
*s* ye shall not be established ... Is 7:9
*S* as I have thought, so shall it ... Is 14:24
*s* they are stricken ... Is 16:7
*S* the princes of Zoan are fools, ... Is 19:11
*S* this iniquity shall not be ... Is 22:14
captivity, and will *s* cover thee ... Is 22:17
He will *s* violently turn and toss ... Is 22:18
*S* your turning of things upside ... Is 29:16
The LORD will *s* deliver us ... Is 36:15
*s* the people is grass ... Is 40:7
thee, saying, *S* God is in thee ... Is 45:14
*S*, shall one say, in the LORD ... Is 45:24
yet *s* my judgment is with the ... Is 49:4
thou shalt *s* clothe thee with ... Is 49:18
*S* he hath borne our griefs, and ... Is 53:4
they shall *s* gather together, but ... Is 54:15
*S* the isles shall wait for me, and ... Is 60:9
*S* I will no more give thy corn to ... Is 62:8
*S* they are my people, children ... Is 63:8
*s* his anger shall turn from me ... Jer 2:35
*S* as a wife treacherously ... Jer 3:20
*s* thou hast greatly deceived this ... Jer 4:10
*s* they swear falsely ... Jer 5:2
I said, *S* these are poor ... Jer 5:4
I will *s* consume them, saith the ... Jer 8:13
*S* our fathers have inherited lies ... Jer 16:19
yet *s* I will make thee a ... Jer 22:6
*s* then shalt thou be ashamed and ... Jer 22:22
*s* thus saith the LORD, So will I ... Jer 24:8
him, saying, Thou shalt *s* die ... Jer 26:8
ye shall *s* bring innocent blood ... Jer 26:15
I have *s* heard Ephraim bemoaning ... Jer 31:18
*S* after that I was turned, I ... Jer 31:19
I will *s* have mercy upon him, ... Jer 31:20
but shall *s* be delivered into the ... Jer 32:4
of his hand, but shalt *s* be taken ... Jer 34:3
We will *s* tell the king of all ... Jer 36:16
Chaldeans shall *s* depart from us ... Jer 37:9
This city shall *s* be given into ... Jer 38:3
wilt thou not *s* put me to death ... Jer 38:15
For I will *s* deliver thee, and ... Jer 39:18
We will *s* perform our vows that ... Jer 44:25
ye will *s* accomplish your vows, ... Jer 44:25
your vows, and *s* perform your vows ... Jer 44:25
*s* stand against you for evil ... Jer 44:29
*S* as Tabor is among the mountains ... Jer 46:18
but thou shalt *s* drink of it ... Jer 49:12
*S* the least of the flock shall ... Jer 49:20
*s* he shall make their habitations ... Jer 49:20
*S* the least of the flock shall ... Jer 50:45
*s* he shall make their habitation ... Jer 50:45
*S* I will fill thee with men, as ... Jer 51:14
of recompences shall *s* requite ... Jer 51:56
*S* against me is he turned ... Lam 3:3
*S*, had I sent thee to them, they ... Eze 3:6
unto the wicked, Thou shalt *s* die ... Eze 3:18
he doth not sin, he shall *s* live ... Eze 3:21
*S*, because thou hast defiled my ... Eze 5:11
*s* in the place where the king ... Eze 17:16
*s* mine oath that he hath despised ... Eze 17:19
he is just, he shall *s* live ... Eze 18:9
he shall *s* die ... Eze 18:13
of his father, he shall *s* live ... Eze 18:17
hath done them, he shall *s* live ... Eze 18:19
lawful and right, he shall *s* live ... Eze 18:21
hath committed, he shall *s* live ... Eze 18:28
*s* with a mighty hand, and with a ... Eze 20:33
he shall *s* deal with him ... Eze 31:11
O wicked man, thou shalt *s* die ... Eze 33:8
righteous, that he shall *s* live ... Eze 33:13
unto the wicked, Thou shalt *s* die ... Eze 33:14
he shall *s* live, he shall not die ... Eze 33:15
he shall *s* live ... Eze 33:16
*s* they that are in the wastes ... Eze 33:27
*s* because my flock became a prey, ... Eze 34:8
*S* in the fire of my jealousy have ... Eze 36:5
*S* the heathen that are about you, ... Eze 36:7
*S* in that day there shall be a ... Eze 38:19
made known that which shall *s* be ... Hos 5:9
*s* they are vanity ... Hos 12:11
*S* the Lord GOD will do nothing, ... Amos 3:7
for Gilgal shall *s* go into ... Amos 5:5
Israel shall *s* be led away ... Amos 7:11
Israel shall *s* go into captivity ... Amos 7:17
*S* I will never forget any of ... Amos 8:7
I will *s* assemble, O Jacob, all ... Mic 2:12
I will *s* gather the remnant of ... Mic 2:12
because it will *s* come, it will ... Hab 2:3
*S* Moab shall be as Sodom, and the ... Zeph 2:9
*S* thou wilt fear me, thou wilt ... Zeph 3:7
*S* thou also art one of them ... Mt 26:73
to Peter, *S* thou art one of them ... Mk 14:70
are most *s* believed among us ... Lk 1:1
Ye will *s* say unto me this ... Lk 4:23
have known *s* that I came out from ... Jn 17:8
*S* blessing I will bless thee, and ... Heb 6:14
things saith, *S* I come quickly ... Rev 22:20

**SURETIES**
or of them that are *s* for debts ... Prov 22:26

**SURETISHIP**
and he that hateth *s* is sure ... Prov 11:15

**SURETY**
Know of a *s* that thy seed shall ... Gen 15:13
Shall I of a *s* bear a child ... Gen 18:13
Behold, of a *s* she is thy wife ... Gen 26:9
I will be *s* for him ... Gen 43:9
For thy servant became *s* for the ... Gen 44:32
down now, put me in a *s* with thee ... Job 17:3
Be *s* for thy servant for good ... Ps 119:122
if thou be *s* for thy friend, if ... Prov 6:1
He that is *s* for a stranger shall ... Prov 11:15
becometh *s* in the presence of his ... Prov 17:18
garment that is *s* for a stranger ... Prov 20:16
garment that is *s* for a stranger ... Prov 27:13
he said, Now I know of a *s* ... Acts 12:11
made a *s* of a better testament ... Heb 7:22

**SURFEITING**
your hearts be overcharged with *s* ... Lk 21:34

**SURMISINGS**
envy, strife, railings, evil *s* ... 1Ti 6:4

**SURNAME**
*s* himself by the name of Israel ... Is 44:5
Lebbaeus, whose *s* was Thaddaeus ... Mt 10:3
for one Simon, whose *s* is Peter ... Acts 10:5
hither Simon, whose *s* is Peter ... Acts 10:32
call for Simon, whose *s* is Peter ... Acts 11:13
mother of John, whose *s* was Mark ... Acts 12:12
with them John, whose *s* was Mark .. Acts 12:25
with them John, whose *s* was Mark .. Acts 15:37

**SURNAMED**
I have *s* thee, though thou hast ... Is 45:4
And Simon he *s* Peter ... Mk 3:16
he *s* them Boanerges, which is, ... Mk 3:17
Satan into Judas *s* Iscariot ... Lk 22:3
called Barsabas, who was *s* Justus ... Acts 1:23
by the apostles was *s* Barnabas ... Acts 4:36
whether Simon, which was *s* Peter ... Acts 10:18
Judas *s* Barsabas, and Silas, chief ... Acts 15:22

**SURPRISED**
fearfulness hath *s* the hypocrites ... Is 33:14
taken, and the strong holds are *s* ... Jer 48:41
the praise of the whole earth *s* ... Jer 51:41

**SUSA** See SHUSHAN.

**SUSANCHITES** (*su'-san-kites*) *Resettled foreigners in Israel.*
the Babylonians, the *S*, the ... Ezr 4:9

**SUSANNA** (*su'-zan'-nah*) *A woman follower of Jesus.*
of Chuza Herod's steward, and *S* ... Lk 8:3

**SUSI** (*su'-si*) *Father of Gaddi.*
of Manasseh, Gaddi the son of *S* ... Num 13:11

**SUSTAIN**
a widow woman there to *s* thee ... 1Kin 17:9
thou *s* them in the wilderness ... Neh 9:21
upon the LORD, and he shall *s* thee ... Ps 55:22
of a man will *s* his infirmity ... Prov 18:14

**SUSTAINED**
and with corn and wine have I *s* him Gen 27:37
for the LORD *s* me ... Ps 3:5
and his righteousness, it *s* him ... Is 59:16

**SUSTENANCE**
left no *s* for Israel, neither ... Judg 6:4
of *s* while he lay at Mahanaim ... 2Sa 19:32
and our fathers found no *s* ... Acts 7:11

**SWADDLED**
those that I have *s* and brought up ... Lam 2:22
not salted at all, nor *s* at all ... Eze 16:4

**SWADDLING**
son, and wrapped him in *s* clothes ... Lk 2:7
the babe wrapped in *s* clothes ... Lk 2:12

**SWADDLINGBAND**
and thick darkness a *s* for it ... Job 38:9

**SWALLOW**
and *s* them up, with all that ... Num 16:30
said, Lest the earth *s* us up also ... Num 16:34
why wilt thou *s* up the ... 2Sa 20:19
me, that I should *s* up or destroy ... 2Sa 20:20
me alone till I *s* down my spittle ... Job 7:19
restore, and shall not *s* it down ... Job 20:18
the LORD shall *s* them up in his ... Ps 21:9
for man would *s* me up ... Ps 56:1
Mine enemies would daily *s* me up ... Ps 56:2
of him that would *s* me up ... Ps 57:3
me, neither let the deep *s* me up ... Ps 69:15
the *s* a nest for herself, where ... Ps 84:3
Let us *s* them up alive as the ... Prov 1:12
as the *s* by flying, so the curse ... Prov 26:2
lips of a fool will *s* up himself ... Eccl 10:12
He will *s* up death in victory ... Is 25:8
Like a crane or a *s*, so did I ... Is 38:14
the *s* observe the time of their ... Jer 8:7
the strangers shall *s* it up ... Hos 8:7
O ye that *s* up the needy, even to ... Amos 8:4
shall drink, and they shall *s* down ... Obad 16
a great fish to *s* up Jonah ... Jonah 1:17
strain at a gnat, and *s* a camel ... Mt 23:24

**SWALLOWED**
but Aaron's rod *s* up their rods ... Ex 7:12
thy right hand, the earth *s* them ... Ex 15:12
*s* them up, and their houses, and ... Num 16:32
*s* them up together with Korah, ... Num 26:10
*s* them up, and their households, ... Deut 11:6
lest the king be *s* up, and all the ... 2Sa 17:16
therefore my words are *s* up ... Job 6:3
He hath *s* down riches, and he ... Job 20:15
speak, surely he shall be *s* up ... Job 37:20
them not say, We have *s* him up ... Ps 35:25
*s* up Dathan, and covered the ... Ps 106:17
Then they had *s* us up quick ... Ps 124:3
they are *s* up of wine, they are ... Is 28:7
they that *s* thee up shall be far ... Is 49:19
he hath *s* me up like a dragon, he ... Jer 51:34
his mouth that which he hath *s* up ... Jer 51:44
The Lord hath *s* up all the ... Lam 2:2
he hath *s* up Israel, he hath ... Lam 2:5
he hath *s* up all her palaces ... Lam 2:5
they say, We have *s* her up ... Lam 2:16
*s* you up on every side, that ye ... Eze 36:3
Israel is *s* up ... Hos 8:8
written, Death is *s* up in victory ... 1Cor 15:54
be *s* up with overmuch sorrow ... 2Cor 2:7
mortality might be *s* up of life ... 2Cor 5:4
*s* up the flood which the dragon ... Rev 12:16

**SWALLOWETH**
the robber *s* up their substance ... Job 5:5
He *s* the ground with fierceness ... Job 39:24

**SWAN**
And the *s*, and the pelican, and the ... Lev 11:18
owl, and the great owl, and the *s* ... Deut 14:16

**SWARE**
because there they *s* both of them ... Gen 21:31
that *s* unto me, saying, Unto thy ... Gen 24:7
*s* to him concerning that matter ... Gen 24:9
and he *s* unto him ... Gen 25:33
which I *s* unto Abraham thy father ... Gen 26:3
the morning, and *s* one to another ... Gen 26:31
Jacob *s* by the fear of his father ... Gen 31:53
And he *s* unto him ... Gen 47:31
the land which he *s* to Abraham ... Gen 50:24
which he *s* unto thy fathers to ... Ex 13:5
as he *s* unto thee and to thy ... Ex 13:11
the land which I *s* unto Abraham ... Ex 33:1
the land which he *s* unto them ... Num 14:16
land which I *s* unto their fathers ... Num 14:23
concerning which I *s* to make you ... Num 14:30
kindled the same time, and he *s* ... Num 32:10
the land which I *s* unto Abraham ... Num 32:11
the LORD *s* unto your fathers ... Deut 1:8
of your words, and was wroth, and *s* .. Deut 1:34
which I *s* to give unto your ... Deut 1:35
the host, as the LORD *s* unto them ... Deut 2:14
*s* that I should not go over ... Deut 4:21
thy fathers which he *s* unto them ... Deut 4:31
land which he *s* unto thy fathers ... Deut 6:10
which the LORD *s* unto thy fathers ... Deut 6:18
land which he *s* unto our fathers ... Deut 6:23
mercy which he *s* unto thy fathers ... Deut 7:12
in the land which he *s* unto thy ... Deut 7:13
the LORD *s* unto your fathers ... Deut 8:1
which he *s* unto thy fathers ... Deut 8:18
which the LORD *s* unto thy fathers ... Deut 9:5
which I *s* unto their fathers to ... Deut 10:11
which the LORD *s* unto your ... Deut 11:9
in the land which the LORD *s* unto ... Deut 11:21
*s* unto our fathers for to give us ... Deut 26:3
in the land which the LORD *s* unto ... Deut 28:11
which the LORD *s* unto thy fathers ... Deut 30:20
land which I *s* unto their fathers ... Deut 31:20
them into the land which I *s* ... Deut 31:21
into the land which I *s* unto them ... Deut 31:23
the land which I *s* unto Abraham ... Deut 34:4
which I *s* unto their fathers to ... Josh 1:6
unto whom the LORD *s* that he ... Josh 5:6
which the LORD *s* unto their ... Josh 5:6
that she hath, as ye *s* unto her ... Josh 6:22
of the congregation *s* unto them ... Josh 9:15
of the oath which we *s* unto them ... Josh 9:20
Moses *s* on that day, saying, ... Josh 14:9
he *s* to give unto their fathers ... Josh 21:43
all that he *s* unto their fathers ... Josh 21:44
land which I *s* unto your fathers ... Judg 2:1
and Saul *s*, As the LORD liveth, he ... 1Sa 19:6
David *s* moreover, and said, Thy ... 1Sa 20:3
And David *s* unto Saul ... 1Sa 24:22
Saul *s* to her by the LORD, saying ... 1Sa 28:10
while it was yet day, David *s* ... 2Sa 3:35
And the king *s* unto him ... 2Sa 19:23
Then the men of David *s* unto him ... 2Sa 21:17
And the king *s*, and said, As the ... 1Kin 1:29
Even as I *s* unto thee by the LORD ... 1Kin 1:30
I *s* to him by the LORD, saying, I ... 1Kin 2:8
Then king Solomon *s* by the LORD ... 1Kin 2:23
And Gedaliah *s* to them, and to ... 2Kin 25:24

they *s* unto the LORD with a loud ...... 2Chr 15:14
And they *s* ...... Ezr 10:5
Unto whom I *s* in my wrath that ...... Ps 95:11
How he *s* unto the LORD, and vowed ...... Ps 132:2
So Zedekiah the king *s* secretly ...... Jer 38:16
the son of Shaphan *s* unto them ...... Jer 40:9
I *s* unto thee, and entered into a ...... Eze 16:8
*s* by him that liveth for ever ...... Dan 12:7
he *s* unto her, Whatsoever thou ...... Mk 6:23
The oath which he *s* to our father ...... Lk 1:73
So I *s* in my wrath, They shall ...... Heb 3:11
to whom *s* he that they should not ...... Heb 3:18
by no greater, he *s* by himself, ...... Heb 6:13
that said unto him, The Lord *s* ...... Heb 7:21
*s* by him that liveth for ever and ...... Rev 10:6

**SWAREST**
to whom thou *s* by thine own self, ...... Ex 32:13
which thou *s* unto their fathers ...... Num 11:12
as thou *s* unto our fathers, a ...... Deut 26:15
thou *s* by the LORD thy God unto ...... 1Kin 1:17
which thou *s* unto David in thy ...... Ps 89:49

**SWARM**
there came a grievous *s* of flies ...... Ex 8:24
by reason of the *s* of flies ...... Ex 8:24
and, behold, there was a *s* of bees ...... Judg 14:8

**SWARMS**
I will send *s* of flies upon thee, ...... Ex 8:21
shall be full of *s* of flies ...... Ex 8:21
that no *s* of flies shall be there ...... Ex 8:22
the *s* of flies may depart from ...... Ex 8:29
he removed the *s* of flies from ...... Ex 8:31

**SWEAR**
Now therefore *s* unto me here by ...... Gen 21:23
And Abraham said, I will *s* ...... Gen 21:24
And I will make thee *s* by the LORD ...... Gen 24:3
And my master made me *s*, saying, ...... Gen 24:37
And Jacob said, *S* to me this day ...... Gen 25:33
And he said, *S* unto me ...... Gen 47:31
My father made me *s*, saying, Lo, ...... Gen 50:5
according as he made thee *s* ...... Gen 50:6
I did *s* to give it to Abraham ...... Ex 6:8
Or if a soul *s*, pronouncing with ...... Lev 5:4
ye shall not *s* by my name falsely ...... Lev 19:12
or *s* an oath to bind his soul ...... Num 30:2
serve him, and shalt *s* by his name ...... Deut 6:13
thou cleave, and *s* by his name ...... Deut 10:20
*s* unto me by the LORD, since I ...... Josh 2:12
oath which thou hast made us *s* ...... Josh 2:17
oath which thou hast made us to *s* ...... Josh 2:20
gods, nor cause to *s* by them ...... Josh 23:7
*S* unto me, that ye will not fall ...... Judg 15:12
Jonathan caused David to *s* again ...... 1Sa 20:17
*S* now therefore unto me by the ...... 1Sa 24:21
*S* unto me by God, that thou wilt ...... 1Sa 30:15
for I *s* by the LORD, if thou go ...... 2Sa 19:7
*s* unto thine handmaid, saying, ...... 1Kin 1:13
Let king Solomon *s* unto me to day ...... 1Kin 1:51
I not make thee to *s* by the LORD ...... 1Kin 2:42
laid upon him to cause him to *s* ...... 1Kin 8:31
be laid upon him to make him *s* ...... 2Chr 6:22
who had made him *s* by God ...... 2Chr 36:13
Israel, to *s* that they should do ...... Ezr 10:5
their hair, and made them *s* by God ...... Neh 13:25
In that day shall he *s*, saying, I ...... Is 3:7
Canaan, and *s* to the LORD of hosts ...... Is 19:18
shall bow, every tongue shall *s* ...... Is 45:23
which *s* by the name of the LORD, ...... Is 48:1
earth shall *s* by the God of truth ...... Is 65:16
And thou shalt *s*, The LORD liveth, ...... Jer 4:2
surely they *s* falsely ...... Jer 5:2
*s* falsely, and burn incense unto ...... Jer 7:9
to *s* by my name, The LORD liveth ...... Jer 12:16
taught my people to *s* by Baal ...... Jer 12:16
I *s* by myself, saith the LORD, ...... Jer 22:5
which thou didst *s* to their ...... Jer 32:22
go ye up to Beth-aven, nor *s* ...... Hos 4:15
They that *s* by the sin of Samaria ...... Amos 8:14
that *s* by the LORD ...... Zeph 1:5
and that *s* by Malcham ...... Zeph 1:5
But I say unto you, *S* not at all ...... Mt 5:34
Neither shalt thou *s* by thy head ...... Mt 5:36
Whosoever shall *s* by the temple ...... Mt 23:16
but whosoever shall *s* by the gold ...... Mt 23:16
Whosoever shall *s* by the altar ...... Mt 23:18
therefore shall *s* by the altar ...... Mt 23:20
whoso shall *s* by the temple, ...... Mt 23:21
And he that shall *s* by heaven ...... Mt 23:22
Then began he to curse and to *s* ...... Mt 26:74
But he began to curse and to *s* ...... Mk 14:71
because he could *s* by no greater ...... Heb 6:13
For men verily *s* by the greater ...... Heb 6:16
*s* not, neither by heaven, neither ...... Jas 5:12

**SWEARERS**
adulterers, and against false *s* ...... Mal 3:5

**SWEARETH**
lieth concerning it, and *s* falsely ...... Lev 6:3
He that *s* to his own hurt, and ...... Ps 15:4
every one that *s* by him shall ...... Ps 63:11
and he that *s*, as he that feareth ...... Eccl 9:2
he that *s* in the earth shall ...... Is 65:16
every one that *s* shall be cut off ...... Zec 5:3
of him that *s* falsely by my name ...... Zec 5:4
but whosoever *s* by the gift that ...... Mt 23:18
*s* by it, and by all things thereon ...... Mt 23:20
*s* by it, and by him that dwelleth ...... Mt 23:21
*s* by the throne of God, and by him ...... Mt 23:22

**SWEARING**
soul sin, and hear the voice of *s* ...... Lev 5:1
for because of *s* the land ...... Jer 23:10
By *s*, and lying, and killing, and ...... Hos 4:2
*s* falsely in making a covenant ...... Hos 10:4

**SWEAT**
In the *s* of thy face shalt thou ...... Gen 3:19
with any thing that causeth *s* ...... Eze 44:18
his *s* was as it were great drops ...... Lk 22:44

**SWEEP**
I will *s* it with the besom of ...... Is 14:23
the hail shall *s* away the refuge ...... Is 28:17
*s* the house, and seek diligently ...... Lk 15:8

**SWEEPING**
a *s* rain which leaveth no food ...... Prov 28:3

**SWEET**
And the LORD smelled a *s* savour ...... Gen 8:21
waters, the waters were made *s* ...... Ex 15:25
anointing oil, and for *s* incense, ...... Ex 25:6
it is a *s* savour, an offering ...... Ex 29:18
for a *s* savour before the LORD ...... Ex 29:25
for a *s* savour, an offering made ...... Ex 29:41
thereon *s* incense every morning ...... Ex 30:7
of *s* cinnamon half so much, even ...... Ex 30:23
of *s* calamus two hundred and fifty ...... Ex 30:23
Moses, Take unto thee *s* spices ...... Ex 30:34
these *s* spices with pure ...... Ex 30:34
*s* incense for the holy place ...... Ex 31:11
oil, and for the *s* incense ...... Ex 35:8
the *s* incense, and the hanging for ...... Ex 35:15
oil, and for the *s* incense ...... Ex 35:28
and the pure incense of *s* spices ...... Ex 37:29
the *s* incense, and the hanging for ...... Ex 39:38
he burnt *s* incense thereon ...... Ex 40:27
of a *s* savour unto the LORD ...... Lev 1:9
of a *s* savour unto the LORD ...... Lev 1:13
of a *s* savour unto the LORD ...... Lev 1:17
of a *s* savour unto the LORD ...... Lev 2:2
of a *s* savour unto the LORD ...... Lev 2:9
burnt on the altar for a *s* savour ...... Lev 2:12
of a *s* savour unto the LORD ...... Lev 3:5
made by fire for a *s* savour ...... Lev 3:16
of *s* incense before the LORD ...... Lev 4:7
for a *s* savour unto the LORD ...... Lev 4:31
it upon the altar for a *s* savour ...... Lev 6:15
for a *s* savour unto the LORD ...... Lev 6:21
a burnt sacrifice for a *s* savour ...... Lev 8:21
were consecrations for a *s* savour ...... Lev 8:28
his hands full of *s* incense ...... Lev 16:12
burn the fat for a *s* savour unto ...... Lev 17:6
fire unto the LORD for a *s* savour ...... Lev 23:13
of *s* savour unto the LORD ...... Lev 23:18
smell the savour of your *s* odours ...... Lev 26:31
the *s* incense, and the daily meat ...... Num 4:16
to make a *s* savour unto the LORD, ...... Num 15:3
for a *s* savour unto the LORD ...... Num 15:7
of a *s* savour unto the LORD ...... Num 15:10
of a *s* savour unto the LORD ...... Num 15:13
of a *s* savour unto the LORD ...... Num 15:14
for a *s* savour unto the LORD, ...... Num 15:24
for a *s* savour unto the LORD ...... Num 18:17
for a *s* savour unto me, shall ye ...... Num 28:2
in mount Sinai for a *s* savour ...... Num 28:6
of a *s* savour unto the LORD ...... Num 28:8
a burnt offering of a *s* savour ...... Num 28:13
of a *s* savour unto the LORD ...... Num 28:24
for a *s* savour unto the LORD ...... Num 28:27
for a *s* savour unto the LORD ...... Num 29:2
for a *s* savour, a sacrifice made ...... Num 29:6
unto the LORD for a *s* savour ...... Num 29:8
of a *s* savour unto the LORD ...... Num 29:13
of a *s* savour unto the LORD ...... Num 29:36
the *s* psalmist of Israel, said, ...... 2Sa 23:1
and to burn before him *s* incense ...... 2Chr 2:4
burnt sacrifices and *s* incense ...... 2Chr 13:11
which was filled with *s* odours ...... 2Chr 16:14
they may offer sacrifices of *s* ...... Ezr 6:10
way, eat the fat, and drink the *s* ...... Neh 8:10
and six months with *s* odours ...... Est 2:12
wickedness be *s* in his mouth ...... Job 20:12
of the valley shall be *s* unto him ...... Job 21:33
Canst thou bind the *s* influences ...... Job 38:31
We took *s* counsel together, and ...... Ps 55:14
My meditation of him shall be *s* ...... Ps 104:34
How *s* are thy words unto my taste ...... Ps 119:103
for they are *s* ...... Ps 141:6
lie down, and thy sleep shall be *s* ...... Prov 3:24
Stolen waters are *s*, and bread ...... Prov 9:17
accomplished is *s* to the soul ...... Prov 13:19
*s* to the soul, and health to the ...... Prov 16:24
Bread of deceit is *s* to a man ...... Prov 20:17
vomit up, and lose thy *s* words ...... Prov 23:8
which is *s* to thy taste ...... Prov 24:13
soul every bitter thing is *s* ...... Prov 27:7
The sleep of a labouring man is *s* ...... Eccl 5:12
Truly the light is *s*, and a ...... Eccl 11:7
and his fruit was *s* to my taste ...... Song 2:3
for *s* is thy voice, and thy ...... Song 2:14
my fingers with *s* smelling myrrh ...... Song 5:5
as a bed of spices, as *s* flowers ...... Song 5:13
dropping *s* smelling myrrh ...... Song 5:13
His mouth is most *s* ...... Song 5:16
that instead of *s* smell there ...... Is 3:24
bitter for *s*, and *s* for bitter ...... Is 5:20
make *s* melody, sing many songs, ...... Is 23:16
bought me no *s* cane with money ...... Is 43:24
their own blood, as with *s* wine ...... Is 49:26
the *s* cane from a far country ...... Jer 6:20
nor your sacrifices *s* unto me ...... Jer 6:20
and my sleep was *s* unto me ...... Jer 31:26
offer *s* savour to all their idols ...... Eze 6:13
set it before them for a *s* savour ...... Eze 16:19
also they made their *s* savour ...... Eze 20:28
accept you with your *s* savour ...... Eze 20:41
an oblation and *s* odours unto him ...... Dan 2:46
the mountains shall drop *s* wine ...... Amos 9:13
*s* wine, but shalt not drink wine ...... Mic 6:15
and Salome, had bought *s* spices ...... Mk 16:1
are unto God a *s* savour of Christ ...... 2Cor 2:15
from you, an odour of a *s* smell ...... Phil 4:18
forth at the same place *s* water ...... Jas 3:11
shall be in thy mouth *s* as honey ...... Rev 10:9
and it was in my mouth *s* as honey ...... Rev 10:10

**SWEETER**
went down, What is *s* than honey ...... Judg 14:18
*s* also than honey and the ...... Ps 19:10
yea, *s* than honey to my mouth ...... Ps 119:103

**SWEETLY**
the worm shall feed *s* on him ...... Job 24:20
for my beloved, that goeth down *s* ...... Song 7:9

**SWEETNESS**
unto them, Should I forsake my *s* ...... Judg 9:11
and out of the strong came forth *s* ...... Judg 14:14
the *s* of the lips increaseth ...... Prov 16:21
so doth the *s* of a man's friend ...... Prov 27:9
it was in my mouth as honey for *s* ...... Eze 3:3

**SWEETSMELLING**
a sacrifice to God for a *s* savour ...... Eph 5:2

**SWELL**
thigh to rot, and thy belly to *s* ...... Num 5:21
bowels, to make thy belly to *s* ...... Num 5:22
bitter, and her belly shall *s* ...... Num 5:27
upon thee, neither did thy foot *s* ...... Deut 8:4

**SWELLED**
not old, and their feet *s* not ...... Neh 9:21

**SWELLING**
shake with the *s* thereof ...... Ps 46:3
*s* out in a high wall, whose ...... Is 30:13
wilt thou do in the *s* of Jordan ...... Jer 12:5
from the *s* of Jordan against the ...... Jer 49:19
come up like a lion from the *s* of ...... Jer 50:44
speak great *s* words of vanity ...... 2Pet 2:18
mouth speaketh great *s* words ...... Jude 16

**SWELLINGS**
backbitings, whisperings, *s* ...... 2Cor 12:20

**SWEPT**
The river of Kishon *s* them away ...... Judg 5:21
Why are thy valiant men *s* away ...... Jer 46:15
is come, he findeth it empty, *s* ...... Mt 12:44
when he cometh, he findeth it *s* ...... Lk 11:25

**SWERVED**
From which some having *s* have ...... 1Ti 1:6

**SWIFT**
earth, as *s* as the eagle flieth ...... Deut 28:49
were as *s* as the roes upon the ...... 1Chr 12:8
are passed away as the *s* ships ...... Job 9:26
He is *s* as the waters ...... Job 24:18
feet that be *s* in running to ...... Prov 6:18
that the race is not to the *s* ...... Eccl 9:11
ye *s* messengers, to a nation ...... Is 18:2
the LORD rideth upon a *s* cloud ...... Is 19:1
and, We will ride upon the *s* ...... Is 30:16
shall they that pursue you be *s* ...... Is 30:16
upon *s* beasts, to my holy ...... Is 66:20
thou art a *s* dromedary traversing ...... Jer 2:23
Let not the *s* flee away, nor the ...... Jer 46:6
flight shall perish from the *s* ...... Amos 2:14
he that is *s* of foot shall not ...... Amos 2:15
bind the chariot to the *s* beast ...... Mic 1:13
I will be a *s* witness against the ...... Mal 3:5
Their feet are *s* to shed blood ...... Rom 3:15
let every man be *s* to hear ...... Jas 1:19
upon themselves *s* destruction ...... 2Pet 2:1

**SWIFTER**
they were *s* than eagles, they ...... 2Sa 1:23
My days are *s* than a weaver's ...... Job 7:6
Now my days are *s* than a post ...... Job 9:25
his horses are *s* than eagles ...... Jer 4:13
Our persecutors are *s* than the ...... Lam 4:19
also are *s* than the leopards ...... Hab 1:8

**SWIFTLY**
his word runneth very *s* ...... Ps 147:15
they shall come with speed *s* ...... Is 5:26
beginning, being caused to fly *s* ...... Dan 9:21
and if ye recompense me, *s* ...... Joel 3:4

**SWIM**
and the iron did *s* ...... 2Kin 6:6
all the night make I my bed to *s* ...... Ps 6:6
spreadeth forth his hands to *s* ...... Is 25:11
waters were risen, waters to *s* in ...... Eze 47:5
lest any of them should *s* out ...... Acts 27:42
*s* should cast themselves first ...... Acts 27:43

**SWIMMEST**
thy blood the land wherein thou *s* ...... Eze 32:6

**SWIMMETH**
as he that *s* spreadeth forth his ...... Is 25:11

**SWINE**
And the *s*, though he divide the ...... Lev 11:7
And the *s*, because it divideth the ...... Deut 14:8

cast ye your pearls before *s* Mt 7:6
them an herd of many *s* feeding Mt 8:30
us to go away into the herd of *s* Mt 8:31
out, they went into the herd of *s* Mt 8:32
the whole herd of *s* ran violently Mt 8:32
a great herd of *s* feeding Mk 5:11
him, saying, Send us into the *s* Mk 5:12
went out, and entered into the *s* Mk 5:13
And they that fed the *s* fled Mk 5:14
devil, and also concerning the *s* Mk 5:16
of many *s* feeding on the mountain Lk 8:32
of the man, and entered into the *s* Lk 8:33
him into his fields to feed *s* Lk 15:15
with the husks that the *s* did eat Lk 15:16

**SWINE'S**
As a jewel of gold in a *s* snout Prov 11:22
the monuments, which eat *s* flesh Is 65:4
as if he offered *s* blood Is 66:3
tree in the midst, eating *s* flesh Is 66:17

**SWOLLEN**
they looked when he should have *s* Acts 28:6

**SWOON**
the sucklings *s* in the streets of Lam 2:11

**SWOONED**
when they *s* as the wounded in the Lam 2:12

**SWORD**
a flaming *s* which turned every Gen 3:24
by thy *s* shalt thou live, and Gen 27:40
as captives taken with the *s* Gen 31:26
brethren, took each man his *s* Gen 34:25
his son with the edge of the *s* Gen 34:26
the hand of the Amorite with my *s* Gen 48:22
us with pestilence, or with the *s* Ex 5:3
to put a *s* in their hand to slay Ex 5:21
I will draw my *s*, my hand shall Ex 15:9
his people with the edge of the *s* Ex 17:13
me from the *s* of Pharaoh Ex 18:4
and I will kill you with the *s* Ex 22:24
Put every man his *s* by his side Ex 32:27
neither shall the *s* go through Lev 26:6
shall fall before you by the *s* Lev 26:7
shall fall before you by the *s* Lev 26:8
And I will bring a *s* upon you Lev 26:25
and will draw out a *s* after you Lev 26:33
shall flee, as fleeing from a *s* Lev 26:36
another, as it were before a *s* Lev 26:37
unto this land, to fall by the *s* Num 14:3
you, and ye shall fall by the *s* Num 14:43
slain with a *s* in the open fields Num 19:16
come out against thee with the *s* Num 20:18
smote him with the edge of the *s* Num 21:24
way, and his *s* drawn in his hand Num 22:23
would there were a *s* in mine hand Num 22:29
way, and his *s* drawn in his hand Num 22:31
son of Beor they slew with the *s* Num 31:8
that city with the edge of the *s* Deut 13:15
thereof, with the edge of the *s* Deut 13:15
thereof with the edge of the *s* Deut 20:13
an extreme burning, and with the *s* Deut 28:22
The *s* without, and terror within, Deut 32:25
If I whet my glittering *s* Deut 32:41
blood, and my *s* shall devour flesh Deut 32:42
who is the *s* of thy excellency Deut 33:29
him with his *s* drawn in his hand Josh 5:13
and ass, with the edge of the *s* Josh 6:21
all fallen on the edge of the *s* Josh 8:24
smote it with the edge of the *s* Josh 8:24
of Israel slew with the *s* Josh 10:11
smote it with the edge of the *s* Josh 10:28
smote it with the edge of the *s* Josh 10:30
smote it with the edge of the *s* Josh 10:32
smote it with the edge of the *s* Josh 10:35
smote it with the edge of the *s* Josh 10:37
smote them with the edge of the *s* Josh 10:39
smote the king thereof with the *s* Josh 11:10
therein with the edge of the *s* Josh 11:11
smote them with the edge of the *s* Josh 11:12
they smote with the edge of the *s* Josh 11:14
of Israel slay with the *s* among Josh 13:22
smote it with the edge of the *s* Josh 19:47
but not with thy *s*, nor with thy Josh 24:12
smitten it with the edge of the *s* Judg 1:8
the city with the edge of the *s* Judg 1:25
the edge of the *s* before Barak Judg 4:15
fell upon the edge of the *s* Judg 4:16
the *s* of Gideon the son of Joash Judg 7:14
The *s* of the LORD, and of Gideon Judg 7:18
The *s* of the LORD, and of Gideon Judg 7:20
every man's *s* against his fellow Judg 7:22
twenty thousand men that drew *s* Judg 8:10
But the youth drew not his *s* Judg 8:20
and said unto him, Draw thy *s* Judg 9:54
smote them with the edge of the *s* Judg 18:27
thousand footmen that drew *s* Judg 20:2
and six thousand men that drew *s* Judg 20:15
hundred thousand men that drew *s* Judg 20:17
all these drew the *s* Judg 20:25
all these drew the *s* Judg 20:35
the city with the edge of the *s* Judg 20:37
five thousand men that drew the *s* Judg 20:46
smote them with the edge of the *s* Judg 20:48
with the edge of the *s*, with the Judg 21:10
that there was neither *s* nor 1Sa 13:22
every man's *s* was against his 1Sa 14:20
the people with the edge of the *s* 1Sa 15:8
said, As thy *s* hath made women 1Sa 15:33
girded his *s* upon his armour 1Sa 17:39
Thou comest to me with a *s* 1Sa 17:45
that the LORD saveth not with *s* 1Sa 17:47
but there was no *s* in the hand of 1Sa 17:50
the Philistine, and took his *s* 1Sa 17:51
and his garments, even to his *s* 1Sa 18:4
here under thine hand spear or *s* 1Sa 21:8
my *s* nor my weapons with me 1Sa 21:8
The *s* of Goliath the Philistine, 1Sa 21:9
gave him the *s* of Goliath the 1Sa 22:10
thou hast given him bread, and a *s* 1Sa 22:13
smote he with the edge of the *s* 1Sa 22:19
and sheep, with the edge of the *s* 1Sa 22:19
men, Gird ye on every man his *s* 1Sa 25:13
And they girded on every man his *s* 1Sa 25:13
and David also girded on his *s* 1Sa 25:13
unto his armourbearer, Draw thy *s* 1Sa 31:4
Therefore Saul took a *s*, and fell 1Sa 31:4
dead, he fell likewise upon his *s* 1Sa 31:5
because they were fallen by the *s* 2Sa 1:12
the *s* of Saul returned not empty 2Sa 1:22
thrust his *s* in his fellow's side 2Sa 2:16
Shall the *s* devour for ever 2Sa 2:26
a staff, or that falleth on the *s* 2Sa 3:29
for the *s* devoureth one as well 2Sa 11:25
Uriah the Hittite with the *s* 2Sa 12:9
hast slain him with the *s* of the 2Sa 12:9
Now therefore the *s* shall never 2Sa 12:10
the city with the edge of the *s* 2Sa 15:14
that day than the *s* devoured 2Sa 18:8
upon it a girdle with a *s* 2Sa 20:8
to the *s* that was in Joab's hand 2Sa 20:10
he being girded with a new *s* 2Sa 21:16
and his hand clave unto the *s* 2Sa 23:10
valiant men that drew the *s* 2Sa 24:9
not slay his servant with the *s* 1Kin 1:51
not put thee to death with the *s* 1Kin 2:8
than he, and slew them with the *s* 1Kin 2:32
And the king said, Bring me a *s* 1Kin 3:24
they brought a *s* before the king 1Kin 3:24
slain all the prophets with the *s* 1Kin 19:1
and slain thy prophets with the *s* 1Kin 19:10
and slain thy prophets with the *s* 1Kin 19:14
the *s* of Hazael shall Jehu slay 1Kin 19:17
the *s* of Jehu shall Elisha slay 1Kin 19:17
hast taken captive with thy *s* 2Kin 6:22
men wilt thou slay with the *s* 2Kin 8:12
smote them with the edge of the *s* 2Kin 10:25
followeth her kill with the *s* 2Kin 11:15
the *s* beside the king's house 2Kin 11:20
to fall by the *s* in his own land 2Kin 19:7
his sons smote him with the *s* 2Kin 19:37
men able to bear buckler and *s* 1Chr 5:18
to his armourbearer, Draw thy *s* 1Chr 10:4
So Saul took a *s*, and fell upon it 1Chr 10:4
dead, he fell likewise on the *s* 1Chr 10:5
hundred thousand men that drew *s* 1Chr 21:5
and ten thousand men that drew *s* 1Chr 21:5
while that the *s* of thine enemies 1Chr 21:12
else three days the *s* of the LORD 1Chr 21:12
having a drawn *s* in his hand 1Chr 21:16
he put up his *s* again into the 1Chr 21:27
of the *s* of the angel of the LORD 1Chr 21:30
evil cometh upon us, as the *s* 2Chr 20:9
slew all his brethren with the *s* 2Chr 21:4
her, let him be slain with the *s* 2Chr 23:14
had slain Athaliah with the *s* 2Chr 23:21
our fathers have fallen by the *s* 2Chr 29:9
bowels slew him there with the *s* 2Chr 32:21
slew their young men with the *s* 2Chr 36:17
the *s* carried he away to Babylon 2Chr 36:20
the kings of the lands, to the *s* Ezr 9:7
every one had his *s* girded by his Neh 4:18
enemies with the stroke of the *s* Est 9:5
servants with the edge of the *s* Job 1:15
servants with the edge of the *s* Job 1:17
But he saveth the poor from the *s* Job 5:15
and in war from the power of the *s* Job 5:20
and he is waited for of the *s* Job 15:22
Be ye afraid of the *s* Job 19:29
bringeth the punishments of the *s* Job 19:29
the glittering *s* cometh out of Job 20:25
be multiplied, it is for the *s* Job 27:14
his life from perishing by the *s* Job 33:18
not, they shall perish by the *s* Job 36:12
turneth he back from the *s* Job 39:22
make his *s* to approach unto him Job 40:19
The *s* of him that layeth at him Job 41:26
he turn not, he will whet his *s* Ps 7:12
from the wicked, which is thy *s* Ps 17:13
Deliver my soul from the *s* Ps 22:20
The wicked have drawn out the *s* Ps 37:14
Their *s* shall enter into their Ps 37:15
As with a *s* in my bones, mine Ps 42:10
land in possession by their own *s* Ps 44:3
bow, neither shall my *s* save me Ps 44:6
Gird thy *s* upon thy thigh, O most Ps 45:3
arrows, and their tongue a sharp *s* Ps 57:4
They shall fall by the *s* Ps 63:10
Who whet their tongue like a *s* Ps 64:3
of the bow, the shield, and the *s* Ps 76:3
his people over also unto the *s* Ps 78:62
Their priests fell by the *s* Ps 78:64
also turned the edge of his *s* Ps 89:43
his servant from the hurtful *s* Ps 144:10
a twoedged *s* in their hand Ps 149:6
wormwood, sharp as a twoedged *s* Prov 5:4
like the piercings of a *s* Prov 12:18
his neighbour is a maul, and a *s* Prov 25:18
every man hath his *s* upon his Song 3:8
ye shall be devoured with the *s* Is 1:20
not lift up *s* against nation Is 2:4
Thy men shall fall by the *s* Is 3:25
unto them shall fall by the *s* Is 13:15
slain, thrust through with a *s* Is 14:19
from the swords, from the drawn *s* Is 21:15
men are not slain with the *s* Is 22:2
strong *s* shall punish leviathan Is 27:1
the Assyrian fall with the *s* Is 31:8
and the *s*, not of a mean man, Is 31:8
but he shall flee from the *s* Is 31:8
For my *s* shall be bathed in Is 34:5
The *s* of the LORD is filled with Is 34:6
to fall by the *s* in his own land Is 37:7
his sons smote him with the *s* Is 37:38
he gave them as the dust to his *s* Is 41:2
hath made my mouth like a sharp *s* Is 49:2
and the famine, and the *s* Is 51:19
will I number you to the *s* Is 65:12
by his *s* will the LORD plead with Is 66:16
your own *s* hath devoured your Jer 2:30
whereas the *s* reacheth unto the Jer 4:10
neither shall we see *s* nor famine Jer 5:12
thou trustedst, with the *s* Jer 5:17
for the *s* of the enemy and fear is Jer 6:25
and I will send a *s* after them Jer 9:16
the young men shall die by the *s* Jer 11:22
for the *s* of the LORD shall Jer 12:12
but I will consume them by the *s* Jer 14:12
unto them, Ye shall not see the *s* Jer 14:13
I sent them not, yet they say, *S* Jer 14:15
By *s* and famine shall those Jer 14:15
because of the famine and the *s* Jer 14:16
then behold the slain with the *s* Jer 14:18
as are for the *s*, to the *s* Jer 15:2
the *s* to slay, and the dogs to Jer 15:3
to the *s* before their enemies Jer 15:9
they shall be consumed by the *s* Jer 16:4
their blood by the force of the *s* Jer 18:21
men be slain by the *s* in battle Jer 18:21
by the *s* before their enemies Jer 19:7
fall by the *s* of their enemies Jer 20:4
and shall slay them with the *s* Jer 20:4
from the pestilence, from the *s* Jer 21:7
smite them with the edge of the *s* Jer 21:7
in this city shall die by the *s* Jer 21:9
And I will send the *s*, the famine, Jer 24:10
because of the *s* that I will send Jer 25:16
because of the *s* which I will Jer 25:27
for I will call for a *s* upon all Jer 25:29
them that are wicked to the *s* Jer 25:31
who slew him with the *s*, and cast Jer 26:23
saith the LORD, with the *s* Jer 27:8
die, thou and thy people, by the *s* Jer 27:13
I will send upon them the *s* Jer 29:17
I will persecute them with the *s* Jer 29:18
*s* found grace in the wilderness Jer 31:2
against it, because of the *s* Jer 32:24
of the king of Babylon by the *s* Jer 32:36
down by the mounts, and by the *s* Jer 33:4
thee, Thou shalt not die by the *s* Jer 34:4
for you, saith the LORD, to the *s* Jer 34:17
in this city shall die by the *s* Jer 38:2
and thou shalt not fall by the *s* Jer 39:18
the son of Shaphan with the *s* Jer 41:2
it shall come to pass, that the *s* Jer 42:16
they shall die by the *s*, by the Jer 42:17
that ye shall die by the *s* Jer 42:22
as are for the *s* to the *s* Jer 43:11
shall even be consumed by the *s* Jer 44:12
even unto the greatest, by the *s* Jer 44:12
have punished Jerusalem, by the *s* Jer 44:13
and have been consumed by the *s* Jer 44:18
Egypt shall be consumed by the *s* Jer 44:27
a small number that escape the *s* Jer 44:28
the *s* shall devour, and it shall Jer 46:10
for the *s* shall devour round Jer 46:14
nativity, from the oppressing *s* Jer 46:16
O thou *s* of the LORD, how long Jer 47:6
the *s* shall pursue thee Jer 48:2
keepeth back his *s* from blood Jer 48:10
and I will send the *s* after them Jer 49:37
for fear of the oppressing *s* they Jer 50:16
A *s* is upon the Chaldeans, saith Jer 50:35
A *s* is upon the liars Jer 50:36
a *s* is upon her mighty men Jer 50:36
A *s* is upon their horses, and upon Jer 50:37
a *s* is upon her treasures Jer 50:37
Ye that have escaped the *s* Jer 51:50
abroad the *s* bereaveth, at home Lam 1:20
my young men are fallen by the *s* Lam 2:21
They that be slain with the *s* are Lam 4:9
of the *s* of the wilderness Lam 5:9
and I will draw out a *s* after them Eze 5:2
fall by the *s* round about thee Eze 5:12
and I will draw out a *s* after them Eze 5:12
and I will bring the *s* upon thee Eze 5:17
even I, will bring a *s* upon you Eze 6:3
escape the *s* among the nations Eze 6:8
for they shall fall by the *s* Eze 6:11
that is near shall fall by the *s* Eze 6:12
The *s* is without, and the Eze 7:15
in the field shall die with the *s* Eze 7:15
Ye have feared the *s* Eze 11:8
and I will bring a *s* upon you Eze 11:8
Ye shall fall by the *s* Eze 11:10
I will draw out the *s* after them Eze 12:14
a few men of them from the *s* Eze 12:16
a *s* upon that land, and say, *S* Eze 14:17
judgments upon Jerusalem, the *s* Eze 14:21
all his bands shall fall by the *s* Eze 17:21
draw forth my *s* out of his sheath Eze 21:3

therefore shall my *s* go forth out ... Eze 21:4
forth my *s* out of his sheath ... Eze 21:5
Say, A *s*, a *s* is sharpened, ... Eze 21:9
this *s* is sharpened, and it is ... Eze 21:11
of the *s* shall be upon my people ... Eze 21:12
what if the *s* contemn even the ... Eze 21:13
let the *s* be doubled the third ... Eze 21:14
third time, the *s* of the slain ... Eze 21:14
it is the *s* of the great men that ... Eze 21:14
of the *s* against all their gates ... Eze 21:15
that the *s* of the king of Babylon ... Eze 21:19
that the *s* may come to Rabbath of ... Eze 21:20
thou, The *s*, the *s* is drawn ... Eze 21:28
daughters, and slew her with the *s* ... Eze 23:10
thy remnant shall fall by the *s* ... Eze 23:25
ye have left shall fall by the *s* ... Eze 24:21
they of Dedan shall fall by the *s* ... Eze 25:13
the field shall be slain by the *s* ... Eze 26:6
He shall slay with the *s* thy ... Eze 26:8
he shall slay thy people by the *s* ... Eze 26:11
by the *s* upon her on every side ... Eze 28:23
I will bring a *s* upon thee ... Eze 29:8
the *s* shall come upon Egypt, and ... Eze 30:4
shall fall with them by the *s* ... Eze 30:5
shall they fall in it by the *s* ... Eze 30:6
of Pi-beseth shall fall by the *s* ... Eze 30:17
to make it strong to hold the *s* ... Eze 30:21
I will cause the *s* to fall out of ... Eze 30:22
Babylon, and put my *s* in his hand ... Eze 30:24
when I shall put my *s* into the ... Eze 30:25
them that be slain with the *s* ... Eze 31:17
with them that be slain by the *s* ... Eze 31:18
I shall brandish my *s* before them ... Eze 32:10
The *s* of the king of Babylon ... Eze 32:11
of them that are slain by the *s* ... Eze 32:20
she is delivered to the *s* ... Eze 32:20
lie uncircumcised, slain by the *s* ... Eze 32:21
of them slain, fallen by the *s* ... Eze 32:22
of them slain, fallen by the *s* ... Eze 32:23
of them slain, fallen by the *s* ... Eze 32:24
uncircumcised, slain by the *s* ... Eze 32:25
uncircumcised, slain by the *s* ... Eze 32:26
them that are slain with the *s* ... Eze 32:28
by them that were slain by the *s* ... Eze 32:29
with them that be slain by the *s* ... Eze 32:30
and all his army slain by the *s* ... Eze 32:31
them that are slain with the *s* ... Eze 32:32
When I bring the *s* upon a land ... Eze 33:2
he seeth the *s* come upon the land ... Eze 33:3
if the *s* come, and take him away, ... Eze 33:4
if the watchman see the *s* come ... Eze 33:6
if the *s* come, and take any person ... Eze 33:6
Ye stand upon your *s*, ye work ... Eze 33:26
in the wastes shall fall by the *s* ... Eze 33:27
*s* in the time of their calamity ... Eze 35:5
fall that are slain with the *s* ... Eze 35:8
that is brought back from the *s* ... Eze 38:8
I will call for a *s* against him ... Eze 38:21
every man's *s* shall be against ... Eze 38:21
so fell they all by the *s* ... Eze 39:23
yet they shall fall by the *s* ... Dan 11:33
not save them by bow, nor by *s* ... Hos 1:7
and I will break the bow and the *s* ... Hos 2:18
*s* for the rage of their tongue ... Hos 7:16
the *s* shall abide on his cities, ... Hos 11:6
they shall fall by the *s* ... Hos 13:16
and when they fall upon the *s* ... Joel 2:8
did pursue his brother with the *s* ... Amos 1:11
young men have I slain with the *s* ... Amos 4:10
the house of Jeroboam with the *s* ... Amos 7:9
Jeroboam shall die by the *s* ... Amos 7:11
thy daughters shall fall by the *s* ... Amos 7:17
slay the last of them with the *s* ... Amos 9:1
thence will I command the *s* ... Amos 9:4
of my people shall die by the *s* ... Amos 9:10
not lift up a *s* against nation ... Mic 4:3
the land of Assyria with the *s* ... Mic 5:6
will I give up to the *s* ... Mic 6:14
the *s* shall devour thy young ... Nah 2:13
lifteth up both the bright *s* ... Nah 3:3
the *s* shall cut thee off, it ... Nah 3:15
also, ye shall be slain by my *s* ... Zeph 2:12
every one by the *s* of his brother ... Hag 2:22
thee as the *s* of a mighty man ... Zec 9:13
the *s* shall be upon his arm, and ... Zec 11:17
Awake, O *s*, against my shepherd, ... Zec 13:7
I came not to send peace, but a *s* ... Mt 10:34
out his hand, and drew his *s* ... Mt 26:51
Put up again thy *s* into his place ... Mt 26:52
the *s* shall perish with the *s* ... Mt 26:52
of them that stood by drew a *s* ... Mk 14:47
a *s* shall pierce through thy own ... Lk 2:35
shall fall by the edge of the *s* ... Lk 21:24
and he that hath no *s*, let him ... Lk 22:36
Lord, shall we smite with the *s* ... Lk 22:49
Simon Peter having a *s* drew it ... Jn 18:10
Put up thy *s* into the sheath ... Jn 18:11
the brother of John with the *s* ... Acts 12:2
doors open, he drew out his *s* ... Acts 16:27
or nakedness, or peril, or *s* ... Rom 8:35
for he beareth not the *s* in vain ... Rom 13:4
the *s* of the Spirit, which is the ... Eph 6:17
and sharper than any twoedged *s* ... Heb 4:12
fire, escaped the edge of the *s* ... Heb 11:34
tempted, were slain with the *s* ... Heb 11:37
his mouth went a sharp twoedged *s* ... Rev 1:16
hath the sharp *s* with two edges ... Rev 2:12
them with the *s* of my mouth ... Rev 2:16
was given unto him a great *s* ... Rev 6:4
part of the earth, to kill with *s* ... Rev 6:8
he that killeth with the *s* must ... Rev 13:10
must be killed with the *s* ... Rev 13:10
beast, which had the wound by a *s* ... Rev 13:14
out of his mouth goeth a sharp *s* ... Rev 19:15
*s* of him that sat upon the horse ... Rev 19:21
which *s* proceeded out of his ... Rev 19:21

**SWORDS**
the Hebrews make them *s* or spears ... 1Sa 13:19
him seven hundred men that drew *s* ... 2Kin 3:26
after their families with their *s* ... Neh 4:13
than oil, yet were they drawn *s* ... Ps 55:21
*s* are in their lips ... Ps 59:7
generation, whose teeth are as *s* ... Prov 30:14
They all hold *s*, being expert in ... Song 3:8
beat their *s* into plowshares ... Is 2:4
For they fled from the *s*, from ... Is 21:15
thrust thee through with their *s* ... Eze 16:40
and dispatch them with their *s* ... Eze 23:47
they shall draw their *s* against ... Eze 28:7
shall draw their *s* against Egypt ... Eze 30:11
By the *s* of the mighty will I ... Eze 32:12
laid their *s* under their heads ... Eze 32:27
shields, all of them handling *s* ... Eze 38:4
Beat your plowshares into *s* ... Joel 3:10
beat their *s* into plowshares ... Mic 4:3
with him a great multitude with *s* ... Mt 26:47
out as against a thief with *s* ... Mt 26:55
with him a great multitude with *s* ... Mk 14:43
out, as against a thief, with *s* ... Mk 14:48
Lord, behold, here are two *s* ... Lk 22:38
out, as against a thief, with *s* ... Lk 22:52

**SWORN**
And said, By myself have I *s* ... Gen 22:16
for he had straitly *s* the ... Ex 13:19
Because the LORD hath *s* that the ... Ex 17:16
about which he hath *s* falsely ... Lev 6:5
which he had *s* unto your fathers ... Deut 7:8
as he hath *s* unto thy fathers ... Deut 13:17
as he hath *s* unto thy fathers, and ... Deut 19:8
himself, as he hath *s* unto thee ... Deut 28:9
as he hath *s* unto thy fathers, to ... Deut 29:13
the land which the LORD hath *s* ... Deut 31:7
*s* unto them by the LORD God of ... Josh 9:18
We have *s* unto them by the LORD ... Josh 9:19
and as the LORD had *s* unto them ... Judg 2:15
the men of Israel had *s* in Mizpeh ... Judg 21:1
seeing we have *s* by the LORD that ... Judg 21:7
for the children of Israel have *s* ... Judg 21:18
therefore I have *s* unto the house ... 1Sa 3:14
forasmuch as we have *s* both of us ... 1Sa 20:42
as the LORD hath *s* to David ... 2Sa 3:9
of Israel had *s* unto them ... 2Sa 21:2
for they had *s* with all their ... 2Chr 15:15
were many in Judah *s* unto him ... Neh 6:18
which thou hadst *s* to give them ... Neh 9:15
unto vanity, nor *s* deceitfully ... Ps 24:4
I have *s* unto David my servant, ... Ps 89:3
Once have I *s* by my holiness that ... Ps 89:35
mad against me are *s* against me ... Ps 102:8
The LORD hath *s*, and will not ... Ps 110:4
I have *s*, and I will perform it, ... Ps 119:106
The LORD hath *s* in truth unto ... Ps 132:11
The LORD of hosts hath *s*, saying, ... Is 14:24
I have *s* by myself, the word is ... Is 45:23
for as I have *s* that the waters ... Is 54:9
so have I *s* that I would not be ... Is 54:9
The LORD hath *s* by his right hand ... Is 62:8
*s* by them that are no gods ... Jer 5:7
which I have *s* unto your fathers ... Jer 11:5
I have *s* by my great name, saith ... Jer 44:26
For I have *s* by myself, saith the ... Jer 49:13
LORD of hosts hath *s* by himself ... Jer 51:14
sight, to them that have *s* oaths ... Eze 21:23
Lord GOD hath *s* by his holiness ... Amos 4:2
The Lord GOD hath *s* by himself ... Amos 6:8
The LORD hath *s* by the excellency ... Amos 8:7
which thou hast *s* unto our ... Mic 7:20
God had *s* with an oath to him ... Acts 2:30
nigh, which God had *s* to Abraham ... Acts 7:17
As I have *s* in my wrath, if they ... Heb 4:3

**SYCAMINE**
ye might say unto this *s* tree ... Lk 17:6

**SYCHAR** (*si'-kar*) See SHECHEM. *A city in Samaria.*
of Samaria, which is called *S* ... Jn 4:5

**SYCHEM** (*si'-kem*) See SHECHEM. *Same as Shechem.*
And were carried over into *S* ... Acts 7:16
the sons of Emmor the father of *S* ... Acts 7:16

**SYCOMORE**
the *s* trees that are in the vale ... 1Kin 10:27
the *s* trees that were in the low ... 1Chr 27:28
cedar trees made he as the *s* ... 2Chr 1:15
the *s* trees that are in the low ... 2Chr 9:27
hail, and their *s* trees with frost ... Ps 78:47
herdman, and a gatherer of *s* fruit ... Amos 7:14
up into a *s* tree to see him ... Lk 19:4

**SYCOMORES**
the *s* are cut down, but we will ... Is 9:10

**SYENE** (*si-e'-ne*) *An Egyptian city.*
from the tower of *S* even unto the ... Eze 29:10
from the tower of *S* shall they ... Eze 30:6

**SYNAGOGUE**
thence, he went into their *s* ... Mt 12:9
he taught them in their *s* ... Mt 13:54
sabbath day he entered into the *s* ... Mk 1:21
there was in their *s* a man with ... Mk 1:23
when they were come out of the *s* ... Mk 1:29
And he entered again into the *s* ... Mk 3:1
cometh one of the rulers of the *s* ... Mk 5:22
he saith unto the ruler of the *s* ... Mk 5:36
the house of the ruler of the *s* ... Mk 5:38
come, he began to teach in the *s* ... Mk 6:2
he went into the *s* on the sabbath ... Lk 4:16
in the *s* were fastened on him ... Lk 4:20
And all they in the *s*, when they ... Lk 4:28
in the *s* there was a man, which ... Lk 4:33
And he arose out of the *s*, and ... Lk 4:38
that he entered into the *s* ... Lk 6:6
nation, and he hath built us a *s* ... Lk 7:5
and he was a ruler of the *s* ... Lk 8:41
the ruler of the *s* answered with ... Lk 13:14
These things said he in the *s* ... Jn 6:59
he should be put out of the *s* ... Jn 9:22
they should be put out of the *s* ... Jn 12:42
I ever taught in the *s*, and in the ... Jn 18:20
Then there arose certain of the *s* ... Acts 6:9
is called the *s* of the Libertines ... Acts 6:9
went into the *s* on the sabbath ... Acts 13:14
rulers of the *s* sent unto them ... Acts 13:15
the Jews were gone out of the *s* ... Acts 13:42
together into the *s* of the Jews ... Acts 14:1
where was a *s* of the Jews ... Acts 17:1
went into the *s* of the Jews ... Acts 17:10
he in the *s* with the Jews ... Acts 17:17
reasoned in the *s* every sabbath ... Acts 18:4
whose house joined hard to the *s* ... Acts 18:7
Crispus, the chief ruler of the *s* ... Acts 18:8
the chief ruler of the *s* ... Acts 18:17
but he himself entered into the *s* ... Acts 18:19
he began to speak boldly in the *s* ... Acts 18:26
And he went into the *s*, and spake ... Acts 19:8
beat in every *s* them that ... Acts 22:19
And I punished them oft in every *s* ... Acts 26:11
are not, but are the *s* of Satan ... Rev 2:9
will make them of the *s* of Satan ... Rev 3:9

**SYNAGOGUE'S**
of the *s* house certain which said ... Mk 5:35
one from the ruler of the *s* house ... Lk 8:49

**SYNAGOGUES**
up all the *s* of God in the land ... Ps 74:8
all Galilee, teaching in their *s* ... Mt 4:23
as the hypocrites do in the *s* ... Mt 6:2
love to pray standing in the *s* ... Mt 6:5
and villages, teaching in their *s* ... Mt 9:35
they will scourge you in their *s* ... Mt 10:17
and the chief seats in the *s* ... Mt 23:6
them shall ye scourge in your *s* ... Mt 23:34
he preached in their *s* throughout ... Mk 1:39
And the chief seats in the *s* ... Mk 12:39
in the *s* ye shall be beaten ... Mk 13:9
And he taught in their *s*, being ... Lk 4:15
he preached in the *s* of Galilee ... Lk 4:44
love the uppermost seats in the *s* ... Lk 11:43
And when they bring you unto the *s* ... Lk 12:11
in one of the *s* on the sabbath ... Lk 13:10
and the highest seats in the *s* ... Lk 20:46
you, delivering you up to the *s* ... Lk 21:12
They shall put you out of the *s* ... Jn 16:2
him letters to Damascus to the *s* ... Acts 9:2
he preached Christ in the *s* ... Acts 9:20
word of God in the *s* of the Jews ... Acts 13:5
read in the *s* every sabbath day ... Acts 15:21
up the people, neither in the *s* ... Acts 24:12

**SYNTYCHE** (*sin'-ti-ke*) *A Christian at Philippi.*
I beseech Euodias, and beseech *S* ... Phil 4:2

**SYRACUSE** (*sir'-a-cuse*) *A city on Sicily.*
And landing at *S*, we tarried there ... Acts 28:12

**SYRIA** (*sir'-e-ah*) See ARAM, SYRIA-DAMASCUS, SYRIA-MAACHAH, SYRIAN. *Nation north of Israel.*
and Ashtaroth, and the gods of *S* ... Judg 10:6
put garrisons in *S* of Damascus ... 2Sa 8:6
Of *S*, and of Moab, and of the ... 2Sa 8:12
vow while I abode at Geshur in *S* ... 2Sa 15:8
Hittites, and for the kings of *S* ... 1Kin 10:29
Israel, and reigned over *S* ... 1Kin 11:25
the son of Hezion, king of *S* ... 1Kin 15:18
anoint Hazael to be king over *S* ... 1Kin 19:15
Ben-hadad the king of *S* gathered ... 1Kin 20:1
Ben-hadad the king of *S* escaped ... 1Kin 20:20
of *S* will come up against thee ... 1Kin 20:22
of the king of *S* said unto him ... 1Kin 20:23
three years without war between *S* ... 1Kin 22:1
out of the hand of the king of *S* ... 1Kin 22:3
But the king of *S* commanded his ... 1Kin 22:31
of the host of the king of *S* ... 2Kin 5:1
LORD had given deliverance unto *S* ... 2Kin 5:1
And the king of *S* said, Go to, go, ... 2Kin 5:5
Then the king of *S* warred against ... 2Kin 6:8
the heart of the king of *S* was ... 2Kin 6:11
So the bands of *S* came no more ... 2Kin 6:23
king of *S* gathered all his host ... 2Kin 6:24
uttermost part of the camp of *S* ... 2Kin 7:5
Ben-hadad the king of *S* was sick ... 2Kin 8:7
king of *S* hath sent me to thee ... 2Kin 8:9
me that thou shalt be king over *S* ... 2Kin 8:13
Hazael king of *S* in Ramoth-gilead ... 2Kin 8:28
fought against Hazael king of *S* ... 2Kin 8:29
because of Hazael king of *S* ... 2Kin 9:14
he fought with Hazael king of *S* ... 2Kin 9:15
Then Hazael king of *S* went up ... 2Kin 12:17
and sent it to Hazael king of *S* ... 2Kin 12:18

into the hand of Hazael king of *S* ........ 2Kin 13:3
the king of *S* oppressed them ........ 2Kin 13:4
for the king of *S* had destroyed ........ 2Kin 13:7
the arrow of deliverance from *S* ........ 2Kin 13:17
then hadst thou smitten *S* till ........ 2Kin 13:19
now thou shalt smite *S* but thrice ........ 2Kin 13:19
But Hazael king of *S* oppressed ........ 2Kin 13:22
So Hazael king of *S* died ........ 2Kin 13:24
against Judah Rezin the king of *S* ........ 2Kin 15:37
Then Rezin king of *S* and Pekah son .. 2Kin 16:5
of *S* recovered Elath to *S* ........ 2Kin 16:6
out of the hand of the king of *S* ........ 2Kin 16:7
Hittites, and for the kings of *S* ........ 2Chr 1:17
and sent to Ben-hadad king of *S* ........ 2Chr 16:2
thou hast relied on the king of *S* ........ 2Chr 16:7
of *S* escaped out of thine hand ........ 2Chr 16:7
push *S* until they be consumed ........ 2Chr 18:10
Now the king of *S* had commanded .. 2Chr 18:30
beyond the sea on this side *S* ........ 2Chr 20:2
Hazael king of *S* at Ramoth-gilead ........ 2Chr 22:5
he fought with Hazael king of *S* ........ 2Chr 22:6
that the host of *S* came up ........ 2Chr 24:23
into the hand of the king of *S* ........ 2Chr 28:5
gods of the kings of *S* help them ........ 2Chr 28:23
Judah, that Rezin the king of *S* ........ Is 7:1
*S* is confederate with Ephraim ........ Is 7:2
the fierce anger of Rezin with *S* ........ Is 7:4
Because *S*, Ephraim, and the son of ........ Is 7:5
For the head of *S* is Damascus ........ Is 7:8
Damascus, and the remnant of *S* ........ Is 17:3
reproach of the daughters of *S* ........ Eze 16:57
*S* was thy merchant by reason of ........ Eze 27:16
Jacob fled into the country of *S* ........ Hos 12:12
the people of *S* shall go into ........ Amos 1:5
And his fame went throughout all *S* ........ Mt 4:24
when Cyrenius was governor of *S* ........ Lk 2:2
of the Gentiles in Antioch and *S* ........ Acts 15:23
And he went through *S* and Cilicia, ... Acts 15:41
brethren, and sailed thence into *S* ........ Acts 18:18
as he was about to sail into *S* ........ Acts 20:3
the left hand, and sailed into *S* ........ Acts 21:3
I came into the regions of *S* ........ Gal 1:21

**SYRIACK** (*sir'-e-ak*) See SYRIAN. *Language of the Syrians.*
the Chaldeans to the king in *S* ........ Dan 2:4

**SYRIA-DAMASCUS** (*sir''-e-ah-da-mas'-cus*) See SYRIA, DAMASCUS. *Same as Damascus.*
Then David put garrisons in *S* ........ 1Chr 18:6

**SYRIA-MAACHAH** (*sir''-e-ah-ma-a-kah*) *A Syrian city-state.*
out of Mesopotamia, and out of *S* ........ 1Chr 19:6

**SYRIAN** (*sir'-e-un*) See ARAMITES, SYRIANS, SYROPHENICIAN.
*1. An inhabitant of Syria.*
of Bethuel the *S* of Padan-aram ........ Gen 25:20
the sister to Laban the *S* ........ Gen 25:20
unto Laban, son of Bethuel the *S* ........ Gen 28:5
away unawares to Laban the *S* ........ Gen 31:20
Laban the *S* in a dream by night ........ Gen 31:24
A *S* ready to perish was my father ........ Deut 26:5
master hath spared Naaman this *S* ........ 2Kin 5:20
was cleansed, saving Naaman the *S* ........ Lk 4:27
*2. The language of Syria.*
to thy servants in the *S* language ........ 2Kin 18:26
was written in the *S* tongue ........ Ezr 4:7
and interpreted in the *S* tongue ........ Ezr 4:7
thy servants in the *S* language ........ Is 36:11

**SYRIANS**
when the *S* of Damascus came to ........ 2Sa 8:5
of Zobah, David slew of the *S* two ........ 2Sa 8:5
the *S* became servants to David, ........ 2Sa 8:6
of the *S* in the valley of salt ........ 2Sa 8:13
hired the *S* of Beth-rehob, and the ........ 2Sa 10:6
the *S* of Zoba, twenty thousand ........ 2Sa 10:6
the *S* of Zoba, and of Rehob, and ........ 2Sa 10:8
put them in array against the *S* ........ 2Sa 10:9
If the *S* be too strong for me, ........ 2Sa 10:11
unto the battle against the *S* ........ 2Sa 10:13
of Ammon saw that the *S* were fled .... 2Sa 10:14
when the *S* saw that they were ........ 2Sa 10:15
brought out the *S* that were ........ 2Sa 10:16
the *S* set themselves in array ........ 2Sa 10:17
And the *S* fled before Israel ........ 2Sa 10:18
seven hundred chariots of the *S* ........ 2Sa 10:18
So the *S* feared to help the ........ 2Sa 10:19
and the *S* fled ........ 1Kin 20:20
slew the *S* with a great slaughter ........ 1Kin 20:21
that Ben-hadad numbered the *S* ........ 1Kin 20:26
but the *S* filled the country ........ 1Kin 20:27
the LORD, Because the *S* have said .... 1Kin 20:28
*S* an hundred thousand footmen in ... 1Kin 20:29
With these shalt thou push the *S* ........ 1Kin 22:11
up in his chariot against the *S* ........ 1Kin 22:35
the *S* had gone out by companies, ........ 2Kin 5:2
for thither the *S* are come down ........ 2Kin 6:9
us fall unto the host of the *S* ........ 2Kin 7:4
to go unto the camp of the *S* ........ 2Kin 7:5
the *S* to hear a noise of chariots ........ 2Kin 7:6
We came to the camp of the *S* ........ 2Kin 7:10
you what the *S* have done to us ........ 2Kin 7:12
king sent after the host of the *S* ........ 2Kin 7:14
which the *S* had cast away in ........ 2Kin 7:15
and spoiled the tents of the *S* ........ 2Kin 7:16
and the *S* wounded Joram ........ 2Kin 8:28
the *S* had given him at Ramah ........ 2Kin 8:29
wounds which the *S* had given him .... 2Kin 9:15
out from under the hand of the *S* ........ 2Kin 13:5
thou shalt smite the *S* in Aphek ........ 2Kin 13:17
the *S* came to Elath, and dwelt ........ 2Kin 16:6
the Chaldees, and bands of the *S* ........ 2Kin 24:2
when the *S* of Damascus came to ........ 1Chr 18:5
of Zobah, David slew of the *S* two ........ 1Chr 18:5
the *S* became David's servants, and .... 1Chr 18:6
put them in array against the *S* ........ 1Chr 19:10
If the *S* be too strong for me, ........ 1Chr 19:12
nigh before the *S* unto the battle ........ 1Chr 19:14
of Ammon saw that the *S* were fled .. 1Chr 19:15
when the *S* saw that they were put .. 1Chr 19:16
drew forth the *S* that were beyond ... 1Chr 19:16
the battle in array against the *S* ........ 1Chr 19:17
But the *S* fled before Israel ........ 1Chr 19:18
David slew of the *S* seven ........ 1Chr 19:18
neither would the *S* help the ........ 1Chr 19:19
against the *S* until the even ........ 2Chr 18:34
and the *S* smote Joram ........ 2Chr 22:5
For the army of the *S* came with a ... 2Chr 24:24
The *S* before, and the Philistines ........ Is 9:12
and for fear of the army of the *S* ........ Jer 35:11
from Caphtor, and the *S* from Kir ........ Amos 9:7

**SYROPHENICIAN** (*sy''-ro-fe-ne'-she-un*) *A citizen of Phenicia in Syria.*
woman was a Greek, a *S* by nation ........ Mk 7:26

**SYRTIS**

# T

**TAANACH** (*ta'-a-nak*) See TANACH. *A Levitical city in Manasseh.*
The king of *T*, one ........ Josh 12:21
towns, and the inhabitants of *T* ........ Josh 17:11
of Beth-shean and her towns, nor *T* .... Judg 1:27
in *T* by the waters of Megiddo ........ Judg 5:19
to him pertained *T* and Megiddo, and . 1Kin 4:12
Beth-shean and her towns, *T* ........ 1Chr 7:29

**TAANATH-SHILOH** (*ta''-a-nath-shi'-lo*) *A city on the border of Benjamin.*
border went about eastward unto *T* ..... Josh 16:6

**TABALIAH** See TEBALIAH.

**TABBAOTH** (*tab'-ba-oth*) *A family of exiles.*
of Hasupha, the children of *T* ........ Ezr 2:43
of Hashupha, the children of *T* ........ Neh 7:46

**TABBATH** (*tab'-bath*) *A city in Issachar.*
border of Abel-meholah, unto *T* ........ Judg 7:22

**TABEAL** (*tab'-e-al*) See TABEEL. *Father of a would-be king of Israel.*
midst of it, even the son of *T* ........ Is 7:6

**TABEEL** (*tab'-e-el*) See TABEAL. *A Persian official in Samaria.*
wrote Bishlam, Mithredath, *T* ........ Ezr 4:7

**TABERAH** (*tab'-e-rah*) *A place in the wilderness of Paran.*
he called the name of the place *T* ........ Num 11:3
And at *T*, and at Massah, and at ........ Deut 9:22

**TABERING**
of doves, *t* upon their breasts ........ Nah 2:7

**TABERNACLE**
thee, after the pattern of the *t* ........ Ex 25:9
the *t* with ten curtains of fine ........ Ex 26:1
and it shall be one *t* ........ Ex 26:6
hair to be a covering upon the *t* ........ Ex 26:7
curtain in the forefront of the *t* ........ Ex 26:9
hang over the backside of the *t* ........ Ex 26:12
the sides of the *t* on this side ........ Ex 26:13
the *t* of shittim wood standing up ........ Ex 26:15
make for all the boards of the *t* ........ Ex 26:17
shalt make the boards for the *t* ........ Ex 26:18
for the second side of the *t* on ........ Ex 26:20
for the sides of the *t* westward ........ Ex 26:22
corners of the *t* in the two sides ........ Ex 26:23
boards of the one side of the *t* ........ Ex 26:26
boards of the other side of the *t* ........ Ex 26:27
the boards of the side of the *t* ........ Ex 26:27
And thou shalt rear up the *t* ........ Ex 26:30
side of the *t* toward the south ........ Ex 26:35
shalt make the court of the *t* ........ Ex 27:9
All the vessels of the *t* in all ........ Ex 27:19
In the *t* of the congregation ........ Ex 27:21
in unto the *t* of the congregation ........ Ex 28:43
door of the *t* of the congregation ........ Ex 29:4
before the *t* of the congregation ........ Ex 29:10
by the door of the *t* of the ........ Ex 29:11
when he cometh into the *t* of the ........ Ex 29:30
by the door of the *t* of the ........ Ex 29:32
*t* of the congregation before the ........ Ex 29:42
the *t* shall be sanctified by my ........ Ex 29:43
the *t* of the congregation ........ Ex 29:44
of the *t* of the congregation ........ Ex 30:16
between the *t* of the congregation ........ Ex 30:18
go into the *t* of the congregation ........ Ex 30:20
thou shalt anoint the *t* of the ........ Ex 30:26
in the *t* of the congregation ........ Ex 30:36
The *t* of the congregation, and the ........ Ex 31:7
and all the furniture of the *t* ........ Ex 31:7
And Moses took the *t*, and pitched ........ Ex 33:7
camp, and called it the *T* of the ........ Ex 33:7
unto the *t* of the congregation ........ Ex 33:7
when Moses went out unto the *t* ........ Ex 33:8
until he was gone into the *t* ........ Ex 33:8
pass, as Moses entered into the *t* ........ Ex 33:9
and stood at the door of the *t* ........ Ex 33:9
cloudy pillar stand at the *t* door ........ Ex 33:10
man, departed not out of the *t* ........ Ex 33:11
The *t*, his tent, and his covering, ........ Ex 35:11
door at the entering in of the *t* ........ Ex 35:15
The pins of the *t*, and the pins of ........ Ex 35:18
work of the *t* of the congregation ........ Ex 35:21
the *t* made ten curtains of fine ........ Ex 36:8
so it became one *t* ........ Ex 36:13
hair for the tent over the *t* ........ Ex 36:14
boards for the *t* of shittim wood ........ Ex 36:20
make for all the boards of the *t* ........ Ex 36:22
And he made boards for the *t* ........ Ex 36:23
And for the other side of the *t* ........ Ex 36:25
for the sides of the *t* westward ........ Ex 36:27
corners of the *t* in the two sides ........ Ex 36:28
boards of the one side of the *t* ........ Ex 36:31
boards of the other side of the *t* ........ Ex 36:32
of the *t* for the sides westward ........ Ex 36:32
an hanging for the *t* door of blue ........ Ex 36:37
door of the *t* of the congregation ........ Ex 38:8
And all the pins of the *t*, and of ........ Ex 38:20
This is the sum of the *t*, even of ........ Ex 38:21
even of the *t* of testimony, as it ........ Ex 38:21
door of the *t* of the congregation ........ Ex 38:30
gate, and all the pins of the *t* ........ Ex 38:31
Thus was all the work of the *t* of ........ Ex 39:32
And they brought the *t* unto Moses ........ Ex 39:33
and the hanging for the *t* door ........ Ex 39:38
vessels of the service of the *t* ........ Ex 39:40
month shalt thou set up the *t* of ........ Ex 40:2
the hanging of the door to the *t* ........ Ex 40:5
*t* of the tent of the congregation ........ Ex 40:6
anointing oil, and anoint the *t* ........ Ex 40:9
door of the *t* of the congregation ........ Ex 40:12
month, that the *t* was reared up ........ Ex 40:17
And Moses reared up the *t*, and ........ Ex 40:18
spread abroad the tent over the *t* ........ Ex 40:19
And he brought the ark into the *t* ........ Ex 40:21
upon the side of the *t* northward ........ Ex 40:22
on the side of the *t* southward ........ Ex 40:24
the hanging at the door of the *t* ........ Ex 40:28
offering by the door of the *t* of ........ Ex 40:29
up the court round about the *t* ........ Ex 40:33
glory of the LORD filled the *t* ........ Ex 40:34
glory of the LORD filled the *t* ........ Ex 40:35
was taken up from over the *t* ........ Ex 40:36
of the LORD was upon the *t* by day ........ Ex 40:38
out of the *t* of the congregation ........ Lev 1:1
will at the door of the *t* of the ........ Lev 1:3
door of the *t* of the congregation ........ Lev 1:5
door of the *t* of the congregation ........ Lev 3:2
kill it before the *t* of the ........ Lev 3:8
kill it before the *t* of the ........ Lev 3:13
bullock unto the door of the *t* of ........ Lev 4:4
and bring it to the *t* of the ........ Lev 4:5
LORD, which is in the *t* of the ........ Lev 4:7
door of the *t* of the congregation ........ Lev 4:7
before the *t* of the congregation ........ Lev 4:14
to the *t* of the congregation ........ Lev 4:16
the LORD, that is in the *t* of the ........ Lev 4:18
door of the *t* of the congregation ........ Lev 4:18
in the court of the *t* of the ........ Lev 6:16
of the *t* of the congregation ........ Lev 6:26
into the *t* of the congregation to ........ Lev 6:30
door of the *t* of the congregation ........ Lev 8:3
door of the *t* of the congregation ........ Lev 8:4
anointing oil, and anointed the *t* ........ Lev 8:10
door of the *t* of the congregation ........ Lev 8:31
*t* of the congregation in seven ........ Lev 8:33
of the *t* of the congregation day ........ Lev 8:35
before the *t* of the congregation ........ Lev 9:5
into the *t* of the congregation ........ Lev 9:23
door of the *t* of the congregation ........ Lev 10:7
go into the *t* of the congregation ........ Lev 10:9
door of the *t* of the congregation ........ Lev 12:6
at the door of the *t* of the ........ Lev 14:11
door of the *t* of the congregation ........ Lev 14:23
door of the *t* of the congregation ........ Lev 15:14
to the door of the *t* of the ........ Lev 15:29
defile my *t* that is among them ........ Lev 15:31
door of the *t* of the congregation ........ Lev 16:7
do for the *t* of the congregation ........ Lev 16:16
the *t* of the congregation when he ........ Lev 16:17
the *t* of the congregation, and the ........ Lev 16:20
into the *t* of the congregation ........ Lev 16:23
for the *t* of the congregation ........ Lev 16:33
door of the *t* of the congregation ........ Lev 17:4
the LORD before the *t* of the LORD ........ Lev 17:4
door of the *t* of the congregation ........ Lev 17:5
door of the *t* of the congregation ........ Lev 17:6
door of the *t* of the congregation ........ Lev 17:9
door of the *t* of the congregation ........ Lev 19:21
in the *t* of the congregation, ........ Lev 24:3
And I will set my *t* among you ........ Lev 26:11
in the *t* of the congregation, on ........ Num 1:1
Levites over the *t* of testimony ........ Num 1:50
they shall bear the *t*, and all the ........ Num 1:50
and shall encamp round about the *t* ... Num 1:50
when the *t* setteth forward, the ........ Num 1:51
when the *t* is to be pitched, the ........ Num 1:51
round about the *t* of testimony ........ Num 1:53
the charge of the *t* of testimony ........ Num 1:53
far off about the *t* of the ........ Num 2:2
Then the *t* of the congregation ........ Num 2:17
before the *t* of the congregation ........ Num 3:7
to do the service of the *t* ........ Num 3:7
of the *t* of the congregation ........ Num 3:8
to do the service of the *t* ........ Num 3:8

shall pitch behind the *t* westward Num 3:23
*t* of the congregation shall be Num 3:25
the congregation shall be the *t* Num 3:25
door of the *t* of the congregation Num 3:25
of the court, which is by the *t* Num 3:26
on the side of the *t* southward Num 3:29
on the side of the *t* northward Num 3:35
shall be the boards of the *t* Num 3:36
before the *t* toward the east Num 3:38
even before the *t* of the Num 3:38
work in the *t* of the congregation Num 4:3
in the *t* of the congregation Num 4:4
in the *t* of the congregation Num 4:15
and the oversight of all the *t* Num 4:16
work in the *t* of the congregation Num 4:23
shall bear the curtains of the *t* Num 4:25
the *t* of the congregation, his Num 4:25
door of the *t* of the congregation Num 4:25
of the court, which is by the *t* Num 4:26
in the *t* of the congregation Num 4:28
work of the *t* of the congregation Num 4:30
in the *t* of the congregation Num 4:31
the boards of the *t*, and the bars Num 4:31
in the *t* of the congregation, Num 4:33
work in the *t* of the congregation Num 4:35
in the *t* of the congregation Num 4:37
work in the *t* of the congregation Num 4:39
in the *t* of the congregation Num 4:41
work in the *t* of the congregation Num 4:43
in the *t* of the congregation Num 4:47
of the *t* the priest shall take Num 5:17
to the door of the *t* of the Num 6:10
door of the *t* of the congregation Num 6:13
door of the *t* of the congregation Num 6:18
that Moses had fully set up the *t* Num 7:1
and they brought them before the *t* Num 7:3
of the *t* of the congregation Num 7:5
*t* of the congregation to speak Num 7:89
before the *t* of the congregation Num 8:9
of the *t* of the congregation Num 8:15
in the *t* of the congregation Num 8:19
the *t* of the congregation before Num 8:22
of the *t* of the congregation Num 8:24
in the *t* of the congregation Num 8:26
on the day that the *t* was reared Num 9:15
reared up the cloud covered the *t* Num 9:15
at even there was upon the *t* as Num 9:15
the cloud was taken up from the *t* Num 9:17
the *t* they rested in their tents Num 9:18
tarried long upon the *t* many days Num 9:19
cloud was a few days upon the *t* Num 9:20
that the cloud tarried upon the *t* Num 9:22
door of the *t* of the congregation Num 10:3
from off the *t* of the testimony Num 10:11
And the *t* was taken down Num 10:17
Merari set forward, bearing the *t* Num 10:17
set up the *t* against they came Num 10:21
unto the *t* of the congregation Num 11:16
and set them round about the *t* Num 11:24
but went not out unto the *t* Num 11:26
unto the *t* of the congregation Num 12:4
and stood in the door of the *t* Num 12:5
the cloud departed from off the *t* Num 12:10
of the LORD appeared in the *t* of Num 14:10
the service of the *t* of the LORD Num 16:9
stood in the door of the *t* of the Num 16:18
door of the *t* of the congregation Num 16:19
you up from about the *t* of Korah Num 16:24
they gat up from the *t* of Korah Num 16:27
toward the *t* of the congregation Num 16:42
before the *t* of the congregation Num 16:43
door of the *t* of the congregation Num 16:50
thou shalt lay them up in the *t* Num 17:4
the LORD in the *t* of witness Num 17:7
Moses went into the *t* of witness Num 17:8
unto the *t* of the LORD shall die Num 17:13
minister before the *t* of witness Num 18:2
and the charge of all the *t* Num 18:3
of the *t* of the congregation Num 18:4
for all the service of the *t* Num 18:4
of the *t* of the congregation Num 18:6
of the *t* of the congregation Num 18:21
nigh the *t* of the congregation Num 18:22
of the *t* of the congregation Num 18:23
in the *t* of the congregation Num 18:31
her blood directly before the *t* Num 19:4
defileth the *t* of the LORD Num 19:13
door of the *t* of the congregation Num 20:6
door of the *t* of the congregation Num 25:6
by the door of the *t* of the Num 27:2
the charge of the *t* of the LORD Num 31:30
the charge of the *t* of the LORD Num 31:47
it into the *t* of the congregation Num 31:54
in the *t* of the congregation Deut 31:14
in the *t* of the congregation Deut 31:14
in the *t* in a pillar of a cloud Deut 31:15
stood over the door of the *t* Deut 31:15
set up the *t* of the congregation Josh 18:1
at the door of the *t* of the Josh 19:51
wherein the LORD's *t* dwelleth Josh 22:19
LORD our God that is before his *t* Josh 22:29
door of the *t* of the congregation 1Sa 2:22
in the midst of the *t* that David 2Sa 6:17
have walked in a tent and in a *t* 2Sa 7:6
took an horn of oil out of the *t* 1Kin 1:39
Joab fled unto the *t* of the LORD 1Kin 2:28
was fled unto the *t* of the LORD 1Kin 2:29
Benaiah came to the *t* of the LORD 1Kin 2:30
the *t* of the congregation, and all 1Kin 8:4
holy vessels that were in the *t* 1Kin 8:4
of the *t* of the congregation with 1Chr 6:32
of the *t* of the house of God 1Chr 6:48
keepers of the gates of the *t* 1Chr 9:19
door of the *t* of the congregation 1Chr 9:21
LORD, namely, the house of the *t* 1Chr 9:23
before the *t* of the LORD in the 1Chr 16:39
to tent, and from one *t* to another 1Chr 17:5
For the *t* of the LORD, which 1Chr 21:29
they shall no more carry the *t* 1Chr 23:26
of the *t* of the congregation 1Chr 23:32
for there was the *t* of the 2Chr 1:3
he put before the *t* of the LORD 2Chr 1:5
which was at the *t* of the 2Chr 1:6
from before the *t* of the 2Chr 1:13
the *t* of the congregation, and all 2Chr 5:5
holy vessels that were in the *t* 2Chr 5:5
of Israel, for the *t* of witness 2Chr 24:6
know that thy *t* shall be in peace Job 5:24
The light shall be dark in his *t* Job 18:6
shall be rooted out of his *t* Job 18:14
It shall dwell in his *t*, because Job 18:15
me, and encamp round about my *t* Job 19:12
with him that is left in his *t* Job 20:26
the secret of God was upon my *t* Job 29:4
If the men of my *t* said not Job 31:31
the clouds, or the noise of his *t* Job 36:29
Lord, who shall abide in thy *t* Ps 15:1
them hath he set a *t* for the sun Ps 19:4
secret of his *t* shall he hide me Ps 27:5
offer in his *t* sacrifices of joy Ps 27:6
I will abide in thy *t* for ever Ps 61:4
In Salem also is his *t*, and his Ps 76:2
that he forsook the *t* of Shiloh Ps 78:60
he refused the *t* of Joseph Ps 78:67
not come into the *t* of my house Ps 132:3
but the *t* of the upright shall Prov 14:11
there shall be a *t* for a shadow Is 4:6
it in truth in the *t* of David Is 16:5
a *t* that shall not be taken down Is 33:20
My *t* is spoiled, and all my cords Jer 10:20
in the *t* of the daughter of Zion Lam 2:4
hath violently taken away his *t* Lam 2:6
My *t* also shall be with them Eze 37:27
which was the breadth of the *t* Eze 41:1
have borne the *t* of your Moloch Amos 5:26
up the *t* of David that is fallen Amos 9:11
Yea, ye took up the *t* of Moloch Acts 7:43
Our fathers had the *t* of witness Acts 7:44
desired to find a *t* for the God Acts 7:46
will build again the *t* of David Acts 15:16
house of this *t* were dissolved 2Cor 5:1
we that are in this *t* do groan 2Cor 5:4
the sanctuary, and of the true *t* Heb 8:2
when he was about to make the *t* Heb 8:5
For there was a *t* made Heb 9:2
the *t* which is called the Holiest Heb 9:3
went always into the first *t* Heb 9:6
as the first *t* was yet standing Heb 9:8
by a greater and more perfect *t* Heb 9:11
sprinkled with blood both the *t* Heb 9:21
no right to eat which serve the *t* Heb 13:10
meet, as long as I am in this *t* 2Pet 1:13
shortly I must put off this my *t* 2Pet 1:14
to blaspheme his name, and his *t* Rev 13:6
the temple of the *t* of the Rev 15:5
the *t* of God is with men, and he Rev 21:3

## TABERNACLES

month shall be the feast of *t* for Lev 23:34
are thy tents, O Jacob, and thy *t* Num 24:5
observe the feast of *t* seven days Deut 16:13
of weeks, and in the feast of *t* Deut 16:16
of release, in the feast of *t* Deut 31:10
of weeks, and in the feast of *t* 2Chr 8:13
They kept also the feast of *t* Ezr 3:4
let not wickedness dwell in thy *t* Job 11:14
The *t* of robbers prosper, and they Job 12:6
shall consume the *t* of bribery Job 15:34
put away iniquity far from thy *t* Job 22:23
unto thy holy hill, and to thy *t* Ps 43:3
place of the *t* of the most High Ps 46:4
of their strength in the *t* of Ham Ps 78:51
The *t* of Edom, and the Ishmaelites Ps 83:6
How amiable are thy *t*, O LORD of Ps 84:1
is in the *t* of the righteous Ps 118:15
We will go into his *t* Ps 132:7
he shall plant the *t* of his Dan 11:45
thorns shall be in their *t* Hos 9:6
will yet make thee to dwell in *t* Hos 12:9
hosts, and to keep the feast of *t* Zec 14:16
not up to keep the feast of *t* Zec 14:18
not up to keep the feast of *t* Zec 14:19
scholar, out of the *t* of Jacob Mal 2:12
wilt, let us make here three *t* Mt 17:4
and let us make three *t* Mk 9:5
and let us make three *t* Lk 9:33
the Jews' feast of *t* was at hand Jn 7:2
country, dwelling in *t* with Isaac Heb 11:9

**TABITHA** (*tab'-ith-ah*) *Woman raised from the dead by Peter.*

Joppa a certain disciple named *T* Acts 9:36
turning him to the body said, *T* Acts 9:40

## TABLE

also make a *t* of shittim wood Ex 25:23
of the staves to bear the *t* Ex 25:27
that the *t* may be borne with them Ex 25:28
thou shalt set upon the *t* Ex 25:30
shalt set the *t* without the vail Ex 26:35
candlestick over against the *t* on Ex 26:35
shalt put the *t* on the north side Ex 26:35
And the *t* and all his vessels, and Ex 30:27
And the *t* and his furniture, and the Ex 31:8
The *t*, and his staves, and all his Ex 35:13
he made the *t* of shittim wood Ex 37:10
for the staves to bear the *t* Ex 37:14
them with gold, to bear the *t* Ex 37:15
the vessels which were upon the *t* Ex 37:16
The *t*, and all the vessels thereof Ex 39:36
And thou shalt bring in the *t* Ex 40:4
he put the *t* in the tent of the Ex 40:22
congregation, over against the *t* Ex 40:24
upon the pure *t* before the LORD Lev 24:6
charge shall be the ark, and the *t* Num 3:31
upon the *t* of shewbread they Num 4:7
gathered their meat under my *t* Judg 1:7
he cometh not unto the king's *t* 1Sa 20:29
arose from the *t* in fierce anger 1Sa 20:34
eat bread at my *t* continually 2Sa 9:7
son shall eat bread alway at my *t* 2Sa 9:10
the king, he shall eat at my *t* 2Sa 9:11
eat continually at the king's *t* 2Sa 9:13
them that did eat at thine own *t* 2Sa 19:28
be of those that eat at thy *t* 1Kin 2:7
that came unto king Solomon's *t* 1Kin 4:27
the *t* of gold, whereupon the 1Kin 7:48
And the meat of his *t*, and the 1Kin 10:5
to pass, as they sat at the *t* 1Kin 13:20
hundred, which eat at Jezebel's *t* 1Kin 18:19
set for him there a bed, and a *t* 2Kin 4:10
tables of shewbread, for every *t* 1Chr 28:16
And the meat of his *t*, and the 2Chr 9:4
set they in order upon the pure *t* 2Chr 13:11
thereof, and the shewbread *t* 2Chr 29:18
there were at my *t* an hundred Neh 5:17
thy *t* should be full of fatness Job 36:16
Thou preparest a *t* before me in Ps 23:5
Let their *t* become a snare before Ps 69:22
God furnish a *t* in the wilderness Ps 78:19
olive plants round about thy *t* Ps 128:3
them upon the *t* of thine heart Prov 3:3
them upon the *t* of thine heart Prov 7:3
she hath also furnished her *t* Prov 9:2
While the king sitteth at his *t* Song 1:12
Prepare the *t*, watch in the Is 21:5
go, write it before them in a *t* Is 30:8
that prepare a *t* for that troop Is 65:11
graven upon the *t* of their heart Jer 17:1
a *t* prepared before it, whereupon Eze 23:41
be filled at my *t* with horses Eze 39:20
This is the *t* that is before the Eze 41:22
and they shall come near to my *t* Eze 44:16
and they shall speak lies at one *t* Dan 11:27
The *t* of the LORD is contemptible Mal 1:7
The *t* of the LORD is polluted Mal 1:12
which fall from their masters' *t* Mt 15:27
yet the dogs under the *t* eat of Mk 7:28
And he asked for a writing *t* Lk 1:63
which fell from the rich man's *t* Lk 16:21
betrayeth me is with me on the *t* Lk 22:21
drink at my *t* in my kingdom, and Lk 22:30
them that sat at the *t* with him Jn 12:2
Now no man at the *t* knew for what Jn 13:28
Let their *t* be made a snare, and a Rom 11:9
be partakers of the Lord's *t* 1Cor 10:21
and of the *t* of devils 1Cor 10:21
was the candlestick, and the *t* Heb 9:2

## TABLES

and I will give thee *t* of stone Ex 24:12
two *t* of testimony, *t* of Ex 31:18
*t* of stone, written with the Ex 31:18
the two *t* of the testimony were Ex 32:15
the *t* were written on both their Ex 32:15
the *t* were the work of God, and Ex 32:16
writing of God, graven upon the *t* Ex 32:16
he cast the *t* out of his hands, Ex 32:19
Hew thee two *t* of stone like unto Ex 34:1
I will write upon these *t* the Ex 34:1
words that were in the first *t* Ex 34:1
he hewed two *t* of stone like unto Ex 34:4
in his hand the two *t* of stone Ex 34:4
he wrote upon the *t* the words of Ex 34:28
two *t* of testimony in Moses' hand Ex 34:29
he wrote them upon two *t* of stone Deut 4:13
he wrote them in two *t* of stone Deut 5:22
mount to receive the *t* of stone Deut 9:9
even the *t* of the covenant which Deut 9:9
two *t* of stone written with the Deut 9:10
LORD gave me the two *t* of stone Deut 9:11
even the *t* of the covenant Deut 9:11
the two *t* of the covenant were in Deut 9:15
And I took the two *t*, and cast them Deut 9:17
Hew thee two *t* of stone like unto Deut 10:1
I will write on the *t* the words Deut 10:2
in the first *t* which thou brakest Deut 10:2
hewed two *t* of stone like unto Deut 10:3
having the two *t* in mine hand Deut 10:3
And he wrote on the *t*, according Deut 10:4
put the *t* in the ark which I had Deut 10:5
the ark save the two *t* of stone 1Kin 8:9
gave gold for the *t* of shewbread 1Chr 28:16
silver for the *t* of silver 1Chr 28:16
He made also ten *t*, and placed 2Chr 4:8
the *t* whereon the shewbread was 2Chr 4:19
two *t* which Moses put therein at 2Chr 5:10
For all *t* are full of vomit and Is 28:8
the gate were two *t* on this side Eze 40:39
two *t* on that side, to slay Eze 40:39
of the north gate, were two *t* Eze 40:40
the porch of the gate, were two *t* Eze 40:40
Four *t* were on this side, and four Eze 40:41

T

four *t* on that side, by the side ............ Eze 40:41
eight *t*, whereupon they slew ............ Eze 40:41
the four *t* were of hewn stone for ............ Eze 40:42
upon the *t* was the flesh of the ............ Eze 40:43
vision, and make it plain upon *t* ............ Hab 2:2
temple, and overthrew the *t* of the ............ Mt 21:12
and pots, brasen vessels, and of *t* ............ Mk 7:4
temple, and overthrew the *t* of the ............ Mk 11:15
money, and overthrew the *t* ............ Jn 2:15
leave the word of God, and serve *t* ............ Acts 6:2
not in *t* of stone, but in fleshly ............ 2Cor 3:3
but in fleshly *t* of the heart ............ 2Cor 3:3
budded, and the *t* of the covenant ............ Heb 9:4

**TABLETS**
and earrings, and rings, and *t* ............ Ex 35:22
bracelets, rings, earrings, and *t* ............ Num 31:50
legs, and the headbands, and the *t* ............ Is 3:20

**TABOR** (*ta'-bor*)
*1. A mountain in Issachar and Zebulun.*
And the coast reacheth to *T* ............ Josh 19:22
saying, Go and draw toward mount *T* .. Judg 4:6
of Abinoam was gone up to mount *T*. Judg 4:12
So Barak went down from mount *T* ... Judg 4:14
men were they whom ye slew at *T* ..... Judg 8:18
*T* and Hermon shall rejoice in thy ............ Ps 89:12
hosts, Surely as *T* is among the ............ Jer 46:18
on Mizpah, and a net spread upon *T* ...... Hos 5:1
*2. A plain in Benjamin.*
thou shalt come to the plain of *T* ............ 1Sa 10:3
*3. A Levitical city in Zebulun.*
her suburbs, *T* with her suburbs ............ 1Chr 6:77

**TABRET**
with mirth, and with songs, with *t* ...... Gen 31:27
place with a psaltery, and a *t* ............ 1Sa 10:5
and aforetime I was as a *t* ............ Job 17:6
And the harp, and the viol, the *t* ............ Is 5:12

**TABRETS**
to meet king Saul, with *t* ............ 1Sa 18:6
The mirth of *t* ceaseth, the noise ............ Is 24:8
lay upon him, it shall be with *t* ............ Is 30:32
shalt again be adorned with thy *t* ............ Jer 31:4
the workmanship of thy *t* and of ............ Eze 28:13

**TABRIMMON** See TABRIMON.

**TABRIMON** (*tab'-rim-on*) *Father of Benhadad, king of Syria.*
them to Ben-hadad, the son of *T* ........ 1Kin 15:18

**TACHES**
thou shalt make fifty *t* of gold ............ Ex 26:6
the curtains together with the *t* ............ Ex 26:6
thou shalt make fifty *t* of brass ............ Ex 26:11
put the *t* into the loops, and ............ Ex 26:11
hang up the vail under the *t* ............ Ex 26:33
his tent, and his covering, his *t* ............ Ex 35:11
And he made fifty *t* of gold ............ Ex 36:13
one unto another with the *t* ............ Ex 36:13
he made fifty *t* of brass to ............ Ex 36:18
tent, and all his furniture, his *t* ............ Ex 39:33

**TACHMONITE** (*tak'-mun-ite*) See HACHMONITE. *Family name of a 'mighty man' of David.*
The *T* that sat in the seat, chief ............ 2Sa 23:8

**TACKLING**
our own hands the *t* of the ship .......... Acts 27:19

**TACKLINGS**
Thy *t* are loosed ............ Is 33:23

**TADMOR** (*tad'-mor*) *A city rebuilt by Solomon.*
*T* in the wilderness, in the land, ............ 1Kin 9:18
he built *T* in the wilderness, and ............ 2Chr 8:4

**TAHAN** (*ta'-han*) See TAHANITES.
*1. A son of Ephraim.*
of *T*, the family of the Tahanites ....... Num 26:35
*2. A descendant of Ephraim.*
and Telah his son, and *T* his son, ........ 1Chr 7:25

**TAHANITES** (*ta'-han-ites*) *Descendants of Tahan 1.*
of Tahan, the family of the *T* ............ Num 26:35

**TAHAPANES** (*ta-hap'-a-neze*) See TAHAPANHES. *A city in Egypt.*
*T* have broken the crown of thy ............ Jer 2:16

**TAHASH** See THAHASH.

**TAHATH** (*ta'-hath*)
*1. An Israelite encampment in the wilderness.*
from Makheloth, and encamped at *T* Num 33:26
And they departed from *T*, and .......... Num 33:27
*2. Father of Uriel.*
*T* his son, Uriel his son, Uzziah ............ 1Chr 6:24
The son of *T*, the son of Assir, ............ 1Chr 6:37
*3. Father of Eladah.*
*T* his son, and Eladah his son, and ....... 1Chr 7:20
*4. Son of Eladah.*
and Eladah his son, and *T* his son, ....... 1Chr 7:20

**TAHCHEMONITE**

**TAHKEMONITE** See TACHMONITE.

**TAHPANHES** (*tah'-pan-heze*) See TAHAPANES, TAHPENES, TEHAPHNEHES. *Same as Tahapanes.*
thus came they even to *T* ............ Jer 43:7
of the LORD unto Jeremiah in *T* ............ Jer 43:8
the entry of Pharaoh's house in *T* ............ Jer 43:9
which dwell at Migdol, and at *T* ............ Jer 44:1
and publish in Noph and in *T* ............ Jer 46:14

**TAHPENES** (*tah'-pe-neze*) See TAHPANHES. *Queen of a pharaoh.*
wife, the sister of *T* the queen ............ 1Kin 11:19
the sister of *T* bare him Genubath ..... 1Kin 11:20
whom *T* weaned in Pharaoh's house. 1Kin 11:20

**TAHREA** (*tah'-re-ah*) See TAREA. *Son of Micah.*
were, Pithon, and Melech, and *T* .......... 1Chr 9:41

**TAHTIM-HODSHI** (*tah''-tim-hod'-shi*) *A district north of Gilead in Bashan.*
to Gilead, and to the land of *T* ............ 2Sa 24:6

**TAIL**
thine hand, and take it by the *t* ............ Ex 4:4
make thee the head, and not the *t* .... Deut 28:13
the head, and thou shalt be the *t* ....... Deut 28:44
firebrands, and turned *t* to *t* ............ Judg 15:4
He moveth his *t* like a cedar ............ Job 40:17
cut off from Israel head and *t* ............ Is 9:14
that teacheth lies, he is the *t* ............ Is 9:15
for Egypt, which the head or *t* ............ Is 19:15
his *t* drew the third part of the ............ Rev 12:4

**TAILS**
in the midst between two *t* ............ Judg 15:4
two *t* of these smoking firebrands ............ Is 7:4
they had *t* like unto scorpions, ............ Rev 9:10
and there were stings in their *t* ............ Rev 9:10
is in their mouth, and in their *t* ............ Rev 9:19
for their *t* were like unto ............ Rev 9:19

**TAKE** See PREFACE.

**TAKEN**
which the LORD God had *t* from man... Gen 2:22
because she was *t* out of Man ............ Gen 2:23
for out of it wast thou *t* ............ Gen 3:19
the ground from whence he was *t* ........ Gen 3:23
shall be *t* on him sevenfold ............ Gen 4:15
the woman was *t* into Pharaoh's ......... Gen 12:15
so I might have *t* her to me to ............ Gen 12:19
that his brother was *t* captive ............ Gen 14:14
I have *t* upon me to speak unto ............ Gen 18:27
I have *t* upon me to speak unto ............ Gen 18:31
for the woman which thou hast *t* ......... Gen 20:3
servants had violently *t* away ............ Gen 21:25
where is he that hath *t* venison ............ Gen 27:33
and hath *t* away thy blessing ............ Gen 27:35
now he hath *t* away my blessing ............ Gen 27:36
that thou hast *t* my husband ............ Gen 30:15
God hath *t* away my reproach ............ Gen 30:23
Jacob hath *t* away all that was ............ Gen 31:1
Thus God hath *t* away the cattle ............ Gen 31:9
which God hath *t* from our father ...... Gen 31:16
as captives *t* with the sword ............ Gen 31:26
Now Rachel had *t* the images ............ Gen 31:34
hast thou *t* us away to die in the ............ Ex 14:11
they shall not be *t* from it ............ Ex 25:15
when the cloud was *t* up from over ...... Ex 40:36
But if the cloud were not *t* up ............ Ex 40:37
not till the day that it was *t* up ............ Ex 40:37
As it was *t* off from the bullock ............ Lev 4:10
as the fat is *t* away from off the ............ Lev 4:31
as the fat of the lamb is *t* away ............ Lev 4:35
or in a thing *t* away by violence, ............ Lev 6:2
the heave shoulder have I *t* of ............ Lev 7:34
that he hath *t* away the stones ............ Lev 14:43
being *t* from the children of ............ Lev 24:8
I have *t* the Levites from among ......... Num 3:12
neither she be *t* with the manner ......... Num 5:13
of Israel, have I *t* them unto me ......... Num 8:16
I have *t* the Levites for all the ............ Num 8:18
when the cloud was *t* up from the ....... Num 9:17
the cloud was *t* up in the morning ...... Num 9:21
by night that the cloud was *t* up ......... Num 9:21
but when it was *t* up, they ............ Num 9:22
that the cloud was *t* up from off ......... Num 10:11
And the tabernacle was *t* down ............ Num 10:17
I have not *t* one ass from them, ......... Num 16:15
I have *t* your brethren the ............ Num 18:6
*t* all his land out of his hand, ............ Num 21:26
the sum of the prey that was *t* ............ Num 31:26
Thy servants have *t* the sum of ............ Num 31:49
(For the men of war had *t* spoil ............ Num 31:53
be *t* from the inheritance of our ............ Num 36:3
so shall it be *t* from the lot of ............ Num 36:3
be *t* away from the inheritance of ....... Num 36:4
But the LORD hath *t* you, and ............ Deut 4:20
a wife, and hath not *t* her ............ Deut 20:7
thou hast *t* them captive, ............ Deut 21:10
When a man hath *t* a wife, and ............ Deut 24:1
When a man hath *t* a new wife ............ Deut 24:5
cheer up his wife which he hath *t* ....... Deut 24:5
neither have I *t* away ought ............ Deut 26:14
*t* away from before thy face ............ Deut 28:31
for they have even *t* of the ............ Josh 7:11
that he that is *t* with the ............ Josh 7:15
and the tribe of Judah was *t* ............ Josh 7:16
and Zabdi was *t* ............ Josh 7:17
of the tribe of Judah, was *t* ............ Josh 7:18
shall be, when ye have *t* the city ............ Josh 8:8
that the ambush had *t* the city ............ Josh 8:21
had heard how Joshua had *t* Ai ............ Josh 10:1
against Jerusalem, and had *t* it ............ Judg 1:8
forasmuch as the LORD hath *t* ............ Judg 11:36
he told not them that he had *t* ............ Judg 14:9
because he had *t* his wife ............ Judg 15:6
of silver that were *t* from thee ............ Judg 17:2
Ye have *t* away my gods which I ....... Judg 18:24
And the ark of God was *t* ............ 1Sa 4:11
are dead, and the ark of God is *t* ............ 1Sa 4:17
tidings that the ark of God was *t* ......... 1Sa 4:19
because the ark of God was *t* ............ 1Sa 4:21
for the ark of God is *t* ............ 1Sa 4:22
which the Philistines had *t* from ............ 1Sa 7:14
near, the tribe of Benjamin was *t* ......... 1Sa 10:20
the family of Matri was *t* ............ 1Sa 10:21
and Saul the son of Kish was *t* ............ 1Sa 10:21
whose ox have I *t* ............ 1Sa 12:3
or whose ass have I *t* ............ 1Sa 12:3
neither hast thou *t* ought of any ............ 1Sa 12:4
And Saul and Jonathan were *t* ............ 1Sa 14:41
And Jonathan was *t* ............ 1Sa 14:42
that was *t* from before the LORD, ............ 1Sa 21:6
in the day when it was *t* away ............ 1Sa 21:6
had *t* the women captives, that ............ 1Sa 30:2
their daughters, were *t* captives ............ 1Sa 30:3
David's two wives were *t* captives ......... 1Sa 30:5
they had *t* out of the land of the ............ 1Sa 30:16
any thing that they had *t* to them ....... 1Sa 30:19
hast *t* his wife to be thy wife, ............ 2Sa 12:9
hast *t* the wife of Uriah the ............ 2Sa 12:10
have *t* the city of waters ............ 2Sa 12:27
thou art *t* in thy mischief, ............ 2Sa 16:8
he was *t* up between the heaven and.... 2Sa 18:9
Now Absalom in his lifetime had *t* ....... 2Sa 18:18
they cannot be *t* with hands ............ 2Sa 23:6
daughter, whom he had *t* to wife ............ 1Kin 7:8
have *t* hold upon other gods, and ............ 1Kin 9:9
*t* Gezer, and burnt it with fire, ............ 1Kin 9:16
Zimri saw that the city was *t* ............ 1Kin 16:18
thou killed, and also *t* possession ......... 1Kin 21:19
the high places were not *t* away ........ 1Kin 22:43
before I be *t* away from thee ............ 2Kin 2:9
thou see me when I am *t* from thee .... 2Kin 2:10
Spirit of the LORD hath *t* him up ......... 2Kin 2:16
And when he had *t* him, and brought. 2Kin 4:20
hast *t* captive with thy sword ............ 2Kin 6:22
the high places were not *t* away ......... 2Kin 12:3
which he had *t* out of the hand of ..... 2Kin 13:25
the high places were not *t* away ......... 2Kin 14:4
king of Israel, Samaria was *t* ............ 2Kin 18:10
whose altars Hezekiah hath *t* away... 2Kin 18:22
for the king of Babylon had *t* ............ 2Kin 24:7
household being *t* for Eleazar ............ 1Chr 24:6
for Eleazar, and one *t* for Ithamar ....... 1Chr 24:6
which he had *t* from mount Ephraim . 2Chr 15:8
were not *t* away out of Israel ............ 2Chr 15:17
which Asa his father had *t* ............ 2Chr 17:2
in that thou hast *t* away the ............ 2Chr 19:3
the high places were not *t* away ........ 2Chr 20:33
which ye have *t* captive of your ......... 2Chr 28:11
had *t* Beth-shemesh ............ 2Chr 28:18
For the king had *t* counsel ............ 2Chr 30:2
Hezekiah *t* away his high places ........ 2Chr 32:12
For they have *t* of their ............ Ezr 9:2
have *t* strange wives of the ............ Ezr 10:2
have *t* strange wives, to increase ......... Ezr 10:10
let all them which have *t* strange ......... Ezr 10:14
end with all the men that had *t* ............ Ezr 10:17
found that had *t* strange wives ............ Ezr 10:18
All these had *t* strange wives ............ Ezr 10:44
had *t* of them bread and wine, ............ Neh 5:15
his son Johanan had *t* the ............ Neh 6:18
who had *t* her for his daughter, ............ Est 2:15
So Esther was *t* unto king ............ Est 2:16
ring, which he had *t* from Haman ............ Est 8:2
gave, and the LORD hath *t* away ............ Job 1:21
he hath also *t* me by my neck, and ....... Job 16:12
and *t* the crown from my head ............ Job 19:9
because he hath violently *t* away ......... Job 20:19
For thou hast *t* a pledge from thy ......... Job 22:6
they are *t* out of the way as all ............ Job 24:24
who hath *t* away my judgment ............ Job 27:2
Iron is *t* out of the earth, and ............ Job 28:2
of affliction have *t* hold upon me ......... Job 30:16
God hath *t* away my judgment ............ Job 34:5
shall be *t* away without hand ............ Job 34:20
they hid is their own foot *t* ............ Ps 9:15
let them be *t* in the devices that ............ Ps 10:2
iniquities have *t* hold upon me ............ Ps 40:12
let them even be *t* in their pride ............ Ps 59:12
They have *t* crafty counsel ............ Ps 83:3
Thou hast *t* away all thy wrath ............ Ps 85:3
Horror hath *t* hold upon me ............ Ps 119:53
Thy testimonies have I *t* as an ............ Ps 119:111
and anguish have *t* hold on me ......... Ps 119:143
shall keep thy foot from being *t* ......... Prov 3:26
and their sleep is *t* away, unless ......... Prov 4:16
thou art *t* with the words of thy ............ Prov 6:2
He hath *t* a bag of money with him .... Prov 7:20
be *t* in their own naughtiness ............ Prov 11:6
which I had *t* under the sun ............ Eccl 2:18
to it, nor any thing *t* from it ............ Eccl 3:14
but the sinner shall be *t* by her ......... Eccl 7:26
fishes that are *t* in an evil net ............ Eccl 9:12
which he had *t* with the tongs ............ Is 6:6
and thine iniquity is *t* away ............ Is 6:7
have *t* evil counsel against thee, ............ Is 7:5
the spoil of Samaria shall be *t* ............ Is 8:4
be broken, and be snared, and be *t* ......... Is 8:15
that his burden shall be *t* away ............ Is 10:27
they have *t* up their lodging at ............ Is 10:29
And gladness is *t* away, and joy out....... Is 16:10
Damascus is *t* away from being a ............ Is 17:1
pangs have *t* hold upon me, as the ......... Is 21:3
Who hath *t* this counsel against ............ Is 23:8
the pit shall be *t* in the snare ............ Is 24:18

and be broken, and snared, and *t* Is 28:13
that shall not be *t* down Is 33:20
whose altars Hezekiah hath *t* away Is 36:7
Thou whom I have *t* from the ends Is 41:9
the prey be *t* from the mighty Is 49:24
of the mighty shall be *t* away Is 49:25
I have *t* out of thine hand the Is 51:22
my people is *t* away for nought Is 52:5
He was *t* from prison and from Is 53:8
and merciful men are *t* away Is 57:1
that the righteous is *t* away from Is 57:1
like the wind, have *t* us away Is 64:6
husband with the wife shall be *t* Jer 6:11
anguish hath *t* hold of us Jer 6:24
ashamed, they are dismayed and *t* Jer 8:9
astonishment hath *t* hold on me Jer 8:21
them, yea, they have *t* root Jer 12:2
for I have *t* away my peace from Jer 16:5
of them shall be *t* up a curse by Jer 29:22
his hand, but shalt surely be *t* Jer 34:3
but shalt be *t* by the hand of the Jer 38:23
the day that Jerusalem was *t* Jer 38:28
he was there when Jerusalem was *t* Jer 38:28
and when they had *t* him, they Jer 39:5
when he had *t* him being bound in Jer 40:1
in your cities that ye have *t* Jer 40:10
Kiriathaim is confounded and *t* Jer 48:1
treasures, thou shalt also be *t* Jer 48:7
gladness is *t* from the plentiful Jer 48:33
Kerioth is *t*, and the strong holds Jer 48:41
the pit shall be *t* in the snare Jer 48:44
for thy sons are *t* captives Jer 48:46
LORD, that he hath *t* against Edom Jer 49:20
anguish and sorrows have *t* her Jer 49:24
hath *t* counsel against you Jer 49:30
say, Babylon is *t*, Bel is Jer 50:2
from thence she shall be *t* Jer 50:9
for thee, and thou art also *t* Jer 50:24
that he hath *t* against Babylon Jer 50:45
that his city is *t* at one end Jer 51:31
How is Sheshach *t* Jer 51:41
Babylon, and her mighty men are *t* Jer 51:56
he hath violently *t* away his Lam 2:6
was *t* in their pits, of whom we Lam 4:20
him, and he shall be *t* in my snare Eze 12:13
Shall wood be *t* thereof to do any Eze 15:3
Thou hast also *t* thy fair jewels Eze 16:17
Moreover thou hast *t* thy sons Eze 16:20
with whom thou hast *t* pleasure Eze 16:37
hath *t* the king thereof, and the Eze 17:12
hath *t* of the king's seed, and Eze 17:13
him, and hath *t* an oath of him Eze 17:13
he hath also *t* the mighty of the Eze 17:13
him, and he shall be *t* in my snare Eze 17:20
neither hath *t* any increase Eze 18:8
upon usury, and hath *t* increase Eze 18:13
That hath *t* off his hand from the Eze 18:17
he was *t* in their pit, and they Eze 19:4
he was *t* in their pit Eze 19:8
the iniquity, that they may be *t* Eze 21:23
ye shall be *t* with the hand Eze 21:24
In thee have they *t* gifts to shed Eze 22:12
thou hast *t* usury and increase, and Eze 22:12
they have *t* the treasure and Eze 22:25
and have *t* vengeance with a Eze 25:15
they have *t* cedars from Lebanon Eze 27:5
he is *t* away in his iniquity Eze 33:6
ye are *t* up in the lips of Eze 36:3
his father Nebuchadnezzar had *t* Dan 5:2
the golden vessels that were *t* Dan 5:3
So Daniel was *t* up out of the den Dan 6:23
they had their dominion *t* away Dan 7:12
the daily sacrifice was *t* away Dan 8:11
when he hath *t* away the multitude Dan 11:12
daily sacrifice shall be *t* away Dan 12:11
of the sea also shall be *t* away Hos 4:3
Because ye have *t* my silver Joel 3:5
of his den, if he have *t* nothing Amos 3:4
earth, and have *t* nothing at all Amos 3:5
be *t* out that dwell in Samaria in Amos 3:12
sword, and have *t* away your horses Amos 4:10
Have we not *t* to us horns by our Amos 6:13
have ye *t* away my glory for ever Mic 2:9
for pangs have *t* thee as a woman Mic 4:9
The LORD hath *t* away thy Zeph 3:15
and the city shall be *t*, and the Zec 14:2
that were *t* with divers diseases Mt 4:24
bridegroom shall be *t* from them Mt 9:15
from him shall be *t* away even Mt 13:12
It is because we have *t* no bread Mt 16:7
of God shall be *t* from you Mt 21:43
the one shall be *t*, and the other Mt 24:40
the one shall be *t*, and the other Mt 24:41
be *t* away even that which he hath Mt 25:29
And when Joseph had *t* the body Mt 27:59
had *t* counsel, they gave large Mt 28:12
shall be *t* away from them Mk 2:20
from him shall be *t* even that Mk 4:25
when he had *t* the five loaves and Mk 6:41
when he had *t* him in his arms, he Mk 9:36
Forasmuch as many have *t* in hand Lk 1:1
mother was *t* with a great fever Lk 4:38
all the night, and have *t* nothing Lk 5:5
of the fishes which they had *t* Lk 5:9
a man which was *t* with a palsy Lk 5:18
shall be *t* away from them Lk 5:35
the piece that was *t* out of the Lk 5:36
from him shall be *t* even that Lk 8:18
for they were *t* with great fear Lk 8:37
there was *t* up of fragments that Lk 9:17
shall not be *t* away from her Lk 10:42
for ye have *t* away the key of Lk 11:52
the one shall be *t*, and the other Lk 17:34
the one shall be *t*, and the other Lk 17:35
the one shall be *t*, and the other Lk 17:36
if I have *t* any thing from any Lk 19:8
he hath shall be *t* away from him Lk 19:26
And some of them would have *t* him Jn 7:44
unto him a woman *t* in adultery Jn 8:3
this woman was *t* in adultery Jn 8:4
had *t* his garments, and was set Jn 13:12
and that they might be *t* away Jn 19:31
seeth the stone *t* away from the Jn 20:1
They have *t* away the Lord out of Jn 20:2
Because they have *t* away my Lord Jn 20:13
the day in which he was *t* up Acts 1:2
while they beheld, he was *t* up Acts 1:9
which is *t* up from you into Acts 1:11
same day that he was *t* up from us Acts 1:22
foreknowledge of God, ye have *t* Acts 2:23
many *t* with palsies, and that were Acts 8:7
his judgment was *t* away Acts 8:33
for his life is *t* from the earth Acts 8:33
when they had *t* security of Jason Acts 17:9
the third loft, and was *t* up dead Acts 20:9
when we had *t* our leave one of Acts 21:6
This man was *t* of the Jews Acts 23:27
Which when they had *t* up, they Acts 27:17
should be saved was then *t* away Acts 27:20
fasting, having *t* nothing Acts 27:33
when they had *t* up the anchors, Acts 27:40
word of God hath *t* none effect Rom 9:6
might be *t* away from among you 1Cor 5:2
There hath no temptation *t* you 1Cor 10:13
Lord, the vail shall be *t* away 2Cor 3:16
being *t* from you for a short time 1Th 2:17
until he be *t* out of the way 2Th 2:7
Let not a widow be *t* into the 1Ti 5:9
who are *t* captive by him at his 2Ti 2:26
For every high priest *t* from Heb 5:1
brute beasts, made to be *t* 2Pet 2:12
And when he had *t* the book Rev 5:8
because thou hast *t* to thee thy Rev 11:17
And the beast was *t*, and with him Rev 19:20

**TAKER**

as with the *t* of usury, so with Is 24:2

**TAKEST**

the water which thou *t* out of the Ex 4:9
When thou *t* the sum of the Ex 30:12
the journey that thou *t* shall not Judg 4:9
if thou *t* heed to fulfil the 1Chr 22:13
thou *t* away their breath, they Ps 104:29
that thou *t* knowledge of him Ps 144:3
labour which thou *t* under the sun Eccl 9:9
our soul, and thou *t* no knowledge Is 58:3
thou *t* up that thou layedst not Lk 19:21

**TAKETH**

guiltless that *t* his name in vain Ex 20:7
guiltless that *t* his name in vain Deut 5:11
not persons, nor *t* reward Deut 10:17
for he *t* a man's life to pledge Deut 24:6
her hand, and *t* him by the secrets Deut 25:11
Cursed be he that *t* reward to Deut 27:25
*t* them, beareth them on her wings Deut 32:11
*t* shall come according to the Josh 7:14
*t* it, to him will I give Achsah Josh 15:16
*t* it, to him will I give Achsah Judg 1:12
*t* away the reproach from Israel 1Sa 17:26
as a man *t* away dung, till it be 1Kin 14:10
*t* it even out of the thorns, and Job 5:5
He *t* the wise in their own Job 5:13
he *t* away, who can hinder him Job 9:12
*t* away the understanding of the Job 12:20
He *t* away the heart of the chief Job 12:24
trembling *t* hold on my flesh Job 21:6
gained, when God *t* away his soul Job 27:8
He *t* it with his eyes Job 40:24
nor *t* up a reproach against his Ps 15:3
nor *t* reward against the innocent Ps 15:5
The LORD *t* my part with them that Ps 118:7
Happy shall he be, that *t* Ps 137:9
he *t* not pleasure in the legs of Ps 147:10
The LORD *t* pleasure in them that Ps 147:11
For the LORD *t* pleasure in his Ps 149:4
which *t* away the life of the Prov 1:19
his spirit than he that *t* a city Prov 16:32
A wicked man *t* a gift out of the Prov 17:23
As he that *t* away a garment in Prov 25:20
is like one that *t* a dog by the Prov 26:17
The spider *t* hold with her hands, Prov 30:28
labour which he *t* under the sun Eccl 1:3
his heart *t* not rest in the night Eccl 2:23
*t* under the sun all the days of Eccl 5:18
and as a sheep that no man *t* up Is 13:14
he *t* up the isles as a very Is 40:15
*t* the cypress and the oak, which Is 44:14
neither is there any that *t* her Is 51:18
it, and *t* hold of my covenant Is 56:6
which *t* strangers instead of her Eze 16:32
of the trumpet, and *t* not warning Eze 33:4
But he that *t* warning shall Eze 33:5
As the shepherd *t* out of the Amos 3:12
Then the devil *t* him up into the Mt 4:5
the devil *t* him up into an Mt 4:8
to fill it up *t* from the garment Mt 9:16
he that *t* not his cross, and Mt 10:38
*t* with himself seven other Mt 12:45
And after six days Jesus *t* Peter Mt 17:1
filled it up *t* away from the old Mk 2:21
*t* away the word that was sown in Mk 4:15
he *t* the father and the mother of Mk 5:40
six days Jesus *t* with him Peter Mk 9:2
And wheresoever he *t* him, he Mk 9:18
he *t* with him Peter and James and Mk 14:33
him that *t* away thy cloke forbid Lk 6:29
of him that *t* away thy goods ask Lk 6:30
*t* away the word out of their Lk 8:12
And, lo, a spirit *t* him, and he Lk 9:39
he *t* from him all his armour Lk 11:22
*t* to him seven other spirits more Lk 11:26
for my lord *t* away from me the Lk 16:3
which *t* away the sin of the world Jn 1:29
No man *t* it from me, but I lay it Jn 10:18
that beareth not fruit he *t* away Jn 15:2
and your joy no man *t* from you Jn 16:22
*t* bread, and giveth them, and fish Jn 21:13
God unrighteous who *t* vengeance Rom 3:5
He *t* the wise in their own 1Cor 3:19
For in eating every one *t* before 1Cor 11:21
no man *t* this honour unto himself Heb 5:4
He *t* away the first, that he may Heb 10:9

**TAKING**

of persons, nor *t* of gifts 2Chr 19:7
I have seen the foolish *t* root Job 5:3
by *t* heed thereto according to Ps 119:9
At the noise of the *t* of Babylon Jer 50:46
the house of Judah by *t* vengeance Eze 25:12
also to go, *t* them by their arms Hos 11:3
Which of you by *t* thought can add Mt 6:27
man is as a man *t* a far journey Mk 13:34
*t* him up into an high mountain, Lk 4:5
which of you with *t* thought can Lk 12:25
*t* up that I laid not down, and Lk 19:22
had spoken of *t* of rest in sleep Jn 11:13
*t* occasion by the commandment, Rom 7:8
*t* occasion by the commandment, Rom 7:11
but *t* my leave of them, I went 2Cor 2:13
*t* wages of them, to do you 2Cor 11:8
*t* the shield of faith, wherewith Eph 6:16
In flaming fire *t* vengeance on 2Th 1:8
*t* the oversight thereof, not by 1Pet 5:2
*t* nothing of the Gentiles 3Jn 7

**TALE**

the *t* of the bricks, which they Ex 5:8
shall ye deliver the *t* of bricks Ex 5:18
gave them in full *t* to the king 1Sa 18:27
should bring them in and out by *t* 1Chr 9:28
our years as a *t* that is told Ps 90:9

**TALEBEARER**

down as a *t* among thy people Lev 19:16
A *t* revealeth secrets Prov 11:13
The words of a *t* are as wounds Prov 18:8
about as a *t* revealeth secrets Prov 20:19
so where there is no *t*, the Prov 26:20
The words of a *t* are as wounds Prov 26:22

**TALENT**

Of a *t* of pure gold shall he make Ex 25:39
Of a *t* of pure gold made he it, Ex 37:24
hundred talents, a *t* for a socket Ex 38:27
the weight whereof was a *t* of 2Sa 12:30
else thou shalt pay a *t* of silver 1Kin 20:39
a *t* of silver, and two changes of 2Kin 5:22
talents of silver, and a *t* of gold 2Kin 23:33
and found it to weigh a *t* of gold 1Chr 20:2
talents of silver and a *t* of gold 2Chr 36:3
there was lifted up a *t* of lead Zec 5:7
which had received the one *t* came Mt 25:24
and went and hid thy *t* in the earth Mt 25:25
Take therefore the *t* from him Mt 25:28
stone about the weight of a *t* Rev 16:21

**TALENTS**

offering, was twenty and nine *t* Ex 38:24
the congregation was an hundred *t* Ex 38:25
of the hundred *t* of silver were Ex 38:27
hundred sockets of the hundred *t* Ex 38:27
of the offering was seventy *t* Ex 38:29
to the king sixscore *t* of gold 1Kin 9:14
gold, four hundred and twenty *t* 1Kin 9:28
twenty *t* of gold, and of spices 1Kin 10:10
threescore and six *t* of gold, 1Kin 10:14
of Shemer for two *t* of silver 1Kin 16:24
and took with him ten *t* of silver 2Kin 5:5
said, Be content, take two *t* 2Kin 5:23
bound two *t* of silver in two bags 2Kin 5:23
gave Pul a thousand *t* of silver 2Kin 15:19
Judah three hundred *t* of silver 2Kin 18:14
of silver and thirty *t* of gold 2Kin 18:14
tribute of an hundred *t* of silver 2Kin 23:33
of Ammon sent a thousand *t* of 1Chr 19:6
an hundred thousand *t* of gold 1Chr 22:14
a thousand thousand *t* of silver 1Chr 22:14
Even three thousand *t* of gold 1Chr 29:4
seven thousand *t* of refined 1Chr 29:4
of God of gold five thousand *t* 1Chr 29:7
and of silver ten thousand *t* 1Chr 29:7
and of brass eighteen thousand *t* 1Chr 29:7
and one hundred thousand *t* of iron 1Chr 29:7
gold, amounting to six hundred *t* 2Chr 3:8
fifty *t* of gold, and brought them 2Chr 8:18
twenty *t* of gold, and of spices 2Chr 9:9
and threescore and six *t* of gold 2Chr 9:13
Israel for an hundred *t* of silver 2Chr 25:6
shall we do for the hundred *t* 2Chr 25:9
same year an hundred *t* of silver 2Chr 27:5
land in an hundred *t* of silver 2Chr 36:3
Unto an hundred *t* of silver Ezr 7:22
fifty *t* of silver, and silver Ezr 8:26

and silver vessels an hundred *t* ............ Ezr 8:26
and of gold an hundred *t* ............ Ezr 8:26
I will pay ten thousand *t* of ............ Est 3:9
which owed him ten thousand *t* ............ Mt 18:24
And unto one he gave five *t* ............ Mt 25:15
that had received the five *t* went ............ Mt 25:16
same, and made them other five *t* ............ Mt 25:16
he that had received five *t* came ............ Mt 25:20
came and brought other five *t* ............ Mt 25:20
thou deliveredst unto me five *t* ............ Mt 25:20
gained beside them five *t* more ............ Mt 25:20
also that had received two *t* came ............ Mt 25:22
thou deliveredst unto me two *t* ............ Mt 25:22
gained two other *t* beside them ............ Mt 25:22
give it unto him which hath ten *t* ............ Mt 25:28

**TALES**
men that carry *t* to shed blood ............ Eze 22:9
words seemed to them as idle *t* ............ Lk 24:11

**TALITHA** (*tal'-ith-ah*) *Aramaic for damsel.*
hand, and said unto her, *T* cumi ............ Mk 5:41

**TALK**
come down and *t* with thee there ............ Num 11:17
this day that God doth *t* with man ............ Deut 5:24
shalt *t* of them when thou sittest ............ Deut 6:7
*T* no more so exceeding proudly ............ 1Sa 2:3
*t* not with us in the Jews' ............ 2Kin 18:26
*t* ye of all his wondrous works ............ 1Chr 16:9
a man full of *t* be justified ............ Job 11:2
and *t* deceitfully for him ............ Job 13:7
he reason with unprofitable *t* ............ Job 15:3
they *t* to the grief of those whom ............ Ps 69:26
My tongue also shall *t* of thy ............ Ps 71:24
all thy work, and *t* of thy doings ............ Ps 77:12
*t* ye of all his wondrous works ............ Ps 105:2
so shall I *t* of thy wondrous ............ Ps 119:27
of thy kingdom, and *t* of thy power ............ Ps 145:11
awakest, it shall *t* with thee ............ Prov 6:22
but the *t* of the lips tendeth ............ Prov 14:23
and their lips *t* of mischief ............ Prov 24:2
the end of his *t* is mischievous ............ Eccl 10:13
yet let me *t* with thee of thy ............ Jer 12:1
and I will there *t* with thee ............ Eze 3:22
this my lord *t* with this my lord ............ Dan 10:17
they might entangle him in his *t* ............ Mt 22:15
I will not *t* much with you ............ Jn 14:30

**TALKED**
Cain *t* with Abel his brother ............ Gen 4:8
and God *t* with him, saying, ............ Gen 17:3
in the place where he *t* with him ............ Gen 35:13
in the place where he *t* with him ............ Gen 35:14
that his brethren *t* with him ............ Gen 45:15
I have *t* with you from heaven ............ Ex 20:22
and the LORD *t* with Moses ............ Ex 33:9
face shone while he *t* with him ............ Ex 34:29
and Moses *t* with them ............ Ex 34:31
The LORD *t* with you face to face ............ Deut 5:4
he went down, and *t* with the woman ............ Judg 14:7
while Saul *t* unto the priest, ............ 1Sa 14:19
as he *t* with them, behold, there ............ 1Sa 17:23
lo, while she yet *t* with the king ............ 1Kin 1:22
pass, as they still went on, and *t* ............ 2Kin 2:11
And while he yet *t* with them ............ 2Kin 6:33
the king *t* with Gehazi the ............ 2Kin 8:4
as he *t* with him, that the king ............ 2Chr 25:16
hear that I have *t* with thee ............ Jer 38:25
*t* with me, and said, O Daniel, I ............ Dan 9:22
the angel that *t* with me said ............ Zec 1:9
that *t* with me with good words ............ Zec 1:13
unto the angel that *t* with me ............ Zec 1:19
the angel that *t* with me went ............ Zec 2:3
the angel that *t* with me came ............ Zec 4:1
spake to the angel that *t* with me ............ Zec 4:4
the angel that *t* with me answered ............ Zec 4:5
angel that *t* with me went forth ............ Zec 5:5
I to the angel that *t* with me ............ Zec 5:10
unto the angel that *t* with me ............ Zec 6:4
While he yet *t* to the people, ............ Mt 12:46
And immediately he *t* with them ............ Mk 6:50
there *t* with him two men, which ............ Lk 9:30
they *t* together of all these ............ Lk 24:14
while he *t* with us by the way, and ............ Lk 24:32
that he *t* with the woman ............ Jn 4:27
as he *t* with him, he went in, and ............ Acts 10:27
*t* a long while, even till break ............ Acts 20:11
they *t* between themselves, saying ............ Acts 26:31
*t* with me, saying unto me, Come ............ Rev 17:1
*t* with me, saying, Come hither, I ............ Rev 21:9
he that *t* with me had a golden ............ Rev 21:15

**TALKERS**
ye are taken up in the lips of *t* ............ Eze 36:3
there are many unruly and vain *t* ............ Titus 1:10

**TALKEST**
me a sign that thou *t* with me ............ Judg 6:17
while thou yet *t* there with the ............ 1Kin 1:14
or, Why *t* thou with her ............ Jn 4:27

**TALKETH**
and his tongue *t* of judgment ............ Ps 37:30
him, and it is he that *t* with thee ............ Jn 9:37

**TALKING**
And he left off *t* with him ............ Gen 17:22
either he is *t*, or he is pursuing ............ 1Kin 18:27
And while they were yet *t* with him ............ Est 6:14
The princes refrained *t*, and laid ............ Job 29:9
of thy people still are *t* against ............ Eze 33:30
them Moses and Elias *t* with him ............ Mt 17:3
and they were *t* with Jesus ............ Mk 9:4

Neither filthiness, nor foolish *t* ............ Eph 5:4
as it were of a trumpet *t* with me ............ Rev 4:1

**TALL**
a people great, and many, and *t* ............ Deut 2:10
A people great, and many, and *t* ............ Deut 2:21
A people great and *t*, the children ............ Deut 9:2
will cut down the *t* cedar trees ............ 2Kin 19:23
cut down the *t* cedars thereof ............ Is 37:24

**TALLER**
people is greater and *t* than we ............ Deut 1:28

**TALMAI** (*tal'-mahee*)
*1. A son of Anak.*
where Ahiman, Sheshai, and *T* ............ Num 13:22
Sheshai, and Ahiman, and *T* ............ Josh 15:14
slew Sheshai, and Ahiman, and *T* ............ Judg 1:10
*2. A king of Geshur.*
the daughter of *T* king of Geshur ............ 2Sa 3:3
But Absalom fled, and went to *T* ............ 2Sa 13:37
the daughter of *T* king of Geshur ............ 1Chr 3:2

**TALMON** (*tal'-mon*) *A Levite in Jerusalem.*
were, Shallum, and Akkub, and *T* ............ 1Chr 9:17
of Ater, the children of *T* ............ Ezr 2:42
of Ater, the children of *T* ............ Neh 7:45
Moreover the porters, Akkub, *T* ............ Neh 11:19
Bakbukiah, Obadiah, Meshullam, *T* ............ Neh 12:25

**TAMAH** (*ta'-mah*) See THAMAH. *A family of exiles.*
of Sisera, the children of *T* ............ Neh 7:55

**TAMAR** (*ta'-mar*) See THAMAR.
*1. Wife of Er.*
his firstborn, whose name was *T* ............ Gen 38:6
Then said Judah to *T* his daughter ............ Gen 38:11
*T* went and dwelt in her father's ............ Gen 38:11
And it was told *T*, saying, Behold ............ Gen 38:13
*T* thy daughter in law hath played ............ Gen 38:24
whom *T* bare unto Judah, of the ............ Ruth 4:12
*T* his daughter in law bare him ............ 1Chr 2:4
*2. A daughter of David.*
a fair sister, whose name was *T* ............ 2Sa 13:1
he fell sick for his sister *T* ............ 2Sa 13:2
And Amnon said unto him, I love *T* ............ 2Sa 13:4
I pray thee, let my sister *T* come ............ 2Sa 13:5
let *T* my sister come, and make me ............ 2Sa 13:6
Then David sent home to *T* ............ 2Sa 13:7
So *T* went to her brother Amnon's ............ 2Sa 13:8
And Amnon said unto *T*, Bring the ............ 2Sa 13:10
*T* took the cakes which she had ............ 2Sa 13:10
*T* put ashes on her head, and rent ............ 2Sa 13:19
So *T* remained desolate in her ............ 2Sa 13:20
he had forced his sister *T* ............ 2Sa 13:22
day that he forced his sister *T* ............ 2Sa 13:32
the concubines, and *T* their sister ............ 1Chr 3:9
*3. A daughter of Absalom.*
and one daughter, whose name was *T* 2Sa 14:27
*4. A city in Judah.*
from *T* even to the waters of ............ Eze 47:19
*T* unto the waters of strife in ............ Eze 48:28

**TAME**
neither could any man *t* him ............ Mk 5:4
But the tongue can no man *t* ............ Jas 3:8

**TAMED**
and of things in the sea, is *t* ............ Jas 3:7
and hath been *t* of mankind ............ Jas 3:7

**TAMMUZ** (*tam'-muz*) *A Syrian god.*
there sat women weeping for *T* ............ Eze 8:14

**TANACH** (*ta'-nak*) See TAANACH. *Same as Taanach.*
Manasseh, *T* with her suburbs, and ............ Josh 21:25

**TANHUMETH** (*tan'-hu-meth*) *Father of Seraiah.*
the son of *T* the Netophathite ............ 2Kin 25:23
Kareah, and Seraiah the son of *T* ............ Jer 40:8

**TANNER**
days in Joppa with one Simon a *t* ............ Acts 9:43
He lodgeth with one Simon a *t* ............ Acts 10:6
of one Simon a *t* by the sea side ............ Acts 10:32

**TAPESTRY**
decked my bed with coverings of *t* ............ Prov 7:16
She maketh herself coverings of *t* ............ Prov 31:22

**TAPHATH** (*ta'-fath*) *A daughter of Solomon.*
which had *T* the daughter of ............ 1Kin 4:11

**TAPPUAH** (*tap'-pu-ah*)
*1. A city in Judah.*
The king of *T*, one ............ Josh 12:17
And Zanoah, and En-gannim, *T* ............ Josh 15:34
*2. A city in Ephraim.*
The border went out from *T* ............ Josh 16:8
Now Manasseh had the land of *T* ............ Josh 17:8
but *T* on the border of Manasseh ............ Josh 17:8
*3. A son of Hebron.*
Korah, and *T*, and Rekem ............ 1Chr 2:43

**TARAH** (*ta'-rah*) *An Israelite encampment in the wilderness.*
from Tahath, and pitched at *T* ............ Num 33:27
And they removed from *T*, and ............ Num 33:28

**TARALAH** (*tar'-a-lah*) *A city in Benjamin.*
And Rekem, and Irpeel, and *T* ............ Josh 18:27

**TARE**
*t* his garments, and lay on the ............ 2Sa 13:31
*t* forty and two children of them ............ 2Kin 2:24

him, straightway the spirit *t* him ............ Mk 9:20
devil threw him down, and *t* him ............ Lk 9:42

**TAREA** (*ta'-re-ah*) See TAHREA. *A son of Micah.*
were, Pithon, and Melech, and *T* ............ 1Chr 8:35

**TARES**
sowed *t* among the wheat, and went ............ Mt 13:25
fruit, then appeared the *t* also ............ Mt 13:26
from whence then hath it *t* ............ Mt 13:27
lest while ye gather up the *t* ............ Mt 13:29
Gather ye together first the *t* ............ Mt 13:30
the parable of the *t* of the field ............ Mt 13:36
but the *t* are the children of the ............ Mt 13:38
As therefore the *t* are gathered ............ Mt 13:40

**TARGET**
legs, and a *t* of brass between his ............ 1Sa 17:6
shekels of gold went to one *t* ............ 1Kin 10:16
of beaten gold went to one *t* ............ 2Chr 9:15

**TARGETS**
made two hundred *t* of beaten gold ............ 1Kin 10:16
made two hundred *t* of beaten gold ............ 2Chr 9:15
had an army of men that bare *t* ............ 2Chr 14:8

**TARPELITES** (*tar'-pel-ites*) *Foreigners resettled in Israel.*
the Apharsathchites, the *T* ............ Ezr 4:9

**TARRIED**
were with him, and *t* all night ............ Gen 24:54
*t* there all night, because the ............ Gen 28:11
and *t* all night in the mount ............ Gen 31:54
when the cloud *t* long upon the ............ Num 9:19
that the cloud *t* upon the ............ Num 9:22
they *t* till they were ashamed ............ Judg 3:25
And Ehud escaped while they *t* ............ Judg 3:26
they *t* until afternoon, and they ............ Judg 19:8
that she *t* a little in the house ............ Ruth 2:7
he *t* seven days, according to the ............ 1Sa 13:8
Saul *t* in the uttermost part of ............ 1Sa 14:2
But David *t* still at Jerusalem ............ 2Sa 11:1
*t* in a place that was far off ............ 2Sa 15:17
and they *t* there ............ 2Sa 15:29
but he *t* longer than the set time ............ 2Sa 20:5
(for he *t* at Jericho,) he said ............ 2Kin 2:18
But David *t* at Jerusalem ............ 1Chr 20:1
she that *t* at home divided the ............ Ps 68:12
While the bridegroom *t*, they all ............ Mt 25:5
marvelled that he *t* so long in ............ Lk 1:21
the child Jesus *t* behind in ............ Lk 2:43
there he *t* with them, and baptized ............ Jn 3:22
that he *t* many days in Joppa with ............ Acts 9:43
And after they had *t* there a space ............ Acts 15:33
Paul after this *t* there yet a ............ Acts 18:18
going before *t* for us at Troas ............ Acts 20:5
at Samos, and *t* at Trogyllium ............ Acts 20:15
disciples, we *t* there seven days ............ Acts 21:4
as we *t* there many days, there ............ Acts 21:10
when he had *t* among them more ............ Acts 25:6
the fourteenth day that ye have *t* ............ Acts 27:33
Syracuse, we *t* there three days ............ Acts 28:12

**TARRIEST**
And now why *t* thou ............ Acts 22:16

**TARRIETH**
his part be that *t* by the stuff ............ 1Sa 30:24
that *t* not for man, nor waiteth ............ Mic 5:7

**TARRY**
*t* all night, and wash your feet, ............ Gen 19:2
*t* with him a few days, until thy ............ Gen 27:44
found favour in thine eyes, *t* ............ Gen 30:27
come down unto me, *t* not ............ Gen 45:9
out of Egypt, and could not *t* ............ Ex 12:39
*T* ye here for us, until we come ............ Ex 24:14
shall *t* abroad out of his tent ............ Lev 14:8
*t* ye also here this night, that I ............ Num 22:19
Why *t* the wheels of his chariots ............ Judg 5:28
I will *t* until thou come again ............ Judg 6:18
*t* all night, and let thine heart ............ Judg 19:6
evening, I pray you *t* all night ............ Judg 19:9
the man would not *t* that night ............ Judg 19:10
Would ye *t* for them till they ............ Ruth 1:13
*T* this night, and it shall be in ............ Ruth 3:13
*t* until thou have weaned him ............ 1Sa 1:23
seven days shalt thou *t*, till I ............ 1Sa 10:8
unto us, *T* until we come to you ............ 1Sa 14:9
*T* at Jericho until your beards be ............ 2Sa 10:5
*T* here to day also, and to morrow ............ 2Sa 11:12
I will *t* in the plain of the ............ 2Sa 15:28
I may not *t* thus with thee ............ 2Sa 18:14
there will not *t* one with thee ............ 2Sa 19:7
unto Elisha, *T* here, I pray thee ............ 2Kin 2:2
him, Elisha, *t* here, I pray thee ............ 2Kin 2:4
And Elijah said unto him, *T* ............ 2Kin 2:6
if we *t* till the morning light, ............ 2Kin 7:9
open the door, and flee, and *t* not ............ 2Kin 9:3
glory of this, and *t* at home ............ 2Kin 14:10
*T* at Jericho until your beards be ............ 1Chr 19:5
lies shall not *t* in my sight ............ Ps 101:7
They that *t* long at the wine ............ Prov 23:30
off, and my salvation shall not *t* ............ Is 46:13
turneth aside to *t* for a night ............ Jer 14:8
though it *t*, wait for it ............ Hab 2:3
will surely come, it will not *t* ............ Hab 2:3
*t* ye here, and watch with me ............ Mt 26:38
*t* ye here, and watch ............ Mk 14:34
And he went in to *t* with them ............ Lk 24:29
but *t* ye in the city of Jerusalem ............ Lk 24:49
him that he would *t* with them ............ Jn 4:40

If I will that he *t* till I come ..... Jn 21:22
If I will that he *t* till I come ..... Jn 21:23
prayed they him to *t* certain days ..... Acts 10:48
him to *t* longer time with them ..... Acts 18:20
were desired to *t* with them seven ..... Acts 28:14
to eat, *t* one for another ..... 1Cor 11:33
but I trust to *t* a while with you ..... 1Cor 16:7
But I will *t* at Ephesus until ..... 1Cor 16:8
But if I *t* long, that thou mayest ..... 1Ti 3:15
come will come, and will not *t* ..... Heb 10:37

**TARRYING**
make no *t*, O my God ..... Ps 40:17
O LORD, make no *t* ..... Ps 70:5

**TARSHISH** (*tar'-shish*) See THARSHISH.
*1. A son of Javan.*
Elishah, and *T*, Kittim, and Dodanim ..... Gen 10:4
Elishah, and *T*, Kittim, and Dodanim ..... 1Chr 1:7
*2. Spain.*
to *T* with the servants of Huram ..... 2Chr 9:21
came the ships of *T* bringing gold ..... 2Chr 9:21
with him to make ships to go to *T* ..... 2Chr 20:36
they were not able to go to *T* ..... 2Chr 20:37
the ships of *T* with an east wind ..... Ps 48:7
The kings of *T* and of the isles ..... Ps 72:10
And upon all the ships of *T* ..... Is 2:16
Howl, ye ships of *T* ..... Is 23:1
Pass ye over to *T* ..... Is 23:6
land as a river, O daughter of *T* ..... Is 23:10
Howl, ye ships of *T* ..... Is 23:14
for me, and the ships of *T* first ..... Is 60:9
of them unto the nations, to *T* ..... Is 66:19
into plates is brought from *T* ..... Jer 10:9
*T* was thy merchant by reason of ..... Eze 27:12
The ships of *T* did sing of thee ..... Eze 27:25
and Dedan, and the merchants of *T* ..... Eze 38:13
*T* from the presence of the LORD ..... Jonah 1:3
and he found a ship going to *T* ..... Jonah 1:3
to go with them unto *T* from the ..... Jonah 1:3
Therefore I fled before unto *T* ..... Jonah 4:2
*3. A prince of Persia.*
was Carshena, Shethar, Admatha, *T* ..... Est 1:14

**TARSHISHAH** See TARSHISH.

**TARSUS** (*tar'-sus*) *Capital of Roman province of Cilicia.*
Judas for one called Saul, of *T* ..... Acts 9:11
Caesarea, and sent him forth to *T* ..... Acts 9:30
Then departed Barnabas to *T* ..... Acts 11:25
I am a man which am a Jew of *T* ..... Acts 21:39
a man which am a Jew, born in *T* ..... Acts 22:3

**TARTAK** (*tar'-tak*) *A god of the Avites.*
And the Avites made Nibhaz and *T* ..... 2Kin 17:31

**TARTAN** (*tar'-tan*) *The commander of the Assyrian army.*
And the king of Assyria sent *T* ..... 2Kin 18:17
the year that *T* came unto Ashdod ..... Is 20:1

**TASK**
have ye not fulfilled your *t* in ..... Ex 5:14
from your bricks of your daily *t* ..... Ex 5:19

**TASKMASTERS**
they did set over them *t* to ..... Ex 1:11
their cry by reason of their *t* ..... Ex 3:7
the same day the *t* of the people ..... Ex 5:6
the *t* of the people went out, and ..... Ex 5:10
the *t* hasted them, saying, Fulfil ..... Ex 5:13
which Pharaoh's *t* had set over ..... Ex 5:14

**TASKS**
Fulfil your works, your daily *t* ..... Ex 5:13

**TASTE**
the *t* of it was like wafers made ..... Ex 16:31
the *t* of it was as the ..... Num 11:8
of it was as the *t* of fresh oil ..... Num 11:8
I did but *t* a little honey with ..... 1Sa 14:43
if I *t* bread, or ought else, till ..... 2Sa 3:35
can thy servant *t* what I eat or ..... 2Sa 19:35
or is there any *t* in the white of ..... Job 6:6
cannot my *t* discern perverse ..... Job 6:30
and the mouth *t* his meat ..... Job 12:11
O *t* and see that the LORD is good ..... Ps 34:8
How sweet are thy words unto my *t*. Ps 119:103
which is sweet to thy *t* ..... Prov 24:13
and his fruit was sweet to my *t* ..... Song 2:3
therefore his *t* remained in him ..... Jer 48:11
herd nor flock, *t* any thing ..... Jonah 3:7
here, which shall not *t* of death ..... Mt 16:28
here, which shall not *t* of death ..... Mk 9:1
here, which shall not *t* of death ..... Lk 9:27
were bidden shall *t* of my supper ..... Lk 14:24
saying, he shall never *t* of death ..... Jn 8:52
*t* not ..... Col 2:21
God should *t* death for every man ..... Heb 2:9

**TASTED**
So none of the people *t* any food ..... 1Sa 14:24
because I *t* a little of this ..... 1Sa 14:29
Belshazzar, whiles he *t* the wine ..... Dan 5:2
and when he had *t* thereof, he ..... Mt 27:34
*t* the water that was made wine ..... Jn 2:9
have *t* of the heavenly gift, and ..... Heb 6:4
have *t* the good word of God, and ..... Heb 6:5
If so be ye have *t* that the Lord ..... 1Pet 2:3

**TASTETH**
trieth words, as the mouth *t* meat ..... Job 34:3

**TATNAI** (*tat'-nahee*) *Persian governor of Samaria.*
At the same time came to them *T* ..... Ezr 5:3
The copy of the letter that *T* ..... Ezr 5:6
Now therefore, *T*, governor beyond ..... Ezr 6:6
Then *T*, governor on this side the ..... Ezr 6:13

**TATTENAI** See TATNAI.

**TATTLERS**
but *t* also and busybodies, ..... 1Ti 5:13

**TAUGHT**
Behold, I have *t* you statutes and ..... Deut 4:5
*t* it the children of Israel ..... Deut 31:22
with them he *t* the men of Succoth ..... Judg 8:16
*t* them how they should fear the ..... 2Kin 17:28
when thou hast *t* them the good ..... 2Chr 6:27
they *t* in Judah, and had the book ..... 2Chr 17:9
cities of Judah, and *t* the people ..... 2Chr 17:9
and such as *t* to sing praise ..... 2Chr 23:13
unto all the Levites that *t* the ..... 2Chr 30:22
the Levites that *t* all Israel ..... 2Chr 35:3
and the Levites that *t* the people ..... Neh 8:9
thou hast *t* me from my youth ..... Ps 71:17
for thou hast *t* me ..... Ps 119:102
when thou hast *t* me thy statutes ..... Ps 119:171
He *t* me also, and said unto me, ..... Prov 4:4
I have *t* thee in the way of ..... Prov 4:11
prophecy that his mother *t* him ..... Prov 31:1
he still *t* the people knowledge ..... Eccl 12:9
me is *t* by the precept of men ..... Is 29:13
being his counsellor hath *t* him ..... Is 40:13
*t* him in the path of judgment, and ..... Is 40:14
*t* him knowledge, and shewed to him ..... Is 40:14
children shall be *t* of the LORD ..... Is 54:13
also *t* the wicked ones thy ways ..... Jer 2:33
they have *t* their tongue to speak ..... Jer 9:5
which their fathers *t* them ..... Jer 9:14
as they *t* my people to swear by ..... Jer 12:16
for thou hast *t* them to be ..... Jer 13:21
because thou hast *t* rebellion ..... Jer 28:16
because he hath *t* rebellion ..... Jer 29:32
though I *t* them, rising up early ..... Jer 32:33
that all women may be *t* not to do ..... Eze 23:48
Ephraim is as an heifer that is *t* ..... Hos 10:11
I *t* Ephraim also to go, taking ..... Hos 11:3
for man *t* me to keep cattle from ..... Zec 13:5
his mouth, and *t* them, saying, ..... Mt 5:2
For he *t* them as one having ..... Mt 7:29
he *t* them in their synagogue, ..... Mt 13:54
the money, and did as they were *t* ..... Mt 28:15
entered into the synagogue, and *t* ..... Mk 1:21
for he *t* them as one that had ..... Mk 1:22
resorted unto him, and he *t* them ..... Mk 2:13
he *t* them many things by parables ..... Mk 4:2
they had done, and what they had *t* ..... Mk 6:30
For he *t* his disciples, and said ..... Mk 9:31
as he was wont, he *t* them again ..... Mk 10:1
And he *t*, saying unto them, Is it ..... Mk 11:17
while he *t* in the temple, How say ..... Mk 12:35
he *t* in their synagogues, being ..... Lk 4:15
*t* them on the sabbath days ..... Lk 4:31
*t* the people out of the ship ..... Lk 5:3
entered into the synagogue and *t* ..... Lk 6:6
as John also *t* his disciples ..... Lk 11:1
thou hast *t* in our streets ..... Lk 13:26
And he *t* daily in the temple ..... Lk 19:47
as he *t* the people in the temple, ..... Lk 20:1
And they shall be all *t* of God ..... Jn 6:45
synagogue, as he *t* in Capernaum ..... Jn 6:59
went up into the temple, and *t* ..... Jn 7:14
cried Jesus in the temple as he *t* ..... Jn 7:28
and he sat down, and *t* them ..... Jn 8:2
treasury, as he *t* in the temple ..... Jn 8:20
but as my Father hath *t* me ..... Jn 8:28
I ever *t* in the synagogue, and in ..... Jn 18:20
grieved that they *t* the people ..... Acts 4:2
temple early in the morning, and *t* ..... Acts 5:21
with the church, and *t* much people ..... Acts 11:26
had *t* many, they returned again ..... Acts 14:21
down from Judaea *t* the brethren ..... Acts 15:1
*t* diligently the things of the ..... Acts 18:25
have *t* you publickly, and from ..... Acts 20:20
*t* according to the perfect manner ..... Acts 22:3
it of man, neither was I *t* it ..... Gal 1:12
Let him that is *t* in the word ..... Gal 6:6
heard him, and have been *t* by him ..... Eph 4:21
in the faith, as ye have been *t* ..... Col 2:7
for ye yourselves are *t* of God to ..... 1Th 4:9
traditions which ye have been *t* ..... 2Th 2:15
faithful word as he hath been *t* ..... Titus 1:9
no lie, and even as it hath *t* you ..... 1Jn 2:27
of Balaam, who *t* Balac to cast a ..... Rev 2:14

**TAUNT**
be a reproach and a proverb, a *t* ..... Jer 24:9
So it shall be a reproach and a *t* ..... Eze 5:15

**TAUNTING**
a *t* proverb against him, and say, ..... Hab 2:6

**TAVERNS**
as Appii forum, and The three *t* ..... Acts 28:15

**TAXATION**
of every one according to his *t* ..... 2Kin 23:35

**TAXED**
but he *t* the land to give the ..... 2Kin 23:35
that all the world should be *t* ..... Lk 2:1
And all went to be *t*, every one ..... Lk 2:3
To be *t* with Mary his espoused ..... Lk 2:5

**TAXES**
of *t* in the glory of the kingdom ..... Dan 11:20

**TAXING**
this *t* was first made when ..... Lk 2:2
of Galilee in the days of the *t* ..... Acts 5:37

**TEACH**
*t* thee what thou shalt say ..... Ex 4:12
will *t* you what ye shall do ..... Ex 4:15
thou shalt *t* them ordinances and ..... Ex 18:20
that thou mayest *t* them ..... Ex 24:12
put in his heart that he may *t* ..... Ex 35:34
that ye may *t* the children of ..... Lev 10:11
To *t* when it is unclean, and when ..... Lev 14:57
unto the judgments, which I *t* you ..... Deut 4:1
but *t* them thy sons, and thy sons' ..... Deut 4:9
that they may *t* their children ..... Deut 4:10
me at that time to *t* you statutes ..... Deut 4:14
which thou shalt *t* them, that ..... Deut 5:31
LORD your God commanded to *t* you ..... Deut 6:1
thou shalt *t* them diligently unto ..... Deut 6:7
ye shall *t* them your children, ..... Deut 11:19
the law which they shall *t* thee ..... Deut 17:11
That they *t* you not to do after ..... Deut 20:18
priests the Levites shall *t* you ..... Deut 24:8
*t* it the children of Israel ..... Deut 31:19
They shall *t* Jacob thy judgments, ..... Deut 33:10
to *t* them war, at the least such ..... Judg 3:2
*t* us what we shall do unto the ..... Judg 13:8
but I will *t* you the good and the ..... 1Sa 12:23
(Also he bade them *t* the children ..... 2Sa 1:18
that thou *t* them the good way ..... 1Kin 8:36
let him *t* them the manner of the ..... 2Kin 17:27
to *t* in the cities of Judah ..... 2Chr 17:7
to *t* in Israel statutes and ..... Ezr 7:10
*t* ye them that know them not ..... Ezr 7:25
*T* me, and I will hold my tongue ..... Job 6:24
Shall not they *t* thee, and tell ..... Job 8:10
the beasts, and they shall *t* thee ..... Job 12:7
to the earth, and it shall *t* thee ..... Job 12:8
Shall any *t* God knowledge ..... Job 21:22
I will *t* you by the hand of God ..... Job 27:11
of years should *t* wisdom ..... Job 32:7
peace, and I shall *t* thee wisdom ..... Job 33:33
That which I see not *t* thou me ..... Job 34:32
*T* us what we shall say unto him ..... Job 37:19
*t* me thy paths ..... Ps 25:4
Lead me in thy truth, and *t* me ..... Ps 25:5
therefore will he *t* sinners in ..... Ps 25:8
and the meek will he *t* his way ..... Ps 25:9
him shall he *t* in the way that he ..... Ps 25:12
*T* me thy way, O LORD, and lead me ..... Ps 27:11
*t* thee in the way which thou ..... Ps 32:8
I will *t* you the fear of the LORD ..... Ps 34:11
hand shall *t* thee terrible things ..... Ps 45:4
Then will I *t* transgressors thy ..... Ps 51:13
Michtam of David, to *t* ..... Ps 60:*t*
*T* me thy way, O LORD ..... Ps 86:11
So *t* us to number our days, that ..... Ps 90:12
and *t* his senators wisdom ..... Ps 105:22
*t* me thy statutes ..... Ps 119:12
*t* me thy statutes ..... Ps 119:26
*T* me, O LORD, the way of thy ..... Ps 119:33
*t* me thy statutes ..... Ps 119:64
*T* me good judgment and knowledge ..... Ps 119:66
*t* me thy statutes ..... Ps 119:68
O LORD, and *t* me thy judgments ..... Ps 119:108
thy mercy, and *t* me thy statutes ..... Ps 119:124
and *t* me thy statutes ..... Ps 119:135
my testimony that I shall *t* them ..... Ps 132:12
*T* me to do thy will ..... Ps 143:10
*t* a just man, and he will increase ..... Prov 9:9
he will *t* us of his ways, and we ..... Is 2:3
Whom shall he *t* knowledge ..... Is 28:9
him to discretion, and doth *t* him ..... Is 28:26
*t* your daughters wailing, and ..... Jer 9:20
they shall *t* no more every man ..... Jer 31:34
they shall *t* my people the ..... Eze 44:23
and whom they might *t* the learning ..... Dan 1:4
and the priests thereof *t* for hire ..... Mic 3:11
he will *t* us of his ways, and we ..... Mic 4:2
the dumb stone, Arise, it shall *t* ..... Hab 2:19
shall *t* men so, he shall be ..... Mt 5:19
*t* them, the same shall be called ..... Mt 5:19
he departed thence to *t* and to ..... Mt 11:1
*t* all nations, baptizing them in ..... Mt 28:19
began again to *t* by the sea side ..... Mk 4:1
he began to *t* in the synagogue ..... Mk 6:2
he began to *t* them many things ..... Mk 6:34
And he began to *t* them, that the ..... Mk 8:31
*t* us to pray, as John also taught ..... Lk 11:1
For the Holy Ghost shall *t* you in ..... Lk 12:12
the Gentiles, and *t* the Gentiles ..... Jn 7:35
born in sins, and dost thou *t* us ..... Jn 9:34
he shall *t* you all things, and ..... Jn 14:26
that Jesus began both to do and *t* ..... Acts 1:1
at all nor *t* in the name of Jesus ..... Acts 4:18
that ye should not *t* in this name ..... Acts 5:28
every house, they ceased not to *t* ..... Acts 5:42
*t* customs, which are not lawful ..... Acts 16:21
as I *t* every where in every ..... 1Cor 4:17
Doth not even nature itself *t* you ..... 1Cor 11:14
by my voice I might *t* others also ..... 1Cor 14:19
that they *t* no other doctrine ..... 1Ti 1:3
But I suffer not a woman to *t* ..... 1Ti 2:12
given to hospitality, apt to *t* ..... 1Ti 3:2
These things command and *t* ..... 1Ti 4:11
These things *t* and exhort ..... 1Ti 6:2
If any man *t* otherwise, and ..... 1Ti 6:3
shall be able to *t* others also ..... 2Ti 2:2
be gentle unto all men, apt to *t* ..... 2Ti 2:24
That they may *t* the young women ..... Titus 2:4
ye have need that one *t* you again ..... Heb 5:12
they shall not *t* every man his ..... Heb 8:11
and ye need not that any man *t* you ..... 1Jn 2:27
herself a prophetess, to *t* ..... Rev 2:20

**TEACHER**
the great, the *t* as the scholar ... 1Chr 25:8
a *t* of lies, that the maker of ... Hab 2:18
that thou art a *t* come from God ... Jn 3:2
a *t* of babes, which hast the form ... Rom 2:20
a *t* of the Gentiles in faith and ... 1Ti 2:7
apostle, and a *t* of the Gentiles ... 2Ti 1:11

**TEACHERS**
more understanding than all my *t* ... Ps 119:99
have not obeyed the voice of my *t* ... Prov 5:13
yet shall not thy *t* be removed ... Is 30:20
but thine eyes shall see thy *t* ... Is 30:20
thy *t* have transgressed against ... Is 43:27
at Antioch certain prophets and *t* ... Acts 13:1
secondarily prophets, thirdly *t* ... 1Cor 12:28
are all *t*? ... 1Cor 12:29
and some, pastors and *t* ... Eph 4:11
Desiring to be *t* of the law ... 1Ti 1:7
shall they heap to themselves *t* ... 2Ti 4:3
to much wine, *t* of good things ... Titus 2:3
for the time ye ought to be *t* ... Heb 5:12
there shall be false *t* among you ... 2Pet 2:1

**TEACHEST**
O LORD, and *t* him out of thy law ... Ps 94:12
*t* the way of God in truth, ... Mt 22:16
but *t* the way of God in truth ... Mk 12:14
*t* rightly, neither acceptest thou ... Lk 20:21
but *t* the way of God truly ... Lk 20:21
that thou *t* all the Jews which ... Acts 21:21
Thou therefore which *t* another ... Rom 2:21
*t* thou not thyself? ... Rom 2:21

**TEACHETH**
He *t* my hands to war ... 2Sa 22:35
Who *t* us more than the beasts of ... Job 35:11
who *t* like him ... Job 36:22
He *t* my hands to war, so that a ... Ps 18:34
he that *t* man knowledge, shall ... Ps 94:10
which *t* my hands to war, and my ... Ps 144:1
his feet, he *t* with his fingers ... Prov 6:13
The heart of the wise *t* his mouth ... Prov 16:23
and the prophet that *t* lies ... Is 9:15
thy God which *t* thee to profit ... Is 48:17
that *t* all men every where ... Acts 21:28
or he that *t*, on teaching ... Rom 12:7
in the words which man's wisdom *t* ... 1Cor 2:13
but which the Holy Ghost *t* ... 1Cor 2:13
him that *t* in all good things ... Gal 6:6
anointing *t* you of all things ... 1Jn 2:27

**TEACHING**
true God, and without a *t* priest ... 2Chr 15:3
*t* them, yet they have not ... Jer 32:33
*t* in their synagogues, and ... Mt 4:23
*t* in their synagogues, and ... Mt 9:35
*t* for doctrines the commandments ... Mt 15:9
people came unto him as he was *t* ... Mt 21:23
daily with you *t* in the temple ... Mt 26:55
*T* them to observe all things ... Mt 28:20
went round about the villages, *t* ... Mk 6:6
*t* for doctrines the commandments ... Mk 7:7
daily with you in the temple *t* ... Mk 14:49
on a certain day, as he was *t* ... Lk 5:17
he was *t* in one of the synagogues ... Lk 13:10
through the cities and villages, *t* ... Lk 13:22
day time he was *t* in the temple ... Lk 21:37
*t* throughout all Jewry, beginning ... Lk 23:5
in the temple, and *t* the people ... Acts 5:25
Barnabas continued in Antioch, *t* ... Acts 15:35
*t* the word of God among them ... Acts 18:11
*t* those things which concern the ... Acts 28:31
or he that teacheth, on *t* ... Rom 12:7
*t* every man in all wisdom ... Col 1:28
*t* and admonishing one another in ... Col 3:16
*t* things which they ought not, ... Titus 1:11
*T* us that, denying ungodliness and ... Titus 2:12

**TEAR**
then I will *t* your flesh with the ... Judg 8:7
Lest he *t* my soul like a lion, ... Ps 7:2
they did *t* me, and ceased not ... Ps 35:15
lest I *t* you in pieces, and there ... Ps 50:22
sword to slay, and the dogs to *t* ... Jer 15:3
Neither shall men *t* themselves ... Jer 16:7
I will *t* them from your arms, and ... Eze 13:20
Your kerchiefs also will I *t* ... Eze 13:21
I, even I, will *t* and go away ... Hos 5:14
the wild beast shall *t* them ... Hos 13:8
and his anger did *t* perpetually ... Amos 1:11
The lion did *t* in pieces enough ... Nah 2:12
fat, and *t* their claws in pieces ... Zec 11:16

**TEARETH**
*t* the arm with the crown of the ... Deut 33:20
He *t* me in his wrath, who hateth ... Job 16:9
He *t* himself in his anger ... Job 18:4
*t* in pieces, and none can deliver ... Mic 5:8
he taketh him, he *t* him ... Mk 9:18
it *t* him that he foameth again, ... Lk 9:39

**TEARS**
thy prayer, I have seen thy *t* ... 2Kin 20:5
besought him with *t* to put away ... Est 8:3
mine eye poureth out *t* unto God ... Job 16:20
I water my couch with my *t* ... Ps 6:6
hold not thy peace at my *t* ... Ps 39:12
My *t* have been my meat day and ... Ps 42:3
put thou my *t* into thy bottle ... Ps 56:8
feedest them with the bread of *t* ... Ps 80:5
givest them *t* to drink in great ... Ps 80:5
soul from death, mine eyes from *t* ... Ps 116:8
They that sow in *t* shall reap in ... Ps 126:5
behold the *t* of such as were ... Eccl 4:1
I will water thee with my *t* ... Is 16:9
wipe away *t* from off all faces ... Is 25:8
thy prayer, I have seen thy *t* ... Is 38:5
and mine eyes a fountain of *t* ... Jer 9:1
that our eyes may run down with *t* ... Jer 9:18
weep sore, and run down with *t* ... Jer 13:17
mine eyes run down with *t* night ... Jer 14:17
weeping, and thine eyes from *t* ... Jer 31:16
night, and her *t* are on her cheeks ... Lam 1:2
Mine eyes do fail with *t*, my ... Lam 2:11
let *t* run down like a river day ... Lam 2:18
neither shall thy *t* run down ... Eze 24:16
the altar of the LORD with *t* ... Mal 2:13
child cried out, and said with *t* ... Mk 9:24
and began to wash his feet with *t* ... Lk 7:38
she hath washed my feet with *t* ... Lk 7:44
humility of mind, and with many *t* ... Acts 20:19
every one night and day with *t* ... Acts 20:31
I wrote unto you with many *t* ... 2Cor 2:4
see thee, being mindful of thy *t* ... 2Ti 1:4
*t* unto him that was able to save ... Heb 5:7
he sought it carefully with *t* ... Heb 12:17
wipe away all *t* from their eyes ... Rev 7:17
wipe away all *t* from their eyes ... Rev 21:4

**TEATS**
They shall lament for the *t* ... Is 32:12
bruised the *t* of their virginity ... Eze 23:3
youth, in bruising thy *t* by the ... Eze 23:21

**TEBAH** (*te'-bah*) *A son of Nahor.*
name was Reumah, she bare also *T* ... Gen 22:24

**TEBALIAH** (*teb-a-li'-ah*) *A sanctuary servant.*
*T* the third, Zechariah the fourth ... 1Chr 26:11

**TEBETH** (*te'-beth*) *Tenth month of the Hebrew year.*
tenth month, which is the month *T* ... Est 2:16

**TEDIOUS**
that I be not further *t* unto thee ... Acts 24:4

**TEETH**
wine, and his *t* white with milk ... Gen 49:12
the flesh was yet between their *t* ... Num 11:33
send the *t* of beasts upon them ... Deut 32:24
fleshhook of three *t* in his hand ... 1Sa 2:13
the *t* of the young lions, are ... Job 4:10
do I take my flesh in my *t* ... Job 13:14
he gnasheth upon me with his *t* ... Job 16:9
am escaped with the skin of my *t* ... Job 19:20
and plucked the spoil out of his *t* ... Job 29:17
his *t* are terrible round about ... Job 41:14
hast broken the *t* of the ungodly ... Ps 3:7
they gnashed upon me with their *t* ... Ps 35:16
and gnasheth upon him with his *t* ... Ps 37:12
whose *t* are spears and arrows, and ... Ps 57:4
Break their *t*, O God, in their ... Ps 58:6
the great *t* of the young lions ... Ps 58:6
he shall gnash with his *t* ... Ps 112:10
not given us as a prey to their *t* ... Ps 124:6
As vinegar to the *t*, and as smoke ... Prov 10:26
whose *t* are as swords, and their ... Prov 30:14
swords, and their jaw *t* as knives ... Prov 30:14
Thy *t* are like a flock of sheep ... Song 4:2
Thy *t* are as a flock of sheep ... Song 6:6
threshing instrument having *t* ... Is 41:15
the children's *t* are set on edge ... Jer 31:29
his *t* shall be set on edge ... Jer 31:30
they hiss and gnash the *t* ... Lam 2:16
broken my *t* with gravel stones ... Lam 3:16
the children's *t* are set on edge ... Eze 18:2
mouth of it between the *t* of it ... Dan 7:5
and it had great iron *t* ... Dan 7:7
whose *t* were of iron, and his ... Dan 7:19
whose *t* are the ... Joel 1:6
are the *t* of a lion ... Joel 1:6
hath the cheek *t* of a great lion ... Joel 1:6
cleanness of *t* in all your cities ... Amos 4:6
err, that bite with their *t* ... Mic 3:5
abominations from between his *t* ... Zec 9:7
shall be weeping and gnashing of *t* ... Mt 8:12
shall be wailing and gnashing of *t* ... Mt 13:42
shall be wailing and gnashing of *t* ... Mt 13:50
shall be weeping and gnashing of *t* ... Mt 22:13
shall be weeping and gnashing of *t* ... Mt 24:51
shall be weeping and gnashing of *t* ... Mt 25:30
with him, cast the same in his *t* ... Mt 27:44
foameth, and gnasheth with his *t* ... Mk 9:18
shall be weeping and gnashing of *t* ... Lk 13:28
they gnashed on him with their *t* ... Acts 7:54
their *t* were as the ... Rev 9:8
were as the *t* of lions ... Rev 9:8

**TEHAPHNEHES** (*te-haf'-ne-heze*) *Same as Tahpannes.*
At *T* also the day shall be ... Eze 30:18

**TEHINNAH** (*te-hin'-nah*) *A descendant of Judah.*
*T* the father of Ir-nahash ... 1Chr 4:12

**TEIL**
as a *t* tree, and as an oak, whose ... Is 6:13

**TEKEL** (*te'-kel*) *Part of the "handwriting of the wall."*
that was written, MENE, MENE, *T* ... Dan 5:25
*T*; Thou art weighed ... Dan 5:27

**TEKOA** (*te'-ko-ah*) See TEKOAH, TEKOITE.
*1. Son of Ashur.*
bare him Ashur the father of *T* ... 1Chr 2:24
the father of *T* had two wives ... 1Chr 4:5
*2. A city in Judah.*
even Beth-lehem, and Etam, and *T* ... 2Chr 11:6
forth into the wilderness of *T* ... 2Chr 20:20
and blow the trumpet in *T* ... Jer 6:1
who was among the herdmen of *T* ... Amos 1:1

**TEKOAH** (*te'-ko-ah*) See TEKOA. *Same as Tekoa 2.*
And Joab sent to *T*, and fetched ... 2Sa 14:2
the woman of *T* spake to the king ... 2Sa 14:4
the woman of *T* said unto the king ... 2Sa 14:9

**TEKOITE** (*te'-ko-ite*) See TEKOITES. *An inhabitant of Tekoa.*
Ira the son of Ikkesh the *T* ... 2Sa 23:26
Ira the son of Ikkesh the *T* ... 1Chr 11:28
was Ira the son of Ikkesh the *T* ... 1Chr 27:9

**TEKOITES** (*te'-ko-ites*)
And next unto them the *T* repaired ... Neh 3:5
After them the *T* repaired another ... Neh 3:27

**TEL-ABIB** (*tel-a'-bib*) *Town of the River Chebar.*
to them of the captivity at *T* ... Eze 3:15

**TELAH** (*te'-lah*) *Father of Tahan.*
*T* his son, and Tahan his son, ... 1Chr 7:25

**TELAIM** (*tel'-a-im*) See TELEM. *A place in Judah.*
together, and numbered them in *T* ... 1Sa 15:4

**TELASSAR** (*te-las'-sar*) See THELASSAR. *A city in Mesopotamia.*
children of Eden which were in *T* ... Is 37:12

**TEL AVIV** See TEL-ABIB.

**TELEM** (*te'-lem*) See TELAIM.
*1. A city in Judah.*
Ziph, and *T*, and Bealoth, ... Josh 15:24
*2. Married a foreigner in exile.*
Shallum, and *T*, and Uri ... Ezr 10:24

**TEL-HARESHA** (*tel-ha-re'-sha*) See TEL-HARSA. *A Babylonian settlement of exiles.*
went up also from Tel-melah, *T* ... Neh 7:61

**TEL-HARSA** (*tel'-har-sah*) See TEL-HARESHA. *Same as Tel-haresha.*
which went up from Tel-melah, *T* ... Ezr 2:59

**TELL**
why didst thou not *t* me that she ... Gen 12:18
*t* the stars, if thou be able to ... Gen 15:5
neither didst thou *t* me, neither ... Gen 21:26
mountains which I will *t* thee of ... Gen 22:2
*t* me, I pray thee ... Gen 24:23
and truly with my master, *t* me ... Gen 24:49
and if not, *t* me ... Gen 24:49
the land which I shall *t* thee of ... Gen 26:2
*t* me, what shall thy wages be ... Gen 29:15
and didst not *t* me, that I might ... Gen 31:27
and I have sent to *t* my lord ... Gen 32:5
*T* me, I pray thee, thy name ... Gen 32:29
*t* me, I pray thee, where they ... Gen 37:16
*t* me them, I pray you ... Gen 40:8
as to *t* the man whether ye had ... Gen 43:6
we cannot *t* who put our money in ... Gen 43:22
ye shall *t* my father of all my ... Gen 45:13
that I may *t* you that which shall ... Gen 49:1
*t* him, Thus saith the LORD God of ... Ex 9:1
that thou mayest *t* in the ears of ... Ex 10:2
word that we did *t* thee in Egypt ... Ex 14:12
and *t* the children of Israel ... Ex 19:3
*t* the priest, saying, It seemeth ... Lev 14:35
they will *t* it to the inhabitants ... Num 14:14
heard *t* that Israel came by the ... Num 21:1
he sheweth me I will *t* thee ... Num 23:3
judgment which they shall *t* thee ... Deut 17:11
thy elders, and they will *t* thee ... Deut 32:7
*t* me now what thou hast done ... Josh 7:19
my mother, and shall I *t* it thee ... Judg 14:16
*T* me, I pray thee, wherein thy ... Judg 16:6
now *t* me, I pray thee, wherewith ... Judg 16:10
*t* me wherewith thou mightest be ... Judg 16:13
*T* us, how was this wickedness ... Judg 20:3
he will *t* thee what thou shalt do ... Ruth 3:4
wilt not redeem it, then *t* me ... Ruth 4:4
*t* us wherewith we shall send it ... 1Sa 6:2
the man of God, to *t* us our way ... 1Sa 9:8
*T* me, I pray thee, where the ... 1Sa 9:18
will *t* thee all that is in thine ... 1Sa 9:19
*T* me, I pray thee, what Samuel ... 1Sa 10:15
*T* me what thou hast done ... 1Sa 14:43
I will *t* thee what the LORD hath ... 1Sa 15:16
soul liveth, O king, I cannot *t* ... 1Sa 17:55
and what I see, that I will *t* thee ... 1Sa 19:3
thee, then would not I *t* it thee ... 1Sa 20:9
David to Jonathan, Who shall *t* me ... 1Sa 20:10
that he would surely *t* Saul ... 1Sa 22:22
I beseech thee, *t* thy servant ... 1Sa 23:11
saying, Lest they should *t* on us ... 1Sa 27:11
I pray thee, *t* me ... 2Sa 1:4
*T* it not in Gath, publish it not ... 2Sa 1:20
*t* my servant David, Thus saith ... 2Sa 7:5
to *t* him that the child was dead ... 2Sa 12:18
if we *t* him that the child is ... 2Sa 12:18
Who can *t* whether GOD will be ... 2Sa 12:22
wilt thou not *t* me ... 2Sa 13:4
thou shalt *t* it to Zadok and ... 2Sa 15:35

*t* David, saying, Lodge not this 2Sa 17:16
Go *t* the king what thou hast seen 2Sa 18:21
that thou shouldest *t* them who 1Kin 1:20
he shall *t* thee what shall become 1Kin 14:3
*t* Jeroboam, Thus saith the LORD 1Kin 14:7
*t* thy lord, Behold, Elijah is 1Kin 18:8
*t* thy lord, Behold, Elijah is 1Kin 18:11
*t* Ahab, and he cannot find thee, 1Kin 18:12
*t* thy lord, Behold, Elijah is 1Kin 18:14
*T* my lord the king, All that thou 1Kin 20:9
*T* him, Let not him that girdeth 1Kin 20:11
*t* me nothing but that which is 1Kin 22:16
Did I not *t* thee that he would 1Kin 22:18
*t* me, what hast thou in the house 2Kin 4:2
may go and *t* the king's household 2Kin 7:9
*T* me, I pray thee, all the great 2Kin 8:4
*t* us now 2Kin 9:12
the city to go to *t* it in Jezreel 2Kin 9:15
*t* Hezekiah the captain of my 2Kin 20:5
*T* the man that sent you to me, 2Kin 22:15
*t* David my servant, Thus saith 1Chr 17:4
Furthermore I *t* thee that the 1Chr 17:10
*t* David, saying, Thus saith the 1Chr 21:10
Did I not *t* thee that he would 2Chr 18:17
*T* ye the man that sent you to me, 2Chr 34:23
I only am escaped alone to *t* thee Job 1:15
I only am escaped alone to *t* thee Job 1:16
I only am escaped alone to *t* thee Job 1:17
I only am escaped alone to *t* thee Job 1:19
*t* thee, and utter words out of Job 8:10
of the air, and they shall *t* thee Job 12:7
Let men of understanding *t* me Job 34:34
I may *t* all my bones Ps 22:17
*t* of all thy wondrous works Ps 26:7
*t* the towers thereof Ps 48:12
that ye may *t* it to the Ps 48:13
I were hungry, I would not *t* thee Ps 50:12
his son's name, if thou canst *t* Prov 30:4
for who can *t* a man what shall be Eccl 6:12
for who can *t* him when it shall Eccl 8:7
a man cannot *t* what shall be Eccl 10:14
shall be after him, who can *t* him Eccl 10:14
hath wings shall *t* the matter Eccl 10:20
*T* me, O thou whom my soul loveth, Song 1:7
ye find my beloved, that ye *t* him Song 5:8
I will *t* you what I will do to my Is 5:5
*t* this people, Hear ye indeed, Is 6:9
and let them *t* thee now, and let Is 19:12
they spring forth I *t* you of them Is 42:9
*T* ye, and bring them near Is 45:21
*t* this, utter it even to the end Is 48:20
then thou shalt *t* them, Thus Jer 15:2
the words that I shall *t* thee Jer 19:2
they *t* every man to his neighbour Jer 23:27
hath a dream, let him *t* a dream Jer 23:28
do *t* them, and cause my people to Jer 23:32
*t* Hananiah, saying, Thus saith Jer 28:13
*t* him, Thus saith the LORD Jer 34:2
*t* the men of Judah and the Jer 35:13
We will surely *t* the king of all Jer 36:16
*T* us now, How didst thou write Jer 36:17
*t* ye it in Arnon, that Moab is Jer 48:20
*t* them, Thus saith the Lord GOD Eze 3:11
*T* them therefore, Thus saith the Eze 12:23
*t* them, Behold, the king of Eze 17:12
Wilt thou not *t* us what these Eze 24:19
*t* thy servants the dream, and we Dan 2:4
Let the king *t* his servants the Dan 2:7
therefore *t* me the dream, and I Dan 2:9
we will *t* the interpretation Dan 2:36
*t* me the visions of my dream that Dan 4:9
*T* ye your children of it, and let Joel 1:3
your children *t* their children Joel 1:3
*T* us, we pray thee, for whose Jonah 1:8
Who can *t* if God will turn and Jonah 3:9
saith unto him, See thou *t* no man Mt 8:4
What I *t* you in darkness, that Mt 10:27
*t* no man that he was Jesus the Mt 16:20
*T* the vision to no man, until the Mt 17:9
*t* him his fault between thee and Mt 18:15
hear them, *t* it unto the church Mt 18:17
*T* ye the daughter of Sion, Behold Mt 21:5
you one thing, which if ye *t* me Mt 21:24
I in like wise will *t* you by what Mt 21:24
Jesus, and said, We cannot *t* Mt 21:27
Neither *t* I you by what authority Mt 21:27
*T* them which are bidden, Behold, Mt 22:4
*T* us therefore, What thinkest Mt 22:17
*T* us, when shall these things be Mt 24:3
that thou *t* us whether thou be Mt 26:63
*t* his disciples that he is risen Mt 28:7
as they went to *t* his disciples Mt 28:9
go *t* my brethren that they go Mt 28:10
fever, and anon they *t* him of her Mk 1:30
*t* them how great things the Lord Mk 5:19
them that they should *t* no man Mk 7:36
nor *t* it to any in the town Mk 8:26
that they should *t* no man of him Mk 8:30
*t* no man what things they had Mk 9:9
began to *t* them what things Mk 10:32
I will *t* you by what authority I Mk 11:29
and said unto Jesus, We cannot *t* Mk 11:33
Neither do I *t* you by what Mk 11:33
*T* us, when shall these things be Mk 13:4
*t* his disciples and Peter that he Mk 16:7
But I *t* you of a truth, many Lk 4:25
And he charged him to *t* no man Lk 5:14
*t* John what things ye have seen Lk 7:22
*T* me therefore, which of them Lk 7:42
should *t* no man what was done Lk 8:56
them to *t* no man that thing Lk 9:21
But I *t* you of a truth, there be Lk 9:27
For I *t* you, that many prophets Lk 10:24
I *t* you, Nay Lk 12:51
I *t* thee, thou shalt not depart Lk 12:59
I *t* you, Nay Lk 13:3
I *t* you, Nay Lk 13:5
I *t* you, I know you not whence ye Lk 13:27
*t* that fox, Behold, I cast out Lk 13:32
I *t* you, in that night there Lk 17:34
I *t* you that he will avenge them Lk 18:8
I *t* you, this man went down to Lk 18:14
I *t* you that, if these should Lk 19:40
*T* us, by what authority doest Lk 20:2
they could not *t* whence it was Lk 20:7
Neither *t* I you by what authority Lk 20:8
I *t* thee, Peter, the cock shall Lk 22:34
Art thou the Christ? *t* us Lk 22:67
And he said unto them, If I *t* you Lk 22:67
but canst not *t* whence it cometh, Jn 3:8
if I *t* you of heavenly things Jn 3:12
is come, he will *t* us all things Jn 4:25
but ye cannot *t* whence I come Jn 8:14
because I *t* you the truth, ye Jn 8:45
thou be the Christ, *t* us plainly Jn 10:24
and again Andrew and Philip *t* Jesus Jn 12:22
Now I *t* you before it come, that, Jn 13:19
Nevertheless I *t* you the truth Jn 16:7
we cannot *t* what he saith Jn 16:18
or did others *t* it thee of me Jn 18:34
*t* me where thou hast laid him, and Jn 20:15
*T* me whether ye sold the land for Acts 5:8
he shall *t* thee what thou Acts 10:6
Who shall *t* thee words, whereby Acts 11:14
who shall also *t* you the same Acts 15:27
in nothing else, but either to *t* Acts 17:21
unto him, *T* me, art thou a Roman Acts 22:27
he hath a certain thing to *t* him Acts 23:17
What is that thou hast to *t* me Acts 23:19
See thou *t* no man that thou hast Acts 23:22
(whether in the body, I cannot *t* 2Cor 12:2
out of the body, I cannot *t* 2Cor 12:2
or out of the body, I cannot *t* 2Cor 12:3
because I *t* you the truth Gal 4:16
*T* me, ye that desire to be under Gal 4:21
of the which I *t* you before Gal 5:21
now *t* you even weeping, that they Phil 3:18
time would fail me to *t* of Gedeon Heb 11:32
I will *t* thee the mystery of the Rev 17:7

**TELLEST**
Thou *t* my wanderings Ps 56:8

**TELLETH**
Also the LORD *t* thee that he will 2Sa 7:11
*t* the king of Israel the words 2Kin 6:12
when he goeth abroad, he *t* it Ps 41:6
he that *t* lies shall not tarry in Ps 101:7
He *t* the number of the stars Ps 147:4
the hands of him that *t* them Jer 33:13
Philip cometh and *t* Andrew Jn 12:22

**TELLING**
Gideon heard the *t* of the dream Judg 7:15
When thou hast made an end of *t* 2Sa 11:19
as he was *t* the king how he had 2Kin 8:5

**TEL-MELAH** (*tel-me'-lah*) *A place where the exiles lived.*
were they which went up from *T* Ezr 2:59
they which went up also from *T* Neh 7:61

**TEMA** (*te'-mah*)
*1. A son of Ishmael.*
Hadar, and Tema, Jetur, Naphish, and Gen 25:15
and Dumah, Massa, Hadad, and *T* 1Chr 1:30
*T* brought water to him that was Is 21:14
Dedan, and *T*, and Buz, and all that Jer 25:23
*2. A city in northern Arabia.*
The troops of *T* looked, the Job 6:19

**TEMAH** See THAMAH.

**TEMAN** (*te'-man*) See TEMANITE.
*1. A son of Eliphaz.*
And the sons of Eliphaz were *T* Gen 36:11
duke *T*, duke Omar, duke Zepho, Gen 36:15
Duke Kenaz, duke *T*, duke Mibzar, Gen 36:42
*T*, and Omar, Zephi, and Gatam, 1Chr 1:36
Duke Kenaz, duke *T*, duke Mibzar, 1Chr 1:53
*2. A race and district of Edom.*
Is wisdom no more in *T* Jer 49:7
against the inhabitants of *T* Jer 49:20
and I will make it desolate from *T* Eze 25:13
But I will send a fire upon *T* Amos 1:12
And thy mighty men, O *T*, shall be Obad 9
God came from *T*, and the Holy One Hab 3:3

**TEMANI** (*te'-ma-ni*) See TEMANITE. *A son of Ashur.*
land of *T* reigned in his stead Gen 36:34

**TEMANITE** (*te'-man-ite*) See TEMANI, TEMANITES. *An inhabitant of Teman 3.*
Eliphaz the *T*, and Bildad the Job 2:11
Then Eliphaz the *T* answered Job 4:1
Then answered Eliphaz the *T* Job 15:1
Then Eliphaz the *T* answered Job 22:1
the LORD said to Eliphaz the *T* Job 42:7
So Eliphaz the *T* and Bildad the Job 42:9

**TEMANITES** (*te'-man-ites*)
of the *T* reigned in his stead 1Chr 1:45

**TEMENI** (*tem'-e-ni*) *A descendant of Caleb.*
bare him Ahuzam, and Hepher, and *T* 1Chr 4:6

**TEMPER**
of oil, to *t* with the fine flour Eze 46:14

**TEMPERANCE**
he reasoned of righteousness, *t* Acts 24:25
Meekness, *t* Gal 5:23
And to knowledge *t* 2Pet 1:6
and to *t* patience 2Pet 1:6

**TEMPERATE**
the mastery is *t* in all things 1Cor 9:25
of good men, sober, just, holy, *t* Titus 1:8
the aged men be sober, grave, *t* Titus 2:2

**TEMPERED**
and cakes unleavened *t* with oil Ex 29:2
*t* together, pure and holy Ex 30:35
but God hath *t* the body together, 1Cor 12:24

**TEMPEST**
For he breaketh me with a *t* Job 9:17
a *t* stealeth him away in the Job 27:20
and brimstone, and an horrible *t* Ps 11:6
escape from the windy storm and *t* Ps 55:8
So persecute them with thy *t* Ps 83:15
strong one, which as a *t* of hail Is 28:2
and great noise, with storm and *t* Is 29:6
fire, with scattering, and *t* Is 30:30
the wind, and a covert from the *t* Is 32:2
O thou afflicted, tossed with *t* Is 54:11
with a *t* in the day of the Amos 1:14
there was a mighty *t* in the sea Jonah 1:4
my sake this great *t* is upon you Jonah 1:12
there arose a great *t* in the sea Mt 8:24
being exceedingly tossed with a *t* Acts 27:18
no small *t* lay on us, all hope Acts 27:20
unto blackness, and darkness, and *t* Heb 12:18
clouds that are carried with a *t* 2Pet 2:17

**TEMPESTUOUS**
shall be very *t* round about him Ps 50:3
for the sea wrought, and was *t* Jonah 1:11
wrought, and was *t* against them Jonah 1:13
there arose against it a *t* wind Acts 27:14

**TEMPLE**
by a post of the *t* of the LORD 1Sa 1:9
God went out in the *t* of the LORD 1Sa 3:3
he did hear my voice out of his *t* 2Sa 22:7
porch before the *t* of the house 1Kin 6:3
house round about, both of the *t* 1Kin 6:5
the *t* before it, was forty cubits 1Kin 6:17
door of the *t* posts of olive tree 1Kin 6:33
the pillars in the porch of the *t* 1Kin 7:21
of the house, to wit, of the *t* 1Kin 7:50
that were in the *t* of the LORD 2Kin 11:10
the *t* to the left corner of the 2Kin 11:11
to the left corner of the *t* 2Kin 11:11
along by the altar and the *t* 2Kin 11:11
the people into the *t* of the LORD 2Kin 11:13
the doors of the *t* of the LORD 2Kin 18:16
to bring forth out of the *t* of 2Kin 23:4
had made in the *t* of the LORD 2Kin 24:13
the priest's office in the *t* that 1Chr 6:10
his head in the *t* of Dagon 1Chr 10:10
up the pillars before the *t* 2Chr 3:17
their form, and set them in the *t* 2Chr 4:7
tables, and placed them in the *t* 2Chr 4:8
the doors of the house of the *t* 2Chr 4:22
from the right side of the *t* to 2Chr 23:10
to the left side of the *t* 2Chr 23:10
along by the altar and the *t* 2Chr 23:10
went into the *t* of the LORD to 2Chr 26:16
not into the *t* of the LORD 2Chr 27:2
that they found in the *t* of the 2Chr 29:16
when Josiah had prepared the *t* 2Chr 35:20
and put them in his *t* at Babylon 2Chr 36:7
But the foundation of the *t* of Ezr 3:6
foundation of the *t* of the LORD Ezr 3:10
the *t* unto the LORD God of Israel Ezr 4:1
of the *t* that was in Jerusalem Ezr 5:14
them into the *t* of Babylon Ezr 5:14
king take out of the *t* of Babylon Ezr 5:14
carry them into the *t* that is in Ezr 5:15
of the *t* which is at Jerusalem Ezr 6:5
unto the *t* which is at Jerusalem Ezr 6:5
in the house of God, within the *t* Neh 6:10
and let us shut the doors of the *t* Neh 6:10
go into the *t* to save his life Neh 6:11
will I worship toward thy holy *t* Ps 5:7
The LORD is in his holy *t* Ps 11:4
he heard my voice out of his *t* Ps 18:6
the LORD, and to enquire in his *t* Ps 27:4
in his *t* doth every one speak of Ps 29:9
O God, in the midst of thy *t* Ps 48:9
of thy house, even of thy holy *t* Ps 65:4
Because of thy *t* at Jerusalem Ps 68:29
thy holy *t* have they defiled Ps 79:1
I will worship toward thy holy *t* Ps 138:2
up, and his train filled the *t* Is 6:1
and to the *t*, Thy foundation shall Is 44:28
from the city, a voice from the *t* Is 66:6
The *t* of the LORD Jer 7:4
The *t* of the LORD Jer 7:4
The *t* of the LORD, are these Jer 7:4
were set before the *t* of the LORD Jer 24:1
our God, the vengeance of his *t* Jer 50:28
the LORD, the vengeance of his *t* Jer 51:11

T

at the door of the *t* of the LORD Eze 8:16
backs toward the *t* of the LORD Eze 8:16
Afterward he brought me to the *t* Eze 41:1
twenty cubits, before the *t* Eze 41:4
hundred cubits, with the inner *t* Eze 41:15
made, and on the wall of the *t* Eze 41:20
The posts of the *t* were squared Eze 41:21
And the *t* and the sanctuary had two Eze 41:23
on them, on the doors of the *t* Eze 41:25
before the *t* were an hundred Eze 42:8
had taken out of the *t* which was Dan 5:2
that were taken out of the *t* of Dan 5:3
the songs of the *t* shall be Amos 8:3
will look again toward thy holy *t* Jonah 2:4
in unto thee, into thine holy *t* Jonah 2:7
you, the Lord from his holy *t* Mic 1:2
But the LORD is in his holy *t* Hab 2:20
upon a stone in the *t* of the LORD Hag 2:15
of the LORD's *t* was laid, Hag 2:18
he shall build the *t* of the LORD Zec 6:12
he shall build the *t* of the LORD Zec 6:13
a memorial in the *t* of the LORD Zec 6:14
and build in the *t* of the LORD Zec 6:15
that the *t* might be built Zec 8:9
shall suddenly come to his *t* Mal 3:1
him on a pinnacle of the *t* Mt 4:5
in the *t* profane the sabbath Mt 12:5
place is one greater than the *t* Mt 12:6
And Jesus went into the *t* of God Mt 21:12
them that sold and bought in the *t* Mt 21:12
and the lame came to him in the *t* Mt 21:14
and the children crying in the *t* Mt 21:15
And when he was come into the *t* Mt 21:23
Whosoever shall swear by the *t* Mt 23:16
shall swear by the gold of the *t* Mt 23:16
or the *t* that sanctifieth the Mt 23:17
And whoso shall swear by the *t* Mt 23:21
whom ye slew between the *t* Mt 23:35
went out, and departed from the *t* Mt 24:1
shew him the buildings of the *t* Mt 24:1
daily with you teaching in the *t* Mt 26:55
I am able to destroy the *t* of God Mt 26:61
the pieces of silver in the *t* Mt 27:5
Thou that destroyest the *t* Mt 27:40
the veil of the *t* was rent in Mt 27:51
into Jerusalem, and into the *t* Mk 11:11
and Jesus went into the *t*, and Mk 11:15
them that sold and bought in the *t* Mk 11:15
carry any vessel through the *t* Mk 11:16
and as he was walking in the *t* Mk 11:27
and said, while he taught in the *t* Mk 12:35
And as he went out of the *t* Mk 13:1
of Olives over against the *t* Mk 13:3
daily with you in the *t* teaching Mk 14:49
I will destroy this *t* that is Mk 14:58
Ah, thou that destroyest the *t* Mk 15:29
the veil of the *t* was rent in Mk 15:38
he went into the *t* of the Lord Lk 1:9
that he tarried so long in the *t* Lk 1:21
he had seen a vision in the *t* Lk 1:22
he came by the Spirit into the *t* Lk 2:27
which departed not from the *t* Lk 2:37
days they found him in the *t* Lk 2:46
and set him on a pinnacle of the *t* Lk 4:9
between the altar and the *t* Lk 11:51
men went up into the *t* to pray Lk 18:10
And he went into the *t*, and began Lk 19:45
And he taught daily in the *t* Lk 19:47
as he taught the people in the *t* Lk 20:1
And as some spake of the *t* Lk 21:5
day time he was teaching in the *t* Lk 21:37
in the morning to him in the *t* Lk 21:38
priests, and captains of the *t* Lk 22:52
I was daily with you in the *t* Lk 22:53
the veil of the *t* was rent in the Lk 23:45
And were continually in the *t* Lk 24:53
found in the *t* those that sold Jn 2:14
he drove them all out of the *t* Jn 2:15
and said unto them, Destroy this *t* Jn 2:19
six years was this *t* in building Jn 2:20
But he spake of the *t* of his body Jn 2:21
Jesus findeth him in the *t* Jn 5:14
feast Jesus went up into the *t* Jn 7:14
cried Jesus in the *t* as he taught Jn 7:28
morning he came again into the *t* Jn 8:2
treasury, as he taught in the *t* Jn 8:20
hid himself, and went out of the *t* Jn 8:59
in the *t* in Solomon's porch Jn 10:23
as they stood in the *t*, What Jn 11:56
in the synagogue, and in the *t* Jn 18:20
daily with one accord in the *t* Acts 2:46
into the *t* at the hour of prayer Acts 3:1
the *t* which is called Beautiful Acts 3:2
of them that entered into the *t* Acts 3:2
to go into the *t* asked an alms Acts 3:3
and entered with them into the *t* Acts 3:8
at the Beautiful gate of the *t* Acts 3:10
priests, and the captain of the *t* Acts 4:1
speak in the *t* to the people all Acts 5:20
into the *t* early in the morning Acts 5:21
priest and the captain of the *t* Acts 5:24
in prison are standing in the *t* Acts 5:25
And daily in the *t*, and in every Acts 5:42
but also that the *t* of the great Acts 19:27
with them entered into the *t* Acts 21:26
Asia, when they saw him in the *t* Acts 21:27
brought Greeks also into the *t* Acts 21:28
that Paul had brought into the *t* Acts 21:29
Paul, and drew him out of the *t* Acts 21:30
even while I prayed in the *t* Acts 22:17
hath gone about to profane the *t* Acts 24:6
in the *t* disputing with any man Acts 24:12
Asia found me purified in the *t* Acts 24:18
the Jews, neither against the *t* Acts 25:8
the Jews caught me in the *t* Acts 26:21
ye not that ye are the *t* of God 1Cor 3:16
If any man defile the *t* of God 1Cor 3:17
for the *t* of God is holy, which 1Cor 3:17
of God is holy, which *t* ye are 1Cor 3:17
ye not that your body is the *t* of 1Cor 6:19
sit at meat in the idol's *t* 1Cor 8:10
live of the things of the *t* 1Cor 9:13
hath the *t* of God with idols 2Cor 6:16
for ye are the *t* of the living 2Cor 6:16
unto an holy *t* in the Lord Eph 2:21
he as God sitteth in the *t* of God 2Th 2:4
make a pillar in the *t* of my God Rev 3:12
serve him day and night in his *t* Rev 7:15
Rise, and measure the *t* of God Rev 11:1
which is without the *t* leave out Rev 11:2
the *t* of God was opened in heaven Rev 11:19
there was seen in his *t* the ark Rev 11:19
another angel came out of the *t* Rev 14:15
out of the *t* which is in heaven Rev 14:17
the *t* of the tabernacle of the Rev 15:5
seven angels came out of the *t* Rev 15:6
the *t* was filled with smoke from Rev 15:8
man was able to enter into the *t* Rev 15:8
the *t* saying to the seven angels Rev 16:1
voice out of the *t* of heaven Rev 16:17
And I saw no *t* therein Rev 21:22
and the Lamb are the *t* of it Rev 21:22

## TEMPLES

him, and smote the nail into his *t* Judg 4:21
dead, and the nail was in his *t* Judg 4:22
pierced and stricken through his *t* Judg 5:26
thy *t* are like a piece of a Song 4:3
are thy *t* within thy locks Song 6:7
his Maker, and buildeth *t* Hos 8:14
have carried into your *t* my Joel 3:5
dwelleth not in *t* made with hands Acts 7:48
dwelleth not in *t* made with hands Acts 17:24

## TEMPORAL

the things which are seen are *t* 2Cor 4:18

## TEMPT

things, that God did *t* Abraham Gen 22:1
wherefore do ye *t* the LORD Ex 17:2
Ye shall not *t* the LORD your God, Deut 6:16
ask, neither will I *t* the LORD Is 7:12
yea, they that *t* God are even Mal 3:15
Thou shalt not *t* the Lord thy God Mt 4:7
Why *t* ye me, ye hypocrites Mt 22:18
said unto them, Why *t* ye me Mk 12:15
Thou shalt not *t* the Lord thy God Lk 4:12
and said unto them, Why *t* ye me Lk 20:23
to *t* the Spirit of the Lord Acts 5:9
Now therefore why *t* ye God Acts 15:10
that Satan *t* you not for your 1Cor 7:5
Neither let us *t* Christ, as some 1Cor 10:9

## TEMPTATION

as in the day of *t* in the Ps 95:8
And lead us not into *t*, but Mt 6:13
and pray, that ye enter not into *t* Mt 26:41
ye and pray, lest ye enter into *t* Mk 14:38
the devil had ended all the *t* Lk 4:13
and in time of *t* fall away Lk 8:13
And lead us not into *t* Lk 11:4
Pray that ye enter not into *t* Lk 22:40
and pray, lest ye enter into *t* Lk 22:46
There hath no *t* taken you but 1Cor 10:13
but will with the *t* also make a 1Cor 10:13
my *t* which was in my flesh ye Gal 4:14
that will be rich fall into *t* 1Ti 6:9
in the day of *t* in the wilderness Heb 3:8
is the man that endureth *t* Jas 1:12
will keep thee from the hour of *t* Rev 3:10

## TEMPTATIONS

the midst of another nation, by *t* Deut 4:34
The great *t* which thine eyes saw, Deut 7:19
The great *t* which thine eyes have Deut 29:3
have continued with me in my *t* Lk 22:28
of mind, and with many tears, and *t* Acts 20:19
joy when ye fall into divers *t* Jas 1:2
in heaviness through manifold *t* 1Pet 1:6
how to deliver the godly out of *t* 2Pet 2:9

## TEMPTED

and because they *t* the LORD Ex 17:7
have *t* me now these ten times, and Num 14:22
your God, as ye *t* him in Massah Deut 6:16
they *t* God in their heart by Ps 78:18
*t* God, and limited the Holy One of Ps 78:41
Yet they *t* and provoked the most Ps 78:56
When your fathers *t* me, proved me Ps 95:9
and *t* God in the desert Ps 106:14
wilderness to be *t* of the devil Mt 4:1
wilderness forty days, *t* of Satan Mk 1:13
Being forty days *t* of the devil Lk 4:2
*t* him, saying, Master, what shall Lk 10:25
Christ, as some of them also *t* 1Cor 10:9
to be *t* above that ye are able 1Cor 10:13
thyself, lest thou also be *t* Gal 6:1
some means the tempter have *t* you 1Th 3:5
he himself hath suffered being *t* Heb 2:18
able to succour them that are *t* Heb 2:18
When your fathers *t* me, proved me Heb 3:9
in all points *t* like as we are Heb 4:15
they were sawn asunder, were *t* Heb 11:37
when he is *t*, I am *t* of God Jas 1:13
for God cannot be *t* with evil Jas 1:13
But every man is *t*, when he is Jas 1:14

## TEMPTER

when the *t* came to him, he said, Mt 4:3
some means the *t* have tempted you 1Th 3:5

## TEMPTETH

with evil, neither *t* he any man Jas 1:13

## TEMPTING

*t* desired him that he would shew Mt 16:1
*t* him, and saying unto him, Is it Mt 19:3
him a question, *t* him, and saying, Mt 22:35
of him a sign from heaven, *t* him Mk 8:11
put away his wife? *t* him Mk 10:2
*t* him, sought of him a sign from Lk 11:16
*t* him, that they might have to Jn 8:6

## TEN

were nine hundred and *t* years Gen 5:14
after Abram had dwelt *t* years in Gen 16:3
Peradventure *t* shall be found Gen 18:32
the servant took *t* camels of the Gen 24:10
hands of *t* shekels weight of gold Gen 24:22
us a few days, at the least *t* Gen 24:55
me, and changed my wages *t* times Gen 31:7
hast changed my wages *t* times Gen 31:41
*t* bulls, twenty she asses Gen 32:15
twenty she asses, and *t* foals Gen 32:15
Joseph's *t* brethren went down to Gen 42:3
*t* asses laden with the good Gen 45:23
*t* she asses laden with corn and Gen 45:23
into Egypt, were threescore and *t* Gen 46:27
for him threescore and *t* days Gen 50:3
lived an hundred and *t* years Gen 50:22
being an hundred and *t* years old Gen 50:26
and threescore and *t* palm trees Ex 15:27
*t* curtains of fine twined linen Ex 26:1
*T* cubits shall be the length of a Ex 26:16
pillars *t*, and their sockets *t* Ex 27:12
the covenant, the *t* commandments Ex 34:28
*t* curtains of fine twined linen Ex 36:8
length of a board was *t* cubits Ex 36:21
pillars *t*, and their sockets *t* Ex 38:12
shall put *t* thousand to flight Lev 26:8
*t* women shall bake your bread in Lev 26:26
and for the female *t* shekels Lev 27:5
and for the female *t* shekels Lev 27:7
One spoon of *t* shekels of gold, Num 7:14
One spoon of gold of *t* shekels Num 7:20
One golden spoon of *t* shekels Num 7:26
One golden spoon of *t* shekels Num 7:32
One golden spoon of *t* shekels Num 7:38
One golden spoon of *t* shekels Num 7:44
One golden spoon of *t* shekels Num 7:50
One golden spoon of *t* shekels Num 7:56
One golden spoon of *t* shekels Num 7:62
One golden spoon of *t* shekels Num 7:68
One golden spoon of *t* shekels Num 7:74
One golden spoon of *t* shekels Num 7:80
weighing *t* shekels apiece, after Num 7:86
nor five days, neither *t* days Num 11:19
gathered least gathered *t* homers Num 11:32
have tempted me now these *t* times Num 14:22
And on the fourth day *t* bullocks Num 29:23
and threescore and *t* palm trees Num 33:9
to perform, even *t* commandments Deut 4:13
the *t* commandments, which the Deut 10:4
with threescore and *t* persons Deut 10:22
two put *t* thousand to flight, Deut 32:30
he came with *t* thousands of Deut 33:2
they are the *t* thousands of Deut 33:17
*t* cities with their villages Josh 15:57
there fell *t* portions to Manasseh Josh 17:5
half tribe of Manasseh, *t* cities Josh 21:5
All the cities were *t* with their Josh 21:26
And with him *t* princes, of each Josh 22:14
being an hundred and *t* years old Josh 24:29
of them in Bezek *t* thousand men Judg 1:4
*t* kings, having their thumbs and Judg 1:7
being an hundred and *t* years old Judg 2:8
at that time about *t* thousand men Judg 3:29
take with thee *t* thousand men of Judg 4:6
he went up with *t* thousand men at Judg 4:10
and *t* thousand men after him Judg 4:14
Then Gideon took *t* men of his Judg 6:27
and there remained *t* thousand Judg 7:3
*t* sons of his body begotten Judg 8:30
*t* persons, reign over you, or Judg 9:2
*t* pieces of silver out of the Judg 9:4
*t* persons, upon one stone Judg 9:5
*t* persons, upon one stone, and Judg 9:18
*t* sons of Jerubbaal might come, Judg 9:24
and he judged Israel *t* years Judg 12:11
rode on threescore and *t* ass colts Judg 12:14
I will give thee *t* shekels of Judg 17:10
we will take *t* men of an hundred Judg 20:10
and a thousand out of *t* thousand Judg 20:10
there came against Gibeah *t* Judg 20:34
they dwelled there about *t* years Ruth 1:4
he took *t* men of the elders of Ruth 4:2
not I better to thee than *t* sons 1Sa 1:8
thousand and threescore and *t* men 1Sa 6:19
and *t* thousand men of Judah 1Sa 15:4
these *t* loaves, and run to the 1Sa 17:17
carry these *t* cheeses unto the 1Sa 17:18
and David his *t* thousands 1Sa 18:7
ascribed unto David *t* thousands 1Sa 18:8
and David his *t* thousands 1Sa 21:11
And David sent out *t* young men 1Sa 25:5

came to pass about *t* days after ... 1Sa 25:38
and David his *t* thousands ... 1Sa 29:5
And the king left *t* women, which ... 2Sa 15:16
thou art worth *t* thousand of us ... 2Sa 18:3
given thee *t* shekels of silver ... 2Sa 18:11
*t* young men that bare Joab's ... 2Sa 18:15
We have *t* parts in the king, and ... 2Sa 19:43
the king took the *t* women his ... 2Sa 20:3
*T* fat oxen, and twenty oxen out of ... 1Kin 4:23
*t* thousand a month by courses ... 1Kin 5:14
*t* thousand that bare burdens, and ... 1Kin 5:15
*t* cubits was the breadth thereof ... 1Kin 6:3
of olive tree, each *t* cubits high ... 1Kin 6:23
part of the other were *t* cubits ... 1Kin 6:24
And the other cherub was *t* cubits ... 1Kin 6:25
of the one cherub was *t* cubits ... 1Kin 6:26
great stones, stones of *t* cubits ... 1Kin 7:10
*t* cubits from the one brim to the ... 1Kin 7:23
*t* in a cubit, compassing the sea ... 1Kin 7:24
And he made *t* bases of brass ... 1Kin 7:27
this manner he made the *t* bases ... 1Kin 7:37
Then made he *t* lavers of brass ... 1Kin 7:38
one of the *t* bases one laver ... 1Kin 7:38
bases, and *t* lavers on the bases ... 1Kin 7:43
to Jeroboam, Take thee *t* pieces ... 1Kin 11:31
will give *t* tribes to thee ... 1Kin 11:31
give it unto thee, even *t* tribes ... 1Kin 11:35
And take with thee *t* loaves ... 1Kin 14:3
took with him *t* talents of silver ... 2Kin 5:5
of gold, and *t* changes of raiment ... 2Kin 5:5
*t* chariots, and *t* thousand ... 2Kin 13:7
in the valley of salt *t* thousand ... 2Kin 14:7
reigned *t* years in Samaria ... 2Kin 15:17
*t* degrees, or go back *t* degrees ... 2Kin 20:9
the shadow to go down *t* degrees ... 2Kin 20:10
shadow return backward *t* degrees ... 2Kin 20:10
the shadow *t* degrees backward ... 2Kin 20:11
even *t* thousand captives, and all ... 2Kin 24:14
*t* men with him, and smote Gedaliah 2Kin 25:25
of Manasseh, by lot, *t* cities ... 1Chr 6:61
*t* thousand men that drew sword ... 1Chr 21:5
*t* thousand drams, and of silver ... 1Chr 29:7
of silver *t* thousand talents, and ... 1Chr 29:7
*t* thousand men to bear burdens, ... 2Chr 2:2
*t* thousand of them to be bearers ... 2Chr 2:18
*t* cubits the height thereof ... 2Chr 4:1
sea of *t* cubits from brim to brim ... 2Chr 4:2
*t* in a cubit, compassing the sea ... 2Chr 4:3
He made also *t* lavers, and put ... 2Chr 4:6
he made *t* candlesticks of gold ... 2Chr 4:7
He made also *t* tables, and placed ... 2Chr 4:8
days the land was quiet *t* years ... 2Chr 14:1
the children of Seir *t* thousand ... 2Chr 25:11
other *t* thousand left alive did ... 2Chr 25:12
*t* thousand measures of wheat ... 2Chr 27:5
and *t* thousand of barley ... 2Chr 27:5
*t* bullocks, an hundred rams, and ... 2Chr 29:32
bullocks and *t* thousand sheep ... 2Chr 30:24
months and *t* days in Jerusalem ... 2Chr 36:9
to fulfil threescore and *t* years ... 2Chr 36:21
a second sort four hundred and *t* ... Ezr 1:10
and with him an hundred and *t* males .. Ezr 8:12
*t* of their brethren with them, ... Ezr 8:24
came, they said unto us *t* times ... Neh 4:12
once in *t* days store of all sorts ... Neh 5:18
to bring one of *t* to dwell in ... Neh 11:1
I will pay *t* thousand talents of ... Est 3:9
The *t* sons of Haman the son of ... Est 9:10
palace, and the *t* sons of Haman ... Est 9:12
let Haman's *t* sons be hanged upon ... Est 9:13
and they hanged Haman's *t* sons ... Est 9:14
These *t* times have ye reproached ... Job 19:3
afraid of *t* thousands of people ... Ps 3:6
and an instrument of *t* strings ... Ps 33:2
years are threescore years and *t* ... Ps 90:10
*t* thousand at thy right hand ... Ps 91:7
Upon an instrument of *t* strings ... Ps 92:3
an instrument of *t* strings will I ... Ps 144:9
*t* thousands in our streets ... Ps 144:13
the wise more than *t* mighty men ... Eccl 7:19
the chiefest among *t* thousand ... Song 5:10
*t* acres of vineyard shall yield ... Is 5:10
dial of Ahaz, *t* degrees backward ... Is 38:8
So the sun returned *t* degrees ... Is 38:8
even *t* men with him, came unto ... Jer 41:1
the *t* men that were with him, and ... Jer 41:2
But *t* men were found among them ... Jer 41:8
And it came to pass after *t* days ... Jer 42:7
the entry of the gate, *t* cubits ... Eze 40:11
breadth of the door was *t* cubits ... Eze 41:2
a walk of *t* cubits breadth inward ... Eze 42:4
the breadth shall be *t* thousand ... Eze 45:1
and the breadth of *t* thousand ... Eze 45:3
the *t* thousand of breadth, shall ... Eze 45:5
cor, which is an homer of *t* baths ... Eze 45:14
for *t* baths are an homer ... Eze 45:14
and of *t* thousand in breadth ... Eze 48:9
toward the west *t* thousand in ... Eze 48:10
toward the east *t* thousand in ... Eze 48:10
length, and *t* thousand in breadth ... Eze 48:13
and the breadth *t* thousand ... Eze 48:13
shall be *t* thousand eastward ... Eze 48:18
and *t* thousand westward ... Eze 48:18
servants, I beseech thee, *t* days ... Dan 1:12
matter, and proved them *t* days ... Dan 1:14
at the end of *t* days their ... Dan 1:15
he found them *t* times better than ... Dan 1:20
and it had *t* horns ... Dan 7:7
unto him, and *t* thousand times ... Dan 7:10
*t* thousand stood before him ... Dan 7:10
of the *t* horns that were in his ... Dan 7:20
the *t* horns out of this kingdom ... Dan 7:24
are *t* kings that shall arise ... Dan 7:24
shall cast down many *t* thousands ... Dan 11:12
forth by an hundred shall leave *t* ... Amos 5:3
if there remain *t* men in one ... Amos 6:9
or with *t* thousands of rivers of ... Mic 6:7
twenty measures, there were but *t* ... Hag 2:16
these threescore and *t* years ... Zec 1:12
and the breadth thereof *t* cubits ... Zec 5:2
that *t* men shall take hold out of ... Zec 8:23
which owed him *t* thousand talents ... Mt 18:24
And when the *t* heard it, they were ... Mt 20:24
heaven be likened unto *t* virgins ... Mt 25:1
it unto him which hath *t* talents ... Mt 25:28
And when the *t* heard it, they ... Mk 10:41
whether he be able with *t* ... Lk 14:31
woman having *t* pieces of silver ... Lk 15:8
there met him *t* men that were ... Lk 17:12
said, Were there not *t* cleansed ... Lk 17:17
And he called his *t* servants ... Lk 19:13
and delivered them *t* pounds ... Lk 19:13
thy pound hath gained *t* pounds ... Lk 19:16
have thou authority over *t* cities ... Lk 19:17
give it to him that hath *t* pounds ... Lk 19:24
unto him, Lord, he hath *t* pounds ... Lk 19:25
and horsemen threescore and *t* ... Acts 23:23
among them more than *t* days ... Acts 25:6
For though ye have *t* thousand ... 1Cor 4:15
than *t* thousand words in an ... 1Cor 14:19
the Lord cometh with *t* thousands ... Jude 14
ye shall have tribulation *t* days ... Rev 2:10
the number of them was *t* thousand ... Rev 5:11
thousand times *t* thousand ... Rev 5:11
*t* horns, and seven crowns upon his ... Rev 12:3
*t* horns, and upon his horns ... Rev 13:1
and upon his horns *t* crowns ... Rev 13:1
having seven heads and *t* horns ... Rev 17:3
hath the seven heads and *t* horns ... Rev 17:7
the *t* horns which thou sawest are ... Rev 17:12
which thou sawest are *t* kings ... Rev 17:12
the *t* horns which thou sawest ... Rev 17:16

**TEND**
diligent *t* only to plenteousness ... Prov 21:5

**TENDER**
unto the herd, and fetcht a calf *t* ... Gen 18:7
Leah was *t* eyed ... Gen 29:17
knoweth that the children are *t* ... Gen 33:13
that the man that is *t* among you ... Deut 28:54
The *t* and delicate woman ... Deut 28:56
as the small rain upon the *t* herb ... Deut 32:2
as the *t* grass springing out of ... 2Sa 23:4
Because thine heart was *t* ... 2Kin 22:19
Solomon my son is young and *t* ... 1Chr 22:5
hath chosen, is yet young and *t* ... 1Chr 29:1
Because thine heart was *t* ... 2Chr 34:27
that the *t* branch thereof will ... Job 14:7
bud of the *t* herb to spring forth ... Job 38:27
O LORD, thy *t* mercies and thy ... Ps 25:6
not thou thy *t* mercies from me ... Ps 40:11
of thy *t* mercies blot out my ... Ps 51:1
to the multitude of thy *t* mercies ... Ps 69:16
he in anger shut up his *t* mercies ... Ps 77:9
let thy *t* mercies speedily ... Ps 79:8
with lovingkindness and *t* mercies ... Ps 103:4
Let thy *t* mercies come unto me, ... Ps 119:77
Great are thy *t* mercies, O LORD ... Ps 119:156
his *t* mercies are over all his ... Ps 145:9
For I was my father's son, *t* ... Prov 4:3
but the *t* mercies of the wicked ... Prov 12:10
the *t* grass sheweth itself, and ... Prov 27:25
the vines with the *t* grape give a ... Song 2:13
for our vines have *t* grapes ... Song 2:15
whether the *t* grape appear, and ... Song 7:12
thou shalt no more be called *t* ... Is 47:1
grow up before him as a *t* plant ... Is 53:2
top of his young twigs a *t* one ... Eze 17:22
*t* love with the prince of the ... Dan 1:9
in the *t* grass of the field ... Dan 4:15
in the *t* grass of the field ... Dan 4:23
When his branch is yet *t*, and ... Mt 24:32
When her branch is yet *t*, and ... Mk 13:28
Through the *t* mercy of our God ... Lk 1:78
is very pitiful, and of *t* mercy ... Jas 5:11

**TENDERHEARTED**
when Rehoboam was young and *t* ... 2Chr 13:7
And be ye kind one to another, *t* ... Eph 4:32

**TENDERNESS**
the ground for delicateness and *t* ... Deut 28:56

**TENDETH**
labour of the righteous *t* to life ... Prov 10:16
As righteousness *t* to life ... Prov 11:19
than is meet, but it *t* to poverty ... Prov 11:24
talk of the lips *t* only to penury ... Prov 14:23
The fear of the LORD *t* to life ... Prov 19:23

**TENONS**
Two *t* shall there be in one board ... Ex 26:17
under one board for his two *t* ... Ex 26:19
under another board for his two *t* ... Ex 26:19
One board had two *t*, equally ... Ex 36:22
under one board for his two *t* ... Ex 36:24
under another board for his two *t* ... Ex 36:24

**TENOR**
according to the *t* of these words ... Gen 43:7
for after the *t* of these words I ... Ex 34:27

**TEN'S**
I will not destroy it for *t* sake ... Gen 18:32

**TENS**
rulers of fifties, and rulers of *t* ... Ex 18:21
rulers of fifties, and rulers of *t* ... Ex 18:25
over fifties, and captains over *t* ... Deut 1:15

**TENT**
and he was uncovered within his *t* ... Gen 9:21
east of Beth-el, and pitched his *t* ... Gen 12:8
unto the place where his *t* had ... Gen 13:3
pitched his *t* toward Sodom ... Gen 13:12
Abram removed his *t* ... Gen 13:18
he sat in the *t* door in the heat ... Gen 18:1
ran to meet them from the *t* door ... Gen 18:2
hastened into the *t* unto Sarah ... Gen 18:6
And he said, Behold, in the *t* ... Gen 18:9
And Sarah heard it in the *t* door ... Gen 18:10
her into his mother Sarah's *t* ... Gen 24:67
pitched his *t* in the valley of ... Gen 26:17
the LORD, and pitched his *t* there ... Gen 26:25
had pitched his *t* in the mount ... Gen 31:25
Jacob's *t*, and into Leah's *t* ... Gen 31:33
Then went he out of Leah's *t* ... Gen 31:33
and entered into Rachel's *t* ... Gen 31:33
And Laban searched all the *t* ... Gen 31:34
pitched his *t* before the city ... Gen 33:18
field, where he had spread his *t* ... Gen 33:19
spread his *t* beyond the tower of ... Gen 35:21
and they came into the *t* ... Ex 18:7
loops, and couple the *t* together ... Ex 26:11
of the curtains of the *t*, the ... Ex 26:12
length of the curtains of the *t* ... Ex 26:13
for the *t* of rams' skins dyed red ... Ex 26:14
an hanging for the door of the *t* ... Ex 26:36
and stood every man at his *t* door ... Ex 33:8
every man in his *t* door ... Ex 33:10
The tabernacle, his *t*, and his ... Ex 35:11
for the *t* over the tabernacle ... Ex 36:14
of brass to couple the *t* together ... Ex 36:18
for the *t* of rams' skins dyed red ... Ex 36:19
*t* of the congregation finished ... Ex 39:32
the tabernacle unto Moses, the *t* ... Ex 39:33
for the *t* of the congregation, ... Ex 39:40
of the *t* of the congregation ... Ex 40:2
of the *t* of the congregation ... Ex 40:6
between the *t* of the congregation ... Ex 40:7
abroad the *t* over the tabernacle ... Ex 40:19
covering of the *t* above upon it ... Ex 40:19
in the *t* of the congregation ... Ex 40:22
in the *t* of the congregation ... Ex 40:24
*t* of the congregation before the ... Ex 40:26
of the *t* of the congregation ... Ex 40:29
between the *t* of the congregation ... Ex 40:30
into the *t* of the congregation ... Ex 40:32
covered the *t* of the congregation ... Ex 40:34
into the *t* of the congregation ... Ex 40:35
abroad out of his *t* seven days ... Lev 14:8
shall be the tabernacle, and the *t* ... Num 3:25
namely, the *t* of the testimony ... Num 9:15
every man in the door of his *t* ... Num 11:10
the law, when a man dieth in a *t* ... Num 19:14
all that come into the *t*, and all ... Num 19:14
and all that is in the *t* ... Num 19:14
water, and sprinkle it upon the *t* ... Num 19:18
the man of Israel into the *t* ... Num 25:8
in the earth in the midst of my *t* ... Josh 7:21
and they ran unto the *t* ... Josh 7:22
and, behold, it was hid in his *t* ... Josh 7:22
them out of the midst of the *t* ... Josh 7:23
his asses, and his sheep, and his *t* ... Josh 7:24
pitched his *t* unto the plain of ... Judg 4:11
fled away on his feet to the *t* of ... Judg 4:17
had turned in unto her into the *t* ... Judg 4:18
her, Stand in the door of the *t* ... Judg 4:20
Heber's wife took a nail of the *t* ... Judg 4:21
And when he came into her *t* ... Judg 4:22
shall she be above women in the *t* ... Judg 5:24
of Israel every man unto his *t* ... Judg 7:8
host of Midian, and came unto a *t* ... Judg 7:13
it, that the *t* lay along ... Judg 7:13
We will not any of us go to his *t* ... Judg 20:8
and they fled every man into his *t* ... 1Sa 4:10
people he sent every man to his *t* ... 1Sa 13:2
but he put his armour in his *t* ... 1Sa 17:54
this day, but have walked in a *t* ... 2Sa 7:6
So they spread Absalom a *t* upon ... 2Sa 16:22
Israel fled every one to his *t* ... 2Sa 18:17
had fled every man to his *t* ... 2Sa 19:8
from the city, every man to his *t* ... 2Sa 20:22
of the camp, they went into one *t* ... 2Kin 7:8
again, and entered into another *t* ... 2Kin 7:8
ark of God, and pitched for it a *t* ... 1Chr 15:1
set it in the midst of the *t* that ... 1Chr 16:1
but have gone from *t* to *t* ... 1Chr 17:5
pitched a *t* for it at Jerusalem ... 2Chr 1:4
and they fled every man to his *t* ... 2Chr 25:22
the *t* which he placed among men ... Ps 78:60
shall the Arabian pitch *t* there ... Is 13:20
removed from me as a shepherd's *t* ... Is 38:12
them out as a *t* to dwell in ... Is 40:22
Enlarge the place of thy *t* ... Is 54:2
to stretch forth my *t* any more ... Jer 10:20
they rise up every man in his *t* ... Jer 37:10

**TENTH**
continually until the *t* month ... Gen 8:5
in the *t* month, on the first day ... Gen 8:5
will surely give the *t* unto thee ... Gen 28:22
In the *t* day of this month they ... Ex 12:3
an omer is the *t* part of an ephah ... Ex 16:36

with the one lamb a *t* deal of ... Ex 29:40
bring for his offering the *t* part ... Lev 5:11
the *t* part of an ephah of fine ... Lev 6:20
three *t* deals of fine flour for a ... Lev 14:10
one *t* deal of fine flour mingled ... Lev 14:21
on the *t* day of the month, ye ... Lev 16:29
two *t* deals of fine flour mingled ... Lev 23:13
two wave loaves of two *t* deals ... Lev 23:17
Also on the *t* day of this seventh ... Lev 23:27
two *t* deals shall be in one cake ... Lev 24:5
on the *t* day of the seventh month ... Lev 25:9
the *t* shall be holy unto the LORD ... Lev 27:32
the *t* part of an ephah of barley ... Num 5:15
On the *t* day Ahiezer the son of ... Num 7:66
*t* deal of flour mingled with the ... Num 15:4
*t* deals of flour mingled with the ... Num 15:6
a meat offering of three *t* deals ... Num 15:9
*t* in Israel for an inheritance ... Num 18:21
even a *t* part of the tithe ... Num 18:26
a *t* part of an ephah of flour for ... Num 28:5
two *t* deals of flour for a meat ... Num 28:9
three *t* deals of flour for a meat ... Num 28:12
two *t* deals of flour for a meat ... Num 28:12
a several *t* deal of flour mingled ... Num 28:13
three *t* deals shall ye offer for ... Num 28:20
bullock, and two *t* deals for a ram ... Num 28:20
A several *t* deal shalt thou offer ... Num 28:21
three *t* deals unto one bullock, ... Num 28:28
two *t* deals unto one ram, ... Num 28:28
A several *t* deal unto one lamb, ... Num 28:29
three *t* deals for a bullock ... Num 29:3
and two *t* deals for a ram, ... Num 29:3
And one *t* deal for one lamb, ... Num 29:4
ye shall have on the *t* day of ... Num 29:7
three *t* deals to a bullock ... Num 29:9
and two *t* deals to one ram, ... Num 29:9
A several *t* deal for one lamb, ... Num 29:10
three *t* deals unto every bullock ... Num 29:14
two *t* deals to each ram of the ... Num 29:14
a several *t* deal to each lamb of ... Num 29:15
even to his *t* generation shall he ... Deut 23:2
even to their *t* generation shall ... Deut 23:3
on the *t* day of the first month ... Josh 4:19
he will take the *t* of your seed ... 1Sa 8:15
He will take the *t* of your sheep ... 1Sa 8:17
year of his reign, in the *t* month ... 2Kin 25:1
in the *t* day of the month, that ... 2Kin 25:1
Jeremiah the *t*, Machbanai the ... 1Chr 12:13
to Jeshua, the *t* to Shecaniah, ... 1Chr 24:11
The *t* to Shimei, he, his sons, and ... 1Chr 25:17
The *t* captain for the *t* month ... 1Chr 27:13
the *t* month to examine the matter ... Ezr 10:16
his house royal in the *t* month ... Est 2:16
But yet in it shall be a *t* ... Is 6:13
Jeremiah from the LORD in the *t* ... Jer 32:1
king of Judah, in the *t* month ... Jer 39:1
year of his reign, in the *t* month ... Jer 52:4
in the *t* day of the month, that ... Jer 52:4
in the *t* day of the month, which ... Jer 52:12
the *t* day of the month, that ... Eze 20:1
in the ninth year, in the *t* month ... Eze 24:1
in the *t* day of the month, the ... Eze 24:1
In the *t* year, in the *t* month ... Eze 29:1
of our captivity, in the *t* month ... Eze 33:21
in the *t* day of the month, in the ... Eze 40:1
contain the *t* part of an homer ... Eze 45:11
the ephah the *t* part of an homer ... Eze 45:11
ye shall offer the *t* part of a ... Eze 45:14
the seventh, and the fast of the *t* ... Zec 8:19
for it was about the *t* hour ... Jn 1:39
also Abraham gave a *t* part of all ... Heb 7:2
Abraham gave the *t* of the spoils ... Heb 7:4
the *t* part of the city fell, and ... Rev 11:13
the *t*, a chrysoprasus ... Rev 21:20

**TENTMAKERS**

by their occupation they were *t* ... Acts 18:3

**TENTS**

the father of such as dwell in *t* ... Gen 4:20
he shall dwell in the *t* of Shem ... Gen 9:27
Abram, had flocks, and herds, and *t* ... Gen 13:5
was a plain man, dwelling in *t* ... Gen 25:27
and into the two maidservants' *t* ... Gen 31:33
man for them which are in his *t* ... Ex 16:16
of Israel shall pitch their *t* ... Num 1:52
of Israel pitched their *t* ... Num 9:17
tabernacle they rested in their *t* ... Num 9:18
of the LORD they abode in their *t* ... Num 9:20
of Israel abode in their *t* ... Num 9:22
of the LORD they rested in the *t* ... Num 9:23
that they dwell in, whether in *t* ... Num 13:19
from the *t* of these wicked men, ... Num 16:26
and stood in the door of their *t* ... Num 16:27
his *t* according to their tribes ... Num 24:2
How goodly are thy *t*, O Jacob, and ... Num 24:5
And ye murmured in your *t*, and said. Deut 1:27
out a place to pitch your *t* in ... Deut 1:33
them, Get you into your *t* again ... Deut 5:30
and their households, and their *t* ... Deut 11:6
in the morning, and go unto thy *t* ... Deut 16:7
and, Issachar, in thy *t* ... Deut 33:18
the people removed from their *t* ... Josh 3:14
return ye, and get you unto your *t* ... Josh 22:4
and they went unto their *t* ... Josh 22:6
sent them away also unto their *t* ... Josh 22:7
with much riches unto your *t* ... Josh 22:8
up with their cattle and their *t* ... Judg 6:5
dwelt in *t* on the east of Nobah ... Judg 8:11
and they spoiled their *t* ... 1Sa 17:53
and Israel, and Judah, abide in *t* ... 2Sa 11:11
every man to his *t*, O Israel ... 2Sa 20:1
king, and went unto their *t* joyful ... 1Kin 8:66
to your *t*, O Israel ... 1Kin 12:16
So Israel departed unto their *t* ... 1Kin 12:16
in the twilight, and left their *t* ... 2Kin 7:7
asses tied, and the *t* as they were ... 2Kin 7:10
spoiled the *t* of the Syrians ... 2Kin 7:16
and the people fled into their *t* ... 2Kin 8:21
of Israel dwelt in their *t* ... 2Kin 13:5
and they fled every man to their *t* ... 2Kin 14:12
king of Judah, and smote their *t* ... 1Chr 4:41
they dwelt in their *t* throughout ... 1Chr 5:10
sent the people away into their *t* ... 2Chr 7:10
every man to your *t*, O Israel, and ... 2Chr 10:16
So all Israel went to their *t* ... 2Chr 10:16
They smote also the *t* of cattle ... 2Chr 14:15
in the gates of the *t* of the LORD ... 2Chr 31:2
and there abode we in *t* three days ... Ezr 8:15
and let none dwell in their *t* ... Ps 69:25
of Israel to dwell in their *t* ... Ps 78:55
to dwell in the *t* of wickedness ... Ps 84:10
But murmured in their *t*, and ... Ps 106:25
that I dwell in the *t* of Kedar ... Ps 120:5
as the *t* of Kedar, as the ... Song 1:5
thy kids beside the shepherds' *t* ... Song 1:8
suddenly are my *t* spoiled ... Jer 4:20
they shall pitch their *t* against ... Jer 6:3
again the captivity of Jacob's *t* ... Jer 30:18
all your days ye shall dwell in *t* ... Jer 35:7
But we have dwelt in *t*, and have ... Jer 35:10
Their *t* and their flocks shall ... Jer 49:29
I saw the *t* of Cushan in ... Hab 3:7
shall save the *t* of Judah first ... Zec 12:7
beasts that shall be in these *t* ... Zec 14:15

**TERAH** (*te'-rah*) See THARA. *Father of Abraham.*

nine and twenty years, and begat *T* ... Gen 11:24
lived after he begat *T* an hundred ... Gen 11:25
*T* lived seventy years, and begat ... Gen 11:26
these are the generations of *T* ... Gen 11:27
*T* begat Abram, Nahor, and Haran ... Gen 11:27
*T* in the land of his nativity ... Gen 11:28
*T* took Abram his son, and Lot the ... Gen 11:31
the days of *T* were two hundred and .. Gen 11:32
and *T* died in Haran ... Gen 11:32
of the flood in old time, even *T* ... Josh 24:2
Serug, Nahor, *T*, ... 1Chr 1:26

**TERAPHIM**

of gods, and made an ephod, and *t* ... Judg 17:5
is in these houses an ephod, and *t* ... Judg 18:14
image, and the ephod, and the *t* ... Judg 18:17
carved image, the ephod, and the *t* ... Judg 18:18
and he took the ephod, and the *t* ... Judg 18:20
and without an ephod, and without *t* ... Hos 3:4

**TERESH** (*te'-resh*) *A servant of King Ahasuerus.*

king's chamberlains, Bigthan and *T* ... Est 2:21
had told of Bigthana and *T* ... Est 6:2

**TERMED**

Thou shalt no more be *t* Forsaken ... Is 62:4
thy land any more be *t* Desolate ... Is 62:4

**TERRACES**

trees *t* to the house of the LORD ... 2Chr 9:11

**TERRESTRIAL**

celestial bodies, and bodies *t* ... 1Cor 15:40
and the glory of the *t* is another ... 1Cor 15:40

**TERRIBLE**

for it is a *t* thing that I will ... Ex 34:10
*t* wilderness, which ye saw by the ... Deut 1:19
is among you, a mighty God and *t* ... Deut 7:21
*t* wilderness, wherein were fiery ... Deut 8:15
a great God, a mighty, and a *t* ... Deut 10:17
*t* things, which thine eyes have ... Deut 10:21
of an angel of God, very *t* ... Judg 13:6
to do for you great things and *t* ... 2Sa 7:23
*t* God, that keepeth covenant and ... Neh 1:5
the LORD, which is great and *t* ... Neh 4:14
great, the mighty, and the *t* God ... Neh 9:32
with God is *t* majesty ... Job 37:22
the glory of his nostrils is *t* ... Job 39:20
his teeth are *t* round about ... Job 41:14
hand shall teach thee *t* things ... Ps 45:4
For the LORD most high is *t* ... Ps 47:2
By *t* things in righteousness wilt ... Ps 65:5
How *t* art thou in thy works ... Ps 66:3
he is *t* in his doing toward the ... Ps 66:5
thou art *t* out of thy holy places ... Ps 68:35
he is *t* to the kings of the earth ... Ps 76:12
them praise thy great and *t* name ... Ps 99:3
Ham, and *t* things by the Red sea ... Ps 106:22
speak of the might of thy *t* acts ... Ps 145:6
*t* as an army with banners ... Song 6:4
*t* as an army with banners ... Song 6:10
lay low the haughtiness of the *t* ... Is 13:11
peeled, to a people *t* from their ... Is 18:2
from a people *t* from their ... Is 18:7
from the desert, from a *t* land ... Is 21:1
the city of the *t* nations shall ... Is 25:3
when the blast of the *t* ones is ... Is 25:4
the branch of the *t* ones shall be ... Is 25:5
the multitude of the *t* ones shall ... Is 29:5
For the *t* one is brought to ... Is 29:20
the prey of the *t* shall be ... Is 49:25
When thou didst *t* things which we ... Is 64:3
thee out of the hand of the *t* ... Jer 15:21
LORD is with me as a mighty *t* one ... Jer 20:11
an oven because of the *t* famine ... Lam 5:10
as the colour of the *t* crystal ... Eze 1:22
upon thee, the *t* of the nations ... Eze 28:7
the *t* of the nations, shall be ... Eze 30:11
the *t* of the nations, have cut ... Eze 31:12
the *t* of the nations, all of them ... Eze 32:12
and the form thereof was *t* ... Dan 2:31
a fourth beast, dreadful and *t* ... Dan 7:7
of the LORD is great and very *t* ... Joel 2:11
the *t* day of the LORD come ... Joel 2:31
They are *t* and dreadful ... Hab 1:7
The LORD will be *t* unto them ... Zeph 2:11
so *t* was the sight, that Moses ... Heb 12:21

**TERRIBLENESS**

outstretched arm, and with great *t* ... Deut 26:8
thee a name of greatness and *t* ... 1Chr 17:21
Thy *t* hath deceived thee, and the ... Jer 49:16

**TERRIBLY**

he ariseth to shake *t* the earth ... Is 2:19
he ariseth to shake *t* the earth ... Is 2:21
the fir trees shall be *t* shaken ... Nah 2:3

**TERRIFIED**

neither be ye *t* because of them ... Deut 20:3
of wars and commotions, be not *t* ... Lk 21:9
But they were *t* and affrighted, and ... Lk 24:37
in nothing *t* by your adversaries ... Phil 1:28

**TERRIFIEST**

dreams, and *t* me through visions ... Job 7:14

**TERRIFY**

let the blackness of the day *t* it ... Job 3:5
from me, and let not his fear *t* me ... Job 9:34
did the contempt of families *t* me ... Job 31:34
as if I would *t* you by letters ... 2Cor 10:9

**TERROR**

the *t* of God was upon the cities ... Gen 35:5
I will even appoint over you *t* ... Lev 26:16
*t* within, shall destroy both the ... Deut 32:25
in all the great *t* which Moses ... Deut 34:12
that your *t* is fallen upon us, and ... Josh 2:9
from God was a *t* to me, and by ... Job 31:23
my *t* shall not make thee afraid, ... Job 33:7
not be afraid for the *t* by night ... Ps 91:5
hosts, shall lop the bough with *t* ... Is 10:33
of Judah shall be a *t* unto Egypt ... Is 19:17
Thine heart shall meditate *t* ... Is 33:18
and from *t* ... Is 54:14
Be not a *t* unto me ... Jer 17:17
I will make thee a *t* to thyself ... Jer 20:4
out arm, and with great *t* ... Jer 32:21
which cause their *t* to be on all ... Eze 26:17
I will make thee a *t*, and thou ... Eze 26:21
thou shalt be a *t*, and never shalt ... Eze 27:36
thou shalt be a *t*, and never shalt ... Eze 28:19
which caused *t* in the land of the ... Eze 32:23
which caused their *t* in the land ... Eze 32:24
though their *t* was caused in the ... Eze 32:25
though they caused their *t* in the ... Eze 32:26
though they were the *t* of the ... Eze 32:27
with their *t* they are ashamed of ... Eze 32:30
For I have caused my *t* in the ... Eze 32:32
rulers are not a *t* to good works ... Rom 13:3
therefore the *t* of the Lord ... 2Cor 5:11
and be not afraid of their *t* ... 1Pet 3:14

**TERRORS**

stretched out arm, and by great *t* ... Deut 4:34
the *t* of God do set themselves in ... Job 6:4
*T* shall make him afraid on every ... Job 18:11
shall bring him to the king of *t* ... Job 18:14
*t* are upon him ... Job 20:25
they are in the *t* of the shadow ... Job 24:17
*T* take hold on him as waters, a ... Job 27:20
*T* are turned upon me ... Job 30:15
the *t* of death are fallen upon me ... Ps 55:4
they are utterly consumed with *t* ... Ps 73:19
I suffer thy *t* I am distracted ... Ps 88:15
thy *t* have cut me off ... Ps 88:16
it suddenly, and *t* upon the city ... Jer 15:8
in a solemn day my *t* round about ... Lam 2:22
*t* by reason of the sword shall be ... Eze 21:12

**TERTIUS** (*tur'-she-us*) *An assistant of Paul.*

I *T*, who wrote this epistle, ... Rom 16:22

**TERTULLUS** (*tur-tul'-lus*) *An orator who opposed Paul.*

and with a certain orator named *T* ... Acts 24:1
*T* began to accuse him, saying, ... Acts 24:2

**TESTAMENT**

For this is my blood of the new *t* ... Mt 26:28
This is my blood of the new *t* ... Mk 14:24
This cup is the new *t* in my blood ... Lk 22:20
This cup is the new *t* in my blood ... 1Cor 11:25
us able ministers of the new *t* ... 2Cor 3:6
away in the reading of the old *t* ... 2Cor 3:14
Jesus made a surety of a better *t* ... Heb 7:22
he is the mediator of the new *t* ... Heb 9:15
that were under the first *t* ... Heb 9:15
For where a *t* is, there must also ... Heb 9:16
For a *t* is of force after men are ... Heb 9:17
*t* was dedicated without blood ... Heb 9:18
This is the blood of the *t* which ... Heb 9:20
in his temple the ark of his *t* ... Rev 11:19

**TESTATOR**

necessity be the death of the *t* ... Heb 9:16
at all while the *t* liveth ... Heb 9:17

**TESTIFIED**
and it hath been *t* to his owner ... Ex 21:29
hath *t* falsely against his ... Deut 19:18
seeing the LORD hath *t* against me ... Ruth 1:21
for thy mouth hath *t* against thee ... 2Sa 1:16
Yet the LORD *t* against Israel, and ... 2Kin 17:13
which he *t* against them ... 2Kin 17:15
and they *t* against them ... 2Chr 24:19
slew thy prophets which *t* against ... Neh 9:26
I *t* against them in the day ... Neh 13:15
Then I *t* against them, and said ... Neh 13:21
the saying of the woman, which *t* ... Jn 4:39
For Jesus himself *t*, that a ... Jn 4:44
he was troubled in spirit, and *t* ... Jn 13:21
And they, when they had *t* and ... Acts 8:25
*t* to the Jews that Jesus was ... Acts 18:5
for as thou hast *t* of me in ... Acts 23:11
*t* the kingdom of God, persuading ... Acts 28:23
because we have *t* of God that he ... 1Cor 15:15
we also have forewarned you and *t* ... 1Th 4:6
for all, to be *t* in due time ... 1Ti 2:6
But one in a certain place *t* ... Heb 2:6
signify, when it *t* beforehand the ... 1Pet 1:11
of God which he hath *t* of his Son ... 1Jn 5:9
*t* of the truth that is in thee, ... 3Jn 3

**TESTIFIEDST**
*t* against them, that thou ... Neh 9:29
*t* against them by thy spirit in ... Neh 9:30

**TESTIFIETH**
the pride of Israel *t* to his face ... Hos 7:10
he hath seen and heard, that he *t* ... Jn 3:32
disciple which *t* of these things ... Jn 21:24
For he *t*, Thou art a priest for ... Heb 7:17
He which *t* these things saith, ... Rev 22:20

**TESTIFY**
but one witness shall not *t* ... Num 35:30
I *t* against you this day that ye ... Deut 8:19
rise up against any man to *t* ... Deut 19:16
that this song shall *t* against ... Deut 31:21
which I *t* among you this day ... Deut 32:46
thou didst *t* against them ... Neh 9:34
thine own lips *t* against thee ... Job 15:6
Israel, and I will *t* against thee ... Ps 50:7
my people, and I will *t* unto thee ... Ps 81:8
thee, and our sins *t* against us ... Is 59:12
our iniquities *t* against us ... Jer 14:7
of Israel doth *t* to his face ... Hos 5:5
*t* in the house of Jacob, saith ... Amos 3:13
*t* against me ... Mic 6:3
that he may *t* unto them, lest ... Lk 16:28
not that any should *t* of man ... Jn 2:25
do know, and *t* that we have seen ... Jn 3:11
and they are they which *t* of me ... Jn 5:39
me it hateth, because I *t* of it ... Jn 7:7
from the Father, he shall *t* of me ... Jn 15:26
And with many other words did he *t* ... Acts 2:40
to *t* that it is he which was ... Acts 10:42
to *t* the gospel of the grace of ... Acts 20:24
the beginning, if they would *t* ... Acts 26:5
For I *t* again to every man that ... Gal 5:3
*t* in the Lord, that ye henceforth ... Eph 4:17
do *t* that the Father sent the Son ... 1Jn 4:14
to *t* unto you these things in the ... Rev 22:16
For I *t* unto every man that ... Rev 22:18

**TESTIFYING**
*T* both to the Jews, and also to ... Acts 20:21
was righteous, God *t* of his gifts ... Heb 11:4
*t* that this is the true grace of ... 1Pet 5:12

**TESTIMONIES**
These are the *t*, and the statutes, ... Deut 4:45
of the LORD your God, and his *t* ... Deut 6:17
to come, saying, What mean the *t* ... Deut 6:20
and his judgments, and his *t* ... 1Kin 2:3
his *t* which he testified against ... 2Kin 17:15
to keep his commandments and his *t* ... 2Kin 23:3
to keep thy commandments, thy *t* ... 1Chr 29:19
keep his commandments, and his *t* ... 2Chr 34:31
unto thy commandments and thy *t* ... Neh 9:34
as keep his covenant and his *t* ... Ps 25:10
most high God, and kept not his *t* ... Ps 78:56
Thy *t* are very sure ... Ps 93:5
they kept his *t*, and the ordinance ... Ps 99:7
Blessed are they that keep his *t* ... Ps 119:2
have rejoiced in the way of thy *t* ... Ps 119:14
for I have kept thy *t* ... Ps 119:22
Thy *t* also are my delight, and my ... Ps 119:24
I have stuck unto thy *t* ... Ps 119:31
Incline my heart unto thy *t* ... Ps 119:36
speak of thy *t* also before kings ... Ps 119:46
and turned my feet unto thy *t* ... Ps 119:59
and those that have known thy *t* ... Ps 119:79
but I will consider thy *t* ... Ps 119:95
for thy *t* are my meditation ... Ps 119:99
Thy *t* have I taken as an heritage ... Ps 119:111
therefore I love thy *t* ... Ps 119:119
that I may know thy *t* ... Ps 119:125
Thy *t* are wonderful ... Ps 119:129
Thy *t* that thou hast commanded ... Ps 119:138
of thy *t* is everlasting ... Ps 119:144
save me, and I shall keep thy *t* ... Ps 119:146
Concerning thy *t*, I have known of ... Ps 119:152
yet do I not decline from thy *t* ... Ps 119:157
My soul hath kept thy *t* ... Ps 119:167
I have kept thy precepts and thy *t* ... Ps 119:168
nor in his statutes, nor in his *t* ... Jer 44:23

**TESTIMONY**
so Aaron laid it up before the *T* ... Ex 16:34
ark the *t* which I shall give thee ... Ex 25:16
put the *t* that I shall give thee ... Ex 25:21
which are upon the ark of the *t* ... Ex 25:22
within the vail the ark of the *t* ... Ex 26:33
of the *t* in the most holy place ... Ex 26:34
the vail, which is before the *t* ... Ex 27:21
vail that is by the ark of the *t* ... Ex 30:6
the mercy seat that is over the *t* ... Ex 30:6
therewith, and the ark of the *t* ... Ex 30:26
put of it before the *t* in the ... Ex 30:36
congregation, and the ark of the *t* ... Ex 31:7
upon mount Sinai, two tables of *t* ... Ex 31:18
tables of the *t* were in his hand ... Ex 32:15
two tables of *t* in Moses' hand ... Ex 34:29
even of the tabernacle of *t* ... Ex 38:21
The ark of the *t*, and the staves ... Ex 39:35
put therein the ark of the *t* ... Ex 40:3
incense before the ark of the *t* ... Ex 40:5
put the *t* into the ark, and set ... Ex 40:20
and covered the ark of the *t* ... Ex 40:21
the mercy seat that is upon the *t* ... Lev 16:13
Without the vail of the *t* ... Lev 24:3
Levites over the tabernacle of *t* ... Num 1:50
round about the tabernacle of *t* ... Num 1:53
the charge of the tabernacle of *t* ... Num 1:53
and cover the ark of *t* with it ... Num 4:5
seat that was upon the ark of *t* ... Num 7:89
namely, the tent of the *t* ... Num 9:15
from off the tabernacle of the *t* ... Num 10:11
of the congregation before the *t* ... Num 17:4
Aaron's rod again before the *t* ... Num 17:10
that bear the ark of the *t* ... Josh 4:16
and this was a *t* in Israel ... Ruth 4:7
crown upon him, and gave him the *t* ... 2Kin 11:12
him the crown, and gave him the *t* ... 2Chr 23:11
the *t* of the LORD is sure, making ... Ps 19:7
For he established a *t* in Jacob ... Ps 78:5
he ordained in Joseph for a *t* ... Ps 81:5
shall I keep the *t* of thy mouth ... Ps 119:88
unto the *t* of Israel, to give ... Ps 122:4
my *t* that I shall teach them, ... Ps 132:12
Bind up the *t*, seal the law among ... Is 8:16
To the law and to the *t* ... Is 8:20
commanded, for a *t* unto them ... Mt 8:4
for a *t* against them and the ... Mt 10:18
commanded, for a *t* unto them ... Mk 1:44
your feet for a *t* against them ... Mk 6:11
for my sake, for a *t* against them ... Mk 13:9
commanded, for a *t* unto them ... Lk 5:14
your feet for a *t* against them ... Lk 9:5
And it shall turn to you for a *t* ... Lk 21:13
and no man receiveth his *t* ... Jn 3:32
He that hath received his *t* hath ... Jn 3:33
But I receive not *t* from man ... Jn 5:34
that the *t* of two men is true ... Jn 8:17
and we know that his *t* is true ... Jn 21:24
to whom also he gave *t*, and said, ... Acts 13:22
which gave *t* unto the word of his ... Acts 14:3
not receive thy *t* concerning me ... Acts 22:18
Even as the *t* of Christ was ... 1Cor 1:6
declaring unto you the *t* of God ... 1Cor 2:1
the *t* of our conscience, that in ... 2Cor 1:12
them that believe (because our *t* ... 2Th 1:10
ashamed of the *t* of our Lord ... 2Ti 1:8
for a *t* of those things which ... Heb 3:5
his translation he had this *t* ... Heb 11:5
of the *t* of Jesus Christ, and of ... Rev 1:2
for the *t* of Jesus Christ ... Rev 1:9
for the *t* which they held ... Rev 6:9
they shall have finished their *t* ... Rev 11:7
Lamb, and by the word of their *t* ... Rev 12:11
have the *t* of Jesus Christ ... Rev 12:17
of the *t* in heaven was opened ... Rev 15:5
brethren that have the *t* of Jesus ... Rev 19:10
for the *t* of Jesus is the spirit ... Rev 19:10

**TETRARCH**
At that time Herod the *t* heard of ... Mt 14:1
and Herod being *t* of Galilee ... Lk 3:1
his brother Philip *t* of Ituraea ... Lk 3:1
and Lysanias the *t* of Abilene ... Lk 3:1
But Herod the *t*, being reproved ... Lk 3:19
Now Herod the *t* heard of all that ... Lk 9:7
been brought up with Herod the *t* ... Acts 13:1

**THADDAEUS** (*thad-de'-us*) See JUDE, LEBBAEUS. *A disciple of Jesus.*
and Lebbaeus, whose surname was *T* ... Mt 10:3
James the son of Alphaeus, and *T* ... Mk 3:18

**THAHASH** (*tha'-hash*) *A son of Reumah.*
bare also Tebah, and Gaham, and *T* ... Gen 22:24

**THAMAH** (*tha'-mah*) See TAMAH. *A family of exiles.*
of Sisera, the children of *T* ... Ezr 2:53

**THAMAR** (*tha'-mar*) See TAMAR. *Mother of Phares and Zarajan; ancestor of Jesus.*
Judas begat Phares and Zara of *T* ... Mt 1:3

**THAN** See PREFACE.

**THANK**
the LORD, and to record, and to *t* ... 1Chr 16:4
delivered first this psalm to *t* ... 1Chr 16:7
And to stand every morning to *t* ... 1Chr 23:30
we *t* thee, and praise thy glorious ... 1Chr 29:13
*t* offerings into the house of the ... 2Chr 29:31
in sacrifices and *t* offerings ... 2Chr 29:31
*t* offerings, and commanded Judah ... 2Chr 33:16
I *t* thee, and praise thee, O thou ... Dan 2:23
I *t* thee, O Father, Lord of ... Mt 11:25
which love you, what *t* have ye ... Lk 6:32
do good to you, what *t* have ye ... Lk 6:33
hope to receive, what *t* have ye ... Lk 6:34
I *t* thee, O Father, Lord of ... Lk 10:21
Doth he *t* that servant because he ... Lk 17:9
I *t* thee, that I am not as other ... Lk 18:11
I *t* thee that thou hast heard me ... Jn 11:41
I *t* my God through Jesus Christ ... Rom 1:8
I *t* God through Jesus Christ our ... Rom 7:25
I *t* my God always on your behalf, ... 1Cor 1:4
I *t* God that I baptized none of ... 1Cor 1:14
I *t* my God, I speak with tongues ... 1Cor 14:18
I *t* my God upon every remembrance ... Phil 1:3
For this cause also *t* we God ... 1Th 2:13
We are bound to *t* God always for ... 2Th 1:3
I *t* Christ Jesus our Lord, who ... 1Ti 1:12
I *t* God, whom I serve from my ... 2Ti 1:3
I *t* my God, making mention of ... Philem 4

**THANKED**
and bowed himself, and *t* the king ... 2Sa 14:22
he *t* God, and took courage ... Acts 28:15
But God be *t*, that ye were the ... Rom 6:17

**THANKFUL**
be *t* unto him, and bless his name ... Ps 100:4
him not as God, neither were *t* ... Rom 1:21
and be ye *t* ... Col 3:15

**THANKFULNESS**
most noble Felix, with all *t* ... Acts 24:3

**THANKING**
heard in praising and *t* the LORD ... 2Chr 5:13

**THANKS**
Therefore I will give *t* unto thee ... 2Sa 22:50
Give *t* unto the LORD, call upon ... 1Chr 16:8
O give *t* unto the LORD ... 1Chr 16:34
we may give *t* to thy holy name ... 1Chr 16:35
to give *t* to the LORD, because ... 1Chr 16:41
prophesied with a harp, to give *t* ... 1Chr 25:3
to minister, and to give *t* ... 2Chr 31:2
and giving *t* unto the LORD ... Ezr 3:11
them, to praise and to give *t* ... Neh 12:24
companies of them that gave *t* ... Neh 12:31
gave *t* went over against them ... Neh 12:38
that gave *t* in the house of God ... Neh 12:40
the grave who shall give thee *t* ... Ps 6:5
Therefore will I give *t* unto thee ... Ps 18:49
give *t* at the remembrance of his ... Ps 30:4
I will give *t* unto thee for ever ... Ps 30:12
I will give thee *t* in the great ... Ps 35:18
Unto thee, O God, do we give *t* ... Ps 75:1
unto thee do we give *t* ... Ps 75:1
pasture will give thee *t* for ever ... Ps 79:13
thing to give *t* unto the LORD ... Ps 92:1
give *t* at the remembrance of his ... Ps 97:12
O give *t* unto the LORD ... Ps 105:1
O give *t* unto the LORD ... Ps 106:1
to give *t* unto thy holy name, and ... Ps 106:47
O give *t* unto the LORD, for he is ... Ps 107:1
O give *t* unto the LORD ... Ps 118:1
O give *t* unto the LORD ... Ps 118:29
give *t* unto thee because of thy ... Ps 119:62
to give *t* unto the name of the ... Ps 122:4
O Give *t* unto the LORD ... Ps 136:1
O give *t* unto the God of gods ... Ps 136:2
O give *t* to the Lord of lords ... Ps 136:3
O give *t* unto the God of heaven ... Ps 136:26
shall give *t* unto thy name ... Ps 140:13
gave *t* before his God, as he did ... Dan 6:10
loaves and the fishes, and gave *t* ... Mt 15:36
And he took the cup, and gave *t* ... Mt 26:27
took the seven loaves, and gave *t* ... Mk 8:6
the cup, and when he had given *t* ... Mk 14:23
gave *t* likewise unto the Lord ... Lk 2:38
face at his feet, giving him *t* ... Lk 17:16
And he took the cup, and gave *t* ... Lk 22:17
And he took bread, and gave *t* ... Lk 22:19
and when he had given *t*, he ... Jn 6:11
after that the Lord had given *t* ... Jn 6:23
gave *t* to God in presence of them ... Acts 27:35
to the Lord, for he giveth God *t* ... Rom 14:6
he eateth not, and giveth God *t* ... Rom 14:6
unto whom not only I give *t* ... Rom 16:4
of for that for which I give *t* ... 1Cor 10:30
And when he had given *t*, he brake ... 1Cor 11:24
say Amen at thy giving of *t* ... 1Cor 14:16
For thou verily givest *t* well ... 1Cor 14:17
But *t* be to God, which giveth us ... 1Cor 15:57
*t* may be given by many on our ... 2Cor 1:11
Now *t* be unto God, which always ... 2Cor 2:14
But *t* be to God, which put the ... 2Cor 8:16
*T* be unto God for his unspeakable ... 2Cor 9:15
Cease not to give *t* for you ... Eph 1:16
but rather giving of *t* ... Eph 5:4
Giving *t* always for all things ... Eph 5:20
We give *t* to God and the Father of ... Col 1:3
Giving *t* unto the Father, which ... Col 1:12
the Lord Jesus, giving *t* to God ... Col 3:17
We give *t* to God always for you ... 1Th 1:2
For what *t* can we render to God ... 1Th 3:9
In every thing give *t* ... 1Th 5:18
to give *t* alway to God for you ... 2Th 2:13
intercessions, and giving of *t* ... 1Ti 2:1
of our lips giving *t* to his name ... Heb 13:15
*t* to him that sat on the throne, ... Rev 4:9
Saying, We give thee *t*, O Lord ... Rev 11:17

**THANKSGIVING**
If he offer it for a *t*, then he... Lev 7:12
offer with the sacrifice of *t*... Lev 7:12
of *t* of his peace offerings... Lev 7:13
of his peace offerings for *t*... Lev 7:15
a sacrifice of *t* unto the LORD... Lev 22:29
to begin the *t* in prayer... Neh 11:17
Mattaniah, which was over the *t*... Neh 12:8
I may publish with the voice of *t*... Ps 26:7
Offer unto God *t*... Ps 50:14
song, and will magnify him with *t*... Ps 69:30
come before his presence with *t*... Ps 95:2
Enter into his gates with *t*... Ps 100:4
sacrifice the sacrifices of *t*... Ps 107:22
offer to thee the sacrifice of *t*... Ps 116:17
Sing unto the LORD with *t*... Ps 147:7
shall be found therein, *t*... Is 51:3
And out of them shall proceed *t*... Jer 30:19
a sacrifice of *t* with leaven... Amos 4:5
unto thee with the voice of *t*... Jonah 2:9
grace might through the *t* of many... 2Cor 4:15
which causeth through us *t* to God... 2Cor 9:11
supplication with *t* let your... Phil 4:6
taught, abounding therein with *t*... Col 2:7
and watch in the same with *t*... Col 4:2
with *t* of them which believe... 1Ti 4:3
refused, if it be received with *t*... 1Ti 4:4
and glory, and wisdom, and *t*... Rev 7:12

**THANKSGIVINGS**
with gladness, both with *t*... Neh 12:27
abundant also by many *t* unto God... 2Cor 9:12

**THANKWORTHY**
For this is *t*, if a man for... 1Pet 2:19

**THANSKGIVING**
and songs of praise and *t* unto God... Neh 12:46

**THARA** (*tha'-rah*) See TERAH. *Greek form of Terah.*
Abraham, which was the son of *T*... Lk 3:34

**THARSHISH** (*thar'-shish*) See TARSHISH.
*1. Ships fitted for long voyages.*
navy of *T* with the navy of Hiram... 1Kin 10:22
in three years came the navy of *T*... 1Kin 10:22
of *T* to go to Ophir for gold... 1Kin 22:48
*2. Son of Bilhan.*
and Chenaanah, and Zethan, and *T*... 1Chr 7:10

**THAT** See PREFACE.

**THE** See PREFACE.

**THEATRE**
rushed with one accord into the *t*... Acts 19:29
not adventure himself into the *t*... Acts 19:31

**THEBES** See THEBEZ.

**THEBEZ** (*the'-bez*) *A city in Ephraim.*
Then went Abimelech to *T*, and... Judg 9:50
to *T*, and encamped against *T*... Judg 9:50
from the wall, that he died in *T*... 2Sa 11:21

**THEE** See PREFACE.

**THEE-WARD**
works have been to *t* very good... 1Sa 19:4

**THEFT**
then he shall be sold for his *t*... Ex 22:3
If the *t* be certainly found in... Ex 22:4

**THEFTS**
adulteries, fornications, *t*... Mt 15:19
*T*, covetousness, wickedness,... Mk 7:22
their fornication, nor of their *t*... Rev 9:21

**THEIR** See PREFACE.

**THEIR'S**
thing in Israel shall be *t*... Eze 44:29

**THEIRS**
stranger in a land that is not *t*... Gen 15:13
and every beast of *t* be ours... Gen 34:23
five times so much as any of *t*... Gen 43:34
be *t* for a perpetual statute... Ex 29:9
for *t* is thine own nakedness... Lev 18:10
wicked men, and touch nothing of *t*. Num 16:26
*t*, every meat offering of *t*... Num 18:9
and every sin offering of *t*... Num 18:9
and every trespass offering of *t*... Num 18:9
for *t* was the first lot... Josh 21:10
for *t* was the lot... 1Chr 6:54
I pray thee, be like one of *t*... 2Chr 18:12
words shall stand, mine, or *t*... Jer 44:28
their multitude, nor of any of *t*... Eze 7:11
the dwellingplaces that are not *t*... Hab 1:6
for *t* is the kingdom of heaven... Mt 5:3
for *t* is the kingdom of heaven... Mt 5:10
of Jesus Christ our Lord, both *t*... 1Cor 1:2
unto all men, as *t* also was... 2Ti 3:9

**THELASAR** (*the-la'-sar*) See TELASSAR. *Same as Telassar.*
children of Eden which were in *T*... 2Kin 19:12

**THEM** See PREFACE.

**THEMSELVES** See PREFACE.

**THEN** See PREFACE.

**THENCE**
from *t* it was parted, and became... Gen 2:10
*t* upon the face of all the earth... Gen 11:8
from *t* did the LORD scatter them... Gen 11:9
he removed from *t* unto a mountain... Gen 12:8
And the men rose up from *t*... Gen 18:16
the men turned their faces from *t*... Gen 18:22
Abraham journeyed from *t* toward... Gen 20:1
take a wife unto my son from *t*... Gen 24:7
And Isaac departed *t*, and pitched... Gen 26:17
And he removed from *t*, and digged... Gen 26:22
he went up from *t* to Beer-sheba... Gen 26:23
fetch me from *t* two good kids of... Gen 27:9
I will send, and fetch thee from *t*... Gen 27:45
take thee a wife from *t* of the... Gen 28:2
to take him a wife from *t*... Gen 28:6
removing from *t* all the speckled... Gen 30:32
thither, and buy for us from *t*... Gen 42:2
with the corn, and departed *t*... Gen 42:26
(from *t* is the shepherd, the... Gen 49:24
cut down from *t* a branch with one... Num 13:23
of Israel cut down from *t*... Num 13:24
From *t* they removed, and pitched... Num 21:12
From *t* they removed, and pitched... Num 21:13
And from *t* they went to Beer... Num 21:16
that *t* he might see the utmost... Num 22:41
and curse me them from *t*... Num 23:13
thou mayest curse me them from *t*... Num 23:27
But if from *t* thou shalt seek the... Deut 4:29
thee out *t* through a mighty hand... Deut 5:15
And he brought us out from *t*... Deut 6:23
From *t* they journeyed unto... Deut 10:7
city shall send and fetch him *t*... Deut 19:12
house, if any man fall from *t*... Deut 22:8
the LORD thy God redeemed thee *t*... Deut 24:18
from *t* will the LORD thy God... Deut 30:4
from *t* will he fetch thee... Deut 30:4
house, and bring out *t* the woman... Josh 6:22
From *t* it passed toward Azmon, and... Josh 15:4
Caleb drove *t* the three sons of... Josh 15:14
he went up *t* to the inhabitants... Josh 15:15
went over from *t* toward Luz... Josh 18:13
And the border was drawn *t*... Josh 18:14
from *t* passeth on along on the... Josh 19:13
and goeth out from *t* to Hukkok... Josh 19:34
from *t* he went against the... Judg 1:11
he expelled *t* the three sons of... Judg 1:20
And he went up *t* to Penuel... Judg 8:8
there went from *t* of the family... Judg 18:11
they passed *t* unto mount Ephraim,... Judg 18:13
from *t* am I... Judg 19:18
of Israel departed *t* at that time... Judg 21:24
they went out from *t* every man to... Judg 21:24
that they might bring from *t* the... 1Sa 4:4
shalt thou go on forward from *t*... 1Sa 10:3
And they ran and fetched him *t*... 1Sa 10:23
took *t* a stone, and slang it, and... 1Sa 17:49
David therefore departed *t*... 1Sa 22:1
David went *t* to Mizpeh of Moab... 1Sa 22:3
And David went up from *t*, and dwelt 1Sa 23:29
to bring up from *t* the ark of God... 2Sa 6:2
fetched *t* a wise woman, and said... 2Sa 14:2
*t* came out a man of the family of... 2Sa 16:5
up from *t* the bones of Saul... 2Sa 21:13
they are come up from *t* rejoicing... 1Kin 1:45
and go not forth *t* any whither... 1Kin 2:36
to Ophir, and fetched from *t* gold... 1Kin 9:28
and went out from *t*, and built... 1Kin 12:25
So he departed *t*, and found Elisha... 1Kin 19:19
there shall not be from *t* any... 2Kin 2:21
And he went up from *t* unto Beth-el... 2Kin 2:23
he went from *t* to mount Carmel,... 2Kin 2:25
from *t* he returned to Samaria... 2Kin 2:25
take *t* every man a beam, and let... 2Kin 6:2
eat and drink, and carried *t* silver... 2Kin 7:8
another tent, and carried *t* also... 2Kin 7:8
And when he was departed *t*... 2Kin 10:15
priests whom ye brought from *t*... 2Kin 17:27
whom they carried away from *t*... 2Kin 17:33
down, and brake them down from *t*.. 2Kin 23:12
And he carried out *t* all the... 2Kin 24:13
to bring up *t* the ark of God the... 1Chr 13:6
took *t* four hundred and fifty... 2Chr 8:18
and they thrust him out from *t*... 2Chr 26:20
the river, be ye far from *t*... Ezr 6:6
yet will I gather them from *t*... Neh 1:9
From *t* she seeketh the prey, and... Job 39:29
ye, depart ye, go ye out from *t*... Is 52:11
be no more *t* an infant of days... Is 65:20
out *t* shall be torn in pieces... Jer 5:6
and take the girdle from *t*... Jer 13:6
hand, yet would I pluck thee *t*... Jer 22:24
shall cause to cease from *t* man... Jer 36:29
to separate himself *t* in the... Jer 37:12
took *t* old cast clouts and old... Jer 38:11
he shall go forth from *t* in peace... Jer 43:12
I will bring thee down from *t*... Jer 49:16
and will destroy from *t* the king... Jer 49:38
from *t* she shall be taken... Jer 50:9
the abominations thereof from *t*... Eze 11:18
give her her vineyards from *t*... Hos 2:15
from *t* go ye to Hamath the great... Amos 6:2
*t* shall mine hand take them... Amos 9:2
heaven, *t* will I bring them down... Amos 9:2
I will search and take them out *t*... Amos 9:3
*t* will I command the serpent, and... Amos 9:3
*t* will I command the sword, and it... Amos 9:4
*t* will I bring thee down, saith... Obad 4
And going on from *t*, he saw other... Mt 4:21
Thou shalt by no means come out *t*... Mt 5:26
And as Jesus passed forth from *t*... Mt 9:9
And when Jesus departed *t*, two... Mt 9:27
and there abide till ye go *t*... Mt 10:11
disciples, he departed *t* to teach... Mt 11:1
And when he was departed *t*... Mt 12:9
it, he withdrew himself from *t*... Mt 12:15
these parables, he departed *t*... Mt 13:53
he departed *t* by ship into a... Mt 14:13
Then Jesus went *t*, and departed... Mt 15:21
And Jesus departed from *t*, and came.. Mt 15:29
his hands on them, and departed *t*... Mt 19:15
he had gone a little farther *t*... Mk 1:19
And he went out from *t*, and came... Mk 6:1
nor hear you, when ye depart *t*... Mk 6:11
from *t* he arose, and went into the... Mk 7:24
And they departed *t*, and passed... Mk 9:30
And he arose from *t*, and cometh... Mk 10:1
into, there abide, and *t* depart... Lk 9:4
thee, thou shalt not depart *t*... Lk 12:59
to us, that would come from *t*... Lk 16:26
Now after two days he departed *t*... Jn 4:43
but went *t* unto a country near to... Jn 11:54
and from *t*, when his father was... Acts 7:4
from *t* they sailed to Cyprus... Acts 13:4
*t* sailed to Antioch, from whence... Acts 14:26
from *t* to Philippi, which is the... Acts 16:12
And he departed *t*, and entered into... Acts 18:7
sailed *t* into Syria, and with him... Acts 18:18
And we sailed *t*, and came the next... Acts 20:15
Rhodes, and from *t* unto Patara... Acts 21:1
And when we had launched from *t*... Acts 27:4
part advised to depart *t* also... Acts 27:12
obtained their purpose, loosing *t*... Acts 27:13
from *t* we fetched a compass, and... Acts 28:13
And from *t*, when the brethren... Acts 28:15
I went from *t* into Macedonia... 2Cor 2:13

**THENCEFORTH**
*t* it shall be accepted for an... Lev 22:27
the sight of all nations from *t*... 2Chr 32:23
it is *t* good for nothing, but to... Mt 5:13
from *t* Pilate sought to release... Jn 19:12

**THEOPHILUS** (*the-of'-il-us*) *To whom the gospel of Luke and the Acts of the Apostles are addressed.*
thee in order, most excellent *T*... Lk 1:3
former treatise have I made, O *T*... Acts 1:1

**THERE** See PREFACE.

**THEREABOUT**
as they were much perplexed *t*... Lk 24:4

**THEREAT**
wash their hands and their feet *t*... Ex 30:19
their hands and their feet *t*... Ex 40:31
and many there be which go in *t*... Mt 7:13

**THEREBY**
*t* shall I know that thou hast... Gen 24:14
them, that ye should be defiled *t*... Lev 11:43
*t* good shall come unto thee... Job 22:21
is deceived *t* is not wise... Prov 20:1
wood shall be endangered *t*... Eccl 10:9
neither shall gallant ship pass *t*... Is 33:21
passeth *t* shall be astonished... Jer 18:16
passeth *t* shall be astonished... Jer 19:8
doth any son of man pass *t*... Jer 51:43
in their sight, and carry out *t*... Eze 12:5
through the wall to carry out *t*... Eze 12:12
he shall not fall *t* in the day... Eze 33:12
iniquity, he shall even die *t*... Eze 33:18
lawful and right, he shall live *t*... Eze 33:19
And Hamath also shall border *t*... Zec 9:2
Son of God might be glorified *t*... Jn 11:4
cross, having slain the enmity *t*... Eph 2:16
unto them which are exercised *t*... Heb 12:11
trouble you, and *t* many be defiled... Heb 12:15
for *t* some have entertained... Heb 13:2
of the word, that ye may grow *t*... 1Pet 2:2

**THEREFORE**
*T* shall a man leave his father and... Gen 2:24
*T* the LORD God sent him forth... Gen 3:23
*T* whosoever slayeth Cain,... Gen 4:15
*T* is the name of it called Babel... Gen 11:9
*T* it shall come to pass, when the... Gen 12:12
now *t* behold thy wife, take her,... Gen 12:19
Thou shalt keep my covenant *t*... Gen 17:9
for *t* are ye come to your servant... Gen 18:5
*T* Sarah laughed within herself,... Gen 18:12
for *t* came they under the shadow... Gen 19:8
*T* the name of the city was called... Gen 19:22
*t* suffered I thee not to touch... Gen 20:6
Now *t* restore the man his wife... Gen 20:7
*T* Abimelech rose early in the... Gen 20:8
Now *t* swear unto me here by God... Gen 21:23
bury *t* thy dead... Gen 23:15
*t* she took a vail, and covered... Gen 24:65
*t* was his name called Edom... Gen 25:30
*t* the name of the city is... Gen 26:33
Now *t* take, I pray thee, thy... Gen 27:3
Now *t*, my son, obey my voice... Gen 27:8
*T* God give thee of the dew of... Gen 27:28
Now *t*, my son, obey my voice... Gen 27:43
shouldest thou *t* serve me for... Gen 29:15
now *t* my husband will love me... Gen 29:32
he hath *t* given me this son also... Gen 29:33
*t* was his name called Levi... Gen 29:34
*t* she called his name Judah... Gen 29:35
*t* called she his name Dan... Gen 30:6
*T* he shall lie with thee to night... Gen 30:15
Now *t* come thou, let us make a... Gen 31:44
*T* was the name of it called... Gen 31:48
*T* the children of Israel eat not... Gen 32:32
for *t* I have seen thy face, as... Gen 33:10

*t* the name of the place is called ... Gen 33:17
*t* let them dwell in the land, and ... Gen 34:21
Come now *t*, and let us slay him, ... Gen 37:20
*t* his name was called Pharez ... Gen 38:29
Now *t* let Pharaoh look out a man ... Gen 41:33
*t* is this distress come upon us ... Gen 42:21
*t*, behold, also his blood is ... Gen 42:22
Now *t* when I come to thy servant ... Gen 44:30
Now *t*, I pray thee, let thy ... Gen 44:33
Now *t* be not grieved, nor angry ... Gen 45:5
now *t*, we pray thee, let thy ... Gen 47:4
Now *t* let me go up, I pray thee, ... Gen 50:5
Now *t* fear ye not ... Gen 50:21
*T* they did set over them ... Ex 1:11
*T* God dealt well with the ... Ex 1:20
Now *t*, behold, the cry of the ... Ex 3:9
Come now *t*, and I will send thee ... Ex 3:10
Now *t* go, and I will be with thy ... Ex 4:12
*t* they cry, saying, Let us go and ... Ex 5:8
*t* ye say, Let us go and do ... Ex 5:17
Go *t* now, and work ... Ex 5:18
Send *t* now, and gather thy cattle, ... Ex 9:19
Now *t* forgive, I pray thee, my ... Ex 10:17
*t* shall ye observe this day in ... Ex 12:17
Thou shalt *t* keep this ordinance ... Ex 13:10
*t* I sacrifice to the LORD all ... Ex 13:15
*t* the name of it was called Marah ... Ex 15:23
*t* he giveth you on the sixth day ... Ex 16:29
Now *t*, if ye will obey my voice ... Ex 19:5
Ye shall keep the sabbath *t* ... Ex 31:14
Now *t* let me alone, that my wrath ... Ex 32:10
*T* now go, lead the people unto ... Ex 32:34
*t* now put off thy ornaments from ... Ex 33:5
Now *t*, I pray thee, if I have ... Ex 33:13
*T* shall ye abide at the door of ... Lev 8:35
Aaron *t* went unto the altar, and ... Lev 9:8
ye shall *t* sanctify yourselves, ... Lev 11:44
ye shall *t* be holy, for I am holy ... Lev 11:45
He shall *t* burn that garment, ... Lev 13:52
*t* shall he wash his flesh in ... Lev 16:4
*T* I said unto the children of ... Lev 17:12
*t* I said unto the children of ... Lev 17:14
Ye shall *t* keep my statutes, and ... Lev 18:5
*t* I do visit the iniquity thereof ... Lev 18:25
Ye shall *t* keep my statutes and my ... Lev 18:26
*T* shall ye keep mine ordinance, ... Lev 18:30
*T* every one that eateth it shall ... Lev 19:8
*T* shall ye observe all my ... Lev 19:37
Sanctify yourselves *t*, and be ye ... Lev 20:7
Ye shall *t* keep all my statutes, ... Lev 20:22
things, and *t* I abhorred them ... Lev 20:23
Ye shall *t* put difference between ... Lev 20:25
*t* they shall be holy ... Lev 21:6
Thou shalt sanctify him *t* ... Lev 21:8
They shall *t* keep mine ordinance, ... Lev 22:9
they bear sin for it, and die *t* ... Lev 22:9
*T* shall ye keep my commandments, ... Lev 22:31
Ye shall not *t* oppress one ... Lev 25:17
*t* the Levites shall be mine ... Num 3:12
*t* the LORD will give you flesh, ... Num 11:18
*t* he hath slain them in the ... Num 14:16
*t* the LORD will not be with you ... Num 14:43
the LORD, *t* they are hallowed ... Num 16:38
*T* thou and thy sons with thee ... Num 18:7
*t* I have said unto them, Among ... Num 18:24
*T* thou shalt say unto them, When ... Num 18:30
*t* ye shall not bring this ... Num 20:12
*T* the people came to Moses, and ... Num 21:7
He sent messengers *t* unto Balaam ... Num 22:5
Come now *t*, I pray thee, curse me ... Num 22:6
come *t*, I pray thee, curse me ... Num 22:17
Now *t*, I pray you, tarry ye also ... Num 22:19
now *t*, if it displease thee, I ... Num 22:34
*T* now flee thou to thy place ... Num 24:11
come *t*, and I will advertise thee ... Num 24:14
Give unto us *t* a possession among ... Num 27:4
Now *t* kill every male among the ... Num 31:17
We have *t* brought an oblation for ... Num 31:50
Defile not *t* the land which ye ... Num 35:34
ye good heed unto yourselves *t* ... Deut 2:4
Now *t* hearken, O Israel, unto the ... Deut 4:1
Keep *t* and do them ... Deut 4:6
Take ye *t* good heed unto ... Deut 4:15
*t* he chose their seed after them, ... Deut 4:37
Know *t* this day, and consider it ... Deut 4:39
Thou shalt keep *t* his statutes ... Deut 4:40
*t* the LORD thy God commanded thee. Deut 5:15
Now *t* why should we die ... Deut 5:25
Ye shall observe to do *t* as the ... Deut 5:32
Hear *t*, O Israel, and observe to ... Deut 6:3
Know *t* that the LORD thy God, he ... Deut 7:9
Thou shalt *t* keep the ... Deut 7:11
*T* thou shalt keep the ... Deut 8:6
Understand *t* this day, that the ... Deut 9:3
Understand *t*, that the LORD thy ... Deut 9:6
I prayed *t* unto the LORD, and said ... Deut 9:26
Circumcise *t* the foreskin of your ... Deut 10:16
Love ye *t* the stranger ... Deut 10:19
*T* thou shalt love the LORD thy ... Deut 11:1
*T* shall ye keep all the ... Deut 11:8
*T* shall ye lay up these my words ... Deut 11:18
*t* they are unclean unto you ... Deut 14:7
*t* I command thee, saying, Thou ... Deut 15:11
*t* I command thee this thing to ... Deut 15:15
Thou shalt *t* sacrifice the ... Deut 16:2
*t* thou shalt surely rejoice ... Deut 16:15
*T* shall they have no inheritance ... Deut 18:2
*t* shall thy camp be holy ... Deut 23:14
*t* I command thee to do this thing ... Deut 24:18
*t* I command thee to do this thing ... Deut 24:22
*T* it shall be, when the LORD thy ... Deut 25:19
thou shalt *t* keep and do them with .. Deut 26:16
*T* it shall be when ye be gone ... Deut 27:4
Thou shalt *t* obey the voice of ... Deut 27:10
*T* shalt thou serve thine enemies ... Deut 28:48
Keep *t* the words of this covenant ... Deut 29:9
*t* choose life, that both thou and ... Deut 30:19
Now *t* write ye this song for you, ... Deut 31:19
Moses *t* wrote this song the same ... Deut 31:22
now *t* arise, go over this Jordan, ... Josh 1:2
Now *t*, I pray you, swear unto me ... Josh 2:12
Now *t* take you twelve men out of ... Josh 3:12
Joshua *t* commanded the priests, ... Josh 4:17
*T* the children of Israel could ... Josh 7:12
In the morning *t* ye shall be ... Josh 7:14
*t* we will flee before them ... Josh 8:6
Joshua *t* sent them forth ... Josh 8:9
now *t* make ye a league with us ... Josh 9:6
*t* now make ye a league with us ... Josh 9:11
now *t* we may not touch them ... Josh 9:19
Now *t* ye are cursed, and there ... Josh 9:23
*t* we were sore afraid of our ... Josh 9:24
*T* the five kings of the Amorites, ... Josh 10:5
Joshua *t* came unto them suddenly, ... Josh 10:9
Now *t* divide this land for an ... Josh 13:7
*t* they gave no part unto the ... Josh 14:4
Now *t* give me this mountain, ... Josh 14:12
Hebron *t* became the inheritance ... Josh 14:14
*t* he had Gilead and Bashan ... Josh 17:1
*T* according to the commandment of ... Josh 17:4
Ye shall *t* describe the land into ... Josh 18:6
*t* the children of Simeon had ... Josh 19:9
*t* the children of Dan went up to ... Josh 19:47
*t* now return ye, and get you unto ... Josh 22:4
*T* we said, Let us now prepare to ... Josh 22:26
*T* said we, that it shall be, when ... Josh 22:28
Be ye *t* very courageous to keep ... Josh 23:6
Take good heed *t* unto yourselves, ... Josh 23:11
*T* it shall come to pass, that as ... Josh 23:15
*t* he blessed you still ... Josh 24:10
Now *t* fear the LORD, and serve him .. Josh 24:14
*t* will we also serve the LORD ... Josh 24:18
Now *t* put away, said he, the ... Josh 24:23
it shall be *t* a witness unto you, ... Josh 24:27
*T* the LORD left those nations, ... Judg 2:23
*T* the anger of the LORD was hot ... Judg 3:8
*t* they took a key, and opened them ... Judg 3:25
*T* on that day he called him ... Judg 6:32
Now *t* go to, proclaim in the ears ... Judg 7:3
*T* when the LORD hath delivered ... Judg 8:7
Now *t*, if ye have done truly and ... Judg 9:16
Now *t* up by night, thou and the ... Judg 9:32
*T* we turn again to thee now, that ... Judg 11:8
now *t* restore those lands again ... Judg 11:13
why *t* did ye not recover them ... Judg 11:26
Now *t* beware, I pray thee, and ... Judg 13:4
now *t* get her for me to wife ... Judg 14:2
*t* I gave her to thy companion ... Judg 15:2
Delilah *t* took new ropes, and ... Judg 16:12
now *t* I will restore it unto thee ... Judg 17:3
now *t* consider what ye have to do ... Judg 18:14
*t* he lodged there again ... Judg 19:7
Now *t* deliver us the men, the ... Judg 20:13
*T* they turned their backs before ... Judg 20:42
*T* they commanded the children of ... Judg 21:20
Wash thyself *t*, and anoint thee, ... Ruth 3:3
spread *t* thy skirt over thine ... Ruth 3:9
*T* the kinsman said unto Boaz, Buy ... Ruth 4:8
*t* she wept, and did not eat ... 1Sa 1:7
*t* Eli thought she had been ... 1Sa 1:13
*T* also I have lent him to the ... 1Sa 1:28
*T* Eli said unto Samuel, Go, lie ... 1Sa 3:9
*t* I have sworn unto the house of ... 1Sa 3:14
*T* neither the priests of Dagon, ... 1Sa 5:5
They sent *t* and gathered all the ... 1Sa 5:8
*T* they sent the ark of God to ... 1Sa 5:10
Now *t* make a new cart, and take ... 1Sa 6:7
Now *t* hearken unto their voice ... 1Sa 8:9
Now *t* get you up ... 1Sa 9:13
*T* it became a proverb, Is Saul ... 1Sa 10:12
Now *t* present yourselves before ... 1Sa 10:19
*T* they enquired of the LORD ... 1Sa 10:22
*T* the men of Jabesh said, To ... 1Sa 11:10
Now *t* stand still, that I may ... 1Sa 12:7
Now *t* behold the king whom ye ... 1Sa 12:13
Now *t* stand and see this great ... 1Sa 12:16
*T* said I, The Philistines will ... 1Sa 13:12
I forced myself *t*, and offered a ... 1Sa 13:12
*T* Saul said unto the LORD God of ... 1Sa 14:41
now *t* hearken thou unto the voice ... 1Sa 15:1
Now *t*, I pray thee, pardon my sin ... 1Sa 15:25
*T* David ran, and stood upon the ... 1Sa 17:51
*T* Saul removed him from him, and ... 1Sa 18:13
now *t* be the king's son in law ... 1Sa 18:22
now *t*, I pray thee, take heed to ... 1Sa 19:2
*T* thou shalt deal kindly with thy ... 1Sa 20:8
*T* he cometh not unto the king's ... 1Sa 20:29
Now *t* what is under thine hand ... 1Sa 21:3
David *t* departed thence, and ... 1Sa 22:1
*T* David enquired of the LORD, ... 1Sa 23:2
Now *t*, O king, come down ... 1Sa 23:20
See *t*, and take knowledge of all ... 1Sa 23:23
*t* they called that place ... 1Sa 23:28
The LORD *t* be judge, and judge ... 1Sa 24:15
Swear now *t* unto me by the LORD, ... 1Sa 24:21
Now *t* know and consider what thou .. 1Sa 25:17
Now *t*, my lord, as the LORD ... 1Sa 25:26
David *t* sent out spies, and ... 1Sa 26:4
now *t* let me smite him, I pray ... 1Sa 26:8
Now *t*, I pray thee, let my lord ... 1Sa 26:19
Now *t*, let not my blood fall to ... 1Sa 26:20
*t* he shall be my servant for ever ... 1Sa 27:12
*T* will I make thee keeper of mine ... 1Sa 28:2
*t* I have called thee, that thou ... 1Sa 28:15
*t* hath the LORD done this thing ... 1Sa 28:18
Now *t*, I pray thee, hearken thou ... 1Sa 28:22
*T* Saul took a sword, and fell upon ... 1Sa 31:4
*T* now let your hands be ... 2Sa 2:7
shall I not *t* now require his ... 2Sa 4:11
*T* he called the name of that ... 2Sa 5:20
*t* will I play before the LORD ... 2Sa 6:21
*T* Michal the daughter of Saul had ... 2Sa 6:23
Now *t* so shalt thou say unto my ... 2Sa 7:8
*t* hath thy servant found in his ... 2Sa 7:27
*T* now let it please thee to bless ... 2Sa 7:29
Thou *t*, and thy sons, and thy ... 2Sa 9:10
Now *t* the sword shall never ... 2Sa 12:10
David *t* besought God for the ... 2Sa 12:16
*t* David said unto his servants, ... 2Sa 12:19
Now *t* gather the rest of the ... 2Sa 12:28
Now *t*, I pray thee, speak unto ... 2Sa 13:13
Now *t* let not my lord the king ... 2Sa 13:33
Now *t* that I am come to speak of ... 2Sa 14:15
*t* the LORD thy God will be with ... 2Sa 14:17
go *t*, bring the young man Absalom ... 2Sa 14:21
was heavy on him, *t* he polled it ... 2Sa 14:26
*T* Absalom sent for Joab, to have ... 2Sa 14:29
*T* he said unto his servants, See, ... 2Sa 14:30
now *t* let me see the king's face ... 2Sa 14:32
Zadok *t* and Abiathar carried the ... 2Sa 15:29
*t* it shall be, that what thing ... 2Sa 15:35
*T* I counsel that all Israel be ... 2Sa 17:11
Now *t* send quickly, and tell David ... 2Sa 17:16
*t* now it is better that thou ... 2Sa 18:3
Now *t* arise, go forth, and speak ... 2Sa 19:7
Now *t* why speak ye not a word of ... 2Sa 19:10
*t*, behold, I am come the first ... 2Sa 19:20
*T* the king said unto Shimei, Thou ... 2Sa 19:23
do *t* what is good in thine eyes ... 2Sa 19:27
What right *t* have I yet to cry ... 2Sa 19:28
*T* the LORD hath recompensed me ... 2Sa 22:25
*T* I will give thanks unto thee, O ... 2Sa 22:50
*t* he would not drink it ... 2Sa 23:17
*t* he was their captain ... 2Sa 23:19
Now *t* come, let me, I pray thee, ... 1Kin 1:12
be thou strong *t*, and shew thyself ... 1Kin 2:2
Do *t* according to thy wisdom, and ... 1Kin 2:6
Now *t* hold him not guiltless ... 1Kin 2:9
Bath-sheba *t* went unto king ... 1Kin 2:19
Now *t*, as the LORD liveth, which ... 1Kin 2:24
Their blood shall *t* return upon ... 1Kin 2:33
*t* the LORD shall return thy ... 1Kin 2:44
Give *t* thy servant an ... 1Kin 3:9
Now *t* command thou that they hew ... 1Kin 5:6
*T* now, LORD God of Israel, keep ... 1Kin 8:25
Let your heart *t* be perfect with ... 1Kin 8:61
*t* hath the LORD brought upon them ... 1Kin 9:9
*t* made he thee king, to do ... 1Kin 10:9
Solomon sought *t* to kill Jeroboam ... 1Kin 11:40
now *t* make thou the grievous ... 1Kin 12:4
*T* king Rehoboam made speed to get 1Kin 12:18
They hearkened *t* to the word of ... 1Kin 12:24
*t* the LORD hath delivered him ... 1Kin 13:26
*T*, behold, I will bring evil upon ... 1Kin 14:10
Arise thou *t*, get thee to thine ... 1Kin 14:12
Now *t* send, and gather to me all ... 1Kin 18:19
Let them *t* give us two bullocks ... 1Kin 18:23
*t* they were stronger than we ... 1Kin 20:23
*t* will I deliver all this great ... 1Kin 20:28
*t* thy life shall go for his life, ... 1Kin 20:42
Hear thou *t* the word of the LORD ... 1Kin 22:19
Now *t*, behold, the LORD hath put ... 1Kin 22:23
Now *t* thus saith the LORD, Thou ... 2Kin 1:4
*t* thou shalt not come down from ... 2Kin 1:6
*t* let my life now be precious in ... 2Kin 1:14
*t* thou shalt not come down off ... 2Kin 1:16
They sent *t* fifty men ... 2Kin 2:17
now *t*, Moab, to the spoil ... 2Kin 3:23
He went in *t*, and shut the door ... 2Kin 4:33
now *t*, I pray thee, take a ... 2Kin 5:15
The leprosy *t* of Naaman shall ... 2Kin 5:27
*T* said he, Take it up to thee ... 2Kin 6:7
*T* the heart of the king of Syria ... 2Kin 6:11
*T* sent he thither horses, and ... 2Kin 6:14
Now *t* come, and let us fall unto ... 2Kin 7:4
now *t* come, that we may go and ... 2Kin 7:9
*t* are they gone out of the camp ... 2Kin 7:12
They took *t* two chariot horses ... 2Kin 7:14
Now *t* take and cast him into the ... 2Kin 9:26
Now *t* call unto me all the ... 2Kin 10:19
now *t* receive no more money of ... 2Kin 12:7
*T* Jehoash king of Israel went up ... 2Kin 14:11
opened not to him, *t* he smote it ... 2Kin 15:16
*t* the king of Assyria shut him up ... 2Kin 17:4
*T* the LORD was very angry with ... 2Kin 17:18
*t* the LORD sent lions among them, ... 2Kin 17:25
*t* he hath sent lions among them, ... 2Kin 17:26
Now *t*, I pray thee, give pledges ... 2Kin 18:23
*t* they have destroyed them ... 2Kin 19:18
Now *t*, O LORD our God, I beseech ... 2Kin 19:19
*T* their inhabitants were of small ... 2Kin 19:26
*t* I will put my hook in thy nose, ... 2Kin 19:28
*T* thus saith the LORD concerning ... 2Kin 19:32
*T* thus saith the LORD God of ... 2Kin 21:12
*t* my wrath shall be kindled ... 2Kin 22:17
Behold *t*, I will gather thee unto ... 2Kin 22:20
*t* he slew him, and turned the ... 1Chr 10:14
*T* came all the elders of Israel ... 1Chr 11:3
*t* they called it the city of ... 1Chr 11:7
*T* he would not drink it ... 1Chr 11:19
*t* they called the name of that ... 1Chr 14:11
*T* David enquired again of God ... 1Chr 14:14
David *t* did as God commanded him . 1Chr 14:16

Now *t* thus shall thou say unto my .... 1Chr 17:7
*T* now, LORD, let the thing that .......... 1Chr 17:23
*t* thy servant hath found in his .......... 1Chr 17:25
Now *t* let it please thee to bless .......... 1Chr 17:27
*t* he smote Israel .......... 1Chr 21:7
Now *t* advise thyself what word I...... 1Chr 21:12
I will *t* now make preparation for...... 1Chr 22:5
Arise *t*, and be doing, and the LORD.. 1Chr 22:16
arise *t*, and build ye the .......... 1Chr 22:19
*t* they were in one reckoning, .......... 1Chr 23:11
*t* Eleazar and Ithamar executed the.... 1Chr 24:2
Now *t*, in the sight of all Israel.......... 1Chr 28:8
Now *t*, our God, we thank thee, and. 1Chr 29:13
Send me now *t* a man cunning to.......... 2Chr 2:7
Now *t* the wheat, and the barley, ........ 2Chr 2:15
The LORD *t* hath performed his .......... 2Chr 6:10
Now *t*, O LORD God of Israel, keep...... 2Chr 6:16
Have respect *t* to the prayer of .......... 2Chr 6:19
Hearken *t* unto the supplications .......... 2Chr 6:21
Now *t* arise, O LORD God, into thy ...... 2Chr 6:41
*t* hath he brought all this evil .......... 2Chr 7:22
*t* made he thee king over them, to ........ 2Chr 9:8
now *t* ease thou somewhat the.......... 2Chr 10:4
*t* have I also left you in the .......... 2Chr 12:5
*t* I will not destroy them, but I.......... 2Chr 12:7
*T* he said unto Judah, Let us.......... 2Chr 14:7
Be ye strong *t*, and let not your .......... 2Chr 15:7
*t* is the host of the king of .......... 2Chr 16:7
*t* from henceforth thou shalt have.......... 2Chr 16:9
*T* the LORD stablished the kingdom..... 2Chr 17:5
*T* the king of Israel gathered .......... 2Chr 18:5
let thy word *t*, I pray thee, be.......... 2Chr 18:12
let them return *t* every man to.......... 2Chr 18:16
*T* hear the word of the LORD.......... 2Chr 18:18
Now *t*, behold, the LORD hath put ...... 2Chr 18:22
*T* they compassed about him to .......... 2Chr 18:31
*t* he said to his chariot man,.......... 2Chr 18:33
*t* is wrath upon thee from before .......... 2Chr 19:2
*t* the name of the same place was ..... 2Chr 20:26
Now hear me *t*, and deliver the.......... 2Chr 28:11
*t* will I sacrifice to them, that .......... 2Chr 28:23
who *t* gave them up to desolation, ...... 2Chr 30:7
*t* the Levites had the charge of .......... 2Chr 30:17
Now *t* let not Hezekiah deceive .......... 2Chr 32:15
*t* there was wrath upon him, and.......... 2Chr 32:25
*t* my wrath shall be poured out.......... 2Chr 34:25
*t* the Levites prepared for .......... 2Chr 35:14
His servants *t* took him out of.......... 2Chr 35:24
*T* he brought upon them the king ..... 2Chr 36:17
*t* were they, as polluted, put .......... Ezr 2:62
*t* have we sent and certified the.......... Ezr 4:14
Now *t*, if it seem good to the.......... Ezr 5:17
Now *t*, Tatnai, governor beyond .......... Ezr 6:6
Now *t* give not your daughters .......... Ezr 9:12
Now *t* let us make a covenant with...... Ezr 10:3
Now *t* make confession unto the.......... Ezr 10:11
*t* we his servants will arise and.......... Neh 2:20
*T* set I in the lower places.......... Neh 4:13
In what place *t* ye hear the sound........ Neh 4:20
*t* we take up corn for them, that.......... Neh 5:2
Come now *t*, and let us take .......... Neh 6:7
Now *t*, O God, strengthen my hands...... Neh 6:9
*T* was he hired, that I should be.......... Neh 6:13
*t* were they, as polluted, put.......... Neh 7:64
*T* thou deliveredst them into the.......... Neh 9:27
*t* leftest thou them in the hand.......... Neh 9:28
*t* gavest thou them into the hand .......... Neh 9:30
Now *t*, our God, the great, the.......... Neh 9:32
*t* I cast forth all the household .......... Neh 13:8
*t* I chased him from me .......... Neh 13:28
*t* was the king very wroth, and his.......... Est 1:12
*t* they were both hanged on a tree.......... Est 2:23
*t* it is not for the king's profit .......... Est 3:8
*T* the Jews of the villages, that.......... Est 9:19
*T* for all the words of this .......... Est 9:26
*t* despise not thou the chastening.......... Job 5:17
*t* my words are swallowed up.......... Job 6:3
Now *t* be content, look upon me.......... Job 6:28
*T* I will not refrain my mouth .......... Job 7:11
*t* I said it, He destroyeth the.......... Job 9:22
*t* see thou mine affliction .......... Job 10:15
Know *t* that God exacteth of thee .......... Job 11:6
*t* shalt thou not exalt them .......... Job 17:4
*T* do my thoughts cause me to.......... Job 20:2
*t* shall no man look for his goods.......... Job 20:21
*T* they say unto God, Depart from....... Job 21:14
*T* snares are round about thee, and..... Job 22:10
*T* am I troubled at his presence .......... Job 23:15
*T* I said, Hearken to me .......... Job 32:10
*T* hearken unto me, ye men of.......... Job 34:10
*T* he knoweth their works, and he.......... Job 34:25
*t* speak what thou knowest.......... Job 34:33
*t* trust thou in him .......... Job 35:14
*T* doth Job open his mouth in vain...... Job 35:16
Men do *t* fear him.......... Job 37:24
*t* have I uttered that I.......... Job 42:3
*T* take unto you now seven .......... Job 42:8
*T* the ungodly shall not stand in.......... Ps 1:5
Be wise now *t*, O ye kings.......... Ps 2:10
for their sakes *t* return thou on .......... Ps 7:7
*T* my heart is glad, and my glory.......... Ps 16:9
*T* hath the LORD recompensed me.......... Ps 18:24
*T* will I give thanks unto thee, O.......... Ps 18:49
*T* shalt thou make them turn their .......... Ps 21:12
*t* will he teach sinners in the .......... Ps 25:8
*t* I shall not slide.......... Ps 26:1
*t* will I offer in his tabernacle .......... Ps 27:6
*t* my heart greatly rejoiceth .......... Ps 28:7
*t* for thy name's sake lead me, and .......... Ps 31:3
*t* the children of men put their.......... Ps 36:7
*t* my heart faileth me.......... Ps 40:12

*t* will I remember thee from the .......... Ps 42:6
*t* God hath blessed thee for ever.......... Ps 45:2
*t* God, thy God, hath anointed .......... Ps 45:7
*t* shall the people praise thee .......... Ps 45:17
*T* will not we fear, though the.......... Ps 46:2
no changes, *t* they fear not God .......... Ps 55:19
Thou *t*, O LORD God of hosts, the.......... Ps 59:5
*t* in the shadow of thy wings will .......... Ps 63:7
*T* pride compasseth them about as.......... Ps 73:6
*T* his people return hither.......... Ps 73:10
*T* the LORD heard this, and was .......... Ps 78:21
*T* their days did he consume in .......... Ps 78:33
upon me, *t* will I deliver him .......... Ps 91:14
*T* he said that he would destroy.......... Ps 106:23
*T* he lifted up his hand against.......... Ps 106:26
*T* was the wrath of the LORD.......... Ps 106:40
*T* he brought down their heart.......... Ps 107:12
*t* shall he lift up the head .......... Ps 110:7
*t* will I call upon him as long as.......... Ps 116:2
I believed, *t* have I spoken .......... Ps 116:10
*t* shall I see my desire upon them .......... Ps 118:7
*t* I hate every false way .......... Ps 119:104
*t* I love thy testimonies .......... Ps 119:119
*T* I love thy commandments above.... Ps 119:127
*T* I esteem all thy precepts.......... Ps 119:128
*t* doth my soul keep them .......... Ps 119:129
*t* thy servant loveth it.......... Ps 119:140
depart from me *t*, ye bloody men ........ Ps 139:19
*T* is my spirit overwhelmed within........ Ps 143:4
*T* shall they eat of the fruit of.......... Prov 1:31
*t* get wisdom .......... Prov 4:7
Hear me now *t*, O ye children, and........ Prov 5:7
*T* shall his calamity come.......... Prov 6:15
*t* he will not spare in the day of .......... Prov 6:34
*T* came I forth to meet thee, .......... Prov 7:15
Hearken unto me now *t*, O ye.......... Prov 7:24
Now *t* hearken unto me, O ye.......... Prov 8:32
*t* a cruel messenger shall be sent........ Prov 17:11
*t* leave off contention, before it.......... Prov 17:14
*t* shall he beg in harvest, and .......... Prov 20:4
*t* meddle not with him that.......... Prov 20:19
thee with mirth, *t* enjoy pleasure .......... Eccl 2:1
*T* I hated life.......... Eccl 2:17
*T* I went about to cause my heart ........ Eccl 2:20
*t* let thy words be few.......... Eccl 5:2
*t* the misery of man is great upon.......... Eccl 8:6
*t* the heart of the sons of men is.......... Eccl 8:11
*T* remove sorrow from thy heart,........ Eccl 11:10
*t* do the virgins love thee.......... Song 1:3
*T* saith the Lord, the LORD of.......... Is 1:24
*T* thou hast forsaken thy people.......... Is 2:6
*t* forgive them not .......... Is 2:9
*T* the Lord will smite with a scab.......... Is 3:17
*T* my people are gone into.......... Is 5:13
*T* hell hath enlarged herself, and.......... Is 5:14
*T* as the fire devoureth the.......... Is 5:24
*T* is the anger of the LORD.......... Is 5:25
*T* the Lord himself shall give you .......... Is 7:14
Now *t*, behold, the Lord bringeth .......... Is 8:7
*T* the LORD shall set up the.......... Is 9:11
*T* the LORD will cut off from.......... Is 9:14
*T* the Lord shall have no joy in.......... Is 9:17
*T* shall the Lord, the Lord of.......... Is 10:16
*T* thus saith the Lord GOD of.......... Is 10:24
*T* with joy shall ye draw water.......... Is 12:3
*T* shall all hands be faint, and .......... Is 13:7
*T* I will shake the heavens, and.......... Is 13:13
*t* the armed soldiers of Moab.......... Is 15:4
*T* the abundance they have gotten, .......... Is 15:7
*T* shall Moab howl for Moab, every.......... Is 16:7
*T* I will bewail with the weeping .......... Is 16:9
*t* shalt thou plant pleasant .......... Is 17:10
*T* are my loins filled with pain.......... Is 21:3
*T* said I, Look away from me .......... Is 22:4
*T* hath the curse devoured the.......... Is 24:6
*t* the inhabitants of the earth .......... Is 24:6
*T* shall the strong people glorify .......... Is 25:3
*t* hast thou visited and destroyed .......... Is 26:14
By this *t* shall the iniquity of.......... Is 27:9
*t* he that made them will not have.......... Is 27:11
*T* thus saith the Lord GOD, Behold .......... Is 28:16
Now *t* be ye not mockers, lest.......... Is 28:22
*T*, behold, I will proceed to do a .......... Is 29:14
*T* thus saith the LORD, who.......... Is 29:22
*T* shall the strength of Pharaoh .......... Is 30:3
*t* have I cried concerning this, .......... Is 30:7
*T* this iniquity shall be to you .......... Is 30:13
*t* shall ye flee .......... Is 30:16
*t* shall they that pursue you be.......... Is 30:16
*t* will the LORD wait, that he may.......... Is 30:18
*t* will he be exalted, that he may.......... Is 30:18
Now *t* give pledges, I pray thee, .......... Is 36:8
*t* they have destroyed them .......... Is 37:19
Now *t*, O LORD our God, save us .......... Is 37:20
*T* their inhabitants were of small.......... Is 37:27
*t* will I put my hook in thy nose,.......... Is 37:29
*T* thus saith the LORD concerning .......... Is 37:33
*t* we will sing my songs to the .......... Is 38:20
*T* he hath poured upon him the.......... Is 42:25
*t* will I give men for thee, and.......... Is 43:4
*t* ye are my witnesses, saith the.......... Is 43:12
*T* I have profaned the princes of .......... Is 43:28
*T* hear now this, thou that art.......... Is 47:8
*T* shall evil come upon thee.......... Is 47:11
*t* shall I not be confounded.......... Is 50:7
*t* have I set my face like a flint.......... Is 50:7
*T* the redeemed of the LORD shall.......... Is 51:11
*T* hear now this, thou afflicted, .......... Is 51:21
Now *t*, what have I here, saith .......... Is 52:5
*T* my people shall know my name.......... Is 52:6
*t* they shall know in that day .......... Is 52:6

*T* will I divide him a portion.......... Is 53:12
*t* thou wast not grieved.......... Is 57:10
*T* is judgment far from us, .......... Is 59:9
*t* his arm brought salvation unto.......... Is 59:16
*T* thy gates shall be open.......... Is 60:11
*t* in their land they shall .......... Is 61:7
*t* mine own arm brought salvation.......... Is 63:5
*t* he was turned to be their enemy.......... Is 63:10
*t* will I measure their former .......... Is 65:7
*T* will I number you to the sword, .......... Is 65:12
*T* thus saith the Lord GOD, Behold .......... Is 65:13
Thou *t* gird up thy loins, and.......... Jer 1:17
know *t* and see that it is an evil.......... Jer 2:19
*t* hast thou also taught the .......... Jer 2:33
*T* the showers have been .......... Jer 3:3
*T* I said, Surely these are poor .......... Jer 5:4
*t* they are become great, and waxen ...... Jer 5:27
*T* I am full of the fury of the.......... Jer 6:11
*t* they shall fall among them that.......... Jer 6:15
*T* hear, ye nations, and know, O.......... Jer 6:18
*T* thus saith the LORD, Behold, I .......... Jer 6:21
*T* will I do unto this house,.......... Jer 7:14
*T* pray not thou for this people,.......... Jer 7:16
*T* thus saith the Lord GOD.......... Jer 7:20
*T* thou shalt speak all these .......... Jer 7:27
*T*, behold, the days come, saith.......... Jer 7:32
*T* will I give their wives unto .......... Jer 8:10
*t* shall they fall among them that.......... Jer 8:12
*T* thus saith the LORD of hosts.......... Jer 9:7
*T* thus saith the LORD of hosts,.......... Jer 9:15
*t* they shall not prosper, and all.......... Jer 10:21
*t* I will bring upon them all the .......... Jer 11:8
*T* thus saith the LORD, Behold, I.......... Jer 11:11
*T* pray not thou for this people,.......... Jer 11:14
*T* thus saith the LORD of the men .......... Jer 11:21
*T* thus saith the LORD of hosts,.......... Jer 11:22
*t* have I hated it.......... Jer 12:8
*T* thou shalt speak unto them this........ Jer 13:12
*T* will I scatter them as the.......... Jer 13:24
*T* will I discover thy skirts upon.......... Jer 13:26
*t* the LORD doth not accept them .......... Jer 14:10
*T* thus saith the LORD concerning .......... Jer 14:15
*T* thou shalt say this word unto .......... Jer 14:17
*t* we will wait upon thee.......... Jer 14:22
*t* will I stretch out my hand .......... Jer 15:6
*T* thus saith the LORD, If thou.......... Jer 15:19
*T* will I cast you out of this.......... Jer 16:13
*T*, behold, the days come, saith.......... Jer 16:14
*T*, behold, I will this once cause .......... Jer 16:21
Now *t* go to, speak to the men of .......... Jer 18:11
*T* thus saith the LORD.......... Jer 18:13
*T* deliver up their children to.......... Jer 18:21
*T*, behold, the days come, saith.......... Jer 19:6
*t* my persecutors shall stumble, .......... Jer 20:11
*T* thus saith the LORD concerning .......... Jer 22:18
*T* thus saith the LORD God of.......... Jer 23:2
*T*, behold, the days come, saith .......... Jer 23:7
*T* thus saith the LORD of hosts .......... Jer 23:15
*T*, behold, I am against the .......... Jer 23:30
*t* they shall not profit this .......... Jer 23:32
*t* thus saith the LORD .......... Jer 23:38
*T*, behold, I, even I, will.......... Jer 23:39
*T* thus saith the LORD of hosts.......... Jer 25:8
*T* thou shalt say unto them, Thus.......... Jer 25:27
*T* prophesy thou against them all.......... Jer 25:30
*T* now amend your ways and your .......... Jer 26:13
*T* hearken not ye to your prophets.......... Jer 27:9
*T* hearken not unto the words of .......... Jer 27:14
*T* thus saith the LORD.......... Jer 28:16
Hear ye *t* the word of the LORD,.......... Jer 29:20
Now *t* why hast thou not reproved.......... Jer 29:27
For *t* he sent unto us in Babylon,.......... Jer 29:28
*T* thus saith the LORD.......... Jer 29:32
*T* fear thou not, O my servant .......... Jer 30:10
*T* all they that devour thee shall .......... Jer 30:16
*t* with lovingkindness have I .......... Jer 31:3
*T* they shall come and sing in the .......... Jer 31:12
*t* my bowels are troubled for him.......... Jer 31:20
*t* thou hast caused all this evil .......... Jer 32:23
*T* thus saith the LORD.......... Jer 32:28
now *t* thus saith the LORD, the .......... Jer 32:36
*T* the word of the LORD came to.......... Jer 34:12
*T* thus saith the LORD.......... Jer 34:17
*T* thus saith the LORD God of.......... Jer 35:17
*T* thus saith the LORD of hosts,.......... Jer 35:19
*T* go thou, and read in the roll,.......... Jer 36:6
*T* all the princes sent Jehudi the.......... Jer 36:14
*T* thus saith the LORD of.......... Jer 36:30
*T* hear now, I pray thee, O my.......... Jer 37:20
*T* the princes said unto the king,.......... Jer 38:4
*t* this thing is come upon you .......... Jer 40:3
now *t* hear the word of the LORD,.......... Jer 42:15
Now *t* know certainly that ye.......... Jer 42:22
*T* now thus saith the LORD, the .......... Jer 44:7
*T* thus saith the LORD of hosts,.......... Jer 44:11
*t* is your land a desolation, and.......... Jer 44:22
*t* this evil is happened unto you, .......... Jer 44:23
*T* hear ye the word of the LORD,.......... Jer 44:26
*t* his taste remained in him, and.......... Jer 48:11
*T*, behold, the days come, saith.......... Jer 48:12
*T* will I howl for Moab, and I will.......... Jer 48:31
*T* mine heart shall sound for Moab.......... Jer 48:36
*T*, behold, the days come, saith.......... Jer 49:2
*T* hear the counsel of the LORD,.......... Jer 49:20
*T* her young men shall fall in her.......... Jer 49:26
*T* thus saith the LORD of hosts,.......... Jer 50:18
*T* shall her young men fall in the .......... Jer 50:30
*T* the wild beasts of the desert .......... Jer 50:39
*T* hear ye the counsel of the LORD .......... Jer 50:45
*t* the nations are mad .......... Jer 51:7
*T* thus saith the LORD.......... Jer 51:36

*T*, behold, the days come, that I ... Jer 51:47
*t* she is removed ... Lam 1:8
*t* she came down wonderfully ... Lam 1:9
*t* he made the rampart and the wall ... Lam 2:8
recall to my mind, *t* have I hope ... Lam 3:21
*t* will I hope in him ... Lam 3:24
*t* hear the word at my mouth, and ... Eze 3:17
*T* thou shalt set thy face toward ... Eze 4:7
*T* thus saith the Lord GOD ... Eze 5:7
*T* thus saith the Lord GOD ... Eze 5:8
*T* the fathers shall eat the sons ... Eze 5:10
*t* will I also diminish thee ... Eze 5:11
*t* have I set it far from them ... Eze 7:20
*T* will I also deal in fury ... Eze 8:18
*T* prophesy against them, prophesy ... Eze 11:4
*T* thus saith the Lord GOD ... Eze 11:7
*T* say, Thus saith the Lord GOD ... Eze 11:16
*T* say, Thus saith the Lord GOD ... Eze 11:17
*T*, thou son of man, prepare thee ... Eze 12:3
Tell them *t*, Thus saith the Lord ... Eze 12:23
*T* say unto them, Thus saith the ... Eze 12:28
*T* thus saith the Lord GOD ... Eze 13:8
spoken vanity, and seen lies, *t* ... Eze 13:8
*T* thus saith the Lord GOD ... Eze 13:13
*T* ye shall see no more vanity, ... Eze 13:23
*T* speak unto them, and say unto ... Eze 14:4
*T* say unto the house of Israel, ... Eze 14:6
*T* thus saith the Lord GOD ... Eze 15:6
*t* I have stretched out my hand ... Eze 16:27
unto thee, *t* thou art contrary ... Eze 16:34
*t* I will gather all thy lovers, ... Eze 16:37
*t* I also will recompense thy way ... Eze 16:43
*t* I took them away as I saw good ... Eze 16:50
*T* thus saith the Lord GOD ... Eze 17:19
*T* I will judge you, O house of ... Eze 18:30
*T*, son of man, speak unto the ... Eze 20:27
*t* shall my sword go forth out of ... Eze 21:4
Sigh *t*, thou son of man, with the ... Eze 21:6
smite *t* upon thy thigh ... Eze 21:12
Thou *t*, son of man, prophesy, and ... Eze 21:14
*T* thus saith the Lord GOD ... Eze 21:24
*t* have I made thee a reproach ... Eze 22:4
*t* I have smitten mine hand at thy ... Eze 22:13
*T* thus saith the Lord GOD ... Eze 22:19
*t* I will gather you into the ... Eze 22:19
*T* have I poured out mine ... Eze 22:31
*T*, O Aholibah, thus saith the ... Eze 23:22
*t* will I give her cup into thine ... Eze 23:31
*T* thus saith the Lord GOD ... Eze 23:35
*t* bear thou also thy lewdness and ... Eze 23:35
*T* thus saith the Lord GOD ... Eze 24:9
*t* I will deliver thee to the men ... Eze 25:4
*t* I will stretch out mine hand ... Eze 25:7
*T*, behold, I will open the side ... Eze 25:9
*T* thus saith the Lord GOD ... Eze 25:13
*T* thus saith the Lord GOD ... Eze 25:16
*T* thus saith the Lord GOD ... Eze 26:3
*T* thus saith the Lord GOD ... Eze 28:6
*t* I will bring strangers upon ... Eze 28:7
*t* I will cast thee as profane out ... Eze 28:16
*t* will I bring forth a fire from ... Eze 28:18
*T* thus saith the Lord GOD ... Eze 29:8
*t* I am against thee, and against ... Eze 29:10
*T* thus saith the Lord GOD ... Eze 29:19
*T* thus saith the Lord GOD ... Eze 30:22
*T* his height was exalted above ... Eze 31:5
*T* thus saith the Lord GOD ... Eze 31:10
I have *t* delivered him into the ... Eze 31:11
I will *t* spread out my net over ... Eze 32:3
*t* thou shalt hear the word at my ... Eze 33:7
*T*, O thou son of man, speak unto ... Eze 33:10
*T*, thou son of man, say unto the ... Eze 33:12
*T*, ye shepherds, hear the word of ... Eze 34:7
*T*, O ye shepherds, hear the word ... Eze 34:9
*T* thus saith the Lord GOD unto ... Eze 34:20
*T* will I save my flock, and they ... Eze 34:22
*T*, as I live, saith the Lord GOD, ... Eze 35:6
*T*, as I live, saith the Lord GOD, ... Eze 35:11
*T* prophesy and say, Thus saith the ... Eze 36:3
*T*, ye mountains of Israel, hear ... Eze 36:4
*T* thus saith the Lord GOD ... Eze 36:5
Prophesy *t* concerning the land of ... Eze 36:6
*T* thus saith the Lord GOD ... Eze 36:7
*T* thou shalt devour men no more, ... Eze 36:14
*T* say unto the house of Israel, ... Eze 36:22
*T* prophesy and say unto them, Thus ... Eze 37:12
*T*, son of man, prophesy and say ... Eze 38:14
*T*, thou son of man, prophesy ... Eze 39:1
*t* hid I my face from them, and ... Eze 39:23
*T* thus saith the Lord GOD ... Eze 39:25
*t* the breadth of the house was ... Eze 41:7
*t* the building was straitened ... Eze 42:6
in by it, *t* it shall be shut ... Eze 44:2
*t* have I lifted up mine hand ... Eze 44:12
*t* he requested of the prince of ... Dan 1:8
*t* stood they before the king ... Dan 1:19
*t* shew me the dream, and the ... Dan 2:6
*t* tell me the dream, and I shall ... Dan 2:9
*t* there is no king, lord, nor ... Dan 2:10
*T* Daniel went in unto Arioch, ... Dan 2:24
*T* at that time, when all the ... Dan 3:7
*t* he spake, and commanded that ... Dan 3:19
*T* because the king's commandment ... Dan 3:22
*T* I make a decree, That every ... Dan 3:29
*T* made I a decree to bring in all ... Dan 4:6
*T* the he goat waxed very great ... Dan 8:8
*t* the curse is poured upon us, and ... Dan 9:11
*T* hath the LORD watched upon the ... Dan 9:14
Now *t*, O our God, hear the prayer ... Dan 9:17
*t* understand the matter, and ... Dan 9:23
Know *t* and understand, that from ... Dan 9:25
*T* I was left alone, and saw this ... Dan 10:8
*t* he shall be grieved, and return, ... Dan 11:30
*t* he shall go forth with great ... Dan 11:44
let her *t* put away her whoredoms ... Hos 2:2
*T*, behold, I will hedge up thy ... Hos 2:6
*T* will I return, and take away my ... Hos 2:9
*T*, behold, I will allure her, and ... Hos 2:14
*T* shall the land mourn, and every ... Hos 4:3
*T* shalt thou fall in the day, and ... Hos 4:5
*t* will I change their glory into ... Hos 4:7
*t* your daughters shall commit ... Hos 4:13
*t* the people that doth not ... Hos 4:14
*t* shall Israel and Ephraim fall in ... Hos 5:5
*t* I will pour out my wrath upon ... Hos 5:10
*T* will I be unto Ephraim as a ... Hos 5:12
*T* have I hewed them by the ... Hos 6:5
*t* it is not God ... Hos 8:6
*t* he will remember their iniquity ... Hos 9:9
*T* shall a tumult arise among thy ... Hos 10:14
*T* turn thou to thy God ... Hos 12:6
*t* shall he leave his blood upon ... Hos 12:14
*T* they shall be as the morning ... Hos 13:3
*t* have they forgotten me ... Hos 13:6
*T* I will be unto them as a lion ... Hos 13:7
*T* also now, saith the LORD, turn ... Joel 2:12
*T* the flight shall perish from ... Amos 2:14
*t* I will punish you for all your ... Amos 3:2
*T* thus saith the Lord GOD ... Amos 3:11
*T* thus will I do unto thee, O ... Amos 4:12
Forasmuch *t* as your treading is ... Amos 5:11
*T* the prudent shall keep silence ... Amos 5:13
*T* the LORD, the God of hosts, the ... Amos 5:16
*T* will I cause you to go into ... Amos 5:27
*T* now shall they go captive with ... Amos 6:7
*t* will I deliver up the city with ... Amos 6:8
Now *t* hear thou the word of the ... Amos 7:16
*T* thus saith the LORD ... Amos 7:17
*T* I fled before unto Tarshish ... Jonah 4:2
*T* now, O LORD, take, I beseech ... Jonah 4:3
*T* I will make Samaria as an heap ... Mic 1:6
*T* I will wail and howl, I will go ... Mic 1:8
*T* shalt thou give presents to ... Mic 1:14
*T* thus saith the LORD ... Mic 2:3
*T* thou shalt have none that shall ... Mic 2:5
*T* night shall be unto you, that ... Mic 3:6
*T* shall Zion for your sake be ... Mic 3:12
*T* will he give them up, until the ... Mic 5:3
*T* also will I make thee sick in ... Mic 6:13
*t* ye shall bear the reproach of ... Mic 6:16
*T* I will look unto the LORD ... Mic 7:7
*T* the law is slacked, and judgment ... Hab 1:4
*t* wrong judgment proceedeth ... Hab 1:4
*t* they rejoice and are glad ... Hab 1:15
*T* they sacrifice unto their net, ... Hab 1:16
Shall they *t* empty their net, and ... Hab 1:17
*T* their goods shall become a ... Zeph 1:13
*T* as I live, saith the LORD of ... Zeph 2:9
*T* wait ye upon me, saith the LORD ... Zeph 3:8
Now *t* thus saith the LORD of ... Hag 1:5
*T* the heaven over you is stayed ... Hag 1:10
*T* say thou unto them, Thus saith ... Zec 1:3
*T* thus saith the LORD ... Zec 1:16
*t* came a great wrath from the ... Zec 7:12
*T* it is come to pass, that as he ... Zec 7:13
*t* love the truth and peace ... Zec 8:19
*t* they went their way as a flock, ... Zec 10:2
*T* have I also made you ... Mal 2:9
*T* take heed to your spirit, and ... Mal 2:15
*t* take heed to your spirit, that ... Mal 2:16
*t* ye sons of Jacob are not ... Mal 3:6
Bring forth *t* fruits meet for ... Mt 3:8
*t* every tree which bringeth not ... Mt 3:10
Whosoever *t* shall break one of ... Mt 5:19
*T* if thou bring thy gift to the ... Mt 5:23
Be ye *t* perfect, even as your ... Mt 5:48
*T* when thou doest thine alms, do ... Mt 6:2
Be not ye *t* like unto them ... Mt 6:8
After this manner *t* pray ye ... Mt 6:9
if *t* thine eye be single, thy ... Mt 6:22
If *t* the light that is in thee be ... Mt 6:23
*T* I say unto you, Take no thought ... Mt 6:25
*T* take no thought, saying, What ... Mt 6:31
Take *t* no thought for the morrow ... Mt 6:34
*T* all things whatsoever ye would ... Mt 7:12
*T* whosoever heareth these sayings ... Mt 7:24
Pray ye *t* the Lord of the harvest ... Mt 9:38
be ye *t* wise as serpents, and ... Mt 10:16
Fear them not *t* ... Mt 10:26
Fear ye not *t*, ye are of more ... Mt 10:31
Whosoever *t* shall confess me ... Mt 10:32
*t* they shall be your judges ... Mt 12:27
*T* speak I to them in parables ... Mt 13:13
Hear ye *t* the parable of the ... Mt 13:18
As *t* the tares are gathered and ... Mt 13:40
them, *T* every scribe which is ... Mt 13:52
*t* mighty works do shew forth ... Mt 14:2
Whosoever *t* shall humble himself ... Mt 18:4
*T* is the kingdom of heaven ... Mt 18:23
The servant *t* fell down, and ... Mt 18:26
What *t* God hath joined together, ... Mt 19:6
what shall we have *t* ... Mt 19:27
When the lord *t* of the vineyard ... Mt 21:40
*T* say I unto you, The kingdom of ... Mt 21:43
Go ye *t* into the highways, and as ... Mt 22:9
Tell us *t*, What thinkest thou ... Mt 22:17
Render *t* unto Caesar the things ... Mt 22:21
*T* in the resurrection whose wife ... Mt 22:28
All *t* whatsoever they bid you ... Mt 23:3
*t* ye shall receive the greater ... Mt 23:14
Whoso *t* shall swear by the altar, ... Mt 23:20
When ye *t* shall see the ... Mt 24:15
Watch *t*: for ye know not ... Mt 24:42
*T* be ye also ready ... Mt 24:44
Watch *t*, for ye know neither the ... Mt 25:13
Thou oughtest *t* to have put my ... Mt 25:27
Take *t* the talent from him, and ... Mt 25:28
*T* when they were gathered ... Mt 27:17
Command *t* that the sepulchre be ... Mt 27:64
Go ye *t*, and teach all nations, ... Mt 28:19
for *t* came I forth ... Mk 1:38
*T* the Son of man is Lord also of ... Mk 2:28
*t* mighty works do shew forth ... Mk 6:14
*T* Herodias had a quarrel against ... Mk 6:19
Whosoever *t* shall be ashamed of ... Mk 8:38
What *t* God hath joined together, ... Mk 10:9
*T* I say unto you, What things ... Mk 11:24
Having yet *t* one son, his ... Mk 12:6
What shall *t* the lord of the ... Mk 12:9
In the resurrection *t*, when they ... Mk 12:23
said unto them, Do ye not *t* err ... Mk 12:24
ye *t* do greatly err ... Mk 12:27
David *t* himself calleth him Lord ... Mk 12:37
Watch ye *t* ... Mk 13:35
*t* also that holy thing which ... Lk 1:35
Bring forth *t* fruits worthy of ... Lk 3:8
every tree *t* which bringeth not ... Lk 3:9
If thou *t* wilt worship me, all ... Lk 4:7
for *t* am I sent ... Lk 4:43
Be ye *t* merciful, as your Father ... Lk 6:36
Tell me *t*, which of them will ... Lk 7:42
Take heed *t* how ye hear ... Lk 8:18
*T* said he unto them, The harvest ... Lk 10:2
pray ye *t* the Lord of the harvest ... Lk 10:2
bid her *t* that she help me ... Lk 10:40
*t* shall they be your judges ... Lk 11:19
*t* when thine eye is single, thy ... Lk 11:34
Take heed *t* that the light which ... Lk 11:35
thy whole body *t* be full of light ... Lk 11:36
*T* also said the wisdom of God, I ... Lk 11:49
*T* whatsoever ye have spoken in ... Lk 12:3
Fear not *t* ... Lk 12:7
*T* I say unto you, Take no thought ... Lk 12:22
Be ye *t* ready also ... Lk 12:40
in them *t* come and be healed, and ... Lk 13:14
a wife, and *t* I cannot come ... Lk 14:20
*t* came his father out, and ... Lk 15:28
If *t* ye have not been faithful in ... Lk 16:11
Then he said, I pray thee *t* ... Lk 16:27
He said *t*, A certain nobleman ... Lk 19:12
What *t* shall the lord of the ... Lk 20:15
Render *t* unto Caesar the things ... Lk 20:25
There were *t* seven brethren ... Lk 20:29
*T* in the resurrection whose wife ... Lk 20:33
David *t* calleth him Lord, how is ... Lk 20:44
go ye not *t* after them ... Lk 21:8
Settle it *t* in your hearts, not ... Lk 21:14
Watch ye *t*, and pray always, that ... Lk 21:36
I will *t* chastise him, and release ... Lk 23:16
Pilate *t*, willing to release ... Lk 23:20
I will *t* chastise him, and let him ... Lk 23:22
*t* am I come baptizing with water ... Jn 1:31
When *t* he was risen from the dead ... Jn 2:22
this my joy *t* is fulfilled ... Jn 3:29
When *t* the Lord knew how the ... Jn 4:1
Jesus *t*, being wearied with his ... Jn 4:6
*T* said the disciples one to ... Jn 4:33
The Jews *t* said unto him that was ... Jn 5:10
*t* did the Jews persecute Jesus, ... Jn 5:16
*T* the Jews sought the more to ... Jn 5:18
*T* they gathered them together, and ... Jn 6:13
When Jesus *t* perceived that they ... Jn 6:15
When the people *t* saw that Jesus ... Jn 6:24
They said *t* unto him, What sign ... Jn 6:30
Jesus *t* answered and said unto ... Jn 6:43
Every man *t* that hath heard, and ... Jn 6:45
The Jews *t* strove among ... Jn 6:52
Many *t* of his disciples, when ... Jn 6:60
*T* said I unto you, that no man ... Jn 6:65
His brethren *t* said unto him, ... Jn 7:3
Moses *t* gave unto you ... Jn 7:22
Many of the people *t*, when they ... Jn 7:40
The Pharisees *t* said unto him ... Jn 8:13
I said *t* unto you, that ye shall ... Jn 8:24
If the Son *t* shall make you free, ... Jn 8:36
ye *t* hear them not, because ye ... Jn 8:47
He went his way *t*, and washed, and ... Jn 9:7
The neighbours *t*, and they which ... Jn 9:8
*T* said they unto him, How were ... Jn 9:10
*T* said some of the Pharisees, ... Jn 9:16
*T* said his parents, He is of age ... Jn 9:23
*t* your sin remaineth ... Jn 9:41
*T* doth my Father love me, because ... Jn 10:17
There was a division *t* again ... Jn 10:19
*T* they sought again to take him ... Jn 10:39
*T* his sisters sent unto him, ... Jn 11:3
he had heard *t* that he was sick ... Jn 11:6
When Jesus *t* saw her weeping, and ... Jn 11:33
Jesus *t* again groaning in himself ... Jn 11:38
Jesus *t* walked no more openly ... Jn 11:54
the Jews *t* knew that he was there ... Jn 12:9
The people *t* that was with him ... Jn 12:17
The Pharisees *t* said among ... Jn 12:19
The same came *t* to Philip ... Jn 12:21
The people *t*, that stood by, and ... Jn 12:29
*T* they could not believe, because ... Jn 12:39
whatsoever I speak *t*, even as the ... Jn 12:50
*t* said he, Ye are not all clean ... Jn 13:11
Simon Peter *t* beckoned to him, ... Jn 13:24
*T*, when he was gone out, Jesus ... Jn 13:31
the world, *t* the world hateth you ... Jn 15:19
*t* said I, that he shall take of ... Jn 16:15
They said *t*, What is this that he ... Jn 16:18

And ye now *t* have sorrow Jn 16:22
Jesus *t*, knowing all things that Jn 18:4
if *t* ye seek me, let these go Jn 18:8
They said *t* unto him, Art not Jn 18:25
The Jews *t* said unto him, It is Jn 18:31
Pilate *t* said unto him, Art thou Jn 18:37
will ye *t* that I release unto you Jn 18:39
Then Pilate *t* took Jesus, and Jn 19:1
Pilate *t* went forth again, and Jn 19:4
When the chief priests *t* and Jn 19:6
When Pilate *t* heard that saying, Jn 19:8
*t* he that delivered me unto thee Jn 19:11
When Pilate *t* heard that saying, Jn 19:13
Then delivered he him *t* unto them Jn 19:16
They said *t* among themselves, Let Jn 19:24
These things *t* the soldiers did Jn 19:24
When Jesus *t* saw his mother, and Jn 19:26
When Jesus *t* had received the Jn 19:30
The Jews *t*, because it was the Jn 19:31
He came *t*, and took the body of Jn 19:38
they Jesus *t* because of the Jews' Jn 19:42
Peter *t* went forth, and that other Jn 20:3
other disciples *t* said unto him Jn 20:25
They cast *t*, and now they were not Jn 21:6
*T* that disciple whom Jesus loved Jn 21:7
When they *t* were come together, Acts 1:6
*T* did my heart rejoice, and my Acts 2:26
*T* being a prophet, and knowing Acts 2:30
*T* being by the right hand of God Acts 2:33
*T* let all the house of Israel Acts 2:36
Repent ye *t*, and be converted, Acts 3:19
*T* they that were scattered abroad Acts 8:4
Repent *t* of this thy wickedness, Acts 8:22
Arise *t*, and get thee down, and go Acts 10:20
*T* came I unto you without Acts 10:29
I ask *t* for what intent ye have Acts 10:29
Send *t* to Joppa, and call hither Acts 10:32
Immediately *t* I sent to thee Acts 10:33
Now *t* are we all here present Acts 10:33
Peter *t* was kept in prison Acts 12:5
Be it known unto you *t*, men and Acts 13:38
Beware *t*, lest that come upon you Acts 13:40
Long time *t* abode they speaking Acts 14:3
When *t* Paul and Barnabas had no Acts 15:2
Now *t* why tempt ye God, to put a Acts 15:10
We have sent *t* Judas and Silas, Acts 15:27
*T* loosing from Troas, we came Acts 16:11
now *t* depart, and go in peace Acts 16:36
*T* many of them believed Acts 17:12
*T* disputed he in the synagogue Acts 17:17
we would know *t* what these things Acts 17:20
Whom *t* ye ignorantly worship, him Acts 17:23
Some *t* cried one thing, and some Acts 19:32
When he *t* was come up again, and Acts 20:11
Take heed *t* unto yourselves, and Acts 20:28
*T* watch, and remember, that by the Acts 20:31
What is it *t* Acts 21:22
Do *t* this that we say to thee Acts 21:23
Now *t* ye with the council signify Acts 23:15
Let them *t*, said he, which among Acts 25:5
*T*, when they were come hither, Acts 25:17
Having *t* obtained help of God, I Acts 26:22
For this cause *t* have I called Acts 28:20
Be it known *t* unto you, that the Acts 28:28
*T* thou art inexcusable, O man, Rom 2:1
Thou *t* which teachest another, Rom 2:21
*T* if the uncircumcision keep the Rom 2:26
*T* by the deeds of the law there Rom 3:20
*T* we conclude that a man is Rom 3:28
*T* it is of faith, that it might Rom 4:16
*t* it was imputed to him for Rom 4:22
*T* being justified by faith, we Rom 5:1
*T* as by the offence of one Rom 5:18
*T* we are buried with him by Rom 6:4
Let not sin *t* reign in your Rom 6:12
There is *t* now no condemnation to Rom 8:1
*T*, brethren, we are debtors, not Rom 8:12
*T* hath he mercy on whom he will Rom 9:18
Behold *t* the goodness and severity Rom 11:22
I beseech you *t*, brethren, by the Rom 12:1
*T* if thine enemy hunger, feed him Rom 12:20
Whosoever *t* resisteth the power, Rom 13:2
Render *t* to all their dues Rom 13:7
*t* love is the fulfilling of the Rom 13:10
let us *t* cast off the works of Rom 13:12
whether we live *t*, or die, we are Rom 14:8
Let us not *t* judge one another Rom 14:13
Let us *t* follow after the things Rom 14:19
I have *t* whereof I may glory Rom 15:17
When *t* I have performed this, and Rom 15:28
I am glad *t* on your behalf Rom 16:19
*T* let no man glory in men 1Cor 3:21
*T* judge nothing before the time, 1Cor 4:5
Purge out *t* the old leaven, that 1Cor 5:7
*T* let us keep the feast, not with 1Cor 5:8
*T* put away from among yourselves 1Cor 5:13
Now *t* there is utterly a fault 1Cor 6:7
*t* glorify God in your body, and in 1Cor 6:20
I say *t* to the unmarried and 1Cor 7:8
I suppose *t* that this is good for 1Cor 7:26
As concerning *t* the eating of 1Cor 8:4
I *t* so run, not as uncertainly 1Cor 9:26
Whether *t* ye eat, or drink, or 1Cor 10:31
ye come together *t* into one place 1Cor 11:20
is it *t* not of the body 1Cor 12:15
is it *t* not of the body 1Cor 12:16
*T* if I know not the meaning of 1Cor 14:11
If *t* the whole church be come 1Cor 14:23
*T* whether it were I or they, so 1Cor 15:11
*T*, my beloved brethren, be ye 1Cor 15:58
Let no man *t* despise him 1Cor 16:11
*t* acknowledge ye them that are 1Cor 16:18
When I *t* was thus minded, did I 2Cor 1:17
*T*, seeing we have this ministry, 2Cor 4:1
I believed, and *t* have I spoken 2Cor 4:13
we also believe, and *t* speak 2Cor 4:13
*T* we are always confident, 2Cor 5:6
Knowing *t* the terror of the Lord, 2Cor 5:11
*T* if any man be in Christ, he is 2Cor 5:17
Having *t* these promises dearly 2Cor 7:1
*T* we were comforted in your 2Cor 7:13
I rejoice *t* that I have 2Cor 7:16
*T*, as ye abound in every thing, 2Cor 8:7
Now *t* perform the doing of it 2Cor 8:11
*T* I thought it necessary to 2Cor 9:5
*T* it is no great thing if his 2Cor 11:15
Most gladly *t* will I rather glory 2Cor 12:9
*T* I take pleasure in infirmities, 2Cor 12:10
*T* I write these things being 2Cor 13:10
is *t* Christ the minister of sin Gal 2:17
He *t* that ministereth to you the Gal 3:5
Know ye *t* that they which are of Gal 3:7
Am I *t* become your enemy, because Gal 4:16
Stand fast *t* in the liberty Gal 5:1
As we have *t* opportunity, let us Gal 6:10
Now *t* ye are no more strangers and Eph 2:19
I *t*, the prisoner of the Lord, Eph 4:1
This I say *t*, and testify in the Eph 4:17
Be ye *t* followers of God, as dear Eph 5:1
Be not ye *t* partakers with them Eph 5:7
*T* as the church is subject unto Eph 5:24
Stand *t*, having your loins girt Eph 6:14
If there be *t* any consolation in Phil 2:1
Him *t* I hope to send presently, Phil 2:23
I sent him *t* the more carefully, Phil 2:28
Receive him *t* in the Lord with Phil 2:29
Let us *t*, as many as be perfect, Phil 3:15
*T*, my brethren dearly beloved and Phil 4:1
As ye have *t* received Christ Col 2:6
Let no man *t* judge you in meat, Col 2:16
Mortify *t* your members which are Col 3:5
Put on *t*, as the elect of God, Col 3:12
*T*, brethren, we were comforted 1Th 3:7
He *t* that despiseth, despiseth 1Th 4:8
*T* let us not sleep, as do others 1Th 5:6
*T*, brethren, stand fast, and hold 2Th 2:15
I exhort *t*, that, first of all, 1Ti 2:1
I will *t* that men pray every 1Ti 2:8
For *t* we both labour and suffer 1Ti 4:10
I will *t* that the younger women 1Ti 5:14
Be not thou *t* ashamed of the 2Ti 1:8
Thou *t*, my son, be strong in the 2Ti 2:1
Thou *t* endure hardness, as a good 2Ti 2:3
*T* I endure all things for the 2Ti 2:10
If a man *t* purge himself from 2Ti 2:21
I charge thee *t* before God 2Ti 4:1
thou *t* receive him, that is, mine Philem 12
For perhaps he *t* departed for a Philem 15
If thou count me *t* a partner Philem 17
*t* God, even thy God, hath Heb 1:9
*T* we ought to give the more Heb 2:1
Let us *t* fear, lest, a promise Heb 4:1
Seeing *t* it remaineth that some Heb 4:6
There remaineth *t* a rest to the Heb 4:9
Let us labour *t* to enter into Heb 4:11
Let us *t* come boldly unto the Heb 4:16
*T* leaving the principles of the Heb 6:1
If *t* perfection were by the Heb 7:11
It was *t* necessary that the Heb 9:23
Having *t*, brethren, boldness to Heb 10:19
Cast not away *t* your confidence, Heb 10:35
*T* sprang there even of one, and Heb 11:12
Let us go forth *t* unto him Heb 13:13
By him *t* let us offer the Heb 13:15
whosoever *t* will be a friend of Jas 4:4
Submit yourselves *t* to God Jas 4:7
*T* to him that knoweth to do good, Jas 4:17
Be patient *t*, brethren, unto the Jas 5:7
Unto you *t* which believe he is 1Pet 2:7
be ye *t* sober, and watch unto 1Pet 4:7
Humble yourselves *t* under the 1Pet 5:6
Ye *t*, beloved, seeing ye know 2Pet 3:17
Let that *t* abide in you, which ye 1Jn 2:24
*t* the world knoweth us not, 1Jn 3:1
*t* speak they of the world, and the 1Jn 4:5
We *t* ought to receive such, that 3Jn 8
I will *t* put you in remembrance, Jude 5
Remember *t* from whence thou art Rev 2:5
Remember *t* how thou hast received Rev 3:3
If *t* thou shalt not watch, I will Rev 3:3
be zealous *t*, and repent Rev 3:19
*T* are they before the throne of Rev 7:15
*T* rejoice, ye heavens, and ye that Rev 12:12
*T* shall her plagues come in one Rev 18:8

**THEREFROM**
that ye turn not aside *t* to the Josh 23:6
he departed not *t* 2Kin 3:3
he departed not *t* 2Kin 13:2

**THEREIN** See PREFACE.

**THEREINTO**
that are in the countries enter *t* Lk 21:21

**THEREOF** See PREFACE.

**THEREON** See PREFACE.

**THEREOUT**
he shall take *t* his handful of Lev 2:2
in the jaw, and there came water *t* Judg 15:19

**THERETO** See PREFACE.

**THEREUNTO**
it, and have sacrificed *t*, and said Ex 32:8
he made *t* four pillars of shittim Ex 36:36
made *t* a crown of gold round Ex 37:11
Also he made *t* a border of an Ex 37:12
and unto all the places nigh *t* Deut 1:7
watching *t* with all perseverance Eph 6:18
know that we are appointed *t* 1Th 3:3
make the comers *t* perfect Heb 10:1
knowing that ye are *t* called 1Pet 3:9

**THEREUPON**
and the mercy seat that is *t* Ex 31:7
colours, and playedst the harlot *t* Eze 16:16
they shall feed *t* Zeph 2:7
man take heed how he buildeth *t* 1Cor 3:10
work abide which he hath built *t* 1Cor 3:14

**THEREWITH**
corn, or the field, be consumed *t* Ex 22:6
tabernacle of the congregation *t* Ex 30:26
*t* he made the sockets to the door Ex 38:30
maketh atonement *t* shall have it Lev 7:7
the ephod, and bound it unto him *t* Lev 8:7
goeth from him, and is defiled *t* Lev 15:32
any beast to defile thyself *t* Lev 18:23
shall not eat to defile himself *t* Lev 22:8
shalt thou eat unleavened bread *t* Deut 16:3
thyself abroad, thou shalt dig *t* Deut 23:13
took it, and slew a thousand men *t* Judg 15:15
took new ropes, and bound him *t* Judg 16:12
any bribe to blind mine eyes *t* 1Sa 12:3
slew him, and cut off his head *t* 1Sa 17:51
thy sword, and thrust me through *t* 1Sa 31:4
so he smote him *t* in the fifth 2Sa 20:10
I have *t* sent Naaman my servant 2Kin 5:6
repaired *t* the house of the LORD 2Kin 12:14
thy sword, and thrust me through *t* 1Chr 10:4
I made, said David, to praise *t* 1Chr 23:5
and he built *t* Geba and Mizpah 2Chr 16:6
than great treasure and trouble *t* Prov 15:16
is, than a stalled ox and hatred *t* Prov 15:17
is a dry morsel, and quietness *t* Prov 17:1
for thee, lest thou be filled *t* Prov 25:16
the sons of man to be exercised *t* Eccl 1:13
to water *t* the wood that bringeth Eccl 2:6
removeth stones shall be hurt *t* Eccl 10:9
itself against him that heweth *t* Is 10:15
and thou shalt prepare thy bread *t* Eze 4:15
oil, and ye shall be satisfied *t* Joel 2:19
state I am, *t* to be content Phil 4:11
and raiment let us be *t* content 1Ti 6:8
*T* bless we God, even the Father Jas 3:9
*t* curse we men, which are made Jas 3:9
and not content *t*, neither doth he 3Jn 10

**THESE** See PREFACE.

**THESSALONIANS** (*thes-sa-lo'-ne-uns*) *The inhabitants of Thessalonica.*
and of the *T*, Aristarchus and Acts 20:4
unto the church of the *T* which is 1Th 1:1
the *T* was written from Athens 1Th s
church of the *T* in God our Father 2Th 1:1
to the *T* was written from Athens 2Th s

**THESSALONICA** (*thes-sa-lo-ni'-cah*) *A city in Macedonia.*
and Apollonia, they came to *T* Acts 17:1
were more noble than those in *T* Acts 17:11
But when the Jews of *T* had Acts 17:13
Aristarchus, a Macedonian of *T* Acts 27:2
For even in *T* ye sent once and Phil 4:16
world, and is departed unto *T* 2Ti 4:10

**THEUDAS** (*thew'-das*) *A false Jewish Messiah.*
For before these days rose up *T* Acts 5:36

**THEY** See PREFACE.

**THICK**
there was a *t* darkness in all the Ex 10:22
Lo, I come unto thee in a *t* cloud Ex 19:9
a *t* cloud upon the mount, and the Ex 19:16
unto the *t* darkness where God was Ex 20:21
trees, and the boughs of *t* trees Lev 23:40
darkness, clouds, and *t* darkness Deut 4:11
of the *t* darkness, with a great Deut 5:22
art waxen fat, thou art grown *t* Deut 32:15
under the *t* boughs of a great oak 2Sa 18:9
waters, and *t* clouds of the skies 2Sa 22:12
the *t* beam were before them 1Kin 7:6
And it was an hand breadth *t* 1Kin 7:26
he would dwell in the *t* darkness 1Kin 8:12
morrow, that he took a *t* cloth 2Kin 8:15
he would dwell in the *t* darkness 2Chr 6:1
branches, and branches of *t* trees Neh 8:15
upon the *t* bosses of his bucklers Job 15:26
*T* clouds are a covering to him, Job 22:14
up the waters in his *t* clouds Job 26:8
watering he wearieth the *t* cloud Job 37:11
*t* darkness a swaddlingband for it Job 38:9
waters and *t* clouds of the skies Ps 18:11
before him his *t* clouds passed Ps 18:12
lifted up axes upon the *t* trees Ps 74:5
as a *t* cloud, thy transgressions, Is 44:22
green tree, and under every *t* oak Eze 6:13
a *t* cloud of incense went up Eze 8:11
was exalted among the *t* branches Eze 19:11
high hill, and all the *t* trees Eze 20:28
and his top was among the *t* boughs Eze 31:3
up his top among the *t* boughs Eze 31:10

up their top among the *t* boughs Eze 31:14
was five cubits *t* round about Eze 41:12
there were *t* planks upon the face Eze 41:25
of the house, and *t* planks Eze 41:26
of *t* darkness, as the morning Joel 2:2
that ladeth himself with *t* clay Hab 2:6
a day of clouds and *t* darkness, Zeph 1:15
people were gathered *t* together Lk 11:29

**THICKER**
shall be *t* than my father's loins 1Kin 12:10
shall be *t* than my father's loins 2Chr 10:10

**THICKET**
a ram caught in a *t* by his horns Gen 22:13
The lion is come up from his *t* Jer 4:7

**THICKETS**
hide themselves in caves, and in *t* 1Sa 13:6
kindle in the *t* of the forest Is 9:18
he shall cut down the *t* of the Is 10:34
they shall go into *t*, and climb up Jer 4:29

**THICKNESS**
the *t* of it was an handbreadth, 2Chr 4:5
the *t* thereof was four fingers Jer 52:21
The *t* of the wall, which was for Eze 41:9
The chambers were in the *t* of the Eze 42:10

**THIEF**
If a *t* be found breaking up, and Ex 22:2
if the *t* be found, let him pay Ex 22:7
If the *t* be not found, then the Ex 22:8
then that *t* shall die Deut 24:7
needy, and in the night is as a *t* Job 24:14
cried after them as after a *t* Job 30:5
When thou sawest a *t*, then thou Ps 50:18
Men do not despise a *t*, if he Prov 6:30
with a *t* hateth his own soul Prov 29:24
As the *t* is ashamed when he is Jer 2:26
the *t* cometh in, and the troop of Hos 7:1
enter in at the windows like a *t* Joel 2:9
enter into the house of the *t* Zec 5:4
in what watch the *t* would come Mt 24:43
out as against a *t* with swords Mt 26:55
Are ye come out, as against a *t* Mk 14:48
where no *t* approacheth, neither Lk 12:33
known what hour the *t* would come Lk 12:39
Be ye come out, as against a *t* Lk 22:52
some other way, the same is a *t* Jn 10:1
The *t* cometh not, but for to Jn 10:10
but because he was a *t*, and had Jn 12:6
so cometh as a *t* in the night 1Th 5:2
day should overtake you as a *t* 1Th 5:4
suffer as a murderer, or as a *t* 1Pet 4:15
will come as a *t* in the night 2Pet 3:10
watch, I will come on thee as a *t* Rev 3:3
Behold, I come as a *t* Rev 16:15

**THIEVES**
rebellious, and companions of *t* Is 1:23
was he found among *t* Jer 48:27
if *t* by night, they will destroy Jer 49:9
If *t* came to thee, if robbers by Obad 5
where *t* break through and steal Mt 6:19
where *t* do not break through nor Mt 6:20
but ye have made it a den of *t* Mt 21:13
there two *t* crucified with him Mt 27:38
The *t* also, which were crucified Mt 27:44
but ye have made it a den of *t* Mk 11:17
And with him they crucify two *t* Mk 15:27
to Jericho, and fell among *t* Lk 10:30
unto him that fell among the *t* Lk 10:36
but ye have made it a den of *t* Lk 19:46
that ever came before me are *t* Jn 10:8
Nor *t*, nor covetous, nor 1Cor 6:10

**THIGH**
I pray thee, thy hand under my *t* Gen 24:2
under the *t* of Abraham his master Gen 24:9
he touched the hollow of his *t* Gen 32:25
of Jacob's *t* was out of joint Gen 32:25
upon him, and he halted upon his *t* Gen 32:31
which is upon the hollow of the *t* Gen 32:32
*t* in the sinew that shrank Gen 32:32
I pray thee, thy hand under my *t* Gen 47:29
the LORD doth make thy *t* to rot Num 5:21
belly to swell, and thy *t* to rot Num 5:22
shall swell, and her *t* shall rot Num 5:27
his raiment upon his right *t* Judg 3:16
took the dagger from his right *t* Judg 3:21
hip and *t* with a great slaughter Judg 15:8
Gird thy sword upon thy *t* Ps 45:3
man hath his sword upon his *t* Song 3:8
make bare the leg, uncover the *t* Is 47:2
was instructed, I smote upon my *t* Jer 31:19
smite therefore upon thy *t* Eze 21:12
it, even every good piece, the *t* Eze 24:4
on his *t* a name written, KING OF Rev 19:16

**THIGHS**
even unto the *t* they shall reach Ex 28:42
joints of thy *t* are like jewels Song 7:1
his belly and his *t* of brass, Dan 2:32

**THIMNATHAH** (*thim'-nath-ah*) See TIMNAH.
*A city in Dan.*
And Elon, and *T*, and Ekron, Josh 19:43

**THIN**
And, behold, seven *t* ears and Gen 41:6
the seven *t* ears devoured the Gen 41:7
behold, seven ears, withered, *t* Gen 41:23
the *t* ears devoured the seven Gen 41:24
And the seven *t* and ill favoured Gen 41:27
did beat the gold into *t* plates Ex 39:3
and there be in it a yellow *t* hair Lev 13:30
certain additions made of *t* work 1Kin 7:29
glory of Jacob shall be made *t* Is 17:4

**THINE** See PREFACE.

**THING**
his kind, cattle, and creeping *t* Gen 1:24
every *t* that creepeth upon the Gen 1:25
over every creeping *t* that Gen 1:26
over every living *t* that moveth Gen 1:28
to every *t* that creepeth upon the Gen 1:30
God saw every *t* that he had made, Gen 1:31
man, and beast, and the creeping *t* Gen 6:7
every *t* that is in the earth Gen 6:17
And of every living *t* of all flesh Gen 6:19
of every creeping *t* of the earth Gen 6:20
of every *t* that creepeth upon the Gen 7:8
every creeping *t* that creepeth Gen 7:14
of every creeping *t* that creepeth Gen 7:21
Noah, and every living *t*, and all Gen 8:1
every living *t* that is with thee Gen 8:17
of every creeping *t* that creepeth Gen 8:17
Every beast, every creeping *t* Gen 8:19
smite any more every *t* living Gen 8:21
Every moving *t* that liveth shall Gen 9:3
will not take any *t* that is thine Gen 14:23
Is any *t* too hard for the LORD Gen 18:14
from Abraham that *t* which I do Gen 18:17
thee concerning this *t* also Gen 19:21
for I cannot do any *t* till thou Gen 19:22
thou, that thou hast done this *t* Gen 20:10
the *t* was very grievous in Gen 21:11
I wot not who hath done this *t* Gen 21:26
neither do thou any *t* unto him Gen 22:12
for because thou hast done this *t* Gen 22:16
The *t* proceedeth from the LORD Gen 24:50
Thou shalt not give me any *t* Gen 30:31
if thou wilt do this *t* for me Gen 30:31
which *t* ought not to be done Gen 34:7
unto them, We cannot do this *t* Gen 34:14
man deferred not to do the *t* Gen 34:19
the *t* which he did displeased the Gen 38:10
kept back any *t* from me but thee Gen 39:9
to any *t* that was under his hand Gen 39:23
This is the *t* which I have spoken Gen 41:28
it is because the *t* is Gen 41:32
the *t* was good in the eyes of Gen 41:37
should do according to this *t* Gen 44:7
them, Why have ye done this *t* Ex 1:18
and said, Surely this *t* is known Ex 2:14
Now when Pharaoh heard this *t* Ex 2:15
LORD shall do this *t* in the land Ex 9:5
the LORD did that *t* on the morrow Ex 9:6
not any green *t* in the trees Ex 10:15
ye shall observe this *t* for an Ex 12:24
there lay a small round *t* Ex 16:14
This is the *t* which the LORD hath Ex 16:16
This is the *t* which the LORD Ex 16:32
for in the *t* wherein they dealt Ex 18:11
What is this *t* that thou doest to Ex 18:14
The *t* that thou doest is not good Ex 18:17
for this *t* is too heavy for thee Ex 18:18
If thou shalt do this *t*, and God Ex 18:23
or any likeness of any *t* that is Ex 20:4
nor any *t* that is thy neighbour's Ex 20:17
or for any manner of lost *t* Ex 22:9
if it be an hired *t*, it came for Ex 22:15
this is the *t* that thou shalt do Ex 29:1
I will do this *t* also that thou Ex 33:17
for it is a terrible *t* that I Ex 34:10
This is the *t* which the LORD Ex 35:4
it is a *t* most holy of the Lev 2:3
it is a *t* most holy of the Lev 2:10
the *t* be hid from the eyes of the Lev 4:13
Or if a soul touch any unclean *t* Lev 5:2
that he hath sinned in that *t* Lev 5:5
that he hath done in the holy *t* Lev 5:16
or in a *t* taken away by violence, Lev 6:2
away, or the *t* which he hath Lev 6:4
or the lost *t* which he found, Lev 6:4
any *t* of all that he hath done in Lev 6:7
any unclean *t* shall not be eaten Lev 7:19
that shall touch any unclean *t* Lev 7:21
or any abominable unclean *t* Lev 7:21
This is the *t* which the LORD Lev 8:5
This is the *t* which the LORD Lev 9:6
of any living *t* which is in the Lev 11:10
*t* that goeth upon all four Lev 11:21
every *t* whereupon any part of Lev 11:35
every creeping *t* that creepeth Lev 11:41
with any creeping *t* that creepeth Lev 11:43
with any manner of creeping *t* Lev 11:44
she shall touch no hallowed *t* Lev 12:4
a skin, or in any *t* made of skin Lev 13:48
in the woof, or in any *t* of skin Lev 13:49
or any *t* of skin, wherein the Lev 13:52
in the woof, or in any *t* of skin Lev 13:53
wash the *t* wherein the plague is Lev 13:54
in the woof, or in any *t* of skin Lev 13:57
or whatsoever *t* of skin it be Lev 13:58
or any *t* of skins, to pronounce Lev 13:59
and every *t*, whereon he sitteth, Lev 15:4
he that sitteth on any *t* whereon Lev 15:6
whosoever toucheth any *t* that was Lev 15:10
every *t* that she lieth upon in Lev 15:20
every *t* also that she sitteth Lev 15:20
whosoever toucheth any *t* that she Lev 15:22
or on any *t* whereon she sitteth, Lev 15:23
This is the *t* which the LORD hath Lev 17:2
the hallowed *t* of the LORD Lev 19:8
not eat any *t* with the blood Lev 19:26
it is a wicked *t* Lev 20:17
wife, it is an unclean *t* Lev 20:21
or by any manner of living *t* that Lev 20:25
flat nose, or any *t* superfluous, Lev 21:18
whoso toucheth any *t* that is Lev 22:4
whosoever toucheth any creeping *t* Lev 22:5
no stranger eat of the holy *t* Lev 22:10
shall not eat of the holy *t* Lev 22:10
man eat of the holy *t* unwittingly Lev 22:14
unto the priest with the holy *t* Lev 22:14
*t* superfluous or lacking in his Lev 22:23
offerings, every *t* upon his day Lev 23:37
as a holy *t* unto the LORD Lev 27:23
Notwithstanding no devoted *t* Lev 27:28
every devoted *t* is most holy unto Lev 27:28
they shall not touch any holy *t* Num 4:15
Seemeth it but a small *t* unto you Num 16:9
Is it a small *t* that thou hast Num 16:13
But if the LORD make a new *t* Num 16:30
Whosoever cometh any *t* near unto Num 17:13
office for every *t* of the altar Num 18:7
Every *t* devoted in Israel shall Num 18:14
Every *t* that openeth the matrix Num 18:15
only, without doing any *t* else Num 20:19
now any power at all to say any *t* Num 22:38
This is the *t* which the LORD hath Num 30:1
Every *t* that may abide the fire, Num 31:23
unto them, If ye will do this *t* Num 32:20
him any *t* without laying of wait Num 35:22
This is the *t* which the LORD doth Num 36:6
The *t* which thou hast spoken is Deut 1:14
Yet in this *t* ye did not believe Deut 1:32
The likeness of any *t* that Deut 4:18
image, or the likeness of any *t* Deut 4:23
image, or the likeness of any *t* Deut 4:25
any such *t* as this great *t* is Deut 4:32
or any likeness of any *t* that is Deut 5:8
or any *t* that is thy neighbour's Deut 5:21
lest thou be a cursed *t* like it Deut 7:26
for it is a cursed *t* Deut 7:26
thou shalt not lack any *t* in it Deut 8:9
What *t* soever I command you, Deut 12:32
and the *t* certain, that such Deut 13:14
of the cursed *t* to thine hand Deut 13:17
shalt not eat any abominable *t* Deut 14:3
every creeping *t* that flieth is Deut 14:19
eat of any *t* that dieth of itself Deut 14:21
because that for this *t* the LORD Deut 15:10
I command thee this *t* to day Deut 15:15
shall there any *t* of the flesh Deut 16:4
true, and the *t* certain, that such Deut 17:4
have committed that wicked *t* Deut 17:5
if the *t* follow not, nor come to Deut 18:22
that is the *t* which the LORD hath Deut 18:22
But if this *t* be true, and the Deut 22:20
keep thee from every wicked *t* Deut 23:9
that he see no unclean *t* in thee Deut 23:14
usury of any *t* that is lent upon Deut 23:19
thou dost lend thy brother any *t* Deut 24:10
I command thee to do this *t* Deut 24:18
I command thee to do this *t* Deut 24:22
*t* which the LORD thy God hath Deut 26:11
which have not known any *t* Deut 31:13
For it is not a vain *t* for you Deut 32:47
through this *t* ye shall prolong Deut 32:47
until every *t* was finished that Josh 4:10
yourselves from the accursed *t* Josh 6:18
when ye take of the accursed *t* Josh 6:18
a trespass in the accursed *t* Josh 7:1
of Judah, took of the accursed *t* Josh 7:1
have even taken of the accursed *t* Josh 7:11
accursed *t* in the midst of thee Josh 7:13
the accursed *t* from among you Josh 7:13
*t* shall be burnt with fire Josh 7:15
of you, and have done this *t* Josh 9:24
Thou knowest the *t* that the LORD Josh 14:6
failed not ought of any good *t* Josh 21:45
a trespass in the accursed *t* Josh 22:20
rather done it for fear of this *t* Josh 22:24
the *t* pleased the children of Josh 22:33
that not one *t* hath failed of all Josh 23:14
not one *t* hath failed thereof Josh 23:14
to another, Who hath done this *t* Judg 6:29
the son of Joash hath done this *t* Judg 6:29
which *t* became a snare unto Judg 8:27
now art thou any *t* better than Judg 11:25
Let this *t* be done for me Judg 11:37
drink, and eat not any unclean *t* Judg 13:4
drink, neither eat any unclean *t* Judg 13:7
She may not eat of any *t* that Judg 13:14
drink, nor eat any unclean *t* Judg 13:14
might put them to shame in any *t* Judg 18:7
of any *t* that is in the earth Judg 18:10
there is no want of any *t* Judg 19:19
unto this man do not so vile a *t* Judg 19:24
But now this shall be the *t* which Judg 20:9
this is the *t* that ye shall do, Judg 21:11
he have finished the *t* this day Ruth 3:18
Behold, I will do a *t* in Israel 1Sa 3:11
What is the *t* that the LORD hath 1Sa 3:17
if thou hide any *t* from me of all 1Sa 3:17
hath not been such a *t* heretofore 1Sa 4:7
But the *t* displeased Samuel, when 1Sa 8:6
stand and see this great *t* 1Sa 12:16
up to us, and we will shew you a *t* 1Sa 14:12
but every *t* that was vile and 1Sa 15:9
told Saul, and the *t* pleased him 1Sa 18:20
light *t* to be a king's son in law 1Sa 18:23

T

my father hide this *t* from me 1Sa 20:2
Saul spake not any *t* that day 1Sa 20:26
But the lad knew not any *t* 1Sa 20:39
Let no man know any *t* of the 1Sa 21:2
impute any *t* unto his servant 1Sa 22:15
I should do this *t* unto my master 1Sa 24:6
not hurt, neither missed we any *t* 1Sa 25:15
This *t* is not good that thou hast 1Sa 26:16
happen to thee for this *t* 1Sa 28:10
done this *t* unto thee this day 1Sa 28:18
nor any *t* that they had taken to 1Sa 30:19
because ye have done this *t* 2Sa 2:6
but one *t* I require of thee, that 2Sa 3:13
was yet a small *t* in thy sight 2Sa 7:19
soul liveth, I will not do this *t* 2Sa 11:11
Let not this *t* displease thee, 2Sa 11:25
But the *t* that David had done 2Sa 11:27
hath done this *t* shall surely die 2Sa 12:5
fourfold, because he did this *t* 2Sa 12:6
will do this *t* before all Israel 2Sa 12:12
What *t* is this that thou hast 2Sa 12:21
hard for him to do any *t* to her 2Sa 13:2
for no such *t* ought to be done in 2Sa 13:12
regard not this *t* 2Sa 13:20
the king take the *t* to his heart 2Sa 13:33
a *t* against the people of God 2Sa 14:13
this *t* as one which is faulty 2Sa 14:13
of this *t* unto my lord the king 2Sa 14:15
the *t* that I shall ask thee 2Sa 14:18
hath thy servant Joab done this *t* 2Sa 14:20
Behold now, I have done this *t* 2Sa 14:21
and they knew not any *t* 2Sa 15:11
that what *t* soever thou shalt 2Sa 15:35
unto me every *t* that ye can hear 2Sa 15:36
and the *t* was not known 2Sa 17:19
lord the king delight in this *t* 2Sa 24:3
Is this *t* done by my lord the 1Kin 1:27
that Solomon had asked this *t* 1Kin 3:10
Because thou hast asked this *t* 1Kin 3:11
was not any *t* hid from the king 1Kin 10:3
commanded him concerning this *t* 1Kin 11:10
for this *t* is from me 1Kin 12:24
And this *t* became a sin 1Kin 12:30
After this *t* Jeroboam returned 1Kin 13:33
this *t* became sin unto the house 1Kin 13:34
to ask a *t* of thee for her son 1Kin 14:5
*t* toward the LORD God of Israel 1Kin 14:13
turned not aside from any *t* that 1Kin 15:5
as if it had been a light *t* for 1Kin 16:31
but this *t* I may not do 1Kin 20:9
And do this *t*, Take the kings away 1Kin 20:24
whether any *t* would come from him 1Kin 20:33
he said, Thou hast asked a hard *t* 2Kin 2:10
this is but a light *t* in the 2Kin 3:18
hath not any *t* in the house 2Kin 4:2
had bid thee do some great *t* 2Kin 5:13
In this *t* the LORD pardon thy 2Kin 5:18
LORD pardon thy servant in this *t* 2Kin 5:18
was sore troubled for this *t* 2Kin 6:11
in heaven, might this *t* be 2Kin 7:2
in heaven, might such a *t* be 2Kin 7:19
even of every good *t* of Damascus 2Kin 8:9
that he should do this great *t* 2Kin 8:13
This is the *t* that ye shall do 2Kin 11:5
unto them, Ye shall not do this *t* 2Kin 17:12
will do the *t* that he hath spoken 2Kin 20:9
It is a light *t* for the shadow to 2Kin 20:10
transgressed in the *t* accursed 1Chr 2:7
it me, that I should do this *t* 1Chr 11:19
for the *t* was right in the eyes 1Chr 13:4
this was a small *t* in thine eyes 1Chr 17:17
let the *t* that thou hast spoken 1Chr 17:23
then doth my lord require this *t* 1Chr 21:3
And God was displeased with this *t* 1Chr 21:7
because I have done this *t* 1Chr 21:8
and whosoever had dedicated any *t* 1Chr 26:28
it was not any *t* accounted of in 2Chr 9:20
for this *t* is done of me 2Chr 11:4
a rage with him because of this *t* 2Chr 16:10
This is the *t* that ye shall do 2Chr 23:4
unclean in any *t* should enter in 2Chr 23:19
for the *t* was done suddenly 2Chr 29:36
the *t* pleased the king and all the 2Chr 30:4
which hath put such a *t* as this Ezr 7:27
And when I heard this *t*, I rent my Ezr 9:3
hope in Israel concerning this *t* Ezr 10:2
that have transgressed in this *t* Ezr 10:13
said, What is this *t* that ye do Neh 2:19
What evil *t* is this that ye do, Neh 13:17
And the *t* pleased the king Est 2:4
the *t* was known to Mordecai, who Est 2:22
And the *t* pleased Haman Est 5:14
every *t* that had befallen him Est 6:13
the *t* seem right before the king, Est 8:5
For the *t* which I greatly feared Job 3:25
Now a *t* was secretly brought to Job 4:12
grant me the *t* that I long for Job 6:8
For now ye are no *t* Job 6:21
This is one *t*, therefore I said Job 9:22
is the soul of every living *t* Job 12:10
And he, as a rotten *t*, consumeth, Job 13:28
bring a clean *t* out of an unclean Job 14:4
is there any secret *t* with thee Job 15:11
Thou shalt also decree a *t* Job 22:28
For he performeth the *t* that is Job 23:14
declared the *t* as it is Job 26:3
and his eye seeth every precious *t* Job 28:10
the *t* that is hid bringeth he Job 28:11
If thou hast any *t* to say Job 33:32
he searcheth after every green *t* Job 39:8
I know that thou canst do every *t* Job 42:2
spoken of me the *t* that is right Job 42:7
spoken of me the *t* which is right Job 42:8
and the people imagine a vain *t* Ps 2:1
One *t* have I desired of the LORD, Ps 27:4
An horse is a vain *t* for safety Ps 33:17
LORD shall not want any good *t* Ps 34:10
I follow the *t* that good is Ps 38:20
every *t* that moveth therein Ps 69:34
no good *t* will he withhold from Ps 84:11
nor alter the *t* that is gone out Ps 89:34
It is a good *t* to give thanks Ps 92:1
set no wicked *t* before mine eyes Ps 101:3
not my heart to any evil *t* Ps 141:4
the desire of every living *t* Ps 145:16
Let every *t* that hath breath Ps 150:6
Wisdom is the principal *t* Prov 4:7
findeth a wife findeth a good *t* Prov 18:22
For it is a pleasant *t* if thou Prov 22:18
the glory of God to conceal a *t* Prov 25:2
soul every bitter *t* is sweet Prov 27:7
The *t* that hath been, it is that Eccl 1:9
there is no new *t* under the sun Eccl 1:9
Is there any *t* whereof it may be Eccl 1:10
To every *t* there is a season, and Eccl 3:1
He hath made every *t* beautiful in Eccl 3:11
to it, nor any *t* taken from it Eccl 3:14
even one *t* befalleth them Eccl 3:19
hasty to utter any *t* before God Eccl 5:2
not seen the sun, nor known any *t* Eccl 6:5
Better is the end of a *t* than the Eccl 7:8
knoweth the interpretation of a *t* Eccl 8:1
stand not in an evil *t* Eccl 8:3
commandment shall feel no evil *t* Eccl 8:5
hath no better *t* under the sun Eccl 8:15
but the dead know not any *t* Eccl 9:5
any *t* that is done under the sun Eccl 9:6
a pleasant *t* it is for the eyes Eccl 11:7
judgment, with every secret *t* Eccl 12:14
Is it a small *t* for you to weary Is 7:13
faileth, there is no green *t* Is 15:6
like a rolling *t* before the Is 17:13
every *t* sown by the brooks, shall Is 19:7
or shall the *t* framed say of him Is 29:16
aside the just for a *t* of nought Is 29:21
do this *t* that he hath spoken Is 38:7
up the isles as a very little *t* Is 40:15
as nothing, and as a *t* of nought Is 41:12
Behold, I will do a new *t* Is 43:19
It is a light *t* that thou Is 49:6
from thence, touch no unclean *t* Is 52:11
in the *t* whereto I sent it Is 55:11
But we are all as an unclean *t* Is 64:6
Who hath heard such a *t* Is 66:8
and see if there be such a *t* Jer 2:10
and see that it is an evil *t* Jer 2:19
horrible *t* is committed in the Jer 5:30
But this *t* commanded I them, Jer 7:23
set up altars to that shameful *t* Jer 11:13
a *t* of nought, and the deceit of Jer 14:14
hath done a very horrible *t* Jer 18:13
For if ye do this *t* indeed Jer 22:4
of Jerusalem an horrible *t* Jer 23:14
hath created a new *t* in the earth Jer 31:22
is there any *t* too hard for me Jer 32:27
that I will perform that good *t* Jer 33:14
he that can do any *t* against you Jer 38:5
Jeremiah, I will ask thee a *t* Jer 38:14
therefore this *t* is come upon you Jer 40:3
Kareah, Thou shalt not do this *t* Jer 40:16
may walk, and the *t* that we may do Jer 42:3
that whatsoever *t* the LORD shall Jer 42:4
nor any *t* for the which he hath Jer 42:21
not this abominable *t* that I hate Jer 44:4
*t* goeth forth out of our own Jer 44:17
What *t* shall I take to witness Lam 2:13
what *t* shall I liken to thee, O Lam 2:13
Is it a light *t* to the house of Eze 8:17
deceived when he hath spoken a *t* Eze 14:9
as if that were a very little *t* Eze 16:47
Seemeth it a small *t* unto you to Eze 34:18
with any *t* that causeth sweat Eze 44:18
every dedicated *t* in Israel shall Eze 44:29
of any *t* that is dead of itself Eze 44:31
that every *t* that liveth, which Eze 47:9
every *t* shall live whither the Eze 47:9
*t* most holy by the border of the Eze 48:12
Chaldeans, The *t* is gone from me Dan 2:5
ye see the *t* is gone from me Dan 2:8
it is a rare *t* that the king Dan 2:11
Arioch made the *t* known to Daniel Dan 2:15
made the *t* known to Hananiah, Dan 2:17
which speak any *t* amiss against Dan 3:29
The same hour was the *t* fulfilled Dan 4:33
shew the interpretation of the *t* Dan 5:15
is the interpretation of the *t* Dan 5:26
The *t* is true, according to the Dan 6:12
a *t* was revealed unto Daniel Dan 10:1
the *t* was true, but the time Dan 10:1
and he understood the *t*, and had Dan 10:1
horrible *t* in the house of Israel Hos 6:10
hath cast off the *t* that is good Hos 8:3
they were counted as a strange *t* Hos 8:12
Ye which rejoice in a *t* of nought Amos 6:13
herd nor flock, taste any *t* Jonah 3:7
unto the Lord a corrupt *t* Mal 1:14
into the city, and told every *t* Mt 8:33
any *t* that they shall ask Mt 18:19
what good *t* shall I do, that I Mt 19:16
and desiring a certain *t* of him Mt 20:20
them, I also will ask you one *t* Mt 21:24
to take any *t* out of his house Mt 24:17
saying, What *t* is this Mk 1:27
neither was any *t* kept secret Mk 4:22
to see her that had done this *t* Mk 5:32
that whatsoever *t* from without Mk 7:18
but if thou canst do any *t* Mk 9:22
said unto him, One *t* thou lackest Mk 10:21
haply he might find any *t* thereon Mk 11:13
to take any *t* out of his house Mk 13:15
neither said they any *t* to any Mk 16:8
and if they drink any deadly *t* Mk 16:18
therefore also that holy *t* which Lk 1:35
see this *t* which is come to pass, Lk 2:15
unto them, I will ask you one *t* Lk 6:9
neither any *t* hid, that shall not Lk 8:17
them to tell no man that *t* Lk 9:21
But one *t* is needful Lk 10:42
how or what *t* ye shall answer Lk 12:11
able to do that *t* which is least Lk 12:26
unto him, Yet lackest thou one *t* Lk 18:22
if I have taken any *t* from any Lk 19:8
them, I will also ask you one *t* Lk 20:3
them it was that should do this *t* Lk 22:23
scrip, and shoes, lacked ye any *t* Lk 22:35
was not any *t* made that was made Jn 1:3
Can there any good *t* come out of Jn 1:46
lest a worse *t* come unto thee Jn 5:14
no man that doeth any *t* in secret Jn 7:4
one *t* I know, that, whereas I was Jn 9:25
Why herein is a marvellous *t* Jn 9:30
If ye shall ask any *t* in my name Jn 14:14
Sayest thou this *t* of thyself Jn 18:34
conceived this *t* in thine heart Acts 5:4
any *t* that is common or unclean Acts 10:14
*t* for a man that is a Jew to keep Acts 10:28
And when he had considered the *t* Acts 12:12
to tell, or to hear some new *t* Acts 17:21
hands, as though he needed any *t* Acts 17:25
Some therefore cried one *t* Acts 19:32
But if ye enquire any *t* Acts 19:39
that they observe no such *t* Acts 21:25
And some cried one *t*, some another Acts 21:34
he hath a certain *t* to tell him Acts 23:17
have I offended any *t* at all Acts 25:8
committed any *t* worthy of death Acts 25:11
certain *t* to write unto my lord Acts 25:26
thought a *t* incredible with you Acts 26:8
Which *t* I also did in Jerusalem Acts 26:10
for this *t* was not done in a Acts 26:26
in my flesh,) dwelleth no good *t* Rom 7:18
Who shall lay any *t* to the charge Rom 8:33
Shall the *t* formed say to him Rom 9:20
continually upon this very *t* Rom 13:6
Owe no man any *t*, but to love one Rom 13:8
esteemeth any *t* to be unclean Rom 14:14
nor any *t* whereby thy brother Rom 14:21
in that *t* which he alloweth Rom 14:22
That in every *t* ye are enriched 1Cor 1:5
that ye all speak the same *t* 1Cor 1:10
not to know any *t* among you 1Cor 2:2
neither is he that planteth any *t* 1Cor 3:7
*t* that I should be judged of you 1Cor 4:3
man think that he knoweth any *t* 1Cor 8:2
it as a *t* offered unto an idol 1Cor 8:7
is it a great *t* if we shall reap 1Cor 9:11
For if I do this *t* willingly 1Cor 9:17
that the idol is any *t*, or that 1Cor 10:19
in sacrifice to idols is any *t* 1Cor 10:19
If any *t* be revealed to another 1Cor 14:30
And if they will learn any *t* 1Cor 14:35
To whom ye forgive any *t*, I 2Cor 2:10
for if I forgave any *t*, to whom I 2Cor 2:10
to think any *t* as of ourselves 2Cor 3:5
us for the selfsame *t* is God 2Cor 5:5
Giving no offence in any *t* 2Cor 6:3
Lord, and touch not the unclean *t* 2Cor 6:17
For behold this selfsame *t* 2Cor 7:11
have boasted any *t* to him of you 2Cor 7:14
as ye abound in every *t*, in 2Cor 8:7
in every *t* to all bountifulness 2Cor 9:11
every high *t* that exalteth itself 2Cor 10:5
great *t* if his ministers also be 2Cor 11:15
For this *t* I besought the Lord 2Cor 12:8
affected always in a good *t* Gal 4:18
circumcision availeth any *t* Gal 5:6
circumcision availeth any *t* Gal 6:15
his hands the *t* which is good Eph 4:28
to their own husbands in every *t* Eph 5:24
spot, or wrinkle, or any such *t* Eph 5:27
whatsoever good *t* any man doeth Eph 6:8
Being confident of this very *t* Phil 1:6
but this one *t* I do, forgetting Phil 3:13
if in any *t* ye be otherwise Phil 3:15
same rule, let us mind the same *t* Phil 3:16
but in every *t* by prayer and Phil 4:6
that we need not to speak any *t* 1Th 1:8
In every *t* give thanks 1Th 5:18
*t* with God to recompense 2Th 1:6
if there be any other *t* that is 1Ti 1:10
That good *t* which was committed 2Ti 1:14
having no evil *t* to say of you Titus 2:8
*t* which is in you in Christ Jesus Philem 6
he was sanctified, an unholy *t* Heb 10:29
It is a fearful *t* to fall into Heb 10:31
provided some better *t* for us Heb 11:40
For it is a good *t* that the heart Heb 13:9
shall receive any *t* of the Lord Jas 1:7
some strange *t* happened unto you 1Pet 4:12
be not ignorant of this one *t* 2Pet 3:8

which *t* is true in him and in you ... 1Jn 2:8
if we ask any *t* according to his ... 1Jn 5:14
the Nicolaitanes, which *t* I hate ... Rev 2:15
of the earth, neither any green *t* ... Rev 9:4
enter into it any *t* that defileth ... Rev 21:27

**THINGS** See PREFACE.

**THINGS'**
For which *t* sake the wrath of God ... Col 3:6

**THINK**
But *t* on me when it shall be well ... Gen 40:14
them marry to whom they *t* best ... Num 36:6
to *t* that all the king's sons are ... 2Sa 13:33
now ye *t* to withstand the kingdom ... 2Chr 13:8
*T* upon me, my God, for good, ... Neh 5:19
that thou and the Jews *t* to rebel ... Neh 6:6
*t* thou upon Tobiah and Sanballat ... Neh 6:14
*T* not with thyself that thou ... Est 4:13
why then should I *t* upon a maid ... Job 31:1
one would *t* the deep to be hoary ... Job 41:32
though a wise man *t* to know it ... Eccl 8:17
so, neither doth his heart *t* so ... Is 10:7
Which *t* to cause my people to ... Jer 23:27
the thoughts that I *t* toward you ... Jer 29:11
thou shalt *t* an evil thought ... Eze 38:10
*t* to change times and laws ... Dan 7:25
if so be that God will *t* upon us ... Jonah 1:6
And I said unto them, If ye *t* good ... Zec 11:12
*t* not to say within yourselves, ... Mt 3:9
*T* not that I am come to destroy ... Mt 5:17
for they *t* that they shall be ... Mt 6:7
Wherefore *t* ye evil in your ... Mt 9:4
*T* not that I am come to send ... Mt 10:34
How *t* ye? ... Mt 18:12
But what *t* ye ... Mt 21:28
Saying, What *t* ye of Christ ... Mt 22:42
as ye *t* not the Son of man cometh ... Mt 24:44
What *t* ye? ... Mt 26:66
what *t* ye? ... Mk 14:64
cometh at an hour when ye *t* not ... Lk 12:40
*t* ye that they were sinners above ... Lk 13:4
for in them ye *t* ye have eternal ... Jn 5:39
Do not *t* that I will accuse you ... Jn 5:45
stood in the temple, What *t* ye ... Jn 11:56
will *t* that he doeth God service ... Jn 16:2
he said, Whom *t* ye that I am ... Acts 13:25
we ought not to *t* that the ... Acts 17:29
I *t* myself happy, king Agrippa, ... Acts 26:2
not to *t* of himself more highly ... Rom 12:3
more highly than he ought to *t* ... Rom 12:3
but to *t* soberly, according as ... Rom 12:3
to *t* of men above that which is ... 1Cor 4:6
For I *t* that God hath set forth ... 1Cor 4:9
But if any man *t* that he behaveth ... 1Cor 7:36
I *t* also that I have the Spirit ... 1Cor 7:40
if any man *t* that he knoweth any ... 1Cor 8:2
which we *t* to be less honourable, ... 1Cor 12:23
If any man *t* himself to be a ... 1Cor 14:37
to *t* any thing as of ourselves ... 2Cor 3:5
wherewith I *t* to be bold against ... 2Cor 10:2
which *t* of us as if we walked ... 2Cor 10:2
let him of himself *t* this again ... 2Cor 10:7
Let such an one *t* this, that, ... 2Cor 10:11
say again, Let no man *t* me a fool ... 2Cor 11:16
lest any man should *t* of me above ... 2Cor 12:6
*t* ye that we excuse ourselves ... 2Cor 12:19
For if a man *t* himself to be ... Gal 6:3
above all that we ask or *t* ... Eph 3:20
meet for me to *t* this of you all ... Phil 1:7
be any praise, *t* on these things ... Phil 4:8
For let not that man *t* that he ... Jas 1:7
Do ye *t* that the scripture saith ... Jas 4:5
Wherein they *t* it strange that ye ... 1Pet 4:4
*t* it not strange concerning the ... 1Pet 4:12
I *t* it meet, as long as I am in ... 2Pet 1:13

**THINKEST**
*T* thou that David doth honour thy ... 2Sa 10:3
*T* thou that David doth honour thy ... 1Chr 19:3
*T* thou this to be right, that ... Job 35:2
him, saying, What *t* thou, Simon ... Mt 17:25
Tell us therefore, What *t* thou ... Mt 22:17
*T* thou that I cannot now pray to ... Mt 26:53
*t* thou, was neighbour unto him ... Lk 10:36
to hear of thee what thou *t* ... Acts 28:22
*t* thou this, O man, that judgest ... Rom 2:3

**THINKETH**
Me *t* the running of the foremost ... 2Sa 18:27
yet the Lord *t* upon me ... Ps 40:17
For as he *t* in his heart, so is ... Prov 23:7
Wherefore let him that *t* he ... 1Cor 10:12
is not easily provoked, *t* no evil ... 1Cor 13:5
If any other man *t* that he hath ... Phil 3:4

**THINKING**
*t* to have brought good tidings, I ... 2Sa 4:10
*t*, David cannot come in ... 2Sa 5:6

**THIRD**
and the morning were the *t* day ... Gen 1:13
the name of the *t* river is ... Gen 2:14
*t* stories shalt thou make it ... Gen 6:16
Then on the *t* day Abraham lifted ... Gen 22:4
on the *t* day that Jacob was fled ... Gen 31:22
commanded he the second, and the *t*. Gen 32:19
And it came to pass on the *t* day ... Gen 34:25
And it came to pass the *t* day ... Gen 40:20
Joseph said unto them the *t* day ... Gen 42:18
children of the *t* generation ... Gen 50:23
In the *t* month, when the children ... Ex 19:1
And be ready against the *t* day ... Ex 19:11
for the *t* day the LORD will come ... Ex 19:11
Be ready against the *t* day ... Ex 19:15
pass on the *t* day in the morning ... Ex 19:16
upon the children unto the *t* ... Ex 20:5
the *t* row a ligure, an agate, and ... Ex 28:19
children's children, unto the *t* ... Ex 34:7
And the *t* row, a ligure, an agate, ... Ex 39:12
*t* day shall be burnt with fire ... Lev 7:17
be eaten at all on the *t* day ... Lev 7:18
if ought remain until the *t* day ... Lev 19:6
it be eaten at all on the *t* day ... Lev 19:7
shall go forward in the *t* rank ... Num 2:24
On the *t* day Eliab the son of ... Num 7:24
upon the children unto the *t* ... Num 14:18
with the *t* part of an hin of oil ... Num 15:6
the *t* part of an hin of wine ... Num 15:7
himself with it on the *t* day ... Num 19:12
he purify not himself the *t* day ... Num 19:12
upon the unclean on the *t* day ... Num 19:19
the *t* part of an hin unto a ram, ... Num 28:14
on the *t* day eleven bullocks, two ... Num 29:20
and your captives on the *t* day ... Num 31:19
upon the children unto the *t* ... Deut 5:9
of the LORD in their *t* generation ... Deut 23:8
of thine increase the *t* year ... Deut 26:12
unto their cities on the *t* day ... Josh 9:17
the *t* lot came up for the ... Josh 19:10
children of Benjamin on the *t* day ... Judg 20:30
called Samuel again the *t* time ... 1Sa 3:8
him Abinadab, and the *t* Shammah ... 1Sa 17:13
sent messengers again the *t* time ... 1Sa 19:21
the field unto the *t* day at even ... 1Sa 20:5
to morrow any time, or the *t* day ... 1Sa 20:12
were come to Ziklag on the *t* day ... 1Sa 30:1
It came even to pass on the *t* day ... 2Sa 1:2
and the *t*, Absalom the son of ... 2Sa 3:3
David sent forth a *t* part of the ... 2Sa 18:2
a *t* part under the hand of ... 2Sa 18:2
a *t* part under the hand of Ittai ... 2Sa 18:2
it came to pass the *t* day after ... 1Kin 3:18
the *t* was seven cubits broad ... 1Kin 6:6
and out of the middle into the *t* ... 1Kin 6:8
people came to Rehoboam the *t* day. 1Kin 12:12
Come to me again the *t* day ... 1Kin 12:12
Even in the *t* year of Asa king of ... 1Kin 15:28
In the *t* year of Asa king of ... 1Kin 15:33
LORD came to Elijah in the *t* year ... 1Kin 18:1
And he said, Do it the *t* time ... 1Kin 18:34
And they did it the *t* time ... 1Kin 18:34
And it came to pass in the *t* year ... 1Kin 22:2
of the *t* fifty with his fifty ... 2Kin 1:13
the *t* captain of fifty went up, ... 2Kin 1:13
A *t* part of you that enter in on ... 2Kin 11:5
a *t* part shall be at the gate of ... 2Kin 11:6
a *t* part at the gate behind the ... 2Kin 11:6
Now it came to pass in the *t* year ... 2Kin 18:1
in the *t* year sow ye, and reap, and ... 2Kin 19:29
on the *t* day thou shalt go up ... 2Kin 20:5
the house of the LORD the *t* day ... 2Kin 20:8
the second, and Shimma the *t* ... 1Chr 2:13
The *t*, Absalom the son of Maachah ... 1Chr 3:2
the *t* Zedekiah, the fourth ... 1Chr 3:15
the second, and Aharah the *t* ... 1Chr 8:1
the second, and Eliphelet the *t* ... 1Chr 8:39
Obadiah the second, Eliab the *t* ... 1Chr 12:9
the second, Jahaziel the *t* ... 1Chr 23:19
The *t* to Harim, the fourth to ... 1Chr 24:8
the second, Jahaziel the *t* ... 1Chr 24:23
The *t* to Zaccur, he, his sons, and ... 1Chr 25:10
the second, Zebadiah the *t* ... 1Chr 26:2
Jehozabad the second, Joah the *t* ... 1Chr 26:4
the second, Tebaliah the *t* ... 1Chr 26:11
The *t* captain of the host for the ... 1Chr 27:5
captain of the host for the *t* ... 1Chr 27:5
came to Rehoboam on the *t* day ... 2Chr 10:12
Come again to me on the *t* day ... 2Chr 10:12
at Jerusalem in the *t* month ... 2Chr 15:10
Also in the *t* year of his reign ... 2Chr 17:7
A *t* part of you entering on the ... 2Chr 23:4
a *t* part shall be at the king's ... 2Chr 23:5
a *t* part at the gate of the ... 2Chr 23:5
both the second year, and the *t* ... 2Chr 27:5
In the *t* month they began to lay ... 2Chr 31:7
on the *t* day of the month Adar ... Ezr 6:15
the *t* part of a shekel for the ... Neh 10:32
In the *t* year of his reign, he ... Est 1:3
Now it came to pass on the *t* day ... Est 5:1
at that time in the *t* month ... Est 8:9
and the name of the *t*, ... Job 42:14
shall Israel be the *t* with Egypt ... Is 19:24
in the *t* year sow ye, and reap, and ... Is 37:30
*t* entry that is in the house of ... Jer 38:14
Thou shalt burn with fire a *t* ... Eze 5:2
and thou shalt take a *t* part ... Eze 5:2
a *t* part thou shalt scatter in ... Eze 5:2
A *t* part of thee shall die with ... Eze 5:12
a *t* part shall fall by the sword ... Eze 5:12
I will scatter a *t* part into all ... Eze 5:12
the *t* the face of a lion, and the ... Eze 10:14
the sword be doubled the *t* time ... Eze 21:14
the eleventh year, in the *t* month ... Eze 31:1
the *t* part of an hin of oil, to ... Eze 46:14
In the *t* year of the reign of ... Dan 1:1
another *t* kingdom of brass, which ... Dan 2:39
shall be the *t* ruler in the ... Dan 5:7
shalt be the *t* ruler in the ... Dan 5:16
be the *t* ruler in the kingdom ... Dan 5:29
In the *t* year of the reign of ... Dan 8:1
In the *t* year of Cyrus king of ... Dan 10:1
in the *t* day he will raise us up, ... Hos 6:2
in the *t* chariot white horses ... Zec 6:3
but the *t* shall be left therein ... Zec 13:8
I will bring the *t* part through ... Zec 13:9
and be raised again the *t* day ... Mt 16:21
the *t* day he shall be raised ... Mt 17:23
And he went out about the *t* hour ... Mt 20:3
the *t* day he shall rise again ... Mt 20:19
the second also, and the *t* ... Mt 22:26
away again, and prayed the *t* time ... Mt 26:44
be made sure until the *t* day ... Mt 27:64
killed, he shall rise the *t* day ... Mk 9:31
the *t* day he shall rise again ... Mk 10:34
and the *t* likewise ... Mk 12:21
And he cometh the *t* time, and saith ... Mk 14:41
And it was the *t* hour, and they ... Mk 15:25
be slain, and be raised the *t* day ... Lk 9:22
watch, or come in the *t* watch ... Lk 12:38
the *t* day I shall be perfected ... Lk 13:32
the *t* day he shall rise again ... Lk 18:33
And again he sent a *t* ... Lk 20:12
And the *t* took her ... Lk 20:31
And he said unto them the *t* time ... Lk 23:22
and the *t* day rise again ... Lk 24:7
to day is the *t* day since these ... Lk 24:21
to rise from the dead the *t* day ... Lk 24:46
the *t* day there was a marriage in ... Jn 2:1
This is now the *t* time that Jesus ... Jn 21:14
He saith unto him the *t* time ... Jn 21:17
he said unto him the *t* time ... Jn 21:17
it is but the *t* hour of the day ... Acts 2:15
Him God raised up the *t* day ... Acts 10:40
and fell down from the *t* loft ... Acts 20:9
at the *t* hour of the night ... Acts 23:23
the *t* day we cast out with our ... Acts 27:19
that he rose again the *t* day ... 1Cor 15:4
an one caught up to the *t* heaven ... 2Cor 12:2
the *t* time I am ready to come to ... 2Cor 12:14
This is the *t* time I am coming to ... 2Cor 13:1
the *t* beast had a face as a man, ... Rev 4:7
And when he had opened the *t* seal ... Rev 6:5
I heard the *t* beast say ... Rev 6:5
the *t* part of trees was burnt up, ... Rev 8:7
the *t* part of the sea became ... Rev 8:8
the *t* part of the creatures which ... Rev 8:9
the *t* part of the ships were ... Rev 8:9
the *t* angel sounded, and there ... Rev 8:10
it fell upon the *t* part of the ... Rev 8:10
the *t* part of the waters became ... Rev 8:11
the *t* part of the sun was smitten ... Rev 8:12
the *t* part of the moon, and the ... Rev 8:12
moon, and the *t* part of the stars ... Rev 8:12
so as the *t* part of them was ... Rev 8:12
day shone not for a *t* part of it ... Rev 8:12
for to slay the *t* part of men ... Rev 9:15
was the *t* part of men killed ... Rev 9:18
behold, the *t* woe cometh quickly ... Rev 11:14
his tail drew the *t* part of the ... Rev 12:4
the *t* angel followed them, saying ... Rev 14:9
the *t* angel poured out his vial ... Rev 16:4
the *t*, a chalcedony ... Rev 21:19

**THIRDLY**
*t* teachers, after that miracles, ... 1Cor 12:28

**THIRST**
our children and our cattle with *t* ... Ex 17:3
against thee, in hunger, and in *t* ... Deut 28:48
heart, to add drunkenness to *t* ... Deut 29:19
and now shall I die for *t*, and fall ... Judg 15:18
to die by famine and by *t*, saying, ... 2Chr 32:11
them out of the rock for their *t* ... Neh 9:15
and gavest them water for their *t* ... Neh 9:20
their winepresses, and suffer *t* ... Job 24:11
in my *t* they gave me vinegar to ... Ps 69:21
the wild asses quench their *t* ... Ps 104:11
their multitude dried up with *t* ... Is 5:13
and their tongue faileth for *t* ... Is 41:17
They shall not hunger nor *t* ... Is 49:10
there is no water, and dieth for *t* ... Is 50:2
unshod, and thy throat from *t* ... Jer 2:25
down from thy glory, and sit in *t* ... Jer 48:18
to the roof of his mouth for *t* ... Lam 4:4
a dry land, and slay her with *t* ... Hos 2:3
nor a *t* for water, but of hearing ... Amos 8:11
virgins and young men faint for *t* ... Amos 8:13
hunger and *t* after righteousness ... Mt 5:6
of this water shall *t* again ... Jn 4:13
I shall give him shall never *t* ... Jn 4:14
give me this water, that I *t* not ... Jn 4:15
believeth on me shall never *t* ... Jn 6:35
and cried, saying, If any man *t* ... Jn 7:37
might be fulfilled, saith, I *t* ... Jn 19:28
if he *t*, give him drink ... Rom 12:20
present hour we both hunger, and *t* ... 1Cor 4:11
watchings often, in hunger and *t* ... 2Cor 11:27
no more, neither *t* any more ... Rev 7:16

**THIRSTED**
the people *t* there for water ... Ex 17:3
they *t* not when he led them ... Is 48:21

**THIRSTETH**
My soul *t* for God, for the living ... Ps 42:2
my soul *t* for thee, my flesh ... Ps 63:1
my soul *t* after thee, as a ... Ps 143:6
Ho, every one that *t*, come ye to ... Is 55:1

**THIRSTY**
for I am *t* ... Judg 4:19
people is hungry, and weary, and *t* ... 2Sa 17:29
*t* land, where no water is ... Ps 63:1
Hungry and *t*, their soul fainted ... Ps 107:5

T

thirsteth after thee, as a *t* land ... Ps 143:6
and if he be *t*, give him water to ... Prov 25:21
As cold waters to a *t* soul ... Prov 25:25
brought water to him that was *t* ... Is 21:14
or as when a *t* man dreameth ... Is 29:8
cause the drink of the *t* to fail ... Is 32:6
the *t* land springs of water ... Is 35:7
pour water upon him that is *t* ... Is 44:3
shall drink, but ye shall be *t* ... Is 65:13
wilderness, in a dry and *t* ground ... Eze 19:13
I was *t*, and ye gave me drink ... Mt 25:35
or *t*, and gave thee drink ... Mt 25:37
I was *t*, and ye gave me no drink ... Mt 25:42

**THIRTEEN**
Ishmael his son was *t* years old ... Gen 17:25
two hundred and threescore and *t* ... Num 3:43
*t* of the firstborn of the ... Num 3:46
*t* young bullocks, two rams, and ... Num 29:13
every bullock of the *t* bullocks ... Num 29:14
*t* cities and their villages ... Josh 19:6
the tribe of Benjamin, *t* cities ... Josh 21:4
of Manasseh in Bashan, *t* cities ... Josh 21:6
were *t* cities with their suburbs ... Josh 21:19
to their families were *t* cities ... Josh 21:33
building his own house *t* years ... 1Kin 7:1
their families were *t* cities ... 1Chr 6:60
of Manasseh in Bashan, *t* cities ... 1Chr 6:62
sons and brethren of Hosah were *t* ... 1Chr 26:11
the length of the gate, *t* cubits ... Eze 40:11

**THIRTEENTH**
in the *t* year they rebelled ... Gen 14:4
The *t* to Huppah, the fourteenth ... 1Chr 24:13
The *t* to Shubael, he, his sons, ... 1Chr 25:20
on the *t* day of the first month ... Est 3:12
even upon the *t* day of the ... Est 3:13
upon the *t* day of the twelfth ... Est 8:12
on the *t* day of the same, when ... Est 9:1
On the *t* day of the month Adar ... Est 9:17
together on the *t* day thereof ... Est 9:18
in the *t* year of his reign ... Jer 1:2
From the *t* year of Josiah the son ... Jer 25:3

**THIRTIETH**
*t* year of Uzziah king of Judah ... 2Kin 15:13
*t* year of Azariah king of Judah ... 2Kin 15:17
*t* year of the captivity of ... 2Kin 25:27
*t* year of the reign of Asa ... 2Chr 15:19
*t* year of the reign of Asa Baasha ... 2Chr 16:1
*t* year of Artaxerxes the king, ... Neh 5:14
*t* year of Artaxerxes king of ... Neh 13:6
*t* year of the captivity of ... Jer 52:31
Now it came to pass in the *t* year ... Eze 1:1

**THIRTY**
*t* years, and begat a son in his ... Gen 5:3
were nine hundred and *t* years ... Gen 5:5
*t* years, and begat sons and ... Gen 5:16
and the height of it *t* cubits ... Gen 6:15
five and *t* years, and begat Salah ... Gen 11:12
And Salah lived *t* years, and begat ... Gen 11:14
four and *t* years, and begat Peleg ... Gen 11:16
*t* years, and begat sons and ... Gen 11:17
And Peleg lived *t* years, and begat ... Gen 11:18
two and *t* years, and begat Serug ... Gen 11:20
And Serug lived *t* years, and begat ... Gen 11:22
there shall *t* be found there ... Gen 18:30
will not do it, if I find *t* there ... Gen 18:30
life of Ishmael, an hundred and *t* ... Gen 25:17
*T* milch camels with their colts, ... Gen 32:15
Joseph was *t* years old when he ... Gen 41:46
his sons and his daughters were *t* ... Gen 46:15
are an hundred and *t* years ... Gen 47:9
life of Levi were an hundred *t* ... Ex 6:16
life of Kohath were an hundred *t* ... Ex 6:18
of Amram were an hundred and *t* ... Ex 6:20
was four hundred and *t* years ... Ex 12:40
*t* years, even the selfsame day it ... Ex 12:41
their master *t* shekels of silver ... Ex 21:32
of one curtain shall be *t* cubits ... Ex 26:8
of one curtain was *t* cubits ... Ex 36:15
*t* shekels, after the shekel of ... Ex 38:24
of her purifying three and *t* days ... Lev 12:4
thy estimation shall be *t* shekels ... Lev 27:4
of the tribe of Manasseh, were *t* ... Num 1:35
of the tribe of Benjamin, were *t* ... Num 1:37
were numbered of them, were *t* ... Num 2:21
were numbered of them, were *t* ... Num 2:23
From *t* years old and upward even ... Num 4:3
From *t* years old and upward until ... Num 4:23
From *t* years old and upward even ... Num 4:30
From *t* years old and upward even ... Num 4:35
From *t* years old and upward even ... Num 4:39
two thousand and six hundred and *t* .. Num 4:40
From *t* years old and upward even ... Num 4:43
From *t* years old and upward even ... Num 4:47
*t* shekels, one silver bowl of ... Num 7:13
*t* shekels, one silver bowl of ... Num 7:19
*t* shekels, one silver bowl of ... Num 7:25
*t* shekels, one silver bowl of ... Num 7:31
*t* shekels, one silver bowl of ... Num 7:37
*t* shekels, a silver bowl of ... Num 7:43
*t* shekels, one silver bowl of ... Num 7:49
*t* shekels, one silver bowl of ... Num 7:55
*t* shekels, one silver bowl of ... Num 7:61
*t* shekels, one silver bowl of ... Num 7:67
*t* shekels, one silver bowl of ... Num 7:73
*t* shekels, one silver bowl of ... Num 7:79
*t* shekels, each bowl seventy ... Num 7:85
they mourned for Aaron *t* days ... Num 20:29
thousand and seven hundred and *t* ... Num 26:7
that were numbered of them, *t* ... Num 26:37
and a thousand seven hundred and *t* Num 26:51
And *t* and two thousand persons in .. Num 31:35
*t* thousand and five hundred sheep ... Num 31:36
And the beeves were *t* and six ... Num 31:38
And the asses were *t* thousand ... Num 31:39
of which the LORD's tribute was *t* ... Num 31:40
*t* thousand and seven thousand and .. Num 31:43
And *t* and six thousand beeves, ... Num 31:44
*t* thousand asses and five hundred, ... Num 31:45
come over the brook Zered, was *t* ... Deut 2:14
in the plains of Moab *t* days ... Deut 34:8
men of Ai smote of them about *t* ... Josh 7:5
Joshua chose out *t* thousand ... Josh 8:3
all the kings *t* and one ... Josh 12:24
he had *t* sons that rode ... Judg 10:4
sons that rode on *t* ass colts ... Judg 10:4
ass colts, and they had *t* cities ... Judg 10:4
And he had *t* sons ... Judg 12:9
*t* daughters, whom he sent abroad, ... Judg 12:9
took in *t* daughters from abroad ... Judg 12:9
sons and *t* nephews, that rode on ... Judg 12:14
that they brought *t* companions to ... Judg 14:11
then I will give you *t* sheets ... Judg 14:12
sheets and *t* change of garments ... Judg 14:12
then shall ye give me *t* sheets ... Judg 14:13
sheets and *t* change of garments ... Judg 14:13
slew *t* men of them, and took their ... Judg 14:19
the field, about *t* men of Israel ... Judg 20:31
the men of Israel about *t* persons ... Judg 20:39
fell of Israel *t* thousand footmen ... 1Sa 4:10
which were about *t* persons ... 1Sa 9:22
and the men of Judah *t* thousand ... 1Sa 11:8
*t* thousand chariots, and six ... 1Sa 13:5
David was *t* years old when he ... 2Sa 5:4
and in Jerusalem he reigned *t* ... 2Sa 5:5
chosen men of Israel, *t* thousand ... 2Sa 6:1
three of the *t* chief went down, ... 2Sa 23:13
He was more honourable than the *t* ... 2Sa 23:23
brother of Joab was one of the *t* ... 2Sa 23:24
*t* and seven in all ... 2Sa 23:39
years reigned he in Hebron, and *t* ... 1Kin 2:11
day was *t* measures of fine flour ... 1Kin 4:22
and the levy was *t* thousand men ... 1Kin 5:13
and the height thereof *t* cubits ... 1Kin 6:2
and the height thereof *t* cubits ... 1Kin 7:2
and the breadth thereof *t* cubits ... 1Kin 7:6
a line of *t* cubits did compass it ... 1Kin 7:23
In the *t* and first year of Asa ... 1Kin 16:23
And in the *t* and eighth year of Asa .. 1Kin 16:29
and there were *t* and two kings with .. 1Kin 20:1
they were two hundred and *t* ... 1Kin 20:15
pavilions, he and the kings, the *t* ... 1Kin 20:16
the king of Syria commanded his *t* ... 1Kin 22:31
Jehoshaphat was *t* and five years ... 1Kin 22:42
*T* and two years old was he when he .. 2Kin 8:17
In the *t* and seventh year of Joash ... 2Kin 13:10
In the *t* and eighth year of ... 2Kin 15:8
of silver and *t* talents of gold ... 2Kin 18:14
began to reign, and he reigned *t* ... 2Kin 22:1
and in Jerusalem he reigned *t* ... 1Chr 3:4
for war, six and *t* thousand men ... 1Chr 7:4
twenty and two thousand and *t* ... 1Chr 7:7
Now three of the *t* captains went ... 1Chr 11:15
he was honourable among the *t* ... 1Chr 11:25
of the Reubenites, and *t* with him, ... 1Chr 11:42
among the *t*, and over the *t* ... 1Chr 12:4
with them with shield and spear *t* ... 1Chr 12:34
and his brethren an hundred and *t* ... 1Chr 15:7
So they hired *t* and two thousand ... 1Chr 19:7
numbered from the age of *t* years ... 1Chr 23:3
by their polls, man by man, was *t* ... 1Chr 23:3
among the *t*, and above the *t* ... 1Chr 27:6
years reigned he in Hebron, and *t* ... 1Chr 29:27
before the house two pillars of *t* ... 2Chr 3:15
a line of *t* cubits did compass it ... 2Chr 4:2
And Asa in the *t* and ninth year of ... 2Chr 16:12
he was *t* and five years old when ... 2Chr 20:31
Jehoram was *t* and two years old ... 2Chr 21:5
*T* and two years old was he when he 2Chr 21:20
*t* years old was he when he died ... 2Chr 24:15
in Jerusalem one and *t* years ... 2Chr 34:1
to the number of *t* thousand ... 2Chr 35:7
*t* chargers of gold, a thousand ... Ezr 1:9
*T* basons of gold, silver basons ... Ezr 1:10
thousand and six hundred and *t* ... Ezr 2:35
of Shobai, in all an hundred *t* ... Ezr 2:42
seven thousand three hundred *t* ... Ezr 2:65
Their horses were seven hundred *t* ... Ezr 2:66
Their camels, four hundred *t* ... Ezr 2:67
three thousand nine hundred and *t* ... Neh 7:38
children of Shobai, an hundred *t* ... Neh 7:45
seven thousand three hundred *t* ... Neh 7:67
Their horses, seven hundred *t* ... Neh 7:68
Their camels, four hundred *t* ... Neh 7:69
hundred and *t* priests' garments ... Neh 7:70
in unto the king these *t* days ... Est 4:11
Take from hence *t* men with thee ... Jer 38:10
from Jerusalem eight hundred *t* ... Jer 52:29
*t* chambers were upon the pavement .. Eze 40:17
one over another, and *t* in order ... Eze 41:6
of forty cubits long and *t* broad ... Eze 46:22
of any God or man for *t* days ... Dan 6:7
of any God or man within *t* days ... Dan 6:12
three hundred and five and *t* days ... Dan 12:12
for my price *t* pieces of silver ... Zec 11:12
I took the *t* pieces of silver, and ... Zec 11:13
hundredfold, some sixty, some *t* ... Mt 13:23
with him for *t* pieces of silver ... Mt 26:15
brought again the *t* pieces of ... Mt 27:3
they took the *t* pieces of silver, ... Mt 27:9
and brought forth, some *t*, and some ... Mk 4:8
began to be about *t* years of age ... Lk 3:23
there, which had an infirmity *t* ... Jn 5:5
five and twenty or *t* furlongs ... Jn 6:19
*t* years after, cannot disannul, ... Gal 3:17

**THIRTYFOLD**
some sixtyfold, some *t* ... Mt 13:8
it, and bring forth fruit, some *t* ... Mk 4:20

**THIS** See PREFACE.

**THISTLE**
The *t* that was in Lebanon sent to ... 2Kin 14:9
in Lebanon, and trode down the *t* ... 2Kin 14:9
The *t* that was in Lebanon sent to ... 2Chr 25:18
in Lebanon, and trode down the *t* ... 2Chr 25:18
the *t* shall come up on their ... Hos 10:8

**THISTLES**
*t* shall it bring forth to thee ... Gen 3:18
Let *t* grow instead of wheat, and ... Job 31:40
grapes of thorns, or figs of *t* ... Mt 7:16

**THITHER**
Oh, let me escape *t*, (is it not a ... Gen 19:20
Haste thee, escape *t* ... Gen 19:22
do any thing till thou be come *t* ... Gen 19:22
thou bring not my son *t* again ... Gen 24:6
only bring not my son *t* again ... Gen 24:8
*t* were all the flocks gathered ... Gen 29:3
which had brought him down *t* ... Gen 39:1
get you down *t*, and buy for us ... Gen 42:2
serve the LORD, until we come *t* ... Ex 10:26
that thou mayest bring in *t* ... Ex 26:33
the manslayer, that he may flee *t* ... Num 35:6
that the slayer may flee *t* ... Num 35:11
any person unawares may flee *t* ... Num 35:15
Thou also shalt not go in *t* ... Deut 1:37
before thee, he shall go in *t* ... Deut 1:38
good and evil, they shall go in *t* ... Deut 1:39
That the slayer might flee *t* ... Deut 4:42
ye seek, and *t* thou shalt come ... Deut 12:5
*t* ye shall bring your burnt ... Deut 12:6
*t* shall ye bring all that I ... Deut 12:11
that every slayer may flee *t* ... Deut 19:3
of the slayer, which shall flee *t* ... Deut 19:4
but thou shalt not go *t* unto the ... Deut 32:52
but thou shalt not go over *t* ... Deut 34:4
not all the people to labour *t* ... Josh 7:3
So there went up *t* of the people ... Josh 7:4
and unwittingly may flee *t* ... Josh 20:3
person at unawares might flee *t* ... Josh 20:9
all Israel went *t* a whoring after ... Judg 8:27
*t* fled all the men and women, and ... Judg 9:51
and they turned in *t*, and said unto ... Judg 18:3
the land went up, and came in *t* ... Judg 18:17
And they turned aside *t*, to go in ... Judg 19:15
the congregation sent *t* twelve ... Judg 21:10
all the Israelites that came *t* ... 1Sa 2:14
ark of the God of Israel about *t* ... 1Sa 5:8
now let us go *t* ... 1Sa 9:6
when thou art come *t* to the city ... 1Sa 10:5
And when they came *t* to the hill ... 1Sa 10:10
if the man should yet come *t* ... 1Sa 10:22
he went *t* to Naioth in Ramah ... 1Sa 19:23
heard it, they went down *t* to him ... 1Sa 22:1
Abiathar brought *t* the ephod to ... 1Sa 30:7
So David went up *t*, and his two ... 2Sa 2:2
they came *t* into the midst of the ... 2Sa 4:6
ready before it was brought *t* ... 1Kin 6:7
he came *t* unto a cave, and lodged ... 1Kin 19:9
and they were divided hither and *t* ... 2Kin 2:8
waters, they parted hither and *t* ... 2Kin 2:14
by, he turned in *t* to eat bread ... 2Kin 4:8
to us, that he shall turn in *t* ... 2Kin 4:10
it fell on a day, that he came *t* ... 2Kin 4:11
cut down a stick, and cast it in *t* ... 2Kin 6:6
for *t* the Syrians are come down ... 2Kin 6:9
Therefore sent he *t* horses ... 2Kin 6:14
And when thou comest *t*, look out ... 2Kin 9:2
Carry *t* one of the priests whom ... 2Kin 17:27
Solomon went up *t* to the brasen ... 2Chr 1:6
and when he came *t*, he did eat no ... Ezr 10:6
the trumpet, resort ye *t* unto us ... Neh 4:20
were gathered *t* unto the work ... Neh 5:16
*t* brought I again the vessels of ... Neh 13:9
womb, and naked shall I return *t* ... Job 1:21
they came *t*, and were ashamed ... Job 6:20
rivers come, *t* they return again ... Eccl 1:7
and with bows shall men come *t* ... Is 7:24
not come *t* the fear of briers ... Is 7:25
that send forth *t* the feet of the ... Is 32:20
from heaven, and returneth not *t* ... Is 55:10
even *t* wentest thou up to offer ... Is 57:7
He shall not return *t* any more ... Jer 22:11
return, *t* shall they not return ... Jer 22:27
a great company shall return *t* ... Jer 31:8
convenient for thee to go, *t* go ... Jer 40:4
went, *t* was their spirit to go ... Eze 1:20
And they shall come *t*, and they ... Eze 11:18
was upon me, and brought me, *t* ... Eze 40:1
And he brought me *t*, and, behold, ... Eze 40:3
because these waters shall come *t* ... Eze 47:9
*t* cause thy mighty ones to come ... Joel 3:11
Herod, he was afraid to go *t* ... Mt 2:22
ran afoot *t* out of all cities, and ... Mk 6:33
*t* will the eagles be gathered ... Lk 17:37
poor widow casting in *t* two mites ... Lk 21:2
and where I am, *t* ye cannot come ... Jn 7:34
and where I am, *t* ye cannot come ... Jn 7:36
and goest thou *t* again ... Jn 11:8

resorted *t* with his disciples ... Jn 18:2
cometh *t* with lanterns and torches ... Jn 18:3
And Philip ran *t* to him, and heard ... Acts 8:30
there came *t* certain Jews from ... Acts 14:19
unto the women which resorted *t* ... Acts 16:13
who coming *t* went into the ... Acts 17:10
Paul at Berea, they came *t* also ... Acts 17:13
he himself would depart shortly *t* ... Acts 25:4

**THITHERWARD**
And they turned *t*, and came to the .. Judg 18:15
way to Zion with their faces *t* ... Jer 50:5
to be brought on my way *t* by you .... Rom 15:24

**THOMAS** (*tom'-us*) See DIDYMUS. *One of the twelve apostles.*
*T*, and Matthew the publican ... Mt 10:3
and Bartholomew, and Matthew, and *T* Mk 3:18
Matthew and *T*, James the son of ... Lk 6:15
Then said *T*, which is called ... Jn 11:16
*T* saith unto him, Lord, we know ... Jn 14:5
But *T*, one of the twelve, called ... Jn 20:24
were within, and *T* with them ... Jn 20:26
Then saith he to *T*, Reach hither ... Jn 20:27
*T* answered and said unto him, My ... Jn 20:28
Jesus saith unto him, *T*, because ... Jn 20:29
*T* called Didymus, and Nathanael of ... Jn 21:2
and John, and Andrew, Philip, and *T* ... Acts 1:13

**THONGS**
And as they bound him with *t* ... Acts 22:25

**THORN**
or bore his jaw through with a *t* ... Job 41:2
As a *t* goeth up into the hand of ... Prov 26:9
Instead of the the *t* shall come ... Is 55:13
nor any grieving *t* of all that ... Eze 28:24
the *t* and the thistle shall come ... Hos 10:8
upright is sharper than a *t* hedge ... Mic 7:4
was given to me a *t* in the flesh ... 2Cor 12:7

**THORNS**
*T* also and thistles shall it bring ... Gen 3:18
If fire break out, and catch in *t* ... Ex 22:6
*t* in your sides, and shall vex you ... Num 33:55
*t* in your eyes, until ye perish ... Josh 23:13
they shall be as *t* in your sides ... Judg 2:3
with the *t* of the wilderness ... Judg 8:7
*t* of the wilderness and briers, and ... Judg 8:16
be all of them as *t* thrust away ... 2Sa 23:6
which took Manasseh among the *t* ... 2Chr 33:11
and taketh it even out of the *t* ... Job 5:5
Before your pots can feel the *t* ... Ps 58:9
are quenched as the fire of *t* ... Ps 118:12
slothful man is as an hedge of *t* ... Prov 15:19
*T* and snares are in the way of the ... Prov 22:5
lo, it was all grown over with *t* ... Prov 24:31
as the crackling of *t* under a pot ... Eccl 7:6
As the lily among *t*, so is my ... Song 2:2
there shall come up briers and *t* ... Is 5:6
holes of the rocks, and upon all *t* ... Is 7:19
it shall even be for briers and *t* ... Is 7:23
the land shall become briers and *t* ... Is 7:24
thither the fear of briers and *t* ... Is 7:25
it shall devour the briers and *t* ... Is 9:18
and it shall burn and devour his *t* ... Is 10:17
briers and *t* against me in battle ... Is 27:4
land of my people shall come up *t* ... Is 32:13
as *t* cut up shall they be burned ... Is 33:12
*t* shall come up in her palaces, ... Is 34:13
fallow ground, and sow not among *t* ... Jer 4:3
have sown wheat, but shall reap *t* ... Jer 12:13
*t* be with thee, and thou dost ... Eze 2:6
I will hedge up thy way with *t* ... Hos 2:6
*t* shall be in their tabernacles ... Hos 9:6
they be folden together as *t* ... Nah 1:10
Do men gather grapes of *t* ... Mt 7:16
And some fell among *t* ... Mt 13:7
the *t* sprung up, and choked them ... Mt 13:7
the *t* is he that heareth the word ... Mt 13:22
they had platted a crown of *t* ... Mt 27:29
And some fell among *t*, and the ... Mk 4:7
the *t* grew up, and choked it, and ... Mk 4:7
are they which are sown among *t* ... Mk 4:18
purple, and platted a crown of *t* ... Mk 15:17
For of *t* men do not gather figs, ... Lk 6:44
And some fell among *t* ... Lk 8:7
the *t* sprang up with it, and ... Lk 8:7
that which fell among *t* are they ... Lk 8:14
the soldiers platted a crown of *t* ... Jn 19:2
forth, wearing the crown of *t* ... Jn 19:5
But that which beareth *t* and ... Heb 6:8

**THOROUGHLY**
and shall cause him to be *t* healed ... Ex 21:19
his images brake they in pieces *t* ... 2Kin 11:18

**THOSE** See PREFACE.

**THOU** See PREFACE.

**THOUGH**
*t* thou wouldest needs be gone, ... Gen 31:30
as *t* I had seen the face of God, ... Gen 33:10
and it was as *t* it budded, and her ... Gen 40:10
*t* he wist it not, yet is he ... Lev 5:17
*t* he divide the hoof, and be ... Lev 11:7
yea, *t* he be a stranger, or a ... Lev 25:35
as *t* it were the corn of the ... Num 18:27
*t* I walk in the imagination of ... Deut 29:19
*t* they have iron chariots, and ... Josh 17:18
chariots, and *t* they be strong ... Josh 17:18
*T* thou detain me, I will not eat ... Judg 13:16
*t* I do them a displeasure ... Judg 15:3
*T* ye have done this, yet will I ... Judg 15:7
*t* I be not like unto one of thine ... Ruth 2:13
*t* it be in Jonathan my son, he ... 1Sa 14:39
thereof, as *t* I shot at a mark ... 1Sa 20:20
*t* it were sanctified this day in ... 1Sa 21:5
as *t* he had not been anointed ... 2Sa 1:21
am this day weak, *t* anointed king ... 2Sa 3:39
as *t* they would have fetched ... 2Sa 4:6
*T* I should receive a thousand ... 2Sa 18:12
*t* he turned not after Absalom ... 1Kin 2:28
(for *t* he was not the firstborn, ... 1Chr 26:10
*t* he be not cleansed according to ... 2Chr 30:19
*t* there were of you cast out unto ... Neh 1:9
(*t* at that time I had not set up ... Neh 6:1
(*t* it was turned to the contrary, ... Est 9:1
*T* thy beginning was small, yet ... Job 8:7
*t* I were righteous, yet would I ... Job 9:15
*T* I were perfect, yet would I not ... Job 9:21
have been as *t* I had not been ... Job 10:19
*t* man be born like a wild ass's ... Job 11:12
*T* he slay me, yet will I trust in ... Job 13:15
*T* the root thereof wax old in the ... Job 14:8
*T* I speak, my grief is not ... Job 16:6
*t* I forbear, what am I eased ... Job 16:6
*t* I intreated for the children's ... Job 19:17
*t* after my skin worms destroy ... Job 19:26
*t* my reins be consumed within me ... Job 19:27
*T* his excellency mount up to the ... Job 20:6
*T* wickedness be sweet in his ... Job 20:12
*t* he hide it under his tongue ... Job 20:12
*T* he spare it, and forsake it not, ... Job 20:13
*T* it be given him to be in safety ... Job 24:23
*t* he hath gained, when God taketh ... Job 27:8
*T* he heap up silver as the dust, ... Job 27:16
*t* they cry in his destruction ... Job 30:24
ones, as *t* they were not hers ... Job 39:16
*t* I walk through the valley of ... Ps 23:4
*T* an host should encamp against ... Ps 27:3
*t* war should rise against me, in ... Ps 27:3
I behaved myself as *t* he had been ... Ps 35:14
*T* he fall, he shall not be ... Ps 37:24
*T* thou hast sore broken us in the ... Ps 44:19
*t* the earth be removed ... Ps 46:2
*t* the mountains be carried into ... Ps 46:2
*T* the waters thereof roar and be ... Ps 46:3
*t* the mountains shake with the ... Ps 46:3
*T* while he lived he blessed his ... Ps 49:18
*T* ye have lien among the pots, ... Ps 68:13
*T* he had commanded the clouds ... Ps 78:23
*t* thou tookest vengeance of their ... Ps 99:8
*T* the LORD be high, yet hath he ... Ps 138:6
*T* I walk in the midst of trouble, ... Ps 138:7
content, *t* thou givest many gifts ... Prov 6:35
*T* hand join in hand, the wicked ... Prov 11:21
*t* hand join in hand, he shall not ... Prov 16:5
*T* thou shouldest bray a fool in a ... Prov 27:22
in his ways, *t* he be rich ... Prov 28:6
for *t* he understand he will not ... Prov 29:19
*t* he live a thousand years twice ... Eccl 6:6
*T* a sinner do evil an hundred ... Eccl 8:12
because *t* a man labour to seek it ... Eccl 8:17
*t* a wise man think to know it, ... Eccl 8:17
*t* your sins be as scarlet, they ... Is 1:18
*t* they be red like crimson, they ... Is 1:18
For *t* thy people Israel be as the ... Is 10:22
*t* thou wast angry with me, thine ... Is 12:1
*t* the Lord give you the bread of ... Is 30:20
*t* fools, shall not err therein ... Is 35:8
thee, *t* thou hast not known me ... Is 45:4
thee, *t* thou hast not known me ... Is 45:5
*T* Israel be not gathered, yet ... Is 49:5
*t* Abraham be ignorant of us, and ... Is 63:16
For *t* thou wash thee with nitre, ... Jer 2:22
*T* thou clothest thyself with ... Jer 4:30
crimson, *t* thou deckest thee with ... Jer 4:30
*t* thou rentest thy face with ... Jer 4:30
*t* they say, The LORD liveth ... Jer 5:2
and *t* the waves thereof toss ... Jer 5:22
*t* they roar, yet can they not ... Jer 5:22
*t* they shall cry unto me, I will ... Jer 11:11
*t* they speak fair words unto thee ... Jer 12:6
*t* our iniquities testify against ... Jer 14:7
*T* Moses and Samuel stood before me .... Jer 15:1
*t* Coniah the son of Jehoiakim ... Jer 22:24
*t* I make a full end of all ... Jer 30:11
*t* ye fight with the Chaldeans, ye ... Jer 32:5
*t* I taught them, rising up early ... Jer 32:33
For *t* ye had smitten the whole ... Jer 37:10
the LORD, *t* it cannot be searched ... Jer 46:23
*t* thou shouldest make thy nest as ... Jer 49:16
*t* their land was filled with sin ... Jer 51:5
*T* Babylon should mount up to ... Jer 51:53
*t* she should fortify the height ... Jer 51:53
But *t* he cause grief, yet will he ... Lam 3:32
*t* briers and thorns be with thee, ... Eze 2:6
*t* they be a rebellious house ... Eze 2:6
*t* they be a rebellious house ... Eze 3:9
*t* they cry in mine ears with a ... Eze 8:18
*t* they be a rebellious house ... Eze 12:3
not see it, *t* he shall die there ... Eze 12:13
*T* these three men, Noah, Daniel, ... Eze 14:14
*T* these three men were in it, as ... Eze 14:16
*T* these three men were in it, as ... Eze 14:18
*T* Noah, Daniel, and Job, were in ... Eze 14:20
*t* thou be sought for, yet shalt ... Eze 26:21
*t* thou set thine heart as the ... Eze 28:2
*t* their terror was caused in the ... Eze 32:25
*t* they caused their terror in the ... Eze 32:26
*t* they were the terror of the ... Eze 32:27
heart, *t* thou knewest all this ... Dan 5:22
*t* we have rebelled against him ... Dan 9:9
*T* thou, Israel, play the harlot, ... Hos 4:15
*t* I have been a rebuker of them ... Hos 5:2
*t* I have redeemed them, yet they ... Hos 7:13
*T* I have bound and strengthened ... Hos 7:15
*t* they have hired among the ... Hos 8:10
*T* they bring up their children, ... Hos 9:12
*t* they bring forth, yet will I ... Hos 9:16
*t* they called them to the most ... Hos 11:7
*T* he be fruitful among his ... Hos 13:15
*T* ye offer me burnt offerings and ... Amos 5:22
*T* they dig into hell, thence ... Amos 9:2
*t* they climb up to heaven, thence ... Amos 9:2
*t* they hide themselves in the top ... Amos 9:3
*t* they be hid from my sight in ... Amos 9:3
*t* they go into captivity before ... Amos 9:4
*T* thou exalt thyself as the eagle ... Obad 4
*t* thou set thy nest among the ... Obad 4
they shall be as *t* they had not ... Obad 16
*t* thou be little among the ... Mic 5:2
*T* they be quiet, and likewise many ... Nah 1:12
*T* I have afflicted thee, I will ... Nah 1:12
not believe, *t* it be told you ... Hab 1:5
*t* it tarry, wait for it ... Hab 2:3
and Zidon, *t* it be very wise ... Zec 9:2
they shall be as *t* I had not cast ... Zec 10:6
*t* all the people of the earth be ... Zec 12:3
*T* all men shall be offended ... Mt 26:33
*T* I should die with thee, yet ... Mt 26:35
*t* many false witnesses came, yet ... Mt 26:60
because his face was as *t* he ... Lk 9:53
*T* he will not rise and give him, ... Lk 11:8
*t* one rose from the dead ... Lk 16:31
*T* I fear not God, nor regard man ... Lk 18:4
him, *t* he bear long with them ... Lk 18:7
he made as *t* he would have gone ... Lk 24:28
(*T* Jesus himself baptized not, ... Jn 4:2
ground, as *t* he heard them not ... Jn 8:6
*T* I bear record of myself, yet my ... Jn 8:14
*t* ye believe not me, believe the ... Jn 10:38
*t* he were dead, yet shall he live ... Jn 11:25
But *t* he had done so many ... Jn 12:37
as *t* by our own power or holiness ... Acts 3:12
*t* they found no cause of death in ... Acts 13:28
*t* a man declare it unto you ... Acts 13:41
as *t* he needed any thing, seeing ... Acts 17:25
*t* he be not far from every one of ... Acts 17:27
as *t* ye would enquire something ... Acts 23:15
as *t* they would enquire somewhat ... Acts 23:20
under colour as *t* they would have ... Acts 27:30
*t* he hath escaped the sea, yet ... Acts 28:4
*t* I have committed nothing ... Acts 28:17
*t* they be not circumcised ... Rom 4:11
which be not as *t* they were ... Rom 4:17
*t* she be married to another man ... Rom 7:3
Not as *t* the word of God hath ... Rom 9:6
*T* the number of the children of ... Rom 9:27
For *t* ye have ten thousand ... 1Cor 4:15
as *t* I would not come to you ... 1Cor 4:18
as *t* I were present, concerning ... 1Cor 5:3
have wives be as *t* they had none ... 1Cor 7:29
that weep, as *t* they wept not ... 1Cor 7:30
rejoice, as *t* they rejoiced not ... 1Cor 7:30
that buy, as *t* they possessed not ... 1Cor 7:30
For *t* there be that are called ... 1Cor 8:5
For *t* I preach the gospel, I have ... 1Cor 9:16
For *t* I be free from all men, yet ... 1Cor 9:19
*T* I speak with the tongues of men ... 1Cor 13:1
*t* I have the gift of prophecy, and ... 1Cor 13:2
*t* I have all faith, so that I ... 1Cor 13:2
*t* I bestow all my goods to feed ... 1Cor 13:3
*t* I give my body to be burned, and ... 1Cor 13:3
but *t* our outward man perish, yet ... 2Cor 4:16
*t* we have known Christ after the ... 2Cor 5:16
as *t* God did beseech you by us ... 2Cor 5:20
For *t* I made you sorry with a ... 2Cor 7:8
I do not repent, *t* I did repent ... 2Cor 7:8
*t* it were but for a season ... 2Cor 7:8
*t* I wrote unto you, I did it not ... 2Cor 7:12
*t* he was rich, yet for your sakes ... 2Cor 8:9
For *t* we walk in the flesh, we do ... 2Cor 10:3
For *t* I should boast somewhat ... 2Cor 10:8
as *t* we reached not unto you ... 2Cor 10:14
But *t* I be rude in speech, yet ... 2Cor 11:6
reproach, as *t* we had been weak ... 2Cor 11:21
For *t* I would desire to glory, I ... 2Cor 12:6
chiefest apostles, *t* I be nothing ... 2Cor 12:11
*t* the more abundantly I love you, ... 2Cor 12:15
For *t* he was crucified through ... 2Cor 13:4
is honest, *t* we be as reprobates ... 2Cor 13:7
But *t* we, or an angel from heaven ... Gal 1:8
*T* it be but a man's covenant, yet ... Gal 3:15
a servant, *t* he be lord of all ... Gal 4:1
*T* I might also have confidence in ... Phil 3:4
Not as *t* I had already attained, ... Phil 3:12
For *t* I be absent in the flesh, ... Col 2:5
as *t* living in the world, are ye ... Col 2:20
*t* I might be much bold in Christ ... Philem 8
*T* he were a Son, yet learned he ... Heb 5:8
salvation, *t* we thus speak ... Heb 6:9
*t* they come out of the loins of ... Heb 7:5
*t* he sought it carefully with ... Heb 12:17
*t* a man say he hath faith, and ... Jas 2:14
which *t* they be so great, and are ... Jas 3:4
*t* now for a season, if need be, ... 1Pet 1:6
*t* it be tried with fire, might be ... 1Pet 1:7
*t* now ye see him not, yet ... 1Pet 1:8
as *t* some strange thing happened ... 1Pet 4:12
*t* ye know them, and be established ... 2Pet 1:12
lady, not as *t* I wrote a new ... 2Jn 5

*t* ye once knew this, how that the ... Jude 5

## THOUGHT

And Abraham said, Because I *t* ... Gen 20:11
saw her, he *t* her to be an harlot ... Gen 38:15
I had not *t* to see thy face ... Gen 48:11
as for you, ye *t* evil against me ... Gen 50:20
which he *t* to do unto his people ... Ex 32:14
I *t* to promote thee unto great ... Num 24:11
unto you, as I *t* to do unto them ... Num 33:56
be not a *t* in thy wicked heart ... Deut 15:9
as he had *t* to have done unto his ... Deut 19:19
I verily *t* that thou hadst ... Judg 15:2
by night, and *t* to have slain me ... Judg 20:5
I *t* to advertise thee, saying, ... Ruth 4:4
therefore Eli *t* she had been ... 1Sa 1:13
for the asses, and take *t* for us ... 1Sa 9:5
But Saul *t* to make David fall by ... 1Sa 18:25
for he *t*, Something hath befallen ... 1Sa 20:26
who *t* that I would have given him ... 2Sa 4:10
Amnon *t* it hard for him to do any ... 2Sa 13:2
Wherefore then hast thou *t* such a ... 2Sa 14:13
and to do what he *t* good ... 2Sa 19:18
new sword, *t* to have slain David ... 2Sa 21:16
went away, and said, Behold, I *t* ... 2Kin 5:11
for he *t* to make him king ... 2Chr 11:22
*t* to win them for himself ... 2Chr 32:1
But they *t* to do me mischief ... Neh 6:2
he *t* scorn to lay hands on ... Est 3:6
Now Haman *t* in his heart, To whom ... Est 6:6
in the *t* of him that is at ease ... Job 12:5
that no *t* can be withholden from ... Job 42:2
We have *t* of thy lovingkindness, ... Ps 48:9
Their inward *t* is, that their ... Ps 49:11
both the inward *t* of every one of ... Ps 64:6
When I *t* to know this, it was too ... Ps 73:16
I *t* on my ways, and turned my feet ... Ps 119:59
thou understandest my *t* afar off ... Ps 139:2
The *t* of foolishness is sin ... Prov 24:9
thyself, or if thou hast *t* evil ... Prov 30:32
not the king, no not in thy *t* ... Eccl 10:20
sworn, saying, Surely as I have *t* ... Is 14:24
the evil that I *t* to do unto them ... Jer 18:8
and thou shalt think an evil *t* ... Eze 38:10
I *t* it good to shew the signs and ... Dan 4:2
the king *t* to set him over the ... Dan 6:3
declareth unto man what is his *t* ... Amos 4:13
the LORD of hosts *t* to do unto us ... Zec 1:6
As I *t* to punish you, when your ... Zec 8:14
So again have I *t* in these days ... Zec 8:15
the LORD, and that *t* upon his name ... Mal 3:16
But while he *t* on these things, ... Mt 1:20
Take no *t* for your life, what ye ... Mt 6:25
Which of you by taking *t* can add ... Mt 6:27
And why take ye *t* for raiment ... Mt 6:28
Therefore take no *t*, saying, What ... Mt 6:31
therefore no *t* for the morrow ... Mt 6:34
take *t* for the things of itself ... Mt 6:34
take no *t* how or what ye shall ... Mt 10:19
take no *t* beforehand what ye ... Mk 13:11
And when he *t* thereon, he wept ... Mk 14:72
Wherefore neither *t* I myself ... Lk 7:7
perceiving the *t* of their heart ... Lk 9:47
take ye no *t* how or what thing ye ... Lk 12:11
he *t* within himself, saying, What ... Lk 12:17
Take no *t* for your life, what ye ... Lk 12:22
which of you with taking *t* can ... Lk 12:25
why take ye *t* for the rest ... Lk 12:26
because they *t* that the kingdom ... Lk 19:11
but they *t* that he had spoken of ... Jn 11:13
For some of them *t*, because Judas ... Jn 13:29
because thou hast *t* that the gift ... Acts 8:20
if perhaps the *t* of thine heart ... Acts 8:22
While Peter *t* on the vision, the ... Acts 10:19
but *t* he saw a vision ... Acts 12:9
But Paul *t* not good to take him ... Acts 15:38
Why should it be *t* a thing ... Acts 26:8
I verily *t* with myself, that I ... Acts 26:9
as a child, I *t* as a child ... 1Cor 13:11
Therefore I *t* it necessary to ... 2Cor 9:5
*t* to the obedience of Christ ... 2Cor 10:5
*t* it not robbery to be equal with ... Phil 2:6
we *t* it good to be left at Athens ... 1Th 3:1
suppose ye, shall he be *t* worthy ... Heb 10:29

## THOUGHTEST

thou *t* that I was altogether such ... Ps 50:21

## THOUGHTS

the *t* of his heart was only evil ... Gen 6:5
there were great *t* of heart ... Judg 5:15
all the imaginations of the *t* ... 1Chr 28:9
the *t* of the heart of thy people ... 1Chr 29:18
In *t* from the visions of the ... Job 4:13
off, even the *t* of my heart ... Job 17:11
Therefore do my *t* cause me to ... Job 20:2
Behold, I know your *t*, and the ... Job 21:27
God is not in all his *t* ... Ps 10:4
the *t* of his heart to all ... Ps 33:11
thy *t* which are to us-ward ... Ps 40:5
all their *t* are against me for ... Ps 56:5
and thy *t* are very deep ... Ps 92:5
The LORD knoweth the *t* of man ... Ps 94:11
In the multitude of my *t* within ... Ps 94:19
I hate vain *t* ... Ps 119:113
precious also are thy *t* unto me ... Ps 139:17
try me, and know my *t* ... Ps 139:23
in that very day his *t* perish ... Ps 146:4
The *t* of the righteous are right ... Prov 12:5
The *t* of the wicked are an ... Prov 15:26
thy *t* shall be established ... Prov 16:3
The *t* of the diligent tend only ... Prov 21:5
way, and the unrighteous man his *t* ... Is 55:7
For my *t* are not your *t*, ... Is 55:8
ways, and my *t* than your *t* ... Is 55:9
their *t* are *t* of iniquity ... Is 59:7
was not good, after their own *t* ... Is 65:2
For I know their works and their *t* ... Is 66:18
thy vain *t* lodge within thee ... Jer 4:14
people, even the fruit of their *t* ... Jer 6:19
have performed the *t* of his heart ... Jer 23:20
For I know the *t* that I think ... Jer 29:11
*t* of peace, and not of evil, to ... Jer 29:11
thy *t* came into thy mind upon thy ... Dan 2:29
mightest know the *t* of thy heart ... Dan 2:30
the *t* upon my bed and the visions ... Dan 4:5
one hour, and his *t* troubled him ... Dan 4:19
his *t* troubled him, so that the ... Dan 5:6
let not thy *t* trouble thee, nor ... Dan 5:10
they know not the *t* of the LORD ... Mic 4:12
And Jesus knowing their *t* said ... Mt 9:4
And Jesus knew their *t*, and said ... Mt 12:25
out of the heart proceed evil *t* ... Mt 15:19
the heart of men, proceed evil *t* ... Mk 7:21
that the *t* of many hearts may be ... Lk 2:35
But when Jesus perceived their *t* ... Lk 5:22
But he knew their *t*, and said to ... Lk 6:8
But he, knowing their *t*, said ... Lk 11:17
why do *t* arise in your hearts ... Lk 24:38
their *t* the mean while accusing ... Rom 2:15
Lord knoweth the *t* of the wise ... 1Cor 3:20
and is a discerner of the *t* ... Heb 4:12
and are become judges of evil *t* ... Jas 2:4

## THOUSAND

thy brother a *t* pieces of silver ... Gen 20:16
about six hundred *t* on foot that ... Ex 12:37
people that day about three *t* men ... Ex 32:28
a *t* seven hundred and threescore ... Ex 38:25
six hundred *t* and three *t* ... Ex 38:26
of the *t* seven hundred seventy and ... Ex 38:28
was seventy talents, and two *t* ... Ex 38:29
of you shall put ten *t* to flight ... Lev 26:8
of Reuben, were forty and six *t* ... Num 1:21
of Simeon, were fifty and nine *t* ... Num 1:23
five *t* six hundred and fifty ... Num 1:25
were threescore and fourteen *t* ... Num 1:27
of Issachar, were fifty and four *t* ... Num 1:29
of Zebulun, were fifty and seven *t* ... Num 1:31
tribe of Ephraim, were forty *t* ... Num 1:33
of Manasseh, were thirty and two *t* ... Num 1:35
Benjamin, were thirty and five *t* ... Num 1:37
of Dan, were threescore and two *t* ... Num 1:39
of Asher, were forty and one *t* ... Num 1:41
Naphtali, were fifty and three *t* ... Num 1:43
were numbered were six hundred *t* ... Num 1:46
six hundred *t* and three *t* ... Num 1:46
were threescore and fourteen *t* ... Num 2:4
thereof, were fifty and four *t* ... Num 2:6
thereof, were fifty and seven *t* ... Num 2:8
camp of Judah were an hundred *t* ... Num 2:9
and fourscore *t* and six *t* ... Num 2:9
thereof, were forty and six *t* ... Num 2:11
of them, were fifty and nine *t* ... Num 2:13
of them, were forty and five *t* ... Num 2:15
camp of Reuben were an hundred *t* ... Num 2:16
*t* and fifty and one *t* ... Num 2:16
numbered of them, were forty *t* ... Num 2:19
of them, were thirty and two *t* ... Num 2:21
of them, were thirty and five *t* ... Num 2:23
an hundred *t* and eight *t* ... Num 2:24
of them, were threescore and two *t* ... Num 2:26
of them, were forty and one *t* ... Num 2:28
of them, were fifty and three *t* ... Num 2:30
the camp of Dan were an hundred *t* ... Num 2:31
and fifty and seven *t* ... Num 2:31
six hundred *t* and three *t* ... Num 2:32
numbered of them were seven *t* ... Num 3:22
month old and upward, were eight *t* ... Num 3:28
a month old and upward, were six *t* ... Num 3:34
and upward, were twenty and two *t* ... Num 3:39
two *t* two hundred and threescore ... Num 3:43
a *t* three hundred and threescore ... Num 3:50
families were two *t* seven hundred ... Num 4:36
of their fathers, were two *t* ... Num 4:40
their families, were three *t* ... Num 4:44
numbered of them, were eight *t* ... Num 4:48
the silver vessels weighed two *t* ... Num 7:85
I am, are six hundred *t* footmen ... Num 11:21
in the plague were fourteen *t* ... Num 16:49
the plague were twenty and four *t* ... Num 25:9
of them were forty and three *t* ... Num 26:7
the Simeonites, twenty and two *t* ... Num 26:14
were numbered of them, forty *t* ... Num 26:18
of them, threescore and sixteen *t* ... Num 26:22
of them, threescore and four *t* ... Num 26:25
numbered of them, threescore *t* ... Num 26:27
numbered of them, fifty and two *t* ... Num 26:34
numbered of them, thirty and two *t* ... Num 26:37
of them were forty and five *t* ... Num 26:41
them, were threescore and four *t* ... Num 26:43
who were fifty and three *t* ... Num 26:47
of them were forty and five *t* ... Num 26:50
children of Israel, six hundred *t* ... Num 26:51
a *t* seven hundred and thirty ... Num 26:51
of them were twenty and three *t* ... Num 26:62
Of every tribe a *t*, throughout ... Num 31:4
a *t* of every tribe, twelve ... Num 31:5
tribe, twelve *t* armed for war ... Num 31:5
a *t* of every tribe, them and ... Num 31:6
war had caught, was six hundred *t* ... Num 31:32
seventy *t* and five *t* sheep, ... Num 31:32
And threescore and twelve *t* beeves ... Num 31:33
And threescore and one *t* asses, ... Num 31:34
two *t* persons in all, of women ... Num 31:35
was in number three hundred *t* ... Num 31:36
and seven and thirty *t* ... Num 31:36
the beeves were thirty and six *t* ... Num 31:38
And the asses were thirty *t* ... Num 31:39
And the persons were sixteen *t* ... Num 31:40
congregation was three hundred *t* ... Num 31:43
and thirty *t* and seven *t* ... Num 31:43
And thirty and six *t* beeves, ... Num 31:44
And thirty *t* asses and five hundred ... Num 31:45
And sixteen *t* persons ... Num 31:46
was sixteen *t* seven hundred and ... Num 31:52
outward a *t* cubits round about ... Num 35:4
on the east side two *t* cubits ... Num 35:5
and on the south side two *t* cubits ... Num 35:5
and on the west side two *t* cubits ... Num 35:5
and on the north side two *t* cubits ... Num 35:5
a *t* times so many more as ye are ... Deut 1:11
commandments to a *t* generations ... Deut 7:9
How should one chase a *t*, and two ... Deut 32:30
and two put ten *t* to flight ... Deut 32:30
about two *t* cubits by measure ... Josh 3:4
About forty *t* prepared for war ... Josh 4:13
about two or three *t* men go up ... Josh 7:3
of the people about three *t* men ... Josh 7:4
out thirty *t* mighty men of valour ... Josh 8:3
And he took about five *t* men ... Josh 8:12
of men and women, were twelve *t* ... Josh 8:25
One man of you shall chase a *t* ... Josh 23:10
slew of them in Bezek ten *t* men ... Judg 1:4
Moab at that time about ten *t* men ... Judg 3:29
take with thee ten *t* men of the ... Judg 4:6
up with ten *t* men at his feet ... Judg 4:10
Tabor, and ten *t* men after him ... Judg 4:14
seen among forty *t* in Israel ... Judg 5:8
of the people twenty and two *t* ... Judg 7:3
and there remained ten *t* ... Judg 7:3
with them, about fifteen *t* men ... Judg 8:10
twenty *t* men that drew sword ... Judg 8:10
that he requested was a *t* ... Judg 8:26
Shechem died also, about a *t* men ... Judg 9:49
of the Ephraimites forty and two *t* ... Judg 12:6
Then three *t* men of Judah went to ... Judg 15:11
it, and slew a *t* men therewith ... Judg 15:15
of an ass have I slain a *t* men ... Judg 15:16
upon the roof about three *t* men ... Judg 16:27
four hundred *t* footmen that drew ... Judg 20:2
of Israel, and an hundred of a *t* ... Judg 20:10
and a *t* out of ten *t* ... Judg 20:10
six *t* men that drew sword, beside ... Judg 20:15
hundred *t* men that drew sword ... Judg 20:17
that day twenty and two *t* men ... Judg 20:21
of Israel again eighteen *t* men ... Judg 20:25
*t* chosen men out of all Israel ... Judg 20:34
that day twenty and five *t* ... Judg 20:35
fell of Benjamin eighteen *t* men ... Judg 20:44
them in the highways five *t* men ... Judg 20:45
Gidom, and slew two *t* men of them ... Judg 20:45
five *t* men that drew the sword ... Judg 20:46
sent thither twelve *t* men of the ... Judg 21:10
in the field about four *t* men ... 1Sa 4:2
fell of Israel thirty *t* footmen ... 1Sa 4:10
he smote of the people fifty *t* ... 1Sa 6:19
of Israel were three hundred *t* ... 1Sa 11:8
and the men of Judah thirty *t* ... 1Sa 11:8
chose him three *t* men of Israel ... 1Sa 13:2
whereof two *t* were with Saul in ... 1Sa 13:2
a *t* were with Jonathan in Gibeah ... 1Sa 13:2
thirty *t* chariots, and six ... 1Sa 13:5
six *t* horsemen, and people as the ... 1Sa 13:5
in Telaim, two hundred *t* footmen ... 1Sa 15:4
footmen, and ten *t* men of Judah ... 1Sa 15:4
coat was five *t* shekels of brass ... 1Sa 17:5
unto the captain of their *t* ... 1Sa 17:18
and made him his captain over a *t* ... 1Sa 18:13
Then Saul took three *t* chosen men ... 1Sa 24:2
great, and he had three *t* sheep ... 1Sa 25:2
sheep, and a *t* goats ... 1Sa 25:2
having three *t* chosen men of ... 1Sa 26:2
chosen men of Israel, thirty *t* ... 2Sa 6:1
David took from him a *t* chariots ... 2Sa 8:4
horsemen, and twenty *t* footmen ... 2Sa 8:4
the Syrians two and twenty *t* men ... 2Sa 8:5
of salt, being eighteen *t* men ... 2Sa 8:13
twenty *t* footmen, and of king ... 2Sa 10:6
and of king Maacah a *t* men ... 2Sa 10:6
and of Ish-tob twelve *t* men ... 2Sa 10:6
forty *t* horsemen, and smote ... 2Sa 10:18
me now choose out twelve *t* men ... 2Sa 17:1
now thou art worth ten *t* of us ... 2Sa 18:3
that day of twenty *t* men ... 2Sa 18:7
Though I should receive a *t* ... 2Sa 18:12
there were a *t* men of Benjamin ... 2Sa 19:17
were in Israel eight hundred *t* ... 2Sa 24:9
of Judah were five hundred *t* men ... 2Sa 24:9
even to Beer-sheba seventy *t* men ... 2Sa 24:15
a *t* burnt offerings did Solomon ... 1Kin 3:4
Solomon had forty *t* stalls of ... 1Kin 4:26
chariots, and twelve *t* horsemen ... 1Kin 4:26
And he spake three *t* proverbs ... 1Kin 4:32
and his songs were a *t* and five ... 1Kin 4:32
Solomon gave Hiram twenty *t* ... 1Kin 5:11
and the levy was thirty *t* men ... 1Kin 5:13
Lebanon, ten *t* a month by courses ... 1Kin 5:14
ten *t* that bare burdens, and ... 1Kin 5:15
fourscore *t* hewers in the ... 1Kin 5:15
which were over the work, three *t* ... 1Kin 5:16
it contained two *t* baths ... 1Kin 7:26
the LORD, two and twenty *t* oxen ... 1Kin 8:63

and an hundred and twenty *t* sheep 1Kin 8:63
and he had a *t* and four hundred 1Kin 10:26
twelve *t* horsemen, whom he 1Kin 10:26
fourscore *t* chosen men, which 1Kin 12:21
I have left me seven *t* in Israel 1Kin 19:18
children of Israel, being seven *t* 1Kin 20:15
an hundred *t* footmen in one day 1Kin 20:29
seven *t* of the men that were left 1Kin 20:30
king of Israel an hundred *t* lambs 2Kin 3:4
lambs, and an hundred *t* rams 2Kin 3:4
six *t* pieces of gold, and ten 2Kin 5:5
and ten chariots, and ten *t* footmen 2Kin 13:7
Edom in the valley of salt ten *t* 2Kin 14:7
gave Pul a *t* talents of silver 2Kin 15:19
I will deliver thee two *t* horses 2Kin 18:23
an hundred fourscore and five *t* 2Kin 19:35
of valour, even ten *t* captives 2Kin 24:14
the men of might, even seven *t* 2Kin 24:16
and craftsmen and smiths a *t* 2Kin 24:16
four and forty *t* seven hundred and 1Chr 5:18
of their camels fifty *t*, and of 1Chr 5:21
fifty *t*, and of asses two *t* 1Chr 5:21
and of men an hundred *t* 1Chr 5:21
the days of David two and twenty *t* 1Chr 7:2
for war, six and thirty *t* men 1Chr 7:4
genealogies fourscore and seven *t* 1Chr 7:5
their genealogies twenty and two *t* 1Chr 7:7
men of valour, was twenty *t* 1Chr 7:9
men of valour, were seventeen *t* 1Chr 7:11
to battle was twenty and six *t* men 1Chr 7:40
the house of their fathers, a *t* 1Chr 9:13
hundred, and the greatest over a *t* 1Chr 12:14
bare shield and spear were six *t* 1Chr 12:24
of valour for the war, seven *t* 1Chr 12:25
Of the children of Levi four *t* 1Chr 12:26
and with him were three *t* 1Chr 12:27
the kindred of Saul, three *t* 1Chr 12:29
the children of Ephraim twenty *t* 1Chr 12:30
half tribe of Manasseh eighteen *t* 1Chr 12:31
all instruments of war, fifty *t* 1Chr 12:33
And of Naphtali a *t* captains 1Chr 12:34
shield and spear thirty and seven *t* 1Chr 12:34
expert in war twenty and eight *t* 1Chr 12:35
to battle, expert in war, forty *t* 1Chr 12:36
battle, an hundred and twenty *t* 1Chr 12:37
he commanded to a *t* generations 1Chr 16:15
David took from him a *t* chariots 1Chr 18:4
seven *t* horsemen, and twenty 1Chr 18:4
horsemen, and twenty *t* footmen 1Chr 18:4
the Syrians two and twenty *t* men 1Chr 18:5
in the valley of salt eighteen *t* 1Chr 18:12
the children of Ammon sent a *t* 1Chr 19:6
two *t* chariots, and the king of 1Chr 19:7
*t* men which fought in chariots 1Chr 19:18
forty *t* footmen, and killed 1Chr 19:18
they of Israel were a *t t* 1Chr 21:5
an hundred *t* men that drew sword 1Chr 21:5
ten *t* men that drew sword 1Chr 21:5
fell of Israel seventy *t* men 1Chr 21:14
LORD an hundred *t* talents of gold 1Chr 22:14
a *t t* talents of silver 1Chr 22:14
man by man, was thirty and eight *t* 1Chr 23:3
four *t* were to set forward the 1Chr 23:4
six *t* were officers and judges 1Chr 23:4
Moreover four *t* were porters 1Chr 23:5
four *t* praised the LORD with the 1Chr 23:5
his brethren, men of valour, a *t* 1Chr 26:30
men of valour, were two *t* 1Chr 26:32
course were twenty and four *t* 1Chr 27:1
his course were twenty and four *t* 1Chr 27:2
likewise were twenty and four *t* 1Chr 27:4
his course were twenty and four *t* 1Chr 27:5
his course were twenty and four *t* 1Chr 27:7
his course were twenty and four *t* 1Chr 27:8
his course were twenty and four *t* 1Chr 27:9
his course were twenty and four *t* 1Chr 27:10
his course were twenty and four *t* 1Chr 27:11
his course were twenty and four *t* 1Chr 27:12
his course were twenty and four *t* 1Chr 27:13
his course were twenty and four *t* 1Chr 27:14
his course were twenty and four *t* 1Chr 27:15
Even three *t* talents of gold, of 1Chr 29:4
seven *t* talents of refined silver 1Chr 29:4
of God of gold five *t* talents 1Chr 29:7
ten *t* drams, and of silver ten 1Chr 29:7
drams, and of silver ten *t* talents 1Chr 29:7
and of brass eighteen *t* talents 1Chr 29:7
one hundred *t* talents of iron 1Chr 29:7
even a *t* bullocks, a *t* 1Chr 29:21
a *t* rams, and a *t* lambs, 1Chr 29:21
offered a *t* burnt offerings upon 2Chr 1:6
and he had a *t* and four hundred 2Chr 1:14
twelve *t* horsemen, which he 2Chr 1:14
ten *t* men to bear burdens, and 2Chr 2:2
fourscore *t* to hew in the 2Chr 2:2
hew in the mountain, and three *t* 2Chr 2:2
twenty *t* measures of beaten wheat 2Chr 2:10
twenty *t* measures of barley, and 2Chr 2:10
twenty *t* baths of wine, and twenty 2Chr 2:10
of wine, and twenty *t* baths of oil 2Chr 2:10
and fifty *t* and three *t* 2Chr 2:17
ten *t* of them to be bearers of 2Chr 2:18
fourscore *t* to be hewers in the 2Chr 2:18
in the mountain, and three *t* 2Chr 2:18
it received and held three *t* baths 2Chr 4:5
two *t* oxen, and an hundred and 2Chr 7:5
and an hundred and twenty *t* sheep 2Chr 7:5
Solomon had four *t* stalls for 2Chr 9:25
and chariots, and twelve *t* horsemen 2Chr 9:25
fourscore *t* chosen men, which 2Chr 11:1
and threescore *t* horsemen 2Chr 12:3
even four hundred *t* chosen men 2Chr 13:3
with eight hundred *t* chosen men 2Chr 13:3
Israel five hundred *t* chosen men 2Chr 13:17
out of Judah three hundred *t* 2Chr 14:8
bows, two hundred and fourscore *t* 2Chr 14:8
with an host of a *t t* 2Chr 14:9
hundred oxen and seven *t* sheep 2Chr 15:11
brought him flocks, seven *t* 2Chr 17:11
hundred rams, and seven *t* 2Chr 17:11
men of valour three hundred *t* 2Chr 17:14
him two hundred and fourscore *t* 2Chr 17:15
hundred *t* mighty men of valour 2Chr 17:16
with bow and shield two hundred *t* 2Chr 17:17
fourscore *t* ready prepared for 2Chr 17:18
them three hundred *t* choice men 2Chr 25:5
He hired also an hundred *t* mighty 2Chr 25:6
of the children of Seir ten *t* 2Chr 25:11
other ten *t* left alive did the 2Chr 25:12
and smote three *t* of them 2Chr 25:13
mighty men of valour were two *t* 2Chr 26:12
three hundred *t* and seven *t* 2Chr 26:13
ten *t* measures of wheat, and ten 2Chr 27:5
of wheat, and ten *t* of barley 2Chr 27:5
twenty *t* in one day, which were 2Chr 28:6
of their brethren two hundred *t* 2Chr 28:8
six hundred oxen and three *t* sheep 2Chr 29:33
to the congregation a *t* bullocks 2Chr 30:24
bullocks and seven *t* sheep 2Chr 30:24
to the congregation a *t* bullocks 2Chr 30:24
*t* bullocks and ten *t* sheep 2Chr 30:24
to the number of thirty *t* 2Chr 35:7
and three *t* bullocks 2Chr 35:7
for the passover offerings two *t* 2Chr 35:8
offerings five *t* small cattle 2Chr 35:9
a *t* chargers of silver, nine and Ezr 1:9
and ten, and other vessels a *t* Ezr 1:10
of gold and of silver were five *t* Ezr 1:11
two *t* an hundred seventy and two Ezr 2:3
two *t* eight hundred and twelve Ezr 2:6
a *t* two hundred fifty and four Ezr 2:7
a *t* two hundred twenty and two Ezr 2:12
of Bigvai, two *t* fifty and six Ezr 2:14
a *t* two hundred fifty and four Ezr 2:31
The children of Senaah, three *t* Ezr 2:35
of Immer, a *t* fifty and two Ezr 2:37
a *t* two hundred forty and seven Ezr 2:38
The children of Harim, a *t* Ezr 2:39
two *t* three hundred and threescore Ezr 2:64
were seven *t* three hundred thirty Ezr 2:65
six *t* seven hundred and twenty Ezr 2:67
one *t* drams of gold, and five Ezr 2:69
five *t* pound of silver, and one Ezr 2:69
basons of gold, of a *t* drams Ezr 8:27
a *t* cubits on the wall unto the Neh 3:13
two *t* an hundred seventy and two Neh 7:8
children of Jeshua and Joab, two *t* Neh 7:11
a *t* two hundred fifty and four Neh 7:12
two *t* three hundred twenty and two Neh 7:17
two *t* threescore and seven Neh 7:19
a *t* two hundred fifty and four Neh 7:34
three *t* nine hundred and thirty Neh 7:38
of Immer, a *t* fifty and two Neh 7:40
a *t* two hundred forty and seven Neh 7:41
The children of Harim, a *t* Neh 7:42
two *t* three hundred and threescore Neh 7:66
were seven *t* three hundred thirty Neh 7:67
six *t* seven hundred and twenty Neh 7:69
to the treasure a *t* drams of gold Neh 7:70
the work twenty *t* drams of gold Neh 7:71
of gold, and two *t* Neh 7:71
gave was twenty *t* drams of gold Neh 7:72
two *t* pounds of silver, and Neh 7:72
I will pay ten *t* talents of Est 3:9
of their foes seventy and five *t* Est 9:16
substance also was seven *t* sheep Job 1:3
three *t* camels, and five hundred Job 1:3
he cannot answer him one of a *t* Job 9:3
an interpreter, one among a *t* Job 33:23
for he had fourteen *t* sheep Job 42:12
six *t* camels, and a *t* yoke Job 42:12
yoke of oxen, and a *t* she asses Job 42:12
and the cattle upon a *t* hills Ps 50:10
in the valley of salt twelve *t* Ps 60:*t*
The chariots of God are twenty *t* Ps 68:17
in thy courts is better than a *t* Ps 84:10
For a *t* years in thy sight are Ps 90:4
A *t* shall fall at thy side, and Ps 91:7
side, and ten *t* at thy right hand Ps 91:7
he commanded to a *t* generations Ps 105:8
he live a *t* years twice told Eccl 6:6
one man among a *t* have I found Eccl 7:28
whereon there hang a *t* bucklers Song 4:4
ruddy, the chiefest among ten *t* Song 5:10
was to bring a *t* pieces of silver Song 8:11
thou, O Solomon, must have a *t* Song 8:12
*t* vines at a *t* silverlings Is 7:23
One *t* shall flee at the rebuke of Is 30:17
and I will give thee two *t* horses Is 36:8
an hundred and fourscore and five *t* Is 37:36
A little one shall become a *t* Is 60:22
in the seventh year three *t* Jews Jer 52:28
all the persons were four *t* Jer 52:30
length of five and twenty *t* reeds Eze 45:1
and the breadth shall be ten *t* Eze 45:1
the length of five and twenty *t* Eze 45:3
and the breadth of ten *t* Eze 45:3
twenty *t* of length, and the ten Eze 45:5
the ten *t* of breadth, shall also Eze 45:5
of the city five *t* broad, and five Eze 45:6
broad, and five and twenty *t* long Eze 45:6
eastward, he measured a *t* cubits Eze 47:3
Again he measured a *t*, and brought Eze 47:4
Again he measured a *t*, and brought Eze 47:4
Afterward he measured a *t* Eze 47:5
twenty *t* reeds in breadth, and in Eze 48:8
twenty *t* in length, and of ten Eze 48:9
in length, and of ten *t* in breadth Eze 48:9
twenty *t* in length, and toward the Eze 48:10
toward the west ten *t* in breadth Eze 48:10
toward the east ten *t* in breadth Eze 48:10
south five and twenty *t* in length Eze 48:10
twenty *t* in length, and ten Eze 48:13
in length, and ten *t* in breadth Eze 48:13
length shall be five and twenty *t* Eze 48:13
and the breadth ten *t* Eze 48:13
And the five *t*, that are left in Eze 48:15
over against the five and twenty *t* Eze 48:15
the north side four *t* and five Eze 48:16
hundred, and the south side four *t* Eze 48:16
and on the east side four *t* Eze 48:16
hundred, and the west side four *t* Eze 48:16
portion shall be ten *t* eastward Eze 48:18
eastward, and ten *t* westward Eze 48:18
twenty *t* by five and twenty Eze 48:20
by five and twenty *t* Eze 48:20
twenty *t* of the oblation toward Eze 48:21
twenty *t* toward the west border, Eze 48:21
city on the north side, four *t* Eze 48:30
And at the east side four *t* Eze 48:32
And at the south side four *t* Eze 48:33
At the west side four *t* and five Eze 48:34
round about eighteen *t* measures Eze 48:35
a great feast to a *t* of his lords Dan 5:1
lords, and drank wine before the *t* Dan 5:1
*t* thousands ministered unto him, Dan 7:10
ten *t* times ten *t* stood Dan 7:10
And he said unto me, Unto two *t* Dan 8:14
there shall be a *t* two hundred Dan 12:11
and cometh to the *t* three hundred Dan 12:12
out by a *t* shall leave an hundred Amos 5:3
*t* persons that cannot discern Jonah 4:11
had eaten were about five *t* men Mt 14:21
they that did eat were four *t* men Mt 15:38
the five loaves of the five *t* Mt 16:9
the seven loaves of the four *t* Mt 16:10
him, which owed him ten *t* talents Mt 18:24
the sea, (they were about two *t* Mk 5:13
the loaves were about five *t* men Mk 6:44
that had eaten were about four *t* Mk 8:9
the five loaves among five *t* Mk 8:19
And when the seven among four *t* Mk 8:20
For they were about five *t* men Lk 9:14
whether he be able with ten *t* to Lk 14:31
cometh against him with twenty *t* Lk 14:31
sat down, in number about five *t* Jn 6:10
unto them about three *t* souls Acts 2:41
of the men was about five *t* Acts 4:4
found it fifty *t* pieces of silver Acts 19:19
four *t* men that were murderers Acts 21:38
reserved to myself seven *t* men Rom 11:4
have ten *t* instructers in Christ 1Cor 4:15
fell in one day three and twenty *t* 1Cor 10:8
than ten *t* words in an unknown 1Cor 14:19
day is with the Lord as a *t* years 2Pet 3:8
years, and a *t* years as one day 2Pet 3:8
them was ten *t* times ten *t* Rev 5:11
four *t* of all the tribes of the Rev 7:4
of Juda were sealed twelve *t* Rev 7:5
of Reuben were sealed twelve *t* Rev 7:5
tribe of Gad were sealed twelve *t* Rev 7:5
of Aser were sealed twelve *t* Rev 7:6
of Nepthalim were sealed twelve *t* Rev 7:6
of Manasses were sealed twelve *t* Rev 7:6
of Simeon were sealed twelve *t* Rev 7:7
of Levi were sealed twelve *t* Rev 7:7
of Issachar were sealed twelve *t* Rev 7:7
of Zabulon were sealed twelve *t* Rev 7:8
of Joseph were sealed twelve *t* Rev 7:8
of Benjamin were sealed twelve *t* Rev 7:8
were two hundred *t t* Rev 9:16
shall prophesy a *t* two hundred Rev 11:3
were slain of men seven *t* Rev 11:13
feed her there a *t* two hundred Rev 12:6
him an hundred forty and four *t* Rev 14:1
the hundred and forty and four *t* Rev 14:3
bridles, by the space of a *t* Rev 14:20
and Satan, and bound him a *t* years Rev 20:2
till the *t* years should be Rev 20:3
and reigned with Christ a *t* years Rev 20:4
until the *t* years were finished Rev 20:5
and shall reign with him a *t* years Rev 20:6
when the *t* years are expired, Rev 20:7
with the reed, twelve *t* furlongs Rev 21:16

**THOUSANDS**

thou the mother of *t* of millions Gen 24:60
such over them, to be rulers of *t* Ex 18:21
over the people, rulers of *t* Ex 18:25
shewing mercy unto *t* of them that Ex 20:6
Keeping mercy for *t*, forgiving Ex 34:7
fathers, heads of *t* in Israel Num 1:16
are heads of the *t* of Israel Num 10:4
O LORD, unto the many *t* of Israel Num 10:36
delivered out of the *t* of Israel Num 31:5
host, with the captains over *t* Num 31:14
which were over *t* of the host Num 31:48
of the host, the captains of *t* Num 31:48
to the LORD, of the captains of *t* Num 31:52
the gold of the captains of *t* Num 31:54
heads over you, captains over *t* Deut 1:15

T

shewing mercy unto *t* of them that .... Deut 5:10
and he came with ten *t* of saints.......... Deut 33:2
and they are the ten *t* of Ephraim..... Deut 33:17
and they are the *t* of Manasseh.......... Deut 33:17
fathers among the *t* of Israel .......... Josh 22:14
unto the heads of the *t* of Israel ......... Josh 22:21
heads of the *t* of Israel which.............. Josh 22:30
will appoint him captains over *t* ............ 1Sa 8:12
LORD by your tribes, and by your *t*...... 1Sa 10:19
his *t*, and David his ten *t* ........................ 1Sa 18:7
have ascribed unto David ten *t*............ 1Sa 18:8
and to me they have ascribed but *t* ....... 1Sa 18:8
saying, Saul hath slain his *t*.................. 1Sa 21:11
and David his ten *t* ................................ 1Sa 21:11
and make you all captains of *t*............ 1Sa 22:7
out throughout all the *t* of Judah......... 1Sa 23:23
passed on by hundreds, and by *t* ........... 1Sa 29:2
dances, saying, Saul slew his *t* ............. 1Sa 29:5
and David his ten *t* .................................. 1Sa 29:5
with him, and set captains of *t*........... 2Sa 18:1
came out by hundreds and by *t*............. 2Sa 18:4
captains of the *t* that were of ............ 1Chr 12:20
consulted with the captains of *t*.......... 1Chr 13:1
of Israel, and the captains over *t* ...... 1Chr 15:25
fathers, the captains over *t*.................. 1Chr 26:26
chief fathers and captains of *t*............ 1Chr 27:1
and the captains over the *t*................... 1Chr 28:1
of Israel, and the captains of *t*............ 1Chr 29:6
all Israel, to the captains of *t*................. 2Chr 1:2
Of Judah, the captains of *t*.................. 2Chr 17:14
and made them captains over *t* ............. 2Chr 25:5
not be afraid of ten *t* of people................... Ps 3:6
twenty thousand, even *t* of angels ......... Ps 68:17
is better unto me than *t* of gold........... Ps 119:72
that our sheep may bring forth *t* .......... Ps 144:13
and ten *t* in our streets........................ Ps 144:13
shewest lovingkindness unto *t*............... Jer 32:18
thousand *t* ministered unto him,........... Dan 7:10
and he shall cast down many ten *t*..... Dan 11:12
be little among the *t* of Judah................. Mic 5:2
LORD be pleased with *t* of rams ............... Mic 6:7
or with ten *t* of rivers of oil.................... Mic 6:7
how many *t* of Jews there are............ Acts 21:20
cometh with ten *t* of his saints ............... Jude 14
ten thousand, and *t* of *t* ......................... Rev 5:11

### THREAD

from a *t* even to a shoelatchet............ Gen 14:23
bound upon his hand a scarlet *t*........... Gen 38:28
had the scarlet *t* upon his hand .......... Gen 38:30
*t* in the window which thou didst ........ Josh 2:18
as a *t* of tow is broken when it.............. Judg 16:9
them from off his arms like a *t* ........... Judg 16:12
Thy lips are like a *t* of scarlet................ Song 4:3

### THREATEN

people, let us straitly *t* them .................. Acts 4:17

### THREATENED

So when they had further *t* them......... Acts 4:21
when he suffered, he *t* not................... 1Pet 2:23

### THREATENING

things unto them, forbearing *t* ................ Eph 6:9

### THREATENINGS

And now, Lord, behold their *t* .............. Acts 4:29
And Saul, yet breathing out *t*.................. Acts 9:1

### THREE

begat Methuselah *t* hundred years........ Gen 5:22
of Enoch were *t* hundred sixty.............. Gen 5:23
And Noah begat *t* sons, Shem, Ham,.... Gen 6:10
the ark shall be *t* hundred cubits.......... Gen 6:15
the *t* wives of his sons with them ......... Gen 7:13
These are the *t* sons of Noah............... Gen 9:19
lived after the flood *t* hundred ............... Gen 9:28
*t* years, and begat sons and ............... Gen 11:13
*t* years, and begat sons and ............... Gen 11:15
*t* hundred and eighteen, and pursued. Gen 14:14
Take me an heifer of *t* years old............ Gen 15:9
old, and a she goat of *t* years old ......... Gen 15:9
a ram of *t* years old, and a .................... Gen 15:9
and, lo, *t* men stood by him .................. Gen 18:2
Make ready quickly *t* measures of........ Gen 18:6
there were *t* flocks of sheep................... Gen 29:2
because I have born him *t* sons............ Gen 29:34
he set *t* days' journey betwixt............... Gen 30:36
came to pass about *t* months after ...... Gen 38:24
And in the vine were *t* branches ......... Gen 40:10
The *t* branches are *t* days.................... Gen 40:12
Yet within *t* days shall Pharaoh ........... Gen 40:13
I had *t* white baskets on my head....... Gen 40:16
The *t* baskets are *t* days...................... Gen 40:18
Yet within *t* days shall Pharaoh ........... Gen 40:19
all together into ward *t* days ............... Gen 42:17
but to Benjamin he gave *t* hundred..... Gen 45:22
and his daughters were thirty and *t*... Gen 46:15
child, she hid him *t* months......................... Ex 2:2
thee, *t* days' journey into the.................... Ex 3:18
*t* days' journey into the desert,................ Ex 5:3
were an hundred thirty and *t* years......... Ex 6:18
*t* years old, when they spake unto............ Ex 7:7
We will go *t* days' journey into ............... Ex 8:27
in all the land of Egypt *t* days ............... Ex 10:22
any from his place for *t* days ................ Ex 10:23
and they went *t* days in the .................. Ex 15:22
And if he do not these *t* unto her......... Ex 21:11
*T* times thou shalt keep a feast ............. Ex 23:14
*T* times in the year all thy males.......... Ex 23:17
*t* branches of the candlestick out......... Ex 25:32
*t* branches of the candlestick out......... Ex 25:32
*T* bowls made like unto almonds,........... Ex 25:33
*t* bowls made like almonds in the .......... Ex 25:33
height thereof shall be *t* cubits................ Ex 27:1
pillars *t*, and their sockets *t*.................... Ex 27:14
pillars *t*, and their sockets *t*.................... Ex 27:15
that day about *t* thousand men ............. Ex 32:28
*t* branches of the candlestick out........... Ex 37:18
*t* branches of the candlestick out........... Ex 37:18
*T* bowls made after the fashion of ........ Ex 37:19
*t* bowls made like almonds in.................. Ex 37:19
*t* cubits the height thereof.......................... Ex 38:1
pillars *t*, and their sockets *t*..................... Ex 38:14
pillars *t*, and their sockets *t*..................... Ex 38:15
*t* thousand and five hundred and........... Ex 38:26
in the blood of her purifying *t* ................ Lev 12:4
*t* tenth deals of fine flour for a............. Lev 14:10
*t* years shall it be as.............................. Lev 19:23
bring forth fruit for *t* years.................... Lev 25:21
shall be *t* shekels of silver........................ Lev 27:6
and nine thousand and *t* hundred......... Num 1:23
*t* thousand and four hundred............... Num 1:43
*t* thousand and five hundred and.......... Num 1:46
and nine thousand and *t* hundred......... Num 2:13
*t* thousand and four hundred............... Num 2:30
*t* thousand and five hundred and.......... Num 2:32
a thousand *t* hundred and...................... Num 3:50
were *t* thousand and two hundred....... Num 4:44
mount of the LORD *t* days' journey ... Num 10:33
them in the *t* days' journey.................. Num 10:33
Come out ye *t* unto the tabernacle ..... Num 12:4
And they *t* came out ............................... Num 12:4
of *t* tenth deals of flour mingled.......... Num 15:9
hast smitten me these *t* times............. Num 22:28
smitten thine ass these *t* times............ Num 22:32
and turned from me these *t* times ..... Num 22:33
blessed them these *t* times.................. Num 24:10
*t* thousand and seven hundred and..... Num 26:7
and four thousand and *t* hundred...... Num 26:25
*t* thousand and four hundred.............. Num 26:47
*t* thousand, all males from a............... Num 26:62
*t* tenth deals of flour for a meat......... Num 28:12
*t* tenth deals shall ye offer for ........... Num 28:20
*t* tenth deals unto one bullock,........... Num 28:28
*t* tenth deals for a bullock, and ........... Num 29:3
*t* tenth deals to a bullock, and............. Num 29:9
*t* tenth deals unto every bullock ....... Num 29:14
was in number *t* hundred thousand .. Num 31:36
was *t* hundred thousand and thirty... Num 31:43
went *t* days' journey in the.................. Num 33:8
*t* years old when he died in mount.... Num 33:39
Ye shall give *t* cities on this.............. Num 35:14
*t* cities shall ye give in the................. Num 35:14
Then Moses severed *t* cities on............... Deut 4:41
At the end of *t* years thou shalt......... Deut 14:28
*T* times in a year shall all thy ........... Deut 16:16
or *t* witnesses, shall he that is ............. Deut 17:6
Thou shalt separate *t* cities for............ Deut 19:2
into *t* parts, that every slayer .............. Deut 19:3
shalt separate *t* cities for thee............. Deut 19:7
then shalt thou add *t* cities more.......... Deut 19:9
more for thee, beside these *t*................ Deut 19:9
or at the mouth of *t* witnesses........... Deut 19:15
for within *t* days ye shall pass............... Josh 1:11
and hide yourselves there *t* days.......... Josh 2:16
mountain, and abode there *t* days......... Josh 2:22
And it came to pass after *t* days ............ Josh 3:2
about two or *t* thousand men go up ...... Josh 7:3
the people about *t* thousand men ........... Josh 7:4
of *t* days after they had made a............ Josh 9:16
drove thence the *t* sons of Anak......... Josh 15:14
and her towns, even *t* countries.......... Josh 17:11
among you *t* men for each tribe ........... Josh 18:4
with her suburbs; *t* cities .................. Josh 21:32
thence the *t* sons of Anak..................... Judg 1:20
their mouth, were *t* hundred men ........... Judg 7:6
By the *t* hundred men that lapped.......... Judg 7:7
and retained those *t* hundred men......... Judg 7:8
he divided the *t* hundred men into ....... Judg 7:16
hundred men into *t* companies ............. Judg 7:16
the *t* companies blew the trumpets ..... Judg 7:20
the *t* hundred blew the trumpets, .......... Judg 7:22
the *t* hundred men that were with........ Judg 8:4
had reigned *t* years over Israel ............ Judg 9:22
and divided them into *t* companies........ Judg 9:43
*t* years, and died, and was buried......... Judg 10:2
coasts of Arnon, *t* hundred years........ Judg 11:26
they could not in *t* days expound......... Judg 14:14
caught *t* hundred foxes, and took.......... Judg 15:4
Then *t* thousand men of Judah went Judg 15:11
thou hast mocked me these *t* times... Judg 16:15
the roof about *t* thousand men............. Judg 16:27
and he abode with him *t* days............... Judg 19:4
with *t* bullocks, and one ephah of.......... 1Sa 1:24
fleshhook of *t* teeth in his hand............ 1Sa 2:13
she conceived, and bare *t* sons............... 1Sa 2:21
asses that were lost *t* days ago ............ 1Sa 9:20
there shall meet thee *t* men going ......... 1Sa 10:3
to Beth-el, one carrying *t* kids............. 1Sa 10:3
carrying *t* loaves of bread..................... 1Sa 10:3
of Israel were *t* hundred thousand......... 1Sa 11:8
put the people in *t* companies.............. 1Sa 11:11
Saul chose him *t* thousand men of......... 1Sa 13:2
of the Philistines in *t* companies........... 1Sa 13:17
the *t* eldest sons of Jesse went............. 1Sa 17:13
the names of his *t* sons that went........ 1Sa 17:13
the *t* eldest followed Saul...................... 1Sa 17:14
And when thou hast stayed *t* days ...... 1Sa 20:19
I will shoot *t* arrows on the side......... 1Sa 20:20
ground, and bowed himself *t* times........ 1Sa 20:41
kept from us about these *t* days............. 1Sa 21:5
Then Saul took *t* thousand chosen ........ 1Sa 24:2
he had *t* thousand sheep, and a.............. 1Sa 25:2
having *t* thousand chosen men of.......... 1Sa 26:2
any water, *t* days and *t* nights ............. 1Sa 30:12
because *t* days agone I fell sick ........... 1Sa 30:13
his *t* sons, and his armourbearer, ........... 1Sa 31:6
his *t* sons fallen in mount Gilboa........... 1Sa 31:8
there were *t* sons of Zeruiah ................... 2Sa 2:18
of Abner's men, so that *t* hundred ........ 2Sa 2:31
*t* years over all Israel and Judah ............... 2Sa 5:5
of Obed-edom the Gittite *t* months........ 2Sa 6:11
to Geshur, and was there *t* years ......... 2Sa 13:38
Absalom there were born *t* sons........... 2Sa 14:27
he took *t* darts in his hand, and........... 2Sa 18:14
me the men of Judah within *t* days....... 2Sa 20:4
in the days of David *t* years..................... 2Sa 21:1
*t* hundred shekels of brass in................. 2Sa 21:16
one of the *t* mighty men with ................. 2Sa 23:9
*t* of the thirty chief went down, ........... 2Sa 23:13
the *t* mighty men brake through.............. 2Sa 23:16
things did these *t* mighty men ............... 2Sa 23:17
son of Zeruiah, was chief among *t*....... 2Sa 23:18
up his spear against *t* hundred............... 2Sa 23:18
them, and had the name among *t* ........ 2Sa 23:18
Was he not most honourable of *t*......... 2Sa 23:19
he attained not unto the first *t* .............. 2Sa 23:19
had the name among *t* mighty men .... 2Sa 23:22
he attained not to the first *t*................. 2Sa 23:23
the LORD, I offer thee *t* things.............. 2Sa 24:12
or wilt thou flee *t* months before.......... 2Sa 24:13
or that there be *t* days' ........................ 2Sa 24:13
*t* years reigned he in Jerusalem ............ 1Kin 2:11
to pass at the end of *t* years ................ 1Kin 2:39
he spake *t* thousand proverbs .............. 1Kin 4:32
*t* thousand and *t* hundred,..................... 1Kin 5:16
court with *t* rows of hewed stone ........ 1Kin 6:36
And there were windows in *t* rows........ 1Kin 7:4
was against light in *t* ranks .................... 1Kin 7:4
was against light in *t* ranks .................... 1Kin 7:5
was with *t* rows of hewed stones .......... 1Kin 7:12
*t* looking toward the north, and .......... 1Kin 7:25
*t* looking toward the west, and............ 1Kin 7:25
*t* looking toward the south, and.......... 1Kin 7:25
*t* looking toward the east ...................... 1Kin 7:25
*t* cubits the height of it.......................... 1Kin 7:27
*t* times in a year did Solomon .............. 1Kin 9:25
he made *t* hundred shields of.............. 1Kin 10:17
*t* pound of gold went to one................. 1Kin 10:17
once in *t* years came the navy of ....... 1Kin 10:22
and *t* hundred concubines....................... 1Kin 11:3
unto them, Depart yet for *t* days.......... 1Kin 12:5
*T* years reigned he in Jerusalem .......... 1Kin 15:2
himself upon the child *t* times............ 1Kin 17:21
they continued *t* years without............... 1Kin 22:1
and they sought *t* days, but found....... 2Kin 2:17
called these *t* kings together ................ 2Kin 3:10
called these *t* kings together ................ 2Kin 3:13
out to him two or *t* eunuchs ................. 2Kin 9:32
But it was so, that in the *t*.................... 2Kin 12:6
In the *t* and twentieth year of ............... 2Kin 13:1
*T* times did Joash beat him, and......... 2Kin 13:25
Samaria, and besieged it *t* years ........... 2Kin 17:5
at the end of *t* years they took ......... 2Kin 18:10
Judah *t* hundred talents of silver......... 2Kin 18:14
*t* years old when he began to............... 2Kin 23:31
he reigned *t* months in Jerusalem ...... 2Kin 23:31
became his servant *t* years.................... 2Kin 24:1
he reigned in Jerusalem *t* months.......... 2Kin 24:8
height of the chapiter *t* cubits............ 2Kin 25:17
the *t* keepers of the door....................... 2Kin 25:18
which *t* were born unto him of the ....... 1Chr 2:3
Abishai, and Joab, and Asahel, *t* .......... 1Chr 2:16
And Segub begat Jair, who had *t*........... 1Chr 2:22
he reigned thirty and *t* years.................... 1Chr 3:4
and Hezekiah, and Azrikam, *t* ............... 1Chr 3:23
Bela, and Becher, and Jediael, *t*............... 1Chr 7:6
his *t* sons, and all his house died.......... 1Chr 10:6
*t* hundred slain by him at one.............. 1Chr 11:11
who was one of the *t* mighties ............ 1Chr 11:12
Now *t* of the thirty captains went ..... 1Chr 11:15
the *t* brake through the host of........... 1Chr 11:18
things did these *t* mightiest................. 1Chr 11:19
of Joab, he was chief of the *t*................ 1Chr 11:20
up his spear against *t* hundred ............ 1Chr 11:20
them, and had a name among the *t* .. 1Chr 11:20
Of the *t*, he was more honourable ..... 1Chr 11:21
he attained not to the first *t*................ 1Chr 11:21
had the name among the *t* mighties . 1Chr 11:24
but attained not to the first *t*............... 1Chr 11:25
and with him were *t* thousand............. 1Chr 12:27
the kindred of Saul, *t* thousand............ 1Chr 12:29
there they were with David *t* days ..... 1Chr 12:39
Obed-edom in his house *t* months ..... 1Chr 13:14
the LORD, I offer thee *t* things ............ 1Chr 21:10
Either *t* years' famine............................ 1Chr 21:12
or *t* months to be destroyed ................ 1Chr 21:12
or else *t* days the sword of the ........... 1Chr 21:12
was Jehiel, and Zetham, and Joel, *t*...... 1Chr 23:8
Shelomith, and Haziel, and Haran, *t* ... 1Chr 23:9
Mahli, and Eder, and Jeremoth, *t*....... 1Chr 23:23
The *t* and twentieth to Delaiah, .......... 1Chr 24:18
fourteen sons and *t* daughters .............. 1Chr 25:5
The *t* and twentieth to Mahazioth,.... 1Chr 25:30
Even *t* thousand talents of gold, .......... 1Chr 29:4
*t* years reigned he in Jerusalem.......... 1Chr 29:27
*t* thousand and six hundred to................ 2Chr 2:2
*t* thousand and six hundred.................. 2Chr 2:17
*t* thousand and six hundred.................. 2Chr 2:18
*t* looking toward the north, and............. 2Chr 4:4
*t* looking toward the west, and.............. 2Chr 4:4
*t* looking toward the south, and............ 2Chr 4:4

*t* looking toward the east ... 2Chr 4:4
received and held *t* thousand baths ... 2Chr 4:5
*t* cubits high, and had set it in ... 2Chr 6:13
And on the *t* and twentieth day of ... 2Chr 7:10
*t* times in the year, even in the ... 2Chr 8:13
*t* hundred shields made he of ... 2Chr 9:16
*t* hundred shekels of gold went to ... 2Chr 9:16
every *t* years once came the ships ... 2Chr 9:21
Come again unto me after *t* days ... 2Chr 10:5
son of Solomon strong, *t* years ... 2Chr 11:17
for *t* years they walked in the ... 2Chr 11:17
He reigned *t* years in Jerusalem ... 2Chr 13:2
out of Judah *t* hundred thousand ... 2Chr 14:8
thousand, and *t* hundred chariots ... 2Chr 14:9
men of valour *t* hundred thousand ... 2Chr 17:14
they were *t* days in gathering of ... 2Chr 20:25
found them *t* hundred thousand ... 2Chr 25:5
smote *t* thousand of them, and took. 2Chr 25:13
*t* hundred thousand and seven ... 2Chr 26:13
hundred oxen and *t* thousand sheep. 2Chr 29:33
from *t* years old and upward, even ... 2Chr 31:16
thousand, and *t* thousand bullocks ... 2Chr 35:7
small cattle, and *t* hundred oxen ... 2Chr 35:8
*t* years old when he began to ... 2Chr 36:2
he reigned *t* months in Jerusalem ... 2Chr 36:2
to reign, and he reigned *t* months ... 2Chr 36:9
*t* hundred seventy and two ... Ezr 2:4
of Bebai, six hundred twenty and *t* ... Ezr 2:11
Bezai, *t* hundred twenty and *t* ... Ezr 2:17
Hashum, two hundred twenty and *t* ... Ezr 2:19
an hundred twenty and *t* ... Ezr 2:21
seven hundred and forty and *t* ... Ezr 2:25
and Ai, two hundred twenty and *t* ... Ezr 2:28
of Harim, *t* hundred and twenty ... Ezr 2:32
Jericho, *t* hundred forty and five ... Ezr 2:34
*t* thousand and six hundred and ... Ezr 2:35
Jeshua, nine hundred seventy and *t* ... Ezr 2:36
were *t* hundred ninety and two ... Ezr 2:58
forty and two thousand *t* hundred ... Ezr 2:64
seven thousand *t* hundred thirty ... Ezr 2:65
With *t* rows of great stones, and a ... Ezr 6:4
and with him *t* hundred males ... Ezr 8:5
and there abode we in tents *t* days ... Ezr 8:15
Jerusalem, and abode there *t* days ... Ezr 8:32
would not come within *t* days ... Ezr 10:8
unto Jerusalem within *t* days ... Ezr 10:9
to Jerusalem, and was there *t* days ... Neh 2:11
*t* hundred seventy and two ... Neh 7:9
two thousand *t* hundred twenty and ... Neh 7:17
*t* hundred twenty and eight ... Neh 7:22
Bezai, *t* hundred twenty and four ... Neh 7:23
Beeroth, seven hundred forty and *t* ... Neh 7:29
and Ai, an hundred twenty and *t* ... Neh 7:32
of Harim, *t* hundred and twenty ... Neh 7:35
Jericho, *t* hundred forty and five ... Neh 7:36
*t* thousand nine hundred and thirty ... Neh 7:38
Jeshua, nine hundred seventy and *t* ... Neh 7:39
were *t* hundred ninety and two ... Neh 7:60
forty and two thousand *t* hundred ... Neh 7:66
seven thousand *t* hundred thirty ... Neh 7:67
and neither eat nor drink *t* days ... Est 4:16
is, the month Sivan, on the *t* ... Est 8:9
slew *t* hundred men at Shushan ... Est 9:15
him seven sons and *t* daughters ... Job 1:2
*t* thousand camels, and five ... Job 1:3
called for their *t* sisters to eat ... Job 1:4
The Chaldeans made out *t* bands ... Job 1:17
Now when Job's *t* friends heard of ... Job 2:11
So these *t* men ceased to answer ... Job 32:1
Also against his *t* friends was ... Job 32:3
in the mouth of these *t* men ... Job 32:5
also seven sons and *t* daughters ... Job 42:13
There are *t* things that are never ... Prov 30:15
There be *t* things which are too ... Prov 30:18
For *t* things the earth is ... Prov 30:21
There be *t* things which go well, ... Prov 30:29
Zoar, an heifer of *t* years old ... Is 15:5
spoken, saying, Within *t* years ... Is 16:14
two or *t* berries in the top of ... Is 17:6
barefoot *t* years for a sign and ... Is 20:3
even unto this day, that is the *t* ... Jer 25:3
Jehudi had read *t* or four leaves ... Jer 36:23
as an heifer of *t* years old ... Jer 48:34
the *t* keepers of the door ... Jer 52:24
year *t* thousand Jews and *t* ... Jer 52:28
In the *t* and twentieth year of ... Jer 52:30
days, *t* hundred and ninety days ... Eze 4:5
*t* hundred and ninety days shalt ... Eze 4:9
Though these *t* men, Noah, Daniel, ... Eze 14:14
Though these *t* men were in it, as ... Eze 14:16
Though these *t* men were in it, as ... Eze 14:18
gate eastward were *t* on this side ... Eze 40:10
on this side, and *t* on that side ... Eze 40:10
they *t* were of one measure ... Eze 40:10
thereof were *t* on this side ... Eze 40:21
on this side and *t* on that side ... Eze 40:21
gate was *t* cubits on this side ... Eze 40:48
side, and *t* cubits on that side ... Eze 40:48
And the side chambers were *t* ... Eze 41:6
round about on their *t* stories ... Eze 41:16
altar of wood was *t* cubits high ... Eze 41:22
against gallery in *t* stories ... Eze 42:3
For they were in *t* stories ... Eze 42:6
*t* gates northward ... Eze 48:31
five hundred: and *t* gates ... Eze 48:32
hundred measures: and *t* gates ... Eze 48:33
five hundred, with their *t* gates ... Eze 48:34
so nourishing them *t* years ... Dan 1:5
And these *t* men, Shadrach, Meshach.. Dan 3:23
Did not we cast *t* men bound into ... Dan 3:24
And over these *t* presidents ... Dan 6:2
upon his knees *t* times a day ... Dan 6:10
maketh his petition *t* times a day ... Dan 6:13
it had *t* ribs in the mouth of it ... Dan 7:5
before whom there were *t* of the ... Dan 7:8
came up, and before whom *t* fell ... Dan 7:20
first, and he shall subdue *t* kings ... Dan 7:24
two thousand and *t* hundred days ... Dan 8:14
Daniel was mourning *t* full weeks ... Dan 10:2
till *t* whole weeks were fulfilled ... Dan 10:3
stand up yet *t* kings in Persia ... Dan 11:2
cometh to the thousand *t* hundred ... Dan 12:12
For *t* transgressions of Damascus, ... Amos 1:3
For *t* transgressions of Gaza, and ... Amos 1:6
For *t* transgressions of Tyrus, and ... Amos 1:9
For *t* transgressions of Edom, and ... Amos 1:11
For *t* transgressions of the ... Amos 1:13
For *t* transgressions of Moab, and ... Amos 2:1
For *t* transgressions of Judah, and ... Amos 2:4
For *t* transgressions of Israel, ... Amos 2:6
and your tithes after *t* years ... Amos 4:4
when there were yet *t* months to ... Amos 4:7
So two or *t* cities wandered unto ... Amos 4:8
the fish *t* days and *t* nights ... Jonah 1:17
great city of *t* days' journey ... Jonah 3:3
*T* shepherds also I cut off in one ... Zec 11:8
For as Jonas was *t* days ... Mt 12:40
*t* nights in the whale's belly ... Mt 12:40
so shall the Son of man be *t* days ... Mt 12:40
*t* nights in the heart of the ... Mt 12:40
hid in *t* measures of meal, till ... Mt 13:33
they continue with me now *t* days ... Mt 15:32
let us make here *t* tabernacles ... Mt 17:4
or *t* witnesses every word may be ... Mt 18:16
For where two or *t* are gathered ... Mt 18:20
of God, and to build it in *t* days ... Mt 26:61
temple, and buildest it in *t* days ... Mt 27:40
After *t* days I will rise again ... Mt 27:63
they have now been with me *t* days ... Mk 8:2
and after *t* days rise again ... Mk 8:31
and let us make *t* tabernacles ... Mk 9:5
for more than *t* hundred pence ... Mk 14:5
within *t* days I will build ... Mk 14:58
temple, and buildest it in *t* days ... Mk 15:29
abode with her about *t* months ... Lk 1:56
that after *t* days they found him ... Lk 2:46
the heaven was shut up *t* years ... Lk 4:25
and let us make *t* tabernacles ... Lk 9:33
Which now of these *t*, thinkest ... Lk 10:36
him, Friend, lend me *t* loaves ... Lk 11:5
*t* against two, and two against ... Lk 12:52
against two, and two against *t* ... Lk 12:52
these *t* years I come seeking ... Lk 13:7
hid in *t* measures of meal, till ... Lk 13:21
two or *t* firkins apiece ... Jn 2:6
in *t* days I will raise it up ... Jn 2:19
and wilt thou rear it up in *t* days ... Jn 2:20
ointment sold for *t* hundred pence ... Jn 12:5
fishes, an hundred and fifty and *t* ... Jn 21:11
unto them about *t* thousand souls ... Acts 2:41
about the space of *t* hours after ... Acts 5:7
up in his father's house *t* months ... Acts 7:20
he was *t* days without sight, and ... Acts 9:9
unto him, Behold, *t* men seek thee ... Acts 10:19
And this was done *t* times ... Acts 11:10
immediately there were *t* men ... Acts 11:11
*t* sabbath days reasoned with them ... Acts 17:2
boldly for the space of *t* months ... Acts 19:8
And there abode *t* months ... Acts 20:3
that by the space of *t* years I ... Acts 20:31
after *t* days he ascended from ... Acts 25:1
lodged us *t* days courteously ... Acts 28:7
after *t* months we departed in a ... Acts 28:11
Syracuse, we tarried there *t* days ... Acts 28:12
as Appii forum, and The *t* taverns ... Acts 28:15
that after *t* days Paul called the ... Acts 28:17
committed, and fell in one day *t* ... 1Cor 10:8
faith, hope, charity, these *t* ... 1Cor 13:13
it be by two, or at the most by *t* ... 1Cor 14:27
Let the prophets speak two or *t* ... 1Cor 14:29
In the mouth of two or *t* ... 2Cor 13:1
Then after *t* years I went up to ... Gal 1:18
but before two or *t* witnesses ... 1Ti 5:19
mercy under two or *t* witnesses ... Heb 10:28
was hid *t* months of his parents, ... Heb 11:23
the earth by the space of *t* years ... Jas 5:17
For there are *t* that bear record ... 1Jn 5:7
and these *t* are one ... 1Jn 5:7
there are *t* that bear witness in ... 1Jn 5:8
and these *t* agree in one ... 1Jn 5:8
*t* measures of barley for a penny ... Rev 6:6
of the trumpet of the *t* angels ... Rev 8:13
By these *t* was the third part of ... Rev 9:18
see their dead bodies *t* days ... Rev 11:9
And after *t* days and an half the ... Rev 11:11
I saw *t* unclean spirits like ... Rev 16:13
city was divided into *t* parts ... Rev 16:19
On the east *t* gates ... Rev 21:13
on the north *t* gates ... Rev 21:13
on the south *t* gates ... Rev 21:13
and on the west *t* gates ... Rev 21:13

## THREEFOLD

a *t* cord is not quickly broken ... Eccl 4:12

## THREESCORE

life which he lived, an hundred *t* ... Gen 25:7
Isaac was *t* years old when she ... Gen 25:26
sons' wives, all the souls were *t* ... Gen 46:26
which came into Egypt, were *t* ... Gen 46:27
the Egyptians mourned for him *t* ... Gen 50:3
were twelve wells of water, and *t* ... Ex 15:27
and a thousand seven hundred and *t* ... Ex 38:25
in the blood of her purifying *t* ... Lev 12:5
of the tribe of Judah, were *t* ... Num 1:27
even of the tribe of Dan, were *t* ... Num 1:39
were numbered of them, were *t* ... Num 2:4
were numbered of them, were *t* ... Num 2:26
and two thousand two hundred and *t* ... Num 3:43
redeemed of the two hundred and *t* ... Num 3:46
a thousand three hundred and *t* ... Num 3:50
that were numbered of them, *t* ... Num 26:22
that were numbered of them, *t* ... Num 26:25
*t* thousand and five hundred ... Num 26:27
were numbered of them, were *t* ... Num 26:43
And *t* and twelve thousand beeves, ... Num 31:33
And *t* and one thousand asses, ... Num 31:34
of the sheep was six hundred and *t* ... Num 31:37
of which the LORD's tribute was *t* ... Num 31:38
of which the LORD's tribute was *t* ... Num 31:39
twelve fountains of water, and *t* ... Num 33:9
*t* cities, all the region of Argob ... Deut 3:4
went down into Egypt with *t* ... Deut 10:22
which are in Bashan, *t* cities ... Josh 13:30
And Adoni-bezek said, *T* and ten ... Judg 1:7
and the elders thereof, even *t* ... Judg 8:14
And Gideon had *t* and ten sons of ... Judg 8:30
sons of Jerubbaal, which are *t* ... Judg 9:2
And they gave him *t* and ten pieces ... Judg 9:4
the sons of Jerubbaal, being *t* ... Judg 9:5
day, and have slain his sons, *t* ... Judg 9:18
That the cruelty done to the *t* ... Judg 9:24
and thirty nephews, that rode on *t* ... Judg 12:14
of the people fifty thousand and *t* ... 1Sa 6:19
that three hundred and *t* men died ... 2Sa 2:31
*t* great cities with walls and ... 1Kin 4:13
flour, and *t* measures of meal, ... 1Kin 4:22
And Solomon had *t* and ten thousand 1Kin 5:15
the length thereof was *t* cubits ... 1Kin 6:2
in one year was six hundred *t* ... 1Kin 10:14
*t* men of the people of the land ... 2Kin 25:19
married when he was *t* years old ... 1Chr 2:21
the towns thereof, even *t* cities ... 1Chr 2:23
forty thousand seven hundred and *t* ... 1Chr 5:18
a thousand and seven hundred and *t*.. 1Chr 9:13
Obed-edom with their brethren, *t* ... 1Chr 16:38
and Judah was four hundred *t* ... 1Chr 21:5
strength for the service, were *t* ... 1Chr 26:8
And Solomon told out *t* and ten ... 2Chr 2:2
And he set *t* and ten thousand of ... 2Chr 2:18
the first measure was *t* cubits ... 2Chr 3:3
in one year was six hundred and *t* ... 2Chr 9:13
eighteen wives, and *t* concubines ... 2Chr 11:21
and eight sons, and *t* daughters ... 2Chr 11:21
chariots, and *t* thousand horsemen ... 2Chr 12:3
the congregation brought, was *t* ... 2Chr 29:32
she kept sabbath, to fulfil *t* ... 2Chr 36:21
of Zaccai, seven hundred and *t* ... Ezr 2:9
two thousand three hundred and *t* ... Ezr 2:64
unto the treasure of the work *t* ... Ezr 2:69
the height thereof *t* cubits ... Ezr 6:3
and the breadth thereof *t* cubits ... Ezr 6:3
and with him an hundred and *t* males .. Ezr 8:10
and Shemaiah, and with them *t* males .. Ezr 8:13
of Zaccai, seven hundred and *t* ... Neh 7:14
of Adonikam, six hundred *t* ... Neh 7:18
of Bigvai, two thousand *t* ... Neh 7:19
two thousand three hundred and *t* ... Neh 7:66
thousand pounds of silver, and *t* ... Neh 7:72
at Jerusalem were four hundred *t* ... Neh 11:6
The days of our years are *t* years ... Ps 90:10
*t* valiant men are about it, of ... Song 3:7
There are *t* queens, and fourscore ... Song 6:8
and within *t* and five years shall ... Is 7:8
*t* men of the people of the land, ... Jer 52:25
He made also posts of *t* cubits ... Eze 40:14
gold, whose height was *t* cubits ... Dan 3:1
took the kingdom, being about *t* ... Dan 5:31
Prince shall be seven weeks, and *t* ... Dan 9:25
And after *t* and two weeks shall ... Dan 9:26
thou hast had indignation these *t* ... Zec 1:12
from Jerusalem about *t* furlongs ... Lk 24:13
to him, and all his kindred, *t* ... Acts 7:14
to go to Caesarea, and horsemen *t* ... Acts 23:23
in all the ship two hundred *t* ... Acts 27:37
into the number under *t* years old ... 1Ti 5:9
*t* days, clothed in sackcloth ... Rev 11:3
a thousand two hundred and *t* days ... Rev 12:6
and his number is six hundred *t* ... Rev 13:18

## THRESH

thou shalt *t* the mountains, and ... Is 41:15
it is time to *t* her ... Jer 51:33
Arise and *t*, O daughter of Zion ... Mic 4:13
thou didst *t* the heathen in anger ... Hab 3:12

## THRESHED

his son Gideon *t* wheat by the ... Judg 6:11
For the fitches are not *t* with a ... Is 28:27
because they have *t* Gilead with ... Amos 1:3

## THRESHETH

that he that *t* in hope should be ... 1Cor 9:10

## THRESHING

your *t* shall reach unto the ... Lev 26:5
and *t* instruments and other ... 2Sa 24:22
had made them like the dust by *t* ... 2Kin 13:7
Now Ornan was *t* wheat ... 1Chr 21:20
the *t* instruments for wood, and ... 1Chr 21:23
O my *t*, and the corn of my floor ... Is 21:10
not threshed with a *t* instrument ... Is 28:27
because he will not ever be *t* it ... Is 28:28

sharp *t* instrument having teeth ........ Is 41:15
Gilead with *t* instruments of iron ........ Amos 1:3

**THRESHINGFLOOR**
And they came to the *t* of Atad........ Gen 50:10
ye do the heave offering of the *t*........ Num 15:20
though it were the corn of the *t*........ Num 18:27
Levites as the increase of the *t*........ Num 18:30
barley to night in the *t*........ Ruth 3:2
And when they came to Nachon's *t*........ 2Sa 6:6
in the *t* of Araunah the Jebusite........ 2Sa 24:18
David said, To buy the *t* of thee........ 2Sa 24:21
So David bought the *t* and the oxen ... 2Sa 24:24
they came unto the *t* of Chidon........ 1Chr 13:9
by the *t* of Ornan the Jebusite........ 1Chr 21:15
in the *t* of Ornan the Jebusite........ 1Chr 21:18
saw David, and went out of the *t*...... 1Chr 21:21
Grant me the place of this *t*........ 1Chr 21:22
in the *t* of Ornan the Jebusite........ 1Chr 21:28
in the *t* of Ornan the Jebusite........ 2Chr 3:1
daughter of Babylon is like a *t*........ Jer 51:33

**THRESHINGFLOORS**
against Keilah, and they rob the *t*........ 1Sa 23:1
like the chaff of the summer *t*........ Dan 2:35

**THRESHINGPLACE**
by the *t* of Araunah the Jebusite........ 2Sa 24:16

**THRESHOLD**
and her hands were upon the *t*........ Judg 19:27
his hands were cut off upon the *t*........ 1Sa 5:4
tread on the *t* of Dagon in Ashdod........ 1Sa 5:5
she came to the *t* of the door........ 1Kin 14:17
he was, to the *t* of the house........ Eze 9:3
and stood over the *t* of the house........ Eze 10:4
from off the *t* of the house........ Eze 10:18
and measured the *t* of the gate........ Eze 40:6
the other *t* of the gate, which........ Eze 40:6
the *t* of the gate by the porch of........ Eze 40:7
of their *t* by my thresholds........ Eze 43:8
worship at the *t* of the gate........ Eze 46:2
under the *t* of the house eastward........ Eze 47:1
all those that leap on the *t*........ Zeph 1:9

**THRESHOLDS**
the ward at the *t* of the gates........ Neh 12:25
of their threshold by my *t*........ Eze 43:8
desolation shall be in the *t*........ Zeph 2:14

**THREW**
*t* stones at him, and cast dust........ 2Sa 16:13
So they *t* her down........ 2Kin 9:33
*t* down the high places and the........ 2Chr 31:1
she *t* in two mites, which make a........ Mk 12:42
a coming, the devil *t* him down........ Lk 9:42
clothes, and *t* dust into the air,........ Acts 22:23

**THREWEST**
persecutors thou *t* into the deeps........ Neh 9:11

**THRICE**
*T* in the year shall all your men........ Ex 34:23
the LORD thy God *t* in the year........ Ex 34:24
And he smote *t*, and stayed........ 2Kin 13:18
now thou shalt smite Syria but *t*........ 2Kin 13:19
cock crow, thou shalt deny me *t*........ Mt 26:34
cock crow, thou shalt deny me *t*........ Mt 26:75
crow twice, thou shalt deny me *t*........ Mk 14:30
crow twice, thou shalt deny me *t*........ Mk 14:72
before that thou shalt *t* deny........ Lk 22:34
cock crow, thou shalt deny me *t*........ Lk 22:61
crow, till thou hast denied me *t*........ Jn 13:38
This was done *t*........ Acts 10:16
*T* was I beaten with rods, once........ 2Cor 11:25
*t* I suffered shipwreck, a night........ 2Cor 11:25
this thing I besought the Lord *t*........ 2Cor 12:8

**THROAT**
their *t* is an open sepulchre........ Ps 5:9
my *t* is dried........ Ps 69:3
speak they through their *t*........ Ps 115:7
And put a knife to thy *t*, if thou........ Prov 23:2
unshod, and thy *t* from thirst........ Jer 2:25
on him, and took him by the *t*........ Mt 18:28
Their *t* is an open sepulchre........ Rom 3:13

**THRONE**
only in the *t* will I be greater........ Gen 41:40
Pharaoh that sitteth upon his *t*........ Ex 11:5
his *t* unto the firstborn of the........ Ex 12:29
sitteth upon the *t* of his kingdom...... Deut 17:18
make them inherit the *t* of glory........ 1Sa 2:8
to set up the *t* of David over........ 2Sa 3:10
I will stablish the *t* of his........ 2Sa 7:13
thy *t* shall be established for........ 2Sa 7:16
and the king and his *t* be guiltless........ 2Sa 14:9
me, and he shall sit upon my *t*........ 1Kin 1:13
me, and he shall sit upon my *t*........ 1Kin 1:17
*t* of my lord the king after him........ 1Kin 1:20
me, and he shall sit upon my *t*........ 1Kin 1:24
who should sit on the *t* of my........ 1Kin 1:27
shall sit upon my *t* in my stead........ 1Kin 1:30
that he may come and sit upon my *t*.. 1Kin 1:35
make his *t* greater than the........ 1Kin 1:37
than the *t* of my lord king David........ 1Kin 1:37
sitteth on the *t* of the kingdom........ 1Kin 1:46
his *t* greater than thy *t*........ 1Kin 1:47
given one to sit on my *t* this day........ 1Kin 1:48
said he) a man on the *t* of Israel........ 1Kin 2:4
upon the *t* of David his father........ 1Kin 2:12
unto her, and sat down on his *t*........ 1Kin 2:19
set me on the *t* of David my........ 1Kin 2:24
and upon his house, and upon his *t*.... 1Kin 2:33
and the *t* of David shall be........ 1Kin 2:45
given him a son to sit on his *t*........ 1Kin 3:6
I will set upon thy *t* in thy room........ 1Kin 5:5
for the *t* where he might judge........ 1Kin 7:7
father, and sit on the *t* of Israel........ 1Kin 8:20
sight to sit on the *t* of Israel........ 1Kin 8:25
Then I will establish the *t* of........ 1Kin 9:5
thee a man upon the *t* of Israel........ 1Kin 9:5
to set thee on the *t* of Israel........ 1Kin 10:9
the king made a great *t* of ivory........ 1Kin 10:18
The *t* had six steps, and the top........ 1Kin 10:19
the top of the *t* was round behind........ 1Kin 10:19
reign, as soon as he sat on his *t*........ 1Kin 16:11
king of Judah sat each on his *t*........ 1Kin 22:10
I saw the LORD sitting on his *t*........ 1Kin 22:19
and set him on his father's *t*........ 2Kin 10:3
shall sit on the *t* of Israel........ 2Kin 10:30
And he sat on the *t* of the kings........ 2Kin 11:19
and Jeroboam sat upon his *t*........ 2Kin 13:13
the *t* of Israel unto the fourth........ 2Kin 15:12
set his *t* above the *t* of the........ 2Kin 25:28
and I will stablish his *t* for ever........ 1Chr 17:12
his *t* shall be established for........ 1Chr 17:14
I will establish the *t* of his........ 1Chr 22:10
Solomon my son to sit upon the *t*........ 1Chr 28:5
Then Solomon sat on the *t* of the........ 1Chr 29:23
and am set on the *t* of Israel........ 2Chr 6:10
sight to sit upon the *t* of Israel........ 2Chr 6:16
I stablish the *t* of thy kingdom........ 2Chr 7:18
in thee to set thee on his *t*........ 2Chr 9:8
the king made a great *t* of ivory........ 2Chr 9:17
And there were six steps to the *t*........ 2Chr 9:18
which were fastened to the *t*........ 2Chr 9:18
Judah sat either of them on his *t*........ 2Chr 18:9
I saw the LORD sitting upon his *t*........ 2Chr 18:18
king upon the *t* of the kingdom........ 2Chr 23:20
unto the *t* of the governor on........ Neh 3:7
sat on the *t* of his kingdom........ Est 1:2
his royal *t* in the royal house........ Est 5:1
He holdeth back the face of his *t*........ Job 26:9
but with kings are they on the *t*........ Job 36:7
satest in the *t* judging right........ Ps 9:4
hath prepared his *t* for judgment........ Ps 9:7
the LORD's *t* is in heaven........ Ps 11:4
Thy *t*, O God, is for ever and ever........ Ps 45:6
upon the *t* of his holiness........ Ps 47:8
build up thy *t* to all generations........ Ps 89:4
are the habitation of thy *t*........ Ps 89:14
his *t* as the days of heaven........ Ps 89:29
his *t* as the sun before me........ Ps 89:36
cast his *t* down to the ground........ Ps 89:44
Thy *t* is established of old........ Ps 93:2
Shall the *t* of iniquity have........ Ps 94:20
are the habitation of his *t*........ Ps 97:2
prepared his *t* in the heavens........ Ps 103:19
of thy body will I set upon thy *t*........ Ps 132:11
also sit upon thy *t* for evermore........ Ps 132:12
for the *t* is established by........ Prov 16:12
A king that sitteth in the *t* of........ Prov 20:8
his *t* is upholden by mercy........ Prov 20:28
his *t* shall be established in........ Prov 25:5
his *t* shall be established for........ Prov 29:14
also the Lord sitting upon a *t*........ Is 6:1
be no end, upon the *t* of David........ Is 9:7
I will exalt my *t* above the stars........ Is 14:13
mercy shall the *t* be established........ Is 16:5
glorious *t* to his father's house........ Is 22:23
there is no *t*, O daughter of the........ Is 47:1
the LORD, The heaven is my *t*........ Is 66:1
they shall set every one his *t* at........ Jer 1:15
call Jerusalem the *t* of the LORD........ Jer 3:17
the kings that sit upon David's *t*........ Jer 13:13
not disgrace the *t* of thy glory........ Jer 14:21
A glorious high *t* from the........ Jer 17:12
sitting upon the *t* of David........ Jer 17:25
that sittest upon the *t* of David........ Jer 22:2
kings sitting upon the *t* of David........ Jer 22:4
sitting upon the *t* of David........ Jer 22:30
that sitteth upon the *t* of David........ Jer 29:16
upon the *t* of the house of Israel........ Jer 33:17
have a son to reign upon his *t*........ Jer 33:21
none to sit upon the *t* of David........ Jer 36:30
will set his *t* upon these stones........ Jer 43:10
And I will set my *t* in Elam........ Jer 49:38
set his *t* above the *t* of the........ Jer 52:32
thy *t* from generation to........ Lam 5:19
heads was the likeness of a *t*........ Eze 1:26
of the *t* was the likeness as the........ Eze 1:26
appearance of the likeness of a *t*........ Eze 10:1
me, Son of man, the place of my *t*........ Eze 43:7
he was deposed from his kingly *t*........ Dan 5:20
his *t* was like the fiery flame,........ Dan 7:9
Nineveh, and he arose from his *t*........ Jonah 3:6
will overthrow the *t* of kingdoms........ Hag 2:22
and shall sit and rule upon his *t*........ Zec 6:13
he shall be a priest upon his *t*........ Zec 6:13
for it is God's *t*........ Mt 5:34
shall sit in the *t* of his glory........ Mt 19:28
heaven, sweareth by the *t* of God........ Mt 23:22
he sit upon the *t* of his glory........ Mt 25:31
him the *t* of his father David........ Lk 1:32
raise up Christ to sit on his *t*........ Acts 2:30
Heaven is my *t*, and earth is my........ Acts 7:49
in royal apparel, sat upon his *t*........ Acts 12:21
But unto the Son he saith, Thy *t*........ Heb 1:8
come boldly unto the *t* of grace........ Heb 4:16
*t* of the Majesty in the heavens........ Heb 8:1
at the right hand of the *t* of God........ Heb 12:2
Spirits which are before his *t*........ Rev 1:4
I grant to sit with me in my *t*........ Rev 3:21
set down with my Father in his *t*........ Rev 3:21
a *t* was set in heaven, and one sat........ Rev 4:2
in heaven, and one sat on the *t*........ Rev 4:2
was a rainbow round about the *t*........ Rev 4:3
And round about the *t* were four........ Rev 4:4
out of the *t* proceeded lightnings........ Rev 4:5
of fire burning before the *t*........ Rev 4:5
before the *t* there was a sea of........ Rev 4:6
and in the midst of the *t*, and........ Rev 4:6
and round about the *t*........ Rev 4:6
thanks to him that sat on the *t*........ Rev 4:9
down before him that sat on the *t*........ Rev 4:10
and cast their crowns before the *t*........ Rev 4:10
on the *t* a book written within........ Rev 5:1
and, lo, in the midst of the *t*........ Rev 5:6
hand of him that sat upon the *t*........ Rev 5:7
of many angels round about the *t*........ Rev 5:11
unto him that sitteth upon the *t*........ Rev 5:13
face of him that sitteth on the *t*........ Rev 6:16
and tongues, stood before the *t*........ Rev 7:9
our God which sitteth upon the *t*........ Rev 7:10
angels stood round about the *t*........ Rev 7:11
fell before the *t* on their faces........ Rev 7:11
are they before the *t* of God........ Rev 7:15
on the *t* shall dwell among them........ Rev 7:15
midst of the *t* shall feed them........ Rev 7:17
altar which was before the *t*........ Rev 8:3
caught up unto God, and to his *t*........ Rev 12:5
it were a new song before the *t*........ Rev 14:3
without fault before the *t* of God........ Rev 14:5
the temple of heaven, from the *t*........ Rev 16:17
worshipped God that sat on the *t*........ Rev 19:4
And a voice came out of the *t*........ Rev 19:5
And I saw a great white *t*, and him.... Rev 20:11
And he that sat upon the *t* said........ Rev 21:5
proceeding out of the *t* of God........ Rev 22:1
but the *t* of God and of the Lamb........ Rev 22:3

**THRONES**
For there are set *t* of judgment........ Ps 122:5
the *t* of the house of David........ Ps 122:5
*t* all the kings of the nations........ Is 14:9
sea shall come down from their *t*........ Eze 26:16
beheld till the *t* were cast down........ Dan 7:9
ye also shall sit upon twelve *t*........ Mt 19:28
sit on *t* judging the twelve........ Lk 22:30
and invisible, whether they be *t*........ Col 1:16
And I saw *t*, and they sat upon them... Rev 20:4

**THRONG**
multitude, lest they should *t* him........ Mk 3:9
Master, the multitude *t* thee........ Lk 8:45

**THRONGED**
people followed him, and *t* him........ Mk 5:24
But as he went the people *t* him........ Lk 8:42

**THRONGING**
Thou seest the multitude *t* thee........ Mk 5:31

**THROUGH**
is filled with violence *t* them........ Gen 6:13
Abram passed *t* the land unto the........ Gen 12:6
walk *t* the land in the length of........ Gen 13:17
I will pass *t* all thy flock to........ Gen 30:32
the land perish not *t* the famine........ Gen 41:36
field, *t* all the land of Egypt........ Ex 10:15
For I will pass *t* the land of........ Ex 12:12
pass *t* to smite the Egyptians........ Ex 12:23
that God led them not *t* the way........ Ex 13:17
*t* the way of the wilderness of........ Ex 13:18
dry ground *t* the midst of the sea........ Ex 14:16
Egyptians *t* the pillar of fire........ Ex 14:24
shall surely be stoned, or shot *t*........ Ex 19:13
lest they break *t* unto the LORD........ Ex 19:21
the people break *t* to come up........ Ex 19:24
shall bore his ear *t* with an aul........ Ex 21:6
*t* the boards from the one end to........ Ex 36:33
If a soul shall sin *t* ignorance........ Lev 4:2
of Israel sin *t* ignorance........ Lev 4:13
done somewhat *t* ignorance against...... Lev 4:22
the common people sin *t* ignorance........ Lev 4:27
sin *t* ignorance, in the holy........ Lev 5:15
seed pass *t* the fire to Molech........ Lev 18:21
shall the sword go *t* your land........ Lev 26:6
*t* which we have gone to search it.... Num 13:32
which we passed *t* to search it........ Num 14:7
And if any soul sin *t* ignorance........ Num 15:27
for him that sinneth *t* ignorance........ Num 15:29
pass, I pray thee, *t* thy country........ Num 20:17
we will not pass *t* the fields........ Num 20:17
or *t* the vineyards, neither will........ Num 20:17
any thing else, go *t* on my feet........ Num 20:19
And he said, Thou shalt not go *t*........ Num 20:20
give Israel passage *t* his border........ Num 20:21
Let me pass *t* thy land........ Num 21:22
Israel to pass *t* his border........ Num 21:23
pierce them *t* with his arrows........ Num 24:8
tent, and thrust both of them *t*........ Num 25:8
Israel, and the woman *t* her belly........ Num 25:8
*t* the counsel of Balaam, to........ Num 31:16
ye shall make it go *t* the fire........ Num 31:23
fire ye shall make go *t* the water........ Num 31:23
passed *t* the midst of the sea........ Num 33:8
we went *t* all that great and........ Deut 1:19
Ye are to pass *t* the coast of........ Deut 2:4
walking *t* this great wilderness........ Deut 2:7
*t* the way of the plain from Elath........ Deut 2:8
Thou art to pass over *t* Ar........ Deut 2:18
Let me pass *t* thy land........ Deut 2:27
only I will pass *t* on my feet........ Deut 2:28
thee out thence *t* a mighty hand........ Deut 5:15
Who led thee *t* that great........ Deut 8:15
hast redeemed *t* thy greatness........ Deut 9:26

thrust it *t* his ear unto the door — Deut 15:17
his daughter to pass *t* the fire — Deut 18:10
how we came *t* the nations which — Deut 29:16
to anger *t* the work of your hands — Deut 31:29
*t* this thing ye shall prolong — Deut 32:47
smite *t* the loins of them that — Deut 33:11
Pass *t* the host, and command the — Josh 1:11
them down by a cord *t* the window — Josh 2:15
that the officers went *t* the host — Josh 3:2
go *t* the land, and describe it — Josh 18:4
walk *t* the land, and describe it, — Josh 18:8
passed *t* the land, and described — Josh 18:9
went up *t* the mountains westward — Josh 18:12
all the people *t* whom we passed — Josh 24:17
That *t* them I may prove Israel, — Judg 2:22
Then Ehud went forth *t* the porch — Judg 3:23
and the travellers walked *t* byways — Judg 5:6
pierced and stricken *t* his temples — Judg 5:26
cried *t* the lattice, Why is his — Judg 5:28
And his young man thrust him *t* — Judg 9:54
walked *t* the wilderness unto the — Judg 11:16
me, I pray thee, pass *t* thy land — Judg 11:17
they went along *t* the wilderness — Judg 11:18
thee, *t* thy land into my place — Judg 11:19
not Israel to pass *t* his coast — Judg 11:20
men *t* all the tribe of Benjamin — Judg 20:12
he passed *t* mount Ephraim, and — 1Sa 9:4
passed *t* the land of Shalisha, — 1Sa 9:4
then they passed *t* the land of — 1Sa 9:4
he passed *t* the land of the — 1Sa 9:4
Michal let David down *t* a window — 1Sa 19:12
sword, and thrust me *t* therewith — 1Sa 31:4
uncircumcised come and thrust me *t* — 1Sa 31:4
walked all that night *t* the plain — 2Sa 2:29
went *t* all Bithron, and they came — 2Sa 2:29
gat them away *t* the plain all — 2Sa 4:7
Saul's daughter looked *t* a window — 2Sa 6:16
and made them pass *t* the brickkiln — 2Sa 12:31
thrust them *t* the heart of — 2Sa 18:14
he went *t* all the tribes of — 2Sa 20:14
*T* the brightness before him were — 2Sa 22:13
For by thee I have run *t* a troop — 2Sa 22:30
the three mighty men brake *t* the — 2Sa 23:16
Go now *t* all the tribes of Israel — 2Sa 24:2
when they had gone *t* all the land — 2Sa 24:8
Ahaziah fell down *t* a lattice in — 2Kin 1:2
The way *t* the wilderness of Edom — 2Kin 3:8
to break *t* even unto the king of — 2Kin 3:26
And Jehu sent *t* all Israel — 2Kin 10:21
made his son to pass *t* the fire — 2Kin 16:3
daughters to pass *t* the fire — 2Kin 17:17
he made his son pass *t* the fire — 2Kin 21:6
to pass *t* the fire to Molech — 2Kin 23:10
For *t* the anger of the LORD it — 2Kin 24:20
sword, and thrust me *t* therewith — 1Chr 10:4
the three brake *t* the host of the — 1Chr 11:18
he went out again *t* the people — 2Chr 19:4
they came *t* the high gate into — 2Chr 23:20
they made a proclamation *t* Judah — 2Chr 24:9
to city *t* the country of Ephraim — 2Chr 30:10
daughters, *t* all the congregation — 2Chr 31:18
the brook that ran *t* the midst of — 2Chr 32:4
*t* the fire in the valley of the — 2Chr 33:6
they prospered *t* the prophesying — Ezr 6:14
so that they went *t* the midst of — Neh 9:11
*t* the street of the city, and — Est 6:9
*t* the street of the city, and — Est 6:11
and terrifiest me *t* visions — Job 7:14
Yet *t* the scent of water it will — Job 14:9
bow of steel shall strike him *t* — Job 20:24
can he judge *t* the dark cloud — Job 22:13
In the dark they dig *t* houses — Job 24:16
he smiteth *t* the proud — Job 26:12
by his light I walked *t* darkness — Job 29:3
I went out to the gate *t* the city — Job 29:7
his nose pierceth *t* snares — Job 40:24
or bore his jaw *t* with a thorn — Job 41:2
whatsoever passeth *t* the paths of — Ps 8:8
*t* the pride of his countenance, — Ps 10:4
For by thee I have run *t* a troop — Ps 18:29
line is gone out *t* all the earth — Ps 19:4
*t* the mercy of the most High he — Ps 21:7
though I walk *t* the valley of the — Ps 23:4
my bones waxed old *t* my roaring — Ps 32:3
*T* thee will we push down our — Ps 44:5
*t* thy name will we tread them — Ps 44:5
*T* God we shall do valiantly — Ps 60:12
*t* the greatness of thy power — Ps 66:3
they went *t* the flood on foot — Ps 66:6
we went *t* fire and *t* water — Ps 66:12
thou didst march *t* the wilderness — Ps 68:7
their tongue walketh *t* the earth — Ps 73:9
the sea, and caused them to pass *t* — Ps 78:13
when he went out *t* the land of — Ps 81:5
Who passing *t* the valley of Baca — Ps 84:6
hast made me glad *t* thy work — Ps 92:4
so he led them *t* the depths — Ps 106:9
the depths, as *t* the wilderness — Ps 106:9
and brought low *t* oppression — Ps 107:39
*T* God we shall do valiantly — Ps 108:13
My knees are weak *t* fasting — Ps 109:24
*t* kings in the day of his wrath — Ps 110:5
neither speak they *t* their throat — Ps 115:7
Thou *t* thy commandments hast made — Ps 119:98
*T* thy precepts I get — Ps 119:104
Israel to pass *t* the midst of it — Ps 136:14
led his people *t* the wilderness — Ps 136:16
my house I looked *t* my casement — Prov 7:6
Passing *t* the street near her — Prov 7:8
Till a dart strike *t* his liver — Prov 7:23

but *t* knowledge shall the just be — Prov 11:9
*T* desire a man, having separated — Prov 18:1
*T* wisdom is an house builded — Prov 24:3
For a dream cometh *t* the — Eccl 5:3
*t* idleness of the hands the house — Eccl 10:18
of the hands the house droppeth *t* — Eccl 10:18
shewing himself *t* the lattice — Song 2:9
And he shall pass *t* Judah — Is 8:8
And they shall pass *t* it, hardly — Is 8:21
*T* the wrath of the LORD of hosts — Is 9:19
that is found shall be thrust *t* — Is 13:15
thrust *t* with a sword, that go — Is 14:19
they wandered *t* the wilderness — Is 16:8
As whirlwinds in the south pass *t* — Is 21:1
Pass *t* thy land as a river, O — Is 23:10
I would go *t* them, I would burn — Is 27:4
But they also have erred *t* wine — Is 28:7
*t* strong drink are out of the way — Is 28:7
prophet have erred *t* strong drink — Is 28:7
are out of the way *t* strong drink — Is 28:7
overflowing scourge shall pass *t* — Is 28:15
overflowing scourge shall pass *t* — Is 28:18
For *t* the voice of the LORD shall — Is 30:31
none shall pass *t* it for ever — Is 34:10
When thou passest *t* the waters — Is 43:2
*t* the rivers, they shall not — Is 43:2
when thou walkest *t* the fire — Is 43:2
when he led them *t* the deserts — Is 48:21
hated, so that no man went *t* thee — Is 60:15
Go *t*, go *t* the gates — Is 62:10
That led them *t* the deep, as an — Is 63:13
that led us *t* the wilderness, — Jer 2:6
*t* a land of deserts and of pits, — Jer 2:6
*t* a land of drought, and of the — Jer 2:6
*t* a land that no man passed — Jer 2:6
a land that no man passed *t* — Jer 2:6
it came to pass *t* the lightness — Jer 3:9
fro *t* the streets of Jerusalem, — Jer 5:1
*t* deceit they refuse to know me, — Jer 9:6
up, so that none can pass *t* them — Jer 9:10
a wilderness, that none passeth *t* — Jer 9:12
all high places *t* the wilderness — Jer 12:12
to bring in no burden *t* the gates — Jer 17:24
to pass *t* the fire unto Molech — Jer 32:35
that are thrust *t* in her streets — Jer 51:4
*t* all her land the wounded shall — Jer 51:52
For *t* the anger of the LORD it — Jer 52:3
that our prayer should not pass *t* — Lam 3:44
stricken *t* for want of the fruits — Lam 4:9
cup also shall pass *t* unto thee — Lam 4:21
and blood shall pass *t* thee — Eze 5:17
be scattered *t* the countries — Eze 6:8
Go *t* the midst of the city, — Eze 9:4
*t* the midst of Jerusalem, and set — Eze 9:4
Go ye after him *t* the city — Eze 9:5
Dig thou *t* the wall in their — Eze 12:5
in the even I digged *t* the wall — Eze 12:7
they shall dig *t* the wall to — Eze 12:12
estranged from me *t* their idols — Eze 14:5
noisome beasts to pass *t* the land — Eze 14:15
that no man may pass *t* because of — Eze 14:15
and say, Sword, go *t* the land — Eze 14:17
it was perfect *t* my comeliness — Eze 16:14
them to pass *t* the fire for them — Eze 16:21
thy nakedness discovered *t* thy — Eze 16:36
thrust thee *t* with their swords — Eze 16:40
and disperse them *t* the countries — Eze 20:23
in that they caused to pass *t* the — Eze 20:26
make your sons to pass *t* the fire — Eze 20:31
me, to pass for them *t* the fire — Eze 23:37
No foot of man shall pass *t* it — Eze 29:11
nor foot of beast shall pass *t* it — Eze 29:11
disperse them *t* the countries — Eze 29:12
disperse them *t* the countries — Eze 30:23
desolate, that none shall pass *t* — Eze 33:28
wandered *t* all the mountains — Eze 34:6
were dispersed *t* the countries — Eze 36:19
passing *t* the land to bury with — Eze 39:14
passengers that pass *t* the land — Eze 39:15
it was made *t* all the house round — Eze 41:19
After he brought me *t* the entry — Eze 46:19
and he brought me *t* the waters — Eze 47:3
and brought me *t* the waters — Eze 47:4
a thousand, and brought me *t* — Eze 47:4
*t* his policy also he shall cause — Dan 8:25
*t* all the countries whither thou — Dan 9:7
by his strength *t* his riches he — Dan 11:2
come, and overflow, and pass *t* — Dan 11:10
no strangers pass *t* her any more — Joel 3:17
you forty years *t* the wilderness — Amos 2:10
for I will pass *t* thee, saith the — Amos 5:17
published *t* Nineveh by the decree — Jonah 3:7
up, and have passed *t* the gate — Mic 2:13
who, if he go *t*, both treadeth — Mic 5:8
be cut down, when he shall pass *t* — Nah 1:12
wicked shall no more pass *t* thee — Nah 1:15
selleth nations *t* her whoredoms — Nah 3:4
families *t* her witchcrafts — Nah 3:4
which shall march *t* the breadth — Hab 1:6
Thou didst march *t* the land in — Hab 3:12
Thou didst strike *t* with his — Hab 3:14
Thou didst walk *t* the sea with — Hab 3:15
*t* the heap of great waters — Hab 3:15
to walk to and fro *t* the earth — Zec 1:10
fro *t* the earth, and, behold, all — Zec 1:11
My cities *t* prosperity shall yet — Zec 1:17
run to and fro *t* the whole earth — Zec 4:10
*t* the two golden pipes empty the — Zec 4:12
their resemblance *t* all the earth — Zec 5:6
might walk to and fro *t* the earth — Zec 6:7

hence, walk to and fro *t* the earth — Zec 6:7
they walked to and fro *t* the earth — Zec 6:7
that no man passed *t* nor returned — Zec 7:14
shall pass *t* them any more — Zec 9:8
drink, and make a noise as *t* wine — Zec 9:15
heart shall rejoice as *t* wine — Zec 10:7
he shall pass *t* the sea with — Zec 10:11
thrust him *t* when he prophesieth — Zec 13:3
bring the third part *t* the fire — Zec 13:9
corrupt, and where thieves break *t* — Mt 6:19
thieves do not break *t* nor steal — Mt 6:20
He casteth out devils *t* the — Mt 9:34
on the sabbath day *t* the corn — Mt 12:1
of a man, he walketh *t* dry places — Mt 12:43
camel to go *t* the eye of a needle — Mt 19:24
that he went *t* the corn fields on — Mk 2:23
ran *t* that whole region round — Mk 6:55
of none effect *t* your tradition — Mk 7:13
*t* the midst of the coasts of — Mk 7:31
thence, and passed *t* Galilee — Mk 9:30
camel to go *t* the eye of a needle — Mk 10:25
carry any vessel *t* the temple — Mk 11:16
*T* the tender mercy of our God — Lk 1:78
shall pierce *t* thy own soul also — Lk 2:35
him *t* all the region round about — Lk 4:14
But he passing *t* the midst of — Lk 4:30
let him down *t* the tiling with — Lk 5:19
that he went *t* the corn fields — Lk 6:1
went *t* the towns, preaching the — Lk 9:6
are subject unto us *t* thy name — Lk 10:17
He casteth out devils *t* Beelzebub — Lk 11:15
I cast out devils *t* Beelzebub — Lk 11:18
of a man, he walketh *t* dry places — Lk 11:24
suffered his house to be broken *t* — Lk 12:39
he went *t* the cities and villages, — Lk 13:22
woe unto him, *t* whom they come — Lk 17:1
that he passed *t* the midst of — Lk 17:11
a camel to go *t* a needle's eye — Lk 18:25
Jesus entered and passed *t* Jericho — Lk 19:1
that all men *t* him might believe — Jn 1:7
the world *t* him might be saved — Jn 3:17
And he must needs go *t* Samaria — Jn 4:4
going *t* the midst of them, and so — Jn 8:59
Now ye are clean *t* the word which — Jn 15:3
keep *t* thine own name those whom — Jn 17:11
Sanctify them *t* thy truth — Jn 17:17
might be sanctified *t* the truth — Jn 17:19
shall believe on me *t* their word — Jn 17:20
ye might have life *t* his name — Jn 20:31
after that he *t* the Holy Ghost — Acts 1:2
his name *t* faith in his name hath — Acts 3:16
I wot that *t* ignorance ye did it, — Acts 3:17
preached *t* Jesus the resurrection — Acts 4:2
when Simon saw that *t* laying on — Acts 8:18
passing *t* he preached in all the — Acts 8:40
that *t* his name whosoever — Acts 10:43
out, and passed on *t* one street — Acts 12:10
when they had gone *t* the isle — Acts 13:6
that *t* this man is preached unto — Acts 13:38
that we must *t* much tribulation — Acts 14:22
the church, they passed *t* Phenice — Acts 15:3
But we believe that *t* the grace — Acts 15:11
And he went *t* Syria and Cilicia, — Acts 15:41
And as they went *t* the cities — Acts 16:4
when they had passed *t* Amphipolis — Acts 17:1
much which had believed *t* grace — Acts 18:27
Paul having passed *t* the upper — Acts 19:1
when he had passed *t* Macedonia — Acts 19:21
he purposed to return *t* Macedonia — Acts 20:3
who said to Paul *t* the Spirit — Acts 21:4
I thank my God *t* Jesus Christ for — Rom 1:8
gave them up to uncleanness *t* the — Rom 1:24
*t* breaking the law dishonourest — Rom 2:23
among the Gentiles *t* you, as it — Rom 2:24
abounded *t* my lie unto his glory — Rom 3:7
grace *t* the redemption that is in — Rom 3:24
propitiation *t* faith in his blood — Rom 3:25
past, *t* the forbearance of God — Rom 3:25
faith, and uncircumcision *t* faith — Rom 3:30
we then make void the law *t* faith — Rom 3:31
*t* the law, but *t* the — Rom 4:13
at the promise of God *t* unbelief — Rom 4:20
with God *t* our Lord Jesus Christ — Rom 5:1
shall be saved from wrath *t* him — Rom 5:9
in God *t* our Lord Jesus Christ — Rom 5:11
For if *t* the offence of one many — Rom 5:15
even so might grace reign *t* — Rom 5:21
but alive unto God *t* Jesus Christ — Rom 6:11
life *t* Jesus Christ our Lord — Rom 6:23
I thank God *t* Jesus Christ our — Rom 7:25
in that it was weak *t* the flesh — Rom 8:3
but if ye *t* the Spirit do mortify — Rom 8:13
conquerors *t* him that loved us — Rom 8:37
but rather *t* their fall salvation — Rom 11:11
obtained mercy *t* their unbelief — Rom 11:30
that *t* your mercy they also may — Rom 11:31
*t* him, and to him, are all things — Rom 11:36
*t* the grace given unto me, to — Rom 12:3
that we *t* patience and comfort of — Rom 15:4
*t* the power of the Holy Ghost — Rom 15:13
*t* Jesus Christ in those things — Rom 15:17
*T* mighty signs and wonders, by the — Rom 15:19
be glory *t* Jesus Christ for ever — Rom 16:27
of Jesus Christ *t* the will of God — 1Cor 1:1
I have begotten you *t* the gospel — 1Cor 4:15
*t* thy knowledge shall the weak — 1Cor 8:11
cloud, and all passed *t* the sea — 1Cor 10:1
For now we see *t* a glass, darkly — 1Cor 13:12
victory *t* our Lord Jesus Christ — 1Cor 15:57
when I shall pass *t* Macedonia — 1Cor 16:5

for I do pass *t* Macedonia ... 1Cor 16:5
have we *t* Christ to God-ward ... 2Cor 3:4
might *t* the thanksgiving of many ... 2Cor 4:15
that ye *t* his poverty might be ... 2Cor 8:9
which causeth *t* us thanksgiving ... 2Cor 9:11
but mighty *t* God to the pulling ... 2Cor 10:4
beguiled Eve *t* his subtilty ... 2Cor 11:3
*t* a window in a basket was I let ... 2Cor 11:33
measure *t* the abundance of the ... 2Cor 12:7
he was crucified *t* weakness ... 2Cor 13:4
For I *t* the law am dead to the ... Gal 2:19
would justify the heathen *t* faith ... Gal 3:8
on the Gentiles *t* Jesus Christ ... Gal 3:14
the promise of the Spirit *t* faith ... Gal 3:14
son, then an heir of God *t* Christ ... Gal 4:7
Ye know how *t* infirmity of the ... Gal 4:13
For we *t* the Spirit wait for the ... Gal 5:5
have confidence in you *t* the Lord ... Gal 5:10
we have redemption *t* his blood ... Eph 1:7
kindness toward us *t* Christ Jesus ... Eph 2:7
For by grace are ye saved *t* faith ... Eph 2:8
For *t* him we both have access by ... Eph 2:18
an habitation of God *t* the Spirit ... Eph 2:22
all, and *t* all, and in you all ... Eph 4:6
*t* the ignorance that is in them ... Eph 4:18
to my salvation *t* your prayer ... Phil 1:19
be done *t* strife or vainglory ... Phil 2:3
but that which is *t* the faith of ... Phil 3:9
hearts and minds *t* Christ Jesus ... Phil 4:7
I can do all things *t* Christ ... Phil 4:13
we have redemption *t* his blood ... Col 1:14
having made peace *t* the blood of ... Col 1:20
In the body of his flesh *t* death ... Col 1:22
any man spoil you *t* philosophy ... Col 2:8
also ye are risen with him *t* the ... Col 2:12
chosen you to salvation *t* ... 2Th 2:13
consolation and good hope *t* grace ... 2Th 2:16
themselves *t* with many sorrows ... 1Ti 6:10
immortality to light *t* the gospel ... 2Ti 1:10
make thee wise unto salvation *t* ... 2Ti 3:15
manifested his word *t* preaching ... Titus 1:3
*t* Jesus Christ our Saviour ... Titus 3:6
for I trust that *t* your prayers I ... Philem 22
salvation perfect *t* sufferings ... Heb 2:10
that *t* death he might destroy him ... Heb 2:14
deliver them who *t* fear of death ... Heb 2:15
*t* the deceitfulness of sin ... Heb 3:13
but followers of them who *t* faith ... Heb 6:12
who *t* the eternal Spirit offered ... Heb 9:14
*t* the offering of the body of ... Heb 10:10
*t* the veil, that is to say, his ... Heb 10:20
*T* faith we understand that the ... Heb 11:3
*T* faith also Sara herself ... Heb 11:11
*T* faith he kept the passover, and ... Heb 11:28
By faith they passed *t* the Red ... Heb 11:29
Who *t* faith subdued kingdoms, ... Heb 11:33
obtained a good report *t* faith ... Heb 11:39
stoned, or thrust *t* with a dart ... Heb 12:20
*t* the blood of the everlasting ... Heb 13:20
in his sight, *t* Jesus Christ ... Heb 13:21
*t* sanctification of the Spirit, ... 1Pet 1:2
are kept by the power of God *t* ... 1Pet 1:5
ye are in heaviness *t* manifold ... 1Pet 1:6
*t* the Spirit unto unfeigned love ... 1Pet 1:22
may be glorified *t* Jesus Christ ... 1Pet 4:11
us *t* the righteousness of God ... 2Pet 1:1
unto you *t* the knowledge of God ... 2Pet 1:2
*t* the knowledge of him that hath ... 2Pet 1:3
that is in the world *t* lust ... 2Pet 1:4
*t* covetousness shall they with ... 2Pet 2:3
they allure *t* the lusts of the ... 2Pet 2:18
*t* much wantonness, those that ... 2Pet 2:18
world *t* the knowledge of the Lord ... 2Pet 2:20
world, that we might live *t* him ... 1Jn 4:9
flying *t* the midst of heaven ... Rev 8:13
of the earth are waxed rich *t* the ... Rev 18:3
may enter in *t* the gates into the ... Rev 22:14

**THROUGHLY**
let us make brick, and burn them *t* ... Gen 11:3
O that my grief were *t* weighed ... Job 6:2
Wash me *t* from mine iniquity, and ... Ps 51:2
They shall *t* glean the remnant of ... Jer 6:9
For if ye *t* amend your ways and ... Jer 7:5
if ye *t* execute judgment between ... Jer 7:5
he shall *t* plead their cause, ... Jer 50:34
I *t* washed away thy blood from ... Eze 16:9
he will *t* purge his floor, and ... Mt 3:12
he will *t* purge his floor, and ... Lk 3:17
but we have been *t* made manifest ... 2Cor 11:6
*t* furnished unto all good works ... 2Ti 3:17

**THROUGHOUT**
plenty *t* all the land of Egypt ... Gen 41:29
went *t* all the land of Egypt ... Gen 41:46
a ruler *t* all the land of Egypt ... Gen 45:8
people were scattered abroad *t* ... Ex 5:12
be blood *t* all the land of Egypt ... Ex 7:19
there was blood *t* all the land of ... Ex 7:21
lice *t* all the land of Egypt ... Ex 8:16
lice *t* all the land of Egypt ... Ex 8:17
beast, *t* all the land of Egypt ... Ex 9:9
may be declared *t* all the earth ... Ex 9:16
of the field, *t* the land of Egypt ... Ex 9:22
the hail smote *t* all the land of ... Ex 9:25
great cry *t* all the land of Egypt ... Ex 11:6
to the LORD *t* your generations ... Ex 12:14
be a continual burnt offering *t* ... Ex 29:42
the LORD *t* your generations ... Ex 30:8
upon it *t* your generations ... Ex 30:10
to his seed *t* their generations ... Ex 30:21
oil unto me *t* your generations ... Ex 30:31
me and you *t* your generations ... Ex 31:13
the sabbath *t* their generations ... Ex 31:16
out from gate to gate *t* the camp ... Ex 32:27
any man be seen *t* all the mount ... Ex 34:3
Ye shall kindle no fire *t* your ... Ex 35:3
it to be proclaimed *t* the camp ... Ex 36:6
so *t* the six branches going out ... Ex 37:19
priesthood *t* their generations ... Ex 40:15
of Israel, *t* all their journeys ... Ex 40:38
generations *t* all your dwellings ... Lev 3:17
for ever *t* their generations ... Lev 7:36
for ever *t* your generations ... Lev 10:9
unto them *t* their generations ... Lev 17:7
*t* your generations in all your ... Lev 23:14
your dwellings *t* your generations ... Lev 23:21
*t* your generations in all your ... Lev 23:31
the trumpet sound *t* all your land ... Lev 25:9
proclaim liberty *t* all the land ... Lev 25:10
that bought it *t* his generations ... Lev 25:30
*t* their generations, after their ... Num 1:42
his own standard, *t* their hosts ... Num 1:52
of Judah pitch *t* their armies ... Num 2:3
and four hundred, *t* their armies ... Num 2:9
hundred and fifty, *t* their armies ... Num 2:16
and an hundred, *t* their armies ... Num 2:24
*t* their hosts were six hundred ... Num 2:32
*t* their families, all the males ... Num 3:39
*t* the houses of their fathers, by ... Num 4:22
*t* their families, and by the house ... Num 4:38
*t* their families, by the house of ... Num 4:40
*t* their families, by the house of ... Num 4:42
for ever *t* your generations ... Num 10:8
of all the camps *t* their hosts ... Num 10:25
the people weep *t* their families ... Num 11:10
garments *t* their generations ... Num 15:38
for ever *t* your generations ... Num 18:23
*t* their fathers' house, all that ... Num 26:2
month *t* the months of the year ... Num 28:14
for every lamb, *t* the seven lambs ... Num 28:21
*t* the seven days, the meat of the ... Num 28:24
unto one lamb, *t* the seven lambs ... Num 28:29
for one lamb, *t* the seven lambs ... Num 29:4
for one lamb, *t* the seven lambs ... Num 29:10
*t* all the tribes of Israel, shall ... Num 31:4
*t* your generations in all your ... Num 35:29
thy God giveth thee, *t* thy tribes ... Deut 16:18
have olive trees *t* all thy coasts ... Deut 28:40
thou trustedst, *t* all thy land ... Deut 28:52
in all thy gates *t* all thy land ... Deut 28:52
sought them *t* all the way ... Josh 2:22
fame was noised *t* all the country ... Josh 6:27
up from Jericho *t* mount Beth-el ... Josh 16:1
prince *t* all the tribes of Israel ... Josh 22:14
led him *t* all the land of Canaan, ... Josh 24:3
he sent messengers *t* all Manasseh ... Judg 6:35
his fellow, even *t* all the host ... Judg 7:22
messengers *t* all mount Ephraim ... Judg 7:24
sent her *t* all the country of the ... Judg 20:6
*t* all the tribes of Israel ... Judg 20:10
deadly destruction *t* all the city ... 1Sa 5:11
sent them *t* all the coasts of ... 1Sa 11:7
blew the trumpet *t* all the land ... 1Sa 13:3
found *t* all the land of Israel ... 1Sa 13:19
out *t* all the thousands of Judah ... 1Sa 23:23
*t* all Edom put he garrisons, and ... 2Sa 8:14
But Absalom sent spies *t* all the ... 2Sa 15:10
strife *t* all the tribes of Israel ... 2Sa 19:9
damsel *t* all the coasts of Israel ... 1Kin 1:3
finished *t* all the parts thereof ... 1Kin 6:38
made a proclamation *t* all Judah ... 1Kin 15:22
land between them to pass *t* it ... 1Kin 18:6
there went a proclamation *t* the ... 1Kin 22:36
of Assyria came up *t* all the land ... 2Kin 17:5
they dwelt in their tents *t* all ... 1Chr 5:10
*t* their castles in their coasts ... 1Chr 6:54
All their cities *t* their families ... 1Chr 6:60
to the sons of Gershom *t* their ... 1Chr 6:62
*t* their families, out of the ... 1Chr 6:63
the number *t* the genealogy of ... 1Chr 7:40
were chief *t* their generations ... 1Chr 9:34
famous *t* the house of their ... 1Chr 12:30
went *t* all Israel, and came to ... 1Chr 21:4
*t* all the coasts of Israel ... 1Chr 21:12
fame and of glory *t* all countries ... 1Chr 22:5
that ruled *t* the house of their ... 1Chr 26:6
went out month by month *t* all the ... 1Chr 27:1
*t* all the land of his dominion ... 2Chr 8:6
*t* all the countries of Judah ... 2Chr 11:23
fro *t* the whole earth, to shew ... 2Chr 16:9
went about *t* all the cities of ... 2Chr 17:9
in the fenced cities *t* all Judah ... 2Chr 17:19
he set judges in the land *t* all ... 2Chr 19:5
and proclaimed a fast *t* all Judah ... 2Chr 20:3
fathers, *t* all Judah and Benjamin ... 2Chr 25:5
for them *t* all the host shields ... 2Chr 26:14
to make proclamation *t* all Israel ... 2Chr 30:5
king and his princes *t* all Israel ... 2Chr 30:6
they did eat *t* the feast seven ... 2Chr 30:22
And thus did Hezekiah *t* all Judah ... 2Chr 31:20
idols *t* all the land of Israel ... 2Chr 34:7
a proclamation *t* all his kingdom ... 2Chr 36:22
a proclamation *t* all his kingdom ... Ezr 1:1
And they made proclamation *t* Judah ... Ezr 10:7
be published *t* all his empire ... Est 1:20
*t* the whole kingdom of Ahasuerus ... Est 3:6
together in their cities *t* all ... Est 9:2
fame went out *t* all the provinces ... Est 9:4
kept *t* every generation, every ... Est 9:28
and moon endure, *t* all generations ... Ps 72:5
thy years are *t* all generations ... Ps 102:24
O LORD, *t* all generations ... Ps 135:13
endureth *t* all generations ... Ps 145:13
places for sin, *t* all thy borders ... Jer 17:3
against him *t* all my mountains ... Eze 38:21
And his fame went *t* all Syria ... Mt 4:24
his fame spread abroad *t* all the ... Mk 1:28
in their synagogues *t* all Galilee ... Mk 1:39
be preached *t* the whole world ... Mk 14:9
sayings were noised abroad *t* all ... Lk 1:65
great famine was *t* all the land ... Lk 4:25
of him went forth *t* all Judaea ... Lk 7:17
*t* all the region round about ... Lk 7:17
that he went *t* every city ... Lk 8:1
published *t* the whole city how ... Lk 8:39
teaching *t* all Jewry, beginning ... Lk 23:5
seam, woven from the top *t* ... Jn 19:23
abroad *t* the regions of Judaea ... Acts 8:1
the churches rest *t* all Judaea ... Acts 9:31
as Peter passed *t* all quarters ... Acts 9:32
And it was known *t* all Joppa ... Acts 9:42
which was published *t* all Judaea ... Acts 10:37
be great dearth *t* all the world ... Acts 11:28
was published *t* all the region ... Acts 13:49
after they had passed *t* Pisidia ... Acts 14:24
Now when they had gone *t* Phrygia ... Acts 16:6
at Ephesus, but almost *t* all Asia ... Acts 19:26
among all the Jews *t* the world ... Acts 24:5
*t* all the coasts of Judaea, and ... Acts 26:20
is spoken of *t* the whole world ... Rom 1:8
might be declared *t* all the earth ... Rom 9:17
in the gospel *t* all the churches ... 2Cor 8:18
church by Christ Jesus *t* all ages ... Eph 3:21
the strangers scattered *t* Pontus ... 1Pet 1:1

**THROW**
ye shall *t* down their altars ... Judg 2:2
*t* down the altar of Baal that thy ... Judg 6:25
battered the wall, to *t* it down ... 2Sa 20:15
And he said, *T* her down ... 2Kin 9:33
to *t* down, to build, and to plant ... Jer 1:10
to *t* down, and to destroy, and to ... Jer 31:28
they shall *t* down thine eminent ... Eze 16:39
*t* down all thy strong holds ... Mic 5:11
shall build, but I will *t* down ... Mal 1:4

**THROWING**
And if he smite him with *t* a stone ... Num 35:17

**THROWN**
his rider hath he *t* into the sea ... Ex 15:1
his rider hath he *t* into the sea ... Ex 15:21
because he hath *t* down his altar ... Judg 6:32
his head shall be *t* to thee over ... 2Sa 20:21
*t* down thine altars, and slain thy ... 1Kin 19:10
*t* down thine altars, and slain thy ... 1Kin 19:14
nor *t* down any more for ever ... Jer 31:40
which are *t* down by the mounts, ... Jer 33:4
are fallen, her walls are *t* down ... Jer 50:15
he hath *t* down in his wrath the ... Lam 2:2
he hath *t* down, and hath not ... Lam 2:17
I will leave thee *t* into the ... Eze 29:5
and the mountains shall be *t* down ... Eze 38:20
and the rocks are *t* down by him ... Nah 1:6
another, that shall not be *t* down ... Mt 24:2
another, that shall not be *t* down ... Mk 13:2
the devil had *t* him in the midst ... Lk 4:35
another, that shall not be *t* down ... Lk 21:6
that great city Babylon be *t* down ... Rev 18:21

**THRUST**
he shall surely *t* you out hence ... Ex 11:1
because they were *t* out of Egypt ... Ex 12:39
she *t* herself unto the wall, and ... Num 22:25
*t* both of them through, the man ... Num 25:8
But if he *t* him of hatred, or ... Num 35:20
But if he *t* him suddenly without ... Num 35:22
to *t* thee out of the way which ... Deut 13:5
because he hath sought to *t* thee ... Deut 13:10
*t* it through his ear unto the ... Deut 15:17
he shall *t* out the enemy from ... Deut 33:27
thigh, and *t* it into his belly ... Judg 3:21
*t* the fleece together, and wringed ... Judg 6:38
Zebul *t* out Gaal and his brethren, ... Judg 9:41
And his young man *t* him through ... Judg 9:54
they *t* out Jephthah, and said unto ... Judg 11:2
that I may *t* out all your right ... 1Sa 11:2
sword, and *t* me through therewith ... 1Sa 31:4
*t* me through, and abuse me ... 1Sa 31:4
*t* his sword in his fellow's side ... 2Sa 2:16
*t* them through the heart of ... 2Sa 18:14
be all of them as thorns *t* away ... 2Sa 23:6
So Solomon *t* out Abiathar from ... 1Kin 2:27
Gehazi came near to *t* her away ... 2Kin 4:27
sword, and *t* me through therewith ... 1Chr 10:4
they *t* him out from thence ... 2Chr 26:20
Thou hast *t* sore at me that I ... Ps 118:13
that is found shall be *t* through ... Is 13:15
*t* through with a sword, that go ... Is 14:19
they that are *t* through in her ... Jer 51:4
*t* thee through with their swords ... Eze 16:40
Because ye have *t* with side ... Eze 34:21
to *t* them out of their possession ... Eze 46:18
Neither shall one *t* another ... Joel 2:8
*t* him through when he prophesieth ... Zec 13:3
*t* him out of the city, and led him ... Lk 4:29
prayed him that he would *t* out a ... Lk 5:3
heaven, shalt be *t* down to hell ... Lk 10:15
of God, and you yourselves *t* out ... Lk 13:28
*t* my hand into his side, I will ... Jn 20:25
thy hand, and *t* it into my side ... Jn 20:27
his neighbour wrong *t* him away ... Acts 7:27

but *t* him from them, and in their ........ Acts 7:39
*t* them into the inner prison, and........ Acts 16:24
now do they *t* us out privily ................ Acts 16:37
were possible, to *t* in the ship.............. Acts 27:39
stoned, or *t* through with a dart .......... Heb 12:20
cloud, *T* in thy sickle, and reap .............. Rev 14:15
he that sat on the cloud *t* in his............ Rev 14:16
*T* in thy sharp sickle, and gather ......... Rev 14:18
the angel *t* in his sickle into.................. Rev 14:19

**THRUSTETH**
God *t* him down, not man ...................... Job 32:13

**THUMB**
upon the *t* of their right hand,................ Ex 29:20
upon the *t* of his right hand, and .......... Lev 8:23
upon the *t* of his right hand, and ......... Lev 14:14
upon the *t* of his right hand, and ......... Lev 14:17
upon the *t* of his right hand, and ......... Lev 14:25
upon the *t* of his right hand, and ......... Lev 14:28

**THUMBS**
upon the *t* of their right hands,............. Lev 8:24
and caught him, and cut off his *t*.......... Judg 1:6
and ten kings, having their *t*................. Judg 1:7

**THUMMIM** (*thum'-mim*) *A symbolic object in the High Priest's breastplate.*
of judgment the Urim and the *T*............. Ex 28:30
the breastplate the Urim and the *T*......... Lev 8:8
And of Levi he said, Let thy *T*.............. Deut 33:8
up a priest with Urim and with *T*.......... Ezr 2:63
stood up a priest with Urim and *T*........ Neh 7:65

**THUNDER**
and the LORD sent *t* and hail, and............ Ex 9:23
the *t* shall cease, neither shall................... Ex 9:29
of heaven shall he *t* upon them ............... 1Sa 2:10
a great *t* on that day upon the.................. 1Sa 7:10
unto the LORD, and he shall send *t* ...... 1Sa 12:17
and the LORD sent *t* and rain that......... 1Sa 12:18
but the *t* of his power who can............. Job 26:14
a way for the lightning of the *t* ............ Job 28:26
or a way for the lightning of *t*.............. Job 38:25
hast thou clothed his neck with *t*......... Job 39:19
the *t* of the captains, and the ............... Job 39:25
or canst thou *t* with a voice like............ Job 40:9
The voice of thy *t* was in the.................. Ps 77:18
thee in the secret place of *t* ..................... Ps 81:7
voice of thy *t* they hasted away.............. Ps 104:7
of the LORD of hosts with *t*...................... Is 29:6
which is, The sons of *t* ............................ Mk 3:17
heard, as it were the noise of *t*............... Rev 6:1
and as the voice of a great *t* .................. Rev 14:2

**THUNDERBOLTS**
hail, and their flocks to hot *t*................. Ps 78:48

**THUNDERED**
but the LORD *t* with a great.................... 1Sa 7:10
The LORD *t* from heaven, and the ........ 2Sa 22:14
The LORD also *t* in the heavens,............. Ps 18:13
by, and heard it, said that it *t*................ Jn 12:29

**THUNDERETH**
he *t* with the voice of his........................ Job 37:4
God *t* marvellously with his voice.......... Job 37:5
the God of glory *t*..................................... Ps 29:3

**THUNDERINGS**
that there be no more mighty *t*............... Ex 9:28
And all the people saw the *t* .................. Ex 20:18
throne proceeded lightnings and *t*.......... Rev 4:5
and there were voices, and *t*.................... Rev 8:5
were lightnings, and voices, and *t* ....... Rev 11:19
and as the voice of mighty *t* .................. Rev 19:6

**THUNDERS**
and the *t* and hail ceased, and the........... Ex 9:33
the *t* were ceased, he sinned yet ............. Ex 9:34
in the morning, that there were *t* .......... Ex 19:16
seven *t* uttered their voices..................... Rev 10:3
when the seven *t* had uttered.................. Rev 10:4
things which the seven *t* uttered ........... Rev 10:4
And there were voices, and *t*................ Rev 16:18

**THUS**
*T* the heavens and the earth were........... Gen 2:1
*T* did Noah ............................................. Gen 6:22
*T* were both the daughters of Lot ....... Gen 19:36
*t* she was reproved ................................ Gen 20:16
*T* they made a covenant at .................... Gen 21:32
saying, *T* spake the man unto me ....... Gen 24:30
she said, If it be so, why am I *t* ........... Gen 25:22
*t* Esau despised his birthright ............ Gen 25:34
If he said *t*, The speckled shall............. Gen 31:8
and if he said *t*, The ringstraked............ Gen 31:8
*T* God hath taken away the cattle ......... Gen 31:9
*T* I was.................................................. Gen 31:40
*T* have I been twenty years in thy....... Gen 31:41
*T* shall ye speak unto my lord.............. Gen 32:4
Thy servant Jacob saith *t* ..................... Gen 32:4
*T* dwelt Esau in mount Seir ................ Gen 36:8
*T* his father wept for him .................... Gen 37:35
and *t* did he unto them ......................... Gen 42:25
*T* saith thy son Joseph, God hath.......... Gen 45:9
*T* shalt thou say unto the........................ Ex 3:14
*T* shalt thou say unto the ....................... Ex 3:15
*T* saith the LORD, Israel is my.............. Ex 4:22
*T* saith the LORD God of Israel, ................ Ex 5:1
*T* saith Pharaoh, I will not give.............. Ex 5:10
dealest thou *t* with thy servants............. Ex 5:15
*T* saith the LORD, In this thou................ Ex 7:17
*T* saith the LORD, Let my people ............. Ex 8:1
*T* saith the LORD, Let my people ............ Ex 8:20
*T* saith the LORD God of the....................... Ex 9:1
*T* saith the LORD God of the..................... Ex 9:13
*T* saith the LORD God of the..................... Ex 10:3
*T* saith the LORD, About midnight .......... Ex 11:4
And *t* shall ye eat it................................. Ex 12:11
*T* did all the children of Israel............... Ex 12:50
hast thou dealt *t* with us......................... Ex 14:11
*T* the LORD saved Israel that day ........... Ex 14:30
*T* shalt thou say to the house of .............. Ex 19:3
*T* thou shalt say unto the........................ Ex 20:22
*t* shalt thou make for all the .................. Ex 26:17
*t* shall it be for them both........................ Ex 26:24
*t* shalt thou do unto Aaron, and to.......... Ex 29:35
*T* saith the LORD God of Israel, ................ Ex 32:27
*t* did he make for all the boards ............. Ex 36:22
*t* he did to both of them in both.............. Ex 36:29
*T* was all the work of the......................... Ex 39:32
*T* did Moses ............................................ Ex 40:16
*T* shall ye separate the children............ Lev 15:31
*T* shall Aaron come into the holy............ Lev 16:3
But *t* do unto them, that they may ..... Num 4:19
*t* were they numbered of him, as......... Num 4:49
*t* shalt thou do unto them, to ................. Num 8:7
*T* shalt thou separate the Levites.......... Num 8:14
*T* shalt thou do unto the Levites.......... Num 8:26
*T* were the journeyings of the ........... Num 10:28
And if thou deal *t* with me.................. Num 11:15
*T* shall it be done for one.................... Num 15:11
*T* speak unto the Levites, and say ..... Num 18:26
*T* ye also shall offer an heave ............ Num 18:28
*T* saith thy brother Israel, Thou.......... Num 20:14
*T* Edom refused to give Israel............. Num 20:21
*T* Israel dwelt in the land of the......... Num 21:31
*T* saith Balak the son of Zippor,.......... Num 22:16
unto Balak, and *t* thou shalt speak...... Num 23:5
Go again unto Balak, and say *t*........... Num 23:16
*T* did your fathers, when I sent........... Num 32:8
But *t* shall ye deal with them................ Deut 7:5
*T* I fell down before the LORD............... Deut 9:25
*T* shalt thou do unto all the ................ Deut 20:15
the LORD done *t* unto this land............. Deut 29:24
Do ye *t* requite the LORD, O .................. Deut 32:6
two men, and hid them, and said *t*......... Josh 2:4
*T* shalt thou do six days........................ Josh 6:3
liest thou *t* upon thy face ...................... Josh 7:10
for *t* saith the LORD God of..................... Josh 7:13
the LORD God of Israel, and *t* .................. Josh 7:20
and *t* have I done .................................... Josh 7:20
for *t* shall the LORD do to all................ Josh 10:25
according to their families was *t*.......... Josh 16:5
*T* they gave to the children of............... Josh 21:13
*t* were all these cities ........................... Josh 21:42
*T* saith the whole congregation of........ Josh 22:16
*T* saith the LORD God of Israel,.............. Josh 24:2
*T* saith the LORD God of Israel, I........... Judg 6:8
him, Why hast thou served us *t* ............ Judg 8:1
*T* was Midian subdued before the.......... Judg 8:28
*T* God rendered the wickedness of.......... Judg 9:56
*T* saith Jephthah, Israel took not ....... Judg 11:15
*T* the children of Ammon were............ Judg 11:33
Why askest thou *t* after my name......... Judg 13:18
And he said unto them, *T* and ............. Judg 18:4
*t* dealeth Micah with me, and hath....... Judg 18:4
*T* they inclosed the Benjamites............ Judg 20:43
*T* saith the LORD, Did I plainly............... 1Sa 2:27
*t* he spake, Come, and let us go to........... 1Sa 9:9
*T* saith the LORD God of Israel, I........... 1Sa 10:18
*T* shall ye say unto the men of .............. 1Sa 11:9
If they say *t* unto us, Tarry ..................... 1Sa 14:9
But if they say *t*, Come up unto ........... 1Sa 14:10
*T* saith the LORD of hosts, I ..................... 1Sa 15:2
*T* shall ye say to David, The king.......... 1Sa 18:25
If he say *t*, It is well ................................ 1Sa 20:7
But if I say *t* unto the young man ....... 1Sa 20:22
*t* shall ye say to him that liveth............. 1Sa 25:6
Wherefore doth my lord *t* pursue ......... 1Sa 26:18
And I will yet be more vile than *t*.......... 2Sa 6:22
*T* saith the LORD, Shalt thou ................... 2Sa 7:5
*T* saith the LORD of hosts, I took............. 2Sa 7:8
*T* shalt thou say unto Joab, Let............ 2Sa 11:25
*T* saith the LORD God of Israel, I............. 2Sa 12:7
*T* saith the LORD, Behold, I will ............ 2Sa 12:11
*t* did he unto all the cities of ............... 2Sa 12:31
But if he *t* say, I have no...................... 2Sa 15:26
*t* said Shimei when he cursed,................ 2Sa 16:7
and to Abiathar the priests, *T* .............. 2Sa 17:15
*t* did Ahithophel counsel Absalom ....... 2Sa 17:15
and *t* and *t* have I counselled............... 2Sa 17:15
for *t* hath Ahithophel counselled........... 2Sa 17:21
Joab, I may not tarry *t* with thee.......... 2Sa 18:14
*t* he said, O my son Absalom, my........... 2Sa 18:33
*T* saith the LORD, I offer thee .............. 2Sa 24:12
also *t* said the king, Blessed be ............ 1Kin 1:48
*T* saith the king, Come forth ................ 1Kin 2:30
*T* said Joab, and *t* he answered............ 1Kin 2:30
*T* they spake before the king................ 1Kin 3:22
*t* gave Solomon to Hiram year by.......... 1Kin 5:11
the LORD done *t* unto this land............... 1Kin 9:8
for *t* saith the LORD, the God of ......... 1Kin 11:31
*T* shalt thou speak unto this............... 1Kin 12:10
*t* shalt thou say unto them, My........... 1Kin 12:10
*T* saith the LORD, Ye shall not go.......... 1Kin 12:24
O altar, altar, *t* saith the LORD ............ 1Kin 13:2
*T* saith the LORD, Forasmuch as............ 1Kin 13:21
*t* and *t* shalt thou say unto her........... 1Kin 14:5
*t* shalt thou say unto her....................... 1Kin 14:5
*T* saith the LORD God of Israel,.............. 1Kin 14:7
*T* did Zimri destroy all the house ....... 1Kin 16:12
For *t* saith the LORD God of................. 1Kin 17:14
said unto him, *T* saith Ben-hadad,........ 1Kin 20:2
*T* speaketh Ben-hadad, saying,.............. 1Kin 20:5
*T* saith the LORD, Hast thou seen ....... 1Kin 20:13
*T* saith the LORD, Even by the ............ 1Kin 20:14
*T* saith the LORD, Because the............. 1Kin 20:28
*T* saith the LORD, Because thou ........... 1Kin 20:42
*T* saith the LORD, Hast thou ................ 1Kin 21:19
*T* saith the LORD, In the place............. 1Kin 21:19
*T* saith the LORD, With these............... 1Kin 22:11
*T* saith the king, Put this fellow ......... 1Kin 22:27
Now therefore *t* saith the LORD,............. 2Kin 1:4
*T* saith the LORD, Is it not ..................... 2Kin 1:6
man of God, *t* hath the king said ......... 2Kin 1:11
*T* saith the LORD, Forasmuch as............. 2Kin 1:16
*T* saith the LORD, I have healed............. 2Kin 2:21
*T* saith the LORD, Make this .................. 2Kin 3:16
For *t* saith the LORD, Ye shall .............. 2Kin 3:17
for *t* saith the LORD, They shall ............ 2Kin 4:43
in, and told his lord, saying, *T*............... 2Kin 5:4
*t* said the maid that is of the.................. 2Kin 5:4
*T* saith the LORD, To morrow about ....... 2Kin 7:1
*T* saith the LORD, I have anointed.......... 2Kin 9:3
*T* saith the LORD God of Israel, I............ 2Kin 9:6
And he said, *T* and *t* spake he to........... 2Kin 9:12
*T* saith the LORD, I have anointed......... 2Kin 9:12
*T* saith the king, Is it peace.................. 2Kin 9:18
*T* saith the king, Is it peace................... 2Kin 9:19
*T* Jehu destroyed Baal out of.............. 2Kin 10:28
*T* did Urijah the priest,........................ 2Kin 16:16
*T* saith the great king, the king ........... 2Kin 18:19
*T* saith the king, Let not....................... 2Kin 18:29
for *t* saith the king of Assyria,.............. 2Kin 18:31
*T* saith Hezekiah, This day is a............. 2Kin 19:3
*T* shall ye say to your master,................ 2Kin 19:6
*T* saith the LORD, Be not afraid.............. 2Kin 19:6
*T* shall ye speak to Hezekiah king ..... 2Kin 19:10
*T* saith the LORD God of Israel,............ 2Kin 19:20
Therefore *t* saith the LORD ................... 2Kin 19:32
*T* saith the LORD, Set thine house ........ 2Kin 20:1
*T* saith the LORD, the God of................... 2Kin 20:5
Therefore *t* saith the LORD God of..... 2Kin 21:12
*T* saith the LORD God of Israel,............ 2Kin 22:15
*T* saith the LORD, Behold, I will ........... 2Kin 22:16
*t* shall ye say to him, *T* saith ............... 2Kin 22:18
*T* saith the LORD God of Israel,............. 2Kin 22:18
*T* all Israel brought up the ark ........... 1Chr 15:28
*T* saith the LORD, Thou shalt not ......... 1Chr 17:4
Now therefore *t* shalt thou say.............. 1Chr 17:7
*T* saith the LORD of hosts, I took .......... 1Chr 17:7
*T* the LORD preserved David .................. 1Chr 18:6
*T* the LORD preserved David................. 1Chr 18:13
*T* saith the LORD, I offer thee............... 1Chr 21:10
*T* saith the LORD, Choose thee............. 1Chr 21:11
and *t* were they divided ........................ 1Chr 24:4
*T* were they divided by lot, one ............ 1Chr 24:5
*T* David the son of Jesse reigned ....... 1Chr 29:26
*T* Solomon made all these vessels........ 2Chr 4:18
*T* all the work that Solomon made......... 2Chr 5:1
*T* Solomon finished the house of.......... 2Chr 7:11
the LORD done *t* unto this land............. 2Chr 7:21
*T* shalt thou answer the people ......... 2Chr 10:10
*t* shalt thou say unto them, My........... 2Chr 10:10
*T* saith the LORD, Ye shall not go ......... 2Chr 11:4
*T* saith the LORD, Ye have ..................... 2Chr 12:5
*T* the children of Israel were.............. 2Chr 13:18
*T* saith the LORD, With these thou..... 2Chr 18:10
*T* saith the king, Put this fellow......... 2Chr 18:26
*T* shall ye do in the fear of the............ 2Chr 19:9
*T* saith the LORD unto you, Be not .... 2Chr 20:15
*T* saith the LORD God of David thy ... 2Chr 21:12
*T* they did day by day, and................. 2Chr 24:11
*T* saith God, Why transgress ye ......... 2Chr 24:20
*T* Joash the king remembered not ..... 2Chr 24:22
*t* did Hezekiah throughout all............. 2Chr 31:20
*T* saith Sennacherib king of ............... 2Chr 32:10
*T* the LORD saved Hezekiah and the.. 2Chr 32:22
*T* saith the LORD God of Israel, .......... 2Chr 34:23
*T* saith the LORD, Behold, I will.......... 2Chr 34:24
*T* saith the LORD God of Israel ........... 2Chr 34:26
*T* saith Cyrus king of Persia, All ....... 2Chr 36:23
*T* saith Cyrus king of Persia, The ............. Ezr 1:2
said *t* unto them, Who hath..................... Ezr 5:3
unto him, wherein was written *t* .............. Ezr 5:7
those elders, and said unto them *t* ........... Ezr 5:9
*t* they returned us answer, saying .......... Ezr 5:11
and therein was a record *t* written............ Ezr 6:2
even *t* be he shaken out, and............... Neh 5:13
Did not your fathers *t*, and did ............. Neh 13:18
*T* cleansed I them from all.................. Neh 13:30
*T* shall there arise too much................... Est 1:18
Then *t* came every maiden unto the ...... Est 2:13
*T* shall it be done to the man................. Est 6:9
*T* shall it be done unto the man ............ Est 6:11
*T* the Jews smote all their...................... Est 9:5
*T* did Job continually ............................. Job 1:5
why then are ye *t* altogether vain ........ Job 27:12
*T* I was as a man that heareth not......... Ps 38:14
*T* will I bless thee while I live ................ Ps 63:4
If I say, I will speak *t* ........................... Ps 73:15
*T* my heart was grieved, and I was........ Ps 73:21
*T* they changed their glory into ............ Ps 106:20
*T* they provoked him to anger with ..... Ps 106:29
*T* were they defiled with their ............. Ps 106:39
that *t* shall the man be blessed............... Ps 128:4
*T* saith the Lord GOD, It shall.................... Is 7:7
For the LORD spake *t* to me with a ........... Is 8:11
Therefore *t* saith the Lord GOD of............ Is 10:24
For *t* hath the Lord said unto me,............... Is 21:6
For *t* hath the Lord said unto me,............ Is 21:16
*T* saith the Lord GOD of hosts, Go ........... Is 22:15
When *t* it shall be in the midst................ Is 24:13

T

Therefore *t* saith the Lord GOD, Is 28:16
Therefore *t* saith the LORD, who Is 29:22
Wherefore *t* saith the Holy One of Is 30:12
For *t* saith the Lord GOD, the Is 30:15
For *t* hath the LORD spoken unto Is 31:4
*T* saith the great king, the king Is 36:4
*T* saith the king, Let not Is 36:14
for *t* saith the king of Assyria, Is 36:16
*T* saith Hezekiah, This day is a Is 37:3
*T* shall ye say unto your master, Is 37:6
*T* saith the LORD, Be not afraid Is 37:6
*T* shall ye speak to Hezekiah king Is 37:10
*T* saith the LORD God of Israel, Is 37:21
Therefore *t* saith the LORD Is 37:33
*T* saith the LORD, Set thine house Is 38:1
*T* saith the LORD, the God of Is 38:5
*T* saith God the LORD, he that Is 42:5
But now *t* saith the LORD that Is 43:1
*T* saith the LORD, your redeemer, Is 43:14
*T* saith the LORD, which maketh a Is 43:16
*T* saith the LORD that made thee, Is 44:2
*T* saith the LORD the King of Is 44:6
*T* saith the LORD, thy redeemer, Is 44:24
*T* saith the LORD to his anointed, Is 45:1
*T* saith the LORD, the Holy One of Is 45:11
*T* saith the LORD, The labour of Is 45:14
For *t* saith the LORD that created Is 45:18
*T* shall they be unto thee with Is 47:15
*T* saith the LORD, thy Redeemer, Is 48:17
*T* saith the LORD, the Redeemer of Is 49:7
*T* saith the LORD, In an Is 49:8
*T* saith the Lord GOD, Behold, I Is 49:22
But *t* saith the LORD, Even the Is 49:25
*T* saith the LORD, Where is the Is 50:1
*T* saith thy Lord the LORD, and thy Is 51:22
For *t* saith the LORD, Ye have Is 52:3
For *t* saith the Lord GOD, My Is 52:4
*T* saith the LORD, Keep ye Is 56:1
For *t* saith the LORD unto the Is 56:4
For *t* saith the high and lofty One Is 57:15
*T* saith the LORD, As the new wine Is 65:8
Therefore *t* saith the Lord GOD, Is 65:13
*T* saith the LORD, The heaven is Is 66:1
For *t* saith the LORD, Behold, I Is 66:12
saying, *T* saith the LORD Jer 2:2
*T* saith the LORD, What iniquity Jer 2:5
For *t* saith the LORD to the men Jer 4:3
For *t* hath the LORD said, The Jer 4:27
*t* shall it be done unto them Jer 5:13
Wherefore *t* saith the LORD God of Jer 5:14
For *t* hath the LORD of hosts said Jer 6:6
*T* saith the LORD of hosts, They Jer 6:9
*T* saith the LORD, Stand ye in the Jer 6:16
Therefore *t* saith the LORD, Jer 6:21
*T* saith the LORD, Behold, a Jer 6:22
*T* saith the LORD of hosts, the Jer 7:3
Therefore *t* saith the Lord GOD Jer 7:20
*T* saith the LORD of hosts, the Jer 7:21
say unto them, *T* saith the LORD Jer 8:4
Therefore *t* saith the LORD of Jer 9:7
Therefore *t* saith the LORD of Jer 9:15
*T* saith the LORD of hosts, Jer 9:17
*T* saith the LORD, Even the Jer 9:22
*T* saith the LORD, Let not the Jer 9:23
*T* saith the LORD, Learn not the Jer 10:2
*T* shall ye say unto them, The Jer 10:11
For *t* saith the LORD, Behold, I Jer 10:18
*T* saith the LORD God of Israel Jer 11:3
Therefore *t* saith the LORD, Jer 11:11
Therefore *t* saith the LORD of the Jer 11:21
Therefore *t* saith the LORD of Jer 11:22
*T* saith the LORD against all mine Jer 12:14
*T* saith the LORD unto me, Go and Jer 13:1
*T* saith the LORD, After this Jer 13:9
*T* saith the LORD God of Israel, Jer 13:12
*T* saith the LORD, Behold, I will Jer 13:13
*T* saith the LORD unto this people Jer 14:10
*T* have they loved to wander, they Jer 14:10
Therefore *t* saith the LORD Jer 14:15
shalt tell them, *T* saith the LORD Jer 15:2
Therefore *t* saith the LORD, If Jer 15:19
For *t* saith the LORD concerning Jer 16:3
For *t* saith the LORD, Enter not Jer 16:5
For *t* saith the LORD of hosts, Jer 16:9
*T* saith the LORD Jer 17:5
*T* said the LORD unto me Jer 17:19
*T* saith the LORD Jer 17:21
saying, *T* saith the LORD Jer 18:11
Therefore *t* saith the LORD Jer 18:13
deal *t* with them in the time of Jer 18:23
*T* saith the LORD, Go and get a Jer 19:1
*T* saith the LORD of hosts, the Jer 19:3
*T* saith the LORD of hosts Jer 19:11
*T* will I do unto this place, Jer 19:12
*T* saith the LORD of hosts, the Jer 19:15
For *t* saith the LORD, Behold, I Jer 20:4
*T* shall ye say to Zedekiah Jer 21:3
*T* saith the LORD God of Israel Jer 21:4
thou shalt say, *T* saith the LORD Jer 21:8
house of David, *t* saith the LORD Jer 21:12
*T* saith the LORD Jer 22:1
*T* saith the LORD Jer 22:3
For *t* saith the LORD unto the Jer 22:6
LORD done *t* unto this great city Jer 22:8
For *t* saith the LORD touching Jer 22:11
Therefore *t* saith the LORD Jer 22:18
*T* saith the LORD, Write ye this Jer 22:30
Therefore *t* saith the LORD God of Jer 23:2
Therefore *t* saith the LORD of Jer 23:15
*T* saith the LORD of hosts, Jer 23:16
*T* shall ye say every one to his Jer 23:35
*T* shalt thou say to the prophet, Jer 23:37
therefore *t* saith the LORD Jer 23:38
*T* saith the LORD, the God of Jer 24:5
surely *t* saith the LORD, So will Jer 24:8
Therefore *t* saith the LORD of Jer 25:8
For *t* saith the LORD God of Jer 25:15
*T* saith the LORD of hosts, the Jer 25:27
*T* saith the LORD of hosts Jer 25:28
*T* saith the LORD of hosts, Behold Jer 25:32
*T* saith the LORD Jer 26:2
say unto them, *T* saith the LORD Jer 26:4
*T* saith the LORD of hosts Jer 26:18
*T* might we procure great evil Jer 26:19
*T* saith the LORD to me Jer 27:2
*T* saith the LORD of hosts, the Jer 27:4
*T* shall ye say unto your masters Jer 27:4
people, saying, *T* saith the LORD Jer 27:16
For *t* saith the LORD of hosts Jer 27:19
*t* saith the LORD of hosts, the Jer 27:21
*T* speaketh the LORD of hosts, the Jer 28:2
people, saying, *T* saith the LORD Jer 28:11
saying, *T* saith the LORD Jer 28:13
For *t* saith the LORD of hosts, Jer 28:14
Therefore *t* saith the LORD Jer 28:16
*T* saith the LORD of hosts, the Jer 29:4
For *t* saith the LORD of hosts, Jer 29:8
For *t* saith the LORD, That after Jer 29:10
Know that *t* saith the LORD of the Jer 29:16
*T* saith the LORD of hosts Jer 29:17
*T* saith the LORD of hosts, the Jer 29:21
*T* shalt thou also speak to Jer 29:24
*T* speaketh the LORD of hosts, the Jer 29:25
*T* saith the LORD concerning Jer 29:31
Therefore *t* saith the LORD Jer 29:32
*T* speaketh the LORD God of Israel Jer 30:2
For *t* saith the LORD Jer 30:5
For *t* saith the LORD, Thy bruise Jer 30:12
*T* saith the LORD Jer 30:18
*T* saith the LORD, The people Jer 31:2
For *t* saith the LORD Jer 31:7
*T* saith the LORD Jer 31:15
*T* saith the LORD Jer 31:16
heard Ephraim bemoaning himself *t* Jer 31:18
*T* saith the LORD of hosts, the Jer 31:23
*T* saith the LORD, which giveth Jer 31:35
*T* saith the LORD Jer 31:37
*T* saith the LORD, Behold, I will Jer 32:3
*T* saith the LORD of hosts, the Jer 32:14
For *t* saith the LORD of hosts, Jer 32:15
Therefore *t* saith the LORD Jer 32:28
now therefore *t* saith the LORD, Jer 32:36
For *t* saith the LORD Jer 32:42
*T* saith the LORD the maker Jer 33:2
For *t* saith the LORD, the God of Jer 33:4
*T* saith the LORD Jer 33:10
*T* saith the LORD of hosts Jer 33:12
For *t* saith the LORD Jer 33:17
*T* saith the LORD Jer 33:20
*t* they have despised my people, Jer 33:24
*T* saith the LORD Jer 33:25
*T* saith the LORD, the God of Jer 34:2
and tell him, *T* saith the LORD Jer 34:2
*T* saith the LORD of thee, Thou Jer 34:4
*T* saith the LORD, the God of Jer 34:13
Therefore *t* saith the LORD Jer 34:17
*T* have we obeyed the voice of Jer 35:8
*T* saith the LORD of hosts, the Jer 35:13
Therefore *t* saith the LORD God of Jer 35:17
*T* saith the LORD of hosts, the Jer 35:18
Therefore *t* saith the LORD of Jer 35:19
king of Judah, *T* saith the LORD Jer 36:29
Therefore *t* saith the LORD of Jer 36:30
*T* saith the LORD, the God of Jer 37:7
*T* shall ye say to the king of Jer 37:7
*T* saith the LORD Jer 37:9
*T* Jeremiah remained in the court Jer 37:21
*T* saith the LORD, He that Jer 38:2
*T* saith the LORD, This city shall Jer 38:3
for *t* he weakeneth the hands of Jer 38:4
*T* saith the LORD of hosts, the Jer 39:16
*T* saith the LORD, the God of Jer 42:9
*T* saith the LORD of hosts, the Jer 42:15
For *t* saith the LORD of hosts, Jer 42:18
*t* came they even to Tahpanhes Jer 43:7
*T* saith the LORD of hosts, the Jer 43:10
*T* saith the LORD of hosts, the Jer 44:2
Therefore now *t* saith the LORD, Jer 44:7
Therefore *t* saith the LORD of Jer 44:11
*T* saith the LORD of hosts, the Jer 44:25
*T* saith the LORD Jer 44:30
*T* saith the LORD, the God of Jer 45:2
*T* shalt thou say unto him, The Jer 45:4
say unto him, The LORD saith *t* Jer 45:4
*T* saith the LORD Jer 47:2
Against Moab *t* saith the LORD of Jer 48:1
For *t* saith the LORD Jer 48:40
*T* far is the judgment of Moab Jer 48:47
The Ammonites, *t* saith the LORD Jer 49:1
*t* saith the LORD of hosts Jer 49:7
For *t* saith the LORD Jer 49:12
shall smite, *t* saith the LORD Jer 49:28
*T* saith the LORD of hosts Jer 49:35
Therefore *t* saith the LORD of Jer 50:18
*T* saith the LORD of hosts Jer 50:33
*T* saith the LORD Jer 51:1
*T* the slain shall fall in the Jer 51:4
For *t* saith the LORD of hosts, Jer 51:33
Therefore *t* saith the LORD Jer 51:36
*T* saith the LORD of hosts Jer 51:58
*T* shall Babylon sink, and shall Jer 51:64
*T* far are the words of Jeremiah Jer 51:64
*T* Judah was carried away captive Jer 52:27
*T* were their faces Eze 1:11
unto them, *T* saith the Lord GOD Eze 2:4
tell them, *T* saith the Lord GOD Eze 3:11
unto them, *T* saith the Lord GOD Eze 3:27
Even *t* shall the children of Eze 4:13
*T* saith the Lord GOD Eze 5:5
Therefore *t* saith the Lord GOD Eze 5:7
Therefore *t* saith the Lord GOD Eze 5:8
*T* shall mine anger be Eze 5:13
*T* saith the Lord GOD to the Eze 6:3
*T* saith the Lord GOD Eze 6:11
*t* will I accomplish my fury upon Eze 6:12
*t* saith the Lord GOD unto the Eze 7:2
*T* saith the Lord GOD Eze 7:5
*T* saith the LORD Eze 11:5
*T* have ye said, O house of Israel Eze 11:5
Therefore *t* saith the Lord GOD Eze 11:7
say, *T* saith the Lord GOD Eze 11:16
say, *T* saith the Lord GOD Eze 11:17
unto them, *T* saith the Lord GOD Eze 12:10
*T* saith the Lord GOD of the Eze 12:19
therefore, *T* saith the Lord GOD Eze 12:23
unto them, *T* saith the Lord GOD Eze 12:28
*T* saith the Lord GOD Eze 13:3
Therefore *t* saith the Lord GOD Eze 13:8
Therefore *t* saith the Lord GOD Eze 13:13
*T* will I accomplish my wrath upon Eze 13:15
And say, *T* saith the Lord GOD Eze 13:18
Wherefore *t* saith the Lord GOD Eze 13:20
unto them, *T* saith the Lord GOD Eze 14:4
of Israel, *T* saith the Lord GOD Eze 14:6
For *t* saith the Lord GOD Eze 14:21
Therefore *t* saith the Lord GOD Eze 15:6
*T* saith the Lord GOD unto Eze 16:3
*T* wast thou decked with gold and Eze 16:13
*t* it was, saith the Lord GOD Eze 16:19
*T* saith the Lord GOD Eze 16:36
For *t* saith the Lord GOD Eze 16:59
And say, *T* saith the Lord GOD Eze 17:3
Say thou, *T* saith the Lord GOD Eze 17:9
Therefore *t* saith the Lord GOD Eze 17:19
*T* saith the Lord GOD Eze 17:22
unto them, *T* saith the Lord GOD Eze 20:3
unto them, *T* saith the Lord GOD Eze 20:5
unto them, *T* saith the Lord GOD Eze 20:27
of Israel, *T* saith the Lord GOD Eze 20:30
of Israel, *t* saith the Lord GOD Eze 20:39
*T* saith the Lord GOD Eze 20:47
land of Israel, *T* saith the LORD Eze 21:3
and say, *T* saith the LORD Eze 21:9
Therefore *t* saith the Lord GOD Eze 21:24
*T* saith the Lord GOD Eze 21:26
*T* saith the Lord GOD concerning Eze 21:28
*T* saith the Lord GOD, The city Eze 22:3
Therefore *t* saith the Lord GOD Eze 22:19
*T* saith the Lord GOD, when the Eze 22:28
*T* were their names Eze 23:4
*T* she committed her whoredoms Eze 23:7
*T* thou calledst to remembrance Eze 23:21
O Aholibah, *t* saith the Lord GOD Eze 23:22
*T* will I make thy lewdness to Eze 23:27
For *t* saith the Lord GOD Eze 23:28
*T* saith the Lord GOD Eze 23:32
Therefore *t* saith the Lord GOD Eze 23:35
*t* have they done in the midst of Eze 23:39
For *t* saith the Lord GOD Eze 23:46
*T* will I cause lewdness to cease Eze 23:48
unto them, *T* saith the Lord GOD Eze 24:3
Wherefore *t* saith the Lord GOD Eze 24:6
Therefore *t* saith the Lord GOD Eze 24:9
of Israel, *T* saith the Lord GOD Eze 24:21
*T* Ezekiel is unto you a sign Eze 24:24
*T* saith the Lord GOD Eze 25:3
For *t* saith the Lord GOD Eze 25:6
*T* saith the Lord GOD Eze 25:8
*T* saith the Lord GOD Eze 25:12
Therefore *t* saith the Lord GOD Eze 25:13
*T* saith the Lord GOD Eze 25:15
Therefore *t* saith the Lord GOD Eze 25:16
Therefore *t* saith the Lord GOD Eze 26:3
For *t* saith the Lord GOD Eze 26:7
*T* saith the Lord GOD to Tyrus Eze 26:15
For *t* saith the Lord GOD Eze 26:19
many isles, *T* saith the Lord GOD Eze 27:3
of Tyrus, *T* saith the Lord GOD Eze 28:2
Therefore *t* saith the Lord GOD Eze 28:6
unto him, *T* saith the Lord GOD Eze 28:12
And say, *T* saith the Lord GOD Eze 28:22
*T* saith the Lord GOD Eze 28:25
and say, *T* saith the Lord GOD Eze 29:3
Therefore *t* saith the Lord GOD Eze 29:8
Yet *t* saith the Lord GOD Eze 29:13
Therefore *t* saith the Lord GOD Eze 29:19
and say, *T* saith the Lord GOD Eze 30:2
*T* saith the LORD Eze 30:6
*T* saith the Lord GOD Eze 30:10
*T* saith the Lord GOD Eze 30:13
*T* will I execute judgments in Eze 30:19
Therefore *t* saith the Lord GOD Eze 30:22
*T* was he fair in his greatness, Eze 31:7
Therefore *t* saith the Lord GOD Eze 31:10
*T* saith the Lord GOD Eze 31:15
To whom art thou *t* like in glory Eze 31:18
*T* saith the Lord GOD Eze 32:3
For *t* saith the Lord GOD Eze 32:11
*T* ye speak, saying, If our Eze 33:10
unto them, *T* saith the Lord GOD Eze 33:25

Say thou *t* unto them, *T* saith Eze 33:27
*T* saith the Lord GOD unto the Eze 34:2
*T* saith the Lord GOD Eze 34:10
For *t* saith the Lord GOD Eze 34:11
O my flock, *t* saith the Lord GOD Eze 34:17
Therefore *t* saith the Lord GOD Eze 34:20
*T* shall they know that I the LORD Eze 34:30
say unto it, *T* saith the Lord GOD Eze 35:3
*T* will I make mount Seir most Eze 35:7
*T* with your mouth ye have boasted Eze 35:13
*T* saith the Lord GOD Eze 35:14
*T* saith the Lord GOD Eze 36:2
and say, *T* saith the Lord GOD Eze 36:3
*T* saith the Lord GOD to the Eze 36:4
Therefore *t* saith the Lord GOD Eze 36:5
the valleys, *T* saith the Lord GOD Eze 36:6
Therefore *t* saith the Lord GOD Eze 36:7
*T* saith the Lord GOD Eze 36:13
of Israel, *T* saith the Lord GOD Eze 36:22
*T* saith the Lord GOD Eze 36:33
*T* saith the Lord GOD Eze 36:37
*T* saith the Lord GOD unto these Eze 37:5
to the wind, *T* saith the Lord GOD Eze 37:9
unto them, *T* saith the Lord GOD Eze 37:12
unto them, *T* saith the Lord GOD Eze 37:19
unto them, *T* saith the Lord GOD Eze 37:21
And say, *T* saith the Lord GOD Eze 38:3
*T* saith the Lord GOD Eze 38:10
unto Gog, *T* saith the Lord GOD Eze 38:14
*T* saith the Lord GOD Eze 38:17
*T* will I magnify myself, and Eze 38:23
Gog, and say, *T* saith the Lord GOD Eze 39:1
*T* shall they cleanse the land Eze 39:16
son of man, *t* saith the Lord GOD Eze 39:17
*T* ye shall be filled at my table Eze 39:20
Therefore *t* saith the Lord GOD Eze 39:25
Son of man, *t* saith the Lord GOD Eze 43:18
*t* shalt thou cleanse and purge it Eze 43:20
of Israel, *T* saith the Lord GOD Eze 44:6
*T* saith the Lord GOD Eze 44:9
*T* saith the Lord GOD Eze 45:9
*T* saith the Lord GOD Eze 45:18
*T* saith the Lord GOD Eze 46:1
*T* shall they prepare the lamb, and Eze 46:15
*T* saith the Lord GOD Eze 46:16
*T* saith the Lord GOD Eze 47:13
*T* Melzar took away the portion of Dan 1:16
he went and said *t* unto him Dan 2:24
said *t* unto him, I have found a Dan 2:25
*T* were the visions of mine head Dan 4:10
He cried aloud, and said *t* Dan 4:14
said *t* unto him, King Darius, Dan 6:6
and they said *t* unto it, Arise, Dan 7:5
*T* he said, The fourth beast shall Dan 7:23
*t* shall he do Dan 11:17
*T* shall he do in the most strong Dan 11:39
*t* judgment springeth up as Hos 10:4
*T* saith the LORD Amos 1:3
*T* saith the LORD Amos 1:6
*T* saith the LORD Amos 1:9
*T* saith the LORD Amos 1:11
*T* saith the LORD Amos 1:13
*T* saith the LORD Amos 2:1
*T* saith the LORD Amos 2:4
*T* saith the LORD Amos 2:6
Is it not even *t*, O ye children Amos 2:11
Therefore *t* saith the Lord GOD Amos 3:11
*T* saith the LORD Amos 3:12
Therefore *t* will I do unto thee, Amos 4:12
For *t* saith the Lord GOD Amos 5:3
For *t* saith the LORD unto the Amos 5:4
God of hosts, the Lord, saith *t* Amos 5:16
*T* hath the Lord GOD shewed unto Amos 7:1
*T* hath the Lord GOD shewed unto Amos 7:4
*T* he shewed me Amos 7:7
For *t* Amos saith, Jeroboam shall Amos 7:11
Therefore *t* saith the LORD Amos 7:17
*T* hath the Lord GOD shewed unto Amos 8:1
*T* saith the Lord GOD concerning Obad 1
Therefore *t* saith the LORD Mic 2:3
*T* saith the LORD concerning the Mic 3:5
*t* shall he deliver us from the Mic 5:6
*T* saith the LORD Nah 1:12
yet *t* shall they be cut down, Nah 1:12
*T* speaketh the LORD of hosts, Hag 1:2
Now therefore *t* saith the LORD of Hag 1:5
*T* saith the LORD of hosts Hag 1:7
For *t* saith the LORD of hosts Hag 2:6
*T* saith the LORD of hosts Hag 2:11
*T* saith the LORD of hosts Zec 1:3
*T* saith the LORD of hosts Zec 1:4
*T* saith the LORD of hosts Zec 1:14
Therefore *t* saith the LORD Zec 1:16
*T* saith the LORD of hosts Zec 1:17
For *t* saith the LORD of hosts Zec 2:8
*T* saith the LORD of hosts Zec 3:7
*T* speaketh the LORD of hosts, Zec 6:12
*T* speaketh the LORD of hosts, Zec 7:9
*T* the land was desolate after Zec 7:14
*T* saith the LORD of hosts Zec 8:2
*T* saith the LORD Zec 8:3
*T* saith the LORD of hosts Zec 8:4
*T* saith the LORD of hosts Zec 8:6
*T* saith the LORD of hosts Zec 8:7
*T* saith the LORD of hosts Zec 8:9
For *t* saith the LORD of hosts Zec 8:14
*T* saith the LORD of hosts Zec 8:19
*T* saith the LORD of hosts Zec 8:20
*T* saith the LORD of hosts Zec 8:23
*T* saith the LORD my God Zec 11:4
*t* saith the LORD of hosts, They Mal 1:4
*t* ye brought an offering Mal 1:13
for *t* it is written by the Mt 2:5
for *t* it becometh us to fulfil Mt 3:15
*T* have ye made the commandment of Mt 15:6
be fulfilled, that *t* it must be Mt 26:54
doth this man *t* speak blasphemies Mk 2:7
*T* hath the Lord dealt with me in Lk 1:25
why hast thou *t* dealt with us Lk 2:48
While he *t* spake, there came a Lk 9:34
*t* saying thou reproachest us also Lk 11:45
Even *t* shall it be in the day Lk 17:30
prayed *t* with himself, God, I Lk 18:11
And when he had *t* spoken, he went Lk 19:28
*t* shall ye say unto him, Because Lk 19:31
answered and said, Suffer ye *t* far Lk 22:51
and having said *t*, he gave up the Lk 23:46
And as they *t* spake, Jesus himself Lk 24:36
And when he had *t* spoken, he Lk 24:40
*T* it is written, and *t* it Lk 24:46
his journey, sat *t* on the well Jn 4:6
When he had *t* spoken, he spat on Jn 9:6
when he *t* had spoken, he cried Jn 11:43
If we let him *t* alone, all men Jn 11:48
When Jesus had *t* said, he was Jn 13:21
And when he had *t* spoken, one of Jn 18:22
And when she had *t* said, she Jn 20:14
And when he had *t* spoken, he Acts 19:41
And when he had *t* spoken, he Acts 20:36
*T* saith the Holy Ghost, So shall Acts 21:11
as he *t* spake for himself, Festus Acts 26:24
And when he had *t* spoken, the king Acts 26:30
And when he had *t* spoken, he took Acts 27:35
it, Why hast thou made me *t* Rom 9:20
*t* are the secrets of his heart 1Cor 14:25
When I therefore was *t* minded 2Cor 1:17
because we *t* judge, that if one 2Cor 5:14
many as be perfect, be *t* minded Phil 3:15
salvation, though we *t* speak Heb 6:9
when these things were *t* ordained Heb 9:6
*t* I saw the horses in the vision, Rev 9:17
be, because thou hast judged *t* Rev 16:5
*T* with violence shall that great Rev 18:21

**THY** See PREFACE.

**THYATIRA** *(thi-a-ti'-rah) A city in Lydia in Asia Minor.*
of purple, of the city of *T* Acts 16:14
and unto Pergamos, and unto *T* Rev 1:11
angel of the church in *T* write Rev 2:18
you I say, and unto the rest in *T* Rev 2:24

**THYINE**
all *t* wood, and all manner vessels Rev 18:12

**THYSELF**
separate *t*, I pray thee, from me Gen 13:9
persons, and take the goods to *t* Gen 14:21
and submit *t* under her hands Gen 16:9
keep that thou hast unto *t* Gen 33:9
exaltest thou *t* against my people Ex 9:17
thou refuse to humble *t* before me Ex 10:3
Get thee from me, take heed to *t* Ex 10:28
why sittest thou *t* alone, and all Ex 18:14
not able to perform it *t* alone Ex 18:18
so shall it be easier for *t* Ex 18:22
Thou shalt not bow down *t* to them Ex 20:5
present *t* there to me in the top Ex 34:2
Take heed to *t*, lest thou make a Ex 34:12
and make an atonement for *t* Lev 9:7
wife, to defile *t* with her Lev 18:20
any beast to defile *t* therewith Lev 18:23
shalt love thy neighbour as *t* Lev 19:18
you, and thou shalt love him as *t* Lev 19:34
that thou bear it not *t* alone Num 11:17
except thou make *t* altogether a Num 16:13
Only take heed to *t*, and keep thy Deut 4:9
shalt not bow down *t* unto them Deut 5:9
greater and mightier than *t* Deut 9:1
Take heed to *t* that thou offer Deut 12:13
Take heed to *t* that thou forsake Deut 12:19
Take heed to *t* that thou be not Deut 12:30
thereof, shalt thou take unto *t* Deut 20:14
go astray, and hide *t* from them Deut 22:1
thou mayest not hide *t* Deut 22:3
by the way, and hide *t* from them Deut 22:4
wherewith thou coverest *t* Deut 22:12
be, when thou wilt ease *t* abroad Deut 23:13
shalt not anoint *t* with the oil Deut 28:40
cut down for *t* there in the land Josh 17:15
Wash *t* therefore, and anoint thee, Ruth 3:3
but make not *t* known unto the man Ruth 3:3
redeem thou my right to *t* Ruth 4:6
take heed to *t* until the morning, 1Sa 19:2
in a secret place, and hide *t* 1Sa 19:2
be in me iniquity, slay me *t* 1Sa 20:8
*t* when the business was in hand 1Sa 20:19
from avenging *t* with thine own 1Sa 25:26
that then thou shalt bestir *t* 2Sa 5:24
to *t* thy people Israel to be a 2Sa 7:24
down on thy bed, and make *t* sick 2Sa 13:5
feign *t* to be a mourner, and put 2Sa 14:2
apparel, and anoint not *t* with oil 2Sa 14:2
thou *t* wouldest have set *t* 2Sa 18:13
wouldest have set *t* against me 2Sa 18:13
thou wilt shew *t* merciful 2Sa 22:26
man thou wilt shew *t* upright 2Sa 22:26
the pure thou wilt shew *t* pure 2Sa 22:27
thou wilt shew *t* unsavoury 2Sa 22:27
strong therefore, and shew *t* a man 1Kin 2:2
and whithersoever thou turnest *t* 1Kin 2:3
and hast not asked for *t* long life 1Kin 3:11
neither hast asked riches for *t* 1Kin 3:11
but hast asked for *t* 1Kin 3:11
Come home with me, and refresh *t* 1Kin 13:7
Arise, I pray thee, and disguise *t* 1Kin 14:2
why feignest thou *t* to be another 1Kin 14:6
hide *t* by the brook Cherith, that 1Kin 17:3
saying, Go, shew *t* unto Ahab 1Kin 18:1
said unto him, Go, strengthen *t* 1Kin 20:22
*t* hast decided it 1Kin 20:40
because thou hast sold *t* to work 1Kin 21:20
into an inner chamber to hide *t* 1Kin 22:25
hast humbled *t* before the LORD 2Kin 22:19
Now therefore advise *t* what word 1Chr 21:12
asked wisdom and knowledge for *t* 2Chr 1:11
into an inner chamber to hide *t* 2Chr 18:24
thou hast joined *t* with Ahaziah 2Chr 20:37
house, which were better than *t* 2Chr 21:13
and thou didst humble *t* before God 2Chr 34:27
thereof, and humbledst *t* before me 2Chr 34:27
Think not with *t* that thou shalt Est 4:13
prepare *t* to the search of their Job 8:8
thou shewest *t* marvellous upon me Job 10:16
and dost thou restrain wisdom to *t* Job 15:8
Acquaint now *t* with him, and be at Job 22:21
hand thou opposest *t* against me Job 30:21
Deck *t* now with majesty and Job 40:10
array *t* with glory and beauty Job 40:10
lift up *t* because of the rage of Ps 7:6
why hidest thou *t* in times of Ps 10:1
thou wilt shew *t* merciful Ps 18:25
man thou wilt shew *t* upright Ps 18:25
the pure thou wilt shew *t* pure Ps 18:26
froward thou wilt shew *t* froward Ps 18:26
Stir up *t*, and awake to my Ps 35:23
Fret not *t* because of evildoers, Ps 37:1
Delight *t* also in the LORD Ps 37:4
fret not *t* because of him who Ps 37:7
fret not *t* in any wise to do evil Ps 37:8
thee, when thou doest well to *t* Ps 49:18
I was altogether such an one as *t* Ps 50:21
Why boastest thou *t* in mischief Ps 52:1
hide not *t* from my supplication Ps 55:1
O turn *t* to us again Ps 60:1
that thou madest strong for *t* Ps 80:15
man whom thou madest strong for *t* Ps 80:17
thou hast turned *t* from the Ps 85:3
wilt thou hide *t* for ever Ps 89:46
whom vengeance belongeth, shew *t* Ps 94:1
Lift up *t*, thou judge of the Ps 94:2
Who coverest *t* with light as with Ps 104:2
Do this now, my son, and deliver *t* Prov 6:3
go, humble *t*, and make sure thy Prov 6:3
Deliver *t* as a roe from the hand Prov 6:5
be wise, thou shalt be wise for *t* Prov 9:12
Fret not *t* because of evil men, Prov 24:19
and make it fit for *t* in the field Prov 24:27
Put not forth *t* in the presence Prov 25:6
Boast not *t* of to morrow Prov 27:1
done foolishly in lifting up *t* Prov 30:32
neither make *t* over wise Eccl 7:16
why shouldest thou destroy *t* Eccl 7:16
*t* likewise hast cursed others Eccl 7:22
hide *t* as it were for a little Is 26:20
at the lifting up of *t* the Is 33:3
thou art a God that hidest *t* Is 45:15
Shake *t* from the dust Is 52:2
loose *t* from the bands of thy Is 52:2
discovered *t* to another than me Is 57:8
didst debase *t* even unto hell Is 57:9
that thou hide not *t* from thine Is 58:7
shalt thou delight *t* in the LORD Is 58:14
to make *t* a glorious name Is 63:14
thou refrain *t* for these things Is 64:12
Which say, Stand by *t*, come not Is 65:5
thou not procured this unto *t* Jer 2:17
thou clothest *t* with crimson Jer 4:30
in vain shalt thou make *t* fair Jer 4:30
sackcloth, and wallow *t* in ashes Jer 6:26
And thou, even *t*, shalt Jer 17:4
I will make thee a terror to *t* Jer 20:4
because thou closest *t* in cedar Jer 22:15
buy it for *t* Jer 32:8
seekest thou great things for *t* Jer 45:5
furnish *t* to go into captivity Jer 46:19
how long wilt thou cut *t* Jer 47:5
put up *t* into thy scabbard, rest, Jer 47:6
give *t* no rest Lam 2:18
Thou hast covered *t* with a cloud Lam 3:44
be drunken, and shalt make *t* naked Lam 4:21
shut *t* within thine house Eze 3:24
madest to *t* images of men, and Eze 16:17
hast defiled *t* in thine idols Eze 22:4
in *t* in the sight of the heathen Eze 22:16
for whom thou didst wash *t* Eze 23:40
deckedst *t* with ornaments, Eze 23:40
thou hast lifted up *t* in height Eze 31:10
thou prepared, and prepare for *t* Eze 38:7
the king, Let thy gifts be to *t* Dan 5:17
But hast lifted up *t* against the Dan 5:23
to chasten *t* before thy God, thy Dan 10:12
O Israel, thou hast destroyed *t* Hos 13:9
Though thou exalt *t* as the eagle Obad 4
of Aphrah roll *t* in the dust Mic 1:10
Now gather *t* in troops, O Mic 5:1
make *t* many as the cankerworm, Nah 3:15
make *t* many as the locusts Nah 3:15
Deliver *t*, O Zion, that dwellest Zec 2:7
be the Son of God, cast *t* down Mt 4:6
time, Thou shalt not forswear *t* Mt 5:33

shew *t* to the priest, and offer .................. Mt 8:4
shalt love thy neighbour as *t*................. Mt 19:19
shalt love thy neighbour as *t*................. Mt 22:39
buildest it in three days, save *t*............. Mt 27:40
shew *t* to the priest, and offer ................ Mk 1:44
shalt love thy neighbour as *t*................. Mk 12:31
Save *t*, and come down from the......... Mk 15:30
of God, cast *t* down from hence................. Lk 4:9
this proverb, Physician, heal *t*................. Lk 4:23
shew *t* to the priest, and offer................. Lk 5:14
when thou *t* beholdest not the ................ Lk 6:42
unto him, Lord, trouble not *t*.................... Lk 7:6
and thy neighbour as *t*......................... Lk 10:27
wherewith I may sup, and gird *t*.............. Lk 17:8
be the king of the Jews, save *t*.............. Lk 23:37
saying, If thou be Christ, save *t*............ Lk 23:39
What sayest thou of *t*.............................. Jn 1:22
these things, shew *t* to the world .............. Jn 7:4
him, Thou bearest record of *t*.................... Jn 8:13
whom makest thou *t*.................................. Jn 8:53
thou, being a man, makest *t* God........... Jn 10:33
that thou wilt manifest *t* unto us............ Jn 14:22
him, Sayest thou this thing of *t*............. Jn 18:34
thou wast young, thou girdedst *t*........... Jn 21:18
near, and join *t* to this chariot............. Acts 8:29
the angel said unto him, Gird *t*............. Acts 12:8
loud voice, saying, Do *t* no harm........ Acts 16:28
purify *t* with them, and be at............... Acts 21:24
but that thou *t* also walkest................. Acts 21:24
by examining of whom *t* mayest .......... Acts 24:8
Thou art permitted to speak for *t*......... Acts 26:1
voice, Paul, thou art beside *t*.............. Acts 26:24
another, thou condemnest *t*...................... Rom 2:1
heart treasurest up unto *t* wrath............... Rom 2:5
art confident that thou *t* art a.............. Rom 2:19
another, teachest thou not *t*.................... Rom 2:21
shalt love thy neighbour as *t*.................. Rom 13:9
have it to *t* before God........................ Rom 14:22
shalt love thy neighbour as *t*.................. Gal 5:14
considering *t*, lest thou also be.................. Gal 6:1
to behave *t* in the house of God............. 1Ti 3:15
exercise *t* rather unto godliness................. 1Ti 4:7
give *t* wholly to them............................... 1Ti 4:15
Take heed unto *t*, and unto the............... 1Ti 4:16
doing this thou shalt both save *t*............ 1Ti 4:16
keep *t* pure............................................... 1Ti 5:22
from such withdraw *t*.................................. 1Ti 6:5
Study to shew *t* approved unto God ...... 2Ti 2:15
In all things shewing *t* a pattern .......... Titus 2:7
shalt love thy neighbour as *t*..................... Jas 2:8

**TIARAS** See HOODS.

**TIBERIAS** (*ti-be'-re-as*) *A city on the Sea of Galilee.*
of Galilee, which is the sea of *T*.................. Jn 6:1
there came other boats from *T*................... Jn 6:23
to the disciples at the sea of *T* ................. Jn 21:1

**TIBERIUS** (*ti-be'-re-us*) See CAESAR. *A Roman emperor.*
year of the reign of *T* Caesar...................... Lk 3:1

**TIBHATH** (*tib'-hath*) *A city in Aram Zobah.*
Likewise from *T*, and from Chun,........ 1Chr 18:8

**TIBNI** (*tib'-ni*) *Son of Ginath.*
followed *T* the son of Ginath............... 1Kin 16:21
that followed *T* the son of Ginath...... 1Kin 16:22
so *T* died, and Omri reigned................. 1Kin 16:22

**TIDAL** (*ti'-dal*) *A king of Goyim.*
of Elam, and *T* king of nations.............. Gen 14:1
with *T* king of nations, and..................... Gen 14:9

**TIDINGS**
when Laban heard the *t* of Jacob........ Gen 29:13
the people heard these evil *t*................... Ex 33:4
when she heard the *t* that the ark......... 1Sa 4:19
told the *t* in the ears of the..................... 1Sa 11:4
they told him the *t* of the men of.............. 1Sa 11:5
upon Saul when he heard those *t*............. 1Sa 11:6
woman alive, to bring *t* to Gath .......... 1Sa 27:11
years old when the *t* came of Saul.......... 2Sa 4:4
thinking to have brought good *t* ........... 2Sa 4:10
have given him a reward for his *t*.......... 2Sa 4:10
that *t* came to David, saying,............... 2Sa 13:30
me now run, and bear the king *t*............ 2Sa 18:19
Thou shalt not bear *t* this day............... 2Sa 18:20
but thou shalt bear *t* another day.......... 2Sa 18:20
but this day thou shalt bear no *t*........... 2Sa 18:20
seeing that thou hast no *t* ready ........... 2Sa 18:22
be alone, there is *t* in his mouth........... 2Sa 18:25
the king said, He also bringeth *t* .......... 2Sa 18:26
a good man, and cometh with good *t*.. 2Sa 18:27
and Cushi said, *T*, my lord the............... 2Sa 18:31
a valiant man, and bringest good *t* ........ 1Kin 1:42
Then *t* came to Joab.................................. 1Kin 2:28
I am sent to thee with heavy *t* .............. 1Kin 14:6
this day is a day of good *t*....................... 2Kin 7:9
to carry *t* unto their idols, and ............. 1Chr 10:9
He shall not be afraid of evil *t*................... Ps 112:7
O Zion, that bringest good *t* ..................... Is 40:9
O Jerusalem, that bringest good *t* ............. Is 40:9
one that bringeth good *t*.......................... Is 41:27
feet of him that bringeth good *t*................. Is 52:7
that bringeth good *t* of good ..................... Is 52:7
me to preach good *t* unto the meek ........ Is 61:1
man who brought *t* to my father............. Jer 20:15
Jerusalem heard *t* of them ..................... Jer 37:5
for they have heard evil *t*........................ Jer 49:23
that thou shalt answer, For the *t* ........... Eze 21:7
But *t* out of the east and out of.......... Dan 11:44
feet of him that bringeth good *t*........... Nah 1:15
and to shew thee these glad *t*................... Lk 1:19
I bring you good *t* of great joy.................. Lk 2:10
shewing the glad *t* of the kingdom............ Lk 8:1
Then *t* of these things came unto....... Acts 11:22
And we declare unto you glad *t*........... Acts 13:32
*t* came unto the chief captain of......... Acts 21:31
bring glad *t* of good things................... Rom 10:15
brought us good *t* of your faith................. 1Th 3:6

**TIE**
*t* the kine to the cart, and bring .............. 1Sa 6:7
heart, and *t* them about thy neck ........ Prov 6:21

**TIED**
they *t* unto it a lace of blue, to............... Ex 39:31
*t* them to the cart, and shut up ............... 1Sa 6:10
voice of man, but horses *t*..................... 2Kin 7:10
man, but horses *t*, and asses *t*............... 2Kin 7:10
ye shall find an ass *t*, and a colt................ Mt 21:2
into it, ye shall find a colt *t*...................... Mk 11:2
found the colt *t* by the door........................ Mk 11:4
entering ye shall find a colt *t*.................... Lk 19:30

**TIGLATH-PILESER** (*tig''-lath-pi-le'-zur*) See TILGATH-PILNESER. *An Assyrian king.*
of Israel came *T* king of Assyria.......... 2Kin 15:29
messengers to *T* king of Assyria.......... 2Kin 16:7
to meet *T* king of Assyria...................... 2Kin 16:10

**TIGRIS** See HIDDEKEL.

**TIKVAH** (*tik'-vah*) See TIKVATH.
*1. Father-in-law of Huldah.*
the wife of Shallum the son of *T*........ 2Kin 22:14
*2. Father of Jahaziah.*
Jahaziah the son of *T* were .................... Ezr 10:15

**TIKVATH** (*tik'-vath*) See TIKVAH. *Same as Tikvah 1.*
the wife of Shallum the son of *T*........ 2Chr 34:22

**TIL**
*t* the Assyrian founded it for .................... Is 23:13

**TILE**
also, son of man, take thee a *t*.................. Eze 4:1

**TILGATH-PILNESER** (*til''-gath-pil-ne'-zur*) See TIGLATH-PILESER. *Same as Tiglath-pileser.*
whom *T* king of Assyria carried............ 1Chr 5:6
the spirit of *T* king of Assyria,............. 1Chr 5:26
*T* king of Assyria came unto him,....... 2Chr 28:20

**TILING**
let him down through the *t* with ............. Lk 5:19

**TILL**
was not a man to *t* the ground................ Gen 2:5
*t* thou return unto the ground ............... Gen 3:19
to *t* the ground from whence he.............. Gen 3:23
any thing *t* thou be come thither........ Gen 19:22
*t* they roll the stone from the.................. Gen 29:8
house, *t* Shelah my son be grown ....... Gen 38:11
give me a pledge, *t* thou send it........... Gen 38:17
*t* thy people pass over, O LORD,............. Ex 15:16
*t* the people pass over, which................. Ex 15:16
no man leave of it *t* the morning........... Ex 16:19
And they laid it up *t* the morning.......... Ex 16:24
*t* Moses had done speaking with ........... Ex 34:33
then they journeyed not *t* the day.......... Ex 40:37
the people journeyed not *t* Miriam..... Num 12:15
them with stones, *t* they die................. Deut 17:5
thee, *t* thou be destroyed..................... Deut 28:45
*t* all the people that were men of .......... Josh 5:6
in the camp, *t* they were whole.............. Josh 5:8
us) *t* we have drawn them from the ...... Josh 8:6
*t* they were consumed, that the .......... Josh 10:20
they tarried *t* they were ashamed ........ Judg 3:25
*t* thou come unto Gaza, and left no ...... Judg 6:4
even *t* thou come to Minnith, even ... Judg 11:33
And Samson lay *t* midnight, and.......... Judg 16:3
her lord was, *t* it was light.................. Judg 19:26
abode there *t* even before God, and..... Judg 21:2
tarry for them *t* they were grown .......... Ruth 1:13
*t* I come to thee, and shew thee .............. 1Sa 10:8
not sit down *t* he come hither.............. 1Sa 16:11
*t* I know what God will do for me ......... 1Sa 22:3
or ought else, *t* the sun be down............ 2Sa 3:35
shall *t* the land for him, and thou .......... 2Sa 9:10
away dung, *t* it be all gone ................ 1Kin 14:10
*t* the blood gushed out upon them....... 1Kin 18:28
they urged him *t* he was ashamed......... 2Kin 2:17
he sat on her knees *t* noon .................. 2Kin 4:20
if we tarry *t* the morning light,............. 2Kin 7:9
*t* he had destroyed him, according....... 2Kin 10:17
*t* thou have consumed them................. 2Kin 13:17
Syria *t* thou hadst consumed it............. 2Kin 13:19
*t* he had filled Jerusalem from............ 2Kin 21:16
helped, *t* he was strong....................... 2Chr 26:15
*t* the work was ended, and until.......... 2Chr 29:34
his people, *t* there was no remedy ..... 2Chr 36:16
*t* there stood up a priest with ................ Ezr 2:63
*t* the matter came to Darius .................... Ezr 5:5
with us *t* thou hadst consumed us......... Ezr 9:14
me over *t* I come into Judah .................. Neh 2:7
*t* we come in the midst among them.... Neh 4:11
the morning *t* the stars appeared ........ Neh 4:21
*t* there stood up a priest with................ Neh 7:65
not be opened *t* after the sabbath ....... Neh 13:19
nor let me alone *t* I swallow down......... Job 7:19
*T* he fill thy mouth with laughing ........... Job 8:21
*t* he shall accomplish, as an .................. Job 14:6
*t* the heavens be no more, they............ Job 14:12
will I wait, *t* my change come............... Job 14:14
*t* I die I will not remove mine ................ Job 27:5
Elihu had waited *t* Job had spoken ........ Job 32:4
his wickedness *t* thou find none .............. Ps 10:15
I turn again *t* they were consumed....... Ps 18:37
*t* every one submit himself with ............. Ps 68:30
*T* a dart strike through his liver .......... Prov 7:23
man keepeth it in *t* afterwards............ Prov 29:11
*t* I might see what was that good ........... Eccl 2:3
nor awake my love, *t* he please............. Song 2:7
nor awake my love, *t* he please.............. Song 3:5
*t* there be no place, that they..................... Is 5:8
until night, *t* wine inflame them ............... Is 5:11
not be purged from you *t* ye die............. Is 22:14
*t* ye be left as a beacon upon the............ Is 30:17
I reckoned *t* morning, that, as a .............. Is 38:13
*t* he have set judgment in the................... Is 42:4
*t* he establish, and *t* he make.................. Is 62:7
in Tophet, *t* there be no place ................. Jer 7:32
them, *t* I have consumed them ................. Jer 9:16
*t* there be no place to bury .................... Jer 19:11
*t* he have performed the thoughts......... Jer 23:20
*t* they be consumed from off the .......... Jer 24:10
and they shall *t* it, and dwell ................. Jer 27:11
will destroy *t* they have enough ............. Jer 49:9
them, *t* I have consumed them ............... Jer 49:37
*t* he had cast them out from his.............. Jer 52:3
put him in prison *t* the day of................ Jer 52:11
*T* the LORD look down, and behold ...... Lam 3:50
*t* thou hast ended the days of thy........... Eze 4:8
for from my youth up even *t* now ......... Eze 4:14
*t* I have caused my fury to rest ........... Eze 24:13
*t* iniquity was found in thee ................ Eze 28:15
*t* ye have scattered them abroad .......... Eze 34:21
*t* the buriers have buried it in.............. Eze 39:15
And ye shall eat fat *t* ye be full ........... Eze 39:19
drink blood *t* ye be drunken, of............. Eze 39:19
*t* a man come over against Hamath .... Eze 47:20
before me, *t* the time be changed............ Dan 2:9
Thou sawest *t* that a stone was............. Dan 2:34
*t* seven times pass over him................... Dan 4:23
*t* thou know that the most High ........... Dan 4:25
*t* his hairs were grown like .................... Dan 4:33
*t* he knew that the most high God....... Dan 5:21
he laboured *t* the going down of .......... Dan 6:14
I beheld *t* the wings thereof were .......... Dan 7:4
I beheld *t* the thrones were cast.............. Dan 7:9
I beheld even *t* the beast was................. Dan 7:11
at all, *t* three whole weeks were............ Dan 10:3
shall prosper *t* the indignation ............. Dan 11:36
sealed *t* the time of the end .................... Dan 12:9
But go thou thy way *t* the end be....... Dan 12:13
*t* they acknowledge their offence,.......... Hos 5:15
*t* he come and rain righteousness....... Hos 10:12
not have stolen *t* they had enough .......... Obad 5
*t* he might see what would become..... Jonah 4:5
gnaw not the bones *t* the morrow......... Zeph 3:3
knew her not *t* she had brought ............. Mt 1:25
*t* it came and stood over where the .......... Mt 2:9
*T* heaven and earth pass, one jot............. Mt 5:18
from the law, *t* all be fulfilled................... Mt 5:18
*t* thou hast paid the uttermost ................ Mt 5:26
there abide *t* ye go thence...................... Mt 10:11
Israel, *t* the Son of man be come........... Mt 10:23
*t* he send forth judgment unto ............... Mt 12:20
of meal, *t* the whole was leavened ........ Mt 13:33
*t* they see the Son of man coming.......... Mt 16:28
*t* seven times?........................................... Mt 18:21
prison, *t* he should pay the debt............ Mt 18:30
*t* he should pay all that was due............ Mt 18:34
*t* I make thine enemies thy .................... Mt 22:44
*t* ye shall say, Blessed is he ................. Mt 23:39
*t* all these things be fulfilled.................. Mt 24:34
there abide *t* ye depart from that .......... Mk 6:10
*t* they have seen the kingdom of............... Mk 9:1
*t* the Son of man were risen from............ Mk 9:9
*t* I make thine enemies thy.................... Mk 12:36
*t* all these things be done...................... Mk 13:30
was in the deserts *t* the day of .................. Lk 1:80
*t* they see the kingdom of God..................... Lk 9:27
I straitened *t* it be accomplished ............ Lk 12:50
*t* thou hast paid the very last.................. Lk 12:59
*t* I shall dig about it, and dung................. Lk 13:8
of meal, *t* the whole was leavened......... Lk 13:21
and seek diligently *t* she find it ............... Lk 15:8
*t* I have eaten and drunken........................ Lk 17:8
said unto them, Occupy *t* I come............ Lk 19:13
*T* I make thine enemies thy ................... Lk 20:43
not pass away, *t* all be fulfilled.............. Lk 21:32
*t* thou hast denied me thrice.................... Jn 13:38
If I will that he tarry *t* I come ................ Jn 21:22
If I will that he tarry *t* I come ............... Jn 21:23
*T* another king arose, which knew....... Acts 7:18
the cities, *t* he came to Caesarea.......... Acts 8:40
even *t* break of day, so he.................... Acts 20:11
*t* we were out of the city ........................ Acts 21:5
nor drink *t* they had killed Paul........... Acts 23:12
nor drink *t* they have killed him.......... Acts 23:21
kept *t* I might send him to Caesar ..... Acts 25:21
prophets, from morning *t* evening........ Acts 28:23
shew the Lord's death *t* he come ........ 1Cor 11:26
*t* he hath put all enemies under.......... 1Cor 15:25
*t* the seed should come to whom............. Gal 3:19
*T* we all come in the unity of the........... Eph 4:13
without offence *t* the day of ................... Phil 1:10
*T* I come, give attendance to.................... 1Ti 4:13
*t* his enemies be made his.................... Heb 10:13
have already hold fast *t* I come............. Rev 2:25
*t* we have sealed the servants of............... Rev 7:3
*t* the seven plagues of the seven............. Rev 15:8
*t* the thousand years should be .............. Rev 20:3

**TILLAGE**
did the work of the field for *t* 1Chr 27:26
tithes in all the cities of our *t* Neh 10:37
Much food is in the *t* of the poor Prov 13:23

**TILLED**
turn unto you, and ye shall be *t* Eze 36:9
And the desolate land shall be *t* Eze 36:34

**TILLER**
but Cain was a *t* of the ground Gen 4:2

**TILLEST**
When thou *t* the ground, it shall Gen 4:12

**TILLETH**
He that *t* his land shall be Prov 12:11
He that *t* his land shall have Prov 28:19

**TILON** (*ti'-lon*) *A descendant of Judah.*
Rinnah, Ben-hanan, and *T* 1Chr 4:20

**TIMAEUS** (*ti-me'-us*) See BARTIMAEUS. *Father of Bartimaeus.*
blind Bartimaeus, the son of *T* Mk 10:46

**TIMBER**
to set them, and in carving of *t* Ex 31:5
the *t* thereof, and all the morter Lev 14:45
to hew *t* like unto the Sidonians 1Kin 5:6
thy desire concerning *t* of cedar 1Kin 5:8
of cedar, and concerning *t* of fir 1Kin 5:8
so they prepared *t* and stones to 1Kin 5:18
on the house with *t* of cedar 1Kin 6:10
the *t* thereof, wherewith Baasha 1Kin 15:22
and hewers of stone, and to buy *t* 2Kin 12:12
builders, and masons, and to buy *t* 2Kin 22:6
*t* of cedars, with masons and 1Chr 14:1
*t* also and stone have I prepared 1Chr 22:14
hewers and workers of stone and *t* 1Chr 22:15
can skill to cut *t* in Lebanon 2Chr 2:8
Even to prepare me *t* in abundance 2Chr 2:9
servants, the hewers that cut *t* 2Chr 2:10
brass, in iron, in stone, and in *t* 2Chr 2:14
the *t* thereof, wherewith Baasha 2Chr 16:6
*t* for couplings, and to floor the 2Chr 34:11
*t* is laid in the walls, and this Ezr 5:8
great stones, and a row of new *t* Ezr 6:4
let *t* be pulled down from his Ezr 6:11
that he may give me *t* to make Neh 2:8
shall lay thy stones and thy *t* Eze 26:12
beam out of the *t* shall answer it Hab 2:11
consume it with the *t* thereof Zec 5:4

**TIMBREL**
of Aaron, took a *t* in her hand Ex 15:20
They take the *t* and harp, and Job 21:12
a psalm, and bring hither the *t* Ps 81:2
sing praises unto him with the *t* Ps 149:3
Praise him with the *t* and dance Ps 150:4

**TIMBRELS**
women went out after her with *t* Ex 15:20
came out to meet him with *t* Judg 11:34
harps, and on psalteries, and on *t* 2Sa 6:5
and with psalteries, and with *t* 1Chr 13:8
were the damsels playing with *t* Ps 68:25

**TIME** See PREFACE.

**TIMES**
he hath supplanted me these two *t* Gen 27:36
me, and changed my wages ten *t* Gen 31:7
thou hast changed my wages ten *t* Gen 31:41
himself to the ground seven *t* Gen 33:3
five *t* so much as any of theirs Gen 43:34
Three *t* thou shalt keep a feast Ex 23:14
Three *t* in the year all thy males Ex 23:17
the blood seven *t* before the LORD Lev 4:6
it seven *t* before the LORD Lev 4:17
thereof upon the altar seven *t* Lev 8:11
cleansed from the leprosy seven *t* Lev 14:7
finger seven *t* before the LORD Lev 14:16
left hand seven *t* before the LORD Lev 14:27
and sprinkle the house seven *t* Lev 14:51
that he come not at all *t* into Lev 16:2
the blood with his finger seven *t* Lev 16:14
upon it with his finger seven *t* Lev 16:19
ye use enchantment, nor observe *t* Lev 19:26
unto thee, seven *t* seven years Lev 25:8
you seven *t* more for your sins Lev 26:18
I will bring seven *t* more plagues Lev 26:21
you yet seven *t* for your sins Lev 26:24
you seven *t* for your sins Lev 26:28
have tempted me now these ten *t* Num 14:22
of the congregation seven *t* Num 19:4
hast smitten me these three *t* Num 22:28
smitten thine ass these three *t* Num 22:32
and turned from me these three *t* Num 22:33
he went not, as at other *t* Num 24:1
blessed them these three *t* Num 24:10
thousand *t* so many more as ye are Deut 1:11
The Emims dwelt therein in *t* past Deut 2:10
and hated him not in *t* past Deut 4:42
Three *t* in a year shall all thy Deut 16:16
divination, or an observer of *t* Deut 18:10
hearkened unto observers of *t* Deut 18:14
ye shall compass the city seven *t* Josh 6:4
after the same manner seven *t* Josh 6:15
they compassed the city seven *t* Josh 6:15
at *t* in the camp of Dan between Judg 13:25
thou hast mocked me these three *t* Judg 16:15
will go out as at other *t* before Judg 16:20
against Gibeah, as at other *t* Judg 20:30
people, and kill, as at other *t* Judg 20:31
and stood, and called as at other *t* 1Sa 3:10
with his hand, as at other *t* 1Sa 18:10
was in his presence, as in *t* past 1Sa 19:7
sat upon his seat, as at other *t* 1Sa 20:25
ground, and bowed himself three *t* 1Sa 20:41
Ye sought for David in *t* past to 2Sa 3:17
of his people Israel at all *t* 1Kin 8:59
three *t* in a year did Solomon 1Kin 9:25
himself upon the child three *t* 1Kin 17:21
And he said, Go again seven *t* 1Kin 18:43
How many *t* shall I adjure thee 1Kin 22:16
and the child sneezed seven *t* 2Kin 4:35
Go and wash in Jordan seven *t* 2Kin 5:10
dipped himself seven *t* in Jordan 2Kin 5:14
have smitten five or six *t* 2Kin 13:19
Three *t* did Joash beat him, and 2Kin 13:25
of ancient *t* that I have formed 2Kin 19:25
through the fire, and observed *t* 2Kin 21:6
that had understanding of the *t* 1Chr 12:32
hundred *t* so many more as they be 1Chr 21:3
the *t* that went over him, and over 1Chr 29:30
three *t* in the year, even in the 2Chr 8:13
in those *t* there was no peace to 2Chr 15:5
How many *t* shall I adjure thee 2Chr 18:15
also he observed *t*, and used 2Chr 33:6
in our cities come at appointed *t* Ezr 10:14
came, they said unto us ten *t* Neh 4:12
unto me four *t* after this sort Neh 6:4
many *t* didst thou deliver them Neh 9:28
at *t* appointed year by year, to Neh 10:34
at *t* appointed, and for the Neh 13:31
to the wise men, which knew the *t* Est 1:13
of Purim in their *t* appointed Est 9:31
These ten *t* have ye reproached me Job 19:3
seeing *t* are not hidden from the Job 24:1
a refuge in *t* of trouble Ps 9:9
thou thyself in *t* of trouble Ps 10:1
of earth, purified seven *t* Ps 12:6
My *t* are in thy hand Ps 31:15
I will bless the LORD at all *t* Ps 34:1
in their days, in the *t* of old Ps 44:1
Trust in him at all *t* Ps 62:8
of old, the years of ancient *t* Ps 77:5
that doeth righteousness at all *t* Ps 106:3
Many *t* did he deliver them Ps 106:43
hath unto thy judgments at all *t* Ps 119:20
Seven *t* a day do I praise thee Ps 119:164
her breasts satisfy thee at all *t* Prov 5:19
A friend loveth at all *t*, and a Prov 17:17
For a just man falleth seven *t* Prov 24:16
a sinner do evil an hundred *t* Eccl 8:12
shall be alone in his appointed *t* Is 14:31
shall be the stability of thy *t* Is 33:6
and of ancient *t*, that I have Is 37:26
from ancient *t* the things that Is 46:10
heaven knoweth her appointed *t* Jer 8:7
of the *t* that are far off Eze 12:27
he found them ten *t* better than Dan 1:20
And he changeth the *t* and the Dan 2:21
heat the furnace one seven *t* more Dan 3:19
let seven *t* pass over him Dan 4:16
till seven *t* pass over him Dan 4:23
seven *t* shall pass over thee, Dan 4:25
seven *t* shall pass over thee, Dan 4:32
upon his knees three *t* a day Dan 6:10
maketh his petition three *t* a day Dan 6:13
ten thousand *t* ten thousand stood Dan 7:10
most High, and think to change *t* Dan 7:25
into his hand until a time and *t* Dan 7:25
and the wall, even in troublous *t* Dan 9:25
that strengthened her in these *t* Dan 11:6
in those *t* there shall many stand Dan 11:14
that it shall be for a time, *t* Dan 12:7
ye not discern the signs of the *t* Mt 16:3
till seven *t* Mt 18:21
say not unto thee, Until seven *t* Mt 18:22
but, Until seventy *t* seven Mt 18:22
against thee seven *t* in a day Lk 17:4
seven *t* in a day turn again to Lk 17:4
until the *t* of the Gentiles be Lk 21:24
you to know the *t* or the seasons Acts 1:7
when the *t* of refreshing shall Acts 3:19
*t* of restitution of all things Acts 3:21
And this was done three *t* Acts 11:10
Who in *t* past suffered all Acts 14:16
determined the *t* before appointed Acts 17:26
the *t* of this ignorance God Acts 17:30
For as ye in *t* past have not Rom 11:30
Of the Jews five *t* received I 2Cor 11:24
in *t* past now preacheth the faith Gal 1:23
Ye observe days, and months, and *t* Gal 4:10
dispensation of the fulness of *t* Eph 1:10
*t* past in the lusts of our flesh Eph 2:3
But of the *t* and the seasons, 1Th 5:1
that in the latter *t* some shall 1Ti 4:1
Which in his *t* he shall shew, who 1Ti 6:15
last days perilous *t* shall come 2Ti 3:1
But hath in due *t* manifested his Titus 1:3
God, who at sundry *t* and in divers Heb 1:1
of the angels said he at any *t* Heb 1:13
manifest in these last *t* for you 1Pet 1:20
was ten thousand *t* ten thousand Rev 5:11
she is nourished for a time, and *t* Rev 12:14

**TIMNA** (*tim'-nah*) See TIMNATH.
*1. Concubine of Eliphaz.*
*T* was concubine to Eliphaz Esau's Gen 36:12
*2. Daughter of Seir.*
and Lotan's sister was *T* Gen 36:22
and *T* was Lotan's sister 1Chr 1:39
*3. A son of Eliphaz.*
Zephi, and Gatam, Kenaz, and *T* 1Chr 1:36

**TIMNAH** (*tim'-nah*) See TIMNA, TIMNATH.
*1. A chief of Edom.*
duke *T*, duke Alvah, duke Jetheth, Gen 36:40
duke *T*, duke Aliah, duke Jetheth, 1Chr 1:51
*2. A city in Judah.*
Cain, Gibeah, and *T* Josh 15:57
*3. A city in Dan.*
Beth-shemesh, and passed on to *T* Josh 15:10
*T* with the villages thereof, 2Chr 28:18

**TIMNATH** (*tim'-nath*) See THIMNATHAH, TIMNAH.
*1. Same as Timnah 2.*
up unto his sheepshearers to *T* Gen 38:12
goeth up to *T* to shear his sheep Gen 38:13
place, which is by the way to *T* Gen 38:14
*2. Same as Timnah 3.*
And Samson went down to *T* Judg 14:1
saw a woman in *T* of the daughters Judg 14:1
I have seen a woman in *T* of the Judg 14:2
and his father and his mother, to *T* Judg 14:5
and came to the vineyards of *T* Judg 14:5

**TIMNATH-HERES** (*tim''-nath-he'-rez*) See TIMNATH-SERAH. *Land near Mount Ephraim.*
border of his inheritance in *T* Judg 2:9

**TIMNATH-SERAH** (*tim''-nath-se'-rah*) See TIMANTH-HERES. *Same as Timnath-heres.*
he asked, even *T* in mount Ephraim Josh 19:50
border of his inheritance in *T* Josh 24:30

**TIMNITE** (*tim'-nite*) *An inhabitant of Timnath.*
Samson, the son in law of the *T* Judg 15:6

**TIMON** (*ti'-mon*) *A leader in the Jerusalem church.*
and Prochorus, and Nicanor, and *T* Acts 6:5

**TIMOTHEOUS**
and Fortunatus, and Achaicus, and *T* 1Cor s

**TIMOTHEUS** (*tim-o'-the-us*) See TIMOTHY. *Same as Timothy.*
disciple was there, named *T* Acts 16:1
but Silas and *T* abode there still Acts 17:14
*T* for to come to him with all Acts 17:15
*T* were come from Macedonia, Paul Acts 18:5
them that ministered unto him, *T* Acts 19:22
and Gaius of Derbe, and *T* Acts 20:4
*T* my workfellow, and Lucius, and Rom 16:21
this cause have I sent unto you *T* 1Cor 4:17
Now if *T* come, see that he may be 1Cor 16:10
us, even by me and Silvanus and *T* 2Cor 1:19
Paul and *T*, the servants of Jesus Phil 1:1
Jesus to send *T* shortly unto you Phil 2:19
will of God, and *T* our brother, Col 1:1
Paul, and Silvanus, and *T*, unto the 1Th 1:1
And sent *T*, our brother, and 1Th 3:2
But now when *T* came from you unto 1Th 3:6
Paul, and Silvanus, and *T*, unto the 2Th 1:1
The second epistle unto *T* 2Ti s

**TIMOTHY** (*tim'-o-thy*) See TIMOTHEUS. *A co-worker with Paul.*
*T* our brother, unto the church of 2Cor 1:1
Unto *T*, my own son in the faith 1Ti 1:2
charge I commit unto thee, son *T* 1Ti 1:18
O *T*, keep that which is committed 1Ti 6:20
The first to *T* was written from 1Ti s
To *T*, my dearly beloved son 2Ti 1:2
*T* our brother, unto Philemon our Philem 1
our brother *T* is set at liberty Heb 13:23
to the Hebrews from Italy by *T* Heb s

**TIN**
the brass, the iron, the *t* Num 31:22
thy dross, and take away all thy *t* Is 1:25
all they are brass, and *t*, and iron Eze 22:18
and brass, and iron, and lead, and *t* Eze 22:20
with silver, iron, *t*, and lead, Eze 27:12

**TINGLE**
every one that heareth it shall *t* 1Sa 3:11
of it, both his ears shall *t* 2Kin 21:12
heareth, his ears shall *t* Jer 19:3

**TINKLING**
making a *t* with their feet Is 3:16
*t* ornaments about their feet Is 3:18
as sounding brass, or a *t* cymbal 1Cor 13:1

**TIP**
put it upon the *t* of the right Ex 29:20
upon the *t* of the right ear of Ex 29:20
put it upon the *t* of Aaron's Lev 8:23
upon the *t* of their right ear Lev 8:24
priest shall put it upon the *t* of Lev 14:14
shall the priest put upon the *t* Lev 14:17
put it upon the *t* of the right Lev 14:25
that is in his hand upon the *t* of Lev 14:28
that he may dip the *t* of his Lk 16:24

**TIPHSAH** (*tif'-sah*)
*1. A city on the Euphrates River.*
from *T* even to Azzah, over all 1Kin 4:24
*2. A city in Judah.*
Then Menahem smote *T* 2Kin 15:16

**TIRAS** (*Ti'-ras*) *A son of Japheth.*
Javan, and Tubal, and Meshech, and *T* Gen 10:2
Javan, and Tubal, and Meshech, and *T* 1Chr 1:5

**TIRATHITES** (*ti'-rath-ites*) *A family of scribes.*
the *T*, the Shimeathites, and ........ 1Chr 2:55

**TIRE**
bind the *t* of thine head upon ........ Eze 24:17

**TIRED**
*t* her head, and looked out at a ........ 2Kin 9:30

**TIRES**
their round *t* like the moon,........ Is 3:18
your *t* shall be upon your heads,........ Eze 24:23

**TIRHAKAH** (*tur-ha'-kah*) *A king of Ethiopia.*
heard say of *T* king of Ethiopia ........ 2Kin 19:9
say concerning *T* king of Ethiopia ........ Is 37:9

**TIRHANAH** (*tur-ha'-nah*) *A son of Caleb.*
concubine, bare Sheber, and *T*........ 1Chr 2:48

**TIRIA** (*tir'-e-ah*) *A descendant of Judah.*
Ziph, and Ziphah, *T*, and Asareel........ 1Chr 4:16

**TIRSHATHA** (*tur'-sha-thah*) *Persian governors of Judah.*
the *T* said unto them, that they........ Ezr 2:63
the *T* said unto them, that they........ Neh 7:65
The *T* gave to the treasure a........ Neh 7:70
And Nehemiah, which is the *T*........ Neh 8:9
that sealed were, Nehemiah, the *T*........ Neh 10:1

**TIRZAH** (*tur'-zah*)
*1. A daughter of Zelophehad.*
and Noah, Hoglah, Milcah, and *T*........ Num 26:33
Noah, and Hoglah, and Milcah, and *T* Num 27:1
For Mahlah, *T*, and Hoglah, and........ Num 36:11
and Noah, Hoglah, Milcah, and *T*........ Josh 17:3
*2. A city in Ephraim.*
The king of *T*, one........ Josh 12:24
arose, and departed, and came to *T*... 1Kin 14:17
building of Ramah, and dwelt in *T*..... 1Kin 15:21
to reign over all Israel in *T*........ 1Kin 15:33
his fathers, and was buried in *T*........ 1Kin 16:6
Baasha to reign over Israel in *T*........ 1Kin 16:8
against him, as he was in *T*........ 1Kin 16:9
of Arza steward of his house in *T*........ 1Kin 16:9
did Zimri reign seven days in *T*........ 1Kin 16:15
with him, and they besieged *T*........ 1Kin 16:17
six years reigned he in *T*........ 1Kin 16:23
the son of Gadi went up from *T*........ 2Kin 15:14
and the coasts thereof from *T*........ 2Kin 15:16
art beautiful, O my love, as *T*........ Song 6:4

**TISHBE** See TISHBITE.

**TISHBITE** (*tish'-bite*) *An inhabitant of Tishbeh.*
And Elijah the *T*, who was of the........ 1Kin 17:1
of the LORD came to Elijah the *T*........ 1Kin 21:17
of the LORD came to Elijah the *T*........ 1Kin 21:28
of the LORD said to Elijah the *T*........ 2Kin 1:3
And he said, It is Elijah the *T*........ 2Kin 1:8
spake by his servant Elijah the *T*........ 2Kin 9:36

**TITHE**
all the *t* of the land, whether of........ Lev 27:30
And concerning the *t* of the herd........ Lev 27:32
LORD, even a tenth part of the *t*........ Num 18:26
thy gates the *t* of thy corn ........ Deut 12:17
Thou shalt truly *t* all the........ Deut 14:22
the *t* of thy corn, of thy wine,........ Deut 14:23
thou shalt bring forth all the *t*........ Deut 14:28
the *t* of all things brought they........ 2Chr 31:5
also brought in the *t* of oxen ........ 2Chr 31:6
the *t* of holy things which were........ 2Chr 31:6
the Levites shall bring up the *t*........ Neh 10:38
all Judah the *t* of the corn ........ Neh 13:12
for ye pay *t* of mint and anise and........ Mt 23:23
for ye *t* mint and rue and all........ Lk 11:42

**TITHES**
And he gave him *t* of all........ Gen 14:20
will at all redeem ought of his *t* ........ Lev 27:31
But the *t* of the children of........ Num 18:24
the *t* which I have given you from.... Num 18:26
unto the LORD of all your *t*........ Num 18:28
and your sacrifices, and your *t* ........ Deut 12:6
and your sacrifices, your *t* ........ Deut 12:11
the *t* of thine increase the third........ Deut 26:12
brought in the offerings and the *t*........ 2Chr 31:12
the *t* of our ground unto the........ Neh 10:37
the *t* in all the cities of our........ Neh 10:37
Levites, when the Levites take *t*........ Neh 10:38
the *t* unto the house of our God........ Neh 10:38
for the firstfruits, and for the *t* ........ Neh 12:44
the *t* of the corn, the new wine,........ Neh 13:5
and your *t* after three years........ Amos 4:4
In *t* and offerings........ Mal 3:8
Bring ye all the *t* into the........ Mal 3:10
I give *t* of all that I possess........ Lk 18:12
have a commandment to take *t* of........ Heb 7:5
from them received *t* of Abraham........ Heb 7:6
And here men that die receive *t*........ Heb 7:8
say, Levi also, who receiveth *t*........ Heb 7:9
payed *t* in Abraham ........ Heb 7:9

**TITHING**
end of *t* all the tithes of thine........ Deut 26:12
year, which is the year of *t*........ Deut 26:12

**TITIUS** See JUSTUS.

**TITIUS JUSTUS** See JUSTUS.

**TITLE**
What *t* is that that I see........ 2Kin 23:17
And Pilate wrote a *t*, and put it on........ Jn 19:19
This *t* then read many of the Jews........ Jn 19:20

**TITLES**
let me give flattering *t* unto man........ Job 32:21
I know not to give flattering *t* ........ Job 32:22

**TITTLE**
one jot or one *t* shall in no wise........ Mt 5:18
than one *t* of the law to fail........ Lk 16:17

**TITUS** (*ti'-tus*) *A co-worker with Paul.*
because I found not *T* my brother........ 2Cor 2:13
comforted us by the coming of *T*........ 2Cor 7:6
more joyed we for the joy of *T*........ 2Cor 7:13
boasting, which I made before *T*........ 2Cor 7:14
Insomuch that we desired *T*........ 2Cor 8:6
care into the heart of *T* for you........ 2Cor 8:16
Whether any do enquire of *T*........ 2Cor 8:23
I desired *T*, and with him I sent a...... 2Cor 12:18
Did *T* make a gain of you........ 2Cor 12:18
a city of Macedonia, by *T*........ 2Cor *s*
Barnabas, and took *T* with me also........ Gal 2:1
But neither *T*, who was with me,........ Gal 2:3
to Galatia, *T* unto Dalmatia........ 2Ti 4:10
To *T*, mine own son after the........ Titus 1:4
It was written to *T*, ordained the........ Titus *s*

**TIZITE** (*ti'-zite*) *Family name of Joha.*
and Joha his brother, the *T*........ 1Chr 11:45

**TO** See PREFACE.

**TOAH** (*to'-ah*) See NAHATH, TOHU. *An ancestor of Samuel.*
the son of Eliel, the son of *T*........ 1Chr 6:34

**TOB** (*tob*) *A district in Syria.*
and dwelt in the land of *T*........ Judg 11:3
Jephthah out of the land of *T*........ Judg 11:5

**TOB-ADONIJAH** (*tob''-ad-o-ni-jah*) *A Levite messenger of King Jehoshaphat.*
and Adonijah, and Tobijah, and *T*........ 2Chr 17:8

**TOBIAH** (*to-bi'-ah*) See TOBIJAH.
*1. A family of exiles.*
of Delaiah, the children of *T*........ Ezr 2:60
of Delaiah, the children of *T*........ Neh 7:62
*2. An Ammonite who opposed Nehemiah.*
*T* the servant, the Ammonite,........ Neh 2:10
*T* the servant, the Ammonite, and........ Neh 2:19
Now *T* the Ammonite was by him, and. Neh 4:3
pass, that when Sanballat, and *T*........ Neh 4:7
to pass, when Sanballat, and *T*........ Neh 6:1
for *T* and Sanballat had hired him........ Neh 6:12
My God, think thou upon *T*........ Neh 6:14
of Judah sent many letters unto *T*........ Neh 6:17
the letters of *T* came unto them........ Neh 6:17
*T* sent letters to put me in fear........ Neh 6:19
of our God, was allied unto *T*........ Neh 13:4
the evil that Eliashib did for *T*........ Neh 13:7
stuff of *T* out of the chamber........ Neh 13:8

**TOBIJAH** (*to-bi'-jah*) See TOBIAH.
*1. A Levite messenger of King Jehoshaphat.*
and Jehonathan, and Adonijah, and *T* 2Chr 17:8
*2. A clan leader of exiles.*
captivity, even of Heldai, of *T*........ Zec 6:10
crowns shall be to Helem, and to *T*........ Zec 6:14

**TOCHEN** (*to'-ken*) *A city in Simeon.*
were, Etam, and Ain, Rimmon, and *T*. 1Chr 4:32

**TODAY**
glorious was the king of Israel *t*........ 2Sa 6:20
*T* thy servant knoweth that I have...... 2Sa 14:22
*T* shall the house of Israel........ 2Sa 16:3

**TOE**
upon the great *t* of their right........ Ex 29:20
upon the great *t* of his right........ Lev 8:23
upon the great *t* of his right........ Lev 14:14
upon the great *t* of his right........ Lev 14:17
upon the great *t* of his right........ Lev 14:25
upon the great *t* of his right........ Lev 14:28

**TOES**
upon the great *t* of their right........ Lev 8:24
cut off his thumbs and his great *t*........ Judg 1:6
thumbs and their great *t* cut off........ Judg 1:7
fingers, and on every foot six *t*........ 2Sa 21:20
*t* were four and twenty, six on........ 1Chr 20:6
whereas thou sawest the feet and *t*........ Dan 2:41
as the *t* of the feet were part of........ Dan 2:42

**TOGARMAH** (*to-gar'-mah*) *A son of Gomer.*
Ashkenaz, and Riphath, and *T*........ Gen 10:3
Ashchenaz, and Riphath, and *T*........ 1Chr 1:6
They of the house of *T* traded in........ Eze 27:14
the house of *T* of the north ........ Eze 38:6

**TOGETHER** See PREFACE.
The rich and poor meet *t*........ Prov 22:2
three are gathered *t* in my name........ Mt 18:20
I have gathered thy children *t*........ Mt 23:37
What therefore God hath joined *t*........ Mk 10:9
And all that believed were *t*........ Acts 2:44
and had gathered the church *t*........ Acts 14:27
we know that all things work *t*........ Rom 8:28
We then, as workers *t* with him........ 2Cor 6:1
yoked *t* with unbelievers........ 2Cor 6:14
the assembling of ourselves *t*........ Heb 10:25

**TOHU** (*to'-hu*) See NAHATH, TOAH. *An ancestor of Samuel.*
the son of Elihu, the son of *T*........ 1Sa 1:1

**TOI** (*to'-i*) See TOU. *King of Hamath.*
When *T* king of Hamath heard that........ 2Sa 8:9
Then *T* sent Joram his son unto........ 2Sa 8:10
for Hadadezer had wars with *T*........ 2Sa 8:10

**TOIL**
*t* of our hands, because of the........ Gen 5:29
he, hath made me forget all my *t*........ Gen 41:51
they *t* not, neither do they spin........ Mt 6:28
they *t* not, they spin not ........ Lk 12:27

**TOILED**
we have *t* all the night, and have ........ Lk 5:5

**TOILING**
And he saw them *t* in rowing........ Mk 6:48

**TOKEN**
This is the *t* of the covenant ........ Gen 9:12
it shall be for a *t* of a covenant........ Gen 9:13
This is the *t* of the covenant,........ Gen 9:17
it shall be a *t* of the covenant ........ Gen 17:11
and this shall be a *t* unto thee........ Ex 3:12
a *t* upon the houses where ye are........ Ex 12:13
shall be for a *t* upon thine hand........ Ex 13:16
to be kept for a *t* against the........ Num 17:10
house, and give me a true *t*........ Josh 2:12
Shew me a *t* for good........ Ps 86:17
betrayed him had given them a *t*........ Mk 14:44
to them an evident *t* of perdition........ Phil 1:28
Which is a manifest *t* of the........ 2Th 1:5
which is the *t* in every epistle........ 2Th 3:17

**TOKENS**
bring forth the *t* of the damsel's........ Deut 22:15
yet these are the *t* of my........ Deut 22:17
the *t* of virginity be not found........ Deut 22:20
and do ye not know their *t*........ Job 21:29
parts are afraid at thy *t*........ Ps 65:8
Who sent *t* and wonders into the........ Ps 135:9
frustrateth the *t* of the liars........ Is 44:25

**TOKHATH** See TIKVATH.

**TOLA** (*to'-lah*) See TOLAITES.
*1. A son of Issachar.*
*T*, and Phuvah, and Job ........ Gen 46:13
of *T*, the family of the Tolaites........ Num 26:23
Now the sons of Issachar were, *T*........ 1Chr 7:1
And the sons of *T* ........ 1Chr 7:2
father's house, to wit, of *T*........ 1Chr 7:2
*2. A judge of Israel.*
defend Israel *T* the son of Puah ........ Judg 10:1

**TOLAD** (*to'-lad*) See EL-TOLAD. *A city in Simeon.*
And at Bilhah, and at Ezem, and at *T*. 1Chr 4:29

**TOLAITES** (*to'-lah-ites*) *Descendants of Tola.*
of Tola, the family of the *T*........ Num 26:23

**TOLD**
Who *t* thee that thou wast naked........ Gen 3:11
*t* his two brethren without........ Gen 9:22
escaped, and *t* Abram the Hebrew........ Gen 14:13
*t* all these things in their ears........ Gen 20:8
the place of which God had *t* him........ Gen 22:3
the place which God had *t* him of........ Gen 22:9
things, that it was *t* Abraham........ Gen 22:20
*t* them of her mother's house........ Gen 24:28
eat, until I have *t* mine errand........ Gen 24:33
the servant *t* Isaac all things........ Gen 24:66
*t* him concerning the well which........ Gen 26:32
her elder son were *t* to Rebekah........ Gen 27:42
Jacob *t* Rachel that he was her........ Gen 29:12
and she ran and *t* her father........ Gen 29:12
he *t* Laban all these things........ Gen 29:13
in that he *t* him not that he fled........ Gen 31:20
it was *t* Laban on the third day........ Gen 31:22
a dream, and he *t* it his brethren........ Gen 37:5
*t* it his brethren, and said,........ Gen 37:9
he *t* it to his father, and to his........ Gen 37:10
And it was *t* Tamar, saying, Behold.... Gen 38:13
months after, that it was *t* Judah........ Gen 38:24
the chief butler *t* his dream to........ Gen 40:9
and Pharaoh *t* them his dream........ Gen 41:8
we *t* him, and he interpreted to us........ Gen 41:12
I *t* this unto the magicians........ Gen 41:24
*t* him all that befell unto them........ Gen 42:29
we *t* him according to the tenor........ Gen 43:7
we *t* him the words of my lord ........ Gen 44:24
*t* him, saying, Joseph is yet........ Gen 45:26
they *t* him all the words of ........ Gen 45:27
*t* Pharaoh, and said, My father and...... Gen 47:1
these things, that one *t* Joseph ........ Gen 48:1
one *t* Jacob, and said, Behold, thy........ Gen 48:2
Moses *t* Aaron all the words of ........ Ex 4:28
*t* Pharaoh, Thus saith the LORD........ Ex 5:1
it was *t* the king of Egypt that........ Ex 14:5
the congregation came and *t* Moses...... Ex 16:22
Moses *t* his father in law all........ Ex 18:8
Moses *t* the words of the people ........ Ex 19:9
*t* the people all the words of the........ Ex 24:3
Moses *t* it unto Aaron, and to his........ Lev 21:24
*t* the people the words of the........ Num 11:24
*t* Moses, and said, Eldad and Medad. Num 11:27
And they *t* him, and said, We came.. Num 13:27
Moses *t* these sayings unto all........ Num 14:39
*T* not I thee, saying, All that........ Num 23:26
Moses *t* the children of Israel ........ Num 29:40
And it be *t* thee, and thou hast ........ Deut 17:4
it was *t* the king of Jericho,........ Josh 2:2
*t* him all things that befell them........ Josh 2:23
it was certainly *t* thy servants........ Josh 9:24
And it was *t* Joshua, saying, The........ Josh 10:17
which our fathers *t* us of........ Judg 6:13
there was a man that *t* a dream........ Judg 7:13
when they *t* it to Jotham, he went........ Judg 9:7
and it was *t* Abimelech........ Judg 9:25

and they *t* Abimelech Judg 9:42
it was *t* Abimelech, that all the Judg 9:47
*t* her husband, saying, A man of Judg 13:6
he was, neither *t* he me his name Judg 13:6
have *t* us such things as these Judg 13:23
*t* his father and his mother, and Judg 14:2
but he *t* not his father or his Judg 14:6
but he *t* not them that he had Judg 14:9
of my people, and hast not *t* it me Judg 14:16
I have not *t* it my father nor my Judg 14:16
on the seventh day, that he *t* her Judg 14:17
she *t* the riddle to the children Judg 14:17
it was *t* the Gazites, saying, Judg 16:2
thou hast mocked me, and *t* me lies Judg 16:10
thou hast mocked me, and *t* me lies Judg 16:13
hast not *t* me wherein thy great Judg 16:15
That he *t* her all his heart, and Judg 16:17
that he had *t* her all his heart Judg 16:18
she *t* her all that the man had Ruth 3:16
For I have *t* him that I will 1Sa 3:13
Samuel *t* him every whit, and hid 1Sa 3:18
*t* it, all the city cried out 1Sa 4:13
the man came in hastily, and *t* Eli 1Sa 4:14
Samuel *t* all the words of the 1Sa 8:10
Now the LORD had *t* Samuel in his 1Sa 9:15
He *t* us plainly that the asses 1Sa 10:16
Samuel spake, he *t* him not 1Sa 10:16
Then Samuel *t* the people the 1Sa 10:25
*t* the tidings in the ears of the 1Sa 11:4
they *t* him the tidings of the men 1Sa 11:5
But he *t* not his father 1Sa 14:1
Then they *t* Saul, saying, Behold, 1Sa 14:33
And Jonathan *t* him, and said, I did 1Sa 14:43
in the morning, it was *t* Samuel 1Sa 15:12
and they *t* Saul, and the thing 1Sa 18:20
And the servants of Saul *t* him 1Sa 18:24
his servants *t* David these words 1Sa 18:26
and Jonathan *t* David, saying, Saul 1Sa 19:2
and Michal David's wife *t* him 1Sa 19:11
*t* him all that Saul had done to 1Sa 19:18
And it was *t* Saul, saying, Behold, 1Sa 19:19
And when it was *t* Saul, he sent 1Sa 19:21
Then they *t* David, saying, Behold 1Sa 23:1
it was *t* Saul that David was come 1Sa 23:7
it was *t* Saul that David was 1Sa 23:13
for it is *t* me that he dealeth 1Sa 23:22
And they *t* David 1Sa 23:25
Philistines, that it was *t* him 1Sa 24:1
came and *t* him all those sayings 1Sa 25:12
one of the young men *t* Abigail 1Sa 25:14
But she *t* not her husband Nabal 1Sa 25:19
wherefore she *t* him nothing 1Sa 25:36
his wife had *t* him these things, 1Sa 25:37
it was *t* Saul that David was fled 1Sa 27:4
unto the young man that *t* him 2Sa 1:5
And the young man that *t* him said 2Sa 1:6
unto the young man that *t* him 2Sa 1:13
they *t* David, saying, That the 2Sa 2:4
with him were come, they *t* Joab 2Sa 3:23
When one *t* me, saying, Behold, 2Sa 4:10
it was *t* king David, saying, The 2Sa 6:12
When they *t* it unto David, he 2Sa 10:5
And when it was *t* David, he 2Sa 10:17
*t* David, and said, I am with child 2Sa 11:5
And when they had *t* David, saying, 2Sa 11:10
*t* David all the things concerning 2Sa 11:18
Joab came to the king, and *t* him 2Sa 14:33
one *t* David, saying, Ahithophel 2Sa 15:31
and a wench went and *t* them 2Sa 17:17
and they went and *t* king David 2Sa 17:17
a lad saw them, and *t* Absalom 2Sa 17:18
*t* king David, and said unto David, 2Sa 17:21
*t* Joab, and said, Behold, I saw 2Sa 18:10
Joab said unto the man that *t* him 2Sa 18:11
the watchman cried, and *t* the king 2Sa 18:25
And it was *t* Joab, Behold, the 2Sa 19:1
they *t* unto all the people, 2Sa 19:8
it was *t* David what Rizpah the 2Sa 21:11
*t* him, and said unto him, Shall 2Sa 24:13
they *t* the king, saying, Behold 1Kin 1:23
it was *t* Solomon, saying, Behold, 1Kin 1:51
it was *t* king Solomon that Joab 1Kin 2:29
they *t* Shimei, saying, Behold, 1Kin 2:39
it was *t* Solomon that Shimei had 1Kin 2:41
that could not be *t* nor numbered 1Kin 8:5
Solomon *t* her all her questions 1Kin 10:3
from the king, which he *t* her not 1Kin 10:3
and, behold, the half was not *t* me 1Kin 10:7
*t* him all the works that the man 1Kin 13:11
them they *t* also to their father 1Kin 13:11
*t* it in the city where the old 1Kin 13:25
which *t* me that I should be king 1Kin 14:2
Was it not *t* my lord what I did 1Kin 18:13
went to meet Ahab, and *t* him 1Kin 18:16
Ahab *t* Jezebel all that Elijah 1Kin 19:1
Ben-hadad sent out, and they *t* him 1Kin 20:17
to meet you, and *t* you these words 2Kin 1:7
Then she came and *t* the man of God 2Kin 4:7
hid it from me, and hath not *t* me 2Kin 4:27
*t* him, saying, The child is not 2Kin 4:31
*t* his lord, saying, Thus and thus 2Kin 5:4
place which the man of God *t* him 2Kin 6:10
And it was *t* him, saying, Behold, 2Kin 6:13
and they *t* them, saying, We came 2Kin 7:10
they *t* it to the king's house 2Kin 7:11
returned, and *t* the king 2Kin 7:15
king asked the woman, she *t* him 2Kin 8:6
and it was *t* him, saying, The man 2Kin 8:7
He *t* me that thou shouldest 2Kin 8:14
And the watchman *t*, saying, The 2Kin 9:18
And the watchman *t*, saying, He 2Kin 9:20
they came again, and *t* him 2Kin 9:36
*t* him, saying, They have brought 2Kin 10:8
*t* the money that was found in the 2Kin 12:10
And they gave the money, being *t* 2Kin 12:11
*t* him the words of Rab-shakeh 2Kin 18:37
And the men of the city *t* him 2Kin 23:17
hast *t* thy servant that thou wilt 1Chr 17:25
*t* David how the men were served 1Chr 19:5
And it was *t* David 1Chr 19:17
Solomon *t* out threescore and ten 2Chr 2:2
which could not be *t* nor numbered 2Chr 5:6
Solomon *t* her all her questions 2Chr 9:2
from Solomon which he *t* her not 2Chr 9:2
of thy wisdom was not *t* me 2Chr 9:6
came some that *t* Jehoshaphat 2Chr 20:2
Shaphan the scribe *t* the king 2Chr 34:18
I *t* them what they should say Ezr 8:17
neither *t* I any man what my God Neh 2:12
had I as yet *t* it to the Jews Neh 2:16
Then I *t* them of the hand of my Neh 2:18
who *t* it unto Esther the queen Est 2:22
not unto them, that they *t* Haman Est 3:4
for he had *t* them that he was a Est 3:4
her chamberlains came and *t* it her Est 4:4
Mordecai *t* him of all that had Est 4:7
*t* Esther the words of Mordecai Est 4:9
they *t* to Mordecai Esther's words Est 4:12
Haman *t* them of the glory of his Est 5:11
that Mordecai had *t* of Bigthana Est 6:2
Haman *t* Zeresh his wife and all Est 6:13
for Esther had *t* what he was unto Est 8:1
men have *t* from their fathers Job 15:18
Shall it be *t* him that I speak Job 37:20
O God, our fathers have *t* us Ps 44:1
*t* Saul, and said unto him, David Ps 52:*t*
known, and our fathers have *t* us Ps 78:3
our years as a tale that is *t* Ps 90:9
he live a thousand years twice *t* Eccl 6:6
it was *t* the house of David, Is 7:2
*t* him the words of Rabshakeh Is 36:22
hath it not been *t* you from the Is 40:21
have not I *t* thee from that time, Is 44:8
who hath *t* it from that time Is 45:21
not been *t* them shall they see Is 52:15
*t* all the words in the ears of Jer 36:20
he *t* them according to all these Jer 38:27
I *t* the dream before them Dan 4:7
and before him I *t* the dream Dan 4:8
and *t* the sum of the matters Dan 7:1
So he *t* me, and made me know the Dan 7:16
the morning which was *t* is true Dan 8:26
the LORD, because he had *t* them Jonah 1:10
not believe, though it be *t* you Hab 1:5
a lie, and have *t* false dreams Zec 10:2
*t* every thing, and what was Mt 8:33
and said unto him that *t* him Mt 12:48
and buried it, and went and *t* Jesus Mt 14:12
*t* unto their lord all that was Mt 18:31
Behold, I have *t* you before Mt 24:25
be *t* for a memorial of her Mt 26:13
lo, I have *t* you Mt 28:7
*t* it in the city, and in the Mk 5:14
they that saw it *t* them how it Mk 5:16
him, and *t* him all the truth Mk 5:33
*t* him all things, both what they Mk 6:30
*t* them, Elias verily cometh first Mk 9:12
*t* them that had been with him, as Mk 16:10
went and *t* it unto the residue Mk 16:13
which were *t* her from the Lord Lk 1:45
was *t* them concerning this child Lk 2:17
were *t* them by the shepherds Lk 2:18
and seen, as it was *t* unto them Lk 2:20
it was *t* him by certain which Lk 8:20
*t* it in the city and in the Lk 8:34
They also which saw it *t* them by Lk 8:36
*t* him all that they had done Lk 9:10
*t* no man in those days any of Lk 9:36
some that *t* him of the Galilaeans Lk 13:1
And they *t* him, that Jesus of Lk 18:37
*t* all these things unto the Lk 24:9
which *t* these things unto the Lk 24:10
they *t* what things were done in Lk 24:35
If I have *t* you earthly things, Jn 3:12
which *t* me all things that ever I Jn 4:29
He *t* me all that ever I did Jn 4:39
*t* him, saying, Thy son liveth Jn 4:51
*t* the Jews that it was Jesus, Jn 5:15
a man that hath *t* you the truth Jn 8:40
I have *t* you already, and ye did Jn 9:27
I *t* you, and ye believed not Jn 10:25
*t* them what things Jesus had done Jn 11:46
were not so, I would have *t* you Jn 14:2
now I have *t* you before it come Jn 14:29
But these things have I *t* you Jn 16:4
may remember that I *t* you of them Jn 16:4
I have *t* you that I am he Jn 18:8
*t* the disciples that she had seen Jn 20:18
the prison, they returned, and *t* Acts 5:22
*t* them, saying, Behold, the men Acts 5:25
it shall be *t* thee what thou must Acts 9:6
*t* how Peter stood before the gate Acts 12:14
the prison *t* this saying to Paul Acts 16:36
the serjeants *t* these words unto Acts 16:38
there it shall be *t* thee of all Acts 22:10
*t* the chief captain, saying, Take Acts 22:26
into the castle, and *t* Paul Acts 23:16
when it was *t* me how that the Acts 23:30
it shall be even as it was *t* me Acts 27:25
when he *t* us your earnest desire, 2Cor 7:7
I *t* you before, and foretell you, 2Cor 13:2
as I have also *t* you in time past Gal 5:21
walk, of whom I have *t* you often Phil 3:18
we *t* you before that we should 1Th 3:4
with you, I *t* you these things 2Th 2:5
How that they *t* you there should Jude 18

**TOLERABLE**

It shall be more *t* for the land Mt 10:15
you, It shall be more *t* for Tyre Mt 11:22
That it shall be more *t* for the Mt 11:24
you, It shall be more *t* for Sodom Mk 6:11
be more *t* in that day for Sodom Lk 10:12
But it shall be more *t* for Tyre Lk 10:14

**TOLL**

again, then will they not pay *t* Ezr 4:13
and *t*, tribute, and custom, was Ezr 4:20
shall not be lawful to impose *t* Ezr 7:24

**TOMB**

grave, and shall remain in the *t* Job 21:32
And laid it in his own new *t* Mt 27:60
up his corpse, and laid it in a *t* Mk 6:29

**TOMBS**

with devils, coming out of the *t* Mt 8:28
ye build the *t* of the prophets Mt 23:29
there met him out of the *t* a man Mk 5:2
Who had his dwelling among the *t* Mk 5:3
was in the mountains, and in the *t* Mk 5:5
abode in any house, but in the *t* Lk 8:27

**TONGS**

the *t* thereof, and the snuffdishes Ex 25:38
the light, and his lamps, and his *t* Num 4:9
and the lamps, and the *t* of gold, 1Kin 7:49
flowers, and the lamps, and the *t* 2Chr 4:21
with the *t* from off the altar Is 6:6
The smith with the *t* both worketh Is 44:12

**TONGUE**

every one after his *t*, after Gen 10:5
am slow of speech, and of a slow *t* Ex 4:10
Israel shall not a dog move his *t* Ex 11:7
a nation whose *t* thou shalt not Deut 28:49
none moved his *t* against any of Josh 10:21
lappeth of the water with his *t* Judg 7:5
by me, and his word was in my *t* 2Sa 23:2
was written in the Syrian *t* Ezr 4:7
and interpreted in the Syrian *t* Ezr 4:7
and bondwomen, I had held my *t* Est 7:4
be hid from the scourge of the *t* Job 5:21
Teach me, and I will hold my *t* Job 6:24
Is there iniquity in my *t* Job 6:30
for now, if I hold my *t*, I shall Job 13:19
thou choosest the *t* of the crafty Job 15:5
though he hide it under his *t* Job 20:12
the viper's *t* shall slay him Job 20:16
wickedness, nor my *t* utter deceit Job 27:4
their *t* cleaved to the roof of Job 29:10
my *t* hath spoken in my mouth Job 33:2
or his *t* with a cord which thou Job 41:1
they flatter with their *t* Ps 5:9
under his *t* is mischief and vanity Ps 10:7
the *t* that speaketh proud things Ps 12:3
With our *t* will we prevail Ps 12:4
He that backbiteth not with his *t* Ps 15:3
and my *t* cleaveth to my jaws Ps 22:15
Keep thy *t* from evil, and thy lips Ps 34:13
And my *t* shall speak of thy Ps 35:28
his *t* talketh of judgment Ps 37:30
my ways, that I sin not with my *t* Ps 39:1
then spake I with my *t*, Ps 39:3
my *t* is the pen of a ready writer Ps 45:1
to evil, and thy *t* frameth deceit Ps 50:19
my *t* shall sing aloud of thy Ps 51:14
Thy *t* deviseth mischiefs Ps 52:2
words, O thou deceitful *t* Ps 52:4
arrows, and their *t* a sharp sword Ps 57:4
Who whet their *t* like a sword Ps 64:3
own *t* to fall upon themselves Ps 64:8
and he was extolled with my *t* Ps 66:17
the *t* of thy dogs in the same Ps 68:23
My *t* also shall talk of thy Ps 71:24
their *t* walketh through the earth Ps 73:9
spoken against me with a lying *t* Ps 109:2
My *t* shall speak of thy word Ps 119:172
lying lips, and from a deceitful *t* Ps 120:2
be done unto thee, thou false *t* Ps 120:3
laughter, and our *t* with singing Ps 126:2
let my *t* cleave to the roof of my Ps 137:6
For there is not a word in my *t* Ps 139:4
A proud look, a lying *t*, and hands Prov 6:17
of the *t* of a strange woman Prov 6:24
The *t* of the just is as choice Prov 10:20
but the froward *t* shall be cut Prov 10:31
but the *t* of the wise is health Prov 12:18
but a lying *t* is but for a moment Prov 12:19
The *t* of the wise useth knowledge Prov 15:2
A wholesome *t* is a tree of life Prov 15:4
in man, and the answer of the *t* Prov 16:1
a liar giveth ear to a naughty *t* Prov 17:4
perverse *t* falleth into mischief Prov 17:20
and life are in the power of the *t* Prov 18:21
a lying *t* is a vanity tossed to Prov 21:6
his *t* keepeth his soul from Prov 21:23
a soft *t* breaketh the bone Prov 25:15
angry countenance a backbiting *t* Prov 25:23
A lying *t* hateth those that are Prov 26:28
he that flattereth with the *t* Prov 28:23
in her *t* is the law of kindness Prov 31:26
honey and milk are under thy *t* Song 4:11

T

because their *t* and their doings ... Is 3:8
destroy the *t* of the Egyptian sea ... Is 11:15
another *t* will he speak to this ... Is 28:11
his *t* as a devouring fire ... Is 30:27
the *t* of the stammerers shall be ... Is 32:4
of a stammering *t*, that thou ... Is 33:19
hart, and the *t* of the dumb sing ... Is 35:6
their *t* faileth for thirst, I the ... Is 41:17
shall bow, every *t* shall swear ... Is 45:23
given me the *t* of the learned ... Is 50:4
every *t* that shall rise against ... Is 54:17
a wide mouth, and draw out the *t* ... Is 57:4
your *t* hath muttered perverseness ... Is 59:3
have taught their *t* to speak lies ... Jer 9:5
Their *t* is as an arrow shot out ... Jer 9:8
and let us smite him with the *t* ... Jer 18:18
The *t* of the sucking child ... Lam 4:4
I will make thy *t* cleave to the ... Eze 3:26
and the *t* of the Chaldeans ... Dan 1:4
the sword for the rage of their *t* ... Hos 7:16
Then shall he say, Hold thy *t* ... Amos 6:10
their *t* is deceitful in their ... Mic 6:12
holdest thy *t* when the wicked ... Hab 1:13
*t* be found in their mouth ... Zeph 3:13
their *t* shall consume away in ... Zec 14:12
and he spit, and touched his *t* ... Mk 7:33
and the string of his *t* was loosed ... Mk 7:35
his *t* loosed, and he spake, and ... Lk 1:64
his finger in water, and cool my *t* ... Lk 16:24
called in the Hebrew *t* Bethesda ... Jn 5:2
field is called in their proper *t* ... Acts 1:19
hear we every man in our own *t* ... Acts 2:8
heart rejoice, and my *t* was glad ... Acts 2:26
spake unto them in the Hebrew *t* ... Acts 21:40
he spake in the Hebrew *t* to them ... Acts 22:2
me, and saying in the Hebrew *t* ... Acts 26:14
every *t* shall confess to God ... Rom 14:11
unknown *t* speaketh not unto men ... 1Cor 14:2
in an unknown *t* edifieth himself ... 1Cor 14:4
except ye utter by the *t* words ... 1Cor 14:9
*t* pray that he may interpret ... 1Cor 14:13
For if I pray in an unknown *t* ... 1Cor 14:14
thousand words in an unknown *t* ... 1Cor 14:19
psalm, hath a doctrine, hath a *t* ... 1Cor 14:26
If any man speak in an unknown *t* ... 1Cor 14:27
that every *t* should confess that ... Phil 2:11
religious, and bridleth not his *t* ... Jas 1:26
Even so the *t* is a little member, ... Jas 3:5
the *t* is a fire, a world of ... Jas 3:6
so is the *t* among our members, ... Jas 3:6
But the *t* can no man tame ... Jas 3:8
let him refrain his *t* from evil ... 1Pet 3:10
us not love in word, neither in *t* ... 1Jn 3:18
blood out of every kindred, and *t* ... Rev 5:9
name in the Hebrew *t* is Abaddon ... Rev 9:11
but in the Greek *t* hath his name ... Rev 9:11
to every nation, and kindred, and *t* ... Rev 14:6
called in the Hebrew *t* Armageddon ... Rev 16:16

**TONGUES**
their families, after their *t* ... Gen 10:20
their families, after their *t* ... Gen 10:31
a pavilion from the strife of *t* ... Ps 31:20
O Lord, and divide their *t* ... Ps 55:9
they lied unto him with their *t* ... Ps 78:36
sharpened their *t* like a serpent ... Ps 140:3
I will gather all nations and *t* ... Is 66:18
they bend their *t* like their bow ... Jer 9:3
saith the LORD, that use their *t* ... Jer 23:31
they shall speak with new *t* ... Mk 16:17
them cloven *t* like as of fire ... Acts 2:3
and began to speak with other *t* ... Acts 2:4
our *t* the wonderful works of God ... Acts 2:11
For they heard them speak with *t* ... Acts 10:46
and they spake with *t*, and ... Acts 19:6
with their *t* they have used ... Rom 3:13
to another divers kinds of *t* ... 1Cor 12:10
another the interpretation of *t* ... 1Cor 12:10
governments, diversities of *t* ... 1Cor 12:28
do all speak with *t* ... 1Cor 12:30
Though I speak with the *t* of men ... 1Cor 13:1
whether there be *t*, they shall ... 1Cor 13:8
I would that ye all spake with *t* ... 1Cor 14:5
than he that speaketh with *t* ... 1Cor 14:5
I come unto you speaking with *t* ... 1Cor 14:6
I speak with *t* more than ye all ... 1Cor 14:18
is written, With men of other *t* ... 1Cor 14:21
Wherefore *t* are for a sign, not ... 1Cor 14:22
one place, and all speak with *t* ... 1Cor 14:23
and forbid not to speak with *t* ... 1Cor 14:39
and kindreds, and people, and *t* ... Rev 7:9
many peoples, and nations, and *t* ... Rev 10:11
of the people and kindreds and *t* ... Rev 11:9
given him over all kindreds, and *t* ... Rev 13:7
and they gnawed their *t* for pain ... Rev 16:10
and multitudes, and nations, and *t* ... Rev 17:15

**TOO**
Is any thing *t* hard for the LORD ... Gen 18:14
be *t* little for the lamb, let him ... Ex 12:4
this thing is *t* heavy for thee ... Ex 18:18
the work to make it, and *t* much ... Ex 36:7
because it is *t* heavy for me ... Num 11:14
Ye take *t* much upon you, seeing ... Num 16:3
ye take *t* much upon you, ye sons ... Num 16:7
for they are *t* mighty for me ... Num 22:6
the cause that is *t* hard for you ... Deut 1:17
was not one city *t* strong for us ... Deut 2:36
his name there be *t* far from thee ... Deut 12:21
And if the way be *t* long for thee ... Deut 14:24
if the place be *t* far from thee ... Deut 14:24
If there arise a matter *t* hard ... Deut 17:8
Ephraim be *t* narrow for thee ... Josh 17:15
of Judah was *t* much for them ... Josh 19:9
of Dan went out *t* little for them ... Josh 19:47
iniquity of Peor *t* little for us ... Josh 22:17
are *t* many for me to give the ... Judg 7:2
Gideon, The people are yet *t* many ... Judg 7:4
that they were *t* strong for him ... Judg 18:26
for I am *t* old to have an husband ... Ruth 1:12
sons of Zeruiah be *t* hard for me ... 2Sa 3:39
If the Syrians be *t* strong for me ... 2Sa 10:11
of Ammon be *t* strong for thee ... 2Sa 10:11
and if that had been *t* little ... 2Sa 12:8
for they were *t* strong for me ... 2Sa 22:18
God of my lord the king say so *t* ... 1Kin 1:36
was *t* little to receive the burnt ... 1Kin 8:64
It is *t* much for you to go up to ... 1Kin 12:28
the journey is *t* great for thee ... 1Kin 19:7
the battle was *t* sore for him ... 2Kin 3:26
with thee is *t* strait for us ... 2Kin 6:1
If the Syrians be *t* strong for me ... 1Chr 19:12
of Ammon be *t* strong for thee ... 1Chr 19:12
But the priests were *t* few ... 2Chr 29:34
shall there arise *t* much contempt ... Est 1:18
things *t* wonderful for me, which ... Job 42:3
for they were *t* strong for me ... Ps 18:17
from him that is *t* strong for him ... Ps 35:10
burden they are *t* heavy for me ... Ps 38:4
this, it was *t* painful for me ... Ps 73:16
or in things *t* high for me ... Ps 131:1
knowledge is *t* wonderful for me ... Ps 139:6
Wisdom is *t* high for a fool ... Prov 24:7
which are *t* wonderful for me ... Prov 30:18
shall even now be *t* narrow by ... Is 49:19
The place is *t* strait for me ... Is 49:20
there is nothing *t* hard for thee ... Jer 32:17
is there any thing *t* hard for me ... Jer 32:27
all things ye are *t* superstitious ... Acts 17:22

**TOOK** See PREFACE.

**TOOKEST**
though thou *t* vengeance of their ... Ps 99:8
*t* thy broidered garments, and ... Eze 16:18

**TOOL**
for if thou lift up thy *t* upon it ... Ex 20:25
and fashioned it with a graving *t* ... Ex 32:4
not lift up any iron *t* upon them ... Deut 27:5
any *t* of iron heard in the house ... 1Kin 6:7

**TOOTH**
Eye for eye, *t* for *t*, hand ... Ex 21:24
he smite out his manservant's *t* ... Ex 21:27
or his maidservant's *t* ... Ex 21:27
breach, eye for eye, *t* for *t* ... Lev 24:20
life, eye for eye, *t* for *t* ... Deut 19:21
of trouble is like a broken *t* ... Prov 25:19
for an eye, and a *t* for a *t* ... Mt 5:38

**TOOTH'S**
let him go free for his *t* sake ... Ex 21:27

**TOP**
whose *t* may reach unto heaven ... Gen 11:4
the *t* of it reached to heaven ... Gen 28:12
and poured oil upon the *t* of it ... Gen 28:18
to morrow I will stand on the *t* ... Ex 17:9
Hur went up to the *t* of the hill ... Ex 17:10
Sinai, on the *t* of the mount ... Ex 19:20
Moses up to the *t* of the mount ... Ex 19:20
was like devouring fire on the *t* ... Ex 24:17
shall be an hole in the *t* of it ... Ex 28:32
the *t* thereof, and the sides ... Ex 30:3
there to me in the *t* of the mount ... Ex 34:2
with pure gold, both the *t* of it ... Ex 37:26
up into the *t* of the mountain ... Num 14:40
presumed to go up unto the hill *t* ... Num 14:44
died there in the *t* of the mount ... Num 20:28
to the *t* of Pisgah, which looketh ... Num 21:20
For from the *t* of the rocks I see ... Num 23:9
to the *t* of Pisgah, and built ... Num 23:14
brought Balaam unto the *t* of Peor ... Num 23:28
Get thee up into the *t* of Pisgah ... Deut 3:27
thy foot unto the *t* of thy head ... Deut 28:35
upon the *t* of the head of him ... Deut 33:16
to the *t* of Pisgah, that is over ... Deut 34:1
the border went up to the *t* of ... Josh 15:8
*t* of the hill unto the fountain ... Josh 15:9
thy God upon the *t* of this rock ... Judg 6:26
stood in the *t* of mount Gerizim, ... Judg 9:7
for him in the *t* of the mountains ... Judg 9:25
down from the *t* of the mountains ... Judg 9:36
gat them up to the *t* of the tower ... Judg 9:51
dwelt in the *t* of the rock Etam ... Judg 15:8
went to the *t* of the rock Etam ... Judg 15:11
carried them up to the *t* of an ... Judg 16:3
with Saul upon the *t* of the house ... 1Sa 9:25
called Saul to the *t* of the house ... 1Sa 9:26
stood on the *t* of an hill afar ... 1Sa 26:13
and stood on the *t* of an hill ... 2Sa 2:25
was come to the *t* of the mount ... 2Sa 15:32
a little past the *t* of the hill ... 2Sa 16:1
a tent upon the *t* of the house ... 2Sa 16:22
were upon the *t* of the pillars ... 1Kin 7:17
chapiters that were upon the *t* ... 1Kin 7:18
the *t* of the pillars were of lily ... 1Kin 7:19
upon the *t* of the pillars was ... 1Kin 7:22
in the *t* of the base was there a ... 1Kin 7:35
on the *t* of the base the ledges ... 1Kin 7:35
were on the *t* of the two pillars ... 1Kin 7:41
were upon the *t* of the pillars ... 1Kin 7:41
the *t* of the throne was round ... 1Kin 10:19
Elijah went up to the *t* of Carmel ... 1Kin 18:42
he sat on the *t* of an hill ... 2Kin 1:9
under him on the *t* of the stairs ... 2Kin 9:13
the altars that were on the *t* of ... 2Kin 23:12
the chapiter that was on the *t* of ... 2Chr 3:15
were on the *t* of the two pillars ... 2Chr 4:12
were on the *t* of the pillars ... 2Chr 4:12
them unto the *t* of the rock ... 2Chr 25:12
them down from the *t* of the rock ... 2Chr 25:12
touched the *t* of the sceptre ... Est 5:2
earth upon the *t* of the mountains ... Ps 72:16
a sparrow alone upon the house *t* ... Ps 102:7
standeth in the *t* of high places ... Prov 8:2
that lieth upon the *t* of a mast ... Prov 23:34
look from the *t* of Amana, from ... Song 4:8
from the *t* of Shenir and Hermon, ... Song 4:8
in the *t* of the mountains ... Is 2:2
in the *t* of the uppermost bough ... Is 17:6
a beacon upon the *t* of a mountain ... Is 30:17
shout from the *t* of the mountains ... Is 42:11
hunger in the *t* of every street ... Lam 2:19
out in the *t* of every street ... Lam 4:1
off the *t* of his young twigs ... Eze 17:4
I will crop off from the *t* of his ... Eze 17:22
she set it upon the *t* of a rock ... Eze 24:7
her blood upon the *t* of a rock ... Eze 24:8
and make her like the *t* of a rock ... Eze 26:4
make thee like the *t* of a rock ... Eze 26:14
his *t* was among the thick boughs ... Eze 31:3
he hath shot up his *t* among the ... Eze 31:10
up their *t* among the thick boughs ... Eze 31:14
Upon the *t* of the mountain the ... Eze 43:12
the *t* of Carmel shall wither ... Amos 1:2
themselves in the *t* of Carmel ... Amos 9:3
in the *t* of the mountains ... Mic 4:1
at the *t* of all the streets ... Nah 3:10
with a bowl upon the *t* of it ... Zec 4:2
which are upon the *t* thereof ... Zec 4:2
in twain from the *t* to the bottom ... Mt 27:51
in twain from the *t* to the bottom ... Mk 15:38
seam, woven from the *t* throughout ... Jn 19:23
leaning upon the *t* of his staff ... Heb 11:21

**TOPAZ**
first row shall be a sardius, a *t* ... Ex 28:17
the first row was a sardius, a *t* ... Ex 39:10
The *t* of Ethiopia shall not equal ... Job 28:19
was thy covering, the sardius, *t* ... Eze 28:13
the ninth, a *t* ... Rev 21:20

**TOPHEL** (*to'-fel*) *A place in the Sinai wilderness.*
the Red sea, between Paran, and *T* ... Deut 1:1

**TOPHET** (*to'-fet*) See TOPHETH. *A place in the valley of Hinnom.*
For *T* is ordained of old ... Is 30:33
have built the high places of *T* ... Jer 7:31
that it shall no more be called *T* ... Jer 7:32
for they shall bury in *T*, till ... Jer 7:32
place shall no more be called *T* ... Jer 19:6
and they shall bury them in *T* ... Jer 19:11
and even make this city as *T* ... Jer 19:12
be defiled as the place of *T* ... Jer 19:13
Then came Jeremiah from *T* ... Jer 19:14

**TOPHETH** (*to'-feth*) See TOPHET. *Same as Tophet.*
And he defiled *T*, which is in the ... 2Kin 23:10

**TOPS**
were the *t* of the mountains seen ... Gen 8:5
in the *t* of the mulberry trees ... 2Sa 5:24
to set upon the *t* of the pillars ... 1Kin 7:16
herb, as the grass on the house *t* ... 2Kin 19:26
in the *t* of the mulberry trees ... 1Chr 14:15
cut off as the *t* of the ears of ... Job 24:24
into the *t* of the ragged rocks, ... Is 2:21
on the *t* of their houses, and in ... Is 15:3
in all the *t* of the mountains, and ... Eze 6:13
upon the *t* of the mountains ... Hos 4:13
*t* of mountains shall they leap ... Joel 2:5

**TORCH**
like a *t* of fire in a sheaf ... Zec 12:6

**TORCHES**
*t* in the day of his preparation ... Nah 2:3
they shall seem like *t*, they ... Nah 2:4
cometh thither with lanterns and *t* ... Jn 18:3

**TORMENT**
hither to *t* us before the time ... Mt 8:29
thee by God, that thou *t* me not ... Mk 5:7
I beseech thee, *t* me not ... Lk 8:28
also come into this place of *t* ... Lk 16:28
because fear hath *t* ... 1Jn 4:18
their *t* was as the *t* of a ... Rev 9:5
was as the *t* of a scorpion ... Rev 9:5
the smoke of their *t* ascendeth up ... Rev 14:11
and lived deliciously, so much *t* ... Rev 18:7
afar off for the fear of her *t* ... Rev 18:10
afar off for the fear of her *t* ... Rev 18:15

**TORMENTED**
sick of the palsy, grievously *t* ... Mt 8:6
for I am *t* in this flame ... Lk 16:24
he is comforted, and thou art *t* ... Lk 16:25
being destitute, afflicted, *t* ... Heb 11:37
that they should be *t* five months ... Rev 9:5
because these two prophets *t* them ... Rev 11:10
and he shall be *t* with fire ... Rev 14:10
prophet are, and shall be *t* day ... Rev 20:10

**TORMENTORS**
wroth, and delivered him to the *t* ........ Mt 18:34

**TORMENTS**
taken with divers diseases and *t* ........ Mt 4:24
he lift up his eyes, being in *t* ........ Lk 16:23

**TORN**
That which was *t* of beasts I ........ Gen 31:39
I said, Surely he is *t* in pieces ........ Gen 44:28
If it be *t* in pieces, then let ........ Ex 22:13
not make good that which was *t* ........ Ex 22:13
that is *t* of beasts in the field ........ Ex 22:31
of that which is *t* with beasts ........ Lev 7:24
or that which was *t* with beasts ........ Lev 17:15
or is *t* with beasts, he shall not ........ Lev 22:8
unto the lion, which hath *t* him ........ 1Kin 13:26
eaten the carcase, nor *t* the ass ........ 1Kin 13:28
their carcases were *t* in the ........ Is 5:25
out thence shall be *t* in pieces ........ Jer 5:6
of itself, or is *t* in pieces ........ Eze 4:14
that is dead of itself, or *t* ........ Eze 44:31
for he hath *t*, and he will heal us ........ Hos 6:1
and ye brought that which was *t* ........ Mal 1:13
when the unclean spirit had *t* him ........ Mk 1:26

**TORTOISE**
mouse, and the *t* after his kind, ........ Lev 11:29

**TORTURED**
and others were *t*, not accepting ........ Heb 11:35

**TOSS**
*t* thee like a ball into a large ........ Is 22:18
the waves thereof *t* themselves ........ Jer 5:22

**TOSSED**
I am *t* up and down as the locust ........ Ps 109:23
a lying tongue is a vanity *t* to ........ Prov 21:6
*t* with tempest, and not comforted, ........ Is 54:11
midst of the sea, *t* with waves ........ Mt 14:24
exceedingly *t* with a tempest ........ Acts 27:18
*t* to and fro, and carried about ........ Eph 4:14
the sea driven with the wind and *t* ........ Jas 1:6

**TOSSINGS**
and I am full of *t* to and fro unto ........ Job 7:4

**TOTTERING**
wall shall ye be, and as a *t* fence ........ Ps 62:3

**TOU** (*to'-u*) See TOI. *Same as Toi.*
Now when *T* king of Hamath heard ........ 1Chr 18:9
(for Hadarezer had war with *T* ........ 1Chr 18:10

**TOUCH**
eat of it, neither shall ye *t* it ........ Gen 3:3
suffered I thee not to *t* her ........ Gen 20:6
the mount, or *t* the border of it ........ Ex 19:12
There shall not an hand *t* it ........ Ex 19:13
Or if a soul *t* any unclean thing, ........ Lev 5:2
Or if he *t* the uncleanness of man ........ Lev 5:3
Whatsoever shall *t* the flesh ........ Lev 6:27
that shall *t* any unclean thing ........ Lev 7:21
and their carcase shall ye not *t* ........ Lev 11:8
whosoever doth *t* them, when they ........ Lev 11:31
she shall *t* no hallowed thing, ........ Lev 12:4
they shall not *t* any holy thing ........ Num 4:15
*t* nothing of theirs, lest ye be ........ Num 16:26
flesh, nor *t* their dead carcase ........ Deut 14:8
now therefore we may not *t* them ........ Josh 9:19
men that they shall not *t* thee ........ Ruth 2:9
he shall not *t* thee any more ........ 2Sa 14:10
Beware that none *t* the young man ........ 2Sa 18:12
But the man that shall *t* them ........ 2Sa 23:7
*T* not mine anointed, and do my ........ 1Chr 16:22
*t* all that he hath, and he will ........ Job 1:11
*t* his bone and his flesh, and he ........ Job 2:5
seven there shall no evil *t* thee ........ Job 5:19
to *t* are as my sorrowful meat ........ Job 6:7
*T* not mine anointed, and do my ........ Ps 105:15
*t* the mountains, and they shall ........ Ps 144:5
from thence, *t* no unclean thing ........ Is 52:11
that *t* the inheritance which I ........ Jer 12:14
men could not *t* their garments ........ Lam 4:14
depart, depart, *t* not ........ Lam 4:15
and with his skirt do *t* bread ........ Hag 2:12
by a dead body *t* any of these ........ Hag 2:13
If I may but *t* his garment ........ Mt 9:21
only *t* the hem of his garment ........ Mt 14:36
pressed upon him for to *t* him ........ Mk 3:10
If I may *t* but his clothes, I ........ Mk 5:28
*t* if it were but the border of ........ Mk 6:56
him, and besought him to *t* him ........ Mk 8:22
to him, that he should *t* them ........ Mk 10:13
whole multitude sought to *t* him ........ Lk 6:19
ye yourselves *t* not the burdens ........ Lk 11:46
infants, that he would *t* them ........ Lk 18:15
Jesus saith unto her, *T* me not ........ Jn 20:17
good for a man not to *t* a woman ........ 1Cor 7:1
Lord, and *t* not the unclean thing ........ 2Cor 6:17
*T* not; taste not ........ Col 2:21
the firstborn should *t* them ........ Heb 11:28
so much as a beast *t* the mountain ........ Heb 12:20

**TOUCHED**
us no hurt, as we have not *t* thee ........ Gen 26:29
he *t* the hollow of his thigh ........ Gen 32:25
because he *t* the hollow of ........ Gen 32:32
The soul which hath *t* any such ........ Lev 22:6
there, and upon him that *t* a bone ........ Num 19:18
and whosoever hath *t* any slain ........ Num 31:19
*t* the flesh and the unleavened ........ Judg 6:21
of men, whose hearts God had *t* ........ 1Sa 10:26
wing of the one *t* the one wall ........ 1Kin 6:27
the other cherub *t* the other wall ........ 1Kin 6:27
their wings *t* one another in the ........ 1Kin 6:27
tree, behold, then an angel *t* him ........ 1Kin 19:5
*t* him, and said, Arise and eat ........ 1Kin 19:7
*t* the bones of Elisha, he revived ........ 2Kin 13:21
near, and *t* the top of the sceptre ........ Est 5:2
for the hand of God hath *t* me ........ Job 19:21
and said, Lo, this hath *t* thy lips ........ Is 6:7
put forth his hand, and *t* my mouth ........ Jer 1:9
creatures that *t* one another ........ Eze 3:13
whole earth, and *t* not the ground ........ Dan 8:5
but he *t* me, and set me upright ........ Dan 8:18
*t* me about the time of the ........ Dan 9:21
And, behold, an hand *t* me, which ........ Dan 10:10
of the sons of men *t* my lips ........ Dan 10:16
*t* me one like the appearance of a ........ Dan 10:18
hand, and *t* him, saying, I will ........ Mt 8:3
he *t* her hand, and the fever left ........ Mt 8:15
him, and *t* the hem of his garment ........ Mt 9:20
Then *t* he their eyes, saying, ........ Mt 9:29
as many as *t* were made perfectly ........ Mt 14:36
*t* them, and said, Arise, and be not ........ Mt 17:7
on them, and *t* their eyes ........ Mt 20:34
*t* him, and saith unto him, I will ........ Mk 1:41
press behind, and *t* his garment ........ Mk 5:27
press, and said, Who *t* my clothes ........ Mk 5:30
thee, and sayest thou, Who *t* me ........ Mk 5:31
as many as *t* him were made whole ........ Mk 6:56
ears, and he spit, and *t* his tongue ........ Mk 7:33
hand, and *t* him, saying, I will ........ Lk 5:13
And he came and *t* the bier ........ Lk 7:14
*t* the border of his garment ........ Lk 8:44
And Jesus said, Who *t* me ........ Lk 8:45
thee, and sayest thou, Who *t* me ........ Lk 8:45
And Jesus said, Somebody hath *t* me ........ Lk 8:46
for what cause she had *t* him ........ Lk 8:47
he *t* his ear, and healed him ........ Lk 22:51
And the next day we *t* at Sidon ........ Acts 27:3
be *t* with the feeling of our ........ Heb 4:15
unto the mount that might be *t* ........ Heb 12:18

**TOUCHETH**
He that *t* this man or his wife ........ Gen 26:11
whosoever *t* the mount shall be ........ Ex 19:12
whatsoever *t* the altar shall be ........ Ex 29:37
whatsoever *t* them shall be holy ........ Ex 30:29
every one that *t* them shall be ........ Lev 6:18
the flesh that *t* any unclean ........ Lev 7:19
whosoever *t* the carcase of them ........ Lev 11:24
every one that *t* them shall be ........ Lev 11:26
whoso *t* their carcase shall be ........ Lev 11:27
but that which *t* their carcase ........ Lev 11:36
he that *t* the carcase thereof ........ Lev 11:39
whosoever *t* his bed shall wash ........ Lev 15:5
he that *t* the flesh of him that ........ Lev 15:7
whosoever *t* any thing that was ........ Lev 15:10
whomsoever he *t* that hath the ........ Lev 15:11
that he *t* which hath the issue, ........ Lev 15:12
whosoever *t* her shall be unclean ........ Lev 15:19
whosoever *t* her bed shall wash ........ Lev 15:21
whosoever *t* any thing that she ........ Lev 15:22
whereon she sitteth, when he *t* it ........ Lev 15:23
whosoever *t* those things shall be ........ Lev 15:27
whoso *t* any thing that is unclean ........ Lev 22:4
Or whosoever *t* any creeping thing ........ Lev 22:5
He that *t* the dead body of any ........ Num 19:11
Whosoever *t* the dead body of any ........ Num 19:13
whosoever *t* one that is slain ........ Num 19:16
he that *t* the water of separation ........ Num 19:21
unclean person *t* shall be unclean ........ Num 19:22
the soul that *t* it shall be ........ Num 19:22
tow is broken when it *t* the fire ........ Judg 16:9
it *t* thee, and thou art troubled ........ Job 4:5
he *t* the hills, and they smoke ........ Ps 104:32
whosoever *t* her shall not be ........ Prov 6:29
wither, when the east wind *t* it ........ Eze 17:10
they break out, and blood *t* blood ........ Hos 4:2
of hosts is he that *t* the land ........ Amos 9:5
for he that *t* you ........ Zec 2:8
you *t* the apple of his eye ........ Zec 2:8
of woman this is that *t* him ........ Lk 7:39
and that wicked one *t* him not ........ 1Jn 5:18

**TOUCHING**
as *t* thee, doth comfort himself, ........ Gen 27:42
make an atonement for him as *t* ........ Lev 5:13
unto the Levites *t* their charge ........ Num 8:26
as *t* the matter which thou and I ........ 1Sa 20:23
As *t* the words which thou hast ........ 2Kin 22:18
that *t* any of the priests and ........ Ezr 7:24
*T* the Almighty, we cannot find ........ Job 37:23
which I have made *t* the king ........ Ps 45:1
song of my beloved *t* his vineyard ........ Is 5:1
them *t* all their wickedness ........ Jer 1:16
*t* the house of the king of Judah, ........ Jer 21:11
For thus saith the LORD *t* Shallum ........ Jer 22:11
for the vision is *t* the whole ........ Eze 7:13
*t* any thing that they shall ask ........ Mt 18:19
But as *t* the resurrection of the ........ Mt 22:31
as *t* the dead, that they rise ........ Mk 12:26
*t* those things whereof ye accuse ........ Lk 23:14
ye intend to do as *t* these men ........ Acts 5:35
As *t* the Gentiles which believe, ........ Acts 21:25
*T* the resurrection of the dead I ........ Acts 24:21
*t* all the things whereof I am ........ Acts 26:2
but as *t* the election, they are ........ Rom 11:28
Now as *t* things offered unto ........ 1Cor 8:1
As *t* our brother Apollos, I ........ 1Cor 16:12
For as *t* the ministering to the ........ 2Cor 9:1
as *t* the law, a Pharisee ........ Phil 3:5
*t* the righteousness which is in ........ Phil 3:6
(*t* whom ye received commandments ........ Col 4:10
But as *t* brotherly love ye need ........ 1Th 4:9
have confidence in the Lord *t* you ........ 2Th 3:4

**TOW**
as a thread of *t* is broken when ........ Judg 16:9
And the strong shall be as *t* ........ Is 1:31
extinct, they are quenched as *t* ........ Is 43:17

**TOWARD**
which goeth *t* the east of Assyria ........ Gen 2:14
going on still *t* the south ........ Gen 12:9
and pitched his tent *t* Sodom ........ Gen 13:12
and said, Look now *t* heaven ........ Gen 15:5
and bowed himself *t* the ground ........ Gen 18:2
up from thence, and looked *t* Sodom ........ Gen 18:16
from thence, and went *t* Sodom ........ Gen 18:22
with his face *t* the ground ........ Gen 19:1
looked *t* Sodom and Gomorrah ........ Gen 19:28
*t* all the land of the plain, and ........ Gen 19:28
from thence *t* the south country ........ Gen 20:1
Egypt, as thou goest *t* Assyria ........ Gen 25:18
from Beer-sheba, and went *t* Haran ........ Gen 28:10
of the flocks *t* the ringstraked ........ Gen 30:40
it was not *t* him as before ........ Gen 31:2
that it is not *t* me as before ........ Gen 31:5
set his face *t* the mount Gilead ........ Gen 31:21
right hand *t* Israel's left hand ........ Gen 48:13
left hand *t* Israel's right hand ........ Gen 48:13
let Moses sprinkle it *t* the ........ Ex 9:8
and Moses sprinkled it up *t* heaven ........ Ex 9:10
Stretch forth thine hand *t* heaven ........ Ex 9:22
stretched forth his rod *t* heaven ........ Ex 9:23
Stretch out thine hand *t* heaven ........ Ex 10:21
stretched forth his hand *t* heaven ........ Ex 10:22
that they looked *t* the wilderness ........ Ex 16:10
*t* the mercy seat shall the faces ........ Ex 25:20
of the tabernacle *t* the south ........ Ex 26:35
*t* the forepart thereof, over ........ Ex 28:27
and bowed his head *t* the earth ........ Ex 34:8
which is *t* the north corner, he ........ Ex 36:25
*t* the forepart of it, over ........ Ex 39:20
lifted up his hand *t* the people ........ Lev 9:22
the part of his head *t* his face ........ Lev 13:41
on the east side *t* the rising of ........ Num 2:3
before the tabernacle *t* the east ........ Num 3:38
that they looked *t* the tabernacle ........ Num 16:42
is before Moab, *t* the sunrising ........ Num 21:11
Pisgah, which looketh *t* Jeshimon ........ Num 21:20
of Peor, that looketh *t* Jeshimon ........ Num 23:28
he set his face *t* the wilderness ........ Num 24:1
fierce anger of the LORD *t* Israel ........ Num 32:14
Jericho eastward, *t* the sunrising ........ Num 34:15
this side Jordan *t* the sunrising ........ Deut 4:41
this side Jordan *t* the sunrising ........ Deut 4:47
eye shall be evil *t* his brother ........ Deut 28:54
*t* the wife of his bosom, and ........ Deut 28:54
*t* the remnant of his children ........ Deut 28:54
her eye shall be evil *t* the ........ Deut 28:56
*t* her son, and *t* her daughter ........ Deut 28:56
*t* her young one that cometh out ........ Deut 28:57
*t* her children which she shall ........ Deut 28:57
unto the great sea *t* the going ........ Josh 1:4
this side Jordan *t* the sunrising ........ Josh 1:15
came down *t* the sea of the plain ........ Josh 3:16
spear that is in thy hand *t* Ai ........ Josh 8:18
he had in his hand *t* the city ........ Josh 8:18
Jordan *t* the rising of the sun ........ Josh 12:1
*t* the sunrising, from Baal-gad ........ Josh 13:5
From thence it passed *t* Azmon ........ Josh 15:4
the border went up *t* Debir from ........ Josh 15:7
and so northward, looking *t* Gilgal ........ Josh 15:7
the border passed *t* the waters of ........ Josh 15:7
*t* the coast of Edom southward ........ Josh 15:21
the border went out *t* the sea to ........ Josh 16:6
went over from thence *t* Luz ........ Josh 18:13
and went forth *t* Geliloth ........ Josh 18:17
passed along *t* the side over ........ Josh 18:18
And their border went up *t* the sea ........ Josh 19:11
turned from Sarid eastward *t* the ........ Josh 19:12
And their border was *t* Jezreel ........ Josh 19:18
turneth *t* the sunrising to ........ Josh 19:27
*t* the north side of Beth-emek ........ Josh 19:27
Judah upon Jordan *t* the sunrising ........ Josh 19:34
took the fords of Jordan *t* Moab ........ Judg 3:28
draw *t* mount Tabor, and take with ........ Judg 4:6
My heart is *t* the governors of ........ Judg 5:9
even the righteous acts *t* the ........ Judg 5:11
Then their anger was abated *t* him ........ Judg 8:3
when the flame went up *t* heaven ........ Judg 13:20
now the day draweth *t* evening ........ Judg 19:9
*t* the side of mount Ephraim ........ Judg 19:18
against Gibeah *t* the sunrising ........ Judg 20:43
fled *t* the wilderness unto the ........ Judg 20:45
valley of Zeboim *t* the wilderness ........ 1Sa 13:18
And he turned from him *t* another ........ 1Sa 17:30
ran *t* the army to meet the ........ 1Sa 17:48
behold, if there be good *t* David ........ 1Sa 20:12
arose out of a place *t* the south ........ 1Sa 20:41
the king's heart was *t* Absalom ........ 2Sa 14:1
*t* the way of the wilderness ........ 2Sa 15:23
of the river of Gad, and *t* Jazer ........ 2Sa 24:5
and his servants coming on *t* him ........ 2Sa 24:20
on the outside *t* the great court ........ 1Kin 7:9
oxen, three looking *t* the north ........ 1Kin 7:25
and three looking *t* the west ........ 1Kin 7:25
and three looking *t* the south ........ 1Kin 7:25
and three looking *t* the east ........ 1Kin 7:25
spread forth his hands *t* heaven ........ 1Kin 8:22
may be open *t* this house night ........ 1Kin 8:29
even *t* the place of which thou ........ 1Kin 8:29

servant shall make *t* this place ........ 1Kin 8:29
when they shall pray *t* this place ........ 1Kin 8:30
if they pray *t* this place ........ 1Kin 8:35
forth his hands *t* this house ........ 1Kin 8:38
shall come and pray *t* this house ........ 1Kin 8:42
shall pray unto the LORD *t* the ........ 1Kin 8:44
*t* the house that I have built for ........ 1Kin 8:44
and pray unto thee *t* their land ........ 1Kin 8:48
*t* the LORD God of Israel in the ........ 1Kin 14:13
Go up now, look *t* the sea ........ 1Kin 18:43
of Judah, I would not look *t* thee ........ 2Kin 3:14
the king went the way *t* the plain ........ 2Kin 25:4
*t* the east, west, north, and south ........ 1Chr 9:24
both *t* the east, and *t* the ........ 1Chr 12:15
*t* the east, and *t* the west ........ 1Chr 12:15
a day, and *t* Asuppim two and two ... 1Chr 26:17
oxen, three looking *t* the north ........ 2Chr 4:4
and three looking *t* the west ........ 2Chr 4:4
and three looking *t* the south ........ 2Chr 4:4
and three looking *t* the east ........ 2Chr 4:4
spread forth his hands *t* heaven ........ 2Chr 6:13
thy servant prayeth *t* this place ........ 2Chr 6:20
they shall make *t* this place ........ 2Chr 6:21
yet if they pray *t* this place ........ 2Chr 6:26
they pray unto thee *t* this city ........ 2Chr 6:34
pray *t* their land, which thou ........ 2Chr 6:38
*t* the city which thou hast chosen ........ 2Chr 6:38
*t* the house which I have built ........ 2Chr 6:38
them whose heart is perfect *t* him ........ 2Chr 16:9
when Judah came *t* the watch tower 2Chr 20:24
done good in Israel, both *t* God ........ 2Chr 24:16
God, and *t* his house ........ 2Chr 24:16
the Levite, the porter *t* the east ........ 2Chr 31:14
mercy endureth for ever *t* Israel ........ Ezr 3:11
against the water gate *t* the east ........ Neh 3:26
upon the wall *t* the dung gate ........ Neh 12:31
king's manner *t* all that knew law ........ Est 1:13
out the golden sceptre *t* Esther ........ Est 8:4
dust upon their heads *t* heaven ........ Job 2:12
and stretch out thine hands *t* him ........ Job 11:13
and stretch her wings *t* the south ........ Job 39:26
will I worship *t* thy holy temple ........ Ps 5:7
Mine eyes are ever *t* the LORD ........ Ps 25:15
up my hands *t* thy holy oracle ........ Ps 28:2
his doing *t* the children of men ........ Ps 66:5
cause thine anger *t* us to cease ........ Ps 85:4
For great is thy mercy *t* me ........ Ps 86:13
his truth *t* the house of Israel ........ Ps 98:3
is his mercy *t* them that fear him ........ Ps 103:11
LORD for all his benefits *t* me ........ Ps 116:12
merciful kindness is great *t* us ........ Ps 117:2
I will worship *t* thy holy temple, ........ Ps 138:2
king's favour is *t* a wise servant ........ Prov 14:35
fly away as an eagle *t* heaven ........ Prov 23:5
The wind goeth *t* the south ........ Eccl 1:6
and if the tree fall *t* the south ........ Eccl 11:3
or *t* the north, in the place ........ Eccl 11:3
Lebanon which looketh *t* Damascus ..... Song 7:4
beloved's, and his desire is *t* me ........ Song 7:10
went up *t* Jerusalem to war ........ Is 7:1
of the Philistines *t* the west ........ Is 11:14
their fear *t* me is taught by the ........ Is 29:13
turned his face *t* the wall ........ Is 38:2
thee with their face *t* the earth ........ Is 49:23
the great goodness *t* the house of ........ Is 63:7
thy bowels and of thy mercies *t* me ........ Is 63:15
shall be known *t* his servants ........ Is 66:14
and his indignation *t* his enemies ........ Is 66:14
the face thereof is *t* the north ........ Jer 1:13
proclaim these words *t* the north ........ Jer 3:12
Set up the standard *t* Zion ........ Jer 4:6
*t* the daughter of my people ........ Jer 4:11
me, and tried mine heart *t* thee ........ Jer 12:3
mind could not be *t* this people ........ Jer 15:1
and perform my good word *t* you ........ Jer 29:10
the thoughts that I think *t* you ........ Jer 29:11
set thine heart *t* the highway ........ Jer 31:21
of the horse gate *t* the east ........ Jer 31:40
fall *t* the north by the river ........ Jer 46:6
scatter them *t* all those winds ........ Jer 49:36
lift up thy hands *t* him for the ........ Lam 2:19
straight, the one *t* the other ........ Eze 1:23
thy face *t* the siege of Jerusalem ........ Eze 4:7
set thy face *t* the mountains of ........ Eze 6:2
than the wilderness *t* Diblath ........ Eze 6:14
gate, that looketh *t* the north ........ Eze 8:3
eyes now the way *t* the north ........ Eze 8:5
up mine eyes the way *t* the north ........ Eze 8:5
house which was *t* the north ........ Eze 8:14
with their backs *t* the temple of ........ Eze 8:16
LORD, and their faces *t* the east ........ Eze 8:16
worshipped the sun *t* the east ........ Eze 8:16
gate, which lieth *t* the north ........ Eze 9:2
I will scatter *t* every wind all ........ Eze 12:14
I make my fury *t* thee to rest ........ Eze 16:42
when I am pacified *t* thee for all ........ Eze 16:63
whose branches turned *t* him ........ Eze 17:6
vine did bend her roots *t* him ........ Eze 17:7
and shot forth her branches *t* him ........ Eze 17:7
shall be scattered *t* all winds ........ Eze 17:21
of man, set thy face *t* the south ........ Eze 20:46
and drop thy word *t* the south ........ Eze 20:46
of man, set thy face *t* Jerusalem ........ Eze 21:2
drop thy word *t* the holy places, ........ Eze 21:2
and mourn one *t* another ........ Eze 24:23
and lift up your eyes *t* your idols ........ Eze 33:25
the gate which looketh *t* the east ........ Eze 40:6
court that looked *t* the north ........ Eze 40:20
the gate that looketh *t* the east ........ Eze 40:22
*t* the north, and *t* the east ........ Eze 40:23

that he brought me *t* the south ........ Eze 40:24
and behold a gate *t* the south ........ Eze 40:24
in the inner court *t* the south ........ Eze 40:27
*t* the south an hundred cubits ........ Eze 40:27
thereof were *t* the utter court ........ Eze 40:31
into the inner court *t* the east ........ Eze 40:32
thereof were *t* the outward court ........ Eze 40:34
thereof were *t* the utter court ........ Eze 40:37
and their prospect was *t* the south ........ Eze 40:44
having the prospect *t* the north ........ Eze 40:44
whose prospect is *t* the south ........ Eze 40:45
is *t* the north is for the priests ........ Eze 40:46
were *t* the place that was left ........ Eze 41:11
one door *t* the north, and another ........ Eze 41:11
and another door *t* the south ........ Eze 41:11
end *t* the west was seventy cubits ........ Eze 41:12
of the separate place *t* the east ........ Eze 41:14
*t* the palm tree on the one side ........ Eze 41:19
the face of a young lion *t* the ........ Eze 41:19
utter court, the way *t* the north ........ Eze 42:1
before the building *t* the north ........ Eze 42:1
and their doors *t* the north ........ Eze 42:4
*t* the utter court on the forepart ........ Eze 42:7
the wall of the court *t* the east ........ Eze 42:10
chambers which were *t* the north ........ Eze 42:11
*t* the south was a door in the ........ Eze 42:12
before the wall *t* the east ........ Eze 42:12
he brought me forth *t* the gate ........ Eze 42:15
gate whose prospect is *t* the east ........ Eze 42:15
the gate that looketh *t* the east ........ Eze 43:1
gate whose prospect is *t* the east ........ Eze 43:4
his stairs shall look *t* the east ........ Eze 43:17
which looketh *t* the east ........ Eze 44:1
*t* the east shall be shut the six ........ Eze 46:1
the gate that looketh *t* the east ........ Eze 46:12
priests, which looked *t* the north ........ Eze 46:19
of the house stood *t* the east ........ Eze 47:1
issue out *t* the east country ........ Eze 47:8
of the land *t* the north side ........ Eze 47:15
*t* the north five and twenty ........ Eze 48:10
*t* the west ten thousand in ........ Eze 48:10
*t* the east ten thousand in ........ Eze 48:10
*t* the south five and twenty ........ Eze 48:10
shall be *t* the north two hundred ........ Eze 48:17
*t* the south two hundred and fifty, ........ Eze 48:17
*t* the east two hundred and fifty, ........ Eze 48:17
*t* the west two hundred and fifty ........ Eze 48:17
of the oblation *t* the east border ........ Eze 48:21
twenty thousand *t* the west border ........ Eze 48:21
to the river *t* the great sea ........ Eze 48:28
the high God hath wrought *t* me ........ Dan 4:2
open in his chamber *t* Jerusalem ........ Dan 6:10
ones *t* the four winds of heaven ........ Dan 8:8
*t* the south, and *t* the east, ........ Dan 8:9
the east, and *t* the pleasant land ........ Dan 8:9
sleep on my face *t* the ground ........ Dan 8:18
my face, and my face *t* the ground ........ Dan 10:9
me, I set my face *t* the ground ........ Dan 10:15
shall be divided *t* the four winds ........ Dan 11:4
face *t* the fort of his own land ........ Dan 11:19
shall return, and come *t* the south ........ Dan 11:29
the LORD *t* the children of Israel ........ Hos 3:1
for judgment is *t* you, because ye ........ Hos 5:1
with his face *t* the east sea ........ Joel 2:20
his hinder part *t* the utmost sea ........ Joel 2:20
will look again *t* thy holy temple ........ Jonah 2:4
go forth *t* the south country ........ Zec 6:6
these that go *t* the north country ........ Zec 6:8
of Israel, shall be *t* the LORD ........ Zec 9:1
in the midst thereof *t* the east ........ Zec 14:4
*t* the west, and there shall be a ........ Zec 14:4
mountain shall remove *t* the north ........ Zec 14:4
north, and half of it *t* the south ........ Zec 14:4
half of them *t* the former sea, and ........ Zec 14:8
half of them *t* the hinder sea ........ Zec 14:8
forth his hand *t* his disciples ........ Mt 12:49
was moved with compassion *t* them ........ Mt 14:14
as it began to dawn *t* the first ........ Mt 28:1
was moved with compassion *t* them ........ Mk 6:34
on earth peace, good will *t* men ........ Lk 2:14
for himself, and is not rich *t* God ........ Lk 12:21
and journeying *t* Jerusalem ........ Lk 13:22
for it is *t* evening, and the day ........ Lk 24:29
and went over the sea *t* Capernaum ........ Jn 6:17
stedfastly *t* heaven as he went up ........ Acts 1:10
go *t* the south unto the way that ........ Acts 8:26
to the Greeks, repentance *t* God ........ Acts 20:21
faith *t* our Lord Jesus Christ ........ Acts 20:21
the fathers, and was zealous *t* God ........ Acts 22:3
And have hope *t* God, which they ........ Acts 24:15
conscience void of offence *t* God ........ Acts 24:16
God, and *t* men ........ Acts 24:16
lieth *t* the south west and north ........ Acts 27:12
to the wind, and made *t* shore ........ Acts 27:40
and so we went *t* Rome ........ Acts 28:14
in their lust one *t* another ........ Rom 1:27
But God commendeth his love *t* us ........ Rom 5:8
but *t* thee, goodness, if thou ........ Rom 11:22
Be of the same mind one *t* another ... Rom 12:16
one *t* another according to Christ ........ Rom 15:5
himself uncomely *t* his virgin ........ 1Cor 7:36
to be brought on my way *t* Judaea ........ 2Cor 1:16
our word *t* you was not yea and nay .. 2Cor 1:18
ye would confirm your love *t* him ........ 2Cor 2:8
is my boldness of speech *t* you ........ 2Cor 7:4
mourning, your fervent mind *t* me ........ 2Cor 7:7
affection is more abundant *t* you ........ 2Cor 7:15
to make all grace abound *t* you ........ 2Cor 9:8
but being absent am bold *t* you ........ 2Cor 10:1
him by the power of God *t* you ........ 2Cor 13:4

was mighty in me *t* the Gentiles ........ Gal 2:8
hath abounded *t* us in all wisdom ........ Eph 1:8
*t* us through Christ Jesus ........ Eph 2:7
supply your lack of service *t* me ........ Phil 2:30
I press *t* the mark for the prize ........ Phil 3:14
Walk in wisdom *t* them that are ........ Col 4:5
and abound in love one *t* another ........ 1Th 3:12
*t* all men, even as we do *t* ........ 1Th 3:12
all men, even as we do *t* you ........ 1Th 3:12
indeed ye do it *t* all the ........ 1Th 4:10
honestly *t* them that are without ........ 1Th 4:12
the weak, be patient *t* all men ........ 1Th 5:14
of you all *t* each other aboundeth ........ 2Th 1:3
of God our Saviour *t* man appeared ........ Titus 3:4
which thou hast *t* the Lord Jesus ........ Philem 5
the Lord Jesus, and *t* all saints ........ Philem 5
dead works, and of faith *t* God ........ Heb 6:1
which ye have shewed *t* his name ........ Heb 6:10
for conscience *t* God endure grief ........ 1Pet 2:19
answer of a good conscience *t* God ........ 1Pet 3:21
then have we confidence *t* God ........ 1Jn 3:21
manifested the love of God *t* us ........ 1Jn 4:9

**TOWEL**

and took a *t*, and girded himself ........ Jn 13:4
to wipe them with the *t* wherewith ........ Jn 13:5

**TOWER**

to, let us build us a city and a *t* ........ Gen 11:4
down to see the city and the *t* ........ Gen 11:5
his tent beyond the *t* of Edar ........ Gen 35:21
peace, I will break down this *t* ........ Judg 8:9
And he beat down the *t* of Penuel ........ Judg 8:17
of the *t* of Shechem heard that ........ Judg 9:46
that all the men of the *t* of ........ Judg 9:47
men of the *t* of Shechem died also ........ Judg 9:49
was a strong *t* within the city ........ Judg 9:51
gat them up to the top of the *t* ........ Judg 9:51
And Abimelech came unto the *t* ........ Judg 9:52
of the *t* to burn it with fire ........ Judg 9:52
horn of my salvation, my high *t* ........ 2Sa 22:3
He is the *t* of salvation for his ........ 2Sa 22:51
And when he came to the *t*, he took ... 2Kin 5:24
a watchman on the *t* in Jezreel ........ 2Kin 9:17
from the *t* of the watchmen to the ........ 2Kin 17:9
from the *t* of the watchmen to the ........ 2Kin 18:8
the watch *t* in the wilderness ........ 2Chr 20:24
even unto the *t* of Meah they ........ Neh 3:1
it, unto the *t* of Hananeel ........ Neh 3:1
piece, and the *t* of the furnaces ........ Neh 3:11
the *t* which lieth out from the ........ Neh 3:25
the east, and the *t* that lieth out ........ Neh 3:26
the great *t* that lieth out ........ Neh 3:27
from beyond the *t* of the furnaces ........ Neh 12:38
the *t* of Hananeel ........ Neh 12:39
the *t* of Meah, even unto the ........ Neh 12:39
of my salvation, and my high *t* ........ Ps 18:2
a strong *t* from the enemy ........ Ps 61:3
my high *t*, and my deliverer ........ Ps 144:2
name of the LORD is a strong *t* ........ Prov 18:10
Thy neck is like the *t* of David ........ Song 4:4
Thy neck is as a *t* of ivory ........ Song 7:4
thy nose is as the *t* of Lebanon ........ Song 7:4
And upon every high *t*, and upon ........ Is 2:15
built a *t* in the midst of it, and ........ Is 5:2
I have set thee for a *t* and a ........ Jer 6:27
*t* of Hananeel unto the gate of ........ Jer 31:38
from the *t* of Syene even unto the ........ Eze 29:10
from the *t* of Syene shall they ........ Eze 30:6
O *t* of the flock, the strong hold ........ Mic 4:8
my watch, and set me upon the *t* ........ Hab 2:1
from the *t* of Hananeel unto the ........ Zec 14:10
a winepress in it, and built a *t* ........ Mt 21:33
for the winefat, and built a *t* ........ Mk 12:1
upon whom the *t* in Siloam fell, ........ Lk 13:4
of you, intending to build a *t* ........ Lk 14:28

**TOWERS**

and make about them walls, and *t* ........ 2Chr 14:7
Moreover Uzziah built *t* in ........ 2Chr 26:9
Also he built *t* in the desert ........ 2Chr 26:10
by cunning men, to be on the *t* ........ 2Chr 26:15
the forests he built castles and *t* ........ 2Chr 27:4
broken, and raised it up to the *t* ........ 2Chr 32:5
tell the *t* thereof ........ Ps 48:12
I am a wall, and my breasts like *t* ........ Song 8:10
they set up the *t* thereof ........ Is 23:13
great slaughter, when the *t* fall ........ Is 30:25
*t* shall be for dens for ever, a ........ Is 32:14
where is he that counted the *t* ........ Is 33:18
of Tyrus, and break down her *t* ........ Eze 26:4
axes he shall break down thy *t* ........ Eze 26:9
and the Gammadims were in thy *t* ........ Eze 27:11
cities, and against the high *t* ........ Zeph 1:16
their *t* are desolate ........ Zeph 3:6

**TOWN**

for her house was upon the *t* wall ........ Josh 2:15
the elders of the *t* trembled at ........ 1Sa 16:4
entering into a *t* that hath gates ........ 1Sa 23:7
a place in some *t* in the country ........ 1Sa 27:5
him that buildeth a *t* with blood ........ Hab 2:12
city or *t* ye shall enter, enquire ........ Mt 10:11
the hand, and led him out of the *t* ........ Mk 8:23
saying, Neither go into the *t* ........ Mk 8:26
nor tell it to any in the *t* ........ Mk 8:26
come out of every *t* of Galilee ........ Lk 5:17
out of the *t* of Bethlehem, where ........ Jn 7:42
the *t* of Mary and her sister ........ Jn 11:1
Jesus was not yet come into the *t* ........ Jn 11:30

**TOWNCLERK**
when the *t* had appeased the ... Acts 19:35

**TOWNS**
these are their names, by their *t* ... Gen 25:16
went and took the small *t* thereof ... Num 32:41
beside unwalled *t* a great many ... Deut 3:5
of Bashan, and all the *t* of Jair ... Josh 13:30
Ekron, with her *t* and her villages ... Josh 15:45
Ashdod with her *t* and her villages ... Josh 15:47
and her villages, Gaza with her *t* ... Josh 15:47
and in Asher Beth-shean and her *t* ... Josh 17:11
and Ibleam and her *t* ... Josh 17:11
the inhabitants of Dor and her *t* ... Josh 17:11
inhabitants of En-dor and her *t* ... Josh 17:11
inhabitants of Taanach and her *t* ... Josh 17:11
inhabitants of Megiddo and her *t* ... Josh 17:11
who are of Beth-shean and her *t* ... Josh 17:16
of Beth-shean and her *t*, nor ... Judg 1:27
nor Taanach and her *t* ... Judg 1:27
the inhabitants of Dor and her *t* ... Judg 1:27
inhabitants of Ibleam and her *t* ... Judg 1:27
inhabitants of Megiddo and her *t* ... Judg 1:27
Israel dwelt in Heshbon and her *t* ... Judg 11:26
and in Aroer and her *t* ... Judg 11:26
to him pertained the *t* of Jair ... 1Kin 4:13
and Aram, with the *t* of Jair ... 1Chr 2:23
the *t* thereof, even threescore ... 1Chr 2:23
in Gilead in Bashan, and in her *t* ... 1Chr 5:16
the *t* thereof, and eastward Naaran ... 1Chr 7:28
Gezer, with the *t* thereof ... 1Chr 7:28
unto Gaza and the *t* thereof ... 1Chr 7:28
of Manasseh, Beth-shean and her *t* ... 1Chr 7:29
Taanach and her *t* ... 1Chr 7:29
Megiddo and her *t* ... 1Chr 7:29
Dor and her *t* ... 1Chr 7:29
Ono, and Lod, with the *t* thereof ... 1Chr 8:12
her *t* out of the hand of the ... 1Chr 18:1
him, Beth-el with the *t* thereof ... 2Chr 13:19
and Jeshanah with the *t* thereof ... 2Chr 13:19
and Ephrain with the *t* thereof ... 2Chr 13:19
that dwelt in the unwalled *t* ... Est 9:19
upon all her *t* all the evil that ... Jer 19:15
*t* without walls for the multitude ... Zec 2:4
them, Let us go into the next *t* ... Mk 1:38
into the *t* of Caesarea Philippi ... Mk 8:27
departed, and went through the *t* ... Lk 9:6
away, that they may go into the *t* ... Lk 9:12

**TRACHONITIS** (*trak-o-ni'-tis*) *A rocky district east of the Jordan.*
of Ituraea and of the region of *T* ... Lk 3:1

**TRADE**
dwell and *t* ye therein, and get you ... Gen 34:10
dwell in the land, and *t* therein ... Gen 34:21
for their *t* hath been to feed ... Gen 46:32
Thy servants' *t* hath been about ... Gen 46:34
sailors, and as many as *t* by sea ... Rev 18:17

**TRADED**
tin, and lead, they *t* in thy fairs ... Eze 27:12
they *t* the persons of men and ... Eze 27:13
*t* in thy fairs with horses ... Eze 27:14
they *t* in thy market wheat of ... Eze 27:17
*t* with the same, and made them ... Mt 25:16

**TRADING**
much every man had gained by *t* ... Lk 19:15

**TRADITION**
transgress the *t* of the elders ... Mt 15:2
the commandment of God by your *t* ... Mt 15:3
of God of none effect by your *t* ... Mt 15:6
holding the *t* of the elders ... Mk 7:3
according to the *t* of the elders ... Mk 7:5
of God, ye hold the *t* of men ... Mk 7:8
God, that ye may keep your own *t* ... Mk 7:9
God of none effect through your *t* ... Mk 7:13
vain deceit, after the *t* of men ... Col 2:8
not after the *t* which he received ... 2Th 3:6
received by *t* from your fathers ... 1Pet 1:18

**TRADITIONS**
zealous of the *t* of my fathers ... Gal 1:14
hold the *t* which ye have been ... 2Th 2:15

**TRAFFICK**
and ye shall *t* in the land ... Gen 42:34
of the *t* of the spice merchants ... 1Kin 10:15
and carried it into a land of *t* ... Eze 17:4
by thy *t* hast thou increased thy ... Eze 28:5
by the iniquity of thy *t* ... Eze 28:18

**TRAFFICKERS**
whose *t* are the honourable of the ... Is 23:8

**TRAIN**
to Jerusalem with a very great *t* ... 1Kin 10:2
*T* up a child in the way he should ... Prov 22:6
up, and his *t* filled the temple ... Is 6:1

**TRAINED**
captive, he armed his *t* servants ... Gen 14:14

**TRAITOR**
Iscariot, which also was the *t* ... Lk 6:16

**TRAITORS**
*T*, heady, highminded, lovers of ... 2Ti 3:4

**TRAMPLE**
dragon shalt thou *t* under feet ... Ps 91:13
mine anger, and *t* them in my fury ... Is 63:3
lest they *t* them under their feet ... Mt 7:6

**TRANCE**
of the Almighty, falling into a *t* ... Num 24:4
of the Almighty, falling into a *t* ... Num 24:16
they made ready, he fell into a *t* ... Acts 10:10
in a *t* I saw a vision, A certain ... Acts 11:5
in the temple, I was in a *t* ... Acts 22:17

**TRANQUILITY**
it may be a lengthening of thy *t* ... Dan 4:27

**TRANSFERRED**
I have in a figure *t* to myself ... 1Cor 4:6

**TRANSFIGURED**
And was *t* before them ... Mt 17:2
and he was *t* before them ... Mk 9:2

**TRANSFORMED**
but be ye *t* by the renewing of ... Rom 12:2
for Satan himself is *t* into an ... 2Cor 11:14
also be *t* as the ministers of ... 2Cor 11:15

**TRANSFORMING**
*t* themselves into the apostles of ... 2Cor 11:13

**TRANSGRESS**
Wherefore now do ye *t* the ... Num 14:41
ye make the LORD's people to *t* ... 1Sa 2:24
Why *t* ye the commandments of the. 2Chr 24:20
servant Moses, saying, If ye *t* ... Neh 1:8
to *t* against our God in marrying ... Neh 13:27
that my mouth shall not *t* ... Ps 17:3
be ashamed which *t* without cause ... Ps 25:3
a piece of bread that man will *t* ... Prov 28:21
and thou saidst, I will not *t* ... Jer 2:20
rebels, and them that *t* against me ... Eze 20:38
Come to Beth-el, and *t* ... Amos 4:4
Why do thy disciples *t* the ... Mt 15:2
Why do ye also *t* the commandment ... Mt 15:3
and circumcision dost *t* the law ... Rom 2:27

**TRANSGRESSED**
I have not *t* thy commandments, ... Deut 26:13
they have also *t* my covenant ... Josh 7:11
because he hath *t* the covenant of ... Josh 7:15
When ye have *t* the covenant of ... Josh 23:16
*t* my covenant which I commanded ... Judg 2:20
And he said, Ye have *t* ... 1Sa 14:33
for I have *t* the commandment of ... 1Sa 15:24
wherein they have *t* against thee ... 1Kin 8:50
but *t* his covenant, and all that ... 2Kin 18:12
who *t* in the thing accursed ... 1Chr 2:7
they *t* against the God of their ... 1Chr 5:25
they had *t* against the LORD ... 2Chr 12:2
for he *t* against the LORD his God ... 2Chr 26:16
naked, and *t* sore against the LORD ... 2Chr 28:19
*t* very much after all the ... 2Chr 36:14
up, and said unto them, Ye have *t* ... Ezr 10:10
many that have *t* in this thing ... Ezr 10:13
because they have *t* the laws ... Is 24:5
and thy teachers have *t* against me ... Is 43:27
of the men that have *t* against me ... Is 66:24
the pastors also *t* against me ... Jer 2:8
ye all have *t* against me, saith ... Jer 2:29
that thou hast *t* against the LORD ... Jer 3:13
and whereby they have *t* against me ... Jer 33:8
the men that have *t* my covenant ... Jer 34:18
We have *t* and have rebelled ... Lam 3:42
their fathers have *t* against me ... Eze 2:3
transgressions, whereby ye have *t* ... Eze 18:31
Yea, all Israel have *t* thy law ... Dan 9:11
they like men have *t* the covenant ... Hos 6:7
because they have *t* against me ... Hos 7:13
because they have *t* my covenant ... Hos 8:1
wherein thou hast *t* against me ... Zeph 3:11
neither *t* I at any time thy ... Lk 15:29

**TRANSGRESSEST**
Why *t* thou the king's commandment ... Est 3:3

**TRANSGRESSETH**
his mouth *t* not in judgment ... Prov 16:10
Yea also, because he *t* by wine ... Hab 2:5
committeth sin *t* also the law ... 1Jn 3:4
Whosoever *t*, and abideth not in ... 2Jn 9

**TRANSGRESSING**
LORD thy God, in *t* his covenant, ... Deut 17:2
In *t* and lying against the LORD, ... Is 59:13

**TRANSGRESSION**
forgiving iniquity and *t* and sin, ... Ex 34:7
mercy, forgiving iniquity and *t* ... Num 14:18
or if in *t* against the LORD, ( ... Josh 22:22
neither evil nor *t* in mine hand ... 1Sa 24:11
away to Babylon for their *t* ... 1Chr 9:1
So Saul died for his *t* which he ... 1Chr 10:13
his reign did cast away in his *t* ... 2Chr 29:19
because of the *t* of those that ... Ezr 9:4
*t* of them that had been carried ... Ezr 10:6
And why dost thou not pardon my *t* ... Job 7:21
have cast them away for their *t* ... Job 8:4
make me to know my *t* and my sin ... Job 13:23
My *t* is sealed up in a bag, and ... Job 14:17
I am clean without *t*, I am ... Job 33:9
my wound is incurable without *t* ... Job 34:6
be innocent from the great *t* ... Ps 19:13
Blessed is he whose *t* is forgiven ... Ps 32:1
The *t* of the wicked saith within ... Ps 36:1
not for my *t*, nor for my sin, O ... Ps 59:3
will I visit their *t* with the rod ... Ps 89:32
Fools, because of their *t* ... Ps 107:17
is snared by the *t* of his lips ... Prov 12:13
He that covereth a *t* seeketh love ... Prov 17:9
He loveth *t* that loveth strife ... Prov 17:19
it is his glory to pass over a *t* ... Prov 19:11
For the *t* of a land many are the ... Prov 28:2
his mother, and saith, It is no *t* ... Prov 28:24
In the *t* of an evil man there is ... Prov 29:6
are multiplied, *t* increaseth ... Prov 29:16
and a furious man aboundeth in *t* ... Prov 29:22
the *t* thereof shall be heavy upon ... Is 24:20
for the *t* of my people was he ... Is 53:8
are ye not children of *t*, a seed ... Is 57:4
and shew my people their *t* ... Is 58:1
them that turn from *t* in Jacob ... Is 59:20
deliver him in the day of his *t* ... Eze 33:12
daily sacrifice by reason of *t* ... Dan 8:12
the *t* of desolation, to give both ... Dan 8:13
thy holy city, to finish the *t* ... Dan 9:24
at Gilgal multiply *t* ... Amos 4:4
For the *t* of Jacob is all this, ... Mic 1:5
What is the *t* of Jacob ... Mic 1:5
to declare unto Jacob his *t* ... Mic 3:8
I give my firstborn for my *t* ... Mic 6:7
passeth by the *t* of the remnant ... Mic 7:18
from which Judas by *t* fell ... Acts 1:25
where no law is, there is no *t* ... Rom 4:15
after the similitude of Adam's *t* ... Rom 5:14
woman being deceived was in the *t* ... 1Ti 2:14
angels was stedfast, and every *t* ... Heb 2:2
for sin is the *t* of the law ... 1Jn 3:4

**TRANSGRESSIONS**
for he will not pardon your *t* ... Ex 23:21
because of their *t* in all their ... Lev 16:16
all their *t* in all their sins, ... Lev 16:21
not forgive your *t* nor your sins ... Josh 24:19
all their *t* wherein they have ... 1Kin 8:50
If I covered my *t* as Adam ... Job 31:33
or if thy *t* be multiplied, what ... Job 35:6
their *t* that they have exceeded ... Job 36:9
out in the multitude of their *t* ... Ps 5:10
the sins of my youth, nor my *t* ... Ps 25:7
I will confess my *t* unto the LORD ... Ps 32:5
Deliver me from all my *t* ... Ps 39:8
thy tender mercies blot out my *t* ... Ps 51:1
For I acknowledge my *t* ... Ps 51:3
as for our *t*, thou shalt purge ... Ps 65:3
far hath he removed our *t* from us ... Ps 103:12
out thy *t* for mine own sake ... Is 43:25
out, as a thick cloud, thy *t* ... Is 44:22
for your *t* is your mother put ... Is 50:1
But he was wounded for our *t* ... Is 53:5
For our *t* are multiplied before ... Is 59:12
for our *t* are with us ... Is 59:12
because their *t* are many, and ... Jer 5:6
her for the multitude of her *t* ... Lam 1:5
The yoke of my *t* is bound by his ... Lam 1:14
hast done unto me for all my *t* ... Lam 1:22
any more with all their *t* ... Eze 14:11
All his *t* that he hath committed ... Eze 18:22
all his *t* that he hath committed ... Eze 18:28
turn yourselves from all your *t* ... Eze 18:30
Cast away from you all your *t* ... Eze 18:31
in that your *t* are discovered, so ... Eze 21:24
Thus ye speak, saying, If our *t* ... Eze 33:10
things, nor with any of their *t* ... Eze 37:23
according to their *t* have I done ... Eze 39:24
For three *t* of Damascus, and for ... Amos 1:3
For three *t* of Gaza, and for four, ... Amos 1:6
For three *t* of Tyrus, and for four ... Amos 1:9
For three *t* of Edom, and for four, ... Amos 1:11
For three *t* of the children of ... Amos 1:13
For three *t* of Moab, and for four, ... Amos 2:1
For three *t* of Judah, and for four ... Amos 2:4
For three *t* of Israel, and for ... Amos 2:6
*t* of Israel upon him I will also ... Amos 3:14
For I know your manifold *t* ... Amos 5:12
for the *t* of Israel were found in ... Mic 1:13
It was added because of *t* ... Gal 3:19
the *t* that were under the first ... Heb 9:15

**TRANSGRESSOR**
and the *t* for the upright ... Prov 21:18
overthroweth the words of the *t* ... Prov 22:12
and wast called a *t* from the womb ... Is 48:8
I destroyed, I make myself a *t* ... Gal 2:18
thou art become a *t* of the law ... Jas 2:11

**TRANSGRESSORS**
But the *t* shall be destroyed ... Ps 37:38
Then will I teach *t* thy ways ... Ps 51:13
be not merciful to any wicked *t* ... Ps 59:5
I beheld the *t*, and was grieved ... Ps 119:158
the *t* shall be rooted out of it ... Prov 2:22
of *t* shall destroy them ... Prov 11:3
but *t* shall be taken in their own ... Prov 11:6
soul of the *t* shall eat violence ... Prov 13:2
but the way of *t* is hard ... Prov 13:15
and increaseth the *t* among men ... Prov 23:28
the fool, and rewardeth *t* ... Prov 26:10
And the destruction of the *t* ... Is 1:28
bring it again to mind, O ye *t* ... Is 46:8
and he was numbered with the *t* ... Is 53:12
and made intercession for the *t* ... Is 53:12
when the *t* are come to the full, ... Dan 8:23
but the *t* shall fall therein ... Hos 14:9
And he was numbered with the *t* ... Mk 15:28
And he was reckoned among the *t* ... Lk 22:37
and are convinced of the law as *t* ... Jas 2:9

**TRANSLATE**
To *t* the kingdom from the house ... 2Sa 3:10

**TRANSLATED**
hath *t* us into the kingdom of his ... Col 1:13
By faith Enoch was *t* that he ... Heb 11:5

T

not found, because God had *t* him ... Heb 11:5

**TRANSLATION**
for before his *t* he had this ... Heb 11:5

**TRANSPARENT**
was pure gold, as it were *t* glass ... Rev 21:21

**TRAP**
ground, and a *t* for him in the way ... Job 18:10
their welfare, let it become a *t* ... Ps 69:22
they set a *t*, they catch men ... Jer 5:26
table be made a snare, and a *t* ... Rom 11:9

**TRAPS**
*t* unto you, and scourges in your ... Josh 23:13

**TRAVAIL**
came to pass in the time of her *t* ... Gen 38:27
all the *t* that had come upon them ... Ex 18:8
and pain, as of a woman in *t* ... Ps 48:6
this sore *t* hath God given to the ... Eccl 1:13
days are sorrows, and his *t* grief ... Eccl 2:23
but to the sinner he giveth *t* ... Eccl 2:26
I have seen the *t*, which God hath ... Eccl 3:10
Again, I considered all *t* ... Eccl 4:4
than both the hands full with *t* ... Eccl 4:6
also vanity, yea, it is a sore *t* ... Eccl 4:8
But those riches perish by evil *t* ... Eccl 5:14
I *t* not, nor bring forth children ... Is 23:4
He shall see of the *t* of his soul ... Is 53:11
thou that didst not *t* with child ... Is 54:1
heard a voice as of a woman in *t* ... Jer 4:31
us, and pain, as of a woman in *t* ... Jer 6:24
take thee, as a woman in *t* ... Jer 13:21
thee, the pain as of a woman in *t* ... Jer 22:23
whether a man doth *t* with child ... Jer 30:6
on his loins, as a woman in *t* ... Jer 30:6
have taken her, as a woman in *t* ... Jer 49:24
him, and pangs as of a woman in *t* ... Jer 50:43
have taken thee as a woman in *t* ... Mic 4:9
of Zion, like a woman in *t* ... Mic 4:10
when she is in *t* hath sorrow ... Jn 16:21
of whom I *t* in birth again until ... Gal 4:19
brethren, our labour and *t* ... 1Th 2:9
as *t* upon a woman with child ... 1Th 5:3
*t* night and day, that we might not ... 2Th 3:8

**TRAVAILED**
and Rachel *t*, and she had hard ... Gen 35:16
And it came to pass, when she *t* ... Gen 38:28
were dead, she bowed herself and *t* ... 1Sa 4:19
Before she *t*, she brought forth ... Is 66:7
for as soon as Zion *t*, she ... Is 66:8

**TRAVAILEST**
forth and cry, thou that *t* not ... Gal 4:27

**TRAVAILETH**
The wicked man *t* with pain all ... Job 15:20
he *t* with iniquity, and hath ... Ps 7:14
be in pain as a woman that *t* ... Is 13:8
as the pangs of a woman that *t* ... Is 21:3
her that *t* with child together ... Jer 31:8
she which *t* hath brought forth ... Mic 5:3
*t* in pain together until now ... Rom 8:22

**TRAVAILING**
now will I cry like a *t* woman ... Is 42:14
The sorrows of a *t* woman shall ... Hos 13:13
*t* in birth, and pained to be ... Rev 12:2

**TRAVEL**
Thou knowest all the *t* that hath ... Num 20:14
and compassed me with gall and *t* ... Lam 3:5
Macedonia, Paul's companions in *t* ... Acts 19:29
to *t* with us with this grace ... 2Cor 8:19

**TRAVELERS**
the *t* walked through byways ... Judg 5:6

**TRAVELLED**
about Stephen *t* as far as Phenice ... Acts 11:19

**TRAVELLER**
there came a *t* unto the rich man, ... 2Sa 12:4
but I opened my doors to the *t* ... Job 31:32

**TRAVELLETH**
thy poverty come as one that *t* ... Prov 6:11
thy poverty come as one that *t* ... Prov 24:34

**TRAVELLING**
O ye *t* companies of Dedanim ... Is 21:13
*t* in the greatness of his ... Is 63:1
is as a man *t* into a far country ... Mt 25:14

**TRAVERSING**
art a swift dromedary *t* her ways ... Jer 2:23

**TREACHEROUS**
the *t* dealer dealeth ... Is 21:2
the *t* dealers have dealt ... Is 24:16
the *t* dealers have dealt very ... Is 24:16
her *t* sister Judah saw it ... Jer 3:7
yet her *t* sister Judah feared not ... Jer 3:8
yet for all this her *t* sister ... Jer 3:10
herself more than *t* Judah ... Jer 3:11
adulterers, an assembly of *t* men ... Jer 9:2
prophets are light and *t* persons ... Zeph 3:4

**TREACHEROUSLY**
of Shechem dealt *t* with Abimelech ... Judg 9:23
the treacherous dealer dealeth *t* ... Is 21:2
treacherous dealers have dealt *t* ... Is 24:16
dealers have dealt very *t* ... Is 24:16
and dealest *t*, and they dealt not ... Is 33:1
and they dealt not *t* with thee ... Is 33:1
thou shalt make an end to deal *t* ... Is 33:1
they shall deal *t* with thee ... Is 33:1
that thou wouldest deal very *t* ... Is 48:8
Surely as a wife *t* departeth from ... Jer 3:20
so have ye dealt *t* with me ... Jer 3:20
have dealt very *t* against me ... Jer 5:11
all they happy that deal very *t* ... Jer 12:1
even they have dealt *t* with thee ... Jer 12:6
her friends have dealt *t* with her ... Lam 1:2
They have dealt *t* against the ... Hos 5:7
have they dealt *t* against me ... Hos 6:7
thou upon them that deal *t* ... Hab 1:13
why do we deal *t* every man ... Mal 2:10
Judah hath dealt *t*, and an ... Mal 2:11
against whom thou hast dealt *t* ... Mal 2:14
let none deal *t* against the wife ... Mal 2:15
your spirit, that ye deal not *t* ... Mal 2:16

**TREACHERY**
and said to Ahaziah, There is *t* ... 2Kin 9:23

**TREAD**
your feet shall *t* shall be yours ... Deut 11:24
all the land that ye shall *t* upon ... Deut 11:25
thou shalt *t* upon their high ... Deut 33:29
sole of your foot shall *t* upon ... Josh 1:3
*t* on the threshold of Dagon in ... 1Sa 5:5
*t* their winepresses, and suffer ... Job 24:11
*t* down the wicked in their place ... Job 40:12
let him *t* down my life upon the ... Ps 7:5
through thy name will we *t* them ... Ps 44:5
is that shall *t* down our enemies ... Ps 60:12
Thou shalt *t* upon the lion and ... Ps 91:13
is that shall *t* down our enemies ... Ps 108:13
this at your hand, to *t* my courts ... Is 1:12
to *t* them down like the mire of ... Is 10:6
my mountains *t* him under foot ... Is 14:25
the treaders shall *t* out no wine ... Is 16:10
The foot shall *t* it down, even ... Is 26:6
for I will *t* them in mine anger, ... Is 63:3
I will *t* down the people in mine ... Is 63:6
shout, as they that *t* the grapes ... Jer 25:30
none shall *t* with shouting ... Jer 48:33
shall he *t* down all thy streets ... Eze 26:11
but ye must *t* down with your feet ... Eze 34:18
shall *t* it down, and break it in ... Dan 7:23
and loveth to *t* out the corn ... Hos 10:11
*t* upon the high places of the ... Mic 1:3
when he shall *t* in our palaces, ... Mic 5:5
thou shalt *t* the olives, but thou ... Mic 6:15
*t* the morter, make strong the ... Nah 3:14
which *t* down their enemies in the ... Zec 10:5
ye shall *t* down the wicked ... Mal 4:3
unto you power to *t* on serpents ... Lk 10:19
shall they *t* under foot forty ... Rev 11:2

**TREADER**
the *t* of grapes him that soweth ... Amos 9:13

**TREADERS**
the *t* shall tread out no wine in ... Is 16:10

**TREADETH**
the ox when he *t* out the corn ... Deut 25:4
*t* upon the waves of the sea ... Job 9:8
morter, and as the potter *t* clay ... Is 41:25
like him that *t* in the winefat ... Is 63:2
*t* upon the high places of the ... Amos 4:13
when he *t* within our borders ... Mic 5:6
if he go through, both *t* down ... Mic 5:8
of the ox that *t* out the corn ... 1Cor 9:9
muzzle the ox that *t* out the corn ... 1Ti 5:18
he *t* the winepress of the ... Rev 19:15

**TREADING**
some *t* winepresses on the sabbath ... Neh 13:15
for the *t* of lesser cattle ... Is 7:25
of *t* down, and of perplexity by ... Is 22:5
as your *t* is upon the poor ... Amos 5:11

**TREASON**
his *t* that he wrought, are they ... 1Kin 16:20
rent her clothes, and cried, *T* ... 2Kin 11:14
her clothes, and cried, *T*, *T* ... 2Kin 11:14
rent her clothes, and said, *T* ... 2Chr 23:13
her clothes, and said, *T*, *T* ... 2Chr 23:13

**TREASURE**
hath given you *t* in your sacks ... Gen 43:23
they built for Pharaoh *t* cities ... Ex 1:11
*t* unto me above all people ... Ex 19:5
shall open unto thee his good *t* ... Deut 28:12
to the *t* of the house of the LORD ... 1Chr 29:8
unto the *t* of the work threescore ... Ezr 2:69
search made in the king's *t* house ... Ezr 5:17
it out of the king's *t* house ... Ezr 7:20
to the *t* a thousand drams of gold ... Neh 7:70
of the fathers gave to the *t* of ... Neh 7:71
to the chambers, into the *t* house ... Neh 10:38
belly thou fillest with thy hid *t* ... Ps 17:14
and Israel for his peculiar *t* ... Ps 135:4
house of the righteous is much *t* ... Prov 15:6
the fear of the LORD than great *t* ... Prov 15:16
There is *t* to be desired and oil ... Prov 21:20
gold, and the peculiar *t* of kings ... Eccl 2:8
the fear of the LORD is his *t* ... Is 33:6
they have taken the *t* and precious ... Eze 22:25
into the *t* house of his god ... Dan 1:2
he shall spoil the *t* of all ... Hos 13:15
For where your *t* is, there will ... Mt 6:21
A good man out of the good *t* of ... Mt 12:35
evil *t* bringeth forth evil things ... Mt 12:35
is like unto *t* hid in a field ... Mt 13:44
forth out of his *t* things new ... Mt 13:52
and thou shalt have *t* in heaven ... Mt 19:21
and thou shalt have *t* in heaven ... Mk 10:21
A good man out of the good *t* of ... Lk 6:45
*t* of his heart bringeth forth ... Lk 6:45
he that layeth up *t* for himself ... Lk 12:21
a *t* in the heavens that faileth ... Lk 12:33
For where your *t* is, there will ... Lk 12:34
and thou shalt have *t* in heaven ... Lk 18:22
who had the charge of all her *t* ... Acts 8:27
But we have this *t* in earthen ... 2Cor 4:7
Ye have heaped *t* together for the ... Jas 5:3

**TREASURED**
it shall not be *t* nor laid up ... Is 23:18

**TREASURER**
by the hand of Mithredath the *t* ... Ezr 1:8
hosts, Go, get thee unto this *t* ... Is 22:15

**TREASURERS**
the *t* which are beyond the river ... Ezr 7:21
I made *t* over the treasuries, ... Neh 13:13
the captains, the judges, the *t* ... Dan 3:2
and captains, the judges, the *t* ... Dan 3:3

**TREASURES**
with me, and sealed up among my *t* ... Deut 32:34
the seas, and of *t* hid in the sand ... Deut 33:19
did he put among the *t* of the ... 1Kin 7:51
he took away the *t* of the house ... 1Kin 14:26
the *t* of the king's house ... 1Kin 14:26
in the *t* of the house of the LORD ... 1Kin 15:18
the *t* of the king's house, and ... 1Kin 15:18
in the *t* of the house of the LORD ... 2Kin 12:18
in the *t* of the king's house, and ... 2Kin 14:14
in the *t* of the king's house, and ... 2Kin 16:8
in the *t* of the king's house ... 2Kin 18:15
and all that was found in his *t* ... 2Kin 20:13
there is nothing among my *t* that ... 2Kin 20:15
the *t* of the house of the LORD ... 2Kin 24:13
the *t* of the king's house, and cut ... 2Kin 24:13
over the *t* of the house of God ... 1Chr 26:20
over the *t* of the dedicated ... 1Chr 26:20
which were over the *t* of the ... 1Chr 26:22
son of Moses, was ruler of the *t* ... 1Chr 26:24
all the *t* of the dedicated things ... 1Chr 26:26
over the king's *t* was Azmaveth ... 1Chr 27:25
put he among the *t* of the house ... 2Chr 5:1
any matter, or concerning the *t* ... 2Chr 8:15
took away the *t* of the house of ... 2Chr 12:9
the *t* of the king's house ... 2Chr 12:9
gold out of the *t* of the house of ... 2Chr 16:2
the *t* of the king's house, the ... 2Chr 25:24
the *t* of the house of the LORD, ... 2Chr 36:18
the *t* of the king, and of his ... 2Chr 36:18
where the *t* were laid up in ... Ezr 6:1
over the chambers for the *t* ... Neh 12:44
and dig for it more than for hid *t* ... Job 3:21
entered into the *t* of the snow ... Job 38:22
hast thou seen the *t* of the hail ... Job 38:22
and searchest for her as for hid *t* ... Prov 2:4
and I will fill their *t* ... Prov 8:21
*T* of wickedness profit nothing ... Prov 10:2
The getting of *t* by a lying ... Prov 21:6
is there any end of their *t* ... Is 2:7
people, and have robbed their *t* ... Is 10:13
their *t* upon the bunches of ... Is 30:6
and all that was found in his *t* ... Is 39:2
there is nothing among my *t* that ... Is 39:4
will give thee the *t* of darkness ... Is 45:3
forth the wind out of his *t* ... Jer 10:13
thy *t* will I give to the spoil ... Jer 15:13
all thy *t* to the spoil, and thy ... Jer 17:3
all the *t* of the kings of Judah ... Jer 20:5
for we have *t* in the field, of ... Jer 41:8
trusted in thy works and in thy *t* ... Jer 48:7
that trusted in her *t*, saying, ... Jer 49:4
a sword is upon her *t* ... Jer 50:37
upon many waters, abundant in *t* ... Jer 51:13
forth the wind out of his *t* ... Jer 51:16
gotten gold and silver into thy *t* ... Eze 28:4
have power over the *t* of gold ... Dan 11:43
Are there yet the *t* of wickedness ... Mic 6:10
and when they had opened their *t* ... Mt 2:11
up for yourselves *t* upon earth ... Mt 6:19
lay up for yourselves *t* in heaven ... Mt 6:20
whom are hid all the *t* of wisdom ... Col 2:3
riches than the *t* in Egypt ... Heb 11:26

**TREASUREST**
impenitent heart *t* up unto ... Rom 2:5

**TREASURIES**
chambers and *t* of the house of God ... 1Chr 9:26
of the *t* thereof, and of the upper ... 1Chr 28:11
of the *t* of the house of God, and ... 1Chr 28:12
of the *t* of the dedicated things ... 1Chr 28:12
and he made himself *t* for silver ... 2Chr 32:27
new wine and the oil unto the *t* ... Neh 13:12
And I made treasurers over the *t* ... Neh 13:13
to bring it into the king's *t* ... Est 3:9
pay to the king's *t* for the Jews ... Est 4:7
he bringeth the wind out of his *t* ... Ps 135:7

**TREASURY**
shall come into the *t* of the LORD ... Josh 6:19
they put into the *t* of the house ... Josh 6:24
the house of the king under the *t* ... Jer 38:11
lawful for to put them into the *t* ... Mt 27:6
And Jesus sat over against the *t* ... Mk 12:41
the people cast money into the *t* ... Mk 12:41
they which have cast into the *t* ... Mk 12:43
casting their gifts into the *t* ... Lk 21:1

These words spake Jesus in the *t* ........ Jn 8:20

**TREATISE**
The former *t* have I made, O ........ Acts 1:1

**TREE**
the fruit *t* yielding fruit after ........ Gen 1:11
the *t* yielding fruit, whose seed ........ Gen 1:12
face of all the earth, and every *t* ........ Gen 1:29
is the fruit of a *t* yielding seed ........ Gen 1:29
*t* that is pleasant to the sight ........ Gen 2:9
the *t* of life also in the midst ........ Gen 2:9
the *t* of knowledge of good and ........ Gen 2:9
Of every *t* of the garden thou ........ Gen 2:16
But of the *t* of the knowledge of ........ Gen 2:17
not eat of every *t* of the garden ........ Gen 3:1
But of the fruit of the *t* which ........ Gen 3:3
saw that the *t* was good for food ........ Gen 3:6
a *t* to be desired to make one ........ Gen 3:6
Hast thou eaten of the *t*, whereof ........ Gen 3:11
be with me, she gave me of the *t* ........ Gen 3:12
thy wife, and hast eaten of the *t* ........ Gen 3:17
and take also of the *t* of life ........ Gen 3:22
to keep the way of the *t* of life ........ Gen 3:24
and rest yourselves under the *t* ........ Gen 18:4
and he stood by them under the *t* ........ Gen 18:8
and of the hazel and chesnut *t* ........ Gen 30:37
thee, and shall hang thee on a *t* ........ Gen 40:19
brake every *t* of the field ........ Ex 9:25
shall eat every *t* which groweth ........ Ex 10:5
and the LORD shewed him a *t* ........ Ex 15:25
land, or of the fruit of the *t* ........ Lev 27:30
that is made of the vine *t* ........ Num 6:4
the hills, and under every green *t* ........ Deut 12:2
with the axe to cut down the *t* ........ Deut 19:5
not cut them down (for the *t* of ........ Deut 20:19
to death, and thou hang him on a *t* .. Deut 21:22
not remain all night upon the *t* ........ Deut 21:23
before thee in the way in any *t* ........ Deut 22:6
When thou beatest thine olive *t* ........ Deut 24:20
he hanged on a *t* until eventide ........ Josh 8:29
take his carcase down from the *t* ........ Josh 8:29
palm *t* of Deborah between Ramah ........ Judg 4:5
and they said unto the olive *t* ........ Judg 9:8
But the olive *t* said unto them, ........ Judg 9:9
And the trees said to the fig *t* ........ Judg 9:10
But the fig *t* said unto them, ........ Judg 9:11
pomegranate *t* which is in Migron ........ 1Sa 14:2
in Gibeah under a *t* in Ramah ........ 1Sa 22:6
buried them under a *t* at Jabesh ........ 1Sa 31:13
under his vine and under his fig *t* ........ 1Kin 4:25
from the cedar *t* that is in ........ 1Kin 4:33
he made two cherubims of olive *t* ........ 1Kin 6:23
oracle he made doors of olive *t* ........ 1Kin 6:31
two doors also were of olive *t* ........ 1Kin 6:32
of the temple posts of olive *t* ........ 1Kin 6:33
And the two doors were of fir *t* ........ 1Kin 6:34
high hill, and under every green *t* ........ 1Kin 14:23
and sat down under a juniper *t* ........ 1Kin 19:4
he lay and slept under a juniper *t* ........ 1Kin 19:5
city, and shall fell every good *t* ........ 2Kin 3:19
the hills, and under every green *t* ........ 2Kin 16:4
high hill, and under every green *t* ........ 2Kin 17:10
vine, and every one of his fig *t* ........ 2Kin 18:31
house he cieled with fir *t* ........ 2Chr 3:5
the hills, and under every green *t* ........ 2Chr 28:4
they were both hanged on a *t* ........ Est 2:23
For there is hope of a *t*, if it ........ Job 14:7
hope hath he removed like a *t* ........ Job 19:10
wickedness shall be broken as a *t* ........ Job 24:20
he shall be like a *t* planted by ........ Ps 1:3
himself like a green bay *t* ........ Ps 37:35
green olive *t* in the house of God ........ Ps 52:8
shall flourish like the palm *t* ........ Ps 92:12
She is a *t* of life to them that ........ Prov 3:18
of the righteous is a *t* of life ........ Prov 11:30
desire cometh, it is a *t* of life ........ Prov 13:12
A wholesome tongue is a *t* of life ........ Prov 15:4
Whoso keepeth the fig *t* shall eat ........ Prov 27:18
if the *t* fall toward the south, ........ Eccl 11:3
in the place where the *t* falleth ........ Eccl 11:3
the almond *t* shall flourish, and ........ Eccl 12:5
As the apple *t* among the trees of ........ Song 2:3
The fig *t* putteth forth her green ........ Song 2:13
thy stature is like to a palm *t* ........ Song 7:7
said, I will go up to the palm *t* ........ Song 7:8
raised thee up under the apple *t* ........ Song 8:5
as a teil *t*, and as an oak, whose ........ Is 6:13
it, as the shaking of an olive *t* ........ Is 17:6
be as the shaking of an olive *t* ........ Is 24:13
as a falling fig from the fig *t* ........ Is 34:4
vine, and every one of his fig *t* ........ Is 36:16
chooseth a *t* that will not rot ........ Is 40:20
the cedar, the shittah *t*, and the ........ Is 41:19
*t*, and the myrtle, and the oil *t* ........ Is 41:19
will set in the desert the fir *t* ........ Is 41:19
the pine, and the box *t* together ........ Is 41:19
I fall down to the stock of a *t* ........ Is 44:19
O forest, and every *t* therein ........ Is 44:23
the thorn shall come up the fir *t* ........ Is 55:13
brier shall come up the myrtle *t* ........ Is 55:13
eunuch say, Behold, I am a dry *t* ........ Is 56:3
with idols under every green *t* ........ Is 57:5
shall come unto thee, the fir *t* ........ Is 60:13
thee, the fir *t*, the pine *t* ........ Is 60:13
for as the days of a *t* are the ........ Is 65:22
gardens behind one *t* in the midst ........ Is 66:17
said, I see a rod of an almond *t* ........ Jer 1:11
every green *t* thou wanderest ........ Jer 2:20
mountain and under every green *t* ........ Jer 3:6
the strangers under every green *t* ........ Jer 3:13
the vine, nor figs on the fig *t* ........ Jer 8:13
one cutteth a *t* out of the forest ........ Jer 10:3
They are upright as the palm *t* ........ Jer 10:5
called thy name, A green olive *t* ........ Jer 11:16
Let us destroy the *t* with the ........ Jer 11:19
For he shall be as a *t* planted by ........ Jer 17:8
mountains, and under every green *t* ........ Eze 6:13
is the vine *t* more than any *t* ........ Eze 15:2
As the vine *t* among the trees of ........ Eze 15:6
waters, and set it as a willow *t* ........ Eze 17:5
LORD have brought down the high *t* ... Eze 17:24
have exalted the low *t* ........ Eze 17:24
*t*, have dried up the green *t* ........ Eze 17:24
have made the dry *t* to flourish ........ Eze 17:24
devour every green *t* in thee ........ Eze 20:47
and every dry *t* ........ Eze 20:47
the rod of my son, as every *t* ........ Eze 21:10
nor any *t* in the garden of God ........ Eze 31:8
the *t* of the field shall yield ........ Eze 34:27
will multiply the fruit of the *t* ........ Eze 36:30
so that a palm *t* was between a ........ Eze 41:18
toward the palm *t* on the one side ........ Eze 41:19
the palm *t* on the other side ........ Eze 41:19
behold a *t* in the midst of the ........ Dan 4:10
The *t* grew, and was strong, and the ... Dan 4:11
and said thus, Hew down the *t* ........ Dan 4:14
The *t* that thou sawest, which ........ Dan 4:20
heaven, and saying, Hew the *t* down ... Dan 4:23
to leave the stump of the *t* roots ........ Dan 4:26
in the fig *t* at her first time ........ Hos 9:10
beauty shall be as the olive *t* ........ Hos 14:6
I am like a green fir *t* ........ Hos 14:8
my vine waste, and barked my fig *t* ........ Joel 1:7
up, and the fig *t* languisheth ........ Joel 1:12
pomegranate *t*, the palm *t* also ........ Joel 1:12
also, and the apple *t* ........ Joel 1:12
for the *t* beareth her fruit, the ........ Joel 2:22
beareth her fruit, the fig *t* ........ Joel 2:22
under his vine and under his fig *t* ........ Mic 4:4
Although the fig *t* shall not ........ Hab 3:17
as yet the vine, and the fig *t* ........ Hag 2:19
the pomegranate, and the olive *t* ........ Hag 2:19
under the vine and under the fig *t* ........ Zec 3:10
Howl, fir *t* ........ Zec 11:2
therefore every *t* which bringeth ........ Mt 3:10
Even so every good *t* bringeth ........ Mt 7:17
but a corrupt *t* bringeth forth ........ Mt 7:17
A good *t* cannot bring forth evil ........ Mt 7:18
neither can a corrupt *t* bring ........ Mt 7:18
Every *t* that bringeth not forth ........ Mt 7:19
Either make the *t* good, and his ........ Mt 12:33
or else make the *t* corrupt ........ Mt 12:33
for the *t* is known by his fruit ........ Mt 12:33
among herbs, and becometh a *t* ........ Mt 13:32
And when he saw a fig *t* in the way ..... Mt 21:19
presently the fig *t* withered away ........ Mt 21:19
soon is the fig *t* withered away ........ Mt 21:20
this which is done to the fig *t* ........ Mt 21:21
Now learn a parable of the fig *t* ........ Mt 24:32
seeing a fig *t* afar off having ........ Mk 11:13
they saw the fig *t* dried up from ........ Mk 11:20
the fig *t* which thou cursedst is ........ Mk 11:21
Now learn a parable of the fig *t* ........ Mk 13:28
every *t* therefore which bringeth ........ Lk 3:9
For a good *t* bringeth not forth ........ Lk 6:43
corrupt *t* bring forth good fruit ........ Lk 6:43
For every *t* is known by his own ........ Lk 6:44
a fig *t* planted in his vineyard ........ Lk 13:6
come seeking fruit on this fig *t* ........ Lk 13:7
and it grew, and waxed a great *t* ........ Lk 13:19
ye might say unto this sycamine *t* ........ Lk 17:6
up into a sycomore *t* to see him ........ Lk 19:4
Behold the fig *t*, and all the ........ Lk 21:29
they do these things in a green *t* ........ Lk 23:31
when thou wast under the fig *t* ........ Jn 1:48
thee, I saw thee under the fig *t* ........ Jn 1:50
whom ye slew and hanged on a *t* ........ Acts 5:30
whom they slew and hanged on a *t* ... Acts 10:39
they took him down from the *t* ........ Acts 13:29
and thou, being a wild olive *t* ........ Rom 11:17
root and fatness of the olive *t* ........ Rom 11:17
olive *t* which is wild by nature ........ Rom 11:24
to nature into a good olive *t* ........ Rom 11:24
be graffed into their own olive *t* ........ Rom 11:24
is every one that hangeth on a *t* ........ Gal 3:13
Can the fig *t*, my brethren, bear ........ Jas 3:12
our sins in his own body on the *t* ........ 1Pet 2:24
I give to eat of the *t* of life ........ Rev 2:7
even as a fig *t* casteth her ........ Rev 6:13
nor on the sea, nor on any *t* ........ Rev 7:1
any green thing, neither any *t* ........ Rev 9:4
river, was there the *t* of life ........ Rev 22:2
the leaves of the *t* were for the ........ Rev 22:2
may have right to the *t* of life ........ Rev 22:14

**TREES**
the fruit of the *t* of the garden ........ Gen 3:2
God amongst the *t* of the garden ........ Gen 3:8
all the *t* that were in the field, ........ Gen 23:17
all the fruit of the *t* which the ........ Ex 10:15
not any green thing in the *t* ........ Ex 10:15
and threescore and ten palm *t* ........ Ex 15:27
planted all manner of *t* for food ........ Lev 19:23
first day the boughs of goodly *t* ........ Lev 23:40
branches of palm *t* ........ Lev 23:40
and the boughs of thick *t* ........ Lev 23:40
the *t* of the field shall yield ........ Lev 26:4
neither shall the *t* of the land ........ Lev 26:20
as the *t* of lign aloes which the ........ Num 24:6
as cedar *t* beside the waters ........ Num 24:6
and threescore and ten palm *t* ........ Num 33:9
not, vineyards and olive *t* ........ Deut 6:11
and barley, and vines, and fig *t* ........ Deut 8:8
not plant thee a grove of any *t* ........ Deut 16:21
the *t* thereof by forcing an ax ........ Deut 20:19
Only the *t* which thou knowest ........ Deut 20:20
that they be not *t* for meat ........ Deut 20:20
Thou shalt have olive *t* ........ Deut 28:40
All thy *t* and fruit of thy land ........ Deut 28:42
of Jericho, the city of palm *t* ........ Deut 34:3
them, and hanged them on five *t* ........ Josh 10:26
upon the *t* until the evening ........ Josh 10:26
and they took them down off the *t* .... Josh 10:27
*t* with the children of Judah into ........ Judg 1:16
and possessed the city of palm *t* ........ Judg 3:13
The *t* went forth on a time to ........ Judg 9:8
and go to be promoted over the *t* ........ Judg 9:9
the *t* said to the fig tree, Come ........ Judg 9:10
and go to be promoted over the *t* ........ Judg 9:11
Then said the *t* unto the vine ........ Judg 9:12
and go to be promoted over the *t* ........ Judg 9:13
said all the *t* unto the bramble ........ Judg 9:14
And the bramble said unto the *t* ........ Judg 9:15
and cut down a bough from the *t* ........ Judg 9:48
messengers to David, and cedar *t* ........ 2Sa 5:11
them over against the mulberry *t* ........ 2Sa 5:23
in the tops of the mulberry *t* ........ 2Sa 5:24
And he spake of *t*, from the cedar ........ 1Kin 4:33
hew me cedar *t* out of Lebanon ........ 1Kin 5:6
So Hiram gave Solomon cedar *t* ........ 1Kin 5:10
fir *t* according to all his desire ........ 1Kin 5:10
figures of cherubims and palm *t* ........ 1Kin 6:29
carvings of cherubims and palm *t* ........ 1Kin 6:32
the cherubims, and upon the palm *t* .... 1Kin 6:32
thereon cherubims and palm *t* ........ 1Kin 6:35
cherubims, lions, and palm *t* ........ 1Kin 7:36
Solomon with cedar *t* and fir *t* ........ 1Kin 9:11
Ophir great plenty of almug *t* ........ 1Kin 10:11
the king made of the almug *t* ........ 1Kin 10:12
there came no such almug *t* ........ 1Kin 10:12
sycomore *t* that are in the vale ........ 1Kin 10:27
water, and felled all the good *t* ........ 2Kin 3:25
cut down the tall cedar *t* thereof ........ 2Kin 19:23
and the choice fir *t* thereof ........ 2Kin 19:23
them over against the mulberry *t* ........ 1Chr 14:14
in the tops of the mulberry *t* ........ 1Chr 14:15
Then shall the *t* of the wood sing ........ 1Chr 16:33
Also cedar *t* in abundance ........ 1Chr 22:4
And over the olive *t* and the ........ 1Chr 27:28
the sycomore *t* that were in the ........ 1Chr 27:28
cedar *t* made he as the sycomore ........ 2Chr 1:15
*t* that are in the vale for ........ 2Chr 1:15
Send me also cedar *t* ........ 2Chr 2:8
fir *t*, and algum *t* ........ 2Chr 2:8
fine gold, and set thereon palm *t* ........ 2Chr 3:5
gold from Ophir, brought algum *t* ........ 2Chr 9:10
the king made of the algum *t* ........ 2Chr 9:11
cedar *t* made he as the sycomore ........ 2Chr 9:27
*t* that are in the low plains in ........ 2Chr 9:27
to Jericho, the city of palm *t* ........ 2Chr 28:15
to bring cedar *t* from Lebanon to ........ Ezr 3:7
branches, and branches of thick *t* ........ Neh 8:15
and fruit *t* in abundance ........ Neh 9:25
firstfruits of all fruit of all *t* ........ Neh 10:35
and the fruit of all manner of *t* ........ Neh 10:37
He lieth under the shady *t* ........ Job 40:21
The shady *t* cover him with their ........ Job 40:22
lifted up axes upon the thick *t* ........ Ps 74:5
and their sycomore *t* with frost ........ Ps 78:47
then shall all the *t* of the wood ........ Ps 96:12
The *t* of the LORD are full of sap ........ Ps 104:16
stork, the fir *t* are her house ........ Ps 104:17
their vines also and their fig *t* ........ Ps 105:33
brake the *t* of their coasts ........ Ps 105:33
fruitful *t*, and all cedars ........ Ps 148:9
I planted *t* in them of all kind ........ Eccl 2:5
the wood that bringeth forth *t* ........ Eccl 2:6
tree among the *t* of the wood ........ Song 2:3
with all *t* of frankincense ........ Song 4:14
as the *t* of the wood are moved ........ Is 7:2
the rest of the *t* of his forest ........ Is 10:19
the fir *t* rejoice at thee, and the ........ Is 14:8
and the choice fir *t* thereof ........ Is 37:24
himself among the *t* of the forest ........ Is 44:14
all the *t* of the field shall clap ........ Is 55:12
be called *t* of righteousness ........ Is 61:3
eat up thy vines and thy fig *t* ........ Jer 5:17
LORD of hosts said, Hew ye down *t* ........ Jer 6:6
upon the *t* of the field, and upon ........ Jer 7:20
the green *t* upon the high hills ........ Jer 17:2
is among the *t* of the forest ........ Eze 15:2
tree among the *t* of the forest ........ Eze 15:6
all the *t* of the field shall know ........ Eze 17:24
high hill, and all the thick *t* ........ Eze 20:28
thy ship boards of fir *t* of Senir ........ Eze 27:5
unto all the *t* of the field ........ Eze 31:4
above all the *t* of the field ........ Eze 31:5
the fir *t* were not like his ........ Eze 31:8
the chesnut *t* were not like his ........ Eze 31:8
so that all the *t* of Eden ........ Eze 31:9
*t* by the waters exalt themselves ........ Eze 31:14
neither their *t* stand up in their ........ Eze 31:14
all the *t* of the field fainted ........ Eze 31:15
and all the *t* of Eden, the choice ........ Eze 31:16
in greatness among the *t* of Eden ........ Eze 31:18
*t* of Eden unto the nether parts ........ Eze 31:18
and upon each post were palm *t* ........ Eze 40:16
and their arches, and their palm *t* ........ Eze 40:22
and it had palm *t*, one on this ........ Eze 40:26
palm *t* were upon the posts ........ Eze 40:31
palm *t* were upon the posts ........ Eze 40:34

T

palm *t* were upon the posts ..... Eze 40:37
was made with cherubims and palm *t*. Eze 41:18
were cherubims and palm *t* made ..... Eze 41:20
the temple, cherubims and palm *t* ..... Eze 41:25
palm *t* on the one side and on the ..... Eze 41:26
were very many *t* on the one side ..... Eze 47:7
side, shall grow all *t* for meat ..... Eze 47:12
destroy her vines and her fig *t* ..... Hos 2:12
tree, even all the *t* of the field ..... Joel 1:12
burned all the *t* of the field ..... Joel 1:19
and your vineyards and your fig *t* ..... Amos 4:9
and your olive *t* increased ..... Amos 4:9
the fir *t* shall be terribly ..... Nah 2:3
fig *t* with the firstripe figs ..... Nah 3:12
myrtle *t* that were in the bottom ..... Zec 1:8
stood among the myrtle *t* answered ..... Zec 1:10
that stood among the myrtle *t* ..... Zec 1:11
And two olive *t* by it, one upon ..... Zec 4:3
What are these two olive *t* upon ..... Zec 4:11
ax is laid unto the root of the *t* ..... Mt 3:10
cut down branches from the *t* ..... Mt 21:8
up, and said, I see men as *t* ..... Mk 8:24
cut down branches off the *t* ..... Mk 11:8
is laid unto the root of the *t* ..... Lk 3:9
Behold the fig tree, and all the *t* ..... Lk 21:29
Took branches of palm *t*, and went ..... Jn 12:13
*t* whose fruit withereth, without ..... Jude 12
earth, neither the sea, nor the *t* ..... Rev 7:3
the third part of *t* was burnt up ..... Rev 8:7
These are the two olive *t* ..... Rev 11:4

**TREMBLE**
hear report of thee, and shall *t* ..... Deut 2:25
faint, fear not, and do not *t* ..... Deut 20:3
lord, and of those that *t* at the ..... Ezr 10:3
place, and the pillars thereof *t* ..... Job 9:6
The pillars of heaven *t*, and are ..... Job 26:11
Thou hast made the earth to *t* ..... Ps 60:2
let the people *t* ..... Ps 99:1
*T*, thou earth, at the presence of ..... Ps 114:7
the keepers of the house shall *t* ..... Eccl 12:3
and the hills did *t*, and their ..... Is 5:25
the man that made the earth to *t* ..... Is 14:16
*T*, ye women that are at ease ..... Is 32:11
the nations may *t* at thy presence ..... Is 64:2
the LORD, ye that *t* at his word ..... Is 66:5
will ye not *t* at my presence, ..... Jer 5:22
at his wrath the earth shall *t* ..... Jer 10:10
*t* for all the goodness and for all ..... Jer 33:9
And the land shall *t* and sorrow ..... Jer 51:29
shall *t* at every moment, and be ..... Eze 26:16
Now shall the isles *t* in the day ..... Eze 26:18
they shall *t* at every moment, ..... Eze 32:10
dominion of my kingdom men *t* ..... Dan 6:26
children shall *t* from the west ..... Hos 11:10
They shall *t* as a bird out of ..... Hos 11:11
all the inhabitants of the land *t* ..... Joel 2:1
the heavens shall *t* ..... Joel 2:10
Shall not the land *t* for this ..... Amos 8:8
of the land of Midian did *t* ..... Hab 3:7
the devils also believe, and *t* ..... Jas 2:19

**TREMBLED**
Isaac *t* very exceedingly, and said ..... Gen 27:33
the people that was in the camp *t* ..... Ex 19:16
of the field of Edom, the earth *t* ..... Judg 5:4
for his heart *t* for the ark of ..... 1Sa 4:13
and the spoilers, they also *t* ..... 1Sa 14:15
of the town *t* at his coming ..... 1Sa 16:4
afraid, and his heart greatly *t* ..... 1Sa 28:5
Then the earth shook and *t* ..... 2Sa 22:8
unto me every one that *t* at the ..... Ezr 9:4
Then the earth shook and *t* ..... Ps 18:7
the earth *t* and shook ..... Ps 77:18
the earth saw, and *t* ..... Ps 97:4
the mountains, and, lo, they *t* ..... Jer 4:24
the whole land *t* at the sound of ..... Jer 8:16
people, nations, and languages, *t* ..... Dan 5:19
The mountains saw thee, and they *t* ..... Hab 3:10
When I heard, my belly *t* ..... Hab 3:16
I *t* in myself, that I might rest ..... Hab 3:16
for they *t* and were amazed ..... Mk 16:8
Then Moses *t*, and durst not behold ..... Acts 7:32
and judgment to come, Felix *t* ..... Acts 24:25

**TREMBLETH**
At this also my heart *t*, and is ..... Job 37:1
He looketh on the earth, and it *t* ..... Ps 104:32
My flesh *t* for fear of thee ..... Ps 119:120
contrite spirit, and *t* at my word ..... Is 66:2

**TREMBLING**
*t* shall take hold upon them ..... Ex 15:15
shall give thee there a *t* heart ..... Deut 28:65
and all the people followed him *t* ..... 1Sa 13:7
there was *t* in the host, in the ..... 1Sa 14:15
so it was a very great *t* ..... 1Sa 14:15
*t* because of this matter, and for ..... Ezr 10:9
Fear came upon me, and *t*, which ..... Job 4:14
*t* taketh hold on my flesh ..... Job 21:6
LORD with fear, and rejoice with *t* ..... Ps 2:11
*t* are come upon me, and horror ..... Ps 55:5
drunken the dregs of the cup of *t* ..... Is 51:17
out of thine hand the cup of *t* ..... Is 51:22
We have heard a voice of *t* ..... Jer 30:5
and drink thy water with *t* ..... Eze 12:18
shall clothe themselves with *t* ..... Eze 26:16
this word unto me, I stood *t* ..... Dan 10:11
When Ephraim spake *t*, he exalted ..... Hos 13:1
I will make Jerusalem a cup of *t* ..... Zec 12:2
But the woman fearing and *t* ..... Mk 5:33
that she was not hid, she came *t* ..... Lk 8:47

And he *t* and astonished said, Lord, ..... Acts 9:6
a light, and sprang in, and came *t* ..... Acts 16:29
and in fear, and in much *t* ..... 1Cor 2:3
with fear and *t* ye received him ..... 2Cor 7:15
to the flesh, with fear and *t* ..... Eph 6:5
your own salvation with fear and *t* ..... Phil 2:12

**TRENCH**
and he came to the *t*, as the host ..... 1Sa 17:20
and Saul lay in the *t*, and the ..... 1Sa 26:5
Saul lay sleeping within the *t* ..... 1Sa 26:7
the city, and it stood in the *t* ..... 2Sa 20:15
he made a *t* about the altar, as ..... 1Kin 18:32
he filled the *t* also with water ..... 1Kin 18:35
up the water that was in the *t* ..... 1Kin 18:38
enemies shall cast a *t* about thee ..... Lk 19:43

**TRESPASS**
and said to Laban, What is my *t* ..... Gen 31:36
the *t* of thy brethren, and their ..... Gen 50:17
forgive the *t* of the servants of ..... Gen 50:17
For all manner of *t*, whether it ..... Ex 22:9
he shall bring his *t* offering ..... Lev 5:6
then he shall bring for his *t* ..... Lev 5:7
If a soul commit a *t*, and sin ..... Lev 5:15
his *t* unto the LORD a ram without ..... Lev 5:15
the sanctuary, for a *t* offering ..... Lev 5:15
with the ram of the *t* offering ..... Lev 5:16
for a *t* offering, unto the priest ..... Lev 5:18
It is a *t* offering ..... Lev 5:19
commit a *t* against the LORD, and ..... Lev 6:2
in the day of his *t* offering ..... Lev 6:5
he shall bring his *t* offering ..... Lev 6:6
for a *t* offering, unto the priest ..... Lev 6:6
offering, and as the *t* offering ..... Lev 6:17
this is the law of the *t* offering ..... Lev 7:1
shall they kill the *t* offering ..... Lev 7:2
it is a *t* offering ..... Lev 7:5
offering is, so is the *t* offering ..... Lev 7:7
of the *t* offering, and of the ..... Lev 7:37
and offer him for a *t* offering ..... Lev 14:12
priest's, so is the *t* offering ..... Lev 14:13
of the blood of the *t* offering ..... Lev 14:14
upon the blood of the *t* offering ..... Lev 14:17
lamb for a *t* offering to be waved ..... Lev 14:21
take the lamb of the *t* offering ..... Lev 14:24
kill the lamb of the *t* offering ..... Lev 14:25
of the blood of the *t* offering ..... Lev 14:25
of the blood of the *t* offering ..... Lev 14:28
he shall bring his *t* offering ..... Lev 19:21
even a ram for a *t* offering ..... Lev 19:21
for him with the ram of the *t* ..... Lev 19:22
them to bear the iniquity of *t* ..... Lev 22:16
fathers, with their *t* which they ..... Lev 26:40
to do a *t* against the LORD, and ..... Num 5:6
he shall recompense his *t* with ..... Num 5:7
kinsman to recompense the *t* unto ..... Num 5:8
let the *t* be recompensed unto the ..... Num 5:8
aside, and commit a *t* against him, ..... Num 5:12
have done *t* against her husband, ..... Num 5:27
the first year for a *t* offering ..... Num 6:12
every *t* offering of theirs, which ..... Num 18:9
to commit *t* against the LORD in ..... Num 31:16
a *t* in the accursed thing ..... Josh 7:1
What *t* is this that ye have ..... Josh 22:16
commit a *t* in the accursed thing ..... Josh 22:20
committed this *t* against the LORD ..... Josh 22:31
any wise return him a *t* offering ..... 1Sa 6:3
What shall be the *t* offering ..... 1Sa 6:4
ye return him for a *t* offering ..... 1Sa 6:8
for a *t* offering unto the LORD ..... 1Sa 6:17
forgive the *t* of thine handmaid ..... 1Sa 25:28
If any man *t* against his ..... 1Kin 8:31
The *t* money and sin money was not ..... 2Kin 12:16
will he be a cause of *t* to Israel ..... 1Chr 21:3
that they *t* not against the LORD ..... 2Chr 19:10
this do, and ye shall not *t* ..... 2Chr 19:10
and Jerusalem for this their *t* ..... 2Chr 24:18
add more to our sins and to our *t* ..... 2Chr 28:13
for our *t* is great, and there is ..... 2Chr 28:13
he *t* yet more against the LORD ..... 2Chr 28:22
of him, and all his sin, and his *t* ..... 2Chr 33:19
rulers hath been chief in this *t* ..... Ezr 9:2
our *t* is grown up unto the ..... Ezr 9:6
been in a great *t* unto this day ..... Ezr 9:7
evil deeds, and for our great *t* ..... Ezr 9:13
to increase the *t* of Israel ..... Ezr 10:10
a ram of the flock for their *t* ..... Ezr 10:19
because they have committed a *t* ..... Eze 15:8
plead with him there for his *t* ..... Eze 17:20
in his *t* that he hath trespassed, ..... Eze 18:24
have committed a *t* against me ..... Eze 20:27
sin offering and the *t* offering ..... Eze 40:39
sin offering, and the *t* offering ..... Eze 42:13
sin offering, and the *t* offering ..... Eze 44:29
priests shall boil the *t* offering ..... Eze 46:20
because of their *t* that they have ..... Dan 9:7
thy brother shall *t* against thee ..... Mt 18:15
If thy brother *t* against thee ..... Lk 17:3
if he *t* against thee seven times ..... Lk 17:4

**TRESPASSED**
hath certainly *t* against the LORD ..... Lev 5:19
trespass which they *t* against me ..... Lev 26:40
unto him against whom he hath *t* ..... Num 5:7
Because ye *t* against me among the .. Deut 32:51
for thou hast *t* ..... 2Chr 26:18
For our fathers have *t*, and done ..... 2Chr 29:6
which *t* against the LORD God of ..... 2Chr 30:7
but Amon *t* more and more ..... 2Chr 33:23
We have *t* against our God, and ..... Ezr 10:2
that he hath *t* against me ..... Eze 17:20

in his trespass that he hath *t* ..... Eze 18:24
because they *t* against me ..... Eze 39:23
whereby they have *t* against me ..... Eze 39:26
that they have *t* against thee ..... Dan 9:7
my covenant, and *t* against my law ..... Hos 8:1

**TRESPASSES**
we are before thee in our *t* ..... Ezr 9:15
an one as goeth on still in his *t* ..... Ps 68:21
all their *t* whereby they have ..... Eze 39:26
For if ye forgive men their *t* ..... Mt 6:14
But if ye forgive not men their *t* ..... Mt 6:15
will your Father forgive your *t* ..... Mt 6:15
not every one his brother their *t* ..... Mt 18:35
in heaven may forgive you your *t* ..... Mk 11:25
which is in heaven forgive your *t* ..... Mk 11:26
not imputing their *t* unto them ..... 2Cor 5:19
he quickened, who were dead in *t* ..... Eph 2:1
him, having forgiven you all *t* ..... Col 2:13

**TRESPASSING**
that he hath done in *t* therein ..... Lev 6:7
against me by *t* grievously ..... Eze 14:13

**TRIAL**
laugh at the *t* of the innocent ..... Job 9:23
Because it is a *t*, and what if the ..... Eze 21:13
How that in a great *t* of ..... 2Cor 8:2
others had *t* of cruel mockings and .... Heb 11:36
That the *t* of your faith, being ..... 1Pet 1:7
the fiery *t* which is to try you ..... 1Pet 4:12

**TRIBE**
the son of Hur, of the *t* of Judah ..... Ex 31:2
son of Ahisamach, of the *t* of Dan ..... Ex 31:6
the son of Hur, of the *t* of Judah ..... Ex 35:30
son of Ahisamach, of the *t* of Dan ..... Ex 35:34
of the *t* of Judah, made all that ..... Ex 38:22
son of Ahisamach, of the *t* of Dan ..... Ex 38:23
of Dibri, of the *t* of Dan ..... Lev 24:11
there shall be a man of every *t* ..... Num 1:4
of the *t* of Reuben ..... Num 1:5
of them, even of the *t* of Reuben ..... Num 1:21
of them, even of the *t* of Simeon ..... Num 1:23
of them, even of the *t* of Gad ..... Num 1:25
of them, even of the *t* of Judah ..... Num 1:27
them, even of the *t* of Issachar ..... Num 1:29
of them, even of the *t* of Zebulun ..... Num 1:31
of them, even of the *t* of Ephraim ..... Num 1:33
them, even of the *t* of Manasseh ..... Num 1:35
them, even of the *t* of Benjamin ..... Num 1:37
of them, even of the *t* of Dan ..... Num 1:39
of them, even of the *t* of Asher ..... Num 1:41
them, even of the *t* of Naphtali ..... Num 1:43
the *t* of their fathers were not ..... Num 1:47
shalt not number the *t* of Levi ..... Num 1:49
him shall be the *t* of Issachar ..... Num 2:5
Then the *t* of Zebulun ..... Num 2:7
by him shall be the *t* of Simeon ..... Num 2:12
Then the *t* of Gad ..... Num 2:14
by him shall be the *t* of Manasseh ..... Num 2:20
Then the *t* of Benjamin ..... Num 2:22
by him shall be the *t* of Asher ..... Num 2:27
Then the *t* of Naphtali ..... Num 2:29
Bring the *t* of Levi near, and ..... Num 3:6
Cut ye not off the *t* of the ..... Num 4:18
of Amminadab, of the *t* of Judah ..... Num 7:12
over the host of the *t* of the ..... Num 10:15
over the host of the *t* of the ..... Num 10:16
over the host of the *t* of the ..... Num 10:19
over the host of the *t* of the ..... Num 10:20
over the host of the *t* of the ..... Num 10:23
over the host of the *t* of the ..... Num 10:24
over the host of the *t* of the ..... Num 10:26
over the host of the *t* of the ..... Num 10:27
of every *t* of their fathers shall ..... Num 13:2
of the *t* of Reuben, Shammua the ..... Num 13:4
Of the *t* of Simeon, Shaphat the ..... Num 13:5
Of the *t* of Judah, Caleb the son ..... Num 13:6
Of the *t* of Issachar, Igal the ..... Num 13:7
Of the *t* of Ephraim, Oshea the ..... Num 13:8
Of the *t* of Benjamin, Palti the ..... Num 13:9
Of the *t* of Zebulun, Gaddiel the ..... Num 13:10
Of the *t* of Joseph, namely, of ..... Num 13:11
of the *t* of Manasseh, Gaddi the ..... Num 13:11
Of the *t* of Dan, Ammiel the son ..... Num 13:12
Of the *t* of Asher, Sethur the son ..... Num 13:13
Of the *t* of Naphtali, Nahbi the ..... Num 13:14
Of the *t* of Gad, Geuel the son of ..... Num 13:15
brethren also of the *t* of Levi ..... Num 18:2
the *t* of thy father, bring thou ..... Num 18:2
Of every *t* a thousand, throughout ..... Num 31:4
of Israel, a thousand of every *t* ..... Num 31:5
to the war, a thousand of every *t* ..... Num 31:6
unto half the *t* of Manasseh the ..... Num 32:33
the nine tribes, and to the half *t* ..... Num 34:13
For the *t* of the children of Gad ..... Num 34:14
the *t* of the children of Gad ..... Num 34:14
half the *t* of Manasseh have ..... Num 34:14
the half *t* have received their ..... Num 34:15
shall take one prince of every *t* ..... Num 34:18
Of the *t* of Judah, Caleb the son ..... Num 34:19
of the *t* of the children of ..... Num 34:20
Of the *t* of Benjamin, Elidad the ..... Num 34:21
the prince of the *t* of the ..... Num 34:22
for the *t* of the children of ..... Num 34:23
the prince of the *t* of the ..... Num 34:24
the prince of the *t* of the ..... Num 34:25
the prince of the *t* of the ..... Num 34:26
the prince of the *t* of the ..... Num 34:27
the prince of the *t* of the ..... Num 34:28
the *t* whereunto they are received ..... Num 36:3

the *t* whereunto they are received ....... Num 36:4
of the *t* of our fathers ....... Num 36:4
The *t* of the sons of Joseph hath ....... Num 36:5
only to the family of the *t* of ....... Num 36:6
of Israel remove from *t* to *t* ....... Num 36:7
of the *t* of his fathers ....... Num 36:7
an inheritance in any *t* of the ....... Num 36:8
the family of the *t* of her father ....... Num 36:8
from one *t* to another *t* ....... Num 36:9
inheritance remained in the *t* of ....... Num 36:12
twelve men of you, one of a *t* ....... Deut 1:23
I unto the half *t* of Manasseh ....... Deut 3:13
the LORD separated the *t* of Levi ....... Deut 10:8
the Levites, and all the *t* of Levi ....... Deut 18:1
and to the half *t* of Manasseh ....... Deut 29:8
man, or woman, or family, or *t* ....... Deut 29:18
and to half the *t* of Manasseh ....... Josh 1:12
of Israel, out of every *t* a man ....... Josh 3:12
the people, out of every *t* a man ....... Josh 4:2
of Israel, out of every *t* a man ....... Josh 4:4
half the *t* of Manasseh, passed ....... Josh 4:12
of the *t* of Judah, took of the ....... Josh 7:1
that the *t* which the LORD taketh ....... Josh 7:14
and the *t* of Judah was taken ....... Josh 7:16
of the *t* of Judah, was taken ....... Josh 7:18
and the half *t* of Manasseh ....... Josh 12:6
and the half *t* of Manasseh, ....... Josh 13:7
Only unto the *t* of Levi he gave ....... Josh 13:14
Moses gave unto the *t* of the ....... Josh 13:15
inheritance unto the *t* of Gad ....... Josh 13:24
unto the half *t* of Manasseh ....... Josh 13:29
*t* of the children of Manasseh by ....... Josh 13:29
But unto the *t* of Levi Moses gave ....... Josh 13:33
nine tribes, and for the half *t* ....... Josh 14:2
an half *t* on the other side ....... Josh 14:3
the *t* of the children of Judah by ....... Josh 15:1
of the *t* of the children of Judah ....... Josh 15:20
the uttermost cities of the *t* of ....... Josh 15:21
*t* of the children of Ephraim by ....... Josh 16:8
also a lot for the *t* of Manasseh ....... Josh 17:1
among you three men for each *t* ....... Josh 18:4
half the *t* of Manasseh, have ....... Josh 18:7
the lot of the *t* of the children ....... Josh 18:11
Now the cities of the *t* of the ....... Josh 18:21
even for the *t* of the children of ....... Josh 19:1
the *t* of the children of Simeon ....... Josh 19:8
the *t* of the children of Issachar ....... Josh 19:23
the *t* of the children of Asher ....... Josh 19:24
of the *t* of the children of Asher ....... Josh 19:31
the *t* of the children of Naphtali ....... Josh 19:39
for the *t* of the children of Dan ....... Josh 19:40
of the *t* of the children of Dan ....... Josh 19:48
the plain out of the *t* of Reuben ....... Josh 20:8
in Gilead out of the *t* of Gad ....... Josh 20:8
Bashan out of the *t* of Manasseh ....... Josh 20:8
had by lot out of the *t* of Judah ....... Josh 21:4
Judah, and out of the *t* of Simeon ....... Josh 21:4
out of the *t* of Benjamin, ....... Josh 21:4
the families of the *t* of Ephraim ....... Josh 21:5
Ephraim, and out of the *t* of Dan ....... Josh 21:5
and out of the half *t* of Manasseh ....... Josh 21:5
the families of the *t* of Issachar ....... Josh 21:6
and out of the *t* of Asher ....... Josh 21:6
out of the *t* of Naphtali, and out ....... Josh 21:6
out of the half *t* of Manasseh in ....... Josh 21:6
had out of the *t* of Reuben ....... Josh 21:7
of Reuben, and out of the *t* of Gad ....... Josh 21:7
Gad, and out of the *t* of Zebulun ....... Josh 21:7
they gave out of the *t* of the ....... Josh 21:9
out of the *t* of the children of ....... Josh 21:9
out of the *t* of Benjamin, Gibeon ....... Josh 21:17
their lot out of the *t* of Ephraim ....... Josh 21:20
And out of the *t* of Dan, Eltekeh ....... Josh 21:23
And out of the half *t* of Manasseh ....... Josh 21:25
out of the other half *t* of ....... Josh 21:27
out of the *t* of Issachar, Kishon ....... Josh 21:28
And out of the *t* of Asher, Mishal ....... Josh 21:30
out of the *t* of Naphtali, Kedesh ....... Josh 21:32
Levites, out of the *t* of Zebulun ....... Josh 21:34
And out of the *t* of Reuben ....... Josh 21:36
And out of the *t* of Gad, Ramoth in ....... Josh 21:38
and the half *t* of Manasseh, ....... Josh 22:1
Now to the one half of the *t* of ....... Josh 22:7
the half *t* of Manasseh returned, ....... Josh 22:9
the half *t* of Manasseh built ....... Josh 22:10
the half *t* of Manasseh have built ....... Josh 22:11
Gad, and to the half *t* of Manasseh ....... Josh 22:13
Gad, and to the half *t* of Manasseh ....... Josh 22:15
the half *t* of Manasseh answered, ....... Josh 22:21
in those days the *t* of the ....... Judg 18:1
or that thou be a priest unto a *t* ....... Judg 18:19
the *t* of Dan until the day of the ....... Judg 18:30
men through all the *t* of Benjamin ....... Judg 20:12
be to day one *t* lacking in Israel ....... Judg 21:3
There is one *t* cut off from ....... Judg 21:6
that a *t* be not destroyed out of ....... Judg 21:17
at that time, every man to his *t* ....... Judg 21:24
the families of the *t* of Benjamin ....... 1Sa 9:21
the *t* of Benjamin was taken ....... 1Sa 10:20
When he had caused the *t* of ....... 1Sa 10:21
widow's son of the *t* of Naphtali ....... 1Kin 7:14
but will give one *t* to thy son ....... 1Kin 11:13
(But he shall have one *t* for my ....... 1Kin 11:32
And unto his son will I give one *t* ....... 1Kin 11:36
of David, but the *t* of Judah only ....... 1Kin 12:20
with the *t* of Benjamin, an ....... 1Kin 12:21
none left but the *t* of Judah only ....... 2Kin 17:18
half the *t* of Manasseh, of ....... 1Chr 5:18
the children of the half *t* of ....... 1Chr 5:23
the half *t* of Manasseh, and ....... 1Chr 5:26
And out of the *t* of Benjamin ....... 1Chr 6:60
were left of the family of that *t* ....... 1Chr 6:61
cities given out of the half *t* ....... 1Chr 6:61
out of the half *t* of Manasseh ....... 1Chr 6:61
families out of the *t* of Issachar ....... 1Chr 6:62
and out of the *t* of Asher ....... 1Chr 6:62
out of the *t* of Naphtali, and out ....... 1Chr 6:62
out of the *t* of Manasseh in ....... 1Chr 6:62
families, out of the *t* of Reuben ....... 1Chr 6:63
of Reuben, and out of the *t* of Gad ....... 1Chr 6:63
Gad, and out of the *t* of Zebulun ....... 1Chr 6:63
of the *t* of the children of Judah ....... 1Chr 6:65
out of the *t* of the children of ....... 1Chr 6:65
out of the *t* of the children of ....... 1Chr 6:65
coasts out of the *t* of Ephraim ....... 1Chr 6:66
And out of the half *t* of Manasseh ....... 1Chr 6:70
family of the half *t* of Manasseh ....... 1Chr 6:71
And out of the *t* of Issachar ....... 1Chr 6:72
And out of the *t* of Asher ....... 1Chr 6:74
And out of the *t* of Naphtali ....... 1Chr 6:76
given out of the *t* of Zebulun ....... 1Chr 6:77
given them out of the *t* of Reuben ....... 1Chr 6:78
And out of the *t* of Gad ....... 1Chr 6:80
of the half *t* of Manasseh ....... 1Chr 12:31
and of the half *t* of Manasseh ....... 1Chr 12:37
sons were named of the *t* of Levi ....... 1Chr 23:14
the half *t* of Manasseh, for every ....... 1Chr 26:32
of the half *t* of Manasseh ....... 1Chr 27:20
Of the half *t* of Manasseh in ....... 1Chr 27:21
and chose not the *t* of Ephraim ....... Ps 78:67
But chose the *t* of Judah, the ....... Ps 78:68
that in what *t* the stranger ....... Eze 47:23
of Phanuel, of the *t* of Aser ....... Lk 2:36
Cis, a man of the *t* of Benjamin ....... Acts 13:21
of Abraham, of the *t* of Benjamin ....... Rom 11:1
of the *t* of Benjamin, an Hebrew ....... Phil 3:5
spoken pertaineth to another *t* ....... Heb 7:13
of which *t* Moses spake nothing ....... Heb 7:14
behold, the Lion of the *t* of Juda ....... Rev 5:5
Of the *t* of Juda were sealed ....... Rev 7:5
Of the *t* of Reuben were sealed ....... Rev 7:5
Of the *t* of Gad were sealed ....... Rev 7:5
Of the *t* of Aser were sealed ....... Rev 7:6
Of the *t* of Nepthalim were sealed ....... Rev 7:6
Of the *t* of Manasses were sealed ....... Rev 7:6
Of the *t* of Simeon were sealed ....... Rev 7:7
Of the *t* of Levi were sealed ....... Rev 7:7
Of the *t* of Issachar were sealed ....... Rev 7:7
Of the *t* of Zabulon were sealed ....... Rev 7:8
Of the *t* of Joseph were sealed ....... Rev 7:8
Of the *t* of Benjamin were sealed ....... Rev 7:8

**TRIBES**
people, as one of the *t* of Israel ....... Gen 49:16
these are the twelve *t* of Israel ....... Gen 49:28
to the twelve *t* of Israel ....... Ex 24:4
they be according to the twelve *t* ....... Ex 28:21
name, according to the twelve *t* ....... Ex 39:14
princes of the *t* of their fathers ....... Num 1:16
who were the princes of the *t* ....... Num 7:2
in his tents according to their *t* ....... Num 24:2
the *t* of their fathers they shall ....... Num 26:55
the *t* concerning the children of ....... Num 30:1
throughout all the *t* of Israel ....... Num 31:4
the chief fathers of the *t* of the ....... Num 32:28
according to the *t* of your ....... Num 33:54
commanded to give unto the nine *t* .. Num 34:13
The two *t* and the half tribe have ....... Num 34:15
other *t* of the children of Israel ....... Num 36:3
but every one of the *t* of the ....... Num 36:9
and known among your *t*, and I will .. Deut 1:13
So I took the chief of your *t* ....... Deut 1:15
tens, and officers among your *t* ....... Deut 1:15
me, even all the heads of your *t* ....... Deut 5:23
all your *t* to put his name there ....... Deut 12:5
LORD shall choose in one of thy *t* ....... Deut 12:14
God giveth thee, throughout thy *t* .... Deut 16:18
hath chosen him out of all thy *t* ....... Deut 18:5
your captains of your *t*, your ....... Deut 29:10
evil out of all the *t* of Israel ....... Deut 29:21
unto me all the elders of your *t* ....... Deut 31:28
the *t* of Israel were gathered ....... Deut 33:5
twelve men out of the *t* of Israel ....... Josh 3:12
unto the number of the *t* of the ....... Josh 4:5
the *t* of the children of Israel ....... Josh 4:8
be brought according to your *t* ....... Josh 7:14
and brought Israel by their *t* ....... Josh 7:16
to their divisions by their *t* ....... Josh 11:23
the *t* of Israel for a possession ....... Josh 12:7
an inheritance unto the nine *t* ....... Josh 13:7
the *t* of the children of Israel ....... Josh 14:1
the hand of Moses, for the nine *t* ....... Josh 14:2
given the inheritance of two *t* ....... Josh 14:3
the children of Joseph were two *t* ....... Josh 14:4
the children of Israel seven *t* ....... Josh 18:2
the *t* of the children of Israel ....... Josh 19:51
the *t* of the children of Israel ....... Josh 21:1
nine cities out of those two *t* ....... Josh 21:16
throughout all the *t* of Israel ....... Josh 22:14
to be an inheritance for your *t* ....... Josh 23:4
all the *t* of Israel to Shechem ....... Josh 24:1
unto them among the *t* of Israel ....... Judg 18:1
even of all the *t* of Israel ....... Judg 20:2
throughout all the *t* of Israel ....... Judg 20:10
the *t* of Israel sent men through ....... Judg 20:12
Who is there among all the *t* of ....... Judg 21:5
What one is there of the *t* of ....... Judg 21:8
made a breach in the *t* of Israel ....... Judg 21:15
the *t* of Israel to be my priest ....... 1Sa 2:28
the smallest of the *t* of Israel ....... 1Sa 9:21
before the LORD by your *t* ....... 1Sa 10:19
all the *t* of Israel to come near ....... 1Sa 10:20
made the head of the *t* of Israel ....... 1Sa 15:17
Then came all the *t* of Israel to ....... 2Sa 5:1
word with any of the *t* of Israel ....... 2Sa 7:7
is of one of the *t* of Israel ....... 2Sa 15:2
throughout all the *t* of Israel ....... 2Sa 15:10
throughout all the *t* of Israel ....... 2Sa 19:9
all the *t* of Israel unto Abel ....... 2Sa 20:14
now through all the *t* of Israel ....... 2Sa 24:2
Israel, and all the heads of the *t* ....... 1Kin 8:1
the *t* of Israel to build an house ....... 1Kin 8:16
and will give ten *t* to thee ....... 1Kin 11:31
chosen out of all the *t* of Israel ....... 1Kin 11:32
give it unto thee, even ten *t* ....... 1Kin 11:35
choose out of all the *t* of Israel ....... 1Kin 14:21
of the *t* of the sons of Jacob ....... 1Kin 18:31
chosen out of all *t* of Israel ....... 2Kin 21:7
Furthermore over the *t* of Israel ....... 1Chr 27:16
the princes of the *t* of Israel ....... 1Chr 27:22
of Israel, the princes of the *t* ....... 1Chr 28:1
and princes of the *t* of Israel ....... 1Chr 29:6
Israel, and all the heads of the *t* ....... 2Chr 5:2
I chose no city among all the *t* ....... 2Chr 6:5
after them out of all the *t* of ....... 2Chr 11:16
chosen out of all the *t* of Israel ....... 2Chr 12:13
chosen before all the *t* of Israel ....... 2Chr 33:7
to the number of the *t* of Israel ....... Ezr 6:17
made the *t* of Israel to dwell in ....... Ps 78:55
one feeble person among their *t* ....... Ps 105:37
Whither the *t* go up, the *t* ....... Ps 122:4
the *t* of the LORD, unto the ....... Ps 122:4
are the stay of the *t* thereof ....... Is 19:13
to raise up the *t* of Jacob ....... Is 49:6
the *t* of thine inheritance ....... Is 63:17
the *t* of Israel his fellows, and ....... Eze 37:19
of Israel according to their *t* ....... Eze 45:8
to the twelve *t* of Israel ....... Eze 47:13
you according to the *t* of Israel ....... Eze 47:21
with you among the *t* of Israel ....... Eze 47:22
Now these are the names of the *t* ....... Eze 48:1
it out of all the *t* of Israel ....... Eze 48:19
As for the rest of the *t*, from ....... Eze 48:23
the *t* of Israel for inheritance ....... Eze 48:29
the names of the *t* of Israel ....... Eze 48:31
among the *t* of Israel have I made ....... Hos 5:9
according to the oaths of the *t* ....... Hab 3:9
of man, as of all the *t* of Israel ....... Zec 9:1
judging the twelve *t* of Israel ....... Mt 19:28
all the *t* of the earth mourn ....... Mt 24:30
judging the twelve *t* of Israel ....... Lk 22:30
Unto which promise our twelve *t* ....... Acts 26:7
to the twelve *t* which are ....... Jas 1:1
four thousand of all the *t* of the ....... Rev 7:4
*t* of the children of Israel ....... Rev 21:12

**TRIBULATION**
When thou art in *t*, and all these ....... Deut 4:30
deliver you in the time of your *t* ....... Judg 10:14
let him deliver me out of all *t* ....... 1Sa 26:24
for when *t* or persecution ariseth ....... Mt 13:21
For then shall be great *t* ....... Mt 24:21
Immediately after the *t* of those ....... Mt 24:29
But in those days, after that *t* ....... Mk 13:24
In the world ye shall have *t* ....... Jn 16:33
that we must through much *t* enter .. Acts 14:22
*T* and anguish, upon every soul of ....... Rom 2:9
knowing that *t* worketh patience ....... Rom 5:3
shall *t*, or distress, or ....... Rom 8:35
patient in *t* ....... Rom 12:12
Who comforteth us in all our *t* ....... 2Cor 1:4
am exceeding joyful in all our *t* ....... 2Cor 7:4
before that we should suffer *t* ....... 1Th 3:4
*t* to them that trouble you ....... 2Th 1:6
your brother, and companion in *t* ....... Rev 1:9
I know thy works, and *t*, and ....... Rev 2:9
and ye shall have *t* ten days ....... Rev 2:10
adultery with her into great *t* ....... Rev 2:22
they which came out of great *t* ....... Rev 7:14

**TRIBULATIONS**
of all your adversities and your *t* ....... 1Sa 10:19
only so, but we glory in *t* also ....... Rom 5:3
that ye faint not at my *t* for you ....... Eph 3:13
persecutions and *t* that ye endure ....... 2Th 1:4

**TRIBUTARIES**
therein shall be *t* unto thee ....... Deut 20:11
dwelt among them, and became *t* ....... Judg 1:30
of Beth-anath became *t* unto them ....... Judg 1:33
prevailed, so that they became *t* ....... Judg 1:35

**TRIBUTARY**
provinces, how is she become *t* ....... Lam 1:1

**TRIBUTE**
bear, and became a servant unto *t* ....... Gen 49:15
levy a *t* unto the LORD of the men ....... Num 31:28
the LORD's *t* of the sheep was six ....... Num 31:37
which the LORD's *t* was threescore ....... Num 31:38
which the LORD's *t* was threescore ....... Num 31:39
of which the LORD's *t* was thirty ....... Num 31:40
And Moses gave the *t*, which was ....... Num 31:41
unto the LORD thy God with a *t* of ....... Deut 16:10
unto this day, and serve under *t* ....... Josh 16:10
that they put the Canaanites to *t* ....... Josh 17:13
that they put the Canaanites to *t* ....... Judg 1:28
And Adoram was over the *t* ....... 2Sa 20:24
the son of Abda was over the *t* ....... 1Kin 4:6
a *t* of bondservice unto this day ....... 1Kin 9:21
sent Adoram, who was over the *t* ....... 1Kin 12:18
put the land to a *t* of an hundred ....... 2Kin 23:33
make to pay *t* until this day ....... 2Chr 8:8
sent Hadoram that was over the *t* ....... 2Chr 10:18

T

Jehoshaphat presents, and *t* silver — 2Chr 17:11
then will they not pay toll, *t* — Ezr 4:13
and toll, *t*, and custom, was paid — Ezr 4:20
even of the *t* beyond the river, — Ezr 6:8
not be lawful to impose toll, *t* — Ezr 7:24
borrowed money for the king's *t* — Neh 5:4
Ahasuerus laid a *t* upon the land — Est 10:1
but the slothful shall be under *t* — Prov 12:24
they that received *t* money came — Mt 17:24
said, Doth not your master pay *t* — Mt 17:24
of the earth take custom or *t* — Mt 17:25
it lawful to give *t* unto Caesar — Mt 22:17
Shew me the *t* money — Mt 22:19
Is it lawful to give *t* to Caesar — Mk 12:14
for us to give *t* unto Caesar — Lk 20:22
and forbidding to give *t* to Caesar — Lk 23:2
For for this cause pay ye *t* also — Rom 13:6
*t* to whom *t* is due — Rom 13:7

**TRICKLETH**
Mine eye *t* down, and ceaseth not, — Lam 3:49

**TRIED**
controversy and every stroke be *t* — Deut 21:5
the word of the LORD is *t* — 2Sa 22:31
when he hath *t* me, I shall come — Job 23:10
is that Job may be *t* unto the end — Job 34:36
as silver *t* in a furnace of earth — Ps 12:6
thou hast *t* me, and shalt find — Ps 17:3
the word of the LORD is *t* — Ps 18:30
hast *t* us, as silver is *t* — Ps 66:10
the word of the LORD *t* him — Ps 105:19
a *t* stone, a precious corner — Is 28:16
me, and *t* mine heart toward thee — Jer 12:3
be purified, and made white, and *t* — Dan 12:10
and will try them as gold is *t* — Zec 13:9
By faith Abraham, when he was *t* — Heb 11:17
for when he is *t*, he shall — Jas 1:12
though it be *t* with fire — 1Pet 1:7
thou hast *t* them which say they — Rev 2:2
you into prison, that ye may be *t* — Rev 2:10
to buy of me gold *t* in the fire — Rev 3:18

**TRIEST**
my God, that thou *t* the heart — 1Chr 29:17
that *t* the reins and the heart, — Jer 11:20
that *t* the righteous, and seest — Jer 20:12

**TRIETH**
For the ear *t* words, as the mouth — Job 34:3
the righteous God *t* the hearts — Ps 7:9
The LORD *t* the righteous — Ps 11:5
but the LORD *t* the hearts — Prov 17:3
men, but God, which *t* our hearts — 1Th 2:4

**TRIMMED**
nor *t* his beard, nor washed his — 2Sa 19:24
virgins arose, and *t* their lamps — Mt 25:7

**TRIMMEST**
Why *t* thou thy way to seek love — Jer 2:33

**TRIUMPH**
daughters of the uncircumcised *t* — 2Sa 1:20
let not mine enemies *t* over me — Ps 25:2
mine enemy doth not *t* over me — Ps 41:11
unto God with the voice of *t* — Ps 47:1
Philistia, *t* thou because of me — Ps 60:8
I will *t* in the works of thy — Ps 92:4
how long shall the wicked *t* — Ps 94:3
holy name, and to *t* in thy praise — Ps 106:47
over Philistia will I *t* — Ps 108:9
always causeth us to *t* in Christ — 2Cor 2:14

**TRIUMPHED**
LORD, for he hath *t* gloriously — Ex 15:1
LORD, for he hath *t* gloriously — Ex 15:21

**TRIUMPHING**
That the *t* of the wicked is short — Job 20:5
of them openly, *t* over them in it — Col 2:15

**TROAS** (*tro'-as*) *A seaport of Phrygia in Asia Minor.*
passing by Mysia came down to *T* — Acts 16:8
Therefore loosing from *T*, we came — Acts 16:11
going before tarried for us at *T* — Acts 20:5
came unto them to *T* in five days — Acts 20:6
when I came to *T* to preach — 2Cor 2:12
that I left at *T* with Carpus — 2Ti 4:13

**TRODDEN**
give the land that he hath *t* upon — Deut 1:36
have *t* shall be thine inheritance — Josh 14:9
thou hast *t* down strength — Judg 5:21
old way which wicked men have *t* — Job 22:15
The lion's whelps have not *t* it — Job 28:8
Thou hast *t* down all them that — Ps 119:118
thereof, and it shall be *t* down — Is 5:5
as a carcase *t* under feet — Is 14:19
*t* down, whose land the rivers — Is 18:2
*t* under foot, whose land the — Is 18:7
Moab shall be *t* down under him, — Is 25:10
even as straw is *t* down for the — Is 25:10
of Ephraim, shall be *t* under feet — Is 28:3
then ye shall be *t* down by it — Is 28:18
I have *t* the winepress alone — Is 63:3
have *t* down thy sanctuary — Is 63:18
they have *t* my portion under foot — Jer 12:10
The Lord hath *t* under foot all my — Lam 1:15
the Lord hath *t* the virgin — Lam 1:15
which ye have *t* with your feet — Eze 34:19
and the host to be *t* under foot — Dan 8:13
now shall she be *t* down as the — Mic 7:10
to be *t* under foot of men — Mt 5:13
and it was *t* down, and the fowls of — Lk 8:5
Jerusalem shall be *t* down of the — Lk 21:24
who hath *t* under foot the Son of — Heb 10:29
winepress was *t* without the city — Rev 14:20

**TRODE**
*t* the grapes, and made merry, and — Judg 9:27
*t* them down with ease over — Judg 20:43
the people *t* upon him in the gate — 2Kin 7:17
for the people *t* upon him in the — 2Kin 7:20
and he *t* her under foot — 2Kin 9:33
in Lebanon, and *t* down the thistle — 2Kin 14:9
in Lebanon, and *t* down the thistle — 2Chr 25:18
that they *t* one upon another — Lk 12:1

**TROGYLLIUM** (*tro-jil'-le-um*) *A coastal town in Ionia in Asia Minor.*
arrived at Samos, and tarried at *T* — Acts 20:15

**TROOP**
And Leah said, A *t* cometh — Gen 30:11
Gad, a *t* shall overcome him — Gen 49:19
Shall I pursue after this *t* — 1Sa 30:8
after Abner, and became one *t* — 2Sa 2:25
and Joab came from pursuing a *t* — 2Sa 3:22
by thee I have run through a *t* — 2Sa 22:30
were gathered together into a *t* — 2Sa 23:11
the *t* of the Philistines pitched — 2Sa 23:13
by thee I have run through a *t* — Ps 18:29
that prepare a table for that *t* — Is 65:11
bring a *t* suddenly upon them — Jer 18:22
the *t* of robbers spoileth without — Hos 7:1
hath founded his *t* in the earth — Amos 9:6

**TROOPS**
The *t* of Tema looked, the — Job 6:19
His *t* come together, and raise up — Job 19:12
by *t* in the harlots' houses — Jer 5:7
as *t* of robbers wait for a man, — Hos 6:9
in *t*, O daughter of *t* — Mic 5:1
he will invade them with his *t* — Hab 3:16

**TROPHIMUS** (*trof'-im-us*) *A companion of Paul.*
and of Asia, Tychicus and *T* — Acts 20:4
him in the city *T* an Ephesian — Acts 21:29
but *T* have I left at Miletum sick — 2Ti 4:20

**TROUBLE**
camp of Israel a curse, and *t* it — Josh 6:18
the LORD shall *t* thee this day — Josh 7:25
and thou art one of them that *t* me — Judg 11:35
Hezekiah, This day is a day of *t* — 2Kin 19:3
in my *t* I have prepared for the — 1Chr 22:14
But when they in their *t* did turn — 2Chr 15:4
and he hath delivered them to *t* — 2Chr 29:8
to affright them, and to *t* them — 2Chr 32:18
and in the time of their *t* — Neh 9:27
let not all the *t* seem little — Neh 9:32
yet *t* came — Job 3:26
neither doth *t* spring out of the — Job 5:6
Yet man is born unto *t*, as the — Job 5:7
is of few days, and full of *t* — Job 14:1
*T* and anguish shall make him — Job 15:24
his cry when *t* cometh upon him — Job 27:9
not I weep for him that was in *t* — Job 30:25
quietness, who then can make *t* — Job 34:29
reserved against the time of *t* — Job 38:23
how are they increased that *t* me — Ps 3:1
oppressed, a refuge in times of *t* — Ps 9:9
consider my *t* which I suffer of — Ps 9:13
hidest thou thyself in times of *t* — Ps 10:1
those that *t* me rejoice when I am — Ps 13:4
LORD hear thee in the day of *t* — Ps 20:1
for *t* is near — Ps 22:11
For in the time of *t* he shall — Ps 27:5
for thou hast considered my *t* — Ps 31:7
upon me, O LORD, for I am in *t* — Ps 31:9
thou shalt preserve me from *t* — Ps 32:7
their strength in the time of *t* — Ps 37:39
will deliver him in time of *t* — Ps 41:1
a very present help in *t* — Ps 46:1
And call upon me in the day of *t* — Ps 50:15
he hath delivered me out of all *t* — Ps 54:7
and refuge in the day of my *t* — Ps 59:16
Give us help from *t* — Ps 60:11
hath spoken, when I was in *t* — Ps 66:14
for I am in *t* — Ps 69:17
They are not in *t* as other men — Ps 73:5
In the day of my *t* I sought the — Ps 77:2
in vanity, and their years in *t* — Ps 78:33
wrath, and indignation, and *t* — Ps 78:49
Thou calledst in *t*, and I — Ps 81:7
In the day of my *t* I will call — Ps 86:7
I will be with him in *t* — Ps 91:15
from me in the day when I am in *t* — Ps 102:2
cried unto the LORD in their *t* — Ps 107:6
cried unto the LORD in their *t* — Ps 107:13
they cry unto the LORD in their *t* — Ps 107:19
their soul is melted because of *t* — Ps 107:26
they cry unto the LORD in their *t* — Ps 107:28
Give us help from *t* — Ps 108:12
I found *t* and sorrow — Ps 116:3
*T* and anguish have taken hold on — Ps 119:143
Though I walk in the midst of *t* — Ps 138:7
I shewed before him my *t* — Ps 142:2
sake bring my soul out of *t* — Ps 143:11
righteous is delivered out of *t* — Prov 11:8
but the just shall come out of *t* — Prov 12:13
the revenues of the wicked is *t* — Prov 15:6
great treasure and *t* therewith — Prov 15:16
time of *t* is like a broken tooth — Prov 25:19
they are a *t* unto me — Is 1:14
and behold *t* and darkness, dimness — Is 8:22
And behold at eveningtide *t* — Is 17:14
For it is a day of *t*, and of — Is 22:5
in *t* have they visited thee — Is 26:16
into the land of *t* and anguish, — Is 30:6
salvation also in the time of *t* — Is 33:2
Hezekiah, This day is a day of *t* — Is 37:3
answer, nor save him out of his *t* — Is 46:7
in vain, nor bring forth for *t* — Is 65:23
the time of their *t* they will say — Jer 2:27
save thee in the time of thy *t* — Jer 2:28
for a time of health, and behold *t* — Jer 8:15
at all in the time of their *t* — Jer 11:12
that they cry unto me for their *t* — Jer 11:14
the saviour thereof in time of *t* — Jer 14:8
the time of healing, and behold *t* — Jer 14:19
it is even the time of Jacob's *t* — Jer 30:7
for in the day of *t* they shall be — Jer 51:2
mine enemies have heard of my *t* — Lam 1:21
is come, the day of *t* is near — Eze 7:7
the foot of man *t* them any more — Eze 32:13
nor the hoofs of beasts *t* them — Eze 32:13
interpretation thereof, *t* thee — Dan 4:19
let not thy thoughts *t* thee — Dan 5:10
and out of the north shall *t* him — Dan 11:44
and there shall be a time of *t* — Dan 12:1
a strong hold in the day of *t* — Nah 1:7
that I might rest in the day of *t* — Hab 3:16
day is a day of wrath, a day of *t* — Zeph 1:15
unto them, Why *t* ye the woman — Mt 26:10
why *t* ye her — Mk 14:6
unto him, Lord, *t* not thyself — Lk 7:6
*t* not the Master — Lk 8:49
shall answer and say, *T* me not — Lk 11:7
that we *t* not them, which from — Acts 15:19
Jews, do exceedingly *t* our city — Acts 16:20
him said, *T* not yourselves — Acts 20:10
such shall have *t* in the flesh — 1Cor 7:28
comfort them which are in any *t* — 2Cor 1:4
of our *t* which came to us in Asia — 2Cor 1:8
but there be some that *t* you — Gal 1:7
were even cut off which *t* you — Gal 5:12
From henceforth let no man *t* me — Gal 6:17
tribulation to them that *t* you — 2Th 1:6
Wherein I suffer *t*, as an evil — 2Ti 2:9
of bitterness springing up *t* you — Heb 12:15

**TROUBLED**
Ye have *t* me to make me to stink — Gen 34:30
the morning that his spirit was *t* — Gen 41:8
for they were *t* at his presence — Gen 45:3
*t* the host of the Egyptians, — Ex 14:24
Joshua said, Why hast thou *t* us — Josh 7:25
My father hath *t* the land — 1Sa 14:29
evil spirit from the LORD *t* him — 1Sa 16:14
Saul, and saw that he was sore *t* — 1Sa 28:21
and all the Israelites were *t* — 2Sa 4:1
he answered, I have not *t* Israel — 1Kin 18:18
Syria was sore *t* for this thing — 2Kin 6:11
of Judah, and *t* them in building, — Ezr 4:4
it toucheth thee, and thou art *t* — Job 4:5
so, why should not my spirit be *t* — Job 21:4
Therefore am I *t* at his presence — Job 23:15
the people shall be *t* at midnight — Job 34:20
didst hide thy face, and I was *t* — Ps 30:7
I am *t* — Ps 38:6
the waters thereof roar and be *t* — Ps 46:3
they were *t*, and hasted away — Ps 48:5
I remembered God, and was *t* — Ps 77:3
I am so *t* that I cannot speak — Ps 77:4
the depths also were *t* — Ps 77:16
them be confounded and *t* for ever — Ps 83:17
anger, and by thy wrath are we *t* — Ps 90:7
Thou hidest thy face, they are *t* — Ps 104:29
the wicked is as a *t* fountain — Prov 25:26
Many days and years shall ye be *t* — Is 32:10
be *t*, ye careless ones — Is 32:11
But the wicked are like the *t* sea — Is 57:20
therefore my bowels are *t* for him — Jer 31:20
my bowels are *t* — Lam 1:20
fail with tears, my bowels are *t* — Lam 2:11
the people of the land shall be *t* — Eze 7:27
sea shall be *t* at thy departure — Eze 26:18
afraid, they shall be *t* in their — Eze 27:35
wherewith his spirit was *t* — Dan 2:1
my spirit was *t* to know the dream — Dan 2:3
and the visions of my head *t* me — Dan 4:5
one hour, and his thoughts *t* him — Dan 4:19
changed, and his thoughts *t* him — Dan 5:6
was king Belshazzar greatly *t* — Dan 5:9
and the visions of my head *t* me — Dan 7:15
Daniel, my cogitations much *t* me — Dan 7:28
their way as a flock, they were *t* — Zec 10:2
had heard these things, he was *t* — Mt 2:3
walking on the sea, they were *t* — Mt 14:26
see that ye be not *t* — Mt 24:6
For they all saw him, and were *t* — Mk 6:50
and rumours of wars, be ye not *t* — Mk 13:7
when Zacharias saw him, he was *t* — Lk 1:12
she was *t* at his saying, and cast — Lk 1:29
careful and *t* about many things — Lk 10:41
he said unto them, Why are ye *t* — Lk 24:38
into the pool, and *t* the water — Jn 5:4
have no man, when the water is *t* — Jn 5:7
groaned in the spirit, and was *t* — Jn 11:33
Now is my soul *t* — Jn 12:27
he was *t* in spirit, and testified, — Jn 13:21
Let not your heart be *t* — Jn 14:1
Let not your heart be *t*, neither — Jn 14:27
out from us have *t* you with words — Acts 15:24
they *t* the people and the rulers — Acts 17:8

We are *t* on every side, yet not ... 2Cor 4:8
but we were *t* on every side ... 2Cor 7:5
And to you who are *t* rest with us ... 2Th 1:7
not soon shaken in mind, or be *t* ... 2Th 2:2
of their terror, neither be *t* ... 1Pet 3:14

### TROUBLEDST
*t* the waters with thy feet, and ... Eze 32:2

### TROUBLER
the *t* of Israel, who transgressed ... 1Chr 2:7

### TROUBLES
many evils and *t* shall befall them ... Deut 31:17
*t* are befallen them, that this ... Deut 31:21
He shall deliver thee in six *t* ... Job 5:19
The *t* of my heart are enlarged ... Ps 25:17
Israel, O God, out of all his *t* ... Ps 25:22
and saved him out of all his *t* ... Ps 34:6
them out of all their *t* ... Ps 34:17
hast shewed me great and sore *t* ... Ps 71:20
For my soul is full of *t* ... Ps 88:3
tongue keepeth his soul from *t* ... Prov 21:23
the former *t* are forgotten ... Is 65:16
and there shall be famines and *t* ... Mk 13:8

### TROUBLEST
why *t* thou the Master any further ... Mk 5:35

### TROUBLETH
an evil spirit from God *t* thee ... 1Sa 16:15
him, Art thou he that *t* Israel ... 1Kin 18:17
about thee, and sudden fear *t* thee ... Job 22:10
heart soft, and the Almighty *t* me ... Job 23:16
he that is cruel *t* his own flesh ... Prov 11:17
He that *t* his own house shall ... Prov 11:29
is greedy of gain *t* his own house ... Prov 15:27
is in thee, and no secret *t* thee ... Dan 4:9
Yet because this widow *t* me ... Lk 18:5
but he that *t* you shall bear his ... Gal 5:10

### TROUBLING
There the wicked cease from *t* ... Job 3:17
the *t* of the water stepped in was ... Jn 5:4

### TROUBLOUS
and the wall, even in *t* times ... Dan 9:25

### TROUGH
and emptied her pitcher into the *t* ... Gen 24:20

### TROUGHS
*t* when the flocks came to drink ... Gen 30:38
filled the *t* to water their ... Ex 2:16

### TROW
I *t* not ... Lk 17:9

### TRUCEBREAKERS
Without natural affection, *t* ... 2Ti 3:3

### TRUE
we are *t* men, thy servants are no ... Gen 42:11
If ye be *t* men, let one of your ... Gen 42:19
And we said unto him, We are *t* men ... Gen 42:31
shall I know that ye are *t* men ... Gen 42:33
no spies, but that ye are *t* men ... Gen 42:34
diligently, and, behold, it be *t* ... Deut 17:4
But if this thing be *t*, and the ... Deut 22:20
house, and give me a *t* token ... Josh 2:12
now it is *t* that I am thy near ... Ruth 3:12
art that God, and thy words be *t* ... 2Sa 7:28
It was a *t* report that I heard in ... 1Kin 10:6
is *t* in the name of the LORD ... 1Kin 22:16
It was a *t* report which I heard ... 2Chr 9:5
hath been without the *t* God ... 2Chr 15:3
and *t* laws, good statutes and ... Neh 9:13
the judgments of the LORD are *t* ... Ps 19:9
Thy word is *t* from the beginning ... Ps 119:160
A *t* witness delivereth souls ... Prov 14:25
But the LORD is the *t* God ... Jer 10:10
said to Jeremiah, The LORD be a *t* ... Jer 42:5
hath executed *t* judgment between ... Eze 18:8
spake and said unto them, Is it *t* ... Dan 3:14
answered and said unto the king, *T* ... Dan 3:24
answered and said, The thing is *t* ... Dan 6:12
the morning which was told is *t* ... Dan 8:26
and the thing was *t*, but the time ... Dan 10:1
Execute *t* judgment, and shew mercy ... Zec 7:9
Master, we know that thou art *t* ... Mt 22:16
Master, we know that thou art *t* ... Mk 12:14
commit to your trust the *t* riches ... Lk 16:11
That was the *t* Light, which ... Jn 1:9
set to his seal that God is *t* ... Jn 3:33
when the *t* worshippers shall ... Jn 4:23
And herein is that saying *t* ... Jn 4:37
of myself, my witness is not *t* ... Jn 5:31
which he witnesseth of me is *t* ... Jn 5:32
you the *t* bread from heaven ... Jn 6:32
that sent him, the same is *t* ... Jn 7:18
myself, but he that sent me is *t* ... Jn 7:28
thy record is not *t* ... Jn 8:13
of myself, yet my record is *t* ... Jn 8:14
yet if I judge, my judgment is *t* ... Jn 8:16
the testimony of two men is *t* ... Jn 8:17
but he that sent me is *t* ... Jn 8:26
John spake of this man were *t* ... Jn 10:41
I am the *t* vine, and my Father is ... Jn 15:1
might know thee the only *t* God ... Jn 17:3
bare record, and his record is *t* ... Jn 19:35
and he knoweth that he saith *t* ... Jn 19:35
we know that his testimony is *t* ... Jn 21:24
wist not that it was *t* which was ... Acts 12:9
yea, let God be *t*, but every man ... Rom 3:4
But as God is *t*, our word toward ... 2Cor 1:18
as deceivers, and yet *t* ... 2Cor 6:8
in righteousness and *t* holiness ... Eph 4:24
*t* yokefellow, help those women ... Phil 4:3
brethren, whatsoever things are *t* ... Phil 4:8
to serve the living and *t* God ... 1Th 1:9
This is a *t* saying, If a man ... 1Ti 3:1
This witness is *t* ... Titus 1:13
of the *t* tabernacle, which the ... Heb 8:2
which are the figures of the *t* ... Heb 9:24
Let us draw near with a *t* heart ... Heb 10:22
testifying that this is the *t* ... 1Pet 5:12
them according to the *t* proverb ... 2Pet 2:22
unto you, which thing is *t* in him ... 1Jn 2:8
past, and the *t* light now shineth ... 1Jn 2:8
that we may know him that is *t* ... 1Jn 5:20
and we are in him that is *t* ... 1Jn 5:20
This is the *t* God, and eternal ... 1Jn 5:20
and ye know that our record is *t* ... 3Jn 12
he that is holy, he that is *t* ... Rev 3:7
*t* witness, the beginning of the ... Rev 3:14
How long, O Lord, holy and *t* ... Rev 6:10
*t* are thy ways, thou King of ... Rev 15:3
Even so, Lord God Almighty, *t* ... Rev 16:7
For *t* and righteous are his ... Rev 19:2
These are the *t* sayings of God ... Rev 19:9
upon him was called Faithful and *T* ... Rev 19:11
for these words are *t* and faithful ... Rev 21:5
These sayings are faithful and *t* ... Rev 22:6

### TRULY
*t* Lamech seventy and sevenfold ... Gen 4:24
*t* with my master, tell me ... Gen 24:49
and deal kindly and *t* with me ... Gen 47:29
but *t* his younger brother shall ... Gen 48:19
But as *t* as I live, all the earth ... Num 14:21
As *t* as I live, saith the LORD, ... Num 14:28
Thou shalt *t* tithe all the ... Deut 14:22
will deal kindly and *t* with thee ... Josh 2:14
*T* the LORD hath delivered into ... Josh 2:24
Now therefore, if ye have done *t* ... Judg 9:16
If ye then have dealt *t* and ... Judg 9:19
but *t* as the LORD liveth, and as ... 1Sa 20:3
For *t* my words shall not be false ... Job 36:4
*T* my soul waiteth upon God ... Ps 62:1
*T* God is good to Israel, even to ... Ps 73:1
O LORD, *t* I am thy servant ... Ps 116:16
they that deal *t* are his delight ... Prov 12:22
*T* the light is sweet, and a ... Eccl 11:7
*T* in vain is salvation hoped for ... Jer 3:23
*t* in the LORD our God is the ... Jer 3:23
*T* this is a grief, and I must bear ... Jer 10:19
that the LORD hath *t* sent him ... Jer 28:9
hath kept my judgments, to deal *t* ... Eze 18:9
But *t* I am full of power by the ... Mic 3:8
The harvest *t* is plenteous, but ... Mt 9:37
Elias *t* shall first come, and ... Mt 17:11
*T* this was the Son of God ... Mt 27:54
The spirit *t* is ready, but the ... Mk 14:38
*T* this man was the Son of God ... Mk 15:39
unto them, The harvest *t* is great ... Lk 10:2
*T* ye bear witness that ye allow ... Lk 11:48
but teachest the way of God *t* ... Lk 20:21
*t* the Son of man goeth, as it was ... Lk 22:22
in that saidst thou *t* ... Jn 4:18
many other signs *t* did Jesus in ... Jn 20:30
For John *t* baptized with water ... Acts 1:5
For Moses *t* said unto the fathers ... Acts 3:22
The prison *t* found we shut with ... Acts 5:23
*T* the signs of an apostle were ... 2Cor 12:12
they *t* were many priests, because ... Heb 7:23
And *t*, if they had been mindful of ... Heb 11:15
*t* our fellowship is with the ... 1Jn 1:3

### TRUMP
O my soul, the sound of the *t* ... Jer 4:19
in Gibeah, and the *t* in Ramah ... Hos 5:8
of an eye, at the last *t* ... 1Cor 15:52
archangel, and with the *t* of God ... 1Th 4:16

### TRUMPET
when the *t* soundeth long, they ... Ex 19:13
the voice of the *t* exceeding loud ... Ex 19:16
the voice of the *t* sounded long ... Ex 19:19
lightnings, and the noise of the *t* ... Ex 20:18
Then shalt thou cause the *t* of ... Lev 25:9
*t* sound throughout all your land ... Lev 25:9
And if they blow but with one *t* ... Num 10:4
when ye hear the sound of the *t* ... Josh 6:5
people heard the sound of the *t* ... Josh 6:20
that he blew a *t* in the mountain ... Judg 3:27
came upon Gideon, and he blew a *t* ... Judg 6:34
he put a *t* in every man's hand, ... Judg 7:16
When I blow with a *t*, I and all ... Judg 7:18
Saul blew the *t* throughout all ... 1Sa 13:3
So Joab blew a *t*, and all the ... 2Sa 2:28
and with the sound of the *t* ... 2Sa 6:15
as ye hear the sound of the *t* ... 2Sa 15:10
And Joab blew the *t*, and the people ... 2Sa 18:16
and he blew a *t*, and said, We have ... 2Sa 20:1
And he blew a *t*, and they retired ... 2Sa 20:22
and blow ye with the *t*, and say, ... 1Kin 1:34
And they blew the *t* ... 1Kin 1:39
Joab heard the sound of the *t* ... 1Kin 1:41
he that sounded the *t* was by me ... Neh 4:18
ye hear the sound of the *t* ... Neh 4:20
he that it is the sound of the *t* ... Job 39:24
the LORD with the sound of a *t* ... Ps 47:5
Blow up the *t* in the new moon, in ... Ps 81:3
him with the sound of the *t* ... Ps 150:3
and when he bloweth a *t*, hear ye ... Is 18:3
that the great *t* shall be blown ... Is 27:13
not, lift up thy voice like a *t* ... Is 58:1
and say, Blow ye the *t* in the land ... Jer 4:5
and hear the sound of the *t* ... Jer 4:21
Jerusalem, and blow the *t* in Tekoa ... Jer 6:1
Hearken to the sound of the *t* ... Jer 6:17
war, nor hear the sound of the *t* ... Jer 42:14
blow the *t* among the nations, ... Jer 51:27
They have blown the *t*, even to ... Eze 7:14
come upon the land, he blow the *t* ... Eze 33:3
heareth the sound of the *t* ... Eze 33:4
He heard the sound of the *t* ... Eze 33:5
the sword come, and blow not the *t* ... Eze 33:6
Set the *t* to thy mouth ... Hos 8:1
Blow ye the *t* in Zion, and sound ... Joel 2:1
Blow the *t* in Zion, sanctify a ... Joel 2:15
and with the sound of the *t* ... Amos 2:2
Shall a *t* be blown in the city, ... Amos 3:6
A day of the *t* and alarm against ... Zeph 1:16
and the Lord GOD shall blow the *t* ... Zec 9:14
do not sound a *t* before thee ... Mt 6:2
angels with a great sound of a *t* ... Mt 24:31
For if the *t* give an uncertain ... 1Cor 14:8
for the *t* shall sound, and the ... 1Cor 15:52
And the sound of a *t*, and the voice ... Heb 12:19
me a great voice, as of a *t* ... Rev 1:10
as it were of a *t* talking with me ... Rev 4:1
of the *t* of the three angels ... Rev 8:13
the sixth angel which had the *t* ... Rev 9:14

### TRUMPETERS
the *t* by the king, and all the ... 2Kin 11:14
It came even to pass, as the *t* ... 2Chr 5:13
singers sang, and the *t* sounded ... 2Chr 29:28
and musicians, and of pipers, and *t* ... Rev 18:22

### TRUMPETS
a memorial of blowing of *t* ... Lev 23:24
Make thee two *t* of silver ... Num 10:2
priests, shall blow with the *t* ... Num 10:8
ye shall blow an alarm with the *t* ... Num 10:9
ye shall blow with the *t* over ... Num 10:10
a day of blowing the *t* unto you ... Num 29:1
the *t* to blow in his hand ... Num 31:6
the ark seven *t* of rams' horns ... Josh 6:4
the priests shall blow with the *t* ... Josh 6:4
let seven priests bear seven *t* of ... Josh 6:6
*t* of rams' horns passed on before ... Josh 6:8
the LORD, and blew with the *t* ... Josh 6:8
the priests that blew with the *t* ... Josh 6:9
going on, and blowing with the *t* ... Josh 6:9
seven priests bearing seven *t* of ... Josh 6:13
continually, and blew with the *t* ... Josh 6:13
going on, and blowing with the *t* ... Josh 6:13
when the priests blew with the *t* ... Josh 6:16
when the priests blew with the *t* ... Josh 6:20
in their hand, and their *t* ... Judg 7:8
then blow ye the *t* also on every ... Judg 7:18
and they blew the *t*, and brake the ... Judg 7:19
And the three companies blew the *t* ... Judg 7:20
the *t* in their right hands to ... Judg 7:20
And the three hundred blew the *t* ... Judg 7:22
top of the stairs, and blew with *t* ... 2Kin 9:13
the land rejoiced, and blew with *t* ... 2Kin 11:14
of silver, snuffers, basons, *t* ... 2Kin 12:13
and with cymbals, and with *t* ... 1Chr 13:8
did blow with the *t* before the ... 1Chr 15:24
sound of the cornet, and with *t* ... 1Chr 15:28
Jahaziel the priests with *t* ... 1Chr 16:6
them Heman and Jeduthun with *t* ... 1Chr 16:42
and twenty priests sounding with *t* ... 2Chr 5:12
lifted up their voice with the *t* ... 2Chr 5:13
the priests sounded *t* before them ... 2Chr 7:6
*t* to cry alarm against you ... 2Chr 13:12
and the priests sounded with the *t* ... 2Chr 13:14
and with shouting, and with *t* ... 2Chr 15:14
*t* unto the house of the LORD ... 2Chr 20:28
the princes and the *t* by the king ... 2Chr 23:13
land rejoiced, and sounded with *t* ... 2Chr 23:13
David, and the priests with the *t* ... 2Chr 29:26
of the LORD began also with the *t* ... 2Chr 29:27
priests in their apparel with *t* ... Ezr 3:10
of the priests' sons with *t* ... Neh 12:35
Zechariah, and Hananiah, with *t* ... Neh 12:41
He saith among the *t*, Ha, ha ... Job 39:25
With *t* and sound of cornet make a ... Ps 98:6
and to them were given seven *t* ... Rev 8:2
angels which had the seven *t* ... Rev 8:6

### TRUST
come and put your *t* in my shadow ... Judg 9:15
whose wings thou art come to *t* ... Ruth 2:12
in him will I *t* ... 2Sa 22:3
buckler to all them that *t* in him ... 2Sa 22:31
Now on whom dost thou *t*, that ... 2Kin 18:20
of Egypt unto all that *t* on him ... 2Kin 18:21
unto me, We *t* in the LORD our God ... 2Kin 18:22
put thy *t* on Egypt for chariots ... 2Kin 18:24
Hezekiah make you *t* in the LORD ... 2Kin 18:30
because they put their *t* in him ... 1Chr 5:20
king of Assyria, Whereon do ye *t* ... 2Chr 32:10
he put no *t* in his servants ... Job 4:18
whose *t* shall be a spider's web ... Job 8:14
he slay me, yet will I *t* in him ... Job 13:15
he putteth no *t* in his saints ... Job 15:15
him that is deceived *t* in vanity ... Job 15:31
therefore *t* thou in him ... Job 35:14
Wilt thou *t* him, because his ... Job 39:11
all they that put their *t* in him ... Ps 2:12
and put your *t* in the LORD ... Ps 4:5
that put their *t* in thee rejoice ... Ps 5:11
my God, in thee do I put my *t* ... Ps 7:1
thy name will put their *t* in thee ... Ps 9:10
In the LORD put I my *t* ... Ps 11:1
for in thee do I put my *t* ... Ps 16:1

T

t in thee from those that rise up Ps 17:7
my strength, in whom I will t. Ps 18:2
to all those that t in him Ps 18:30
Some t in chariots, and some in Ps 20:7
O my God, I t in thee Ps 25:2
for I put my t in thee Ps 25:20
IN thee, O LORD, do I put my t. Ps 31:1
but I t in the LORD Ps 31:6
t in thee before the sons of men Ps 31:19
none of them that t in him shall Ps 34:22
t under the shadow of thy wings Ps 36:7
T in the LORD, and do good Ps 37:3
t also in him Ps 37:5
save them, because they t in him Ps 37:40
and fear, and shall t in the LORD Ps 40:3
man that maketh the LORD his t. Ps 40:4
For I will not t in my bow Ps 44:6
They that t in their wealth, and Ps 49:6
I t in the mercy of God for ever Ps 52:8
but I will t in thee Ps 55:23
I am afraid, I will t in thee Ps 56:3
his word, in God I have put my t Ps 56:4
In God have I put my t. Ps 56:11
I will t in the covert of thy Ps 61:4
T in him at all times Ps 62:8
T not in oppression, and become Ps 62:10
in the LORD, and shall t in him Ps 64:10
In thee, O LORD, do I put my t. Ps 71:1
thou art my t from my youth Ps 71:5
I have put my t in the Lord GOD, Ps 73:28
in him will I t. Ps 91:2
and under his wings shalt thou t Ps 91:4
O Israel, t thou in the LORD Ps 115:9
O house of Aaron, t in the LORD Ps 115:10
that fear the LORD, t in the LORD Ps 115:11
It is better to t in the LORD Ps 118:8
It is better to t in the LORD Ps 118:9
for I t in thy word Ps 119:42
They that t in the LORD shall be Ps 125:1
in thee is my t Ps 141:8
for in thee do I t Ps 143:8
my shield, and he in whom I t Ps 144:2
Put not your t in princes Ps 146:3
T in the LORD with all thine Prov 3:5
That thy t may be in the LORD, I Prov 22:19
but he that putteth his t in the Prov 28:25
but whoso putteth his t in the Prov 29:25
unto them that put their t in him Prov 30:5
her husband doth safely t in her Prov 31:11
I will t, and not be afraid Is 12:2
poor of his people shall t in it Is 14:32
T ye in the LORD for ever Is 26:4
to t in the shadow of Egypt Is 30:2
the t in the shadow of Egypt your Is 30:3
t in oppression and perverseness, Is 30:12
t in chariots, because they are Is 31:1
now on whom dost thou t, that Is 36:5
of Egypt to all that t in him Is 36:6
to me, We t in the LORD our God Is 36:7
put thy t on Egypt for chariots Is 36:9
Hezekiah make you t in the LORD Is 36:15
that t in graven images, that say Is 42:17
let him t in the name of the LORD Is 50:10
me, and on mine arm shall they t Is 51:5
but he that putteth his t in me Is 57:13
they t in vanity, and speak lies Is 59:4
T ye not in lying words, saying, Jer 7:4
ye t in lying words, that cannot Jer 7:8
called by my name, wherein ye t Jer 7:14
and t ye not in any brother Jer 9:4
makest this people to t in a lie Jer 28:15
and he caused you to t in a lie Jer 29:31
because thou hast put thy t in me Jer 39:18
and all them that t in him Jer 46:25
and let thy widows t in me Jer 49:11
But thou didst t in thine own Eze 16:15
if he t to his own righteousness, Eze 33:13
because thou didst t in thy way Hos 10:13
t in the mountain of Samaria, Amos 6:1
T ye not in a friend, put ye not Mic 7:5
and he knoweth them that t in him Nah 1:7
they shall t in the name of the Zeph 3:12
in his name shall the Gentiles t Mt 12:21
t in riches to enter into the Mk 10:24
commit to your t the true riches Lk 16:11
you, even Moses, in whom ye t Jn 5:45
in him shall the Gentiles t Rom 15:12
for I t to see you in my journey, Rom 15:24
but I t to tarry a while with you 1Cor 16:7
that we should not t in ourselves 2Cor 1:9
in whom we t that he will yet 2Cor 1:10
I t ye shall acknowledge even to 2Cor 1:13
such t have we through Christ to 2Cor 3:4
I t also are made manifest in 2Cor 5:11
If any man t to himself that he 2Cor 10:7
But I t that ye shall know that 2Cor 13:6
But I t in the Lord Jesus to send Phil 2:19
But I t in the Lord that I also Phil 2:24
whereof he might t in the flesh Phil 3:4
to be put in t with the gospel 1Th 2:4
God, which was committed to my t 1Ti 1:11
because we t in the living God, 1Ti 4:10
nor t in uncertain riches, but in 1Ti 6:17
that which is committed to thy t 1Ti 6:20
for I t that through your prayers Philem 22
And again, I will put my t in him Heb 2:13
for we t we have a good Heb 13:18
but I t to come unto you, and 2Jn 12
But I t I shall shortly see thee, 3Jn 14

**TRUSTED**

gods, their rock in whom they t Deut 32:37
But Sihon t not Israel to pass Judg 11:20
because they t unto the liers in Judg 20:36
He t in the LORD God of Israel 2Kin 18:5
But I have t in thy mercy Ps 13:5
Our fathers t in thee Ps 22:4
they t, and thou didst deliver Ps 22:4
they t in thee, and were not Ps 22:5
He t on the LORD that he would Ps 22:8
I have t also in the LORD Ps 26:1
my heart t in him, and I am helped Ps 28:7
But I t in thee, O LORD Ps 31:14
because we have t in his holy Ps 33:21
own familiar friend, in whom I t Ps 41:9
but t in the abundance of his Ps 52:7
in God, and t not in his salvation Ps 78:22
For thou hast t in thy wickedness Is 47:10
forgotten me, and t in falsehood Jer 13:25
because thou hast t in thy works Jer 48:7
that t in her treasures, saying, Jer 49:4
his servants that t in him Dan 3:28
she t not in the LORD Zeph 3:2
He t in God Mt 27:43
him all his armour wherein he t Lk 11:22
t in themselves that they were Lk 18:9
But we t that it had been he Lk 24:21
his glory, who first t in Christ Eph 1:12
In whom ye also t, after that ye Eph 1:13
who t in God, adorned themselves, 1Pet 3:5

**TRUSTEDST**

walls come down, wherein thou t Deut 28:52
thy fenced cities, wherein thou t Jer 5:17
the land of peace, wherein thou t Jer 12:5

**TRUSTEST**

confidence is this wherein thou t 2Kin 18:19
thou t upon the staff of this 2Kin 18:21
God in whom thou t deceive thee 2Kin 19:10
confidence is this wherein thou t Is 36:4
thou t in the staff of this Is 36:6
Let not thy God, in whom thou t Is 37:10

**TRUSTETH**

he t that he can draw up Jordan Job 40:23
For the king t in the LORD Ps 21:7
but he that t in the LORD Ps 32:10
blessed is the man that t in him Ps 34:8
for my soul t in thee Ps 57:1
blessed is the man that t in thee Ps 84:12
save thy servant that t in thee Ps 86:2
so is every one that t in them Ps 115:8
so is every one that t in them Ps 135:18
He that t in his riches shall Prov 11:28
whoso t in the LORD, happy is he Prov 16:20
He that t in his own heart is a Prov 28:26
because he t in thee Is 26:3
Cursed be the man that t in man Jer 17:5
is the man that t in the LORD Jer 17:7
the maker of his work t therein Hab 2:18
t in God, and continueth in 1Ti 5:5

**TRUSTING**

his heart is fixed, t in the LORD Ps 112:7

**TRUSTY**

removeth away the speech of the t Job 12:20

**TRUTH**

my master of his mercy and his t Gen 24:27
all the mercies, and of all the t Gen 32:10
whether there be any t in you Gen 42:16
men, such as fear God, men of t Ex 18:21
and abundant in goodness and t Ex 34:6
and, behold, if it be t, and the Deut 13:14
a God of t and without iniquity, Deut 32:4
and serve him in sincerity and in t Josh 24:14
If in t ye anoint me king over Judg 9:15
serve him in t with all your 1Sa 12:24
Of a t women have been kept from 1Sa 21:5
LORD shew kindness and t unto you 2Sa 2:6
mercy and t be with thee 2Sa 15:20
me in t with all their heart 1Kin 2:4
as he walked before thee in t 1Kin 3:6
of the LORD in thy mouth is t 1Kin 17:24
Of a t, LORD, the kings of 2Kin 19:17
I have walked before thee in t 2Kin 20:3
good, if peace and t be in my days 2Kin 20:19
t to me in the name of the LORD 2Chr 18:15
t before the LORD his God 2Chr 31:20
with words of peace and t Est 9:30
I know it is so of a t Job 9:2
and speaketh the t in his heart Ps 15:2
Lead me in thy t, and teach me Ps 25:5
t unto such as keep his covenant Ps 25:10
and I have walked in thy t Ps 26:3
shall it declare thy t Ps 30:9
hast redeemed me, O LORD God of t Ps 31:5
and all his works are done in t Ps 33:4
thy t from the great congregation Ps 40:10
thy t continually preserve me Ps 40:11
O send out thy light and thy t Ps 43:3
ride prosperously because of t Ps 45:4
thou desirest t in the inward Ps 51:6
cut them off in thy t Ps 54:5
send forth his mercy and his t Ps 57:3
heavens, and thy t unto the clouds Ps 57:10
may be displayed because of the t Ps 60:4
O prepare mercy and t, which may Ps 61:7
in the t of thy salvation Ps 69:13
with the psaltery, even thy t Ps 71:22
Mercy and t are met together Ps 85:10
T shall spring out of the earth Ps 85:11
I will walk in thy t Ps 86:11
and plenteous in mercy and t Ps 86:15
t shall go before thy face Ps 89:14
thou swarest unto David in thy t Ps 89:49
his t shall be thy shield and Ps 91:4
and the people with his t Ps 96:13
his t toward the house of Israel Ps 98:3
his t endureth to all generations Ps 100:5
thy t reacheth unto the clouds Ps 108:4
ever and ever, and are done in t Ps 111:8
the t of the LORD endureth for Ps 117:2
I have chosen the way of t Ps 119:30
take not the word of t utterly Ps 119:43
and thy law is the t Ps 119:142
and all thy commandments are t Ps 119:151
LORD hath sworn in t unto David Ps 132:11
thy lovingkindness and for thy t Ps 138:2
to all that call upon him in t Ps 145:18
which keepeth t for ever Ps 146:6
Let not mercy and t forsake thee Prov 3:3
For my mouth shall speak t Prov 8:7
He that speaketh t sheweth forth Prov 12:17
The lip of t shall be established Prov 12:19
t shall be to them that devise Prov 14:22
By mercy and t iniquity is purged Prov 16:6
Mercy and t preserve the king Prov 20:28
the certainty of the words of t Prov 22:21
of t to them that send unto thee Prov 22:21
Buy the t, and sell it not Prov 23:23
was upright, even words of t Eccl 12:10
Of a t many houses shall be Is 5:9
the Holy One of Israel, in t Is 10:20
he shall sit upon it in t in the Is 16:5
of old are faithfulness and t Is 25:1
which keepeth the t may enter in Is 26:2
Of a t, LORD, the kings of Is 37:18
I have walked before thee in t Is 38:3
the pit cannot hope for thy t Is 38:18
children shall make known thy t Is 38:19
shall be peace and t in my days Is 39:8
shall bring forth judgment unto t Is 42:3
or let them hear, and say, It is t Is 43:9
the God of Israel, but not in t Is 48:1
justice, nor any pleadeth for t Is 59:4
for t is fallen in the street, and Is 59:14
Yea, t faileth Is 59:15
and I will direct their work in t Is 61:8
bless himself in the God of t Is 65:16
earth shall swear by the God of t Is 65:16
swear, The LORD liveth, in t Jer 4:2
judgment, that seeketh the t Jer 5:1
are not thine eyes upon the t Jer 5:3
t is perished, and is cut off from Jer 7:28
valiant for the t upon the earth Jer 9:3
and will not speak the t Jer 9:5
for of a t the LORD hath sent me Jer 26:15
them the abundance of peace and t Jer 33:6
Of a t it is, that your God is a Dan 2:47
of heaven, all whose works are t Dan 4:37
and asked him the t of all this Dan 7:16
know the t of the fourth beast Dan 7:19
it cast down the t to the ground Dan 8:12
iniquities, and understand thy t Dan 9:13
is noted in the scripture of t Dan 10:21
And now will I shew thee the t Dan 11:2
the land, because there is no t Hos 4:1
Thou wilt perform the t to Jacob Mic 7:20
shall be called a city of t Zec 8:3
and I will be their God, in t Zec 8:8
every man the t to his neighbour Zec 8:16
execute the judgment of t Zec 8:16
therefore love the t and peace Zec 8:19
The law of t was in his mouth, and Mal 2:6
Of a t thou art the Son of God Mt 14:33
And she said, T, Lord Mt 15:27
and teachest the way of God in t Mt 22:16
before him, and told him all the t Mk 5:33
but teachest the way of God in t Mk 12:14
Master, thou hast said the t Mk 12:32
But I tell you of a t, many Lk 4:25
But I tell you of a t, there be Lk 9:27
Of a t I say unto you, that he Lk 12:44
Of a t I say unto you, that this Lk 21:3
Of a t this fellow also was with Lk 22:59
the Father,) full of grace and t Jn 1:14
grace and t came by Jesus Christ Jn 1:17
But he that doeth t cometh to the Jn 3:21
the Father in spirit and in t Jn 4:23
worship him in spirit and in t Jn 4:24
and he bare witness unto the t Jn 5:33
This is of a t that prophet that Jn 6:14
Of a t this is the Prophet Jn 7:40
And ye shall know the t, and the Jn 8:32
the t shall make you free Jn 8:32
a man that hath told you the t Jn 8:40
beginning, and abode not in the t Jn 8:44
because there is no t in him Jn 8:44
And because I tell you the t Jn 8:45
And if I say the t, why do ye not Jn 8:46
unto him, I am the way, the t Jn 14:6
Even the Spirit of t Jn 14:17
the Father, even the Spirit of t Jn 15:26
Nevertheless I tell you the t Jn 16:7
Howbeit when he, the Spirit of t Jn 16:13
he will guide you into all t Jn 16:13
Sanctify them through thy t Jn 17:17

thy word is *t* — Jn 17:17
might be sanctified through the *t* — Jn 17:19
I should bear witness unto the *t* — Jn 18:37
that is of the *t* heareth my voice — Jn 18:37
Pilate saith unto him, What is *t* — Jn 18:38
For of a *t* against thy holy child — Acts 4:27
Of a *t* I perceive that God is no — Acts 10:34
but speak forth the words of *t* — Acts 26:25
who hold the *t* in unrighteousness — Rom 1:18
Who changed the *t* of God into a — Rom 1:25
*t* against them which commit such — Rom 2:2
contentious, and do not obey the *t* — Rom 2:8
knowledge and of the *t* in the law — Rom 2:20
For if the *t* of God hath more — Rom 3:7
I say the *t* in Christ, I lie not, — Rom 9:1
the circumcision for the *t* of God — Rom 15:8
bread of sincerity and *t* — 1Cor 5:8
iniquity, but rejoiceth in the *t* — 1Cor 13:6
report that God is in you of a *t* — 1Cor 14:25
but by manifestation of the *t* — 2Cor 4:2
By the word of *t*, by the power of — 2Cor 6:7
we spake all things to you in *t* — 2Cor 7:14
I made before Titus, is found a *t* — 2Cor 7:14
As the *t* of Christ is in me, no — 2Cor 11:10
for I will say the *t* — 2Cor 12:6
against the *t*, but for the *t* — 2Cor 13:8
that the *t* of the gospel might — Gal 2:5
according to the *t* of the gospel — Gal 2:14
that ye should not obey the *t* — Gal 3:1
enemy, because I tell you the *t* — Gal 4:16
you that ye should not obey the *t* — Gal 5:7
after that ye heard the word of *t* — Eph 1:13
But speaking the *t* in love — Eph 4:15
by him, as the *t* is in Jesus — Eph 4:21
speak every man *t* with his — Eph 4:25
goodness and righteousness and *t* — Eph 5:9
your loins girt about with *t* — Eph 6:14
way, whether in pretence, or in *t* — Phil 1:18
the word of the *t* of the gospel — Col 1:5
it, and knew the grace of God in *t* — Col 1:6
word of men, but as it is in *t* — 1Th 2:13
received not the love of the *t* — 2Th 2:10
be damned who believed not the *t* — 2Th 2:12
of the Spirit and belief of the *t* — 2Th 2:13
come unto the knowledge of the *t* — 1Ti 2:4
apostle, (I speak the *t* in Christ — 1Ti 2:7
the pillar and ground of the *t* — 1Ti 3:15
them which believe and know the *t* — 1Ti 4:3
minds, and destitute of the *t* — 1Ti 6:5
rightly dividing the word of *t* — 2Ti 2:15
Who concerning the *t* have erred — 2Ti 2:18
to the acknowledging of the *t* — 2Ti 2:25
to come to the knowledge of the *t* — 2Ti 3:7
so do these also resist the *t* — 2Ti 3:8
turn away their ears from the *t* — 2Ti 4:4
of the *t* which is after godliness — Titus 1:1
of men, that turn from the *t* — Titus 1:14
received the knowledge of the *t* — Heb 10:26
begat he us with the word of *t* — Jas 1:18
not, and lie not against the *t* — Jas 3:14
if any of you do err from the *t* — Jas 5:19
the *t* through the Spirit unto — 1Pet 1:22
be established in the present *t* — 2Pet 1:12
way of *t* shall be evil spoken of — 2Pet 2:2
darkness, we lie, and do not the *t* — 1Jn 1:6
ourselves, and the *t* is not in us — 1Jn 1:8
is a liar, and the *t* is not in him — 1Jn 2:4
you because ye know not the *t* — 1Jn 2:21
it, and that no lie is of the *t* — 1Jn 2:21
you of all things, and is *t* — 1Jn 2:27
but in deed and in *t* — 1Jn 3:18
we know that we are of the *t* — 1Jn 3:19
Hereby know we the spirit of *t* — 1Jn 4:6
witness, because the Spirit is *t* — 1Jn 5:6
children, whom I love in the *t* — 2Jn 1
all they that have known the *t* — 2Jn 1
the Son of the Father, in *t* — 2Jn 3
of thy children walking in *t* — 2Jn 4
Gaius, whom I love in the *t* — 3Jn 1
of the *t* that is in thee, even as — 3Jn 3
even as thou walkest in the *t* — 3Jn 3
hear that my children walk in *t* — 3Jn 4
might be fellowhelpers to the *t* — 3Jn 8
of all men, and of the *t* itself — 3Jn 12

**TRUTH'S**
for thy mercy, and for thy *t* sake — Ps 115:1
For the *t* sake, which dwelleth in — 2Jn 2

**TRY**
I will *t* them for thee there — Judg 7:4
to *t* him, that he might know all — 2Chr 32:31
morning, and *t* him every moment — Job 7:18
Doth not the ear *t* words — Job 12:11
his eyes behold, his eyelids *t* — Ps 11:4
*t* my reins and my heart — Ps 26:2
*t* me, and know my thoughts — Ps 139:23
thou mayest know and *t* their way — Jer 6:27
I will melt them, and *t* them — Jer 9:7
I *t* the reins, even to give every — Jer 17:10
*t* our ways, and turn again to the — Lam 3:40
to *t* them, and to purge, and to — Dan 11:35
will *t* them as gold is tried — Zec 13:9
the fire shall *t* every man's work — 1Cor 3:13
the fiery trial which is to *t* you — 1Pet 4:12
but *t* the spirits whether they — 1Jn 4:1
to *t* them that dwell upon the — Rev 3:10

**TRYING**
that the *t* of your faith worketh — Jas 1:3

**TRYPHAENA** See TRYPHENA.

**TRYPHENA** (*tri-fe'-nah*) *A Christian in Rome.*
Salute *T* and Tryphosa, who labour — Rom 16:12

**TRYPHOSA** (*tri-fo'-sah*) *A Christian in Rome.*
Salute Tryphena and *T*, who labour — Rom 16:12

**TUBAL** (*tu'-bal*)
*1. A son of Japeth.*
Magog, and Madai, and Javan, and *T* — Gen 10:2
Magog, and Madai, and Javan, and *T* — 1Chr 1:5
*2. Migrants to Sicily and Spain.*
and Lud, that draw the bow, to *T* — Is 66:19
Javan, *T*, and Meshech, they were — Eze 27:13
There is Meshech, *T*, and all her — Eze 32:26
the chief prince of Meshech and *T* — Eze 38:2
the chief prince of Meshech and *T* — Eze 38:3
the chief prince of Meshech and *T* — Eze 39:1

**TUBAL-CAIN** (*tu'-bal-cain*) *Son of Lamech.*
And Zillah, she also bare *T* — Gen 4:22
and the sister of *T* was Naamah — Gen 4:22

**TUMBLED**
a cake of barley bread *t* into the — Judg 7:13

**TUMULT**
What meaneth the noise of this *t* — 1Sa 4:14
me thy servant, I saw a great *t* — 2Sa 18:29
thy *t* is come up into mine ears, — 2Kin 19:28
waves, and the *t* of the people — Ps 65:7
the *t* of those that rise up — Ps 74:23
For, lo, thine enemies make a *t* — Ps 83:2
noise of the *t* the people fled — Is 33:3
thy rage against me, and thy *t* — Is 37:29
with the noise of a great *t* he — Jer 11:16
Therefore shall a *t* arise among — Hos 10:14
and Moab shall die with *t*, with — Amos 2:2
that a great *t* from the LORD — Zec 14:13
but that rather a *t* was made — Mt 27:24
of the synagogue, and seeth the *t* — Mk 5:38
not know the certainty for the *t* — Acts 21:34
with multitude, nor with *t* — Acts 24:18

**TUMULTS**
behold the great *t* in the midst — Amos 3:9
stripes, in imprisonments, in *t* — 2Cor 6:5
whisperings, swellings, *t* — 2Cor 12:20

**TUMULTUOUS**
a *t* noise of the kingdoms of — Is 13:4
of stirs, a *t* city, a joyous city — Is 22:2
crown of the head of the *t* ones — Jer 48:45

**TURN**
*t* in, I pray you, into your — Gen 19:2
that I may *t* to the right hand, — Gen 24:49
until thy brother's fury *t* away — Gen 27:44
brother's anger *t* away from thee — Gen 27:45
And Moses said, I will now *t* aside — Ex 3:3
children of Israel, that they *t* — Ex 14:2
enemies *t* their backs unto thee — Ex 23:27
*T* from thy fierce wrath, and — Ex 32:12
Or if the raw flesh *t* again — Lev 13:16
*T* ye not unto idols, nor make to — Lev 19:4
To morrow *t* you, and get you into — Num 14:25
we will not *t* to the right hand — Num 20:17
we will not *t* into the fields, or — Num 21:22
the ass, to *t* her into the way — Num 22:23
where was no way to *t* either to — Num 22:26
For if ye *t* away from after him, — Num 32:15
your border shall *t* from the — Num 34:4
*T* you, and take your journey, and — Deut 1:7
*t* you, and take your journey into — Deut 1:40
*t* you northward — Deut 2:3
I will neither *t* unto the right — Deut 2:27
if thou *t* to the LORD thy God, and — Deut 4:30
ye shall not *t* aside to the right — Deut 5:32
For they will *t* away thy son from — Deut 7:4
ye *t* aside, and serve other gods, — Deut 11:16
but *t* aside out of the way which — Deut 11:28
because he hath spoken to *t* you — Deut 13:5
that the LORD may *t* from the — Deut 13:17
Then shalt thou *t* it into money — Deut 14:25
thou shalt *t* in the morning, and — Deut 16:7
that his heart *t* not away — Deut 17:17
that he *t* not aside from the — Deut 17:20
dig therewith, and shalt *t* back — Deut 23:13
in thee, and *t* away from thee — Deut 23:14
LORD thy God will *t* thy captivity — Deut 30:3
if thou *t* unto the LORD thy God — Deut 30:10
But if thine heart *t* away — Deut 30:17
then will they *t* unto other gods, — Deut 31:20
*t* aside from the way which I have — Deut 31:29
*t* not from it to the right hand — Josh 1:7
to *t* away this day from following — Josh 22:16
But that ye must *t* away this day — Josh 22:18
to *t* from following the LORD — Josh 22:23
*t* this day from following the — Josh 22:29
that ye *t* not aside therefrom to — Josh 23:6
strange gods, then he will *t* — Josh 24:20
*T* in, my lord, *t* in to me — Judg 4:18
Therefore we *t* again to thee now, — Judg 11:8
let us *t* in into this city of the — Judg 19:11
We will not *t* aside hither into — Judg 19:12
we any of us *t* into his house — Judg 20:8
Naomi said, *T* again, my daughters — Ruth 1:11
*T* again, my daughters, go your — Ruth 1:12
*t* aside, sit down here — Ruth 4:1
yet *t* not aside from following — 1Sa 12:20
And *t* ye not aside — 1Sa 12:21
*t* thee; behold, I am — 1Sa 14:7
*t* again with me, that I may — 1Sa 15:25
*t* again with me, that I may — 1Sa 15:30
footmen that stood about him, *T* — 1Sa 22:17
*T* thou, and fall upon the priests — 1Sa 22:18
*T* thee aside to thy right hand or — 2Sa 2:21
But Asahel would not *t* aside from — 2Sa 2:21
*T* thee aside from following me — 2Sa 2:22
Howbeit he refused to *t* aside — 2Sa 2:23
none can *t* to the right hand or — 2Sa 14:19
Let him *t* to his own house, and — 2Sa 14:24
*t* the counsel of Ahithophel into — 2Sa 15:31
unto him, *T* aside, and stand here — 2Sa 18:30
*t* back again, that I may die in — 2Sa 19:37
shall *t* again to thee, and confess — 1Kin 8:33
*t* from their sin, when thou — 1Kin 8:35
shall at all *t* from following me — 1Kin 9:6
for surely they will *t* away your — 1Kin 11:2
people *t* again unto their lord — 1Kin 12:27
nor *t* again by the same way that — 1Kin 13:9
nor *t* again to go by the way that — 1Kin 13:17
*t* thee eastward, and hide thyself — 1Kin 17:3
*T* thine hand, and carry me out of — 1Kin 22:34
*t* again unto the king that sent — 2Kin 1:6
to us, that he shall *t* in thither — 2Kin 4:10
*t* thee behind me — 2Kin 9:18
*t* thee behind me — 2Kin 9:19
*T* ye from your evil ways, and keep — 2Kin 17:13
How then wilt thou *t* away the — 2Kin 18:24
I will *t* thee back by the way by — 2Kin 19:28
*T* again, and tell Hezekiah the — 2Kin 20:5
to *t* the kingdom of Saul to him, — 1Chr 12:23
*t* away from them, and come upon — 1Chr 14:14
*t* from their sin, when thou dost — 2Chr 6:26
they are carried captive, and *t* — 2Chr 6:37
*t* not away the face of thine — 2Chr 6:42
face, and *t* from their wicked ways — 2Chr 7:14
But if ye *t* away, and forsake my — 2Chr 7:19
did *t* unto the LORD God of Israel — 2Chr 15:4
*T* thine hand, that thou mayest — 2Chr 18:33
*t* away from following the LORD — 2Chr 25:27
fierce wrath may *t* away from us — 2Chr 29:10
*t* again unto the LORD God of — 2Chr 30:6
of his wrath may *t* away from you — 2Chr 30:8
For if ye *t* again unto the LORD, — 2Chr 30:9
will not *t* away his face from you — 2Chr 30:9
would not *t* his face from him — 2Chr 35:22
But if ye *t* unto me, and keep my — Neh 1:9
*t* their reproach upon their own — Neh 4:4
against them to *t* them to thee — Neh 9:26
Now when every maid's *t* was come — Est 2:12
Now when the *t* of Esther, the — Est 2:15
which of the saints wilt thou *t* — Job 5:1
*T* from him, that he may rest, — Job 14:6
is in one mind, and who can *t* him — Job 23:13
They *t* the needy out of the way — Job 24:4
man shall *t* again unto dust — Job 34:15
how long will ye *t* my glory into — Ps 4:2
If he *t* not, he will whet his — Ps 7:12
neither did I *t* again till they — Ps 18:37
shalt thou make them *t* their back — Ps 21:12
shall remember and *t* unto the LORD — Ps 22:27
*T* thee unto me, and have mercy — Ps 25:16
nor such as *t* aside to lies — Ps 40:4
Thou makest us to *t* back from the — Ps 44:10
then shall mine enemies *t* back — Ps 56:9
O *t* thyself to us again — Ps 60:1
*t* unto me according to the — Ps 69:16
*T* us again, O God, and cause thy — Ps 80:3
*T* us again, O God of hosts, and — Ps 80:7
*T* us again, O LORD God of hosts, — Ps 80:19
*T* us, O God of our salvation, and — Ps 85:4
but let them not *t* again to folly — Ps 85:8
O *t* unto me, and have mercy upon — Ps 86:16
the work of them that *t* aside — Ps 101:3
that they *t* not again to cover — Ps 104:9
to *t* away his wrath, lest he — Ps 106:23
*T* away mine eyes from beholding — Ps 119:37
*T* away my reproach which I fear — Ps 119:39
those that fear thee *t* unto me — Ps 119:79
As for such as *t* aside unto their — Ps 125:5
*T* again our captivity, O LORD, as — Ps 126:4
sake *t* not away the face of thine — Ps 132:10
he will not *t* from it — Ps 132:11
*T* you at my reproof — Prov 1:23
by it, *t* from it, and pass away — Prov 4:15
*T* not to the right hand nor to — Prov 4:27
is simple, let him *t* in hither — Prov 9:4
is simple, let him *t* in hither — Prov 9:16
he *t* away his wrath from him — Prov 24:18
shame, and thine infamy *t* not away. — Prov 25:10
but wise men *t* away wrath — Prov 29:8
the dust, and all *t* to dust again — Eccl 3:20
and the shadows flee away, *t* — Song 2:17
*T* away thine eyes from me, for — Song 6:5
I will *t* my hand upon thee, and — Is 1:25
To *t* aside the needy from — Is 10:2
every man *t* to his own people — Is 13:14
out, and who shall *t* it back — Is 14:27
they shall *t* the rivers far away — Is 19:6
He will surely violently *t* — Is 22:18
she shall *t* to her hire, and shall — Is 23:17
that *t* the battle to the gate — Is 28:6
*t* aside the just for a thing of — Is 29:21
*t* aside out of the path, cause — Is 30:11
when ye *t* to the right hand, and — Is 30:21
hand, and when ye *t* to the left — Is 30:21
*T* ye unto him from whom the — Is 31:6
How then wilt thou *t* away the — Is 36:9
I will *t* thee back by the way by — Is 37:29

If thou *t* away thy foot from the ... Is 58:13
to Zion, and unto them that *t* from ... Is 59:20
her occasion who can *t* her away ... Jer 2:24
surely his anger shall *t* from me ... Jer 2:35
all these things, *T* thou unto me ... Jer 3:7
*T*, O backsliding children, saith ... Jer 3:14
and shalt not *t* away from me ... Jer 3:19
neither will I *t* back from it ... Jer 4:28
*t* back thine hand as a ... Jer 6:9
shall he *t* away, and not return ... Jer 8:4
he *t* it into the shadow of death, ... Jer 13:16
*t* from their evil, I will repent ... Jer 18:8
to *t* away thy wrath from them ... Jer 18:20
I will *t* back the weapons of war ... Jer 21:4
*T* ye again now every one from his ... Jer 25:5
*t* every man from his evil way, ... Jer 26:3
I will *t* away your captivity, and ... Jer 29:14
for I will *t* their mourning into ... Jer 31:13
*t* thou me, and I shall be turned ... Jer 31:18
*t* again, O virgin of Israel ... Jer 31:21
*t* again to these thy cities ... Jer 31:21
that I will not *t* away from them ... Jer 32:40
ear to *t* from their wickedness ... Jer 44:5
*t* back, dwell deep, O inhabitants ... Jer 49:8
shall *t* every one to his people ... Jer 50:16
iniquity, to *t* away thy captivity ... Lam 2:14
To *t* aside the right of a man ... Lam 3:35
our ways, and *t* again to the LORD ... Lam 3:40
*T* thou us unto thee, O LORD, and ... Lam 5:21
he *t* not from his wickedness, nor ... Eze 3:19
man doth *t* from his righteousness ... Eze 3:20
thou shalt not *t* thee from one ... Eze 4:8
My face will I *t* also from them ... Eze 7:22
but *t* thee yet again, and thou ... Eze 8:6
*T* thee yet again, and thou shalt ... Eze 8:13
*t* thee yet again, and thou shalt ... Eze 8:15
*t* yourselves from your idols ... Eze 14:6
*t* away your faces from all your ... Eze 14:6
But if the wicked will *t* from all ... Eze 18:21
*t* yourselves from all your ... Eze 18:30
wherefore *t* yourselves, and live ... Eze 18:32
wicked of his way to *t* from it ... Eze 33:9
if he do not *t* from his way ... Eze 33:9
that the wicked *t* from his way ... Eze 33:11
*t* ye, *t* ye from your evil ways ... Eze 33:11
if he *t* from his sin, and do that ... Eze 33:14
But if the wicked *t* from his ... Eze 33:19
I will *t* unto you, and ye shall be ... Eze 36:9
I will *t* thee back, and put hooks ... Eze 38:4
to *t* thine hand upon the desolate ... Eze 38:12
I will *t* thee back, and leave but ... Eze 39:2
our God, that we might *t* from our ... Dan 9:13
After this shall he *t* his face ... Dan 11:18
he shall cause it to *t* upon him ... Dan 11:18
Then he shall *t* his face toward ... Dan 11:19
they that *t* many to righteousness ... Dan 12:3
their doings to *t* unto their God ... Hos 5:4
Therefore *t* thou to thy God ... Hos 12:6
with you words, and *t* to the LORD ... Hos 14:2
*t* ye even to me with all your ... Joel 2:12
and *t* unto the LORD your God ... Joel 2:13
I will not *t* away the punishment ... Amos 1:3
I will not *t* away the punishment ... Amos 1:6
I will *t* mine hand against Ekron ... Amos 1:8
I will not *t* away the punishment ... Amos 1:9
I will not *t* away the punishment ... Amos 1:11
I will not *t* away the punishment ... Amos 1:13
I will not *t* away the punishment ... Amos 2:1
I will not *t* away the punishment ... Amos 2:4
I will not *t* away the punishment ... Amos 2:6
*t* aside the way of the meek ... Amos 2:7
*t* judgment to wormwood ... Amos 5:7
they *t* aside the poor in the gate ... Amos 5:12
I will *t* your feasts into ... Amos 8:10
let them *t* every one from his ... Jonah 3:8
Who can tell if God will *t* ... Jonah 3:9
*t* away from his fierce anger, ... Jonah 3:9
He will *t* again, he will have ... Mic 7:19
them, and *t* away their captivity ... Zeph 2:7
For then will I *t* to the people a ... Zeph 3:9
when I *t* back your captivity ... Zeph 3:20
*T* ye unto me, saith the LORD of ... Zec 1:3
I will *t* unto you, saith the LORD ... Zec 1:3
*T* ye now from your evil ways, and ... Zec 1:4
*T* you to the strong hold, ye ... Zec 9:12
with their children, and *t* again ... Zec 10:9
I will *t* mine hand upon the ... Zec 13:7
did *t* many away from iniquity ... Mal 2:6
that *t* aside the stranger from ... Mal 3:5
he shall *t* the heart of the ... Mal 4:6
cheek, *t* to him the other also ... Mt 5:39
borrow of thee *t* not thou away ... Mt 5:42
feet, and *t* again and rend you ... Mt 7:6
him that is in the field not *t* ... Mk 13:16
shall he *t* to the Lord their God ... Lk 1:16
to *t* the hearts of the fathers to ... Lk 1:17
if not, it shall *t* to you again ... Lk 10:6
times in a day *t* again to thee ... Lk 17:4
it shall *t* to you for a testimony ... Lk 21:13
seeking to *t* away the deputy from ... Acts 13:8
life, lo, we *t* to the Gentiles ... Acts 13:46
*t* from these vanities unto the ... Acts 14:15
to *t* them from darkness to light, ... Acts 26:18
*t* to God, and do works meet for ... Acts 26:20
shall *t* away ungodliness from ... Rom 11:26
when it shall *t* to the Lord ... 2Cor 3:16
how *t* ye again to the weak and ... Gal 4:9
For I know that this shall *t* to ... Phil 1:19
from such *t* away ... 2Ti 3:5
they shall *t* away their ears from ... 2Ti 4:4
of men, that *t* from the truth ... Titus 1:14
if we *t* away from him that ... Heb 12:25
we *t* about their whole body ... Jas 3:3
to *t* from the holy commandment ... 2Pet 2:21
over waters to *t* them to blood ... Rev 11:6

**TURNED**

a flaming sword which *t* every way ... Gen 3:24
the men *t* their faces from thence ... Gen 18:22
they *t* in unto him, and entered ... Gen 19:3
*t* in to a certain Adullamite, ... Gen 38:1
he *t* unto her by the way, and said ... Gen 38:16
he *t* himself about from them, and ... Gen 42:24
LORD saw that he *t* aside to see ... Ex 3:4
it was *t* again as his other flesh ... Ex 4:7
the rod which was *t* to a serpent ... Ex 7:15
and they shall be *t* to blood ... Ex 7:17
were in the river were *t* to blood ... Ex 7:20
And Pharaoh *t* and went into his ... Ex 7:23
he *t* himself, and went out from ... Ex 10:6
the LORD *t* a mighty strong west ... Ex 10:19
servants was *t* against the people ... Ex 14:5
They have *t* aside quickly out of ... Ex 32:8
And Moses *t*, and went down from the ... Ex 32:15
And he *t* again into the camp ... Ex 33:11
the hair in the plague is *t* white ... Lev 13:3
the hair thereof be not *t* white ... Lev 13:4
it have *t* the hair white, and ... Lev 13:10
it is all *t* white ... Lev 13:13
if the plague be *t* into white ... Lev 13:17
and the hair thereof be *t* white ... Lev 13:20
in the bright spot be *t* white ... Lev 13:25
because ye are *t* away from the ... Num 14:43
wherefore Israel *t* away from him ... Num 20:21
And they *t* and went up by the way ... Num 21:33
the ass *t* aside out of the way, ... Num 22:23
*t* from me these three times ... Num 22:33
unless she had *t* from me, surely ... Num 22:33
LORD may be *t* away from Israel ... Num 25:4
hath *t* my wrath away from the ... Num 25:11
*t* again unto Pi-hahiroth, which ... Num 33:7
And they *t* and went up into the ... Deut 1:24
Then we *t*, and took our journey ... Deut 2:1
Elath, and from Ezion-gaber, we *t* ... Deut 2:8
Then we *t*, and went up the way to ... Deut 3:1
they are quickly *t* aside out of ... Deut 9:12
So I *t* and came down from the ... Deut 9:15
ye had *t* aside quickly out of the ... Deut 9:16
I *t* myself and came down from the ... Deut 10:5
but the LORD thy God *t* the curse ... Deut 23:5
that they are *t* unto other gods ... Deut 31:18
but *t* their backs before their ... Josh 7:12
So the LORD *t* from the fierceness ... Josh 7:26
*t* back upon the pursuers ... Josh 8:20
city ascended, then they *t* again ... Josh 8:21
And Joshua at that time *t* back ... Josh 11:10
*t* from Sarid eastward toward the ... Josh 19:12
they *t* quickly out of the way ... Judg 2:17
But he himself *t* again from the ... Judg 3:19
when he had *t* in unto her into ... Judg 4:18
the children of Israel *t* again ... Judg 8:33
he *t* aside to see the carcase of ... Judg 14:8
and *t* tail to tail, and put a ... Judg 15:4
they *t* in thither, and said unto ... Judg 18:3
they *t* thitherward, and came to ... Judg 18:15
So they *t* and departed, and put the ... Judg 18:21
they *t* their faces, and said unto ... Judg 18:23
were too strong for him, he *t* ... Judg 18:26
they *t* aside thither, to go in and ... Judg 19:15
And when the men of Israel *t* again ... Judg 20:41
Therefore they *t* their backs ... Judg 20:42
And they *t* and fled toward the ... Judg 20:45
But six hundred men *t* and fled to ... Judg 20:47
the men of Israel *t* again upon ... Judg 20:48
the man was afraid, and *t* himself ... Ruth 3:8
And he *t* aside, and sat down ... Ruth 4:1
*t* not aside to the right hand or ... 1Sa 6:12
but *t* aside after lucre, and took ... 1Sa 8:3
shalt be *t* into another man ... 1Sa 10:6
that when he had *t* his back to go ... 1Sa 10:9
one company *t* unto the way that ... 1Sa 13:17
another company *t* the way to ... 1Sa 13:18
another company *t* to the way of ... 1Sa 13:18
even they also *t* to be with the ... 1Sa 14:21
and whithersoever he *t* himself ... 1Sa 14:47
for he is *t* back from following ... 1Sa 15:11
as Samuel *t* about to go away, he ... 1Sa 15:27
So Samuel *t* again after Saul ... 1Sa 15:31
he *t* from him toward another, and ... 1Sa 17:30
And Doeg the Edomite *t*, and he fell ... 1Sa 22:18
So David's young men *t* their way ... 1Sa 25:12
the bow of Jonathan *t* not back ... 2Sa 1:22
in going he *t* not to the right ... 2Sa 2:19
he *t* aside, and stood still ... 2Sa 18:30
the victory that day was *t* into ... 2Sa 19:2
*t* not again until I had consumed ... 2Sa 22:38
howbeit the kingdom is *t* about ... 1Kin 2:15
for Joab had *t* after Adonijah, ... 1Kin 2:28
though he *t* not after Absalom ... 1Kin 2:28
the king *t* his face about, and ... 1Kin 8:14
So she *t* and went to her own ... 1Kin 10:13
his wives *t* away his heart ... 1Kin 11:3
that his wives *t* away his heart ... 1Kin 11:4
because his heart was *t* from the ... 1Kin 11:9
*t* not aside from any thing that ... 1Kin 15:5
that thou hast *t* their heart back ... 1Kin 18:37
and, behold, a man *t* aside ... 1Kin 20:39
*t* away his face, and would eat no ... 1Kin 21:4
they *t* aside to fight against him ... 1Kin 22:32
that they *t* back from pursuing ... 1Kin 22:33
he *t* not aside from it, doing ... 1Kin 22:43
the messengers *t* back unto him ... 2Kin 1:5
unto them, Why are ye now *t* back ... 2Kin 1:5
he *t* back, and looked on them, and ... 2Kin 2:24
he *t* in thither to eat bread ... 2Kin 4:8
he *t* into the chamber, and lay ... 2Kin 4:11
So he *t* and went away in a rage ... 2Kin 5:12
when the man *t* again from his ... 2Kin 5:26
Joram *t* his hands, and fled, and ... 2Kin 9:23
So the king of Assyria *t* back ... 2Kin 15:20
*t* he from the house of the LORD ... 2Kin 16:18
Then he *t* his face to the wall, ... 2Kin 20:2
*t* not aside to the right hand or ... 2Kin 22:2
And as Josiah *t* himself, he spied ... 2Kin 23:16
that *t* to the LORD with all his ... 2Kin 23:25
Notwithstanding the LORD *t* not ... 2Kin 23:26
*t* his name to Jehoiakim, and took ... 2Kin 23:34
then he *t* and rebelled against him ... 2Kin 24:1
*t* the kingdom unto David the son ... 1Chr 10:14
Ornan *t* back, and saw the ... 1Chr 21:20
And the king *t* his face, and ... 2Chr 6:3
So she *t*, and went away to her own ... 2Chr 9:12
the wrath of the LORD *t* from him ... 2Chr 12:12
they *t* back again from pursuing ... 2Chr 18:32
Egypt, but they *t* from them, and ... 2Chr 20:10
have *t* away their faces from the ... 2Chr 29:6
of the LORD, and *t* their backs ... 2Chr 29:6
*t* his name to Jehoiakim ... 2Chr 36:4
*t* the heart of the king of ... Ezr 6:22
God for this matter be *t* from us ... Ezr 10:14
*t* back, and entered by the gate of ... Neh 2:15
neither *t* they from their wicked ... Neh 9:35
howbeit our God *t* the curse into ... Neh 13:2
(though it was *t* to the contrary, ... Est 9:1
the month which was *t* unto them ... Est 9:22
paths of their way are *t* aside ... Job 6:18
*t* me over into the hands of the ... Job 16:11
whom I loved are *t* against me ... Job 19:19
Yet his meat in his bowels is *t* ... Job 20:14
under it is *t* up as it were fire ... Job 28:5
Terrors are *t* upon me ... Job 30:15
My harp also is *t* to mourning ... Job 30:31
If my step hath *t* out of the way ... Job 31:7
Because they *t* back from him, and ... Job 34:27
it is *t* round about by his ... Job 37:12
It is *t* as clay to the seal ... Job 38:14
sorrow is *t* into joy before him ... Job 41:22
slingstones are *t* with him into ... Job 41:28
the LORD *t* the captivity of Job, ... Job 42:10
When mine enemies are *t* back ... Ps 9:3
The wicked shall be *t* into hell ... Ps 9:17
Thou hast *t* for me my mourning ... Ps 30:11
my moisture is *t* into the drought ... Ps 32:4
let them be *t* back and brought to ... Ps 35:4
Our heart is not *t* back, neither ... Ps 44:18
He *t* the sea into dry land ... Ps 66:6
which hath not *t* away my prayer ... Ps 66:20
let them be *t* backward, and put to ... Ps 70:2
Let them be *t* back for a reward ... Ps 70:3
*t* back in the day of battle ... Ps 78:9
many a time *t* he his anger away, ... Ps 78:38
Yea, they *t* back and tempted God, ... Ps 78:41
had *t* their rivers into blood ... Ps 78:44
But *t* back, and dealt unfaithfully ... Ps 78:57
they were *t* aside like a ... Ps 78:57
and *t* my hand against their ... Ps 81:14
thou hast *t* thyself from the ... Ps 85:3
Thou hast also *t* the edge of his ... Ps 89:43
He *t* their heart to hate his ... Ps 105:25
He *t* their waters into blood, and ... Ps 105:29
Which *t* the rock into a standing ... Ps 114:8
*t* my feet unto thy testimonies ... Ps 119:59
When the LORD *t* again the ... Ps 126:1
and *t* back that hate Zion ... Ps 129:5
I *t* myself to behold wisdom, and ... Eccl 2:12
whither is thy beloved *t* aside ... Song 6:1
all this his anger is not *t* away ... Is 5:25
all this his anger is not *t* away ... Is 9:12
all this his anger is not *t* away ... Is 9:17
all this his anger is not *t* away ... Is 9:21
all this his anger is not *t* away ... Is 10:4
with me, thine anger is *t* away ... Is 12:1
hath he *t* into fear unto me ... Is 21:4
wheel *t* about upon the cummin ... Is 28:27
Lebanon shall be *t* into a ... Is 29:17
thereof shall be *t* into pitch ... Is 34:9
Then Hezekiah *t* his face toward ... Is 38:2
They shall be *t* back, they shall ... Is 42:17
a deceived heart hath *t* him aside ... Is 44:20
rebellious, neither *t* away back ... Is 50:5
we have *t* every one to his own ... Is 53:6
judgment is *t* away backward, and ... Is 59:14
therefore he was *t* to be their ... Is 63:10
how then art thou *t* into the ... Jer 2:21
for they have *t* their back unto ... Jer 2:27
sister Judah hath not *t* unto me ... Jer 3:10
of the LORD is not *t* back from us ... Jer 4:8
have *t* away these things, and your ... Jer 5:25
houses shall be *t* unto others ... Jer 6:12
every one *t* to his course, as the ... Jer 8:6
They are *t* back to the iniquities ... Jer 11:10
then they should have *t* them from ... Jer 23:22
and all faces are *t* into paleness ... Jer 30:6
turn thou me, and I shall be *t* ... Jer 31:18
Surely after that I was *t* ... Jer 31:19
they have *t* unto me the back, and ... Jer 32:33
But afterward they *t*, and caused ... Jer 34:11
And ye were now *t*, and had done ... Jer 34:15
But ye *t* and polluted my name, and ... Jer 34:16
the mire, and they are *t* away back ... Jer 38:22
seen them dismayed and *t* away back ... Jer 46:5

for they also are *t* back, and are Jer 46:21
how hath Moab *t* the back with Jer 48:39
they have *t* them away on the Jer 50:6
for my feet, he hath *t* me back Lam 1:13
mine heart is *t* within me Lam 1:20
Surely against me is he *t* Lam 3:3
He hath *t* aside my ways, and Lam 3:11
Our inheritance is *t* to strangers Lam 5:2
our dance is *t* into mourning Lam 5:15
thee, O LORD, and we shall be *t* Lam 5:21
they *t* not when they went Eze 1:9
they *t* not when they went Eze 1:12
they *t* not when they went Eze 1:17
they *t* not as they went, but to Eze 10:11
they *t* not as they went Eze 10:11
also *t* not from beside them Eze 10:16
whose branches *t* toward him Eze 17:6
she is *t* unto me Eze 26:2
He *t* about to the west side, and Eze 42:19
thy fury be *t* away from thy city Dan 9:16
was *t* in me into corruption Dan 10:8
vision my sorrows are *t* upon me Dan 10:16
Ephraim is a cake not *t* Hos 7:8
mine heart is *t* within me Hos 11:8
for mine anger is *t* away from him Hos 14:4
The sun shall be *t* into darkness Joel 2:31
for ye have *t* judgment into gall, Amos 6:12
that they *t* from their evil way Jonah 3:10
For the LORD hath *t* away the Nah 2:2
right hand shall be *t* unto thee Hab 2:16
them that are *t* back from the Zeph 1:6
yet ye *t* not to me, saith the Hag 2:17
Then I *t*, and lifted up mine eyes, Zec 5:1
And I *t*, and lifted up mine eyes, Zec 6:1
All the land shall be *t* as a Zec 14:10
he *t* aside into the parts of Mt 2:22
But Jesus *t* him about, and when he Mt 9:22
But he *t*, and said unto Peter, Get Mt 16:23
*t* him about in the press, and said Mk 5:30
But when he had *t* about and looked Mk 8:33
they *t* back again to Jerusalem, Lk 2:45
*t* him about, and said unto the Lk 7:9
he *t* to the woman, and said unto Lk 7:44
But he *t*, and rebuked them, and Lk 9:55
he *t* him unto his disciples, and Lk 10:23
and he *t*, and said unto them, Lk 14:25
*t* back, and with a loud voice Lk 17:15
And the Lord *t*, and looked upon Lk 22:61
Then Jesus *t*, and saw them Jn 1:38
your sorrow shall be *t* into joy Jn 16:20
she *t* herself back, and saw Jesus Jn 20:14
She *t* herself, and saith unto him, Jn 20:16
The sun shall be *t* into darkness Acts 2:20
in their hearts *t* back again into Acts 7:39
Then God *t*, and gave them up to Acts 7:42
Saron saw him, and *t* to the Lord Acts 9:35
believed, and *t* unto the Lord Acts 11:21
among the Gentiles are *t* to God Acts 15:19
But Paul, being grieved, *t* Acts 16:18
These that have *t* the world Acts 17:6
*t* away much people, saying that Acts 19:26
how ye *t* to God from idols to 1Th 1:9
have *t* aside unto vain jangling 1Ti 1:6
are already *t* aside after Satan 1Ti 5:15
are in Asia be *t* away from me 2Ti 1:15
truth, and shall be *t* unto fables 2Ti 4:4
*t* to flight the armies of the Heb 11:34
which is lame be *t* out of the way Heb 12:13
yet are they *t* about with a very Jas 3:4
your laughter be *t* to mourning Jas 4:9
The dog is *t* to his own vomit 2Pet 2:22
I *t* to see the voice that spake Rev 1:12
And being *t*, I saw seven golden Rev 1:12

**TURNEST**
and whithersoever thou *t* thyself 1Kin 2:3
That thou *t* thy spirit against Job 15:13
Thou *t* man to destruction Ps 90:3

**TURNETH**
the soul that *t* after such as Lev 20:6
whose heart *t* away this day from Deut 29:18
when Israel *t* their backs before Josh 7:8
*t* toward the sunrising to Josh 19:27
And then the coast *t* to Ramah Josh 19:29
and the coast *t* to Hosah Josh 19:29
then the coast *t* westward to Josh 19:34
neither *t* he back from the sword Job 39:22
He *t* rivers into a wilderness, and Ps 107:33
He *t* the wilderness into a Ps 107:35
of the wicked he *t* upside down Ps 146:9
A soft answer *t* away wrath Prov 15:1
whithersoever it *t*, it prospereth Prov 17:8
he *t* it whithersoever he will Prov 21:1
As the door *t* upon his hinges, so Prov 26:14
He that *t* away his ear from Prov 28:9
beasts, and *t* not away for any Prov 30:30
south, and *t* about unto the north Eccl 1:6
that *t* aside by the flocks of thy Song 1:7
For the people *t* not unto him Is 9:13
*t* it upside down, and scattereth Is 24:1
that *t* wise men backward, and Is 44:25
as a wayfaring man that *t* aside Jer 14:8
*t* herself to flee, and fear hath Jer 49:24
yea, she sigheth, and *t* backward Lam 1:8
he *t* his hand against me all the Lam 3:3
But when the righteous *t* away Eze 18:24
When a righteous man *t* away from Eze 18:26
when the wicked man *t* away from Eze 18:27
and *t* away from all his Eze 18:28
day that he *t* from his wickedness Eze 33:12
When the righteous *t* from his Eze 33:18
*t* the shadow of death into the Amos 5:8

**TURNING**
wiping it, and *t* it upside down 2Kin 21:13
gate, and at the *t* of the wall, and 2Chr 26:9
hardened his heart from *t* unto 2Chr 36:13
the armoury at the *t* of the wall Neh 3:19
from the *t* of the wall unto the Neh 3:20
of Azariah unto the *t* of the wall Neh 3:24
over against the *t* of the wall Neh 3:25
For the *t* away of the simple Prov 1:32
Surely your *t* of things upside Is 29:16
two leaves apiece, two *t* leaves Eze 41:24
*t* away he hath divided our fields Mic 2:4
But Jesus *t* unto them said, Lk 23:28
*t* about, seeth the disciple whom Jn 21:20
in *t* away every one of you from Acts 3:26
*t* him to the body said, Tabitha, Acts 9:40
variableness, neither shadow of *t* Jas 1:17
*t* the cities of Sodom and Gomorrah 2Pet 2:6
*t* the grace of our God into Jude 4

**TURTLE**
the voice of the *t* is heard in Song 2:12
and the *t* and the crane and the Jer 8:7

**TURTLEDOVE**
a ram of three years old, and a *t* Gen 15:9
and a young pigeon, or a *t* Lev 12:6
thy *t* unto the multitude of the Ps 74:19

**TURTLEDOVES**
he shall bring his offering of *t* Lev 1:14
which he hath committed, two *t* Lev 5:7
if he be not able to bring two *t* Lev 5:11
And two *t*, or two young pigeons, Lev 14:22
he shall offer the one of the *t* Lev 14:30
day he shall take to him two *t* Lev 15:14
the law of the Lord, A pair of *t* Lk 2:24

**TURTLES**
lamb, then she shall bring two *t* Lev 12:8
day she shall take unto her two *t* Lev 15:29
eighth day he shall bring two *t* Num 6:10

**TUTORS**
But is under *t* and governors until Gal 4:2

**TWAIN**
my son in law in the one of the *t* 1Sa 18:21
and shut the door upon them *t* 2Kin 4:33
with *t* he covered his face, and Is 6:2
with *t* he covered his feet, and Is 6:2
his feet, and with *t* he did fly Is 6:2
me, when they cut the calf in *t* Jer 34:18
both *t* shall come forth out of Eze 21:19
thee to go a mile, go with him *t* Mt 5:41
they *t* shall be one flesh Mt 19:5
Wherefore they are no more *t* Mt 19:6
Whether of them *t* did the will of Mt 21:31
Whether of the *t* will ye that I Mt 27:21
in *t* from the top to the bottom Mt 27:51
they *t* shall be one flesh Mk 10:8
so then they are no more *t* Mk 10:8
in *t* from the top to the bottom Mk 15:38
make in himself of *t* one new man Eph 2:15

**TWELFTH**
On the *t* day Ahira the son of Num 7:78
oxen before him, and he with the *t* 1Kin 19:19
In the *t* year of Joram the son of 2Kin 8:25
In the *t* year of Ahaz king of 2Kin 17:1
king of Judah, in the *t* month 2Kin 25:27
to Eliashib, the *t* to Jakim, 1Chr 24:12
The *t* to Hashabiah, he, his sons, 1Chr 25:19
The *t* captain for the *t* 1Chr 27:15
in the *t* year he began to purge 2Chr 34:3
on the *t* day of the first month Ezr 8:31
in the *t* year of king Ahasuerus, Est 3:7
month to month, to the *t* month Est 3:7
the thirteenth day of the *t* month Est 3:13
the thirteenth day of the *t* month Est 8:12
Now in the *t* month, that is, the Est 9:1
king of Judah, in the *t* month Jer 52:31
in the *t* day of the month, the Eze 29:1
the *t* year, in the *t* month Eze 32:1
came to pass also in the *t* year Eze 32:17
in the *t* year of our captivity Eze 33:21
the *t*, an amethyst Rev 21:20

**TWELVE**
Seth were nine hundred and *t* years Gen 5:8
*T* years they served Chedorlaomer, Gen 14:4
*t* princes shall he beget, and I Gen 17:20
*t* princes according to their Gen 25:16
Now the sons of Jacob were *t* Gen 35:22
said, Thy servants are *t* brethren Gen 42:13
We be *t* brethren, sons of our Gen 42:32
these are the *t* tribes of Israel Gen 49:28
where were *t* wells of water, and Ex 15:27
*t* pillars, according to the Ex 24:4
to the *t* tribes of Israel Ex 24:4
of the children of Israel, *t* Ex 28:21
they be according to the *t* tribes Ex 28:21
of the children of Israel, *t* Ex 39:14
name, according to the *t* tribes Ex 39:14
flour, and bake *t* cakes thereof Lev 24:5
princes of Israel, being *t* men Num 1:44
six covered wagons, and *t* oxen Num 7:3
*t* chargers of silver Num 7:84
*t* silver bowls, *t* spoons of Num 7:84
The golden spoons were *t*, full of Num 7:86
were *t* bullocks, the rams *t* Num 7:87
the lambs of the first year *t* Num 7:87
of the goats for sin offering *t* Num 7:87
the house of their fathers *t* rods Num 17:2
fathers' houses, even *t* rods Num 17:6
ye shall offer *t* young bullocks Num 29:17
tribe, *t* thousand armed for war Num 31:5
threescore and *t* thousand beeves, Num 31:33
tribute was threescore and *t* Num 31:38
in Elim were *t* fountains of water Num 33:9
I took *t* men of you, one of a Deut 1:23
Now therefore take you *t* men out Josh 3:12
Take you *t* men out of the people, Josh 4:2
*t* stones, and ye shall carry them Josh 4:3
Then Joshua called the *t* men Josh 4:4
took up *t* stones out of the midst Josh 4:8
Joshua set up *t* stones in the Josh 4:9
those *t* stones, which they took Josh 4:20
were *t* thousand, even all the men Josh 8:25
*t* cities with their villages Josh 18:24
*t* cities with their villages Josh 19:15
of the tribe of Zebulun, *t* cities Josh 21:7
were by their lot *t* cities Josh 21:40
into *t* pieces, and sent her into Judg 19:29
the congregation sent thither *t* Judg 21:10
went over by number *t* of Benjamin 2Sa 2:15
*t* of the servants of David 2Sa 2:15
of Ish-tob *t* thousand men 2Sa 10:6
me now choose out *t* thousand men 2Sa 17:1
Solomon had *t* officers over all 1Kin 4:7
chariots, and *t* thousand horsemen 1Kin 4:26
a line of *t* cubits did compass 1Kin 7:15
It stood upon *t* oxen, three 1Kin 7:25
one sea, and *t* oxen under the sea 1Kin 7:44
*t* lions stood there on the one 1Kin 10:20
*t* thousand horsemen, whom he 1Kin 10:26
on him, and rent it in *t* pieces 1Kin 11:30
to reign over Israel, *t* years 1Kin 16:23
And Elijah took *t* stones, 1Kin 18:31
who was plowing with *t* yoke of 1Kin 19:19
king of Judah, and reigned *t* years 2Kin 3:1
Manasseh was *t* years old when he 2Kin 21:1
of the tribe of Zebulun, *t* cities 1Chr 6:63
the gates were two hundred and *t* 1Chr 9:22
and his brethren an hundred and *t* 1Chr 15:10
with his brethren and sons were *t* 1Chr 25:9
his sons, and his brethren, were *t* 1Chr 25:10
his sons, and his brethren, were *t* 1Chr 25:11
his sons, and his brethren, were *t* 1Chr 25:12
his sons, and his brethren, were *t* 1Chr 25:13
his sons, and his brethren, were *t* 1Chr 25:14
his sons, and his brethren, were *t* 1Chr 25:15
his sons, and his brethren, were *t* 1Chr 25:16
his sons, and his brethren, were *t* 1Chr 25:17
his sons, and his brethren, were *t* 1Chr 25:18
his sons, and his brethren, were *t* 1Chr 25:19
his sons, and his brethren, were *t* 1Chr 25:20
his sons, and his brethren, were *t* 1Chr 25:21
his sons, and his brethren, were *t* 1Chr 25:22
his sons, and his brethren, were *t* 1Chr 25:23
his sons, and his brethren, were *t* 1Chr 25:24
his sons, and his brethren, were *t* 1Chr 25:25
his sons, and his brethren, were *t* 1Chr 25:26
his sons, and his brethren, were *t* 1Chr 25:27
his sons, and his brethren, were *t* 1Chr 25:28
his sons, and his brethren, were *t* 1Chr 25:29
his sons, and his brethren, were *t* 1Chr 25:30
his sons, and his brethren, were *t* 1Chr 25:31
*t* thousand horsemen, which he 2Chr 1:14
It stood upon *t* oxen, three 2Chr 4:4
One sea, and *t* oxen under it 2Chr 4:15
*t* lions stood there on the one 2Chr 9:19
chariots, and *t* thousand horsemen 2Chr 9:25
With *t* hundred chariots, and 2Chr 12:3
Manasseh was *t* years old when he 2Chr 33:1
two thousand eight hundred and *t* Ezr 2:6
of Jorah, an hundred and *t* Ezr 2:18
*t* he goats, according to the Ezr 6:17
Then I separated *t* of the chief Ezr 8:24
*t* bullocks for all Israel, ninety Ezr 8:35
*t* he goats for a sin offering Ezr 8:35
*t* years, I and my brethren have Neh 5:14
of Hariph, an hundred and *t* Neh 7:24
after that she had been *t* months Est 2:12
in the valley of salt *t* thousand Ps 60:*t*
*t* brasen bulls that were under Jer 52:20
a fillet of *t* cubits did compass Jer 52:21
the altar shall be *t* cubits long Eze 43:16
*t* broad, square in the four Eze 43:16
to the *t* tribes of Israel Eze 47:13
At the end of *t* months he walked Dan 4:29
with an issue of blood *t* years Mt 9:20
called unto him his *t* disciples Mt 10:1
names of the *t* apostles are these Mt 10:2
These *t* Jesus sent forth, and Mt 10:5
end of commanding his *t* disciples Mt 11:1
that remained *t* baskets full Mt 14:20
ye also shall sit upon *t* thrones Mt 19:28
judging the *t* tribes of Israel Mt 19:28
the *t* disciples apart in the way Mt 20:17
Then one of the *t*, called Judas Mt 26:14
was come, he sat down with the *t* Mt 26:20
spake, lo, Judas, one of the *t* Mt 26:47
me more than *t* legions of angels Mt 26:53
And he ordained *t*, that they Mk 3:14
the *t* asked of him the parable Mk 4:10
had an issue of blood *t* years Mk 5:25
for she was of the age of *t* years Mk 5:42
And he called unto him the *t* Mk 6:7
they took up *t* baskets full of Mk 6:43
They say unto him, *T* Mk 8:19

And he sat down, and called the *t* Mk 9:35
And he took again the *t*, and began Mk 10:32
went out unto Bethany with the *t* Mk 11:11
And Judas Iscariot, one of the *t* Mk 14:10
the evening he cometh with the *t* Mk 14:17
unto them, It is one of the *t* Mk 14:20
spake, cometh Judas, one of the *t* Mk 14:43
And when he was *t* years old Lk 2:42
and of them he chose *t*, whom also Lk 6:13
and the *t* were with him, Lk 8:1
about *t* years of age, and she lay Lk 8:42
having an issue of blood *t* years Lk 8:43
called his *t* disciples together Lk 9:1
to wear away, then came the *t* Lk 9:12
that remained to them *t* baskets Lk 9:17
Then he took unto him the *t* Lk 18:31
being of the number of the *t* Lk 22:3
down, and the *t* apostles with him Lk 22:14
judging the *t* tribes of Israel Lk 22:30
was called Judas, one of the *t* Lk 22:47
filled *t* baskets with the Jn 6:13
Then said Jesus unto the *t* Jn 6:67
them, Have not I chosen you *t* Jn 6:70
betray him, being one of the *t* Jn 6:71
Are there not *t* hours in the day Jn 11:9
But Thomas, one of the *t*, called Jn 20:24
Then the *t* called the multitude Acts 6:2
and Jacob begat the *t* patriarchs Acts 7:8
And all the men were about *t* Acts 19:7
that there are yet but *t* days Acts 24:11
Unto which promise our *t* tribes Acts 26:7
was seen of Cephas, then of the *t* 1Cor 15:5
to the *t* tribes which are Jas 1:1
of Juda were sealed *t* thousand Rev 7:5
of Reuben were sealed *t* thousand Rev 7:5
of Gad were sealed *t* thousand Rev 7:5
of Aser were sealed *t* thousand Rev 7:6
Nepthalim were sealed *t* thousand Rev 7:6
Manasses were sealed *t* thousand Rev 7:6
of Simeon were sealed *t* thousand Rev 7:7
of Levi were sealed *t* thousand Rev 7:7
Issachar were sealed *t* thousand Rev 7:7
of Zabulon were sealed *t* thousand Rev 7:8
of Joseph were sealed *t* thousand Rev 7:8
Benjamin were sealed *t* thousand Rev 7:8
upon her head a crown of *t* stars Rev 12:1
had *t* gates, and at the gates Rev 21:12
gates, and at the gates *t* angels Rev 21:12
the *t* tribes of the children of Rev 21:12
of the city had *t* foundations Rev 21:14
of the *t* apostles of the Lamb Rev 21:14
the reed, *t* thousand furlongs Rev 21:16
the *t* gates were *t* pearls Rev 21:21
which bare *t* manner of fruits, and Rev 22:2

## TWENTIETH

*t* day of the month, was the earth Gen 8:14
*t* day of the month at even Ex 12:18
it came to pass on the *t* day of Num 10:11
in the *t* year of Jeroboam king of 1Kin 15:9
*t* year of king Jehoash the 2Kin 12:6
*t* year of Joash the son of 2Kin 13:1
in the *t* year of Jotham the son 2Kin 15:30
seven and *t* day of the month, that 2Kin 25:27
to Pethahiah, the *t* to Jehezekel, 1Chr 24:16
to Jachin, the two and 1Chr 24:17
to Jachin, the two and *t* to Gamul, 1Chr 24:17
*t* to Delaiah, the four and 1Chr 24:18
Delaiah, the four and *t* to Maaziah 1Chr 24:18
The *t* to Eliathah, he, his sons, 1Chr 25:27
*t* to Hothir, he, his sons, and his 1Chr 25:28
*t* to Giddalti, he, his sons, and 1Chr 25:29
*t* to Mahazioth, he, his sons, and 1Chr 25:30
*t* to Romamti-ezer, he, his sons, 1Chr 25:31
*t* day of the seventh month he 2Chr 7:10
on the *t* day of the month Ezr 10:9
the month Chisleu, in the *t* year Neh 1:1
in the *t* year of Artaxerxes the Neh 2:1
from the *t* year even unto the two Neh 5:14
on the three and *t* day thereof Est 8:9
*t* year, the word of the LORD hath Jer 25:3
three and *t* year of Nebuchadrezzar Jer 52:30
five and *t* day of the month, that Jer 52:31
*t* year, in the first month, in Eze 29:17
*t* year of our captivity, in the Eze 40:1
*t* day of the first month, as I Dan 10:4
*t* day of the sixth month, in the Hag 1:15
*t* day of the month, came the word Hag 2:1
*t* day of the ninth month, in the Hag 2:10
*t* day of the ninth month, even Hag 2:18
*t* day of the month, saying, Hag 2:20
*t* day of the eleventh month, Zec 1:7

## TWENTY

shall be an hundred and *t* years Gen 6:3
nine and *t* years, and begat Terah Gen 11:24
there shall be *t* found there Gen 18:31
hundred and seven and *t* years old Gen 23:1
This *t* years have I been with Gen 31:38
Thus have I been *t* years in thy Gen 31:41
*t* he goats, two hundred ewes, and Gen 32:14
two hundred ewes, and *t* rams, Gen 32:14
*t* she asses, and ten foals Gen 32:15
for *t* pieces of silver Gen 37:28
*t* cubits, and the breadth of one Ex 26:2
*t* boards on the south side Ex 26:18
of silver under the *t* boards Ex 26:19
side there shall be *t* boards Ex 26:20
the *t* pillars thereof and their Ex 27:10
their *t* sockets shall be of brass Ex 27:10
his *t* pillars and their *t* Ex 27:11
shall be an hanging of *t* cubits Ex 27:16
(a shekel is *t* gerahs Ex 30:13
from *t* years old and above, shall Ex 30:14
The length of one curtain was *t* Ex 36:9
*t* boards for the south side Ex 36:23
silver he made under the *t* boards Ex 36:24
north corner, he made *t* boards Ex 36:25
Their pillars were *t*, and their Ex 38:10
and their brasen sockets *t* Ex 38:10
cubits, their pillars were *t* Ex 38:11
and their sockets of brass *t* Ex 38:11
*t* cubits was the length, and the Ex 38:18
the gold of the offering, was *t* Ex 38:24
from *t* years old and upward, for Ex 38:26
shall be of the male from *t* years Lev 27:3
years old even unto *t* years old Lev 27:5
shall be of the male *t* shekels Lev 27:5
*t* gerahs shall be the shekel Lev 27:25
From *t* years old and upward, all Num 1:3
from *t* years old and upward, by Num 1:18
every male from *t* years old Num 1:20
every male from *t* years old Num 1:22
from *t* years old and upward, all Num 1:24
from *t* years old and upward, all Num 1:26
from *t* years old and upward, all Num 1:28
from *t* years old and upward, all Num 1:30
from *t* years old and upward, all Num 1:32
from *t* years old and upward, all Num 1:34
from *t* years old and upward, all Num 1:36
from *t* years old and upward, all Num 1:38
from *t* years old and upward, all Num 1:40
from *t* years old and upward, all Num 1:42
from *t* years old and upward, all Num 1:45
a month old and upward, were *t* Num 3:39
were numbered of them, were *t* Num 3:43
(the shekel is *t* gerahs Num 3:47
was an hundred and *t* shekels Num 7:86
of the peace offerings were *t* Num 7:88
from *t* and five years old and Num 8:24
neither ten days, nor *t* days Num 11:19
from *t* years old and upward, which Num 14:29
the sanctuary, which is *t* gerahs Num 18:16
that died in the plague were *t* Num 25:9
from *t* years old and upward, Num 26:2
from *t* years old and upward Num 26:4
the families of the Simeonites, *t* Num 26:14
that were numbered of them were *t* Num 26:62
from *t* years old and upward, shall Num 32:11
And Aaron was an hundred and *t* Num 33:39
hundred and *t* years old this day Deut 31:2
and *t* years old when he died Deut 34:7
all the cities are *t* and nine, Josh 15:32
*t* and two cities with their Josh 19:30
*t* years he mightily oppressed the Judg 4:3
And there returned of the people *t* Judg 7:3
*t* thousand men that drew sword Judg 8:10
And he judged Israel *t* and three Judg 10:2
a Gileadite, and judged Israel *t* Judg 10:3
even *t* cities, and unto the plain Judg 11:33
days of the Philistines *t* years Judg 15:20
And he judged Israel *t* years Judg 16:31
at that time out of the cities *t* Judg 20:15
of the Israelites that day *t* Judg 20:21
of the Benjamites that day *t* Judg 20:35
fell that day of Benjamin were *t* Judg 20:46
for it was *t* years 1Sa 7:2
made, was about *t* men, within as 1Sa 14:14
to Hebron, and *t* men with him 2Sa 3:20
horsemen, and *t* thousand footmen 2Sa 8:4
the Syrians two and *t* thousand men 2Sa 8:5
had fifteen sons and *t* servants 2Sa 9:10
*t* thousand footmen, and of king 2Sa 10:6
that day of *t* thousand men 2Sa 18:7
sons and his *t* servants with him 2Sa 19:17
six toes, four and *t* in number 2Sa 21:20
the end of nine months and *t* days 2Sa 24:8
*t* oxen out of the pastures, and an 1Kin 4:23
Solomon gave Hiram *t* thousand 1Kin 5:11
and *t* measures of pure oil 1Kin 5:11
and the breadth thereof *t* cubits 1Kin 6:2
*t* cubits was the length thereof, 1Kin 6:3
he built *t* cubits on the sides of 1Kin 6:16
forepart was *t* cubits in length 1Kin 6:20
*t* cubits in breadth 1Kin 6:20
*t* cubits in the height thereof 1Kin 6:20
*t* thousand oxen, and an hundred and 1Kin 8:63
and an hundred and *t* thousand sheep 1Kin 8:63
to pass at the end of *t* years 1Kin 9:10
then king Solomon gave Hiram *t* 1Kin 9:11
*t* talents, and brought it to king 1Kin 9:28
*t* talents of gold, and of spices 1Kin 10:10
reigned were two and *t* years 1Kin 14:20
over all Israel in Tirzah, *t* 1Kin 15:33
In the *t* and sixth year of Asa 1Kin 16:8
him, and killed him, in the *t* 1Kin 16:10
In the *t* and seventh year of Asa 1Kin 16:15
reigned over Israel in Samaria *t* 1Kin 16:29
and there a wall fell upon *t* 1Kin 20:30
and he reigned *t* and five years in 1Kin 22:42
*t* loaves of barley, and full ears 2Kin 4:42
*t* years old was Ahaziah when he 2Kin 8:26
over Israel in Samaria was *t* 2Kin 10:36
He was *t* and five years old when 2Kin 14:2
he began to reign, and reigned *t* 2Kin 14:2
In the *t* and seventh year of 2Kin 15:1
in Samaria, and reigned *t* years 2Kin 15:27
*t* years old was he when he began 2Kin 15:33
*T* years old was Ahaz when he 2Kin 16:2
*T* and five years old was he when 2Kin 18:2
and he reigned *t* and nine years in 2Kin 18:2
Amon was *t* and two years old when 2Kin 21:19
Jehoahaz was *t* and three years old 2Kin 23:31
Jehoiakim was *t* and five years old 2Kin 23:36
Zedekiah was *t* and one years old 2Kin 24:18
*t* cities in the land of Gilead 1Chr 2:22
*t* thousand and six hundred 1Chr 7:2
reckoned by their genealogies *t* 1Chr 7:7
was *t* thousand and two hundred 1Chr 7:9
apt to the war and to battle was *t* 1Chr 7:40
and of his father's house *t* 1Chr 12:28
children of Ephraim *t* thousand 1Chr 12:30
And of the Danites expert in war *t* 1Chr 12:35
battle, an hundred and *t* thousand 1Chr 12:37
and his brethren an hundred and *t* 1Chr 15:5
and his brethren two hundred and *t* 1Chr 15:6
horsemen, and *t* thousand footmen 1Chr 18:4
the Syrians two and *t* thousand men 1Chr 18:5
fingers and toes were four and *t* 1Chr 20:6
Of which, *t* and four thousand were 1Chr 23:4
the LORD, from the age of *t* years 1Chr 23:24
were numbered from *t* years old 1Chr 23:27
the year, of every course were *t* 1Chr 27:1
and in his course were *t* and four 1Chr 27:2
in his course likewise were *t* 1Chr 27:4
and in his course were *t* and four 1Chr 27:5
and in his course were *t* and four 1Chr 27:7
and in his course were *t* and four 1Chr 27:8
and in his course were *t* and four 1Chr 27:9
and in his course were *t* and four 1Chr 27:10
and in his course were *t* and four 1Chr 27:11
and in his course were *t* and four 1Chr 27:12
and in his course were *t* and four 1Chr 27:13
and in his course were *t* and four 1Chr 27:14
and in his course were *t* and four 1Chr 27:15
number of them from *t* years old 1Chr 27:23
*t* thousand measures of beaten 2Chr 2:10
*t* thousand measures of barley, and 2Chr 2:10
*t* thousand baths of wine, and 2Chr 2:10
wine, and *t* thousand baths of oil 2Chr 2:10
cubits, and the breadth *t* cubits 2Chr 3:3
*t* cubits, and the height was an 2Chr 3:4
and the height was an hundred and *t* 2Chr 3:4
*t* cubits, and the breadth thereof 2Chr 3:8
and the breadth thereof *t* cubits 2Chr 3:8
the cherubims were *t* cubits long 2Chr 3:11
spread themselves forth *t* cubits 2Chr 3:13
*t* cubits the length thereof, and 2Chr 4:1
*t* cubits the breadth thereof, and 2Chr 4:1
*t* priests sounding with trumpets 2Chr 5:12
Solomon offered a sacrifice of *t* 2Chr 7:5
and an hundred and *t* thousand sheep 2Chr 7:5
to pass at the end of *t* years 2Chr 8:1
*t* talents of gold, and of spices 2Chr 9:9
and begat *t* and eight sons, and 2Chr 11:21
fourteen wives, and begat *t* 2Chr 13:21
began to reign, and he reigned *t* 2Chr 20:31
Amaziah was *t* and five years old 2Chr 25:1
began to reign, and he reigned *t* 2Chr 25:1
he numbered them from *t* years old 2Chr 25:5
Jotham was *t* and five years old 2Chr 27:1
*t* years old when he began to 2Chr 27:8
Ahaz was *t* years old when he 2Chr 28:1
*t* thousand in one day, which were 2Chr 28:6
*t* years old, and he reigned nine 2Chr 29:1
nine and *t* years in Jerusalem 2Chr 29:1
and the Levites from *t* years old 2Chr 31:17
*t* years old when he began to 2Chr 33:21
Jehoahaz was *t* and three years old 2Chr 36:2
Jehoiakim was *t* and five years old 2Chr 36:5
*t* years old when he began to 2Chr 36:11
of silver, nine and *t* knives, Ezr 1:9
children of Bebai, six hundred *t* Ezr 2:11
Azgad, a thousand two hundred *t* Ezr 2:12
of Bezai, three hundred *t* Ezr 2:17
children of Hashum, two hundred *t* Ezr 2:19
of Beth-lehem, an hundred *t* Ezr 2:21
The men of Anathoth, an hundred *t* Ezr 2:23
of Ramah and Gaba, six hundred *t* Ezr 2:26
The men of Michmas, an hundred *t* Ezr 2:27
of Beth-el and Ai, two hundred *t* Ezr 2:28
of Harim, three hundred and *t* Ezr 2:32
Hadid, and Ono, seven hundred *t* Ezr 2:33
children of Asaph, an hundred *t* Ezr 2:41
six thousand seven hundred and *t* Ezr 2:67
from *t* years old and upward, to Ezr 3:8
the son of Bebai, and with him *t* Ezr 8:11
his brethren and their sons, *t* Ezr 8:19
two hundred and *t* Nethinims Ezr 8:20
Also *t* basons of gold, of a Ezr 8:27
So the wall was finished in the *t* Neh 6:15
children of Bebai, six hundred *t* Neh 7:16
two thousand three hundred *t* Neh 7:17
of Hashum, three hundred *t* Neh 7:22
of Bezai, three hundred *t* Neh 7:23
The men of Anathoth, an hundred *t* Neh 7:27
of Ramah and Gaba, six hundred *t* Neh 7:30
men of Michmas, an hundred and *t* Neh 7:31
of Beth-el and Ai, an hundred *t* Neh 7:32
of Harim, three hundred and *t* Neh 7:35
Hadid, and Ono, seven hundred *t* Neh 7:37
thousand seven hundred and *t* asses Neh 7:69
the work *t* thousand drams of gold Neh 7:71
gave was *t* thousand drams of gold Neh 7:72
Now in the *t* and fourth day of Neh 9:1
Gabbai, Sallai, nine hundred *t* Neh 11:8
of the house were eight hundred *t* Neh 11:12
men of valour, an hundred *t* Neh 11:14
hundred and seven and *t* provinces Est 1:1
India unto Ethiopia, an hundred *t* Est 8:9
all the Jews, to the hundred *t* Est 9:30

chariots of God are *t* thousand — Ps 68:17
*t* years old when he began to — Jer 52:1
three thousand Jews and three and *t* — Jer 52:28
be by weight, *t* shekels a day — Eze 4:10
*t* men, with their backs toward — Eze 8:16
door of the gate five and *t* men — Eze 11:1
*t* cubits, door against door — Eze 40:13
and the breadth five and *t* cubits — Eze 40:21
and the breadth five and *t* cubits — Eze 40:25
long, and five and *t* cubits broad — Eze 40:29
*t* cubits long, and five cubits — Eze 40:30
long, and five and *t* cubits broad — Eze 40:33
and the breadth five and *t* cubits — Eze 40:36
length of the porch was *t* cubits — Eze 40:49
and the breadth, *t* cubits — Eze 41:2
the length thereof, *t* cubits — Eze 41:4
*t* cubits, before the temple — Eze 41:4
chambers was the wideness of *t* — Eze 41:10
Over against the *t* cubits which — Eze 42:3
*t* thousand reeds, and the breadth — Eze 45:1
*t* thousand, and the breadth of ten — Eze 45:3
*t* thousand of length, and the ten — Eze 45:5
for a possession for *t* chambers — Eze 45:5
*t* thousand long, over against the — Eze 45:6
And the shekel shall be *t* gerahs — Eze 45:12
*t* shekels, five and *t* shekels — Eze 45:12
*t* thousand reeds in breadth, and — Eze 48:8
*t* thousand in length, and of ten — Eze 48:9
*t* thousand in length, and toward — Eze 48:10
five and *t* thousand in length — Eze 48:10
*t* thousand in length, and ten — Eze 48:13
*t* thousand, and the breadth ten — Eze 48:13
*t* thousand, shall be a profane — Eze 48:15
*t* thousand by five and — Eze 48:20
thousand by five and *t* thousand — Eze 48:20
*t* thousand of the oblation toward — Eze 48:21
*t* thousand toward the west border — Eze 48:21
*t* princes, which should be over — Dan 6:1
Persia withstood me one and *t* days — Dan 10:13
one came to an heap of *t* measures — Hag 2:16
of the press, there were but *t* — Hag 2:16
the length thereof is *t* cubits — Zec 5:2
against him with *t* thousand — Lk 14:31
*t* or thirty furlongs, they see — Jn 6:19
were about an hundred and *t* — Acts 1:15
And sounded, and found it *t* fathoms — Acts 27:28
in one day three and *t* thousand — 1Cor 10:8
the throne were four and *t* seats — Rev 4:4
*t* elders sitting, clothed in — Rev 4:4
*t* elders fall down before him — Rev 4:10
*t* elders fell down before the — Rev 5:8
*t* elders fell down and worshipped — Rev 5:14
*t* elders, which sat before God on — Rev 11:16
*t* elders and the four beasts fell — Rev 19:4

**TWENTY'S**
I will not destroy it for *t* sake — Gen 18:31

**TWICE**
dream was doubled unto Pharaoh *t* — Gen 41:32
it shall be *t* as much as they — Ex 16:5
day they gathered *t* as much bread — Ex 16:22
with his rod he smote the rock *t* — Num 20:11
avoided out of his presence *t* — 1Sa 18:11
which had appeared unto him *t* — 1Kin 11:9
himself there, not once nor *t* — 2Kin 6:10
without Jerusalem once or *t* — Neh 13:20
For God speaketh once, yea *t* — Job 33:14
will not answer: yea, *t* — Job 40:5
also the LORD gave Job *t* as much — Job 42:10
*t* have I heard this — Ps 62:11
he live a thousand years *t* told — Eccl 6:6
night, before the cock crow *t* — Mk 14:30
unto him, Before the cock crow *t* — Mk 14:72
I fast *t* in the week, I give — Lk 18:12
*t* dead, plucked up by the roots — Jude 12

**TWIGS**
off the top of his young *t* — Eze 17:4
top of his young *t* a tender one — Eze 17:22

**TWILIGHT**
David smote them from the *t* even — 1Sa 30:17
And they rose up in the *t*, to go — 2Kin 7:5
they arose and fled in the *t* — 2Kin 7:7
stars of the *t* thereof be dark — Job 3:9
the adulterer waiteth for the *t* — Job 24:15
In the *t*, in the evening, in the — Prov 7:9
and carry it forth in the *t* — Eze 12:6
I brought it forth in the *t* — Eze 12:7
bear upon his shoulder in the *t* — Eze 12:12

**TWINED**
with ten curtains of fine *t* linen — Ex 26:1
fine *t* linen of cunning work — Ex 26:31
fine *t* linen, wrought with — Ex 26:36
hangings for the court of fine *t* — Ex 27:9
fine *t* linen, wrought with — Ex 27:16
five cubits of fine *t* linen — Ex 27:18
fine *t* linen, with cunning work — Ex 28:6
and scarlet, and fine *t* linen — Ex 28:8
and of scarlet, and of fine *t* linen — Ex 28:15
made ten curtains of fine *t* linen — Ex 36:8
and scarlet, and fine *t* linen — Ex 36:35
fine *t* linen, of needlework — Ex 36:37
of the court were of fine *t* linen — Ex 38:9
round about were of fine *t* linen — Ex 38:16
and scarlet, and fine *t* linen — Ex 38:18
and scarlet, and fine *t* linen — Ex 39:2
and scarlet, and fine *t* linen — Ex 39:5
and scarlet, and fine *t* linen — Ex 39:8
and purple, and scarlet, and *t* linen — Ex 39:24
and linen breeches of fine *t* linen — Ex 39:28
And a girdle of fine *t* linen — Ex 39:29

**TWINKLING**
in the *t* of an eye, at the last — 1Cor 15:52

**TWINS**
behold, there were *t* in her womb — Gen 25:24
that, behold, *t* were in her womb — Gen 38:27
whereof every one bear *t*, and none — Song 4:2
like two young roes that are *t* — Song 4:5
whereof every one beareth *t* — Song 6:6
like two young roes that are *t* — Song 7:3

**TWO** See PREFACE.

**TWOEDGED**
mouth, and a *t* sword in their hand — Ps 149:6
as wormwood, sharp as a *t* sword — Prov 5:4
and sharper than any *t* sword — Heb 4:12
of his mouth went a sharp *t* sword — Rev 1:16

**TWOFOLD**
ye make him *t* more the child of — Mt 23:15

**TYCHICUS** (*tik'-ik-us*) *A co-worker with Paul.*
and of Asia, *T* and Trophimus — Acts 20:4
know my affairs, and how I do, *T* — Eph 6:21
from Rome unto the Ephesians by *T* — Eph s
my state shall *T* declare unto you — Col 4:7
from Rome to the Colossians by *T* — Col s
And *T* have I sent to Ephesus — 2Ti 4:12
send Artemas unto thee, or *T* — Titus 3:12

**TYRANNUS** (*ti-ran'-nus*) *An Ephesian schoolmaster.*
daily in the school of one *T* — Acts 19:9

**TYRE** (*tire*) See TYRUS. *A coastal city of Phoenicia.*
to Ramah, and to the strong city *T* — Josh 19:29
Hiram king of *T* sent messengers — 2Sa 5:11
And came to the strong hold of *T* — 2Sa 24:7
Hiram king of *T* sent his servants — 1Kin 5:1
sent and fetched Hiram out of *T* — 1Kin 7:13
and his father was a man of *T* — 1Kin 7:14
(Now Hiram the king of *T* had — 1Kin 9:11
Hiram came out from *T* to see the — 1Kin 9:12
Now Hiram king of *T* sent — 1Chr 14:1
they of *T* brought much cedar wood — 1Chr 22:4
sent to Huram the king of *T* — 2Chr 2:3
the king of *T* answered in writing — 2Chr 2:11
Dan, and his father was a man of *T* — 2Chr 2:14
them of Zidon, and to them of *T* — Ezr 3:7
There dwelt men of *T* also therein — Neh 13:16
the daughter of *T* shall be there — Ps 45:12
with the inhabitants of *T* — Ps 83:7
behold Philistia, and *T*, with — Ps 87:4
The burden of *T* — Is 23:1
sorely pained at the report of *T* — Is 23:5
hath taken this counsel against *T* — Is 23:8
that *T* shall be forgotten seventy — Is 23:15
years shall *T* sing as an harlot — Is 23:15
years, that the LORD will visit *T* — Is 23:17
what have ye to do with me, O *T* — Joel 3:4
done in you, had been done in *T* — Mt 11:21
It shall be more tolerable for *T* — Mt 11:22
and departed into the coasts of *T* — Mt 15:21
and they about *T* and Sidon, a great — Mk 3:8
and went into the borders of *T* — Mk 7:24
departing from the coasts of *T* — Mk 7:31
and from the sea coast of *T* — Lk 6:17
mighty works had been done in *T* — Lk 10:13
it shall be more tolerable for *T* — Lk 10:14
highly displeased with them of *T* — Acts 12:20
sailed into Syria, and landed at *T* — Acts 21:3
we had finished our course from *T* — Acts 21:7

**TYRIAN** See TYRE.

**TYRUS** (*ti'-rus*) See TYRE. *Same as Tyre.*
And all the kings of *T*, and all the — Jer 25:22
Ammonites, and to the king of *T* — Jer 27:3
Philistines, and to cut off from *T* — Jer 47:4
because that *T* hath said against — Eze 26:2
Behold, I am against thee, O *T* — Eze 26:3
they shall destroy the walls of *T* — Eze 26:4
Behold, I will bring upon *T* — Eze 26:7
Thus saith the Lord GOD to *T* — Eze 26:15
man, take up a lamentation for *T* — Eze 27:2
And say unto *T*, O thou that art — Eze 27:3
O *T*, thou hast said, I am of — Eze 27:3
thy wise men, O *T*, that were in — Eze 27:8
thee, saying, What city is like *T* — Eze 27:32
of man, say unto the prince of *T* — Eze 28:2
a lamentation upon the king of *T* — Eze 28:12
serve a great service against *T* — Eze 29:18
he no wages, nor his army, for *T* — Eze 29:18
Ephraim, as I saw *T*, is planted — Hos 9:13
For three transgressions of *T* — Amos 1:9
will send a fire on the wall of *T* — Amos 1:10
*T*, and Zidon, though it be very — Zec 9:2
*T* did build herself a strong hold — Zec 9:3

# U

**UCAL** (*u'-cal*) *An obscure name.*
Ithiel, even unto Ithiel and *U* — Prov 30:1

**UEL** (*u'-el*) *Married a foreigner in exile.*
Maadai, Amram, and *U*, — Ezr 10:34

**ULAI** (*u'-lahee*) *A river near Susa.*
and I was by the river of *U* — Dan 8:2
voice between the banks of *U* — Dan 8:16

**ULAM** (*u'-lam*)
*1. A son of Sheresh.*
and his sons were *U* and Rakem — 1Chr 7:16
And the sons of *U* — 1Chr 7:17
*2. A son of Eshek.*
*U* his firstborn, Jehush the — 1Chr 8:39
the sons of *U* were mighty men of — 1Chr 8:40

**ULLA**
And the sons of *U* — 1Chr 7:39

**UMMAH** (*um'-mah*) *A city in Asher.*
*U* also, and Aphek, and Rehob — Josh 19:30

**UNACCUSTOMED**
as a bullock *u* to the yoke — Jer 31:18

**UNADVISEDLY**
so that he spake *u* with his lips — Ps 106:33

**UNAWARES**
Jacob stole away *u* to Laban the — Gen 31:20
thou hast stolen away *u* to me — Gen 31:26
which killeth any person at *u* — Num 35:11
any person *u* may flee thither — Num 35:15
which should kill his neighbour *u* — Deut 4:42
slayer that killeth any person *u* — Josh 20:3
person at *u* might flee thither — Josh 20:9
destruction come upon him at *u* — Ps 35:8
and so that day come upon you *u* — Lk 21:34
of false brethren *u* brought in — Gal 2:4
some have entertained angels *u* — Heb 13:2
there are certain men crept in *u* — Jude 4

**UNBELIEF**
works there because of their *u* — Mt 13:58
said unto them, Because of your *u* — Mt 17:20
he marvelled because of their *u* — Mk 6:6
help thou mine *u* — Mk 9:24
and upbraided them with their *u* — Mk 16:14
shall their *u* make the faith of — Rom 3:3
at the promise of God through *u* — Rom 4:20
because of *u* they were broken off — Rom 11:20
if they abide not still in *u* — Rom 11:23
obtained mercy through their *u* — Rom 11:30
God hath concluded them all in *u* — Rom 11:32
because I did it ignorantly in *u* — 1Ti 1:13
in any of you an evil heart of *u* — Heb 3:12
could not enter in because of *u* — Heb 3:19
entered not in because of *u* — Heb 4:6
fall after the same example of *u* — Heb 4:11

**UNBELIEVERS**
him his portion with the *u* — Lk 12:46
brother, and that before the *u* — 1Cor 6:6
in those that are unlearned, or *u* — 1Cor 14:23
unequally yoked together with *u* — 2Cor 6:14

**UNBELIEVING**
But the *u* Jews stirred up the — Acts 14:2
For the *u* husband is sanctified — 1Cor 7:14
the *u* wife is sanctified by the — 1Cor 7:14
But if the *u* depart, let him — 1Cor 7:15
are defiled and *u* is nothing pure — Titus 1:15
But the fearful, and *u*, and the — Rev 21:8

**UNBLAMEABLE**
death, to present you holy and *u* — Col 1:22
hearts *u* in holiness before God — 1Th 3:13

**UNBLAMEABLY**
*u* we behaved ourselves among you — 1Th 2:10

**UNCERTAIN**
if the trumpet give an *u* sound — 1Cor 14:8
highminded, nor trust in *u* riches — 1Ti 6:17

**UNCERTAINLY**
I therefore so run, not as *u* — 1Cor 9:26

**UNCHANGEABLE**
ever, hath an *u* priesthood — Heb 7:24

**UNCIRCUMCISED**
the *u* man child whose flesh of — Gen 17:14
give our sister to one that is *u* — Gen 34:14
Pharaoh hear me, who am of *u* lips — Ex 6:12
the LORD, Behold, I am of *u* lips — Ex 6:30
for no *u* person shall eat thereof — Ex 12:48
count the fruit thereof as *u* — Lev 19:23
years shall it be as *u* unto you — Lev 19:23
if then their *u* hearts be humbled — Lev 26:41
for they were *u*, because they had — Josh 5:7
take a wife of the *u* Philistines — Judg 14:3
and fall into the hand of the *u* — Judg 15:18
over unto the garrison of these *u* — 1Sa 14:6
for who is this *u* Philistine — 1Sa 17:26
this *u* Philistine shall be as one — 1Sa 17:36
lest these *u* come and thrust me — 1Sa 31:4
the daughters of the *u* triumph — 2Sa 1:20
lest these *u* come and abuse me — 1Chr 10:4
no more come into thee the *u* — Is 52:1
behold, their ear is *u*, and they — Jer 6:10
which are circumcised with the *u* — Jer 9:25
for all these nations are *u* — Jer 9:26
of Israel are *u* in the heart — Jer 9:26
of the *u* by the hand of strangers — Eze 28:10
shalt lie in the midst of the *u* — Eze 31:18
down, and be thou laid with the *u* — Eze 32:19
they are gone down, they lie *u* — Eze 32:21
which are gone down *u* into the — Eze 32:24
all of them *u*, slain by the sword — Eze 32:25
all of them *u*, slain by the sword — Eze 32:26
mighty that are fallen of the *u* — Eze 32:27
be broken in the midst of the *u* — Eze 32:28
they shall lie with the *u* — Eze 32:29
they lie *u* with them that be — Eze 32:30
be laid in the midst of the *u* — Eze 32:32

*u* in heart, and *u* in flesh ........ Eze 44:7
*u* in heart, nor *u* in flesh ........ Eze 44:9
*u* in heart and ears, ye do always ........ Acts 7:51
Saying, Thou wentest in to men *u* ........ Acts 11:3
faith which he had yet being *u* ........ Rom 4:11
Abraham, which he had being yet *u* ........ Rom 4:12
let him not become *u* ........ 1Cor 7:18

## UNCIRCUMCISION

law, thy circumcision is made *u* ........ Rom 2:25
Therefore if the *u* keep the ........ Rom 2:26
shall not his *u* be counted for ........ Rom 2:26
shall not *u* which is by nature, ........ Rom 2:27
by faith, and *u* through faith ........ Rom 3:30
only, or upon the *u* also ........ Rom 4:9
he was in circumcision, or in *u* ........ Rom 4:10
Not in circumcision, but in *u* ........ Rom 4:10
Is any called in *u* ........ 1Cor 7:18
*u* is nothing, but the keeping of ........ 1Cor 7:19
of the *u* was committed unto me ........ Gal 2:7
availeth any thing, nor *u* ........ Gal 5:6
availeth any thing, nor *u* ........ Gal 6:15
who are called *U* by that which is ........ Eph 2:11
the *u* of your flesh, hath he ........ Col 2:13
Greek nor Jew, circumcision nor *u* ........ Col 3:11

## UNCLE

the sons of Uzziel the *u* of Aaron ........ Lev 10:4
Either his *u*, or his uncle's son, ........ Lev 25:49
Saul's *u* said unto him and to his ........ 1Sa 10:14
And Saul's *u* said, Tell me, I pray ........ 1Sa 10:15
And Saul said unto his *u*, He told ........ 1Sa 10:16
Abner, the son of Ner, Saul's *u* ........ 1Sa 14:50
David's *u* was a counsellor ........ 1Chr 27:32
of Abihail the *u* of Mordecai ........ Est 2:15
thine *u* shall come unto thee ........ Jer 32:7
a man's *u* shall take him up, and ........ Amos 6:10

## UNCLEAN

Or if a soul touch any *u* thing ........ Lev 5:2
it be a carcase of an *u* beast ........ Lev 5:2
or a carcase of *u* cattle ........ Lev 5:2
the carcase of *u* creeping things ........ Lev 5:2
he also shall be *u*, and guilty ........ Lev 5:2
any *u* thing shall not be eaten ........ Lev 7:19
soul that shall touch any *u* thing ........ Lev 7:21
of man, or any *u* beast, or any ........ Lev 7:21
or any abominable *u* thing ........ Lev 7:21
holy and unholy, and between *u* ........ Lev 10:10
he is *u* unto you ........ Lev 11:4
he is *u* unto you ........ Lev 11:5
he is *u* unto you ........ Lev 11:6
he is *u* to you ........ Lev 11:7
they are *u* to you ........ Lev 11:8
And for these ye shall be *u* ........ Lev 11:24
of them shall be *u* until the even ........ Lev 11:24
clothes, and be *u* until the even ........ Lev 11:25
cheweth the cud, are *u* unto you ........ Lev 11:26
one that toucheth them shall be *u* ........ Lev 11:26
on all four, those are *u* unto you ........ Lev 11:27
carcase shall be *u* until the even ........ Lev 11:27
clothes, and be *u* until the even ........ Lev 11:28
they are *u* unto you ........ Lev 11:28
These also shall be *u* unto you ........ Lev 11:29
These are *u* to you among all that ........ Lev 11:31
shall be *u* until the even ........ Lev 11:31
dead, doth fall, it shall be *u* ........ Lev 11:32
it shall be *u* until the even ........ Lev 11:32
whatsoever is in it shall be *u* ........ Lev 11:33
such water cometh shall be *u* ........ Lev 11:34
in every such vessel shall be *u* ........ Lev 11:34
their carcase falleth shall be *u* ........ Lev 11:35
for they are *u*, and shall be ........ Lev 11:35
and shall be *u* unto you ........ Lev 11:35
toucheth their carcase shall be *u* ........ Lev 11:36
thereon, it shall be *u* unto you ........ Lev 11:38
thereof shall be *u* until the even ........ Lev 11:39
clothes, and be *u* until the even ........ Lev 11:40
clothes, and be *u* until the even ........ Lev 11:40
ye make yourselves *u* with them ........ Lev 11:43
make a difference between the *u* ........ Lev 11:47
then she shall be *u* seven days ........ Lev 12:2
for her infirmity shall she be *u* ........ Lev 12:2
then she shall be *u* two weeks ........ Lev 12:5
look on him, and pronounce him *u* ........ Lev 13:3
the priest shall pronounce him *u* ........ Lev 13:8
the priest shall pronounce him *u* ........ Lev 13:11
for he is *u* ........ Lev 13:11
appeareth in him, he shall be *u* ........ Lev 13:14
flesh, and pronounce him to be *u* ........ Lev 13:15
for the raw flesh is *u* ........ Lev 13:15
the priest shall pronounce him *u* ........ Lev 13:20
the priest shall pronounce him *u* ........ Lev 13:22
the priest shall pronounce him *u* ........ Lev 13:25
the priest shall pronounce him *u* ........ Lev 13:27
the priest shall pronounce him *u* ........ Lev 13:30
he is *u* ........ Lev 13:36
He is a leprous man, he is *u* ........ Lev 13:44
shall pronounce him utterly *u* ........ Lev 13:44
lip, and shall cry, *U*, *u* ........ Lev 13:45
he is *u* ........ Lev 13:46
it is *u* ........ Lev 13:51
it is *u* ........ Lev 13:55
it clean, or to pronounce it *u* ........ Lev 13:59
is in the house be not made *u* ........ Lev 14:36
into an *u* place without the city ........ Lev 14:40
without the city into an *u* place ........ Lev 14:41
it is *u* ........ Lev 14:44
out of the city into an *u* place ........ Lev 14:45
shut up shall be *u* until the even ........ Lev 14:46
To teach when it is *u*, and when it ........ Lev 14:57
because of his issue he is *u* ........ Lev 15:2
lieth that hath the issue, is *u* ........ Lev 15:4
whereon he sitteth, shall be *u* ........ Lev 15:4
in water, and be *u* until the even ........ Lev 15:5
in water, and be *u* until the even ........ Lev 15:6
in water, and be *u* until the even ........ Lev 15:7
in water, and be *u* until the even ........ Lev 15:8
that hath the issue shall be *u* ........ Lev 15:9
him shall be *u* until the even ........ Lev 15:10
in water, and be *u* until the even ........ Lev 15:10
in water, and be *u* until the even ........ Lev 15:11
in water, and be *u* until the even ........ Lev 15:16
water, and be *u* until the even ........ Lev 15:17
in water, and be *u* until the even ........ Lev 15:18
her shall be *u* until the even ........ Lev 15:19
upon in her separation shall be *u* ........ Lev 15:20
that she sitteth upon shall be *u* ........ Lev 15:20
in water, and be *u* until the even ........ Lev 15:21
in water, and be *u* until the even ........ Lev 15:22
he shall be *u* until the even ........ Lev 15:23
him, he shall be *u* seven days ........ Lev 15:24
bed whereon he lieth shall be *u* ........ Lev 15:24
she shall be *u* ........ Lev 15:25
she sitteth upon shall be *u* ........ Lev 15:26
toucheth those things shall be *u* ........ Lev 15:27
in water, and be *u* until the even ........ Lev 15:27
him that lieth with her that is *u* ........ Lev 15:33
in water, and be *u* until the even ........ Lev 17:15
brother's wife, it is an *u* thing ........ Lev 20:21
between clean beasts and *u* ........ Lev 20:25
and between *u* fowls ........ Lev 20:25
I have separated from you as *u* ........ Lev 20:25
any thing that is *u* by the dead ........ Lev 22:4
thing, whereby he may be made *u* ........ Lev 22:5
any such shall be *u* until even ........ Lev 22:6
And if it be any *u* beast, of which ........ Lev 27:11
And if it be of an *u* beast ........ Lev 27:27
not make himself *u* for his father ........ Num 6:7
be *u* by reason of a dead body ........ Num 9:10
the firstling of *u* beasts shalt ........ Num 18:15
priest shall be *u* until the even ........ Num 19:7
shall be *u* until the even ........ Num 19:8
clothes, and be *u* until the even ........ Num 19:10
of any man shall be *u* seven days ........ Num 19:11
sprinkled upon him, he shall be *u* ........ Num 19:13
the tent, shall be *u* seven days ........ Num 19:14
no covering bound upon it, is *u* ........ Num 19:15
or a grave, shall be *u* seven days ........ Num 19:16
for an *u* person they shall take ........ Num 19:17
upon the *u* on the third day ........ Num 19:19
But the man that shall be *u* ........ Num 19:20
he is *u* ........ Num 19:20
separation shall be *u* until even ........ Num 19:21
whatsoever the *u* person toucheth ........ Num 19:22
person toucheth shall be *u* ........ Num 19:22
toucheth it shall be *u* until even ........ Num 19:22
the *u* and the clean may eat ........ Deut 12:15
the *u* and the clean shall eat of ........ Deut 12:22
therefore they are *u* unto you ........ Deut 14:7
not the cud, it is *u* unto you ........ Deut 14:8
it is *u* unto you ........ Deut 14:10
thing that flieth is *u* unto you ........ Deut 14:19
the *u* and the clean person shall ........ Deut 15:22
that he see no *u* thing in thee ........ Deut 23:14
away ought thereof for any *u* use ........ Deut 26:14
the land of your possession be *u* ........ Josh 22:19
drink, and eat not any *u* thing ........ Judg 13:4
drink, neither eat any *u* thing ........ Judg 13:7
strong drink, nor eat any *u* thing ........ Judg 13:14
that none which was *u* in any ........ 2Chr 23:19
is an *u* land with the filthiness ........ Ezr 9:11
bring a clean thing out of an *u* ........ Job 14:4
and their life is among the *u* ........ Job 36:14
good and to the clean, and to the *u* ........ Eccl 9:2
because I am a man of *u* lips ........ Is 6:5
the midst of a people of *u* lips ........ Is 6:5
the *u* shall not pass over it ........ Is 35:8
thee the uncircumcised and the *u* ........ Is 52:1
out from thence, touch no *u* thing ........ Is 52:11
But we are all as an *u* thing ........ Is 64:6
it is *u* ........ Lam 4:15
shewed difference between the *u* ........ Eze 22:26
them to discern between the *u* ........ Eze 44:23
they shall eat *u* things in ........ Hos 9:3
If one that is *u* by a dead body ........ Hag 2:13
touch any of these, shall it be *u* ........ Hag 2:13
answered and said, It shall be *u* ........ Hag 2:13
that which they offer there is *u* ........ Hag 2:14
the *u* spirit to pass out of the ........ Zec 13:2
gave them power against *u* spirits ........ Mt 10:1
When the *u* spirit is gone out of ........ Mt 12:43
synagogue a man with an *u* spirit ........ Mk 1:23
when the *u* spirit had torn him, ........ Mk 1:26
commandeth he even the *u* spirits ........ Mk 1:27
*u* spirits, when they saw him, ........ Mk 3:11
they said, He hath an *u* spirit ........ Mk 3:30
the tombs a man with an *u* spirit ........ Mk 5:2
out of the man, thou *u* spirit ........ Mk 5:8
the *u* spirits went out, and ........ Mk 5:13
and gave them power over *u* spirits ........ Mk 6:7
young daughter had an *u* spirit ........ Mk 7:25
which had a spirit of an *u* devil ........ Lk 4:33
power he commandeth the *u* spirits ........ Lk 4:36
that were vexed with *u* spirits ........ Lk 6:18
(For he had commanded the *u* ........ Lk 8:29
And Jesus rebuked the *u* spirit ........ Lk 9:42
When the *u* spirit is gone out of ........ Lk 11:24
which were vexed with *u* spirits ........ Acts 5:16
For *u* spirits, crying with loud ........ Acts 8:7
any thing that is common or *u* ........ Acts 10:14
not call any man common or *u* ........ Acts 10:28
for nothing common or *u* hath at ........ Acts 11:8
that there is nothing *u* of itself ........ Rom 14:14
that esteemeth any thing to be *u* ........ Rom 14:14
to him it is *u* ........ Rom 14:14
else were your children *u* ........ 1Cor 7:14
Lord, and touch not the *u* thing ........ 2Cor 6:17
nor *u* person, nor covetous man, ........ Eph 5:5
of an heifer sprinkling the *u* ........ Heb 9:13
I saw three *u* spirits like frogs ........ Rev 16:13
foul spirit, and a cage of every *u* ........ Rev 18:2

## UNCLEANNESS

Or if he touch the *u* of man ........ Lev 5:3
whatsoever *u* it be that a man ........ Lev 5:3
the LORD, having his *u* upon him ........ Lev 7:20
unclean thing, as the *u* of man ........ Lev 7:21
that is to be cleansed from his *u* ........ Lev 14:19
this shall be his *u* in his issue ........ Lev 15:3
from his issue, it is his *u* ........ Lev 15:3
her *u* shall be as the days of her ........ Lev 15:25
as the *u* of her separation ........ Lev 15:26
the LORD for the issue of her *u* ........ Lev 15:30
children of Israel from their *u* ........ Lev 15:31
that they die not in their *u* ........ Lev 15:31
because of the *u* of the children ........ Lev 16:16
them in the midst of their *u* ........ Lev 16:16
hallow it from the *u* of the ........ Lev 16:19
as she is put apart for her *u* ........ Lev 18:19
the LORD, having his *u* upon him ........ Lev 22:3
or a man of whom he may take *u* ........ Lev 22:5
whatsoever *u* he hath ........ Lev 22:5
to *u* with another instead of thy ........ Num 5:19
his *u* is yet upon him ........ Num 19:13
of *u* that chanceth him by night ........ Deut 23:10
he hath found some *u* in her ........ Deut 24:1
for she was purified from her *u* ........ 2Sa 11:4
brought out all the *u* that they ........ 2Chr 29:16
one end to another with their *u* ........ Ezr 9:11
me as the *u* of a removed woman ........ Eze 36:17
According to their *u* and according ........ Eze 39:24
of Jerusalem for sin and for *u* ........ Zec 13:1
of dead men's bones, and of all *u* ........ Mt 23:27
God also gave them up to *u* ........ Rom 1:24
your members servants to *u* ........ Rom 6:19
and have not repented of the *u* ........ 2Cor 12:21
Adultery, fornication, *u*, ........ Gal 5:19
to work all *u* with greediness ........ Eph 4:19
But fornication, and all *u* ........ Eph 5:3
fornication, *u*, inordinate ........ Col 3:5
was not of deceit, nor of *u* ........ 1Th 2:3
For God hath not called us unto *u* ........ 1Th 4:7
after the flesh in the lust of *u* ........ 2Pet 2:10

## UNCLEANNESSES

also save you from all your *u* ........ Eze 36:29

## UNCLE'S

a man shall lie with his *u* wife ........ Lev 20:20
he hath uncovered his *u* nakedness ........ Lev 20:20
Either his uncle, or his *u* son ........ Lev 25:49
that is, Esther, his *u* daughter ........ Est 2:7
So Hanameel mine *u* son came to me ........ Jer 32:8
the field of Hanameel my *u* son ........ Jer 32:9
the sight of Hanameel mine *u* son ........ Jer 32:12

## UNCLOTHED

not for that we would be *u* ........ 2Cor 5:4

## UNCOMELY

himself *u* toward his virgin ........ 1Cor 7:36
our *u* parts have more abundant ........ 1Cor 12:23

## UNCONDEMNED

They have beaten us openly *u* ........ Acts 16:37
a man that is a Roman, and *u* ........ Acts 22:25

## UNCORRUPTIBLE

changed the glory of the *u* God ........ Rom 1:23

## UNCORRUPTNESS

in doctrine shewing *u*, gravity, ........ Titus 2:7

## UNCOVER

*U* not your heads, neither rend ........ Lev 10:6
kin to him, to *u* their nakedness ........ Lev 18:6
of thy mother, shalt thou not *u* ........ Lev 18:7
thou shalt not *u* her nakedness ........ Lev 18:7
father's wife shalt thou not *u* ........ Lev 18:8
their nakedness thou shalt not *u* ........ Lev 18:9
their nakedness thou shalt not *u* ........ Lev 18:10
thou shalt not *u* her nakedness ........ Lev 18:11
Thou shalt not *u* the nakedness of ........ Lev 18:12
Thou shalt not *u* the nakedness of ........ Lev 18:13
Thou shalt not *u* the nakedness of ........ Lev 18:14
Thou shalt not *u* the nakedness of ........ Lev 18:15
thou shalt not *u* her nakedness ........ Lev 18:15
Thou shalt not *u* the nakedness of ........ Lev 18:16
Thou shalt not *u* the nakedness of ........ Lev 18:17
daughter, to *u* her nakedness ........ Lev 18:17
to *u* her nakedness, beside the ........ Lev 18:18
unto a woman to *u* her nakedness ........ Lev 18:19
and shall *u* her nakedness ........ Lev 20:18
thou shalt not *u* the nakedness of ........ Lev 20:19
garments, shall not *u* his head ........ Lev 21:10
*u* the woman's head, and put the ........ Num 5:18
*u* his feet, and lay thee down ........ Ruth 3:4
*u* thy locks, make bare the leg, ........ Is 47:2
*u* the thigh, pass over the rivers ........ Is 47:2
for he shall *u* the cedar work ........ Zeph 2:14

## UNCOVERED

and he was *u* within his tent ........ Gen 9:21
hath *u* his father's nakedness ........ Lev 20:11
he hath *u* his sister's nakedness ........ Lev 20:17
she hath *u* the fountain of her ........ Lev 20:18

he hath *u* his uncle's nakedness Lev 20:20
he hath *u* his brother's nakedness Lev 20:21
*u* his feet, and laid her down Ruth 3:7
of Israel today, who *u* himself 2Sa 6:20
even with their buttocks *u* Is 20:4
and horsemen, and Kir *u* the shield Is 22:6
Thy nakedness shall be *u*, yea, Is 47:3
I have *u* his secret places, and he Jer 49:10
and thine arm shall be *u*, and thou Eze 4:7
also, and let thy foreskin be *u* Hab 2:16
they *u* the roof where he was Mk 2:4
her head *u* dishonoureth her head 1Cor 11:5
that a woman pray unto God *u* 1Cor 11:13

**UNCOVERETH**

for he *u* his near kin Lev 20:19
because he *u* his father's skirt Deut 27:20
fellows shamelessly *u* himself 2Sa 6:20

**UNCTION**

But ye have an *u* from the Holy 1Jn 2:20

**UNDEFILED**

Blessed are the *u* in the way Ps 119:1
my sister, my love, my dove, my *u* Song 5:2
My dove, my *u* is but one Song 6:9
us, who is holy, harmless, *u* Heb 7:26
honourable in all, and the bed *u* Heb 13:4
*u* before God and the Father is Jas 1:27
inheritance incorruptible, and *u* 1Pet 1:4

**UNDER**

*u* the firmament from the waters Gen 1:7
Let the waters *u* the heaven be Gen 1:9
the breath of life, from *u* heaven Gen 6:17
that were *u* the whole heaven, Gen 7:19
and submit thyself *u* her hands Gen 16:9
and rest yourselves *u* the tree Gen 18:4
and he stood by them *u* the tree Gen 18:8
came they *u* the shadow of my roof Gen 19:8
the child *u* one of the shrubs Gen 21:15
I pray thee, thy hand *u* my thigh Gen 24:2
the servant put his hand *u* the Gen 24:9
Jacob hid them *u* the oak which Gen 35:4
buried beneath Beth-el *u* an oak Gen 35:8
to any thing that was *u* his hand Gen 39:23
lay up corn *u* the hand of Pharaoh Gen 41:35
I pray thee, thy hand *u* my thigh Gen 47:29
of the deep that lieth *u*, Gen 49:25
I will bring you out from *u* the Ex 6:6
which bringeth you out from *u* the Ex 6:7
took a stone, and put it *u* him Ex 17:12
of Amalek from *u* heaven Ex 17:14
from *u* the hand of the Egyptians Ex 18:10
that is in the water *u* the earth Ex 20:4
with a rod, and he die *u* his hand Ex 21:20
hateth thee lying *u* his burden Ex 23:5
and builded an altar *u* the hill Ex 24:4
there was *u* his feet as it were a Ex 24:10
there shall be a knop *u* two Ex 25:35
a knop *u* two branches of the same Ex 25:35
a knop *u* two branches of the same Ex 25:35
of silver *u* the twenty boards Ex 26:19
two sockets *u* one board for his Ex 26:19
two sockets *u* another board for Ex 26:19
two sockets *u* one board Ex 26:21
two sockets *u* another board Ex 26:21
two sockets *u* one board Ex 26:25
two sockets *u* another board Ex 26:25
hang up the vail *u* the taches Ex 26:33
thou shalt put it *u* the compass Ex 27:5
thou make to it *u* the crown of it Ex 30:4
he made *u* the twenty boards Ex 36:24
two sockets *u* one board for his Ex 36:24
two sockets *u* another board for Ex 36:24
two sockets *u* one board Ex 36:26
two sockets *u* another board Ex 36:26
*u* every board two sockets Ex 36:30
a knop *u* two branches of the same Ex 37:21
a knop *u* two branches of the same Ex 37:21
a knop *u* two branches of the same Ex 37:21
gold for it *u* the crown thereof Ex 37:27
*u* the compass thereof beneath Ex 38:4
toucheth any thing that was *u* him Lev 15:10
it shall be seven days *u* the dam Lev 22:27
of whatsoever passeth *u* the rod Lev 27:32
*u* the custody and charge of the Num 3:36
their charge shall be *u* the hand Num 4:28
*u* the hand of Ithamar the son of Num 4:33
is *u* the sacrifice of the peace Num 6:18
*u* the hand of Ithamar the son of Num 7:8
clave asunder that was *u* them Num 16:31
the LORD, she fell down *u* Balaam Num 22:27
men of war which are *u* our charge Num 31:49
their armies *u* the hand of Moses Num 33:1
that are *u* the whole heaven Deut 2:25
*u* Ashdoth-pisgah eastward Deut 3:17
came near and stood *u* the mountain Deut 4:11
all nations *u* the whole heaven Deut 4:19
plain, *u* the springs of Pisgah Deut 4:49
destroy their name from *u* heaven Deut 7:24
blot out their name from *u* heaven Deut 9:14
the hills, and *u* every green tree Deut 12:2
of Amalek from *u* heaven Deut 25:19
the earth that is *u* thee shall be Deut 28:23
blot out his name from *u* heaven Deut 29:20
of my tent, and the silver *u* it Josh 7:21
in his tent, and the silver *u* it Josh 7:22
to the Hivite *u* Hermon in the Josh 11:3
valley of Lebanon *u* mount Hermon Josh 11:17
from the south, *u* Ashdoth-pisgah Josh 12:3
from Baal-gad *u* mount Hermon unto Josh 13:5
unto this day, and serve *u* tribute Josh 16:10
and set it up there *u* an oak Josh 24:26
gathered their meat *u* my table Judg 1:7
he did gird it *u* his raiment upon Judg 3:16
that day *u* the hand of Israel Judg 3:30
she dwelt *u* the palm tree of Judg 4:5
sat *u* an oak which was in Ophrah, Judg 6:11
brought it out unto him *u* the oak Judg 6:19
to God this people were *u* my hand Judg 9:29
*u* whose wings thou art come to Ruth 2:12
them, until they came *u* Beth-car 1Sa 7:11
*u* a pomegranate tree which is in 1Sa 14:2
therefore what is *u* thine hand 1Sa 21:3
is no common bread *u* mine hand 1Sa 21:4
is there not here *u* thine hand 1Sa 21:8
abode in Gibeah *u* a tree in Ramah 1Sa 22:6
buried them *u* a tree at Jabesh, 1Sa 31:13
spear smote him *u* the fifth rib 2Sa 2:23
smote him there *u* the fifth rib 2Sa 3:27
and they smote him *u* the fifth rib 2Sa 4:6
were therein, and put them *u* saws 2Sa 12:31
*u* harrows of iron, and *u* axes 2Sa 12:31
of the people *u* the hand of Joab 2Sa 18:2
a third part *u* the hand of 2Sa 18:2
a third part *u* the hand of Ittai 2Sa 18:2
the mule went *u* the thick boughs 2Sa 18:9
the mule that was *u* him went away 2Sa 18:9
and darkness was *u* his feet 2Sa 22:10
Thou hast enlarged my steps *u* me 2Sa 22:37
yea, they are fallen *u* my feet 2Sa 22:39
against me hast thou subdued *u* me 2Sa 22:40
bringeth down the people *u* me 2Sa 22:48
safely, every man *u* his vine 1Kin 4:25
*u* his fig tree, from Dan even to 1Kin 4:25
put them *u* the soles of his feet 1Kin 5:3
*u* the brim of it round about 1Kin 7:24
*u* the laver were undersetters 1Kin 7:30
*u* the borders were four wheels 1Kin 7:32
one sea, and twelve oxen *u* the sea 1Kin 7:44
even *u* the wings of the cherubims 1Kin 8:6
and found him sitting *u* an oak 1Kin 13:14
high hill, and *u* every green tree 1Kin 14:23
lay it on wood, and put no fire *u* 1Kin 18:23
lay it on wood, and put no fire *u* 1Kin 18:23
of your gods, but put no fire *u* 1Kin 18:25
sat down *u* a juniper tree 1Kin 19:4
slept *u* a juniper tree, behold, 1Kin 19:5
revolted from *u* the hand of Judah 2Kin 8:20
Yet Edom revolted from *u* the hand 2Kin 8:22
put it *u* him on the top of the 2Kin 9:13
and he trode her *u* foot 2Kin 9:33
from *u* the hand of the Syrians 2Kin 13:5
the name of Israel from *u* heaven 2Kin 14:27
the hills, and *u* every green tree 2Kin 16:4
the brasen oxen that were *u* it 2Kin 16:17
from *u* the hand of Pharaoh king 2Kin 17:7
high hill, and *u* every green tree 2Kin 17:10
their bones *u* the oak in Jabesh 1Chr 10:12
of the LORD remaineth *u* curtains 1Chr 17:1
*u* Aaron their father, as the LORD 1Chr 24:19
the sons of Asaph *u* the hands of 1Chr 25:2
*u* the hands of their father 1Chr 25:3
All these were *u* the hands of 1Chr 25:6
it was *u* the hand of Shelomith, 1Chr 26:28
them from twenty years old and *u* 1Chr 27:23
*u* it was the similitude of oxen, 2Chr 4:3
One sea, and twelve oxen *u* it 2Chr 4:15
even *u* the wings of the cherubims 2Chr 5:7
were brought *u* at that time 2Chr 13:18
from *u* the dominion of Judah 2Chr 21:8
So the Edomites revolted from *u* 2Chr 21:10
did Libnah revolt from *u* his hand 2Chr 21:10
*u* the hand of Hananiah, one of 2Chr 26:11
*u* their hand was an army, three 2Chr 26:13
the hills, and *u* every green tree 2Chr 28:4
to keep *u* the children of Judah 2Chr 28:10
were overseers *u* the hand of 2Chr 31:13
the beast that was *u* me to pass Neh 2:14
made booths, and sat *u* the booths Neh 8:17
the proud helpers do stoop *u* him Job 9:13
though he hide it *u* his tongue Job 20:12
are formed from *u* the waters Job 26:5
and the cloud is not rent *u* them Job 26:8
*u* it is turned up as it were fire Job 28:5
and seeth *u* the whole heaven Job 28:24
*u* the nettles they were gathered Job 30:7
He directeth it *u* the whole Job 37:3
He lieth *u* the shady trees, in Job 40:21
whatsoever is *u* the whole heaven Job 41:11
Sharp stones are *u* him Job 41:30
hast put all things *u* his feet Ps 8:6
*u* his tongue is mischief and Ps 10:7
hide me *u* the shadow of thy wings Ps 17:8
and darkness was *u* his feet Ps 18:9
Thou hast enlarged my steps *u* me Ps 18:36
they are fallen *u* my feet Ps 18:38
thou hast subdued *u* me those that Ps 18:39
me, and subdueth the people *u* me Ps 18:47
trust *u* the shadow of thy wings Ps 36:7
them *u* that rise up against us Ps 44:5
whereby the people fall *u* thee Ps 45:5
He shall subdue the people *u* us Ps 47:3
us, and the nations *u* our feet Ps 47:3
*u* the shadow of the Almighty Ps 91:1
*u* his wings shalt thou trust Ps 91:4
dragon shalt thou trample *u* feet Ps 91:13
into subjection *u* their hand Ps 106:42
adders' poison is *u* their lips Ps 140:3
who subdueth my people *u* me Ps 144:2
the slothful shall be *u* tribute Prov 12:24
he take away thy bed from *u* thee Prov 22:27
labour which he taketh *u* the sun Eccl 1:3
there is no new thing *u* the sun Eccl 1:9
all things that are done *u* heaven Eccl 1:13
the works that are done *u* the sun Eccl 1:14
which they should do *u* the heaven Eccl 2:3
and there was no profit *u* the sun Eccl 2:11
the work that is wrought *u* the Eccl 2:17
which I had taken *u* the sun Eccl 2:18
have shewed myself wise *u* the sun Eccl 2:19
the labour which I took *u* the sun Eccl 2:20
he hath laboured *u* the sun Eccl 2:22
to every purpose *u* the heaven Eccl 3:1
moreover I saw *u* the sun the Eccl 3:16
that are done *u* the sun Eccl 4:1
evil work that is done *u* the sun Eccl 4:3
and I saw vanity *u* the sun Eccl 4:7
the living which walk *u* the sun Eccl 4:15
evil which I have seen *u* the sun Eccl 5:13
*u* the sun all the days of his Eccl 5:18
evil which I have seen *u* the sun Eccl 6:1
what shall be after him *u* the sun Eccl 6:12
the crackling of thorns *u* a pot Eccl 7:6
every work that is done *u* the sun Eccl 8:9
hath no better thing *u* the sun Eccl 8:15
which God giveth him *u* the sun Eccl 8:15
the work that is done *u* the sun Eccl 8:17
things that are done *u* the sun Eccl 9:3
any thing that is done *u* the sun Eccl 9:6
he hath given thee *u* the sun Eccl 9:9
which thou takest *u* the sun Eccl 9:9
saw *u* the sun, that the race is Eccl 9:11
wisdom have I seen also *u* the sun Eccl 9:13
evil which I have seen *u* the sun Eccl 10:5
I sat down *u* his shadow with Song 2:3
His left hand is *u* my head Song 2:6
honey and milk are *u* thy tongue Song 4:11
His left hand should be *u* my head Song 8:3
I raised thee up *u* the apple tree Song 8:5
and let this ruin be *u* thy hand Is 3:6
shall bow down *u* the prisoners Is 10:4
and they shall fall *u* the slain Is 10:4
*u* his glory he shall kindle a Is 10:16
the worm is spread *u* thee Is 14:11
as a carcase trodden *u* feet Is 14:19
my mountains tread him *u* foot Is 14:25
meted out and trodden *u* foot Is 18:7
defiled *u* the inhabitants thereof Is 24:5
Moab shall be trodden down *u* him Is 25:10
Ephraim, shall be trodden *u* feet Is 28:3
*u* falsehood have we hid ourselves Is 28:15
and hatch, and gather *u* her shadow Is 34:15
with idols *u* every green tree Is 57:5
valleys *u* the clifts of the rocks Is 57:5
spread sackcloth and ashes *u* him Is 58:5
*u* every green tree thou wanderest Jer 2:20
*u* every green tree, and there hath Jer 3:6
the strangers *u* every green tree Jer 3:13
earth, and from *u* these heavens Jer 10:11
have trodden my portion *u* foot Jer 12:10
that will not put their neck *u* Jer 27:8
nations that bring their neck *u* Jer 27:11
Bring your necks *u* the yoke of Jer 27:12
shall the flocks pass again *u* the Jer 33:13
house of the king *u* the treasury Jer 38:11
*u* thine armholes *u* the cords Jer 38:12
They that fled stood *u* the shadow Jer 48:45
bulls that were *u* the bases Jer 52:20
The Lord hath trodden *u* foot all Lam 1:15
To crush *u* his feet all the Lam 3:34
from *u* the heavens of the LORD Lam 3:66
*U* his shadow we shall live among Lam 4:20
Our necks are *u* persecution Lam 5:5
and the children fell *u* the wood Lam 5:13
they had the hands of a man *u* Eze 1:8
*u* the firmament were their wings Eze 1:23
*u* every green tree Eze 6:13
*u* every thick oak, the place Eze 6:13
even *u* the cherub, and fill thine Eze 10:2
of a man's hand *u* their wings Eze 10:8
*u* the God of Israel by the river Eze 10:20
hands of a man was *u* their wings Eze 10:21
and the roots thereof were *u* him Eze 17:6
*u* it shall dwell all fowl of Eze 17:23
will cause you to pass *u* the rod Eze 20:37
and burn also the bones *u* it Eze 24:5
*u* his branches did all the beasts Eze 31:6
*u* his shadow dwelt all great Eze 31:6
that dwelt *u* his shadow in the Eze 31:17
laid their swords *u* their heads Eze 32:27
from *u* these chambers was the Eze 42:9
places *u* the rows round about Eze 46:23
waters issued out from *u* the Eze 47:1
the waters came down from *u* from Eze 47:1
of the field had shadow *u* it Dan 4:12
let the beasts get away from *u* it Dan 4:14
*u* which the beasts of the field Dan 4:21
of the kingdom *u* the whole heaven Dan 7:27
and the host to be trodden *u* foot Dan 8:13
for *u* the whole heaven hath not Dan 9:12
gone a whoring from *u* their God Hos 4:12
*u* oaks and poplars and elms, Hos 4:13
They that dwell *u* his shadow Hos 14:7
The seed is rotten *u* their clods Joel 1:17
Behold, I am pressed *u* you Amos 2:13
bread have laid a wound *u* thee Obad 7
sat *u* it in the shadow, till he Jonah 4:5
mountains shall be molten *u* him Mic 1:4
*u* his vine and *u* his fig tree Mic 4:4
man his neighbour *u* the vine Zec 3:10

*u* the vine and *u* the fig tree ........ Zec 3:10
for they shall be ashes *u* the ........ Mal 4:3
thereof, from two years old and *u* ........ Mt 2:16
and to be trodden *u* foot of men ........ Mt 5:13
put it *u* a bushel, but on a ........ Mt 5:15
they trample them *u* their feet ........ Mt 7:6
thou shouldest come *u* my roof ........ Mt 8:8
For I am a man *u* authority ........ Mt 8:9
authority, having soldiers *u* me ........ Mt 8:9
her chickens *u* her wings, and ye ........ Mt 23:37
be put *u* a bushel, or *u* a bed ........ Mk 4:21
air may lodge *u* the shadow of it ........ Mk 4:32
shake off the dust *u* your feet ........ Mk 6:11
yet the dogs *u* the table eat of ........ Mk 7:28
thou shouldest enter *u* my roof ........ Lk 7:6
I also am a man set *u* authority ........ Lk 7:8
having *u* me soldiers, and I say ........ Lk 7:8
a vessel, or putteth it *u* a bed ........ Lk 8:16
neither *u* a bushel, but on a ........ Lk 11:33
doth gather her brood *u* her wings ........ Lk 13:34
out of the one part *u* heaven ........ Lk 17:24
unto the other part *u* heaven ........ Lk 17:24
when thou wast *u* the fig tree ........ Jn 1:48
I saw thee *u* the fig tree, ........ Jn 1:50
men, out of every nation *u* heaven ........ Acts 2:5
name *u* heaven given among men ........ Acts 4:12
an eunuch of great authority *u* ........ Acts 8:27
and bound themselves *u* a curse ........ Acts 23:12
bound ourselves *u* a great curse ........ Acts 23:14
from thence, we sailed *u* Cyprus ........ Acts 27:4
suffering us, we sailed *u* Crete ........ Acts 27:7
running *u* a certain island which ........ Acts 27:16
*u* colour as though they would ........ Acts 27:30
Gentiles, that they are all *u* sin ........ Rom 3:9
poison of asps is *u* their lips ........ Rom 3:13
saith to them who are *u* the law ........ Rom 3:19
not *u* the law, but *u* grace ........ Rom 6:14
not *u* the law, but *u* grace ........ Rom 6:15
but I am carnal, sold *u* sin ........ Rom 7:14
bruise Satan *u* your feet shortly ........ Rom 16:20
not be brought *u* the power of any ........ 1Cor 6:12
is not *u* bondage in such cases ........ 1Cor 7:15
to them that are *u* the law ........ 1Cor 9:20
as *u* the law, that I might gain ........ 1Cor 9:20
gain them that are *u* the law ........ 1Cor 9:20
but *u* the law to Christ,) that I ........ 1Cor 9:21
But I keep *u* my body, and bring it ........ 1Cor 9:27
all our fathers were *u* the cloud ........ 1Cor 10:1
are commanded to be *u* obedience ........ 1Cor 14:34
hath put all enemies *u* his feet ........ 1Cor 15:25
he hath put all things *u* his feet ........ 1Cor 15:27
he saith all things are put *u* him ........ 1Cor 15:27
which did put all things *u* him ........ 1Cor 15:27
him that put all things *u* him ........ 1Cor 15:28
In Damascus the governor *u* Aretas ........ 2Cor 11:32
works of the law are *u* the curse ........ Gal 3:10
hath concluded all *u* sin, that ........ Gal 3:22
came, we were kept *u* the law ........ Gal 3:23
we are no longer *u* a schoolmaster ........ Gal 3:25
But is *u* tutors and governors ........ Gal 4:2
were in bondage *u* the elements of ........ Gal 4:3
made of a woman, made *u* the law, ........ Gal 4:4
redeem them that were *u* the law ........ Gal 4:5
ye that desire to be *u* the law ........ Gal 4:21
the Spirit, ye are not *u* the law ........ Gal 5:18
And hath put all things *u* his feet ........ Eph 1:22
in earth, and things *u* the earth ........ Phil 2:10
every creature which is *u* heaven ........ Col 1:23
the number *u* threescore years old ........ 1Ti 5:9
as are *u* the yoke count their own ........ 1Ti 6:1
things in subjection *u* his feet ........ Heb 2:8
he put all in subjection *u* him ........ Heb 2:8
nothing that is not put *u* him ........ Heb 2:8
see not yet all things put *u* him ........ Heb 2:8
(for *u* it the people received the ........ Heb 7:11
that were *u* the first testament ........ Heb 9:15
mercy *u* two or three witnesses ........ Heb 10:28
who hath trodden *u* foot the Son ........ Heb 10:29
or sit here *u* my footstool ........ Jas 2:3
*u* the mighty hand of God, that he ........ 1Pet 5:6
*u* darkness unto the judgment of ........ Jude 6
neither *u* the earth, was able to ........ Rev 5:3
*u* the earth, and such as are in ........ Rev 5:13
I saw *u* the altar the souls of ........ Rev 6:9
shall they tread *u* foot forty ........ Rev 11:2
the sun, and the moon *u* her feet ........ Rev 12:1

## UNDERGIRDING
up, they used helps, *u* the ship ........ Acts 27:17

## UNDERNEATH
on the two sides of the ephod *u* ........ Ex 28:27
on the two sides of the ephod *u* ........ Ex 39:20
*u* are the everlasting arms ........ Deut 33:27

## UNDERSETTERS
and the four corners thereof had *u* ........ 1Kin 7:30
under the laver were *u* molten ........ 1Kin 7:30
there were four *u* to the four ........ 1Kin 7:34
the *u* were of the very base ........ 1Kin 7:34

## UNDERSTAND
that they may not *u* one another's ........ Gen 11:7
that thou canst *u* a dream to ........ Gen 41:15
then ye shall *u* that these men ........ Num 16:30
*U* therefore this day, that the ........ Deut 9:3
*U* therefore, that the LORD thy ........ Deut 9:6
whose tongue thou shalt not *u* ........ Deut 28:49
for we *u* it ........ 2Kin 18:26
the LORD made me *u* in writing by ........ 1Chr 28:19
the women, and those that could *u* ........ Neh 8:3
caused the people to *u* the law ........ Neh 8:7
and caused them to *u* the reading ........ Neh 8:8
even to *u* the words of the law ........ Neh 8:13
cause me to *u* wherein I have ........ Job 6:24
*u* what he would say unto me ........ Job 23:5
thunder of his power who can *u* ........ Job 26:14
neither do the aged *u* judgment ........ Job 32:9
Also can any *u* the spreadings of ........ Job 36:29
see if there were any that did *u* ........ Ps 14:2
Who can *u* his errors ........ Ps 19:12
see if there were any that did *u* ........ Ps 53:2
know not, neither will they *u* ........ Ps 82:5
neither doth a fool *u* this ........ Ps 92:6
*U*, ye brutish among the people ........ Ps 94:8
things, even they shall *u* the ........ Ps 107:43
Make me to *u* the way of thy ........ Ps 119:27
I *u* more than the ancients, ........ Ps 119:100
To *u* a proverb, and the ........ Prov 1:6
Then shalt thou *u* the fear of the ........ Prov 2:5
Then shalt thou *u* righteousness ........ Prov 2:9
O ye simple, *u* wisdom ........ Prov 8:5
of the prudent is to *u* his way ........ Prov 14:8
and he will *u* knowledge ........ Prov 19:25
how can a man then *u* his own way ........ Prov 20:24
Evil men *u* not judgment ........ Prov 28:5
that seek the LORD *u* all things ........ Prov 28:5
for though he *u* he will not ........ Prov 29:19
people, Hear ye indeed, but *u* not ........ Is 6:9
*u* with their heart, and convert, ........ Is 6:10
whom shall he make to *u* doctrine ........ Is 28:9
a vexation only to *u* the report ........ Is 28:19
of the rash shall *u* knowledge ........ Is 32:4
tongue, that thou canst not *u* ........ Is 33:19
for we *u* it ........ Is 36:11
*u* together, that the hand of the ........ Is 41:20
and believe me, and *u* that I am he ........ Is 43:10
their hearts, that they cannot *u* ........ Is 44:18
they are shepherds that cannot *u* ........ Is 56:11
is the wise man, that may *u* this ........ Jer 9:12
whose words thou canst not *u* ........ Eze 3:6
make this man to *u* the vision ........ Dan 8:16
but he said unto me, *U*, O son of ........ Dan 8:17
our iniquities, and *u* thy truth ........ Dan 9:13
therefore *u* the matter, and ........ Dan 9:23
Know therefore and *u*, that from ........ Dan 9:25
*u* the words that I speak unto ........ Dan 10:11
thou didst set thine heart to *u* ........ Dan 10:12
I am come to make thee *u* ........ Dan 10:14
they that *u* among the people ........ Dan 11:33
and none of the wicked shall *u* ........ Dan 12:10
but the wise shall *u* ........ Dan 12:10
people that doth not *u* shall fall ........ Hos 4:14
wise, and he shall *u* these things ........ Hos 14:9
neither *u* they his counsel ........ Mic 4:12
they hear not, neither do they *u* ........ Mt 13:13
ye shall hear, and shall not *u* ........ Mt 13:14
should *u* with their heart, and ........ Mt 13:15
and said unto them, Hear, and *u* ........ Mt 15:10
Do not ye yet *u*, that whatsoever ........ Mt 15:17
Do ye not yet *u*, neither remember ........ Mt 16:9
How is it that ye do not *u* that I ........ Mt 16:11
place, (whoso readeth, let him *u* ........ Mt 24:15
hearing they may hear, and not *u* ........ Mk 4:12
unto me every one of you, and *u* ........ Mk 7:14
perceive ye not yet, neither *u* ........ Mk 8:17
them, How is it that ye do not *u* ........ Mk 8:21
not, (let him that readeth *u* ........ Mk 13:14
neither *u* I what thou sayest ........ Mk 14:68
see, and hearing they might not *u* ........ Lk 8:10
that they might *u* the scriptures ........ Lk 24:45
Why do ye not *u* my speech ........ Jn 8:43
nor *u* with their heart, and be ........ Jn 12:40
Because that thou mayest *u* ........ Acts 24:11
ye shall hear, and shall not *u* ........ Acts 28:26
*u* with their heart, and should be ........ Acts 28:27
they that have not heard shall *u* ........ Rom 15:21
Wherefore I give you to *u* ........ 1Cor 12:3
*u* all mysteries, and all knowledge ........ 1Cor 13:2
ye may *u* my knowledge in the ........ Eph 3:4
But I would ye should *u*, brethren ........ Phil 1:12
Through faith we *u* that the ........ Heb 11:3
of the things that they *u* not ........ 2Pet 2:12

## UNDERSTANDEST
what *u* thou, which is not in us ........ Job 15:9
thou *u* my thought afar off ........ Ps 139:2
not, neither *u* what they say ........ Jer 5:15
and said, *U* thou what thou readest ........ Acts 8:30

## UNDERSTANDETH
*u* all the imaginations of the ........ 1Chr 28:9
God *u* the way thereof, and he ........ Job 28:23
*u* not, is like the beasts that ........ Ps 49:20
They are all plain to him that *u* ........ Prov 8:9
knowledge is easy unto him that *u* ........ Prov 14:6
glorieth glory in this, that he *u* ........ Jer 9:24
*u* it not, then cometh the wicked ........ Mt 13:19
he that heareth the word, and *u* it ........ Mt 13:23
There is none that *u*, there is ........ Rom 3:11
for no man *u* him ........ 1Cor 14:2
seeing he *u* not what thou sayest ........ 1Cor 14:16

## UNDERSTANDING
spirit of God, in wisdom, and in *u* ........ Ex 31:3
spirit of God, in wisdom, in *u* ........ Ex 35:31
*u* to know how to work all manner ........ Ex 36:1
Take you wise men, and *u* ........ Deut 1:13
your *u* in the sight of the ........ Deut 4:6
nation is a wise and *u* people ........ Deut 4:6
neither is there any *u* in them ........ Deut 32:28
and she was a woman of good *u* ........ 1Sa 25:3
an *u* heart to judge thy people ........ 1Kin 3:9
for thyself *u* to discern judgment ........ 1Kin 3:11
given thee a wise and an *u* heart ........ 1Kin 3:12
*u* exceeding much, and largeness of ........ 1Kin 4:29
he was filled with wisdom, and *u* ........ 1Kin 7:14
were men that had *u* of the times ........ 1Chr 12:32
the LORD give thee wisdom and *u* ........ 1Chr 22:12
son, endued with prudence and *u* ........ 2Chr 2:12
sent a cunning man, endued with *u* ........ 2Chr 2:13
who had *u* in the visions of God ........ 2Chr 26:5
and for Elnathan, men of *u* ........ Ezr 8:16
us they brought us a man of *u* ........ Ezr 8:18
and all that could hear with *u* ........ Neh 8:2
one having knowledge, and having *u*. ........ Neh 10:28
But I have *u* as well as you ........ Job 12:3
and in length of days *u* ........ Job 12:12
and strength, he hath counsel and *u* ........ Job 12:13
and taketh away the *u* of the aged ........ Job 12:20
thou hast hid their heart from *u* ........ Job 17:4
the spirit of my *u* causeth me to ........ Job 20:3
by his *u* he smiteth through the ........ Job 26:12
and where is the place of *u* ........ Job 28:12
and where is the place of *u* ........ Job 28:20
and to depart from evil is *u* ........ Job 28:28
of the Almighty giveth them *u* ........ Job 32:8
hearken unto me, ye men of *u* ........ Job 34:10
If now thou hast *u*, hear this ........ Job 34:16
Let men of *u* tell me, and let a ........ Job 34:34
declare, if thou hast *u* ........ Job 38:4
or who hath given *u* to the heart ........ Job 38:36
neither hath he imparted to her *u* ........ Job 39:17
or as the mule, which have no *u* ........ Ps 32:9
sing ye praises with *u* ........ Ps 47:7
of my heart shall be of *u* ........ Ps 49:3
a good *u* have all they that do ........ Ps 111:10
Give me *u*, and I shall keep thy ........ Ps 119:34
give me *u*, that I may learn thy ........ Ps 119:73
I have more *u* than all my ........ Ps 119:99
Through thy precepts I get *u* ........ Ps 119:104
give me *u*, that I may know thy ........ Ps 119:125
it giveth *u* unto the simple ........ Ps 119:130
give me *u*, and I shall live ........ Ps 119:144
give me *u* according to thy word ........ Ps 119:169
his *u* is infinite ........ Ps 147:5
to perceive the words of *u* ........ Prov 1:2
a man of *u* shall attain unto wise ........ Prov 1:5
wisdom, and apply thine heart to *u* ........ Prov 2:2
and liftest up thy voice for *u* ........ Prov 2:3
his mouth cometh knowledge and *u* ........ Prov 2:6
preserve thee, *u* shall keep thee ........ Prov 2:11
good *u* in the sight of God and man ........ Prov 3:4
and lean not unto thine own *u* ........ Prov 3:5
wisdom, and the man that getteth *u* ........ Prov 3:13
by *u* hath he established the ........ Prov 3:19
of a father, and attend to know *u* ........ Prov 4:1
Get wisdom, get *u* ........ Prov 4:5
and with all thy getting get *u* ........ Prov 4:7
wisdom, and bow thine ear to my *u* ........ Prov 5:1
adultery with a woman lacketh *u* ........ Prov 6:32
and call *u* thy kinswoman ........ Prov 7:4
the youths, a young man void of *u* ........ Prov 7:7
and *u* put forth her voice ........ Prov 8:1
and, ye fools, be ye of an *u* heart ........ Prov 8:5
I am *u* ........ Prov 8:14
as for him that wanteth *u* ........ Prov 9:4
and go in the way of *u* ........ Prov 9:6
and the knowledge of the holy is *u* ........ Prov 9:10
and as for him that wanteth *u* ........ Prov 9:16
him that hath *u* wisdom is found ........ Prov 10:13
the back of him that is void of *u* ........ Prov 10:13
but a man of *u* hath wisdom ........ Prov 10:23
but a man of *u* holdeth his peace ........ Prov 11:12
vain persons is void of *u* ........ Prov 12:11
Good *u* giveth favour ........ Prov 13:15
is slow to wrath is of great *u* ........ Prov 14:29
in the heart of him that hath *u* ........ Prov 14:33
him that hath *u* seeketh knowledge ........ Prov 15:14
but a man of *u* walketh uprightly ........ Prov 15:21
he that heareth reproof getteth *u* ........ Prov 15:32
to get *u* rather to be chosen than ........ Prov 16:16
*U* is a wellspring of life unto ........ Prov 16:22
A man void of *u* striketh hands, ........ Prov 17:18
Wisdom is before him that hath *u* ........ Prov 17:24
a man of *u* is of an excellent ........ Prov 17:27
his lips is esteemed a man of *u* ........ Prov 17:28
A fool hath no delight in *u* ........ Prov 18:2
he that keepeth *u* shall find good ........ Prov 19:8
and reprove one that hath *u* ........ Prov 19:25
but a man of *u* will draw it out ........ Prov 20:5
the way of *u* shall remain in the ........ Prov 21:16
There is no wisdom nor *u* nor ........ Prov 21:30
also wisdom, and instruction, and *u* ........ Prov 23:23
and by *u* it is established ........ Prov 24:3
the vineyard of the man void of *u* ........ Prov 24:30
but by a man of *u* and knowledge ........ Prov 28:2
that hath *u* searcheth him out ........ Prov 28:11
The prince that wanteth *u* is also ........ Prov 28:16
man, and have not the *u* of a man ........ Prov 30:2
wise, nor yet riches to men of *u* ........ Eccl 9:11
him, the spirit of wisdom and *u* ........ Is 11:2
quick *u* in the fear of the LORD ........ Is 11:3
for it is a people of no *u* ........ Is 27:11
the *u* of their prudent men shall ........ Is 29:14
him that framed it, He had no *u* ........ Is 29:16
erred in spirit shall come to *u* ........ Is 29:24
and shewed to him the way of *u* ........ Is 40:14
there is no searching of his *u* ........ Is 40:28
is there knowledge nor *u* to say ........ Is 44:19
feed you with knowledge and *u* ........ Jer 3:15
children, and they have none *u* ........ Jer 4:22
O foolish people, and without *u* ........ Jer 5:21
stretched out the heaven by his *u* ........ Jer 51:15

with thine *u* thou hast gotten Eze 28:4
*u* science, and such as had ability Dan 1:4
Daniel had *u* in all visions and Dan 1:17
And in all matters of wisdom and *u* Dan 1:20
and knowledge to them that know *u* Dan 2:21
mine *u* returned unto me, and I Dan 4:34
the days of thy father light and *u* Dan 5:11
spirit, and knowledge, and *u* Dan 5:12
is in thee, and that light and *u* Dan 5:14
*u* dark sentences, shall stand up Dan 8:23
forth to give thee skill and *u* Dan 9:22
the thing, and had *u* of the vision Dan 10:1
And some of them of *u* shall fall Dan 11:35
and idols according to their own *u* Hos 13:2
there is none *u* in him Obad 7
*u* out of the mount of Esau Obad 8
said, Are ye also yet without *u* Mt 15:16
them, Are ye so without *u* also Mk 7:18
all the heart, and with all the *u* Mk 12:33
having had perfect *u* of all Lk 1:3
him were astonished at his *u* Lk 2:47
Then opened he their *u*, that they Lk 24:45
Without *u*, covenantbreakers, Rom 1:31
to nothing the *u* of the prudent 1Cor 1:19
prayeth, but my *u* is unfruitful 1Cor 14:14
and I will pray with the *u* also 1Cor 14:15
and I will sing with the *u* also 1Cor 14:15
rather speak five words with my *u* 1Cor 14:19
Brethren, be not children in *u* 1Cor 14:20
be ye children, but in *u* be men 1Cor 14:20
The eyes of your *u* being Eph 1:18
Having the *u* darkened, being Eph 4:18
but *u* what the will of the Lord Eph 5:17
peace of God, which passeth all *u* Phil 4:7
will in all wisdom and spiritual *u* Col 1:9
riches of the full assurance of *u* Col 2:2
*u* neither what they say, nor 1Ti 1:7
Lord give thee *u* in all things 2Ti 2:7
is come, and hath given us an *u* 1Jn 5:20
Let him that hath *u* count the Rev 13:18

**UNDERSTOOD**
they knew not that Joseph *u* them Gen 42:23
they were wise, that they *u* this Deut 32:29
they *u* that the ark of the LORD 1Sa 4:6
*u* that Saul was come in very deed 1Sa 26:4
all Israel *u* that day that it was 2Sa 3:37
because they had *u* the words that Neh 8:12
*u* of the evil that Eliashib did Neh 13:7
this, mine ear hath heard and *u* it Job 13:1
have I uttered that I *u* not Job 42:3
then *u* I their end Ps 73:17
I heard a language that I *u* not Ps 81:5
Our fathers *u* not thy wonders in Ps 106:7
have ye not *u* from the Is 40:21
They have not known nor *u* Is 44:18
at the vision, but none *u* it Dan 8:27
*u* by books the number of the Dan 9:2
and he *u* the thing, and had Dan 10:1
And I heard, but I *u* not Dan 12:8
Have ye *u* all these things Mt 13:51
Then *u* they how that he bade them Mt 16:12
Then the disciples *u* that he Mt 17:13
When Jesus *u* it, he said unto Mt 26:10
But they *u* not that saying, and Mk 9:32
they *u* not the saying which he Lk 2:50
But they *u* not this saying, and it Lk 9:45
they *u* none of these things Lk 18:34
They *u* not that he spake to them Jn 8:27
but they *u* not what things they Jn 10:6
These things *u* not his disciples Jn 12:16
his brethren would have *u* how Acts 7:25
but they *u* not Acts 7:25
having *u* that he was a Roman Acts 23:27
when he *u* that he was of Cilicia Acts 23:34
being *u* by the things that are Rom 1:20
I *u* as a child, I thought as a 1Cor 13:11
by the tongue words easy to be *u* 1Cor 14:9
are some things hard to be *u* 2Pet 3:16

**UNDERTAKE**
oppressed; *u* for me Is 38:14

**UNDERTOOK**
the Jews *u* to do as they had Est 9:23

**UNDO**
to *u* the heavy burdens, and to let Is 58:6
at that time I will *u* all that Zeph 3:19

**UNDONE**
thou art *u*, O people of Chemosh Num 21:29
he left nothing *u* of all that the Josh 11:15
for I am *u* Is 6:5
done, and not to leave the other *u* Mt 23:23
done, and not to leave the other *u* Lk 11:42

**UNDRESSED**
gather the grapes of thy vine *u* Lev 25:5
the grapes in it of thy vine *u* Lev 25:11

**UNEQUAL**
are not your ways *u* Eze 18:25
are not your ways *u* Eze 18:29

**UNEQUALLY**
Be ye not *u* yoked together with 2Cor 6:14

**UNFAITHFUL**
Confidence in an *u* man in time of Prov 25:19

**UNFAITHFULLY**
dealt *u* like their fathers Ps 78:57

**UNFEIGNED**
by the Holy Ghost, by love *u* 2Cor 6:6
a good conscience, and of faith *u* 1Ti 1:5
the *u* faith that is in thee 2Ti 1:5
unto *u* love of the brethren 1Pet 1:22

**UNFRUITFUL**
choke the word, and he becometh *u* Mt 13:22
choke the word, and it becometh *u* Mk 4:19
but my understanding is *u* 1Cor 14:14
with the *u* works of darkness Eph 5:11
uses, that they be not *u* Titus 3:14
*u* in the knowledge of our Lord 2Pet 1:8

**UNGIRDED**
he *u* his camels, and gave straw and Gen 24:32

**UNGODLINESS**
from heaven against all *u* Rom 1:18
and shall turn away *u* from Jacob Rom 11:26
they will increase unto more *u* 2Ti 2:16
Teaching us that, denying *u* Titus 2:12

**UNGODLY**
the floods of *u* men made me 2Sa 22:5
Shouldest thou help the *u* 2Chr 19:2
God hath delivered me to the *u* Job 16:11
and to princes, Ye are *u* Job 34:18
not in the counsel of the *u* Ps 1:1
The *u* are not so Ps 1:4
Therefore the *u* shall not stand Ps 1:5
but the way of the *u* shall perish Ps 1:6
hast broken the teeth of the *u* Ps 3:7
the floods of *u* men made me Ps 18:4
my cause against an *u* nation Ps 43:1
Behold, these are the *u*, who Ps 73:12
An *u* man diggeth up evil Prov 16:27
An *u* witness scorneth judgment Prov 19:28
on him that justifieth the *u* Rom 4:5
in due time Christ died for the *u* Rom 5:6
lawless and disobedient, for the *u* 1Ti 1:9
be saved, where shall the *u* 1Pet 4:18
the flood upon the world of the *u* 2Pet 2:5
those that after should live *u* 2Pet 2:6
of judgment and perdition of *u* men 2Pet 3:7
*u* men, turning the grace of our Jude 4
to convince all that are *u* among Jude 15
*u* deeds which they have Jude 15
deeds which they have *u* committed Jude 15
all their hard speeches which *u* Jude 15
walk after their own *u* lusts Jude 18

**UNHOLY**
put difference between holy and *u* Lev 10:10
the ungodly and for sinners, for *u* 1Ti 1:9
to parents, unthankful, *u* 2Ti 3:2
an *u* thing, and hath done despite Heb 10:29

**UNICORN**
as it were the strength of a *u* Num 23:22
as it were the strength of a *u* Num 24:8
Will the *u* be willing to serve Job 39:9
Canst thou bind the *u* with his Job 39:10
Lebanon and Sirion like a young *u* Ps 29:6
thou exalt like the horn of an *u* Ps 92:10

**UNICORNS**
his horns are like the horns of *u* Deut 33:17
heard me from the horns of the *u* Ps 22:21
the *u* shall come down with them, Is 34:7

**UNITE**
*u* my heart to fear thy name Ps 86:11

**UNITED**
mine honour, be not thou *u* Gen 49:6

**UNITY**
brethren to dwell together in *u* Ps 133:1
Endeavouring to keep the *u* of the Eph 4:3
we all come in the *u* of the faith Eph 4:13

**UNJUST**
me from the deceitful and *u* man Ps 43:1
the hope of *u* men perisheth Prov 11:7
*u* gain increaseth his substance, Prov 28:8
An *u* man is an abomination to the Prov 29:27
but the *u* knoweth no shame Zeph 3:5
rain on the just and on the *u* Mt 5:45
the lord commended the *u* steward Lk 16:8
he that is *u* in the least is Lk 16:10
in the least is *u* also in much Lk 16:10
said, Hear what the *u* judge saith Lk 18:6
as other men are, extortioners, *u* Lk 18:11
the dead, both of the just and *u* Acts 24:15
another, go to law before the *u* 1Cor 6:1
for sins, the just for the *u* 1Pet 3:18
to reserve the *u* unto the day of 2Pet 2:9
He that is *u*, let him be *u* Rev 22:11

**UNJUSTLY**
How long will ye judge *u*, and Ps 82:2
of uprightness will he deal *u* Is 26:10

**UNKNOWN**
this inscription, TO THE *U* GOD Acts 17:23
For he that speaketh in an *u* 1Cor 14:2
He that speaketh in an *u* tongue 1Cor 14:4
in an *u* tongue pray that he may 1Cor 14:13
For if I pray in an *u* tongue 1Cor 14:14
ten thousand words in an *u* tongue 1Cor 14:19
If any man speak in an *u* tongue 1Cor 14:27
As *u*, and yet well known 2Cor 6:9
was *u* by face unto the churches Gal 1:22

**UNLADE**
the ship was to *u* her burden Acts 21:3

**UNLAWFUL**
Ye know how that it is an *u* thing Acts 10:28
day to day with their *u* deeds 2Pet 2:8

**UNLEARNED**
and perceived that they were *u* Acts 4:13
the *u* say Amen at thy giving of 1Cor 14:16
and there come in those that are *u* 1Cor 14:23
one that believeth not, or one *u* 1Cor 14:24
*u* questions avoid, knowing that 2Ti 2:23
understood, which they that are *u* 2Pet 3:16

**UNLEAVENED**
them a feast, and did bake *u* bread Gen 19:3
roast with fire, and *u* bread Ex 12:8
Seven days shall ye eat *u* bread Ex 12:15
observe the feast of *u* bread Ex 12:17
at even, ye shall eat *u* bread Ex 12:18
habitations shall ye eat *u* bread Ex 12:20
they baked *u* cakes of the dough Ex 12:39
Seven days thou shalt eat *u* bread Ex 13:6
*U* bread shall be eaten seven days Ex 13:7
shalt keep the feast of *u* bread Ex 23:15
(thou shalt eat *u* bread seven Ex 23:15
*u* bread, and cakes *u* Ex 29:2
wafers *u* anointed with oil Ex 29:2
*u* bread that is before the LORD Ex 29:23
The feast of *u* bread shalt thou Ex 34:18
Seven days thou shalt eat *u* bread Ex 34:18
it shall be *u* cakes of fine flour Lev 2:4
or *u* wafers anointed with oil Lev 2:4
pan, it shall be of fine flour *u* Lev 2:5
with *u* bread shall it be eaten in Lev 6:16
*u* cakes mingled with oil, and Lev 7:12
*u* wafers anointed with oil, and Lev 7:12
two rams, and a basket of *u* bread Lev 8:2
And out of the basket of *u* bread Lev 8:26
the LORD, he took one *u* cake Lev 8:26
feast of *u* bread unto the LORD Lev 23:6
seven days ye must eat *u* bread Lev 23:6
And a basket of *u* bread, cakes of Num 6:15
wafers of *u* bread anointed with Num 6:15
LORD, with the basket of *u* bread Num 6:17
one *u* cake out of the basket, and Num 6:19
one *u* wafer, and shall put them Num 6:19
keep it, and eat it with *u* bread Num 9:11
seven days shall *u* bread be eaten Num 28:17
shalt thou eat *u* bread therewith Deut 16:3
Six days thou shalt eat *u* bread Deut 16:8
in the feast of *u* bread, and in Deut 16:16
*u* cakes, and parched corn in the Josh 5:11
*u* cakes of an ephah of flour Judg 6:19
the *u* cakes, and lay them upon Judg 6:20
touched the flesh and the *u* cakes Judg 6:21
consumed the flesh and the *u* cakes Judg 6:21
it, and did bake *u* bread thereof 1Sa 28:24
but they did eat of the *u* bread 2Kin 23:9
meat offering, and for the *u* cakes 1Chr 23:29
even in the feast of *u* bread 2Chr 8:13
of *u* bread in the second month 2Chr 30:13
of *u* bread seven days with great 2Chr 30:21
the feast of *u* bread seven days 2Chr 35:17
kept the feast of *u* bread seven Ezr 6:22
*u* bread shall be eaten Eze 45:21
of *u* bread the disciples came to Mt 26:17
of the passover, and of *u* bread Mk 14:1
And the first day of *u* bread Mk 14:12
the feast of *u* bread drew nigh Lk 22:1
Then came the day of *u* bread Lk 22:7
(Then were the days of *u* bread Acts 12:3
after the days of *u* bread Acts 20:6
ye may be a new lump, as ye are *u* 1Cor 5:7
but with the *u* bread of sincerity 1Cor 5:8

**UNLESS**
*u* he wash his flesh with water Lev 22:6
*u* she had turned from me, surely Num 22:33
*u* thou hadst spoken, surely then 2Sa 2:27
*u* I had believed to see the Ps 27:13
*U* the LORD had been my help, my Ps 94:17
*U* thy law had been my delights, I Ps 119:92
*u* they cause some to fall Prov 4:16
*u* ye have believed in vain 1Cor 15:2

**UNLOOSE**
am not worthy to stoop down and *u* Mk 1:7
whose shoes I am not worthy to *u* Lk 3:16
latchet I am not worthy to *u* Jn 1:27

**UNMARRIED**
I say therefore to the *u* and 1Cor 7:8
if she depart, let her remain *u* 1Cor 7:11
He that is *u* careth for the 1Cor 7:32
The *u* woman careth for the things 1Cor 7:34

**UNMERCIFUL**
natural affection, implacable, *u* Rom 1:31

**UNMINDFUL**
Rock that begat thee thou art *u* Deut 32:18

**UNMOVABLE**
brethren, be ye stedfast, *u* 1Cor 15:58

**UNMOVEABLE**
stuck fast, and remained *u* Acts 27:41

**UNNI**
and Shemiramoth, and Jehiel, and *U* 1Chr 15:18
and Shemiramoth, and Jehiel, and *U* 1Chr 15:20
Also Bakbukiah and *U*, their Neh 12:9

**UNOCCUPIED**
days of Jael, the highways were *u* Judg 5:6

**UNPERFECT**
did see my substance, yet being *u* Ps 139:16

**UNPREPARED**
come with me, and find you *u* 2Cor 9:4

**UNPROFITABLE**
Should he reason with *u* talk Job 15:3
cast ye the *u* servant into outer Mt 25:30

you, say, We are *u* servants .................... Lk 17:10
way, they are together become *u*......... Rom 3:12
for they are *u* and vain .......................... Titus 3:9
Which in time past was to thee *u* ....... Philem 11
for that is *u* for you ............................ Heb 13:17

**UNPROFITABLENESS**
for the weakness and *u* thereof ............ Heb 7:18

**UNPUNISHED**
hand, the wicked shall not be *u*.......... Prov 11:21
join in hand, he shall not be *u*............ Prov 16:5
glad at calamities shall not be *u*.......... Prov 17:5
A false witness shall not be *u*.............. Prov 19:5
A false witness shall not be *u*.............. Prov 19:9
name, and should ye be utterly *u*......... Jer 25:29
Ye shall not be *u* ................................. Jer 25:29
will not leave thee altogether *u*............ Jer 30:11
will I not leave thee wholly *u*................ Jer 46:28
he that shall altogether go *u* ............... Jer 49:12
thou shalt not go *u*, but thou ................ Jer 49:12

**UNQUENCHABLE**
burn up the chaff with *u* fire ................... Mt 3:12
chaff he will burn with fire *u* .................. Lk 3:17

**UNREASONABLE**
to me *u* to send a prisoner .................. Acts 25:27
that we may be delivered from *u*............. 2Th 3:2

**UNREBUKEABLE**
this commandment without spot, *u*....... 1Ti 6:14

**UNREPROVEABLE**
and unblameable and *u* in his sight ....... Col 1:22

**UNRIGHTEOUS**
the wicked to be an *u* witness ................. Ex 23:1
riseth up against me as the *u* ................. Job 27:7
wicked, out of the hand of the *u* ............. Ps 71:4
unto them that decree *u* decrees.............. Is 10:1
way, and the *u* man his thoughts............. Is 55:7
not been faithful in the *u* mammon ......... Lk 16:11
Is God *u* who taketh vengeance.............. Rom 3:5
Know ye not that the *u* shall not.......... 1Cor 6:9
For God is not *u* to forget your ............ Heb 6:10

**UNRIGHTEOUSLY**
do such things, and all that do *u* ....... Deut 25:16

**UNRIGHTEOUSNESS**
Ye shall do no *u* in judgment............... Lev 19:15
Ye shall do no *u* in judgment............... Lev 19:35
my rock, and there is no *u* in him.......... Ps 92:15
him that buildeth his house by *u*.......... Jer 22:13
friends of the mammon of *u*...................... Lk 16:9
same is true, and no *u* is in him............... Jn 7:18
*u* of men, who hold the truth in.......... Rom 1:18
of men, who hold the truth in *u*.......... Rom 1:18
Being filled with all *u*, .......................... Rom 1:29
do not obey the truth, but obey *u*.......... Rom 2:8
But if our *u* commend the...................... Rom 3:5
as instruments of *u* unto sin................. Rom 6:13
Is there *u* with God ................................ Rom 9:14
hath righteousness with *u*................... 2Cor 6:14
of *u* in them that perish ......................... 2Th 2:10
the truth, but had pleasure in *u* ........... 2Th 2:12
For I will be merciful to their *u*............ Heb 8:12
And shall receive the reward of *u*......... 2Pet 2:13
Bosor, who loved the wages of *u* ........... 2Pet 2:15
sins, and to cleanse us from all *u* ............ 1Jn 1:9
All *u* is sin ............................................... 1Jn 5:17

**UNRIPE**
shake off his *u* grape as the vine.......... Job 15:33

**UNRULY**
brethren, warn them that are *u*............. 1Th 5:14
children not accused of riot or *u* ............ Titus 1:6
For there are many *u* and vain ........... Titus 1:10
it is an *u* evil, full of deadly ........................ Jas 3:8

**UNSATIABLE**
Assyrians, because thou wast *u*........... Eze 16:28

**UNSAVOURY**
froward thou wilt shew thyself *u* ......... 2Sa 22:27
Can that which is *u* be eaten..................... Job 6:6

**UNSEARCHABLE**
Which doeth great things and *u* ................. Job 5:9
and his greatness is *u* ........................... Ps 145:3
depth, and the heart of kings is *u* ....... Prov 25:3
how *u* are his judgments, and his ...... Rom 11:33
Gentiles the *u* riches of Christ.................. Eph 3:8

**UNSEEMLY**
with men working that which is *u*....... Rom 1:27
Doth not behave itself *u*, seeketh ........ 1Cor 13:5

**UNSHOD**
Withhold thy foot from being *u*............... Jer 2:25

**UNSKILFUL**
is *u* in the word of righteousness........... Heb 5:13

**UNSPEAKABLE**
Thanks be unto God for his *u* gift ....... 2Cor 9:15
into paradise, and heard *u* words......... 2Cor 12:4
believing, ye rejoice with joy *u* ............... 1Pet 1:8

**UNSPOTTED**
to keep himself *u* from the world........... Jas 1:27

**UNSTABLE**
*U* as water, thou shalt not excel........... Gen 49:4
minded man is *u* in all his ways ................ Jas 1:8
beguiling *u* souls ................................... 2Pet 2:14
*u* wrest, as they do also the .................. 2Pet 3:16

**UNSTOPPED**
the ears of the deaf shall be *u* .................... Is 35:5

**UNTAKEN**
day remaineth the same vail *u*.............. 2Cor 3:14

**UNTEMPERED**
others daubed it with *u* morter............. Eze 13:10
them which daub it with *u* morter....... Eze 13:11
that ye have daubed with *u* morter..... Eze 13:14
that have daubed it with *u* morter....... Eze 13:15
have daubed them with *u* morter......... Eze 22:28

**UNTHANKFUL**
for he is kind unto the *u* ............................ Lk 6:35
disobedient to parents, *u* .............................. 2Ti 3:2

**UNTIL**
continually *u* the tenth month................. Gen 8:5
*u* the waters were dried up from ............. Gen 8:7
*u* they have done drinking..................... Gen 24:19
*u* I have told mine errand ..................... Gen 24:33
grew *u* he became very great................. Gen 26:13
*u* thy brother's fury turn away ............ Gen 27:44
*U* thy brother's anger turn away......... Gen 27:45
*u* I have done that which I have......... Gen 28:15
*u* all the flocks be gathered...................... Gen 29:8
with Laban, and stayed there *u* now.... Gen 32:4
him *u* the breaking of the day ............ Gen 32:24
*u* he came near to his brother................ Gen 33:3
*u* I come unto my lord unto Seir......... Gen 33:14
held his peace *u* they were come.......... Gen 34:5
by her, *u* his lord came home............... Gen 39:16
very much, *u* he left numbering .......... Gen 41:49
cattle from our youth even *u* now...... Gen 46:34
between his feet, *u* Shiloh come......... Gen 49:10
the foundation thereof even *u* now......... Ex 9:18
serve the LORD, *u* we come thither....... Ex 10:26
ye shall keep it up *u* the.......................... Ex 12:6
of it remain *u* the morning ................... Ex 12:10
that which remaineth of it *u* the........... Ex 12:10
the first day *u* the seventh day............ Ex 12:15
*u* the one and twentieth day of the....... Ex 12:18
door of his house *u* the morning........... Ex 12:22
of them left of it *u* the morning .......... Ex 16:20
for you to be kept *u* the morning .......... Ex 16:23
*u* they came to a land inhabited............ Ex 16:35
*u* they came unto the borders of............ Ex 16:35
his hands were steady *u* the going ........ Ex 17:12
my sacrifice remain *u* the morning........ Ex 23:18
*u* thou be increased, and inherit............ Ex 23:30
for us, *u* we come again unto you ......... Ex 24:14
*u* he was gone into the tabernacle........... Ex 33:8
took the vail off, *u* he came out ............. Ex 34:34
*u* he went in to speak with him ........... Ex 34:35
not leave any of it *u* the morning ......... Lev 7:15
*u* the days of your consecration ............. Lev 8:33
them shall be unclean *u* the even ........ Lev 11:24
clothes, and be unclean *u* the even ..... Lev 11:25
shall be unclean *u* the even.................. Lev 11:27
clothes, and be unclean *u* the even ..... Lev 11:28
dead, shall be unclean *u* the even ........ Lev 11:31
and it shall be unclean *u* the even....... Lev 11:32
shall be unclean *u* the even.................. Lev 11:39
clothes, and be unclean *u* the even ..... Lev 11:40
clothes, and be unclean *u* the even ..... Lev 11:40
*u* the days of her purifying be............... Lev 12:4
up shall be unclean *u* the even............. Lev 14:46
water, and be unclean *u* the even............ Lev 15:5
water, and be unclean *u* the even............ Lev 15:6
water, and be unclean *u* the even............ Lev 15:7
water, and be unclean *u* the even............ Lev 15:8
him shall be unclean *u* the even........... Lev 15:10
water, and be unclean *u* the even.......... Lev 15:10
water, and be unclean *u* the even.......... Lev 15:11
water, and be unclean *u* the even.......... Lev 15:16
water, and be unclean *u* the even.......... Lev 15:17
water, and be unclean *u* the even.......... Lev 15:18
her shall be unclean *u* the even............ Lev 15:19
water, and be unclean *u* the even.......... Lev 15:21
water, and be unclean *u* the even.......... Lev 15:22
he shall be unclean *u* the even ............ Lev 15:23
water, and be unclean *u* the even.......... Lev 15:27
*u* he come out, and have made an......... Lev 16:17
water, and be unclean *u* the even.......... Lev 17:15
if ought remain *u* the third day.............. Lev 19:6
with thee all night *u* the morning........ Lev 19:13
of the holy things, *u* he be clean........... Lev 22:4
any such shall be unclean *u* even .......... Lev 22:6
leave none of it *u* the morrow .............. Lev 22:30
*u* the selfsame day that ye have........... Lev 23:14
yet of old fruit *u* the ninth year .......... Lev 25:22
*u* her fruits come in ye shall eat........... Lev 25:22
bought it *u* the year of jubile ............... Lev 25:28
upward even *u* fifty years old, ................ Num 4:3
upward *u* fifty years old shalt.............. Num 4:23
*u* the days be fulfilled, in the ................ Num 6:5
appearance of fire, *u* the morning........ Num 9:15
*u* it come out at your nostrils, ........... Num 11:20
people, from Egypt even *u* now.......... Num 14:19
*u* your carcases be wasted in the....... Num 14:33
shall be unclean *u* the even................. Num 19:7
and shall be unclean *u* the even ........... Num 19:8
clothes, and be unclean *u* the even ... Num 19:10
shall be unclean *u* even ...................... Num 19:21
it shall be unclean *u* even ................... Num 19:22
*u* we have passed thy borders.............. Num 20:17
way, *u* we be past thy borders............. Num 21:22
*u* there was none left him alive........... Num 21:35
not lie down *u* he eat of the prey ...... Num 23:24
*u* Asshur shall carry thee away ......... Num 24:22
*u* all the generation, that had ........... Num 32:13
*u* we have brought them unto their.. Num 32:17
*u* the children of Israel have ............. Num 32:18
*u* he hath driven out his enemies....... Num 32:21
die not, *u* he stand before the............ Num 35:12
in the city of his refuge *u* the ............ Num 35:28
*u* the death of the priest.................... Num 35:32
*u* ye came into this place ...................... Deut 1:31
*u* we were come over the brook........... Deut 2:14
*u* all the generation of the men........... Deut 2:14
the host, *u* they were consumed .......... Deut 2:15
*u* I shall pass over Jordan into ............ Deut 2:29
we smote him *u* none was left to........... Deut 3:3
*U* the LORD have given rest unto......... Deut 3:20
*u* they also possess the land................ Deut 3:20
*u* they that are left, and hide.............. Deut 7:20
destruction, *u* they be destroyed.......... Deut 7:23
*u* thou have destroyed them ............... Deut 7:24
*u* ye came unto this place, ye ................. Deut 9:7
even *u* it was as small as dust .............. Deut 9:21
*u* ye came into this place .................... Deut 11:5
remain all night *u* the morning ............ Deut 16:4
war with thee, *u* it be subdued........... Deut 20:20
it shall be with thee *u* thy .................... Deut 22:2
*u* thou be destroyed.............................. Deut 28:20
and *u* thou perish quickly..................... Deut 28:20
*u* he have consumed thee from off.... Deut 28:21
shall pursue thee *u* thou perish .......... Deut 28:22
upon thee, *u* thou be destroyed........... Deut 28:24
neck, *u* he have destroyed thee.......... Deut 28:48
of thy land, *u* thou be destroyed......... Deut 28:51
sheep, *u* he have destroyed thee ........ Deut 28:51
*u* thy high and fenced walls come..... Deut 28:52
upon thee, *u* thou be destroyed........... Deut 28:61
in a book, *u* they were finished, ......... Deut 31:24
of this song, *u* they were ended ......... Deut 31:30
*U* the LORD have given your.................. Josh 1:15
*u* the pursuers be returned.................... Josh 2:16
*u* the pursuers were returned ............... Josh 2:22
*u* all the people were passed ................ Josh 3:17
*u* every thing was finished that............. Josh 4:10
*u* ye were passed over, as the............... Josh 4:23
before us, *u* we were gone over ........... Josh 4:23
*u* we were passed over, that their........... Josh 5:1
*u* the day I bid you shout ..................... Josh 6:10
ark of the LORD *u* the eventide .............. Josh 7:6
*u* ye take away the accursed thing ...... Josh 7:13
*u* they were consumed, that all............. Josh 8:24
*u* he had utterly destroyed all............... Josh 8:26
Ai he hanged on a tree *u* eventide ....... Josh 8:29
stayed, *u* the people had avenged....... Josh 10:13
upon the trees *u* the evening .............. Josh 10:26
which remain *u* this very day............... Josh 10:27
*u* he had left him none remaining ...... Josh 10:33
*u* they left them none remaining ........... Josh 11:8
*u* they had destroyed them, ................ Josh 11:14
among the Israelites *u* this day........... Josh 13:13
that city, *u* he stand before the............. Josh 20:6
*u* the death of the high priest................ Josh 20:6
of blood, *u* he stood before the............. Josh 20:9
we are not cleansed *u* this day........... Josh 22:17
*u* ye perish from off this good ............. Josh 23:13
*u* he have destroyed you from off........ Josh 23:15
*u* they had destroyed Jabin king .......... Judg 4:24
*u* that I Deborah arose, that I................. Judg 5:7
*u* I come unto thee, and bring ............... Judg 6:18
I will tarry *u* thou come again.............. Judg 6:18
*u* we shall have made ready a kid...... Judg 13:15
priests to the tribe of Dan *u* the.......... Judg 18:30
And they tarried *u* afternoon ................... Judg 19:8
her all the night *u* the morning.......... Judg 19:25
up and wept before the LORD *u* even Judg 20:23
LORD, and fasted that day *u* even .... Judg 20:26
So they two went *u* they came to ....... Ruth 1:19
even from the morning *u* now................ Ruth 2:7
she gleaned in the field *u* even............ Ruth 2:17
*u* they have ended all my harvest........ Ruth 2:21
*u* he shall have done eating and ........... Ruth 3:3
lie down *u* the morning........................ Ruth 3:13
she lay at his feet *u* the morning......... Ruth 3:14
*u* thou know how the matter will........ Ruth 3:18
*u* he have finished the thing this......... Ruth 3:18
I will not go up *u* the child be .............. 1Sa 1:22
tarry *u* thou have weaned him................ 1Sa 1:23
her son suck *u* she weaned him.............. 1Sa 1:23
Samuel lay *u* the morning, and.............. 1Sa 3:15
*u* they came under Beth-car .................. 1Sa 7:11
the people will not eat *u* he come......... 1Sa 9:13
slew the Ammonites *u* the heat of...... 1Sa 11:11
unto us, Tarry *u* we come to you.......... 1Sa 14:9
that eateth any food *u* evening............. 1Sa 14:24
spoil them *u* the morning light, ........... 1Sa 14:36
Havilah *u* thou comest to Shur............... 1Sa 15:7
against them *u* they be consumed ....... 1Sa 15:18
see Saul *u* the day of his death ............ 1Sa 15:35
*u* thou come to the valley, and to........ 1Sa 17:52
heed to thyself *u* the morning.................. 1Sa 19:2
*u* he came to Naioth in Ramah............. 1Sa 19:23
with another, *u* David exceeded ........... 1Sa 20:41
less or more, *u* the morning light ......... 1Sa 25:36
*u* they had no more power to weep....... 1Sa 30:4
and wept, and fasted *u* even .................. 2Sa 1:12
were sojourners there *u* this day............. 2Sa 4:3
from Geba *u* thou come to Gazer........... 2Sa 5:25
Tarry at Jericho *u* your beards be.......... 2Sa 10:5
*u* all the people had done passing ........ 2Sa 15:24
*u* there come word from you to............ 2Sa 15:28
*u* there be not one small stone............. 2Sa 17:13
befell thee from thy youth *u* now .......... 2Sa 19:7
*u* the day he came again in peace........ 2Sa 19:24
from the beginning of harvest *u*........... 2Sa 21:10

turned not again *u* I had consumed ... 2Sa 22:38
Philistines *u* his hand was weary ... 2Sa 23:10
*u* he had made an end of building ... 1Kin 3:1
name of the LORD, *u* those days ... 1Kin 3:2
*u* the LORD put them under the ... 1Kin 5:3
*u* he had finished all the house ... 1Kin 6:22
*u* I came, and mine eyes had seen ... 1Kin 10:7
*u* he had cut off every male in ... 1Kin 11:16
was in Egypt *u* the death of ... 1Kin 11:40
*u* he had destroyed him, according ... 1Kin 15:29
*u* the day that the LORD sendeth ... 1Kin 17:14
of Baal from morning even *u* noon ... 1Kin 18:26
they prophesied *u* the time of the ... 1Kin 18:29
*u* thou have consumed them ... 1Kin 22:11
of affliction, *u* I come in peace ... 1Kin 22:27
*u* an ass's head was sold for ... 2Kin 6:25
another, Why sit we here *u* we die ... 2Kin 7:3
she left the land, even *u* now ... 2Kin 8:6
stedfastly, *u* he was ashamed ... 2Kin 8:11
in of the gate *u* the morning ... 2Kin 10:8
*u* he left him none remaining ... 2Kin 10:11
*u* he had cast them out of his ... 2Kin 17:20
*U* the LORD removed Israel out of ... 2Kin 17:23
*U* I come and take you away to a ... 2Kin 18:32
*u* he had cast them out from his ... 2Kin 24:20
in their steads *u* the captivity ... 1Chr 5:22
*u* Solomon had built the house of ... 1Chr 6:32
*u* it was a great host, like the ... 1Chr 12:22
Tarry at Jericho *u* your beards be ... 1Chr 19:5
*u* thou hast finished all the work ... 1Chr 28:20
make to pay tribute *u* this day ... 2Chr 8:8
of the LORD, and *u* it was finished ... 2Chr 8:16
*u* I came, and mine eyes had seen ... 2Chr 9:6
*u* his disease was exceeding great ... 2Chr 16:12
push Syria *u* they be consumed ... 2Chr 18:10
affliction, *u* I return in peace ... 2Chr 18:26
against the Syrians *u* the even ... 2Chr 18:34
*u* thy bowels fall out by reason ... 2Chr 21:15
the chest, *u* they had made an end ... 2Chr 24:10
all this continued *u* the burnt ... 2Chr 29:28
ended, and *u* the other priests had ... 2Chr 29:34
*u* they had utterly destroyed them ... 2Chr 31:1
offerings and the fat *u* night ... 2Chr 35:14
*u* the wrath of the LORD arose ... 2Chr 36:16
his sons *u* the reign of the ... 2Chr 36:20
*u* the land had enjoyed her ... 2Chr 36:21
even *u* the reign of Darius king ... Ezr 4:5
*u* another commandment shall be ... Ezr 4:21
since that time even *u* now hath ... Ezr 5:16
*u* ye weigh them before the chief ... Ezr 8:29
I sat astonied *u* the evening ... Ezr 9:4
*u* the fierce wrath of our God for ... Ezr 10:14
be opened *u* the sun be hot ... Neh 7:3
gate from the morning *u* midday ... Neh 8:3
even *u* the days of Johanan the ... Neh 12:23
*u* thy wrath be past, that thou ... Job 14:13
*u* the day and night come to an end ... Job 26:10
*u* his iniquity be found to be ... Ps 36:2
*u* these calamities be overpast ... Ps 57:1
*u* I have shewed thy strength unto ... Ps 71:18
*U* I went into the sanctuary of ... Ps 73:17
*u* the pit be digged for the ... Ps 94:13
and to his labour *u* the evening ... Ps 104:23
*U* the time that his word came ... Ps 105:19
*u* I make thine enemies thy ... Ps 110:1
*u* he see his desire upon his ... Ps 112:8
*u* that he have mercy upon us ... Ps 123:2
*U* I find out a place for the LORD ... Ps 132:5
our fill of love *u* the morning ... Prov 7:18
*U* the day break, and the shadows ... Song 2:17
*u* I had brought him into my ... Song 3:4
*U* the day break, and the shadows ... Song 4:6
nor awake my love, *u* he please ... Song 8:4
that continue *u* night, till wine ... Is 5:11
*U* the cities be wasted without ... Is 6:11
*u* the indignation be overpast ... Is 26:20
*U* the spirit be poured upon us ... Is 32:15
*U* I come and take you away to a ... Is 36:17
have laid up in store *u* this day ... Is 39:6
*u* the righteousness thereof go ... Is 62:1
*u* he have executed, and till he ... Jer 23:20
*u* the very time of his land come ... Jer 27:7
*u* I have consumed them by his ... Jer 27:8
there shall they be *u* the day ... Jer 27:22
*u* he have done it ... Jer 30:24
*u* he have performed the intents ... Jer 30:24
there shall he be *u* I visit him ... Jer 32:5
*u* all the roll was consumed in ... Jer 36:23
*u* all the bread in the city were ... Jer 37:21
*u* the day that Jerusalem was ... Jer 38:28
*u* there be an end of them ... Jer 44:27
every day a portion *u* the day of ... Jer 52:34
*u* he come whose right it is ... Eze 21:27
*u* he came to me in the morning ... Eze 33:22
shall not be shut *u* the evening ... Eze 46:2
*u* thou know that the most High ... Dan 4:32
*U* the Ancient of days came, and ... Dan 7:22
be given into his hand *u* a time ... Dan 7:25
even *u* the consummation, and that ... Dan 9:27
the dough, *u* it be leavened ... Hos 7:4
*u* the time that she which ... Mic 5:3
*u* he plead my cause, and execute ... Mic 7:9
*u* the day that I rise up to the ... Zeph 3:8
from David *u* the carrying away ... Mt 1:17
be thou there *u* I bring thee word ... Mt 2:13
was there *u* the death of Herod ... Mt 2:15
*u* now the kingdom of heaven ... Mt 11:12
and the law prophesied *u* John ... Mt 11:13
it would have remained *u* this day ... Mt 11:23
both grow together *u* the harvest ... Mt 13:30
*u* the Son of man be risen again ... Mt 17:9
say not unto thee, *U* seven times ... Mt 18:22
but, *U* seventy times seven ... Mt 18:22
*u* the day that Noe entered into ... Mt 24:38
knew not *u* the flood came, and ... Mt 24:39
*u* that day when I drink it new ... Mt 26:29
be made sure *u* the third day ... Mt 27:64
among the Jews *u* this day ... Mt 28:15
*u* that day that I drink it new in ... Mk 14:25
the whole land *u* the ninth hour ... Mk 15:33
*u* the day that these things shall ... Lk 1:20
*u* the time come when ye shall say ... Lk 13:35
that which is lost, *u* he find it ... Lk 15:4
law and the prophets were *u* John ... Lk 16:16
*u* the day that Noe entered into ... Lk 17:27
*u* the times of the Gentiles be ... Lk 21:24
*u* it be fulfilled in the kingdom ... Lk 22:16
*u* the kingdom of God shall come ... Lk 22:18
all the earth *u* the ninth hour ... Lk 23:44
*u* ye be endued with power from on ... Lk 24:49
hast kept the good wine *u* now ... Jn 2:10
*u* they called the parents of him ... Jn 9:18
*U* the day in which he was taken ... Acts 1:2
*U* I make thy foes thy footstool ... Acts 2:35
Whom the heaven must receive *u* ... Acts 3:21
ago I was fasting *u* this hour ... Acts 10:30
fifty years, *u* Samuel the prophet ... Acts 13:20
continued his speech *u* midnight ... Acts 20:7
*u* that an offering should be ... Acts 21:26
conscience before God *u* this day ... Acts 23:1
eat nothing *u* we have slain Paul ... Acts 23:14
(For *u* the law sin was in the ... Rom 5:13
travaileth in pain together *u* now ... Rom 8:22
*u* the fulness of the Gentiles be ... Rom 11:25
*u* the Lord come, who both will ... 1Cor 4:5
will tarry at Ephesus *u* Pentecost ... 1Cor 16:8
for *u* this day remaineth the same ... 2Cor 3:14
governors *u* the time appointed of ... Gal 4:2
again *u* Christ be formed in you ... Gal 4:19
the earnest of our inheritance *u* ... Eph 1:14
gospel from the first day *u* now ... Phil 1:5
it *u* the day of Jesus Christ ... Phil 1:6
*u* he be taken out of the way ... 2Th 2:7
*u* the appearing of our Lord Jesus ... 1Ti 6:14
*u* I make thine enemies thy ... Heb 1:13
imposed on them *u* the time of ... Heb 9:10
*u* he receive the early and latter ... Jas 5:7
*u* the day dawn, and the day star ... 2Pet 1:19
is in darkness even *u* now ... 1Jn 2:9
*u* their fellowservants also and ... Rev 6:11
*u* the words of God shall be ... Rev 17:17
again *u* the thousand years were ... Rev 20:5

**UNTIMELY**
Or as an hidden *u* birth I had not ... Job 3:16
like the *u* birth of a woman, that ... Ps 58:8
that an *u* birth is better than he ... Eccl 6:3
as a fig tree casteth her *u* figs ... Rev 6:13

**UNTO** See PREFACE.

**UNTOWARD**
yourselves from this *u* generation ... Acts 2:40

**UNWALLED**
beside *u* towns a great many ... Deut 3:5
that dwelt in the *u* towns ... Est 9:19
go up to the land of *u* villages ... Eze 38:11

**UNWASHEN**
but to eat with *u* hands defileth ... Mt 15:20
defiled, that is to say, with *u* ... Mk 7:2
but eat bread with *u* hands ... Mk 7:5

**UNWEIGHED**
And Solomon left all the vessels *u* ... 1Kin 7:47

**UNWISE**
the LORD, O foolish people and *u* ... Deut 32:6
he is an *u* son ... Hos 13:13
both to the wise, and to the *u* ... Rom 1:14
Wherefore be ye not *u*, but ... Eph 5:17

**UNWITTINGLY**
if a man eat of the holy thing *u* ... Lev 22:14
unawares and *u* may flee thither ... Josh 20:3
because he smote his neighbour *u* ... Josh 20:5

**UNWORTHILY**
and drink this cup of the Lord, *u* ... 1Cor 11:27
For he that eateth and drinketh *u* ... 1Cor 11:29

**UNWORTHY**
judge yourselves *u* of everlasting ... Acts 13:46
are ye *u* to judge the smallest ... 1Cor 6:2

**UP** See PREFACE.

**UPBRAID**
Zalmunna, with whom ye did *u* me ... Judg 8:15
Then began he to *u* the cities ... Mt 11:20

**UPBRAIDED**
*u* them with their unbelief and ... Mk 16:14

**UPBRAIDETH**
to all men liberally, and *u* not ... Jas 1:5

**UPHARSIN** (*u-far'-sin*) See PERES. *Part of the 'handwriting on the wall.'*
*MENE, MENE, TEKEL, U* ... Dan 5:25

**UPHAZ** (*u'-faz*) *A place in southern Arabia.*
from Tarshish, and gold from *U* ... Jer 10:9
were girded with fine gold of *U* ... Dan 10:5

**UPHELD**
and my fury, it *u* me ... Is 63:5

**UPHOLD**
*u* me with thy free spirit ... Ps 51:12
Lord is with them that *u* my soul ... Ps 54:4
*U* me according unto thy word, ... Ps 119:116
but honour shall *u* the humble in ... Prov 29:23
I will *u* thee with the right hand ... Is 41:10
Behold my servant, whom I *u* ... Is 42:1
wondered that there was none to *u* ... Is 63:5
They also that *u* Egypt shall fall ... Eze 30:6

**UPHOLDEN**
Thy words have *u* him that was ... Job 4:4
and his throne is *u* by mercy ... Prov 20:28

**UPHOLDEST**
thou *u* me in mine integrity, and ... Ps 41:12

**UPHOLDETH**
but the LORD *u* the righteous ... Ps 37:17
for the LORD *u* him with his hand ... Ps 37:24
thy right hand *u* me ... Ps 63:8
The LORD *u* all that fall, and ... Ps 145:14

**UPHOLDING**
*u* all things by the word of his ... Heb 1:3

**UPON** See PREFACE.

**UPPER**
on the *u* door post of the houses, ... Ex 12:7
put a covering upon his *u* lip ... Lev 13:45
or the *u* millstone to pledge ... Deut 24:6
And he gave her the *u* springs ... Josh 15:19
unto Beth-horon the *u* ... Josh 16:5
And Caleb gave her the *u* springs ... Judg 1:15
his *u* chamber that was in Samaria ... 2Kin 1:2
by the conduit of the *u* pool ... 2Kin 18:17
the top of the *u* chamber of Ahaz ... 2Kin 23:12
Beth-horon the nether, and the *u* ... 1Chr 7:24
of the *u* chambers thereof, and of ... 1Chr 28:11
he overlaid the *u* chambers with ... 2Chr 3:9
Also he built Beth-horon the *u* ... 2Chr 8:5
the *u* watercourse of Gihon ... 2Chr 32:30
the *u* pool in the highway of the ... Is 7:3
the *u* pool in the highway of the ... Is 36:2
Now the *u* chambers were shorter ... Eze 42:5
lodge in the *u* lintels of it ... Zeph 2:14
shew you a large *u* room furnished ... Mk 14:15
shew you a large *u* room furnished ... Lk 22:12
in, they went up into an *u* room ... Acts 1:13
they laid her in an *u* chamber ... Acts 9:37
brought him into the *u* chamber ... Acts 9:39
the *u* coasts came to Ephesus ... Acts 19:1
were many lights in the *u* chamber ... Acts 20:8

**UPPERMOST**
in the *u* basket there was of all ... Gen 40:17
berries in the top of the *u* bough ... Is 17:6
an *u* branch, which they left ... Is 17:9
love the *u* rooms at feasts, and ... Mt 23:6
and the *u* rooms at feasts ... Mk 12:39
for ye love the *u* seats in the ... Lk 11:43

**UPRIGHT**
my sheaf arose, and also stood *u* ... Gen 37:7
the floods stood *u* as an heap ... Ex 15:8
of your yoke, and made you go *u* ... Lev 26:13
the LORD liveth, thou hast been *u* ... 1Sa 29:6
I was also *u* before him, and have ... 2Sa 22:24
with the *u* man thou wilt shew ... 2Sa 22:26
man thou wilt shew thyself *u* ... 2Sa 22:26
for the Levites were more *u* in ... 2Chr 29:34
and that man was perfect and *u* ... Job 1:1
an *u* man, one that feareth God, ... Job 1:8
an *u* man, one that feareth God, ... Job 2:3
If thou wert pure and *u* ... Job 8:6
the just *u* man is laughed to ... Job 12:4
*U* men shall be astonied at this, ... Job 17:8
God, which saveth the *u* in heart ... Ps 7:10
privily shoot at the *u* in heart ... Ps 11:2
his countenance doth behold the *u* ... Ps 11:7
I was also *u* before him, and I ... Ps 18:23
with an *u* man thou wilt shew ... Ps 18:25
man thou wilt shew thyself *u* ... Ps 18:25
then shall I be *u*, and I shall be ... Ps 19:13
but we are risen, and stand *u* ... Ps 20:8
Good and *u* is the LORD ... Ps 25:8
joy, all ye that are *u* in heart ... Ps 32:11
for praise is comely for the *u* ... Ps 33:1
righteousness to the *u* in heart ... Ps 36:10
slay such as be of *u* conversation ... Ps 37:14
LORD knoweth the days of the *u* ... Ps 37:18
the perfect man, and behold the *u* ... Ps 37:37
the *u* shall have dominion over ... Ps 49:14
all the *u* in heart shall glory ... Ps 64:10
To shew that the LORD is *u* ... Ps 92:15
all the *u* in heart shall follow ... Ps 94:15
and gladness for the *u* in heart ... Ps 97:11
heart, in the assembly of the *u* ... Ps 111:1
of the *u* shall be blessed ... Ps 112:2
Unto the *u* there ariseth light in ... Ps 112:4
O LORD, and *u* are thy judgments ... Ps 119:137
them that are *u* in their hearts ... Ps 125:4
the *u* shall dwell in thy presence ... Ps 140:13
For the *u* shall dwell in the land ... Prov 2:21
of the LORD is strength to the *u* ... Prov 10:29
of the *u* shall guide them ... Prov 11:3
of the *u* shall deliver them ... Prov 11:6
of the *u* the city is exalted ... Prov 11:11
but such as are *u* in their way ... Prov 11:20
mouth of the *u* shall deliver them ... Prov 12:6

keepeth him that is *u* in the way Prov 13:6
of the *u* shall flourish Prov 14:11
prayer of the *u* is his delight Prov 15:8
The highway of the *u* is to depart Prov 16:17
and the transgressor for the *u* Prov 21:18
but as for the *u*, he directeth Prov 21:29
but the *u* shall have good things Prov 28:10
The bloodthirsty hate the *u* Prov 29:10
he that is *u* in the way is Prov 29:27
I found, that God hath made man *u* Eccl 7:29
and that which was written was *u* Eccl 12:10
the *u* love thee Song 1:4
thou, most *u*, dost weigh the path Is 26:7
They are *u* as the palm tree, but Jer 10:5
but he touched me, and set me *u* Dan 8:18
I speak unto thee, and stand *u* Dan 10:11
whole kingdom, and *u* ones with him Dan 11:17
and there is none *u* among men Mic 7:2
the most *u* is sharper than a Mic 7:4
is lifted up is not *u* in him Hab 2:4
a loud voice, Stand *u* on thy feet Acts 14:10

**UPRIGHTLY**
He that walketh *u*, and worketh Ps 15:2
do ye judge *u*, O ye sons of men Ps 58:1
the congregation I will judge *u* Ps 75:2
he withhold from them that walk *u* Ps 84:11
is a buckler to them that walk *u* Prov 2:7
He that walketh *u* walketh surely Prov 10:9
a man of understanding walketh *u* Prov 15:21
Whoso walketh *u* shall be saved Prov 28:18
righteously, and speaketh *u* Is 33:15
and they abhor him that speaketh *u* Amos 5:10
do good to him that walketh *u* Mic 2:7
*u* according to the truth of the Gal 2:14

**UPRIGHTNESS**
or for the *u* of thine heart, dost Deut 9:5
and in *u* of heart with thee 1Kin 3:6
in integrity of heart, and in *u* 1Kin 9:4
the heart, and hast pleasure in *u* 1Chr 29:17
in the *u* of mine heart I have 1Chr 29:17
thy hope, and the *u* of thy ways Job 4:6
shall be of the *u* of my heart Job 33:3
thousand, to shew unto man his *u* Job 33:23
judgment to the people in *u* Ps 9:8
Let integrity and *u* preserve me Ps 25:21
ever, and are done in truth and *u* Ps 111:8
will praise thee with *u* of heart Ps 119:7
lead me into the land of *u* Ps 143:10
Who leave the paths of *u*, to walk Prov 2:13
walketh in his *u* feareth the LORD Prov 14:2
is the poor that walketh in his *u* Prov 28:6
The way of the just is *u* Is 26:7
in the land of *u* will he deal Is 26:10
beds, each one walking in his *u* Is 57:2

**UPRISING**
knowest my downsitting and mine *u* Ps 139:2

**UPROAR**
noise of the city being in an *u* 1Kin 1:41
there be an *u* among the people Mt 26:5
lest there be an *u* of the people Mk 14:2
and set all the city on an *u* Acts 17:5
in question for this day's *u* Acts 19:40
after the *u* was ceased, Paul Acts 20:1
that all Jerusalem was in an *u* Acts 21:31
before these days madest an *u* Acts 21:38

**UPSIDE**
wiping it, and turning it *u* down 2Kin 21:13
of the wicked he turneth *u* down Ps 146:9
it waste, and turneth it *u* down Is 24:1
*u* down shall be esteemed as the Is 29:16
world *u* down are come hither also Acts 17:6

**UPWARD**
Fifteen cubits *u* did the waters Gen 7:20
from twenty years old and *u* Ex 38:26
From twenty years old and *u* Num 1:3
names, from twenty years old and *u* Num 1:18
male from twenty years old and *u* Num 1:20
male from twenty years old and *u* Num 1:22
names, from twenty years old and *u* Num 1:24
names, from twenty years old and *u* Num 1:26
names, from twenty years old and *u* Num 1:28
names, from twenty years old and *u* Num 1:30
names, from twenty years old and *u* Num 1:32
names, from twenty years old and *u* Num 1:34
names, from twenty years old and *u* Num 1:36
names, from twenty years old and *u* Num 1:38
names, from twenty years old and *u* Num 1:40
names, from twenty years old and *u* Num 1:42
from twenty years old and *u* Num 1:45
old and *u* shalt thou number them Num 3:15
the males, from a month old and *u* Num 3:22
the males, from a month old and *u* Num 3:28
the males, from a month old and *u* Num 3:34
the males from a month old and *u* Num 3:39
of Israel from a month old and *u* Num 3:40
of names, from a month old and *u* Num 3:43
*u* even until fifty years old, all Num 4:3
*u* until fifty years old shalt Num 4:23
*u* even unto fifty years old shalt Num 4:30
*u* even unto fifty years old, Num 4:35
*u* even unto fifty years old, Num 4:39
*u* even unto fifty years old, Num 4:43
*u* even unto fifty years old, Num 4:47
*u* they shall go in to wait upon Num 8:24
from twenty years old and *u* Num 14:29
from twenty years old and *u* Num 26:2
from twenty years old and *u* Num 26:4
all males from a month old and *u* Num 26:62
Egypt, from twenty years old and *u* Num 32:11
to Akrabbim, from the rock, and *u* Judg 1:36
*u* he was higher than any of the 1Sa 9:2
people from his shoulders and *u* 1Sa 10:23
were able to put on armour, and *u* 2Kin 3:21
root downward, and bear fruit *u* 2Kin 19:30
from the age of thirty years and *u* 1Chr 23:3
from the age of twenty years and *u* 1Chr 23:24
males, from three years old and *u* 2Chr 31:16
from twenty years old and *u* 2Chr 31:17
from twenty years old and *u* Ezr 3:8
unto trouble, as the sparks fly *u* Job 5:7
the spirit of man that goeth *u* Eccl 3:21
king and their God, and look *u* Is 8:21
root downward, and bear fruit *u* Is 37:31
mine eyes fail with looking *u* Is 38:14
and their wings were stretched *u* Eze 1:11
appearance of his loins even *u* Eze 1:27
and from his loins even *u*, as the Eze 8:2
still *u* to the side chambers Eze 41:7
still *u* round about the house Eze 41:7
breadth of the house was still *u* Eze 41:7
altar and *u* shall be four horns Eze 43:15
you, consider from this day and *u* Hag 2:15
Consider now from this day and *u* Hag 2:18

**UR** (*ur*)
*1. A district in Mesopotamia.*
nativity, in *U* of the Chaldees Gen 11:28
with them from *U* of the Chaldees Gen 11:31
thee out of *U* of the Chaldees Gen 15:7
forth out of *U* of the Chaldees Neh 9:7
*2. Father of Eliphal.*
Hararite, Eliphal the son of *U* 1Chr 11:35

**URBANE** (*ur'-bane*) *A Christian in Rome.*
Salute *U*, our helper in Christ, Rom 16:9

**URBANUS** See URBANE.

**URGE**
began to *u* him vehemently Lk 11:53

**URGED**
And he *u* him, and he took it Gen 33:11
*u* him, so that his soul was vexed Judg 16:16
depart, his father in law *u* him Judg 19:7
when they *u* him till he was 2Kin 2:17
And he *u* him to take it 2Kin 5:16
he *u* him, and bound two talents of 2Kin 5:23

**URGENT**
Egyptians were *u* upon the people Ex 12:33
the king's commandment was *u* Dan 3:22

**URI** (*u'-ri*)
*1. Father of Bezaleel.*
by name Bezaleel the son of *U* Ex 31:2
by name Bezaleel the son of *U* Ex 35:30
And Bezaleel the son of *U*, the son Ex 38:22
And Hur begat *U* 1Chr 2:20
and *U* begat Bezaleel 1Chr 2:20
altar, that Bezaleel the son of *U* 2Chr 1:5
*2. Father of Geber.*
Geber the son of *U* was in the 1Kin 4:19
Shallum, and Telem, and *U* Ezr 10:24

**URIAH** (*u-ri'-ah*) See URIAH'S, URIAS, URIJAH.
*1. Husband of Bathsheba.*
Eliam, the wife of *U* the Hittite 2Sa 11:3
saying, Send me *U* the Hittite 2Sa 11:6
And Joab sent *U* to David 2Sa 11:6
when *U* was come unto him, David 2Sa 11:7
And David said to *U*, Go down to 2Sa 11:8
*U* departed out of the king's 2Sa 11:8
But *U* slept at the door of the 2Sa 11:9
*U* went not down unto his house, 2Sa 11:10
unto his house, David said unto *U* 2Sa 11:10
*U* said unto David, The ark, and 2Sa 11:11
And David said to *U*, Tarry here to 2Sa 11:12
So *U* abode in Jerusalem that day, 2Sa 11:12
Joab, and sent it by the hand of *U* 2Sa 11:14
Set ye *U* in the forefront of the 2Sa 11:15
that he assigned *U* unto a place 2Sa 11:16
and *U* the Hittite died also 2Sa 11:17
Thy servant *U* the Hittite is dead 2Sa 11:21
thy servant *U* the Hittite is dead 2Sa 11:24
when the wife of *U* heard that 2Sa 11:26
heard that *U* her husband was dead 2Sa 11:26
thou hast killed *U* the Hittite 2Sa 12:9
hast taken the wife of *U* the 2Sa 12:10
*U* the Hittite 2Sa 23:39
in the matter of *U* the Hittite 1Kin 15:5
*U* the Hittite, Zabad the son of 1Chr 11:41
*2. A rebuilder of Jerusalem's wall.*
Meremoth the son of *U* the priest Ezr 8:33
*3. A priest who aided Isaiah.*
*U* the priest, and Zechariah the Is 8:2

**URIAH'S** (*u-ri'-ahz*) *Refers to Uriah 1.*
child that *U* wife bare unto David 2Sa 12:15

**URIAS** (*u-ri'-as*) *Greek form of Uriah 1.*
her that had been the wife of *U* Mt 1:6

**URIEL** (*u'-re-el*)
*1. Son of Tahath.*
*U* his son, Uzziah his son, and 1Chr 6:24
*U* the chief, and his brethren an 1Chr 15:5
and for the Levites, for *U* 1Chr 15:11
*2. Father of Micaiah.*
the daughter of *U* of Gibeah 2Chr 13:2

**URIJAH** (*u-ri'-jah*) See URIAH.
*1. A priest in Jerusalem.*
king Ahaz sent to *U* the priest 2Kin 16:10
*U* the priest built an altar 2Kin 16:11
so *U* the priest made it against 2Kin 16:11
king Ahaz commanded *U* the priest 2Kin 16:15
Thus did *U* the priest, according 2Kin 16:16
*2. A priest who rebuilt the wall.*
repaired Meremoth the son of *U* Neh 3:4
of *U* the son of Koz another piece Neh 3:21
*3. A priest who aided Ezra.*
and Shema, and Anaiah, and *U* Neh 8:4
*4. A prophet killed by Jehoiakim.*
LORD, *U* the son of Shemaiah of Jer 26:20
but when *U* heard it, he was Jer 26:21
they fetched forth *U* out of Egypt Jer 26:23

**URIM** (*u'-rim*) *A symbolic object in the High Priest's breastplate.*
the breastplate of judgment the *U* Ex 28:30
he put in the breastplate the *U* Lev 8:8
the judgment of *U* before the LORD Num 27:21
thy *U* be with thy holy one, whom Deut 33:8
not, neither by dreams, nor by *U* 1Sa 28:6
there stood up a priest with *U* Ezr 2:63
there stood up a priest with *U* Neh 7:65

**US** See PREFACE.

**USE**
may be used in any other *u* Lev 7:24
neither shall ye *u* enchantment Lev 19:26
that thou mayest *u* them for the Num 10:2
after which ye *u* to go a whoring Num 15:39
ought thereof for any unclean *u* Deut 26:14
of Judah the *u* of the bow 2Sa 1:18
could *u* both the right hand and 1Chr 12:2
according to the *u* of every 1Chr 28:15
that *u* their tongues, and say, He Jer 23:31
As yet they shall *u* this speech Jer 31:23
vain shalt thou *u* many medicines Jer 46:11
they shall no more *u* it as a Eze 12:23
shall *u* this proverb against thee Eze 16:44
that ye *u* this proverb concerning Eze 18:2
more to *u* this proverb in Israel Eze 18:3
of the two ways, to *u* divination Eze 21:21
for them which despitefully *u* you Mt 5:44
*u* not vain repetitions, as the Mt 6:7
for them which despitefully *u* you Lk 6:28
to *u* them despitefully, and to Acts 14:5
*u* into that which is against Rom 1:26
the natural *u* of the woman Rom 1:27
mayest be made free, *u* it rather 1Cor 7:21
they that *u* this world, as not 1Cor 7:31
thus minded, did I *u* lightness 2Cor 1:17
we *u* great plainness of speech 2Cor 3:12
present I should *u* sharpness 2Cor 13:10
only *u* not liberty for an Gal 5:13
is good to the *u* of edifying Eph 4:29
is good, if a man *u* it lawfully 1Ti 1:8
then let them *u* the office of a 1Ti 3:10
but *u* a little wine for thy 1Ti 5:23
and meet for the master's *u* 2Ti 2:21
even those who by reason of *u* Heb 5:14
*U* hospitality one to another 1Pet 4:9

**USED**
ox hath *u* to push in time past Ex 21:36
may be *u* in any other use Lev 7:24
for so *u* the young men to do Judg 14:10
whom he had *u* as his friend Judg 14:20
*u* divination and enchantments, and 2Kin 17:17
*u* enchantments, and dealt with 2Kin 21:6
times, and *u* enchantments, and *u* 2Chr 33:6
*u* witchcraft, and dealt with a 2Chr 33:6
A wild ass *u* to the wilderness, Jer 2:24
of the land have *u* oppression Eze 22:29
to thine envy which thou hast *u* Eze 35:11
*u* similitudes, by the ministry of Hos 12:10
and of the Pharisees *u* to fast Mk 2:18
in the same city *u* sorcery Acts 8:9
Many of them also which *u* curious Acts 19:19
they *u* helps, undergirding the Acts 27:17
their tongues they have *u* deceit Rom 3:13
we have not *u* this power 1Cor 9:12
But I have *u* none of these things 1Cor 9:15
at any time *u* we flattering words 1Th 2:5
For they that have *u* the office 1Ti 3:13
companions of them that were so *u* Heb 10:33

**USES**
good works for necessary *u* Titus 3:14

**USEST**
as thou *u* to do unto those that Ps 119:132

**USETH**
or that *u* divination, or an Deut 18:10
brought which the king *u* to wear Est 6:8
of the wise *u* knowledge aright Prov 15:2
The poor *u* intreaties Prov 18:23
that *u* his neighbour's service Jer 22:13
every one that *u* proverbs shall Eze 16:44
For every one that *u* milk is Heb 5:13

**USING**
all are to perish with the *u* Col 2:22
not *u* your liberty for a cloke of 1Pet 2:16

**USURER**
thou shalt not be to him as a *u* Ex 22:25

**USURP**
nor to *u* authority over the man, 1Ti 2:12

**USURY**
neither shalt thou lay upon him *u* Ex 22:25
Take thou no *u* of him, or Lev 25:36

not give him thy money upon *u* ... Lev 25:37
not lend upon *u* to thy brother ... Deut 23:19
*u* of money, *u* of victuals, ... Deut 23:19
*u* of any thing that is lent upon ... Deut 23:19
of any thing that is lent upon *u* ... Deut 23:19
stranger thou mayest lend upon *u* ... Deut 23:20
thou shalt not lend upon *u* ... Deut 23:20
and said unto them, Ye exact *u* ... Neh 5:7
pray you, let us leave off this *u* ... Neh 5:10
putteth not out his money to *u* ... Ps 15:5
He that by *u* and unjust gain ... Prov 28:8
as with the taker of *u* ... Is 24:2
so with the giver of *u* to him ... Is 24:2
I have neither lent on *u* ... Jer 15:10
nor men have lent to me on *u* ... Jer 15:10
that hath not given forth upon *u* ... Eze 18:8
Hath given forth upon *u*, and hath ... Eze 18:13
hath not received *u* nor increase ... Eze 18:17
thou hast taken *u* and increase, and ... Eze 22:12
have received mine own with *u* ... Mt 25:27
have required mine own with *u* ... Lk 19:23

**US-WARD**
and thy thoughts which are to *u* ... Ps 40:5
of his power to *u* who believe ... Eph 1:19
but is longsuffering to *u* ... 2Pet 3:9

**UTHAI** (*u'-thahee*)
*1. Son of Ammihud.*
*U* the son of Ammihud, the son of ... 1Chr 9:4
*2. A clan leader with Ezra.*
*U*, and Zabbud, and with them ... Ezr 8:14

**UTMOST**
of my progenitors unto the *u* ... Gen 49:26
of Arnon, which is in the *u* coast ... Num 22:36
see the *u* part of the people ... Num 22:41
shalt see but the *u* part of them ... Num 23:13
the land of Judah, unto the *u* sea ... Deut 34:2
and all that are in the *u* corners ... Jer 9:26
and all that are in the *u* corners ... Jer 25:23
them that are in the *u* corners ... Jer 49:32
against her from the *u* border ... Jer 50:26
his hinder part toward the *u* sea ... Joel 2:20
for she came from the *u* parts of ... Lk 11:31

**UTTER**
if he do not *u* it, then he shall ... Lev 5:1
if ye *u* not this our business ... Josh 2:14
if thou *u* this our business, then ... Josh 2:20
awake, awake, *u* a song ... Judg 5:12
whom I appointed to *u* destruction ... 1Kin 20:42
*u* words out of their heart ... Job 8:10
a wise man *u* vain knowledge ... Job 15:2
nor my tongue *u* deceit ... Job 27:4
my lips shall *u* knowledge clearly ... Job 33:3
I will *u* dark sayings of old ... Ps 78:2
How long shall they *u* and speak ... Ps 94:4
Who can *u* the mighty acts of the ... Ps 106:2
My lips shall *u* praise, when thou ... Ps 119:171
They shall abundantly *u* the ... Ps 145:7
but a false witness will *u* lies ... Prov 14:5
heart shall *u* perverse things ... Prov 23:33
man cannot *u* it ... Eccl 1:8
hasty to *u* any thing before God ... Eccl 5:2
to *u* error against the LORD, to ... Is 32:6
*u* it even to the end of the earth ... Is 48:20
I will *u* my judgments against ... Jer 1:16
*u* his voice from his holy ... Jer 25:30
*u* a parable unto the rebellious ... Eze 24:3
thereof were toward the *u* court ... Eze 40:31
thereof were toward the *u* court ... Eze 40:37
brought me forth into the *u* court ... Eze 42:1
which was for the *u* court ... Eze 42:3
toward the *u* court on the ... Eze 42:7
in the *u* court was fifty cubits ... Eze 42:8
goeth into them from the *u* court ... Eze 42:9
the holy place into the *u* court ... Eze 42:14
they go forth into the *u* court ... Eze 44:19
even into the *u* court to the ... Eze 44:19
them not out into the *u* court ... Eze 46:20
brought me forth into the *u* court ... Eze 46:21
*u* gate by the way that looketh ... Eze 47:2
the LORD shall *u* his voice before ... Joel 2:11
*u* his voice from Jerusalem ... Joel 3:16
*u* his voice from Jerusalem ... Amos 1:2
flood he will make an *u* end of ... Nah 1:8
he will make an *u* end ... Nah 1:9
shall be no more *u* destruction ... Zec 14:11
I will *u* things which have been ... Mt 13:35
except ye *u* by the tongue words ... 1Cor 14:9
it is not lawful for a man to *u* ... 2Cor 12:4

**UTTERANCE**
as the Spirit gave them *u* ... Acts 2:4
ye are enriched by him, in all *u* ... 1Cor 1:5
in every thing, in faith, and *u* ... 2Cor 8:7
that *u* may be given unto me, that ... Eph 6:19
would open unto us a door of *u* ... Col 4:3

**UTTERED**
or *u* ought out of her lips, ... Num 30:6
and that which she *u* with her lips ... Num 30:8
Jephthah *u* all his words before ... Judg 11:11
and the most High *u* his voice ... 2Sa 22:14
before me, and *u* my words to him ... Neh 6:19
To whom hast thou *u* words ... Job 26:4
therefore have I *u* that I ... Job 42:3
he *u* his voice, the earth melted ... Ps 46:6
Which my lips have *u*, and my mouth .. Ps 66:14
have they *u* their voice, from ... Jer 48:34
a noise of their voice is *u* ... Jer 51:55
the deep *u* his voice, and lifted ... Hab 3:10
with groanings which cannot be *u* ... Rom 8:26
things to say, and hard to be *u* ... Heb 5:11
seven thunders *u* their voices ... Rev 10:3
seven thunders had *u* their voices ... Rev 10:4
things which the seven thunders *u* ... Rev 10:4

**UTTERETH**
For thy mouth *u* thine iniquity, ... Job 15:5
Day unto day *u* speech, and night ... Ps 19:2
she *u* her voice in the streets ... Prov 1:20
in the city she *u* her words ... Prov 1:21
he that *u* a slander, is a fool ... Prov 10:18
A fool *u* all his mind ... Prov 29:11
When he *u* his voice, there is a ... Jer 10:13
When he *u* his voice, there is a ... Jer 51:16
he *u* his mischievous desire ... Mic 7:3

**UTTERING**
*u* from the heart words of ... Is 59:13

**UTTERLY**
for I will *u* put out the ... Ex 17:14
If her father *u* refuse to give ... Ex 22:17
only, he shall be *u* destroyed ... Ex 22:20
but thou shalt *u* overthrow them ... Ex 23:24
shall pronounce him *u* unclean ... Lev 13:44
I abhor them, to destroy them *u* ... Lev 26:44
that soul shall *u* be cut off ... Num 15:31
then I will *u* destroy their ... Num 21:2
they *u* destroyed them and their ... Num 21:3
But if her husband hath *u* made ... Num 30:12
*u* destroyed the men, and the women. Deut 2:34
we *u* destroyed them, as we did ... Deut 3:6
*u* destroying the men, women, and ... Deut 3:6
that ye shall soon *u* perish from ... Deut 4:26
upon it, but shall *u* be destroyed ... Deut 4:26
smite them, and *u* destroy them ... Deut 7:2
but thou shalt *u* detest it ... Deut 7:26
and thou shalt *u* abhor it ... Deut 7:26
Ye shall *u* destroy all the places ... Deut 12:2
of the sword, destroying it *u* ... Deut 13:15
But thou shalt *u* destroy them ... Deut 20:17
ye will *u* corrupt yourselves ... Deut 31:29
Sihon and Og, whom ye *u* destroyed ... Josh 2:10
they *u* destroyed all that was in ... Josh 6:21
until he had *u* destroyed all the ... Josh 8:26
taken Ai, and had *u* destroyed it ... Josh 10:1
the king thereof he *u* destroyed ... Josh 10:28
therein he *u* destroyed that day ... Josh 10:35
but destroyed it *u*, and all the ... Josh 10:37
*u* destroyed all the souls that ... Josh 10:39
but *u* destroyed all that breathed ... Josh 10:40
of the sword, *u* destroying them ... Josh 11:11
he *u* destroyed them, as Moses the ... Josh 11:12
that he might destroy them *u* ... Josh 11:20
them *u* with their cities ... Josh 11:21
but did not *u* drive them out ... Josh 17:13
Zephath, and *u* destroyed it ... Judg 1:17
and did not *u* drive them out ... Judg 1:28
that thou hadst *u* hated her ... Judg 15:2
Ye shall *u* destroy every male, and ... Judg 21:11
*u* destroy all that they have, and ... 1Sa 15:3
*u* destroyed all the people with ... 1Sa 15:8
good, and would not *u* destroy them ... 1Sa 15:9
and refuse, that they destroyed *u* ... 1Sa 15:9
and the rest we have *u* destroyed ... 1Sa 15:15
*u* destroy the sinners the ... 1Sa 15:18
have *u* destroyed the Amalekites ... 1Sa 15:20
should have been *u* destroyed ... 1Sa 15:21
his people Israel *u* to abhor him ... 1Sa 27:12
the heart of a lion, shall *u* melt ... 2Sa 17:10
they shall be *u* burned with fire ... 2Sa 23:7
also were not able *u* to destroy ... 1Kin 9:21
all lands, by destroying them *u* ... 2Kin 19:11
and destroyed them *u* unto this day ... 1Chr 4:41
*u* to slay and destroy them ... 2Chr 20:23
until they had *u* destroyed them ... 2Chr 31:1
that my fathers *u* destroyed ... 2Chr 32:14
thou didst not *u* consume them ... Neh 9:31
fall, he shall not be *u* cast down ... Ps 37:24
they are *u* consumed with terrors ... Ps 73:19
will I not *u* take from him ... Ps 89:33
O forsake me not *u* ... Ps 119:8
word of truth *u* out of my mouth ... Ps 119:43
for love, it would *u* be contemned ... Song 8:7
And the idols he shall *u* abolish ... Is 2:18
man, and the land be *u* desolate ... Is 6:11
the LORD shall *u* destroy the ... Is 11:15
be *u* emptied, and *u* spoiled ... Is 24:3
The earth is *u* broken down ... Is 24:19
he hath *u* destroyed them, he hath ... Is 34:2
to all lands by destroying them *u* ... Is 37:11
and the young men shall *u* fall ... Is 40:30
The LORD hath *u* separated me from ... Is 56:3
those nations shall be *u* wasted ... Is 60:12
for every brother will *u* supplant ... Jer 9:4
I will *u* pluck up and destroy that ... Jer 12:17
Hast thou *u* rejected Judah ... Jer 14:19
will *u* forget you, and I will ... Jer 23:39
will *u* destroy them, and make them ... Jer 25:9
and should ye be *u* unpunished ... Jer 25:29
*u* destroy after them, saith the ... Jer 50:21
her up as heaps, and destroy her *u* ... Jer 50:26
destroy ye *u* all her host ... Jer 51:3
of Babylon shall be *u* broken ... Jer 51:58
But thou hast *u* rejected us ... Lam 5:22
Slay *u* old and young, both maids, ... Eze 9:6
shall it not *u* wither, when the ... Eze 17:10
make themselves *u* bald for thee ... Eze 27:31
make the land of Egypt *u* waste ... Eze 29:10
destroy, and *u* to make away many ... Dan 11:44
but I will *u* take them away ... Hos 1:6
the king of Israel *u* be cut off ... Hos 10:15
saving that I will not *u* destroy ... Amos 9:8
and say, We be *u* spoiled ... Mic 2:4
he is *u* cut off ... Nah 1:15
I will *u* consume all things from ... Zeph 1:2
his right eye shall be *u* darkened ... Zec 11:17
there is *u* a fault among you ... 1Cor 6:7
shall *u* perish in their own ... 2Pet 2:12
she shall be *u* burned with fire ... Rev 18:8

**UTTERMOST**
in the *u* edge of another curtain ... Ex 26:4
in the *u* side of another curtain ... Ex 36:11
the *u* edge of the curtain in the ... Ex 36:17
were in the *u* parts of the camp ... Num 11:1
a city in the *u* of thy border ... Num 20:16
even unto the *u* sea shall your ... Deut 11:24
was the *u* part of the south coast ... Josh 15:1
the sea at the *u* part of Jordan ... Josh 15:5
the *u* cities of the tribe of the ... Josh 15:21
Saul tarried in the *u* part of ... 1Sa 14:2
from the *u* part of the one wing ... 1Kin 6:24
the *u* part of the other were ten ... 1Kin 6:24
the *u* part of the camp of Syria ... 2Kin 7:5
came to the *u* part of the camp ... 2Kin 7:8
out unto the *u* part of the heaven ... Neh 1:9
the *u* parts of the earth for thy ... Ps 2:8
They also that dwell in the *u* ... Ps 65:8
dwell in the *u* parts of the sea ... Ps 139:9
the *u* part of the rivers of Egypt ... Is 7:18
From the *u* part of the earth have ... Is 24:16
thou hast paid the *u* farthing ... Mt 5:26
for she came from the *u* parts of ... Mt 12:42
from the *u* part of the earth to ... Mk 13:27
the earth to the *u* part of heaven ... Mk 13:27
unto the *u* part of the earth ... Acts 1:8
I will know the *u* of your matter ... Acts 24:22
wrath is come upon them to the *u* ... 1Th 2:16
the *u* that come unto God by him ... Heb 7:25

**UZ** (*uz*)
*1. A son of Aram.*
*U*, and Hul, and Gether, and Mash ... Gen 10:23
are these; *U*, and Aran ... Gen 36:28
Arphaxad, and Lud, and Aram, and *U* 1Chr 1:17
of Dishan; *U*, and Aran ... 1Chr 1:42
There was a man in the land of *U* ... Job 1:1
and all the kings of the land of *U* ... Jer 25:20
that dwellest in the land of *U* ... Lam 4:21

**UZAI** (*u'-zahee*) *Father of Palal.*
Palal the son of *U*, over against ... Neh 3:25

**UZAL** (*u'-zal*) *A son of Joktan.*
And Hadoram, and *U*, and Diklah, ... Gen 10:27
Hadoram also, and *U*, and Diklah, ... 1Chr 1:21

**UZZA** (*uz'-zah*) See UZZAH.
*1. Name of the burial ground of Manasseh and Amon.*
his own house, in the garden of *U* ... 2Kin 21:18
his sepulchre in the garden of *U* ... 2Kin 21:26
*2. Son of Shimei.*
son, Shimei his son, *U* his son, ... 1Chr 6:29
*3. A brother of Ahihud.*
Gera, he removed them, and begat *U* ... 1Chr 8:7
*4. Touched the Ark and died.*
and *U* and Ahio drave the cart ... 1Chr 13:7
*U* put forth his hand to hold the ... 1Chr 13:9
of the LORD was kindled against *U* ... 1Chr 13:10
had made a breach upon *U* ... 1Chr 13:11
*5. A family of Nethinims.*
The children of *U*, the children ... Ezr 2:49
of Gazzam, the children of *U* ... Neh 7:51

**UZZAH** (*uz'-zah*) See UZZA. *Same as Uzza 4.*
and *U* and Ahio, the sons of ... 2Sa 6:3
*U* put forth his hand to the ark ... 2Sa 6:6
of the LORD was kindled against *U* ... 2Sa 6:7
the LORD had made a breach upon *U* ... 2Sa 6:8

**UZZEN-SHEERAH** See UZZEN-SHERAH.

**UZZEN-SHERAH** (*uz''-zen-she'-rah*) *A city in Ephraim.*
the nether, and the upper, and *U* ... 1Chr 7:24

**UZZI** (*uz'-zi*)
*1. A son of Bukki.*
begat Bukki, and Bukki begat *U* ... 1Chr 6:5
*U* begat Zerahiah, and Zerahiah ... 1Chr 6:6
*U* his son, Zerahiah his son, ... 1Chr 6:51
The son of Zerahiah, the son of *U* ... Ezr 7:4
*2. Father of Izrahiah.*
*U*, and Rephaiah, and Jeriel, and ... 1Chr 7:2
And the sons of *U* ... 1Chr 7:3
*3. Son of Bela.*
Ezbon, and *U*, and Uzziel, and ... 1Chr 7:7
*4. A family of exiles.*
of Jeroham, and Elah the son of *U* ... 1Chr 9:8
*5. An overseer of Levites.*
Jerusalem was *U* the son of Bani ... Neh 11:22
*6. A priest descended from Jedaiah.*
of Jedaiah, *U* ... Neh 12:19
and Shemaiah, and Eleazar, and *U* ... Neh 12:42

**UZZIA** (*uz-zi'-ah*) *A 'mighty man' of David.*
*U* the Ashterathite, Shama and ... 1Chr 11:44

**UZZIAH** (*uz-zi'-ah*)
*1. A king of Judah.*
thirtieth year of *U* king of Judah ... 2Kin 15:13
year of Jotham the son of *U* ... 2Kin 15:30
son of *U* king of Judah to reign ... 2Kin 15:32
to all that his father *U* had done ... 2Kin 15:34
all the people of Judah took *U* ... 2Chr 26:1
Sixteen years old was *U* when he ... 2Chr 26:3
And the Ammonites gave gifts to *U* ... 2Chr 26:8

Moreover *U* built towers in ........ 2Chr 26:9
Moreover *U* had an host of ........ 2Chr 26:11
*U* prepared for them throughout........ 2Chr 26:14
And they withstood *U* the king........ 2Chr 26:18
It appertaineth not unto thee, *U*........ 2Chr 26:18
*U* was wroth, and had........ 2Chr 26:19
*U* the king was a leper unto the........ 2Chr 26:21
Now the rest of the acts of *U*........ 2Chr 26:22
So *U* slept with his fathers, and........ 2Chr 26:23
to all that his father *U* did........ 2Chr 27:2
and Jerusalem in the days of *U*........ Is 1:1
In the year that king *U* died I........ Is 6:1
the son of Jotham, the son of *U*........ Is 7:1
son of Beeri, in the days of *U*........ Hos 1:1
in the days of *U* king of Judah........ Amos 1:1
in the days of *U* king of Judah........ Zec 14:5

*2. Son of Uriel.*
*U* his son, and Shaul his son........ 1Chr 6:24

*3. Father of Jehonathan.*
was Jehonathan the son of *U*........ 1Chr 27:25

*4. Married a foreigner in exile.*
and Shemaiah, and Jehiel, and *U*........ Ezr 10:21

*5. A family of exiles.*
Athaiah the son of *U*, the son of........ Neh 11:4

**UZZIEL** (*uz-zi'-el*)
*1. A son of Kohath.*
Amram, and Izhar, and Hebron, and *U*.. Ex 6:18
And the sons of *U*........ Ex 6:22
the sons of *U* the uncle of Aaron,........ Lev 10:4
Amram, and Izehar, Hebron, and *U*.... Num 3:19
shall be Elizaphan the son of *U*........ Num 3:30
Amram, Izhar, and Hebron, and *U*........ 1Chr 6:2
Izhar, and Hebron, and *U*........ 1Chr 6:18
Of the sons of *U*........ 1Chr 15:10
Amram, Izhar, Hebron, and *U*........ 1Chr 23:12
Of the sons of *U*........ 1Chr 23:20
Of the sons of *U*........ 1Chr 24:24

*2. A son of Ishi.*
and Neariah, and Rephaiah, and *U*...... 1Chr 4:42

*3. A son of Bela.*
Ezbon, and Uzzi, and *U*, and Jerimoth. 1Chr 7:7

*4. A sanctuary servant.*
Bukkiah, Mattaniah, *U*, Shebuel,........ 1Chr 25:4

*5. A Levite who cleansed the Temple.*
Shemaiah, and *U*........ 2Chr 29:14

*6. A repairer of Jerusalem's wall.*
repaired *U* the son of Harhaiah........ Neh 3:8

**UZZIELITES** (*uz-zi'-el-ites*) *Descendants of Uzziel 1.*
and the family of the *U*........ Num 3:27
the Hebronites, and the *U*........ 1Chr 26:23

# V

**VAGABOND**
a *v* shalt thou be in the earth........ Gen 4:12
be a fugitive and a *v* in the earth........ Gen 4:14
Then certain of the *v* Jews........ Acts 19:13

**VAGABONDS**
Let his children be continually *v*........ Ps 109:10

**VAIL**
therefore she took a *v*, and........ Gen 24:65
from her, and covered her with a *v*.... Gen 38:14
away, and laid by her *v* from her........ Gen 38:19
And thou shalt make a *v* of blue........ Ex 26:31
hang up the *v* under the taches........ Ex 26:33
the *v* the ark of the testimony........ Ex 26:33
the *v* shall divide unto you........ Ex 26:33
shalt set the table without the *v*........ Ex 26:35
of the congregation without the *v*........ Ex 27:21
the *v* that is by the ark of the........ Ex 30:6
with them, he put a *v* on his face........ Ex 34:33
speak with him, he took the *v* off........ Ex 34:34
Moses put the *v* upon his face........ Ex 34:35
seat, and the *v* of the covering,........ Ex 35:12
And he made a *v* of blue, and purple.... Ex 36:35
and the sockets of the *v*........ Ex 38:27
skins, and the *v* of the covering,........ Ex 39:34
and cover the ark with the *v*........ Ex 40:3
set up the *v* of the covering, and........ Ex 40:21
northward, without the *v*........ Ex 40:22
of the congregation before the *v*........ Ex 40:26
before the *v* of the sanctuary........ Lev 4:6
the LORD, even before the *v*........ Lev 4:17
the *v* before the mercy seat........ Lev 16:2
small, and bring it within the *v*........ Lev 16:12
and bring his blood within the *v*........ Lev 16:15
he shall not go in unto the *v*........ Lev 21:23
Without the *v* of the testimony,........ Lev 24:3
shall take down the covering *v*........ Num 4:5
of the altar, and within the *v*........ Num 18:7
Bring the *v* that thou hast upon........ Ruth 3:15
And he made the *v* of blue, and........ 2Chr 3:14
the *v* that is spread over all........ Is 25:7
which put a *v* over his face, that........ 2Cor 3:13
this day remaineth the same *v*........ 2Cor 3:14
which *v* is done away in Christ........ 2Cor 3:14
the *v* is upon their heart........ 2Cor 3:15
the *v* shall be taken away........ 2Cor 3:16

**VAILS**
linen, and the hoods, and the *v*........ Is 3:23

**VAIN**
and let them not regard *v* words........ Ex 5:9
the name of the LORD thy God in *v*........ Ex 20:7
that taketh his name in *v*........ Ex 20:7
and ye shall sow your seed in *v*........ Lev 26:16
your strength shall be spent in *v*........ Lev 26:20
the name of the LORD thy God in *v*.... Deut 5:11
that taketh his name in *v*........ Deut 5:11
For it is not a *v* thing for you........ Deut 32:47
wherewith Abimelech hired *v*........ Judg 9:4
were gathered *v* men to Jephthah........ Judg 11:3
then should ye go after *v* things........ 1Sa 12:21
for they are *v*........ 1Sa 12:21
Surely in *v* have I kept all that........ 1Sa 25:21
servants, as one of the *v* fellows........ 2Sa 6:20
they followed vanity, and became *v*.. 2Kin 17:15
sayest, (but they are but *v* words........ 2Kin 18:20
there are gathered unto him *v* men..... 2Chr 13:7
be wicked, why then labour I in *v*........ Job 9:29
For he knoweth *v* men........ Job 11:11
For *v* man would be wise, though........ Job 11:12
a wise man utter *v* knowledge........ Job 15:2
Shall *v* words have an end........ Job 16:3
How then comfort ye me in *v*........ Job 21:34
why then are ye thus altogether *v*........ Job 27:12
doth Job open his mouth in *v*........ Job 35:16
her labour is in *v* without fear........ Job 39:16
Behold, the hope of him is in *v*........ Job 41:9
and the people imagine a *v* thing........ Ps 2:1
I have not sat with *v* persons........ Ps 26:4
An horse is a *v* thing for safety........ Ps 33:17
every man walketh in a *v* shew........ Ps 39:6
surely they are disquieted in *v*........ Ps 39:6
for *v* is the help of man........ Ps 60:11
and become not *v* in robbery........ Ps 62:10
I have cleansed my heart in *v*........ Ps 73:13
hast thou made all men in *v*........ Ps 89:47
for *v* is the help of man........ Ps 108:12
I hate *v* thoughts........ Ps 119:113
they labour in *v* that build it........ Ps 127:1
the watchman waketh but in *v*........ Ps 127:1
It is *v* for you to rise up early,........ Ps 127:2
thine enemies take thy name in *v*........ Ps 139:20
Surely in *v* the net is spread in........ Prov 1:17
followeth *v* persons is void of........ Prov 12:11
*v* persons shall have poverty........ Prov 28:19
and take the name of my God in *v*...... Prov 30:9
is deceitful, and beauty is *v*........ Prov 31:30
all the days of his *v* life which........ Eccl 6:12
Bring no more *v* oblations........ Is 1:13
For the Egyptians shall help in *v*........ Is 30:7
(but they are but *v* words) I have........ Is 36:5
it, he created it not in *v*........ Is 45:18
seed of Jacob, Seek ye me in *v*........ Is 45:19
Then I said, I have laboured in *v*........ Is 49:4
my strength for nought, and in *v*........ Is 49:4
They shall not labour in *v*........ Is 65:23
after vanity, and are become *v*........ Jer 2:5
In *v* have I smitten your children........ Jer 2:30
Truly in *v* is salvation hoped for........ Jer 3:23
How long shall thy *v* thoughts........ Jer 4:14
in *v* shalt thou make thyself fair........ Jer 4:30
the founder melteth in *v*........ Jer 6:29
Lo, certainly in *v* made he it........ Jer 8:8
the pen of the scribes is in *v*........ Jer 8:8
the customs of the people are *v*........ Jer 10:3
they make you *v*........ Jer 23:16
in *v* shalt thou use many........ Jer 46:11
none shall return in *v*........ Jer 50:9
and the people shall labour in *v*........ Jer 51:58
Thy prophets have seen *v* and........ Lam 2:14
eyes as yet failed for our *v* help........ Lam 4:17
that I have not said in *v* that I........ Eze 6:10
more any *v* vision nor flattering........ Eze 12:24
Have ye not seen a *v* vision........ Eze 13:7
they comfort in *v*........ Zec 10:2
have said, It is *v* to serve God........ Mal 3:14
use not *v* repetitions, as the........ Mt 6:7
But in *v* they do worship me,........ Mt 15:9
Howbeit in *v* do they worship me,........ Mk 7:7
and the people imagine *v* things........ Acts 4:25
but became *v* in their........ Rom 1:21
for he beareth not the sword in *v*........ Rom 13:4
of the wise, that they are *v*........ 1Cor 3:20
you, unless ye have believed in *v*........ 1Cor 15:2
was bestowed upon me was not in *v*. 1Cor 15:10
risen, then is our preaching *v*........ 1Cor 15:14
and your faith is also *v*........ 1Cor 15:14
be not raised, your faith is *v*........ 1Cor 15:17
labour is not in *v* in the Lord........ 1Cor 15:58
receive not the grace of God in *v*........ 2Cor 6:1
you should be in *v* in this behalf........ 2Cor 9:3
I should run, or had run, in *v*........ Gal 2:2
the law, then Christ is dead in *v*........ Gal 2:21
ye suffered so many things in *v*........ Gal 3:4
if it be yet in *v*........ Gal 3:4
bestowed upon you labour in *v*........ Gal 4:11
Let us not be desirous of *v* glory........ Gal 5:26
no man deceive you with *v* words........ Eph 5:6
Christ, that I have not run in *v*........ Phil 2:16
neither laboured in *v*........ Phil 2:16
*v* deceit, after the tradition of........ Col 2:8
in unto you, that it was not in *v*........ 1Th 2:1
you, and our labour be in *v*........ 1Th 3:5
have turned aside unto *v* jangling........ 1Ti 1:6
*v* babblings, and oppositions of........ 1Ti 6:20
But shun profane and *v* babblings........ 2Ti 2:16
*v* talkers and deceivers, specially........ Titus 1:10
for they are unprofitable and *v*........ Titus 3:9
heart, this man's religion is *v*........ Jas 1:26
O *v* man, that faith without works........ Jas 2:20
that the scripture saith in *v*........ Jas 4:5
from your *v* conversation received........ 1Pet 1:18

**VAINGLORY**
be done through strife or *v*........ Phil 2:3

**VAINLY**
*v* puffed up by his fleshly mind,........ Col 2:18

**VAIZATHA** See VAJEZATHA.

**VAJEZATHA** (*va-jez'-a-thah*) *A son of Haman.*
and Arisai, and Aridai, and *V*........ Est 9:9

**VALE**
together in the *v* of Siddim........ Gen 14:3
with them in the *v* of Siddim........ Gen 14:8
the *v* of Siddim was full of........ Gen 14:10
sent him out of the *v* of Hebron........ Gen 37:14
plain, in the hills, and in the *v*........ Deut 1:7
and of the south, and of the *v*........ Josh 10:40
sycomore trees that are in the *v*........ 1Kin 10:27
that are in the *v* for abundance........ 2Chr 1:15
mountains, in the cities of the *v*........ Jer 33:13

**VALIANT**
saw any strong man, or any *v* man........ 1Sa 14:52
in playing, and a mighty *v* man........ 1Sa 16:18
only be thou *v* for me, and fight........ 1Sa 18:17
to Abner, Art not thou a *v* man........ 1Sa 26:15
All the *v* men arose, and went all........ 1Sa 31:12
hands be strengthened, and be ye *v*........ 2Sa 2:7
where he knew that *v* men were........ 2Sa 11:16
be courageous, and be *v*........ 2Sa 13:28
And he also that is *v*, whose heart........ 2Sa 17:10
they which be with him are *v* men........ 2Sa 17:10
of Jehoiada, the son of a *v* man........ 2Sa 23:20
*v* men that drew the sword........ 2Sa 24:9
for thou art a *v* man, and bringest........ 1Kin 1:42
of *v* men, men able to bear........ 1Chr 5:18
they were *v* men of might in their........ 1Chr 7:2
of Issachar were *v* men of might........ 1Chr 7:5
They arose, all the *v* men........ 1Chr 10:12
the son of a *v* man of Kabzeel,........ 1Chr 11:22
Also the *v* men of the armies were.... 1Chr 11:26
mighty men, and with all the *v* men... 1Chr 28:1
with an army of *v* men of war........ 2Chr 13:3
of the LORD, that were *v* men........ 2Chr 26:17
in one day, which were all *v* men........ 2Chr 28:6
hundred threescore and eight *v* men.... Neh 11:6
threescore *v* men are about it, of........ Song 3:7
are about it, of the *v* of Israel........ Song 3:7
down the inhabitants like a *v* man........ Is 10:13
their *v* ones shall cry without........ Is 33:7
but they are not *v* for the truth........ Jer 9:3
Why are thy *v* men swept away........ Jer 46:15
red, the *v* men are in scarlet........ Nah 2:3
waxed *v* in fight, turned to........ Heb 11:34

**VALIANTEST**
twelve thousand men of the *v*........ Judg 21:10

**VALIANTLY**
and Israel shall do *v*........ Num 24:18
behave ourselves *v* for our people........ 1Chr 19:13
Through God we shall do *v*........ Ps 60:12
Through God we shall do *v*........ Ps 108:13
right hand of the LORD doeth *v*........ Ps 118:15
right hand of the LORD doeth *v*........ Ps 118:16

**VALLEY**
at the *v* of Shaveh, which is the........ Gen 14:17
his tent in the *v* of Gerar........ Gen 26:17
Isaac's servants digged in the *v*........ Gen 26:19
and the Canaanites dwelt in the *v*..... Num 14:25
and pitched in the *v* of Zared........ Num 21:12
And from Bamoth in the *v*, that is.... Num 21:20
they went up unto the *v* of Eshcol...... Num 32:9
and came unto the *v* of Eshcol........ Deut 1:24
unto the river Arnon half the *v*........ Deut 3:16
So we abode in the *v* over against........ Deut 3:29
in the *v* over against Beth-peor,........ Deut 4:46
down the heifer unto a rough *v*........ Deut 21:4
the heifer's neck there in the *v*........ Deut 21:4
heifer that is beheaded in the *v*........ Deut 21:6
and the plain of the *v* of Jericho........ Deut 34:3
he buried him in a *v* in the land........ Deut 34:6
brought them unto the *v* of Achor........ Josh 7:24
The *v* of Achor, unto this day........ Josh 7:26
now there was a *v* between them........ Josh 8:11
night into the midst of the *v*........ Josh 8:13
and thou, Moon, in the *v* of Ajalon..... Josh 10:12
south of Chinneroth, and in the *v*........ Josh 11:2
unto the *v* of Mizpeh eastward........ Josh 11:8
all the land of Goshen, and the *v*........ Josh 11:16
of Israel, and the *v* of the same........ Josh 11:16
even unto Baal-gad in the *v* of........ Josh 11:17
from Baal-gad in the *v* of Lebanon...... Josh 12:7
in the mount of the *v*,........ Josh 13:19
And in the *v*, Beth-aram, and........ Josh 13:27
toward Debir from the *v* of Achor........ Josh 15:7
the border went up by the *v* of........ Josh 15:8
before the *v* of Hinnom westward........ Josh 15:8
of the *v* of the giants northward........ Josh 15:8
And in the *v*, Eshtaol, and Zoreah,..... Josh 15:33
of the *v* have chariots of iron........ Josh 17:16
they who are of the *v* of Jezreel........ Josh 17:16
before the *v* of the son of Hinnom..... Josh 18:16
which is in the *v* of the giants........ Josh 18:16
and descended to the *v* of Hinnom..... Josh 18:16
Beth-hoglah, and the *v* of Keziz,........ Josh 18:21

are in the v of Jiphthah-el Josh 19:14
to the v of Jiphthah-el toward Josh 19:27
and in the south, and in the v Judg 1:9
out the inhabitants of the v Judg 1:19
suffer them to come down to the v Judg 1:34
he was sent on foot into the v Judg 5:15
and pitched in the v of Jezreel Judg 6:33
by the hill of Moreh, in the v Judg 7:1
Midian was beneath him in the v Judg 7:8
of the east lay along in the v Judg 7:12
loved a woman in the v of Sorek Judg 16:4
it was in the v that lieth by Judg 18:28
their wheat harvest in the v 1Sa 6:13
the border that looketh to the v 1Sa 13:18
of Amalek, and laid wait in the v 1Sa 15:5
and pitched by the v of Elah 1Sa 17:2
there was a v between them 1Sa 17:3
of Israel, were in the v of Elah 1Sa 17:19
until thou come to the v 1Sa 17:52
thou slewest in the v of Elah 1Sa 21:9
were on the other side of the v 1Sa 31:7
themselves in the v of Rephaim 2Sa 5:18
themselves in the v of Rephaim 2Sa 5:22
of the Syrians in the v of salt 2Sa 8:13
pitched in the v of Rephaim 2Sa 23:13
some mountain, or into some v 2Kin 2:16
Make this v full of ditches 2Kin 3:16
yet that v shall be filled with 2Kin 3:17
in the v of salt ten thousand 2Kin 14:7
which is in the v of the children 2Kin 23:10
the father of the v of Charashim 1Chr 4:14
even unto the east side of the v 1Chr 4:39
were in the v saw that they fled 1Chr 10:7
encamped in the v of Rephaim 1Chr 11:15
themselves in the v of Rephaim 1Chr 14:9
spread themselves abroad in the v 1Chr 14:13
the v of salt eighteen thousand 1Chr 18:12
in the v of Zephathah at Mareshah 2Chr 14:10
themselves in the v of Berachah 2Chr 20:26
The v of Berachah, unto this day 2Chr 20:26
people, and went to the v of salt 2Chr 25:11
the corner gate, and at the v gate 2Chr 26:9
in the v of the son of Hinnom 2Chr 28:3
in the v of the son of Hinnom 2Chr 33:6
the west side of Gihon, in the v 2Chr 33:14
came to fight in the v of Megiddo 2Chr 35:22
out by night by the gate of the v Neh 2:13
and entered by the gate of the v Neh 2:15
The v gate repaired Hanun, and the Neh 3:13
Beer-sheba unto the v of Hinnom Neh 11:30
Lod, and Ono, the v of craftsmen Neh 11:35
The clods of the v shall be sweet Job 21:33
He paweth in the v, and rejoiceth Job 39:21
the v of the shadow of death Ps 23:4
smote of Edom in the v of salt Ps 60:t
and mete out the v of Succoth Ps 60:6
the v of Baca make it a well Ps 84:6
and mete out the v of Succoth Ps 108:7
ravens of the v shall pick it out Prov 30:17
nuts to see the fruits of the v Song 6:11
ears in the v of Rephaim Is 17:5
The burden of the v of vision Is 22:1
God of hosts in the v of vision Is 22:5
which is on the head of the fat v Is 28:4
be wroth as in the v of Gibeon Is 28:21
Every v shall be exalted, and Is 40:4
As a beast goeth down into the v Is 63:14
the v of Achor a place for the Is 65:10
see thy way in the v, know what Jer 2:23
which is in the v of the son of Jer 7:31
nor the v of the son of Hinnom, Jer 7:32
of Hinnom, but the v of slaughter Jer 7:32
go forth unto the v of the son of Jer 19:2
nor The v of the son of Hinnom, Jer 19:6
of Hinnom, but The v of slaughter Jer 19:6
thee, O inhabitant of the v Jer 21:13
the whole v of the dead bodies, Jer 31:40
which are in the v of the son of Jer 32:35
and in the cities of the v Jer 32:44
off with the remnant of their v Jer 47:5
the v also shall perish, and the Jer 48:8
in the valleys, thy flowing v Jer 49:4
of the v which was full of bones Eze 37:1
were very many in the open v Eze 37:2
the v of the passengers on the Eze 39:11
shall call it The v of Hamon-gog Eze 39:11
buried it in the v of Hamon-gog Eze 39:15
bow of Israel in the v of Jezreel Hos 1:5
the v of Achor for a door of hope Hos 2:15
down into the v of Jehoshaphat Joel 3:2
come up to the v of Jehoshaphat Joel 3:12
multitudes in the v of decision Joel 3:14
Lord is near in the v of decision Joel 3:14
and shall water the v of Shittim Joel 3:18
the stones thereof into the v Mic 1:6
Hadadrimmon in the v of Megiddon Zec 12:11
and there shall be a very great v Zec 14:4
flee to the v of the mountains Zec 14:5
for the v of the mountains shall Zec 14:5
Every v shall be filled, and every Lk 3:5

## VALLEYS
As the v are they spread forth, Num 24:6
and depths that spring out of v Deut 8:7
it is a land of hills and v Deut 11:11
Jordan, in the hills, and in the v Josh 9:1
In the mountains, and in the v Josh 12:8
hills, but he is not God of the v 1Kin 20:28
put to flight all them of the v 1Chr 12:15
v was Shaphat the son of Adlai 1Chr 27:29
To dwell in the cliffs of the v Job 30:6
will he harrow the v after thee Job 39:10
the v also are covered over with Ps 65:13
they go down by the v unto the Ps 104:8
He sendeth the springs into the v Ps 104:10
of Sharon, and the lily of the v Song 2:1
all of them in the desolate v Is 7:19
that thy choicest v shall be full Is 22:7
are on the head of the fat v of Is 28:1
fountains in the midst of the v Is 41:18
slaying the children in the v Is 57:5
Wherefore gloriest thou in the v Jer 49:4
hills, to the rivers, and to the v Eze 6:3
the mountains like doves of the v Eze 7:16
in all the v his branches are Eze 31:12
fill the v with thy height Eze 32:5
in thy hills, and in thy v Eze 35:8
hills, to the rivers, and to the v Eze 36:4
hills, to the rivers, and to the v Eze 36:6
the v shall be cleft, as wax Mic 1:4

## VALOUR
armed, all the mighty men of v Josh 1:14
thereof, and the mighty men of v Josh 6:2
thirty thousand mighty men of v Josh 8:3
him, and all the mighty men of v Josh 10:7
men, all lusty, and all men of v Judg 3:29
with thee, thou mighty man of v Judg 6:12
Gileadite was a mighty man of v Judg 11:1
men from their coasts, men of v Judg 18:2
all these were men of v Judg 20:44
all these were men of v Judg 20:46
Jeroboam was a mighty man of v 1Kin 11:28
he was also a mighty man in v 2Kin 5:1
and all the mighty men of v 2Kin 24:14
and Jahdiel, mighty men of v 1Chr 5:24
of their fathers, mighty men of v 1Chr 7:7
of their fathers, mighty men of v 1Chr 7:9
of their fathers, mighty men of v 1Chr 7:11
house, choice and mighty men of v 1Chr 7:40
sons of Ulam were mighty men of v 1Chr 8:40
for they were all mighty men of v 1Chr 12:21
mighty men of v for the war 1Chr 12:25
a young man mighty of v 1Chr 12:28
and eight hundred, mighty men of v. 1Chr 12:30
for they were mighty men of v 1Chr 26:6
and his brethren, men of v 1Chr 26:30
men of v at Jazer of Gilead 1Chr 26:31
And his brethren, men of v 1Chr 26:32
chosen men, being mighty men of v 2Chr 13:3
all these were mighty men of v 2Chr 14:8
the men of war, mighty men of v 2Chr 17:13
men of v three hundred thousand 2Chr 17:14
hundred thousand mighty men of v 2Chr 17:16
Eliada a mighty man of v, and with 2Chr 17:17
of v out of Israel for an hundred 2Chr 25:6
mighty men of v were two thousand 2Chr 26:12
cut off all the mighty men of v 2Chr 32:21
their brethren, mighty men of v Neh 11:14

## VALUE
priest, and the priest shall v him Lev 27:8
that vowed shall the priest v him Lev 27:8
And the priest shall v it, whether Lev 27:12
ye are all physicians of no v Job 13:4
ye are of more v than many Mt 10:31
of the children of Israel did v Mt 27:9
ye are of more v than many Lk 12:7

## VALUED
be v at fifty shekels of silver Lev 27:16
It cannot be v with the gold of Job 28:16
shall it be v with pure gold Job 28:19
the price of him that was v Mt 27:9

## VALUEST
as thou v it, who art the priest, Lev 27:12

## VANIAH
(*va-ni'-ah*) *Married a foreigner in exile.*
V, Meremoth, Eliashib, Ezr 10:36

## VANISH
What time they wax warm, they v Job 6:17
heavens shall v away like smoke Is 51:6
be knowledge, it shall v away 1Cor 13:8
and waxeth old is ready to v away Heb 8:13

## VANISHED
is their wisdom v Jer 49:7
and he v out of their sight Lk 24:31

## VANISHETH
the cloud is consumed and v away Job 7:9
for a little time, and then v away Jas 4:14

## VANITIES
provoked me to anger with their v Deut 32:21
of Israel to anger with their v 1Kin 16:13
of Israel to anger with their v 1Kin 16:26
hated them that regard lying v Ps 31:6
Vanity of v, saith the Preacher, Eccl 1:2
saith the Preacher, vanity of v Eccl 1:2
words there are also divers v Eccl 5:7
Vanity of v, saith the preacher Eccl 12:8
graven images, and with strange v Jer 8:19
the stock is a doctrine of v Jer 10:8
Are there any among the v of the Jer 14:22
lying v forsake their own mercy Jonah 2:8
from these v unto the living God Acts 14:15

## VANITY
and they followed v, and became 2Kin 17:15
am I made to possess months of v Job 7:3
for my days are v Job 7:16
him that is deceived trust in v Job 15:31
for v shall be his recompence Job 15:31
mischief, and bring forth v Job 15:35
If I have walked with v, or if my Job 31:5
Surely God will not hear v Job 35:13
how long will ye love v, and seek Ps 4:2
under his tongue is mischief and v Ps 10:7
They speak v every one with his Ps 12:2
not lifted up his soul unto v Ps 24:4
at his best state is altogether v Ps 39:5
surely every man is v Ps 39:11
he come to see me, he speaketh v Ps 41:6
Surely men of low degree are v Ps 62:9
are altogether lighter than v Ps 62:9
their days did he consume in v Ps 78:33
thoughts of man, that they are v Ps 94:11
away mine eyes from beholding v Ps 119:37
Man is like to v Ps 144:4
Whose mouth speaketh v, and their Ps 144:8
children, whose mouth speaketh v Ps 144:11
Wealth gotten by v shall be Prov 13:11
a lying tongue is a v tossed to Prov 21:6
that soweth iniquity shall reap v Prov 22:8
Remove far from me v and lies Prov 30:8
V of vanities, saith the Preacher Eccl 1:2
saith the Preacher, v of vanities Eccl 1:2
all is v Eccl 1:2
and, behold, all is v and vexation Eccl 1:14
and, behold, this also is v Eccl 2:1
and, behold, all was v and vexation Eccl 2:11
in my heart, that this also is v Eccl 2:15
for all is v and vexation of Eccl 2:17
This is also v Eccl 2:19
This also is v and a great evil Eccl 2:21
This is also v Eccl 2:23
This also is v and vexation of Eccl 2:26
for all is v Eccl 3:19
This is also v and vexation of Eccl 4:4
and I saw v under the sun Eccl 4:7
This is also v, yea, it is a sore Eccl 4:8
Surely this also is v and vexation Eccl 4:16
this is also v Eccl 5:10
this is v, and it is an evil Eccl 6:2
For he cometh in with v, and Eccl 6:4
this is also v and vexation of Eccl 6:9
be many things that increase v Eccl 6:11
this also is v Eccl 7:6
have I seen in the days of my v Eccl 7:15
this is also v Eccl 8:10
There is a v which is done upon Eccl 8:14
I said that this also is v Eccl 8:14
all the days of the life of thy v Eccl 9:9
the sun, all the days of thy v Eccl 9:9
All that cometh is v Eccl 11:8
for childhood and youth are v Eccl 11:10
V of vanities, saith the preacher Eccl 12:8
all is v Eccl 12:8
draw iniquity with cords of v Is 5:18
the nations with the sieve of v Is 30:28
to him less than nothing, and v Is 40:17
the judges of the earth as v Is 40:23
Behold, they are all v Is 41:29
a graven image are all of them v Is 44:9
v shall take them Is 57:13
of the finger, and speaking v Is 58:9
they trust in v, and speak lies Is 59:4
from me, and have walked after v Jer 2:5
They are v, and the work of errors Jer 10:15
fathers have inherited lies, v Jer 16:19
me, they have burned incense to v Jer 18:15
They are v, the work of errors Jer 51:18
They have seen v and lying Eze 13:6
Because ye have spoken v, and seen Eze 13:8
be upon the prophets that see v Eze 13:9
Therefore ye shall see no more v Eze 13:23
Whiles they see v unto thee Eze 21:29
with untempered morter, seeing v Eze 22:28
surely they are v Hos 12:11
shall weary themselves for very v Hab 2:13
For the idols have spoken v Zec 10:2
creature was made subject to v Rom 8:20
walk, in the v of their mind, Eph 4:17
speak great swelling words of v 2Pet 2:18

## VAPORS
he causeth the v to ascend from Jer 10:13
he causeth the v to ascend from Jer 51:16

## VAPOUR
rain according to the v thereof Job 36:27
the cattle also concerning the v Job 36:33
blood, and fire, and v of smoke Acts 2:19
It is even a v, that appeareth Jas 4:14

## VAPOURS
He causeth the v to ascend from Ps 135:7
and hail; snow, and v Ps 148:8

## VARIABLENESS
of lights, with whom is no v Jas 1:17

## VARIANCE
set a man at v against his father Mt 10:35
Idolatry, witchcraft, hatred, v Gal 5:20

## VASHNI
(*vash'-ni*) *A son of Samuel.*
the firstborn V, and Abiah 1Chr 6:28

## VASHTI
(*vash'-ti*) *A Persian queen, succeeded by Esther.*
Also V the queen made a feast for Est 1:9
To bring V the queen before the Est 1:11
But the queen V refused to come Est 1:12
unto the queen V according to law Est 1:15

V the queen hath not done wrong Est 1:16
V the queen to be brought in Est 1:17
That V come no more before king Est 1:19
was appeased, he remembered V Est 2:1
the king be queen instead of V Est 2:4
and made her queen instead of V Est 2:17

**VAUNT**
lest Israel v themselves against Judg 7:2

**VAUNTETH**
charity v not itself, is not 1Cor 13:4

**VEDAN** See DAN.

**VEHEMENT**
fire, which hath a most v flame Song 8:6
that God prepared a v east wind Jonah 4:8
what v desire, yea, what zeal, 2Cor 7:11

**VEHEMENTLY**
But he spake the more v, If I Mk 14:31
the stream beat v upon that house Lk 6:48
which the stream did beat v Lk 6:49
the Pharisees began to urge him v Lk 11:53
and scribes stood and v accused him Lk 23:10

**VEIL**
the walls took away my v from me Song 5:7
the v of the temple was rent in Mt 27:51
the v of the temple was rent in Mk 15:38
the v of the temple was rent in Lk 23:45
entereth into that within the v Heb 6:19
And after the second v, the Heb 9:3
consecrated for us, through the v Heb 10:20

**VEIN**
there is a v for the silver Job 28:1

**VENGEANCE**
v shall be taken on him sevenfold Gen 4:15
To me belongeth v, and recompence Deut 32:35
I will render v to mine enemies, Deut 32:41
will render v to his adversaries, Deut 32:43
as the LORD hath taken v for thee Judg 11:36
shall rejoice when he seeth the v Ps 58:10
O LORD God, to whom v belongeth Ps 94:1
to whom v belongeth, shew thyself Ps 94:1
tookest v of their inventions Ps 99:8
To execute v upon the heathen, and Ps 149:7
he will not spare in the day of v Prov 6:34
For it is the day of the LORD's v Is 34:8
behold, your God will come with v Is 35:4
I will take v, and I will not meet Is 47:3
on the garments of v for clothing Is 59:17
LORD, and the day of v of our God Is 61:2
For the day of v is in mine heart Is 63:4
heart, let me see thy v on them Jer 11:20
heart, let me see thy v on them Jer 20:12
the Lord GOD of hosts, a day of v Jer 46:10
for it is the v of the LORD Jer 50:15
take v upon her Jer 50:15
in Zion the v of the LORD our God Jer 50:28
LORD our God, the v of his temple Jer 50:28
this is the time of the LORD's v Jer 51:6
because it is the v of the LORD Jer 51:11
of the LORD, the v of his temple Jer 51:11
thy cause, and take v for thee Jer 51:36
Thou hast seen all their v Lam 3:60
cause fury to come up to take v Eze 24:8
the house of Judah by taking v Eze 25:12
I will lay my v upon Edom by the Eze 25:14
and they shall know my v, saith Eze 25:14
have taken v with a despiteful Eze 25:15
I will execute great v upon them Eze 25:17
when I shall lay my v upon them Eze 25:17
And I will execute v in anger Mic 5:15
will take v on his adversaries Nah 1:2
For these be the days of v Lk 21:22
yet v suffereth not to live Acts 28:4
Is God unrighteous who taketh v Rom 3:5
for it is written, V is mine Rom 12:19
In flaming fire taking v on them 2Th 1:8
V belongeth unto me, I will Heb 10:30
suffering the v of eternal fire Jude 7

**VENISON**
Esau, because he did eat of his v Gen 25:28
to the field, and take me some v Gen 27:3
went to the field to hunt for v Gen 27:5
Bring me v, and make me savoury Gen 27:7
I pray thee, sit and eat of my v Gen 27:19
me, and I will eat of my son's v Gen 27:25
arise, and eat of his son's v Gen 27:31
where is he that hath taken v Gen 27:33

**VENOM**
dragons, and the cruel v of asps Deut 32:33

**VENOMOUS**
saw the v beast hang on his hand Acts 28:4

**VENT**
belly is as wine which hath no v Job 32:19

**VENTURE**
a certain man drew a bow at a v 1Kin 22:34
a certain man drew a bow at a v 2Chr 18:33

**VERIFIED**
so shall your words be v, and ye Gen 42:20
let thy word, I pray thee, be v 1Kin 8:26
God of Israel, let thy word be v 2Chr 6:17

**VERILY**
We are v guilty concerning our Gen 42:21
V my sabbaths ye shall keep Ex 31:13
I v thought that thou hadst Judg 15:2
V our lord king David hath made 1Kin 1:43
V she hath no child, and her 2Kin 4:14
but I will v buy it for the full 1Chr 21:24
are v estranged from me Job 19:13
the land, and v thou shalt be fed Ps 37:3
v every man at his best state is Ps 39:5
V there is a reward for the Ps 58:11
v he is a God that judgeth in the Ps 58:11
But v God hath heard me Ps 66:19
V I have cleansed my heart in Ps 73:13
V thou art a God that hidest Is 45:15
V it shall be well with thy Jer 15:11
v I will cause the enemy to Jer 15:11
For v I say unto you, Till heaven Mt 5:18
V I say unto thee, Thou shalt by Mt 5:26
V I say unto you, They have their Mt 6:2
V I say unto you, They have their Mt 6:5
V I say unto you, They have their Mt 6:16
V I say unto you, I have not Mt 8:10
V I say unto you, It shall be Mt 10:15
for v I say unto you, Ye shall Mt 10:23
v I say unto you, he shall in no Mt 10:42
V I say unto you, Among them that Mt 11:11
For v I say unto you, That many Mt 13:17
V I say unto you, There be some Mt 16:28
for v I say unto you, If ye have Mt 17:20
V I say unto you, Except ye be Mt 18:3
v I say unto you, he rejoiceth Mt 18:13
V I say unto you, Whatsoever ye Mt 18:18
V I say unto you, That a rich man Mt 19:23
V I say unto you, That ye which Mt 19:28
V I say unto you, If ye have Mt 21:21
V I say unto you, That the Mt 21:31
V I say unto you, All these Mt 23:36
v I say unto you, There shall not Mt 24:2
V I say unto you, This generation Mt 24:34
V I say unto you, That he shall Mt 24:47
V I say unto you, I know you not Mt 25:12
V I say unto you, Inasmuch as ye Mt 25:40
V I say unto you, Inasmuch as ye Mt 25:45
V I say unto you, Wheresoever Mt 26:13
V I say unto you, that one of you Mt 26:21
V I say unto thee, That this Mt 26:34
V I say unto you, All sins shall Mk 3:28
V I say unto you, It shall be Mk 6:11
v I say unto you, There shall no Mk 8:12
V I say unto you, That there be Mk 9:1
them, Elias v cometh first, and Mk 9:12
v I say unto you, he shall not Mk 9:41
V I say unto you, Whosoever shall Mk 10:15
V I say unto you, There is no man Mk 10:29
For v I say unto you, That Mk 11:23
V I say unto you, That this poor Mk 12:43
V I say unto you, that this Mk 13:30
V I say unto you, Wheresoever Mk 14:9
V I say unto you, One of you Mk 14:18
V I say unto you, I will drink no Mk 14:25
V I say unto thee, That this day, Mk 14:30
V I say unto you, No prophet is Lk 4:24
v I say unto you, It shall be Lk 11:51
v I say unto you, that he shall Lk 12:37
v I say unto you, Ye shall not Lk 13:35
V I say unto you, Whosoever shall Lk 18:17
V I say unto you, There is no man Lk 18:29
V I say unto you, This generation Lk 21:32
V I say unto thee, To day shalt Lk 23:43
And he saith unto him, V, v, Jn 1:51
and said unto him, V, v Jn 3:3
Jesus answered, V, v Jn 3:5
V, v, I say unto thee, We Jn 3:11
and said unto them, V, v Jn 5:19
V, v, I say unto you, He Jn 5:24
V, v, I say unto you, The Jn 5:25
answered them and said, V, v Jn 6:26
Jesus said unto them, V, v Jn 6:32
V, v, I say unto you, He Jn 6:47
Jesus said unto them, V, v Jn 6:53
Jesus answered them, V, v Jn 8:34
V, v, I say unto you, If a Jn 8:51
Jesus said unto them, V, v Jn 8:58
V, v, I say unto you, He Jn 10:1
Jesus unto them again, V, v Jn 10:7
V, v, I say unto you, Except Jn 12:24
V, v, I say unto you, The Jn 13:16
V, v, I say unto you, He Jn 13:20
and testified, and said, V, v Jn 13:21
V, v, I say unto thee, The Jn 13:38
V, v, I say unto you, He Jn 14:12
V, v, I say unto you, That Jn 16:20
V, v, I say unto you, Jn 16:23
V, v, I say unto thee, When Jn 21:18
nay v; but let them Acts 16:37
John v baptized with the baptism Acts 19:4
I am v a man which am a Jew, born Acts 22:3
I v thought with myself, that I Acts 26:9
For circumcision v profiteth Rom 2:25
Yes v, their sound went into all Rom 10:18
It hath pleased them v Rom 15:27
For I v, as absent in body, but 1Cor 5:3
V that, when I preach the gospel, 1Cor 9:18
For thou v givest thanks well, 1Cor 14:17
v righteousness should have been Gal 3:21
For v, when we were with you, we 1Th 3:4
For v he took not on him the Heb 2:16
Moses v was faithful in all his Heb 3:5
For men v swear by the greater Heb 6:16
v they that are of the sons of Heb 7:5
For there is v a disannulling of Heb 7:18
Then v the first covenant had Heb 9:1
For they v for a few days Heb 12:10
Who v was foreordained before the 1Pet 1:20
in him v is the love of God 1Jn 2:5

**VERITY**
The works of his hands are v Ps 111:7
of the Gentiles in faith and v 1Ti 2:7

**VERMILION**
with cedar, and painted with v Jer 22:14
the Chaldeans pourtrayed with v Eze 23:14

**VERY**
made, and, behold, it was v good Gen 1:31
And Cain was v wroth, and his Gen 4:5
the woman that she was v fair Gen 12:14
Abram was v rich in cattle, in Gen 13:2
because their sin is v grievous Gen 18:20
the thing was v grievous in Gen 21:11
the damsel was v fair to look Gen 24:16
and grew until he became v great Gen 26:13
thou be my v son Esau or not Gen 27:21
he said, Art thou my v son Esau Gen 27:24
And Isaac trembled v exceedingly Gen 27:33
grieved, and they were v wroth Gen 34:7
v ill favoured and leanfleshed, Gen 41:19
for it shall be v grievous Gen 41:31
v much, until he left numbering Gen 41:49
for the famine was v sore Gen 47:13
and it was a v great company Gen 50:9
a great and v sore lamentation Gen 50:10
multiplied, and waxed v mighty Ex 1:20
only ye shall not go v far away Ex 8:28
shall be a v grievous murrain Ex 9:3
in v deed for this cause have I Ex 9:16
it to rain a v grievous hail Ex 9:18
v grievous, such as there was Ex 9:24
v grievous were they Ex 10:14
was v great in the land of Egypt Ex 11:3
and herds, even v much cattle Ex 12:38
shalt beat some of it v small Ex 30:36
if any man die v suddenly by him, Num 6:9
the people with a v great plague Num 11:33
(Now the man Moses was v meek Num 12:3
the cities are walled, and v great Num 13:28
And Moses was v wroth, and said Num 16:15
promote thee unto v great honour Num 22:17
had a v great multitude of cattle Num 32:1
the LORD was v angry with Aaron Deut 9:20
stamped it, and ground it v small Deut 9:21
which are v far off from thee Deut 20:15
the words of this law v plainly Deut 27:8
shall get up above thee v high Deut 28:43
and thou shalt come down v low Deut 28:43
v delicate, his eye shall be evil Deut 28:54
But the word is v nigh unto thee Deut 30:14
for they are a v froward Deut 32:20
v courageous, that thou mayest Josh 1:7
rose up upon an heap v far from Josh 3:16
go not v far from the city, but Josh 8:4
From a v far country thy servants Josh 9:9
by reason of the v long journey Josh 9:13
us, saying, We are v far from you Josh 9:22
them with a v great slaughter Josh 10:20
which remain until this v day Josh 10:27
with horses and chariots v many Josh 11:4
there remaineth yet v much land Josh 13:1
with v much cattle, with silver, Josh 22:8
with iron, and with v much raiment Josh 22:8
Be ye therefore v courageous to Josh 23:6
and Eglon was a v fat man Judg 3:17
with a v great slaughter Judg 11:33
thou hast brought me v low Judg 11:35
of an angel of God, v terrible Judg 13:6
land, and, behold, it is v good Judg 18:9
hath dealt v bitterly with me Ruth 1:20
men was v great before the LORD 1Sa 2:17
Now Eli was v old, and heard all 1Sa 2:22
there was a v great slaughter 1Sa 4:10
city with a v great destruction 1Sa 5:9
the hand of God was v heavy there 1Sa 5:11
so it was a v great trembling 1Sa 14:15
there was a v great discomfiture 1Sa 14:20
and the people were v faint 1Sa 14:31
And Saul was v wroth, and the 1Sa 18:8
that he behaved himself v wisely 1Sa 18:15
have been to thee-ward v good 1Sa 19:4
but if he be v wroth, then be 1Sa 20:7
me that he dealeth v subtilly 1Sa 23:22
and the man was v great, and he had 1Sa 25:2
But the men were v good unto us 1Sa 25:15
For in v deed, as the LORD God of 1Sa 25:34
within him for he was v drunken 1Sa 25:36
that Saul was come in v deed 1Sa 26:4
v pleasant hast thou been unto me 2Sa 1:26
there was a v sore battle that 2Sa 2:17
Then was Abner v wroth for the 2Sa 3:8
the woman was v beautiful to look 2Sa 11:2
bare unto David, and it was v sick 2Sa 12:15
and Jonadab was a v subtil man 2Sa 13:3
all these things, he was v wroth 2Sa 13:21
and all his servants wept v sore 2Sa 13:36
laid a v great heap of stones 2Sa 18:17
Now Barzillai was a v aged man 2Sa 19:32
for he was a v great man 2Sa 19:32
for I have done v foolishly 2Sa 24:10
And the damsel was v fair, and 1Kin 1:4
and he also was a v goodly man 1Kin 1:6
and the king was v old 1Kin 1:15
were of the v base itself 1Kin 7:34
to Jerusalem with a v great train 1Kin 10:2
v much gold, and precious stones 1Kin 10:2

of spices *v* great store, and 1Kin 10:10
I have been *v* jealous for the 1Kin 19:10
I have been *v* jealous for the 1Kin 19:14
he did *v* abominably in following 1Kin 21:26
of Israel, that it was *v* bitter 2Kin 14:26
the LORD was *v* angry with Israel 2Kin 17:18
shed innocent blood *v* much 2Kin 21:16
*v* able men for the work of the 1Chr 9:13
brought David *v* much brass 1Chr 18:8
for I have done *v* foolishly 1Chr 21:8
for *v* great are his mercies 1Chr 21:13
the sons of Rehabiah were *v* many 1Chr 23:17
But will God in *v* deed dwell with 2Chr 6:18
a *v* great congregation, from the 2Chr 7:8
with a *v* great company, and camels 2Chr 9:1
and they carried away *v* much spoil 2Chr 14:13
with *v* many chariots and horsemen 2Chr 16:8
they made a *v* great burning for 2Chr 16:14
of Israel, who did *v* wickedly 2Chr 20:35
the LORD delivered a *v* great host 2Chr 24:24
month, a *v* great congregation 2Chr 30:13
had given him substance *v* much 2Chr 32:29
and raised it up a *v* great height 2Chr 33:14
transgressed *v* much after all the 2Chr 36:14
unto him out of Israel a *v* great Ezr 10:1
for the people wept *v* sore Ezr 10:1
We have dealt *v* corruptly against Neh 1:7
Then I was *v* sore afraid, Neh 2:2
stopped, then they were *v* wroth Neh 4:7
I was *v* angry when I heard their Neh 5:6
there was *v* great gladness Neh 8:17
therefore was the king *v* wroth Est 1:12
she asses, and a *v* great household Job 1:3
saw that his grief was *v* great Job 2:13
*v* aged men, much elder than thy Job 15:10
said, I am young, and ye are *v* old Job 32:6
their inward part is *v* wickedness Ps 5:9
into that *v* destruction let him Ps 35:8
a *v* present help in trouble Ps 46:1
it shall be *v* tempestuous round Ps 50:3
is *v* high, who hast done great Ps 71:19
for we are brought *v* low Ps 79:8
thou establish in the *v* heavens Ps 89:2
and thy thoughts are *v* deep Ps 92:5
Thy testimonies are *v* sure Ps 93:5
O LORD my God, thou art *v* great Ps 104:1
*v* few, and strangers in it Ps 105:12
I am afflicted *v* much Ps 119:107
are righteous and *v* faithful Ps 119:138
Thy word is *v* pure Ps 119:140
for I am brought *v* low Ps 142:6
in that *v* day his thoughts perish Ps 146:4
his word runneth *v* swiftly Ps 147:15
a matter separateth *v* friends Prov 17:9
dropping in a *v* rainy day Prov 27:15
left unto us a *v* small remnant Is 1:9
a vineyard in a *v* fruitful hill Is 5:1
For yet a *v* little while, and the Is 10:25
he is *v* proud Is 16:6
and the remnant shall be *v* small Is 16:14
have dealt *v* treacherously Is 24:16
Is it not yet a *v* little while Is 29:17
he will be *v* gracious unto thee Is 30:19
because they are *v* strong Is 31:1
behold the land that is *v* far off Is 33:17
up the isles as a *v* little thing Is 40:15
hast thou *v* heavily laid thy yoke Is 47:6
wouldest deal *v* treacherously Is 48:8
exalted and extolled, and be *v* high Is 52:13
Be not wroth *v* sore, O LORD, Is 64:9
thy peace, and afflict us *v* sore Is 64:12
be ye *v* desolate, saith the LORD Jer 2:12
I am pained at my *v* heart Jer 4:19
dealt *v* treacherously against me Jer 5:11
happy that deal *v* treacherously Jer 12:1
breach, with a *v* grievous blow Jer 14:17
hath done a *v* horrible thing Jer 18:13
making him *v* glad Jer 20:15
One basket had *v* good figs Jer 24:2
other basket had *v* naughty figs Jer 24:2
the good figs, *v* good Jer 24:3
*v* evil, that cannot be eaten, Jer 24:3
until the *v* time of his land come Jer 27:7
wine and summer fruits *v* much Jer 40:12
Egypt is like a *v* fair heifer Jer 46:20
thou art *v* wroth against us Lam 5:22
against me, even unto this *v* day Eze 2:3
as if that were a *v* little thing Eze 16:47
made *v* glorious in the midst of Eze 27:25
thou art unto them as a *v* lovely Eze 33:32
there were *v* many in the open Eze 37:2
and, lo, they were *v* dry Eze 37:2
and set me upon a *v* high mountain Eze 40:2
were *v* many trees on the one side Eze 47:7
and there shall be a *v* great Eze 47:9
*v* furious, and commanded to Dan 2:12
Then the king arose *v* early in Dan 6:19
a mouth that spake *v* great things Dan 7:20
the he goat waxed *v* great Dan 8:8
up to battle with a *v* great Dan 11:25
for his camp is *v* great Joel 2:11
the LORD is great and *v* terrible Joel 2:11
even *v* dark, and no brightness in Amos 5:20
exceedingly, and he was *v* angry Jonah 4:1
people shall labour in the *v* fire Hab 2:13
weary themselves for *v* vanity Hab 2:13
I am *v* sore displeased with the Zec 1:15
his staff in his hand for *v* age Zec 8:4
and Zidon, though it be *v* wise Zec 9:2
it, and be *v* sorrowful, and Ekron Zec 9:5
there shall be a *v* great valley Zec 14:4
But the *v* hairs of your head are Mt 10:30
was made whole from that *v* hour Mt 15:28
child was cured from that *v* hour Mt 17:18
what was done, they were *v* sorry Mt 18:31
a *v* great multitude spread their Mt 21:8
they shall deceive the *v* elect Mt 24:24
box of *v* precious ointment Mt 26:7
began to be sorrowful and *v* heavy Mt 26:37
days the multitude being *v* great Mk 8:1
ointment of spikenard *v* precious Mk 14:3
be sore amazed, and to be *v* heavy Mk 14:33
*v* early in the morning the first Mk 16:2
for it was *v* great Mk 16:4
of all things from the *v* first Lk 1:3
shake off the *v* dust from your Lk 9:5
Even the *v* dust of your city, Lk 10:11
But even the *v* hairs of your head Lk 12:7
thou hast paid the *v* last mite Lk 12:59
he heard this, he was *v* sorrowful Lk 18:23
for he was *v* rich Lk 18:23
Jesus saw that he was *v* sorrowful Lk 18:24
hast been faithful in a *v* little Lk 19:17
were *v* attentive to hear him Lk 19:48
*v* early in the morning, they came Lk 24:1
indeed that this is the *v* Christ Jn 7:26
taken in adultery, in the *v* act Jn 8:4
*v* costly, and anointed the feet of Jn 12:3
believe me for the *v* works' sake Jn 14:11
proving that this is *v* Christ Acts 9:22
And he became *v* hungry, and would Acts 10:10
that *v* worthy deeds are done unto Acts 24:2
no wrong, as thou *v* well knowest Acts 25:10
But Esaias is *v* bold, and saith, I Rom 10:20
continually upon this *v* thing Rom 13:6
But with me it is a *v* small thing 1Cor 4:3
and your zeal hath provoked *v* many 2Cor 9:2
behind the *v* chiefest apostles 2Cor 11:5
I behind the *v* chiefest apostles 2Cor 12:11
I will *v* gladly spend and be spent 2Cor 12:15
Being confident of this *v* thing Phil 1:6
to esteem them *v* highly in love 1Th 5:13
the *v* God of peace sanctify you 1Th 5:23
he sought me out *v* diligently 2Ti 1:17
at Ephesus, thou knowest *v* well 2Ti 1:18
not the *v* image of the things, Heb 10:1
turned about with a *v* small helm Jas 3:4
that the Lord is *v* pitiful Jas 5:11

**VESSEL**

But the earthen *v* wherein it is Lev 6:28
whether it be any *v* of wood Lev 11:32
skin, or sack, whatsoever *v* it be Lev 11:32
And every earthen *v*, whereinto any Lev 11:33
in every such *v* shall be unclean Lev 11:34
an earthen *v* over running water Lev 14:5
an earthen *v* over running water Lev 14:50
the *v* of earth, that he toucheth Lev 15:12
every *v* of wood shall be rinsed Lev 15:12
take holy water in an earthen *v* Num 5:17
And every open *v*, which hath no Num 19:15
water shall be put thereto in a *v* Num 19:17
thou shalt not put any in thy *v* Deut 23:24
were sanctified this day in the *v* 1Sa 21:5
pray thee, a little water in a *v* 1Kin 17:10
unto her son, Bring me yet a *v* 2Kin 4:6
unto her, There is not a *v* more 2Kin 4:6
them in pieces like a potter's *v* Ps 2:9
I am like a broken *v* Ps 31:12
come forth a *v* for the finer Prov 25:4
*v* that is broken in pieces Is 30:14
*v* into the house of the LORD Is 66:20
the *v* that he made of clay was Jer 18:4
so he made it again another *v* Jer 18:4
as one breaketh a potter's *v* Jer 19:11
is he a *v* wherein is no pleasure Jer 22:28
ye shall fall like a pleasant *v* Jer 25:34
and put them in an earthen *v* Jer 32:14
not been emptied from *v* to *v* Jer 48:11
like a *v* wherein is no pleasure Jer 48:38
me, he hath made me an empty *v* Jer 51:34
and fitches, and put them in one *v* Eze 4:9
a pin of it to hang any *v* thereon Eze 15:3
as a *v* wherein is no pleasure Hos 8:8
carry any *v* through the temple Mk 11:16
a candle, covereth it with a *v* Lk 8:16
there was set a *v* full of vinegar Jn 19:29
for he is a chosen *v* unto me Acts 9:15
a certain *v* descending unto him, Acts 10:11
the *v* was received up again into Acts 10:16
saw a vision, A certain *v* descend Acts 11:5
lump to make one *v* unto honour Rom 9:21
possess his *v* in sanctification 1Th 4:4
he shall be a *v* unto honour 2Ti 2:21
the wife, as unto the weaker *v* 1Pet 3:7

**VESSELS**

best fruits in the land in your *v* Gen 43:11
*v* of wood, and in *v* of stone Ex 7:19
he make it, with all these *v* Ex 25:39
all the *v* thereof thou shalt make Ex 27:3
All the *v* of the tabernacle in Ex 27:19
And the table and all his *v* Ex 30:27
and the candlestick and his *v* Ex 30:27
of burnt offering with all his *v* Ex 30:28
and his staves, and all his *v* Ex 35:13
grate, his staves, and all his *v* Ex 35:16
he made the *v* which were upon the Ex 37:16
made he it, and all the *v* thereof Ex 37:24
And he made all the *v* of the altar Ex 38:3
all the *v* thereof made he of Ex 38:3
it, and all the *v* of the altar, Ex 38:30
The table, and all the *v* thereof Ex 39:36
in order, and all the *v* thereof Ex 39:37
brass, his staves, and all his *v* Ex 39:39
all the *v* of the service of the Ex 39:40
hallow it, and all the *v* thereof Ex 40:9
the burnt offering, and all his *v* Ex 40:10
anointed the altar and all his *v* Lev 8:11
and over all the *v* thereof Num 1:50
tabernacle, and all the *v* thereof Num 1:50
the *v* of the sanctuary wherewith Num 3:31
thereof, and all the *v* thereof Num 3:36
and all the oil *v* thereof Num 4:9
all the *v* thereof within a Num 4:10
put upon it all the *v* thereof Num 4:14
basons, all the *v* of the altar Num 4:14
all the *v* of the sanctuary, as Num 4:15
sanctuary, and in the *v* thereof Num 4:16
the altar and all the *v* thereof Num 7:1
all the silver *v* weighed two Num 7:85
come nigh the *v* of the sanctuary Num 18:3
upon the tent, and upon all the *v* Num 19:18
gold, and *v* of brass and iron, are Josh 6:19
the *v* of brass and of iron, they Josh 6:24
thou art athirst, go unto the *v* Ruth 2:9
for the bread is spent in our *v* 1Sa 9:7
the *v* of the young men are holy, 1Sa 21:5
brought with him *v* of silver 2Sa 8:10
and *v* of gold, and *v* of brass 2Sa 8:10
beds, and basons, and earthen *v* 2Sa 17:28
and all these *v*, which Hiram made 1Kin 7:45
Solomon left all the *v* unweighed 1Kin 7:47
Solomon made all the *v* that 1Kin 7:48
the silver, and the gold, and the *v* 1Kin 7:51
all the holy *v* that were in the 1Kin 8:4
Solomon's drinking *v* were of gold 1Kin 10:21
all the *v* of the house of the 1Kin 10:21
*v* of silver, and *v* of gold, 1Kin 10:25
the LORD, silver, and gold, and *v* 1Kin 15:15
borrow thee *v* abroad of all thy 2Kin 4:3
all thy neighbours, even empty *v* 2Kin 4:3
shalt pour out into all those *v* 2Kin 4:4
sons, who brought the *v* to her 2Kin 4:5
when the *v* were full, that she 2Kin 4:6
the way was full of garments and *v* 2Kin 7:15
any *v* of gold 2Kin 12:13
or *v* of silver, of the money that 2Kin 12:13
all the *v* that were found in the 2Kin 14:14
all the *v* that were made for Baal 2Kin 23:4
cut in pieces all the *v* of gold 2Kin 24:13
all the *v* of brass wherewith they 2Kin 25:14
of all these *v* was without weight 2Kin 25:16
the charge of the ministering *v* 1Chr 9:28
were appointed to oversee the *v* 1Chr 9:29
and the pillars, and the *v* of brass 1Chr 18:8
with him all manner of *v* of gold 1Chr 18:10
of the LORD, and the holy *v* of God 1Chr 22:19
nor any *v* of it for the service 1Chr 23:26
for all the *v* of service in the 1Chr 28:13
all these *v* in great abundance 2Chr 4:18
Solomon made all the *v* that were 2Chr 4:19
all the holy *v* that were in the 2Chr 5:5
all the drinking *v* of king 2Chr 9:20
all the *v* of the house of the 2Chr 9:20
*v* of silver, and *v* of gold, 2Chr 9:24
dedicated, silver, and gold, and *v* 2Chr 15:18
whereof were made *v* for the house 2Chr 24:14
even *v* to minister, and to offer 2Chr 24:14
and spoons, and *v* of gold and silver 2Chr 24:14
all the *v* that were found in the 2Chr 25:24
the *v* of the house of God 2Chr 28:24
cut in pieces the *v* of the house 2Chr 28:24
offering, with all the *v* thereof 2Chr 29:18
table, with all the *v* thereof 2Chr 29:18
Moreover all the *v*, which king 2Chr 29:19
also carried of the *v* of the 2Chr 36:7
with the goodly *v* of the house of 2Chr 36:10
all the *v* of the house of God, 2Chr 36:18
all the goodly *v* thereof 2Chr 36:19
their hands with *v* of silver Ezr 1:6
the *v* of the house of the LORD Ezr 1:7
and ten, and other *v* a thousand Ezr 1:10
All the *v* of gold and of silver Ezr 1:11
the *v* also of gold and silver of Ezr 5:14
And said unto him, Take these *v* Ezr 5:15
silver *v* of the house of God, Ezr 6:5
The *v* also that are given thee Ezr 7:19
the silver, and the gold, and the *v* Ezr 8:25
silver *v* an hundred talents, and Ezr 8:26
two *v* of fine copper, precious as Ezr 8:27
the *v* are holy also Ezr 8:28
the silver, and the gold, and the *v* Ezr 8:30
the *v* weighed in the house of our Ezr 8:33
where are the *v* of the sanctuary, Neh 10:39
the frankincense, and the *v* Neh 13:5
I again the *v* of the house of God Neh 13:9
they gave them drink in *v* of gold Est 1:7
(the *v* being diverse one from Est 1:7
even in *v* of bulrushes upon the Is 18:2
all *v* of small quantity, from the Is 22:24
quantity, from the *v* of cups Is 22:24
even to all the *v* of flagons Is 22:24
that bear the *v* of the LORD Is 52:11
abominable things is in their *v* Is 65:4
they returned with their *v* empty Jer 14:3
the *v* of the LORD's house shall Jer 27:16
that the *v* which are left in the Jer 27:18
of the *v* that remain in this city Jer 27:19
concerning the *v* that remain in Jer 27:21
all the *v* of the LORD's house Jer 28:3

to bring again the *v* of the ... Jer 28:6
and oil, and put them in your *v* ... Jer 40:10
to wander, and shall empty his *v* ... Jer 48:12
their curtains, and all their *v* ... Jer 49:29
all the *v* of brass wherewith they ... Jer 52:18
of all these *v* was without weight ... Jer 52:20
men and *v* of brass in thy market ... Eze 27:13
with part of the *v* of the house ... Dan 1:2
he brought the *v* into the ... Dan 1:2
silver *v* which his father ... Dan 5:2
*v* that were taken out of the ... Dan 5:3
they have brought the *v* of his ... Dan 5:23
with their precious *v* of silver ... Dan 11:8
the treasure of all pleasant *v* ... Hos 13:15
draw out fifty *v* out of the press ... Hag 2:16
down, and gathered the good into *v* ... Mt 13:48
oil in their *v* with their lamps ... Mt 25:4
of cups, and pots, brasen *v* ... Mk 7:4
with much longsuffering the *v* of ... Rom 9:22
of his glory on the *v* of mercy ... Rom 9:23
have this treasure in earthen *v* ... 2Cor 4:7
there are not only *v* of gold ... 2Ti 2:20
all the *v* of the ministry ... Heb 9:21
as the *v* of a potter shall they ... Rev 2:27
wood, and all manner *v* of ivory ... Rev 18:12
all manner *v* of most precious ... Rev 18:12

### VESTMENTS
Bring forth *v* for all the ... 2Kin 10:22
And he brought them forth *v* ... 2Kin 10:22

### VESTRY
said unto him that was over the *v* ... 2Kin 10:22

### VESTURE
upon the four quarters of thy *v* ... Deut 22:12
them, and cast lots upon my *v* ... Ps 22:18
as a *v* shalt thou change them, and ... Ps 102:26
upon my *v* did they cast lots ... Mt 27:35
for my *v* they did cast lots ... Jn 19:24
as a *v* shalt thou fold them up, ... Heb 1:12
clothed with a *v* dipped in blood ... Rev 19:13
And he hath on his *v* and on his ... Rev 19:16

### VESTURES
and arrayed him in *v* of fine linen ... Gen 41:42

### VEX
Thou shalt neither *v* a stranger ... Ex 22:21
sister, to *v* her, to uncover her ... Lev 18:18
in your land, ye shall not *v* him ... Lev 19:33
*V* the Midianites, and smite them ... Num 25:17
For they *v* you with their wiles, ... Num 25:18
shall *v* you in the land wherein ... Num 33:55
how will he then *v* himself ... 2Sa 12:18
for God did *v* them with all ... 2Chr 15:6
How long will ye *v* my soul ... Job 19:2
*v* them in his sore displeasure ... Ps 2:5
*v* it, and let us make a breach ... Is 7:6
and Judah shall not *v* Ephraim ... Is 11:13
I will also *v* the hearts of many ... Eze 32:9
thee, and awake that shall *v* thee ... Hab 2:7
hands to *v* certain of the church ... Acts 12:1

### VEXATION
shall send upon thee cursing, *v* ... Deut 28:20
all is vanity and *v* of spirit ... Eccl 1:14
that this also is *v* of spirit ... Eccl 1:17
*v* of spirit, and there was no ... Eccl 2:11
for all is vanity and *v* of spirit ... Eccl 2:17
of the *v* of his heart, wherein he ... Eccl 2:22
also is vanity and *v* of spirit ... Eccl 2:26
is also vanity and *v* of spirit ... Eccl 4:4
full with travail and *v* of spirit ... Eccl 4:6
also is vanity and *v* of spirit ... Eccl 4:16
is also vanity and *v* of spirit ... Eccl 6:9
shall not be such as was in her *v* ... Is 9:1
and it shall be a *v* only to ... Is 28:19
and shall howl for *v* of spirit ... Is 65:14

### VEXATIONS
but great *v* were upon all the ... 2Chr 15:5

### VEXED
and the Egyptians *v* us, and our ... Num 20:15
that oppressed them and *v* them ... Judg 2:18
And that year they *v* and oppressed ... Judg 10:8
so that his soul was *v* unto death ... Judg 16:16
he turned himself, he *v* them ... 1Sa 14:47
And Amnon was so *v*, that he fell ... 2Sa 13:2
for her soul is *v* within her ... 2Kin 4:27
hand of their enemies, who *v* them ... Neh 9:27
the Almighty, who hath *v* my soul ... Job 27:2
for my bones are *v* ... Ps 6:2
My soul is also sore *v* ... Ps 6:3
mine enemies be ashamed and sore *v* ... Ps 6:10
rebelled, and *v* his holy Spirit ... Is 63:10
which art infamous and much *v* ... Eze 22:5
thee have they *v* the fatherless ... Eze 22:7
and have *v* the poor and needy ... Eze 22:29
is grievously *v* with a devil ... Mt 15:22
for he is lunatick, and sore *v* ... Mt 17:15
they that were *v* with unclean ... Lk 6:18
them which were *v* with unclean ... Acts 5:16
*v* with the filthy conversation of ... 2Pet 2:7
*v* his righteous soul from day to ... 2Pet 2:8

### VIAL
Then Samuel took a *v* of oil ... 1Sa 10:1
poured out his *v* upon the earth ... Rev 16:2
poured out his *v* upon the sea ... Rev 16:3
poured out his *v* upon the rivers ... Rev 16:4
poured out his *v* upon the sun ... Rev 16:8
his *v* upon the seat of the beast ... Rev 16:10
*v* upon the great river Euphrates ... Rev 16:12
poured out his *v* into the air ... Rev 16:17

### VIALS
golden *v* full of odours, which ... Rev 5:8
golden *v* full of the wrath of God ... Rev 15:7
pour out the *v* of the wrath of ... Rev 16:1
angels which had the seven *v* ... Rev 17:1
angels which had the seven *v* full ... Rev 21:9

### VICTORY
the *v* that day was turned into ... 2Sa 19:2
LORD wrought a great *v* that day ... 2Sa 23:10
and the LORD wrought a great *v* ... 2Sa 23:12
the power, and the glory, and the *v* .. 1Chr 29:11
holy arm, hath gotten him the *v* ... Ps 98:1
He will swallow up death in *v* ... Is 25:8
he send forth judgment unto *v* ... Mt 12:20
Death is swallowed up in *v* ... 1Cor 15:54
O grave, where is thy *v* ... 1Cor 15:55
which giveth us the *v* through our ... 1Cor 15:57
this is the *v* that overcometh the ... 1Jn 5:4
had gotten the *v* over the beast ... Rev 15:2

### VICTUAL
prepared for themselves any *v* ... Ex 12:39
to fetch *v* for the people, that ... Judg 20:10
provided *v* for king Solomon ... 1Kin 4:27
captains in them, and store of *v* ... 2Chr 11:11
and he gave them *v* in abundance ... 2Chr 11:23

### VICTUALS
Sodom and Gomorrah, and all their *v* Gen 14:11
nor lend him thy *v* for increase ... Lev 25:37
usury of money, usury of *v* ... Deut 23:19
the people, saying, Prepare you *v* ... Josh 1:11
Take *v* with you for the journey, ... Josh 9:11
And the men took of their *v* ... Josh 9:14
the people took *v* in their hand ... Judg 7:8
and a suit of apparel, and thy *v* ... Judg 17:10
the LORD for him, and gave him *v* ... 1Sa 22:10
which provided *v* for the king ... 1Kin 4:7
him an house, and appointed him *v* ... 1Kin 11:18
any *v* on the sabbath day to sell ... Neh 10:31
in the day wherein they sold *v* ... Neh 13:15
captain of the guard gave him *v* ... Jer 40:5
for then had we plenty of *v* ... Jer 44:17
the villages, and buy themselves *v* ... Mt 14:15
round about, and lodge, and get *v* ... Lk 9:12

### VIEW
Go *v* the land, even Jericho ... Josh 2:1
saying, Go up and *v* the country ... Josh 7:2
went, and stood to *v* afar off ... 2Kin 2:7
were to *v* at Jericho saw him ... 2Kin 2:15

### VIEWED
And the men went up and *v* Ai ... Josh 7:2
I *v* the people, and the priests, ... Ezr 8:15
*v* the walls of Jerusalem, which ... Neh 2:13
*v* the wall, and turned back, and ... Neh 2:15

### VIGILANT
the husband of one wife, *v* ... 1Ti 3:2
Be sober, be *v* ... 1Pet 5:8

### VILE
brother should seem *v* unto thee ... Deut 25:3
unto this man do not so *v* a thing ... Judg 19:24
his sons made themselves *v* ... 1Sa 3:13
but every thing that was *v* ... 1Sa 15:9
And I will yet be more *v* than thus ... 2Sa 6:22
and reputed *v* in your sight ... Job 18:3
Behold, I am *v* ... Job 40:4
In whose eyes a *v* person is ... Ps 15:4
The *v* person shall be no more ... Is 32:5
For the *v* person will speak ... Is 32:6
forth the precious from the *v* ... Jer 15:19
and will make them like *v* figs ... Jer 29:17
for I am become *v* ... Lam 1:11
estate shall stand up a *v* person ... Dan 11:21
for thou art *v* ... Nah 1:14
filth upon thee, and make thee *v* ... Nah 3:6
gave them up unto *v* affections ... Rom 1:26
Who shall change our *v* body ... Phil 3:21
in also a poor man in *v* raiment ... Jas 2:2

### VILELY
of the mighty is *v* cast away ... 2Sa 1:21

### VILER
they were *v* than the earth ... Job 30:8

### VILEST
when the *v* men are exalted ... Ps 12:8

### VILLAGE
Go into the *v* over against you, ... Mt 21:2
way into the *v* over against you ... Mk 11:2
went throughout every city and *v* ... Lk 8:1
went, and entered into a *v* of the ... Lk 9:52
And they went to another *v* ... Lk 9:56
that he entered into a certain *v* ... Lk 10:38
And as he entered into a certain *v* ... Lk 17:12
Go ye into the *v* over against you ... Lk 19:30
same day to a *v* called Emmaus ... Lk 24:13
And they drew nigh unto the *v* ... Lk 24:28

### VILLAGES
out of the houses, out of the *v* ... Ex 8:13
But the houses of the *v* which ... Lev 25:31
Heshbon, and in all the *v* thereof ... Num 21:25
and they took the *v* thereof ... Num 21:32
the *v* thereof, and called it Nobah ... Num 32:42
the cities and the *v* thereof ... Josh 13:23
families, the cities, and their *v* ... Josh 13:28
are twenty and nine, with their *v* ... Josh 15:32
fourteen cities with their *v* ... Josh 15:36
sixteen cities with their *v* ... Josh 15:41
nine cities with their *v* ... Josh 15:44
Ekron, with her towns and her *v* ... Josh 15:45
lay near Ashdod, with their *v* ... Josh 15:46
Ashdod with her towns and her *v* ... Josh 15:47
Gaza with her towns and her *v* ... Josh 15:47
eleven cities with their *v* ... Josh 15:51
nine cities with their *v* ... Josh 15:54
ten cities with their *v* ... Josh 15:57
six cities with their *v* ... Josh 15:59
two cities with their *v* ... Josh 15:60
six cities with their *v* ... Josh 15:62
all the cities with their *v* ... Josh 16:9
twelve cities with their *v* ... Josh 18:24
fourteen cities with their *v* ... Josh 18:28
thirteen cities and their *v* ... Josh 19:6
four cities and their *v* ... Josh 19:7
all the *v* that were round about ... Josh 19:8
twelve cities with their *v* ... Josh 19:15
these cities with their *v* ... Josh 19:16
sixteen cities with their *v* ... Josh 19:22
families, the cities and their *v* ... Josh 19:23
twenty and two cities with their *v* ... Josh 19:30
these cities with their *v* ... Josh 19:31
nineteen cities with their *v* ... Josh 19:38
families, the cities and their *v* ... Josh 19:39
these cities with their *v* ... Josh 19:48
the *v* thereof, gave they to Caleb ... Josh 21:12
The inhabitants of the *v* ceased ... Judg 5:7
inhabitants of his *v* in Israel ... Judg 5:11
of fenced cities, and of country *v* ... 1Sa 6:18
And their *v* were, Etam, and Ain, ... 1Chr 4:32
all their *v* that were round about ... 1Chr 4:33
the *v* thereof, they gave to Caleb ... 1Chr 6:56
that dwelt in the *v* of the ... 1Chr 9:16
by their genealogy in their *v* ... 1Chr 9:22
brethren, which were in their *v* ... 1Chr 9:25
in the cities, and in the *v* ... 1Chr 27:25
and Shocho with the *v* thereof ... 2Chr 28:18
and Timnah with the *v* thereof ... 2Chr 28:18
Gimzo also and the *v* thereof ... 2Chr 28:18
one of the *v* in the plain of Ono ... Neh 6:2
And for the *v*, with their fields, ... Neh 11:25
in the *v* thereof, and at Dibon, and ... Neh 11:25
in the *v* thereof, and at Jekabzeel ... Neh 11:25
Jekabzeel, and in the *v* thereof, ... Neh 11:25
Beer-sheba, and in the *v* thereof, ... Neh 11:27
at Mekonah, and in the *v* thereof, ... Neh 11:28
Zanoah, Adullam, and in their *v* ... Neh 11:30
at Azekah, and in the *v* thereof ... Neh 11:30
Aija, and Beth-el, and in their *v* ... Neh 11:31
and from the *v* of Netophathi ... Neh 12:28
them *v* round about Jerusalem ... Neh 12:29
Therefore the Jews of the *v* ... Est 9:19
in the lurking places of the *v* ... Ps 10:8
let us lodge in the *v* ... Song 7:11
the *v* that Kedar doth inhabit ... Is 42:11
go up to the land of unwalled *v* ... Eze 38:11
with his staves the head of his *v* ... Hab 3:14
went about all the cities and *v* ... Mt 9:35
away, that they may go into the *v* ... Mt 14:15
And he went round about the *v* ... Mk 6:6
round about, and into the *v* ... Mk 6:36
whithersoever he entered, into *v* ... Mk 6:56
he went through the cities and *v* ... Lk 13:22
in many *v* of the Samaritans ... Acts 8:25

### VILLANY
For the vile person will speak *v* ... Is 32:6
they have committed *v* in Israel ... Jer 29:23

### VINE
dream, behold, a *v* was before me ... Gen 40:9
in the *v* were three branches ... Gen 40:10
Binding his foal unto the *v* ... Gen 49:11
his ass's colt unto the choice *v* ... Gen 49:11
the grapes of thy *v* undressed ... Lev 25:5
grapes in it of thy *v* undressed ... Lev 25:11
that is made of the *v* tree ... Num 6:4
their *v* is of the *v* of Sodom ... Deut 32:32
Then said the trees unto the *v* ... Judg 9:12
the *v* said unto them, Should I ... Judg 9:13
of any thing that cometh of the *v* ... Judg 13:14
safely, every man under his *v* ... 1Kin 4:25
gather herbs, and found a wild *v* ... 2Kin 4:39
eat ye every man of his own *v* ... 2Kin 18:31
*v* dressers in the mountains, and ... 2Chr 26:10
off his unripe grape as the *v* ... Job 15:33
hast brought a *v* out of Egypt ... Ps 80:8
and behold, and visit this *v* ... Ps 80:14
*v* by the sides of thine house ... Ps 128:3
to see whether the *v* flourished ... Song 6:11
shall be as clusters of the *v* ... Song 7:8
let us see if the *v* flourish ... Song 7:12
and planted it with the choicest *v* ... Is 5:2
languish, and the *v* of Sibmah ... Is 16:8
weeping of Jazer the *v* of Sibmah ... Is 16:9
the *v* languisheth, all the ... Is 24:7
fields, for the fruitful *v* ... Is 32:12
the leaf falleth off from the *v* ... Is 34:4
and eat ye every one of his *v* ... Is 36:16
Yet I had planted thee a noble *v* ... Jer 2:21
plant of a strange *v* unto me ... Jer 2:21
the remnant of Israel as a *v* ... Jer 6:9
there shall be no grapes on the *v* ... Jer 8:13
O *v* of Sibmah, I will weep for ... Jer 48:32
What is the *v* tree more than any ... Eze 15:2
As the *v* tree among the trees of ... Eze 15:6
a spreading *v* of low stature ... Eze 17:6

so it became a *v*, and brought ... Eze 17:6
this *v* did bend her roots toward ... Eze 17:7
that it might be a goodly *v* ... Eze 17:8
mother is like a *v* in thy blood ... Eze 19:10
Israel is an empty *v*, he bringeth ... Hos 10:1
as the corn, and grow as the *v* ... Hos 14:7
He hath laid my *v* waste, and ... Joel 1:7
The *v* is dried up, and the fig ... Joel 1:12
the *v* do yield their strength ... Joel 2:22
shall sit every man under his *v* ... Mic 4:4
out, and marred their *v* branches ... Nah 2:2
yea, as yet the *v*, and the fig ... Hag 2:19
man his neighbour under the *v* ... Zec 3:10
the *v* shall give her fruit, and ... Zec 8:12
neither shall your *v* cast her ... Mal 3:11
henceforth of this fruit of the *v* ... Mt 26:29
no more of the fruit of the *v* ... Mk 14:25
not drink of the fruit of the *v* ... Lk 22:18
I am the true *v*, and my Father is ... Jn 15:1
itself, except it abide in the *v* ... Jn 15:4
I am the *v*, ye are the branches ... Jn 15:5
either a *v*, figs? ... Jas 3:12
clusters of the *v* of the earth ... Rev 14:18
and gathered the *v* of the earth ... Rev 14:19

**VINEDRESSERS**
of the poor of the land to be *v* ... 2Kin 25:12
shall be your plowmen and your *v* ... Is 61:5
of the poor of the land for *v* ... Jer 52:16
howl, O ye *v*, for the wheat and ... Joel 1:11

**VINEGAR**
and shall drink no *v* of wine ... Num 6:3
or *v* of strong drink, neither ... Num 6:3
bread, and dip thy morsel in the *v* ... Ruth 2:14
my thirst they gave me *v* to drink ... Ps 69:21
As *v* to the teeth, and as smoke to ... Prov 10:26
as *v* upon nitre, so is he that ... Prov 25:20
They gave him *v* to drink mingled ... Mt 27:34
a spunge, and filled it with *v* ... Mt 27:48
ran and filled a spunge full of *v* ... Mk 15:36
coming to him, and offering him *v* ... Lk 23:36
there was set a vessel full of *v* ... Jn 19:29
and they filled a spunge with *v* ... Jn 19:29
therefore had received the *v* ... Jn 19:30

**VINES**
of seed, or of figs, or of *v* ... Num 20:5
A land of wheat, and barley, and *v* ... Deut 8:8
He destroyed their *v* with hail ... Ps 78:47
He smote their *v* also and their ... Ps 105:33
the *v* with the tender grape give ... Song 2:13
little foxes, that spoil the *v* ... Song 2:15
for our *v* have tender grapes ... Song 2:15
*v* at a thousand silverlings ... Is 7:23
they shall eat up thy *v* and thy ... Jer 5:17
Thou shalt yet plant *v* upon the ... Jer 31:5
And I will destroy her *v* and her ... Hos 2:12
neither shall fruit be in the *v* ... Hab 3:17

**VINEYARD**
an husbandman, and he planted a *v* ... Gen 9:20
cause a field or *v* to be eaten ... Ex 22:5
and of the best of his own *v* ... Ex 22:5
manner thou shalt deal with thy *v* ... Ex 23:11
And thou shalt not glean thy *v* ... Lev 19:10
thou gather every grape of thy *v* ... Lev 19:10
six years thou shalt prune thy *v* ... Lev 25:3
sow thy field, nor prune thy *v* ... Lev 25:4
man is he that hath planted a *v* ... Deut 20:6
not sow thy *v* with divers seeds ... Deut 22:9
hast sown, and the fruit of thy *v* ... Deut 22:9
comest into thy neighbour's *v* ... Deut 23:24
gatherest the grapes of thy *v* ... Deut 24:21
thou shalt plant a *v*, and shalt ... Deut 28:30
Naboth the Jezreelite had a *v* ... 1Kin 21:1
Naboth, saying, Give me thy *v* ... 1Kin 21:2
thee for it a better *v* than it ... 1Kin 21:2
unto him, Give me thy *v* for money ... 1Kin 21:6
I will give thee another *v* for it ... 1Kin 21:6
I will not give thee my *v* ... 1Kin 21:6
I will give thee the *v* of Naboth ... 1Kin 21:7
take possession of the *v* of ... 1Kin 21:15
to the *v* of Naboth the Jezreelite ... 1Kin 21:16
behold, he is in the *v* of Naboth ... 1Kin 21:18
the *v* which thy right hand hath ... Ps 80:15
by the *v* of the man void of ... Prov 24:30
of her hands she planteth a *v* ... Prov 31:16
but mine own *v* have I not kept ... Song 1:6
Solomon had a *v* at Baal-hamon ... Song 8:11
he let out the *v* unto keepers ... Song 8:11
My *v*, which is mine, is before me ... Song 8:12
Zion is left as a cottage in a *v* ... Is 1:8
for ye have eaten up the *v* ... Is 3:14
song of my beloved touching his *v* ... Is 5:1
My wellbeloved hath a *v* in a very ... Is 5:1
I pray you, betwixt me and my *v* ... Is 5:3
could have been done more to my *v* ... Is 5:4
tell you what I will do to my *v* ... Is 5:5
For the *v* of the LORD of hosts is ... Is 5:7
ten acres of *v* shall yield one ... Is 5:10
sing ye unto her, A *v* of red wine ... Is 27:2
Many pastors have destroyed my *v* ... Jer 12:10
house, nor sow seed, nor plant *v* ... Jer 35:7
neither have we *v*, nor field, nor ... Jer 35:9
the field, and as plantings of a *v* ... Mic 1:6
to hire labourers into his *v* ... Mt 20:1
a day, he sent them into his *v* ... Mt 20:2
Go ye also into the *v*, and ... Mt 20:4
unto them, Go ye also into the *v* ... Mt 20:7
the lord of the *v* saith unto his ... Mt 20:8
said, Son, go work to day in my *v* ... Mt 21:28
householder, which planted a *v* ... Mt 21:33
him, and cast him out of the *v* ... Mt 21:39
lord therefore of the *v* cometh ... Mt 21:40
will let out his *v* unto other ... Mt 21:41
A certain man planted a *v* ... Mk 12:1
husbandmen of the fruit of the *v* ... Mk 12:2
him, and cast him out of the *v* ... Mk 12:8
therefore the lord of the *v* do ... Mk 12:9
and will give the *v* unto others ... Mk 12:9
had a fig tree planted in his *v* ... Lk 13:6
said he unto the dresser of his *v* ... Lk 13:7
A certain man planted a *v* ... Lk 20:9
give him of the fruit of the *v* ... Lk 20:10
Then said the lord of the *v* ... Lk 20:13
So they cast him out of the *v* ... Lk 20:15
the lord of the *v* do unto them ... Lk 20:15
and shall give the *v* to others ... Lk 20:16
who planteth a *v*, and eateth not ... 1Cor 9:7

**VINEYARDS**
us inheritance of fields and *v* ... Num 16:14
the fields, or through the *v* ... Num 20:17
into the fields, or into the *v* ... Num 21:22
the LORD stood in a path of the *v* ... Num 22:24
which thou diggedst not, *v* ... Deut 6:11
Thou shalt plant *v*, and dress them ... Deut 28:39
of the *v* and oliveyards which ye ... Josh 24:13
the fields, and gathered their *v* ... Judg 9:27
and unto the plain of the *v* ... Judg 11:33
and came to the *v* of Timnath ... Judg 14:5
the standing corn, with the *v* ... Judg 15:5
Go and lie in wait in the *v* ... Judg 21:20
dances, then come ye out of the *v* ... Judg 21:21
will take your fields, and your *v* ... 1Sa 8:14
tenth of your seed, and of your *v* ... 1Sa 8:15
give every one of you fields and *v* ... 1Sa 22:7
garments, and oliveyards, and *v* ... 2Kin 5:26
and wine, a land of bread and *v* ... 2Kin 18:32
year sow ye, and reap, and plant *v* ... 2Kin 19:29
over the *v* was Shimei the ... 1Chr 27:27
over the increase of the *v* for ... 1Chr 27:27
We have mortgaged our lands, *v* ... Neh 5:3
and that upon our lands and *v* ... Neh 5:4
for other men have our lands and *v* ... Neh 5:5
this day, their lands, their *v* ... Neh 5:11
of all goods, wells digged, *v* ... Neh 9:25
he beholdeth not the way of the *v* ... Job 24:18
And sow the fields, and plant *v* ... Ps 107:37
I planted me *v* ... Eccl 2:4
they made me the keeper of the *v* ... Song 1:6
of camphire in the *v* of En-gedi ... Song 1:14
Let us get up early to the *v* ... Song 7:12
in the *v* there shall be no ... Is 16:10
and wine, a land of bread and *v* ... Is 36:17
year sow ye, and reap, and plant *v* ... Is 37:30
and they shall plant *v*, and eat the ... Is 65:21
*v* shall be possessed again in ... Jer 32:15
the land of Judah, and gave them *v* ... Jer 39:10
and shall build houses, and plant *v* ... Eze 28:26
I will give her her *v* from thence ... Hos 2:15
when your gardens and your *v* ... Amos 4:9
ye have planted pleasant *v* ... Amos 5:11
in all *v* shall be wailing ... Amos 5:17
and they shall plant *v*, and drink ... Amos 9:14
and they shall plant *v*, but not ... Zeph 1:13

**VINTAGE**
threshing shall reach unto the *v* ... Lev 26:5
the *v* shall reach unto the sowing ... Lev 26:5
better than the *v* of Abi-ezer ... Judg 8:2
they gather the *v* of the wicked ... Job 24:6
made their *v* shouting to cease ... Is 16:10
grapes when the *v* is done ... Is 24:13
for the *v* shall fail, the ... Is 32:10
thy summer fruits and upon thy *v* ... Jer 48:32
as the grapegleanings of the *v* ... Mic 7:1
the forest of the *v* is come down ... Zec 11:2

**VIOL**
And the harp, and the *v*, the tabret ... Is 5:12
That chant to the sound of the *v* ... Amos 6:5

**VIOLATED**
Her priests have *v* my law ... Eze 22:26

**VIOLENCE**
and the earth was filled with *v* ... Gen 6:11
is filled with *v* through them ... Gen 6:13
or in a thing taken away by *v* ... Lev 6:2
thou savest me from *v* ... 2Sa 22:3
him that loveth *v* his soul hateth ... Ps 11:5
for I have seen *v* and strife in ... Ps 55:9
ye weigh the *v* of your hands in ... Ps 58:2
their soul from deceit and *v* ... Ps 72:14
*v* covereth them as a garment ... Ps 73:6
and drink the wine of *v* ... Prov 4:17
but *v* covereth the mouth of the ... Prov 10:6
but *v* covereth the mouth of the ... Prov 10:11
of the transgressors shall eat *v* ... Prov 13:2
A man that doeth *v* to the blood ... Prov 28:17
because he had done no *v*, neither ... Is 53:9
the act of *v* is in their hands ... Is 59:6
*V* shall no more be heard in thy ... Is 60:18
*v* and spoil is heard in her ... Jer 6:7
I spake, I cried out, I cried *v* ... Jer 20:8
do no *v* to the stranger, the ... Jer 22:3
and for oppression, and for *v* ... Jer 22:17
The *v* done to me and to my flesh ... Jer 51:35
*v* in the land, ruler against ... Jer 51:46
*V* is risen up into a rod of ... Eze 7:11
crimes, and the city is full of *v* ... Eze 7:23
they have filled the land with *v* ... Eze 8:17
because of the *v* of all them that ... Eze 12:19
pledge, hath spoiled none by *v* ... Eze 18:7
poor and needy, hath spoiled by *v* ... Eze 18:12
pledge, neither hath spoiled by *v* ... Eze 18:16
spoiled his brother by *v* ... Eze 18:18
filled the midst of thee with *v* ... Eze 28:16
remove *v* and spoil, and execute ... Eze 45:9
for the *v* against the children of ... Joel 3:19
saith the LORD, who store up *v* ... Amos 3:10
cause the seat of *v* to come near ... Amos 6:3
For thy *v* against thy brother ... Obad 10
from the *v* that is in their hands ... Jonah 3:8
covet fields, and take them by *v* ... Mic 2:2
rich men thereof are full of *v* ... Mic 6:12
even cry out unto thee of *v* ... Hab 1:2
for spoiling and *v* are before me ... Hab 1:3
They shall come all for *v* ... Hab 1:9
for the *v* of the land, of the ... Hab 2:8
For the *v* of Lebanon shall cover ... Hab 2:17
for the *v* of the land, of the ... Hab 2:17
fill their masters' houses with *v* ... Zeph 1:9
they have done *v* to the law ... Zeph 3:4
one covereth *v* with his garment ... Mal 2:16
the kingdom of heaven suffereth *v* ... Mt 11:12
Do *v* to no man, neither accuse ... Lk 3:14
and brought them without *v* ... Acts 5:26
soldiers for the *v* of the people ... Acts 21:35
with great *v* took him away out of ... Acts 24:7
broken with the *v* of the waves ... Acts 27:41
Quenched the *v* of fire, escaped ... Heb 11:34
Thus with *v* shall that great city ... Rev 18:21

**VIOLENT**
hast delivered me from the *v* man ... 2Sa 22:49
his *v* dealing shall come down ... Ps 7:16
hast delivered me from the *v* man ... Ps 18:48
the assemblies of *v* men have ... Ps 86:14
preserve me from the *v* man ... Ps 140:1
preserve me from the *v* man ... Ps 140:4
evil shall hunt the *v* man to ... Ps 140:11
A *v* man enticeth his neighbour, ... Prov 16:29
*v* perverting of judgment and ... Eccl 5:8
and the *v* take it by force ... Mt 11:12

**VIOLENTLY**
servants had *v* taken away ... Gen 21:25
restore that which he took *v* away ... Lev 6:4
thine ass shall be *v* taken away ... Deut 28:31
because he hath *v* taken away an ... Job 20:19
they *v* take away flocks, and feed ... Job 24:2
He will surely *v* turn and toss ... Is 22:18
And he hath *v* taken away his ... Lam 2:6
the whole herd of swine ran *v* ... Mt 8:32
the herd ran *v* down a steep place ... Mk 5:13
the herd ran *v* down a steep place ... Lk 8:33

**VIOLS**
the grave, and the noise of thy *v* ... Is 14:11
will not hear the melody of thy *v* ... Amos 5:23

**VIPER**
come the young and old lion, the *v* ... Is 30:6
is crushed breaketh out into a *v* ... Is 59:5
there came a *v* out of the heat, ... Acts 28:3

**VIPER'S**
the *v* tongue shall slay him ... Job 20:16

**VIPERS**
said unto them, O generation of *v* ... Mt 3:7
O generation of *v*, how can ye, ... Mt 12:34
Ye serpents, ye generation of *v* ... Mt 23:33
of him, O generation of *v* ... Lk 3:7

**VIRGIN**
was very fair to look upon, a *v* ... Gen 24:16
that when the *v* cometh forth to ... Gen 24:43
And for his sister a *v*, that is ... Lev 21:3
but he shall take a *v* of his own ... Lev 21:14
an evil name upon a *v* of Israel ... Deut 22:19
If a damsel that is a *v* be ... Deut 22:23
a man find a damsel that is a *v* ... Deut 22:28
both the young man and the *v* ... Deut 32:25
for she was a *v* ... 2Sa 13:2
for my lord the king a young *v* ... 1Kin 1:2
The *v* the daughter of Zion hath ... 2Kin 19:21
a *v* shall conceive, and bear a son ... Is 7:14
more rejoice, O thou oppressed *v* ... Is 23:12
The *v*, the daughter of Zion, hath ... Is 37:22
O *v* daughter of Babylon, sit on ... Is 47:1
For as a young man marrieth a *v* ... Is 62:5
for the *v* daughter of my people ... Jer 14:17
the *v* of Israel hath done a very ... Jer 18:13
shalt be built, O *v* of Israel ... Jer 31:4
Then shall the *v* rejoice in the ... Jer 31:13
O *v* of Israel, turn again to ... Jer 31:21
up into Gilead, and take balm, O *v* ... Jer 46:11
the Lord hath trodden the *v* ... Lam 1:15
thee, O *v* daughter of Zion ... Lam 2:13
Lament like a *v* girded with ... Joel 1:8
The *v* of Israel is fallen ... Amos 5:2
a *v* shall be with child, and shall ... Mt 1:23
To a *v* espoused to a man whose ... Lk 1:27
if a *v* marry, she hath not sinned ... 1Cor 7:28
also between a wife and a *v* ... 1Cor 7:34
himself uncomely toward his *v* ... 1Cor 7:36
his heart that he will keep his *v* ... 1Cor 7:37
you as a chaste *v* to Christ ... 2Cor 11:2

**VIRGINITY**
And he shall take a wife in her *v* ... Lev 21:13
the tokens of the damsel's *v* unto ... Deut 22:15
are the tokens of my daughter's *v* ... Deut 22:17
the tokens of *v* be not found for ... Deut 22:20
the mountains, and bewail my *v* ... Judg 11:37

bewailed her v upon the mountains .. Judg 11:38
they bruised the teats of their v ... Eze 23:3
they bruised the breasts of her v ... Eze 23:8
an husband seven years from her v ... Lk 2:36

**VIRGIN'S**
and the v name was Mary ... Lk 1:27

**VIRGINS**
money according to the dowry of v ... Ex 22:17
four hundred young v, that had ... Judg 21:12
daughters that were v apparelled ... 2Sa 13:18
fair young v sought for the king ... Est 2:2
young v unto Shushan the palace ... Est 2:3
in his sight more than all the v ... Est 2:17
when the v were gathered together ... Est 2:19
the v her companions that follow ... Ps 45:14
therefore do the v love thee ... Song 1:3
concubines, and v without number ... Song 6:8
up young men, nor bring up v ... Is 23:4
her v are afflicted, and she is in ... Lam 1:4
my v and my young men are gone ... Lam 1:18
the v of Jerusalem hang down ... Lam 2:10
my v and my young men are fallen ... Lam 2:21
In that day shall the fair v ... Amos 8:13
of heaven be likened unto ten v ... Mt 25:1
Then all those v arose, and ... Mt 25:7
Afterward came also the other v ... Mt 25:11
same man had four daughters, v ... Acts 21:9
Now concerning v I have no ... 1Cor 7:25
for they are v ... Rev 14:4

**VIRTUE**
that v had gone out of him ... Mk 5:30
for there went v out of him ... Lk 6:19
perceive that v is gone out of me ... Lk 8:46
if there be any v, and if there be ... Phil 4:8
that hath called us to glory and v ... 2Pet 1:3
diligence, add to your faith v ... 2Pet 1:5
and to v knowledge ... 2Pet 1:5

**VIRTUOUS**
doth know that thou art a v woman .. Ruth 3:11
A v woman is a crown to her ... Prov 12:4
Who can find a v woman ... Prov 31:10

**VIRTUOUSLY**
Many daughters have done v ... Prov 31:29

**VISAGE**
his v was so marred more than any ... Is 52:14
Their v is blacker than a coal ... Lam 4:8
the form of his v was changed ... Dan 3:19

**VISIBLE**
heaven, and that are in earth, v ... Col 1:16

**VISION**
the LORD came unto Abram in a v ... Gen 15:1
make myself known unto him in a v .. Num 12:6
which saw the v of the Almighty ... Num 24:4
which saw the v of the Almighty, ... Num 24:16
there was no open v ... 1Sa 3:1
Samuel feared to shew Eli the v ... 1Sa 3:15
words, and according to all this v ... 2Sa 7:17
words, and according to all this v ... 1Chr 17:15
in the v of Isaiah the prophet ... 2Chr 32:32
chased away as a v of the night ... Job 20:8
in a v of the night, when deep ... Job 33:15
thou spakest in v to thy holy one ... Ps 89:19
Where there is no v, the people ... Prov 29:18
The v of Isaiah the son of Amoz, ... Is 1:1
A grievous v is declared unto me ... Is 21:2
The burden of the valley of v ... Is 22:1
GOD of hosts in the valley of v ... Is 22:5
they err in v, they stumble in ... Is 28:7
shall be as a dream of a night v ... Is 29:7
the v of all is become unto you ... Is 29:11
they prophesy unto you a false v ... Jer 14:14
they speak a v of their own heart ... Jer 23:16
also find no v from the LORD ... Lam 2:9
for the v is touching the whole ... Eze 7:13
they seek a v of the prophet ... Eze 7:26
according to the v that I saw in ... Eze 8:4
brought me in a v by the Spirit ... Eze 11:24
So the v that I had seen went up ... Eze 11:24
are prolonged, and every v faileth ... Eze 12:22
at hand, and the effect of every v ... Eze 12:23
vain v nor flattering divination ... Eze 12:24
The v that he seeth is for many ... Eze 12:27
Have ye not seen a vain v ... Eze 13:7
appearance of the v which I saw ... Eze 43:3
even according to the v that I ... Eze 43:3
the visions were like the v that ... Eze 43:3
revealed unto Daniel in a night v ... Dan 2:19
and said, I saw in my v by night ... Dan 7:2
Belshazzar a v appeared unto me ... Dan 8:1
And I saw in a v ... Dan 8:2
and I saw in a v, and I was by the ... Dan 8:2
spake, How long shall be the v ... Dan 8:13
I, even I Daniel, had seen the v ... Dan 8:15
make this man to understand the v ... Dan 8:16
time of the end shall be the v ... Dan 8:17
the v of the evening and the ... Dan 8:26
wherefore shut thou up the v ... Dan 8:26
and I was astonished at the v ... Dan 8:27
seen in the v at the beginning ... Dan 9:21
the matter, and consider the v ... Dan 9:23
and to seal up the v and prophecy, ... Dan 9:24
and had understanding of the v ... Dan 10:1
And I Daniel alone saw the v ... Dan 10:7
that were with me saw not the v ... Dan 10:7
left alone, and saw this great v ... Dan 10:8
for yet the v is for many days ... Dan 10:14
by the v my sorrows are turned ... Dan 10:16
themselves to establish the v ... Dan 11:14
The v of Obadiah ... Obad 1
you, that ye shall not have a v ... Mic 3:6
The book of the v of Nahum the ... Nah 1:1
answered me, and said, Write the v ... Hab 2:2
For the v is yet for an appointed ... Hab 2:3
be ashamed every one of his v ... Zec 13:4
Tell the v to no man, until the ... Mt 17:9
he had seen a v in the temple ... Lk 1:22
they had also seen a v of angels ... Lk 24:23
and to him said the Lord in a v ... Acts 9:10
hath seen in a v a man named ... Acts 9:12
He saw in a v evidently about the ... Acts 10:3
doubted in himself what this v ... Acts 10:17
While Peter thought on the v ... Acts 10:19
and in a trance I saw a v, A ... Acts 11:5
but thought he saw a v ... Acts 12:9
a v appeared to Paul in the night ... Acts 16:9
And after he had seen the v ... Acts 16:10
Lord to Paul in the night by a v ... Acts 18:9
disobedient unto the heavenly v ... Acts 26:19
And thus I saw the horses in the v ... Rev 9:17

**VISIONS**
unto Israel in the v of the night ... Gen 46:2
in the v of Iddo the seer against ... 2Chr 9:29
had understanding in the v of God ... 2Chr 26:5
thoughts from the v of the night ... Job 4:13
and terrifiest me through v ... Job 7:14
were opened, and I saw v of God ... Eze 1:1
brought me in the v of God to ... Eze 8:3
which see v of peace for her, and ... Eze 13:16
In the v of God brought he me ... Eze 40:2
the v were like the vision that I ... Eze 43:3
Daniel had understanding in all v ... Dan 1:17
the v of thy head upon thy bed, ... Dan 2:28
the v of my head troubled me ... Dan 4:5
tell me the v of my dream that I ... Dan 4:9
Thus were the v of mine head in ... Dan 4:10
I saw in the v of my head upon my ... Dan 4:13
v of his head upon his bed ... Dan 7:1
After this I saw in the night v ... Dan 7:7
I saw in the night v, and, behold, ... Dan 7:13
the v of my head troubled me ... Dan 7:15
prophets, and I have multiplied v ... Hos 12:10
your young men shall see v ... Joel 2:28
and your young men shall see v ... Acts 2:17
I will come to v and revelations ... 2Cor 12:1

**VISIT**
and God will surely v you, and ... Gen 50:24
saying, God will surely v you ... Gen 50:25
saying, God will surely v you ... Ex 13:19
I v I will v their sin upon ... Ex 32:34
therefore I do v the iniquity ... Lev 18:25
thou shalt v thy habitation, and ... Job 5:24
shouldest v him every morning ... Job 7:18
awake to v all the heathen ... Ps 59:5
heaven, and behold, and v this vine ... Ps 80:14
Then will I v their transgression ... Ps 89:32
O v me with thy salvation ... Ps 106:4
years, that the LORD will v Tyre ... Is 23:17
neither shall they v it ... Jer 3:16
Shall I not v for these things ... Jer 5:9
Shall I not v for these things ... Jer 5:29
at the time that I v them they ... Jer 6:15
Shall I not v them for these ... Jer 9:9
their iniquity, and v their sins ... Jer 14:10
v me, and revenge me of my ... Jer 15:15
I will v upon you the evil of ... Jer 23:2
be until the day that I v them ... Jer 27:22
at Babylon I will v you, and ... Jer 29:10
there shall he be until I v him ... Jer 32:5
him, the time that I will v him ... Jer 49:8
come, the time that I will v thee ... Jer 50:31
he will v thine iniquity, O ... Lam 4:22
I will v upon her the days of ... Hos 2:13
their iniquity, and v their sins ... Hos 8:13
iniquity, he will v their sins ... Hos 9:9
v the transgressions of Israel ... Amos 3:14
will also v the altars of Beth-el ... Amos 3:14
the LORD their God shall v them ... Zeph 2:7
which shall not v those that be ... Zec 11:16
it came into his heart to v his ... Acts 7:23
at the first did v the Gentiles ... Acts 15:14
v our brethren in every city ... Acts 15:36
To v the fatherless and widows in ... Jas 1:27

**VISITATION**
be visited after the v of all men ... Num 16:29
thy v hath preserved my spirit ... Job 10:12
what will ye do in the day of v ... Is 10:3
in the time of their v they shall ... Jer 8:12
time of their v they shall perish ... Jer 10:15
even the year of their v ... Jer 11:23
them, even the year of their v ... Jer 23:12
upon them, and the time of their v ... Jer 46:21
upon Moab, the year of their v ... Jer 48:44
day is come, the time of their v ... Jer 50:27
time of their v they shall perish ... Jer 51:18
The days of v are come, the days ... Hos 9:7
of thy watchmen and thy v cometh ... Mic 7:4
knewest not the time of thy v ... Lk 19:44
glorify God in the day of v ... 1Pet 2:12

**VISITED**
the LORD v Sarah as he had said, ... Gen 21:1
me, saying, I have surely v you ... Ex 3:16
LORD had v the children of Israel ... Ex 4:31
or if they be v after the ... Num 16:29
that Samson v his wife with a kid ... Judg 15:1
of Moab how that the LORD had v ... Ruth 1:6
And the LORD v Hannah, so that she ... 1Sa 2:21
is not so, he hath v in his anger ... Job 35:15
thou hast v me in the night ... Ps 17:3
he shall not be v with evil ... Prov 19:23
after many days shall they be v ... Is 24:22
therefore hast thou v and ... Is 26:14
LORD, in trouble have they v thee ... Is 26:16
Thou shalt be v of the LORD of ... Is 29:6
this is the city to be v ... Jer 6:6
them away, and have not v them ... Jer 23:2
After many days thou shalt be v ... Eze 38:8
for the LORD of hosts hath v his ... Zec 10:3
I was sick, and ye v me ... Mt 25:36
and in prison, and ye v me not ... Mt 25:43
for he hath v and redeemed his ... Lk 1:68
dayspring from on high hath v us ... Lk 1:78
and, That God hath v his people ... Lk 7:16

**VISITEST**
the son of man, that thou v him ... Ps 8:4
Thou v the earth, and waterest it ... Ps 65:9
the son of man, that thou v him ... Heb 2:6

**VISITETH**
and when he v, what shall I answer ... Job 31:14

**VISITING**
v the iniquity of the fathers ... Ex 20:5
v the iniquity of the fathers ... Ex 34:7
v the iniquity of the fathers ... Num 14:18
v the iniquity of the fathers ... Deut 5:9

**VOCATION**
of the v wherewith ye are called ... Eph 4:1

**VOICE** See PREFACE.
the v of thy brother's blood ... Gen 4:10
and said, The v is Jacob's v ... Gen 27:22
Beware of him, and obey his v ... Ex 23:21
the people answered with one v ... Ex 24:3
ye heard the v of the words ... Deut 4:12
Did ever people hear the v of God ... Deut 4:33
and after the fire a still small v ... 1Kin 19:12
into the v of them that weep ... Job 30:31
After it a v roareth ... Job 37:4
with the v of his excellency ... Job 37:4
not stay them when his v is heard ... Job 37:4
marvellously with his v ... Job 37:5
thou lift up thy v to the clouds ... Job 38:34
My v shalt thou hear in the ... Ps 5:3
house of God, with the v of joy ... Ps 42:4
To day if ye will hear his v ... Ps 95:7
my v is to the sons of man ... Prov 8:4
unto thee at the v of thy cry ... Is 30:19
The v of him that crieth in the ... Is 40:3
the v of weeping shall be no more ... Is 65:19
heard in her, nor the v of crying ... Is 65:19
When he uttereth his v, there is ... Jer 10:13
as the v of the Almighty God when ... Eze 10:5
his v was like a noise of many ... Eze 43:2
The v of one crying in the ... Mt 3:3
lo a v from heaven, saying, This ... Mt 3:17
behold a v out of the cloud, ... Mt 17:5
The v of one crying in the ... Mk 1:3
The v of one crying in the ... Lk 3:4
I am the v of one crying in the ... Jn 1:23
hear the v of the Son of God ... Jn 5:25
for they know his v ... Jn 10:4
This v came not because of me, ... Jn 12:30
that is of the truth heareth my v ... Jn 18:37
him stood speechless, hearing a v ... Acts 9:7
saying, It is the v of a god ... Acts 12:22
that by my v I might teach others ... 1Cor 14:19
To day if ye will hear his v ... Heb 3:7
To day if ye will hear his v ... Heb 3:15
Whose v then shook the earth ... Heb 12:26
his v as the sound of many waters ... Rev 1:15
if any man hear my v, and open the ... Rev 3:20

**VOICES**
before God, and lifted up their v ... Judg 21:2
all the people lifted up their v ... 1Sa 11:4
And they lifted up their v ... Lk 17:13
And they were instant with loud v ... Lk 23:23
the v of them and of the chief ... Lk 23:23
nor yet the v of the prophets ... Acts 13:27
had done, they lifted up their v ... Acts 14:11
word, and then lifted up their v ... Acts 22:22
so many kinds of v in the world ... 1Cor 14:10
lightnings and thunderings and v ... Rev 4:5
and there were v, and thunderings, ... Rev 8:5
v of the trumpet of the three ... Rev 8:13
seven thunders uttered their v ... Rev 10:3
thunders had uttered their v ... Rev 10:4
and there were great v in heaven ... Rev 11:15
and there were lightnings, and v ... Rev 11:19
And there were v, and thunders, and . Rev 16:18

**VOID**
the earth was without form, and v ... Gen 1:2
them v on the day he heard them ... Num 30:12
her husband hath made them v ... Num 30:12
it, or her husband may make it v ... Num 30:13
v after that he hath heard them ... Num 30:15
they are a nation v of counsel ... Deut 32:28
in a v place in the entrance of ... 1Kin 22:10
they sat in a v place at the ... 2Chr 18:9
Thou hast made v the covenant of ... Ps 89:39
for they have made v thy law ... Ps 119:126
a young man v of understanding, ... Prov 7:7
of him that is v of understanding ... Prov 10:13
He that is v of wisdom despiseth ... Prov 11:12

persons is *v* of understanding... Prov 12:11
A man *v* of understanding striketh... Prov 17:18
of the man *v* of understanding... Prov 24:30
it shall not return unto me *v*... Is 55:11
and, lo, it was without form, and *v*... Jer 4:23
I will make *v* the counsel of... Jer 19:7
She is empty, and *v*, and waste... Nah 2:10
*v* of offence toward God, and... Acts 24:16
Do we then make *v* the law through... Rom 3:31
the law be heirs, faith is made *v*... Rom 4:14
any man should make my glorying *v*... 1Cor 9:15

**VOLUME**
in the *v* of the book it is... Ps 40:7
I come (in the *v* of the book it... Heb 10:7

**VOLUNTARILY**
peace offerings *v* unto the LORD... Eze 46:12

**VOLUNTARY**
his own *v* will at the door of the... Lev 1:3
or a *v* offering, it shall be... Lev 7:16
a *v* burnt offering or peace... Eze 46:12
of your reward in a *v* humility... Col 2:18

**VOMIT**
and he shall *v* them up again... Job 20:15
thou hast eaten shalt thou *v* up... Prov 23:8
thou be filled therewith, and *v* it... Prov 25:16
As a dog returneth to his *v*... Prov 26:11
a drunken man staggereth in his *v*... Is 19:14
For all tables are full of *v*... Is 28:8
Moab also shall wallow in his *v*... Jer 48:26
dog is turned to his own *v* again... 2Pet 2:22

**VOMITED**
it *v* out Jonah upon the dry land... Jonah 2:10

**VOMITETH**
the land itself *v* out her... Lev 18:25

**VOPHSI** (*vof'-si*) *A spy sent to the Promised Land.*
of Naphtali, Nahbi the son of *V*... Num 13:14

**VOW**
And Jacob vowed a *v*, saying, If... Gen 28:20
and where thou vowedst a *v* unto me Gen 31:13
sacrifice of his offering be a *v*... Lev 7:16
unto the LORD to accomplish his *v*... Lev 22:21
but for a *v* it shall not be... Lev 22:23
a man shall make a singular *v*... Lev 27:2
separate themselves to *v*... Num 6:2
a *v* of a Nazarite, to... Num 6:2
All the days of the *v* of his... Num 6:5
according to the *v* which he vowed... Num 6:21
or a sacrifice in performing a *v*... Num 15:3
for a sacrifice in performing a *v*... Num 15:8
And Israel vowed a *v* unto the LORD... Num 21:2
If a man *v* a... Num 30:2
a *v* unto the LORD... Num 30:2
If a woman also *v* a... Num 30:3
a *v* unto the LORD... Num 30:3
And her father hear her *v*, and her... Num 30:4
shall make her *v* which she vowed... Num 30:8
But every *v* of a widow, and of her... Num 30:9
Every *v*, and every binding oath to... Num 30:13
vows which ye *v* unto the LORD... Deut 12:11
of the LORD thy God for any *v*... Deut 23:18
When thou shalt *v* a... Deut 23:21
a *v* unto the LORD thy God... Deut 23:21
But if thou shalt forbear to *v*... Deut 23:22
Jephthah vowed a *v* unto the LORD... Judg 11:30
to his *v* which he had vowed... Judg 11:39
And she vowed a *v*, and said, O LORD... 1Sa 1:11
the yearly sacrifice, and his *v*... 1Sa 1:21
pray thee, let me go and pay my *v*... 2Sa 15:7
For thy servant vowed a *v* while I... 2Sa 15:8
thee shall the *v* be performed... Ps 65:1
*V*, and pay unto the LORD your God... Ps 76:11
When thou vowest a *v* unto God... Eccl 5:4
is it that thou shouldest not *v*... Eccl 5:5
than that thou shouldest *v*... Eccl 5:5
oblation; yea, they shall *v*... Is 19:21
a *v* unto the LORD... Is 19:21
for he had a *v*... Acts 18:18
four men which have a *v* on them... Acts 21:23

**VOWED**
And Jacob *v* a vow, saying, If God... Gen 28:20
that *v* shall the priest value him... Lev 27:8
law of the Nazarite who hath *v*... Num 6:21
according to the vow which he *v*... Num 6:21
Israel *v* a vow unto the LORD, and... Num 21:2
had at all an husband, when she *v*... Num 30:6
he shall make her vow which she *v*... Num 30:8
if she *v* in her husband's house,... Num 30:10
thou hast *v* unto the LORD thy God... Deut 23:23
Jephthah *v* a vow unto the LORD,... Judg 11:30
to his vow which he had *v*... Judg 11:39
she *v* a vow, and said, O LORD of... 1Sa 1:11
which I have *v* unto the LORD, in... 2Sa 15:7
For thy servant *v* a vow while I... 2Sa 15:8
*v* unto the mighty God of Jacob... Ps 132:2
pay that which thou hast *v*... Eccl 5:4
perform our vows that we have *v*... Jer 44:25
I will pay that that I have *v*... Jonah 2:9

**VOWEDST**
where thou *v* a vow unto me... Gen 31:13

**VOWEST**
nor any of thy vows which thou *v*... Deut 12:17
When thou *v* a vow unto God, defer... Eccl 5:4

**VOWETH**
hath in his flock a male, and *v*... Mal 1:14

**VOWS**
offer his oblation for all his *v*... Lev 22:18
your gifts, and beside all your *v*... Lev 23:38
in your set feasts, beside your *v*... Num 29:39
then all her *v* shall stand... Num 30:4
not any of her *v*, or of her bonds... Num 30:5
then her *v* shall stand, and her... Num 30:7
then all her *v* shall stand... Num 30:11
out of her lips concerning her *v*... Num 30:12
then he establisheth all her *v*... Num 30:14
offerings of your hand, and your *v*... Deut 12:6
all your choice *v* which ye vow... Deut 12:11
nor any of thy *v* which thou... Deut 12:17
things which thou hast, and thy *v*... Deut 12:26
thee, and thou shalt pay thy *v*... Job 22:27
I will pay my *v* before them that... Ps 22:25
pay thy *v* unto the most High... Ps 50:14
Thy *v* are upon me, O God... Ps 56:12
For thou, O God, hast heard my *v*... Ps 61:5
that I may daily perform my *v*... Ps 61:8
I will pay thee my *v*,... Ps 66:13
I will pay my *v* unto the LORD now... Ps 116:14
I will pay my *v* unto the LORD now... Ps 116:18
this day have I payed my *v*... Prov 7:14
holy, and after *v* to make enquiry... Prov 20:25
and what, the son of my *v*... Prov 31:2
perform our *v* that we have vowed... Jer 44:25
ye will surely accomplish your *v*... Jer 44:25
and surely perform your *v*... Jer 44:25
unto the LORD, and made *v*... Jonah 1:16
thy solemn feasts, perform thy *v*... Nah 1:15

**VOYAGE**
that this *v* will be with hurt... Acts 27:10

**VULTURE**
And the *v*, and the kite after his... Lev 11:14
kite, and the *v* after his kind,... Deut 14:13

**VULTURE'S**
which the *v* eye hath not seen... Job 28:7

**VULTURES**
there shall the *v* also be... Is 34:15

# W

**WADI ZERED** See ZERED.

**WAFER**
one *w* out of the basket of the... Ex 29:23
a cake of oiled bread, and one *w*... Lev 8:26
the basket, and one unleavened *w*... Num 6:19

**WAFERS**
of it was like *w* made with honey... Ex 16:31
*w* unleavened anointed with oil... Ex 29:2
or unleavened *w* anointed with oil... Lev 2:4
unleavened *w* anointed with oil,... Lev 7:12
*w* of unleavened bread anointed... Num 6:15

**WAG**
be astonished, and *w* his head... Jer 18:16
*w* their head at the daughter of... Lam 2:15
by her shall hiss, and *w* his hand... Zeph 2:15

**WAGES**
tell me, what shall thy *w* be... Gen 29:15
And he said, Appoint me thy *w*... Gen 30:28
me, and changed my *w* ten times... Gen 31:7
thus, The speckled shall be thy *w*... Gen 31:8
thou hast changed my *w* ten times... Gen 31:41
for me, and I will give thee thy *w*... Ex 2:9
the *w* of him that is hired shall... Lev 19:13
his neighbour's service without *w*... Jer 22:13
yet had he no *w*, nor his army,... Eze 29:18
and it shall be the *w* for his army... Eze 29:19
he that earneth *w* earneth *w*... Hag 1:6
oppress the hireling in his *w*... Mal 3:5
and be content with your *w*... Lk 3:14
And he that reapeth receiveth *w*... Jn 4:36
For the *w* of sin is death... Rom 6:23
taking *w* of them, to do you... 2Cor 11:8
son of Bosor, who loved the *w* of... 2Pet 2:15

**WAGGING**
by reviled him, *w* their heads,... Mt 27:39
*w* their heads, and saying, Ah,... Mk 15:29

**WAGON**
a *w* for two of the princes, and... Num 7:3

**WAGONS**
take you *w* out of the land of... Gen 45:19
and Joseph gave them *w*, according... Gen 45:21
when he saw the *w* which Joseph... Gen 45:27
in the *w* which Pharaoh had sent... Gen 46:5
before the LORD, six covered *w*... Num 7:3
And Moses took the *w* and the oxen,... Num 7:6
Two *w* and four oxen he gave unto... Num 7:7
And four *w* and eight oxen he gave... Num 7:8
against thee with chariots, *w*... Eze 23:24

**WAIL**
*w* for the multitude of Egypt, and... Eze 32:18
Therefore I will *w* and howl, I... Mic 1:8
the earth shall *w* because of him... Rev 1:7

**WAILED**
and them that wept and *w* greatly... Mk 5:38

**WAILING**
and fasting, and weeping, and *w*... Est 4:3
will I take up a weeping and *w*... Jer 9:10
make haste, and take up a *w* for us... Jer 9:18
For a voice of *w* is heard out of... Jer 9:19
mouth, and teach your daughters *w*... Jer 9:20
neither shall there be *w* for them... Eze 7:11
bitterness of heart and bitter *w*... Eze 27:31
in their *w* they shall take up a... Eze 27:32
*W* shall be in all streets... Amos 5:16
are skilful of lamentation to *w*... Amos 5:16
And in all vineyards shall be *w*... Amos 5:17
I will make a *w* like the dragons,... Mic 1:8
there shall be *w* and gnashing of... Mt 13:42
there shall be *w* and gnashing of... Mt 13:50
fear of her torment, weeping and *w*... Rev 18:15
heads, and cried, weeping and *w*... Rev 18:19

**WAIT**
And if a man lie not in *w*, but God... Ex 21:13
they shall *w* on their priest's... Num 3:10
in to *w* upon the service of the... Num 8:24
or hurl at him by laying of *w*... Num 35:20
him any thing without laying of *w*... Num 35:22
lie in *w* for him, and rise up... Deut 19:11
ye shall lie in *w* against the... Josh 8:4
their liers in *w* on the west of... Josh 8:13
in *w* for him in the top of the... Judg 9:25
thee, and lie in *w* in the field... Judg 9:32
they laid *w* against Shechem in... Judg 9:34
were with him, from lying in *w*... Judg 9:35
laid *w* in the field, and looked,... Judg 9:43
laid *w* for him all night in the... Judg 16:2
Now there were men lying in *w*... Judg 16:9
there were liers in *w* abiding in... Judg 16:12
set liers in *w* round about Gibeah... Judg 20:29
the liers in *w* of Israel came... Judg 20:33
in *w* which they had set beside... Judg 20:36
And the liers in *w* hasted, and... Judg 20:37
the liers in *w* drew themselves... Judg 20:37
men of Israel and the liers in *w*... Judg 20:38
lie in *w* in the vineyards... Judg 21:20
how he laid *w* for him in the way,... 1Sa 15:2
Amalek, and laid *w* in the valley... 1Sa 15:5
servant against me, to lie in *w*... 1Sa 22:8
rise against me, to lie in *w*... 1Sa 22:13
what should I *w* for the LORD any... 2Kin 6:33
Because their office was to *w* on... 1Chr 23:28
and did not then *w* by course... 2Chr 5:11
the Levites *w* upon their business... 2Chr 13:10
and of such as lay in *w* by the way... Ezr 8:31
of my appointed time will I *w*... Job 14:14
If I *w*, the grave is mine house... Job 17:13
or if I have laid *w* at my... Job 31:9
abide in the covert to lie in *w*... Job 38:40
He lieth in *w* secretly as a lion... Ps 10:9
he lieth in *w* to catch the poor... Ps 10:9
let none that *w* on thee be... Ps 25:3
on thee do I *w* all the day... Ps 25:5
for I *w* on thee... Ps 25:21
*W* on the LORD... Ps 27:14
*w*, I say, on the LORD... Ps 27:14
the LORD, and *w* patiently for him... Ps 37:7
but those that *w* upon the LORD... Ps 37:9
*W* on the LORD, and keep his way,... Ps 37:34
And now, Lord, what *w* I for... Ps 39:7
and I will *w* on thy name... Ps 52:9
my steps, when they *w* for my soul... Ps 56:6
lo, they lie in *w* for my soul... Ps 59:3
his strength will I *w* upon thee... Ps 59:9
My soul, *w* thou only upon God... Ps 62:5
eyes fail while I *w* for my God... Ps 69:3
Let not them that *w* on thee... Ps 69:6
they that lay *w* for my soul take... Ps 71:10
These *w* all upon thee... Ps 104:27
so our eyes *w* upon the LORD our... Ps 123:2
*w* for the LORD, my soul doth *w*... Ps 130:5
The eyes of all *w* upon thee... Ps 145:15
with us, let us lay *w* for blood... Prov 1:11
they lay *w* for their own blood... Prov 1:18
lieth in *w* at every corner... Prov 7:12
wicked are to lie in *w* for blood... Prov 12:6
but *w* on the LORD, and he shall... Prov 20:22
She also lieth in *w* as for a prey... Prov 23:28
Lay not *w*, O wicked man, against... Prov 24:15
I will *w* upon the LORD, that... Is 8:17
And therefore will the LORD *w*... Is 30:18
are all they that *w* for him... Is 30:18
But they that *w* upon the LORD... Is 40:31
and the isles shall *w* for his law... Is 42:4
not be ashamed that *w* for me... Is 49:23
the isles shall *w* upon me... Is 51:5
we *w* for light, but behold... Is 59:9
Surely the isles shall *w* for me... Is 60:9
they lay *w*, as he that setteth... Jer 5:26
but in heart he layeth his *w*... Jer 9:8
therefore we will *w* upon thee... Jer 14:22
was unto me as a bear lying in *w*... Lam 3:10
is good unto them that *w* for him... Lam 3:25
quietly *w* for the salvation of... Lam 3:26
they laid *w* for us in the... Lam 4:19
as troops of robbers *w* for a man... Hos 6:9

W

an oven, whiles they lie in *w* Hos 7:6
and *w* on thy God continually Hos 12:6
they all lie in *w* for blood Mic 7:2
I will *w* for the God of my Mic 7:7
though it tarry, *w* for it Hab 2:3
Therefore *w* ye upon me, saith the Zeph 3:8
that a small ship should *w* on him Mk 3:9
Laying *w* for him, and seeking to Lk 11:54
unto men that *w* for their lord Lk 12:36
but *w* for the promise of the Acts 1:4
And when the Jews laid *w* for him Acts 20:3
me by the lying in *w* of the Jews Acts 20:19
son heard of their lying in *w* Acts 23:16
for there lie in *w* for him of Acts 23:21
that the Jews laid *w* for the man Acts 23:30
laying *w* in the way to kill him Acts 25:3
then do we with patience *w* for it Rom 8:25
let us *w* on our ministering Rom 12:7
they which *w* at the altar are 1Cor 9:13
For we through the Spirit *w* for Gal 5:5
whereby they lie in *w* to deceive Eph 4:14
to *w* for his Son from heaven, 1Th 1:10

### WAITED
I have *w* for thy salvation, O Gen 49:18
*w* for the king by the way, and 1Kin 20:38
and she *w* on Naaman's wife 2Kin 5:2
then they *w* on their office 1Chr 6:32
they that *w* with their children 1Chr 6:33
Who hitherto *w* in the king's gate 1Chr 9:18
the priests *w* on their offices 2Chr 7:6
These *w* on the king, beside those 2Chr 17:19
the porters *w* at every gate 2Chr 35:15
priests and for the Levites that *w* Neh 12:44
the companies of Sheba *w* for them Job 6:19
and he is *w* for of the sword Job 15:22
Unto me men gave ear, and *w* Job 29:21
they *w* for me as for the rain Job 29:23
when I *w* for light, there came Job 30:26
Now Elihu had *w* till Job had Job 32:4
Behold, I *w* for your words Job 32:11
When I had *w*, (for they spake not Job 32:16
I *w* patiently for the LORD Ps 40:1
they *w* not for his counsel Ps 106:13
The wicked have *w* for me to Ps 119:95
we have *w* for him, and he will Is 25:9
we have *w* for him, we will be Is 25:9
O LORD, have we *w* for thee Is 26:8
we have *w* for thee Is 33:2
Now when she saw that she had *w* Eze 19:5
of Maroth *w* carefully for good Mic 1:12
*w* upon me knew that it was the Zec 11:11
which also *w* for the kingdom of Mk 15:43
the people *w* for Zacharias, and Lk 1:21
who also himself *w* for the Lk 23:51
of them that *w* on him continually Acts 10:7
And Cornelius *w* for them, and had Acts 10:24
Now while Paul *w* for them at Acts 17:16
of God *w* in the days of Noah 1Pet 3:20

### WAITETH
the adulterer *w* for the twilight Job 24:15
Our soul *w* for the LORD Ps 33:20
Truly my soul *w* upon God Ps 62:1
Praise *w* for thee, O God, in Sion Ps 65:1
My soul *w* for the Lord more than Ps 130:6
so he that *w* on his master shall Prov 27:18
prepared for him that *w* for him Is 64:4
Blessed is he that *w*, and cometh Dan 12:12
nor *w* for the sons of men Mic 5:7
expectation of the creature *w* for Rom 8:19
the husbandman *w* for the precious Jas 5:7

### WAITING
cease *w* upon the service thereof Num 8:25
*w* at the posts of my doors Prov 8:34
*w* for the consolation of Israel Lk 2:25
for they were all *w* for him Lk 8:40
*w* for the moving of the water Jn 5:3
*w* for the adoption, to wit, the Rom 8:23
*w* for the coming of our Lord 1Cor 1:7
and into the patient *w* for Christ 2Th 3:5

### WAKE
sleep a perpetual sleep, and not *w* Jer 51:39
sleep a perpetual sleep, and not *w* Jer 51:57
*w* up the mighty men, let all the Joel 3:9
us, that, whether we *w* or sleep 1Th 5:10

### WAKED
*w* me, as a man that is wakened Zec 4:1

### WAKENED
Let the heathen be *w*, and come up Joel 3:12
a man that is *w* out of his sleep Zec 4:1

### WAKENETH
he *w* morning by morning Is 50:4
he *w* mine ear to hear as the Is 50:4

### WAKETH
city, the watchman *w* but in vain Ps 127:1
I sleep, but my heart *w* Song 5:2

### WAKING
Thou holdest mine eyes *w* Ps 77:4

### WALK
*w* through the land in the length Gen 13:17
*w* before me, and be thou perfect Gen 17:1
me, The LORD, before whom I *w* Gen 24:40
my fathers Abraham and Isaac did *w* Gen 48:15
whether they will *w* in my law Ex 16:4
them the way wherein they must *w* Ex 18:20
*w* abroad upon his staff, then Ex 21:19
neither shall ye *w* in their Lev 18:3
mine ordinances, to *w* therein Lev 18:4
ye shall not *w* in the manners of Lev 20:23
If ye *w* in my statutes, and keep Lev 26:3
I will *w* among you, and will be Lev 26:12
if ye *w* contrary unto me, and will Lev 26:21
but will *w* contrary unto me Lev 26:23
Then will I also *w* contrary unto Lev 26:24
unto me, but *w* contrary unto me Lev 26:27
Then I will *w* contrary unto you Lev 26:28
Ye shall *w* in all the ways which Deut 5:33
to *w* in his ways, and to fear him Deut 8:6
*w* after other gods, and serve them Deut 8:19
to *w* in all his ways, and to love Deut 10:12
to *w* in all his ways, and to Deut 11:22
Ye shall *w* after the LORD your Deut 13:4
thy God commanded thee to *w* in Deut 13:5
thy God, and to *w* ever in his ways Deut 19:9
to *w* in his ways, and to keep his Deut 26:17
LORD thy God, and *w* in his ways Deut 28:9
though I *w* in the imagination of Deut 29:19
to *w* in his ways, and to keep his Deut 30:16
*w* through the land, and describe Josh 18:8
to *w* in all his ways, and to keep Josh 22:5
the way of the LORD to *w* therein Judg 2:22
sit in judgment, and *w* by the way Judg 5:10
should *w* before me for ever 1Sa 2:30
he shall *w* before mine anointed 1Sa 2:35
thy sons *w* not in thy ways 1Sa 8:5
to *w* in his ways, to keep his 1Kin 2:3
to *w* before me in truth with all 1Kin 2:4
And if thou wilt *w* in my ways 1Kin 3:14
as thy father David did *w* 1Kin 3:14
if thou wilt *w* in my statutes, and 1Kin 6:12
all my commandments to *w* in them 1Kin 6:12
that *w* before thee with all their 1Kin 8:23
that they *w* before me as thou 1Kin 8:25
good way wherein they should *w* 1Kin 8:36
to *w* in all his ways, and to keep 1Kin 8:58
to *w* in his statutes, and to keep 1Kin 8:61
And if thou wilt *w* before me 1Kin 9:4
wilt *w* in my ways, and do that is 1Kin 11:38
been a light thing for him to *w* 1Kin 16:31
But Jehu took no heed to *w* in the 2Kin 10:31
to *w* after the LORD, and to keep 2Kin 23:3
that *w* before thee with all their 2Chr 6:14
heed to their way to *w* in my law 2Chr 6:16
good way, wherein they should *w* 2Chr 6:27
to *w* in thy ways, so long as they 2Chr 6:31
thee, if thou wilt *w* before me 2Chr 7:17
to *w* after the LORD, and to keep 2Chr 34:31
ought ye not to *w* in the fear of Neh 5:9
to *w* in God's law, which was Neh 10:29
The wicked *w* on every side, when Ps 12:8
though I *w* through the valley of Ps 23:4
I will *w* in mine integrity Ps 26:11
*W* about Zion, and go round about Ps 48:12
that I may *w* before God in the Ps 56:13
God, and refused to *w* in his law Ps 78:10
they *w* on in darkness Ps 82:5
from them that *w* uprightly Ps 84:11
I will *w* in thy truth Ps 86:11
they shall *w*, O LORD, in the Ps 89:15
my law, and *w* not in my judgments Ps 89:30
I will *w* within my house with a Ps 101:2
feet have they, but they *w* not Ps 115:7
I will *w* before the LORD in the Ps 116:9
who *w* in the law of the LORD Ps 119:1
they *w* in his ways Ps 119:3
And I will *w* at liberty Ps 119:45
Though I *w* in the midst of Ps 138:7
know the way wherein I should *w* Ps 143:8
*w* not thou in the way with them Prov 1:15
buckler to them that *w* uprightly Prov 2:7
to *w* in the ways of darkness Prov 2:13
That thou mayest *w* in the way of Prov 2:20
Then shalt thou *w* in thy way Prov 3:23
the living which *w* under the sun Eccl 4:15
that knoweth to *w* before the Eccl 6:8
*w* in the ways of thine heart, and Eccl 11:9
ways, and we will *w* in his paths Is 2:3
let us *w* in the light of the LORD Is 2:5
*w* with stretched forth necks and Is 3:16
not *w* in the way of this people Is 8:11
That *w* to go down into Egypt, and Is 30:2
*w* ye in it, when ye turn to the Is 30:21
but the redeemed shall *w* there Is 35:9
and they shall *w*, and not faint Is 40:31
and spirit to them that *w* therein Is 42:5
for they would not *w* in his ways Is 42:24
*w* in the light of your fire, and Is 50:11
brightness, but we *w* in darkness Is 59:9
neither shall they *w* any more Jer 3:17
shall *w* with the house of Israel Jer 3:18
*w* therein, and ye shall find rest Jer 6:16
they said, We will not *w* therein Jer 6:16
into the field, nor *w* by the way Jer 6:25
neither *w* after other gods to Jer 7:6
*w* after other gods whom ye know Jer 7:9
*w* ye in all the ways that I have Jer 7:23
neighbour will *w* with slanders Jer 9:4
which *w* in the imagination of Jer 13:10
*w* after other gods, to serve them Jer 13:10
behold, ye *w* every one after the Jer 16:12
but we will *w* after our own Jer 18:12
to *w* in paths, in a way not cast Jer 18:15
commit adultery, and *w* in lies Jer 23:14
to *w* in my law, which I have set Jer 26:4
I will cause them to *w* by the Jer 31:9
shew us the way wherein we may *w* Jer 42:3
is desolate, the foxes *w* upon it Lam 5:18
That they may *w* in my statutes, Eze 11:20
*W* ye not in the statutes of your Eze 20:18
*w* in my statutes, and keep my Eze 20:19
*w* in the statutes of life, Eze 33:15
I will cause men to *w* upon you Eze 36:12
cause you to *w* in my statutes, and Eze 36:27
they shall also *w* in my judgments Eze 37:24
before the chambers was a *w* of Eze 42:4
those that *w* in pride he is able Dan 4:37
to *w* in his laws, which he set Dan 9:10
They shall *w* after the LORD Hos 11:10
and the just shall *w* in them Hos 14:9
they shall *w* every one in his Joel 2:8
Can two *w* together, except they Amos 3:3
ways, and we will *w* in his paths Mic 4:2
For all people will *w* every one Mic 4:5
we will *w* in the name of the LORD Mic 4:5
and to *w* humbly with thy God Mic 6:8
Ahab, and ye *w* in their counsels Mic 6:16
they shall stumble in their *w* Nah 2:5
Thou didst *w* through the sea with Hab 3:15
he will make me to *w* upon mine Hab 3:19
that they shall *w* like blind men Zeph 1:17
whom the LORD hath sent to *w* to Zec 1:10
If thou wilt *w* in my ways Zec 3:7
to *w* among these that stand by Zec 3:7
sought to go that they might *w* to Zec 6:7
*w* to and fro through the earth Zec 6:7
and they shall *w* up and down in his Zec 10:12
or to say, Arise, and *w* Mt 9:5
their sight, and the lame *w* Mt 11:5
maimed to be whole, the lame to *w* Mt 15:31
Arise, and take up thy bed, and *w* Mk 2:9
Why *w* not thy disciples according Mk 7:5
or to say, Rise up and *w* Lk 5:23
that the blind see, the lame *w* Lk 7:22
the men that *w* over them are not Lk 11:44
Nevertheless I must *w* to day Lk 13:33
which desire to *w* in long robes Lk 20:46
ye have one to another, as ye *w* Lk 24:17
him, Rise, take up thy bed, and *w* Jn 5:8
unto me, Take up thy bed, and *w* Jn 5:11
unto thee, Take up thy bed, and *w* Jn 5:12
for he would not *w* in Jewry Jn 7:1
me shall not *w* in darkness Jn 8:12
If any man *w* in the day, he Jn 11:9
But if a man *w* in the night Jn 11:10
*W* while ye have the light, lest Jn 12:35
Christ of Nazareth rise up and *w* Acts 3:6
we had made this man to *w* Acts 3:12
nations to *w* in their own ways Acts 14:16
neither to *w* after the customs Acts 21:21
but who also *w* in the steps of Rom 4:12
also should *w* in newness of life Rom 6:4
who *w* not after the flesh, but Rom 8:1
who *w* not after the flesh, but Rom 8:4
Let us *w* honestly, as in the day Rom 13:13
are ye not carnal, and *w* as men 1Cor 3:3
called every one, so let him *w* 1Cor 7:17
(For we *w* by faith, not by sight 2Cor 5:7
will dwell in them, and *w* in them 2Cor 6:16
For though we *w* in the flesh 2Cor 10:3
*W* in the Spirit, and ye shall not Gal 5:16
let us also *w* in the Spirit Gal 5:25
as many as *w* according to this Gal 6:16
ordained that we should *w* in them Eph 2:10
beseech you that ye *w* worthy of Eph 4:1
*w* not as other Gentiles *w* Eph 4:17
*w* in love, as Christ also hath Eph 5:2
*w* as children of light Eph 5:8
See then that ye *w* circumspectly Eph 5:15
let us *w* by the same rule, let us Phil 3:16
mark them which *w* so as ye have Phil 3:17
(For many *w*, of whom I have told Phil 3:18
That ye might *w* worthy of the Col 1:10
Jesus the Lord, so *w* ye in him Col 2:6
*W* in wisdom toward them that are Col 4:5
That ye would *w* worthy of God 1Th 2:12
received of us how ye ought to *w* 1Th 4:1
That ye may *w* honestly toward 1Th 4:12
some which *w* among you disorderly 2Th 3:11
But chiefly them that *w* after the 2Pet 2:10
*w* in darkness, we lie, and do not 1Jn 1:6
But if we *w* in the light, as he 1Jn 1:7
in him ought himself also so to *w* 1Jn 2:6
that we *w* after his commandments 2Jn 6
the beginning, ye should *w* in it 2Jn 6
hear that my children *w* in truth 3Jn 4
who should *w* after their own Jude 18
they shall *w* with me in white Rev 3:4
neither can see, nor hear, nor *w* Rev 9:20
his garments, lest he *w* naked Rev 16:15
saved shall *w* in the light of it Rev 21:24

### WALKED
Enoch *w* with God after he begat Gen 5:22
And Enoch *w* with God Gen 5:24
generations, and Noah *w* with God Gen 6:9
her maidens *w* along by the Ex 2:5
But the children of Israel *w* upon Ex 14:29
also they have *w* contrary unto me Lev 26:40
that I also have *w* contrary unto Lev 26:41
For the children of Israel *w* Josh 5:6
the way which their fathers *w* in Judg 2:17
the travellers *w* through byways Judg 5:6
*w* through the wilderness unto the Judg 11:16
his sons *w* not in his ways, but 1Sa 8:3
I have *w* before you from my 1Sa 12:2

his men *w* all that night through 2Sa 2:29
but have *w* in a tent and in a 2Sa 7:6
all the places wherein I have *w* 2Sa 7:7
*w* upon the roof of the king's 2Sa 11:2
according as he *w* before thee in 1Kin 3:6
me as thou hast *w* before me 1Kin 8:25
before me, as David thy father *w* 1Kin 9:4
have not *w* in my ways, to do that 1Kin 11:33
he *w* in all the sins of his 1Kin 15:3
*w* in the way of his father, and in 1Kin 15:26
*w* in the way of Jeroboam, and in 1Kin 15:34
thou hast *w* in the way of 1Kin 16:2
For he *w* in all the way of 1Kin 16:26
he *w* in all the ways of Asa his 1Kin 22:43
*w* in the way of his father, and in 1Kin 22:52
and *w* in the house to and fro 2Kin 4:35
he *w* in the way of the kings of 2Kin 8:18
he *w* in the way of the house of 2Kin 8:27
made Israel sin, but *w* therein 2Kin 13:6
but he *w* therein 2Kin 13:11
But he *w* in the way of the kings 2Kin 16:3
*w* in the statutes of the heathen, 2Kin 17:8
but *w* in the statutes of Israel 2Kin 17:19
For the children of Israel *w* in 2Kin 17:22
how I have *w* before thee in truth 2Kin 20:3
he *w* in all the way that his 2Kin 21:21
all the way that his father *w* in 2Kin 21:21
*w* not in the way of the LORD 2Kin 21:22
*w* in all the way of David his 2Kin 22:2
I have *w* with all Israel, spake I 1Chr 17:6
thee whithersoever thou hast *w* 1Chr 17:8
my law, as thou hast *w* before me 2Chr 6:16
before me, as David thy father *w* 2Chr 7:17
years they *w* in the way of David 2Chr 11:17
because he *w* in the first ways of 2Chr 17:3
*w* in his commandments, and not 2Chr 17:4
he *w* in the way of Asa his father 2Chr 20:32
he *w* in the way of the kings of 2Chr 21:6
Because thou hast not *w* in the 2Chr 21:12
But hast *w* in the way of the 2Chr 21:13
He also *w* in the ways of the 2Chr 22:3
He *w* also after their counsel, and 2Chr 22:5
For he *w* in the ways of the kings 2Chr 28:2
*w* in the ways of David his father 2Chr 34:2
Mordecai *w* every day before the Est 2:11
by his light I *w* through darkness Job 29:3
If I have *w* with vanity, or if my Job 31:5
mine heart *w* after mine eyes, and Job 31:7
or hast thou *w* in the search of Job 38:16
for I have *w* in mine integrity Ps 26:1
and I have *w* in thy truth Ps 26:3
*w* unto the house of God in Ps 55:14
they *w* in their own counsels Ps 81:12
me, and Israel had *w* in my ways Ps 81:13
In the way wherein I *w* have they Ps 142:3
The people that *w* in darkness Is 9:2
as my servant Isaiah hath *w* naked Is 20:3
how I have *w* before thee in truth Is 38:3
have *w* after vanity, and are Jer 2:5
*w* after things that do not profit Jer 2:8
but *w* in the counsels and in the Jer 7:24
served, and after whom they have *w* Jer 8:2
my voice, neither *w* therein Jer 9:13
But have *w* after the imagination Jer 9:14
their ear, but *w* every one in the Jer 11:8
have *w* after other gods, and have Jer 16:11
thy voice, neither *w* in thy law Jer 32:23
nor *w* in my law, nor in my Jer 44:10
nor *w* in his law, nor in his Jer 44:23
statutes, they have not *w* in them Eze 5:6
have not *w* in my statutes, Eze 5:7
for ye have not *w* in my statutes Eze 11:12
hast thou not *w* after their ways Eze 16:47
Hath *w* in my statutes, and hath Eze 18:9
judgments, hath *w* in my statutes Eze 18:17
they *w* not in my statutes, and Eze 20:13
*w* not in my statutes, but Eze 20:16
they *w* not in my statutes, Eze 20:21
Thou hast *w* in the way of thy Eze 23:31
thou hast *w* up and down in the Eze 28:14
At the end of twelve months he *w* Dan 4:29
because he willingly *w* after the Hos 5:11
the which their fathers have *w* Amos 2:4
the lion, even the old lion, *w* Nah 2:11
trees, and said, We have *w* to Zec 1:11
So they *w* to and fro through the Zec 6:7
he *w* with me in peace and equity, Mal 2:6
that we have *w* mournfully before Mal 3:14
he *w* on the water, to go to Jesus Mt 14:29
Now as he *w* by the sea of Galilee Mk 1:16
the damsel arose, and *w* Mk 5:42
form unto two of them, as they *w* Mk 16:12
And looking upon Jesus as he *w* Jn 1:36
whole, and took up his bed, and *w* Jn 5:9
went back, and *w* no more with him Jn 6:66
these things Jesus *w* in Galilee Jn 7:1
And Jesus *w* in the temple in Jn 10:23
Jesus therefore *w* no more openly Jn 11:54
And he leaping up stood, and *w* Acts 3:8
mother's womb, who never had *w* Acts 14:8
And he leaped and *w* Acts 14:10
as if we *w* according to the flesh 2Cor 10:2
*w* we not in the same spirit 2Cor 12:18
*w* we not in the same steps 2Cor 12:18
But when I saw that they *w* not Gal 2:14
Wherein in time past ye *w* Eph 2:2
In the which ye also *w* some time Col 3:7
when we *w* in lasciviousness, 1Pet 4:3
also so to walk, even as he *w* 1Jn 2:6

**WALKEDST**
and *w* whither thou wouldest Jn 21:18

**WALKEST**
when thou *w* by the way, and when Deut 6:7
thou *w* by the way Deut 11:19
*w* abroad any whither, that thou 1Kin 2:42
when thou *w* through the fire, Is 43:2
that thou thyself also *w* orderly Acts 21:24
now *w* thou not charitably Rom 14:15
thee, even as thou *w* in the truth 3Jn 3

**WALKETH**
What man is this that *w* in the Gen 24:65
For the LORD thy God *w* in the Deut 23:14
behold, the king *w* before you 1Sa 12:2
own feet, and he *w* upon a snare Job 18:8
he *w* in the circuit of heaven Job 22:14
of iniquity, and *w* with wicked men Job 34:8
Blessed is the man that *w* not in Ps 1:1
He that *w* uprightly, and worketh Ps 15:2
Surely every man *w* in a vain shew Ps 39:6
their tongue *w* through the earth Ps 73:9
the pestilence that *w* in darkness Ps 91:6
he that *w* in a perfect way, he Ps 101:6
who *w* upon the wings of the wind Ps 104:3
that *w* in his ways Ps 128:1
man, *w* with a froward mouth Prov 6:12
that *w* uprightly *w* surely Prov 10:9
He that *w* with wise men shall be Prov 13:20
He that *w* in his uprightness Prov 14:2
man of understanding *w* uprightly Prov 15:21
the poor that *w* in his integrity Prov 19:1
The just man *w* in his integrity Prov 20:7
poor that *w* in his uprightness Prov 28:6
Whoso *w* uprightly shall be saved Prov 28:18
but whoso *w* wisely, he shall be Prov 28:26
but the fool *w* in darkness Eccl 2:14
he that is a fool *w* by the way Eccl 10:3
He that *w* righteously, and Is 33:15
that *w* in darkness, and hath no Is 50:10
which *w* in a way that was not Is 65:2
in man that *w* to direct his steps Jer 10:23
*w* after the imagination of his Jer 23:17
heart *w* after the heart of their Eze 11:21
do good to him that *w* uprightly Mic 2:7
he *w* through dry places, seeking Mt 12:43
he *w* through dry places, seeking Lk 11:24
for he that *w* in darkness knoweth Jn 12:35
every brother that *w* disorderly 2Th 3:6
*w* about, seeking whom he may 1Pet 5:8
*w* in darkness, and knoweth not 1Jn 2:11
who *w* in the midst of the seven Rev 2:1

**WALKING**
*w* in the garden in the cool of Gen 3:8
he knoweth thy *w* through this Deut 2:7
*w* in the statutes of David his 1Kin 3:3
in *w* in the way of Jeroboam, and 1Kin 16:19
and fro in the earth, and from *w* up Job 1:7
and fro in the earth, and from *w* up Job 2:2
or the moon *w* in brightness Job 31:26
princes *w* as servants upon the Eccl 10:7
forth necks and wanton eyes, *w* Is 3:16
And he did so, *w* naked and barefoot Is 20:2
each one *w* in his uprightness Is 57:2
revolters, *w* with slanders Jer 6:28
*w* in the midst of the fire, and Dan 3:25
If a man *w* in the spirit and Mic 2:11
*w* by the sea of Galilee, saw two Mt 4:18
went unto them, *w* on the sea Mt 14:25
disciples saw him *w* on the sea Mt 14:26
*w* upon the sea, and would have Mk 6:48
when they saw him *w* upon the sea Mk 6:49
and said, I see men as trees, *w* Mk 8:24
as he was *w* in the temple, there Mk 11:27
*w* in all the commandments and Lk 1:6
they see Jesus *w* on the sea Jn 6:19
with them into the temple, *w* Acts 3:8
And all the people saw him *w* Acts 3:9
*w* in the fear of the Lord, and in Acts 9:31
not *w* in craftiness, nor handling 2Cor 4:2
*w* after their own lusts, 2Pet 3:3
found of thy children *w* in truth 2Jn 4
*w* after their own lusts Jude 16

**WALL**
selfwill they digged down a *w* Gen 49:6
whose branches run over the *w* Gen 49:22
the waters were a *w* unto them on Ex 14:22
the waters were a *w* unto them on Ex 14:29
in sight are lower than the *w* Lev 14:37
no *w* round about them shall be Lev 25:31
a *w* being on this side, and a *w* Num 22:24
she thrust herself unto the *w* Num 22:25
Balaam's foot against the *w* Num 22:25
reach from the *w* of the city Num 35:4
for her house was upon the town *w* Josh 2:15
and she dwelt upon the *w* Josh 2:15
the *w* of the city shall fall down Josh 6:5
that the *w* fell down flat, so Josh 6:20
smite David even to the *w* with it 1Sa 18:11
even to the *w* with the javelin 1Sa 19:10
he smote the javelin into the *w* 1Sa 19:10
times, even upon a seat by the *w* 1Sa 20:25
They were a *w* unto us both by 1Sa 25:16
any that pisseth against the *w* 1Sa 25:22
any that pisseth against the *w* 1Sa 25:34
his body to the *w* of Beth-shan 1Sa 31:10
his sons from the *w* of Beth-shan 1Sa 31:12
that they would shoot from the *w* 2Sa 11:20
a millstone upon him from the *w* 2Sa 11:21
why went ye nigh the *w* 2Sa 11:21
from off the *w* upon thy servants 2Sa 11:24
the roof over the gate unto the *w* 2Sa 18:24
were with Joab battered the *w* 2Sa 20:15
be thrown to thee over the *w* 2Sa 20:21
by my God have I leaped over a *w* 2Sa 22:30
the *w* of Jerusalem round about 1Kin 3:1
that springeth out of the *w* 1Kin 4:33
against the *w* of the house he 1Kin 6:5
for without in the *w* of the house 1Kin 6:6
wing of the one touched the one *w* 1Kin 6:27
other cherub touched the other *w* 1Kin 6:27
posts were a fifth part of the *w* 1Kin 6:31
tree, a fourth part of the *w* 1Kin 6:33
the *w* of Jerusalem, and Hazor, and 1Kin 9:15
him that pisseth against the *w* 1Kin 14:10
not one that pisseth against a *w* 1Kin 16:11
there a *w* fell upon twenty and 1Kin 20:30
him that pisseth against the *w* 1Kin 21:21
eat Jezebel by the *w* of Jezreel 1Kin 21:23
for a burnt offering upon the *w* 2Kin 3:27
chamber, I pray thee, on the *w* 2Kin 4:10
Israel was passing by upon the *w* 2Kin 6:26
and he passed by upon the *w* 2Kin 6:30
him that pisseth against the *w* 2Kin 9:8
her blood was sprinkled on the *w* 2Kin 9:33
brake down the *w* of Jerusalem 2Kin 14:13
of the people that are on the *w* 2Kin 18:26
me to the men which sit on the *w* 2Kin 18:27
Then he turned his face to the *w* 2Kin 20:2
reaching to the *w* of the house 2Chr 3:11
reaching to the *w* of the house 2Chr 3:12
brake down the *w* of Jerusalem 2Chr 25:23
and brake down the *w* of Gath 2Chr 26:6
the *w* of Jabneh, and the 2Chr 26:6
the *w* of Ashdod, and built cities 2Chr 26:6
gate, and at the turning of the *w* 2Chr 26:9
on the *w* of Ophel he built much 2Chr 27:3
up all the *w* that was broken 2Chr 32:5
the towers, and another *w* without 2Chr 32:5
of Jerusalem that were on the *w* 2Chr 32:18
a *w* without the city of David 2Chr 33:14
and brake down the *w* of Jerusalem 2Chr 36:19
this house, and to make up this *w* Ezr 5:3
and to give us a *w* in Judah Ezr 9:9
the *w* of Jerusalem also is broken Neh 1:3
for the *w* of the city, and for the Neh 2:8
by the brook, and viewed the *w* Neh 2:15
us build up the *w* of Jerusalem Neh 2:17
Jerusalem unto the broad *w* Neh 3:8
on the *w* unto the dung gate Neh 3:13
the *w* of the pool of Siloah by Neh 3:15
armoury at the turning of the *w* Neh 3:19
from the turning of the *w* unto Neh 3:20
Azariah unto the turning of the *w* Neh 3:24
over against the turning of the *w* Neh 3:25
out, even unto the *w* of Ophel Neh 3:27
heard that we builded the *w* Neh 4:1
even break down their stone *w* Neh 4:3
So built we the *w* Neh 4:6
all the *w* was joined together Neh 4:6
we are not able to build the *w* Neh 4:10
in the lower places behind the *w* Neh 4:13
we returned all of us to the *w* Neh 4:15
They which builded on the *w* Neh 4:17
and we are separated upon the *w* Neh 4:19
I continued in the work of this *w* Neh 5:16
heard that I had builded the *w* Neh 6:1
which cause thou buildest the *w* Neh 6:6
So the *w* was finished in the Neh 6:15
when the *w* was built, and I had Neh 7:1
at the dedication of the *w* of Neh 12:27
people, and the gates, and the *w* Neh 12:30
the princes of Judah upon the *w* Neh 12:31
upon the *w* toward the dung gate Neh 12:31
David, at the going up of the *w* Neh 12:37
the half of the people upon the *w* Neh 12:38
furnaces even unto the broad *w* Neh 12:38
them, Why lodge ye about the *w* Neh 13:21
by my God have I leaped over a *w* Ps 18:29
as a bowing *w* shall ye be Ps 62:3
as an high *w* in his own conceit Prov 18:11
the stone *w* thereof was broken Prov 24:31
behold, he standeth behind our *w* Song 2:9
If she be a *w*, we will build upon Song 8:9
I am a *w*, and my breasts like Song 8:10
tower, and upon every fenced *w* Is 2:15
and break down the *w* thereof Is 5:5
ye broken down to fortify the *w* Is 22:10
ones is as a storm against the *w* Is 25:4
to fall, swelling out in a high *w* Is 30:13
of the people that are on the *w* Is 36:11
me to the men that sit upon the *w* Is 36:12
turned his face toward the *w* Is 38:2
We grope for the *w* like the blind Is 59:10
this people a fenced brasen *w* Jer 15:20
a fire in the *w* of Damascus Jer 49:27
the *w* of Babylon shall fall Jer 51:44
the *w* of the daughter of Zion Lam 2:8
the rampart and the *w* to lament Lam 2:8
O *w* of the daughter of Zion, let Lam 2:18
set it for a *w* of iron between Eze 4:3
I looked, behold a hole in the *w* Eze 8:7
me, Son of man, dig now in the *w* Eze 8:8
and when I had digged in the *w* Eze 8:8
pourtrayed upon the *w* round about Eze 8:10
thou through the *w* in their sight Eze 12:5
through the *w* with mine hand Eze 12:7
the *w* to carry out thereby Eze 12:12
and one built up a *w*, and, lo, Eze 13:10

when the *w* is fallen, shall it ... Eze 13:12
the *w* that ye have daubed with ... Eze 13:14
I accomplish my wrath upon the *w* ... Eze 13:15
The *w* is no more, neither they ... Eze 13:15
she saw men pourtrayed upon the *w* .. Eze 23:14
every *w* shall fall to the ground ... Eze 38:20
behold a *w* on the outside of the ... Eze 40:5
he measured the *w* of the house ... Eze 41:5
they entered into the *w* which was ... Eze 41:6
not hold in the *w* of the house ... Eze 41:6
The thickness of the *w*, which was ... Eze 41:9
the *w* of the building was five ... Eze 41:12
by all the *w* round about within ... Eze 41:17
made, and on the *w* of the temple ... Eze 41:20
the *w* that was without over ... Eze 42:7
*w* of the court toward the east ... Eze 42:10
before the *w* toward the east ... Eze 42:12
it had a *w* round about, five ... Eze 42:20
the *w* between me and them, they ... Eze 43:8
of the *w* of the king's palace ... Dan 5:5
shall be built again, and the *w* ... Dan 9:25
thy way with thorns, and make a *w* ... Hos 2:6
shall climb the *w* like men of war ... Joel 2:7
they shall run upon the *w* ... Joel 2:9
will send a fire on the *w* of Gaza ... Amos 1:7
send a fire on the *w* of Tyrus ... Amos 1:10
kindle a fire in the *w* of Rabbah ... Amos 1:14
and leaned his hand on the *w* ... Amos 5:19
upon a *w* made by a plumbline ... Amos 7:7
shall make haste to the *w* thereof ... Nah 2:5
sea, and her *w* was from the sea ... Nah 3:8
the stone shall cry out of the *w* ... Hab 2:11
will be unto her a *w* of fire ... Zec 2:5
let him down by the *w* in a basket ... Acts 9:25
shall smite thee, thou whited *w* ... Acts 23:3
a basket was I let down by the *w* ... 2Cor 11:33
middle *w* of partition between us ... Eph 2:14
And had a *w* great and high, and had Rev 21:12
the *w* of the city had twelve ... Rev 21:14
gates thereof, and the *w* thereof ... Rev 21:15
And he measured the *w* thereof ... Rev 21:17
of the *w* of it was of jasper ... Rev 21:18
the foundations of the *w* of the ... Rev 21:19

### WALLED
sell a dwelling house in a *w* city ... Lev 25:29
*w* city shall be established for ... Lev 25:30
in the land, and the cities are *w* ... Num 13:28
are great and *w* up to heaven ... Deut 1:28

### WALLOW
sackcloth, and *w* thyself in ashes ... Jer 6:26
*w* yourselves in the ashes, ye ... Jer 25:34
Moab also shall *w* in his vomit ... Jer 48:26
they shall *w* themselves in the ... Eze 27:30

### WALLOWED
Amasa *w* in blood in the midst of ... 2Sa 20:12
fell on the ground, and *w* foaming ... Mk 9:20

### WALLOWING
was washed to her *w* in the mire ... 2Pet 2:22

### WALLS
if the plague be in the *w* of the ... Lev 14:37
be spread in the *w* of the house ... Lev 14:39
cities were fenced with high *w* ... Deut 3:5
fenced *w* come down, wherein thou . Deut 28:52
threescore great cities with *w* ... 1Kin 4:13
against the *w* of the house round ... 1Kin 6:5
be fastened in the *w* of the house ... 1Kin 6:6
he built the *w* of the house ... 1Kin 6:15
house, and the *w* of the cieling ... 1Kin 6:15
the *w* with boards of cedar ... 1Kin 6:16
he carved all the *w* of the house ... 1Kin 6:29
the way of the gate between two *w* ... 2Kin 25:4
brake down the *w* of Jerusalem ... 2Kin 25:10
to overlay the *w* of the houses ... 1Chr 29:4
the *w* thereof, and the doors ... 2Chr 3:7
and graved cherubims on the *w* ... 2Chr 3:7
the nether, fenced cities, with *w* ... 2Chr 8:5
cities, and make about them *w* ... 2Chr 14:7
and have set up the *w* thereof ... Ezr 4:12
the *w* set up again, then will ... Ezr 4:13
the *w* thereof set up, by this ... Ezr 4:16
and timber is laid in the *w* ... Ezr 5:8
this house, and to make up these *w* ... Ezr 5:9
viewed the *w* of Jerusalem, which ... Neh 2:13
heard that the *w* of Jerusalem ... Neh 4:7
Which make oil within their *w* ... Job 24:11
build thou the *w* of Jerusalem ... Ps 51:18
go about it upon the *w* thereof ... Ps 55:10
Peace be within thy *w*, and ... Ps 122:7
that is broken down, and without *w*. Prov 25:28
the keepers of the *w* took away my ... Song 5:7
of vision, breaking down the *w* ... Is 22:5
also a ditch between the two *w* ... Is 22:11
fort of thy *w* shall he bring down ... Is 25:12
salvation will God appoint for *w* ... Is 26:1
thy *w* are continually before me ... Is 49:16
mine house and within my *w* a place ... Is 56:5
of strangers shall build up thy *w* ... Is 60:10
thou shalt call thy *w* Salvation ... Is 60:18
I have set watchmen upon thy *w* ... Is 62:6
against all the *w* thereof round ... Jer 1:15
brasen *w* against the whole land ... Jer 1:18
Go ye up upon her *w*, and destroy ... Jer 5:10
which besiege you without the *w* ... Jer 21:4
by the gate betwixt the two *w* ... Jer 39:4
and brake down the *w* of Jerusalem ... Jer 39:8
are fallen, her *w* are thrown down ... Jer 50:15
standard upon the *w* of Babylon ... Jer 51:12
The broad *w* of Babylon shall be ... Jer 51:58
way of the gate between the two *w* ... Jer 52:7
brake down all the *w* of Jerusalem ... Jer 52:14
of the enemy the *w* of her palaces ... Lam 2:7
they shall destroy the *w* of Tyrus ... Eze 26:4
set engines of war against thy *w* ... Eze 26:9
thy *w* shall shake at the noise of ... Eze 26:10
and they shall break down thy *w* ... Eze 26:12
army were upon thy *w* round about ... Eze 27:11
shields upon thy *w* round about ... Eze 27:11
are talking against thee by the *w* ... Eze 33:30
all of them dwelling without *w* ... Eze 38:11
the building, with the *w* thereof ... Eze 41:13
the *w* thereof, were of wood ... Eze 41:22
like as were made upon the *w* ... Eze 41:25
day that thy *w* are to be built ... Mic 7:11
*w* for the multitude of men ... Zec 2:4
By faith the *w* of Jericho fell ... Heb 11:30

### WANDER
when God caused me to *w* from my ... Gen 20:13
your children shall *w* in the ... Num 14:33
he made them *w* in the wilderness ... Num 32:13
the blind to *w* out of the way ... Deut 27:18
causeth them to *w* in a wilderness ... Job 12:24
unto God, they *w* for lack of meat ... Job 38:41
Lo, then would I *w* far off ... Ps 55:7
Let them *w* up and down for meat, ... Ps 59:15
and causeth them to *w* in the ... Ps 107:40
O let me not *w* from thy ... Ps 119:10
they shall *w* every one to his ... Is 47:15
people, Thus have they loved to *w* ... Jer 14:10
that shall cause him to *w* ... Jer 48:12
they shall *w* from sea to sea, and ... Amos 8:12

### WANDERED
*w* in the wilderness of Beer-sheba ... Gen 21:14
of Israel *w* in the wilderness ... Josh 14:10
They *w* in the wilderness in a ... Ps 107:4
they *w* through the wilderness ... Is 16:8
They have *w* as blind men in the ... Lam 4:14
when they fled away and *w*, they ... Lam 4:15
My sheep *w* through all the ... Eze 34:6
or three cities *w* unto one city ... Amos 4:8
they *w* about in sheepskins and ... Heb 11:37
they *w* in deserts, and in ... Heb 11:38

### WANDERERS
LORD, that I will send unto him *w* ... Jer 48:12
they shall be *w* among the nations ... Hos 9:17

### WANDEREST
and under every green tree thou *w* ... Jer 2:20

### WANDERETH
He *w* abroad for bread, saying, ... Job 15:23
The man that *w* out of the way of ... Prov 21:16
As a bird that *w* from her nest ... Prov 27:8
so is a man that *w* from his place ... Prov 27:8
bewray not him that *w* ... Is 16:3
none shall gather up him that *w* ... Jer 49:5

### WANDERING
and, behold, he was *w* in the field ... Gen 37:15
As the bird by *w*, as the swallow ... Prov 26:2
the eyes than the *w* of the desire ... Eccl 6:9
as a *w* bird cast out of the nest, ... Is 16:2
*w* about from house to house ... 1Ti 5:13
*w* stars, to whom is reserved the ... Jude 13

### WANDERINGS
Thou tellest my *w* ... Ps 56:8

### WANT
nakedness, and in *w* of all things ... Deut 28:48
for she shall eat them for *w* of ... Deut 28:57
a place where there is no *w* of ... Judg 18:10
there is no *w* of any thing ... Judg 19:19
the rock for *w* of a shelter ... Job 24:8
For *w* and famine they were ... Job 30:3
seen any perish for *w* of clothing ... Job 31:19
I shall not *w* ... Ps 23:1
for there is no *w* to them that ... Ps 34:9
LORD shall not *w* any good thing ... Ps 34:10
and thy *w* as an armed man ... Prov 6:11
but fools die for *w* of wisdom ... Prov 10:21
is destroyed for *w* of judgment ... Prov 13:23
the belly of the wicked shall *w* ... Prov 13:25
but in the *w* of people is the ... Prov 14:28
every one that is hasty only to *w* ... Prov 21:5
the rich, shall surely come to *w* ... Prov 22:16
and thy *w* as an armed man ... Prov 24:34
shall fail, none shall *w* her mate ... Is 34:16
David shall never *w* a man to sit ... Jer 33:17
shall the priests the Levites *w* a ... Jer 33:18
the son of Rechab shall not *w* a ... Jer 35:19
stricken through for *w* of the ... Lam 4:9
That they may *w* bread and water, ... Eze 4:17
*w* of bread in all your places ... Amos 4:6
but she of her *w* did cast in all ... Mk 12:44
and he began to be in *w* ... Lk 15:14
may be a supply for their *w* ... 2Cor 8:14
also may be a supply for your *w* ... 2Cor 8:14
supplieth the *w* of the saints ... 2Cor 9:12
Not that I speak in respect of *w* ... Phil 4:11

### WANTED
we have *w* all things, and have ... Jer 44:18
And when they *w* wine, the mother ... Jn 2:3
when I was present with you, and *w* .. 2Cor 11:9

### WANTETH
for his need, in that which he *w* ... Deut 15:8
as for him that *w* understanding ... Prov 9:4
as for him that *w* understanding ... Prov 9:16
of words there *w* not sin ... Prov 10:19
The prince that *w* understanding ... Prov 28:16
so that he *w* nothing for his soul ... Eccl 6:2
round goblet, which *w* not liquor ... Song 7:2

### WANTING
let none be *w* ... 2Kin 10:19
whosoever shall be *w*, he shall ... 2Kin 10:19
with words, yet they are *w* to him ... Prov 19:7
that which is *w* cannot be ... Eccl 1:15
in the balances, and art found *w* ... Dan 5:27
in order the things that are *w* ... Titus 1:5
that nothing be *w* unto them ... Titus 3:13
be perfect and entire, *w* nothing ... Jas 1:4

### WANTON
*w* eyes, walking and mincing as ... Is 3:16
begun to wax *w* against Christ ... 1Ti 5:11
pleasure on the earth, and been *w* ... Jas 5:5

### WANTONNESS
not in chambering and *w*, not in ... Rom 13:13
of the flesh, through much *w* ... 2Pet 2:18

### WANTS
let all thy *w* lie upon me ... Judg 19:20
and he that ministered to my *w* ... Phil 2:25

### WAR
That these made *w* with Bera king ... Gen 14:2
when there falleth out any *w* ... Ex 1:10
the people repent when they see *w* ... Ex 13:17
The LORD is a man of *w* ... Ex 15:3
sworn that the LORD will have *w* ... Ex 17:16
There is a noise of *w* in the camp ... Ex 32:17
able to go forth to *w* in Israel ... Num 1:3
that were able to go forth to *w* ... Num 1:20
that were able to go forth to *w* ... Num 1:22
that were able to go forth to *w* ... Num 1:24
that were able to go forth to *w* ... Num 1:26
that were able to go forth to *w* ... Num 1:28
that were able to go forth to *w* ... Num 1:30
that were able to go forth to *w* ... Num 1:32
that were able to go forth to *w* ... Num 1:34
that were able to go forth to *w* ... Num 1:36
that were able to go forth to *w* ... Num 1:38
that were able to go forth to *w* ... Num 1:40
that were able to go forth to *w* ... Num 1:42
able to go forth to *w* in Israel ... Num 1:45
if ye go to *w* in your land ... Num 10:9
are able to go to *w* in Israel ... Num 26:2
Arm some of yourselves unto the *w* ... Num 31:3
of Israel, shall ye send to the *w* ... Num 31:4
twelve thousand armed for *w* ... Num 31:5
And Moses sent them to the *w* ... Num 31:6
of Eleazar the priest, to the *w* ... Num 31:6
men of *w* which went to the battle ... Num 31:21
them that took the *w* upon them ... Num 31:27
men of *w* which went out to battle ... Num 31:28
which the men of *w* had caught ... Num 31:32
of them that went out to *w* ... Num 31:36
of *w* which are under our charge ... Num 31:49
(For the men of *w* had taken spoil ... Num 31:53
Shall your brethren go to *w* ... Num 32:6
go armed before the LORD to *w* ... Num 32:20
pass over, every man armed for *w* ... Num 32:27
on every man his weapons of *w* ... Deut 1:41
the generation of the men of *w* ... Deut 2:14
all the men of *w* were consumed ... Deut 2:16
all that are meet for the *w* ... Deut 3:18
by signs, and by wonders, and by *w* ... Deut 4:34
but will make *w* against thee ... Deut 20:12
in making *w* against it to take it ... Deut 20:19
the city that maketh *w* with thee ... Deut 20:20
forth to *w* against thine enemies ... Deut 21:10
wife, he shall not go out to *w* ... Deut 24:5
for *w* passed over before the LORD ... Josh 4:13
were males, even all the men of *w* ... Josh 5:4
all the people that were men of *w* ... Josh 5:6
compass the city, all ye men of *w* ... Josh 6:3
all the people of *w* with thee ... Josh 8:1
arose, and all the people of *w* ... Josh 8:3
people of *w* that were with him ... Josh 8:11
Gibeon, and made *w* against it ... Josh 10:5
and all the people of *w* with him ... Josh 10:7
the men of *w* which went with him ... Josh 10:24
and all the people of *w* with him ... Josh 11:7
Joshua made *w* a long time with ... Josh 11:18
And the land rested from *w* ... Josh 11:23
even so is my strength now, for *w* ... Josh 14:11
And the land had rest from *w* ... Josh 14:15
because he was a man of *w* ... Josh 17:1
to go up to *w* against them ... Josh 22:12
might know, to teach them *w* ... Judg 3:2
judged Israel, and went out to *w* ... Judg 3:10
then was *w* in the gates ... Judg 5:8
of Ammon made *w* against Israel ... Judg 11:4
of Ammon made *w* against Israel ... Judg 11:5
doest me wrong to *w* against me ... Judg 11:27
men appointed with weapons of *w* ... Judg 18:11
appointed with their weapons of *w* ... Judg 18:16
were appointed with weapons of *w* ... Judg 18:17
all these were men of *w* ... Judg 20:17
not to each man his wife in the *w* ... Judg 21:22
and to make his instruments of *w* ... 1Sa 8:12
there was sore *w* against the ... 1Sa 14:52
mighty valiant man, and a man of *w* .. 1Sa 16:18
he a man of *w* from his youth ... 1Sa 17:33
and Saul set him over the men of *w* ... 1Sa 18:5
And there was *w* again ... 1Sa 19:8
all the people together to *w* ... 1Sa 23:8
the Philistines make *w* against me ... 1Sa 28:15
and the weapons of *w* perished ... 2Sa 1:27
Now there was long *w* between the ... 2Sa 3:1

while there was *w* between the 2Sa 3:6
did, and how the *w* prospered 2Sa 11:7
all the things concerning the *w* 2Sa 11:18
matters of the *w* unto the king 2Sa 11:19
and thy father is a man of *w* 2Sa 17:8
had yet *w* again with Israel 2Sa 21:15
He teacheth my hands to *w* 2Sa 22:35
and shed the blood of *w* in peace 1Kin 2:5
put the blood of *w* upon his 1Kin 2:5
but they were men of *w*, and his 1Kin 9:22
there was *w* between Rehoboam and 1Kin 14:30
there was *w* between Rehoboam and 1Kin 15:6
there was *w* between Abijam and 1Kin 15:7
there was *w* between 1Kin 15:16
there was *w* between 1Kin 15:32
or whether they be come out for *w* 1Kin 20:18
years without *w* between Syria 1Kin 22:1
Joram the son of Ahab to the *w* 2Kin 8:28
hand of Jehoahaz his father by *w* 2Kin 13:25
ten thousand, and took Selah by *w* 2Kin 14:7
Israel came up to Jerusalem to *w* 2Kin 16:5
counsel and strength for the *w* 2Kin 18:20
all that were strong and apt for *w* 2Kin 24:16
all the men of *w* fled by night by 2Kin 25:4
that was set over the men of *w* 2Kin 25:19
they made *w* with the Hagarites 1Chr 5:10
shoot with bow, and skilful in *w* 1Chr 5:18
that went out to the *w* 1Chr 5:18
they made *w* with the Hagarites, 1Chr 5:19
slain, because the *w* was of God 1Chr 5:22
were bands of soldiers for *w* 1Chr 7:4
soldiers, fit to go out for *w* 1Chr 7:11
of them that were apt to the *w* 1Chr 7:40
the mighty men, helpers of the *w* 1Chr 12:1
men of *w* fit for the battle, that 1Chr 12:8
that were ready armed to the *w* 1Chr 12:23
hundred, ready armed to the *w* 1Chr 12:24
mighty men of valour for the *w* 1Chr 12:25
went forth to battle, expert in *w* 1Chr 12:33
with all instruments of *w* 1Chr 12:33
of the Danites expert in *w* twenty 1Chr 12:35
went forth to battle, expert in *w* 1Chr 12:36
instruments of *w* for the battle 1Chr 12:37
All these men of *w*, that could 1Chr 12:38
(for Hadarezer had *w* with Tou 1Chr 18:10
that there arose *w* at Gezer with 1Chr 20:4
there was *w* again with the 1Chr 20:5
And yet again there was *w* at Gath 1Chr 20:6
because thou hast been a man of *w* 1Chr 28:3
If thy people go out to *w* against 2Chr 6:34
but they were men of *w*, and chief 2Chr 8:9
there was *w* between Abijah and 2Chr 13:2
with an army of valiant men of *w* 2Chr 13:3
he had no *w* in those years 2Chr 14:6
there was no more *w* unto the five 2Chr 15:19
made no *w* against Jehoshaphat 2Chr 17:10
and the men of *w*, mighty men of 2Chr 17:13
thousand ready prepared for the *w* 2Chr 17:18
and we will be with thee in the *w* 2Chr 18:3
son of Ahab king of Israel to *w* 2Chr 22:5
choice men, able to go forth to *w* 2Chr 25:5
men, that went out to *w* by bands 2Chr 26:11
that made *w* with mighty power, to 2Chr 26:13
against them that came from the *w* 2Chr 28:12
set captains of *w* over the people 2Chr 32:6
put captains of *w* in all the 2Chr 33:14
the house wherewith I have *w* 2Chr 35:21
in *w* from the power of the sword Job 5:20
changes and *w* are against me Job 10:17
against the day of battle and *w* Job 38:23
He teacheth my hands to *w* Ps 18:34
though *w* should rise against me, Ps 27:3
butter, but *w* was in his heart Ps 55:21
thou the people that delight in *w* Ps 68:30
but when I speak, they are for *w* Ps 120:7
are they gathered together for *w* Ps 140:2
which teacheth my hands to *w* Ps 144:1
and with good advice make *w* Prov 20:18
counsel thou shalt make thy *w* Prov 24:6
a time of *w*, and a time of peace Eccl 3:8
there is no discharge in that *w* Eccl 8:8
is better than weapons of *w* Eccl 9:18
hold swords, being expert in *w* Song 3:8
shall they learn *w* any more Is 2:4
The mighty man, and the man of *w* Is 3:2
the sword, and thy mighty in the *w* Is 3:25
toward Jerusalem to *w* against it Is 7:1
and from the grievousness of *w* Is 21:15
I have counsel and strength for *w* Is 36:5
is come forth to make *w* with thee Is 37:9
they that *w* against thee shall be Is 41:12
stir up jealousy like a man of *w* Is 42:13
of the trumpet, the alarm of *w* Jer 4:19
Prepare ye *w* against her Jer 6:4
array as men for *w* against thee Jer 6:23
of Babylon maketh *w* against us Jer 21:2
of *w* that are in your hands Jer 21:4
and against great kingdoms, of *w* Jer 28:8
the hands of the men of *w* that Jer 38:4
saw them, and all the men of *w* Jer 39:4
were found there, and the men of *w* Jer 41:3
of Ahikam, even mighty men of *w* Jer 41:16
of Egypt, where we shall see no *w* Jer 42:14
mighty and strong men for the *w* Jer 48:14
of *w* to be heard in Rabbah of the Jer 49:2
all the men of *w* shall be cut off Jer 49:26
all her men of *w* shall be cut off Jer 50:30
art my battle ax and weapons of *w* Jer 51:20
the men of *w* are affrighted Jer 51:32
up, and all the men of *w* fled Jer 52:7
had the charge of the men of *w* Jer 52:25
company make for him in the *w* Eze 17:17
engines of *w* against thy walls Eze 26:9
were in thine army, thy men of *w* Eze 27:10
merchandise, and all thy men of *w* Eze 27:27
to hell with their weapons of *w* Eze 32:27
mighty men, and with all men of *w* Eze 39:20
same horn made *w* with the saints Dan 7:21
unto the end of the *w* desolations Dan 9:26
climb the wall like men of *w* Joel 2:7
Prepare *w*, wake up the mighty men Joel 3:9
let all the men of *w* draw near Joel 3:9
by securely as men averse from *w* Mic 2:8
they even prepare *w* against him Mic 3:5
shall they learn *w* any more Mic 4:3
going to make *w* against another Lk 14:31
his men of *w* set him at nought Lk 23:11
we do not *w* after the flesh 2Cor 10:3
by them mightest *w* a good warfare 1Ti 1:18
your lusts that *w* in your members Jas 4:1
ye fight and *w*, yet ye have not, Jas 4:2
lusts, which *w* against the soul 1Pet 2:11
pit shall make *w* against them Rev 11:7
And there was *w* in heaven Rev 12:7
went to make *w* with the remnant Rev 12:17
who is able to make *w* with him Rev 13:4
him to make *w* with the saints Rev 13:7
These shall make *w* with the Lamb Rev 17:14
he doth judge and make *w* Rev 19:11
gathered together to make *w* Rev 19:19

**WARD**
he put them in *w* in the house of Gen 40:3
and they continued a season in *w* Gen 40:4
him in the *w* of his lord's house Gen 40:7
put me in *w* in the captain of the Gen 41:10
all together into *w* three days Gen 42:17
And they put him in *w*, that the Lev 24:12
And they put him in *w*, because it Num 15:34
keep the house, and put them in *w* 2Sa 20:3
kept the *w* of the house of Saul 1Chr 12:29
And they cast lots, *w* against 1Chr 25:8
against *w*, as well 1Chr 25:8
of the going up, *w* against *w* 1Chr 26:16
man of God, *w* over against *w* Neh 12:24
were porters keeping the *w* at the Neh 12:25
porters kept the *w* of their God Neh 12:45
the *w* of the purification, Neh 12:45
and I am set in my *w* whole nights Is 21:8
a captain of the *w* was there Jer 37:13
And they put him in *w* in chains Eze 19:9
past the first and the second *w* Acts 12:10

**WARDROBE**
son of Harhas, keeper of the *w* 2Kin 22:14
son of Hasrah, keeper of the *w* 2Chr 34:22

**WARDS**
the house of the tabernacle, by *w* 1Chr 9:23
having *w* one against another, to 1Chr 26:12
appointed the *w* of the priests and Neh 13:30

**WARE**
*w* or any victuals on the sabbath Neh 10:31
brought fish, and all manner of *w* Neh 13:16
sellers of all kind of *w* lodged Neh 13:20
*w* no clothes, neither abode in Lk 8:27
They were *w* of it, and fled unto Acts 14:6
Of whom be thou *w* also 2Ti 4:15

**WARES**
Gather up thy *w* out of the land, Jer 10:17
multitude of the *w* of thy making Eze 27:16
multitude of the *w* of thy making Eze 27:18
When thy *w* went forth out of the Eze 27:33
cast forth the *w* that were in the Jonah 1:5

**WARFARE**
their armies together for *w* 1Sa 28:1
that her *w* is accomplished, that Is 40:2
Who goeth a *w* any time at his own 1Cor 9:7
weapons of our *w* are not carnal 2Cor 10:4
by them mightest war a good *w* 1Ti 1:18

**WARM**
and the flesh of the child waxed *w* 2Kin 4:34
What time they wax *w*, they vanish Job 6:17
How thy garments are *w*, when he Job 37:17
but how can one be *w* alone Eccl 4:11
will take thereof, and *w* himself Is 44:15
himself, and saith, Aha, I am *w* Is 44:16
there shall not be a coal to *w* at Is 47:14
clothe you, but there is none *w* Hag 1:6

**WARMED**
if he were not *w* with the fleece Job 31:20
and *w* himself at the fire Mk 14:54
and they *w* themselves Jn 18:18
stood with them, and *w* himself Jn 18:18
And Simon Peter stood and *w* himself Jn 18:25
them, Depart in peace, be ye *w* Jas 2:16

**WARMETH**
the earth, and *w* them in the dust, Job 39:14
he *w* himself, and saith, Aha, I am Is 44:16

**WARMING**
And when she saw Peter *w* himself Mk 14:67

**WARN**
ye shall even *w* them that they 2Chr 19:10
nor speakest to *w* the wicked from Eze 3:18
Yet if thou *w* the wicked, and he Eze 3:19
if thou *w* the righteous man Eze 3:21
blow the trumpet, and *w* the people Eze 33:3
at my mouth, and *w* them from me Eze 33:7
to *w* the wicked from his way Eze 33:8
if thou *w* the wicked of his way Eze 33:9
I ceased not to *w* every one night Acts 20:31
but as my beloved sons I *w* you 1Cor 4:14
*w* them that are unruly, comfort 1Th 5:14

**WARNED**
*w* him of, and saved himself there, 2Kin 6:10
Moreover by them is thy servant *w* Ps 19:11
surely live, because he is *w* Eze 3:21
trumpet, and the people be not *w* Eze 33:6
being *w* of God in a dream that Mt 2:12
being *w* of God in a dream, he Mt 2:22
who hath *w* you to flee from the Mt 3:7
who hath *w* you to flee from the Lk 3:7
was *w* from God by an holy angel Acts 10:22
being *w* of God of things not seen Heb 11:7

**WARNING**
To whom shall I speak, and give *w* Jer 6:10
my mouth, and give them *w* from me Eze 3:17
and thou givest him not *w*, nor Eze 3:18
because thou hast not given him *w* Eze 3:20
of the trumpet, and taketh not *w* Eze 33:4
of the trumpet, and took not *w* Eze 33:5
But he that taketh *w* shall Eze 33:5
*w* every man, and teaching every Col 1:28

**WARP**
Whether it be in the *w*, or woof Lev 13:48
or in the skin, either in the *w* Lev 13:49
in the garment, either in the *w* Lev 13:51
that garment, whether *w* or woof Lev 13:52
in the garment, either in the *w* Lev 13:53
out of the skin, or out of the *w* Lev 13:56
in the garment, either in the *w* Lev 13:57
And the garment, either *w*, or woof Lev 13:58
woollen or linen, either in the *w* Lev 13:59

**WARRED**
they *w* against the Midianites, as Num 31:7
Moses divided from the men that *w* Num 31:42
*w* against Israel, and sent and Josh 24:9
of the acts of Jeroboam, how he *w* 1Kin 14:19
besieged Samaria, and *w* against it 1Kin 20:1
he shewed, and how he *w* 1Kin 22:45
king of Syria *w* against Israel 2Kin 6:8
he did, and his might, how he *w* 2Kin 14:28
*w* against the Philistines, and 2Chr 26:6

**WARRETH**
No man that *w* entangleth himself 2Ti 2:4

**WARRING**
king of Assyria *w* against Libnah 2Kin 19:8
king of Assyria *w* against Libnah Is 37:8
*w* against the law of my mind, and Rom 7:23

**WARRIOR**
of the *w* is with confused noise Is 9:5

**WARRIORS**
chosen men, which were *w* 1Kin 12:21
thousand chosen men, which were *w*. 2Chr 11:1

**WARS**
in the book of the *w* of the LORD Num 21:14
had not known all the *w* of Canaan Judg 3:1
for Hadadezer had *w* with Toi 2Sa 8:10
of the LORD his God for the *w* 1Kin 5:3
abundantly, and hast made great *w* 1Chr 22:8
there were *w* between 2Chr 12:15
from henceforth thou shalt have *w* 2Chr 16:9
the acts of Jotham, and all his *w* 2Chr 27:7
He maketh *w* to cease unto the end Ps 46:9
hear of *w* and rumours of *w* Mt 24:6
hear of *w* and rumours of *w* Mk 13:7
But when ye shall hear of *w* Lk 21:9
From whence come *w* and fightings Jas 4:1

**WAS** See PREFACE.

**WASH**
*w* your feet, and rest yourselves Gen 18:4
*w* your feet, and ye shall rise up Gen 19:2
camels, and water to *w* his feet Gen 24:32
down to *w* herself at the river Ex 2:5
let them *w* their clothes, Ex 19:10
and shalt *w* them with water Ex 29:4
*w* the inwards of him, and his legs Ex 29:17
foot also of brass, to *w* withal Ex 30:18
and his sons shall *w* their hands Ex 30:19
they shall *w* with water, that Ex 30:20
So they shall *w* their hands Ex 30:21
and *w* them with water Ex 40:12
and put water there, to *w* withal Ex 40:30
and his legs shall he *w* in water Lev 1:9
But he shall *w* the inwards Lev 1:13
thou shalt *w* that whereon it was Lev 6:27
he did *w* the inwards and the legs, Lev 9:14
of them shall *w* his clothes Lev 11:25
of them shall *w* his clothes Lev 11:28
carcase of it shall *w* his clothes Lev 11:40
carcase of it shall *w* his clothes Lev 11:40
he shall *w* his clothes, and be Lev 13:6
he shall *w* his clothes, and be Lev 13:34
priest shall command that they *w* Lev 13:54
of skin it be, which thou shalt *w* Lev 13:58
be cleansed shall *w* his clothes Lev 14:8
*w* himself in water, that he may Lev 14:8
he shall *w* his clothes, also he Lev 14:9
also he shall *w* his flesh in Lev 14:9
in the house shall *w* his clothes Lev 14:47
in the house shall *w* his clothes Lev 14:47

W

his bed shall *w* his clothes Lev 15:5
the issue shall *w* his clothes Lev 15:6
the issue shall *w* his clothes Lev 15:7
then he shall *w* his clothes Lev 15:8
those things shall *w* his clothes Lev 15:10
he shall *w* his clothes, and bathe Lev 15:11
*w* his clothes, and bathe his flesh Lev 15:13
then he shall *w* all his flesh in Lev 15:16
her bed shall *w* his clothes Lev 15:21
she sat upon shall *w* his clothes Lev 15:22
shall *w* his clothes, and bathe Lev 15:27
shall he *w* his flesh in water Lev 16:4
he shall *w* his flesh with water Lev 16:24
the scapegoat shall *w* his clothes Lev 16:26
burneth them shall *w* his clothes Lev 16:28
he shall both *w* his clothes Lev 17:15
But if he *w* them not, nor bathe Lev 17:16
unless he *w* his flesh with water Lev 22:6
let them *w* their clothes, and so Num 8:7
the priest shall *w* his clothes Num 19:7
her shall *w* his clothes in water Num 19:8
of the heifer shall *w* his clothes Num 19:10
*w* his clothes, and bathe himself Num 19:19
of separation shall *w* his clothes Num 19:21
ye shall *w* your clothes on the Num 31:24
shall *w* their hands over the Deut 21:6
he shall *w* himself with water Deut 23:11
*W* thyself therefore, and anoint Ruth 3:3
*w* the feet of the servants of my 1Sa 25:41
down to thy house, and *w* thy feet 2Sa 11:8
*w* in Jordan seven times, and thy 2Kin 5:10
may I not *w* in them, and be clean 2Kin 5:12
then, when he saith to thee, *W* 2Kin 5:13
and five on the left, to *w* in them 2Chr 4:6
sea was for the priests to *w* in 2Chr 4:6
If I *w* myself with snow water, and Job 9:30
I will *w* mine hands in innocency Ps 26:6
*W* me throughly from mine iniquity Ps 51:2
*w* me, and I shall be whiter than Ps 51:7
he shall *w* his feet in the blood Ps 58:10
*W* you, make you clean Is 1:16
For though thou *w* thee with nitre Jer 2:22
*w* thine heart from wickedness, Jer 4:14
for whom thou didst *w* thyself Eze 23:40
anoint thine head, and *w* thy face Mt 6:17
for they *w* not their hands when Mt 15:2
except they *w* their hands oft, Mk 7:3
from the market, except they *w* Mk 7:4
began to *w* his feet with tears, Lk 7:38
*w* in the pool of Siloam, (which Jn 9:7
Go to the pool of Siloam, and *w* Jn 9:11
began to *w* the disciples' feet, Jn 13:5
him, Lord, dost thou *w* my feet Jn 13:6
him, Thou shalt never *w* my feet Jn 13:8
If I *w* thee not, thou hast no Jn 13:8
needeth not save to *w* his feet Jn 13:10
ye also ought to *w* one another's Jn 13:14
*w* away thy sins, calling on the Acts 22:16

**WASHED**
them water, and they *w* their feet Gen 43:24
he *w* his face, and went out, and Gen 43:31
he *w* his garments in wine, and his Gen 49:11
and they *w* their clothes Ex 19:14
his sons *w* their hands and their Ex 40:31
came near unto the altar, they *w* Ex 40:32
and his sons, and *w* them with water Lev 8:6
he *w* the inwards and the legs in Lev 8:21
on the plague, after that it is *w* Lev 13:55
it shall be *w* the second time Lev 13:58
shall be *w* with water, and be Lev 15:17
purified, and they *w* their clothes Num 8:21
they *w* their feet, and did eat and Judg 19:21
David arose from the earth, and *w* 2Sa 12:20
nor *w* his clothes, from the day 2Sa 19:24
one *w* the chariot in the pool of 1Kin 22:38
and they *w* his armour 1Kin 22:38
the burnt offering they *w* in them 2Chr 4:6
When I *w* my steps with butter, and Job 29:6
vain, and *w* my hands in innocency Ps 73:13
eyes, and yet is not *w* from their Prov 30:12
I have *w* my feet Song 5:3
*w* with milk, and fitly set Song 5:12
When the Lord shall have *w* away Is 4:4
neither wast thou *w* in water to Eze 16:4
Then *w* I thee with water Eze 16:9
I throughly *w* away thy blood from Eze 16:9
where they *w* the burnt offering Eze 40:38
*w* his hands before the multitude, Mt 27:24
but she hath *w* my feet with tears Lk 7:44
he had not first *w* before dinner Lk 11:38
He went his way therefore, and *w* Jn 9:7
and I went and *w*, and I received Jn 9:11
put clay upon mine eyes, and I *w* Jn 9:15
He that is *w* needeth not save to Jn 13:10
So after he had *w* their feet Jn 13:12
Lord and Master, have *w* your feet Jn 13:14
whom when they had *w*, they laid Acts 9:37
of the night, and *w* their stripes Acts 16:33
but ye are *w*, but ye are 1Cor 6:11
if she have *w* the saints' feet, 1Ti 5:10
our bodies *w* with pure water Heb 10:22
the sow that was *w* to her 2Pet 2:22
*w* us from our sins in his own Rev 1:5
have *w* their robes, and made them Rev 7:14

**WASHEST**
thou *w* away the things which grow Job 14:19

**WASHING**
somewhat dark after the *w* of it Lev 13:56
the roof he saw a woman *w* herself 2Sa 11:2
that every one put them off for *w* Neh 4:23
shorn, which came up from the *w* Song 4:2
of sheep which go up from the *w* Song 6:6
as the *w* of cups, and pots, brasen Mk 7:4
of men, as the *w* of pots and cups Mk 7:8
out of them, and were *w* their nets Lk 5:2
cleanse it with the *w* of water by Eph 5:26
by the *w* of regeneration, and Titus 3:5

**WASHINGS**
in meats and drinks, and divers *w* Heb 9:10

**WASHPOT**
Moab is my *w* Ps 60:8
Moab is my *w* Ps 108:9

**WAST**
Who told thee that thou *w* naked Gen 3:11
for out of it *w* thou taken Gen 3:19
of God, and thou *w* pleased with me Gen 33:10
manner when thou *w* his butler Gen 40:13
remember that thou *w* a servant in Deut 5:15
thou shalt remember that thou *w* a Deut 15:15
that thou *w* a bondman in Egypt Deut 16:12
because thou *w* a stranger in his Deut 23:7
that thou *w* a bondman in Egypt Deut 24:18
thou shalt remember that thou *w* a Deut 24:22
behind thee, when thou *w* faint Deut 25:18
of Egypt, which thou *w* afraid of Deut 28:60
with whose maidens thou *w* Ruth 3:2
When thou *w* little in thine own 1Sa 15:17
*w* thou not made the head of the 1Sa 15:17
How *w* thou not afraid to stretch 2Sa 1:14
thou *w* slain in thine high places 2Sa 1:25
thou *w* he that leddest out and 2Sa 5:2
thou *w* he that leddest out and 1Chr 11:2
or *w* thou made before the hills Job 15:7
Where *w* thou when I laid the Job 38:4
thou it, because thou *w* then born Job 38:21
thou *w* a God that forgavest them, Ps 99:8
Jordan, that thou *w* driven back Ps 114:5
though thou *w* angry with me, Is 12:1
wherein thou *w* made to serve Is 14:3
spoilest, and thou *w* not spoiled Is 33:1
Since thou *w* precious in my sight Is 43:4
*w* called a transgressor from the Is 48:8
of youth, when thou *w* refused Is 54:6
therefore thou *w* not grieved Is 57:10
as thou *w* ashamed of Assyria Jer 2:36
O Babylon, and thou *w* not aware Jer 50:24
in the day thou *w* born thy navel Eze 16:4
neither *w* thou washed in water to Eze 16:4
thou *w* not salted at all, nor Eze 16:4
but thou *w* cast out in the open Eze 16:5
in the day that thou *w* born Eze 16:5
thee when thou *w* in thy blood Eze 16:6
thee when thou *w* in thy blood Eze 16:6
is grown, whereas thou *w* naked Eze 16:7
Thus *w* thou decked with gold and Eze 16:13
thou *w* exceeding beautiful, and Eze 16:13
of thy youth, when thou *w* naked Eze 16:22
bare, and *w* polluted in thy blood Eze 16:22
because thou *w* unsatiable Eze 16:28
yet thou *w* not satisfied herewith Eze 16:29
thou *w* corrupted more than they Eze 16:47
in the place where thou *w* created Eze 21:30
thou *w* not purged, thou shalt not Eze 24:13
that *w* inhabited of seafaring men Eze 26:17
which *w* strong in the sea, she and Eze 26:17
thou *w* replenished, and made very Eze 27:25
in the day that thou *w* created Eze 28:13
thou *w* upon the holy mountain of Eze 28:14
Thou *w* perfect in thy ways from Eze 28:15
from the day that thou *w* created Eze 28:15
even thou *w* as one of them Obad 11
Thou also *w* with Jesus of Galilee Mt 26:69
thou also *w* with Jesus of Mk 14:67
when thou *w* under the fig tree, I Jn 1:48
Thou *w* altogether born in sins, Jn 9:34
say unto thee, When thou *w* young Jn 21:18
for thou *w* slain, and hast Rev 5:9
God Almighty, which art, and *w* Rev 11:17
O Lord, which art, and *w*, and Rev 16:5

**WASTE**
And I will make your cities *w* Lev 26:31
be desolate, and your cities *w* Lev 26:33
have laid them *w* even unto Nophah Num 21:30
in the *w* howling wilderness Deut 32:10
The barrel of meal shall not *w* 1Kin 17:14
lay *w* fenced cities into ruinous 2Kin 19:25
of wickedness *w* them any more 1Chr 17:9
my fathers' sepulchres, lieth *w* Neh 2:3
we are in, how Jerusalem lieth *w* Neh 2:17
in former time desolate and *w* Job 30:3
satisfy the desolate and *w* ground Job 38:27
laid *w* his dwelling place Ps 79:7
boar out of the wood doth *w* it Ps 80:13
And I will lay it *w* Is 5:6
the *w* places of the fat ones Is 5:17
in the night Ar of Moab is laid *w* Is 15:1
the night Kir of Moab is laid *w* Is 15:1
for it is laid *w*, so that there Is 23:1
for your strength is laid *w* Is 23:14
the earth empty, and maketh it *w* Is 24:1
The highways lie *w*, the wayfaring Is 33:8
to generation it shall lie *w* Is 34:10
have laid *w* all the nations Is 37:18
*w* defenced cities into ruinous Is 37:26
I will make *w* mountains and hills, Is 42:15
they that made thee *w* shall go Is 49:17
For thy *w* and thy desolate places, Is 49:19
he will comfort all her *w* places Is 51:3
ye *w* places of Jerusalem Is 52:9
thee shall build the old *w* places Is 58:12
and they shall repair the *w* cities Is 61:4
our pleasant things are laid *w* Is 64:11
yelled, and they made his land *w* Jer 2:15
and thy cities shall be laid *w* Jer 4:7
should this city be laid *w* Jer 27:17
for Noph shall be *w* and desolate Jer 46:19
a desolation, a reproach, a *w* Jer 49:13
*w* and utterly destroy after them, Jer 50:21
Moreover I will make thee *w* Eze 5:14
the cities shall be laid *w* Eze 6:6
that your altars may be laid *w* Eze 6:6
are inhabited shall be laid *w* Eze 12:20
and he laid *w* their cities Eze 19:7
be replenished, now she is laid *w* Eze 26:2
of Egypt shall be desolate and *w* Eze 29:9
make the land of Egypt utterly *w* Eze 29:10
*w* shall be desolate forty years Eze 29:12
and I will make the land *w* Eze 30:12
I will lay thy cities *w*, and thou Eze 35:4
and the *w* and desolate and ruined Eze 36:35
so shall the *w* cities be filled Eze 36:38
Israel, which have been always *w* Eze 38:8
He hath laid my vine *w*, and barked Joel 1:7
of Israel shall be laid *w* Amos 7:9
and they shall build the *w* cities Amos 9:14
they shall *w* the land of Assyria Mic 5:6
She is empty, and void, and *w* Nah 2:10
thee, and say, Nineveh is laid *w* Nah 3:7
I made their streets *w*, that none Zeph 3:6
houses, and this house lie *w* Hag 1:4
Because of mine house that is *w* Hag 1:9
his heritage *w* for the dragons of Mal 1:3
saying, To what purpose is this *w* Mt 26:8
Why was this *w* of the ointment Mk 14:4

**WASTED**
carcases be *w* in the wilderness Num 14:33
the Kenite shall be *w*, until Num 24:22
of the men of war were *w* out from Deut 2:14
And the barrel of meal *w* not 1Kin 17:16
*w* the country of the children of 1Chr 20:1
they that *w* us required of us Ps 137:3
cities be *w* without inhabitant Is 6:11
the sea, and the river shall be *w* Is 19:5
those nations shall be utterly *w* Is 60:12
and they are *w* and desolate, as at Jer 44:6
midst of the cities that are *w* Eze 30:7
The field is *w*, the land mourneth Joel 1:10
for the corn is *w* Joel 1:10
there *w* his substance with Lk 15:13
unto him that he had *w* his goods Lk 16:1
the church of God, and *w* it Gal 1:13

**WASTENESS**
trouble and distress, a day of *w* Zeph 1:15

**WASTER**
brother to him that is a great *w* Prov 18:9
I have created the *w* to destroy Is 54:16

**WASTES**
And they shall build the old *w* Is 61:4
thereof shall be perpetual *w* Jer 49:13
they that inhabit those *w* of the Eze 33:24
in the *w* shall fall by the sword Eze 33:27
to the valleys, to the desolate *w* Eze 36:4
and the *w* shall be builded Eze 36:10
cities, and the *w* shall be builded Eze 36:33

**WASTETH**
But man dieth, and *w* away Job 14:10
the destruction that *w* at noonday Ps 91:6
He that *w* his father, and chaseth Prov 19:26

**WASTING**
*w* and destruction are in their Is 59:7
*w* nor destruction within thy Is 60:18

**WATCH**
The LORD *w* between me and thee, Gen 31:49
that in the morning *w* the LORD Ex 14:24
in the beginning of the middle *w* Judg 7:19
and they had but newly set the *w* Judg 7:19
of the host in the morning *w* 1Sa 11:11
to *w* him, and to slay him in the 1Sa 19:11
kept the *w* lifted up his eyes 2Sa 13:34
of the *w* of the king's house 2Kin 11:5
shall ye keep the *w* of the house 2Kin 11:6
even they shall keep the *w* of the 2Kin 11:7
the *w* tower in the wilderness 2Chr 20:24
shall keep the *w* of the LORD 2Chr 23:6
*W* ye, and keep them, until ye Ezr 8:29
set a *w* against them day and night Neh 4:9
of Jerusalem, every one in his *w* Neh 7:3
that thou settest a *w* over me Job 7:12
dost thou not *w* over my sin Job 14:16
is past, and as a *w* in the night Ps 90:4
I *w*, and am as a sparrow alone Ps 102:7
than they that *w* for the morning Ps 130:6
than they that *w* for the morning Ps 130:6
Set a *w*, O LORD, before my mouth Ps 141:3
*w* in the watchtower, eat, drink Is 21:5
all that *w* for iniquity are cut Is 29:20
a leopard shall *w* over their Jer 5:6
so will I *w* over them, to build, Jer 31:28
I will *w* over them for evil, and Jer 44:27
of Babylon, make the *w* strong Jer 51:12
*w* the way, make thy loins strong, Nah 2:1
I will stand upon my *w*, and set me Hab 2:1
will *w* to see what he will say Hab 2:1

in the fourth *w* of the night Mt 14:25
*W* therefore Mt 24:42
in what *w* the thief would come Mt 24:43
*W* therefore, for ye know neither Mt 25:13
tarry ye here, and *w* with me Mt 26:38
could ye not *w* with me one hour Mt 26:40
*W* and pray, that ye enter not into Mt 26:41
said unto them, Ye have a *w* Mt 27:65
sealing the stone, and setting a *w* Mt 27:66
some of the *w* came into the city, Mt 28:11
about the fourth *w* of the night Mk 6:48
Take ye heed, *w* and pray Mk 13:33
and commanded the porter to *w* Mk 13:34
*W* ye therefore Mk 13:35
I say unto you I say unto all, *W* Mk 13:37
tarry ye here, and *w* Mk 14:34
couldest not thou *w* one hour Mk 14:37
*W* ye and pray, lest ye enter into Mk 14:38
keeping *w* over their flock by Lk 2:8
if he shall come in the second *w* Lk 12:38
or come in the third *w* Lk 12:38
*W* ye therefore, and pray always, Lk 21:36
Therefore *w*, and remember, that by. Acts 20:31
*W* ye, stand fast in the faith, 1Cor 16:13
*w* in the same with thanksgiving Col 4:2
but let us *w* and be sober 1Th 5:6
But *w* thou in all things, endure 2Ti 4:5
for they *w* for your souls, as Heb 13:17
therefore sober, and *w* unto prayer 1Pet 4:7
If therefore thou shalt not *w* Rev 3:3

**WATCHED**
they *w* the house to kill him Ps 59:*t*
All my familiars *w* for my halting Jer 20:10
that like as I have *w* over them Jer 31:28
in our watching we have *w* for a Lam 4:17
hath the LORD *w* upon the evil Dan 9:14
thief would come, he would have *w* Mt 24:43
And sitting down they *w* him there Mt 27:36
And they *w* him, whether he would Mk 3:2
And the scribes and Pharisees *w* him Lk 6:7
thief would come, he would have *w* Lk 12:39
the sabbath day, that they *w* him Lk 14:1
And they *w* him, and sent forth Lk 20:20
they *w* the gates day and night to Acts 9:24

**WATCHER**
head upon my bed, and, behold, a *w* Dan 4:13
And whereas the king saw a *w* Dan 4:23

**WATCHERS**
that *w* come from a far country, Jer 4:16
matter is by the decree of the *w* Dan 4:17

**WATCHES**
appoint *w* of the inhabitants of Neh 7:3
were over against them in the *w* Neh 12:9
meditate on thee in the night *w* Ps 63:6
Mine eyes prevent the night *w* Ps 119:148
in the beginning of the *w* pour Lam 2:19

**WATCHETH**
The wicked *w* the righteous, and Ps 37:32
it *w* for thee Eze 7:6
Blessed is he that *w*, and keepeth Rev 16:15

**WATCHFUL**
Be *w*, and strengthen the things Rev 3:2

**WATCHING**
sat upon a seat by the wayside *w* 1Sa 4:13
*w* daily at my gates, waiting at Prov 8:34
in our *w* we have watched for a Lam 4:17
*w* Jesus, saw the earthquake, and Mt 27:54
lord when he cometh shall find *w* Lk 12:37
*w* thereunto with all perseverance Eph 6:18

**WATCHINGS**
in tumults, in labours, in *w* 2Cor 6:5
in *w* often, in hunger and thirst, 2Cor 11:27

**WATCHMAN**
the *w* went up to the roof over 2Sa 18:24
the *w* cried, and told the king 2Sa 18:25
the *w* saw another man running 2Sa 18:26
the *w* called unto the porter, and 2Sa 18:26
the *w* said, Me thinketh the 2Sa 18:27
there stood a *w* on the tower in 2Kin 9:17
the *w* told, saying, The messenger 2Kin 9:18
the *w* told, saying, He came even 2Kin 9:20
city, the *w* waketh but in vain Ps 127:1
Lord said unto me, Go, set a *w* Is 21:6
He calleth to me out of Seir, *W* Is 21:11
*W*, what of the night Is 21:11
The *w* said, The morning cometh, Is 21:12
I have made thee a *w* unto the Eze 3:17
coasts, and set him for their *w* Eze 33:2
But if the *w* see the sword come, Eze 33:6
I have set thee a *w* unto the Eze 33:7
The *w* of Ephraim was with my God Hos 9:8

**WATCHMAN'S**
will I require at the *w* hand Eze 33:6

**WATCHMEN**
the *w* of Saul in Gibeah of 1Sa 14:16
tower of the *w* to the fenced city 2Kin 17:9
tower of the *w* to the fenced city 2Kin 18:8
The *w* that go about the city Song 3:3
The *w* that went about the city Song 5:7
Thy *w* shall lift up the voice Is 52:8
His *w* are blind Is 56:10
I have set *w* upon thy walls, O Is 62:6
Also I set *w* over you, saying, Jer 6:17
that the *w* upon the mount Ephraim Jer 31:6
the watch strong, set up the *w* Jer 51:12
the day of thy *w* and thy Mic 7:4

**WATCHTOWER**
Prepare the table, watch in the *w* Is 21:5
upon the *w* in the daytime Is 21:8

**WATER**
went out of Eden to *w* the garden Gen 2:10
a fountain of *w* in the wilderness Gen 16:7
Let a little *w*, I pray you, be Gen 18:4
and took bread, and a bottle of *w* Gen 21:14
the *w* was spent in the bottle, and Gen 21:15
her eyes, and she saw a well of *w* Gen 21:19
went, and filled the bottle with *w* Gen 21:19
Abimelech because of a well of *w* Gen 21:25
of *w* at the time of the evening Gen 24:11
time that women go out to draw *w* Gen 24:11
I stand here by the well of *w* Gen 24:13
of the city come out to draw *w* Gen 24:13
drink a little *w* of thy pitcher Gen 24:17
I will draw *w* for thy camels also Gen 24:19
ran again unto the well to draw *w* Gen 24:20
*w* to wash his feet, and the men's Gen 24:32
Behold, I stand by the well of *w* Gen 24:43
the virgin cometh forth to draw *w* Gen 24:43
a little *w* of thy pitcher to Gen 24:43
down unto the well, and drew *w* Gen 24:45
Isaac digged again the wells of *w* Gen 26:18
found there a well of springing *w* Gen 26:19
herdmen, saying, The *w* is ours Gen 26:20
and said unto him, We have found *w* Gen 26:32
*w* ye the sheep, and go and feed Gen 29:7
then we *w* the sheep Gen 29:8
was empty, there was no *w* in it Gen 37:24
Joseph's house, and gave them *w* Gen 43:24
Unstable as *w*, thou shalt not Gen 49:4
Because I drew him out of the *w* Ex 2:10
and they came and drew *w*, and filled Ex 2:16
troughs to *w* their father's flock Ex 2:16
also drew *w* enough for us, and Ex 2:19
shalt take of the *w* of the river Ex 4:9
the *w* which thou takest out of Ex 4:9
lo, he goeth out unto the *w* Ex 7:15
to drink of the *w* of the river Ex 7:18
and upon all their pools of *w* Ex 7:19
not drink of the *w* of the river Ex 7:21
about the river for *w* to drink Ex 7:24
not drink of the *w* of the river Ex 7:24
lo, he cometh forth to the *w* Ex 8:20
it raw, nor sodden at all with *w* Ex 12:9
in the wilderness, and found no *w* Ex 15:22
where were twelve wells of *w* Ex 15:27
there was no *w* for the people to Ex 17:1
Give us *w* that we may drink Ex 17:2
the people thirsted there for *w* Ex 17:3
and there shall come *w* out of it Ex 17:6
that is in the *w* under the earth Ex 20:4
shall bless thy bread, and thy *w* Ex 23:25
and shalt wash them with *w* Ex 29:4
and thou shalt put *w* therein Ex 30:18
they shall wash with *w*, that Ex 30:20
powder, and strawed it upon the *w* Ex 32:20
neither eat bread, nor drink *w* Ex 34:28
the altar, and shalt put *w* therein Ex 40:7
congregation, and wash them with *w* Ex 40:12
put *w* there, to wash withal Ex 40:30
and his legs shall he wash in *w* Lev 1:9
the inwards and the legs with *w* Lev 1:13
be both scoured, and rinsed in *w* Lev 6:28
his sons, and washed them with *w* Lev 8:6
the inwards and the legs in *w* Lev 8:21
is done, it must be put into *w* Lev 11:32
that on which such *w* cometh shall Lev 11:34
pit, wherein there is plenty of *w* Lev 11:36
But if any *w* be put upon the seed Lev 11:38
an earthen vessel over running *w* Lev 14:5
was killed over the running *w* Lev 14:6
his hair, and wash himself in *w* Lev 14:8
also he shall wash his flesh in *w* Lev 14:9
an earthen vessel over running *w* Lev 14:50
slain bird, and in the running *w* Lev 14:51
the bird, and with the running *w* Lev 14:52
clothes, and bathe himself in *w* Lev 15:5
clothes, and bathe himself in *w* Lev 15:6
clothes, and bathe himself in *w* Lev 15:7
clothes, and bathe himself in *w* Lev 15:8
clothes, and bathe himself in *w* Lev 15:10
and hath not rinsed his hands in *w* Lev 15:11
clothes, and bathe himself in *w* Lev 15:11
of wood shall be rinsed in *w* Lev 15:12
and bathe his flesh in running *w* Lev 15:13
he shall wash all his flesh in *w* Lev 15:16
shall be washed with *w*, and be Lev 15:17
shall both bathe themselves in *w* Lev 15:18
clothes, and bathe himself in *w* Lev 15:21
clothes, and bathe himself in *w* Lev 15:22
clothes, and bathe himself in *w* Lev 15:27
shall he wash his flesh in *w* Lev 16:4
flesh with *w* in the holy place Lev 16:24
clothes, and bathe his flesh in *w* Lev 16:26
clothes, and bathe his flesh in *w* Lev 16:28
clothes, and bathe himself in *w* Lev 17:15
unless he wash his flesh with *w* Lev 22:6
take holy *w* in an earthen vessel Num 5:17
shall take, and put it into the *w* Num 5:17
bitter *w* that causeth the curse Num 5:18
bitter *w* that causeth the curse Num 5:19
this *w* that causeth the curse Num 5:22
blot them out with the bitter *w* Num 5:23
bitter *w* that causeth the curse Num 5:24
the *w* that causeth the curse Num 5:24
cause the woman to drink the *w* Num 5:26
he hath made her to drink the *w* Num 5:27
that the *w* that causeth the curse Num 5:27
Sprinkle *w* of purifying upon them Num 8:7
and he shall bathe his flesh in *w* Num 19:7
her shall wash his clothes in *w* Num 19:8
and bathe his flesh in *w* Num 19:8
of Israel for a *w* of separation Num 19:9
because the *w* of separation was Num 19:13
running *w* shall be put thereto in Num 19:17
take hyssop, and dip it in the *w* Num 19:18
clothes, and bathe himself in *w* Num 19:19
the *w* of separation hath not been Num 19:20
that he that sprinkleth the *w* of Num 19:21
he that toucheth the *w* of Num 19:21
And there was no *w* for the Num 20:2
neither is there any *w* to drink Num 20:5
and it shall give forth his *w* Num 20:8
forth to them *w* out of the rock Num 20:8
we fetch you *w* out of this rock Num 20:10
the *w* came out abundantly, and the Num 20:11
This is the *w* of Meribah Num 20:13
we drink of the *w* of the wells Num 20:17
if I and my cattle drink of thy *w* Num 20:19
my word at the *w* of Meribah Num 20:24
no bread, neither is there any *w* Num 21:5
together, and I will give them *w* Num 21:16
He shall pour the *w* out of his Num 24:7
me at the *w* before their eyes Num 27:14
that is the *w* of Meribah in Num 27:14
purified with the *w* of separation Num 31:23
ye shall make go through the *w* Num 31:23
Elim were twelve fountains of *w* Num 33:9
where was no *w* for the people to Num 33:14
also buy *w* of them for money Deut 2:6
give me *w* for money, that I may Deut 2:28
good land, a land of brooks of *w* Deut 8:7
and drought, where there was no *w* Deut 8:15
who brought thee forth *w* out of Deut 8:15
neither did eat bread nor drink *w* Deut 9:9
neither eat bread, nor drink *w* Deut 9:18
how he made the *w* of the Red sea Deut 11:4
drinketh *w* of the rain of heaven Deut 11:11
shall pour it upon the earth as *w* Deut 12:16
shalt pour it upon the earth as *w* Deut 12:24
pour it upon the ground as *w* Deut 15:23
with *w* in the way, when ye came Deut 23:4
on, he shall wash himself with *w* Deut 23:11
thy wood unto the drawer of thy *w* Deut 29:11
up the *w* of the Red sea for you Josh 2:10
to the brink of the *w* of Jordan Josh 3:8
were dipped in the brim of the *w* Josh 3:15
the people melted, and became as *w* Josh 7:5
drawers of *w* unto all the Josh 9:21
drawers of *w* for the house of my Josh 9:23
drawers of *w* for the congregation Josh 9:27
the fountain of the *w* of Nephtoah Josh 15:9
give me also springs of *w* Josh 15:19
unto the *w* of Jericho on the east Josh 16:1
give me also springs of *w* Judg 1:15
I pray thee, a little *w* to drink Judg 4:19
the clouds also dropped *w* Judg 5:4
in the places of drawing *w* Judg 5:11
He asked *w*, and she gave him milk Judg 5:25
of the fleece, a bowl full of *w* Judg 6:38
bring them down unto the *w* Judg 7:4
down the people unto the *w* Judg 7:5
lappeth of the *w* with his tongue Judg 7:5
down upon their knees to drink *w* Judg 7:6
the jaw, and there came *w* thereout. Judg 15:19
together to Mizpeh, and drew *w* 1Sa 7:6
young maidens going out to draw *w* 1Sa 9:11
I then take my bread, and my *w* 1Sa 25:11
at his bolster, and the cruse of *w* 1Sa 26:11
the cruse of *w* from Saul's 1Sa 26:12
the cruse of *w* that was at his 1Sa 26:16
and they made him drink *w* 1Sa 30:11
eaten no bread, nor drunk any *w* 1Sa 30:12
are as *w* spilt on the ground, 2Sa 14:14
They be gone over the brook of *w* 2Sa 17:20
Arise, and pass quickly over the *w* 2Sa 17:21
the beginning of harvest until *w* 2Sa 21:10
the *w* of the well of Beth-lehem 2Sa 23:15
drew *w* out of the well of 2Sa 23:16
bread nor drink *w* in this place 1Kin 13:8
saying, Eat no bread, nor drink *w* 1Kin 13:9
drink *w* with thee in this place 1Kin 13:16
eat no bread nor drink *w* there 1Kin 13:17
that he may eat bread and drink *w* 1Kin 13:18
bread in his house, and drank *w* 1Kin 13:19
drunk *w* in the place, of the 1Kin 13:22
thee, Eat no bread, and drink no *w* 1Kin 13:22
as a reed is shaken in the *w* 1Kin 14:15
a little *w* in a vessel, that I 1Kin 17:10
cave, and fed them with bread and *w*. 1Kin 18:4
the land, unto all fountains of *w* 1Kin 18:5
fed them with bread and *w* 1Kin 18:13
and said, Fill four barrels with *w* 1Kin 18:33
the *w* ran round about the altar 1Kin 18:35
he filled the trench also with *w* 1Kin 18:35
licked up the *w* that was in the 1Kin 18:38
and a cruse of *w* at his head 1Kin 19:6
with *w* of affliction, until I 1Kin 22:27
but the *w* is naught, and the 2Kin 2:19
and there was no *w* for the host 2Kin 3:9
which poured *w* on the hands of 2Kin 3:11
valley shall be filled with *w* 2Kin 3:17
good tree, and stop all wells of *w* 2Kin 3:19
there came *w* by the way of Edom, 2Kin 3:20

and the country was filled with *w* 2Kin 3:20
and the sun shone upon the *w* 2Kin 3:22
the Moabites saw the *w* on the 2Kin 3:22
they stopped all the wells of *w* 2Kin 3:25
beam, the ax head fell into the *w* 2Kin 6:5
*w* before them, that they may eat 2Kin 6:22
a thick cloth, and dipped it in *w* 2Kin 8:15
brought *w* into the city, are they 2Kin 20:20
the *w* of the well of Beth-lehem 1Chr 11:17
drew *w* out of the well of 1Chr 11:18
with *w* of affliction, until I 2Chr 18:26
of Assyria come, and find much *w* 2Chr 32:4
he did eat no bread, nor drink *w* Ezr 10:6
the *w* gate toward the east Neh 3:26
street that was before the *w* gate Neh 8:1
the *w* gate from the morning until Neh 8:3
and in the street of the *w* gate Neh 8:16
broughtest forth *w* for them out Neh 9:15
gavest them *w* for their thirst Neh 9:20
even unto the *w* gate eastward Neh 12:37
of Israel with bread and with *w* Neh 13:2
can the flag grow without *w* Job 8:11
If I wash myself with snow *w* Job 9:30
the scent of *w* it will bud Job 14:9
which drinketh iniquity like *w* Job 15:16
Thou hast not given *w* to the Job 22:7
who drinketh up scorning like *w* Job 34:7
he maketh small the drops of *w* Job 36:27
a tree planted by the rivers of *w* Ps 1:3
I *w* my couch with my tears Ps 6:6
I am poured out like *w*, and all my Ps 22:14
hart panteth after the *w* brooks Ps 42:1
and thirsty land, where no *w* is Ps 63:1
river of God, which is full of *w* Ps 65:9
we went through fire and through *w* Ps 66:12
as showers that *w* the earth Ps 72:6
The clouds poured out *w* Ps 77:17
shed like *w* round about Jerusalem Ps 79:3
came round about me daily like *w* Ps 88:17
the wilderness into a standing *w* Ps 107:35
it come into his bowels like *w* Ps 109:18
turned the rock into a standing *w* Ps 114:8
no fountains abounding with *w* Prov 8:24
is as when one letteth out *w* Prov 17:14
the heart of man is like deep *w* Prov 20:5
of the LORD, as the rivers of *w* Prov 21:1
be thirsty, give him *w* to drink Prov 25:21
As in *w* face answereth to face, Prov 27:19
earth that is not filled with *w* Prov 30:16
I made me pools of *w* Eccl 2:6
to *w* therewith the wood that Eccl 2:6
dross, thy wine mixed with *w* Is 1:22
and as a garden that hath no *w* Is 1:30
of bread, and the whole stay of *w* Is 3:1
with joy shall ye draw *w* out of Is 12:3
for the bittern, and pools of *w* Is 14:23
I will *w* thee with my tears, O Is 16:9
brought *w* to him that was thirsty Is 21:14
walls for the *w* of the old pool Is 22:11
I will *w* it every moment Is 27:3
or to take *w* withal out of the Is 30:14
the *w* of affliction, yet shall Is 30:20
as rivers of *w* in a dry place, as Is 32:2
and the thirsty land springs of *w* Is 35:7
I have digged, and drunk *w* Is 37:25
When the poor and needy seek *w* Is 41:17
make the wilderness a pool of *w* Is 41:18
and the dry land springs of *w* Is 41:18
For I will pour *w* upon him that Is 44:3
as willows by the *w* courses Is 44:4
he drinketh no *w*, and is faint Is 44:12
springs of *w* shall he guide them Is 49:10
stinketh, because there is no *w* Is 50:2
garden, and like a spring of *w* Is 58:11
arm, dividing the *w* before them Is 63:12
cisterns, that can hold no *w* Jer 2:13
given us *w* of gall to drink, Jer 8:14
give them *w* of gall to drink Jer 9:15
thy loins, and put it not in *w* Jer 13:1
came to the pits, and found no *w* Jer 14:3
and make them drink the *w* of gall Jer 23:15
And in the dungeon there was no *w* Jer 38:6
eye, mine eye runneth down with *w* Lam 1:16
pour out thine heart like *w* Lam 2:19
of *w* for the destruction of the Lam 3:48
We have drunken our *w* for money Lam 5:4
shalt drink also *w* by measure Eze 4:11
and they shall drink by measure Eze 4:16
That they may want bread and *w* Eze 4:17
and all knees shall be weak as *w* Eze 7:17
drink thy *w* with trembling and Eze 12:18
drink their *w* with astonishment, Eze 12:19
thou washed in *w* to supple thee Eze 16:4
Then washed I thee with *w* Eze 16:9
that he might *w* it by the furrows Eze 17:7
and all knees shall be weak as *w* Eze 21:7
set it on, and also pour *w* into it Eze 24:3
and thy dust in the midst of the *w* Eze 26:12
in their height, all that drink *w* Eze 31:14
best of Lebanon, all that drink *w* Eze 31:16
I will also *w* with thy blood the Eze 32:6
will I sprinkle clean *w* upon you Eze 36:25
us pulse to eat, and *w* to drink Dan 1:12
that give me my bread and my *w* Hos 2:5
out my wrath upon them like *w* Hos 5:10
is cut off as the foam upon the *w* Hos 10:7
shall *w* the valley of Shittim Joel 3:18
unto one city, to drink *w* Amos 4:8
of bread, nor a thirst for *w* Amos 8:11
let them not feed, nor drink *w* Jonah 3:7
is of old like a pool of *w* Nah 2:8
overflowing of the *w* passed by Hab 3:10
out of the pit wherein is no *w* Zec 9:11
you with *w* unto repentance Mt 3:11
went up straightway out of the *w* Mt 3:16
*w* only in the name of a disciple Mt 10:42
bid me come unto thee on the *w* Mt 14:28
of the ship, he walked on the *w* Mt 14:29
into the fire, and oft into the *w* Mt 17:15
a tumult was made, he took *w* Mt 27:24
I indeed have baptized you with *w* Mk 1:8
coming up out of the *w*, he saw Mk 1:10
a cup of *w* to drink in my name Mk 9:41
you a man bearing a pitcher of *w* Mk 14:13
all, I indeed baptize you with *w* Lk 3:16
thou gavest me no *w* for my feet Lk 7:44
and they were filled with *w* Lk 8:23
the wind and the raging of the *w* Lk 8:24
he commandeth even the winds and *w* Lk 8:25
dip the tip of his finger in *w* Lk 16:24
meet you, bearing a pitcher of *w* Lk 22:10
them, saying, I baptize with *w* Jn 1:26
am I come baptizing with *w* Jn 1:31
he that sent me to baptize with *w* Jn 1:33
them, Fill the waterpots with *w* Jn 2:7
tasted the *w* that was made wine Jn 2:9
servants which drew the *w* knew Jn 2:9
thee, Except a man be born of *w* Jn 3:5
because there was much *w* there Jn 3:23
a woman of Samaria to draw *w* Jn 4:7
he would have given thee living *w* Jn 4:10
then hast thou that living *w* Jn 4:11
of this *w* shall thirst again Jn 4:13
the *w* that I shall give him shall Jn 4:14
but the *w* that I shall give him Jn 4:14
*w* springing up into everlasting Jn 4:14
unto him, Sir, give me this *w* Jn 4:15
Galilee, where he made the *w* wine Jn 4:46
waiting for the moving of the *w* Jn 5:3
into the pool, and troubled the *w* Jn 5:4
after the troubling of the *w* Jn 5:4
when the *w* is troubled, to put me Jn 5:7
shall flow rivers of living *w* Jn 7:38
that he poureth *w* into a bason Jn 13:5
came there out blood and *w* Jn 19:34
For John truly baptized with *w* Acts 1:5
way, they came unto a certain *w* Acts 8:36
the eunuch said, See, here is *w* Acts 8:36
and they went down both into the *w* Acts 8:38
they were come up out of the *w* Acts 8:39
Can any man forbid *w*, that these Acts 10:47
said, John indeed baptized with *w* Acts 11:16
with the washing of *w* by the word Eph 5:26
Drink no longer *w*, but use a 1Ti 5:23
of calves and of goats, with *w* Heb 9:19
and our bodies washed with pure *w* Heb 10:22
forth at the same place sweet *w* Jas 3:11
can no fountain both yield salt *w* Jas 3:12
is, eight souls were saved by *w* 1Pet 3:20
These are wells without *w* 2Pet 2:17
out of the *w* and in the *w* 2Pet 3:5
then was, being overflowed with *w* 2Pet 3:6
This is he that came by *w* 1Jn 5:6
not by *w* only, but by *w* 1Jn 5:6
in earth, the spirit, and the *w* 1Jn 5:8
clouds they are without *w* Jude 12
*w* as a flood after the woman Rev 12:15
the *w* thereof was dried up, that Rev 16:12
fountain of the *w* of life freely Rev 21:6
me a pure river of *w* of life Rev 22:1
let him take the *w* of life freely Rev 22:17

**WATERCOURSE**

also stopped the upper *w* of Gihon 2Chr 32:30
Who hath divided a *w* for the Job 38:25

**WATERED**

*w* the whole face of the ground Gen 2:6
that it was well *w* every where Gen 13:10
of that well they *w* the flocks Gen 29:2
*w* the sheep, and put the stone Gen 29:3
*w* the flock of Laban his mother's Gen 29:10
and helped them, and *w* their flock Ex 2:17
enough for us, and *w* the flock Ex 2:19
watereth shall be *w* also himself Prov 11:25
and thou shalt be like a *w* garden Is 58:11
their soul shall be as a *w* garden Jer 31:12
I have planted, Apollos *w* 1Cor 3:6

**WATEREDST**

*w* it with thy foot, as a garden Deut 11:10

**WATEREST**

Thou visitest the earth, and *w* it Ps 65:9
Thou *w* the ridges thereof Ps 65:10

**WATERETH**

He *w* the hills from his chambers Ps 104:13
he that *w* shall be watered also Prov 11:25
but *w* the earth, and maketh it Is 55:10
any thing, neither he that *w* 1Cor 3:7
planteth and he that *w* are one 1Cor 3:8

**WATERFLOOD**

Let not the *w* overflow me Ps 69:15

**WATERING**

flocks in the gutters in the *w* Gen 30:38
Also by *w* he wearieth the thick Job 37:11
the stall, and lead him away to *w* Lk 13:15

**WATERPOT**

The woman then left her *w* Jn 4:28

**WATERPOTS**

were set there six *w* of stone Jn 2:6
unto them, Fill the *w* with water Jn 2:7

**WATERS**

God moved upon the face of the *w* Gen 1:2
a firmament in the midst of the *w* Gen 1:6
it divide the *w* from the *w* Gen 1:6
divided the *w* which were under Gen 1:7
under the firmament from the *w* Gen 1:7
Let the *w* under the heaven be Gen 1:9
together of the *w* called he Seas Gen 1:10
Let the *w* bring forth abundantly Gen 1:20
which the *w* brought forth Gen 1:21
fill the *w* in the seas, and let Gen 1:22
bring a flood of *w* upon the earth Gen 6:17
the flood of *w* was upon the earth Gen 7:6
because of the *w* of the flood Gen 7:7
that the *w* of the flood were upon Gen 7:10
the *w* increased, and bare up the Gen 7:17
And the *w* prevailed, and were Gen 7:18
ark went upon the face of the *w* Gen 7:18
the *w* prevailed exceedingly upon Gen 7:19
cubits upward did the *w* prevail Gen 7:20
the *w* prevailed upon the earth an Gen 7:24
over the earth, and the *w* asswaged Gen 8:1
the *w* returned from off the earth Gen 8:3
and fifty days the *w* were abated Gen 8:3
the *w* decreased continually until Gen 8:5
until the *w* were dried up from Gen 8:7
to see if the *w* were abated from Gen 8:8
for the *w* were on the face of the Gen 8:9
so Noah knew that the *w* were Gen 8:11
the *w* were dried up from off the Gen 8:13
off any more by the *w* of a flood Gen 9:11
the *w* shall no more become a Gen 9:15
upon the *w* which are in the river Ex 7:17
thine hand upon the *w* of Egypt Ex 7:19
smote the *w* that were in the Ex 7:20
all the *w* that were in the river Ex 7:20
out his hand over the *w* of Egypt Ex 8:6
dry land, and the *w* were divided Ex 14:21
the *w* were a wall unto them on Ex 14:22
that the *w* may come again upon Ex 14:26
the *w* returned, and covered the Ex 14:28
the *w* were a wall unto them on Ex 14:29
the *w* were gathered together Ex 15:8
they sank as lead in the mighty *w* Ex 15:10
again the *w* of the sea upon them Ex 15:19
could not drink of the *w* of Marah Ex 15:23
which when he had cast into the *w* Ex 15:25
the *w* were made sweet Ex 15:25
and they encamped there by the *w* Ex 15:27
ye eat of all that are in the *w* Lev 11:9
hath fins and scales in the *w* Lev 11:9
rivers, of all that move in the *w* Lev 11:10
living thing which is in the *w* Lev 11:10
hath no fins nor scales in the *w* Lev 11:12
creature that moveth in the *w* Lev 11:46
not drink of the *w* of the well Num 21:22
and as cedar trees beside the *w* Num 24:6
and his seed shall be in many *w* Num 24:7
is in the *w* beneath the earth Deut 4:18
is in the *w* beneath the earth Deut 5:8
to Jotbath, a land of rivers of *w* Deut 10:7
eat of all that are in the *w* Deut 14:9
Israel at the *w* of Meribah-kadesh Deut 32:51
didst strive at the *w* of Meribah Deut 33:8
shall rest in the *w* of Jordan Josh 3:13
that the *w* of Jordan shall be cut Josh 3:13
the *w* that come down from above Josh 3:13
That the *w* which came down from Josh 3:16
That the *w* of Jordan were cut off Josh 4:7
the *w* of Jordan were cut off Josh 4:7
that the *w* of Jordan returned Josh 4:18
the *w* of Jordan from before you Josh 4:23
the *w* of Jordan from before the Josh 5:1
together at the *w* of Merom Josh 11:5
them by the *w* of Merom suddenly Josh 11:7
passed toward the *w* of En-shemesh Josh 15:7
out to the well of *w* of Nephtoah Josh 18:15
in Taanach by the *w* of Megiddo Judg 5:19
before them the *w* unto Beth-barah Judg 7:24
took the *w* unto Beth-barah and Judg 7:24
before me, as the breach of *w* 2Sa 5:20
and have taken the city of *w* 2Sa 12:27
pavilions round about him, dark *w* 2Sa 22:12
he drew me out of many *w* 2Sa 22:17
it together, and smote the *w* 2Kin 2:8
fell from him, and smote the *w* 2Kin 2:14
and when he also had smitten the *w* 2Kin 2:14
forth unto the spring of the *w* 2Kin 2:21
the LORD, I have healed these *w* 2Kin 2:21
So the *w* were healed unto this 2Kin 2:22
better than all the *w* of Israel 2Kin 5:12
ye every one the *w* of his cistern 2Kin 18:31
I have digged and drunk strange *w* 2Kin 19:24
hand like the breaking forth of *w* 1Chr 14:11
his mighty men to stop the *w* of 2Chr 32:3
as a stone into the mighty *w* Neh 9:11
are poured out like the *w* Job 3:24
sendeth *w* upon the fields Job 5:10
remember it as *w* that pass away Job 11:16
Behold, he withholdeth the *w* Job 12:15
As the *w* fail from the sea, and Job 14:11
The *w* wear the stones Job 14:19
and abundance of *w* cover thee Job 22:11
He is swift as the *w* Job 24:18
and heat consume the snow *w* Job 24:19
are formed from under the *w* Job 26:5
He bindeth up the *w* in his thick Job 26:8
hath compassed the *w* with bounds Job 26:10
Terrors take hold on him as *w* Job 27:20
even the *w* forgotten of the foot Job 28:4

and he weigheth the *w* by measure Job 28:25
My root was spread out by the *w* Job 29:19
me as a wide breaking in of *w* Job 30:14
breadth of the *w* is straitened Job 37:10
for the overflowing of *w*, or a Job 38:25
The *w* are hid as with a stone, and Job 38:30
abundance of *w* may cover thee Job 38:34
round about him were dark *w* Ps 18:11
Then the channels of *w* were seen Ps 18:15
took me, he drew me out of many *w* Ps 18:16
he leadeth me beside the still *w* Ps 23:2
voice of the LORD is upon the *w* Ps 29:3
the LORD is upon many *w* Ps 29:3
*w* they shall not come nigh unto Ps 32:6
He gathereth the *w* of the sea Ps 33:7
Though the *w* thereof roar and be Ps 46:3
away as *w* which run continually Ps 58:7
for the *w* are come in unto my Ps 69:1
I am come into deep *w*, where the Ps 69:2
hate me, and out of the deep *w* Ps 69:14
*w* of a full cup are wrung out to Ps 73:10
the heads of the dragons in the *w* Ps 74:13
The *w* saw thee, O God, the *w* Ps 77:16
sea, and thy path in the great *w* Ps 77:19
he made the *w* to stand as an heap Ps 78:13
caused *w* to run down like rivers Ps 78:16
that the *w* gushed out, and the Ps 78:20
I proved thee at the *w* of Meribah Ps 81:7
mightier than the noise of many *w* Ps 93:4
beams of his chambers in the *w* Ps 104:3
the *w* stood above the mountains Ps 104:6
He turned their *w* into blood Ps 105:29
the rock, and the *w* gushed out Ps 105:41
the *w* covered their enemies Ps 106:11
him also at the *w* of strife Ps 106:32
that do business in great *w* Ps 107:23
the flint into a fountain of *w* Ps 114:8
Rivers of *w* run down mine eyes, Ps 119:136
Then the *w* had overwhelmed us, Ps 124:4
Then the proud *w* had gone over Ps 124:5
out the earth above the *w* Ps 136:6
me, and deliver me out of great *w* Ps 144:7
his wind to blow, and the *w* flow Ps 147:18
ye *w* that be above the heavens Ps 148:4
Drink *w* out of thine own cistern, Prov 5:15
running *w* out of thine own well Prov 5:15
rivers of *w* in the streets Prov 5:16
that the *w* should not pass his Prov 8:29
Stolen *w* are sweet, and bread Prov 9:17
of a man's mouth are as deep *w* Prov 18:4
As cold *w* to a thirsty soul, so Prov 25:25
who hath bound the *w* in a garment Prov 30:4
Cast thy bread upon the *w* Eccl 11:1
of gardens, a well of living *w* Song 4:15
eyes of doves by the rivers of *w* Song 5:12
Many *w* cannot quench love, Song 8:7
the *w* of Shiloah that go softly Is 8:6
up upon them the *w* of the river Is 8:7
the LORD, as the *w* cover the sea Is 11:9
For the *w* of Nimrim shall be Is 15:6
For the *w* of Dimon shall be full Is 15:9
like the rushing of mighty *w* Is 17:12
rush like the rushing of many *w* Is 17:13
vessels of bulrushes upon the *w* Is 18:2
the *w* shall fail from the sea, and Is 19:5
nets upon the *w* shall languish Is 19:8
together the *w* of the lower pool Is 22:9
by great *w* the seed of Sihor, the Is 23:3
a flood of mighty *w* overflowing Is 28:2
the *w* shall overflow the hiding Is 28:17
streams of *w* in the day of the Is 30:25
are ye that sow beside all *w* Is 32:20
his *w* shall be sure Is 33:16
the wilderness shall *w* break out Is 35:6
one the *w* of his own cistern Is 36:16
Who hath measured the *w* in the Is 40:12
When thou passest through the *w* Is 43:2
sea, and a path in the mighty *w* Is 43:16
because I give *w* in the Is 43:20
come forth out of the *w* of Judah Is 48:1
he caused the *w* to flow out of Is 48:21
rock also, and the *w* gushed out Is 48:21
the sea, the *w* of the great deep Is 51:10
this is as the *w* of Noah unto me Is 54:9
for as I have sworn that the *w* of Is 54:9
that thirsteth, come ye to the *w* Is 55:1
whose *w* cast up mire and dirt Is 57:20
spring of water, whose *w* fail not Is 58:11
the fire causeth the *w* to boil Is 64:2
me the fountain of living *w* Jer 2:13
of Egypt, to drink the *w* of Sihor Jer 2:18
to drink the *w* of the river Jer 2:18
As a fountain casteth out her *w* Jer 6:7
Oh that my head were *w*, and mine Jer 9:1
and our eyelids gush out with *w* Jer 9:18
a multitude of *w* in the heavens Jer 10:13
sent their little ones to the *w* Jer 14:3
me as a liar, and as *w* that fail Jer 15:18
be as a tree planted by the *w* Jer 17:8
LORD, the fountain of living *w* Jer 17:13
or shall the cold flowing *w* that Jer 18:14
the rivers of *w* in a straight way Jer 31:9
by the great *w* that are in Gibeon Jer 41:12
whose *w* are moved as the rivers Jer 46:7
his *w* are moved like the rivers Jer 46:8
*w* rise up out of the north, and Jer 47:2
for the *w* also of Nimrim shall be Jer 48:34
A drought is upon her *w* Jer 50:38
O thou that dwellest upon many *w* Jer 51:13
a multitude of *w* in the heavens Jer 51:16
her waves do roar like great *w* Jer 51:55
*W* flowed over mine head Lam 3:54
wings, like the noise of great *w* Eze 1:24
he placed it by great *w*, and set Eze 17:5
planted in a good soil by great *w* Eze 17:8
in thy blood, planted by the *w* Eze 19:10
of branches by reason of many *w* Eze 19:10
thee, and great *w* shall cover thee Eze 26:19
have brought thee into great *w* Eze 27:26
depths of the *w* thy merchandise Eze 27:34
The *w* made him great, the deep Eze 31:4
because of the multitude of *w* Eze 31:5
for his root was by great *w* Eze 31:7
the *w* exalt themselves for their Eze 31:14
and the great *w* were stayed Eze 31:15
and troubledst the *w* with thy feet Eze 32:2
thereof from beside the great *w* Eze 32:13
Then will I make their *w* deep Eze 32:14
and to have drunk of the deep *w* Eze 34:18
voice was like a noise of many *w* Eze 43:2
*w* issued out from under the Eze 47:1
the *w* came down from under from Eze 47:1
there ran out *w* on the right side Eze 47:2
and he brought me through the *w* Eze 47:3
the *w* were to the ancles Eze 47:3
and brought me through the *w* Eze 47:4
the *w* were to the knees Eze 47:4
the *w* were to the loins Eze 47:4
for the *w* were risen Eze 47:5
*w* to swim in, a river that could Eze 47:5
These *w* issue out toward the east Eze 47:8
the sea, the *w* shall be healed Eze 47:8
because these *w* shall come Eze 47:9
because their *w* they they issued Eze 47:12
even to the *w* of strife in Kadesh Eze 47:19
unto the *w* of strife in Kadesh Eze 48:28
which was upon the *w* of the river Dan 12:6
which was upon the *w* of the river Dan 12:7
for the rivers of *w* are dried up Joel 1:20
rivers of Judah shall flow with *w* Joel 3:18
that calleth for the *w* of the sea Amos 5:8
But let judgment run down as *w* Amos 5:24
that calleth for the *w* of the sea Amos 9:6
The *w* compassed me about, even to Jonah 2:5
as the *w* that are poured down a Mic 1:4
that had the *w* round about it, Nah 3:8
Draw thee *w* for the siege, Nah 3:14
the LORD, as the *w* cover the sea Hab 2:14
through the heap of great *w* Hab 3:15
that living *w* shall go out from Zec 14:8
the sea, and perished in the *w* Mt 8:32
him into the fire, and into the *w* Mk 9:22
journeyings often, in perils of *w* 2Cor 11:26
his voice as the sound of many *w* Rev 1:15
them unto living fountains of *w* Rev 7:17
and upon the fountains of *w* Rev 8:10
part of the *w* became wormwood Rev 8:11
and many men died of the *w* Rev 8:11
have power over *w* to turn them to Rev 11:6
heaven, as the voice of many *w* Rev 14:2
and the sea, and the fountains of *w* Rev 14:7
upon the rivers and fountains of *w* Rev 16:4
And I heard the angel of the *w* say Rev 16:5
whore that sitteth upon many *w* Rev 17:1
The *w* which thou sawest, where Rev 17:15
and as the voice of many *w* Rev 19:6

## WATERSPOUTS
unto deep at the noise of thy *w* Ps 42:7

## WATERSPRINGS
and the *w* into dry ground Ps 107:33
water, and dry ground into *w* Ps 107:35

## WAVE
shalt *w* them for a Ex 29:24
them for a *w* offering Ex 29:24
and *w* it for a Ex 29:26
it for a *w* offering before Ex 29:26
the breast of the *w* offering Ex 29:27
for a *w* offering before the LORD Lev 7:30
For the *w* breast and the heave Lev 7:34
waved them for a *w* offering Lev 8:27
waved it for a *w* offering before Lev 8:29
for a *w* offering before the LORD Lev 9:21
the *w* breast and heave shoulder Lev 10:14
the *w* breast shall they bring Lev 10:15
to *w* it for a *w* offering Lev 10:15
*w* them for a Lev 14:12
them for a *w* offering before Lev 14:12
the priest shall *w* them for a Lev 14:24
for a *w* offering before the LORD Lev 14:24
he shall *w* the sheaf before the Lev 23:11
the sabbath the priest shall *w* it Lev 23:11
ye *w* the sheaf an he lamb without Lev 23:12
the sheaf of the *w* offering Lev 23:15
two *w* loaves of two tenth deals Lev 23:17
the priest shall *w* them with the Lev 23:20
for a *w* offering before the LORD Lev 23:20
shall *w* the offering before the Num 5:25
the priest shall *w* them for a Num 6:20
for a *w* offering before the LORD Num 6:20
for the priest, with the *w* breast Num 6:20
with all the *w* offerings of the Num 18:11
shall be thine, as the *w* breast Num 18:18
For he that wavereth is like a *w* Jas 1:6

## WAVED
of the heave offering, which is *w* Ex 29:27
that the breast may be *w* for a Lev 7:30
*w* them for a wave offering before Lev 8:27
*w* it for a wave offering before Lev 8:29
the right shoulder Aaron *w* for a Lev 9:21
for a trespass offering to be *w* Lev 14:21

## WAVERETH
For he that *w* is like a wave of Jas 1:6

## WAVERING
profession of our faith without *w* Heb 10:23
let him ask in faith, nothing *w* Jas 1:6

## WAVES
When the *w* of death compassed me, 2Sa 22:5
and treadeth upon the *w* of the sea Job 9:8
here shall thy proud *w* be stayed Job 38:11
all thy *w* and thy billows are gone Ps 42:7
of the seas, the noise of their *w* Ps 65:7
hast afflicted me with all thy *w* Ps 88:7
when the *w* thereof arise, thou Ps 89:9
the floods lift up their *w* Ps 93:3
yea, than the mighty *w* of the sea Ps 93:4
which lifteth up the *w* thereof Ps 107:25
so that the *w* thereof are still Ps 107:29
righteousness as the *w* of the sea Is 48:18
divided the sea, whose *w* roared Is 51:15
though the *w* thereof toss Jer 5:22
the sea when the *w* thereof roar Jer 31:35
the multitude of the *w* thereof Jer 51:42
when her *w* do roar like great Jer 51:55
the sea causeth his *w* to come up Eze 26:3
billows and thy *w* passed over me Jonah 2:3
and shall smite the *w* in the sea Zec 10:11
the ship was covered with the *w* Mt 8:24
midst of the sea, tossed with *w* Mt 14:24
the *w* beat into the ship, so that Mk 4:37
the sea and the *w* roaring Lk 21:25
broken with the violence of the *w* Acts 27:41
Raging *w* of the sea, foaming out Jude 13

## WAX
And my wrath shall *w* hot, and I Ex 22:24
my wrath may *w* hot against them Ex 32:10
why doth thy wrath *w* hot against Ex 32:11
not the anger of my lord *w* hot Ex 32:22
or stranger *w* rich by thee Lev 25:47
that dwelleth by him *w* poor Lev 25:47
place, and his eyes began to *w* dim 1Sa 3:2
What time they *w* warm, they Job 6:17
root thereof *w* old in the earth Job 14:8
my heart is like *w* Ps 22:14
as *w* melteth before the fire, so Ps 68:2
The hills melted like *w* at the Ps 97:5
all of them shall *w* old like a Ps 102:26
fatness of his flesh shall *w* lean Is 17:4
neither shall his face now *w* pale Is 29:22
they all shall *w* old as a garment Is 50:9
the earth shall *w* old like a Is 51:6
our hands *w* feeble Jer 6:24
as *w* before the fire, and as the Mic 1:4
the love of many shall *w* cold Mt 24:12
yourselves bags which *w* not old Lk 12:33
begun to *w* wanton against Christ 1Ti 5:11
men and seducers shall *w* worse 2Ti 3:13
they all shall *w* old as doth a Heb 1:11

## WAXED
After I am *w* old shall I have Gen 18:12
And the man *w* great, and went Gen 26:13
the famine *w* sore in the land of Gen 41:56
multiplied, and *w* exceeding mighty Ex 1:7
multiplied, and *w* very mighty Ex 1:20
and when the sun *w* hot, it melted Ex 16:21
*w* louder and louder, Moses spake, Ex 19:19
and Moses' anger *w* hot, and he cast Ex 32:19
Moses, Is the LORD's hand *w* short Num 11:23
Thy raiment *w* not old upon thee, Deut 8:4
But Jeshurun *w* fat, and kicked Deut 32:15
round about, that Joshua *w* old Josh 23:1
hath many children is *w* feeble 1Sa 2:5
but David *w* stronger and stronger, 2Sa 3:1
and the house of Saul *w* weaker 2Sa 3:1
and David *w* faint 2Sa 21:15
and the flesh of the child *w* warm 2Kin 4:34
So David *w* greater and greater 1Chr 11:9
But Abijah *w* mighty, and married 2Chr 13:21
Jehoshaphat *w* great exceedingly 2Chr 17:12
But Jehoiada *w* old, and was full 2Chr 24:15
their clothes *w* not old, and their Neh 9:21
for this man Mordecai *w* greater Est 9:4
my bones *w* old through my roaring Ps 32:3
Damascus is *w* feeble, and turneth Jer 49:24
of them, and his hands *w* feeble Jer 50:43
the he goat *w* very great Dan 8:8
which *w* exceeding great, toward Dan 8:9
it *w* great, even to the host of Dan 8:10
this people's heart is *w* gross Mt 13:15
*w* strong in spirit, and was in the Lk 1:80
*w* strong in spirit, filled with Lk 2:40
*w* it grew, and *w* a great tree Lk 13:19
Then Paul and Barnabas *w* bold Acts 13:46
heart of this people is *w* gross Acts 28:27
*w* valiant in fight, turned to Heb 11:34
*w* rich through the abundance of Rev 18:3

## WAXEN
because the cry of them is *w* Gen 19:13
If thy brother be *w* poor, and hath Lev 25:25
And if thy brother be *w* poor Lev 25:35
that dwelleth by thee be *w* poor Lev 25:39
clothes are not *w* old upon you Deut 29:5
thy shoe is not *w* old upon thy Deut 29:5
and filled themselves, and *w* fat Deut 31:20
thou art *w* fat, thou art grown Deut 32:15
children of Israel were *w* strong Josh 17:13

W

they are become great, and *w* rich... Jer 5:27
They are *w* fat, they shine... Jer 5:28
*w* great, and thou art come to... Eze 16:7

**WAXETH**
it *w* old because of all mine... Ps 6:7
*w* old is ready to vanish away... Heb 8:13

**WAXING**
*w* confident by my bonds, are much... Phil 1:14

**WAY** See PREFACE.

**WAYFARING**
he saw a *w* man in the street of... Judg 19:17
to dress for the *w* man that was... 2Sa 12:4
lie waste, the *w* man ceaseth... Is 33:8
the *w* men, though fools, shall... Is 35:8
a lodging place of *w* men... Jer 9:2
as a *w* man that turneth aside to... Jer 14:8

**WAYMARKS**
Set thee up *w*, make thee high... Jer 31:21

**WAYS**
rise up early, and go on your *w*... Gen 19:2
*w* hide their eyes from the man... Lev 20:4
your high *w* shall be desolate... Lev 26:22
But if he shall any *w* make them... Num 30:15
Ye shall walk in all the *w* which... Deut 5:33
LORD thy God, to walk in his *w*... Deut 8:6
thy God, to walk in all his *w*... Deut 10:12
your God, to walk in all his *w*... Deut 11:22
thy God, and to walk ever in his *w*... Deut 19:9
be thy God, and to walk in his *w*... Deut 26:17
way, and flee before thee seven *w*... Deut 28:7
LORD thy God, and walk in his *w*... Deut 28:9
them, and flee seven *w* before them. Deut 28:25
thou shalt not prosper in thy *w*... Deut 28:29
LORD thy God, to walk in his *w*... Deut 30:16
for all his *w* are judgment... Deut 32:4
your God, and to walk in all his *w*... Josh 22:5
And his sons walked not in his *w*... 1Sa 8:3
and thy sons walk not in thy *w*... 1Sa 8:5
himself wisely in all his *w*... 1Sa 18:14
For I have kept the *w* of the LORD... 2Sa 22:22
LORD thy God, to walk in his *w*... 1Kin 2:3
And if thou wilt walk in my *w*... 1Kin 3:14
to every man according to his *w*... 1Kin 8:39
unto him, to walk in all his *w*... 1Kin 8:58
have not walked in my *w*... 1Kin 11:33
thee, and wilt walk in my *w*... 1Kin 11:38
in all the *w* of Asa his father... 1Kin 22:43
saying, Turn ye from your evil *w*... 2Kin 17:13
man according unto all his *w*... 2Chr 6:30
may fear thee, to walk in thy *w*... 2Chr 6:31
face, and turn from their wicked *w*... 2Chr 7:14
of the acts of Abijah, and his *w*... 2Chr 13:22
the first *w* of his father David... 2Chr 17:3
lifted up in the *w* of the LORD... 2Chr 17:6
the *w* of Jehoshaphat thy father... 2Chr 21:12
nor in the *w* of Asa king of Judah... 2Chr 21:12
in the *w* of the house of Ahab... 2Chr 22:3
his *w* before the LORD his God... 2Chr 27:6
Jotham, and all his wars, and his *w*... 2Chr 27:7
For he walked in the *w* of the... 2Chr 28:2
rest of his acts and of all his *w*... 2Chr 28:26
the nations of those lands any *w*... 2Chr 32:13
walked in the *w* of David his... 2Chr 34:2
hope, and the uprightness of thy *w*... Job 4:6
maintain mine own *w* before him... Job 13:15
desire not the knowledge of thy *w*... Job 21:14
that thou makest thy *w* perfect... Job 22:3
the light shall shine upon thy *w*... Job 22:28
they know not the *w* thereof... Job 24:13
yet his eyes are upon their *w*... Job 24:23
Lo, these are parts of his *w*... Job 26:14
me the *w* of their destruction... Job 30:12
Doth not he see my *w*, and count... Job 31:4
man to find according to his *w*... Job 34:11
his eyes are upon the *w* of man... Job 34:21
would not consider any of his *w*... Job 34:27
He is the chief of the *w* of God... Job 40:19
His *w* are always grievous... Ps 10:5
For I have kept the *w* of the LORD... Ps 18:21
Shew me thy *w*, O LORD... Ps 25:4
I said, I will take heed to my *w*... Ps 39:1
will I teach transgressors thy *w*... Ps 51:13
me, and Israel had walked in my *w*... Ps 81:13
in whose heart are the *w* of them... Ps 84:5
thee, to keep thee in all thy *w*... Ps 91:11
and they have not known my *w*... Ps 95:10
He made known his *w* unto Moses... Ps 103:7
they walk in his *w*... Ps 119:3
O that my *w* were directed to keep... Ps 119:5
and have respect unto thy *w*... Ps 119:15
I have declared my *w*, and thou... Ps 119:26
I thought on my *w*, and turned my... Ps 119:59
for all my *w* are before thee... Ps 119:168
turn aside unto their crooked *w*... Ps 125:5
that walketh in his *w*... Ps 128:1
shall sing in the *w* of the LORD... Ps 138:5
and art acquainted with all my *w*... Ps 139:3
LORD is righteous in all his *w*... Ps 145:17
So are the *w* of every one that is... Prov 1:19
to walk in the *w* of darkness... Prov 2:13
Whose *w* are crooked, and they... Prov 2:15
In all thy *w* acknowledge him, and... Prov 3:6
Her *w* are *w* of pleasantness,... Prov 3:17
and choose none of his *w*... Prov 3:31
let all thy *w* be established... Prov 4:26
her *w* are moveable, that thou... Prov 5:6
For the *w* of man are before the... Prov 5:21
consider her *w*, and be wise... Prov 6:6
not thine heart decline to her *w*... Prov 7:25
blessed are they that keep my *w*... Prov 8:32
who go right on their *w*... Prov 9:15
perverteth his *w* shall be known... Prov 10:9
perverse in his *w* despiseth him... Prov 14:2
end thereof are the *w* of death... Prov 14:12
shall be filled with his own *w*... Prov 14:14
All the *w* of a man are clean in... Prov 16:2
When a man's *w* please the LORD,... Prov 16:7
end thereof are the *w* of death... Prov 16:25
to pervert the *w* of judgment... Prov 17:23
he that despiseth his *w* shall die... Prov 19:16
Lest thou learn his *w*, and get a... Prov 22:25
and let thine eyes observe my *w*... Prov 23:26
than he that is perverse in his *w*... Prov 28:6
in his *w* shall fall at once... Prov 28:18
women, nor thy *w* to that which... Prov 31:3
well to the *w* of her household... Prov 31:27
walk in the *w* of thine heart, and... Eccl 11:9
in the broad *w* I will seek him... Song 3:2
and he will teach us of his *w*... Is 2:3
for they would not walk in his *w*... Is 42:24
and I will direct all his *w*... Is 45:13
They shall feed in the *w*, and... Is 49:9
neither are your *w* my *w*... Is 55:8
so are my *w* higher than your *w*... Is 55:9
I have seen his *w*, and will heal... Is 57:18
me daily, and delight to know my *w*... Is 58:2
honour him, not doing thine own *w*... Is 58:13
thou made us to err from thy *w*... Is 63:17
those that remember thee in thy *w*... Is 64:5
Yea, they have chosen their own *w*... Is 66:3
swift dromedary traversing her *w*... Jer 2:23
also taught the wicked ones thy *w*... Jer 2:33
In the *w* hast thou sat for them,... Jer 3:2
hast scattered thy *w* to the... Jer 3:13
saith the LORD, Stand ye in the *w*... Jer 6:16
the God of Israel, Amend your *w*... Jer 7:3
For if ye throughly amend your *w*... Jer 7:5
walk ye in all the *w* that I have... Jer 7:23
learn the *w* of my people, to... Jer 12:16
they return not from their *w*... Jer 15:7
mine eyes are upon all their *w*... Jer 16:17
give every man according to his *w*... Jer 17:10
from his evil way, and make your *w*... Jer 18:11
in their *w* from the ancient paths... Jer 18:15
as slippery *w* in the darkness... Jer 23:12
Therefore now amend your *w*... Jer 26:13
upon all the *w* of the sons of men... Jer 32:19
give every one according to his *w*... Jer 32:19
The *w* of Zion do mourn, because... Lam 1:4
inclosed my *w* with hewn stone... Lam 3:9
He hath turned aside my *w*... Lam 3:11
Let us search and try our *w*... Lam 3:40
judge thee according to thy *w*... Eze 7:3
I will recompense thy *w* upon thee... Eze 7:4
judge thee according to thy *w*... Eze 7:8
thee according to thy *w* and thine... Eze 7:9
comfort you, when ye see their *w*... Eze 14:23
thou not walked after their *w*... Eze 16:47
more than they in all thy *w*... Eze 16:47
Then thou shalt remember thy *w*... Eze 16:61
that he should return from his *w*... Eze 18:23
are not your *w* unequal... Eze 18:25
of Israel, are not my *w* equal... Eze 18:29
are not your *w* unequal... Eze 18:29
every one according to his *w*... Eze 18:30
And there shall ye remember your *w*.. Eze 20:43
not according to your wicked *w*... Eze 20:44
son of man, appoint thee two *w*... Eze 21:19
the way, at the head of the two *w*... Eze 21:21
according to thy *w*, and according... Eze 24:14
Thou wast perfect in thy *w* from... Eze 28:15
turn ye, turn ye from your evil *w*... Eze 33:11
judge you every one after his *w*... Eze 33:20
shall ye remember your own evil *w*... Eze 36:31
and confounded for your own *w*... Eze 36:32
are truth, and his *w* judgment... Dan 4:37
breath is, and whose are all thy *w*... Dan 5:23
and I will punish them for their *w*... Hos 4:9
a snare of a fowler in all his *w*... Hos 9:8
punish Jacob according to his *w*... Hos 12:2
for the *w* of the LORD are right,... Hos 14:9
shall march every one on his *w*... Joel 2:7
and he will teach us of his *w*... Mic 4:2
against another in the broad *w*... Nah 2:4
his *w* are everlasting... Hab 3:6
Consider your *w*... Hag 1:5
Consider your *w*... Hag 1:7
Turn ye now from your evil *w*... Zec 1:4
to do unto us, according to our *w*... Zec 1:6
If thou wilt walk in my *w*... Zec 3:7
as ye have not kept my *w*, but... Mal 2:9
went their *w* into the city, and... Mt 8:33
made light of it, and went their *w*... Mt 22:5
in a place where two *w* met... Mk 11:4
face of the Lord to prepare his *w*... Lk 1:76
the rough *w* shall be made smooth... Lk 3:5
Go your *w*... Lk 10:3
go your *w* out into the streets of... Lk 10:10
went their *w* to the Pharisees... Jn 11:46
made known to me the *w* of life... Acts 2:28
pervert the right *w* of the Lord... Acts 13:10
nations to walk in their own *w*... Acts 14:16
and misery are in their *w*... Rom 3:16
and his *w* past finding out... Rom 11:33
of my *w* which be in Christ... 1Cor 4:17
and they have not known my *w*... Heb 3:10
man is unstable in all his *w*... Jas 1:8
the rich man fade away in his *w*... Jas 1:11
shall follow their pernicious *w*... 2Pet 2:2
just and true are thy *w*, thou King... Rev 15:3
to the seven angels, Go your *w*... Rev 16:1

**WAYSIDE**
sat upon a seat by the *w* watching... 1Sa 4:13
they have spread a net by the *w*... Ps 140:5

**WE** See PREFACE.

**WEAK**
whether they be strong or *w*... Num 13:18
never dried, then shall I be *w*... Judg 16:7
were occupied, then shall I be *w*... Judg 16:11
go from me, and I shall become *w*... Judg 16:17
And I am this day *w*, though... 2Sa 3:39
*w* handed, and will make him afraid... 2Sa 17:2
and let not your hands be *w*... 2Chr 15:7
hast strengthened the *w* hands... Job 4:3
for I am *w*... Ps 6:2
My knees are *w* through fasting... Ps 109:24
Art thou also become *w* as we... Is 14:10
Strengthen ye the *w* hands... Is 35:3
and all knees shall be *w* as water... Eze 7:17
How *w* is thine heart, saith the... Eze 16:30
and all knees shall be *w* as water... Eze 21:7
let the *w* say, I am strong... Joel 3:10
is willing, but the flesh is *w*... Mt 26:41
is ready, but the flesh is *w*... Mk 14:38
ye ought to support the *w*... Acts 20:35
And being not *w* in faith, he... Rom 4:19
in that it was *w* through the... Rom 8:3
Him that is *w* in the faith... Rom 14:1
another, who is *w*, eateth herbs... Rom 14:2
or is offended, or is made *w*... Rom 14:21
to bear the infirmities of the *w*... Rom 15:1
God hath chosen the *w* things of... 1Cor 1:27
we are *w*, but ye are strong... 1Cor 4:10
conscience being *w* is defiled... 1Cor 8:7
stumblingblock to them that are *w*... 1Cor 8:9
is *w* be emboldened to eat those... 1Cor 8:10
shall the *w* brother perish... 1Cor 8:11
and wound their *w* conscience... 1Cor 8:12
To the *w* became I as *w*... 1Cor 9:22
as *w*, that I might gain the *w*... 1Cor 9:22
For this cause many are *w*... 1Cor 11:30
but his bodily presence is *w*... 2Cor 10:10
reproach, as though we had been *w*.. 2Cor 11:21
Who is *w*, and I am not *w*... 2Cor 11:29
for when I am *w*, then am I strong... 2Cor 12:10
in me, which to you-ward is not *w*... 2Cor 13:3
For we also are *w* in him, but we... 2Cor 13:4
For we are glad, when we are *w*... 2Cor 13:9
God, how turn ye again to the *w*... Gal 4:9
the feebleminded, support the *w*... 1Th 5:14

**WEAKEN**
ground, which didst *w* the nations... Is 14:12

**WEAKENED**
land *w* the hands of the people of... Ezr 4:4
hands shall be *w* from the work... Neh 6:9
He *w* my strength in the way... Ps 102:23

**WEAKENETH**
*w* the strength of the mighty... Job 12:21
for thus he *w* the hands of the... Jer 38:4

**WEAKER**
house of Saul waxed *w* and *w*... 2Sa 3:1
the wife, as unto the *w* vessel... 1Pet 3:7

**WEAKNESS**
the *w* of God is stronger than men... 1Cor 1:25
And I was with you in *w*, and in... 1Cor 2:3
it is sown in *w*... 1Cor 15:43
my strength is made perfect in *w*... 2Cor 12:9
though he was crucified through *w*... 2Cor 13:4
going before for the *w* and... Heb 7:18
out of *w* were made strong, waxed... Heb 11:34

**WEALTH**
And all their *w*, and all their... Gen 34:29
mine hand hath gotten me this *w*... Deut 8:17
that giveth thee power to get *w*... Deut 8:18
her husband's, a mighty man of *w*... Ruth 2:1
in all the *w* which God shall give... 1Sa 2:32
even of all the mighty men of *w*... 2Kin 15:20
and thou hast not asked riches, *w*... 2Chr 1:11
and I will give thee riches, and *w*... 2Chr 1:12
their peace or their *w* for ever... Ezr 9:12
seeking the *w* of his people, and... Est 10:3
They spend their days in *w*... Job 21:13
I rejoiced because my *w* was great... Job 31:25
not increase thy *w* by their price... Ps 44:12
They that trust in their *w*... Ps 49:6
and leave their *w* to others... Ps 49:10
*W* and riches shall be in his house... Ps 112:3
strangers be filled with thy *w*... Prov 5:10
The rich man's *w* is his strong... Prov 10:15
*W* gotten by vanity shall be... Prov 13:11
the *w* of the sinner is laid up... Prov 13:22
The rich man's *w* is his strong... Prov 18:11
*W* maketh many friends... Prov 19:4
whom God hath given riches and *w*... Eccl 5:19
to whom God hath given riches, *w*... Eccl 6:2
the *w* of all the heathen round... Zec 14:14
that by this craft we have our *w*... Acts 19:25
own, but every man another's *w*... 1Cor 10:24

**WEALTHY**
broughtest us out into a *w* place... Ps 66:12
get you up unto the *w* nation... Jer 49:31

**WEANED**
And the child grew, and was *w* ............ Gen 21:8
the same day that Isaac was *w*............ Gen 21:8
not go up until the child be *w*............ 1Sa 1:22
tarry until thou have *w* him............ 1Sa 1:23
gave her son suck until she *w* him....... 1Sa 1:23
And when she had *w* him, she took....... 1Sa 1:24
whom Tahpenes *w* in Pharaoh's.......... 1Kin 11:20
a child that is *w* of his mother............ Ps 131:2
my soul is even as a *w* child............ Ps 131:2
the *w* child shall put his hand on............ Is 11:8
them that are *w* from the milk............ Is 28:9
Now when she had *w* Lo-ruhamah......... Hos 1:8

**WEAPON**
smite him with an hand *w* of wood... Num 35:18
shalt have a paddle upon thy *w*......... Deut 23:13
man having his *w* in his hand............ 2Chr 23:10
and with the other hand held a *w*......... Neh 4:17
He shall flee from the iron *w*............ Job 20:24
No *w* that is formed against thee............ Is 54:17
with his destroying *w* in his hand............ Eze 9:1
man a slaughter *w* in his hand............ Eze 9:2

**WEAPONS**
take, I pray thee, thy *w*, thy............ Gen 27:3
girded on every man his *w* of war....... Deut 1:41
men appointed with *w* of war............ Judg 18:11
men appointed with their *w* of war... Judg 18:16
that were appointed with *w* of war... Judg 18:17
brought my sword nor my *w* with me.. 1Sa 21:8
fallen, and the *w* of war perished......... 2Sa 1:27
every man with his *w* in his hand........ 2Kin 11:8
every man with his *w* in his hand........ 2Kin 11:11
every man with his *w* in his hand........ 2Chr 23:7
Wisdom is better than *w* of war........ Eccl 9:18
the *w* of his indignation, to............ Is 13:5
I will turn back the *w* of war............ Jer 21:4
thee, every one with his *w*............ Jer 22:7
forth the *w* of his indignation............ Jer 50:25
Thou art my battle ax and *w* of war..... Jer 51:20
down to hell with their *w* of war...... Eze 32:27
shall set on fire and burn the *w*............ Eze 39:9
they shall burn the *w* with fire............ Eze 39:10
with lanterns and torches and *w*............ Jn 18:3
(For the *w* of our warfare are not........ 2Cor 10:4

**WEAR**
Thou wilt surely *w* away, both............ Ex 18:18
The woman shall not *w* that which.... Deut 22:5
Thou shalt not *w* a garment of.......... Deut 22:11
incense, to *w* an ephod before me.......... 1Sa 2:28
persons that did *w* a linen ephod......... 1Sa 22:18
brought which the king useth to *w*......... Est 6:8
The waters *w* the stones............ Job 14:19
own bread, and *w* our own apparel............ Is 4:1
shall *w* out the saints of the............ Dan 7:25
neither shall they *w* a rough............ Zec 13:4
they that *w* soft clothing are in............ Mt 11:8
And when the day began to *w* away...... Lk 9:12

**WEARETH**
to him that *w* the gay clothing............ Jas 2:3

**WEARIED**
so that they *w* themselves to find....... Gen 19:11
offering, nor *w* thee with incense............ Is 43:23
thou hast *w* me with thine............ Is 43:24
Thou art *w* in the multitude of............ Is 47:13
Thou art *w* in the greatness of............ Is 57:10
for my soul is *w* because of............ Jer 4:31
the footmen, and they have *w* thee........ Jer 12:5
thou trustedst, they *w* thee............ Jer 12:5
She hath *w* herself with lies, and......... Eze 24:12
and wherein have I *w* thee............ Mic 6:3
Ye have *w* the LORD with your............ Mal 2:17
Yet ye say, Wherein have we *w* him.... Mal 2:17
being *w* with his journey, sat............ Jn 4:6
against himself, lest ye be *w*............ Heb 12:3

**WEARIETH**
by watering he *w* the thick cloud......... Job 37:11
the foolish *w* every one of them.......... Eccl 10:15

**WEARINESS**
and much study is a *w* of the flesh..... Eccl 12:12
said also, Behold, what a *w* is it............ Mal 1:13
In *w* and painfulness, in watchings... 2Cor 11:27

**WEARING**
priest in Shiloh, *w* an ephod............ 1Sa 14:3
*w* the crown of thorns, and the............ Jn 19:5
of *w* of gold, or of putting on of............ 1Pet 3:3

**WEARISOME**
*w* nights are appointed to me............ Job 7:3

**WEARY**
I am *w* of my life because of the......... Gen 27:46
thee, when thou wast faint and *w*..... Deut 25:18
for he was fast asleep and *w*............ Judg 4:21
bread unto thy men that are *w*............ Judg 8:15
people that were with him, came *w*..... 2Sa 16:14
will come upon him while he is *w*.......... 2Sa 17:2
said, The people is hungry, and *w*......... 2Sa 17:29
Philistines until his hand was *w*............ 2Sa 23:10
and there the *w* be at rest............ Job 3:17
My soul is *w* of my life............ Job 10:1
But now he hath made me *w*............ Job 16:7
not given water to the *w* to drink............ Job 22:7
I am *w* with my groaning............ Ps 6:6
thine inheritance, when it was *w*............ Ps 68:9
I am *w* of my crying............ Ps 69:3
neither be *w* of his correction............ Prov 3:11
lest he be *w* of thee, and so hate........ Prov 25:17
I am *w* to bear them............ Is 1:14
None shall be *w* nor stumble among........ Is 5:27
it a small thing for you to *w* men............ Is 7:13
but will ye *w* my God also............ Is 7:13
that Moab is *w* on the high place............ Is 16:12
ye may cause the *w* to rest............ Is 28:12
of a great rock in a *w* land............ Is 32:2
earth, fainteth not, neither is *w*............ Is 40:28
the youths shall faint and be *w*............ Is 40:30
they shall run, and not be *w*............ Is 40:31
but thou hast been *w* of me............ Is 43:22
they are a burden to the *w* beast............ Is 46:1
a word in season to him that is *w*............ Is 50:4
seek her will not *w* themselves............ Jer 2:24
I am *w* with holding in............ Jer 6:11
*w* themselves to commit iniquity............ Jer 9:5
I am *w* with repenting............ Jer 15:6
I was *w* with forbearing, and I............ Jer 20:9
For I have satiated the *w* soul............ Jer 31:25
in the fire, and they shall be *w*............ Jer 51:58
and they shall be *w*............ Jer 51:64
the people shall *w* themselves for......... Hab 2:13
by her continual coming she *w* me......... Lk 18:5
And let us not be *w* in well doing............ Gal 6:9
brethren, be not *w* in well doing............ 2Th 3:13

**WEASEL**
the *w*, and the mouse, and the............ Lev 11:29

**WEATHER**
Fair *w* cometh out of the north............ Job 37:22
taketh away a garment in cold *w*...... Prov 25:20
ye say, It will be fair *w*............ Mt 16:2
morning, It will be foul *w* to day............ Mt 16:3

**WEAVE**
flax, and they that *w* networks............ Is 19:9
eggs, and *w* the spider's web............ Is 59:5

**WEAVER**
and in fine linen, and of the *w*............ Ex 35:35
I have cut off like a *w* my life............ Is 38:12

**WEAVER'S**
of his spear was like a *w* beam............ 1Sa 17:7
of whose spear was like a *w* beam......... 2Sa 21:19
hand was a spear like a *w* beam........ 1Chr 11:23
spear staff was like a *w* beam............ 1Chr 20:5
days are swifter than a *w* shuttle............ Job 7:6

**WEAVEST**
If thou *w* the seven locks of my........ Judg 16:13

**WEB**
seven locks of my head with the *w*... Judg 16:13
pin of the beam, and with the *w*........ Judg 16:14
whose trust shall be a spider's *w*............ Job 8:14
eggs, and weave the spider's *w*............ Is 59:5

**WEBS**
Their *w* shall not become garments.......... Is 59:6

**WEDDING**
them that were bidden to the *w*............ Mt 22:3
The *w* is ready, but they which............ Mt 22:8
the *w* was furnished with guests............ Mt 22:10
man which had not on a *w* garment....... Mt 22:11
in hither not having a *w* garment............ Mt 22:12
when he will return from the *w*............ Lk 12:36
thou art bidden of any man to a *w*........ Lk 14:8

**WEDGE**
a *w* of gold of fifty shekels............ Josh 7:21
the *w* of gold, and his sons, and............ Josh 7:24
a man than the golden *w* of Ophir.......... Is 13:12

**WEDLOCK**
judge thee, as women that break *w*.... Eze 16:38

**WEEDS**
the *w* were wrapped about my head... Jonah 2:5

**WEEK**
Fulfil her *w*, and we will give............ Gen 29:27
Jacob did so, and fulfilled her *w*......... Gen 29:28
the covenant with many for one *w*......... Dan 9:27
in the midst of the *w* he shall............ Dan 9:27
toward the first day of the *w*............ Mt 28:1
morning the first day of the *w*............ Mk 16:2
early the first day of the *w*............ Mk 16:9
I fast twice in the *w*, I give............ Lk 18:12
Now upon the first day of the *w*............ Lk 24:1
The first day of the *w* cometh............ Jn 20:1
being the first day of the *w*............ Jn 20:19
And upon the first day of the *w*............ Acts 20:7
Upon the first day of the *w* let............ 1Cor 16:2

**WEEKS**
thou shalt observe the feast of *w*.......... Ex 34:22
then she shall be unclean two *w*............ Lev 12:5
the LORD, after your *w* be out............ Num 28:26
Seven *w* shalt thou number unto......... Deut 16:9
seven *w* from such time as thou......... Deut 16:9
of *w* unto the LORD thy God with a.. Deut 16:10
bread, and in the feast of *w*............ Deut 16:16
bread, and in the feast of *w*............ 2Chr 8:13
us the appointed *w* of the harvest............ Jer 5:24
Seventy *w* are determined upon thy.... Dan 9:24
the Prince shall be seven *w*............ Dan 9:25
and threescore and two *w*............ Dan 9:25
two *w* shall Messiah be cut off............ Dan 9:26
Daniel was mourning three full *w*......... Dan 10:2
till three whole *w* were fulfilled............ Dan 10:3

**WEEP**
mourn for Sarah, and to *w* for her........ Gen 23:2
and he sought where to *w*............ Gen 43:30
*w* throughout their families............ Num 11:10
for they *w* unto me, saying, Give....... Num 11:13
aileth the people that they *w*............ 1Sa 11:5
until they had no more power to *w*....... 1Sa 30:4
*w* over Saul, who clothed you in............ 2Sa 1:24
*w* for the child, while it was............ 2Sa 12:21
rend thy clothes, and *w* before me.... 2Chr 34:27
mourn not, nor *w*............ Neh 8:9
and his widows shall not *w*............ Job 27:15
Did not I *w* for him that was in............ Job 30:25
into the voice of them that *w*............ Job 30:31
A time to *w*, and a time to laugh............ Eccl 3:4
to Dibon, the high places, to *w*............ Is 15:2
I will *w* bitterly, labour not to............ Is 22:4
thou shalt *w* no more............ Is 30:19
of peace shall *w* bitterly............ Is 33:7
of tears, that I might *w* day............ Jer 9:1
my soul shall *w* in secret places............ Jer 13:17
and mine eye shall *w* sore, and run...... Jer 13:17
*W* ye not for the dead, neither............ Jer 22:10
but *w* sore for him that goeth............ Jer 22:10
I will *w* for thee with the............ Jer 48:32
For these things I *w*............ Lam 1:16
neither shalt thou mourn nor *w*............ Eze 24:16
ye shall not mourn nor *w*............ Eze 24:23
they shall *w* for thee with............ Eze 27:31
Awake, ye drunkards, and *w*............ Joel 1:5
*w* between the porch and the altar,...... Joel 2:17
it not at Gath, *w* ye not at all............ Mic 1:10
Should I *w* in the fifth month,............ Zec 7:3
them, Why make ye this ado, and *w*..... Mk 5:39
Blessed are ye that *w* now............ Lk 6:21
for ye shall mourn and *w*............ Lk 6:25
on her, and said unto her, *W* not............ Lk 7:13
but he said, *W* not............ Lk 8:52
*w* not for me, but *w* for............ Lk 23:28
goeth unto the grave to *w* there............ Jn 11:31
I say unto you, That ye shall *w*............ Jn 16:20
Paul answered, What mean ye to *w*.. Acts 21:13
rejoice, and *w* with them that *w*........ Rom 12:15
And they that *w*, as though they......... 1Cor 7:30
Be afflicted, and mourn, and *w*............ Jas 4:9
Go to now, ye rich men, *w*............ Jas 5:1
the elders saith unto me, *W* not............ Rev 5:5
merchants of the earth shall *w*............ Rev 18:11

**WEEPEST**
to her, Hannah, why *w* thou............ 1Sa 1:8
say unto her, Woman, why *w* thou........ Jn 20:13
saith unto her, Woman, why *w* thou..... Jn 20:15

**WEEPETH**
was told Joab, Behold, the king *w*......... 2Sa 19:1
And Hazael said, Why *w* my lord......... 2Kin 8:12
He that goeth forth and *w*, bearing....... Ps 126:6
She *w* sore in the night, and her............ Lam 1:2

**WEEPING**
who were *w* before the door of the..... Num 25:6
so the days of *w* and mourning for..... Deut 34:8
her along *w* behind her to Bahurim....... 2Sa 3:16
they went up, *w* as they went up.......... 2Sa 15:30
the noise of the *w* of the people............ Ezr 3:13
and when he had confessed, *w*............ Ezr 10:1
among the Jews, and fasting, and *w*........ Est 4:3
My face is foul with *w*, and on my...... Job 16:16
LORD hath heard the voice of my *w*............ Ps 6:8
*w* may endure for a night, but joy............ Ps 30:5
bread, and mingled my drink with *w*..... Ps 102:9
one shall howl, *w* abundantly............ Is 15:3
Luhith with *w* shall they go it up............ Is 15:5
I will bewail with the *w* of Jazer............ Is 16:9
the Lord GOD of hosts call to *w*............ Is 22:12
the voice of *w* shall be no more............ Is 65:19
was heard upon the high places, *w*......... Jer 3:21
the mountains will I take up a *w*............ Jer 9:10
They shall come with *w*, and with............ Jer 31:9
Ramah, lamentation, and bitter *w*......... Jer 31:15
Rahel *w* for her children refused............ Jer 31:15
Refrain thy voice from *w*, and............ Jer 31:16
meet them, *w* all along as he went......... Jer 41:6
of Luhith continual *w* shall go up............ Jer 48:5
weep for thee with the *w* of Jazer........ Jer 48:32
of Judah together, going and *w*............ Jer 50:4
there sat women *w* for Tammuz............ Eze 8:14
heart, and with fasting, and with *w*...... Joel 2:12
of the LORD with tears, with *w*............ Mal 2:13
a voice heard, lamentation, and *w*............ Mt 2:18
Rachel *w* for her children, and............ Mt 2:18
there shall be *w* and gnashing of............ Mt 8:12
there shall be *w* and gnashing of............ Mt 22:13
there shall be *w* and gnashing of............ Mt 24:51
there shall be *w* and gnashing of............ Mt 25:30
And stood at his feet behind him *w*............ Lk 7:38
There shall be *w* and gnashing of.......... Lk 13:28
When Jesus therefore saw her *w*............ Jn 11:33
the Jews also *w* which came with............ Jn 11:33
stood without at the sepulchre *w*............ Jn 20:11
and all the widows stood by him *w*...... Acts 9:39
you often, and now tell you even *w*......... Phil 3:18
for the fear of her torment, *w*............ Rev 18:15
dust on their heads, and cried, *w*......... Rev 18:19

**WEIGH**
found it to *w* a talent of gold,............ 1Chr 20:2
until ye *w* them before the chief............ Ezr 8:29
ye *w* the violence of your hands............ Ps 58:2
dost *w* the path of the just............ Is 26:7
*w* silver in the balance, and hire............ Is 46:6
then take thee balances to *w*............ Eze 5:1

**WEIGHED**
Abraham *w* to Ephron the silver, Gen 23:16
the silver vessels *w* two thousand Num 7:85
and by him actions are *w* 1Sa 2:3
his spear's head *w* six hundred 1Sa 17:7
he *w* the hair of his head at two 2Sa 14:26
the weight of whose spear *w* three 2Sa 21:16
*w* unto them the silver, and the Ezr 8:25
I even *w* unto their hand six Ezr 8:26
the vessels *w* in the house of our Ezr 8:33
O that my grief were throughly *w* Job 6:2
silver be *w* for the price thereof Job 28:15
Let me be *w* in an even balance, Job 31:6
*w* the mountains in scales, and the Is 40:12
*w* him the money, even seventeen Jer 32:9
*w* him the money in the balances Jer 32:10
Thou art *w* in the balances, and Dan 5:27
So they *w* for my price thirty Zec 11:12

**WEIGHETH**
he *w* the waters by measure Job 28:25
but the LORD *w* the spirits Prov 16:2

**WEIGHING**
charger of silver *w* an hundred Num 7:85
*w* ten shekels apiece, after the Num 7:86

**WEIGHT**
golden earring of half a shekel *w* Gen 24:22
hands of ten shekels *w* of gold Gen 24:22
of his sack, our money in full *w* Gen 43:21
of each shall there be a like *w* Ex 30:34
in judgment, in meteyard, in *w* Lev 19:35
deliver you your bread again by *w* Lev 26:26
the *w* thereof was an hundred and Num 7:13
the *w* whereof was an hundred and Num 7:19
the *w* whereof was an hundred and Num 7:25
charger of the *w* of an hundred Num 7:31
the *w* whereof was an hundred and Num 7:37
charger of the *w* of an hundred Num 7:43
the *w* whereof was an hundred and Num 7:49
charger of the *w* of an hundred Num 7:55
the *w* whereof was an hundred and Num 7:61
the *w* whereof was an hundred and Num 7:67
the *w* whereof was an hundred and Num 7:73
the *w* whereof was an hundred and Num 7:79
shalt have a perfect and just *w* Deut 25:15
wedge of gold of fifty shekels *w* Josh 7:21
the *w* of the golden earrings that Judg 8:26
the *w* of the coat was five 1Sa 17:5
the *w* whereof was a talent of 2Sa 12:30
shekels after the king's *w* 2Sa 14:26
the *w* of whose spear weighed 2Sa 21:16
hundred shekels of brass in *w* 2Sa 21:16
neither was the *w* of the brass 1Kin 7:47
Now the *w* of gold that came to 1Kin 10:14
all these vessels was without *w* 2Kin 25:16
six hundred shekels of gold by *w* 1Chr 21:25
and brass in abundance without *w* 1Chr 22:3
and of brass and iron without *w* 1Chr 22:14
of gold by *w* for things of gold 1Chr 28:14
all instruments of silver by *w* 1Chr 28:14
Even the *w* for the candlesticks 1Chr 28:15
by *w* for every candlestick, and 1Chr 28:15
the candlesticks of silver by *w* 1Chr 28:15
by *w* he gave gold for the tables 1Chr 28:16
he gave gold by *w* for every bason 1Chr 28:17
likewise silver by *w* for every 1Chr 28:17
of incense refined gold by *w* 1Chr 28:18
the *w* of the nails was fifty 2Chr 3:9
for the *w* of the brass could not 2Chr 4:18
Now the *w* of gold that came to 2Chr 9:13
the Levites the *w* of the silver Ezr 8:30
By number and by *w* of every one Ezr 8:34
all the *w* was written at that Ezr 8:34
To make the *w* for the winds Job 28:25
but a just *w* is his delight Prov 11:1
A just *w* and balance are the Prov 16:11
all these vessels was without *w* Jer 52:20
thou shalt eat shall be by *w* Eze 4:10
and they shall eat bread by *w* Eze 4:16
he cast the *w* of lead upon the Zec 5:8
aloes, about an hundred pound *w* Jn 19:39
exceeding and eternal *w* of glory 2Cor 4:17
let us lay aside every *w* Heb 12:1
stone about the *w* of a talent Rev 16:21

**WEIGHTIER**
have omitted the *w* matters of the Mt 23:23

**WEIGHTS**
Just balances, just *w*, a just Lev 19:36
not have in thy bag divers *w* Deut 25:13
all the *w* of the bag are his work Prov 16:11
Divers *w*, and divers measures, Prov 20:10
Divers *w* are an abomination unto Prov 20:23
and with the bag of deceitful *w* Mic 6:11

**WEIGHTY**
A stone is heavy, and the sand *w* Prov 27:3
For his letters, say they, are *w* 2Cor 10:10

**WELFARE**
And he asked them of their *w* Gen 43:27
they asked each other of their *w* Ex 18:7
king David, to enquire of his *w* 1Chr 18:10
the *w* of the children of Israel Neh 2:10
my *w* passeth away as a cloud Job 30:15
should have been for their *w* Ps 69:22
seeketh not the *w* of this people Jer 38:4

**WELL**
If thou doest *w*, shalt thou not Gen 4:7
and if thou doest not *w*, sin lieth Gen 4:7
that it may be *w* with me for thy Gen 12:13
he entreated Abram *w* for her sake Gen 12:16
that it was *w* watered every where Gen 13:10
Wherefore the *w* was called Gen 16:14
were old and *w* stricken in age Gen 18:11
her eyes, and she saw a *w* of water Gen 21:19
Abimelech because of a *w* of water Gen 21:25
me, that I have digged this *w* Gen 21:30
was old, and *w* stricken in age Gen 24:1
down without the city by a *w* of Gen 24:11
I stand here by the *w* of water Gen 24:13
and she went down to the *w* Gen 24:16
again unto the *w* to draw water Gen 24:20
ran out unto the man, unto the *w* Gen 24:29
he stood by the camels at the *w* Gen 24:30
And I came this day unto the *w* Gen 24:42
Behold, I stand by the *w* of water Gen 24:43
and she went down unto the *w* Gen 24:45
from the way of the *w* Lahai-roi Gen 24:62
and Isaac dwelt by the *w* Lahai-roi Gen 25:11
found there a *w* of springing Gen 26:19
he called the name of the *w* Esek Gen 26:20
And they digged another *w*, and Gen 26:21
from thence, and digged another *w* Gen 26:22
there Isaac's servants digged a *w* Gen 26:25
the *w* which they had digged Gen 26:32
behold a *w* in the field, and, lo, Gen 29:2
for out of that *w* they watered Gen 29:2
And he said unto them, Is he *w* Gen 29:6
And they said, He is *w* Gen 29:6
was beautiful and *w* favoured Gen 29:17
and I will deal *w* with thee Gen 32:9
whether it be *w* with thy brethren Gen 37:14
and *w* with the flocks Gen 37:14
a goodly person, and *w* favoured Gen 39:6
me when it shall be *w* with thee Gen 40:14
the river seven *w* favoured kine Gen 41:2
did eat up the seven *w* favoured Gen 41:4
kine, fatfleshed and *w* favoured Gen 41:18
and said, Is your father *w* Gen 43:27
and it pleased Pharaoh *w*, and his Gen 45:16
even a fruitful bough by a *w* Gen 49:22
God dealt *w* with the midwives Ex 1:20
and he sat down by a *w* Ex 2:15
I know that he can speak *w* Ex 4:14
And Moses said, Thou hast spoken *w* Ex 10:29
as *w* the stranger, as he that is Lev 24:16
as *w* for the stranger, as for one Lev 24:22
for it was *w* with us in Egypt Num 11:18
for we are *w* able to overcome it Num 13:30
that is the *w* whereof the LORD Num 21:16
sang this song, Spring up, O *w* Num 21:17
The princes digged the *w*, the Num 21:18
not drink of the waters of the *w* Num 21:22
of the sons of Joseph hath said *w* Num 36:5
hear the small as *w* as the great Deut 1:17
And the saying pleased me *w* Deut 1:23
as *w* as unto you, and until they Deut 3:20
day, that it may go *w* with thee Deut 4:40
maidservant may rest as *w* as thou Deut 5:14
and that it may go *w* with thee Deut 5:16
they have *w* said all that they Deut 5:28
that it might be *w* with them Deut 5:29
and that it may be *w* with you Deut 5:33
that it may be *w* with thee Deut 6:3
that it may be *w* with thee Deut 6:18
but shalt *w* remember what the Deut 7:18
that it may go *w* with thee Deut 12:25
thee, that it may go *w* with thee Deut 12:28
house, because he is *w* with thee Deut 15:16
They have *w* spoken that which Deut 18:17
that it may go *w* with thee Deut 19:13
heart faint as *w* as his heart Deut 20:8
that it may be *w* with thee Deut 22:7
as *w* the stranger, as he that was Josh 8:33
went out to the *w* of waters of Josh 18:15
and pitched beside the *w* of Harod Judg 7:1
if ye have dealt *w* with Jerubbaal Judg 9:16
for she pleaseth me *w* Judg 14:3
and she pleased Samson *w* Judg 14:7
as *w* the men of every city, as Judg 20:48
thee, that it may be *w* with thee Ruth 3:1
thee the part of a kinsman, *w* Ruth 3:13
said Saul to his servant, *W* said 1Sa 9:10
with his hand, and thou shalt be *w* 1Sa 16:16
me now a man that can play *w* 1Sa 16:17
so Saul was refreshed, and was *w* 1Sa 16:23
it pleased David *w* to be the 1Sa 18:26
came to a great *w* that is in 1Sa 19:22
If he say thus, It is *w* 1Sa 20:7
that thou hast dealt *w* with me 1Sa 24:18
enemy, will he let him go *w* away 1Sa 24:19
I know *w* that thou shalt surely 1Sa 24:20
shall have dealt *w* with my lord 1Sa 25:31
And he said, *W* 2Sa 3:13
him again from the *w* of Sirah 2Sa 3:26
as *w* to the women as men, to 2Sa 6:19
devoureth one as *w* as another 2Sa 11:25
And the saying pleased Absalom *w* 2Sa 17:4
which had a *w* in his court 2Sa 17:18
that they came up out of the *w* 2Sa 17:21
and said unto the king, All is *w* 2Sa 18:28
day, then it had pleased thee *w* 2Sa 19:6
the water of the *w* of Beth-lehem 2Sa 23:15
water out of the *w* of Beth-lehem 2Sa 23:16
And Bath-sheba said, *W* 1Kin 2:18
thou didst *w* that it was in thine 1Kin 8:18
answered and said, It is *w* spoken 1Kin 18:24
And she said, It shall be *w* 2Kin 4:23
say unto her, Is it *w* with thee 2Kin 4:26
is it *w* with thy husband 2Kin 4:26
is it *w* with the child 2Kin 4:26
And she answered, It is *w* 2Kin 4:26
to meet him, and said, Is all *w* 2Kin 5:21
And he said, All is *w* 2Kin 5:22
said one to another, We do not *w* 2Kin 7:9
and one said unto him, Is all *w* 2Kin 9:11
Because thou hast done *w* in 2Kin 10:30
and it shall be *w* with you 2Kin 25:24
the water of the *w* of Beth-lehem 1Chr 11:17
water out of the *w* of Beth-lehem 1Chr 11:18
as *w* the small as the great, the 1Chr 25:8
as *w* the small as the great, 1Chr 26:13
thou didst *w* in that it was in 2Chr 6:8
and also in Judah things went *w* 2Chr 12:12
as *w* to the great as to the small 2Chr 31:15
valley, even before the dragon *w* Neh 2:13
I have understanding as *w* as you Job 12:3
Mark *w*, O Job, hearken unto me Job 33:31
Mark ye *w* her bulwarks, consider Ps 48:13
when thou doest *w* to thyself Ps 49:18
my steps had *w* nigh slipped Ps 73:2
So they did eat, and were *w* filled Ps 78:29
the valley of Baca make it a *w* Ps 84:6
As *w* the singers as the players Ps 87:7
Thou hast dealt *w* with thy Ps 119:65
be, and it shall be *w* with thee Ps 128:2
and that my soul knoweth right *w* Ps 139:14
running waters out of thine own *w* Prov 5:15
of a righteous man is a *w* of life Prov 10:11
When it goeth *w* with the Prov 11:10
but with the *w* advised is wisdom Prov 13:10
man looketh *w* to his going Prov 14:15
Then I saw, and considered it *w* Prov 24:32
flocks, and look *w* to thy herds Prov 27:23
There be three things which go *w* Prov 30:29
She looketh *w* to the ways of her Prov 31:27
be *w* with them that fear God Eccl 8:12
it shall not be *w* with the wicked Eccl 8:13
a *w* of living waters, and streams Song 4:15
Learn to do *w* Is 1:17
that it shall be *w* with him Is 3:10
instead of *w* set hair baldness Is 3:24
of wines on the lees *w* refined Is 25:6
they could not *w* strengthen their Is 33:23
The LORD is *w* pleased for his Is 42:21
LORD unto me, Thou hast *w* seen Jer 1:12
you, that it may be *w* unto you Jer 7:23
it shall be *w* with thy remnant Jer 15:11
thee *w* in the time of evil Jer 15:11
and then it was *w* with him Jer 22:15
then it was *w* with him Jer 22:16
so it shall be *w* unto thee Jer 38:20
look *w* to him, and do him no harm Jer 39:12
and I will look *w* unto thee Jer 40:4
and it shall be *w* with you Jer 40:9
that it may be *w* with us, when we Jer 42:6
we plenty of victuals, and were *w* Jer 44:17
bones under it, and make it boil *w* Eze 24:5
consume the flesh, and spice it *w* Eze 24:10
can play *w* on an instrument Eze 33:32
said unto me, Son of man, mark *w* Eze 44:5
mark *w* the entering in of the Eze 44:5
inherit it, one as *w* as another Eze 47:14
but *w* favoured, and skilful in all Dan 1:4
which I have made; *w* Dan 3:15
LORD, Doest thou *w* to be angry Jonah 4:4
Doest thou *w* to be angry for the Jonah 4:9
I do *w* to be angry, even unto Jonah 4:9
these days to do *w* unto Jerusalem Zec 8:15
Son, in whom I am *w* pleased Mt 3:17
to do *w* on the sabbath days Mt 12:12
in whom my soul is *w* pleased Mt 12:18
*w* did Esaias prophesy of you, Mt 15:7
Son, in whom I am *w* pleased Mt 17:5
*W* done, thou good and faithful Mt 25:21
*W* done, good and faithful servant Mt 25:23
Son, in whom I am *w* pleased Mk 1:11
*W* hath Esaias prophesied of you Mk 7:6
Full *w* ye reject the commandment Mk 7:9
saying, He hath done all things *w* Mk 7:37
that he had answered them *w* Mk 12:28
And the scribe said unto him, *W* Mk 12:32
both were now *w* stricken in years Lk 1:7
my wife *w* stricken in years Lk 1:18
in thee I am *w* pleased Lk 3:22
when all men shall speak *w* of you Lk 6:26
And if it bear fruit, *w* Lk 13:9
And he said unto him, *W*, thou good Lk 19:17
said, Master, thou hast *w* said Lk 20:39
and when men have *w* drunk, then Jn 2:10
Now Jacob's *w* was there Jn 4:6
his journey, sat thus on the *w* Jn 4:6
to draw with, and the *w* is deep Jn 4:11
father Jacob, which gave us the *w* Jn 4:12
a *w* of water springing up into Jn 4:14
said unto her, Thou hast *w* said Jn 4:17
Say we not *w* that thou art a Jn 8:48
Lord, if he sleep, he shall do *w* Jn 11:12
and ye say *w* Jn 13:13
but if *w*, why smitest thou me Jn 18:23
thou hast *w* done that thou art Acts 10:33
the Holy Ghost as *w* as we Acts 10:47
ye keep yourselves, ye shall do *w* Acts 15:29
Fare ye *w* Acts 15:29
Which was *w* reported of by the Acts 16:2
no wrong, as thou very *w* knowest Acts 25:10
*W* spake the Holy Ghost by Esaias Acts 28:25
in *w* doing seek for glory Rom 2:7
*W*; because of unbelief Rom 11:20

he will keep his virgin, doeth *w* 1Cor 7:37
giveth her in marriage doeth *w* 1Cor 7:38
as *w* as other apostles, and as the 1Cor 9:5
of them God was not *w* pleased 1Cor 10:5
For thou verily givest thanks *w* 1Cor 14:17
As unknown, and yet *w* known 2Cor 6:9
ye might *w* bear with him 2Cor 11:4
zealously affect you, but not *w* Gal 4:17
Ye did run *w* Gal 5:7
And let us not be weary in *w* doing Gal 6:9
That it may be *w* with thee Eph 6:3
Notwithstanding ye have *w* done Phil 4:14
for this is *w* pleasing unto the Col 3:20
brethren, be not weary in *w* doing 2Th 3:13
One that ruleth *w* his own house 1Ti 3:4
children and their own houses *w* 1Ti 3:12
used the office of a deacon *w* 1Ti 3:13
*W* reported of for good works 1Ti 5:10
Let the elders that rule *w* be 1Ti 5:17
at Ephesus, thou knowest very *w* 2Ti 1:18
and to please them *w* in all things Titus 2:9
preached, as *w* as unto them Heb 4:2
such sacrifices God is *w* pleased Heb 13:16
thy neighbour as thyself, ye do *w* Jas 2:8
thou doest *w* Jas 2:19
for the praise of them that do *w* 1Pet 2:14
that with *w* doing ye may put to 1Pet 2:15
but if, when ye do *w*, and suffer 1Pet 2:20
ye are, as long as ye do *w* 1Pet 3:6
be so, that ye suffer for *w* doing 1Pet 3:17
of their souls to him in *w* doing 1Pet 4:19
Son, in whom I am *w* pleased 2Pet 1:17
whereunto ye do *w* that ye take 2Pet 1:19
a godly sort, thou shalt do *w* 3Jn 6

**WELLBELOVED**
A bundle of myrrh is my *w* unto me Song 1:13
Now will I sing to my *w* a song of Is 5:1
My *w* hath a vineyard in a very Is 5:1
yet therefore one son, his *w* Mk 12:6
Salute my *w* Epaenetus, who is the Rom 16:5
The elder unto the *w* Gaius 3Jn 1

**WELLFAVOURED**
of the whoredoms of the *w* harlot Nah 3:4

**WELLPLEASING**
a sacrifice acceptable, *w* to God Phil 4:18
you that which is *w* in his sight Heb 13:21

**WELL'S**
great stone was upon the *w* mouth Gen 29:2
rolled the stone from the *w* mouth Gen 29:3
upon the *w* mouth in his place Gen 29:3
roll the stone from the *w* mouth Gen 29:8
rolled the stone from the *w* mouth Gen 29:10
a covering over the *w* mouth 2Sa 17:19

**WELLS**
For all the *w* which his father's Gen 26:15
Isaac digged again the *w* of water Gen 26:18
where were twelve *w* of water Ex 15:27
we drink of the water of the *w* Num 20:17
*w* digged, which thou diggedst not Deut 6:11
good tree, and stop all *w* of water 2Kin 3:19
they stopped all the *w* of water 2Kin 3:25
in the desert, and digged many *w* 2Chr 26:10
goods, *w* digged, vineyards, and Neh 9:25
water out of the *w* of salvation Is 12:3
These are *w* without water, clouds 2Pet 2:17

**WELLSPRING**
Understanding is a *w* of life unto Prov 16:22
the *w* of wisdom as a flowing Prov 18:4

**WEN**
broken, or maimed, or having a *w* Lev 22:22

**WENCH**
and a *w* went and told them 2Sa 17:17

**WENT** See PREFACE.

**WENTEST**
because thou *w* up to thy father's Gen 49:4
when thou *w* out of Seir, when Judg 5:4
when thou *w* to fight with the Judg 8:1
which thou *w* to seek are found 1Sa 10:2
with thee whithersoever thou *w* 2Sa 7:9
why *w* thou not with thy friend 2Sa 16:17
Wherefore *w* not thou with me, 2Sa 19:25
when thou *w* forth before thy Ps 68:7
even thither *w* thou up to offer Is 57:7
thou *w* to the king with ointment, Is 57:9
when thou *w* after me in the Jer 2:2
even the way which thou *w* Jer 31:21
Thou *w* forth for the salvation of Hab 3:13
Thou *w* in to men uncircumcised, Acts 11:3

**WEPT**
him, and lift up her voice, and *w* Gen 21:16
And Esau lifted up his voice, and *w* Gen 27:38
and lifted up his voice, and *w* Gen 29:11
and they *w* Gen 33:4
Thus his father *w* for him Gen 37:35
himself about from them, and *w* Gen 42:24
into his chamber, and *w* there Gen 43:30
And he *w* aloud Gen 45:2
his brother Benjamin's neck, and *w* Gen 45:14
and Benjamin *w* upon his neck Gen 45:14
all his brethren, and *w* upon them Gen 45:15
*w* on his neck a good while Gen 46:29
*w* upon him, and kissed him Gen 50:1
Joseph *w* when they spake unto him. Gen 50:17
and, behold, the babe *w* Ex 2:6
children of Israel also *w* again Num 11:4
for ye have *w* in the ears of the Num 11:18
have *w* before him, saying, Why Num 11:20
and the people *w* that night Num 14:1
ye returned and *w* before the LORD Deut 1:45
the children of Israel *w* for Deut 34:8
lifted up their voice, and *w* Judg 2:4
And Samson's wife *w* before him Judg 14:16
she *w* before him the seven days, Judg 14:17
*w* before the LORD until even, and Judg 20:23
came unto the house of God, and *w* Judg 20:26
lifted up their voices, and *w* sore Judg 21:2
they lifted up their voice, and *w* Ruth 1:9
lifted up their voice, and *w* again Ruth 1:14
therefore she *w*, and did not eat 1Sa 1:7
prayed unto the LORD, and *w* sore 1Sa 1:10
lifted up their voices, and *w* 1Sa 11:4
*w* one with another, until David 1Sa 20:41
And Saul lifted up his voice, and *w* 1Sa 24:16
him lifted up their voice and *w* 1Sa 30:4
And they mourned, and *w*, and fasted 2Sa 1:12
voice, and *w* at the grave of Abner 2Sa 3:32
and all the people *w* 2Sa 3:32
all the people *w* again over him 2Sa 3:34
was yet alive, I fasted and *w* 2Sa 12:22
and lifted up their voice and *w* 2Sa 13:36
and all his servants *w* very sore 2Sa 13:36
all the country *w* with a loud 2Sa 15:23
*w* as he went up, and had his head 2Sa 15:30
the chamber over the gate, and *w* 2Sa 18:33
and the man of God *w* 2Kin 8:11
*w* over his face, and said, O my 2Kin 13:14
And Hezekiah *w* sore 2Kin 20:3
rent thy clothes, and *w* before me 2Kin 22:19
their eyes, *w* with a loud voice Ezr 3:12
for the people *w* very sore Ezr 10:1
these words, that I sat down and *w* Neh 1:4
For all the people *w*, when they Neh 8:9
they lifted up their voice, and *w* Job 2:12
When I *w*, and chastened my soul Ps 69:10
there we sat down, yea, we *w* Ps 137:1
And Hezekiah *w* sore Is 38:3
he *w*, and made supplication unto Hos 12:4
And he went out, and *w* bitterly Mt 26:75
seeth the tumult, and them that *w* Mk 5:38
And when he thought thereon, he *w* Mk 14:72
with him, as they mourned and *w* Mk 16:10
mourned to you, and ye have not *w* Lk 7:32
And all *w*, and bewailed her Lk 8:52
he beheld the city, and *w* over it, Lk 19:41
And Peter went out, and *w* bitterly Lk 22:62
Jesus *w* Jn 11:35
and as she *w*, she stooped down, and Jn 20:11
And they all *w* sore, and fell on Acts 20:37
that weep, as though they *w* not 1Cor 7:30
I *w* much, because no man was Rev 5:4

**WERE** See PREFACE.

**WERT**
If thou *w* pure and upright Job 8:6
O that thou *w* as my brother, that Song 8:1
*w* graffed in among them, and with Rom 11:17
For if thou *w* cut out of the Rom 11:24
*w* graffed contrary to nature into Rom 11:24
I would thou *w* cold or hot Rev 3:15

**WEST**
his tent, having Beth-el on the *w* Gen 12:8
thou shalt spread abroad to the *w* Gen 28:14
turned a mighty strong *w* wind Ex 10:19
*w* side shall be hangings of fifty Ex 27:12
for the *w* side were hangings of Ex 38:12
On the *w* side shall be the Num 2:18
this shall be your *w* border Num 34:6
on the *w* side two thousand cubits Num 35:5
of the LORD, possess thou the *w* Deut 33:23
and Ai, on the *w* side of Ai Josh 8:9
on the *w* side of the city Josh 8:12
in wait on the *w* of the city Josh 8:13
and in the borders of Dor on the *w* Josh 11:2
Canaanite on the east and on the *w* Josh 11:3
on this side Jordan on the *w* Josh 12:7
the *w* border was to the great sea Josh 15:12
this was the *w* quarter Josh 18:14
and the border went out on the *w* Josh 18:15
reacheth to Asher on the *w* side Josh 19:34
and three looking toward the *w* 1Kin 7:25
the porters, toward the east, *w* 1Chr 9:24
toward the east, and toward the *w* 1Chr 12:15
and three looking toward the *w* 2Chr 4:4
the *w* side of the city of David 2Chr 32:30
on the *w* side of Gihon, in the 2Chr 33:14
from the east, nor from the *w* Ps 75:6
As far as the east is from the *w* Ps 103:12
from the east, and from the *w* Ps 107:3
of the Philistines toward the *w* Is 11:14
east, and gather thee from the *w* Is 43:5
rising of the sun, and from the *w* Is 45:6
from the north and from the *w* Is 49:12
the name of the LORD from the *w* Is 59:19
the *w* was seventy cubits broad Eze 41:12
He turned about to the *w* side Eze 42:19
from the *w* side westward, and from Eze 45:7
from the *w* border unto the east Eze 45:7
The *w* side also shall be the Eze 47:20
This is the *w* side Eze 47:20
for these are his sides east and *w* Eze 48:1
the east side unto the *w* side Eze 48:2
east side even unto the *w* side Eze 48:3
the east side unto the *w* side Eze 48:4
the east side unto the *w* side Eze 48:5
east side even unto the *w* side Eze 48:6
the east side unto the *w* side Eze 48:7
the east side unto the *w* side Eze 48:8
the east side unto the *w* side Eze 48:8
toward the *w* ten thousand in Eze 48:10
the *w* side four thousand and five Eze 48:16
toward the *w* two hundred and fifty Eze 48:17
thousand toward the *w* border Eze 48:21
the east side unto the *w* side Eze 48:23
the east side unto the *w* side Eze 48:24
the east side unto the *w* side Eze 48:25
the east side unto the *w* side Eze 48:26
the east side unto the *w* side Eze 48:27
At the *w* side four thousand and Eze 48:34
an he goat came from the *w* on the Dan 8:5
children shall tremble from the *w* Hos 11:10
country, and from the *w* country Zec 8:7
toward the east and toward the *w* Zec 14:4
shall come from the east and *w* Mt 8:11
east, and shineth even unto the *w* Mt 24:27
ye see a cloud rise out of the *w* Lk 12:54
come from the east, and from the *w* Lk 13:29
and lieth toward the south *w* Acts 27:12
and north *w* Acts 27:12
and on the *w* three gates Rev 21:13

**WESTERN**
And as for the *w* border, ye shall Num 34:6

**WESTWARD**
and southward, and eastward, and *w*. Gen 13:14
*w* thou shalt make six boards Ex 26:22
tabernacle, for the two sides *w* Ex 26:27
tabernacle *w* he made six boards Ex 36:27
of the tabernacle for the sides *w* Ex 36:32
pitch behind the tabernacle *w* Num 3:23
Pisgah, and lift up thine eyes *w* Deut 3:27
were on the side of Jordan *w* Josh 5:1
before the valley of Hinnom *w* Josh 15:8
from Baalah *w* unto mount Seir Josh 15:10
goeth down *w* to the coast of Josh 16:3
Tappuah *w* unto the river Kanah Josh 16:8
went up through the mountains *w* Josh 18:12
and reacheth to Carmel *w*, and to Josh 19:26
coast turneth *w* to Aznoth-tabor Josh 19:34
brethren on this side Jordan *w* Josh 22:7
off, even unto the great sea *w* Josh 23:4
*w* Gezer, with the towns thereof 1Chr 7:28
and Hosah the lot came forth *w* 1Chr 26:16
At Parbar *w*, four at the causeway 1Chr 26:18
of Israel on this side Jordan *w* 1Chr 26:30
of the city, from the west side *w* Eze 45:7
was a place on the two sides *w* Eze 46:19
eastward, and ten thousand *w* Eze 48:18
*w* over against the five and twenty Eze 48:21
I saw the ram pushing *w*, and Dan 8:4

**WET**
They are *w* with the showers of Job 24:8
let it be *w* with the dew of Dan 4:15
let it be *w* with the dew of Dan 4:23
they shall *w* thee with the dew of Dan 4:25
his body was *w* with the dew of Dan 4:33
his body was *w* with the dew of Dan 5:21

**WHALE**
Am I a sea, or a *w*, that thou Job 7:12
and thou art as a *w* in the seas Eze 32:2

**WHALE'S**
and three nights in the *w* belly Mt 12:40

**WHALES**
And God created great *w*, and every Gen 1:21

**WHAT** See PREFACE.

**WHATSOEVER**
*w* Adam called every living Gen 2:19
*w* creepeth upon the earth, after Gen 8:19
*w* thou hast in the city, bring Gen 19:12
*w* God hath said unto thee, do Gen 31:16
*w* they did there, he was the doer Gen 39:22
*w* openeth the womb among the Ex 13:2
of his life *w* is laid upon him Ex 21:30
*w* toucheth the altar shall be Ex 29:37
*w* toucheth them shall be holy Ex 30:29
*w* uncleanness it be that a man Lev 5:3
do good, *w* it be that a man shall Lev 5:4
*W* shall touch the flesh thereof Lev 6:27
*W* soul it be that eateth any Lev 7:27
*W* parteth the hoof, and is Lev 11:3
*w* hath fins and scales in the Lev 11:9
*W* hath no fins nor scales in the Lev 11:12
*w* goeth upon his paws, among all Lev 11:27
upon *w* any of them, when they are Lev 11:32
*w* vessel it be, wherein any work Lev 11:32
*w* is in it shall be unclean Lev 11:33
*W* goeth upon the belly, and Lev 11:42
*w* goeth upon all four, or Lev 11:42
or *w* hath more feet among all Lev 11:42
or *w* thing of skin it be, which Lev 13:58
*w* she sitteth upon shall be Lev 15:26
*W* man there be of the house of Lev 17:8
*w* man there be of the house of Lev 17:10
*w* man there be of the children of Lev 17:13
For *w* man he be that hath a Lev 21:18
*w* uncleanness he hath Lev 22:5
*W* he be of the house of Israel, Lev 22:18
But *w* hath a blemish, that shall Lev 22:20
For *w* soul it be that shall not Lev 23:29
*w* soul it be that doeth any work Lev 23:30
even of *w* passeth under the rod, Lev 27:32
*w* any man giveth the priest, it Num 5:10

*w* is first ripe in the land, Num 18:13
*w* the unclean person toucheth Num 19:22
I will do *w* thou sayest unto me Num 22:17
*w* he sheweth me I will tell thee Num 23:3
then *w* proceeded out of her lips Num 30:12
nor unto *w* the LORD our God Deut 2:37
every man *w* is right in his own Deut 12:8
*w* thy soul lusteth after, Deut 12:15
flesh, *w* thy soul lusteth after Deut 12:20
gates *w* thy soul lusteth after Deut 12:21
*w* hath not fins and scales ye may Deut 14:10
for *w* thy soul lusteth after Deut 14:26
or for *w* thy soul desireth Deut 14:26
do thou unto us *w* seemeth good Judg 10:15
that *w* cometh forth of the doors Judg 11:31
Do *w* seemeth good unto thee 1Sa 14:36
*W* thy soul desireth, I will even 1Sa 20:4
*w* cometh to thine hand unto thy 1Sa 25:8
as *w* the king did pleased all the 2Sa 3:36
thy servants are ready to do *w* my 2Sa 15:15
*w* thou shalt require of me, that 2Sa 19:38
*w* plague, *w* sickness 1Kin 8:37
*w* she asked, beside that which 1Kin 10:13
that *w* is pleasant in thine eyes, 1Kin 20:6
*w* sore or *w* sickness 2Chr 6:28
*w* she asked, beside that which 2Chr 9:12
*w* shall seem good to thee, and to Ezr 7:18
*w* more shall be needful for the Ezr 7:20
that *w* Ezra the priest, the Ezr 7:21
*W* is commanded by the God of Ezr 7:23
*w* she desired was given her to go Est 2:13
that they may do *w* he commandeth Job 37:12
*w* is under the whole heaven is Job 41:11
and *w* he doeth shall prosper Ps 1:3
*w* passeth through the paths of Ps 8:8
he hath done *w* he hath pleased Ps 115:3
*W* the LORD pleased, that did he Ps 135:6
*w* mine eyes desired I kept not Eccl 2:10
*w* God doeth, it shall be for ever Eccl 3:14
for he doeth *w* pleaseth him Eccl 8:3
*W* thy hand findeth to do, do it Eccl 9:10
*w* I command thee thou shalt speak Jer 1:7
that *w* thing the LORD shall Jer 42:4
But we will certainly do *w* thing Jer 44:17
for *w* is more than these cometh Mt 5:37
Therefore all things *w* ye would Mt 7:12
into *w* city or town ye shall Mt 10:11
oath to give her *w* she would ask Mt 14:7
by *w* thou mightest be profited by Mt 15:5
that *w* entereth in at the mouth Mt 15:17
*w* thou shalt bind on earth shall Mt 16:19
*w* thou shalt loose on earth shall Mt 16:19
have done unto him *w* they listed Mt 17:12
*W* ye shall bind on earth shall be Mt 18:18
*w* ye shall loose on earth shall Mt 18:18
*w* is right I will give you Mt 20:4
*w* is right, that shall ye receive Mt 20:7
*w* ye shall ask in prayer, Mt 21:22
All therefore *w* they bid you Mt 23:3
all things *w* I have commanded you Mt 28:20
the damsel, Ask of me *w* thou wilt Mk 6:22
*W* thou shalt ask of me, I will Mk 6:23
by *w* thou mightest be profited by Mk 7:11
that *w* thing from without Mk 7:18
have done unto him *w* they listed Mk 9:13
sell *w* thou hast, and give to the Mk 10:21
do for us *w* we shall desire Mk 10:35
he shall have *w* he saith Mk 11:23
but *w* shall be given you in that Mk 13:11
*w* we have heard done in Capernaum Lk 4:23
*w* house ye enter into, there Lk 9:4
into *w* house ye enter, first say, Lk 10:5
into *w* city ye enter, and they Lk 10:8
But into *w* city ye enter, and they Lk 10:10
*w* thou spendest more, when I come Lk 10:35
Therefore *w* ye have spoken in Lk 12:3
*W* he saith unto you, do it Jn 2:5
made whole of *w* disease he had Jn 5:4
*w* thou wilt ask of God, God will Jn 11:22
*w* I speak therefore, even as the Jn 12:50
*w* ye shall ask in my name, that Jn 14:13
*w* I have said unto you Jn 14:26
friends, if ye do *w* I command you Jn 15:14
that *w* ye shall ask of the Father Jn 15:16
but *w* he shall hear, that shall Jn 16:13
*W* ye shall ask the Father in my Jn 16:23
*w* thou hast given me are of thee Jn 17:7
things *w* he shall say unto you Acts 3:22
For to do *w* thy hand and thy Acts 4:28
for *w* is not of faith is sin Rom 14:23
For *w* things were written Rom 15:4
that ye assist her in *w* business Rom 16:2
*W* is sold in the shambles, that 1Cor 10:25
*w* is set before you, eat, asking 1Cor 10:27
or *w* ye do, do all to the glory 1Cor 10:31
(*w* they were, it maketh no matter Gal 2:6
for *w* a man soweth, that shall he Gal 6:7
for *w* doth make manifest is light Eph 5:13
Knowing that *w* good thing any man Eph 6:8
*w* things are true Phil 4:8
*w* things are honest Phil 4:8
*w* things are just Phil 4:8
*w* things are pure Phil 4:8
*w* things are lovely Phil 4:8
*w* things are of good report Phil 4:8
in *w* state I am, therewith to be Phil 4:11
*w* ye do in word or deed, do all Col 3:17
*w* ye do, do it heartily, as to Col 3:23
*w* we ask, we receive of him 1Jn 3:22
For *w* is born of God overcometh 1Jn 5:4
*w* we ask, we know that we have 1Jn 5:15
thou doest faithfully *w* thou 3Jn 5
of *w* craft he be, shall be found Rev 18:22
neither *w* worketh abomination, or Rev 21:27

**WHEAT**

went in the days of *w* harvest Gen 30:14
But the *w* and the rie were not Ex 9:32
of the firstfruits of *w* harvest Ex 34:22
the best of the wine, and of the *w* Num 18:12
A land of *w*, and barley, and vines, Deut 8:8
with the fat of kidneys of *w* Deut 32:14
threshed *w* by the winepress Judg 6:11
after, in the time of *w* harvest Judg 15:1
of barley harvest and of *w* harvest Ruth 2:23
their *w* harvest in the valley 1Sa 6:13
Is it not *w* harvest to day 1Sa 12:17
though they would have fetched *w* 2Sa 4:6
basons, and earthen vessels, and *w* 2Sa 17:28
of *w* for food to his household 1Kin 5:11
Now Ornan was threshing *w* 1Chr 21:20
the *w* for the meat offering 1Chr 21:23
thousand measures of beaten *w* 2Chr 2:10
Now therefore the *w*, and the 2Chr 2:15
and ten thousand measures of *w* 2Chr 27:5
offerings of the God of heaven, *w* Ezr 6:9
and to an hundred measures of *w* Ezr 7:22
Let thistles grow instead of *w* Job 31:40
also with the finest of the *w* Ps 81:16
thee with the finest of the *w* Ps 147:14
in a mortar among *w* with a pestle Prov 27:22
heap of *w* set about with lilies Song 7:2
and cast in the principal *w* Is 28:25
They have sown *w*, but shall reap Jer 12:13
What is the chaff to the *w* Jer 23:28
the goodness of the LORD, for *w* Jer 31:12
have treasures in the field, of *w* Jer 41:8
Take thou also unto thee *w* Eze 4:9
traded in thy market *w* of Minnith Eze 27:17
part of an ephah of an homer of *w* Eze 45:13
O ye vinedressers, for the *w* Joel 1:11
And the floors shall be full of *w* Joel 2:24
and ye take from him burdens of *w* Amos 5:11
sabbath, that we may set forth *w* Amos 8:5
yea, and sell the refuse of the *w* Amos 8:6
gather his *w* into the garner Mt 3:12
came and sowed tares among the *w* Mt 13:25
ye root up also the *w* with them Mt 13:29
but gather the *w* into my barn Mt 13:30
will gather the *w* into his garner Lk 3:17
he said, An hundred measures of *w* Lk 16:7
you, that he may sift you as *w* Lk 22:31
Except a corn of *w* fall into the Jn 12:24
and cast out the *w* into the sea Acts 27:38
bare grain, it may chance of *w* 1Cor 15:37
say, A measure of *w* for a penny Rev 6:6
wine, and oil, and fine flour, and *w* Rev 18:13

**WHEATEN**

of *w* flour shalt thou make them Ex 29:2

**WHEEL**

and the height of a *w* was a cubit 1Kin 7:32
was like the work of a chariot *w* 1Kin 7:33
O my God, make them like a *w* Ps 83:13
and bringeth the *w* over them Prov 20:26
or the *w* broken at the cistern Eccl 12:6
neither is a cart *w* turned about Is 28:27
break it with the *w* of his cart Is 28:28
behold one *w* upon the earth by Eze 1:15
were a *w* in the middle of a *w* Eze 1:16
one *w* by one cherub, and another Eze 10:9
another *w* by another cherub Eze 10:9
as if a *w* had been in the midst Eze 10:10
had been in the midst of a *w* Eze 10:10
unto them in my hearing, O *w* Eze 10:13

**WHEELS**

And took off their chariot *w* Ex 14:25
Why tarry the *w* of his chariots Judg 5:28
And every base had four brasen *w* 1Kin 7:30
And under the borders were four *w* 1Kin 7:32
the axletrees of the *w* were 1Kin 7:32
the work of the *w* was like the 1Kin 7:33
and their *w* like a whirlwind Is 5:28
he wrought a work on the *w* Jer 18:3
and at the rumbling of his *w* Jer 47:3
The appearance of the *w* and their Eze 1:16
went, the *w* went by them Eze 1:19
the earth, the *w* were lifted up Eze 1:19
the *w* were lifted up over against Eze 1:20
the living creature was in the *w* Eze 1:20
the *w* were lifted up over against Eze 1:21
the living creature was in the *w* Eze 1:21
the noise of the *w* over against Eze 3:13
and said, Go in between the *w* Eze 10:2
Take fire from between the *w* Eze 10:6
he went in, and stood beside the *w* Eze 10:6
looked, behold the four *w* by the Eze 10:9
the appearance of the *w* was as Eze 10:9
hands, and their wings, and the *w* Eze 10:12
even the *w* that they four had Eze 10:12
As for the *w*, it was cried unto Eze 10:13
went, the *w* went by them Eze 10:16
the same *w* also turned not from Eze 10:16
the *w* also were beside them, and Eze 10:19
their wings, and the *w* beside them Eze 11:22
thee with chariots, wagons, and *w* Eze 23:24
of the horsemen, and of the *w* Eze 26:10
flame, and his *w* as burning fire Dan 7:9
noise of the rattling of the *w* Nah 3:2

**WHELP**

Judah is a lion's *w* Gen 49:9
of Dan he said, Dan is a lion's *w* Deut 33:22
old lion, walked, and the lion's *w* Nah 2:11

**WHELPS**

bear robbed of her *w* in the field 2Sa 17:8
the stout lion's *w* are scattered Job 4:11
The lion's *w* have not trodden it, Job 28:8
a bear robbed of her *w* meet a man Prov 17:12
they shall yell as lions' *w* Jer 51:38
nourished her *w* among young lions Eze 19:2
And she brought up one of her *w* Eze 19:3
then she took another of her *w* Eze 19:5
a bear that is bereaved of her *w* Hos 13:8
tear in pieces enough for his *w* Nah 2:12

**WHEN** See PREFACE.

**WHENCE**

the ground from *w* he was taken Gen 3:23
Sarai's maid, *w* camest thou Gen 16:8
unto the land from *w* thou camest Gen 24:5
unto them, My brethren, *w* be ye Gen 29:4
and he said unto them, *W* come ye Gen 42:7
*W* should I have flesh to give Num 11:13
from *w* thou mayest see them Num 23:13
Lest the land *w* thou broughtest Deut 9:28
from *w* ye came out, where thou Deut 11:10
me, but I wist not *w* they were Josh 2:4
and from *w* come ye Josh 9:8
unto the city from *w* he fled Josh 20:6
but I asked him not *w* he was Judg 13:6
said unto him, *W* comest thou Judg 17:9
and *w* comest thou Judg 19:17
men, whom I know not *w* they be 1Sa 25:11
and *w* art thou 1Sa 30:13
said unto him, From *w* comest thou 2Sa 1:3
man that told him, *W* art thou 2Sa 1:13
unto him, *W* comest thou, Gehazi 2Kin 5:25
help thee, *w* shall I help thee 2Kin 6:27
from *w* came they unto thee 2Kin 20:14
From all places *w* ye shall return Neh 4:12
said unto Satan, *W* comest thou Job 1:7
unto Satan, From *w* comest thou Job 2:2
Before I go *w* I shall not return, Job 10:21
go the way *w* I shall not return Job 16:22
*W* then cometh wisdom Job 28:20
the hills, from *w* cometh my help Ps 121:1
the place from *w* the rivers come Eccl 1:7
from *w* come the young and old lion Is 30:6
from *w* came they unto thee Is 39:3
shalt not know from *w* it riseth Is 47:11
look unto the rock *w* ye are hewn Is 51:1
hole of the pit *w* ye are digged Is 51:1
bring you again into the place *w* Jer 29:14
and *w* comest thou Jonah 1:8
*w* shall I seek comforters for Nah 3:7
into my house from *w* I came out Mt 12:44
from *w* then hath it tares Mt 13:27
*W* hath this man this wisdom, and Mt 13:54
*W* then hath this man all these Mt 13:56
*W* should we have so much bread in Mt 15:33
The baptism of John, *w* was it Mt 21:25
From *w* hath this man these things Mk 6:2
From *w* can a man satisfy these Mk 8:4
and *w* is he then his son Mk 12:37
*w* is this to me, that the mother Lk 1:43
return unto my house *w* I came out Lk 11:24
unto you, I know you not *w* ye are Lk 13:25
tell you, I know you not *w* ye are Lk 13:27
that they could not tell *w* it was Lk 20:7
saith unto him, *W* knowest thou me Jn 1:48
made wine, and knew not *w* it was Jn 2:9
but canst not tell *w* it cometh Jn 3:8
from *w* then hast thou that living Jn 4:11
*W* shall we buy bread, that these Jn 6:5
Howbeit we know this man *w* he is Jn 7:27
cometh, no man knoweth *w* he is Jn 7:27
both know me, and ye know *w* I am Jn 7:28
for I know *w* I came, and whither I Jn 8:14
but ye cannot tell *w* I come Jn 8:14
fellow, we know not from *w* he is Jn 9:29
that ye know not from *w* he is Jn 9:30
and saith unto Jesus, *W* art thou Jn 19:9
from *w* they had been recommended Acts 14:26
from *w* also we look for the Phil 3:20
that country from *w* they came out Heb 11:15
from *w* also he received him in a Heb 11:19
From *w* come wars and fightings Jas 4:1
therefore from *w* thou art fallen Rev 2:5
and *w* came they Rev 7:13

**WHENSOEVER**

*w* the stronger cattle did Gen 30:41
*w* ye will ye may do them good Mk 14:7
*W* I take my journey into Spain, I Rom 15:24

**WHERE**

land of Havilah, *w* there is gold Gen 2:11
and said unto him, *W* art thou Gen 3:9
unto Cain, *W* is Abel thy brother Gen 4:9
unto the place *w* his tent had Gen 13:3
that it was well watered every *w* Gen 13:10
the place *w* thou art northward Gen 13:14
unto him, *W* is Sarah thy wife Gen 18:9
*W* are the men which came in to Gen 19:5
place *w* he stood before the LORD Gen 19:27
dwell *w* it pleaseth thee Gen 20:15
the voice of the lad *w* he is Gen 21:17
but *w* is the lamb for a burnt Gen 22:7
*w* is he that hath taken venison, Gen 27:33
*w* thou anointedst the pillar, and Gen 31:13

*w* thou vowedst a vow unto me ... Gen 31:13
*w* he had spread his tent, at the ... Gen 33:19
in the place *w* he talked with him ... Gen 35:13
in the place *w* he talked with him ... Gen 35:14
of the place *w* God spake with him ... Gen 35:15
*w* Abraham and Isaac sojourned ... Gen 35:27
thee, *w* they feed their flocks ... Gen 37:16
*W* is the harlot, that was openly ... Gen 38:21
a place *w* the king's prisoners ... Gen 39:20
the place *w* Joseph was bound ... Gen 40:3
and he sought *w* to weep ... Gen 43:30
unto his daughters, And *w* is he ... Ex 2:20
get you straw *w* ye can find it ... Ex 5:11
*w* the children of Israel were, ... Ex 9:26
a token upon the houses *w* ye are ... Ex 12:13
a house *w* there was not one dead ... Ex 12:30
*w* were twelve wells of water, and ... Ex 15:27
*w* he encamped at the mount of God ... Ex 18:5
unto the thick darkness *w* God was ... Ex 20:21
in all places *w* I record my name ... Ex 20:24
and the breadth fifty every *w* ... Ex 27:18
*w* I will meet you, to speak there ... Ex 29:42
*w* I will meet with thee ... Ex 30:6
*w* I will meet with thee ... Ex 30:36
*w* the ashes are poured out, and ... Lev 4:12
*w* the ashes are poured out shall ... Lev 4:12
kill it in the place *w* they kill ... Lev 4:24
*w* they kill the burnt offering ... Lev 4:33
In the place *w* the burnt offering ... Lev 6:25
In the place *w* they kill the ... Lev 7:2
slay the lamb in the place *w* he ... Lev 14:13
in the place *w* the cloud abode, ... Num 9:17
*w* Ahiman, Sheshai, and Talmai, the. Num 13:22
testimony, *w* I will meet with you ... Num 17:4
*w* was no way to turn either to ... Num 22:26
*w* was no water for the people to ... Num 33:14
be in the place *w* his lot falleth ... Num 33:54
*w* thou hast seen how that the ... Deut 1:31
and drought, *w* there was no water ... Deut 8:15
*w* thou sowedst thy seed, and ... Deut 11:10
by the way *w* the sun goeth down, ... Deut 11:30
*w* he sojourned, and come with all ... Deut 18:6
thy gates, *w* it liketh him best ... Deut 23:16
*W* are their gods, their rock in ... Deut 32:37
out of the place *w* the priests' ... Josh 4:3
*w* ye shall lodge this night ... Josh 4:3
them unto the place *w* they lodged ... Josh 4:8
in the place *w* the feet of the ... Josh 4:9
*w* he bowed, there he fell down ... Judg 5:27
*w* be all his miracles which our ... Judg 6:13
*W* is now thy mouth, wherewith ... Judg 9:38
sojourn *w* he could find a place ... Judg 17:8
I go to sojourn *w* I may find a ... Judg 17:9
a place *w* there is no want of any ... Judg 18:10
of the man's house *w* her lord was ... Judg 19:26
again in array in the place *w* ... Judg 20:22
forth out of the place *w* she was ... Ruth 1:7
*w* thou lodgest, I will lodge ... Ruth 1:16
*W* thou diest, will I die, and ... Ruth 1:17
*W* hast thou gleaned to day ... Ruth 2:19
and *w* wroughtest thou ... Ruth 2:19
mark the place *w* he shall lie ... Ruth 3:4
*w* the ark of God was, and Samuel ... 1Sa 3:3
*w* there was a great stone ... 1Sa 6:14
the city *w* the man of God was ... 1Sa 9:10
pray thee, *w* the seer's house is ... 1Sa 9:18
of God, *w* is the garrison of the ... 1Sa 10:5
when we saw that they were no *w* ... 1Sa 10:14
holes *w* they had hid themselves ... 1Sa 14:11
my father in the field *w* thou art ... 1Sa 19:3
and said, *W* are Samuel and David ... 1Sa 19:22
come to the place *w* thou didst ... 1Sa 20:19
and see his place *w* his haunt is ... 1Sa 23:22
places *w* he hideth himself ... 1Sa 23:23
by the way, *w* was a cave ... 1Sa 24:3
to the place *w* Saul had pitched ... 1Sa 26:5
David beheld the place *w* Saul lay ... 1Sa 26:5
now see *w* the king's spear is, and ... 1Sa 26:16
*w* those that were left behind ... 1Sa 30:9
to all the places *w* David himself ... 1Sa 30:31
to the place *w* Asahel fell down ... 2Sa 2:23
the king said unto him, *W* is he ... 2Sa 9:4
*w* he knew that valiant men were ... 2Sa 11:16
*w* he worshipped God, behold, ... 2Sa 15:32
said, And *w* is thy master's son ... 2Sa 16:3
in some place *w* he shall be found ... 2Sa 17:12
said, *W* is Ahimaaz and Jonathan ... 2Sa 17:20
*W* the people of Israel were slain ... 2Sa 18:7
*w* the Philistines had hanged them ... 2Sa 21:12
*w* Elhanan the son of Jaare-oregim ... 2Sa 21:19
*w* was a man of great stature, ... 2Sa 21:20
*w* was a piece of ground full of ... 2Sa 23:11
the place *w* the officers were ... 1Kin 4:28
for the throne *w* he might judge ... 1Kin 7:7
his house *w* he dwelt had another ... 1Kin 7:8
told it in the city *w* the old ... 1Kin 13:25
*w* he abode, and laid him upon his ... 1Kin 17:19
In the place *w* dogs licked the ... 1Kin 21:19
*W* is the LORD God of Elijah ... 2Kin 2:14
to Shunem, *w* was a great woman ... 2Kin 4:8
the place *w* we dwell with thee is ... 2Kin 6:1
us a place there, *w* we may dwell ... 2Kin 6:2
And the man of God said, *W* fell it ... 2Kin 6:6
spy *w* he is, that I may send and ... 2Kin 6:13
*W* are the gods of Hamath, and of ... 2Kin 18:34
*w* are the gods of Sepharvaim, ... 2Kin 18:34
*W* is the king of Hamath, and the ... 2Kin 19:13
*w* the women wove hangings for the .. 2Kin 23:7
defiled the high places *w* the ... 2Kin 23:8
*w* the Jebusites were, the ... 1Chr 11:4
*w* was a parcel of ground full of ... 1Chr 11:13
abroad unto our brethren every *w* ... 1Chr 13:2
*w* was a man of great stature, ... 1Chr 20:6
*w* the LORD appeared unto David ... 2Chr 3:1
*w* the LORD commanded, saying, The . 2Chr 25:4
*w* they were servants to him and ... 2Chr 36:20
in any place *w* he sojourneth ... Ezr 1:4
*w* the treasures were laid up in ... Ezr 6:1
builded, the place *w* they offered ... Ezr 6:3
*w* are the vessels of the ... Neh 10:39
*w* aforetime they laid the meat ... Neh 13:5
*W* were white, green, and blue, ... Est 1:6
*w* is he, that durst presume in ... Est 7:5
or *w* were the righteous cut off ... Job 4:7
if not, *w*, and who is he ... Job 9:24
*w* the light is as darkness ... Job 10:22
in a wilderness *w* there is no way ... Job 12:24
giveth up the ghost, and *w* is he ... Job 14:10
abroad for bread, saying, *W* is it ... Job 15:23
And *w* is now my hope ... Job 17:15
have seen him shall say, *W* is he ... Job 20:7
*W* is the house of the prince ... Job 21:28
*w* are the dwelling places of the ... Job 21:28
Oh that I knew *w* I might find him ... Job 23:3
*w* he doth work, but I cannot ... Job 23:9
a place for gold *w* they fine it ... Job 28:1
But *w* shall wisdom be found ... Job 28:12
*w* is the place of understanding ... Job 28:12
*w* is the place of understanding ... Job 28:20
*w* the workers of iniquity may ... Job 34:22
*W* is God my maker, who giveth ... Job 35:10
place, *w* there is no straitness ... Job 36:16
*W* wast thou when I laid the ... Job 38:4
*W* is the way *w* light dwelleth ... Job 38:19
darkness, *w* is the place thereof, ... Job 38:19
to rain on the earth, *w* no man is ... Job 38:26
*w* the slain are, there is she ... Job 39:30
*w* all the beasts of the field ... Job 40:20
*w* their voice is not heard ... Ps 19:3
the place *w* thine honour dwelleth ... Ps 26:8
say unto me, *W* is thy God ... Ps 42:3
say daily unto me, *W* is thy God ... Ps 42:10
they in great fear, *w* no fear was ... Ps 53:5
and thirsty land, *w* no water is ... Ps 63:1
deep mire, *w* there is no standing ... Ps 69:2
waters, *w* the floods overflow me ... Ps 69:2
the heathen say, *W* is their God ... Ps 79:10
*w* I heard a language that I ... Ps 81:5
*w* she may lay her young, even ... Ps 84:3
*w* are thy former lovingkindnesses ... Ps 89:49
*W* the birds make their nests ... Ps 104:17
the wilderness, *w* there is no way ... Ps 107:40
heathen say, *W* is now their God ... Ps 115:2
*W* no counsel is, the people fall ... Prov 11:14
*W* no oxen are, the crib is clean ... Prov 14:4
is a dinner of herbs *w* love is ... Prov 15:17
*W* no wood is, there the fire ... Prov 26:20
so *w* there is no talebearer, the ... Prov 26:20
*W* there is no vision, the people ... Prov 29:18
hasteth to his place *w* he arose ... Eccl 1:5
*W* the word of a king is, there is ... Eccl 8:4
in the city *w* they had so done ... Eccl 8:10
in the place *w* the tree falleth, ... Eccl 11:3
*w* thou feedest, *w* thou makest ... Song 1:7
*w* there were a thousand vines at ... Is 7:23
*w* will ye leave your glory ... Is 10:3
*W* are they ... Is 19:12
*w* are thy wise men ... Is 19:12
to Ariel, the city *w* David dwelt ... Is 29:1
in every place *w* the grounded ... Is 30:32
*W* is the scribe ... Is 33:18
*w* is the receiver ... Is 33:18
*w* is he that counted the towers ... Is 33:18
*w* each lay, shall be grass with ... Is 35:7
*W* are the gods of Hamath and ... Is 36:19
*w* are the gods of Sepharvaim ... Is 36:19
*W* is the king of Hamath, and the ... Is 37:13
these, *w* had they been ... Is 49:21
*W* is the bill of your mother's ... Is 50:1
*w* is the fury of the oppressor ... Is 51:13
their bed *w* thou sawest it ... Is 57:8
*W* is he that brought them up out ... Is 63:11
*w* is he that put his holy Spirit ... Is 63:11
*w* is thy zeal and thy strength, ... Is 63:15
*w* our fathers praised thee, is ... Is 64:11
*w* is the house that ye build unto ... Is 66:1
*w* is the place of my rest ... Is 66:1
*W* is the LORD that brought us up ... Jer 2:6
passed through, and *w* no man dwelt ... Jer 2:6
priests said not, *W* is the LORD ... Jer 2:8
But *w* are thy gods that thou hast ... Jer 2:28
see *w* thou hast not been lien ... Jer 3:2
*w* is the good way, and walk ... Jer 6:16
*w* I set my name at the first, and ... Jer 7:12
from the place *w* I had hid it ... Jer 13:7
*w* is the flock that was given ... Jer 13:20
*w* I will not shew you favour ... Jer 16:13
*W* is the word of the LORD ... Jer 17:15
country, *w* ye were not born ... Jer 22:26
in the land *w* ye be strangers ... Jer 35:7
and let no man know *w* ye be ... Jer 36:19
*W* are now your prophets which ... Jer 37:19
for hunger in the place *w* he is ... Jer 38:9
*w* he gave judgment upon him ... Jer 39:5
*w* we shall see no war, nor hear ... Jer 42:14
*w* he gave judgment upon him ... Jer 52:9
their mothers, *W* is corn and wine ... Lam 2:12
I sat *w* they sat, and remained ... Eze 3:15
the place *w* they did offer sweet ... Eze 6:13
*w* was the seat of the image of ... Eze 8:3
the countries *w* they shall come ... Eze 11:16
*w* ye have been scattered, and I ... Eze 11:17
*W* is the daubing wherewith ye ... Eze 13:12
wither in the furrows *w* it grew ... Eze 17:10
surely in the place *w* the king ... Eze 17:16
out of the country *w* they sojourn ... Eze 20:38
in the place *w* thou wast created ... Eze 21:30
deliver them out of all places *w* ... Eze 34:12
*w* they washed the burnt offering ... Eze 40:38
*w* the priests that approach unto ... Eze 42:13
*w* I will dwell in the midst of ... Eze 43:7
This is the place *w* the priests ... Eze 46:20
*w* they shall bake the meat ... Eze 46:20
*w* the ministers of the house ... Eze 46:24
So he came near *w* I stood ... Dan 8:17
that in the place *w* it was said ... Hos 1:10
*w* is any other that may save thee ... Hos 13:10
among the people, *W* is their God ... Joel 2:17
the earth, *w* no gin is for him ... Amos 3:5
unto me, *W* is the LORD thy God ... Mic 7:10
*W* is the dwelling of the lions, ... Nah 2:11
*w* the lion, even the old lion, ... Nah 2:11
place is not known *w* they are ... Nah 3:17
fame in every land *w* they have ... Zeph 3:19
Your fathers, *w* are they ... Zec 1:5
I be a father, *w* is mine honour ... Mal 1:6
and if I be a master, *w* is my fear ... Mal 1:6
or, *W* is the God of judgment ... Mal 2:17
*W* is he that is born King of the ... Mt 2:2
he demanded of them *w* Christ ... Mt 2:4
stood over *w* the young child was ... Mt 2:9
*w* moth and rust doth corrupt, and ... Mt 6:19
*w* thieves break through and steal ... Mt 6:19
*w* neither moth nor rust doth ... Mt 6:20
*w* thieves do not break through ... Mt 6:20
For *w* your treasure is, there ... Mt 6:21
of man hath not *w* to lay his head ... Mt 8:20
*w* they had not much earth ... Mt 13:5
For *w* two or three are gathered ... Mt 18:20
reaping *w* thou hast not sown, and ... Mt 25:24
gathering *w* thou hast not strawed ... Mt 25:24
knewest that I reap *w* I sowed not ... Mt 25:26
gather *w* I have not strawed ... Mt 25:26
*W* wilt thou that we prepare for ... Mt 26:17
*w* the scribes and the elders were ... Mt 26:57
see the place *w* the Lord lay ... Mt 28:6
into a mountain *w* Jesus had ... Mt 28:16
they uncovered the roof *w* he was ... Mk 2:4
ground, *w* it had not much earth ... Mk 4:5
the way side, *w* the word is sown ... Mk 4:15
entereth in *w* the damsel was ... Mk 5:40
were sick, *w* they heard he was ... Mk 6:55
*W* their worm dieth not, and the ... Mk 9:44
*W* their worm dieth not, and the ... Mk 9:46
*W* their worm dieth not, and the ... Mk 9:48
without in a place *w* two ways met ... Mk 11:4
standing *w* it ought not, (let him ... Mk 13:14
*W* wilt thou that we go and prepare ... Mk 14:12
*W* is the guestchamber ... Mk 14:14
*w* I shall eat the passover with ... Mk 14:14
of Joses beheld *w* he was laid ... Mk 15:47
behold the place *w* they laid him ... Mk 16:6
went forth, and preached every *w* ... Mk 16:20
*w* he had been brought up ... Lk 4:16
found the place *w* it was written ... Lk 4:17
said unto them, *W* is your faith ... Lk 8:25
the gospel, and healing every *w* ... Lk 9:6
of man hath not *w* to lay his head ... Lk 9:58
as he journeyed, came *w* he was ... Lk 10:33
no room *w* to bestow my fruits ... Lk 12:17
*w* no thief approacheth, neither ... Lk 12:33
For *w* your treasure is, there ... Lk 12:34
but *w* are the nine ... Lk 17:17
they answered and said unto him, *W* ... Lk 17:37
*W* wilt thou that we prepare ... Lk 22:9
into the house *w* he entereth in ... Lk 22:10
*W* is the guestchamber ... Lk 22:11
*w* I shall eat the passover with ... Lk 22:11
Jordan, *w* John was baptizing ... Jn 1:28
Master,) *w* dwellest thou ... Jn 1:38
saw *w* he dwelt, and abode with him ... Jn 1:39
The wind bloweth *w* it listeth ... Jn 3:8
the place *w* men ought to worship ... Jn 4:20
Galilee, *w* he made the water wine ... Jn 4:46
the place *w* they did eat bread ... Jn 6:23
of man ascend up *w* he was before ... Jn 6:62
at the feast, and said, *W* is he ... Jn 7:11
*w* I am, thither ye cannot come ... Jn 7:34
*w* I am, thither ye cannot come ... Jn 7:36
town of Bethlehem, *w* David was ... Jn 7:42
*w* are those thine accusers ... Jn 8:10
they unto him, *W* is thy Father ... Jn 8:19
Then said they unto him, *W* is he ... Jn 9:12
place *w* John at first baptized ... Jn 10:40
still in the same place *w* he was ... Jn 11:6
in that place *w* Martha met him ... Jn 11:30
when Mary was come *w* Jesus was ... Jn 11:32
And said, *W* have ye laid him ... Jn 11:34
the place *w* the dead was laid ... Jn 11:41
that, if any man knew *w* he were ... Jn 11:57
*w* Lazarus was which had been dead ... Jn 12:1
*w* I am, there shall also my ... Jn 12:26
that *w* I am, there ye may be also ... Jn 14:3
hast given me, be with me *w* I am ... Jn 17:24
*w* was a garden, into the which he ... Jn 18:1
*W* they crucified him, and two ... Jn 19:18
for the place *w* Jesus was ... Jn 19:20
Now in the place *w* he was ... Jn 19:41
we know not *w* they have laid him ... Jn 20:2
*w* the body of Jesus had lain ... Jn 20:12

I know not *w* they have laid him Jn 20:13
tell me *w* thou hast laid him, and Jn 20:15
when the doors were shut *w* the Jn 20:19
*w* abode both Peter, and James, and Acts 1:13
all the house *w* they were sitting Acts 2:2
the place was shaken *w* they were Acts 4:31
of Madian, *w* he begat two sons Acts 7:29
for the place *w* thou standest is Acts 7:33
went every *w* preaching the word Acts 8:4
come unto the house *w* I was Acts 11:11
*w* many were gathered together Acts 12:12
our brethren in every city *w* we Acts 15:36
*w* prayer was wont to be made Acts 16:13
*w* was a synagogue of the Jews Acts 17:1
all men every *w* to repent Acts 17:30
*w* we abode seven days Acts 20:6
*w* they were gathered together Acts 20:8
men every *w* against the people Acts 21:28
seat, *w* I ought to be judged Acts 25:10
into a place *w* two seas met Acts 27:41
*W* we found brethren, and were Acts 28:14
we know that every *w* it is spoken Acts 28:22
*W* is boasting then Rom 3:27
for *w* no law is, there is no Rom 4:15
But *w* sin abounded, grace did Rom 5:20
that in the place *w* it was said Rom 9:26
not *w* Christ was named, lest I Rom 15:20
*W* is the wise 1Cor 1:20
*w* is the scribe 1Cor 1:20
*w* is the disputer of this world 1Cor 1:20
I teach every *w* in every church 1Cor 4:17
were an eye, *w* were the hearing 1Cor 12:17
were hearing, *w* were the smelling 1Cor 12:17
all one member, *w* were the body 1Cor 12:19
O death, *w* is thy sting 1Cor 15:55
O grave, *w* is thy victory 1Cor 15:55
*w* the Spirit of the Lord is, 2Cor 3:17
*W* is then the blessedness ye Gal 4:15
every *w* and in all things I am Phil 4:12
*w* Christ sitteth on the right Col 3:1
*W* there is neither Greek nor Jew, Col 3:11
therefore that men pray every *w* 1Ti 2:8
For *w* a testament is, there must Heb 9:16
Now *w* remission of these is, Heb 10:18
For *w* envying and strife is, there Jas 3:16
*w* shall the ungodly and the sinner 1Pet 4:18
*W* is the promise of his coming 2Pet 3:4
*w* thou dwellest Rev 2:13
even *w* Satan's seat is Rev 2:13
slain among you, *w* Satan dwelleth Rev 2:13
*w* also our Lord was crucified Rev 11:8
*w* she hath a place prepared of Rev 12:6
*w* she is nourished for a time, and Rev 12:14
*w* the whore sitteth, are peoples, Rev 17:15
*w* the beast and the false prophet Rev 20:10

## WHEREABOUT

of the business *w* I send thee 1Sa 21:2

## WHEREAS

*W* thou hast searched all my stuff Gen 31:37
*w* he was not worthy of death, Deut 19:6
*w* ye were as the stars of heaven Deut 28:62
*w* I have rewarded thee evil 1Sa 24:17
*W* I have not dwelt in any house 2Sa 7:6
*W* thou camest but yesterday, 2Sa 15:20
*W* it was in thine heart to build 1Kin 8:18
now *w* my father did lade you with 1Kin 12:11
*w* now thou shalt smite Syria but 2Kin 13:19
For *w* my father put a heavy yoke 2Chr 10:11
for *w* we have offended against 2Chr 28:13
*W* our substance is not cut down, Job 22:20
*w* also he that is born in his Eccl 4:14
*W* thou hast prayed to me against Is 37:21
*W* thou hast been forsaken and Is 60:15
*w* the sword reacheth unto the Jer 4:10
*w* ye say, The LORD saith it Eze 13:7
*w* thou wast naked and bare Eze 16:7
*w* none followeth thee to commit Eze 16:34
*w* the LORD was there Eze 35:10
*w* it lay desolate in the sight of Eze 36:34
*w* thou sawest the feet and toes, Dan 2:41
*w* thou sawest iron mixed with Dan 2:43
*w* the king saw a watcher and an Dan 4:23
*w* they commanded to leave the Dan 4:26
*w* four stood up for it, four Dan 8:22
*W* Edom saith, We are impoverished Mal 1:4
that, *w* I was blind, now I see Jn 9:25
for *w* there is among you envying, 1Cor 3:3
*W* ye know not what shall be on Jas 4:14
*w* they speak against you as 1Pet 2:12
*w* they speak evil of you, as of 1Pet 3:16
*W* angels, which are greater in 2Pet 2:11

## WHEREBY

*w* shall I know that I shall Gen 15:8
drinketh, and *w* indeed he divineth Gen 44:5
*w* he may be made unclean, or a Lev 22:5
*w* an atonement shall be made for Num 5:8
*w* they murmur against you Num 17:5
*w* the LORD thy God brought thee Deut 7:19
doings, *w* thou hast forsaken me Deut 28:20
*w* Jonathan knew that it was 1Sa 20:33
*w* the people fall under thee Ps 45:5
*w* they have made thee glad Ps 45:8
*w* thou didst confirm thine Ps 68:9
when for all the causes *w* Jer 3:8
*w* the kings of Judah come in, and Jer 17:19
this is his name *w* he shall be Jer 23:6
*w* they have sinned against me Jer 33:8
*w* they have sinned Jer 33:8
*w* they have transgressed against Jer 33:8
*w* ye have transgressed Eze 18:31
judgments *w* they should not live Eze 20:25
all their trespasses *w* they have Eze 39:26
by the steps *w* they went up to it Eze 40:49
the way of the gate *w* he came in Eze 46:9
*w* ye shall inherit the land Eze 47:13
*w* they have reproached my people, Zeph 2:8
the angel, *W* shall I know this Lk 1:18
*w* the dayspring from on high hath Lk 1:78
among men, *w* we must be saved Acts 4:12
*w* thou and all thy house shall be Acts 11:14
there being no cause *w* we may Acts 19:40
adoption, *w* we cry, Abba, Father Rom 8:15
nor any thing *w* thy brother Rom 14:21
*W*, when ye read, ye may Eph 3:4
*w* they lie in wait to deceive Eph 4:14
*w* ye are sealed unto the day of Eph 4:30
according to the working *w* he is Phil 3:21
*w* we may serve God acceptably Heb 12:28
*W* are given unto us exceeding 2Pet 1:4
*W* the world that then was, being 2Pet 3:6
*w* we know that it is the last 1Jn 2:18

## WHEREFORE

*w* it is said, Even as Nimrod the Gen 10:9
*W* the well was called Gen 16:14
*W* did Sarah laugh, saying, Shall Gen 18:13
*W* she said unto Abraham, Cast out Gen 21:10
*W* he called that place Beer-sheba Gen 21:31
*w* standest thou without Gen 24:31
*W* come ye to me, seeing ye hate Gen 26:27
*w* then hast thou beguiled me Gen 29:25
*W* didst thou flee away secretly, Gen 31:27
yet *w* hast thou stolen my gods Gen 31:30
*W* is it that thou dost ask after Gen 32:29
*w* he slew him also Gen 38:10
*W* look ye so sadly to day Gen 40:7
*W* dealt ye so ill with me, as to Gen 43:6
*W* have ye rewarded evil for good Gen 44:4
*W* saith my lord these words Gen 44:7
*W* shall we die before thine eyes, Gen 47:19
*w* they sold not their lands Gen 47:22
*w* the name of it was called Gen 50:11
*W* smitest thou thy fellow Ex 2:13
*W* do ye, Moses and Aaron, let the Ex 5:4
*W* have ye not fulfilled your task Ex 5:14
*W* dealest thou thus with thy Ex 5:15
*w* hast thou so evil entreated Ex 5:22
*W* say unto the children of Israel Ex 6:6
*w* hast thou dealt thus with us, Ex 14:11
unto Moses, *W* criest thou unto me Ex 14:15
*W* the people did chide with Moses Ex 17:2
*w* do ye tempt the LORD Ex 17:2
*W* is this that thou hast brought Ex 17:3
*w* the LORD blessed the sabbath Ex 20:11
*W* the children of Israel shall Ex 31:16
*W* should the Egyptians speak, and Ex 32:12
*W* have ye not eaten the sin Lev 10:17
*w* the priest shall pronounce him Lev 13:25
*W* ye shall do my statutes, and Lev 25:18
*w* are we kept back, that we may Num 9:7
*W* hast thou afflicted thy servant Num 11:11
*w* have I not found favour in thy Num 11:11
*w* then were ye not afraid to Num 12:8
*w* hath the LORD brought us unto Num 14:3
*W* now do ye transgress the Num 14:41
*w* then lift ye up yourselves Num 16:3
*w* have ye made us to come up out Num 20:5
*w* Israel turned away from him Num 20:21
*W* have ye brought us up out of Num 21:5
*W* it is said in the book of the Num 21:14
*W* they that speak in proverbs say Num 21:27
*W* hast thou smitten thine ass Num 22:32
*w* camest thou not unto me Num 22:37
*W* say, Behold, I give unto him my Num 25:12
*W*, said they, if we have found Num 32:5
*w* discourage ye the heart of the Num 32:7
*W* it shall come to pass, if ye Deut 7:12
*W* Levi hath no part nor Deut 10:9
*W* I command thee, saying, Thou Deut 19:7
*W* hath the LORD done thus unto Deut 29:24
*W* the name of the place is called Josh 5:9
*w* the hearts of the people melted Josh 7:5
*w* hast thou at all brought this Josh 7:7
*w* liest thou thus upon thy face Josh 7:10
*W* the name of that place was Josh 7:26
*W* our elders and all the Josh 9:11
*W* have ye beguiled us, saying, We Josh 9:22
*W* Adoni-zedek king of Jerusalem Josh 10:3
*W* I also said, I will not drive Judg 2:3
*w* I will deliver you no more Judg 10:13
*W* I have not sinned against thee, Judg 11:27
*W* passedst thou over to fight Judg 12:1
*w* then are ye come up unto me Judg 12:3
*w* he called the name thereof Judg 15:19
*w* they called that place Judg 18:12
*W* she went forth out of the place Ruth 1:7
*W* it came to pass, when the time 1Sa 1:20
*W* the sin of the young men was 1Sa 2:17
*W* kick ye at my sacrifice and at 1Sa 2:29
*W* the LORD God of Israel saith, I 1Sa 2:30
*W* hath the LORD smitten us to day 1Sa 4:3
*W* ye shall make images of your 1Sa 6:5
*W* then do ye harden your hearts, 1Sa 6:6
*w* then speakest thou so to me 1Sa 9:21
*w* he put forth the end of the rod 1Sa 14:27
*W* then didst thou not obey the 1Sa 15:19
*W* Saul sent messengers unto Jesse 1Sa 16:19
*W* when Saul saw that he behaved 1Sa 18:15
*W* Saul said to David, Thou shalt 1Sa 18:21
*W* David arose and went, he and his 1Sa 18:27
*w* then wilt thou sin against 1Sa 19:5
*W* they say, Is Saul also among 1Sa 19:24
*W* cometh not the son of Jesse to 1Sa 20:27
*W* now send and fetch him unto me, 1Sa 20:31
unto him, *W* shall he be slain 1Sa 20:32
*w* then have ye brought him to me 1Sa 21:14
*w* he came down into a rock, and 1Sa 23:25
*W* Saul returned from pursuing 1Sa 23:28
*W* hearest thou men's words, 1Sa 24:9
*w* the LORD reward thee good for 1Sa 24:19
*W* let the young men find favour 1Sa 25:8
*w* she told him nothing, less or 1Sa 25:36
*w* then hast thou not kept thy 1Sa 26:15
*W* doth my lord thus pursue after 1Sa 26:18
*w* Ziklag pertaineth unto the 1Sa 27:6
*w* then layest thou a snare for my 1Sa 28:9
*W* then dost thou ask of me, 1Sa 28:16
*W* now return, and go in peace, 1Sa 29:7
*W* now rise up early in the 1Sa 29:10
*w* that place was called 2Sa 2:16
*w* should I smite thee to the 2Sa 2:22
*w* Abner with the hinder end of 2Sa 2:23
*W* hast thou gone in unto my 2Sa 3:7
*W* they said, The blind and the 2Sa 5:8
*W* thou art great, O LORD God 2Sa 7:22
*W* Hanun took David's servants, and 2Sa 10:4
*W* approached ye so nigh unto the 2Sa 11:20
*W* hast thou despised the 2Sa 12:9
now he is dead, *w* should I fast 2Sa 12:23
*W* then hast thou thought such a 2Sa 14:13
*W* have thy servants set my field 2Sa 14:31
to say, *W* am I come from Geshur 2Sa 14:32
*W* goest thou also with us 2Sa 15:19
then say, *W* hast thou done so 2Sa 16:10
*W* wilt thou run, my son, seeing 2Sa 18:22
*w* then are ye the last to bring 2Sa 19:12
*W* wentest not thou with me, 2Sa 19:25
*w* then should thy servant be yet 2Sa 19:35
*w* then be ye angry for this 2Sa 19:42
*W* David said unto the Gibeonites, 2Sa 21:3
*W* is my lord the king come to his 2Sa 24:21
*W* his servants said unto him, Let 1Kin 1:2
*W* Nathan spake unto Bath-sheba 1Kin 1:11
*W* is this noise of the city being 1Kin 1:41
*W* the LORD said unto Solomon, 1Kin 11:11
*W* the king hearkened not unto the 1Kin 12:15
*w* all Israel made Omri, the 1Kin 16:16
*W* he said unto the messengers of 1Kin 20:9
*w* he said unto the driver of his 1Kin 22:34
*W* wilt thou go to him to day 2Kin 4:23
*W* he went again to meet him, and 2Kin 4:31
*w* consider, I pray you, and see 2Kin 5:7
*W* hast thou rent thy clothes 2Kin 5:8
*W* they arose and fled in the 2Kin 7:7
*w* came this mad fellow to thee 2Kin 9:11
*W* they came again, and told him 2Kin 9:36
*W* they spake to the king of 2Kin 17:26
*w* lift up thy prayer for the 2Kin 19:4
*w* that place is called Perez-uzza 1Chr 13:11
*W* Hanun took David's servants, and 1Chr 19:4
*W* Joab departed, and went 1Chr 21:4
*W* David blessed the LORD before 1Chr 29:10
*W* all the men of Israel assembled 2Chr 5:3
*W* now let the fear of the LORD be 2Chr 19:7
*W* he did evil in the sight of the 2Chr 22:4
*w* their anger was greatly kindled 2Chr 25:10
*W* the anger of the LORD was 2Chr 25:15
*W* the LORD his God delivered him 2Chr 28:5
*W* the wrath of the LORD was upon 2Chr 29:8
*w* their brethren the Levites did 2Chr 29:34
*W* the LORD brought upon them the 2Chr 33:11
*W* the king said unto me, Why is Neh 2:2
*w* Haman sought to destroy all the Est 3:6
*W* they called these days Purim Est 9:26
*W* is light given to him that is Job 3:20
shew me *w* thou contendest with me Job 10:2
*W* then hast thou brought me forth Job 10:18
*W* do I take my flesh in my teeth, Job 13:14
*W* hidest thou thy face, and Job 13:24
*W* are we counted as beasts, and Job 18:3
*W* do the wicked live, become old, Job 21:7
*w* I was afraid, and durst not shew Job 32:6
*W*, Job, I pray thee, hear my Job 33:1
*W* I abhor myself, and repent in Job 42:6
*W* doth the wicked contemn God Ps 10:13
*W* hidest thou thy face, and Ps 44:24
*W* should I fear in the days of Ps 49:5
*W* should the heathen say, Where Ps 79:10
*w* hast thou made all men in vain Ps 89:47
*W* should the heathen say, Where Ps 115:2
*W* is there a price in the hand of Prov 17:16
*W* I perceive that there is Eccl 3:22
*W* I praised the dead which are Eccl 4:2
*w* should God be angry at thy Eccl 5:6
*w*, when I looked that it should Is 5:4
*W* it shall come to pass, that Is 10:12
*W* my bowels shall sound like an Is 16:11
*W* glorify ye the LORD in the Is 24:15
*W* hear the word of the LORD, ye Is 28:14
*W* the Lord said, Forasmuch as Is 29:13
*W* thus saith the Holy One of Is 30:12
*w* lift up thy prayer for the Is 37:4
*W*, when I came, was there no man Is 50:2
*W* do ye spend money for that Is 55:2
*W* have we fasted, say they, and Is 58:3
*w* have we afflicted our soul, and Is 58:3
*W* art thou red in thine apparel, Is 63:2
*W* I will yet plead with you, Jer 2:9
*W* will ye plead with me Jer 2:29
*w* say my people, We are lords Jer 2:31

W a lion out of the forest shall ... Jer 5:6
W thus saith the LORD God of ... Jer 5:14
W doeth the LORD our God all ... Jer 5:19
W doth the way of the wicked ... Jer 12:1
w are all they happy that deal ... Jer 12:1
W come these things upon me ... Jer 13:22
W hath the LORD pronounced all ... Jer 16:10
W came I forth out of the womb to ... Jer 20:18
W hath the LORD done thus unto ... Jer 22:8
w are they cast out, he and his ... Jer 22:28
W their way shall be unto them as ... Jer 23:12
w should this city be laid waste ... Jer 27:17
w do I see every man with his ... Jer 30:6
W dost thou prophesy, and say, ... Jer 32:3
W the princes were wroth with ... Jer 37:15
w should he slay thee, that all ... Jer 40:15
W my fury and mine anger was ... Jer 44:6
W commit ye this great evil ... Jer 44:7
W have I seen them dismayed and ... Jer 46:5
W gloriest thou in the valleys, ... Jer 49:4
W, behold, the days come, saith ... Jer 51:52
W doth a living man complain, a ... Lam 3:39
W dost thou forget us for ever, ... Lam 5:20
W, as I live, saith the Lord GOD ... Eze 5:11
W I will bring the worst of the ... Eze 7:24
W thus saith the Lord GOD ... Eze 13:20
W, O harlot, hear the word of the ... Eze 16:35
w turn yourselves, and live ye ... Eze 18:32
W I caused them to go forth out ... Eze 20:10
W I gave them also statutes that ... Eze 20:25
W say unto the house of Israel, ... Eze 20:30
say unto thee, W sighest thou ... Eze 21:7
W I have delivered her into the ... Eze 23:9
W thus saith the Lord GOD ... Eze 24:6
W say unto them, Thus saith the ... Eze 33:25
W I poured my fury upon them for ... Eze 36:18
w I have consumed them in mine ... Eze 43:8
W at that time certain Chaldeans ... Dan 3:8
W, O king, let my counsel be ... Dan 4:27
W king Darius signed the writing ... Dan 6:9
w shut thou up the vision ... Dan 8:26
Knowest thou w I come unto thee ... Dan 10:20
w should they say among the ... Joel 2:17
W they cried unto the LORD, and ... Jonah 1:14
w lookest thou upon them that ... Hab 1:13
Yet ye say, W ... Mal 2:14
And w one ... Mal 2:15
W, if God so clothe the grass of ... Mt 6:30
W by their fruits ye shall know ... Mt 7:20
W think ye evil in your hearts ... Mt 9:4
W it is lawful to do well on the ... Mt 12:12
W I say unto you, All manner of ... Mt 12:31
little faith, w didst thou doubt ... Mt 14:31
W if thy hand or thy foot offend ... Mt 18:8
W they are no more twain, but one ... Mt 19:6
W ye be witnesses unto yourselves ... Mt 23:31
W, behold, I send unto you ... Mt 23:34
W if they shall say unto you, ... Mt 24:26
unto him, Friend, w art thou come ... Mt 26:50
W that field was called, The ... Mt 27:8
W neither thought I myself worthy ... Lk 7:7
W I say unto thee, Her sins, ... Lk 7:47
W then gavest not thou my money ... Lk 19:23
w would ye hear it again ... Jn 9:27
W of these men which have ... Acts 1:21
W, brethren, look ye out among ... Acts 6:3
what is the cause w ye are come ... Acts 10:21
W he saith also in another psalm, ... Acts 13:35
W my sentence is, that we trouble ... Acts 15:19
the more part knew not w they ... Acts 19:32
W if Demetrius, and the craftsmen ... Acts 19:38
W I take you to record this day, ... Acts 20:26
that he might know w they cried ... Acts 22:24
w he was accused of the Jews ... Acts 22:30
the cause w they accused him ... Acts 23:28
w he sent for him the oftener, and ... Acts 24:26
W I have brought him forth before ... Acts 25:26
w I beseech thee to hear me ... Acts 26:3
W, sirs, be of good cheer ... Acts 27:25
W I pray you to take some meat ... Acts 27:34
W God also gave them up to ... Rom 1:24
W, as by one man sin entered into ... Rom 5:12
W, my brethren, ye also are ... Rom 7:4
W the law is holy, and the ... Rom 7:12
W? Because they sought ... Rom 9:32
W ye must needs be subject, not ... Rom 13:5
W receive ye one another, as ... Rom 15:7
W I beseech you, be ye followers ... 1Cor 4:16
W, if meat make my brother to ... 1Cor 8:13
W let him that thinketh he ... 1Cor 10:12
W, my dearly beloved, flee from ... 1Cor 10:14
W whosoever shall eat this bread, ... 1Cor 11:27
W, my brethren, when ye come ... 1Cor 11:33
W I give you to understand, that ... 1Cor 12:3
W let him that speaketh in an ... 1Cor 14:13
W tongues are for a sign, not to ... 1Cor 14:22
W, brethren, covet to prophesy, ... 1Cor 14:39
W I beseech you that ye would ... 2Cor 2:8
W we labour, that, whether ... 2Cor 5:9
W henceforth know we no man after. 2Cor 5:16
W come out from among them ... 2Cor 6:17
W, though I wrote unto you, I did ... 2Cor 7:12
W shew ye to them, and before the ... 2Cor 8:24
W? because I love ... 2Cor 11:11
W then serveth the law ... Gal 3:19
W the law was our schoolmaster to ... Gal 3:24
W thou art no more a servant, but ... Gal 4:7
W I also, after I heard of your ... Eph 1:15
W remember, that ye being in time ... Eph 2:11
W I desire that ye faint not at ... Eph 3:13
W he saith, When he ascended up ... Eph 4:8
W putting away lying, speak every ... Eph 4:25
W he saith, Awake thou that ... Eph 5:14
W be ye not unwise, but ... Eph 5:17
W take unto you the whole armour ... Eph 6:13
W God also hath highly exalted ... Phil 2:9
W, my beloved, as ye have always ... Phil 2:12
W if ye be dead with Christ from ... Col 2:20
W we would have come unto you, ... 1Th 2:18
W when we could no longer forbear ... 1Th 3:1
W comfort one another with these ... 1Th 4:18
W comfort yourselves together, and ... 1Th 5:11
W also we pray always for you, ... 2Th 1:11
W I put thee in remembrance that ... 2Ti 1:6
W rebuke them sharply, that they ... Titus 1:13
W, though I might be much bold in ... Philem 8
W in all things it behoved him to ... Heb 2:17
W, holy brethren, partakers of ... Heb 3:1
W (as the Holy Ghost saith, To ... Heb 3:7
W I was grieved with that ... Heb 3:10
W he is able also to save them to ... Heb 7:25
w it is of necessity that this ... Heb 8:3
W when he cometh into the world, ... Heb 10:5
w God is not ashamed to be called ... Heb 11:16
W seeing we also are compassed ... Heb 12:1
W lift up the hands which hang ... Heb 12:12
W we receiving a kingdom which ... Heb 12:28
W Jesus also, that he might ... Heb 13:12
W, my beloved brethren, let every ... Jas 1:19
W lay apart all filthiness and ... Jas 1:21
W he saith, God resisteth the ... Jas 4:6
W gird up the loins of your mind, ... 1Pet 1:13
W laying aside all malice, and all ... 1Pet 2:1
W also it is contained in the ... 1Pet 2:6
W let them that suffer according ... 1Pet 4:19
W the rather, brethren, give ... 2Pet 1:10
W I will not be negligent to put ... 2Pet 1:12
W, beloved, seeing that ye look ... 2Pet 3:14
And w slew he him ... 1Jn 3:12
W, if I come, I will remember his ... 3Jn 10
said unto me, W didst thou marvel ... Rev 17:7

## WHEREIN

w there is life, I have given ... Gen 1:30
w is the breath of life, from ... Gen 6:17
flesh, w is the breath of life ... Gen 7:15
the land w thou art a stranger, ... Gen 17:8
to the land w thou hast sojourned ... Gen 21:23
the land w thou art a stranger ... Gen 28:4
the land w they were strangers ... Gen 36:7
Jacob dwelt in the land w his ... Gen 37:1
w they made them serve, was with ... Ex 1:14
pilgrimage, w they were strangers ... Ex 6:4
the houses, w they shall eat it ... Ex 12:7
for in the thing w they dealt ... Ex 18:11
them the way w they must walk ... Ex 18:20
w shall he sleep ... Ex 22:27
For w shall it be known here that ... Ex 33:16
w he hath sinned, come to his ... Lev 4:23
his ignorance w he erred and wist ... Lev 5:18
But the earthen vessel w it is ... Lev 6:28
w any work is done, it must be ... Lev 11:32
w there is plenty of water, shall ... Lev 11:36
All the days w the plague shall ... Lev 13:46
thing of skin, w the plague is ... Lev 13:52
wash the thing w the plague is ... Lev 13:54
thou shalt burn that w the plague ... Lev 13:57
w ye dwelt, shall ye not do ... Lev 18:3
w we have done foolishly ... Num 12:11
and w we have sinned ... Num 12:11
w is no blemish, and upon which ... Num 19:2
all their cities w they dwelt ... Num 31:10
vex you in the land w ye dwell ... Num 33:55
not pollute the land w ye are ... Num 35:33
which ye shall inhabit, w I dwell ... Num 35:34
A land w thou shalt eat bread ... Deut 8:9
w were fiery serpents, and ... Deut 8:15
w the nations which ye shall ... Deut 12:2
w the LORD thy God hath blessed ... Deut 12:7
or sheep, w is blemish, or any ... Deut 17:1
w thou trustedst, throughout all ... Deut 28:52
the wilderness w they chased them ... Josh 8:24
into the cave w they had been hid ... Josh 10:27
w the LORD's tabernacle dwelleth, ... Josh 22:19
to destroy the land w the ... Josh 22:33
us in all the way w we went ... Josh 24:17
see w his great strength lieth, ... Judg 16:5
w thy great strength lieth, and ... Judg 16:6
hast not told me w thy great ... Judg 16:15
the LORD is your way w ye go ... Judg 18:6
w the jewels of gold were, and put ... 1Sa 6:15
see w this sin hath been this day ... 1Sa 14:38
In all the places w I have walked ... 2Sa 7:7
in all w my father was afflicted ... 1Kin 2:26
w is the covenant of the LORD, ... 1Kin 8:21
the good way w they should walk ... 1Kin 8:36
all their transgressions w they ... 1Kin 8:50
w the man of God is buried ... 1Kin 13:31
w Jehoiada the priest instructed ... 2Kin 12:2
w the LORD commanded, saying, The . 2Kin 14:6
in their cities w they dwelt ... 2Kin 17:29
is this w thou trustest ... 2Kin 18:19
w this passover was holden to the ... 2Kin 23:23
Now these are the things w ... 2Chr 3:3
w is the covenant of the LORD, ... 2Chr 6:11
the good way, w they should walk ... 2Chr 6:27
w Solomon had built the house of ... 2Chr 8:1
the places w he built high places ... 2Chr 33:19
unto him, w was written thus ... Ezr 5:7
W was written, It is reported ... Neh 6:6
light in the way w they should go ... Neh 9:12
and the way w they should go ... Neh 9:19
in the day w they sold victuals ... Neh 13:15
all the things w the king had ... Est 5:11
W the king granted the Jews which ... Est 8:11
As the days w the Jews rested ... Est 9:22
Let the day perish w I was born ... Job 3:3
of the ice, and w the snow is hid ... Job 6:16
me to understand w I have erred ... Job 6:24
the wilderness, w there is no man ... Job 38:26
mount Zion, w thou hast dwelt ... Ps 74:2
the days w thou hast afflicted us ... Ps 90:15
the years w we have seen evil ... Ps 90:15
w all the beasts of the forest do ... Ps 104:20
w are things creeping innumerable ... Ps 104:25
In the way w I walked have they ... Ps 142:3
to know the way w I should walk ... Ps 143:8
all my labour w I have laboured ... Eccl 2:19
w I have shewed myself wise under ... Eccl 2:19
w he hath laboured under the sun ... Eccl 2:22
worketh in that w he laboureth ... Eccl 3:9
there is a time w one man ruleth ... Eccl 8:9
for w is he to be accounted of ... Is 2:22
from the hard bondage w thou wast ... Is 14:3
w shall go no galley with oars, ... Is 33:21
is this w thou trustest ... Is 36:4
w thou hast laboured from thy ... Is 47:12
did choose that w I delighted not ... Is 65:12
w thou trustedst, with the sword ... Jer 5:17
w ye trust, and unto the place ... Jer 7:14
w thou trustedst, they wearied ... Jer 12:5
things w there is no profit ... Jer 16:19
Cursed be the day w I was born ... Jer 20:14
let not the day w my mother bare ... Jer 20:14
is he a vessel w is no pleasure ... Jer 22:28
way, w they shall not stumble ... Jer 31:9
Take in thine hand the roll w ... Jer 36:14
Now the pit w Ishmael had cast ... Jer 41:9
may shew us the way w we may walk .. Jer 42:3
like a vessel w is no pleasure ... Jer 48:38
a land w no man dwelleth, neither ... Jer 51:43
the countries w ye are scattered ... Eze 20:34
w ye have been scattered ... Eze 20:41
doings, w ye have been defiled ... Eze 20:43
w she had played the harlot in ... Eze 23:19
into a city w is made a breach ... Eze 26:10
blood the land w thou swimmest ... Eze 32:6
w they have sinned, and will ... Eze 37:23
w your fathers have dwelt ... Eze 37:25
their garments w they minister ... Eze 42:14
their garments w they ministered ... Eze 44:19
w she burned incense to them, and ... Hos 2:13
as a vessel w is no pleasure ... Hos 8:8
w are more than sixscore thousand .. Jonah 4:11
and w have I wearied thee ... Mic 6:3
w thou hast transgressed against ... Zeph 3:11
out of the pit w is no water ... Zec 9:11
Yet ye say, W hast thou loved us ... Mal 1:2
W have we despised thy name ... Mal 1:6
ye say, W have we polluted thee ... Mal 1:7
Yet ye say, W have we wearied him ... Mal 2:17
But ye said, W shall we return ... Mal 3:7
But ye say, W have we robbed thee ... Mal 3:8
w most of his mighty works were ... Mt 11:20
the hour w the Son of man cometh ... Mt 25:13
they let down the bed w the sick ... Mk 2:4
w thou hast been instructed ... Lk 1:4
me in the days w he looked on me ... Lk 1:25
him all his armour w he trusted ... Lk 11:22
w never man before was laid ... Lk 23:53
w was never man yet laid ... Jn 19:41
in our own tongue, w we were born ... Acts 2:8
into this land, w ye now dwell ... Acts 7:4
W were all manner of fourfooted ... Acts 10:12
for w thou judgest another, thou ... Rom 2:1
faith into this grace w we stand ... Rom 5:2
that being dead w we were held ... Rom 7:6
the same calling w he was called ... 1Cor 7:20
w he is called, therein abide ... 1Cor 7:24
ye have received, and w ye stand ... 1Cor 15:1
that w they glory, they may be ... 2Cor 11:12
For what is it w ye were inferior ... 2Cor 12:13
w he hath made us accepted in the ... Eph 1:6
W he hath abounded toward us in ... Eph 1:8
W in time past ye walked ... Eph 2:2
not drunk with wine, w is excess ... Eph 5:18
w ye were also careful, but ye ... Phil 4:10
w also ye are risen with him ... Col 2:12
W I suffer trouble, as an evil ... 2Ti 2:9
W God, willing more abundantly to ... Heb 6:17
w was the candlestick, and the ... Heb 9:2
w was the golden pot that had ... Heb 9:4
W ye greatly rejoice, though now ... 1Pet 1:6
w few, that is, eight souls were ... 1Pet 3:20
W they think it strange that ye ... 1Pet 4:4
the true grace of God w ye stand ... 1Pet 5:12
w the heavens being on fire shall ... 2Pet 3:12
earth, w dwelleth righteousness ... 2Pet 3:13
even in those days w Antipas was ... Rev 2:13
w were made rich all that had ... Rev 18:19

## WHEREINSOEVER

Howbeit w any is bold, (I speak ... 2Cor 11:21

## WHEREINTO

w any of them falleth, whatsoever ... Lev 11:33
I bring into the land w he went ... Num 14:24
save that one w his disciples ... Jn 6:22

## WHEREOF

w I commanded thee that thou ... Gen 3:11
w any of the blood is brought ... Lev 6:30
in the skin w there is a hot ... Lev 13:24

W

*w* men bring an offering unto the Lev 27:9
camps, in the midst *w* I dwell Num 5:3
the weight *w* was an hundred and Num 7:19
the weight *w* was an hundred and Num 7:25
the weight *w* was an hundred and Num 7:37
the weight *w* was an hundred and Num 7:49
the weight *w* was an hundred and Num 7:61
the weight *w* was an hundred and Num 7:67
the weight *w* was an hundred and Num 7:73
the weight *w* was an hundred and Num 7:79
that is the well *w* the LORD spake Num 21:16
*w* he spake unto thee, saying, Let Deut 13:2
*w* thou canst not be healed Deut 28:27
by the way *w* I spake unto thee, Deut 28:68
*w* the LORD spake in that day Josh 14:12
*w* I spake unto you by the hand of Josh 20:2
*w* they were possessed, according Josh 22:9
*w* Samuel spake, he told him not 1Sa 10:16
*w* two thousand were with Saul in 1Sa 13:2
the weight *w* was a talent of gold 2Sa 12:30
sick of his sickness *w* he died 2Kin 13:14
*w* the LORD had said unto them, Ye 2Kin 17:12
the length *w* was according to the 2Chr 3:8
upon the place *w* thou hast said 2Chr 6:20
*w* were made vessels for the house 2Chr 24:14
*w* the LORD had said, In Jerusalem 2Chr 33:4
*w* one went on the right hand upon Neh 12:31
the poison *w* drinketh up my Job 6:4
the streams *w* shall make glad the Ps 46:4
into the midst *w* they are fallen Ps 57:6
*w* we are glad Ps 126:3
there any thing *w* it may be said Eccl 1:10
*w* every one bear twins, and none Song 4:2
*w* every one beareth twins, and Song 6:6
*w* ye say, It shall be delivered Jer 32:36
*w* ye say, It is desolate without Jer 32:43
*w* ye were afraid, shall follow Jer 42:16
destitute of that *w* it was full Eze 32:15
this is the day *w* I have spoken Eze 39:8
*w* the word of the LORD came to Dan 9:2
*w* she hath said, These are my Hos 2:12
those things *w* ye accuse him Lk 23:14
raised up, *w* we all are witnesses Acts 2:32
*w* we are witnesses Acts 3:15
new doctrine, *w* thou speakest, is Acts 17:19
*w* he hath given assurance unto Acts 17:31
*w* they were informed concerning Acts 21:24
all these things, *w* we accuse him Acts 24:8
the things *w* they now accuse me Acts 24:13
of these things *w* these accuse me Acts 25:11
things *w* I am accused of the Jews Acts 26:2
by works, he hath *w* to glory Rom 4:2
those things *w* ye are now ashamed Rom 6:21
I have therefore *w* I may glory Rom 15:17
the things *w* ye wrote unto me 1Cor 7:1
*w* ye had notice before, that the 2Cor 9:5
*W* I was made a minister, Eph 3:7
*w* he might trust in the flesh Phil 3:4
*w* ye heard before in the word of Col 1:5
*w* I Paul am made a minister Col 1:23
*W* I am made a minister, according Col 1:25
what they say, nor *w* they affirm 1Ti 1:7
*w* cometh envy, strife, railings, 1Ti 6:4
the world to come, *w* we speak Heb 2:5
*W* the Holy Ghost also is a Heb 10:15
*w* all are partakers, then are ye Heb 12:8
*w* they have no right to eat which Heb 13:10
*w* ye have heard that it should 1Jn 4:3

**WHEREON**

the land *w* thou liest, to thee Gen 28:13
for the place *w* thou standest is Ex 3:5
and also the ground *w* they are Ex 8:21
thou shalt wash that *w* it was Lev 6:27
*w* he lieth that hath the issue, Lev 15:4
*w* he sitteth, shall be unclean Lev 15:4
*w* he sat that hath the issue Lev 15:6
*w* is the seed of copulation, Lev 15:17
or on any thing *w* she sitteth Lev 15:23
all the bed *w* he lieth shall be Lev 15:24
Every bed *w* she lieth all the Lev 15:26
Every place *w* the soles of your Deut 11:24
for the place *w* thou standest is Josh 5:15
Surely the land *w* thy feet have Josh 14:9
*w* they set down the ark of the 1Sa 6:18
the tables *w* the shewbread was 2Chr 4:19
*W* do ye trust, that ye abide in 2Chr 32:10
fallen upon the bed *w* Esther was Est 7:8
him to be in safety, *w* he resteth Job 24:23
*w* there hang a thousand bucklers, Song 4:4
*w* if a man lean, it will go into Is 36:6
the sticks *w* thou writest shall Eze 37:20
find a colt tied, *w* never man sat Mk 11:2
the hill *w* their city was built Lk 4:29
them, and took up that *w* he lay Lk 5:25
a colt tied, *w* yet never man sat Lk 19:30
reap that *w* ye bestowed no labour Jn 4:38

**WHERESOEVER**

to his foot, *w* the priest looketh Lev 13:12
sojourn *w* thou canst sojourn 2Kin 8:1
*w* any breach shall be found 2Kin 12:5
*W* I have walked with all Israel, 1Chr 17:6
or go *w* it seemeth convenient Jer 40:5
*w* the children of men dwell, the Dan 2:38
For *w* the carcase is, there will Mt 24:28
*W* this gospel shall be preached Mt 26:13
*w* he taketh him, he teareth him Mk 9:18
*W* this gospel shall be preached Mk 14:9
*w* he shall go in, say ye to the Mk 14:14
*W* the body is, thither will the Lk 17:37

**WHERETO**

*w* might the strength of their Job 30:2
prosper in the thing *w* I sent it Is 55:11
*w* we have already attained, let Phil 3:16

**WHEREUNTO**

of the tribe *w* they are received Num 36:3
of the tribe *w* they are received Num 36:4
perish from off the land *w* ye go Deut 4:26
*w* the ark of the LORD hath come 2Chr 8:11
*w* the king advanced him, are they Est 10:2
*w* I may continually resort Ps 71:3
But to the land *w* they desire to Jer 22:27
*w* I will not do any more the like Eze 5:9
What is the high place *w* ye go Eze 20:29
But *w* shall I liken this Mt 11:16
*W* shall we liken the kingdom of Mk 4:30
*W* then shall I liken the men of Lk 7:31
and *w* shall I resemble it Lk 13:18
*W* shall I liken the kingdom of Lk 13:20
doubted of them *w* this would grow Acts 5:24
Saul for the work *w* I have called Acts 13:2
nigh *w* was the city of Lasea Acts 27:8
*w* ye desire again to be in Gal 4:9
*W* I also labour, striving Col 1:29
*W* he called you by our gospel, to 2Th 2:14
*W* I am ordained a preacher, and an 1Ti 2:7
doctrine, *w* thou hast attained 1Ti 4:6
*w* thou art also called, and hast 1Ti 6:12
*W* I am appointed a preacher, and 2Ti 1:11
*w* also they were appointed 1Pet 2:8
The like figure *w* even baptism 1Pet 3:21
*w* ye do well that ye take heed, 2Pet 1:19

**WHEREUPON**

every thing *w* any part of their Lev 11:35
the pillars *w* the house standeth Judg 16:26
of gold, *w* the shewbread was, 1Kin 7:48
*W* the king took counsel, and made 1Kin 12:28
*W* the princes of Israel and the 2Chr 12:6
*W* are the foundations thereof Job 38:6
*w* he was, to the threshold of the Eze 9:3
*w* thou hast set mine incense and Eze 23:41
that *w* they set their minds, Eze 24:25
*w* they slew their sacrifices Eze 40:41
*w* also they laid the instruments Eze 40:42
the piece *w* it rained not Amos 4:7
*W* he promised with an oath to Mt 14:7
*W* certain Jews from Asia found me Acts 24:18
*W* as I went to Damascus with Acts 26:12
*W*, O king Agrippa, I was not Acts 26:19
*W* neither the first testament was Heb 9:18

**WHEREWITH**

blessing *w* his father blessed him Gen 27:41
*w* the Egyptians oppress them Ex 3:9
thine hand, *w* thou shalt do signs Ex 4:17
the bread *w* I have fed you in the Ex 16:32
*w* thou smotest the river, take in Ex 17:5
things *w* the atonement was made Ex 29:33
of the sanctuary *w* they minister Num 3:31
*w* the odd number of them is to be Num 3:48
thereof, *w* they minister unto it Num 4:9
*w* they minister in the sanctuary, Num 4:12
*w* they minister about it, even Num 4:14
*w* they that were burnt had Num 16:39
*w* they have beguiled you in the Num 25:18
her bond *w* she hath bound her Num 30:4
every bond *w* she hath bound her Num 30:4
or of her bonds *w* she hath bound Num 30:5
of her lips, *w* she bound her soul Num 30:6
her bonds *w* she bound her soul Num 30:7
*w* she bound her soul, of none Num 30:8
*w* they have bound their souls, Num 30:9
every bond *w* she bound her soul Num 30:11
*w* he may die, and he die, he is a Num 35:17
*w* he may die, and he die, he is a Num 35:18
*w* a man may die, seeing him not, Num 35:23
*w* the LORD was wroth against you Deut 9:19
of that *w* the LORD thy God hath Deut 15:14
vesture, *w* thou coverest thyself Deut 22:12
*w* thine enemies shall distress Deut 28:53
*w* thine enemies shall distress Deut 28:55
*w* thine enemy shall distress thee Deut 28:57
of thine heart *w* thou shalt fear Deut 28:67
*w* Moses the man of God blessed Deut 33:1
*w* he stretched out the spear, Josh 8:26
Oh my Lord, *w* shall I save Israel Judg 6:15
*w* Abimelech hired vain and light Judg 9:4
*w* by me they honour God and man, Judg 9:9
*w* thou saidst, Who is Abimelech, Judg 9:38
*w* thou mightest be bound to Judg 16:6
thee, *w* thou mightest be bound Judg 16:10
tell me *w* thou mightest be bound Judg 16:13
tell us *w* we shall send it to his 1Sa 6:2
*w* they have forsaken me, and 1Sa 8:8
for *w* should he reconcile himself 1Sa 29:4
so that the hatred *w* he hated her 2Sa 13:15
than the love *w* he had loved her 2Sa 13:15
*w* shall I make the atonement, 2Sa 21:3
*w* I have made supplication before 1Kin 8:59
thereof, *w* Baasha had builded 1Kin 15:22
in his sin *w* he made Israel to 1Kin 15:26
by his provocation *w* he provoked 1Kin 15:30
in his sin *w* he made Israel to 1Kin 15:34
in his sin *w* he made Israel to 1Kin 16:26
for the provocation *w* thou hast 1Kin 21:22
And the LORD said unto him, *W* 1Kin 22:22
his might *w* he fought against 2Kin 13:12
beside his sin *w* he made Judah to 2Kin 21:16
*w* his anger was kindled against 2Kin 23:26
of brass *w* they ministered 2Kin 25:14
*w* Solomon made the brasen sea, and 1Chr 18:8
after the numbering *w* David his 2Chr 2:17
thereof, *w* Baasha was building 2Chr 16:6
And the LORD said unto him, *W* 2Chr 18:20
against the house *w* I have war 2Chr 35:21
*w* thou didst testify against them Neh 9:34
or with speeches *w* he can do no Job 15:3
*w* they have reproached thee, O Ps 79:12
*W* thine enemies have reproached, Ps 89:51
*w* they have reproached the Ps 89:51
*w* he hath girded himself Ps 93:1
for a girdle *w* he is girded Ps 109:19
So shall I have *w* to answer him Ps 119:42
*W* the mower filleth not his hand Ps 129:7
king Solomon with the crown *w* his Song 3:11
This is the rest *w* ye may cause Is 28:12
*w* the servants of the king of Is 37:6
*w* I said I would benefit them Jer 18:10
*w* their enemies, and they that Jer 19:9
*w* ye fight against the king of Jer 21:4
this is the name *w* she shall be Jer 33:16
of brass *w* they ministered Jer 52:18
*w* the LORD hath afflicted me in Lam 1:12
the daubing *w* ye have daubed it Eze 13:12
*w* ye there hunt the souls to make Eze 13:20
*w* I fed thee, thou hast even set Eze 16:19
his labour *w* he served against it Eze 29:20
*w* they shall lament her Eze 32:16
for their idols *w* they had Eze 36:18
*w* they slew the burnt offering Eze 40:42
*w* his spirit was troubled, and his Dan 2:1
*W* shall I come before the LORD, Mic 6:6
this shall be the plague *w* the Zec 14:12
*w* the LORD will smite the heathen Zec 14:18
him for the fear *w* he feared me Mal 2:5
his savour, *w* shall it be salted Mt 5:13
blasphemies *w* soever they shall Mk 3:28
his saltness, *w* will ye season it Mk 9:50
savour, *w* shall it be seasoned Lk 14:34
unto him, Make ready *w* I may sup Lk 17:8
with the towel *w* he was girded Jn 13:5
that the love *w* thou hast loved Jn 17:26
things *w* one may edify another Rom 14:19
by the comfort *w* we ourselves are 2Cor 1:4
but by the consolation *w* he was 2Cor 7:7
*w* I think to be bold against some 2Cor 10:2
*w* Christ hath made us free Gal 5:1
for his great love *w* he loved us Eph 2:4
of the vocation *w* ye are called Eph 4:1
*w* ye shall be able to quench all Eph 6:16
for all the joy *w* we joy for your 1Th 3:9
*w* he was sanctified, an unholy Heb 10:29

**WHEREWITHAL**

*W* shall a young man cleanse his Ps 119:9
or, *W* shall we be clothed Mt 6:31

**WHET**

If I *w* my glittering sword, and Deut 32:41
he turn not, he will *w* his sword Ps 7:12
Who *w* their tongue like a sword, Ps 64:3
be blunt, and he do not *w* the edge Eccl 10:10

**WHETHER**

see *w* they have done altogether Gen 18:21
to wit *w* the LORD had made his Gen 24:21
*w* thou be my very son Esau or not Gen 27:21
*w* stolen by day, or stolen by Gen 31:39
see *w* it be well with thy Gen 37:14
know now *w* it be thy son's coat Gen 37:32
*w* there be any truth in you Gen 42:16
as to tell the man *w* ye had yet a Gen 43:6
Egypt, and see *w* they be yet alive Ex 4:18
*w* he be a stranger, or born in Ex 12:19
*w* they will walk in my law, or no Ex 16:4
*w* it be beast or man, it shall Ex 19:13
*W* he have gored a son, or have Ex 21:31
*w* it be ox, or ass, or sheep Ex 22:4
to see *w* he have put his hand Ex 22:8
*w* it be for ox, for ass, for Ex 22:9
*w* ox or sheep, that is male Ex 34:19
*w* it be a male or female, he Lev 3:1
*w* he hath seen or known of it Lev 5:1
*w* it be a carcase of an unclean Lev 5:2
*w* it be of fowl or of beast, in Lev 7:26
*w* it be any vessel of wood, or Lev 11:32
*w* it be oven, or ranges for pots, Lev 11:35
*w* it be a woollen garment, or a Lev 13:47
*W* it be in the warp, or woof Lev 13:48
*w* in a skin, or in any thing made Lev 13:48
*w* warp or woof, in woollen or in Lev 13:52
*w* it be bare within or without Lev 13:55
*w* his flesh run with his issue, Lev 15:3
*w* it be one of your own country, Lev 16:29
*w* it be one of your own country, Lev 17:15
*w* she be born at home, or born Lev 18:9
*w* it be cow or ewe, ye shall not Lev 22:28
value it, *w* it be good or bad Lev 27:12
estimate it, *w* it be good or bad Lev 27:14
*w* it be ox, or sheep Lev 27:26
*w* of the seed of the land, or of Lev 27:30
not search *w* it be good or bad Lev 27:33
*w* it was by day or by night that Num 9:21
Or *w* it were two days, or a month Num 9:22
thou shalt see now *w* my word Num 11:23
*w* they be strong or weak, few or Num 13:18
dwell in, *w* it be good or bad Num 13:19
*w* in tents, or in strong holds Num 13:19
*w* it be fat or lean Num 13:20
*w* there be wood therein, or not Num 13:20
*w* he be born in the land, or a Num 15:30
*w* it be of men or beasts, shall Num 18:15

*w* there hath been any such thing Deut 4:32
heart, *w* thou wouldest keep his Deut 8:2
to know *w* ye love the LORD your Deut 13:3
a sacrifice, *w* it be ox or sheep Deut 18:3
*w* they be young ones, or eggs, and Deut 22:6
*w* he be of thy brethren, or of Deut 24:14
*w* the gods which your fathers Josh 24:15
*w* they will keep the way of the Judg 2:22
to know *w* they would hearken unto Judg 3:4
*W* is better for you, either that Judg 9:2
that we may know *w* our way which Judg 18:5
not young men, *w* poor or rich Ruth 3:10
Who can tell *w* GOD will be 2Sa 12:22
*w* in death or life, even there 2Sa 15:21
*W* they be come out for peace, 1Kin 20:18
or *w* they be come out for war, 1Kin 20:18
*w* any thing would come from him 1Kin 20:33
of Baal-zebub the god of Ekron *w* 2Kin 1:2
*w* with many, or with them that 2Chr 14:11
*w* small or great 2Chr 15:13
*w* man or woman 2Chr 15:13
their seed, *w* they were of Israel Ezr 2:59
*w* it be so, that a decree was Ezr 5:17
*w* it be unto death, or to Ezr 7:26
their seed, *w* they were of Israel Neh 7:61
to see *w* Mordecai's matters would Est 3:4
*w* man or woman, shall come unto Est 4:11
who knoweth *w* thou art come to Est 4:14
*w* it be done against a nation, or Job 34:29
*w* thou refuse, or *w* thou Job 34:33
*w* for correction, or for his land Job 37:13
*w* his work be pure Prov 20:11
and *w* it be right Prov 20:11
*w* he rage or laugh, there is no Prov 29:9
who knoweth *w* he shall be a wise Eccl 2:19
is sweet, *w* he eat little or much Eccl 5:12
thou knowest not *w* shall prosper Eccl 11:6
or *w* they both shall be alike Eccl 11:6
*w* it be good, or *w* it be Eccl 12:14
to see *w* the vine flourished, and Song 6:11
*w* the tender grape appear, and the Song 7:12
see *w* a man doth travail with Jer 30:6
*W* it be good, or *w* it be Jer 42:6
*w* they will hear, or *w* they Eze 2:5
*w* they will hear, or *w* they Eze 2:7
*w* they will hear, or *w* they Eze 3:11
or torn, *w* it be fowl or beast Eze 44:31
For *w* is easier, to say, Thy sins Mt 9:5
*W* of them twain did the will of Mt 21:31
for *w* is greater, the gold, or Mt 23:17
for *w* is greater, the gift, or Mt 23:19
that thou tell us *w* thou be the Mt 26:63
*W* of the twain will ye that I Mt 27:21
let us see *w* Elias will come to Mt 27:49
*W* is it easier to say to the sick Mk 2:9
*w* he would heal him on the Mk 3:2
let us see *w* Elias will come to Mk 15:36
he asked him *w* he had been any Mk 15:44
*w* he were the Christ, or not Lk 3:15
*W* is easier, to say, Thy sins be Lk 5:23
*w* he would heal on the sabbath Lk 6:7
*w* he have sufficient to finish it Lk 14:28
consulteth *w* he be able with ten Lk 14:31
For *w* is greater, he that sitteth Lk 22:27
he asked *w* the man were a Lk 23:6
*w* it be of God Jn 7:17
or *w* I speak of myself Jn 7:17
*W* he be a sinner or no, I know Jn 9:25
shew *w* of these two thou hast Acts 1:24
*W* it be right in the sight of God Acts 4:19
Tell me *w* ye sold the land for so Acts 5:8
*w* they were men or women, he Acts 9:2
And called, and asked *w* Simon Acts 10:18
daily, *w* those things were so Acts 17:11
heard *w* there be any Holy Ghost Acts 19:2
I asked him *w* he would go to Acts 25:20
*w* of sin unto death, or of Rom 6:16
*w* prophecy, let us prophesy Rom 12:6
For *w* we live, we live unto the Rom 14:8
*w* we die, we die unto the Lord Rom 14:8
*w* we live therefore, or die, we Rom 14:8
I know not *w* I baptized any other 1Cor 1:16
*W* Paul, or Apollos, or Cephas, or 1Cor 3:22
*w* thou shalt save thy husband 1Cor 7:16
*w* thou shalt save thy wife 1Cor 7:16
*w* in heaven or in earth, (as 1Cor 8:5
*W* therefore ye eat, or drink, or 1Cor 10:31
*w* we be Jews or Gentiles 1Cor 12:13
*w* we be bond or free 1Cor 12:13
*w* one member suffer, all the 1Cor 12:26
but *w* there be prophecies, they 1Cor 13:8
*w* there be tongues, they shall 1Cor 13:8
*w* there be knowledge, it shall 1Cor 13:8
*w* pipe or harp, except they give 1Cor 14:7
Therefore *w* it were I or they, so 1Cor 15:11
*w* we be afflicted, it is for your 2Cor 1:6
or *w* we be comforted, it is for 2Cor 1:6
*w* ye be obedient in all things 2Cor 2:9
*w* present or absent, we may be 2Cor 5:9
he hath done, *w* it be good or bad 2Cor 5:10
For *w* we be beside ourselves, it 2Cor 5:13
or *w* we be sober, it is for your 2Cor 5:13
*W* any do enquire of Titus, he is 2Cor 8:23
(*w* in the body, I cannot tell 2Cor 12:2
or *w* out of the body, I cannot 2Cor 12:2
(*w* in the body, or out of the 2Cor 12:3
yourselves, *w* ye be in the faith 2Cor 13:5
of the Lord, *w* he be bond or free Eph 6:8
*w* in pretence, or in truth, Phil 1:18
*w* it be by life, or by death Phil 1:20
that *w* I come and see you, or else Phil 1:27
*w* they be thrones, or dominions, Col 1:16
*w* they be things in earth, or Col 1:20
*w* we wake or sleep, we should 1Th 5:10
*w* by word, or our epistle 2Th 2:15
*w* it be to the king, as supreme 1Pet 2:13
try the spirits *w* they are of God 1Jn 4:1

**WHICH** See PREFACE.

**WHILE**

*W* the earth remaineth, seedtime Gen 8:22
*w* he lingered, the men laid hold Gen 19:16
*w* he yet lived, eastward, unto Gen 25:6
*w* he yet spake with them, Rachel Gen 29:9
*w* Joseph made himself known unto Gen 45:1
and wept on his neck a good *w* Gen 46:29
*w* my glory passeth by, that I Ex 33:22
thee with my hand *w* I pass by Ex 33:22
face shone *w* he talked with him Ex 34:29
*w* he doeth somewhat against any Lev 4:27
the *w* that it is shut up shall be Lev 14:46
*w* she lieth desolate without them Lev 26:43
*w* the flesh was yet between their Num 11:33
*w* the children of Israel were in Num 15:32
*w* I meet the LORD yonder Num 23:15
*w* he was zealous for my sake Num 25:11
*w* his heart is hot, and overtake Deut 19:6
*w* I am yet alive with you this Deut 31:27
*w* the children of Israel wandered Josh 14:10
And Ehud escaped *w* they tarried Judg 3:26
*W* Israel dwelt in Heshbon and her Judg 11:26
seven days, *w* their feast lasted Judg 14:17
it came to pass within a *w* after Judg 15:1
that beheld *w* Samson made sport Judg 16:27
*w* the flesh was in seething, with 1Sa 2:13
*w* the ark abode in Kirjath-jearim 1Sa 7:2
on,) but stand thou still a *w* 1Sa 9:27
*w* Saul talked unto the priest, 1Sa 14:19
thou shalt not only *w* yet I live 1Sa 20:14
the *w* that David was in the hold 1Sa 22:4
all the *w* they were in Carmel 1Sa 25:7
all the *w* we were with them 1Sa 25:16
*w* he dwelleth in the country of 1Sa 27:11
*w* there was war between the house 2Sa 3:6
to eat meat *w* it was yet day 2Sa 3:35
house for a great *w* to come 2Sa 7:19
*w* the child was yet alive, we 2Sa 12:18
for the child, *w* it was alive 2Sa 12:21
*W* the child was yet alive, I 2Sa 12:22
*w* they were in the way, that 2Sa 13:30
vow *w* I abode at Geshur in Syria 2Sa 15:8
Giloh, *w* he offered sacrifices 2Sa 15:12
will come upon him *w* he is weary 2Sa 17:2
*w* he was yet alive in the midst 2Sa 18:14
sustenance *w* he lay at Mahanaim 2Sa 19:32
thine enemies, *w* they pursue thee 2Sa 24:13
*w* thou yet talkest there with the 1Kin 1:14
*w* she yet talked with the king, 1Kin 1:22
*w* he yet spake, behold, Jonathan 1Kin 1:42
*w* thine handmaid slept, and laid 1Kin 3:20
the house, *w* it was in building 1Kin 6:7
Solomon his father *w* he yet lived 1Kin 12:6
And it came to pass after a *w* 1Kin 17:7
And it came to pass in the mean *w* 1Kin 18:45
*w* he yet talked with them, behold 2Kin 6:33
*w* he yet kept himself close 1Chr 12:1
house for a great *w* to come 1Chr 17:17
*w* that the sword of thine enemies 1Chr 21:12
Solomon his father *w* he yet lived 2Chr 10:6
*w* the land is yet before us 2Chr 14:7
is with you, *w* ye be with him 2Chr 15:2
*w* he was wroth with the priests, 2Chr 26:19
*w* he was yet young, he began to 2Chr 34:3
*w* they stand by, let them shut Neh 7:3
*w* Mordecai sat in the king's gate Est 2:21
*w* they were yet talking with him, Est 6:14
*W* he was yet speaking, there came Job 1:16
*W* he was yet speaking, there came Job 1:17
*W* he was yet speaking, there came Job 1:18
rain it upon him *w* he is eating Job 20:23
They are exalted for a little *w* Job 24:24
All the *w* my breath is in me, and Job 27:3
*w* there is none to deliver Ps 7:2
*w* they took counsel together Ps 31:13
For yet a little *w*, and the wicked Ps 37:10
*w* the wicked is before me Ps 39:1
*w* I was musing the fire burned Ps 39:3
*w* they continually say unto me, Ps 42:3
*w* they say daily unto me, Where Ps 42:10
Though *w* he lived he blessed his Ps 49:18
Thus will I bless thee *w* I live Ps 63:4
mine eyes fail *w* I wait for my Ps 69:3
but *w* their meat was yet in their Ps 78:30
*w* I suffer thy terrors I am Ps 88:15
to my God *w* I have my being Ps 104:33
*W* I live will I praise the LORD Ps 146:2
unto my God *w* I have any being Ps 146:2
*W* as yet he had not made the Prov 8:26
Chasten thy son *w* there is hope Prov 19:18
She riseth also *w* it is yet night Prov 31:15
is in their heart *w* they live Eccl 9:3
*w* the evil days come not, nor the Eccl 12:1
*W* the sun, or the light, or the Eccl 12:2
*W* the king sitteth at his table, Song 1:12
For yet a very little *w*, and the Is 10:25
*w* it is yet in his hand he eateth Is 28:4
Is it not yet a very little *w* Is 29:17
ye the LORD *w* he may be found Is 55:6
call ye upon him *w* he is near Is 55:6
have possessed it but a little *w* Is 63:18
*w* they are yet speaking, I will Is 65:24
*w* ye look for light, he turn it Jer 13:16
sun is gone down *w* it was yet day Jer 15:9
*w* he was yet shut up in the court Jer 33:1
*w* he was shut up in the court of Jer 39:15
Now *w* he was not yet gone back, Jer 40:5
yet a little *w*, and the time of Jer 51:33
*w* they sought their meat to Lam 1:19
*w* they were slaying them, and I Eze 9:8
*W* the word was in the king's Dan 4:31
for yet a little *w*, and I will Hos 1:4
For *w* they be folden together as Nah 1:10
*w* they are drunken as drunkards, Nah 1:10
Yet once, it is a little *w* Hag 2:6
away *w* they stand upon their feet Zec 14:12
But *w* he thought on these things, Mt 1:20
*W* he spake these things unto them Mt 9:18
*W* he yet talked to the people, Mt 12:46
in himself, but dureth for a *w*, Mt 13:21
But *w* men slept, his enemy came Mt 13:25
lest *w* ye gather up the tares, ye Mt 13:29
*w* he sent the multitudes away Mt 14:22
*W* he yet spake, behold, a bright Mt 17:5
*w* they abode in Galilee, Jesus Mt 17:22
*W* the Pharisees were gathered Mt 22:41
*W* the bridegroom tarried, they Mt 25:5
And *w* they went to buy, the Mt 25:10
ye here, *w* I go and pray yonder Mt 26:36
*w* he yet spake, lo, Judas, one of Mt 26:47
after a *w* came unto him they that Mt 26:73
*w* he was yet alive, After three Mt 27:63
and stole him away *w* we slept Mt 28:13
rising up a great *w* before day Mk 1:35
*w* the bridegroom is with them Mk 2:19
*W* he yet spake, there came from Mk 5:35
into a desert place, and rest a *w* Mk 6:31
*w* he sent away the people Mk 6:45
*w* he taught in the temple, How Mk 12:35
Sit ye here, *w* I shall pray Mk 14:32
*w* he yet spake, cometh Judas, one Mk 14:43
whether he had been any *w* dead Mk 15:44
that *w* he executed the priest's Lk 1:8
*w* they were there, the days were Lk 2:6
*w* the bridegroom is with them Lk 5:34
no root, which for a *w* believe Lk 8:13
*W* he yet spake, there cometh one Lk 8:49
*W* he thus spake, there came a Lk 9:34
But *w* they wondered every one at Lk 9:43
they had a great *w* ago repented Lk 10:13
*w* the other is yet a great way Lk 14:32
And he would not for a *w* Lk 18:4
And *w* he yet spake, behold a Lk 22:47
after a little *w* another saw him, Lk 22:58
*w* he yet spake, the cock crew Lk 22:60
*w* they communed together and Lk 24:15
*w* he talked with us by the way, Lk 24:32
*w* he opened to us the scriptures Lk 24:32
*w* they yet believed not for joy, Lk 24:41
*w* I was yet with you, that all Lk 24:44
*w* he blessed them, he was parted Lk 24:51
In the mean *w* his disciples Jn 4:31
but *w* I am coming, another Jn 5:7
Yet a little *w* am I with you, and Jn 7:33
of him that sent me, *w* it is day Jn 9:4
Yet a little *w* is the light with Jn 12:35
Walk *w* ye have the light, lest Jn 12:35
*W* ye have light, believe in the Jn 12:36
yet a little *w* I am with you Jn 13:33
Yet a little *w*, and the world Jn 14:19
A little *w*, and ye shall not see Jn 16:16
and again, a little *w*, and ye shall Jn 16:16
that he saith unto us, A little *w* Jn 16:17
and again, a little *w*, and ye shall Jn 16:17
is this that he saith, A little *w* Jn 16:18
of that I said, A little *w* Jn 16:19
and again, a little *w*, and ye shall Jn 16:19
*W* I was with them in the world, I Jn 17:12
*w* they beheld, he was taken up Acts 1:9
*w* they looked stedfastly toward Acts 1:10
Dorcas made, *w* she was with them Acts 9:39
but *w* they made ready, he fell Acts 10:10
Now *w* Peter doubted in himself Acts 10:17
*W* Peter thought on the vision, Acts 10:19
*W* Peter yet spake these words, Acts 10:44
ye know how that a good *w* ago God Acts 15:7
Now *w* Paul waited for them at Acts 17:16
this tarried there yet a good *w* Acts 18:18
*w* Apollos was at Corinth, Paul Acts 19:1
and eaten, and talked a long *w* Acts 20:11
even *w* I prayed in the temple, I Acts 22:17
*w* I stood before the council, Acts 24:20
*W* he answered for himself, Acts 25:8
*w* the day was coming on, Paul Acts 27:33
after they had looked a great *w* Acts 28:6
their thoughts the mean *w* Rom 2:15
*w* we were yet sinners, Christ Rom 5:8
*w* her husband liveth, she be Rom 7:3
For *w* one saith, I am of Paul 1Cor 3:4
eat no flesh *w* the world standeth 1Cor 8:13
but I trust to tarry a *w* with you 1Cor 16:7
*W* we look not at the things which 2Cor 4:18
*w* we seek to be justified by Gal 2:17
in pleasure is dead *w* she liveth 1Ti 5:6
which *w* some coveted after, they 1Ti 6:10
daily, *w* it is called To day Heb 3:13
*W* it is said, To day if ye will Heb 3:15
*w* as the first tabernacle was yet Heb 9:8
at all *w* the testator liveth Heb 9:17
For yet a little *w*, and he that Heb 10:37
*W* they behold your chaste 1Pet 3:2

*w* the ark was a preparing, 1Pet 3:20
after that ye have suffered a *w* 1Pet 5:10
deceivings *w* they feast with you 2Pet 2:13
*W* they promise them liberty, they 2Pet 2:19

### WHILES
*W* they see vanity unto thee, Eze 21:29
*w* they divine a lie unto thee, to Eze 21:29
*w* they minister in the gates of Eze 44:17
*w* he tasted the wine, commanded Dan 5:2
*w* I was speaking, and praying, and Dan 9:20
*w* I was speaking in prayer, even Dan 9:21
like an oven, *w* they lie in wait Hos 7:6
*w* thou art in the way with him Mt 5:25
*W* it remained, was it not thine Acts 5:4
*W* by the experiment of this 2Cor 9:13

### WHILST
put to death *w* it is yet morning Judg 6:31
*w* I leave it, and come down to you Neh 6:3
*W* it is yet in his greenness, and Job 8:12
*w* ye searched out what to say Job 32:11
own nets, *w* that I withal escape Ps 141:10
*W* their children remember their Jer 17:2
*w* we are at home in the body, we 2Cor 5:6
*w* he remembereth the obedience of 2Cor 7:15
*w* ye were made a gazingstock both Heb 10:33
*w* ye became companions of them Heb 10:33

### WHIP
A *w* for the horse, a bridle for Prov 26:3
The noise of a *w*, and the noise of Nah 3:2

### WHIPS
father hath chastised you with *w* 1Kin 12:11
father also chastised you with *w* 1Kin 12:14
my father chastised you with *w* 2Chr 10:11
my father chastised you with *w* 2Chr 10:14

### WHIRLETH
it *w* about continually, and the Eccl 1:6

### WHIRLWIND
take up Elijah into heaven by a *w* 2Kin 2:1
Elijah went up by a *w* into heaven 2Kin 2:11
Out of the south cometh the *w* Job 37:9
LORD answered Job out of the *w* Job 38:1
the LORD unto Job out of the *w* Job 40:6
shall take them away as with a *w* Ps 58:9
and your destruction cometh as a *w* Prov 1:27
As the *w* passeth, so is the Prov 10:25
flint, and their wheels like a *w* Is 5:28
like a rolling thing before the *w* Is 17:13
the *w* shall take them away as Is 40:24
away, and the *w* shall scatter them Is 41:16
and with his chariots like a *w* Is 66:15
and his chariots shall be as a *w* Jer 4:13
a *w* of the LORD is gone forth in Jer 23:19
forth in fury, even a grievous *w* Jer 23:19
a great *w* shall be raised up from Jer 25:32
the *w* of the LORD goeth forth Jer 30:23
forth with fury, a continuing *w* Jer 30:23
a *w* came out of the north, a Eze 1:4
shall come against him like a *w* Dan 11:40
wind, and they shall reap the *w* Hos 8:7
with the *w* out of the floor Hos 13:3
a tempest in the day of the *w* Amos 1:14
the LORD hath his way in the *w* Nah 1:3
came out as a *w* to scatter me Hab 3:14
But I scattered them with a *w* Zec 7:14

### WHIRLWINDS
As *w* in the south pass through Is 21:1
and shall go with *w* of the south Zec 9:14

### WHISPER
All that hate me *w* together Ps 41:7
speech shall *w* out of the dust Is 29:4

### WHISPERED
David saw that his servants *w* 2Sa 12:19

### WHISPERER
a *w* separateth chief friends Prov 16:28

### WHISPERERS
*w*, Rom 1:29

### WHISPERINGS
wraths, strifes, backbitings, *w* 2Cor 12:20

### WHIT
and all the spoil thereof every *w* Deut 13:16
And Samuel told him every *w* 1Sa 3:18
every *w* whole on the sabbath day Jn 7:23
his feet, but is clean every *w* Jn 13:10
not a *w* behind the very chiefest 2Cor 11:5

### WHITE
every one that had some *w* in it Gen 30:35
pilled *w* strakes in them Gen 30:37
made the *w* appear which was in Gen 30:37
I had three *w* baskets on my head Gen 40:16
wine, and his teeth *w* with milk Gen 49:12
and it was like coriander seed, *w* Ex 16:31
hair in the plague is turned *w* Lev 13:3
If the bright spot be *w* in the Lev 13:4
the hair thereof be not turned *w* Lev 13:4
if the rising be *w* in the skin Lev 13:10
and it have turned the hair *w* Lev 13:10
it is all turned *w* Lev 13:13
turn again, and be changed unto *w* Lev 13:16
if the plague be turned into *w* Lev 13:17
of the boil there be a *w* rising Lev 13:19
or a bright spot, *w* Lev 13:19
and the hair thereof be turned *w* Lev 13:20
there be no *w* hairs therein, and Lev 13:21
that burneth have a *w* bright spot Lev 13:24
somewhat reddish, or *w* Lev 13:24
in the bright spot be turned *w* Lev 13:25
there be no *w* hair in the bright Lev 13:26
bright spots, even *w* bright spots Lev 13:38
skin of their flesh be darkish *w* Lev 13:39
bald forehead, a *w* reddish sore Lev 13:42
be *w* reddish in his bald head Lev 13:43
Miriam became leprous, *w* as snow Num 12:10
Speak, ye that ride on *w* asses Judg 5:10
his presence a leper as *w* as snow 2Kin 5:27
being arrayed in *w* linen 2Chr 5:12
Where were *w*, green, and blue, Est 1:6
a pavement of red, and blue, and *w* Est 1:6
in royal apparel of blue and *w* Est 8:15
any taste in the *w* of an egg Job 6:6
it was *w* as snow in Salmon Ps 68:14
Let thy garments be always *w* Eccl 9:8
My beloved is *w* and ruddy, the Song 5:10
they shall be as *w* as snow Is 1:18
in the wine of Helbon, and *w* wool Eze 27:18
sit, whose garment was *w* as snow Dan 7:9
and to purge, and to make them *w* Dan 11:35
Many shall be purified, and made *w* Dan 12:10
the branches thereof are made *w* Joel 1:7
there red horses, speckled, and *w* Zec 1:8
And in the third chariot *w* horses Zec 6:3
the *w* go forth after them Zec 6:6
not make one hair *w* or black Mt 5:36
and his raiment was *w* as the light Mt 17:2
and his raiment *w* as snow Mt 28:3
shining, exceeding *w* as snow Mk 9:3
as no fuller on earth can *w* them Mk 9:3
side, clothed in a long *w* garment Mk 16:5
was altered, and his raiment was *w* Lk 9:29
for they are *w* already to harvest Jn 4:35
And seeth two angels in *w* sitting Jn 20:12
men stood by them in *w* apparel Acts 1:10
*w* like wool, as *w* as snow Rev 1:14
manna, and will give him a *w* stone Rev 2:17
and they shall walk with me in *w* Rev 3:4
shall be clothed in *w* raiment Rev 3:5
*w* raiment, that thou mayest be Rev 3:18
sitting, clothed in *w* raiment Rev 4:4
And I saw, and behold a *w* horse Rev 6:2
*w* robes were given unto every one Rev 6:11
the Lamb, clothed with *w* robes Rev 7:9
which are arrayed in *w* robes Rev 7:13
made them *w* in the blood of the Rev 7:14
And I looked, and behold a *w* cloud Rev 14:14
*w* linen, and having their breasts Rev 15:6
arrayed in fine linen, clean and *w* Rev 19:8
opened, and behold a *w* horse Rev 19:11
heaven followed him upon *w* horses Rev 19:14
clothed in fine linen, *w* Rev 19:14
And I saw a great *w* throne Rev 20:11

### WHITED
for ye are like unto *w* sepulchres Mt 23:27
God shall smite thee, thou *w* wall Acts 23:3

### WHITER
me, and I shall be *w* than snow Ps 51:7
than snow, they were *w* than milk Lam 4:7

### WHITHER
and *w* wilt thou go Gen 16:8
at every place *w* we shall come Gen 20:13
thee in all places *w* thou goest Gen 28:15
and *w* goest thou Gen 32:17
and I, *w* shall I go Gen 37:30
thee a place *w* he shall flee Ex 21:13
of the land *w* thou goest, lest it Ex 34:12
*w* I bring you, shall ye not do Lev 18:3
*w* I bring you to dwell therein Lev 20:22
unto the land *w* thou sentest us Num 13:27
come into the land *w* I bring you Num 15:18
city of his refuge, *w* he was fled Num 35:25
city of his refuge, *w* he was fled Num 35:26
*W* shall we go up Deut 1:28
all the kingdoms *w* thou passest Deut 3:21
in the land *w* ye go to possess it Deut 4:5
land *w* ye go over to possess it Deut 4:14
*w* the LORD shall lead you Deut 4:27
in the land *w* ye go to possess it Deut 6:1
land *w* thou goest to possess it Deut 7:1
the land, *w* ye go to possess it Deut 11:8
*w* thou goest in to possess it, is Deut 11:10
*w* ye go to possess it, is a land Deut 11:11
land *w* thou goest to possess it Deut 11:29
*w* thou goest to possess them, and Deut 12:29
thou shalt let her go *w* she will Deut 21:14
*w* thou shalt go forth abroad Deut 23:12
land *w* thou goest to possess it Deut 23:20
*w* thou goest to possess it Deut 28:21
among all nations *w* the LORD Deut 28:37
land *w* thou goest to possess it Deut 28:63
*w* the LORD thy God hath driven Deut 30:1
*w* the LORD thy God hath scattered Deut 30:3
land *w* thou goest to possess it Deut 30:16
*w* thou passest over Jordan to go Deut 30:18
as long as ye live in the land *w* Deut 31:13
*w* they go to be among them, and Deut 31:16
*w* ye go over Jordan to possess it Deut 32:47
die in the mount *w* thou goest up Deut 32:50
*w* the men went I wot not Josh 2:5
and the old man said, *W* goest thou Judg 19:17
for *w* thou goest, I will go Ruth 1:16
him and to his servant, *W* went ye 1Sa 10:14
*W* have ye made a road to day 1Sa 27:10
And David said, *W* shall I go up 2Sa 2:1
*w* shall I cause my shame to go 2Sa 13:13
seeing I go *w* I may, return thou, 2Sa 15:20
*w* they went down 2Sa 17:18
and go not forth thence any *w* 1Kin 2:36
out, and walkest abroad any *w* 1Kin 2:42
land *w* they were carried captives 1Kin 8:47
*w* my lord hath not sent to seek 1Kin 18:10
shall carry thee *w* I know not 1Kin 18:12
*w* he is gone down to possess it 1Kin 21:18
And he said, Thy servant went no *w* 2Kin 5:25
land *w* they are carried captive 2Chr 6:37
*w* they have carried them captives 2Chr 6:38
*w* he had fled from the presence 2Chr 10:2
And the rulers knew not *w* I went Neh 2:16
*W* the tribes go up, the tribes of Ps 122:4
*W* shall I go from thy spirit Ps 139:7
or *w* shall I flee from thy Ps 139:7
in the grave, *w* thou goest Eccl 9:10
*W* is thy beloved gone, O thou Song 6:1
*w* is thy beloved turned aside Song 6:1
*w* we flee for help to be Is 20:6
the places *w* I have driven them Jer 8:3
unto thee, *W* shall we go forth Jer 15:2
the lands *w* he had driven them Jer 16:15
*w* the LORD had sent him to Jer 19:14
place *w* they have led him captive Jer 22:12
countries *w* I have driven them Jer 23:3
all countries *w* I had driven them Jer 23:8
in all places *w* I shall drive Jer 24:9
seek the peace of the city *w* I Jer 29:7
the places *w* I have driven you Jer 29:14
the nations *w* I have driven them Jer 29:18
nations *w* I have scattered thee Jer 30:11
*w* I have driven them in mine Jer 32:37
*w* it seemeth good and convenient Jer 40:4
of all places *w* they were driven Jer 40:12
in the place *w* ye desire to go and Jer 42:22
*w* they had been driven, to dwell Jer 43:5
*w* ye be gone to dwell, that ye Jer 44:8
a prey in all places *w* thou goest Jer 45:5
the nations *w* I have driven thee Jer 46:28
there shall be no nation *w* the Jer 49:36
*w* the spirit was to go, they went Eze 1:12
the Gentiles, *w* I will drive them Eze 4:13
remember me among the nations *w* Eze 6:9
but to the place *w* the head Eze 10:11
among the heathen *w* they come Eze 12:16
the people *w* they were scattered Eze 29:13
*w* they went, they profaned my Eze 36:20
among the heathen, they *w* went Eze 36:21
among the heathen, *w* ye went Eze 36:22
*w* they be gone, and will gather Eze 37:21
shall live *w* the river cometh Eze 47:9
countries *w* thou hast driven them Dan 9:7
of the place *w* ye have sold them Joel 3:7
Then said I, *W* goest thou Zec 2:2
*W* do these bear the ephah Zec 5:10
and place, *w* he himself would come Lk 10:1
unto the village, *w* they went Lk 24:28
whence it cometh, and *w* it goeth Jn 3:8
ship was at the land *w* they went Jn 6:21
*W* will he go, that we shall not Jn 7:35
I know whence I came, and *w* I go Jn 8:14
tell whence I come, and *w* I go Jn 8:14
*w* I go, ye cannot come Jn 8:21
he saith, *W* I go, ye cannot come Jn 8:22
darkness knoweth not *w* he goeth Jn 12:35
the Jews, *W* I go, ye cannot come Jn 13:33
said unto him, Lord, *w* goest thou Jn 13:36
*W* I go, thou canst not follow me Jn 13:36
*w* I go ye know, and the way ye Jn 14:4
Lord, we know not *w* thou goest Jn 14:5
of you asketh me, *W* goest thou Jn 16:5
temple, *w* the Jews always resort Jn 18:20
and walkedst *w* thou wouldest Jn 21:18
carry thee *w* thou wouldest not Jn 21:18
*W* the forerunner is for us Heb 6:20
went out, not knowing *w* he went Heb 11:8
and knoweth not *w* he goeth 1Jn 2:11

### WHITHERSOEVER
thou mayest prosper *w* thou goest Josh 1:7
thy God is with thee *w* thou goest Josh 1:9
*w* thou sendest us, we will go Josh 1:16
*W* they went out, the hand of the Judg 2:15
*w* he turned himself, he vexed 1Sa 14:47
And David went out *w* Saul sent him 1Sa 18:5
Keilah, and went *w* they could go 1Sa 23:13
And I was with thee *w* thou wentest 2Sa 7:9
LORD preserved David *w* he went 2Sa 8:6
LORD preserved David *w* he went 2Sa 8:14
doest, and *w* thou turnest thyself 1Kin 2:3
*w* thou shalt send them, and shall 1Kin 8:44
he prospered *w* he went forth 2Kin 18:7
been with thee *w* thou hast walked 1Chr 17:8
LORD preserved David *w* he went 1Chr 18:6
LORD preserved David *w* he went 1Chr 18:13
*w* the king's commandment and his Est 4:3
*w* the king's commandment and his Est 8:17
*w* it turneth, it prospereth Prov 17:8
he turneth it *w* he will Prov 21:1
*W* the spirit was to go, they went Eze 1:20
or on the left, *w* thy face is set Eze 21:16
*w* the rivers shall come, shall Eze 47:9
I will follow thee *w* thou goest Mt 8:19
*w* he entered, into villages, or Mk 6:56
I will follow thee *w* thou goest Lk 9:57
may bring me on my journey *w* I go 1Cor 16:6
helm, *w* the governor listeth Jas 3:4
which follow the Lamb *w* he goeth Rev 14:4

**WHO** See PREFACE.

**WHOLE**
watered the *w* face of the ground Gen 2:6
compasseth the *w* land of Havilah Gen 2:11
compasseth the *w* land of Ethiopia Gen 2:13
that were under the *w* heaven Gen 7:19
were on the face of the *w* earth Gen 8:9
and of them was the *w* earth Gen 9:19
the *w* earth was of one language, Gen 11:1
upon the face of the *w* earth Gen 11:4
Is not the *w* land before thee Gen 13:9
so the *w* age of Jacob was an Gen 47:28
covered the face of the *w* earth Ex 10:15
and the *w* assembly of the Ex 12:6
the *w* congregation of the Ex 16:2
to kill this *w* assembly with Ex 16:3
as Aaron spake unto the *w* Ex 16:10
the *w* mount quaked greatly Ex 19:18
burn the *w* ram upon the altar Ex 29:18
the *w* rump, it shall he take off Lev 3:9
Even the *w* bullock shall he carry Lev 4:12
if the *w* congregation of Israel Lev 4:13
he shall offer one out of the *w* Lev 7:14
Moses burnt the *w* ram upon the Lev 8:21
the *w* house of Israel, bewail the Lev 10:6
within a *w* year after it is sold Lev 25:29
the charge of the *w* congregation Num 3:7
thou shalt gather the *w* assembly Num 8:9
of a *w* piece shalt thou make them Num 10:2
But even a *w* month, until it come Num 11:20
that they may eat a *w* month Num 11:21
the *w* congregation said unto them Num 14:2
you, according to your *w* number Num 14:29
even the *w* congregation, into the Num 20:1
Israel, even the *w* congregation, Num 20:22
that are under the *w* heaven Deut 2:25
all nations under the *w* heaven Deut 4:19
of the LORD thy God of *w* stones Deut 27:6
that the *w* land thereof is Deut 29:23
*w* burnt sacrifice upon thine Deut 33:10
in the camp, till they were *w* Josh 5:8
of Moses, an altar of *w* stones Josh 8:31
not to go down about a *w* day Josh 10:13
So Joshua took the *w* land Josh 11:23
the *w* congregation of the Josh 18:1
the *w* congregation of the Josh 22:12
Thus saith the *w* congregation of Josh 22:16
with the *w* congregation of Israel Josh 22:18
and was there four *w* months Judg 19:2
the *w* congregation sent some to Judg 21:13
because my life is yet *w* in me 2Sa 1:9
good to the *w* house of Benjamin 2Sa 3:19
even among the *w* multitude of 2Sa 6:19
the *w* family is risen against 2Sa 14:7
the *w* house he overlaid with gold 1Kin 6:22
also the *w* altar that was by the 1Kin 6:22
the *w* kingdom out of his hand 1Kin 11:34
For the *w* house of Ahab shall 2Kin 9:8
blessed the *w* congregation of 2Chr 6:3
and sought him with their *w* desire 2Chr 15:15
to and fro throughout the *w* earth 2Chr 16:9
The *w* number of the chief of the 2Chr 26:12
the *w* assembly took counsel to 2Chr 30:23
them, according to the *w* law 2Chr 33:8
The *w* congregation together was Ezr 2:64
The *w* congregation together was Neh 7:66
the *w* kingdom of Ahasuerus Est 3:6
he woundeth, and his hands make *w* Job 5:18
and seeth under the *w* heaven Job 28:24
Or who hath disposed the *w* world Job 34:13
directeth it under the *w* heaven Job 37:3
is under the *w* heaven is mine Job 41:11
thee, O LORD, with my *w* heart Ps 9:1
situation, the joy of the *w* earth Ps 48:2
offering and *w* burnt offering Ps 51:19
let the *w* earth be filled with Ps 72:19
of the LORD of the *w* earth Ps 97:5
he brake the *w* staff of bread Ps 105:16
praise the LORD with my *w* heart Ps 111:1
and that seek him with the *w* heart Ps 119:2
With my *w* heart have I sought Ps 119:10
shall observe it with my *w* heart Ps 119:34
thy favour with my *w* heart Ps 119:58
keep thy precepts with my *w* heart Ps 119:69
I cried with my *w* heart Ps 119:145
will praise thee with my *w* heart Ps 138:1
and *w*, as those that go down into Prov 1:12
but the *w* disposing thereof is of Prov 16:33
shewed before the *w* congregation Prov 26:26
the conclusion of the *w* matter Eccl 12:13
for this is the *w* duty of man Eccl 12:13
the *w* head is sick Is 1:5
and the *w* heart faint Is 1:5
the *w* stay of bread Is 3:1
and the *w* stay of water Is 3:1
the *w* earth is full of his glory Is 6:3
his *w* work upon mount Zion Is 10:12
to destroy the *w* land Is 13:5
The *w* earth is at rest, and is Is 14:7
that is purposed upon the *w* earth Is 14:26
*w* Palestina, because the rod of Is 14:29
*w* Palestina, art dissolved Is 14:31
and I am set in my ward *w* nights Is 21:8
even determined upon the *w* earth Is 28:22
The God of the *w* earth shall he Is 54:5
brasen walls against the *w* land Jer 1:18
turned unto me with her *w* heart Jer 3:10
for the *w* land is spoiled Jer 4:20
The *w* land shall be desolate Jer 4:27
The *w* city shall flee for the Jer 4:29
even the *w* seed of Ephraim Jer 7:15
the *w* land trembled at the sound Jer 8:16
the *w* land is made desolate, Jer 12:11
unto me the *w* house of Israel Jer 13:11
the *w* house of Judah, saith the Jer 13:11
man of contention to the *w* earth Jer 15:10
that cannot be made *w* again Jer 19:11
return unto me with their *w* heart Jer 24:7
this *w* land shall be a desolation Jer 25:11
the *w* valley of the dead bodies, Jer 31:40
my *w* heart and with my *w* soul Jer 32:41
the *w* house of the Rechabites Jer 35:3
the *w* army of the Chaldeans that Jer 37:10
I will pluck up, even this *w* land Jer 45:4
of the *w* earth cut in asunder Jer 50:23
praise of the *w* earth surprised Jer 51:41
her *w* land shall be confounded, Jer 51:47
of beauty, The joy of the *w* earth Lam 2:15
the *w* remnant of thee will I Eze 5:10
touching the *w* multitude thereof Eze 7:13
And their *w* body, and their backs, Eze 10:12
Behold, when it was *w*, it was Eze 15:5
beasts of the *w* earth with thee Eze 32:4
When the *w* earth rejoiceth, I Eze 35:14
bones are the *w* house of Israel Eze 37:11
mercy upon the *w* house of Israel Eze 39:25
they may keep the *w* form thereof Eze 43:11
the top of the mountain the *w* Eze 43:12
be for the *w* house of Israel Eze 45:6
mountain, and filled the *w* earth Dan 2:35
over the *w* province of Babylon Dan 2:48
should be over the *w* kingdom Dan 6:1
to set him over the *w* realm Dan 6:3
and shall devour the *w* earth Dan 7:23
of the kingdom under the *w* heaven Dan 7:27
west on the face of the *w* earth Dan 8:5
for under the *w* heaven hath not Dan 9:12
till three *w* weeks were fulfilled Dan 10:3
the strength of his *w* kingdom Dan 11:17
away captive the *w* captivity Amos 1:6
up the *w* captivity to Edom Amos 1:9
against the *w* family which I Amos 3:1
unto the Lord of the *w* earth Mic 4:13
but the *w* land shall be devoured Zeph 1:18
run to and fro through the *w* earth Zec 4:10
stand by the Lord of the *w* earth Zec 4:14
over the face of the *w* earth Zec 5:3
robbed me, even this *w* nation Mal 3:9
not that thy *w* body should be Mt 5:29
not that thy *w* body should be Mt 5:30
thy *w* body shall be full of light Mt 6:22
thy *w* body shall be full of Mt 6:23
the *w* herd of swine ran violently Mt 8:32
the *w* city came out to meet Jesus Mt 8:34
They that be *w* need not a Mt 9:12
touch his garment, I shall be *w* Mt 9:21
thy faith hath made thee *w* Mt 9:22
woman was made *w* from that hour Mt 9:22
and it was restored *w*, like as the Mt 12:13
the *w* multitude stood on the Mt 13:2
of meal, till the *w* was leavened Mt 13:33
as touched were made perfectly *w* Mt 14:36
was made *w* from that very hour Mt 15:28
dumb to speak, the maimed to be *w* Mt 15:31
if he shall gain the *w* world Mt 16:26
shall be preached in the *w* world Mt 26:13
unto him the *w* band of soldiers Mt 27:27
They that are *w* have no need of Mk 2:17
hand was restored *w* as the other Mk 3:5
the *w* multitude was by the sea on Mk 4:1
but his clothes, I shall be *w* Mk 5:28
thy faith hath made thee *w* Mk 5:34
in peace, and be *w* of thy plague Mk 5:34
ran through that *w* region round Mk 6:55
many as touched him were made *w* Mk 6:56
man, if he shall gain the *w* world Mk 8:36
thy faith hath made thee *w* Mk 10:52
more than all *w* burnt offerings Mk 12:33
preached throughout the *w* world Mk 14:9
the *w* council, and bound Jesus, and Mk 15:1
and they call together the *w* band Mk 15:16
the *w* land until the ninth hour Mk 15:33
the *w* multitude of the people Lk 1:10
They that are *w* need not a Lk 5:31
hand was restored *w* as the other Lk 6:10
the *w* multitude sought to touch Lk 6:19
found the servant *w* that had been Lk 7:10
Then the *w* multitude of the Lk 8:37
published throughout the *w* city Lk 8:39
thy faith hath made thee *w* Lk 8:48
only, and she shall be made *w* Lk 8:50
if he gain the *w* world, and lose Lk 9:25
thy *w* body also is full of light Lk 11:34
If thy *w* body therefore be full Lk 11:36
the *w* shall be full of light, as Lk 11:36
of meal, till the *w* was leavened Lk 13:21
thy faith hath made thee *w* Lk 17:19
the *w* multitude of the disciples Lk 19:37
dwell on the face of the *w* earth Lk 21:35
the *w* multitude of them arose, and Lk 23:1
himself believed, and his *w* house Jn 4:53
*w* of whatsoever disease he had Jn 5:4
unto him, Wilt thou be made *w* Jn 5:6
And immediately the man was made *w* Jn 5:9
answered them, He that made me *w* Jn 5:11
unto him, Behold, thou art made *w* Jn 5:14
was Jesus, which had made him *w* Jn 5:15
every whit *w* on the sabbath day Jn 7:23
that the *w* nation perish not Jn 11:50
man, by what means he is made *w* Acts 4:9
this man stand here before you *w* Acts 4:10
saying pleased the *w* multitude Acts 6:5
Jesus Christ maketh thee *w* Acts 9:34
that a *w* year they assembled Acts 11:26
sabbath day came almost the *w* Acts 13:44
and elders, with the *w* church Acts 15:22
the *w* city was filled with Acts 19:29
Paul dwelt two *w* years in his own Acts 28:30
spoken of throughout the *w* world Rom 1:8
know that the *w* creation groaneth Rom 8:22
mine host, and of the *w* church Rom 16:23
leaven leaveneth the *w* lump 1Cor 5:6
If the *w* body were an eye, where 1Cor 12:17
If the *w* were hearing, where were 1Cor 12:17
If therefore the *w* church be come 1Cor 14:23
he is a debtor to do the *w* law Gal 5:3
leaven leaveneth the *w* lump Gal 5:9
Of whom the *w* family in heaven and Eph 3:15
From whom the *w* body fitly joined Eph 4:16
Put on the *w* armour of God, that Eph 6:11
take unto you the *w* armour of God Eph 6:13
and I pray God your *w* spirit 1Th 5:23
be stopped, who subvert *w* houses Titus 1:11
whosoever shall keep the *w* law Jas 2:10
and able also to bridle the *w* body Jas 3:2
and we turn about their *w* body Jas 3:3
that it defileth the *w* body Jas 3:6
also for the sins of the *w* world 1Jn 2:2
the *w* world lieth in wickedness 1Jn 5:19
which deceiveth the *w* world Rev 12:9
of the earth and of the *w* world Rev 16:14

**WHOLESOME**
A *w* tongue is a tree of life Prov 15:4
and consent not to *w* words 1Ti 6:3

**WHOLLY**
it shall be *w* burnt Lev 6:22
for the priest shall be *w* burnt Lev 6:23
thou shalt not *w* reap the corners Lev 19:9
they are *w* given unto him out of Num 3:9
spread over it a cloth *w* of blue Num 4:6
For they are *w* given unto me from Num 8:16
they have not *w* followed me Num 32:11
for they have *w* followed the LORD Num 32:12
because he hath *w* followed the Deut 1:36
but I *w* followed the LORD my God Josh 14:8
because thou hast *w* followed the Josh 14:9
because that he *w* followed the Josh 14:14
I had *w* dedicated the silver unto Judg 17:3
a burnt offering *w* unto the LORD 1Sa 7:9
will be *w* at thy commandment 1Chr 28:21
being *w* at ease and quiet Job 21:23
that thou art *w* gone up to the Is 22:1
thee a noble vine, *w* a right seed Jer 2:21
she is *w* oppression in the midst Jer 6:6
it shall be *w* carried away Jer 13:19
If ye *w* set your faces to enter Jer 42:15
I not leave thee *w* unpunished Jer 46:28
but it shall be *w* desolate Jer 50:13
and all the house of Israel *w* Eze 11:15
and it shall rise up *w* as a flood Amos 8:8
it shall rise up *w* like a flood Amos 9:5
saw the city *w* given to idolatry Acts 17:16
very God of peace sanctify you *w* 1Th 5:23
give thyself *w* to them 1Ti 4:15

**WHOM** See PREFACE.

**WHOMSOEVER**
With *w* thou findest thy gods, let Gen 31:32
With *w* of thy servants it be Gen 44:9
*w* he toucheth that hath the issue Lev 15:11
of *w* I say unto thee, This shall Judg 7:4
So *w* the LORD our God shall drive Judg 11:24
of men, and giveth it to *w* he will Dan 4:17
of men, and giveth it to *w* he will Dan 4:25
of men, and giveth it to *w* he will Dan 4:32
he appointeth over it *w* he will Dan 5:21
to *w* the Son will reveal him Mt 11:27
but on *w* it shall fall, it will Mt 21:44
*W* I shall kiss, that same is he Mt 26:48
*W* I shall kiss, that same is he Mk 14:44
them one prisoner, *w* they desired Mk 15:6
and to *w* I will I give it Lk 4:6
For unto *w* much is given, of him Lk 12:48
but on *w* it shall fall, it will Lk 20:18
He that receiveth *w* I send Jn 13:20
that on *w* I lay hands, he may Acts 8:19
*w* ye shall approve by your 1Cor 16:3

**WHORE**
daughter, to cause her to be a *w* Lev 19:29
shall not take a wife that is a *w* Lev 21:7
profane herself by playing the *w* Lev 21:9
to play the *w* in her father's Deut 22:21
There shall be no *w* of the Deut 23:17
shalt not bring the hire of a *w* Deut 23:18
played the *w* against him, and went Judg 19:2
For a *w* is a deep ditch Prov 23:27
seed of the adulterer and the *w* Is 57:3
Thou hast played the *w* also with Eze 16:28
*w* that sitteth upon many waters Rev 17:1
thou sawest, where the *w* sitteth Rev 17:15
the beast, these shall hate the *w* Rev 17:16
for he hath judged the great *w* Rev 19:2

**WHOREDOM**
behold, she is with child by *w* Gen 38:24
lest the land fall to *w*, and the Lev 19:29
to commit *w* with Molech, from Lev 20:5
*w* with the daughters of Moab Num 25:1
through the lightness of her *w* Jer 3:9

neighings, the lewdness of thy *w* Jer 13:27
men, and didst commit *w* with them... Eze 16:17
unto thee on every side for thy *w* Eze 16:33
and commit ye *w* after their Eze 20:30
and poured their *w* upon her Eze 23:8
and they defiled her with their *w* Eze 23:17
thy *w* brought from the land of Eze 23:27
they, nor their kings, by their *w* Eze 43:7
Now let them put away their *w* Eze 43:9
the land hath committed great *w* Hos 1:2
they shall commit *w*, and shall not Hos 4:10
*W* and wine and new wine take away.. Hos 4:11
your daughters shall commit *w* Hos 4:13
your daughters when they commit *w*... Hos 4:14
they have committed *w* continually Hos 4:18
now, O Ephraim, thou committest *w* Hos 5:3
there is the *w* of Ephraim Hos 6:10

**WHOREDOMS**

forty years, and bear your *w* Num 14:33
so long as the *w* of thy mother 2Kin 9:22
like to the *w* of the house of 2Chr 21:13
hast polluted the land with thy *w* Jer 3:2
Is this of thy *w* a small matter Eze 16:20
thy *w* thou hast not remembered Eze 16:22
passed by, and multiplied thy *w* Eze 16:25
and hast increased thy *w*, to Eze 16:26
in thee from other women in thy *w* Eze 16:34
none followeth thee to commit *w* Eze 16:34
through thy *w* with thy lovers Eze 16:36
And they committed *w* in Egypt Eze 23:3
they committed *w* in their youth Eze 23:3
she committed her *w* with them Eze 23:7
left she her *w* brought from Egypt Eze 23:8
in her *w* more than her sister in Eze 23:11
more than her sister in her *w* Eze 23:11
And that she increased her *w* Eze 23:14
So she discovered her *w*, and Eze 23:18
Yet she multiplied her *w*, in Eze 23:19
of thy *w* shall be discovered Eze 23:29
both thy lewdness and thy *w* Eze 23:29
thou also thy lewdness and thy *w* Eze 23:35
Will they now commit *w* with her Eze 23:43
Go, take unto thee a wife of *w* Hos 1:2
and children of *w* Hos 1:2
put away her *w* out of her sight Hos 2:2
for they be the children of *w* Hos 2:4
for the spirit of *w* hath caused Hos 4:12
for the spirit of *w* is in the Hos 5:4
the *w* of the wellfavoured harlot Nah 3:4
selleth nations through her *w* Nah 3:4

**WHOREMONGER**

For this ye know, that no *w* Eph 5:5

**WHOREMONGERS**

For *w*, for them that defile 1Ti 1:10
but *w* and adulterers God will Heb 13:4
abominable, and murderers, and *w* Rev 21:8
are dogs, and sorcerers, and *w* Rev 22:15

**WHORE'S**

and thou hadst a *w* forehead Jer 3:3

**WHORES**

They give gifts to all *w* Eze 16:33
themselves are separated with *w* Hos 4:14

**WHORING**

they go a *w* after their gods, and Ex 34:15
daughters go a *w* after their gods Ex 34:16
thy sons go a *w* after their gods Ex 34:16
after whom they have gone a *w* Lev 17:7
off, and all that go a *w* after him Lev 20:5
to go a *w* after them, I will even Lev 20:6
after which ye use to go a *w* Num 15:39
go a *w* after the gods of the Deut 31:16
but they went a *w* after other Judg 2:17
Israel went thither a *w* after it Judg 8:27
went a *w* after Baalim, and made Judg 8:33
went a *w* after the gods of the 1Chr 5:25
of Jerusalem to go a *w*, like to 2Chr 21:13
all them that go a *w* from thee Ps 73:27
works, and went a *w* with their own... Ps 106:39
which go a *w* after their idols Eze 6:9
hast gone a *w* after the heathen Eze 23:30
they have gone a *w* from under Hos 4:12
thou hast gone a *w* from thy God Hos 9:1

**WHORISH**

For by means of a *w* woman a man.... Prov 6:26
I am broken with their *w* heart Eze 6:9
the work of an imperious *w* woman.... Eze 16:30

**WHOSE**

*w* seed is in itself, upon the Gen 1:11
*w* seed was in itself, after his Gen 1:12
All in *w* nostrils was the breath Gen 7:22
*w* top may reach unto heaven Gen 11:4
an Egyptian, *w* name was Hagar Gen 16:1
the uncircumcised man child *w* Gen 17:14
*w* name was Reumah, she bare also... Gen 22:24
And said, *W* daughter art thou Gen 24:23
the Canaanites, in *w* land I dwell Gen 24:37
her, and said, *W* daughter art thou.... Gen 24:47
asketh thee, saying, *W* art thou Gen 32:17
and *w* are these before thee Gen 32:17
Adullamite, *w* name was Hirah Gen 38:1
Canaanite, *w* name was Shuah Gen 38:2
his firstborn, *w* name was Tamar Gen 38:6
*w* these are, am I with child Gen 38:25
*w* are these, the signet, and Gen 38:25
but the man in *w* hand the cup is Gen 44:17
*w* branches run over the wall Gen 49:22
*w* name is Jealous, is a jealous Ex 34:14
every one *w* heart stirred him up, Ex 35:21
all the women *w* heart stirred Ex 35:26
*w* heart made them willing to Ex 35:29
in *w* heart the LORD had put Ex 36:2
even every one *w* heart stirred Ex 36:2
the man *w* hair is fallen off his Lev 13:40
*w* hand is not able to get that Lev 14:32
of him *w* seed goeth from him, and..... Lev 15:32
*w* blood was brought in to make Lev 16:27
upon *w* head the anointing oil was Lev 21:10
or a man *w* seed goeth from him Lev 22:4
*w* father was an Egyptian, went Lev 24:10
the man *w* eyes are open hath said Num 24:3
the man *w* eyes are open hath said... Num 24:15
a land *w* stones are iron Deut 8:9
out of *w* hills thou mayest dig Deut 8:9
*w* land the LORD thy God giveth Deut 19:1
a nation *w* tongue thou shalt not Deut 28:49
*w* heart turneth away this day Deut 29:18
the Amorites, in *w* land ye dwell Josh 24:15
the captain of *w* host was Sisera, Judg 4:2
the Amorites, in *w* land ye dwell Judg 6:10
*w* name he called Abimelech Judg 8:31
of the Danites, *w* name was Manoah.. Judg 13:2
of Sorek, *w* name was Delilah Judg 16:4
mount Ephraim, *w* name was Micah... Judg 17:1
him in *w* sight I shall find grace Ruth 2:2
the reapers, *W* damsel is this Ruth 2:5
under *w* wings thou art come to Ruth 2:12
kindred, with *w* maidens thou wast Ruth 3:2
*w* name was Kish, the son of Abiel 1Sa 9:1
*w* name was Saul, a choice young 1Sa 9:2
of men, *w* hearts God had touched 1Sa 10:26
*w* ox have I taken 1Sa 12:3
or *w* ass have I taken 1Sa 12:3
or of *w* hand have I received any 1Sa 12:3
*w* height was six cubits and a span 1Sa 17:4
*w* name was Jesse 1Sa 17:12
host, Abner, *w* son is this youth 1Sa 17:55
Enquire thou *w* son the stripling 1Sa 17:56
*W* son art thou, thou young man 1Sa 17:58
*w* possessions were in Carmel 1Sa 25:2
*w* name was Rizpah, the daughter 2Sa 3:7
his behalf, saying, *W* is the land 2Sa 3:12
*w* name is called by the name of 2Sa 6:2
of Saul a servant *w* name was Ziba 2Sa 9:2
had a young son, *w* name was Micha... 2Sa 9:12
a fair sister, *w* name was Tamar 2Sa 13:1
*w* name was Jonadab, the son of 2Sa 13:3
*w* name was Tamar 2Sa 14:27
*w* name was Shimei, the son of 2Sa 16:5
in *w* stead thou hast reigned 2Sa 16:8
*w* heart is as the heart of a lion 2Sa 17:10
*w* name was Ithra an Israelite, 2Sa 17:25
*w* name was Sheba, the son of 2Sa 20:1
the weight of *w* spear weighed 2Sa 21:16
the staff of *w* spear was like a 2Sa 21:19
Then spake the woman *w* the living... 1Kin 3:26
to his ways, *w* heart thou knowest 1Kin 8:39
*w* mother's name was Zeruah, a 1Kin 11:26
Then a lord on *w* hand the king 2Kin 7:2
on *w* hand he leaned to have the 2Kin 7:17
*w* son he had restored to life, 2Kin 8:1
*w* son he had restored to life, 2Kin 8:5
into *w* hand they delivered the 2Kin 12:15
*w* high places and *w* altars 2Kin 18:22
*W* sisters were Zeruiah, and 1Chr 2:16
another wife, *w* name was Atarah 1Chr 2:26
an Egyptian, *w* name was Jarha 1Chr 2:34
*w* number was in the days of David...... 1Chr 7:2
*w* sister's name was Maachah 1Chr 7:15
*w* wife's name was Maachah 1Chr 8:29
*w* names are these, Azrikam, 1Chr 8:38
*w* wife's name was Maachah 1Chr 9:35
*w* names are these, Azrikam, 1Chr 9:44
*w* faces were like the faces of 1Chr 12:8
cherubims, *w* name is called on it 1Chr 13:6
*w* spear staff was like a weaver's 1Chr 20:5
*w* fingers and toes were four and 1Chr 20:6
*w* brethren were strong men, Elihu 1Chr 26:7
his ways, *w* heart thou knowest 2Chr 6:30
*w* heart is perfect toward him 2Chr 16:9
LORD was there, *w* name was Oded..... 2Chr 28:9
with all them *w* spirit God had Ezr 1:5
*w* name was Sheshbazzar, whom he Ezr 5:14
*w* habitation is in Jerusalem, Ezr 7:15
*w* names are these, Eliphelet, Ezr 8:13
*w* name was Mordecai, the son of Est 2:5
in the land of Uz, *w* name was Job Job 1:1
light given to a man *w* way is hid Job 3:23
*w* foundation is in the dust, Job 4:19
*W* harvest the hungry eateth up, Job 5:5
*W* hope shall be cut off Job 8:14
*w* trust shall be a spider's web Job 8:14
into *w* hand God bringeth Job 12:6
In *w* hand is the soul of every Job 12:10
*w* foundation was overflown with a.... Job 22:16
and *w* spirit came from thee Job 26:4
*w* fathers I would have disdained Job 30:1
Out of *w* womb came the ice Job 38:29
*W* house I have made the Job 39:6
In *w* eyes a vile person is Ps 15:4
*w* belly thou fillest with thy hid Ps 17:14
In *w* hands is mischief, and their Ps 26:10
Blessed is he *w* transgression is Ps 32:1
is forgiven, *w* sin is covered Ps 32:1
in *w* spirit there is no guile Ps 32:2
*w* mouth must be held in with bit Ps 32:9
is the nation *w* God is the LORD Ps 33:12
in *w* mouth are no reproofs Ps 38:14
*w* teeth are spears and arrows, and Ps 57:4
*w* spirit was not stedfast with Ps 78:8
*w* name alone is JEHOVAH, art the Ps 83:18
Blessed is the man *w* strength is Ps 84:5
in *w* heart are the ways of them Ps 84:5
*W* feet they hurt with fetters Ps 105:18
*W* mouth speaketh vanity, and their.... Ps 144:8
*w* mouth speaketh vanity, and their.... Ps 144:11
is that people, *w* God is the LORD Ps 144:15
*w* hope is in the LORD his God Ps 146:5
*W* ways are crooked, and they Prov 2:15
*W* hatred is covered by deceit, Prov 26:26
*w* teeth are as swords, and their Prov 30:14
For there is a man *w* labour is in Eccl 2:21
*w* heart is snares and nets, and her Eccl 7:26
shall be as an oak *w* leaf fadeth Is 1:30
*w* breath is in his nostrils Is 2:22
*W* arrows are sharp, and all their Is 5:28
*w* substance is in them, when they Is 6:13
*w* graven images did excel them of Is 10:10
captives, *w* captives they were Is 14:2
*w* land the rivers have spoiled Is 18:2
*w* land the rivers have spoiled, Is 18:7
*w* antiquity is of ancient days Is 23:7
*w* merchants are princes Is 23:8
*w* traffickers are the honourable Is 23:8
peace, *w* mind is stayed on thee Is 26:3
*w* glorious beauty is a fading Is 28:1
*w* breaking cometh suddenly at an Is 30:13
*w* fire is in Zion, and his furnace Is 31:9
*w* high places and *w* altars Is 36:7
Chaldeans, *w* cry is in the ships Is 43:14
*w* right hand I have holden, to Is 45:1
the people in *w* heart is my law Is 51:7
divided the sea, *w* waves roared Is 51:15
eternity, *w* name is Holy Is 57:15
*w* waters cast up mire and dirt Is 57:20
of water, *w* waters fail not Is 58:11
a nation *w* language thou knowest Jer 5:15
*w* heart departeth from the LORD Jer 17:5
the LORD, and *w* hope the LORD is Jer 17:7
*w* roofs they have burned incense Jer 19:13
hand of them *w* face thou fearest Jer 22:25
upon *w* roofs they have offered Jer 32:29
for all *w* wickedness I have hid Jer 33:5
*w* name was Irijah, the son of Jer 37:13
shall know *w* words shall stand, Jer 44:28
*w* waters are moved as the rivers Jer 46:7
*w* name is the LORD of hosts, Jer 46:18
*w* name is the LORD of hosts Jer 48:15
they *w* judgment was not to drink Jer 49:12
*w* name is the LORD of hosts Jer 51:57
*w* words thou canst not understand Eze 3:6
But as for them *w* heart walketh Eze 11:21
*w* branches turned toward him, and Eze 17:6
*w* oath he despised Eze 17:16
*w* covenant he brake, even with Eze 17:16
in *w* sight I made myself known Eze 20:9
in *w* sight I brought them out Eze 20:14
in *w* sight I brought them forth Eze 20:22
*w* day is come, when iniquity Eze 21:25
more, until he come *w* right it is Eze 21:27
*w* day is come, when their Eze 21:29
*w* flesh is as the flesh of asses, Eze 23:20
*w* issue is like the issue of Eze 23:20
to the pot *w* scum is therein, and Eze 24:6
*w* scum is not gone out of it Eze 24:6
*W* graves are set in the sides of Eze 32:23
*w* appearance was like the Eze 40:3
*w* prospect is toward the south, Eze 40:45
the chamber *w* prospect is toward Eze 40:46
me forth toward the gate *w* Eze 42:15
*w* prospect is toward the east Eze 43:4
*w* leaf shall not fade, neither Eze 47:12
*w* dwelling is not with flesh Dan 2:11
*w* name was Belteshazzar, Art thou Dan 2:26
*w* brightness was excellent, stood Dan 2:31
*w* height was threescore cubits, Dan 3:1
upon *w* bodies the fire had no Dan 3:27
me, *w* name was Belteshazzar, Dan 4:8
*w* name was Belteshazzar, was Dan 4:19
*w* height reached unto the heaven, Dan 4:20
*W* leaves were fair, and the fruit Dan 4:21
upon *w* branches the fowls of the Dan 4:21
*w* dominion is an everlasting Dan 4:34
all *w* works are truth, and his Dan 4:37
the God in *w* hand thy breath is, Dan 5:23
*w* are all thy ways, hast thou not Dan 5:23
*w* garment was white as snow, and Dan 7:9
*w* teeth were of iron, and his Dan 7:19
*w* look was more stout than his Dan 7:20
*w* kingdom is an everlasting Dan 7:27
*w* name was called Belteshazzar Dan 10:1
*w* loins were girded with fine Dan 10:5
*w* teeth are the teeth of a lion, Joel 1:6
*w* height was like the height of Amos 2:9
*w* name is The God of hosts Amos 5:27
of the rock, *w* habitation is high Obad 3
that we may know for *w* cause this.... Jonah 1:7
for *w* cause this evil is upon us Jonah 1:8
*w* goings forth have been from of Mic 5:2
*w* rampart was the sea, and her Nah 3:8
Behold the man *w* name is The Zec 6:12
*W* possessors slay them, and hold Zec 11:5
*w* shoes I am not worthy to bear Mt 3:11
*W* fan is in his hand, and he will Mt 3:12
Lebbaeus, *w* surname was Thaddaeus.... Mt 10:3
*W* is this image and superscription Mt 22:20
Therefore in the resurrection *w* Mt 22:28

*w* son is he? Mt 22:42
the latchet of *w* shoes I am not Mk 1:7
*w* young daughter had an unclean Mk 7:25
*W* is this image and superscription Mk 12:16
*w* wife shall she be of them Mk 12:23
to a man *w* name was Joseph Lk 1:27
in Jerusalem, *w* name was Simeon Lk 2:25
the latchet of *w* shoes I am not Lk 3:16
*W* fan is in his hand, and he will Lk 3:17
there was a man *w* right hand was Lk 6:6
then *w* shall those things be, Lk 12:20
*w* blood Pilate had mingled with Lk 13:1
*W* image and superscription hath it Lk 20:24
*w* wife of them is she Lk 20:33
*w* name was Cleopas, answering Lk 24:18
sent from God, *w* name was John Jn 1:6
*w* shoe's latchet I am not worthy Jn 1:27
*w* son was sick at Capernaum Jn 4:46
*w* father and mother we know Jn 6:42
*w* own the sheep are not, seeth Jn 10:12
*w* brother Lazarus was sick Jn 11:2
his kinsman *w* ear Peter cut off Jn 18:26
cast lots for it, *w* it shall be Jn 19:24
*W* soever sins ye remit, they are Jn 20:23
*w* soever sins ye retain, they are Jn 20:23
young man's feet, *w* name was Saul Acts 7:58
for one Simon, *w* surname is Peter Acts 10:5
*w* house is by the sea side Acts 10:6
hither Simon, *w* surname is Peter Acts 10:32
for Simon, *w* surname is Peter Acts 11:13
of John, *w* surname was Mark Acts 12:12
them John, *w* surname was Mark Acts 12:25
a Jew, *w* name was Bar-jesus Acts 13:6
*w* shoes of his feet I am not Acts 13:25
them John, *w* surname was Mark Acts 15:37
*w* heart the Lord opened, that she Acts 16:14
*w* house joined hard to the Acts 18:7
of God, *w* I am, and whom I serve, Acts 27:23
of the island, *w* name was Publius Acts 28:7
*w* sign was Castor and Pollux Acts 28:11
*w* praise is not of men, but of Rom 2:29
*w* damnation is just Rom 3:8
*W* mouth is full of cursing and Rom 3:14
Blessed are they *w* iniquities are Rom 4:7
forgiven, and *w* sins are covered Rom 4:7
*W* are the fathers, and of whom as Rom 9:5
*w* praise is in the gospel 2Cor 8:18
*w* end shall be according to their 2Cor 11:15
before *w* eyes Jesus Christ hath Gal 3:1
*W* end is destruction Phil 3:19
*w* God is their belly Phil 3:19
*w* glory is in their shame, who Phil 3:19
*w* names are in the book of life Phil 4:3
*w* coming is after the working of 2Th 2:9
*W* mouths must be stopped, who Titus 1:11
*w* house are we, if we hold fast Heb 3:6
*w* carcases fell in the wilderness Heb 3:17
*w* end is to be burned Heb 6:8
But he *w* descent is not counted Heb 7:6
*w* builder and maker is God Heb 11:10
*W* voice then shook the earth Heb 12:26
*w* faith follow, considering the Heb 13:7
*w* blood is brought into the Heb 13:11
by *w* stripes ye were healed 1Pet 2:24
*W* adorning let it not be that 1Pet 3:3
*w* daughters ye are, as long as ye 1Pet 3:6
*w* judgment now of a long time 2Pet 2:3
trees *w* fruit withereth, without Jude 12
*w* name in the Hebrew tongue is Rev 9:11
*w* names are not written in the Rev 13:8
*w* deadly wound was healed Rev 13:12
*w* names were not written in the Rev 17:8
from *w* face the earth and the Rev 20:11

**WHOSO**

*W* sheddeth man's blood, by man Gen 9:6
*w* toucheth their carcase shall be Lev 11:27
*w* toucheth any thing that is Lev 22:4
*W* killeth any person, the Num 35:30
*W* killeth his neighbour Deut 19:4
*w* followeth her, let him be slain 2Chr 23:14
*W* offereth praise glorifieth me Ps 50:23
*W* privily slandereth his Ps 101:5
*W* is wise, and will observe these Ps 107:43
But *w* hearkeneth unto me shall Prov 1:33
But *w* committeth adultery with a Prov 6:32
For *w* findeth me findeth life, and Prov 8:35
*W* is simple, let him turn in Prov 9:4
*W* is simple, let him turn in Prov 9:16
*W* loveth instruction loveth Prov 12:1
*W* despiseth the word shall be Prov 13:13
*w* trusteth in the LORD, happy is Prov 16:20
*W* mocketh the poor reproacheth Prov 17:5
*W* rewardeth evil for good, evil Prov 17:13
*W* findeth a wife findeth a good Prov 18:22
*w* provoketh him to anger sinneth Prov 20:2
*W* curseth his father or his Prov 20:20
*W* stoppeth his ears at the cry of Prov 21:13
*W* keepeth his mouth and Prov 21:23
*W* boasteth himself of a false Prov 25:14
*W* diggeth a pit shall fall Prov 26:27
*W* keepeth the fig tree shall eat Prov 27:18
*W* keepeth the law is a wise son Prov 28:7
*W* causeth the righteous to go Prov 28:10
but *w* confesseth and forsaketh Prov 28:13
*W* walketh uprightly shall be Prov 28:18
*W* robbeth his father or his Prov 28:24
but *w* walketh wisely, he shall be Prov 28:26
*W* loveth wisdom rejoiceth his Prov 29:3
*W* is partner with a thief hateth Prov 29:24
but *w* putteth his trust in the Prov 29:25
*w* pleaseth God shall escape from Eccl 7:26
*W* keepeth the commandment shall Eccl 8:5
*w* breaketh an hedge, a serpent Eccl 10:8
*W* removeth stones shall be hurt Eccl 10:9
*w* falleth not down and worshippeth Dan 3:6
*w* falleth not down and worshippeth Dan 3:11
that *w* will not come up of all Zec 14:17
*w* shall receive one such little Mt 18:5
But *w* shall offend one of these Mt 18:6
*w* marrieth her which is put away Mt 19:9
*W* therefore shall swear by the Mt 23:20
*w* shall swear by the temple, Mt 23:21
(*w* readeth, let him understand Mt 24:15
*W* curseth father or mother, let Mk 7:10
*W* eateth my flesh, and drinketh my Jn 6:54
But *w* looketh into the perfect Jas 1:25
But *w* keepeth his word, in him 1Jn 2:5
But *w* hath this world's good, and 1Jn 3:17

**WHOSOEVER**

Therefore *w* slayeth Cain, Gen 4:15
for *w* eateth leavened bread from Ex 12:15
for *w* eateth that which is Ex 12:19
*w* toucheth the mount shall be Ex 19:12
*W* lieth with a beast shall surely Ex 22:19
*W* compoundeth any like it Ex 30:33
or *w* putteth any of it upon a Ex 30:33
*W* shall make like unto that, to Ex 30:38
for *w* doeth any work therein, Ex 31:14
*w* doeth any work in the sabbath Ex 31:15
*W* hath any gold, let them break Ex 32:24
*W* hath sinned against me, him Ex 32:33
*w* doeth work therein shall be put Ex 35:2
*w* is of a willing heart, let him Ex 35:5
For *w* eateth the fat of the beast Lev 7:25
*w* toucheth the carcase of them Lev 11:24
*w* beareth ought of the carcase of Lev 11:25
*w* doth touch them, when they be Lev 11:31
*w* toucheth his bed shall wash his Lev 15:5
*w* toucheth any thing that was Lev 15:10
*w* toucheth her shall be unclean Lev 15:19
*w* toucheth her bed shall wash his Lev 15:21
*w* toucheth any thing that she sat Lev 15:22
*w* toucheth those things shall be Lev 15:27
*w* eateth it shall be cut off Lev 17:14
For *w* shall commit any of these Lev 18:29
*w* lieth carnally with a woman, Lev 19:20
*W* he be of the children of Israel Lev 20:2
*W* he be of thy seed in their Lev 21:17
*W* he be of all your seed among Lev 22:3
Or *w* toucheth any creeping thing, Lev 22:5
*w* offereth a sacrifice of peace Lev 22:21
*W* curseth his God shall bear his Lev 24:15
and *w* is defiled by the dead Num 5:2
or *w* be among you in your Num 15:14
*W* cometh any thing near unto the Num 17:13
*W* toucheth the dead body of any Num 19:13
*w* toucheth one that is slain with Num 19:16
*w* hath killed any person, and Num 31:19
*w* hath touched any slain, purify Num 31:19
that *w* will not hearken unto my Deut 18:19
*W* he be that doth rebel against Josh 1:18
that *w* shall go out of the doors Josh 2:19
*w* shall be with thee in the house Josh 2:19
that *w* killeth any person at Josh 20:9
*W* is fearful and afraid, let him Judg 7:3
*W* cometh not forth after Saul and 1Sa 11:7
*W* getteth up to the gutter, and 2Sa 5:8
*W* saith ought unto thee, bring 2Sa 14:10
that *w* heareth it will say, There 2Sa 17:9
*w* would, he consecrated him, and 1Kin 13:33
*w* shall be wanting, he shall not 2Kin 10:19
that *w* heareth of it, both his 2Kin 21:12
*W* smiteth the Jebusites first 1Chr 11:6
*w* had dedicated any thing, it was 1Chr 26:28
so that *w* cometh to consecrate 2Chr 13:9
That *w* would not seek the LORD 2Chr 15:13
*w* else cometh into the house, he 2Chr 23:7
*w* remaineth in any place where he Ezr 1:4
that *w* shall alter this word, let Ezr 6:11
*w* will not do the law of thy God, Ezr 7:26
that *w* would not come within Ezr 10:8
king's provinces, do know, that *w* Est 4:11
*w* toucheth her shall not be Prov 6:29
*w* is deceived thereby is not wise Prov 20:1
*W* hideth her hideth the wind, and Prov 27:16
*w* shall gather together against Is 54:15
*w* goeth therein shall not know Is 59:8
this place, the which *w* heareth Jer 19:3
Then *w* heareth the sound of the Eze 33:4
*W* shall read this writing, and Dan 5:7
that *w* shall ask a petition of Dan 6:7
that *w* shall call on the name of Joel 2:32
*W* therefore shall break one of Mt 5:19
but *w* shall do and teach them, the Mt 5:19
*w* shall kill shall be in danger Mt 5:21
That *w* is angry with his brother Mt 5:22
*w* shall say to his brother, Raca, Mt 5:22
but *w* shall say, Thou fool, shall Mt 5:22
That *w* looketh on a woman to lust Mt 5:28
*W* shall put away his wife, let Mt 5:31
That *w* shall put away his wife, Mt 5:32
*w* shall marry her that is Mt 5:32
but *w* shall smite thee on thy Mt 5:39
*w* shall compel thee to go a mile, Mt 5:41
Therefore *w* heareth these sayings Mt 7:24
*w* shall not receive you, nor hear Mt 10:14
*W* therefore shall confess me Mt 10:32
But *w* shall deny me before men, Mt 10:33
*w* shall give to drink unto one of Mt 10:42
*w* shall not be offended in me Mt 11:6
*w* speaketh a word against the Son Mt 12:32
but *w* speaketh against the Holy Mt 12:32
For *w* shall do the will of my Mt 12:50
For *w* hath, to him shall be given Mt 13:12
but *w* hath not, from him shall be Mt 13:12
*W* shall say to his father or his Mt 15:5
For *w* will save his life shall Mt 16:25
*w* will lose his life for my sake Mt 16:25
*W* therefore shall humble himself Mt 18:4
*W* shall put away his wife, except Mt 19:9
but *w* will be great among you, Mt 20:26
*w* will be chief among you, let Mt 20:27
*w* shall fall on this stone shall Mt 21:44
*w* shall exalt himself shall be Mt 23:12
*W* shall swear by the temple, it Mt 23:16
but *w* shall swear by the gold of Mt 23:16
*W* shall swear by the altar, it is Mt 23:18
but *w* sweareth by the gift that Mt 23:18
For *w* shall do the will of God, Mk 3:35
*w* shall not receive you, nor hear Mk 6:11
*W* will come after me, let him Mk 8:34
For *w* will save his life shall Mk 8:35
but *w* shall lose his life for my Mk 8:35
*W* therefore shall be ashamed of Mk 8:38
*W* shall receive one of such Mk 9:37
*w* shall receive me, receiveth not Mk 9:37
For *w* shall give you a cup of Mk 9:41
*w* shall offend one of these Mk 9:42
*W* shall put away his wife, and Mk 10:11
*W* shall not receive the kingdom Mk 10:15
but *w* will be great among you, Mk 10:43
*w* of you will be the chiefest, Mk 10:44
That *w* shall say unto this Mk 11:23
*W* cometh to me, and heareth my Lk 6:47
*w* shall not be offended in me Lk 7:23
for *w* hath, to him shall be given Lk 8:18
*w* hath not, from him shall be Lk 8:18
*w* will not receive you, when ye Lk 9:5
For *w* will save his life shall Lk 9:24
but *w* will lose his life for my Lk 9:24
For *w* shall be ashamed of me and Lk 9:26
*W* shall receive this child in my Lk 9:48
*w* shall receive me receiveth him Lk 9:48
*W* shall confess me before men, Lk 12:8
*w* shall speak a word against the Lk 12:10
For *w* exalteth himself shall be Lk 14:11
*w* doth not bear his cross, and Lk 14:27
*w* he be of you that forsaketh not Lk 14:33
*W* putteth away his wife, and Lk 16:18
*w* marrieth her that is put away Lk 16:18
*W* shall seek to save his life Lk 17:33
*w* shall lose his life shall Lk 17:33
*W* shall not receive the kingdom Lk 18:17
*W* shall fall upon that stone Lk 20:18
That *w* believeth in him should Jn 3:15
that *w* believeth in him should Jn 3:16
*W* drinketh of this water shall Jn 4:13
But *w* drinketh of the water that Jn 4:14
*w* then first after the troubling Jn 5:4
*W* committeth sin is the servant Jn 8:34
*w* liveth and believeth in me shall Jn 11:26
that *w* believeth on me should not Jn 12:46
that *w* killeth you will think Jn 16:2
*w* maketh himself a king speaketh Jn 19:12
that *w* shall call on the name of Acts 2:21
that through his name *w* believeth Acts 10:43
*w* among you feareth God, to you Acts 13:26
O man, *w* thou art that judgest Rom 2:1
*w* believeth on him shall not be Rom 9:33
*W* believeth on him shall not be Rom 10:11
For *w* shall call upon the name of Rom 10:13
*W* therefore resisteth the power, Rom 13:2
Wherefore *w* shall eat this bread, 1Cor 11:27
*w* of you are justified by the law Gal 5:4
shall bear his judgment, *w* he be Gal 5:10
For *w* shall keep the whole law, Jas 2:10
*w* therefore will be a friend of Jas 4:4
*W* denieth the Son, the same hath 1Jn 2:23
*W* committeth sin transgresseth 1Jn 3:4
*W* abideth in him sinneth not 1Jn 3:6
*w* sinneth hath not seen him, 1Jn 3:6
*W* is born of God doth not commit 1Jn 3:9
*w* doeth not righteousness is not 1Jn 3:10
*W* hateth his brother is a 1Jn 3:15
*W* shall confess that Jesus is the 1Jn 4:15
*W* believeth that Jesus is the 1Jn 5:1
We know that *w* is born of God 1Jn 5:18
*W* transgresseth, and abideth not 2Jn 9
*w* receiveth the mark of his name Rev 14:11
*w* was not found written in the Rev 20:15
and *w* loveth and maketh a lie Rev 22:15
*w* will, let him take the water of Rev 22:17

**WHY**

said unto Cain, *W* art thou wroth Gen 4:6
*w* is thy countenance fallen Gen 4:6
*w* didst thou not tell me that she Gen 12:18
*W* saidst thou, She is my sister Gen 12:19
said, If it be so, *w* am I thus Gen 25:22
*w* should I be deprived also of Gen 27:45
*W* do ye look one upon another Gen 42:1
for *w* should we die in thy Gen 47:15
*W* have ye done this thing, and Ex 1:18
*w* is it that ye have left the man Ex 2:20
sight, *w* the bush is not burnt Ex 3:3
*w* is it that thou hast sent me Ex 5:22
*W* have we done this, that we have Ex 14:5
unto them, *W* chide ye with me Ex 17:2
*w* sittest thou thyself alone, and Ex 18:14
*w* doth thy wrath wax hot against Ex 32:11
*W* came we forth out of Egypt Num 11:20

And *w* have ye brought up the ... Num 20:4
*W* should the name of our father ... Num 27:4
Now therefore *w* should we die ... Deut 5:25
this is the cause *w* Joshua did ... Josh 5:4
said, *W* hast thou troubled us ... Josh 7:25
*W* hast thou given me but one lot ... Josh 17:14
*w* have ye done this ... Judg 2:2
*W* abodest thou among the ... Judg 5:16
*w* did Dan remain in ships ... Judg 5:17
*W* is his chariot so long in ... Judg 5:28
*W* tarry the wheels of his ... Judg 5:28
*w* then is all this befallen us ... Judg 6:13
*W* hast thou served us thus, that ... Judg 8:1
for *w* should we serve him ... Judg 9:28
*w* are ye come unto me now when ye Judg 11:7
*w* therefore did ye not recover ... Judg 11:26
*W* askest thou thus after my name, .. Judg 13:18
*W* are ye come up against us ... Judg 15:10
*w* is this come to pass in Israel, ... Judg 21:3
*w* will ye go with me ... Ruth 1:11
*w* then call ye me Naomi, seeing ... Ruth 1:21
*W* have I found grace in thine ... Ruth 2:10
to her, Hannah, *w* weepest thou ... 1Sa 1:8
and *w* eatest thou not ... 1Sa 1:8
and *w* is thy heart grieved ... 1Sa 1:8
unto them, *W* do ye such things ... 1Sa 2:23
it shall be known to you *w* his ... 1Sa 6:3
*W* are ye come out to set your ... 1Sa 17:8
*W* camest thou down hither ... 1Sa 17:28
*W* hast thou deceived me so, and ... 1Sa 19:17
*w* should I kill thee ... 1Sa 19:17
*w* should my father hide this ... 1Sa 20:2
for *w* shouldest thou bring me to ... 1Sa 20:8
*W* art thou alone, and no man with ... 1Sa 21:1
*W* have ye conspired against me, ... 1Sa 22:13
for *w* should thy servant dwell in ... 1Sa 27:5
saying, *W* hast thou deceived me ... 1Sa 28:12
*W* hast thou disquieted me, to ... 1Sa 28:15
*w* is it that thou hast sent him ... 2Sa 3:24
*W* build ye not me an house of ... 2Sa 7:7
*w* then didst thou not go down ... 2Sa 11:10
*w* went ye nigh the wall ... 2Sa 11:21
*W* art thou, being the king's son, ... 2Sa 13:4
him, *W* should he go with thee ... 2Sa 13:26
*W* should this dead dog curse my ... 2Sa 16:9
*w* wentest thou not with thy ... 2Sa 16:17
*w* didst thou not smite him there ... 2Sa 18:11
Now therefore *w* speak ye not a ... 2Sa 19:10
*W* are ye the last to bring the ... 2Sa 19:11
*W* speakest thou any more of thy ... 2Sa 19:29
*w* should the king recompense it ... 2Sa 19:36
*W* have our brethren the men of ... 2Sa 19:41
*w* then did ye despise us, that ... 2Sa 19:43
*w* wilt thou swallow up the ... 2Sa 20:19
but *w* doth my lord the king ... 2Sa 24:3
in saying, *W* hast thou done so ... 1Kin 1:6
*w* then doth Adonijah reign ... 1Kin 1:13
*w* dost thou ask Abishag the ... 1Kin 2:22
*W* then hast thou not kept the ... 1Kin 2:43
*W* hath the LORD done thus unto ... 1Kin 9:8
*w* feignest thou thyself to be ... 1Kin 14:6
*W* is thy spirit so sad, that thou ... 1Kin 21:5
them, *W* are ye now turned back ... 2Kin 1:5
*W* sit we here until we die ... 2Kin 7:3
And Hazael said, *W* weepeth my lord. 2Kin 8:12
*W* repair ye not the breaches of ... 2Kin 12:7
for *w* shouldest thou meddle to ... 2Kin 14:10
*W* have ye not built me an house ... 1Chr 17:6
*w* then doth my lord require this ... 1Chr 21:3
*w* will he be a cause of trespass ... 1Chr 21:3
*W* hath the LORD done thus unto ... 2Chr 7:21
*W* hast thou not required of the ... 2Chr 24:6
*W* transgress ye the commandments 2Chr 24:20
*W* hast thou sought after the gods ... 2Chr 25:15
*w* shouldest thou be smitten ... 2Chr 25:16
*w* shouldest thou meddle to thine ... 2Chr 25:19
*W* should the kings of Assyria ... 2Chr 32:4
*w* should damage grow to the hurt ... Ezr 4:22
for *w* should there be wrath ... Ezr 7:23
*W* is thy countenance sad, seeing ... Neh 2:2
*w* should not my countenance be ... Neh 2:3
*w* should the work cease, whilst I ... Neh 6:3
*W* is the house of God forsaken ... Neh 13:11
*W* lodge ye about the wall ... Neh 13:21
*W* transgressest thou the king's ... Est 3:3
to know what it was, and *w* it was ... Est 4:5
*W* died I not from the womb ... Job 3:11
*w* did I not give up the ghost ... Job 3:11
*W* did the knees prevent me ... Job 3:12
or *w* the breasts that I should ... Job 3:12
*W* is light given to a man whose ... Job 3:23
*w* hast thou set me as a mark ... Job 7:20
*w* dost thou not pardon my ... Job 7:21
wicked, *w* then labour I in vain ... Job 9:29
*W* doth thine heart carry thee ... Job 15:12
*W* do ye persecute me as God, and ... Job 19:22
*W* persecute we him, seeing the ... Job 19:28
*w* should not my spirit be ... Job 21:4
*W*, seeing times are not hidden ... Job 24:1
*w* then are ye thus altogether ... Job 27:12
*w* then should I think upon a maid ... Job 31:1
*W* dost thou strive against him ... Job 33:13
*W* do the heathen rage, and the ... Ps 2:1
*W* standest thou afar off, O LORD ... Ps 10:1
*w* hidest thou thyself in times of ... Ps 10:1
my God, *w* hast thou forsaken me ... Ps 22:1
*w* art thou so far from helping me ... Ps 22:1
*W* art thou cast down, O my soul ... Ps 42:5
*w* art thou disquieted in me ... Ps 42:5
my rock, *W* hast thou forgotten me ... Ps 42:9
*w* go I mourning because of the ... Ps 42:9
*W* art thou cast down, O my soul ... Ps 42:11
*w* art thou disquieted within me ... Ps 42:11
*w* dost thou cast me off ... Ps 43:2
*W* go I mourning because of the ... Ps 43:2
*W* art thou cast down, O my soul ... Ps 43:5
*w* art thou disquieted within me ... Ps 43:5
Awake, *w* sleepest thou, O Lord ... Ps 44:23
*W* boastest thou thyself in ... Ps 52:1
*W* leap ye, ye high hills ... Ps 68:16
*w* hast thou cast us off for ever ... Ps 74:1
*w* doth thine anger smoke against ... Ps 74:1
*W* withdrawest thou thy hand, even ... Ps 74:11
*W* hast thou then broken down her ... Ps 80:12
*w* castest thou off my soul ... Ps 88:14
*w* hidest thou thy face from me ... Ps 88:14
*w* wilt thou, my son, be ravished ... Prov 5:20
*w* should he take away thy bed ... Prov 22:27
and *w* was I then more wise ... Eccl 2:15
*w* shouldest thou destroy thyself ... Eccl 7:16
*w* shouldest thou die before thy ... Eccl 7:17
for *w* should I be as one that ... Song 1:7
*W* should ye be stricken any more ... Is 1:5
*W* sayest thou, O Jacob, and ... Is 40:27
*w* hast thou made us to err from ... Is 63:17
*w* is he spoiled ... Jer 2:14
*W* trimmest thou thy way to seek ... Jer 2:33
*W* gaddest thou about so much to ... Jer 2:36
*W* then is this people of ... Jer 8:5
*W* do we sit still ... Jer 8:14
*W* have they provoked me to anger ... Jer 8:19
*w* then is not the health of the ... Jer 8:22
*w* shouldest thou be as a stranger ... Jer 14:8
*W* shouldest thou be as a man ... Jer 14:9
*w* hast thou smitten us, and there ... Jer 14:19
*W* is my pain perpetual, and my ... Jer 15:18
*W* hast thou prophesied in the ... Jer 26:9
*W* will ye die, thou and thy people ... Jer 27:13
Now therefore *w* hast thou not ... Jer 29:27
*W* criest thou for thine ... Jer 30:15
*W* hast thou written therein, ... Jer 36:29
*W* are thy valiant men swept away ... Jer 46:15
*w* then doth their king inherit ... Jer 49:1
Yet say ye, *W* ... Eze 18:19
for *w* will ye die, O house of ... Eze 18:31
for *w* will ye die, O house of ... Eze 33:11
for *w* should he see your faces ... Dan 1:10
*W* is the decree so hasty from the ... Dan 2:15
unto him, *W* hast thou done this ... Jonah 1:10
Now *w* dost thou cry out aloud ... Mic 4:9
*W* dost thou shew me iniquity, and ... Hab 1:3
*W*? saith the LORD ... Hag 1:9
*w* do we deal treacherously every ... Mal 2:10
*w* take ye thought for raiment ... Mt 6:28
*w* beholdest thou the mote that is ... Mt 7:3
*W* are ye fearful, O ye of little ... Mt 8:26
*W* eateth your Master with ... Mt 9:11
*W* do we and the Pharisees fast oft ... Mt 9:14
*W* speakest thou unto them in ... Mt 13:10
*W* do thy disciples transgress the ... Mt 15:2
*W* do ye also transgress the ... Mt 15:3
*w* reason ye among yourselves, ... Mt 16:8
*W* then say the scribes that Elias ... Mt 17:10
*W* could not we cast him out ... Mt 17:19
*W* did Moses then command to give ... Mt 19:7
unto him, *W* callest thou me good ... Mt 19:17
*W* stand ye here all the day idle ... Mt 20:6
*W* did ye not then believe him ... Mt 21:25
*W* tempt ye me, ye hypocrites ... Mt 22:18
unto them, *W* trouble ye the woman ... Mt 26:10
And the governor said, *W*, what ... Mt 27:23
my God, *w* hast thou forsaken me ... Mt 27:46
*W* doth this man thus speak ... Mk 2:7
*W* reason ye these things in your ... Mk 2:8
*W* do the disciples of John and of ... Mk 2:18
*w* do they on the sabbath day that ... Mk 2:24
unto them, *W* are ye so fearful ... Mk 4:40
*w* troublest thou the Master any ... Mk 5:35
*W* make ye this ado, and weep ... Mk 5:39
him, *W* walk not thy disciples ... Mk 7:5
*W* doth this generation seek after ... Mk 8:12
*W* reason ye, because ye have no ... Mk 8:17
*W* say the scribes that Elias must ... Mk 9:11
*W* could not we cast him out ... Mk 9:28
unto him, *W* callest thou me good ... Mk 10:18
man say unto you, *W* do ye this ... Mk 11:3
*W* then did ye not believe him ... Mk 11:31
said unto them, *W* tempt ye me ... Mk 12:15
*W* was this waste of the ointment ... Mk 14:4
*w* trouble ye her ... Mk 14:6
Then Pilate said unto them, *W* ... Mk 15:14
my God, *w* hast thou forsaken me ... Mk 15:34
*w* hast thou thus dealt with us ... Lk 2:48
*W* do ye eat and drink with ... Lk 5:30
*W* do the disciples of John fast ... Lk 5:33
*W* do ye that which is not lawful ... Lk 6:2
*w* beholdest thou the mote that is ... Lk 6:41
*w* call ye me, Lord, Lord, and do ... Lk 6:46
*w* take ye thought for the rest ... Lk 12:26
*w* even of yourselves judge ye not ... Lk 12:57
*w* cumbereth it the ground ... Lk 13:7
unto him, *W* callest thou me good ... Lk 18:19
man ask you, *W* do ye loose him ... Lk 19:31
unto them, *W* loose ye the colt ... Lk 19:33
*W* then believed ye him not ... Lk 20:5
and said unto them, *W* tempt ye me ... Lk 20:23
And said unto them, *W* sleep ye ... Lk 22:46
said unto them the third time, *W* ... Lk 23:22
*W* seek ye the living among the ... Lk 24:5
said unto them, *W* are ye troubled ... Lk 24:38
*w* do thoughts arise in your ... Lk 24:38
*W* baptizest thou then, if thou be ... Jn 1:25
or, *W* talkest thou with her ... Jn 4:27
*W* go ye about to kill me ... Jn 7:19
*W* have ye not brought him ... Jn 7:45
*W* do ye not understand my speech ... Jn 8:43
the truth, *w* do ye not believe me ... Jn 8:46
*W* herein is a marvellous thing, ... Jn 9:30
*w* hear ye him ... Jn 10:20
*W* was not this ointment sold for ... Jn 12:5
*w* cannot I follow thee now ... Jn 13:37
*W* askest thou me ... Jn 18:21
but if well, *w* smitest thou me ... Jn 18:23
unto her, Woman, *w* weepest thou ... Jn 20:13
unto her, Woman, *w* weepest thou ... Jn 20:15
*w* stand ye gazing up into heaven ... Acts 1:11
of Israel, *w* marvel ye at this ... Acts 3:12
or *w* look ye so earnestly on us, ... Acts 3:12
*W* did the heathen rage, and the ... Acts 4:25
*w* hath Satan filled thine heart ... Acts 5:3
*w* hast thou conceived this thing ... Acts 5:4
*w* do ye wrong one to another ... Acts 7:26
Saul, Saul, *w* persecutest thou me ... Acts 9:4
Sirs, *w* do ye these things ... Acts 14:15
Now therefore *w* tempt ye God ... Acts 15:10
Saul, Saul, *w* persecutest thou me ... Acts 22:7
And now *w* tarriest thou ... Acts 22:16
*W* should it be thought a thing ... Acts 26:8
Saul, Saul, *w* persecutest thou me ... Acts 26:14
*w* yet am I also judged as a ... Rom 3:7
man seeth, *w* doth he yet hope for ... Rom 8:24
unto me, *W* doth he yet find fault ... Rom 9:19
it, *W* hast thou made me thus ... Rom 9:20
But *w* dost thou judge thy brother ... Rom 14:10
or *w* dost thou set at nought thy ... Rom 14:10
*w* dost thou glory, as if thou ... 1Cor 4:7
*W* do ye not rather take wrong ... 1Cor 6:7
*w* do ye not rather suffer ... 1Cor 6:7
for *w* is my liberty judged of ... 1Cor 10:29
*w* am I evil spoken of for that ... 1Cor 10:30
*w* are they then baptized for the ... 1Cor 15:29
*w* stand we in jeopardy every hour ... 1Cor 15:30
*w* compellest thou the Gentiles to ... Gal 2:14
*w* do I yet suffer persecution ... Gal 5:11
the rudiments of the world, *w* ... Col 2:20

**WICKED**

But the men of Sodom were *w* ... Gen 13:13
destroy the righteous with the *w* ... Gen 18:23
to slay the righteous with the *w* ... Gen 18:25
the righteous should be as the *w* ... Gen 18:25
was *w* in the sight of the LORD ... Gen 38:7
and I and my people are *w* ... Ex 9:27
put not thine hand with the *w* to ... Ex 23:1
for I will not justify the *w* ... Ex 23:7
it is a *w* thing ... Lev 20:17
from the tents of these *w* men ... Num 16:26
be not a thought in thy *w* heart ... Deut 15:9
which have committed that *w* thing ... Deut 17:5
then keep thee from every *w* thing ... Deut 23:9
the righteous, and condemn the *w* ... Deut 25:1
if the *w* man be worthy to be ... Deut 25:2
the *w* shall be silent in darkness ... 1Sa 2:9
Wickedness proceedeth from the *w* ... 1Sa 24:13
Then answered all the *w* men ... 1Sa 30:22
as a man falleth before *w* men ... 2Sa 3:34
when *w* men have slain a righteous ... 2Sa 4:11
thy servants, condemning the *w* ... 1Kin 8:32
wrought *w* things to provoke the ... 2Kin 17:11
thy servants, by requiting the *w* ... 2Chr 6:23
face, and turn from their *w* ways ... 2Chr 7:14
that *w* woman, had broken up the ... 2Chr 24:7
turned they from their *w* works ... Neh 9:35
and enemy is this *w* Haman ... Est 7:6
by letters that his *w* device ... Est 9:25
There the *w* cease from troubling ... Job 3:17
of the *w* shall come to nought ... Job 8:22
destroyeth the perfect and the *w* ... Job 9:22
is given into the hand of the *w* ... Job 9:24
If I be *w*, why then labour I in ... Job 9:29
shine upon the counsel of the *w* ... Job 10:3
Thou knowest that I am not *w* ... Job 10:7
If I be *w*, woe unto me ... Job 10:15
But the eyes of the *w* shall fail ... Job 11:20
The *w* man travaileth with pain ... Job 15:20
me over into the hands of the *w* ... Job 16:11
light of the *w* shall be put out ... Job 18:5
such are the dwellings of the *w* ... Job 18:21
the triumphing of the *w* is short ... Job 20:5
every hand of the *w* shall come ... Job 20:22
the portion of a *w* man from God ... Job 20:29
Wherefore do the *w* live, become ... Job 21:7
counsel of the *w* is far from me ... Job 21:16
is the candle of the *w* put out ... Job 21:17
are the dwelling places of the *w* ... Job 21:28
That the *w* is reserved to the day ... Job 21:30
old way which *w* men have trodden ... Job 22:15
counsel of the *w* is far from me ... Job 22:18
they gather the vintage of the *w* ... Job 24:6
Let mine enemy be as the *w* ... Job 27:7
the portion of a *w* man with God ... Job 27:13
And I brake the jaws of the *w* ... Job 29:17
Is not destruction to the *w* ... Job 31:3
iniquity, and walketh with *w* men ... Job 34:8
fit to say to a king, Thou art *w* ... Job 34:18
He striketh them as *w* men in the ... Job 34:26
because of his answers for *w* men ... Job 34:36
preserveth not the life of the *w* ... Job 36:6
fulfilled the judgment of the *w* ... Job 36:17
that the *w* might be shaken out of ... Job 38:13
from the *w* their light is ... Job 38:15

tread down the *w* in their place ... Job 40:12
of the *w* come to an end ... Ps 7:9
God is angry with the *w* every day ... Ps 7:11
thou hast destroyed the *w* ... Ps 9:5
the *w* is snared in the work of ... Ps 9:16
The *w* shall be turned into hell, ... Ps 9:17
The *w* in his pride doth persecute ... Ps 10:2
For the *w* boasteth of his heart's ... Ps 10:3
The *w*, through the pride of his ... Ps 10:4
Wherefore doth the *w* contemn God ... Ps 10:13
Break thou the arm of the *w* ... Ps 10:15
the *w* bend their bow, they make ... Ps 11:2
but the *w* and him that loveth ... Ps 11:5
Upon the *w* he shall rain snares, ... Ps 11:6
The *w* walk on every side, when ... Ps 12:8
From the *w* that oppress me, from ... Ps 17:9
deliver my soul from the *w* ... Ps 17:13
of the *w* have inclosed me ... Ps 22:16
and will not sit with the *w* ... Ps 26:5
When the *w*, even mine enemies and ... Ps 27:2
Draw me not away with the *w* ... Ps 28:3
let the *w* be ashamed, and let them ... Ps 31:17
Many sorrows shall be to the *w* ... Ps 32:10
Evil shall slay the *w* ... Ps 34:21
of the *w* saith within my heart ... Ps 36:1
not the hand of the *w* remove me ... Ps 36:11
who bringeth *w* devices to pass ... Ps 37:7
while, and the *w* shall not be ... Ps 37:10
The *w* plotteth against the just, ... Ps 37:12
The *w* have drawn out the sword, ... Ps 37:14
better than the riches of many *w* ... Ps 37:16
the arms of the *w* shall be broken ... Ps 37:17
But the *w* shall perish, and the ... Ps 37:20
The *w* borroweth, and payeth not ... Ps 37:21
seed of the *w* shall be cut off ... Ps 37:28
The *w* watcheth the righteous, and ... Ps 37:32
when the *w* are cut off, thou ... Ps 37:34
I have seen the *w* in great power ... Ps 37:35
the end of the *w* shall be cut off ... Ps 37:38
he shall deliver them from the *w* ... Ps 37:40
bridle, while the *w* is before me ... Ps 39:1
But unto the *w* God saith, What ... Ps 50:16
of the oppression of the *w* ... Ps 55:3
The *w* are estranged from the womb ... Ps 58:3
his feet in the blood of the *w* ... Ps 58:10
merciful to any *w* transgressors ... Ps 59:5
from the secret counsel of the *w* ... Ps 64:2
so let the *w* perish at the ... Ps 68:2
my God, out of the hand of the *w* ... Ps 71:4
I saw the prosperity of the *w* ... Ps 73:3
unto the multitude of the *w* ... Ps 74:19
and to the *w*, Lift not up the horn ... Ps 75:4
all the *w* of the earth shall ... Ps 75:8
of the *w* also will I cut off ... Ps 75:10
and accept the persons of the *w* ... Ps 82:2
rid them out of the hand of the *w* ... Ps 82:4
behold and see the reward of the *w* ... Ps 91:8
When the *w* spring as the grass, ... Ps 92:7
of the *w* that rise up against me ... Ps 92:11
LORD, how long shall the *w* ... Ps 94:3
how long shall the *w* triumph ... Ps 94:3
until the pit be digged for the *w* ... Ps 94:13
them out of the hand of the *w* ... Ps 97:10
I will set no *w* thing before mine ... Ps 101:3
I will not know a *w* person ... Ps 101:4
destroy all the *w* of the land ... Ps 101:8
that I may cut off all *w* doers ... Ps 101:8
earth, and let the *w* be no more ... Ps 104:35
the flame burned up the *w* ... Ps 106:18
For the mouth of the *w* and the ... Ps 109:2
Set thou a *w* man over him ... Ps 109:6
The *w* shall see it, and be grieved ... Ps 112:10
the desire of the *w* shall perish ... Ps 112:10
of the *w* that forsake thy law ... Ps 119:53
The bands of the *w* have robbed me ... Ps 119:61
The *w* have waited for me to ... Ps 119:95
The *w* have laid a snare for me ... Ps 119:110
all the *w* of the earth like dross ... Ps 119:119
Salvation is far from the *w* ... Ps 119:155
For the rod of the *w* shall not ... Ps 125:3
cut asunder the cords of the *w* ... Ps 129:4
Surely thou wilt slay the *w* ... Ps 139:19
see if there be any *w* way in me ... Ps 139:24
O LORD, from the hands of the *w* ... Ps 140:4
not, O LORD, the desires of the *w* ... Ps 140:8
further not his *w* device ... Ps 140:8
to practise *w* works with men that ... Ps 141:4
Let the *w* fall into their own ... Ps 141:10
but all the *w* will he destroy ... Ps 145:20
but the way of the *w* he turneth ... Ps 146:9
he casteth the *w* down to the ... Ps 147:6
in the frowardness of the *w* ... Prov 2:14
But the *w* shall be cut off from ... Prov 2:22
of the desolation of the *w* ... Prov 3:25
the LORD is in the house of the *w* ... Prov 3:33
Enter not into the path of the *w* ... Prov 4:14
The way of the *w* is as darkness ... Prov 4:19
shall take the *w* himself, and he ... Prov 5:22
a *w* man, walketh with a froward ... Prov 6:12
that deviseth *w* imaginations ... Prov 6:18
he that rebuketh a *w* man getteth ... Prov 9:7
away the substance of the *w* ... Prov 10:3
covereth the mouth of the *w* ... Prov 10:6
but the name of the *w* shall rot ... Prov 10:7
covereth the mouth of the *w* ... Prov 10:11
the fruit of the *w* to sin ... Prov 10:16
heart of the *w* is little worth ... Prov 10:20
The fear of the *w*, it shall come ... Prov 10:24
passeth, so is the *w* no more ... Prov 10:25
years of the *w* shall be shortened ... Prov 10:27
expectation of the *w* shall perish ... Prov 10:28
but the *w* shall not inhabit the ... Prov 10:30
of the *w* speaketh frowardness ... Prov 10:32
but the *w* shall fall by his own ... Prov 11:5
When a *w* man dieth, his ... Prov 11:7
the *w* cometh in his stead ... Prov 11:8
and when the *w* perish, there is ... Prov 11:10
overthrown by the mouth of the *w* ... Prov 11:11
The *w* worketh a deceitful work ... Prov 11:18
the *w* shall not be unpunished ... Prov 11:21
the expectation of the *w* is wrath ... Prov 11:23
much more the *w* and the sinner ... Prov 11:31
but a man of *w* devices will he ... Prov 12:2
the counsels of the *w* are deceit ... Prov 12:5
The words of the *w* are to lie in ... Prov 12:6
The *w* are overthrown, and are not ... Prov 12:7
tender mercies of the *w* are cruel ... Prov 12:10
The *w* desireth the net of evil ... Prov 12:12
The *w* is snared by the ... Prov 12:13
but the *w* shall be filled with ... Prov 12:21
the way of the *w* seduceth them ... Prov 12:26
but a *w* man is loathsome, and ... Prov 13:5
lamp of the *w* shall be put out ... Prov 13:9
A *w* messenger falleth into ... Prov 13:17
but the belly of the *w* shall want ... Prov 13:25
The house of the *w* shall be ... Prov 14:11
a man of *w* devices is hated ... Prov 14:17
the *w* at the gates of the ... Prov 14:19
The *w* is driven away in his ... Prov 14:32
the revenues of the *w* is trouble ... Prov 15:6
The sacrifice of the *w* is an ... Prov 15:8
The way of the *w* is an ... Prov 15:9
The thoughts of the *w* are an ... Prov 15:26
but the mouth of the *w* poureth ... Prov 15:28
The LORD is far from the *w* ... Prov 15:29
even the *w* for the day of evil ... Prov 16:4
A *w* doer giveth heed to false ... Prov 17:4
He that justifieth the *w*, and he ... Prov 17:15
A *w* man taketh a gift out of the ... Prov 17:23
When the *w* cometh, then cometh ... Prov 18:3
to accept the person of the *w* ... Prov 18:5
the mouth of the *w* devoureth ... Prov 19:28
A wise king scattereth the *w* ... Prov 20:26
heart, and the plowing of the *w* ... Prov 21:4
of the *w* shall destroy them ... Prov 21:7
The soul of the *w* desireth evil ... Prov 21:10
considereth the house of the *w* ... Prov 21:12
the *w* for their wickedness ... Prov 21:12
The *w* shall be a ransom for the ... Prov 21:18
sacrifice of the *w* is abomination ... Prov 21:27
when he bringeth it with a *w* mind ... Prov 21:27
A *w* man hardeneth his face ... Prov 21:29
O *w* man, against the dwelling of ... Prov 24:15
but the *w* shall fall into ... Prov 24:16
neither be thou envious at the *w* ... Prov 24:19
candle of the *w* shall be put out ... Prov 24:20
He that saith unto the *w*, Thou ... Prov 24:24
Take away the *w* from before the ... Prov 25:5
the *w* is as a troubled fountain ... Prov 25:26
a *w* heart are like a potsherd ... Prov 26:23
The *w* flee when no man pursueth ... Prov 28:1
that forsake the law praise the *w* ... Prov 28:4
but when the *w* rise, a man is ... Prov 28:12
so is a *w* ruler over the poor ... Prov 28:15
When the *w* rise, men hide ... Prov 28:28
but when the *w* beareth rule ... Prov 29:2
but the *w* regardeth not to know ... Prov 29:7
to lies, all his servants are *w* ... Prov 29:12
When the *w* are multiplied, ... Prov 29:16
the way is abomination to the *w* ... Prov 29:27
judge the righteous and the *w* ... Eccl 3:17
there is a *w* man that prolongeth ... Eccl 7:15
Be not over much *w*, neither be ... Eccl 7:17
And so I saw the *w* buried, who had ... Eccl 8:10
it shall not be well with the *w* ... Eccl 8:13
according to the work of the *w* ... Eccl 8:14
again, there be *w* men, to whom it ... Eccl 8:14
to the righteous, and to the *w* ... Eccl 9:2
Woe unto the *w* ... Is 3:11
Which justify the *w* for reward ... Is 5:23
of his lips shall he slay the *w* ... Is 11:4
evil, and the *w* for their iniquity ... Is 13:11
hath broken the staff of the *w* ... Is 14:5
Let favour be shewed to the *w* ... Is 26:10
he deviseth *w* devices to destroy ... Is 32:7
peace, saith the LORD, unto the *w* ... Is 48:22
And he made his grave with the *w* ... Is 53:9
Let the *w* forsake his way, and the ... Is 55:7
But the *w* are like the troubled ... Is 57:20
no peace, saith my God, to the *w* ... Is 57:21
also taught the *w* ones thy ways ... Jer 2:33
among my people are found *w* men ... Jer 5:26
they overpass the deeds of the *w* ... Jer 5:28
for the *w* are not plucked away ... Jer 6:29
doth the way of the *w* prosper ... Jer 12:1
thee out of the hand of the *w* ... Jer 15:21
all things, and desperately *w* ... Jer 17:9
grievously upon the head of the *w* ... Jer 23:19
give them that are *w* to the sword ... Jer 25:31
with pain upon the head of the *w* ... Jer 30:23
When I say unto the *w*, Thou shalt ... Eze 3:18
to warn the *w* from his *w* way ... Eze 3:18
the same *w* man shall die in his ... Eze 3:18
Yet if thou warn the *w*, and he ... Eze 3:19
wickedness, nor from his *w* way ... Eze 3:19
to the *w* of the earth for a spoil ... Eze 7:21
behold the *w* abominations that ... Eze 8:9
give *w* counsel in this city ... Eze 11:2
strengthened the hands of the *w* ... Eze 13:22
should not return from his *w* way ... Eze 13:22
of the *w* shall be upon him ... Eze 18:20
But if the *w* will turn from all ... Eze 18:21
at all that the *w* should die ... Eze 18:23
abominations that the *w* man doeth ... Eze 18:24
when the *w* man turneth away from ... Eze 18:27
not according to your *w* ways ... Eze 20:44
from thee the righteous and the *w* ... Eze 21:3
from thee the righteous and the *w* ... Eze 21:4
profane *w* prince of Israel, whose ... Eze 21:25
of them that are slain, of the *w* ... Eze 21:29
the land into the hand of the *w* ... Eze 30:12
When I say unto the *w* ... Eze 33:8
O *w* man, thou shalt surely die ... Eze 33:8
speak to warn the *w* from his way ... Eze 33:8
that *w* man shall die in his ... Eze 33:8
if thou warn the *w* of his way to ... Eze 33:9
no pleasure in the death of the *w* ... Eze 33:11
but that the *w* turn from his way ... Eze 33:11
as for the wickedness of the *w* ... Eze 33:12
Again, when I say unto the *w* ... Eze 33:14
If the *w* restore the pledge, give ... Eze 33:15
But if the *w* turn from his ... Eze 33:19
but the *w* shall do wickedly ... Dan 12:10
none of the *w* shall understand ... Dan 12:10
wickedness in the house of the *w* ... Mic 6:10
them pure with the *w* balances ... Mic 6:11
and will not at all acquit the *w* ... Nah 1:3
against the LORD, a *w* counsellor ... Nah 1:11
for the *w* shall no more pass ... Nah 1:15
for the *w* doth compass about the ... Hab 1:4
holdest thy tongue when the *w* ... Hab 1:13
head out of the house of the *w* ... Hab 3:13
and the stumblingblocks with the *w* ... Zeph 1:3
between the righteous and the *w* ... Mal 3:18
And ye shall tread down the *w* ... Mal 4:3
other spirits more *w* than himself ... Mt 12:45
it be also unto this *w* generation ... Mt 12:45
it not, then cometh the *w* one ... Mt 13:19
are the children of the *w* one ... Mt 13:38
sever the *w* from among the just, ... Mt 13:49
A *w* and adulterous generation ... Mt 16:4
O thou *w* servant, I forgave thee ... Mt 18:32
miserably destroy those *w* men ... Mt 21:41
answered and said unto him, Thou *w* ... Mt 25:26
other spirits more *w* than himself ... Lk 11:26
will I judge thee, thou *w* servant ... Lk 19:22
by *w* hands have crucified and ... Acts 2:23
a matter of wrong or *w* lewdness ... Acts 18:14
among yourselves that *w* person ... 1Cor 5:13
all the fiery darts of the *w* ... Eph 6:16
enemies in your mind by *w* works ... Col 1:21
And then shall that *W* be revealed ... 2Th 2:8
from unreasonable and *w* men ... 2Th 3:2
the filthy conversation of the *w* ... 2Pet 2:7
led away with the error of the *w* ... 2Pet 3:17
ye have overcome the *w* one ... 1Jn 2:13
and ye have overcome the *w* one ... 1Jn 2:14
as Cain, who was of that *w* one ... 1Jn 3:12
that *w* one toucheth him not ... 1Jn 5:18

## WICKEDLY

I pray you, brethren, do not so *w* ... Gen 19:7
in doing *w* in the sight of the ... Deut 9:18
nay, I pray you, do not so *w* ... Judg 19:23
But if ye shall still do *w* ... 1Sa 12:25
have not *w* departed from my God ... 2Sa 22:22
I have sinned, and I have done *w* ... 2Sa 24:17
hath done *w* above all that the ... 2Kin 21:11
have done amiss, and have dealt *w* ... 2Chr 6:37
king of Israel, who did very *w* ... 2Chr 20:35
mother was his counsellor to do *w* ... 2Chr 22:3
done right, but we have done *w* ... Neh 9:33
Will ye speak *w* for God ... Job 13:7
Yea, surely God will not do *w* ... Job 34:12
have not *w* departed from my God ... Ps 18:21
speak *w* concerning oppression ... Ps 73:8
hath done *w* in the sanctuary ... Ps 74:3
iniquity, we have done *w* ... Ps 106:6
For they speak against thee *w* ... Ps 139:20
iniquity, and have done *w*, and have ... Dan 9:5
we have sinned, we have done *w* ... Dan 9:15
such as do *w* against the covenant ... Dan 11:32
but the wicked shall do *w* ... Dan 12:10
the proud, yea, and all that do *w* ... Mal 4:1

## WICKEDNESS

God saw that the *w* of man was ... Gen 6:5
how then can I do this great *w* ... Gen 39:9
it is *w* ... Lev 18:17
and the land become full of *w* ... Lev 19:29
a wife and her mother, it is *w* ... Lev 20:14
that there be no *w* among you ... Lev 20:14
but for the *w* of these nations ... Deut 9:4
but for the *w* of these nations ... Deut 9:5
of this people, nor to their *w* ... Deut 9:27
any such *w* as this is among you ... Deut 13:11
that hath wrought *w* in the sight ... Deut 17:2
because of the *w* of thy doings ... Deut 28:20
God rendered the *w* of Abimelech ... Judg 9:56
Israel, Tell us, how was this *w* ... Judg 20:3
What *w* is this that is done among ... Judg 20:12
and see that your *w* is great ... 1Sa 12:17
ye have done all this *w* ... 1Sa 12:20
*W* proceedeth from the wicked ... 1Sa 24:13
the *w* of Nabal upon his own head ... 1Sa 25:39
doer of evil according to his *w* ... 2Sa 3:39
of *w* afflict them any more ... 2Sa 7:10
but if *w* shall be found in him, ... 1Kin 1:52
Thou knowest all the *w* which ... 1Kin 2:44
return thy *w* upon thine own head ... 1Kin 2:44
perversely, we have committed *w* ... 1Kin 8:47

W

work *w* in the sight of the LORD 1Kin 21:25
he wrought much *w* in the sight of 2Kin 21:6
children of *w* waste them any more 1Chr 17:9
they that plow iniquity, and sow *w* Job 4:8
he seeth *w* also Job 11:11
away, and let not *w* dwell in thy Job 11:14
Though *w* be sweet in his mouth, Job 20:12
Is not thy *w* great Job 22:5
*w* shall be broken as a tree Job 24:20
My lips shall not speak *w* Job 27:4
it from God, that he should do *w* Job 34:10
Thy *w* may hurt a man as thou art Job 35:8
not a God that hath pleasure in *w* Ps 5:4
their inward part is very *w* Ps 5:9
Oh let the *w* of the wicked come Ps 7:9
seek out his *w* till thou find Ps 10:15
according to the *w* of their Ps 28:4
lovest righteousness, and hatest *w* Ps 45:7
and strengthened himself in his *w* Ps 52:7
*W* is in the midst thereof Ps 55:11
for *w* is in their dwellings, and Ps 55:15
Yea, in heart ye work *w* Ps 58:2
than to dwell in the tents of *w* Ps 84:10
nor the son of *w* afflict him Ps 89:22
shall cut them off in their own *w* Ps 94:23
for the *w* of them that dwell Ps 107:34
For they eat the bread of *w* Prov 4:17
*w* is an abomination to my lips Prov 8:7
Treasures of *w* profit nothing Prov 10:2
wicked shall fall by his own *w* Prov 11:5
man shall not be established by *w* Prov 12:3
but *w* overthroweth the sinner Prov 13:6
wicked is driven away in his *w* Prov 14:32
abomination to kings to commit *w* Prov 16:12
the wicked for their *w* Prov 21:12
his *w* shall be shewed before the Prov 26:26
mouth, and saith, I have done no *w* Prov 30:20
of judgment, that *w* was there Eccl 3:16
that prolongeth his life in his *w* Eccl 7:15
things, and to know the *w* of folly Eccl 7:25
neither shall *w* deliver those Eccl 8:8
For *w* burneth as the fire Is 9:18
For thou hast trusted in thy *w* Is 47:10
and to smite with the fist of *w* Is 58:4
to loose the bands of *w*, to undo Is 58:6
against them touching all their *w* Jer 1:16
Thine own *w* shall correct thee, Jer 2:19
with thy whoredoms and with thy *w* Jer 3:2
wash thine heart from *w*, that Jer 4:14
this is thy *w*, because it is Jer 4:18
waters, so she casteth out her *w* Jer 6:7
it for the *w* of my people Israel Jer 7:12
no man repented him of his *w* Jer 8:6
for the *w* of them that dwell Jer 12:4
for I will pour their *w* upon them Jer 14:16
We acknowledge, O LORD, our *w* Jer 14:20
and confounded for all thy *w* Jer 22:22
in my house have I found their *w* Jer 23:11
that none doth return from his *w* Jer 23:14
for all whose *w* I have hid my Jer 33:5
Because of their *w* which they Jer 44:3
their ear to turn from their *w* Jer 44:5
forgotten the *w* of your fathers Jer 44:9
the *w* of the kings of Judah, and Jer 44:9
the *w* of their wives, and your own Jer 44:9
of their wives, and your own *w* Jer 44:9
the *w* of your wives, which they Jer 44:9
Let all their *w* come before thee Lam 1:22
wicked, and he turn not from his *w* Eze 3:19
into *w* more than the nations Eze 5:6
is risen up into a rod of *w* Eze 7:11
it came to pass after all thy *w* Eze 16:23
Before thy *w* was discovered, as Eze 16:57
the *w* of the wicked shall be upon Eze 18:20
from his *w* that he hath committed Eze 18:27
I have driven him out for his *w* Eze 31:11
as for the *w* of the wicked, he Eze 33:12
day that he turneth from his *w* Eze 33:12
But if the wicked turn from his *w* Eze 33:19
discovered, and the *w* of Samaria Hos 7:1
that I remember all their *w* Hos 7:2
make the king glad with their *w* Hos 7:3
All their *w* is in Gilgal Hos 9:15
for the *w* of their doings I will Hos 9:15
Ye have plowed *w*, ye have reaped Hos 10:13
unto you because of your great *w* Hos 10:15
for their *w* is great Joel 3:13
for their *w* is come up before me Jonah 1:2
of *w* in the house of the wicked Mic 6:10
hath not thy *w* passed continually Nah 3:19
And he said, This is *w* Zec 5:8
shall call them, The border of *w* Mal 1:4
yea, they that work *w* are set up Mal 3:15
But Jesus perceived their *w* Mt 22:18
Thefts, covetousness, *w*, deceit, Mk 7:22
part is full of ravening and *w* Lk 11:39
Repent therefore of this thy *w* Acts 8:22
man, if there be any *w* in him Acts 25:5
unrighteousness, fornication, *w* Rom 1:29
with the leaven of malice and *w* 1Cor 5:8
spiritual *w* in high places Eph 6:12
and the whole world lieth in *w* 1Jn 5:19

## WIDE

shalt open thine hand *w* unto him Deut 15:8
thine hand *w* unto thy brother Deut 15:11
and good, and the land was *w* 1Chr 4:40
mouth *w* as for the latter rain Job 29:23
me as a *w* breaking in of waters Job 30:14
opened their mouth *w* against me Ps 35:21
open thy mouth *w*, and I will fill Ps 81:10
*w* sea, wherein are things Ps 104:25
but he that openeth *w* his lips Prov 13:3
a brawling woman and in a *w* house Prov 21:9
a brawling woman and in a *w* house. Prov 25:24
against whom make ye a *w* mouth Is 57:4
saith, I will build me a *w* house Jer 22:14
be set *w* open unto thine enemies Nah 3:13
for *w* is the gate, and broad is Mt 7:13

## WIDENESS

*w* of twenty cubits round about Eze 41:10

## WIDOW

Remain a *w* at thy father's house, Gen 38:11
Ye shall not afflict any *w* Ex 22:22
A *w*, or a divorced woman, or Lev 21:14
if the priest's daughter be a *w* Lev 22:13
But every vow of a *w*, and of her Num 30:9
judgment of the fatherless and *w* Deut 10:18
and the fatherless, and the *w* Deut 14:29
and the fatherless, and the *w* Deut 16:11
and the fatherless, and the *w* Deut 16:14
for the fatherless, and for the *w* Deut 24:19
for the fatherless, and for the *w* Deut 24:20
for the fatherless, and for the *w* Deut 24:21
the fatherless, and the *w* Deut 26:12
to the fatherless, and to the *w* Deut 26:13
of the stranger, fatherless, and *w* Deut 27:19
answered, I am indeed a *w* woman 2Sa 14:5
a *w* woman, even he lifted up his 1Kin 11:26
I have commanded a *w* woman there. 1Kin 17:9
the *w* woman was there gathering 1Kin 17:10
upon the *w* with whom I sojourn 1Kin 17:20
and doeth not good to the *w* Job 24:21
caused the eyes of the *w* to fail Job 31:16
They slay the *w* and the stranger, Ps 94:6
be fatherless, and his wife a *w* Ps 109:9
he relieveth the fatherless and *w* Ps 146:9
establish the border of the *w* Prov 15:25
the fatherless, plead for the *w* Is 1:17
the cause of the *w* come unto them Is 1:23
I shall not sit as a *w*, neither Is 47:8
the fatherless, and the *w* Jer 7:6
the fatherless, nor the *w* Jer 22:3
how is she become as a *w* Lam 1:1
vexed the fatherless and the *w* Eze 22:7
they take for their wives a *w* Eze 44:22
or a *w* that had a priest before Eze 44:22
And oppress not the *w*, nor the Zec 7:10
the hireling in his wages, the *w* Mal 3:5
And there came a certain poor *w* Mk 12:42
That this poor *w* hath cast more Mk 12:43
she was a *w* of about fourscore and Lk 2:37
Sidon, unto a woman that was a *w* Lk 4:26
son of his mother, and she was a *w* Lk 7:12
there was a *w* in that city Lk 18:3
Yet because this *w* troubleth me Lk 18:5
he saw also a certain poor *w* Lk 21:2
that this poor *w* hath cast in Lk 21:3
But if any *w* have children or 1Ti 5:4
Now she that is a *w* indeed 1Ti 5:5
Let not a *w* be taken into the 1Ti 5:9
heart, I sit a queen, and am no *w* Rev 18:7

## WIDOWHOOD

and put on the garments of her *w* Gen 38:19
day of their death, living in *w* 2Sa 20:3
day, the loss of children, and *w* Is 47:9
the reproach of thy *w* any more Is 54:4

## WIDOW'S

she put her *w* garments off from Gen 38:14
nor take a *w* raiment to pledge Deut 24:17
He was a *w* son of the tribe of 1Kin 7:14
they take the *w* ox for a pledge Job 24:3
I caused the *w* heart to sing for Job 29:13

## WIDOWS

and your wives shall be *w*, and your Ex 22:24
Thou hast sent *w* away empty Job 22:9
and his *w* shall not weep Job 27:15
fatherless, and a judge of the *w* Ps 68:5
their *w* made no lamentation Ps 78:64
mercy on their fatherless and *w* Is 9:17
that *w* may be their prey, and that Is 10:2
Their *w* are increased to me above Jer 15:8
of their children, and be *w* Jer 18:21
and let thy *w* trust in me Jer 49:11
fatherless, our mothers are as *w* Lam 5:3
her many *w* in the midst thereof Eze 22:25
many *w* were in Israel in the days Lk 4:25
because their *w* were neglected in Acts 6:1
all the *w* stood by him weeping, Acts 9:39
he had called the saints and *w* Acts 9:41
therefore to the unmarried and *w* 1Cor 7:8
Honour *w* that are *w* indeed 1Ti 5:3
But the younger *w* refuse 1Ti 5:11
or woman that believeth have *w* 1Ti 5:16
relieve them that are *w* indeed 1Ti 5:16
*w* in their affliction, and to keep Jas 1:27

## WIDOWS'

for ye devour *w* houses, and for a Mt 23:14
Which devour *w* houses, and for a Mk 12:40
Which devour *w* houses, and for a Lk 20:47

## WIFE

and shall cleave unto his *w* Gen 2:24
were both naked, the man and his *w* Gen 2:25
his *w* hid themselves from the Gen 3:8
hearkened unto the voice of thy *w* Gen 3:17
to his *w* did the LORD God make Gen 3:21
And Adam knew Eve his *w* Gen 4:1
And Cain knew his *w* Gen 4:17
And Adam knew his *w* again Gen 4:25
ark, thou, and thy sons, and thy *w* Gen 6:18
went in, and his sons, and his *w* Gen 7:7
the sons of Noah, and Noah's *w* Gen 7:13
forth of the ark, thou, and thy *w* Gen 8:16
went forth, and his sons, and his *w* Gen 8:18
the name of Abram's *w* was Sarai Gen 11:29
and the name of Nahor's *w*, Milcah, Gen 11:29
in law, his son Abram's *w* Gen 11:31
And Abram took Sarai his *w* Gen 12:5
that he said unto Sarai his *w* Gen 12:11
they shall say, This is his *w* Gen 12:12
because of Sarai Abram's *w* Gen 12:17
not tell me that she was thy *w* Gen 12:18
I might have taken her to me to *w* Gen 12:19
now therefore behold thy *w* Gen 12:19
and they sent him away, and his *w* Gen 12:20
up out of Egypt, he, and his *w* Gen 13:1
Now Sarai Abram's *w* bare him no Gen 16:1
Sarai Abram's *w* took Hagar her Gen 16:3
to her husband Abram to be his *w* Gen 16:3
unto Abraham, As for Sarai thy *w* Gen 17:15
Sarah thy *w* shall bear thee a son Gen 17:19
unto him, Where is Sarah thy *w* Gen 18:9
Sarah thy *w* shall have a son Gen 18:10
Lot, saying, Arise, take thy *w* Gen 19:15
hand, and upon the hand of his *w* Gen 19:16
But his *w* looked back from behind Gen 19:26
And Abraham said of Sarah his *w* Gen 20:2
for she is a man's *w* Gen 20:3
therefore restore the man his *w* Gen 20:7
and she became my *w* Gen 20:12
and restored him Sarah his *w* Gen 20:14
healed Abimelech, and his *w* Gen 20:17
because of Sarah Abraham's *w* Gen 20:18
his mother took him a *w* out of Gen 21:21
Abraham buried Sarah his *w* in the Gen 23:19
that thou shalt not take a *w* unto Gen 24:3
take a *w* unto my son Isaac Gen 24:4
thou shalt take a *w* unto my son Gen 24:7
the *w* of Nahor, Abraham's brother Gen 24:15
Sarah my master's *w* bare a son to Gen 24:36
Thou shalt not take a *w* to my son Gen 24:37
kindred, and take a *w* unto my son Gen 24:38
thou shalt take a *w* for my son of Gen 24:40
let her be thy master's son's *w* Gen 24:51
took Rebekah, and she became his *w* Gen 24:67
Then again Abraham took a *w* Gen 25:1
Abraham buried, and Sarah his *w* Gen 25:10
old when he took Rebekah to *w* Gen 25:20
intreated the LORD for his *w* Gen 25:21
him, and Rebekah his *w* conceived Gen 25:21
of the place asked him of his *w* Gen 26:7
for he feared to say, She is my *w* Gen 26:7
was sporting with Rebekah his *w* Gen 26:8
Behold, of a surety she is thy *w* Gen 26:9
lightly have lien with thy *w* Gen 26:10
*w* shall surely be put to death Gen 26:11
to *w* Judith the daughter of Beeri Gen 26:34
if Jacob take a *w* of the Gen 27:46
Thou shalt not take a *w* of the Gen 28:1
take thee a *w* from thence of the Gen 28:2
to take him a *w* from thence Gen 28:6
Thou shalt not take a *w* of the Gen 28:6
sister of Nebajoth, to be his *w* Gen 28:9
said unto Laban, Give me my *w* Gen 29:21
him Rachel his daughter to *w* also Gen 29:28
gave him Bilhah her handmaid to *w* Gen 30:4
her maid, and gave her Jacob to *w* Gen 30:9
saying, Get me this damsel to *w* Gen 34:4
I pray you give her him to *w* Gen 34:8
but give me the damsel to *w* Gen 34:12
the son of Adah the *w* of Esau Gen 36:10
son of Bashemath the *w* of Esau Gen 36:10
were the sons of Adah Esau's *w* Gen 36:12
the sons of Bashemath Esau's *w* Gen 36:13
the daughter of Zibeon, Esau's *w* Gen 36:14
the sons of Bashemath Esau's *w* Gen 36:17
the sons of Aholibamah Esau's *w* Gen 36:18
the daughter of Anah, Esau's *w* Gen 36:18
Judah took a *w* for Er his Gen 38:6
Onan, Go in unto thy brother's *w* Gen 38:8
he went in unto his brother's *w* Gen 38:9
daughter of Shuah Judah's *w* died Gen 38:12
she was not given unto him to *w* Gen 38:14
that his master's *w* cast her eyes Gen 39:7
and said unto his master's *w* Gen 39:8
but thee, because thou art his *w* Gen 39:9
master heard the words of his *w* Gen 39:19
he gave him to *w* Asenath the Gen 41:45
Ye know that my *w* bare me two Gen 44:27
The sons of Rachel Jacob's *w* Gen 46:19
buried Abraham and Sarah his *w* Gen 49:31
buried Isaac and Rebekah his *w* Gen 49:31
took to *w* a daughter of Levi Ex 2:1
And Moses took his *w* and his sons, Ex 4:20
Jochebed his father's sister to *w* Ex 6:20
sister of Naashon, to *w* Ex 6:23
of the daughters of Putiel to *w* Ex 6:25
in law, took Zipporah, Moses' *w* Ex 18:2
his *w* unto Moses into the Ex 18:5
am come unto thee, and thy *w* Ex 18:6
shalt not covet thy neighbour's *w* Ex 20:17
then his *w* shall go out with him Ex 21:3
If his master have given him a *w* Ex 21:4
the *w* and her children shall be Ex 21:4
say, I love my master, my *w* Ex 21:5
If he take him another *w* Ex 21:10
surely endow her to be his *w* Ex 22:16

father's *w* shalt thou not uncover Lev 18:8
thou shalt not approach to his *w* Lev 18:14
she is thy son's *w* Lev 18:15
the nakedness of thy brother's *w* Lev 18:16
shalt thou take a *w* to her sister Lev 18:18
carnally with thy neighbour's *w* Lev 18:20
adultery with another man's *w* Lev 20:10
adultery with his neighbour's *w* Lev 20:10
*w* hath uncovered his father's Lev 20:11
And if a man take a *w* and her Lev 20:14
man shall lie with his uncle's *w* Lev 20:20
a man shall take his brother's *w* Lev 20:21
not take a *w* that is a whore Lev 21:7
And he shall take a *w* in her Lev 21:13
a virgin of his own people to *w* Lev 21:14
them, If any man's *w* go aside Num 5:12
him, and he be jealous of his *w* Num 5:14
him, and he be jealous of his *w* Num 5:14
man bring his *w* unto the priest Num 5:15
when a *w* goeth aside to another Num 5:29
him, and he be jealous over his *w* Num 5:30
name of Amram's *w* was Jochebed Num 26:59
Moses, between a man and his *w* Num 30:16
shall be *w* unto one of the family Num 36:8
thou desire thy neighbour's *w* Deut 5:21
or the *w* of thy bosom, or thy Deut 13:6
is there that hath betrothed a *w* Deut 20:7
thou wouldest have her to thy *w* Deut 21:11
husband, and she shall be thy *w* Deut 21:13
If any man take a *w*, and go in Deut 22:13
my daughter unto this man to *w* Deut 22:16
and she shall be his *w* Deut 22:19
he hath humbled his neighbour's *w* Deut 22:24
of silver, and she shall be his *w* Deut 22:29
man shall not take his father's *w* Deut 22:30
When a man hath taken a *w* Deut 24:1
she may go and be another man's *w* Deut 24:2
die, which took her to be his *w* Deut 24:3
not take her again to be his *w* Deut 24:4
When a man hath taken a new *w* Deut 24:5
shall cheer up his *w* which he Deut 24:5
the *w* of the dead shall not marry Deut 25:5
unto her, and take her to him to *w* Deut 25:5
like not to take his brother's *w* Deut 25:7
then let his brother's *w* go up to Deut 25:7
Then shall his brother's *w* come Deut 25:9
the *w* of the one draweth near for Deut 25:11
he that lieth with his father's *w* Deut 27:20
Thou shalt betroth a *w*, and Deut 28:30
toward the *w* of his bosom, and Deut 28:54
I give Achsah my daughter to *w* Josh 15:16
gave him Achsah his daughter to *w* Josh 15:17
I give Achsah my daughter to *w* Judg 1:12
gave him Achsah his daughter to *w* Judg 1:13
the *w* of Lapidoth, she judged Judg 4:4
of Jael the *w* of Heber the Kenite Judg 4:17
Then Jael Heber's *w* took a nail Judg 4:21
Jael the *w* of Heber the Kenite be Judg 5:24
And Gilead's *w* bare him sons Judg 11:2
his *w* was barren, and bare not Judg 13:2
Manoah arose, and went after his *w*. Judg 13:11
and Manoah and his *w* looked on Judg 13:19
his *w* looked on it, and fell on Judg 13:20
to Manoah and to his *w* Judg 13:21
And Manoah said unto his *w* Judg 13:22
But his *w* said unto him, If the Judg 13:23
now therefore get her for me to *w* Judg 14:2
to take a *w* of the uncircumcised Judg 14:3
that they said unto Samson's *w* Judg 14:15
Samson's *w* wept before him, and Judg 14:16
But Samson's *w* was given to his Judg 14:20
Samson visited his *w* with a kid Judg 15:1
go in to my *w* into the chamber Judg 15:1
because he had taken his *w* Judg 15:6
his daughter unto Benjamin to *w* Judg 21:1
be he that giveth a *w* to Benjamin Judg 21:18
catch you every man his *w* of the Judg 21:21
not to each man his *w* in the war Judg 21:22
the country of Moab, he, and his *w* Ruth 1:1
and the name of his *w* Naomi Ruth 1:2
the *w* of the dead, to raise up Ruth 4:5
the *w* of Mahlon, have I purchased Ruth 4:10
have I purchased to be my *w* Ruth 4:10
Boaz took Ruth, and she was his *w* Ruth 4:13
he gave to Peninnah his *w* 1Sa 1:4
and Elkanah knew Hannah his *w* 1Sa 1:19
And Eli blessed Elkanah and his *w* 1Sa 2:20
his daughter in law, Phinehas' *w* 1Sa 4:19
the name of Saul's *w* was Ahinoam 1Sa 14:50
Merab, her will I give thee to *w* 1Sa 18:17
unto Adriel the Meholathite to *w* 1Sa 18:19
gave him Michal his daughter to *w* 1Sa 18:27
and Michal David's *w* told him 1Sa 19:11
and the name of his *w* Abigail 1Sa 25:3
young men told Abigail, Nabal's *w* 1Sa 25:14
his *w* had told him these things, 1Sa 25:37
Abigail, to take her to him to *w* 1Sa 25:39
thee, to take thee to him to *w* 1Sa 25:40
of David, and became his *w* 1Sa 25:42
Michal his daughter, David's *w* 1Sa 25:44
the Carmelitess, Nabal's *w* 1Sa 27:3
Abigail the *w* of Nabal the 1Sa 30:5
save to every man his *w* and his 1Sa 30:22
Abigail Nabal's *w* the Carmelite 2Sa 2:2
of Abigail the *w* of Nabal the 2Sa 3:3
Ithream, by Eglah David's *w* 2Sa 3:5
saying, Deliver me my *w* Michal 2Sa 3:14
the *w* of Uriah the Hittite 2Sa 11:3
and to drink, and to lie with my *w* 2Sa 11:11
when the *w* of Uriah heard that 2Sa 11:26
to his house, and she became his *w* 2Sa 11:27
hast taken his *w* to be thy *w* 2Sa 12:9
hast taken the *w* of Uriah the 2Sa 12:10
of Uriah the Hittite to be thy *w* 2Sa 12:10
that Uriah's *w* bare unto David 2Sa 12:15
David comforted Bath-sheba his *w* 2Sa 12:24
me Abishag the Shunammite to *w* 1Kin 2:17
to Adonijah thy brother to *w* 1Kin 2:21
the daughter of Solomon to *w* 1Kin 4:11
the daughter of Solomon to *w* 1Kin 4:15
daughter, whom he had taken to *w* 1Kin 7:8
unto his daughter, Solomon's *w* 1Kin 9:16
so that he gave him to *w* the 1Kin 11:19
the sister of his own *w* 1Kin 11:19
And Jeroboam said to his *w* 1Kin 14:2
not known to be the *w* of Jeroboam 1Kin 14:2
And Jeroboam's *w* did so, and arose, 1Kin 14:4
the *w* of Jeroboam cometh to ask a 1Kin 14:5
said, Come in, thou *w* of Jeroboam 1Kin 14:6
And Jeroboam's *w* arose, and 1Kin 14:17
that he took to *w* Jezebel the 1Kin 16:31
But Jezebel his *w* came to him 1Kin 21:5
Jezebel his *w* said unto him, Dost 1Kin 21:7
whom Jezebel his *w* stirred up 1Kin 21:25
and she waited on Naaman's *w* 2Kin 5:2
the daughter of Ahab was his *w* 2Kin 8:18
Give thy daughter to my son to *w* 2Kin 14:9
the *w* of Shallum the son of 2Kin 22:14
begat children of Azubah his *w* 1Chr 2:18
then Abiah Hezron's *w* bare him 1Chr 2:24
Jerahmeel had also another *w* 1Chr 2:26
the name of the *w* of Abishur was 1Chr 2:29
to Jarha his servant to *w* 1Chr 2:35
the sixth, Ithream by Eglah his *w* 1Chr 3:3
his *w* Jehudijah bare Jered the 1Chr 4:18
the sons of his *w* Hodiah the 1Chr 4:19
Machir took to *w* the sister of 1Chr 7:15
Maachah the *w* of Machir bare a 1Chr 7:16
And when he went in to his *w* 1Chr 7:23
And he begat of Hodesh his *w* 1Chr 8:9
My *w* shall not dwell in the house 2Chr 8:11
of Jerimoth the son of David to *w* 2Chr 11:18
he had the daughter of Ahab to *w* 2Chr 21:6
the *w* of Jehoiada the priest, ( 2Chr 22:11
Give thy daughter to my son to *w* 2Chr 25:18
the *w* of Shallum the son of 2Chr 34:22
which took a *w* of the daughters Ezr 2:61
of Barzillai the Gileadite to *w* Neh 7:63
for his friends, and Zeresh his *w* Est 5:10
Then said Zeresh his *w* and all his Est 5:14
And Haman told Zeresh his *w* Est 6:13
wise men and Zeresh his *w* unto him Est 6:13
Then said his *w* unto him, Dost Job 2:9
My breath is strange to my *w* Job 19:17
Then let my *w* grind unto another, Job 31:10
be fatherless, and his *w* a widow Ps 109:9
Thy *w* shall be as a fruitful vine Ps 128:3
rejoice with the *w* of thy youth Prov 5:18
goeth in to his neighbour's *w* Prov 6:29
Whoso findeth a *w* findeth a good Prov 18:22
the contentions of a *w* are a Prov 19:13
a prudent *w* is from the LORD Prov 19:14
Live joyfully with the *w* whom Eccl 9:9
the children of the married *w* Is 54:1
a *w* of youth, when thou wast Is 54:6
They say, If a man put away his *w* Jer 3:1
Surely as a *w* treacherously Jer 3:20
neighed after his neighbour's *w* Jer 5:8
husband with the *w* shall be taken Jer 6:11
Thou shalt not take thee a *w* Jer 16:2
But as a *w* that committeth Eze 16:32
hath defiled his neighbour's *w* Eze 18:6
and defiled his neighbour's *w* Eze 18:11
not defiled his neighbour's *w* Eze 18:15
with his neighbour's *w* Eze 22:11
and at even my *w* died Eze 24:18
every one his neighbour's *w* Eze 33:26
take unto thee a *w* of whoredoms Hos 1:2
for she is not my *w*, neither am I Hos 2:2
Syria, and Israel served for a *w* Hos 12:12
and for a *w* he kept sheep Hos 12:12
Thy *w* shall be an harlot in the Amos 7:17
the *w* of thy youth, against whom Mal 2:14
and the *w* of thy covenant Mal 2:14
against the *w* of his youth Mal 2:15
her that had been the *w* of Urias Mt 1:6
not to take unto thee Mary thy *w* Mt 1:20
him, and took unto him his *w* Mt 1:24
Whosoever shall put away his *w* Mt 5:31
whosoever shall put away his *w* Mt 5:32
sake, his brother Philip's *w* Mt 14:3
him to be sold, and his *w*, and Mt 18:25
to put away his *w* for every cause Mt 19:3
mother, and shall cleave to his *w* Mt 19:5
Whosoever shall put away his *w* Mt 19:9
case of the man be so with his *w* Mt 19:10
or father, or mother, or *w* Mt 19:29
his brother shall marry his *w* Mt 22:24
first, when he had married a *w* Mt 22:25
left his *w* unto his brother Mt 22:25
whose *w* shall she be of the seven Mt 22:28
his *w* sent unto him, saying, Have Mt 27:19
sake, his brother Philip's *w* Mk 6:17
for thee to have thy brother's *w* Mk 6:18
for a man to put away his *w* Mk 10:2
and mother, and cleave to his *w* Mk 10:7
Whosoever shall put away his *w* Mk 10:11
or father, or mother, or *w* Mk 10:29
leave his *w* behind him, and leave Mk 12:19
his brother should take his *w* Mk 12:19
and the first took a *w*, and dying Mk 12:20
whose *w* shall she be of them Mk 12:23
for the seven had her to *w* Mk 12:23
his *w* was of the daughters of Lk 1:5
thy *w* Elisabeth shall bear thee a Lk 1:13
my *w* well stricken in years Lk 1:18
days his *w* Elisabeth conceived Lk 1:24
be taxed with Mary his espoused *w* Lk 2:5
Herodias his brother Philip's *w* Lk 3:19
Joanna the *w* of Chuza Herod's Lk 8:3
another said, I have married a *w* Lk 14:20
not his father, and mother, and *w* Lk 14:26
Whosoever putteth away his *w* Lk 16:18
Remember Lot's *w* Lk 17:32
or parents, or brethren, or *w* Lk 18:29
any man's brother die, having a *w* Lk 20:28
his brother should take his *w* Lk 20:28
and the first took a *w*, and died Lk 20:29
And the second took her to *w* Lk 20:30
whose *w* of them is she Lk 20:33
for seven had her to *w* Lk 20:33
Mary the *w* of Cleophas, and Mary Jn 19:25
Ananias, with Sapphira his *w* Acts 5:1
his *w* also being privy to it, and Acts 5:2
of three hours after, when his *w* Acts 5:7
from Italy, with his *w* Priscilla Acts 18:2
Felix came with his *w* Drusilla Acts 24:24
one should have his father's *w* 1Cor 5:1
let every man have his own *w* 1Cor 7:2
render unto the *w* due benevolence 1Cor 7:3
also the *w* unto the husband 1Cor 7:3
The *w* hath not power of her own 1Cor 7:4
power of his own body, but the *w* 1Cor 7:4
Let not the *w* depart from her 1Cor 7:10
not the husband put away his *w* 1Cor 7:11
hath a *w* that believeth not 1Cor 7:12
husband is sanctified by the *w* 1Cor 7:14
the unbelieving *w* is sanctified 1Cor 7:14
For what knowest thou, O *w* 1Cor 7:16
whether thou shalt save thy *w* 1Cor 7:16
Art thou bound unto a *w* 1Cor 7:27
Art thou loosed from a *w* 1Cor 7:27
seek not a *w* 1Cor 7:27
world, how he may please his *w* 1Cor 7:33
is difference also between a *w* 1Cor 7:34
The *w* is bound by the law as long 1Cor 7:39
power to lead about a sister, a *w* 1Cor 9:5
the husband is the head of the *w* Eph 5:23
that loveth his *w* loveth himself Eph 5:28
and shall be joined unto his *w* Eph 5:31
so love his *w* even as himself Eph 5:33
the *w* see that she reverence her Eph 5:33
blameless, the husband of one *w* 1Ti 3:2
deacons be the husbands of one *w* 1Ti 3:12
old, having been the *w* of one man 1Ti 5:9
blameless, the husband of one *w* Titus 1:6
giving honour unto the *w* 1Pet 3:7
his *w* hath made herself ready Rev 19:7
shew thee the bride, the Lamb's *w* Rev 21:9

**WIFE'S**

And Adam called his *w* name Eve Gen 3:20
they will slay me for my *w* sake Gen 20:11
his *w* name was Mehetabel, the Gen 36:39
of thy father's *w* daughter Lev 18:11
his *w* sons grew up, and they Judg 11:2
his *w* name was Mehetabel, the 1Chr 1:50
whose *w* name was Maachah 1Chr 8:29
Jehiel, whose *w* name was Maachah 1Chr 9:35
he saw his *w* mother laid, and sick Mt 8:14
But Simon's *w* mother lay sick of Mk 1:30
Simon's *w* mother was taken with a Lk 4:38

**WILD**

And he will be a *w* man Gen 16:12
will also send *w* beasts among you Lev 26:22
the *w* goat, and the pygarg Deut 14:5
the pygarg, and the *w* ox Deut 14:5
to the *w* beasts of the earth 1Sa 17:46
men upon the rocks of the *w* goats 1Sa 24:2
was as light of foot as a *w* roe 2Sa 2:18
gather herbs, and found a *w* vine 2Kin 4:39
gathered thereof *w* gourds his lap 2Kin 4:39
there passed by a *w* beast that 2Kin 14:9
there passed by a *w* beast that 2Chr 25:18
Doth the *w* ass bray when he hath Job 6:5
man be born like a *w* ass's colt Job 11:12
as *w* asses in the desert, go they Job 24:5
*w* goats of the rock bring forth Job 39:1
Who hath sent out the *w* ass free Job 39:5
loosed the bands of the *w* ass Job 39:5
or that the *w* beast may break Job 39:15
the *w* beasts of the field are Ps 50:11
the *w* beast of the field doth Ps 80:13
the *w* asses quench their thirst Ps 104:11
are a refuge for the *w* goats Ps 104:18
and it brought forth *w* grapes Is 5:2
grapes, brought it forth *w* grapes Is 5:4
But *w* beasts of the desert shall Is 13:21
the *w* beasts of the islands shall Is 13:22
dens for ever, a joy of *w* asses Is 32:14
The *w* beasts of the desert shall Is 34:14
with the *w* beasts of the island Is 34:14
the streets, as a *w* bull in a net Is 51:20
A *w* ass used to the wilderness, Jer 2:24
the *w* asses did stand in the high Jer 14:6
Therefore the *w* beasts of the Jer 50:39
the *w* beasts of the islands shall Jer 50:39
his dwelling was with the *w* asses Dan 5:21
Assyria, a *w* ass alone by himself Hos 8:9
the *w* beast shall tear them Hos 13:8

his meat was locusts and *w* honey........... Mt 3:4
and he did eat locusts and *w* honey......... Mk 1:6
and was with the *w* beasts...................... Mk 1:13
*w* beasts, and creeping things, and..... Acts 10:12
*w* beasts, and creeping things, and..... Acts 11:6
being a *w* olive tree, wert.................... Rom 11:17
olive tree which is *w* by nature.......... Rom 11:24

**WILDERNESS**
unto El-paran, which is by the *w*......... Gen 14:6
by a fountain of water in the *w*.......... Gen 16:7
wandered in the *w* of Beer-sheba........ Gen 21:14
and he grew, and dwelt in the *w*......... Gen 21:20
And he dwelt in the *w* of Paran .......... Gen 21:21
that found the mules in the *w* ............ Gen 36:24
into this pit that is in the *w*............... Gen 37:22
three days' journey into the *w* ................ Ex 3:18
Go into the *w* to meet Moses.................. Ex 4:27
may hold a feast unto me in the *w*.......... Ex 5:1
that they may serve me in the *w*.............. Ex 7:16
go three days' journey into the *w*........... Ex 8:27
to the LORD your God in the *w* ............... Ex 8:28
the way of the *w* of the Red sea........... Ex 13:18
in Etham, in the edge of the *w*............ Ex 13:20
the land, the *w* hath shut them in.......... Ex 14:3
taken us away to die in the *w*............... Ex 14:11
than that we should die in the *w*........... Ex 14:12
they went out into the *w* of Shur.......... Ex 15:22
and they went three days in the *w*.......... Ex 15:22
of Israel came unto the *w* of Sin.............. Ex 16:1
against Moses and Aaron in the *w*.......... Ex 16:2
have brought us forth into this *w*............ Ex 16:3
that they looked toward the *w*................ Ex 16:10
upon the face of the *w* there lay............ Ex 16:14
wherewith I have fed you in the *w*........ Ex 16:32
journeyed from the *w* of Sin.................... Ex 17:1
and his wife unto Moses into the *w*........ Ex 18:5
day came they into the *w* of Sinai........... Ex 19:1
of Sinai, and had pitched in the *w*.......... Ex 19:2
unto the LORD, in the *w* of Sinai........... Lev 7:38
him go for a scapegoat into the *w*....... Lev 16:10
the hand of a fit man into the *w*.......... Lev 16:21
he shall let go the goat in the *w* ......... Lev 16:22
unto Moses in the *w* of Sinai................. Num 1:1
numbered them in the *w* of Sinai........ Num 1:19
in the *w* of Sinai, and they had no........ Num 3:4
unto Moses in the *w* of Sinai............... Num 3:14
unto Moses in the *w* of Sinai................ Num 9:1
month at even in the *w* of Sinai.......... Num 9:5
journeys out of the *w* of Sinai........... Num 10:12
cloud rested in the *w* of Paran .......... Num 10:12
how we are to encamp in the *w*.......... Num 10:31
and pitched in the *w* of Paran........... Num 12:16
sent them from the *w* of Paran............ Num 13:3
land from the *w* of Zin unto Rehob.. Num 13:21
of Israel, unto the *w* of Paran............ Num 13:26
would God we had died in this *w*........ Num 14:2
he hath slain them in the *w*............... Num 14:16
which I did in Egypt and in the *w*..... Num 14:22
get you into the *w* by the way of...... Num 14:25
carcases shall fall in this *w*................. Num 14:29
they shall fall in this *w*.................... Num 14:32
shall wander in the *w* forty years...... Num 14:33
your carcases be wasted in the *w*........ Num 14:33
in this *w* they shall be consumed,...... Num 14:35
children of Israel were in the *w*........ Num 15:32
and honey, to kill us in the *w*........... Num 16:13
of the LORD into this *w*, that we......... Num 20:4
up out of Egypt to die in the *w*.......... Num 21:5
in the *w* which is before Moab,........... Num 21:11
which is in the *w* that cometh out.... Num 21:13
from the *w* they went to Mattanah... Num 21:18
out against Israel into the *w*............. Num 21:23
but he set his face toward the *w*......... Num 24:1
of Israel in the *w* of Sinai................. Num 26:64
They shall surely die in the *w*............ Num 26:65
Our father died in the *w*, and he......... Num 27:3
Meribah in Kadesh in the *w* of Zin... Num 27:14
them wander in the *w* forty years..... Num 32:13
yet again leave them in the *w*............. Num 32:15
which is in the edge of the *w* ............. Num 33:6
the midst of the sea into the *w*............ Num 33:8
days' journey in the *w* of Etham ......... Num 33:8
sea, and encamped in the *w* of Sin.... Num 33:11
their journey out of the *w* of Sin...... Num 33:12
and pitched in the *w* of Sinai............. Num 33:15
and pitched in the *w* of Zin............... Num 33:36
*w* of Zin along by the coast of............ Num 34:3
on this side Jordan in the *w*................ Deut 1:1
all that great and terrible *w*................ Deut 1:19
And in the *w*, where thou hast seen... Deut 1:31
the *w* by the way of the Red sea ......... Deut 1:40
the *w* by the way of the Red sea........... Deut 2:1
thy walking through this great *w*.......... Deut 2:7
by the way of the *w* of Moab ............... Deut 2:8
I sent messengers out of the *w* of....... Deut 2:26
Namely, Bezer in the *w*, in the............ Deut 4:43
thee these forty years in the *w*.............. Deut 8:2
through that great and terrible *w*....... Deut 8:15
Who fed thee in the *w* with manna.... Deut 8:16
LORD thy God to wrath in the *w*............. Deut 9:7
them out to slay them in the *w*............ Deut 9:28
And what he did unto you in the *w*.... Deut 11:5
from the *w* and Lebanon, from the... Deut 11:24
have led you forty years in the *w*......... Deut 29:5
land, and in the waste howling *w*...... Deut 32:10
Meribah-kadesh, in the *w* of Zin........ Deut 32:51
From the *w* and this Lebanon even.............. Josh 1:4
of war, died in the *w* by the way.............. Josh 5:4
people that were born in the *w* by......... Josh 5:5
walked forty years in the *w*.................... Josh 5:6
them, and fled by the way of the *w*..... Josh 8:15
the people that fled to the *w*................. Josh 8:20
in the *w* wherein they chased them..... Josh 8:24
and in the springs, and in the *w*........... Josh 12:8
of Israel wandered in the *w*............... Josh 14:10
the *w* of Zin southward was the........... Josh 15:1
In the *w*, Beth-arabah, Middin, and... Josh 15:61
to the *w* that goeth up from................... Josh 16:1
were at the *w* of Beth-aven................. Josh 18:12
they assigned Bezer in the *w* upon....... Josh 20:8
ye dwelt in the *w* a long season........... Josh 24:7
of Judah into the *w* of Judah................ Judg 1:16
flesh with the thorns of the *w* ................ Judg 8:7
of the city, and thorns of the *w*............. Judg 8:16
through the *w* unto the Red sea.......... Judg 11:16
they went along through the *w*.......... Judg 11:18
from the *w* even unto Jordan............. Judg 11:22
of Israel unto the way of the *w*........... Judg 20:42
fled toward the *w* unto the rock........ Judg 20:45
fled to the *w* unto the rock................ Judg 20:47
with all the plagues in the *w*.................... 1Sa 4:8
the valley of Zeboim toward the *w*...... 1Sa 13:18
left those few sheep in the *w*................ 1Sa 17:28
abode in the *w* in strong holds.............. 1Sa 23:14
in a mountain in the *w* of Ziph.............. 1Sa 23:14
David was in the *w* of Ziph in a........... 1Sa 23:15
and his men were in the *w* of Maon.... 1Sa 23:24
a rock, and abode in the *w* of Maon.... 1Sa 23:25
after David in the *w* of Maon............... 1Sa 23:25
David is in the *w* of En-gedi.................... 1Sa 24:1
and went down to the *w* of Paran.......... 1Sa 25:1
David heard in the *w* that Nabal............ 1Sa 25:4
out of the *w* to salute our master........ 1Sa 25:14
that this fellow hath in the *w*............... 1Sa 25:21
and went down to the *w* of Ziph............... 1Sa 26:2
to seek David in the *w* of Ziph.............. 1Sa 26:2
But David abode in the *w*, and he......... 1Sa 26:3
Saul came after him into the *w*............. 1Sa 26:3
by the way of the *w* of Gibeon.............. 2Sa 2:24
over, toward the way of the *w*.............. 2Sa 15:23
will tarry in the plain of the *w*............. 2Sa 15:28
as be faint in the *w* may drink............... 2Sa 16:2
this night in the plains of the *w*........... 2Sa 17:16
and weary, and thirsty, in the *w*........... 2Sa 17:29
buried in his own house in the *w*........... 1Kin 2:34
And Baalath, and Tadmor in the *w*....... 1Kin 9:18
went a day's journey into the *w*............ 1Kin 19:4
on thy way to the *w* of Damascus..... 1Kin 19:15
The way through the *w* of Edom........... 2Kin 3:8
of the *w* from the river Euphrates.......... 1Chr 5:9
Bezer in the *w* with her suburbs,......... 1Chr 6:78
the hold to the *w* men of might.......... 1Chr 12:8
LORD, which Moses made in the *w*.... 1Chr 21:29
of the LORD had made in the *w*.............. 2Chr 1:3
And he built Tadmor in the *w*............... 2Chr 8:4
the brook, before the *w* of Jeruel....... 2Chr 20:16
and went forth into the *w* of Tekoa.. 2Chr 20:20
toward the watch tower in the *w*...... 2Chr 20:24
of God laid upon Israel in the *w*........ 2Chr 24:9
forsookest them not in the *w*................ Neh 9:19
didst thou sustain them in the *w*.......... Neh 9:21
came a great wind from the *w*............... Job 1:19
in a *w* where there is no way............... Job 12:24
the *w* yieldeth food for them and........... Job 24:5
fleeing into the *w* in former time............ Job 30:3
on the *w*, wherein there is no man...... Job 38:26
Whose house I have made the *w*.............. Job 39:6
voice of the LORD shaketh the *w*............... Ps 29:8
the LORD shaketh the *w* of Kadesh.......... Ps 29:8
far off, and remain in the *w*................... Ps 55:7
when he was in the *w* of Judah................ Ps 63:*t*
drop upon the pastures of the *w*........... Ps 65:12
thou didst march through the *w*.............. Ps 68:7
in the *w* shall bow before him............... Ps 72:9
to the people inhabiting the *w*............ Ps 74:14
He clave the rocks in the *w*.................. Ps 78:15
provoking the most High in the *w*......... Ps 78:17
Can God furnish a table in the *w*.......... Ps 78:19
oft did they provoke him in the *w*......... Ps 78:40
guided them in the *w* like a flock.......... Ps 78:52
in the day of temptation in the *w*............ Ps 95:8
I am like a pelican of the *w*.................. Ps 102:6
the depths, as through the *w*............... Ps 106:9
But lusted exceedingly in the *w*........... Ps 106:14
them, to overthrow them in the *w*......... Ps 106:26
in the *w* in a solitary way.................... Ps 107:4
He turneth rivers into a *w*................... Ps 107:33
He turneth the *w* into a standing......... Ps 107:35
causeth them to wander in the *w*.......... Ps 107:40
led his people through the *w*.............. Ps 136:16
It is better to dwell in the *w*.............. Prov 21:19
of the *w* like pillars of smoke................ Song 3:6
is this that cometh up from the *w*.......... Song 8:5
That made the world as a *w*.................... Is 14:17
of the land from Sela to the *w*................. Is 16:1
they wandered through the *w*.................... Is 16:8
it for them that dwell in the *w*............. Is 23:13
forsaken, and left like a *w*..................... Is 27:10
the *w* be a fruitful field, and the.......... Is 32:15
judgment shall dwell in the *w*............... Is 32:16
Sharon is like a *w*.................................. Is 33:9
The *w* and the solitary place shall............. Is 35:1
for in the *w* shall waters break.............. Is 35:6
voice of him that crieth in the *w*.............. Is 40:3
I will make the *w* a pool of water.......... Is 41:18
I will plant in the *w* the cedar............... Is 41:19
Let the *w* and the cities thereof............... Is 42:11
I will even make a way in the *w*............. Is 43:19
because I give waters in the *w*.............. Is 43:20
up the sea, I make the rivers a *w*............. Is 50:2
and he will make her *w* like Eden............ Is 51:3
the deep, as an horse in the *w*............... Is 63:13
are a *w*, Zion is a *w*................................ Is 64:10
thou wentest after me in the *w*.................. Jer 2:2
Egypt, that led us through the *w*.............. Jer 2:6
A wild ass used to the *w*, that................. Jer 2:24
Have I been a *w* unto Israel.................... Jer 2:31
for them, as the Arabian in the *w*............. Jer 3:2
the *w* toward the daughter of my........... Jer 4:11
lo, the fruitful place was a *w*.................. Jer 4:26
Oh that I had in the *w* a lodging.............. Jer 9:2
of the *w* a lamentation, because............. Jer 9:10
and is burned up like a *w*, that.............. Jer 9:12
corners, that dwell in the *w*.................. Jer 9:26
my pleasant portion a desolate *w*.......... Jer 12:10
all high places through the *w*.............. Jer 12:12
passeth away by the wind of the *w*...... Jer 13:24
the parched places in the *w*.................... Jer 17:6
yet surely I will make thee a *w*................. Jer 22:6
places of the *w* are dried up................ Jer 23:10
of the sword found grace in the *w*........... Jer 31:2
and be like the heath in the *w*................ Jer 48:6
of the nations shall be a *w*................... Jer 50:12
a desolation, a dry land, and a *w*.......... Jer 51:43
like the ostriches in the *w*...................... Lam 4:3
they laid wait for us in the *w*............... Lam 4:19
because of the sword of the *w*.................. Lam 5:9
than the *w* toward Diblath..................... Eze 6:14
And now she is planted in the *w*.......... Eze 19:13
Egypt, and brought them into the *w*... Eze 20:10
rebelled against me in the *w*............... Eze 20:13
out my fury upon them in the *w*........... Eze 20:13
up my hand unto them in the *w*............ Eze 20:15
I make an end of them in the *w*........... Eze 20:17
said unto their children in the *w*........ Eze 20:18
my anger against them in the *w*........... Eze 20:21
mine hand unto them also in the *w*..... Eze 20:23
you into the *w* of the people................ Eze 20:35
in the *w* of the land of Egypt............... Eze 20:36
were brought Sabeans from the *w*........ Eze 23:42
will leave thee thrown into the *w*.......... Eze 29:5
they shall dwell safely in the *w*........... Eze 34:25
she was born, and make her as a *w*........ Hos 2:3
her, and bring her into the *w*................. Hos 2:14
found Israel like grapes in the *w*............ Hos 9:10
I did know thee in the *w*, in the............. Hos 13:5
the LORD shall come up from the *w*.... Hos 13:15
devoured the pastures of the *w*............. Joel 1:19
devoured the pastures of the *w*............. Joel 1:20
them, and behind them a desolate *w*...... Joel 2:3
the pastures of the *w* do spring............ Joel 2:22
and Edom shall be a desolate *w*.............. Joel 3:19
led you forty years through the *w*..... Amos 2:10
and offerings in the *w* forty years...... Amos 5:25
of Hemath unto the river of the *w*...... Amos 6:14
a desolation, and dry like a *w*.......... Zeph 2:13
waste for the dragons of the *w*................ Mal 1:3
preaching in the *w* of Judaea.................. Mt 3:1
The voice of one crying in the *w*.............. Mt 3:3
the *w* to be tempted of the devil................ Mt 4:1
went ye out into the *w* to see................. Mt 11:7
we have so much bread in the *w*.......... Mt 15:33
The voice of one crying in the *w*............. Mk 1:3
John did baptize in the *w*...................... Mk 1:4
the spirit driveth him into the *w*............ Mk 1:12
he was there in the *w* forty days............ Mk 1:13
men with bread here in the *w*................. Mk 8:4
the son of Zacharias in the *w*.................. Lk 3:2
The voice of one crying in the *w*.............. Lk 3:4
was led by the Spirit into the *w*............... Lk 4:1
And he withdrew himself into the *w*....... Lk 5:16
went ye out into the *w* for to see.......... Lk 7:24
driven of the devil into the *w*................. Lk 8:29
leave the ninety and nine in the *w*.......... Lk 15:4
the voice of one crying in the *w*.............. Jn 1:23
lifted up the serpent in the *w*................. Jn 3:14
fathers did eat manna in the *w*................ Jn 6:49
unto a country near to the *w*................... Jn 11:54
there appeared to him in the *w* of........ Acts 7:30
Red sea, and in the *w* forty years......... Acts 7:36
*w* with the angel which spake to........... Acts 7:38
the space of forty years in the *w*.......... Acts 7:42
tabernacle of witness in the *w*.............. Acts 7:44
he their manners in the *w*.................... Acts 13:18
leddest out into the *w* four................... Acts 21:38
for they were overthrown in the *w*..... 1Cor 10:5
in the city, in perils in the *w*........... 2Cor 11:26
in the day of temptation in the *w*.......... Heb 3:8
whose carcases fell in the *w*.................. Heb 3:17
And the woman fled into the *w*............. Rev 12:6
that she might fly into the *w*.............. Rev 12:14
me away in the spirit into the *w*........... Rev 17:3

**WILES**
For they vex you with their *w*........... Num 25:18
stand against the *w* of the devil............. Eph 6:11

**WILFULLY**
For if we sin *w* after that we................ Heb 10:26

**WILILY**
They did work *w*, and went and made.. Josh 9:4

**WILL** See PREFACE.

**WILLETH**
So then it is not of him that *w*............ Rom 9:16

**WILLING**
the woman will not be *w* to follow....... Gen 24:5
will not be *w* to follow thee................. Gen 24:8
whosoever is of a *w* heart......................... Ex 35:5
every one whom his spirit made *w*........ Ex 35:21

women, as many as were *w* hearted ..... Ex 35:22
a *w* offering unto the LORD ..... Ex 35:29
whose heart made them *w* to bring ..... Ex 35:29
a perfect heart and with a *w* mind ..... 1Chr 28:9
workmanship every *w* skilful man ..... 1Chr 28:21
who then is *w* to consecrate his ..... 1Chr 29:5
the unicorn be *w* to serve thee ..... Job 39:9
Thy people shall be *w* in the day ..... Ps 110:3
If ye be *w* and obedient, ye shall ..... Is 1:19
not *w* to make her a publick ..... Mt 1:19
the spirit indeed is *w*, but the ..... Mt 26:41
*w* to content the people, released ..... Mk 15:15
*w* to justify himself, said unto ..... Lk 10:29
Saying, Father, if thou be *w* ..... Lk 22:42
*w* to release Jesus, spake again ..... Lk 23:20
ye were *w* for a season to rejoice ..... Jn 5:35
*w* to shew the Jews a pleasure, ..... Acts 24:27
*w* to do the Jews a pleasure, ..... Acts 25:9
*w* to save Paul, kept them from ..... Acts 27:43
*w* to shew his wrath, and to make ..... Rom 9:22
*w* rather to be absent from the ..... 2Cor 5:8
power they were *w* of themselves ..... 2Cor 8:3
For if there be first a *w* mind ..... 2Cor 8:12
we were *w* to have imparted unto ..... 1Th 2:8
to distribute, *w* to communicate ..... 1Ti 6:18
*w* more abundantly to shew unto ..... Heb 6:17
in all things *w* to live honestly ..... Heb 13:18
not *w* that any should perish, but ..... 2Pet 3:9

**WILLINGLY**
of every man that giveth it *w* ..... Ex 25:2
when the people *w* offered ..... Judg 5:2
themselves *w* among the people ..... Judg 5:9
answered, We will *w* give them ..... Judg 8:25
of the king's work, offered *w* ..... 1Chr 29:6
rejoiced, for that they offered *w* ..... 1Chr 29:9
heart they offered *w* to the LORD ..... 1Chr 29:9
to offer so *w* after this sort ..... 1Chr 29:14
of mine heart I have *w* offered ..... 1Chr 29:17
here, to offer *w* unto thee ..... 1Chr 29:17
who *w* offered himself unto the ..... 2Chr 17:16
princes gave *w* unto the people ..... 2Chr 35:8
beside all that was *w* offered ..... Ezr 1:6
of every one that *w* offered a ..... Ezr 3:5
offering *w* for the house of their ..... Ezr 7:16
that *w* offered themselves to ..... Neh 11:2
flax, and worketh *w* with her hands.. Prov 31:13
For he doth not afflict *w* nor ..... Lam 3:33
because he *w* walked after the ..... Hos 5:11
Then they *w* received him into the ..... Jn 6:21
was made subject to vanity, not *w* ..... Rom 8:20
For if I do this thing *w*, I have ..... 1Cor 9:17
be as it were of necessity, but *w* ..... Philem 14
thereof, not by constraint, but *w* ..... 1Pet 5:2
For this they *w* are ignorant of, ..... 2Pet 3:5

**WILLOW**
waters, and set it as a *w* tree ..... Eze 17:5

**WILLOWS**
of thick trees, and *w* of the brook ..... Lev 23:40
the *w* of the brook compass him ..... Job 40:22
upon the *w* in the midst thereof ..... Ps 137:2
carry away to the brook of the *w* ..... Is 15:7
as *w* by the water courses ..... Is 44:4

**WILT**
if thou *w* take the left hand, ..... Gen 13:9
what *w* thou give me, seeing I go ..... Gen 15:2
and whither *w* thou go ..... Gen 16:8
*W* thou also destroy the righteous ..... Gen 18:23
*w* thou also destroy and not spare ..... Gen 18:24
*w* thou destroy all the city for ..... Gen 18:28
*w* thou slay also a righteous ..... Gen 20:4
thou *w* not deal falsely with me ..... Gen 21:23
saying, But if thou *w* give it ..... Gen 23:13
unto her, *W* thou go with this man .... Gen 24:58
That thou *w* do us no hurt, as we ..... Gen 26:29
if thou *w* do this thing for me, I ..... Gen 30:31
What *w* thou give me, that thou ..... Gen 38:16
*W* thou give me a pledge, till ..... Gen 38:17
If thou *w* send our brother with ..... Gen 43:4
But if thou *w* not send him, we ..... Gen 43:5
the hand of him whom thou *w* send ..... Ex 4:13
if thou *w* not let my people go, ..... Ex 8:21
them go, and *w* hold them still, ..... Ex 9:2
that thou *w* not let them go ..... Ex 9:17
How long *w* thou refuse to humble ..... Ex 10:3
if thou *w* not redeem it, then ..... Ex 13:13
If thou *w* diligently hearken to ..... Ex 15:26
*w* do that which is right in his ..... Ex 15:26
*w* give ear to his commandments, ..... Ex 15:26
Thou *w* surely wear away, both ..... Ex 18:18
if thou *w* make me an altar of ..... Ex 20:25
if thou *w* forgive their sin ..... Ex 32:32
me know whom thou *w* send with me . Ex 33:12
*w* thou put out the eyes of these ..... Num 16:14
*w* thou be wroth with all the ..... Num 16:22
If thou *w* indeed deliver this ..... Num 21:2
when thou *w* ease thyself abroad, ..... Deut 23:13
if thou *w* not hearken unto the ..... Deut 28:15
If thou *w* not observe to do all ..... Deut 28:58
away, so that thou *w* not hear ..... Deut 30:17
what *w* thou do unto thy great ..... Josh 7:9
Caleb said unto her, What *w* thou ..... Judg 1:14
If thou *w* go with me, then I will ..... Judg 4:8
but if thou *w* not go with me, ..... Judg 4:8
If thou *w* save Israel by mine ..... Judg 6:36
thou *w* save Israel by mine hand ..... Judg 6:37
*W* not thou possess that which ..... Judg 11:24
if thou *w* offer a burnt offering, ..... Judg 13:16
If thou *w* redeem it, redeem it ..... Ruth 4:4
but if thou *w* not redeem it, then ..... Ruth 4:4
if thou *w* indeed look on the ..... 1Sa 1:11
but *w* give unto thine handmaid a ..... 1Sa 1:11
How long *w* thou be drunken ..... 1Sa 1:14
*w* thou deliver them into the hand ..... 1Sa 14:37
How long *w* thou mourn for Saul, ..... 1Sa 16:1
wherefore then *w* thou sin against ..... 1Sa 19:5
if thou *w* take that, take it ..... 1Sa 21:9
that thou *w* not cut off my seed ..... 1Sa 24:21
that thou *w* not destroy my name ..... 1Sa 24:21
know and consider what thou *w* do ..... 1Sa 25:17
that thou *w* neither kill me, nor ..... 1Sa 30:15
*w* thou deliver them into mine ..... 2Sa 5:19
*w* thou not tell me ..... 2Sa 13:4
Joab said, Wherefore *w* thou run ..... 2Sa 18:22
why *w* thou swallow up the ..... 2Sa 20:19
thou *w* shew thyself merciful ..... 2Sa 22:26
man thou *w* shew thyself upright ..... 2Sa 22:26
the pure thou *w* shew thyself pure ..... 2Sa 22:27
with the froward thou *w* shew ..... 2Sa 22:27
the afflicted people thou *w* save ..... 2Sa 22:28
or *w* thou flee three months ..... 2Sa 24:13
if thou *w* walk in my ways, to ..... 1Kin 3:14
if thou *w* walk in my statutes, and ..... 1Kin 6:12
if thou *w* walk before me, as ..... 1Kin 9:4
thee, and *w* keep my statutes and my .. 1Kin 9:4
if thou *w* hearken unto all that I ..... 1Kin 11:38
*w* walk in my ways, and do that is ..... 1Kin 11:38
If thou *w* be a servant unto this ..... 1Kin 12:7
*w* serve them, and answer them, and.. 1Kin 12:7
If thou *w* give me half thine ..... 1Kin 13:8
*W* thou go with me to battle to ..... 1Kin 22:4
*w* thou go with me against Moab to ..... 2Kin 3:7
Wherefore *w* thou go to him to day ..... 2Kin 4:23
I know the evil that thou *w* do ..... 2Kin 8:12
strong holds *w* thou set on fire ..... 2Kin 8:12
their young men *w* thou slay with ..... 2Kin 8:12
*w* dash their children, and rip up ..... 2Kin 8:12
How then *w* thou turn away the ..... 2Kin 18:24
*w* thou deliver them into mine ..... 1Chr 14:10
that thou *w* build him an house ..... 1Chr 17:25
if thou *w* walk before me, as ..... 2Chr 7:17
of Judah, *W* thou go with me to ..... 2Chr 18:3
our affliction, then thou *w* hear ..... 2Chr 20:9
O our God, *w* thou not judge them ... 2Chr 20:12
But if thou *w* go, do it, be ..... 2Chr 25:8
and when *w* thou return ..... Neh 2:6
the king unto her, What *w* thou ..... Est 5:3
with thee, *w* thou be grieved ..... Job 4:2
which of the saints *w* thou turn ..... Job 5:1
How long *w* thou not depart from ..... Job 7:19
How long *w* thou speak these ..... Job 8:2
I know that thou *w* not hold me ..... Job 9:28
*w* thou bring me into dust again ..... Job 10:9
thou *w* not acquit me from mine ..... Job 10:14
*W* thou break a leaf driven to and ..... Job 13:25
*w* thou pursue the dry stubble ..... Job 13:25
thou *w* have a desire to the work ..... Job 14:15
that thou *w* bring me to death ..... Job 30:23
*w* thou condemn him that is most ..... Job 34:17
*W* thou hunt the prey for the lion ..... Job 38:39
*W* thou trust him, because his ..... Job 39:11
or *w* thou leave thy labour to him ..... Job 39:11
*W* thou believe him, that he will ..... Job 39:12
*W* thou also disannul my judgment ..... Job 40:8
*w* thou condemn me, that thou ..... Job 40:8
*w* thou take him for a servant for ..... Job 41:4
*W* thou play with him as with a ..... Job 41:5
or *w* thou bind him for thy ..... Job 41:5
thou, LORD, *w* bless the righteous ..... Ps 5:12
with favour *w* thou compass him as ..... Ps 5:12
his heart, Thou *w* not require it ..... Ps 10:13
thou *w* prepare their heart ..... Ps 10:17
thou *w* cause thine ear to hear ..... Ps 10:17
How long *w* thou forget me, O LORD ..... Ps 13:1
how long *w* thou hide thy face ..... Ps 13:1
For thou *w* not leave my soul in ..... Ps 16:10
neither *w* thou suffer thine Holy ..... Ps 16:10
Thou *w* shew me the path of life ..... Ps 16:11
upon thee, for thou *w* hear me ..... Ps 17:6
thou *w* shew thyself merciful ..... Ps 18:25
man thou *w* shew thyself upright ..... Ps 18:25
the pure thou *w* shew thyself pure ..... Ps 18:26
thou *w* shew thyself froward ..... Ps 18:26
For thou *w* save the afflicted ..... Ps 18:27
but *w* bring down high looks ..... Ps 18:27
For thou *w* light my candle ..... Ps 18:28
LORD, how long *w* thou look on ..... Ps 35:17
thou *w* hear, O Lord my God ..... Ps 38:15
thou *w* not deliver him unto the ..... Ps 41:2
thou *w* make all his bed in his ..... Ps 41:3
heart, O God, thou *w* not despise ..... Ps 51:17
*w* not thou deliver my feet from ..... Ps 56:13
*W* not thou, O God, which hadst ..... Ps 60:10
Thou *w* prolong the king's life ..... Ps 61:6
in righteousness *w* thou answer us ..... Ps 65:5
*w* thou be angry for ever ..... Ps 79:5
how long *w* thou be angry against ..... Ps 80:4
if thou *w* hearken unto me ..... Ps 81:8
*W* thou be angry with us for ever ..... Ps 85:5
*w* thou draw out thine anger to ..... Ps 85:5
*W* thou not revive us again ..... Ps 85:6
for thou *w* answer me ..... Ps 86:7
*W* thou shew wonders to the dead ..... Ps 88:10
*w* thou hide thyself for ever ..... Ps 89:46
O when *w* thou come unto me ..... Ps 101:2
*W* not thou, O God, who hast cast ..... Ps 108:11
*w* not thou, O God, go forth with ..... Ps 108:11
saying, When *w* thou comfort me ..... Ps 119:82
when *w* thou execute judgment on ..... Ps 119:84
of trouble, thou *w* revive me ..... Ps 138:7
Surely thou *w* slay the wicked, O ..... Ps 139:19
if thou *w* receive my words, and ..... Prov 2:1
why *w* thou, my son, be ravished ..... Prov 5:20
How long *w* thou sleep, O sluggard ..... Prov 6:9
when *w* thou arise out of thy ..... Prov 6:9
*W* thou set thine eyes upon that ..... Prov 23:5
Thou *w* keep him in perfect peace, ..... Is 26:3
thou *w* ordain peace for us ..... Is 26:12
forth, thou *w* debate with it ..... Is 27:8
How then *w* thou turn away the ..... Is 36:9
to night *w* thou make an end of me ..... Is 38:12
to night *w* thou make an end of me ..... Is 38:13
so *w* thou recover me, and make me ..... Is 38:16
*w* thou call this a fast, and an ..... Is 58:5
*W* thou refrain thyself for these ..... Is 64:12
*w* thou hold thy peace, and afflict ..... Is 64:12
*W* thou not from this time cry ..... Jer 3:4
If thou *w* return, O Israel, saith ..... Jer 4:1
and if thou *w* put away thine ..... Jer 4:1
thou art spoiled, what *w* thou do ..... Jer 4:30
then how *w* thou do in the ..... Jer 12:5
What *w* thou say when he shall ..... Jer 13:21
*w* thou not be made clean ..... Jer 13:27
*w* thou be altogether unto me as a ..... Jer 15:18
How long *w* thou go about, O thou ..... Jer 31:22
*w* thou not surely put me to death ..... Jer 38:15
*w* thou not hearken unto me ..... Jer 38:15
If thou *w* assuredly go forth unto ..... Jer 38:17
But if thou *w* not go forth to the ..... Jer 38:18
how long *w* thou cut thyself ..... Jer 47:5
thou *w* bring the day that thou ..... Lam 1:21
*w* thou destroy all the residue of ..... Eze 9:8
*w* thou make a full end of the ..... Eze 11:13
*W* thou judge them, son of man, ..... Eze 20:4
son of man, *w* thou judge them ..... Eze 20:4
*w* thou judge, *w* thou judge the ..... Eze 22:2
*w* thou judge Aholah and Aholibah ..... Eze 23:36
*W* thou not tell us what these ..... Eze 24:19
*W* thou yet say before him that ..... Eze 28:9
*W* thou not shew us what thou ..... Eze 37:18
what *w* thou give ..... Hos 9:14
thou *w* cast all their sins into ..... Mic 7:19
Thou *w* perform the truth to Jacob ..... Mic 7:20
shall I cry, and thou *w* not hear ..... Hab 1:2
of violence, and thou *w* not save ..... Hab 1:2
I said, Surely thou *w* fear me ..... Zeph 3:7
thou *w* receive instruction ..... Zeph 3:7
how long *w* thou not have mercy on .... Zec 1:12
If thou *w* walk in my ways ..... Zec 3:7
if thou *w* keep my charge, then ..... Zec 3:7
if thou *w* fall down and worship me ..... Mt 4:9
Or how *w* thou say to thy brother, ..... Mt 7:4
him, saying, Lord, if thou *w* ..... Mt 8:2
*W* thou then that we go and gather ..... Mt 13:28
be it unto thee even as thou *w* ..... Mt 15:28
if thou *w*, let us make here three ..... Mt 17:4
but if thou *w* enter into life, ..... Mt 19:17
If thou *w* be perfect, go and sell ..... Mt 19:21
And he said unto her, What *w* thou ..... Mt 20:21
Where *w* thou that we prepare for ..... Mt 26:17
not as I will, but as thou *w* ..... Mt 26:39
and saying unto him, If thou *w* ..... Mk 1:40
Ask of me whatsoever thou *w* ..... Mk 6:22
What *w* thou that I should do unto ..... Mk 10:51
Where *w* thou that we go and ..... Mk 14:12
not what I will, but what thou *w* ..... Mk 14:36
If thou therefore *w* worship me ..... Lk 4:7
him, saying, Lord, if thou *w* ..... Lk 5:12
*w* thou that we command fire to ..... Lk 9:54
What *w* thou that I shall do unto ..... Lk 18:41
Where *w* thou that we prepare ..... Lk 22:9
*w* thou rear it up in three days ..... Jn 2:20
unto him, *W* thou be made whole ..... Jn 5:6
now, whatsoever thou *w* ask of God ..... Jn 11:22
*W* thou lay down thy life for my ..... Jn 13:38
how is it that thou *w* manifest ..... Jn 14:22
*w* thou at this time restore again ..... Acts 1:6
Because thou *w* not leave my soul ..... Acts 2:27
neither *w* thou suffer thine Holy ..... Acts 2:27
*W* thou kill me, as thou diddest ..... Acts 7:28
what *w* thou have me to do ..... Acts 9:6
*w* thou not cease to pervert the ..... Acts 13:10
*W* thou go up to Jerusalem, and ..... Acts 25:9
Thou *w* say then unto me, Why doth . Rom 9:19
Thou *w* say then, The branches ..... Rom 11:19
*W* thou then not be afraid of the ..... Rom 13:3
knowing that thou *w* also do more ..... Philem 21
But *w* thou know, O vain man, that ..... Jas 2:20

**WIMPLES**
apparel, and the mantles, and the *w* ..... Is 3:22

**WIN**
thought to *w* them for himself ..... 2Chr 32:1
but dung, that I may *w* Christ ..... Phil 3:8

**WIND**
God made a *w* to pass over the ..... Gen 8:1
the east *w* sprung up after them ..... Gen 41:6
thin, and blasted with the east *w* ..... Gen 41:23
ears blasted with the east *w* ..... Gen 41:27
the LORD brought an east *w* upon ..... Ex 10:13
the east *w* brought the locusts ..... Ex 10:13
turned a mighty strong west *w* ..... Ex 10:19
by a strong east *w* all that night ..... Ex 14:21
Thou didst blow with thy *w* ..... Ex 15:10
went forth a *w* from the LORD ..... Num 11:31
was seen upon the wings of the *w* ..... 2Sa 22:11
heaven was black with clouds and *w* 1Kin 18:45
strong *w* rent the mountains, and ..... 1Kin 19:11
but the LORD was not in the *w* ..... 1Kin 19:11

after the *w* an earthquake 1Kin 19:11
the LORD, Ye shall not see *w* 2Kin 3:17
there came a great *w* from the Job 1:19
that is desperate, which are as *w* Job 6:26
O remember that my life is *w* Job 7:7
of thy mouth be like a strong *w* Job 8:2
and fill his belly with the east *w* Job 15:2
They are as stubble before the *w* Job 21:18
The east *w* carrieth him away, and Job 27:21
they pursue my soul as the *w* Job 30:15
Thou liftest me up to the *w* Job 30:22
quieteth the earth by the south *w* Job 37:17
but the *w* passeth, and cleanseth Job 37:21
the east *w* upon the earth Job 38:24
chaff which the *w* driveth away Ps 1:4
did fly upon the wings of the *w* Ps 18:10
small as the dust before the *w* Ps 18:42
Let them be as chaff before the *w* Ps 35:5
ships of Tarshish with an east *w* Ps 48:7
He caused an east *w* to blow in Ps 78:26
power he brought in the south *w* Ps 78:26
a *w* that passeth away, and cometh Ps 78:39
as the stubble before the *w* Ps 83:13
For the *w* passeth over it, and it Ps 103:16
walketh upon the wings of the *w* Ps 104:3
and raiseth the stormy *w*, which Ps 107:25
he bringeth the *w* out of his Ps 135:7
he causeth his *w* to blow, and the Ps 147:18
stormy *w* fulfilling his word Ps 148:8
his own house shall inherit the *w* Prov 11:29
is like clouds and *w* without rain Prov 25:14
The north *w* driveth away rain Prov 25:23
Whosoever hideth her hideth the *w* Prov 27:16
hath gathered the *w* in his fists Prov 30:4
The *w* goeth toward the south, and Eccl 1:6
the *w* returneth again according Eccl 1:6
he that hath laboured for the *w* Eccl 5:16
observeth the *w* shall not sow Eccl 11:4
Awake, O north *w* Song 4:16
of the wood are moved with the *w* Is 7:2
with his mighty *w* shall he shake Is 11:15
of the mountains before the *w* Is 17:13
have as it were brought forth *w* Is 26:18
he stayeth his rough *w* in the day Is 27:8
the day of the east *w* Is 27:8
be as an hiding place from the *w* Is 32:2
the *w* shall carry them away, and Is 41:16
their molten images are *w* Is 41:29
but the *w* shall carry them all Is 57:13
and our iniquities, like the *w* Is 64:6
snuffeth up the *w* at her pleasure Jer 2:24
A dry *w* of the high places in the Jer 4:11
Even a full *w* from those places Jer 4:12
And the prophets shall become *w* Jer 5:13
bringeth forth the *w* out of his Jer 10:13
away by the *w* of the wilderness Jer 13:24
snuffed up the *w* like dragons Jer 14:6
with an east *w* before the enemy Jer 18:17
The *w* shall eat up all thy Jer 22:22
up against me, a destroying *w* Jer 51:1
bringeth forth the *w* out of his Jer 51:16
part thou shalt scatter in the *w* Eze 5:2
I will scatter toward every *w* all Eze 12:14
and a stormy *w* shall rend it Eze 13:11
it with a stormy *w* in my fury Eze 13:13
when the east *w* toucheth it Eze 17:10
the east *w* dried up her fruit Eze 19:12
the east *w* hath broken thee in Eze 27:26
he unto me, Prophesy unto the *w* Eze 37:9
son of man, and say to the *w* Eze 37:9
the *w* carried them away, that no Dan 2:35
The *w* hath bound her up in her Hos 4:19
For they have sown the *w*, and they Hos 8:7
Ephraim feedeth on *w* Hos 12:1
and followeth after the east *w* Hos 12:1
an east *w* shall come Hos 13:15
the *w* of the LORD shall come up Hos 13:15
the mountains, and createth the *w* Amos 4:13
sent out a great *w* into the sea Jonah 1:4
God prepared a vehement east *w* Jonah 4:8
faces shall sup up as the east *w* Hab 1:9
and the *w* was in their wings Zec 5:9
A reed shaken with the *w* Mt 11:7
for the *w* was contrary Mt 14:24
But when he saw the *w* boisterous Mt 14:30
come into the ship, the *w* ceased Mt 14:32
And there arose a great storm of *w* Mk 4:37
And he arose, and rebuked the *w* Mk 4:39
the *w* ceased, and there was a Mk 4:39
of man is this, that even the *w* Mk 4:41
for the *w* was contrary unto them Mk 6:48
and the *w* ceased Mk 6:51
A reed shaken with the *w* Lk 7:24
down a storm of *w* on the lake Lk 8:23
Then he arose, and rebuked the *w* Lk 8:24
And when ye see the south *w* blow Lk 12:55
The *w* bloweth where it listeth, Jn 3:8
by reason of a great *w* that blew Jn 6:18
heaven as of a rushing mighty *w* Acts 2:2
the *w* not suffering us, we sailed Acts 27:7
And when the south *w* blew softly Acts 27:13
arose against it a tempestuous *w* Acts 27:14
and could not bear up into the *w* Acts 27:15
hoised up the mainsail to the *w* Acts 27:40
and after one day the south *w* blew Acts 28:13
about with every *w* of doctrine Eph 4:14
wave of the sea driven with the *w* Jas 1:6
when she is shaken of a mighty *w* Rev 6:13
that the *w* should not blow on the Rev 7:1

**WINDING**
they went up with *w* stairs into 1Kin 6:8
a *w* about still upward to the Eze 41:7
for the *w* about of the house went Eze 41:7

**WINDOW**
A *w* shalt thou make to the ark, Gen 6:16
that Noah opened the *w* of the ark Gen 8:6
the Philistines looked out at a *w* Gen 26:8
them down by a cord through the *w* Josh 2:15
line of scarlet thread in the *w* Josh 2:18
bound the scarlet line in the *w* Josh 2:21
of Sisera looked out at a *w* Judg 5:28
Michal let David down through a *w* 1Sa 19:12
daughter looked through a *w* 2Sa 6:16
her head, and looked out at a *w* 2Kin 9:30
And he lifted up his face to the *w* 2Kin 9:32
And he said, Open the *w* eastward 2Kin 13:17
out at a *w* saw king David dancing 1Chr 15:29
For at the *w* of my house I looked Prov 7:6
there sat in a *w* a certain young Acts 20:9
through a *w* in a basket was I let 2Cor 11:33

**WINDOWS**
the *w* of heaven were opened Gen 7:11
the *w* of heaven were stopped, and Gen 8:2
house he made *w* of narrow lights 1Kin 6:4
there were *w* in three rows, and 1Kin 7:4
and posts were square, with the *w* 1Kin 7:5
the LORD would make *w* in heaven 2Kin 7:2
the LORD should make *w* in heaven 2Kin 7:19
look out of the *w* be darkened Eccl 12:3
wall, he looketh forth at the *w* Song 2:9
for the *w* from on high are open, Is 24:18
And I will make thy *w* of agates Is 54:12
cloud, and as the doves to their *w* Is 60:8
For death is come up into our *w* Jer 9:21
chambers, and cutteth him out *w* Jer 22:14
there were narrow *w* to the little Eze 40:16
*w* were round about inward Eze 40:16
And their *w*, and their arches, and Eze 40:22
And there were *w* in it and in the Eze 40:25
thereof round about, like those *w* Eze 40:25
and there were *w* in it and in the Eze 40:29
and there were *w* therein and in the Eze 40:33
and the *w* to it round about Eze 40:36
The door posts, and the narrow *w* Eze 41:16
and from the ground up to the *w* Eze 41:16
and the *w* were covered Eze 41:16
And there were narrow *w* and palm Eze 41:26
his *w* being open in his chamber Dan 6:10
enter in at the *w* like a thief Joel 2:9
their voice shall sing in the *w* Zeph 2:14
will not open you the *w* of heaven Mal 3:10

**WINDS**
To make the weight for the *w* Job 28:25
I will scatter into all *w* them Jer 49:32
four *w* from the four quarters of Jer 49:36
scatter them toward all those *w* Jer 49:36
will I scatter into all the *w* Eze 5:10
a third part into all the *w* Eze 5:12
shall be scattered toward all *w* Eze 17:21
Come from the four *w*, O breath, Eze 37:9
the four *w* of the heaven strove Dan 7:2
ones toward the four *w* of heaven Dan 8:8
toward the four *w* of heaven Dan 11:4
as the four *w* of the heaven Zec 2:6
the *w* blew, and beat upon that Mt 7:25
the *w* blew, and beat upon that Mt 7:27
Then he arose, and rebuked the *w* Mt 8:26
of man is this, that even the *w* Mt 8:27
his elect from the four *w* Mt 24:31
his elect from the four *w* Mk 13:27
for he commandeth even the *w* Lk 8:25
because the *w* were contrary Acts 27:4
great, and are driven of fierce *w* Jas 3:4
without water, carried about of *w* Jude 12
holding the four *w* of the earth Rev 7:1

**WINDY**
hasten my escape from the *w* storm Ps 55:8

**WINE**
And he drank of the *w*, and was Gen 9:21
Noah awoke from his *w* Gen 9:24
of Salem brought forth bread and *w* Gen 14:18
let us make our father drink *w* Gen 19:32
their father drink *w* that night Gen 19:33
make him drink *w* this night also Gen 19:34
father drink *w* that night also Gen 19:35
and he brought him *w*, and he drank. Gen 27:25
the earth, and plenty of corn and *w* Gen 27:28
corn and *w* have I sustained him Gen 27:37
he washed his garments in *w* Gen 49:11
His eyes shall be red with *w* Gen 49:12
an hin of *w* for a drink offering Ex 29:40
Do not drink *w* nor strong drink, Lev 10:9
offering thereof shall be of *w* Lev 23:13
He shall separate himself from *w* Num 6:3
and shall drink no vinegar of *w* Num 6:3
that the Nazarite may drink *w* Num 6:20
the fourth part of an hin of *w* Num 15:5
the third part of an hin of *w* Num 15:7
a drink offering half an hin of *w* Num 15:10
the oil, and all the best of the *w* Num 18:12
shalt thou cause the strong *w* to Num 28:7
half an hin of *w* unto a bullock Num 28:14
of thy land, thy corn, and thy *w* Deut 7:13
gather in thy corn, and thy *w* Deut 11:14
tithe of thy corn, or of thy *w* Deut 12:17
the tithe of thy corn, of thy *w* Deut 14:23
for oxen, or for sheep, or for *w* Deut 14:26
gathered in thy corn and thy *w* Deut 16:13
also of thy corn, of thy *w* Deut 18:4
but shalt neither drink of the *w* Deut 28:39
not leave thee either corn, *w* Deut 28:51
have ye drunk *w* or strong drink Deut 29:6
Their *w* is the poison of dragons, Deut 32:33
drank the *w* of their drink Deut 32:38
shall be upon a land of corn and *w* Deut 33:28
*w* bottles, old, and rent, and bound Josh 9:4
And these bottles of *w*, which we Josh 9:13
unto them, Should I leave my *w* Judg 9:13
drink not *w* nor strong drink, and Judg 13:4
now drink no *w* nor strong drink, Judg 13:7
let her drink *w* or strong drink Judg 13:14
*w* also for me, and for thy Judg 19:19
put away thy *w* from thee 1Sa 1:14
neither *w* nor strong drink 1Sa 1:15
ephah of flour, and a bottle of *w* 1Sa 1:24
and another carrying a bottle of *w* 1Sa 10:3
with bread, and a bottle of *w* 1Sa 16:20
loaves, and two bottles of *w* 1Sa 25:18
when the *w* was gone out of Nabal, 1Sa 25:37
piece of flesh, and a flagon of *w* 2Sa 6:19
Amnon's heart is merry with *w* 2Sa 13:28
summer fruits, and a bottle of *w* 2Sa 16:1
and the *w*, that such as be faint 2Sa 16:2
own land, a land of corn and *w* 2Kin 18:32
and the fine flour, and the *w* 1Chr 9:29
figs, and bunches of raisins, and *w* 1Chr 12:40
piece of flesh, and a flagon of *w* 1Chr 16:3
of the vineyards for the *w* 1Chr 27:27
and twenty thousand baths of *w* 2Chr 2:10
and the barley, the oil, and the *w* 2Chr 2:15
store of victual, and of oil and *w* 2Chr 11:11
the firstfruits of corn, *w* 2Chr 31:5
for the increase of corn, and *w* 2Chr 32:28
the God of heaven, wheat, salt, *w* Ezr 6:9
and to an hundred baths of *w* Ezr 7:22
the king, that *w* was before him Neh 2:1
and I took up the *w*, and gave it Neh 2:1
the money, and of the corn, the *w* Neh 5:11
and had taken of them bread and *w* Neh 5:15
ten days store of all sorts of *w* Neh 5:18
of all manner of trees, of *w* Neh 10:37
of the corn, of the new *w* Neh 10:39
the tithes of the corn, the new *w* Neh 13:5
tithe of the corn and the new *w* Neh 13:12
as also *w*, grapes, and figs, and Neh 13:15
royal *w* in abundance, according Est 1:7
of the king was merry with *w* Est 1:10
unto Esther at the banquet of *w* Est 5:6
second day at the banquet of *w* Est 7:2
of *w* in his wrath went into the Est 7:7
the place of the banquet of *w* Est 7:8
drinking *w* in their eldest Job 1:13
drinking *w* in their eldest Job 1:18
my belly is as *w* which hath no Job 32:19
their corn and their *w* increased Ps 4:7
us to drink the *w* of astonishment Ps 60:3
there is a cup, and the *w* is red Ps 75:8
man that shouteth by reason of *w* Ps 78:65
*w* that maketh glad the heart of Ps 104:15
shall burst out with new *w* Prov 3:10
and drink the *w* of violence Prov 4:17
she hath mingled her *w* Prov 9:2
drink of the *w* which I have Prov 9:5
*W* is a mocker, strong drink is Prov 20:1
he that loveth *w* and oil shall not Prov 21:17
They that tarry long at the *w* Prov 23:30
they that go to seek mixed *w* Prov 23:30
thou upon the *w* when it is red Prov 23:31
it is not for kings to drink *w* Prov 31:4
*w* unto those that be of heavy Prov 31:6
mine heart to give myself unto *w* Eccl 2:3
drink thy *w* with a merry heart Eccl 9:7
for laughter, and *w* maketh merry Eccl 10:19
for thy love is better than *w* Song 1:2
remember thy love more than *w* Song 1:4
much better is thy love than *w* Song 4:10
I have drunk my *w* with my milk Song 5:1
like the best *w* for my beloved Song 7:9
cause thee to drink of spiced *w* Song 8:2
dross, thy *w* mixed with water Is 1:22
until night, till *w* inflame them Is 5:11
viol, the tabret, and pipe, and *w* Is 5:12
them that are mighty to drink *w* Is 5:22
tread out no *w* in their presses Is 16:10
eating flesh, and drinking *w* Is 22:13
The new *w* mourneth, the vine Is 24:7
shall not drink *w* with a song Is 24:9
is a crying for *w* in the streets Is 24:11
ye unto her, A vineyard of red *w* Is 27:2
of them that are overcome with *w* Is 28:1
they also have erred through *w* Is 28:7
drink, they are swallowed up of *w* Is 28:7
they are drunken, but not with *w* Is 29:9
own land, a land of corn and *w* Is 36:17
their own blood, as with sweet *w* Is 49:26
and drunken, but not with *w* Is 51:21
yea, come, buy *w* and milk without Is 55:1
Come ye, say they, I will fetch *w* Is 56:12
stranger shall not drink thy *w* Is 62:8
As the new *w* is found in the Is 65:8
bottle shall be filled with *w* Jer 13:12
bottle shall be filled with *w* Jer 13:12
like a man whom *w* hath overcome Jer 23:9
Take the *w* cup of this fury at my Jer 25:15
of the LORD, for wheat, and for *w* Jer 31:12
chambers, and give them *w* to drink Jer 35:2
of the Rechabites pots full of *w* Jer 35:5

and I said unto them, Drink ye *w* ... Jer 35:5
But they said, We will drink no *w* ... Jer 35:6
us, saying, Ye shall drink no *w* ... Jer 35:6
to drink no *w* all our days, we, ... Jer 35:8
commanded his sons not to drink *w* ... Jer 35:14
but ye, gather ye *w*, and summer ... Jer 40:10
unto Mizpah, and gathered *w* ... Jer 40:12
I have caused *w* to fail from the ... Jer 48:33
the nations have drunken of her *w* ... Jer 51:7
their mothers, Where is corn and *w* ... Lam 2:12
in the *w* of Helbon, and white wool ... Eze 27:18
Neither shall any priest drink *w* ... Eze 44:21
meat, and of the *w* which he drank ... Dan 1:5
nor with the *w* which he drank ... Dan 1:8
the *w* that they should drink ... Dan 1:16
drank *w* before the thousand ... Dan 5:1
whiles he tasted the *w*, ... Dan 5:2
They drank *w*, and praised the gods ... Dan 5:4
concubines, have drunk *w* in them ... Dan 5:23
came flesh nor *w* in my mouth ... Dan 10:3
know that I gave her corn, and *w* ... Hos 2:8
my *w* in the season thereof, and ... Hos 2:9
shall hear the corn, and the *w* ... Hos 2:22
other gods, and love flagons of *w* ... Hos 3:1
Whoredom and *w* and new ... Hos 4:11
new *w* take away the heart ... Hos 4:11
made him sick with bottles of *w* ... Hos 7:5
assemble themselves for corn and *w* ... Hos 7:14
the new *w* shall fail in her ... Hos 9:2
They shall not offer *w* offerings ... Hos 9:4
shall be as the *w* of Lebanon ... Hos 14:7
and howl, all ye drinkers of *w* ... Joel 1:5
because of the new *w* ... Joel 1:5
the new *w* is dried up, the oil ... Joel 1:10
I will send you corn, and *w* ... Joel 2:19
and the fats shall overflow with *w* ... Joel 2:24
an harlot, and sold a girl for *w* ... Joel 3:3
mountains shall drop down new *w* ... Joel 3:18
they drink the *w* of the condemned ... Amos 2:8
ye gave the Nazarites *w* to drink ... Amos 2:12
but ye shall not drink *w* of them ... Amos 5:11
That drink *w* in bowls, and anoint ... Amos 6:6
the mountains shall drop sweet *w* ... Amos 9:13
vineyards, and drink the *w* thereof ... Amos 9:14
I will prophesy unto thee of *w* ... Mic 2:11
with oil; and sweet *w* ... Mic 6:15
but shalt not drink *w* ... Mic 6:15
because he transgresseth by *w* ... Hab 2:5
but not drink the *w* thereof ... Zeph 1:13
upon the corn, and upon the new *w* ... Hag 1:11
do touch bread, or pottage, or *w* ... Hag 2:12
and make a noise as through *w* ... Zec 9:15
men cheerful, and new *w* the maids ... Zec 9:17
heart shall rejoice as through *w* ... Zec 10:7
do men put new *w* into old bottles ... Mt 9:17
the *w* runneth out, and the bottles ... Mt 9:17
they put new *w* into new bottles ... Mt 9:17
putteth new *w* into old bottles ... Mk 2:22
else the new *w* doth burst the ... Mk 2:22
the *w* is spilled, and the bottles ... Mk 2:22
but new *w* must be put into new ... Mk 2:22
him to drink *w* mingled with myrrh ... Mk 15:23
drink neither *w* nor strong drink ... Lk 1:15
putteth new *w* into old bottles ... Lk 5:37
else the new *w* will burst the ... Lk 5:37
But new *w* must be put into new ... Lk 5:38
old *w* straightway desireth new ... Lk 5:39
eating bread nor drinking *w* ... Lk 7:33
his wounds, pouring in oil and *w* ... Lk 10:34
And when they wanted *w*, the mother ... Jn 2:3
saith unto him, They have no *w* ... Jn 2:3
tasted the water that was made *w* ... Jn 2:9
beginning doth set forth good *w* ... Jn 2:10
hast kept the good *w* until now ... Jn 2:10
where he made the water *w* ... Jn 4:46
saying, These men are full of new *w* ... Acts 2:13
to eat flesh, nor to drink *w* ... Rom 14:21
And be not drunk with *w*, wherein ... Eph 5:18
Not given to *w*, no striker, not ... 1Ti 3:3
not given to much *w*, not greedy ... 1Ti 3:8
but use a little *w* for thy ... 1Ti 5:23
not soon angry, not given to *w* ... Titus 1:7
accusers, not given to much *w* ... Titus 2:3
lusts, excess of *w*, revellings, ... 1Pet 4:3
thou hurt not the oil and the *w* ... Rev 6:6
made all nations drink of the *w* ... Rev 14:8
of the *w* of the wrath of God ... Rev 14:10
*w* of the fierceness of his wrath ... Rev 16:19
with the *w* of her fornication ... Rev 17:2
all nations have drunk of the *w* ... Rev 18:3
ointments, and frankincense, and *w* ... Rev 18:13

**WINEBIBBER**
Behold a man gluttonous, and a *w* ... Mt 11:19
Behold a gluttonous man, and a *w* ... Lk 7:34

**WINEBIBBERS**
Be not among *w* ... Prov 23:20

**WINEFAT**
like him that treadeth in the *w* ... Is 63:2
it, and digged a place for the *w* ... Mk 12:1

**WINEPRESS**
and as the fulness of the *w* ... Num 18:27
and as the increase of the *w* ... Num 18:30
out of thy floor, and out of thy *w* ... Deut 15:14
Gideon threshed wheat by the *w* ... Judg 6:11
Zeeb they slew at the *w* of Zeeb ... Judg 7:25
of the barnfloor, or out of the *w* ... 2Kin 6:27
of it, and also made a *w* therein ... Is 5:2
I have trodden the *w* alone ... Is 63:3
the daughter of Judah, as in a *w* ... Lam 1:15
the *w* shall not feed them, and the ... Hos 9:2
round about, and digged a *w* in it ... Mt 21:33
the great *w* of the wrath of God ... Rev 14:19
the *w* was trodden without the ... Rev 14:20
city, and blood came out of the *w* ... Rev 14:20
and he treadeth the *w* of the ... Rev 19:15

**WINEPRESSES**
some treading *w* on the sabbath ... Neh 13:15
their walls, and tread their *w* ... Job 24:11
caused wine to fail from the *w* ... Jer 48:33
of Hananeel unto the king's *w* ... Zec 14:10

**WINES**
a feast of *w* on the lees, of fat ... Is 25:6
of *w* on the lees well refined ... Is 25:6

**WING**
was the one *w* of the cherub ... 1Kin 6:24
cubits the other *w* of the cherub ... 1Kin 6:24
the uttermost part of the one *w* ... 1Kin 6:24
so that the *w* of the one touched ... 1Kin 6:27
the *w* of the other cherub touched ... 1Kin 6:27
one *w* of the one cherub was five ... 2Chr 3:11
the other *w* was likewise five ... 2Chr 3:11
reaching to the *w* of the other ... 2Chr 3:11
one *w* of the other cherub was ... 2Chr 3:12
the other *w* was five cubits also, ... 2Chr 3:12
joining to the *w* of the other ... 2Chr 3:12
there was none that moved the *w* ... Is 10:14
shall dwell all fowl of every *w* ... Eze 17:23

**WINGED**
every *w* fowl after his kind ... Gen 1:21
the likeness of any *w* fowl that ... Deut 4:17

**WINGS**
and how I bare you on eagles' *w* ... Ex 19:4
stretch forth their *w* on high ... Ex 25:20
the mercy seat with their *w* ... Ex 25:20
spread out their *w* on high ... Ex 37:9
covered with their *w* over the ... Ex 37:9
cleave it with the *w* thereof ... Lev 1:17
her young, spreadeth abroad her *w* ... Deut 32:11
them, beareth them on her *w* ... Deut 32:11
under whose *w* thou art come to ... Ruth 2:12
was seen upon the *w* of the wind ... 2Sa 22:11
forth the *w* of the cherubims ... 1Kin 6:27
their *w* touched one another in ... 1Kin 6:27
even under the *w* of the cherubims ... 1Kin 8:6
spread forth their two *w* over the ... 1Kin 8:7
that spread out their *w*, and ... 1Chr 28:18
the *w* of the cherubims were ... 2Chr 3:11
The *w* of these cherubims spread ... 2Chr 3:13
even under the *w* of the cherubims ... 2Chr 5:7
their *w* over the place of the ark ... 2Chr 5:8
the goodly *w* unto the peacocks ... Job 39:13
or *w* and feathers unto the ostrich ... Job 39:13
stretch her *w* toward the south ... Job 39:26
hide me under the shadow of thy *w* ... Ps 17:8
he did fly upon the *w* of the wind ... Ps 18:10
trust under the shadow of thy *w* ... Ps 36:7
said, Oh that I had *w* like a dove ... Ps 55:6
in the shadow of thy *w* will I ... Ps 57:1
will trust in the covert of thy *w* ... Ps 61:4
shadow of thy *w* will I rejoice ... Ps 63:7
yet shall ye be as the *w* of a ... Ps 68:13
under his *w* shalt thou trust ... Ps 91:4
walketh upon the *w* of the wind ... Ps 104:3
If I take the *w* of the morning, ... Ps 139:9
certainly make themselves *w* ... Prov 23:5
that which hath *w* shall tell the ... Eccl 10:20
each one had six *w* ... Is 6:2
the stretching out of his *w* shall ... Is 8:8
Woe to the land shadowing with *w* ... Is 18:1
shall mount up with *w* as eagles ... Is 40:31
Give *w* unto Moab, that it may ... Jer 48:9
and shall spread his *w* over Moab ... Jer 48:40
and spread his *w* over Bozrah ... Jer 49:22
faces, and every one had four *w* ... Eze 1:6
under their *w* on their four sides ... Eze 1:8
four had their faces and their *w* ... Eze 1:8
Their *w* were joined one to ... Eze 1:9
their *w* were stretched upward ... Eze 1:11
two *w* of every one were joined ... Eze 1:11
firmament were their *w* straight ... Eze 1:23
I heard the noise of their *w* ... Eze 1:24
they stood, they let down their *w* ... Eze 1:24
stood, and had let down their *w* ... Eze 1:25
*w* of the living creatures that ... Eze 3:13
*w* was heard even to the outer ... Eze 10:5
of a man's hand under their *w* ... Eze 10:8
backs, and their hands, and their *w* ... Eze 10:12
*w* to mount up from the earth ... Eze 10:16
the cherubims lifted up their *w* ... Eze 10:19
faces apiece, and every one four *w* ... Eze 10:21
hands of a man was under their *w* ... Eze 10:21
did the cherubims lift up their *w* ... Eze 11:22
A great eagle with great *w* ... Eze 17:3
another great eagle with great *w* ... Eze 17:7
was like a lion, and had eagle's *w* ... Dan 7:4
I beheld till the *w* thereof were ... Dan 7:4
the back of it four *w* of a fowl ... Dan 7:6
wind hath bound her up in her *w* ... Hos 4:19
women, and the wind was in their *w* ... Zec 5:9
had *w* like the *w* of a stork ... Zec 5:9
arise with healing in his *w* ... Mal 4:2
her chickens under her *w*, and ye ... Mt 23:37
doth gather her brood under her *w* ... Lk 13:34
had each of them six *w* about him ... Rev 4:8
the sound of their *w* was as the ... Rev 9:9
were given two *w* of a great eagle ... Rev 12:14

**WINK**
and what do thy eyes *w* at, ... Job 15:12
neither let them *w* with the eye ... Ps 35:19

**WINKED**
times of this ignorance God *w* at ... Acts 17:30

**WINKETH**
He *w* with his eyes, he speaketh ... Prov 6:13
He that *w* with the eye causeth ... Prov 10:10

**WINNETH**
and he that *w* souls is wise ... Prov 11:30

**WINNOWED**
which hath been *w* with the shovel ... Is 30:24

**WINNOWETH**
he *w* barley to night in the ... Ruth 3:2

**WINTER**
and cold and heat, and summer and *w* ... Gen 8:22
thou hast made summer and *w* ... Ps 74:17
the *w* is past, the rain is over ... Song 2:11
of the earth shall *w* upon them ... Is 18:6
I will smite the *w* house with the ... Amos 3:15
in summer and in *w* shall it be ... Zec 14:8
that your flight be not in the *w* ... Mt 24:20
that your flight be not in the *w* ... Mk 13:18
of the dedication, and it was *w* ... Jn 10:22
haven was not commodious to *w* in ... Acts 27:12
attain to Phenice, and there to *w* ... Acts 27:12
*w* with you, that ye may bring me ... 1Cor 16:6
Do thy diligence to come before *w* ... 2Ti 4:21
for I have determined there to *w* ... Titus 3:12

**WINTERED**
which had *w* in the isle, whose ... Acts 28:11

**WINTERHOUSE**
sat in the *w* in the ninth month ... Jer 36:22

**WIPE**
I will *w* Jerusalem as a man ... 2Kin 21:13
*w* not out my good deeds that I ... Neh 13:14
the Lord GOD will *w* away tears ... Is 25:8
did *w* them with the hairs of her ... Lk 7:38
on us, we do *w* off against you ... Lk 10:11
feet, and to *w* them with the towel ... Jn 13:5
God shall *w* away all tears from ... Rev 7:17
God shall *w* away all tears from ... Rev 21:4

**WIPED**
his reproach shall not be *w* away ... Prov 6:33
*w* them with the hairs of her head ... Lk 7:44
*w* his feet with her hair, whose ... Jn 11:2
and *w* his feet with her hair ... Jn 12:3

**WIPETH**
wipe Jerusalem as a man *w* a dish ... 2Kin 21:13
*w* her mouth, and saith, I have ... Prov 30:20

**WIPING**
*w* it, and turning it upside down ... 2Kin 21:13

**WIRES**
thin plates, and cut it into *w* ... Ex 39:3

**WISDOM**
have filled with the spirit of *w* ... Ex 28:3
him with the spirit of God, in *w* ... Ex 31:3
are wise hearted I have put *w* ... Ex 31:6
them up in *w* spun goats' hair ... Ex 35:26
him with the spirit of God, in *w* ... Ex 35:31
hath he filled with *w* of heart ... Ex 35:35
man, in whom the LORD put *w* ... Ex 36:1
in whose heart the LORD had put *w* ... Ex 36:2
for this is your *w* and your ... Deut 4:6
Nun was full of the spirit of *w* ... Deut 34:9
according to the *w* of an angel of ... 2Sa 14:20
went unto all the people in her *w* ... 2Sa 20:22
Do therefore according to thy *w* ... 1Kin 2:6
saw that the *w* of God was in him ... 1Kin 3:28
And God gave Solomon *w* and ... 1Kin 4:29
Solomon's *w* excelled the *w* ... 1Kin 4:30
country, and all the *w* of Egypt ... 1Kin 4:30
people to hear the *w* of Solomon ... 1Kin 4:34
earth, which had heard of his *w* ... 1Kin 4:34
And the LORD gave Solomon *w* ... 1Kin 5:12
and he was filled with *w*, and ... 1Kin 7:14
of Sheba had seen all Solomon's *w* ... 1Kin 10:4
own land of thy acts and of thy *w* ... 1Kin 10:6
thy *w* and prosperity exceedeth the ... 1Kin 10:7
before thee, and that hear thy *w* ... 1Kin 10:8
of the earth for riches and for *w* ... 1Kin 10:23
sought to Solomon, to hear his *w* ... 1Kin 10:24
and all that he did, and his *w* ... 1Kin 11:41
Only the LORD give thee *w* ... 1Chr 22:12
Give me now *w* and knowledge, that ... 2Chr 1:10
but hast asked *w* and knowledge for ... 2Chr 1:11
*W* and knowledge is granted unto ... 2Chr 1:12
Sheba had seen the *w* of Solomon ... 2Chr 9:3
land of thine acts, and of thy *w* ... 2Chr 9:5
of thy *w* was not told me ... 2Chr 9:6
before thee, and hear thy *w* ... 2Chr 9:7
kings of the earth in riches and *w* ... 2Chr 9:22
of Solomon, to hear his *w* ... 2Chr 9:23
after the *w* of thy God, that is ... Ezr 7:25
they die, even without *w* ... Job 4:21
is *w* driven quite from me ... Job 6:13
would shew thee the secrets of *w* ... Job 11:6
people, and *w* shall die with you ... Job 12:2
With the ancient is *w* ... Job 12:12
With him is *w* and strength, he ... Job 12:13
With him is strength and *w* ... Job 12:16
and it should be your *w* ... Job 13:5
dost thou restrain *w* to thyself ... Job 15:8

W

thou counseled him that hath no *w* ... Job 26:3
But where shall *w* be found ... Job 28:12
the price of *w* is above rubies ... Job 28:18
Whence then cometh *w* ... Job 28:20
the fear of the LORD, that is *w* ... Job 28:28
multitude of years should teach *w* ... Job 32:7
should say, We have found out *w* ... Job 32:13
peace, and I shall teach thee *w* ... Job 33:33
and his words were without *w* ... Job 34:35
he is mighty in strength and *w* ... Job 36:5
Who hath put *w* in the inward ... Job 38:36
Who can number the clouds in *w* ... Job 38:37
God hath deprived her of *w* ... Job 39:17
Doth the hawk fly by thy *w* ... Job 39:26
mouth of the righteous speaketh *w* ... Ps 37:30
My mouth shall speak of *w* ... Ps 49:3
part thou shalt make me to know *w* ... Ps 51:6
we may apply our hearts unto *w* ... Ps 90:12
In *w* hast thou made them all ... Ps 104:24
and teach his senators *w* ... Ps 105:22
of the LORD is the beginning of *w* ... Ps 111:10
To him that by *w* made the heavens ... Ps 136:5
To know *w* and instruction ... Prov 1:2
To receive the instruction of *w* ... Prov 1:3
but fools despise *w* and ... Prov 1:7
*W* crieth without ... Prov 1:20
thou incline thine ear unto *w* ... Prov 2:2
For the LORD giveth *w* ... Prov 2:6
up sound *w* for the righteous ... Prov 2:7
When *w* entereth into thine heart, ... Prov 2:10
Happy is the man that findeth *w* ... Prov 3:13
The LORD by *w* hath founded the ... Prov 3:19
keep sound *w* and discretion ... Prov 3:21
Get *w*, get understanding ... Prov 4:5
*W* is the principal thing ... Prov 4:7
therefore get *w* ... Prov 4:7
have taught thee in the way of *w* ... Prov 4:11
My son, attend unto my *w*, and bow ... Prov 5:1
Say unto *w*, Thou art my sister ... Prov 7:4
Doth not *w* cry ... Prov 8:1
O ye simple, understand *w* ... Prov 8:5
For *w* is better than rubies ... Prov 8:11
I *w* dwell with prudence, and find ... Prov 8:12
Counsel is mine, and sound *w* ... Prov 8:14
*W* hath builded her house, she ... Prov 9:1
of the LORD is the beginning of *w* ... Prov 9:10
hath understanding *w* is found ... Prov 10:13
but fools die for want of *w* ... Prov 10:21
but a man of understanding hath *w* .. Prov 10:23
of the just bringeth forth *w* ... Prov 10:31
but with the lowly is *w* ... Prov 11:2
He that is void of *w* despiseth ... Prov 11:12
be commended according to his *w* ... Prov 12:8
but with the well advised is *w* ... Prov 13:10
A scorner seeketh *w*, and findeth ... Prov 14:6
The *w* of the prudent is to ... Prov 14:8
*W* resteth in the heart of him ... Prov 14:33
joy to him that is destitute of *w* ... Prov 15:21
the LORD is the instruction of *w* ... Prov 15:33
better is it to get *w* than gold ... Prov 16:16
in the hand of a fool to get *w* ... Prov 17:16
*W* is before him that hath ... Prov 17:24
and intermeddleth with all *w* ... Prov 18:1
the wellspring of *w* as a flowing ... Prov 18:4
He that getteth *w* loveth his own ... Prov 19:8
There is no *w* nor understanding ... Prov 21:30
cease from thine own *w* ... Prov 23:4
will despise the *w* of thy words ... Prov 23:9
also *w*, and instruction, and ... Prov 23:23
Through *w* is an house builded ... Prov 24:3
*W* is too high for a fool ... Prov 24:7
knowledge of *w* be unto thy soul ... Prov 24:14
Whoso loveth *w* rejoiceth his ... Prov 29:3
The rod and reproof give *w* ... Prov 29:15
I neither learned *w*, nor have the ... Prov 30:3
She openeth her mouth with *w* ... Prov 31:26
search out by *w* concerning all ... Eccl 1:13
have gotten more *w* than all they ... Eccl 1:16
heart had great experience of *w* ... Eccl 1:16
And I gave my heart to know *w* ... Eccl 1:17
For in much *w* is much grief ... Eccl 1:18
yet acquainting mine heart with *w* ... Eccl 2:3
also my *w* remained with me ... Eccl 2:9
And I turned myself to behold *w* ... Eccl 2:12
Then I saw that *w* excelleth folly ... Eccl 2:13
is a man whose labour is in *w* ... Eccl 2:21
a man that is good in his sight *w* ... Eccl 2:26
*W* is good with an inheritance ... Eccl 7:11
For *w* is a defence, and money is a ... Eccl 7:12
that *w* giveth life to them that ... Eccl 7:12
*W* strengtheneth the wise more ... Eccl 7:19
All this have I proved by *w* ... Eccl 7:23
and to search, and to seek out *w* ... Eccl 7:25
a man's *w* maketh his face to ... Eccl 8:1
I applied mine heart to know *w* ... Eccl 8:16
nor device, nor knowledge, nor *w* ... Eccl 9:10
This *w* have I seen also under the ... Eccl 9:13
he by his *w* delivered the city ... Eccl 9:15
*W* is better than strength ... Eccl 9:16
the poor man's *w* is despised ... Eccl 9:16
*W* is better than weapons of war ... Eccl 9:18
him that is in reputation for *w* ... Eccl 10:1
his *w* faileth him, and he saith to ... Eccl 10:3
but *w* is profitable to direct ... Eccl 10:10
hand I have done it, and by my *w* ... Is 10:13
rest upon him, the spirit of *w* ... Is 11:2
for the *w* of their wise men shall ... Is 29:14
And *w* and knowledge shall be the ... Is 33:6
Thy *w* and thy knowledge, it hath ... Is 47:10
and what *w* is in them ... Jer 8:9
not the wise man glory in his *w* ... Jer 9:23
established the world by his *w* ... Jer 10:12
Is *w* no more in Teman ... Jer 49:7
is their *w* vanished ... Jer 49:7
established the world by his *w* ... Jer 51:15
With thy *w* and with thine ... Eze 28:4
By thy great *w* and by thy traffick ... Eze 28:5
against the beauty of thy *w* ... Eze 28:7
sealest up the sum, full of *w* ... Eze 28:12
thou hast corrupted thy *w* by ... Eze 28:17
favoured, and skilful in all *w* ... Dan 1:4
and skill in all learning and *w* ... Dan 1:17
And in all matters of *w* and ... Dan 1:20
*w* to Arioch the captain of the ... Dan 2:14
for *w* and might are his ... Dan 2:20
he giveth *w* unto the wise, and ... Dan 2:21
my fathers, who hast given me *w* ... Dan 2:23
any *w* that I have more than any ... Dan 2:30
light and understanding and *w* ... Dan 5:11
like the *w* of the gods, was found ... Dan 5:11
excellent *w* is found in thee ... Dan 5:14
the man of *w* shall see thy name ... Mic 6:9
But *w* is justified of her ... Mt 11:19
earth to hear the *w* of Solomon ... Mt 12:42
said, Whence hath this man this *w* ... Mt 13:54
what *w* is this which is given ... Mk 6:2
disobedient to the *w* of the just ... Lk 1:17
strong in spirit, filled with *w* ... Lk 2:40
And Jesus increased in *w* and ... Lk 2:52
But *w* is justified of all her ... Lk 7:35
earth to hear the *w* of Solomon ... Lk 11:31
Therefore also said the *w* of God ... Lk 11:49
For I will give you a mouth and *w* ... Lk 21:15
full of the Holy Ghost and *w* ... Acts 6:3
were not able to resist the *w* ... Acts 6:10
*w* in the sight of Pharaoh king of ... Acts 7:10
in all the *w* of the Egyptians ... Acts 7:22
depth of the riches both of the *w* ... Rom 11:33
not with *w* of words, lest the ... 1Cor 1:17
I will destroy the *w* of the wise ... 1Cor 1:19
made foolish the *w* of this world ... 1Cor 1:20
For after that in the *w* of God ... 1Cor 1:21
God the world by *w* knew not God ... 1Cor 1:21
sign, and the Greeks seek after *w* ... 1Cor 1:22
the power of God, and the *w* of God ... 1Cor 1:24
who of God is made unto us *w* ... 1Cor 1:30
with excellency of speech or of *w* ... 1Cor 2:1
with enticing words of man's *w* ... 1Cor 2:4
should not stand in the *w* of men ... 1Cor 2:5
Howbeit we speak *w* among them ... 1Cor 2:6
yet not the *w* of this world, nor ... 1Cor 2:6
But we speak the *w* of God in a ... 1Cor 2:7
in a mystery, even the hidden *w* ... 1Cor 2:7
the words which man's *w* teacheth ... 1Cor 2:13
For the *w* of this world is ... 1Cor 3:19
given by the Spirit the word of *w* ... 1Cor 12:8
sincerity, not with fleshly *w* ... 2Cor 1:12
hath abounded toward us in all *w* ... Eph 1:8
may give unto you the spirit of *w* ... Eph 1:17
the church the manifold *w* of God ... Eph 3:10
knowledge of his will in all *w* ... Col 1:9
and teaching every man in all *w* ... Col 1:28
are hid all the treasures of *w* ... Col 2:3
a shew of *w* in will worship ... Col 2:23
dwell in you richly in all *w* ... Col 3:16
Walk in *w* toward them that are ... Col 4:5
If any of you lack *w*, let him ask ... Jas 1:5
his works with meekness of *w* ... Jas 3:13
This *w* descendeth not from above, ... Jas 3:15
But the *w* that is from above is ... Jas 3:17
Paul also according to the *w* ... 2Pet 3:15
to receive power, and riches, and *w* ... Rev 5:12
Blessing, and glory, and *w*, and ... Rev 7:12
Here is *w* ... Rev 13:18
And here is the mind which hath *w* ... Rev 17:9

## WISE

tree to be desired to make one *w* ... Gen 3:6
Egypt, and all the *w* men thereof ... Gen 41:8
look out a man discreet and *w* ... Gen 41:33
none so discreet and *w* as thou art ... Gen 41:39
Pharaoh also called the *w* men ... Ex 7:11
If thou afflict them in any *w* ... Ex 22:23
for the gift blindeth the *w* ... Ex 23:8
speak unto all that are *w* hearted ... Ex 28:3
are *w* hearted I have put wisdom ... Ex 31:6
every *w* hearted among you shall ... Ex 35:10
all the women that were *w* hearted ... Ex 35:25
every *w* hearted man, in whom the ... Ex 36:1
every *w* hearted man, in whose ... Ex 36:2
And all the *w* men, that wrought ... Ex 36:4
every *w* hearted man among them ... Ex 36:8
but ye shall in no *w* eat of it ... Lev 7:24
thou shalt in any *w* rebuke thy ... Lev 19:17
the field will in any *w* redeem it ... Lev 27:19
On this *w* ye shall bless the ... Num 6:23
Take you *w* men, and understanding, ... Deut 1:13
*w* men, and known, and made them ... Deut 1:15
Surely this great nation is a *w* ... Deut 4:6
gift doth blind the eyes of the *w* ... Deut 16:19
Thou shalt in any *w* set him king ... Deut 17:15
shalt in any *w* bury him that day ... Deut 21:23
shalt in any *w* let the dam go ... Deut 22:7
O that they were *w*, that they ... Deut 32:29
in any *w* keep yourselves from the ... Josh 6:18
Else if ye do in any *w* go back ... Josh 23:12
Her *w* ladies answered her, yea, ... Judg 5:29
but in any *w* return him a ... 1Sa 6:3
and fetched thence a *w* woman ... 2Sa 14:2
and my lord is *w*, according to the ... 2Sa 14:20
Then cried a *w* woman out of the ... 2Sa 20:16
for thou art a *w* man, and knowest ... 1Kin 2:9
lo, I have given thee a *w* ... 1Kin 3:12
living child, and in no *w* slay it ... 1Kin 3:26
living child, and in no *w* slay it ... 1Kin 3:27
a *w* son over this great people ... 1Kin 5:7
howbeit let me go in any *w* ... 1Kin 11:22
a *w* counsellor, they cast lots ... 1Chr 26:14
counsellor, a *w* man, and a scribe ... 1Chr 27:32
given to David the king a *w* son ... 2Chr 2:12
Then the king said to the *w* men ... Est 1:13
Then said his *w* men and Zeresh his ... Est 6:13
He taketh the *w* in their own ... Job 5:13
He is *w* in heart, and mighty in ... Job 9:4
For vain man would be *w*, though ... Job 11:12
Should a *w* man utter vain ... Job 15:2
Which *w* men have told from their ... Job 15:18
I cannot find one *w* man among you .. Job 17:10
as he that is *w* may be profitable ... Job 22:2
Great men are not always *w* ... Job 32:9
Hear my words, O ye *w* men ... Job 34:2
let a *w* man hearken unto me ... Job 34:34
not any that are *w* of heart ... Job 37:24
Be *w* now therefore, O ye kings ... Ps 2:10
LORD is sure, making *w* the simple ... Ps 19:7
he hath left off to be *w*, and to ... Ps 36:3
not thyself in any *w* to do evil ... Ps 37:8
For he seeth that *w* men die ... Ps 49:10
and ye fools, when will ye be *w* ... Ps 94:8
Whoso is *w*, and will observe these ... Ps 107:43
A *w* man will hear, and will ... Prov 1:5
shall attain unto *w* counsels ... Prov 1:5
the words of the *w*, and their dark ... Prov 1:6
Be not *w* in thine own eyes ... Prov 3:7
The *w* shall inherit glory ... Prov 3:35
consider her ways, and be *w* ... Prov 6:6
Hear instruction, and be *w* ... Prov 8:33
rebuke a *w* man, and he will love ... Prov 9:8
Give instruction to a *w* man ... Prov 9:9
If thou be *w*, thou shalt ... Prov 9:12
thou shalt be *w* for thyself ... Prov 9:12
A *w* son maketh a glad father ... Prov 10:1
gathereth in summer is a *w* son ... Prov 10:5
The *w* in heart will receive ... Prov 10:8
*W* men lay up knowledge ... Prov 10:14
he that refraineth his lips is *w* ... Prov 10:19
be servant to the *w* of heart ... Prov 11:29
and he that winneth souls is *w* ... Prov 11:30
that hearkeneth unto counsel is *w* ... Prov 12:15
but the tongue of the *w* is health ... Prov 12:18
A *w* son heareth his father's ... Prov 13:1
The law of the *w* is a fountain of ... Prov 13:14
walketh with *w* men shall ... Prov 13:20
men shall be *w* ... Prov 13:20
Every *w* woman buildeth her house ... Prov 14:1
lips of the *w* shall preserve them ... Prov 14:3
A *w* man feareth, and departeth ... Prov 14:16
crown of the *w* is their riches ... Prov 14:24
favour is toward a *w* servant ... Prov 14:35
The tongue of the *w* useth ... Prov 15:2
The lips of the *w* disperse ... Prov 15:7
neither will he go unto the *w* ... Prov 15:12
A *w* son maketh a glad father ... Prov 15:20
The way of life is above to the *w* ... Prov 15:24
of life abideth among the *w* ... Prov 15:31
but a *w* man will pacify it ... Prov 16:14
The *w* in heart shall be called ... Prov 16:21
The heart of the *w* teacheth his ... Prov 16:23
A *w* servant shall have rule over ... Prov 17:2
a *w* man than an hundred stripes ... Prov 17:10
holdeth his peace, is counted *w* ... Prov 17:28
and the ear of the *w* seeketh ... Prov 18:15
mayest be *w* in thy latter end ... Prov 19:20
is deceived thereby is not *w* ... Prov 20:1
A *w* king scattereth the wicked, ... Prov 20:26
is punished, the simple is made *w* ... Prov 21:11
when the *w* is instructed, he ... Prov 21:11
and oil in the dwelling of the *w* ... Prov 21:20
A *w* man scaleth the city of the ... Prov 21:22
ear, and hear the words of the *w* ... Prov 22:17
My son, if thine heart be *w* ... Prov 23:15
Hear thou, my son, and be *w* ... Prov 23:19
he that begetteth a *w* child shall ... Prov 23:24
A *w* man is strong ... Prov 24:5
For by *w* counsel thou shalt make ... Prov 24:6
These things also belong to the *w* ... Prov 24:23
so is a *w* reprover upon an ... Prov 25:12
lest he be *w* in his own conceit ... Prov 26:5
Seest thou a man *w* in his own ... Prov 26:12
My son, be *w*, and make my heart ... Prov 27:11
Whoso keepeth the law is a *w* son ... Prov 28:7
The rich man is *w* in his own ... Prov 28:11
but *w* men turn away wrath ... Prov 29:8
If a *w* man contendeth with a ... Prov 29:9
but a *w* man keepeth it in till ... Prov 29:11
earth, but they are exceeding *w* ... Prov 30:24
The *w* man's eyes are in his head ... Eccl 2:14
and why was I then more *w* ... Eccl 2:15
*w* more than of the fool for ever ... Eccl 2:16
And how dieth the *w* man ... Eccl 2:16
he shall be a *w* man or a fool ... Eccl 2:19
shewed myself *w* under the sun ... Eccl 2:19
a *w* child than an old and foolish ... Eccl 4:13
For what hath the *w* more than the ... Eccl 6:8
The heart of the *w* is in the ... Eccl 7:4
to hear the rebuke of the *w* ... Eccl 7:5
oppression maketh a *w* man mad ... Eccl 7:7
neither make thyself over *w* ... Eccl 7:16
Wisdom strengtheneth the *w* more ... Eccl 7:19
I said, I will be *w* ... Eccl 7:23
Who is as the *w* man ... Eccl 8:1

a *w* man's heart discerneth both ... Eccl 8:5
though a *w* man think to know it, ... Eccl 8:17
that the righteous, and the *w* ... Eccl 9:1
neither yet bread to the *w* ... Eccl 9:11
was found in it a poor *w* man ... Eccl 9:15
The words of *w* men are heard in ... Eccl 9:17
A *w* man's heart is at his right ... Eccl 10:2
The words of a *w* man's mouth are ... Eccl 10:12
because the preacher was *w* ... Eccl 12:9
The words of the *w* are as goads ... Eccl 12:11
them that are *w* in their own eyes ... Is 5:21
the counsel of the *w* counsellors ... Is 19:11
Pharaoh, I am the son of the *w* ... Is 19:11
where are thy *w* men ... Is 19:12
of their *w* men shall perish ... Is 29:14
Yet he also is *w*, and will bring ... Is 31:2
that turneth *w* men backward ... Is 44:25
they are *w* to do evil, but to do ... Jer 4:22
How do ye say, We are *w*, and the ... Jer 8:8
The *w* men are ashamed, they are ... Jer 8:9
Who is the *w* man, that may ... Jer 9:12
Let not the *w* man glory in his ... Jer 9:23
all the *w* men of the nations ... Jer 10:7
priest, nor counsel from the *w* ... Jer 18:18
her princes, and upon her *w* men ... Jer 50:35
drunk her princes, and her *w* men ... Jer 51:57
thy *w* men, O Tyrus, that were in ... Eze 27:8
the *w* men thereof were in thee ... Eze 27:9
destroy all the *w* men of Babylon ... Dan 2:12
that the *w* men should be slain ... Dan 2:13
to slay the *w* men of Babylon ... Dan 2:14
the rest of the *w* men of Babylon ... Dan 2:18
he giveth wisdom unto the *w* ... Dan 2:21
to destroy the *w* men of Babylon ... Dan 2:24
Destroy not the *w* men of Babylon ... Dan 2:24
hath demanded cannot the *w* men ... Dan 2:27
over all the *w* men of Babylon ... Dan 2:48
the *w* men of Babylon before me ... Dan 4:6
forasmuch as all the *w* men of my ... Dan 4:18
said to the *w* men of Babylon, ... Dan 5:7
Then came in all the king's *w* men ... Dan 5:8
And now the *w* men, the astrologers ... Dan 5:15
they that be *w* shall shine as the ... Dan 12:3
but the *w* shall understand ... Dan 12:10
Who is *w*, and he shall understand ... Hos 14:9
destroy the *w* men out of Edom ... Obad 8
and Zidon, though it be very *w* ... Zec 9:2
of Jesus Christ was on this *w* ... Mt 1:18
there came *w* men from the east to ... Mt 2:1
he had privily called the *w* men ... Mt 2:7
that he was mocked of the *w* men ... Mt 2:16
diligently enquired of the *w* men ... Mt 2:16
shall in no *w* pass from the law ... Mt 5:18
I will liken him unto a *w* man ... Mt 7:24
be ye therefore *w* as serpents ... Mt 10:16
he shall in no *w* lose his reward ... Mt 10:42
hast hid these things from the *w* ... Mt 11:25
I in like *w* will tell you by what ... Mt 21:24
prophets, and *w* men, and scribes ... Mt 23:34
*w* servant, whom his lord hath ... Mt 24:45
And five of them were *w*, and five ... Mt 25:2
But the *w* took oil in their ... Mt 25:4
And the foolish said unto the *w* ... Mt 25:8
But the *w* answered, saying, Not ... Mt 25:9
I will not deny thee in any *w* ... Mk 14:31
hast hid these things from the *w* ... Lk 10:21
*w* steward, whom his lord shall ... Lk 12:42
could in no *w* lift up herself ... Lk 13:11
child shall in no *w* enter therein ... Lk 18:17
to me I will in no *w* cast out ... Jn 6:37
on this *w* shewed he himself ... Jn 21:1
And God spake on this *w*, That his ... Acts 7:6
to corruption, he said on this *w* ... Acts 13:34
which ye shall in no *w* believe ... Acts 13:41
both to the *w*, and to the unwise ... Rom 1:14
Professing themselves to be *w* ... Rom 1:22
No, in no *w*: ... Rom 3:9
is of faith speaketh on this *w* ... Rom 10:6
lest ye should be *w* in your own ... Rom 11:25
Be not *w* in your own conceits ... Rom 12:16
you *w* unto that which is good ... Rom 16:19
To God only *w*, be glory through ... Rom 16:27
will destroy the wisdom of the *w* ... 1Cor 1:19
Where is the *w* ... 1Cor 1:20
how that not many *w* men after the ... 1Cor 1:26
of the world to confound the *w* ... 1Cor 1:27
as a *w* masterbuilder, I have laid ... 1Cor 3:10
you seemeth to be *w* in this world ... 1Cor 3:18
become a fool, that he may be *w* ... 1Cor 3:18
He taketh the *w* in their own ... 1Cor 3:19
knoweth the thoughts of the *w* ... 1Cor 3:20
sake, but ye are *w* in Christ ... 1Cor 4:10
there is not a *w* man among you ... 1Cor 6:5
I speak as to *w* men ... 1Cor 10:15
among themselves, are not *w* ... 2Cor 10:12
seeing ye yourselves are *w* ... 2Cor 11:19
not as fools, but as *w*, ... Eph 5:15
invisible, the only *w* God ... 1Ti 1:17
which are able to make thee *w* ... 2Ti 3:15
of the seventh day on this *w* ... Heb 4:4
Who is a *w* man and endued with ... Jas 3:13
To the only *w* God our Saviour, be ... Jude 25
there shall in no *w* enter into it ... Rev 21:27

**WISELY**
Come on, let us deal *w* with them ... Ex 1:10
sent him, and behaved himself *w* ... 1Sa 18:5
behaved himself *w* in all his ways ... 1Sa 18:14
that he behaved himself very *w* ... 1Sa 18:15
*w* than all the servants of Saul ... 1Sa 18:30
And he dealt *w*, and dispersed of ... 2Chr 11:23
of charmers, charming never so *w* ... Ps 58:5
for they shall *w* consider of his ... Ps 64:9
behave myself *w* in a perfect way ... Ps 101:2
a matter *w* shall find good ... Prov 16:20
The righteous man *w* considereth ... Prov 21:12
but whoso walketh *w*, he shall be ... Prov 28:26
not enquire *w* concerning this ... Eccl 7:10
steward, because he had done *w* ... Lk 16:8

**WISER**
For he was *w* than all men ... 1Kin 4:31
maketh us *w* than the fowls of ... Job 35:11
hast made me *w* than mine enemies ... Ps 119:98
a wise man, and he will be yet *w* ... Prov 9:9
The sluggard is *w* in his own ... Prov 26:16
Behold, thou art *w* than Daniel ... Eze 28:3
*w* than the children of light ... Lk 16:8
foolishness of God is *w* than men ... 1Cor 1:25

**WISH**
according to thy *w* in God's stead ... Job 33:6
and put to shame that *w* me evil ... Ps 40:14
they have more than heart could *w* ... Ps 73:7
For I could *w* that myself were ... Rom 9:3
and this also we *w*, even your ... 2Cor 13:9
I *w* above all things that thou ... 3Jn 2

**WISHED**
*w* in himself to die, and said, It ... Jonah 4:8
of the stern, and *w* for the day ... Acts 27:29

**WISHING**
to sin by *w* a curse to his soul ... Job 31:30

**WIST**
for they *w* not what it was ... Ex 16:15
that Moses *w* not that the skin of ... Ex 34:29
though he *w* it not, yet is he ... Lev 5:17
*w* it not, and it shall be forgiven ... Lev 5:18
but I *w* not whence they were ... Josh 2:4
but he *w* not that there were ... Josh 8:14
he *w* not that the LORD was ... Judg 16:20
For he *w* not what to say ... Mk 9:6
neither *w* they what to answer ... Mk 14:40
*w* ye not that I must be about my ... Lk 2:49
that was healed *w* not who it was ... Jn 5:13
*w* not that it was true which was ... Acts 12:9
I *w* not, brethren, that he was ... Acts 23:5

**WIT**
to *w* whether the LORD had made ... Gen 24:21
to *w* what would be done to him ... Ex 2:4
to *w*, for Machir the firstborn of ... Josh 17:1
David not knowing thereof, to *w* ... 1Kin 2:32
for the doors of the house, to *w* ... 1Kin 7:50
he saddled for him the ass, to *w* ... 1Kin 13:23
not from after them, to *w* ... 2Kin 10:29
of their father's house, to *w* ... 1Chr 7:2
Israel after their number, to *w* ... 1Chr 27:1
To *w*, the two pillars, and the ... 2Chr 4:12
the LORD is not with Israel, to *w* ... 2Chr 25:7
Then Amaziah separated them, to *w* ... 2Chr 25:10
for the burnt offerings, to *w* ... 2Chr 31:3
possession in their cities, to *w* ... Neh 11:3
purifications accomplished, to *w* ... Est 2:12
To *w*, Jerusalem, and the cities of ... Jer 25:18
serve himself of them, to *w* ... Jer 34:9
To *w*, the prophets of Israel ... Eze 13:16
waiting for the adoption, to *w* ... Rom 8:23
To *w*, that God was in Christ, ... 2Cor 5:19
we do you to *w* of the grace of ... 2Cor 8:1

**WITCH**
Thou shalt not suffer a *w* to live ... Ex 22:18
of times, or an enchanter, or a *w* ... Deut 18:10

**WITCHCRAFT**
For rebellion is as the sin of *w* ... 1Sa 15:23
and used enchantments, and used *w* ... 2Chr 33:6
Idolatry, *w*, hatred, variance, ... Gal 5:20

**WITCHCRAFTS**
Jezebel and her *w* are so many ... 2Kin 9:22
I will cut off *w* out of thine ... Mic 5:12
harlot, the mistress of *w* ... Nah 3:4
and families through her *w* ... Nah 3:4

**WITH** See PREFACE.

**WITHAL**
and bowls thereof, to cover *w* ... Ex 25:29
for the staves to bear it *w* ... Ex 30:4
his foot also of brass, to wash *w* ... Ex 30:18
of the sanctuary, to make it *w* ... Ex 36:3
bowls, and his covers to cover *w* ... Ex 37:16
for the staves to bear it *w* ... Ex 37:27
sides of the altar, to bear it *w* ... Ex 38:7
and put water there, to wash *w* ... Ex 40:30
be that a man shall be defiled *w* ... Lev 5:3
to reconcile *w* in the holy place ... Lev 6:30
feet, to leap *w* upon the earth ... Lev 11:21
be holy to praise the LORD *w* ... Lev 19:24
the bowls, and covers to cover *w* ... Num 4:7
in their right hands to blow *w* ... Judg 7:20
*w* of a beautiful countenance, and ... 1Sa 16:12
*w* how he had slain all the ... 1Kin 19:1
that Manasseh had provoked him *w*. ... 2Kin 23:26
overlay the walls of the houses *w* ... 1Chr 29:4
to minister, and to offer *w* ... 2Chr 24:14
to shoot arrows and great stones *w* ... 2Chr 26:15
man *w* whom the king delighteth to ... Est 6:9
a potsherd to scrape himself *w* ... Job 2:8
own nets, whilst that I *w* escape ... Ps 141:10
they shall *w* be fitted in thy ... Prov 22:18
or to take water *w* out of the pit ... Is 30:14
that thou shalt sow the ground *w* ... Is 30:23
baptized *w* shall ye be baptized ... Mk 10:39
*w* it shall be measured to you ... Lk 6:38
not *w* to signify the crimes laid ... Acts 25:27
is given to every man to profit *w* ... 1Cor 12:7
*W* praying also for us, that God ... Col 4:3
And *w* they learn to be idle, ... 1Ti 5:13
But *w* prepare me also a lodging ... Philem 22

**WITHDRAW**
unto the priest, *W* thine hand ... 1Sa 14:19
If God will not *w* his anger ... Job 9:13
*W* thine hand far from me ... Job 13:21
That he may *w* man from his ... Job 33:17
*W* thy foot from thy neighbour's ... Prov 25:17
also from this *w* not thine hand ... Eccl 7:18
neither shall thy moon *w* itself ... Is 60:20
the stars shall *w* their shining ... Joel 2:10
the stars shall *w* their shining ... Joel 3:15
that ye *w* yourselves from every ... 2Th 3:6
from such *w* thyself ... 1Ti 6:5

**WITHDRAWEST**
Why *w* thou thy hand, even thy ... Ps 74:11

**WITHDRAWETH**
He *w* not his eyes from the ... Job 36:7

**WITHDRAWN**
have *w* the inhabitants of their ... Deut 13:13
but my beloved had *w* himself ... Song 5:6
he hath not *w* his hand from ... Lam 2:8
that hath *w* his hand from ... Eze 18:8
he hath *w* himself from them ... Hos 5:6
he was *w* from them about a ... Lk 22:41

**WITHDREW**
*w* the shoulder, and hardened their ... Neh 9:29
Nevertheless I *w* mine hand ... Eze 20:22
knew it, he *w* himself from thence ... Mt 12:15
But Jesus *w* himself with his ... Mk 3:7
he *w* himself into the wilderness, ... Lk 5:16
but when they were come, he *w* ... Gal 2:12

**WITHER**
his leaf also shall not *w* ... Ps 1:3
the grass, and *w* as the green herb ... Ps 37:2
the reeds and flags shall *w* ... Is 19:6
thing sown by the brooks, shall *w* ... Is 19:7
blow upon them, and they shall *w* ... Is 40:24
and the herbs of every field *w* ... Jer 12:4
off the fruit thereof, that it *w* ... Eze 17:9
it shall *w* in all the leaves of ... Eze 17:9
shall it not utterly *w*, when the ... Eze 17:10
it shall *w* in the furrows where ... Eze 17:10
and the top of Carmel shall *w* ... Amos 1:2

**WITHERED**
And, behold, seven ears, *w* ... Gen 41:23
heart is smitten, and *w* like grass ... Ps 102:4
and I am *w* like grass ... Ps 102:11
for the hay is *w* away, the grass ... Is 15:6
When the boughs thereof are *w* ... Is 27:11
it is *w*, it is become like a ... Lam 4:8
her strong rods were broken and *w* ... Eze 19:12
all the trees of the field, are *w* ... Joel 1:12
because joy is *w* away from the ... Joel 1:12
for the corn is *w* ... Joel 1:17
piece whereupon it rained not *w* ... Amos 4:7
and it smote the gourd that it *w* ... Jonah 4:7
was a man which had his hand *w* ... Mt 12:10
they had no root, they *w* away ... Mt 13:6
And presently the fig tree *w* away ... Mt 21:19
How soon is the fig tree *w* away ... Mt 21:20
a man there which had a *w* hand ... Mk 3:1
unto the man which had the *w* hand ... Mk 3:3
because it had no root, it *w* away ... Mk 4:6
which thou cursedst is *w* away ... Mk 11:21
was a man whose right hand was *w* ... Lk 6:6
to the man which had the *w* hand ... Lk 6:8
it *w* away, because it lacked ... Lk 8:6
impotent folk, of blind, halt, *w* ... Jn 5:3
cast forth as a branch, and is *w* ... Jn 15:6

**WITHERETH**
it *w* before any other herb ... Job 8:12
the evening it is cut down, and *w* ... Ps 90:6
which *w* afore it groweth up ... Ps 129:6
The grass *w*, the flower fadeth ... Is 40:7
The grass *w*, the flower fadeth ... Is 40:8
but it *w* the grass, and the flower ... Jas 1:11
The grass *w*, and the flower ... 1Pet 1:24
trees whose fruit *w*, without ... Jude 12

**WITHHELD**
for I also *w* thee from sinning ... Gen 20:6
seeing thou hast not *w* thy son ... Gen 22:12
this thing, and hast not *w* thy son ... Gen 22:16
who hath *w* from thee the fruit of ... Gen 30:2
If I have *w* the poor from their ... Job 31:16
I *w* not my heart from any joy ... Eccl 2:10

**WITHHELDEST**
*w* not thy manna from their mouth, ... Neh 9:20

**WITHHOLD**
none of us shall *w* from thee his ... Gen 23:6
for he will not *w* me from thee ... 2Sa 13:13
but who can *w* himself from ... Job 4:2
*W* not thou thy tender mercies ... Ps 40:11
no good thing will he *w* from them ... Ps 84:11
*W* not good from them to whom it ... Prov 3:27
*W* not correction from the child ... Prov 23:13
in the evening *w* not thine hand ... Eccl 11:6
*W* thy foot from being unshod, and ... Jer 2:25

**WITHHOLDEN**
seeing the LORD hath *w* thee from....... 1Sa 25:26
thou hast *w* bread from the hungry....... Job 22:7
from the wicked their light is *w*.......... Job 38:15
no thought can be *w* from thee.............. Job 42:2
hast not *w* the request of his.................... Ps 21:2
Therefore the showers have been *w*......... Jer 3:3
your sins have *w* good things from......... Jer 5:25
hath not *w* the pledge, neither............. Eze 18:16
the drink offering is *w* from the............ Joel 1:13
also I have *w* the rain from you,.......... Amos 4:7

**WITHHOLDETH**
he *w* the waters, and they dry up........ Job 12:15
there is that *w* more than is meet...... Prov 11:24
He that *w* corn, the people shall....... Prov 11:26
now ye know what *w* that he might....... 2Th 2:6

**WITHIN**
in the ark, and shalt pitch it *w*............ Gen 6:14
and he was uncovered *w* his tent......... Gen 9:21
Therefore Sarah laughed *w* herself..... Gen 18:12
be fifty righteous *w* the city................ Gen 18:24
Sodom fifty righteous *w* the city.......... Gen 18:26
children struggled together *w* her....... Gen 25:22
of the men of the house there *w*....... Gen 39:11
Yet *w* three days shall Pharaoh.......... Gen 40:13
Yet *w* three days shall Pharaoh.......... Gen 40:19
thy stranger that is *w* thy gates.......... Ex 20:10
overlay it with pure gold, *w*................ Ex 25:11
thither *w* the vail the ark of the............. Ex 26:33
he overlaid it with pure gold *w*................. Ex 37:2
not brought in *w* the holy place............ Lev 10:18
whether it be bare *w* or without............ Lev 13:55
house to be scraped *w* round about...... Lev 14:41
all times into the holy place *w*.............. Lev 16:2
small, and bring it *w* the vail.................. Lev 16:12
and bring his blood *w* the vail.............. Lev 16:15
then he may redeem it *w* a whole........ Lev 25:29
*w* a full year may he redeem it.............. Lev 25:29
if it be not redeemed *w* the space....... Lev 25:30
gathered together *w* your cities.......... Lev 26:25
all the vessels thereof *w* a.................. Num 4:10
thing of the altar, and *w* the vail........ Num 18:7
thy stranger that is *w* thy gates.......... Deut 5:14
the Levite that is *w* your gates.......... Deut 12:12
Thou mayest not eat *w* thy gates........ Deut 12:17
and the Levite that is *w* thy gates...... Deut 12:18
And the Levite that is *w* thy gates.... Deut 14:27
and shalt lay it up *w* thy gates.......... Deut 14:28
the widow, which are *w* thy gates........ Deut 14:29
*w* any of thy gates in thy land.............. Deut 15:7
Thou shalt eat it *w* thy gates.............. Deut 15:22
the passover *w* any of thy gates.......... Deut 16:5
and the Levite that is *w* thy gates...... Deut 16:11
the widow, that are *w* thy gates......... Deut 16:14
*w* any of thy gates which the LORD.... Deut 17:2
of controversy *w* thy gates.................. Deut 17:8
he shall not come *w* the camp............ Deut 23:10
that are in thy land *w* thy gates.......... Deut 24:14
that they may eat *w* thy gates............ Deut 26:12
The stranger that is *w* thee shall........ Deut 28:43
thy stranger that is *w* thy gates.......... Deut 31:12
The sword without, and terror *w*......... Deut 32:25
for *w* three days ye shall pass............ Josh 1:11
their inheritance was *w* the................. Josh 19:1
*w* the inheritance of them.................... Josh 19:9
All the cities of the Levites *w*............ Josh 21:41
pitchers, and lamps *w* the pitchers...... Judg 7:16
was a strong tower *w* the city............ Judg 9:51
but came not *w* the border of Moab.. Judg 11:18
ye not recover them *w* that time........ Judg 11:26
me *w* the seven days of the feast....... Judg 14:12
it came to pass *w* a while after............. Judg 15:1
camest not *w* the days appointed......... 1Sa 13:11
*w* as it were an half acre of land.......... 1Sa 14:14
Nabal's heart was merry *w* him for....... 1Sa 25:36
things, that his heart died *w* him......... 1Sa 25:37
Saul lay sleeping *w* the trench............ 1Sa 26:7
ark of God dwelleth *w* curtains.............. 2Sa 7:2
me the men of Judah *w* three days......... 2Sa 20:4
the house *w* with boards of cedar......... 1Kin 6:15
he even built them for it *w*................... 1Kin 6:16
the house *w* was carved with knops... 1Kin 6:18
oracle he prepared in the house *w*........ 1Kin 6:19
the house *w* with pure gold.................. 1Kin 6:21
And *w* the oracle he made two.............. 1Kin 6:23
the cherubims *w* the inner house.......... 1Kin 6:27
and palm trees and open flowers, *w*.... 1Kin 6:29
house he overlaid with gold, *w*.............. 1Kin 6:30
had another court *w* the porch............. 1Kin 7:8
hewed stones, sawed with saws, *w*........ 1Kin 7:9
And the mouth of it *w* the chapiter...... 1Kin 7:31
for her soul is vexed *w* her.................... 2Kin 4:27
he had sackcloth *w* upon his flesh......... 2Kin 6:30
told it to the king's house *w*................ 2Kin 7:11
and he that cometh *w* the ranges......... 2Kin 11:8
he overlaid it *w* with pure gold.............. 2Chr 3:4
sedition *w* the same of old time.............. Ezr 4:15
would not come *w* three days................. Ezr 10:8
unto Jerusalem *w* three days.................. Ezr 10:9
his servant lodge *w* Jerusalem.............. Neh 4:22
*w* the temple, and let us shut the.......... Neh 6:10
arrows of the Almighty are *w* me............ Job 6:4
his soul *w* him shall mourn.................. Job 14:22
though my reins be consumed *w* me... Job 19:27
but keep it still *w* his mouth................ Job 20:13
it is the gall of asps *w* him.................. Job 20:14
Which make oil *w* their walls................ Job 24:11
the spirit *w* me constraineth me........... Job 32:18
of the wicked saith *w* my heart............. Ps 36:1
My heart was hot *w* me............................ Ps 39:3
yea, thy law is *w* my heart...................... Ps 40:8
hid thy righteousness *w* my heart....... Ps 40:10
my God, my soul is cast down *w* me......... Ps 42:6
and why art thou disquieted *w* me......... Ps 42:11
and why art thou disquieted *w* me.......... Ps 43:5
king's daughter is all glorious *w*............ Ps 45:13
and renew a right spirit *w* me............... Ps 51:10
My heart is sore pained *w* me................. Ps 55:4
*w* me thy comforts delight my soul....... Ps 94:19
I will walk *w* my house with a................. Ps 101:2
deceit shall not dwell *w* my house......... Ps 101:7
and all that is *w* me, bless his............... Ps 103:1
and my heart is wounded *w* me........... Ps 109:22
Our feet shall stand *w* thy gates........... Ps 122:2
Peace be *w* thy walls............................... Ps 122:7
and prosperity *w* thy palaces................. Ps 122:7
I will now say, Peace be *w* thee............. Ps 122:8
my spirit was overwhelmed *w* me.......... Ps 142:3
is my spirit overwhelmed *w* me.............. Ps 143:4
my heart *w* me is desolate...................... Ps 143:4
hath blessed thy children *w* thee......... Ps 147:13
thing if thou keep them *w* thee.......... Prov 22:18
lips, and layeth up deceit *w* him........ Prov 26:24
a little city, and few men *w* it................. Eccl 9:14
thou hast doves' eyes *w* thy locks......... Song 4:1
of a pomegranate *w* thy locks............... Song 4:3
are thy temples *w* thy locks.................. Song 6:7
*w* threescore and five years shall................. Is 7:8
*W* three years, as the years of an.......... Is 16:14
*W* a year, according to the years............ Is 21:16
with my spirit *w* me will I seek................. Is 26:9
*w* my walls a place and a name.................. Is 56:5
nor destruction *w* thy borders................. Is 60:18
he that put his holy Spirit *w* him........... Is 63:11
thy vain thoughts lodge *w* thee................ Jer 4:14
Mine heart *w* me is broken because......... Jer 23:9
*W* two full years will I bring.................... Jer 28:3
*w* the space of two full years................ Jer 28:11
mine heart is turned *w* me..................... Lam 1:20
of fire round about *w* it, from................ Eze 1:27
and it was written *w* and without........... Eze 2:10
Go, shut thyself *w* thine house.............. Eze 3:24
and the pestilence and the famine *w*..... Eze 7:15
and I will put a new spirit *w* you.......... Eze 11:19
divination *w* the house of Israel........... Eze 12:24
and a new spirit will I put *w* you......... Eze 36:26
And I will put my spirit *w* you............. Eze 36:27
porch of the gate *w* was one reed.......... Eze 40:7
also the porch of the gate *w*.................. Eze 40:8
to their posts *w* the gate round............ Eze 40:16
*w* were hooks, an hand broad,............... Eze 40:43
of the side chambers that were *w*.......... Eze 41:9
and by all the wall round about *w*....... Eze 41:17
gates of the inner court, and *w*............. Eze 44:17
of any God or man *w* thirty days.......... Dan 6:12
but *w* few days he shall be.................... Dan 11:20
mine heart is turned *w* me..................... Hos 11:8
When my soul fainted *w* me I................ Jonah 2:7
pot, and as flesh *w* the caldron................ Mic 3:3
and when he treadeth *w* our borders........ Mic 5:6
Her princes *w* her are roaring............... Zeph 3:3
formeth the spirit of man *w* him............. Zec 12:1
And think not to say *w* yourselves.......... Mt 3:9
of the scribes said *w* themselves............. Mt 9:3
For she said *w* herself, If I may............ Mt 9:21
but *w* they are full of extortion............ Mt 23:25
first that which is *w* the cup................ Mt 23:26
but are *w* full of dead men's.................. Mt 23:27
but *w* ye are full of hypocrisy and......... Mt 23:28
they so reasoned *w* themselves............... Mk 2:8
For from *w*, out of the heart of.............. Mk 7:21
All these evil things come from *w*........... Mk 7:23
that had indignation *w* themselves......... Mk 14:4
*w* three days I will build another.......... Mk 14:58
and begin not to say *w* yourselves.......... Lk 3:8
him saw it, he spake *w* himself.............. Lk 7:39
him began to say *w* themselves............... Lk 7:49
he from *w* shall answer and say,............. Lk 11:7
without make that which is *w* also....... Lk 11:40
And he thought *w* himself, saying,....... Lk 12:17
Then the steward said *w* himself........... Lk 16:3
the kingdom of God is *w* you............... Lk 17:21
but afterward he said *w* himself.............. Lk 18:4
ground, and thy children *w* thee.......... Lk 19:44
Did not our heart burn *w* us................. Lk 24:32
days again his disciples were *w*............. Jn 20:26
we had opened, we found no man *w*... Acts 5:23
we ourselves groan *w* ourselves.......... Rom 8:23
do not ye judge them that are *w*........ 1Cor 5:12
were fightings, *w* were fears.............. 2Cor 7:5
entereth into that *w* the veil................. Heb 6:19
and they were full of eyes *w*.................. Rev 4:8
on the throne a book written *w*............. Rev 5:1

**WITHOUT**
And the earth was *w* form, and void...... Gen 1:2
pitch it within and *w* with pitch........... Gen 6:14
and told his two brethren *w*................... Gen 9:22
him forth, and set him *w* the city....... Gen 19:16
made his camels to kneel down *w*......... Gen 24:11
wherefore standest thou *w*................... Gen 24:31
Joseph is *w* doubt rent in pieces.......... Gen 37:33
*w* thee shall no man lift up his............. Gen 41:44
for it was *w* number............................ Gen 41:49
Your lamb shall be *w* blemish.................. Ex 12:5
shall she go out free *w* money.............. Ex 21:11
*w* shalt thou overlay it, and shalt......... Ex 25:11
shalt set the table *w* the vail................. Ex 26:35
of the congregation *w* the vail.............. Ex 27:21
bullock, and two rams *w* blemish........... Ex 29:1
thou burn with fire *w* the camp............ Ex 29:14
and pitched it *w* the camp.................... Ex 33:7
which was *w* the camp.......................... Ex 33:7
it with pure gold within and *w*............... Ex 37:2
tabernacle northward, *w* the vail.......... Ex 40:22
let him offer a male *w* blemish............... Lev 1:3
shall bring it a male *w* blemish.............. Lev 1:10
he shall offer it *w* blemish...................... Lev 3:1
he shall offer it *w* blemish...................... Lev 3:6
a young bullock *w* blemish unto.............. Lev 4:3
*w* the camp unto a clean place............. Lev 4:12
forth the bullock *w* the camp................ Lev 4:21
of the goats, a male *w* blemish............. Lev 4:23
of the goats, a female *w* blemish.......... Lev 4:28
shall bring it a female *w* blemish.......... Lev 4:32
a ram *w* blemish out of the flocks.......... Lev 5:15
he shall bring a ram *w* blemish............. Lev 5:18
a ram *w* blemish out of the flock,........... Lev 6:6
carry forth the ashes *w* the camp......... Lev 6:11
he burnt with fire *w* the camp............... Lev 8:17
*w* blemish, and offer them before........... Lev 9:2
*w* blemish, for a burnt offering............... Lev 9:3
he burnt with fire *w* the camp.............. Lev 9:11
eat it *w* leaven beside the altar............. Lev 10:12
*w* the camp shall his habitation............. Lev 13:46
whether it be bare within or *w*.............. Lev 13:55
shall take two he lambs *w* blemish...... Lev 14:10
lamb of the first year *w* blemish........... Lev 14:10
into an unclean place *w* the city........... Lev 14:40
the dust that they scrape off *w*............ Lev 14:41
shall one carry forth *w* the camp.......... Lev 16:27
at your own will a male *w* blemish........ Lev 22:19
ye wave the sheaf an he lamb *w*........... Lev 23:12
lambs *w* blemish of the first year......... Lev 23:18
*W* the vail of the testimony, in.............. Lev 24:3
him that hath cursed *w* the camp.......... Lev 24:14
while she lieth desolate *w* them........... Lev 26:43
*w* the camp shall ye put them................ Num 5:3
so, and put them out *w* the camp........... Num 5:4
*w* blemish for a burnt offering.............. Num 6:14
year *w* blemish for a sin offering.......... Num 6:14
one ram *w* blemish for peace................... Num 6:14
ignorance *w* the knowledge of the.... Num 15:24
stone him with stones *w* the camp.... Num 15:35
brought him *w* the camp....................... Num 15:36
bring thee a red heifer *w* spot............... Num 19:2
he may bring her forth *w* the camp.... Num 19:3
lay them up *w* the camp in a clean..... Num 19:9
*w* doing any thing else, go.................... Num 20:19
the first year *w* spot day by day.......... Num 28:3
lambs of the first year *w* spot............... Num 28:9
lambs of the first year *w* spot............. Num 28:11
they shall be unto you *w* blemish....... Num 28:19
they shall be unto you *w* blemish).... Num 28:31
lambs of the first year *w* blemish......... Num 29:2
they shall be unto you *w* blemish.......... Num 29:8
they shall be *w* blemish........................ Num 29:13
lambs of the first year *w* spot............ Num 29:17
lambs of the first year *w* blemish....... Num 29:20
lambs of the first year *w* blemish....... Num 29:23
lambs of the first year *w* spot............ Num 29:26
lambs of the first year *w* blemish....... Num 29:29
lambs of the first year *w* blemish....... Num 29:32
lambs of the first year *w* blemish....... Num 29:36
forth to meet them *w* the camp............ Num 31:13
do ye abide *w* the camp seven days.. Num 31:19
ye shall measure from *w* the city........ Num 35:5
he thrust him suddenly *w* enmity........ Num 35:22
him any thing *w* laying of wait........... Num 35:22
*w* the border of the city of his............ Num 35:26
*w* the borders of the city of his.......... Num 35:27
thou shalt eat bread *w* scarceness......... Deut 8:9
have a place also *w* the camp............. Deut 23:12
shall not marry *w* unto a stranger........ Deut 25:5
*w* iniquity, just and right is he............. Deut 32:4
The sword *w*, and terror within,........ Deut 32:25
that he will *w* fail drive out................. Josh 3:10
left them *w* the camp of Israel.............. Josh 6:23
*w* driving them out hastily..................... Judg 2:23
and their camels were *w* number........... Judg 6:5
and their camels were *w* number......... Judg 7:12
If thou shalt *w* fail deliver the............ Judg 11:30
left thee this day *w* a kinsman............. Ruth 4:14
blood, to slay David *w* a cause............... 1Sa 19:5
them, and *w* fail recover all.................. 1Sa 30:8
riseth, even a morning *w* clouds............. 2Sa 23:4
for *w* in the wall of the house he.......... 1Kin 6:6
and open flowers, within and *w*............ 1Kin 6:29
overlaid with gold, within and *w*.......... 1Kin 6:30
sawed with saws, within and *w*.............. 1Kin 7:9
oracle, and they were not seen *w*............ 1Kin 8:8
three years *w* war between Syria.......... 1Kin 22:1
Jehu appointed fourscore men *w*....... 2Kin 10:24
them, Have her forth *w* the ranges.... 2Kin 11:15
the house, and the king's entry *w*....... 2Kin 16:18
Am I now come up *w* the LORD........... 2Kin 18:25
he burned them *w* Jerusalem in the..... 2Kin 23:4
*w* Jerusalem, unto the brook............... 2Kin 23:6
of all these vessels was *w* weight...... 2Kin 25:16
but Seled died *w* children.................. 1Chr 2:30
and Jether died *w* children................. 1Chr 2:32
nor offer burnt offerings *w* cost.......... 1Chr 21:24
and brass in abundance *w* weight......... 1Chr 22:3
and of brass and iron *w* weight........... 1Chr 22:14
but they were not seen *w*...................... 2Chr 5:9
the people were *w* number that........... 2Chr 12:3
Israel hath been *w* the true God.......... 2Chr 15:3
*w* a teaching priest............................... 2Chr 15:3
a teaching priest, and *w* law................ 2Chr 15:3
and departed *w* being desired............. 2Chr 21:20

set it *w* at the gate of the house 2Chr 24:8
fountains which were *w* the city 2Chr 32:3
to the towers, and another wall *w* 2Chr 32:5
built a wall *w* the city of David 2Chr 33:14
be given them day by day *w* fail Ezr 6:9
salt *w* prescribing how much Ezr 7:22
and we are not able to stand *w* Ezr 10:13
lodged *w* Jerusalem once or twice Neh 13:20
him, to destroy him *w* cause Job 2:3
for ever *w* any regarding it Job 4:20
they die, even *w* wisdom Job 4:21
marvellous things *w* number Job 5:9
is unsavoury be eaten *w* salt Job 6:6
shuttle, and are spent *w* hope Job 7:6
Can the rush grow up *w* mire Job 8:11
can the flag grow *w* water Job 8:11
yea, and wonders *w* number Job 9:10
and multiplieth my wounds *w* cause Job 9:17
*w* any order, and where the light Job 10:22
thou lift up thy face *w* spot Job 11:15
They grope in the dark *w* light Job 12:25
the naked to lodge *w* clothing Job 24:7
cause him to go naked *w* clothing Job 24:10
thou helped him that is *w* power Job 26:2
I went mourning *w* the sun Job 30:28
clothing, or any poor *w* covering Job 31:19
eaten the fruits thereof *w* money Job 31:39
I am clean *w* transgression, I am Job 33:9
is incurable *w* transgression Job 34:6
mighty shall be taken away *w* hand Job 34:20
in pieces mighty men *w* number Job 34:24
Job hath spoken *w* knowledge Job 34:35
and his words were *w* wisdom Job 34:35
he multiplieth words *w* knowledge Job 35:16
and they shall die *w* knowledge Job 36:12
counsel by words *w* knowledge Job 38:2
her labour is in vain *w* fear Job 39:16
not his like, who is made *w* fear Job 41:33
that hideth counsel *w* knowledge Job 42:3
him that *w* cause is mine enemy Ps 7:4
ashamed which transgress *w* cause Ps 25:3
that did see me *w* fled from me Ps 31:11
For *w* cause have they hid for me Ps 35:7
which *w* cause they have digged Ps 35:7
the eye that hate me *w* a cause Ps 35:19
and prepare themselves *w* my fault Ps 59:4
They that hate me *w* a cause are Ps 69:4
caterpillers, and that *w* number, Ps 105:34
and fought against me *w* a cause Ps 109:3
perversely with me *w* a cause Ps 119:78
have persecuted me *w* a cause Ps 119:161
privily for the innocent *w* cause Prov 1:11
Wisdom crieth *w* Prov 1:20
Strive not with a man *w* cause Prov 3:30
He shall die *w* instruction Prov 5:23
shall he be broken *w* remedy Prov 6:15
Now is she *w*, now in the streets, Prov 7:12
fair woman which is *w* discretion Prov 11:22
*W* counsel purposes are Prov 15:22
than great revenues *w* right Prov 16:8
that the soul be *w* knowledge Prov 19:2
man saith, There is a lion *w* Prov 22:13
who hath wounds *w* cause Prov 23:29
Prepare thy work *w*, and make it Prov 24:27
against thy neighbour *w* cause Prov 24:28
is like clouds and wind *w* rain Prov 25:14
that is broken down, and *w* walls Prov 25:28
be destroyed, and that *w* remedy Prov 29:1
serpent will bite *w* enchantment Eccl 10:11
concubines, and virgins *w* number Song 6:8
when I should find thee *w* Song 8:1
even great and fair, *w* inhabitant Is 5:9
and opened her mouth *w* measure Is 5:14
the cities be wasted *w* inhabitant Is 6:11
and the houses *w* man Is 6:11
*W* me they shall bow down under Is 10:4
their valiant ones shall cry *w* Is 33:7
am I now come up *w* the LORD Is 36:10
nor confounded world *w* end Is 45:17
and ye shall be redeemed *w* money Is 52:3
Assyrian oppressed them *w* cause Is 52:4
milk *w* money and *w* price Is 55:1
cities are burned *w* inhabitant Jer 2:15
have forgotten me days *w* number Jer 2:32
be laid waste, *w* an inhabitant Jer 4:7
the earth, and, lo, it was *w* form Jer 4:23
people, and *w* understanding Jer 5:21
Judah desolate, *w* an inhabitant Jer 9:11
to cut off the children from *w* Jer 9:21
will I give to the spoil *w* price Jer 15:13
which besiege you *w* the walls Jer 21:4
his neighbour's service *w* wages Jer 22:13
shall be desolate *w* an inhabitant Jer 26:9
It is desolate *w* man or beast Jer 32:43
ye say shall be desolate *w* man Jer 33:10
*w* beast, even in the cities of Jer 33:10
that are desolate, *w* man Jer 33:10
*w* inhabitant, and *w* beast, Jer 33:10
place, which is desolate *w* man Jer 33:12
*w* beast, and in all the cities Jer 33:12
a desolation *w* an inhabitant Jer 34:22
offerings unto her, *w* our men Jer 44:19
*w* an inhabitant, as at this day Jer 44:22
waste and desolate *w* an inhabitant Jer 46:19
desolate, *w* any to dwell therein Jer 48:9
nation, that dwelleth *w* care Jer 49:31
a desolation *w* an inhabitant Jer 51:29
and an hissing, *w* an inhabitant Jer 51:37
of all these vessels was *w* weight Jer 52:20
they are gone *w* strength before Lam 1:6

ceaseth not, *w* any intermission, Lam 3:49
me sore, like a bird, *w* cause Lam 3:52
and it was written within and *w* Eze 2:10
The sword is *w*, and the pestilence Eze 7:15
*w* cause all that I have done in Eze 14:23
even *w* great power or many people Eze 17:9
of life, *w* committing iniquity Eze 33:15
all of them dwelling *w* walls Eze 38:11
forefront of the inner court *w* Eze 40:19
And at the side *w*, as one goeth up Eze 40:40
*w* the inner gate were the Eze 40:44
which was for the side chamber *w* Eze 41:9
even unto the inner house, and *w* Eze 41:17
the wall round about within and *w* Eze 41:17
upon the face of the porch *w* Eze 41:25
the wall that was *w* over against Eze 42:7
of the house, *w* the sanctuary Eze 43:21
*w* blemish for a sin offering Eze 43:22
offer a young bullock *w* blemish Eze 43:23
a ram out of the flock *w* blemish Eze 43:23
a ram out of the flock, *w* blemish Eze 43:25
take a young bullock *w* blemish Eze 45:18
seven rams *w* blemish daily the Eze 45:23
way of the porch of that gate *w* Eze 46:2
day shall be six lambs *w* blemish Eze 46:4
blemish, and a ram *w* blemish Eze 46:4
be a young bullock *w* blemish Eze 46:6
they shall be *w* blemish Eze 46:6
lamb of the first year *w* blemish Eze 46:13
led me about the way *w* unto the Eze 47:2
that a stone was cut out *w* hands Dan 2:34
cut out of the mountain *w* hands Dan 2:45
but he shall be broken *w* hand Dan 8:25
*w* his own reproach he shall cause Dan 11:18
shall abide many days *w* a king Hos 3:4
and *w* a prince Hos 3:4
*w* a sacrifice Hos 3:4
*w* an image, and *w* an ephod, Hos 3:4
and *w* teraphim Hos 3:4
the troop of robbers spoileth *w* Hos 7:1
also is like a silly dove *w* heart Hos 7:11
*w* number, whose teeth are the Joel 1:6
shall be inhabited as towns *w* Zec 2:4
is angry with his brother *w* a Mt 5:22
fall on the ground *w* your Father Mt 10:29
mother and his brethren stood *w* Mt 12:46
mother and thy brethren stand *w* Mt 12:47
*w* a parable spake he not unto Mt 13:34
them, A prophet is not *w* honour Mt 13:57
Are ye also yet *w* understanding Mt 15:16
Now Peter sat *w* in the palace Mt 26:69
but was *w* in desert places Mk 1:45
and his mother, and, standing *w* Mk 3:31
thy brethren *w* seek for thee Mk 3:32
but unto them that are *w*, all Mk 4:11
But *w* a parable spake he not unto Mk 4:34
them, A prophet is not *w* honour Mk 6:4
There is nothing from *w* a man Mk 7:15
Are ye so *w* understanding also Mk 7:18
from *w* entereth into the man Mk 7:18
*w* in a place where two ways met Mk 11:4
I will build another made *w* hands Mk 14:58
praying *w* at the time of incense Lk 1:10
enemies might serve him *w* fear Lk 1:74
is like a man that *w* a foundation Lk 6:49
mother and thy brethren stand *w* Lk 8:20
*w* make that which is within also Lk 11:40
the door, and ye begin to stand *w* Lk 13:25
he die *w* children, that his Lk 20:28
took a wife, and died *w* children Lk 20:29
them, When I sent you *w* purse Lk 22:35
*w* him was not any thing made that Jn 1:3
He that is *w* sin among you, let Jn 8:7
for *w* me ye can do nothing Jn 15:5
law, They hated me *w* a cause Jn 15:25
But Peter stood at the door *w* Jn 18:16
now the coat was *w* seam, woven Jn 19:23
But Mary stood *w* at the sepulchre Jn 20:11
standing *w* before the doors Acts 5:23
and brought them *w* violence Acts 5:26
And he was three days *w* sight Acts 9:9
came I unto you *w* gainsaying Acts 10:29
but prayer was made *w* ceasing of Acts 12:5
he left not himself *w* witness Acts 14:17
*w* any delay on the morrow I sat Acts 25:17
that *w* ceasing I make mention of Rom 1:9
so that they are *w* excuse Rom 1:20
*W* understanding, covenantbreakers Rom 1:31
*w* natural affection, implacable, Rom 1:31
For as many as have sinned *w* law Rom 2:12
law shall also perish *w* law Rom 2:12
make the faith of God *w* effect Rom 3:3
of God *w* the law is manifested Rom 3:21
by faith *w* the deeds of the law Rom 3:28
imputeth righteousness *w* works Rom 4:6
For when we were yet *w* strength Rom 5:6
For *w* the law sin was dead Rom 7:8
For I was alive *w* the law once Rom 7:9
how shall they hear *w* a preacher Rom 10:14
calling of God are *w* repentance Rom 11:29
Let love be *w* dissimulation Rom 12:9
ye have reigned as kings *w* us 1Cor 4:8
do to judge them also that are *w* 1Cor 5:12
But them that are *w* God judgeth 1Cor 5:13
that a man doeth is *w* the body 1Cor 6:18
I would have you *w* carefulness 1Cor 7:32
upon the Lord *w* distraction 1Cor 7:35
the gospel of Christ *w* charge 1Cor 9:18
To them that are *w* law 1Cor 9:21
as *w* law 1Cor 9:21

being not *w* law to God 1Cor 9:21
I might gain them that are *w* law 1Cor 9:21
neither is the man *w* the woman 1Cor 11:11
neither the woman *w* the man 1Cor 11:11
even things *w* life giving sound, 1Cor 14:7
none of them is *w* signification 1Cor 14:10
that he may be with you *w* fear 1Cor 16:10
*w* were fightings, within were 2Cor 7:5
not boast of things *w* our measure 2Cor 10:13
boasting of things *w* our measure 2Cor 10:15
Beside those things that are *w* 2Cor 11:28
*w* blame before him in love Eph 1:4
at that time ye were *w* Christ Eph 2:12
no hope, and *w* God in the world Eph 2:12
throughout all ages, world *w* end Eph 3:21
it should be holy and *w* blemish Eph 5:27
*w* offence till the day of Christ Phil 1:10
bold to speak the word *w* fear Phil 1:14
Do all things *w* murmurings Phil 2:14
*w* rebuke, in the midst of a Phil 2:15
the circumcision made *w* hands Col 2:11
in wisdom toward them that are *w* Col 4:5
Remembering *w* ceasing your work 1Th 1:3
cause also thank we God *w* ceasing 1Th 2:13
honestly toward them that are *w* 1Th 4:12
Pray *w* ceasing 1Th 5:17
holy hands, *w* wrath and doubting 1Ti 2:8
a good report of them which are *w* 1Ti 3:7
*w* controversy great is the 1Ti 3:16
*w* preferring one before another 1Ti 5:21
thou keep this commandment *w* spot 1Ti 6:14
that *w* ceasing I have remembrance 2Ti 1:3
*W* natural affection, 2Ti 3:3
But *w* thy mind would I do nothing Philem 14
tempted like as we are, yet *w* sin Heb 4:15
*W* father Heb 7:3
*w* mother, *w* descent, having Heb 7:3
*w* descent Heb 7:3
*w* all contradiction the less is Heb 7:7
inasmuch as not *w* an oath he was Heb 7:20
those priests were made *w* an oath Heb 7:21
not *w* blood, which he offered for Heb 9:7
offered himself *w* spot to God Heb 9:14
testament was dedicated *w* blood Heb 9:18
*w* shedding of blood is no Heb 9:22
second time *w* sin unto salvation Heb 9:28
of our faith *w* wavering Heb 10:23
died *w* mercy under two or three Heb 10:28
But *w* faith it is impossible to Heb 11:6
that they *w* us should not be made Heb 11:40
But if ye be *w* chastisement Heb 12:8
*w* which no man shall see the Lord Heb 12:14
conversation be *w* covetousness Heb 13:5
for sin, are burned *w* the camp Heb 13:11
own blood, suffered *w* the gate Heb 13:12
therefore unto him *w* the camp Heb 13:13
he shall have judgment *w* mercy Jas 2:13
shew me thy faith *w* thy works Jas 2:18
that faith *w* works is dead Jas 2:20
For as the body *w* the spirit is Jas 2:26
so faith *w* works is dead also Jas 2:26
fruits, *w* partiality Jas 3:17
partiality, and *w* hypocrisy Jas 3:17
who *w* respect of persons judgeth 1Pet 1:17
of Christ, as of a lamb *w* blemish 1Pet 1:19
blemish and *w* spot 1Pet 1:19
they also may *w* the word be won 1Pet 3:1
one to another *w* grudging 1Pet 4:9
These are wells *w* water, clouds 2Pet 2:17
in peace, *w* spot, and blameless 2Pet 3:14
you, feeding themselves *w* fear Jude 12
clouds they are *w* water, carried Jude 12
*w* fruit, twice dead, plucked up Jude 12
which is *w* the temple leave out Rev 11:2
for they are *w* fault before the Rev 14:5
which is poured out *w* mixture Rev 14:10
winepress was trodden *w* the city Rev 14:20
For *w* are dogs, and sorcerers, and Rev 22:15

**WITHS**
green *w* that were never dried Judg 16:7
green *w* which had not been dried Judg 16:8
And he brake the *w*, as a thread of Judg 16:9

**WITHSTAND**
behold, I went out to *w* thee Num 22:32
and could not *w* them 2Chr 13:7
now ye think to *w* the kingdom of 2Chr 13:8
so that none is able to *w* thee 2Chr 20:6
and no man could *w* them Est 9:2
against him, two shall *w* him Eccl 4:12
the arms of the south shall not *w* Dan 11:15
shall there be any strength to *w* Dan 11:15
what was I, that I could *w* God Acts 11:17
may be able to *w* in the evil day Eph 6:13

**WITHSTOOD**
they *w* Uzziah the king, and said 2Chr 26:18
of the kingdom of Persia *w* me one Dan 10:13
name by interpretation) *w* them Acts 13:8
I *w* him to the face, because he Gal 2:11
Now as Jannes and Jambres *w* Moses 2Ti 3:8
for he hath greatly *w* our words 2Ti 4:15

**WITNESS**
that they may be a *w* unto me Gen 21:30
and let it be for a *w* between me Gen 31:44
said, This heap is a *w* between me Gen 31:48
God is *w* betwixt me and thee Gen 31:50
This heap be *w* Gen 31:52
and this pillar be *w* Gen 31:52
false *w* against thy neighbour Ex 20:16

W

then let him bring it for *w* ... Ex 22:13
the wicked to be an unrighteous *w* ... Ex 23:1
the voice of swearing, and is a *w* ... Lev 5:1
and there be no *w* against her ... Num 5:13
the LORD in the tabernacle of *w* ... Num 17:7
went into the tabernacle of *w* ... Num 17:8
before the tabernacle of *w* ... Num 18:2
but one *w* shall not testify ... Num 35:30
earth to *w* against you this day, ... Deut 4:26
false *w* against thy neighbour ... Deut 5:20
but at the mouth of one *w* he ... Deut 17:6
One *w* shall not rise up against a ... Deut 19:15
If a false *w* rise up against any ... Deut 19:16
if the *w* be a false *w* ... Deut 19:18
that this song may be a *w* for me ... Deut 31:19
shall testify against them as a *w* ... Deut 31:21
may be there for a *w* against thee ... Deut 31:26
But that it may be a *w* between us ... Josh 22:27
but it is a *w* between us and you ... Josh 22:28
for it shall be a *w* between us ... Josh 22:34
this stone shall be a *w* unto us ... Josh 24:27
shall be therefore a *w* unto you ... Josh 24:27
The LORD be *w* between us ... Judg 11:10
*w* against me before the LORD, and ... 1Sa 12:3
them, The LORD is *w* against you ... 1Sa 12:5
and his anointed is *w* this day ... 1Sa 12:5
And they answered, He is *w* ... 1Sa 12:5
to bear *w* against him, saying, ... 1Kin 21:10
Israel, for the tabernacle of *w* ... 2Chr 24:6
wrinkles, which is a *w* against me ... Job 16:8
up in me beareth *w* to my face ... Job 16:8
my *w* is in heaven, and my record ... Job 16:19
the eye saw me, it gave *w* to me ... Job 29:11
and as a faithful *w* in heaven ... Ps 89:37
A false *w* that speaketh lies, and ... Prov 6:19
but a false *w* deceit ... Prov 12:17
A faithful *w* will not lie ... Prov 14:5
but a false *w* will utter lies ... Prov 14:5
A true *w* delivereth souls ... Prov 14:25
but a deceitful *w* speaketh lies ... Prov 14:25
A false *w* shall not be unpunished ... Prov 19:5
A false *w* shall not be unpunished ... Prov 19:9
An ungodly *w* scorneth judgment ... Prov 19:28
A false *w* shall perish ... Prov 21:28
Be not a *w* against thy neighbour ... Prov 24:28
A man that beareth false *w* ... Prov 25:18
countenance doth *w* against them ... Is 3:9
for a *w* unto the LORD of hosts in ... Is 19:20
given him for a *w* to the people ... Is 55:4
even I know, and am a *w*, saith the ... Jer 29:23
faithful *w* between us, if we do ... Jer 42:5
thing shall I take to *w* for thee ... Lam 2:13
let the Lord GOD be *w* against you ... Mic 1:2
the LORD hath been *w* between thee ... Mal 2:14
I will be a swift *w* against the ... Mal 3:5
fornications, thefts, false *w* ... Mt 15:19
Thou shalt not bear false *w* ... Mt 19:18
world for a *w* unto all nations ... Mt 24:14
sought false *w* against Jesus, to ... Mt 26:59
is it which these *w* against thee ... Mt 26:62
many things they *w* against thee ... Mt 27:13
Do not steal, Do not bear false *w* ... Mk 10:19
all the council sought for *w* ... Mk 14:55
For many bare false *w* against him ... Mk 14:56
but their *w* agreed not together ... Mk 14:56
bare false *w* against him, saying, ... Mk 14:57
so did their *w* agree together ... Mk 14:59
is it which these *w* against thee ... Mk 14:60
many things they *w* against thee ... Mk 15:4
And all bare him *w*, and wondered at ... Lk 4:22
Truly ye bear *w* that ye allow the ... Lk 11:48
Do not steal, Do not bear false *w* ... Lk 18:20
said, What need we any further *w* ... Lk 22:71
The same came for a *w* ... Jn 1:7
to bear *w* of the Light, that all ... Jn 1:7
was sent to bear *w* of that Light ... Jn 1:8
John bare *w* of him, and cried, ... Jn 1:15
and ye receive not our *w* ... Jn 3:11
Jordan, to whom thou barest *w* ... Jn 3:26
Ye yourselves bear me *w*, that I ... Jn 3:28
If I bear *w* of myself ... Jn 5:31
of myself, my *w* is not true ... Jn 5:31
is another that beareth *w* of me ... Jn 5:32
I know that the *w* which he ... Jn 5:32
John, and he bare *w* unto the truth ... Jn 5:33
have greater *w* than that of John ... Jn 5:36
bear *w* of me, that the Father ... Jn 5:36
hath sent me, hath borne *w* of me ... Jn 5:37
I am one that bear *w* of myself ... Jn 8:18
that sent me beareth *w* of me ... Jn 8:18
Father's name, they bear *w* of me ... Jn 10:25
And ye also shall bear *w*, because ... Jn 15:27
spoken evil, bear *w* of the evil ... Jn 18:23
I should bear *w* unto the truth ... Jn 18:37
a *w* with us of his resurrection ... Acts 1:22
great power gave the apostles *w* ... Acts 4:33
tabernacle of *w* in the wilderness ... Acts 7:44
To him give all the prophets *w* ... Acts 10:43
he left not himself without *w* ... Acts 14:17
knoweth the hearts, bare them *w* ... Acts 15:8
the high priest doth bear me *w* ... Acts 22:5
For thou shalt be his *w* unto all ... Acts 22:15
so must thou bear *w* also at Rome ... Acts 23:11
a *w* both of these things which ... Acts 26:16
For God is my *w*, whom I serve ... Rom 1:9
their conscience also bearing *w* ... Rom 2:15
itself beareth *w* with our spirit ... Rom 8:16
bearing me *w* in the Holy Ghost ... Rom 9:1
Thou shalt not bear false *w* ... Rom 13:9
God is *w* ... 1Th 2:5
This *w* is true ... Titus 1:13
God also bearing them *w*, both ... Heb 2:4
the Holy Ghost also is a *w* to us ... Heb 10:15
by which he obtained *w* that he ... Heb 11:4
of them shall be a *w* against you ... Jas 5:3
a *w* of the sufferings of Christ, ... 1Pet 5:1
and we have seen it, and bear *w* ... 1Jn 1:2
it is the Spirit that beareth *w* ... 1Jn 5:6
are three that bear *w* in earth ... 1Jn 5:8
If we receive the *w* of men ... 1Jn 5:9
the *w* of God is greater ... 1Jn 5:9
for this is the *w* of God which he ... 1Jn 5:9
Son of God hath the *w* in himself ... 1Jn 5:10
Which have borne *w* of thy charity ... 3Jn 6
Christ, who is the faithful *w* ... Rev 1:5
the Amen, the faithful and true *w* ... Rev 3:14
were beheaded for the *w* of Jesus ... Rev 20:4

**WITNESSED**

the men of Belial *w* against him ... 1Kin 21:13
being *w* by the law and the ... Rom 3:21
Pilate *w* a good confession ... 1Ti 6:13
of whom it is *w* that he liveth ... Heb 7:8

**WITNESSES**

be put to death by the mouth of *w* ... Num 35:30
of two *w*, or three *w* ... Deut 17:6
The hands of the *w* shall be first ... Deut 17:7
at the mouth of two *w* ... Deut 19:15
or at the mouth of three *w* ... Deut 19:15
Ye are *w* against yourselves that ... Josh 24:22
And they said, We are *w* ... Josh 24:22
Ye are *w* this day, that I have ... Ruth 4:9
ye are *w* this day ... Ruth 4:10
and the elders, said, We are *w* ... Ruth 4:11
Thou renewest thy *w* against me ... Job 10:17
for false *w* are risen up against ... Ps 27:12
False *w* did rise up ... Ps 35:11
took unto me faithful *w* to record ... Is 8:2
let them bring forth their *w* ... Is 43:9
Ye are my *w*, saith the LORD, and ... Is 43:10
therefore ye are my *w*, saith the ... Is 43:12
ye are even my *w* ... Is 44:8
and they are their own *w* ... Is 44:9
evidence, and sealed it, and took *w* ... Jer 32:10
in the presence of the *w* that ... Jer 32:12
the field for money, and take *w* ... Jer 32:25
take *w* in the land of Benjamin, ... Jer 32:44
in the mouth of two or three *w* ... Mt 18:16
Wherefore ye be *w* unto yourselves ... Mt 23:31
yea, though many false *w* came ... Mt 26:60
At the last came two false *w* ... Mt 26:60
what further need have we of *w* ... Mt 26:65
saith, What need we any further *w* ... Mk 14:63
And ye are *w* of these things ... Lk 24:48
ye shall be *w* unto me both in ... Acts 1:8
raised up, whereof we all are *w* ... Acts 2:32
whereof we are *w* ... Acts 3:15
we are his *w* of these things ... Acts 5:32
And set up false *w*, which said, ... Acts 6:13
the *w* laid down their clothes at ... Acts 7:58
we are *w* of all things which he ... Acts 10:39
but unto *w* chosen before of God, ... Acts 10:41
who are his *w* unto the people ... Acts 13:31
and we are found false *w* of God ... 1Cor 15:15
In the mouth of two or three *w* ... 2Cor 13:1
Ye are *w*, and God also, how holily ... 1Th 2:10
but before two or three *w* ... 1Ti 5:19
a good profession before many *w* ... 1Ti 6:12
hast heard of me among many *w* ... 2Ti 2:2
mercy under two or three *w* ... Heb 10:28
about with so great a cloud of *w* ... Heb 12:1
I will give power unto my two *w* ... Rev 11:3

**WITNESSETH**

witness which he *w* of me is true ... Jn 5:32
the Holy Ghost *w* in every city ... Acts 20:23

**WITNESSING**

*w* both to small and great, saying ... Acts 26:22

**WIT'S**

man, and are at their *w* end ... Ps 107:27

**WITTINGLY**

head, guiding his hands *w* ... Gen 48:14

**WITTY**

out knowledge of *w* inventions ... Prov 8:12

**WIVES**

And Lamech took unto him two *w* ... Gen 4:19
And Lamech said unto his *w* ... Gen 4:23
ye *w* of Lamech, hearken unto my ... Gen 4:23
they took them *w* of all which ... Gen 6:2
wife, and thy sons' *w* with thee ... Gen 6:18
his wife, and his sons' *w* with him ... Gen 7:7
the three *w* of his sons with them ... Gen 7:13
sons, and thy sons' *w* with thee ... Gen 8:16
his wife, and his sons' *w* with him ... Gen 8:18
And Abram and Nahor took them *w* ... Gen 11:29
took unto the *w* which he had ... Gen 28:9
Give me my *w* and my children, for ... Gen 30:26
set his sons and his *w* upon camels ... Gen 31:17
take other *w* beside my daughters ... Gen 31:50
up that night, and took his two *w* ... Gen 32:22
take their daughters to us for *w* ... Gen 34:21
their *w* took they captive, and ... Gen 34:29
Esau took his *w* of the daughters ... Gen 36:2
And Esau took his *w*, and his sons, ... Gen 36:6
sons of Zilpah, his father's *w* ... Gen 37:2
your little ones, and for your *w* ... Gen 45:19
and their little ones, and their *w* ... Gen 46:5
loins, besides Jacob's sons' *w* ... Gen 46:26
come not at your *w* ... Ex 19:15
your *w* shall be widows, and your ... Ex 22:24
which are in the ears of your *w* ... Ex 32:2
to fall by the sword, that our *w* ... Num 14:3
door of their tents, and their *w* ... Num 16:27
Our little ones, our *w*, our ... Num 32:26
But your *w*, and your little ones, ... Deut 3:19
shall he multiply *w* to himself ... Deut 17:17
If a man have two *w*, one beloved, ... Deut 21:15
Your little ones, your *w*, and thy ... Deut 29:11
Your *w*, your little ones, and your ... Josh 1:14
their daughters to be their *w* ... Judg 3:6
for he had many *w* ... Judg 8:30
How shall we do for *w* for them ... Judg 21:7
give them of our daughters to *w* ... Judg 21:7
they gave them *w* which they had ... Judg 21:14
How shall we do for *w* for them ... Judg 21:16
not give them *w* of our daughters ... Judg 21:18
Benjamin did so, and took them *w* ... Judg 21:23
they took them *w* of the women of ... Ruth 1:4
And he had two *w* ... 1Sa 1:2
they were also both of them his *w* ... 1Sa 25:43
even David with his two *w* ... 1Sa 27:3
and their *w*, and their sons, and ... 1Sa 30:3
David's two *w* were taken captives ... 1Sa 30:5
and David rescued his two *w* ... 1Sa 30:18
up thither, and his two *w* also ... 2Sa 2:2
*w* out of Jerusalem, after he was ... 2Sa 5:13
thy master's *w* into thy bosom, and ... 2Sa 12:8
I will take thy *w* before thine ... 2Sa 12:11
he shall lie with thy *w* in the ... 2Sa 12:11
daughters, and the lives of thy *w* ... 2Sa 19:5
And he had seven hundred *w* ... 1Kin 11:3
his *w* turned away his heart ... 1Kin 11:3
that his *w* turned away his heart ... 1Kin 11:4
did he for all his strange *w* ... 1Kin 11:8
thy *w* also and thy children, even ... 1Kin 20:3
thy silver, and thy gold, and thy *w* ... 1Kin 20:5
for he sent unto me for my *w* ... 1Kin 20:7
the *w* of the sons of the prophets ... 2Kin 4:1
king's mother, and the king's *w* ... 2Kin 24:15
the father of Tekoa had two *w* ... 1Chr 4:5
for they had many *w* and sons ... 1Chr 7:4
Hushim and Baara were his *w* ... 1Chr 8:8
And David took more *w* at Jerusalem ... 1Chr 14:3
of Absalom above all his *w* ... 2Chr 11:21
(for he took eighteen *w*, and ... 2Chr 11:21
And he desired many *w* ... 2Chr 11:23
mighty, and married fourteen *w* ... 2Chr 13:21
with their little ones, their *w* ... 2Chr 20:13
people, and thy children, and thy *w* ... 2Chr 21:14
house, and his sons also, and his *w* ... 2Chr 21:17
And Jehoiada took for him two *w* ... 2Chr 24:3
our *w* are in captivity for this ... 2Chr 29:9
of all their little ones, their *w* ... 2Chr 31:18
have taken strange *w* of the ... Ezr 10:2
our God to put away all the *w* ... Ezr 10:3
and have taken strange *w*, to ... Ezr 10:10
the land, and from the strange *w* ... Ezr 10:11
them which have taken strange *w* ... Ezr 10:14
*w* by the first day of the first ... Ezr 10:17
found that had taken strange *w* ... Ezr 10:18
that they would put away their *w* ... Ezr 10:19
All these had taken strange *w* ... Ezr 10:44
some of them had *w* by whom they ... Ezr 10:44
sons, and your daughters, your *w* ... Neh 4:14
of their *w* against their brethren ... Neh 5:1
unto the law of God, their *w* ... Neh 10:28
the *w* also and the children ... Neh 12:43
Jews that had married *w* of Ashdod ... Neh 13:23
our God in marrying strange *w* ... Neh 13:27
all the *w* shall give to their ... Est 1:20
be spoiled, and their *w* ravished ... Is 13:16
with their fields and *w* together ... Jer 6:12
will I give their *w* unto others ... Jer 8:10
none to bury them, them, their *w* ... Jer 14:16
let their *w* be bereaved of their ... Jer 18:21
Take ye *w*, and beget sons and ... Jer 29:6
take *w* for your sons, and give ... Jer 29:6
adultery with their neighbours' *w* ... Jer 29:23
no wine all our days, we, our *w* ... Jer 35:8
So they shall bring out all thy *w* ... Jer 38:23
and the wickedness of their *w* ... Jer 44:9
and the wickedness of your *w* ... Jer 44:9
*w* had burned incense unto other ... Jer 44:15
your *w* have both spoken with your ... Jer 44:25
they take for their *w* a widow ... Eze 44:22
the king, and his princes, his *w* ... Dan 5:2
the king, and his princes, his *w* ... Dan 5:3
and thou, and thy lords, thy *w* ... Dan 5:23
them, their children, and their *w* ... Dan 6:24
of David apart, and their *w* apart ... Zec 12:12
of Nathan apart, and their *w* apart ... Zec 12:12
of Levi apart, and their *w* apart ... Zec 12:13
of Shimei apart, and their *w* apart ... Zec 12:13
family apart, and their *w* apart ... Zec 12:14
suffered you to put away your *w* ... Mt 19:8
eat, they drank, they married *w* ... Lk 17:27
all brought us on our way, with *w* ... Acts 21:5
that both they that have *w* be as ... 1Cor 7:29
*W*, submit yourselves unto your ... Eph 5:22
so let the *w* be to their own ... Eph 5:24
Husbands, love your *w*, even as ... Eph 5:25
love their *w* as their own bodies ... Eph 5:28
*W*, submit yourselves unto your ... Col 3:18
Husbands, love your *w*, and be not ... Col 3:19
Even so must their *w* be grave ... 1Ti 3:11
Likewise, ye *w*, be in subjection ... 1Pet 3:1
won by the conversation of the *w* ... 1Pet 3:1

**WIVES'**
old *w* fables, and exercise thyself ..... 1Ti 4:7

**WIZARD**
a familiar spirit, or that is a *w* ..... Lev 20:27
with familiar spirits, or a *w* ..... Deut 18:11

**WIZARDS**
spirits, neither seek after *w* ..... Lev 19:31
have familiar spirits, and after *w* ..... Lev 20:6
had familiar spirits, and the *w* ..... 1Sa 28:3
have familiar spirits, and the *w* ..... 1Sa 28:9
dealt with familiar spirits and *w* ..... 2Kin 21:6
with familiar spirits, and the *w* ..... 2Kin 23:24
with a familiar spirit, and with *w* ..... 2Chr 33:6
unto *w* that peep, and that mutter ..... Is 8:19
familiar spirits, and to the *w* ..... Is 19:3

**WOE**
*W* to thee, Moab ..... Num 21:29
And they said, *W* unto us ..... 1Sa 4:7
*W* unto us ..... 1Sa 4:8
If I be wicked, *w* unto me ..... Job 10:15
*W* is me, that I sojourn in Mesech ..... Ps 120:5
Who hath *w* ..... Prov 23:29
but *w* to him that is alone when ..... Eccl 4:10
*W* to thee, O land, when thy king ..... Eccl 10:16
*W* unto their soul ..... Is 3:9
*W* unto the wicked ..... Is 3:11
*W* unto them that join house to ..... Is 5:8
*W* unto them that rise up early in ..... Is 5:11
*W* unto them that draw iniquity ..... Is 5:18
*W* unto them that call evil good, ..... Is 5:20
*W* unto them that are wise in ..... Is 5:21
*W* unto them that are mighty to ..... Is 5:22
Then said I, *W* is me ..... Is 6:5
*W* unto them that decree ..... Is 10:1
*W* to the multitude of many people ..... Is 17:12
*W* to the land shadowing with ..... Is 18:1
leanness, my leanness, *w* unto me ..... Is 24:16
*W* to the crown of pride, to the ..... Is 28:1
*W* to Ariel, to Ariel, the city ..... Is 29:1
*W* unto them that seek deep to ..... Is 29:15
*W* to the rebellious children, ..... Is 30:1
*W* to them that go down to Egypt ..... Is 31:1
*W* to thee that spoilest, and thou ..... Is 33:1
*W* unto him that striveth with his ..... Is 45:9
*W* unto him that saith unto his ..... Is 45:10
*W* unto us ..... Jer 4:13
her hands, saying, *W* is me now ..... Jer 4:31
*W* unto us ..... Jer 6:4
*W* is me for my hurt ..... Jer 10:19
*W* unto thee, O Jerusalem ..... Jer 13:27
*W* is me, my mother, that thou ..... Jer 15:10
*W* unto him that buildeth his ..... Jer 22:13
*W* be unto the pastors that ..... Jer 23:1
Thou didst say, *W* is me now ..... Jer 45:3
*W* unto Nebo ..... Jer 48:1
*W* be unto thee, O Moab ..... Jer 48:46
*w* unto them ..... Jer 50:27
*w* unto us, that we have sinned ..... Lam 5:16
lamentations, and mourning, and *w* ..... Eze 2:10
*W* unto the foolish prophets, that ..... Eze 13:3
*W* to the women that sew pillows ..... Eze 13:18
*w*, *w* unto thee ..... Eze 16:23
*W* to the bloody city, to the pot ..... Eze 24:6
*W* to the bloody city ..... Eze 24:9
Howl ye, *W* worth the day ..... Eze 30:2
*W* be to the shepherds of Israel ..... Eze 34:2
*W* unto them ..... Hos 7:13
*w* also to them when I depart from ..... Hos 9:12
*W* unto you that desire the day of ..... Amos 5:18
*W* to them that are at ease in ..... Amos 6:1
*W* to them that devise iniquity, ..... Mic 2:1
*W* is me ..... Mic 7:1
*W* to the bloody city ..... Nah 3:1
*W* to him that increaseth that ..... Hab 2:6
*W* to him that coveteth an evil ..... Hab 2:9
*W* to him that buildeth a town ..... Hab 2:12
*W* unto him that giveth his ..... Hab 2:15
*W* unto him that saith to the wood ..... Hab 2:19
*W* unto the inhabitants of the sea ..... Zeph 2:5
*W* to her that is filthy and ..... Zeph 3:1
*W* to the idol shepherd that ..... Zec 11:17
*W* unto thee, Chorazin ..... Mt 11:21
*w* unto thee, Bethsaida ..... Mt 11:21
*W* unto the world because of ..... Mt 18:7
but *w* to that man by whom the ..... Mt 18:7
But *w* unto you, scribes and ..... Mt 23:13
*W* unto you, scribes and Pharisees, ..... Mt 23:14
*W* unto you, scribes and Pharisees, ..... Mt 23:15
*W* unto you, ye blind guides, ..... Mt 23:16
*W* unto you, scribes and Pharisees, ..... Mt 23:23
*W* unto you, scribes and Pharisees, ..... Mt 23:25
*W* unto you, scribes and Pharisees, ..... Mt 23:27
*W* unto you, scribes and Pharisees, ..... Mt 23:29
*w* unto them that are with child, ..... Mt 24:19
but *w* unto that man by whom the ..... Mt 26:24
But *w* to them that are with child ..... Mk 13:17
but *w* to that man by whom the Son .. Mk 14:21
But *w* unto you that are rich ..... Lk 6:24
*W* unto you that are full ..... Lk 6:25
*W* unto you that laugh now ..... Lk 6:25
*W* unto you, when all men shall ..... Lk 6:26
*W* unto thee, Chorazin ..... Lk 10:13
*w* unto thee, Bethsaida ..... Lk 10:13
But *w* unto you, Pharisees ..... Lk 11:42
*W* unto you, Pharisees ..... Lk 11:43
*W* unto you, scribes and Pharisees, ..... Lk 11:44
*W* unto you also, ye lawyers ..... Lk 11:46
*W* unto you for ye build the ..... Lk 11:47
*W* unto you, lawyers ..... Lk 11:52
but *w* unto him, through whom they ..... Lk 17:1
But *w* unto them that are with ..... Lk 21:23
but *w* unto that man by whom he is ..... Lk 22:22
*w* is unto me, if I preach not the ..... 1Cor 9:16
*W* unto them ..... Jude 11
saying with a loud voice, *W*, *w* ..... Rev 8:13
with a loud voice, *W*, *w*, *w* ..... Rev 8:13
One *w* is past ..... Rev 9:12
The second *w* is past ..... Rev 11:14
the third *w* cometh quickly ..... Rev 11:14
*W* to the inhabiters of the earth ..... Rev 12:12

**WOEFUL**
neither have I desired the *w* day ..... Jer 17:16

**WOES**
there come two *w* more hereafter ..... Rev 9:12

**WOLF**
Benjamin shall ravin as a *w* ..... Gen 49:27
The *w* also shall dwell with the ..... Is 11:6
The *w* and the lamb shall feed ..... Is 65:25
a *w* of the evenings shall spoil ..... Jer 5:6
sheep are not, seeth the *w* coming ..... Jn 10:12
and the *w* catcheth them, and ..... Jn 10:12

**WOLVES**
are like *w* ravening the prey ..... Eze 22:27
more fierce than the evening *w* ..... Hab 1:8
her judges are evening *w* ..... Zeph 3:3
but inwardly they are ravening *w* ..... Mt 7:15
forth as sheep in the midst of *w* ..... Mt 10:16
I send you forth as lambs among *w* ..... Lk 10:3
grievous *w* enter in among you ..... Acts 20:29

**WOMAN**
had taken from man, made he a *w* ..... Gen 2:22
she shall be called *W*, because ..... Gen 2:23
And he said unto the *w*, Yea, hath ..... Gen 3:1
the *w* said unto the serpent, We ..... Gen 3:2
And the serpent said unto the *w* ..... Gen 3:4
when the *w* saw that the tree was ..... Gen 3:6
The *w* whom thou gavest to be with ... Gen 3:12
And the LORD God said unto the *w* ..... Gen 3:13
the *w* said, The serpent beguiled ..... Gen 3:13
put enmity between thee and the *w* ..... Gen 3:15
Unto the *w* he said, I will ..... Gen 3:16
thou art a fair *w* to look upon ..... Gen 12:11
the *w* that she was very fair ..... Gen 12:14
the *w* was taken into Pharaoh's ..... Gen 12:15
for the *w* which thou hast taken ..... Gen 20:3
Peradventure the *w* will not be ..... Gen 24:5
if the *w* will not be willing to ..... Gen 24:8
Peradventure the *w* will not ..... Gen 24:39
let the same be the *w* whom the ..... Gen 24:44
Shaul the son of a Canaanitish *w* ..... Gen 46:10
the *w* conceived, and bare a son ..... Ex 2:2
the *w* took the child, and nursed ..... Ex 2:9
But every *w* shall borrow of her ..... Ex 3:22
Shaul the son of a Canaanitish *w* ..... Ex 6:15
every *w* of her neighbour, jewels ..... Ex 11:2
hurt a *w* with child, so that her ..... Ex 21:22
If an ox gore a man or a *w* ..... Ex 21:28
that he hath killed a man or a *w* ..... Ex 21:29
unto the LORD, every man and *w* ..... Ex 35:29
Let neither man nor *w* make any ..... Ex 36:6
If a *w* have conceived seed, and ..... Lev 12:2
If a man or *w* have a plague upon ..... Lev 13:29
If a man also or a *w* have in the ..... Lev 13:38
The *w* also with whom man shall ..... Lev 15:18
if a *w* have an issue, and her ..... Lev 15:19
if a *w* have an issue of her blood ..... Lev 15:25
an issue, of the man, and of the *w* ..... Lev 15:33
not uncover the nakedness of a *w* ..... Lev 18:17
unto a *w* to uncover her nakedness ..... Lev 18:19
neither shall any *w* stand before ..... Lev 18:23
whosoever lieth carnally with a *w* ..... Lev 19:20
mankind, as he lieth with a *w* ..... Lev 20:13
if a *w* approach unto any beast, ..... Lev 20:16
thereto, thou shalt kill the *w* ..... Lev 20:16
lie with a *w* having her sickness ..... Lev 20:18
A man also or *w* that hath a ..... Lev 20:27
a *w* put away from her husband ..... Lev 21:7
A widow, or a divorced *w*, or ..... Lev 21:14
And the son of an Israelitish *w* ..... Lev 24:10
and this son of the Israelitish *w* ..... Lev 24:10
When a man or *w* shall commit any ..... Num 5:6
shall set the *w* before the LORD ..... Num 5:18
her by an oath, and say unto the *w* ..... Num 5:19
the *w* with an oath of cursing ..... Num 5:21
the priest shall say unto the *w* ..... Num 5:21
the *w* shall say, Amen, amen ..... Num 5:22
he shall cause the *w* to drink the ..... Num 5:24
cause the *w* to drink the water ..... Num 5:26
the *w* shall be a curse among her ..... Num 5:27
if the *w* be not defiled, but be ..... Num 5:28
shall set the *w* before the LORD, ..... Num 5:30
this *w* shall bear her iniquity ..... Num 5:31
When either man or *w* shall ..... Num 6:2
Ethiopian *w* whom he had married ..... Num 12:1
for he had married an Ethiopian *w* ..... Num 12:1
*w* in the sight of Moses, and in ..... Num 25:6
and the *w* through her belly ..... Num 25:8
was slain with the Midianitish *w* ..... Num 25:14
*w* that was slain was Cozbi ..... Num 25:15
If a *w* also vow a vow unto the ..... Num 30:3
kill every *w* that hath known man ..... Num 31:17
an Hebrew man, or an Hebrew *w* ..... Deut 15:12
thy God giveth thee, man or *w* ..... Deut 17:2
bring forth that man or that *w* ..... Deut 17:5
gates, even that man or that *w* ..... Deut 17:5
among the captives a beautiful *w* ..... Deut 21:11
The *w* shall not wear that which ..... Deut 22:5
upon her, and say, I took this *w* ..... Deut 22:14
with a *w* married to an husband ..... Deut 22:22
that lay with the *w*, and the *w* ..... Deut 22:22
delicate *w* among you, which would. Deut 28:56
should be among you man, or *w* ..... Deut 29:18
the *w* took the two men, and hid ..... Josh 2:4
was in the city, both man and *w* ..... Josh 6:21
house, and bring out thence the *w* ..... Josh 6:22
sell Sisera into the hand of a *w* ..... Judg 4:9
a certain *w* cast a piece of a ..... Judg 9:53
men say not of me, A *w* slew him ..... Judg 9:54
thou art the son of a strange *w* ..... Judg 11:2
of the LORD appeared unto the *w* ..... Judg 13:3
Then the *w* came and told her ..... Judg 13:6
the *w* as she sat in the field ..... Judg 13:9
the *w* made haste, and ran, and ..... Judg 13:10
the man that spakest unto the *w* ..... Judg 13:11
I said unto the *w* let her beware ..... Judg 13:13
the *w* bare a son, and called his ..... Judg 13:24
saw a *w* in Timnath of the ..... Judg 14:1
I have seen a *w* in Timnath of the ..... Judg 14:2
Is there never a *w* among the ..... Judg 14:3
went down, and talked with the *w* ..... Judg 14:7
his father went down unto the *w* ..... Judg 14:10
that he loved a *w* in the valley ..... Judg 16:4
Then came the *w* in the dawning of . Judg 19:26
the *w* his concubine was fallen ..... Judg 19:27
husband of the *w* that was slain ..... Judg 20:4
every *w* that hath lain by man ..... Judg 21:11
the *w* was left of her two sons and ..... Ruth 1:5
and, behold, a *w* lay at his feet ..... Ruth 3:8
know that thou art a virtuous *w* ..... Ruth 3:11
that a *w* came into the floor ..... Ruth 3:14
The LORD make the *w* that is come ..... Ruth 4:11
shall give thee of this young *w* ..... Ruth 4:12
I am a *w* of a sorrowful spirit ..... 1Sa 1:15
So the *w* went her way, and did eat ..... 1Sa 1:18
So the *w* abode, and gave her son ..... 1Sa 1:23
I am the *w* that stood by thee ..... 1Sa 1:26
*w* for the loan which is lent to ..... 1Sa 2:20
but slay both man and *w*, infant and ..... 1Sa 15:3
son of the perverse rebellious *w* ..... 1Sa 20:30
she was a *w* of good understanding ..... 1Sa 25:3
and left neither man nor *w* alive ..... 1Sa 27:9
saved neither man nor *w* alive ..... 1Sa 27:11
Seek me a *w* that hath a familiar ..... 1Sa 28:7
there is a *w* that hath a familiar ..... 1Sa 28:7
and they came to the *w* by night ..... 1Sa 28:8
the *w* said unto him, Behold, thou ..... 1Sa 28:9
Then said the *w*, Whom shall I ..... 1Sa 28:11
when the *w* saw Samuel, she cried ..... 1Sa 28:12
the *w* spake to Saul, saying, Why ..... 1Sa 28:12
the *w* said unto Saul, I saw gods ..... 1Sa 28:13
the *w* came unto Saul, and saw that ..... 1Sa 28:21
his servants, together with the *w* ..... 1Sa 28:23
the *w* had a fat calf in the house ..... 1Sa 28:24
with a fault concerning this *w* ..... 2Sa 3:8
roof he saw a *w* washing herself ..... 2Sa 11:2
the *w* was very beautiful to look ..... 2Sa 11:2
sent and enquired after the *w* ..... 2Sa 11:3
the *w* conceived, and sent and told ..... 2Sa 11:5
did not a *w* cast a piece of a ..... 2Sa 11:21
said, Put now this *w* out from me ..... 2Sa 13:17
and fetched thence a wise *w* ..... 2Sa 14:2
but be as a *w* that had a long ..... 2Sa 14:2
when the *w* of Tekoah spake to the ..... 2Sa 14:4
answered, I am indeed a widow *w* ..... 2Sa 14:5
And the king said unto the *w* ..... 2Sa 14:8
the *w* of Tekoah said unto the ..... 2Sa 14:9
Then the *w* said, Let thine ..... 2Sa 14:12
the *w* said, Wherefore then hast ..... 2Sa 14:13
king answered and said unto the *w* ..... 2Sa 14:18
the *w* said, Let my lord the king ..... 2Sa 14:18
the *w* answered and said, As thy ..... 2Sa 14:19
she was a *w* of a fair countenance ..... 2Sa 14:27
the *w* took and spread a covering ..... 2Sa 17:19
came to the *w* to the house ..... 2Sa 17:20
the *w* said unto them, They be ..... 2Sa 17:20
cried a wise *w* out of the city ..... 2Sa 20:16
the *w* said, Art thou Joab ..... 2Sa 20:17
the *w* said unto Joab, Behold, his ..... 2Sa 20:21
Then the *w* went unto all the ..... 2Sa 20:22
And the one *w* said, O my lord, I ..... 1Kin 3:17
this *w* dwell in one house ..... 1Kin 3:17
that this *w* was delivered also ..... 1Kin 3:18
And the other *w* said, Nay ..... 1Kin 3:22
Then spake the *w* whose the living ..... 1Kin 3:26
name was Zeruah, a widow *w* ..... 1Kin 11:26
feign herself to be another *w* ..... 1Kin 14:5
a widow *w* there to sustain thee ..... 1Kin 17:9
the widow *w* was there gathering ..... 1Kin 17:10
things, that the son of the *w* ..... 1Kin 17:17
the *w* said to Elijah, Now by this ..... 1Kin 17:24
Now there cried a certain *w* of ..... 2Kin 4:1
to Shunem, where was a great *w* ..... 2Kin 4:8
the *w* conceived, and bare a son at ..... 2Kin 4:17
wall, there cried a *w* unto him ..... 2Kin 6:26
This *w* said unto me, Give thy son ..... 2Kin 6:28
the king heard the words of the *w* ..... 2Kin 6:30
Then spake Elisha unto the *w* ..... 2Kin 8:1
the *w* arose, and did after the ..... 2Kin 8:2
that the *w* returned out of the ..... 2Kin 8:3
body to life, that, behold, the *w* ..... 2Kin 8:5
My lord, O king, this is the *w* ..... 2Kin 8:5
And when the king asked the *w* ..... 2Kin 8:6
said, Go, see now this cursed *w* ..... 2Kin 9:34
one of Israel, both man and *w* ..... 1Chr 16:3
The son of a *w* of the daughters ..... 2Chr 2:14
small or great, whether man or *w* ..... 2Chr 15:13
sons of Athaliah, that wicked *w* ..... 2Chr 24:7

that whosoever, whether man or *w* ... Est 4:11
is born of a *w* is of few days ... Job 14:1
and he which is born of a *w* ... Job 15:14
he be clean that is born of a *w* ... Job 25:4
heart have been deceived by a *w* ... Job 31:9
and pain, as of a *w* in travail ... Ps 48:6
like the untimely birth of a *w* ... Ps 58:8
maketh the barren *w* to keep house ... Ps 113:9
deliver thee from the strange *w* ... Prov 2:16
a strange *w* drop as an honeycomb ... Prov 5:3
son, be ravished with a strange *w* ... Prov 5:20
To keep thee from the evil *w* ... Prov 6:24
of the tongue of a strange *w* ... Prov 6:24
For by means of a whorish *w* a man ... Prov 6:26
with a *w* lacketh understanding ... Prov 6:32
may keep thee from the strange *w* ... Prov 7:5
there met him a *w* with the attire ... Prov 7:10
A foolish *w* is clamorous ... Prov 9:13
A gracious *w* retaineth honour ... Prov 11:16
so is a fair *w* which is without ... Prov 11:22
A virtuous *w* is a crown to her ... Prov 12:4
Every wise *w* buildeth her house ... Prov 14:1
a pledge of him for a strange *w* ... Prov 20:16
housetop, than with a brawling *w* ... Prov 21:9
with a contentious and an angry *w* ... Prov 21:19
a strange *w* is a narrow pit ... Prov 23:27
housetop, than with a brawling *w* ... Prov 25:24
a pledge of him for a strange *w* ... Prov 27:13
day and a contentious *w* are alike ... Prov 27:15
is the way of an adulterous *w* ... Prov 30:20
For an odious *w* when she is ... Prov 30:23
Who can find a virtuous *w* ... Prov 31:10
but a *w* that feareth the LORD, ... Prov 31:30
find more bitter than death the *w* ... Eccl 7:26
but a *w* among all those have I ... Eccl 7:28
be in pain as a *w* that travaileth ... Is 13:8
the pangs of a *w* that travaileth ... Is 21:3
Like as a *w* with child, that ... Is 26:17
will I cry like a travailing *w* ... Is 42:14
or to the *w*, What hast thou ... Is 45:10
Can a *w* forget her sucking child, ... Is 49:15
hath called thee as a *w* forsaken ... Is 54:6
a voice as of a *w* in travail ... Jer 4:31
of Zion to a comely and delicate *w* ... Jer 6:2
us, and pain, as of a *w* in travail ... Jer 6:24
take thee, as a *w* in travail ... Jer 13:21
the pain as of a *w* in travail ... Jer 22:23
as a *w* in travail, and all faces ... Jer 30:6
the *w* with child and her that ... Jer 31:8
earth, A *w* shall compass a man ... Jer 31:22
to cut off from you man and *w* ... Jer 44:7
as the heart of a *w* in her pangs ... Jer 48:41
as the heart of a *w* in her pangs ... Jer 49:22
have taken her, as a *w* in travail ... Jer 49:24
and pangs as of a *w* in travail ... Jer 50:43
will I break in pieces man and *w* ... Jer 51:22
is as a menstruous *w* among them ... Lam 1:17
work of an imperious whorish *w* ... Eze 16:30
hath come near to a menstruous *w* ... Eze 18:6
as they go in unto a *w* that ... Eze 23:44
as the uncleanness of a removed *w* ... Eze 36:17
love a *w* beloved of her friend, ... Hos 3:1
travailing *w* shall come upon him ... Hos 13:13
have taken thee as a *w* in travail ... Mic 4:9
of Zion, like a *w* in travail ... Mic 4:10
this is a *w* that sitteth in the ... Zec 5:7
on a *w* to lust after her hath ... Mt 5:28
And, behold, a *w*, which was ... Mt 9:20
the *w* was made whole from that ... Mt 9:22
like unto leaven, which a *w* took ... Mt 13:33
a *w* of Canaan came out of the ... Mt 15:22
answered and said unto her, O *w* ... Mt 15:28
And last of all the *w* died also ... Mt 22:27
There came unto him a *w* having an ... Mt 26:7
unto them, Why trouble ye the *w* ... Mt 26:10
also this, that this *w* hath done ... Mt 26:13
And a certain *w*, which had an ... Mk 5:25
But the *w* fearing and trembling, ... Mk 5:33
For a certain *w*, whose young ... Mk 7:25
The *w* was a Greek, a ... Mk 7:26
if a *w* shall put away her husband ... Mk 10:12
last of all the *w* died also ... Mk 12:22
at meat, there came a *w* having an ... Mk 14:3
unto a *w* that was a widow ... Lk 4:26
a *w* in the city, which was a ... Lk 7:37
what manner of *w* this is that ... Lk 7:39
And he turned to the *w*, and said ... Lk 7:44
unto Simon, Seest thou this *w* ... Lk 7:44
but this *w* since the time I came ... Lk 7:45
but this *w* hath anointed my feet ... Lk 7:46
And he said to the *w*, Thy faith ... Lk 7:50
a *w* having an issue of blood ... Lk 8:43
when the *w* saw that she was not ... Lk 8:47
a certain *w* named Martha received ... Lk 10:38
a certain *w* of the company lifted ... Lk 11:27
there was a *w* which had a spirit ... Lk 13:11
her to him, and said unto her, *W* ... Lk 13:12
And ought not this *w*, being a ... Lk 13:16
It is like leaven, which a *w* took ... Lk 13:21
Either what *w* having ten pieces ... Lk 15:8
Last of all the *w* died also ... Lk 20:32
And he denied him, saying, *W* ... Lk 22:57
Jesus saith unto her, *W*, what ... Jn 2:4
There cometh a *w* of Samaria to ... Jn 4:7
Then saith the *w* of Samaria unto ... Jn 4:9
of me, which am a *w* of Samaria ... Jn 4:9
The *w* saith unto him, Sir, thou ... Jn 4:11
The *w* saith unto him, Sir, give ... Jn 4:15
The *w* answered and said, I have no ... Jn 4:17
The *w* saith unto him, Sir, I ... Jn 4:19
Jesus saith unto her, *W*, believe ... Jn 4:21
The *w* saith unto him, I know that ... Jn 4:25
that he talked with the *w* ... Jn 4:27
The *w* then left her waterpot, and ... Jn 4:28
on him for the saying of the *w* ... Jn 4:39
And said unto the *w*, Now we ... Jn 4:42
unto him a *w* taken in adultery ... Jn 8:3
this *w* was taken in adultery, in ... Jn 8:4
the *w* standing in the midst ... Jn 8:9
up himself, and saw none but the *w* ... Jn 8:10
he said unto her, *W* ... Jn 8:10
A *w* when she is in travail hath ... Jn 16:21
he saith unto his mother, *W* ... Jn 19:26
And they say unto her, *W*, why ... Jn 20:13
Jesus saith unto her, *W*, why ... Jn 20:15
this *w* was full of good works and ... Acts 9:36
Timotheus, the son of a certain *w* ... Acts 16:1
a certain *w* named Lydia, a seller ... Acts 16:14
a *w* named Damaris, and others with ... Acts 17:34
leaving the natural use of the *w* ... Rom 1:27
For the *w* which hath an husband ... Rom 7:2
good for a man not to touch a *w* ... 1Cor 7:1
let every *w* have her own husband ... 1Cor 7:2
the *w* which hath an husband that ... 1Cor 7:13
The unmarried *w* careth for the ... 1Cor 7:34
and the head of the *w* is the man ... 1Cor 11:3
But every *w* that prayeth or ... 1Cor 11:5
For if the *w* be not covered, let ... 1Cor 11:6
for a *w* to be shorn or shaven ... 1Cor 11:6
but the *w* is the glory of the man ... 1Cor 11:7
For the man is not of the *w* ... 1Cor 11:8
but the *w* of the man ... 1Cor 11:8
was the man created for the *w* ... 1Cor 11:9
but the *w* for the man ... 1Cor 11:9
For this cause ought the *w* to ... 1Cor 11:10
neither is the man without the *w* ... 1Cor 11:11
neither the *w* without the man, in ... 1Cor 11:11
For as the *w* is of the man ... 1Cor 11:12
even so is the man also by the *w* ... 1Cor 11:12
is it comely that a *w* pray unto ... 1Cor 11:13
But if a *w* have long hair, it is ... 1Cor 11:15
sent forth his Son, made of a *w* ... Gal 4:4
heir with the son of the free *w* ... Gal 4:30
as travail upon a *w* with child ... 1Th 5:3
Let the *w* learn in silence with ... 1Ti 2:11
But I suffer not a *w* to teach ... 1Ti 2:12
but the *w* being deceived was in ... 1Ti 2:14
If any man or *w* that believeth ... 1Ti 5:16
thou sufferest that *w* Jezebel ... Rev 2:20
a *w* clothed with the sun, and the ... Rev 12:1
the dragon stood before the *w* ... Rev 12:4
the *w* fled into the wilderness, ... Rev 12:6
he persecuted the *w* which brought ... Rev 12:13
to the *w* were given two wings of ... Rev 12:14
water as a flood after the *w* ... Rev 12:15
And the earth helped the *w* ... Rev 12:16
the dragon was wroth with the *w* ... Rev 12:17
I saw a *w* sit upon a scarlet ... Rev 17:3
the *w* was arrayed in purple and ... Rev 17:4
I saw the *w* drunken with the ... Rev 17:6
tell thee the mystery of the *w* ... Rev 17:7
mountains, on which the *w* sitteth ... Rev 17:9
the *w* which thou sawest is that ... Rev 17:18

**WOMANKIND**

not lie with mankind, as with *w* ... Lev 18:22

**WOMAN'S**

his pledge from the *w* hand ... Gen 38:20
according as the *w* husband will ... Ex 21:22
the Israelitish *w* son blasphemed ... Lev 24:11
the LORD, and uncover the *w* head ... Num 5:18
offering out of the *w* hand ... Num 5:25
shall a man put on a *w* garment ... Deut 22:5
this *w* child died in the night ... 1Kin 3:19

**WOMB**

her, Two nations are in thy *w* ... Gen 25:23
behold, there were twins in her *w* ... Gen 25:24
Leah was hated, he opened her *w* ... Gen 29:31
from thee the fruit of the *w* ... Gen 30:2
hearkened to her, and opened her *w* ... Gen 30:22
that, behold, twins were in her *w* ... Gen 38:27
of the breasts, and of the *w* ... Gen 49:25
whatsoever openeth the *w* among ... Ex 13:2
instead of such as open every *w* ... Num 8:16
he cometh out of his mother's *w* ... Num 12:12
also bless the fruit of thy *w* ... Deut 7:13
be a Nazarite unto God from the *w* ... Judg 13:5
the *w* to the day of his death ... Judg 13:7
unto God from my mother's *w* ... Judg 16:17
there yet any more sons in my *w* ... Ruth 1:11
but the LORD had shut up her *w* ... 1Sa 1:5
the LORD had shut up her *w* ... 1Sa 1:6
Naked came I out of my mother's *w* ... Job 1:21
not up the doors of my mother's *w* ... Job 3:10
Why died I not from the *w* ... Job 3:11
brought me forth out of the *w* ... Job 10:18
carried from the *w* to the grave ... Job 10:19
The *w* shall forget him ... Job 24:20
he that made me in the *w* make him ... Job 31:15
did not one fashion us in the *w* ... Job 31:15
guided her from my mother's *w* ... Job 31:18
as if it had issued out of the *w* ... Job 38:8
Out of whose *w* came the ice ... Job 38:29
art he that took me out of the *w* ... Ps 22:9
I was cast upon thee from the *w* ... Ps 22:10
wicked are estranged from the *w* ... Ps 58:3
have I been holden up from the *w* ... Ps 71:6
from the *w* of the morning ... Ps 110:3
the fruit of the *w* is his reward ... Ps 127:3
hast covered me in my mother's *w* ... Ps 139:13
and the barren *w* ... Prov 30:16
and what, the son of my *w* ... Prov 31:2
he came forth of his mother's *w* ... Eccl 5:15
the *w* of her that is with child ... Eccl 11:5
no pity on the fruit of the *w* ... Is 13:18
thee, and formed thee from the *w* ... Is 44:2
and he that formed thee from the *w* ... Is 44:24
which are carried from the *w* ... Is 46:3
called a transgressor from the *w* ... Is 48:8
LORD hath called me from the *w* ... Is 49:1
me from the *w* to be his servant ... Is 49:5
compassion on the son of her *w* ... Is 49:15
to bring forth, and shut the *w* ... Is 66:9
out of the *w* I sanctified thee ... Jer 1:5
Because he slew me not from the *w* ... Jer 20:17
her *w* to be always great with me ... Jer 20:17
forth out of the *w* to see labour ... Jer 20:18
the fire all that openeth the *w* ... Eze 20:26
from the birth, and from the *w* ... Hos 9:11
give them a miscarrying *w* ... Hos 9:14
even the beloved fruit of their *w* ... Hos 9:16
his brother by the heel in the *w* ... Hos 12:3
so born from their mother's *w* ... Mt 19:12
Ghost, even from his mother's *w* ... Lk 1:15
thou shalt conceive in thy *w* ... Lk 1:31
of Mary, the babe leaped in her *w* ... Lk 1:41
and blessed is the fruit of thy *w* ... Lk 1:42
the babe leaped in my *w* for joy ... Lk 1:44
before he was conceived in the *w* ... Lk 2:21
the *w* shall be called holy to the ... Lk 2:23
Blessed is the *w* that bare thee ... Lk 11:27
second time into his mother's *w* ... Jn 3:4
from his mother's *w* was carried ... Acts 3:2
a cripple from his mother's *w* ... Acts 14:8
yet the deadness of Sarah's *w* ... Rom 4:19
separated me from my mother's *w* ... Gal 1:15

**WOMBS**

the *w* of the house of Abimelech ... Gen 20:18
the *w* that never bare, and the ... Lk 23:29

**WOMEN**

the *w* also, and the people ... Gen 14:16
with Sarah after the manner of *w* ... Gen 18:11
even the time that *w* go out to ... Gen 24:11
for the custom of *w* is upon me ... Gen 31:35
lifted up his eyes, and saw the *w* ... Gen 33:5
of a midwife to the Hebrew *w* ... Ex 1:16
Because the Hebrew *w* are not as ... Ex 1:19
not as the Egyptian *w* ... Ex 1:19
to thee a nurse of the Hebrew *w* ... Ex 2:7
all the *w* went out after her with ... Ex 15:20
And they came, both men and *w* ... Ex 35:22
all the *w* that were wise hearted ... Ex 35:25
all the *w* whose heart stirred ... Ex 35:26
of the *w* assembling, which ... Ex 38:8
ten *w* shall bake your bread in ... Lev 26:26
took all the *w* of Midian captives ... Num 31:9
Have ye saved all the *w* alive ... Num 31:15
But all the *w* children, that have ... Num 31:18
of *w* that had not known man by ... Num 31:35
destroyed the men, and the *w* ... Deut 2:34
utterly destroying the men, *w* ... Deut 3:6
But the *w*, and the little ones, and ... Deut 20:14
the people together, men, and *w* ... Deut 31:12
fell that day, both of men and *w* ... Josh 8:25
of Israel, with the *w*, and the ... Josh 8:35
Blessed above *w* shall Jael the ... Judg 5:24
shall she be above *w* in the tent ... Judg 5:24
also, about a thousand men and *w* ... Judg 9:49
and thither fled all the men and *w* ... Judg 9:51
the house was full of men and *w* ... Judg 16:27
about three thousand men and *w* ... Judg 16:27
the edge of the sword, with the *w* ... Judg 21:10
alive of the *w* of Jabesh-gilead ... Judg 21:14
seeing the *w* are destroyed out of ... Judg 21:16
took them wives of the *w* of Moab ... Ruth 1:4
the *w* said unto Naomi, Blessed be ... Ruth 4:14
the *w* her neighbours gave it a ... Ruth 4:17
how they lay with the *w* that ... 1Sa 2:22
*w* that stood by her said unto her ... 1Sa 4:20
thy sword hath made *w* childless ... 1Sa 15:33
thy mother be childless among *w* ... 1Sa 15:33
that the *w* came out of all cities ... 1Sa 18:6
the *w* answered one another as ... 1Sa 18:7
kept themselves at least from *w* ... 1Sa 21:4
Of a truth *w* have been kept from ... 1Sa 21:5
edge of the sword, both men and *w* ... 1Sa 22:19
And had taken the *w* captives ... 1Sa 30:2
wonderful, passing the love of *w* ... 2Sa 1:26
Israel, as well to the *w* as men ... 2Sa 6:19
And the king left ten *w*, which ... 2Sa 15:16
voice of singing men and singing *w* ... 2Sa 19:35
took the ten *w* his concubines ... 2Sa 20:3
Then came there two *w*, that were ... 1Kin 3:16
king Solomon loved many strange *w* ... 1Kin 11:1
*w* of the Moabites, Ammonites, ... 1Kin 11:1
and rip up their *w* with child ... 2Kin 8:12
all the *w* therein that were with ... 2Kin 15:16
where the *w* wove hangings for the ... 2Kin 23:7
brethren two hundred thousand, *w* ... 2Chr 28:8
the singing *w* spake of Josiah in ... 2Chr 35:25
hundred singing men and singing *w* ... Ezr 2:65
great congregation of men and *w* ... Ezr 10:1
and five singing men and singing *w* ... Neh 7:67
the congregation both of men and *w* ... Neh 8:2
midday, before the men and the *w* ... Neh 8:3
him did outlandish *w* cause to sin ... Neh 13:26
the *w* in the royal house which ... Est 1:9
shall come abroad unto all *w* ... Est 1:17
the palace, to the house of the *w* ... Est 2:3

chamberlain, keeper of the *w* ... Est 2:3
custody of Hegai, keeper of the *w* ... Est 2:8
best place of the house of the *w* ... Est 2:9
according to the manner of the *w* ... Est 2:12
things for the purifying of the *w* ... Est 2:12
of the *w* unto the king's house ... Est 2:13
into the second house of the *w* ... Est 2:14
chamberlain, the keeper of the *w* ... Est 2:15
king loved Esther above all the *w* ... Est 2:17
and old, little children and *w* ... Est 3:13
them, both little ones and *w* ... Est 8:11
as one of the foolish *w* speaketh ... Job 2:10
in all the land were no *w* found ... Job 42:15
were among thy honourable *w* ... Ps 45:9
mouth of strange *w* is a deep pit ... Prov 22:14
Thine eyes shall behold strange *w* ... Prov 23:33
Give not thy strength unto *w* ... Prov 31:3
*w* singers, and the delights of the ... Eccl 2:8
know not, O thou fairest among *w* ... Song 1:8
beloved, O thou fairest among *w* ... Song 5:9
gone, O thou fairest among *w* ... Song 6:1
oppressors, and *w* rule over them ... Is 3:12
in that day seven *w* shall take ... Is 4:1
day shall Egypt be like unto *w* ... Is 19:16
the *w* come, and set them on fire ... Is 27:11
Rise up, ye *w* that are at ease ... Is 32:9
ye be troubled, ye careless *w* ... Is 32:10
Tremble, ye *w* that are at ease ... Is 32:11
the *w* knead their dough, to make ... Jer 7:18
ye, and call for the mourning *w* ... Jer 9:17
and send for cunning *w*, that they ... Jer 9:17
hear the word of the LORD, O ye *w* ... Jer 9:20
all the *w* that are left in the ... Jer 38:22
those *w* shall say, Thy friends ... Jer 38:22
had committed unto him men, and *w* ... Jer 40:7
even mighty men of war, and the *w* ... Jer 41:16
Even men, and *w*, and children, and ... Jer 43:6
all the *w* that stood by, a great ... Jer 44:15
people, to the men, and to the *w* ... Jer 44:20
all the people, and to all the *w* ... Jer 44:24
and they shall become as *w* ... Jer 50:37
they became as *w* ... Jer 51:30
Shall the *w* eat their fruit, and ... Lam 2:20
The hands of the pitiful *w* have ... Lam 4:10
They ravished the *w* in Zion ... Lam 5:11
there sat *w* weeping for Tammuz ... Eze 8:14
maids, and little children, and *w* ... Eze 9:6
Woe to the *w* that sew pillows to ... Eze 13:18
from other *w* in thy whoredoms ... Eze 16:34
as *w* that break wedlock and shed ... Eze 16:38
upon thee in the sight of many *w* ... Eze 16:41
Son of man, there were two *w* ... Eze 23:2
and she became famous among *w* ... Eze 23:10
and unto Aholibah, the lewd *w* ... Eze 23:44
the manner of *w* that shed blood ... Eze 23:45
that all *w* may be taught not to ... Eze 23:48
shall give him the daughter of *w* ... Dan 11:17
his fathers, nor the desire of *w* ... Dan 11:37
their *w* with child shall be ... Hos 13:16
up the *w* with child of Gilead ... Amos 1:13
The *w* of my people have ye cast ... Mic 2:9
people in the midst of thee are *w* ... Nah 3:13
and, behold, there came out two *w* ... Zec 5:9
old *w* dwell in the streets of ... Zec 8:4
houses rifled, and the *w* ravished ... Zec 14:2
Among them that are born of *w* ... Mt 11:11
about five thousand men, beside *w* ... Mt 14:21
were four thousand men, beside *w* ... Mt 15:38
Two *w* shall be grinding at the ... Mt 24:41
many *w* were there beholding afar ... Mt 27:55
angel answered and said unto the *w* ... Mt 28:5
There were also *w* looking on afar ... Mk 15:40
many other *w* which came up with ... Mk 15:41
blessed art thou among *w* ... Lk 1:28
and said, Blessed art thou among *w* ... Lk 1:42
Among those that are born of *w* ... Lk 7:28
And certain *w*, which had been ... Lk 8:2
Two *w* shall be grinding together ... Lk 17:35
great company of people, and of *w* ... Lk 23:27
the *w* that followed him from ... Lk 23:49
the *w* also, which came with him ... Lk 23:55
other *w* that were with them, ... Lk 24:10
certain *w* also of our company ... Lk 24:22
it even so as the *w* had said ... Lk 24:24
and supplication, with the *w* ... Acts 1:14
Lord, multitudes both of men and *w* ... Acts 5:14
*w* committed them to prison ... Acts 8:3
they were baptized, both men and *w* ... Acts 8:12
way, whether they were men or *w* ... Acts 9:2
up the devout and honourable *w* ... Acts 13:50
spake unto the *w* which resorted ... Acts 16:13
and of the chief *w* not a few ... Acts 17:4
of honourable *w* which were Greeks ... Acts 17:12
into prisons both men and *w* ... Acts 22:4
for even their *w* did change the ... Rom 1:26
Let your *w* keep silence in the ... 1Cor 14:34
for it is a shame for *w* to speak ... 1Cor 14:35
help those *w* which laboured with ... Phil 4:3
that *w* adorn themselves in modest ... 1Ti 2:9
But (which becometh *w* professing ... 1Ti 2:10
The elder *w* as mothers ... 1Ti 5:2
that the younger *w* marry, bear ... 1Ti 5:14
captive silly *w* laden with sins ... 2Ti 3:6
The aged *w* likewise, that they be ... Titus 2:3
may teach the young *w* to be sober ... Titus 2:4
*W* received their dead raised to ... Heb 11:35
in the old time the holy *w* also ... 1Pet 3:5
And they had hair as the hair of *w* ... Rev 9:8
which were not defiled with *w* ... Rev 14:4

**WOMEN'S**
before the court of the *w* house ... Est 2:11

**WOMENSERVANTS**
and oxen, and menservants, and *w* ... Gen 20:14
flocks, and menservants, and *w* ... Gen 32:5
took his two wives, and his two *w* ... Gen 32:22

**WON**
Out of the spoils *w* in battles ... 1Chr 26:27
harder to be *w* than a strong city ... Prov 18:19
be *w* by the conversation of the ... 1Pet 3:1

**WONDER**
and giveth thee a sign or a *w* ... Deut 13:1
And the sign or the *w* come to pass ... Deut 13:2
upon thee for a sign and for a *w* ... Deut 28:46
the *w* that was done in the land ... 2Chr 32:31
I am as a *w* unto many ... Ps 71:7
*w* upon Egypt and upon Ethiopia ... Is 20:3
Stay yourselves, and *w* ... Is 29:9
even a marvellous work and a *w* ... Is 29:14
and the prophets shall *w* ... Jer 4:9
and regard, and *w* marvellously ... Hab 1:5
and they were filled with *w* ... Acts 3:10
Behold, ye despisers, and *w* ... Acts 13:41
appeared a great *w* in heaven ... Rev 12:1
appeared another *w* in heaven ... Rev 12:3
that dwell on the earth shall *w* ... Rev 17:8

**WONDERED**
*w* that there was no intercessor ... Is 59:16
I *w* that there was none to uphold ... Is 63:5
for they are men *w* at ... Zec 3:8
Insomuch that the multitude *w* ... Mt 15:31
themselves beyond measure, and *w* ... Mk 6:51
all they that heard it *w* at those ... Lk 2:18
*w* at the gracious words which ... Lk 4:22
And they being afraid *w*, saying ... Lk 8:25
But while they *w* every one at all ... Lk 9:43
and the people *w* ... Lk 11:14
yet believed not for joy, and *w* ... Lk 24:41
Moses saw it, he *w* at the sight ... Acts 7:31
he continued with Philip, and *w* ... Acts 8:13
all the world *w* after the beast ... Rev 13:3
I *w* with great admiration ... Rev 17:6

**WONDERFUL**
the LORD will make thy plagues *w* ... Deut 28:59
thy love to me was *w*, passing the ... 2Sa 1:26
about to build shall be *w* great ... 2Chr 2:9
things too *w* for me, which I knew ... Job 42:3
are thy *w* works which thou hast ... Ps 40:5
his *w* works that he hath done ... Ps 78:4
for his *w* works to the children ... Ps 107:8
for his *w* works to the children ... Ps 107:15
for his *w* works to the children ... Ps 107:21
for his *w* works to the children ... Ps 107:31
He hath made his *w* works to be ... Ps 111:4
Thy testimonies are *w* ... Ps 119:129
Such knowledge is too *w* for me ... Ps 139:6
things which are too *w* for me ... Prov 30:18
and his name shall be called *W* ... Is 9:6
for thou hast done *w* things ... Is 25:1
which is *w* in counsel, and ... Is 28:29
A *w* and horrible thing is ... Jer 5:30
and in thy name done many *w* works ... Mt 7:22
scribes saw the *w* things that he ... Mt 21:15
in our tongues the *w* works of God ... Acts 2:11

**WONDERFULLY**
when he had wrought *w* among them ... 1Sa 6:6
for I am fearfully and *w* made ... Ps 139:14
therefore she came down *w* ... Lam 1:9
and he shall destroy *w*, and shall ... Dan 8:24

**WONDERING**
the man *w* at her held his peace, ... Gen 24:21
*w* in himself at that which was ... Lk 24:12
is called Solomon's, greatly *w* ... Acts 3:11

**WONDEROUSLY**
and the angel did *w* ... Judg 13:19

**WONDERS**
smite Egypt with all my *w* which I ... Ex 3:20
do all those *w* before Pharaoh ... Ex 4:21
my *w* in the land of Egypt ... Ex 7:3
that my *w* may be multiplied in ... Ex 11:9
did all these *w* before Pharaoh ... Ex 11:10
fearful in praises, doing *w* ... Ex 15:11
by temptations, by signs, and by *w* ... Deut 4:34
And the LORD shewed signs and *w* ... Deut 6:22
eyes saw, and the signs, and the *w* ... Deut 7:19
and with signs, and with *w* ... Deut 26:8
In all the signs and the *w* ... Deut 34:11
the LORD will do *w* among you ... Josh 3:5
works that he hath done, his *w* ... 1Chr 16:12
*w* upon Pharaoh, and on all his ... Neh 9:10
thy *w* that thou didst among them ... Neh 9:17
yea, and *w* without number ... Job 9:10
I will remember thy *w* of old ... Ps 77:11
Thou art the God that doest *w* ... Ps 77:14
his *w* that he had shewed them ... Ps 78:11
his *w* in the field of Zoan ... Ps 78:43
Wilt thou shew *w* to the dead ... Ps 88:10
Shall thy *w* be known in the dark ... Ps 88:12
And the heavens shall praise thy *w* ... Ps 89:5
heathen, his *w* among all people ... Ps 96:3
his *w*, and the judgments of his ... Ps 105:5
them, and *w* in the land of Ham ... Ps 105:27
understood not thy *w* in Egypt ... Ps 106:7
of the LORD, and his *w* in the deep ... Ps 107:24
*w* into the midst of thee, O Egypt ... Ps 135:9
To him who alone doeth great *w* ... Ps 136:4
for *w* in Israel from the LORD of ... Is 8:18
*w* in the land of Egypt, even unto ... Jer 32:20
of Egypt with signs, and with *w* ... Jer 32:21
*w* that the high God hath wrought ... Dan 4:2
and how mighty are his *w* ... Dan 4:3
*w* in heaven and in earth, who hath ... Dan 6:27
shall it be to the end of these *w* ... Dan 12:6
I will shew *w* in the heavens and ... Joel 2:30
and shall shew great signs and *w* ... Mt 24:24
rise, and shall shew signs and *w* ... Mk 13:22
him, Except ye see signs and *w* ... Jn 4:48
I will shew *w* in heaven above, and ... Acts 2:19
of God among you by miracles and *w*. ... Acts 2:22
and many *w* and signs were done by ... Acts 2:43
*w* may be done by the name of thy ... Acts 4:30
*w* wrought among the people ... Acts 5:12
of faith and power, did great *w* ... Acts 6:8
out, after that he had shewed *w* ... Acts 7:36
*w* to be done by their hands ... Acts 14:3
*w* God had wrought among the ... Acts 15:12
Through mighty signs and *w* ... Rom 15:19
in all patience, in signs, and *w* ... 2Cor 12:12
all power and signs and lying *w* ... 2Th 2:9
witness, both with signs and *w* ... Heb 2:4
And he doeth great *w*, so that he ... Rev 13:13

**WONDROUS**
him, talk ye of all his *w* works ... 1Chr 16:9
and consider the *w* works of God ... Job 37:14
the *w* works of him which is ... Job 37:16
and tell of all thy *w* works ... Ps 26:7
have I declared thy *w* works ... Ps 71:17
Israel, who only doeth *w* things ... Ps 72:18
name is near thy *w* works declare ... Ps 75:1
and believed not for his *w* works ... Ps 78:32
thou art great, and doest *w* things ... Ps 86:10
talk ye of all his *w* works ... Ps 105:2
*W* works in the land of Ham, and ... Ps 106:22
that I may behold *w* things out of ... Ps 119:18
so shall I talk of thy *w* works ... Ps 119:27
of thy majesty, and of thy *w* works ... Ps 145:5
us according to all his *w* works ... Jer 21:2

**WONDROUSLY**
God, that hath dealt *w* with you ... Joel 2:26

**WONT**
But if the ox were *w* to push with ... Ex 21:29
was I ever *w* to do so unto thee ... Num 22:30
and his men were *w* to haunt ... 1Sa 30:31
They were *w* to speak in old time, ... 2Sa 20:18
more than it was *w* to be heated ... Dan 3:19
*w* to release unto the people a ... Mt 27:15
and, as he was *w*, he taught them ... Mk 10:1
he came out, and went, as he was *w* ... Lk 22:39
where prayer was *w* to be made ... Acts 16:13

**WOOD**
Make thee an ark of gopher *w* ... Gen 6:14
clave the *w* for the burnt ... Gen 22:3
Abraham took the *w* of the burnt ... Gen 22:6
he said, Behold the fire and the *w* ... Gen 22:7
there, and laid the *w* in order ... Gen 22:9
laid him on the altar upon the *w* ... Gen 22:9
of Egypt, both in vessels of *w* ... Ex 7:19
and badgers' skins, and shittim *w* ... Ex 25:5
shall make an ark of shittim *w* ... Ex 25:10
shalt make staves of shittim *w* ... Ex 25:13
also make a table of shittim *w* ... Ex 25:23
make the staves of shittim *w* ... Ex 25:28
of shittim *w* standing up ... Ex 26:15
thou shalt make bars of shittim *w* ... Ex 26:26
of shittim *w* overlaid with gold ... Ex 26:32
hanging five pillars of shittim *w* ... Ex 26:37
shalt make an altar of shittim *w* ... Ex 27:1
the altar, staves of shittim *w* ... Ex 27:6
of shittim *w* shalt thou make it ... Ex 30:1
make the staves of shittim *w* ... Ex 30:5
and badgers' skins, and shittim *w* ... Ex 35:7
*w* for any work of the service ... Ex 35:24
to set them, and in carving of *w* ... Ex 35:33
for the tabernacle of shittim *w* ... Ex 36:20
And he made bars of shittim *w* ... Ex 36:31
four pillars of shittim *w* ... Ex 36:36
made the ark of shittim *w* ... Ex 37:1
And he made staves of shittim *w* ... Ex 37:4
And he made the table of shittim *w* ... Ex 37:10
he made the staves of shittim *w* ... Ex 37:15
the incense altar of shittim *w* ... Ex 37:25
he made the staves of shittim *w* ... Ex 37:28
of burnt offering of shittim *w* ... Ex 38:1
he made the staves of shittim *w* ... Ex 38:6
lay the *w* in order upon the fire ... Lev 1:7
in order upon the *w* that is on ... Lev 1:8
*w* that is on the fire which is ... Lev 1:12
upon the *w* that is upon the fire ... Lev 1:17
which is upon the *w* that is on ... Lev 3:5
and burn him on the *w* with fire ... Lev 4:12
shall burn *w* on it every morning ... Lev 6:12
whether it be any vessel of *w* ... Lev 11:32
birds alive and clean, and cedar *w* ... Lev 14:4
he shall take it, and the cedar *w* ... Lev 14:6
the house two birds, and cedar *w* ... Lev 14:49
And he shall take the cedar *w* ... Lev 14:51
living bird, and with the cedar *w* ... Lev 14:52
every vessel of *w* shall be rinsed ... Lev 15:12
lean, whether there be *w* therein ... Num 13:20
And the priest shall take cedar *w* ... Num 19:6
hair, and all things made of *w* ... Num 31:20
him with an hand weapon of *w* ... Num 35:18
gods, the work of men's hands, *w* ... Deut 4:28

mount, and make thee an ark of w ..... Deut 10:1
And I made an ark of shittim w ..... Deut 10:3
As when a man goeth into the w ..... Deut 19:5
his neighbour to hew w ..... Deut 19:5
shalt thou serve other gods, w ..... Deut 28:36
thy fathers have known, even w ..... Deut 28:64
from the hewer of thy w unto the ..... Deut 29:11
abominations, and their idols, w ..... Deut 29:17
but let them be hewers of w ..... Josh 9:21
being bondmen, and hewers of w ..... Josh 9:23
made them that day hewers of w ..... Josh 9:27
then get thee up to the w country ..... Josh 17:15
for it is a w, and thou shalt cut ..... Josh 17:18
a burnt sacrifice with the w of ..... Judg 6:26
and they clave the w of the cart ..... 1Sa 6:14
all they of the land came to a w ..... 1Sa 14:25
the people were come into the w ..... 1Sa 14:26
in the wilderness of Ziph in a w ..... 1Sa 23:15
and went to David into the w ..... 1Sa 23:16
and David abode in the w, and ..... 1Sa 23:18
with us in strong holds in the w ..... 1Sa 23:19
of instruments made of fir w ..... 2Sa 6:5
battle was in the w of Ephraim ..... 2Sa 18:6
the w devoured more people that ..... 2Sa 18:8
him into a great pit in the w ..... 2Sa 18:17
instruments of the oxen for w ..... 2Sa 24:22
covered them on the inside with w ..... 1Kin 6:15
cut it in pieces, and lay it on w ..... 1Kin 18:23
the other bullock, and lay it on w ..... 1Kin 18:23
And he put the w in order, and cut ..... 1Kin 18:33
in pieces, and laid him on the w ..... 1Kin 18:33
the burnt sacrifice, and on the w ..... 1Kin 18:33
the burnt sacrifice, and the w ..... 1Kin 18:38
forth two she bears out of the w ..... 2Kin 2:24
came to Jordan, they cut down w ..... 2Kin 6:4
but the work of men's hands, w ..... 2Kin 19:18
Then shall the trees of the w ..... 1Chr 16:33
the threshing instruments for w ..... 1Chr 21:23
brought much cedar w to David ..... 1Chr 22:4
of iron, and w for things of w ..... 1Chr 29:2
we will cut w out of Lebanon, as ..... 2Chr 2:16
scribe stood upon a pulpit of w ..... Neh 8:4
for the w offering, to bring it ..... Neh 10:34
for the w offering, at times ..... Neh 13:31
as straw, and brass as rotten w ..... Job 41:27
boar out of the w doth waste it ..... Ps 80:13
As the fire burneth a w, and as ..... Ps 83:14
all the trees of the w rejoice ..... Ps 96:12
found it in the fields of the w ..... Ps 132:6
cleaveth w upon the earth ..... Ps 141:7
Where no w is, there the fire ..... Prov 26:20
to burning coals, and w to fire ..... Prov 26:21
to water therewith the w that ..... Eccl 2:6
he that cleaveth w shall be ..... Eccl 10:9
tree among the trees of the w ..... Song 2:3
a chariot of the w of Lebanon ..... Song 3:9
as the trees of the w are moved ..... Is 7:2
up itself, as if it were no w ..... Is 10:15
pile thereof is fire and much w ..... Is 30:33
but the work of men's hands, w ..... Is 37:19
up the w of their graven image ..... Is 45:20
for w brass, and for stones iron ..... Is 60:17
thy mouth fire, and this people w ..... Jer 5:14
The children gather w, and the ..... Jer 7:18
Thou hast broken the yokes of w ..... Jer 28:13
her with axes, as hewers of w ..... Jer 46:22
our w is sold unto us ..... Lam 5:4
and the children fell under the w ..... Lam 5:13
Shall w be taken thereof to do ..... Eze 15:3
of the countries, to serve w ..... Eze 20:32
Heap on w, kindle the fire, ..... Eze 24:10
shall take no w out of the field ..... Eze 39:10
door, cieled with w round about ..... Eze 41:16
The altar of w was three cubits ..... Eze 41:22
and the walls thereof, were of w ..... Eze 41:22
silver, of brass, of iron, of w ..... Dan 5:4
and gold, of brass, iron, w ..... Dan 5:23
which dwell solitarily in the w ..... Mic 7:14
Woe unto him that saith to the w ..... Hab 2:19
Go up to the mountain, and bring w ..... Hag 1:8
an hearth of fire among the w ..... Zec 12:6
gold, silver, precious stones, w ..... 1Cor 3:12
gold and of silver, but also of w ..... 2Ti 2:20
and brass, and stone, and of w ..... Rev 9:20
silk, and scarlet, and all thyine w ..... Rev 18:12
manner vessels of most precious w ..... Rev 18:12

## WOODS

the wilderness, and sleep in the w ..... Eze 34:25

## WOOF

Whether it be in the warp, or w ..... Lev 13:48
either in the warp, or in the w ..... Lev 13:49
either in the warp, or in the w ..... Lev 13:51
that garment, whether warp or w ..... Lev 13:52
either in the warp, or in the w ..... Lev 13:53
out of the warp, or out of the w ..... Lev 13:56
either in the warp, or in the w ..... Lev 13:57
And the garment, either warp, or w ..... Lev 13:58
linen, either in the warp, or w ..... Lev 13:59

## WOOL

put a fleece of w in the floor ..... Judg 6:37
hundred thousand rams, with the w ..... 2Kin 3:4
He giveth snow like w ..... Ps 147:16
She seeketh w, and flax, and ..... Prov 31:13
like crimson, they shall be as w ..... Is 1:18
and the worm shall eat them like w ..... Is 51:8
in the wine of Helbon, and white w ..... Eze 27:18
fat, and ye clothe you with the w ..... Eze 34:3
no w shall come upon them, whiles ..... Eze 44:17
hair of his head like the pure w ..... Dan 7:9
me my bread and my water, my w ..... Hos 2:5
thereof, and will recover my w ..... Hos 2:9
goats, with water, and scarlet w ..... Heb 9:19
and his hairs were white like w ..... Rev 1:14

## WOOLLEN

is in, whether it be a w garment ..... Lev 13:47
of linen, or of w ..... Lev 13:48
in w or in linen, or any thing of ..... Lev 13:52
in a garment of w or linen ..... Lev 13:59
of linen and w come upon thee ..... Lev 19:19
garment of divers sorts, as of w ..... Deut 22:11

## WORD See PREFACE.

unto the w which I command you ..... Deut 4:2
but by every w that proceedeth ..... Deut 8:3
But the w is very nigh unto thee, ..... Deut 30:14
the w of the LORD was precious in ..... 1Sa 3:1
By the w of the LORD were the ..... Ps 33:6
heed thereto according to thy w ..... Ps 119:9
Thy w have I hid in mine heart, ..... Ps 119:11
Thy w is a lamp unto my feet, and ..... Ps 119:105
For there is not a w in my tongue ..... Ps 139:4
a w spoken in due season, how ..... Prov 15:23
A w fitly spoken is like apples ..... Prov 25:11
Hear the w of the LORD ..... Is 66:5
ye that tremble at his w ..... Is 66:5
for every man's w shall be his ..... Jer 23:36
the w that I shall speak shall ..... Eze 12:25
house, will I say the w, and will ..... Eze 12:25
dry bones, hear the w of the LORD ..... Eze 37:4
but by every w that proceedeth ..... Mt 4:4
cast out the spirits with his w ..... Mt 8:16
That every idle w that men shall ..... Mt 12:36
The sower soweth the w ..... Mk 4:14
In the beginning was the W ..... Jn 1:1
the W was with God ..... Jn 1:1
and the W was God ..... Jn 1:1
the W was made flesh, and dwelt ..... Jn 1:14
the w which ye hear is not mine, ..... Jn 14:24
w which I have spoken unto you ..... Jn 15:3
thy w is truth ..... Jn 17:17
they spake the w of God with ..... Acts 4:31
and to the ministry of the w ..... Acts 6:4
went every where preaching the w ..... Acts 8:4
on all them which heard the w ..... Acts 10:44
But the w of God grew and ..... Acts 12:24
in that they received the w with ..... Acts 17:11
The w is nigh thee, even in thy ..... Rom 10:8
the kingdom of God is not in w ..... 1Cor 4:20
our w toward you was not yea and ..... 2Cor 1:18
all the law is fulfilled in one w ..... Gal 5:14
the washing of water by the w ..... Eph 5:26
the Spirit, which is the w of God ..... Eph 6:17
And whatsoever ye do in w or deed ..... Col 3:17
it is sanctified by the w of God ..... 1Ti 4:5
Preach the w ..... 2Ti 4:2
For the w of God is quick, and ..... Heb 4:12
with meekness the engrafted w ..... Jas 1:21
But be ye doers of the w, and not ..... Jas 1:22
But the w of the Lord endureth ..... 1Pet 1:25
desire the sincere milk of the w ..... 1Pet 2:2
have handled, of the W of life ..... 1Jn 1:1
children, let us not love in w ..... 1Jn 3:18
by the w of their testimony ..... Rev 12:11

## WORD'S

For thy w sake, and according to ..... 2Sa 7:21
ariseth for the w sake, ..... Mk 4:17

## WORDS See PREFACE.

And these w, which I command thee ..... Deut 6:6
w that were in the first tables ..... Deut 10:2
lay up these my w in your heart ..... Deut 11:18
will put my w in his mouth ..... Deut 18:18
These are the w of the covenant, ..... Deut 29:1
Let the w of my mouth, and the ..... Ps 19:14
The w of a talebearer are as ..... Prov 26:22
Add thou not unto his w, lest he ..... Prov 30:6
The w of a wise man's mouth are ..... Eccl 10:12
sought to find out acceptable w ..... Eccl 12:10
was upright, even w of truth ..... Eccl 12:10
Hear ye the w of this covenant, ..... Jer 11:2
not the w of this covenant ..... Jer 11:3
he shall speak great w against ..... Dan 7:25
For by thy w thou shalt be ..... Mt 12:37
by thy w thou shalt be condemned ..... Mt 12:37
but my w shall not pass away ..... Mt 24:35
but my w shall not pass away ..... Mk 13:31
shall be ashamed of me and of my w ..... Lk 9:26
And they remembered his w, ..... Lk 24:8
thou hast the w of eternal life ..... Jn 6:68
a man love me, he will keep my w ..... Jn 14:23
them the w which thou gavest me ..... Jn 17:8
five w with my understanding ..... 1Cor 14:19
comfort one another with these w ..... 1Th 4:18
Hold fast the form of sound w ..... 2Ti 1:13
for these w are true and faithful ..... Rev 21:5
w of the prophecy of this book ..... Rev 22:18
w of the book of this prophecy ..... Rev 22:19

## WORK

God ended his w which he had made ..... Gen 2:2
from all his w which he had made ..... Gen 2:2
from all his w which God created ..... Gen 2:3
shall comfort us concerning our w ..... Gen 5:29
Let there more w be laid upon the ..... Ex 5:9
of your w shall be diminished ..... Ex 5:11
Go therefore now, and w ..... Ex 5:18
no manner of w shall be done in ..... Ex 12:16
Israel saw that great w which the ..... Ex 14:31
walk, and the w that they must do ..... Ex 18:20
thou labour, and do all thy w ..... Ex 20:9
in it thou shalt not do any w ..... Ex 20:10
Six days thou shalt do thy w ..... Ex 23:12
a paved w of a sapphire stone ..... Ex 24:10
of beaten w shalt thou make them, ..... Ex 25:18
of beaten w shall the candlestick ..... Ex 25:31
be one beaten w of pure gold ..... Ex 25:36
of cunning w shalt thou make them ..... Ex 26:1
and fine twined linen of cunning w ..... Ex 26:31
fine twined linen, with cunning w ..... Ex 28:6
same, according to the w thereof ..... Ex 28:8
With the w of an engraver in ..... Ex 28:11
of wreathen w shalt thou make ..... Ex 28:14
of judgment with cunning w ..... Ex 28:15
after the w of the ephod thou ..... Ex 28:15
ends of wreathen w of pure gold ..... Ex 28:22
w round about the hole of it ..... Ex 28:32
to w in gold, and in silver, and in ..... Ex 31:4
to w in all manner of workmanship ..... Ex 31:5
for whosoever doeth any w therein ..... Ex 31:14
Six days may w be done ..... Ex 31:15
doeth any w in the sabbath day ..... Ex 31:15
And the tables were the w of God ..... Ex 32:16
art shall see the w of the LORD ..... Ex 34:10
Six days thou shalt w, but on the ..... Ex 34:21
Six days shall w be done, but on ..... Ex 35:2
whosoever doeth w therein shall ..... Ex 35:2
to the w of the tabernacle of the ..... Ex 35:21
wood for any w of the service ..... Ex 35:24
to bring for all manner of w ..... Ex 35:29
to w in gold, and in silver, and in ..... Ex 35:32
to make any manner of cunning w ..... Ex 35:33
to w all manner of ..... Ex 35:35
all manner of w ..... Ex 35:35
even of them that do any w ..... Ex 35:35
and of those that devise cunning w ..... Ex 35:35
to w all manner of ..... Ex 36:1
of w for the service of the ..... Ex 36:1
up to come unto the w to do it ..... Ex 36:2
of Israel had brought for the w ..... Ex 36:3
all the w of the sanctuary ..... Ex 36:4
man from his w which they made ..... Ex 36:4
enough for the service of the w ..... Ex 36:5
more w for the offering of the ..... Ex 36:6
for all the w to make it, and too ..... Ex 36:7
the w of the tabernacle made ten ..... Ex 36:8
of cunning w made he them ..... Ex 36:8
cherubims made he it of cunning w ..... Ex 36:35
of beaten w made he the ..... Ex 37:17
it was one beaten w of pure gold ..... Ex 37:22
according to the w of the ..... Ex 37:29
the w in all the w of the holy ..... Ex 38:24
to w it in the blue, and in the ..... Ex 39:3
in the fine linen, with cunning w ..... Ex 39:3
same, according to the w thereof ..... Ex 39:5
made the breastplate of cunning w ..... Ex 39:8
like the w of the ephod ..... Ex 39:8
of wreathen w of pure gold ..... Ex 39:15
the robe of the ephod of woven w ..... Ex 39:22
fine linen of woven w for Aaron ..... Ex 39:27
Thus was all the w of the ..... Ex 39:32
children of Israel made all the w ..... Ex 39:42
And Moses did look upon all the w ..... Ex 39:43
So Moses finished the w ..... Ex 40:33
it be, wherein any w is done ..... Lev 11:32
or in any w that is made of skin ..... Lev 13:51
do no w at all, whether it be one ..... Lev 16:29
Six days shall w be done ..... Lev 23:3
ye shall do no w therein ..... Lev 23:3
ye shall do no servile w therein ..... Lev 23:7
ye shall do no servile w therein ..... Lev 23:8
ye shall do no servile w therein ..... Lev 23:21
Ye shall do no servile w therein ..... Lev 23:25
ye shall do no w in that same day ..... Lev 23:28
that doeth any w in that same day ..... Lev 23:30
Ye shall do no manner of w ..... Lev 23:31
ye shall do no servile w therein ..... Lev 23:35
ye shall do no servile w therein ..... Lev 23:36
to do the w in the tabernacle of ..... Num 4:3
to do the w of the tabernacle of ..... Num 4:23
to do the w of the tabernacle of ..... Num 4:30
for the w in the tabernacle of ..... Num 4:35
for the w in the tabernacle of ..... Num 4:39
for the w in the tabernacle of ..... Num 4:43
this w of the candlestick was of ..... Num 8:4
the flowers thereof, was beaten w ..... Num 8:4
do no manner of servile w therein ..... Num 28:18
ye shall do no servile w ..... Num 28:25
ye shall do no servile w ..... Num 28:26
ye shall do no servile w ..... Num 29:1
ye shall not do any w therein ..... Num 29:7
ye shall do no servile w, and ye ..... Num 29:12
ye shall do no servile w therein ..... Num 29:35
all w of goats' hair, and all ..... Num 31:20
the w of men's hands, wood and ..... Deut 4:28
shalt labour, and do all thy w ..... Deut 5:13
in it thou shalt not do any w ..... Deut 5:14
God may bless thee in all the w ..... Deut 14:29
thou shalt do no w with the ..... Deut 15:19
thou shalt do no w therein ..... Deut 16:8
thee in all the w of thine hands ..... Deut 24:19
the w of the hands of the ..... Deut 27:15
to bless all the w of thine hand ..... Deut 28:12
in every w of thine hand, in the ..... Deut 30:9
anger through the w of your hands ..... Deut 31:29
He is the Rock, his w is perfect ..... Deut 32:4
accept the w of his hands ..... Deut 33:11
They did w wilily, and went and ..... Josh 9:4
his w out of the field at even ..... Judg 19:16
The LORD recompense thy w ..... Ruth 2:12
your asses, and put them to his w ..... 1Sa 8:16

be that the LORD will *w* for us ... 1Sa 14:6
officers which were over the *w* ... 1Kin 5:16
the people that wrought in the *w* ... 1Kin 5:16
gold fitted upon the carved *w* ... 1Kin 6:35
porch, which was of the like *w* ... 1Kin 7:8
cunning to *w* all works in brass ... 1Kin 7:14
Solomon, and wrought all his *w* ... 1Kin 7:14
And nets of checker *w* ... 1Kin 7:17
and wreaths of chain *w* ... 1Kin 7:17
were of lily *w* in the porch ... 1Kin 7:19
the top of the pillars was lily *w* ... 1Kin 7:22
so was the *w* of the pillars ... 1Kin 7:22
the *w* of the bases was on this ... 1Kin 7:28
certain additions made of thin *w* ... 1Kin 7:29
was round after the *w* of the base ... 1Kin 7:31
the *w* of the wheels was like the ... 1Kin 7:33
was like the *w* of a chariot wheel ... 1Kin 7:33
made an end of doing all the *w* ... 1Kin 7:40
So was ended all the *w* that king ... 1Kin 7:51
that were over Solomon's *w* ... 1Kin 9:23
the people that wrought in the *w* ... 1Kin 9:23
to anger with the *w* of his hands ... 1Kin 16:7
thou hast sold thyself to *w* evil ... 1Kin 21:20
which did sell himself to *w* ... 1Kin 21:25
the hands of them that did the *w* ... 2Kin 12:11
but the *w* of men's hands, wood and 2Kin 19:18
the hand of the doers of the *w* ... 2Kin 22:5
give it to the doers of the *w* ... 2Kin 22:5
the hand of them that do the *w* ... 2Kin 22:9
and the wreathen *w*, and ... 2Kin 25:17
the second pillar with wreathen *w* ... 2Kin 25:17
dwelt with the king for his *w* ... 1Chr 4:23
all the *w* of the place most holy ... 1Chr 6:49
very able men for the *w* of the ... 1Chr 9:13
were over the *w* of the service, ... 1Chr 9:19
they were employed in that *w* day ... 1Chr 9:33
as every day's *w* required ... 1Chr 16:37
cunning men for every manner of *w*. 1Chr 22:15
were to set forward the *w* of the ... 1Chr 23:4
that did the *w* for the service of ... 1Chr 23:24
the *w* of the service of the house ... 1Chr 23:28
over them that did the *w* of the ... 1Chr 27:26
for all the *w* of the service of ... 1Chr 28:13
thou hast finished all the *w* for ... 1Chr 28:20
and tender, and the *w* is great ... 1Chr 29:1
for all manner of *w* to be made by ... 1Chr 29:5
with the rulers of the king's *w* ... 1Chr 29:6
a man cunning to *w* in gold ... 2Chr 2:7
man of Tyre, skilful to *w* in gold ... 2Chr 2:14
overseers to set the people a *w* ... 2Chr 2:18
he made two cherubims of image *w* ... 2Chr 3:10
like the *w* of the brim of a cup ... 2Chr 4:5
Huram finished the *w* that he was ... 2Chr 4:11
Thus all the *w* that Solomon made ... 2Chr 5:1
make no servants for his *w* ... 2Chr 8:9
Now all the *w* of Solomon was ... 2Chr 8:16
for your *w* shall be rewarded ... 2Chr 15:7
of Ramah, and let his *w* cease ... 2Chr 16:5
gave it to such as did the *w* of ... 2Chr 24:12
the *w* was perfected by them, and ... 2Chr 24:13
till the *w* was ended, and until ... 2Chr 29:34
in every *w* that he began in the ... 2Chr 31:21
which were the *w* of the hands of ... 2Chr 32:19
And the men did the *w* faithfully ... 2Chr 34:12
of all that wrought the *w* in any ... 2Chr 34:13
the treasure of the *w* threescore ... Ezr 2:69
to set forward the *w* of the house ... Ezr 3:8
Then ceased the *w* of the house of ... Ezr 4:24
and this *w* goeth fast on, and ... Ezr 5:8
Let the *w* of this house of God ... Ezr 6:7
in the *w* of the house of God ... Ezr 6:22
is this a *w* of one day or two ... Ezr 10:13
nor to the rest that did the *w* ... Neh 2:16
their hands for this good *w* ... Neh 2:18
necks to the *w* of their Lord ... Neh 3:5
for the people had a mind to *w* ... Neh 4:6
them, and cause the *w* to cease ... Neh 4:11
to the wall, every one unto his *w* ... Neh 4:15
of my servants wrought in the *w* ... Neh 4:16
one of his hands wrought in the *w* ... Neh 4:17
The *w* is great and large, and we ... Neh 4:19
So we laboured in the *w* ... Neh 4:21
I continued in the *w* of this wall ... Neh 5:16
were gathered thither unto the *w* ... Neh 5:16
saying, I am doing a great *w* ... Neh 6:3
why should the *w* cease, whilst I ... Neh 6:3
shall be weakened from the *w* ... Neh 6:9
this *w* was wrought of our God ... Neh 6:16
of the fathers gave unto the *w* ... Neh 7:70
gave to the treasure of the *w* ... Neh 7:71
for all the *w* of the house of our ... Neh 10:33
their brethren that did the *w* of ... Neh 11:12
and the singers, that did the *w* ... Neh 13:10
hast blessed the *w* of his hands ... Job 1:10
looketh for the reward of his *w* ... Job 7:2
despise the *w* of thine hands ... Job 10:3
a desire to the *w* of thine hands ... Job 14:15
On the left hand, where he doth *w* ... Job 23:9
desert, go they forth to their *w* ... Job 24:5
For the *w* of a man shall he ... Job 34:11
they all are the *w* of his hands ... Job 34:19
Then he sheweth them their *w* ... Job 36:9
Remember that thou magnify his *w* ... Job 36:24
that all men may know his *w* ... Job 37:7
the *w* of thy fingers, the moon and ... Ps 8:3
snared in the *w* of his own hands ... Ps 9:16
them after the *w* of their hands ... Ps 28:4
what *w* thou didst in their days, ... Ps 44:1
Yea, in heart ye *w* wickedness ... Ps 58:2
to every man according to his *w* ... Ps 62:12

and shall declare the *w* of God ... Ps 64:9
*w* thereof at once with axes ... Ps 74:6
I will meditate also of all thy *w* ... Ps 77:12
Let thy *w* appear unto thy ... Ps 90:16
establish thou the *w* of our hands ... Ps 90:17
the *w* of our hands establish thou ... Ps 90:17
hast made me glad through thy *w* ... Ps 92:4
me, proved me, and saw my *w* ... Ps 95:9
I hate the *w* of them that turn ... Ps 101:3
heavens are the *w* of thy hands ... Ps 102:25
Man goeth forth unto his *w* ... Ps 104:23
His *w* is honourable and glorious ... Ps 111:3
and gold, the *w* of men's hands ... Ps 115:4
It is time for thee, LORD, to *w* ... Ps 119:126
and gold, the *w* of men's hands ... Ps 135:15
works with men that *w* iniquity ... Ps 141:4
I muse on the *w* of thy hands ... Ps 143:5
The wicked worketh a deceitful *w* ... Prov 11:18
the weights of the bag are his *w* ... Prov 16:11
his *w* is brother to him that is a ... Prov 18:9
his doings, whether his *w* be pure ... Prov 20:11
as for the pure, his *w* is right ... Prov 21:8
Prepare thy *w* without, and make it .. Prov 24:27
to the man according to his *w* ... Prov 24:29
because the *w* that is wrought ... Eccl 2:17
the *w* that God maketh from the ... Eccl 3:11
for every purpose and for every *w* ... Eccl 3:17
evil *w* that is done under the sun ... Eccl 4:3
all travail, and every right *w* ... Eccl 4:4
destroy the *w* of thine hands ... Eccl 5:6
Consider the *w* of God ... Eccl 7:13
*w* that is done under the sun ... Eccl 8:9
evil *w* is not executed speedily ... Eccl 8:11
according to the *w* of the wicked ... Eccl 8:14
to the *w* of the righteous ... Eccl 8:14
Then I beheld all the *w* of God ... Eccl 8:17
the *w* that is done under the sun ... Eccl 8:17
for there is no *w*, nor device, ... Eccl 9:10
shall bring every *w* into judgment ... Eccl 12:14
the *w* of the hands of a cunning ... Song 7:1
they worship the *w* of their own ... Is 2:8
they regard not the *w* of the LORD ... Is 5:12
him make speed, and hasten his *w* ... Is 5:19
his whole *w* upon mount Zion ... Is 10:12
the *w* of his hands, neither shall ... Is 17:8
Moreover they that *w* in fine flax ... Is 19:9
Egypt to err in every *w* thereof ... Is 19:14
shall there be any *w* for Egypt ... Is 19:15
and Assyria the *w* of my hands ... Is 19:25
he may do his *w*, his strange *w* ... Is 28:21
a marvellous *w* among this people ... Is 29:14
this people, even a marvellous *w* ... Is 29:14
for shall the *w* say of him that ... Is 29:16
the *w* of mine hands, in the midst ... Is 29:23
the help of them that *w* iniquity ... Is 31:2
and his heart will *w* iniquity ... Is 32:6
the *w* of righteousness shall be ... Is 32:17
but the *w* of men's hands, wood and ... Is 37:19
is with him, and his *w* before him ... Is 40:10
of nothing, and your *w* of nought ... Is 41:24
I will *w*, and who shall let it ... Is 43:13
or thy *w*, He hath no hands ... Is 45:9
concerning the *w* of my hands ... Is 45:11
the LORD, and my *w* with my God ... Is 49:4
forth an instrument for his *w* ... Is 54:16
the *w* of my hands, that I may be ... Is 60:21
and I will direct their *w* in truth ... Is 61:8
is with him, and his *w* before him ... Is 62:11
and we all are the *w* of thy hand ... Is 64:8
their former *w* into their bosom ... Is 65:7
long enjoy the *w* of their hands ... Is 65:22
the *w* of the hands of the workman ... Jer 10:3
the *w* of the workman, and of the ... Jer 10:9
they are all the *w* of cunning men ... Jer 10:9
are vanity, and the *w* of errors ... Jer 10:15
sabbath day, neither do ye any *w* ... Jer 17:22
sabbath day, to do no *w* therein ... Jer 17:24
he wrought a *w* on the wheels ... Jer 18:3
and giveth him not for his *w* ... Jer 22:13
for thy *w* shall be rewarded, ... Jer 31:16
Great in counsel, and mighty in *w* ... Jer 32:19
anger with the *w* of their hands ... Jer 32:30
the *w* of the LORD deceitfully ... Jer 48:10
for this is the *w* of the Lord GOD ... Jer 50:25
recompense her according to her *w* ... Jer 50:29
in Zion the *w* of the LORD our God ... Jer 51:10
They are vanity, the *w* of errors ... Jer 51:18
according to the *w* of their hands ... Lam 3:64
the *w* of the hands of the potter ... Lam 4:2
their *w* was like unto the colour ... Eze 1:16
their *w* was as it were a wheel in ... Eze 1:16
wood be taken thereof to do any *w* ... Eze 15:3
Is it meet for any *w* ... Eze 15:4
was whole, it was meet for no *w* ... Eze 15:5
shall it be meet yet for any *w* ... Eze 15:5
thee also with broidered *w* ... Eze 16:10
linen, and silk, and broidered *w* ... Eze 16:13
the *w* of an imperious whorish ... Eze 16:30
Fine linen with broidered *w* from ... Eze 27:7
emeralds, purple, and broidered *w* ... Eze 27:16
in blue clothes, and broidered *w* ... Eze 27:24
ye *w* abomination, and ye defile ... Eze 33:26
with him he shall *w* deceitfully ... Dan 11:23
is a city of them that *w* iniquity ... Hos 6:8
all of it the *w* of the craftsmen ... Hos 13:2
any more to the *w* of our hands ... Hos 14:3
and *w* evil upon their beds ... Mic 2:1
more worship the *w* of thine hands ... Mic 5:13
for I will *w* a ... Hab 1:5
a *w* in your days ... Hab 1:5

maker of his *w* trusteth therein ... Hab 2:18
revive thy *w* in the midst of the ... Hab 3:2
for he shall uncover the cedar *w* ... Zeph 2:14
did *w* in the house of the LORD of ... Hag 1:14
of the land, saith the LORD, and *w* ... Hag 2:4
so is every *w* of their hands ... Hag 2:14
they that *w* wickedness are set up ... Mal 3:15
from me, ye that *w* iniquity ... Mt 7:23
go *w* to day in my vineyard ... Mt 21:28
she hath wrought a good *w* upon me ... Mt 26:10
And he could there do no mighty *w* ... Mk 6:5
servants, and to every man his *w* ... Mk 13:34
she hath wrought a good *w* on me ... Mk 14:6
six days in which men ought to *w* ... Lk 13:14
that sent me, and to finish his *w* ... Jn 4:34
Father worketh hitherto, and I *w* ... Jn 5:17
that we might *w* the works of God ... Jn 6:28
unto them, This is the *w* of God ... Jn 6:29
what dost thou *w* ... Jn 6:30
said unto them, I have done one *w* ... Jn 7:21
I must *w* the works of him that ... Jn 9:4
night cometh, when no man can *w* ... Jn 9:4
For a good *w* we stone thee not ... Jn 10:33
I have finished the *w* which thou ... Jn 17:4
this counsel or this *w* be of men ... Acts 5:38
Saul for the *w* whereunto I have ... Acts 13:2
for I *w* a ... Acts 13:41
a *w* in your days ... Acts 13:41
a *w* which ye shall in no wise ... Acts 13:41
for the *w* which they fulfilled ... Acts 14:26
and went not with them to the *w* ... Acts 15:38
we had much *w* to come by the boat Acts 27:16
Which shew the *w* of the law ... Rom 2:15
did *w* in our members to bring ... Rom 7:5
we know that all things *w* ... Rom 8:28
For he will finish the *w*, and cut ... Rom 9:28
because a short *w* will the Lord ... Rom 9:28
otherwise *w* is no more *w* ... Rom 11:6
For meat destroy not the *w* of God ... Rom 14:20
Every man's *w* shall be made ... 1Cor 3:13
every man's *w* of what sort it is ... 1Cor 3:13
If any man's *w* abide which he ... 1Cor 3:14
If any man's *w* shall be burned, ... 1Cor 3:15
are not ye my *w* in the Lord ... 1Cor 9:1
abounding in the *w* of the Lord ... 1Cor 15:58
for he worketh the *w* of the Lord ... 1Cor 16:10
may abound to every good *w* ... 2Cor 9:8
But let every man prove his own *w* ... Gal 6:4
for the *w* of the ministry, for ... Eph 4:12
to *w* all uncleanness with ... Eph 4:19
*w* in you will perform it until ... Phil 1:6
*w* out your own salvation with ... Phil 2:12
Because for the *w* of Christ he ... Phil 2:30
being fruitful in every good *w* ... Col 1:10
without ceasing your *w* of faith ... 1Th 1:3
to *w* with your own hands, as we ... 1Th 4:11
the *w* of faith with power ... 2Th 1:11
of iniquity doth already *w* ... 2Th 2:7
you in every good word and *w* ... 2Th 2:17
you, that if any would not *w* ... 2Th 3:10
that with quietness they *w* ... 2Th 3:12
of a bishop, he desireth a good *w* ... 1Ti 3:1
diligently followed every good *w* ... 1Ti 5:10
and prepared unto every good *w* ... 2Ti 2:21
do the *w* of an evangelist, make ... 2Ti 4:5
deliver me from every evil *w* ... 2Ti 4:18
and unto every good *w* reprobate ... Titus 1:16
to be ready to every good *w* ... Titus 3:1
not unrighteous to forget your *w* ... Heb 6:10
in every good *w* to do his will ... Heb 13:21
let patience have her perfect *w* ... Jas 1:4
hearer, but a doer of the *w* ... Jas 1:25
is confusion and every evil *w* ... Jas 3:16
according to every man's *w* ... 1Pet 1:17
man according as his *w* shall be ... Rev 22:12

## WORKER

was a man of Tyre, a *w* in brass ... 1Kin 7:14

## WORKERS

Moreover the *w* with familiar ... 2Kin 23:24
*w* of stone and timber, and all ... 1Chr 22:15
punishment to the *w* of iniquity ... Job 31:3
in company with the *w* of iniquity ... Job 34:8
where the *w* of iniquity may hide ... Job 34:22
thou hatest all *w* of iniquity ... Ps 5:5
from me, all ye *w* of iniquity ... Ps 6:8
Have all the *w* of iniquity no ... Ps 14:4
with the *w* of iniquity, which ... Ps 28:3
There are the *w* of iniquity ... Ps 36:12
envious against the *w* of iniquity ... Ps 37:1
Have the *w* of iniquity no ... Ps 53:4
Deliver me from the *w* of iniquity ... Ps 59:2
insurrection of the *w* of iniquity ... Ps 64:2
when all the *w* of iniquity do ... Ps 92:7
all the *w* of iniquity shall be ... Ps 92:9
all the *w* of iniquity boast ... Ps 94:4
for me against the *w* of iniquity ... Ps 94:16
them forth with the *w* of iniquity ... Ps 125:5
and the gins of the *w* of iniquity ... Ps 141:9
shall be to the *w* of iniquity ... Prov 10:29
shall be to the *w* of iniquity ... Prov 21:15
from me, all ye *w* of iniquity ... Lk 13:27
are all *w* of miracles ... 1Cor 12:29
as *w* together with him, beseech ... 2Cor 6:1
are false apostles, deceitful *w* ... 2Cor 11:13
Beware of dogs, beware of evil *w* ... Phil 3:2
fellow *w* unto the kingdom of God ... Col 4:11

## WORKETH

all these things *w* God oftentimes ... Job 33:29
*w* righteousness, and speaketh the ... Ps 15:2

He that *w* deceit shall not dwell ... Ps 101:7
The wicked *w* a deceitful work ... Prov 11:18
and a flattering mouth *w* ruin ... Prov 26:28
*w* willingly with her hands ... Prov 31:13
What profit hath he that *w* in ... Eccl 3:9
the tongs both *w* in the coals ... Is 44:12
*w* it with the strength of his ... Is 44:12
*w* righteousness, those that ... Is 64:5
he *w* signs and wonders in heaven ... Dan 6:27
them, My Father *w* hitherto ... Jn 5:17
*w* righteousness, is accepted with ... Acts 10:35
peace, to every man that *w* good ... Rom 2:10
Now to him that *w* is the reward ... Rom 4:4
But to him that *w* not, but ... Rom 4:5
Because the law *w* wrath ... Rom 4:15
that tribulation *w* patience ... Rom 5:3
Love *w* no ill to his neighbour ... Rom 13:10
the same God which *w* all in all ... 1Cor 12:6
But all these *w* that one and the ... 1Cor 12:11
for he *w* the work of the Lord, as ... 1Cor 16:10
So then death *w* in us, but life ... 2Cor 4:12
*w* for us a far more exceeding and ... 2Cor 4:17
For godly sorrow *w* repentance to ... 2Cor 7:10
the sorrow of the world *w* death ... 2Cor 7:10
*w* miracles among you, doeth he it ... Gal 3:5
but faith which *w* by love ... Gal 5:6
to the purpose of him who *w* all ... Eph 1:11
the spirit that now *w* in the ... Eph 2:2
to the power that *w* in us ... Eph 3:20
God which *w* in you both to will ... Phil 2:13
working, which *w* in me mightily ... Col 1:29
which effectually *w* also in you ... 1Th 2:13
trying of your faith *w* patience ... Jas 1:3
For the wrath of man *w* not the ... Jas 1:20
neither whatsoever *w* abomination ... Rev 21:27

**WORKFELLOW**

Timotheus my *w*, and Lucius, and ... Rom 16:21

**WORKING**

like a sharp rasor, *w* deceitfully ... Ps 52:2
*w* salvation in the midst of the ... Ps 74:12
in counsel, and excellent in *w* ... Is 28:29
east shall be shut the six *w* days ... Eze 46:1
where, the Lord *w* with them, and ... Mk 16:20
men with men *w* that which is ... Rom 1:27
*w* death in me by that which is ... Rom 7:13
And labour, *w* with our own hands ... 1Cor 4:12
have not we power to forbear *w* ... 1Cor 9:6
To another the *w* of miracles ... 1Cor 12:10
according to the *w* of his mighty ... Eph 1:19
by the effectual *w* of his power ... Eph 3:7
according to the effectual *w* in ... Eph 4:16
*w* with his hands the thing which ... Eph 4:28
according to the *w* whereby he is ... Phil 3:21
striving according to his *w* ... Col 1:29
the *w* of Satan with all power ... 2Th 2:9
*w* not at all, but are busybodies ... 2Th 3:11
his will, *w* in you that which is ... Heb 13:21
*w* miracles, which go forth unto ... Rev 16:14

**WORKMAN**

the engraver, and of the cunning *w* ... Ex 35:35
Dan, an engraver, and a cunning *w* ... Ex 38:23
work of the hands of a cunning *w* ... Song 7:1
The *w* melteth a graven image, and ... Is 40:19
*w* to prepare a graven image ... Is 40:20
the work of the hands of the *w* ... Jer 10:3
from Uphaz, the work of the *w* ... Jer 10:9
the *w* made it ... Hos 8:6
for the *w* is worthy of his meat ... Mt 10:10
a *w* that needeth not to be ... 2Ti 2:15

**WORKMANSHIP**

knowledge, and in all manner of *w* ... Ex 31:3
to work in all manner of *w* ... Ex 31:5
knowledge, and in all manner of *w* ... Ex 35:31
according to all the *w* thereof ... 2Kin 16:10
of *w* every willing skilful man ... 1Chr 28:21
the *w* of thy tabrets and of thy ... Eze 28:13
For we are his *w*, created in ... Eph 2:10

**WORKMEN**

But they gave that to the *w* ... 2Kin 12:14
the money to be bestowed on *w* ... 2Kin 12:15
Moreover there are *w* with thee in ... 1Chr 22:15
the number of the *w* according to ... 1Chr 25:1
*w* wrought, and the work ... 2Chr 24:13
*w* that had the oversight of the ... 2Chr 34:10
they gave it to the *w* that ... 2Chr 34:10
and to the hand of the *w* ... 2Chr 34:17
to set forward the *w* in the house ... Ezr 3:9
and the *w*, they are of men ... Is 44:11
with the *w* of like occupation ... Acts 19:25

**WORKMEN'S**

and her right hand to the *w* hammer .. Judg 5:26

**WORK'S**

highly in love for their *w* sake ... 1Th 5:13

**WORKS**

let the people from their *w* ... Ex 5:4
them, saying, Fulfil your *w* ... Ex 5:13
serve them, nor do after their *w* ... Ex 23:24
To devise cunning *w*, to work in ... Ex 31:4
And to devise curious *w*, to work ... Ex 35:32
hath sent me to do all these *w* ... Num 16:28
thee in all the *w* of thy hand ... Deut 2:7
that can do according to thy *w* ... Deut 3:24
God shall bless thee in all thy *w* ... Deut 15:10
in all the *w* of thine hands, ... Deut 16:15
had known all the *w* of the LORD ... Josh 24:31
seen all the great *w* of the LORD ... Judg 2:7
nor yet the *w* which he had done ... Judg 2:10
According to all the *w* which they ... 1Sa 8:8
because his *w* have been to ... 1Sa 19:4
and cunning to work all *w* in brass ... 1Kin 7:14
told him all the *w* that the man ... 1Kin 13:11
with all the *w* of their hands ... 2Kin 22:17
talk ye of all his wondrous *w* ... 1Chr 16:9
marvellous *w* that he hath done ... 1Chr 16:12
his marvellous *w* among all ... 1Chr 16:24
even all the *w* of this pattern ... 1Chr 28:19
the LORD hath broken thy *w* ... 2Chr 20:37
Hezekiah prospered in all his *w* ... 2Chr 32:30
with all the *w* of their hands ... 2Chr 34:25
according to these their *w* ... Neh 6:14
turned they from their wicked *w* ... Neh 9:35
Therefore he knoweth their *w* ... Job 34:25
and consider the wondrous *w* of God .. Job 37:14
the wondrous *w* of him which is ... Job 37:16
dominion over the *w* of thy hands ... Ps 8:6
shew forth all thy marvellous *w* ... Ps 9:1
they have done abominable *w* ... Ps 14:1
and tell of all thy wondrous *w* ... Ps 26:7
they regard not the *w* of the LORD ... Ps 28:5
all his *w* are done in truth ... Ps 33:4
he considereth all their *w* ... Ps 33:15
are thy wonderful *w* which thou ... Ps 40:5
behold the *w* of the LORD, what ... Ps 46:8
How terrible art thou in thy *w* ... Ps 66:3
Come and see the *w* of God ... Ps 66:5
have I declared thy wondrous *w* ... Ps 71:17
GOD, that I may declare all thy *w* ... Ps 73:28
is near thy wondrous *w* declare ... Ps 75:1
I will remember the *w* of the LORD ... Ps 77:11
his wonderful *w* that he hath done ... Ps 78:4
God, and not forget the *w* of God ... Ps 78:7
And forgat his *w*, and his wonders ... Ps 78:11
believed not for his wondrous *w* ... Ps 78:32
there any *w* like unto thy *w* ... Ps 86:8
triumph in the *w* of thy hands ... Ps 92:4
O LORD, how great are thy *w* ... Ps 92:5
all his *w* in all places of his ... Ps 103:22
satisfied with the fruit of thy *w* ... Ps 104:13
O LORD, how manifold are thy *w* ... Ps 104:24
the LORD shall rejoice in his *w* ... Ps 104:31
talk ye of all his wondrous *w* ... Ps 105:2
marvellous *w* that he hath done ... Ps 105:5
They soon forgat his *w* ... Ps 106:13
Wondrous *w* in the land of Ham, and . Ps 106:22
the heathen, and learned their *w* ... Ps 106:35
they defiled with their own *w* ... Ps 106:39
for his wonderful *w* to the ... Ps 107:8
for his wonderful *w* to the ... Ps 107:15
for his wonderful *w* to the ... Ps 107:21
declare his *w* with rejoicing ... Ps 107:22
These see the *w* of the LORD ... Ps 107:24
for his wonderful *w* to the ... Ps 107:31
The *w* of the LORD are great, ... Ps 111:2
his wonderful *w* to be remembered ... Ps 111:4
his people the power of his *w* ... Ps 111:6
The *w* of his hands are verity and ... Ps 111:7
and declare the *w* of the LORD ... Ps 118:17
so shall I talk of thy wondrous *w* ... Ps 119:27
forsake not the *w* of thine own ... Ps 138:8
marvellous are thy *w* ... Ps 139:14
to practise wicked *w* with men ... Ps 141:4
I meditate on all thy *w* ... Ps 143:5
shall praise thy *w* to another ... Ps 145:4
thy majesty, and of thy wondrous *w* ... Ps 145:5
tender mercies are over all his *w* ... Ps 145:9
All thy *w* shall praise thee, O ... Ps 145:10
his ways, and holy in all his *w* ... Ps 145:17
of tapestry, with carved *w* ... Prov 7:16
of his way, before his *w* of old ... Prov 8:22
Commit thy *w* unto the LORD, and ... Prov 16:3
to every man according to his *w* ... Prov 24:12
let her own *w* praise her in the ... Prov 31:31
I have seen all the *w* that are ... Eccl 1:14
I made me great *w* ... Eccl 2:4
Then I looked on all the *w* that ... Eccl 2:11
a man should rejoice in his own *w* ... Eccl 3:22
and the wise, and their *w*, are in ... Eccl 9:1
for God now accepteth thy *w* ... Eccl 9:7
not the *w* of God who maketh all ... Eccl 11:5
also hast wrought all our *w* in us ... Is 26:12
their *w* are in the dark, and they ... Is 29:15
their *w* are nothing ... Is 41:29
thy righteousness, and thy *w* ... Is 57:12
cover themselves with their *w* ... Is 59:6
their *w* are *w* of iniquity ... Is 59:6
For I know their *w* and their ... Is 66:18
worshipped the *w* of their own ... Jer 1:16
because ye have done all these *w* ... Jer 7:13
according to all his wondrous *w* ... Jer 21:2
to anger with the *w* of your hands ... Jer 25:6
provoke me to anger with the *w* of ... Jer 25:7
according to the *w* of their own ... Jer 25:14
wrath with the *w* of your hands ... Jer 44:8
thou hast trusted in thy *w* ... Jer 48:7
down, and your *w* may be abolished ... Eze 6:6
of heaven, all whose *w* are truth ... Dan 4:37
in all his *w* which he doeth ... Dan 9:14
will never forget any of their *w* ... Amos 8:7
And God saw their *w*, that they ... Jonah 3:10
all the *w* of the house of Ahab, ... Mic 6:16
that they may see your good *w* ... Mt 5:16
in thy name done many wonderful *w* ... Mt 7:22
in the prison the *w* of Christ ... Mt 11:2
most of his mighty *w* were done ... Mt 11:20
for if the mighty *w*, which were ... Mt 11:21
for if the mighty *w*, which have ... Mt 11:23
this wisdom, and these mighty *w* ... Mt 13:54
he did not many mighty *w* there ... Mt 13:58
therefore mighty *w* do shew forth ... Mt 14:2
every man according to his *w* ... Mt 16:27
but do not ye after their *w* ... Mt 23:3
But all their *w* they do for to be ... Mt 23:5
that even such mighty *w* are ... Mk 6:2
therefore mighty *w* do shew forth ... Mk 6:14
for if the mighty *w* had been done ... Lk 10:13
the mighty *w* that they had seen ... Lk 19:37
shew him greater *w* than these ... Jn 5:20
for the *w* which the Father hath ... Jn 5:36
the same *w* that I do, bear ... Jn 5:36
that we might work the *w* of God ... Jn 6:28
may see the *w* that thou doest ... Jn 7:3
that the *w* thereof are evil ... Jn 7:7
ye would do the *w* of Abraham ... Jn 8:39
but that the *w* of God should be ... Jn 9:3
I must work the *w* of him that ... Jn 9:4
the *w* that I do in my Father's ... Jn 10:25
Many good *w* have I shewed you ... Jn 10:32
which of those *w* do ye stone me ... Jn 10:32
If I do not the *w* of my Father ... Jn 10:37
ye believe not me, believe the *w* ... Jn 10:38
dwelleth in me, he doeth the *w* ... Jn 14:10
the *w* that I do shall he do also ... Jn 14:12
greater *w* than these shall he do ... Jn 14:12
the *w* which none other man did ... Jn 15:24
tongues the wonderful *w* of God ... Acts 2:11
rejoiced in the *w* of their own ... Acts 7:41
this woman was full of good *w* ... Acts 9:36
Known unto God are all his *w* from .. Acts 15:18
God, and do *w* meet for repentance ... Acts 26:20
what law? of *w*? ... Rom 3:27
if Abraham were justified by *w* ... Rom 4:2
imputeth righteousness without *w* ... Rom 4:6
to election might stand, not of *w* ... Rom 9:11
as it were by the *w* of the law ... Rom 9:32
by grace, then is it no more of *w* ... Rom 11:6
But if it be of *w*, then is it no ... Rom 11:6
rulers are not a terror to good *w* ... Rom 13:3
cast off the *w* of darkness ... Rom 13:12
end shall be according to their *w* ... 2Cor 11:15
not justified by the *w* of the law ... Gal 2:16
and not by the *w* of the law ... Gal 2:16
for by the *w* of the law shall no ... Gal 2:16
ye the Spirit by the *w* of the law ... Gal 3:2
doeth he it by the *w* of the law ... Gal 3:5
For as many as are of the *w* of ... Gal 3:10
Now the *w* of the flesh are ... Gal 5:19
Not of *w*, lest any man should ... Eph 2:9
in Christ Jesus unto good *w* ... Eph 2:10
with the unfruitful *w* of darkness ... Eph 5:11
enemies in your mind by wicked *w* ... Col 1:21
professing godliness) with good *w* ... 1Ti 2:10
Well reported of for good *w* ... 1Ti 5:10
Likewise also the good *w* of some ... 1Ti 5:25
good, that they be rich in good *w* ... 1Ti 6:18
calling, not according to our *w* ... 2Ti 1:9
furnished unto all good *w* ... 2Ti 3:17
reward him according to his *w* ... 2Ti 4:14
but in *w* they deny him, being ... Titus 1:16
thyself a pattern of good *w* ... Titus 2:7
people, zealous of good *w* ... Titus 2:14
Not by *w* of righteousness which ... Titus 3:5
be careful to maintain good *w* ... Titus 3:8
good *w* for necessary uses ... Titus 3:14
heavens are the *w* of thine hands ... Heb 1:10
set him over the *w* of thy hands ... Heb 2:7
me, and saw my *w* forty years ... Heb 3:9
although the *w* were finished from ... Heb 4:3
the seventh day from all his *w* ... Heb 4:4
also hath ceased from his own *w* ... Heb 4:10
of repentance from dead *w* ... Heb 6:1
dead *w* to serve the living God ... Heb 9:14
to provoke unto love and to good *w* .. Heb 10:24
say he hath faith, and have not *w* ... Jas 2:14
Even so faith, if it hath not *w* ... Jas 2:17
say, Thou hast faith, and I have *w* ... Jas 2:18
shew me thy faith without thy *w* ... Jas 2:18
I will shew thee my faith by my *w* ... Jas 2:18
man, that faith without *w* is dead ... Jas 2:20
Abraham our father justified by *w* ... Jas 2:21
thou how faith wrought with his *w* ... Jas 2:22
by *w* was faith made perfect ... Jas 2:22
how that by *w* a man is justified ... Jas 2:24
Rahab the harlot justified by *w* ... Jas 2:25
so faith without *w* is dead also ... Jas 2:26
his *w* with meekness of wisdom ... Jas 3:13
they may by your good *w*, which ... 1Pet 2:12
the *w* that are therein shall be ... 2Pet 3:10
might destroy the *w* of the devil ... 1Jn 3:8
Because his own *w* were evil ... 1Jn 3:12
I know thy *w*, and thy labour, and ... Rev 2:2
and repent, and do the first *w* ... Rev 2:5
I know thy *w*, and tribulation, and ... Rev 2:9
I know thy *w*, and where thou ... Rev 2:13
I know thy *w*, and charity, and ... Rev 2:19
faith, and thy patience, and thy *w* ... Rev 2:19
one of you according to your *w* ... Rev 2:23
keepeth my *w* unto the end, to him ... Rev 2:26
I know thy *w*, that thou hast a ... Rev 3:1
found thy *w* perfect before God ... Rev 3:2
I know thy *w* ... Rev 3:8
I know thy *w*, that thou art ... Rev 3:15
not of the *w* of their hands ... Rev 9:20
and their *w* do follow them ... Rev 14:13
Great and marvellous are thy *w* ... Rev 15:3
her double according to her *w* ... Rev 18:6
the books, according to their *w* ... Rev 20:12

every man according to their *w* ... Rev 20:13

**WORKS'**

believe me for the very *w* sake ... Jn 14:11

**WORLD**

and he hath set the *w* upon them ... 1Sa 2:8
of the *w* were discovered, at the ... 2Sa 22:16
the *w* also shall be stable, that ... 1Chr 16:30
darkness, and chased out of the *w* ... Job 18:18
Or who hath disposed the whole *w* ... Job 34:13
the face of the *w* in the earth ... Job 37:12
judge the *w* in righteousness ... Ps 9:8
hand, O LORD, from men of the *w* ... Ps 17:14
the foundations of the *w* were ... Ps 18:15
their words to the end of the *w* ... Ps 19:4
the ends of the *w* shall remember ... Ps 22:27
the *w*, and they that dwell therein ... Ps 24:1
of the *w* stand in awe of him ... Ps 33:8
ear, all ye inhabitants of the *w* ... Ps 49:1
for the *w* is mine, and the fulness ... Ps 50:12
the ungodly, who prosper in the *w* ... Ps 73:12
the lightnings lightened the *w* ... Ps 77:18
as for the *w* and the fulness ... Ps 89:11
hadst formed the earth and the *w* ... Ps 90:2
the *w* also is stablished, that it ... Ps 93:1
the *w* also shall be established ... Ps 96:10
judge the *w* with righteousness ... Ps 96:13
His lightnings enlightened the *w* ... Ps 97:4
the *w*, and they that dwell therein ... Ps 98:7
shall he judge the *w*, and the ... Ps 98:9
highest part of the dust of the *w* ... Prov 8:26
he hath set the *w* in their heart ... Eccl 3:11
will punish the *w* for their evil ... Is 13:11
That made the *w* as a wilderness, ... Is 14:17
the face of the *w* with cities ... Is 14:21
All ye inhabitants of the *w* ... Is 18:3
the *w* upon the face of the earth ... Is 23:17
the *w* languisheth and fadeth away, ... Is 24:4
the inhabitants of the *w* will ... Is 26:9
the inhabitants of the *w* fallen ... Is 26:18
fill the face of the *w* with fruit ... Is 27:6
the *w*, and all things that come ... Is 34:1
with the inhabitants of the *w* ... Is 38:11
nor confounded *w* without end ... Is 45:17
proclaimed unto the end of the *w* ... Is 62:11
of the *w* men have not heard ... Is 64:4
established the *w* by his wisdom ... Jer 10:12
and all the kingdoms of the *w* ... Jer 25:26
established the *w* by his wisdom ... Jer 51:15
and all the inhabitants of the *w* ... Lam 4:12
at his presence, yea, the *w* ... Nah 1:5
him all the kingdoms of the *w* ... Mt 4:8
Ye are the light of the *w* ... Mt 5:14
forgiven him, neither in this *w* ... Mt 12:32
neither in the *w* to come ... Mt 12:32
and the care of this *w*, and the ... Mt 13:22
from the foundation of the *w* ... Mt 13:35
The field is the *w* ... Mt 13:38
the harvest is the end of the *w* ... Mt 13:39
shall it be in the end of this *w* ... Mt 13:40
shall it be at the end of the *w* ... Mt 13:49
if he shall gain the whole *w* ... Mt 16:26
Woe unto the *w* because of ... Mt 18:7
coming, and of the end of the *w* ... Mt 24:3
shall be preached in all the *w* ... Mt 24:14
beginning of the *w* to this time ... Mt 24:21
you from the foundation of the *w* ... Mt 25:34
shall be preached in the whole *w* ... Mt 26:13
alway, even unto the end of the *w* ... Mt 28:20
And the cares of this *w*, and the ... Mk 4:19
man, if he shall gain the whole *w* ... Mk 8:36
in the *w* to come eternal life ... Mk 10:30
preached throughout the whole *w* ... Mk 14:9
unto them, Go ye into all the *w* ... Mk 16:15
which have been since the *w* began ... Lk 1:70
that all the *w* should be taxed ... Lk 2:1
of the *w* in a moment of time ... Lk 4:5
if he gain the whole *w*, and lose ... Lk 9:25
shed from the foundation of the *w* ... Lk 11:50
the nations of the *w* seek after ... Lk 12:30
for the children of this *w* are in ... Lk 16:8
in the *w* to come life everlasting ... Lk 18:30
The children of this *w* marry ... Lk 20:34
accounted worthy to obtain that *w* ... Lk 20:35
every man that cometh into the *w* ... Jn 1:9
He was in the *w* ... Jn 1:10
the *w* was made by him, and the ... Jn 1:10
by him, and the *w* knew him not ... Jn 1:10
taketh away the sin of the *w* ... Jn 1:29
For God so loved the *w*, that he ... Jn 3:16
into the *w* to condemn the *w* ... Jn 3:17
but that the *w* through him might ... Jn 3:17
that light is come into the *w* ... Jn 3:19
the Christ, the Saviour of the *w* ... Jn 4:42
that should come into the *w* ... Jn 6:14
heaven, and giveth life unto the *w* ... Jn 6:33
I will give for the life of the *w* ... Jn 6:51
things, shew thyself to the *w* ... Jn 7:4
The *w* cannot hate you ... Jn 7:7
saying, I am the light of the *w* ... Jn 8:12
ye are of this *w* ... Jn 8:23
I am not of this *w* ... Jn 8:23
I speak to the *w* those things ... Jn 8:26
As long as I am in the *w* ... Jn 9:5
I am the light of the *w* ... Jn 9:5
Since the *w* began was it not ... Jn 9:32
judgment I am come into this *w* ... Jn 9:39
sanctified, and sent into the *w* ... Jn 10:36
he seeth the light of this *w* ... Jn 11:9
God, which should come into the *w* ... Jn 11:27
behold, the *w* is gone after him ... Jn 12:19
*w* shall keep it unto life eternal ... Jn 12:25
Now is the judgment of this *w* ... Jn 12:31
the prince of this *w* be cast out ... Jn 12:31
I am come a light into the *w* ... Jn 12:46
for I came not to judge the *w* ... Jn 12:47
but to save the *w* ... Jn 12:47
out of this *w* unto the Father ... Jn 13:1
loved his own which were in the *w* ... Jn 13:1
whom the *w* cannot receive, ... Jn 14:17
while, and the *w* seeth me no more ... Jn 14:19
unto us, and not unto the *w* ... Jn 14:22
not as the *w* giveth, give I unto ... Jn 14:27
for the prince of this *w* cometh ... Jn 14:30
But that the *w* may know that I ... Jn 14:31
If the *w* hate you, ye know that ... Jn 15:18
If ye were of the *w* ... Jn 15:19
the *w* would love his own ... Jn 15:19
but because ye are not of the *w* ... Jn 15:19
I have chosen you out of the *w* ... Jn 15:19
therefore the *w* hateth you ... Jn 15:19
he will reprove the *w* of sin ... Jn 16:8
the prince of this *w* is judged ... Jn 16:11
lament, but the *w* shall rejoice ... Jn 16:20
joy that a man is born into the *w* ... Jn 16:21
the Father, and am come into the *w* ... Jn 16:28
again, I leave the *w*, and go to ... Jn 16:28
In the *w* ye shall have ... Jn 16:33
I have overcome the *w* ... Jn 16:33
I had with thee before the *w* was ... Jn 17:5
which thou gavest me out of the *w* ... Jn 17:6
I pray not for the *w*, but for ... Jn 17:9
And now I am no more in the *w* ... Jn 17:11
but these are in the *w* ... Jn 17:11
While I was with them in the *w* ... Jn 17:12
and these things I speak in the *w* ... Jn 17:13
the *w* hath hated them ... Jn 17:14
because they are not of the *w* ... Jn 17:14
even as I am not of the *w* ... Jn 17:14
shouldest take them out of the *w* ... Jn 17:15
They are not of the *w* ... Jn 17:16
even as I am not of the *w* ... Jn 17:16
As thou hast sent me into the *w* ... Jn 17:18
have I also sent them into the *w* ... Jn 17:18
that the *w* may believe that thou ... Jn 17:21
that the *w* may know that thou ... Jn 17:23
me before the foundation of the *w* ... Jn 17:24
the *w* hath not known thee ... Jn 17:25
him, I spake openly to the *w* ... Jn 18:20
My kingdom is not of this *w* ... Jn 18:36
if my kingdom were of this *w* ... Jn 18:36
for this cause came I into the *w* ... Jn 18:37
I suppose that even the *w* itself ... Jn 21:25
holy prophets since the *w* began ... Acts 3:21
great dearth throughout all the *w* ... Acts 11:28
works from the beginning of the *w* ... Acts 15:18
These that have turned the *w* ... Acts 17:6
God that made the *w* and all things .. Acts 17:24
*w* in righteousness by that man ... Acts 17:31
all Asia and the *w* worshippeth ... Acts 19:27
all the Jews throughout the *w* ... Acts 24:5
spoken of throughout the whole *w* ... Rom 1:8
of the *w* are clearly seen ... Rom 1:20
then how shall God judge the *w* ... Rom 3:6
all the *w* may become guilty ... Rom 3:19
he should be the heir of the *w* ... Rom 4:13
by one man sin entered into the *w* ... Rom 5:12
until the law sin was in the *w* ... Rom 5:13
words unto the ends of the *w* ... Rom 10:18
of them be the riches of the *w* ... Rom 11:12
them be the reconciling of the *w* ... Rom 11:15
And be not conformed to this *w* ... Rom 12:2
was kept secret since the *w* began ... Rom 16:25
where is the disputer of this *w* ... 1Cor 1:20
made foolish the wisdom of this *w* ... 1Cor 1:20
God the *w* by wisdom knew not God . 1Cor 1:21
of the *w* to confound the wise ... 1Cor 1:27
*w* to confound the things which ... 1Cor 1:27
And base things of the *w*, and ... 1Cor 1:28
yet not the wisdom of this *w* ... 1Cor 2:6
nor of the princes of this *w* ... 1Cor 2:6
before the *w* unto our glory ... 1Cor 2:7
of the princes of this *w* knew ... 1Cor 2:8
received, not the spirit of the *w* ... 1Cor 2:12
you seemeth to be wise in this *w* ... 1Cor 3:18
For the wisdom of this *w* is ... 1Cor 3:19
or Apollos, or Cephas, or the *w* ... 1Cor 3:22
are made a spectacle unto the *w* ... 1Cor 4:9
we are made as the filth of the *w* ... 1Cor 4:13
with the fornicators of this *w* ... 1Cor 5:10
must ye needs go out of the *w* ... 1Cor 5:10
that the saints shall judge the *w* ... 1Cor 6:2
if the *w* shall be judged by you, ... 1Cor 6:2
And they that use this *w*, as not ... 1Cor 7:31
fashion of this *w* passeth away ... 1Cor 7:31
for the things that are of the *w* ... 1Cor 7:33
careth for the things of the *w* ... 1Cor 7:34
that an idol is nothing in the *w* ... 1Cor 8:4
eat no flesh while the *w* standeth ... 1Cor 8:13
whom the ends of the *w* are come ... 1Cor 10:11
not be condemned with the *w* ... 1Cor 11:32
so many kinds of voices in the *w* ... 1Cor 14:10
had our conversation in the *w* ... 2Cor 1:12
In whom the god of this *w* hath ... 2Cor 4:4
reconciling the *w* unto himself ... 2Cor 5:19
the sorrow of the *w* worketh death ... 2Cor 7:10
us from this present evil *w* ... Gal 1:4
under the elements of the *w* ... Gal 4:3
by whom the *w* is crucified unto ... Gal 6:14
unto me, and I unto the *w* ... Gal 6:14
before the foundation of the *w* ... Eph 1:4
that is named, not only in this *w* ... Eph 1:21
according to the course of this *w* ... Eph 2:2
no hope, and without God in the *w* ... Eph 2:12
of the *w* hath been hid in God ... Eph 3:9
all ages, *w* without end ... Eph 3:21
rulers of the darkness of this *w* ... Eph 6:12
whom ye shine as lights in the *w* ... Phil 2:15
unto you, as it is in all the *w* ... Col 1:6
men, after the rudiments of the *w* ... Col 2:8
from the rudiments of the *w* ... Col 2:20
why, as though living in the *w* ... Col 2:20
came into the *w* to save sinners ... 1Ti 1:15
Gentiles, believed on in the *w* ... 1Ti 3:16
we brought nothing into this *w* ... 1Ti 6:7
them that are rich in this *w* ... 1Ti 6:17
Christ Jesus before the *w* began ... 2Ti 1:9
me, having loved this present *w* ... 2Ti 4:10
lie, promised before the *w* began ... Titus 1:2
and godly, in this present *w* ... Titus 2:12
in the firstbegotten into the *w* ... Heb 1:6
put in subjection the *w* to come ... Heb 2:5
from the foundation of the *w* ... Heb 4:3
and the powers of the *w* to come ... Heb 6:5
since the foundation of the *w* ... Heb 9:26
*w* hath he appeared to put away ... Heb 9:26
when he cometh into the *w* ... Heb 10:5
by the which he condemned the *w* ... Heb 11:7
(Of whom the *w* was not worthy ... Heb 11:38
keep himself unspotted from the *w* ... Jas 1:27
the poor of this *w* rich in faith ... Jas 2:5
tongue is a fire, a *w* of iniquity ... Jas 3:6
of the *w* is enmity with God ... Jas 4:4
of the *w* is the enemy of God ... Jas 4:4
before the foundation of the *w* ... 1Pet 1:20
your brethren that are in the *w* ... 1Pet 5:9
that is in the *w* through lust ... 2Pet 1:4
And spared not the old *w*, but ... 2Pet 2:5
flood upon the *w* of the ungodly ... 2Pet 2:5
*w* through the knowledge of the ... 2Pet 2:20
Whereby the *w* that then was, ... 2Pet 3:6
also for the sins of the whole *w* ... 1Jn 2:2
Love not the *w*, neither the ... 1Jn 2:15
the things that are in the *w* ... 1Jn 2:15
If any man love the *w*, the love ... 1Jn 2:15
For all that is in the *w*, the ... 1Jn 2:16
of the Father, but is of the *w* ... 1Jn 2:16
the *w* passeth away, and the lust ... 1Jn 2:17
therefore the *w* knoweth us not, ... 1Jn 3:1
my brethren, if the *w* hate you ... 1Jn 3:13
prophets are gone out into the *w* ... 1Jn 4:1
even now already is it in the *w* ... 1Jn 4:3
in you, than he that is in the *w* ... 1Jn 4:4
They are of the *w* ... 1Jn 4:5
therefore speak they of the *w* ... 1Jn 4:5
and the *w* heareth them ... 1Jn 4:5
his only begotten Son into the *w* ... 1Jn 4:9
Son to be the Saviour of the *w* ... 1Jn 4:14
as he is, so are we in this *w* ... 1Jn 4:17
is born of God overcometh the *w* ... 1Jn 5:4
the victory that overcometh the *w* ... 1Jn 5:4
Who is he that overcometh the *w* ... 1Jn 5:5
the whole *w* lieth in wickedness ... 1Jn 5:19
deceivers are entered into the *w* ... 2Jn 7
which shall come upon all the *w* ... Rev 3:10
The kingdoms of this *w* are become ... Rev 11:15
which deceiveth the whole *w* ... Rev 12:9
all the *w* wondered after the ... Rev 13:3
from the foundation of the *w* ... Rev 13:8
of the earth and of the whole *w* ... Rev 16:14
life from the foundation of the *w* ... Rev 17:8

**WORLDLY**

*w* lusts, we should live soberly, ... Titus 2:12
divine service, and a *w* sanctuary ... Heb 9:1

**WORLD'S**

But whoso hath this *w* good ... 1Jn 3:17

**WORLDS**

by whom also he made the *w* ... Heb 1:2
faith we understand that the *w* ... Heb 11:3

**WORM**

neither was there any *w* therein ... Ex 16:24
to the *w*, Thou art my mother, and ... Job 17:14
the *w* shall feed sweetly on him ... Job 24:20
How much less man, that is a *w* ... Job 25:6
and the son of man, which is a *w* ... Job 25:6
But I am a *w*, and no man ... Ps 22:6
the *w* is spread under thee, and ... Is 14:11
thou *w* Jacob, and ye men of Israel ... Is 41:14
the *w* shall eat them like wool ... Is 51:8
for their *w* shall not die, ... Is 66:24
But God prepared a *w* when the ... Jonah 4:7
Where their *w* dieth not, and the ... Mk 9:44
Where their *w* dieth not, and the ... Mk 9:46
Where their *w* dieth not, and the ... Mk 9:48

**WORMS**

until the morning, and it bred *w* ... Ex 16:20
for the *w* shall eat them ... Deut 28:39
My flesh is clothed with *w* ... Job 7:5
after my skin *w* destroy this body ... Job 19:26
dust, and the *w* shall cover them ... Job 21:26
under thee, and the *w* cover thee ... Is 14:11
their holes like *w* of the earth ... Mic 7:17
and he was eaten of *w*, and gave up .. Acts 12:23

**WORMWOOD**

you a root that beareth gall and *w* ... Deut 29:18
But her end is bitter as *w* ... Prov 5:4
them, even this people, with *w* ... Jer 9:15

Behold, I will feed them with *w* Jer 23:15
he hath made me drunken with *w* Lam 3:15
affliction and my misery, the *w* Lam 3:19
Ye who turn judgment to *w* Amos 5:7
the name of the star is called *W* Rev 8:11
third part of the waters became *w* Rev 8:11

## WORSE

now will we deal *w* with thee Gen 19:9
that will be *w* unto thee than all 2Sa 19:7
did *w* than all that were before 1Kin 16:25
was put to the *w* before Israel 2Kin 14:12
were put to the *w* before Israel 1Chr 19:16
were put to the *w* before Israel 1Chr 19:19
be put to the *w* before the enemy 2Chr 6:24
was put to the *w* before the Israel 2Chr 25:22
to do *w* than the heathen, whom 2Chr 33:9
they did *w* than their fathers Jer 7:26
ye have done *w* than your fathers Jer 16:12
why should he see your faces *w* Dan 1:10
garment, and the rent is made *w* Mt 9:16
of that man is *w* than the first Mt 12:45
error shall be *w* than the first Mt 27:64
the old, and the rent is made *w* Mk 2:21
bettered, but rather grew *w* Mk 5:26
of that man is *w* than the first Lk 11:26
well drunk, then that which is *w* Jn 2:10
lest a *w* thing come unto thee Jn 5:14
if we eat not, are we the *w* 1Cor 8:8
not for the better, but for the *w* 1Cor 11:17
faith, and is *w* than an infidel 1Ti 5:8
and seducers shall wax *w* and *w* 2Ti 3:13
the latter end is *w* with them 2Pet 2:20

## WORSHIP

I and the lad will go yonder and *w* Gen 22:5
and *w* ye afar off Ex 24:1
For thou shalt *w* no other god Ex 34:14
shouldest be driven to *w* them Deut 4:19
*w* them, I testify against you Deut 8:19
and serve other gods, and *w* them Deut 11:16
*w* before the LORD thy God Deut 26:10
*w* other gods, and serve them Deut 30:17
his face to the earth, and did *w* Josh 5:14
up out of his city yearly to *w* 1Sa 1:3
with me, that I may *w* the LORD 1Sa 15:25
that I may *w* the LORD thy God 1Sa 15:30
go and serve other gods, and *w* them 1Kin 9:6
people went to *w* before the one 1Kin 12:30
the house of Rimmon to *w* there 2Kin 5:18
shall ye fear, and him shall ye *w* 2Kin 17:36
Ye shall *w* before this altar in 2Kin 18:22
*w* the LORD in the beauty of 1Chr 16:29
go and serve other gods, and *w* them 2Chr 7:19
Ye shall *w* before one altar, and 2Chr 32:12
in thy fear will I *w* toward thy Ps 5:7
the nations shall *w* before thee Ps 22:27
be fat upon earth shall eat and *w* Ps 22:29
*w* the LORD in the beauty of Ps 29:2
and *w* thou him Ps 45:11
All the earth shall *w* thee Ps 66:4
shalt thou *w* any strange god Ps 81:9
come and *w* before thee, O Lord Ps 86:9
O come, let us *w* and bow down Ps 95:6
O *w* the LORD in the beauty of Ps 96:9
*w* him, all ye gods Ps 97:7
our God, and *w* at his footstool Ps 99:5
our God, and *w* at his holy hill Ps 99:9
we will *w* at his footstool Ps 132:7
I will *w* toward thy holy temple, Ps 138:2
they *w* the work of their own Is 2:8
made each one for himself to *w* Is 2:20
shall *w* the LORD in the holy Is 27:13
Ye shall *w* before this altar Is 36:7
they fall down, yea, they *w* Is 46:6
and arise, princes also shall *w* Is 49:7
all flesh come to *w* before me Is 66:23
in at these gates to *w* the LORD Jer 7:2
to *w* them, shall even be as this Jer 13:10
to *w* them, and provoke me not to Jer 25:6
which come to *w* in the LORD's Jer 26:2
did we make her cakes to *w* her Jer 44:19
he shall *w* at the threshold of Eze 46:2
the people of the land shall *w* at Eze 46:3
*w* shall go out by the way of the Eze 46:9
down and *w* the golden image that Dan 3:5
fall down and *w* the golden image Dan 3:10
nor *w* the golden image which thou Dan 3:12
nor *w* the golden image which I Dan 3:14
*w* the image which I have made Dan 3:15
but if ye *w* not, ye shall be cast Dan 3:15
nor *w* the golden image which thou Dan 3:18
might not serve nor *w* any god Dan 3:28
thou shalt no more *w* the work of Mic 5:13
them that *w* the host of heaven Zeph 1:5
and them that *w* and that swear by Zeph 1:5
and men shall *w* him, every one Zeph 2:11
from year to year to *w* the King Zec 14:16
unto Jerusalem to *w* the King Zec 14:17
in the east, and are come to *w* him Mt 2:2
that I may come and *w* him also Mt 2:8
if thou wilt fall down and *w* me Mt 4:9
Thou shalt *w* the Lord thy God, and Mt 4:10
But in vain they do *w* me, Mt 15:9
Howbeit in vain do they *w* me Mk 7:7
If thou therefore wilt *w* me Lk 4:7
Thou shalt *w* the Lord thy God, and Lk 4:8
then shalt thou have *w* in the Lk 14:10
is the place where men ought to *w* Jn 4:20
yet at Jerusalem, *w* the Father Jn 4:21
Ye *w* ye know not what Jn 4:22
we know what we *w* Jn 4:22
shall *w* the Father in spirit Jn 4:23
the Father seeketh such to *w* him Jn 4:23
they that *w* him must Jn 4:24
must *w* him in spirit Jn 4:24
that came up to *w* at the feast Jn 12:20
gave them up to *w* the host of Acts 7:42
figures which ye made to *w* them Acts 7:43
and had come to Jerusalem for to *w* Acts 8:27
Whom therefore ye ignorantly *w* Acts 17:23
men to *w* God contrary to the law Acts 18:13
I went up to Jerusalem for to *w* Acts 24:11
so *w* I the God of my fathers, Acts 24:14
down on his face he will *w* God 1Cor 14:25
which *w* God in the spirit, and Phil 3:3
indeed a shew of wisdom in will *w* Col 2:23
let all the angels of God *w* him Heb 1:6
*w* before thy feet, and to know Rev 3:9
*w* him that liveth for ever and Rev 4:10
that they should not *w* devils Rev 9:20
the altar, and them that *w* therein Rev 11:1
dwell upon the earth shall *w* him Rev 13:8
therein to *w* the first beast Rev 13:12
*w* the image of the beast should Rev 13:15
*w* him that made heaven, and earth, Rev 14:7
voice, If any man *w* the beast Rev 14:9
who *w* the beast and his image, and Rev 14:11
shall come and *w* before thee Rev 15:4
And I fell at his feet to *w* him Rev 19:10
*w* God Rev 19:10
I fell down to *w* before the feet Rev 22:8
*w* God Rev 22:9

## WORSHIPPED

down his head, and *w* the LORD Gen 24:26
*w* the LORD, and blessed the LORD Gen 24:48
he *w* the LORD, bowing himself to Gen 24:52
then they bowed their heads and *w* Ex 4:31
And the people bowed the head and *w* Ex 12:27
them a molten calf, and have *w* it Ex 32:8
and all the people rose up and *w* Ex 33:10
his head toward the earth, and *w* Ex 34:8
*w* them, either the sun, or moon, Deut 17:3
*w* them, gods whom they knew not, Deut 29:26
interpretation thereof, that he *w* Judg 7:15
*w* before the LORD, and returned, 1Sa 1:19
And he *w* the LORD there 1Sa 1:28
and Saul *w* the LORD 1Sa 15:31
into the house of the LORD, and *w* 2Sa 12:20
top of the mount, where he *w* God 2Sa 15:32
upon other gods, and have *w* them 1Kin 9:9
have *w* Ashtoreth the goddess of 1Kin 11:33
served Baal, and *w* him 1Kin 16:31
*w* him, and provoked to anger the 1Kin 22:53
*w* all the host of heaven, and 2Kin 17:16
*w* all the host of heaven, and 2Kin 21:3
that his father served, and *w* them 2Kin 21:21
heads, and *w* the LORD, and the king 1Chr 29:20
ground upon the pavement, and *w* 2Chr 7:3
gods, and *w* them, and served them 2Chr 7:22
And all the congregation *w* 2Chr 29:28
with him bowed themselves, and *w* 2Chr 29:29
and they bowed their heads and *w* 2Chr 29:30
*w* all the host of heaven, and 2Chr 33:3
*w* the LORD with their faces to Neh 8:6
and *w* the LORD their God Neh 9:3
fell down upon the ground, and *w* Job 1:20
in Horeb, and *w* the molten image Ps 106:19
*w* the works of their own hands Jer 1:16
have sought, and whom they have *w* Jer 8:2
have served them, and have *w* them Jer 16:11
*w* other gods, and served them Jer 22:9
they *w* the sun toward the east Eze 8:16
*w* Daniel, and commanded that they Dan 2:46
down and *w* the golden image that Dan 3:7
mother, and fell down, and *w* him Mt 2:11
*w* him, saying, Lord, if thou wilt Mt 8:2
*w* him, saying, My daughter is Mt 9:18
*w* him, saying, Of a truth thou Mt 14:33
*w* him, saying, Lord, help me Mt 15:25
*w* him, saying, Lord, have Mt 18:26
and held him by the feet, and *w* him Mt 28:9
And when they saw him, they *w* him Mt 28:17
Jesus afar off, he ran and *w* him, Mk 5:6
him, and bowing their knees *w* him Mk 15:19
And they *w* him, and returned to Lk 24:52
Our fathers *w* in this mountain Jn 4:20
And he *w* him Jn 9:38
fell down at his feet, and *w* him Acts 10:25
the city of Thyatira, which *w* God Acts 16:14
Neither is *w* with men's hands, as Acts 17:25
named Justus, one that *w* God Acts 18:7
the truth of God into a lie, and *w* Rom 1:25
that is called God, or that is *w* 2Th 2:4
and *w*, leaning upon the top of his Heb 11:21
*w* him that liveth for ever and Rev 5:14
throne on their faces, and *w* God, Rev 7:11
fell upon their faces, and *w* God, Rev 11:16
they *w* the dragon which gave Rev 13:4
they *w* the beast, saying, Who is Rev 13:4
and upon them which *w* his image Rev 16:2
*w* God that sat on the throne, Rev 19:4
beast, and them that *w* his image Rev 19:20
God, and which had not *w* the beast Rev 20:4

## WORSHIPPER

but if any man be a *w* of God Jn 9:31
is a *w* of the great goddess Diana Acts 19:35

## WORSHIPPERS

he might destroy the *w* of Baal 2Kin 10:19
all the *w* of Baal came, so that 2Kin 10:21
vestments for all the *w* of Baal 2Kin 10:22
Baal, and said unto the *w* of Baal 2Kin 10:23
the LORD, but the *w* of Baal only 2Kin 10:23
when the true *w* shall worship the Jn 4:23
because that the *w* once purged Heb 10:2

## WORSHIPPETH

and the host of heaven *w* thee Neh 9:6
yea, he maketh a god, and *w* it Is 44:15
*w* it, and prayeth unto it, and Is 44:17
*w* shall the same hour be cast Dan 3:6
And whoso falleth not down and *w* Dan 3:11
whom all Asia and the world *w* Acts 19:27

## WORSHIPPING

as he was *w* in the house of 2Kin 19:37
fell before the LORD, *w* the LORD 2Chr 20:18
as he was *w* in the house of Is 37:38
*w* him, and desiring a certain Mt 20:20
*w* of angels, intruding into those Col 2:18

## WORST

I will bring the *w* of the heathen Eze 7:24

## WORTH

it is *w* he shall give it me for a Gen 23:9
the land is *w* four hundred Gen 23:15
unto him the *w* of thy estimation Lev 27:23
for he hath been *w* a double hired Deut 15:18
but now thou art *w* ten thousand 2Sa 18:3
give thee the *w* of it in money 1Kin 21:2
liar, and make my speech nothing *w* Job 24:25
heart of the wicked is little *w* Prov 10:20
Howl ye, Woe *w* the day Eze 30:2

## WORTHIES

He shall recount his *w* Nah 2:5

## WORTHILY

do thou *w* in Ephratah, and be Ruth 4:11

## WORTHY

I am not *w* of the least of all Gen 32:10
shall he that is *w* of death be Deut 17:6
whereas he was not *w* of death Deut 19:6
have committed a sin *w* of death Deut 21:22
in the damsel no sin *w* of death Deut 22:26
the wicked man be *w* to be beaten Deut 25:2
unto Hannah he gave a *w* portion 1Sa 1:5
the LORD liveth, ye are *w* to die 1Sa 26:16
the LORD, who is *w* to be praised 2Sa 22:4
If he will shew himself a *w* man 1Kin 1:52
for thou art *w* of death 1Kin 2:26
the LORD, who is *w* to be praised Ps 18:3
saying, This man is *w* to die Jer 26:11
This man is not *w* to die Jer 26:16
I, whose shoes I am not *w* to bear Mt 3:11
I am not *w* that thou shouldest Mt 8:8
for the workman is *w* of his meat Mt 10:10
enter, enquire who in it is *w* Mt 10:11
And if the house be *w*, let your Mt 10:13
but if it be not *w*, let your Mt 10:13
more than me is not *w* of me Mt 10:37
more than me is not *w* of me Mt 10:37
after me, is not *w* of me Mt 10:38
they which were bidden were not *w* Mt 22:8
shoes I am not *w* to stoop down Mk 1:7
therefore fruits *w* of repentance Lk 3:8
whose shoes I am not *w* to unloose Lk 3:16
That he was *w* for whom he should Lk 7:4
for I am not *w* that thou Lk 7:6
I myself *w* to come unto thee Lk 7:7
for the labourer is *w* of his hire Lk 10:7
and did commit things *w* of stripes Lk 12:48
am no more *w* to be called thy son Lk 15:19
am no more *w* to be called thy son Lk 15:21
accounted *w* to obtain that world Lk 20:35
that ye may be accounted *w* to Lk 21:36
nothing *w* of death is done unto Lk 23:15
latchet I am not *w* to unloose Jn 1:27
that they were counted *w* to Acts 5:41
of his feet I am not *w* to loose Acts 13:25
his charge *w* of death or of bonds Acts 23:29
that very *w* deeds are done unto Acts 24:2
committed any thing *w* of death Acts 25:11
had committed nothing *w* of death Acts 25:25
nothing *w* of death or of bonds Acts 26:31
commit such things are *w* of death Rom 1:32
of this present time are not *w* to Rom 8:18
beseech you that ye walk *w* of the Eph 4:1
That ye might walk *w* of the Lord Col 1:10
That ye would walk *w* of God 1Th 2:12
counted *w* of the kingdom of God 2Th 1:5
would count you *w* of this calling 2Th 1:11
*w* of all acceptation, that Christ 1Ti 1:15
saying and *w* of all acceptation 1Ti 4:9
be counted *w* of double honour 1Ti 5:17
The labourer is *w* of his reward 1Ti 5:18
their own masters *w* of all honour 1Ti 6:1
*w* of more glory than Moses Heb 3:3
suppose ye, shall he be thought *w* Heb 10:29
(Of whom the world was not *w* Heb 11:38
Do not they blaspheme that *w* name Jas 2:7
for they are *w* Rev 3:4
Thou art *w*, O Lord, to receive Rev 4:11
Who is *w* to open the book, and to Rev 5:2
no man was found *w* to open Rev 5:4
Thou art *w* to take the book, and Rev 5:9
*W* is the Lamb that was slain to Rev 5:12
for they are *w* Rev 16:6

## WOT

I *w* not who hath done this thing Gen 21:26
*w* ye not that such a man as I can Gen 44:15

we *w* not what is become of him — Ex 32:1
we *w* not what is become of him — Ex 32:23
for I *w* that he whom thou — Num 22:6
whither the men went I *w* not — Josh 2:5
I *w* that through ignorance ye did — Acts 3:17
we *w* not what is become of him — Acts 7:40
*W* ye not what the scripture saith — Rom 11:2
yet what I shall choose I *w* not — Phil 1:22

**WOTTETH**

my master *w* not what is with me — Gen 39:8

**WOULD**

Adam to see what he *w* call them — Gen 2:19
Who *w* have said unto Abraham, — Gen 21:7
I *w* it might be according to thy — Gen 30:34
he besought us, and we *w* not hear — Gen 42:21
and ye *w* not hear — Gen 42:22
we certainly know that he *w* say — Gen 43:7
his father, his father *w* die — Gen 44:22
to wit what *w* be done to him — Ex 2:4
neither *w* he let the people go — Ex 8:32
neither *w* he let the children of — Ex 9:35
so that he *w* not let the children — Ex 10:20
heart, and he *w* not let them go — Ex 10:27
so that he *w* not let the children — Ex 11:10
when Pharaoh *w* hardly let us go, — Ex 13:15
*W* to God we had died by the hand — Ex 16:3
*w* God that all the LORD's people — Num 11:29
that the LORD *w* put his spirit — Num 11:29
*W* God that we had died in the — Num 14:2
or *w* God we had died in this — Num 14:2
*W* God that we had died when our — Num 20:3
Sihon *w* not suffer Israel to pass — Num 21:23
If Balak *w* give me his house full — Num 22:18
I *w* there were a sword in mine — Num 22:29
mine hand, for now *w* I kill thee — Num 22:29
If Balak *w* give me his house full — Num 24:13
Notwithstanding ye *w* not go up — Deut 1:26
ye *w* not hear, but rebelled — Deut 1:43
but the LORD *w* not hearken to — Deut 1:45
Heshbon *w* not let us pass by him — Deut 2:30
for your sakes, and *w* not hear me — Deut 3:26
in them, that they *w* fear me — Deut 5:29
because he *w* keep the oath which — Deut 7:8
because ye *w* not be obedient unto — Deut 8:20
LORD had said he *w* destroy you — Deut 9:25
the LORD *w* not destroy thee — Deut 10:10
thy God *w* not hearken unto Balaam — Deut 23:5
and it *w* be sin in thee — Deut 23:21
which *w* not adventure to set the — Deut 28:56
shalt say, *W* God it were even — Deut 28:67
shalt say, *W* God it were morning — Deut 28:67
I *w* scatter them into corners — Deut 32:26
I *w* make the remembrance of them — Deut 32:26
that they *w* consider their latter — Deut 32:29
that he *w* not shew them the land — Josh 5:6
their fathers that he *w* give us — Josh 5:6
*w* to God we had been content, and — Josh 7:7
Canaanites *w* dwell in that land — Josh 17:12
But I *w* not hearken unto Balaam — Josh 24:10
Canaanites *w* dwell in that land — Judg 1:27
for they *w* not suffer them to — Judg 1:34
But the Amorites *w* dwell in mount — Judg 1:35
yet they *w* not hearken unto their — Judg 2:17
to know whether they *w* hearken — Judg 3:4
them alive, I *w* not slay you — Judg 8:19
I *w* desire a request of you — Judg 8:24
that ye *w* give me every man the — Judg 8:24
*w* to God this people were under — Judg 9:29
then *w* I remove Abimelech — Judg 9:29
of Edom *w* not hearken thereto — Judg 11:17
but he *w* not consent — Judg 11:17
he *w* not have received a burnt — Judg 13:23
neither *w* he have shewed us all — Judg 13:23
nor *w* as at this time have told — Judg 13:23
rent him as he *w* have rent a kid — Judg 14:6
But her father *w* not suffer him — Judg 15:1
But the man *w* not tarry that — Judg 19:10
But the men *w* not hearken to him — Judg 19:25
*w* not hearken to the voice of — Judg 20:13
*W* ye tarry for them till they — Ruth 1:13
*w* ye stay for them from having — Ruth 1:13
then he *w* answer him, Nay — 1Sa 2:16
because the LORD *w* slay them — 1Sa 2:25
for now *w* the LORD have — 1Sa 13:13
*w* not utterly destroy them — 1Sa 15:9
*w* let him go no more home to his — 1Sa 18:2
then *w* not I tell it thee — 1Sa 20:9
*w* not put forth their hand to — 1Sa 22:17
that he *w* surely tell Saul — 1Sa 22:22
but I *w* not stretch forth mine — 1Sa 26:23
But his armourbearer *w* not — 1Sa 31:4
But Asahel *w* not turn aside from — 2Sa 2:21
as though they *w* have fetched — 2Sa 4:6
who thought that I *w* have given — 2Sa 4:10
So David *w* not remove the ark of — 2Sa 6:10
that they *w* shoot from the wall — 2Sa 11:20
I *w* moreover have given unto thee — 2Sa 12:8
but he *w* not, neither did he eat — 2Sa 12:17
he *w* not hearken unto our voice — 2Sa 12:18
Howbeit he *w* not hearken unto her — 2Sa 13:14
But he *w* not hearken unto her — 2Sa 13:16
howbeit he *w* not go, but blessed — 2Sa 13:25
hand of the man that *w* destroy me — 2Sa 14:16
but he *w* not come to him — 2Sa 14:29
the second time, he *w* not come — 2Sa 14:29
unto me, and I *w* do him justice — 2Sa 15:4
I *w* have given thee ten shekels — 2Sa 18:11
yet *w* I not put forth mine hand — 2Sa 18:12
*w* God I had died for thee, O — 2Sa 18:33
Oh that one *w* give me drink of — 2Sa 23:15
nevertheless he *w* not drink — 2Sa 23:16
therefore he *w* not drink it — 2Sa 23:17
The LORD said that he *w* dwell in — 1Kin 8:12
whosoever *w*, he consecrated him, — 1Kin 13:33
as great as *w* contain two — 1Kin 18:32
whether any thing *w* come from him — 1Kin 20:33
away his face, and *w* eat no bread — 1Kin 21:4
Did I not tell thee that he *w* — 1Kin 22:18
But Jehoshaphat *w* not — 1Kin 22:49
when the LORD *w* take up Elijah — 2Kin 2:1
I *w* not look toward thee, nor see — 2Kin 3:14
*W* God my lord were with the — 2Kin 5:3
for he *w* recover him of his — 2Kin 5:3
if the LORD *w* make windows in — 2Kin 7:2
Yet the LORD *w* not destroy Judah — 2Kin 8:19
*w* not destroy them, neither cast — 2Kin 13:23
But Amaziah *w* not hear — 2Kin 14:11
the LORD said not that he *w* blot — 2Kin 14:27
Notwithstanding they *w* not hear — 2Kin 17:14
*w* not hear them, nor do them — 2Kin 18:12
which the LORD *w* not pardon — 2Kin 24:4
But his armourbearer *w* not — 1Chr 10:4
Oh that one *w* give me drink of — 1Chr 11:17
but David *w* not drink of it, but — 1Chr 11:18
Therefore he *w* not drink it — 1Chr 11:19
said that they *w* do so — 1Chr 13:4
neither *w* the Syrians help the — 1Chr 19:19
he *w* increase Israel like to the — 1Chr 27:23
The LORD hath said that he *w* — 2Chr 6:1
the king *w* not hearken unto them — 2Chr 10:16
that he *w* not destroy him — 2Chr 12:12
That whosoever *w* not seek the — 2Chr 15:13
he *w* not prophesy good unto me — 2Chr 18:17
Howbeit the LORD *w* not destroy — 2Chr 21:7
but they *w* not give ear — 2Chr 24:19
But Amaziah *w* not hear — 2Chr 25:20
but they *w* not hearken — 2Chr 33:10
Nevertheless Josiah *w* not turn — 2Chr 35:22
that whosoever *w* not come within — Ezr 10:8
that they *w* put away their wives — Ezr 10:19
*w* go into the temple to save his — Neh 6:11
that *w* have put me in fear — Neh 6:14
they might do with them as they *w* — Neh 9:24
their neck, and *w* not hear — Neh 9:29
yet *w* they not give ear — Neh 9:30
that we *w* not give our daughters — Neh 10:30
that we *w* not buy it of them on — Neh 10:31
that we *w* leave the seventh year, — Neh 10:31
Mordecai's matters *w* stand — Est 3:4
To whom *w* the king delight to do — Est 6:6
and province that *w* assault them — Est 8:11
did what they *w* unto those that — Est 9:5
that they *w* keep these two days — Est 9:27
I *w* seek unto God, and unto God — Job 5:8
unto God *w* I commit my cause — Job 5:8
For now it *w* be heavier than the — Job 6:3
that God *w* grant me the thing — Job 6:8
Even that it *w* please God to — Job 6:9
that he *w* let loose his hand, and — Job 6:9
I *w* harden myself in sorrow — Job 6:10
I *w* not live alway — Job 7:16
surely now he *w* awake for thee, — Job 8:6
yet *w* I not answer — Job 9:15
but I *w* make supplication to my — Job 9:15
yet *w* I not believe that he had — Job 9:16
perfect, yet *w* I not know my soul — Job 9:21
I *w* despise my life — Job 9:21
Then *w* I speak, and not fear him — Job 9:35
But oh that God *w* speak, and open — Job 11:5
that he *w* shew thee the secrets — Job 11:6
For vain man *w* be wise, though — Job 11:12
Surely I *w* speak to the Almighty, — Job 13:3
Oh that ye *w* altogether hold your — Job 13:5
But I *w* strengthen you with my — Job 16:5
I *w* order my cause before him, and — Job 23:4
I *w* know the words which — Job 23:5
the words which he *w* answer me — Job 23:5
understand what he *w* say unto me — Job 23:5
but he *w* put strength in me — Job 23:6
he *w* fain flee out of his hand — Job 27:22
whose fathers I *w* have disdained — Job 30:1
*w* root out all mine increase — Job 31:12
Oh that one *w* hear me — Job 31:35
is, that the Almighty *w* answer me — Job 31:35
Surely I *w* take it upon my — Job 31:36
I *w* declare unto him the number — Job 31:37
as a prince *w* I go near unto him — Job 31:37
my maker *w* soon take me away — Job 32:22
*w* not consider any of his ways — Job 34:27
Even so *w* he have removed thee — Job 36:16
one *w* think the deep to be hoary — Job 41:32
on the LORD that he *w* deliver him — Ps 22:8
their hearts, Ah, so *w* we have it — Ps 35:25
if I *w* declare and speak of them, — Ps 40:5
I were hungry, I *w* not tell thee — Ps 50:12
else *w* I give it — Ps 51:16
for then *w* I fly away, and be at — Ps 55:6
then *w* I wander far off, and — Ps 55:7
I *w* hasten my escape from the — Ps 55:8
then I *w* have hid myself from him — Ps 55:12
for man *w* swallow me up — Ps 56:1
Mine enemies *w* daily swallow me — Ps 56:2
of him that *w* swallow me up — Ps 57:3
they that *w* destroy me, being — Ps 69:4
But my people *w* not hearken to my — Ps 81:11
and Israel *w* none of me — Ps 81:11
he said that he *w* destroy them — Ps 106:23
Oh that men *w* praise the LORD for — Ps 107:8
Oh that men *w* praise the LORD for — Ps 107:15
Oh that men *w* praise the LORD for — Ps 107:21
Oh that men *w* praise the LORD for — Ps 107:31
have said that I *w* keep thy words — Ps 119:57
there was no man that *w* know me — Ps 142:4
counsel, and *w* none of my reproof — Prov 1:25
They *w* none of my counsel — Prov 1:30
*w* not let him go, until I had — Song 3:4
find thee without, I *w* kiss thee — Song 8:1
I *w* lead thee, and bring thee into — Song 8:2
mother's house, who *w* instruct me — Song 8:2
I *w* cause thee to drink of spiced — Song 8:2
if a man *w* give all the substance — Song 8:7
it *w* utterly be contemned — Song 8:7
who *w* set the briers and thorns — Is 27:4
I *w* go through them — Is 27:4
I *w* burn them together — Is 27:4
yet they *w* not hear — Is 28:12
and ye *w* not — Is 30:15
for they *w* not walk in his ways, — Is 42:24
that I *w* not be wroth with thee — Is 54:9
When I *w* comfort myself against — Jer 8:18
Who *w* not fear thee, O King of — Jer 10:7
but they *w* not hear — Jer 13:11
wherewith I said I *w* benefit them — Jer 18:10
yet *w* I pluck thee thence — Jer 22:24
but ye *w* not hear, saith the LORD — Jer 29:19
king that he *w* not burn the roll — Jer 36:25
but he *w* not hear them — Jer 36:25
that he *w* not cause me to return — Jer 38:26
*w* they not leave some gleaning — Jer 49:9
We *w* have healed Babylon, but she — Jer 51:9
*w* not have believed that the — Lam 4:12
they *w* have hearkened unto thee — Eze 3:6
that I *w* do this evil unto them — Eze 6:10
hope that they *w* confirm the word — Eze 13:6
me, and *w* not hearken unto me — Eze 20:8
I *w* pour out my fury upon them in — Eze 20:13
that I *w* not bring them into the — Eze 20:15
I *w* pour out my fury upon them, — Eze 20:21
that I *w* scatter them among the — Eze 20:23
that I *w* bring thee against them — Eze 38:17
he *w* not defile himself with the — Dan 1:8
certainty that ye *w* gain the time — Dan 2:8
the king that he *w* give him time — Dan 2:16
that he *w* shew the king the — Dan 2:16
That they *w* desire mercies of the — Dan 2:18
whom he *w* he slew — Dan 5:19
and whom he *w* he kept alive — Dan 5:19
and whom he *w* he set up — Dan 5:19
and whom he *w* he put down — Dan 5:19
Then I *w* know the truth of the — Dan 7:19
that he *w* accomplish seventy — Dan 9:2
When I *w* have healed Israel, then — Hos 7:1
High, none at all *w* exalt him — Hos 11:7
*w* they not have stolen till they — Obad 5
*w* they not leave some grapes — Obad 5
had said that he *w* do unto them — Jonah 3:10
see what *w* become of the city — Jonah 4:5
as he cried, and they *w* not hear — Zec 7:13
I *w* not hear, saith the LORD of — Zec 7:13
that *w* shut the doors for nought — Mal 1:10
*w* not be comforted, because they — Mt 2:18
from him that *w* borrow of thee — Mt 5:42
all things whatsoever ye *w* that — Mt 7:12
they besought him that he *w* — Mt 8:34
they *w* have repented long ago in — Mt 11:21
it *w* have remained until this day — Mt 11:23
ye *w* not have condemned the — Mt 12:7
we *w* see a sign from thee — Mt 12:38
when he *w* have put him to death, — Mt 14:5
to give her whatsoever she *w* ask — Mt 14:7
he *w* shew them a sign from heaven — Mt 16:1
which *w* take account of his — Mt 18:23
And he *w* not — Mt 18:30
and they *w* not come — Mt 22:3
we *w* not have been partakers with — Mt 23:30
how often *w* I have gathered thy — Mt 23:37
under her wings, and ye *w* not — Mt 23:37
in what watch the thief *w* come — Mt 24:43
he *w* have watched — Mt 24:43
*w* not have suffered his house to — Mt 24:43
people a prisoner, whom they *w* — Mt 27:15
tasted thereof, he *w* not drink — Mt 27:34
whether he *w* heal him on the — Mk 3:2
and calleth unto him whom he *w* — Mk 3:13
he besought him much that he *w* — Mk 5:10
against him, and *w* have killed him — Mk 6:19
sat with him, he *w* not reject her — Mk 6:26
the sea, and *w* have passed by them — Mk 6:48
house, and *w* have no man know it — Mk 7:24
she besought him that he *w* cast — Mk 7:26
he *w* not that any man should know — Mk 9:30
we *w* that thou shouldest do for — Mk 10:35
What *w* ye that I should do for — Mk 10:36
*w* not suffer that any man should — Mk 11:16
father, how he *w* have him called — Lk 1:62
That he *w* grant unto us, that we, — Lk 1:74
prayed him that he *w* thrust out a — Lk 5:3
whether he *w* heal on the sabbath — Lk 6:7
as ye *w* that men should do to you — Lk 6:31
beseeching him that he *w* come — Lk 7:3
him that he *w* eat with him — Lk 7:36
*w* have known who and what manner — Lk 7:39
they besought him that he *w* not — Lk 8:31
they besought him that he *w* — Lk 8:32
him that he *w* come into his house — Lk 8:41
as though he *w* go to Jerusalem — Lk 9:53
place, whither he himself *w* come — Lk 10:1
that he *w* send forth labourers — Lk 10:2
known what hour the thief *w* come — Lk 12:39

he *w* have watched, and not have ........ Lk 12:39
how often *w* I have gathered thy ........ Lk 13:34
under her wings, and ye *w* not ........ Lk 13:34
he *w* fain have filled his belly ........ Lk 15:16
And he was angry, and *w* not go in ........ Lk 15:28
so that they which *w* pass from ........ Lk 16:26
to us, that *w* come from thence ........ Lk 16:26
And he *w* not for a while ........ Lk 18:4
*w* not lift up so much as his eyes ........ Lk 18:13
infants, that he *w* touch them ........ Lk 18:15
which *w* not that I should reign ........ Lk 19:27
the stones *w* immediately cry out ........ Lk 19:40
were about him saw what *w* follow ........ Lk 22:49
as though he *w* have gone further ........ Lk 24:28
Jesus *w* go forth into Galilee ........ Jn 1:43
he *w* have given thee living water ........ Jn 4:10
him that he *w* tarry with them ........ Jn 4:40
besought him that he *w* come down ........ Jn 4:47
Moses, ye *w* have believed me ........ Jn 5:46
for he himself knew what he *w* do ........ Jn 6:6
of the fishes as much as they *w* ........ Jn 6:11
perceived that they *w* come ........ Jn 6:15
for he *w* not walk in Jewry, ........ Jn 7:1
some of them *w* have taken him ........ Jn 7:44
ye *w* do the works of Abraham ........ Jn 8:39
were your Father, ye *w* love me ........ Jn 8:42
wherefore *w* ye hear it again ........ Jn 9:27
him, saying, Sir, we *w* see Jesus ........ Jn 12:21
it were not so, I *w* have told you ........ Jn 14:2
ye *w* rejoice, because I said, I ........ Jn 14:28
world, the world *w* love his own ........ Jn 15:19
we *w* not have delivered him up ........ Jn 18:30
then *w* my servants fight, that I ........ Jn 18:36
he *w* raise up Christ to sit on ........ Acts 2:30
of them whereunto this *w* grow ........ Acts 5:24
yet he promised that he *w* give it ........ Acts 7:5
For he supposed his brethren *w* ........ Acts 7:25
God by his hand *w* deliver them ........ Acts 7:25
*w* have set them at one again, ........ Acts 7:26
To whom our fathers *w* not obey ........ Acts 7:39
desired Philip that he *w* come up ........ Acts 8:31
desiring him that he *w* not delay ........ Acts 9:38
very hungry, and *w* have eaten ........ Acts 10:10
heart they *w* cleave unto the Lord ........ Acts 11:23
when Herod *w* have brought him ........ Acts 12:6
*w* have done sacrifice with the ........ Acts 14:13
Him *w* Paul have to go forth with ........ Acts 16:3
*w* have killed himself, supposing ........ Acts 16:27
we *w* know therefore what these ........ Acts 17:20
reason *w* that I should bear with ........ Acts 18:14
when Paul *w* have entered in unto ........ Acts 19:30
desiring him that he *w* not ........ Acts 19:31
*w* have made his defence unto the ........ Acts 19:33
because he *w* not spend the time ........ Acts 20:16
when he *w* not be persuaded, we ........ Acts 21:14
because he *w* have known the ........ Acts 22:30
saying that they *w* neither eat ........ Acts 23:12
as though ye *w* enquire something ........ Acts 23:15
as though they *w* enquire somewhat. Acts 23:20
when I *w* have known the cause ........ Acts 23:28
*w* have judged according to our ........ Acts 24:6
that he *w* send for him to ........ Acts 25:3
that he himself *w* depart shortly ........ Acts 25:4
him whether he *w* go to Jerusalem ........ Acts 25:20
I *w* also hear the man myself ........ Acts 25:22
the beginning, if they *w* testify ........ Acts 26:5
I *w* to God, that not only thou, ........ Acts 26:29
under colour as though they *w* ........ Acts 27:30
*w* have let me go, because there ........ Acts 28:18
Now I *w* not have you ignorant, ........ Rom 1:13
good man some *w* even dare to die ........ Rom 5:7
for what I *w*, that do I not ........ Rom 7:15
If then I do that which I *w* not ........ Rom 7:16
For the good that I *w* I do not ........ Rom 7:19
but the evil which I *w* not ........ Rom 7:19
Now if I do that I *w* not, it is ........ Rom 7:20
when I *w* do good, evil is present ........ Rom 7:21
For I *w* not, brethren, that ye ........ Rom 11:25
but yet I *w* have you wise unto ........ Rom 16:19
they *w* not have crucified the ........ 1Cor 2:8
I *w* to God ye did reign, that we ........ 1Cor 4:8
as though I *w* not come to you ........ 1Cor 4:18
For I *w* that all men were even as ........ 1Cor 7:7
But I *w* have you without ........ 1Cor 7:32
I *w* not that ye should be ........ 1Cor 10:1
I *w* not that ye should have ........ 1Cor 10:20
But I *w* have you know, that the ........ 1Cor 11:3
For if we *w* judge ourselves, we ........ 1Cor 11:31
I *w* not have you ignorant ........ 1Cor 12:1
I *w* that ye all spake with ........ 1Cor 14:5
For we *w* not, brethren, have you ........ 2Cor 1:8
that I *w* not come again to you in ........ 2Cor 2:1
ye *w* confirm your love toward him ........ 2Cor 2:8
not for that we *w* be unclothed ........ 2Cor 5:4
that we *w* receive the gift ........ 2Cor 8:4
so he *w* also finish in you the ........ 2Cor 8:6
that they *w* go before unto you, ........ 2Cor 9:5
as if I *w* terrify you by letters ........ 2Cor 10:9
*W* to God ye could bear with me a ........ 2Cor 11:1
For though I *w* desire to glory, I ........ 2Cor 12:6
I shall not find you such as I *w* ........ 2Cor 12:20
found unto you such as ye *w* not ........ 2Cor 12:20
*w* pervert the gospel of Christ ........ Gal 1:7
Only they *w* that we should ........ Gal 2:10
This only *w* I learn of you, ........ Gal 3:2
foreseeing that God *w* justify the ........ Gal 3:8
ye *w* have plucked out your own ........ Gal 4:15
they *w* exclude you, that ye might ........ Gal 4:17
I *w* they were even cut off which ........ Gal 5:12
ye cannot do the things that ye *w* ........ Gal 5:17
That he *w* grant you, according to ........ Eph 3:16
But I *w* ye should understand, ........ Phil 1:12
To whom God *w* make known what is . Col 1:27
For I *w* that ye knew what great ........ Col 2:1
that God *w* open unto us a door of ........ Col 4:3
because we *w* not be chargeable ........ 1Th 2:9
That ye *w* walk worthy of God, who ........ 1Th 2:12
Wherefore we *w* have come unto you .. 1Th 2:18
so ye *w* abound more and more ........ 1Th 4:1
But I *w* not have you to be ........ 1Th 4:13
that our God *w* count you worthy ........ 2Th 1:11
you, that if any *w* not work ........ 2Th 3:10
Whom I *w* have retained with me, ........ Philem 13
without thy mind *w* I do nothing ........ Philem 14
then *w* he not afterward have ........ Heb 4:8
For then *w* they not have ceased ........ Heb 10:2
for the time *w* fail me to tell of ........ Heb 11:32
when he *w* have inherited the ........ Heb 12:17
they *w* no doubt have continued ........ 1Jn 2:19
I *w* not write with paper and ink ........ 2Jn 12
and forbiddeth them that *w* ........ 3Jn 10
I *w* thou wert cold or hot ........ Rev 3:15
cause that as many as *w* not ........ Rev 13:15

## WOULDEST

*w* thou take away my son's ........ Gen 30:15
though thou *w* needs be gone, ........ Gen 31:30
Peradventure thou *w* take by force ........ Gen 31:31
behold, hitherto thou *w* not hear ........ Ex 7:16
*w* forbear to help him, thou shalt ........ Ex 23:5
heart, whether thou *w* keep his ........ Deut 8:2
that thou *w* have her to thy wife ........ Deut 21:11
because thou *w* not obey the voice ........ Deut 28:62
Caleb said unto her, What *w* thou ........ Josh 15:18
that thou *w* not suffer the ........ 2Sa 14:11
thou thyself *w* have set thyself ........ 2Sa 18:13
And the king said, What *w* thou ........ 1Kin 1:16
that thou *w* deliver thy servant ........ 1Kin 18:9
*w* thou be spoken for to the king, ........ 2Kin 4:13
thing, *w* thou not have done it ........ 2Kin 5:13
*w* thou smite those whom thou hast ........ 2Kin 6:22
Oh that thou *w* bless me indeed, ........ 1Chr 4:10
that thou *w* keep me from evil, ........ 1Chr 4:10
that thou *w* put thy name there ........ 2Chr 6:20
whom thou *w* not let Israel invade ........ 2Chr 20:10
*w* not thou be angry with us till ........ Ezr 9:14
that thou *w* send me unto Judah, ........ Neh 2:5
If thou *w* seek unto God betimes, ........ Job 8:5
Oh that thou *w* hide me in the ........ Job 14:13
that thou *w* keep me secret, until ........ Job 14:13
that thou *w* appoint me a set time ........ Job 14:13
for I knew that thou *w* deal very ........ Is 48:8
Oh that thou *w* rend the heavens, ........ Is 64:1
that thou *w* come down ........ Is 64:1
that thou *w* send him to my ........ Lk 16:27
thou *w* have asked of him, and he ........ Jn 4:10
thee, that, if thou *w* believe ........ Jn 11:40
and walkedst whither thou *w* ........ Jn 21:18
and carry thee whither thou *w* not ........ Jn 21:18
*w* bring down Paul to morrow into ........ Acts 23:20
I pray thee that thou *w* hear us ........ Acts 24:4
Sacrifice and offering thou *w* not ........ Heb 10:5
and offering for sin thou *w* not ........ Heb 10:8

## WOUND

*w* for *w*, stripe for stripe ........ Ex 21:25
I *w*, and I heal ........ Deut 32:39
the blood ran out of the *w* into ........ 1Kin 22:35
my *w* is incurable without ........ Job 34:6
But God shall *w* the head of his ........ Ps 68:21
he shall *w* the heads over many ........ Ps 110:6
A *w* and dishonour shall he get ........ Prov 6:33
The blueness of a *w* cleanseth ........ Prov 20:30
and healeth the stroke of their *w* ........ Is 30:26
my *w* is grievous ........ Jer 10:19
my *w* incurable, which refuseth to ........ Jer 15:18
incurable, and thy *w* is grievous ........ Jer 30:12
thee with the *w* of an enemy ........ Jer 30:14
his sickness, and Judah saw his *w* ........ Hos 5:13
heal you, nor cure you of your *w* ........ Hos 5:13
bread have laid a *w* under thee ........ Obad 7
For her *w* is incurable ........ Mic 1:9
thy *w* is grievous ........ Nah 3:19
*w* it in linen clothes with the ........ Jn 19:40
*w* him up, and carried him out, and ........ Acts 5:6
*w* their weak conscience, ye sin ........ 1Cor 8:12
and his deadly *w* was healed ........ Rev 13:3
beast, whose deadly *w* was healed ........ Rev 13:12
beast, which had the *w* by a sword ........ Rev 13:14

## WOUNDED

He that is *w* in the stones, or ........ Deut 23:1
were overthrown and *w* ........ Judg 9:40
the *w* of the Philistines fell ........ 1Sa 17:52
he was sore *w* of the archers ........ 1Sa 31:3
*w* them, that they could not arise ........ 2Sa 22:39
him, so that in smiting he *w* him ........ 1Kin 20:37
for I am *w* ........ 1Kin 22:34
and the Syrians *w* Joram ........ 2Kin 8:28
him, and he was *w* of the archers ........ 1Chr 10:3
for I am *w* ........ 2Chr 18:33
for I am sore *w* ........ 2Chr 35:23
and the soul of the *w* crieth out ........ Job 24:12
I have *w* them that they were not ........ Ps 18:38
suddenly shall they be *w* ........ Ps 64:7
grief of those whom thou hast *w* ........ Ps 69:26
needy, and my heart is *w* within me ........ Ps 109:22
For she hath cast down many *w* ........ Prov 7:26
but a *w* spirit who can bear ........ Prov 18:14
me, they smote me, they *w* me ........ Song 5:7
hath cut Rahab, and *w* the dragon ........ Is 51:9
But he was *w* for our ........ Is 53:5
for I have *w* thee with the wound ........ Jer 30:14
remained but *w* men among them ........ Jer 37:10
all her land the *w* shall groan ........ Jer 51:52
when they swooned as the *w* in the ........ Lam 2:12
sound of thy fall, when the *w* cry ........ Eze 26:15
the *w* shall be judged in the ........ Eze 28:23
the groanings of a deadly *w* man ........ Eze 30:24
the sword, they shall not be *w* ........ Joel 2:8
Those with which I was *w* in the ........ Zec 13:6
*w* him in the head, and sent him ........ Mk 12:4
*w* him, and departed, leaving him ........ Lk 10:30
they *w* him also, and cast him out ........ Lk 20:12
fled out of that house naked and *w* ........ Acts 19:16
his heads as it were *w* to death ........ Rev 13:3

## WOUNDEDST

thou *w* the head out of the house ........ Hab 3:13

## WOUNDETH

he *w*, and his hands make whole ........ Job 5:18

## WOUNDING

for I have slain a man to my *w* ........ Gen 4:23

## WOUNDS

to be healed in Jezreel of the *w* ........ 2Kin 8:29
to be healed in Jezreel of the *w* ........ 2Kin 9:15
in Jezreel because of the *w* which ........ 2Chr 22:6
and multiplieth my *w* without cause ........ Job 9:17
My *w* stink and are corrupt because ........ Ps 38:5
in heart, and bindeth up their *w* ........ Ps 147:3
words of a talebearer are as *w* ........ Prov 18:8
who hath *w* without cause ........ Prov 23:29
words of a talebearer are as *w* ........ Prov 26:22
Faithful are the *w* of a friend ........ Prov 27:6
but *w*, and bruises, and putrifying ........ Is 1:6
me continually is grief and *w* ........ Jer 6:7
and I will heal thee of thy *w* ........ Jer 30:17
What are these *w* in thine hands ........ Zec 13:6
And went to him, and bound up his *w*. Lk 10:34

## WOVE

where the women *w* hangings for ........ 2Kin 23:7

## WOVEN

it shall have a binding of *w* work ........ Ex 28:32
the robe of the ephod of *w* work ........ Ex 39:22
of fine linen of *w* work for Aaron ........ Ex 39:27
*w* from the top throughout ........ Jn 19:23

## WRAP

than that he can *w* himself in it ........ Is 28:20
so they *w* it up ........ Mic 7:3

## WRAPPED

*w* herself, and sat in an open ........ Gen 38:14
it is here *w* in a cloth behind ........ 1Sa 21:9
that he *w* his face in his mantle, ........ 1Kin 19:13
*w* it together, and smote the ........ 2Kin 2:8
His roots are *w* about the heap, ........ Job 8:17
of his stones are *w* together ........ Job 40:17
it is *w* up for the slaughter ........ Eze 21:15
the weeds were *w* about my head ........ Jonah 2:5
he *w* it in a clean linen cloth, ........ Mt 27:59
*w* him in the linen, and laid him ........ Mk 15:46
*w* him in swaddling clothes, and ........ Lk 2:7
the babe *w* in swaddling clothes ........ Lk 2:12
*w* it in linen, and laid it in a ........ Lk 23:53
but *w* together in a place by ........ Jn 20:7

## WRATH

that his *w* was kindled ........ Gen 39:19
and their *w*, for it was cruel ........ Gen 49:7
thou sentest forth thy *w*, which ........ Ex 15:7
my *w* shall wax hot, and I will ........ Ex 22:24
that my *w* may wax hot against ........ Ex 32:10
why doth thy *w* wax hot against ........ Ex 32:11
Turn from thy fierce *w*, and repent ........ Ex 32:12
lest *w* come upon all the people ........ Lev 10:6
that there be no *w* upon the ........ Num 1:53
the *w* of the LORD was kindled ........ Num 11:33
for there is *w* gone out from the ........ Num 16:46
that there be no *w* any more upon ........ Num 18:5
hath turned my *w* away from the ........ Num 25:11
thy God to *w* in the wilderness ........ Deut 9:7
Horeb ye provoked the LORD to *w* ........ Deut 9:8
ye provoked the LORD to *w* ........ Deut 9:22
then the LORD's *w* be kindled ........ Deut 11:17
in his anger, and in his *w* ........ Deut 29:23
of their land in anger, and in *w* ........ Deut 29:28
that I feared the *w* of the enemy ........ Deut 32:27
lest *w* be upon us, because of the ........ Josh 9:20
*w* fell on all the congregation of ........ Josh 22:20
his fierce *w* upon Amalek, ........ 1Sa 28:18
if so be that the king's *w* arise ........ 2Sa 11:20
for great is the *w* of the LORD ........ 2Kin 22:13
therefore my *w* shall be kindled ........ 2Kin 22:17
the fierceness of his great *w* ........ 2Kin 23:26
because there fell *w* for it ........ 1Chr 27:24
my *w* shall not be poured out upon ........ 2Chr 12:7
the *w* of the LORD turned from him .. 2Chr 12:12
therefore is *w* upon thee from ........ 2Chr 19:2
so *w* come upon you, and upon your ........ 2Chr 19:10
*w* came upon Judah and Jerusalem ........ 2Chr 24:18
for the fierce *w* of the LORD is ........ 2Chr 28:11
there is fierce *w* against Israel ........ 2Chr 28:13
Wherefore the *w* of the LORD was ........ 2Chr 29:8
that his fierce *w* may turn away ........ 2Chr 29:10
of his *w* may turn away from you ........ 2Chr 30:8
therefore there was *w* upon him ........ 2Chr 32:25
so that the *w* of the LORD came ........ 2Chr 32:26
for great is the *w* of the LORD ........ 2Chr 34:21
therefore my *w* shall be poured ........ 2Chr 34:25
until the *w* of the LORD arose ........ 2Chr 36:16

provoked the God of heaven unto *w* Ezr 5:12
for why should there be *w* against Ezr 7:23
his *w* is against all them that Ezr 8:22
until the fierce *w* of our God for Ezr 10:14
yet ye bring more *w* upon Israel Neh 13:18
arise too much contempt and *w* Est 1:18
when the *w* of king Ahasuerus was Est 2:1
then was Haman full of *w* Est 3:5
his *w* went into the palace garden Est 7:7
Then was the king's *w* pacified Est 7:10
For *w* killeth the foolish man, and Job 5:2
me secret, until thy *w* be past Job 14:13
He teareth me in his *w*, who Job 16:9
also kindled his *w* against me Job 19:11
for *w* bringeth the punishments of Job 19:29
cast the fury of his *w* upon him Job 20:23
flow away in the day of his *w* Job 20:28
drink of the *w* of the Almighty Job 21:20
be brought forth to the day of *w* Job 21:30
Then was kindled the *w* of Elihu Job 32:2
against Job was his *w* kindled Job 32:2
three friends was his *w* kindled Job 32:3
three men, then his *w* was kindled Job 32:5
the hypocrites in heart heap up *w* Job 36:13
Because there is *w*, beware lest Job 36:18
Cast abroad the rage of thy *w* Job 40:11
My *w* is kindled against thee, and Job 42:7
shall he speak unto them in his *w* Ps 2:5
when his *w* is kindled but a Ps 2:12
shall swallow them up in his *w* Ps 21:9
Cease from anger, and forsake *w* Ps 37:8
O LORD, rebuke me not in thy *w* Ps 38:1
upon me, and in *w* they hate me Ps 55:3
both living, and in his *w* Ps 58:9
Consume them in *w*, consume them, Ps 59:13
Surely the *w* of man shall praise Ps 76:10
the remainder of *w* shalt thou Ps 76:10
The *w* of God came upon them, and Ps 78:31
and did not stir up all his *w* Ps 78:38
the fierceness of his anger, *w* Ps 78:49
Pour out thy *w* upon the heathen Ps 79:6
Thou hast taken away all thy *w* Ps 85:3
Thy *w* lieth hard upon me, and thou Ps 88:7
Thy fierce *w* goeth over me Ps 88:16
shall thy *w* burn like fire Ps 89:46
and by thy *w* are we troubled Ps 90:7
our days are passed away in thy *w* Ps 90:9
to thy fear, so is thy *w* Ps 90:11
Unto whom I sware in my *w* that Ps 95:11
of thine indignation and thy *w* Ps 102:10
in the breach, to turn away his *w* Ps 106:23
Therefore was the *w* of the LORD Ps 106:40
through kings in the day of his *w* Ps 110:5
when their *w* was kindled against Ps 124:3
against the *w* of mine enemies Ps 138:7
Riches profit not in the day of *w* Prov 11:4
expectation of the wicked is *w* Prov 11:23
A fool's *w* is presently known Prov 12:16
He that is slow to *w* is of great Prov 14:29
but his *w* is against him that Prov 14:35
A soft answer turneth away *w* Prov 15:1
The *w* of a king is as messengers Prov 16:14
The king's *w* is as the roaring of Prov 19:12
A man of great *w* shall suffer Prov 19:19
and a reward in the bosom strong *w*. Prov 21:14
his name, who dealeth in proud *w* Prov 21:24
and he turn away his *w* from him Prov 24:18
but a fool's *w* is heavier than Prov 27:3
*W* is cruel, and anger is Prov 27:4
but wise men turn away *w* Prov 29:8
so the forcing of *w* bringeth Prov 30:33
sorrow and *w* with his sickness Eccl 5:17
Through the *w* of the LORD of Is 9:19
of my *w* will I give him a charge Is 10:6
LORD cometh, cruel both with *w* Is 13:9
in the *w* of the LORD of hosts, and Is 13:13
in *w* with a continual stroke Is 14:6
and his pride, and his *w* Is 16:6
In a little *w* I hid my face from Is 54:8
for in my *w* I smote thee, but in Is 60:10
forsaken the generation of his *w* Jer 7:29
at his *w* the earth shall tremble, Jer 10:10
and to turn away thy *w* from them Jer 18:20
anger, and in fury, and in great *w* Jer 21:5
and in my fury, and in great *w* Jer 32:37
In that ye provoke me unto *w* with Jer 44:8
I know his *w*, saith the LORD Jer 48:30
Because of the *w* of the LORD it Jer 50:13
in his *w* the strong holds of the Lam 2:2
affliction by the rod of his *w* Lam 3:1
for *w* is upon all the multitude Eze 7:12
for my *w* is upon all the Eze 7:14
in the day of the *w* of the LORD Eze 7:19
I accomplish my *w* upon the wall Eze 13:15
against thee in the fire of my *w* Eze 21:31
blow upon you in the fire of my *w* Eze 22:21
them with the fire of my *w* Eze 22:31
in the fire of my *w* have I spoken Eze 38:19
out my *w* upon them like water Hos 5:10
anger, and took him away in my *w* Hos 13:11
and he kept his *w* for ever Amos 1:11
he reserveth *w* for his enemies Nah 1:2
in *w* remember mercy Hab 3:2
was thy *w* against the sea, that Hab 3:8
That day is a day of *w*, a day of Zeph 1:15
them in the day of the LORD's *w* Zeph 1:18
a great *w* from the LORD of hosts Zec 7:12
your fathers provoked me to *w* Zec 8:14
you to flee from the *w* to come Mt 3:7
you to flee from the *w* to come Lk 3:7
these things, were filled with *w* Lk 4:28
the land, and *w* upon this people Lk 21:23
but the *w* of God abideth on him Jn 3:36
sayings, they were full of *w* Acts 19:28
For the *w* of God is revealed from Rom 1:18
*w* against the day of *w* Rom 2:5
*w* against the day of *w* Rom 2:5
unrighteousness, indignation and *w* Rom 2:8
Because the law worketh *w* Rom 4:15
shall be saved from *w* through him Rom 5:9
if God, willing to shew his *w* Rom 9:22
of *w* fitted to destruction Rom 9:22
but rather give place unto *w* Rom 12:19
a revenger to execute *w* upon him Rom 13:4
needs be subject, not only for *w* Rom 13:5
hatred, variance, emulations, *w* Gal 5:20
were by nature the children of *w* Eph 2:3
not the sun go down upon your *w* Eph 4:26
Let all bitterness, and *w*, and Eph 4:31
of these things cometh the *w* of Eph 5:6
provoke not your children to *w* Eph 6:4
For which things' sake the *w* of Col 3:6
anger, *w*, malice, blasphemy, Col 3:8
delivered us from the *w* to come 1Th 1:10
for the *w* is come upon them to 1Th 2:16
God hath not appointed us to *w* 1Th 5:9
lifting up holy hands, without *w* 1Ti 2:8
So I sware in my *w*, They shall Heb 3:11
he said, As I have sworn in my *w* Heb 4:3
not fearing the *w* of the king Heb 11:27
to hear, slow to speak, slow to *w* Jas 1:19
For the *w* of man worketh not the Jas 1:20
throne, and from the *w* of the Lamb Rev 6:16
the great day of his *w* is come Rev 6:17
thy *w* is come, and the time of the Rev 11:18
down unto you, having great *w* Rev 12:12
wine of the *w* of her fornication Rev 14:8
drink of the wine of the *w* of God Rev 14:10
great winepress of the *w* of God Rev 14:19
in them is filled up the *w* of God Rev 15:1
golden vials full of the *w* of God Rev 15:7
of the *w* of God upon the earth Rev 16:1
wine of the fierceness of his *w* Rev 16:19
wine of the *w* of her fornication Rev 18:3
fierceness and *w* of Almighty God Rev 19:15

**WRATHFUL**
let thy *w* anger take hold of them Ps 69:24
A *w* man stirreth up strife Prov 15:18

**WRATHS**
there be debates, envyings, *w* 2Cor 12:20

**WREATH**
rows of pomegranates on each *w* 2Chr 4:13

**WREATHED**
they are *w*, and come up upon my Lam 1:14

**WREATHEN**
of *w* work shalt thou make them, Ex 28:14
fasten the *w* chains to the ouches Ex 28:14
the ends of *w* work of pure gold Ex 28:22
thou shalt put the two *w* chains Ex 28:24
the other two ends of the two *w* Ex 28:25
the ends, of *w* work of pure gold Ex 39:15
they put the two *w* chains of gold Ex 39:17
the two ends of the two *w* chains Ex 39:18
the *w* work, and pomegranates upon 2Kin 25:17
had the second pillar with *w* work 2Kin 25:17

**WREATHS**
work, and *w* of chain work, for the 1Kin 7:17
the two *w* to cover the two 2Chr 4:12
hundred pomegranates on the two *w*. 2Chr 4:13

**WREST**
decline after many to *w* judgment Ex 23:2
Thou shalt not *w* the judgment of Ex 23:6
Thou shalt not *w* judgment Deut 16:19
Every day they *w* my words Ps 56:5
that are unlearned and unstable *w* 2Pet 3:16

**WRESTLE**
For we *w* not against flesh and Eph 6:12

**WRESTLED**
have I *w* with my sister, and I Gen 30:8
there *w* a man with him until the Gen 32:24
out of joint, as he *w* with him Gen 32:25

**WRESTLINGS**
With great *w* have I wrestled with Gen 30:8

**WRETCHED**
O *w* man that I am Rom 7:24
and knowest not that thou art *w* Rev 3:17

**WRETCHEDNESS**
and let me not see my *w* Num 11:15

**WRING**
*w* off his head, and burn it on the Lev 1:15
*w* off his head from his neck, but Lev 5:8
of the earth shall *w* them out Ps 75:8

**WRINGED**
*w* the dew out of the fleece, a Judg 6:38

**WRINGING**
the *w* of the nose bringeth forth Prov 30:33

**WRINKLE**
church, not having spot, or *w* Eph 5:27

**WRINKLES**
And thou hast filled me with *w* Job 16:8

**WRITE**
*W* this for a memorial in a book, Ex 17:14
I will *w* upon these tables the Ex 34:1
unto Moses, *W* thou these words Ex 34:27
the priest shall *w* these curses Num 5:23
*w* thou every man's name upon his Num 17:2
thou shalt *w* Aaron's name upon Num 17:3
thou shalt *w* them upon the posts Deut 6:9
I will *w* on the tables the words Deut 10:2
thou shalt *w* them upon the door Deut 11:20
that he shall *w* him a copy of Deut 17:18
then let him *w* her a bill of Deut 24:1
*w* her a bill of divorcement, and Deut 24:3
thou shalt *w* upon them all the Deut 27:3
thou shalt *w* upon the stones all Deut 27:8
Now therefore *w* ye this song for Deut 31:19
the prophet, the son of Amoz, *w* 2Chr 26:22
that we might *w* the names of the Ezr 5:10
we make a sure covenant, and *w* it Neh 9:38
*W* ye also for the Jews, as it Est 8:8
*w* them upon the table of thine Prov 3:3
*w* them upon the table of thine Prov 7:3
roll, and *w* in it with a man's pen Is 8:1
that *w* grievousness which they Is 10:1
be few, that a child may *w* them Is 10:19
*w* it before them in a table, and Is 30:8
*W* ye this man childless, a man Jer 22:30
*W* thee all the words that I have Jer 30:2
parts, and *w* it in their hearts Jer 31:33
*w* therein all the words that I Jer 36:2
How didst thou *w* all these words Jer 36:17
*w* in it all the former words that Jer 36:28
*w* thee the name of the day, even Eze 24:2
*w* upon it, For Judah, and for the Eze 37:16
*w* upon it, For Joseph, the stick Eze 37:16
*w* it in their sight, that they Eze 43:11
*W* the vision, and make it plain Hab 2:2
Moses suffered to *w* a bill of Mk 10:4
to *w* unto thee in order, most Lk 1:3
and sit down quickly, and *w* fifty Lk 16:6
Take thy bill, and *w* fourscore Lk 16:7
the law, and the prophets, did *w* Jn 1:45
*W* not, The King of the Jews Jn 19:21
But that we *w* unto them, that Acts 15:20
certain thing to *w* unto my lord Acts 25:26
had, I might have somewhat to *w* Acts 25:26
I *w* not these things to shame you 1Cor 4:14
that the things that I *w* unto you 1Cor 14:37
For we *w* none other things unto 2Cor 1:13
For to this end also did I *w* 2Cor 2:9
is superfluous for me to *w* to you 2Cor 9:1
being absent now I *w* to them 2Cor 13:2
Therefore I *w* these things being 2Cor 13:10
Now the things which I *w* unto you Gal 1:20
To *w* the same things to you, to Phil 3:1
ye need not that I *w* unto you 1Th 4:9
ye have no need that I *w* unto you 1Th 5:1
so I *w* 2Th 3:17
These things *w* I unto thee 1Ti 3:14
mind, and *w* them in their hearts Heb 8:10
and in their minds will I *w* them Heb 10:16
beloved, I now *w* unto you 2Pet 3:1
And these things *w* we unto you 1Jn 1:4
these things *w* I unto you 1Jn 2:1
I *w* no new commandment unto you, 1Jn 2:7
a new commandment I *w* unto you 1Jn 2:8
I *w* unto you, little children, 1Jn 2:12
I *w* unto you, fathers, because ye 1Jn 2:13
I *w* unto you, young men, because 1Jn 2:13
I *w* unto you, little children, 1Jn 2:13
Having many things to *w* unto you 2Jn 12
I would not *w* with paper 2Jn 12
I had many things to *w*, but I 3Jn 13
not with ink and pen *w* unto thee 3Jn 13
to *w* unto you of the common Jude 3
was needful for me to *w* unto you Jude 3
*w* in a book, and send it unto the Rev 1:11
*W* the things which thou hast seen Rev 1:19
angel of the church of Ephesus *w* Rev 2:1
angel of the church in Smyrna *w* Rev 2:8
angel of the church in Pergamos *w* Rev 2:12
angel of the church in Thyatira *w* Rev 2:18
angel of the church in Sardis *w* Rev 3:1
of the church in Philadelphia *w* Rev 3:7
I will *w* upon him the name of my Rev 3:12
I will *w* upon him my new name Rev 3:12
of the church of the Laodiceans *w* Rev 3:14
their voices, I was about to *w* Rev 10:4
thunders uttered, and *w* them not Rev 10:4
from heaven saying unto me, *W* Rev 14:13
And he saith unto me, *W*, Blessed Rev 19:9
And he said unto me, *W* Rev 21:5

**WRITER**
they that handle the pen of the *w* Judg 5:14
my tongue is the pen of a ready *w* Ps 45:1

**WRITER'S**
with a *w* inkhorn by his side Eze 9:2
which had the *w* inkhorn by his Eze 9:3

**WRITEST**
For thou *w* bitter things against Job 13:26
the sticks whereon thou *w* shall Eze 37:20

**WRITETH**
when he *w* up the people, that Ps 87:6

**WRITING**
the *w* was the *w* of God, Ex 32:16
pure gold, and wrote upon it a *w* Ex 39:30
tables, according to the first *w* Deut 10:4
when Moses had made an end of *w* Deut 31:24
in *w* by his hand upon me, even 1Chr 28:19
the king of Tyre answered in *w* 2Chr 2:11
there came a *w* to him from Elijah 2Chr 21:12
according to the *w* of David king 2Chr 35:4

according to the *w* of Solomon his ...... 2Chr 35:4
his kingdom, and put it also in *w* ...... 2Chr 36:22
his kingdom, and put it also in *w* ...... Ezr 1:1
the *w* of the letter was written ...... Ezr 4:7
according to the *w* thereof ...... Est 1:22
according to the *w* thereof ...... Est 3:12
The copy of the *w* for a ...... Est 3:14
he gave him the copy of the *w* of ...... Est 4:8
for the *w* which is written in the ...... Est 8:8
according to the *w* thereof ...... Est 8:9
to the Jews according to their *w* ...... Est 8:9
The copy of the *w* for a ...... Est 8:13
two days according to their *w* ...... Est 9:27
The *w* of Hezekiah king of Judah, ...... Is 38:9
in the *w* of the house of Israel ...... Eze 13:9
Whosoever shall read this *w* ...... Dan 5:7
but they could not read the *w* ...... Dan 5:8
me, that they should read this *w* ...... Dan 5:15
now if thou canst read the *w* ...... Dan 5:16
I will read the *w* unto the king ...... Dan 5:17
and this *w* was written ...... Dan 5:24
this is the *w* that was written, ...... Dan 5:25
the decree, and sign the *w* ...... Dan 6:8
king Darius signed the *w* and the ...... Dan 6:9
Daniel knew that the *w* was signed ...... Dan 6:10
him give her a *w* of divorcement ...... Mt 5:31
to give a *w* of divorcement ...... Mt 19:7
And he asked for a *w* table ...... Lk 1:63
the *w* was, JESUS ...... Jn 19:19

**WRITINGS**

But if ye believe not his *w* ...... Jn 5:47

**WRITTEN**

and commandments which I have *w* .... Ex 24:12
stone, *w* with the finger of God ...... Ex 31:18
the tables were *w* on both their ...... Ex 32:15
side and on the other were they *w* ...... Ex 32:15
out of thy book which thou hast *w* ...... Ex 32:32
and they were of them that were *w* .. Num 11:26
of stone *w* with the finger of God ...... Deut 9:10
on them was *w* according to all ...... Deut 9:10
this law that are *w* in this book ...... Deut 28:58
which is not *w* in the book of ...... Deut 28:61
all the curses that are *w* in this ...... Deut 29:20
are *w* in this book of the law ...... Deut 29:21
curses that are *w* in this book ...... Deut 29:27
his statutes which are *w* in this ...... Deut 30:10
to all that is *w* therein ...... Josh 1:8
as it is *w* in the book of the law ...... Josh 8:31
that is *w* in the book of the law ...... Josh 8:34
Is not this *w* in the book of ...... Josh 10:13
to do all that is *w* in the book ...... Josh 23:6
it is *w* in the book of Jasher ...... 2Sa 1:18
as it is *w* in the law of Moses, ...... 1Kin 2:3
are they not *w* in the book of the ...... 1Kin 11:41
they are *w* in the book of the ...... 1Kin 14:19
are they not *w* in the book of the ...... 1Kin 14:29
are they not *w* in the book of the ...... 1Kin 15:7
are they not *w* in the book of the ...... 1Kin 15:23
are they not *w* in the book of the ...... 1Kin 15:31
are they not *w* in the book of the ...... 1Kin 16:5
are they not *w* in the book of the ...... 1Kin 16:14
are they not *w* in the book of the ...... 1Kin 16:20
are they not *w* in the book of the ...... 1Kin 16:27
as it was *w* in the letters which ...... 1Kin 21:11
are they not *w* in the book of the ...... 1Kin 22:39
are they not *w* in the book of the ...... 1Kin 22:45
are they not *w* in the book of the ...... 2Kin 1:18
are they not *w* in the book of the ...... 2Kin 8:23
are they not *w* in the book of the ...... 2Kin 10:34
are they not *w* in the book of the ...... 2Kin 12:19
are they not *w* in the book of the ...... 2Kin 13:8
are they not *w* in the book of the ...... 2Kin 13:12
according unto that which is *w* in ...... 2Kin 14:6
are they not *w* in the book of the ...... 2Kin 14:15
are they not *w* in the book of the ...... 2Kin 14:18
are they not *w* in the book of the ...... 2Kin 14:28
are they not *w* in the book of the ...... 2Kin 15:6
they are *w* in the book of the ...... 2Kin 15:11
they are *w* in the book of the ...... 2Kin 15:15
are they not *w* in the book of the ...... 2Kin 15:21
they are *w* in the book of the ...... 2Kin 15:26
they are *w* in the book of the ...... 2Kin 15:31
are they not *w* in the book of the ...... 2Kin 15:36
are they not *w* in the book of the ...... 2Kin 16:19
are they not *w* in the book of the ...... 2Kin 20:20
are they not *w* in the book of the ...... 2Kin 21:17
are they are not *w* in the book of ...... 2Kin 21:25
all that which is *w* concerning us ...... 2Kin 22:13
covenant that were *w* in this book ...... 2Kin 23:3
as it is *w* in the book of this ...... 2Kin 23:21
*w* in the book that Hilkiah the ...... 2Kin 23:24
are they not *w* in the book of the ...... 2Kin 23:28
are they not *w* in the book of the ...... 2Kin 24:5
these *w* by name came in the days ...... 1Chr 4:41
they were *w* in the book of the ...... 1Chr 9:1
that is *w* in the law of the LORD ...... 1Chr 16:40
they are *w* in the book of Samuel ...... 1Chr 29:29
are they not *w* in the book of ...... 2Chr 9:29
are they not *w* in the book of ...... 2Chr 12:15
are *w* in the story of the prophet ...... 2Chr 13:22
they are *w* in the book of the ...... 2Chr 16:11
they are *w* in the book of Jehu ...... 2Chr 20:34
as it is *w* in the law of Moses, ...... 2Chr 23:18
they are *w* in the story of the ...... 2Chr 24:27
but did as it is *w* in the law in ...... 2Chr 25:4
are they not *w* in the book of the ...... 2Chr 25:26
they are *w* in the book of the ...... 2Chr 27:7
they are *w* in the book of the ...... 2Chr 28:26
time in such sort as it was *w* ...... 2Chr 30:5
passover otherwise than it was *w* ...... 2Chr 30:18
as it is *w* in the law of the LORD ...... 2Chr 31:3
they are *w* in the vision of ...... 2Chr 32:32
they are *w* in the book of the ...... 2Chr 33:18
they are *w* among the sayings of ...... 2Chr 33:19
after all that is *w* in this book ...... 2Chr 34:21
are *w* in the book which they have ... 2Chr 34:24
covenant which are *w* in this book ... 2Chr 34:31
as it is *w* in the book of Moses ...... 2Chr 35:12
they are *w* in the lamentations ...... 2Chr 35:25
was *w* in the law of the LORD ...... 2Chr 35:26
they are *w* in the book of the ...... 2Chr 35:27
they are *w* in the book of the ...... 2Chr 36:8
as it is *w* in the law of Moses ...... Ezr 3:2
feast of tabernacles, as it is *w* ...... Ezr 3:4
letter was *w* in the Syrian tongue ...... Ezr 4:7
unto him, wherein was *w* thus ...... Ezr 5:7
and therein was a record thus *w* ...... Ezr 6:2
as it is *w* in the book of Moses ...... Ezr 6:18
all the weight was *w* at that time ...... Ezr 8:34
Wherein was *w*, It is reported ...... Neh 6:6
at the first, and found *w* therein, ...... Neh 7:5
they found *w* in the law which the ...... Neh 8:14
trees, to make booths, as it is *w* ...... Neh 8:15
our God, as it is *w* in the law ...... Neh 10:34
as it is *w* in the law, and the ...... Neh 10:36
were *w* in the book of the ...... Neh 12:23
and therein was found *w*, that the ...... Neh 13:1
let it be *w* among the laws of the ...... Est 1:19
it was *w* in the book of the ...... Est 2:23
let it be *w* that they may be ...... Est 3:9
there was *w* according to all that ...... Est 3:12
name of king Ahasuerus was it *w* ...... Est 3:12
And it was found *w*, that Mordecai ...... Est 6:2
let it be *w* to reverse the ...... Est 8:5
which is *w* in the king's name ...... Est 8:8
it was *w* according to all that ...... Est 8:9
and as Mordecai had *w* unto them ...... Est 9:23
and it was *w* in the book ...... Est 9:32
are they not *w* in the book of the ...... Est 10:2
Oh that my words were now *w* ...... Job 19:23
that mine adversary had *w* a book ...... Job 31:35
volume of the book it is *w* of me ...... Ps 40:7
not be *w* with the righteous ...... Ps 69:28
This shall be *w* for the ...... Ps 102:18
in thy book all my members were *w* ... Ps 139:16
execute upon them the judgment *w* ...... Ps 149:9
Have not I *w* to thee excellent ...... Prov 22:20
and that which was *w* was upright .... Eccl 12:10
even every one that is *w* among ...... Is 4:3
Behold, it is *w* before me ...... Is 65:6
of Judah is *w* with a pen of iron ...... Jer 17:1
from me shall be *w* in the earth ...... Jer 17:13
even all that is *w* in this book ...... Jer 25:13
which thou hast *w* from my mouth ...... Jer 36:6
saying, Why hast thou *w* therein ...... Jer 36:29
when he had *w* these words in a ...... Jer 45:1
words that are *w* against Babylon ...... Jer 51:60
and it was *w* within and without ...... Eze 2:10
there was *w* therein lamentations, ...... Eze 2:10
neither shall they be *w* in the ...... Eze 13:9
and this writing was *w* ...... Dan 5:24
And this is the writing that was *w* ...... Dan 5:25
the oath that is *w* in the law of ...... Dan 9:11
As it is *w* in the law of Moses, ...... Dan 9:13
that shall be found *w* in the book ...... Dan 12:1
I have *w* to him the great things ...... Hos 8:12
a book of remembrance was *w* ...... Mal 3:16
for thus it is *w* by the prophet ...... Mt 2:5
But he answered and said, It is *w* ...... Mt 4:4
for it is *w*, He shall give his ...... Mt 4:6
said unto him, It is *w* again ...... Mt 4:7
for it is *w*, Thou shalt worship ...... Mt 4:10
For this is he, of whom it is *w* ...... Mt 11:10
And said unto them, It is *w* ...... Mt 21:13
of man goeth as it is *w* of him ...... Mt 26:24
for it is *w*, I will smite the ...... Mt 26:31
up over his head his accusation *w* ...... Mt 27:37
As it is *w* in the prophets, ...... Mk 1:2
of you hypocrites, as it is *w* ...... Mk 7:6
how it is *w* of the Son of man, ...... Mk 9:12
they listed, as it is *w* of him ...... Mk 9:13
saying unto them, Is it not *w* ...... Mk 11:17
indeed goeth, as it is *w* of him ...... Mk 14:21
for it is *w*, I will smite the ...... Mk 14:27
of his accusation was *w* over ...... Mk 15:26
(As it is *w* in the law of the ...... Lk 2:23
As it is *w* in the book of the ...... Lk 3:4
answered him, saying, It is *w* ...... Lk 4:4
for it is *w*, Thou shalt worship ...... Lk 4:8
For it is *w*, He shall give his ...... Lk 4:10
he found the place where it was *w* ...... Lk 4:17
This is he, of whom it is *w* ...... Lk 7:27
your names are *w* in heaven ...... Lk 10:20
unto him, What is *w* in the law ...... Lk 10:26
all things that are *w* by the ...... Lk 18:31
Saying unto them, It is *w* ...... Lk 19:46
said, What is this then that is *w* ...... Lk 20:17
which are *w* may be fulfilled ...... Lk 21:22
that this that is *w* must yet be ...... Lk 22:37
a superscription also was *w* over ...... Lk 23:38
which were *w* in the law of Moses, ...... Lk 24:44
And said unto them, Thus it is *w* ...... Lk 24:46
remembered that it was *w*, The ...... Jn 2:17
as it is *w*, He gave them bread ...... Jn 6:31
It is *w* in the prophets, And they ...... Jn 6:45
It is also *w* in your law, that ...... Jn 8:17
Is it not *w* in your law, I said, ...... Jn 10:34
as it is *w*, ...... Jn 12:14
that these things were *w* of him ...... Jn 12:16
fulfilled that is *w* in their law ...... Jn 15:25
it was *w* in Hebrew, and Greek, and ...... Jn 19:20
What I have *w* I have *w* ...... Jn 19:22
which are not *w* in this book ...... Jn 20:30
But these are *w*, that ye might ...... Jn 20:31
if they should be *w* every one ...... Jn 21:25
the books that should be *w* ...... Jn 21:25
For it is *w* in the book of Psalms ...... Acts 1:20
as it is *w* in the book of the ...... Acts 7:42
fulfilled all that was *w* of him ...... Acts 13:29
as it is also *w* in the second ...... Acts 13:33
as it is *w*, ...... Acts 15:15
Gentiles which believe, we have *w* ...... Acts 21:25
for it is *w*, Thou shalt not speak ...... Acts 23:5
all things which are *w* in the law ...... Acts 24:14
as it is *w*, The just shall live ...... Rom 1:17
work of the law *w* in their hearts ...... Rom 2:15
Gentiles through you, as it is *w* ...... Rom 2:24
as it is *w*, That thou mightest be ...... Rom 3:4
As it is *w*, There is none ...... Rom 3:10
(As it is *w*, I have made thee a ...... Rom 4:17
Now it was not *w* for his sake ...... Rom 4:23
As it is *w*, For thy sake we are ...... Rom 8:36
As it is *w*, Jacob have I loved, ...... Rom 9:13
As it is *w*, Behold, I lay in Sion ...... Rom 9:33
as it is *w*, How beautiful are the ...... Rom 10:15
(According as it is *w*, God hath ...... Rom 11:8
as it is *w*, There shall come out ...... Rom 11:26
for it is *w*, Vengeance is mine ...... Rom 12:19
For it is *w*, As I live, saith the ...... Rom 14:11
but, as it is *w*, The reproaches ...... Rom 15:3
For whatsoever things were *w* ...... Rom 15:4
aforetime were *w* for our learning ...... Rom 15:4
as it is *w*, For this cause I will ...... Rom 15:9
I have *w* the more boldly unto you ... Rom 15:15
But as it is *w*, To whom he was ...... Rom 15:21
*W* to the Romans from Corinthus, ...... Rom *s*
For it is *w*, I will destroy the ...... 1Cor 1:19
That, according as it is *w* ...... 1Cor 1:31
But as it is *w*, Eye hath not seen ...... 1Cor 2:9
For it is *w*, He taketh the wise ...... 1Cor 3:19
of men above that which is *w* ...... 1Cor 4:6
But now I have *w* unto you not to ...... 1Cor 5:11
For it is *w* in the law of Moses, ...... 1Cor 9:9
our sakes, no doubt, this is *w* ...... 1Cor 9:10
neither have I *w* these things ...... 1Cor 9:15
as it is *w*, The people sat down ...... 1Cor 10:7
they are *w* for our admonition, ...... 1Cor 10:11
In the law it is *w*, With men of ...... 1Cor 14:21
And so it is *w*, The first man Adam ... 1Cor 15:45
to pass the saying that is *w* ...... 1Cor 15:54
was *w* from Philippi by Stephanus ...... 1Cor *s*
are our epistle *w* in our hearts ...... 2Cor 3:2
*w* not with ink, but with the ...... 2Cor 3:3
if the ministration of death, *w* ...... 2Cor 3:7
of faith, according as it is *w* ...... 2Cor 4:13
As it is *w*, He that had gathered ...... 2Cor 8:15
(As it is *w*, He hath dispersed ...... 2Cor 9:9
Corinthians was *w* from Philippi ...... 2Cor *s*
for it is *w*, Cursed is every one ...... Gal 3:10
not in all things which are *w* in ...... Gal 3:10
for it is *w*, Cursed is every one ...... Gal 3:13
For it is *w*, that Abraham had two ...... Gal 4:22
For it is *w*, Rejoice, thou barren ...... Gal 4:27
*w* unto you with mine own hand ...... Gal 6:11
Unto the Galatians *w* from Rome ...... Gal *s*
*W* from Rome unto the Ephesians by ...... Eph *s*
It was *w* to the Philippians from ...... Phil *s*
*W* from Rome to the Colossians by ...... Col *s*
Thessalonians was *w* from Athens ...... 1Th *s*
Thessalonians was *w* from Athens ...... 2Th *s*
The first to Timothy was *w* from ...... 1Ti *s*
was *w* from Rome, when Paul was ...... 2Ti *s*
It was *w* to Titus, ordained the ...... Titus *s*
I Paul have *w* it with mine own ...... Philem 19
*W* from Rome to Philemon, by ...... Philem *s*
volume of the book it is *w* of me ...... Heb 10:7
firstborn, which are *w* in heaven ...... Heb 12:23
for I have *w* a letter unto you in ...... Heb 13:22
*W* to the Hebrews from Italy by ...... Heb *s*
Because it is *w*, Be ye holy ...... 1Pet 1:16
I have *w* briefly, exhorting, and ...... 1Pet 5:12
given unto him hath *w* unto you ...... 2Pet 3:15
I have *w* unto you, fathers, ...... 1Jn 2:14
I have *w* unto you, young men, ...... 1Jn 2:14
I have not *w* unto you because ye ...... 1Jn 2:21
These things have I *w* unto you ...... 1Jn 2:26
These things have I *w* unto you ...... 1Jn 5:13
those things which are *w* therein ...... Rev 1:3
and in the stone a new name *w* ...... Rev 2:17
sat on the throne a book *w* within ...... Rev 5:1
whose names are not *w* in the book ...... Rev 13:8
name *w* in their foreheads ...... Rev 14:1
And upon her forehead was a name *w*. Rev 17:5
whose names were not *w* in the ...... Rev 17:8
and he had a name *w*, that no man ...... Rev 19:12
vesture and on his thigh a name *w* ...... Rev 19:16
things which were *w* in the books ...... Rev 20:12
whosoever was not found *w* in the ...... Rev 20:15
names *w* thereon, which are the ...... Rev 21:12
but they which are *w* in the ...... Rev 21:27
plagues that are *w* in this book ...... Rev 22:18
things which are *w* in this book ...... Rev 22:19

**WRONG**

unto Abram, My *w* be upon thee ...... Gen 16:5
and he said to him that did the *w* ...... Ex 2:13
against him that which is *w* ...... Deut 19:16
thou doest me *w* to war against me .. Judg 11:27
there is no *w* in mine hands ...... 1Chr 12:17
He suffered no man to do them *w* ...... 1Chr 16:21

hath not done *w* to the king only ... Est 1:16
Behold, I cry out of *w*, but I am ... Job 19:7
He suffered no man to do them *w* ... Ps 105:14
and do no *w*, do no violence to the ... Jer 22:3
and his chambers by *w* ... Jer 22:13
O LORD, thou hast seen my *w* ... Lam 3:59
therefore *w* judgment proceedeth ... Hab 1:4
and said, Friend, I do thee no *w* ... Mt 20:13
And seeing one of them suffer *w* ... Acts 7:24
why do ye *w* one to another ... Acts 7:26
his neighbour *w* thrust him away ... Acts 7:27
a matter of *w* or wicked lewdness ... Acts 18:14
to the Jews have I done no *w* ... Acts 25:10
Why do ye not rather take *w* ... 1Cor 6:7
Nay, ye do *w*, and defraud, and that ... 1Cor 6:8
for his cause that had done the *w* ... 2Cor 7:12
nor for his cause that suffered *w* ... 2Cor 7:12
forgive me this *w* ... 2Cor 12:13
But he that doeth *w* shall receive ... Col 3:25
for the *w* which he hath done ... Col 3:25

**WRONGED**
we have *w* no man, we have ... 2Cor 7:2
If he hath *w* thee, or oweth thee ... Philem 18

**WRONGETH**
sinneth against me *w* his own soul ... Prov 8:36

**WRONGFULLY**
which ye *w* imagine against me ... Job 21:27
mine enemies *w* rejoice over me ... Ps 35:19
that hate me *w* are multiplied ... Ps 38:19
destroy me, being mine enemies *w* ... Ps 69:4
they persecute me *w* ... Ps 119:86
have oppressed the stranger *w* ... Eze 22:29
God endure grief, suffering *w* ... 1Pet 2:19

**WROTE**
Moses *w* all the words of the LORD ... Ex 24:4
he *w* upon the tables the words of ... Ex 34:28
*w* upon it a writing, like to the ... Ex 39:30
And Moses *w* their goings out ... Num 33:2
he *w* them upon two tables of ... Deut 4:13
he *w* them in two tables of stone ... Deut 5:22
he *w* on the tables, according to ... Deut 10:4
Moses *w* this law, and delivered it ... Deut 31:9
Moses therefore *w* this song the ... Deut 31:22
he *w* there upon the stones a copy ... Josh 8:32
which he *w* in the presence of the ... Josh 8:32
Joshua *w* these words in the book ... Josh 24:26
*w* it in a book, and laid it up ... 1Sa 10:25
that David *w* a letter to Joab, and ... 2Sa 11:14
he *w* in the letter, saying, Set ... 2Sa 11:15
So she *w* letters in Ahab's name ... 1Kin 21:8
she *w* in the letters, saying ... 1Kin 21:9
Jehu *w* letters, and sent to ... 2Kin 10:1
Then he *w* a letter the second ... 2Kin 10:6
commandment, which he *w* for you .. 2Kin 17:37
*w* them before the king, and the ... 1Chr 24:6
*w* letters also to Ephraim and ... 2Chr 30:1
He *w* also letters to rail on the ... 2Chr 32:17
*w* they unto him an accusation ... Ezr 4:6
the days of Artaxerxes *w* Bishlam ... Ezr 4:7
Shimshai the scribe *w* a letter ... Ezr 4:8
Then *w* Rehum the chancellor, and ... Ezr 4:9
which he *w* to destroy the Jews ... Est 8:5
he *w* in the king Ahasuerus' name ... Est 8:10
Mordecai *w* these things, and sent ... Est 9:20
*w* with all authority, to confirm ... Est 9:29
Baruch *w* from the mouth of ... Jer 36:4
I *w* them with ink in the book ... Jer 36:18
the words which Baruch *w* at the ... Jer 36:27
who *w* therein from the mouth of ... Jer 36:32
So Jeremiah *w* in a book all the ... Jer 51:60
*w* over against the candlestick ... Dan 5:5
saw the part of the hand that *w* ... Dan 5:5
king Darius *w* unto all people ... Dan 6:25
then he *w* the dream, and told the ... Dan 7:1
your heart he *w* you this precept ... Mk 10:5
Moses *w* unto us, If a man's ... Mk 12:19
asked for a writing table, and *w* ... Lk 1:63
Moses *w* unto us, If any man's ... Lk 20:28
for he *w* of me ... Jn 5:46
with his finger *w* on the ground ... Jn 8:6
stooped down, and *w* on the ground ... Jn 8:8
Pilate *w* a title, and put it on ... Jn 19:19
these things, and *w* these things ... Jn 21:24
they *w* letters by them after this ... Acts 15:23
pass into Achaia, the brethren *w* ... Acts 18:27
he *w* a letter after this manner ... Acts 23:25
who *w* this epistle, salute you in ... Rom 16:22
I *w* unto you in an epistle not to ... 1Cor 5:9
the things whereof ye *w* unto me ... 1Cor 7:1
I *w* this same unto you, lest ... 2Cor 2:3
anguish of heart I *w* unto you ... 2Cor 2:4
Wherefore, though I *w* unto you ... 2Cor 7:12
(as I *w* afore in few words ... Eph 3:3
in thy obedience I *w* unto thee ... Philem 21
lady, not as though I *w* a new ... 2Jn 5
I *w* unto the church ... 3Jn 9

**WROTH**
And Cain was very *w*, and his ... Gen 4:5
said unto Cain, Why art thou *w* ... Gen 4:6
And Jacob was *w*, and chode with ... Gen 31:36
were grieved, and they were very *w* ... Gen 34:7
Pharaoh was *w* against two of his ... Gen 40:2
Pharaoh was *w* with his servants ... Gen 41:10
and Moses was *w* with them ... Ex 16:20
And Moses was very *w* ... Num 16:15
wilt thou be *w* with all the ... Num 16:22
Moses was *w* with the officers of ... Num 31:14
the voice of your words, and was *w* ... Deut 1:34
But the LORD was *w* with me for ... Deut 3:26
wherewith the LORD was *w* against ... Deut 9:19
that to morrow he will be *w* with ... Josh 22:18
And Saul was very *w*, and the saying ... 1Sa 18:8
but if he be very *w*, then be sure ... 1Sa 20:7
the Philistines were *w* with him ... 1Sa 29:4
Then was Abner very *w* for the ... 2Sa 3:8
all these things, he was very *w* ... 2Sa 13:21
moved and shook, because he was *w* ... 2Sa 22:8
But Naaman was *w*, and went away ... 2Kin 5:11
the man of God was *w* ... 2Kin 13:19
Then Asa was *w* with the seer, and .. 2Chr 16:10
Then Uzziah was *w*, and had a ... 2Chr 26:19
while he was *w* with the priests ... 2Chr 26:19
of your fathers was *w* with Judah ... 2Chr 28:9
we builded the wall, he was *w* ... Neh 4:1
be stopped, then they were very *w* ... Neh 4:7
therefore was the king very *w* ... Est 1:12
those which kept the door, were *w* ... Est 2:21
and were shaken, because he was *w* ... Ps 18:7
the LORD heard this, and was *w* ... Ps 78:21
When God heard this, he was *w* ... Ps 78:59
was *w* with his inheritance ... Ps 78:62
thou hast been *w* with thine ... Ps 89:38
he shall be *w* as in the valley of ... Is 28:21
I was *w* with my people, I have ... Is 47:6
that I would not be *w* with thee ... Is 54:9
ever, neither will I be always *w* ... Is 57:16
of his covetousness was I *w* ... Is 57:17
I hid me, and was *w*, and he went on ... Is 57:17
behold, thou art *w* ... Is 64:5
Be not *w* very sore, O LORD ... Is 64:9
the princes were *w* with Jeremiah ... Jer 37:15
thou art very *w* against us ... Lam 5:22
of the wise men, was exceeding *w* ... Mt 2:16
And his lord was *w*, and delivered ... Mt 18:34
the king heard thereof, he was *w* ... Mt 22:7
the dragon was *w* with the woman ... Rev 12:17

**WROUGHT**
because he had *w* folly in Israel ... Gen 34:7
what things I have *w* in Egypt ... Ex 10:2
twined linen, *w* with needlework ... Ex 26:36
twined linen, *w* with needlework ... Ex 27:16
Then *w* Bezaleel and Aholiab, and ... Ex 36:1
that *w* all the work of the ... Ex 36:4
hearted man among them that *w* the ... Ex 36:8
they *w* onyx stones inclosed in ... Ex 39:6
they have *w* confusion ... Lev 20:12
and of Israel, What hath God *w* ... Num 23:23
gold of them, even all *w* jewels ... Num 31:51
such abomination is *w* among you ... Deut 13:14
that hath *w* wickedness in the ... Deut 17:2
such abomination is *w* in Israel ... Deut 17:4
which hath not been *w* with ... Deut 21:3
she hath *w* folly in Israel ... Deut 22:21
the evils which they shall have *w* ... Deut 31:18
because he hath *w* folly in Israel ... Josh 7:15
folly that they have *w* in Israel ... Judg 20:10
mother in law with whom she had *w*. Ruth 2:19
name with whom I *w* to day is Boaz .. Ruth 2:19
when he had *w* wonderfully among ... 1Sa 6:6
LORD hath *w* salvation in Israel ... 1Sa 11:13
who hath *w* this great salvation ... 1Sa 14:45
for he hath *w* with God this day ... 1Sa 14:45
the LORD *w* a great salvation for ... 1Sa 19:5
Otherwise I should have *w* ... 2Sa 18:13
the LORD *w* a great victory that ... 2Sa 23:10
the LORD *w* a great victory ... 2Sa 23:12
the people that *w* in the work ... 1Kin 5:16
king Solomon, and *w* all his work ... 1Kin 7:14
the brim thereof was *w* like the ... 1Kin 7:26
the people that *w* in the work ... 1Kin 9:23
Zimri, and his treason that he *w* ... 1Kin 16:20
But Omri *w* evil in the eyes of ... 1Kin 16:25
he *w* evil in the sight of the ... 2Kin 3:2
that *w* upon the house of the LORD ... 2Kin 12:11
*w* wicked things to provoke the ... 2Kin 17:11
he *w* much wickedness in the sight ... 2Kin 21:6
house of them that *w* fine linen ... 1Chr 4:21
he set masons to hew *w* stones to ... 1Chr 22:2
linen, and *w* cherubims thereon ... 2Chr 3:14
he *w* that which was evil in the ... 2Chr 21:6
the LORD, and also such as *w* iron ... 2Chr 24:12
the workmen *w*, and the work ... 2Chr 24:13
*w* that which was good ... 2Chr 31:20
he *w* much evil in the sight of ... 2Chr 33:6
that *w* in the house of the LORD ... 2Chr 34:10
that *w* the work in any manner of ... 2Chr 34:13
half of my servants *w* in the work ... Neh 4:16
one of his hands *w* in the work ... Neh 4:17
that this work was *w* of our God ... Neh 6:16
and had *w* great provocations ... Neh 9:18
they *w* great provocations ... Neh 9:26
the hand of the LORD hath *w* this ... Job 12:9
who can say, Thou hast *w* iniquity ... Job 36:23
which thou hast *w* for them that ... Ps 31:19
her clothing is of *w* gold ... Ps 45:13
that which thou hast *w* for us ... Ps 68:28
How he had *w* his signs in Egypt ... Ps 78:43
curiously *w* in the lowest parts ... Ps 139:15
all the works that my hands had *w* ... Eccl 2:11
because the work that is *w* under ... Eccl 2:17
for thou also hast *w* all our ... Is 26:12
we have not *w* any deliverance in ... Is 26:18
Who hath *w* and done it, calling ... Is 41:4
seeing she hath *w* lewdness with ... Jer 11:15
he *w* a work on the wheels ... Jer 18:3
But I *w* for my name's sake, that ... Eze 20:9
But I *w* for my name's sake, that ... Eze 20:14
*w* for my name's sake, that it ... Eze 20:22
when I have *w* with you for my ... Eze 20:44
against it, because they *w* for me ... Eze 29:20
the high God hath *w* toward me ... Dan 4:2
for the sea *w*, and was tempestuous. Jonah 1:11
for the sea *w*, and was tempestuous. Jonah 1:13
which have *w* his judgment ... Zeph 2:3
These last have *w* but one hour ... Mt 20:12
for she hath *w* a good work upon ... Mt 26:10
mighty works are *w* by his hands ... Mk 6:2
she hath *w* a good work on me ... Mk 14:6
manifest, that they are *w* in God ... Jn 3:21
wonders *w* among the people ... Acts 5:12
wonders God had *w* among the ... Acts 15:12
craft, he abode with them, and *w* ... Acts 18:3
God *w* special miracles by the ... Acts 19:11
what things God had *w* among the ... Acts 21:19
*w* in me all manner of ... Rom 7:8
which Christ hath not *w* by me ... Rom 15:18
Now he that hath *w* us for the ... 2Cor 5:5
what carefulness it *w* in you ... 2Cor 7:11
were *w* among you in all patience ... 2Cor 12:12
(For he that *w* effectually in ... Gal 2:8
Which he *w* in Christ, when he ... Eph 1:20
but *w* with labour and travail ... 2Th 3:8
*w* righteousness, obtained ... Heb 11:33
thou how faith *w* with his works ... Jas 2:22
have *w* the will of the Gentiles ... 1Pet 4:3
not those things which we have *w* ... 2Jn 8
that *w* miracles before him ... Rev 19:20

**WROUGHTEST**
and where *w* thou ... Ruth 2:19

**WRUNG**
the blood thereof shall be *w* out ... Lev 1:15
*w* out at the bottom of the altar ... Lev 5:9
of a full cup are *w* out to them ... Ps 73:10
cup of trembling, and *w* them out ... Is 51:17

# X

**XERXES** See AHASUERUS.

**XERXES'** See AHASUERUS'.

# Y

**YAH** See JAH.

**YARN**
brought out of Egypt, and linen *y* ... 1Kin 10:28
received the linen *y* at a price ... 1Kin 10:28
brought out of Egypt, and linen *y* ... 2Chr 1:16
received the linen *y* at a price ... 2Chr 1:16

**YE** See PREFACE.

**YEA** See PREFACE.

**YEAR**
six hundredth *y* of Noah's life ... Gen 7:11
in the six hundredth and first *y* ... Gen 8:13
in the thirteenth *y* they rebelled ... Gen 14:4
fourteenth *y* came Chedorlaomer ... Gen 14:5
at this set time in the next *y* ... Gen 17:21
in the same *y* an hundredfold ... Gen 26:12
for all their cattle for that *y* ... Gen 47:17
When that *y* was ended, they came ... Gen 47:18
they came unto him the second *y* ... Gen 47:18
the first month of the *y* to you ... Ex 12:2
blemish, a male of the first *y* ... Ex 12:5
in his season from *y* to *y* ... Ex 13:10
in his season from *y* to *y* ... Ex 13:10
But the seventh *y* thou shalt let ... Ex 23:11
keep a feast unto me in the *y* ... Ex 23:14
which is in the end of the *y* ... Ex 23:16
Three times in the *y* all thy ... Ex 23:17
out from before thee in one *y* ... Ex 23:29
first *y* day by day continually ... Ex 29:38
in a *y* with the blood of the sin ... Ex 30:10
once in the *y* shall he make ... Ex 30:10
Thrice in the *y* shall all your ... Ex 34:23
the LORD thy God thrice in the *y* ... Ex 34:24
the first month in the second *y* ... Ex 40:17
and a lamb, both of the first *y* ... Lev 9:3
the first *y* for a burnt offering ... Lev 12:6
of the first *y* without blemish ... Lev 14:10
for all their sins once a *y* ... Lev 16:34
But in the fourth *y* all the fruit ... Lev 19:24
in the fifth *y* shall ye eat of ... Lev 19:25
without blemish of the first *y* ... Lev 23:12
without blemish of the first *y* ... Lev 23:18
two lambs of the first *y* for a ... Lev 23:19
unto the LORD seven days in the *y* ... Lev 23:41
But in the seventh *y* shall be a ... Lev 25:4
for it is a *y* of rest unto the ... Lev 25:5
And ye shall hallow the fiftieth *y* ... Lev 25:10
shall that fiftieth *y* be unto you ... Lev 25:11
In the *y* of this jubile ye shall ... Lev 25:13
What shall we eat the seventh *y* ... Lev 25:20
blessing upon you in the sixth *y* ... Lev 25:21
And ye shall sow the eighth *y* ... Lev 25:22
of old fruit until the ninth *y* ... Lev 25:22
bought it until the *y* of jubile ... Lev 25:28

within a whole y after it is sold .... Lev 25:29
within a full y may he redeem it .... Lev 25:29
within the space of a full y .... Lev 25:30
shall go out in the y of jubile .... Lev 25:33
serve thee unto the y of jubile .... Lev 25:40
y that he was sold to him unto .... Lev 25:50
sold to him unto the y of jubile .... Lev 25:50
few years unto the y of jubile .... Lev 25:52
shall go out in the y of jubile .... Lev 25:54
his field from the y of jubile .... Lev 27:17
even unto the y of the jubile .... Lev 27:18
even unto the y of the jubile .... Lev 27:23
In the y of the jubile the field .... Lev 27:24
in the second y after they were .... Num 1:1
first y for a trespass offering .... Num 6:12
one he lamb of the first y .... Num 6:14
first y without blemish for a sin .... Num 6:14
one ram, one lamb of the first y .... Num 7:15
goats, five lambs of the first y .... Num 7:17
one ram, one lamb of the first y .... Num 7:21
goats, five lambs of the first y .... Num 7:23
one ram, one lamb of the first y .... Num 7:27
goats, five lambs of the first y .... Num 7:29
one ram, one lamb of the first y .... Num 7:33
goats, five lambs of the first y .... Num 7:35
one ram, one lamb of the first y .... Num 7:39
goats, five lambs of the first y .... Num 7:41
one ram, one lamb of the first y .... Num 7:45
goats, five lambs of the first y .... Num 7:47
one ram, one lamb of the first y .... Num 7:51
goats, five lambs of the first y .... Num 7:53
one ram, one lamb of the first y .... Num 7:57
goats, five lambs of the first y .... Num 7:59
one ram, one lamb of the first y .... Num 7:63
goats, five lambs of the first y .... Num 7:65
one ram, one lamb of the first y .... Num 7:69
goats, five lambs of the first y .... Num 7:71
one ram, one lamb of the first y .... Num 7:75
goats, five lambs of the first y .... Num 7:77
one ram, one lamb of the first y .... Num 7:81
goats, five lambs of the first y .... Num 7:83
the lambs of the first y twelve .... Num 7:87
the lambs of the first y sixty .... Num 7:88
the first month of the second y .... Num 9:1
were two days, or a month, or a y .... Num 9:22
the second month, in the second y .... Num 10:11
even forty days, each day for a y .... Num 14:34
of the first y for a sin offering .... Num 15:27
two lambs of the first y without .... Num 28:3
lambs of the first y without spot .... Num 28:9
lambs of the first y without spot .... Num 28:11
throughout the months of the y .... Num 28:14
and seven lambs of the first y .... Num 28:19
ram, seven lambs of the first y .... Num 28:27
of the first y without blemish .... Num 29:2
and seven lambs of the first y .... Num 29:8
and fourteen lambs of the first y .... Num 29:13
lambs of the first y without spot .... Num 29:17
of the first y without blemish .... Num 29:20
of the first y without blemish .... Num 29:23
lambs of the first y without spot .... Num 29:26
of the first y without blemish .... Num 29:29
of the first y without blemish .... Num 29:32
of the first y without blemish .... Num 29:36
in the fortieth y after the .... Num 33:38
it came to pass in the fortieth y .... Deut 1:3
from the beginning of the y even .... Deut 11:12
y even unto the end of the y .... Deut 11:12
field bringeth forth y by y .... Deut 14:22
field bringeth forth y by y .... Deut 14:22
of thine increase the same y .... Deut 14:28
heart, saying, The seventh y .... Deut 15:9
the y of release, is at hand .... Deut 15:9
then in the seventh y thou shalt .... Deut 15:12
y by y in the place which the .... Deut 15:20
by y in the place which the LORD .... Deut 15:20
Three times in a y shall all thy .... Deut 16:16
he shall be free at home one y .... Deut 24:5
of thine increase the third y .... Deut 26:12
which is the y of tithing .... Deut 26:12
the solemnity of the y of release .... Deut 31:10
of the land of Canaan that y .... Josh 5:12
that y they vexed and oppressed .... Judg 10:8
the Gileadite four days in a y .... Judg 11:40
ten shekels of silver by the y .... Judg 17:10
And as he did so y by y .... 1Sa 1:7
brought it to him from y to y .... 1Sa 2:19
he went from y to y in circuit .... 1Sa 7:16
Saul reigned one y .... 1Sa 13:1
of the Philistines was a full y .... 1Sa 27:7
after the y was expired, at the .... 2Sa 11:1
David three years, y after y .... 2Sa 21:1
his month in a y made provision .... 1Kin 4:7
gave Solomon to Hiram y by y .... 1Kin 5:11
eightieth y after the children of .... 1Kin 6:1
in the fourth y of Solomon's .... 1Kin 6:1
In the fourth y was the .... 1Kin 6:37
And in the eleventh y, in the .... 1Kin 6:38
three times in a y did Solomon .... 1Kin 9:25
one y was six hundred threescore .... 1Kin 10:14
and mules, a rate y by y .... 1Kin 10:25
in the fifth y of king Rehoboam .... 1Kin 14:25
Now in the eighteenth y of king .... 1Kin 15:1
in the twentieth y of Jeroboam .... 1Kin 15:9
the second y of Asa king of Judah .... 1Kin 15:25
Even in the third y of Asa king .... 1Kin 15:28
In the third y of Asa king of .... 1Kin 15:33
sixth y of Asa king of Judah .... 1Kin 16:8
seventh y of Asa king of Judah, .... 1Kin 16:10
seventh y of Asa king of Judah .... 1Kin 16:15
first y of Asa king of Judah .... 1Kin 16:23
eighth y of Asa king of Judah .... 1Kin 16:29
came to Elijah in the third y .... 1Kin 18:1
for at the return of the y the .... 1Kin 20:22
to pass at the return of the y .... 1Kin 20:26
And it came to pass in the third y .... 1Kin 22:2
fourth y of Ahab king of Israel .... 1Kin 22:41
in Samaria the seventeenth y of .... 1Kin 22:51
second y of Jehoram the son of .... 2Kin 1:17
in Samaria the eighteenth y of .... 2Kin 3:1
in the fifth y of Joram the son .... 2Kin 8:16
In the twelfth y of Joram the son .... 2Kin 8:25
and he reigned one y in Jerusalem .... 2Kin 8:26
in the eleventh y of Joram the .... 2Kin 9:29
the seventh y Jehoiada sent and .... 2Kin 11:4
In the seventh y of Jehu Jehoash .... 2Kin 12:1
twentieth y of king Jehoash the .... 2Kin 12:6
twentieth y of Joash the son of .... 2Kin 13:1
seventh y of Joash king of Judah .... 2Kin 13:10
land at the coming in of the y .... 2Kin 13:20
In the second y of Joash son of .... 2Kin 14:1
In the fifteenth y of Amaziah the .... 2Kin 14:23
seventh y of Jeroboam king of .... 2Kin 15:1
eighth y of Azariah king of Judah .... 2Kin 15:8
thirtieth y of Uzziah king of .... 2Kin 15:13
thirtieth y of Azariah king of .... 2Kin 15:17
In the fiftieth y of Azariah king .... 2Kin 15:23
fiftieth y of Azariah king of .... 2Kin 15:27
in the twentieth y of Jotham the .... 2Kin 15:30
In the second y of Pekah the son .... 2Kin 15:32
In the seventeenth y of Pekah the .... 2Kin 16:1
In the twelfth y of Ahaz king of .... 2Kin 17:1
Assyria, as he had done y by y .... 2Kin 17:4
In the ninth y of Hoshea the king .... 2Kin 17:6
it came to pass in the third y of .... 2Kin 18:1
in the fourth y of king Hezekiah .... 2Kin 18:9
which was the seventh y of Hoshea .... 2Kin 18:9
even in the sixth y of Hezekiah .... 2Kin 18:10
that is the ninth y of Hoshea .... 2Kin 18:10
fourteenth y of king Hezekiah did .... 2Kin 18:13
Ye shall eat this y such things .... 2Kin 19:29
in the second y that which .... 2Kin 19:29
and in the third y sow ye, and reap .... 2Kin 19:29
the eighteenth y of king Josiah .... 2Kin 22:3
the eighteenth y of king Josiah .... 2Kin 23:23
him in the eighth y of his reign .... 2Kin 24:12
pass in the ninth y of his reign .... 2Kin 25:1
the eleventh y of king Zedekiah .... 2Kin 25:2
which is the nineteenth y of king .... 2Kin 25:8
thirtieth y of the captivity of .... 2Kin 25:27
king of Babylon in the y that he .... 2Kin 25:27
that after the y was expired .... 1Chr 20:1
In the fortieth y of the reign of .... 1Chr 26:31
all the months of the y, of every .... 1Chr 27:1
in the fourth y of his reign .... 2Chr 3:2
feasts, three times in the y .... 2Chr 8:13
Solomon in one y was six hundred .... 2Chr 9:13
and mules, a rate y by y .... 2Chr 9:24
that in the fifth y of king .... 2Chr 12:2
Now in the eighteenth y of king .... 2Chr 13:1
in the fifteenth y of the reign .... 2Chr 15:10
thirtieth y of the reign of Asa .... 2Chr 15:19
thirtieth y of the reign of Asa .... 2Chr 16:1
ninth y of his reign was diseased .... 2Chr 16:12
one and fortieth y of his reign .... 2Chr 16:13
Also in the third y of his reign .... 2Chr 17:7
and he reigned one y in Jerusalem .... 2Chr 22:2
in the seventh y Jehoiada .... 2Chr 23:1
house of your God from y to y .... 2Chr 24:5
came to pass at the end of the y .... 2Chr 24:23
of Ammon gave him the same y an .... 2Chr 27:5
pay unto him, both the second y .... 2Chr 27:5
He in the first y of his reign .... 2Chr 29:3
For in the eighth y of his reign .... 2Chr 34:3
in the twelfth y he began to .... 2Chr 34:3
in the eighteenth y of his reign .... 2Chr 34:8
In the eighteenth y of the reign .... 2Chr 35:19
when the y was expired, king .... 2Chr 36:10
Now in the first y of Cyrus king .... 2Chr 36:22
Now in the first y of Cyrus king .... Ezr 1:1
Now in the second y of their .... Ezr 3:8
So it ceased unto the second y of .... Ezr 4:24
But in the first y of Cyrus the .... Ezr 5:13
In the first y of Cyrus the king .... Ezr 6:3
which was in the sixth y of the .... Ezr 6:15
in the seventh y of Artaxerxes .... Ezr 7:7
was in the seventh y of the king .... Ezr 7:8
month Chisleu, in the twentieth y .... Neh 1:1
in the twentieth y of Artaxerxes .... Neh 2:1
the twentieth y even unto the two .... Neh 5:14
thirtieth y of Artaxerxes the .... Neh 5:14
that we would leave the seventh y .... Neh 10:31
at times appointed y by y .... Neh 10:34
at times appointed y by y .... Neh 10:34
all fruit of all trees, y by y .... Neh 10:35
thirtieth y of Artaxerxes king of .... Neh 13:6
In the third y of his reign .... Est 1:3
in the seventh y of his reign .... Est 2:16
Nisan, in the twelfth y of king .... Est 3:7
to their appointed time every y .... Est 9:27
be joined unto the days of the y .... Job 3:6
crownest the y with thy goodness .... Ps 65:11
In the y that king Uzziah died I .... Is 6:1
In the y that king Ahaz died was .... Is 14:28
In the y that Tartan came unto .... Is 20:1
the Lord said unto me, Within a y .... Is 21:16
add ye y to y .... Is 29:1
the y of recompences for the .... Is 34:8
the fourteenth y of king Hezekiah .... Is 36:1
Ye shall eat this y such as .... Is 37:30
the second y that which springeth .... Is 37:30
and in the third y sow ye, and reap .... Is 37:30
the acceptable y of the LORD .... Is 61:2
the y of my redeemed is come .... Is 63:4
in the thirteenth y of his reign .... Jer 1:2
unto the end of the eleventh y of .... Jer 1:3
even the y of their visitation .... Jer 11:23
be careful in the y of drought .... Jer 17:8
even the y of their visitation, .... Jer 23:12
people of Judah in the fourth y .... Jer 25:1
of Judah, that was the first y of .... Jer 25:1
From the thirteenth y of Josiah .... Jer 25:3
that is the three and twentieth y .... Jer 25:3
And it came to pass the same y .... Jer 28:1
king of Judah, in the fourth y .... Jer 28:1
this y thou shalt die, because .... Jer 28:16
the same y in the seventh month .... Jer 28:17
tenth y of Zedekiah king of Judah .... Jer 32:1
eighteenth y of Nebuchadrezzar .... Jer 32:1
it came to pass in the fourth y .... Jer 36:1
it came to pass in the fifth y of .... Jer 36:9
In the ninth y of Zedekiah king .... Jer 39:1
And in the eleventh y of Zedekiah .... Jer 39:2
in the fourth y of Jehoiakim the .... Jer 45:1
y of Jehoiakim the son of Josiah .... Jer 46:2
the y of their visitation, saith .... Jer 48:44
a rumour shall both come one y .... Jer 51:46
in another y shall come a rumour .... Jer 51:46
in the fourth y of his reign .... Jer 51:59
pass in the ninth y of his reign .... Jer 52:4
the eleventh y of king Zedekiah .... Jer 52:5
which was the nineteenth y of .... Jer 52:12
in the seventh y three thousand .... Jer 52:28
In the eighteenth y of .... Jer 52:29
twentieth y of Nebuchadrezzar .... Jer 52:30
thirtieth y of the captivity of .... Jer 52:31
king of Babylon in the first y of .... Jer 52:31
came to pass in the thirtieth y .... Eze 1:1
which was the fifth y of king .... Eze 1:2
appointed thee each day for a y .... Eze 4:6
And it came to pass in the sixth y .... Eze 8:1
it came to pass in the seventh y .... Eze 20:1
Again in the ninth y, in the .... Eze 24:1
it came to pass in the eleventh y .... Eze 26:1
In the tenth y, in the tenth .... Eze 29:1
pass in the seven and twentieth y .... Eze 29:17
it came to pass in the eleventh y .... Eze 30:20
it came to pass in the eleventh y .... Eze 31:1
it came to pass in the twelfth y .... Eze 32:1
to pass also in the twelfth y .... Eze 32:17
in the twelfth y of our captivity .... Eze 33:21
twentieth y of our captivity, in .... Eze 40:1
in the beginning of the y .... Eze 40:1
in the fourteenth y after that .... Eze 40:1
of the first y without blemish .... Eze 46:13
shall be his to the y of liberty .... Eze 46:17
In the third y of the reign of .... Dan 1:1
unto the first y of king Cyrus .... Dan 1:21
in the second y of the reign of .... Dan 2:1
In the first y of Belshazzar king .... Dan 7:1
In the third y of the reign of .... Dan 8:1
In the first y of Darius the son .... Dan 9:1
In the first y of his reign I .... Dan 9:2
In the third y of Cyrus king of .... Dan 10:1
in the first y of Darius the Mede .... Dan 11:1
offerings, with calves of a y old .... Mic 6:6
In the second y of Darius the .... Hag 1:1
in the second y of Darius the .... Hag 1:15
month, in the second y of Darius .... Hag 2:10
month, in the second y of Darius .... Zec 1:1
Sebat, in the second y of Darius .... Zec 1:7
in the fourth y of king Darius .... Zec 7:1
y to y to worship the King .... Zec 14:16
y at the feast of the passover .... Lk 2:41
Now in the fifteenth y of the .... Lk 3:1
the acceptable y of the Lord .... Lk 4:19
Lord, let it alone this y also .... Lk 13:8
being the high priest that same y .... Jn 11:49
but being high priest that y .... Jn 11:51
was the high priest that same y .... Jn 18:13
that a whole y they assembled .... Acts 11:26
And he continued there a y .... Acts 18:11
but also to be forward a y ago .... 2Cor 8:10
that Achaia was ready a y ago .... 2Cor 9:2
high priest alone once every y .... Heb 9:7
every y with blood of others .... Heb 9:25
y by y continually make the .... Heb 10:1
which they offered y by y .... Heb 10:1
again made of sins every y .... Heb 10:3
a city, and continue there a y .... Jas 4:13
and a day, and a month, and a y .... Rev 9:15

## YEARLY

as a y hired servant shall he be .... Lev 25:53
went y to lament the daughter of .... Judg 11:40
y in a place which is on the .... Judg 21:19
up out of his city y to worship .... 1Sa 1:3
unto the LORD the y sacrifice .... 1Sa 1:21
husband to offer the y sacrifice .... 1Sa 2:19
for there is a y sacrifice there .... 1Sa 20:6
to charge ourselves y with the .... Neh 10:32
the fifteenth day of the same, y .... Est 9:21

## YEARN

his bowels did y upon his brother .... Gen 43:30

## YEARNED

for her bowels y upon her son .... 1Kin 3:26

## YEAR'S

feast of ingathering at the y end .... Ex 34:22
(for it was at every y end that .... 2Sa 14:26

**YEARS** See PREFACE.
unto him that is an hundred y old... Gen 17:17
shall Sarah, that is ninety y old... Gen 17:17
I will serve thee seven y for... Gen 29:18
served with him yet seven other y... Gen 29:30
these forty y in the wilderness... Deut 8:2
led you forty y in the wilderness... Deut 29:5
For a thousand y in thy sight are... Ps 90:4
began to be about thirty y of age... Lk 3:23
much goods laid up for many y... Lk 12:19
sea, and in the wilderness forty y... Acts 7:36
days, and months, and times, and y... Gal 4:10
is with the Lord as a thousand y... 2Pet 3:8
and a thousand y as one day... 2Pet 3:8

**YEARS'**
came to pass at the seven y end... 2Kin 8:3
Either three y famine... 1Chr 21:12

**YELL**
they shall y as lions' whelps... Jer 51:38

**YELLED**
young lions roared upon him, and y... Jer 2:15

**YELLOW**
and there be in it a y thin hair... Lev 13:30
not, and there be in it no y hair... Lev 13:32
priest shall not seek for y hair... Lev 13:36
and her feathers with y gold... Ps 68:13

**YES**
He saith, Y... Mt 17:25
she answered and said unto him, Y... Mk 7:28
Y, of the Gentiles also... Rom 3:29
Y verily, their sound went into... Rom 10:18

**YESTERDAY**
your task in making brick both y... Ex 5:14
son of Jesse to meat, neither y... 1Sa 20:27
Whereas thou camest but y... 2Sa 15:20
Surely I have seen y the blood of... 2Kin 9:26
(For we are but of y, and know... Job 8:9
are but as y when it is past... Ps 90:4
Y at the seventh hour the fever... Jn 4:52
as thou diddest the Egyptian y... Acts 7:28
Jesus Christ the same y, and to... Heb 13:8

**YESTERNIGHT**
Behold, I lay y with my father... Gen 19:34
of your father spake unto me y... Gen 31:29
of my hands, and rebuked thee y... Gen 31:42

**YET** See PREFACE.

**YIELD**
y unto thee her strength... Gen 4:12
he shall y royal dainties... Gen 49:20
that it may y unto you the... Lev 19:25
And the land shall y her fruit... Lev 25:19
and the land shall y her increase... Lev 26:4
of the field shall y their fruit... Lev 26:4
land shall not y her increase... Lev 26:20
trees of the land y their fruits... Lev 26:20
and that the land y not her fruit... Deut 11:17
but y yourselves unto the LORD,... 2Chr 30:8
shall the earth y her increase... Ps 67:6
and our land shall y her increase... Ps 85:12
which may y fruits of increase... Ps 107:37
fair speech she caused him to y... Prov 7:21
of vineyard shall y one bath... Is 5:10
seed of an homer shall y an ephah... Is 5:10
of the field shall y her fruit... Eze 34:27
and the earth shall y her increase... Eze 34:27
y your fruit to my people of... Eze 36:8
the bud shall y no meal... Hos 8:7
if so be it y, the strangers... Hos 8:7
the vine do y their strength... Joel 2:22
and the fields shall y no meat... Hab 3:17
did y fruit that sprang up and... Mk 4:8
But do not thou y unto them... Acts 23:21
Neither y ye your members as... Rom 6:13
but y yourselves unto God, as... Rom 6:13
that to whom ye y yourselves... Rom 6:16
even so now y your members... Rom 6:19
can no fountain both y salt water... Jas 3:12

**YIELDED**
y up the ghost, and was gathered... Gen 49:33
blossoms, and y almonds... Num 17:8
y their bodies, that they might... Dan 3:28
with a loud voice, y up the ghost... Mt 27:50
and choked it, and it y no fruit... Mk 4:7
at his feet, and y up the ghost... Acts 5:10
for as ye have y your members... Rom 6:19
and y her fruit every month... Rev 22:2

**YIELDETH**
it y much increase unto the kings... Neh 9:37
the wilderness y food for them... Job 24:5
the root of the righteous y fruit... Prov 12:12
it y the peaceable fruit of... Heb 12:11

**YIELDING**
forth grass, the herb y seed... Gen 1:11
the fruit tree y fruit after his... Gen 1:11
herb y seed after his kind, and... Gen 1:12
his kind, and the tree y fruit... Gen 1:12
is the fruit of a tree y seed... Gen 1:29
for y pacifieth great offences... Eccl 10:4
neither shall cease from y fruit... Jer 17:8

**YIRON** See IRON.

**YOKE**
break his y from off thy neck... Gen 27:40
I have broken the bands of your y... Lev 26:13
and upon which never came y... Num 19:2
and which hath not drawn in the y... Deut 21:3
he shall put a y of iron upon thy... Deut 28:48
on which there hath come no y... 1Sa 6:7
And he took a y of oxen, and hewed... 1Sa 11:7
which a y of oxen might plow... 1Sa 14:14
Thy father made our y grievous... 1Kin 12:4
his heavy y which he put upon us,... 1Kin 12:4
Make the y which thy father did... 1Kin 12:9
Thy father made our y heavy... 1Kin 12:10
heavy y, I will add to your y... 1Kin 12:11
My father made your y heavy... 1Kin 12:14
and I will add to your y... 1Kin 12:14
with twelve y of oxen before him... 1Kin 19:19
took a y of oxen, and slew them,... 1Kin 19:21
Thy father made our y grievous... 2Chr 10:4
his heavy y that he put upon us,... 2Chr 10:4
Ease somewhat the y that thy... 2Chr 10:9
Thy father made our y heavy... 2Chr 10:10
my father put a heavy y upon you... 2Chr 10:11
you, I will put more to your y... 2Chr 10:11
My father made your y heavy... 2Chr 10:14
camels, and five hundred y of oxen... Job 1:3
camels, and a thousand y of oxen... Job 42:12
hast broken the y of his burden... Is 9:4
his y from off thy neck, and the... Is 10:27
the y shall be destroyed because... Is 10:27
then shall his y depart from off... Is 14:25
hast thou very heavily laid thy y... Is 47:6
go free, and that ye break every y... Is 58:6
away from the midst of thee the y... Is 58:9
of old time I have broken thy y... Jer 2:20
have altogether broken the y... Jer 5:5
the y of the king of Babylon... Jer 27:8
the y of the king of Babylon... Jer 27:11
the y of the king of Babylon... Jer 27:12
I have broken the y of the king... Jer 28:2
for I will break the y of the... Jer 28:4
Hananiah the prophet took the y... Jer 28:10
Even so will I break the y of... Jer 28:11
the y from off the neck of the... Jer 28:12
I have put a y of iron upon the... Jer 28:14
break his y from off thy neck... Jer 30:8
a bullock unaccustomed to the y... Jer 31:18
the husbandman and his y of oxen... Jer 51:23
The y of my transgressions is... Lam 1:14
that he bear the y in his youth... Lam 3:27
have broken the bands of their y... Eze 34:27
that take off the y on their jaws... Hos 11:4
will I break his y from off thee... Nah 1:13
Take my y upon you, and learn of... Mt 11:29
For my y is easy, and my burden is... Mt 11:30
I have bought five y of oxen... Lk 14:19
to put a y upon the neck of the... Acts 15:10
again with the y of bondage... Gal 5:1
y count their own masters worthy... 1Ti 6:1

**YOKED**
Be ye not unequally y together... 2Cor 6:14

**YOKEFELLOW**
And I intreat thee also, true y... Phil 4:3

**YOKES**
Make thee bonds and y, and put them... Jer 27:2
Thou hast broken the y of wood... Jer 28:13
shalt make for them y of iron... Jer 28:13
shall break there the y of Egypt... Eze 30:18

**YONDER**
and I and the lad will go y... Gen 22:5
and scatter thou the fire y... Num 16:37
offering, while I meet the LORD y... Num 23:15
with them on y side Jordan... Num 32:19
Behold, y is that Shunammite... 2Kin 4:25
mountain, Remove hence to y place... Mt 17:20
Sit ye here, while I go and pray y... Mt 26:36

**YOU** See PREFACE.

**YOUNG**
wounding, and a y man to my hurt... Gen 4:23
that which the y men have eaten... Gen 14:24
and a turtledove, and a y pigeon... Gen 15:9
and good, and gave it unto a y man... Gen 18:7
the house round, both old and y... Gen 19:4
and took two of his y men with him... Gen 22:3
And Abraham said unto his y men... Gen 22:5
Abraham returned unto his y men... Gen 22:19
she goats have not cast their y... Gen 31:38
and herds with y are with me... Gen 33:13
the y man deferred not to do the... Gen 34:19
there was there with us a y man... Gen 41:12
Moses said, We will go with our y... Ex 10:9
There shall nothing cast their y... Ex 23:26
he sent y men of the children of... Ex 24:5
Take one y bullock, and two rams... Ex 29:1
a y man, departed not out of the... Ex 33:11
of turtledoves, or of y pigeons... Lev 1:14
a y bullock without blemish unto... Lev 4:3
offer a y bullock for the sin... Lev 4:14
or two y pigeons, unto the LORD... Lev 5:7
or two y pigeons, then he that... Lev 5:11
Take thee a y calf for a sin... Lev 9:2
a y pigeon, or a turtledove, for... Lev 12:6
two turtles, or two y pigeons... Lev 12:8
or two y pigeons, such as he is... Lev 14:22
turtledoves, or of the y pigeons... Lev 14:30
or two y pigeons, and come before... Lev 15:14
or two y pigeons, and bring them... Lev 15:29
with a y bullock for a sin... Lev 16:3
kill it and her y both in one day... Lev 22:28
one y bullock, and two rams... Lev 23:18
or two y pigeons, to the priest,... Num 6:10
One y bullock, one ram, one lamb... Num 7:15
One y bullock, one ram, one lamb... Num 7:21
One y bullock, one ram, one lamb... Num 7:27
One y bullock, one ram, one lamb... Num 7:33
One y bullock, one ram, one lamb... Num 7:39
One y bullock, one ram, one lamb... Num 7:45
One y bullock, one ram, one lamb... Num 7:51
One y bullock, one ram, one lamb... Num 7:57
One y bullock, one ram, one lamb... Num 7:63
One y bullock, one ram, one lamb... Num 7:69
One y bullock, one ram, one lamb... Num 7:75
One y bullock, one ram, one lamb... Num 7:81
Then let them take a y bullock... Num 8:8
another y bullock shalt thou take... Num 8:8
And there ran a y man, and told... Num 11:27
of Moses, one of his y men... Num 11:28
y bullock for a burnt offering... Num 15:24
and lift up himself as a y lion... Num 23:24
two y bullocks, and one ram, seven... Num 28:11
two y bullocks, and one ram, and... Num 28:19
two y bullocks, one ram, seven... Num 28:27
one y bullock, one ram, and seven... Num 29:2
one y bullock, one ram, and seven... Num 29:8
thirteen y bullocks, two rams, and... Num 29:13
ye shall offer twelve y bullocks... Num 29:17
ground, whether they be y ones... Deut 22:6
and the dam sitting upon the y... Deut 22:6
shalt not take the dam with the y... Deut 22:6
the dam go, and take the y to thee... Deut 22:7
the old, nor shew favour to the y... Deut 28:50
toward her y one that cometh out... Deut 28:57
her nest, fluttereth over her y... Deut 32:11
shall destroy both the y man... Deut 32:25
in the city, both man and woman, y... Josh 6:21
the y men that were spies went in... Josh 6:23
him, Take thy father's y bullock... Judg 6:25
caught a y man of the men of... Judg 8:14
unto the y man his armourbearer... Judg 9:54
his y man thrust him through, and... Judg 9:54
a y lion roared against him... Judg 14:5
for so used the y men to do... Judg 14:10
And there was a y man out of... Judg 17:7
the y man was unto him as one of... Judg 17:11
the y man became his priest, and... Judg 17:12
the voice of the y man the Levite... Judg 18:3
the house of the y man the Levite... Judg 18:15
for the y man which is with thy... Judg 19:19
four hundred y virgins, that had... Judg 21:12
have I not charged the y men that... Ruth 2:9
that which the y men have drawn... Ruth 2:9
glean, Boaz commanded his y men... Ruth 2:15
Thou shalt keep fast by my y men... Ruth 2:21
as thou followedst not y men... Ruth 3:10
shall give thee of this y woman... Ruth 4:12
and the child was y... 1Sa 1:24
Wherefore the sin of the y men... 1Sa 2:17
and your goodliest y men, and your... 1Sa 8:16
name was Saul, a choice y man... 1Sa 9:2
they found y maidens going out to... 1Sa 9:11
the y man that bare his armour... 1Sa 14:1
Jonathan said to the y man that... 1Sa 14:6
Whose son art thou, thou y man... 1Sa 17:58
But if I say thus unto the y man... 1Sa 20:22
if the y men have kept themselves... 1Sa 21:4
the vessels of the y men are holy... 1Sa 21:5
And David sent out ten y men... 1Sa 25:5
men, and David said unto the y men... 1Sa 25:5
Ask thy y men, and they will shew... 1Sa 25:8
Wherefore let the y men find... 1Sa 25:8
And when David's y men came... 1Sa 25:9
So David's y men turned their way... 1Sa 25:12
But one of the y men told Abigail... 1Sa 25:14
saw not the y men of my lord... 1Sa 25:25
the y men that follow my lord... 1Sa 25:27
and let one of the y men come over... 1Sa 26:22
I am a y man of Egypt, servant to... 1Sa 30:13
of them, save four hundred y men... 1Sa 30:17
said unto the y man that told him... 2Sa 1:5
the y man that told him said, As... 2Sa 1:6
said unto the y man that told him... 2Sa 1:13
And David called one of the y men... 2Sa 1:15
Let the y men now arise, and play... 2Sa 2:14
lay thee hold on one of the y men... 2Sa 2:21
And David commanded his y men... 2Sa 4:12
And Mephibosheth had a y son... 2Sa 9:12
all the y men the king's sons... 2Sa 13:32
the y man that kept the watch... 2Sa 13:34
bring the y man Absalom again... 2Sa 14:21
summer fruit for the y men to eat... 2Sa 16:2
gently for my sake with the y man... 2Sa 18:5
that none touch the y man Absalom... 2Sa 18:12
ten y men that bare Joab's armour... 2Sa 18:15
Is the y man Absalom safe... 2Sa 18:29
Is the y man Absalom safe... 2Sa 18:32
do thee hurt, be as that y man is... 2Sa 18:32
for my lord the king a y virgin... 1Kin 1:2
Solomon seeing the y man that he... 1Kin 11:28
consulted with the y men that... 1Kin 12:8
the y men that were grown up with... 1Kin 12:10
after the counsel of the y men... 1Kin 12:14
Even by the y men of the princes... 1Kin 20:14
Then he numbered the y men of the... 1Kin 20:15
the y men of the princes of the... 1Kin 20:17
So these y men of the princes of... 1Kin 20:19
me, I pray thee, one of the y men... 2Kin 4:22
to me from mount Ephraim two y... 2Kin 5:22
LORD opened the eyes of the y man... 2Kin 6:17
their y men wilt thou slay with... 2Kin 8:12
So the y man, even the y man... 2Kin 9:4

even the y man the prophet, went 2Kin 9:4
a y man mighty of valour, and of 1Chr 12:28
David said, Solomon my son is y 1Chr 22:5
alone God hath chosen, is yet y 1Chr 29:1
took counsel with the y men that 2Chr 10:8
the y men that were brought up 2Chr 10:10
after the advice of the y men 2Chr 10:14
of Solomon, when Rehoboam was y 2Chr 13:7
himself with a y bullock and seven 2Chr 13:9
of his reign, while he was yet y 2Chr 34:3
who slew their y men with the 2Chr 36:17
compassion upon y man or maiden 2Chr 36:17
both y bullocks, and rams, and Ezr 6:9
Let there be fair y virgins Est 2:2
gather together all the fair y Est 2:3
cause to perish, all Jews, both y Est 3:13
mules, camels, and y dromedaries Est 8:10
house, and it fell upon the y men Job 1:19
lion, and the teeth of the y lions Job 4:10
Yea, y children despised me Job 19:18
The y men saw me, and hid Job 29:8
Buzite answered and said, I am y Job 32:6
fill the appetite of the y lions Job 38:39
when his y ones cry unto God, Job 38:41
they bring forth their y ones Job 39:3
Their y ones are in good liking, Job 39:4
is hardened against her y ones Job 39:16
Her y ones also suck up blood Job 39:30
as it were a y lion lurking in Ps 17:12
and Sirion like a y unicorn Ps 29:6
The y lions do lack, and suffer Ps 34:10
I have been y, and now am old Ps 37:25
the great teeth of the y lions Ps 58:6
The fire consumed their y men Ps 78:63
y he brought him to feed Jacob Ps 78:71
herself, where she may lay her y Ps 84:3
the y lion and the dragon shalt Ps 91:13
The y lions roar after their prey Ps 104:21
shall a y man cleanse his way Ps 119:9
to the y ravens which cry Ps 147:9
Both y men, and maidens Ps 148:12
to the y man knowledge and Prov 1:4
a y man void of understanding, Prov 7:7
The glory of y men is their Prov 20:29
the y eagles shall eat it Prov 30:17
Rejoice, O y man, in thy youth Eccl 11:9
beloved is like a roe or a y hart Song 2:9
be thou like a roe or a y hart Song 2:17
like two y roes that are twins Song 4:5
like two y roes that are twins Song 7:3
to a y hart upon the mountains of Song 8:14
they shall roar like y lions Is 5:29
that a man shall nourish a y cow Is 7:21
shall have no joy in their y men Is 9:17
the y lion and the fatling Is 11:6
their y ones shall lie down Is 11:7
shall dash the y men to pieces Is 13:18
and the Ethiopians captives, y Is 20:4
neither do I nourish up y men Is 23:4
anguish, from whence come the y Is 30:6
upon the shoulders of y asses Is 30:6
the y asses that ear the ground Is 30:24
the y lion roaring on his prey, Is 31:4
his y men shall be discomfited Is 31:8
gently lead those that are with y Is 40:11
the y men shall utterly fall Is 40:30
For as a y man marrieth a virgin, Is 62:5
The y lions roared upon him, and Jer 2:15
the assembly of y men together Jer 6:11
the y men from the streets Jer 9:21
the y men shall die by the sword Jer 11:22
of the y men a spoiler at noonday Jer 15:8
let their y men be slain by the Jer 18:21
for the y of the flock and of the Jer 31:12
rejoice in the dance, both y men Jer 31:13
his chosen y men are gone down to Jer 48:15
Therefore her y men shall fall in Jer 49:26
Therefore shall her y men fall in Jer 50:30
and spare ye not her y men Jer 51:3
will I break in pieces old and y Jer 51:22
will I break in pieces the y man Jer 51:22
against me to crush my y men Lam 1:15
my y men are gone into captivity Lam 1:18
for the life of thy y children Lam 2:19
The y and the old lie on the Lam 2:21
my y men are fallen by the sword Lam 2:21
they give suck to their y ones Lam 4:3
the y children ask bread, and no Lam 4:4
They took the y men to grind Lam 5:13
the y men from their musick Lam 5:14
Slay utterly old and y, both maids Eze 9:6
off the top of his y twigs Eze 17:4
top of his y twigs a tender one Eze 17:22
her whelps among y lions Eze 19:2
it became a y lion, and it learned Eze 19:3
her whelps, and made him a y lion Eze 19:5
the lions, he became a y lion Eze 19:6
all of them desirable y men Eze 23:6
all of them desirable y men Eze 23:12
all of them desirable y men Eze 23:23
The y men of Aven and of Pi-beseth Eze 30:17
of the field bring forth their y Eze 31:6
Thou art like a y lion of the Eze 32:2
with all the y lions thereof, Eze 38:13
the face of a y lion toward the Eze 41:19
a y bullock for a sin offering Eze 43:19
thou shalt offer a y bullock Eze 43:23
shall also prepare a y bullock Eze 43:25
thou shalt take a y bullock Eze 45:18
be a y bullock without blemish Eze 46:6
as a y lion to the house of Judah Hos 5:14
your y men shall see visions Joel 2:28
of your y men for Nazarites Amos 2:11
will a y lion cry out of his den, Amos 3:4
your y men have I slain with the Amos 4:10
virgins and y men faint for thirst Amos 8:13
as a y lion among the flocks of Mic 5:8
the feeding place of the y lions Nah 2:11
sword shall devour thy y lions Nah 2:13
her y children also were dashed Nah 3:10
him, Run, speak to this y man Zec 2:4
shall make the y men cheerful Zec 9:17
a voice of the roaring of y lions Zec 11:3
off, neither shall seek the y one Zec 11:16
search diligently for the y child Mt 2:8
stood over where the y child was Mt 2:9
they saw the y child with Mary Mt 2:11
Arise, and take the y child Mt 2:13
seek the y child to destroy him Mt 2:13
he arose, he took the y child Mt 2:14
Arise, and take the y child Mt 2:20
which sought the y child's life Mt 2:20
And he arose, and took the y child Mt 2:21
The y man saith unto him, All Mt 19:20
But when the y man heard that Mt 19:22
whose y daughter had an unclean Mk 7:25
they brought y children to him, Mk 10:13
followed him a certain y man Mk 14:51
the y men laid hold on him Mk 14:51
they saw a y man sitting on the Mk 16:5
of turtledoves, or two y pigeons Lk 2:24
Y man, I say unto thee, Arise Lk 7:14
Jesus, when he had found a y ass Jn 12:14
I say unto thee, When thou wast y Jn 21:18
your y men shall see visions, and Acts 2:17
the y men arose, wound him up, and Acts 5:6
the y men came in, and found her Acts 5:10
they cast out their y children Acts 7:19
their clothes at a y man's feet Acts 7:58
a certain y man named Eutychus Acts 20:9
And they brought the y man alive Acts 20:12
Bring this y man unto the chief Acts 23:17
me to bring this y man unto thee Acts 23:18
captain then let the y man depart Acts 23:22
may teach the y women to be sober Titus 2:4
Y men likewise exhort to be sober Titus 2:6
y men, because ye have overcome 1Jn 2:13
y men, because ye are strong, and 1Jn 2:14

**YOUNGER**

knew what his y son had done unto Gen 9:24
And the firstborn said unto the y Gen 19:31
the firstborn said unto the y Gen 19:34
the y arose, and lay with him Gen 19:35
And the y, she also bare a son, and Gen 19:38
and the elder shall serve the y Gen 25:23
and put them upon Jacob her y son Gen 27:15
sent and called Jacob her y son Gen 27:42
and the name of the y was Rachel Gen 29:16
years for Rachel thy y daughter Gen 29:18
country, to give the y before the Gen 29:26
and said, Is this your y brother Gen 43:29
Ephraim's head, who was the y Gen 48:14
but truly his y brother shall be Gen 48:19
son of Kenaz, Caleb's y brother Judg 1:13
son of Kenaz, Caleb's y brother Judg 3:9
is not her y sister fairer than Judg 15:2
and the name of the y Michal 1Sa 14:49
over against their y brethren 1Chr 24:31
But now they that are y than I Job 30:1
thy y sister, that dwelleth at Eze 16:46
thy sisters, thine elder and thy y Eze 16:61
the y of them said to his father, Lk 15:12
not many days after the y son Lk 15:13
among you, let him be as the y Lk 22:26
her, The elder shall serve the y Rom 9:12
and the y men as brethren 1Ti 5:1
the y as sisters, with all purity 1Ti 5:2
But the y widows refuse 1Ti 5:11
therefore that the y women marry 1Ti 5:14
Likewise, ye y, submit yourselves 1Pet 5:5

**YOUNGEST**

the y is this day with our father Gen 42:13
except your y brother come hither Gen 42:15
But bring your y brother unto me Gen 42:20
the y is this day with our father Gen 42:32
bring your y brother unto me Gen 42:34
the y according to his youth Gen 43:33
cup, in the sack's mouth of the y Gen 44:2
at the eldest, and left at the y Gen 44:12
Except your y brother come down Gen 44:23
if our y brother be with us, then Gen 44:26
except our y brother be with us Gen 44:26
in his y son shall he set up the Josh 6:26
the y son of Jerubbaal was left Judg 9:5
said, There remaineth yet the y 1Sa 16:11
And David was the y 1Sa 17:14
gates thereof in his y son Segub 1Kin 16:34
save Jehoahaz, the y of his sons 2Chr 21:17
his y son king in his stead 2Chr 22:1

**YOUR** See PREFACE.

**YOURS**

of all the land of Egypt is y Gen 45:20
your feet shall tread shall be y Deut 11:24
men answered her, Our life for y Josh 2:14
for the battle is not y, but 2Chr 20:15
strangers in a land that is not y Jer 5:19
for y is the kingdom of God Lk 6:20
my saying, they will keep y also Jn 15:20
For all things are y 1Cor 3:21
all are y 1Cor 3:22
by any means this liberty of y 1Cor 8:9
have refreshed my spirit and y 1Cor 16:18
for I seek not y, but you 2Cor 12:14

**YOURSELVES**

feet, and rest y under the tree Gen 18:4
be not grieved, nor angry with y Gen 45:5
Gather y together, that I may Gen 49:1
Gather y together, and hear, ye Gen 49:2
about, saying, Take heed to y Ex 19:12
ye shall not make to y according Ex 30:37
Consecrate y to day to the LORD, Ex 32:29
Ye shall not make y abominable Lev 11:43
shall ye make y unclean with them Lev 11:43
ye shall therefore sanctify y Lev 11:44
neither shall ye defile y with Lev 11:44
Defile not ye y in any of these Lev 18:24
and that ye defile not y therein Lev 18:30
idols, nor make to y molten gods Lev 19:4
Sanctify y therefore, and be ye Lev 20:7
Sanctify y against to morrow, and Num 11:18
wherefore then lift ye up y above Num 16:3
Separate y from among this Num 16:21
Arm some of y unto the war, and Num 31:3
lying with him, keep alive for y Num 31:18
touched any slain, purify both y Num 31:19
ye good heed unto y therefore Deut 2:4
ye therefore good heed unto y Deut 4:15
Lest ye corrupt y, and make you a Deut 4:16
Take heed unto y, lest ye forget Deut 4:23
in the land, and shall corrupt y Deut 4:25
Take heed to y, that your heart Deut 11:16
nations and mightier than y Deut 11:23
ye shall not cut y, nor make any Deut 14:1
present y in the tabernacle of Deut 31:14
death ye will utterly corrupt y Deut 31:29
hide y there three days, until Josh 2:16
said unto the people, Sanctify y Josh 3:5
in any wise keep y from the Josh 6:18
thing, lest ye make y accursed Josh 6:18
Sanctify y against to morrow Josh 7:13
shall ye take for a prey unto y Josh 8:2
serve them, nor bow y unto them Josh 23:7
Take good heed therefore unto y Josh 23:11
other gods, and bowed y to them Josh 23:16
Ye are witnesses against y that Josh 24:22
that ye will not fall upon me y Judg 15:12
to make y fat with the chiefest 1Sa 2:29
quit y like men, O ye Philistines 1Sa 4:9
quit y like men, and fight 1Sa 4:9
Now therefore present y before 1Sa 10:19
Disperse y among the people, and 1Sa 14:34
sanctify y, and come with me to 1Sa 16:5
Choose you one bullock for y 1Kin 18:25
unto his servants, Set y in array 1Kin 20:12
other gods, nor bow y to them 2Kin 17:35
sanctify y, both ye and your 1Chr 15:12
set y, stand ye still, and see the 2Chr 20:17
me, ye Levites, sanctify now y 2Chr 29:5
have consecrated y unto the LORD 2Chr 29:31
but yield y unto the LORD, and 2Chr 30:8
to give over y to die by famine 2Chr 32:11
prepare y by the houses of your 2Chr 35:4
kill the passover, and sanctify y 2Chr 35:6
separate y from the people of the Ezr 10:11
unto your sons, or for y Neh 13:25
that ye make y strange to me Job 19:3
ye will magnify y against me Job 19:5
Behold, all ye y have seen it Job 27:12
offer up for y a burnt offering Job 42:8
Associate y, O ye people, and ye Is 8:9
gird y, and ye shall be broken in Is 8:9
gird y, and ye shall be broken in Is 8:9
Stay y, and wonder Is 29:9
Assemble y and come Is 45:20
Remember this, and shew y men Is 46:8
All ye, assemble y, and hear Is 48:14
them that are in darkness, Shew y Is 49:9
your iniquities have ye sold y Is 50:1
that compass y about with sparks Is 50:11
LORD, Ye have sold y for nought Is 52:3
Against whom do ye sport y Is 57:4
Enflaming y with idols under Is 57:5
in their glory shall ye boast y Is 61:6
Circumcise y to the LORD, and take Jer 4:4
together, and say, Assemble y Jer 4:5
gather y to flee out of the midst Jer 6:1
assemble y, and let us enter into Jer 8:14
king and to the queen, Humble y Jer 13:18
Take heed to y, and bear no burden Jer 17:21
wallow y in the ashes, ye Jer 25:34
bring innocent blood upon y Jer 26:15
Deceive not y, saying, The Jer 37:9
to dwell, that ye might cut y off Jer 44:8
Put y in array against Babylon Jer 50:14
Repent, and turn y from your idols Eze 14:6
Repent, and turn y from all your Eze 18:30
wherefore turn y, and live ye Eze 18:32
defile not y with the idols of Eze 20:7
nor defile y with their idols Eze 20:18
ye pollute y with all your idols, Eze 20:31
ye shall lothe y in your own Eze 20:43
shall lothe y in your own sight Eze 36:31
beast of the field, Assemble y Eze 39:17
gather y on every side to my Eze 39:17
my charge in my sanctuary for y Eze 44:8
Sow to y in righteousness, reap Hos 10:12
Gird y, and lament, ye priests Joel 1:13
Assemble y, and come, all ye Joel 3:11

gather y together round about ............ Joel 3:11
Assemble y upon the mountains of...... Amos 3:9
of your god, which ye made to y........ Amos 5:26
Gather y together, yea, gather.............. Zeph 2:1
did drink, did not ye eat for y............ Zec 7:6
for y, and drink for y.......................... Zec 7:6
And think not to say within y.............. Mt 3:9
Lay not up for y treasures upon........... Mt 6:19
But lay up for y treasures in............... Mt 6:20
faith, why reason ye among y............. Mt 16:8
for ye neither go in y, neither.............. Mt 23:13
more the child of hell than y................ Mt 23:15
Wherefore ye be witnesses unto y........ Mt 23:31
to them that sell, and buy for y........... Mt 25:9
Come ye y apart into a desert.............. Mk 6:31
ye disputed among y by the way........... Mk 9:33
Have salt in y, and have peace one....... Mk 9:50
But take heed to y................................ Mk 13:9
and begin not to say within y................. Lk 3:8
ye y touch not the burdens with........... Lk 11:46
ye entered not in y, and them that....... Lk 11:52
provide y bags which wax not old,........ Lk 12:33
ye y like unto men that wait for........... Lk 12:36
why even of y judge ye not what.......... Lk 12:57
of God, and you y thrust out................ Lk 13:28
Make to y friends of the mammon......... Lk 16:9
they which justify y before men............ Lk 16:15
Take heed to y...................................... Lk 17:3
Go shew y unto the priests.................... Lk 17:14
And take heed to y, lest at any............ Lk 21:34
Take this, and divide it among y........... Lk 22:17
weep not for me, but weep for y.......... Lk 23:28
Ye y bear me witness, that I said.......... Jn 3:28
unto them, Murmur not among y........... Jn 6:43
ye enquire among y of that I said......... Jn 16:19
midst of you, as ye y also know........... Acts 2:22
Save y from this untoward..................... Acts 2:40
take heed to y what ye intend to......... Acts 5:35
judge y unworthy of everlasting............ Acts 13:46
from which if ye keep y, ye shall.......... Acts 15:29
embracing him said, Trouble not y....... Acts 20:10
Take heed therefore unto y................... Acts 20:28
ye y know, that these hands have........ Acts 20:34
Likewise reckon ye also y to be........... Rom 6:11
but yield y unto God, as those............. Rom 6:13
whom ye yield y servants to obey......... Rom 6:16
Dearly beloved, avenge not y............... Rom 12:19
from among y that wicked person......... 1Cor 5:13
rather suffer y to be defrauded............. 1Cor 6:7
that ye may give y to fasting................. 1Cor 7:5
Judge in y........................................... 1Cor 11:13
That ye submit y unto such.................. 1Cor 16:16
in you, yea, what clearing of y............. 2Cor 7:11
y to be clear in this matter.................. 2Cor 7:11
gladly, seeing ye y are wise................. 2Cor 11:19
Examine y, whether ye be in the.......... 2Cor 13:5
and that not of y.................................. Eph 2:8
Speaking to y in psalms and hymns..... Eph 5:19
Submitting y one to another in............ Eph 5:21
submit y unto your own husbands,....... Eph 5:22
submit y unto your own husbands,....... Col 3:18
For y, brethren, know our.................... 1Th 2:1
for y know that we are appointed......... 1Th 3:3
for ye y are taught of God to............... 1Th 4:9
For y know perfectly that the day......... 1Th 5:2
Wherefore comfort y together.............. 1Th 5:11
And be at peace among y.................... 1Th 5:13
that which is good, both among y......... 1Th 5:15
that ye withdraw y from every.............. 2Th 3:6
For y know how ye ought to follow....... 2Th 3:7
knowing in y that ye have in................ Heb 10:34
as being y also in the body.................. Heb 13:3
the rule over you, and submit y........... Heb 13:17
Are ye not then partial in y.................. Jas 2:4
Submit y therefore to God.................... Jas 4:7
Humble y in the sight of the Lord......... Jas 4:10
not fashioning y according to the......... 1Pet 1:14
Submit y to every ordinance of............. 1Pet 2:13
arm y likewise with the same mind....... 1Pet 4:1
have fervent charity among y............... 1Pet 4:8
younger, submit y unto the elder.......... 1Pet 5:5
Humble y therefore under the.............. 1Pet 5:6
children, keep y from idols................... 1Jn 5:21
Look to y, that we lose not those.......... 2Jn 8
building up y on your most holy........... Jude 20
Keep y in the love of God,................... Jude 21
gather y together unto the supper....... Rev 19:17

**YOUTH**

of man's heart is evil from his y............ Gen 8:21
the youngest according to his y............ Gen 43:33
cattle from our y even until now.......... Gen 46:34
her father's house, as in her y.............. Lev 22:13
in her father's house in her y............... Num 30:3
being yet in her y in her...................... Num 30:16
But the y drew not his sword................ Judg 8:20
he feared, because he was yet a y........ Judg 8:20
for thou art but a y, and he a man....... 1Sa 17:33
and he a man of war from his y............ 1Sa 17:33
for he was but a y, and ruddy, and....... 1Sa 17:42
host, Abner, whose son is this y........... 1Sa 17:55
befell thee from thy y until now........... 2Sa 19:7
servant fear the LORD from my y......... 1Kin 18:12
to possess the iniquities of my y.......... Job 13:26
are full of the sin of his y.................... Job 20:11
As I was in the days of my y................. Job 29:4
Upon my right hand rise the y............... Job 30:12
(For from my y he was brought up........ Job 31:18
shall return to the days of his y........... Job 33:25
They die in y, and their life is.............. Job 36:14
Remember not the sins of my y............. Ps 25:7
thou art my trust from my y.................. Ps 71:5
thou hast taught me from my y............. Ps 71:17
and ready to die from my y up.............. Ps 88:15
The days of his y hast thou.................. Ps 89:45
so that thy y is renewed like the........... Ps 103:5
thou hast the dew of thy y.................... Ps 110:3
so are children of the y....................... Ps 127:4
have they afflicted me from my y.......... Ps 129:1
have they afflicted me from my y.......... Ps 129:2
be as plants grown up in their y........... Ps 144:12
forsaketh the guide of her y................. Prov 2:17
and rejoice with the wife of thy y......... Prov 5:18
Rejoice, O young man, in thy y............. Eccl 11:9
cheer thee in the days of thy y............. Eccl 11:9
for childhood and y are vanity.............. Eccl 11:10
thy Creator in the days of thy y............ Eccl 12:1
thou hast laboured from thy y............... Is 47:12
even thy merchants, from thy y............. Is 47:15
shalt forget the shame of thy y............. Is 54:4
grieved in spirit, and a wife of y............ Is 54:6
thee, the kindness of thy y................... Jer 2:2
thou art the guide of my y.................... Jer 3:4
labour of our fathers from our y............ Jer 3:24
from our y even unto this day, and........ Jer 3:25
hath been thy manner from thy y.......... Jer 22:21
I did bear the reproach of my y............ Jer 31:19
done evil before me from their y........... Jer 32:30
Moab hath been at ease from his y........ Jer 48:11
that he bear the yoke in his y............... Lam 3:27
for from my y up even till now.............. Eze 4:14
not remembered the days of thy y......... Eze 16:22
not remembered the days of thy y......... Eze 16:43
with thee in the days of thy y............... Eze 16:60
committed whoredoms in their y........... Eze 23:3
for in her y they lay with her,............... Eze 23:8
to remembrance the days of her y......... Eze 23:19
remembrance the lewdness of thy y....... Eze 23:21
Egyptians for the paps of thy y............. Eze 23:21
there, as in the days of her y................ Hos 2:15
for the husband of her y...................... Joel 1:8
me to keep cattle from my y................. Zec 13:5
between thee and the wife of thy y........ Mal 2:14
against the wife of his y....................... Mal 2:15
things have I kept from my y up............ Mt 19:20
these have I observed from my y........... Mk 10:20
these have I kept from my y up............. Lk 18:21
My manner of life from my y................ Acts 26:4
Let no man despise thy y...................... 1Ti 4:12

**YOUTHFUL**

Flee also y lusts.................................. 2Ti 2:22

**YOUTHS**

ones, I discerned among the y............... Prov 7:7
Even the y shall faint and be................. Is 40:30

**YOU-WARD**

world, and more abundantly to y.......... 2Cor 1:12
which to y is not weak, but is.............. 2Cor 13:3
of God which is given me to y............... Eph 3:2

# Z

**ZAANAIM** (*za-an-a'-im*) See ZAANANNIM. *A plain in Naphtali.*

his tent unto the plain of Z................... Judg 4:11

**ZAANAN** (*za'-an-an*) See ZENAN. *A city of Judah.*

the inhabitant of Z came not................. Mic 1:11

**ZA-ANANNIM** See ZAANAIM.

**ZAANANNIM** (*za-an-an'-nim*) *Same as Zaanaim.*

was from Heleph, from Allon to Z........ Josh 19:33

**ZAAVAN** (*za'-av-an*) See ZAVAN. *A son of Ezer.*

Bilhan, and Z, and Akan...................... Gen 36:27

**ZABAD** (*za'-bad*) See JOSABAD, JOZACHAR.

*1. A son of Nathan.*

begat Nathan, and Nathan begat Z..... 1Chr 2:36
Z begat Ephlal, and Ephlal begat......... 1Chr 2:37

*2. Son of Tahath.*

Z his son, and Shuthelah his son,......... 1Chr 7:21

*3. A "mighty man" of David.*

the Hittite, Z the son of Ahlai,............. 1Chr 11:41

*4. A son of Shimeath.*

Z the son of Shimeath an..................... 2Chr 24:26

*5. A son of Zattu.*

Mattaniah, and Jeremoth, and Z........... Ezr 10:27

*6. A son of Hashum.*

Mattenai, Mattathah, Z, Eliphelet......... Ezr 10:33

*7. A son of Nebo.*

Jeiel, Mattithiah, Z, Zebina,................. Ezr 10:43

**ZABBAI** (*zab'-bahee*) See ZACCAI.

*1. Married a foreigner in exile.*

Jehohanan, Hananiah, Z, and Athlai.... Ezr 10:28

*2. Father of Baruch.*

After him Baruch the son of Z.............. Neh 3:20

**ZABBUD** (*zab'-bud*) See ZACCUR. *An exile with Ezra.*

Uthai, and Z, and with them seventy.... Ezr 8:14

**ZABDI** (*zab'-di*) See ZACCHUR, ZICHRI.

*1. Father of Carmi.*

the son of Carmi, the son of Z.............. Josh 7:1
and Z was taken.................................. Josh 7:17
the son of Carmi, the son of Z.............. Josh 7:18

*2. Son of Shimhi.*

And Jakim, and Zichri, and Z................ 1Chr 8:19

*3. A storekeeper in David's court.*

wine cellars was Z the Shiphmite....... 1Chr 27:27

*4. A Levite.*

the son of Micha, the son of Z............. Neh 11:17

**ZABDIEL** (*zab'-de-el*)

*1. Father of Jashobeam.*

month was Jashobeam the son of Z.... 1Chr 27:2

*2. An overseer of priests.*

and their overseer was Z, the son....... Neh 11:14

**ZABUD** (*za'-bud*) *A family of exiles.*

Z the son of Nathan was principal......... 1Kin 4:5

**ZABULON** (*zab'-u-lon*) See ZEBULUN. *Greek form of Zebulon.*

sea coast, in the borders of Z............... Mt 4:13
The land of Z, and the land of.............. Mt 4:15
Of the tribe of Z were sealed............... Rev 7:8

**ZACCAI** (*zac'-cahee*) See ZABBAI. *A family of exiles.*

The children of Z, seven hundred.......... Ezr 2:9
The children of Z, seven hundred.......... Neh 7:14

**ZACCHAEUS** (*zak-ke'-us*) *A tax collector visited by Jesus.*

behold, there was a man named Z.......... Lk 19:2
and saw him, and said unto him, Z........ Lk 19:5
Z stood, and said unto the Lord............ Lk 19:8

**ZACCHUR** (*zac'-cur*) See ZACCUR. *Father of Shimei.*

Z his son, Shimei his son...................... 1Chr 4:26

**ZACCUR** (*zac'-cur*) See ZABBUD, ZABDI, ZACCHUR, ZICHRI.

*1. Father of Shammua.*

of Reuben, Shammua the son of Z...... Num 13:4

*2. A sanctuary servant.*

Beno, and Shoham, and Z, and Ibri... 1Chr 24:27

*3. A son of Asaph.*

Z, and Joseph, and Nethaniah, and...... 1Chr 25:2
The third to Z, he, his sons, and........... 1Chr 25:10
the son of Michaiah, the son of Z....... Neh 12:35

*4. A rebuilder of Jerusalem's wall.*

to them builded Z the son of Imri.......... Neh 3:2

*5. A Levite who renewed the covenant.*

Z, Sherebiah, Shebaniah,..................... Neh 10:12

*6. Father of Hanan.*

to them was Hanan the son of Z......... Neh 13:13

**ZACHARIAH** (*zak-a-ri'-ah*) See ZECHARIAH.

*1. A king of Israel.*

Z his son reigned in his stead............. 2Kin 14:29
of Azariah king of Judah did Z............ 2Kin 15:8
And the rest of the acts of Z............... 2Kin 15:11

*2. Father of Abi.*

also was Abi, the daughter of Z........... 2Kin 18:2

**ZACHARIAS** (*zak'-a-ri'-as*) See ZECHARIAH.

*1. Son of Barachias.*

the blood of Z son of Barachias........... Mt 23:35
blood of Abel unto the blood of Z......... Lk 11:51

*2. Father of John the Baptist.*

Judaea, a certain priest named Z.......... Lk 1:5
when Z saw him, he was troubled,......... Lk 1:12
angel said unto him, Fear not, Z........... Lk 1:13
Z said unto the angel, Whereby........... Lk 1:18
And the people waited for Z................. Lk 1:21
And entered into the house of Z........... Lk 1:40
and they called him Z, after the........... Lk 1:59
his father Z was filled with the............ Lk 1:67
the son of Z in the wilderness.............. Lk 3:2

**ZACHER** (*za'-kur*) See ZECHARIAH. *Father of Gibeon.*

And Gedor, and Ahio, and Z................. 1Chr 8:31

**ZADOK** (*za'-dok*) See ZADOK'S.

*1. A priest in David's time.*

Z the son of Ahitub, and Ahimelech...... 2Sa 8:17
lo Z also, and all the Levites................. 2Sa 15:24
And the king said unto Z, Carry........... 2Sa 15:25
king said also unto Z the priest............ 2Sa 15:27
Z therefore and Abiathar carried........... 2Sa 15:29
hast thou not there with thee Z........... 2Sa 15:35
house, thou shalt tell it to Z................ 2Sa 15:35
Then said Hushai unto Z and to............ 2Sa 17:15
Then said Ahimaaz the son of Z........... 2Sa 18:19
the son of Z yet again to Joab.............. 2Sa 18:22
running of Ahimaaz the son of Z.......... 2Sa 18:27
And king David sent to Z and to........... 2Sa 19:11
and Z and Abiathar were the priests..... 2Sa 20:25
But Z the priest, and Benaiah the.......... 1Kin 1:8
Z the priest, and Benaiah the son.......... 1Kin 1:26
Call me Z the priest, and Nathan........... 1Kin 1:32
let Z the priest and Nathan the............. 1Kin 1:34
So Z the priest, and Nathan the............. 1Kin 1:38
Z the priest took an horn of oil............. 1Kin 1:39
hath sent with him Z the priest............. 1Kin 1:44
Z the priest and Nathan the................. 1Kin 1:45
Z the priest did the king put in............. 1Kin 2:35
Azariah the son of Z the priest............ 1Kin 4:2
and Z and Abiathar were the priests..... 1Kin 4:4
And Ahitub begat Z.............................. 1Chr 6:8
and Z begat Ahimaaz............................ 1Chr 6:8
Z his son, Ahimaaz his son.................... 1Chr 6:53
And David called for Z and Abiathar 1Chr 15:11
Z the priest, and his brethren the....... 1Chr 16:39
Z the son of Ahitub, and Abimelech. 1Chr 18:16

both Z of the sons of Eleazar, and....... 1Chr 24:3
Z the priest, and Ahimelech the.......... 1Chr 24:6
presence of David the king, and Z..... 1Chr 24:31
of the Aaronites, Z.............................. 1Chr 27:17
chief governor, and Z to be priest...... 1Chr 29:22
of the house of Z answered him......... 2Chr 31:10
The son of Shallum, the son of Z............ Ezr 7:2
these are the sons of Z among the....... Eze 40:46
Levites that be of the seed of Z.......... Eze 43:19
the Levites, the sons of Z..................... Eze 44:15
are sanctified of the sons of Z............. Eze 48:11
*2. Father of Jerusha.*
was Jerusha, the daughter of Z......... 2Kin 15:33
was Jerushah, the daughter of Z......... 2Chr 27:1
*3. Son of Ahitub.*
And Ahitub begat Z.............................. 1Chr 6:12
begat Zadok, and Z begat Shallum,..... 1Chr 6:12
son of Meshullam, the son of Z........... 1Chr 9:11
*4. A warrior in David's army.*
And Z, a young man mighty of......... 1Chr 12:28
*5. The son of Baana.*
them repaired Z the son of Baana.......... Neh 3:4
*6. A priest who rebuilt the wall.*
After them repaired Z the son of.......... Neh 3:29
*7. A renewer of the covenant.*
Meshezabeel, Z, Jaddua,...................... Neh 10:21
*8. A son of Meraioth.*
son of Meshullam, the son of Z........... Neh 11:11
*9. A Temple servant.*
Z the scribe, and of the Levites,.......... Neh 13:13

**ZADOKITES** See ZADOK'S.

**ZADOK'S** (*za'-doks*) *Refers to Zadok 1.*
their two sons, Ahimaaz Z son............. 2Sa 15:36

**ZAHAM** (*za'-ham*) *A son of Rehoboam.*
Jeush, and Shamariah, and Z............. 2Chr 11:19

**ZAIR** (*za'-ur*) *A city in Edom.*
So Joram went over to Z, and all........ 2Kin 8:21

**ZALAPH** (*za'-laf*) *Father of Hanun.*
and Hanun the sixth son of Z............... Neh 3:30

**ZALMON** (*zal'-mon*) See ILAI, SALMON.
*1. A hill in Ephraim.*
Abimelech gat him up to mount Z....... Judg 9:48
*2. A "mighty man" of David.*
Z the Ahohite, Maharai the .................. 2Sa 23:28

**ZALMONAH** (*zal'-mo-nah*) *An Israelite encampment in the wilderness.*
from mount Hor, and pitched in Z..... Num 33:41
And they departed from Z, and.......... Num 33:42

**ZALMUNNA** (*zal-mun'-nah*) *A Midianite king.*
and I am pursuing after Zebah and Z... Judg 8:5
Z now in thine hand, that we................. Judg 8:6
Z into mine hand, then I will................. Judg 8:7
Z were in Karkor, and their hosts....... Judg 8:10
Z fled, he pursued after them, and...... Judg 8:12
two kings of Midian, Zebah and Z....... Judg 8:12
and said, Behold Zebah and Z.............. Judg 8:15
Z now in thine hand, that we............... Judg 8:15
Then said he unto Zebah and Z............ Judg 8:18
Z said, Rise thou, and fall upon........... Judg 8:21
Gideon arose, and slew Zebah and Z.. Judg 8:21
their princes as Zebah, and as Z........... Ps 83:11

**ZAMZUMMIMS** (*zam-zum'-mims*) See ZUZIMS. *A tribe in Canaan.*
and the Ammonites call them Z........... Deut 2:20

**ZAMZUMMITES** See ZAMZUMMIMS.

**ZANOAH** (*za-no'-ah*)
*1. A city on the plain of Judah.*
And Z, and En-gannim........................ Josh 15:34
Hanun, and the inhabitants of Z............ Neh 3:13
Z, Adullam, and in their villages,......... Neh 11:30
*2. A city in the hills of Judah.*
And Jezreel, and Jokdeam, and Z....... Josh 15:56
*3. A descendant of Caleb.*
and Jekuthiel the father of Z............... 1Chr 4:18

**ZAPHENATH-PANEAH** See ZAPHNATH-PAANEAH.

**ZAPHNATH-PAANEAH** (*zaf''-nath-pa-a-ne'-ah*) *Name given to Joseph by Pharaoh.*
And Pharaoh called Joseph's name Z. Gen 41:45

**ZAPHON** (*za'-fon*) *A city in Gad.*
and Succoth, and Z.............................. Josh 13:27

**ZARA** (*za'-rah*) See ZARAH, ZERAH. *Greek form of Zarah; an ancestor of Jesus.*
Judas begat Phares and Z of Thamar....... Mt 1:3

**ZARAH** (*za'-rah*) See ZARA, ZERAH. *A son of Judah.*
and his name was called Z.................... Gen 38:30
Onan, and Shelah, and Pharez, and Z Gen 46:12

**ZAREAH** (*za'-re-ah*) See ZAREATHITES, ZORAH. *A city in Judah.*
And at En-rimmon, and at Z, and at .. Neh 11:29

**ZAREATHITES** (*za'-re-ath-ites*) See ZORATHITES. *Descendants of Shobal.*
of them came the Z, and the................. 1Chr 2:53

**ZARED** (*za'-red*) See ZERED. *A brook near the Dead Sea.*
and pitched in the valley of Z............ Num 21:12

**ZAREPHATH** (*zar'-e-fath*) See SAREPTA. *A city in Phoenicia.*
Arise, get thee to Z, which..................... 1Kin 17:9
So he arose and went to Z.................... 1Kin 17:10
of the Canaanites, even unto Z.............. Obad 20

**ZARETAN** (*zar'-e-tan*) See ZARTANAH, ZEREDATHAH. *A city in Ephraim.*
the city Adam, that is beside Z............ Josh 3:16

**ZARETHAN** See ZARTHAN.

**ZARETH-SHAHAR** (*za''-reth-sha'-har*) *A city in Reuben.*
Z in the mount of the valley,............... Josh 13:19

**ZARHITES** (*zar'-hites*)
*1. Descendants of Zerah, the Simeonite.*
Of Zerah, the family of the Z............. Num 26:13
and he took the family of the Z........... Josh 7:17
the family of the Z man by man........... Josh 7:17
Sibbecai the Hushathite, of the Z....... 1Chr 27:11
the Netophathite, of the Z.................. 1Chr 27:13
*2. Descendants of Zerah, son of Judah.*
of Zerah, the family of the Z............. Num 26:20

**ZARTANAH** (*zar'-ta-nah*) See ZARETAN, ZARTHAN. *Same as Zaretan.*
which is by Z beneath Jezreel,............. 1Kin 4:12

**ZARTHAN** (*zar'-than*) See ZARETAN, ZARTANAH. *Same as Zaretan.*
clay ground between Succoth and Z... 1Kin 7:46

**ZATTHU** (*zath'-u*) See ZATTU. *A renewer of the covenant.*
Parosh, Pahath-moab, Elam, Z............ Neh 10:14

**ZATTU** (*zat'-tu*) See ZATTHU. *A family of exiles.*
The children of Z, nine hundred .............. Ezr 2:8
And of the sons of Z.............................. Ezr 10:27
The children of Z, eight hundred.......... Neh 7:13

**ZAVAN** (*za'-van*) See ZAAVAN. *Son of Ezer.*
Bilhan, and Z, and Jakan...................... 1Chr 1:42

**ZAZA** (*za'-zah*) *A son of Jonathan.*
Peleth, and Z........................................ 1Chr 2:33

**ZEAL**
his *z* to the children of Israel................ 2Sa 21:2
with me, and see my *z* for the LORD.. 2Kin 10:16
the *z* of the LORD of hosts shall......... 2Kin 19:31
For the *z* of thine house hath.................. Ps 69:9
My *z* hath consumed me, because...... Ps 119:139
The *z* of the LORD of hosts will.................. Is 9:7
the *z* of the LORD of hosts shall.............. Is 37:32
and was clad with *z* as a cloke............... Is 59:17
where is thy *z* and thy strength,.............. Is 63:15
I the LORD have spoken it in my *z*......... Eze 5:13
The *z* of thine house hath eaten.............. Jn 2:17
record that they have a *z* of God......... Rom 10:2
what vehement desire, yea, what *z*...... 2Cor 7:11
your *z* hath provoked very many.......... 2Cor 9:2
Concerning *z*, persecuting the................ Phil 3:6
that he hath a great *z* for you................ Col 4:13

**ZEALOT** See ZELOTES.

**ZEALOUS**
while he was *z* for my sake among... Num 25:11
because he was *z* for his God........... Num 25:13
and they are all *z* of the law............... Acts 21:20
was *z* toward God, as ye all are........... Acts 22:3
as ye are *z* of spiritual gifts.............. 1Cor 14:12
being more exceedingly *z* of the............ Gal 1:14
peculiar people, *z* of good works........ Titus 2:14
be *z* therefore, and repent...................... Rev 3:19

**ZEALOUSLY**
They *z* affect you, but not well.............. Gal 4:17
But it is good to be *z* affected ............... Gal 4:18

**ZEBADIAH** (*zeb-ad-i'-ah*)
*1. Grandson of Elpael.*
And Z, and Arad, and Ader,................. 1Chr 8:15
*2. A son of Elpael.*
Z, and Meshullam, and Hezeki.............. 1Chr 8:17
*3. A warrior in David's army.*
And Joelah, and Z, the sons of............ 1Chr 12:7
*4. A Levite gatekeeper.*
Z the third, Jathniel the fourth,........... 1Chr 26:2
*5. A son of Asahel.*
of Joab, and Z his son after him.......... 1Chr 27:7
*6. A messenger for King Jehoshaphat.*
and Nethaniah, and Z.......................... 2Chr 17:8
*7. Son of Ishmael.*
Z the son of Ishmael, the ruler........... 2Chr 19:11
*8. A family of exiles.*
Z the son of Michael, and with him......... Ezr 8:8
*9. Married a foreigner in exile.*
Hanani, and Z...................................... Ezr 10:20

**ZEBAH** (*ze'-bah*) *A king of Midian.*
faint, and I am pursuing after Z............ Judg 8:5
Succoth said, Are the hands of Z........... Judg 8:6
when the LORD hath delivered Z............ Judg 8:7
Now Z and Zalmunna were.................. Judg 8:10
And when Z and Zalmunna fled, he.... Judg 8:12
took the two kings of Midian, Z.......... Judg 8:12
men of Succoth, and said, Behold Z.... Judg 8:15
me, saying, Are the hands of Z............ Judg 8:15
Then said he unto Z and Zalmunna,... Judg 8:18
Then Z and Zalmunna said, Rise.......... Judg 8:21
And Gideon arose, and slew Z............ Judg 8:21
yea, all their princes as Z.................... Ps 83:11

**ZEBAIM** (*ze-ba'-im*) *Residence of some exiles in Babylonia.*
the children of Pochereth of Z................ Ezr 2:57
the children of Pochereth of Z.............. Neh 7:59

**ZEBEDEE** (*zeb'-e-dee*) See ZEBEDEE'S. *Father of James and John.*
two brethren, James the son of Z........... Mt 4:21
in a ship with Z their father..................... Mt 4:21
James the son of Z, and John his............ Mt 10:2
him Peter and the two sons of Z.......... Mt 26:37
thence, he saw James the son of Z......... Mk 1:19
they left their father Z in the................. Mk 1:20
And James the son of Z, and John......... Mk 3:17
And James and John, the sons of Z..... Mk 10:35
James, and John, the sons of Z................ Lk 5:10
Cana in Galilee, and the sons of Z.......... Jn 21:2

**ZEBEDEE'S** (*zeb'-e-dees*)
of Z children with her sons.................... Mt 20:20
and the mother of Z children................. Mt 27:56

**ZEBIDAH** See ZEBUDAH.

**ZEBINA** (*ze-bi'-nah*) *Married a foreigner in exile.*
Jeiel, Mattithiah, Zabad, Z................... Ezr 10:43

**ZEBOIIM** (*ze-boy'-im*) See ZEBOIM. *City destroyed with Sodom and Gomorrah.*
of Admah, and Shemeber king of Z...... Gen 14:2
king of Admah, and the king of Z......... Gen 14:8

**ZEBOIM** (*ze-bo'-im*) See ZEBOIIM.
*1. Same as Zeboiim.*
and Gomorrah, and Admah, and Z...... Gen 10:19
Gomorrah, Admah, and Z................... Deut 29:23
how shall I set thee as Z........................ Hos 11:8
*2. A city in Benjamin.*
valley of Z toward the wilderness........ 1Sa 13:18
Hadid, Z, Neballat,............................... Neh 11:34

**ZEBUDAH** (*ze-bu'-dah*) *Mother of King Jehoiakim.*
And his mother's name was Z............ 2Kin 23:36

**ZEBUL** (*ze'-bul*) *A ruler of Shechem.*
and Z his officer.................................... Judg 9:28
when Z the ruler of the city.................. Judg 9:30
Gaal saw the people, he said to Z........ Judg 9:36
Z said unto him, Thou seest the.......... Judg 9:36
Then said Z unto him, Where is.......... Judg 9:38
Z thrust out Gaal and his brethren....... Judg 9:41

**ZEBULONITE** (*zeb'-u-lon-ite*) See ZEBULONITES. *A descendant of Zebulun 1.*
And after him Elon, a Z, judged......... Judg 12:11
And Elon the Z died, and was buried Judg 12:12

**ZEBULUN** (*zeb'-u-lun*) See ZABULON, ZEBULONITE, ZEBULONITES.
*1. A son of Jacob.*
and she called his name Z.................... Gen 30:20
Levi, and Judah, and Issachar, and Z. Gen 35:23
And the sons of Z................................. Gen 46:14
Z shall dwell at the haven of the......... Gen 49:13
Issachar, Z, and Benjamin,..................... Ex 1:3
Levi, and Judah, Issachar, and Z.......... 1Chr 2:1
*2. Descendants of Zebulun.*
Of Z; Eliab the........................................ Num 1:9
Of the children of Z, by their.............. Num 1:30
of them, even of the tribe of Z.............. Num 1:31
Then the tribe of Z................................. Num 2:7
be captain of the children of Z.............. Num 2:7
prince of the children of Z.................... Num 7:24
of Z was Eliab the son of Helon......... Num 10:16
Of the tribe of Z, Gaddiel the.............. Num 13:10
Of the sons of Z after their................. Num 26:26
of the tribe of the children of Z.......... Num 34:25
Reuben, Gad, and Asher, and Z.......... Deut 27:13
And of Zebulun he said, Rejoice, Z... Deut 33:18
of Z according to their families........... Josh 19:10
of Z according to their families........... Josh 19:16
to Beth-dagon, and reacheth to Z....... Josh 19:27
reacheth to Z on the south side,......... Josh 19:34
of Gad, and out of the tribe of Z.......... Josh 21:7
Levites, out of the tribe of Z............... Josh 21:34
Neither did Z drive out the.................... Judg 1:30
Naphtali and of the children of Z.......... Judg 4:6
And Barak called Z and Naphtali to.... Judg 4:10
out of Z they that handle the pen........ Judg 5:14
Z and Naphtali were a people that....... Judg 5:18
messengers unto Asher, and unto Z.... Judg 6:35
in Aijalon in the country of Z............ Judg 12:12
of Gad, and out of the tribe of Z.......... 1Chr 6:63
were given out of the tribe of Z............ 1Chr 6:77
Of Z, such as went forth to................. 1Chr 12:33
them, even unto Issachar and Z.......... 1Chr 12:40
Of Z, Ishmaiah the son of Obadiah..... 1Chr 27:19
Ephraim and Manasseh even unto Z. 2Chr 30:10
of Z humbled themselves, and came. 2Chr 30:11
and Manasseh, Issachar, and Z.......... 2Chr 30:18
their council, the princes of Z............... Ps 68:27
lightly afflicted the land of Z.......................... Is 9:1
unto the west side, Z a portion............ Eze 48:26
And by the border of Z, from the......... Eze 48:27
gate of Issachar, one gate of Z............ Eze 48:33

**ZEBULUNITES** (*zeb'-u-lun-ites*) *Descendants of Zebulun.*
Z according to those that were.......... Num 26:27

**ZECHARIAH** (*zek-a-ri'-ah*) See ZACCUR, ZACHARIAH, ZACHARIAS, ZACHER.
*1. A chief Reubenite.*
were the chief, Jeiel, and Z.................... 1Chr 5:7

*2. A Levite gatekeeper.*
Z the son of Meshelemiah was ........ 1Chr 9:21
Z the firstborn, Jediael the........ 1Chr 26:2
Then for Z his son, a wise........ 1Chr 26:14
was Abijah, the daughter of Z........ 2Chr 29:1
*3. A Benjamite.*
And Gedor, and Ahio, and Z, and........ 1Chr 9:37
*4. A Levite musician.*
brethren of the second degree, Z........ 1Chr 15:18
And Z, and Aziel, and Shemiramoth, 1Chr 15:20
Asaph the chief, and next to him Z..... 1Chr 16:5
*5. A Tabernacle priest.*
and Nethaneel, and Amasai, and Z.... 1Chr 15:24
*6. A son of Isshiah.*
sons of Isshiah; Z........ 1Chr 24:25
*7. Son of Hosah.*
Tebaliah the third, Z the fourth........ 1Chr 26:11
*8. A chief of Manasseh.*
in Gilead, Iddo the son of Z........ 1Chr 27:21
*9. A messenger of King Jehoshaphat.*
Ben-hail, and to Obadiah, and to Z...... 2Chr 17:7
*10. Father of Jehaziel.*
Then upon Jahaziel the son of Z........ 2Chr 20:14
*11. A son of Jehoshaphat.*
Azariah, and Jehiel, and Z........ 2Chr 21:2
*12. Son of Jehoida.*
the Spirit of God came upon Z the.... 2Chr 24:20
*13. A prophet in King Uzziah's time.*
And he sought God in the days of Z... 2Chr 26:5
*14. A Levite who cleansed the Temple.*
Z, and Mattaniah........ 2Chr 29:13
*15. An overseer of the Temple repairs.*
and Z and Meshullam, of the sons of 2Chr 34:12
*16. A prince of Judah.*
Hilkiah and Z and Jehiel, rulers of....... 2Chr 35:8
*17. A prophet in Judah.*
Z the son of Iddo, prophesied........ Ezr 5:1
the prophet and Z the son of Iddo........ Ezr 6:14
came the word of the LORD unto Z........ Zec 1:1
came the word of the LORD unto Z........ Zec 1:7
Z in the fourth day of the ninth........ Zec 7:1
the word of the LORD came unto Z........ Zec 7:8
*18. A son of Pharosh.*
sons of Pharosh; Z........ Ezr 8:3
*19. A son of Bebai.*
Z the son of Bebai, and with him........ Ezr 8:11
Elnathan, and for Nathan, and for Z........ Ezr 8:16
*20. Married a foreigner in exile.*
Mattaniah, Z, and Jehiel, and Abdi,...... Ezr 10:26
*21. A prince who aided Ezra.*
and Hashum, and Hashbadana, Z........ Neh 8:4
*22. A descendant of Pharez.*
the son of Uzziah, the son of Z........ Neh 11:4
*23. A son of Shiloni.*
the son of Joiarib, the son of Z........ Neh 11:5
*24. Father of a resettler in Jerusalem.*
the son of Amzi, the son of Z........ Neh 11:12
*25. A priest in Joiakim's time.*
Of Iddo, Z........ Neh 12:16
*26. A priest who dedicated the wall.*
Z the son of Jonathan, the son of....... Neh 12:35
Miniamin, Michaiah, Elioenai, Z........ Neh 12:41
*27. Son of Jeberechiah.*
and Z the son of Jeberechiah........ Is 8:2

**ZECHER** See ZACHER.

**ZEDAD** (*ze'-dad*) *A place near Hamath.*
forth of the border shall be to Z........ Num 34:8
way of Hethlon, as men go to Z........ Eze 47:15

**ZEDEKIAH** (*zed-e-ki'-ah*) See MATTANIAH, ZEDEKIAH'S, ZIDKIJAH.
*1. A false prophet.*
Z the son of Chenaanah made him.... 1Kin 22:11
But Z the son of Chenaanah went..... 1Kin 22:24
Z the son of Chenaanah had made.... 2Chr 18:10
Then Z the son of Chenaanah came. 2Chr 18:23
*2. Name given to Mattaniah by Nebuchadnezzar.*
stead, and changed his name to Z...... 2Kin 24:17
Z was twenty and one years old........ 2Kin 24:18
that Z rebelled against the king........ 2Kin 24:20
unto the eleventh year of king Z........ 2Kin 25:2
the sons of Z before his eyes........ 2Kin 25:7
eyes, and put out the eyes of Z........ 2Kin 25:7
the second Jehoiakim, the third Z....... 1Chr 3:15
made Z his brother king over........ 2Chr 36:10
Z was one and twenty years old........ 2Chr 36:11
Z the son of Josiah king of Judah........ Jer 1:3
when king Z sent unto him Pashur........ Jer 21:1
unto them, Thus shall ye say to Z........ Jer 21:3
I will deliver Z king of Judah........ Jer 21:7
So will I give Z the king of........ Jer 24:8
to Jerusalem unto Z king of Judah........ Jer 27:3
I spake also to Z king of Judah........ Jer 27:12
of the reign of Z king of Judah........ Jer 28:1
(whom Z king of Judah sent unto........ Jer 29:3
the tenth year of Z king of Judah........ Jer 32:1
For Z king of Judah had shut him........ Jer 32:3
Z king of Judah shall not escape........ Jer 32:4
And he shall lead Z to Babylon........ Jer 32:5
speak to Z king of Judah, and tell........ Jer 34:2
of the LORD, O Z king of Judah........ Jer 34:4
unto Z king of Judah in Jerusalem........ Jer 34:6
after that the king Z had made a........ Jer 34:8
Z king of Judah and his princes........ Jer 34:21
king Z the son of Josiah reigned........ Jer 37:1
Z the king sent Jehucal the son........ Jer 37:3
Then Z the king sent, and took him..... Jer 37:17
Jeremiah said unto king Z........ Jer 37:18
Then Z the king commanded that........ Jer 37:21
Then Z the king said, Behold, he........ Jer 38:5
Then Z the king sent, and took........ Jer 38:14
Then Jeremiah said unto Z........ Jer 38:15
So Z the king sware secretly unto........ Jer 38:16
Then said Jeremiah unto Z........ Jer 38:17
Z the king said unto Jeremiah, I........ Jer 38:19
Then said Z unto Jeremiah, Let no........ Jer 38:24
the ninth year of Z king of Judah........ Jer 39:1
And in the eleventh year of Z........ Jer 39:2
that when Z the king of Judah saw........ Jer 39:4
overtook Z in the plains of........ Jer 39:5
of Z in Riblah before his eyes........ Jer 39:6
as I gave Z king of Judah into........ Jer 44:30
of the reign of Z king of Judah........ Jer 49:34
when he went with Z the king of........ Jer 51:59
Z was one and twenty years old........ Jer 52:1
that Z rebelled against the king........ Jer 52:3
unto the eleventh year of king Z........ Jer 52:5
overtook Z in the plains of........ Jer 52:8
the sons of Z before his eyes........ Jer 52:10
Then he put out the eyes of Z........ Jer 52:11
*3. Grandson of Jehoiakim.*
Jeconiah his son, Z his son........ 1Chr 3:16
*4. A false prophet denounced by Jeremiah.*
of Z the son of Maaseiah, which........ Jer 29:21
saying, The LORD make thee like Z...... Jer 29:22
*5. A prince of Judah.*
Z the son of Hananiah, and all the........ Jer 36:12

**ZEDEKIAH'S** (*zed-e-ki'-ahs*) *Refers to Zedekiah 2.*
Moreover he put out Z eyes........ Jer 39:7

**ZEEB** (*ze'-eb*) *A Midianite prince.*
of the Midianites, Oreb and Z........ Judg 7:25
Z they slew at the winepress of........ Judg 7:25
they slew at the winepress of Z........ Judg 7:25
Z to Gideon on the other side........ Judg 7:25
the princes of Midian, Oreb and Z........ Judg 8:3
their nobles like Oreb, and like Z........ Ps 83:11

**ZELA** See ZELAH.

**ZELAH** (*ze'-lah*) *A city in Benjamin.*
And Z, Eleph, and Jebusi, which is..... Josh 18:28
in the country of Benjamin in Z........ 2Sa 21:14

**ZELEK** (*ze'-lek*) *A "mighty man" of David.*
Z the Ammonite, Nahari the........ 2Sa 23:37
Z the Ammonite, Naharai the........ 1Chr 11:39

**ZELOPHEHAD** (*ze-lo'-fe-had*) *Son of Hepher.*
Z the son of Hepher had no sons,...... Num 26:33
of the daughters of Z were Mahlah... Num 26:33
Then came the daughters of Z........ Num 27:1
The daughters of Z speak right........ Num 27:7
Z our brother unto his daughters........ Num 36:2
concerning the daughters of Z........ Num 36:6
Moses, so did the daughters of Z....... Num 36:10
and Noah, the daughters of Z........ Num 36:11
But Z, the son of Hepher, the son........ Josh 17:3
and the name of the second was Z...... 1Chr 7:15
and Z had daughters........ 1Chr 7:15

**ZELOTES** (*ze-lo-teze*) See CANAANITE, SIMON. *Surname of Simon, disciple of Jesus.*
of Alphaeus, and Simon called Z........ Lk 6:15
the son of Alphaeus, and Simon Z........ Acts 1:13

**ZELZAH** (*zel'-zah*) *A city in Benjamin.*
in the border of Benjamin at Z........ 1Sa 10:2

**ZEMARAIM** (*zem-a-ra'-im*) See ZEMARITE.
*1. A city in Benjamin.*
And Beth-arabah, and Z........ Josh 18:22
*2. A mountain in Ephraim.*
And Abijah stood up upon mount Z... 2Chr 13:4

**ZEMARITE** *A descendant of Canaan.*
And the Arvadite, and the Z........ Gen 10:18
And the Arvadite, and the Z........ 1Chr 1:16

**ZEMIRA** (*ze-mi'-rah*) *A son of Becher.*
Z, and Joash, and Eliezer, and........ 1Chr 7:8

**ZEMIRAH** See ZEMIRA.

**ZENAN** (*ze'-nan*) See ZAANAN. *A city in Judah.*
Z, and Hadashah, and Migdal-gad,..... Josh 15:37

**ZENAS** (*ze'-nas*) *A Christian lawyer.*
Bring Z the lawyer and Apollos on..... Titus 3:13

**ZEPHANIAH** (*zef-a-ni'-ah*)
*1. A priest in exile.*
Z the second priest, and the three...... 2Kin 25:18
Z the son of Maaseiah the priest,........ Jer 21:1
to Z the son of Maaseiah the........ Jer 29:25
Z the priest read this letter in........ Jer 29:29
Z the son of Maaseiah the priest........ Jer 37:3
Z the second priest, and the three........ Jer 52:24
*2. An ancestor of Samuel.*
the son of Azariah, the son of Z........ 1Chr 6:36
*3. A prophet.*
came unto Z the son of Cushi........ Zeph 1:1
*4. Son of Josiah the priest.*
the house of Josiah the son of Z........ Zec 6:10
Jedaiah, and to Hen the son of Z........ Zec 6:14

**ZEPHATH** (*ze'-fath*) See HORMAH. *A city in Simeon.*
the Canaanites that inhabited Z........ Judg 1:17

**ZEPHATHAH** (*zef'-a-thah*) *A valley in Judah.*
in the valley of Z at Mareshah........ 2Chr 14:10

**ZEPHI** (*ze'-fi*) See ZEPHO. *Son of Eliphaz.*
Teman, and Omar, Z, and Gatam,........ 1Chr 1:36

**ZEPHO** (*ze'-fo*) See ZEPHI. *Same as Zephi.*
of Eliphaz were Teman, Omar, Z........ Gen 36:11
duke Teman, duke Omar, duke Z........ Gen 36:15

**ZEPHON** (*ze'-fon*) See ZEPHONITES, ZIPHION. *A son of Gad.*
of Z, the family of the........ Num 26:15

**ZEPHONITES** (*zef'-on-ites*) *Descendants of Zephon.*
of Zephon, the family of the Z........ Num 26:15

**ZER** (*zur*) *A city in Naphtali.*
the fenced cities are Ziddim, Z........ Josh 19:35

**ZERAH** (*ze'-rah*) See EZRAHITE, ZARAH, ZARHITES, ZOHAR.
*1. A son of Reuel.*
and Z, Shammah, and Mizzah........ Gen 36:13
duke Z, duke Shammah........ Gen 36:17
Nahath, Z, Shammah, and Mizzah....... 1Chr 1:37
*2. Father of Jobab.*
Jobab the son of Z of Bozrah........ Gen 36:33
Jobab the son of Z of Bozrah........ 1Chr 1:44
*3. Son of Judah.*
of Z, the family of the Zarhites........ Num 26:20
the son of Zabdi, the son of Z........ Josh 7:1
the son of Zabdi, the son of Z........ Josh 7:18
with him, took Achan the son of Z...... Josh 7:24
son of Z commit a trespass in the...... Josh 22:20
in law bare him Pharez and Z........ 1Chr 2:4
And the sons of Z........ 1Chr 2:6
And of the sons of Z........ 1Chr 9:6
children of Z the son of Judah........ Neh 11:24
*4. A son of Simeon.*
Of Z, the family of the Zarhites........ Num 26:13
were, Nemuel, and Jamin, Jarib, Z....... 1Chr 4:24
*5. Son of Iddo.*
Z his son, Jeaterai his son........ 1Chr 6:21
*6. Father of Ethni.*
The son of Ethni, the son of Z........ 1Chr 6:41
*7. An Ethiopian king.*
there came out against them Z the..... 2Chr 14:9

**ZERAHIAH** (*zer-a-hi'-ah*)
*1. An ancestor of Ezra.*
And Uzzi begat Z, and Z........ 1Chr 6:6
Z, and Z begat Meraioth,........ 1Chr 6:6
his son, Uzzi his son, Z his son,........ 1Chr 6:51
The son of Z, the son of Uzzi,........ Ezr 7:4
*2. Father of Elihoenai.*
Elihoenai the son of Z, and with........ Ezr 8:4

**ZERAHITE** See ZARHITES.

**ZERED** (*ze'-red*) See ZARED. *Same as Zared.*
I, and get you over the brook Z........ Deut 2:13
And we went over the brook Z........ Deut 2:13
we were come over the brook Z........ Deut 2:14

**ZEREDA** (*zer'-e-dah*) *A city north of Mt. Ephraim.*
son of Nebat, an Ephrathite of Z........ 1Kin 11:26

**ZEREDAH** See ZEREDATHAH.

**ZEREDATHAH** (*ze-red'-a-thah*) See ZARTHAN, ZERERATH. *A city in Manasseh.*
clay ground between Succoth and Z... 2Chr 4:17

**ZERERAH** See ZERERATH.

**ZERERATH** (*zer'-e-rath*) See ZARTHAN, ZEREDATHAH. *A district in Manasseh.*
host fled to Beth-shittah in Z........ Judg 7:22

**ZERESH** (*ze'-resh*) *Wife of Haman.*
for his friends, and Z his wife........ Est 5:10
Then said Z his wife and all his........ Est 5:14
And Haman told Z his wife and all........ Est 6:13
Z his wife unto him, If Mordecai........ Est 6:13

**ZERETH** (*ze'-reth*) *A descendant of Judah.*
And the sons of Helah were, Z........ 1Chr 4:7

**ZERETH-SHAHAR** See ZARETH-SHAHAR.

**ZERI** (*ze'-ri*) See IZRI. *Son of Jeduthun.*
Gedaliah, and Z, and Jeshaiah,........ 1Chr 25:3

**ZEROR** (*ze'-ror*) *Ancestor of King Saul.*
the son of Abiel, the son of Z........ 1Sa 9:1

**ZERUAH** (*ze-ru'-ah*) *Mother of Jeroboam I.*
whose mother's name was Z........ 1Kin 11:26

**ZERUBBABEL** (*ze-rub'-ba-bel*) See SHESHBAZZAR, ZOROBABEL. *A leader of a group of exiles.*
And the sons of Pedaiah were, Z........ 1Chr 3:19
and the sons of Z........ 1Chr 3:19
Which came with Z........ Ezr 2:2
Z the son of Shealtiel, and his........ Ezr 3:2
began Z the son of Shealtiel, and........ Ezr 3:8
Then they came to Z, and to the........ Ezr 4:2
But Z, and Jeshua, and the rest of........ Ezr 4:3
Then rose up Z the son of........ Ezr 5:2
Who came with Z, Jeshua, Nehemiah.... Neh 7:7
up with Z the son of Shealtiel........ Neh 12:1
And all Israel in the days of Z........ Neh 12:47
unto Z the son of Shealtiel........ Hag 1:1
Then Z the son of Shealtiel, and........ Hag 1:12
spirit of Z the son of Shealtiel........ Hag 1:14
Speak now to Z the son of........ Hag 2:2

Yet now be strong, O Z, saith the.......... Hag 2:4
Speak to Z, governor of Judah,............. Hag 2:21
of hosts, will I take thee, O Z............. Hag 2:23
is the word of the LORD unto Z.............. Zec 4:6
before Z thou shalt become a................ Zec 4:7
The hands of Z have laid the................ Zec 4:9
in the hand of Z with those seven......... Zec 4:10

**ZERUIAH** (*ze-ru-i'-ah*) *Sister of David.*
and to Abishai the son of Z.................. 1Sa 26:6
And Joab the son of Z, and the.............. 2Sa 2:13
there were three sons of Z there........... 2Sa 2:18
the sons of Z be too hard for me........... 2Sa 3:39
Joab the son of Z was over the.............. 2Sa 8:16
Now Joab the son of Z perceived........... 2Sa 14:1
the son of Z unto the king.................... 2Sa 16:9
I to do with you, ye sons of Z.............. 2Sa 16:10
sister to Z Joab's mother...................... 2Sa 17:25
the hand of Abishai the son of Z........... 2Sa 18:2
But Abishai the son of Z answered......... 2Sa 19:21
I to do with you, ye sons of Z.............. 2Sa 19:22
the son of Z succoured him.................. 2Sa 21:17
the brother of Joab, the son of Z........... 2Sa 23:18
armourbearer to Joab the son of Z......... 2Sa 23:37
conferred with Joab the son of Z.......... 1Kin 1:7
what Joab the son of Z did to me.......... 1Kin 2:5
priest, and for Joab the son of Z........... 1Kin 2:22
Whose sisters were Z, and Abigail........ 1Chr 2:16
And the sons of Z................................ 1Chr 2:16
Joab the son of Z went first up............ 1Chr 11:6
armourbearer of Joab the son of Z.... 1Chr 11:39
Abishai the son Z slew of the............ 1Chr 18:12
Joab the son of Z was over the.......... 1Chr 18:15
son of Ner, and Joab the son of Z...... 1Chr 26:28
Joab the son of Z began to number... 1Chr 27:24

**ZETHAM** (*ze'-tham*) *A descendant of Laadan.*
the chief was Jehiel, and Z.................. 1Chr 23:8
Z, and Joel his brother, which............ 1Chr 26:22

**ZETHAN** (*ze'-than*) *A son of Bilhan.*
and Ehud, and Chenaanah, and Z.......... 1Chr 7:10

**ZETHAR** (*ze'-thar*) *A servant of King Ahasuerus.*
Harbona, Bigtha, and Abagtha, Z............ Est 1:10

**ZEUS** See MERCURIUS.

**ZIA** (*zi'-ah*) *A Gadite in Bashan.*
Sheba, and Jorai, and Jachan, and Z... 1Chr 5:13

**ZIBA** (*zi'-bah*) *A servant of King Saul.*
Saul a servant whose name was Z.......... 2Sa 9:2
king said unto him, Art thou Z.............. 2Sa 9:2
Z said unto the king, Jonathan.............. 2Sa 9:3
Z said unto the king, Behold, he............ 2Sa 9:4
Then the king called to Z.................... 2Sa 9:9
Now Z had fifteen sons and twenty....... 2Sa 9:10
Then said Z unto the king,................... 2Sa 9:11
all that dwelt in the house of Z............ 2Sa 9:12
Z the servant of Mephibosheth met........ 2Sa 16:1
And the king said unto Z, What............ 2Sa 16:2
Z said, The asses be for the.................. 2Sa 16:2
Z said unto the king, Behold, he........... 2Sa 16:3
Then said the king to Z, Behold,........... 2Sa 16:4
Z said, I humbly beseech thee............... 2Sa 16:4
Z the servant of the house of............... 2Sa 19:17
said, Thou and Z divide the land......... 2Sa 19:29

**ZIBEON** (*zib'-e-un*)
*1. Grandfather of Adah.*
Anah the daughter of Z the Hivite........ Gen 36:2
of Anah the daughter of Z.................. Gen 36:14
*2. A son of Seir.*
Lotan, and Shobal, and Z, and Anah,. Gen 36:20
And these are the children of Z.......... Gen 36:24
he fed the asses of Z his father........... Gen 36:24
duke Lotan, duke Shobal, duke Z........ Gen 36:29
Lotan, and Shobal, and Z, and Anah,.. 1Chr 1:38
And the sons of Z.............................. 1Chr 1:40

**ZIBIA** (*zib'-e-ah*) *Son of Hodesh.*
of Hodesh his wife, Jobab, and Z.......... 1Chr 8:9

**ZIBIAH** (*zib'-e-ah*) *Mother of King Jehoash.*
mother's name was Z of Beer-sheba.... 2Kin 12:1
name also was Z of Beer-sheba........... 2Chr 24:1

**ZICHRI** (*zik'-ri*) See ZITHRI.
*1. A son of Izhar.*
Korah, and Nepheg, and Z..................... Ex 6:21
*2. A Benjamite.*
And Jakim, and Z, and Zabdi,.............. 1Chr 8:19
*3. Son of Shishak.*
And Abdon, and Z, and Hanan,............ 1Chr 8:23
*4. Son of Jeroham.*
And Jaresiah, and Eliah, and Z............ 1Chr 8:27
*5. Son of Asaph.*
the son of Micah, the son of Z............. 1Chr 9:15
*6. Descendant of Eliezer.*
Z his son, and Shelomith his son........ 1Chr 26:25
*7. Father of Eliezer.*
was Eliezer the son of Z.................... 1Chr 27:16
*8. Father of Amasiah.*
next him was Amasiah the son of Z.. 2Chr 17:16
*9. Father of Elishaphat.*
and Elishaphat the son of Z............... 2Chr 23:1
*10. A "mighty man" of Ephraim.*
And Z, a mighty man of Ephraim,....... 2Chr 28:7
*11. Father of Joel.*
Joel the son of Z was their.................. Neh 11:9
*12. A priest with Zerubbabel.*
Of Abijah, Z...................................... Neh 12:17

**ZICRI** See ZICHRI.

**ZIDDIM** (*zid'-dim*) *A city in Naphtali.*
And the fenced cities are Z................. Josh 19:35

**ZIDKIJAH** (*zid-ki'-jah*) See ZEDEKIAH. *A clan leader who renewed the covenant.*
the son of Hachaliah, and Z................. Neh 10:1

**ZIDON** (*zi'-don*)
*1. A city in Asher.*
and his border shall be unto Z............ Gen 49:13
them, and chased them unto great Z... Josh 11:8
and Kanah, even unto great Z........... Josh 19:28
Accho, nor the inhabitants of Z.......... Judg 1:31
gods of Syria, and the gods of Z......... Judg 10:6
because it was far from Z.................. Judg 18:28
came to Dan-jaan, and about to Z........ 2Sa 24:6
Zarephath, which belongeth to Z......... 1Kin 17:9
and drink, and oil, unto them of Z......... Ezr 3:7
thou whom the merchants of Z................ Is 23:2
Be thou ashamed, O Z.......................... Is 23:4
oppressed virgin, daughter of Z............ Is 23:12
of Tyrus, and all the kings of Z.......... Jer 25:22
of Tyrus, and to the king of Z.............. Jer 27:3
Z every helper that remaineth.............. Jer 47:4
The inhabitants of Z and Arvad............ Eze 27:8
of man, set thy face against Z........... Eze 28:21
Behold, I am against thee, O Z.......... Eze 28:22
ye to do with me, O Tyre, and Z.......... Joel 3:4
Tyrus, and Z, though it be very............ Zec 9:2
*2. A son of Canaan.*
Canaan begat Z his firstborn, and........ 1Chr 1:13

**ZIDONIANS** (*zi-do'-ne-uns*) See SIDONIANS. *Inhabitants of Zidon.*
The Z also, and the Amalekites, and. Judg 10:12
after the manner of the Z.................... Judg 18:7
and they were far from the Z............... Judg 18:7
Moabites, Ammonites, Edomites, Z...... 1Kin 11:1
Ashtoreth the goddess of the Z........... 1Kin 11:5
Ashtoreth the goddess of the Z.......... 1Kin 11:33
daughter of Ethbaal king of the Z...... 1Kin 16:31
the abomination of the Z, and for...... 2Kin 23:13
for the Z and they of Tyre brought..... 1Chr 22:4
north, all of them, and all the Z.......... Eze 32:30

**ZIF** (*zif*) *Second month of the Hebrew year.*
reign over Israel, in the month Z.......... 1Kin 6:1
of the LORD laid, in the month Z.......... 1Kin 6:37

**ZIHA** (*zi'-hah*)
*1. A family of exiles.*
the children of Z, the children.............. Ezr 2:43
the children of Z, the children............. Neh 7:46
*2. An overseer of Temple servants.*
and Z and Gispa were over the........... Neh 11:21

**ZIKLAG** (*zik'-lag*) *A city in Judah.*
And Z, and Madmannah....................... Josh 15:31
And Z, and Beth-marcaboth, and.......... Josh 19:5
Then Achish gave him Z that day.......... 1Sa 27:6
wherefore Z pertaineth unto the........... 1Sa 27:6
were come to Z on the third day........... 1Sa 30:1
south, and Z, and smitten Z................. 1Sa 30:1
and we burned Z with fire.................... 1Sa 30:14
And when David came to Z, he sent... 1Sa 30:26
and David had abode two days in Z........ 2Sa 1:1
hold of him, and slew him in Z............. 2Sa 4:10
at Bethuel, and at Hormah, and at Z.. 1Chr 4:30
are they that came to David to Z........ 1Chr 12:1
As he went to Z, there fell to............. 1Chr 12:20
And at Z, and at Mekonah.................. Neh 11:28

**ZILLAH** (*zil'-lah*) *A wife of Lamech.*
Adah, and the name of the other Z...... Gen 4:19
And Z, she also bare Tubal-cain,.......... Gen 4:22
said unto his wives, Adah and Z.......... Gen 4:23

**ZILLETHAI** See ZILTHAI.

**ZILPAH** (*zil'-pah*) *Handmaid of Leah.*
Leah Z his maid for an handmaid........ Gen 29:24
left bearing, she took Z her maid......... Gen 30:9
Z Leah's maid bare Jacob a son.......... Gen 30:10
Z Leah's maid bare Jacob a second...... Gen 30:12
And the sons of Z, Leah's handmaid.. Gen 35:26
of Bilhah, and with the sons of Z.......... Gen 37:2
These are the sons of Z, whom........... Gen 46:18

**ZILTHAI** (*zil'-thahee*)
*1. Son of Shimhi.*
And Elienai, and Z, and Eliel,............. 1Chr 8:20
*2. A warrior in David's army.*
and Jozabad, and Elihu, and Z........... 1Chr 12:20

**ZIMMAH** (*zim'-mah*)
*1. A son of Jahath.*
son, Jahath his son, Z his son,............. 1Chr 6:20
*2. A Gershonite.*
The son of Ethan, the son of Z............ 1Chr 6:42
*3. Father of Joah.*
Joah the son of Z, and Eden the........ 2Chr 29:12

**ZIMRAN** (*zim'-ran*) *A son of Abraham.*
And she bare him Z, and Jokshan, and Gen 25:2
she bare Z, and Jokshan, and Medan,. 1Chr 1:32

**ZIMRI** (*zim'-ri*)
*1. A Simeonite.*
with the Midianitish woman, was Z.. Num 25:14
*2. A king of Israel.*
And his servant Z, captain of half........ 1Kin 16:9
Z went in and smote him, and killed. 1Kin 16:10
Thus did Z destroy all the house....... 1Kin 16:12
did Z reign seven days in Tirzah........ 1Kin 16:15
Z hath conspired, and hath also......... 1Kin 16:16
when Z saw that the city was............ 1Kin 16:18
Now the rest of the acts of Z............. 1Kin 16:20
Had Z peace, who slew his master....... 2Kin 9:31
*3. A son of Zerah.*
Z, and Ethan, and Heman, and Calcol,. 1Chr 2:6
*4. Son of Jehoadah.*
begat Alemeth, and Azmaveth, and Z. 1Chr 8:36
and Z begat Moza,............................. 1Chr 8:36
begat Alemeth, and Azmaveth, and Z. 1Chr 9:42
and Z begat Moza............................. 1Chr 9:42
*5. An unspecified place.*
And all the kings of Z, and all the........ Jer 25:25

**ZIN** (*zin*) *A wilderness south of Judah.*
the wilderness of Z unto Rehob......... Num 13:21
desert of Z in the first month.............. Num 20:1
my commandment in the desert of Z Num 27:14
in Kadesh in the wilderness of Z......... Num 27:14
and pitched in the wilderness of Z...... Num 33:36
of Z along by the coast of Edom.......... Num 34:3
of Akrabbim, and pass on to Z............ Num 34:4
in the wilderness of Z........................ Deut 32:51
of Edom the wilderness of Z.............. Josh 15:1
and passed along to Z, and................ Josh 15:3

**ZINA** (*zi'-nah*) *A son of Shimei.*
sons of Shimei were, Jahath, Z........... 1Chr 23:10

**ZION** (*zi'-un*) See SION, ZION'S. *A term for Jerusalem.*
David took the strong hold of Z............. 2Sa 5:7
of the city of David, which is Z............. 1Kin 8:1
daughter of Z hath despised thee....... 2Kin 19:21
they that escape out of mount Z........ 2Kin 19:31
David took the castle of Z................... 1Chr 11:5
of the city of David, which is Z............. 2Chr 5:2
my king upon my holy hill of Z................ Ps 2:6
to the LORD, which dwelleth in Z............ Ps 9:11
in the gates of the daughter of Z........... Ps 9:14
of Israel were come out of Z................ Ps 14:7
and strengthen thee out of Z............... Ps 20:2
of the whole earth, is mount Z.............. Ps 48:2
Let mount Z rejoice, let the................. Ps 48:11
Walk about Z, and go round about........ Ps 48:12
Out of Z, the perfection of.................... Ps 50:2
good in thy good pleasure unto Z......... Ps 51:18
of Israel were come out of Z................ Ps 53:6
For God will save Z, and will............... Ps 69:35
this mount Z, wherein thou hast............. Ps 74:2
and his dwelling place in Z................... Ps 76:2
the mount Z which he loved................. Ps 78:68
of them in Z appeareth before God......... Ps 84:7
The LORD loveth the gates of Z.............. Ps 87:2
of Z it shall be said, This and............... Ps 87:5
Z heard, and was glad......................... Ps 97:8
The LORD is great in Z........................ Ps 99:2
shalt arise, and have mercy upon Z..... Ps 102:13
When the LORD shall build up Z........ Ps 102:16
declare the name of the LORD in Z....... Ps 102:21
the rod of thy strength out of Z.......... Ps 110:2
in the LORD shall be as mount Z.......... Ps 125:1
turned again the captivity of Z........... Ps 126:1
LORD shall bless thee out of Z............. Ps 128:5
and turned back that hate Z................ Ps 129:5
For the LORD hath chosen Z............... Ps 132:13
descended upon the mountains of Z...... Ps 133:3
and earth bless thee out of Z............... Ps 134:3
Blessed be the LORD out of Z............. Ps 135:21
we wept, when we remembered Z........... Ps 137:1
Sing us one of the songs of Z.............. Ps 137:3
reign for ever, even thy God, O Z........ Ps 146:10
praise thy God, O Z........................... Ps 147:12
let the children of Z be joyful.............. Ps 149:2
Go forth, O ye daughters of Z............ Song 3:11
the daughter of Z is left as a.................. Is 1:8
Z shall be redeemed with judgment.......... Is 1:27
for out of Z shall go forth the................. Is 2:3
the daughters of Z are haughty............... Is 3:16
of the head of the daughters of Z........... Is 3:17
pass, that he that is left in Z.................. Is 4:3
the filth of the daughters of Z................. Is 4:4
every dwelling place of mount Z.............. Is 4:5
hosts, which dwelleth in mount Z............ Is 8:18
his whole work upon mount Z............... Is 10:12
O my people that dwellest in Z............. Is 10:24
the mount of the daughter of Z............. Is 10:32
and shout, thou inhabitant of Z............. Is 12:6
That the LORD hath founded Z.............. Is 14:32
the mount of the daughter of Z............... Is 16:1
of the LORD of hosts, the mount Z............ Is 18:7
of hosts shall reign in mount Z.............. Is 24:23
I lay in Z for a foundation a................ Is 28:16
be, that fight against mount Z............... Is 29:8
shall dwell in Z at Jerusalem................ Is 30:19
come down to fight for mount Z............. Is 31:4
the LORD, whose fire is in Z.................. Is 31:9
he hath filled Z with judgment............... Is 33:5
The sinners in Z are afraid.................. Is 33:14
Look upon Z, the city of our................. Is 33:20
for the controversy of Z...................... Is 34:8
and come to Z with songs and............... Is 35:10
The virgin, the daughter of Z................ Is 37:22
they that escape out of mount Z............ Is 37:32
O Z, that bringest good tidings,............. Is 40:9
The first shall say to Z, Behold,............ Is 41:27
in Z for Israel my glory...................... Is 46:13
But Z said, The LORD hath.................. Is 49:14
For the LORD shall comfort Z.................. Is 51:3
and come with singing unto Z................ Is 51:11
of the earth, and say unto Z................. Is 51:16
put on thy strength, O Z........................ Is 52:1
thy neck, O captive daughter of Z............ Is 52:2

that saith unto Z, Thy God ........ Is 52:7
when the LORD shall bring again Z ........ Is 52:8
And the Redeemer shall come to Z ........ Is 59:20
The Z of the Holy One of Israel ........ Is 60:14
appoint unto them that mourn in Z ........ Is 61:3
Say ye to the daughter of Z ........ Is 62:11
Z is a wilderness, Jerusalem a ........ Is 64:10
for as soon as Z travailed ........ Is 66:8
family, and I will bring you to Z ........ Jer 3:14
Set up the standard toward Z ........ Jer 4:6
the voice of the daughter of Z ........ Jer 4:31
the daughter of Z to a comely ........ Jer 6:2
war against thee, O daughter of Z ........ Jer 6:23
Is not the LORD in Z ........ Jer 8:19
of wailing is heard out of Z ........ Jer 9:19
hath thy soul lothed Z ........ Jer 14:19
Z shall be plowed like a field, ........ Jer 26:18
an Outcast, saying, This is Z ........ Jer 30:17
let us go up to Z unto the LORD ........ Jer 31:6
come and sing in the height of Z ........ Jer 31:12
They shall ask the way to Z with ........ Jer 50:5
to declare in Z the vengeance of ........ Jer 50:28
let us declare in Z the work of ........ Jer 51:10
they have done in Z in your sight ........ Jer 51:24
shall the inhabitant of Z say ........ Jer 51:35
The ways of Z do mourn, because ........ Lam 1:4
from the daughter of Z all her ........ Lam 1:6
Z spreadeth forth her hands, and ........ Lam 1:17
of Z with a cloud in his anger ........ Lam 2:1
tabernacle of the daughter of Z ........ Lam 2:4
and sabbaths to be forgotten in Z ........ Lam 2:6
the wall of the daughter of Z ........ Lam 2:8
daughter of Z sit upon the ground ........ Lam 2:10
thee, O virgin daughter of Z ........ Lam 2:13
Lord, O wall of the daughter of Z ........ Lam 2:18
The precious sons of Z, ........ Lam 4:2
and hath kindled a fire in Z ........ Lam 4:11
is accomplished, O daughter of Z ........ Lam 4:22
They ravished the women in Z ........ Lam 5:11
Because of the mountain of Z ........ Lam 5:18
Blow ye the trumpet in Z, and ........ Joel 2:1
Blow the trumpet in Z, sanctify a ........ Joel 2:15
Be glad then, ye children of Z ........ Joel 2:23
for in mount Z and in Jerusalem ........ Joel 2:32
The LORD also shall roar out of Z ........ Joel 3:16
the LORD your God dwelling in Z ........ Joel 3:17
for the LORD dwelleth in Z ........ Joel 3:21
said, The LORD will roar from Z ........ Amos 1:2
Woe to them that are at ease in Z ........ Amos 6:1
But upon mount Z shall be ........ Obad 17
Z to judge the mount of Esau ........ Obad 21
of the sin to the daughter of Z ........ Mic 1:13
They build up Z with blood ........ Mic 3:10
Therefore shall Z for your sake ........ Mic 3:12
for the law shall go forth of Z ........ Mic 4:2
them in mount Z from henceforth ........ Mic 4:7
strong hold of the daughter of Z ........ Mic 4:8
to bring forth, O daughter of Z ........ Mic 4:10
and let our eye look upon Z ........ Mic 4:11
Arise and thresh, O daughter of Z ........ Mic 4:13
Sing, O daughter of Z ........ Zeph 3:14
and to Z, Let not thine hands be ........ Zeph 3:16
for Z with a great jealousy ........ Zec 1:14
and the LORD shall yet comfort Z ........ Zec 1:17
Deliver thyself, O Z, that ........ Zec 2:7
Sing and rejoice, O daughter of Z ........ Zec 2:10
I was jealous for Z with great ........ Zec 8:2
I am returned unto Z, and will ........ Zec 8:3
Rejoice greatly, O daughter of Z ........ Zec 9:9
and raised up thy sons, O Z ........ Zec 9:13

**ZION'S** (*zi'-uns*)
For Z sake will I not hold my ........ Is 62:1

**ZIOR** (*zi'-or*) *A city in Judah.*
which is Hebron, and Z ........ Josh 15:54

**ZIPH** (*zif*) See ZIPHITES.
*1. A city in southeast Judah.*
Z, and Telem, and Bealoth, ........ Josh 15:24
a mountain in the wilderness of Z ........ 1Sa 23:14
in the wilderness of Z in a wood ........ 1Sa 23:15
arose, and went to Z before Saul ........ 1Sa 23:24
went down to the wilderness of Z ........ 1Sa 26:2
seek David in the wilderness of Z ........ 1Sa 26:2
And Gath, and Mareshah, and Z ........ 2Chr 11:8
*2. A city in Judah near Carmel.*
Maon, Carmel, and Z, and Juttah, ........ Josh 15:55
*3. A descendant of Caleb.*
which was the father of Z ........ 1Chr 2:42
*4. A son of Jehalaleel.*
Z, and Ziphah, Tiria, and Asareel ........ 1Chr 4:16

**ZIPHAH** (*zi'-fah*) *A son of Jehalaleel.*
Ziph, and Z, Tiria, and Asareel ........ 1Chr 4:16

**ZIPHIMS** (*zif'-ims*) See ZIPHITES. *Same as Ziphites.*
A Psalm of David, when the Z came ........ Ps 54:*t*

**ZIPHION** (*zif'-e-on*) See ZEPHON. *A son of Gad.*
Z, and Haggi, Shuni, and Ezbon, Eri ... Gen 46:16

**ZIPHITES** (*zif'-ites*) See ZIPHIMS. *Inhabitants of Ziph.*
Then came up the Z to Saul to ........ 1Sa 23:19
the Z came unto Saul to Gibeah, ........ 1Sa 26:1

**ZIPHRON** (*zif'-ron*) *A place in northern Palestine.*
And the border shall go on to Z ........ Num 34:9

**ZIPPOR** (*zip'-por*) *Father of Balak.*
Balak the son of Z saw all that ........ Num 22:2
Balak the son of Z was king of ........ Num 22:4
said unto God, Balak the son of Z ........ Num 22:10
Thus saith Balak the son of Z ........ Num 22:16
hearken unto me, thou son of Z ........ Num 23:18
Then Balak the son of Z, king of ........ Josh 24:9
better than Balak the son of Z ........ Judg 11:25

**ZIPPORAH** (*zip-po'-rah*) *Wife of Moses.*
and he gave Moses Z his daughter ........ Ex 2:21
Then Z took a sharp stone, and cut ........ Ex 4:25
Moses' father in law, took Z ........ Ex 18:2

**ZITHRI** (*zith'-ri*) See ZICHRI. *A son of Uzziel.*
Mishael, and Elzaphan, and Z ........ Ex 6:22

**ZIV** See ZIF.

**ZIZ** (*ziz*) *A place in Judah.*
they come up by the cliff of Z ........ 2Chr 20:16

**ZIZA** (*zi'-zah*) See ZIZAH.
*1. Son of Ziphi.*
Z the son of Shiphi, the son of ........ 1Chr 4:37
*2. A son of Rehoboam.*
bare him Abijah, and Attai, and Z ........ 2Chr 11:20

**ZIZAH** (*zi'-zah*) See ZINA, ZIZA. *Son of Shimei.*
was the chief, and Z the second ........ 1Chr 23:11

**ZOAN** (*zo'-an*) *An Egyptian city.*
seven years before Z in Egypt ........ Num 13:22
land of Egypt, in the field of Z ........ Ps 78:12
and his wonders in the field of Z ........ Ps 78:43
Surely the princes of Z are fools ........ Is 19:11
The princes of Z are become fools ........ Is 19:13
For his princes were at Z ........ Is 30:4
desolate, and will set fire in Z ........ Eze 30:14

**ZOAR** (*zo'-ar*) *A Canaanite city.*
of Egypt, as thou comest unto Z ........ Gen 13:10
and the king of Bela, which is Z ........ Gen 14:2
the king of Bela (the same is Z ........ Gen 14:8
the name of the city was called Z ........ Gen 19:22
the earth when Lot entered into Z ........ Gen 19:23
And Lot went up out of Z, and dwelt. ........ Gen 19:30
for he feared to dwell in Z ........ Gen 19:30
the city of palm trees, unto Z ........ Deut 34:3
his fugitives shall flee unto Z ........ Is 15:5
from Z even unto Horonaim, as an ........ Jer 48:34

**ZOBA** (*zo'-bah*) See ZOBAH. *A district in northern Syria.*
Beth-rehob, and the Syrians of Z ........ 2Sa 10:6
and the Syrians of Z, and of Rehob, ........ 2Sa 10:8

**ZOBAH** (*zo'-bah*) See ZOBA. *Same as Zoba.*
Edom, and against the kings of Z ........ 1Sa 14:47
the son of Rehob, king of Z ........ 2Sa 8:3
to succour Hadadezer king of Z ........ 2Sa 8:5
son of Rehob, king of Z ........ 2Sa 8:12
Igal the son of Nathan of Z ........ 2Sa 23:36
from his lord Hadadezer king of Z ........ 1Kin 11:23
a band, when David slew them of Z ........ 1Kin 11:24
Hadarezer king of Z unto Hamath ........ 1Chr 18:3
came to help Hadarezer king of Z ........ 1Chr 18:5
the host of Hadarezer king of Z ........ 1Chr 18:9
out of Syria-maachah, and out of Z ........ 1Chr 19:6

**ZOBEBAH** (*zo-be'-bah*) *A daughter of Coz.*
And Coz begat Anub, and Z, and the ........ 1Chr 4:8

**ZOHAR** (*zo'-har*) See ZERAH, ZEROR.
*1. Father of Ephron.*
for me to Ephron the son of Z ........ Gen 23:8
Ephron the son of Z the Hittite ........ Gen 25:9
*2. Son of Simeon.*
Jamin, and Ohad, and Jachin, and Z ... Gen 46:10
Jamin, and Ohad, and Jachin, and Z ........ Ex 6:15

**ZOHELETH** (*zo'-he-leth*) *A stone near En-rogel.*
and fat cattle by the stone of Z ........ 1Kin 1:9

**ZOHETH** (*zo'heth*) *Son of Ishi.*
And the sons of Ishi were, Z ........ 1Chr 4:20

**ZOPHAH** (*zo'-fah*) *Son of Helem.*
Z, and Imna, and Shelesh, and Amal .. 1Chr 7:35
The sons of Z ........ 1Chr 7:36

**ZOPHAI** (*zo'-fahee*) See ZUPH. *Brother of Samuel.*
Z his son, and Nahath his son, ........ 1Chr 6:26

**ZOPHAR** (*zo'-far*)
the Shuhite, and Z the Naamathite ........ Job 2:11
Then answered Z the Naamathite, ........ Job 11:1
Then answered Z the Naamathite, ........ Job 20:1
Z the Naamathite went, and did ........ Job 42:9

**ZOPHIM** (*zo'-fim*) *A peak on Mt. Pisgah.*
brought him into the field of Z ........ Num 23:14

**ZORAH** (*zo'-rah*) See ZAREAH, ZORATHITES, ZOREAH, ZORITES. *A city in Judah.*
coast of their inheritance was Z ........ Josh 19:41
And there was a certain man of Z ........ Judg 13:2
in the camp of Dan between Z ........ Judg 13:25
him up, and buried him between Z ........ Judg 16:31
coasts, men of valour, from Z ........ Judg 18:2
came unto their brethren to Z ........ Judg 18:8
family of the Danites, out of Z ........ Judg 18:11
And Z, and Aijalon, and Hebron, ........ 2Chr 11:10

**ZORATHITES** (*zo'-rath-ites*) *Descendants of Shobal.*
These are the families of the Z ........ 1Chr 4:2

**ZOREAH** (*zo'-re-ah*) *Same as Zorah.*
And in the valley, Eshtaol, and Z ........ Josh 15:33

**ZORITES** (*zo'-rites*) See ZAREATHITES, ZORATHITES. *Descendants of Salma.*
half of the Manahethites, the Z ........ 1Chr 2:54

**ZOROBABEL** (*zo-rob'-a-bel*) See ZERUBBABEL. *Father of Abiud; ancestor of Jesus.*
and Salathiel begat Z ........ Mt 1:12
And Z begat Abiud ........ Mt 1:13
of Rhesa, which was the son of Z ........ Lk 3:27

**ZUAR** (*zu'-ar*) *Father of Nethaneel.*
Nethaneel the son of Z ........ Num 1:8
Nethaneel the son of Z shall be ........ Num 2:5
second day Nethaneel the son of Z ........ Num 7:18
of Nethaneel the son of Z ........ Num 7:23
was Nethaneel the son of Z ........ Num 10:15

**ZUPH** (*zuf*)
*1. An ancestor of Samuel.*
the son of Tohu, the son of Z ........ 1Sa 1:1
The son of Z, the son of Elkanah, ........ 1Chr 6:35
*2. A district in Jerusalem.*
they were come to the land of Z ........ 1Sa 9:5

**ZUPHITE** See ZUPH.

**ZUR** (*zur*)
*1. Father of Cozbi.*
was Cozbi, the daughter of Z ........ Num 25:15
namely, Evi, and Rekem, and Z ........ Num 31:8
of Midian, Evi, and Rekem, and Z ........ Josh 13:21
*2. Son of Jehiel.*
And his firstborn son Abdon, and Z ........ 1Chr 8:30
his firstborn son Abdon, then Z ........ 1Chr 9:36

**ZURIEL** (*zu'-re-el*) *Son of Abihail.*
Merari was Z the son of Abihail ........ Num 3:35

**ZURISHADDAI** (*zu-re-shad'-da-i*) *Father of Shelumiel.*
Shelumiel the son of Z ........ Num 1:6
shall be Shelumiel the son of Z ........ Num 2:12
fifth day Shelumiel the son of Z ........ Num 7:36
of Shelumiel the son of Z ........ Num 7:41
Simeon was Shelumiel the son of Z .. Num 10:19

**ZUZIMS** (*zu'-zims*) See ZAMZUMMIMS. *A tribe in the land of Ham.*
the Z in Ham, and the Emims in ........ Gen 14:5

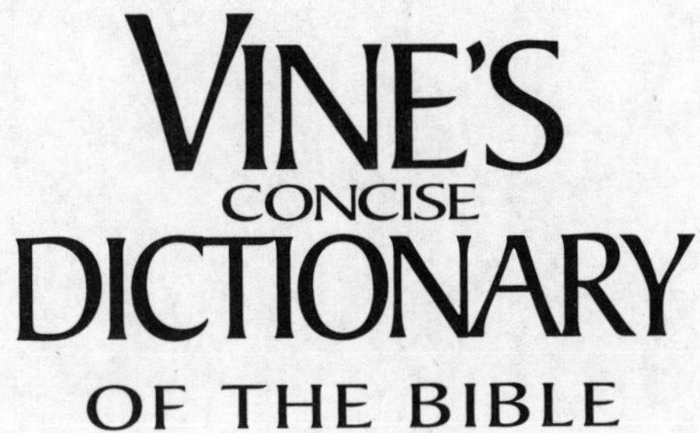
VINE'S
CONCISE
DICTIONARY
OF THE BIBLE

# VINE'S CONCISE DICTIONARY OF THE BIBLE

# Foreword

*Vine's Concise Dictionary of the Bible* combines in one handy volume condensed versions of W. E. Vine's *Expository Dictionary of New Testament Words* and *Nelson's Expository Dictionary of the Old Testament* by Merrill Unger and William White, Jr. For the first time these popular works are blended into one continuous presentation.

The book is organized alphabetically by English words. These words represent the key vocabulary of biblical theology as well as other terms of interpretive importance, colorful in background, rich in cultural significance, or obscure to modern readers. Articles that treat both Hebrew-Aramaic and Greek terms are subdivided by Testament and are further subdivided by part of speech: Verb, Noun, Adjective, etc.

The key Hebrew, Aramaic, and Greek words that underlie the English words are spelled in a simplified system of transliteration, according to the tables that follow. Each word is also keyed to the widely-used numbering system of James Strong's *Exhaustive Concordance*. This cross-indexing is ideal for readers who wish to study every biblical reference to any Hebrew, Aramaic, or Greek word treated in this volume or who wish to see the word spelled in the original language or in a more exacting system of transliteration.

Each entry exposits or explains the meaning of the terms represented by the English words. The insights applied to specific biblical passages allow this book to function as an alphabetical commentary on the Bible.

This handy edition of two popular reference books is a valuable resource, making available to those with no training in biblical languages rich and interesting insights from God's Word.

The Publisher

# A

## ABASE

***tapeinoo*** *(5013)* signifies "to make low, bring low," (a) of bringing to the ground, making level, reducing to a plain, as in Luke 3:5; (b) metaphorically in the active voice, to bring to a humble condition, "to abase," 2 Cor. 11:7, and in the passive, "to be abased," Phil. 4:12; in Matt. 23:12; Luke 14:11; 18:14, the KJV has "shall be abased." It is translated "humble yourselves" in the middle voice sense in Jas. 4:10; 1 Pet. 5:6; "humble," in Matt. 18:4; 2 Cor. 12:21 and Phil. 2:8.

## ABBA

***abba*** (5) is an Aramaic word, found in Mark 14:36; Rom. 8:15 and Gal. 4:6. In the Gemara (a Rabbinical commentary on the Mishna, the traditional teaching of the Jews) it is stated that slaves were forbidden to address the head of the family by this title. It approximates to a personal name, in contrast to "Father," with which it is always joined in the NT. This is probably due to the fact that, ***abba*** having practically become a proper name, Greek-speaking Jews added the Greek word ***pater***, "father," from the language they used. ***abba*** is the word framed by the lips of infants, and betokens unreasoning trust; "father" expresses an intelligent apprehension of the relationship. The two together express the love and intelligent confidence of the child.

## ABIDE, ABODE

**A. Verbs.**

1. ***meno*** *(3306)*, used (a) of place, e.g., Matt. 10:11, metaphorically 1 John 2:19, is said of God, 1 John 4:15; Christ, John 6:56; 15:4, etc.; the Holy Spirit, John 1:32–33; 14:17; believers, John 6:56; 15:4; 1 John 4:15, etc.; the Word of God, 1 John 2:14; the truth, 2 John 2, etc.; (b) of time; it is said of believers, John 21:22–23; Phil. 1:25; 1 John 2:17; Christ, John 12:34; Heb. 7:24; the Word of God, 1 Pet. 1:23; sin, John 9:41; cities, Matt. 11:23; Heb. 13:14; bonds and afflictions, Acts 20:23; (c) of qualities; faith, hope, love, 1 Cor. 13:13; Christ's love, John 15:10; afflictions, Acts 20:23; brotherly love, Heb. 13:1; the love of God, 1 John 3:17; the truth, 2 John 2.

2. ***epimeno*** *(1961)*, "to abide in, continue in, tarry," is a strengthened form of ***meno*** (***epi***, "intensive"), sometimes indicating perseverance in continuing, whether in evil, Rom. 6:1; 11:23, or good, Rom. 11:22; 1 Tim. 4:16.

3. ***katameno*** *(2650)*, ***kata***, "down" (intensive), and No. 1, is used in Acts 1:13. The word may signify "constant residence," but more probably indicates "frequent resort." In 1 Cor. 16:6, it denotes "to wait."

4. ***parameno*** *(3887)*, "to remain beside," "to continue near," came to signify simply "to continue," e.g., negatively, of the Levitical priests, Heb. 7:23. In Phil. 1:25, the apostle uses both the simple verb ***meno*** and the compound ***parameno*** (some mss. have ***sumparameno***), to express his confidence that he will "abide," and "continue to abide," with the saints. In 1 Cor. 16:6 some mss. have this word. In Jas. 1:25, of steadfast continuance in the law of liberty.

5. ***hupomeno*** *(5278)*, lit., "to abide under," signifies "to remain in a place instead of leaving it, to stay behind," e.g., Luke 2:43; Acts 17:14; or "to persevere," Matt. 10:22; 24:13; Mark 13:13; in each of which latter it is used with the phrase "unto the end"; or "to endure bravely and trustfully," e.g., Heb. 12:2–3, 7, suggesting endurance under what would be burdensome. See also Jas. 1:12; 5:11; 1 Pet. 2:20.

6. ***prosmeno*** *(4357)*, "to abide still longer, continue with" is used (a) of place, Matt. 15:32; Mark 8:2; Acts 18:18; 1 Tim. 1:3; (b) metaphorically, "of cleaving unto a person," Acts 11:23, indicating persistent loyalty; of continuing in a thing, Acts 13:43; 1 Tim. 5:5.

**B. Noun.**

***mone*** *(3438)*, "an abode" (akin to No. 1), is found in John 14:2, "mansions," and 14:23, "abode."

## ABOLISH

***katargeo*** *(2673)*, lit., "to reduce to inactivity" (***kata***, "down," ***argos***, "inactive"), is translated "abolish" in Eph. 2:15 and 2 Tim. 1:10. It is rendered "is abolished" in the KJV of 2 Cor. 3:13. In this and similar words not loss of being is implied, but loss of well being.

The barren tree was cumbering the ground, making it useless for the purpose of its existence, Luke 13:7; the unbelief of the Jews could not "make of none effect" the faithfulness of God, Rom. 3:3; the preaching of the gospel could not "make of none effect" the moral enactments of the Law, 3:31; the Law could not make the promise of "none effect," 4:14; Gal.

3:17; the effect of the identification of the believer with Christ in His death is to render inactive his body in regard to sin, Rom. 6:6; the death of a woman's first husband discharges her from the law of the husband, that is, it makes void her status as his wife in the eyes of the law, 7:2; in that sense the believer has been discharged from the Law, 7:6; God has chosen things that are not "to bring to nought things that are," i.e., to render them useless for practical purposes, 1 Cor. 1:28; the princes of this world are "brought to nought," i.e., their wisdom becomes ineffective, 2:6; the use for which the human stomach exists ceases with man's death, 6:13; knowledge, prophesyings, and that which was in part were to be "done away," 1 Cor. 13:8, 10, i.e., they were to be rendered of no effect after their temporary use was fulfilled; when the apostle became a man he did away with the ways of a child, v. 11; God is going to abolish all rule and authority and power, i.e., He is going to render them inactive, 1 Cor. 15:24; the last enemy that shall be abolished, or reduced to inactivity, is death, v. 26; the glory shining in the face of Moses, "was passing away," 2 Cor. 3:7, the transitoriness of its character being of a special significance; so in vv. 11, 13; the veil upon the heart of Israel is "done away" in Christ, v. 14; those who seek justification by the Law are "severed" from Christ, they are rendered inactive in relation to Him, Gal. 5:4; the essential effect of the preaching of the Cross would become inoperative by the preaching of circumcision, 5:11; by the death of Christ the barrier between Jew and Gentile is rendered inoperative as such, Eph. 2:15; the Man of Sin is to be reduced to inactivity by the manifestation of the Lord's ***parousia*** with His people, 2 Thess. 2:8; Christ has rendered death inactive for the believer, 2 Tim. 1:10, death becoming the means of a more glorious life, with Christ; the Devil is to be reduced to inactivity through the death of Christ, Heb. 2:14.

## ABOMINABLE, ABOMINATION

### *Old Testament*

#### A. Noun.

***to'ebah*** (8441), "abomination; loathsome, detestable thing."

First, ***to'ebah*** defines something or someone as essentially unique in the sense of being "dangerous," "sinister," and "repulsive" to another individual, Gen. 43:32. To the Egyptians, eating bread with foreigners was repulsive because of their cultural or social differences, cf. Gen. 46:34; Ps. 88:8. Another clear illustration of this essential clash of disposition appears in Prov. 29:27. When used with reference to God, this nuance of the word describes people, things, acts, relationships, and characteristics that are "detestable" to Him because they are contrary to His nature. Things related to death and idolatry are loathsome to God, Deut. 14:3. People with habits loathsome to God are themselves detestable to Him, Deut. 22:5. Directly opposed to ***to'ebah*** are such reactions as "delight" and "loveth," Prov. 15:8–9.

Second, ***to'ebah*** is used in some contexts to describe pagan practices and objects, Deut. 7:25–26. In other contexts, ***to'ebah*** describes the repeated failures to observe divine regulations, Ezek. 5:7, 9. ***to'ebah*** may represent the pagan cultic practices themselves, as in Deut. 12:31, or the people who perpetrate such practices, Deut. 18:12. If Israelites are guilty of such idolatry, however, their fate will be worse than exile: death by stoning, Deut. 17:2–5.

Third, ***to'ebah*** is used in the sphere of jurisprudence and of family or tribal relationships. Certain acts or characteristics are destructive of societal and familial harmony; both such things and the people who do them are described by ***to'ebah***, Prov. 6:16–19. God says, "The scorner is an abomination to men," Prov. 24:9 because he spreads his bitterness among God's people, disrupting unity and harmony.

#### B. Verb.

***ta'ab*** (8581), "to abhor, treat as abhorrent, cause to be an abomination, act abominably." This verb occurs 21 times, and the first occurrence is in Deut. 7:26.

### *New Testament*

#### A. Adjectives.

1. ***athemitos*** (*111*) occurs in Acts 10:28, "unlawful," and 1 Pet. 4:3, "abominable" (***a***, negative, ***themitos***, an adjective from ***themis***, "law").

2. ***bdeluktos*** (*947*), Titus 1:16, is said of deceivers who profess to know God, but deny Him by their works.

#### B. Noun.

***bdelugma*** (*946*), akin to A, No. 2 denotes an "object of disgust, an abomination." This is said of the image to be set up by Antichrist, Matt. 24:15; Mark 13:14; of that which is highly esteemed amongst men, in contrast to its real character in the sight of God, Luke 16:15. The constant association with idolatry suggests that what is highly esteemed among men constitutes an idol in the human heart. In Rev. 21:27, entrance is forbidden into the Holy City on the part of the unclean, or one who "maketh an abomination and a lie." It is also used of the contents of the golden cup in the hand of the evil woman described in Rev. 17:4, and of the name ascribed to her in the following verse.

## ABSTAIN, ABSTINENCE

***apecho*** (*568*), "to hold oneself from," in the NT, invariably refers to evil practices, moral and ceremonial, Acts 15:20, 29; 1 Thess. 4:3; 5:22; 1 Tim. 4:3; 1 Pet. 2:11.

## ABUNDANCE, ABUNDANT, ABUNDANTLY, ABOUND

### A. Nouns.

1. ***hadrotes*** (*100*), which, in 2 Cor. 8:20, in reference to the gifts from the church at Corinth for poor saints in Judea, is derived from ***hadros***, "thick, fat, full-grown, rich." In regard, therefore, to the offering in 2 Cor. 8:20 the thought is that of bountiful giving, a fat offering, not mere "abundance."

2. ***perisseia*** (*4050*), "an exceeding measure, something above the ordinary," is used four times; Rom. 5:17, "of abundance of grace"; 2 Cor. 8:2, "of abundance of joy"; 2 Cor. 10:15, of the extension of the apostle's sphere of service through the practical fellowship of the saints at Corinth; in Jas. 1:21 it is rendered, metaphorically, "overflowing," KJV "superfluity," with reference to wickedness. Some would render it "residuum," or "what remains."

3. ***perisseuma*** (*4051*) denotes "abundance" in a slightly more concrete form, 2 Cor. 8:13–14, where it stands for the gifts in kind supplied by the saints. In Matt. 12:34 and Luke 6:45 it is used of the "abundance" of the heart; in Mark 8:8, of the broken pieces left after feeding the multitude "that remained over."

4. ***huperbole*** (*5236*), lit., "a throwing beyond," denotes "excellence, exceeding greatness," of the power of God in His servants, 2 Cor. 4:7; of the revelations given to Paul, 12:7; with the preposition ***kata***, the phrase signifies "exceeding," Rom. 7:13; "still more excellent," 1 Cor. 12:31; "exceedingly," 2 Cor. 1:8; "beyond measure," Gal. 1:13; and, in a more extended phrase, "more and more exceedingly," 2 Cor. 4:17.

### B. Verbs.

1. ***perisseuo*** (*4052*), akin to A, Nos. 2 and 3, is used intransitively (a) "of exceeding a certain number, or measure, to be over, to remain," of the fragments after feeding the multitude, Luke 9:17; John 6:12–13; "to exist in abundance"; as of wealth, Luke 12:15; 21:4; of food, 15:17. In this sense it is used also of consolation, 2 Cor. 1:5, of the effect of a gift sent to meet the need of saints, 2 Cor. 9:12; of rejoicing, Phil. 1:26; of what comes or falls to the lot of a person in large measure, as of the grace of God and the gift by the grace of Christ, Rom. 5:15, of the sufferings of Christ, 2 Cor. 1:5.

(b) "to redound to, or to turn out abundantly for something," as of the liberal effects of poverty, 2 Cor. 8:2; in Rom. 3:7, argumentatively of the effects of the truth of God, as to whether God's truthfulness becomes more conspicuous and His glory is increased through man's untruthfulness; of numerical increase, Acts 16:5.

(c) "to be abundantly furnished, to abound in a thing," as of material benefits, Luke 12:15; Phil. 4:18 of spiritual gifts; 1 Cor. 14:12, or "to be pre-eminent, to excel, to be morally better off," as regards partaking of certain meats; 1 Cor. 8:8, "are we the better," "to abound" in hope, Rom. 15:13; the work of the Lord, 1 Cor. 15:58; faith and grace, 2 Cor. 8:7; thanksgiving, Col. 2:7; walking so as to please God, Phil. 1:9; 1 Thess. 4:1, 10; of righteousness, Matt. 5:20; of the Gospel, as the ministration of righteousness, 2 Cor. 3:9, "exceed."

It is used transitively, in the sense of "to make to abound," e.g., to provide a person richly so that he has "abundance," as of spiritual truth, Matt. 13:12; the right use of what God has entrusted to us, 25:29; the power of God in conferring grace, 2 Cor. 9:8; Eph. 1:8; to "make abundant" or to cause to excel, as of the effect of grace in regard to thanksgiving, 2 Cor. 4:15; His power to make us "to abound" in love, 1 Thess. 3:12.

2. ***huperperisseuo*** (*5248*), a strengthened form of No. 1, signifies "to abound exceedingly," Rom. 5:20, of the operation of grace; 2 Cor. 7:4, in the middle voice, of the apostle's joy in the saints.

3. ***pleonazo*** (*4121*), from ***pleion***, or ***pleon***, "more" (greater in quantity), akin to ***pleo***, "to fill," signifies, (a) intransitively, "to superabound," of a trespass or sin, Rom. 5:20; of grace, Rom. 6:1; 2 Cor. 4:15; of spiritual fruit, Phil. 4:17; of love, 2 Thess. 1:3; of various fruits, 2 Pet. 1:8; of the gathering of the manna, 2 Cor. 8:15, "had . . . over"; (b) transitively, "to make to increase," 1 Thess. 3:12.

4. ***huperpleonazo*** (*5250*), a strengthened form of No. 3, signifying "to abound exceedingly," is used in 1 Tim. 1:14, of the grace of God.

5. ***plethuno*** (*4129*), a lengthened form of ***pletho***, "to fill," akin to No. 3, and to ***plethos***, "a multitude," signifies "to increase, to multiply," and, in the passive voice, "to be multiplied."

## ACCEPT, ACCEPTED, ACCEPTABLE

**A. Verbs.**

1. ***dechomai*** (*1209*) signifies "to accept," by a deliberate and ready reception of what is offered (cf. No. 4), e.g., 1 Thess. 2:13; 2 Cor. 8:17; 11:4.

2. ***apodechomai*** (*588*), consisting of ***apo***, "from," intensive, and No. 1, expresses ***dechomai*** more strongly, signifying "to receive heartily, to welcome," Luke 8:40 (KJV, "gladly received"); Acts 2:41; 18:27; 24:3; 28:30.

3. ***prosdechomai*** (*4327*), ***pros***, "to," and No. 1, "to accept favorably, or receive to oneself," is used of things future, in the sense of expecting; with the meaning of "accepting," it is used negatively in Heb. 11:35, "not accepting their deliverance"; of receiving, e.g., Luke 15:2; Rom. 16:2; Phil. 2:29.

**B. Adjectives.**

The following adjectives are translated "acceptable," or in some cases "accepted."

1. ***dektos*** (*1184*), akin to No. 1, denotes "a person or thing who has been regarded favorably," Luke 4:19, 24; Acts 10:35; 2 Cor. 6:2 (in this verse No. 3 is used in the second place); Phil. 4:18.

2. ***apodektos*** (*587*), a strengthened form of No. 1 (***apo***, "from," used intensively), signifies "acceptable," in the sense of what is pleasing and welcome, 1 Tim. 2:3; 5:4.

3. ***euprosdektos*** (*2144*), a still stronger form of No. 1, signifies a "very favorable acceptance" (***eu***, "well," ***pros***, "towards," No. 1), Rom. 15:16, 31; 2 Cor. 6:2; 8:12; 1 Pet. 2:5.

4. ***euarestos*** (*2101*), ***eu***, "well," ***arestos***, "pleasing," is rendered "acceptable," in the KJV of Rom. 12:1–2; 14:18; in 2 Cor. 5:9, "accepted"; Eph. 5:10. The RV usually has "well-pleasing"; so KJV and RV in Phil. 4:18; Col. 3:20; in Titus 2:9, "please well," KJV, Heb. 13:21.

**D. Nouns.**

1. ***apodoche*** (*594*), akin to B, No. 2, signifies "worthy to be received with approbation, acceptation," 1 Tim. 1:15; 4:9. The phrase in 1:15 is found in a writing in the 1st century expressing appreciation of a gift from a princess.

2. ***charis*** (*5485*), "grace," indicating favor on the part of the giver, "thanks" on the part of the receiver, is rendered "acceptable" in 1 Pet. 2:19–20.

## ACCESS

***prosagoge*** (*4318*), lit., "a leading or bringing into the presence of," denotes "access," with which is associated the thought of freedom to enter through the assistance or favor of another. It is used three times, Rom. 5:2; Eph. 2:18; 3:12.

## ACCOMPANY

***propempo*** (*4311*), translated "accompanied," in Acts 20:38, KJV, lit. means "to send forward"; hence of assisting a person on a journey either (a) in the sense of fitting him out with the requisites for it, or (b) actually "accompanying" him for part of the way. The former seems to be indicated in Rom. 15:24 and 1 Cor. 16:6, and v. 11, where the RV has "set him forward." So in 2 Cor. 1:16 and Titus 3:13, and of John's exhortation to Gaius concerning traveling evangelists, "whom thou wilt do well to set forward on their journey worthily of God," 3 John 6, RV. While personal "accompaniment" is not excluded, practical assistance seems to be generally in view, as indicated by Paul's word to Titus to set forward Zenas and Apollos on their journey and to see "that nothing be wanting unto them." In regard to the parting of Paul from the elders of Ephesus at Miletus, personal "accompaniment" is especially in view, perhaps not without the suggestion of assistance, Acts 20:38, RV "brought him on his way"; "accompaniment" is also indicated in 21:5; "they all with wives and children brought us on our way, till we were out of the city." In Acts 15:3, both ideas perhaps are suggested.

## ACCOMPLISH, ACCOMPLISHMENT

**A. Verbs.**

1. ***exartizo*** (*1822*), "to fit out," (from ***ek***, "out," and a verb derived from ***artos***, "a joint"), means "to furnish completely," 2 Tim. 3:17, or "to accomplish," Acts 21:5, there said of a number of days, as if to render the days complete by what was appointed for them.

2. ***pleroo*** (*4137*), "to fulfill, to complete, carry out to the full" (as well as to fill), is translated "perfect" in Rev. 3:2, KJV; RV, "I have found no works of thine fulfilled before My God"; "accomplish" in Luke 9:31.

3. ***teleo*** (*5055*), "to finish, to bring to an end," frequently signifies, not merely to terminate a thing, but to carry out a thing to the full. It is used especially in the Apocalypse, where it occurs eight times, and is rendered "finish" in 10:7; 11:7, and in the RV of 15:1, which rightly translates it "(in them) is finished (the wrath of God)." So in v. 8; in 17:17, RV, "accomplish," and "finish" in 20:3, 5, 7; in Luke 2:39, RV, "accomplish," for KJV, performed.

4. ***epiteleo*** (*2005*), ***epi***, "up," intensive, and No. 3, is a strengthened form of that verb, in the sense of "accomplishing." The fuller mean-

ing is "to accomplish perfectly"; in Rom. 15:28, RV, "accomplish"; "perfecting" in 2 Cor. 7:1; "complete" in 8:6 and 11; "completion" in the latter part of this 11th verse, which is better than "performance"; "perfected" in Gal. 3:3; "perfect" in Phil. 1:6. In Heb. 8:5 the margin rightly has "complete" instead of "make," with regard to the tabernacle. In Heb. 9:6 it is translated "accomplish" and in 1 Pet. 5:9.

5. ***teleioo*** *(5048)*, though distinct grammatically from ***teleo***, has much the same meaning. The main distinction is that ***teleo*** more frequently signifies "to fulfill." ***teleioo***, more frequently signifies, "to make perfect," one of the chief features of the Epistle to the Hebrews, where it occurs nine times. It is rendered "accomplish" in the RV of John 4:34; 5:36; 17:4, and Acts 20:24.

6. ***pletho*** *(4130)*, "to fulfill," is translated "accomplished" in the KJV of Luke 1:23; 2:6, 21–22 (RV, "fulfilled").

## ACCORD

### A. Adverb.

***homothumadon*** *(3661)*, "of one mind," occurs eleven times, ten in the Acts, 1:14; 2:46; 4:24; 5:12; 7:57; 8:6; 12:20; 15:25; 18:12, 19:29, and the other in Rom. 15:6, where, for KJV, "with one mind," the RV has "with one accord," as throughout the Acts.

### B. Adjectives.

*"Of one's own accord."*

1. ***authairetos*** *(830)*, from autos, "self," and ***haireomai***, "to choose, self-chosen, voluntary, of one's own accord," occurs in 2 Cor. 8:3 and 17, of the churches of Macedonia as to their gifts for the poor saints in Judea, and of Titus in his willingness to go and exhort the church in Corinth concerning the matter. In 8:3 the RV translates it "(gave) of their own accord," consistently with the rendering in v. 17.

2. ***sumpsuchos*** *(4861)*, lit., "fellow-souled or minded," occurs in Phil. 2:2, "of one accord."

## ACCURATELY

***akribos*** *(199)* is correctly translated in the RV of Luke 1:3, "having traced the course of all things accurately" (KJV, "having had perfect understanding"). It is used in Matt. 2:8, of Herod's command to the wise men as to searching for the young Child (RV, "carefully"; KJV, "diligently"); in Acts 18:25, of Apollos' teaching of "the things concerning Jesus" (RV, "carefully"; KJV, "diligently"); in Eph. 5:15, of the way in which believers are to walk (RV, "carefully"; KJV, "circumspectly"); in 1 Thess. 5:2, of the knowledge gained by the saints through the apostle's teaching concerning the Day of the Lord (RV and KJV, "perfectly"). The word expresses that "accuracy" which is the outcome of carefulness. It is connected with ***akros***, "pointed."

## ACCUSATION, ACCUSE

### A. Nouns.

1. ***aitia*** *(156)* probably has the primary meaning of "a cause, especially an occasion of something evil, hence a charge, an accusation." It is used in a forensic sense, of (a) an accusation, Acts 25:18 (RV, "charge"), 27; (b) a crime, Matt. 27:37; Mark 15:26, John 18:38; 19:4, 6; Acts 13:28; 23:28; 28:18.

2. ***aitioma*** *(157)*, "an accusation," expressing No. 1 more concretely, is found in Acts 25:7, RV, "charges," for KJV, "complaints."

3. ***enklema*** *(1462)* is "an accusation made in public," but not necessarily before a tribunal. That is the case in Acts 23:29, "laid to his charge." In 25:16 it signifies a matter of complaint; hence, the RV has "the matter laid against him" (KJV, "crime").

4. ***kategoria*** *(2724)*, "an accusation," is found in John 18:29; 1 Tim. 5:19 and Titus 1:6, lit., "not under accusation." This and the verb ***kategoreo***, "to accuse," and the noun ***kategoros***, "an accuser" (see below), all have chiefly to do with judicial procedure, as distinct from ***diaballo***, "to slander." It is derived from ***agora***, "a place of public speaking," prefixed by ***kata***, "against"; hence, it signifies a speaking against a person before a public tribunal. It is the opposite to ***apologia***, "a defense."

### B. Verbs.

1. ***diaballo*** *(1225)*, used in Luke 16:1, in the passive voice, lit. signifies "to hurl across," and suggests a verbal assault. It stresses the act rather than the author, as in the case of ***aitia*** and ***kategoria***. ***diabolos*** is connected.

2. ***enkaleo*** *(1458)*, "to bring a charge against, or to come forward as an accuser against," lit. denotes "to call in," i.e., "to call (something) in or against (someone)"; hence, "to call to account, to accuse," Acts 19:38, RV (KJV, "implead"); in v. 40, "accused" (KJV, "call in question"). It is used in four other places in the Acts, 23:28–29; 26:2, 7, and elsewhere in Rom. 8:33, "shall lay to the charge."

3. ***epereazo*** *(1908)*, besides its more ordinary meaning, "to insult, treat abusively, despitefully," Luke 6:28, has the forensic significance "to accuse falsely," and is used with this meaning in 1 Pet. 3:16, RV, "revile."

4. ***kategoreo*** *(2723)*, "to speak against, accuse" (cf. A, No. 4), is used (a) in a general way, "to accuse," e.g., Luke 6:7, RV, "how to accuse"; Rom. 2:15; Rev. 12:10; (b) before a judge, e.g.,

Matt. 12:10; Mark 15:4 (RV, "witness against"); Acts 22:30; 25:16. In Acts 24:19, RV renders it "make accusation," for the KJV, "object."

5. ***sukophanteo*** (*4811*), (Eng., "sycophant") means (a) "to accuse wrongfully"; Luke 3:14 (KJV and RV, margin); RV, "exact wrongfully"; (b) "to exact money wrongfully, to take anything by false accusation," Luke 19:8, and the RV text of 3:14.

## ACCUSER

1. ***diabolos*** (*1228*), "an accuser," is used 34 times as a title of Satan, the Devil (the English word is derived from the Greek); once of Judas, John 6:70, who, in his opposition to God, acted the part of the Devil. Apart from John 6:70, men are never spoken of as devils. It is always to be distinguished from ***daimon***, "a demon." It is found three times, 1 Tim. 3:11; 2 Tim. 3:3; Titus 2:3, of false accusers, slanderers.

2. ***kategoros*** (*2725*), "an accuser," is used in John 8:10; Acts 23:30, 35; 24:8; 25:16, 18. In Rev. 12:10, it is used of Satan.

## ACKNOWLEDGE (-MENT)

### A. Verb.

***epiginosko*** (*1921*) signifies (a) "to know thoroughly"; (b) "to acknowledge," 1 Cor. 14:37 (RV, "take knowledge of"); 16:18; 2 Cor. 1:13–14.

### B. Noun.

***epignosis*** (*1922*), akin to A, "full, or thorough knowledge, discernment, recognition," is translated "acknowledging" in the KJV of 2 Tim. 2:25; Titus 1:1 and Philem. 6 (in all three, RV, "knowledge," properly, "thorough knowledge"). In Col. 2:2, KJV, "acknowledgement," RV, "that they may know" (i.e., "unto the full knowledge).

## ACQUAINTANCE

1. ***gnostos*** (*1110*), signifies "known, or knowable"; hence, "one's acquaintance"; it is used in this sense, in the plural, in Luke 2:44 and 23:49.

2. ***idios*** (*2398*), "one's own," is translated "acquaintance" in the KJV of Acts 24:23, "friends" (RV).

## ADD

1. ***prostithemi*** (*4369*), "to put to," "to add, or to place beside." In Gal. 3:19, "What then is the law? It was "added" because of transgressions." There is no contradiction of what is said in v. 15, the meaning is not that something had been 'added' to the promise with a view to complete it, which the apostle denies, but that something had been given "in addition" to the promise, as in Rom. 5:20, "The law came in beside."

2. ***epidiatasso*** (*1928*), lit., "to arrange in addition," is used in Gal. 3:15 ("addeth," or rather, "ordains something in addition"). If no one does such a thing in the matter of a human covenant, how much more is a covenant made by God inviolable! The Judaizers by their "addition" violated this principle, and, by proclaiming the divine authority for what they did, they virtually charged God with a breach of promise. He gave the Law, indeed, but neither in place of the promise nor to supplement it.

## ADJURE

1. ***horkizo*** (*3726*), "to cause to swear, to lay under the obligation of an oath" (***horkos***, Mark 5:7; Acts 19:13), is connected with the Heb. word for a thigh, cf. Gen. 24:2, 9; 47:29. Some mss. have this word in 1 Thess. 5:27. The most authentic have No. 3 (below).

2. ***exorkizo*** (*1844*), an intensive form of No. 1, signifies "to appeal by an oath, to adjure," Matt. 26:63.

3. ***enorkizo*** (*1722* and *3726*), "to put under (or bind by) an oath," is translated "adjure" in the RV of 1 Thess. 5:27 (KJV, "charge").

## ADMONITION, ADMONISH

### A. Noun.

***nouthesia*** (*3559*), lit., "a putting in mind," is used in 1 Cor. 10:11, of the purpose of the Scriptures; in Eph. 6:4, of that which is ministered by the Lord; and in Titus 3:10, of that which is to be administered for the correction of one who creates trouble in the church. ***nouthesia*** is "the training by word," whether of encouragement, or, if necessary, by reproof or remonstrance. In contrast to this, the synonymous word ***paideia*** stresses training by act, though both words are used in each respect.

### B. Verbs.

1. ***noutheteo*** (*3560*), cf. the noun above, means "to put in mind, admonish," Acts 20:31 (KJV, "warn"); Rom. 15:14; 1 Cor. 4:14 (KJV, "warn"); Col. 1:28 (KJV, "warning"); Col. 3:16; 1 Thess. 5:12, 14 (KJV, "warn"); 2 Thess. 3:15.

It is used, (a) of instruction, (b) of warning. It is thus distinguished from ***paideuo***, "to correct by discipline, to train by act," Heb. 12:6; cf. Eph. 6:4.

2. ***chrematizo*** (*5537*), primarily, "to transact business," then, "to give advice to enquirers" (especially of official pronouncements of magistrates), or "a response to those consulting an oracle," came to signify the giving of a divine "admonition" or instruction or warning, in a

general way; "admonished" in Heb. 8:5, KJV (RV, "warned"). Elsewhere it is translated by the verb "to warn."

## ADOPTION

***huiothesia*** (*5206*), from ***huios***, "a son," and ***thesis***, "a placing," signifies the place and condition of a son given to one to whom it does not naturally belong. The word is used by the apostle Paul only.

In Rom. 8:15, believers are said to have received "the Spirit of adoption," that is, the Holy Spirit who, given as the Firstfruits of all that is to be theirs, produces in them the realization of sonship and the attitude belonging to sons. In Gal. 4:5 they are said to receive "the adoption of sons," i.e., sonship bestowed in distinction from a relationship consequent merely upon birth; here two contrasts are presented, (1) between the sonship of the believer and the unoriginated sonship of Christ, (2) between the freedom enjoyed by the believer and bondage, whether of Gentile natural condition, or of Israel under the Law. In Eph. 1:5 they are said to have been foreordained unto "adoption as sons" through Jesus Christ. In Rom. 8:23 the "adoption" of the believer is set forth as still future, as it there includes the redemption of the body, when the living will be changed and those who have fallen asleep will be raised. In Rom. 9:4 "adoption" is spoken of as belonging to Israel, in accordance with the statement in Exod. 4:12, "Israel is My Son," cf. Hos. 11:1. Israel was brought into a special relation with God, a collective relationship, not enjoyed by other nations, Deut. 14:1; Jer. 31:9, etc.

## ADULTERER (-ESS), ADULTEROUS, ADULTERY

### A. Nouns.

1. ***moichos*** (*3432*) denotes one "who has unlawful intercourse with the spouse of another," Luke 18:11; 1 Cor. 6:9; Heb. 13:4. As to Jas. 4:4, see below.

2. ***moichalis*** (*3428*), "an adulteress," is used (a) in the natural sense, 2 Pet. 2:14; Rom. 7:3; (b) in the spiritual sense, Jas. 4:4; here the RV rightly omits the word "adulterers." It was added by a copyist. As in Israel the breach of their relationship with God through their idolatry, was described as "adultery" or "harlotry" (e.g., Ezek. 16:15, etc.; 23:43), so believers who cultivate friendship with the world, thus breaking their spiritual union with Christ, are spiritual "adulteresses," having been spiritually united to Him as wife to husband, Rom. 7:4. It is used adjectivally to describe the Jewish people in transferring their affections from God, Matt. 12:39; 16:4; Mark 8:38.

3. ***moicheia*** (*3430*), "adultery," is found in Matt. 15:19; Mark 7:21; John 8:3 (KJV only).

### B. Verbs.

1. ***moichao*** (*3429*), used in the middle voice in the NT, is said of men in Matt. 5:32; 19:9; Mark 10:11; of women in Mark 10:12.

2. ***moicheuo*** (*3431*) is used in Matt. 5:27–28, 32 (in v. 32 some texts have No. 1); 19:18; Mark 10:19; Luke 16:18; 18:20; John 8:4; Rom. 2:22; 13:9; Jas. 2:11; in Rev. 2:22, metaphorically, of those who are by a Jezebel's solicitations drawn away to idolatry.

## ADVANTAGE

1. ***opheleo*** (*5623*) signifies "to be useful, do good, profit," Rom. 2:25; with a negative, "to be of no use, to effect nothing," Matt. 27:24; John 6:63, "profiteth"; 12:19, "prevail"; in Luke 9:25, KJV, "(what is a man) advantaged?" RV, "profited."

2. ***pleonekteo*** (*4122*), lit., "to seek to get more" (***pleon***, "more," ***echo***, "to have"); hence, "to get an advantage of, to take advantage of." In 2 Cor. 7:2 the KJV has "defrauded," the RV, "took advantage of"; in 1 Thess. 4:6, KJV, "defraud," RV, "wrong." In the other three places the RV consistently translates it by the verb "to take advantage of," 2 Cor. 2:11, of Satan's effort to gain an "advantage" over the church, through their neglect to restore the backslider; in 2 Cor. 12:17–18, KJV, "make a gain of."

## ADVERSARY

### A. Noun.

***antidikos*** (*476*), firstly, "an opponent in a lawsuit," Matt. 5:25 (twice); Luke 12:58; 18:3, is also used to denote "an adversary or an enemy," without reference to legal affairs, and this is perhaps its meaning in 1 Pet. 5:8, where it is used of the Devil. Some would regard the word as there used in a legal sense, since the Devil accuses men before God.

### B. Verb.

***antikeimai*** (*480*) is, lit., "to lie opposite to, to be set over against." In addition to its legal sense it signifies "to withstand"; the present participle of the verb with the article, which is equivalent to a noun, signifies "an adversary," e.g., Luke 13:17; 21:15; 1 Cor. 16:9; Phil. 1:28; 1 Tim. 5:14. This construction is used of the Man of Sin, in 2 Thess. 2:4, and is translated "He that opposeth," where, adopting the noun form, we might render by "the opponent and self-exalter against. . . ." In Gal. 5:17 it is used of the antagonism between the Holy Spirit and the flesh in the believer; in 1 Tim. 1:10, of anything, in addition to persons, that is opposed to the doctrine of Christ. In these two places the word is rendered "contrary to."

## ADVICE, ADVISE

1. ***gnome*** (*1106*), "to know, perceive," firstly means "the faculty or knowledge, reason"; then, "that which is thought or known, one's mind." Under this heading there are various meanings: (1) a view, judgment, opinion, 1 Cor. 1:10; Philem. 14; Rev. 17:13, 17; (2) an opinion as to what ought to be done, either (a) by oneself, and so a resolve, or purpose, Acts 20:3; or (b) by others, and so, judgment, advice, 1 Cor. 7:25, 40; 2 Cor. 8:10.

2. ***boule*** (*1012*), from a root meaning "a will," hence "a counsel, a piece of advice," is to be distinguished from ***gnome; boule*** is the result of determination, ***gnome*** is the result of knowledge; (a) counsel of God, in Luke 7:30; Acts 2:23; 4:28; 13:36; 20:27; Eph. 1:11; Heb. 6:17; (b) counsel of men, Luke 23:51; Acts 27:12, 42; 1 Cor. 4:5.

## AFFECTION (-S), AFFECTED

**A. Nouns.**

1. ***pathos*** (*3806*), from ***pascho***, "to suffer," primarily denotes whatever one suffers or experiences in any way; hence, "an affection of the mind, a passionate desire." Used by the Greeks of either good or bad desires, it is always used in the NT of the latter, Rom. 1:26 (KJV, "affections," RV, "passions"); Col. 3:5 (KJV, "inordinate affection," RV, "passion"); 1 Thess. 4:5 (KJV, "lust," RV, "passion").

2. ***splanchna*** (*4698*), lit., "the bowels," which were regarded by the Greeks as the seat of the more violent passions, by the Hebrews as the seat of the tender "affections"; hence the word denotes "tender mercies" and is rendered "affections" in 2 Cor. 6:12 (KJV, "bowels"); "inward affection," 2 Cor. 7:15. Cf. ***epithumia***, "desire."

3. ***pathema*** (*3804*), Gal. 5:24.

**B. Adjectives.**

1. ***astorgos*** (*794*) signifies "without natural affection" especially of parents for children and children for parents, Rom. 1:31; 2 Tim. 3:3.

2. ***philostorgos*** (*5387*), "tenderly loving" (from ***philos***, "friendly," ***storge***, see No. 1), is used in Rom. 12:10, RV, "tenderly affectioned" (KJV, "kindly affectioned").

## AFFLICT (-ED), AFFLICTION

**A. Verbs.**

1. ***kakopatheo*** (*2553*), from ***kakos***, "evil," ***pathos***, "suffering," signifies "to suffer hardship." So the RV in 2 Tim. 2:9; and 4:5; in Jas. 5:13, "suffer" (KJV, "afflicted).

2. ***thlibo*** (*2346*), "to suffer affliction, to be troubled," has reference to sufferings due to the pressure of circumstances, or the antagonism of persons, 1 Thess. 3:4; 2 Thess. 1:6–7; "straitened," in Matt. 7:14 (RV); "throng," Mark 3:9; "afflicted," 2 Cor. 1:6; 7:5 (RV); 1 Tim. 5:10; Heb. 11:37; "pressed," 2 Cor. 4:8. Both the verb and the noun (see B, No. 4), when used of the present experience of believers, refer almost invariably to that which comes upon them from without.

3. ***talaiporeo*** (*5003*), "to be afflicted," is used in Jas. 4:9, in the middle voice ("afflict yourselves").

**B. Nouns.**

1. ***kakopatheia*** (*2552*), from ***kakos***, "evil," and ***pascho***, "to suffer" is rendered "suffering" in Jas. 5:10, RV (KJV, "suffering affliction").

2. ***kakosis*** (*2561*), "affliction, ill treatment," is used in Acts 7:34.

3. ***pathema*** (*3804*), "affliction." The word is frequent in Paul's epistles and is found three times in Hebrews, four in 1 Peter; it is used (a) of "afflictions," Rom. 8:18, etc.; of Christ's "sufferings," 1 Pet. 1:11; 5:1; Heb. 2:9; of those as shared by believers, 2 Cor. 1:5; Phil. 3:10; 1 Pet. 4:13; 5:1; (b) of "an evil emotion, passion," Rom. 7:5; Gal. 5:24.

4. ***thlipsis*** (*2347*) primarily means "a pressing, pressure," (see A, No. 4), anything which burdens the spirit. In two passages in Paul's Epistles it is used of future retribution, in the way of "affliction," Rom. 2:9; 2 Thess. 1:6. In Matt. 24:9.

## AFOREPROMISED

***proepangellomai*** (*4279*), "to promise before," is translated by the one word "aforepromised," in the RV of 2 Cor. 9:5; in Rom. 1:2, "promised afore."

## AGE

1. ***aion*** (*165*), "an age, era," signifies a period of indefinite duration, or time viewed in relation to what takes place in the period.

The phrases containing this word should not be rendered literally, but consistently with its sense of indefinite duration. Thus ***eis ton aiona*** does not mean "unto the age" but "for ever" (see, e.g., Heb. 5:6). The Greeks contrasted that which came to an end with that which was expressed by this phrase, which shows that they conceived of it as expressing interminable duration.

The word occurs most frequently in the Gospel of John, the Hebrews and Revelation. It is sometimes wrongly rendered "world." It is a characteristic word of John's gospel.

2. ***genea*** (*1074*), In some contexts, the meaning focuses from people to the time in which they lived, the word means "an age," i.e., a period ordinarily occupied by each successive generation, say, of thirty or forty years, Acts 14:16; 15:21; Eph. 3:5; Col. 1:26; see also, e.g., Gen. 15:16. In Eph. 3:21 ***genea*** is combined with ***aion*** in a remarkable phrase in a doxology.

3. ***helikia*** (*2244*), primarily "an age," as a certain length of life, John 9:21, 23, or beyond a certain stage of life, Heb. 11:11.

## AGED

1. ***presbutes*** (*4246*), "an elderly man," is a longer form of ***presbus***, the comparative degree of which is ***presbuteros***, "a senior, elder," both of which, as also the verb ***presbeuo***, "to be elder, to be an ambassador," are derived from ***proeisbaino***, "to be far advanced." The noun is found in Luke 1:18, "an old man"; Titus 2:2, "aged men," and Philem. 9, where the RV marg., "Paul an ambassador," is to be accepted, the original almost certainly being ***presbeutes*** (not ***presbutes***), "an ambassador." So he describes himself in Eph. 6:20. As Lightfoot points out, he is hardly likely to have made his age a ground of appeal to Philemon, who, if he was the father of Archippus, cannot have been much younger than Paul himself.

2. ***presbutis*** (*4247*), "an aged woman," Titus 23.

## AGREE, AGREEMENT

### A. Verbs.

1. ***sumphoneo*** (*4856*), lit., "to sound together," in the NT of the "agreement" (a) of persons concerning a matter, Matt. 18:19; 20:2, 13; Acts 5:9; (b) of the writers of Scripture, Acts 15:15; (c) of things that are said to be congruous in their nature, Luke 5:36.

2. ***suntithemi*** (*4934*), lit., "to put together," in the middle voice, means "to make an agreement, or to assent to"; translated "covenanted" in Luke 22:5; "agreed" in John 9:22, and Acts 23:20; "assented" in Acts 24:9.

### B. Nouns.

1. ***gnome*** (*1106*), "mind, will," is used with ***poieo***, "to make," in the sense of "to agree," Rev. 17:17 (twice), lit., "to do His mind, and to make one mind"; RV, "to come to one mind," KJV, "to agree.

2. ***sunkatathesis*** (*4783*), 2 Cor. 6:16.

## ALIEN

***allotrios*** (*245*), primarily, "belonging to another" (the opposite to ***idios***, "one's own"), came to mean "foreign, strange, not of one's own family, alien, an enemy"; "aliens" in, Heb. 11:34, elsewhere "strange," etc.

## ALIENATE

***apallotrioo*** (*526*) consists of ***apo***, "from," and the above; it signifies "to be rendered an alien, to be alienated." In Eph. 2:12 the RV corrects to the verbal form "alienated," for the noun "aliens"; elsewhere in Eph. 4:18 and Col. 1:21; the condition of the unbeliever is presented in a threefold state of "alienation," (a) from the commonwealth of Israel, (b) from the life of God, (c) from God Himself.

## ALLEGORY

***allegoreo*** (*238*), translated in Gal. 4:24 "contain an allegory," came to signify "to speak," not according to the primary sense of the word, but so that the facts stated are applied to illustrate principles.

## ALMIGHTY

***pantokrator*** (*3841*), "almighty, or ruler of all," is used of God only, and is found, in the Epistles, only in 2 Cor. 6:18, where the title is suggestive in connection with the context; elsewhere only in the Apocalypse, nine times. In one place, 19:6, the KJV has "omnipotent"; RV, "(the Lord our God,) the Almighty."

## ALMS, ALMSDEEDS

***eleemosune*** (*1654*), connected with ***eleemon***, "merciful," signifies (a) "mercy, pity, particularly in giving alms," Matt. 6:1 (see below), 2–4; Acts 10:2; 24:17; (b) the benefaction itself, the "alms" (the effect for the cause), Luke 11:41; 12:33; Acts 3:2–3, 10; 9:36, "almsdeeds"; 10:2, 4, 31.

## ALTAR

### *Old Testament*

***mizbeach*** (4196), "altar." This word signifies a raised place where a sacrifice was made, as in Gen. 8:20 (its first biblical appearance). In later references, this word may refer to a table upon which incense was burned, Exod. 30:1.

At Sinai, God directed Israel to fashion altars of valuable woods and metals. This taught them that true worship required man's best and that it was to conform exactly to God's directives; God, not man, initiated and controlled worship. The altar that stood before the holy place, Exod. 27:1–8, and the altar of incense within the holy place, Exod. 30:1–10, had "horns." These horns had a vital function in some offerings, Lev. 4:30; 16:18,. For example, the sacrificial animal may have been bound to these horns in order to allow its blood to drain away completely, Ps. 118:27.

***mizbeach*** is also used of pagan altars, Exod. 34:13.

*New Testament*

1. ***thusiasterion*** (*2379*), derived from ***thusiazo***, "to sacrifice." Accordingly it denotes an "altar" for the sacrifice of victims, though it was also used for the "altar" of incense, e.g., Luke 1:11. In the NT this word is reserved for the "altar" of the true God, Matt. 5:23–24; 23:18–20, 35; Luke 11:51; 1 Cor. 9:13; 10:18, in contrast to ***bomos***, No. 2, below.

2. ***bomos*** (*1041*), properly, "an elevated place," always denotes either a pagan "altar" or an "altar" reared without divine appointment. In the NT the only place where this is found is Acts 17:23, as this is the only mention of such.

## AMAZE, AMAZEMENT

### A. Nouns.

1. ***ekstasis*** (*1611*) is, lit., "a standing out." Eng. "ecstasy" is a transliteration. It is translated "amazement" in Acts 3:10. It was said of any displacement, and especially, with reference to the mind, of that alteration of the normal condition by which the person is thrown into a state of surprise or fear, or both; Acts 10:10; 11:5; 22:17.

2. ***thambos*** (*2285*), "amazement, wonder," is probably connected with a root signifying "to render immovable"; it is frequently associated with terror as well as astonishment, as with the verb in Acts 9:6. It occurs in Luke 4:36; 5:9; Acts 3:10.

### B. Verbs.

1. ***existemi*** (*1839*), akin to A, No. 1, lit. means "to stand out from." Like the noun, this is used with two distinct meanings: (a) in the sense of amazement, the word should be invariably rendered "amazed," as in the RV, e.g., in the case of Simon Magus (for KJV, "bewitched"), Acts 8:9 and 11. It is used, in the passive voice, of Simon himself in the 13th v., RV, "he was amazed," for KJV, "wondered." "Amaze" is preferable to "astonish" throughout; (b) in Mark 3:21 and 2 Cor. 5:13 it is used with its other meaning of being beside oneself.

2. ***ekplesso*** (*1605*), lit., "to strike out," signifies "to be exceedingly struck in mind, to be astonished" (***ek***, intensive). The English "astonish" should be used for this verb, and "amaze" for ***existemi***, as in the RV; see Matt. 19:25; Luke 2:48; 9:43.

## AMBASSADOR, AMBASSAGE

### A. Verb.

***presbeuo*** (*4243*) denotes (a) "to be elder or eldest, prior in birth or age"; (b) "to be an ambassador," 2 Cor. 5:20, and Eph. 6:20. There is a suggestion that to be an "ambassador" for Christ involves the experience suggested by the word "elder." Elder men were chosen as "ambassadors."

### B. Noun.

***presbeia*** (*4242*), primarily, "age, eldership, rank," hence, "an embassy or ambassage," is used in Luke 14:32; in 19:14, RV, "ambassage," for KJV, "message."

## AMEN

***amen*** (*281*) is transliterated from Hebrew into both Greek and English. Its meanings may be seen in such passages as Deut. 7:9, 'the faithful (the Amen) God,' Isa. 49:7, 'Jehovah that is faithful.' 65:16, 'the God of truth,' marg., 'the God of Amen.' And if God is faithful His testimonies and precepts are "sure (***amen***)," Ps. 19:7; 111:7, as are also His warnings, Hos. 5:9, and promises, Isa. 33:16; 55:3. 'Amen' is used of men also, e.g., Prov. 25:13.

Once in the NT 'Amen' is a title of Christ, Rev. 3:14, because through Him the purposes of God are established, 2 Cor. 1:20.

The early Christian churches followed the example of Israel in associating themselves audibly with the prayers and thanksgivings offered on their behalf, 1 Cor. 14:16, where the article 'the' points to a common practice. Moreover this custom conforms to the pattern of things in the Heavens, see Rev. 5:14, etc.

The Lord Jesus often used 'Amen,' translated 'verily,' to introduce new revelations of the mind of God. Matt. 16:28; Mark 9:1; Luke 18:29.

## ANEW

***anothen*** (*509*), lit., "from above," in the phrase rendered "anew" in the RV (KJV, "again") of John 3:3, 7.

## ANGEL

*Old Testament*

***mal'ak*** (4397), "messenger; angel." The word ***mal'ak*** denotes someone sent over a great distance by an individual, Gen. 32:3, or by a community, Num. 21:21, in order to communicate a message. Often several messengers are sent together, 2 Kings 1:2. The introductory formula of the message borne by the ***mal'ak*** often contains the phrase "Thus says . . . ," or "This is what . . . says," signifying the authority of the messenger in giving the message of his master, Judg. 11:15.

As a representative of a king, the ***mal'ak*** might have performed the function of a diplomat. In 1 Kings 20:1ff., we read that Ben-hadad sent messengers with the terms of surrender.

These passages confirm the important place of the ***mal'ak***. Honor to the messenger signified honor to the sender, and the opposite was also true. David took personally the insult of Nabal, 1 Sam. 25:14ff.; and when Hanun, king of Ammon, humiliated David's servants, 2 Sam. 10:4ff., David was quick to dispatch his forces against the Ammonites.

God also sent messengers. First, there are the prophetic messengers, 2 Chron. 36:15–16. Haggai called himself "the messenger of the Lord," ***mal'ak Yahweh***.

There were also angelic messengers. The English word *angel* is etymologically related to the Greek word ***angelos,*** whose translation is similar to the Hebrew: "messenger" or "angel." The angel is a supernatural messenger of the Lord sent with a particular message. Two angels came to Lot at Sodom, Gen. 19:1. The angels were also commissioned to protect God's people, Ps. 91:11.

Third, and most significant, are the phrases ***mal'ak Yahweh,*** "the angel of the Lord," and ***mal'ak 'elohim***, "the angel of God." The phrase is always used in the singular. It denotes an angel who had mainly a saving and protective function, Exod. 23:23. He might also bring about destruction, 1 Chron. 21:16.

The relation between the Lord and the "angel of the Lord" is often so close that it is difficult to separate the two, Gen. 16:7ff.; 21:17ff.; 22:11ff.; 31:11ff.; Exod. 3:2ff.; Judg. 6:11ff.; 13:21ff. This identification has led some interpreters to conclude that the "angel of the Lord" was the pre-incarnate Christ.

### *New Testament*

***angelos*** (*32*), "a messenger," sent whether by God or by man or by Satan, is also used of a guardian or representative in Rev. 1:20, cf. Matt. 18:10; Acts 12:15 (where it is better understood as 'ghost'), but most frequently of an order of created beings, superior to man, Heb. 2:7; Ps. 8:5, belonging to Heaven, Matt. 24:36; Mark 12:25, and to God, Luke 12:8, and engaged in His service, Ps. 103:20. "Angels" are spirits, Heb. 1:14, i.e., they have not material bodies as men have; they are either human in form, or can assume the human form when necessary, cf. Luke 24:4, with v. 23, Acts 10:3 with v. 30.

## ANGER, ANGRY

### *Old Testament*

#### A. Verb.

***charah*** (2734), "to get angry, be angry." In the causative stem, ***charah*** means "to become heated with work" or "with zeal for work," Neh. 3:20.

#### B. Noun.

***charon*** (*2740*), "burning anger." This word refers exclusively to divine anger as that which is "burning." ***charon*** first appears in Exod. 32:12: "Turn from thy fierce wrath [***charon***], and repent of this evil against thy people."

### *New Testament*

#### A. Noun.

***orge*** (*3709*), originally any "natural impulse, or desire, or disposition," came to signify "anger," as the strongest of all passions. It is used of the wrath of man, Eph. 4:31; Col. 3:8; 1 Tim. 2:8; Jas. 1:19–20; the displeasure of human governments, Rom. 13:4–5; the sufferings of the Jews at the hands of the Gentiles, Luke 21:23; the terrors of the Law, Rom. 4:15; "the anger" of the Lord Jesus, Mark 3:5; God's "anger" with Israel in the wilderness, in a quotation from the OT, Heb. 3:11; 4:3; God's present "anger" with the Jews nationally, Rom. 9:22; 1 Thess. 2:16; His present "anger" with those who disobey the Lord Jesus in His gospel, John 3:36; God's purposes in judgment, Matt. 3:7; Luke 3:7; Rom. 1:18; 2:5, 8; 3:5; 5:9; 12:19; Eph. 2:3; 5:6; Col. 3:6; 1 Thess. 1:10; 5:9.

*Notes:* (1) ***thumos***, "wrath" (not translated "anger"), is to be distinguished from ***orge***, in this respect, that ***thumos*** indicates a more agitated condition of the feelings, an outburst of wrath from inward indignation, while ***orge*** suggests a more settled or abiding condition of mind, frequently with a view to taking revenge. ***orge*** is less sudden in its rise than ***thumos***, but more lasting in its nature. ***thumos*** expresses more the inward feeling, ***orge*** the more active emotion. ***thumos*** may issue in revenge, though it does not necessarily include it. It is characteristic that it quickly blazes up and quickly subsides, though that is not necessarily implied in each case.

(2) ***parorgismos***, a strengthened form of ***orge***, and used in Eph. 4:26, RV margin, "provocation," points especially to that which provokes the wrath, and suggests a less con-

tinued state than No. (1). "The first keenness of the sense of provocation must not be cherished, though righteous resentment may remain" (Westcott). The preceding verb, ***orgizo***, in this verse implies a just occasion for the feeling. This is confirmed by the fact that it is a quotation from Ps. 4:4 (Sept.), where the Hebrew word signifies to quiver with strong emotion.

***thumos*** is found eighteen times in the NT, ten of which are in the Apocalypse, in seven of which the reference is to the wrath of God; so in Rom. 2:8, RV, "wrath (***thumos***) and indignation" (***orge***); the order in the KJV is inaccurate. Everywhere else the word ***thumos*** is used in a bad sense. In Gal. 5:20, it follows the word "jealousies," which when smoldering in the heart break out in wrath. ***thumos*** and ***orge*** are coupled in two places in the Apocalypse, 16:19, "the fierceness (***thumos***) of His wrath" (***orge***); and 19:15, "the fierceness of the wrath of Almighty God."

(3) ***aganaktesis*** originally signified "physical pain or irritation" (probably from ***agan***, "very much," and ***achomai***, "to grieve"), hence, "annoyance, vexation," and is used in 2 Cor. 7:11, "indignation."

### B. Verbs.

1. ***orgizo*** (*3710*), "to provoke, to arouse to anger," is used in the middle voice in the eight places where it is found, and signifies "to be angry, wroth"; of individuals, in Matt. 5:22; of nations, Rev. 11:18; of Satan as the Dragon, 12:17.

2. ***parorgizo*** (*3949*) is "to arouse to wrath, provoke"; Rom. 10:19, "will I anger"; Eph. 6:4, "provoke to wrath."

3. ***cholao*** (*5520*), connected with ***chole***, "gall, bile," which became used metaphorically to signify bitter anger, means "to be enraged," John 7:23.

## ANGUISH

### A. Nouns.

1. ***stenochoria*** (*4730*), lit., "narrowness of place," metaphorically came to mean the "distress arising from that condition, anguish." It is used in the plural, of various forms of distress, 2 Cor. 6:4 and 12:10, and of "anguish" or distress in general, Rom. 2:9; 8:35, RV, "anguish" for KJV, "distress." The opposite state, of being in a large place, and so metaphorically in a state of joy, is represented by the word ***platusmos*** in certain Psalms as, e.g., Ps. 118:5; see also 2 Sam. 22:20.

2. ***sunoche*** (*4928*), lit., "a holding together, or compressing," was used of the narrowing of a way. It is found only in its metaphorical sense, of "straits, distress, anguish," Luke 21:25, "distress of nations," and 2 Cor. 2:4, "anguish of heart."

### B. Verbs.

1. ***stenochoreo*** (*4729*), akin to A, No. 1, lit., "to crowd into a narrow space," or, in the passive voice "to be pressed for room," hence, metaphorically, "to be straitened," 2 Cor. 4:8 and 6:12.

2. ***sunecho*** (*4912*), akin to A, No. 2, lit., "to hold together," is used physically of being held, or thronged, Luke 8:45; 19:43; 22:63; of being taken with a malady, Matt. 4:24; Luke 4:38; Acts 28:8; with fear, Luke 8:37; of being straitened or pressed in spirit with desire, Luke 12:50; Acts 18:5; Phil. 1:23; with the love of Christ, 2 Cor. 5:14. In one place it is used of the stopping of their ears by those who killed Stephen.

3. ***odunao*** (*3600*), in the middle and passive voices, signifies "to suffer pain, be in anguish, be greatly distressed" (akin to ***odune***, "pain, distress"); it is rendered "sorrowing" in Luke 2:48; in 16:24–25, RV, "in anguish," for KJV, "tormented"; in Acts 20:38, "sorrowing."

## ANOINT, ANOINTING

#### *Old Testament*

### A. Verb.

***mashach*** (4886), "to anoint, smear, consecrate." Gen. 31:13 illustrates the idea of anointing something or someone as an act of consecration. The basic meaning of the word, however, is simply to "smear" an oily or viscous substance on an object, Exod. 29:2; Isa. 21:5; Jer. 22:14.

The Old Testament most commonly uses ***mashach*** to indicate "anointing" in the sense of a special setting apart for an office or function. Thus, Elisha was "anointed" to be a prophet, 1 Kings 19:16. More typically, kings were "anointed" for their office, 1 Sam. 16:12; 1 Kings 1:39.

### B. Noun.

***mashiach*** (*4899*), "anointed one." A word that is important both to Old Testament and New Testament understandings is the noun ***mashiach***, which gives us the term *messiah*. As is true of the verb, ***mashiach*** implies an anointing for a special office or function. Thus, David refused to harm Saul because Saul was "the Lord's anointed," 1 Sam. 24:6. The Psalms often express the messianic ideals attached to the Davidic line by using the phrase "the Lord's anointed," Ps. 2:2; 18:50; 89:38, 51.

The New Testament title of *Christ* is derived from the Greek ***christos*** which is exactly equivalent to the Hebrew ***mashiach,*** for it is also rooted in the idea of "to smear with oil." So the term *Christ* emphasizes the special anointing of Jesus of Nazareth for His role as God's chosen one.

### *New Testament*

**A. Verbs.**

1. ***aleipho*** (*218*) is a general term used for "an anointing" of any kind, whether of physical refreshment after washing, e.g., in the NT, Matt. 6:17; Luke 7:38, 46; John 11:2; 12:3; or of the sick, Mark 6:13; Jas. 5:14; or a dead body, Mark 16:1. The material used was either oil, or ointment, as in Luke 7:38, 46.

2. ***chrio*** (*5548*) is more limited in its use than No. 1; it is confined to "sacred and symbolical anointings"; Luke 4:18; Acts 4:27; 10:38; Heb. 1:9. The title Christ signifies "The Anointed One," The word (***christos***) is rendered "(His) Anointed" in Acts 4:26, RV. Once it is said of believers, 2 Cor. 1:21. Among the Greeks it was used in other senses than the ceremonial, but in the Scriptures it is not found in connection with secular matters.

**B. Noun.**

***chrisma*** (*5545*), the corresponding noun to No. 2, above, signifies "an unguent, or an anointing." It was prepared from oil and aromatic herbs. It is used only metaphorically in the NT; by metonymy, of the Holy Spirit, 1 John 2:20, 27, twice. The RV translates it "anointing" in all three places, instead of the KJV "unction" and "anointing."

That believers have "an anointing from the Holy One" indicates that this anointing renders them holy, separating them to God. The passage teaches that the gift of the Holy Spirit is the all-efficient means of enabling believers to possess a knowledge of the truth.

## ANOTHER

***allos*** (*243*) and ***heteros*** (*2087*) have a difference in meaning, which is to be observed in numerous passages. ***allos*** expresses a numerical difference and denotes "another of the same sort"; ***heteros*** expresses a qualitative difference and denotes "another of a different sort." Christ promised to send "another Comforter" (***allos***, "another like Himself," not ***heteros***), John 14:16. Paul speaks of "a different gospel (***heteros***), which is not another" (***allos***, another like the one he preached), Gal. 1:6–7.

## ANSWER

**A. Nouns.**

***apologia*** (*627*), a "verbal defense, a speech in defense," is sometimes translated "answer," in the KJV, Acts 25:16; 1 Cor. 9:3; 2 Tim. 4:16, all which the RV corrects to "defense." See Acts 22:1; Phil. 1:7, 16; 2 Cor. 7:11, "clearing." Once it signifies an "answer," 1 Pet. 3:15. Cf. B, No. 4.

**B. Verb.**

***apologeomai*** (*626*), cf. above, lit., "to talk oneself off from" (***apo***, "from," ***lego***, "to speak"), "to answer by way of making a defense for oneself" (besides its meaning "to excuse," Rom. 2:15; 2 Cor. 12:19), is translated "answer" in Luke 12:11; 21:14; in Acts 19:33, KJV and RV both have "made defense"; in Acts 24:10; 25:8; 26:1–2, the RV has the verb to make a defense, for the KJV, "to answer," and in 26:24 for the KJV, "spake for himself."

## ANTICHRIST

***antichristos*** (*500*) can mean either "against Christ" or "instead of Christ," or perhaps, combining the two, "one who, assuming the guise of Christ, opposes Christ" (Westcott). The word is found only in John's epistles, (a) of the many "antichrists" who are forerunners of the "Antichrist" himself, 1 John 2:18, 22; 2 John 7; (b) of the evil power which already operates anticipatively of the "Antichrist," 1 John 4:3; cf. 2 Thess. 2; Rev. 13.

## APOSTLE, APOSTLESHIP

1. ***apostolos*** (*652*) is, lit., "one sent forth." The word is used of the Lord Jesus to describe His relation to God, Heb. 3:1; see John 17:3. The twelve disciples chosen by the Lord for special training were so called, Luke 6:13; 9:10. Paul, though he had seen the Lord Jesus, 1 Cor. 9:1; 15:8, had not 'companied with' the Twelve 'all the time' of His earthly ministry, and hence was not eligible for a place among them, according to Peter's description of the necessary qualifications, Acts 1:22. Paul was commissioned directly, by the Lord Himself, after His Ascension, to carry the gospel to the Gentiles.

It also can refer to those who are not the Twelve, or Paul; Barnabas and others; Acts 14:4, 14; in Rom. 16:7; 2 Cor. 8:23; Phil. 2:25; 1 Thess. 2:6.

2. ***apostole*** (*651*), "a sending, a mission," signifies an apostleship, Acts 1:25; Rom. 1:5; 1 Cor. 9:2; Gal. 2:8.

## APPEAR, APPEARING

**A. Verbs.**

1. ***phaino*** (*5316*) signifies, in the active voice, "to shine"; in the passive, "to be brought forth into light, to become evident, to appear." In Rom. 7:13, concerning sin, the RV has "might be shewn to be," for KJV, "appear."

It is used of the "appearance" of Christ to the disciples, Mark 16:9; of His future "appearing" in glory as the Son of Man, spoken of as a sign to the world, Matt. 24:30; there the genitive is subjective, the sign being the "appearing" of Christ Himself; of Christ as the light, John 1:5; of John the Baptist, 5:35; of the "appearing" of an angel of the Lord, either visibly, Matt. 1:20, or in a dream, 2:13; of a star, 2:7; of men who make an outward show, Matt. 6:5; 6:18 (see the RV); 23:27–28; 2 Cor. 13:7; of tares, Matt. 13:26; of a vapor, Jas. 4:14; of things physical in general, Heb. 11:3; used impersonally in Matt. 9:33, "it was never so seen"; also of what appears to the mind, and so in the sense of to think, Mark 14:64, or to seem, Luke 24:11 (RV, appeared).

2. ***epiphaino*** (*2014*), a strengthened form of No. 1 but differing in meaning, ***epi*** signifying "upon," is used in the active voice with the meaning "to give light," Luke 1:79; in the passive voice, "to appear, become visible." It is said of heavenly bodies, e.g., the stars, Acts 27:20 (RV, "shone"); metaphorically, of things spiritual, the grace of God, Titus 2:11; the kindness and the love of God, 3:4.

3. ***anaphaino*** (*398*), ***ana***, "forth, or up," perhaps originally a nautical term, "to come up into view," hence, in general, "to appear suddenly," is used in the passive voice, in Luke 19:11, of the Kingdom of God; active voice, in Acts 21:3, "to come in sight of," RV; "having sighted" would be a suitable rendering (KJV, "having discovered).

4. ***phaneroo*** (*5319*), akin to No. 1, signifies, in the active voice, "to manifest"; in the passive voice, "to be manifested"; so, regularly, in the RV, instead of "to appear." See 2 Cor. 7:12; Col. 3:4; Heb. 9:26; 1 Pet. 5:4; 1 John 2:28; 3:2; Rev. 3:18. To be manifested, in the Scriptural sense of the word, is more than to "appear." A person may "appear" in a false guise or without a disclosure of what he truly is; to be manifested is to be revealed in one's true character; this is especially the meaning of ***phaneroo***, see, e.g., John 3:21; 1 Cor. 4:5; 2 Cor. 5:10–11; Eph. 5:13.

5. ***emphanizo*** (*1718*), from ***en***, "in," intensive, and ***phaino***, "to shine," is used, either of "physical manifestation," Matt. 27:53; Heb. 9:24; cf. John 14:22, or, metaphorically, of "the manifestation of Christ" by the Holy Spirit in the spiritual experience of believers who abide in His love, John 14:21. It has another, secondary meaning, "to make known, signify, inform." This is confined to the Acts, where it is used five times, 23:15, 22; 24:1; 25:2, 15. There is perhaps a combination of the two meanings in Heb. 11:14, i.e., to declare by oral testimony and to "manifest" by the witness of the life.

### B. Nouns.

1. ***apokalupsis*** (*602*), lit., "an uncovering, unveiling," denotes "a revelation, or appearing" (Eng., apocalypse). It is translated "the appearing" in 1 Pet. 1:7, KJV (RV, "revelation").

2. ***epiphaneia*** (*2015*), "epiphany," lit., "a shining forth," was used of the "appearance" of a god to men, and of an enemy to an army in the field, etc. In the NT it occurs of (a) the advent of the Savior when the Word became flesh, 2 Tim. 1:10; (b) the coming of the Lord Jesus into the air to the meeting with His saints, 1 Tim. 6:14; 2 Tim. 4:1, 8; (c) the shining forth of the glory of the Lord Jesus, Matt. 24:27.

## APPEARANCE

### A. Noun.

***eidos*** (*1491*), properly "that which strikes the eye, that which is exposed to view," signifies the "external appearance, form, or shape," and in this sense is used of the Holy Spirit in taking bodily form, as a dove, Luke 3:22; of Christ, 9:29, "the fashion of His countenance." Christ used it, negatively, of God the Father, when He said "Ye have neither heard His voice at any time, nor seen His form," John 5:37. Thus it is used with reference to each person of the Trinity. Probably the same meaning attaches to the word in the apostle's statement, "We walk by faith, not by sight (***eidos***)," 2 Cor. 5:7. It has a somewhat different significance in 1 Thess. 5:22, in the exhortation, "Abstain from every form of evil," i.e., every sort or kind of evil.

### B. Verb.

***phantazo*** (*5324*), "to make visible," is used in its participial form (middle voice), with the neuter article, as equivalent to a noun, and is translated "appearance," RV, for KJV, "sight," Heb. 12:21.

## APPOINT, APPOINTED

1. ***histemi*** (*2476*), "to make to stand," means "to appoint," in Acts 17:31, of the day in which God will judge the world by Christ. In Acts 1:23, with reference to Joseph and Barnabas, the RV has "put forward"; for these were not both "appointed" in the accepted sense of the term, but simply singled out, in order that it might be made known which of them the Lord had chosen.

2. ***kathistemi*** (*2525*), a strengthened form of No. 1, usually signifies "to appoint a person to a position." In this sense the verb is often translated "to make" or "to set," in appointing

a person to a place of authority, e.g., a servant over a household, Matt. 24:45, 47; 25:21, 23; Luke 12:42, 44; a judge, Luke 12:14; Acts 7:27, 35; a governor, Acts 7:10; man by God over the work of His hands, Heb. 2:7. It is rendered "appoint," with reference to the so-called seven deacons in Acts 6:3. The RV translates it by "appoint" in Titus 1:5, instead of "ordain," of the elders whom Titus was to "appoint" in every city in Crete. Not a formal ecclesiastical ordination is in view, but the "appointment," for the recognition of the churches, of those who had already been raised up and qualified by the Holy Spirit, and had given evidence of this in their life and service (see No. 9). It is used of the priests of old, Heb. 5:1; 7:28; 8:3 (RV, "appointed").

3. ***tithemi*** (*5087*), "to put," is used of "appointment" to any form of service. Christ used it of His followers, John 15:16 (RV, "appointed" for KJV, "ordained"). "I set you" would be more in keeping with the metaphor of grafting. The verb is used by Paul of his service in the ministry of the gospel, 1 Tim. 1:12 (RV, "appointing" for "putting"); 2:7 (RV, "appointed" for "ordained"); and 2 Tim. 1:11 (RV, "appointing" for "putting"); of the overseers, or bishops, in the local church at Ephesus.

4. ***diatithemi*** (*1303*), a strengthened form of No. 3, is used in the middle voice only. The Lord used it of His disciples with reference to the kingdom which is to be theirs hereafter, and of Himself in the same respect, as that which has been "appointed" for Him by His Father, Luke 22:29.

5. ***tasso*** (*5021*), "to place in order, arrange," signifies "to appoint," e.g., of the place where Christ had "appointed" a meeting with His disciples after His resurrection, Matt. 28:16; of positions of military and civil authority over others, whether "appointed" by men, Luke 7:8, or by God, Rom. 13:1, "ordained." It is said of those who, having believed the gospel, "were ordained to eternal life," Acts 13:48. The house of Stephanas at Corinth had "set themselves" to the ministry of the saints (KJV, "addicted"), 1 Cor. 16:15. Other instances of the arranging of special details occur in Acts 15:2; 22:10; 28:23.

6. ***diatasso*** (*1299*), a strengthened form of No. 5, frequently denotes "to arrange, appoint, prescribe," e.g., of what was "appointed" for tax collectors to collect, Luke 3:13; of the tabernacle, as "appointed" by God for Moses to make, Acts 7:44; of the arrangements "appointed" by Paul with regard to himself and his travelling companions, Acts 20:13; of what the apostle "ordained" in all the churches in regard to marital conditions, 1 Cor. 7:17; of what the Lord "ordained" in regard to the support of those who proclaimed the gospel, 1 Cor. 9:14; of the Law as divinely "ordained," or administered, through angels, by Moses, Gal. 3:19.

7. ***suntasso*** (*4929*), ***sun***, "with," and No. 5, lit., "to arrange together with," hence "to appoint, prescribe," is used twice, in Matt. 26:19 of what the Lord "appointed" for His disciples, and in 27:10, in a quotation concerning the price of the potter's field.

8. ***protasso*** (*4384*), ***pro***, "before," and No. 5, "to appoint before," is used in Acts 17:26 (RV, "appointed"), of the seasons arranged by God for nations, and the bounds of their habitation.

9. ***cheirotoneo*** (*5500*), primarily used of voting in the Athenian legislative assembly and meaning "to stretch forth the hands," is not to be taken in its literal sense; it could not be so taken in its compound ***procheirotoneo***, "to choose before, appoint" since it is said of God, Acts 10:41.

10. ***procheirizo*** (*4400*), "at hand," signifies (a) "to deliver up, appoint," Acts 3:20 (RV, "appointed"); (b) in the middle voice, "to take into one's hand, to determine, appoint beforehand," translated "appointed" in Acts 22:14, RV (for KJV, "hath chosen"), and "to appoint" in 26:16 (for KJV, "to make").

11. ***horizo*** (*3724*), (Eng., "horizon"), lit., "to mark by a limit," hence, "to determine, ordain," is used of Christ as ordained of God to be a judge of the living and the dead, Acts 17:31; of His being "marked out" as the Son of God, Rom. 1:4; of divinely appointed seasons, Acts 17:26, "having determined."

## APPREHEND

***katalambano*** (*2638*) properly signifies "to lay hold of"; then, "to lay hold of so as to possess as one's own, to appropriate." Hence it has the same twofold meaning as the Eng. "to apprehend"; (a), "to seize upon, take possession of," (1) with a beneficial effect, as of "laying hold" of the righteousness which is of faith, Rom. 9:30 (not there a matter of attainment, as in the Eng. versions, but of appropriation); of the obtaining of a prize, 1 Cor. 9:24 (RV, "attain"); of the apostle's desire "to apprehend," or "lay hold of," that for which he was apprehended by Christ, Phil. 3:12–13; (2) with a detrimental effect, e.g., of demon power, Mark 9:18; of human action in seizing upon a person, John 8:3–4; metaphorically, with the added idea of overtaking, of spiritual darkness in coming upon people, John 12:35; of the Day of the Lord, in suddenly coming upon unbelievers as a thief, 1 Thess. 5:4; (b), "to lay hold of" with the mind, to understand, perceive, e.g., metaphorically, of darkness with regard to light, John 1:5, though possibly here the sense is that of (a) as in 12:35; of mental perception, Acts 4:13; 10:34; 25:25; Eph. 3:18.

## APPROACH

### A. Verb.

***engizo*** (*1448*), "to draw near, to approach," from ***engus***, "near," is used (a) of place and position, literally and physically, Matt. 21:1; Mark 11:1; Luke 12:33; 15:25; figuratively, of drawing near to God, Matt. 15:8; Heb. 7:19; Jas. 4:8; (b) of time, with reference to things that are imminent, as the kingdom of heaven, Matt. 3:2; 4:17; 10:7.

### B. Adjective.

***aprositos*** (*676*), "unapproachable, inaccessible," in 1 Tim. 6:16, of the light in which God dwells (KJV, "which no man can approach unto"; RV, "unapproachable").

## APPROVE, APPROVED

### A. Verbs.

1. ***dokimazo*** (*1381*), primarily, of metals; signifies "to prove," e.g., 1 John 4:1, more frequently to prove with a view to approval, e.g., Rom. 1:28, KJV, "they did not like to retain God in their knowledge"; RV, "they refused"; marg., "did not approve," the true meaning. Their refusal was not the outcome of ignorance; they had the power to make a deliberate choice; they willfully disapproved of having God in their knowledge; Rom. 2:18; 14:22; 1 Cor. 16:3; 2 Cor. 8:22; Phil. 1:10; 1 Thess. 2:4.

2. ***sunistemi*** (*4921*), lit., "to set together," hence signifies "to set one person or thing with another by way of presenting and commending." This meaning is confined to Romans and 2 Corinthians. The saints at Corinth had "approved themselves in everything to be pure," in the matter referred to, 2 Cor. 7:11. The word often denotes "to commend," so as to meet with approval, Rom. 3:5; 5:8; 16:1; 2 Cor. 4:2; 6:4 (RV); 10:18; 12:11, etc.

3. ***apodeiknumi*** (*584*), lit., "to point out, to exhibit," "to show," is used once in the sense of proving by demonstration, and so bringing about an "approval." The Lord Jesus was "a Man approved of God by mighty works and wonders and signs," Acts 2:22.

### B. Adjective.

***dokimos*** (*1384*), akin to ***dechomai***, "to receive," always signifies "approved"; so the RV everywhere, e.g., in Jas. 1:12 for KJV, "when he is tried."

## ARCHANGEL

***archangelos*** (*743*) A being of exalted rank, named Michael, 1 Thess. 4:16 and Jude 9; cf. also Rev. 12:7; cf. also Rom. 8:38; Eph. 1:21; Col. 1:16. In 1 Thess. 4:16 the meaning seems to be that the voice of the Lord Jesus will be of the character of an "archangelic" shout.

## ARISE, AROSE, AROUSE, RAISE, RISE, ROUSE

1. ***anistemi*** (*450*), "to stand up or to make to stand up," is used (a) of a physical change of position, Mark 1:35; Luke 4:29; Matt. 26:62. (b) metaphorically, of "rising" up antagonistically against persons, e.g. of officials against people, Acts 5:17; of a seditious leader, 5:36, of the "rising" up of Satan, Mark 3:26; of false teachers, Acts 20:30; (c) of "rising" to a position of preeminence or power; e.g., of Christ as a prophet, Acts 3:22; 7:37. (d) of a spiritual awakening from lethargy, Eph. 5:14; (e) of resurrection from the dead: (1) of Christ, Mark 8:31; 9:9–10, 31; 10:34; (2) of believers, John 6:39–40; 1 Thess. 4:16; of unbelievers, Matt. 12:41.

2. ***exanistemi*** (*1817*), a strengthened form of No. 1, signifies "to raise up," Mark 12:19; Luke 20:28; intransitively, "to rise up, Acts 15:5.

3. ***egeiro*** (*1453*) is frequently used in the NT in the sense of "raising" (active voice), or "rising" (middle and passive voices): (a) from sitting, lying, sickness, e.g., Matt. 2:14; 9:5, 7, 19; Jas. 5:15; Rev. 11:1; (b) of causing to appear, or, in the passive, appearing, or raising up so as to occupy a place in the midst of people, Matt. 3:9; 11:11; Mark 13:22; Acts 13:22. It is thus said of Christ in Acts 13:23; cf. No. 1, (c); (c) of rousing, stirring up, or "rising" against, Matt. 24:7; Mark 13:8; (d) of "raising buildings," John 2:19–20; (e) of "raising or rising" from the dead; (1) of Christ, Matt. 16:21; and frequently elsewhere (but not in Phil., 2 Thess., 1 Tim., Titus, Jas., 2 Pet., 1, 2, 3 John, and Jude); (2) of Christ's "raising" the dead, Matt. 11:5; Mark 5:41; Luke 7:14; John 12:1, 9, 17; (3) of the act of the disciples, Matt. 10:8; (4) of the resurrection of believers, Matt. 27:52; John 5:21; 1 Cor. 15:15–16, 29, 32, 35, 42–44 52; 2 Cor. 1:9; 4:14; of unbelievers, Matt. 12:42 (cf. v. 41, No. 1).

4. ***diegeiro*** (*1326*), a strengthened form of No. 3, signifies "to rouse, to awaken from sleep." The active voice is not used intransitively. In Matt. 1:24, RV, "Joseph arose from his sleep," the passive participle is, lit., "being aroused." In Mark 4:39 (KJV, "he arose," RV, "he awoke"), the lit. rendering is "he being awakened." In John 6:18 the imperfect tense of the passive voice is used, and the rendering should be, "the sea was being aroused."

5. ***anatello*** *(393)*, "to arise," is used especially of things in the natural creation, Matt. 4:16; in Heb. 7:14 metaphorically, of the Incarnation of Christ.

## ARK

### *Old Testament*

***'aron*** (727), "ark; coffin; chest; box." In Gen. 50:26, this word represents a coffin or sarcophagus, In 2 Kings 12:9, this is a chest with a hole in its lid. In most occurrences, ***'aron*** refers to the "ark of the covenant." This piece of furniture functioned primarily as a container. As such the word is often modified by divine names or attributes. The divine name first modifies ***'aron*** in 1 Sam. 3:3. ***'aron*** is first modified by God's covenant name, ***Yahweh,*** in Josh. 4:5. Judg. 20:27 is the first appearance of the "ark" as the ark of the covenant of ***'elohim***. First Samuel 5:11 uses the phrase "the ark of the God [***'elohim***] of Israel," and 1 Chron. 15:12 employs "the ark of the Lord [***Yahweh***] God [***'elohim***] of Israel."

As such, the ark contained the memorials of God's great redemptive acts—the tablets upon which were inscribed the Ten Commandments, an omer or two quarts of manna, and Aaron's rod. By Solomon's day, only the stone tablets remained in the ark, 1 Kings 8:9. This chest was also called "the ark of the testimony," Exod. 25:22, which indicates that the two tablets were evidence of divine redemption, for description, see Exodus 25:10–22.

In addition to containing memorials of divine redemption, the ark represented the presence of God. To be before it was to be in God's presence, Num. 10:35, although His presence was not limited to the ark (cf. 1 Sam. 4:3–11; 7:2, 6). The ark ceased to have this sacramental function when Israel began to regard it as a magical box with sacred power (a ***palladium***).

God promised to meet Moses at the ark, Exod. 25:22. Thus, the ark functioned as a place where divine revelation was received, Lev. 1:1; 16:2; Num. 7:89. The ark served as an instrument through which God guided and defended Israel during the wilderness wandering, Num. 10:11. Finally, it was upon this ark that the highest of Israel's sacraments, the blood of atonement, was presented and received, Lev. 16:2ff.

### *New Testament*

***kibotos*** (2787), "a wooden box, a chest," is used of (a) Noah's vessel, Matt. 24:38; Luke 17:27; Heb. 11:7; 1 Pet. 3:20; (b) the "ark" of the covenant in the tabernacle, Heb. 9:4; (c) the "ark" seen in vision in the heavenly temple, Rev. 11:19.

## ARM

***zeroa'*** (2220) means "arm," a part of the body, Deut. 33:20. The word refers to arms in Gen. 49:24, In some passages, ***zeroa'*** refers especially to the forearm, Isa. 17:5. Elsewhere, "shoulder," 2 Kings 9:24. In Num. 6:19 ***zeroa'*** is used of an animal's shoulder, cf. Deut. 18:3.

***zeroa'*** connotes the "seat of strength," Ps. 18:34. In Job 26:2, the poor are described as the arm that has no strength. God's strength is figured by anthropomorphisms (attributing to Him human bodily parts), such as His "stretched out arm," Deut. 4:34, or His "strong arm," Jer. 21:5. In Isa. 30:30, the word seems to represent lightning bolts, cf. Job 40:9.

The arm is frequently a symbol of strength, both of man, 1 Sam. 2:31, and of God, Ps. 71:18. In Ezek. 22:6 ***zeroa'*** may be translated "power." A third nuance is "help," Ps. 83:8. The word can also represent political or military forces, Dan. 11:15; cf. Ezek. 17:9.

## ARMS (weapons), ARMOR, TO ARM

### A. Nouns.

1. ***hoplon*** *(3696)*, originally any tool or implement for preparing a thing, became used in the plural for "weapons of warfare." Once in the NT it is used of actual weapons, John 18:3; elsewhere, metaphorically, of (a) the members of the body as instruments of unrighteousness and as instruments of righteousness, Rom. 6:13; (b) the "armor" of light, Rom. 13:12; the "armor" of righteousness, 2 Cor. 6:7; the weapons of the Christian's warfare, 2 Cor. 10:4.

2. ***panoplia*** *(3833)*, (Eng., "panoply"), lit., "all armor, full armor,," is used (a) of literal "armor," Luke 11:22; (b) of the spiritual helps supplied by God for overcoming the temptations of the Devil, Eph. 6:11, 13.

### B. Verbs.

1. ***hoplizo*** *(3695)*, "to arm oneself," is used in 1 Pet. 4:1, in an exhortation "to arm" ourselves with the same mind as that of Christ in regard to His sufferings.

2. ***kathoplizo*** *(2528)* is an intensive form, "to furnish fully with arms," Luke 11:21, lit., "a strong man fully armed."

## ASHAMED (to be), SHAME

### A. Verbs.

1. ***aischuno*** *(153)*, always used in the passive voice, signifies (a) "to have a feeling of fear or shame which prevents a person from doing a thing," e.g., Luke 16:3; (b) "the feeling of shame arising from something that has

been done," e.g., 2 Cor. 10:8; Phil. 1:20; 1 John 2:28, of the possibility of being "ashamed" before the Lord Jesus at His judgment seat in His Parousia with His saints; in 1 Pet. 4:16, of being ashamed of suffering as a Christian.

2. ***epaischunomai*** (*1870*), a strengthened form of No. 1, is used only in the sense (b) in the preceding paragraph. It is said of being "ashamed" of persons, Mark 8:38; Luke 9:26; the gospel, Rom. 1:16; former evil doing, Rom. 6:21; "the testimony of our Lord," 2 Tim. 1:8; suffering for the gospel, v. 12; rendering assistance and comfort to one who is suffering for the gospel's sake, v. 16. It is used in Heb., of Christ in calling those who are sanctified His brethren, 2:11, and of God in His not being "ashamed" to be called the God of believers, 11:16.

3. ***kataischuno*** (*2617*), another strengthened form, is used (a) in the active voice, "to put to shame," e.g., Rom. 5:5; 1 Cor. 1:27 (KJV, "confound"); 11:4–5 ("dishonoreth"), and v. 22; (b) in the passive voice, Rom. 9:33; 10:11; 2 Cor. 7:14; 1 Pet. 2:6; 3:16.

### B. Noun.

1. ***aischune*** (*152*), "shame," akin to A, No. 1, signifies (a) subjectively, the confusion of one who is "ashamed" of anything, a sense of "shame," Luke 14:9; those things which "shame" conceals, 2 Cor. 4:2; (b) objectively, ignominy, that which is visited on a person by the wicked, Heb. 12:2; that which should arise from guilt, Phil. 3:19; (c) concretely, a thing to be "ashamed" of, Rev. 3:18; Jude 13, where the word is in the plural, lit., "basenesses," "disgraces."

## ASHERAH

***'asherah*** (842) refers to a cultic object representing the presence of the Canaanite goddess Asherah. When the people of Israel entered Palestine, they were to have nothing to do with the idolatrous religions of its inhabitants, but destroy the ***'asherim,*** Exod. 34:13. This cult object was manufactured from wood, Judg. 6:26; 1 Kings 14:15, and it could be burned, Deut. 12:3. Some scholars conclude that it was a sacred pole set up near an altar to Baal. Since there was only one goddess with this name, the plural (***'asherim***) probably represents her several "poles."

***'asherah*** signifies the name of the goddess herself: "Now therefore send, and gather to me all Israel unto mount Carmel, and the prophets of Baal four hundred and fifty, and the prophets of the groves [***'asherah***] four hundred, which eat at Jezebel's table," 1 Kings 18:19. The Canaanites believed that ***'asherah*** ruled the sea, was the mother of all the gods including Baal, and sometimes was his deadly enemy.

## ASK

#### *Old Testament*

### A. Verb.

***sha'al*** (7592), "to ask, inquire, consult." Since prayer often includes petition, ***sha'al*** is sometimes used in the sense of "praying for" something: "Pray for the peace of Jerusalem," Ps. 122:6. In the idiomatic phrase, "to ask another of his welfare," it carries the sense of a greeting, cf. Exod. 18:7; Judg. 18:15; 1 Sam. 10:4. Frequently, it is used to indicate someone's asking for God's direction or counsel, Josh. 9:14; Isa. 30:2. In Ps. 109:10 it is used to indicate a begging.

### B. Noun.

***she'ol*** (7585), "place of the dead." Often incorrectly translated "hell" in the KJV, ***she'ol*** was not understood to be a place of punishment, but simply the ultimate resting place of all mankind, Gen. 37:35. Thus, it was thought to be the land of no return, Job 16:22; 17:14–16. It was a place to be dreaded, not only because it meant the end of physical life on earth, but also because there was no praise of God there, Ps. 6:5. Deliverance from it was a blessing, Ps. 30:3.

***she'ol*** is translated variously in the English versions: "hell, pit, grave" (KJV); "netherworld" (NAB). Some versions simply give the transliteration, Sheol" (RSV, JB, NASB).

#### *New Testament*

### A. Verbs.

1. ***aiteo*** (*154*), "to ask," is to be distinguished from No. 2. ***aiteo*** more frequently suggests the attitude of a suppliant, the petition of one who is lesser in position than he to whom the petition is made; e.g., in the case of men in asking something from God, Matt. 7:7; a child from a parent, Matt. 7:9–10; a subject from a king, Acts 12:20.

2. ***erotao*** (*2065*) more frequently suggests that the petitioner is on a footing of equality or familiarity with the person whom he requests. It is used of a king in making request from another king, Luke 14:32; of the Pharisee who "desired" Christ that He would eat with him, an indication of the inferior conception he had of Christ, Luke 7:36; cf. 11:37; John 9:15; 18:19.

In this respect it is significant that the Lord Jesus never used ***aiteo*** in the matter of making request to the Father. "The consciousness of His equal dignity, of His potent and prevailing intercession, speaks out in this, that as often as He asks, or declares that He will ask anything of the Father, it is always ***erotao***, an asking, that is, upon equal terms, John 14:16; 16:26; 17:9, 15, 20, never ***aiteo***, that He uses. Martha, on the contrary, plainly reveals her poor unworthy conception of His person, that . . . she ascribes that ***aiteo*** to Him which He never ascribes to Himself, John 11:22" (Trench, *Syn.* Sec. xl).

3. ***eperotao*** (*1905*), a strengthened form of No. 2, is frequently used in the synoptic Gospels, but only twice in the Gospel of John, 18:7, 21. In Rom. 10:20 it is rendered "asked of" (KJV, "asked after"). The more intensive character of the "asking" may be observed in Luke 2:46; 3:14; 6:9; 17:20; 20:21, 27, 40; 22:64, 23:3, 6, 9. In Matt. 16:1, it virtually signifies to demand (its meaning in later Greek).

### B. Noun.

***aitema*** (*155*), akin to No. 1, lit., "that which has been asked for," is used in Luke 23:24, RV, "what they asked for" (KJV, "required"); Phil. 4:6, "requests"; 1 John 5:15, petitions.

## ASLEEP, SLEEP

### A. Verbs.

1. ***katheudo*** (*2518*), "to go to sleep," is chiefly used of natural "sleep," and is found most frequently in the Gospels, especially Matthew and Luke. With reference to death it is found in the Lord's remark concerning Jairus' daughter, Matt. 9:24; Mark 5:39; Luke 8:52. In the epistles of Paul it is used as follows: (a) of natural "sleep," e.g., 1 Thess. 5:7; (b) of carnal indifference to spiritual things on the part of believers, Eph. 5:14; 1 Thess. 5:6, 10 (as in Mark 13:36), a condition of insensibility to divine things involving conformity to the world.

2. ***koimaomai*** (*2837*) is used of natural "sleep," Matt. 28:13; Luke 22:45; John 11:12; Acts 12:6; of the death of the body, but only of such as are Christ's; yet never of Christ Himself, though He is "the firstfruits of them that have fallen asleep," 1 Cor. 15:20, of saints who departed before Christ came, Matt. 27:52; Acts 13:36; of Lazarus, while Christ was yet upon the earth, John 11:11; of believers since the Ascension, 1 Thess. 4:13–15, and Acts 7:60; 1 Cor. 7:39; 11:30; 15:6, 18, 51; 2 Pet. 3:4.

In Paul's writings, it is evident the word 'sleep,' where applied to the departed Christians, is not intended to convey the idea that the spirit is unconscious, but the physical frame is dissolved and returns to the dust.

### B. Noun.

***hupnos*** (*5278*) is never used of death. In five places in the NT it is used of physical "sleep"; in Rom. 13:11, metaphorically, of a slumbering state of soul, i.e., of spiritual conformity to the world, out of which believers are warned to awake.

## ASSEMBLE

1. ***sunago*** (*4863*), "to assemble," is used of the "gathering together" of people or things; in Luke 12:17–18.

2. ***sunalizo*** (*4871*), "to gather together, to assemble," with the suggestion of a crowded meeting. The corresponding adjective is ***hales***, "thronged," is used in Acts 1:4.

3. ***sunerchomai*** (*4905*), "to come together," is once rendered "assemble," Mark 14:53, KJV. It is frequently used of "coming together," especially of the "gathering" of a local church, 1 Cor. 11:17–18, 20, 33–34; 14:23, 26; it is rendered "resorted" in Acts 16:13, KJV, where the RV adheres to the lit. rendering, "came together."

## ASSEMBLY

### *Old Testament*

### A. Noun.

***qahal*** (6951), "assembly; company." In many contexts, the word means an assembly gathered to plan or execute war. One of the first of these is Gen. 49:6. In 1 Kings 12:3 (RSV), "all the assembly of Israel" asked Rehoboam to ease the tax burden imposed by Solomon. When Rehoboam refused, they withdrew from him and rejected their feudal (military) allegiance to him. For the application of ***qahal*** to an army, see Ezek. 17:17.

Quite often, ***qahal*** is used to denote a gathering to judge or deliberate. This emphasis first appears in Ezek. 23:45–47, where the "company" judges and executes judgment. In many passages, the word signifies an assembly representing a larger group, 1 Chron. 13:1–2, RSV. Here, "the whole assembly" of Israel refers to the assembled leaders, cf. 2 Chron. 1:2. Thus, in Lev. 4:13 we find that the sin of the whole congregation of Israel can escape the notice of the "assembly" (the judges or elders who represent the congregation).

Sometimes ***qahal*** represents all the males of Israel who were eligible to bring sacrifices to the Lord, Deut. 23:1, RSV. The only eligible members of the assembly were men who were religiously bound together under the covenant, who were neither strangers (living in Israel temporarily) nor sojourners (permanent non-Hebrew residents), Num. 15:15. In Num. 16:3 and 33, it is clear that the "assembly" was the worshiping, voting community, cf. 18:4.

Elsewhere, the word ***qahal*** is used to signify all the people of Israel. The whole congregation of the sons of Israel complained that Moses had brought them forth into the wilderness to kill the whole assembly with hunger, Exod. 16:31. The first occurrence of the word also bears the connotation of a large group, Gen. 28:3.

### B. Verb.

***qahal*** (6950), "to gather." It means "to gather" as a ***qahal*** for conflict or war, for religious purposes, and for judgment, 1 Kings 8:1.

#### *New Testament*

1. ***ekklesia*** (*1577*), "a calling out of," was used among the Greeks of a body of citizens "gathered" to discuss the affairs of state, Acts 19:39. In Acts 7:38 it is used of Israel; in 19:32, 41, of a riotous mob. It has two applications to companies of Christians, (a) to the whole company of the redeemed throughout the present era, the company of which Christ said, "I will build My Church," Matt. 16:18, and which is further described as "the Church which is His Body," Eph. 1:22; 5:23, (b) in the singular number (e.g., Matt. 18:17, RV marg., "congregation"), to a company consisting of professed believers, e.g., Acts 20:28; 1 Cor. 1:2; Gal. 1:13; 1 Thess. 1:1; 2 Thess. 1:1; 1 Tim. 3:5, and in the plural, with reference to churches in a district.

2. ***paneguris*** (*3831*), "any kind of assembly," denoted, among the Greeks, an assembly of the people in contrast to the council of national leaders, or a "gathering" of the people in honor of a god, or for some public festival, such as the Olympic games. The word is used in Heb. 12:23, coupled with the word "church," as applied to all believers who form the body of Christ.

## ASSURANCE, ASSURE, ASSUREDLY

### A. Nouns.

1. ***pistis*** (*4102*), "faith," has the secondary meaning of "an assurance or guarantee," e.g., Acts 17:31; by raising Christ from the dead, God has given "assurance" that the world will be judged by Him (the KJV margin, "offered faith" does not express the meaning). Cf. 1 Tim. 5:12, where "faith" means "pledge."

2. ***plerophoria*** (*4136*), "a fullness, abundance," also means "full assurance, entire confidence"; lit., a "full-carrying." Some explain it as full fruitfulness (cf. RV, "fullness" in Heb. 6:11). In 1 Thess. 1:5 it describes the willingness and freedom of spirit enjoyed by those who brought the gospel to Thessalonica; in Col. 2:2, the freedom of mind and confidence resulting from an understanding in Christ; in Heb. 6:11 (KJV, "full assurance," RV, "fullness"), the engrossing effect of the expectation of the fulfillment of God's promises; in Heb. 10:22, the character of the faith by which we are to draw near to God.

3. ***hupostasis*** (*5287*), lit., "a standing under, support," hence, an "assurance," is so rendered in Heb. 11:1, RV, for KJV, "substance." It here may signify a title-deed, as giving a guarantee, or reality.

### B. Verbs.

1. ***pistoo*** (*4104*), "to trust or give assurance to" (cf. A, No. 1), has a secondary meaning, in the passive voice, "to be assured of," 2 Tim. 3:14.

2. ***plerophoreo*** (*4135*), akin to A, No. 2, "to bring in full measure, to fulfill," also signifies "to be fully assured," Rom. 4:21, RV, of Abraham's faith. In 14:5 it is said of the apprehension of the will of God. So in Col. 4:12 in the best mss. In these three places it is used subjectively, with reference to an effect upon the mind. For its other and objective use, referring to things external.

3. ***peitho*** (*3782*), "to persuade," is rendered "assure" in 1 John 3:19 (marg., "persuade"), where the meaning is that of confidence toward God consequent upon loving in deed and in truth.

## ATONE, ATONEMENT

#### *Old Testament*

### A. Verb.

***kapar*** (3722), "to cover over, atone, propitiate, pacify." This root is found in the Hebrew language at all periods of its history, and perhaps is best known from the term ***Yom Kippur,*** "Day of Atonement."

Most uses of the word, however, involve the theological meaning of "covering over," often with the blood of a sacrifice, in order to atone for some sin. It is not clear whether this means that the "covering over" hides the sin from God's sight or implies that the sin is wiped away in this process.

As might be expected, this word occurs more frequently in the Book of Leviticus than in any other book, since Leviticus deals with the ritual sacrifices that were made to atone for sin. For example, Lev. 4:13–21 gives instructions for bringing a young bull to the tent of meeting for a sin offering. After the elders laid their hands on the bull (to transfer the people's sin to the bull), the bull was killed. The priest then brought some of the blood of the bull into the tent of meeting and sprinkled it seven times before the veil. Some of the blood was put on the horns of the altar and the rest of the blood was poured at the base of the altar of burnt offering. The fat of the bull was then burned on the altar. The bull itself was to be burned outside the camp. By means of this ritual, "the priest shall make an atonement [***kapar***] for them, and it shall be forgiven them," Lev. 4:20.

Sometimes atonement for sin was made apart from or without blood offerings. During his vision-call experience, Isaiah's lips were touched with a coal of fire taken from the altar by one of the seraphim. With that, he was told, "Thy sin is purged [***kapar***]" Isa. 6:7. The English versions translate the word variously as "purged" (KJV, JB); "forgiven" (RSV, NASB, TEV); and "wiped away" (NEB). In another passage, Scripture says that the guilt or iniquity of Israel would be "purged" (KJV, NEB) by the destruction of the implements of idolatrous worship, Isa. 27:9. In this case, the RSV renders ***kapar*** as "expiated," while the NASB and TEV translate it as "forgiven."

### B. Noun.

***kapporet*** (3727), "mercy seat; throne of mercy." This noun form of ***kapar*** has been variously interpreted by the English versions as "mercy seat" (KJV, RSV); "cover" (NEB); "lid" (TEV); "throne of mercy" (JB); and "throne" (Knox). It refers to a slab of gold that rested on top of the ark of the covenant. Images of two cherubims stood on this slab, facing each other. This slab of gold represented the throne of God and symbolized His real presence in the worship shrine.

#### *New Testament*

***katallage*** (*2643*), translated "atonement" in the KJV of Rom. 5:11, signifies, not "atonement," but "reconciliation," as in the RV. See also Rom. 11:15; 2 Cor. 5:18–19. The corresponding NT words are ***hilasmos***, "propitiation," 1 John 2:2; 4:10, and ***hilasterion***, Rom. 3:25; Heb. 9:5, "mercy-seat," the covering of the ark of the covenant. These describe the means (in and through the person and work of the Lord Jesus Christ, in His death on the cross by the shedding of His blood in His vicarious sacrifice for sin) by which God shows mercy to sinners.

## ATTAIN

1. ***katantao*** (*2658*), a strengthened form of ***antao***, "to come opposite to," signifies "to reach, to arrive at." It is used in its local significance several times in the Acts, e.g. 27:12.

In its metaphorical sense of "attaining" to something it is used in three places: Acts 26:7, of the fulfillment of the promise of God made to the ancestors of Israel, to which promise the twelve tribes "hope to attain" (RV); in Eph. 4:13, of "attaining" to the unity of the faith and of the knowledge of the Son of God; in Phil. 3:11, of the paramount aims of the apostle's life, "if by any means," he says, "I might attain unto the resurrection from the dead," not the physical resurrection, which is assured to all believers hereafter, but to the present life of identification with Christ in His resurrection. For the metaphorical sense in 1 Cor. 10:11 and 14:36.

2. ***katalambano*** (*2638*), "to seize, to apprehend," whether physically or mentally, is rendered "attain" in the sense of making something one's own, appropriating a thing, Rom. 9:30, said of the Gentiles, who through the gospel have "attained" to, or laid hold of, the righteousness which is of faith, in contrast to the present condition of Israel; in 1 Cor. 9:24, of securing a prize.

3. ***phthano*** (*5348*), "to anticipate," also means "to reach, attain to a thing"; negatively of Israel. The only other passage where it has this significance is Phil. 3:16, "we have attained."

4. ***tunchano*** (*5177*), "to reach, meet with," signifies "to attain to," in Luke 20:35, RV (for KJV, obtain).

## AUSTERE

***austeros*** (*840*), akin to ***auo***, "to dry up" (Eng., "austere"), primarily denotes "stringent to the taste," like new wine not matured by age, unripe fruit, etc., hence, "harsh, severe," Luke 19:21–22.

## AUTHOR

1. ***aitios*** (*159*), an adjective, denotes "that which causes something." This and No. 2 are both translated "author" in Hebrews. ***aitios***, in Heb. 5:9, describes Christ as the "Author of eternal salvation unto all them that obey Him." He is the concrete and active cause of our salvation. He has not merely caused or effected it, He is, as His name, "Jesus," implies, our salvation itself, Luke 2:30; 3:6.

2. ***archegos*** (*747*), translated "Prince" in Acts 3:15 and 5:31, but "Author" in Heb. 2:10, RV, "Captain," RV marg., and KJV, and "Author" in 12:2, primarily signifies "one who takes a lead in, or provides the first occasion of, anything." That Christ is the Prince of life signifies, as Chrysostom says, that "the life He

had was not from another; the Prince or Author of life must be He who has life from Himself." But the word does not necessarily combine the idea of the source or originating cause with that of leader. In Heb. 12:2 where Christ is called the "Author and Perfecter of faith," He is represented as the one who takes precedence in faith and is thus the perfect exemplar of it. The pronoun "our" does not correspond to anything in the original, and may well be omitted. Christ in the days of His flesh trod undeviatingly the path of faith, and as the Perfecter has brought it to a perfect end in His own person. Thus He is the leader of all others who tread that path.

## AUTHORITY

### A. Noun.

1. ***exousia*** (*1849*) denotes "authority" (from the impersonal verb ***exesti***, "it is lawful"). From the meaning of "leave or permission," or liberty of doing as one pleases, it passed to that of "the ability or strength with which one is endued," then to that of the "power of authority," the right to exercise power, e.g., Matt. 9:6; 21:23; 2 Cor. 10:8; or "the power of rule or government," the power of one whose will and commands must be obeyed by others, e.g., Matt. 28:18; John 17:2; Jude 25; Rev. 12:10; 17:13; more specifically of apostolic "authority," 2 Cor. 10:8; 13:10; the "power" of judicial decision, John 19:10; of "managing domestic affairs," Mark 13:34. By metonymy, or name-change (the substitution of a suggestive word for the name of the thing meant), it stands for "that which is subject to authority or rule," Luke 4:6 (RV, "authority," for the KJV "power"); or, as with the English "authority," "one who possesses authority, a ruler, magistrate," Rom. 13:1–3; Luke 12:11; Titus 3:1; or "a spiritual potentate," e.g., Eph. 3:10; 6:12; Col. 1:16; 2:10, 15; 1 Pet. 3:22. The RV usually translates it "authority."

### B. Verbs.

1. ***exousiazo*** (*1850*), akin to A, signifies "to exercise power," Luke 22:25; 1 Cor. 6:12; 7:4 (twice).

2. ***katexousiazo*** (*2175*), "to exercise authority upon," is used in Matt. 20:25, and Mark 10:42.

## AVENGE, AVENGER

### *Old Testament*

### A. Verb.

***naqam*** (5358), "to avenge, take vengeance, punish." Lamech's sword song is a scornful challenge to his fellows and a blatant attack on the justice of God, Gen. 4:23–24.

The Lord reserves vengeance as the sphere of His own action: "To me belongeth vengeance, and recompense . . . for he will avenge the blood of his servants, and will render vengeance to his adversaries," Deut. 32:35, 43. The law therefore forbade personal vengeance, Lev. 19:18. Hence the Lord's people commit their case to Him, as David, 1 Sam. 24:12.

The Lord uses men to take vengeance, Num. 31:2–3. Vengeance for Israel is the Lord's vengeance.

The law stated, "And if a man smite his servant, or his maid, with a rod, and he die under his hand; he shall be surely punished," Exod. 21:20. In Israel, this responsibility was given to the "avenger of blood," Deut. 19:6. He was responsible to preserve the life and personal integrity of his nearest relative.

When a man was attacked because he was God's servant, he could rightly call for vengeance on his enemies, Judg. 16:28.

In the covenant, God warned that His vengeance may fall on His own people, Lev. 26:25; Isa. 1:24.

### B. Noun.

***naqam*** (5359), "vengeance." The noun is first used in the Lord's promise to Cain, Gen. 4:15.

In some instances a man may call for "vengeance" on his enemies, such as when another man has committed adultery with his wife, Prov. 6:34.

The prophets frequently speak of God's "vengeance" on His enemies: Isa. 59:17; Mic. 5:15; Nah. 1:2. It will come at a set time, Isa. 34:8.

Isaiah brings God's "vengeance" and redemption together in the promise of messianic salvation, Isa. 61:1–2. When Jesus announced that this was fulfilled in Himself, He stopped short of reading the last clause; but His sermon clearly anticipated that "vengeance" would come on Israel for rejecting Him, Isa. 63:4.

### *New Testament*

### A. Verb.

***ekdikeo*** (*1556*), ***ek***, "from," ***dike***, "justice," i.e., that which proceeds from justice, means (a) "to vindicate a person's right," (b) "to avenge a thing." With the meaning (a), it is used in the parable of the unjust judge, Luke 18:3, 5, of the "vindication" of the rights of the widow; with the meaning (b) it is used in Rev. 6:10 and 19:2, of the act of God in "avenging" the blood of the saints; in 2 Cor. 10:6, of the apostle's readiness to use his apostolic authority in punishing disobedience on the part of his readers; here the RV substitutes "avenge" for the KJV, "revenge"; in Rom. 12:19 of "avenging" oneself, against which the believer is warned.

**B. Nouns.**

1. ***ekdikos*** (*1558*), primarily, "without law," then, "one who exacts a penalty from a person, an avenger, a punisher," is used in Rom. 13:4 of a civil authority in the discharge of his function of executing wrath on the evildoer (KJV, wrongly, "revenger"); in 1 Thess. 4:6, of God as the avenger of the one who wrongs his brother, here particularly in the matter of adultery.

2. ***ekdikesis*** (*1557*), vengeance," is used with the verb ***poieo***, "to make," i.e., to avenge, in Luke 18:7–8; Acts 7:24; twice it is used in statements that "vengeance" belongs to God, Rom. 12:19; Heb. 10:30. In 2 Thess. 1:8 it is said of the act of divine justice which will be meted out to those who know not God and obey not the gospel, when the Lord comes in flaming fire at His second advent, though with no element of vindictiveness.

## AVOID

1. ***ekklino*** (*1578*), "to turn away from, to turn aside," lit., "to bend out of" (***ek***, "out," ***klino***, "to bend"), is used in Rom. 3:12, of the sinful condition of mankind, KJV, "gone out of the way," RV, "turned aside"; in Rom. 16:17, of turning away from those who cause offenses and occasions of stumbling (KJV, "avoid"); in 1 Pet. 3:11 of turning away from evil (KJV, "eschew").

2. ***ektrepo*** (*1624*), lit., "to turn or twist out," is used in the passive voice in Heb. 12:13, "that which is lame be not turned out of the way" (or rather, "put out of joint"); in the sense of the middle voice (though passive in form) of turning aside, or turning away from, 2 Tim. 4:4 (KJV, "shall be turned unto fables," RV, "shall turn aside"); in 1 Tim. 1:6, of those who, having swerved from the faith, have turned aside unto vain talking; in 5:15, of those who have turned aside after Satan; in 6:20, RV, of "turning away from (KJV, 'avoiding') profane babblings and oppositions of the knowledge which is falsely so called."

3. ***paraiteomai*** (*3868*), lit., "to ask aside," signifies (a) "to beg of (or from) another," Mark 15:6, in the most authentic mss.; (b) "to deprecate," (1) "to entreat (that) not," Heb. 12:19; (2) "to refuse, decline, avoid," 1 Tim. 4:7; 5:11; 2 Tim. 2:23; Titus 3:10 (see No. 4 for v. 9); Heb. 12:25; (c) "to beg off, ask to be excused," Luke 14:18–19 (some would put Heb. 12:25 here).

4. ***periistemi*** (*4026*), in the active voice, means "to stand around," John 11:42; Acts 25:7; in the middle voice, "to turn oneself about," for the purpose of avoiding something, "to avoid, shun," said of profane babblings, 2 Tim. 2:16; of foolish questions, genealogies, strife, etc., Titus 3:9 (KJV, "avoid").

5. ***stello*** (*4724*), "to place," sometimes signifies, in the middle voice, "to take care against a thing, to avoid," 2 Cor. 8:20; in 2 Thess. 3:6, "of withdrawing from a person."

## AWAKE

1. ***egeiro*** (*1453*) is used, (a) in the active voice, of "arousing a person from sleep" in Matt. 8:25 of the act of the disciples in awaking the Lord; in Acts 12:7, of the awaking of Peter, RV, "awake him"; (b) in the passive voice, with a middle significance, of the virgins, in "arousing themselves" from their slumber, Matt. 25:7; in Rom. 13:11, and Eph. 5:14, metaphorically, "of awaking from a state of moral sloth.

2. ***diegeiro*** (*1326*), is used of "awaking from natural sleep," Matt. 1:24; Mark 4:38; of the act of the disciples in "awaking" the Lord, Luke 8:24.

3. ***eknepho*** (*1594*), primarily, "to return to one's sense from drunkenness, to become sober," in the NT in 1 Cor. 15:34, "Awake up righteously and sin not" (RV), suggesting a return to soberness of mind from the stupor consequent upon the influence of evil doctrine.

4. ***exupnizo*** (*1852*), "to rouse a person out of sleep," is used metaphorically, in John 11:11.

5. ***diagregoreo*** (*1235*), "to watch intensely" is used in Luke 9:32, RV, "were fully awake." KJV "were awake."

# B

## BAAL, MASTER

***ba'al*** (1167), "master; baal." The word ***ba'al*** occurs 84 times in the Hebrew Old Testament, 15 times with the meaning of "husband" and 50 times as a reference to a deity.

The primary meaning of ***ba'al*** is "possessor." Isaiah's use of ***ba'al*** in parallel with ***qanah*** clarifies this basic significance of ***ba'al***, Isa. 1:3. Man may be the owner [ba'al] of an animal, Exod. 22:10, a house, Exod. 22:7, a cistern, Exod. 21:34, or even a wife, Exod. 21:3.

A secondary meaning, "husband," is clearly indicated by the phrase ***ba'al ha-ishshah***, literally, "owner of the woman," Exod. 21:22. The meaning of ***ba'al*** is closely related to ***ish*** "man," as is seen in 2 Sam. 11:26.

The word ***ba'al*** with another noun may signify a peculiar characteristic or quality, Gen. 37:19; the KJV offers a literal translation of the Hebrew—"master of dreams"—as an alternative.

Thirdly, the word ***ba'al*** may denote any deity other than the God of Israel. Baal was a common name given to the god of fertility in Canaan. In the Canaanite city of Ugarit, Baal was especially recognized as the god of fertility. The Old Testament records that Baal was "the god" of the Canaanites. The Israelites worshiped Baal during the time of the judges, Judg. 6:25–32, and of King Ahab. Elijah stood as the opponent of the Baal priests at Mount Carmel, 1 Kings 18:21ff. Many cities made Baal a local god and honored him with special acts of worship: Baal-peor, Num. 25:5, Baal-berith at Shechem, Judg. 8:33, Baal-zebub, 2 Kings 1:2–16, at Ekron, Baal-zephon, Num. 33:7, and Baal-hermon, Judg. 3:3.

## BABBLER, BABBLINGS

1. ***spermologos*** (*4691*), "a babbler," is used in Acts 17:18. Primarily an adjective, it came to be used as a noun signifying a crow, or some other bird, picking up seeds (***sperma***, "a seed," ***lego***, "to collect"). Then it seems to have been used of a man accustomed to hang about the streets and markets, picking up scraps which fall from loads; hence a parasite, who lives at the expense of others, a hanger on.

Metaphorically it became used of a man who picks up scraps of information and retails them secondhand, a plagiarist, or of those who make a show, in unscientific style, of knowledge obtained from misunderstanding lectures.

2. ***kenophonia*** (*2757*), "babbling" (from ***kenos***, "empty," and ***phone***, "a sound"), signifies empty discussion, discussion on useless subjects, 1 Tim. 6:20 and 2 Tim. 2:16.

## BABY

1. ***brephos*** (*1025*) denotes (a) "an unborn child," as in Luke 1:41, 44; (b) "a newborn child, or an infant still older," Luke 2:12, 16; 18:15; Acts 7:19; 2 Tim. 3:15; 1 Pet. 2:2.

2. ***nepios*** (*3516*), lit., "without the power of speech," denotes "a little child," the literal meaning having been lost in the general use of the word. It is used (a) of "infants," Matt. 21:16; (b) metaphorically, of the unsophisticated in mind and trustful in disposition, Matt. 11:25 and Luke 10:21, where it stands in contrast to the wise; of those who are possessed merely of natural knowledge, Rom. 2:20; 1 Cor. 3:1; Heb. 5:13; Gal. 4:3; Eph. 4:14. "Immaturity" is always associated with this word.

## BACKBITER, BACKBITING

***katalalos*** (*2637*), a "backbiter," and ***katalalia*** (*2636*), "backbiting." ***katalalos*** is used in Rom. 1:30. ***katalalia*** is translated "evil speaking" in 1 Pet. 2:1, "backbiting" in 2 Cor. 12:20.

## BAD

1. ***kakos*** (*2556*) indicates the lack in a person or thing of those qualities which should be possessed; it means "bad in character" (a) morally, by way of thinking, feeling or acting, e.g., Mark 7:21, "thoughts"; 1 Cor. 15:33, "company"; Col. 3:5, "desire"; 1 Tim. 6:10, "all kinds of evil"; 1 Pet. 3:9, "evil for evil"; (b) in the sense of what is injurious or baneful, e.g., the tongue as "a restless evil," Jas. 3:8; "evil beasts," Titus 1:12; "harm," Acts 16:28; once it is translated "bad," 2 Cor. 5:10. It is the opposite of ***agathos***, "good."

2. ***poneros*** (*4190*), connected with ***ponos***, "labor," expresses especially the "active form of evil," and is practically the same in meaning as (b), under No. 1. It is used, e.g., of thoughts, Matt. 15:19 (cf. ***kakos***, in Mark 7:21); of speech, Matt. 5:11 (cf. ***kakos***, in 1 Pet. 3:10); and of acts, 2 Tim. 4:18. Where ***kakos*** and ***poneros*** are put

together, ***kakos*** is always put first and signifies "bad in character, base," ***poneros***, "bad in effect, malignant": see 1 Cor. 5:8, and Rev. 16:2. ***kakos*** has a wider meaning, ***poneros*** a stronger meaning. ***poneros*** alone is used of Satan and might well be translated "the malignant one," e.g., Matt. 5:37 and five times in 1 John (2:13–14; 3:12; 5:18–19, RV); of demons, e.g., Luke 7:21. Once it is translated bad, Matt. 22:10.

3. ***sapros*** (*4550*), "corrupt, rotten" (akin to ***sepo***, "to rot"), of trees and fruit; Luke 6:43; of certain fish, Matt. 13:48; of defiling speech, Eph. 4:29.

## BAPTISM, BAPTIST, BAPTIZE

### A. Nouns.

1. ***baptisma*** (*908*), "baptism," consisting of the processes of immersion, submersion and emergence (from ***bapto***, "to dip"), is used (a) of John's "baptism," (b) of Christian "baptism"; (c) of the overwhelming afflictions and judgments to which the Lord voluntarily submitted on the cross, e.g., Luke 12:50; (d) of the sufferings His followers would experience, not of a vicarious character, but in fellowship with the sufferings of their Master. Some mss. have the word in Matt. 20:22–23; it is used in Mark 10:38–39, with this meaning.

2. ***baptismos*** (*909*), as distinct from ***baptisma*** (the ordinance), is used of the "ceremonial washing of articles," Mark 7:4, 8, in some texts; Heb. 9:10; once in a general sense, Heb. 6:2.

3. ***baptistes*** (*910*), "a baptist," is used only of John the Baptist, and only in the Synoptists, 14 times.

### B. Verb.

***baptizo*** (*907*), "to baptize," primarily a frequentative form of ***bapto***, "to dip," was used among the Greeks to signify the dyeing of a garment, or the drawing of water by dipping a vessel into another, etc. Plutarchus uses it of the drawing of wine by dipping the cup into the bowl (*Alexis*, 67) and Plato, metaphorically, of being overwhelmed with questions (*Euthydemus*, 277 D).

It is used in the NT in Luke 11:38 of washing oneself. In the early chapters of the four Gospels and in Acts 1:5; 11:16; 19:4, it is used of the rite performed by John the Baptist who called upon the people to repent that they might receive remission of sins. Those who obeyed came "confessing their sins," thus acknowledging their unfitness to be in the Messiah's coming kingdom. Distinct from this is the "baptism" enjoined by Christ, Matt. 28:19, a "baptism" to be undergone by believers, thus witnessing to their identification with Him in death, burial and resurrection, e.g., Acts 19:5; Rom. 6:3–4; 1 Cor. 1:13–17; 12:13; Gal. 3:27; Col. 2:12. The phrase in Matt. 28:19, "baptizing them into the Name" (RV; cf. Acts 8:16, RV), would indicate that the "baptized" person was closely bound to, or became the property of, the one into whose name he was "baptized."

In Acts 22:16 it is used in the middle voice, in the command given to Saul of Tarsus, "arise and be baptized," the significance of the middle voice form being "get thyself baptized." The experience of those who were in the ark at the time of the Flood was a figure or type of the facts of spiritual death, burial, and resurrection, Christian "baptism" being an ***antitupos***, "a corresponding type," a "like figure," 1 Pet. 3:21. Likewise the nation of Israel was figuratively baptized when made to pass through the Red Sea under the cloud, 1 Cor. 10:2. The verb is used metaphorically also in two distinct senses: firstly, of "baptism" by the Holy Spirit, which took place on the Day of Pentecost; secondly, of the calamity which would come upon the nation of the Jews, a "baptism" of the fire of divine judgment for rejection of the will and word of God, Matt. 3:11; Luke 3:16.

## BARBARIAN, BARBAROUS

***barbaros*** (*915*) properly meant "one whose speech is rude, or harsh"; the word is onomatopoeic, indicating in the sound the uncouth character represented by the repeated syllable "bar-bar." Hence it signified one who speaks a strange or foreign language. See 1 Cor. 14:11. It then came to denote any foreigner ignorant of the Greek language and culture. After the Persian war it acquired the sense of rudeness and brutality. In Acts 28:2, 4, it is used unreproachfully of the inhabitants of Malta, who were of Phoenician origin. So in Rom. 1:14, where it stands in distinction from Greeks, and in implied contrast to both Greeks and Jews. Cf. the contrasts in Col. 3:11, where all such distinctions are shown to be null and void in Christ. "Berber" stood similarly in the language of the Egyptians for all non-Egyptian peoples.

## BARREN

***steiros*** (*4723*), from a root ***ster***– meaning "hard, firm" (hence Eng., "sterile"), signifies "barren, not bearing children," of natural state, Luke, 1:7, 36; 23:29; and of spiritual state, Gal. 4:27.

## BASE, BASER

1. ***agenes*** (*36*), "of low birth," hence denoted "that which is of no reputation, of no account," 1 Cor. 1:28, "the base things of the world," i.e., those which are of no account or fame in the world's esteem. That the neuter plural of the adjective bears reference to persons is clear from verse 26.

2. ***tapeinos*** (*5011*), primarily "that which is low, and does not rise far from the ground," metaphorically, signifies "lowly, of no degree." So the RV in 2 Cor. 10:1. Cf. Luke 1:52 and Jas. 1:9, "of low degree."

3. ***agoraios*** (*60*), translated in the KJV of Acts 17:5 "of the baser sort," RV, "of the rabble," signifies, lit., "relating to the market place"; hence, frequenting markets, and so sauntering about idly. It is also used of affairs usually transacted in the market-place, and hence of judicial assemblies, Acts 19:38.

## BASTARD

***nothos*** (*3541*) denotes "an illegitimate child, one born out of lawful wedlock," Heb. 12:8.

## BEAR

(*in the sense of "carrying, supporting"*)

1. ***bastazo*** (*941*) signifies "to support as a burden." It is used with the meaning (a) "to take up," John 10:31; (b) "to carry" something, Matt. 3:11; (c) "to bear" a burden, whether physically, as of the cross, John 19:17, or metaphorically in respect of sufferings endured in the cause of Christ, Luke 14:27; (d) to "bear" by way of carrying off, John 12:6.

2. ***phero*** (*5342*), "to bring or bear," is translated in the RV by the latter verb in Luke 23:26; John 2:8 (twice); 12:24; 15:2 (twice); Heb. 13:13.

3. ***anaphero*** (*399*), No. 2, with ***ana***, up, is used of "leading persons up to a higher place," and, in this respect, of the Lord's ascension, Luke 24:51. It is used twice of the Lord's propitiatory sacrifice, in His bearing sins on the cross, Heb. 9:28 and 1 Pet. 2:24.

4. ***ekphero*** (*1627*), No. 2, with ***ek***, "out," is used, literally, "of carrying something forth, or out," e.g., a garment, Luke 15:22; sick folk, Acts 5:15; a corpse, Acts 5:6; 9–10; of the impossibility of "carrying" anything out from this world at death, 1 Tim. 6:7.

5. ***periphero*** (*4064*), No. 2, with ***peri***, "about," signifies "to carry about, or bear about," and is used literally, of carrying the sick Mark 6:55, or of physical sufferings endured in fellowship with Christ, 2 Cor. 4:10; metaphorically, of being "carried" about by different evil doctrines, Eph. 4:14; Heb. 13:9; Jude 12.

6. ***hupophero*** (*5297*), lit., "to bear up under," is best rendered by "endure," as 1 Cor. 10:13, RV, of enduring temptations; of "enduring" persecutions, 2 Tim. 3; grief, 1 Pet. 2:19.

7. ***phoreo*** (*5409*), a frequentative form of ***phero***, is to be distinguished from it as denoting, not a simple act of bearing, but a continuous or habitual condition, e.g., of the civil authority in "bearing" the sword as symbolic of execution, Rom. 13:4; of a natural state of bodily existence in this life, spoken of as "the image of the earthy," and the spiritual body of the believer hereafter, "the image of the heavenly," 1 Cor. 15:49, the word "image" denoting the actual form and not a mere similitude.

8. ***tropophoreo*** (*5159*), from ***tropos***, "a manner," and ***phoreo***, "to endure," is found in Acts 13:18, where some ancient authorities have the verb ***trophophoreo***, "He bare them as a nursing father," (from ***trophos***, "a feeder, a nurse," and ***phoreo***, "to carry").

9. ***airo*** (*142*) signifies here (a) "to suspend, to keep in suspense," John 10:24; (b) "to take away what is attached to anything, to remove," as of Christ, in taking (or "bearing," marg.) away the sin of the world, John 1:29

10. ***anechomai*** (*430*) signifies "to hold up against a thing and so to bear with," e.g., Matt. 17:7; 1 Cor. 4:12; 2 Cor. 11:1, 4, 19–20; Heb. 13:22, etc.

11. ***makrothumeo*** (*3114*), "to be long-tempered," is translated "is longsuffering over" in Luke 18:7, RV (KJV, "bear long with").

## BEAST

1. ***zoon*** (*2226*) primarily denotes "a living being" (***zoe***, "life"). The Eng., "animal," is the equivalent, stressing the fact of life as the characteristic feature. In Heb. 13:11 the KJV and the RV translate it "beasts" ("animals" would be quite suitable). In 2 Pet. 2:12 and Jude 10, the KJV has "beasts," the RV "creatures." In the Apocalypse, where the word is found some 20 times, and always of those beings which stand before the throne of God, who give glory and honor and thanks to Him, 4:6, and act in perfect harmony with His counsels, 5:14; 6:1–7, e.g., the word "beasts" is most unsuitable; the RV, "living creatures," should always be used; it gives to ***zoon*** its appropriate significance.

2. ***therion*** (*2342*), to be distinguished from ***zoon***, almost invariably denotes "a wild beast." In Acts 28:4, "venomous beast" is used of the viper which fastened on Paul's hand. ***zoon*** stresses the vital element, ***therion*** the bestial. The idea of a "beast" of prey is not always present. Once, in Heb. 12:20, it is used

of the animals in the camp of Israel, such, e.g., as were appointed for sacrifice.

***therion***, in the sense of wild "beast," is used in the Apocalypse for the two antichristian potentates who are destined to control the affairs of the nations with Satanic power in the closing period of the present era, 11:7; 13:1–18; 14:9, 11; 15:2; 16:2, 10, 13; 17:3–17; 19:19–20; 20:4, 10.

## BEAUTIFUL

1. ***horaios*** (*5611*) describes "that which is seasonable, produced at the right time," as of the prime of life, or the time when anything is at its loveliest and best (from ***hora***, "a season," a period fixed by natural laws and revolutions, and so the best season of the year). It is used of the outward appearance of whited sepulchres in contrast to the corruption within Matt. 23:27; of the Jerusalem gate called "Beautiful," Acts 3:2, 10; of the feet of those that bring glad tidings, Rom. 10:15.

2. ***asteios*** (*791*), connected with ***astu***, "a city," was used primarily "of that which befitted the town, town-bred" (corresponding Eng. words are "polite," "polished," connected with ***polis***, "a town"; cf. "urbane," from Lat., ***urbs***, "a city"). Among Greek writers it is set in contrast to ***agroikos***, "rustic," and ***aischros***, "base," and was used, e.g., of clothing. It is found in the NT only of Moses, Acts 7:20, "(exceeding) fair," lit., "fair (to God)," and Heb. 11:23, "goodly" (KJV, "proper").

## BECKON

1. ***neuo*** (*3506*), lit., "to give a nod, to signify by a nod," is used in John 13:24, of Peter's beckoning to John to ask the Lord of whom He had been speaking; in Acts 24:10, of the intimation given by Felix to Paul to speak.

2. ***dianeuo*** (*1269*), "to express one's meaning by a sign" (No. 1, with ***dia***, "through," used intensively), is said of the act of Zacharias, Luke 1:22.

3. ***kataneuo*** (*2656*), No. 1, with ***kata***, "down," intensive, is used of the fishermen-partners in Luke 5:7, "beckoned."

## BECOME (to be fitting)

### A. Verb.

***prepo*** (*4241*) means "to be conspicuous among a number, to be eminent, distinguished by a thing," hence, "to be becoming, seemly, fit"; 1 Tim. 2:10; Titus 2:1; Heb. 7:26.

### B. Adjective.

***hieroprepes*** (*2412*), from ***hieros***, "sacred," with the adjectival form of ***prepo***, denotes "suited to a sacred character, that which is befitting in persons, actions or things consecrated to God," Titus 2:3.

## BEFIT, BEFITTING

1. ***prepo*** (*4241*) is translated "befit" in Titus 2:1, RV (KJV, "become").

2. ***aneko*** (*433*), primarily, "to have arrived at, reached to, pertained to," came to denote "what is due to a person, one's duty, what is befitting." It is used ethically in the NT; Eph. 5:4, RV, "are (not) befitting," for KJV, "are (not) convenient"; Col. 3:18, concerning the duty of wives towards husbands, RV, "as is fitting," for KJV, "as it is fit." In Philem. 8, the participle is used with the article, signifying "that which is befitting," RV (KJV, "that which is convenient").

## BEG, BEGGAR, BEGGARLY

### A. Verbs.

1. ***epaiteo*** (*1871*), a strengthened form of ***aiteo***, is used in Luke 16:3.

2. ***prosaiteo*** (*4319*), lit., "to ask besides," "to ask earnestly, to importune, continue asking," is said of the blind beggar in John 9:8. In Mark 10:46 and Luke 18:35 certain mss. have this verb; the most authentic have ***prosaites***, "a beggar," a word used in John 9:8.

### B. Adjective.

***ptochos*** (*4434*), an adjective describing "one who crouches and cowers," is used as a noun, "a beggar," Luke 14:13, 21 ("poor"); 16:20, 22; as an adjective, "beggarly" in Gal. 4:9, i.e., poverty-stricken (condition), powerless to enrich, metaphorically descriptive of the religion of the Jews.

## BEGET, BEAR (of begetting), BORN

### A. Verbs.

1. ***gennao*** (*1080*), "to beget," in the passive voice, "to be born," is chiefly used of men or women "begetting" children, Matt. 1:2–16; Luke 1:13, 57. In Gal. 4:24, it is used allegorically, to contrast Jews under bondage to the Law, and spiritual Israel, KJV, "gendereth," RV, "bearing children," to contrast the natural birth of Ishmael and the supernatural birth of Isaac. In Matt. 1:20 it is used of conception. It is used of the act of God in the birth of Christ, Acts 13:33; Heb. 1:5; 5:5, quoted from Psalm 2:7, none of which indicate that Christ became the Son of God at His birth.

It is used metaphorically (a) of the gracious act of God in conferring upon those who believe the nature and disposition of "children," imparting to them spiritual life, John 3:3, 5, 7; 1 John 2:29; 3:9; 4:7; 5:1, 4, 18; (b) of one who by means of preaching the gospel becomes the human instrument in the impartation of spiritual life, 1 Cor. 4:15; Philem. 10; (c) in 2 Pet. 2:12, with reference to the evil men whom the apostle is describing, the RV rightly has "born mere animals"; (d) in the sense of gendering strife, 2 Tim. 2:23.

2. ***anagennao*** (*313*), ***ana***, "again, or from above," with No. 1, is found in 1 Pet. 1:3, 23.

3. ***apokueo*** (*616*), "to give birth to," Jas. 1:18.

4. ***tikto*** (*5088*), "to bring forth," (a) lit. Luke 1:57; John 16:21; Heb. 11:11; Rev. 12:2, 4, or, (b) metaphorically in Jas. 1:15.

**B. Noun.**

***genos*** (*1085*), "a generation, kind, stock," is used in the dative case, with the article, to signify "by race," in Acts 18:2 and 24, RV, for the KJV, "born."

**C. Adjectives.**

1. ***gennetos*** (*1084*), "born" (related to ***gennao***, verb No. 1), is used in Matt. 11:11 and Luke 7:28 in the phrase "born of women," a periphrasis for "men," and suggestive of frailty.

2. ***artigennetos*** (*738*), "newborn" (***arti***, "newly, recently," and No. 1), is used in 1 Pet. 2:2.

## BEGUILE

1. ***apatao*** (*538*), "to deceive," is rendered "beguiled" in the RV of 1 Tim. 2:14.

2. ***exapatao*** (*1818*), a strengthened form of No. 1, is rendered "beguile," 2 Cor. 11:3; the more adequate rendering would be "as the serpent thoroughly beguiled Eve." So in 1 Tim. 2:14, in the best mss., this stronger form is used of Satan's deception of Eve, lit., "thoroughly beguiled"; the simpler verb, No. 1, is used of Adam. In each of these passages the strengthened form is used. So of the influence of sin, Rom. 7:11 (RV, "beguile"); of self-deception, 1 Cor. 3:18 (RV, "deceive"); of evil men who cause divisions, Rom. 16:18 (RV, "beguile"); of deceitful teachers, 2 Thess. 2:3 (RV, "beguile").

3. ***paralogizomai*** (*3884*), lit. and primarily, "to reckon wrong," hence means "to reason falsely." Col. 2:4; Jas. 1:22.

4. ***deleazo*** (*1185*) originally meant "to catch by a bait" (from ***delear***, "a bait"); hence "to beguile, entice by blandishments": in Jas. 1:14, "entice"; in 2 Pet. 2:14, KJV, "beguile"; in v. 18, KJV, "allure"; RV, "entice" in both.

## BEHAVE, BEHAVIOR

**A. Verb.**

***anastrepho*** (*390*), "to turn back, return" (***ana***, "back," ***strepho***, "to turn"), hence, "to move about in a place, to sojourn," and, in the middle and passive voices, "to conduct oneself," indicating one's manner of life and character; 1 Tim. 3:15; Eph. 2:3; 2 Cor. 1:12.

**B. Noun.**

***anastrophe*** (*391*), lit., "a turning back" (cf. Verb, above), is translated "manner of life," "living," etc. in the RV, for KJV, "conversation," Gal. 1:13; Eph. 4:22; 1 Tim. 4:12; Heb. 13:7; Jas. 3:13; 1 Pet. 1:15, 18; 2:1 ("behavior"); 3:1, 2, 16 (ditto); 2 Pet. 2:7; 3:11.

**C. Adjective.**

***kosmios*** (*2887*), "orderly, modest," is translated "orderly" in 1 Tim. 3:2, RV, for KJV, "of good behavior." Both have "modest" in 1 Tim. 2:9.

## BEHOLD, BEHELD

1. ***horao*** (*3708*), with its aorist form ***eidon***, "to see" (in a few places the KJV uses the verb "to behold"), is said (a) of bodily vision, e.g., Mark 6:38; John 1:18, 46; (b) of mental perception, e.g., Rom. 15:21; Col. 2:18; (c) of taking heed, e.g., Matt. 8:4; 1 Thess. 5:15; (d) of experience, as of death, Luke 2:26; Heb. 11:5; life, John 3:36; corruption, Acts 2:27; (e) of caring for, Matt. 27:4; Acts 18:15 (here the form ***opsomai*** is used).

2. ***blepo*** (*991*) is also used of (a) bodily and (b) mental vision, (a) "to perceive," e.g., Matt. 13:13; (b) "to take heed," e.g., Mark 13:23, 33; it indicates greater vividness than ***horao***, expressing a more intent, earnest contemplation; in Luke 6:41, of "beholding" the mote in a brother's eye; Luke 24:12, of "beholding" the linen clothes in the empty tomb; Acts 1:9, of the gaze of the disciples when the Lord ascended. The greater earnestness is sometimes brought out by the rendering "regardest," Matt. 22:16.

3. ***emblepo*** (*1689*), from ***en***, "in" (intensive), and No. 2, (not to be rendered literally), expresses "earnest looking," e.g., in the Lord's command to "behold" the birds of the heaven, with the object of learning lessons of faith from them, Matt. 6:26. See also 19:26; Mark 8:25; 10:21, 27; 14:67; Luke 20:17; 22:61; John 1:36; of the Lord's looking upon Peter, John 1:42; Acts 1:11; 22:11.

4. ***ide*** and ***idou*** (*2396* and *2400*) are imperative moods, active and middle voices, respectively, of ***eidon***, "to see," calling attention to what may be seen or heard or mentally apprehended in any way. These are regularly rendered "behold." See especially the Gospels, Acts and the Apocalypse.

5. ***epide*** (*1896***), a strengthened form of No. 4 (with ***epi***, "upon," prefixed), is used in Acts 4:29 of the entreaty made to the Lord to "behold" the threatenings of persecutors.

6. ***theoreo*** (*2334*), from ***theoros***, "a spectator," is used of one who looks at a thing with interest and for a purpose, usually indicating the careful observation of details; this marks the distinction from No. 2; see, e.g., Mark 15:47; Luke 10:18; 23:35; John 20:6 (RV, "beholdeth," for KJV, "seeth"); so in verses 12 and 14; "consider," in Heb. 7:4. It is used of experience, in the sense of partaking of, in John 8:51; 17:24.

7. ***anatheoreo*** (*333*), ***ana***, "up" (intensive), and No. 6, "to view with interest, consider contemplatively," is translated "beheld," in Acts 17:23, RV, "observed"; "considering" in Heb. 13:7.

8. ***theaomai*** (*2300*), "to behold, view attentively, contemplate," had, in earlier Greek usage, the sense of a wondering regard. This idea was gradually lost. It signifies a more earnest contemplation than the ordinary verbs for "to see," "a careful and deliberate vision which interprets its object," and is more frequently rendered "behold" in the RV than the KJV. Both translate it by "behold" in Luke 23:55 (of the sepulchre); "we beheld," in John 1:14, of the glory of the Son of God; "beheld," RV, in John 1:32; Acts 1:11; 1 John 1:1 (more than merely seeing); 4:12, 14.

9. ***atenizo*** (*816*) from ***atenes***, "strained, intent," denotes "to gaze upon," "beholding earnestly," or "steadfastly" in Acts 14:9; 23:1.

10. ***katanoeo*** (*2657*), a strengthened form of ***noeo***, "to perceive," (***kata***, intensive), denotes "the action of the mind in apprehending certain facts about a thing"; hence, "to consider"; "behold," Acts 7:31–32; Jas. 1:23–24.

11. ***katoptrizo*** (*2734*), from ***katoptron***, "a mirror," in the active voice, signifies "to make to reflect, to mirror"; in the middle voice "to reflect as a mirror"; so the RV in 2 Cor. 3:18, for KJV, "beholding as in a glass."

## BELIAL

***belial*** (*955*) came to be a proper name for Satan. There may be an indication of this in Nahum 1:15, where the word translated "the wicked one" is *Belial*.

The oldest form of the word is "Beliar," possibly from a phrase signifying "Lord of the forest," or perhaps simply a corruption of the form "Belial," due to harsh Syriac pronunciation. In the NT, in 2 Cor. 6:15, it is set in contrast to Christ and represents a personification of the system of impure worship connected especially with the cult of Aphrodite.

## BELIEF, BELIEVE, BELIEVERS

B

### *Old Testament*

### A. Verb.

***'aman*** (539), "to be firm, endure, be faithful, be true, stand fast, trust, have belief, believe." In the passive stem, ***'aman*** has several emphases. First, it indicates that a subject is "lasting" or "enduring," which is its meaning in Deut. 28:59. It also signifies the element of being "firm" or "trustworthy." In Isa. 22:23, ***'aman*** refers to a "firm" place, a place into which a peg will be driven so that it will be immovable. The peg will remain firmly anchored, even though it is pushed so hard that it breaks off at the point of entry, Isa. 22:25. The Bible also speaks of "faithful" people who fulfill their obligations, cf. 1 Sam. 22:14; Prov. 25:13.

The meaning "trustworthy" also occurs, Prov. 11:13; cf. Isa. 8:2. An office-bearer may be conceived as an "entrusted one," Job 12:20

In Gen. 42:20 Joseph requests that his brothers bring Benjamin to him; "so shall your words be verified," cf. 1 Kings 8:26; Hos. 5:9. In Hos. 11:12, ***'aman*** contrasts Judah's actions ("faithful") with those of Ephraim and Israel ("deceit"). So here ***'aman*** represents both "truthfulness" and "faithfulness," cf. Ps. 78:37; Jer. 15:18. The word may be rendered "true" in several passages, 1 Kings 8:26; 2 Chron. 1:9; 6:17.

***'aman*** refers to what God has done ("faithfulness"), rather than what He will do ("trustworthy"), because He has already proved Himself faithful by keeping the covenant, Deut. 7:9.

Even more often, this stem connotes a psychological or mental certainty, as in Job 29:24. Considering something to be trustworthy is an act of full trusting or believing. This is the emphasis in the first biblical occurrence of ***'aman***, Gen. 15:6. The meaning here is that Abram was full of trust and confidence in God, and that he did not fear Him (v. 1). It was not primarily in God's words that he believed, but in God Himself. Nor does the text tell us that Abram believed God so as to accept what He said as "true" and "trustworthy," cf. Gen. 45:26, but simply that he believed in God. In other words, Abram came to experience a personal relationship to God rather than an impersonal relationship with His promises, Exod. 4:9.

A more precise sense of ***'aman*** does appear sometimes: "That they may believe that the Lord . . . hath appeared unto thee," Exod. 4:5; cf. 1 Kings 10:7.

In other instances, ***'aman*** has a cultic use, by which the worshiping community affirms its identity with what the worship leader says, 1 Chron. 16:32. The "God of the ***'amen***," 2 Chron. 20:20; Isa. 65:16, is the God who always accomplishes what He says; He is a "God who is faithful."

## B. Noun.

***'emunah*** (530), "firmness; faithfulness; truth; honesty; official obligation," Exod. 17:12; Isa. 33:6: 1 Chron. 9:22. The most frequent sense of ***'emunah*** is "faithfulness," 1 Sam. 26:23.

The essential meaning of ***'emunah*** is "established" or "lasting," "continuing," "certain," cf. 2 Sam. 7:16; Isa. 16:5. Thus, the phrase frequently rendered "with lovingkindness and truth" should be rendered "with perpetual (faithful) lovingkindness," cf. Josh. 2:14. He who sows righteousness earns a "true" or "lasting" reward, Prov. 11:18, a reward on which he can rely.

Quite often, this word means "truthfulness," as when it is contrasted to false swearing, lying, Jer. 5:1; cf. Jer. 5:2. Here ***'emunah*** signifies the condition of being faithful to God's covenant, practicing truth, or doing righteousness. On the other hand, the word can represent the abstract idea of "truth," Jer. 7:28. ***'emunah*** means "true"—the personal sense, which identifies a subject as honest, trustworthy, faithful, truthful (Prov. 12:22); and the factual sense, which identifies a subject as being factually true (cf. Prov. 12:27), as opposed to that which is false.

In other contexts, ***'emunah*** embraces other aspects of the concept of truth, Ps. 98:3. Here the emphasis is on truth as a subjective quality, defined personally. In a similar sense, one can both practice, Gen. 47:29, and speak the "truth," 2 Sam. 7:28.

## C. Adverb.

***'amen*** (543), "truly; genuinely; amen; so be it." The term ***'amen*** is used 30 times as an adverb. This Hebrew word usually appears as a response to a curse that has been pronounced upon someone, as the one accursed accepts the curse upon himself. By so doing, he binds himself to fulfill certain conditions or else be subject to the terms of the curse, cf. Deut. 29:15–26.

Although signifying a voluntary acceptance of the conditions of a covenant, the ***'amen*** was sometimes pronounced with coercion. Even in these circumstances, the one who did not pronounce it received the punishment embodied in the curse, Num. 5:22; Neh. 5:1–13; Jer. 18:6.

In 1 Kings 1:36, ***'amen*** is noncovenantal. It functions as an assertion of a person's agreement with the intent of a speech just delivered.

### *New Testament*

## A. Verb.

***pisteuo*** (*4100*), "to believe," also "to be persuaded of," and hence, "to place confidence in, to trust," signifies, in this sense of the word, reliance upon, not mere credence. It is most frequent in the writings of the apostle John, especially the Gospel. He does not use the noun (see below). For the Lord's first use of the verb, see 1:50. Of the writers of the Gospels, Matthew uses the verb ten times, Mark ten, Luke nine, John ninety-nine. In Acts 5:14 the present participle of the verb is translated "believers."

## B. Noun.

***pistis*** (*4102*), "faith," is translated "belief" in Rom. 10:17; 2 Thess. 2:13. Its chief significance is a conviction respecting God and His Word and the believer's relationship to Him.

## C. Adjective.

***pistos*** (*4103*), (a) in the active sense means "believing, trusting"; (b) in the passive sense, "trusty, faithful, trustworthy." It is translated "believer" in 2 Cor. 6:15; "them that believe" in 1 Tim. 4:12, RV (KJV, "believers"); in 1 Tim. 5:16, "if any woman that believeth," lit. "if any believing woman." So in 6:2, "believing masters." In 1 Pet. 1:21 the RV, following the most authentic mss., gives the noun form, "are believers in God" (KJV, "do believe in God"). In John 20:27 it is translated "believing." It is best understood with significance (a), above, e.g., in Gal. 3:9; Acts 16:1; 2 Cor. 6:15; Titus 1:6; it has significance (b), e.g., in 1 Thess. 5:24; 2 Thess. 3:3.

*Notes:* (1) The corresponding negative verb is ***apisteo***, 2 Tim. 2:13, KJV, "believe not" RV, "are faithless," in contrast to the statement "He abideth faithful."

(2) The negative noun ***apistia***, "unbelief," is used twice in Matthew (13:58); 17:20), three times in Mark (6:6; 9:24; 16:14), four times in Romans (3:3; 4:20; 11:20, 23); elsewhere in 1 Tim. 1:13 and Heb. 3:12, 19.

(3) The adjective ***apistos*** is translated "unbelievers" in 1 Cor. 6:6, and 2 Cor. 6:14; in v. 15, RV, "unbeliever" (KJV, "infidel"); so in 1 Tim. 5:8; "unbelieving" in 1 Cor. 7:12–15; 14:22–24; 2 Cor. 4:4; Titus 1:15; Rev. 21:8; "that believe not" in 1 Cor. 10:27. In the Gospels it is translated "faithless" in Matt. 17:17; Mark 9:19; Luke 9:41; John 20:27, but in Luke 12:46, RV,

"unfaithful," KJV, "unbelievers." Once it is translated "incredible," Acts 26:8.

(4) ***plerophoreo***, in Luke 1:1 (KJV, "are most surely believed," lit., "have had full course"), the RV renders "have been fulfilled."

## BELLY

1. ***koilia*** (*2836*), from ***koilos***, "hollow" (Lat., ***coelum***, "heaven," is connected), denotes the entire physical cavity, but most frequently was used to denote "the womb." In John 7:38 it stands metaphorically for the innermost part of man, the soul, the heart.

2. ***gaster*** (*1064*), (cf. Eng., "gastritis"), is used much as No. 1, but in Titus 1:12, by synecdoche (a figure of speech in which the part is put for the whole, or vice versa), it is used to denote "gluttons," RV, for KJV, "bellies."

## BELOVED

**A. Adjective.**

***agapetos*** (*27*), from ***agapao***, "to love," is used of Christ as loved by God, e.g., Matt. 3:17; of believers (ditto), e.g., Rom. 1:7; of believers, one of another, 1 Cor. 4:14; often, as a form of address, e.g., 1 Cor. 10:14. Whenever the KJV has "dearly beloved," the RV has "beloved"; so, "well beloved" in 3 John 1; in 1 John 2:7, KJV, "brethren" (***adelphos***), the RV has "beloved," according to the mss. which have ***agapetos***.

**B. Verb.**

***agapao*** (*25*), in its perfect participle passive form, is translated "beloved" in Rom. 9:25; Eph. 1:6; Col. 3:12; 1 Thess. 1:4; 2 Thess. 2:13. In Jude 1 the best texts have this verb (RV); the KJV, "sanctified" follows those which have ***hagiazo***.

## BENEFIT, BENEFACTOR

1. ***euergesia*** (*2108*), lit., "good work" (***eu***, "well," ***ergon***, "work"), is found in Acts 4:9, "good deed," and 1 Tim. 6:2, "benefit."

2. ***euergetes*** (*2110*), "a benefactor," expresses the agent, Luke 22:25.

3. ***charis*** (*5485*), "grace," is once rendered "benefit," 2 Cor. 1:15; it stresses the character of the "benefit," as the effect of the gracious disposition of the benefactor.

4. ***agathon*** (*18*), the neuter of ***agathos***, used as a noun in Philem. 14, is translated "benefit," KJV; RV, "goodness."

## BENEVOLENCE

***eunoia*** (*2133*), "good will" (***eu***, "well," ***nous***, "the mind"), is rendered "benevolence" in 1 Cor. 7:3, KJV. The RV, following the texts which have ***opheilen*** ("due"), has "her due," a more comprehensive expression; in Eph. 6:7, "good will."

## BEREAVED, BEREFT

1. ***aporphanizomai*** (*642*), lit., "to be rendered an orphan" (***apo***, "from," with the thought of separation, and ***orphanos***, "an orphan"), is used metaphorically in 1 Thess. 2:17 (KJV, "taken from"; RV, "bereaved"), in the sense of being "bereft" of the company of the saints through being compelled to leave them (cf. the similes in 7 and 11). The word has a wider meaning than that of being an orphan.

2. ***apostereo*** (*650*), "to rob, defraud, deprive," is used in 1 Tim. 6:5, in the passive voice, of being deprived or "bereft" (of the truth), with reference to false teachers (KJV, destitute).

## BESET

***euperistatos*** (*2139*), used in Heb. 12:1, and translated "which doth so easily beset," lit. signifies "standing well (i.e., easily) around," "standing," i.e., easily encompassing. It describes sin as having advantage in favor of its prevailing.

## BESIDE ONESELF (to be)

1. ***existemi*** (*1839*), primarily and lit. means "to put out of position, displace": hence, (a) "to amaze," Luke 24:22 (for KJV, "make . . . astonished"); Acts 8:9, 11 (KJV, "bewitched"); or "to be amazed, astounded," Matt. 12:23; Mark 6:51; (b) "to be out of one's mind, to be beside oneself," Mark 3:21; 2 Cor. 5:13, in the latter of which it is contrasted with ***sophroneo***, "to be of a sound mind, sober."

2. ***mainomai*** (*3105*), "to be mad, to rave," is said of one who so speaks that he appears to be out of his mind, Acts 26:24, translated "thou art beside thyself," KJV; RV, "thou art mad." In v. 25; John 10:20; Acts 12:15; 1 Cor. 14:23, both versions use the verb to be mad.

## BEST

1. ***protos*** (*4413*) is one of two words translated "best" in the KJV, but the only one so rendered in the RV. In Luke 15:22 "the best (robe)" is, lit., "the first (robe)," i.e., chief, principal, first in rank or quality.

2. ***meizon*** (*3187*), "greater," is translated "best" in 1 Cor. 12:31, "the best gifts," greater, not in quality, but in importance and value. It is the comparative degree of ***megas***, "great"; the superlative, ***megistos***, is used only in 2 Pet. 1:4.

## BETRAY, BETRAYER

**A. Verb.**

***paradidomi*** (*3860*), "to betray," lit., "to give over," is used either (a) in the sense of delivering a person or thing to be kept by another, to commend, e.g., Acts 28:16; (b) to deliver to prison or judgment, e.g., Matt. 4:12; 1 Tim. 1:20; (c) to deliver over treacherously by way of "betrayal," Matt. 17:22 (RV, "delivered"); 26:16; John 6:64 etc.; (d) to hand on, deliver, e.g., 1 Cor. 11:23; (e) to allow of something being done, said of the ripening of fruit, Mark 4:29, RV, "is ripe" (marg., "alloweth").

**B. Noun.**

***prodotes*** (*4273*), "a betrayer" (akin to A), is translated "betrayers" in Acts 7:52; "traitor," "traitors," in Luke 6:16 and 2 Tim. 3:4.

## BETTER

1. ***kreisson*** (*2909*), from ***kratos***, "strong" (which denotes power in activity and effect), serves as the comparative degree of ***agathos***, "good" (good or fair, intrinsically). ***kreisson*** is especially characteristic of the Epistle to the Hebrews, where it is used 12 times; it indicates what is (a) advantageous or useful, 1 Cor. 7:9, 38; 11:17; Heb. 11:40; 12:24; 2 Pet. 2:21; Phil. 1:23, where it is coupled with ***mallon***, "more," and ***pollo***, "much, by far," "very far better" (RV); (b) excellent, Heb. 1:4; 6:9; 7:7, 19, 22; 8:6; 9:23; 10:34; 11:16, 35.

2. ***kalon mallon***, the neuter of ***kalos***, with ***mallon***, "more," is used in Mark 9:42, "it were better (lit., 'much better') for him if a great millstone were hanged about his neck." In verses 43, 45, 47, ***kalos*** is used alone (RV, "good," for KJV, "better").

## BEWAIL

1. ***klaio*** (*2799*), "to wail," whether with tears or any external expression of grief, is regularly translated "weep" in the RV; once in the KJV it is rendered "bewail," Rev. 18:9.

2. ***kopto*** (*2875*), primarily, "to beat, smite"; then, "to cut off," Matt. 21:8; Mark 11:8, is used in the middle voice, of beating oneself, beating the breast, as a token of grief; hence, "to bewail," Matt. 11:17 (RV, "mourn," for KJV, "lament"); 24:30, "mourn"; Rev. 1:7 (RV, "mourn"; KJV, "wail"); in Luke 8:52; 23:27 "bewail"; in Rev. 18:9, "wail" (for KJV, "lament").

3. ***pentheo*** (*3996*) denotes "to lament, mourn," especially for the dead; in 2 Cor. 12:21, RV, "mourn" (KJV, "bewail"). See also Rev. 18:11, 15, 19.

## BEWARE

1. ***blepo*** (*991*), "to see," is applied to mental vision, and is sometimes used by way of warning "to take heed" against an object, Mark 8:15; 12:38; Acts 13:40; Phil. 3:2 (three times); in Col. 2:8, RV, "take heed."

2. ***prosecho*** (*4337*), lit., "to hold to" (***pros***, "to," ***echo***, "to have, to hold"), hence, "to turn one's mind or attention to a thing by being on one's guard against it," is translated "beware" in Matt. 7:15; 10:17; 16:6, 11–12; Luke 12:1; 20:46.

3. ***phulasso*** (*5442*), "to guard, watch, keep," is used, in the middle voice, of being "on one's guard against" (the middle v. stressing personal interest in the action), Luke 12:15, "beware of," RV, "keep yourselves from," as in Acts 21:25; in 2 Tim. 4:15, "be thou ware"; in 2 Pet. 3:17, "beware."

## BEWITCH

1. ***baskaino*** (*940*), primarily, "to slander, to prate about anyone"; then "to bring evil on a person by feigned praise, or mislead by an evil eye, and so to charm, bewitch" (Eng., "fascinate" is connected), is used figuratively in Gal. 3:1, of leading into evil doctrine.

2. ***existemi*** (*1839*) is rendered "bewitch" in Acts 8:9, 11, KJV, concerning Simon the sorcerer; it does not mean "to bewitch," as in the case of the preceding verb, but "to confuse, amaze" (RV).

## BILL

1. ***biblion*** (*975*), primarily "a small book, a scroll, or any sheet on which something has been written"; hence, in connection with ***apostasion***, "divorce," signifies "a bill of divorcement," Matt. 19:7 (KJV, "writing"); Mark 10:4.

2. ***gramma*** (*1121*), from ***grapho***, "to write" (Eng., "graph, graphic," etc.), in Luke 16:6, KJV, is translated "bill." It lit. signifies that which is drawn, a picture; hence, a written document; hence, a "bill," or bond, or note of hand, showing the amount of indebtedness.

## BIND, BINDING

### *Old Testament*

***'asar*** (631), "to bind, imprison, tie, gird, to harness," Gen. 39:20. The common word for "tying up" for security and safety, ***'asar*** is often used to indicate the tying up of horses and donkeys, 2 Kings 7:10. Similarly, oxen are "harnessed" to carts, 1 Sam. 6:7, 10. Frequently, ***'asar*** is used to describe the "binding" of prisoners with cords and various fetters, Gen. 42:24; Judg. 15:10, 12–13. Samson misled Delilah as she probed for the secret of his strength, telling her to "bind" him with bowstrings, Judg. 16:7, and new ropes, Judg. 16:11, none of which could hold him.

Used in an abstract sense, ***'asar*** refers to those who are spiritually "bound," Ps. 146:7; Isa. 49:9; 61:1 or a man who is emotionally "captivated" by a woman's hair, Song of Sol.

7:5. Only in Num. 30 does it refer to the binding of an oath.

### *New Testament*

1. ***deo*** (*1210*), "to bind," is used (a) literally, of any sort of "binding," Acts 22:5; 24:27; (b) figuratively, of the Word of God, as not being "bound," 2 Tim. 2:9; Paul speaks of himself, in Acts 20:22, as being "bound in the spirit," i.e. compelled by his convictions, under the constraining power of the Spirit of God, to go to Jerusalem. A wife is said to be "bound" to her husband, Rom. 7:2; 1 Cor. 7:39; and the husband to the wife, 1 Cor. 7:27. The Lord's words to the apostle Peter in Matt. 16:19, as to "binding," and to all the disciples in 18:18.

2. ***perideo*** (*4019*), ***peri***, "around," with No. 1, "to bind around," is used in John 11:44 of the napkin around the face of Lazarus.

3. ***hupodeo*** (*5265*), ***hupo***, "under," with No. 1, "to bind underneath," is used of binding of sandals, Acts 12:8; rendered "shod" in Mark 6:9 and Eph. 6:15.

4. ***katadeo*** (*2611*), ***kata***, "down," with No. 1, "to bind or tie down, or bind up," is used in Luke 10:34 of the act of the good Samaritan.

5. ***sundeo*** (*4887*), ***sun***, "together," and No. 1, "to bind together," implying association, is used in Heb. 13:3 of those bound together in confinement.

6. ***desmeuo*** or ***desmeo*** (*1195*) signifies "to put in fetters or any kind of bond," Luke 8:29; Acts 22:4, or "to bind a burden upon a person," Matt. 23:4. The verb is connected with No. 1.

## BIRTHRIGHT

***prototokia*** (*4415*), a birthright" (from ***protos***, "first," ***tikto***, "to beget"), is found in Heb. 12:16, with reference to Esau. The "birthright" involved preeminence and authority, Gen. 27:29; 49:3. Another right was that of the double portion, Deut. 21:17; 1 Chron. 5:1–2. Connected with the "birthright" was the progenitorship of the Messiah. Esau transferred his "birthright" to Jacob for a paltry mess of pottage, profanely despising this last spiritual privilege, Gen. 25 and 27. In the history of the nation God occasionally set aside the "birthright," to show that the objects of His choice depended not on the will of the flesh, but on His own authority. Thus Isaac was preferred to Ishmael, Jacob to Esau, Joseph to Reuben, David to his elder brethren, Solomon to Adonijah.

## BISHOP (Overseer)

1. ***episkopos*** (*1985*), lit., "an overseer," whence Eng. "bishop," which has precisely the same meaning, is found in Acts 20:28; Phil. 1:1; 1 Tim. 3:2; Titus 1:7; 1 Pet. 2:25.

2. ***episkope*** (*1984*), besides its meaning, "visitation," e.g., 1 Pet. 2:12, is rendered "office," in Acts 1:20, RV (KJV, "bishoprick"); in 1 Tim. 3:1 "the office of a bishop," lit., "(if any one seeketh) overseership," there is no word representing office.

## BITTER, BITTERLY, BITTERNESS

### A. Adjective.

***pikros*** (*4089*), from a root ***pik***–, meaning "to cut, to prick," hence, lit., "pointed, sharp, keen, pungent to the sense of taste, smell, etc.," is found in Jas. 3:11, 14. In v. 11 it has its natural sense, with reference to water; in v. 14 it is used metaphorically of jealousy, RV.

### B. Verb.

***pikraino*** (*4087*), related to A, signifies, in the active voice, "to be bitter," Col. 3:19, or "to embitter, irritate, or to make bitter," Rev. 10:9; the passive voice, "to be made bitter," is used in Rev. 8:11; 10:10.

### C. Noun.

***pikria*** (*4088*) denotes "bitterness." It is used in Acts 8:23, metaphorically, of a condition of extreme wickedness, "gall of bitterness" or "bitter gall"; in Rom. 3:14, of evil speaking; in Eph. 4:31, of "bitter" hatred; in Heb. 12:15, in the same sense, metaphorically, of a root of "bitterness," producing "bitter" fruit.

### D. Adverb.

***pikros*** (*4090*), "bitterly," is used of the poignant grief of Peter's weeping for his denial of Christ, Matt. 26:75; Luke 22:62.

## BLACK, BLACKNESS

1. ***gnophos*** (*1105*), Heb. 12:18, "blackness, gloom," seems to have been associated with the idea of a tempest. It is related to ***skotos***, "darkness."

2. ***zophos*** (*2217*), akin to No. 1, especially "the gloom of the regions of the lost," is used four times; 2 Pet. 2:4, "darkness" (RV); 2:17, RV, "blackness," for KJV, "mist"; Jude 6, "darkness"; v. 13, "blackness," suggesting a kind of emanation.

## BLAME, BLAMELESS

### A. Verb.

***momaomai*** (*3469*), "to find fault with, to blame, or calumniate," is used in 2 Cor. 6:3, of the ministry of the gospel; in 8:20, of the ministration of financial help.

**B. Adjectives.**

1. ***amomos*** *(299)*: See BLEMISH, B.

2. ***amometos*** *(298)*, translated in Phil. 2:15 "without blemish" (KJV, "without rebuke"), is rendered "blameless" in 2 Pet. 3:14 (KJV and RV).

3. ***amemptos*** *(273)*, is translated "unblameable" in 1 Thess. 3:13; "blameless," in Luke 1:6; Phil. 2:15; 3:6; "faultless" in Heb. 8:7.

**C. Adverb.**

***amemptos*** *(274)*, in 1 Thess. 2:10, "unblameably"; in 5:23, "without blame," KJV, "blameless," is said of believers at the judgment-seat of Christ in His Parousia (His presence after His coming), as the outcome of present witness and steadfastness.

## BLASPHEME, BLASPHEMY, BLASPHEMER, BLASPHEMOUS

**A. Noun.**

***blasphemia*** *(988)*, either from ***blax***, "sluggish, stupid," or, probably, from ***blapto***, "to injure," and ***pheme***, "speech," (Eng. "blasphemy") is so translated thirteen times in the RV, but "railing" in Matt. 15:19; Mark 7:22; Eph. 4:31; Col. 3:8; 1 Tim. 6:4; Jude 9. The word "blasphemy" is practically confined to speech defamatory of the Divine Majesty.

**B. Verb.**

***blasphemeo*** *(987)*, "to blaspheme, rail at or revile," is used (a) in a general way, of any contumelious speech, reviling, calumniating, railing at, etc., as of those who railed at Christ, e.g., Matt. 27:39; Mark 15:29; Luke 22:65 (RV, "reviling"); 23:39; (b) of those who speak contemptuously of God or of sacred things, e.g., Matt. 9:3; Mark 3:28; Rom. 2:24; 1 Tim. 1:20; 6:1; Rev. 13:6; 16:9, 11, 21; "hath spoken blasphemy," Matt. 26:65; "rail at," 2 Pet. 2:10; Jude 8, 10; "railing," 2 Pet. 2:12; "slanderously reported," Rom. 3:8; "be evil spoken of," Rom. 14:16; 1 Cor. 10:30; 2 Pet. 2:2; "speak evil of," Titus 3:2; 1 Pet. 4:4; "being defamed," 1 Cor. 4:13. The verb (in the present participial form) is translated "blasphemers" in Acts 19:37; in Mark 2:7, "blasphemeth," RV, for KJV, "speaketh blasphemies."

There is no noun in the original representing the English "blasphemer." This is expressed either by the verb, or by the adjective ***blasphemos***.

**C. Adjective.**

***blasphemos*** *(989)*, "abusive, speaking evil," is translated "blasphemous," in Acts 6:11, 13; "a blasphemer," 1 Tim. 1:13; "railers," 2 Tim. 3:2, RV; "railing," 2 Pet. 2:11.

## BLEMISH

**A. Noun.**

***momos*** *(3470)*, akin to ***momaomai***, signifies "a shame, a moral disgrace," metaphorical of the licentious, 2 Pet. 2:13.

**B. Adjective.**

***amomos*** *(299)*, "without blemish"; is always so rendered in the RV, Eph. 1:4; 5:27; Phil. 2:15; Col. 1:22; Heb. 9:14; 1 Pet. 1:19; Jude 24; Rev. 14:5.

## BLESS, BLESSED, BLESSEDNESS, BLESSING

### *Old Testament*

**A. Verb.**

***barak*** (1288), "to kneel, bless, be blessed, curse." ***barak*** occurs about 330 times in the Bible, first in Gen. 1:22, when God blesses creation. ***barak*** is used again of man, Gen. 5:2; Gen. 9:1; Gen. 12:2–3. The covenant promise called the nations to seek the "blessing," cf. Isa. 2:2–4, but made it plain that the initiative in blessing rests with God, and that Abraham and his seed were the instruments of it, Num. 6:23–27. The passive form of ***barak*** is used in pronouncing God's "blessing on men," Gen. 14:19; 9:26; 14:20. ***barak*** was also a common form of greeting, 1 Sam. 13:10.

**B. Nouns.**

***berakah*** (1293), "blessing," used in conjunction with the verb ***barak***, Gen. 12:2. When expressed by men, a "blessing" was a wish or prayer for favorable circumstance, Gen. 28:4. Patriarchs customarily extended this wish or prayer upon their children before they died: Jacob's, Gen. 49; Moses', Deut. 33:1ff. Blessing was the opposite of a cursing (***qelalah***), Gen. 27:12; 33:11; Neh. 9:5.

The Lord's "blessing" rests on those who are faithful to Him, Deut. 11:27. His blessing brings righteousness, Ps. 24:5, life, Ps. 133:3, prosperity, 2 Sam. 7:29, and salvation, Ps. 3:8. The "blessing" is portrayed as a rain or dew, Ezek. 34:26; cf. Ps. 84:6. In the fellowship of the saints, the Lord commands His "blessing," Ps. 133:3. In a few cases, the Lord made people to be a "blessing" to others. Abraham is a blessing to the nations, Gen. 12:2. His descendants are expected to become a blessing to the nations, Isa. 19:24; Zech. 8:13.

***'asher*** (835), "blessed; happy," mostly in Psalms and Proverbs. Basically, this word connotes the state of "prosperity" or "happiness" that comes when a superior bestows his favor (blessing) on one. In most passages, the one bestowing favor is God Himself, Deut. 33:29;

Job 5:17–18; 5:22. A human can call another blessed, 1 Kings 10:8.

*New Testament*

**A. Verbs.**

1. ***eulogeo*** (*2127*), lit., "to speak well of," signifies, (a) "to praise, to celebrate with praises," of that which is addressed to God, acknowledging His goodness, with desire for His glory, Luke 1:64; 2:28; 24:51, 53; Jas. 3:9; (b) "to invoke blessings upon a person," e.g., Luke 6:28; Rom. 12:14. The present participle passive, "blessed, praised," is especially used of Christ in Matt. 21:9; 23:39, and the parallel passages; also in John 12:13; (c) "to consecrate a thing with solemn prayers, to ask God's blessing on a thing," e.g., Luke 9:16; 1 Cor. 10:16; (d) "to cause to prosper, to make happy, to bestow blessings on," said of God, e.g., in Acts 3:26; Gal. 3:9; Eph. 1:3.

2. ***eneulogeomai*** (*1757*), "to bless," is used in the passive voice, Acts 3:25, and Gal. 3:8. The prefix ***en*** apparently indicates the person on whom the blessing is conferred.

3. ***makarizo*** (*3106*), from a root ***mak***–, meaning "large, lengthy," found also in ***makros***, "long," ***mekos***, "length," hence denotes "to pronounce happy, blessed," Luke 1:48 and Jas. 5:11.

**B. Adjectives.**

1. ***eulogetos*** (*2128*), akin to A, 1, means "blessed, praised"; it is applied only to God, Mark 14:61; Luke 1:68; Rom. 1:25; 9:5; 2 Cor. 1:3; 11:31; Eph. 1:3; 1 Pet. 1:3.

2. ***makarios*** (*3107*), akin to A, No. 3, is used in the beatitudes in Matt. 5 and Luke 6, is especially frequent in the Gospel of Luke, and is found seven times in Revelation, 1:3; 14:13; 16:15; 19:9; 20:6; 22:7, 14. It is said of God twice, 1 Tim. 1:11; 6:15. In the beatitudes the Lord indicates not only the characters that are "blessed," but the nature of that which is the highest good.

**C. Nouns.**

1. ***eulogia*** (*2129*), akin to A, 1, lit., "good speaking, praise," is used of (a) God and Christ, Rev. 5:12–13; 7:12; (b) the invocation of blessings, benediction, Heb. 12:17; Jas. 3:10; (c) the giving of thanks, 1 Cor. 10:16; (d) a blessing, a benefit bestowed, Rom. 15:29; Gal. 3:14; Eph. 1:3; Heb. 6:7; of a monetary gift sent to needy believers, 2 Cor. 9:5–6; (e) in a bad sense, of fair speech, Rom. 16:18, RV, where it is joined with ***chrestologia***, "smooth speech," the latter relating to the substance, ***eulogia*** to the expression.

2. ***makarismos*** (*3109*), akin to A, 3, "blessedness," indicates an ascription of blessing rather than a state; hence in Rom. 4:6, where the KJV renders it as a noun, "(describeth) the blessedness"; the RV rightly puts "(pronounceth) blessing." So v. 9. In Gal. 4:15 the KJV has "blessedness," RV, "gratulation." The Galatian believers had counted themselves happy when they heard and received the gospel. Had they lost that opinion?

## BLIND, BLINDNESS

**A. Verbs.**

1. ***tuphloo*** (*5186*), "to blind," from a root ***tuph***–, "to burn, smoke"; is used metaphorically, of the dulling of the intellect, John 12:40; 2 Cor. 4:4; 1 John 2:11.

2. ***poroo*** (*4456*) signifies "to harden" (from ***poros***, "a thick skin, a hardening"); rendered "blinded," KJV, in Rom. 11:7 and 2 Cor. 3:14 (RV, "hardened"); cf. 4:4.

**B. Adjective.**

***tuphlos*** (*5185*), "blind," is used both physically and metaphorically, chiefly in the Gospels; elsewhere four times; physically, Acts 13:11; metaphorically, Rom. 2:19; 2 Pet. 1:9; Rev. 3:17. The word is frequently used as a noun, signifying "a blind man."

**C. Noun.**

***porosis*** (*4457*), akin to A. No. 2, primarily means "a covering with a callus," a "hardening," Rom. 11:25 and Eph. 4:18, RV for KJV, "blindness"; Mark 3:5, RV, for KJV, "hardness." It is metaphorical of a dulled spiritual perception.

## BLOOD

*Old Testament*

***dam*** (1818), "blood," is used to denote the "blood" of animals, birds, and men, never of fish. In Gen. 9:4, "blood" is synonymous with "life," also Lev. 3:17. Only infrequently does this word mean "blood-red," a color, 2 Kings 3:22. In two passages, ***dam*** represents "wine," Gen. 49:11; cf. Deut. 32:14. ***dam*** can mean "blood shed by violence," Num. 35:33. "Blood" can also mean "death," Ezek. 5:17. Next, ***dam*** may connote an act by which a human life is taken, Deut. 17:8; Gen. 9:6; Lev. 17:3–4.

In judicial language, "to stand against one's blood" means to stand before a court and against the accused as a plaintiff, witness, or judge, Lev. 19:16. The phrase, "his blood be on his head," signifies that the guilt and punishment for a violent act shall be on the perpetrator, Lev. 20:9.

Animal blood could take the place of a sinner's blood in atoning (covering) for sin, Lev. 17:11. Adam's sin merited death and brought death on all his posterity, Rom. 5:12; so the offering of an animal in substitution not only typified the payment of that penalty, but it symbolized that the perfect offering would bring life for Adam and all others represented by the sacrifice, Heb. 10:4. The animal sacrifice prefigured and typologically represented the blood of Christ, who made the great and only effective substitutionary atonement, and whose offering was the only offering that gained life for those whom He represented. The shedding of His "blood" seals the covenant of life between God and man, Matt. 26:28.

### *New Testament*

### A. Nouns.

1. ***haima*** (*129*), (hence Eng., prefix ***hem***—), besides its natural meaning, stands, (a) in conjunction with ***sarx***, "flesh," "flesh and blood," Matt. 16:17; 1 Cor. 15:50; Gal. 1:16; the original has the opposite order, blood and flesh, in Eph. 6:12 and Heb. 2:14; this phrase signifies, by ***synecdoche***, "man, human beings." It stresses the limitations of humanity; the two are essential elements in man's physical being; "the life of the flesh is in the blood," Lev. 17:11; (b) for human generation, John 1:13; (c) for "blood" shed by violence, e.g., Matt. 23:35; Rev. 17:6; (d) for the "blood" of sacrificial victims, e.g., Heb. 9:7; of the "blood" of Christ, which betokens His death by the shedding of His "blood" in expiatory sacrifice; to drink His "blood" is to appropriate the saving effects of His expiatory death, John 6:53. As "the life of the flesh is in the blood," Lev. 17:11, and was forfeited by sin, life eternal can be imparted only by the expiation made, in the giving up of the life by the sinless Savior.

2. ***haimatekchusia*** (*130*) denotes "shedding of blood," Heb. 9:22.

### B. Verb.

***haimorrhoeo*** (*131*), from ***haima***, "blood," ***rheo***, "to flow" (Eng., "hemorrhage"), signifies "to suffer from a flow of blood," Matt. 9:20.

## BLOT OUT

***exaleipho*** (*1813*), from ***ek***, "out," used intensively, and ***aleipho***, "to wipe," signifies "to wash, or to smear completely." Hence, metaphorically, in the sense of removal, "to wipe away, wipe off, obliterate"; Acts 3:19, of sins; Col. 2:14, of writing; Rev. 3:5, of a name in a book; Rev. 7:17; 21:4, of tears.

## BOAST, BOASTER, BOASTFUL

### A. Verbs.

1. ***kauchaomai*** (*2744*), and its related words ***katakauchaomai***, "to glory or boast" and the nouns ***kauchesis*** and ***kauchema***, translated "boast," and "boasting," in the KJV, are always translated "glory," and "glorying" in the RV, e.g., 2 Cor. 10:15; 11:10, 17; Eph. 2:9.

2. ***megalaucheo*** (*3166*), from ***megala***, "great things," and ***aucheo***, "to lift up the neck," hence, "to boast," is found in some texts of Jas. 3:5. The most authentic mss. have the two words separated. It indicates any kind of haughty speech which stirs up strife or provokes others.

### B. Nouns.

1. ***alazon*** (*213*), "a boaster," Rom. 1:30 and 2 Tim. 3:2, KJV, "boasters," RV, "boastful," primarily signifies "a wanderer about the country" (from ***ale***, "wandering"), "a vagabond," hence, "an impostor."

2. ***alazoneia*** (*212*), the practice of an ***alazon***, denotes quackery; hence, "arrogant display, or boastings," Jas. 4:16, RV, "vauntings"; in 1 John 2:16, RV, "vainglory"; KJV, "pride."

## BODY, BODILY

### A. Nouns.

***soma*** (*4983*) is "the body as a whole, the instrument of life," whether of man living, e.g., Matt. 6:22, or dead, Matt. 27:52; or in resurrection, 1 Cor. 15:44; or of beasts, Heb. 13:11; of grain, 1 Cor. 15:37–38; of the heavenly hosts, 1 Cor. 15:40. In Rev. 18:13 it is translated "slaves." In its figurative uses the essential idea is preserved.

Sometimes the word stands, by *synecdoche*, for "the complete man," Matt. 5:29; 6:22; Rom. 12:1; Jas. 3:6; Rev. 18:13. Sometimes the person is identified with his or her "body," Acts 9:37; 13:36, and this is so even of the Lord Jesus, John 19:40 with 42.

The word is also used for physical nature, as distinct from ***pneuma***, "the spiritual nature," e.g., 1 Cor. 5:3, and from ***psuche***, "the soul," e.g., 1 Thess. 5:23.

It is also used metaphorically, of the mystic body of Christ, with reference to the whole church, e.g., Eph. 1:23; Col. 1:18, 22, 24; also of a local church, 1 Cor. 12:27.

### B. Adjectives.

1. ***sussomos*** (*4954*), ***sun***, "with," and A, No. 1., means "united in the same body," Eph. 3:6, of the church.

2. ***somatikos*** (*4984*), "bodily," is used in Luke 3:22, of the Holy Spirit in taking a bodily shape; in 1 Tim. 4:8 of bodily exercise.

**C. Adverb.**

***somatikos*** (*4985*), "bodily, corporeally," is used in Col. 2:9.

## BOLD, BOLDNESS, BOLDLY

**A. Verbs.**

1. ***tharreo*** (*2292*), a later form of ***tharseo***, is connected with ***thero***, "to be warm" (warmth of temperament being associated with confidence); hence, "to be confident, bold, courageous"; RV, invariably, "to be of good courage"; 2 Cor. 5:6, 8 (KJV, "to be confident"); 7:16 (KJV, "to have confidence"); 10:1–2 (KJV, "to be bold"); Heb. 13:6, KJV, "boldly"; RV, "with good courage" (lit., "being courageous").

2. ***parrhesiazomai*** (*3955*), "to speak boldly, or freely," primarily had reference to speech, but acquired the meaning of "being bold, or waxing bold," 1 Thess. 2:2; in Acts 13:46, RV, "spake out boldly" (the aorist participle here signifies "waxing bold"); Acts 9:27, 29, "preached boldly" (see also 18:26; 19:8); in 26:26, "speak freely."

3. ***tolmao*** (*5111*) signifies "to dare to do, or to bear, something terrible or difficult"; hence, "to be bold, to bear oneself boldly, deal boldly"; it is translated "be bold" in 2 Cor. 10:2, as contrasted with ***tharreo*** in verse 1, and the first line of verse 2, "shew courage"; in 10:12, RV, "are not bold to," for KJV, "dare not make ourselves of." ***tharreo*** denotes confidence in one's own powers, and has reference to character; ***tolmao*** denotes boldness in undertaking and has reference to manifestation.

4. ***apotolmao*** (*662*), ***apo*** (intensive), with No. 3, means "to be very bold, to speak out boldly," and is used in Rom. 10:20.

**B. Noun.**

***parrhesia*** (*3954*), from ***pas***, "all," ***rhesis***, "speech," denotes (a), primarily, "freedom of speech, unreservedness of utterance," Acts 4:29, 31; 2 Cor. 3:12; 7:4; Philem. 8; or "to speak without ambiguity, plainly," John 10:24; or "without figures of speech," John 16:25; (b) "the absence of fear in speaking boldly; hence, confidence, cheerful courage, boldness, without any connection necessarily with speech"; the RV has "boldness" in the following; Acts 4:13; Eph. 3:12; 1 Tim. 3:13; Heb. 3:6; 4:16; 10:19, 35; 1 John 2:28; 3:21; 4:17; 5:14; (c) the deportment by which one becomes conspicuous, John 7:4; 11:54, acts openly, or secures publicity, Col. 2:15.

**C. Adverb.**

***tolmeroteros*** (*5112*), the comparative degree of ***tolmeros***, means "the more boldly," Rom. 15:15; in some texts, ***tolmeroteron***.

## BOND

1. ***desmos*** (*1199*), from ***deo***, "to bind"; (a) "bonds" of a prisoner, Luke 8:29; (b) a figurative sense for "a condition of imprisonment," Phil. 1:7, 13.

2. ***desmios*** (*1198*), "a binding," denotes "a prisoner," e.g., Acts 25:14, RV, for the KJV, "in bonds"; Heb. 13:3, "them that are in bonds." Paul speaks of himself as a prisoner of Christ, Eph. 3:1; 2 Tim. 1:8; Philem. 1, 9; "in the Lord," Eph. 4:1.

3. ***sundesmos*** (*4886*), "that which binds together" (***sun***, "with," and No. 1), is said of "the bond of iniquity," Acts 8:23; "the bond of peace," Eph. 4:3; "the bond of perfectness," Col. 3:14 (figurative of the ligaments of the body); elsewhere; Col. 2:19, "bands," figuratively of the bands which unite the church, the body of Christ.

## BONDAGE

**A. Noun.**

***douleia*** (*1397*), akin to ***deo***, "to bind," primarily "the condition of being a slave," came to denote any kind of bondage, as, e.g., of the condition of creation, Rom. 8:21; of that fallen condition of man himself which makes him dread God, v. 15, and fear death, Heb. 2:15; of the condition imposed by the Mosaic Law, Gal. 4:24.

**B. Verbs.**

1. ***douleuo*** (*1398*), "to serve as a slave, to be a slave, to be in bondage," is frequently used without any association of slavery, e.g., Acts 20:19; Rom. 6:6; 7:6; 12:11; Gal. 5:13.

2. ***douloo*** (*1402*), different from No. 1, in being transitive instead of intransitive, signifies "to make a slave of, to bring into bondage," Acts 7:6; 1 Cor. 9:19, RV; in the passive voice, "to be brought under bondage," 2 Pet. 2:19; "to be held in bondage," Gal. 4:3 (lit., "were reduced to bondage"); Titus 2:3, "of being enslaved to wine"; Rom. 6:18, "of service to righteousness" (lit., "were made bondservants"). As with the purchased slave there were no limitations either in the kind or the time of service, so the life of the believer is to be lived in continuous obedience to God.

3. ***doulagogeo*** (*1396*), "to bring into bondage" (from A, above, and ***ago***, "to bring"), is used in 1 Cor. 9:27, concerning the body, RV, "bondage," for KJV, "subjection."

4. ***katadouloo*** (*2615*), "to bring into bondage," occurs in 2 Cor. 11:20; Gal. 2:4.

## BONDMAN, BONDMAID

***doulos*** (*1401*), from ***deo***, "to bind," "a slave," originally the lowest term in the scale of servitude, came also to mean "one who gives himself up to the will of another," e.g., 1 Cor. 7:23; Rom. 6:17, 20, and became the most common and general word for "servant," as in Matt. 8:9, without any idea of bondage. In calling himself, however, a "bondslave of Jesus Christ," e.g., Rom. 1:1, the apostle Paul intimates (1) that he had been formerly a "bondslave" of Satan, and (2) that, having been bought by Christ, he was now a willing slave, bound to his new Master.

The feminine, ***doule***, signifies "a handmaid," Luke 1:38, 48; Acts 2:18.

## BOOK

### *Old Testament*

***sepher*** (5612), "book; document; writing." The most common translation of ***sepher*** is "book." A manuscript was written, Exod. 32:32; Deut. 17:18, and sealed, Isa. 29:11, to be read by the addressee, 2 Kings 22:16. The sense of ***sepher*** is similar to "scroll" (***megillah***): "Therefore go thou, and read in the roll [***sepher***] which thou hast written from my mouth, the words of the Lord in the ears of the people in the Lord's house upon the fasting day: and also thou shalt read them in the ears of all Judah that come out of their cities" (Jer. 36:6). ***sepher*** is also closely related to "book" (***siphra***) (Ps. 56:8).

Many "books" are named in the Old Testament: of remembrance, Mal. 3:16; of life, Ps. 69:28, of Jasher, Josh. 10:13, of generations, Gen. 5:1, of the Lord, of chronicles, 2 Chron. 24:27. Prophets wrote "books" in their lifetime, Nah. 1:1. Jeremiah had several "books" written in addition to his letters to the exiles, Jer. 36. In this context, we learn about the nature of writing a "book," Jer. 36:32. Ezekiel was commanded to eat a "book," Ezek. 2:8—3:1 as a symbolic act of God's judgment on and restoration of Judah.

***sepher*** can also signify "a letter," Jer. 29:1. The contents of the ***sepher*** varied. It might contain a written order, a commission, a request, or a decree, Esth. 8:10; Deut. 24:1; Jer. 32:14.

### *New Testament*

1. ***biblos*** (*976*) (Eng. "Bible") was the inner part, or rather the cellular substance, of the stem of the papyrus (Eng. "paper"). It came to denote the paper made from this plant in Egypt, and then a written "book," roll, or volume. It is used in referring to "books" of Scripture, the "book," or scroll, of Matthew's Gospel, Matt. 1:1; the Pentateuch, as the "book" of Moses, Mark 12:26; Isaiah, as "the book of the words of Isaiah," Luke 3:4; the Psalms, Luke 20:42 and Acts 1:20; "the prophets," Acts 7:42; to "the Book of Life," Phil. 4:3; Rev. 3:5; 20:15. Once only it is used of secular writings, Acts 19:19.

2. ***biblion*** (*975*), "a scroll or a small book." It is used in Luke 4:17, 20, of the "book" of Isaiah; in John 20:30, of the Gospel of John; in Gal. 3:10 and Heb. 10:7, of the whole of the OT; in Heb. 9:19, of the "book" of Exodus; in Rev. 1:11; 22:7, 9–10, 18 (twice), 19, of the Apocalypse; in John 21:25 and 2 Tim. 4:13, of "books" in general; in Rev. 13:8; 17:8; 20:12; 21:27, of the "Book" of Life; in Rev. 20:12, of other "books" to be opened in the Day of Judgment, containing, it would seem, the record of human deeds. In Matt. 19:7 and Mark 10:4 the word is used of a bill of divorcement.

3. ***biblaridion*** (*974*), another diminutive of No. 1, is always rendered "little book," in Rev. 10:2, 9–10. Some texts have it also in verse 8, instead of ***biblion***.

## BOSOM

### *Old Testament*

***cheq*** (2436), "bosom; lap; base." The word represents the "outer front of one's body" where beloved ones, infants, and animals are pressed closely, Num. 11:12; Gen. 16:5; Deut. 28:56. In a figurative inward sense, Ps. 35:13; cf. Job 19:27; 1 Kings 22:35. ***cheq*** represents a fold of one's garment above the belt, often rendered "lap" in the modern versions Exod. 4:6; Prov. 16:33; 2 Sam. 12:3. Finally, ***cheq*** means the "base of the altar," as described in Ezek. 43:13–17.

### *New Testament*

***kolpos*** (*2859*) signifies (a) "the front of the body between the arms"; hence, to recline in the "bosom" was said of one who so reclined at table that his head covered, as it were, the "bosom" of the one next to him, John 13:23. Hence, figuratively, it is used of a place of blessedness with another, as with Abraham in paradise, Luke 16:22–23 (plural in v. 23), from the custom of reclining at table in the "bosom," a place of honor; of the Lord's eternal and essential relation with the Father, in all its blessedness and affection as intimated in the phrase, "The Only-begotten Son, which is in the bosom of the Father" (John 1:18); (b) "of the bosom of a garment, the hollow formed by the upper forepart of a loose garment, bound by a girdle and used for carrying or keeping things"; thus figuratively of repaying one liberally, Luke 6:38; cf. Isa. 65:6; Jer. 39:18; (c) "of an inlet of the sea," because of its shape, like a bosom, Acts 27:39.

## BOTTOM, BOTTOMLESS

**A. Adverb.**

***kato*** (*2736*). From ***kata***, it signifies to be "down," or "below," another spacial object, Matt. 4:6; 27:51; Mark 14:66; 15:38; Luke 4:9; John 8:3; Acts 2:19; 20:9.

**B. Adjective.**

***abussos*** (*12*), "bottomless"; Eng., "bath," is used as a noun denoting the abyss (KJV, "bottomless pit"). It describes an immeasurable depth, the underworld, the lower regions, the abyss of Sheol. In Rom. 10:7, quoted from Deut. 30:13, the abyss (the abode of the lost dead) is substituted for the sea (the change in the quotation is due to the facts of the death and resurrection of Christ); the KJV has "deep" here and in Luke 8:31; the reference is to the lower regions as the abode of demons, out of which they can be let loose, Rev. 11:7; 17:8, it is found seven times in the Apocalypse, 9:1–2, 11; 11:7; 17:8; 20:1, 3; in 9:1, 2.

## BOUND (to be)

(a) *of obligation:*

***opheilo*** (*3784*), "to owe, whether of a debt or any obligation," is translated "we are bound," in 2 Thess. 1:3 and 2:13 (the apostle expressing his obligation to give thanks for his readers).

(b) *of binding*:

***perikeimai*** (*4029*), lit., "to lie around," "to be compassed," is used of binding fetters around a person, Acts 28:20; in Mark 9:42, and Luke 17:2, to hang about a person's neck; in Heb. 5:2, to compass about, metaphorically of infirmities; in 12:1, of those who have witness borne to their faith.

## BOUNTY, BOUNTIFULLY

1. ***eulogia*** (*2129*), "a blessing," has the meaning of "bounty" in 2 Cor. 9:5, of the offering sent by the church at Corinth to their needy brethren in Judea.

2. ***haplotes*** (*572*), from ***haplous***, "simple, single," is translated "bountifulness" in 2 Cor. 9:11, KJV; RV, "liberality" (marg., "singleness"); cf. 8:2; 9:13; from sincerity of mind springs "liberality." The thought of sincerity is present in Rom. 12:8; 2 Cor. 11:3; Eph. 6:5; Col. 3:22.

3. ***charis*** (*5485*), "grace," is rendered, "bounty" in 1 Cor. 16:3, RV, (KJV, "liberality"), by metonymy for a material gift.

4. ***hadrotes*** (*100*), lit. "fatness," is used of a monetary gift, in 2 Cor. 8:20, KJV, "abundance," RV, "bounty."

## BOW, BOWED (Verb)

### *Old Testament*

***kara'*** (3766), "to bow, bow down, bend the knee," Gen. 49:9. "Bow" could be a common stance of body, Judg. 7:5–6; or worship to deity, 1 Kings 8:54; Ezra 9:5; Isa. 45:23; cf. Phil. 2:10. To "bow down upon" a woman was an euphemism for sexual intercourse, Job 31:10; for birthing, 1 Sam. 4:19; in old age, Job 4:4.

### *New Testament*

1. ***kampto*** (*2578*), "to bend," is used especially of bending the knees in religious veneration, Rom. 11:4; 14:11; Eph. 3:14; Phil. 2:10.

2. ***sunkampto*** (*4781*) signifies "to bend completely together, to bend down by compulsory force," Rom. 11:10.

3. ***sunkupto*** (*4794*), "to bow together," is said, in Luke 13:11, of the woman crippled with a physical infirmity.

4. ***klino*** (*2827*), "to incline, to bow down," is used of the women who in their fright "bowed" their faces to the earth at the Lord's empty tomb, Luke 24:5; of the act of the Lord on the cross immediately before giving up His Spirit. What is indicated in the statement "He bowed His head," is not the helpless dropping of the head after death, but the deliberate putting of His head into a position of rest, John 19:30. The verb is deeply significant here. The Lord reversed the natural order. The same verb is used in His statement in Matt. 8:20 and Luke 9:58, "the Son of Man hath not where to lay His head." It is used, too, of the decline of day, Luke 9:12; 24:29; of turning enemies to flight, Heb. 11:34.

## BOWELS

***splanchnon*** (*4698*), always in the plural, properly denotes "the physical organs of the intestines," and is once used in this respect, Acts 1:18. The RV substitutes the following for the word "bowels": "affections," 2 Cor. 6:12; "affection," 2 Cor. 7:15; "tender mercies," Phil. 1:8; 2:1; "a heart (of compassion)," Col. 3:12; "heart," Philem. 12, 20; "hearts," Philem. 7; "compassion," 1 John 3:17. The word is rendered "tender" in the KJV and RV of Luke 1:78, in connection with the word "mercy."

## BOY

***pais*** (*3816*) denotes "a boy" (in contrast to ***paidion***, a diminutive of ***pais***, and to ***teknon***, "a child"). With reference to Christ, instead of the KJV "child," the RV suitably translates otherwise as follows: Luke 2:43, "the boy Jesus"; Acts 4:27, 30, "Thy Holy Servant, Jesus." So in the case of others, Matt. 17:18 and Luke 9:42 ("boy").

## BRAIDED (KJV, BROIDED)

***plegma*** (*4117*) signifies "what is woven" (from ***pleko***, "to weave, plait"), whether a net or basket (Josephus uses it of the ark of bulrushes in which the infant Moses was laid), or of a web, plait, braid. It is used in 1 Tim. 2:9, of "braided hair," which the Vulgate signifies as "ringlets, curls."

## BRANDED

***kausteriazo*** (*2743*), "to burn in with a branding iron" (cf. Eng., "caustic"), is found, in the best mss., in 1 Tim. 4:2, RV "branded." Others have ***kauteriazo*** (from ***kauterion***, "a branding-iron," Eng., "cauterize"), to mark by "branding," an act not quite so severe as that indicated by the former. The reference is to apostates whose consciences are "branded" with the effects of their sin.

## BRASS, BRAZEN

1. ***chalkos*** (*5475*), primarily, "copper," became used for metals in general, later was applied to bronze, a mixture of copper and tin, then, by metonymy, to any article made of these metals, e.g., money, Matt. 10:9; Mark 6:8; 12:41, or a sounding instrument, 1 Cor. 13:1, figurative of a person destitute of love. See Rev. 18:12.

2. ***chalkeos*** (*5470*), "made of brass or bronze," is used of idols, Rev. 9:20.

3. ***chalkion*** (*5473*) is used in Mark 7:4 of "brazen vessels."

4. ***chalkolibanon*** (*5474*) is used of "white or shining copper or bronze," and describes the feet of the Lord, in Rev. 1:15 and 2:18.

5. ***chalkeus*** (*5471*) denotes "a coppersmith," 2 Tim. 4:14.

## BRAWLER

1. ***paroinos*** (*3943*), an adjective, lit., "tarrying at wine" (***para***, "at," ***oinos***, "wine"), "given to wine," 1 Tim. 3:3 and Titus 1:7, KJV, probably has the secondary sense, of the effects of wine-bibbing, viz., abusive brawling. Hence RV, "brawler."

2. ***amachos*** (*269*), an adjective, lit., "not fighting" (***a***, negative, ***mache***, "a fight"), came to denote, metaphorically, "not contentious," 1 Tim. 3:3, and Titus 3:2, RV, for KJV, "not a brawler," "not brawlers."

## BREAK, BREAKER, BREAKING, BRAKE

### A. Verbs.

1. ***klao*** or ***klazo*** (*2806*), "to break, to break off pieces," is used of "breaking bread," (a) of the Lord's act in providing for people, Matt. 14:19; 15:36; Mark 8:6, 19; (b) of the "breaking of bread" in the Lord's Supper, Matt. 26:26; Mark 14:22; Luke 22:19; Acts 20:7; 1 Cor. 10:16; 11:24; (c) of an ordinary meal, Acts 2:46; 20:11; 27:35; (d) of the Lord's act in giving evidence of His resurrection, Luke 24:30.

2. ***ekklao*** (*1575*), ***ek***, "off," and No. 1, "to break off," is used metaphorically of branches, Rom. 11:17, 19–20.

3. ***kataklao*** (*2622*), ***kata***, "down," and No. 1, is used in Mark 6:41 and Luke 9:16, of Christ's "breaking" loaves for the multitudes.

4. ***luo*** (*3089*), "to loosen," especially by way of deliverance, sometimes has the meaning of "breaking, destructively," e.g., of "breaking" commandments, not only infringing them, but loosing the force of them, rendering them not binding, Matt. 5:19; John 5:18; of "breaking" the Law of Moses, John 7:23; Scripture, John 10:35; of the "breaking up" of a ship, Acts 27:41; of the "breaking down" of the middle wall of partition, Eph. 2:14; of the marriage tie, 1 Cor. 7:27.

5. ***rhegnumi*** (*4486*), "to tear, rend, as of garments, etc.," is translated "break" in the KJV, of Matt. 9:17, of wine-skins (RV, "burst"); as in Mark 2:22 and Luke 5:37; "break forth" in Gal. 4:27.

6. ***diarrhegnumi*** (*1284*), ***dia***, "through" (intensive), and No. 5, "to burst asunder, to rend, cleave," is said of the rending of garments, Matt. 26:65; Mark 14:63; Acts 14:14; of the "breaking" of a net, Luke 5:6; of fetters, 8:29.

7. ***katagnumi*** (*2608*), ***kata***, "down" (intensive), and No. 5, is used of the "breaking" of a bruised reed, Matt. 12:20, and of the "breaking" of the legs of those who were crucified, John 19:31, 32, 33.

8. ***diorusso*** (*1358*), lit., "to dig through" (***dia***, "through," ***orusso***, "to dig"), is used of the act of thieves in "breaking" into a house, Matt. 6:19, 20; 24:43; Luke 12:39.

9. ***exorusso*** (*1846*), lit., "to dig out" (cf. No. 8), is used of the "breaking up" of part of a roof, Mark 2:4, and, in a vivid expression, of plucking out the eyes, Gal. 4:15.

### B. Nouns.

1. ***parabasis*** (*3847*), "a transgression" (***para***, "across," ***baino***, "to go"), is translated "breaking" in Rom. 2:23, KJV; RV, "transgres-

sion"; KJV and RV ditto in 4:15; 5:14; Gal. 3:19; 1 Tim. 2:14; Heb. 2:2; 9:15.

2. ***parabates*** (*3848*), "a transgressor" (cf. No. 1), is translated "breaker," Rom. 2:25, KJV; RV, "transgressor." In v. 27 the KJV turns it into a verb, "dost transgress." See Gal. 2:18; Jas. 2:9, 11.

## BREASTPLATE

***thorax*** (*2382*), primarily, "the breast," denotes "a breastplate or corselet," consisting of two parts and protecting the body on both sides, from the neck to the middle. It is used metaphorically of righteousness, Eph. 6:14; of faith and love, 1 Thess. 5:8, with perhaps a suggestion of the two parts, front and back, which formed the coat of mail (an alternative term for the word in the NT sense); elsewhere in Rev. 9:9, 17.

## BREATH, BREATHE

### *Old Testament*

***hebel*** (1892), "breath; vanity; idol."

First, the word represents human "breath" as a transitory thing, Job 7:16. Second, ***hebel*** means something meaningless and purposeless, Eccl. 1:2. Third, this word signifies a worthless "idol," Deut. 32:21.

### *New Testament*

**A. Nouns.**

1. ***pnoe*** (*4157*), akin to ***pneo***, "to blow," lit., "a blowing," signifies (a) "breath, the breath of life," Acts 17:25; (b) "wind," Acts 2:2.

2. ***pneuma*** (*4151*), "spirit," also denotes "breath," Rev. 11:11 and 13:15, RV. In 2 Thess. 2:8, the KJV has "spirit" for RV, breath.

**B. Verbs.**

1. ***empneo*** (*1709*), lit., "to breathe in, or on," is used in Acts 9:1, indicating that threatening and slaughter were, so to speak, the elements from which Saul drew and expelled his breath.

2. ***emphusao*** (*1720*), "to breathe upon," is used of the symbolic act of the Lord Jesus in breathing upon His apostles the communication of the Holy Spirit, John 20:22.

## BRIDE, BRIDECHAMBER, BRIDEGROOM

***numphe*** (3565) (Eng. "nymph") "a bride, or young wife," John 3:29; Rev. 18:23; 21:2, 9; 22:17, is probably connected with the Latin ***nubo***, "to veil"; the "bride" was often adorned with embroidery and jewels (see Rev. 21:2), and was led veiled from her home to the "bridegroom." Hence the secondary meaning of "daughter-in-law," Matt. 10:35; Luke 12:53. For the relationship between Christ and a local church, under this figure, see 2 Cor. 11:2; regarding the whole church, Eph. 5:23–32; Rev. 22:17.

***numphios*** (*3566*), "a bridegroom," occurs fourteen times in the gospels, and in Rev. 18:23. "The friend of the bridegroom," John 3:29, is distinct from "the sons of the bridechamber" who were numerous. When John the Baptist speaks of "the friend of the Bridegroom," he uses language according to the customs of the Jews.

***numphon*** (*3567*), signifies (a) "the room or dining hall in which the marriage ceremonies were held," Matt. 22:10; some mss. have ***gamos***, "a wedding," here; (b) "the chamber containing the bridal bed," "the sons of the bridechamber" being the friends of the bridegroom, who had the charge of providing what was necessary for the nuptials, Matt. 9:15; Mark 2:19; Luke 5:34.

## BRIGHT, BRIGHTNESS

**A. Adjective.**

***lampros*** (*2986*), "shining, brilliant, bright," is used of the clothing of an angel, Acts 10:30 and Rev. 15:6; symbolically, of the clothing of the saints in glory, Rev. 19:8, RV, in the best texts (KJV, "white"); of Christ as the Morning Star, 22:16; of the water of life, 22:1, KJV, "clear."

**B. Noun.**

***lamprotes*** (*2987*), "brightness," akin to A, above is found in Acts 26:13.

## BRIMSTONE

1. ***theion*** (*2303*) originally denoted "fire from heaven." It is connected with sulphur. Places touched by lightning were called ***theia***, and, as lightning leaves a sulphurous smell, and sulphur was used in pagan purifications, it received the name of ***theion*** Luke 17:29; Rev. 9:17–18; 14:10; 19:20; 20:10; 21:8.

2. ***theiodes*** (*2306*), akin to No. 1, signifies "brimstone-like, or consisting of brimstone," Rev. 9:17.

## BROTHER, BRETHREN, BROTHERHOOD, BROTHERLY

### *Old Testament*

***'ach*** (251), "brother." ***'ach*** means "male sibling," i.e., a "brother," Gen. 4:2; ; a full brother or a half-brother, Gen. 37:14. ***'ach*** means a "blood relative," such as a nephew or grandson, Gen. 9:25; 14:16; 29:12. ***'achim*** (plural) means "tribe," Judg. 1:3. The word ***'ach*** is used of a fellow tribesman, Gen. 31:32. Elsewhere it describes a fellow countryman, Exod. 2:11, or simply a fellow human being, Gen. 9:5–6. ***'ach*** connotes "companion" or "colleague"—that is, a brother by choice, 2 Kings 9:2; cf. Isa. 41:6; Num. 8:26, or by circumstance, Gen. 9:5–6. Somewhat along this line is the covenantal use of the word as a synonym for "ally," Num. 20:14 and 1 Kings 9:13. ***'ach*** can also be a term of polite address, Gen. 29:4

*New Testament*

***adelphos*** (*80*) denotes "a brother, or near kinsman"; in the plural, "a community based on identity of origin or life." It is used of:—

(1) male children of the same parents, Matt. 1:2; 14:3; (2) male descendants of the same parents, Acts 7:23, 26; Heb. 7:5; (3) male children of the same mother, Matt. 13:55; 1 Cor. 9:5; Gal. 1:19; (4) people of the same nationality, Acts 3:17, 22; Rom. 9:3. With "men" (***aner***, "male"), prefixed, it is used in addresses only, Acts 2:29, 37, etc.; (5) any man, a neighbor, Luke 10:29; Matt. 5:22; 7:3; (6) persons united by a common interest, Matt. 5:47; (7) persons united by a common calling, Rev. 22:9; (8) mankind, Matt. 25:40; Heb. 2:17; (9) the disciples, and so, by implication, all believers, Matt. 28:10; John 20:17; (10) believers, apart from sex, Matt. 23:8; Acts 1:15; Rom. 1:13; 1 Thess. 1:4; Rev. 19:10 (the word "sisters" is used of believers, only in 1 Tim. 5:2); (11) believers, with ***aner***, "male," prefixed, and with "or sister" added, 1 Cor. 7:14 (RV), 15; Jas. 2:15, male as distinct from female, Acts 1:16; 15:7, 13, but not 6:3.

## BRUISE

***thrauo*** (*2352*), "to smite through, shatter," is used in Luke 4:18, "them that are bruised," i.e., broken by calamity.

## BRUTE

***alogos*** (*249*), translated "brute" in the KJV of 2 Pet. 2:12 and Jude 10, signifies "without reason," RV, though, as J. Hastings points out, "brute beasts" is not at all unsuitable, as "brute" is from Latin ***brutus***, which means "dull, irrational"; in Acts 25:27 it is rendered "unreasonable."

## BUFFET

1. ***kolaphizo*** (*2852*) signifies "to strike with clenched hands, to buffet with the fist" (***kolaphos***, "a fist"), Matt. 26:67; Mark 14:65; 1 Cor. 4:11; 2 Cor. 12:7; 1 Pet. 2:20.

2. ***hupopiazo*** (*5299*), lit., "to strike under the eye," hence, to beat the face black and blue (to give a black eye), is used metaphorically, and translated "buffet" in 1 Cor. 9:27 (KJV, "keep under"), of Paul's suppressive treatment of his body, in order to keep himself spiritually fit (RV marg., "bruise"); so RV marg. in Luke 18:5, of the persistent widow, text, "wear out" (KJV, "weary").

## BUILD, BUILDER, BUILDING

*Old Testament*

### A. Verb.

***banah*** (1129), "to build, establish, construct, rebuild." ***banah*** means to construct, fashion, or manufacture a new object, Gen. 2:22; 4:17; 8:20; Ezek. 27:5; 1 Kings 15:22; ***banah*** can also refer to "rebuilding"; Josh. 6:26; ***banah*** also means "having children," Gen. 16:2; Deut. 25:9; or "to found a dynasty," 2 Sam. 7:27.

### B. Nouns.

***ben*** (1121), "son." ***bat*** (1323), "daughter, " derived from the verb, see above. ***ben*** and ***bat*** means a "male or female offspring," Gen. 3:16; 5:4; 49:11. The words ***ben*** and ***bat*** can signify "descendants" in general—daughters, sons, granddaughters, and grandsons, Gen. 31:28; cf. v. 43. The phrase, "my son," may be used by a superior to a subordinate as a term of familiar address, Josh. 7:19. A special use of "my son" is a teacher's speaking to a disciple, referring to intellectual or spiritual sonship, Prov. 1:10. ***ben*** can also be used in an adoption formula, Ps. 2:7; Hos. 11:1.

The Bible also refers to the heavenly court as the "sons of God," Job 1:6. God called the elders of Israel the "sons [KJV, "children"] of the Most High," Ps. 82:6. In Gen. 6:2, the phrase "sons of God" is variously understood as members of the heavenly court, the spiritual disciples of God (the sons of Seth), and the boastful among mankind.

***ben*** may signify "young men" in general, Prov. 7:7. A city may be termed a "mother" and its inhabitants its "sons," Ps. 147:13. ***ben*** is sometimes used to mean a single individual, Gen. 18:7. The phrase "son of man" is used in this sense—God is asked to save the poor individuals, not the children of the poor, Ps. 72:4. ***ben*** may also denote a member of a group, 1 Kings 20:35; cf. Amos 7:14, or someone worthy of a certain fate, Deut. 21:18. Used figuratively, "son of" can mean "something belonging to"—e.g., "the arrow [literally, "the son of a bow"] cannot make him flee," Job 41:28.

*New Testament*

### A. Verbs.

1. ***oikodomeo*** (*3618*), lit., "to build a house," hence, to build anything, e.g., Matt. 7:24; Luke 4:29; 6:48, RV, "well builded" (last clause of verse); John 2:20; is frequently used figura-

tively, e.g., Acts 20:32 (some mss. have No. 3 here); Gal. 2:18; especially of edifying, Acts 9:31; Rom. 15:20; 1 Cor. 10:23; 14:4; 1 Thess. 5:11 (RV). In 1 Cor. 8:10 it is translated "emboldened" (marg., "builded up"). The participle with the article (equivalent to a noun) is rendered "builder," Matt. 21:42; Acts 4:11; 1 Pet. 2:7.

2. ***anoikodomeo*** (*456*) signifies "to build again," Acts 15:16.

3. ***epoikodomeo*** (*2026*) signifies "to build upon," 1 Cor. 3:10, 12, 14; Eph. 2:20; Jude 20; or up, Acts 20:32; Col. 2:7.

4. ***sunoikodomeo*** (*4925*), "to build together," is used in Eph. 2:22, metaphorically, of the church, as a spiritual dwelling-place for God.

**B. Nouns.**

1. ***oikodome*** (*3619*), "a building, or edification," is used (a) literally, e.g., Matt. 24:1; Mark 13:1–2; (b) figuratively, e.g., Rom. 14:19 (lit., "the things of building up"); 15:2 of a local church as a spiritual building, 1 Cor. 3:9, or the whole church, the body of Christ, Eph. 2:21. It expresses the strengthening effect of teaching, 1 Cor. 14:3, 5, 12, 26; 2 Cor. 10:8; 12:19; 13:10, or other ministry, Eph. 4:12, 16, 29 (the idea conveyed is progress resulting from patient effort). It is also used of the believer's resurrection body, 2 Cor. 5:1.

2. ***endomesis*** (*1739*), "a thing built, structure," is used of the wall of the heavenly city, Rev. 21:18 (some suggest that the word means "a fabric"; others, "a roofing or coping"; these interpretations are questionable; the probable significance is "a building").

## BURDEN, BURDENED, BURDENSOME

**A. Nouns.**

1. ***baros*** (*922*) denotes "a weight, anything pressing on one physically," Matt. 20:12, or "that makes a demand on one's resources," whether material, 1 Thess. 2:6 (to be burdensome), or spiritual, Gal. 6:2; Rev. 2:24, or religious, Acts 15:28. In one place it metaphorically describes the future state of believers as "an eternal weight of glory," 2 Cor. 4:17.

2. ***phortion*** (*5413*), lit., "something carried" (from ***phero***, "to bear"), is always used metaphorically (except in Acts 27:10, of the lading of a ship); of that which, though "light," is involved in discipleship of Christ, Matt. 11:30; of tasks imposed by the scribes, Pharisees and lawyers, Matt. 23:4; Luke 11:46; of that which will be the result, at the judgment-seat of Christ, of each believer's work, Gal. 6:5.

**B. Verbs.**

1. ***bareo*** (*916*), akin to A, No. 1, is used of the effect of drowsiness, "were heavy," Matt. 26:43; Mark 14:40; Luke 9:32; of the effects of gluttony, Luke 21:34 ("overcharged"); of the believer's present physical state in the body, 2 Cor. 5:4; of persecution, 2 Cor. 1:8; of a charge upon material resources, 1 Tim. 5:16 (RV).

2. ***epibareo*** (*1912*), "to burden heavily," is said of material resources, 1 Thess. 2:9 (RV); 2 Thess. 3:8, RV, "burden," KJV, "be chargeable to," of the effect of spiritual admonition and discipline, 2 Cor. 2:5, RV, "press heavily," KJV, "overcharge.

3. ***katabareo*** (*2599*), "to weigh down," "overload," is used of material charges, in 2 Cor. 12:16.

**C. Adjective.**

***abares*** (*4*), "without weight" (***a***,) negative, and ***baros***, "see" A, No. 1), is used in 2 Cor. 11:9, lit. "I kept myself burdensomeless."

## BURN, BURNING

***Old Testament***

**A. Verb.**

***saraph*** (8313), "to burn." Since burning is the main characteristic of fire, the term ***saraph*** is usually used to describe the destroying of objects of all kinds, Josh. 6:24; Judg. 9:52; 1 Sam. 30:1; Jer. 36:25, 27–28; Amos 2:1.

Interestingly, ***saraph*** is never used for the "burning" of a sacrifice on the altar, although a few times it designates the disposal of refuse, unused sacrificial parts, and some diseased parts. The "burning" of a red heifer was for the purpose of producing ashes for purification, Lev. 19:5, 8.

**B. Nouns.**

***saraph*** (8314), "burning one; fiery being." In Num. 21:6, 8, the term ***saraph*** describes the serpents that attacked the Israelites in the wilderness. They are referred to as "fiery" serpents. A "fiery" flying serpent appears in Isa. 14:29, as well as in Isa. 30:6.

***seraphim*** (8314), "burning, noble." ***seraphim*** refers to the ministering beings in Isa. 6:2, 6, and may imply either a serpentine form (albeit with wings, human hands, and voices) or beings that have a "glowing" quality about them. One of the ***seraphim*** ministered to Isaiah by bringing a glowing coal from the altar.

***New Testament***

**A. Verbs.**

1. ***kaio*** (*2545*), "to set fire to, to light"; in the passive voice, "to be lighted, to burn," Matt.

5:15; John 15:6; Heb. 12:18; Rev. 4:5; 8:8, 10; 19:20; 21:8; 1 Cor. 13:3, is used metaphorically of the heart, Luke 24:32; of spiritual light, Luke 12:35; John 5:35.

2. ***katakaio*** *(2618)*, from ***kata***, "down" (intensive), and No. 1, signifies "to burn up, burn utterly," as of chaff, Matt. 3:12; Luke 3:17; tares, Matt. 13:30, 40; the earth and its works, 2 Pet. 3:10; trees and grass, Rev. 8:7. This form should be noted in Acts 19:19; 1 Cor. 3:15; Heb. 13:11, Rev. 17:16. In each place the full rendering "burn utterly" might be used, as in Rev. 18:8.

3. ***ekkaio*** *(1572)*, from ***ek***, out (intensive), and No. 1, lit., "to burn out," in the passive voice, "to be kindled, burn up," is used of the lustful passions of men, Rom. 1:27.

4. ***puroomai*** *(4448)*, from ***pur***, "fire, to glow with heat," is said of the feet of the Lord, in the vision in Rev. 1:15; it is translated "fiery" in Eph. 6:16 (of the darts of the evil one); used metaphorically of the emotions, in 1 Cor. 7:9; 2 Cor. 11:29; elsewhere literally, of the heavens, 2 Pet. 3:12; of gold, Rev. 3:18 (RV, "refined").

**B. Nouns.**

1. ***kausis*** *(2740)*, akin to A, No. 1 (Eng., "caustic"), is found in Heb. 6:8, lit. "whose end is unto burning."

2. ***kauson*** *(2742)* is rendered "burning heat" in Jas. 1:11, KJV (RV, "scorching).

3. ***purosis*** *(4451)*, akin to A. No. 4, is used literally in Rev. 18:9, 18; metaphorically in 1 Pet. 4:12, "fiery trial."

## TO BURN INCENSE

**A. Verb.**

***qatar*** (6999), "to burn incense, cause to rise up in smoke." ***qatar*** means "offering true offerings" every time it appears in the causative stem, cf. Hos. 4:13; 11:2; 2 Chron. 13:11. Offerings are burned in order to change the thing offered into smoke (the ethereal essence of the offering), which would ascend to God as a pleasing or placating savor.

Such offerings represent both the giving of the thing offered and a vicarious substitution of the offering for the offerer, cf. John 17:19; Eph. 5:2. Because of man's sinfulness, Gen. 8:21; Rom. 5:12, he was unable to initiate a relationship with God. Therefore, God Himself told man what was necessary in order to worship and serve Him. God specified that only the choicest of one's possessions could be offered, and the best of the offering belonged to Him, Lev. 4:10. Only His priests were to offer sacrifices, 2 Kings 16:13. All offerings were to be made at the designated place; after the conquest, this was the central sanctuary, Lev. 17:6.

**B. Nouns.**

***qetorel*** (7004), "incense." The word represents "perfume" in Prov. 27:9.

***qitter*** means "incense." This word appears once in the Old Testament, in Jer. 44:21. Another noun, ***qetorah***, also means "incense." This word's only appearance is in Deut. 33:10. ***qitor*** refers to "smoke; vapor." This word does not refer to the smoke of an offering, but to other kinds of smoke or vapor. The reference in Ps. 148:8 ("vapor") is one of its four biblical occurrences. ***muqtar*** means "the kindling of incense." The word is used only once, Mal. 1:11.

***miqteret*** means "censer; incense." The word occurs twice. ***miqteret*** represents a "censer"—a utensil in which coals are carried—in 2 Chron. 26:19. The word refers to "incense" in Ezek. 8:11. ***meqatterah*** refers to "incense altar." The word occurs once, 2 Chron. 26:19. ***miqtar*** means a "place of sacrificial smoke; altar." The word appears once, Exod. 30:1.

## BURNT (offering)

***holokautoma*** (3646) denotes "a whole burnt offering" (***holos***, "whole," ***kautos***, for ***kaustos***, a verbal adjective from ***kaio***, "to burn"), i.e., "a victim," the whole of which is burned, as in Ex. 30:20; Lev. 5:12; 23:8, 25, 27. It is used in Mark 12:33, by the scribe who questioned the Lord as to the first commandment in the Law and in Heb. 10:6, 8, RV "whole burnt offerings."

## BURST (asunder)

***lakeo*** or ***lasko*** (2997), primarily, "to crack, or crash," denotes "to burst asunder with a crack, crack open" (always of making a noise), is used in Acts 1:18.

## BUSINESS

**A. Nouns.**

1. ***chreia*** *(5532)*, translated "business" in Acts 6:3, of the distribution of funds, signifies "a necessity, a need," and is used in this place concerning duty or business.

2. ***ergasia*** *(2039)* denotes "a business," Acts 19:24, 25, RV, KJV, "gain" and "craft" (from ***ergon***, "work").

**B. Adjective.**

***idios*** *(2398)* expresses "what is one's own" (hence, Eng. "idiot," in a changed sense, lit., "a person with his own opinions"); the neuter plural with the article (***ta idia***) signifies "one's own things." In 1 Thess. 4:11, the noun is not expressed in the original but is supplied in the English versions by "business," "your own business." For the same phrase, otherwise expressed, see John 1:11, "His own (things)";

16:32 and 19:27, "his own (home)"; Acts 21:6, "home." In Luke 2:49, the phrase "in My Father's house" (RV), "about My Father's business" (KJV), is, lit., "in the (things, the neuter plural of the article) of My Father."

## BUSYBODY

### A. Verb.

***periergazomai*** (*4020*), lit., "to be working round about, instead of at one's own business," signifies to take more pains than enough about a thing, to waste one's labor, to be meddling with, or bustling about, other people's matters. This is found in 2 Thess. 3:11, where, following the verb ***ergazomai***, "to work," it forms a ***paronomasia***. This may be produced in a free rendering: "some who are not busied in their own business, but are overbusied in that of others."

### B. Adjective.

***periergos*** (*4021*), akin to A, denoting "taken up with trifles," is used of magic arts in Acts 19:19; "busybodies" in 1 Tim. 5:13, i.e., meddiing in other persons' affairs.

### C. Noun.

***allotrioepiskopos*** (*244*), from ***allotrios***, "belonging to another person," and ***episkopos***, "an overseer," translated "busybody" in the KJV of 1 Pet. 4:15, "meddler," RV, was a legal term for a charge brought against Christians as being hostile to civilized society, their purpose being to make Gentiles conform to Christian standards. Some explain it as a pryer into others' affairs.

## BUY, BOUGHT

### *Old Testament*

***qanah*** (7069), "to get, acquire, create, buy." ***qanah*** expresses a basic meaning of God's "creating" or "bringing into being," Gen. 4:1; 14:19,22. In Deut. 32:6, God is called the "father" who "created" Israel; a father begets or "creates," rather than "acquires" children. In the Wisdom version of the Creation story, Ps 139:13; Prov. 8:22–36. ***qanah*** is used several times to express God's redeeming activity in behalf of Israel, again reflecting "creativity" rather than "purchase," Exod. 15:16; See also Ps. 74:2; 78:54. ***qanah*** also means frequently "make a purchase agreement with another," Gen. 47:20; Exod. 21:2.

### *New Testament*

***agorazo*** (*59*), primarily, "to frequent the market-place," the ***agora***, hence "to do business there, to buy or sell," is used lit., e.g., in Matt. 14:15. Figuratively Christ is spoken of as having bought His redeemed, making them His property at the price of His blood (i.e., His death through the shedding of His blood in expiation for their sins), 1 Cor. 6:20; 7:23; 2 Pet. 2:1; see also Rev. 5:9; 14:3–4 (not as KJV, "redeemed"). ***agorazo*** does not mean "to redeem."

C

## CALL, CALLED, CALLING

### *Old Testament*

**A. Verb.**

***qara'*** (7121), "to call, call out, recite."

***qara'*** may signify the "specification of a name." Naming a thing is frequently an assertion of sovereignty over it, which is the case in the first use of ***qara'***, Gen. 1:5. God's act of creating, "naming," and numbering includes the stars, Ps. 147:4, and all other things, Isa. 40:26. He allowed Adam to "name" the animals as a concrete demonstration of man's relative sovereignty over them, Gen. 2:19. Divine sovereignty and election are extended over all generations, for God "called" them all from the beginning, Isa. 41:4; cf. Amos 5:8. "Calling" or "naming" an individual may specify the individual's primary characteristic, Gen. 27:36; it may consist of a confession or evaluation, Isa. 58:13; 60:14; and it may recognize an eternal truth, Isa. 7:14.

This verb also is used to indicate "calling to a specific task," Exod. 2:7.

To "call" on God's name is to summon His aid, Gen. 4:26. The "calling" on God's name is clearly not the beginning of prayer, Gen. 4:7ff. The sense of "summoning" God to one's aid was surely in Abraham's mind when he "called upon" God's name, Gen. 12:8. "Calling" in this sense constitutes a prayer prompted by recognized need and directed to One who is able and willing to respond, Ps. 145:18; Isa. 55:6.

Basically, ***qara'*** means "to call out loudly" in order to get someone's attention so that contact can be initiated, Job 5:11. Often this verb represents sustained communication, paralleling "to say" (***'amar***), as in Gen. 3:9. ***qara'*** can also mean "to call out a warning," Lev. 13:45.

***qara'*** may mean "to shout" or "to call out loudly." Goliath "shouted," 1 Sam. 17:8.

***qara'*** may also mean "to proclaim" or "to announce," Judg. 21:13; Esth. 6:9. In prophetic literature, ***qara'*** is a technical term for "declaring" a prophetic message: "For the saying which he *cried* by the word of the Lord . . . shall surely come to pass," 1 Kings 13:32.

Another major emphasis of ***qara'*** is "to summon," Gen. 12:18. Often the summons is in the form of a friendly invitation, Exod. 2:20. The participial form of ***qara'*** is used to denote "invited guests," 1 Sam. 9:13, NASB. This verb is also used in judicial contexts, to mean being "summoned to court," Deut. 25:8. ***qara'*** is used of mustering an army, Judg. 8:1.

***qara'*** means "to dictate," Jer. 36:18.

**B. Noun.**

***miqra'*** (4744), "public worship service; convocation." The word implies the product of an official summons to worship ("convocation"). In one of its 23 appearances, ***miqra'*** refers to Sabbaths as "convocation days" (Lev. 23:2).

### *New Testament*

**A. Verbs.**

1. ***kaleo*** (*2564*), derived from the root ***kal***—, whence Eng. "call" and "clamor," is used (a) with a personal object, "to call anyone, invite, summon," e.g., Matt. 20:8; 25:14; it is used particularly of the divine call to partake of the blessings of redemption, e.g., Rom. 8:30; 1 Cor. 1:9; 1 Thess. 2:12; Heb. 9:15; cf. B and C, below; (b) of nomenclature or vocation, "to call by a name, to name"; in the passive voice, "to be called by a name, to bear a name." Thus it suggests either vocation or destination; the context determines which, e.g., Rom. 9:25–26.

2. ***eiskaleo*** (*1528*), lit., "to call in," hence, "to invite" (***eis***, "in," and No. 1), is found in Acts 10:23.

3. ***epikaleo*** (*1941*), ***epi***, "upon," and No. 1., denotes (a) "to surname"; (b) "to be called by a person's name"; hence it is used of being declared to be dedicated to a person, as to the Lord, Acts 15:17 (from Amos 9:12); Jas. 2:7; (c) "to call a person by a name by charging him with an offense," as the Pharisees charged Christ with doing His works by the help of Beelzebub, Matt. 10:25 (the most authentic reading has ***epikaleo***, for ***kaleo***); (d) "to call upon, invoke"; in the middle voice, "to call upon for oneself" (i.e., on one's behalf), Acts 7:59, or "to call upon a person as a witness," 2 Cor. 1:23, or to appeal to an authority, Acts 25:11, etc.; (e) "to call upon by way of adoration, making use of the Name of the Lord," Acts 2:21; Rom. 10:12–14; 2 Tim. 2:22.

4. ***metakaleo*** (*3333*), ***meta***, implying "change," and No. 1, "to call from one place to another, to summon," is used in the middle

voice only, "to call for oneself, to send for, call hither," Acts 7:14; 10:32; 20:17; 24:25.

5. ***proskaleo*** (*4341*), ***pros***, "to," and No. 1, signifies (a) "to call to oneself, to bid to come"; it is used only in the middle voice, e.g., Matt. 10:1; Acts 5:40; Jas. 5:14; (b) "God's call to Gentiles through the gospel," Acts 2:39; (c) the divine call in entrusting men with the preaching of the gospel," Acts 13:2; 16:10.

6. ***sunkaleo*** (*4779*) signifies "to call together," Mark 15:16; Luke 9:1; 15:6, 9; 23:13; Acts 5:21; 10:24; 28:17.

7. ***aiteo*** (*154*), "to ask," is translated "called for" in Acts 16:29 ("he called for lights").

8. ***phoneo*** (*5455*), "to sound" (Eng., "phone"), is used of the crowing of a cock, e.g., Matt. 26:34; John 13:38; of "calling" out with a clear or loud voice, to cry out, e.g. Mark 1:26 (some mss. have ***krazo*** here); Acts 16:28; of "calling" to come to oneself, e.g., Matt. 20:32; Luke 19:15; of "calling" forth, as of Christ's call to Lazarus to come forth from the tomb, John 12:17; of inviting, e.g., Luke 14:12; of "calling" by name, with the implication of the pleasure taken in the possession of those "called," e.g., John 10:3; 13:13.

9. ***lego*** (*3004*), "to speak," is used of all kinds of oral communication, e.g. "to call, to call by name," to surname, Matt. 1:16; 26:36; John 4:5; 11:54; 15:15; Rev. 2:2, RV, "call themselves," etc.

10. ***epilego*** (*1951*), ***epi*** "upon," and No. 9, signifies "to call in addition," i.e., by another name besides that already intimated, John 5:2; for its other meaning in Acts 15:40, see CHOOSE.

11. ***chrematizo*** (*5337*), occasionally means "to be called or named," Acts 11:26 (of the name "Christians") and Rom. 7:3, the only places where it has this meaning. Its primary significance, "to have business dealings with," led to this. They "were (publicly) called" Christians, because this was their chief business.

12. ***eipon*** (*3004*), "to say, speak," akin to 9 above, means "to call by a certain appellation," John 10:35.

13. ***krino*** (*2919*), "to judge," is translated "to call in question," in Acts 23:6; 24:21.

### B. Noun.

***klesis*** (*2821*), "a calling" (akin to A, No. 1), is always used in the NT of that "calling" the origin, nature and destiny of which are heavenly (the idea of invitation being implied); it is used especially of God's invitation to man to accept the benefits of salvation, Rom. 11:29; 1 Cor. 1:26; 7:20 (said there of the condition in which the "calling" finds one); Eph. 1:18, "His calling"; Phil. 3:14, the "high calling"; 2 Thess. 1:11 and 2 Pet. 1:10, "your calling"; 2 Tim. 1:9, a "holy calling"; Heb. 3:1, a "heavenly calling"; Eph. 4:1, "the calling wherewith ye were called"; 4:4, "in one hope of your calling."

### C. Adjective.

***kletos*** (*2822*), "called, invited," is used, (a) "of the call of the gospel," Matt. 20:16; 22:14, not there "an effectual call," as in the Epistles, Rom. 1:1, 6–7; 8:28; 1 Cor. 1:2, 24; Jude 1; Rev. 17:14; in Rom. 1:7 and 1 Cor. 1:2 the meaning is "saints by calling"; (b) of "an appointment to apostleship," Rom. 1:1; 1 Cor. 1:1.

## CAMP

***machaneh*** (*4264*), "camp; encampment; host." Those who travel were called "campers," or in most versions (KJV, RSV, NASB) a "company" or "group" (NIV), as in Gen. 32:8. Naaman stood before Elisha "with all his company," 2 Kings 5:15 NASB, NEB, "retinue." Jacob "encamped" by the Jabbok with his retinue, Gen. 32:10. The name ***Mahanaim***, Gen. 32:2, "camps," owes its origin to Jacob's experience with the angels, calling it God's camp, Gen. 32:2.

Usage of ***machaneh*** varies according to context. First, it signifies a nation set over against another, Exod. 14:20. Second, the word refers to a division concerning the Israelites; each of the tribes had a special "encampment" in relation to the tent of meeting, Num. 1:52. Third, the word "camp" is used to describe the whole people of Israel, Exod. 19:16.

## CANAAN; CANAANITE

***kena'an*** (*3667*), "Canaan"; ***kena'ani*** (*3669*), "Canaanite; merchant." "Canaan" is first used of a person in Gen. 9:18; later it referenced an area, from Sidon to Gaza, to Sodom, west of the Jordan, Gen. 15:18–20; cf. Exod. 3:8, 17; Josh. 3:10. "Canaanite" is a general term for all the descendants of "Canaan," Deut. 7:1. It is interchanged with Amorite in Gen. 15:16. "Canaanite" also refers to one specific people in Canaan, Num. 13:29; cf. Josh. 5:1; 2 Sam. 24:7. These peoples were traders, Prov. 31:24; Job 41:6.

Gen. 9:25–27 stamps a theological significance on "Canaan" from the beginning. Noah prophetically placed this curse on "Canaan" because his father had stared at Noah's nakedness and reported it grossly to his brothers. Ham's sin, deeply rooted in his youngest son, is observable in the Canaanites, Lev. 18:3. The command to destroy the "Canaanites" was very specific, Deut. 7:2–6. But, too often the house of David and Judah "built them high places, 1 Kings 14:23–24; cf. 2 Kings 16:3–4; 21:1–15. "Canaanite" became synonymous with religious and moral perversions of every kind, Zech. 14:21, cf. Rev. 21:27.

## CAPTAIN

1. ***chiliarchos*** (*5506*), denoting "a commander of 1000 soldiers," was the Greek word for the Persian vizier, and for the Roman military tribune, the commander of a Roman cohort, e.g., John 18:12; Acts 21:31–33, 37. One such commander was constantly in charge of the Roman garrison in Jerusalem. The word became used also for any military commander, e.g., a "captain" or "chief captain," Mark 6:21; Rev. 6:15; 19:18.

2. ***strategos*** (*4755*), originally the commander of an army (from ***stratos***, "an army," and ***ago***, "to lead"), came to denote "a civil commander, a governor" (Latin, ***duumvir***), the highest magistrate, or any civil officer in chief command, Acts 16:20, 22, 35–36, 38; also the "chief captain" of the Temple, himself Levite, having command of the Levites who kept guard in and around the Temple, Luke 22:4, 52; Acts 4:1; 5:24, 26. Cf. Jer. 20:1.

3. ***archegos*** (*747*): Acts 3:15; 5:31; Heb. 2:10; 12:2.

## CAPTIVE, CAPTIVITY

### A. Nouns.

1. ***aichmalotos*** (*164*), lit., "one taken by the spear," a verbal adjective, from ***halonai***, "to be captured," hence denotes "a captive," Luke 4:18.

2. ***aichmalosia*** (*161*), "captivity," the abstract noun in contrast to No. 1, the concrete, is found in Rev. 13:10 and Eph. 4:8, where "He led captivity captive," seems to be an allusion to the triumphal procession by which a victory was celebrated, the "captives" taken forming part of the procession. See Judg. 5:12. The quotation is from Ps. 68:18, and probably is a forceful expression for Christ's victory, through His death, over the hostile powers of darkness. An alternative suggestion is that at His ascension Christ transferred the redeemed Old Testament saints from Sheol to His own presence in glory.

### B. Verbs.

1. ***aichmaloteuo*** (*162*) signifies (a) "to be a prisoner of war," (b) "to make a prisoner of war." The latter meaning is the only one used in the NT, Eph. 4:8.

2. ***aichmalotizo*** (*163*), practically synonymous with No. 1, denotes either "to lead away captive," Luke 21:24, or "to subjugate, to bring under control," said of the effect of the Law in one's members in bringing the person into captivity under the law of sin, Rom. 7:23; or of subjugating the thoughts to the obedience of Christ, 2 Cor. 10:5; or of those who took captive "silly women laden with sins," 2 Tim. 3:6.

3. ***zogreo*** (*2221*), lit. signifies "to take men alive," Luke 5:10, there of the effects of the work of the gospel; in 2 Tim. 2:26 it is said of the power of Satan to lead men astray. The verse should read "and that they may recover themselves out of the snare of the Devil (having been taken captive by him), unto the will of God." This is the probable meaning rather than "to take alive or for life."

## CARE (noun and verb), CAREFUL, CAREFULLY, CAREFULNESS

### A. Nouns.

1. ***merimna*** (*3308*), probably connected with ***merizo***, "to draw in different directions, distract," hence signifies "that which causes this, a care, especially an anxious care," Matt. 13:22; Mark 4:19; Luke 8:14; 21:34; 2 Cor. 11:28 (RV, "anxiety for"), 1 Pet. 5:7 (RV, "anxiety").

2. ***spoude*** (*4710*), primarily "haste, zeal, diligence," hence means "earnest care, carefulness," 2 Cor. 7:11–12; 8:16 (RV, "earnest care," in each place). ***merimna*** conveys the thought of anxiety, ***spoude***, of watchful interest and earnestness.

### B. Verbs.

1. ***merimnao*** (*3309*), akin to A No. 1, signifies "to be anxious about, to have a distracting care," e.g., Matt. 6:25, 28, RV, "be anxious," for KJV, "take thought"; 10:19; Luke 10:41 (RV, "anxious," for KJV, "careful"); 12:11 (RV, "anxious"); to be careful for, 1 Cor. 7:32–34; to have a care for, 1 Cor. 12:25; to care for, Phil. 2:20; "be anxious," Phil. 4:6, RV.

2. ***melei*** (*3199*), the third person sing. of ***melo***, used impersonally, signifies that "something is an object of care," especially the care of forethought and interest, rather than anxiety, Matt. 22:16; Mark 4:38; 12:14; Luke 10:40; John 10:13; 12:6; Acts 18:17; 1 Cor. 9:9 (RV, "Is it for the oxen that God careth?" The KJV seriously misses the point. God does "care" for oxen, but there was a divinely designed significance in the OT passage, relating to the service of preachers of the gospel); 7:21; 1 Pet. 5:7.

3. ***epimeleomai*** (*1959*) signifies "to take care of," involving forethought and provision (***epi*** indicating "the direction of the mind toward the object cared for"), Luke 10:34–35, of the Good Samaritan's care for the wounded man, and in 1 Tim. 3:5, of a bishop's (or overseer's) care of a church—a significant association of ideas.

4. ***phrontizo*** (*5431*), "to think, consider, be thoughtful" (from ***phren***, "the mind"), is translated "be careful" in Titus 3:8.

5. ***phroneo*** (*5426*), translated "be careful," in Phil. 4:10, KJV [RV, "(ye did) take thought"], has a much wider range of meaning than No. 5, and denotes to be minded, in whatever way.

### C. Adverb.

***spoudaioteros***, (*4708*), the comparative adverb corresponding to A, No. 2, signifies "the more diligently," Phil. 2:28.

## CARNAL, CARNALLY

1. ***sarkikos*** (*4559*), from ***sarx***, "flesh," signifies (a) "having the nature of flesh," i.e., sensual, controlled by animal appetites, governed by human nature, instead of by the Spirit of God, 1 Cor. 3:3 (for v. 1, see below; same mss. have it in v. 4); having its seat in the animal nature, or excited by it, 1 Pet. 2:11, "fleshly"; or as the equivalent of "human," with the added idea of weakness, figuratively of the weapons of spiritual warfare, "of the flesh" (KJV, "carnal"), 2 Cor. 10:4; or with the idea of unspirituality, of human wisdom, "fleshly," 2 Cor. 1:12; (b) "pertaining to the flesh" (i.e., the body), Rom. 15:27; 1 Cor. 9:11.

2. ***sarkinos*** (*4560*), (a) "consisting of flesh," 2 Cor. 3:3; (b) "pertaining to the natural, transient life of the body," Heb. 7:16; (c) given up to the flesh, Rom. 7:14. It is hard to distinguish 1 & 2 in 1 Cor. 3:1 and some other passages.

## CARPENTER

***tekton*** (*5405*) denotes any craftsman, but especially a worker in wood, a carpenter, Matt. 13:55; Mark 6:3.

## CATCH

1. ***harpazo*** (*726*), "to snatch or catch away," is said of the act of the Spirit of the Lord in regard to Philip in Acts 8:39; of Paul in being "caught" up to paradise, 2 Cor. 12:2, 4; of the rapture of the saints at the return of the Lord, 1 Thess. 4:17; of the rapture of the man child in the vision of Rev. 12:5. This verb conveys the idea of force suddenly exercised, as in Matt. 11:12, "take (it) by force"; 12:29, "spoil" (some mss. have ***diarpazo*** here), in 13:19, RV, "snatcheth"; for forceful seizure, see also John 6:15; 10:12 28–29; Acts 23:10; in Jude 23, RV, "snatching."

2. ***lambano*** (*2983*), "to receive," is once used of "catching" by fraud, circumventing, 2 Cor. 12:16. In Matt. 21:39 and Mark 12:3, RV "took," for KJV "caught."

3. ***agreuo*** (*4*), "to take by hunting" (from ***agra***, "a hunt, a catch"), is used metaphorically, of the Pharisees and Herodians in seeking to catch Christ in His talk, Mark 12:13.

4. ***sunarpazo*** (*4884*), ***sun***, used intensively, and No. 1, "to snatch, to seize, to keep a firm grip of," is used only by Luke, and translated "caught" in the KJV of Luke 8:29, of demon-possession; in Acts 6:12, of the act of the elders and scribes in seizing Stephen, RV, more suitably, "seized." So in Acts 19:29. In 27:15, it is used of the effects of wind upon a ship.

5. ***sullambano*** (*4815*), ***sun***, and No. 2, "to seize," is used, similarly to No. 6, in Acts 26:21, of the act of the Jews in seizing Paul in the temple.

6. ***epilambano*** (*1949*), "to lay hold" (***epi***, intensive, and No. 2), Acts 16:19.

## CEASE

***Old Testament***

### A. Verbs.

***chadal*** (2308), "to cease, come to an end, desist, forbear, lack." ***chadal*** means "coming to an end." Thus, Sarah's capacity for childbearing had long since "ceased" before an angel informed her that she was to have a son, Gen. 18:11. The Mosaic law made provision for the poor, since they would "never cease out of the land," Deut. 15:11; Matt. 26:11. In Exod. 14:12, this verb is better translated "let us alone" for the literal "cease from us."

***shabat*** (7673), "to rest, cease." The basic and most frequent meaning of ***shabat*** is shown in Gen. 8:22; Jer. 31:36. We find a variety of senses: "put away," Exod. 12:15; "be lacking," Lev. 2:13; "put down," 2 Kings 23:5; "eliminate," Lev. 26:6.

### B. Noun.

***shabbat*** (7676), "the sabbath," the seventh day of rest, Exod. 23:12. A man's "rest" was to include his animals and servants, Exod. 23:12; 31:17; 34:21. There is also a sabbath year, Lev. 25:2,4. The "sabbath" was a "day of worship," Lev. 23:3, as well as a "day of rest and refreshment" for man, Exod. 23:12. God "rested and was refreshed," Exod. 31:17. The "sabbath" was the covenant sign of God's lordship over the creation. By observing the "sabbath," Israel confessed that they were God's redeemed people, subject to His lordship to obey the whole of His law. They were His stewards to show mercy with kindness and liberality to all, Exod. 23:12; Lev. 25.

The prophets rebuked Israel for their neglect of the sabbath, Isa. 1:13; Jer. 17:21–27; Ezek. 20:12–24; Amos 8:5. They also proclaimed "sabbath" observance as a blessing in the messianic age and a sign of its fullness,

Isa. 56:2–4; 58:13; 66:23; Ezek. 44:24; 45:17; 46:1, 3–4, 12. The length of the Babylonian Captivity was determined by the extent of Israel's abuse of the sabbatical year, 2 Chron. 36:21; cf. Lev. 26:34–35.

*New Testament*

**A. Verbs.**

1. ***pauo*** *(3973)*, "to stop, to make an end," is used chiefly in the middle voice in the NT, signifying "to come to an end, to take one's rest, a willing cessation" (in contrast to the passive voice which denotes a forced cessation); Luke 5:4, of a discourse; 8:24, of a storm, 11:1, of Christ's prayer; Acts 5:42, of teaching and preaching; 6:13, of speaking against; 13:10, of evil doing; 20:1, of an uproar; 20:31, of admonition; 21:32, of a scourging; 1 Cor. 13:8, of tongues; Eph. 1:16, of giving thanks; Col. 1:9, of prayer; Heb. 10:2, of sacrifices; 1 Pet. 4:1, of "ceasing" from sin. It is used in the active voice in 1 Pet. 3:10, "let him cause his tongue to cease from evil."

2. ***dialeipo*** *(1257)*, lit., "to leave between," i.e., "to leave an interval, whether of space or time," (***dia***, "between," ***leipo***, "to leave"); hence, "to intermit, desist, cease," in Luke 7:45 is used of the kissing of the Lord's feet.

3. ***hesuchazo*** *(2270)*, "to be quiet, still, at rest," is said of Paul's friends in Caesarea, in "ceasing" to persuade him not to go to Jerusalem, Acts 21:14; it is used of silence (save in Luke 23:56 and 1 Thess. 4:11) in Luke 14:4 and Acts 11:18.

4. ***kopazo*** *(2869)*, "to cease through being spent with toil, to cease raging" (from ***kopos***, "labor, toil," ***kopiao***, "to labor"), is said of the wind only, Matt. 14:32; Mark 4:39; 6:51.

5. ***aphiemi*** *(863)*, "to let go," is translated "let us cease to" in Heb. 6:1.

6. ***katapauo*** *(2664)*, "to rest" (***kata***, "down," intensive, and No. 1), is so translated in Heb. 4:10, for the KJV "hath ceased."

**B. Adjective.**

***adialeiptos*** *(88)*, "unceasing" (from ***a***, negative, ***dia***, "through," ***leipo***, "to leave"), is used of "incessant" heart pain, Rom. 9:2, KJV, "continual," RV, "unceasing," and in 2 Tim. 1:3, of remembrance in prayer; the meaning in each place is not that of unbroken continuity, but without the omission of any occasion.

**C. Adverb.**

***adialeiptos*** *(89)*, "unceasingly, without ceasing," is used with the same significance as the adjective, not of what is not interrupted, but of that which is constantly recurring; in Rom. 1:9 and 1 Thess. 5:17, of prayer; in 1 Thess. 1:3, of the remembrance of the work, labor and patience of saints; in 1 Thess. 2:13, of thanksgiving.

## CENSER

1. ***thumiaterion*** *(2369)*, "a vessel for burning incense," 2 Chron. 26:19; Ezek. 8:11, is found in Heb. 9:4.

2. ***libanotos*** *(3031)* denotes "frankincense," the gum of the ***libanos***, "the frankincense tree"; in a secondary sense, "a vessel in which to burn incense," Rev. 8:3, 5.

## CENTURION

1. ***hekatontarchos*** *(1543)*, "a centurion," denotes a military officer commanding from 50 to 100 men, according to the size of the legion of which it was a part (***hekaton***, "a hundred," ***archo***, "to rule"), e.g., Matt. 8:5, 8., cf. Acts 10:1, 22.

2. ***kenturion*** *(2760)* is a Greek transliteration of the Latin ***centurio***, signifying practically the same as No. 1, Mark 15:39, 44–45.

## CERTAIN, CERTAINTY, CERTAINLY, CERTIFY

**A. Noun.**

***asphaleia*** *(803)*, primarily, "not liable to fall, steadfast, firm," hence denoting "safety," Acts 5:23, and 1 Thess. 5:3, has the further meaning, "certainty," Luke 1:4.

**B. Adjective.**

***asphales*** *(804)*, safe, is translated "certainty," Acts 21:34; 22:30; "certain," Acts 25:26; "safe," Phil. 3:1; "sure," Heb. 6:19.

## CHAMBERING

***koite*** *(2845)*, primarily a place in which to lie down, hence, "a bed, especially the marriage bed"; denotes, in Rom. 13:13, "illicit intercourse."

## CHAMBERLAIN

***ho epi tou koitonos***, lit., "the (one) over the bedchamber," denotes "a chamberlain," an officer who had various duties in the houses of kings and nobles. The importance of the position is indicated by the fact that the people of Tyre and Sidon sought the favor of Herod Agrippa through the mediation of Blastus, Acts 12:20.

## CHARGE (Nouns, Adjective and Verbs), CHARGEABLE

**A. Nouns.**

(a) *With the meaning of "an accusation."*

1. ***aitia*** *(156)*, "a cause, accusation," is rendered "charges" in Acts 25:27 (KJV, crimes); cf. v. 18.

2. ***aitioma*** (*157*), in some texts ***aitiama***, denotes "a charge," Acts 25:7.

3. ***enklema*** (*1462*), Acts 23:29; 25:16.

(b) *With the meaning of "something committed or bestowed."*

4. ***kleros*** (*2819*), "a lot, allotment, heritage" (whence Eng. "clergy"), is translated in 1 Pet. 5:3.

5. ***opsonion*** (*3800*), (from ***opson***, "meat," and ***oneomai***, "to buy"), primarily signified whatever is brought to be eaten with bread provisions, supplies for an army, soldier's pay, "charges," 1 Cor. 9:7, of the service of a soldier. It is rendered "wages" in Luke 3:14; Rom. 6:23; 2 Cor. 11:8.

6. ***parangelia*** (*3852*), "a proclamation, a command or commandment," is strictly used of commands received from a superior and transmitted to others, Acts 5:28; 16:24; 1 Thess. 4:2; 1 Tim. 1:5,18.

**B. Adjective.**

***adapanos*** (*77*), lit., "without expense," is used in 1 Cor. 9:18, "without charge" (of service in the gospel).

**C. Verbs.**

1. ***diamarturomai*** (*1263*), a strengthened form of ***marturomai*** (***dia***, "through," intensive), is used in the middle voice; primarily it signifies to testify through and through, bear a solemn witness; hence, "to charge earnestly," 1 Tim. 5:21; 2 Tim. 2:14; 4:1.

2. ***diastellomai*** (*1291*), lit., "to draw asunder," signifies "to admonish, order, charge," Matt. 16:20; Mark 5:43; 7:36 (twice); 8:15; 9:9. In Acts 15:24 it is translated "gave commandment"; in Heb. 12:20, KJV, "commanded," RV, "enjoined."

3. ***embrimaomai*** (*1690*), (from ***en***, "in," intensive, and ***brime***, "strength"), primarily signifies "to snort with anger, as of horses." Used of men it signifies "to fret, to be painfully moved"; then, "to express indignation against"; hence, "to rebuke sternly, to charge strictly," Matt. 9:30; Mark 1:43, it is rendered "murmured against" in Mark 14:5; "groaned" in John 11:33; "groaning" in v. 38.

4. ***entellomai*** (*1781*), to order, command, enjoin (from ***en***, in, used intensively, and ***teleo***, to fulfill), is translated by the verb to give charge, Matt. 4:6; 17:9 (AV); Luke 4:10.

5. ***epitimao*** (*2008*), signifies (a) to put honour upon; (b) to adjudge, to find fault with, rebuke; hence to charge, or rather, to charge strictly (***epi***, intensive), e.g., Matt. 12:16; Mark 3:12, "charged much"; Mark 8:30.

6. ***parangello*** (*3853*), lit., "to announce beside," "to hand on an announcement from one to another," usually denotes "to command, to charge," Luke 5:14; 8:56; 1 Cor. 7:10 (KJV, "command"), "give charge," RV; 11:17, "in giving you this charge," RV; 1 Tim. 1:3; 6:13, RV, and 6:17. It is rendered by the verb "to charge" in the RV of Acts 1:4; 4:18; 5:28; 15:5; 1 Thess. 4:11. See Acts 5:28 under A, No. 6.

7. ***proaitiaomai*** (*4256*), "to accuse beforehand, to have already brought a charge," is used in Rom. 3:9, "we before laid to the charge."

## CHASTE

***hagnos*** (*53*) signifies (a) "pure from every fault, immaculate," 2 Cor. 7:11 (KJV, "clear"); Phil. 4:8; 1 Tim. 5:22; Jas. 3:17; 1 John 3:3 (in all which the RV rendering is "pure"), and 1 Pet. 3:2, "chaste"; (b) "pure from carnality, modest," 2 Cor. 11:2, RV, "pure"; Titus 2:5, "chaste."

## CHASTEN, CHASTENING, CHASTISE, CHASTISEMENT

**A. Verb.**

***paideuo*** (*3811*) primarily denotes "to train children," suggesting the broad idea of education (***pais***, "a child"), Acts 7:22; 22:3; see also Titus 2:12, "instructing" (RV), here of a training gracious and firm; grace, which brings salvation, employs means to give us full possession of it, hence, "to chastise," this being part of the training, whether (a) by correcting with words, reproving, and admonishing, 1 Tim. 1:20 (RV, "be taught"); 2 Tim. 2:25, or (b) by "chastening" by the infliction of evils and calamities, 1 Cor. 11:32; 2 Cor. 6:9; Heb. 12:6–7, 10; Rev. 3:19. The verb also has the meaning "to chastise with blows, to scourge," said of the command of a judge, Luke 23:16, 22.

**B. Noun.**

***paideia*** (*3809*) denotes "the training of a child, including instruction"; hence, "discipline, correction," "chastening," Eph. 6:4, RV (KJV, "nurture"), suggesting the Christian discipline that regulates character; so in Heb. 12:5, 7, 8 (in v. 8, KJV, "chastisement," the RV corrects to "chastening"); in 2 Tim. 3:16, "instruction."

## CHEER, CHEERFUL, CHEERFULLY, CHEERFULNESS

**A. Verbs.**

1. ***euthumeo*** (*2114*) signifies, in the active voice, "to put in good spirits, to make cheerful," "mind or passion"; or, intransitively, "to be cheerful," Acts 27:22, 25; Jas. 5:13 (RV, "cheerful," for KJV, "merry").

2. ***tharseo*** (*2293*), "to be of good courage, of good cheer," is used only in the imperative mood, in the NT; "be of good cheer," Matt. 9:2, 22; 14:27; Mark 6:50; 10:49; Luke 8:48; John 16:33; Acts 23:11.

**B. Adjectives.**

1. ***euthumos*** (*2115*) means "of good cheer" (see A, No. 1), Acts 27:36.

2. ***hilaros*** (*2431*), from ***hileos***, "propitious," signifies that readiness of mind, that joyousness, which is prompt to do anything; hence, "cheerful" (cf. Eng., "hilarious"), 2 Cor. 9:7.

**C. Adverb.**

***euthumos*** (*2115*), cheerfully (see A, No. 1), Acts 24:10.

**D. Noun.**

***hilarotes*** (*2432*), "cheerfulness" (akin to B, No. 2), is used in Rom. 12:8, in connection with showing mercy.

## CHERISH

***thalpo*** (*2282*) primarily means "to heat, to soften by heat"; then, "to keep warm;" metaphorically, "to cherish with tender love, to foster with tender care"; in Eph. 5:29 of Christ and the church; in 1 Thess. 2:7 of saints care.

## CHERUBIM

***cheroubim*** (3742) are regarded by some as the ideal representatives of redeemed animate creation. In the tabernacle and Temple they were represented by the two golden figures of two-winged living creatures. The first reference to the "cherubim" is in Gen. 3:24. The presence of the "cherubim" suggests that redeemed men, restored to God on God's conditions, would have access to the Tree of Life, see Rev. 22:14. Certain other references in the OT give clear indication that angelic beings are upon occasion in view, e.g., Ps. 18:10; Ezek. 28:4. So with the vision of the cherubim in Ezek. 10:1–20; 11:22. In the NT the word is found in Heb. 9:5, where the reference is to the ark in the tabernacle, and the thought is suggested of those who minister to the manifestation of the glory of God.

## CHIEF, CHIEFEST, CHIEFLY

**A. Adjective.**

***protos*** (*4413*) denotes "the first," whether in time or place. It is translated "chief" in Mark 6:21, RV, of men of Galilee, in Acts 13:50, of men in a city; in 28:7, of the "chief" man in the island of Melita; in 17:4, of "chief" women in a city; in 28:17, of Jews; in 1 Tim. 1:15–16, of a sinner. In the following, where the KJV has "chief," or "chiefest," the RV renderings are different: Matt. 20:27 and Mark 10:44, "first"; Luke 19:47 and Acts 25:2, "principal men"; Acts 16:12, said of Philippi, "the first (city) of the district," RV, for incorrect KJV, "the chief city of that part of Macedonia." Amphipolis was the "chief" city of that part. ***protos*** here must mean the first in the direction in which the apostle came.

**B. Nouns.**

1. ***kephalaion*** (*2774*), denotes the chief point or principal thing in a subject, Heb. 8:1, "the chief point is this" (KJV, "the sum"); elsewhere in Acts 22:28 (of principal, as to money), "(a great) sum."

2. ***archiereus*** (*749*), "a chief priest, high priest," is frequent in the gospels, Acts and Hebrews, but there only in the NT. It is used of Christ, e.g., in Heb. 2:17; 3:1; of "chief" priests, including ex-high-priests and members of their families, e.g., Matt. 2:4; Mark 8:31.

3. ***archipoimen*** (*750*), "a chief shepherd," is said of Christ only, 1 Pet. 5:4. Modern Greeks use it of tribal chiefs.

4. ***architelones*** (*754*) denotes "a chief tax-collector, or publican," Luke 19:2.

5. ***akrogoniaios*** (*204*) denotes "a chief corner-stone" (from ***akros***, "highest, extreme," ***gonia***, "a corner, angle"), Eph. 2:20 and 1 Pet. 2:6.

6. ***protokathedria*** (*4410*), "a sitting in the first or chief seat," is found in Matt. 23:6; Mark 12:39; Luke 11:43; 20:46.

7. ***protoklisia*** (*4411*), "the first reclining place, the chief place at table," Matt. 23:6; Mark 12:39 (as with No. 6); Luke 14:7–8; 20:46.

8. ***chiliarchos*** (*5506*) denotes "a chief captain," Mark 6:21.

9. ***asiarches*** (*775*), "an Asiarch," was one of certain officers elected by various cities in the province of Asia, whose function consisted in celebrating, partly at their own expense, the public games and festivals; in Acts 19:31, RV, the word is translated "chief officers of Asia" (KJV, "chief of Asia").

10. ***archon*** (*758*), "a ruler," is rendered "chief" in the KJV of Luke 14:1 (RV, "ruler"); "chief rulers," in John 12:42, RV, "rulers (of the people)," i.e., of members of the Sanhedrin; "chief," in Luke 11:15 (RV, "prince"), in reference to Beelzebub, the prince of demons.

11. ***archisunagogos*** (*752*), "a ruler of a synagogue," translated "chief ruler of the synagogue," in Acts 18:8, 17, KJV, was the administrative officer supervising the worship.

## C. Verb.

***hegeomai*** *(2233)*, "to lead the way, to preside, rule, be the chief," is used of the ambition "to be chief" among the disciples of Christ, Luke 22:26; of Paul as the "chief" speaker in gospel testimony at Lystra, Acts 14:12; of Judas and Silas, as chief (or rather, "leading") men among the brethren at Jerusalem, Acts 15:22.

# CHILD, CHILDREN, CHILDBEARING, CHILDISH, CHILDLESS

1. ***teknon*** *(5043)*, "a child" (akin to ***tikto***, "to beget, bear"), is used in both the natural and the figurative senses. In contrast to ***huios***, "son" (see below), it gives prominence to the fact of birth, whereas ***huios*** stresses the dignity and character of the relationship. Figuratively, ***teknon*** is used of "children" of (a) God, John 1:12; (b) light, Eph. 5:8; (c) obedience, 1 Pet. 1:14; (d) a promise, Rom. 9:8; Gal. 4:28; (e) the Devil, 1 John 3:10; (f) wrath, Eph. 2:3; (g) cursing, 2 Pet. 2:14; (h) spiritual relationship, 2 Tim. 2:1; Philem. 10.

2. ***teknion*** *(5040)*, "a little child," a diminutive of No. 1, is used only figuratively in the NT, and always in the plural. It is found frequently in 1 John, see 2:1, 12, 28; 3:7, 18; 4:4; 5:21; elsewhere, once in John's Gospel, 13:33, once in Paul's epistles, Gal. 4:19. It is a term of affection by a teacher to his disciples.

3. ***huios*** *(5207)*, "a son," is always so translated in the RV, except in the phrase "children of Israel," e.g., Matt. 27:9; and with reference to a foal, Matt. 21:5.

4. ***pais*** *(3816)* signifies (a) "a child in relation to descent," (b) "a boy or girl in relation to age," (c) "a servant, attendant, maid, in relation to condition." As an instance of (a) see Matt. 21:15, "children," and Acts 20:12 (RV, "lad"). In regard to (b) the RV has "boy" in Matt. 17:18 and Luke 9:42. In Luke 2:43 it is used of the Lord Jesus. In regard to (c), see Matt. 8:6, 8, 13, etc. As to (a) note Matt. 2:16, RV, male children.

5. ***paidion*** *(3813)*, a diminutive of 4. above, signifies "a little or young child"; it is used of an infant just born, John 16:21, of a male child recently born, e.g., Matt. 2:8; Heb. 11:23; of a more advanced child, Mark 9:24; of a son, John 4:49; of a girl, Mark 5:39, 40, 41; in the plural, of "children," e.g., Matt. 14:21. It is used metaphorically of believers who are deficient in spiritual understanding, 1 Cor. 14:20, and in affectionate and familiar address by the Lord to His disciples, almost like the Eng., "lads," John 21:5.

6. ***paidarion*** *(3808)*, another diminutive of 4. above, is used of "boys and girls," in Matt. 11:16 (the best texts have ***paidiois*** here), and a "lad," John 6:9; the tendency in colloquial Greek was to lose the diminutive character of the word.

7. ***nepios*** *(3516)*, lit., "not-speaking" (from ***ne***, a negative, and ***epos***, a word) is rendered "childish" in 1 Cor. 13:11.

8. ***monogenes*** *(3439)*, lit., "only-begotten," is translated "only child" in Luke 9:38.

9. ***teknogonia*** *(5042)*, "to beget," denotes "bearing children," implying the duties of motherhood, 1 Tim. 2:15.

## B. Verbs.

1. ***nepiazo*** *(3515)*, "to be a baby," is used in 1 Cor. 14:20, "(in malice) be ye babes" (akin to No. 7, above).

2. ***teknotropheo*** *(5044)*, "to rear young," (***teknon***, and ***trepho***, "to rear"), signifies "to bring up children," 1 Tim. 5:10.

3. ***teknogoneo*** *(5041)*, "to bear children" (***teknon***, and ***gennao***, "to beget"), see No. 9 above, is found in 1 Tim. 5:14.

## C. Adjectives.

1. ***enkuos*** *(1471)* denotes "great with child" (***en***, "in," and ***kuo***, "to conceive"), Luke 2:5.

2. ***philoteknos*** *(5388)*, (from ***phileo***, "to love," and ***teknon***), signifies "loving one's children," Titus 2:4.

3. ***ateknos*** *(815)*, (from ***a***, negative, and ***teknon***), signifies "childless," Luke 20:28–30.

# CHOICE, CHOOSE, CHOSEN

### *Old Testament*

## A. Verb.

***bachar*** (977), "to choose." ***bachar*** is often used with a man as the subject, Gen. 13:11. In more than half of the occurrences, God is the subject of ***bachar***, Num. 16:5. Neh. 9:7–8 describes God's "choosing" (election) of persons as far back as Abram. ***bachar*** is used 30 times in Deuteronomy, all but twice referring to God's "choice" of Israel or something in Israel's life, Deut. 4:37; 14:1–2. God's choices shaped the history of Israel; His "choice" led to their redemption from Egypt, Deut. 7:7–8, sent Moses and Aaron to work miracles in Egypt, Ps. 105:26–27, and gave them the Levites "to bless in the name of the Lord," Deut. 21:5, and many more examples, Deut. 12:5; 2 Chron. 6:5, 21. Men and women are called to respond to God's election, Deut. 30:19; cf. Josh. 24:22.

## B. Noun.

***bachir*** (972), "chosen ones." Another noun, ***bachir,*** is used 13 times, always of the Lord's "chosen ones": "Saul, whom the Lord did choose," 2 Sam. 21:6; "ye children of Jacob, his chosen ones," 1 Chron. 16:13.

*New Testament*

**A. Verbs.**

1. ***eklego*** *(1586)*, "to pick out, select," means, in the middle voice, "to choose for oneself," not necessarily implying the rejection of what is not chosen, but "choosing" with the subsidiary ideas of kindness or favor or love, Mark 13:20; Luke 6:13; 9:35 (RV); 10:42; 14:7; John 6:70; 13:18; 15:16, 19; Acts 1:2, 24; 6:5; 13:17; 15:22, 25; in 15:7 it is rendered "made choice"; 1 Cor. 1:27–28; Eph. 1:4; Jas. 2:5.

2. ***epilego*** *(1951)*, in the middle voice, signifies "to choose," either in addition or in succession to another. It has this meaning in Acts 15:40, of Paul's choice of Silas.

3. ***cheirotoneo*** *(5500)*, Acts 14:23; 2 Cor. 8:19.

4. ***procheirotoneo*** *(4401)* signifies "to choose before," Acts 10:41, where it is used of a choice made before by God.

**B. Adjective.**

***eklektos*** *(1588)*, akin to A, No. 1, signifies "chosen out, select," e.g., Matt. 22:14; Luke 23:35; Rom. 16:13 (perhaps in the sense of "eminent"), Rev. 17:14. In 1 Pet. 2:4, 9, the RV translates it "elect."

**C. Noun.**

***ekloge*** *(1589)*, akin to A, No. 1 and B, "a picking out, choosing" (Eng., "eclogue"), is translated "chosen" in Acts 9:15, lit., "he is a vessel of choice unto Me." In the six other places where this word is found it is translated "election."

## CHRIST

***christos*** (5547), "anointed," translates, in the Sept., the word "Messiah," a term applied to mere humans with a special office, Lev. 4:3, 5, 16; Ps. 105:15. A king of Israel was "the anointed of the Lord," 1 Sam. 2:10, 35; 2 Sam. 1:14; Ps. 2:2; 18:50; Hab. 3:13; Isa. 45:1.

The title ***ho Christos***, in the NT is frequently used with the article, of the Lord Jesus, as an appellative rather than a title, e.g., Matt. 2:4; Acts 2:31; without the article, Luke 2:11; 23:2; John 1:41.

It is added as an appellative to the proper name "Jesus," e.g., John 17:3, the only time when the Lord so spoke of Himself; Acts 9:34; 1 Cor. 3:11; 1 John 5:6. It is distinctly a proper name in many passages, whether with the article, e.g., Matt. 1:17; 11:2; Rom. 7:4, 9:5; 15:19; 1 Cor. 1:6, or without the article, Mark 9:41; Rom. 6:4; 8:9, 17; 1 Cor. 1:12; Gal. 2:16. The single title ***Christos*** is sometimes used without the article to signify the One who by His Holy Spirit and power indwells believers and molds their character in conformity to His likeness, Rom. 8:10; Gal. 2:20; 4:19; Eph. 3:17. As to the use or absence of the article, the title with the article specifies the Lord Jesus as "the Christ"; the title without the article stresses His character and His relationship with believers. Again, speaking generally, when the title is the subject of a sentence it has the article; when it forms part of the predicate the article is absent.

## CHRISTS (FALSE)

***pseudochristos*** (5580) denotes "one who falsely lays claim to the name and office of the Messiah," Matt. 24:24; Mark 13:22.

## CHRISTIAN

***christianos*** (5546), "Christian," a word formed after the Roman style, signifying an adherent of Jesus, was first applied to such by the Gentiles and is found in Acts 11:26; 26:28; 1 Pet. 4:16.

Though the word rendered "were called" in Acts 11:26 might be used of a name adopted by oneself or given by others, the "Christians" do not seem to have adopted it for themselves in the times of the apostles. In 1 Pet. 4:16, the apostle is speaking from the point of view of the persecutor, cf. "as a thief," "as a murderer." Nor is it likely that the appellation was given by Jews. As applied by Gentiles there was no doubt an implication of scorn, as in Agrippa's statement in Acts 26:28, though after Bible times, a title of honor.

## CIRCUMCISION, UNCIRCUMCISION, CIRCUMCISE

*Old Testament*

***mul*** (4135), "to circumcise, cut off." The physical act of circumcision was introduced by God as a sign of the Abrahamic covenant, Gen. 17:10–11, NIV. It was a permanent "cutting off" of the foreskin of the male organ, and as such was a reminder of the perpetuity of the covenantal relationship. Israel was enjoined to be faithful in "circumcising" all males; each male baby was to be "circumcised" on the eighth day, Gen. 17:12; Lev. 12:3.

To be figuratively circumcised in the "heart" (or inner self), was to not be obstinate, but to respond to God's will, and be obedient, Deut. 10:16, NIV; cf. 30:6; Jer. 4:4. Few occurrences of the verb differ from the physical and the spiritual usage of "to circumcise." ***mul*** in the Book of Psalms has the meaning of "to cut off, destroy," Ps. 118:10, NIV; cf. vv. 11–12. In the English versions, the verb is rendered "to circumcise," "to destroy" (KJV), as well as "to cut off" and "to wither" (RSV, NASB, NIV).

*New Testament*

**A. Nouns.**

1. ***peritome*** (*4061*), lit., "a cutting round, circumcision" (the verb is ***peritemno***), was a rite enjoined by God upon Abraham and his male descendants and dependents, as a sign of the covenant made with him, Gen. 17; Acts 7:8; Rom. 4:11. Hence Israelites termed Gentiles "the uncircumcised," Judg. 15:18; 2 Sam. 1:20. So in the NT, but without the suggestion of contempt, e.g., Rom. 2:26; Eph. 2:11.

The rite had a moral significance, Ex. 6:12, 30, where it is metaphorically applied to the lips; so to the ear, Jer. 6:10, and the heart, Deut. 30:6; Jer. 4:4. Cf. Jer. 9:25–26. It refers to the state of "circumcision," in Rom. 2:25–28; 3:1; 4:10; 1 Cor. 7:19; Gal. 5:6; 6:15; Col. 3:11.

In the economy of grace no account is taken of any ordinance performed on the flesh; the old racial distinction is ignored in the preaching of the gospel, and faith is the sole condition upon which the favor of God in salvation is to be obtained, Rom. 10:11–13; 1 Cor. 7:19. See also Rom. 4:9–12.

Upon the preaching of the gospel to, and the conversion of, Gentiles, a sect of Jewish believers arose who argued that the gospel, without the fulfillment of "circumcision," would make void the Law and make salvation impossible, Acts 15:1. Hence this party was known as "the circumcision," Acts 10:45; 11:2; Gal. 2:12; Col. 4:11; Titus 1:10 (the term being used by metonymy, the abstract being put for the concrete, as with the application of the word to Jews generally, Rom. 3:30; 4:9, 12; 15:8; Gal. 2:7–9; Eph. 2:11). It is used metaphorically and spiritually of believers with reference to the act, Col. 2:11 and Rom. 2:29; to the condition, Phil. 3:3.

2. ***akrobustia*** (*203*), "uncircumcision," is used (a) of the physical state, in contrast to the act of "circumcision," Acts 11:3 (lit., "having uncircumcision"); Rom. 2:25–26; 4:10–11 ("though they be in uncircumcision," RV), 12; 1 Cor. 7:18–19; Gal. 5:6; 6:15; Col. 3:11; (b) by metonymy, for Gentiles, e.g., Rom. 2:26–27; 3:30; 4:9; Gal. 2:7; Eph. 2:11; (c) in a metaphorical or transferred sense, of the moral condition in which the corrupt desires of the flesh still operate, Col. 2:13.

**B. Adjective.**

***aperitmetos*** (*564*), "uncircumcised" (***a***, negative, ***peri***, "around," ***temno***, "to cut"), is used in Acts 7:51, metaphorically, of "heart and ears."

**C. Verb.**

***peritemno*** (*4059*), "to circumcise," is used (a) lit., e.g., Luke 1:59; 2:21; of receiving circumcision, Gal. 5:2–3; 6:13, RV; (b) metaphorically, of spiritual circumcision, Col. 2:11.

## CITIZEN, CITIZENSHIP

1. ***polites*** (*4177*), "a member of a city or state, or the inhabitant of a country or district," Luke 15:15, is used elsewhere in Luke 19:14; Acts 21:39, and, in the most authentic mss., in Heb. 8:11 (where some texts have ***plesion***, "a neighbor"). Apart from Heb. 8:11, the word occurs only in the writings of Luke (himself a Greek).

2. ***sumpolites*** (*4847*), ***sun***, "with," and No. 1, denotes "a fellow-citizen," i.e., possessing the same "citizenship," Eph. 2:19, used metaphorically in a spiritual sense.

3. ***politeia*** (*4174*) signifies (a) "the relation in which a citizen stands to the state, the condition of a citizen, citizenship," Acts 22:28, "with a great sum obtained I this citizenship" (KJV, "freedom"). While Paul's "citizenship" of Tarsus was not of advantage outside that city, yet his Roman "citizenship" availed throughout the Roman Empire and, besides private rights, included (1) exemption from all degrading punishments; (2) a right of appeal to the emperor after a sentence; (3) a right to be sent to Rome for trial before the emperor if charged with a capital offense. Paul's father might have obtained "citizenship" (1) by manumission; (2) as a reward of merit; (3) by purchase; the contrast implied in Acts 22:28 is perhaps against the last mentioned; (b) "a civil polity, the condition of a state, a commonwealth," said of Israel, Eph. 2:12.

4. ***politeuma*** (*4175*) signifies "the condition, or life, of a citizen, citizenship"; it is said of the heavenly status of believers, Phil. 3:20.

## CITY

*Old Testament*

***'ir*** (5892), "city; town; village; quarter [of a city]." The word suggests a "village." An unwalled village is represented by the Hebrew word ***chatser. qiryat***, a synonym of ***'ir***, is an Aramaic loan-word.

But ***'ir*** and its synonym do not necessarily suggest a walled city. This usage is seen in Deut. 3:5, where ***'ir*** may be a city standing in the open country (perhaps surrounded by dirt or stone ramparts for protection): "All these cities were fenced with high walls, gates, and bars; beside unwalled towns a great many." A comparison of Lev. 25:29 and Lev. 25:31 shows that ***'ir*** can be used as synonym of ***chatser:***

"And if a man sell a dwelling house in a walled city, then he may redeem it within a whole year after it is sold;.but the houses of the villages [***chatser***] which have no wall round about them shall be counted as the fields of the country . . ."

***'ir*** can signify not only a "village consisting of permanent houses" but also one in a permanent place, even though the dwellings are tents, 1 Sam. 15:5. As a rule, there are no political overtones to the word; ***'ir*** simply represents the "place where people dwell on a permanent basis." At some points, however, ***'ir*** represents a political entity, 1 Sam. 15:5; 30:29. This word can also represent "those who live in a given town," 1 Sam. 4:13. ***'ir*** can also signify only "a part of a city," such as a stronghold, 2 Sam. 5:7. Ancient cities (especially larger ones) were sometimes divided into sections (quarters) by walls, in order to make it more difficult to capture them. This suggests that, by the time of the statement just cited, ***'ir*** normally implied a "walled city."

### *New Testament*

***polis*** (*4172*), primarily "a town enclosed with a wall"; of the heavenly Jerusalem, the abode and community of the redeemed, Heb. 11:10, 16; 12:22; 13:14; Rev. 3:12; 21:2, 14, 19; its inhabitants, Matt. 8:34; 12:25; 21:10; Mark 1:33; Acts 13:44.

## CLANGING

***alalazo*** (*214*), in the NT, in Mark 5:38, of wailing mourners; in 1 Cor. 13:1, of the "clanging" of cymbals.

## CLEAN, CLEANNESS, CLEANSE, CLEANSING

### *Old Testament*

### A. Verb.

***taher*** (2891), "to be clean, pure." Since the fall of Adam and Eve, none of their offspring is clean in the sight of the holy God, Prov. 20:9; Job 4:17. There is hope, however, because God promised penitent Israel: "And I will cleanse them from all their iniquity, whereby they have sinned against me . . ." Jer. 33:8; Ezek. 37:23.

God required that His people observe purification rites when they came into His presence for worship. On the Day of Atonement, for example, prescribed ceremonies were performed to "cleanse" the altar from "the uncleanness of the children of Israel" and to "hallow it," Lev. 16:17–19; cf. Exod. 29:36ff. The priests were to be purified before they performed their sacred tasks. Moses was directed to "take the Levites . . . and cleanse them," Num. 8:6; cf. Lev. 8:5–13. After they had been held captive in the unclean land of Babylon, ". . . the priests and the Levites purified themselves, and purified the people, and the gates, and the wall [of the rebuilt city of Jerusalem]," Neh. 12:30. Some cleansing rites required blood as the purifying agent, Lev. 16:19. Sacrifices were offered to make atonement for a mother after childbirth, Lev. 12:8.

### B. Adjective.

***tahor*** (2889), "clean; pure." The word denotes the absence of impurity, filthiness, defilement, or imperfection. It is applied concretely to substances that are genuine or unadulterated as well as describing an unstained condition of a spiritual or ceremonial nature. Gold is a material frequently said to be free of baser ingredients. Thus the ark of the covenant, the incense altar, and the porch of the temple and many other items were "overlaid with pure gold," Exod. 25:11; 37:11, 26; 2 Chron. 3:4.

God demands that His people have spiritual and moral purity, unsullied by sin, Job 14:4; Ps. 51:10. In sharp contrast with mankind's polluted nature and actions, "the words of the Lord are pure words . . ." Ps. 12:6. The Lord is "of purer eyes than to behold evil," Hab. 1:13.

The people of the old covenant were told that "he that toucheth the dead body of any man shall be unclean seven days," Num. 19:11. A priest was not to defile himself "for the dead among his people" except "for his kin, that is near unto him," Lev. 21:1–2. This relaxation of the rule was even denied the high priest and a Nazarite during "all the days that he separateth himself unto the Lord," Num. 6:6ff. Also cleansing was necessary for childbirth and menstrual period, Lev. 15:1–18. To be ceremonially "clean," the Israelite also had to abstain from eating certain animals and even from touching them, Lev. 11; Deut. 14:3–21. After the Israelites settled in the Promised Land, some modifications were made in the regulations, Deut. 12:15, 22; 15:22.

Purification rites frequently involved the use of water in washing his body, and many things that were around him, including clothing, Lev. 15:27; Num. 19:18. However, the rites were not meritorious deeds, earning God's favor and forgiveness. Nor did the ceremonies serve their intended purpose if performed mechanically. Unless the rites expressed a person's contrite and sincere desire to be cleansed from the defilement of sin, they were an abomination to God and only aggravated a person's guilt. Anyone who appeared before Him in ritual and ceremony with "hands . . .

full of blood," Isa. 1:15, and did not plead for cleansing of his crimes was judged to be as wicked as the people of Sodom and Gomorrah. Zion's hope lay in this cleansing by means of an offering: "And they shall bring all your brethren for an offering unto the Lord out of all nations upon horses . . . as the children of Israel bring an offering in a clean vessel into the house of the Lord," Isa. 66:20.

### *New Testament*

**A. Adjective.**

***katharos*** (*2513*), "free from impure admixture, without blemish, spotless," is used (a) physically, e.g., Matt. 23:26; 27:59; John 13:10 (where the Lord, speaking figuratively, teaches that one who has been entirely "cleansed," needs not radical renewal, but only to be "cleansed" from every sin into which he may fall); 15:3; Heb. 10:22; Rev. 15:6; 19:8, 14; 21:18, 21; (b) in a Levitical sense, Rom. 14:20; Titus 1:15, "pure"; (c) ethically, with the significance free from corrupt desire, from guilt, Matt. 5:8; John 13:10–11; Acts 20:26; 1 Tim. 1:5; 3:9; 2 Tim. 1:3; 2:22; Titus 1:15; Jas. 1:27; blameless, innocent (a rare meaning for this word), Acts 18:6; (d) in a combined Levitical and ethical sense ceremonially, Luke 11:41, "all things are clean unto you."

**B. Verbs.**

1. ***katharizo*** (*2511*), akin to A, signifies (1) "to make clean, to cleanse" (a) from physical stains and dirt, as in the case of utensils, Matt. 23:25 (figuratively in verse 26); from disease, as of leprosy, Matt. 8:2; (b) in a moral sense, from the defilement of sin, Acts 15:9; 2 Cor. 7:1; Heb. 9:14; Jas. 4:8, "cleanse" from the guilt of sin, Eph. 5:26; 1 John 1:7; (2) "to pronounce clean in a Levitical sense," Mark 7:19, RV; Acts 10:15; 11:9; "to consecrate by cleansings," Heb. 9:22, 23; 10:2.

2. ***diakatharizo*** (*1245*), "to cleanse thoroughly," is used in Matt. 3:12, RV.

**C. Nouns.**

1. ***katharismos*** (*2512*), akin to A, denotes "cleansing," (a) both the action and its results, in the Levitical sense, Mark 1:44; Luke 2:22, "purification"; 5:14, "cleansing"; John 2:6; 3:25, "purifying"; (b) in the moral sense, from sins, Heb. 1:3; 2 Pet. 1:9.

2. ***katharotes*** (*2514*), akin to B, "cleanness, purity," is used in the Levitical sense in Heb. 9:13, RV, "cleanness."

## CLEAR, CLEARING, CLEARLY

**A. Verb.**

***krustallizo*** (*2929*), "to shine like crystal, to be of crystalline brightness, or transparency," is found in Rev. 21:11, "clear as crystal," or transitive, so speaking of Christ.

**B. Adjective.**

***lampros*** (*2986*) is said of crystal, Rev. 22:1.

C

## CLEAVE, CLAVE

### *Old Testament*

***dabaq*** (1692), "to cling, cleave, keep close"; used of a man and wife, Gen. 2:24, of a sword, 2 Sam. 23:10; of clothing, Jer. 13:11; of a tongue, Job 29:10; of a body prone in the dirt, Ps. 119:25.

The figurative use of ***dabaq*** in the sense of "loyalty" and "affection" is based on the physical closeness of the persons involved, such as a husband's closeness to his wife, Gen. 2:24, Shechem's affection for Dinah, Gen. 34:3, or Ruth's staying with Naomi, Ruth 1:14. "Cleaving" to God is equivalent to "loving" God, Deut. 30:20.

### *New Testament*

1. ***kollao*** (*2853*), "to join fast together, to glue, cement," is primarily said of metals and other materials (from ***kolla***, "glue"). In the NT it is used only in the passive voice, with reflexive force, in the sense of "cleaving unto," as of cleaving to one's wife, Matt. 19:5; some mss. have the intensive verb No. 2, here; 1 Cor. 6:16–17, "joined." In the corresponding passage in Mark 10:7, the most authentic mss. omit the sentence. In Luke 10:11 it is used of the "cleaving" of dust to the feet; in Acts 5:13; 8:29; 9:26; 10:28; 17:34, in the sense of becoming associated with a person so as to company with him, or be on his side, said, in the last passage, of those in Athens who believed: in Rom. 12:9, ethically, of "cleaving" to that which is good.

2. ***proskollao*** (*4347*), in the passive voice, used reflexively, "to cleave unto," is found in Eph. 5:31 (KJV "joined to").

## CLEMENCY

***epieikeia*** (*1932*), "mildness, gentleness, kindness" (what Matthew Arnold has called "sweet reasonableness"), is translated "clemency" in Acts 24:4; elsewhere, in 2 Cor. 10:1, of the gentleness of Christ.

## CLOKE (Pretense)

1. ***epikalumma*** (*1942*) is "a covering, a means of hiding"; hence, "a pretext, a cloke, for wickedness," 1 Pet. 2:16.

2. ***prophasis*** (*4392*), probably, from ***pro***, and ***phemi***, "to say," is rendered "cloke" (of covetousness) in 1 Thess. 2:5; "excuse" in John 15:22 (KJV "cloke"); "pretense" in Matt. 23:14; Mark 12: 40; Luke 20:47 (KJV "show"); Phil. 1:18;

"color" in Acts 27:30. It signifies the assuming of something so as to disguise one's real motives.

## CLOSE (Verb)

***kammuo*** (*2576*), denotes "to close down"; hence, "to shut the eyes," in stubbornness Matt. 13:15 and Acts 28:27.

## COLLECTION

***logia*** (*3048*), akin to ***lego***, "to collect," is used in 1 Cor. 16:1, 2.

## COLT

***polos*** (*4454*), "a foal," whether "colt or filly," had the general significance of "a young creature"; in Matt. 21:2, and parallel passages, "an ass's colt."

## TO COME NEAR, APPROACH

***nagash*** (5066), "to approach, draw near, bring," Gen. 18:23. The word is often used to describe ordinary "contact" of one person with another, Gen. 27:22; 43:19. Sometimes ***nagash*** describes "contact" for the purpose of sexual intercourse, Exod. 19:15. More frequently, it is used to speak of the priests "coming into the presence of" God, Ezek. 44:13, or of the priests' "approach" to the altar, Exod. 30:20. Opposing armies are said "to draw near" to battle each other, Judg. 20:23. Inanimate objects, such as the close-fitting scales of the crocodile, are said to be so "near" to each other that no air can come between them, Job 41:16. Sometimes the word is used to speak of "bringing" an offering to the altar, Mal. 1:7.

## TO COME UP, ASCEND

### A. Verb.

***'alah*** (5927), "to go up, ascend, offer up." Basically, ***'alah*** suggests movement from a lower to a higher place, Gen. 2:6; Isa. 14:13. This word may mean "to take a journey," Gen. 13:1. "To extend, reach," is another meaning, Josh. 18:12. It can also mean general linear movement with no particular focus on ascending, Gen. 44:17; Ezra 2:1. The verb became a technical term for "making a pilgrimage," Exod. 34:24 or "going up" before the Lord; in a secular context, compare Joseph's "going up" before Pharaoh, Gen. 46:31.

Another special use of ***'alah*** is "to overpower" (literally, "to go up from"). For example, the Pharaoh feared the Israelites lest in a war they join the enemy, fight against Egypt, and "overpower" the land, Exod. 1:10. "To go up" may also be used of "increasing in strength," as the lion that becomes strong from his prey: The lion "goes up from his prey," Gen. 49:9; cf. Deut. 28:43.

***'alah*** can be used also of the "increasing" of wrath, 2 Sam. 11:20, the "ascent" of an outcry before God, Exod. 2:23. Sometimes "go up" means "placed," even when the direction is downward, as when placing a yoke upon an ox, Num. 19:2, or going to one's grave, Job 5:26. This may be an illustration of how Hebrew verbs can sometimes mean their opposite. The verb is also used of "recording" a census, 1 Chron. 27:24.

***'alah*** signifies "presenting an offering" to God, especially the whole burnt offering, Lev. 14:20; Isa. 57:6.

### B. Nouns.

***'elyon*** (5945), "the upper; the highest." The use of ***'elyon*** in Gen. 40:17 means "the upper" as opposed to "the lower." Where referring to or naming God, ***'elyon*** means "the highest," Gen. 14:18.

***ma'alah*** (4699), "step; procession; pilgrimage." ***ma'alah*** signifies a "step" or "stair," cf. Exod. 20:26. The word can also mean "procession," Ps. 84:6.

## COMELINESS, COMELY

### A. Noun.

***euschemosune*** (*2157*), "elegance of figure, gracefulness, comeliness" (***eu***, "well," ***schema***, "a form"), is found in this sense in 1 Cor. 12:23.

### B. Adjective.

***euschemon*** (*2158*), akin to A, "elegant in figure, well formed, graceful," is used in 1 Cor. 12:24, of parts of the body (see above); in 1 Cor. 7:35 RV, "(that which is) seemly," KJV, "comely"; "honourable," Mark 15:43; Acts 13:50; 17:12.

## COMFORT, COMFORTER, COMFORTLESS

### A. Nouns.

1. ***paraklesis*** (*3874*), means "a calling to one's side"; hence, either "an exhortation, or consolation, comfort," e.g., Luke 2:25 (here "looking for the consolation of Israel" is equivalent to waiting for the coming of the Messiah); 6:24; Acts 9:31; Rom. 15:4–5; 1 Cor. 14:3, "exhortation"; 2 Cor. 1:3, 4–7; 7:4, 7, 13; 2 Thess. 2:16; Philem. 7. In 2 Thess. 2:16 it combines encouragement with alleviation of grief. The RV changes "consolation" into "comfort," except in Luke 2:25; 6:24; Acts 15:31; in Heb. 6:18, "encouragement"; in Acts 4:36, "exhortation." RV (KJV, consolation").

2. ***paramuthia*** (*3889*), primarily "a speaking closely to anyone"; hence denotes "consolation, comfort," with a greater degree of tenderness than No. 1, 1 Cor. 14:3.

3. ***paramuthion*** (*3890*) has the same meaning as No. 2, the difference being that ***paramuthia*** stresses the process or progress of the act, ***paramuthion*** the instrument as used by the agent, Phil. 2:1.

4. ***parakletos*** (*3875*), lit., "called to one's side," i.e., to one's aid, is primarily a verbal adjective, and suggests the capability or adaptability for giving aid. It was used in a court of justice to denote a legal assistant, counsel for the defense, an advocate; then, generally, one who pleads another's cause, an intercessor, advocate, as in 1 John 2:1, of the Lord Jesus. In the widest sense, it signifies a "succorer, comforter," John 14:16. In 14:26; 15:26; 16:7.

**B. Verbs.**

1. ***parakaleo*** (*3870*) has the same variety of meanings as Noun, No. 1, above, e.g., Matt. 2:18; 1 Thess. 3:2, 7; 4:18. In 2 Cor. 13:11, it signifies "to be comforted" (so the RV).

2. ***sumparakaleo*** (*4837*), ***sun***, "with," and No. 1, signifies "to comfort together," Rom. 1:12.

3. ***paramutheomai*** (*3888*), akin to Noun No. 2, "to soothe, console, encourage," is translated, in John 11:31, "comforted", in v. 19, RV, "console." In 1 Thess. 2:11 and 5:14, RV, "encourage," as the sense there is that of stimulating to the earnest discharge of duties.

## COMING (Noun)

***parousia*** (*3952*), lit., "a presence," ***para***, "with," and ***ousia***, "being" (from ***eimi***, "to be"), denotes both an "arrival" and a consequent "presence with." For instance, in a papyrus letter a lady speaks of the necessity of her parousia in a place in order to attend to matters relating to her property there. Paul speaks of his ***parousia*** in Philippi, Phil. 2:12 (in contrast to his ***apousia***, "his absence"). ***parousia*** is used to describe the presence of Christ with His disciples on the Mount of Transfiguration, 2 Pet. 1:16. When used of the return of Christ, at the rapture of the church, it signifies, not merely His momentary "coming" for His saints, but His presence with them from that moment until His revelation and manifestation to the world. In some passages the word gives prominence to the beginning of that period, the course of the period being implied, 1 Cor. 15:23; 1 Thess. 4:15; 5:23; 2 Thess. 2:1; Jas. 5:7–8; 2 Pet. 3:4. In some, the course is prominent, Matt. 24:3, 37; 1 Thess. 3:13; 1 John 2:28; in others the conclusion of the period, Matt. 24:27; 2 Thess. 2:8.

The word is also used of the Lawless One, the Man of Sin, his access to power and his doings in the world during his ***parousia***, 2 Thess. 2:9. In addition to Phil. 2:12 (above), it is used in the same way of the apostle, or his companions, in 1 Cor. 16:17; 2 Cor. 7:6–7; 10:10; Phil. 1:26; of the Day of God, 2 Pet. 3:12.

## COMMAND (Verbs)

### *Old Testament*

***tsawah*** (6680), "to command," refers to verbal communication by which a superior "orders" or "commands" a subordinate. The word implies the content of what was said, Gen. 12:20. This order defines an action relevant to a specific situation. ***tsawah*** can also connote "command" in the sense of the establishment of a rule by which a subordinate is to act in every recurring similar situation, Gen. 2:16. In this case, the word does not contain the content of the action but focuses on the action itself.

The verb ***tsawah*** can be used of a commission or charge, such as the act of "commanding," "telling," or "sending" someone to do a particular task, Gen. 32:4; 49:30. One of the recurring formulas in the Bible is "X did all that Y commanded him," Ruth 3:6. This means that she carried out Naomi's "orders."

The most frequent subject of this verb is God. However, He is not to be questioned or "commanded" to explain the work of His hands, Isa. 45:11. He tells Israel that His "commands" are unique, requiring an inner commitment and not just external obedience, as the commands of men do, Gen. 29:13; Exod. 25:22; Lev. 7:38; cf. 17:1ff.; Ps. 33:9. He also issues "orders" through and to the prophets, Jer. 27:4, who explain, apply, and speak His "commands," Jer. 1:17.

### *New Testament*

1. ***diatasso*** (*1299*) signifies "to set in order, appoint, command," Matt. 11:1; Luke 8:55; 17:9–10; Acts 18:2; 23:31; "gave order," 1 Cor. 16:1, RV. So in Acts 24:23, where it is in the middle voice.

2. ***epo*** (*2036*) denotes "to speak" (connected with ***eipon***, "to say"); hence, among various renderings, "to bid, command," Matt. 4:3; Mark 5:43; 8:7; Luke 4:3; 19:15.

3. ***entello*** (*1781*) signifies "to enjoin upon, to charge with"; it is used in the middle voice in the sense of commanding, Matt. 19:7; 28:20; Mark 10:3; 13:34; John 8:5; 15:14, 17; Acts 13:47; Heb. 9:20; 11:22, "gave commandment."

4. ***epitasso*** (*2004*) signifies to appoint over, put in charge (***epi***, "over," ***tasso***, "to appoint"); then, "to put upon one as a duty, to enjoin," Mark 1:27; 6:27, 39; 9:25; Luke 4:36; 8:25, 31; 14:22; Acts 23:2; Philem. 8.

5. ***keleuo*** (*2753*), "to urge, incite, order," suggests a stronger injunction than No. 6, Matt. 14:9, 19; 15:35; 18:25; 27:58, 64; Luke 18:40; Acts 4:15 (frequently in Acts, not subsequently in the NT).

6. ***parangello*** (*3853*), "to announce beside," "to pass on an announcement," hence denotes "to give the word, order, give a charge, command", e.g., Mark 6:8; Luke 8:29; 9:21; Acts 5:28; 2 Thess. 3:4, 6, 10, 12.

7. ***prostasso*** (*4367*) denotes "to arrange or set in order towards"; hence "to prescribe, give command," Matt. 1:24; 8:4; Mark 1:44; Luke 5:14; Acts 10:33, 48.

## COMMANDMENT

### *Old Testament*

***mitswah*** (4687), "commandment." This noun occurs 181 times in the Old Testament. Its first occurrence is in Gen. 26:5, where ***mitswah*** is synonymous with ***choq*** ("statute") and ***torah*** ("law"): "Because that Abraham obeyed my voice, and kept my charge, my *commandments,* my statutes, and my laws."

In the Pentateuch, God is always the Giver of the ***mitswah***, Deut. 8:1–2. The "commandment" was to be heard and kept, Exod. 15:26; Deut. 4:2; 11:13 Any failure to do so signified a covenantal breach, Num. 15:31, transgression, 2 Chron. 24:20, and apostasy, 1 Kings 18:18. Outside the Pentateuch, "commandments" are given by kings, 1 Kings 2:43, fathers, Jer. 35:14, people, Isa. 29:13, and teachers of wisdom, Prov. 6:20; cf. 5:13. The plural of ***mitswah*** often denotes a "body of laws" given by divine revelation, Ps. 119:9.

### *New Testament*

1. ***diatagma*** (*1297*) signifies "that which is imposed by decree or law," Heb. 11:23. It stresses the concrete character of the "commandment" more than ***epitage*** (No. 4).

2. ***entole*** (*1785*), akin to No. 3, above, denotes, in general, "an injunction, charge, precept, commandment." It is the most frequent term, and is used of moral and religious precepts, e.g., Matt. 5:19; it is frequent in the Gospels, especially that of John, and in his Epistles. See also, e.g., Acts 17:15; Rom. 7:8–13; 13:9; 1 Cor. 7:19; Eph. 2:15; Col. 4:10.

3. ***entalma*** (*1778*), akin to No. 2, marks more especially "the thing commanded, a commission"; in Matt. 15:9; Mark 7:7; Col. 2:22, RV, "precepts," KJV, "commandments."

4. ***epitage*** (*2003*), akin to No. 4, above, stresses "the authoritativeness of the command"; it is used in Rom. 16:26; 1 Cor. 7:6, 25; 2 Cor. 8:8; 1 Tim. 1:1; Tit. 1:3; 2:15.

## COMMEND, COMMENDATION

### *A. Verbs.*

1. ***epaineo*** (*1867*), "to praise," is an intensive form of ***aineo***, Luke 16:8. It is elsewhere translated by the verb "to praise," in the RV, Rom. 15:11; 1 Cor. 11:2, 17, 22.

2. ***paradidomi*** (*3860*), lit., to give or deliver over," is said of "commending," or "committing," servants of God to Him (KJV, "recommend), Acts 14:26; 15:40.

3. ***paratithemi*** (*3908*), lit., "to put near," denotes "to place with someone, entrust, commit." In the sense of commending, it is said (a) of the Lord Jesus in "commending" His spirit into the Father's hands, Luke 23:46; (b) of "commending" disciples to God, Acts 14:23; (c) of "commending" elders to God, Acts 20:32. Cf. No. 2.

4. ***paristemi*** (*3936*), lit., "to place near, set before," is used of "self-commendation," 1 Cor. 8:8.

5. ***sunistemi*** (*4921*), or ***sunistano*** (*4921*), lit., "to place together," denotes "to introduce one person to another, represent as worthy," e.g., Rom. 3:5; 5:8; 16:1; 2 Cor. 4:2; 6:4; 10:18; 12:11. In 2 Cor. 3:1; 5:12 and 10:12, the verb ***sunistano*** is used.

### B. Adjective.

***sustatikos*** (*4956*), akin to A, No. 5, lit., "placing together," hence, "commendatory," is used of letters of "commendation," 2 Cor. 3:1, lit., "commendatory letters."

## COMMIT, COMMISSION

### A. Verbs.

1. ***paradidomi*** (*3860*), "to give over," is often rendered by the verb "to commit," e.g., to prison, Acts 8:3; to the grace of God, Acts 14:26; to God, 1 Pet. 2:23; by God to pits of darkness, 2 Pet. 2:4.

2. ***pisteuo*** (*4100*) signifies "to entrust, commit to," Luke 16:11; 1 Tim. 1:11, "committed to (my) trust."

3. ***tithemi*** (*5087*), "to put, place," signifies, in the middle voice, "to put for oneself, assign, place in," 2 Cor. 5:19, "having committed (unto us)."

4. ***paratithemi*** (*3908*), signifies "to entrust, commit to one's charge," e.g., in Luke 12:48; 1 Tim. 1:18; 2 Tim. 2:2; 1 Pet. 4:19 (KJV, "commit the keeping").

### B. Nouns.

***paratheke*** (*3866*) (akin to 4. above), "a putting with, a deposit," 2 Tim. 1:12, "that which He hath committed unto me," RV, marg., lit., "my deposit" (perhaps, "my deposit with Him"), the latter in 1 Tim. 6:20, where "guard that which is committed unto thee" is, lit., "guard the deposit," and 2 Tim. 1:14, "that good thing which was committed unto thee," i.e., the good deposit; RV, marg., "the good deposit."

## COMMON, COMMONLY

### A. Adjective.

***koinos*** (*2834*) denotes (a) "common, belonging to several" (Lat., ***communis***), said of things had in common, Acts 2:44; 4:32; of faith, Titus 1:4; of salvation, Jude 3; it stands in contrast to ***idios***, "one's own"; (b) "ordinary, belonging to the generality, as distinct from what is peculiar to the few," hence the application to religious practices of Gentiles in contrast with those of Jews; or of the ordinary people in contrast with those of the Pharisees; hence the meaning "unhallowed, profane," Levitically unclean (Lat., ***profanus***), said of hands, Mark 7:2 (KJV, "defiled,") RV marg., "common"; of animals, ceremonially unclean, Acts 10:14; 11:8; of a man, 10:28; of meats, Rom. 14:14, "unclean"; of the blood of the covenant, as viewed by an apostate, Heb. 10:29, "unholy" (RV, marg., "common"); of everything unfit for the holy city, Rev. 21:27, RV, "unclean" (marg., "common"). Some mss. have the verb here.

### B. Verb.

***koinoo*** (*2840*), "to make, or count, common," has this meaning in Acts 10:15; 11:9.

## COMMUNICATE, COMMUNICATION

### A. Verbs.

1. ***koinoneo*** (*2841*) is used in two senses, (a) "to have a share in," Rom. 15:27; 1 Tim. 5:22; Heb. 2:14; 1 Pet. 4:13; 2 John 11; (b) "to give a share to, go shares with," Rom. 12:13, RV, "communicating," for KJV, "distributing"; Gal. 6:6, "communicate"; Phil. 4:15, KJV, "did communicate," RV, "had fellowship with."

2. ***sunkoinoneo*** (*4790*), "to share together with" (***sun*** "and" No. 1), is translated "communicated with" in Phil. 4:14; "have fellowship with," Eph. 5:11; "be . . . partakers of," Rev. 18:4 (RV, "have fellowship"). The thought is that of sharing with others what one has, in order to meet their needs.

### B. Nouns.

1. ***koinonia*** (*2842*), akin to A (which see), is translated in Heb. 13:16 "to communicate," lit., "be not forgetful of good deed and of fellowship"; "fellowship" (KJV, "communication") in Philem. 6, RV.

2. ***logos*** (*3056*), "a word, that which is spoken" (***lego***, "to speak"), is used in the plural with reference to a conversation; "communication," Luke 24:17. Elsewhere with this significance the RV renders it "speech," Matt. 5:37; Eph. 4:29.

### C. Adjective.

***koinonikos*** (*2843*), akin to A, No. 1 and B, No. 1, means "apt, or ready, to communicate," 1 Tim. 6:18.

## COMMUNION

### A. Noun.

***koinonia*** (*2842*), "a having in common (***koinos***), partnership, fellowship," denotes (a) the share which one has in anything, a participation, fellowship recognized and enjoyed; thus it is used of the common experiences and interests of Christian men, Acts 2:42; Gal. 2:9; of participation in the knowledge of the Son of God, 1 Cor. 1:9; of sharing in the realization of the effects of the blood (i.e., the death) of Christ and the body of Christ, as set forth by the emblems in the Lord's Supper, 1 Cor. 10:16; of participation in what is derived from the Holy Spirit, 2 Cor. 13:14 (RV, "communion"); Phil. 2:1; of participation in the sufferings of Christ, Phil. 3:10; of sharing in the resurrection life possessed in Christ, and so of fellowship with the Father and the Son, 1 John 1:3, 6–7; negatively, of the impossibility of "communion" between light and darkness, 2 Cor. 6:14; (b) fellowship manifested in acts, the practical effects of fellowship with God, wrought by the Holy Spirit in the lives of believers as the outcome of faith, Philem. 6, and finding expression in joint ministration to the needy, Rom. 15:26; 2 Cor. 8:4; 9:13; Heb. 13:16, and in the furtherance of the Gospel by gifts, Phil. 1:5.

### B. Adjective.

***koinonos*** (*2844*), "having in common," is rendered "have communion with (the altar),"—the altar standing by metonymy for that which is associated with it—in 1 Cor. 10:18, RV (for KJV, "are partakers of"), and in v. 20, for KJV, "have fellowship with (demons)."

## COMPANION

***Old Testament***

### A. Nouns.

***rea'*** (7453), "friend; companion." A ***rea'*** is a "personal friend" with whom one shares confidences and to whom one feels very close, Exod. 33:11. In this sense, the word is a synonym of *'ah*, "brother," and of *qarob*, "kin," Exod. 32:27. *rea'* also means "marriage partner," Song of Sol. 5:16; or paramour, Jer. 3:1, cf. Hosea's wife.

*rea'* is also a *neighbor*, the person with whom one associates regularly or casually without establishing close relations, Exod. 20:16. The prophets charged Israel with breaking the commandment regarding respect for one's neighbor, Isa. 3:5; Jer. 5:8; 22:13; Ezek. 18:6. *rea'* can also mean "friend," Prov. 19:4. Here the "friend" is a person whose association is not long-lasting, whose friendship is superficial.

*re'eh* also means "friend," Judg. 11:27; 1 Kings 4:5. The noun *ra'yah* means "beloved companion; bride." *ra'yah* occurs many times in the Song of Solomon: 1:9, 15; 2:2, 10, 13; 4:1, 7; 5:2; 6:4. *re'ut* refers to a "fellow woman."

**B. Verb.**

*ra'ah* (7462), "to associate with." This word appears in Prov. 22:24: "Make no friendship with an angry man; and with a furious man thou shalt not go . . ."

*New Testament*

*koinonos* (*2844*) is rendered "companions" in the KJV of Heb. 10:33 (RV "partakers"). So *sunkoinonos* in Rev. 1:9, KJV, "companion"; RV, "partaker with you."

## COMPASS

1. *kukleuo* (*2944v*) denotes "to encircle, surround," and is found in the best texts in John 10:24, "came round about," and Rev. 20:9, of a camp surrounded by foes; some mss. have No. 2 in each place.

2. *kukloo* (*2944*), (cf. Eng., cycle"), signifies "to move in a circle, to compass about," as of a city "encompassed" by armies, Luke 21:20; Heb. 11:30; in Acts 14:20, "stood round about.

3. *perikukloo* (*4033*), *peri*, "about," with No. 2, is used in Luke 19:43, "shall compass . . . round."

## COMPASSION, COMPASSIONATE

*Old Testament*

**A. Verb.**

*racham* (7355), "to have compassion, be merciful, pity." *racham* is used in God's promise to declare His name to Moses, with a special focus on His love, Exod. 33:19; Ps. 25:6; Isa. 54:7–8.

**B. Nouns.**

*rechem* (7358), "bowels; womb; mercy." The first use of *rechem* is in its primary meaning of "womb": "The Lord had fast closed up all the wombs of the house of Abimelech," Gen. 20:18. The word is personified in Judg. 5:30: "Have they not divided the prey; to every man a damsel or two . . . ?" In another figurative sense, the KJV reads in 1 Kings 3:26: "Her bowels yearned upon her son," which the NIV translates more idiomatically: "[She] was filled with compassion for her son." The greatest frequency is in this figurative sense of "tender love," such as a mother has for the child she has borne.

*rachamim* (7356), "bowels; mercies; compassion." This noun, always used in the plural intensive, occurs in Gen. 43:14: "And God Almighty give you mercy [NASB, "compassion"]." In Gen. 43:30, it is used of Joseph's feelings toward Benjamin: "His bowels did yearn upon his brother." (NIV, "He was deeply moved at the sight of his brother.") *rachamim* is most often used of God, as by David in 2 Sam. 24:14: "Let us fall now into the hand of the Lord; for his mercies are great . . ." We have the equivalent Aramaic word in Daniel's request to his friends: "That they would desire mercies of the God of heaven concerning this secret . . ." Dan. 2:18.

**C. Adjective.**

*rachum* (7349), "compassionate; merciful," Exod. 34:6.

*New Testament*

**A. Verbs.**

1. *oikteiro* (*3627*), "to have pity, a feeling of distress through the ills of others," is used of God's compassion, Rom. 9:15.

2. *splanchnizomai* (*4697*), "to be moved as to one's inwards (*splanchna*), to be moved with compassion, to yearn with compassion," is frequently recorded of Christ towards the multitude and towards individual sufferers, Matt. 9:36; 14:14; 15:32; 18:27; 20:34; Mark 1:41; 6:34; 8:2; 9:22 (of the appeal of a father for a demon-possessed son); Luke 7:13; 10:33; of the father in the parable of the Prodigal Son, 15:20.

3. *sumpatheo* (*4834*), "to suffer with another, to be affected similarly" (Eng., "sympathy"), to have "compassion" upon, Heb. 10:34, of "compassionating" those in prison, is translated "be touched with" in Heb. 4:15, of Christ as the High Priest.

4. *eleeo* (*1653*), "to have mercy (*eleos*, "mercy"), to show kindness, by beneficence, or assistance," is translated "have compassion" in Matt. 18:33 (KJV); Mark 5:19 and Jude 22.

5. *metriopatheo* (*3356*) is rendered "have compassion," in Heb. 5:2, KJV.

**B. Nouns.**

1. ***oiktirmos*** (*3628*), akin to A, No. 1, is used with ***splanchna*** (see below), "the viscera, the inward parts," as the seat of emotion, the "heart," Phil. 2:1; Col. 3:12, "a heart of compassion" (KJV, "bowels of mercies"). In Heb. 10:28 it is used with ***choris***, "without," (lit., "without compassions"). It is translated "mercies" in Rom. 12:1 and 2 Cor. 1:3.

2. ***splanchnon*** (*4698*), always used in the plural, is suitably rendered "compassion" in the RV of Col. 3:12 and 1 John 3:17; "compassions" in Phil. 2:1, Cf. A, No. 2.

**C. Adjective.**

***sumpathes*** (*4835*) denotes suffering with, "compassionate," 1 Pet. 3:8.

## COMPEL

1. ***anankazo*** (*315*) denotes "to put constraint upon (from ***ananke***, 'necessity'), to constrain, whether by threat, entreaty, force or persuasion"; Christ "constrained" the disciples to get into a boat, Matt. 14:22; Mark 6:45; the servants of the man who made a great supper were to constrain people to come in, Luke 14:23 (RV, "constrain"); Saul of Tarsus "strove" to make saints blaspheme, Acts 26:11, RV (KJV, "compelled"); Titus, though a Greek, was not "compelled" to be circumcised, Gal. 2:3, as Galatian converts were, 6:12, RV; Peter was "compelling" Gentiles to live as Jews, Gal. 2:14; Paul was "constrained" to appeal to Caesar, Acts 28:19, and was "compelled" by the church at Corinth to become foolish in speaking of himself, 2 Cor. 12:11.

2. ***angareuo*** (*29*), "to dispatch as an ***angaros***" (a Persian courier kept at regular stages with power of impressing men into service), and hence, in general, "to impress into service," is used of "compelling" a person to go a mile, Matt. 5:41; of the impressing of Simon to bear Christ's cross, Matt. 27:32; Mark 15:21.

## COMPLAINER, COMPLAINT

1. ***mempsimoiros*** (*3202*) denotes "one who complains," lit., "complaining of one's lot," Jude 16.

2. ***momphe*** (*3437*), denotes "blame," "an occasion of complaint," Col. 3:13.

3. ***aitioma*** (*157v*), "a charge," is translated "complaints" in Acts 25:7, KJV.

## COMPLETE, COMPLETION, COMPLETELY

1. ***epiteleo*** (*2005*), "to complete," Rom. 15:28.

2. ***exartizo*** (*1822*), "to fit out," lit., "exactly right,", is said of the equipment of the man of God, 2 Tim. 3:17, "furnished completely" (KJV, "thoroughly furnished"); elsewhere in Acts 21:5, "accomplished.

3. ***sunteleo*** (*4931*), "to end together, bring quite to an end," is said (a) of the "completion" of a period of days, Luke 4:2; Acts 21:27; (b) of "completing" something; some mss. have it in Matt. 7:28, of the Lord, in ending His discourse (the best mss. have ***teleo***, "to finish"); of God, in finishing a work, Rom. 9:28, in making a new covenant, Heb. 8:8, marg., "accomplish"; of the fulfillment of things foretold, Mark 13:4; of the Devil's temptation of the Lord, Luke 4:13.

4. ***pleroo*** (*4137*), "to fill" (in the passive voice, "to be made full"), is translated "complete" in the KJV of Col. 2:10 (RV, "made full"; cf. v. 9).

5. ***plerophoreo*** (*4135*), "to be fully assured," is translated "complete" in Col. 4:12.

## CONCEITS

1. ***en heautois***, lit., "in yourselves," is used with ***phronimos***, "wise," in Rom. 11:25, "(wise) in your own conceits (i.e., opinions)."

2. ***par' heautois***, (***para***, "with, in the estimation of"), in Rom. 12:16 has the same rendering as No. 1.

## CONCEIVE

1. ***gennao*** (*1080*), "to conceive, beget," Matt. 1:20.

2. ***sullambano*** (*4815*), lit., "to take together," is used (a) of a woman, to "conceive," Luke 1:24, 31, 36; in the passive voice. Luke 2:21; (b) metaphorically, of the impulse of lust in the human heart, enticing to sin, Jas. 1:15.

## CONCISION

***katatome*** (*2699*), lit., "a cutting off," "a mutilation," is a term found in Phil. 3:2.

## CONCLUDE

***sumbibazo*** (*4822*), lit., "to make to come together," is translated "concluding" in Acts 16:10.

## CONCORD

***sumphonesis*** (*4857*), lit., "a sounding together"; cf. Eng., "symphony," is found in 2 Cor. 6:15.

## CONDEMN, CONDEMNATION

**A. Verbs.**

1. ***kataginosko*** (*2607*), "to know something against," hence, "to think ill of, to condemn," is said, in Gal. 2:11, of Peter's conduct (RV, "stood condemned"), he being "self-condemned" as the result of an exercised and enlightened conscience, and "condemned" in the sight of

others; so of "self-condemnation" due to an exercise of heart, 1 John 3:20–21.

2. ***katadikazo*** (*2613*) signifies "to exercise right or law against anyone"; hence, "to pronounce judgment, to condemn," Matt. 12:7, 37; Luke 6:37; Jas. 5:6.

3. ***krino*** (*2919*), "to distinguish, choose, give an opinion upon, judge," sometimes denotes "to condemn," e.g., Acts 13:27; Rom. 2:27; Jas. 5:9 (in the best mss.). Cf. No. 1, below.

4. ***katakrino*** (*2632*), a strengthened form of No. 3, signifies "to give judgment against, pass sentence upon"; hence, "to condemn," implying (a) the fact of a crime, e.g., Rom. 2:1; 14:23; 2 Pet. 2:6; some mss. have it in Jas. 5:9; (b) the imputation of a crime, as in the "condemnation" of Christ by the Jews, Matt. 20:18; Mark 14:64. It is used metaphorically of "condemning" by a good example, Matt. 12:41–42; Luke 11:31–32; Heb. 11:7.

### B. Nouns.

1. ***krima*** (*2917*) denotes (a) "the sentence pronounced, a verdict, a condemnation, the decision resulting from an investigation," e.g., Mark 12:40; Luke 23:40; 1 Tim. 3:6; Jude 4; (b) "the process of judgment leading to a decision," 1 Pet. 4:17 ("judgment"), where ***krisis*** (see No. 3, below) might be expected. In Luke 24:20, "to be condemned" translates the phrase ***eis krima***, "unto condemnation" (i.e., unto the pronouncement of the sentence of "condemnation"). For the rendering "judgment," see, e.g., Rom. 11:33; 1 Cor. 11:34; Gal. 5:10; Jas. 3:1. In these (a) the process leading to a decision and (b) the pronouncement of the decision, the verdict, are to be distinguished. In 1 Cor. 6:7 the word means a matter for judgment, a lawsuit.

2. ***katakrima*** (*2631*), cf. No. 4, above, is "the sentence pronounced, the condemnation" with a suggestion of the punishment following; it is found in Rom. 5:16, 18; 8:1.

3. ***krisis*** (*2920*) (a) denotes "the process of investigation, the act of distinguishing and separating" (as distinct from ***krima***, see No. 1 above); hence "a judging, a passing of judgment upon a person or thing"; it has a variety of meanings, such as judicial authority, John 5:22, 27; justice, Acts 8:33; Jas. 2:13; a tribunal, Matt. 5:21–22; a trial, John 5:24; 2 Pet. 2:4; a judgment, 2 Pet. 2:11; Jude 9; by metonymy, the standard of judgment, just dealing, Matt. 12:18, 20; 23:23; Luke 11:42; divine judgment executed, 2 Thess. 1:5; Rev. 16:7; (b) sometimes it has the meaning "condemnation."

4. ***katakrisis*** (*2633*), a strengthened form of No. 3, denotes "a judgment against, condemnation," with the suggestion of the process leading to it, as of "the ministration of condemnation," 2 Cor. 3:9; in 7:3, "to condemn," more lit., "with a view to condemnation."

### C. Adjective.

***autokatakritos*** (*843*), "self-condemned," i.e., on account of doing himself what he condemns in others, is used in Titus 3:11.

## CONDUCT

### A. Noun.

***agoge*** (*72*), from ***ago***, "to lead," properly denotes "a teaching"; then, figuratively, "a training, discipline," and so, the life led, a way or course of life, conduct, 2 Tim. 3:10, RV, "conduct"; KJV, "manner of life."

### B. Verbs.

1. ***kathistemi*** (*2525*), lit., "to stand down or set down," has, among its various meanings, "the significance of bringing to a certain place, conducting," Acts 17:15 (so the Sept. in Josh. 6:23; 1 Sam. 5:3; 2 Chron. 28:15).

2. ***propempo*** (*4311*) signifies "to set forward, conduct," 1 Cor. 16:11.

## CONFER, CONFERENCE

1. ***prosanatithemi*** (*4323*), lit., "to put before," i.e., "to lay a matter before others so as to obtain counsel or instruction," is used of Paul's refraining from consulting human beings, Gal. 1:16.

2. ***sullaleo*** (*4814*), "to speak together with," is translated "conferred" in Acts 25:12; elsewhere of talking with Matt. 17:3; Mark 9:4; Luke 4:36; 9:30; "communed" in Luke 22:4.

3. ***sumballo*** (*4820*), lit., "to throw together," is used of "conversation, to discourse or consult together, confer," Acts 4:15.

## CONFESS, CONFESSION

#### *Old Testament*

***yadah*** (3034), "to confess, praise, give thanks." ***yadah*** overlaps in meaning with a number of other Hebrew words implying public "praise," and "thanksgiving," such as ***halal*** (whence ***halleluyah***). Humans are occasionally the object of ***yadah***; but usually God is the object. Praise inevitably entails confession of sin, but also a pronouncement of forgiveness by God.

Often the direct object of ***yadah*** is the "name" of Yahweh, e.g., Ps. 105:1; Isa. 12:4; 1 Chron. 16:8. In one sense, this idiom is simply synonymous with praising Yahweh. In another sense, however, it introduces the entire dimension evoked by the "name" in biblical usage. It reminds us that the holy God cannot be directly approached by fallen man, but only through His "name"—i.e., His Word and reputation, an anticipation of the incarnation. God reveals Himself only in His "name," especially in the sanctuary where He "causes His name to dwell" (a phrase especially frequent in Deuteronomy).

The vista of ***yadah*** expands both vertically and horizontally—vertically to include all creation, and horizontally stretching forward to that day when praise and thanksgiving shall be eternal, e.g., Ps. 29; 95:10; 96:7–9; 103:19–22.

*New Testament*

**A. Verbs.**

1. ***homologeo*** *(3670)*, lit., "to speak the same thing," "to assent, accord, agree with," denotes, (a) "to confess, declare, admit," John 1:20; e.g., Acts 24:14; Heb. 11:13; (b) "to confess by way of admitting oneself guilty of what one is accused of, the result of inward conviction," 1 John 1:9; (c) "to declare openly by way of speaking out freely, such confession being the effect of deep conviction of facts," Matt. 7:23; 10:32 (twice) and Luke 12:8; John 9:22; 12:42; Acts 23:8; Rom. 10:9–10 ("confession is made"); 1 Tim. 6:12 (RV); Titus 1:16; 1 John 2:23; 4:2, 15; 2 John 7 (in John's epistle it is the necessary antithesis to Gnostic docetism); Rev. 3:5, in the best mss. (some have No. 2 here); (d) "to confess by way of celebrating with praise," Heb. 13:15; (e) "to promise," Matt. 14:7.

2. ***exomologeo*** *(1843)*, (***ek***, "out," intensive, and No. 1), and accordingly stronger than No. 1, "to confess forth," i.e., "freely, openly," is used (a) "of a public acknowledgment or confession of sins," Matt. 3:6; Mark 1:5; Acts 19:18; Jas. 5:16; (b) "to profess or acknowledge openly," Matt. 11:25 (translated "thank," but indicating the fuller idea); Phil. 2:11 (some mss. have it in Rev. 3:5: see No. 1); (c) "to confess by way of celebrating, giving praise," Rom. 14:11; 15:9. In Luke 10:21, it is translated "I thank," the true meaning being "I gladly acknowledge." In Luke 22:6 it signifies to consent (RV), for KJV, "promised."

**B. Noun.**

***homologia*** *(3671)*, akin to A, No. 1, denotes "confession, by acknowledgment of the truth," 2 Cor. 9:13; 1 Tim. 6:12–13; Heb. 3:1; 4:14; 10:23 (KJV, incorrectly, "profession," except in 1 Tim. 6:13).

## CONFIDENCE (Noun, or Verb with "have"), CONFIDENT (-LY)

**A. Nouns.**

1. ***pepoithesis*** *(4006)*, akin to ***peitho***, B, No. 1 below, denotes "persuasion, assurance, confidence," 2 Cor. 1:15; 3:4, KJV, "trust"; 8:22; 10:2; Eph. 3:12; Phil. 3:4.

2. ***hupostasis*** *(5287)*, lit., "a standing under" (***hupo***, "under," ***stasis***, "a standing"), "that which stands, or is set, under, a foundation, beginning"; hence, the quality of confidence which leads one to stand under, endure, or undertake anything, 2 Cor. 9:4; 11:17; Heb. 3:14. Twice in Heb. it signifies "substance," 1:3 (KJV, "Person") and 11:1.

3. ***parrhesia*** *(3954)*, often rendered "confidence" in the KJV, is in all such instances rendered "boldness" in the RV, Acts 28:31; Heb. 3:6; 1 John 2:28; 3:21; 5:14.

**B. Verbs.**

***peitho*** *(3982)*, "to persuade," or, intransitively, "to have confidence, to be confident" (cf. A, No. 1), has this meaning in the following, Rom. 2:19; 2 Cor. 2:3; Gal. 5:10; Phil. 1:6, 14 (RV, "being confident," for KJV, "waxing confident"), 25; 3:3–4; 2 Thess. 3:4; Philem. 21.

## CONFIRM, CONFIRMATION

**A. Verbs.**

1. ***bebaioo*** *(950)*, "to make firm, establish, make secure" (the connected adjective ***bebaios*** signifies "stable, fast, firm"), is used of "confirming" a word, Mark 16:20; promises, Rom. 15:8; the testimony of Christ, 1 Cor. 1:6; the saints by the Lord Jesus Christ, 1 Cor. 1:8; the saints by God, 2 Cor. 1:21 ("stablisheth"); in faith, Col. 2:7; the salvation spoken through the Lord and "confirmed" by the apostles, Heb. 2:3; the heart by grace, Heb. 13:9 ("stablished").

2. ***episterizo*** *(1991)*, "to make to lean upon, strengthen" (***epi***, "upon," ***sterix***, "a prop, support"), is used of "confirming" souls Acts 14:22, brethren, 15:32; churches, 15:41; disciples, 18:23, in some mss. ("stablishing," RV, "strengthening," KJV); the most authentic mss. have ***sterizo*** in 18:23.

3. ***kuroo*** *(2964)*, "to make valid, ratify, impart authority or influence" (from ***kuros***, "might," ***kurios***, "mighty, a head, as supreme in authority"), is used of spiritual love, 2 Cor. 2:8; a human covenant, Gal. 3:15.

4. ***prokuroo*** *(4300)*, (***pro***, "before," and No. 3), "to confirm or ratify before," is said of the divine confirmation of a promise given originally to Abraham, Gen. 12, and "confirmed" by the vision of the furnace and torch, Gen. 15, by the birth of Isaac, Gen. 21, and by the oath of God, Gen. 22, all before the giving of the Law, Gal. 3:17.

**B. Noun.**

***bebaiosis*** *(951)*, akin to A, No. 1, is used in two senses (a) "of firmness, establishment," said of the "confirmation" of the gospel, Phil.

1:7; (b) "of authoritative validity imparted," said of the settlement of a dispute by an oath to produce confidence, Heb. 6:16. The word is found frequently in the papyri of the settlement of a business transaction.

## CONFLICT (Noun)

1. ***agon*** (*73*), from ***ago***, "to lead," signifies (a) "a place of assembly," especially the place where the Greeks assembled for the Olympic and Pythian games; (b) "a contest of athletes," metaphorically, 1 Tim. 6:12; 2 Tim. 4:7, "fight"; Heb. 12:1, "race"; hence, (c) "the inward conflict of the soul"; inward "conflict" is often the result, or the accompaniment, of outward "conflict," Phil. 1:30; 1 Thess. 2:2, implying a contest against spiritual foes, as well as human adversaries; so Col. 2:1.

2. ***athlesis*** (*119*) denotes "a combat, contest of athletes"; hence, "a struggle, fight," Heb. 10:32, with reference to affliction.

## CONFORMED, CONFORMABLE

**A. Verb.**

***summorphizo*** (*4833v*), "to make of like form with another person or thing, to render like" (***sun***, "with," ***morphe***, "a form"), is found in Phil. 3:10, focusing on death of the carnal self.

**B. Adjective.**

***summorphos*** (*4832*), akin to A, signifies "having the same form as another, conformed to"; (a) of the "conformity" of children of God "to the image of His Son," Rom. 8:29; (b), of their future physical "conformity" to His body of glory, Phil. 3:21.

## CONFOUND, CONFUSE, CONFUSION

**A. Nouns.**

1. ***akatastasia*** (*181*), "instability," (***a***, negative, ***kata***, "down," ***stasis***, "a standing"), denotes "a state of disorder, disturbance, confusion, tumult," 1 Cor. 14:33; Jas. 3:16, "revolution or anarchy"; translated "tumults" in Luke 21:9 (KJV, "commotions"); 2 Cor. 6:5; 12:20.

2. ***sunchusis*** (*4799*), "a pouring or mixing together," hence "a disturbance, confusion, a tumultuous disorder, as of riotous persons," is found in Acts 19:29.

**B. Verb.**

***suncheo*** (*4797*), or ***sunchunno*** or ***sunchuno*** (the verb form of A., No. 2), lit., "to pour together, commingle," hence (said of persons), means "to trouble or confuse, to stir up," Acts 19:32 (said of the mind); "to be in confusion," 21:31, RV (KJV, "was in an uproar"); 21:27, "stirred up"; Acts 2:6; 9:22, "confounded.

## CONFUTE

***diakatelenchomai*** (*1246*), "to confute powerfully," with a focus on ascribing moral blame, Acts 18:28.

## CONGREGATION

### *Old Testament*

***'edah*** (5712), "congregation," it is similar to the Greek words ***sunagoge*** and ***ekklesia***. The most general meaning of ***'edah*** is "group," whether of animals, Judg. 14:8; Ps. 68:30; Hos. 7:12—or of people, such as the righteous, Ps. 1:5, the evildoers, Ps. 22:16, and the nations, Ps. 7:7.

***mo'ed*** (4150), "appointed place of meeting; meeting." The word ***mo'ed*** keeps its basic meaning of "appointed," but varies as to what is agreed upon or appointed according to the context: the time, the place, or the meeting itself. The usage of the verb in Amos 3:3 is illuminating: "Can two walk together, except they be agreed?"

The meaning of ***mo'ed*** is fixed within the context of Israel's religion. First, the prescribed festivals came to be known as the "appointed times" or the set feasts, Lev. 23:15ff.

The word ***mo'ed*** also signifies a "fixed place," though not frequent, Job 30:23; Isa. 14:13.

***'ohel mo'ed*** means "tent of meeting," it signifies that the Lord has an "appointed, fixed place," Exod. 28:43; cf. Rev. 15:5.

### *New Testament*

1. ***ekklesia*** (*1577*) is translated "congregation" in Heb. 2:12, RV, instead of the usual rendering "church."

2. ***sunagoge*** (*4864*) is translated "congregation" in Acts 13:43, KJV (RV, "synagogue).

## CONQUER, CONQUEROR

1. ***nikao*** (*3528*), "to overcome" (its usual meaning), is translated "conquering" and "to conquer" in Rev. 6:2.

2. ***hupernikao*** (*5245*), "to be more than conqueror" (***huper***, "over," and No. 1), "to gain a surpassing victory," is found in Rom. 8:37, lit., "we are hyper-conquerors," i.e., we are preeminently victorious.

## CONSCIENCE

***suneidesis*** (*4893*), lit., "a knowing with," i.e., "a co-knowledge (with oneself), the witness borne to one's conduct by conscience, that faculty by which we apprehend the will of God, as that which is designed to govern our lives"; hence (a) the sense of guiltiness before God; Heb. 10:2; (b) that process of thought which distinguishes what it considers morally good or bad, commending the good, condemning the bad, and so prompting to do the former, and avoid the latter; Rom. 2:15 (bearing witness with God's law); 9:1; 2 Cor. 1:12; acting in a certain way because "conscience" requires it, Rom. 13:5; so as not to cause scruples of "conscience" in another, 1 Cor. 10:28–29; not calling a thing in question unnecessarily, as if conscience demanded it, 1 Cor. 10:25, 27; "commending oneself to every man's conscience," 2 Cor. 4:2; cf. 5:11. There may be a "conscience" not strong enough to distinguish clearly between the lawful and the unlawful, 1 Cor. 8:7, 10, 12 (some regard consciousness as the meaning here). The phrase "conscience toward God," in 1 Pet. 2:19, signifies a "conscience" (or perhaps here, a consciousness) so controlled by the apprehension of God's presence, that the person realizes that griefs are to be borne in accordance with His will. Heb. 9:9 teaches that sacrifices under the Law could not so perfect a person that he could regard himself as free from guilt.

For various descriptions of "conscience" see Acts 23:1; 24:16; 1 Cor. 8:7; 1 Tim. 1:5, 19; 3:9; 4:2; 2 Tim. 1:3; Titus 1:15; Heb. 9:14; 10:22; 13:18; 1 Pet. 3:16, 21.

## CONSENT

### A. Verbs.

1. ***exomologeo*** (*1843*), "to agree openly, to acknowledge outwardly, or fully," is translated "consented" in the RV of Luke 22:6 (KJV, promised).

2. ***sumphemi*** (*4852*), lit., "to speak with," hence, "to express agreement with," is used of "consenting" to the Law, agreeing that it is good, Rom. 7:16.

3. ***suneudokeo*** (*4909*), lit., "to think well with," to take pleasure with others in anything, to approve of, to assent, is used in Luke 11:48, of "consenting" to the evil deeds of predecessors (KJV, "allow"); in Rom. 1:32, of "consenting" in doing evil; in Acts 8:1; 22:20, of "consenting" to the death of another. All these are cases of "consenting" to evil things. In 1 Cor. 7:12–13, it is used of an unbelieving wife's "consent" to dwell with her converted husband, and of an unbelieving husband's "consent" to dwell with a believing wife (KJV, "be pleased"; RV, "be content").

### B. Phrases.

1. ***apo mias***, lit., "from one," is found in Luke 14:18, some word like "consent" being implied; e.g., "with one consent."

2. ***ek sumphonou***, lit., "from (or by) agreement" (***sun***, "with," ***phone***, "a sound"), i.e., "by consent," is found in 1 Cor. 7:5.

## CONSIDER

C

1. ***eidon*** (Aor. of *3708*), used as the aorist tense of ***horao***, "to see," is translated "to consider" in Acts 15:6, of the gathering of the apostles and elders regarding the question of circumcision in relation to the gospel.

2. ***suneidon*** (*4894*), ***sun***, with, and No. 1, used as the aorist tense of ***sunorao***, to see with one view, to be aware, conscious, as the result of mental perception, is translated "considered" in Acts 12:12, of Peter's consideration of the circumstances of his deliverance from.

3. ***katamanthano*** (*2648*), lit., "to learn thoroughly," hence, "to note accurately, consider well," is used in the Lord's exhortation to "consider" the lilies. Matt. 6:28.

4. ***noeo*** (*3539*), "to perceive with the mind" (***nous***), "think about, ponder," is translated "consider," only in Paul's exhortation to Timothy in 2 Tim. 2:7.

5. ***katanoeo*** (*2657*), "to perceive clearly" (***kata***, intensive, and No. 4), "to understand fully, consider closely," is used of not "considering" thoroughly the beam in one's own eye, Matt. 7:3 and Luke 6:41 (KJV, "perceivest"); of carefully "considering" the ravens, Luke 12:24; the lilies, v. 27; of Peter's full "consideration" of his vision, Acts 11:6; of Abraham's careful "consideration" of his own body, and Sarah's womb, as dead, and yet accepting by faith God's promise, Rom. 4:19 (RV); of "considering" fully the Apostle and High Priest of our confession, Heb. 3:1; of thoughtfully "considering" one another to provoke unto love and good works, Heb. 10:24. It is translated by the verbs "behold," Acts 7:31–32; Jas. 1:23–24; "perceive," Luke 20:23; "discover," Acts 27:39.

6. ***logizomai*** (*3049*) signifies "to take account of," 2 Cor. 10:7 (RV, "consider," KJV, "think"), the only place where the RV translates it "consider."

7. ***theoreo*** (*2334*), Heb 7:4.

8. ***anatheoreo*** (*333*), "to consider carefully," Heb 13:7.

9. ***analogizomai*** (*357*), "to consider," occurs in Heb. 12:3.

## CONSIST

***sunistemi*** (*4921*), (***sun***, "with," ***histemi*** "to stand"), denotes, in its intransitive sense, "to stand with or fall together, to be constituted, to be compact"; it is said of the universe as upheld by the Lord, Col. 1:17, lit., "by Him all things stand together," i.e., "consist."

## CONSOLATION, CONSOLE

### A. Nouns.

1. ***paraklesis*** (*3874*) is translated "consolation," in both KJV and RV, in Luke 2:25; 6:24;

Acts 15:31; in 1 Cor. 14:3, KJV, "exhortation," RV, "comfort"; in the following the KJV has "consolation," the RV, "comfort," Rom. 15:5; 2 Cor. 1:6–7; 7:7; Phil. 2:1; 2 Thess. 2:16; Philem. 7; in Acts 4:36, RV, "exhortation"; in Heb. 6:18, RV, "encouragement."

2. ***paramuthia*** (*3889*), "a comfort, consolation," 1 Cor. 14:3.

3. ***paramuthion*** (*3890*), "an encouragement, consolation," Phil. 2:1, RV, in the phrase "consolation of love."

**B. Verb.**

***paramutheomai*** (*3888*), "to speak soothingly to," is translated "console," John 11:19, RV; in v. 31 "were comforting"; in 1 Thess. 2:11 and 5:14, KJV, "comforted" and "comfort," RV, "encouraged" and "encourage."

## CONSTRAIN, CONSTRAINT

**A. Verbs.**

1. ***anankazo*** (*315*), Gal. 6:12.

2. ***sunecho*** (*4912*), "to hold together, confine, secure, to hold fast" (***echo***, "to have or hold"), "to constrain," is said (a) of the effect of the word of the Lord upon Paul, Acts 18:5 (KJV, "was pressed in spirit," RV, "was constrained by the word"); of the effect of the love of Christ, 2 Cor. 5:14; (b) of being taken with a disease, Matt. 4:24; Luke 4:38; Acts 28:8; with fear, Luke 8:37; (c) of thronging or holding in a person, Luke 8:45; being straitened, Luke 12:50; being in a strait betwixt two, Phil. 1:23; keeping a city in on every side, Luke 19:43; keeping a tight hold on a person, as the men who seized the Lord Jesus did, after bringing Him into the High Priest's house, Luke 22:63; (d) of stopping the ears in refusal to listen, Acts 7:57. Luke uses the word nine times out of its twelve occurrences in the NT.

**B. Adverb.**

***anankastos*** (*317*), akin to A, No. 1, "by force, unwillingly, by constraint," is used in 1 Pet. 5:2.

## CONSULT, CONSULTATION

**A. Verbs.**

1. ***bouleuo*** (*1011*), used in the middle voice, means (a) "to consult," Luke 14:31; (b) "to resolve," John 12:10, KJV, "consulted"; RV, took counsel."

2. ***sumbouleuo*** (*4823*), "to take counsel together," is translated "consulted together," in Matt. 26:4.

**B. Noun.**

***sumboulion*** (*4824*), a word of the Graeco-Roman period (akin to A, No. 2), "counsel, advice," is translated "consultation" in Mark 15:1.

## CONSUME

1. ***analisko*** (*355*), "to use up, spend up, especially in a bad sense, to destroy," is said of the destruction of persons, (a) literally, Luke 9:54 and the RV marg. of 2 Thess. 2:8 (text, "shall slay"); (b) metaphorically, Gal. 5:15 "(that) ye be not consumed (one of another)."

2. ***katanalisko*** (*2654*), "to consume utterly, wholly" (***kata***, intensive), is said, in Heb. 12:29, of God as "a consuming fire."

3. ***aphanizo*** (*853*), lit., "to cause to disappear, put out of sight," came to mean "to do away with" (***a***, negative, ***phaino***, "to cause to appear"), said of the destructive work of moth and rust, Matt. 6:19–20.

## CONTEND (-ING)

1. ***athleo*** (*118*), "to engage in a contest" (cf. Eng., "athlete"), "to contend in public games," is used in 2 Tim. 2:5.

2. ***epagonizomai*** (*1864*) signifies "to contend about a thing, as a combatant" (***epi***, "upon or about," intensive, ***agon***, "a contest"), "to contend earnestly," Jude 3. The word "earnestly" is added to convey the intensive force of the preposition.

## CONTENT (to be), CONTENTMENT

**A. Verb.**

***arkeo*** (*174*) primarily signifies "to be sufficient, to be possessed of sufficient strength, to be strong, to be enough for a thing"; hence, "to defend, ward off"; in the middle voice, "to be satisfied, contented with," Luke 3:14, with wages; 1 Tim. 6:8, with food and raiment; Heb. 13:5, with "such things as ye have"; negatively of Diotrephes, in 3 John 10, "not content therewith."

**B. Adjective.**

***autarkes*** (*842*), as found in the papyri writings, means "sufficient in oneself" (***autos***, "self," ***arkeo***, "see" A), "self-sufficient, adequate, needing no assistance"; hence, "content," Phil. 4:11.

**C. Noun.**

***autarkeia*** (*841*), "contentment, satisfaction with what one has," is found in 1 Tim. 6:6. For its other meaning "sufficiency," in 2 Cor. 9:8.

## CONTENTION, CONTENTIOUS

**A. Nouns.**

1. ***eris*** (*2054*), "strife, quarrel, especially rivalry, contention, wrangling," as in the church

in Corinth, 1 Cor. 1:11, is translated "contentions" in Titus 3:9, KJV.

2. ***paroxusmos*** (*3948*), (Eng., "paroxysm"), lit., "a sharpening," hence "a sharpening of the feeling, or action," denotes an incitement, a sharp contention, Acts 15:39, the effect of irritation; elsewhere in Heb. 10:24, "provoke," unto love.

3. ***philoneikia*** (*5379*), lit., "love of strife," signifies "eagerness to contend"; hence, a "contention," said of the disciples, Luke 22:24. Cf. B, 2.

**B. Adjectives.**

1. ***amachos*** (*269*), lit., "not fighting," primarily signifying "invincible," came to mean "not contentious," 1 Tim. 3:3, RV; Titus 3:2 (KJV, "not a brawler," "no brawlers").

2. ***philoneikos*** (*5380*), akin to A, No. 3, is used in 1 Cor. 11:16.

## CONTRADICT, CONTRADICTION

**A. Verb.**

***antilego*** (*483*), lit., "to speak against," is translated "contradict" in Acts 13:45.

**B. Noun.**

***antilogia*** (*485*), akin to A, is translated "contradiction" in the KJV of Heb. 7:7; 12:3, "dispute," and "gainsaying."

## CONTRARY

**A. Verb.**

***antikeimai*** (*480*), "to be contrary," (***anti***, "against," ***keimai***, "to lie"), Gal. 5:17; 1 Tim. 1:10.

**B. Adjectives.**

1. ***enantios*** (*1727*), "over against," place, Mark 15:39; metaphorically, opposed as an adversary, antagonistic, Acts 26:9; 1 Thess. 2:15; Titus 2:8; Acts 28:17.

2. ***hupenantios*** (*5227*), (***hupo***, "under," and No. 1), opposite to, is used of "that which is contrary to persons," Col. 2:14, and as a noun, "adversaries," Heb. 10:27.

## CONTRIBUTION

***koinonia*** (*2842*) is twice rendered "contribution," Rom. 15:26, and 2 Cor. 9:13, RV, (KJV, "distribution).

## CONVENIENT, CONVENIENTLY

**A. Adjective.**

***eukairos*** (*2121*), lit., "well-timed," hence signifies "timely, opportune, convenient"; it is said of a certain day, Mark 6:21; elsewhere, Heb. 4:16, "in time of need."

**B. Adverb.**

***eukairos*** (*2122*), "conveniently," Mark 14:11, is used elsewhere in 2 Tim. 4:2, "in season."

**C. Verbs.**

1. ***aneko*** (*433*) is rendered "befitting" in Eph. 5:4, for KJV, "convenient"; so in Philem. 8.

2. ***katheko*** (*2520*), "to be fitting," is so translated in Rom. 1:28, RV; KJV, "(not) convenient"; in Acts 22:22, "it is (not) fit."

## CONVERT, CONVERSION

**A. Verbs.**

1. ***strepho*** (*4762*), "to turn," is translated "be converted" in Matt. 18:3, KJV.

2. ***epistrepho*** (*1994*), "to turn about, turn towards" (***epi***, "towards" and No. 1), is used transitively, and so rendered "convert" (of causing a person to turn) in Jas. 5:19–20. Elsewhere, where the KJV translates this verb, either in the middle voice and intransitive use, or the passive, the RV adheres to the middle voice significance, and translates by "turn again," Matt. 13:15; Mark 4:12; Luke 22:32; Acts 3:19; 28:27.

**B. Noun.**

***epistrophe*** (*1995*), akin to A, No. 2, "a turning about, or round, conversion," is found in Acts 15:3. The word implies "a turning from and a turning to"; corresponding to these are repentance and faith; cf. "turned to God from idols," 1 Thess. 1:9. Divine grace is the efficient cause, human agency the responding effect.

## CONVICT (including the KJV, "convince")

1. ***elencho*** (*1651*) signifies (a) "to convict, confute, refute," usually with the suggestion of putting the convicted person to shame; see Matt. 18:15, where more than telling the offender his fault is in view; it is used of "convicting" of sin, John 8:46; 16:8; gainsayers in regard to the faith, Titus 1:9; transgressors of the Law, Jas. 2:9; some texts have the verb in John 8:9; (b) "to reprove," 1 Cor. 14:24, RV (for KJV, "convince"), for the unbeliever is there viewed as being reproved for, or "convicted" of, his sinful state; so in Luke 3:19; it is used of reproving works, John 3:20; Eph. 5:11, 13; 1 Tim. 5:20; 2 Tim. 4:2; Titus 1:13; 2:15; all these speak of reproof by word of mouth. In Heb. 12:5 and Rev. 3:19, the word is used of reproving by action.

2. ***exelencho*** (*1827*), an intensive form of No. 1, "to convict thoroughly," is used of the Lord's future "conviction" of the ungodly, Jude 15.

## COPY

***hupodeigma*** *(5262)*, (from ***hupo***, "under," ***deiknumi***, "to show"), properly denotes "what is shown below or privately"; it is translated "example," Heb. 8:5, KJV (RV, "copy"). It signifies (a) a sign suggestive of anything, the delineation or representation of a thing, and so, a figure, "copy"; in Heb. 9:23 the RV has "copies," for the KJV, "patterns"; (b) an example for imitation, John 13:15; Jas. 5:10; for warning, Heb. 4:11; 2 Pet. 2:6 (KJV "ensample").

## CORBAN

***korban*** *(2878)* signifies (a) "an offering," and was a Hebrew term for any sacrifice, whether by the shedding of blood or otherwise; (b) "a gift offered to God," Mark 7:11. Jews were much addicted to rash vows; a saying of the rabbis was, "It is hard for the parents, but the law is clear, vows must be kept."

## CORNER, CORNERSTONE

1. ***gonia*** *(1137)*, "an angle" (Eng., "*coin*"), signifies (a) "an external angle," as of the "corner" of a street, Matt. 6:5; or of a building, 21:42; Mark 12:10; Luke 20:17; Acts 4:11; 1 Pet. 2:7, "the corner stone or head-stone of the corner"; or the four extreme limits of the earth, Rev. 7:1; 20:8; (b) "an internal corner," a secret place, Acts 26:26.

2. ***arche*** *(746)*, "a beginning" (its usual meaning), "first in time, order, or place," is used to denote the extremities or "corners" of a sheet, Acts 10:11; 11:5.

## CORRECT, CORRECTION, CORRECTOR, CORRECTING

### A. Nouns.

1. ***diorthoma*** *(1357v)* signifies "a reform, amendment, correction," lit., "a making straight." In Acts 24:2, lit., "reformations come about (or take place, lit., 'become')," the RV has "evils are corrected," KJV, "worthy deeds are done"; there is no word for "worthy" or for "deeds" in the original. Some texts have ***katorthoma***, which has the same meaning.

2. ***epanorthosis*** *(1882)*, lit., "a restoration to an upright or right state" (***epi***, "to," ***ana***, "up, or again," and ***orthoo***, see No. 1), hence, "correction," is used of the Scripture in 2 Tim. 3:16, referring to improvement of life and character.

3. ***paideutes*** *(3810)* has two meanings, corresponding to the two meanings of the verb ***paideuo*** (see below) from which it is derived, (a) "a teacher, preceptor, corrector," Rom. 2:20 (KJV, "instructor"), (b) "a chastiser," Heb. 12:9, rendered "to chasten" (KJV, "which corrected"; lit., "chastisers").

### B. Verb.

***paideuo*** *(381)*, "to train up a child" (***pais***), is rendered "correcting in 2 Tim. 2:25, RV, KJV, "instructing.

## CORRUPT, verb and adjective. CORRUPTION, CORRUPTIBLE, INCORRUPTION, INCORRUPTIBLE

### A. Verbs.

1. ***kapeleuo*** *(2585)* primarily signifies "to be a retailer, to peddle, to hucksterize" (from ***kapelos***, "an inn-keeper, a petty retailer, especially of wine, a huckster, peddler," in contrast to ***emporos***, "a merchant"); hence, "to get base gain by dealing in anything," and so, more generally, "to do anything for sordid personal advantage." It is found in 2 Cor. 2:17, with reference to the ministry of the gospel. The significance can be best ascertained by comparison and contrast with the verb ***doloo*** in 4:2 (likewise there only in the NT), "to handle deceitfully." The meanings are not identical. While both involve the deceitful dealing of adulterating the word of truth, ***kapeleuo*** has the broader significance of doing so in order to make dishonest gain. Those to whom the apostle refers in 2:17 are such as make merchandise of souls through covetousness, cf. Titus 1:11; 2 Pet. 2:3, 14–15; Jude 11, 16; Ezek. 13:19; accordingly "hucksterizing" would be the most appropriate rendering in this passage, while "handling deceitfully" is the right meaning in 4:2.

2. ***phtheiro*** *(5351)* signifies "to destroy by means of corrupting," and so "bringing into a worse state"; (a) with this significance it is used of the effect of evil company upon the manners of believers, and so of the effect of association with those who deny the truth and hold false doctrine, 1 Cor. 15:33 (this was a saying of the pagan poet Menander, which became a well known proverb); in 2 Cor. 7:2, of the effects of dishonorable dealing by bringing people to want (a charge made against the apostle); in 11:3, of the effects upon the minds (or thoughts) of believers by "corrupting" them "from the simplicity and the purity that is toward Christ"; in Eph. 4:22, intransitively, of the old nature in waxing "corrupt," "morally decaying, on the way to final ruin" (Moule), "after the lusts of deceit"; in Rev. 19:2, metaphorically, of the Babylonish harlot, in "corrupting" the inhabitants of the earth by her false religion.

(b) With the significance of destroying, it is used of marring a local church by leading it away from that condition of holiness of life and purity of doctrine in which it should abide, 1 Cor. 3:17 (KJV, "defile"), and of God's retributive destruction of the offender who is guilty of this sin (id.); of the effects of the work of false and abominable teachers upon themselves, 2 Pet. 2:12 (some texts have ***kataphtheiro***; KJV, "shall utterly perish"), and Jude 10.

3. ***diaphtheiro*** (*1311*), (***dia***, "through," intensive, and No. 2), "to corrupt utterly, through and through," is said of men "corrupted in mind," whose wranglings result from the doctrines of false teachers, 1 Tim. 6:5 (the KJV wrongly renders it as an adjective, "corrupt"). It is translated "destroyeth" instead of "corrupteth," in the RV of Luke 12:33, of the work of a moth, in Rev. 8:9, of the effect of divine judgments hereafter upon navigation; in 11:18, of the divine retribution of destruction upon those who have destroyed the earth; in 2 Cor. 4:16 it is translated "is decaying," said of the human body.

4. ***kataphtheiro*** (*2704*), (***kata***, "down," intensive, and No. 2), is said of men who are reprobate concerning the faith, "corrupted in mind" (KJV, "corrupt"), 2 Tim. 3:8. For 2 Pet. 2:12, RV, "shall be destroyed," see No. 2.

**B. Nouns.**

1. ***phthora*** (*5356*), connected with ***phtheiro***, No. 2, above, signifies "a bringing or being brought into an inferior or worse condition, a destruction or corruption." It is used (a) physically, (1) of the condition of creation, as under bondage, Rom. 8:21; (2) of the effect of the withdrawal of life, and so of the condition of the human body in burial, 1 Cor. 15:42; (3) by metonymy, of anything which is liable to "corruption," 1 Cor. 15:50; (4) of the physical effects of merely gratifying the natural desires and ministering to one's own needs or lusts, Gal. 6:8, to the flesh in contrast to the Spirit, "corruption" being antithetic to "eternal life"; (5) of that which is naturally short-lived and transient, Col. 2:22, "perish"; (b) of the death and decay of beasts, 2 Pet. 2:12, RV, "destroyed" (first part of verse; lit., "unto . . . destruction"); (c) ethically, with a moral significance, (1) of the effect of lusts, 2 Pet. 1:4; (2) of the effect upon themselves of the work of false and immoral teachers, 2 Pet. 2:12, RV, "destroying"; KJV, "corruption," and verse 19.

2. ***diaphthora*** (*1312*), an intensified form of No. 1, "utter or thorough corruption," referring in the NT to physical decomposition and decay, is used six times, five of which refer, negatively, to the body of God's "Holy One," after His death, which body, by reason of His absolute holiness, could not see "corruption," Acts 2:27, 31; 13:34–35, 37; once it is used of a human body, that of David, which, by contrast, saw "corruption," Acts 13:36.

3. ***aphtharsia*** (*861*), "incorruption," (***a***, negative, with A, No. 2), is used (a) of the resurrection body, 1 Cor. 15:42, 50, 53–54; (b) of a condition associated with glory and honor and life, including perhaps a moral significance, Rom. 2:7; 2 Tim. 1:10; this is wrongly translated "immortality" in the KJV; (c) of love to Christ, that which is sincere and undiminishing, Eph. 6:24 (translated "uncorruptness").

4. ***aphthoria*** (*5356d*), similar to No. 3, "uncorruptness, free from (moral) taint," is said of doctrine, Titus 2:7 (some texts have ***adiaphthoria***, the negative form of No. 2, above).

**C. Adjectives.**

1. ***phthartos*** (*5349*), "corruptible," akin to A, No. 2, is used (a) of man as being mortal, liable to decay (in contrast to God), Rom. 1:23; (b) of man's body as death-doomed, 1 Cor. 15:53–54; (c) of a crown of reward at the Greek games, 1 Cor. 9:25; (d) of silver and gold, as specimens or "corruptible" things, 1 Pet. 1:18; (e) of natural seed, 1 Pet. 1:23.

2. ***apthartos*** (*862*), "not liable to corruption or decay, incorruptible" (***a***, negative, and A, No. 2), is used of (a) God, Rom. 1:23; 1 Tim. 1:17 (KJV, "immortal"); (b) the raised dead, 1 Cor. 15:52; (c) rewards given to the saints hereafter, metaphorically described as a "crown," 1 Cor. 9:25; (d) the eternal inheritance of the saints, 1 Pet. 1:4; (e) the Word of God, as incorruptible" seed, 1 Pet. 1:23; (f) a meek and quiet spirit, metaphorically spoken of as "incorruptible" apparel, 1 Pet. 3:4.

## COST, COSTLINESS, COSTLY

**A. Nouns.**

1. ***dapane*** (*1160*), "expense, cost" (from ***dapto***, "to tear"; from a root ***dap***—meaning "to divide"), is found in Luke 14:28, in the Lord's illustration of counting the "cost" of becoming His disciple.

2. ***timiotes*** (*5094*), "costliness" (from ***timios***, "valued at great price, precious"; see No. 3, below), is connected with ***time***, "honor, price," and used in Rev. 18:19, in reference to Babylon.

**B. Adjectives.**

1. ***timios*** (*5093*), akin to A, No. 2, is translated "costly" in 1 Cor. 3:12, of "costly" stones, in a metaphorical sense (KJV, "precious"). Cf. Rev. 17:4; 18:12, 16; 21:19.

2. ***poluteles*** (*4185*), primarily, "the very end or limit" (from ***polus***, "much," ***telos***, "revenue"),

with reference to price, of highest "cost," very expensive, is said of spikenard, Mark 14:3; raiment, 1 Tim. 2:9; metaphorically, of a meek and quiet spirit, 1 Pet. 3:4, "of great price"; cf. No. 1 and A, No. 2, above.

3. ***polutimos*** *(4186)*, lit., "of great value" (see A, No. 2 and B, No. 1), is used of a pearl, Matt. 13:46; of spikenard, John 12:3 (RV, "very precious," KJV "very costly"). The comparative ***polutimo*** (v.l. ***io***) ***teros***, "much more precious," is used in 1 Pet. 1:7.

## COUNCIL

1. ***sumboulion*** *(4824)*, "a uniting in counsel," denotes (a) "counsel" which is given, taken and acted upon, e.g., Matt. 12:14, RV, "took counsel," for KJV, "held a council"; 22:15; hence (b) "a council," an assembly of counsellors or persons in consultation, Acts 25:12, of the "council" with which Festus conferred concerning Paul. The governors and procurators of provinces had a board of advisers or assessors, with whom they took "counsel," before pronouncing judgment.

2. ***sunedrion*** *(4892)*, properly, "a settling together" (***sun***, "together," ***hedra***, "a seat"), hence, (a) "any assembly or session of persons deliberating or adjusting"; Prov. 22:10; Jer. 15:17, etc.; in the NT, e.g., Matt. 10:17; Mark 13:9; John 11:47, in particular, it denoted (b) "the Sanhedrin," the Great Council at Jerusalem, consisting of 71 members, namely, prominent members of the families of the high priest, elders and scribes. The Jews trace the origin of this to Num. 11:16. The more important causes came up before this tribunal. The Roman rulers of Judea permitted the Sanhedrin to try such cases, and even to pronounce sentence of death, with the condition that such a sentence should be valid only if confirmed by the Roman procurator. In John 11:47, it is used of a meeting of the Sanhedrin; in Acts 4:15, of the place of meeting.

## COUNSEL

### *Old Testament*

### A. Verb.

***ya'as*** (3289), "to advise, counsel, consult." While ***ya'as*** most often describes the "giving of good advice," Num. 24:14, the opposite is sometimes true, 2 Chron. 22:3. The idea of "decision" is expressed in Isa. 23:9.

### B. Noun.

***yo'es*** (3289), "counselor," means one who gives counsel; as messiah, Isa. 9:6; or as counsel for political and military leaders, 2 Sam. 15:12; 1 Chron. 13:1.

### *New Testament*

### A. Nouns.

1. ***boule*** *(1012)*, Luke 23:51.

2. ***sumboulos*** *(4825)*, "a councillor with," occurs in Rom. 11:34.

### B. Verbs.

1. ***bouleuo*** *(1011)*, "to take counsel, to resolve," is used in the middle voice in the NT, "took counsel" in Acts 5:33, KJV (RV translates ***boulomai***); both in 27:39; in Luke 14:31, RV "take counsel" (KJV, "consulteth"); in John 11:53, KJV and RV (so the best mss.); 12:10, RV, "took counsel," for KJV, "consulted"; in 2 Cor. 1:17 (twice), "purpose."

2. ***sumbouleuo*** *(4823)*, in the active voice, "to advise, to counsel," John 18:14, "gave counsel"; in Rev. 3:18, "I counsel"; in the middle voice, "to take counsel, consult," Matt. 26:4, RV, "took counsel together," for KJV, "consulted"; Acts 9:23, "took counsel" (RV adds "together"); in some mss. John 11:53.

## COUNTENANCE

1. ***opsis*** *(3799)*: only Rev. 1:16 has "countenance."

2. ***prosopon*** *(4383)*, is translated "countenance" in Luke 9:29; Acts 2:28, and in the KJV of 2 Cor. 3:7 (RV, "face").

3. ***eidea*** *(2397)*, Matt. 28:3.

## COURAGE

### A. Noun.

***tharsos*** (2294), akin to ***tharseo***, "to be of good cheer," is found in Acts 28:15.

### B. Verb.

***tharreo*** (2292) is translated by some form of the verb "to be of good courage," in the RV in five of the six places where it is used: 2 Cor. 5:6, "being of good courage" (KJV, "we are . . . confident"); 5:8, "we are of good courage" (KJV, "we are confident"); 7:16, "I am of good courage" (KJV, "I have confidence"); 10:1, "I am of good courage" (KJV, "I am bold"); 10:2, "show courage" (KJV, "be bold"); Heb. 13:6, "with good courage," lit., "being of good courage" (KJV, "boldly").

## COURT

### *Old Testament*

***chatser*** (2691), "court; enclosure, settlement." The ***chatser*** ("settlement") was a place where people lived without an enclosure to protect them, Lev. 25:31. ***chatser*** also denotes a "settlement" of people outside the city wall, as a new quarter of the city, 2 Kings 22:14. The

Book of Joshua includes Israel's victories in Canaan's major cities as well as the suburbs: "Ain, Remmon, and Ether, and Ashan; four cities and their villages . . ." Josh. 19:7; cf. 15:45, 47; 21:12.

The predominant usage of ***chatser*** is "court," whether of a house, a palace, or the temple. Each house generally had a courtyard surrounded by a wall or else one adjoined several homes, 2 Sam. 17:18; Ps. 84:3,10; 116:19.

### *New Testament*

***aule*** (*833*), primarily, "an uncovered space around a house, enclosed by a wall, where the stables were," hence was used to describe (a) "the courtyard of a house"; in the OT it is used of the "courts" of the tabernacle and Temple; in this sense it is found in the NT in Rev. 11:2; (b) "the courts in the dwellings of well-to-do folk," which usually had two, one exterior, between the door and the street (called the ***proaulion***, or "porch," Mark 14:68.), the other, interior, surrounded by the buildings of the dwellings, as in Matt. 26:69 (in contrast to the room where the judges were sitting); Mark 14:66; Luke 22:55; KJV, "hall"; RV "court" gives the proper significance, Matt. 26:3, 58; Mark 14:54; 15:16 (RV, "Praetorium"); Luke 11:21; John 18:15. It is here to be distinguished from the Praetorium, translated "palace."

## COURTEOUS, COURTEOUSLY

1. ***philophronos*** (*5390*), lit., "friendly," or, more fully, "with friendly thoughtfulness" (***philos***, "friend," ***phren***, "the mind"), is found in Acts 28:7, of the hospitality showed by Publius to Paul and his fellow-shipwrecked travelers.

2. ***philanthropos*** (*5364*), Acts 27:3, (cf. Eng., "philanthropically").

## COUSIN

***anepsios*** (*431*), in Col. 4:10 denotes a "cousin," not "nephew."

## COVENANT (Noun and Verb)

### *Old Testament*

***berit*** (1285), "covenant; league; confederacy." ***berit*** refers to a political agreement; within Israel, 2 Sam. 3:12–13, 21; 5:3, or between nations, 1 Kings 15:19.

***berit*** means "covenant," as a binding agreement between two parties, either individuals or nations, Gen. 21:32; 1 Sam. 18:3; 20:8, 16–18, 42; Ezek. 17:13.

In Israel, the kingship was based on "covenant": ". . . David made a covenant [KJV, "league"] with them [the elders of Israel] in Hebron before the Lord . . ." 2 Sam. 5:3. The "covenant" was based on their knowledge that God had appointed him, 2 Sam. 5:2; thus they became David's subjects, cf. 2 Kings 11:4, 17.

The great majority of occurrences of ***berit*** are of God's "covenants" with men, as in Gen. 6:18 above. The verbs used are important: "I will *establish* my covenant," Gen. 6:18—literally, "cause to stand" or "confirm." "I will *make* my covenant," Gen. 17:2, RSV. "He *declared* to you his covenant," Deut. 4:13. "My covenant which I *commanded* them . . ." Josh. 7:11. "I have *remembered* my covenant. Wherefore . . . I will bring you out from under the burdens of the Egyptians," Exod. 6:5–6. God will not reject Israel for their disobedience so as "to destroy them utterly, and to *break* my covenant with them . . ." Lev. 26:44. "He will not . . . forget the covenant . . . which he *sware* unto them," Deut. 4:31.

"Covenant" is parallel or equivalent to the Hebrew words ***dabar*** ("word"), ***hoq*** ("statute"), ***piqqud***, "precepts"—Ps. 103:18, NASB, ***'edah***, "testimony"—Ps. 25:10, ***torah***, "law"—Ps. 78:10, and ***hesed***, "lovingkindness"—Deut. 7:9, NASB. These words emphasize the authority and grace of God in making and keeping the "covenant," and the specific responsibility of man under the covenant. The words of the "covenant" were written in a book, Exod. 24:4, 7; Deut. 31:24–26, and on stone tablets, Exod. 34:28.

Men "enter into," Deut. 29:12, or "join," Jer. 50:5, God's "covenant." They are to obey, Gen. 12:4, and "observe carefully" all the commandments of the "covenant." Deut. 4:6. But above all, the "covenant" calls Israel to "love the Lord thy God with all thine heart, and with all thy soul, and with all thy might," Deut. 6:5. God's "covenant" is a relationship of love and loyalty between the Lord and His chosen people.

The use of "Old Testament" and "New Testament" as the names for the two sections of the Bible indicates that God's "covenant" is central to the entire book. The Bible relates God's "covenant" purpose, that man be joined to Him in loving service and know eternal fellowship with Him through the redemption that is in Jesus Christ.

### *New Testament*

***diatheke*** (*1242*) primarily signifies "a disposition of property by will or otherwise." In its use in the Sept., it is the rendering of a Hebrew word meaning a "covenant" or agreement, from a verb signifying "to cut or divide," in allusion to a sacrificial custom in connection with "covenant-making," e.g., Gen. 15:10, "divided" Jer. 34:18–19. In contradistinction to the English word "covenant" (lit., "a coming together"), which signifies a mutual undertaking between two parties or more, each binding himself to fulfill obligations, it does not in itself contain the idea of joint obligation, it mostly signifies an obligation undertaken by a single person. For instance, in Gal. 3:17 it is used as an alternative to a "promise" (vv. 16–18). God enjoined upon Abraham the rite of circumcision, but His promise to Abraham, here called a "covenant," was not conditional upon the observance of circumcision, though a penalty attached to its nonobservance.

"The NT uses of the word may be analyzed as follows: (a) a promise or undertaking, human or divine, Gal. 3:15; (b) a promise or undertaking on the part of God, Luke 1:72; Acts 3:25; Rom. 9:4; 11:27; Gal. 3:17 Eph. 2:12; Heb. 7:22; 8:6, 8, 10; 10:16; (c) an agreement, a mutual undertaking, between God and Israel, see Deut. 29–30 (described as a 'commandment,' Heb. 7:18, cf. v. 22); Heb. 8:9; 9:20; (d) by metonymy, the token of the covenant, or promise, made to Abraham, Acts 7:8, (e) by metonymy, the record of the covenant, 2 Cor. 3:14; Heb. 9:4; cf. Rev. 11:19; (f) the basis, established by the death of Christ, on which the salvation of men is secured, Matt. 26:28; Mark 14:24; Luke 22:20; 1 Cor. 11:25; 2 Cor. 3:6; Heb. 10:29; 12:24; 13:20.

"This covenant is called the 'new,' Heb. 9:15, the 'second,' 8:7, the 'better,' 7:22. In Heb. 9:16–17, the translation is much disputed. There does not seem to be any sufficient reason for departing in these verses from the word used everywhere else.

## COVENANT-BREAKERS

***asunthetos*** (*802*), signifies "not covenant-keeping," i.e., refusing to abide by "covenants" made, "covenant-breaking," faithless, Rom. 1:31.

## COVET, COVETOUS, COVETOUSNESS

### A. Verbs.

1. ***epithumeo*** (*1937*), "to fix the desire upon," whether things good or bad; hence, "to long for, lust after, covet," is used with the meaning "to covet evilly" in Acts 20:33, of "coveting money and apparel"; so in Rom. 7:7; 13:9.

2. ***zeloo*** (*2206*) is rendered "covet earnestly," in 1 Cor. 12:31, KJV; RV, "desire earnestly," as in 14:39 (KJV "covet").

3. ***orego*** (*3713*), "to stretch after," is rendered "covet after" in 1 Tim. 6:10, KJV; RV, "reaching after."

### B. Nouns.

1. ***epithumetes*** (*1938*), "a luster after" (akin to A, No. 1), is translated in 1 Cor. 10:6, in verbal form, "should not lust after."

2. ***epithumia*** (*1939*) denotes "coveting," Rom. 7:7–8, RV; KJV, "lust" and "concupiscence"; the commandment here referred to convicted him of sinfulness in his desires for unlawful objects besides that of gain.

3. ***pleonexia*** (*4124*), "covetousness," lit., "a desire to have more," always in a bad sense, is used in a general way in Mark 7:22 (plural, lit., "covetings," i.e., various ways in which "covetousness" shows itself); Rom. 1:29; Eph. 5:3; 1 Thess. 2:5. Elsewhere it is used, (a) of material possessions, Luke 12:15; 2 Pet. 2:3; 2 Cor. 9:5 (RV, "extortion"), lit., "as (a matter of) extortion" i.e., a gift which betrays the giver's unwillingness to bestow what is due; (b) of sensuality, Eph. 4:19, "greediness"; Col. 3:5 (where it is called "idolatry"); 2 Pet. 2:14 (KJV, "covetous practices").

### C. Adjectives.

1. ***pleonektes*** (*4123*), lit., "(eager) to have more" (see B, No. 3), i.e., to have what belongs to others; hence, "greedy of gain, covetous," 1 Cor. 5:10–11; 6:10; Eph. 5:5 ("covetous man").

2. ***philarguros*** (*5366*), lit., "money-loving," is rendered "covetous" in the KJV of Luke 16:14 and 2 Tim. 3:2; RV, "lovers of money," the wider and due significance.

3. ***aphilarguros*** (*866*), No. 2, with negative prefix, is translated "without covetousness" in Heb. 13:5, KJV; RV, "free from the love of money." In 1 Tim. 3:3, the KJV has "not covetous," the RV, "no lover of money."

## CRAFTINESS, CRAFTY

### A. Noun.

***panourgia*** (*3834*), lit., "all-working," i.e., doing everything (***pan***, "all," ***ergon***, "work"), hence, "unscrupulous conduct, craftiness," is always used in a bad sense in the NT, Luke 20:23; 1 Cor. 3:19; 2 Cor. 4:2; 11:3; Eph. 4:14, KJV, "cunning craftiness."

### B. Adjective.

***panourgos*** (*3835*), "cunning, crafty," is found in 2 Cor. 12:16, where the apostle is really quoting an accusation made against him by his detractors.

### C. Noun.

***dolos*** (*1388*), primarily, "a bait," hence, "fraud, guile, deceit," Mark 14:1.

## CREATE, CREATION, CREATOR, CREATURE

### *Old Testament*

***bara'*** (1254), "to create, make," The verb expresses creation out of nothing, Gen. 1:1; cf. Gen. 2:3; Isa. 40:26; 42:5. All other verbs for "creating" allow a much broader range of meaning, including forming an existing thing, or establishing an existing thing; they have both divine and human subjects, and are used in contexts where bringing something or someone into existence is not the issue.

Objects of the verb include the heavens and earth, Gen. 1:1; Isa. 40:26; 42:5; 45:18; 65:17; man, Gen. 1:27; 5:2; 6:7; Deut. 4:32; Ps. 89:47; Isa. 43:7; 45:12; Israel Isa. 43:1; Mal. 2:10; a new thing, Jer. 31:22; cloud and smoke, Isa. 4:5; north and south, Ps. 89:12; salvation and righteousness, Isa. 45:8; speech, Isa. 57:19; darkness, Isa. 45:7; wind, Amos 4:13; and a new heart, Ps. 51:10. A careful study of the passages where ***bara'*** occurs shows that in the few nonpoetic uses (primarily in Genesis), the writer uses scientifically precise language to demonstrate that God brought the object or concept into being from previously nonexistent material. Isa 45–65 has a special focus on Yahweh as Creator, and so powerful and able to deliver, Isa. 43:16–21; 44:12–20; 45:12; 46:1–7; 65:17–25.

Though a precisely correct technical term to suggest cosmic, material creation from nothing, ***bara'*** is a rich theological vehicle for communicating the sovereign power of God, who originates and regulates all things to His glory.

***qanah*** (7069), "to get, acquire, earn," and so as a figurative extension, this verb means "create," Gen. 14:19, 22.

***'asah*** (6213), "to create, do, make," Only when ***'asah*** is parallel to ***bara'*** that we can be sure that it implies creation, Gen. 2:3, and then ***'asah*** may have a focus of manipulating existing material. But one must exhibit caution, it is unwarranted to overly refine the meaning of ***'asah*** to suggest that it means creation from something, as opposed to creation from nothing. Only context can determine its special nuance. It can mean either, depending upon the situation.

### *New Testament*

**A. Verb.**

***ktizo*** (*2936*), used among the Greeks to mean the founding of a place, a city or colony, signifies, in Scripture, "to create," always of the act of God, whether (a) in the natural creation, Mark 13:19; Rom. 1:25 (where the title "The Creator" translates the article with the aorist participle of the verb); 1 Cor. 11:9; Eph. 3:9; Col. 1:16; 1 Tim. 4:3; Rev. 4:11; 10:6, or (b) in the spiritual creation, Eph. 2:10, 15; 4:24; Col. 3:10.

**B. Nouns.**

1. ***ktisis*** (*2937*), primarily "the act of creating," or "the creative act in process," has this meaning in Rom. 1:20 and Gal. 6:15. Like the English word "creation," it also signifies the product of the "creative" act, the "creature," as in Mark 16:15, RV; Rom. 1:25; 8:19; Col. 1:15 etc.; in Heb. 9:11, KJV, "building." In Mark 16:15 and Col. 1:23 its significance has special reference to mankind in general. As to its use in Gal. 6:15 and 2 Cor. 5:17, in the former, apparently, the reference is to the creative act of God, whereby a man is introduced into the blessing of salvation, in contrast to circumcision done by human hands, which the Judaizers claimed was necessary to that end. In 2 Cor. 5:17 the reference is to what the believer is in Christ; in consequence of the creative act he has become a new creature.

2. ***ktistma*** (*2938*) has the concrete sense, "the created thing, the creature, the product of the creative act," 1 Tim. 4:4; Jas. 1:18; Rev. 5:13; 8:9.

3. ***ktistes*** (*2939*), among the Greeks, the founder of a city, etc., denotes in Scripture "the Creator," 1 Pet. 4:19 (cf. Rom. 1:20, under B, No. 1, above).

## CROSS, CRUCIFY

**A. Noun.**

***stauros*** (*4716*) denotes, primarily, "an upright pale or stake." On such malefactors were nailed for execution. Both the noun and the verb ***stauroo***, "to fasten to a stake or pale," are originally to be distinguished from the ecclesiastical form of a two beamed "cross." The shape of the latter had its origin in ancient Chaldea, and was used as the symbol of the god Tammuz (being in the shape of the mystic Tau, the initial of his name) in that country and in adjacent lands, including Egypt. By the middle of the 3rd cent. A.D. the churches had either departed from, or had travestied, certain doctrines of the Christian faith. In order to increase the prestige of the apostate ecclesiastical system pagans were received into the churches apart from regeneration by faith, and were permitted largely to retain their pagan signs and symbols. Hence the Tau or T, in its most frequent form, with the cross-piece lowered, was adopted to stand for the "cross" of Christ.

The method of execution was borrowed by the Greeks and Romans from the Phoenicians. The ***stauros*** denotes (a) "the cross, or stake itself," e.g., Matt. 27:32; (b) "the crucifixion suffered," e.g., 1 Cor. 1:17–18, where "the word of the cross," RV, stands for the gospel; Gal. 5:11, where crucifixion is metaphorically used of the renunciation of the world, that characterizes the true Christian life; 6:12, 14; Eph. 2:16; Phil. 3:18.

The judicial custom by which the condemned person carried his stake to the place of execution, was applied by the Lord to those sufferings by which His faithful followers were to express their fellowship with Him, e.g., Matt. 10:38.

### B. Verbs.

1. ***stauroo*** (*4717*) signifies (a) "the act of crucifixion," e.g., Matt. 20:19; (b) metaphorically, "the putting off of the flesh with its passions and lusts," a condition fulfilled in the case of those who are "of Christ Jesus," Gal. 5:24, RV; so of the relationship between the believer and the world, 6:14.

2. ***sustauroo*** (*4957*), "to crucify with," is used (a) of actual "crucifixion" in company with another, Matt. 27:44; Mark 15:32; John 19:32; (b) metaphorically, of spiritual identification with Christ in His death, Rom. 6:6, and Gal. 2:20.

3. ***anastauroo*** (*388*) (***ana***, again) is used in Heb. 6:6 of Hebrew apostates, who as merely nominal Christians, in turning back to Judaism, were thereby virtually guilty of "crucifying" Christ again.

4. ***prospegnumi*** (*4362*), "to fix or fasten to anything" (***pros***, "to," ***pegnumi***, "to fix"), is used of the "crucifixion" of Christ, Acts 2:23.

## CROWN (Noun and Verb)

### A. Nouns.

1. ***stephanos*** (*4735*), primarily, "that which surrounds, as a wall or crowd" (from ***stepho***, "to encircle"), denotes (a) "the victor's crown," the symbol of triumph in the games or some such contest; hence, by metonymy, a reward or prize; (b) "a token of public honor" for distinguished service, military prowess, etc., or of nuptial joy, or festal gladness, especially at the parousia of kings. It was woven as a garland of oak, ivy, parsley, myrtle, or olive, or in imitation of these in gold. In some passages the reference to the games is clear, 1 Cor. 9:25; 2 Tim. 4:8 ("crown of righteousness"); it may be so in 1 Pet. 5:4, where the fadeless character of "the crown of glory" is set in contrast to the garlands of earth. In other passages it stands as an emblem of life, joy, reward and glory, Phil. 4:1; 1 Thess. 2:19; Jas. 1:12 ("crown of life"); Rev. 2:10 (ditto); 3:11; 4:4, 10: of triumph, 6:2; 9:7; 12:1; 14:14.

It is used of "the crown of thorns" which the soldiers plaited and put on Christ's head, Matt. 27:29; Mark 15:17; John 19:2, 5. At first sight this might be taken as an alternative for ***diadema***, "a kingly crown."

2. ***diadema*** (*1238*) is never used as ***stephanos*** is; it is always the symbol of kingly or imperial dignity, and is translated "diadem" instead of "crown" in the RV, of the claims of the Dragon, Rev. 12:3; 13:1; 19:12.

### B. Verb.

***stephanoo*** (*4737*), "to crown," conforms in meaning to ***stephanos;*** it is used of the reward of victory in the games, in 2 Tim. 2:5; of the glory and honor bestowed by God upon man in regard to his position in creation, Heb. 2:7; of the glory and honor bestowed upon the Lord Jesus in His exaltation, v. 9.

## CRY (Noun and Verb), CRYING

### *Old Testament*

***tsa'aq*** (6817), "to cry, cry out, call." This word is often used in the sense of "crying out" for help, Gen. 41:55; Exod. 14:10; Isa. 46:7.

***za'aq*** (2199), "to cry, cry out, call." ***za'aq*** is perhaps most frequently used to indicate the "crying out" for aid in time of emergency, especially "crying out" for divine aid, Judg. 3:9, 15; 6:7; 10:10; Jer. 11:12; Jonah 1:5. That ***za'aq*** means more than a normal speaking volume is indicated in appeals to the king, 2 Sam. 19:28.

The word may imply a "crying out" in distress, 1 Sam. 4:13, a "cry" of horror, 1 Sam. 5:10, or a "cry" of sorrow, 2 Sam. 13:19. Used figuratively, it is said that "the stone shall cry out of the wall," Hab. 2:11 of a house that is built by means of evil gain.

### *New Testament*

### A. Nouns.

1. ***krauge*** (*2906*), an onomatopoeic word, is used in Matt. 25:6; Luke 1:42 (some mss. have ***phone***); Acts 23:9, RV, "clamor"; Eph. 4:31, "clamor"; Heb. 5:7; Rev. 21:4, "crying." Some mss. have it in Rev. 14:18 (the most authentic have ***phone***).

2. ***boe*** (*995*), especially "a cry for help," an onomatopoeic word (cf. Eng., "boo"), connected with ***boao*** (see B, No. 1), is found in Jas. 5:4.

**B. Verbs.**

1. ***boao*** (*994*), akin to A, No. 2, signifies (a) "to raise a cry," whether of joy, Gal. 4:27, or vexation, Acts 8:7; (b) "to speak with a strong voice," Matt. 3:3; Mark 1:3; 15:34; Luke 3:4; 9:38 (some mss. have ***anaboao*** here: see No. 2); John 1:23; Acts 17:6; 25:24 (some mss. have ***epiboao***, No. 3, here); (c) "to cry out for help," Luke 18:7, 38.

2. ***anaboao*** (*310*), ***ana***, "up," intensive, and No. 1, "to lift up the voice, cry out," is said of Christ at the moment of His death, a testimony to His supernatural power in giving up His life, Matt. 27:46; in some mss. in Mark 15:8, of the shouting of a multitude; in some mss. in Luke 9:38, of the "crying" out of a man in a company (see No. 1).

3. ***epiboao*** (*1916*), ***epi***, "upon," intensive, and No. 1, "to cry out, exclaim vehemently," is used in some mss. in Acts 25:24 (see No. 1.)

4. ***krazo*** (*2896*), akin to A, No. 1, "to cry out," an onomatopoeic word, used especially of the "cry" of the raven; then, of any inarticulate cries, from fear, pain etc.; of the "cry" of a Canaanitish woman, Matt. 15:22 (so the best mss., instead of ***kraugazo***); of the shouts of the children in the Temple, Matt. 21:15; of the people who shouted for Christ to be crucified, 27:23; Mark 15:13–14; of the "cry" of Christ on the Cross at the close of His sufferings, Matt. 27:50; Mark 15:39 (see No. 2, above).

5. ***anakrazo*** (*349*), ***ana***, "up," intensive, and No. 4, signifies "to cry out loudly," Mark 1:23; 6:49; Luke 4:33; 8:28; 23:18.

6. ***kraugazo*** (*2905*), a stronger form of No. 4, "to make a clamor or outcry" (A, No. 1), is used in Matt. 12:19, in a prophecy from Isaiah of Christ; in Luke 4:41 (in the best mss., instead of ***krazo***); John 11:43; 12:13 (in the best mss.); 18:40; 19:6, 12, 15; Acts 22:23.

## CRYSTAL

**A. Noun.**

***krustallos*** (*2930*), from ***kruos***, "ice," and hence properly anything congealed and transparent, denotes "crystal," a kind of precious stone, Rev. 4:6; 22:1. Rock crystal is pure quartz; it crystallizes in hexagonal prisms, each with a pyramidical apex.

**B. Verb.**

***krustallizo*** (*2929*), "to be of crystalline brightness and transparency, to shine like crystal," is found in Rev. 21:11, where it is said of Christ as the "Light-giver" (***phoster***) of the heavenly city (not ***phos***, "light," RV and KJV). Possibly there the verb has a transitive force, "to transform into crystal splendor," as of the effect of Christ upon His saints.

## CUBIT

### *Old Testament*

***'ammah*** (520), "cubit," a primary unit of linear measurement in the Old Testament, possibly based on the Egyptian system. A "cubit" ordinarily was the distance from one's elbow to the tip of the middle finger.

There was an official "cubit" in Egypt. In fact, there were both a shorter "cubit" (17.6 inches) and a longer "cubit" (20.65 inches). The Siloam inscription states that the Siloam tunnel was 1,200 "cubits" long. This divided by its measurement in feet (1,749) demonstrates that as late as Hezekiah's day, cf. 2 Chron. 32:4, the "cubit" was about 17.5 inches or the shorter Egyptian cubit. Ezekiel probably used the Babylonian "cubit" in describing the temple. The Egyptian shorter cubit is only about three inches shorter than the longer cubit; on the other hand, the Babylonian shorter cubit was about four-fifths the length of the official royal "cubit," about a handbreadth shorter: "And behold a wall on the outside of the house round about, and in the man's hand a measuring reed of six cubits long by the cubit and a handbreadth . . ." Ezek. 40:5. In other words, it was the width of seven palms rather than six.

### *New Testament*

***pechus*** (*4083*), Matt. 6:27; Luke 12:25; John 21:8; Rev. 21:17; see also above.

## CUP

***poterion*** (*4221*), a diminutive of ***poter***, denotes, primarily, a "drinking vessel"; hence, "a cup" (a) literal, as, e.g., in Matt. 10:42. The "cup" of blessing, 1 Cor. 10:16, is so named from the third (the fourth according to Edersheim) "cup" in the Jewish Passover feast, over which thanks and praise were given to God. This connection is not to be rejected on the ground that the church at Corinth was unfamiliar with Jewish customs. That the contrary was the case, see 5:7; (b) figurative, of one's lot or experience, joyous or sorrowful (frequent in the Psalms; cf. Ps. 116:18, "cup of salvation"); in the NT it is used most frequently of the sufferings of Christ, Matt. 20:22–23; 26:39; Mark 10:38–39; 14:36; Luke 22:42; John 18:11; also of the evil deeds of Babylon, Rev. 17:4; 18:6; of divine punishments to be inflicted, Rev. 14:10; 16:19. Cf. Ps. 11:6; 75:8; Isa. 51:17; Jer. 25:15; Ezek. 23:32–34; Zech. 12:2.

## CURSE, CURSING (Noun and Verb), CURSED, ACCURSED

*Old Testament*

**A. Verbs.**

***qalal*** (7043), "to be trifling, light, swift; to curse." The idea of "to be swifter" is expressed in 2 Sam. 1:23; 1 Sam. 18:23.

***qalal*** frequently includes the idea of "cursing" or "scorning or mocking, Exod. 21:17; 1 Sam. 17:43; Job 24:18; Isa 65:20.

The causative form of the verb sometimes expressed the idea of "lightening, lifting a weight," and so being in an easier circumstance, 1 Sam. 6:5; Exod. 18:22.

***'arar*** (779), "to curse," usually parallel with "bless." The two "curses" in Gen. 3 are in bold contrast to the two blessings ("And God blessed them . . .") in Gen. 1. The covenant with Abraham includes: "I will bless them that bless thee, and curse [different root] him that curseth thee . . ." Gen. 12:3. Compare Jeremiah's "Cursed be the man that trusteth in man" and "Blessed is the man that trusteth in the Lord," Jer. 17:5, 7.

God alone truly "curses." It is a revelation of His justice, in support of His claim to absolute obedience. Men may claim God's "curses" by committing their grievances to God and trusting in His righteous judgment, cf. Ps. 109:26–31; Christ alone redeems from the curse of the law, Gal. 3:13.

**B. Noun.**

***'alah*** (423), "curse; oath." ***'alah*** basically refers to "the execution of a proper oath to legalize a covenant or agreement." As a noun, ***'alah*** refers to the "oath" itself, Gen. 24:41; Lev. 5:1. So ***'alah*** functions as a "curse" sanctioning a pledge or commission, and it can close an agreement or covenant. On the other hand, the word sometimes represents a "curse" against someone else, whether his identity is known or not.

*New Testament*

**A. Nouns.**

1. ***ara*** (*685*), in its most usual meaning, "a malediction, cursing" (its other meaning is "a prayer"), is used in Rom. 3:14.

2. ***katara*** (*2671*), ***kata***, "down," intensive, and No. 1, denotes an "execration, imprecation, curse," uttered out of malevolence, Jas. 3:10; 2 Pet. 2:14; or pronounced by God in His righteous judgment, as upon a land doomed to barrenness, Heb. 6:8; upon those who seek for justification by obedience, in part or completely, to the Law, Gal. 3:10, 13; in this 13th verse it is used concretely of Christ, as having "become a curse" for us, i.e., by voluntarily undergoing on the cross the appointed penalty of the "curse." He thus was identified, on our behalf, with the doom of sin.

3. ***anathema*** (*33*), transliterated from the Greek, is frequently used in the Sept., where it translates the Heb. ***cherem***, "a thing devoted to God," whether (a) for His service, as the sacrifices, Lev. 27:28 (cf. ***anathema***, a votive offering, gift), or (b) for its destruction, as an idol, Deut. 7:26, or a city, Josh. 6:17. Later it acquired the more general meaning of "the disfavor of Jehovah," e.g., Zech. 14:11. This is the meaning in the NT. It is used of (a) the sentence pronounced, Acts 23:14 (lit., "cursed themselves with a curse"; (b) of the object on which the "curse" is laid, "accursed"; in the following, the RV keeps to the word "anathema," Rom. 9:3; 1 Cor. 12:3; 16:22; Gal. 1:8–9, all of which the KJV renders by "accursed" except 1 Cor. 16:22, where it has "Anathema." In Gal. 1:8–9, the apostle declares in the strongest manner that the gospel he preached was the one and only way of salvation, and that to preach another was to nullify the death of Christ.

4. ***katathema*** (*2652*), or, as in some mss., the longer form ***katanathema***, is stronger than No. 3 (***kata***, intensive), and denotes, by metonymy, "an accursed thing" (the object "cursed" being put for the "curse" pronounced), Rev. 22:3.

**B. Verbs.**

1. ***anathematizo*** (*332*), akin to No. 3, signifies "to declare anathema," i.e., "devoted to destruction, accursed, to curse," Mark 14:71, or "to bind by a curse," Acts 23:12, 14, 21.

2. ***katanathematizo*** (*2653*), a strengthened form of No. 1, denotes "to utter curses against," Matt. 26:74; cf. Mark's word concerning the same occasion (No. 1).

3. ***kataraomai*** (*2672*), akin to A, No. 2, primarily signifies "to pray against, to wish evil against a person or thing"; hence "to curse," Matt. 25:41; Mark 11:21; Luke 6:28; Rom. 12:14; Jas. 3:9. Some mss. have it in Matt. 5:44.

**C. Adjectives.**

1. ***epikataratos*** (*1944*), "cursed, accursed" (***epi*** "upon," and A, No. 2), is used in Gal. 3:10, 13.

2. ***eparatos*** (*1883a*), "accursed," is found, in the best mss., in John 7:49, RV, "accursed," instead of No. 1.

## CUSTOM (Usage), ACCUSTOM (Verb)

**A. Nouns.**

1. ***ethos*** (*1485*) denotes (a) "a custom, usage, prescribed by law," Acts 6:14; 15:1; 25:16; "a rite

or ceremony," Luke 2:42; (b) a "custom, habit, manner," Luke 22:39; John 19:40; Heb. 10:25 (KJV, "manner").

2. ***sunetheia*** (*4914*), (***sun***, "with," ***ethos***, see No. 1), denotes (a) "an intercourse, intimacy," a meaning not found in the NT; (b) "a custom, customary usage," John 18:39; 1 Cor. 11:16; "or force of habit," 1 Cor. 8:7, RV, "being used to" (some mss. here have ***suneidsis***, "conscience"; whence KJV, "with conscience of").

**B. Verbs.**

1. ***ethizo*** (*1480*), akin to A, No. 1, signifies "to accustom," or in the passive voice, "to be accustomed." In the participial form it is equivalent to a noun, "custom, Luke 2:27.

2. ***etho*** (*1486*), "to be accustomed," as in the case of No. 1, is used in the passive participle as a noun, signifying "a custom," Luke 4:16; Acts 17:2 (KJV, "manner"; RV, "custom"); in Matt. 17:15 and Mark 10:1, "was wont."

C

# D

## DAILY (Adjective)

1. ***epiousios*** (*1967*) is found in Matt. 6:11 and Luke 11:3. Its derivation likely is from ***epi***, and ***eimi***, "to go," so then, (bread) for going on, i.e., for the morrow and after, or (bread) coming (for us).

2. ***ephemeros*** (*2184*) signifies "for the day," cf. Eng., "ephemeral," Jas. 2:15.

3. ***kathemerinos*** (2522) means, lit., "according to the day," so, "day by day, daily," Acts 6:1.

## DAINTY

***liparos*** (*3045*) properly signifies "oily, or anointed with oil" (from ***lipos***, "grease," connected with ***aleipho***, "to anoint"); it is said of things which pertain to delicate and sumptuous living; hence, "dainty," Rev. 18:14.

## DAMSEL

1. ***korasion*** (*2877*), a diminutive of ***kore***, "a girl," denotes "a little girl" (properly a colloquial word, often used disparagingly, but not so in later writers); in the NT it is used only in familiar conversation, Matt. 9:24–25 (KJV, "maid"); 14:11; Mark 5:41–42; 6:22, 28.

2. ***paidion*** (*3813*), a diminutive of ***pais***, denotes "a young child (male or female)" in the KJV of Mark 5:39–41.

3. ***paidiske*** (*3814*) denotes "a young girl, or a female slave"; "damsel," KJV, in John 18:17; Acts 12:13; 16:16; RV "maid" in each case.

## DANCE

***orcheo*** (*3738*), (cf. Eng., "orchestra"), probably originally signified "to lift up," as of the feet; hence, "to leap with regularity of motion." It is always used in the middle voice, Matt. 11:17; 14:6; Mark 6:22; Luke 7:32. The performance by the daughter of Herodias is the only clear instance of artistic dancing, a form introduced from Greek customs.

## DANGER, DANGEROUS

### A. Verb.

***kinduneuo*** (*2793*) properly signifies "to run a risk, face danger," but is used in the NT in the sense of "being in danger, jeopardy," Acts 19:27, 40. It is translated "were in jeopardy" in Luke 8:23, and "stand we in jeopardy," 1 Cor. 15:30.

### B. Adjectives.

1. ***enochos*** (*1777*), lit., "held in, contained in," hence, "bound under obligation to, liable to, subject to," is used in the sense of being in "danger" of the penal effect of a misdeed, i.e., in a forensic sense, signifying the connection of a person with (a) his crime, "guilty of an eternal sin," Mark 3:29, RV; (b) the trial or tribunal, as a result of which sentence is passed, Matt. 5:21–22, "the judgment," "the council"; ***enochos*** here has the obsolete sense of control; (c) the penalty itself, 5:22, "the hell of fire," and, with the translation "worthy" (KJV, "guilty"), of the punishment determined to be inflicted on Christ, Matt. 26:66 and Mark 14:64, "death"; (d) the person or thing against whom or which the offense is committed 1 Cor. 11:27, "guilty," the crime being against "the body and blood of the Lord"; Jas. 2:10, "guilty" of an offense against all the Law, because of a breach of one commandment.

2. ***episphales*** (*2000*), lit., "prone to fall," hence, "insecure, dangerous," is used in Acts 27:9.

## DARE, DARING, DURST

### A. Verb.

***tolmao*** (*5111*) signifies "to dare," (a) in the sense of not dreading or shunning through fear, Matt. 22:46; Mark 12:34; Mark 15:43, "boldly," lit., "having dared, went in"; Luke 20:40; John 21:12; Acts 5:13; 7:32; Rom. 15:18; 2 Cor. 10:2, RV, "show courage," (KJV, "be bold"); 10:12, RV, "are (not) bold," 11:21; Phil. 1:14, "are bold"; Jude 9; (b) in the sense of bearing, enduring, bringing oneself to do a thing, Rom. 5:7; 1 Cor. 6:1. Cf. ***apotolmao***, "to be very bold," Rom. 10:20.

### B. Adjective.

***tolmetes*** (*5113*), akin to A, "daring," is used in 2 Pet. 2:10, RV, "daring" (KJV "presumptuous"), "shameless and irreverent daring."

## DARK, DARKEN, DARKLY, DARKNESS

### A. Adjectives.

1. ***skoteinos*** (*4652*), "full of darkness, or covered with darkness," is translated "dark" in Luke 11:36; "full of darkness," in Matt. 6:23 and Luke 11:34, where the physical condition is figurative of the moral. The group of ***skot***— words

is derived from a root ***ska***—, meaning "to cover." The same root is to be found in ***skene***, "a tent."

2. ***auchmeros*** (*850*), from ***auchmos***, "drought produced by excessive heat," hence signifies "dry, murky, dark," 2 Pet. 1:19.

### B. Nouns.

1. ***skotia*** (*4653*) is used (a) of physical darkness, "dark," John 6:17, lit., "darkness had come on," and 20:1, lit., "darkness still being"; (b) of secrecy, in general, whether what is done therein is good or evil, Matt. 10:27; Luke 12:3; (c) of spiritual or moral "darkness," emblematic of sin, as a condition of moral or spiritual depravity, Matt. 4:16; John 1:5; 8:12; 12:35, 46; 1 John 1:5; 2:8–9, 11.

2. ***skotos*** (*4655*), an older form than No. 1, grammatically masculine, is found in some mss. in Heb. 12:18.

3. ***skotos*** (*4655*), the equivalent of No. 1; (a) of "physical darkness," Matt. 27:45; 2 Cor. 4:6; (b) of "intellectual darkness," Rom. 2:19 (cf. C, No. 1); (c) of "blindness," Acts 13:11; (d) by metonymy, of the "place of punishment," e.g., Matt. 8:12; 2 Pet. 2:17; Jude 13; (e) metaphorically, of "moral and spiritual darkness," e.g., Matt. 6:23; Luke 1:79; 11:35; John 3:19; Acts 26:18; 2 Cor. 6:14; Eph. 6:12; Col. 1:13; 1 Thess. 5:4–5; 1 Pet. 2:9; 1 John 1:6; (f) by metonymy, of "those who are in moral or spiritual darkness," Eph. 5:8; (g) of "evil works," Rom. 13:12; Eph. 5:11, (h) of the "evil powers that dominate the world," Luke 22:53; (i) "of secrecy" [as in No. 1, (b)].

4. ***zophos*** (*2217*) denotes "the gloom of the nether world," hence, "thick darkness, darkness that may be felt"; it is rendered "darkness" in Heb. 12:18; 2 Pet. 2:4 and Jude 6; in 2 Pet. 2:17, RV, "blackness," KJV, "mists"; in Jude 13, RV and KJV, blackness.

### C. Verbs.

1. ***skotizo*** (*4654*), "to deprive of light, to make dark," is used in the NT in the passive voice only, (a) of the heavenly bodies Matt. 24:29; Mark 13:24; Rev. 8:12; (b) metaphorically, of the mind, Rom. 1:21; 11:10; (some mss. have it in Luke 23:45).

2. ***skotoo*** (*4656*), "to darken," is used (a) of the heavenly bodies, Rev. 9:2; 16:10; (b) metaphorically, of the mind, Eph. 4:18.

## DAUGHTER, DAUGHTER-IN-LAW

1. ***thugater*** (*2364*), "a daughter," (etymologically, Eng., "daughter" is connected), is used of (a) the natural relationship (frequent in the gospels); (b) spiritual relationship to God, 2 Cor. 6:18; (c) the inhabitants of a city or region, Matt. 21:5; John 12:15 ("of Zion"); (d) the women who followed Christ to Calvary, Luke 23:28; (e) women of Aaron's posterity, Luke 1:5.

2. ***thugatrion*** (*2365*), a diminutive of No. 1, denotes "a little daughter," Mark 5:23; 7:25.

3. ***parthenos*** (*3933*), "a maiden, virgin," e.g., Matt. 1:23, signifies a virgin-daughter in 1 Cor. 7:36–38 (RV); in Rev. 14:4, it is used of chaste persons.

4. ***numphe*** (*3565*), (Eng., "nymph"), denotes "a bride," John 3:29; also "a daughter-in-law," Matt. 10:35; Luke 12:53.

D

## DAY

### *Old Testament*

***yom*** (3117), "daylight; day; time; moment; year." ***yom*** has several meanings. The word represents the period of "daylight," Gen. 8:22. The word denotes a period of twenty-four hours, Gen. 39:10. ***yom*** can also signify a period of time of unspecified duration, Gen. 2:3. Another nuance appears in Gen. 2:17, where the word represents a "point of time" or "a moment." Finally, when used in the plural, the word may represent "year," Exod. 13:10.

***yom*** can mean "first," as in a series, Gen. 25:31. It may also mean "one day," or "about this day," Gen. 39:11. When used with the definite article ***ha***, the noun may mean "today," as it does in Gen. 4:14, or refer to some particular "day," 1 Sam. 1:4, and the "daytime," Neh. 4:16.

The "day of the Lord" is used to denote both the end of the age (eschatologically) or some occurrence during the present age (non-eschatologically). It may be a day of either judgment or blessing, or both, cf. Isa. 2.

It is noteworthy that Hebrew people did not divide the period of daylight into regular hourly periods, whereas nighttime was divided into three watches, Exod. 14:24; Judg. 7:19. The beginning of a "day" is sometimes said to be dusk, Esth. 4:16, and sometimes dawn, Deut. 28:66–67.

### *New Testament*

### A. Nouns.

1. ***hemera*** (*2250*), "a day," is used of (a) the period of natural light, Gen. 1:5; Prov. 4:18; Mark 4:35; (b) the same, but figuratively, for a period of opportunity for service, John 9:4; Rom. 13:13; (c) one period of alternate light and darkness, Gen. 1:5; Mark 1:13; (d) a period of undefined length marked by certain characteristics, Rom. 2:5; (e) an appointed time, Ecc. 8:6; Eph. 4:30; (f) of a time of life, Luke 1:17–18 ("years").

As the "day" throws light upon things that have been in darkness, the word is often associated with the passing of judgment upon circumstances, 1 Cor. 4:3; Rev. 1:10.

The phrases "the day of Christ," Phil. 1:10; 2:16; "the day of Jesus Christ," 1:6; "the day of the Lord Jesus," 1 Cor. 5:5; 2 Cor. 1:14; "the day of our Lord Jesus Christ," 1 Cor. 1:8, denote the time of the Parousia of Christ with His saints, subsequent to the Rapture, 1 Thess. 4:16–17. In 2 Pet. 1:19 this is spoken of simply as the day.

In the NT "the day of the Lord" is mentioned in 1 Thess. 5:2 and 2 Thess. 2:2, RV, where the apostle's warning is that the church at Thessalonica should not be deceived by thinking that "the Day of the Lord is now present." This period will not begin till the circumstances mentioned in verses 3 and 4 take place.

2. ***auge*** (*827*), "brightness, bright, shining, as of the sun"; hence, "the beginning of daylight," is translated "break of day" in Acts 20:11.

**B. Adverb.**

***ennucha*** (*1773***), lit., "in night," signifies "very early, yet in the night," "a great while before day," Mark 1:35.

## DAYSPRING

***anatole*** (*395*), lit., "a rising up," is used of the rising of the sun and stars; it chiefly means the east, as in Matt. 2:1, etc.; rendered "dayspring" in Luke 1:78.

## DAY-STAR

***phosphoros*** (*5459*), (Eng., "phosphorus," lit., "light-bearing," is used of the morning star, as the light-bringer, 2 Pet. 1:19, where it indicates the arising of the light of Christ as the personal fulfillment, in the hearts of believers, of the prophetic Scriptures concerning His coming to receive them to Himself.

## DEACON

***diakonos*** (*1249*), (Eng., "deacon"), primarily denotes a "servant," whether as doing servile work, or as an attendant rendering free service, without particular reference to its character. It occurs in the NT of domestic servants, John 2:5, 9; the civil ruler, Rom. 13:4; Christ, Rom. 15:8; Gal. 2:17; the followers of Christ in relation to their Lord, John 12:26; Eph. 6:21; Col. 1:7; 4:7; the followers of Christ in relation to one another, Matt. 20:26; 23:11, Mark 9:35; 10:43; the servants of Christ in the work of preaching and teaching, 1 Cor. 3:5; 2 Cor. 3:6; 6:4; 11:23; Eph. 3:7; Col. 1:23, 25; 1 Thess. 3:2; 1 Tim. 4:6; those who serve in the churches, Rom. 16:1 (used of a woman here only in NT); Phil. 1:1; 1 Tim. 3:8, 12; false apostles, servants of Satan, 2 Cor. 11:15.

***diakonos*** is, generally speaking, to be distinguished from ***doulos***, "a bondservant, slave"; ***diakonos*** views a servant in relationship to his work, ***doulos*** views him in relationship to his master. See, e.g., Matt. 22:2–14; those who bring in the guests (vv. 3–4, 6, 8, 10) are ***douloi***; those who carry out the king's sentence (v. 13) are ***diakonoi***.

## DEAD

**A. Noun and Adjective.**

***nekros*** (*3498*) is used of (a) the death of the body, cf. Jas. 2:26, its most frequent sense: (b) the actual spiritual condition of unsaved men, Matt. 8:22; John 5:25; Eph. 2:1, 5; 5:14; Phil. 3:11; Col. 2:13; cf. Luke 15:24: (c) the ideal spiritual condition of believers in regard to sin, Rom. 6:11: (d) a church in declension, inasmuch as in that state it is inactive and barren, Rev. 3:1: (e) sin, which apart from law cannot produce a sense of guilt, Rom. 7:8: (f) the body of the believer in contrast to his spirit, Rom. 8:10: (g) the works of the Law, inasmuch as, however good in themselves, Rom. 7:13, they cannot produce life, Heb. 6:1; 9:14: (h) the faith that does not produce works, Jas. 2:17, 26; cf. v. 20.

**B. Verbs.**

1. ***nekroo*** (*3499*), "to put to death," is used in the active voice in the sense of destroying the strength of, depriving of power, with reference to the evil desires which work in the body, Col. 3:5. In the passive voice it is used of Abraham's body as being "as good as dead," Rom. 4:19 with Heb. 11:12.

2. ***thanatoo*** (*2289*), "to put to death," Matt. 10:21.

## DEADLY

1. ***thanatephoros*** (*2287*), lit., "death-bearing, deadly," is used in Jas. 3:8.

2. ***thanasimos*** (*2286*), from ***thanatos*** (akin to No. 1), "belonging to death, or partaking of the nature of death," is used in Mark 16:18.

## HALF DEAD

***hemithanes*** (*2253*), from ***hemi***, "half," and ***thnesko***, "to die," is used in Luke 10:30.

## DEADNESS

***nekrosis*** (*3500*), "a putting to death," is rendered "dying" in 2 Cor. 4:10; "deadness" in Rom. 4:19, i.e., the state of being virtually "dead."

## DEAR

1. ***timios*** (*5093*), from ***time***, "honor, price," signifies (a), primarily, "accounted as of great price, precious, costly," 1 Cor. 3:12; Rev. 17:4; 18:12, 16; 21:19, and in the superlative degree, 18:12; 21:11; the comparative degree is found in 1 Pet. 1:7 (***polutimoteros***, in the most authentic mss., "much more precious"); (b) in the metaphorical sense, "held in honor, esteemed, very dear," Acts 5:34, "had in honor," RV (KJV, "had in reputation"); so in Heb. 13:4, RV, "let marriage be had in honor"; KJV, "is honorable"; Acts 20:24, "dear," negatively of Paul's estimate of his life; Jas. 5:7, "precious" (of fruit); 1 Pet. 1:19, "precious" (of the blood of Christ); 2 Pet. 1:4 (of God's promises).

2. ***entimos*** (*1784*), "held in honor" (***time***, see above), "precious, dear," is found in Luke 7:2, of the centurion's servant; 14:8, "more honorable"; Phil. 2:29, "honor" (KJV, "reputation"), of devoted servants of Christ, in 1 Pet. 2:4, 6, "precious," of stones, metaphorically.

3. ***agapetos*** (27), from ***agape***, "love," signifies "beloved"; it is rendered "very dear" in 1 Thess. 2:8 (KJV, "dear"), of the affection of Paul and his fellow workers for the saints at Thessalonica; in Eph. 5:1 and Col. 1:7, KJV, "dear"; RV, "beloved."

## DEATH, DEATH-STROKE (See also DIE)

### *Old Testament*

***mawet*** (4194), "death," the opposite of "life," Deut. 30:19. "Death" is the natural end of human life on this earth; it is an aspect of God's judgment on man, Gen. 2:17. Hence all men die, Num. 16:29. The Old Testament uses "death" in phrases such as "the day of death," Gen. 27:2, and "the year of death," Isa. 6:1, or to mark an event as occurring before, Gen. 27:7, 10, or after, Gen. 26:18, someone's passing away.

"Death" may also come upon someone in a violent manner, as an execution of justice, Deut. 21:22–23. Saul declared David to be a "son of death" because he intended to have David killed, 1 Sam. 20:31; cf. Prov. 16:14. In one of his experiences, David composed a psalm expressing how close an encounter he had had with death, 2 Sam. 22:5–6; cf. Ps. 18:5–6. Isaiah predicted the Suffering Servant was to die a violent death, Isa. 53:9.

Finally, the word ***mawet*** denotes the "realm of the dead" or ***she'ol***. This place of death has gates, Ps. 9:13; 107:18, and chambers, Prov. 7:27; the path of the wicked leads to this abode, Prov. 5:5.

Isaiah expected "death" to be ended when the Lord's full kingship would be established, Isa. 25:8. Paul argued on the basis of Jesus' resurrection that this event had already taken place, 1 Cor. 15:54, but John looked forward to the hope of the resurrection when God would wipe away our tears, Rev. 21:4.

### *New Testament*

#### A. Nouns

1. ***thanatos*** (*2288*), "death," is used in Scripture of:

(a) the separation of the soul (the spiritual part of man) from the body (the material part), the latter ceasing to function and turning to dust, e.g., John 11:13; Heb. 2:15; 5:7; 7:23. In Heb. 9:15, the KJV, "by means of death" is inadequate; the RV, "a death having taken place" is in keeping with the subject. In Rev. 13:3, 12, the RV, "death-stroke" (KJV, "deadly wound") is, lit., "the stroke of death."

(b) the separation of man from God; Adam died on the day he disobeyed God, Gen. 2:17, and hence all mankind are born in the same spiritual condition, Rom. 5:12, 14, 17, 21, from which, however, those who believe in Christ are delivered, John 5:24; 1 John 3:14. "Death" is the opposite of life; it never denotes nonexistence. As spiritual life is "conscious existence in communion with God," so spiritual "death" is "conscious existence in separation from God."

2. ***anairesis*** (*336*), another word for "death," lit. signifies "a taking up or off," as of the taking of a life, or "putting to death"; it is found in Acts 8:1, of the murder of Stephen. Some mss. have it in 22:20.

3. ***teleute*** (*5054*), "an end, limit," hence, "the end of life, death," is used of the "death" of Herod, Matt. 2:15.

#### B. Adjective.

***epithanatios*** (*1935*), "doomed to death" (***epi***, "upon," ***thanatos***, A, No. 1), is said of the apostles, in 1 Cor. 4:9.

#### C. Verbs.

1. ***thanatoo*** (*2289*), "to put to death" (akin to A, No. 1), in Matt. 10:21; Mark 13:12; Luke 21:16, is translated "shall . . . cause (them) to be put to death." It is used of the death of Christ in Matt. 26:59; 27:1; Mark 14:55 and 1 Pet. 3:18. In Rom. 7:4 (passive voice) it is translated "ye . . . were made dead," RV (for KJV, "are become"), with reference to the change from bondage to the Law to union with Christ; in 8:13, "mortify," of the act of the believer in regard to the deeds of the body; in 8:36, "are killed"; so in 2 Cor. 6:9.

2. ***anaireo*** (*337*), lit., "to take or lift up or away" (see A, No. 2), hence, "to put to death," is usually translated "to kill or slay"; in two places "put to death," Luke 23:32; Acts 26:10. It is used 17 times, with this meaning, in Acts.

3. ***apago*** (*520*), lit., "to lead away" (***apo***, "away," ***ago***, "to lead"), is used especially in a judicial sense, "to put to death," e.g., Acts 12:19.

4. ***apokteino*** (*615*), to kill, is so translated in the RV, for the KJV, "put to death," in Mark 14:1; Luke 18:33; in John 11:53; 12:10 and 18:31, RV, "put to death."

## DEBT

1. ***opheile*** (*3782*), "that which is owed," is translated "debt" in Matt. 18:32; in the plural, "dues," Rom. 13:7; "(her) due," 1 Cor. 7:3, of conjugal duty: some texts here have ***opheilomenen*** (***eunoian***) "due (benevolence)," KJV; the context confirms the RV.

2. ***opheilema*** (*3783*), a longer form of No. 1, expressing a "debt" more concretely, is used (a) literally, of that which is legally due, Rom. 4:4; (b) metaphorically, of sin as a "debt," because it demands expiation, and thus payment by way of punishment, Matt. 6:12.

3. ***daneion*** (*1156*), "a loan," is translated "debt" in Matt. 18:27.

## DEBTOR

1. ***opheiletes*** (*3781*), "one who owes anything to another," primarily in regard to money; in Matt. 18:24, "who owed" (lit., "one was brought, a debtor to him of ten thousand talents"). The slave could own property, and so become a "debtor" to his master, who might seize him for payment. It is used metaphorically, (a) of a person who is under an obligation, Rom. 1:14, of Paul, in the matter of preaching the gospel; in Rom. 8:12, of believers, to mortify the deeds of the body; in Rom. 15:27, of gentile believers, to assist afflicted Jewish believers; in Gal. 5:3, of those who would be justified by circumcision, to do the whole Law: (b) of those who have not yet made amends to those whom they have injured, Matt. 6:12, "our debtors"; of some whose disaster was liable to be regarded as a due punishment, Luke 13:4.

2. ***chreopheiletes*** (*5533*), lit., "a debt-ower" (***chreos***, "a loan, a debt," and No. 1), is found in Luke 7:41, of the two "debtors" mentioned in the Lord's parable addressed to Simon the Pharisee, and in 16:5, of the "debtors" in the parable of the unrighteous steward. This parable indicates a system of credit in the matter of agriculture.

## DECAY

1. ***palaioo*** (*3822*), "to make old" (***palaios***), is translated in Heb. 8:13, firstly, "hath made . . . old," secondly (passive voice), RV "is becoming old" (KJV, "decayeth"); "wax old," Luke 12:33 and Heb. 1:11.

2. ***diaphtheiro*** (*1311*), "to destroy utterly," as used in 2 Cor. 4:16 (here in the passive voice, lit., "is being destroyed"), is rendered "is decaying" (RV, for KJV, "perish").

## DECEASE

### A. Noun.

***exodos*** (*1841*), (Eng., "exodus"), lit. signifies "a way out"; hence, "a departure," especially from life, "a decease"; in Luke 9:31, of the Lord's death, "which He was about to accomplish"; in 2 Pet. 1:15, of Peter's death; "departure" in Heb. 11:22, RV.

### B. Verb.

***teleutao*** (*5053*), lit., "to end," is used intransitively and translated "deceased" in Matt. 22:25.

## DECEIT, DECEITFUL, DECEITFULLY, DECEITFULNESS, DECEIVE, DECEIVABLENESS

### *Old Testament*

***shaw'*** (7723), "deceit; deception; malice; falsity; vanity; emptiness," often used in a legal context, Exod. 23:1; Ps. 31:6; Job 15:31.

### *New Testament*

### A. Nouns.

1. ***apate*** (*539*), "deceit or deceitfulness" (akin to ***apatao***, "to cheat, deceive, beguile"), that which gives a false impression, whether by appearance, statement or influence, is said of riches, Matt. 13:22; Mark 4:19; of sin, Heb. 3:13. The phrase in Eph. 4:22, "deceitful lusts," KJV, "lusts of deceit," RV, signifies lusts excited by "deceit," of which "deceit" is the source of strength, not lusts "deceitful" in themselves. In 2 Thess. 2:10, "all deceit of unrighteousness," RV, signifies all manner of unscrupulous words and deeds designed to "deceive" (see Rev. 13:13–15). In Col. 2:8, "vain deceit" suggests that "deceit" is void of anything profitable.

2. ***dolos*** (*1388*), primarily "a bait, snare"; hence, "craft, deceit, guile," is translated "deceit" in Mark 7:22; Rom. 1:29.

### B. Adjective.

***dolios*** (*1386*), "deceitful," is used in 2 Cor. 11:13, of false apostles as "deceitful workers"; cf. A, No. 2.

C. Verbs.

1. ***apatao*** *(538)*, "to beguile, deceive" (see A, No. 1), is used (a) of those who "deceive" "with empty words," belittling the true character of the sins mentioned, Eph. 5:6; (b) of the fact that Adam was "not beguiled," 1 Tim. 2:14, RV.

2. ***exapatao*** *(1818)*, ***ek*** (***ex***), intensive, and No. 1, signifies "to beguile thoroughly, to deceive wholly," 1 Tim. 2:14, RV.

3. ***phrenapatao*** *(5422)*, lit., "to deceive in one's mind" (***phren***, "the mind," and No. 1), "to deceive by fancies," is used in Gal. 6:3, with reference to self-conceit, which is "self-deceit," a sin against common sense.

4. ***dolioo*** *(1387)*, "to lure," as by a bait (see A, No. 2), is translated "have used deceit" in Rom. 3:13.

5. ***doloo*** *(1389)*, a short form of No. 4, primarily signifies "to ensnare"; hence, "to corrupt," especially by mingling the truths of the Word of God with false doctrines or notions, and so handling it "deceitfully," 2 Cor. 4:2.

6. ***planao*** *(4105)*, in the passive form sometimes means "to go astray, wander," Matt. 18:12; 1 Pet. 2:25; Heb. 11:38; frequently active, "to deceive, by leading into error, to seduce," e.g., Matt. 24:4, 5, 11, 24; John 7:12, "leadeth astray," RV (cf. 1 John 3:7). In Rev. 12:9 the present participle is used with the definite article, as a title of the Devil, "the Deceiver," lit., "the deceiving one." Often it has the sense of "deceiving oneself," e.g., 1 Cor. 6:9; 15:33; Gal. 6:7; Jas. 1:16, "be not deceived," RV, "do not err," KJV.

7. ***paralogizomai*** *(3884)*, lit., "to reason amiss," Col. 2:4; Jas. 1:22.

## DECEIVER

1. ***planos*** *(4108)* is, properly, an adjective, signifying "wandering, or leading astray, seducing," 1 Tim. 4:1, "seducing (spirits)," used as a noun, it denotes an impostor of the vagabond type, and so any kind of "deceiver" or corrupter, Matt. 27:63; 2 Cor. 6:8; 2 John 7 (twice), in the last of which the accompanying definite article necessitates the translation "the deceiver," RV.

2. ***phrenapates*** *(5423)*, akin to C, No. 3, under DECEIVE, lit., "a mind-deceiver," is used in Titus 1:10.

## DECENTLY

***euschemonos*** *(2156)* denotes "gracefully, becomingly, in a seemly manner" (***eu***, "well," ***schema***, "a form, figure"); "honestly," in Rom. 13:13, in contrast to the shamefulness of gentile social life; in 1 Thess. 4:12, the contrast is to idleness and its concomitant evils and the resulting bad testimony to unbelievers; in 1 Cor. 14:40, "decently," where the contrast is to disorder in oral testimony in the churches.

## DECIDE, DECISION

A. Verb.

***diakrino*** *(1252)* primarily signifies "to make a distinction," hence, "to decide, especially judicially, to decide a dispute, to give judgment," 1 Cor. 6:5, KJV, "judge"; RV, "decide," where church members are warned against procuring decisions by litigation in the world's law courts.

B. Nouns.

1. ***diagnosis*** *(1233)*, transliterated in English, primarily denotes "a discrimination" (***dia***, "apart," ***ginosko***, "to know"), hence, "a judicial decision," which is its meaning in Acts 25:21, RV, "for the decision of the Emperor" (KJV, "hearing").

2. ***diakrisis*** *(1253)*, "a distinguishing," and so "a decision" (see A), signifies "discerning" in 1 Cor. 12:10; Heb. 5:14, lit., "unto a discerning of good and evil" (translated "to discern"); in Rom. 14:1.

## DECLARE, DECLARATION

A. Verbs.

1. ***anangello*** *(312)* signifies "to announce, report, bring back tidings." Possibly the ***ana*** carries the significance of upward, i.e., heavenly, as characteristic of the nature of the tidings. In the following, either the KJV or the RV translates the word by the verb "to declare"; in John 4:25, RV, "declare," KJV, "tell"; in 16:13–15, RV, "declare," KJV, "shew"; in Acts 15:4, RV, "rehearsed," KJV, "declared"; in 19:18, RV, "declaring," KJV, "shewed" (a reference, perhaps, to the destruction of their idols, in consequence of their new faith); in 20:20, RV, "declaring," KJV, "have shewed"; in 1 John 1:5, RV, "announce," KJV, "declare."

2. ***apangello*** *(518)* signifies "to announce or report from a person or place"; hence, "to declare, publish"; it is rendered "declare" in Luke 8:47; Heb. 2:12; 1 John 1:3. It is very frequent in the Gospels and Acts; elsewhere, other than the last two places mentioned, only in 1 Thess. 1:9 and 1 John 1:2.

3. ***diangello*** *(1229)*, lit., "to announce through," hence, "to declare fully, or far and wide," Acts 21:26, RV (KJV, "to signify"); in Luke 9:60, RV, "publish abroad" (for KJV, "preach"), giving the verb its fuller significance; so in Rom. 9:17, for KJV, "declared."

4. ***katangello*** *(2605)*, lit., "to report down," is ordinarily translated "to preach"; "declare" in Acts 17:23, KJV (RV, "set forth"); in 1 Cor. 2:1,

RV, "proclaiming," for KJV, "declaring." It is nowhere translated by "declare" in the RV.

5. ***parangello*** (*3853*) lit., "to announce beside," Acts 10:42.

**B. Noun.**

***endeixis*** (*1732*), "a showing, pointing out," is said of the "showing forth" of God's righteousness, in Rom. 3:25–26, KJV, "to declare"; RV, "to show," and "(for) the showing." In 2 Cor. 8:24, "proof"; Phil. 1:28, "an evident token."

## DECREASE (Verb)

***elattoo*** (*1642*) signifies "to make less or inferior, in quality, position or dignity"; "madest . . . lower" and "hast made . . . lower," in Heb. 2:7, 9. In John 3:30, it is used in the middle voice, in John the Baptist's "I must decrease," indicating the special interest he had in his own "decrease," i.e., in authority and popularity.

## DECREE (Noun and Verb)

***dogma*** (*1378*), transliterated in English, primarily denoted "an opinion or judgment" (from ***dokeo***, "to be of opinion"), hence, an "opinion expressed with authority, a doctrine, ordinance, decree"; "decree," Luke 2:1; Acts 16:4; 17:7; in the sense of ordinances, Eph. 2:15; Col. 2:14.

## DEDICATE, DEDICATION

**A. Verb.**

***enkainizo*** (*1457*) primarily means "to make new, to renew," so then, to initiate or "dedicate," Heb. 9:18, with reference to the first covenant, as not "dedicated" without blood; in 10:20, of Christ's "dedication" of the new and living way (KJV, "consecrated"; RV, "dedicated").

**B. Noun.**

***enkainia*** (*1456*), akin to A, "dedication," became used particularly for the annual eight days' feast beginning on the 25th of Chisleu (mid. of Dec.), instituted by Judas Maccabaeus, 164 B.C., to commemorate the cleansing of the Temple from the pollutions of Antiochus Epiphanes; hence it was called the Feast of the Dedication, John 10:22.

## DEED, DEEDS

1. ***ergon*** (*2041*) denotes "a work" (Eng., "work" is etymologically akin), "deed, act." When used in the sense of a "deed or act," the idea of "working" is stressed, e.g., Rom. 15:18; it frequently occurs in an ethical sense of human actions, good or bad, e.g., Matt. 23:3; 26:10; John 3:20–21; Rom. 2:7, 15; 1 Thess. 1:3; 2 Thess. 1:11, etc.; sometimes in a less concrete sense, e.g., Titus 1:16; Jas. 1:25 (RV that worketh, lit., of work).

2. ***praxis*** (*4234*) denotes "a doing, transaction, a deed the action of which is looked upon as incomplete and in progress"; in Matt. 16:27, RV, "deeds," for KJV, "works"; in Luke 23:51, "deed"; in v. 41, the verb is used; Acts 19:18; Rom. 8:13; Col. 3:9. In Rom. 12:4 it denotes an "action," business, or function, translated "office."

## DEEP (Noun and Adjective), DEEPNESS, DEEPLY, DEPTH

**A. Nouns.**

1. ***bathos*** (*899*) is used (a) naturally, in Matt. 13:5, "deepness"; Mark 4:5, KJV, "depth," RV, "deepness"; Luke 5:4, of "deep" water; Rom. 8:39 (contrasted with ***hupsoma***, "height"); (b) metaphorically, in Rom. 11:33, of God's wisdom and knowledge; in 1 Cor. 2:10, of God's counsels; in Eph. 3:18, of the dimensions of the sphere of the activities of God's counsels, and of the love of Christ which occupies that sphere; in 2 Cor. 8:2, of "deep" poverty; some mss. have it in Rev. 2:24.

2. ***buthos*** (*1037*), "a depth," is used in the NT only in the natural sense, of the sea 2 Cor. 11:25.

**B. Adjective and Adverb.**

***bathus*** (*901*), akin to A, No. 1, "deep," is said in John 4:11, of a well; in Acts 20:9, of sleep; in Rev. 2:24 the plural is used, of the "deep things," the evil designs and workings, of Satan.

**C. Verb.**

***bathuno*** (*900*), "to deepen, make deep," is used in Luke 6:48.

## DEFAME

***dusphemeo*** (*1418* and *5346*), lit., "to speak injuriously" (from ***dus***—, an inseparable prefix signifying "opposition, injury, etc.," and ***phemi***, "to speak"), is translated "defamed," 1 Cor. 4:13.

## DEFENSE

**A. Noun.**

***apologia*** (*627*), a speech made in defense, Acts 22:1.

**B. Verb.**

***apologeomai*** (*626*), lit., "to talk oneself off," Luke 12:11.

## DEFILE, DEFILEMENT

### A. Verbs.

1. ***koinoo*** (*2840*) denotes (a) "to make common"; hence, in a ceremonial sense, "to render unholy, unclean, to defile," Matt. 15:11, 18, 20; Mark 7:15, 18, 20, 23; Acts 21:28 (RV, "defiled"; KJV, "polluted"); Heb. 9:13 (RV, "them that have been defiled," KJV, "the unclean"); (b) "to count unclean," Acts 10:15; 11:9.

2. ***miaino*** (*3392*), primarily, "to stain, to tinge or dye with another color," as in the staining of a glass, hence, "to pollute, contaminate, soil, defile," is used (a) of "ceremonial defilement," John 18:28; (b) of "moral defilement," Titus 1:15 (twice); Heb. 12:15; "of moral and physical defilement," Jude 8.

3. ***moluno*** (*3435*) properly denotes "to besmear," as with mud or filth, "to befoul." It is used in the figurative sense, of a conscience "defiled" by sin, 1 Cor. 8:7; of believers who have kept themselves (their "garments") from "defilement," Rev. 3:4.

4. ***spiloo*** (*4695*), "to make a stain or spot," and so "to defile," is used in Jas. 3:6 of the "defiling" effects of an evil use of the tongue; in Jude 23, "spotted," with reference to moral "defilement."

### B. Nouns.

1. ***miasma*** (*3393*), whence the Eng. word, denotes "defilement" (akin to A, No. 2), and is found in 2 Pet. 2:20, AV, "pollutions," RV, "defilements," the vices of the ungodly which contaminate a person in his intercourse with the world.

2. ***miasmos*** (*3394*), also akin to A, No. 2, primarily denotes "the act of defiling," the process, in contrast to the "defiling" thing (No. 1). It is found in 2 Pet. 2:10 (KJV, "uncleanness," RV, "defilement").

3. ***molusmos*** (*3436*), akin to A, No. 3, denotes "defilement," in the sense of an action by which anything is "defiled," 2 Cor. 7:1.

### C. Adjective.

***koinos*** (*2839*), akin to A, No. 1, common, and, from the idea of coming into contact with everything, "defiled," is used in the ceremonial sense in Mark 7:2.

## DEFRAUD

1. ***apostereo*** (*650*) signifies "to rob, despoil, defraud," Mark 10:19; 1 Cor. 6:8; 7:5 (of that which is due to the condition of natural relationship of husband and wife); in the middle voice, "to allow oneself to be defrauded," 1 Cor. 6:7; in the passive voice, "bereft," 1 Tim. 6:5.

2. ***pleonekteo*** (*4122*), translated "defraud" in 1 Thess. 4:6.

## DELAY

### A. Verbs.

1. ***okneo*** (*3635*), akin to ***oknos***, "a shrinking, to be loath or slow to do a thing, to hesitate, delay," is used in Acts 9:38.

2. ***chronizo*** (*5549*), from ***chronos***, "time," lit. means "to while away time," i.e., by way of lingering, tarrying, "delaying"; "delayeth," Matt. 24:48; Luke 12:45, "tarried" Matt. 25:5; "tarried so long," Luke 1:21; "will (not) tarry," Heb. 10:37.

### B. Noun.

***anabole*** (*311*) lit. signifies "that which is thrown up" (***ana***, "up," ***ballo***, "to throw"); hence "a delay," Acts 25:17.

## DELICATELY (live)

### A. Verbs.

***truphao*** (*5171*), from ***thrupto***, "to enervate," signifies "to lead a voluptuous life, to give oneself up to pleasure," Jas. 5:5, RV, "ye have lived delicately"; KJV, "ye have lived in pleasure."

### B. Noun.

***truphe*** (*5172*), akin to A, "luxuriously," "delicately," Luke 7:25, and denotes effeminacy, softness; "to revel" in 2 Pet. 2:13.

## DELIGHT IN

***sunedomai*** (*4913*), lit., "to rejoice with (anyone), to delight in (a thing) with (others)," signifies "to delight with oneself inwardly in a thing," in Rom. 7:22.

## DELIVER, DELIVERANCE, DELIVERER

#### *Old Testament*

### A. Verbs.

***nathan*** (5414), "to deliver, give, place, set up, lay, make, do"; first, ***nathan*** represents the action by which something is set going or actuated. Achsah asked her father Caleb to "give" her a blessing, such as a tract of land with abundant water, as her dowry; she wanted him to "transfer" it from his possession to hers, Josh. 15:19. There is a technical use of this verb without an object: Moses instructs Israel to "give" generously to the man in desperate need, Deut. 15:10. In some instances, ***nathan*** can mean to "send forth," as in "sending forth" a fragrance, Song of Sol. 1:12.

***nathan*** also has a technical meaning in the area of jurisprudence, meaning to hand something over to someone—for example, "to pay," Gen. 23:9, or "to loan," Deut. 15:10. A girl's parent or someone else in a responsible position may "give" her to a man to be his wife, Gen.

16:3, as well as presenting a bride price, Gen. 34:12, and dowry, 1 Kings 9:16. The verb also is used of "giving" or "granting" a request, Gen. 15:2.

Sometimes, ***nathan*** can be used to signify "putting" ("placing") someone into custody, 2 Sam. 14:7; Jer. 37:4. This same basic sense may be applied to "dedicating" ("handing over") something or someone to God, such as the first-born son, Exod. 22:29. Levites are those who have been "handed over" in this way, Num. 3:9. "To give something into someone's hand" is to "commit" it to his care, Gen. 9:2; 2 Sam. 16:8; or transfer control Deut. 7:24. "To give one's heart" to something or someone is "to be concerned about it"; Pharaoh was not "concerned" about ("did not set his heart to") Moses' message from God, Exod. 7:23. "To put [give] something into one's heart" is to give one ability and concern to do something; thus God "put" it in the heart of the Hebrew craftsmen to teach others, Exod. 36:2.

***nathan*** can be used of "giving" or "ascribing" glory and praise to God, Josh. 7:19. ***nathan*** can focus on a result or effect, so "yield" fruit, Deut. 25:19. In some passages, this verb means "to procure" ("to set up"), as when God "gave" ("procured, set up") favor for Joseph, Gen. 39:21. The word can be used of sexual activity, too, Lev. 18:23.

"To give one's face to" is to focus one's attention on something, as when Jehoshaphat was afraid of the alliance of the Transjordanian kings and "set [his face] to seek the Lord," 2 Chron. 20:3. This same phrase can merely mean "to be facing someone or something," cf. Gen. 30:40. "To give one's face against" is a hostile action, Lev. 17:10.

***yasha'*** (3467), "to deliver, help," with a special focus of being delivered from danger, Isa. 30:15.

## B. Nouns.

***yeshu'ah*** (3444), "deliverance." "Salvation" in the Old Testament is not understood as a salvation from sin, since the word denotes broadly anything from which "deliverance" must be sought: distress, war, servitude, or enemies. There are both human and divine deliverers, but the word ***yeshu'ah*** rarely refers to human "deliverance." A couple of exceptions are when Jonathan brought respite to the Israelites from the Philistine pressure, 1 Sam. 14:45, and when Joab and his men were to help one another in battle, 2 Sam. 10:11. "Deliverance" is generally used with God as the subject, Deut. 32:15; cf. Isa. 12:2. He worked many wonders on behalf of His people, Ps. 98:1. ***yeshu'ah*** occurs either in the context of rejoicing, Ps. 9:14, or prayer for "deliverance," Ps. 69:29.

Many personal names contain a form of the root, such as *Joshua* ("the Lord is help"), *Isaiah* ("the Lord is help"), and *Jesus* (a Greek form of ***yeshu'ah***).

***yesha'*** (3468), "deliverance," Ps. 50:23.

***teshu'ah*** (8668), "deliverance," Isa. 45:17.

### *New Testament*

## A. Verbs.

1. ***didomi*** (*1325*), "to give," is translated "delivered" in Luke 7:15; RV, "gave"; so 19:13.

2. ***anadidomi*** (*325*), "to deliver over, give up," is used of "delivering" the letter mentioned in Acts 23:33.

3. ***apodidomi*** (*591*), "to give away," hence, "to give back or up," is used in Pilate's command for the Lord's body to be "given up," Matt. 27:58; in the sense of "giving back," of the Lord's act in giving a healed boy back to his father, Luke 9:42.

4. ***epididomi*** (*1929*), lit., "to give upon or in addition," as from oneself to another, hence, "to deliver over," is used of the "delivering" of the scroll of Isaiah to Christ in the synagogue, Luke 4:17; of the "delivering" of the epistle from the elders at Jerusalem to the church at Antioch, Acts 15:30.

5. ***paradidomi*** (*3860*), "to deliver over," in Rom. 6:17, RV, "that form of teaching whereunto ye were delivered," the figure being that of a mold which gives its shape to what is cast in it (not as the KJV). In Rom. 8:32 it is used of God in "delivering" His Son to expiatory death; so 4:25; see Mark 9:31; of Christ in "delivering" Himself up, Gal. 2:20; Eph. 5:2, 25. In Mark 1:14, RV, it is used of "delivering" John the Baptist to prison.

6. ***rhuomai*** (*4506*), "to rescue from, to preserve from," and so, "to deliver," the word by which it is regularly translated, is largely synonymous with ***sozo***, "to save," though the idea of "rescue from" is predominant in ***rhuomai*** (see Matt. 27:43), that of "preservation from," in ***sozo***. In Rom. 11:26 the present participle is used with the article, as a noun, "the Deliverer." This is the construction in 1 Thess. 1:10, where Christ is similarly spoken of. Here the KJV wrongly has "which delivered" (the tense is not past); RV, "which delivereth"; the translation might well be (as in Rom. 11:26), "our Deliverer," that is, from the retributive calamities with which God will visit men at the end of the present age. From that wrath believers are to be "delivered." The verb is used with ***apo***, "away from," in Matt. 6:13; Luke 11:4 (in some mss.); so also in 11:4; Rom. 15:31; 2 Thess.

3:2; 2 Tim. 4:18; and with ***ek***, "from, out of," in Luke 1:74; Rom. 7:24; 2 Cor. 1:10; Col. 1:13, from bondage; in 2 Pet. 2:9, from temptation, in 2 Tim. 3:11, from persecution; but ***ek*** is used of ills impending, in 2 Cor. 1:10; in 2 Tim. 4:17, ***ek*** indicates that the danger was more imminent than in v. 18, where ***apo*** is used. Accordingly the meaning "out of the midst of" cannot be pressed in 1 Thess. 1:10.

**B. Nouns.**

1. ***apolutrosis*** *(629)* denotes "redemption" (***apo***, "from," ***lutron***, "a price of release"). In Heb. 11:35 it is translated "deliverance"; usually the release is effected by the payment of a ransom, or the required price, the ***lutron*** (ransom).

2. ***aphesis*** *(859)* denotes "a release, from bondage, imprisonment, etc." (the corresponding verb is ***aphiemi***, "to send away, let go"); in Luke 4:18 it is used of "liberation" from captivity (KJV, "deliverance," RV, "release").

3. ***lutrotes*** *(3086)*, "a redeemer, one who releases" (see No. 1), is translated "deliverer" in Acts 7:35.

**C. Verbal Adjective.**

***ekdotos*** *(1560)*, lit., "given up," so "delivered up" (to enemies, or to the power or will of someone), is used of Christ in Acts 2:23.

## DELUDE, DELUSION

**A. Verb.**

***paralogizomai*** *(3884)* lit., "to reason amiss," Col. 2:4; Jas. 1:22.

**B. Noun.**

***plane*** *(4106)*, lit., "a wandering," whereby those who are led astray roam hither and thither, is always used in the NT, of mental straying, wrong opinion, error in morals or religion, 2 Thess. 2:11.

## DEMON, DEMONIAC

**A. Nouns.**

1. ***daimon*** *(1142)*, "a demon," signified, among pagan Greeks, an inferior deity, whether good or bad. In the NT it denotes "an evil spirit." It is used in Matt. 8:31, mistranslated "devils."

2. ***daimonion*** *(1140)*, not a diminutive of ***daimon***, No. 1, but the neuter of the adjective ***daimonios***, pertaining to a demon, is also mistranslated "devil," "devils." In Acts 17:18, it denotes an inferior pagan deity. "Demons" are the spiritual agents acting in all idolatry. The idol itself is nothing, but every idol has a "demon" associated with it who induces idolatry, with its worship and sacrifices, 1 Cor. 10:20–21; Rev. 9:20; cf. Deut. 32:17; Isa. 13:21; 34:14; 65:3, 11. They disseminate errors among men, and seek to seduce believers, 1 Tim. 4:1.

Acting under Satan (cf. Rev. 16:13–14), "demons" are permitted to afflict with bodily disease, Luke 13:16. Being unclean they tempt human beings with unclean thoughts, Matt. 10:1; Mark 5:2; 7:25; Luke 8:27–29; Rev. 16:13; 18:2, e.g. They differ in degrees of wickedness, Matt. 12:45. They will instigate the rulers of the nations at the end of this age to make war against God and His Christ, Rev. 16:14.

**B. Verb.**

***daimonizomai*** *(1139)* signifies "to be possessed of a demon, to act under the control of a demon." Those who were thus afflicted expressed the mind and consciousness of the "demon" or "demons" indwelling them, e.g., Luke 8:28. The verb is found chiefly in Matt. and Mark; Matt. 4:24; 8:16, 28, 33; 9:32; 12:22; 15:22; Mark 1:32; 5:15–16, 18; elsewhere in Luke 8:36 and John 10:21, "him that hath a devil (demon)."

**C. Adjective.**

***daimoniodes*** *(1141)* signifies "proceeding from, or resembling, a demon," Jas. 3:15.

## DENY

1. ***arneomai*** *(720)* signifies (a) "to say . . . not, to contradict," e.g., Mark 14:70; John 1:20; 18:25, 27; 1 John 2:22; (b) "to deny" by way of disowning a person, as, e.g., the Lord Jesus as master, e.g., Matt. 10:33; Luke 12:9; John 13:38 (in the best mss.); 2 Tim. 2:12; or, on the other hand, of Christ Himself, "denying" that a person is His follower, Matt. 10:33; 2 Tim. 2:12; or to "deny" the Father and the Son, by apostatizing and by disseminating pernicious teachings, to "deny" Jesus Christ as master and Lord by immorality under a cloak of religion, 2 Pet. 2:1; Jude 4; (c) "to deny oneself," either in a good sense, by disregarding one's own interests, Luke 9:23, or in a bad sense, to prove false to oneself, to act quite unlike oneself, 2 Tim. 2:13; (d) to "abrogate, forsake, or renounce a thing," whether evil, Titus 2:12, or good, 1 Tim. 5:8; 2 Tim. 3:5; Rev. 2:13; 3:8; (e) "not to accept, to reject" something offered, Acts 3:14; 7:35, "refused"; Heb. 11:24 "refused."

2. ***aparneomai*** *(533)*, a strengthened form of No. 1, with ***apo***, "from," prefixed (Lat., ***abnego***), means (a) "to deny utterly," to abjure, to affirm that one has no connection with a person, as in Peter's denial of Christ, Matt. 26:34–35, 75; Mark 14:30–31, 72; Luke 22:34, 61 (some mss.

have it in John 13:38). This stronger form is used in the Lord's statements foretelling Peter's "denial," and in Peter's assurance of fidelity; the simple verb (No. 1) is used in all the records of his actual denial.

## DESERT (Noun and Adjective)

### A. Noun.

***eremia*** (*2047*), primarily "a solitude, an uninhabited place," in contrast to a town or village, is translated "deserts" in Heb. 11:38; "the wilderness" in Matt. 15:33, KJV, "a desert place," RV; so in Mark 8:4; "wilderness" in 2 Cor. 11:26. It does not always denote a barren region, void of vegetation; it is often used of a place uncultivated, but fit for pasturage.

### B. Adjective.

***eremos*** (*2048*), used as a noun, has the same meaning as ***eremia***, in Luke 5:16 and 8:29, RV, "deserts," for KJV, "wilderness"; in Matt. 24:26 and John 6:31, RV, "wilderness," for KJV, "desert." As an adjective, it denotes (a), with reference to persons, "deserted," desolate, deprived of the friends and kindred, e.g. of a woman deserted by a husband, Gal 4:21; (b) so of a city, as Jerusalem, Matt. 23:38; or uninhabited places, "desert," e.g., Matt. 14:13, 15; Acts 8:26; in Mark 1:35.

## DESIRE (Noun and Verb), DESIROUS

### A. Nouns.

1. ***epithumia*** (*1939*), "a desire, craving, longing, mostly of evil desires," frequently translated "lust," is used in the following, of good "desires": of the Lord's "wish" concerning the last Passover, Luke 22:15, of Paul's "desire" to be with Christ, Phil. 1:23; of his "desire" to see the saints at Thessalonica again, 1 Thess. 2:17.

With regard to evil "desires," in Col. 3:5 the RV has "desire," for the KJV, "concupiscence"; in 1 Thess. 4:5, RV, "lust," for KJV, "concupiscence"; there the preceding word ***pathos*** is translated "passion," RV, for KJV, "lust"; also in Col. 3:5 ***pathos*** and ***epithumia*** are associated, RV, "passion," for KJV, "inordinate affection." ***epithumia*** is combined with ***pathema***, in Gal. 5:24; for the KJV, "affections and lusts," the RV has "passions, and the lusts thereof." ***epithumia*** is the more comprehensive term, including all manner of "lusts and desires"; ***pathema*** denotes suffering; in the passage in Gal. 5:24 the sufferings are those produced by yielding to the flesh; ***pathos*** points more to the evil state from which "lusts" spring.

2. ***eudokia*** (*2107*), lit., "good pleasure" (***eu***, "well," ***dokeo***, "to seem"), implies a gracious purpose, a good object being in view, with the idea of a resolve, showing the willingness with which the resolve is made. It is often translated "good pleasure," e.g., Eph. 1:5, 9; Phil. 2:13; in Phil. 1:15, "good will"; in Rom. 10:1, "desire."

3. ***epipothesis*** (*1972*), "an earnest desire, a longing for" (***epi***, "upon," intensive, ***potheo***, "to desire"), is found in 2 Cor. 7:7, 11, KJV, "earnest desire," and "vehement desire"; RV, "longing" in both places.

4. ***epipothia*** (*1974*), with the same meaning as No. 3, is used in Rom. 15:23, RV, "longing," KJV, "great desire."

5. ***thelema*** (*2307*) denotes "a will, that which is willed" (akin to B, No. 4). It is rendered "desires," in Eph. 2:3.

### B. Verbs.

1. ***epithumeo*** (*1937*), "to desire earnestly" (as with A, No. 1), stresses the inward impulse rather than the object desired. It is translated "to desire" in Luke 16:21; 17:22; 22:15; 1 Tim. 3:1; Heb. 6:11; 1 Pet. 1:12; Rev. 9:6.

2. ***homeiromai*** or ***himeiromai*** (*2442*), "to have a strong affection for, a yearning after," is found in 1 Thess. 2:8, "being affectionately desirous of you." It is probably derived from a root indicating remembrance.

3. ***orego*** (*3713*), "to reach or stretch out," is used only in the middle voice, signifying the mental effort of stretching oneself out for a thing, of longing after it, with stress upon the object desired; it is translated "desire" in Heb. 11:16; in 1 Tim. 3:1, RV, "seeketh," for KJV, "desireth"; in 1 Tim. 6:10, RV, "reached after," for KJV, "coveted after." In Heb. 11:16, a suitable rendering would be "reach after."

4. ***thelo*** (*2309*), "to will, to wish," implying volition and purpose, frequently a determination, is most usually rendered "to will." It is translated "to desire" in the RV of the following: Matt. 9:13; 12:7; Mark 6:19; Luke 10:29; 14:28; 23:20; Acts 24:27; 25:9; Gal. 4:17; 1 Tim. 5:11; Heb. 12:17; 13:18.

5. ***boulomai*** (*1014*), "to wish, to will deliberately," expresses more strongly than ***thelo*** (No. 6) the deliberate exercise of the will; it is translated "to desire" in the RV of the following: Acts 22:30; 23:38; 27:43; 28:18; 1 Tim. 2:8; 5:14; 6:9 and Jude 5.

6. ***zeloo*** (*2206*), "to have a zeal for, to be zealous towards," whether in a good or evil sense, the former in 1 Cor. 14:1, concerning spiritual gifts RV, "desire earnestly," KJV, "desire"; in an evil sense, in Jas. 4:2, RV, "covet," for KJV, "desire to have."

## DESOLATE (Verb and Adjective), DESOLATION

### Old Testament

***shamem*** (8074), "to be desolate, astonished, appalled, devastated, ravaged." ***shamem*** often expresses the idea of to "devastate" or "ravage": "I will destroy her vines," Hos. 2:12. What one sees sometimes is so horrible that it "horrifies" or "appalls," Job 21:5.

### New Testament

**A. Verbs.**

1. ***eremoo*** *(2049)* signifies "to make desolate, lay waste." From the primary sense of "making quiet" comes that of "making lonely." It is used only in the passive voice in the NT; in Rev. 17:16, "shall make desolate" is, lit., "shall make her desolated"; in 18:17, 19, "is made desolate"; in Matt. 12:25 and Luke 11:17, "is brought to desolation."

**B. Adjectives.**

1. ***eremos*** *(2048)* is translated "desolate" in the Lord's words against Jerusalem, Matt. 23:38; some mss. have it in Luke 13:35; in reference to the habitation of Judas, Acts 1:20, and to Sarah, from whom, being barren, her husband had turned, Gal. 4:27.

2. ***orphanos*** *(3737)* (Eng., "orphan"; Lat., "***orbus***"), signifies "bereft of parents or of a father." In Jas. 1:27 it is translated "fatherless." It was also used in the general sense of being "friendless or desolate," John 14:18.

**C. Noun.**

***eremosis*** *(2050)*, akin to A, No. 1, denotes "desolation," (a) in the sense of "making desolate," e.g., in the phrase "the abomination of desolation," Matt. 24:15; Mark 13:14; the genitive is objective, "the abomination that makes desolate"; (b) with stress upon the effect of the process, Luke 21:20, with reference to the "desolation" of Jerusalem.

## DESPAIR

1. ***exaporeo*** *(1820)* "to be utterly without a way," so "to be quite at a loss, without resource, in despair." It is used in 2 Cor. 1:8, with reference to life; in 4:8, in the sentence "perplexed, yet not unto (KJV, 'in') despair," the word "perplexed" translates the verb ***aporeo***, and the phrase "unto despair" translates the intensive form ***exaporeo***, a play on the words.

2. ***apelpizo*** *(560)*, lit., "to hope away," i.e., "to give up in despair, to despair," is used in Luke 6:35.

## DESPISE, DESPISER

### Old Testament

***ma'as*** (3988), "to reject, refuse, despise." God will not force man to do His will, so He sometimes must "reject" him, Hos. 4:6. Although God had chosen Saul to be king, Saul's response caused a change in God's attitude, 1 Sam. 15:23; likewise, as a creature of free choice, man may "reject" God, Isa. 7:15–16. When the things that God requires are done with the wrong motives or attitudes, God "despises" such actions, Amos 5:21.

### New Testament

**A. Verbs.**

1. ***exoutheneo*** *(1848)*, "to make of no account" (***ex***, "out," ***oudeis***, "nobody," alternatively written, ***outheis***), "to regard as nothing, to despise utterly, to treat with contempt." This is usually translated to "set at nought," Luke 18:9, RV, KJV, "despised." So in Rom. 14:3. Both have "set at nought" in Luke 23:11; Acts 4:11; Rom. 14:10. Both have "despise" in 1 Cor. 16:11; Gal. 4:14, and 1 Thess. 5:20; in 2 Cor. 10:10, RV, "of no account," for KJV, "contemptible"; in 1 Cor. 1:28, KJV and RV, "despised."

2. ***kataphroneo*** *(2706)*, lit., "to think down upon or against anyone," hence signifies "to think slightly of, to despise," Matt. 6:24; 18:10; Luke 16:13; Rom. 2:4; 1 Cor. 11:22; 1 Tim. 4:12; 6:2; Heb. 12:2; 2 Pet. 2:10.

3. ***periphroneo*** *(4065)* lit. denotes "to think round a thing, to turn over in the mind"; hence, "to have thoughts beyond, to despise," Titus 2:15.

**B. Adjective.**

***atimos*** *(820)*, "without honor," is translated as a verb in 1 Cor. 4:10, KJV, "are despised"; RV, "have dishonor," lit., "(we are) without honor"; "without honor" in Matt. 13:57; Mark 6:4.

**C. Noun.**

***kataphronetes*** *(2707)*, lit., "one who thinks down against," hence, "a despiser" (see A, No. 2), is found in Acts 13:41.

## DESPITE, DESPITEFUL, DESPITEFULLY (use)

1. ***enubrizo*** *(1796)*, "to treat insultingly, with contumely" (***en***, intensive, ***hubrizo***, "to insult"; some connect it with ***huper***, "above, over," Lat. ***super***, which suggests the insulting disdain of one who considers himself superior), is translated "hath done despite" in Heb. 10:29.

D

2. ***epereazo*** *(1908)*, A text variant in Matt. 5:44, and found in Luke 6:28, where the KJV and RV have "despitefully use"; in 1 Pet. 3:16, KJV, "falsely accuse," RV, "revile."

## DESTITUTE (be, etc.)

1. ***apostereo*** *(650)*, signifies to "rob or steal," Jas. 5:4.

2. ***hustereo*** *(5302)*, primarily, "to be behind, to be last," hence, "to lack, fail of, come short of," is translated "being destitute" in Heb. 11:37.

3. ***leipo*** *(3007)* signifies "to leave, forsake"; in the passive voice, "to be left, forsaken, destitute"; in Jas. 2:15, KJV, "destitute," RV, "be in lack."

## DESTROY, DESTROYER, DESTRUCTION, DESTRUCTIVE

### *Old Testament*

***shamad*** (8045), "to destroy, annihilate, exterminate." This word always expresses complete "destruction" or "annihilation." While the word is often used to express literal "destruction" of people, Deut. 2:12; Judg. 21:16, ***shamad*** frequently is part of an open threat or warning given to the people of Israel, promising "destruction" if they forsake God for idols, cf. Deut. 4:25–26. This word also expresses the complete "destruction" of the pagan high places, Hos. 10:8, of Baal and his images, 2 Kings 10:28.

***shachat*** (7843), "to corrupt, spoil, ruin, mar, destroy," Gen. 6:11–12, 17. Anything that is good can be "corrupted" or "spoiled," such as Jeremiah's loincloth, Jer. 13:7, a vineyard, Jer. 12:10, cities, Gen. 13:10, and a temple, Lam. 2:6. ***shachat*** has the meaning of "to waste" when used of words that are inappropriately spoken, Prov. 23:8. ***shachat*** is used frequently by the prophets in the sense of "to corrupt morally," Isa. 1:4; Ezek. 23:11; Zeph. 3:7.

### *New Testament*

**A. Verbs.**

1. ***apollumi*** *(622)*, a strengthened form of ***ollumi***, signifies "to destroy utterly"; in middle voice, "to perish." The idea is not extinction but ruin, loss, not of being, but of well-being. This is clear from its use, as, e.g., of the marring of wine skins, Luke 5:37; of lost sheep, i.e., lost to the shepherd, metaphorical of spiritual destitution, Luke 15:4, 6, etc.; the lost son, 15:24; of the perishing of food, John 6:27; of gold, 1 Pet. 1:7. So of persons, Matt. 2:13, "destroy"; 8:25, "perish"; 22:7; 27:20; of the loss of well-being in the case of the unsaved hereafter, Matt. 10:28; Luke 13:3, 5; John 3:16 (v. 15 in some mss.); 10:28; 17:12; Rom. 2:12; 1 Cor. 15:18; 2 Cor. 2:15, "are perishing"; 4:3; 2 Thess. 2:10; Jas. 4:12; 2 Pet. 3:9.

2. ***katargeo*** *(2673)* lit., "to reduce to inactivity," 1 Cor. 6:13.

3. ***kathaireo*** *(2507)*, "to cast down, pull down by force, etc.," is translated "to destroy" in Acts 13:19. In Acts 19:27, KJV, "should be destroyed," the RV suitably has "should be deposed."

4. ***luo*** *(3089)*, "to loose, dissolve, sever, break, demolish," is translated "destroy," in 1 John 3:8, of the works of the Devil.

5. ***kataluo*** *(2647)*, ***kata***, "down," intensive, and No. 4, "to destroy utterly, to overthrow completely," is rendered "destroy," in Matt. 5:17, twice, of the Law; Matt. 24:2; 26:61; 27:40; Mark 13:2; 14:58; 15:29; Luke 21:6, of the Temple; in Acts 6:14, of Jerusalem; in Gal. 2:18, of the Law as a means of justification; in Rom. 14:20 (KJV, "destroy," RV, "overthrow"), of the marring of a person's spiritual well-being (in v. 15 ***apollumi***, No. 1, is used in the same sense); in Acts 5:38 and 39 (RV, "overthrow") of the failure of purposes; in 2 Cor. 5:1, of the death of the body ("dissolved).

6. ***olothreuo*** *(3645)*, "to destroy," especially in the sense of slaying, is found in Heb. 11:28, where the RV translates the present participle with the article by the noun "destroyer." See B, below.

7. ***exolothreuo*** *(1842)*, ***ek***, "out of" (intensive), and No. 6, "to destroy utterly to slay wholly," is found in Acts 3:23, RV, "utterly destroyed," referring to the "destruction" of one who would refuse to hearken to the voice of God through Christ.

**B. Nouns.**

(I) *(Personal: DESTROYER)*

***olothreutes*** *(3644)*, akin to A, No. 6, "a destroyer," is found in 1 Cor. 10:10.

(II) *(Abstract: DESTRUCTION)*

1. ***apoleia*** *(684)*, akin to A, No. 1, and likewise indicating "loss of well-being, not of being," is used (a) of things, signifying their waste, or ruin; of ointment, Matt. 26:8; Mark 14:4; of money, Acts 8:20 ("perish"); (b) of persons, signifying their spiritual and eternal perdition, Matt. 7:13; John 17:12; 2 Thess. 2:3, where "son of perdition" signifies the proper destiny of the person mentioned; metaphorically of men persistent in evil, Rom. 9:22, where "fitted" is in the middle voice, indicating that the vessels of wrath fitted themselves for "destruction," of the adversaries of the Lord's people, Phil. 1:28 ("perdition"); of pro-

fessing Christians, really enemies of the cross of Christ, Phil. 3:19 (RV, "perdition"); of those who are subjects of foolish and hurtful lusts, 1 Tim. 6:9.

2. ***kathairesis*** *(2506)*, akin to A, No. 3, "a taking down, a pulling down," is used three times in 2 Cor., "casting down" in the RV in each place; in 10:4 (KJV, "pulling down"); in 10:8 and 13:10 (KJV, "destruction").

3. ***olethros*** *(3639)*, "ruin, destruction," akin to A, No. 6, always translated "destruction," is used in 1 Cor. 5:5, of the effect upon the physical condition of an erring believer for the purpose of his spiritual profit; in 1 Thess. 5:3 and 2 Thess. 1:9, of the effect of the divine judgments upon men at the ushering in of the Day of the Lord and the revelation of the Lord Jesus; in 1 Tim. 6:9, of the consequences of the indulgence of the flesh, referring to physical "ruin" and possibly that of the whole being, the following word ***apoleia*** (see No. 1) stressing the final, eternal and irrevocable character of the ruin.

4. ***suntrimma*** *(4938)*, "a breaking in pieces, shattering," Rom. 3:16, from Isa. 59:7.

## DETERMINE, DETERMINATE

1. ***krino*** *(2919)*, primarily "to separate," hence, "to be of opinion, approve, esteem," Rom. 14:5, also "to determine, resolve, decree," is used in this sense in Acts 3:13; 20:16; 25:25; 27:1; 1 Cor. 2:2; 2 Cor. 2:1; Titus 3:12.

2. ***horizo*** *(3724)* denotes "to bound, to set a boundary" (Eng., "horizon"); hence, "to mark out definitely, determine"; it is translated "to determine" in Luke 22:22, of the foreordained pathway of Christ; Acts 11:29, of a "determination" to send relief; 17:26, where it is used of fixing the bounds of seasons. In Acts 2:23 the verb is translated "determinate," with reference to counsel. Here the verbal form might have been adhered to by the translation "determined"; that is to say, in the sense of "settled."

In Rom. 1:4 it is translated "declared," where the meaning is that Christ was marked out as the Son of God by His resurrection and that of others. In Acts 10:42 and 17:31 it has its other meaning of "ordain," that is, "to appoint by determined counsel."

3. ***proorizo*** *(4309)*, ***pro***, "beforehand," and No. 2, denotes "to mark out beforehand, to determine before, foreordain"; in Acts 4:28, KJV, "determined before," RV, "foreordained"; so the RV in 1 Cor. 2:7, KJV, "ordained," in Rom. 8:29–30 and Eph. 1:5, 11, KJV, "predestinate," RV, "foreordain."

## DEVICE

1. ***enthumesis*** *(1761)*, "a cogitation, an inward reasoning" (generally, evil surmising or supposition), is formed from ***en***, "in," and ***thumos***, "strong feeling, passion"; Eng., "fume" is akin; the root, ***thu***, signifies "to rush, rage."

2. ***noema*** *(3540)* denotes "thought, that which is thought out"; hence, "a purpose, device"; translated "devices" in 2 Cor. 2:11; "minds" in 2 Cor. 3:14; 4:4; 11:3; in 2 Cor. 10:5, "thought"; in Phil. 4:7, KJV, "minds," RV, "thoughts."

## DEVIL, DEVILISH

***diabolos*** *(1228)*, "an accuser, a slanderer" (from ***diaballo***, "to accuse, to malign"), is one of the names of Satan. From it the English word "Devil" is derived, and should be applied only to Satan, as a proper name. ***daimon***, "a demon," is frequently, but wrongly, translated "devil"; it should always be translated "demon," as in the RV margin. There is one "Devil," there are many demons. Being the malignant enemy of God and man, he accuses man to God, Job 1:6–11; 2:1–5; Rev. 12:9, 10, and God to man, Gen. 3. He afflicts men with physical sufferings, Acts 10:38. Being himself sinful, 1 John 3:8, he instigated man to sin, Gen. 3, and tempts man to do evil, Eph. 4:27; 6:11, encouraging him thereto by deception, Eph. 2:2. Death having been brought into the world by sin, the "Devil" had the power of death, but Christ through His own death, has triumphed over him, and will bring him to nought, Heb. 2:14; his power over death is intimated in his struggle with Michael over the body of Moses, Jude 9. Judas, who gave himself over to the "Devil," was so identified with him, that the Lord described him as such, John 6:70 (see 13:2). As the "Devil" raised himself in pride against God and fell under condemnation, so believers are warned against similar sin, 1 Tim. 3:6; for them he lays snares, v. 7, seeking to devour them as a roaring lion, 1 Pet. 5:8; those who fall into his snare may be recovered therefrom unto the will of God, 2 Tim. 2:26, "having been taken captive by him (i.e., by the 'Devil')"; "by the Lord's servant" is an alternative, which some regard as confirmed by the use of ***zogreo*** ("to catch alive") in Luke 5:10; but the general use is that of taking captive in the usual way. If believers resist he will flee from them, Jas. 4:7. His fury and malignity will be especially exercised at the end of the present age, Rev. 12:12. His doom is the lake of fire, Matt. 25:41; Rev. 20:10.

The noun is applied to slanderers, false accusers, 1 Tim. 3:11; 2 Tim. 3:3; Titus 2:3.

## DEVISED (cunningly)

***sophizo*** (*4679*), from ***sophos***, "wise" (connected etymologically with ***sophes***, "tasty"), in the active voice signifies "to make wise," 2 Tim. 3:15. In the New Testament it means, "to play the sophist, to devise cleverly," it is used with this meaning in the passive voice in 2 Pet. 1:16, "cunningly devised fables."

## DEVOUT

1. ***eulabes*** (*2126*), lit., "taking hold well" (***eu***, "well," ***lambano***, "to take hold"), primarily, "cautious," signifies in the NT, "careful as to the realization of the presence and claims of God, reverencing God, pious, devout"; in Luke 2:25 it is said of Simeon; in Acts 2:5, of certain Jews; in 8:2, of those who bore Stephen's body to burial; of Ananias, 22:12 (see No. 2).

2. ***eusebes*** (*2152*), from ***eu***, "well," ***sebomai***, "to reverence," the root ***seb***— signifying "sacred awe," describes "reverence" exhibited especially in actions, reverence or awe well directed. Among the Greeks it was used, e.g., of practical piety towards parents. In the NT it is used of a pious attitude towards God, Acts 10:2, 7; (in some mss. in 22:12); "godly," in 2 Pet. 2:9.

## DIADEM

***diadema*** (*1238*) is derived from ***diadeo***, "to bind round." It was the kingly ornament for the head; among the Greeks and Romans it was the distinctive badge of royalty. The word is found in Rev. 12:3; 13:1; 19:12, where it symbolizes the rule respectively of the Dragon, the Beast, and Christ.

## DIE, DEAD (to be, become), DYING

### *Old Testament*

***mot*** (4191), "to die, kill," i.e., "lose one's life," with special reference to animate, physical death, Gen. 33:13; Job 14:8. Occasionally, ***mot*** is used figuratively of land, Gen. 47:19, or wisdom, Job 12:2. Then, too, there is the unique hyperbolic expression that Nabal's heart had "died" within him, indicating that he was overcome with great fear, 1 Sam. 25:37.

In the usual causative stem, this verb can mean "to cause to die" or "to kill"; God is the one who "puts to death" and gives life, Deut. 32:39.

God is clearly the ultimate Ruler of life and death, cf. Deut. 32:39. This idea is especially clear in the Creation account, in which God tells man that he will surely die if he eats of the forbidden fruit, Gen. 2:17. Apparently there was no death before this time. When Adam and Eve ate of the fruit, both spiritual and physical death came upon Adam and Eve and their descendants, cf. Rom. 5:12.

### *New Testament*

1. ***thnesko*** (*2348*), "to die" (in the perf. tense, "to be dead"), in the NT is always used of physical "death," except in 1 Tim. 5:6, where it is metaphorically used of the loss of spiritual life.

2. ***apothnesko*** (*599*), lit., "to die off or out," is used (a) of the separation of the soul from the body, i.e., the natural "death" of human beings, e.g., Matt. 9:24; Rom. 7:2; by reason of descent from Adam, 1 Cor. 15:22; or of violent "death," whether of men or animals; with regard to the latter it is once translated "perished," Matt. 8:32; of vegetation, Jude 12; of seeds, John 12:24; 1 Cor. 15:36; it is used of "death" as a punishment in Israel under the Law, in Heb. 10:28; (b) of the separation of man from God, all who are descended from Adam not only "die" physically, owing to sin, see (a) above, but are naturally in the state of separation from God, 2 Cor. 5:14. From this believers are freed both now and eternally, John 6:50; 11:26, through the "death" of Christ, Rom. 5:8, e.g.; unbelievers, who "die" physically as such, remain in eternal separation from God, John 8:24. Believers have spiritually "died" to the Law as a means of life, Gal. 2:19; Col. 2:20; to sin, Rom. 6:2, and in general to all spiritual association with the world and with that which pertained to their unregenerate state, Col. 3:3, because of their identification with the "death" of Christ, Rom. 6:8 (see No. 3, below). As life never means mere existence, so "death," the opposite of life, never means non-existence.

3. ***sunapothnesko*** (*4880*), "to die with, to die together," is used of association in physical "death," Mark 14:31; in 2 Cor. 7:3, the apostle declares that his love to the saints makes separation impossible, whether in life or in "death." It is used once of association spiritually with Christ in His "death," 2 Tim. 2:11. See No. 2 (b).

4. ***teleutao*** (*5053*), "to end," hence, "to end one's life," is used (a) of the "death" of the body, Matt. 2:19; 9:18; 15:4, where "die the death" means "surely die," RV, marg., lit., "let him end by death"; Mark 7:10; Matt. 22:25, "deceased"; Luke 7:2; John 11:39, some mss. have verb No. 1 here; Acts 2:29; 7:15; Heb. 11:22 (RV, "his end was nigh"); (b) of the gnawings of conscience in self reproach, under the symbol of a worm, Mark 9:48 (vv. 44 and 46, KJV).

## DIGNITY, DIGNITIES

***doxa*** (*1391*) primarily denotes "an opinion, estimation, repute"; in the NT, always "good opinion, praise, honor, glory, an appearance commanding respect, magnificence, excellence, manifestation of glory"; hence, of angelic powers, in respect of their state as commanding recognition, "dignities," 2 Pet. 2:10; Jude 8.

## DILIGENCE, DILIGENT, DILIGENTLY

### A. Nouns.

1. ***ergasia*** (*2039*), (a) lit., "a working" (akin to ***ergon***, "work"), is indicative of a process, in contrast to the concrete, ***ergon***, e.g., Eph. 4:19, lit., "unto a working" (RV marg., "to make a trade of"); contrast ***ergon*** in v. 12; (b) "business," Acts 19:25, RV (for KJV, "craft"); or gain got by "work," Acts 16:16, 19; 19:24; (c) endeavor, pains, "diligence," Luke 12:58.

2. ***spoude*** (*4710*), "earnestness, zeal," or sometimes "the haste accompanying this," Mark 6:25; Luke 1:39.

### B. Verb.

***spoudazo*** (*4704*) has meanings corresponding to A, No. 2; it signifies "to hasten to do a thing, to exert oneself, endeavor, give diligence"; in Gal. 2:10, of remembering the poor, KJV, "was forward," RV, "was zealous"; in Eph. 4:3, of keeping the unity of the Spirit, KJV "endeavoring," RV, "giving diligence"; in 1 Thess. 2:17, of going to see friends, "endeavored"; in 2 Tim. 4:9; 4:21, "do thy diligence"; in the following the RV uses the verb "to give diligence": 2 Tim. 2:15, KJV, "study"; Titus 3:12, KJV, "be diligent"; Heb. 4:11, of keeping continuous Sabbath rest, KJV, "let us labor"; in 2 Pet. 1:10, of making our calling and election sure; in 2 Pet. 1:15, of enabling believers to call Scripture truth to remembrance, KJV, "endeavour"; in 2 Pet. 3:14, of being found in peace without fault and blameless, when the Lord comes, KJV, be diligent.

### C. Adjectives.

1. ***spoudaios*** (*4705*), akin to A, No. 2 and B, No. 1, primarily signifies "in haste"; hence, diligent, earnest, zealous, 2 Cor. 8:22, KJV, "diligent, RV, "earnest."

2. ***spoudaioteros*** (*4707*), the comparative degree of No. 1, 2 Cor. 8:22.

### D. Adverbs.

1. ***spoudaios*** (*4709*), "speedily, earnestly, diligently," is translated "earnestly" in the RV of Luke 7:4 (KJV, "instantly"); "diligently" in Titus 3:13.

2. ***spoudaioteros*** (*4708*), the comparative degree of No. 1, "more diligently," is used in Phil. 2:28.

## DINE, DINNER

### A. Verb.

***aristao*** (*709*), primarily, "to breakfast" (see B), was later used also with the meaning "to dine," e.g., Luke 11:37; in John 21:12, 15, RV, "break your fast," and "had broken their fast," for KJV, "dine"; obviously there it was the first meal in the day.

### B. Noun.

***ariston*** (*712*), primarily, "the first food," taken early in the morning before work; the meal in the Pharisee's house, in Luke 11:37, was a breakfast or early meal; the dinner was called ***deipnon***. Later the breakfast was called ***akratisma*** (not in NT), and dinner, ***ariston***, as in Matt. 22:4; Luke 11:38; 14:12.

## DIP, DIPPED, DIPPETH

1. ***bapto*** (*911*), "to immerse, dip" (derived from a root signifying "deep"), also signified "to dye," which is suggested in Rev. 19:13, of the Lord's garment "dipped (i.e. dyed) in blood," also Luke 16:24; John 13:26.

2. ***embapto*** (*1686*), ***en***, "in," and No. 1, "to dip into," is used of the act of Judas in "dipping" his hand with that of Christ in the dish, Matt. 26:23; Mark 14:20.

## DISANNUL, DISANNULLING

### A. Verbs.

1. ***atheteo*** (*114*) signifies "to put as of no value" (***a***, negative and ***theton***, "what is placed," from ***tithemi***, "to put, place"); hence, (a) "to act towards anything as though it were annulled"; e.g., to deprive a law of its force by opinions or acts contrary to it, Gal. 3:15, KJV, "disannulleth," RV, "maketh void"; (b) "to thwart the efficacy of anything, to nullify, to frustrate it," Luke 7:30, "rejected"; 1 Cor. 1:19, "will I reject"; to make void, Gal. 2:21; to set at nought, Jude 8, RV (KJV, "despised"); the parallel passage, in 2 Pet. 2:10, has ***kataphroneo***. In Mark 6:26, the thought is that of breaking faith with.

2. ***akuroo*** (*208*), "to deprive of authority," hence, "to make of none effect," Matt. 15:6; Mark 7:13, with reference to the commandment or word of God, RV, "to make void," is translated "disannul" in Gal. 3:17, of the inability of the Law to deprive of force God's covenant with Abraham. This verb stresses the effect of the act, while No. 1 stresses the attitude of the rejecter.

**B. Noun.**

***athetesis*** (*115*), akin to A, No. 1, "a setting aside, abolition," is translated "disannulling" in Heb. 7:18, with reference to a commandment; in 9:26 "to put away," with reference to sin, lit., "for a putting away."

## DISBELIEVE

***apisteo*** (*569*), "to be unbelieving" (***a***, negative, ***pistis***, "faith"); is translated "believed not," etc., in the KJV (except in 1 Pet. 2:7, "be disobedient"); "disbelieve" (or "disbelieved") in the RV, in Mark 16:11, 16; Luke 24:11, 41; Acts 28:24; "disbelieve" is the best rendering, implying that the unbeliever has had a full opportunity of believing and has rejected it.

## DISCERN, DISCERNER, DISCERNMENT

### *Old Testament*

***nakar*** (5234), "to discern, regard, recognize, pay attention to, be acquainted with." The basic meaning of the term is a "physical apprehension," whether through sight, touch, or hearing. Darkness sometimes makes "recognition" impossible, Ruth 3:14. People are often "recognized" by their voices, Judg. 18:3. ***nakar*** sometimes has the meaning of "pay attention to," a special kind of "recognition," Ruth 2:19. The sense of "to distinguish" is seen in Ezra 3:13.

### *New Testament*

**A. Verbs.**

1. ***anakrino*** (*350*), "to distinguish, or separate out so as to investigate (***krino***) by looking throughout (***ana***, intensive) objects or particulars," hence signifies "to examine, scrutinize, question, to hold a preliminary judicial examination preceding the trial proper" (this first examination, implying more to follow, is often present in the non-legal uses of the word), e.g. Luke 23:14; figuratively, in 1 Cor. 4:3; it is said of searching the Scriptures in Acts 17:11; of "discerning" or determining the excellence or defects of a person or thing, e.g., 1 Cor. 2:14, KJV, "discerned"; RV, "judged"; in 1 Cor. 10:27, "asking (no) question" (i.e., not raising the question as to whether the meat is the residue from an idolatrous sacrifice). Except in Luke 23:14, this word is found only in Acts and 1 Cor.

2. ***diakrino*** (*1252*) signifies "to separate, discriminate"; then, "to learn by discriminating, to determine, decide." It is translated "discern" in Matt. 16:3, of discriminating between the varying conditions of the sky (see No. 3, below, in Luke 12:56), and in 1 Cor. 11:29, with reference to partaking of the bread and the cup of the Lord's Supper unworthily, by not "discerning" or discriminating what they represent; in v. 31, the RV has "discerned," for the KJV, "would judge," of trying oneself, "discerning" one's condition, and so judging any evil before the Lord; in 14:29, regarding oral testimony in a gathering of believers, it is used of "discerning" what is of the Holy Spirit, RV, "discern" (KJV, "judge").

3. ***dokimazo*** (*1381*) signifies "to test, prove, scrutinize," so as "to decide." It is translated "discern" in the KJV of Luke 12:56.

**B. Noun.**

***diakrisis*** (*1253*), cf. A, No. 2, "a distinguishing, a clear discrimination, discerning, judging," is translated "discernings" in 1 Cor. 12:10, of "discerning" spirits, judging by evidence whether they are evil or of God. In Heb. 5:14 the phrase consisting of pros, with this noun, lit., "towards a discerning," is translated "to discern," said of those who are capable of discriminating between good and evil. In Rom. 14:1 the word has its other sense of decision or judgment, and the phrase "doubtful disputations" is, lit., "judgments of reasonings."

**C. Adjective.**

***kritikos*** (*2924*) signifies "that which relates to judging (***krino***, "to judge"), fit for, or skilled in, judging" (Eng., "critical"), found in Heb. 4:12, of the Word of God as "quick to discern the thoughts and intents of the heart," (lit., "critical of, etc."), i.e., discriminating and passing judgment on the thoughts and feelings.

## DISCIPLE

**A. Nouns.**

1. ***mathetes*** (*3101*), lit., "a learner" (from ***manthano***, "to learn," from a root ***math***—, indicating thought accompanied by endeavor), in contrast to ***didaskalos***, "a teacher"; hence it denotes "one who follows one's teaching," as the "disciples" of John, Matt. 9:14; of the Pharisees, Matt. 22:16; of Moses, John 9:28; it is used of the "disciples" of Jesus (a) in a wide sense, of Jews who became His adherents, John 6:66; Luke 6:17, some being secretly so, John 19:38; (b) especially of the twelve apostles, Matt. 10:1; Luke 22:11, e.g.; (c) of all who manifest that they are His "disciples" by abiding in His Word, and so be an adherent, John 8:31.

2. ***mathetria*** (*3102*), "a female disciple," is said of Tabitha, Acts 9:36.

3. ***summathetes*** (*4827*) means "a fellow disciple" (***sun***, with, and No. 1), John 11:16.

**B. Verb.**

***matheteuo*** (*3100*) is used in the active voice, intransitively, in some mss., in Matt. 27:57, in the sense of being the "disciple" of a person; here, however, the best mss. have the passive voice, lit., "had been made a disciple," as in Matt. 13:52, RV, "who hath been made a disciple." It is used in this transitive sense in the active voice in 28:19 and Acts 14:21.

## DISCIPLINE

***sophronismos*** (*4995*), from ***sophron***, lit., "saving the mind," primarily, "an admonishing or calling to soundness of mind, or to self-control," is used in 2 Tim. 1:7, KJV, "a sound mind"; RV, "discipline."

## DISCREET, DISCREETLY

**A. Adjective.**

***sophron*** (*4998*), "of sound mind self-controlled," is translated "sober-minded," in its four occurrences in the RV, 1 Tim. 3:2 (KJV, "sober"); Titus 1:8 (KJV, "sober"); 2:2 (KJV, "temperate"); 2:5 (KJV, "discreet").

**B. Adverb.**

***nounechos*** (*3562*), lit., "mind-possessing" (***nous***, "mind, understanding," ***echo***, "to have"), hence denotes "discreetly, sensibly prudently." Mark 12:34.

## DISEASE, DISEASED (BE)

**A. Nouns.**

1. ***astheneia*** (*769*), lit., "lacking strength" (***a***, negative, ***sthenos***, "strength"), "weakness, infirmity," is translated "diseases" in Matt. 8:17, RV, for KJV, "sicknesses," and in Acts 28:9. Its usual rendering is "infirmity" or "infirmities"; "sickness," in John 11:4.

2. ***malakia*** (*3119*) primarily denotes "softness"; hence, "debility, disease." It is found in Matthew only, 4:23; 9:35; 10:1.

3. ***nosos*** (*3554*), akin to Lat. ***nocere***, "to injure" (Eng., "noxious"), is the regular word for "disease, sickness," Matt. 4:23; 8:17; 9:35; 10:1, RV, "disease," KJV, "sickness"; in Matt. 4:24; Mark 1:34; Luke 4:40; 6:17; 9:1; Acts 19:12, KJV and RV render it "diseases." In Luke 7:21, KJV has "infirmities." The most authentic mss. omit the word in Mark 3:15.

4. ***nosema*** (*3553*), an alternative form of No. 3, is found in some mss. in John 5:4.

**B. Verbs.**

1. ***astheneo*** (*770*), akin to A, No. 1, "to lack strength, to be weak, sick," is translated "were diseased" in John 6:2, KJV (RV, "were sick).

2. ***echo kakos*** lit., "to have badly," i.e., "to be ill or in an evil case," is used in Matt. 14:35 (KJV, "were diseased," RV, "were sick"); so in Mark 1:32; Luke 7:2.

D

## DISHONESTY

***aischune*** (*152*), "shame," so the RV in 2 Cor. 4:2 (for KJV, "dishonesty"), is elsewhere rendered "shame," Luke 14:9; Phil. 3:19; Heb. 12:2; Jude 13; Rev. 3:18.

## DISHONOR

**A. Noun.**

***atimia*** (*819*), from ***a***, negative, ***time***, "honor," denotes "dishonor, ignominy, disgrace," in Rom. 1:26, "vile passions" (RV), lit., 'passions of dishonor;' in Rom. 9:21, "dishonor," of vessels designed for meaner household purposes (in contrast to ***time***, "honor," as in 2 Tim. 2:20); in 1 Cor. 11:14, said of long hair, if worn by men, RV, "dishonor," for KJV, "shame," in contrast to ***doxa***, glory, v. 15; so in 1 Cor. 15:43, of the "sowing" of the natural body, and in 2 Cor. 6:8, of the apostle Paul's ministry.

**B. Verb.**

1. ***atimazo*** (*818*) akin to A, signifies "to dishonour, treat shamefully, insult," whether in word, John 8:49, or deed, Mark 12:4; Luke 20:11, RV "handled (him) shamefully," (RV "entreated . . . shamefully"); Rom. 1:24; 2:23, "dishonorest"; Jas. 2:6, RV, "ye have dishonored (the poor)," (KJV, "despised"); in the passive voice, to suffer dishonor, Acts 5:41 (KJV, "suffer shame").

## TO BE DISMAYED

***chatat*** (2865), "to be dismayed, shattered, broken, terrified." ***chatat*** is often used in parallelism with the Hebrew term for "fear," cf. Deut. 31:8; Josh. 8:1; 1 Sam. 17:11. Similarly, ***chatat*** is frequently used in parallelism with "to be ashamed," Isa. 20:5; Jer. 8:9.

## DISOBEDIENCE, DISOBEDIENT

**A. Nouns.**

1. ***apeitheia*** (*543*), lit., "the condition of being unpersuadable," denotes "obstinacy, obstinate rejection of the will of God"; hence, "disobedience"; Eph. 2:2; 5:6; Col. 3:6, and in the RV of Rom. 11:30, 32 and Heb. 4:6, 11 (for KJV, "unbelief"), speaking of Israel, past and present.

2. ***parakoe*** (*3876*), primarily, "hearing amiss," hence signifies "a refusal to hear"; hence, "an act of disobedience," Rom. 5:19;

2 Cor. 10:6; Heb. 2:2. It is broadly to be distinguished from No. 1, as an act from a condition, though ***parakoe*** itself is the effect, in transgression, of the condition of failing or refusing to hear. Carelessness in attitude is the precursor of actual "disobedience." In the OT "disobedience" is frequently described as "a refusing to hear," e.g., Jer. 11:10; 35:17; cf. Acts 7:57.

### B. Adjective.

***apeithes*** (*545*), akin to A, No. 1, signifies "unwilling to be persuaded, spurning belief, disobedient," Luke 1:17; Acts 26:19; Rom. 1:30; 2 Tim. 3:2; Titus 1:16; 3:3.

### C. Verb.

***apeitheo*** (*544*), akin to A, No. 1, and B, "to refuse to be persuaded, to refuse belief, to be disobedient," is translated "disobedient," or by the verb "to be disobedient," in the RV of Acts 14:2 (KJV, "unbelieving"), and 19:9 (KJV, "believed not"); it is absent from the most authentic mss. in Acts 17:5; in John 3:36 "obeyeth not," RV (KJV, "believeth not"); in Rom. 2:8 "obey not"; in 10:21, "disobedient"; in 11:30, 31, "were disobedient" (KJV, "have not believed"); so in 15:31; Heb. 3:18; 11:31; in 1 Pet. 2:8, "disobedient"; so in 3:20; in 3:1 and 4:17, "obey not."

## DISORDERLY

### A. Adjective.

***ataktos*** (*813*) signifies "not keeping order"; it was especially a military term, denoting "not keeping rank, insubordinate"; it is used in 1 Thess. 5:14, describing certain church members who manifested an insubordinate spirit, whether by excitability or officiousness or idleness.

### B. Adverb.

***ataktos*** (*814*) signifies "disorderly, with slackness" (like soldiers not keeping rank) 2 Thess. 3:6; in v. 11 it is said of those in the church who refused to work, and became busybodies (cf. 1 Tim. 5:13).

### C. Verb.

***atakteo*** (*812*) signifies "to be out of rank, out of one's place, undisciplined, to behave disorderly": in the military sense, "to break rank"; negatively in 2 Thess. 3:7, of the example set by the apostle and his fellow missionaries, in working for their bread while they were at Thessalonica so as not to burden the saints.

## DISPENSATION

***oikonomia*** (*3622*) primarily signifies "the management of a household or of household affairs" (***oikos***, "a house," ***nomos***, "a law"); then the management or administration of the property of others, and so "a stewardship," Luke 16:2–4; elsewhere only in the epistles of Paul, who applies it (a) to the responsibility entrusted to him of preaching the gospel, 1 Cor. 9:17 (RV, "stewardship," KJV, "dispensation"); (b) to the stewardship committed to him "to fulfill the Word of God," the fulfillment being the unfolding of the completion of the divinely arranged and imparted cycle of truths which are consummated in the truth relating to the church as the body of Christ, Col. 1:25 (RV and KJV, "dispensation"); so in Eph. 3:2, of the grace of God given him as a stewardship ("dispensation") in regard to the same "mystery"; (c) in Eph. 1:10 and 3:9, it is used of the arrangement or administration by God, by which in "the fullness of the times" (or seasons) God will sum up all things in the heavens and on earth in Christ.

## DISPERSE, DISPERSION

### A. Verbs.

1. ***dialuo*** (*1262*), "to dissolve," is used in Acts 5:36 of the breaking up and dispersion of a company of men.

2. ***skorpizo*** (*4650*), "to scatter," is used in Matt. 12:30; Luke 11:23; John 10:12; 16:32; in the RV of 2 Cor. 9:9, "scattered abroad" (KJV, "he hath dispersed abroad"), of one who liberally dispenses benefits.

3. ***diaskorpizo*** (*1287*), ***dia***, "through," and No. 2, signifies "to scatter abroad," in Matt. 26:31; Mark 14:27, metaphorically of sheep; in Luke 1:51, of the proud; in John 11:52, of the "scattering" of the children of God; in Acts 5:37, of the followers of Judas of Galilee.

4. ***diaspeiro*** (*1289*), "to scatter abroad" (***dia***, "through," ***speiro***, "to sow"), is used in Acts 8:1, 4; 11:19.

### B. Noun.

***diaspora*** (*1290*), akin to A, No. 4, "a scattering, a dispersion," was used of the Jews who from time to time had been scattered among the Gentiles, John 7:35; later with reference to Jews, so "scattered," who had professed, or actually embraced, the Christian faith, "the Dispersion," Jas. 1:1, RV; especially of believers who were converts from Judaism and "scattered" throughout certain districts, "sojourners of the Dispersion," 1 Pet. 1:1, RV.

## DISPLEASED

1. ***aganakteo*** (*23*), from ***agan***, "much," and ***achomai***, "to grieve," primarily meant "to feel a violent irritation, physically"; it was used,

too, of the fermenting of wine hence, metaphorically, "to show signs of grief, to be displeased, to be grieved, vexed"; it is translated "sore displeased" in Matt. 21:15, KJV; "much displeased," in Mark 10:14, 41; the RV always renders it "to be moved with, or to have, indignation," as the KJV elsewhere, Matt. 20:24; 26:8; Mark 14:4; Luke 13:14.

2. ***prosochthizo*** (*4360*), "to be wroth or displeased with" (***pros***, "toward," or "with," ***ochtheo***, "to be sorely vexed"), is used in Heb. 3:10, 17 (KJV, "grieved"; RV, "displeased"). "Grieved" does not adequately express the righteous anger of God intimated in the passage.

3. ***thumomacheo*** (*2371*), lit., "to fight with great animosity," hence, "to be very angry, to be highly displeased," is said of Herod's "displeasure" with the Tyrians and Sidonians, Acts 12:20.

## DISPOSITION

***diatage*** (*1296*), an ordinance, e.g., Rom. 13:2 (cf. ***diatasso***, "to appoint, ordain"), is rendered "disposition" in Acts 7:53; cf. Deut. 33:2. In Acts 7:53 Stephen mentions the angels to stress the majesty of the Law.

## DISPUTATION

1. ***zetesis*** (*2214*) denotes, firstly, "a seeking" (***zeteo***, "to seek"), then, "a debate, dispute, questioning," Acts 15:2, 7.

2. ***dialogismos*** (*1261*) is translated "disputations" in Rom. 14:1.

## DISPUTE, DISPUTER, DISPUTING

### A. Nouns.

1. ***dialogismos*** (*1261*) denotes, primarily, "an inward reasoning, an opinion" (***dia***, "through," suggesting separation, ***logismos***, "a reasoning"), e.g., Luke 2:35; 5:22; 6:8; then, "a deliberating, questioning," Luke 24:38; (more strongly) "a disputing," Phil. 2:14; 1 Tim. 2:8 (KJV, "doubtings"); in Rom. 14:1, "disputations"; marg., "(not for decisions) of doubts" (lit., "not unto discussions or doubts," which is perhaps a suitable rendering).

2. ***logomachia*** (*3055*) denotes "a dispute about words" (***logos***, "a word," ***mache***, "a fight"), or about trivial things, 1 Tim. 6:4, RV, "disputes," KJV, "strifes."

3. ***antilogia*** (*485*) denotes "a gainsaying, contradiction" (***anti***, "against," ***lego***, "to speak"), Heb. 6:16; 7:7; 12:3; Jude 11.

4. ***suzetetes*** (*4804*), from ***sun***, "with," ***zeteo***, "to seek," denotes "a disputer," 1 Cor. 1:20, where the reference is especially to a learned "disputant," a sophist.

### B. Verbs.

1. ***dialegomai*** (*1256*), akin to A No. 1, primarily signifies "to think different things with oneself, to ponder"; then, with other persons, "to converse, argue, dispute"; it is translated "to dispute" in Mark 9:34 (for v. 33, see No. 2), the RV and KJV "had disputed" is somewhat unsuitable here, for the delinquency was not that they had wrangled, but that they had reasoned upon the subject at all; in Acts 17:17, KJV (RV, "reasoned," as in the KJV of 18:4, 19); in 19:8–9 (RV, "reasoning"); in 24:12, "disputing"; in Jude 9, "disputed."

2. ***dialogizomai*** (*1260*), akin to A, No. 1, "to bring together different reasons, to reckon them up, to reason, discuss," in Mark 9:33 is translated "ye disputed among yourselves," KJV; RV, "were reasoning."

3. ***suzeteo*** (*4802*), akin to A, No. 4, lit., "to seek or examine together," signifies "to discuss," but is translated "to dispute" in Acts 6:9, and 9:29; elsewhere only in Mark and Luke.

## DISSENSION

***stasis*** (*4714*), akin to ***histemi***, "to stand," denotes (a) "a standing, stability," Heb. 9:8, "(while as the first tabernacle) is yet standing"; (b) "an insurrection, uproar," Mark 15:7; Luke 23:19, 25; Acts 19:40; 24:5; (c) "a dissension," Acts 15:2; 23:7, 10.

## DISSIMULATION, DISSEMBLE

### A. Noun.

***hupokrisis*** (*5272*), primarily, "a reply," came to mean "the acting of a stageplayer," because such answered one another in dialogue; hence the meaning "dissembling or pretense." It is translated "dissimulation" in Gal. 2:13 (see B).

### B. Verb.

***sunupokrinomai*** (*4942*), lit., "to join in acting the hypocrite," in pretending to act from one motive, whereas another motive really inspires the act. So in Gal. 2:13, Peter with other believing Jews, in separating from believing Gentiles at Antioch, pretended that the motive was loyalty to the Law of Moses, whereas really it was fear of the Judaizers.

### C. Adjective.

***anupokritos*** (*505*), from ***a***, negative, ***n***, euphonic, and an adjectival form corresponding to A, signifies "unfeigned"; it is said of love, 2 Cor. 6:6; 1 Pet. 1:22; Rom. 12:9, KJV, "without dissimulation," RV, "without hypocrisy"; of faith, 1 Tim. 1:5; 2 Tim. 1:5, "unfeigned"; of the wisdom that is from above, Jas. 3:17, "without hypocrisy."

D

## DISTRESS, DISTRESSED

*Old Testament*

**A. Nouns.**

***tsarah*** (6869), "distress; straits," in a psychological or spiritual sense, which is its meaning in Gen. 42:21.

***tsar*** (6862), "distress." This word also occurs mostly in poetry. In Prov. 24:10, ***tsar*** means "scarcity" or the "distress" caused by scarcity. The emphasis of the noun is sometimes on the feeling of "dismay" arising from a distressful situation, Job 7:11. In this usage the word ***tsar*** represents a psychological or spiritual status. In Isa. 5:30, the word describes conditions that cause distress, cf. Isa. 30:20.

**B. Verb.**

***tsarar*** (6887), "to wrap, tie up, be narrow, be distressed, be in pangs of birth," Judg. 11:7.

**C. Adjective.**

***tsar*** (6862), "narrow," Num. 22:26.

*New Testament*

**A. Noun.**

***ananke*** (*318*) denotes (a) "a necessity," imposed whether by external circumstances, e.g., Luke 23:17, or inward pressure, e.g., 1 Cor. 9:16; (b) "straits, distress," Luke 21:23; 1 Cor. 7:26; 1 Thess. 3:7; the last two refer to the lack of material things.

**B. Verbs.**

1. ***basanizo*** (*928*), properly signifies "to test by rubbing on the touchstone" (***basanos***, "a touchstone"), then, "to question by applying torture"; hence "to vex, torment"; in the passive voice, "to be harassed, distressed"; it is said of men struggling in a boat against wind and waves, Matt. 14:24, RV, "distressed" (KJV, "tossed"); Mark 6:48, RV, "distressed" (KJV, toiling).

2. ***kataponeo*** (*2669*), primarily, "to tire down with toil, exhaust with labor" (***kata***, "down," ***ponos***, "labor"), hence signifies "to afflict, oppress"; in the passive voice, "to be oppressed, much distressed"; it is translated "oppressed" in Acts 7:24, and "sore distressed" in 2 Pet. 2:7, RV, (KJV, "vexed").

## DISTRIBUTE, DISTRIBUTION

**A. Verb.**

***diadidomi*** (*1239*), lit., "to give through," (***dia***, "through," ***didomi***, "to give"), as from one to another, "to deal out," is said of "distributing" to the poor, Luke 18:22; Acts 4:35.

**B. Adjective.**

***eumetadotos*** (*2130*), "ready to impart" (***eu***, "well," ***meta***, "with," ***didomi***, "to give": see A, is used in 1 Tim. 6:18, "ready to distribute."

## DIVERS

**A. Adjectives.**

1. ***diaphoros*** (*1313*) is rendered divers in Heb. 9:10.

2. ***poikilos*** (*4164*) denotes "parti-colored, variegated" (***poikillo*** means "to make bright, various colors," hence "divers"), Matt. 4:24; Mark 1:34; Luke 4:40; 2 Tim. 3:6; Titus 3:3; Heb. 2:4 (RV, "manifold"), 13:9; Jas. 1:2 (RV, "manifold"); in 1 Pet. 1:6 and 4:10, "manifold," both KJV and RV.

**B. Adverb.**

***polutropos*** (*4187*) means "in many ways," Heb. 1:1.

## DIVIDE, DIVIDER, DIVIDING

*Old Testament*

**A. Verb.**

***chalaq*** (2505), "to divide, share, plunder, assign, distribute." The sense of "dividing" or "allotting" is found in Deut. 4:19, where the sun, moon, and stars are said to have been "allotted" to all peoples by God. A similar use is seen in Deut. 29:26, where God is said not to have "allotted" false gods to His people.

***chalaq*** is used in the legal sense of "sharing" an inheritance in Prov. 17:2. The word is used three times in reference to "sharing" the spoils of war in 1 Sam. 30:24.

This verb describes the "division" of the people of Israel, as one half followed Tibni and the other half followed Omri, 1 Kings 16:21.

**B. Noun.**

***cheleq*** (2506), "portion; territory." It has a variety of meanings, such as "booty" of war, Gen. 14:24, a "portion" of food, Lev. 6:17, a "tract" of land, Josh. 18:5, a spiritual "possession" or blessing, Ps. 73:26, and a chosen "pattern" or "life-style," Ps. 50:18.

*New Testament*

**A. Verbs.**

1. ***aphorizo*** (*873*), lit., "to mark off by boundaries or limits" (***apo***, "from," ***horizo***, "to determine, mark out"), denotes "to separate"; "divideth," Matt. 25:32.

2. ***diaireo*** (*1244*), lit., "to take asunder," "to divide into parts, to distribute," is found in Luke 15:12 and 1 Cor. 12:11.

3. ***diakrino*** (*1252*), "to separate," discriminate, hence, "to be at variance with oneself, to

be divided in one's mind," is rendered "divided" in Jas. 2:4, RV; KJV, "partial."

4. ***merizo*** (*3307*), akin to ***meros***, "a part, to part, divide into," in the middle voice means "to divide anything with another, to share with." The usual meaning is "to divide," Matt. 12:25, 26; Mark 3:24–26; 6:41; Luke 12:13 (middle voice); Rom. 12:3, "hath dealt"; 1 Cor. 1:13; Heb. 7:2, RV (KJV, "gave a part"). Elsewhere with other meanings, 1 Cor. 7:17, 34; 2 Cor. 10:13.

5. ***diamerizo*** (*1266*), ***dia***, "through," and No. 4, "to divide through," i.e., "completely, to divide up," is translated "to divide" in Luke 11:17–18; 12:52–53; 22:17; "parted" in Matt. 27:35; Mark 15:24; Luke 23:34; John 19:24; Acts 2:45; in Acts 2:3, KJV, "cloven," RV, "parting asunder."

6. ***orthotomeo*** (*3718*), lit., "to cut straight" (***orthos***, "straight," ***temno***, "to cut"), is found in 2 Tim. 2:15, KJV, "rightly dividing," RV, "handling aright," used figuratively, means teaching Scripture accurately.

### B. Nouns.

1. ***meristes*** (*3312*), "a divider," is found in Luke 12:14.

2. ***merismos*** (*3311*), akin to No. 1, primarily denotes "a division, partition" (***meros***, "a part"); hence, (a) "a distribution," Heb. 2:4, "gifts"; (b) likely means, "an active dividing or separation," Heb. 4:12.

## DIVINATION, (TO) DIVINE

### *Old Testament*

***qasam*** (7080), "to divine, practice divination." Divination was a pagan parallel to prophesying, and so forbidden, Deut. 18:10, 14–15. It is a seeking after the will of the gods, in an effort to learn their future action or divine blessing on some proposed future action, Josh. 13:22, likely demons, 1 Cor. 10:20. The pagan practice of divination might involve: sacrifice, Num. 23:1ff.; speaking to the spirits of the dead, 1 Sam. 28:8; shaking of arrows; or studying the livers of sacrificed animals, Ezek. 21:21.

### *New Testament*

***puthon*** (*4436*), (Eng., "python"), in Greek mythology was the name of the Pythian serpent or dragon, Acts 16:16; which here refers to being possessed by a demon instigating the cult of Apollo.

## DIVINE

### A. Adjective.

***theios*** (*2304*), "divine" (from ***theos***, "God"), is used of the power of God, 2 Pet. 1:3, and of His nature, v. 4, in each place, as that which proceeds from Himself. In Acts 17:29 it is used as a noun with the definite article, to denote "the Godhead," the Deity (i.e., the one true God). This word, instead of ***theos***, was purposely used by the apostle in speaking to Greeks on Mars Hill, as in accordance with Greek usage.

### B. Noun.

***latreia*** (*2999*), akin to ***latreuo***, "to serve," primarily, any service for hire denotes in Scripture the service of God according to the requirements of the Levitical Law, Rom. 9:4; Heb. 9:1, 6, "divine service." It is used in the more general sense of service to God, in John 16:2; Rom. 12:1.

## DIVINITY

***theiotes*** (*2305*), divinity, the RV rendering in Rom. 1:20 (KJV, "Godhead"), is derived from ***theios***, and is to be distinguished from ***theotes***, in Col. 2:9, "Godhead." In Rom. 1:20 the apostle "is declaring how much of God may be known from the revelation of Himself which He has made in nature, from those vestiges of Himself which men may everywhere trace in the world around them. Yet it is not the personal God whom any man may learn to know by these aids; He can be known only by the revelation of Himself in His Son; . . . But in the second passage, Col. 2:9, Paul is declaring that in the Son there dwells all the fullness of absolute Godhead."

## DIVORCE, DIVORCEMENT

### A. Verb.

***apoluo*** (*630*), "to let loose from, let go free" (***apo***, "from," ***luo***, "to loose"), is translated "is divorced" in the KJV of Matt. 5:32 (RV, "is put away"); it is further used of "divorce" in Matt. 1:19; 19:3, 7–9; Mark 10:2, 4 11; Luke 16:18. The Lord also used it of the case of a wife putting away her husband, Mark 10:12, a usage among Greeks and Romans, not among Jews.

### B. Noun.

***apostasion*** (*647*), primarily, "a defection," lit., "a standing off," denotes in the NT, "a writing or bill of divorcement," Matt. 5:31; 19:7; Mark 10:4.

## DOCTRINE

1. ***didache*** (*1322*), denotes "teaching," either (a) that which is taught, e.g., Matt. 7:28, KJV, "doctrine," RV, "teaching"; Titus 1:9, RV; Rev. 2:14–15, 24, or (b) the act of teaching, instruction, e.g., Mark 4:2, KJV, "doctrine," RV,

"teaching" the RV has "the doctrine" in Rom. 16:17.

2. ***didaskalia*** (*1319*) denotes, as No. 1 (from which, however, it is to be distinguished), (a) "that which is taught, doctrine," Matt. 15:9; Mark 7:7; Eph. 4:14; Col. 2:22; 1 Tim. 1:10; 4:1, 6; 6:1, 3; 2 Tim. 4:3; Titus 1:9 ("doctrine," in last part of verse: see also No. 1); 2:1, 10; (b) "teaching, instruction," Rom. 12:7, "teaching"; 15:4, "learning," 1 Tim. 4:13, KJV, "doctrine," RV, "teaching"; v. 16, KJV, "the doctrine," RV, (correctly) "thy teaching; 5:17, KJV, "doctrine," RV "teaching"; 2 Tim. 3:10, 16 ("doctrine"); Titus 2:7, "thy doctrine."

## DOG

1. ***kuon*** (*2965*) is used in two senses, (a) natural, Matt. 7:6; Luke 16:21; 2 Pet. 2:22; (b) metaphorical, Phil. 3:2; Rev. 22:15, of those whose moral impurity will exclude them from the New Jerusalem.

2. ***kunarion*** (*2952*), a diminutive of No. 1, "a little dog, a puppy," is used in Matt. 15:26–27; Mark 7:27, 28.

## DOMINION (have . . . over)

### A. Nouns.

1. ***kratos*** (*2904*), "force, strength, might," more especially "manifested power," is derived from a root ***kra***–, "to perfect, to complete": "creator" is probably connected. It also signifies "dominion," and is so rendered frequently in doxologies, 1 Pet. 4:11; 5:11; Jude 25; Rev. 1:6; 5:13 (RV); in 1 Tim. 6:16, and Heb. 2:14 it is translated "power."

2. ***kuriotes*** (*2963*) denotes "lordship" (***kurios***, "a lord"), "power, dominion," whether angelic or human, Eph. 1:21; Col. 1:16; 2 Pet. 2:10 (RV, for KJV, "government"); Jude 8. In Eph. and Col. it indicates a grade in the angelic orders, in which it stands second.

### B. Verbs.

1. ***kurieuo*** (*2961*), "to be lord over, rule over, have dominion over" (akin to A, No. 2), is used of (a) divine authority over men, Rom. 14:9, "might be Lord"; (b) human authority over men, Luke 22:25, "lordship," 1 Tim. 6:15, "lords"; (c) the permanent immunity of Christ from the "dominion" of death, Rom. 6:9; (d) the deliverance of the believer from the "dominion" of sin, Rom. 6:14; (e) the "dominion" of law over men, Rom. 7:1; (f) the "dominion" of a person over the faith of other believers, 2 Cor. 1:24 (RV, "lordship").

2. ***katakurieuo*** (*2634*), ***kata***, "down" (intensive), and No. 1, "to exercise, or gain, dominion over, to lord it over," is used of (a) the "lordship" of gentile rulers, Matt. 20:25, KJV, "exercise dominion," RV, "lord it," Mark 10:42, KJV, "exercise lordship," RV, "lord it"; (b) the power of demons over men, Acts 19:16, KJV, "overcame," RV, "mastered"; (c) of the evil of elders in "lording" it over the saints under their spiritual care, 1 Pet. 5:3.

## DOOR

***thura*** (*2374*), "a door, gate" (Eng., "door" is connected), is used (a) literally, e.g., Matt. 6:6; 27:60; (b) metaphorically, of Christ, John 10:7, 9; of faith, by acceptance of the gospel, Acts 14:27; of "openings" for preaching and teaching the Word of God, 1 Cor. 16:9; 2 Cor. 2:12; Col. 4:3; Rev. 3:8; of "entrance" into the Kingdom of God, Matt. 25:10; Luke 13:24–25; of Christ's "entrance" into a repentant believer's heart, Rev. 3:20; of the nearness of Christ's second advent, Matt. 24:33; Mark 13:29; cf. Jas. 5:9; of "access" to behold visions relative to the purposes of God, Rev. 4:1.

## DOTE

***noseo*** (*3552*) signifies "to be ill, to be ailing," whether in body or mind; hence, "to be taken with such a morbid interest in a thing as is tantamount to a disease, to dote," 1 Tim. 6:4.

## DOUBLE-MINDED

***dipsuchos*** (*1374*) lit. means "two-souled," hence, "double-minded," Jas. 1:8; 4:8.

## DOUBLE-TONGUED

***dilogos*** (*1351*) primarily means "saying the same thing twice, or given to repetition"; hence, "saying a thing to one person and giving a different view of it to another, double-tongued," 1 Tim. 3:8.

## DOUBT (be in, make to), DOUBTFUL, DOUBTING

### A. Verbs.

1. ***aporeo*** (*639*), always used in the middle voice, lit. means "to be without a way" (***a***, negative, ***poros***, "a way, transit"), "to be without resources, embarrassed, in doubt, perplexity, at a loss," as was Herod regarding John the Baptist, Mark 6:20 (RV, following the most authentic mss., "was much perplexed"); as the disciples were, regarding the Lord's betrayal, John 13:22, "doubting"; and regarding the absence of His body from the tomb, Luke 24:4, "were perplexed"; as was Festus, about the nature of the accusations brought against Paul, Acts 25:20, KJV "doubted," RV, "being perplexed"; as Paul was, in his experiences of trial

2 Cor. 4:8, "perplexed," and, as to the attitude of the believers of the churches in Galatia towards Judaistic errors, Gal. 4:20, KJV, "I stand in doubt," RV, "I am perplexed." Perplexity is the main idea.

2. ***diaporeo*** (*1280*), ***dia***, "asunder" (intensive), and No. 1, signifies "to be thoroughly perplexed," with a perplexity amounting to despair, Acts 2:12; 5:24 and 10:17, KJV, "were in doubt," "doubted," RV, "were (was) perplexed." See also Luke 9:7 (some mss. have it in Luke 24:4, where the most authentic have No. 1).

3. ***diakrino*** (*1252*): in Acts 11:12, KJV, "nothing doubting," RV, "making no distinction"; in Jude 22, RV, "who are in doubt"; in Jas. 1:6, KJV, "wavereth," RV, "doubteth." This verb suggests, not so much weakness of faith, as lack of it (contrast, Nos. 4 and 5).

4. ***distazo*** (*1365*), "to stand in two ways," implying "uncertainty which way to take," is used in Matt. 14:31 and 28:17; said of believers whose faith is small.

5. ***meteorizo*** (*3349*), (Eng., "meteor"), signifying "in mid air, raised on high," was primarily used of putting a ship out to sea, or of "raising" fortifications, in the NT used metaphorically, of "being anxious," through a "distracted" state of mind, of "wavering" between hope and fear, Luke 12:29.

6. ***psuchen airo***, lit., "to raise the breath, or to lift the soul," signifies "to hold in suspense," RV of John 10:24 (KJV, "make us to doubt"), suggestive of "an objective suspense due to lack of light," through a failure of their expectations, rather than, subjectively, through unbelief. The meaning may thus be, "How long dost Thou raise our expectations without satisfying them?"

### B. Noun.

***dialogismos*** (*1261*) expresses reasoning or questioning hesitation, 1 Tim. 2:8.

## DOVE, TURTLE-DOVE

1. ***peristera*** (*4058*) denotes "a dove or pigeon," Matt. 3:16; 10:16 (indicating its proverbial harmlessness); 21:12; Mark 1:10; 11:15; Luke 2:24 ("pigeons"); 3:22; John 1:32; 2:14, 16.

2. ***trugon*** (*5167*) denotes "a turtledove" (from ***truzo***, "to murmur, to coo"), Luke 2:24.

## DRAGON

***drakon*** (*1404*) denoted "a mythical monster, a dragon"; also a large serpent, so called because of its keen power of sight (from a root ***derk***—, signifying "to see"). Twelve times in the Apocalypse it is used of the Devil 12:3–4, 7, 9, 13, 16–17; 13:2, 4, 11; 16:13; 20:2.

## DRAW (Away, Back, Nigh, On, Out, Up)

(A) *In the sense of "dragging, pulling, or attracting":*

1. ***spao*** (*4685*), "to draw or pull," is used, in the middle voice of "drawing" a sword from its sheath, Mark 11:47; Acts 16:27.

2. ***anaspao*** (*385*), ***ana***, "up," and No. 1, "to draw up," is used of "drawing" up an animal out of a pit, Luke 14:5 (RV, "draw up"; KJV, "pull out"), and of the "drawing" up of the sheet into heaven, in the vision in Acts 11:10.

3. ***apospao*** (*645*), ***apo***, "from," and No. 1, "to draw away," lit., "to wrench away from," is used of a sword, Matt. 26:51, of "drawing" away disciples into error, Acts 20:30; of Christ's "withdrawal" from the disciples, in Gethsemane, Luke 22:41, KJV, "was withdrawn," RV, "was parted" (or "was reft away from them"); of "parting" from a company, Acts 21:1 (KJV, "were gotten," RV, "were parted").

4. ***antleo*** (*501*) signified, primarily, "to draw out a ship's bilgewater, to bale or pump out" (from ***antlos***, "bilge-water"), hence, "to draw water" in any way (***ana***, "up" and a root, ***tel***—, "to lift, bear"), John 2:8–9; 4:7, 15.

5. ***exelko*** (*1828*), "to draw away, or lure forth," is used metaphorically in Jas. 1:14, of being "drawn away" by lust. As in hunting or fishing the game is "lured" from its haunt, so man's lust "allures" him from the safety of his self-restraint.

9. ***anatassomai*** (*392*), "to arrange in order," is used in Luke 1:1, RV, "to draw up."

(B) *In the sense of "approaching or withdrawing":*

1. ***engizo*** (*1448*), "to come near, draw nigh" (akin to ***engus***, "near"), is translated by the verb "draw near or nigh," in the RV, Luke 12:33, KJV, "approacheth"; Heb. 10:25, KJV, "approaching"; Luke 18:35; 19:29, 37; Acts 22:6, KJV, "was come nigh"; Luke 7:12 "came nigh"; Acts 9:3, "came near."

2. ***proserchomai*** (*4334*) is translated "draw near" in Heb. 4:16; 7:25, RV, and 10:22, KJV and RV; in Acts 7:31, "drew near."

3. ***prosago*** (*4317*), used transitively, "to bring to"; intransitively, "to draw near," is so rendered in Acts 27:27.

4. ***hupostello*** (*5288*), "to draw back, withdraw," perhaps a metaphor from lowering a sail and so slackening the course, and hence of being remiss in holding the truth; in the active voice, rendered "drew back" in Gal. 2:12, RV (KJV, "withdrew"); in the middle, in Heb. 10:38, "shrink back" RV (KJV, "draw back"); the prefix ***hupo***, "underneath," is here suggestive of stealth. In v. 39 the correspond-

ing noun, ***hupostole***, is translated "of them that shrink back," RV; KJV, "draw back" (lit., "of shrinking back"). In Acts 20:20, 27, "shrank," RV.

5. ***epiphosko*** (*2020*), "to dawn" (lit., "to make to shine upon"), is said of the approach of the Sabbath, Luke 23:54; cf. Matt. 28:1.

## DREAM (noun and verb), DREAMER

### *Old Testament*

**A. Noun.**

***chalom*** (2472), "dream." It is used of the ordinary dreams of sleep, Job 7:14. The most significant use of this word, however, is with reference to prophetic "dreams" and/or "visions," Deut. 13:1ff.

**B. Verb.**

***chalam*** (2492), "to become healthy or strong; to dream." The meaning, "to become healthy," applies only to animals though "to dream" is used of human dreams, Gen. 28:12.

### *New Testament*

**A. Nouns.**

1. ***onar*** (*3677*) is "a vision in sleep," in distinction from a waking vision, Matt. 1:20; 2:12–13, 19, 22; 27:19.

2. ***enupnion*** (*1798*), is, lit., "what appears in sleep," an ordinary "dream," Acts 2:17.

**B. Verb.**

***enupniazo*** (*1797*), akin to A, No. 2, is used in Acts 2:17, in the passive voice in a phrase (according to the most authentic mss.) which means "shall be given up to dream by dreams," translated "shall dream dreams" metaphorically in Jude 8, of being given over to sensuous "dreamings."

## DRIFT

***pararheo*** (*3901*), lit., "to flow past, glide by," is used in Heb. 2:1, where the significance is to find oneself "flowing" or "passing by," without giving due heed to a thing, here "the things that were heard," or perhaps the salvation of which they spoke; hence the RV, "lest haply we drift away from them," for KJV, "let them slip."

## DRUNK, (-EN, be), DRUNKARD, DRUNKENNESS

### *Old Testament*

***shatah*** (8354) means "to drink," related to both creatures and things Gen. 9:21; 24:19; Ps. 50:13. Priests were commanded to practice a partial fast when they served before God—they were not to drink wine or strong drink, Lev. 10:9. They and all Israel were to eat no unclean thing. These conditions were stricter for Nazirites, who lived constantly before God, Num. 6:3; cf. Judg. 13:4; 1 Sam. 1:15. The phrase, "eating and drinking," may also signify life in general; 1 Kings 4:20; cf. Eccl. 2:24; 5:18; Jer. 22:15.

### *New Testament*

**A. Verbs.**

1. ***methuo*** (*3184*) signifies "to be drunk with wine" (from ***methu***, "mulled wine"; hence Eng., "mead, honey-wine"); originally it denoted simply "a pleasant drink." The verb is used of "being intoxicated" in Matt. 24:49; Acts 2:15; 1 Cor. 11:21; 1 Thess. 5:7*b*; metaphorically, of the effect upon men of partaking of the abominations of the Babylonish system, Rev. 17:2; of being in a state of mental "intoxication," through the shedding of men's blood profusely, v. 6.

2. ***methusko*** (*3182*) signifies "to make drunk, or to grow drunk" (an inceptive verb, marking the process or the state expressed in No. 1), "to become intoxicated," Luke 12:45; Eph. 5:18; 1 Thess. 5:7*a*.

**B. Adjective.**

***methusos*** (*3183*), "drunken," is used as noun, in the singular, in 1 Cor. 5:11, and in the plural, in 6:10, "drunkard," "drunkards."

**C. Noun.**

***methe*** (*3178*), "strong drink" (akin to ***methu***, "wine," see under A. 1, above), denotes "drunkenness, habitual intoxication," Luke 21:34; Rom. 13:13; Gal. 5:21.

## DULL

**A. Adjective.**

***nothros*** (*3576*), "slow, sluggish, indolent, dull" (the etymology is uncertain), is translated "dull" in Heb. 5:11 (in connection with ***akoe***, "hearing"; lit., "in hearings"); "sluggish," in 6:12.

**B. Adverb.**

***bareos*** (*917*), "heavily, with difficulty" (***barus***, "heavy"), is used with ***akouo***, "to hear," in Matt. 13:15, and Acts 28:27, from Isa. 6:10, lit., "to hear heavily, to be dull of hearing."

## DUMB

**A. Adjectives.**

1. ***alalos*** (*216*), lit., "speechless," is found in Mark 7:37; 9:17, 25.

2. ***aphonos*** (*880*), lit., "voiceless, or soundless," has reference to voice, Acts 8:32; 1 Cor.

12:2; 2 Pet. 2:16, while ***alalos*** has reference to words. In 1 Cor. 14:10 it is used metaphorically of the significance of voices or sounds, "without signification."

**B. Verb.**

***siopao*** (*4623*), from ***siope***, "silence, to be silent," is used of Zacharias' "dumbness," Luke 1:20.

## DUNG

1. ***skubalon*** (*4657*) denotes "refuse," whether (a) "excrement," that which is cast out from the body, or (b) "the leavings of a feast," that which is thrown away from the table, Phil. 3:8.

2. ***koprion*** (*2874d*), "manure," Luke 13:8, used in the plural with ***ballo***, "to throw," is translated by the verb "to dung." Some mss. have the accusative case of the noun ***kopria***, "a dunghill."

## DWELL, DWELLERS, DWELLING (place)

### *Old Testament*

**A. Verbs.**

***yashab*** (3427), "to dwell, sit, abide, inhabit, remain." ***yashab*** is first used in Gen. 4:16, in its most common connotation of "to dwell." The word has the sense of "to remain"; Gen. 38:11; and it is used of God in a similar sense, Lam. 5:19.

***yashab*** is sometimes combined with other words to form expressions in common usage. For example, Deut. 17:18; cf. 1 Kings 1:13, 17, 24 carries the meaning "begins to reign"; or "to decide a case," Ruth 4:1–2. "Sit thou at my right hand," Ps. 110:1, means to assume a ruling position as deputy. "There will I sit to judge all the heathen," Joel 3:12, was a promise of eschatological judgment. "To sit in the dust" or "to sit on the ground," Isa. 47:1, was a sign of humiliation and grief.

***yashab*** is often used figuratively of God. The sentences, "I saw the Lord sitting on his throne," 1 Kings 22:19; "He that sitteth in the heavens shall laugh," Ps. 2:4; and "God sitteth upon the throne of his holiness," Ps. 47:8, all describe God as the exalted Ruler over the universe.

The word is also used to describe man's being in God's presence, Ps. 27:4; cf. Ps. 23:6; Exod. 15:17.

***shakan*** (7931), "to dwell, inhabit, settle down, abide." ***shakan*** is first used in the sense of "to dwell" in Gen. 9:27; and of God, Exod. 25:8. ***shakan*** is a word from nomadic life, meaning "to live in a tent.," Num. 24:2, where it refers to temporary "camping," but it can also refer to being permanently "settled," Ps. 102:28. God promised to give Israel security, 2 Sam. 7:10.

**B. Noun.**

***mishkan*** (4908), "dwelling place; tent." This word occurs nearly 140 times, and often refers to the wilderness "tabernacle," Exod. 25:9. ***mishkan*** was also used later to refer to the "temple." This usage probably prepared the way for the familiar term ***shekinah***.

**C. Participle.**

***yashab*** (3427), "remaining; inhabitant." This participle is sometimes used as a simple adjective: ". . . Jacob was a plain man, *dwelling* in tents," Gen. 25:27. But the word is more often used as in Gen. 19:25: ". . . All the *inhabitants* of the cities."

### *New Testament*

**A. Verbs.**

1. ***oikeo*** (*3611*), "to dwell" (from ***oikos***, "a house"), "to inhabit as one's abode," is derived from the Sanskrit, ***vic***, "a dwelling place" (the Eng. termination "—wick" is connected). It is used (a) of God as "dwelling" in light, 1 Tim. 6:16; (b) of the "indwelling" of the Spirit of God in the believer, Rom. 8:9, 11, or in a church, 1 Cor. 3:16; (c) of the "indwelling" of sin, Rom. 7:20; (d) of the absence of any good thing in the flesh of the believer, Rom. 7:18; (e) of the "dwelling" together of those who are married, 1 Cor. 7:12–13.

2. ***katoikeo*** (*2730*), ***kata***, "down," and No. 1, the most frequent verb with this meaning, properly signifies "to settle down in a dwelling, to dwell fixedly in a place." Besides its literal sense, it is used of (a) the "indwelling" of the totality of the attributes and powers of the Godhead in Christ, Col. 1:19; 2:9; (b) the "indwelling" of Christ in the hearts of believers ("may make a home in your hearts"), Eph. 3:17; (c) the "dwelling" of Satan in a locality, Rev. 2:13; (d) the future "indwelling" of righteousness in the new heavens and earth, 2 Pet. 3:13. It is translated "dwellers" in Acts 1:19; 2:9; "inhabitants" in Rev. 17:2, KJV (RV, "they that dwell"), "inhabiters" in Rev. 8:13 and 12:12, KJV (RV, "them that dwell").

3. ***katoikizo*** (*2730*), "to cause to dwell," is said of the act of God concerning the Holy Spirit in Jas. 4:5, RV (some mss. have No. 2).

4. ***enoikeo*** (*1774*), lit., "to dwell in" (***en***, "in," and No. 1), is used, with a spiritual significance only, of (a) the "indwelling" of God in believers, 2 Cor. 6:16; (b) the "indwelling" of the

Holy Spirit, Rom. 8:11; 2 Tim. 1:14; (c) the "indwelling" of the Word of Christ, Col. 3:16; (d) the "indwelling" of faith, 2 Tim. 1:5; (e) the "indwelling" of sin in the believer, Rom. 7:17.

5. ***perioikeo*** *(4039)*, ***peri***, "around," and No. 1, "to dwell around, be a neighbor," is used in Luke 1:65.

6. ***sunoikeo*** *(4924)*, ***sun***, "with," and No. 1, "to dwell with," is used in 1 Pet. 3:7.

7. ***enkatoikeo*** *(1460)*, ***en***, "in," and No. 2, "to dwell among," is used in 2 Pet. 2:8.

8. ***meno*** *(3306)*, "to abide, remain," is translated "to dwell," in the KJV of John 1:38–39; 6:56; 14:10, 17; Acts 28:16. The RV adheres throughout to the verb "to abide."

9. ***skenoo*** *(4637)*, "to pitch a tent" (***skene***), "to tabernacle," John 1:14; Rev. 7:15; 12:12; 13:6; 21:3.

10. ***kataskenoo*** *(2681)*, "to pitch one's tent" (***kata***, "down," ***skene***, "a tent"), is translated "lodge" in Matt. 13:32; Mark 4:32; Luke 13:19; in Acts 2:26, RV, "dwell," KJV, "rest."

## B. Nouns.

1. ***paroikia*** *(3940)* denotes "a sojourning," Acts 13:17, lit., "in the sojourning," translated "when they sojourned," RV (KJV, "dwelt as strangers"); in 1 Pet. 1:17, "sojourning."

2. ***katoikesis*** *(2731)*, akin to A, No. 2, "a dwelling, a habitation," is used in Mark 5:3.

# E

## EACH OTHER

***allelon*** (*240*), a reciprocal pronoun, preceded by the preposition ***meta***, "with," signifies "with each other," Luke 23:12, RV, for KJV, "together." Similarly in 24:14 ***pros allelous***, where ***pros*** suggests greater intimacy.

## EAGLE

***aetos*** (*105*), "an eagle" (also a vulture), is perhaps connected with ***aemi***, "to blow," as of the wind, on account of its wind-like flight. In Matt. 24:28 and Luke 17:37 the vultures are probably intended. The "eagle" is mentioned elsewhere in the NT in Rev. 4:7; 8:13 (RV); 12:14. There are eight species in Palestine.

## EAR (of the body)

1. ***ous*** (*3775*), Latin ***auris***, Hebrew ***'ozen*** (241), is used (a) of the physical organ, e.g., Luke 4:21; Acts 7:57; in Acts 11:22, in the plural with ***akouo***, "to hear," lit., "was heard into the ears of someone," i.e., came to the knowledge of; similarly, in the singular, Matt. 10:27, in familiar private conversation; in Jas. 5:4 the phrase is used with ***eiserchomai***, "to enter into"; in Luke 1:44, with ***ginomai***, "to become, to come"; in Luke 12:3, with ***lalein***, "to speak" and ***pros***, "to"; (b) metaphorically, of the faculty of perceiving with the mind, understanding and knowing, Matt. 13:16; frequently with ***akouo***, "to hear," e.g., Matt. 11:15; 13:9, 43; Rev. 2 and 3, at the close of each of the messages to the churches, in Matt. 13:15 and Acts 28:27, with ***bareos***, "heavily," of being slow to understand and obey; with a negative in Mark 8:18; Rom. 11:8; in Luke 9:44 the lit. meaning is "put those words into your ears," i.e., take them into your mind and keep them there; in Acts 7:51 it is used with ***aperitmetos***, "uncircumcised." As seeing is metaphorically associated with conviction, so hearing is with obedience (***hupakoe***, lit., "hearing under"; the Eng., "obedience" is etymologically "hearing over against," i.e., with response in the hearer).

2. ***otion*** (*5621*), a diminutive of No. 1, but without the diminutive force, it being a common tendency in everyday speech to apply a diminutive form to most parts of the body, is used in Matt. 26:51; Mark 14:47 (in some mss.); Luke 22:51; John 18:10 (in some mss.) and v. 26, all with reference to the "ear" of Malchus.

3. ***akoe*** (*189*), "hearing," denotes (a) the sense of "hearing," e.g., 1 Cor. 12:17; 2 Pet. 2:8; (b) that which is "heard," a report, e.g., Matt. 4:24; (c) the physical organ, Mark 7:35, standing for the sense of "hearing"; so in Luke 7:1, RV, for KJV, "audience"; Acts 17:20; 2 Tim. 4:3–4 (in v. 3, lit., "being tickled as to the ears"); (d) a message or teaching, John 12:38; Rom. 10:16–17; Gal. 3:2, 5; 1 Thess. 2:13; Heb. 4:2, RV, "(the word) of hearing," for KJV, "(the word) preached."

## EARNEST (Noun)

***arrabon*** (*728*), originally, "earnest-money" deposited by the purchaser and forfeited if the purchase was not completed, was probably a Phoenician word, introduced into Greece. In general usage it came to denote "a pledge" or "earnest" of any sort; in the NT it is used only of that which is assured by God to believers; it is said of the Holy Spirit as the divine "pledge" of all their future blessedness, 2 Cor. 1:22; 5:5; in Eph. 1:14, particularly of their eternal inheritance.

## EARNEST, EARNESTNESS, EARNESTLY

### A. Noun.

***spoude*** (*4710*), "to hasten," denotes "haste," Mark 6:25; Luke 1:39; hence, "earnestness," 2 Cor. 8:7, RV, for KJV, "diligence," and v. 8, for KJV, "forwardness"; in 7:12, "earnest care," for KJV, "care"; in 8:16, earnest care.

### B. Adjective.

***spoudaios*** (*4705*), akin to A, denotes "active, diligent, earnest," 2 Cor. 8:22 RV, "earnest," for KJV, "diligent"; in the latter part of the verse the comparative degree, ***spoudaioteros***, is used, RV, "more earnest," for KJV, "more diligent"; in v. 17, RV, in the superlative sense, "very earnest," for KJV, "more forward."

### C. Adverbs.

1. ***ektenos*** (*1619*), "earnestly" (***ek***, "out," ***teino***, "to stretch"; Eng., "tension," etc.), is used in Acts 12:5, "earnestly," RV, for KJV, "without ceasing" (some mss. have the adjective ***ektenes***, "earnest"); in 1 Pet. 1:22, "fervently." The idea suggested is that of not relaxing in effort, or acting in a right spirit.

2. ***ektenesteron*** (*1617*), the comparative degree of No. 1, used as an adverb in this neuter

form, denotes "more earnestly, fervently," Luke 22:44.

3. ***spoudaios*** (*4709*), akin to B, signifies "with haste," or "with zeal, earnestly," Luke 7:4, RV, "earnestly," for KJV, "instantly"; in 2 Tim. 1:17, RV, and Titus 3:13, "diligently"; in Phil. 2:28, the comparative ***spoudaioteros***, RV, "the more diligently," KJV, "the more carefully."

**D. Adverbial Phrase.**

***en ekteneia***, lit., "in earnestness," cf. C, No. 1, is translated "earnestly" in Acts 26:7, RV, for KJV, "instantly."

## EARTH

### *Old Testament*

***'erets*** (776), "earth; land." ***'erets*** may be translated "earth," the temporal scene of human activity, experience, and history. The material world had a beginning when God "made the earth by His power," "formed it," and "spread it out," Isa. 40:28; 42:5; 45:12, 18; Jer. 27:5; 51:15. Because He did so, it follows that "the earth is the Lord's," Ps. 24:1; Deut. 10:1; Exod. 9:29; Neh. 9:6.

God formed the earth to be inhabited, Isa. 45:18. Having "authority over the earth" by virtue of being its Maker, He decreed to "let the earth sprout vegetation: of every kind," Job 34:13; Gen. 1:11. It was never to stop its productivity, for "while the earth stands, seedtime and harvest, and cold and heat, and summer and winter, and day and night shall not cease," Gen. 8:22. "The earth is full of God's riches" and mankind can "multiply and fill the earth and subdue it," Ps. 104:24; Gen. 1:28; 9:1. Let no one think that the earth is an independent, self-contained mechanism, for "the Lord reigns" as He "sits on the vault of the earth" from where "He sends rain on the earth," Ps. 97:1; Isa. 40:22; 1 Kings 17:14; Ps. 104:4. What the Creator formed "in the beginning" is also to have an end, for He will "create a new heaven and a new earth," Isa. 65:17; 66:22.

The Hebrew word ***'erets*** also occurs frequently in the phrase "heaven and earth" or "earth and heaven." In other words, the Scriptures teach that our terrestrial planet is a part of an all-embracing cosmological framework which we call the universe, Ps. 121:2; 124:8; 134:3. ***'erets*** also means a smaller part of the whole earth, translated by words like *land*, *country*, *ground*, and *soil*, which transfer its meanings into our language. Quite frequently, it refers to an area occupied by a nation or tribe, Gen. 47:13; Zech. 2:5; 2 Kings 5:2, 4; Judg. 21:21.

The Hebrew noun may also be translated "the ground," Job 2:13; Amos 3:5; Gen. 24:52; Ezek. 43:14. When God executes judgment, "He brings down the wicked to the ground," Ps. 147:6, NASB.

### *New Testament*

1. ***ge*** (*1093*) denotes (a) "earth as arable land," e.g., Matt. 13:5, 8, 23; in 1 Cor. 15:47 it is said of the "earthly" material of which "the first man" was made, suggestive of frailty; (b) "the earth as a whole, the world," in contrast, whether to the heavens, e.g., Matt. 5:18, 35, or to heaven, the abode of God, e.g., Matt. 6:19, where the context suggests the "earth" as a place characterized by mutability and weakness; in Col. 3:2 the same contrast is presented by the word "above"; in John 3:31 (RV, "of the earth," for KJV, "earthly") it describes one whose origin and nature are "earthly" and whose speech is characterized thereby, in contrast with Christ as the One from heaven; in Col. 3:5 the physical members are said to be "upon the earth," as a sphere where, as potential instruments of moral evils, they are, by metonymy, spoken of as the evils themselves; (c) "the inhabited earth," e.g., Luke 21:35; Acts 1:8; 8:33; 10:12; 11:6; 17:26; 22:22; Heb. 11:13; Rev. 13:8. In the following the phrase "on the earth" signifies "among men," Luke 12:49; 18:8; John 17:4, (d) "a country, territory," e.g. Luke 4:25; John 3:22; (e) "the ground," e.g., Matt. 10:29; Mark 4:26, RV, "(upon the) earth," for KJV, "(into the) ground"; (f) "land," e.g., Mark 4:1; John 21:8–9, 11. Cf. Eng. words beginning with *ge*—, e.g., "geodetic," "geodesy," "geology," "geometry," "geography."

2. ***oikoumene*** (*3625*), the present participle, passive voice, of ***oikeo***, "to dwell, inhabit," denotes the "inhabited earth." It is translated "world" in every place where it has this significance, except in Luke 21:26, KJV, where it is translated "earth."

## EARTHEN, EARTHLY, EARTHY

1. ***ostrakinos*** (*3749*) signifies "made of earthenware or clay," 2 Tim. 2:20, "of earth"; 2 Cor. 4:7, "earthen."

2. ***epigeios*** (*1919*), "on earth," is rendered "earthly" in John 3:12; 2 Cor. 5:1; Phil. 3:19; Jas. 3:15; in Phil. 2:10, "on earth," RV; "terrestrial" in 1 Cor. 15:40 (twice).

3. ***choikos*** (*5517*) denotes "earthy," made of earth, from ***chous***, "soil, earth thrown down or heaped up," 1 Cor. 15:47–49.

4. ***katachthonios*** (*2709*), "under the earth, subterranean" (***kata***, "down," ***chthon***, "the ground," from a root signifying that which is deep), is used in Phil. 2:10.

## EASE, EASED

**A. Verb.**

***anapauo*** (*373*) signifies "to cause or permit one to cease from any labor or movement" so as to recover strength. It implies previous toil and care. Its chief significance is that of taking, or causing to take, rest; it is used in the middle voice in Luke 12:19, "take (thine) ease," indicative of unnecessary, self-indulgent relaxation. In the papyri it is used technically, as an agricultural term.

**B. Noun.**

***anesis*** (*425*) denotes "a letting loose, relaxation, easing"; it is connected with ***aniemi***, "to loosen, relax" (***ana***, "back," and ***hiemi***, "to send"). It signifies "rest," not from toil, but from endurance and suffering. Thus it is said (a) of a "less vigorous" condition in imprisonment, Acts 24:23, "indulgence," AV, "liberty"; (b) "relief" from anxiety, 2 Cor. 2:13; 7:5, "relief" (KJV, "rest"), (c) "relief" from persecutions, 2 Thess. 1:7, "rest"; (d) of "relief" from the sufferings of poverty, 2 Cor. 8:13, "be eased," lit., "(that there should be) easing for others (trouble to you)."

## EAST

***anatole*** (*395*), primarily "a rising," as of the sun and stars, corresponds to ***anatello***, "to make to rise," or, intransitively, "to arise," which is also used of the sunlight, as well as of other objects in nature. In Luke 1:78 it is used metaphorically of Christ as "the Dayspring," the One through whom light came into the world, shining immediately into Israel, to dispel the darkness which was upon all nations. Cf. Mal. 4:2. Elsewhere it denotes the "east," as the quarter of the sun's rising, Matt. 2:1–2, 9; 8:11; 24:27; Luke 13:29; Rev. 7:2; 16:12; 21:13. The "east" in general stands for that side of things upon which the rising of the sun gives light. In the heavenly city itself, Rev. 21:13, the reference to the "east" gate points to the outgoing of the influence of the city "eastward."

## EASTER

***pascha*** (*3957*), mistranslated "Easter" in Acts 12:4, KJV, denotes the Passover (RV). The phrase "after the Passover" signifies after the whole festival was at an end. The term "Easter" is not of Christian origin. It is another form of *Astarte*, one of the titles of the Chaldean goddess, the queen of heaven. The festival of Pasch held by Christians in post-apostolic times was a continuation of the Jewish feast, but was not instituted by Christ, nor was it connected with Lent. From this Pasch the pagan festival of "Easter" was quite distinct and was introduced into the apostate Western religion, as part of the attempt to adapt pagan festivals to Christianity.

## EASY, EASIER, EASILY

1. ***chrestos*** (*5543*) primarily signifies "fit for use, able to be used" (akin to ***chraomai***, "to use"), hence, "good, virtuous, mild, pleasant" (in contrast to what is hard, harsh, sharp, bitter). It is said (a) of the character of God as "kind, gracious," Luke 6:35; 1 Pet. 2:3; "good," Rom. 2:4, where the neuter of the adjective is used as a noun, "the goodness"; of the yoke of Christ, Matt. 11:30, "easy" (a suitable rendering would be "kindly"); (c) of believers, Eph. 4:32; (d) of things, as wine, Luke 5:39.

2. ***eukopoteros*** (*2123*), the comparative degree of ***eukopos***, "easy, with easy labor," hence, of that which is "easier to do," is found in the Synoptics only, Matt. 9:5; 19:24; Mark 2:9; 10:25; Luke 5:23; 16:17; 18:25.

## EAT, EAT WITH, EATING

### *Old Testament*

**A. Verb.**

***'akal*** (398), "to eat, feed, consume, devour." Essentially, this root refers to the "consumption of food by man or animals," Gen. 3:6. The function of eating is presented along with seeing, hearing, and smelling as one of the basic functions of living, Deut. 4:28. Before Christ, certain foods could not be eaten, Gen. 1:29; 9:3; Lev. 11; Deut. 14. This verb is often used figuratively, "to destroy," Gen. 3:17; Isa. 1:7; Deut. 18:1; Isa. 3:10.

The word can refer not only to "eating" but to the entire concept "room and board," 2 Sam. 9:11, 13, the special act of "feasting," Eccl. 10:16, or the entire activity of "earning a living," Amos 7:12; cf. Gen. 3:19. "To eat another's flesh," used figuratively, means "killing him," Ps. 27:2.

Unlike the pagan deities, Deut. 32:37–38, God "eats" no food, Ps. 50:13; although as a "consuming" fire, Deut. 4:24, He is ready to defend His own honor and glory. He "consumes" evil and the sinner.

**B. Noun.**

***'okel*** (400), "food," as that which is physically consumed, Gen. 41:35; Ps. 104:21; 145:15. A related noun, ***'aklah***, also means "food."

### *New Testament*

**A. Verbs.**

1. ***esthio*** (*2068*) signifies "to eat" (as distinct from ***pino***, "to drink"); cf. Eng., "edible"; in

Heb. 10:27, metaphorically, "devour"; it is said of the ordinary use of food and drink, 1 Cor. 9:7; 11:22; of partaking of food at table, e.g., Mark 2:16; of reveling, Matt. 24:49; Luke 12:45.

2. ***phago*** (*5315*), "to eat, devour, consume," is obsolete in the present and other tenses, but supplies certain tenses which are wanting in No. 1, above. In Luke 8:55 the KJV has "(to give her) meat," the RV "(that something be given her) to eat." The idea that this verb combines both "eating" and "drinking," while No. 1 differentiates the one from the other, is not borne out in the NT. The word is very frequent in the Gospels and is used eleven times in 1 Cor. See also No. 3.

3. ***trogo*** (*5176*), primarily, "to gnaw, to chew," stresses the slow process; it is used metaphorically of the habit of spiritually feeding upon Christ, John 6:54, 56–58 (the aorists here do not indicate a definite act, but view a series of acts seen in perspective); of the constant custom of "eating" in certain company, John 13:18; of a practice unduly engrossing the world, Matt. 24:38.

4. ***geuo*** (*1089*), primarily, "to cause to taste, to give one a taste of," is used in the middle voice and denotes (a) "to taste," its usual meaning; (b) "to take food, to eat," Acts 10:10; 20:11; 23:14; the meaning to taste must not be pressed in these passages, the verb having acquired the more general meaning. As to whether Acts 20:11 refers to the Lord's Supper or to an ordinary meal, the addition of the words "and eaten" is perhaps a sufficient indication that the latter is referred to here, whereas v. 7, where the single phrase "to break bread" is used, refers to the Lord's Supper. A parallel instance is found in Acts 2:43, 46. In the former verse the phrase "the breaking of bread," unaccompanied by any word about taking food, clearly stands for the Lord's Supper; whereas in v. 46 the phrase "breaking bread at home" is immediately explained by "they did take their food," indicating their ordinary meals.

5. ***bibrosko*** (*977*), "to eat," is derived from a root, ***bor–***, "to devour" (likewise seen in the noun ***broma***, "food, meat"; cf. Eng., "carnivorous," "voracious," from Lat. ***vorax***). This verb is found in John 6:13. The difference between this and ***phago***, No. 2, above, may be seen perhaps in the fact that whereas in the Lord's question to Philip in v. 5, ***phago*** intimates nothing about a full supply, the verb ***bibrosko***, in v. 13, indicates that the people had been provided with a big meal, of which they had partaken eagerly.

6. ***sunesthio*** (*4906*), "to eat with," is found in Luke 15:2; Acts 10:41; 11:3; 1 Cor. 5:11; Gal. 2:12.

### B. Nouns.

1. ***brosis*** (*1035*), akin to A, No. 5, denotes (a) "the act of eating," e.g., Rom. 14:17; said of rust, Matt. 6:19–20; or, more usually (b) "that which is eaten, food" (like ***broma***, "food"), "meat," John 4:32; 6:27, 55; Col. 2:16; Heb. 12:16 ("morsel of meat"); "food," 2 Cor. 9:10; "eating," 1 Cor. 8:4.

2. ***prosphagion*** (*4371*), primarily "a dainty or relish" (especially cooked fish), to be eaten with bread (***pros***, "to," and A, No. 2), then, "fish" in general, is used in John 21:5.

### C. Adjective.

***brosimos*** (*1034*), akin to A, No. 5, and B., signifying "eatable," is found in Luke 24:41, RV, appropriately, "to eat," for the KJV, "meat."

## EDIFICATION, EDIFY, EDIFYING

### A. Noun.

***oikodome*** (*3619*) denotes (a) "the act of building" (***oikos***, "a home," and ***demo***, "to build"); this is used only figuratively in the NT, in the sense of edification, the promotion of spiritual growth (lit., "the things of building up"), Rom. 14:19; 15:2; 1 Cor. 14:3, 5, 12, 26, e.g.; (b) "a building, edifice," whether material, Matt. 24:1, e.g., or figurative, of the future body of the believer, 2 Cor. 5:1, or of a local church, 1 Cor. 3:9, or the whole church, "the body of Christ," Eph. 2:21.

### B. Verb.

***oikodomeo*** (*3618*), lit., "to build a house" (see above), (a) usually signifies "to build," whether literally, or figuratively; the present participle, lit., "the (ones) building," is used as a noun, "the builders," in Matt. 21:42; Mark 12:10; Luke 20:17; Acts 4:11 (in some mss.; the most authentic have the noun ***oikodomos***;) 1 Pet. 2:7; (b) is used metaphorically, in the sense of "edifying," promoting the spiritual growth and development of character of believers, by teaching or by example, suggesting such spiritual progress as the result of patient labor. It is said (1) of the effect of this upon local churches, Acts 9:31; 1 Cor. 14:4; (2) of the individual action of believers towards each other, 1 Cor. 8:1; 10:23; 14:17; 1 Thess. 5:11; (3) of an individual in regard to himself, 1 Cor. 14:4. In 1 Cor. 8:10, where it is translated "emboldened," the apostle uses it with pathetic irony, of the action of a brother in "building up" his brother who had a weak conscience, causing him to compromise his scruples; "strengthened," or "confirmed," would be suitable renderings.

## EFFECT (of none)

1. ***akuroo*** *(208)* signifies "to render void, deprive of force and authority." It is used of making "void" the Word of God, Matt. 15:6; Mark 7:13 (KJV, "making of none effect"), and of the promise of God to Abraham as not being deprived of authority by the Law 430 years after, Gal. 3:17.

2. ***katargeo*** *(2673)*, "to reduce to inactivity, to render useless," is translated "to make of none effect," in Rom. 3:3, 31; 4:14; Gal. 3:17.

3. ***kenoo*** *(2758)*, "to make empty, to empty," is translated "should be made of none effect" in 1 Cor. 1:17, KJV (RV "made void"); it is used (a) of the Cross of Christ, there; (b) of Christ, in emptying Himself, Phil. 2:7; (c) of faith, Rom. 4:14; (d) of the apostle Paul's glorying in the gospel ministry, 1 Cor. 9:15; (e) of his glorying on behalf of the church at Corinth, 2 Cor. 9:3.

## EFFECTUAL

**A. Adjective.**

***energes*** *(1756)* denotes "active, powerful in action" (***en***, "in," ***ergon***, "work"; Eng. "energy"; the word "work" is derived from the same root). It is translated "effectual" in 1 Cor. 16:9, of the door opened for the gospel in Ephesus, and made "effectual" in the results of entering it; and in Philem. 6, of the fellowship of Philemon's faith "in the knowledge of every good thing" (RV). In Heb. 4:12 it describes the Word of God as "active," RV (KJV, "powerful"), i.e., full of power to achieve results.

**B. Verb.**

***energeo*** *(1754)*, "to put forth power, be operative, to work" (its usual meaning), is rendered by the verb "to work effectually," or "to be effectual," in the KJV of 2 Cor. 1:6; Gal. 2:8 and 1 Thess. 2:13; in each case the RV translates it by the simple verb "to work" (past tense, "wrought"). In Jas. 5:16 the RV omits the superfluous word "effectual," and translates the sentence "the supplication of a righteous man availeth much in its working," the verb being in the present participial form. Here the meaning may be "in its inworking," i.e., in the effect produced in the praying man, bringing him into line with the will of God, as in the case of Elijah.

## EFFEMINATE

***malakos*** *(3120)*, "soft, soft to the touch" (Lat., ***mollis***, Eng., "mollify," "emollient," etc.), is used (a) of clothing, Matt. 11:8 (twice); Luke 7:25; (b) metaphorically, in a bad sense, 1 Cor. 6:9, "effeminate," not simply of a male who practices forms of lewdness, but persons in general, who are guilty of addiction to sins of the flesh, voluptuous.

## EFFULGENCE

***apaugasma*** *(541)*, "radiance, effulgence," is used of light shining from a luminous body (***apo***, "from," and ***auge***, "brightness"). The word is found in Heb. 1:3, where it is used of the Son of God as "being the effulgence of His glory."

E

## ELDER, ELDEST

### *Old Testament*

***zaqen*** (2204, 2205), "old man; old woman; elder; old," can refer to a person of old age, one in the very latter stage of life, opposite of being "young," Gen. 18:11; 19:4; Josh. 6:21; 1 Kings 12:8; Jer. 31:13.

The word ***zaqen*** has a more specialized use with the sense of "elder," a man, with gifts of leadership, wisdom, and justice; his duties varied to include religious, civic, and judicial activities, Josh. 23:2; 1 Kings 12:8; Ezek. 8:1.

***zaqan*** means "beard," i.e., the uncut, untrimmed hair on the face of a Hebrew man, Ps. 133:2.

### *New Testament*

**A. Adjectives.**

1. ***presbuteros*** *(4245)*, an adjective, the comparative degree of ***presbus***, "an old man, an elder," is used (a) of age, whether of the "elder" of two persons, Luke 15:25, or more, John 8:9, "the eldest," or of a person advanced in life, a senior, Acts 2:17; in Heb. 11:2, the "elders" are the forefathers in Israel so in Matt. 15:2; Mark 7:3, 5 the feminine of the adjective is used of "elder" women in the churches, 1 Tim. 5:2, not in respect of position but in seniority of age; (b) of rank or positions of responsibility, (1) among Gentiles, as in the Sept. of Gen. 50:7; Num. 22:7, (2) in the Jewish nation, firstly, those who were the heads or leaders of the tribes and families, as of the seventy who assisted Moses, Num. 11:16; Deut. 27:1, and those assembled by Solomon; secondly, members of the Sanhedrin, consisting of the chief priests, "elders" and scribes, learned in Jewish law, e.g., Matt. 16:21; 26:47; thirdly, those who managed public affairs in the various cities, Luke 7:3; (3) in the Christian churches those who, being raised up and qualified by the work of the Holy Spirit, were appointed to have the spiritual care of, and to exercise oversight over, the churches. To these the term "bishops," ***episkopoi***, or "overseers," is applied (see Acts 20, v. 17 with v. 28, and Titus 1:5 and 7), the latter term indicating the nature of their

work, ***presbuteroi*** their maturity of spiritual experience. The divine arrangement seen throughout the NT was for a plurality of these to be appointed in each church, Acts 14:23; 20:17; Phil. 1:1; 1 Tim. 5:17; Titus 1:5. The duty of "elders" is described by the verb ***episkopeo***. They were appointed according as they had given evidence of fulfilling the divine qualifications, Titus 1:6 to 9; cf. 1 Tim. 3:1–7 and 1 Pet. 5:2; (4) the twenty-four "elders" enthroned in heaven around the throne of God, Rev. 4:4, 10; 5:5–14; 7:11, 13; 11:16; 14:3; 19:4. The number twenty-four is representative of earthly conditions. The word "elder" is nowhere applied to angels.

2. ***sumpresbuteros*** (*4850*), "a fellow-elder" (***sun***, "with"), is used in 1 Pet. 5:1.

**B. Noun.**

***presbuterion*** (*4244*), "an assembly of aged men," denotes (a) the Council or Senate among the Jews, Luke 22:66; Acts 22:5; (b) the "elders" or bishops in a local church, 1 Tim. 4:14, "the presbytery." For their functions see A, No. 1, (3).

## ELECT, ELECTED, ELECTION

**A. Adjectives.**

1. ***eklektos*** (*1588*) lit. signifies "picked out, chosen," and is used of (a) Christ, the "chosen" of God, as the Messiah, Luke 23:35, and metaphorically as a "living Stone," "a chief corner Stone," 1 Pet. 2:4, 6; some mss. have it in John 1:34, instead of ***huios***, "Son"; (b) angels, 1 Tim. 5:21, as "chosen" to be of especially high rank in administrative association with God, or as His messengers to human beings, doubtless in contrast to fallen angels (see 2 Pet. 2:4 and Jude 6); (c) believers (Jews or Gentiles), Matt. 24:22, 24, 31; Mark 13:20, 22, 27; Luke 18:7; Rom. 8:33; Col. 3:12; 2 Tim. 2:10; Titus 1:1; 1 Pet. 1:1; 2:9 (as a spiritual race); Matt. 20:16; 22:14 and Rev. 17:14, "chosen"; individual believers are so mentioned in Rom. 16:13; 2 John 1, 13.

Believers were "chosen" "before the foundation of the world" (cf. "before times eternal," 2 Tim. 1:9), in Christ, Eph. 1:4, to adoption, Eph. 1:5; good works, 2:10; conformity to Christ, Rom. 8:29; salvation from the delusions of the Antichrist and the doom of the deluded, 2 Thess. 2:13; eternal glory, Rom. 9:23.

The source of their "election" is God's grace, not human will, Eph. 1:4, 5; Rom. 9:11; 11:5. They are given by God the Father to Christ as the fruit of His death, all being foreknown and foreseen by God, John 17:6 and Rom. 8:29. While Christ's death was sufficient for all men, and is effective in the case of the "elect," yet men are treated as responsible, being capable of the will and power to choose. For the rendering "being chosen as firstfruits," an alternative reading in 2 Thess. 2:13.

2. ***suneklektos*** (*4899*) means "elect together with," 1 Pet. 5:13.

**B. Noun.**

***ekloge*** (*1589*) denotes "a picking out, selection" (Eng., "eclogue"), then, "that which is chosen"; in Acts 9:15, said of the "choice" of God of Saul of Tarsus, the phrase is, lit., "a vessel of choice." It is used four times in Romans; in 9:11, of Esau and Jacob, where the phrase "the purpose . . . according to election" is virtually equivalent to "the electing purpose"; in 11:5, the "remnant according to the election of grace" refers to believing Jews, saved from among the unbelieving nation; so in v. 7; in v. 28, "the election" may mean either the "act of choosing" or the "chosen" ones; the context, speaking of the fathers, points to the former, the choice of the nation according to the covenant of promise. In 1 Thess. 1:4, "your election" refers not to the church collectively, but to the individuals constituting it; the apostle's assurance of their "election" gives the reason for his thanksgiving. Believers are to give "the more diligence to make their calling and election sure," by the exercise of the qualities and graces which make them fruitful in the knowledge of God, 2 Pet. 1:10.

## ELOQUENT

***logios*** (*3052*), an adjective, from ***logos***, "a word," primarily meant "learned, a man skilled in literature and the arts," and could communicate the learning effectively, Acts 18:24.

## EMBRACE

1. ***aspazomai*** (*782*) lit. signifies "to draw to oneself"; hence, "to greet, salute, welcome," the ordinary meaning, e.g., in Rom. 16, where it is used 21 times. It also signifies "to bid farewell," e.g., Acts 20:1, RV, "took leave of" (KJV, "embraced"). A "salutation or farewell" was generally made by embracing and kissing.

2. ***sumperilambano*** (*4843*), lit., "to take around with," (***sun***, "with" ***peri*** "around," ***lambano***, "to take"), "to embrace," is used in Acts 20:10, in connection with Paul's recovery of Eutychus.

## EMPEROR

***sebastos*** (*4575*), "august, reverent," the masculine gender of an adjective (from ***sebas***, "reverential awe"), became used as the title of the Roman emperor, Acts 25:21, 25, RV, for KJV, "Augustus"; then, taking its name from the emperor, it became a title of honor applied to certain legions or cohorts or battalions, marked for their valor, Acts 27:1.

## EMPTY

### A. Verb.

***kenoo*** *(2758)*, "to empty," is so translated in Phil. 2:7, RV, for KJV, "made . . . of no reputation." The clauses which follow the verb are exegetical of its meaning, especially the phrases "the form of a servant," and "the likeness of men." Christ did not "empty" Himself of Godhood. For other occurrences of the word, see Rom. 4:14; 1 Cor. 1:17; 9:15; 2 Cor. 9:3.

### B. Adjective.

***kenos*** *(2756)* expresses the "hollowness" of anything, the "absence," especially of quality, of that which otherwise might be possessed. It is used (a) literally, Mark 12:3; Luke 1:53; 20:10–11; (b) metaphorically, of imaginations, Acts 4:25; of words which convey erroneous teachings, Eph. 5:6; of deceit, Col. 2:8; of a person whose professed faith is not accompanied by works, Jas. 2:20; negatively, concerning the grace of God, 1 Cor. 15:10; of refusal to receive it, 2 Cor. 6:1; of faith, 1 Cor. 15:14; of preaching (id.); and other forms of Christian activity and labor, 1 Cor. 15:58; Gal. 2:2; Phil. 2:16; 1 Thess. 2:1; 3:5.

## ENCHANTER

***'ashap*** (825), "enchanter, " the ***ashipu*** offered incantations to deliver a person from evil magical forces (demons). The sick often underwent actual surgery while the incantations were spoken, Dan. 1:20.

## ENCOURAGE, ENCOURAGEMENT

### A. Verbs.

1. ***protrepo*** *(4389)*, "to urge forward, persuade," is used in Acts 18:27 in the middle voice, RV, "encouraged," indicating their particular interest in giving Apollos the "encouragement" mentioned; the KJV, "exhorting," wrongly connects the verb.

2. ***paramutheomai*** *(3888)*, from ***para***, "with," and ***muthos***, "counsel, advice," is translated "encouraging" in 1 Thess. 2:11, RV, and "encourage" in 5:14, RV, there signifying to stimulate to the discharge of the ordinary duties of life. In John 11:19, 31, it means "to comfort."

### B. Noun.

***paraklesis*** *(3874)*, "a calling to one's aid" (***para***, "by the side," ***kaleo***, "to call"), then, "an exhortation, encouragement," is translated "encouragement" in Heb. 6:18, RV, for KJV, "consolation"; it is akin to ***parakaleo***, "to beseech or exhort, encourage, comfort," and ***parakletos***, "a paraclete or advocate."

## END, ENDING

#### *Old Testament*

### A. Nouns.

***'ephes*** (657), "end; not; nothing; only," often referring to the outer, end part of a space or limit, Prov. 30:4; cf. Ps. 72:8. In other contexts, ***'ephes*** means the "territory" of the nations other than Israel, as an "outer region, from the writer's point of view, " Deut. 33:17; Ps. 2:8; 22:27.

***'epec*** also is used to express "nonexistence," as a state or condition, or refer to non-person, translated "not" or "no," 2 Sam. 9:3; "none" or "no one," Isa 45:6. This word can also mean "nothing" in the sense of "powerlessness" and "worthlessness," Isa. 40:17, or "nothing other than" or "only," Num. 22:35.

***qets*** (7093), "end," denotes the "end of a person" or "death," Gen. 6:13; Ps. 39:4; "end" as the state of "being annihilated," Job 28:3; "end," of a period of time, 2 Chron. 18:2; cf. Gen. 4:3; "end" of a boundary or limit of a space, Ps. 119:96.

***qatseh*** (7097), "end; border; extremity," in the sense of the limit or boundary of a space, Exod. 13:20; Deut. 30:4. ***qatseh*** can also signify an "end," of a time or sequence, Gen. 8:3.

***qatsah*** (7098), "end; border; edge; extremity," refers primarily to concrete objects, Job 26:14, so translate, "fringe."

***'acharit*** (319), "hind-part; end; issue; outcome; posterity," used spatially, the word identifies the "remotest and most distant part of something," Ps. 139:9. The most frequent emphasis of the word is "outcome," Deut. 11:12. A slight shift of meaning occurs in Dan. 8:23, where ***'acharit*** is applied to time in a relative or comparative sense. In some passages, ***'acharit*** represents the "ultimate outcome" of a person's life, Num. 23:10, In other passages, ***'acharit*** refers to "all that comes afterwards," Jer. 31:17. In Amos 9:1, ***'acharit*** is used of the "rest" (remainder) of one's fellows. Both conclusion and result are apparent in passages such as Isa. 41:22, where the word represents the "end" or "result" of a matter.

Another nuance of ***'acharit*** indicates the "last" or the "least in importance," Jer. 50:12. The fact that ***'acharit*** used with "day" or "years" may signify either "a point at the end of time" or "a period of the end time," referring to a near or possibly far time, an issue much debated, but unfortunately the meaning of this word does not definitively answer this debate, but rather involves other theological issues, Isa. 2:2; Dan. 10:14.

**B. Adverb.**

***'ephes*** (657), "howbeit; notwithstanding; however; without cause." This word's first occurrence is in Num. 13:28: "*Nevertheless* the people be strong that dwell in the land. . . ."

*New Testament*

**A. Nouns.**

1. ***telos*** (*5056*) signifies (a) "the limit," either at which a person or thing ceases to be what he or it was up to that point, or at which previous activities were ceased, 2 Cor. 3:13; 1 Pet. 4:7; (b) "the final issue or result" of a state or process, e.g., Luke 1:33; in Rom. 10:4, Christ is described as "the end of the Law unto righteousness to everyone that believeth"; this is best explained by Gal. 3:23–26; cf. Jas. 5:11; the following more especially point to the issue or fate of a thing, Matt. 26:58; Rom. 6:21; 2 Cor. 11:15; Phil. 3:19; Heb. 6:8; 1 Pet. 1:9; (c) "a fulfillment," Luke 22:37, KJV, "(have) an end"; (d) "the utmost degree" of an act, as of the love of Christ towards His disciples, John 13:1; (e) "the aim or purpose" of a thing, 1 Tim. 1:5; (f) "the last" in a succession or series, Rev. 1:8 (KJV, only, "ending"); 21:6; 22:13.

2. ***sunteleia*** (*4930*) signifies "a bringing to completion together" (***sun*** "with," ***teleo***, "to complete," akin to No. 1), marking the "completion" or consummation of the various parts of a scheme, Matt. 13:39–40, 49; 24:3; 28:20. The word does not denote a termination, but the heading up of events to the appointed climax. ***aion*** is not the world, but a period or epoch or era in which events take place. In Heb. 9:26, the word translated "world" (KJV) is in the plural, and the phrase is "the consummation of the ages." It was at the heading up of all the various epochs appointed by divine counsels that Christ was manifested (i.e., in His Incarnation) "to put away sin by the sacrifice of Himself."

**B. Verbs.**

1. ***teleo*** (*5055*), "to complete, finish, bring to an end," is translated "had made an end," in Matt. 11:1.

2. ***sunteleo*** (*4931*), cf. A, No. 2, signifies (a) "to bring to an end, finish completely" (***sun***, "together," imparting a perfective significance to ***teleo***), Matt. 7:28 (in some mss.); Luke 4:2, 13; Acts 21:27, RV, "completed"; (b) "to bring to fulfillment," Mark 13:4; Rom. 9:28; (c) "to effect, make," Heb. 8:8.

**C. Adjective.**

***eschatos*** (*2078*), "last, utmost, extreme," is used as a noun (a) of time, rendered "end" in Heb. 1:2, RV, "at the 'end' of these days," i.e., at the "end" of the period under the Law, for KJV, "in these last days"; so in 1 Pet. 1:20, "at the end of the times." In 2 Pet. 2:20, the plural, ***ta eschata***, lit., "the last things," is rendered "the latter end," KJV, (RV, "the last state"); the same phrase is used in Matt. 12:45; Luke 11:26; (b) of place, Acts 13:47, KJV, "ends (of the earth)," RV, "uttermost part."

## ENDURE, ENDURING

**A. Verbs.**

1. ***meno*** (*3306*), "to abide," is rendered "to endure" in the KJV of John 6:27 and 1 Pet. 1:25 (RV, "abideth"); Heb. 10:34, KJV, "enduring (substance)," RV, "abiding."

2. ***hupomeno*** (*5278*), a strengthened form of No. 1, denotes "to abide under, to bear up courageously" (under suffering), Matt. 10:22; 24:13; Mark 13:13; Rom. 12:12, translated "patient"; 1 Cor. 13:7; 2 Tim. 2:10, 12 (KJV, "suffer"); Heb. 10:32; 12:2–3, 7; Jas. 1:12; 5:11; 1 Pet. 2:20, "ye shall take it patiently." It has its other significance, "to tarry, wait for, await," in Luke 2:43; Acts 17:14 (in some mss., Rom. 8:24).

3. ***phero*** (*5342*), "to bear," is translated "endured" in Rom. 9:22 and Heb. 12:20.

4. ***hupophero*** (*5297*), a strengthened form of No. 3, "to bear or carry," by being under, is said metaphorically of "enduring" temptation, 1 Cor. 10:13, KJV, "bear"; persecutions, 2 Tim. 3:11; griefs, 1 Pet. 2:19.

5. ***anecho*** (*430*), "to hold up" (***ana***, "up," ***echo***, "to hold or have"), always in the middle voice in the NT, is rendered "endure" in 2 Thess. 1:4, of persecutions and tribulations; in 2 Tim. 4:3, of sound doctrine.

6. ***kartereo*** (*2594*), "to be steadfast, patient," is used in Heb. 11:27, "endured," of Moses in relation to Egypt.

7. ***makrothumeo*** (*3114*), "to be longtempered" (***makros***, "long," ***thumos***, "mind"), is rendered "patiently endured" in Heb. 6:15, said of Abraham. See B, below.

**B. Noun.**

***hupomone*** (*5281*), "patience," lit., "a remaining under" (akin to A, No. 2), is translated "patient enduring" in 2 Cor. 1:6, RV, for KJV, "enduring."

## ENEMY

*Old Testament*

***'oyeb*** (341), "enemy." ***'oyeb*** refers to both individuals and nations, Gen. 22:17; Exod. 23:4; Ps.

38:19; or, one might be an "enemy" of God, Nah. 1:2.

***tsar*** (6862), "adversary; enemy; foe," a general designation for "enemy": a nation, 2 Sam. 24:13, or, more rarely, an individual, cf. Gen. 14:20; Ps. 3:1. The Lord may also be the "enemy" of His sinful people as His judgment comes upon them, cf. Deut. 32:41–43; Lam. 2:4.

The word ***tsar*** has several synonyms: ***'oyeb***, "enemy," cf. Lam. 2:5; ***sone'***, "hater," Ps. 44:7; ***rodep***, "persecutor," Ps. 119:157; ***'arits***, "tyrant; oppressor," Job 6:23.

*New Testament*

***echthros*** (*2190*), an adjective, primarily denoting "hated" or "hateful" (akin to ***echthos***, "hate"; perhaps associated with ***ekos***, "outside"), hence, in the active sense, denotes "hating, hostile"; it is used as a noun signifying an "enemy," adversary, and is said (a) of the Devil, Matt. 13:39; Luke 10:19; (b) of death, 1 Cor. 15:26; (c) of the professing believer who would be a friend of the world, thus making himself an enemy of God, Jas. 4:4; (d) of men who are opposed to Christ, Matt. 13:25, 28; 22:44; Mark 12:36; Luke 19:27; 20:43; Acts 2:35; Rom. 11:28; Phil. 3:18; Heb. 1:13; 10:13; or to His servants, Rev. 11:5, 12; to the nation of Israel, Luke 1:71, 74; 19:43; (e) of one who is opposed to righteousness, Acts 13:10; (f) of Israel in its alienation from God, Rom. 11:28; (g) of the unregenerate in their attitude toward God, Rom. 5:10; Col. 1:21; (h) of believers in their former state, 2 Thess. 3:15; (i) of foes, Matt. 5:43–44; 10:36; Luke 6:27, 35; Rom. 12:20; 1 Cor. 15:25; of the apostle Paul because he told converts "the truth," Gal. 4:16.

## ENGRAVE

***entupoo*** (*1795*), "to imprint, engrave," is used of the "engraving" of the Law on the two stones, or tablets, 2 Cor. 3:7.

## ENLIGHTEN

***photizo*** (*5461*), from ***phos***, "light," (a), used intransitively, signifies "to give light, shine," Rev. 22:5; (b), used transitively, "to enlighten, illumine," is rendered "enlighten" in Eph. 1:18, metaphorically of spiritual "enlightenment"; so John 1:9, i.e., "lighting every man" (by reason of His coming); Eph. 3:9, "to make (all men) see"; Heb. 6:4, "were enlightened"; 10:32, RV, "enlightened," KJV, "illuminated."

## ENOUGH

### A. Adjectives.

1. ***arketos*** (*713*), "sufficient," akin to ***arkeo*** (see B, No. 1), is rendered "enough" in Matt. 10:25; "sufficient" in Matt. 6:34; "suffice" in 1 Pet. 4:3, lit., "(is) sufficient."

2. ***hikanos*** (*2425*), "sufficient, competent, fit" (akin to ***hikano*** and ***hiko***, "to reach, attain" and ***hikanoo***, "to make sufficient"), is translated "enough" in Luke 22:38, of the Lord's reply to Peter concerning the swords.

### B. Verbs.

1. ***arkeo*** (*714*), "to ward off"; hence, "to aid, assist"; then, "to be strong enough," i.e., "to suffice, to be enough" (cf. A, No. 1), is translated "be enough" in Matt. 25:9.

2. ***apecho*** (*568*), lit., "to hold off from, to have off or out" (***apo***, "from," ***echo***, "to have"), i.e., "to have in full, to have received," is used impersonally in Mark 14:41, "it is enough," in the Lord's words to His slumbering disciples in Gethsemane.

## ENROLL, ENROLLMENT

### A. Verb.

***apographo*** (*583*) primarily signifies "to write out, to copy"; then, "to enroll, to inscribe," as in a register. It is used of a census, Luke 2:1, RV, "be enrolled," for KJV, "be taxed"; in the middle voice, vv. 3, 5, to enroll oneself, KJV, "be taxed." Confirmation that this census (not taxation) was taken in the dominions of the Roman Empire is given by the historians Tacitus and Suetonius. Augustus himself drew up a sort of Roman Doomsday Book, a Rationarium, afterwards epitomized into a Breviarium, to include the allied kingdoms, appointing twenty commissioners to draw up the lists. In Heb. 12:23 the members of the church of the firstborn are said to be "enrolled," RV.

### B. Noun.

***apographe*** (*582*) primarily denotes "a written copy," or, as a law term, "a deposition"; then, "a register, census, enrollment," Luke 2:2; Acts 5:37.

## ENSAMPLE

1. ***tupos*** (*5179*) primarily denoted "a blow" (from a root ***tup***–, seen also in ***tupto***, "to strike"), hence, (a) an impression, the mark of a "blow," John 20:25; (b) the "impress" of a seal, the stamp made by a die, a figure, image, Acts 7:43; (c) a "form" or mold, Rom. 6:17 (see RV); (d) the sense or substance of a letter, Acts 23:25; (e) "an ensample," pattern, Acts 7:44; Heb. 8:5, "pattern"; in an ethical sense, 1 Cor. 10:6; Phil. 3:17; 1 Thess. 1:7; 2 Thess. 3:9; 1 Tim. 4:12, RV, "ensample"; Titus 2:7, RV, "ensample," for KJV, "pattern"; 1 Pet. 5:3; in a doctrinal sense, a type, Rom. 5:14.

2. ***hupotuposis*** (*5296*), "an outline, sketch," akin to ***hupotupoo***, "to delineate," is used metaphorically to denote a "pattern," an "ensample," 1 Tim. 1:16, RV, "ensample," for KJV, "pattern"; 2 Tim. 1:13, RV, "pattern," for KJV, "form."

3. ***hupodeigma*** (*5262*), lit., "that which is shown" (from ***hupo***, "under," and ***deiknumi***, "to show"), hence, (a) "a figure, copy," Heb. 8:5, RV, "copy," for KJV, "example"; 9:23; (b) "an example," whether for imitation, John 13:15; Jas. 5:10, or for warning, Heb. 4:11; 2 Pet. 2:6, RV, "example."

## ENSLAVED

***douloo*** (*1402*), "to make a slave of," is rendered "enslaved" (to much wine) in Titus 2:3, RV, for KJV, "given to."

## ENTANGLE

1. ***empleko*** (*1707*), "to weave in," hence, metaphorically, to be involved, entangled in, is used in the passive voice in 2 Tim. 2:4, "entangleth himself"; 2 Pet. 2:20, "are entangled."

2. ***enecho*** (*1758*), "to hold in," is said (a) of being "entangled" in a yoke of bondage, such as Judaism, Gal. 5:1. Some mss. have the word in 2 Thess. 1:4, the most authentic have ***anecho***, "to endure"; (b) with the meaning to set oneself against, be urgent against, said of the plotting of Herodias against John the Baptist, Mark 6:19, RV, "set herself against," KJV, "had a quarrel against"; of the effort of the scribes and Pharisees to provoke the Lord to say something which would provide them with a ground of accusation against Him, Luke 11:53.

## ENTERTAIN

***xenizo*** (*3579*) signifies (a) "to receive as a guest" (***xenos***, "a guest") rendered "entertained" in Acts 28:7, RV, for KJV, "lodged"; in Heb. 13:2, "have entertained"; (b) "to be astonished by the strangeness of a thing," Acts 17:20; 1 Pet. 4:4, 12.

## ENTICE, ENTICING

**A. Verb.**

***deleazo*** (*1185*), primarily, "to lure by a bait" (from ***delear***, "a bait"), is used metaphorically in Jas. 1:14, of the "enticement" of lust; in 2 Pet. 2:14, of seducers, RV, "enticing," for KJV, "beguiling"; in v. 18, RV, "entice (in)," for AV, "allure (through)."

**B. Adjective.**

***peithos*** (*3981*), "apt to persuade" (from ***peitho***, "to persuade"), is used in 1 Cor. 2:4, KJV, "enticing," RV, "persuasive."

## ENVY, ENVYING

**A. Noun.**

***phthonos*** (*5355*), "envy," is the feeling of displeasure produced by witnessing or hearing of the advantage or prosperity of others; this evil sense always attaches to this word, Matt. 27:18; Mark 15:10; Rom. 1:29; Gal. 5:21; Phil. 1:15; 1 Tim. 6:4; Titus 3:3; 1 Pet. 2:1; so in Jas. 4:5, where the question is rhetorical and strongly remonstrative, signifying that the Spirit (or spirit) which God made to dwell in us was certainly not so bestowed that we should be guilty of "envy."

**B. Verbs.**

1. ***phthoneo*** (*5354*), "to envy" (akin to A.), is used in Gal. 5:26.

2. ***zeloo*** (*2206*) denotes "to be zealous, moved with jealousy," Acts 7:9 and 17:5, RV, "moved with jealousy" (KJV, "moved with envy"); both have "envieth" in 1 Cor. 13:4.

## EPILEPTIC

***seleniazo*** (*4583*), lit., "to be moon struck" (from ***selene***, "the moon"), is used in the passive voice with active significance, RV, "epileptic," for KJV, "lunatick," Matt. 4:24; 17:15; the corresponding English word is "lunatic." Epilepsy was supposed to be influenced by the moon.

## EPISTLE

***epistole*** (*1992*), primarily "a message" (from ***epistello***, "to send to"), hence, "a letter, an epistle," is used in the singular, e.g., Acts 15:30; in the plural, e.g., Acts 9:2; 2 Cor. 10:10. Epistle is a less common word for a letter. A letter affords a writer more freedom, both in subject and expression, than does a formal treatise. A letter is usually occasional, that is, it is written in consequence of some circumstance which requires to be dealt with promptly. The style of a letter depends largely on the occasion that calls it forth. "A broad line is to be drawn between the letter and the epistle. The one is essentially a spontaneous product dominated throughout by the image of the reader, his sympathies and interests, instinct also with the writer's own soul: it is virtually one half of an imaginary dialogue, the suppressed responses of the other party shaping the course of what is actually written . . . the other has a general aim, addressing all and sundry whom it may concern: it is like a public speech and looks towards publication" (J. V. Bartlet).

## EQUAL, EQUALITY

### A. Adjective.

***isos*** *(2470)*, "the same in size, number, quality," etc., is translated "equal" in John 5:18; Phil. 2:6; in the latter the word is in the neuter plural, lit., "equalities"; in the RV the words are translated 'on an equality with God,' instead of 'equal with God,' as in the KJV. The change is of great importance to the right interpretation of the whole passage.

### B. Nouns.

1. ***isotes*** *(2471)*, "equality" (akin to A.), is translated "equality" in 2 Cor. 8:14, twice; in Col. 4:1, with the article, "that which is . . . equal," i.e. equity, fairness.

2. ***sunelikiotes*** *(4915)* denotes "one of the same age, an equal in age" (***sun***, "with," ***helikia***, "an age"), "a contemporary," Gal. 1:14, RV, "of mine own age," for KJV "mine equals," the reference being to the apostle's good standing among his fellow students in the rabbinical schools; cf. Acts 22:3.

## ERR

1. ***planao*** *(4105)*, in the active voice, signifies "to cause to wander, lead astray, deceive" (***plane***, "a wandering"; cf. Eng., "planet"); in the passive voice, "to be led astray, to err." It is translated "err," in Matt. 22:29; Mark 12:24, 27; Heb. 3:10; Jas. 1:16 (KJV, "do not err," RV, "be not deceived"); 5:19.

2. ***apoplanao*** *(635)*, "to cause to wander away from, to lead astray from" (***apo***, "from," and No. 1), is used metaphorically of leading into error, Mark 13:22, KJV, "seduce," RV "lead astray"; 1 Tim. 6:10, in the passive voice, KJV, "have erred," RV, "have been led astray."

3. ***astocheo*** *(795)*, "to miss the mark, fail," is used only in the Pastoral Epistles, 1 Tim. 1:6, "having swerved"; 6:21 and 2 Tim. 2:18, "have erred."

## ERROR

1. ***plane*** *(4106)*, akin to ***planao***, "a wandering, a forsaking of the right path, see Jas. 5:20, whether in doctrine, 2 Pet. 3:17; 1 John 4:6, or in morals, Rom. 1:27; 2 Pet. 2:18; Jude 11, though, in Scripture, doctrine and morals are never divided by any sharp line. See also Matt. 27:64, where it is equivalent to fraud." "Errors" in doctrine are not infrequently the effect of relaxed morality, and vice versa.

2. ***agnoema*** *(51)*, "a sin of ignorance," is used in the plural in Heb. 9:7.

## ESCAPE

### *Old Testament*

***malat*** (4422), "to escape, slip away, deliver, give birth," its most common use of this word is to express the "escaping" from any kind of danger, such as an enemy, Isa. 20:6, a trap, 2 Kings 10:24, or a temptress, Eccl. 7:26. It may also mean to "save, deliver from destruction," 2 Kings 23:18. ***malat*** is used once in the sense of "delivering (birthing) a child," Isa. 66:7.

E

### *New Testament*

### A. Verbs.

1. ***pheugo*** *(5343)*, "to flee" (Lat., ***fuga***, "flight," etc.; cf. Eng., "fugitive, subterfuge"), is rendered "escape" in Matt. 23:33; Heb. 11:34.

2. ***apopheugo*** *(668)*, "to flee away from" (***apo***, "from," and No. 1), is used in 2 Pet. 1:4; 2:18, 20.

3. ***diapheugo*** *(1309)*, lit., "to flee through," is used of the "escaping" of prisoners from a ship, Acts 27:42. For the word in v. 44, see No. 5.

4. ***ekpheugo*** *(1628)*, "to flee out of a place" (***ek***, "out of," and No. 1), is said of the "escape" of prisoners, Acts 16:27; of Sceva's sons, "fleeing" from the demoniac, 19:16; of Paul's escape from Damascus, 2 Cor. 11:33; elsewhere with reference to the judgments of God, Luke 21:36; Rom. 2:3; Heb. 2:3; 12:25; 1 Thess. 5:3.

5. ***diasozo*** *(1295)*, in the active voice, "to bring safely through a danger" (***dia***, "through," intensive, ***sozo***, "to save"), to make completely whole, to heal, Luke 7:3; to bring "safe," Acts 23:24; "to save," 27:43; in the passive voice, Matt. 14:36, "were made whole"; 1 Pet. 3:20. It is also used in the passive voice, signifying "to escape," said of shipwrecked mariners, Acts 27:44; 28:1, 4.

### B. Noun.

***ekbasis*** *(1545)*, "a way out," denotes (a) "an escape," 1 Cor. 10:13, used with the definite article and translated "the way of escape," as afforded by God in case of temptation; (b) "an issue or result," Heb. 13:7.

## ESPOUSED

1. ***harmozo*** *(718)*, "to fit, join" (from ***hamnos***, "a joint, joining"; the root ***ar***—, signifying "to fit," is in evidence in various languages; cf. ***arthron***, "a joint," ***arithmos***, "a number," etc.), is used in the middle voice, of marrying or giving in marriage; in 2 Cor. 11:2 it is rendered "espoused," metaphorically of the relationship established between Christ and the local church, through the apostle's instrumentality. The thought may be that of "fitting" or "join-

ing" to one husband, the middle voice expressing the apostle's interest or desire in doing so.

2. ***mnesteuo*** (*3423*), "to woo and win, to espouse or promise in marriage," is used in the passive voice in Matt. 1:18; Luke 1:27; 2:5, all with reference to the Virgin Mary, RV, "betrothed," for KJV, "espoused," in each case.

## ESTABLISH

1. ***sterizo*** (*4741*), "to fix, make fast, to set" (from ***sterix***, "a prop"), is used of "establishing" or "stablishing" (i.e., the confirmation) of persons; the apostle Peter was called by the Lord to "establish" his brethren, Luke 22:32, translated "strengthen"; Paul desired to visit Rome that the saints might be "established," Rom. 1:11; cf. Acts 8:23; so with Timothy at Thessalonica, 1 Thess. 3:2; the "confirmation" of the saints is the work of God, Rom. 16:25, "to stablish (you)"; 1 Thess. 3:13, "stablish (your hearts)"; 2 Thess. 2:17, "stablish them (in every good work and word)"; 1 Pet. 5:10, "stablish"; the means used to effect the "confirmation" is the ministry of the Word of God, 2 Pet. 1:12, "are established (in the truth which is with you)"; James exhorts Christians to "stablish" their hearts, Jas. 5:8; cf. Rev. 3:2, RV.

2. ***stereoo*** (*4732*), "to make firm, or solid" (akin to ***stereos***, "hard, firm, solid"; cf. Eng., "stereotype"), is used only in Acts, (a) physically, 3:7, "received strength"; 3:16, "hath made strong"; (b) metaphorically, of establishment in the faith, 16:5, RV, "strengthened," for KJV established.

3. ***histemi*** (*2476*), "to cause to stand," is translated "establish" in Rom. 3:31; 10:3; Heb. 10:9.

4. ***bebaioo*** (*950*), "to confirm," is rendered "stablish," 2 Cor. 1:21; "stablished," Col. 2:7; "be established," Heb. 13:9.

## ESTATE, STATE

1. ***euschemon*** (*2158*), signifying "elegant, graceful, comely" (***eu***, "well," ***schema***, "figure, fashion"), is used (a) in a moral sense, seemly, becoming, 1 Cor. 7:35; (b) in a physical sense, comely, 1 Cor. 12:24; (c) with reference to social degree, influential, a meaning developed in later Greek, and rendered of "honorable estate" in the RV of Mark 15:43; Acts 13:50; 17:12 (for KJV, "honorable").

2. ***tapeinosis*** (*5014*) denotes "abasement, humiliation, low estate" (from ***tapeinos***, "lowly"), Luke 1:48, "low estate"; Acts 8:33, "humiliation"; Phil. 3:21, RV, "of humiliation," for KJV, "vile"; Jas. 1:10, "is made low," lit., "in his low estate."

3. ***hupsos*** (*5311*), signifying "height," is rendered "(in his) high estate," Jas. 1:9, RV, for KJV, "in that he is exalted"; "on high," Luke 1:78; 24:49; Eph. 4:8; "height," Eph. 3:18; Rev. 21:16.

## ESTEEM

1. ***hegeomai*** (*2233*) signifies "to lead"; then, "to lead before the mind, to suppose, consider, esteem"; translated "esteem" in Phil. 2:3, KJV, RV, "counting"; in 1 Thess. 5:13, "esteem"; in Heb. 11:26, KJV, "esteeming," RV, "accounting."

2. ***krino*** (*2919*) signifies "to separate, choose"; then, "to approve, esteem"; translated "esteemeth" in Rom. 14:5 (twice), said of days; here the word "alike" (KJV) is rightly omitted in the RV, the meaning being that every day is especially regarded as sacred.

3. ***logizomai*** (*3049*), "to reckon," is translated "esteemeth" in Rom. 14:14 (RV, "accounteth").

## ETERNAL

1. ***aion*** (*165*), "an age," is translated "eternal" in Eph. 3:11, lit., "(purpose) of the ages," and 1 Tim. 1:17, lit. "(king) of the ages."

2. ***aionios*** (*166*) describes "duration," either undefined but not endless, as in Rom. 16:25; 2 Tim. 1:9; Titus 1:2; or undefined because it is endless as in Rom. 16:26, and the other sixty-six places in the NT.

The predominant meaning of ***aionios***, that with which it is used everywhere in the NT, save the places noted above, may be seen in 2 Cor. 4:18, where it is set in contrast with ***proskairos***, lit., "for a season," and in Philem. 15, where only in the NT it is used without a noun. Moreover it is used of persons and things which are in their nature endless, as, e.g., of God, Rom. 16:26; of His power, 1 Tim. 6:16, and of His glory, 1 Pet. 5:10; of the Holy Spirit, Heb. 9:14; of the redemption effected by Christ, Heb. 9:12, and of the consequent salvation of men, 5:9, as well as of His future rule, 2 Pet. 1:11, which is elsewhere declared to be without end, Luke 1:33; of the life received by those who believe in Christ, John 3:16, concerning whom He said, "they shall never perish," 10:28, and of the resurrection body, 2 Cor. 5:1, elsewhere said to be "immortal," 1 Cor. 15:53, in which that life will be finally realized, Matt. 25:46; Titus 1:2.

## EUNUCH

### A. Noun.

***eunouchos*** (*2135*) denotes (a) "an emasculated man, a eunuch," Matt. 19:12; (b) in the 3rd instance in that verse, "one naturally incapacitated for, or voluntarily abstaining from, wedlock"; (c) one such, in a position of high authority in a court, "a chamberlain," Acts 8:27–39.

**B. Verb.**

***eunouchizo*** (*2134*), "to make a eunuch" (from A), is used in Matt. 19:12, as under (b) in A; and in the passive voice, "were made eunuchs," probably an allusion by the Lord to the fact that there were eunuchs in the courts of the Herods, as would be well known to His hearers.

## EVANGELIST

***euangelistes*** (*2099*), lit., "a messenger of good," denotes a "preacher of the gospel," Acts 21:8; Eph. 4:11, which makes clear the distinctiveness of the function in the churches; 2 Tim. 4:5.

## EVER, FOREVER, EVERMORE

### *Old Testament*

***'olam*** (5769), "eternity; remotest time; perpetuity," usually signifies "remotest time" or "remote time." In 1 Chron. 16:36, God is described as blessed "from everlasting to everlasting" (KJV, "for ever and ever"), or from the most distant past time to the most distant future time. In passages where God is viewed as the One who existed before the creation was brought into existence, ***'olam*** may mean: (1) "at the very beginning," Isa. 46:9; or (2) "from eternity, from the pre-creation, till now," Ps. 25:6. In other passages, the word means "from (in) olden times," Gen. 6:4. In Isa. 42:14, the word is used hyperbolically meaning "for a long time." In Josh. 24:2, the word means "formerly; in ancient times." When used with the negative, ***'olam*** can mean "never," Isa. 63:19.

With the preposition ***'ad***, the word can mean "into the indefinite future," Deut. 23:3. The same construction can signify "as long as one lives," 1 Sam. 1:22. This construction then sets forth an extension into the indefinite future, beginning from the time of the speaker.

In the largest number of its occurrences, ***'olam*** appears with the preposition ***le***. This construction is weaker and less dynamic in emphasis than the previous phrase, insofar as it envisions a "simple duration." This difference emerges in 1 Kings 2:33, where both phrases occur. ***Le'olam*** is applied to the curse set upon the dead Joab and his descendants. The other more dynamic phrase (***'ad 'olam***), applied to David and his descendants, emphasizes the ever-continued, ever-acting presence of the blessing extended into the "indefinite future." In Exod. 21:6 the phrase ***le 'olam*** means "as long as one lives," Gen. 3:22.

The same emphasis on "simple duration" pertains when ***o'olam*** is used in passages such as Ps. 61:8, where it appears by itself. In Gen. 9:16, the word (used absolutely) means the "most distant future." In other places, the word means "without beginning, without end, and ever-continuing," Isa. 26:4.

### *New Testament*

**A. Adverbs.**

1. ***pantote*** (*3842*), "at all times, always" (from ***pas***, "all"), is translated "ever" in Luke 15:31; John 18:20; 1 Thess. 4:17; 5:15; 2 Tim. 3:7; Heb. 7:25; "evermore" in John 6:34; in 1 Thess. 5:16, RV, "alway," for KJV, "evermore." It there means "on all occasions," as, e.g., in 1 Thess. 1:2; 3:6; 5:15; 2 Thess. 1:3, 11; 2:13.

2. ***aei*** (*104*), "ever," is used (a) of continuous time, signifying "unceasingly, perpetually," Acts 7:51; 2 Cor. 4:11; 6:10; Titus 1:12; Heb. 3:10; (b) of successive occurrences, signifying "on every occasion," 1 Pet. 3:15; 2 Pet. 1:12. Some texts have the word in Mark 15:8.

**B. Phrases.**

The following phrases are formed in connection with ***aion***, "an age": they are idiomatic expressions betokening undefined periods and are not to be translated literally: (a) ***eis aiona***, lit., "unto an age," Jude 13, "for ever"; (b) ***eis ton aiona***, lit., "unto the age," "for ever" (or, with a negative, "never"), Matt. 21:19; Mark 3:29; 11:14; Luke 1:55; John 4:14; 6:51, 58; 8:35 (twice), 51–52; 10:28; 11:26; 12:34; 13:8; 14:16; 1 Cor. 8:13; 2 Cor. 9:9; Heb. 5:6; 6:20; 7:17, 21, 24, 28; 1 Pet. 1:25; 1 John 2:17; 2 John 2; (c) ***eis tous aionas***, lit., "unto the ages," "for ever," Matt. 6:13 (KJV only); Luke 1:33; Rom. 1:25; 9:5; 11:36; 16:27 (some mss. have the next phrase here); 2 Cor. 11:31; Heb. 13:8; (d) ***eis tous aionas ton aionon***, lit. "unto the ages of the ages," "for ever and ever," or "for evermore," Gal. 1:5; Phil. 4:20; 1 Tim. 1:17; 2 Tim. 4:18; Heb. 13:21; 1 Pet. 4:11; 5:11 [(c) in some mss.]; Rev. 1:6 [(c) in some mss.]; 1:18, "for evermore"; 4:9–10; 5:13; 7:12; 10:6; 11:15; 15:7; 19:3; 20:10; 22:5; (e) ***eis aionas aionon***, lit., "unto ages of ages," "for ever and ever," Rev. 14:11; (f) ***eis ton aiona tou aionos***, lit., "unto the age of the age," "for ever and ever," Heb. 1:8; (g) ***tou aionos ton aionon***, lit., "of the age of the ages," "for ever and ever," Eph. 3:21; (h) ***eis pantas tous aionas***, lit., "unto all the ages," Jude 25 ("for evermore," RV; "ever," KJV); (i) ***eis hemeran aionos***, lit., "unto a day of an age," "for ever," 2 Pet. 3:18.

## EVERLASTING

1. ***aidios*** (*126*) denotes "everlasting" (from ***aei***, "ever"), Rom. 1:20, RV, "everlasting," for

KJV, "eternal"; Jude 6, KJV and RV "everlasting." ***aionios*** should always be translated "eternal," and ***aidios***, "everlasting."

## EVIDENT, EVIDENTLY

### A. Adjectives.

1. ***delos*** (*1212*), properly signifying "visible, clear to the mind, evident," is translated "evident" in Gal. 3:11 and 1 Cor. 15:27, RV (KJV, "manifest"); "bewrayeth," Matt. 26:73; "certain," 1 Tim. 6:7, KJV.

2. ***katadelos*** (*2612*), a strengthened form of No. 1, "quite manifest, evident," is used in Heb. 7:15 (KJV, "more evident"). For the preceding verse see No. 3.

3. ***prodelos*** (*4271*), "manifest beforehand" (***pro***, "before," and No. 1), is used in Heb. 7:14 in the sense of "clearly evident." So in 1 Tim. 5:24–25, RV, "evident," for KJV, "open beforehand," and "manifest beforehand." The ***pro*** is somewhat intensive.

### B. Adverb.

***phaneros*** (*5320*), manifestly, is rendered "openly" in Mark 1:45; "publicly" in John 7:10, RV (opposite to "in secret"); in Acts 10:3, RV, "openly," for KJV, evidently.

## EVIL, EVIL-DOER

### A. Adjectives.

1. ***kakos*** (*2556*) stands for "whatever is evil in character, base," in distinction (wherever the distinction is observable) from ***poneros*** (see No. 2), which indicates "what is evil in influence and effect, malignant." ***kakos*** is the wider term and often covers the meaning of ***poneros***. ***kakos*** is antithetic to ***kalos***, "fair, advisable, good in character," and to ***agathos***, "beneficial, useful, good in act"; hence it denotes what is useless, incapable, bad; ***poneros*** is essentially antithetic to ***chrestos***, "kind, gracious, serviceable"; hence it denotes what is destructive, injurious, evil. As evidence that ***poneros*** and ***kakos*** have much in common, though still not interchangeable, each is used of thoughts, cf. Matt. 15:19 with Mark 7:21; of speech, Matt. 5:11 with 1 Pet. 3:10; of actions, 2 Tim. 4:18 with 1 Thess. 5:15; of man, Matt. 18:32 with 24:48.

The use of ***kakos*** may be broadly divided as follows: (a) of what is morally or ethically "evil," whether of persons, e.g., Matt. 21:41; 24:48; Phil. 3:2; Rev. 2:2, or qualities, emotions, passions, deeds, e.g., Mark 7:21; John 18:23, 30; Rom. 1:30; 3:8; 7:19, 21; 13:4; 14:20; 16:19; 1 Cor. 13:5; 2 Cor. 13:7; 1 Thess. 5:15; 1 Tim. 6:10; 2 Tim. 4:14; 1 Pet. 3:9, 12; (b) of what is injurious, destructive, baneful, pernicious, e.g., Luke 16:25; Acts 16:28; 28:5; Titus 1:12; Jas. 3:8; Rev. 16:2, where ***kakos*** and ***poneros*** come in that order, "noisome and grievous." See B, No. 3.

2. ***poneros*** (*4190*), akin to ***ponos***, "labor, toil," denotes "evil that causes labor, pain, sorrow, malignant evil" (see No. 1); it is used (a) with the meaning bad, worthless, in the physical sense, Matt. 7:17–18; in the moral or ethical sense, "evil," wicked; of persons, e.g., Matt. 7:11; Luke 6:45; Acts 17:5; 2 Thess. 3:2; 2 Tim. 3:13; of "evil" spirits, e.g., Matt. 12:45; Luke 7:21; Acts 19:12–13, 15–16; of a generation, Matt. 12:39, 45; 16:4; Luke 11:29; of things, e.g., Matt. 5:11; 6:23; 20:15; Mark 7:22; Luke 11:34; John 3:19; 7:7; Acts 18:14; Gal. 1:4; Col. 1:21; 1 Tim. 6:4; 2 Tim. 4:18; Heb. 3:12; 10:22; Jas. 2:4; 4:16; 1 John 3:12; 2 John 11; 3 John 10; (b) with the meaning toilsome, painful, Eph. 5:16; 6:13; Rev. 16:2.

3. ***phaulos*** (*5337*) primarily denotes "slight, trivial, blown about by every wind"; then, "mean, common, bad," in the sense of being worthless, paltry or contemptible, belonging to a low order of things; in John 5:29, those who have practiced "evil" things, RV, "ill" (***phaula***), are set in contrast to those who have done good things (***agatha***); the same contrast is presented in Rom. 9:11 and 2 Cor. 5:10, in each of which the most authentic mss. have ***phaulos*** for ***kakos***; he who practices "evil" things (RV, "ill") hates the light, John 3:20; jealousy and strife are accompanied by "every vile deed," Jas. 3:16. It is used as a noun in Titus 2:8 (see B, No. 4).

### B. Nouns.

1. ***kakia*** (*2549*), primarily, "badness" in quality (akin to A, No. 1), denotes (a) "wickedness, depravity, malignity," e.g., Acts 8:22, "wickedness"; Rom. 1:29, "maliciousness"; in Jas. 1:21, KJV, "naughtiness"; (b) "the evil of trouble, affliction," Matt. 6:34, only, and here alone translated "evil."

2. ***poneros*** (*4190*), the adjective (A, No. 2), is used as a noun, (a) of Satan as the "evil" one, Matt. 5:37; 6:13; 13:19, 38; Luke 11:4 (in some texts); John 17:15; Eph. 6:16; 2 Thess. 3:3; 1 John 2:13–14; 3:12; 5:18–19; (b) of human beings, Matt. 5:45; (probably v. 39); 13:49; 22:10; Luke 6:35; 1 Cor. 5:13; (c) neuter, "evil (things)," Matt. 9:4; 12:35; Mark 7:23; Luke 3:19; "that which is evil," Luke 6:45; Rom. 12:9; Acts 28:21, "harm."

3. ***kakon*** (*2556*), the neuter of A, No. 1, is used with the article, as a noun, e.g., Acts 23:9; Rom. 7:21; Heb. 5:14; in the plural, "evil things," e.g., 1 Cor. 10:6; 1 Tim. 6:10, "all kinds of evil," RV.

4. ***phaulon*** *(5337)*, the neuter of A, No. 3, is used as a noun in Titus 2:8.

5. ***kakopoios*** *(2555)*, properly the masculine gender of the adjective, denotes an "evil-doer" (***kakon***, "evil," ***poieo***, "to do"), 1 Pet. 2:12, 14; 4:15; in some mss. in 3:16 and John 18:30 (so the KJV).

## C. Verbs.

1. ***kakoo*** *(2559)*, "to ill-treat" (akin to A, No. 1), is rendered "to entreat evil" in Acts 7:6, 19; "made (them) evil affected," 14:2.

2. ***kakopoieo*** *(2554)* signifies "to do evil" (cf. B, No. 5), Mark 3:4 (RV, "to do harm"); so, Luke 6:9; in 3 John 11, "doeth evil"; in 1 Pet. 3:17, "evil doing."

## D. Adverb.

***kakos*** *(2560)*, "badly, evilly," akin to A, No. 1, is used in the physical sense, "to be sick," e.g., Matt. 4:24; Mark 1:32, 34; Luke 5:31. In Matt. 21:41 this adverb is used with the adjective, "He will miserably destroy those miserable men," more lit., "He will evilly destroy those men (evil as they are)," with stress on the adjective; (b) in the moral sense, "to speak evilly," John 18:23; Acts 23:5; to ask evilly, Jas. 4:3.

# EVIL SPEAKING

1. ***blasphemia*** *(988)* is translated "evil speaking" in Eph. 4:31, KJV (RV, railing).

2. ***katalalia*** *(2636)*, "evil speaking," 1 Pet. 2:1.

# EXALT, EXALTED

### *Old Testament*

## A. Verb.

***rum*** (7311), "to be high, exalted," means either the "state of being on a higher plane," Gen. 7:17, or "movement in an upward direction," Gen. 14:22. Used of men, this verb may refer to their "physical stature," Deut. 1:28. ***rum*** also means to give great honor and status to another, Ps. 12:8; Isa. 52:13. Another meaning is found in Ezek. 31:4, this verb is used of "making a plant grow larger," or raising a child, so rear a child, Isa. 1:2. The word sometimes means "to take up away from, remove," Lev 2:9; Isa. 57:14. ***rum*** also means to "be haughty," and so have improper "raised opinion" about oneself, and thus have a moral flaw of arrogance, 2 Sam. 22:28. When referring to the voice, ***rum*** means to "cry aloud," Deut. 27:14.

The raising of the hand serves as a symbol of power and strength and signifies being "mighty" or "triumphant," Deut. 32:27. To raise one's hand against someone is to rebel against him, 1 Kings 11:26. The raising of one's horn suggests the picture of a wild ox standing in all its strength. This is a picture of "triumph" over one's enemies, 1 Sam. 2:1. Raising one's head may be a public gesture of "triumph and supremacy," Ps. 110:7. Raising the head also came to signify "to mark with distinction," "to give honor to," Ps. 3:3. To raise one's eyes or heart is to be "proud" and "arrogant," Deut. 8:14.

## B. Nouns.

***rum*** (7312), "height; haughtiness." Physical height, Prov. 25:3; improper pride, Isa. 2:11.

***marom*** (4791), "higher plane; height; high social position." Job 16:19 and Isa. 33:5 contain the word with the meaning of "the height" as the abode of God. Job 5:11 uses the word to refer to "a high social position." ***marom*** can also signify improper pride, or "self-exaltation," 2 Kings 19:22; Ps. 73:8.

### *New Testament*

## A. Verbs.

1. ***hupsoo*** *(5312)*, "to lift up" (akin to ***hupsos***, "height"), is used (a) literally of the "lifting" up of Christ in His crucifixion, John 3:14; 8:28; 12:32, 34; illustratively, of the serpent of brass, John 3:14; (b) figuratively, of spiritual privileges bestowed on a city, Matt. 11:23; Luke 10:15; of "raising" to dignity and happiness, Luke 1:52; Acts 13:17; of haughty self-exaltation, and, contrastingly, of being "raised" to honor, as a result of self-humbling, Matt. 23:12; Luke 14:11; 18:14; of spiritual "uplifting" and revival, Jas. 4:10; 1 Pet. 5:6; of bringing into the blessings of salvation through the gospel, 2 Cor. 11:7; (c) with a combination of the literal and metaphorical, of the "exaltation" of Christ by God the Father, Acts 2:33; 5:31.

2. ***huperupsoo*** *(5251)*, "to exalt highly" (***huper***, "over," and No. 1), is used of Christ, as in No. 1, (c), in Phil. 2:9.

3. ***epairo*** *(1869)*, "to lift up" (***epi***, "up," ***airo***, "to raise"), is said (a) literally, of a sail, Acts 27:40; hands, Luke 24:50; 1 Tim. 2:8; heads, Luke 21:28; eyes, Matt. 17:8, etc.; (b) metaphorically, of "exalting" oneself, being "lifted up" with pride, 2 Cor. 10:5; 11:20.

4. ***huperairo*** *(5229)*, "to raise over" (***huper***, "above," and ***airo***, see No. 3), is used in the middle voice, of "exalting" oneself exceedingly, 2 Cor. 12:7; 2 Thess. 2:4.

## B. Adjective.

***hupselos*** *(5308)*, "high, lofty," is used metaphorically in Luke 16:15, as a noun with the article, RV, "that which is exalted," KJV, "that which is highly esteemed."

## EXAMINATION, EXAMINE

**A. Noun.**

***anakrisis*** *(351)*, from ***ana***, "up or through," and ***krino***, "to distinguish," was a legal term among the Greeks, denoting the preliminary investigation for gathering evidence for the information of the judges, Acts 25:26.

**B. Verbs.**

1. ***anakrino*** *(350)*, "to examine, investigate," is used (a) of searching or enquiry, Acts 17:11; 1 Cor. 9:3; 10:25, 27; (b) of reaching a result of the enquiry, judging, 1 Cor. 2:14–15; 4:3–4; 14:24; (c) forensically, of examining by torture, Luke 23:14; Acts 4:9; 12:19; 24:8; 28:18.

2. ***anetazo*** *(426)*, "to examine judicially," is used in Acts 22:24, 29.

3. ***dokimazo*** *(1381)*, "to prove, test, approve," is rendered "examine" in 1 Cor. 11:28, KJV (RV, prove).

4. ***peirazo*** *(3985)*, "to tempt, try," is rendered "examine" in 2 Cor. 13:5, KJV (RV, try).

## EXAMPLE

**A. Nouns.**

1. ***deigma*** *(1164)*, primarily "a thing shown, a specimen" (akin to ***deiknumi***, "to show"), denotes an "example" given as a warning, Jude 7.

2. ***hupogrammos*** *(5261)*, lit., "an underwriting" (from ***hupographo***, "to write under, to trace letters" for copying by scholars); hence, "a writing-copy, an example," 1 Pet. 2:21, said of what Christ left for believers, by His sufferings (not expiatory, but exemplary), that they might "follow His steps."

**B. Verbs.**

1. ***deigmatizo*** *(1165)*, "to make a show of, to expose" (akin to A, No. 1), is translated "to make a public example," in Matt. 1:19 (some mss. have the strengthened form ***paradeigmatizo*** here; "put . . . to an open shame," Heb. 6:6,); in Col. 2:15, "made a show of."

2. ***hupodeiknumi*** *(5263)*, primarily, "to show secretly" (***hupo***, "under," ***deiknumi***, "to show"), "to show by tracing out" (akin to A, No. 1); hence, "to teach, to show by example," Acts 20:35, RV, "I gave you an example," for KJV, "I showed you." Elsewhere, "to warn," Matt. 3:7; Luke 3:7; 12:5, RV, for KJV, "forewarn"; "to show," Luke 6:47; Acts 9:16.

## EXCEED, EXCEEDING, EXCEEDINGLY

**A. Verbs.**

1. ***huperballo*** *(5235)*, "to throw over or beyond" (***huper***, "over," ***ballo***, "to throw"), is translated "exceeding" in 2 Cor. 9:14; Eph. 1:19; 2:7; "excelleth" (RV, "surpasseth") in 2 Cor. 3:10; "passeth" in Eph. 3:19 ("surpasseth" might be the meaning here).

2. ***perisseuo*** *(4052)*, "to be over and above, over a certain number or measure, to abound, exceed," is translated "exceed" in Matt. 5:20; 2 Cor. 3:9.

**B. Adverbs and Adverbial Phrases.**

1. ***sphodra*** *(4970)*, properly the neuter plural of ***sphodros***, "excessive, violent" (from a root indicating restlessness), signifies "very, very much, exceedingly," Matt. 2:10; 17:6, "sore"; 17:23; 18:31, RV, "exceeding," for KJV, "very"; 19:25; 26:22; 27:54, RV, "exceedingly" for KJV, "greatly"; Mark 16:4, "very"; Luke 18:23 (ditto); Acts 6:7, RV, "exceedingly," for KJV, greatly; Rev. 16:21.

2. ***sphodros*** *(4971)*, "exceedingly," is used in Acts 27:18.

3. ***perissos*** *(4057)*, akin to A. 2., is used in Matt. 27:23, RV, "exceedingly," for KJV, "the more"; Mark 10:26, RV, "exceedingly," for KJV, "out of measure"; in Acts 26:11, "exceedingly." In Mark 15:14, the most authentic mss. have this word (RV, "exceedingly") for No. 4 (KJV, "the more exceedingly").

4. ***perissoteros*** *(4056)*, akin to A. 2., "abundantly, exceedingly," Gal. 1:14, "more exceedingly"; 1 Thess. 2:17.

5. ***huperekperissou*** *(5528* and *1537* and *4053)* denotes "superabundantly" (***huper***, "over," ***ek***, "from," ***perissos***, "abundant"); in 1 Thess. 3:10, "exceedingly"; Eph. 3:20, "exceeding abundantly." Another form, ***huperekperissos*** (***huper***, "and" ***ek*** and No. 3), is used in 1 Thess. 5:13 (in the best mss.), "exceeding highly." Cf. the verb ***huperperisseuo***, "to abound more exceedingly," Rom. 5:21; in 2 Cor. 7:4, "I overflow (with joy)," RV, for KJV, "I am exceeding (joyful)."

## EXCEL, EXCELLENCY, EXCELLENT

**A. Verbs.**

1. ***perisseuo*** *(4052)*, "to be over and above," is rendered "abound" in 1 Cor. 14:12, RV, for KJV, "excel."

2. ***huperecho*** *(5242)*, lit., "to have over" (***huper***, "over," ***echo***, "to have"), is translated "excellency" in Phil. 3:8, "the surpassingness" (Moule); the phrase could be translated "the surpassing thing, which consists in the knowledge of Christ Jesus," and this is the probable meaning. This verb is used three times in Philippians, here and in 2:3; 4:7. See also Rom. 13:1; 1 Pet. 2:13.

3. ***diaphero*** *(1308)*, "to differ," is used in the neuter plural of the present participle with the

article, in Phil. 1:10, "the things that are excellent."

**B. Nouns.**

1. ***huperbole*** (*5236*), lit., "a throwing beyond," hence, "a surpassing, an excellence," is translated "excellency" in 2 Cor. 4:7, KJV; RV, "exceeding greatness." It always betokens preeminence.

2. ***huperoche*** (*5247*), akin to A, No. 2, strictly speaking, "the act of overhanging" (***huper***, and ***echo***, "to hold") or "the thing which overhangs," hence, "superiority, preeminence," is translated "excellency (of speech)" in 1 Cor. 2:1; elsewhere, in 1 Tim. 2:2, RV, "high place," for KJV, "authority."

**C. Adjectives.**

1. ***megaloprepes*** (*3169*) signifies "magnificent, majestic, that which is becoming to a great man" (from ***megas***, "great," and ***prepo***, "to be fitting or becoming"), in 2 Pet. 1:17, "excellent."

2. ***diaphoroteros*** (*1313**), comparative degree of ***diaphoros***, "excellent," akin to A, No. 3, is used twice, in Heb. 1:4, "more excellent (name)," and 8:6, "more excellent (ministry)." For the positive degree see Rom. 12:6; Heb. 9:10.

3. ***pleion*** (*4119*), "more, greater," the comparative degree of ***polus***, "much," is translated "more excellent" in Heb. 11:4, of Abel's sacrifice; ***pleion*** is used sometimes of that which is superior by reason of inward worth, cf. 3:3, "more (honor)"; in Matt. 6:25, of the life in comparison with meat.

4. ***kratistos*** (*2903*), "mightiest, noblest, best," the superlative degree of ***kratus***, "strong" (cf. ***kratos***, "strength"), is used as a title of honor and respect, "most excellent," Luke 1:3 (Theophilus was quite possibly a man of high rank); Acts 23:26; 24:3 and 26:25, RV, for KJV, "most noble."

## EXCESS

1. ***akrasia*** (*192*) lit. denotes "want of strength," hence, "want of self-control, incontinence," Matt. 23:25, "excess"; 1 Cor. 7:5, "incontinency."

2. ***anachusis*** (*401*), lit., "a pouring out, overflowing" (akin to ***anacheo***, "to pour out"), is used metaphorically in 1 Pet. 4:4, "excess," said of the riotous conduct described in v. 3.

## EXCHANGE

**A. Noun.**

***antallagma*** (465), "the price received as an equivalent of, or in exchange for, an article, an exchange" (***anti***, "instead of," ***allasso***, "to change," akin to ***allos***, "another"), hence denotes the price at which the "exchange" is effected, Matt. 16:26; Mark 8:37. Connected with this is the conception of atonement, as in the word ***lutron***, "a ransom."

**B. Verb.**

***metallasso*** (*3337*) denotes (a) "to exchange," ***meta***, "with," implying change, and ***allasso*** (see A), Rom. 1:25, of "exchanging" the truth for a lie, RV, for KJV, "changed"; (b) "to change," v. 26, a different meaning from that in the preceding verse.

## EXCUSE

**A. Adjective (negative).**

***anapologetos*** (*379*), "without excuse, inexcusable" (***a***, negative, ***n***, euphonic, and ***apologeomai***, see B, No. 1, below), is used, Rom. 1:20, "without excuse," of those who reject the revelation of God in creation; 2:1, RV, for KJV, "inexcusable," of the Jew who judges the Gentile.

**B. Verbs.**

1. ***apologeomai*** (*626*), lit., "to speak oneself off," hence "to plead for oneself," and so, in general, (a) "to defend," as before a tribunal; in Rom. 2:15, RV, "excusing them," means one "excusing" others (not themselves); the preceding phrase "one with another" signifies one person with another, not one thought with another; it may be paraphrased, "their thoughts with one another, condemning or else excusing one another"; conscience provides a moral standard by which men judge one another; (b) "to excuse" oneself, 2 Cor. 12:19.

2. ***paraiteomai*** (*3868*) is used in the sense of "begging off, asking to be excused or making an excuse," in Luke 14:18 (twice) and v. 19. In the first part of v. 18 the verb is used in the middle voice, "to make excuse" (acting in imagined self-interest); in the latter part and in v. 19 it is in the passive voice, "have me excused."

## EXERCISE

**A. Verb.**

***gumnazo*** (*1128*) primarily signifies "to exercise naked" (from ***gumnos***, "naked"); then, generally, "to exercise, to train the body or mind" (Eng., "gymnastic"), 1 Tim. 4:7, with a view to godliness; Heb. 5:14, of the senses, so as to discern good and evil; 12:11, of the effect of chastening, the spiritual "exercise producing the fruit of righteousness"; 2 Pet. 2:14, of certain evil teachers with hearts "exercised in covetousness," RV.

**B. Noun.**

***gumnasia*** (*1129*) primarily denotes "gymnastic exercise" (akin to A), 1 Tim. 4:8, where the immediate reference is probably not to mere physical training for games but to discipline of the body such as that to which the apostle refers in 1 Cor. 9:27, though there may be an allusion to the practices of asceticism.

## EXHORT, EXHORTATION

**A. Verbs.**

1. ***parakaleo*** (*3870*), primarily, "to call to a person" (***para***, "to the side," ***kaleo***, "to call"), denotes (a) "to call on, entreat"; (b) to admonish, exhort, to urge one to pursue some course of conduct (always prospective, looking to the future, in contrast to the meaning to comfort, which is retrospective, having to do with trial experienced), translated "exhort" in the RV of Phil. 4:2; 1 Thess. 4:10; Heb. 13:19, 22, for KJV, "beseech"; in 1 Tim. 5:1, for KJV, "intreat"; in 1 Thess. 5:11, for KJV, "comfort"; "exhorted" in 2 Cor. 8:6 and 12:18, for KJV, "desired"; in 1 Tim. 1:3, for KJV, "besought.

2. ***paraineo*** (*3867*), primarily, "to speak of near" (***para***, "near," and ***aineo***, "to tell of, speak of," then, "to recommend"), hence, "to advise, exhort, warn," is used in Acts 27:9, "admonished," and v. 22, "I exhort."

3. ***protrepo*** (*4389*), lit., "to turn forward, propel" (***pro***, "before," ***trepo***, "to turn"); hence, "to impel morally, to urge forward, encourage," is used in Acts 18:27, RV, "encouraged him" (Apollos), with reference to his going into Achaia; KJV, "exhorting the disciples"; while the encouragement was given to Apollos, a letter was written to the disciples in Achaia to receive him.

**B. Noun.**

***paraklesis*** (*3874*), akin to A, No. 1, primarily "a calling to one's side," and so "to one's aid," hence denotes (a) an appeal, "entreaty," 2 Cor. 8:4; (b) encouragement, "exhortation," e.g., Rom. 12:8; in Acts 4:36, RV, "exhortation," for KJV, "consolation"; (c) "consolation and comfort," e.g., Rom. 15:4.

## EXORCIST

***exorkistes*** (*1845*) denotes (a) "one who administers an oath"; (b) "an exorcist" (akin to ***exorkizo***, "to adjure," from ***orkos***, "an oath"), "one who employs a formula of conjuration for the expulsion of demons," Acts 19:13. The practice of "exorcism" was carried on by strolling Jews, who used their power in the recitation of particular names.

## EXPECT, EXPECTATION

**A. Verbs.**

1. ***ekdechomai*** (*1551*), lit. and primarily, "to take or receive from" (***ek***, "from," ***dechomai***, "to receive"), hence denotes "to await, expect," the only sense of the word in the NT; it suggests a reaching out in readiness to receive something; "expecting," Heb. 10:13; "expect," 1 Cor. 16:11, RV (KJV, "look for"); to wait for, John 5:3 (KJV only); Acts 17:16; 1 Cor. 11:33, RV (KJV, "tarry for"); Jas. 5:7; to wait, 1 Pet. 3:20 in some mss.; "looked for," Heb. 11:10.

2. ***prosdokao*** (*4328*), "to watch toward, to look for, expect" (***pros***, "toward," ***dokeo***, "to think": ***dokao*** "does not exist"), is translated "expecting" in Matt. 24:50 and Luke 12:46, RV (KJV, "looketh for"); Luke 3:15, "were in expectation"; Acts 3:5, "expecting" (KJV and RV); 28:6 (twice), "expected that," RV (KJV, "looked when") and "when they were long in expectation" (KJV, "after they had looked a great while").

**B. Nouns.**

1. ***apokaradokia*** (*603*), primarily "a watching with outstretched head" (***apo***, "from," ***kara***, "the head," and ***dokeo***, "to look, to watch"), signifies "strained expectancy, eager longing," the stretching forth of the head indicating an "expectation" of something from a certain place, Rom. 8:19 and Phil. 1:20. The prefix ***apo*** suggests "abstraction and absorption" (Lightfoot), i.e., abstraction from anything else that might engage the attention, and absorption in the object expected "till the fulfillment is realized" (Alford). The intensive character of the noun, in comparison with No. 2 (below), is clear from the contexts; in Rom. 8:19 it is said figuratively of the creation as waiting for the revealing of the sons of God ("waiting" translates the verb ***apekdechomai***, a strengthened form of A, No. 1. In Phil. 1:20 the apostle states it as his "earnest expectation" and hope, that, instead of being put to shame, Christ shall be magnified in his body, "whether by life, or by death," suggesting absorption in the person of Christ, abstraction from aught that hinders.

2. ***prosdokia*** (*4329*), "a watching for, expectation" (akin to A, No. 2, which see), is used in the NT only of the "expectation" of evil, Luke 21:26, RV, "expectation," KJV, "looking for," regarding impending calamities; Acts 12:11, "the expectation" of the execution of Peter. 3. ***ekdoche*** (*1561*), primarily "a receiving from,"

hence, "expectation" (akin to A, No. 1), is used in Heb. 10:27 (RV, "expectation"; KJV, "looking for"), of judgment.

## EXPERIENCE (without), EXPERIMENT

1. ***apeiros*** (*552*), "without experience" (***a***, negative, ***peira***, "a trial, experiment") is used in Heb. 5:13, RV, "without experience," KJV, "unskillful," with reference to "the word of righteousness."

2. ***dokime*** (*1382*) means (a) "the process of proving"; it is rendered "experiment" in 2 Cor. 9:13, KJV, RV, "the proving (of you)"; in 8:2, KJV, "trial," RV, "proof"; (b) "the effect of proving, approval, approvedness," RV, "probation," Rom. 5:4 (twice), for KJV, "experience"; KJV and RV, "proof" in 2 Cor. 2:9; 13:3 and Phil. 2:22.

## EXPLAIN

***diasapheo*** (*1285*), "to make clear, explain fully" (***dia*** "through," intensive, and ***saphes***, "clear"), is translated "explain" in Matt. 13:36 RV (KJV, "declare") translates ***phrazo***; in 18:31, "told."

## EXPOUND

1. ***ektithemi*** (*1620*), "to set out, expose" (***ek***, "out," ***tithemi***, "to place"), is used (a) literally, Acts 7:21; (b) metaphorically, in the middle voice, to set forth, "expound," of circumstances, Acts 11:4; of the way of God, 18:26; of the kingdom of God, 28:23.

2. ***epiluo*** (*1956*), primarily, "to loose, release," a strengthened form of ***luo***, "to loose," signifies "to solve, explain, expound," Mark 4:34, "expounded"; in Acts 19:39, of settling a controversy, RV, "it shall be settled," for KJV, "it shall be determined."

3. ***diermeneuo*** (*1329*), "to interpret fully" (***dia*** "through," intensive, ***hermeneuo***, "to interpret"); (Eng., "hermeneutics"), is translated, "He expounded" in Luke 24:27, KJV, RV, "interpreted"; in Acts 9:36, "by interpretation," lit., "being interpreted"; see also 1 Cor. 12:30; 14:5, 13, 27.

## EXTORT, EXTORTION, EXTORTIONER

### A. Verb.

***prasso*** (*4238*), "to practice," has the special meaning "extort" in Luke 3:13, RV (KJV, "exact"). In Luke 19:23 it is translated "required"; it may be that the master, in addressing the slothful servant, uses the word "extort" or "exact" (as in 3:13), in accordance with the character attributed to him by the servant.

### B. Nouns.

1. ***harpage*** (*724*) denotes "pillage, plundering, robbery, extortion" (akin to ***harpazo***, "to seize, carry off by force," and ***harpagmos***, "a thing seized, or the act of seizing"; from the root ***arp***, seen in Eng., "rapacious"; an associated noun, with the same spelling, denoted a rake, or hook for drawing up a bucket); it is translated "extortion" in Matt. 23:25; Luke 11:39, RV, KJV, "ravening"; Heb. 10:34, "spoiling."

2. ***pleonexia*** (*4124*), "covetousness, desire for advantage," is rendered "extortion" in 2 Cor. 9:5.

### C. Adjective.

***harpax*** (*727*), "rapacious" (akin to No. 1), is translated as a noun, "extortioners," in Luke 18:11; 1 Cor. 5:10–11; 6:10; in Matt. 7:15 "ravening" (of wolves).

## EYE

### *Old Testament*

***'ayin*** (5869), "eye; well; surface; appearance; spring of water." First, the word represents the bodily part, "eye," Gen. 13:10. The expression "between the eyes" means "on the forehead," as a part of the body, Exod. 13:9.

***'ayin*** is often used in connection with expressions of "seeing," Gen. 45:12. The expression "to lift up one's eyes," means to look up and see an object in front of one's view, Gen. 13:10. "Lifting up one's eyes" may also be an act expressing "desire," "longing," Gen. 39:7. The "eyes" may be used in gaining or seeking a judgment, in the sense of "seeing intellectually," "making an evaluation," or "seeking an evaluation or proof of faithfulness," Gen. 44:21.

"Eyes" are used figuratively of mental and spiritual abilities, acts and states. So the "opening of the eyes" in Gen. 3:5 (the first occurrence) means to become autonomous by setting standards of good and evil for oneself. In passages such as Prov. 4:25, "eye" represents a moral faculty. The phrase, "in the eye of," means "in one's view or opinion," Gen. 16:4. Another phrase, "from the eyes of," may signify that a thing or matter is "hidden" from one's knowledge, Num. 5:13. In Exod. 10:5, the word represents the "visible surface of the earth." Lev. 13:5 uses ***'ayin*** to represent "one's appearance." A "gleam or sparkle" is described in the phrase, "to give its eyes," KJV "giveth his colour," Prov. 23:31.

***Ma'yan*** (4599), "spring," means a body of water that naturally comes from the ground as compared to a stored body of water in a well or cistern, Gen. 7:11. This spring may occasionally refer to the life-giving elements which water of course has, Ps 87:7; Lev. 11:36.

### *New Testament*

1. ***ophthalmos*** (*3788*), akin to ***opsis***, "sight," probably from a root signifying "penetration, sharpness" (Curtius, *Gk. Etym.*) (cf. Eng., "ophthalmia," etc.). is used (a) of the physical organ, e.g., Matt. 5:38; of restoring sight, e.g., Matt. 20:33; of God's power of vision, Heb. 4:13; 1 Pet. 3:12; of Christ in vision, Rev. 1:14; 2:18; 19:12; of the Holy Spirit in the unity of Godhood with Christ, Rev. 5:6; (b) metaphorically, of ethical qualities, evil, Matt. 6:23; Mark 7:22 (by metonymy, for envy); singleness of motive, Matt. 6:22; Luke 11:34; as the instrument of evil desire, "the principal avenue of temptation," 1 John 2:16; of adultery, 2 Pet. 2:14; (c) metaphorically, of mental vision, Matt. 13:15; John 12:40; Rom. 11:8; Gal. 3:1, where the metaphor of the "evil eye" is altered to a different sense from that of bewitching (the posting up or placarding of an "eye" was used as a charm, to prevent mischief); by gospel-preaching Christ had been, so to speak, placarded before their "eyes"; the question may be paraphrased, "What evil teachers have been malignly fascinating you?"; Eph. 1:18, of the "eyes of the heart," as a means of knowledge.

2. ***trumalia*** (*5168*) is used of the "eye" of a needle, Mark 10:25 (from ***trume***, "a hole," ***truo***, "to wear away").

## EYE-SERVICE

***ophthalmodoulia*** (*3787*) denotes "service performed only under the master's eye," diligently performed when he is looking, but neglected in his absence, Eph. 6:6 and Col. 3:22.

## EYEWITNESS

1. ***autoptes*** (*845*) signifies "seeing with one's own eyes," Luke 1:2.

2. ***epoptes*** (*2030*), primarily "an overseer" (***epi***, "over"), then, a "spectator, an eyewitness" of anything, is used in 2 Pet. 1:16 of those who were present at the transfiguration of Christ, with a possible focus that this is sight which observes a revelation not given to all.

# F

## FABLE

***muthos*** *(3454)* primarily signifies "speech, conversation." The first syllable comes from a root ***mu***—, signifying "to close, keep secret, be dumb"; whence, ***muo***, "to close" (eyes, mouth) and ***musterion***, "a secret, a mystery"; hence, "a story, narrative, fable, fiction" (Eng., "myth"). The word is used of Gnostic errors and of Jewish and profane fables and genealogies, in 1 Tim. 1:4; 4:7; 2 Tim. 4:4; Titus 1:14; of fiction, in 2 Pet. 1:16.

***muthos*** is to be contrasted with ***aletheia***, "truth," and with ***logos***, "a story, a narrative purporting to set forth facts," e.g., Matt. 28:15, a "saying" (i.e., an account, story, in which actually there is a falsification of facts); Luke 5:15, RV, "report."

## FACE

### *Old Testament*

***panim*** (6440), "face." In its most basic meaning, this noun refers to the "face," on the head of a person, Gen. 17:3. Also ***panim*** means "the look on one's face," or one's "countenance," often with a focus on the person himself, Gen. 4:5; Deut. 7:10. ***panim*** can also be used of the surface or visible side of a thing, Gen. 1:2; Exod. 26:9.

This noun is sometimes used anthropomorphically of God; the Bible speaks of God as though He had a "face": ". . . For therefore I have seen thy face, as though I had seen the face of God," Gen. 33:10. The Bible clearly teaches that God is a spiritual being and ought not to be depicted by an image or any likeness whatever, Exod. 20:4.

### *New Testament*

1. ***prosopon*** *(4383)* denotes "the countenance," lit., "the part towards the eyes" (from ***pros***, "towards," ***ops***, "the eye"), and is used (a) of the "face," Matt. 6:16–17; 2 Cor. 3:7, 2nd part (KJV, "countenance"); in 2 Cor. 10:7, in the RV, "things that are before your face" (KJV, "outward appearance"), the phrase is figurative of superficial judgment; (b) of the look, i.e., the "face," which by its various movements affords an index of inward thoughts and feelings, e g., Luke 9:51, 53; 1 Pet. 3:12; (c) the presence of a person, the "face" being the noblest part, e.g., Acts 3:13, RV, "before the face of," KJV, "in the presence of"; 5:41, "presence"; 2 Cor. 2:10, "person"; 1 Thess. 2:17 (first part), "presence"; 2 Thess. 1:9, RV, "face," KJV, "presence"; Rev. 12:14, "face"; (d) the person himself, e.g., Gal. 1:22; 1 Thess. 2:17 (second part); (e) the appearance one presents by his wealth or poverty, his position or state, Matt. 22:16; Mark 12:14; Gal. 2:6; Jude 16; (f) the outward appearance of inanimate things, Matt. 16:3; Luke 12:56; 21:35; Acts 17:26.

2. ***opsis*** *(3799)* is primarily "the act of seeing"; then, (a) "the face"; of the body of Lazarus, John 11:44; of the "countenance" of Christ in a vision, Rev. 1:16; (b) the "outward appearance" of a person or thing, John 7:24.

## FACTION, FACTIOUS

***erithia*** (or ***—eia***) *(2052)* denotes "ambition, self-seeking, rivalry," self-will being an underlying idea in the word; hence it denotes "party-making." It is derived, not from ***eris***, "strife," but from ***erithos***, "a hireling"; hence the meaning of "seeking to win followers," "factions," so rendered in the RV of 2 Cor. 12:20, KJV, "strifes"; not improbably the meaning here is rivalries, or base ambitions (all the other words in the list express abstract ideas rather than factions); Gal. 5:20; Phil. 1:17 (RV; KJV, v. 16, "contention"); 2:3 (KJV, "strife"); Jas. 3:14, 16; in Rom. 2:8 it is translated as an adjective, "factious" (KJV, "contentious"). The order "strife, jealousy, wrath, faction," is the same in 2 Cor. 12:20 and Gal. 5:20. "Faction" is the fruit of jealousy. Cf. the synonymous adjective ***hairetikos***, Titus 3:10, causing division (marg., "factious"), not necessarily "heretical," in the sense of holding false doctrine.

## FADE (away)

**A. Verb.**

***maraino*** *(3133)* was used (a) to signify "to quench a fire," and in the passive voice, of the "dying out of a fire"; hence (b) in various relations, in the active voice, "to quench, waste, wear out"; in the passive, "to waste away"; Jas. 1:11, of the "fading" away of a rich man, as illustrated by the flower of the field.

**B. Adjectives (negative).**

1. ***amarantos*** *(263)*, "unfading" (***a***, negative, and A, above), whence the "amaranth," an unfading flower, a symbol of perpetuity, is used in 1 Pet. 1:4 of the believer's inheritance, "that fadeth not away."

2. ***amarantinos*** (*262*) primarily signifies "composed of amaranth" (see No. 1); hence, "unfading," 1 Pet. 5:4, of the crown of glory promised to faithful elders.

## FAIL

**A. Verbs.**

1. ***ekleipo*** (*1587*), "to leave out" (***ek***, "out," ***leipo***, "to leave"), used intransitively, means "to leave off, cease, fail"; it is said of the cessation of earthly life, Luke 16:9; of faith, 22:32; of the light of the sun, 23:45 (in the best mss.); of the years of Christ, Heb. 1:12.

2. ***epileipo*** (*1952*), "not to suffice for a purpose" (***epi***, over), is said of insufficient time, in Heb. 11:32.

3. ***pipto*** (*4098*), "to fall," is used of the law of God in its smallest detail, in the sense of losing its authority or ceasing to have force, Luke 16:17. In 1 Cor. 13:8 it is used of love (some mss. have ***ekpipto***, "to fall off").

**B. Adjective.**

***anekleiptos*** (*413*), "unfailing" (***a***, negative, and A, No. 1), is rendered "that faileth not," in Luke 12:33. In a Greek document dated A.D. 42, some contractors undertake to provide "unfailing" heat for a bath during the current year.

## FAIN

1. ***boulomai*** (*1014*), "to will deliberately, wish, desire, be minded," implying the deliberate exercise of volition (contrast No. 3), is translated "would fain" in Philem. 13 (in the best mss.).

2. ***epithumeo*** (*1937*), "to set one's heart upon, desire," is translated "would fain" in Luke 15:16, of the Prodigal Son.

3. ***thelo*** (*2309*), "to wish, to design to do anything," expresses the impulse of the will rather than the intention (see No. 1); the RV translates it "would fain" in Luke 13:31, of Herod's desire to kill Christ, KJV, "will (kill)"; in 1 Thess. 2:18, of the desire of the missionaries to return to the church in Thessalonica.

## FAINT

1. ***ekluo*** (*1590*) denotes (a) "to loose, release" (***ek***, "out," ***luo***, "to loose"); (b) "to unloose," as a bow-string, "to relax," and so, "to enfeeble," and is used in the passive voice with the significance "to be faint, grow weary," (1) of the body, Matt. 15:32; (some mss. have it in 9:36); Mark 8:3; (2) of the soul, Gal. 6:9 (last clause), in discharging responsibilities in obedience to the Lord; in Heb. 12:3, of becoming weary in the strife against sin; in v. 5, under the chastening hand of God.

2. ***enkakeo*** or ***ekkakeo*** (*1573*), "to lack courage, lose heart, be fainthearted" (***en***, "in," ***kakos***, "base"), is said of prayer, Luke 18:1; of gospel ministry, 2 Cor. 4:1, 16; of the effect of tribulation, Eph. 3:13; as to well doing, 2 Thess. 3:13, "be not weary" (KJV marg., "fain not"). Some mss. have this word in Gal. 6:9 (No. 1).

3. ***kamno*** (*2577*) primarily signified "to work"; then, as the effect of continued labor, "to be weary"; it is used in Heb. 12:3, of becoming "weary" (see also No. 1), RV, "wax not weary"; in Jas. 5:15, of sickness; some mss. have it in Rev. 2:3, KJV, "hast (not) fainted," RV, "grown weary."

## FAINTHEARTED

***oligopsuchos*** (*3642*), lit., "small-souled," denotes "despondent"; then, "fainthearted," 1 Thess. 5:14, RV, for the incorrect KJV, "feeble-minded."

## FAIR

1. ***asteios*** (*791*), lit., "of the city" (from ***astu***, "a city"; like Lat. ***urbanus***, from ***urbs***, "a city"; Eng., "urbane"; similarly, "polite," from ***polis***, "a town"), hence, "fair, elegant" (used in the papyrus writings of clothing), is said of the external form of a child, Acts 7:20, of Moses "(exceeding) fair," lit., "fair to God"; Heb. 11:23 (RV, "goodly," KJV, "proper").

2. ***eudia*** (*2105*) denotes "fair weather," Matt. 16:2, (from ***eudios***, "calm"; from ***eu***, "good," and ***dios***, "divine"), among the pagan Greeks, akin to the name for the god Zeus, or Jupiter. Some would derive ***dios*** and the Latin ***deus*** (god) and ***dies*** (day) from a root meaning "bright."

## FAITH, FAITHFULNESS

### *Old Testament*

***'emunah*** (530), The basic meaning of ***'emunah*** is "certainty" and "faithfulness," 1 Sam. 26:23. But generally, the Person to whom one is "faithful" is the Lord Himself, 2 Chron. 19:9. The Lord has manifested His "faithfulness" to His people, Deut. 32:4. All his works reveal his "faithfulness," Ps. 33:4. His commandments are an expression of his "faithfulness," Ps. 119:86; those who seek them are found on the road of "faithfulness," Ps. 119:30. The Lord looks for those who seek to do His will with all their hearts. Their ways are established and His blessing rests on them, Prov. 28:20.

Man's acts, Prov. 12:22, and speech, 12:17, must reflect his favored status with God. As in the marriage relationship, "faithfulness" is not optional. For the relation to be established, the two parties are required to respond to each other in "faithfulness," Jer. 5:1; cf. Isa.

59:4; Jer. 7:28; 9:3. Hosea portrays God's relation to Israel as a marriage and states God's promise of "faithfulness" to Israel (where several Hebrew words describe faithfulness), Hos. 2:19–20.

### *New Testament*

***pistis*** (*4102*), primarily, "firm persuasion," a conviction based upon hearing (akin to ***peitho***, "to persuade"), is used in the NT always of "faith in God or Christ, or things spiritual."

The word is used of (a) trust, e.g., Rom. 3:25; 1 Cor. 2:5; 15:14, 17; 2 Cor. 1:24; Gal. 3:23; Phil. 1:25; 2:17; 1 Thess. 3:2; 2 Thess. 1:3; 3:2; (b) trust-worthiness, e.g., Matt. 23:23; Rom. 3:3, RV, "the faithfulness of God"; Gal. 5:22 (RV, "faithfulness"); Titus 2:10, "fidelity"; (c) by metonymy, what is believed, the contents of belief, the "faith," Acts 6:7; 14:22; Gal. 1:23; 3:25 [contrast 3:23, under (a)]; 6:10; Phil. 1:27; 1 Thess. 3:10; Jude 3, 20 (and perhaps 2 Thess. 3:2); (d) a ground for "faith," an assurance, Acts 17:31 (not as in KJV, marg., "offered faith"); (e) a pledge of fidelity, plighted "faith," 1 Tim. 5:12.

The main elements in "faith" in its relation to the invisible God, as distinct from "faith" in man, are especially brought out in the use of this noun and the corresponding verb, ***pisteuo***; they are (1) a firm conviction, producing a full acknowledgement of God's revelation or truth, e.g., 2 Thess. 2:11–12; (2) a personal surrender to Him, John 1:12; (3) a conduct inspired by such surrender, 2 Cor. 5:7. Prominence is given to one or other of these elements according to the context. All this stands in contrast to belief in its purely natural exercise, which consists of an opinion held in good "faith" without necessary reference to its proof. The object of Abraham's "faith" was not God's promise (that was the occasion of its exercise); his "faith" rested on God Himself, Rom. 4:17, 20–21.

## FAITH (of little)

***oligopistos*** (*3640*), lit., "little of faith" (***oligos***, "little," ***pistis***, "faith"), is used only by the Lord, and as a tender rebuke, for anxiety, Matt. 6:30 and Luke 12:28; for fear, Matt. 8:26; 14:31; 16:8.

## FAITHFUL, FAITHFULLY, FAITHLESS

1. ***pistos*** (*4103*), a verbal adjective, akin to ***peitho***, is used in two senses, (a) passive, "faithful, to be trusted, reliable," said of God, e.g., 1 Cor. 1:9; 10:13; 2 Cor. 1:18 (KJV, "true"); 2 Tim. 2:13; Heb. 10:23; 11:11; 1 Pet. 4:19; 1 John 1:9; of Christ, e.g., 2 Thess. 3:3; Heb. 2:17; 3:2; Rev. 1:5; 3:14; 19:11; of the words of God, e.g., Acts 13:34, "sure"; 1 Tim. 1:15; 3:1 (KJV, "true"); 4:9; 2 Tim. 2:11; Titus 1:9; 3:8; Rev. 21:5; 22:6; of servants of the Lord, Matt. 24:45; 25:21, 23; Acts 16:15; 1 Cor. 4:2, 17; 7:25; Eph. 6:21; Col. 1:7; 4:7, 9; 1 Tim. 1:12; 3:11; 2 Tim. 2:2; Heb. 3:5; 1 Pet. 5:12; 3 John 5; Rev. 2:13; 17:14; of believers, Eph. 1:1; Col. 1:2; (b) active, signifying "believing, trusting, relying," e.g., Acts 16:1 (feminine); 2 Cor. 6:15; Gal. 3:9 seems best taken in this respect, as the context lays stress upon Abraham's "faith" in God, rather than upon his "faithfulness." In John 20:27 the context requires the active sense, as the Lord is reproaching Thomas for his want of "faith." See No. 2.

2. ***apistos*** (*571*) is used with meanings somewhat parallel to No. 1; (a) "untrustworthy" (***a***, negative, and No. 1), not worthy of confidence or belief, is said of things "incredible," Acts 26:8 (b) "unbelieving, distrustful," used as a noun, "unbeliever," Luke 12:46; 1 Tim. 5:8 (RV, for KJV, "infidel"); in Titus 1:15 and Rev. 21:8, "unbelieving"; "faithless" in Matt. 17:17; Mark 9:19; Luke 9:41; John 20:27. The word is most frequent in 1 and 2 Corinthians.

## FALL, FALLEN, FALLING, FELL

### A. Nouns.

1. ***ptosis*** (*4431*); "a fall" (akin to B, No. 1), is used (a) literally, of the "overthrow of a building," Matt. 7:27; (b) metaphorically, Luke 2:34, of the spiritual "fall" of those in Israel who would reject Christ; the word "again" in the KJV of the next clause is misleading; the "rising up" (RV) refers to those who would acknowledge and receive Him, a distinct class from those to whom the "fall" applies. The "fall" would be irretrievable, cf. (a); such a lapse as Peter's is not in view.

2. ***paraptoma*** (*3900*), primarily "a false step, a blunder" (***para***, "aside," ***pipto***, "to fall"), then "a lapse from uprightness, a sin, a moral trespass, misdeed," is translated "fall" in Rom. 11:11–12, of the sin and "downfall" of Israel in their refusal to acknowledge God's claims and His Christ; by reason of this the offer of salvation was made to Gentiles.

3. ***apostasia*** (*646*), "a defection, revolt, apostasy," is used in the NT of religious apostasy; in Acts 21:21, it is translated "to forsake," lit., "thou teachest apostasy from Moses." In 2 Thess. 2:3 "the falling away" signifies apostasy from the faith. In papyri documents it is used politically of rebels.

### B. Verbs.

1. ***pipto*** (*4098*), "to fall," is used (a) of descent, to "fall" down from, e.g., Matt. 10:29; 13:4; (b) of a lot, Acts 1:26; (c) of "falling" under judgment, Jas. 5:12 (cf. Rev. 18:2, RV); (d) of

persons in the act of prostration, to prostrate oneself, e.g., Matt. 17:6; John 18:6; Rev. 1:17; in homage and worship, e.g., Matt. 2:11; Mark 5:22; Rev. 5:14; 19:4; (e) of things, "falling" into ruin, or failing, e.g., Matt. 7:25; Luke 16:17, RV, "fall," for KJV, "fail"; Heb. 1:30; (f), of "falling" in judgment upon persons, as of the sun's heat, Rev. 7:16, RV, "strike," KJV, "light"; of a mist and darkness, Acts 13:11.

2. ***apopipto*** (*634*), "to fall from" (***apo***, "from"), is used in Acts 9:18, of the scales which "fell" from the eyes of Saul of Tarsus.

3. ***ekpipto*** (*1601*), to fall out of (***ek***, "out," and No. 1), is used in the NT, literally, of flowers that wither in the course of nature, Jas. 1:11; 1 Pet. 1:24; of a ship not under control, Acts 27:17, 26, 29, 32; of shackles loosed from a prisoner's wrist, 12:7; figuratively, of the Word of God (the expression of His purpose), which cannot "fall" away from the end to which it is set, Rom. 9:6; of the believer who is warned lest he "fall" away from the course in which he has been confirmed by the Word of God, 2 Pet. 3:17. So of those who seek to be justified by law, Gal. 5:4, "ye are fallen away from grace." Some mss. have this verb in Mark 13:25, for No. 1; so in Rev. 2:5.

4. ***empipto*** (*1706*), "to fall into, or among" (***en***, "in," and No. 1), is used (a) literally, Matt. 12:11; Luke 6:39 (some mss. have No. 1 here); 10:36; some mss. have it in 14:5; (b) metaphorically, into condemnation, 1 Tim. 3:6; reproach, 3:7; temptation and snare, 6:9; the hands of God in judgment, Heb. 10:13.

5. ***epipipto*** (*1968*), "to fall upon" (***epi***, "upon," and No. 1), is used (a) literally, Mark 3:10, "pressed upon"; Acts 20:10, 37; (b) metaphorically, of fear, Luke 1:12; Acts 19:17; Rev. 11:11 (No. 1, in some mss.); reproaches, Rom. 15:3; of the Holy Spirit, Acts 8:16; 10:44; 11:15.

6. ***katapipto*** (*2667*), "to fall down" (***kata***, "down," and No. 1), is used in Luke 8:6 (in the best mss.); Acts 26:14; 28:6.

7. ***parapipto*** (*3895*), akin to A, No. 2, properly, "to fall in one's way" (***para***, "by"), signifies "to fall away" (from adherence to the realities and facts of the faith), Heb. 6:6.

8. ***peripipto*** (*4045*), "to fall around" (***peri***, "around"), hence signifies to "fall" in with, or among, to light upon, come across, Luke 10:30, "among (robbers)"; Acts 27:41.

## FALSE, FALSEHOOD, FALSELY

### *Old Testament*

***sheqer*** (8267), "falsehood; lie." In about thirty-five passages, ***sheqer*** describes the nature of "deceptive speech": "to speak," Isa. 59:3, "to teach," Isa. 9:15, "to prophesy," Jer. 14:14, and "to lie," Mic. 2:11. It may also indicate a "deceptive character," as expressed in one's acts: "to deal treacherously," 2 Sam. 18:13, and "to deal falsely," Hos. 7:1. Thus ***sheqer*** defines a way of life that goes contrary to the law of God, Ps. 119:29–30; cf. vv. 104, 118, 128. The Old Testament saint was instructed to avoid "deception" and the liar, Exod. 23:7; cf. Prov. 13:5.

### *New Testament*

**A. Adjectives.**

1. ***pseudes*** (*5571*), is used of "false witnesses," Acts 6:13; "false apostles," Rev. 2:2, RV, "false," KJV, "liars"; Rev. 21:8, "liars."

2. ***pseudonumos*** (*5581*), "under a false name" (No. 1, and ***onoma***, "a name"; Eng., "pseudonym"), is said of the knowledge professed by the propagandists of various heretical cults, 1 Tim. 6:20.

**B. Noun.**

***pseudos*** (*5579*), "a falsehood" (akin to A, No. 1), is so translated in Eph. 4:25, RV (KJV, "lying"); in 2 Thess. 2:9, "lying wonders" is lit. "wonders of falsehood," i.e., wonders calculated to deceive; it is elsewhere rendered "lie," John 8:44; Rom. 1:25; 2 Thess. 2:11; 1 John 2:21, 27; Rev. 14:5, RV; 21:27; 22:15.

**C. Verb.**

***pseudo*** (*5574*), "to deceive by lies," is used in the middle voice, translated "to say . . . falsely," in Matt. 5:11; it is elsewhere rendered "to lie," Acts 5:3–4; Rom. 9:1; 2 Cor. 11:31; Gal. 1:20; Col. 3:9; 1 Tim. 2:7.

## FAME

**A. Noun.**

***pheme*** (*5345*) originally denoted "a divine voice, an oracle"; hence, "a saying or report" (akin to ***phemi***, "to say," from a root meaning "to shine, to be clear"; hence, Lat., ***fama***, Eng., "fame"), is rendered "fame" in Matt. 9:26 and Luke 4:14.

**B. Verb.**

***diaphemizo*** (*1310*) signifies "to spread abroad a matter," Matt. 28:15, RV; Mark 1:45, RV (from ***dia***, "throughout," and ***phemi***, "to say"); hence, "to spread abroad one's fame," Matt. 9:31. All the passages under this heading relate to the testimony concerning Christ in the days of His flesh.

## FAMILY

### *Old Testament*

***mishpachah*** (4940), "family; clan, kind." ***mishpachah*** basically means persons or creatures that are associated with each other, so refer to "kinds," of animals, Gen. 8:19; or all members of a group who were related by blood and who still felt a sense of consanguinity belonged to the "clan" or "the extended family," or "immediate family," 1 Sam. 9:21; Lev. 25:48–49; Josh. 6:23; or a "major tribal division, Num. 1–4; 26; or the "families" of the nations, Ps. 22:28; 96:7; cf. Gen. 10:5; 12:3.

*New Testament*

1. ***oikos*** (*3624*) signifies (a) "a dwelling, a house" (akin to ***oikeo***, to dwell); (b) "a household, family," translated "family" in 1 Tim. 5:4, RV, for KJV, "at home."

2. ***patria*** (*3965*), primarily "an ancestry, lineage," signifies in the NT "a family or tribe"; it is used of the "family" of David, Luke 2:4, RV, for KJV, "lineage"; in the wider sense of "nationalities, races," Acts 3:25, RV, "families," for KJV, "kindreds"; in Eph. 3:15, RV, "every family," for KJV, "the whole family," the reference being to all those who are spiritually related to God the Father, He being the Author of their spiritual relationship to Him as His children.

## FARE, FAREWELL

1. ***euphraino*** (*2165*), in the active voice, signifies "to cheer, gladden," 2 Cor. 2:2; in the passive, "to rejoice, make merry"; translated "faring sumptuously" in Luke 16:19, especially of food (RV, marg., "living in mirth and splendor").

2. ***rhonnumi*** (*4517*), "to strengthen, to be strong," is used in the imperative mood as a formula at the end of letters, signifying "Farewell," Acts 15:29.

3. ***chairo*** (*5463*), "to joy, rejoice, be glad," is used in the imperative mood in salutations, (a) on meeting, "Hail," e.g., Matt. 26:49; or with ***lego***, "to say, to give a greeting," 2 John 11; in letters, "greeting," e.g., Acts 15:23; (b) at parting, the underlying thought being joy, 2 Cor. 13:11.

## FASHION

### A. Nouns.

1. ***eidos*** (*1491*), "that which is seen, an appearance," is translated "fashion" in Luke 9:29, of the Lord's countenance at the Transfiguration.

2. ***prosopon*** (*4383*), "the face, countenance," is translated "fashion" in Jas. 1:11, of the flower of grass.

3. ***schema*** (*4976*), "a figure, fashion" (akin to ***echo***, "to have"), is translated "fashion" in 1 Cor. 7:31, of the world, signifying that which comprises the manner of life, actions, etc. of humanity in general; in Phil. 2:8 it is used of the Lord in His being found "in fashion" as a man.

4. ***tupos*** (*5179*), "a type, figure, example," is translated "fashion" in the KJV of Acts 7:44, RV, "figure," said of the tabernacle.

### B. Verbs.

1. ***metaschematizo*** (*3345*), "to change in fashion or appearance" (***meta***, "after," here implying change, ***schema***, see A, No. 3), is rendered "shall fashion anew" in Phil. 3:21, RV; KJV, "shall change," of the bodies of believers as changed or raised at the Lord's return; in 2 Cor. 11:13, 14, 15, the RV uses the verb "to fashion oneself," for KJV, to transform, of Satan and his human ministers, false apostles; in 1 Cor. 4:6 it is used by way of a rhetorical device, with the significance of transferring by a figure.

2. ***suschematizo*** (*4964*), "to give the same figure or appearance as, to conform to" (***sun***, "with," ***schema***, cf. No. 1), used in the passive voice, signifies "to fashion oneself, to be fashioned," Rom. 12:2, RV, "be not fashioned according to," for KJV, "be not conformed to"; 1 Pet. 1:14, "(not) fashioning yourselves."

### C. Adjective.

***summorphos*** (*4832*), "having like form with" (***sun***, "with," ***morphe***, "form"), is used in Rom. 8:29 and Phil. 3:21 (KJV, "fashioned," RV, "conformed").

## FAST, FASTING

### A. Nouns.

1. ***nesteia*** (*3521*), "a fasting, fast" (from ***ne***, a negative prefix, and ***esthio***, "to eat"), is used (a) of voluntary abstinence from food, Luke 2:37; Acts 14:23 (some mss. have it in Matt. 17:21 and Mark 9:29); "fasting" had become a common practice among Jews, and was continued among Christians; in Acts 27:9, "the Fast" refers to the Day of Atonement, Lev. 16:29; that time of the year would be one of dangerous sailing; (b) of involuntary abstinence (perhaps voluntary is included), consequent upon trying circumstances, 2 Cor. 6:5; 11 27.

2. ***nestis*** (*3523*), "not eating" (see No. 1), "fasting," is used of lack of food, Matt. 15:32; Mark 8:3.

### B. Verb.

***nesteuo*** (*3522*), "to fast, to abstain from eating" (akin to A, Nos. 1 and 2), is used of voluntary "fasting," Matt. 4:2; 6:16, 17, 18; 9:14, 15; Mark 2:18, 19, 20; Luke 5:33, 34, 35; 18:12; Acts 13:2, 3. Some of these passages show that teachers to whom scholars or disciples were attached gave them special instructions as to "fasting." Christ taught the need of purity and simplicity of motive.

**C. Adjectives.**

***asitos*** (*777*), "without food" (***a***, negative, ***sitos***, "corn, food"), is used in Acts 27:33, "fasting."

***asphalizo*** (*805*), "to make secure, safe, firm" (akin to ***asphales***, "safe"), (***a***, negative, and ***sphallo***, "to trip up"), is translated "make . . . fast," in Acts 16:24, of prisoners' feet in the stocks. In Matt. 27:64, 65, 66, it is rendered "to make sure."

## FATHER

### *Old Testament*

***'ab*** (1), "father; grandfather; forefather; ancestor." Basically, ***'ab*** relates to the familial relationship represented by the word "father," Gen. 2:24. ***'ab*** also means "grandfather" and/or "great-grandfather," as in Gen. 28:2,13; 1 Kings 19:4; "forefather," Jer. 35:6. ***'ab*** can also mean "founder of a class or station," such as a trade, Gen. 4:20, and a title of respect, usually applied to an older person, like, "sir," with a focus on relationship 1 Sam. 24:11; 2 Kings 2:12; 6:21; Jer. 3:4. In Gen. 45:8, the noun is used of an "advisor." In conjunction with ***bayit*** ("house"), the word ***'ab*** may mean "family," Exod. 6:25; 12:3.

God is described as the "father" of Israel, Deut. 32:6. Mal. 2:10 tells us that God is the "father" of all people. He is especially the "protector" or "father" of the fatherless, Ps. 68:5. As the "father" of a king, God especially aligns Himself to that man and his kingdom, 2 Sam. 7:14; Ps. 2:7. One of the Messiah's enthronement names is "Eternal Father," Isa. 9:6.

### *New Testament*

**A. Noun.**

***pater*** (*3962*), from a root signifying "a nourisher, protector, upholder" (Lat., ***pater***, Eng., "father," are akin), is used (a) of the nearest ancestor, e.g., Matt. 2:22; (b) of a more remote ancestor, the progenitor of the people, a "forefather," e.g., Matt. 3:9; 23:30; 1 Cor. 10:1; the patriarchs, 2 Pet. 3:4; (c) one advanced in the knowledge of Christ, 1 John 2:13; (d) metaphorically, of the originator of a family or company of persons animated by the same spirit as himself, as of Abraham, Rom. 4:11, 12, 16, 17, 18, or of Satan, John 8:38, 41, 44; (e) of one who, as a preacher of the gospel and a teacher, stands in a "father's" place, caring for his spiritual children, 1 Cor. 4:15 (not the same as a mere title of honor, which the Lord prohibited, Matt. 23:9); (f) of the members of the Sanhedrin, as of those who exercised religious authority over others, Acts 7:2; 22:1; (g) of God in relation to those who have been born anew (John 1:12, 13), and so are believers, Eph 2:18; 4:6 (cf. 2 Cor. 6:18), and imitators of their "Father," Matt. 5:45, 48; 6:1, 4, 6, 8, 9, etc. Christ never associated Himself with them by using the personal pronoun "our"; He always used the singular, "My Father"; His relationship being unoriginated and essential, whereas theirs is by grace and regeneration, e.g., Matt. 11:27; 25:34; John 20:17; Rev. 2:27; 3:5, 21; so the apostles spoke of God as the "Father" of the Lord Jesus Christ, e.g., Rom. 15:6; 2 Cor. 1:3; 11:31; Eph. 1:3; Heb. 1:5; 1 Pet. 1:3; Rev. 1:6; (h) of God, as the "Father" of lights, i.e., the Source or Giver of whatsoever provides illumination, physical and spiritual, Jas. 1:17; of mercies, 2 Cor. 1:3; of glory, Eph. 1:17; (i) of God, as Creator, Heb. 12:9, cf. Zech. 12:1.

**B. Adjectives.**

1. ***patroos*** (*3971*) signifies "of one's fathers," or "received from one's fathers" (akin to A), Acts 22:3; 24:14; 28:17.

2. ***patrikos*** (*3967*), "from one's fathers, or ancestors," is said of that which is handed down from one's "forefathers," Gal. 1:14.

3. ***apator*** (*540*), "without father," signifies, in Heb. 7:3, i.e., with no recorded genealogy.

4. ***patroparadotos*** (*3970*), "handed down from one's fathers," is used in 1 Pet. 1:18.

## FATHERLESS

***orphanos*** (*3737*), properly, "an orphan," is rendered "fatherless" in Jas. 1:27; "desolate" in John 14:18, for KJV, "comfortless."

## FAULT, FAULTLESS

**A. Noun.**

***aition*** (*158*), properly the neuter of ***aitios***, causative of, responsible for, is used as a noun, "a crime, a legal ground for punishment," translated "fault" in Luke 23:4, 14; in v. 22, cause.

**B. Adjective.**

***amemptos*** (*273*), "without blame," is rendered "faultless," in Heb. 8:7.

**C. Verbs.**

1. ***memphomai*** (*3201*), "to blame," is translated "to find fault" in Rom. 9:19 and Heb. 8:8. Some mss. have the verb in Mark 7:2.

2. ***elencho*** (*1651*), "to convict, reprove, rebuke," is translated "shew (him) his fault" in Matt. 18:15.

## FAVOR, FAVORED

### *Old Testament*

#### A. Noun.

***ratson*** (7522), "favor; goodwill; acceptance; will; desire; pleasure." ***ratson*** represents a concrete reaction of the superior to an inferior. When used of God, ***ratson*** may represent that which is shown in His blessings, Deut. 33:16. Thus Isaiah speaks of the day, year, or time of divine "favor"—in other words, the day of the Lord when all the blessings of the covenant shall be heaped upon God's people, Isa. 49:8; 58:5; 61:2. This word represents the position one enjoys before a superior who is favorably disposed toward him, Exod. 28:38.

***ratson*** also signifies a voluntary or arbitrary decision, Ezra 10:11. When a man does according to his own "will," he does "what he desires," Dan. 8:4. In Ps. 145:16, the word ***ratson*** means "one's desire" or "what one wants," cf. Esth. 1:8.

#### B. Verb.

***ratsah*** (7521), "to be pleased with," Gen. 33:10, (see A. above).

### *New Testament*

#### A. Noun.

***charis*** (*5485*) denotes (a) objectively, "grace in a person, graciousness," (b) subjectively, (1) "grace on the part of a giver, favor, kindness," (2) "a sense of favor received, thanks." It is rendered "favor" in Luke 1:30; 2:52; Acts 2:47; 7:10, 46; 24:27 and 25:9, RV (for KJV, "pleasure"); 25:3.

#### B. Verb.

***charitoo*** (*5487*), akin to A, to endow with ***charis***, primarily signified "to make graceful or gracious," and came to denote, in Hellenistic Greek, "to cause to find favor," Luke 1:28, "highly favored"; in Eph. 1:6, it is translated "made . . . accepted," KJV, "freely bestowed," RV (lit., "graced"); it does not here mean to endue with grace. Grace implies more than favor; grace is a free gift, favor may be deserved or gained.

## FEAR, FEARFUL, FEARFULNESS

### *Old Testament*

#### A. Verb.

***yare'*** (3372), "to be afraid, stand in awe, fear." Basically, this verb connotes the psychological reaction of "fear, dread, anxiety." ***yare'*** may indicate being afraid of something or someone, or simply in the state of fear, Gen. 32:11; cf. 19:30. Used of a person in an exalted position, ***yare'*** connotes "standing in awe," Gen. 22:12, 17; Exod. 14:31; 20:20.

#### B. Nouns.

***mora'*** (4172), "fear." The noun ***mora'***, is used exclusively of the fear of being before a superior kind of being. Usually it is used to describe the reaction evoked in men by God's mighty works of destruction and sovereignty, Deut. 4:24. Hence, the word represents a very strong "fear" or "terror." In the singular, this word emphasizes the divine acts themselves. ***mora'*** may suggest the reaction of animals to men, Gen. 9:2, and of the nations to conquering Israel, Deut. 11:25.

***yir'ah*** (3374), "fear; reverence," of men, Deut. 2:25; of things, Isa. 7:25; of situations, Jonah 1:10; and of God, Jonah 1:12; it may also mean "reverence" of God, Gen. 20:11.

### *New Testament*

#### A. Nouns.

1. ***phobos*** (*5401*) first had the meaning of "flight," that which is caused by being scared; then, "that which may cause flight," (a) "fear, dread, terror," always with this significance in the four Gospels; also e.g., in Acts 2:43; 19:17; 1 Cor. 2:3; 1 Tim. 5:20 (lit., "may have fear"); Heb. 2:15; 1 John 4:18; Rev. 11:11; 18:10, 15; by metonymy, that which causes "fear," Rom. 13:3; 1 Pet. 3:14, RV, "(their) fear," KJV "(their) terror," an adaptation of the Sept. of Isa. 8:12, "fear not their fear"; hence some take it to mean, as there, "what they fear," but in view of Matt. 10:28, e.g., it seems best to understand it as that which is caused by the intimidation of adversaries; (b) "reverential fear," (1) of God, as a controlling motive of the life, in matters spiritual and moral, not a mere "fear" of His power and righteous retribution, but a wholesome dread of displeasing Him, a "fear" which banishes the terror that shrinks from His presence, Rom. 8:15, and which influences the disposition and attitude of one whose circumstances are guided by trust in God, through the indwelling Spirit of God, Acts 9:31; Rom. 3:18; 2 Cor. 7:1; Eph. 5:21 (RV, "the fear of Christ"); Phil. 2:12; 1 Pet. 1:17 (a comprehensive phrase: the reverential "fear" of God will inspire a constant carefulness in dealing with others in His "fear"); 3:2, 15; the association of "fear and trembling," as, e.g., in Phil. 2:12, has in the Sept. a much sterner import, e.g., Gen. 9:2; Exod. 15:16; Deut. 2:25; 11:25; Ps. 55:5; Isa. 19:16; (2) of superiors, e.g., Rom. 13:7; 1 Pet. 2:18.

2. ***deilia*** (*1167*), "fearfulness" (from ***deos***, "fright"), is rightly rendered "fearfulness" in

2 Tim. 1:7, RV (for KJV, "fear"). That spirit is not given us of God. The word denotes "cowardice and timidity" and is never used in a good sense, as No. 1 is.

3. ***eulabeia*** (*2124*) signifies, firstly, "caution"; then, "reverence, godly fear," Heb. 5:7; 12:28.

### B. Adjectives.

1. ***phoberos*** (*5398*), "fearful" (akin to A, No. 1), is used only in the active sense in the NT, i.e., causing "fear," terrible, Heb. 10:27, 31; 12:21, RV, "fearful," for KJV, "terrible."

2. ***deilos*** (*1169*), "cowardly" (see A, No. 2), "timid," is used in Matt. 8:26; Mark 4:40; Rev. 21:8 (here "the fearful" are first in the list of the transgressors).

3. ***ekphobos*** (*1630*), signifies "frightened outright" (***ek***, "out," intensive, and A, No. 1), Heb. 12:21 (with ***eimi***, "I am"), "I exceedingly fear" (see No. 4); Mark 9:6, "sore afraid."

4. ***entromos*** (*1790*), "trembling with fear" (***en***, "in," intensive, and ***tremo***, "to tremble, quake"; Eng., "tremor," etc.), is used with ***ginomai***, "to become," in Acts 7:32, "trembled"; 16:29, RV, "trembling for fear"; with ***eimi***, "to be," in Heb. 12:21, "quake" (some mss. have ***ektromos*** here). The distinction between No. 3 and No. 4, as in Heb. 12:21, would seem to be that ***ekphobos*** stresses the intensity of the "fear," ***entromos*** the inward effect, "I inwardly tremble (or quake)."

### C. Adverb.

***aphobos*** (*880*) denotes "without fear" (***a***, negative, and A, No. 1), and is said of serving the Lord, Luke 1:74; of being among the Lord's people as His servant, 1 Cor. 16:10; of ministering the Word of God, Phil. 1:14; of the evil of false spiritual shepherds, Jude 12.

### D. Verbs.

1. ***phobeo*** (*5399*), in earlier Greek, "to put to flight" (see A, No. 1), in the NT is always in the passive voice, with the meanings either (a) "to fear, be afraid," its most frequent use, e.g., Acts 23:10, according to the best mss. (see No. 2); or (b) "to show reverential fear" [see A, No. 1, (b)], (1) of men, Mark 6:20; Eph. 5:33, RV, "fear," for KJV, "reverence"; (2) of God, e.g., Acts 10:2, 22; 13:16, 26; Col. 3:22 (RV, "the Lord"); 1 Pet. 2:17; Rev. 14:7; 15:4; 19:5; (a) and (b) are combined in Luke 12:4, 5, where Christ warns His followers not to be afraid of men, but to "fear" God.

2. ***eulabeomai*** (*2125*), "to be cautious, to beware" (see A, No. 3), signifies to act with the reverence produced by holy "fear," Heb. 11:7, "moved with godly fear."

## FEAST

### *Old Testament*

***chag*** (2282), "feast; festal sacrifice." This word refers especially to a "feast observed by a pilgrimage," Exod. 10:9; three are referred to in Ezek. 45:17; Hos. 2:11.

There are two unique uses of ***chag***. First, Aaron proclaimed a "feast to the Lord" at the foot of Mt. Sinai. This "feast" involved no pilgrimage but was celebrated with burnt offerings, communal meals, singing, and dancing. The whole matter was displeasing to God, Exod. 32:5–7.

In two passages, ***chag*** represents the "sacrificial animal," Ps. 118:27; cf. Exod. 23:18.

### *New Testament*

### A. Nouns.

1. ***heorte*** (*1859*), "a feast or festival," is used (a) especially of those of the Jews, and particularly of the Passover; the word is found mostly in John's gospel (seventeen times); apart from the Gospels it is used in this way only in Acts 18:21; (b) in a more general way, in Col. 2:16, KJV, "holy day," RV, "a feast day."

2. ***deipnon*** (*1173*) denotes (a) "the chief meal of the day," dinner or supper, taken at or towards evening; in the plural "feasts," Matt. 23:6; Mark 6:21; 12:39; Luke 20:46; otherwise translated "supper," Luke 14:12, 16, 17, 24; John 12:2; 13:2, 4; 21:20; 1 Cor. 11:21 (of a social meal); (b) "the Lord's Supper," 1 Cor. 11:20; (c) "the supper or feast" which will celebrate the marriage of Christ with His spiritual Bride, at the inauguration of His Kingdom, Rev. 19:9; (d) figuratively, of that to which the birds of prey will be summoned after the overthrow of the enemies of the Lord at the termination of the war of Armageddon, 19:17, cf. Ezek. 39:4, 17–20.

3. ***doche*** (*1403*), "a reception feast, a banquet" (from ***dechomai***, "to receive"), Luke 5:29; 14:13 (not the same as No 2; see v. 12).

4. ***gamos*** (*1062*), "a wedding," especially a wedding "feast" (akin to ***gameo***, "to marry"); it is used in the plural in the following passages (the RV rightly has "marriage feast" for the KJV, "marriage," or "wedding"), Matt. 22:2, 3, 4, 9 (in verses 11, 12, it is used in the singular, in connection with the wedding garment); 25:10; Luke 12:36; 14:8; in the following it signifies a wedding itself, John 2:1, 2; Heb. 13:4; and figuratively in Rev. 19:7, of the marriage of the Lamb; in v. 9 it is used in connection with the supper, the wedding supper (or what in English is termed "breakfast"), not the wedding itself, as in v. 7.

5. ***agape*** (*26*), "love," is used in the plural in Jude 12, signifying "love feasts," RV (KJV, "feasts of charity"); in the corresponding passage, 2 Pet. 2:13, the most authentic mss. have the word ***apate***, in the plural, "deceivings."

**B. Verb.**

***heortizo*** (*1858*), "to keep festival" (akin to A, No. 1) is translated "let us keep the feast," in 1 Cor. 5:8. This is not the Lord's Supper, nor the Passover, but has reference to the continuous life of the believer as a festival or holy-day, in freedom from "the leaven of malice and wickedness, but with the unleavened bread of sincerity and truth."

## FEEBLE

***asthenes*** (*772*), "without strength," is translated "feeble" in 1 Cor. 12:22, of members of the body.

## FEEL, FEELING, FELT

1. ***ginosko*** (*1097*), "to know, perceive," is translated "she felt (in her body)," of the woman with the issue of blood, Mark 5:29, i.e., she became aware of the fact.

2. ***phroneo*** (*5426*), "to think, to be minded," is translated "I felt" in the RV of 1 Cor. 13:11 (for KJV, I understood).

3. ***pselaphao*** (*5584*), "to feel or grope about" (from ***psao***, "to touch"), expressing the motion of the hands over a surface, so as to "feel" it, is used (a) metaphorically, of seeking after God, Acts 17:27; (b) literally, of physical handling or touching, Luke 24:39 with 1 John 1:1; Heb. 12:18.

4. ***sumpatheo*** (*4834*), "to have a fellow-feeling for or with," is rendered "touched with the feeling of" in Heb. 4:15; "have compassion" in 10:34.

5. ***apalgeo*** (*524*) signifies "to cease to feel pain for" (***apo***, "from," ***algeo***, "to feel pain"; cf. Eng., "neuralgia"); hence, to be callous, "past feeling," insensible to honor and shame, Eph. 4:19.

## FEIGN, FEIGNED

**A. Verb.**

***hupokrinomai*** (*5271*) primarily denotes "to answer"; then, "to answer on the stage, play a part," and so, metaphorically, "to feign, pretend," Luke 20:20.

**B. Adjective.**

***plastos*** (*4112*) primarily denotes "formed, molded" (from ***plasso***, to mold; Eng., "plastic"); then, metaphorically, "made up, fabricated, feigned," 2 Pet. 2:3.

## FELLOWSHIP

**A. Nouns.**

1. ***koinonia*** (*2842*), (a) "communion, fellowship, sharing in common" (from ***koinos***, "common"), is translated "communion" in 1 Cor. 10:16; Philem. 6, RV, "fellowship," for KJV, "communication"; it is most frequently translated "fellowship"; (b) "that which is the outcome of fellowship, a contribution," e.g., Rom. 15:26; 2 Cor. 8:4.

2. ***metoche*** (*3352*), "partnership," is translated "fellowship" in 2 Cor. 6:4.

3. ***koinonos*** (*2844*) denotes "a partaker" or "partner" (akin to No. 1); in 1 Cor. 10:20 it is used with ***ginomai***, "to become," "that ye should have communion with," RV (KJV, fellowship with).

**B. Verbs.**

1. ***koinoneo*** (*2841*), "to have fellowship," is so translated in Phil. 4:15, RV, for KJV, "did communicate."

2. ***sunkoinoneo*** (*4790*), "to have fellowship with or in" (***sun***, "with," and No. 1), is used in Eph. 5:11; Phil. 4:14, RV, "ye had fellowship," for KJV, "ye did communicate"; Rev. 18:4, RV, "have (no) fellowship with," for KJV, "be (not) partakers of."

## FERVENT, FERVENTLY

**A. Adjective.**

***ektenes*** (*1618*) denotes "strained, stretched" (***ek***, "out," ***teino***, "to stretch"); hence, metaphorically, "fervent," 1 Pet. 4:8. Some mss. have it in Acts 12:5, for the adverb (see B).

**B. Adverb.**

***ektenos*** (*1619*), "fervently" (akin to A), is said of love, in 1 Pet. 1:22; of prayer, in some mss., Acts 12:5; for the comparative degree in Luke 22:44.

**C. Verb.**

***zeo*** (*2204*), "to be hot, to boil" (Eng. "zeal" is akin), is metaphorically used of "fervency" of spirit, Acts 18:25; Rom. 12:11.

## FIGHT

### *Old Testament*

**A. Verb.**

***lacham*** (3898), "to fight, do battle, engage in combat," commonly used in the context of "armies engaged in pitched battle" against each other, Num. 21:23; Josh. 10:5; Judg. 11:5, or "hand-to-hand combat," 1 Sam. 17:32–33. Frequently, God "fights" the battle for Israel, Deut. 20:4. Instead of swords, words spoken by a lying tongue are often used "to fight" against God's servants, Ps. 109:2.

**B. Noun.**

***milchamah*** (4421), "battle; war," so referring to either a pitched attack by two opposing armies as a single event, or many battles over a period of time, "war," Gen. 14:8.

***New Testament***

**A. Nouns.**

1. ***agon*** (*73*), akin to ***ago***, "to lead," primarily "a gathering," then, "a place of assembly," and hence, "a contest, conflict," is translated "fight" in 1 Tim. 6:12; 2 Tim. 4:7.

2. ***athlesis*** (*119*) is translated "fight" in Heb. 10:32, KJV.

**B. Verbs.**

1. ***agonizomai*** (*75*), from A, No. 1, denotes (a) "to contend" in the public games, 1 Cor. 9:25 ("striveth in the games," RV); (b) "to fight, engage in conflict," John 18:36; (c) metaphorically, "to contend" perseveringly against opposition and temptation, 1 Tim. 6:12; 2 Tim. 4:7 (cf. A, No. 1; in regard to the meaning there, the evidence of *Koine* inscriptions is against the idea of games-contests); to strive as in a contest for a prize, straining every nerve to attain to the object Luke 13:24; to put forth every effort, involving toil, Col. 1:29; 1 Tim. 4:10 (some mss. have ***oneidizomai*** here, "to suffer reproach"); to wrestle earnestly in prayer, Col. 4:12.

2. ***pukteuo*** (*4438*), "to box" (from ***puktes***, "a pugilist"), one of the events in the Olympic games, is translated "fight" in 1 Cor. 9:26.

3. ***machomai*** (*3164*), "to fight," is so rendered in Jas. 4:2 (cf. "fightings," v. 1, see below), and translated "strive" in 2 Tim. 2:24; "strove" in John 6:52; Acts 7:26.

4. ***theriomacheo*** (*2341*) signifies "to fight with wild beasts" (***therion***, "a beast," and No. 3), 1 Cor. 15:32. Some think that the apostle was condemned to fight with wild beasts; if so, he would scarcely have omitted it from 2 Cor. 11:23—end.

## FIGHTING

**A. Noun.**

***mache*** (*3163*), "a fight, strife" (akin to B, No. 3, under FIGHT, *New Testament*), is always used in the plural in the NT, and translated "fightings" in 2 Cor. 7:5; Jas. 4:1; and Titus 3:9, RV (for KJV, "strivings"); "strifes in 2 Tim. 2:23.

**B. Adjective.**

***theomachos*** (*2314*), "fighting against God" (***theos***, "God," and A, occurs in Acts 5:39 (KJV, "to fight"), lit., "God-fighters."

## FIGURE

1. ***tupos*** (*5179*), "a type, figure, pattern," is translated "figures" (i.e., representations of gods) in Acts 7:43; in the RV of v. 44 (for KJV, "fashion") and in Rom. 5:14, of Adam as a "figure of Christ."

2. ***antitupos*** (*499*), an adjective, used as a noun, denotes, lit., "a striking back"; metaphorically, "resisting, adverse"; then, in a passive sense, "struck back"; in the NT metaphorically, "corresponding to," (a) a copy of an archetype (***anti***, "corresponding to, and No. 1), i.e., the event or person or circumstance corresponding to the type, Heb. 9:24, RV, "like in pattern" (KJV, "the figure of"), of the tabernacle which, with its structure and appurtenances, was a pattern of that "holy place," "Heaven itself," "the true," into which Christ entered, "to appear before the face of God for us." The earthly tabernacle anticipatively represented what is now made good in Christ; it was a "figure" or "parable" (9:9), "for the time now present," RV, i.e., pointing to the present time, not "then present," KJV (see below); (b) "a corresponding type," 1 Pet. 3:21, said of baptism; the circumstances of the flood, the ark and its occupants, formed a type, and baptism forms "a corresponding type" (not an antitype), each setting forth the spiritual realities of the death, burial, and resurrection of believers in their identification with Christ. It is not a case of type and antitype, but of two types, that in Genesis, the type, and baptism, the corresponding type.

3. ***parabole*** (*3850*), "a casting or placing side by side" (***para***, "beside," ***ballo***, "to throw") with a view to comparison or resemblance, a parable, is translated "figure" in the KJV of Heb. 9:9 (RV, "a parable for the time now present") and 11:19, where the return of Isaac was (parabolically, in the lit. sense of the term) figurative of resurrection (RV, "parable"). See No. 2 (a).

## FILL, FILL UP

***Old Testament***

**A. Verb.**

***male'*** (4390), "to fill, fulfill, overflow, ordain, endow." ***male'*** means "to be full" in the sense of having something done to one, Gen. 6:13; 2 Kings 4:6. Used transitively, this verb means the act or state of "filling something," Gen. 1:22; Exod. 40:34. ***male'*** is sometimes used in the sense "coming to an end," 1 Kings 2:27. In a different but related nuance, the verb signifies "to confirm," someone's word, 1 Kings 1:14. This verb is used to signify filling something to the full extent of what is necessary, in the sense of being "successfully completed," Isa. 40:2.

***male'*** is used of "filling to overflowing," Josh. 3:15. A special nuance appears when the verb is used with "heart"; in such cases, it means "to presume," Esth. 7:5; Jer. 4:5. The word often has a special meaning in conjunction with "hand." ***male'*** can connote "endow," (often with an office, or a power), Exod. 28:3; Judg. 17:5; Ezek. 43:26. In military contexts, "to fill one's hand" is to prepare for battle, or prepare to wield a weapon, 2 Sam. 23:7; 2 Kings 9:24; Jer. 51:11.

## B. Adjective.

***male'*** (4390), "full," Deut. 6:11; Ruth 1:21.

### *New Testament*

## A. Verbs.

1. ***pleroo*** (*4137*) denotes (1) "to make full, to fill to the full"; in the passive voice, "to be filled, made full"; it is used (1) of things: a net, Matt. 13:48; a building, John 12:3; Acts 2:2; a city, Acts 5:28; needs, Phil. 4:19, KJV "supply," RV, "fulfill"; metaphorically, of valleys, Luke 3:5; figuratively, of a measure of iniquity, Matt. 23:32; (2) of persons: (a) of the members of the church, the body of Christ, as filled by Him, Eph. 1:23 ("all things in all the members"); 4:10; in 3:19, of their being filled "into" (***eis***), RV, "unto," KJV, "with" (all the fullness of God); of their being "made full" in Him, Col. 2:10 (RV, for KJV, "complete"); (b) of Christ Himself: with wisdom, in the days of His flesh, Luke 2:40; with joy, in His return to the Father, Acts 2:28; (c) of believers: with the Spirit, Eph. 5:18; with joy, Acts 13:52; 2 Tim. 1:4; with joy and peace, Rom. 15:13, [from these are to be distinguished those passages which speak of joy as being fulfilled or completed, which come under FULFILL, John 3:29; 15:11 (RV); 16:24 (RV); Phil. 2:2; 1 John 1:4 (RV); 2 John 12 (RV)]; with knowledge, Rom. 15:14; with comfort, 2 Cor. 7:4; with the fruits of righteousness, Phil. 1:11 (Gk. "fruit"); with the knowledge of God's will, Col. 1:9; with abundance through material supplies by fellow believers, Phil. 4:18; (d) of the hearts of believers as the seat of emotion and volition, John 16:6 (sorrow); Acts 5:3 (deceitfulness); (e) of the unregenerate who refuse recognition of God, Rom. 1:29; (II), "to accomplish, complete, fulfill."

2. ***anapleroo*** (*378*), "to fill up adequately, completely" (***ana***, "up," and No. 1), is twice translated by the verbs "to fill, to fill up," in 1 Cor. 14:16, RV (for KJV, "occupieth"), of a believer as a member of an assembly, who "fills" the position or condition (not one who "fills" it by assuming it) of being unable to understand the language of him who had the gift of tongues; in 1 Thess. 2:16, "to fill up their sins," of the Jews who persisted in their course of antagonism and unbelief.

3. ***antanapleroo*** (*466*), "to fill up in turn" (or "on one's part"; ***anti***, "corresponding to," and No. 2), is used in Col. 1:24, of the apostle's responsive devotion to Christ in "filling" up, or undertaking on his part a full share of, the sufferings which follow after the sufferings of Christ, and are experienced by the members of His Body, the church. "The point of the apostle's boast is that Christ, the sinless Master, should have left something for Paul, the unworthy servant, to suffer" (Lightfoot, on Col., p. 165).

4. ***sumpleroo*** (*4845*), "to fill completely" (***sun***, "with," and No. 1), is used in the passive voice (a) of a boat filling with water, and, by metonymy, of the occupants themselves, Luke 8:23 (RV, "were filling"); (b) of "fulfilling," with regard to time, "when the days were well-nigh come," RV, for KJV, "when the time was come," Luke 9:51; Acts 2:1.

5. ***pimplemi*** (*4130*) and ***pletho*** (*4130*), lengthened forms of ***pleo***, "to fill" (***pletho*** supplies certain tenses of ***pimplemi***), is used (1) of things; boats, with fish, Luke 5:7; a sponge, with vinegar, Matt. 27:48 (some mss. have this verb in John 19:29); a city, with confusion, Acts 19:29; a wedding, with guests, Matt. 22:10; (2) of persons (only in Luke's writings): (a) with the Holy Spirit, Luke 1:15, 41, 67; Acts 2:4; 4:8, 31; 9:17; 13:9; (b) with emotions: wrath, Luke 4:28; fear, 5:26; madness, 6:11; wonder, amazement, Acts 3:10; jealousy, 5:17, RV, for KJV, "indignation," and 13:45 (KJV, "envy"). For its other significance, "to complete."

6. ***empiplemi*** (*1705*) or ***empletho*** (as in No. 5), "to fill full, to satisfy," is used (a) of "filling" the hungry, Luke 1:53; John 6:12; of the abundance of the rich, Luke 6:25; (b) metaphorically, of a company of friends, Rom. 15:24, RV, "satisfied," for KJV, "filled.

7. ***empiplao*** (*1705v*), an alternative form of No. 6, is found in Acts 14:17, "filling (your hearts)," of God's provision for mankind.

## B. Noun.

***pleroma*** (*4138*), fullness, has two meanings, (a) in the active sense, "that which fills up," a piece of undressed cloth on an old garment, Matt. 9:16; Mark 2:21, lit., "the filling" (RV, "that which should fill it up"), i.e., "the patch," which is probably the significance; (b) "that which has been completed, the fullness," e.g., Mark 8:20.

## FILTH

1. ***perikatharma*** *(4027)* denotes "offscouring, refuse" (lit., "cleanings," i.e., that which is thrown away in cleansing; from ***perikathairo***, "to purify all around." It is used in 1 Cor. 4:13 much in this sense (not of sacrificial victims), "the filth of the world" representing "the most abject and despicable men," i.e., the scum or rubbish of humanity.

2. ***rhupos*** *(4509)* denotes "dirt, filth," 1 Pet. 3:21.

## FILTHINESS, FILTHY (to make)

**A. Nouns.**

1. ***aischrotes*** *(151)*, "baseness" (from ***aischos***, "shame, disgrace"), is used in Eph, 5:4, of obscenity, all that is contrary to purity.

2. ***rhuparia*** *(4507)* denotes "dirt, filth," and is used metaphorically of moral "defilement" in Jas. 1:21.

3. ***molusmos*** *(3436)*, "a soiling, defilement," is used in 2 Cor. 7:1.

4. ***aselgeia*** *(766)*, "wantonness, licentiousness, lasciviousness," is translated "filthy (conversation)," in 2 Pet. 2:7, KJV; RV, lascivious (life).

**B. Adjectives.**

1. ***aischros*** *(150)*, "base, shameful" (akin to A, No. 1), is used of "base gain," "filthy (lucre)," Titus 1:11, and translated "shame" in 1 Cor. 11:6, with reference to a woman with shorn hair; in 14:35, of oral utterances of women in a church gathering (RV, "shameful"); in Eph. 5:12, of mentioning the base and bestial practices of those who live lascivious lives.

2. ***aischrokerdes*** *(146)*, "greedy of base gain" (No. 1, and ***kerdos***, "gain"), is used in 1 Tim. 3:8 and Titus 1:7, "greedy of filthy lucre"; some mss. have it also in 1 Tim. 3:3.

3. ***rhuparos*** *(4508)*, akin to A, No. 2, is said of shabby clothing, Jas. 2:2: metaphorically, of moral "defilement," Rev. 22:11 (in the best mss.).

**C. Adverb.**

***aischrokerdos*** *(147)*, "eagerness for base gain" (akin to B, No. 2), is used in 1 Pet. 5:2, "for filthy lucre."

**D. Verb.**

***rhupaino*** *(4510v)*, "to make filthy, defile" (from A, No. 2), is used in the passive voice, in an ethical sense, in Rev. 22:11 (cf. B, No. 3, in the same verse), "let him be made filthy," RV. The tense (the aorist) marks the decisiveness of that which is decreed. Some texts have ***rhupareuomai***, here, with the same meaning; some have ***rhupoo***, in the middle voice, "to make oneself filthy."

## FINISH

1. ***teleo*** *(5055)*, "to bring to an end" (***telos***, "an end"), in the passive voice, "to be finished," is translated by the verb "to finish" in Matt. 13:53; 19:1; 26:1; John 19:28, where the RV "are . . . finished" brings out the force of the perfect tense (the same word as in v. 30, "It is finished"), which is missed in the KJV; the word was in His heart before He uttered it, 2 Tim. 4:7; Rev. 10:7; 11:7; 20:3, RV, "should be finished" (KJV, "fulfilled"), 5, 7, RV, "finished" (KJV, "expired"). In Rev. 15:1 the verb is rightly translated "is finished." In 15:8 the RV, "should be finished" corrects the KJV, "were fulfilled."

2. ***teleioo*** *(5048)*, akin to the adjective ***teleios***, "complete, perfect," and to No. 1, denotes "to bring to an end" in the sense of completing or perfecting, and is translated by the verb "to finish" in John 4:34; 5:36; 17:4; Acts 20:24.

3. ***ekteleo*** *(1615)*, lit., "to finish out," i.e., "completely" (***ek***, "out," intensive, and No. 1) is used in Luke 14:29, 30.

4. ***epiteleo*** *(2005)*, "to bring through to an end," is rendered "finish" in 2 Cor. 8:6, KJV (RV, "complete").

5. ***sunteleo*** *(4931)*, "to bring to fulfillment, to effect," is translated "finishing" (KJV, "will finish") in Rom. 9:28.

## FIRM

1. ***bebaios*** *(949)*, "firm, steadfast, secure" (from ***baino***, "to go"), is translated "firm" in Heb. 3:6, of the maintenance of the boldness of the believer's hope, and in 3:14, RV, of "the beginning of our confidence" (KJV, "steadfast).

2. ***stereos*** *(4731)*, "solid, hard, stiff," is translated "firm" in 2 Tim. 2:19; 1 Pet. 5:9.

## FIRST-BEGOTTEN, FIRSTBORN

### *Old Testament*

***bekor*** (1060), "firstborn." The word represents the "firstborn" individual in a family, Gen. 25:13; or fig. Num. 3:46; or quality animal, Exod. 11:5; Lev. 27:26. The "oldest" or "firstborn" son, Exod. 6:14, had special privileges within the family. He received the family blessing, which meant spiritual and social leadership and a double portion of the father's possessions—or twice what all the other sons received, Deut. 21:17. Israel was God's "firstborn," enjoying a privileged position and blessings over other nations, Exod. 4:22; Jer. 31:9.

***bikkurim*** (1061), "first fruits," produce offered to God, Num. 28:26; at festivals, Lev. 23:20; Num. 28:26.

### *New Testament*

***prototokos*** (*4416*), "firstborn" (from ***protos***, "first," and ***tikto***, "to beget"), is used of Christ as born of the Virgin Mary, Luke 2:7; further, in His relationship to the Father, expressing His priority to, and preeminence over, creation, not in the sense of being the "first" to be born. It is used occasionally of superiority of position in the OT, see Exod. 4:22; Deut. 21:16, 17, the prohibition being against the evil of assigning the privileged position of the "firstborn" to one born subsequently to the "first" child.

The five passages in the NT relating to Christ may be set forth chronologically thus: (a) Col. 1:15, where His eternal relationship with the Father is in view, and the clause means both that He was the "Firstborn" before all creation and that He Himself produced creation (the genitive case being objective, as v. 16 makes clear); (b) Col. 1:18 and Rev. 1:5, in reference to His resurrection; (c) Rom. 8:29, His position in relationship to the church; (d) Heb. 1:6, RV, His second advent (the RV "when He again bringeth in," puts "again" in the right place, the contrast to His first advent, at His birth, being implied); cf. Ps. 89:27. The word is used in the plural, in Heb. 11:28, of the firstborn sons in the families of the Egyptians, and in 12:23, of the members of the Church.

## FIRSTFRUIT(S)

***aparche*** (*536*) denotes, primarily, "an offering of firstfruits"; in sacrifices, "to offer firstfruits." "Though the English word is plural in each of its occurrences save Rom. 11:16, the Greek word is always singular. Two Hebrew words are thus translated, one meaning the "chief" or "principal part," e.g., Num. 18:12; Prov. 3:9; the other, "the earliest ripe of the crop or of the tree," e.g., Exod. 23:16; Neh. 10:35; they are found together, e.g., in Exod. 23:19, "the first of the firstfruits."

The term is applied in things spiritual, (a) to the presence of the Holy Spirit with the believer as the firstfruits of the full harvest of the Cross, Rom. 8:23; (b) to Christ Himself in resurrection in relation to all believers who have fallen asleep, 1 Cor. 15:20, 23; (c) to the earliest believers in a country in relation to those of their countrymen subsequently converted, Rom. 16:5; 1 Cor. 16:15; (d) to the believers of this age in relation to the whole of the redeemed, 2 Thess. 2:13.

## FISH

1. ***ichthus*** (*2486*) denotes "a fish," Matt. 7:10; Mark 6:38, etc.; apart from the Gospels, only in 1 Cor. 15:39.

2. ***ichthudion*** (*2485*) is a diminutive of No. 1, "a little fish," Matt. 15:34; Mark 8:7.

3. ***opsarion*** (*3795*) is a diminutive of ***opson***, "cooked meat," or "a relish, a dainty dish, especially of fish"; it denotes "a little fish," John 6:9, 11; 21:9, 10, 13.

## FIT (Adjective and Verb), FITLY, FITTING

### A. Adjectives.

1. ***euthetos*** (*2111*), "ready for use, fit, well adapted," lit., "well placed" (***eu***, "well," ***tithemi***, "to place"), is used (a) of persons, Luke 9:62, negatively, of one who is not fit for the kingdom of God; (b) of things, Luke 14:35, of salt that has lost its savor; rendered "meet" in Heb. 6:7, of herbs.

2. ***arestos*** (*701*), "pleasing" (akin to ***aresko***, "to please"), is translated "(it is not) fit," RV (KJV, "reason"), in Acts 6:2.

### B. Verbs.

1. ***aneko*** (*433*), properly, "to have come up to" (***ana***, "up," and ***heko***, "to arrive"), is translated "is fitting," in Col. 3:18, RV.

2. ***katheko*** (*2520*), "to come or reach down to" (***kata***, "down"), hence, "to befit, be proper," is translated "is (not fit)" in Acts 22:22; in Rom. 1:28, RV, "fitting" (KJV, "convenient").

3. ***katartizo*** (*2675*), "to make fit, to equip, prepare" (***kata***, "down," ***artos***, "a joint"), is rendered "fitted" in Rom. 9:22, of vessels of wrath; here the middle voice signifies that those referred to "fitted" themselves for destruction (as illustrated in the case of Pharaoh, the self-hardening of whose heart is accurately presented in the RV in the first part of the series of incidents in the Exodus narrative, which records Pharaoh's doings; only after repeated and persistent obstinacy on his part is it recorded that God hardened his heart.)

4. ***sunarmologeo*** (*4883*), "to fit or frame together" (***sun***, "with," ***harmos***, "a joint, in building," and ***lego***, "to choose"), is used metaphorically of the various parts of the church as a building, Eph. 2:21, "fitly framed together"; also of the members of the church as the body of Christ, 4:16, RV, "fitly framed . . . together."

## FLATTERY (-ING)

***kolakia*** (or *-eia*) (*2850*), akin to ***kolakeuo***, "to flatter," is used in 1 Thess. 2:5 of "words of flattery" (RV), adopted as "a cloke of covetousness," i.e., words which "flattery" uses, not simply as an effort to give pleasure, but with motives of self-interest.

## FLEE, FLED

### *Old Testament*

***barach*** (1272), "to flee, pass through," means to move from one place to another, often to escape danger or unfavorable circumstance, Gen. 16:6; 1 Sam. 20:1; Job 20:24. In its figurative use, the word describes days "fleeing" away, Job 9:25, or frail man "fleeing" like a shadow, Job 14:2. A rather paradoxical use is found in Song of Sol. 8:14, in which "flee" must mean "come quickly."

***nus*** (5127), "to flee, escape, take flight, depart." ***nus*** is the common word for "fleeing" from an enemy or danger, Gen. 39:12; Num. 16:34; Josh. 10:6. The word is also used to describe "escape," as in Jer. 46:6 and Amos 9:1. In a figurative use, the word describes the "disappearance" of physical strength, Deut. 34:7, the "fleeing" of evening shadows, Song of Sol. 2:17, and the "fleeing away" of sorrow, Isa. 35:10.

### *New Testament*

1. ***pheugo*** (*5343*), "to flee from or away" (Lat., ***fugio***; Eng., "fugitive," etc.), besides its literal significance, is used metaphorically, (a) transitively, of "fleeing" fornication, 1 Cor. 6:18; idolatry, 10:14; evil doctrine, questionings, disputes of words, envy, strife, railings, evil surmisings, wranglings, and the love of money, 1 Tim. 6:11; youthful lusts, 2 Tim. 2:22; (b) intransitively, of the "flight" of physical matter, Rev. 16:20; 20:11; of death, 9:6; cf. also Acts 14:6; 16:27; Heb. 6:18; 12:25.

## FLESH

### *Old Testament*

***basar*** (1320), "flesh; meat; male sex organ." The word means the "meaty part plus the skin" of men or animal, often referring to the entire organ of the body called "the skin," Num. 11:33; Deut. 14:8; Job 10:11, or the "edible part," of animals, cooked or raw, 1 Sam. 2:13,15; Dan. 10:3. ***basar*** can also be a specific organ of the body, the "male sex organ," Lev 15:2.

Flesh represents the "physical aspect" of man or animals as contrasted with the spirit, soul, or heart (the nonphysical aspect), Num. 16:22. It means collectively "all mankind"; Deut. 5:26, or "all creatures," Gen. 6:17. Flesh also means "blood relative," Gen. 29:14; 37:27; Lev. 18:6.

### *New Testament*

***sarx*** (*4561*) has a wider range of meaning in the NT than ***basar*** in the OT. Its uses in the NT may be analyzed as follows: (a) "the substance of the body," whether of beasts or of men, 1 Cor. 15:39; (b) "the human body," 2 Cor. 10:3a; Gal. 2:20; Phil. 1:22; (c) by synecdoche, of "mankind," in the totality of all that is essential to manhood, i.e., spirit, soul, and body, Matt. 24:22; John 1:13; Rom. 3:20; (d) by synecdoche, of "the holy humanity" of the Lord Jesus, in the totality of all that is essential to manhood, i.e., spirit, soul, and body John 1:14; 1 Tim. 3:16; 1 John 4:2; 2 John 7, in Heb. 5:7, "the days of His flesh," i.e., His past life on earth in distinction from His present life in resurrection; (e) by synecdoche, for "the complete person," John 6:51–57; 2 Cor. 7:5; Jas. 5:3; (f) "the weaker element in human nature," Matt. 26:41; Rom. 6:19; 8:3a; (g) "the unregenerate state of men," Rom. 7:5; 8:8, 9; (h) "the seat of sin in man" (but this is not the same thing as in the body), 2 Pet. 2:18; 1 John 2:16; (i) "the lower and temporary element in the Christian," Gal. 3:3; 6:8, and in religious ordinances, Heb. 9:10; (j) "the natural attainments of men," 1 Cor. 1:26; 2 Cor. 10:2, 3b; (k) "circumstances," 1 Cor. 7:28; the externals of life, 2 Cor. 7:1; Eph. 6:5; Heb. 9:13; (1) by metonymy, "the outward and seeming," as contrasted with the spirit, the inward and real, John 6:63; 2 Cor. 5:16; (m) "natural relationship, consanguine," 1 Cor. 10:18; Gal. 4:23, or marital, Matt. 19:5.

In Matt. 26:41; Rom. 8:4, 13; 1 Cor. 5:5; Gal. 6:8 (not the Holy Spirit, here), "flesh" is contrasted with spirit, in Rom. 2:28, 29, with heart and spirit; in Rom. 7:25, with the mind; cf. Col. 2:1, 5. It is coupled with the mind in Eph. 2:3, and with the spirit in 2 Cor. 7:1.

## FLESHLY, FLESHY

1. ***sarkikos*** (*4559*), akin to ***sarx***, under FLESH, signifies (a) associated with or pertaining to, "the flesh, carnal," Rom. 15:27; 1 Cor. 9:11; (b) of "the nature of the flesh, sensual," translated "fleshly" in 2 Cor. 1:12, of wisdom, in 1 Pet. 2:11, of lusts; in 2 Cor. 10:4, negatively, of the weapons of the Christian's warfare, RV, "of the flesh" (KJV, "carnal").

2. ***sarkinos*** (*4560*) denotes "of the flesh, fleshly" (the termination ***–inos*** signifying the substance or material of a thing); in 2 Cor. 3:3, RV, "(tables that are hearts) of flesh," KJV, fleshly (tables), etc.

## FLOCK

### *Old Testament*

***tso'n*** (6629), "flock; small cattle; sheep; goats." The primary meaning of ***tso'n*** is "small cattle," (so, "sheep, goats, flocks") to be distinguished from ***baqar*** ("herd, large four-footed mammals"); sheep only, 1 Sam. 25:2; or to both sheep and goats, Gen. 30:33. In the metaphorical usage of ***tso'n***, the imagery of a "multitude" may apply to people, Ps. 100:3; cf. Ps. 23; 79:13; Isa 53:6; Ezek. 36:38; Mic. 7:14.

### *New Testament*

1. ***poimne*** (*4167*), akin to ***poimen***, "a shepherd," denotes "a flock" (properly, of sheep), Matt. 26:31; Luke 2:8; 1 Cor. 9:7; metaphorically, of Christ's followers, John 10:16.

2. ***poimnion*** (*4168*), possibly a diminutive of No. 1, is used in the NT only metaphorically, of a group of Christ's disciples, Luke 12:32; of local churches cared for by elders, Acts 20:28, 29; 1 Pet. 5:2, 3.

## FLOOD

### A. Noun.

***kataklusmos*** (*2627*), "a deluge" (Eng., "cataclysm"), akin to ***katakluzo***, "to inundate," 2 Pet. 3:6, is used of the "flood" in Noah's time, Matt. 24:38, 39; Luke 17:27; 2 Pet. 2:5; cf. also Luke 6:4; Matt. 7:25, 27; in Rev. 12:15, 16.

### B. Adjective.

***potamophoretos*** (*4216*) signifies "carried away by a stream or river," Rev. 12:15, RV, "carried away by the stream" (KJV, "of the flood").

## FOLLOW, FOLLOW AFTER

1. ***akoloutheo*** (*190*), to be an ***akolouthos***, "a follower," or "companion" (from the prefix ***a***, here expressing "union, likeness," and ***keleuthos***, "a way"; hence, "one going in the same way"), is used (a) frequently in the literal sense, e.g., Matt. 4:25; (b) metaphorically, of "discipleship," e.g., Mark 8:34; 9:38; 10:21. It is used 77 times in the Gospels, of "following" Christ, and only once otherwise, Mark 14:13.

2. ***exakoloutheo*** (*1811*), "to follow up, or out to the end" (***ek***, "out," used intensively, and No. 1), is used metaphorically, and only by the apostle Peter in his second epistle: in 1:16, of cunningly devised fables; 2:2 of lascivious doings; 2:15, of the way of Balaam.

3. ***epakoloutheo*** (*1872*), "to follow after, close upon" (***epi***, "upon," and No. 1). is used of signs "following" the preaching of the gospel, Mark 16:20; of "following" good works, 1 Tim. 5:10; of sins "following" after those who are guilty of them, 5:24; of "following" the steps of Christ, 1 Pet. 2:21.

4. ***katakoloutheo*** (*2628*), "to follow behind or intently after" (***kata***, "after," used intensively, and No. 1), is used of the women on their way to Christ's tomb, Luke 23:55; of the demon-possessed maid in Philippi in "following" the missionaries, Acts 16:17.

5. ***parakoloutheo*** (*3877*) lit. signifying "to follow close up, or side by side," hence, "to accompany, to conform to" (***para***, "beside," and No. 1), is used of signs accompanying "them that believe," Mark 16:17; of tracing the course of facts, Luke 1:3, RV; of "following" the good doctrine, 1 Tim. 4:6, RV (KJV, "attained"); similarly of "following" teaching so as to practice it, 2 Tim. 3:10, RV, "didst follow" (KJV, "hast fully known").

6. ***sunakoloutheo*** (*4870*), "to follow along with, to accompany a leader" (***sun***, "with," and No. 1), is given its true rendering in the RV of Mark 5:37, "He suffered no man to follow with Him"; in 14:51, of the young man who "followed with" Christ (inferior mss. have No. 1 here); Luke 23:49, of the women who "followed with" Christ from Galilee.

7. ***dioko*** (*1377*) denotes (a) "to drive away," Matt. 23:34; (b) "to pursue without hostility, to follow, follow after," said of righteousness, Rom. 9:30; the Law, 9:31; 12:13, hospitality ("given to") lit., "pursuing" (as one would a calling), the things which make for peace, 14:19; love, 1 Cor. 14:1; that which is good, 1 Thess. 5:15; righteousness, godliness, faith, love, patience, meekness, 1 Tim. 6:11; righteousness, faith, love, peace, 2 Tim. 2:22; peace and sanctification, Heb. 12:14; peace, 1 Pet. 3:11; (c) "to follow on" (used intransitively), Phil. 3:12, 14, RV, "I press on"; "follow after," is an inadequate meaning.

8. ***katadioko*** (*2614*), "to follow up or closely," with the determination to find (***kata***, "down," intensive, giving the idea of a hard, persistent search, and No. 7), Mark 1:36, "followed after (Him)," is said of the disciples in going to find the Lord who had gone into a desert place to pray. The verb is found, e.g., in 1 Sam. 30:22; Ps. 23:6, and with hostile intent in Gen. 31:36.

## FOLLY

***anoia*** (*454*) lit. signifies "without understanding" (***a***, negative, ***nous***, "mind"); hence, "folly," or, rather, "senselessness," 2 Tim. 3:9; in Luke 6:11 it denotes violent or mad rage, "madness."

## FOOL, FOOLISH, FOOLISHLY, FOOLISHNESS

### *Old Testament*

***'ewil*** (191), "fool," This word describes a person who lacks wisdom; indeed, wisdom is beyond his grasp, Prov. 24:7. In another nuance, "fool" is a morally undesirable individual who despises wisdom and discipline, Prov. 1:7; 15:5.

He mocks guilt, Prov. 14:9, and is quarrelsome, Prov. 20:3, and licentious, Prov. 7:22. Trying to give him instruction is futile, Prov. 16:22.

***'iwwelet*** (200), "foolishness; stupidity." This noun can mean "foolishness" in the sense of violating God's law, or "sin," Ps. 38:5. The word also describes the activities and life-style of the man who ignores the instructions of wisdom, Prov. 5:23. In another nuance, the noun means "thoughtless." Hence ***'iwwelet*** describes the way a young person is prone to act, Prov. 22:15 and the way any fool or stupid person chatters, Prov. 15:2.

***nebalah*** (5039), "foolishness; senselessness; impropriety; stupidity." This abstract noun is most often used as a word for a serious sin, Gen. 34:7, which is of course a disregard for God's will.

### *New Testament*

**A. Adjectives.**

1. ***aphron*** (*878*) signifies "without reason" (***a***, negative, ***phren***, "the mind"), "want of mental sanity and sobriety, a reckless and inconsiderate habit of mind" (Hort), or "the lack of commonsense perception of the reality of things natural and spiritual . . . or the imprudent ordering of one's life in regard to salvation"; it is mostly translated "foolish" or "foolish ones" in the RV; Luke 11:40; 12:20; Rom. 2:20; 1 Cor. 15:36; 2 Cor. 11:16 (twice), 19 (contrasted with ***phronimos***, "prudent"); 12:6, 11; Eph. 5:17; 1 Pet. 2:15.

2. ***anoetos*** (*453*) signifies "not understanding" (***a***, negative, ***noeo***, "to perceive, understand"), not applying ***nous***, "the mind," Luke 24:25; in Rom. 1:14 and Gal. 3:1, 3 it signifies "senseless," an unworthy lack of understanding; sometimes it carries a moral reproach (in contrast with ***sophron***, "sober-minded, self-controlled") and describes one who does not govern his lusts, Titus 3:3; in 1 Tim. 6:9 it is associated with evil desires, lusts.

3. ***moros*** (*3474*) primarily denotes "dull, sluggish"; hence, "stupid, foolish"; it is used (a) of persons, Matt. 5:22, "Thou fool"; here the word means morally worthless, a scoundrel, a more serious reproach than "Raca"; the latter scorns a man's mind and calls him stupid; ***moros*** scorns his heart and character; hence the Lord's more severe condemnation; in 7:26, "a foolish man"; 23:17, 19, "fools"; 25:2, 3, 8, "foolish"; in 1 Cor. 3:18, "a fool"; the apostle Paul uses it of himself and his fellow-workers, in 4:10, "fools" (i.e., in the eyes of opponents); (b) of things, 2 Tim. 2:23, "foolish and ignorant questionings"; so Titus 3:9; in 1 Cor. 1:25, "the foolishness of God," not ***moria***, "foolishness" as a personal quality (see C, No. 1), but adjectivally, that which is considered by the ignorant as a "foolish" policy or mode of dealing, lit., "the foolish (thing)"; so in v. 27, "the foolish (things) of the world."

4. ***asunetos*** (*801*) denotes "without discernment," or "understanding" (***a***, negative, ***suniemi***, "to understand"); hence "senseless," as in the RV of Rom. 1:21 (KJV, "foolish"), of the heart; in 10:19, KJV, "foolish," RV, "void of understanding."

**B. Verb.**

***moraino*** (*3471*) is used (a) in the causal sense, "to make foolish," 1 Cor. 1:20; (b) in the passive sense, "to become foolish," Rom. 1:22; in Matt. 5:13 and Luke 14:34 it is said of salt that has lost its flavor, becoming tasteless.

**C. Nouns.**

1. ***moria*** (*3472*) denotes "foolishness" (akin to A, No. 3 and B, No. 1), and is used in 1 Cor. 1:18, 21, 23; 2:14; 3:19.

2. ***aphrosune*** (*877*), "senselessness," is translated "foolishness" in Mark 7:22; 2 Cor. 11:1, 17, 21, "foolishness," RV (KJV "folly" and "foolishly").

## FOOTSTOOL

***hupopodion*** (*5286*), from ***hupo***, "under," and ***pous***, "a foot," is used (a) literally in Jas. 2:3, (b) metaphorically, of the earth as God's "footstool," Matt. 5:35.

## FORBEAR, FORBEARANCE

**A. Verbs.**

1. ***anecho*** (*430*), "to hold up" (***ana***, "up," ***echo***, "to have or hold"), is used in the middle voice in the NT, signifying "to bear with, endure"; it is rendered "forbearing (one another)" in Eph. 4:2 and Col. 3:13.

2. ***aniemi*** (*447*), lit., "to send up or back" (***ana***, "up," ***hiemi***, "to send"), hence, "to relax, loosen," or, metaphorically, "to desist from," is translated "forbearing" (threatening) in Eph. 6:9 ("giving up your threatening," T. K. Abbott).

3. ***pheidomai*** (*5339*), "to spare" (its usual meaning), "to refrain from doing something," is rendered "I forbear" in 2 Cor. 12:6.

4. ***stego*** (*4722*) properly denotes "to protect by covering"; then, "to conceal"; then, by covering, "to bear up under"; it is translated "forbear" in 1 Thess. 3:1, 5.

**B. Noun.**

***anoche*** (*463*), "a holding back" (akin to A, No. 1), denotes "forbearance," a delay of punishment, Rom. 2:4; 3:25, in both places of God's "forbearance" with men, in the latter passage His "forbearance" is the ground, not of His forgiveness, but of His praetermission of sins,

His withholding punishment. In 2:4 it represents a suspense of wrath which must eventually be exercised unless the sinner accepts God's conditions; in 3:25 it is connected with the passing over of sins in times past, previous to the atoning work of Christ.

### C. Adjectives.

1. ***anexikakos*** (*420*) denotes "patiently forbearing evil," lit., "patient of wrong," (from ***anecho***, A, No. 1 and ***kakos***, "evil"), "enduring"; it is rendered "forbearing" in 2 Tim. 2:24.

2. ***epieikes*** (*1933*), an adjective (from ***epi***, used intensively, and ***eikos***, "reasonable"), is used as a noun with the article in Phil. 4:5, and translated "forbearance" in the RV.

## FORBID, FORBADE

***koluo*** (*2967*), "to hinder, restrain, withhold, forbid" (akin to ***kolos***, "docked, lopped, clipped"), is most usually translated "to forbid," often an inferior rendering to that of hindering or restraining, e.g., 1 Thess. 2:16; Luke 23:2; 2 Pet. 2:16, where the RV has "stayed"; in Acts 10:47 "forbid." In Luke 6:29, the RV has "withhold not (thy coat also)."

## FORCE

***harpazo*** (*726*), "to snatch away, carry off by force," Matt. 11:12, "men of violence (KJV 'the violent') take it by force," the meaning being, as determined by the preceding clause, that those who are possessed of eagerness and zeal, instead of yielding to the opposition of religious foes, such as the scribes and Pharisees, press their way into the kingdom, so as to possess themselves of it. It is elsewhere similarly rendered in John 6:15, of those who attempted to seize the Lord, and in Acts 23:10, of the chief captain's command to the soldiers to rescue Paul.

## FOREFATHER

1. ***progonos*** (*4269*), an adjective, primarily denoting "born before" (***pro***, "before," and ***ginomai***, "to become"), is used as a noun in the plural, 2 Tim. 1:3, "forefathers" (in 1 Tim. 5:4, "parents").

2. ***propator*** (*4253* and *3962*), "a forefather" (***pro***, "before," ***pater***, "a father"), is used of Abraham in Rom. 4:1.

## FOREKNOW, FOREKNOWLEDGE

### A. Verb.

***proginosko*** (*4267*), "to know before" (***pro***, "before," ***ginosko***, "to know"), is used (a) of divine knowledge, concerning (1) Christ, 1 Pet. 1:20, RV, "foreknown" (KJV, "foreordained"); (2) Israel as God's earthly people, Rom. 11:2; (3) believers, Rom. 8:29; "the foreknowledge" of God is the basis of His foreordaining counsels; (b) of human knowledge, (1) of persons, Acts 26:5; (2) of facts, 2 Pet. 3:17.

### B. Noun.

***prognosis*** (*4268*), "a foreknowledge" (akin to A.), is used only of divine "foreknowledge," Acts 2:23; 1 Pet. 1:2. "Foreknowledge" is one aspect of omniscience; it is implied in God's warnings, promises and predictions. See Acts 15:18. God's "foreknowledge" involves His electing grace, but this does not preclude human will. He "foreknows" the exercise of faith which brings salvation. The apostle Paul stresses especially the actual purposes of God rather than the ground of the purposes, see, e.g., Gal. 1:16; Eph. 1:5, 11. The divine counsels will ever be unthwartable.

## FORERUNNER

***prodromos*** (*4274*), an adjective signifying "running forward, going in advance," is used as a noun, of "those who were sent before to take observations," acting as scouts, especially in military matters; or of "one sent before a king" to see that the way was prepared, Isa. 40:3; (cf. Luke 9:52; and, of John the Baptist, Matt. 11:10, etc.). In the NT it is said of Christ in Heb. 6:20, as going in advance of His followers who are to be where He is, when He comes to receive them to Himself.

## FORESEE, FORESEEN

1. ***proorao*** (*4308*), with the aorist form ***proeidon*** (used to supply tenses lacking in ***proorao***), "to see before" (***pro***, "before," ***horao***, "to see"), is used with reference (a) to the past, of seeing a person before, Acts 21:29; (b) to the future, in the sense of "foreseeing" a person or thing, Acts 2:25, with reference to Christ and the Father, RV, "beheld" (here the middle voice is used).

2. ***proeidon*** (*4275*), an aorist tense form without a present, "to foresee," is used of David, as foreseeing Christ, in Acts 2:31, RV, "foreseeing" (KJV, "seeing before"); in Gal. 3:8 it is said of the Scripture, personified, personal activity being attributed to it by reason of its divine source (cf. v. 22). "What saith the Scripture?" was a common formula among the Rabbis.

3. ***problepo*** (*4265*), from ***pro***, "before," and ***blepo***, "to see, perceive," is translated "having provided" in Heb. 11:40 (middle voice), marg., "foreseen," which is the lit. meaning of the verb, as with Eng. "provide."

## FORETELL

***prolego*** (*4302*), with the aorist form ***proeipon***, and a perfect form ***proeireka*** (from ***proereo***), signifies (1) "to declare openly" or "plainly," or "to say" or "tell beforehand" (***pro***, "before," ***lego***, "to say"), translated in 2 Cor. 13:2 (in the first sentence), RV, "I have said beforehand," KJV, "I told . . . before," in the next sentence, KJV, "I foretell," RV, "I do say beforehand" (marg., "plainly"); not prophecy is here in view, but a warning given before and repeated; (2) "to speak before, of prophecy," as "foretelling" the future, Mark 13:23, KJV, "have foretold," RV, "have told . . . beforehand"; Acts 1:16 (of the prophecy concerning Judas); Rom. 9:29; 2 Pet. 3:2; Jude 17; some inferior mss. have it in Heb. 10:15.

## FOREWARN

***prolego*** (*4302*), with verbal forms as mentioned above, is translated "I forewarn" and "I did forewarn," in the RV of Gal. 5:21, KJV, "I tell (you) before" and "I have told (you) in time past"; here, however, as in 2 Cor. 13:2 and 1 Thess. 3:4 (see below), the RV marg., "plainly" is to be preferred to "beforehand" or "before"; the meaning in Gal. 5:21 is not so much that Paul prophesied the result of the practice of the evils mentioned but that he had told them before of the consequence and was now repeating his warning, as leaving no possible room for doubt or misunderstanding; in 1 Thess. 3:4, the subject told before was the affliction consequent upon the preaching of the Gospel; in 1 Thess. 4:6, "we forewarned," the warning was as to the consequences of whatsoever violates chastity.

## FORFEIT

***zemioo*** (*2210*), in the active voice signifies "to damage"; in the passive, "to suffer loss, forfeit," Matt. 16:26 and Mark 8:36, of the "life," RV; KJV, and RV marg., "soul"; in each place the RV has "forfeit," for A.V., "lose"; Luke 9:25, "his own self" (RV, "forfeit," KJV, "be cast away"; here the preceding word "lose" translates ***apollumi***, "to destroy"). What is in view here is the act of "forfeiting" what is of the greatest value, not the casting away by divine judgment, though that is involved, but losing or penalizing one's own self, with spiritual and eternal loss. The word is also used in 1 Cor. 3:15; 2 Cor. 7:9; Phil. 3:8.

## FORGET, FORGETFUL

### *Old Testament*

***shakach*** (7911), "to forget," can mean simply to forget information or feelings related to that information, Gen. 27:45. But "to forget," can also mean, "to not take action, implying a lack of relationship, Lam. 5:20; Hos. 4:6.

### *New Testament*

**A. Verbs.**

1. ***lanthano*** (*2990*), "to escape notice," is translated "they (wilfully) forget" in 2 Pet. 3:5, RV, lit., "this escapes them (i.e., their notice, wilfully on their part)," KJV, "they willingly are ignorant of"; in v. 8, RV, "forget not," lit., "let not this one thing escape you" (your notice), KJV, "be not ignorant of."

2. ***epilanthanomai*** (*1950*), "to forget, or neglect" (***epi***, "upon," used intensively, and No. 1), is said (a) negatively of God, indicating His remembrance of sparrows, Luke 12:6, and of the work and labor of love of His saints, Heb. 6:10; (b) of the disciples regarding taking bread, Matt. 16:5: Mark 8:14; (c) of Paul regarding "the things which are behind," Phil. 3:13; (d) of believers, as to showing love to strangers, Heb. 13:2, RV, and as to doing good and communicating, v. 16; (e) of a person who after looking at himself in a mirror, forgets what kind of person he is, Jas. 1:24; cf. also Heb. 12:5.

**B. Nouns.**

1. ***lethe*** (*3024*), "forgetfulness" (from ***letho***, "to forget," an old form of ***lanthano***, see A, No. 1; cf. Eng. "lethal," "lethargy," and the mythical river "Lethe," which was supposed to cause forgetfulness of the past to those who drank of it), is used with ***lambano***, "to take," in 2 Pet. 1:9, "having forgotten," lit., "having taken forgetfulness" (cf. 2 Tim. 1:5, lit., "having taken reminder"), a periphrastic expression for a single verb.

2. ***epilesmone*** (*1953*), "forgetfulness" (akin to A, No. 2), is used in Jas. 1:25, "a forgetful hearer," RV, "a hearer that forgetteth," lit., "a hearer of forgetfulness," i.e., a hearer characterized by "forgetfulness."

## FORGIVE, FORGAVE, FORGIVENESS

### *Old Testament*

***calach*** (5545), "to forgive." The basic meaning undergoes no change throughout the Old Testament. God is always the subject of "forgiveness." No other Old Testament verb means "to forgive," although several verbs include "forgiveness" in the range of meanings given a particular context, e.g., ***naca'*** and ***'awon*** in Exod. 32:32; ***kapar*** in Ezek. 16:63.

The verb occurs throughout the Old Testament. Most occurrences of ***calach*** are in the sacrificial laws of Leviticus and Numbers. In the typology of the Old Testament, sacrifices foreshadowed the accomplished work of Jesus Christ, and the Old Testament believer was assured of "forgiveness" based on sacrifice:, Num. 15:25, 28; Lev. 4:26; cf. vv. 20, 31, 35; 5:10, 13, 16, 18. The mediators of the atonement were the priests who offered the sacrifice. The sacrifice was ordained by God to promise ultimate "forgiveness" in God's sacrifice of His own Son. Moreover, sacrifice was appropriately connected to atonement, as there is no forgiveness without the shedding of blood, Lev. 4:20; cf. Heb. 9:22. When the temple was destroyed and sacrifices ceased, God sent the prophetic word that He graciously would restore Israel out of exile and "forgive" its sins, Jer. 31:34.

### *New Testament*

**A. Verbs.**

1. ***aphiemi*** (*863*), primarily, "to send forth, send away" (***apo***, "from," ***hiemi***, "to send"), denotes, besides its other meanings, "to remit or forgive" (a) debts, Matt. 6:12; 18:27, 32, these being completely cancelled; (b) sins, e.g., Matt. 9:2, 5, 6; 12:31, 32; Acts 8:22 ("the thought of thine heart"); Rom. 4:7; Jas. 5:15; 1 John 1:9; 2:12. In this latter respect the verb, like its corresponding noun (below), firstly signifies the remission of the punishment due to sinful conduct, the deliverance of the sinner from the penalty divinely, and therefore righteously, imposed; secondly, it involves the complete removal of the cause of offense; such remission is based upon the vicarious and propitiatory sacrifice of Christ. In the OT atoning sacrifice and "forgiveness" are often associated, e.g., Lev. 4:20, 26.

Human "forgiveness" is to be strictly analogous to divine "forgiveness," e.g., Matt. 6:12. If certain conditions are fulfilled, there is no limitation to Christ's law of "forgiveness," Matt. 18:21, 22. The conditions are repentance and confession, Matt. 18:15–17; Luke 17:3.

As to limits to the possibility of divine "forgiveness," see Matt. 12:32; 1 John 5:16.

2. ***charizomai*** (*5483*), "to bestow a favor unconditionally," is used of the act of "forgiveness," whether divine, Eph. 4:32; Col. 2:13; 3:13; or human, Luke 7:42, 43 (debt); 2 Cor. 2:7, 10; 12:13; Eph. 4:32 (1st mention). Paul uses this word frequently, but No. 1 only, in Rom. 4:7, in this sense of the word.

**B. Noun.**

***aphesis*** (*859*) denotes "a dismissal, release" (akin to A, No. 1); it is used of the remission of sins, and translated "forgiveness" in Mark 3:29; Eph. 1:7; Col. 1:14, and in the KJV of Acts 5:31; 13:38; 26:18, in each of which the RV has "remission." Eleven times it is followed by "of sins," and once by "of trespasses." It is never used of the remission of sins in the Sept., but is especially connected with the Year of Jubilee (Lev. 25:10, etc.). Cf. the RV of Luke 4:18, "release" (KJV, "liberty"). For the significance in connection with remission of sins and the propitiatory sacrifice of Christ, see A, No. 1.

## FORM (Noun)

1. ***morphe*** (*3444*) denotes "the special or characteristic form or feature" of a person or thing; it is used with particular significance in the NT, only of Christ, in Phil. 2:6, 7, in the phrases "being in the form of God," and "taking the form of a servant." ***morphe*** is therefore properly the nature or essence, not in the abstract, but as actually subsisting in the individual, and retained as long as the individual itself exists. . . . Thus in the passage before us ***morphe theou*** is the Divine nature actually and inseparably subsisting in the Person of Christ. . . . For the interpretation of 'the form of God' it is sufficient to say that (1) it includes the whole nature and essence of Deity, and is inseparable from them, since they could have no actual existence without it; and (2) that it does not include in itself anything 'accidental' or separable, such as particular modes of manifestation, or conditions of glory and majesty, which may at one time be attached to the 'form,' at another separated from it . . ." (Gifford).

The definition above mentioned applies to its use in Mark 16:12, as to the particular ways in which the Lord manifested Himself.

2. ***morphosis*** (*3446*), "a form or outline," denotes, in the NT, "an image or impress, an outward semblance," Rom. 2:20, of knowledge of the truth; 2 Tim. 3:5, of godliness. It is thus to be distinguished from ***morphe*** (No. 1).

3. ***tupos*** (*5179*), "the representation or pattern" of anything, is rendered "form" in Rom. 6:17, "that form (or mold) of teaching whereunto ye were delivered," RV. The metaphor is that of a cast or frame into which molten material is poured so as to take its shape. The Gospel is the mould; those who are obedient to its teachings become conformed to Christ, whom it presents. In Acts 23:25, it is used of a letter, RV, "form" (KJV, "manner"), with reference to the nature of the contents.

4. ***eidos*** (*1491*), lit., "that which is seen," "an appearance or external form," is rendered "form" in the RV of Luke 3:22, of the Holy Spirit's appearance at the baptism of Christ; in John 5:37, in the Lord's testimony concerning the Father; in Luke 9:29 it is said of Christ Himself; it is translated "sight" in 2 Cor. 5:7,

the Christian being guided by what he knows to be true, though unseen; in 1 Thess. 5:22 Christians are exhorted to abstain from "every form of evil," RV (the KJV, "appearance" is inadequate), i.e., from every kind of evil.

## FORM (Verb)

### *Old Testament*

***yatsar*** (3335), "to form, mold, fashion." ***yatsar*** is a technical potter's word, and it is often used in connection with the potter at work, Isa. 29:16; Jer. 18:4, 6. The word is sometimes used as a general term of "craftsmanship or handiwork," whether molding, carving, or casting, Isa. 44:9–10, 12. The word may be used to express the "forming of plans in one's mind, Ps. 94:20. ***yatsar*** is frequently used to describe God's creative activity, whether literally or figuratively. Thus, God "formed" not only man, Gen. 2:7–8, but the animals, Gen. 2:19. God also "formed" the nation of Israel, Isa. 27:11; 45:9, 11; Israel was "formed" as God's special servant even from the womb, Isa. 44:2, 24; 49:5. While yet in the womb, Jeremiah was "formed" to be a prophet, Jer. 1:5. God "formed" locusts as a special visual lesson for Amos, Amos 7:1; the great sea monster, Leviathan, was "formed" to play in the seas, Ps. 104:26.

### *New Testament*

**A. Verbs.**

1. ***morphoo*** (*3445*), like the noun ***morphe***, refers, not to the external and transient, but to the inward and real; it is used in Gal. 4:19, expressing the necessity of a change in character and conduct to correspond with inward spiritual condition, so that there may be moral conformity to Christ.

2. ***plasso*** (*4111*), "to mold, to shape," was used of the artist who wrought in clay or wax (Eng., "plastic," "plasticity"), and occurs in Rom. 9:20; 1 Tim. 2:13.

**B. Noun.**

***plasma*** (*4110*) denotes "anything molded or shaped into a form" (akin to A, No. 2), Rom. 9:20, "the thing formed."

## FORNICATION, FORNICATOR

**A. Nouns.**

1. ***porneia*** (*4202*) is used (a) of "illicit sexual intercourse," in John 8:41; Acts 15:20, 29; 21:25; 1 Cor. 5:1; 6:13, 18; 2 Cor. 12:21; Gal. 5:19; Eph. 5:3; Col. 3:5; 1 Thess. 4:3; Rev. 2:21; 9:21; in the plural in 1 Cor. 7:2; in Matt. 5:32 and 19:9 it stands for, or includes, adultery; it is distinguished from it in 15:19 and Mark 7:21; (b) metaphorically, of "the association of pagan idolatry with doctrines of, and professed adherence to, the Christian faith," Rev. 14:8; 17:2, 4; 18:3; 19:2; some suggest this as the sense in 2:21.

2. ***pornos*** (*4205*) denotes "a man who indulges in fornication, a fornicator," 1 Cor. 5:9, 10, 11; 6:9; Eph. 5:5, RV; 1 Tim. 1:10, RV; Heb. 12:16; 13:4, RV; Rev. 21:8 and 22:15, RV (KJV, "whoremonger").

**B. Verbs.**

1. ***porneuo*** (*4203*) "to commit fornication," is used (a) literally, Mark 10:19; 1 Cor. 6:18; 10:8; Rev. 2:14, 20, see Nouns A. 1. (a) and (b) above; (b) metaphorically, Rev. 17:2; 18:3, 9.

2. ***ekporneuo*** (*1608*), a strengthened form of No. 1 (***ek***, used intensively), "to give oneself up to fornication," implying excessive indulgence, Jude 7.

## FORSAKE

### *Old Testament*

***'azab*** (5800), "to leave, forsake, abandon, leave behind, be left over, let go." Basically ***'azab*** means "to depart from something," or "to leave," Gen. 2:24. A special nuance of the word is "to leave in the lurch," Num. 10:31. The word also carries the meaning "forsake," implying the severing or straining of a relationship, Isa. 7:16; 54:6–7; 62:4. A second emphasis of ***'azab*** is "to leave behind," meaning to allow something to remain while one leaves the scene, Gen. 39:6,12.

In a somewhat different nuance, the word means to "let someone or something alone with a problem," Exod. 23:5. Used figuratively, ***'azab*** means to "put distance between" in a spiritual or intellectual sense: "Cease from anger, and forsake wrath . . . ," Ps. 37:8. The third emphasis of the word is "to be left over, a remainder," of physical collection or mass, Lev. 19:10.

Finally, ***'azab*** can mean "to let go" or "allow to leave," Ps. 49:10. A different nuance occurs in Ruth 2:16, where the verb means "to let something lie" on the ground. ***'azab*** can also mean "to give up," Prov. 28:13, "to set free," as in 2 Chron. 28:14, to "allow someone to do something," as in 2 Chron. 32:31; Neh. 5:10. ***'azab*** is sometimes used in a judicial technical sense of "being free," Deut. 32:36.

### *New Testament*

**A. Verbs.**

1. ***kataleipo*** (*2641*), a strengthened form of ***leipo***, "to leave," signifies (a) "to leave, to leave behind," e.g., Matt. 4:13; (b) "to leave remaining, reserve," e.g., Luke 10:40; (c) "to forsake,"

in the sense of abandoning, translated "to forsake" in the RV of Luke 5:28 and Acts 6:2; in Heb. 11:27 and 2 Pet. 2:15, KJV and RV. In this sense it is translated "to leave," in Mark 10:7; 14:52; Luke 15:4; Eph. 5:31.

2. ***enkataleipo*** (*1459*), from ***en***, "in," and No. 1, denotes (a) "to leave behind, among, leave surviving," Rom. 9:29; (b) "to forsake, abandon, leave in straits, or helpless," said by, or of, Christ, Matt. 27:46; Mark 15:34; Acts 2:27, 31 (No. 1 in some mss.); of men, 2 Cor. 4:9; 2 Tim. 4:10, 16; by God, Heb. 13:5; of things, by Christians (negatively), Heb. 10:25.

3. ***aphiemi*** (*863*) sometimes has the significance of "forsaking," Mark 1:18; 14:50 (RV, "left"); so Luke 5:11.

4. ***apotasso*** (*657*), primarily, "to set apart" (***apo***, off, "from," ***tasso***, "to arrange"), is used in the middle voice, meaning (a) "to take leave of," e.g., Mark 6:46, (b) "to renounce, forsake," Luke 14:33, KJV, "forsaketh," RV, "renounceth" ("all that he hath").

**B. Noun.**

***apostasia*** (*646*), "an apostasy, defection, revolt," always in NT of religious defection, is translated "to forsake" in Acts 2:2 lit., "(thou teachest) apostasy (from Moses)"; in 2 Thess. 2:3, "falling away."

## FORSWEAR

***epiorkeo*** (*1964*) signifies "to swear falsely, to undo one's swearing, forswear oneself" (***epi***, "against," ***orkos***, "an oath"), Matt. 5:33.

## FOUNDATION (to lay), FOUNDED

**A. Nouns.**

1. ***themelios***, or ***themelion*** (*2310*) is properly an adjective denoting "belonging to a foundation" (connected with ***tithemi***, "to place"). It is used (1) as a noun, with ***lithos***, "a stone," understood, in Luke 6:48, 49; 14:29; Heb. 11:10; Rev. 21:14, 19; (2) as a neuter noun in Acts 16:26, and metaphorically, (a) of "the ministry of the gospel and the doctrines of the faith," Rom. 15:20; 1 Cor. 3:10, 11, 12; Eph. 2:20, where the "of" is not subjective (i.e., consisting of the apostles and prophets), but objective, (i.e., laid by the apostles, etc.); so in 2 Tim. 2:19, where "the foundation of God" is "the foundation laid by God,"—not the Church (which is not a "foundation"), but Christ Himself, upon whom the saints are built; Heb. 6:1; (b) "of good works," 1 Tim. 6:19.

2. ***katabole*** (*2602*), lit., "a casting down," is used (a) of "conceiving seed," Heb. 11:11; (b) of "a foundation," as that which is laid down, or in the sense of founding; metaphorically, of "the foundation of the world"; in this respect two phrases are used, (1) "from the foundation of the world," Matt. 25:34 (in the most authentic mss. in 13:35 there is no phrase representing "of the world"); Luke 11:50; Heb. 4:3; 9:26; Rev. 13:8; 17:8; (2) "before the foundation of the world," John 17:24; Eph. 1:4; 1 Pet. 1:20. The latter phrase looks back to the past eternity.

**B. Verb.**

***themelioo*** (*2311*), "to lay a foundation, to found" (akin to A, No. 1), is used (a) literally, Matt. 7:25; Luke 6:48; Heb. 1:10; (b) metaphorically, Eph. 3:17, "grounded (in love)"; Col. 1:23 (ditto, "in the faith"); 1 Pet. 5:10, KJV, "settle."

## FOUNTAIN

***pege*** (*4077*), "a spring or fountain," is used of (a) "an artificial well," fed by a spring, John 4:6; (b) metaphorically (in contrast to such a well), "the indwelling Spirit of God," 4:14; (c) "springs," metaphorically in 2 Pet. 2:17, RV, for KJV, "wells"; (d) "natural fountains or springs," Jas. 3:11, 12; Rev. 8:10; 14:7; 16:4; (e) metaphorically, "eternal life and the future blessings accruing from it," Rev. 7:17; 21:6; (f) "a flow of blood," Mark 5:29.

## FRAME (Verb)

1. ***katartizo*** (*2675*), "to fit, to render complete," is translated "have been framed" in Heb. 11:3, of the worlds or ages.

2. ***sunarmologeo*** (*4883*), "to fit or frame together" (***sun***, "with," ***harmos***, "a joint," ***lego***, "to choose"), is used metaphorically of the church as a spiritual temple, the parts being "fitly framed together," Eph. 2:21; as a body, 4:16, RV, "fitly framed," (for KJV, "fitly joined").

## FRANKINCENSE

***libanos*** (*2030*), Matt. 2:11; Rev. 18:13, from a Semitic verb signifying "to be white," is a vegetable resin, bitter and glittering, obtained by incisions in the bark of the *arbor thuris*, "the incense tree." The Indian variety is called *looban*.

## FRAUD

***aphustereo*** (*575* and *5302*), "to keep back, deprive" (***apo***, "from," ***hustereo***, "to be lacking"), is used in Jas. 5:4, "is kept back by fraud" (some mss. have ***apostereo***, "to defraud"). The word is found in a papyrus writing of A.D. 42, of a bath insufficiently warmed.

## FREE, FREEDOM, FREELY, FREEMAN, FREEDMAN, FREEWOMAN

**A. Adjective.**

***eleutheros*** (*1658*), primarily of "freedom to go wherever one likes," is used (a) of "freedom from restraint and obligation" in general, Matt. 17:26; Rom. 7:3; 1 Cor. 7:39, RV, "free," of the second marriage of a woman; 9:1, 19; 1 Pet. 2:16; from the Law, Gal. 4:26; from sin, John 8:36; with regard to righteousness, Rom. 6:20 (i.e., righteousness laid no sort of bond upon them, they had no relation to it); (b) in a civil sense, "free" from bondage or slavery, John 8:33; 1 Cor. 7:21, 22, 2nd part (for v. 22, 1st part, see C, No. 2); 12:13; Gal. 3:28; Eph. 6:8; Rev. 13:16; 19:18; as a noun, "freeman," Col. 3:11, RV; Rev. 6:15; "freewoman," Gal. 4:22, 23, 30, and v. 31. RV.

**B. Verb.**

***eleutheroo*** (*1659*), "to make free" (akin to A), is used of deliverance from (a) sin, John 8:32, 36; Rom. 6:18, 22; (b) the Law, Rom. 8:2; Gal. 5:1 (see, however under C); (c) the bondage of corruption, Rom. 8:21.

**C. Nouns.**

1. ***eleutheria*** (*1657*), "liberty" (akin to A and B), is rendered "freedom" in Gal. 5:1, "with freedom did Christ set us free." The combination of the noun with the verb stresses the completeness of the act, the aorist (or point) tense indicating both its momentary and comprehensive character; it was done once for all. The RV margin "for freedom" gives perhaps the preferable meaning, i.e., "not to bring us into another form of bondage did Christ liberate us from that in which we were born, but in order to make us free from bondage."

The word is twice rendered "freedom" in the RV of Gal. 5:13 (KJV, "liberty"). The phraseology is that of manumission from slavery, which among the Greeks was effected by a legal fiction, according to which the manumitted slave was purchased by a god; as the slave could not provide the money, the master paid it into the temple treasury in the presence of the slave, a document being drawn up containing the words "for freedom." No one could enslave him again, as he was the property of the god. Hence the word ***apeleutheros***, No. 2. The word is also translated "freedom" in 1 Pet. 2:16, RV. In 2 Cor. 3:17 the word denotes "freedom" of access to the presence of God.

2. ***apeleutheros*** (*558*), "a freed man" (***apo***, "from," and A), is used in 1 Cor. 7:22, "the Lord's freedman."

**D. Adverb.**

***dorean*** (*1432*), from ***dorea***, "a gift" is used as an adverb in the sense "freely," in Matt. 10:8; Rom. 3:24; 2 Cor. 11:7 (RV, "for nought"); Rev. 21:6; 22:17. Here the prominent thought is the grace of the Giver.

## FRIEND (make one's)

### *Old Testament*

***rea'*** (7453), "friend; companion; fellow." The word refers to a "friend" in 2 Sam. 13:3: "But Amnon had a friend, whose name was Jonadab." The word may be used of a husband, Jer. 3:20, or a beloved one, Song of Sol. 5:16.

In another sense, ***rea'*** may be used of any person with whom one has reciprocal relations: "And they said every one to his fellow, Come, and let us cast lots . . . ," Jonah 1:7. The word also appears in such phrases as "one another," found in Gen. 11:3: "And they said *one to another* . . . ," cf. Gen. 31:49.

Other related nouns that appear less frequently are ***re'eh***, which means "friend" about 5 times, e.g., 1 Kings 4:5; and ***re'ah***, which means "companion or attendant," Judg. 11:38; Ps. 45:14.

### *New Testament*

**A. Nouns.**

1. ***philos*** (*5384*), primarily an adjective, denoting "loved, dear, or friendly," became used as a noun, (a) masculine, Matt. 11:19; fourteen times in Luke (once feminine, 15:9); six in John; three in Acts; two in James, 2:23, "the friend of God"; 4:4, "a friend of the world"; 3 John 14 (twice); (b) feminine, Luke 15:9, "her friends."

2. ***hetairos*** (*2083*), "a comrade, companion, partner," is used as a term of kindly address in Matt. 20:13; 22:12; 26:50. This, as expressing comradeship, is to be distinguished from No. 1, which is a term of endearment.

**B. Verb.**

***peitho*** (*3982*), "to persuade, influence," is rendered "having made . . . their friend" in Acts 12:20, of the folks of Tyre and Sidon in winning the good will of Blastus, Herod's chamberlain, possibly with bribes.

## FRIENDSHIP

***philia*** (*5373*), akin to ***philos***, "a friend" (see above), is rendered in Jas. 4:4, "the friendship (of the world)." It involves "the idea of loving as well as being loved" (Mayor); cf. the verb in John 15:19.

## FRUIT (bear), FRUITFUL, UNFRUITFUL

### *Old Testament*

**A. Noun.**

***peri*** (6529), "fruit; reward; price; earnings; product; result." First, ***peri*** represents the mature edible product of a plant, Gen. 1:11; Ps. 107:34. Second, ***peri*** means "offspring," or the "fruit of a womb," of any creature, Gen. 1:22;

Deut. 7:13. Third, the "product" or "result," of an action Ps. 58:11; Prov. 31:16,31.

**B. Verb.**

***parah*** (6504), "to be fruitful, bear fruit," Gen. 1:22.

*New Testament*

**A. Noun.**

***karpos*** (*2590*), "fruit," is used (I) of the fruit of trees, fields, the earth, that which is produced by the inherent energy of a living organism, e.g., Matt. 7:17; Jas. 5:7, 18; plural, e.g., in Luke 12:17 and 2 Tim. 2:6; of the human body, Luke 1:42; Acts 2:30; (II), metaphorically, (a) of works or deeds, "fruit" being the visible expression of power working inwardly and invisibly, the character of the "fruit" being evidence of the character of the power producing it, Matt. 7:16. The invisible power of the Holy Spirit in those who are brought into living union with Christ (John 15:2–8, 16) produces "the fruit of the Spirit," Gal. 5:22. So in Phil. 1:11, marg., "fruit of righteousness." In Heb. 12:11, "the fruit of righteousness" is described as "peaceable fruit," the outward effect of divine chastening; "the fruit of righteousness is sown in peace," Jas. 3:18, i.e., the seed contains the fruit; those who make peace, produce a harvest of righteousness; in Eph. 5:9, "the fruit of the light" (RV, and see context) is seen in "goodness and righteousness and truth," as the expression of the union of the Christian with God; for God is good, Mark 10:18, the Son is "the righteous One," Acts 7:52, the Spirit is "the Spirit of truth," John 16:13; (b) of advantage, profit, consisting (1) of converts as the result of evangelistic ministry, John 4:36; Rom. 1:13; Phil. 1:22; (2) of sanctification, through deliverance from a life of sin and through service to God, Rom. 6:22, in contrast to (3) the absence of anything regarded as advantageous as the result of former sins, v. 21; (4) of the reward for ministration to servants of God, Phil. 4:17; (5) of the effect of making confession to God's Name by the sacrifice of praise, Heb. 13:15.

**B. Adjective.**

***akarpos*** (*175*), "unfruitful" (***a***, negative, and ***karpos*** above), is used figuratively (a) of "the word of the Kingdom," rendered "unfruitful" in the case of those influenced by the cares of the world and the deceitfulness of riches, Matt. 13:22; Mark 4:19; (b) of the understanding of one praying with a "tongue," which effected no profit to the church without an interpretation of it, 1 Cor. 14:14; (c) of the works of darkness, Eph. 5:11; (d) of believers who fail "to maintain good works," indicating the earning of one's living so as to do good works to others, Titus 3:14; of the effects of failing to supply in one's faith the qualities of virtue, knowledge, temperance, patience, godliness, love of the brethren, and love, 2 Pet. 1:8. In Jude 12 it is rendered "without fruit," of ungodly men, who oppose the gospel while pretending to uphold it, depicted as "autumn trees."

**C. Verb.**

***karpophoreo*** (*2592*), "to bear or bring forth fruit," is used (a) in the natural sense, of the "fruit of the earth," Mark 4:28; (b) metaphorically, of conduct, or that which takes effect in conduct, Matt. 13:23; Mark 4:20; Luke 8:15; Rom. 7:4, 5 (the latter, of evil "fruit," borne "unto death," of activities resulting from a state of alienation from God); Col. 1:6 in the middle voice; Col. 1:10.

## FULFILL, FULFILLING, FULFILLMENT

**A. Verbs.**

1. ***pleroo*** (*4137*) signifies (1) "to fill"; (2) "to fulfill, complete," (a) of time, e.g., Mark 1:15; Luke 21:24; John 7:8 (KJV, "full come"); Acts 7:23, RV, "he was well-nigh forty years old" (KJV, "was full" etc.), lit., "the time of forty years was fulfilled to him"; v. 30, KJV, "were expired"; 9:23; 24:27 (KJV, "after two years"; RV, "when two years were fulfilled"); (b) of number, Rev. 6:11; (c) of good pleasure, 2 Thess. 1:11; (d) of joy, Phil. 2:2; in the passive voice, "to be fulfilled," John 3:29 and 17:13; in the following the verb is rendered "fulfilled" in the RV, for the KJV, "full," John 15:11; 16:24; 1 John 1:4; 2 John 12; (e) of obedience, 2 Cor. 10:6; (f) of works, Rev. 3:2; (g) of the future Passover, Luke 22:16; (h) of sayings, prophecies, etc., e.g., Matt. 1:22 (twelve times in Matt., two in Mark, four in Luke, eight in John, two in Acts); Jas. 2:23; in Col. 1:25 the word signifies to preach "fully," to complete the ministry of the Gospel appointed.

2. ***anapleroo*** (*378*), "to fill up fill completely" (***ana***, "up, up to," and No. 1), is used (a) of Isaiah's prophecy of Israel's rejection of God, fulfilled in the rejection of His Son, Matt. 13:14; (b) of the status of a person in a church, RV, "filleth the place," for KJV, "occupieth the room," 1 Cor. 14:16; (c) of an adequate supply of service, 1 Cor. 16:17, "supplied"; Phil. 2:30, "to supply"; (d) of sins, 1 Thess. 2:16; (e) of the law of Christ; Gal. 6:2.

3. ***teleo*** (*5055*), "to end" (akin to ***telos***, "an end"), signifies, among its various meanings, "to give effect to," and is translated "fulfill," of

the Law, intentionally, Jas. 2:8, or unconsciously, Rom. 2:27; of the prophetic Scriptures concerning the death of Christ, Acts 13:29; prohibitively, of the lust of the flesh, Gal. 5:16.

4. ***sunteleo*** (*4931*), "to complete," is translated "fulfilled" in the KJV of Mark 13:4 (RV, "accomplished).

5. ***teleioo*** (*5048*), "to bring to an end, fulfill," is rendered "to fulfill," of days. Luke 2:43; of the Scripture, John 19:28.

6. ***plerophoreo*** (*4135*), "to bring in full measure," from ***pleroo*** (see No. 1), and ***phoreo***, "to bring"; hence, "to fulfill," of circumstances relating to Christ, Luke 1:1, RV, "have been fulfilled" (KJV "are most surely believed"); of evangelical ministry, 2 Tim. 4:5, "fulfill" (KJV, "make full proof"); so in v. 17, RV, "fully proclaimed" (KJV, "fully known").

7. ***ekpleroo*** (*1603*), a strengthened form of No. 1, occurs in Acts 13:33.

**B. Nouns.**

1. ***pleroma*** (*4138*) stands for the result of the action expressed in ***pleroo***, "to fill." It is used to signify (a) "that which has been completed, the complement, fullness," e.g., John 1:16; Eph. 1:23; some suggest that the "fullness" here points to the body as the filled receptacle of the power of Christ (words terminating in *—**ma*** are frequently concrete in character.

2. ***teleiosis*** (*5058*), a fulfillment, is so rendered in Luke 1:45, akin to A. 3.

## FULL

**A. Adjectives.**

1. ***pleres*** (*4134*) denotes "full," (a) in the sense of "being filled," materially, Matt. 14:20; 15:37; Mark 8:19 (said of baskets "full" of bread crumbs); of leprosy, Luke 5;12; spiritually, of the Holy Spirit, Luke 4:1; Acts 6:3; 7:55; 11:24; grace and truth, John 1:14; faith, Acts 6:5; grace and power, 6:8; of the effects of spiritual life and qualities, seen in good works, Acts 9:36; in an evil sense, of guile and villany, Acts 13:10; wrath, 19:28; (b) in the sense of "being complete," "full corn in the ear," Mark 4:28; of a reward hereafter, 2 John 8.

2. ***mestos*** (*3324*) probably akin to a root signifying "to measure," hence conveys the sense of "having full measure," (a) of material things, a vessel, John 19:29; a net, 21:11; (b) metaphorically, of thoughts and feelings, exercised (1) in evil things, hypocrisy, Matt. 23:28; envy, murder, strife, deceit, malignity, Rom. 1:29; the utterances of the tongue, Jas. 3:8; adultery, 2 Pet. 2:14; (2) in virtues, goodness, Rom. 15:14; mercy, etc., Jas. 3:17.

**B. Verb.**

***gemo*** (*1073*), "to be full, to be heavily laden with," was primarily used of a ship; it is chiefly used in the NT of evil contents, such as extortion and excess, Matt. 23:25; dead men's bones, v. 27; extortion and wickedness, Luke 11:39; cursing, Rom. 3:14; blasphemy, Rev. 17:3; abominations, v. 4; of divine judgments 15:17; 21:9; (RV, "laden," KJV, "full"); of good things, 4:6, 8; 5:8.

## FULLER

***gnapheus*** (*102*), akin to ***knapto***, "to card wool," denotes "a clothcarder, or dresser" (***gnaphos***, "the prickly teasel-cloth"; hence, "a carding comb"); it is used of the raiment of the Lord in Mark 9:3.

## FULLNESS

***pleroma*** (*4138*) denotes "fullness," that of which a thing is "full"; it is thus used of the grace and truth manifested in Christ, John 1:16; of all His virtues and excellencies, Eph. 4:13; "the blessing of Christ," Rom. 15:29, RV (not as KJV); the conversion and restoration of Israel, Rom. 11:12; the completion of the number of Gentiles who receive blessing through the gospel, v. 25; the complete products of the earth, 1 Cor. 10:26; the end of an appointed period, Gal. 4:4; Eph. 1:10; God, in the completeness of His Being, Eph. 3:19; Col. 1:19; 2:9; the church as the complement of Christ, Eph. 1:23. In Mark 6:43, "basketfuls," RV, is, lit., "fullnesses of baskets."

## FURNISH

***exartizo*** (*1822*), "to fit out, to prepare perfectly, to complete for a special purpose" (***ex***, "out," used intensively, and ***artios***, "joined," ***artos***, "a joint"), is used of "accomplishing" days, Acts 21:5, i.e., of "terminating" a space of time; of being "completely furnished," by means of the Scriptures, for spiritual service, 2 Tim. 3:17.

# G

## GAIN (Noun and Verb)

### A. Nouns.

1. ***ergasia*** (*2039*) signifies (a) "work, working, performance" (from ***ergon***, "work"), Eph. 4:19; in Luke 12:58, "diligence"; (b) "business or gain got by work," Acts 16:16, 19; in 19:24, 25, the RV adheres to the meaning "business" (KJV, "gain" and "craft").

2. ***porismos*** (*4200*) primarily denotes "a providing" (akin to ***porizo***, "to procure"), then, "a means of gain," 1 Tim. 6:5 (RV, "a way of gain"); 6:6.

3. ***kerdos*** (*2771*), "gain" (akin to ***kerdaino***, see below), occurs in Phil. 1:21; 3:7; Titus 1:11.

### B. Verbs.

1. ***kerdaino*** (*2770*), akin to A, No. 3, signifies (I), literally, (a) "to gain something," Matt. 16:26; 25:16 (in the best mss.), 17, 20, 22; Mark 8:36; Luke 9:25; (b) "to get gain, make a profit," Jas. 4:13; (II), metaphorically, (a) "to win persons," said (1) of "gaining" an offending brother who by being told privately of his offense, and by accepting the representations, is won from alienation and from the consequences of his fault, Matt. 18:15; (2) of winning souls into the kingdom of God by the gospel, 1 Cor. 9:19, 20 (twice), 21, 22, or by godly conduct, 1 Pet. 3:1 (RV, "gained"); (3) of so practically appropriating Christ to oneself that He becomes the dominating power in and over one's whole being and circumstances, Phil. 3:8 (RV, "gain"); (b) "to gain things," said of getting injury and loss, Acts 27:21, RV, "gotten."

2. ***diapragmateuomai*** (*1281*) signifies "to gain by trading," Luke 19:15 (from ***dia***, "through," used intensively, and ***pragmateuomai***, "to busy oneself, to be engaged in business").

3. ***peripoieo*** (*4046*), "to save for oneself, gain," is in the middle voice in the best mss. in Luke 17:33, RV, gain.

## GAINSAY, GAINSAYER, GAINSAYING

### A. Verbs.

1. ***antilego*** (*483*), "to contradict, oppose," lit., "say against," is translated "gainsaying" in Rom. 10:21 and Titus 2:9, RV (KJV, "answering again"), of servants in regard to masters; in Titus 1:9 "gainsayers."

2. ***anteipon*** (*483*), which serves as an aorist tense of No. 1, is rendered "gainsay" in Luke 21:15; "say against" in Acts 4:14.

### B. Noun.

***antilogia*** (*485*), akin to A, No. 1, is rendered "gainsaying," in Heb. 12:3, RV, and Jude 11. Opposition in act seems to be implied in these two places; though this sense has been questioned by some, it is confirmed by instances from the papyri.

### C. Adjective.

***anantirrhetos*** (*368*), lit., "not to be spoken against" (***a***, negative, ***n***, euphonic, ***anti***, "against," ***rhetos***, "spoken"), is rendered "cannot be gainsaid" in Acts 19:36, RV.

### D. Adverb.

***anantirrhetos*** (*369*), corresponding to C, is translated "without gainsaying" in Acts 10:29; it might be rendered "unquestioningly."

## GARNER

***apotheke*** (*596*), "a storehouse, granary" (from ***apo***, "away," and ***tithemi***, "to put"), is translated "garner" in Matt. 3:12 and Luke 3:17.

## GARNISH

***kosmeo*** (*2885*) is translated by the verb "to garnish" in Matt. 12:44; 23:29; Luke 11:25; and in the KJV of Rev. 21:19.

## GAZINGSTOCK

***theatrizo*** (*2301*) signifies "to make a spectacle" (from ***theatron***, "a theater, spectacle, show"); it is used in the passive voice in Heb. 10:33, "being made a gazingstock."

## GENEALOGY

### A. Noun.

***genealogia*** (*1076*) is used in 1 Tim. 1:4 and Titus 3:9, with reference to such "genealogies" as are found in Philo, Josephus and the book of Jubilees, by which Jews traced their descent from the patriarchs and their families, and perhaps also to Gnostic "genealogies" and orders of aeons and spirits. Amongst the Greeks, as well as other nations, mythological stories gathered round the birth and "genealogy" of their heroes. Probably Jewish "genealogical" tales crept into Christian communities. Hence the warnings to Timothy and Titus.

### B. Verb.

***genealogeo*** (*1075*), "to reckon or trace a genealogy" (from ***genea***, "a race," and ***lego***, "to choose, pick out"), is used, in the passive voice, of Melchizedek in Heb. 7:6.

### C. Adjective (negative).

***agenealogetos*** (*35*), denoting "without recorded pedigree" (***a***, negative, and an adjectival form from B), is rendered "without genealogy" in Heb. 7:3. The narrative in Gen. 14 is so framed in facts and omissions as to foreshadow the person of Christ.

## GENERATION

***Old Testament***

***dor*** (1755), "generation." First the concrete meaning of "generation" is the "period during which people live," Gen. 7:1. A ***dor*** is roughly the period of time from one's birth to one's maturity, which in the Old Testament corresponds to a period of about 40 years, Num. 14:33 cf. also Exod. 20:5; Deut. 7:9. The psalmist recognized the obligation of one "generation" to the "generations" to come," Ps. 71:17–18; 145:4.

***New Testament***

1. ***genea*** (*1074*), "generation," Acts 8:33.

2. ***genesis*** (*1078*) denotes "an origin, a lineage, or birth," translated "generation" in Matt. 1:1.

## GENTILES

### A. Nouns.

1. ***ethnos*** (*1484*), whence Eng., "heathen," denotes, firstly, "a multitude or company"; then, "a multitude of people of the same nature or genus, a nation, people"; it is used in the singular, of the Jews, e.g., Luke 7:5; 23:2; John 11:48, 50–52; in the plural, of nations (Heb., ***goiim***) other than Israel, e.g., Matt. 4:15; Rom. 3:29; 11:11; 15:10; Gal. 2:8; occasionally it is used of gentile converts in distinction from Jews, e.g., Rom. 11:13; 16:4; Gal. 2:12, 14; Eph. 3:1.

2. ***hellen*** (*1672*) originally denoted the early descendants of Thessalian Hellas; then, Greeks as opposed to barbarians, Rom. 1:14. It became applied to such Gentiles as spoke the Greek language, e.g., Gal. 2:3; 3:28. Since that was the common medium of intercourse in the Roman Empire, Greek and Gentile became more or less interchangeable terms. For this term the RV always adheres to the word "Greeks," e.g., John 7:35; Rom. 2:9, 10; 3:9; 1 Cor. 10:32, where the local church is distinguished from Jews and Gentiles; 12:13.

### B. Adjective.

***ethnikos*** (*1482*) is used as noun, and translated "Gentiles" in the RV of Matt. 5:47; 6:7; "the Gentile" in 18:17 (KJV, "an heathen man"); "the Gentiles" in 3 John 7, KJV and RV.

### C. Adverb.

***ethnikos*** (*1483*), "in Gentile fashion, in the manner of Gentiles," is used in Gal. 2:14, "as do the Gentiles," RV.

## GENTLE, GENTLENESS, GENTLY

### A. Adjectives.

1. ***epieikes*** (*1933*), from ***epi***, "unto," and ***eikos***, "likely," denotes "seemly, fitting"; hence, "equitable, fair, moderate, forbearing, not insisting on the letter of the law"; it expresses that considerateness that looks "humanely and reasonably at the facts of a case"; it is rendered "gentle" in 1 Tim. 3:3, RV (KJV, "patient"), in contrast to contentiousness; in Titus 3:2, "gentle," in association with meekness, in Jas. 3:17, as a quality of the wisdom from above, in 1 Pet. 2:18, in association with the good; for the RV rendering "forbearance" in Phil. 4:5.

2. ***epios*** (*2261*), "mild, gentle," was frequently used by Greek writers as characterizing a nurse with trying children or a teacher with refractory scholars, or of parents toward their children. In 1 Thess. 2:7, the apostle uses it of the conduct of himself and his fellow missionaries towards the converts at Thessalonica (cf. 2 Cor. 11:13, 20); in 2 Tim. 2:24, of the conduct requisite for a servant of the Lord.

### B. Noun.

***epieikeia*** (*1932*), or ***epieikia***, denotes "fairness, moderation, gentleness," "sweet reasonableness" (Matthew Arnold); it is said of Christ, 2 Cor. 10:1, where it is coupled with ***prautes***, "meekness"; for its meaning in Acts 24:4.

## GHOST (give up the)

1. ***ekpneo*** (*1606*), lit., "to breathe out," "to expire," is used in the NT, without an object, "soul" or "life" being understood, Mark 15:37, 39, and Luke 23:46, of the death of Christ. In Matt. 27:50 and John 19:30, where different verbs are used, the act is expressed in a way which stresses it as of His own volition: in the former, "Jesus . . . yielded up His spirit (***pneuma***)"; in the latter, "He gave up His spirit."

2. ***ekpsucho*** (*1634*), "to expire," lit., "to breathe out the soul (or life), to give up the

ghost" (***ek***, "out," ***psuche***, "the soul"), is used in Acts 5:5, 10; 12:23.

## GIFT, GIVING

1. ***doron*** (*1435*), akin to ***didomi***, "to give," is used (a) of "gifts" presented as an expression of honor, Matt. 2:11; (b) of "gifts" for the support of the temple and the needs of the poor, Matt. 15:5; Mark 7:11; Luke 21:1, 4; (c) of "gifts" offered to God, Matt. 5:23, 24; 8:4; 23:18, 19; Heb. 5:1; 8:3, 4; 9:9; 11:4; (d) of salvation by grace as the "gift" of God, Eph. 2:8; (e) of "presents" for mutual celebration of an occasion, Rev. 11:10.

2. ***dorea*** (*1431*) denotes "a free gift," stressing its gratuitous character; it is always used in the NT of a spiritual or supernatural gift, John 4:10; Acts 8:20; 11:17; Rom. 5:15; 2 Cor. 9:15; Eph. 3:7; Heb. 6:4; in Eph. 4:7, "according to the measure of the gift of Christ," the "gift" is that given by Christ; in Acts 2:28, "the gift of the Holy Ghost," the clause is epexegetical, the "gift" being the Holy Ghost Himself; cf. 10:45; 11:17, and the phrase, "the gift of righteousness," Rom. 5:17.

3. ***dorema*** (*1434*): "gift," Rom. 5:16; Jas. 1:17.

4. ***doma*** (*1390*) lends greater stress to the concrete character of the "gift," than to its beneficent nature, Matt. 7:11; Luke 11:13; Eph. 4:8; Phil. 4:17.

5. ***dosis*** (*1394*) denotes, properly, "the act of giving," Phil. 4:15, euphemistically referring to "gifts" as a matter of debt and credit accounts; then, objectively, "a gift," Jas. 1:17.

6. ***charisma*** (*5486*), "a gift of grace, a gift involving grace" (***charis***) on the part of God as the donor, is used (a) of His free bestowments upon sinners, Rom. 5:15, 16; 6:23; 11:29; (b) of His endowments upon believers by the operation of the Holy Spirit in the churches, Rom. 12:6; 1 Cor. 1:7; 12:4, 9, 28, 30, 31; 1 Tim. 4:14; 2 Tim. 1:6; 1 Pet. 4:10; (c) of that which is imparted through human instruction, Rom. 1:11; (d) of the natural "gift" of continence, consequent upon the grace of God as Creator, 1 Cor. 7:7; (e) of gracious deliverances granted in answer to the prayers of fellow believers, 2 Cor. 1:11.

7. ***merismos*** (*3311*), "a dividing" (from ***meros***, "a part"), is translated "gifts" in Heb. 2:4, "gifts of the Holy Ghost" (marg., "distributions"); in 4:12, "dividing."

## GIRD, GIRDED, GIRT (about, up)

1. ***zonnumi*** (*2224*), or ***zonnuo***, "to gird" in the middle voice, "to gird oneself," is used of the long garments worn in the east, John 21:18; Acts 12:8 (***perizonnumi*** in some mss.).

2. ***anazonnumi*** (*328*), "to gird up" (***ana***, "up," and No. 1), is used metaphorically of the loins of the mind, 1 Pet. 1:13; cf. Luke 12:35 (see No. 4). The figure is taken from the circumstances of the Israelites as they ate the Passover in readiness for their journey, Exod. 12:11; the Christian is to have his mental powers alert in expectation of Christ's coming. The verb is in the middle voice, indicating the special interest the believer is to take in so doing.

3. ***diazonnumi*** (*1241*), "to gird round," i.e., firmly (***dia***, "throughout," used intensively), is used of the Lord's act in "girding" Himself with a towel, John 13:4, 5, and of Peter's girding himself with his coat, 21:7.

4. ***perizonnumi*** (*4024*), "to gird around or about," is used (a) literally, of "girding" oneself for service, Luke 12:37; 17:8; for rapidity of movement, Acts 12:8; (b) figuratively, of the condition for service on the part of the followers of Christ, Luke 12:35; Eph. 6:14; (c) emblematically, of Christ's priesthood, Rev. 1:13, indicative of majesty of attitude and action, the middle voice suggesting the particular interest taken by Christ in "girding" Himself thus; so of the action of the angels mentioned in 15:6.



## GIRDLE

***zone*** (*2223*), Eng., "zone," denotes "a belt or girdle," Matt. 3:4; Mark 1:6; Acts 21:11; Rev. 1:13; 15:6; it was often hollow, and hence served as a purse, Matt. 10:9; Mark 6:8.

## GIVE

1. ***didomi*** (*1325*), "to give," is used with various meanings according to the context; it is said, e.g., of seed "yielding fruit," Mark 4:7, 8; of "giving" (i.e., exercising) diligence, Luke 12:58; of giving lots, Acts 1:26, RV (KJV, "gave forth"); of "rendering" vengeance, 2 Thess. 1:8; of "striking or smiting" Christ, John 18:22 (lit., "gave a blow") and 19:3 (lit., "they gave Him blows"); of "putting" a ring on the hand, Luke 15:22; of Paul's "adventuring" himself into a place, Acts 19:31. (In Rev. 17:13 some mss. have ***diadidomi***, "to divide").

2. ***apodidomi*** (*591*) signifies "to give up or back, to restore, return, render what is due, to pay, give an account" (***apo***, "back," and No. 1), e.g., of an account. Matt. 5:26; 12:36; Luke 16:2; Acts. 19:40; Heb. 13:17; 1 Pet. 4:5; of wages, etc., e.g., Matt. 18:25–34; 20:8; of conjugal duty, 1 Cor. 7:3; of a witness, Acts 4:33; frequently of recompensing or rewarding, 1 Tim. 5:4; 2 Tim. 4:8, 14; 1 Pet. 3:9; Rev. 18:6; 22:12. In the middle voice it is used of "giving" up what is one's own; hence, "to sell," Acts 5:8; 7:9; Heb. 12:16.

3. ***epididomi*** (*1929*) signifies (a) "to give by handing, to hand" (***epi***, "over"), e.g., Matt. 7:9,

10; Luke 4:17; 24:30, here of the Lord's act in "handing" the broken loaf to the two at Emmaus, an act which was the means of the revelation of Himself as the crucified and risen Lord; the simple verb, No. 1, is used of His "handing" the bread at the institution of the Lord's Supper, Matt. 26:26; Mark 14:22; Luke 22:19; this meaning of the verb ***epididomi*** is found also in Acts 15:30, "they delivered"; (b) "to give in, give way," Acts 27:15, RV, "we gave way to it."

4. ***metadidomi*** (*3330*), "to give a share of, impart" (***meta***, "with"), as distinct from "giving." The apostle Paul speaks of "sharing" some spiritual gift with Christians at Rome, Rom. 1:11, "that I may impart," and exhorts those who minister in things temporal, to do so as "sharing," and that generously, 12:8, "he that giveth"; so in Eph. 4:28; Luke 3:11; in 1 Thess. 2:8 he speaks of himself and his fellow missionaries as having been well pleased to impart to the converts both God's gospel and their own souls (i.e., so "sharing" those with them as to spend themselves and spend out their lives for them).

5. ***paradidomi*** (*3860*), "to give or hand over," is said of "giving" up the ghost, John 19:30; of "giving" persons up to evil, Acts 7:42; Rom. 1:24, 26; of "giving" one's body to be burned, 1 Cor. 13:3; of Christ's "giving" Himself up to death, Gal. 2:20; Eph. 5:2, 25.

6. ***prodidomi*** (*4272*), "to give before, or first" (***pro***, "before"), is found in Rom. 11:35.

7. ***charizomai*** (*5483*) primarily denotes "to show favor or kindness," as in Gal. 3:18, RV, "hath granted" (KJV, "gave"); then, to "give" freely, bestow graciously; in this sense it is used almost entirely of that which is "given" by God, Acts 27:24, "God hath granted thee all them that sail with thee" (RV); in Rom. 8:32, "shall . . . freely give"; 1 Cor. 2:12, "are freely given"; Phil. 1:29, "it hath been granted" (said of believing on Christ and suffering for Him); 2:9, "hath given" (said of the name of Jesus as "given" by God); Philem. 22, "I shall be granted unto you" (RV). In Luke 7:21, it is said in regard to the blind, upon whom Christ "bestowed" sight (RV). The only exceptions, in this sense of the word, as to divinely imparted "gifts," are Acts 3:14, of the "granting" of Barabbas by Pilate to the Jews, and Acts 25:11, 16, of the "giving" up of a prisoner to his accusers or to execution.

8. ***parecho*** (*3930*), in the active voice, signifies "to afford, furnish, provide, supply" (lit., "to hold out or towards"; ***para***, "near," ***echo***, "to hold"); it is translated "hath given" in Acts 17:31; "giveth" in 1 Tim. 6:17 (in the sense of affording); in Col. 4:1, RV, "render" (KJV, "give").

9. ***doreo*** (*143*), akin to No. 1, and used in the middle voice, "to bestow, make a gift of," is translated in the RV by the verb "to grant," instead of the KJV, "to give," Mark 15:45; 2 Pet. 1:3, 4.

## GLAD (be, make), GLADLY

### A. Verbs.

1. ***chairo*** (*5463*) is the usual word for "rejoicing, being glad"; it is rendered by the verb "to be glad" in Mark 14:11; Luke 15:32; 22:5; 23:8; John 8:56; 11:15; 20:20; Acts 11:23; 13:48; in the following the RV has "to rejoice" for KJV, "to be glad," Rom. 16:19; 1 Cor. 16:17; 2 Cor. 13:9; 1 Pet. 4:13; Rev. 19:7.

2. ***agalliao*** (*21*), "to exult, rejoice greatly," is chiefly used in the middle voice (active in Luke 1:47; some mss. have the passive in John 5:35, "to be made glad"). It conveys the idea of jubilant exultation, spiritual "gladness," Matt. 5:12, "be exceeding glad," the Lord's command to His disciples; Luke 1:47, in Mary's song; 10:21, of Christ's exultation ("rejoiced"); cf. Acts 2:26, "(My tongue) was glad," KJV (RV, "rejoiced"); John 8:56, of Abraham; Acts 16:34, RV, "rejoiced greatly" (of the Philippian jailor); 1 Pet. 1:6, 8; 4:13 ("with exceeding joy"), of believers in general; in Rev. 19:7, RV, "be exceeding glad" (KJV, "rejoice").

3. ***euphraino*** (*2165*), "to cheer, gladden," is rendered "maketh . . . glad" in 2 Cor. 2:2.

### B. Adverbs.

1. ***hedeos*** (*2234*), "gladly" (from ***hedus***, "sweet"), is used in Mark 6:20; 12:37; 2 Cor. 11:19.

2. ***hedista*** (*2236*), the superlative degree of No. 1, "most gladly, most delightedly, with great relish," is rendered "most gladly" in 2 Cor. 12:9, and in v. 15 (RV; KJV, "very gladly").

3. ***asmenos*** (*780*), "with delight, delightedly, gladly," is found in Acts 21:17.

## GLADNESS

1. ***chara*** (*5479*), "joy, delight" (akin to A, No. 1 above), is rendered "gladness" in the KJV of Mark 4:16; Acts 12:14 and Phil. 2:29 (RV "joy," as elsewhere in both versions).

2. ***agalliasis*** (*20*), "exultation, exuberant joy" (akin to A, No. 2), is translated "gladness" in Luke 1:14; Acts 2:6; Heb. 1:9; "joy" in Luke 1:44; "exceeding joy" in Jude 24. It indicates a more exultant "joy" than No. 1.

3. ***euphrosune*** (*2167*), "good cheer, joy, mirth, gladness of heart" (akin to A, No. 3), from ***eu***, "well," and ***phren***, "the mind," is ren-

dered "gladness" in Acts 2:28, RV (KJV, "joy") and 14:17.

## GLORIFY

1. ***doxazo*** (*1392*) primarily denotes "to suppose" (from ***doxa***, "an opinion"); in the NT (a) "to magnify, extol, praise," especially of "glorifying"; God, i.e., ascribing honor to Him, acknowledging Him as to His being, attributes and acts, i.e., His glory, e.g., Matt. 5:16; 9:8; 15:31; Rom. 15:6, 9; Gal. 1:24; 1 Pet. 4:16; the Word of the Lord, Acts 13:48; the Name of the Lord, Rev. 15:4; also of "glorifying" oneself, John 8:54; Rev. 18:7; (b) "to do honor to, to make glorious," e.g., Rom. 8:30; 2 Cor. 3:10; 1 Pet. 1:8, "full of glory," passive voice (lit., "glorified"); said of Christ, e.g., John 7:39; 8:54, RV, "glorifieth," for KJV, "honor" and "honoreth" (which would translate ***timao***, "to honor"); of the Father, e.g., John 13:31, 32; 21:19; 1 Pet. 4:11; of "glorifying" one's ministry, Rom. 11:13, RV, "glorify" (KJV, "magnify"); of a member of the body, 1 Cor. 12:26, "be honored" (RV marg., "be glorified").

God manifests all His goodness in the Son by glorifying Him, John 12:28, Christ so glorifies the Father, John 17:1, 4; or the Father is glorified in Him, 13:31; 14:13; 15:8. When ***doxazo*** is predicated of Christ, it means simply that His innate glory is brought to light, cf. John 11:4; so 7:39; 12:16, 23; 13:31; 17:1, 5.

2. ***endoxazo*** (*1740*), No. 1 prefixed by ***en***, "in," signifies, in the passive voice, "to be glorified," i.e., to exhibit one's glory; it is said of God, regarding His saints in the future, 2 Thess. 1:10, and of the name of the Lord Jesus as "glorified" in them in the present, v. 12.

3. ***sundoxazo*** (*4888*), "to glorify together" (***sun***, "with"), is used in Rom. 8:17.

## GLORY, GLORIOUS

### *Old Testament*

***tip'eret*** (8597), "glory; beauty; ornament; distinction; pride." The word represents "beauty," Exod. 28:2; or "adornment," Isa. 4:2. ***tip'eret*** (or ***tip'arah***) means "glory" in several instances. The word is used of one's rank. A crown of "glory" is a crown which, by its richness, indicates high rank, Prov. 4:9; 16:31; Isa. 62:3. In another related nuance, the noun is used of God, to emphasize His rank, renown, and inherent "beauty," 1 Chron. 29:11; used of a nation, Lam. 2:1. In Isa. 10:12, the word represents a raising of oneself to a high rank in one's own eyes, and so be improper pride.

***kabod*** is another common word for "glory." which often means to be in a state of high status, Josh. 7:19; or speaking honor toward another of high status, whether God or mankind, Prov. 11:16. ***kabod*** also can mean, "great wealth," or related "reward," Gen. 31:1; Num. 24:11. It can also mean a "ruler," with a special focus on a person of high regard and possibly wealth, Esth. 1:4, or a display of power as in a miracle, with a special focus that this act of power produces awe in those who see it, Exod. 16:7. ***kabod*** is a title of God, as one who is "totally awesome," and so glorious, filling a space with divine light whenever he is present, Ps 106:20; cf. Exod. 29:43.

G

### *New Testament*

**A. Nouns.**

1. ***doxa*** (*1391*), "glory" (from ***dokeo***, "to seem"), primarily signifies an opinion, estimate, and hence, the honor resulting from a good opinion. It is used (I) (a) of the nature and acts of God in self-manifestation, i.e., what He essentially is and does, as exhibited in whatever way He reveals Himself in these respects, and particularly in the person of Christ, in whom essentially His "glory" has ever shone forth and ever will do, John 17:5, 24; Heb. 1:3; it was exhibited in the character and acts of Christ in the days of His flesh, John 1:14; John 2:11; at Cana both His grace and His power were manifested, and these constituted His "glory," so also in the resurrection of Lazarus 11:4, 40; the "glory" of God was exhibited in the resurrection of Christ, Rom. 6:4, and in His ascension and exaltation, 1 Pet. 1:21, likewise on the Mount of Transfiguration, 2 Pet. 1:17. In Rom. 1:23 His "everlasting power and Divinity" are spoken of as His "glory," i.e., His attributes and power as revealed through creation; in Rom. 3:23 the word denotes the manifested perfection of His character, especially His righteousness, of which all men fall short; in Col. 1:11 "the might of His glory" signifies the might which is characteristic of His "glory"; in Eph. 1:6, 12, 14, "the praise of the glory of His grace" and "the praise of His glory" signify the due acknowledgement of the exhibition of His attributes and ways; in Eph. 1:17, "the Father of glory" describes Him as the source from whom all divine splendor and perfection proceed in their manifestation, and to whom they belong; (b) of the character and ways of God as exhibited through Christ to and through believers, 2 Cor. 3:18 and 4:6; (c) of the state of blessedness into which believers are to enter hereafter through being brought into the likeness of Christ, e.g., Rom. 8:18, 21;

Phil. 3:21 (RV, "the body of His glory"); 1 Pet. 5:1, 10; Rev. 21:11; (d) brightness or splendor, (1) supernatural, emanating from God (as in the *shekinah* "glory," in the pillar of cloud and in the Holy of Holies, e.g., Exod. 16:10; 25:22), Luke 2:9; Acts 22:11; Rom. 9:4; 2 Cor. 3:7; Jas. 2:1; in Titus 2:13 it is used of Christ's return, "the appearing of the glory of our great God and Savior Jesus Christ" (RV); cf. Phil. 3:21, above; (2) natural, as of the heavenly bodies, 1 Cor. 15:40, 41; (II) of good reputation, praise, honor, Luke 14:10 (RV, "glory," for KJV, "worship"); John 5:41 (RV, "glory," for KJV, "honor"); 7:18; 8:50; 12:43 (RV, "glory," for KJV, "praise"); 2 Cor. 6:8 (RV, "glory," for KJV "honor"); Phil. 3:19; Heb. 3:3; in 1 Cor. 11:7, of man as representing the authority of God, and of woman as rendering conspicuous the authority of man; in 1 Thess. 2:6, "glory" probably stands, by metonymy, for material gifts, an honorarium, since in human estimation "glory" is usually expressed in things material.

2. ***kleos*** (*2811*), "good report, fame, renown," is used in 1 Pet. 2:20. The word is derived from a root signifying "hearing"; hence, the meaning "reputation."

**B. Adjective.**

***endoxos*** (*1741*) signifies (a) "held in honor," "of high repute," 1 Cor. 4:10, RV "have glory" (KJV, "are honorable"); (b) "splendid, glorious," said of apparel, Luke 7:25, "gorgeously"; of the works of Christ, 13:17; of the church, Eph. 5:27.

## GLORY (to boast), GLORYING

**A. Verbs.**

1. ***kauchaomai*** (*2744*), "to boast or glory," is always translated in the RV by the verb "to glory," where the KJV uses the verb "to boast" (see, e.g., Rom. 2:17, 23; 2 Cor. 7:14; 9:2; 10:8, 13, 15, 16); it is used (a) of "vainglorying," e.g., 1 Cor. 1:29; 3:21; 4:7; 2 Cor. 5:12; 11:12, 18; Eph. 2:9; (b) of "valid glorying," e.g., Rom. 5:2, "rejoice"; 5:3, 11 (RV, "rejoice"); 1 Cor. 1:31; 2 Cor. 9:2; 10:8, 12:9; Gal. 6:14; Phil. 3:3 and Jas. 1:9, RV, "glory" (KJV, "rejoice").

2. ***katakauchaomai*** (*2620*), a strengthened form of No. 1 (***kata***, intensive), signifies "to boast against, exult over," Rom. 11:18, RV, "glory" (KJV, "boast"); Jas. 2:13, RV, "glorieth" (KJV, "rejoiceth"); 3:14, "glory (not).

3. ***enkauchaomai***, ***en***, "in," and No. 1, "to glory in," is found, in the most authentic mss., in 2 Thess. 1:4.

**B. Nouns.**

1. ***kauchema*** (*2745*), akin to A, No. 1, denotes "that in which one glories, a matter or ground of glorying," Rom. 4:2 and Phil. 2:16, RV, "whereof to glory" (for Rom. 3:27, see No. 2); in the following the meaning is likewise "a ground of glorying": 1 Cor. 5:6; 9:15, "glorying," 16, "to glory of"; 2 Cor. 1:14 RV; 9:3, RV; Gal. 6:4, RV (KJV, "rejoicing"); Phil. 1:26 (ditto); Heb. 3:6 (ditto). In 2 Cor. 5:12 and 9:3 the word denotes the boast itself, yet as distinct from the act (see No. 2).

2. ***kauchesis*** (*2746*) denotes "the act of boasting," Rom. 3:27; 15:17, RV, "(my) glorying" (KJV, "whereof I may glory"); 1 Cor. 15:31, RV, "glorying"; 2 Cor. 1:12 (ditto); 7:4, 14 (KJV, "boasting"); 8:24; 11:10, and 17 (ditto); 1 Thess. 2:19 (KJV, "rejoicing"); Jas. 4:16 (ditto). The distinction between this and No. 1 is to be observed in 2 Cor. 8:24, speaking of the apostle's act of "glorying" in the liberality of the Corinthians, while in 9:3 he exhorts them not to rob him of the ground of his "glorying" (No. 1). Some take the word in 2 Cor. 1:12 (see above) as identical with No. 1, a boast, but there seems to be no reason for regarding it as different from its usual sense, No. 2.

## GOAL

***skopos*** (*4649*), primarily, "a watcher" (from ***skopeo***, "to look at"; Eng., "scope"), denotes "a mark on which to fix the eye," and is used metaphorically of an aim or object in Phil. 3:14, RV, "goal" (KJV, "mark").

## GOAT

1. ***eriphos*** (*2056*) denotes "a kid or goat," Matt. 25:32 (RV, marg., "kids"); Luke 15:29, "a kid"; some mss. have No. 2 here, indicating a sneer on the part of the elder son, that his father had never given him even a tiny kid.

2. ***eriphion*** (*2055*), a diminutive of No. 1, is used in Matt. 25:33. In v. 32 ***eriphos*** is purely figurative; in v. 33, where the application is made, though metaphorically, the change to the diminutive is suggestive of the contempt which those so described bring upon themselves by their refusal to assist the needy.

3. ***tragos*** (*5131*) denotes "a he-goat," Heb. 9:12, 13, 19; 10:4, the male prefiguring the strength by which Christ laid down His own life in expiatory sacrifice.

## GOAT-DEMONS

***sa'ir*** (8163), "goat-demons; goat-idols." This word occurs 4 times in biblical Hebrew. In its first biblical appearance, the word represents "goat-demons" (some scholars translate it "goat-idols"): "And they shall no more offer their sacrifices unto devils [NASB, "goat demons"], after whom they have gone a whoring,"

Lev. 17:7. This passage demonstrates that the word represents beings that were objects of pagan worship.

## GOD

### *Old Testament*

***'el*** (410), "God, god," A term of supreme power and divinity, which can refer to the true God, Gen. 33:20; or to false gods, such as "*El*," the chief Canaanite god. Names with ***'el*** as one of their components were common in the Near East in the second millennium B.C. The names Methusael, Gen. 4:18, and Ishmael, Gen. 16:11, come from a very early period. When the true God is called "El," he reveals himself in power and enters into a covenant relationship with His people, Ps. 7:11; 85:8; Isa. 43:12; 46:9. The name of ***'el*** was commonly used by the Israelites to denote supernatural provision or power; or negatively, punishment.

***'elah*** (426), "god." This Aramaic word is the equivalent of the Hebrew ***'eloah.*** It is a general term for "God" in the Aramaic passages of the Old Testament, and it is a cognate form of the word ***'allah,*** the designation of deity used by the Arabs, Ezra 4:24—7:26; Jer. 10:11; Dan. 2:11.

***'eloah*** (433), "god," (singular version of the common plural form ***'elohim***), The word ***'eloah*** is predominant in poetry rather than prose literature, and this is especially true of the Book of Job. Some scholars have suggested that the author of Job deliberately chose a description for godhead that avoided the historical associations found in a phrase such as "the God of Bethel," Gen. 31:13, or "God of Israel," Exod. 24:10. But even the Book of Job is by no means historically neutral, since places and peoples are mentioned in introducing the narrative, cf. Job 1:1, 15, 17. Perhaps the author considered ***'eloah*** a suitable term for poetry and used it accordingly with consistency. This is also apparently the case in Ps. 18:31, where ***'eloah*** is found instead of ***'el***, as in the parallel passage of 2 Sam. 22:32. ***'eloah*** also appears as a term for God in Ps. 50:22; 139:19; and Prov. 30:5. Although ***'eloah*** as a divine name is rarely used outside Job, its literary history extends from at least the second millennium B.C., as in Deut. 32:15, to the fifth century B.C., as in Neh. 9:17.

***'el shadday*** (410, 7706), "God Almighty," A title of the true God, which has a focus on the power, and all-surpassing provision of God, Gen. 17:1; ***'el shadday,*** is the God who will keep His promises, and the power to see His will is done, Gen. 49:26; see also Exod. 3:15, 6:3. In the early Mosaic era, the new redemptive name of "God" and the formulation of the Sinai covenant made ***'el shadday*** largely obsolete as a designation of deity. Subsequently, the name occurs about 35 times in the Old Testament, most of which are in the Book of Job. Occasionally, the name is used synonymously with the name of God, Yahweh, Ruth 1:21; Ps. 91:1–2, to emphasize the power and might of "God."

***'el 'olam*** (410, 5769), "God of eternity; God the everlasting; God for ever," Ps. 90:2. The name ***'el 'olam*** was associated predominantly with Beer-sheba, Gen. 21:25–34. Abraham planted a commemorative tree in Beer-sheba and invoked the name of the Lord as ***'el 'olam***.

### *New Testament*

***theos*** (*2316*), (I) in the polytheism of the Greeks, denoted "a god or deity," e.g., Acts 14:11; 19:26; 28:6; 1 Cor. 8:5; Gal. 4:8.

(II) (a) Hence the word was appropriated by Jews and retained by Christians to denote "the one true God."

In the NT, these and all the other divine attributes are predicated of Him. To Him are ascribed, e.g., His unity, or monism, e.g., Mark 12:29; 1 Tim. 2:5; self-existence, John 5:26; immutability, Jas. 1:17; eternity, Rom. 1:20; universality, Matt. 10:29; Acts 17:26–28; almighty power Matt. 19:26; infinite knowledge, Acts 2:23; 15:18; Rom. 11:33, creative power, Rom. 11:36; 1 Cor. 8:6; Eph. 3:9; Rev. 4:11; 10:6; absolute holiness, 1 Pet. 1:15; 1 John 1:5; righteousness, John 17:25; faithfulness, 1 Cor. 1:9; 10:13; 1 Thess. 5:24; 2 Thess. 3:3; 1 John 1:9; love, 1 John 4:8, 16; mercy, Rom. 9:15, 18; truthfulness, Titus 1:2; Heb. 6:18.

(b) The divine attributes are likewise indicated or definitely predicated of Christ, e.g., Matt. 20:18–19; John 1:1–3; 1:18, RV, marg.; 5:22–29; 8:58; 14:6; 17:22–24; 20:28; Rom. 1:4; 9:5; Phil. 3:21; Col. 1:15; 2:3; Titus 2:13, RV; Heb. 1:3; 13:8; 1 John 5:20; Rev. 22:12, 13.

(c) Also of the Holy Spirit, e.g., Matt. 28:19; Luke 1:35; John 14:16; 15:26; 16:7–14; Rom. 8:9, 26; 1 Cor. 12:11; 2 Cor. 13:14.

(d) ***theos*** is used with and without the definite article, but that point cuts no figure in the Greek idiom. As to this latter it is usual to employ the article with a proper name, when mentioned a second time. There are, of course, exceptions to this, as when the absence of the article serves to lay stress upon, or give precision to, the character or nature of what is expressed in the noun. A notable instance of this is in John 1:1, "and the Word was God"; here a double stress is on ***theos***, by the absence of

G

the article and by the emphatic position. To translate it literally, "a god was the Word," is entirely misleading. Where two or more epithets are applied to the same person or thing, one article usually serves for both (the exceptions being when a second article lays stress upon different aspects of the same person or subject, e.g., Rev. 1:17). In Titus 2:13 the RV correctly has "our great God and Savior Jesus Christ"; so in 2 Pet. 1:1 (cf. 1:11; 3:18).

In the following titles God is described by certain of His attributes; the God of glory, Acts 7:2; of peace, Rom. 15:33; 16:20; Phil. 4:9; 1 Thess. 5:23; Heb. 13:20; of love and peace, 2 Cor. 13:11; of patience and comfort, Rom. 15:5; of all comfort, 2 Cor. 1:3; of hope, Rom. 15:13; of all grace, 1 Pet. 5:10. These describe Him, not as in distinction from other persons, but as the source of all these blessings; hence the employment of the definite article. In such phrases as "the God of a person," e.g., Matt. 22:32, the expression marks the relationship in which the person stands to God and God to him.

(e) The phrase "the things of God" (translated literally or otherwise) stands for (1) His interests, Matt. 16:23; Mark 8:33; (2) His counsels, 1 Cor. 2:11; (3) things which are due to Him, Matt. 22:21; Mark 12:17; Luke 20:25. The phrase "things pertaining to God," Rom. 15:17; Heb. 2:17; 5:1, describes, in the Heb. passages, the sacrificial service of the priest; in the Rom. passage the gospel ministry as an offering to God.

(III) The word is used of divinely appointed judges in Israel, as representing God in His authority, John 10:34, quoted from Ps. 82:6, which indicates that God Himself sits in judgment on those whom He has appointed. The application of the term to the Devil, 2 Cor. 4:4, and the belly, Phil. 3:19, virtually places these instances under (I).

## GOD (without)

***atheos*** (*112*), cf. Eng., "atheist," primarily signifies "godless" (***a***, negative), i.e., destitute of God; in Eph. 2:12 the phrase indicates, not only that the Gentiles were void of any true recognition of God, and hence became morally "godless," Rom. 1:19–32, but that being given up by God, they were excluded from communion with God and from the privileges granted to Israel (see the context and cf. Gal. 4:8).

## GODDESS

***thea*** (*2299*) is found in Acts 19:27 (in some mss. in vv. 35, 37).

## GODLINESS, GODLY

### A. Nouns.

1. ***eusebeia*** (*2150*), from ***eu***, "well," and ***sebomai***, "to be devout," denotes that piety which, characterized by a Godward attitude, does that which is well-pleasing to Him. This and the corresponding adjective and adverb (see below) are frequent in the Pastoral Epistles, but do not occur in previous epistles of Paul. The apostle Peter has the noun four times in his 2nd Epistle, 1:3, 6, 7; 3:11. Elsewhere it occurs in Acts 3:12; 1 Tim. 2:2; 3:16; 4:7, 8; 6:3, 5, 6, 11; 2 Tim. 3:5; Titus 1:1. In 1 Tim. 6:3 "the doctrine which is according to godliness" signifies that which is consistent with "godliness," in contrast to false teachings; in Titus 1:1, "the truth which is according to godliness" is that which is productive of "godliness"; in 1 Tim. 3:16, "the mystery of godliness" is "godliness" as embodied in, and communicated through, the truths of the faith concerning Christ; in 2 Pet. 3:11, the word is in the plural, signifying acts of "godliness."

2. ***theosebeia*** (*2317*) denotes "the fear or reverence of God," from ***theos***, "god," and ***sebomai*** (see No. 1), 1 Tim. 2:10.

### B. Adjective.

***eusebes*** (*2152*), akin to A, No. 1, denotes "pious, devout, godly," indicating reverence manifested in actions; it is rendered "godly" in 2 Pet. 2:9.

### C. Adverb.

***eusebos*** (*2153*) denotes "piously, godly"; it is used with the verb "to live" (of manner of life) in 2 Tim. 3:12; Titus 2:12.

## GOLD, GOLDEN

*Old Testament*

***zahab*** (2091), "gold," a precious metal, often used to make ornaments, or as units of money. ***zahab*** can refer to "gold ore," or "gold in its raw state," Gen. 2:11; Exod. 25:11; Job 23:10; or in bars, pieces, or lumps, Gen. 13:2; Job 28:17; Ezek. 27:22. ***zahab*** is also used for the color "gold," Zech. 4:12.

*New Testament*

### A. Nouns.

1. ***chrusos*** (*5557*) is used (a) of "coin," Matt. 10:9; Jas. 5:3; (b) of "ornaments," Matt. 23:16, 17; Jas. 5:3 (perhaps both coin and ornaments); Rev. 18:12; some mss. have it instead of No. 2 in 1 Cor. 3:12; (c) of "images," Acts 17:29; (d) of "the metal in general," Matt. 2:11; Rev. 9:7 (some mss. have it in Rev. 18:16).

2. ***chrusion*** (5553), a diminutive of No. 1, is used (a) of "coin," primarily smaller than those in No. 1 (a), Acts 3:6; 20:33; 1 Pet. 1:18; (b) of "ornaments," 1 Pet. 3:3, and the following (in which some mss. have No. 1), 1 Tim. 2:9; Rev. 17:4; 18:16; (c) of "the metal in general," Heb. 9:4; 1 Pet. 1:7; Rev. 21:18, 21; metaphorically, (d) of "sound doctrine and its effects," 1 Cor. 3:12; (e) of "righteousness of life and conduct," Rev. 3:18.

**B. Adjective.**

***chruseos*** (*5552*) denotes "golden," i.e., made of, or overlaid with, gold, 2 Tim. 2:20; Heb. 9:4, and fifteen times in the Apocalypse.

## GOOD, GOODLY, GOODNESS

### *Old Testament*

**A. Adjective.**

***tob*** (2896), "good; favorable; festive; pleasing; pleasant; well; better; right; best." This adjective denotes "good" in every sense of that word. For example, ***tob*** is used in the sense "pleasant" or "delightful," Gen. 49:15; or as in Gen. 40:16, "favorable" or "in one's favor." God is described as One who is "good," or One who gives "delight" and "pleasure," Ps. 73:28. ***tob*** often qualifies a common object or activity. When the word is used in this sense, no ethical overtones are intended, 1 Sam. 19:4; 25:15; 1 Kings 12:7; Gen. 2:18. Elsewhere ***tob*** is applied to an evaluation of one's well-being or of the well-being of a situation or thing, Gen. 1:4.

***tob*** is used to describe land and agriculture, Exod. 3:8; 1 Sam. 8:14. ***tob*** is used to describe men or women. Sometimes it is used of an "elite corps" of people, 1 Sam. 8:16, 27. In other passages, ***tob*** describes physical appearance, Gen. 24:16. Dying "at a good old age" describes "advanced age," rather than moral accomplishment, but a time when due to divine blessings one is fulfilled and satisfied, Gen. 15:15. ***tob*** indicates that a given word, act, or circumstance contributes positively to the condition of a situation, Gen. 40:16; The judgment may be ethical, Neh. 5:9. The word may also represent "agreement" or "concurrence," Gen. 24:50.

**B. Verbs.**

***yatab*** (3190), "to be good, do well, be glad, please, do good," This word means to do an activity which is favorable to a circumstance, of quality deemed of value, or of what is right according to a standard: Gen. 4:7; "to deal well," Exod. 1:20; "to play [a musical instrument] well," 1 Sam. 16:17; "to adorn, make beautiful," 2 Kings 9:30; and "to inquire diligently," Deut. 17:4.

***tob*** (2896), "good." This word in Hebrew has about the same very broad range of meanings as it does in English. It means generally, "that which is valuable according to a standard, be it things, or events, Gen. 1:4,31. As a positive term, with a basic meaning of "good," with a focus on the emotional attitude which one responds to a favorable circumstance; the word is used to express many nuances of that which is "good," such as a "glad" heart, Judg. 18:20, "pleasing," words Gen. 34:18, and a "cheerful" face, Prov. 15:13.

### *New Testament*

**A. Adjectives.**

1. ***agathos*** (*18*) describes that which, being "good" in its character or constitution, is beneficial in its effect; it is used (a) of things physical, e.g., a tree, Matt. 7:17; ground, Luke 8:8; (b) in a moral sense, frequently of persons and things. God is essentially, absolutely and consummately "good," Matt. 19:17; Mark 10:18; Luke 18:19. To certain persons the word is applied in Matt. 20:15; 25:21, 23; Luke 19:17; 23:50; John 7:12; Acts 11:24; Titus 2:5; in a general application, Matt. 5:45; 12:35; Luke 6:45; Rom. 5:7; 1 Pet. 2:18.

The neuter of the adjective with the definite article signifies that which is "good," lit., "the good," as being morally honorable, pleasing to God, and therefore beneficial. Christians are to prove it, Rom. 12:2; to cleave to it, 12:9; to do it, 13:3; Gal. 6:10; 1 Pet. 3:11 (here, and here only, the article is absent); John 5:29 (here, the neuter plural is used, "the good things"); to work it, Rom. 2:10; Eph. 4:28; 6:8; to follow after it, 1 Thess. 5:15; to be zealous of it, 1 Pet. 3:13; to imitate it, 3 John 11; to overcome evil with it, Rom. 12:21. Governmental authorities are ministers of "good," i.e., that which is salutary, suited to the course of human affairs, Rom. 13:4. In Philem. 14, "thy goodness," RV (lit., "thy good"), means "thy benefit." As to Matt. 19:17, "why askest thou Me concerning that which is good?" the RV follows the most ancient mss.

The neuter plural is also used of material "goods," riches, etc., Luke 1:53; 12:18, 19; 16:25; Gal. 6:6 (of temporal supplies); in Rom. 10:15; Heb. 9:11; 10:1, the "good" things are the benefits provided through the sacrifice of Christ, in regard both to those conferred through the gospel and to those of the coming messianic kingdom.

2. ***kalos*** (*2570*) denotes that which is intrinsically "good," and so, "goodly, fair, beautiful," as (a) of that which is well adapted to its circumstances or ends, e.g., fruit, Matt. 3:10; a tree, 12:33; ground, 13:8, 23; fish, 13:48; the Law,

Rom. 7:16; 1 Tim. 1:8; every creature of God, 1 Tim. 4:4; a faithful minister of Christ and the doctrine he teaches, 4:6; (b) of that which is ethically good, right, noble, honorable e.g., Gal. 4:18; 1 Tim. 5:10, 25; 6:18; Titus 2:7, 14; 3:8, 14. The word does not occur in the Apocalypse, nor indeed after 1 Peter.

Christians are to "take thought for things honorable" (***kalos***), 2 Cor. 8:21, RV; to do that which is honorable, 13:7; not to be weary in well doing, Gal. 6:9; to hold fast "that which is good," 1 Thess. 5:21; to be zealous of good works, Titus 2:14; to maintain them, 3:8; to provoke to them, Heb. 10:24; to bear testimony by them, 1 Pet. 2:12. ***kalos*** and ***agathos*** occur together in Luke 8:15; Rom. 7:18; 1 Thess. 5:15.

3. ***chrestos*** (*5543*), said of things, "that which is pleasant," said of persons, "kindly, gracious," is rendered "good" in 1 Cor. 15:33, "goodness" in Rom. 2:4.

**B. Nouns.**

1. ***chrestotes*** (*5544*), akin to A, No. 3, denotes "goodness" (a) in the sense of what is upright, righteous, Rom. 3:12 (translated "good"); (b) in the sense of kindness of heart or act, said of God, Rom. 2:4; 11:22 (thrice); Eph. 2:7 ("kindness"); Titus 3:4 ("kindness"); said of believers and rendered "kindness," 2 Cor. 6:6; Col. 3:12; Gal. 5:22 (RV; KJV, "gentleness"). It signifies "not merely goodness as a quality, rather it is goodness in action, goodness expressing itself in deeds; yet not goodness expressing itself in indignation against sin, for it is contrasted with severity in Rom. 11:22, but in grace and tenderness and compassion."

2. ***agathosune*** (*19*), "goodness," signifies that moral quality which is described by the adjective ***agathos*** (see A, No. 1). It is used, in the NT, of regenerate persons, Rom. 15:14; Gal. 5:22; Eph. 5:9; 2 Thess. 1:11; in the last, the phrase "every desire of goodness" (RV; the addition of "His" in the KJV is an interpolation; there is no pronoun in the original) may be either subjective, i.e., desire characterized by "goodness," "good" desire, or objective, i.e., desire after "goodness," to be and do good.

Trench, following Jerome, distinguishes between ***chrestotes*** and ***agathosune*** in that the former describes the kindlier aspects of "goodness," Luke 7:37–50, the latter includes also the sterner qualities by which doing "good" to others is not necessarily by gentle means, Matt. 21:12, 13; 23:13–29.

3. ***eupoiia*** (*2140*), "beneficence, doing good," is translated as a verb in Heb. 13:16, "to do good."

**C. Adverbs.**

1. ***kalos*** (*2573*), "well, finely," is used in some mss. in Matt. 5:44, with ***poieo***, "to do," and translated "do good." In Jas. 2:3 it is rendered "in a good place" (KJV marg., "well" or "seemly").

2. ***eu*** (*2095*), "well," used with ***poieo***, is translated "do . . . good" in Mark 14:7.

**D. Verbs (to do, or be, good).**

1. ***agathopoieo*** (*15*), from A, No. 1, and ***poieo***, "to do," is used (a) in a general way, "to do well," 1 Pet. 2:15, 20; 3:6, 17; 3 John 11; (b) with pointed reference "to the benefit of another," Luke 6:9, 33, 35; in Mark 3:4 the parts of the word are separated in some mss. Some mss. have it in Acts 14:17, for No. 2.

2. ***agathourgeo*** (*14*), for ***agathoergeo***, "to do good" (from A, No. 1, and ***ergon***, "a work"), is used in Acts 14:17 (in the best mss.; see No. 1), where it is said of God's beneficence towards man, and 1 Tim. 6:18, where it is enjoined upon the rich.

3. ***euergeteo*** (*2109*), "to bestow a benefit, to do good" (***eu***, "well," and a verbal form akin to ***ergon***), is used in Acts 10:38.

## GOODMAN

***oikodespotes*** (*3617*) denotes "the master of a house," "a householder." It occurs only in the Synoptics, and there 12 times. It is rendered "goodman" in Luke 22:11, where "of the house" is put separately; in Matt. 20:11, where the KJV has "the goodman of the house" for the one word; in 24:43; Mark 14:14; Luke 12:39.

## GOODS

1. For the neuter plural of ***agathos***, used as a noun, "goods," see Luke 12:18, 19, where alone this word is so rendered.

2. ***huparxis*** (*5223*), primarily, "subsistence," then, "substance, property, goods" (akin to ***huparcho***, "to exist, be, belong to"), is translated "goods" in Acts 2:45; "possession." RV (KJV, "substance") in Heb. 10:34.

3. ***bios*** (*979*), which denotes (a) "life, lifetime," (b) "livelihood, living, means of living," is translated "goods" in 1 John 3:17, RV (KJV, "good).

4. ***skeuos*** (*4632*), "a vessel," denotes "goods" in Matt. 12:29; Mark 3:27; Luke 17:31, RV (KJV, stuff).

## GORGEOUS, GORGEOUSLY

***lampros*** (*2986*), "bright, splendid," is rendered "gorgeous" in Luke 23:11 of the apparel in which Herod and his soldiers arrayed Christ.

## GOSPEL (Noun and Verb: to preach)

### A. Noun.

***euangelion*** (*2098*) originally denoted a reward for good tidings; later, the idea of reward dropped, and the word stood for "the good news" itself. The Eng. word "gospel," i.e. "good message," is the equivalent of ***euangelion*** (Eng., "evangel"). In the NT it denotes the "good tidings" of the kingdom of God and of salvation through Christ, to be received by faith, on the basis of His expiatory death, His burial, resurrection, and ascension, e.g., Acts 15:7; 20:24; 1 Pet. 4:17. Apart from those references and those in the gospels of Matthew and Mark, and Rev. 14:6, the noun is confined to Paul's epistles. The apostle uses it of two associated yet distinct things, (a) of the basic facts of the death, burial and resurrection of Christ, e.g., 1 Cor. 15:1–3; (b) of the interpretation of these facts, e.g., Rom. 2:16; Gal. 1:7, 11; 2:2; in (i.) the "gospel" is viewed historically, in (ii.) doctrinally, with reference to the interpretation of the facts, as is sometimes indicated by the context.

The following phrases describe the subjects or nature or purport of the message; it is the "gospel" of God, Mark 1:14; Rom. 1:1; 15:16; 2 Cor. 11:7; 1 Thess. 2:2, 9; 1 Pet. 4:17; God, concerning His Son, Rom. 1:1–3; His Son, Rom. 1:9; Jesus Christ, the Son of God, Mark 1:1; our Lord Jesus, 2 Thess. 1:8; Christ, Rom. 15:19, etc.; the glory of Christ, 2 Cor. 4:4; the grace of God, Acts 20:24; the glory of the blessed God, 1 Tim. 1:11; your salvation, Eph. 1:13; peace, Eph. 6:15. Cf. also "the gospel of the Kingdom," Matt. 4:23; 9:35; 24:14; "an eternal gospel," Rev. 14:6.

In Gal. 2:14, "the truth of the gospel" denotes, not the true "gospel," but the true teaching of it, in contrast to perversions of it.

The following expressions are used in connection with the "gospel": (a) with regard to its testimony; (1) ***kerusso***, "to preach it as a herald, e.g., Matt. 4:23; Gal. 2:2; (2) ***laleo***, "to speak," 1 Thess. 2:2; (3) ***diamarturomai***, "to testify (thoroughly)," Acts 20:24; (4) ***euangelizo***, "to preach," e.g., 1 Cor. 15:1; 2 Cor. 11:7; Gal. 1:11 (see B, No. 1 below); (5) ***katangello***, "to proclaim," 1 Cor. 9:14; (6) ***douleuo eis***, "to serve unto" ("in furtherance of"), Phil. 2:22; (7) ***sunathleo en***, "to labor with in," Phil. 4:3; (8) ***hierourgeo***, "to minister," Rom. 15:16; (9) ***pleroo***, "to preach fully," Rom. 15:19; (10) ***sunkakopatheo***, "to suffer hardship with," 2 Tim. 1:8; (b) with regard to its reception or otherwise: ***dechomai***, "to receive," 2 Cor. 11:4; ***hupakouo***, "to hearken to, or obey," Rom. 10:16; 2 Thess. 1:8; ***pisteuo en***, "to believe in," Mark 1:15; ***metastrepho***, "to pervert," Gal. 1:7.

### B. Verbs.

1. ***euangelizo*** (*2097*), "to bring or announce glad tidings" (Eng., "evangelize"), is used (a) in the active voice in Rev. 10:7 ("declared") and 14:6 ("to proclaim," RV, KJV, "to preach"); (b) in the passive voice, of matters to be proclaimed as "glad tidings," Luke 16:16; Gal. 1:11; 1 Pet. 1:25; of persons to whom the proclamation is made, Matt. 11:5; Luke 7:22; Heb. 4:2, 6; 1 Pet. 4:6; (c) in the middle voice, especially of the message of salvation, with a personal object, either of the person preached, e.g., Acts 5:42; 11:20; Gal. 1:16, or, with a preposition, of the persons evangelized, e.g., Acts 13:32, "declare glad tidings"; Rom. 1:15; Gal. 1:8; with an impersonal object, e.g., "the word," Acts 8:4; "good tidings," 8:12; "the word of the Lord," 15:35; "the gospel," 1 Cor. 15:1; 2 Cor. 11:7; "the faith," Gal. 1:23; "peace," Eph. 2:17; "the unsearchable riches of Christ," 3:8.

2. ***proeuangelizomai*** (*4283*), "to announce glad tidings beforehand," is used in Gal. 3:8.

## GOVERNMENT

***kubernesis*** (*2941*), from ***kubernao***, "to guide" (whence Eng., "govern"), denotes (a) "steering, pilotage"; (b) metaphorically, "governments or governings," said of those who act as guides in a local church, 1 Cor. 12:28.

## GOVERNOR

### A. Nouns.

1. ***hegemon*** (2232) is a term used (a) for "rulers" generally, Mark 13:9; 1 Pet. 2:14; translated "princes" (i.e., leaders) in Matt. 2:6; (b) for the Roman procurators, referring, in the gospels to Pontius Pilate, e.g., Matt. 27:2; Luke 20:20 (so designated by Tacitus, *Annals*, xv. 44); to Felix, Acts 23:26. Technically the procurator was a financial official under a proconsul or propraetor, for collecting the imperial revenues, but entrusted also with magisterial powers for decisions of questions relative to the revenues. In certain provinces, of which Judea was one (the procurator of which was dependent on the legate of Syria), he was the general administrator and supreme judge, with sole power of life and death. Such a governor was a person of high social standing. Felix, however, was an ex-slave, a freedman, and his appointment to Judea could not but be regarded by the Jews as an insult to the nation. The headquarters of the governor of Judea was Caesarea, which was made a garrison town.

2. ***ethnarches*** (*1481*), "an ethnarch," lit. "a ruler of a nation" (***ethnos***, "a people," ***arche***, "rule"), is translated "governor" in 2 Cor. 11:32; it describes normally the ruler of a nation possessed of separate laws and customs among those of a different race. Eventually it denoted a ruler of a province, superior to a tetrarch, but inferior to a king (e.g., Aretas).

3. ***oikonomos*** (*3623*), lit., "one who rules a house" (***oikos***, "a house," ***nomos***, "a law"), Gal. 4:2, denotes a superior servant responsible for the family housekeeping, the direction of other servants, and the care of the children under age.

4. ***architriklinos*** (*755*), from ***arche***, "rule," and ***triklinos***, "a room with three couches," denotes "the ruler of a feast," John 2:8, RV (KJV, "the governor of the feast"), a man appointed to see that the table and couches were duly placed and the courses arranged, and to taste the food and wine.

**B. Verbs.**

1. ***hegeomai*** (*2233*), akin to A, No. 1, is used in the present participle to denote "a governor," lit., "(one) governing," Matt. 2:6; Acts 7:10.

2. ***hegemoneuo*** (*2230*), to be a ***hegemon***, "to lead the way," came to signify to be "a governor of a province"; it is used of Quirinius, governor of Syria, Luke 2:2.

## GRACE

1. ***charis*** (*5485*) has various uses, (a) objective, that which bestows or occasions pleasure, delight, or causes favorable regard; it is applied, e.g., to beauty, or gracefulness of person, Luke 2:40; act, 2 Cor. 8:6, or speech, Luke 4:22, RV, "words of grace" (KJV, "gracious words"); Col. 4:6; (b) subjective, (1) on the part of the bestower, the friendly disposition from which the kindly act proceeds, graciousness, loving-kindness, goodwill generally, e.g., Acts 7:10; especially with reference to the divine favor or "grace," e.g., Acts 14:26; in this respect there is stress on its freeness and universality, its spontaneous character, as in the case of God's redemptive mercy, and the pleasure or joy He designs for the recipient; thus it is set in contrast with debt, Rom. 4:4, 16, with works, 11:6, and with law, John 1:17; see also, e.g., Rom. 6:14, 15; Gal. 5:4; (2) on the part of the receiver, a sense of the favor bestowed, a feeling of gratitude, e.g., Rom. 6:17 ("thanks"); in this respect it sometimes signifies "to be thankful," e.g., Luke 17:9 ("doth he thank the servant?" lit., "hath he thanks to"); 1 Tim. 1:12; (c) in another objective sense, the effect of "grace," the spiritual state of those who have experienced its exercise, whether (1) a state of "grace," e.g., Rom. 5:2; 1 Pet. 5:12; 2 Pet. 3:18, or (2) a proof thereof in practical effects, deeds of "grace," e.g., 1 Cor. 16:3, RV, "bounty" (KJV, "liberality"); 2 Cor. 8:6, 19 (in 2 Cor. 9:8 it means the sum of earthly blessings); the power and equipment for ministry, e.g., Rom. 1:5; 12:6; 15:15; 1 Cor. 3:10; Gal. 2:9; Eph. 3:2, 7.

To be in favor with is to find "grace" with, e.g., Acts 2:47; hence it appears in this sense at the beginning and the end of several epistles, where the writer desires "grace" from God for the readers, e.g., Rom. 1:7; 1 Cor. 1:3; in this respect it is connected with the imperative mood of the word ***chairo***, "to rejoice," a mode of greeting among Greeks, e.g., Acts 15:23; Jas. 1:1 (marg.); 2 John 10, 11, RV, "greeting" (KJV, "God speed").

The fact that "grace" is received both from God the Father, 2 Cor. 1:12, and from Christ, Gal. 1:6; Rom. 5:15 (where both are mentioned), is a testimony to the deity of Christ. See also 2 Thess. 1:12, where the phrase "according to the grace of our God and the Lord Jesus Christ" is to be taken with each of the preceding clauses, "in you," "and ye in Him."

In Jas. 4:6, "But He giveth more grace" (Greek, "a greater grace," RV, marg.), the statement is to be taken in connection with the preceding verse, which contains two remonstrating, rhetorical questions, "Think ye that the Scripture speaketh in vain?" and "Doth the Spirit (the Holy Spirit) which He made to dwell in us long unto envying?" (see the RV). The implied answer to each is "it cannot be so." Accordingly, if those who are acting so flagrantly, as if it were so, will listen to the Scripture instead of letting it speak in vain, and will act so that the Holy Spirit may have His way within, God will give even "a greater grace," namely, all that follows from humbleness and from turning away from the world.

2. ***euprepeia*** (*2143*), "comeliness, goodly appearance," is said of the outward appearance of the flower of the grass, Jas. 1:11.

## GRACIOUS, TO BE GRACIOUS, SHOW FAVOR

### *Old Testament*

**A. Verb.**

***chanan*** (2603), "to be gracious, considerate; to show favor," Gen. 33:5. ***chanan*** may express "generosity," a gift from the heart, Ps. 37:21. God especially is the source of undeserved "favor," Gen. 33:11, and He is asked repeatedly for such "gracious" acts as only He can do, Num. 6:25; Gen. 43:29. God's "favor" is especially seen in His deliverance from one's enemies or surrounding evils, Ps. 77:9; Amos 5:15.

However, God extends His "graciousness" in His own sovereign way and will, to whomever He chooses, Exod. 33:19.

**B. Noun.**

***chen*** (2580), "favor; grace." The basic meaning of ***chen*** is "favor." Whatever is "pleasant and agreeable" can be described by this word. When a woman is said to have ***chen***, she is a "gracious" woman, Prov. 11:16; or the word may have the negative association of being "beautiful without sense," Prov. 31:30. A person's speech may be characterized by "graciousness," Prov. 22:11; cf. Ps. 45:2. ***chen*** also denotes the response to whatever is "agreeable," Gen. 39:21; Exod. 3:21; Ruth 2:10.

**C. Adjective.**

***channun*** (2587), "gracious," Exod. 34:6.

***New Testament***

***chrestos*** (*5543*) is rendered "gracious" in 1 Pet. 2:3, as an attribute of the Lord.

## GRAVE (Noun)

1. ***mnemeion*** (*3419*) primarily denotes "a memorial" (akin to ***mnaomai***, "to remember"), then, "a monument" (the significance of the word rendered "tombs," KJV, "sepulchres," in Luke 11:47), anything done to preserve the memory of things and persons; it usually denotes a tomb, and is translated either "tomb" or "sepulchre" or "grave." Apart from the Gospels, it is found only in Acts 13:29. Among the Hebrews it was generally a cavern, closed by a door or stone, often decorated. Cf. Matt. 23:29.

2. ***mnema*** (*3418*), akin to No. 1, like which it signified "a memorial" or "record of a thing or a dead person," then "a sepulchral monument," and hence "a tomb"; it is rendered "graves" in the KJV of Rev. 11:9 (RV, "a tomb"); "tomb" or "tombs," Mark 5:3, 5 (some mss. have No. 1, as in 15:46, KJV, "sepulchre") and 16:2 (KJV, "sepulchre"); Luke 8:27; Acts 2:29 and 7:16 (KJV, "sepulchre").

## GRAVE (Adjective)

***semnos*** (*4518*) first denoted "reverend, august, venerable" (akin to ***sebomai***, "to reverence"); then, "serious, grave," whether of persons, 1 Tim. 3:8, 11 (deacons and their wives); Titus 2:2 (aged men); or things, Phil. 4:8, RV, "honorable" (marg., "reverend"), KJV, "honest."

## GRAVEN

***charagma*** (*5480*), from ***charasso***, "to engrave" (akin to ***charakter***, "an impress," RV, marg., of Heb. 1:3), denotes (a) "a mark" or "stamp," e.g., Rev. 13:16, 17; 14:9, 11; 16:2; 19:20; 20:4; 15:2 in some mss.; (b) "a thing graven," Acts 17:29.

## GREAT

***Old Testament***

**A. Verbs.**

***kabed*** (3515), "to be heavy, weighty, burdensome, dull, honored, glorious." ***kabed*** basically means to be "heavy, or weighty," so "rich," Gen. 13:2; then, by figurative extension, "being honored" or "glorious." The word includes negative as well as positive aspects. Thus, calamity is "heavier than the sand of the sea," Job 6:3, and the hand of God is "very heavy" in punishing the Philistines, 1 Sam. 5:11. "To honor" or "glorify" anything is to add something which it does not have in itself, or that which others can give. Children are commanded to "honor" their parents, Exod. 20:12; Deut. 5:16; Balak promised "honor" to Balaam, Num. 22:17.

***kabed*** is also the Hebrew word for "liver," Exod. 29:13, an organ of the body.

***rabab*** (7231), "to be numerous, great, large, powerful." ***rabab*** can also mean "to be great" in size, prestige, or power, or number, cf. Gen. 18:20; Job 33:12; Ps. 49:16. With a subject indicating time, this verb implies "lengthening," Gen. 38:12, and with special subjects the word may imply "extension of space," Deut. 14:24.

**B. Nouns.**

***rob*** (7230), "multitude; abundance." This noun has numerical implications apparent in its first biblical appearance, Gen. 16:10. When applied to time or distance, ***rob*** indicates a "large amount" or "long," Josh. 9:13. In several passages, ***rob*** means "great" or "greatness," Isa. 63:1.

***rab*** (7227), "chief." This word is a transliteration of the Akkadian ***rab***, an indication of "military rank" similar to our word ***general***, Jeremiah 39:9–13.

**C. Adjective.**

***rab*** (7227), "many; great; large; prestigious; powerful." First, this word represents plurality in number or amount, whether applied to people or to things. ***rab*** is applied to people in Gen. 26:14; or things, 13:6; or groups, Exod. 5:5; or collections or masses, Num. 20:11; or land, 1 Sam. 26:13. The phrase "many waters" is a fixed phrase meaning the "sea," Isa. 23:2–3. Used in conjunction with "days" or "years," ***rab*** means "long," Gen. 21:34.

***New Testament***

1. ***megas*** (*3173*) is used (a) of external form, size, measure, e.g., of a stone, Matt. 27:60; fish,

John 21:11; (b) of degree and intensity, e.g., of fear, Mark 4:41; wind, John 6:18; Rev. 6:13, RV, "great" (KJV, "mighty"); of a circumstance, 1 Cor. 9:11; 2 Cor. 11:15; in Rev. 5:2, 12, the RV has "great" (KJV, "loud"), of a voice; (c) of rank, whether of persons, e.g., God, Titus 2:13; Christ as a "great Priest," Heb. 10:21, RV; Diana, Acts 19:27, Simon Magus, Acts 8:9 "(some) great one"; in the plural "great ones," Matt. 20:25; Mark 10:42, those who hold positions of authority in gentile nations; or of things, e.g., a mystery, Eph. 5:32.

2. ***polus*** (*4183*), "much, many, great," is used of number, e.g., Luke 5:6; Acts 11:21; degree, e.g., of harvest, Matt. 9:37; mercy, 1 Pet. 1:3, RV "great" (KJV, "abundant"); glory, Matt. 24:30; joy, Philem. 7, RV, "much" (KJV, "great"); peace, Acts 24:2. The best mss. have it in Acts 8:8 (RV, "much"), of joy.

3. ***hikanos*** (*2425*), lit., "reaching to" (from ***hikano***, "to reach"), denotes "sufficient, competent, fit," and is sometimes rendered "great," e.g., of number (of people), Mark 10:46; of degree (of light), Acts 22:6.

4. ***helikos*** (*2245*) primarily denotes "as big as, as old as" (akin to ***helikia***, "an age"); then, as an indirect interrogation, "what, what size, how great, how small" (the context determines the meaning), said of a spiritual conflict, Col. 2:1, KJV, "what great (conflict) I have"; RV, "how greatly (I strive)"; of much wood as kindled by a little fire, Jas. 3:5 (twice in the best mss.), "how much (wood is kindled by) how small (a fire)," RV, said metaphorically of the use of the tongue. Some mss. have No. 4 in Gal. 6:11; the most authentic have No. 5.

5. ***pelikos*** (*4080*), primarily a direct interrogative, "how large? how great?" is used in exclamations, indicating magnitude, like No. 4 (No. 6 indicates quantity), in Gal. 6:11, of letter characters; in Heb. 7:4, metaphorically, of the distinguished character of Melchizedek.

6. ***posos*** (*4214*), an adjective of number, magnitude, degree etc., is rendered "how great" in Matt. 6:23.

7. ***hosos*** (*3745*), "how much, how many," is used in the neuter plural to signify how great things, Mark 5:19, 20; Luke 8:39 (twice); Acts 9:16, KJV (RV, "how many things"); in Rev. 21:16 (in the best mss.), "as great as," RV (KJV, "as large as," said of length).

8. ***tosoutos*** (*5118*), "so great, so many, so much," of quantity, size, etc., is rendered "so great," in Matt. 8:10, and Luke 7:9, of faith; Matt. 15:33, of a multitude; Heb. 12:1, of a cloud of witnesses; Rev. 18:17, of riches.

9. ***telikoutos*** (*5082*), "so great," is used in the NT of things only, a death, 2 Cor. 1:10; salvation, Heb. 2:3; ships, Jas. 3:4; an earthquake, Rev. 16:18, KJV, "so mighty," corrected in the RV to "so great."

## GREATER

1. ***meizon*** (*3187*) is the comparative degree of ***megas***, e.g., Matt. 11:11; in Matt. 13:32, the RV rightly has "greater than" (KJV, "the greatest among"); 23:17; in Luke 22:26, RV, "the greater (among you)" (KJV, "greatest"); in Jas. 3:1, RV, "the heavier (marg., greater) judgment" (KJV, "the greater condemnation"); it is used in the neuter plural in John 1:50, "greater things"; in 14:12, "greater works" (lit., "greater things"); in 1 Cor. 12:31, RV, "the greater," KJV, "the best."

2. ***meizoteros*** (*3186*), a double comparative of ***megas*** (cf. No. 1, above), is used in 3 John 4, of joy.

3. ***pleion*** (*4119*), the comparative of ***polus***, is used (a) as an adjective, "greater, more," e.g., Acts 15:28; (b) as a noun, e.g., Matt. 12:41, "a greater (than Jonah)"; v. 42, "a greater (than Solomon)"; in these instances the neuter ***pleion***, "something greater," is "a fixed or stereotyped form" of the word; in 1 Cor. 15:6, "the greater part" (masculine plural); (c) as an adverb, e.g., Matt. 5:20, lit., "(except your righteousness abound) more greatly (than of scribes and Pharisees)"; so 26:53, "more"; Luke 9:13.

4. ***perissoteros*** (*4055*), the comparative of ***perissos***, "over and above, abundant," signifies "more abundant, greater," e.g., of condemnation, Mark 12:40; Luke 20:47.

## GREATEST

1. ***megas*** (*3173*), "the greatest," in Acts 8:10 and Heb. 8:11. The whole phrase, lit., "from small to great," is equivalent to the Eng. idiom "one and all."

2. ***meizon*** (*3187*), the comparative of No. 1, is sometimes translated "greatest"; besides the two cases given under GREATER, No. 1, where the RV corrects the KJV, "greatest" to "greater" (Matt. 13:32 and Luke 22:26), the RV itself has "greatest" for this comparative in the following, and relegates "greater" to the margin Matt. 18:1, 4; 23:11; Mark 9:34; Luke 9:46; 22:24.

## GREEN

1. ***chloros*** (*5515*), akin to ***chloe***, "tender foliage" (cf. the name "Chloe," 1 Cor. 1:11, and Eng., "chlorine"), denotes (a) "pale green," the color of young grass, Mark 6:39; Rev. 8:7; 9:4, "green thing"; hence, (b) "pale," Rev. 6:8, the color of the horse whose rider's name is Death.

2. ***hugros*** (*5200*) denotes "wet, moist" (the opposite of ***xeros***, "dry"); said of wood, sappy,

"green," Luke 23:31, i.e., if they thus by the fire of their wrath treated Christ, the guiltless, holy, the fruitful, what would be the fate of the perpetrators, who were like the dry wood, exposed to the fire of divine wrath.

## GREET, GREETING

### A. Verbs.

1. ***aspazomai*** (*782*) signifies "to greet welcome," or "salute." In the KJV it is chiefly rendered by either of the verbs "to greet" or "to salute." In two passages the renderings vary otherwise; in Acts 20:1, of bidding farewell, KJV, "embraced them"; in Heb. 11:13, of welcoming promises, KJV, "embraced," RV, "greeted." The verb is used as a technical term for conveying "greetings" at the close of a letter, often by an amanuensis, e.g., Rom. 16:22, the only instance of the use of the first person in this respect in the NT; see also 1 Cor. 16:19, 20; 2 Cor. 13:13; Phil. 4:22; Col. 4:10–15; 1 Thess. 5:26; 2 Tim. 4:21; Titus 3:15; Philem. 23; Heb. 13:24; 1 Pet. 5:13, 14; 2 John 13. This special use is largely illustrated in the papyri, one example of this showing how keenly the absence of the greeting was felt.

2. ***chairo*** (*5463*), "to rejoice," is thrice used as a formula of salutation in Acts 15:23, KJV, "send greeting," RV, "greeting"; so 23:26; Jas. 1:1. In 2 John 10, 11, the RV substitutes the phrase (to give) "greeting," for the KJV (to bid) "God speed."

### B. Noun.

***aspamos*** (*783*), a salutation, is always so rendered in the RV; KJV, "greetings" in Matt. 23:7; Luke 11:43; 20:46, it is used (a) orally in those instances and in Mark 12:38; Luke 1:29, 41, 44; (b) in written salutations, 1 Cor. 16:21 (cf. A, No. 1, in v. 20); Col. 4:18; 2 Thess. 3:17.

## GRIEF, GRIEVE

### A. Noun.

***lupe*** (*3077*) signifies "pain," of body or mind; it is used in the plural in 1 Pet. 2:19 only, RV, "griefs" (KJV, "grief"); here, however, it stands, by metonymy, for "things that cause sorrow, grievances"; hence Tyndale's rendering, "grief," for Wycliffe's "sorews"; everywhere else it is rendered "sorrow," except in Heb. 12:11, where it is translated "grievous" (lit., "of grief").

### B. Verbs.

1. ***lupeo*** (*3076*), akin to A, denotes (a), in the active voice, "to cause pain, or grief, to distress, grieve," e.g., 2 Cor. 2:2 (twice, active and passive voices); v. 5 (twice), RV, "hath caused sorrow" (KJV, "have caused grief," and "grieved"); 7:8, "made (you) sorry"; Eph. 4:30, of grieving the Holy Spirit of God (as indwelling the believer); (b) in the passive voice, "to be grieved, to be made sorry, to be sorry, sorrowful," e.g., Matt. 14:9, RV, "(the king) was grieved" (KJV, "was sorry"); Mark 10:22, RV, "(went away) sorrowful" (KJV, "grieved"); John 21:17, "(Peter) was grieved," Rom. 14:15, "(if . . . thy brother) is grieved"; 2 Cor. 2:4, "(not that) ye should be made sorry," RV, KJV, "ye should be grieved."

2. ***sunlupeo*** (*4818*), or ***sullupeo***, is used in the passive voice in Mark 3:5, "to be grieved" or afflicted together with a person, said of Christ's "grief" at the hardness of heart of those who criticized His healing on the Sabbath day; it here seems to suggest the sympathetic nature of His grief because of their self-injury. Some suggest that the ***sun*** indicates the mingling of "grief" with His anger.

G

3. ***stenazo*** (*4727*), "to groan" (of an inward, unexpressed feeling of sorrow), is translated "with grief" in Heb. 13:17 (marg. "groaning"). It is rendered "sighed" in Mark 7:34; "groan," in Rom. 8:23; 2 Cor. 5:2, 4; "murmur," in Jas. 5:9, RV (KJV, "grudge").

## GRIEVOUS, GRIEVOUSLY

### A. Adjectives.

1. ***barus*** (*926*) denotes "heavy, burdensome"; it is always used metaphorically in the NT, and is translated "heavy" in Matt. 23:4, of Pharisaical ordinances; in the comparative degree "weightier," 23:23, of details of the law of God; "grievous," metaphorically of wolves, in Acts 20:29; of charges, 25:7; negatively of God's commandments, 1 John 5:3 (causing a burden on him who fulfills them); in 2 Cor. 10:10, "weighty," of Paul's letters.

2. ***poneros*** (*4190*), "painful, bad," is translated "grievous" in Rev. 16:2, of a sore inflicted retributively.

3. ***dusbastaktos*** (*1419*), "hard to be borne" (from ***dus***, an inseparable prefix, like Eng. "mis-," and "un-," indicating "difficulty, injuriousness, opposition," etc., and ***bastazo***, "to bear"), is used in Luke 11:46 and, in some mss., in Matt. 23:4, "grievous to be borne"; in the latter the RV marg. has "many ancient authorities omit."

4. ***chalepos*** (*5467*), "hard," signifies (a) "hard to deal with," Matt. 8:28; (b) "hard to bear, grievous," 2 Tim. 3:1, RV, "grievous" (KJV, "perilous"), said of a characteristic of the last days of this age.

**B. Adverbs.**

1. ***deinos*** *(1171)*, akin to ***deos***, "fear," signifies (a) "terribly," Matt. 8:6, "grievously (tormented)"; (b) "vehemently," Luke 11:53.

2. ***kakos*** *(2560)*, "badly, ill," is translated "grievously (vexed)," in Matt. 15:22.

## GROAN, GROANING

**A. Verbs.**

1. ***embrimaomai*** *(1690)*, from ***en***, "in," and ***brime***, "strength," is rendered "groaned" in John 11:33 (preferable to the RV marg., "He had indignation"); so in v. 38. The Lord was deeply moved doubtless with the combination of circumstances, present and in the immediate future. Indignation does not here seem to express His feelings.

2. ***stenazo*** *(4727)*, "groan," Mark 7:34.

3. ***sustenazo*** *(4959)*, "to groan together" (***sun***, "with," and No. 2) is used of the Creation in Rom. 8:22. In v. 23, No. 2 is used.

**B. Noun.**

***stenagmos*** *(4726)*, akin to A No. 2, is used in Acts 7:34.

## GROSS (to wax)

***pachuno*** *(3975)*, from ***pachus***, "thick," signifies "to thicken, fatten"; in the passive voice, "to grow fat"; metaphorically said of the heart, to wax gross or dull, Matt. 13:15; Acts 28:27.

## GROUND, GROUNDED

**A. Nouns.**

1. ***ge*** *(1093)*, "the earth, land," etc., often denotes "the ground," e.g., Matt. 10:29; Mark 8:6.

2. ***edaphos*** *(1475)*, "a bottom, base," is used of the "ground" in Acts 22:7, suggestive of that which is level and hard. Cf. B, No. 1, below.

3. ***chora*** *(5561)*, "land, country," is used of property, "ground," in Luke 12:16, "the ground (of a certain rich man)."

4. ***chorion*** *(5564)*, a diminutive of No. 3, "a piece of land, a place, estate," is translated "parcel of ground" in John 4:5.

5. ***hedraioma*** *(1477)*, "a support, bulwark, stay" (from ***hedraios***, "steadfast, firm"; from ***hedra***, "a seat"), is translated "ground" in 1 Tim. 3:15 (said of a local church); the RV marg., "stay" is preferable.

**B. Verbs.**

1. ***edaphizo*** *(1474)*, akin to A, No. 2.

2. ***themelioo*** *(2311)* signifies "to lay the foundation of, to found" (akin to ***themelios***, "a foundation"; from ***tithemi***, "to put"), and is rendered "grounded" in Eph. 3:17, said of the condition of believers with reference to the love of Christ; in Col. 1:23, of their continuance in the faith.

## GROW

1. ***auxano*** *(837)*, "to grow or increase," of the growth of that which lives, naturally or spiritually, is used (a) transitively, signifying to make to increase, said of giving the increase, 1 Cor. 3:6, 7; 2 Cor. 9:10, the effect of the work of God, according to the analogy of His operations in nature; "to grow, become greater," e.g. of plants and fruit, Matt. 6:28; used in the passive voice in 13:32 and Mark 4:8, "increase"; in the active in Luke 12:27; 13:19; of the body, Luke 1:80; 2:40; of Christ, John 3:30, "increase"; of the work of the gospel of God, Acts 6:7, "increased"; 12:24; 19:20; of people, Acts 7:17; of faith, 2 Cor. 10:15 (passive voice), RV, "groweth" (KJV, "is increased"); of believers individually, Eph. 4:15; Col. 1:6, RV, 10 (passive voice), "increasing"; 1 Pet. 2:2; 2 Pet. 3:18; of the church, Col. 2:19; of churches, Eph. 2:21.

2. ***mekunomai*** *(3373)*, "to grow long, lengthen, extend" (from ***mekos***, "length"), is used of the "growth" of plants, in Mark 4:27.

3. ***huperauxano*** *(5232)*, "to increase beyond measure," is used of faith and love, in their living and practical effects, 2 Thess. 1:3. Lightfoot compares this verb and the next in the verse (***pleonazo***, "to abound") in that the former implies "an internal, organic growth, as of a tree," the latter "a diffusive or expansive character, as of a flood irrigating the land."

4. ***sunauxano*** *(4885)*, "to grow together," is in Matt. 13:30.

5. ***phuo*** *(5453)*, "to produce," is rendered "grew" (passive voice) in Luke 8:6.

6. ***sumphuo*** *(4855)* is used in Luke 8:7, RV, "grow with."

## GUARD (Noun and Verb)

**A. Nouns.**

1. ***koustodia*** *(2892)*; "a guard," (Latin, ***custodia***, Eng., "custodian"), is used of the soldiers who "guarded" Christ's sepulchre, Matt. 27:65, 66 and 28:11, and is translated "(ye have) a guard," "the guard (being with them)," and "(some of) the guard," RV, KJV, ". . . a watch," "(setting a) watch," and ". . . the watch." This was the Temple guard, stationed under a Roman officer in the tower of Antonia, and having charge of the high priestly vestments. Hence the significance of Pilate's words "Ye have a guard."

2. ***spekoulator*** *(4688)*, Latin, ***speculator***, primarily denotes "a lookout officer," or "scout," but, under the emperors, "a member of the

bodyguard"; these were employed as messengers, watchers and executioners; ten such officers were attached to each legion; such a guard was employed by Herod Antipas, Mark 6:27, RV, "a soldier of his guard" (KJV, "executioner").

3. ***phulax*** (*5441*), "a guard, keeper" (akin to ***phulasso***, "to guard, keep"), is translated "keepers" in Acts 5:23; in 12:6, 19, RV, "guards" (KJV, "keepers").

**B. Verbs.**

1. ***phulasso*** (*5442*), "to guard, watch, keep" (akin to A, No. 3), is rendered by the verb "to guard" in the RV (KJV, "to keep") of Luke 11:21; John 17:12; Acts 12:4; 28:16; 2 Thess. 3:3; 1 Tim. 6:20; 2 Tim. 1:12, 14; 1 John 5:21; Jude 24. In Luke 8:29, "was kept under guard, RV (KJV, kept).

2. ***diaphulasso*** (*1314*), a strengthened form of No. 1 (***dia***, "through," used intensively), "to guard carefully, defend," is found in Luke 4:10, RV, "to guard" (KJV, "to keep").

3. ***phroureo*** (*5432*), a military term, "to keep by guarding, to keep under guard," as with a garrison (***phrouros***, "a guard, or garrison"), is used, (a) of blocking up every way of escape, as in a siege; (b) of providing protection against the enemy, as a garrison does; see 2 Cor. 11:32, "guarded." KJV, "kept," i.e., kept the city, "with a garrison." It is used of the security of the Christian until the end, 1 Pet. 1:5, RV, "are guarded," and of the sense of that security that is his when he puts all his matters into the hand of God, Phil. 4:7, RV, "shall guard." In these passages the idea is not merely that of protection, but of inward garrisoning as by the Holy Spirit; in Gal. 3:23 ("were kept in ward"), it means rather a benevolent custody and watchful guardianship in view of worldwide idolatry (cf. Isa. 5:2).

## GUARDIAN

***epitropos*** (*2012*), lit., "one to whose care something is committed," is rendered "guardians" in Gal. 4:2, RV, KJV, "tutors" (in Matt. 20:8 and Luke 8:3, "steward"). The corresponding verb, ***epitrepo***, is translated "permit, give leave, suffer"; see 1 Cor. 14:34; 16:7; 1 Tim. 2:12. An allied noun, ***epitrope***, is translated "commission" in Acts 26:12, and refers to delegated authority over persons. This usage of cognate words suggests that the ***epitropos*** was a superior servant responsible for the persons composing the household, whether children or slaves.

## GUEST

***anakeimai*** (*345*), "to recline at table," frequently rendered "to sit at meat," is used in its present participial form (lit., "reclining ones") as a noun denoting "guests," in Matt. 22:10, 11.

## GUEST-CHAMBER

***kataluma*** (*2646*), akin to ***kataluo***, signifies (a) "an inn, lodging-place," Luke 2:7; (b) "a guest-room," Mark 14:14; Luke 22:11. The word is used of the place where travelers and their beasts untied their packages, girdles and sandals. The two passages in the NT concern a room in a private house, which the owner readily placed at the disposal of Jesus and His disciples for the celebration of the Passover.

## GUILE

***dolos*** (*1388*), "a bait, snare, deceit," is rendered "guile" in John 1:47, negatively of Nathanael; Acts 13:10, RV, KJV, "subtlety" (of Bar-Jesus); 2 Cor. 12:16, in a charge made against Paul by his detractors, of catching the Corinthian converts by "guile" (the apostle is apparently quoting the language of his critics); 1 Thess. 2:3, negatively, of the teaching of the apostle and his fellow missionaries; 1 Pet. 2:1, of that from which Christians are to be free; 2:22, of the guileless speech of Christ; 3:10, of the necessity that the speech of Christians should be guileless. See also Matt. 26:4; Mark 7:22; 14:1.

## GUILELESS (WITHOUT GUILE)

1. ***adolos*** (*97*), "without guile," "pure, unadulterated," is used metaphorically of the teaching of the Word of God, 1 Pet. 2:2, RV. It is used in the papyri writings of seed, corn, wheat, oil, wine, etc.

2. ***akakos*** (*172*), lit., "without evil," signifies "simple, guileless," Rom. 16:18, "simple," of believers (perhaps = unsuspecting, or, rather, innocent, free from admixture of evil); in Heb. 7:26, RV, "guileless" (KJV, "harmless"), the character of Christ (more lit., "free from evil").

## GUILTLESS

### *Old Testament*

**A. Verb.**

***naqah*** (5352), "to be pure, innocent." The verb is most often used to mean being "free" (with the preposition ***min*** [from]) an obligation, Gen. 24:8, 41; Num. 5:31; from punishment, Exod. 21:19; Num. 5:28. The verb also appears with the legal connotation of "innocence," Ps. 19:13. The punishment of the person who is not "acquitted" is also expressed by a negation of the verb ***naqah***: "The Lord will not hold anyone guiltless who misuses his name," Exod. 20:7.

**B. Adjective.**

***naqi*** (5355), "innocent," Ps. 15:5.

***New Testament***

***anaitios*** *(338)*, "innocent, guiltless" (***a***, negative, ***n***, euphonic, ***aitia***, "a charge of crime"), is translated "blameless" in Matt. 12:5, KJV, "guiltless" in v. 7; RV, "guiltless" in each place.

## GUILTY (Adjective)

***enochos*** *(1777)*, lit., "held in, bound by, liable to a charge or action at law," Mark 3:29.

## GULF

***chasma*** *(5490)*, akin to ***chasko***, "to yawn" (Eng., "chasm"), is found in Luke 16:26.

# H

## HADES

***hades*** (*86*), "the region of departed spirits of the lost" (but including the blessed dead in periods preceding the ascension of Christ). It has been thought by some that the word etymologically meant "the unseen" (from ***a***, negative, and ***eido***, "to see"), but this derivation is questionable; a more probable derivation is from ***hado***, signifying "all-receiving." It corresponds to "Sheol" in the OT. In the KJV of the OT and NT; it has been unhappily rendered "hell," e.g., Ps. 16:10; or "the grave," e.g., Gen. 37:35; or "the pit," Num. 16:30, 33; in the NT the revisers have always used the rendering "hades"; in the OT, they have not been uniform in the translation, e.g. in Isa. 14:15 "hell" (marg., "Sheol"); usually they have "Sheol" in the text and "the grave" in the margin. It never denotes the grave, nor is it the permanent region of the lost; in point of time it is, for such, intermediate between decease and the doom of Gehenna. For the condition, see Luke 16:23–31.

## HAIR

***thrix*** (*2359*) denotes the "hair," whether of beast, as of the camel's "hair" which formed the raiment of John the Baptist, Matt. 3:4; Mark 1:6; or of man. Regarding the latter (a) it is used to signify the minutest detail, as that which illustrates the exceeding care and protection bestowed by God upon His children, Matt. 10:30; Luke 12:7; 21:18; Acts 27:34; (b) as the Jews swore by the "hair," the Lord used the natural inability to make one "hair" white or black, as one of the reasons for abstinence from oaths, Matt. 5:36; (c) while long "hair" is a glory to a woman, and to wear it loose or dishevelled is a dishonor, yet the woman who wiped Christ's feet with her "hair" (in place of the towel which Simon the Pharisee omitted to provide), despised the shame in her penitent devotion to the Lord (slaves were accustomed to wipe their masters' feet), Luke 7:38, 44 (RV, "hair"); see also John 11:2; 12:3; (d) the dazzling whiteness of the head and "hair" of the Son of Man in the vision of Rev. 1 (v. 14) is suggestive of the holiness and wisdom of "the Ancient of Days"; (e) the long "hair" of the spirit-beings described as locusts in Rev. 9:8 is perhaps indicative of their subjection to their satanic master (cf. 1 Cor. 11:10, RV); (f) Christian women are exhorted to refrain from adorning their "hair" for outward show, 1 Pet. 3:3.

## HALLELUJAH

***hallelouia*** (*239*) signifies "Praise ye Jah." In the NT it is found in Rev. 19:1, 3, 4, 6, as the keynote in the song of the great multitude in heaven. See PRAISE.

## HALLOW

***hagiazo*** (*37*), "to make holy" (from ***hagios***, "holy"), signifies to set apart for God, to sanctify, to make a person or thing the opposite of ***koinos***, "common"; it is translated "hallowed," with reference to the name of God the Father in the Lord's Prayer, Matt. 6:9; Luke 11:2.

## HAND

### *Old Testament*

***yad*** (3027), "hand; side; border; alongside; hand-measure; portion; arm (rest); monument; manhood (male sex organ); power; rule." The primary sense of this word is "hand," as a part of the body which can grasp, extend, do things, etc. Gen. 3:22; Num. 35:17. ***yad*** also means "human," Dan. 8:25; cf. Job 34:20, and is used of God as a figure of speech, Jer. 16:21. In several passages, ***yad*** is used in the sense of "power" or "rule," 1 Sam. 23:7; cf. Prov. 18:21.

***yad*** is employed in several other noteworthy phrases. The "lifting of the hand" may be involved in "taking an oath," Gen. 14:22; Prov. 11:21. "Putting one's hand on one's mouth" is a gesture of silence, Prov. 30:32; or submission, 1 Chron. 29:24; or entrusting, Gen. 42:37.

***yad*** represents the location, *beside,* 2 Sam. 15:2; or "border," of a land, 2 Chron. 21:16; or "bank," of a river, Dan. 10:4. ***yad*** also means a part or fraction of something, Gen. 43:34. Other meanings include "support," 1 Kings 7:35ff., an "arm rest," 1 Kings 10:19, and a "monument" or "stele," 1 Sam. 15:12. ***yad*** sometimes represents the "male sex organ," Isa. 57:8; cf. v. 10; 6:2; 7:20.

### *New Testament*

***cheir*** (*5495*), "the hand," is used, besides its ordinary significance, (a) in the idiomatic phrases, "by the hand of," "at the hand of," etc., to signify "by the agency of," Acts 5:12; 7:35; 17:25; 14:3; Gal. 3:19 (cf. Lev. 26:46); Rev. 19:2; (b) metaphorically, for the power of God, e.g., Luke 1:66; 23:46; John 10:28, 29; Acts 11:21;

13:11; Heb. 1:10; 2:7; 10:31; (c) by metonymy, for power, e.g., Matt. 17:22; Luke 24:7; John 10:39; Acts 12:11.

## HANDED DOWN

***patroparadotos*** (*3970*), an adjective, denoting "handed down from one's fathers," 1 Pet. 1:18.

## HANDS (made by, not made with)

1. ***cheiropoietos*** (*5499*), "made by hand," of human handiwork, is said of the temple in Jerusalem, Mark 14:58; temples in general, Acts 7:48 (RV, "houses"); 17:24; negatively, of the heavenly and spiritual tabernacle, Heb. 9:11; of the holy place in the earthly tabernacle, v. 24; of circumcision, Eph. 2:11.

2. ***acheiropoietos*** (*886*), "not made by hands" (***a***, negative, and No. 1), is said of an earthly temple, Mark 14:58; of the resurrection body of believers, metaphorically as a house, 2 Cor. 5:1; metaphorically, of spiritual circumcision, Col. 2:11.

## HANDLE

1. ***pselaphao*** (*5584*), "to feel, touch, handle," is rendered by the latter verb in Luke 24:39, in the Lord's invitation to the disciples to accept the evidence of His resurrection in His being bodily in their midst; in 1 John 1:1, in the apostle's testimony (against the Gnostic error that Christ had been merely a phantom) that he and his fellow apostles had handled Him.

2. ***thingano*** (2345) signifies (a) "to touch, to handle" (though "to handle" is rather stronger than the actual significance compared with No 1). In Col. 2:21 the RV renders it "touch," and the first verb (***hapto***, "to lay hold of") "handle," i.e., "handle not, nor taste, nor touch"; "touch" is the appropriate rendering; in Heb. 12:20 it is said of a beast's touching Mount Sinai; (b) "to touch by way of injuring," Heb. 11:28.

3. ***orthotomeo*** (*3718*), "to cut straight," as in road-making, is used metaphorically in 2 Tim. 2:15, of "handling aright (the word of truth)," RV (KJV, "rightly dividing"). The stress is on ***orthos***; the Word of God is to be "handled" strictly along the lines of its teaching. If the metaphor is taken from plowing, cutting a straight furrow, the word would express a careful cultivation, the Word of God viewed as ground designed to give the best results from its ministry and in the life.

## HARD, HARDEN, HARDENING, HARDNESS

### A. Adjectives.

1. ***skleros*** (*4642*), from ***skello***, "to dry," signifies "trying, exacting."

2. ***duskolos*** (*1422*) primarily means "hard to satisfy with food" (***dus***, a prefix like Eng., ***un***— or ***mis***—, indicating "difficulty, opposition, injuriousness," etc., the opposite of, ***eu***, "well," and ***kolon***, "food"); hence, "difficult," Mark 10:24, of the "difficulty," for those who trust in riches, to enter into the Kingdom of God.

### B. Nouns.

1. ***sklerotes*** (*4643*), akin to A, No. 1, is rendered "hardness" in Rom. 2:5.

2. ***porosis*** (*4457*) denotes "a hardening," a covering with a ***poros***, a kind of stone, indicating "a process" (from ***poroo***, C, No. 1), and is used metaphorically of dulled spiritual perception, Mark 3:5, RV, "at the hardening of their hearts"; Rom. 11:25, RV, "a hardening" (KJV, "blindness"), said of the state of Israel; Eph. 4:8, RV, "hardening," of the heart of Gentiles.

### C. Verbs.

1. ***poroo*** (*4456*), "to make hard, callous, to petrify" (akin to B, No. 2), is used metaphorically, of the heart, Mark 6:52; 8:17; John 12:40; of the mind (or thoughts), 2 Cor. 3:14, of those in Israel who refused the revealed will and ways of God in the gospel, as also in Rom. 11:7, RV, "hardened" (KJV, "blinded"), in both places.

2. ***skleruno*** (*4645*), "to make dry or hard" (akin to A, No. 1 and B, No. 1), is used in Acts 19:9; in Rom. 9:18, illustrated by the case of Pharaoh; in Heb. 3:8, 13, 15; 4:7, warnings against the "hardening" of the heart.

## HARDSHIP (to suffer)

1. ***kakopatheo*** (*2553*), "to suffer evil," is translated "suffer hardship" in three places in the RV, 2 Tim. 2:3 (in some mss.; see No. 2), KJV, "endure hardness"; 2:9, KJV, "suffer trouble"; 4:5, KJV, "endure affliction"; in Jas. 5:13, RV, "suffering" (KJV, "afflicted").

2. ***sunkakopatheo*** (*4777*), "to suffer hardship with," is so rendered in 2 Tim. 1:8, RV, KJV, "be thou partaker of the afflictions" (of the gospel), and, in the best mss., in 2:3, "suffer hardship with me."

## HARLOT

### *Old Testament*

***zanah*** (2181), "to go a whoring, commit fornication, be a harlot, serve other gods." This word describes sexual misconduct on the part of a female in the Old Testament (occasionally a male), Deut. 31:16. ***zanah*** became, then, the common term for spiritual backsliding. The act of harloting after strange gods was more than changing gods, however. This was especially true when Israel went after the Canaanite gods, for the worship of these pagan deities involved actual prostitution with cult prostitutes connected with the Canaanite shrines. In the Old Testament sometimes the use of the phrase "go a whoring after" gods implies an individual's involvement with cult prostitutes, Exod. 34:15–16.

The Book of Hosea, in which Hosea's wife Gomer became unfaithful and most likely was involved in such cult prostitution, again illustrates not only Hosea's heartbreak but also God's own heartbreak because of the unfaithfulness of his wife, Israel. Israel's unfaithfulness appears in Hos. 9:1: "Rejoice not, O Israel, for joy, as other people: for thou hast gone a whoring from thy God, thou hast loved a reward upon every cornfloor."

*New Testament*

***porne*** (*4204*), "a prostitute, harlot" (from ***pernemi***, "to sell"), is used (a) literally, in Matt. 21:31, 32, of those who were the objects of the mercy shown by Christ; in Luke 15:30, of the life of the Prodigal; in 1 Cor. 6:15, 16, in a warning to the Corinthian church against the prevailing licentiousness which had made Corinth a byword; in Heb. 11:31 and Jas. 2:25, of Rahab; (b) metaphorically, of mystic Babylon, Rev. 17:1, 5 (KJV, "harlots"), 15, 16; 19:2, RV, for KJV, "whore."

## HARM

**A. Nouns.**

1. ***kakos*** (*2556*), "evil," is rendered "harm" in Acts 16:28; 28:5.

2. ***poneros*** (*4190*), "evil," generally of a more malignant sort than No. 1, is translated "harm" in Acts 28:21.

**B. Verb.**

1. ***kakoo*** (2559), "to do evil to a person" (akin to A, No. 1), is rendered "harm" in 1 Pet. 3:13, and in the RV of Acts 18:10 (KJV, "hurt").

2. ***kakopoieo*** (*2554*), "to do harm" (A, No. 1, and ***poieo***, "to do"), is so rendered in the RV of Mark 3:4 and Luke 6:9 (KJV, "to do evil"), with reference to the moral character of what is done; in 1 Pet. 3:17, "evil doing"; 3 John 11, "doeth evil."

## HARMLESS

1. ***akeraios*** (*185*), lit., "unmixed, with absence of foreign mixture" (from ***a***, negative, and ***kerannumi***, "to mix"), "pure," is used metaphorically in the NT of what is guileless, sincere, Matt. 10:16, "harmless" (marg., "simple"), i.e., with the simplicity of a single eye, discerning what is evil, and choosing only what glorifies God; Rom. 16:19, "simple (unto that which is evil)," KJV marg., "harmless"; Phil. 2:15, "harmless," KJV marg., "sincere."

2. ***akakos*** (*172*), the negative of ***kakos***, is rendered "harmless" in Heb. 7:26 (RV, "guileless"), of the character of Christ as a High Priest; in Rom. 16:18, RV, "innocent," KJV, "simple."

## HARVEST

***therismos*** (*2326*), akin to ***therizo***, "to reap," is used (a) of "the act of harvesting," John 4:35; (b) "the time of harvest," figuratively, Matt. 13:30, 39; Mark 4:29; (c) "the crop," figuratively, Matt. 9:37, 38; Luke 10:2; Rev. 14:15. The beginning of "harvest" varied according to natural conditions, but took place on the average about the middle of April in the eastern lowlands of Palestine, in the latter part of the month in the coast plains and a little later in high districts. Barley "harvest" usually came first and then wheat. "Harvesting" lasted about seven weeks, and was the occasion of festivities.

## HATE, HATEFUL, HATER, HATRED

*Old Testament*

***A. Verb.***

***sane'*** (8130), "to hate, come to hate" (or weakened sense) "set against." The strong sense of the word typifies the emotion of intense jealousy, or bitter disdain, which could plot murder and torture, Gen. 37:18ff. In a weaker sense, ***sane'*** signifies "being set against," Exod. 18:21; or unloved, or lesser loved, Deut. 22:16.

**B. Noun.**

***sin'ah*** (8135), "hatred," Num. 35:20.

*New Testament*

**A. Verb.**

***miseo*** (*3404*), "to hate," is used especially (a) of malicious and unjustifiable feelings towards others, whether towards the innocent or by mutual animosity, e.g., Matt. 10:22; 24:10; Luke 6:22, 27; 19:14; John 3:20, of "hating" the light (metaphorically); 7:7; 15:18, 19, 23–25; Titus 3:3; 1 John 2:9, 11; 3:13, 15; 4:20; Rev. 18:2, where "hateful" translates the perfect participle passive voice of the verb, lit., "hated," or "having been hated"; (b) of a right feeling of aversion from what is evil; said of wrongdoing, Rom. 7:15; iniquity, Heb. 1:9; "the garment (figurative) spotted by the flesh," Jude 23; "the works of the Nicolaitans," Rev. 2:6 (and v. 15, in some mss.; see the KJV); (c) of relative preference for one thing over another, by way of expressing either aversion from, or disregard for, the claims of one person or thing relatively to those of another, Matt. 6:24, and Luke 16:13, as to the impossibility of serving two masters; Luke 14:26, as to the claims of parents relatively to those of Christ; John 12:25, of disregard for one's life relatively to the claims of Christ; Eph. 5:29, negatively, of one's flesh, i.e. of one's own, and therefore a man's wife as one with him.

### B. Adjective.

***stugetos*** (*4767*), "hateful" (from ***stugeo***, "to hate," not found in the NT), is used in Titus 3:3.

### C. Nouns.

1. ***echthra*** (*2189*), "hatred," Rom. 8:7.
2. ***theostuges*** (*2319*), from ***theos***, "God," and ***stugeo*** (see B), is used in Rom. 1:30, KJV, and RV, marg., "haters of God," RV, "hateful to God"; the former rendering is appropriate to what is expressed by the next words, "insolent," "haughty," but the RV text seems to give the true meaning. Lightfoot quotes from the Epistle of Clement of Rome, in confirmation of this, "those who practice these things are hateful to God."

## HAUGHTY

***huperephanos*** (*5244*), "showing oneself above others" (***huper***, "over," ***phainomai***, "to appear"), though often denoting preeminent, is always used in the NT in the evil sense of "arrogant, disdainful, haughty"; it is rendered "haughty" in Rom. 1:30 and 2 Tim. 3:2, RV, KJV, "proud," but "proud" in both versions in Luke 1:51; Jas. 4:6, and 1 Pet. 5:5; in the last two it is set in opposition to ***tapeinos***, "humble, lowly."

## HEAD

### *Old Testament*

### A. Nouns.

***ro'sh*** (7218), "head; top; first; sum." This word often represents a "head," a bodily part, Gen. 40:20; Dan. 2:32; 7:9. To "lift up one's own head" may be a sign of declaring one's innocence, Job 10:15. This same figure of speech may indicate an intention to begin a war, the most violent form of self-assertion, Ps. 83:2. Used transitively (i.e., to lift up someone else's "head"), this word may connote restoring someone to a previous position: "Yet within three days shall Pharaoh lift up thine head, and restore thee unto thy place . . . ," Gen. 40:13. It can also denote the release of someone from prison, 2 Kings 25:27.

The word can connote unity, representing every individual in a given group, Judg. 5:30; or a total in a group, Num. 1:2.

***ro'sh*** sometimes means "leader," Exod. 18:25; 2 Kings 25:18. When used of things, ***ro'sh*** means "point" or "beginning of a space," Gen. 11:4;. In Gen. 47:31, the word denotes the "head" of a bed, or where one lays his "head." In 1 Kings 8:8, ***ro'sh*** refers to the ends of poles, Ezek. 16:25; cf. Dan. 7:1; headwaters, Gen. 2:10; the "head" of the stars is a star located at the zenith of the sky, Job 22:12. The "head" cornerstone occupies a place of primary importance. It is the stone by which all the other stones are measured; it is the chief cornerstone, Ps. 118:22.

This word may have a temporal significance, meaning "beginning" or "first of a series," 1 Chron. 16:7.

***re'shit*** (7225), "beginning; first; choicest." The abstract word ***re'shit*** corresponds to the temporal and estimative sense of ***ro'sh***. ***re'shit*** connotes the "beginning" of a fixed period of time, Deut. 11:12; of one's life, Job 42:12; of creation, Gen. 1:1. Estimatively, this word can mean the "first" or "choicest," Exod. 23:19; Dan. 11:41.

Used substantively, the word can mean "first fruits," as the first of a harvest time, Lev. 2:12; of an offering, Num. 15:20.

### B. Adjective.

***ri'shon*** (7223), "first; foremost; preceding; former." It denotes the "first" in a temporal sequence, Gen. 8:13; or first of rank, Ezra 9:2.

A second meaning of this adjective is "preceding" or "former," Gen. 13:4; used locally in Gen. 33:2.

### *New Testament*

***kephale*** (*2776*), besides its natural significance, is used (a) figuratively in Rom. 12:20, of heaping coals of fire on a "head"; in Acts 18:6, "Your blood be upon your own heads," i.e., "your blood-guiltiness rest upon your own persons," a mode of expression frequent in the OT, and perhaps here directly connected with Ezek. 3:18, 20; 33:6, 8; see also Lev. 20:16; 2 Sam. 1:16; 1 Kings 2:37; (b) metaphorically, of the authority or direction of God in relation to Christ, of Christ in relation to believing men, of the husband in relation to the wife, 1 Cor. 11:3; of Christ in relation to the Church, Eph. 1:22; 4:15; 5:23; Col. 1:18; 2:19; of Christ in relation to principalities and powers, Col. 2:10. As to 1 Cor. 11:10, taken in connection with the context, the word "authority" probably stands, by metonymy, for a sign of authority (RV), the angels being witnesses of the preeminent relationship as established by God in the creation of man as just mentioned, with the spiritual significance regarding the position of Christ in relation to the Church; cf. Eph. 3:10; it is used of Christ as the foundation of the spiritual building set forth by the Temple, with its "corner stone," Matt. 21:42; symbolically also of the imperial rulers of the Roman power, as seen in the apocalyptic visions, Rev. 13:1, 3; 17:3, 7, 9.

## HEAL, HEALING

### *Old Testament*

***rapa'*** (7495), "to heal," i.e., "restoring to normal," an act which God typically performs, Ps. 6:2; Jer. 17:14; or restoring food or drink, 2 Kings 2:22; Ezek. 47:8; even pottery is "healed" or restored, Jer. 19:11.

A large number of the uses of ***rapa'*** express the "healing," as a figure of the act of God's grace and forgiveness, as well as the nation's repentance, Jer. 51:8–9.

### *New Testament*

**A. Verbs.**

1. ***therapeuo*** (*2323*) primarily signifies "to serve as a ***therapon***, an attendant"; then, "to care for the sick, to treat, cure, heal" (Eng., "therapeutics"). It is chiefly used in Matthew and Luke, once in John (5:10), and, after the Acts, only Rev. 13:3 and 12.

2. ***iaomai*** (*4390*), "to heal," is used (a) of physical treatment 22 times; in Matt. 5:28, KJV, "made whole," RV, "healed"; so in Acts 9:34; (b) figuratively, of spiritual "healing," Matt. 13:15; John 12:40; Acts 28:27; Heb. 12:13; 1 Pet. 2:24; possibly, Jas. 5:16 includes both (a) and (b); some mss. have the word, with sense (b), in Luke 4:18. Apart from this last, Luke, the physician, uses the word fifteen times.

3. ***sozo*** (*4982*), "to save," is translated by the verb "to heal" in the KJV of Mark 5:23 and Luke 8:36 (RV, "to make whole"; so KJV frequently); the idea is that of saving from disease and its effects.

4. ***diasozo*** (*1295*), "to save thoroughly" (***dia***, "through," and No. 3), is translated "heal" in Luke 7:3, KJV (RV, "save").

**B. Nouns.**

1. ***therapeia*** (*2322*), akin to A, No. 1, primarily denotes "care, attention," Luke 12:42; then, "medical service, healing" (Eng., "therapy"), Luke 9:11; Rev. 22:2, of the effects of the leaves of the tree of life, perhaps here with the meaning "health."

2. ***iama*** (*2386*), akin to A, No. 2, formerly signified "a means of healing"; in the NT, "a healing" (the result of the act), used in the plural, in 1 Cor. 12:9, 28, 30, RV, "healings"; of divinely imparted gifts in the churches in apostolic times.

3. ***iasis*** (*2392*), akin to A, No. 2, stresses the process as reaching completion, Luke 13:32, "cures," of the acts of Christ in the days of His flesh; Acts 4:22, 30, "to heal," lit. 'unto healing.'

## HEAR, HEARING

### *Old Testament*

**A. Verb.**

***shama'*** (8085), "to hear, hearken, listen, obey, publish." Basically, this verb means to "hear" something with one's ears, Gen. 37:17; or eavesdropping, Gen. 18:10; or "listening," Gen. 37:6; 1 Chron. 28:2. ***shama'*** may also imply to "gain knowledge" or to "get knowledge," Jer. 37:5; or "come into knowledge about," Num. 9:8.

"Hearing," often means to listen and respond to a message or information: spiritually, Num. 24:4; or obey outright, Gen. 22:18.

To have a "hearing heart" is to have "discernment" or "understanding," 1 Kings 3:9. Certainly when Moses told Israel's judges to "hear" cases, he meant more than listening with one's ear. He meant for them to examine the merits of a case, so as to render a just decision, Deut. 1:16.

**B. Nouns.**

***shema'*** (8088), "report," Gen. 29:13. ***shem-u'ah*** (8052), "revelation; something heard," Isa. 28:9.

### *New Testament*

**A. Verbs.**

1. ***akouo*** (*191*), the usual word denoting "to hear," is used (a) intransitively, e.g., Matt. 11:15; Mark 4:23; (b) transitively when the object is expressed, sometimes in the accusative case, sometimes in the genitive.

2. ***eisakouo*** (*1522*), "to listen to" (***eis***, to, and No. 1), has two meanings, (a) "to hear and to obey," 1 Cor. 14:21, "they will not hear"; (b) "to hear so as to answer," of God's answer to prayer, Matt. 6:7; Luke 1:13; Acts 10:31; Heb. 5:7.

3. ***diakouo*** (*1251*), "to hear through, hear fully" (***dia***, "through," and No. 1), is used technically, of "hearing" judicially, in Acts 23:35, of Felix in regard to the charges against Paul.

4. ***epakouo*** (*1873*), "to listen to, hear with favor, at or upon an occasion" (***epi***, "upon," and No. 1), is used in 2 Cor. 6:2 (RV, "hearken").

5. ***epakroaomai*** (*1874*), "to listen attentively to" (***epi***, used intensively, and a verb akin to No. 1), is used in Acts 16:25, "(the prisoners) were listening to (them)," RV, expressive of rapt attention.

6. ***proakouo*** (*4257*) signifies "to hear before" (***pro***), Col. 1:5, where Lightfoot suggests that the preposition contrasts what they heard before, the true gospel, with the false gospel of their recent teachers.

7. ***parakouo*** (*3878*) primarily signifies "to overhear, hear amiss or imperfectly" (***para***, "beside, amiss," and No. 1); then (in the NT) "to hear without taking heed, to neglect to hear," Matt. 18:17 (twice); in Mark 5:36 the best mss. have this verb, which the RV renders "not heeding" (marg., "overhearing"); some mss. have No. 1, KJV, "hearing." It seems obvious that the Lord paid no attention to those from the ruler's house and their message that his daughter was dead.

**B. Nouns.**

1. ***akoe*** (*189*), akin to A, No. 1, denotes (a) "the sense of hearing," 1 Cor. 12:17; 2 Pet. 2:8; a combination of verb and noun is used in phrases which have been termed Hebraic as they express somewhat literally an OT phraseology, e.g., "By hearing ye shall hear," Matt. 13:14; Acts 28:26, RV, a mode of expression conveying emphasis; (b) "the organ of hearing," Mark 7:35, "ears"; Luke 7:1, RV, "ears," for KJV, "audience"; Acts 17:20; 2 Tim. 4:3, 4; Heb. 5:11, "dull of hearing," lit., "dull as to ears"; (c) "a thing heard, a message or teaching," John 12:38, "report"; Rom. 10:16; 1 Thess. 2:13, "the word of the message," lit. "the word of hearing" (KJV, "which ye heard"); Heb. 4:2, "the word of hearing," RV, for KJV, "the word preached"; in a somewhat similar sense, "a rumor, report," Matt. 4:24; 14:1; Mark 1:28, KJV, "fame," RV, "report"; Matt. 24:6; Mark 13:7, "rumors (of wars)"; (d) "the receiving of a message," Rom. 10:17, something more than the mere sense of "hearing" [see (a)]; so with the phrase "the hearing of faith," Gal. 3:2, 5, which it seems better to understand so than under (c).

## HEART, HEARTILY

### *Old Testament*

***leb*** (3820), "heart; mind; midst." ***leb*** and its synonym ***lebab***, often means the inner person, with a focus on the psychological aspects of the mind and heart, which also includes decision making ability, Gen. 6:5,6. "Heart" may refer to the organ of the body, 2 Sam. 18:14, and can be used of the inner man, i.e., that part of man which thinks, lives, has a personality, and most of all responds to God, Deut. 30:14; cf. Prov. 23:7; Joel 2:13.

The "heart" is regarded as the seat of emotions, Deut. 6:5; for joy, Judg. 16:25; or fear and sorrow, 1 Sam. 4:13, and also as the seat of conscience and moral character, 2 Sam. 24:10. The "heart" is the fountain of man's deeds, 1 Kings 3:6; Isa. 38:3. A "pure heart," Ps. 24:4, can stand in God's presence. God controls the "heart." Because of his natural "heart," man's only hope is in the promise of God, Ezek. 36:26; it can be cleaned, Ps. 51:10; the heart can be tested, Ps. 86:11; yet a man cannot understand his own "heart," Jer. 17:9; it can become hard, Deut. 30:6.

***leb*** may also refer to the inner part or middle of a space, Exod. 15:8; or heaven, Deut. 4:11.

### *New Testament*

***kardia*** (*2588*), "the heart" (Eng., "cardiac," etc.), the chief organ of physical life ("for the life of the flesh is in the blood," Lev. 17:11), occupies the most important place in the human system. By an easy transition the word came to stand for man's entire mental and moral activity, both the rational and the emotional elements. In other words, the heart is used figuratively for the hidden springs of the personal life. The Bible describes human depravity as in the 'heart,' because sin is a principle which has its seat in the center of man's inward life, and then 'defiles' the whole circuit of his action, Matt. 15:19, 20. On the other hand, Scripture regards the heart as the sphere of Divine influence, Rom. 2:15; Acts 15:9. . . . The heart, as lying deep within, contains 'the hidden man,' 1 Pet. 3:4, the real man. It represents the true character but conceals it.

As to its usage in the NT it denotes (a) the seat of physical life, Acts 14:17; Jas. 5:5; (b) the seat of moral nature and spiritual life, the seat of grief, John 14:1; Rom. 9:2; 2 Cor. 2:4; joy, John 16:22; Eph. 5:19; the desires, Matt. 5:28; 2 Pet. 2:14; the affections, Luke 24:32; Acts 21:13; the perceptions, John 12:40; Eph. 4:18; the thoughts, Matt. 9:4; Heb. 4:12; the understanding, Matt. 13:15; Rom. 1:21; the reasoning powers, Mark 2:6; Luke 24:38; the imagination, Luke 1:51; conscience, Acts 2:37; 1 John 3:20; the intentions, Heb. 4:12, cf. 1 Pet. 4:1; purpose, Acts 11:23; 2 Cor. 9:7; the will, Rom. 6:17; Col. 3:15; faith, Mark 11:23; Rom. 10:10; Heb. 3:12.

2. ***psuche*** (*5590*), the soul, or life, is rendered "heart" in Eph. 6:6 (marg., "soul"), "doing the will of God from the heart." In Col. 3:23, a form of the word ***psuche*** preceded by ***ek***, from, lit., "from (the) soul," is rendered "heartily."

### HEART (hardness of)

***sklerokardia*** (*4641*), "hardness of heart" (***skleros***, "hard," and ***kardia***), is used in Matt. 19:8; Mark 10:5; 16:14.

### HEART (knowing the)

***kardiognostes*** (*2589*), "a knower of hearts" (***kardia*** and ***ginosko***, "to know"), is used in Acts 1:24; 15:8.

### HEAVEN, HEAVENLY (-IES)

***Old Testament***

***shamayim*** (8064), "heavens; heaven; sky." First, ***shamayim*** is the usual Hebrew word for the "sky" and the "realm of the sky," where birds fly, Deut. 4:17; or just above the surface of earth, 2 Sam. 18:9; or very high, near God's realm, heaven, 1 Chron. 21:16. Second, this word represents an area farther removed from the earth's surface, the place of the windows of heaven from which precipitation comes, Gen. 8:2; Deut. 28:12. Third, ***shamayim*** also represents the realm in which the sun, moon, and stars are located, Gen. 1:14; Ps. 104:2; Isa. 34:4. Fourth, the phrase "heaven and earth," may denote the entire creation, the totality of the whole, Gen. 1:1. Fifth, "heaven" is the dwelling place of God, Ps. 2:4; cf. Deut. 4:39; 10:14.

***New Testament***

**A. Noun.**

***ouranos*** (*3772*), probably akin to ***ornumi***, "to lift, to heave," is used in the NT (a) of "the aerial heavens," e.g., Matt. 6:26; 8:20; Acts 10:12; 11:6 (RV, "heaven," in each place, KJV, "air"); Jas. 5:18; (b) "the sidereal," e.g., Matt. 24:29, 35; Mark 13:25, 31; Heb. 11:12, RV, "heaven," KJV, "sky"; Rev. 6:14; 20:11; they, (a) and (b), were created by the Son of God, Heb. 1:10, as also by God the Father, Rev. 10:6; (c) "the eternal dwelling place of God," Matt. 5:16; 12:50; Rev. 3:12; 11:13; 16:11; 20:9. From thence the Son of God descended to become incarnate, John 3:13, 31; 6:38, 42. In His ascension Christ "passed through the heavens," Heb. 4:14, RV; He "ascended far above all the heavens," Eph. 4:10, and was "made higher than the heavens," Heb. 7:26; He "sat down on the right hand of the throne of the Majesty in the heavens," Heb. 8:1; He is "on the right hand of God," having gone into heaven, 1 Pet. 3:22. Since His ascension it is the scene of His present life and activity, e.g., Rom. 8:34; Heb. 9:24. From thence the Holy Spirit descended at Pentecost, 1 Pet. 1:12. It is the abode of the angels, e.g., Matt. 18:10; 22:30; cf. Rev. 3:5. Thither Paul was "caught up," whether in the body or out of the body, he knew not, 2 Cor. 12:2. It is to be the eternal dwelling place of the saints in resurrection glory, 2 Cor. 5:1. From thence Christ will descend to the air to receive His saints at the Rapture, 1 Thess. 4:16; Phil. 3:20, 21, and will subsequently come with His saints and with His holy angels at His second advent, Matt. 24:30; 2 Thess. 1:7. In the present life "heaven" is the region of the spiritual Citizenship of believers, Phil. 3:20. The present "heavens," with the earth, are to pass away, 2 Pet. 3:10, "being on fire," v. 12 (see v. 7); Rev. 20:11, and new "heavens" and earth are to be created, 2 Pet. 3:13; Rev. 21:1, with Isa. 65:17.

H

**B. Adjectives.**

1. ***ouranios*** (*3770*), signifying "of heaven, heavenly," corresponding to ***ouranos*** above, is used (a) as an appellation of God the Father, Matt. 6:14, 26, 32, "your heavenly Father"; 15:13, "My heavenly Father"; (b) as descriptive of the holy angels, Luke 2:13; (c) of the vision seen by Paul, Acts 26:19.

2. ***epouranios*** (*2032*), "heavenly," what pertains to, or is in, heaven (***epi***, in the sense of "pertaining to," not here, "above"), has meanings corresponding to some of the meanings of ***ouranos*** above. It is used (a) of God the Father, Matt. 18:35; (b) of the place where Christ "sitteth at the right hand of God" (i.e., in a position of divine authority), Eph. 1:20; and of the present position of believers in relationship to Christ, 2:6; where they possess "every spiritual blessing," 1:3; (c) of Christ as "the Second Man," and all those who are related to Him spiritually, 1 Cor. 15:48; (d) of those whose sphere of activity or existence is above, or in contrast to that of earth, of "principalities and powers," Eph. 3:10; of "spiritual hosts of wickedness," 6:12, RV, "in heavenly places," for KJV, "in high places"; (e) of the Holy Spirit, Heb. 6:4; (f) of "heavenly things," as the subjects of the teaching of Christ, John 3:12, and as consisting of the spiritual and "heavenly" sanctuary and "true tabernacle" and all that appertains thereto in relation to Christ and His sacrifice as antitypical of the earthly tabernacle and sacrifices under the Law, Heb. 8:5; 9:23; (g) of the "calling" of believers, Heb. 3:1; (h) of heaven as the abode of the saints, "a better country" than that of earth, Heb. 11:16, and of the spiritual Jerusalem, 12:22; (i) of the kingdom of Christ in its future manifestation, 2 Tim. 4:18; (j) of all beings and things, animate and inanimate, that are "above the earth," Phil. 2:10; (k) of the resurrection and glorified bodies of believers, 1 Cor. 15:49; (l) of the "heav-

enly orbs," 1 Cor. 15:40 ("celestial," twice, and so rendered here only).

### C. Adverb.

***ouranothen*** (3771), formed from ***ouranos*** above, and denoting "from heaven," is used of (a) the aerial heaven, Acts 14:17; (b) heaven, as the uncreated sphere of God's abode, 26:13.

## HEAVY, HEAVINESS

### A. Noun.

***lupe*** (*3077*), "grief, sorrow," is rendered "heaviness" in the KJV of Rom. 9:2; 2 Cor. 2:1 (RV, "sorrow," in both places).

### B. Verb.

1. ***lupeo*** (*3076*), "to distress, grieve" (akin to ***lupe*** above), is rendered "are in heaviness" in 1 Pet. 1:6, KJV (RV, "have been put to grief"); here, as frequently, it is in the passive voice.

2. ***bareo*** (*916*), always in the passive voice in the NT, is rendered "were heavy" in Matt. 26:43; Mark 14:40; Luke 9:32.

### C. Adjective.

***barus*** (*926*), "heavy" (akin to B, No. 2), is so rendered in Matt. 23:4.

## HEED (to give, to take)

1. ***blepo*** (*991*), "to look," see, usually implying more especially an intent, earnest contemplation, is rendered "take heed" in Matt. 24:4; Mark 4:24; 13:5, 9, 23, 33; Luke 8:18; 21:8; 1 Cor. 3:10; 8:9; 10:12; Gal. 5:15; Col. 2:8 (KJV, "beware"); 4:17; Heb. 3:12.

2. ***horao*** (*3708*), "to see," usually expressing the sense of vision, is rendered "take heed" in Matt. 16:6; 18:10, KJV (RV, "see"); Mark 8:15; Luke 12:15; Acts 22:26 (KJV only).

3. ***prosecho*** (*4337*), lit., "to hold to," signifies "to turn to, turn one's attention to"; hence, "to give heed"; it is rendered "take heed" in Matt. 6:1; Luke 17:3; 21:34; Acts 5:35; 20:28; 2 Pet. 1:19; to give heed to, in Acts 8:6, 10; in v. 11 (KJV, "had regard to"); 16:14 (KJV, "attended unto"); 1 Tim. 1:4; 4:1, 13 (KJV, "give attendance to"); Titus 1:14; Heb. 2:1, lit., "to give heed more earnestly."

4. ***epecho*** (*1907*), lit., "to hold upon," then, "to direct towards, to give attention to," is rendered "gave heed," in Acts 3:5; "take heed," in 1 Tim. 4:16.

## HEIR

### A. Noun.

1. ***kleronomos*** (*2818*) lit. denotes "one who obtains a lot or portion (***kleros***, "a lot," ***nemomai***, "to possess"), especially of an inheritance. The NT usage may be analyzed as under: (a) the person to whom property is to pass on the death of the owner, Matt. 21:38; Mark 12:7; Luke 20:14; Gal. 4:1; (b) one to whom something has been assigned by God, on possession of which, however, he has not yet entered, as Abraham, Rom. 4:13, 14; Heb. 6:17; Christ, Heb. 1:2; the poor saints, Jas. 2:5; (c) believers, inasmuch as they share in the new order of things to be ushered in at the return of Christ, Rom. 8:17; Gal. 3:29; 4:7; Titus 3:7; (d) one who receives something other than by merit, as Noah, Heb. 11:7.

2. ***sunkleronomos*** (*4789*), "a joint-heir, co-inheritor" (***sun***, "with," and No. 1), is used of Isaac and Jacob as participants with Abraham in the promises of God, Heb. 11:9; of husband and wife who are also united in Christ, 1 Pet. 3:7; of Gentiles who believe, as participants in the gospel with Jews who believe, Eph. 3:6; and of all believers as prospective participants with Christ in His glory, as recompense for their participation in His sufferings, Rom. 8:17.

### B. Verb.

***kleronomeo*** (*2816*), "to be an heir to, to inherit" (see A, No. 1), is rendered "shall (not) inherit with" in Gal. 4:30, RV, KJV, "shall (not) be heir with"; in Heb. 1:14, RV, "shall inherit," KJV, "shall be heirs of."

## HELL

1. ***geenna*** (*1067*) represents the Hebrew ***gehinnom*** (the valley of Tophet) and a corresponding Aramaic word; it is found twelve times in the NT, eleven of which are in the Synoptists, in every instance as uttered by the Lord Himself, Matt. 5:22; 18:8, 9; Mark 9:43–47.

## HELMET

***perikephalaia*** (*4030*), from ***peri***, "around," and ***kephale***, "a head," is used figuratively in Eph. 6:17, with reference to salvation, and 1 Thess. 5:8, where it is described as "the hope of salvation."

## HELP, HOLPEN

### *Old Testament*

***'azar*** (5826), "to help, assist, aid." Help or aid comes from a variety of sources: Thirty-two kings "helped" Ben-hadad, 1 Kings 20:6; one city "helps" another, Josh. 10:33; even false gods are believed to be of "help," 2 Chron. 28:23. Of course, the greatest source of help is God Himself; He is "the helper of the fatherless," Ps. 10:14. God promises: "I will help thee," Isa. 41:10; "and the Lord shall help them, and deliver them . . . ," Ps. 37:40.

### *New Testament*

**A. Nouns.**

1. ***antilepsis*** or ***antilempsis*** (*484*) properly signifies "a laying hold of, an exchange" (***anti***, "in exchange," or, in its local sense, "in front," and ***lambano***, "to take, lay hold of," so as to support); then, "a help" (akin to B, No. 1); it is mentioned in 1 Cor. 12:28, as one of the ministrations in the local church, by way of rendering assistance, perhaps especially of "help" ministered to the weak and needy. So Theophylact defines the injunction in 1 Thess. 5:14, "support the weak"; cf. Acts 20:35.

2. ***boetheia*** (*996*), from ***boe***, "a shout," and ***theo***, "to run," denotes "help, succour," Heb. 4:16, lit., "(grace) unto (timely) help"; in Acts 27:17, where the plural is used, the term is nautical, "frapping."

3. ***epikouria*** (*1947*) strictly denotes such aid as is rendered by an ***epikouros***, "an ally, an auxiliary"; Paul uses it in his testimony to Agrippa, "having therefore obtained the help that is from God," Acts 26:22, RV.

**B. Verbs.**

1. ***antilambano*** (*482*), lit., "to take instead of, or in turn" (akin to A, No. 1), is used in the middle voice, and rendered "He hath holpen" in Luke 1:54; "to help," RV, "to support," KJV, in Acts 20:35; its other meaning, "to partake of," is used of partaking of things, 1 Tim. 6:2, "that partake of," for KJV, "partakers of."

2. ***sullambano*** (*4815*), "to assist, take part with" (***sun***, "with," and ***lambano***), is used, in the middle voice, of rendering help in what others are doing, Luke 5:7, of bringing in a catch of fish; in Phil. 4:3, in an appeal to Synzygus ("yokefellow") to help Euodia and Syntyche (v. 2).

3. ***sunantizambano*** (*4878*) signifies "to lake hold with at the side for assistance" (***sun***, "with," and No. 1); hence, "to take a share in, help in bearing, to help in general." It is used, in the middle voice in Martha's request to the Lord to bid her sister help her, Luke 10:40; and of the ministry of the Holy Spirit in helping our infirmities, Rom. 8:26.

4. ***boetheo*** (*997*), "to come to the aid of anyone, to succour" (akin to A, No. 2), is used in Matt. 15:25; Mark 9:22, 24; Acts 16:9; 21:28; 2 Cor. 6:2, "did I succour"; Heb. 2:18, "to succour"; Rev. 12:16.

5. ***sumballo*** (*4820*), lit., "to throw together" (***sun***, "with," ***ballo***, "to throw"), is used in the middle voice in Acts 18:27, of helping or benefiting believers by discussion or ministry of the Word of God.

6. ***sunupourgeo*** (*4943*) denotes "to help together," 2 Cor. 1:11.

7. ***sunergeo*** (*4903*), "to help in work, to cooperate, be a co-worker," is rendered "that helpeth with" in 1 Cor. 16:16.

## HELPER, FELLOW-HELPER

1. ***boethos*** (*998*), an adjective, akin to A, No. 2, and B, No. 4, under HELP, signifying "helping," is used as a noun in Heb. 13:6, of God as the helper of His saints.

2. ***sunergos*** (*4904*), an adjective, akin to B, No. 7, under HELP, "a fellow worker," is translated "helper" in the KJV of Rom. 16:3, 9; 2 Cor. 1:24, "helpers"; in 2 Cor. 8:23, KJV, "fellow helper; so the plural in 3 John 8.

## HERESY

***hairesis*** (*139*) denotes "a choosing, choice" (from ***haireomai***, "to choose"); then came to mean in NT, "a sect" that leads to divisions, Acts 5:17; 15:5; 24:5, 14; 26:5; 28:22; "heresies" in 1 Cor. 11:19.

## HERETICAL

***hairetikos*** (*141*), akin to the above, primarily denotes "capable of choosing" (***haireomai***); hence, "causing division by a party spirit, factious," Titus 3:10, RV, "heretical."

## HERITAGE

***kleroo*** (*2820*), primarily, "to cast lots" or "to choose by lot," then, "to assign a portion," is used in the passive voice in Eph. 1:11, "we were made a heritage."

## HERO

**A. Nouns.**

***gibbor*** (1368), "mighty one." In the context of battle, the word is better understood to refer to the category of proven, effective, warriors, Josh. 1:14; 2 Sam. 23. The phrase ***gibbor chayil*** may also refer to a man of a high social class, the landed man who had military responsibilities, such as Saul, 1 Sam. 9:1.

The king symbolized the strength of his kingdom. He had to lead his troops in battle, and as commander he was expected to be a "hero." Early in David's life, he was recognized as a "hero," 1 Sam. 18:7; so also of God, Ps. 45:3; or Messiah, Isa. 9:6.

Israel's God was a mighty God, Isa. 10:21. He had the power to deliver, Zeph. 3:17.

***geber*** (181), "man," i.e., an adult male, 1 Chron. 23:3.

**B. Verb.**

***gabar*** (1396), "to be strong," Job 21:7.

**C. Adjective.**

***gibbor*** (1368), "strong," often referring to physical strength or prowess, 1 Sam. 14:52; lion, Prov. 30:30; hunter, Gen. 10:9; unique race, Gen. 6:1–4.

## HIDE, HID, HIDDEN

### *Old Testament*

***satar*** (5641), "to conceal, hide, shelter." ***satar*** has the sense of "separation," in some passages, Gen. 31:49; or take refuge, 1 Sam. 23:19; or shelter from danger, Jer. 36:26.

### *New Testament*

**A. Verbs.**

1. ***krupto*** *(2928)*, "to cover, conceal, keep secret" (Eng., "crypt," "cryptic," etc.), is used (a) in its physical significance, e.g., Matt. 5:14; 13:44; 25:18 (some mss. have No. 2); (b) metaphorically, e.g., Matt. 11:25 (some mss. have No. 2 here); 13:35, RV, "(things) hidden"; KJV, "(things) which have been kept secret"; Luke 18:34; 19:42; John 19:38, "secretly."

2. ***apokrupto*** *(613)*, "to conceal from, to keep secret" (***apo***, "from," and No. 1), is used metaphorically, in Luke 10:21, of truths "hidden" from the wise and prudent and revealed to babes; 1 Cor. 2:7, of God's wisdom; Eph. 3:9, of the mystery of the unsearchable riches of Christ, revealed through the gospel; Col. 1:26, of the mystery associated with the preceding.

3. ***enkrupto*** *(1470)*, "to hide in anything" (***en***, "in," and No. 1), is used in Matt. 13:33, of leaven "hidden" in meal.

4. ***perikrupto*** *(4032)* signifies "to hide by placing something around, to conceal entirely, to keep hidden" (***peri***, "around," used intensively, and No. 1), Luke 1:24.

**B. Adjectives.**

1. ***kruptos*** *(2927)*, akin to A, No. 1, "hidden, secret," is translated "hid" in Matt. 10:26; Mark 4:22; Luke 8:17, RV, for KJV, "secret"; 12:2 (last part); in 1 Cor. 4:5, "hidden (things of darkness)"; 2 Cor. 4:2, "hidden (things of shame)"; 1 Pet. 3:4, "hidden (man of the heart)."

2. ***apokruphos*** *(614)*, "hidden away from" (corresponding to A, No. 2; cf. Eng., "apocryphal"), is translated, "made (KJV, kept) secret," in Mark 4:22; in Luke 8:17, RV, "secret," for KJV, "hid"; in Col. 2:3, RV, "hidden," KJV, "hid."

## HIGH (from on, most), HIGHLY

### *Old Testament*

**A. Adjective.**

***gaboah*** (1364), "high; exalted." This word means "lofty, tall in dimension," Gen. 7:19; of a man's height, 1 Sam. 9:2; cf. 16:7; of horns, Dan. 8:2. The word also means "high or exalted in station," and so have much recognition or status, Ezek. 21:26; Eccl. 5:8. ***gaboah*** may be used self-exaltation, or "haughtiness," 1 Sam. 2:3.

***'elyon*** (5945), "high; top; uppermost; highest; upper; height." This word indicates the "uppermost" (as opposed to the lower) of a spacial position, an elevation, Gen. 40:16–17; Ezek. 42:5. A figurative use of the word appears in 2 Chron. 7:21, where it modifies the dynasty (house) of Solomon. The messianic Davidic king will be God's firstborn, "higher than the kings of the earth," Ps. 89:27. This word is frequently used in a name ***el 'elyon*** of God; it describes Him as the Most High, the "highest" and only Supreme Being. The emphasis here is on divine supremacy, Gen. 14:18.

Also the figurative use of ***'elyon*** to describe the "house" or dynasty of Israel takes an unusual turn in 1 Kings 9:8, where the kingdom is said to be the "height" of astonishment.

**B. Verb.**

***gabah*** (1362), "to be high, exalted, lofty." This verb, which occurs 38 times in the Bible, has cognates in Akkadian, Aramaic, and Arabic. Its meanings parallel those of the adjective. It may mean "to be high, lofty." In this sense, it is used of trees, Ezek. 19:11, the heavens, Job 35:5, and a man, 1 Sam. 10:23. It may mean "to be exalted" in dignity and honor, Job 36:7. Or it may simply mean "to be lofty," used in the positive sense of "being encouraged," 2 Chron. 17:6, or in the negative sense of "being haughty or proud," 2 Chron. 26:16.

**C. Noun.**

***gobah*** (1363), "height; exaltation; grandeur; haughtiness; pride." This noun, which occurs 17 times in biblical Hebrew, refers to the "height" of things, 2 Chron. 3:4; exaltation, Job 40:10; haughtiness or pride, 2 Chron. 32:26.

### *New Testament*

**A. Adjectives.**

1. ***hupselos*** *(5308)*, "high, lofty," is used (a) naturally, of mountains, Matt. 4:8; 17:1; Mark 9:2; Rev. 21:10; of a wall, Rev. 21:12; (b) figuratively, of the arm of God, Acts 13:17; of heaven, "on high," plural, lit., "in high (places)," Heb. 1:3; (c) metaphorically, Luke

16:15, RV, "exalted" (KJV, "highly esteemed"); Rom. 11:20, in the best texts, "high-minded" [lit., "mind (not) high things"]; 12:16.

2. ***hupsistos*** (*5310*), "most high," is a superlative degree, the positive not being in use; it is used of God in Luke 1:32, 35, 76; 6:35, in each of which the RV has "the most High," for KJV, "the highest," KJV and RV in Mark 5:7; Luke 8:28; Acts 7:48; 16:17; Heb. 7:1.

**B. Nouns.**

1. ***hupsos*** (*5311*), "height," is used with ***ex*** (***ek***) "from," in the phrase "on high," Luke 1:78; 24:49; with ***eis***, "in" or "into," Eph. 4:8.

2. ***hupsoma*** (*5313*), "high thing," 2 Cor. 10:5; in Rom. 8:39, "height."

## HIGH PLACE

***bamah*** (1116), "high place." ***bamah*** is a pagan worship center, often in a geographically elevated spot, an evil place to be destroyed, Lev. 26:30. Not every literal ***bamah*** was a cultic high place; the word may simply refer to a geographically elevated place, with no denotation of a worship center, Amos 4:13; Mic. 3:12. Before the temple was built, Solomon worshiped the Lord at the great ***bamah*** of Gideon, 1 Kings 3:4. This was permissible until the temple was constructed; however, history demonstrates that Israel soon adopted these "high places" for pagan customs. The ***bamah*** was found in the cities of Samaria, 2 Kings 23:19, in the cities of Judah, 2 Chron. 21:11, and even in Jerusalem, 2 Kings 23:13. The ***bamah*** was a place of cult prostitution, Amos 2:7–8.

## HIGH-MINDED

1. ***tuphoo*** (*5187*) properly means "to wrap in smoke" (from ***tuphos***, "smoke"; metaphorically, for "conceit"); it is used in the passive voice, metaphorically in 1 Tim. 3:6, "puffed up," RV (KJV, "lifted up with pride"); so 6:4, KJV, "proud," and 2 Tim. 3:4, KJV, "highminded."

2. ***hupselophroneo*** (*5309*), "to be highminded," is used in 1 Tim. 6:17.

## HINDER, HINDRANCE

**Verbs.**

1. ***enkopto*** (*1465*), lit., "to cut into" (***en***, "in," ***kopto***, "to cut"), was used of "impeding" persons by breaking up the road, or by placing an obstacle sharply in the path; hence, metaphorically, of "detaining" a person unnecessarily, Acts 24:4, of "hindrances" in the way of reaching others, Rom. 15:22; or returning to them, 1 Thess. 2:18; of "hindering" progress in the Christian life, Gal. 5:7.

2. ***koluo*** (*2967*), "to hinder, forbid, restrain," is translated "to hinder" in Luke 11:52; Acts 8:36; Rom. 1:13, RV (KJV, "was let"); Heb. 7:23, RV (KJV, "were not suffered").

3. ***diakoluo*** (*1254*), a strengthened form of No. 2, "to hinder thoroughly," is used in Matt. 3:14, of John the Baptist's endeavor to "hinder" Christ from being baptized, KJV, "forbad," RV, "would have hindered," lit., "was hindering."

## HIRED SERVANT, HIRELING

1. ***misthotos*** (*3411*), an adjective denoting "hired," is used as a noun, signifying "one who is hired," "hired servants," Mark 1:20; "hireling," John 10:12, 13; here, it expresses, not only one who has no real interest in his duty (that may or may not be present in its use in Mark 1:20, and in ***misthios***, No. 2), but one who is unfaithful in the discharge of it; that sense attaches always to the word rendered "hireling."

2. ***misthios*** (*3407*), an adjective, akin to No. 1, and similarly signifying "a hired servant," is used in Luke 15:17, 19 (in some texts, v. 21).

## HOLINESS, HOLY, HOLILY

### *Old Testament*

**A. Adjective.**

***qadosh*** (6918), "holy." In the Old Testament ***qadosh*** has a strongly religious connotation. In one sense the word describes an object or place or day to be "holy" with the meaning of "devoted" or "dedicated" to a particular purpose, Num. 5:17. Particularly the sabbath day is "devoted" as a day of rest, Isa. 58:13–14.

God has dedicated Israel as His people. They are "holy" by their relationship to the "holy" God. All of the people are in a sense "holy," as members of the covenant community, irrespective of their faith and obedience, Num. 16:3. God's intent was to use this "holy" nation as a "holy," royal priesthood amongst the nations, Exod. 19:6. The priests were chosen to officiate at the Holy Place of the tabernacle/temple. Because of their function as intermediaries between God and Israel and because of their proximity to the temple, they were dedicated by God to the office of priest, with instructions for a holy life, Lev. 21:6–8; Ps. 106:16.

The Old Testament clearly and emphatically teaches that God is "holy." He is "the Holy One of Israel," Isa. 1:4, the "holy God," Isa. 5:16, and "the Holy One," Isa. 40:25. His name is "Holy," 1 Sam. 2:2; Zech. 14:5, cf. Isa. 6:3.

## B. Verb.

***qadesh*** (6942), or ***qadash*** (6942), "to be holy; to sanctify," Exod. 29:37; Lev. 6:18; 2 Chron. 29:5.

## C. Nouns.

***qodesh*** (6944), "holiness; holy thing; sanctuary"; "holiness," Exod. 15:11; "holy thing," Num. 4:15; and "sanctuary," Exod. 36:4.

Another noun, ***qadesh***, means "temple-prostitute" or "sodomite," with a focus on one set apart (here negatively) for a special purpose, Deut. 23:17.

### *NewTestament*

## A. Nouns.

1. ***hagiasmos*** (*38*), translated "holiness" in the KJV of Rom. 6:19, 22; 1 Thess. 4:7; 1 Tim. 2:15; Heb. 12:14, is always rendered "sanctification" in the RV. It signifies (a) separation to God, 1 Cor. 1:30; 2 Thess. 2:13; 1 Pet. 1:2; (b) the resultant state, the conduct befitting those so separated, 1 Thess. 4:3, 4, 7, and the four other places mentioned above.

2. ***hagiosune*** (*42*) denotes the manifestation of the quality of "holiness" in personal conduct; (a) it is used in Rom. 1:4, of the absolute "holiness" of Christ in the days of His flesh, which distinguished Him from all merely human beings; this (which is indicated in the phrase "the spirit of holiness") and (in vindication of it) His resurrection from the dead, marked Him out as (He was "declared to be") the Son of God; (b) believers are to be "perfecting holiness in the fear of God," 2 Cor. 7:1, i.e., bringing "holiness" to its predestined end, whereby (c) they may be found "unblameable in holiness" in the Parousia of Christ, 1 Thess. 3:13.

3. ***hagiotes*** (*41*), "sanctity," the abstract quality of "holiness," is used (a) of God, Heb. 12:10; (b) of the manifestation of it in the conduct of the apostle Paul and his fellowlaborers, 2 Cor. 1:12.

4. ***hosiotes*** (*3742*) is to be distinguished from No. 3, as denoting that quality of "holiness" which is manifested in those who have regard equally to grace and truth; it involves a right relation to God; it is used in Luke 1:75 and Eph. 4:24, and in each place is associated with righteousness.

## B. Adjectives.

1. ***hagios*** (*40*), akin to A, Nos. 1 and 2, which are from the same root as ***hagnos*** (found in ***hazo***, "to venerate"), fundamentally signifies "separated" (among the Greeks, dedicated to the gods), and hence, in Scripture in its moral and spiritual significance, separated from sin and therefore consecrated to God, sacred.

(a) It is predicated of God (as the absolutely "Holy" One, in His purity, majesty and glory): of the Father, e.g., Luke 1:49; John 17:11; 1 Pet. 1:15, 16; Rev. 4:8; 6:10; of the Son, e.g., Luke 1:35; Acts 3:14; 4:27, 30; 1 John 2:20; of the Spirit, e.g., Matt. 1:18 and frequently in all the Gospels, Acts, Romans, 1 and 2 Cor., Eph., 1 Thess.; also in 2 Tim. 1:14; Titus 3:5; 1 Pet. 1:12; 2 Pet. 1:21; Jude 20.

(b) It is used of men and things (see below) in so far as they are devoted to God. Indeed the quality, as attributed to God, is often presented in a way which involves divine demands upon the conduct of believers. These are called ***hagioi***, "saints," i.e., "sanctified" or "holy" ones.

This sainthood is not an attainment, it is a state into which God in grace calls men; yet believers are called to sanctify themselves (consistently with their calling, 2 Tim. 1:9), cleansing themselves from all defilement, forsaking sin, living a "holy" manner of life, 1 Pet. 1:15; 2 Pet. 3:11, and experiencing fellowship with God in His holiness. The saints are thus figuratively spoken of as "a holy temple," 1 Cor. 3:17 (a local church); Eph. 2:21 (the whole Church), cf. 5:27; "a holy priesthood," 1 Pet. 2:5; "a holy nation," 2:9.

The adjective is also used of the outer part of the tabernacle, Heb. 9:2 (RV, "the holy place"); of the inner sanctuary, 9:3, RV, "the Holy of Holies"; 9:4, "a holy place," RV; v. 25 (plural), of the presence of God in heaven, where there are not two compartments as in the tabernacle, all being "the holy place"; 9:8, 12 (neuter plural); 10:19, "the holy place," RV (KJV, "the holiest," neut. plural); of the city of Jerusalem, Rev. 11:2; its temple, Acts 6:13; of the faith, Jude 20; of the greetings of saints, 1 Cor. 16:20; of angels, e.g., Mark 8:38; of apostles and prophets, Eph. 3:5; of the future heavenly Jerusalem, Rev. 21:2, 10; 22:19.

2. ***hosios*** (*3741*), akin to A, No. 4, signifies "religiously right, holy," as opposed to what is unrighteous or polluted. It is commonly associated with righteousness (see A, No. 4). It is used of God, Rev. 15:4; 16:5; and of the body of the Lord Jesus, Acts 2:27; 13:35, citations from Ps. 16:10.

## C. Adverb.

***hosios*** (*3743*), akin to A, No. 4, and B, No. 2, "holily," i.e., pure from evil conduct, and observant of God's will, is used in 1 Thess. 2:10, of the conduct of the apostle and his fellow missionaries.

**D. Verb.**

***hagiazo*** (*37*), "to hallow, sanctify," in the passive voice, "to be made holy, be sanctified," is translated "let him be made holy" in Rev. 22:11, the aorist or point tense expressing the definiteness and completeness of the divine act; elsewhere it is rendered by the verb "to sanctify."

## HONEST, HONESTLY, HONESTY

**A. Adjective.**

***kalos*** (*2570*), "good, admirable, becoming," has also the ethical meaning of what is "fair, right, honorable, of such conduct as deserves esteem"; it is translated "honest" [cf. Latin *honestus* (from *honos*, "honor")], which has the same double meaning as "honest" in the KJV, namely, regarded with honor, honorable, and bringing honor, becoming; in Luke 8:15 (KJV, and RV), "an honest and good (***agathos***) heart"; Rom. 12:17; 2 Cor. 8:21 and 13:7, RV, "honorable" (KJV, "honest"), of things which are regarded with esteem; in 1 Pet. 2:12, of behavior, RV, "seemly," KJV, "honest" (i.e., becoming).

**B. Adverbs.**

1. ***kalos*** (*2573*), corresponding to A, ***kalos*** above, is used in Heb. 13:18, "honestly," i.e., honorably.

2. ***euschemonos*** (*2156*), "becomingly, decently," is rendered "honestly" in Rom. 13:13, where it is set in contrast with the confusion of gentile social life, and in 1 Thess. 4:12, of the manner of life of believers as a witness to "them that are without"; in 1 Cor. 14:40, "decently," in contrast with confusion in the churches.

**C. Noun.**

***semnotes*** (*4587*) denotes "gravity, dignified seriousness"; it is rendered "honesty" in the KJV of 1 Tim. 2:2, RV, "gravity."

## HONOR (Noun and Verb)

### *Old Testament*

**A. Verbs.**

***kabed*** (3513), "to honor," i.e., give high praise and status to another, in word and deed, Deut. 5:16.

***hadar*** (1921), "to honor, prefer, exalt oneself, behave arrogantly"; honor, Exod. 23:3; to behave arrogantly, Prov. 25:6.

**B. Nouns.**

***kabod*** (3519), "honor; glory; great quantity; multitude; wealth; reputation [majesty]; splendor." ***kabod*** refers to the great physical weight or "quantity" of a thing, Nah. 2:9. ***kabod*** often refers to both "wealth" and significant and positive "reputation"; wealth, Gen. 31:1; majesty, 45:13. So also in Ps. 85:9 is the idea of richness or abundance.

***kabod*** can also have an abstract emphasis of "glory." When used in the sense of "honor" or "importance," cf. Gen. 45:13, there are two nuances of the word. First, ***kabod*** can emphasize the position of an individual within the sphere in which he lives, Prov. 11:16. This "honor" can be lost through wrong actions or attitudes, Prov. 26:1, 8 and evidenced in proper actions, Prov. 20:3; 25:2. This emphasis then is on a relationship between personalities. Second, there is a suggestion of nobility in many uses of the word, such as "honor" that belongs to a royal family, 1 Kings 3:13. Thus, ***kabod*** can be used of the social distinction and position of respect enjoyed by nobility.

When applied to God, the word represents a quality corresponding to Him and by which He is recognized. Joshua commanded Achan to give glory to God, to recognize His importance, worth, and significance, Josh. 7:19. In this and similar instances "giving honor" refers to saying something; what Achan was to do was to tell the truth. In other passages giving honor to God is a cultic recognition and confession of God as God, Ps. 29:1.

***hadar*** (1926), "honor; splendor." First, ***hadar*** refers to "splendor" in nature," Lev. 23:40. Second, this word is a counterpart to Hebrew words for "glory" and "dignity." Thus ***hadar*** means not so much overwhelming beauty as a combination of physical attractiveness and social position. The Messiah is said to have "no form nor [majesty]; and when we shall see him, there is no beauty that we should desire him," Isa. 53:2. Mankind is crowned with "glory and honor" in the sense of superior desirability (for God) and rank, Ps. 8:5. In the case of earthly kings their beauty or brilliance usually arises from their surroundings, Ezek. 27:10–11.

The noun ***hadarah*** means "majesty; splendor; exaltation; adornment," Ps. 29:2.

**C. Adjective.**

***kabed*** (3515), "heavy; numerous; severe; rich." The adjective ***kabed*** occurs about 40 times. Basically this adjective connotes "heavy." In Exod. 17:12 the word is used of physical weight: "But Moses' hands were heavy; and they took a stone, and put it under him, and he sat thereon; and Aaron and Hur stayed up his hands. . . ." This adjective bears the connotation of heaviness as an enduring, ever-present quality, a lasting thing, Ps. 38:4. A task can be described as "heavy," Exod. 18:18.

Moses argued his inability to lead God's people out of Egypt because he was "slow of speech, and of a slow tongue"; his speech or tongue was not smooth-flowing but halting, Exod. 4:10. Another nuance of this word appears in Exod. 7:14, where it is applied to Pharaoh's refusing heart.

A second series of passages uses this word of something that falls upon or overcomes one. So God sent upon Egypt a "heavy" hail, Exod. 9:18, a "great" swarm of insects, 8:24, "numerous" locusts, and a "severe" pestilence, 9:3. The first appearance of the word belongs to this category: "the famine was [severe] in the land" of Egypt, Gen. 12:10.

Used with a positive connotation, ***kabed*** can describe the amount of "riches," Gen. 13:2; or a collection of persons, Gen. 50:9.

### *New Testament*

### A. Noun.

***time*** (*5092*), primarily "a valuing," hence, objectively, (a) "a price paid or received," e.g., Matt. 27:6, 9; Acts 4:34; 5:2, 3; 7:16, RV, "price" (KJV, "sum"); 19:19; 1 Cor. 6:20; 7:23; (b) of "the preciousness of Christ" unto believers, 1 Pet. 2:7, RV, i.e., the honor and inestimable value of Christ as appropriated by believers, who are joined, as living stones, to Him the cornerstone; (c) in the sense of value, of human ordinances, valueless against the indulgence of the flesh, or, perhaps of no value in attempts at asceticism, Col. 2:23; (d) "honor, esteem," (1) used in ascriptions of worship to God, 1 Tim. 1:17; 6:16; Rev. 4:9, 11; 5:13; 7:12; to Christ, 5:12, 13; (2) bestowed upon Christ by the Father, Heb. 2:9; 2 Pet. 1:17; (3) bestowed upon man, Heb. 2:7; (4) bestowed upon Aaronic priests, Heb. 5:4; (5) to be the reward hereafter of "the proof of faith" on the part of tried saints, 1 Pet. 1:7, RV; (6) used of the believer who as a vessel is "meet for the Master's use," 2 Tim. 2:21; (7) to be the reward of patience in well-doing, Rom. 2:7, and of working good (a perfect life to which man cannot attain, so as to be justified before God thereby), 2:10; (8) to be given to all to whom it is due, Rom. 13:7 (see 1 Pet. 2:17, under B, below); (9) as an advantage to be given by believers one to another instead of claiming it for self, Rom. 12:10; (10) to be given to elders that rule well ("double honor"), 1 Tim. 5:17 (here the meaning may be an honorarium); (11) to be given by servants to their master, 1 Tim. 6:1; (12) to be given to wives by husbands, 1 Pet. 3:7; (13) said of the husband's use of the wife, in contrast to the exercise of the passion of lust, 1 Thess. 4:4 (some regard the "vessel" here as the believer's body); (14) of that bestowed upon; parts of the body, 1 Cor. 12:23, 24; (15) of that which belongs to the builder of a house in contrast to the house itself, Heb. 3:3; (16) of that which is not enjoyed by a prophet in his own country, John 4:44; (17) of that bestowed by the inhabitants of Melita upon Paul and his fellow-passengers, in gratitude for his benefits of healing, Acts 28:10; (18) of the festive honor to be possessed by nations, and brought into the Holy City, the heavenly Jerusalem, Rev. 21:26 (in some mss., v. 24); (19) of honor bestowed upon things inanimate, a potter's vessel, Rom. 9:21; 2 Tim. 2:20.

### B. Verb.

***timao*** (*5091*), "to honor" (akin to A, above), is used of (a) valuing Christ at a price, Matt. 27:9, cf. A, above, (a); (b) "honoring" a person: (1) the "honor" done by Christ to the Father, John 8:49; (2) "honor" bestowed by the Father upon him who serves Christ, John 12:26; (3) the duty of all to "honor" the Son equally with the Father, 5:23; (4) the duty of children to "honor" their parents, Matt. 15:4; 19:19; Mark 7:10; 10:19; Luke 18:20; Eph. 6:2; (5) the duty of Christians to "honor" the king, and all men, 1 Pet. 2:17; (6) the respect and material assistance to be given to widows "that are widows indeed," 1 Tim. 5:3; (7) the "honor" done to Paul and his companions by the inhabitants of Melita, Acts 28:10; (8) mere lip profession of "honor" to God, Matt. 15:8: Mark 7:6.

## HONORABLE, WITHOUT HONOR

1. ***endoxos*** (*1741*) denotes (a) "held in honor," "of high repute," 1 Cor. 4:10, KJV "(are) honorable," RV, "(have) glory," in contrast to ***atimos***, "without honor."

2. ***entimos*** (*1784*), lit., "in honor," is used of the centurion's servant in Luke 7:2. "dear" (RV marg., "precious . . . or honorable"): of self-sacrificing servants of the Lord, said of Epaphroditus, Phil. 2:29, RV "(hold such) in honor" (KJV, "in reputation"; marg., "honor such"); of Christ, as a precious stone, 1 Pet. 2:4, 6 (RV marg., "honorable").

3. ***euschemon*** (*2158*) signifies "elegant, comely, of honorable position," KJV, "honorable," RV, "of honorable estate," Mark 15:43; Acts 13:50; 17:12; for other renderings in 1 Cor. 7:35 and 12:24.

4. ***timios*** (*5093*), "precious, valuable, honorable" (akin to ***time***, "honor"; see No. 2), is used of marriage in Heb. 13:4, KJV, as a statement, "(marriage) is honorable (in all)," RV, as an exhortation, "let (marriage) be had in honor (among all)."

5. ***kalos*** (*2570*), "good, fair," is translated "honorable" in Rom. 12:17; 2 Cor. 8:21; 13:7, RV (KJV, "honest").

## HOPE (Noun and Verb), HOPE (for)

### A. Noun.

***elpis*** (*1680*), in the NT, "favorable and confident expectation." It has to do with the unseen and the future, Rom. 8:24, 25. "Hope" describes (a) the happy anticipation of good (the most frequent significance), e.g., Titus 1:2; 1 Pet. 1:21; (b) the ground upon which "hope" is based, Acts 16:19; Col. 1:27, "Christ in you the hope of glory"; (c) the object upon which the "hope" is fixed, e.g., 1 Tim. 1:1.

Various phrases are used with the word "hope," in Paul's epistles and speeches: (1) Acts 23:6, "the hope and resurrection of the dead"; this has been regarded as a hendiadys (one by means of two), i.e., the "hope" of the resurrection; but the ***kai***, "and," is epexegetic, defining the "hope," namely, the resurrection; (2) Acts 26:6, 7, "the hope of the promise (i.e., the fulfillment of the promise) made unto the fathers"; (3) Gal. 5:5, "the hope of righteousness"; i.e., the believer's complete conformity to God's will, at the coming of Christ; (4) Col. 1:23, "the hope of the Gospel," i.e., the "hope" of the fulfillment of all the promises presented in the gospel; cf. 1:5; (5) Rom. 5:2, "(the) hope of the glory of God," i.e., as in Titus 2:13, "the blessed hope and appearing of the glory of our great God and Savior Jesus Christ"; cf. Col. 1:27; (6) 1 Thess. 5:8, "the hope of salvation," i.e., of the rapture of believers, to take place at the opening of the Parousia of Christ; (7) Eph. 1:18, "the hope of His (God's) calling," i.e., the prospect before those who respond to His call in the gospel; (8) Eph. 4:4, "the hope of your calling," the same as (7), but regarded from the point of view of the called; (9) Titus 1:2, and 3:7, "the hope of eternal life," i.e., the full manifestation and realization of that life which is already the believer's possession; (10) Acts 28:20, "the hope of Israel," i.e., the expectation of the coming of the Messiah.

In Rom. 15:13 God is spoken of as "the God of hope," i.e., He is the author, not the subject, of it. "Hope" is a factor in salvation, Rom. 8:24; it finds its expression in endurance under trial, which is the effect of waiting for the coming of Christ, 1 Thess. 1:3; it is "an anchor of the soul," staying it amidst the storms of this life, Heb. 6:18, 19; it is a purifying power, "every one that hath this hope set on Him (Christ) purifieth himself, even as He is pure," 1 John 3:3, RV (the apostle John's one mention of "hope").

### B. Verbs.

1. ***elpizo*** (*1679*), "to hope," is not infrequently translated in the KJV, by the verb "to trust"; the RV adheres to some form of the verb "to hope," e.g., John 5:45, "Moses, on whom ye have set your hope"; 2 Cor. 1:10, "on whom we have set our hope"; so in 1 Tim. 4:10; 5:5; 6:17; see also, e.g., Matt. 12:21; Luke 24:21; Rom. 15:12, 24.

The verb is followed by three prepositions: (1) ***eis***, rendered "on" in John 5:45 (as above); the meaning is really "in" as in 1 Pet. 3:5, "who hoped in God"; the "hope" is thus said to be directed to, and to center in, a person; (2) ***epi***, "on," Rom. 15:12, "On Him shall the Gentiles hope," RV; so 1 Tim. 4:10; 5:5 (in the best mss.); 6:17, RV; this expresses the ground upon which "hope" rests; (3) ***en***, "in," 1 Cor. 15:19, "we have hoped in Christ," RV, more lit., "we are (men) that have hoped in Christ," the preposition expresses that Christ is not simply the ground upon whom, but the sphere and element in whom, the "hope" is placed. The form of the verb (the perfect participle with the verb to be, lit., "are having hoped") stresses the character of those who "hope," more than the action; "hope" characterizes them, showing what sort of persons they are.

2. ***proelpizo*** (*4276*), "to hope before" (***pro***, "before," and No. 1), is found in Eph. 1:12.

3. ***apelpizo*** (*560*), lit., "to hope from," Luke 6:35.

## HORN

***keras*** (*2768*), "a horn," is used in the plural, as the symbol of strength, (a) in the apocalyptic visions; (1) on the head of the Lamb as symbolic of Christ, Rev. 5:6; (2) on the heads of beasts as symbolic of national potentates, Rev. 12:3; 13:1, 11; 17:3, 7, 12, 16 (cf. Dan. 7:8; 8:9; Zech. 1:18, etc.); (3) at the corners of the golden altar, Rev. 9:13 (cf. Exod. 30:2; the horns were of one piece with the altar, as in the case of the brazen altar, 27:2, and were emblematic of the efficacy of the ministry connected with it); (b) metaphorically, in the singular, "a horn of salvation," Luke 1:69.

## HORSE

***hippos*** (*2462*), apart from the fifteen occurrences in the Apocalypse, occurs only in Jas. 3:3; in the Apocalypse "horses" are seen in visions in 6:2, 4, 5, 8; 9:7, 9, 17 (twice); 14:20; 19:11, 14, 19, 21; otherwise in 18:13; 19:18.

## HOSANNA

***hosanna*** (*5614*), in the Hebrew, means "save, we pray." The word seems to have become an utterance of praise rather than of prayer, though originally, probably, a cry for help. The people's cry at the Lord's triumphal entry into Jerusalem (Matt. 21:9, 15; Mark 11:9, 10; John

12:13) was taken from Ps. 118, which was recited at the Feast of Tabernacles in the great Hallel (Psalms 113 to 118).

## HOSPITALITY

**A. Noun.**

***philoxenia*** (*5381*), "love of strangers" (***philos***, "loving," ***xenos***, "a stranger"), is used in Rom. 12:13; Heb. 13:2, lit. "(be not forgetful of) hospitality.

**B. Adjective.**

***philoxenos*** (*5382*), "hospitable," occurs in 1 Tim. 3:2; Titus 1:8; 1 Pet. 4:9.

## HOST (of angels, etc.)

### *Old Testament*

**A. Noun.**

***tsaba'*** (6633), "host; military service; war; army; service; labor; forced labor; conflict." This word involves several interrelated ideas: a group; impetus; difficulty; and force. These ideas undergird the general concept of "service" which one does for or under a superior rather than for himself. ***tsaba'*** is usually applied to "military service" but is sometimes used of "work" in general (under or for a superior). In Num. 1:2–3 the word means "military service." Num. 31:14 uses ***tsaba'*** of the actual battling itself. The word can also represent an "army," Num. 31:48. In Num. 1, 2, and 10, where ***tsaba'*** occurs with regard to a census of Israel, it is possibly suggested that this was a military census by which God organized His "army" to march through the wilderness.

That ***tsaba'*** can refer to a "group" for any purpose, Ps. 68:11; of stars, Zeph. 1:5; Deut. 4:19; or angels, 1 Kings 22:19; Dan. 8:10–11. Another meaning of the phrase "the host(s) of heaven" is simply "the numberless stars," Jer. 33:22; including all heavenly bodies, Ps. 33:6. The meaning "nonmilitary service in behalf of a superior" emerges in Num. 4:2–3. In Job 7:1 the word represents the burdensome everyday "toil" of mankind. In Job 14:14 ***tsaba'*** seems to represent "forced labor." In Dan. 10:1 the word is used for "conflict."

**B. Verb.**

***tsaba'*** (6633), "to wage war, to muster an army, to serve in worship," Num. 31:7; or muster an army, 2 Kings 25:19; or serving in worship, Num. 4:23.

### *New Testament*

***stratia*** (*4756*), "an army," is used of angels, Luke 2:13; of stars, Acts 7:42.

## HOT

***zestos*** (*2200*), "boiling hot" (from ***zeo***, "to boil, be hot, fervent"; cf. Eng., "zest"), is used, metaphorically, in Rev. 3:15, 16.

## HOUR

***hora*** (*5610*), whence Lat., ***hora***, Eng., "hour," primarily denoted any time or period, especially a season. In the NT it is used to denote (a) "a part of the day," especially a twelfth part of day or night, an "hour," e.g., Matt. 8:13; Acts 10:3, 9; 23:23; Rev. 9:15; in 1 Cor. 15:30, "every hour" stands for "all the time"; in some passages it expresses duration, e.g., Matt. 20:12; 26:40; Luke 22:59; inexactly, in such phrases as "for a season," John 5:35; 2 Cor. 7:8; "for an hour," Gal. 2:5; "for a short season," 1 Thess. 2:17, RV (KJV, "for a short time," lit., "for the time of an hour"); (b) "a period more or less extended," e.g., 1 John 2:18, "it is the last hour," RV; (C) "a definite point of time," e.g., Matt. 26:45, "the hour is at hand"; Luke 1:10; 10:21; 14:17, lit., "at the hour of supper"; Acts 16:18; 22:13; Rev. 3:3; 11:13; 14:7; a point of time when an appointed action is to begin, Rev. 14:15; in Rom. 13:11, "it is high time," lit., "it is already an hour," indicating that a point of time has come later than would have been the case had responsibility been realized. In 1 Cor. 4:11, it indicates a point of time previous to which certain circumstances have existed.

## HOUSE

***oikos*** (*3624*) denotes (a) "a house, a dwelling," e.g., Matt. 9:6, 7; 11:8; it is used of the Tabernacle, as the House of God, Matt. 12:4, and the Temple similarly, e.g., Matt. 21:13; Luke 11:51, KJV, "temple," RV, "sanctuary"; John 2:16, 17; called by the Lord "your house" in Matt. 23:38 and Luke 13:35 (some take this as the city of Jerusalem); metaphorically of Israel as God's house, Heb. 3:2, 5, where "his house" is not Moses', but God's; of believers, similarly, v. 6, where Christ is spoken of as "over God's House" (the word "own" is rightly omitted in the RV); Heb. 10:21; 1 Pet. 2:5; 4:17; of the body, Matt. 12:44; Luke 11:24; (b) by metonymy, of the members of a household or family, e.g., Luke 10:5; Acts 7:10; 11:14; 1 Tim. 3:4, 5, 12; 2 Tim. 1:16; 4:19, RV (KJV, "household"); Titus 1:11 (plural); of a local church, 1 Tim. 3:15; of the descendants of Jacob (Israel) and David, e.g., Matt. 10:6; Luke 1:27, 33; Acts 2:36; 7:42.

## HOUSEHOLD

**A. Nouns.**

1. ***oikos*** (*3624*) is translated "household" in Acts 16:15; 1 Cor. 1:16; in the KJV of 2 Tim. 4:19 (RV, "house").

2. ***oikia*** (*3614*) is translated "household" in Phil. 4:22.

3. ***oiketeia*** (*3610d*) denotes "a household of servants," Matt. 24:45 (some mss. have No. 4 here).

4. ***therapeia*** (*2322*), "service, care, attention," is also used in the collective sense of "a household," in Luke 12:42 (see No. 3).

### B. Adjectives.

1. ***oikeios*** (*3609*), akin to A, No. 1, primarily signifies "of, or belonging to, a house," hence, "of persons, one's household, or kindred," as in 1 Tim. 5:8, RV, "household," KJV "house," marg., "kindred"; in Eph. 2:19, "the household of God" denotes the company of the redeemed; in Gal. 6:10, it is called "the household of the faith," RV.

2. ***oikiakos*** (*3615*), from A, No. 2, denotes "belonging to one's household, one's own"; it is used in Matt. 10:25, 36.

## HOUSEHOLDER

### A. Noun.

***oikodespotes*** (*3617*), "a master of a house" appears in Matt. 10:25; Luke 13:25, and 14:21, where the context shows that the authority of the "householder" is stressed; "goodman of the house," is used in Matt. 24:43; Mark 14:14; and Luke 12:39; "householder" is the rendering in Matt. 13:27, 52; 20:1; 21:33.

### B. Verb.

***oikodespoteo*** (*3616*), corresponding to A, "to rule a house," is used in 1 Tim. 5:14.

## HOWL

***ololuzo*** (*3649*), an onomatopoeic verb (expressing its significance in its sound), "to cry aloud"; it is found in Jas. 5:1 in an exhortation to the godless rich.

## HUMBLE (Adjective and Verb)

#### *Old Testament*

### A. Verbs.

***kana'*** (3665), "to be humble, to humble, subdue," used in subduing enemies, 2 Sam. 8:1; 1 Chron. 17:10; Ps. 81:14. "To humble oneself" before God in repentance is a common theme and need in the life of ancient Israel, Lev. 26:41; 2 Chron. 7:14; 12:6–7, 12.

***shapel*** (8213), "to be low, become low; sink down; be humiliated; be abased," generally used in a figurative sense. ***shapel*** rarely denotes a literal lowness. Even in passages where the meaning may be taken literally, the prophet communicates a spiritual truth, Isa. 10:33; 40:4. Isaiah particularly presented Judah's sin as one of rebellion, self-exaltation, and pride, 2:17; 3:16–17. Pride and self-exaltation have no place in the life of the godly, as the Lord "brings low" a person, a city, and a nation, 1 Sam. 2:7.

### B. Nouns.

Some nouns related to this verb occur infrequently. ***shepel*** refers to a "low condition, low estate." This word appears twice, Ps. 136:23; Eccl. 10:6. The noun ***shiplah*** means a "humiliated state." This noun occurs once: "When it shall hail, coming down on the forest; and the city shall be low in a low place," Isa. 32:19; the city is leveled completely. ***shepelah*** means "lowland." This word is used most often as a technical designation for the low-lying hills of the Judean hill country, cf. Deut. 1:7; Josh. 9:1. ***shiplut*** refers to a "sinking." This noun's single appearance is in Eccl. 10:18.

### C. Adjective.

***shapal*** (8217), means "low; humble." This word means "low" in Ezek. 17:24: "And all the trees of the field shall know that I the Lord have brought down the high tree, have exalted the low tree. . . ." In Isa. 57:15 ***shapal*** refers to "humble": ". . . I dwell in the high and holy place, with him also that is of a contrite and humble spirit, to revive the spirit of the humble, and to revive the heart of the contrite ones."

#### *New Testament*

### A. Adjectives.

1. ***tapeinos*** (*5011*) primarily signifies "low-lying." It is used always in a good sense in the NT, metaphorically, to denote (a) "of low degree, brought low," Luke 1:52; Rom. 12:16, KJV, "(men) of low estate," RV, "(things that are) lowly" (i.e., of low degree); 2 Cor. 7:6, KJV, "cast down," RV, "lowly"; the preceding context shows that this occurrence belongs to (a); Jas. 1:9, "of low degree"; (b) humble in spirit, Matt. 11:29; 2 Cor. 10:1, RV, "lowly," KJV "base"; Jas. 4:6; 1 Pet. 5:5.

2. ***tapeinophron***, "humble-minded" (***phren***, "the mind"), 1 Pet. 3:8.

### B. Verb.

***tapeinoo*** (*5013*), akin to A, signifies "to make low," (a) literally, "of mountains and hills," Luke 3:5 (passive voice); (b) metaphorically, in the active voice, Matt. 18:4; 23:12 (2nd part); Luke 14:11 (2nd part); 18:14 (2nd part); 2 Cor. 11:7 ("abasing"); 12:21; Phil. 2:8; in the passive voice, Matt. 23:12 (1st part), RV, "shall be humbled," KJV, "shall be abased"; Luke 14:11; 18:14; Phil. 4:12, "to be abased"; in the passive, with middle voice sense, Jas. 4:10, "humble yourselves"; 1 Pet. 5:6.

## TO BE HUMBLED, AFFLICTED

### A. Verb.

***'anah*** (6031), "to be afflicted, be bowed down, be humbled, be meek." ***'anah*** often expresses harsh and painful treatment. Sarai "dealt hardly" with Hagar, Gen. 16:6. When Joseph was sold as a slave, his feet were hurt with fetters, Ps. 105:18. Frequently the verb expresses the idea that God sends affliction for disciplinary purposes, 1 Kings 11:39; Ps. 90:15.

### B. Noun.

***'ani*** (6041), "poor; humble; meek." Especially in later Israelite history, just before the Exile and following, this noun came to have a special connection with those faithful ones who were being abused, taken advantage of, by the rich, Isa. 29:19; 32:7; Amos 2:7. The prophet Zephaniah's reference to them as the "meek of the earth," Zeph. 2:3 set the stage for Jesus' concern and ministry to the "poor" and the "meek," Matt. 5:3, 5; Luke 4:18; cf. Isa. 61:1.

## HUMBLENESS OF MIND, HUMILITY

***tapeinophrosune*** (*5012*), "lowliness of mind," is rendered "humility of mind" in Acts 20:19, KJV (RV, "lowliness of mind"); in Eph. 4:2, "lowliness"; in Phil. 2:3, "lowliness of mind"; in Col. 2:18, 23, of a false "humility"; in Col. 3:12, KJV, "humbleness of mind," RV, "humility"; 1 Pet. 5:5, "humility."

## HUMILIATION

***tapeinosis*** (*5014*), akin to ***tapeinos***, is rendered "low estate" in Luke 1:48; "humiliation," Acts 8:33; Phil. 3:21, RV "(the body of our) humiliation," KJV, "(our) vile (body)"; Jas. 1:10, where "in that he is made low," is, lit., "in his humiliation."

## HUNGER (Noun and Verb), HUNGERED, HUNGRY

### A. Noun.

***limos*** (*3042*) has the meanings "famine" and "hunger"; "hunger" in Luke 15:17; 2 Cor. 11:27; in Rev. 6:8, RV "famine" (KJV, "hunger").

### B. Verb.

***peinao*** (*3983*), "to hunger, be hungry, hungered," is used (a) literally, e.g., Matt. 4:2; 12:1; 21:18; Rom. 12:20; 1 Cor. 11:21, 34; Phil. 4:12; Rev. 7:16; Christ identifies Himself with His saints in speaking of Himself as suffering in their sufferings in this and other respects, Matt. 25:35, 42; (b) metaphorically, Matt. 5:6; Luke 6:21, 25; John 6:35.

### C. Adjective.

***prospeinos*** (*4361*) signifies "hungry" (***pros***, "intensive," ***peina***, "hunger"), Acts 10:10, KJV, "very hungry," RV, "hungry."

## HURT (Noun and Verb), HURTFUL

### A. Verbs

1. ***adikeo*** (*91*) signifies, intransitively, "to do wrong, do hurt, act unjustly" (***a***, negative, and ***dike***, "justice"), transitively, "to wrong, hurt or injure a person." It is translated "to hurt" in the following: (a), intransitively, Rev. 9:19; (b) transitively, Luke 10:19; Rev. 2:11 (passive); 6:6; 7:2, 3; 9:4, 10; 11:5.

2. ***blapto*** (*984*) signifies "to injure, mar, do damage to," Mark 16:18, "shall (in no wise) hurt (them)"; Luke 4:35, "having done (him no) hurt," RV. ***adikeo*** stresses the unrighteousness of the act, ***blapto*** stresses the injury done.

3. ***kakoo*** (*2559*), "to do evil to anyone," Acts 7:6.

### B. Adjective.

***blaberos*** (*983*), akin to A, No. 2, signifies "hurtful," 1 Tim. 6:9, said of lusts.

## HUSBANDMAN

***georgos*** (*1092*), from ***ge***, "land, ground," and ***ergo*** (or ***erdo***), "to do" (Eng., "George"), denotes (a) "a husbandman," a tiller of the ground, 2 Tim. 2:6; Jas. 5:7; (b) "a vinedresser," Matt. 21:33–35, 38, 40, 41; Mark 12:1, 2, 7, 9; Luke 20:9, 10, 14, 16; John 15:1, where Christ speaks of the Father as the "Husbandman," Himself as the Vine, His disciples as the branches, the object being to bear much fruit, life in Christ producing the fruit of the Spirit, i.e., character and ways in conformity to Christ.

## HYMN (Noun and Verb)

### A. Noun.

***humnos*** (*5215*) denotes "a song of praise addressed to God" (Eng., "hymn"), Eph. 5:19; Col. 3:16, in each of which the punctuation should probably be changed; in the former "speaking to one another" goes with the end of v. 18, and should be followed by a semicolon; similarly in Col. 3:16, the first part of the verse should end with the words "admonishing one another," where a semicolon should be placed.

### B. Verb.

***humneo*** (*5214*), akin to A, is used (a) transitively, Matt. 26:30; Mark 14:26, where the "hymn" was that part of the Hallel consisting of Psalms 113–118; (b) intransitively, where the verb itself is rendered "to sing praises" or "praise," Acts 16:25; Heb. 2:12. The Psalms are called, in general, "hymns," by Philo; Josephus calls them "songs and hymns."

## HYPOCRISY

***hupokrisis*** *(5272)* primarily denotes "a reply, an answer" (akin to ***hupokrinomai***, "to answer"); then, "play-acting," as the actors spoke in dialogue; hence, "pretence, hypocrisy"; it is translated "hypocrisy" in Matt. 23:28; Mark 12:15; Luke 12:1; 1 Tim. 4:2; the plural in 1 Pet. 2:1. For Gal. 2:13 and ***anupokritos***, "without hypocrisy," in Jas. 3:17.

## HYPOCRITE

***hupokrites*** *(5273)*, corresponding to the above, primarily denotes "one who answers"; then, "a stage-actor"; it was a custom for Greek and Roman actors to speak in large masks with mechanical devices for augmenting the force of the voice; hence the word became used metaphorically of "a dissembler, a hypocrite." It is found only in the Synoptists, and always used by the Lord, fifteen times in Matthew; elsewhere, Mark 7:6; Luke 6:42; 11:44 (in some mss.); 12:56; 13:15.

## HYSSOP

***hussopos*** *(5301)*, a bunch of which was used in ritual sprinklings, is found in Heb. 9:19; in John 19:29 the reference is apparently to a branch or rod of "hyssop," upon which a sponge was put and offered to the Lord on the cross.

# I

## IDLE

***argos*** (*692*) denotes "inactive, idle, unfruitful, barren" (***a***, negative, and ***ergon***, "work"); it is used (a) literally, Matt. 20:3, 6; 1 Tim. 5:13 (twice); Titus 1:12, RV, "idle (gluttons); 2 Pet. 1:8, RV, "idle," KJV, "barren"; (b) metaphorically in the sense of "ineffective, worthless," as of a word, Matt. 12:36; of faith unaccompanied by works, Jas. 2:20 (some mss. have ***nekra***, "dead").

## IDOL

### *Old Testament*

***terapim*** (8655), "idol; household idol; cultic mask; divine symbol." ***terapim*** first appears in Gen. 31:19. Hurrian law of this period recognized "household idols" as deeds to the family's succession and goods. To understand the ***terapim*** [here a plural of "majesty"] of 1 Sam. 19:13 as a "household idol" is difficult, in view of verse 11, where it is said to be in David's private quarters. In Judg. 18:14–17 ***terapim*** appears to be distinguished from idols: ". . . there is in these houses an ephod, and ***terapim***, and a graven image, and a molten image?" ***terapim*** may signify an "idol," a "cultic mask," or perhaps a "symbol of the divine presence," Judg. 18:31.

***'elil*** (457), "idol; gods; nought; vain." This disdainful word signifies an "idol" or "false god," Lev. 19:4; 26:1; Ps. 96:5. Second, ***'elil*** can mean "nought" or "vain." 1 Chron. 16:26 might well be rendered: "For all the gods of the people are nought." This nuance appears clearly in Job 13:4.

***gillulim*** (1544), "idols." Of the 48 occurrences of this word, all but 9 appear in Ezekiel. This word for "idols" is a disdainful word and may originally have meant "dung pellets," Lev. 26:30. This word and others for "idol" exhibit the horror and scorn that biblical writers felt toward them. In passages such as Isa. 66:3 the word for "idol," ***'awen***, means "uncanny or wickedness." Jer. 50:38 evidences the word ***'emim***, which means "fright or horror." The word ***'elil*** appears for "idol" in Lev. 19:4; it means "nothingness or feeble." 1 Kings 15:13 uses the Hebrew word, ***mipletset***, meaning a "horrible thing, a cause of trembling."

### *New Testament*

***eidolon*** (*1497*), primarily "a phantom or likeness" (from ***eidos***, "an appearance," lit., "that which is seen"), or "an idea, fancy," denotes in the NT (a) "an idol," an image to represent a false god, Acts 7:41; 1 Cor. 12:2; Rev. 9:20; (b) "the false god" worshipped in an image, Acts 15:20; Rom. 2:22; 1 Cor. 8:4, 7; 10:19; 2 Cor. 6:16; 1 Thess. 1:9; 1 John 5:21.

The corresponding Heb. word denotes "vanity," Jer. 14:22; 18:15; "thing of nought," Lev. 19:4, marg., cf. Eph. 4:17. Hence what represented a deity to the Gentiles, was to Paul a "vain thing," Acts 14:15; "nothing in the world," 1 Cor. 8:4; 10:19. Jeremiah calls the idol a "scarecrow" ("pillar in a garden," 10:5, marg.), and Isaiah, 44:9–20, etc., and Habakkuk, 2:18, 19 and the Psalmist, 115:4–8, etc., are all equally scathing. It is important to notice, however, that in each case the people of God are addressed. When he speaks to idolaters, Paul, knowing that no man is won by ridicule, adopts a different line, Acts 14:15–18; 17:16, 21–31.

## IDOLS (full of)

***kateidolos*** (*2712*), an adjective denoting "full of idols" (***kata***, "throughout," and ***eidolon***), is said of Athens in Acts 17:16, RV, and KJV, marg. (KJV, "wholly given to idolatry").

## IDOLS (offered to, sacrificed to)

1. ***eidolothutos*** (*1494*) is an adjective signifying "sacrificed to idols" (***eidolon***, as above, and ***thuo***, "to sacrifice"), Acts 15:29; 21:25; 1 Cor. 8:1, 4, 7, 10; 10:19 (in all these the RV substitutes "sacrificed" for the KJV); Rev. 2:14, 20 (in these the RV and KJV both have "sacrificed"). Some inferior mss. have this adjective in 1 Cor. 10:28; see No. 2. The flesh of the victims, after sacrifice, was eaten or sold.

2. ***nierothutos***, "offered in sacrifice" (***hieros***, "sacred," and ***thuo***, "to sacrifice"), is found in the best mss. in 1 Cor. 10:28 (see No. 1).

## IDOLATER

***eidololatres*** (*1496*), an "idolater" (from ***eidolon***, and ***latris***, "a hireling"), is found in 1 Cor. 5:10, 11; 6:9; 10:7; the warning is to believers against turning away from God to idolatry, whether "openly or secretly, consciously or unconsciously"; Eph. 5:5; Rev. 21:8; 22:15.

## IDOLATRY

***eidololatria*** (or ***-eia***) (*1495*), whence Eng., "idolatry," (from ***eidolon***, and ***latreia***, "service"), is found in 1 Cor. 10:14; Gal. 5:20; Col. 3:5; and, in the plural, in 1 Pet. 4:3.

Heathen sacrifices were sacrificed to demons, 1 Cor. 10:19; there was a dire reality in the cup and table of demons and in the involved communion with demons. In Rom. 1:22–25, "idolatry," the sin of the mind against God (Eph. 2:3), and immorality, sins of the flesh, are associated, and are traced to lack of the acknowledgment of God and of gratitude to Him. An "idolater" is a slave to the depraved ideas his idols represent, Gal. 4:8, 9; and thereby, to divers lusts, Titus 3:3.

## IGNORANCE, IGNORANT, IGNORANTLY

### A. Nouns.

1. ***agnoia*** (*52*), lit., "want of knowledge or perception" (akin to ***agnoeo***, "to be ignorant"), denotes "ignorance" on the part of the Jews regarding Christ, Acts 3:17; of Gentiles in regard to God, 17:30; Eph. 4:18 (here including the idea of willful blindness: see Rom. 1:28, not the "ignorance" which mitigates guilt); 1 Pet. 1:14, of the former unregenerate condition of those who became believers (RV, "in ***the time of*** your ignorance").

2. ***agnosia*** (*56*) denotes "ignorance" as directly opposed to ***gnosis***, which signifies "knowledge" as a result of observation and experience (***a***, negative, ***ginosko***, "to know"; cf. Eng., "agnostic"); 1 Cor. 15:34 ("no knowledge"); 1 Pet. 2:15. In both these passages reprehensible "ignorance" is suggested.

3. ***agnoema*** (*51*), "a sin of ignorance," occurs in Heb. 9:7, "errors" (RV marg., "ignorances"). For the corresponding verb in Heb. 5:2 see B, No. 1. What is especially in view in these passages is unwitting error. For Israel a sacrifice was appointed, greater in proportion to the culpability of the guilty, greater, for instance, for a priest or ruler than for a private person. Sins of "ignorance," being sins, must be expiated. A believer guilty of a sin of "ignorance" needs the efficacy of the expiatory sacrifice of Christ, and finds "grace to help." Yet, as the conscience of the believer receives enlightenment, what formerly may have been done in "ignorance" becomes a sin against the light and demands a special confession, to receive forgiveness, 1 John 1:8, 9.

### B. Verbs.

1. ***agnoeo*** (*50*), signifies (a) "to be ignorant, not to know," either intransitively, 1 Cor. 14:38 (in the 2nd occurrence in this verse, the RV text translates the active voice, the margin the passive); 1 Tim. 1:13, lit., "being ignorant (I did it)"; Heb. 5:2, "ignorant"; or transitively, 2 Pet. 2:12, KJV, "understand not," RV, "are ignorant (of)"; Acts 13:27, "knew (Him) not"; 17:23, RV, "(what ye worship) in ignorance," for KJV, "(whom ye) ignorantly (worship)," lit., "(what) not knowing (ye worship"; also rendered by the verb "to be ignorant that," or "to be ignorant of," Rom. 1:13; 10:3; 11:25; 1 Cor. 10:1; 12:1; 2 Cor. 1:8; 2:11; 1 Thess. 4:13; to know not, Rom. 2:4; 6:3; 7:1; to be unknown (passive voice), 2 Cor. 6:9; Gal. 1:22; (b) "not to understand," Mark 9:32; Luke 9:45.

## IMAGE



1. ***eikon*** (*1504*) denotes "an image"; the word involves the two ideas of representation and manifestation. "The idea of perfection does not lie in the word itself, but must be sought from the context" (Lightfoot); the following instances clearly show any distinction between the imperfect and the perfect likeness.

The word is used (1) of an "image" or a coin (not a mere likeness), Matt. 22:20; Mark 12:16; Luke 20:24; so of a statue or similar representation (more than a resemblance), Rom. 1:23; Rev. 13:14, 15 (thrice); 14:9, 11; 15:2; 16:2; 19:20; 20:4; of the descendants of Adam as bearing his image, 1 Cor. 15:49, each a representation derived from the prototype; (2) of subjects relative to things spiritual, Heb. 10:1, negatively of the Law as having "a shadow of the good things to come, not the very image of the things," i.e., not the essential and substantial form of them; the contrast has been likened to the difference between a statue and the shadow cast by it; (3) of the relations between God the Father, Christ, and man, (a) of man as he was created as being a visible representation of God, 1 Cor. 11:7, a being corresponding to the original; the condition of man as a fallen creature has not entirely effaced the "image"; he is still suitable to bear responsibility, he still has Godlike qualities, such as love of goodness and beauty, none of which are found in a mere animal; in the Fall man ceased to be a perfect vehicle for the representation of God; God's grace in Christ will yet accomplish more than what Adam lost; (b) of regenerate persons, in being moral representations of what God is, Col. 3:10; cf. Eph. 4:24; (c) of believers, in their glorified state, not merely as resembling Christ but representing Him, Rom. 8:29; 1 Cor. 15:49; here the perfection is the work of divine grace; believers are yet to represent, not something like Him, but what He is in Himself, both in His spiritual body and in His moral character; (d) of Christ in relation to God, 2 Cor. 4:4, "the image of God," i.e., essentially and absolutely the perfect expression and representation of the Archetype, God the Father; in Col. 1:15, "the image of the invisible God" gives the additional thought suggested by the word "invisible," that Christ is the visible representation and manifestation of God to created beings; the likeness expressed in this manifestation is involved in the essential relations in the Godhead, and is therefore unique and perfect; "he that hath seen Me hath seen the Father," John 14:9. "The epithet 'invisible' . . . must not be confined to the apprehension of the bodily senses, but will include the cognizance of the inward eye also" (Lightfoot).

2. ***charakter*** (*5481*) denotes, firstly, "a tool for graving" (from ***charasso***, "to cut into, to engross"; cf. Eng., "character," "characteristic"); then, "a stamp" or "impress," as on a coin or a seal, in which case the seal or die which makes an impression bears the "image" produced by it, and, *vice versa*, all the features of the "image" correspond respectively with those of the instrument producing it. In the NT it is used metaphorically in Heb. 1:3, of the Son of God as "the very image (marg., 'the impress') of His substance."

## IMAGINATION

1. ***logismos*** (*3053*), "a reasoning, a thought" (akin to ***logizomai***, "to count, reckon"), is translated "thoughts" in Rom. 2:15, suggestive of evil intent, not of mere reasonings; "imaginations" in 2 Cor. 10:5. The word suggests the contemplation of actions as a result of the verdict of conscience.

2. ***dialogismos*** (*1261*), ***dia***, and No. 1, is rendered "imaginations" in Rom. 1:21, carrying with it the idea of evil purposes.

3. ***dianoia*** (*1271*), strictly, "a thinking over," denotes "the faculty of thinking"; then, "of knowing"; hence, "the understanding," and in general, "the mind," and so, "the faculty of moral reflection"; it is rendered "imagination" in Luke 1:51, "the imagination of their heart" signifying their thoughts and ideas.

## IMITATE, IMITATOR

**A. Verb.**

***mimeomai*** (*3401*), "a mimic, an actor" (Eng., "mime," etc.), is always translated "to imitate" in the RV, for KJV, "to follow," (a) of imitating the conduct of missionaries, 2 Thess. 3:7, 9; the faith of spiritual guides, Heb. 13:7; (b) that which is good, 3 John 11. The verb is always used in exhortations, and always in the continuous tense, suggesting a constant habit or practice.

**B. Nouns.**

1. ***mimetes*** (*3402*), akin to A, "an imitator," so the RV for KJV, "follower," is always used in a good sense in the NT. In 1 Cor. 4:16; 11:1; Eph. 5:1; Heb. 6:12, it is used in exhortations, accompanied by the verb ***ginomai***, "to be, become," and in the continuous tense (see A) except in Heb. 6:12, where the aorist or momentary tense indicates a decisive act with permanent results; in 1 Thess. 1:6; 2:14, the accompanying verb is in the aorist tense, referring to the definite act of conversion in the past. These instances, coupled with the continuous tenses referred to, teach that what we became at conversion we must diligently continue to be thereafter.

2. ***summimetes*** (*4831*) denotes "a fellow imitator" (***sun***, "with," and No. 1), Phil. 3:17, RV, "imitators together" (KJV, "followers together").

## IMMORTAL, IMMORTALITY

***athanasia*** (*110*), lit., "deathlessness," is rendered "immortality" in 1 Cor. 15:53, 54, of the glorified body of the believer; 1 Tim. 6:16, of the nature of God. In the NT ***athanasia*** expresses more than deathlessness, it suggests the quality of the life enjoyed, as is clear from 2 Cor. 5:4; for the believer what is mortal is to be "swallowed up of life."

## IMMUTABLE, IMMUTABILITY

***ametathetos*** (*276*), an adjective signifying "immutable" (***a***, negative, ***metatithemi***, "to change"), Heb. 6:18, where the "two immutable things" are the promise and the oath. In v. 17 the word is used in the neuter with the article, as a noun, denoting "the immutability," with reference to God's counsel. Examples from the papyri show that the word was used as a technical term in connection with wills. The connotation adds considerably to the force of Heb. 6:17ff.

## IMPEDIMENT

***mogilalos*** (*3424*) denotes "speaking with difficulty," "stammering," Mark 7:32.

## IMPENITENT

***ametanoetos*** (*279*), lit., "without change of mind," is used in Rom. 2:5, "impenitent" (or "unrepentant"). Moulton and Milligan show from the papyri writings that the word is also used "in a passive sense, 'not affected by change of mind,' like ***ametameletos*** in Rom. 11:29," "without repentance."

## IMPLANTED

***emphutos*** (*1721*), "implanted," or "rooted" (from ***emphuo***, "to implant"), is used in Jas. 1:21, RV, "implanted," for KJV, "engrafted," of the Word of God, as the "rooted word," i.e., a word whose property it is to root itself like a seed in the heart. "The KJV seems to identify it with ***emphuteuton***, which however would be out of place here, since the word is sown, not grafted, in the heart" (Mayor).

## IMPORTUNITY

***anaidia*** (or ***anaideia***) (*335*), denotes "shamelessness, importunity" (***a***, negative, ***n***, euphonic, and ***aidos***, "shame, modesty"), and is used in the Lord's illustration concerning the need of earnestness and perseverance in prayer, Luke 11:8. If shameless persistence can obtain a boon from a neighbor, then certainly earnest prayer will receive our Father's answer.

## IMPOSED

***epikeimai*** (*1945*) denotes "to be placed on, to lie on," (a) literally, as of the stone on the sepulchre of Lazarus, John 11:38; of the fish on the fire of coals, 21:9; (b) figuratively, of a tempest (to press upon), Acts 27:20; of a necessity laid upon the apostle Paul, 1 Cor. 9:16; of the pressure of the multitude upon Christ to hear Him, Luke 5:1, "pressed upon"; of the insistence of the chief priests, rulers and people that Christ should be crucified, Luke 23:23, "were instant"; of carnal ordinances "imposed" under the Law until a time of reformation, brought in through the High Priesthood of Christ, Heb. 9:10.

## IMPOSSIBLE

### A. Adjective.

***adunatos*** (*102*), from ***a***, negative, and ***dunatos***, "able, strong," is used (a) of persons, Acts 14:8, "impotent"; figuratively, Rom. 15:1, "weak"; (b) of things, "impossible," Matt. 19:26; Mark 10:27; Luke 18:27; Heb. 6:4, 18; 10:4; 11:6; in Rom. 8:3, "for what the Law could not do," is, more lit., "the inability of the law"; the meaning may be either "the weakness of the Law," or "that which was impossible for the Law"; the latter is perhaps preferable; literalism is ruled out here, but the sense is that the Law could neither justify nor impart life.

### B. Verb.

***adunateo*** (*101*) signifies "to be impossible" (corresponding to A, No. 1), "unable"; in the NT it is used only of things, Matt. 17:20.

## IMPOSTORS

***goes*** (*1114*) primarily denotes "a wailer" (***goao***, "to wail"); hence, from the howl in which spells were chanted, "a wizard, sorcerer, enchanter," and hence, "a juggler, cheat, impostor," rendered "impostors" in 2 Tim. 3:13.

## IMPUTE

1. ***logizomai*** (*3049*), "to reckon, take into account," or, metaphorically, "to put down to a person's account," is never rendered in the RV by the verb "to impute." In the following, where the KJV has that rendering, the RV uses the verb "to reckon," which is far more suitable, Rom. 4:6, 8, 11, 22, 23, 24; 2 Cor. 5:19; Jas. 2:23.

2. ***ellogao***, or ***-eo*** (*1677*) (the ***-ao*** termination is the one found in the *Koine*, the language covering the NT period), denotes "to charge to one's account, to lay to one's charge," and is translated "imputed" in Rom. 5:13. In Philem. 18 the verb is rendered "put (that) to (mine) account."

## INCENSE (burn)

### A. Noun.

***thumiama*** (*2368*) denotes "fragrant stuff for burning, incense" (from ***thuo***, "to offer in sacrifice"), Luke 1:10, 11; in the plural, Rev. 5:8 and 18:13, RV (KJV, "odors"); 8:3, 4, signifying "frankincense" here. In connection with the tabernacle, the "incense" was to be prepared from stacte, onycha, and galbanum, with pure frankincense, an equal weight of each; imitation for private use was forbidden, Exod. 30:34–38.

### B. Verb.

***thumiao*** (*2370*), "to burn incense" (see A), is found in Luke 1:9.

## INCREASE (Verb)

1. ***perisseo*** (*4052*), "to be over and above, to abound," is translated "increased" in Acts 16:5, of churches; "increase" in the KJV of 1 Thess. 4:10 (RV, abound).

2. ***pleonazo*** (*4121*), "to make to abound," is translated "make (you) to increase" in 1 Thess. 3:12.

3. ***prokopto*** (*4278*) is translated by the verb "to increase" in Luke 2:52 and in the KJV of 2 Tim. 2:16 (RV, "will proceed further").

4. ***prostithemi*** (*4369*), "to put to, add to," is translated "increase" in Luke 17:5.

## INDEBTED (to be)

***opheilo*** (*3784*), "to owe, to be a debtor," is translated "is indebted" in Luke 11:4. Luke does not draw a parallel between our forgiving and God's; he speaks of God's forgiving sins, of our forgiving "debts," moral debts, probably not excluding material debts.

## INDIGNATION

### A. Noun.

***aganaktesis*** (*24*) is rendered "indignation" in 2 Cor. 7:11.

### B. Verb.

***aganakteo*** (*23*), "to be indignant, to be moved with indignation" (from ***agan***, "much," ***achomai***, "to grieve"), is translated "were moved with indignation" of the ten disciples against James and John, Matt. 20:24; in Mark 10:41, RV (KJV, "they began to be much displeased"); in Matt. 21:15, of the chief priests and scribes, against Christ and the children, RV, "they were moved with indignation" (KJV, "they were sore displeased"); in 26:8, of the disciples against the woman who anointed Christ's feet, "they had indignation"; so Mark 14:4; in Mark 10:14, of Christ, against the disciples, for rebuking the children, "He was moved with indignation," RV (KJV, "he was much displeased"); in Luke 13:14, of the ruler of the synagogue against Christ for healing on the Sabbath, "being moved with indignation," RV, KJV, "(answered) with indignation."

## INDULGENCE

1. ***anesis*** (*425*), "a loosening, relaxation of strain" (akin to ***aniemi***, "to relax, loosen"), is translated "indulgence" in Acts 24:23, RV (KJV, "liberty"), in the command of Felix to the centurion, to moderate restrictions upon Paul. In the NT it always carries the thought of relief from tribulation or persecution; so 2 Thess. 1:7, "rest"; in 2 Cor. 2:13 and 7:5 it is rendered "relief," RV (KJV, "rest"); in 8:13, "eased."

2. ***plesmone*** (*4140*), "a filling up, satiety" (akin to ***pimplemi***, "to fill"), is translated "indulgence (of the flesh)" in Col. 2:23, RV (KJV, "satisfying").

## INFERIOR

***hettaomai***, or ***hessaomai*** (2274), "to be less or inferior," is used in the passive voice, and translated "ye were made inferior," in 2 Cor. 12:13, RV, for KJV, "ye were inferior," i.e., were treated with less consideration than other churches, through his independence in not receiving gifts from them. In 2 Pet. 2:19, 20 it signifies to be overcome, in the sense of being subdued and enslaved.

## INFIRMITY

1. ***ostheneia*** (*769*), lit., "want of strength" (***a***, negative, ***sthenos***, "strength"), "weakness," indicating inability to produce results, is most frequently translated "infirmity," or "infirmities"; in Rom. 8:26, the RV has "infirmity" (KJV, "infirmities"); in 2 Cor. 12:5, 9, 10, "weaknesses" and in 11:30, "weakness" (KJV, "infirmities"); in Luke 13:11 the phrase "a spirit of infirmity" attributes her curvature directly to satanic agency. The connected phraseology is indicative of trained medical knowledge on the part of the writer.

2. ***asthenema*** (*771*), akin to No. 1, is found in the plural in Rom. 15:1, "infirmities," i.e., those scruples which arise through weakness of faith. The strong must support the infirmities of the weak (***adunatos***) by submitting to self-restraint.

## INFORM

1. ***emphanizo*** (*1718*), "to manifest, exhibit," in the middle and passive voices, "to appear, also signifies to declare, make known," and is translated "informed" in Acts 24:1; 25:2, 15.

2. ***katecheo*** (2727) primarily denotes "to resound" (***kata***, "down," ***echos*** "a sound"); then, "to sound down the ears, to teach by word of mouth, instruct, inform" (Eng., "catechize, catechumen"); it is rendered, in the passive voice, by the verb "to inform," in Acts 21:21, 24.

## INHERIT, INHERITANCE

### *Old Testament*

### A. Verb.

***nachal*** (5157), "to inherit, get possession of, take as a possession." Usually this term means to take a possession, and not inherit, Deut. 21:16; Prov. 28:10.

### B. Noun.

***nachalah*** (5159), "possession; property; inheritance." The basic translation of ***nachalah*** is "inheritance," 1 Kings 21:3. The word more appropriately refers to a "possession" to which one has received the legal claim, Num. 26:56; Josh. 11:23; 1 Kings 21:3–4; Ruth 4:10.

Metaphorically, Israel is said to be God's "possession," Deut. 4:20. Within the special covenantal status Israel experienced the blessing that its children were a special gift from the Lord, Ps. 127:3. However, the Lord abandoned Israel as His "possession" to the nations, cf. Isa. 47:6, and permitted a remnant of the "possession" to return, Mic. 7:18.

### New Testament

**A. Verbs.**

1. ***kleronomeo*** (*2816*) strictly means "to receive by lot" (***kleros***, "a lot," ***nemomai***, "to possess"); then, in a more general sense, "to possess oneself of, to receive as one's own, to obtain." The following list shows how in the NT the idea of inheriting broadens out to include all spiritual good provided through and in Christ, and particularly all that is contained in the hope grounded on the promises of God.

The verb is used of the following objects:

(a) birthright, that into the possession of which one enters in virtue of sonship, not because of a price paid or of a task accomplished, Gal. 4:30; Heb. 1:4; 12:17:

(b) that which is received as a gift, in contrast with that which is received as the reward of law-keeping, Heb. 1:14; 6:12 ("through," i.e., "through experiences that called for the exercise of faith and patience," but not "on the ground of the exercise of faith and patience").

(c) the reward of that condition of soul which forbears retaliation and self-vindication, and expresses itself in gentleness of behavior. . . . Matt. 5:5.

(d) the reward (in the coming age, Mark 10:30) of the acknowledgment of the paramountcy of the claims of Christ, Matt. 19:29. In the three accounts given of this incident, see Mark 10:17–31; Luke 18:18–30, the words of the question put to the Lord are, in Matthew, "that I may have," in Mark and Luke, "that I may inherit." In the report of the Lord's word to Peter in reply to his subsequent question, Matthew has "inherit eternal life," while Mark and Luke have "receive eternal life." It seems to follow that the meaning of the word "inherit" is here ruled by the words "receive" and "have," with which it is interchanged in each of the three Gospels, i.e., the less common word "inherit" is to be regarded as equivalent to the more common words "receive" and "have." Cf. Luke 10:25:

(e) the reward of those who have shown kindness to the "brethren" of the Lord in their distress, Matt. 25:34:

2. ***kleroo*** (*2820*) is used in the passive voice in Eph. 1:11, KJV, "we have obtained an inheritance"; RV, "we were made a heritage."

**B. Nouns.**

1. ***kleronomia*** (*2817*), "a lot" (see A), properly "an inherited property, an inheritance." It is always rendered inheritance in NT, but only in a few cases in the Gospels has it the meaning ordinarily attached to that word in English, i.e., that into possession of which the heir enters only on the death of an ancestor. The NT usage may be set out as follows: (a) that property in real estate which in ordinary course passes from father to son on the death of the former, Matt. 21:38; Mark 12:7; Luke 12:13; 20:14; (b) a portion of an estate made the substance of a gift, Acts 7:5; Gal. 3:18, which also is to be included under (c); (c) the prospective condition and possessions of the believer in the new order of things to be ushered in at the return of Christ, Acts 20:32; Eph. 1:14; 5:5; Col. 3:24; Heb. 9:15; 1 Pet. 1:4; (d) what the believer will be to God in that age, Eph. 1:18.

2. ***kleros*** (*2819*), (whence Eng., "clergy"), denotes (a) "a lot," given or cast (the latter as a means of obtaining divine direction), Matt. 27:35; Mark 15:24; Luke 23:24; John 19:24; Acts 1:26; (b) "a person's share" in anything, Acts 1:17, RV, "portion" (KJV, "part"); 8:21, "lot"; (c) "a charge" (lit., "charges") "allotted," to elders, 1 Pet. 5:3, RV [KJV, "(God's) heritage"]; the figure is from portions of lands allotted to be cultivated; (d) "an inheritance," as in No. 1 (c); Acts 26:18; Col. 1:12.

## INIQUITY

### Old Testament

**A. Verb.**

***'awah*** (5753), "to do iniquity," ***'awah*** is often used as a synonym of ***chata'***, "to sin," as in Ps. 106:6.

**B. Nouns.**

***'awon*** (5771), "iniquity; guilt; punishment." The most basic meaning of ***'awon*** is "iniquity." The word signifies an offense, intentional or not, against God's law. This meaning is also most basic to the word ***chatta't***, "sin," Isa. 6:7.

"Iniquity" as an offense to God's holiness is punishable. The individual is warned that the Lord punishes man's transgression, Jer. 31:30. There is also a collective sense in that the one is responsible for the many, Exod. 20:5. No generation, however, was to think that it bore God's judgment for the "iniquity" of another generation, Ezek. 18:19–20.

Israel went into captivity for the sin of their fathers and for their own sins, Ezek. 39:23.

Serious as "iniquity" is in the covenantal relationship between the Lord and His people, the people are reminded that He is a living God who willingly forgives "iniquity," Exod. 34:7; Ps. 32:5; 51:2.

The usage of ***'awon*** includes the whole area of sin, judgment, and "punishment" for sin. The Old Testament teaches that God's forgiveness of "iniquity" extends to the actual sin, the guilt of sin, God's judgment upon that sin, and God's punishment of the sin, Ps. 32:2.

***'awen*** (205), "iniquity; misfortune." The meaning of "misfortune" comes to expression in the devices of the wicked against the righteous. The psalmist expected "misfortune" to come upon him, Ps. 41:6. ***'awen*** in this sense is synonymous with ***'ed***, "disaster," Job 18:12. In a real sense ***'awen*** is part of human existence, and as such the word is identical with ***'amal***, "toil," as in Ps. 90:10.

***'awen*** in a deeper sense characterizes the way of life of those who are without God, Isa. 32:6. The being of man is corrupted by "iniquity." Though all of mankind is subject to ***'awen*** ("toil"), there are those who delight in causing difficulties and "misfortunes" for others by scheming, lying, and acting deceptively, Ps. 7:14; cf. Job 15:35.

Those who are involved in the ways of darkness are the "workers of iniquity," the doers of evil or the creators of "misfortune" and disaster. Synonyms for ***'awen*** with this sense are ***ra'***, "evil," and ***rasha'***, "wicked," opposed to "righteousness" and "justice." They seek the downfall of the just, Ps. 141:9. The qualitative aspect of the word comes to the best expression in the verbs with ***'awen***. The wicked work, speak, beget, think, devise, gather, reap, and plow ***'awen***, and it is revealed ("comes forth") by the misfortune that comes upon the righteous. Ultimately when Israel's religious festivals, Isa. 1:13, and legislation, Isa. 10:1, were affected by their apostate way of life, they had reduced themselves to the Gentile practices and way of life. The prophetic hope lay in the period after the purification of Israel, when the messianic king would introduce a period of justice and righteousness, Isa. 32, and the evil men would be shown up for their folly and ungodliness.

***New Testament***

1. ***anomia*** (*458*), lit., "lawlessness" (***a***, negative, ***nomos***, "law"), is used in a way which indicates the meaning as being lawlessness or wickedness. Its usual rendering in the NT is "iniquity," which lit. means unrighteousness. It is used (a) of iniquity in general, Matt. 7:23; 13:41; 23:28; 24:12; Rom. 6:19 (twice); 2 Cor. 6:14, RV, "iniquity" (KJV, "unrighteousness"); 2 Thess. 2:3, in some mss.; the KJV and RV follow those which have ***hamartia***, "(man of) sin"; 2:7, RV, "lawlessness" (KJV, "iniquity"); Titus 2:14; Heb. 1:9; 1 John 3:4 (twice), RV, "(doeth) . . . lawlessness" and "lawlessness" (KJV, "transgresseth the law" and "transgression of the law"); (b) in the plural, of acts or manifestations of lawlessness, Rom. 4:7; Heb. 10:17 (some inferior mss. have it in 8:12, for the word ***hamartia***).

2. ***adikia*** (*93*) denotes "unrighteousness," lit., "unrightness" (***a***, negative, ***dike***, "right"), a condition of not being right, whether with God, according to the standard of His holiness and righteousness, or with man, according to the standard of what man knows to be right by his conscience. In Luke 16:8 and 18:6, the phrases lit. are, "the steward of unrighteousness" and "the judge of injustice," the subjective genitive describing their character; in 18:6 the meaning is "injustice" and so perhaps in Rom. 9:14. The word is usually translated "unrighteousness," but is rendered "iniquity" in Luke 13:27; Acts 1:18; 8:23; 1 Cor. 13:6, KJV (RV, "unrighteousness"); so in 2 Tim. 2:19; Jas. 3:6.

3. ***adikema*** (*92*) denotes "a wrong, injury, misdeed" (akin to No. 2; from ***adikeo***, "to do wrong"), the concrete act, in contrast to the general meaning of No. 2, and translated "a matter of wrong," in Acts 18:14; "wrongdoing," 24:20 (KJV, "evil-doing"); "iniquities," Rev. 18:5.

4. ***poneria*** (*4189*), akin to ***poneo***, "to toil," denotes "wickedness," and is so translated in Matt. 22:18; Mark 7:22 (plural); Luke 11:39; Rom. 1:29; 1 Cor. 5:8; Eph. 6:12; in Acts 3:26, "iniquities."

5. ***paranomia*** (*3892*), "lawbreaking" (***para***, "against," ***nomos***, "law"), denotes "transgression," so rendered in 2 Pet. 2:16, for KJV, "iniquity."

## INJURE, INJURIOUS

### A. Verb.

***adikeo*** (*91*) is usually translated either "to hurt," or by some form of the verb "to do wrong." In the KJV of Gal. 4:12, it is rendered "ye have (not) injured me."

### B. Adjective.

***hubristes*** (*5197*), "a violent, insolent man," is translated "insolent" in Rom. 1:30, RV, for KJV, "despiteful"; in 1 Tim. 1:13, "injurious."

## INNOCENT

1. ***athoos*** (*121*) primarily denotes "unpunished" (***a***, negative, ***thoe***, "a penalty"); then, "innocent," Matt. 27:4, "innocent blood," i.e., the blood of an "innocent" person, the word "blood" being used both by synecdoche (a part standing for the whole), and by metonymy (one thing standing for another), i.e., for death by execution (some mss. have ***dikaion***, "righteous"); v. 24, where Pilate speaks of himself as "innocent."

2. ***akakos*** (*172*), lit., "not bad," denotes "guileless, innocent," Rom. 16:18, RV, "innocent" (KJV, "simple"); "harmless" in Heb. 7:26.

## INQUIRE, INQUIRY (make)

### A. Verbs.

1. ***punthanomai*** (*4441*), "to inquire," is translated "inquired" in Matt. 2:4, and Acts 21:33, RV (KJV, "demanded"); in Luke 15:26; 18:36 and Acts 4:7 (KJV, "asked"); "inquired" (KJV, "inquired") in John 4:52; "inquire" (KJV, "inquire") in Acts 23:20; in Acts 23:34 it denotes "to learn by inquiry," KJV, and RV, "when (he) understood"; elsewhere it is rendered by the verb "to ask," Acts 10:18, 29; 23:19.

2. ***zeteo*** (*2212*), "to seek," is rendered "inquire" in John 16:19; "inquire . . . for" in Acts 9:11.

3. ***dierotao*** (*1331*), "to find by inquiry, to inquire through to the end" (***dia***, intensive, ***erotao***, "to ask") is used in Acts 10:17.

4. ***exetazo*** (*1833*), "to examine, seek out, inquire thoroughly," is translated "inquire" in Matt. 10:11, KJV (RV, "search out"); in John 21:12, "durst inquire," RV [KJV, "(durst) ask"]; in Matt. 2:8, RV, "search out" (KJV, "search").

### B. Noun.

***zetesis*** (*2214*) primarily denotes "a search"; then, "an inquiry, a questioning, debate"; it forms part of a phrase translated by the verb "to inquire," in Acts 25:20, RV, "how to inquire," lit. "(being perplexed as to) the inquiry."

## INSPIRATION OF GOD, INSPIRED OF GOD

***theopneustos*** (*2315*), "inspired by God" (***theos***, "God," ***pneo***, "to breathe"), is used in 2 Tim. 3:16, of the Scriptures as distinct from non-inspired writings.

## INSTRUCT, INSTRUCTION, INSTRUCTOR

### *Old Testament*

### A. Noun.

***musar*** (4148), "instruction; chastisement; warning." One of the major purposes of the wisdom literature was to teach wisdom and ***musar***, Prov. 1:2. ***musar*** is discipline, but more; it teaches how to live correctly in the fear of the Lord, so that the wise man learns his lesson before temptation and testing, Prov. 24:32. When ***musar*** as "instruction" has been given, but was not observed, the ***musar*** as "chastisement" or "discipline" may be the next step, Prov. 22:15.

Careful attention to "instruction" brings honor, Prov. 1:9, life, Prov. 4:13, and wisdom, Prov. 8:33, and above all it pleases God, Prov. 8:35. Discipline from parents and leaders are an example of God's discipline, Jer. 5:3; 35:13; Isa. 53:5.

### B. Verb.

***yasar*** (3256), "to discipline," cf. Prov. 19:18.

### *New Testament*

### A. Verbs.

1. ***katecheo*** (2727), "to teach orally, inform, instruct," is translated by the verb "to instruct" in Luke 1:4; Acts 18:25 (RV marg., "taught by word of mouth"); Rom. 2:18; 1 Cor. 14:19, RV (KJV, "teach").

2. ***paideuo*** (*3811*), "to train children, teach," is rendered "was instructed," in Acts 7:22, RV (KJV, "learned"); "instructing" in 2 Tim. 2:25, KJV (RV, "correcting"); Titus 2:12, RV, "instructing" (KJV, "teaching"). The verb is used of the family discipline, as in Heb. 12:6, 7, 10; cf. 1 Cor. 11:32; 2 Cor. 6:9; Rev. 3:19. In 1 Tim. 1:20 (passive voice) it is translated "might be taught," RV (KJV, "may learn"), but, however the passage is to be understood, it is clear that not the impartation of knowledge but severe discipline is intended. In Luke 23:16, 22, Pilate, since he had declared the Lord guiltless of the charge brought against Him, and hence could not punish Him, weakly offered, as a concession to the Jews, to 'chastise, ***paideuo***, Him, and let Him go.'

3. ***matheteuo*** (*3100*), used transitively, "to make a disciple," is translated "which is instructed" in Matt. 13:52, KJV (RV, "who hath been made a disciple").

4. ***probibazo*** (*4264*), "to lead forward, lead on" (the causal of ***probaino***, "to go forward"; ***pro***, "forward," ***bibazo***, "to lift up"), is used in the passive voice in Matt. 14:8, and translated, KJV, "being before instructed," RV, "being put forward." Some mss. have it in Acts 19:33, instead of No. 5.

5. ***sumbibazo*** (*4822*), to join, knit, unite" (***sun***, "with"), then, "to compare," and so, "to prove," hence, "to teach, instruct," is so rendered in 1 Cor. 2:16; it is found in the best mss. in Acts 19:33 (RV marg., "instructed").

### B. Nouns.

(INSTRUCTION)

***paideia*** (*3809*), "training, instruction," is translated "instruction" in 2 Tim. 3:16.

(INSTRUCTOR)

1. ***paidagogos*** (*3807*), "a guide," or "guardian" or "trainer of boys," lit., "a child-leader" (***pais***, "a boy, or child," ***ago***, "to lead"), "a tutor," is translated "instructors" in 1 Cor. 4:15, KJV (RV, "tutors"); here the thought is that of pas-

tors rather than teachers; in Gal. 3:24, 25, KJV, "schoolmaster" (RV, "tutor,"), but here the idea of instruction is absent.

2. ***paideutes*** (*3810*), akin to A, No. 2, denotes (a) "an instructor, a teacher," Rom. 2:20, KJV, "an instructor" (RV, "a corrector"); (b) "one who disciplines, corrects, chastens," Heb. 12:9, RV, "to chasten" [KJV, "which corrected" (lit., "correctors")]. In (a) the discipline of the school is in view; in (b) that of the family.

## INSTRUMENTS

***hoplon*** (*3696*), "a tool, instrument, weapon," is used metaphorically in Rom. 6:13 of the members of the body as "instruments" (marg., "weapons"), negatively, of unrighteousness, positively, of righteousness.

## INSURRECTION

### A. Nouns.

1. ***stasis*** (*4714*), akin to ***histemi***, "to make to stand," denotes (a) primarily, "a standing or place," Heb. 9:8; (b) "an insurrection, sedition," translated "insurrection" in Mark 15:7; "insurrections" in Acts 24:5, RV (KJV, "sedition"); in Luke 23:19, 25 (KJV "sedition"), "riot," Acts 19:40, RV (KJV, "uproar"); (c) "a dissension," Acts 15:2; in Acts 23:7, 10, "dissension."

2. ***stasiastes*** (*4955v*) denotes "a rebel, revolutionist, one who stirs up sedition" (from ***stasiazo***, "to stir up sedition"), Mark 15:7, "had made insurrection."

### B. Verb.

***katephistemi*** (*2721*) signifies "to rise up against"; lit., "to cause to stand forth against," Acts 18:12.

## INTEND

1. ***boulomai*** (*1014*), "to will, wish, desire, purpose" (expressing a fixed resolve, the deliberate exercise of volition), is translated "intend" in Acts 5:28, and "intending" in 12:4.

2. ***thelo*** (*2309*), "to will, be willing, desire" (less strong, and more frequent than No. 1), is translated "intending" in Luke 14:28, KJV (RV, "desiring").

## INTENT

1. ***ennoia*** (*1771*), primarily "a thinking, idea, consideration," denotes "purpose, intention, design" (***en***, in, ***nous***, mind); it is rendered "intents" in Heb. 4:12; "mind," in 1 Pet. 4:1.

2. ***logos*** (*3056*), "a word, account, etc.," sometimes denotes "a reason, cause; intent," e.g., Matt. 5:32, "cause"; it is rendered "intent" in Acts 10:29.

## INTERCESSIONS

### A. Noun.

***enteuxis*** (*1783*) primarily denotes "a lighting upon, meeting with" (akin to B); then, "a conversation"; hence, "a petition," a meaning frequent in the papyri; it is a technical term for approaching a king, and so for approaching God in "intercession"; it is rendered "prayer" in 1 Tim. 4:5; in the plural in 2:1 (i.e., seeking the presence and hearing of God on behalf of others).

### B. Verbs.

1. ***entunchano*** (*1793*), primarily "to fall in with, meet with in order to converse"; then, "to make petition," especially "to make intercession, plead with a person," either for or against others; (a) against, Acts 25:24, "made suit to (me)," RV [KJV, "have dealt with (me)"], i.e., against Paul; in Rom. 11:2, of Elijah in "pleading" with God, RV (KJV, "maketh intercession to"), against Israel; (b) for, in Rom. 8:27, of the intercessory work of the Holy Spirit for the saints; v. 34, of the similar intercessory work of Christ; so Heb. 7:25.

2. ***huperentunchano*** (*5241*), "to make a petition" or "intercede on behalf of another" (***huper***, "on behalf of," and No. 1), is used in Rom. 8:26 of the work of the Holy Spirit in making "intercession."

## INTEREST

***tokos*** (*5110*), primarily "a bringing forth, birth" (from ***tikto***, "to beget"), then, "an offspring," is used metaphorically of the produce of money lent out, "interest," usury, Matt. 25:27; Luke 19:23.

## INTERPRET, INTERPRETATION, INTERPRETER

### A. Verbs.

1. ***hermeneuo*** (*2059*), (cf. Eng., "hermeneutics"), and is used of explaining the meaning of words in a different language, John 1:38.

2. ***diermeneuo*** (*1329*), a strengthened form of No. 1 (***dia***, "through," used intensively), signifies "to interpret fully, to explain." In Luke 24:27, it is used of Christ in interpreting to the two on the way to Emmaus "in all the Scriptures the things concerning Himself," RV, "interpreted" (KJV, "expounded"); in Acts 9:36, it is rendered "is by interpretation," lit., "being interpreted" (of Tabitha, as meaning Dorcas); in 1 Cor. 12:30 and 14:5, 13, 27, it is used with reference to the temporary gift of tongues in the churches; this gift was inferior in character to that of prophesying unless he who spoke in a "tongue" interpreted his words, 14:5; he

was, indeed, to pray that he might interpret, v. 13; only two, or at the most three, were to use the gift in a gathering, and that "in turn" (RV); one was to interpret; in the absence of an interpreter, the gift was not to be exercised, v. 27.

3. ***methermeneuo*** (*3177*), "to change or translate from one language to another (***meta***, implying change, and No. 1), to interpret," is always used in the passive voice in the NT, "being interpreted," of interpreting the names, Immanuel, Matt. 1:23; Golgotha, Mark 15:22; Barnabas, Acts 4:36; in Acts 13:8, of Elymas, the verb is rendered "is . . . by interpretation," lit., "is interpreted"; it is used of interpreting or translating sentences in Mark 5:41; 15:34; in the best mss., John 1:38 (Rabbi, interpreted as "Master"); v. 41 (Messiah, interpreted as "Christ"); see No. 1.

**B. Nouns.**

(INTERPRETATION)

1. ***hermeneia*** (or ***-ia***) (*2058*), akin to A, No. 1, is used in 1 Cor. 12:10; 14:26 (see A, No. 2).

2. ***epilusis*** (*1955*), from ***epiluo***, "to loose, solve, explain," denotes "a solution, explanation," lit., "a release" (***epi***, "up," ***luo***, "to loose"), 2 Pet. 1:20, "(of private) interpretation"; i.e., the writers of Scripture did not put their own construction upon the "God-breathed" words they wrote.

(INTERPRETER)

***diermeneutes*** (*1328*), lit., "a thorough interpreter" (cf. A, No. 2), is used in 1 Cor. 14:28 (some mss. have ***hermeneutes***).

## INTERROGATION

***eperotema*** (*1906*), primarily a question or inquiry, denotes "a demand or appeal," 1 Pet. 3:21, RV (KJV, "answer"). Some take the word to indicate that baptism affords a good conscience, an appeal against the accuser.

## INTRUST

***pisteuo*** (*4100*), "to believe," also means "to entrust," and in the active voice is translated "to commit," in Luke 16:11; John 2:24; in the passive voice, "to be intrusted with," Rom. 3:2, RV, "they were intrusted with" (KJV, "unto them were committed"), of Israel and the oracles of God; 1 Cor. 9:17, RV, "I have . . . intrusted to me" (KJV, "is committed unto me"), of Paul and the stewardship of the gospel; so Gal. 2:7; Titus 1:3; in 1 Thess. 2:4, where he associates with himself his fellow missionaries, RV, "to be intrusted with" (KJV, "to be put in trust with").

## INVISIBLE

***aoratos*** (*517*), lit., "unseen" (***a***, negative, ***horao***, "to see"), is translated "invisible" in Rom. 1:20, of the power and divinity of God; of God Himself, Col. 1:15; 1 Tim. 1:17; Heb. 11:27; of things unseen, Col. 1:16.

## INWARD (man, part), INWARDLY

1. ***eso*** (*2080*), "within, inward," is used adjectivally in Rom. 7:22, "(the) inward (man)"; 2 Cor. 4:16, with "man" expressed in the preceding clause, but not repeated in the original, "(our) inward (man)" (some mss. have ***esothen***, "from within"); Eph. 3:16, RV, "(the) inward (man)" (KJV, "inner").

2. ***esothen*** (*2081*) is used in Luke 11:39, as a noun with the article, "part" being understood, "(your) inward part"; in Matt. 7:15 it has its normal use as an adverb, "inwardly."

## ITCHING

***knetho*** (*2833*), "to scratch, tickle," is used in the passive voice, metaphorically, of an eagerness to hear, in 2 Tim. 4:3, lit., "itched (as to the hearing)," of those who, not enduring sound doctrine, heap to themselves teachers.

J

## JEALOUS, JEALOUSY

### *Old Testament*

**A. Verb.**

***qana'*** (7065), "to be jealous; to be zealous." At the inter-human level ***qana'*** has a strongly competitive sense. In its most positive sense the word means "to be filled with righteous zeal or jealousy." The law provides that a husband who suspects his wife of adultery can bring her to a priest, who will administer a test of adultery, Num. 5:12–31. ***qana'***, then, in its most basic sense is the act of advancing one's rights to the exclusion of the rights of others: ". . . Ephraim shall not envy Judah, and Judah shall not vex Ephraim," Isa. 11:13. Saul sought to murder the Gibeonite enclave "in his zeal to the children of Israel and Judah," 2 Sam. 21:2. Next, the word signifies the attitude of envy toward an opponent. Rachel in her barren state "envied her sister," Gen. 30:1, and in the state of envy approached Jacob, Gen. 26:14. The Bible contains a strong warning against being envious of sinners, who might prosper and be powerful today, but will be no more tomorrow, Prov. 3:31, NIV; cf. Ps. 37:1.

In man's relation to God, the act of zeal is more positively viewed as the act of the advancement of God and His glory over against substitutes. The tribe of Levi received the right to service because "he was zealous for his God," Num. 25:13; 1 Kings 19:10. However, the sense of ***qana'*** is "to make jealous," that is, "to provoke to anger," Deut. 32:16.

**B. Noun.**

***qin'ah*** (7068), "ardor; zeal; jealousy," Deut. 29:20.

**C. Adjective.**

***qanna'*** (7067), "jealous." This adjective occurs 6 times in the Old Testament. The word refers directly to the attributes of God's justice and holiness, as He is the sole object of human worship and does not tolerate man's sin, Exod. 20:5. The adjective ***qanno'*** also means "jealous," Josh. 24:19; Nah. 1:2.

### *New Testament*

**A. Noun.**

***zelos*** (*2205*), "zeal, jealousy," is rendered "jealousy" in the RV (KJV, "envying") in Rom. 13:13; 1 Cor. 3:3; Jas. 3:14, 16; in 2 Cor. 12:20 (KJV, "envyings"); in Gal. 5:20, KJV, ("emulations"); in Acts 5:17 (KJV, "indignation"); in 13:45 (KJV, "envy"); in 2 Cor. 11:2 it is used in the phrase "with a godly jealousy."

**B. Verbs.**

1. ***zeloo*** (*2206*), akin to A, "to be jealous, to burn with jealousy" (otherwise, to seek or desire eagerly), is rendered "moved with jealousy," in Acts 7:9 and 17:5 (KJV, "moved with envy"); in 1 Cor. 13:4, "envieth (not)"; in Jas. 4:2, RV marg. (KJV, "desire to have").

2. ***parazeloo*** (*3863*), "to provoke to jealousy" (***para***, "beside," used intensively, and No. 1), is found in Rom. 10:19 and 11:11, of God's dealings with Israel through his merciful dealings with Gentiles; in 11:14, RV, "I may provoke to jealousy" (KJV, ". . . emulation"), of the apostle's evangelical ministry to Gentiles with a view to stirring his fellow nationals to a sense of their need and responsibilities regarding the gospel; in 1 Cor. 10:22, of the provocation of God on the part of believers who compromise their divine relationship by partaking of the table of demons; in Gal. 5:20, of the works of the flesh.

## JESTING

***eutrapelia*** (*2160*) properly denotes "wit, facetiousness, versatility" (lit., "easily turning," from ***eu***, "well," ***trepo***, "to turn"); by New Testament times it certainly deteriorated, and it came to denote "coarse jesting, ribaldry," as in Eph. 5:4.

## JESUS

***Iesous*** (*2424*) is a transliteration of the Heb. "Joshua," meaning "Jehovah is salvation," i.e., "is the Savior," "a common name among the Jews, e.g., Ex. 17:9; Luke 3:29 (RV); Col. 4:11. It was given to the Son of God in Incarnation as His personal name, in obedience to the command of an angel to Joseph, the husband of His Mother, Mary, shortly before He was born, Matt. 1:21. By it He is spoken of throughout the Gospel narratives generally, but not without exception, as in Mark 16:19, 20; Luke 7:13, and a dozen other places in that Gospel, and a few in John.

"Jesus Christ" occurs only in Matt. 1:1, 18; 16:21, marg.; Mark 1:1; John 1:17; 17:3. In Acts the name "Jesus" is found frequently. "Lord

Jesus" is the normal usage, as in Acts 8:16; 19:5, 17; see also the reports of the words of Stephen, 7:59, of Ananias, 9:17, and of Paul, 16:31; though both Peter, 10:36, and Paul, 16:18, also used "Jesus Christ."

In the Epistles of James, Peter, John and Jude, the personal name is not once found alone, but in Rev. eight times (RV), 1:9; 12:17; 14:12; 17:6; 19:10 (twice); 20:4; 22:16.

In the Epistles of Paul "Jesus" appears alone just thirteen times, and in the Hebrews eight times; in the latter the title "Lord" is added once only, at 13:20. In the Epistles of James, Peter, John, and Jude, who had companied with the Lord in the days of His flesh, "Jesus Christ" is the invariable order (RV) of the Name and Title, for this was the order of their experience; as "Jesus" they knew Him first, that He was Messiah they learned in His resurrection. But Paul came to know Him first in the glory of heaven, Acts 9:1–6, and his experience being thus the reverse of theirs, the reverse order, "Christ Jesus," is frequent in his letters, but, with the exception of Acts 24:24, does not occur elsewhere in the RV.

## JEW(-S) (live as do the), JEWESS, JEWISH, JEWRY, JEWS' RELIGION

### A. Adjectives.

1. ***ioudaios*** (*2453*), is used (a) adjectivally, with the lit. meaning, "Jewish," sometimes with the addition of ***aner***, "a man," Acts 10:28; 22:3; in 21:39 with ***anthropos***, in some mss. (a man in the generic sense); the best mss. omit the phrase here; in 13:6, lit., "a Jewish false-prophet"; in John 3:22, with the word ***chora***, "land" or "country," signifying "Judean," lit., "Judean country"; used by metonymy for the people of the country; (b) as a noun, "a Jew, Jews," e.g., Matt. 2:2; Mark 7:3. The name "Jew" is primarily tribal (from Judah). It is first found in 2 Kings 16:6, as distinct from Israel, of the northern kingdom. After the Captivity it was chiefly used to distinguish the race from Gentiles, e.g., John 2:6; Acts 14:1; Gal. 2:15, where it denotes Christians of "Jewish" race; it distinguishes Jews from Samaritans, in John 4:9; from proselytes, in Acts 2:10. The word is most frequent in John's gospel and the Acts, John 3:25; 5:10; 7:13; 9:22; Rom. 2:28, 29.

It also denotes Judea, e.g., Matt. 2:1; Luke 1:5; John 4:3, the word "country" being understood [cf. (a) above]. In Luke 23:5 and John 7:1, where the KJV has "Jewry," the RV translates it as usual, "Judea."

2. ***ioudaikos*** (*2451*) denotes "Jewish," Titus 1:14.

### B. Noun.

***ioudaismos*** (*2454*), "Judaism," denotes "the Jews' religion," Gal. 1:13, 14, and stands, not for their religious beliefs, but for their religious practices, not as instituted by God, but as developed and extended from these by the traditions of the Pharisees and scribes. In the Apocrypha it denotes comprehensively "the Government, laws, institutions and religion of the Jews."

### C. Verb.

***ioudaizo*** (*2450*), lit., "to Judaize," i.e., to conform to "Jewish" religious practices and manners, is translated "to live as do the Jews," in Gal. 2:14.

### D. Adverb.

***ioudaikos*** (*2452*), "in Jewish fashion," is translated "as do the Jews," in Gal. 2:14.



## JOIN

1. ***kollao*** (*2853*), primarily, "to glue or cement together," then, generally, "to unite, to join firmly," is used in the passive voice signifying "to join oneself to, to be joined to," Luke 15:15; Acts 5:13; 8:29; 9:26; 10:28, RV (KJV, "to keep company with"); 1 Cor. 6:16, 17; elsewhere, "to cleave to," Luke 10:11; Acts 17:34; Rom. 12:9.

2. ***proskollao*** (*4347*), "to stick to," a strengthened form of No. 1, with ***pros***, "to," intensive, is used in the passive voice, reflexively, in a metaphorical sense, with the meanings (a) "to join oneself to," in Acts 5:36; (b) "to cleave to," of the husband with regard to the wife, Matt. 19:5; Mark 10:7; in Eph. 5:31.

3. ***su(n)zeugnumi*** (*4801*), "to yoke together," is used metaphorically of union in wedlock, in Matt. 19:6; Mark 10:9.

## JOINT

1. ***harmos*** (*719*), "a joining, joint" (akin to ***harmozo***, "to fit, join"), is found in Heb. 4:12, figuratively (with the word "marrow") of the inward moral and spiritual being of man, as just previously expressed literally in the phrase "soul and spirit."

2. ***haphe*** (*860*), "a ligature, joint" (akin to ***hapto***, "to fit, to fasten"), occurs in Eph. 4:16 and Col. 2:19.

## JOT

***iota*** (*2503*), from the Heb. ***yodh***, the smallest Hebrew letter, mentioned to express the fact that not a single item of the Law will pass away or remain unfulfilled.

## JOURNEY (Noun and Verb), JOURNEYINGS

### A. Nouns.

1. ***hodos*** (*3598*), "a way, path, road," used of a traveler's way, a "journey," is rendered "journey" in Matt. 10:13; Mark 6:8; Luke 2:44, "a day's journey" (probably to Beeroth, six miles north of Jerusalem); 9:3; 11:6; Acts 1:12, "a Sabbath day's journey," i.e., the journey which a Jew was allowed to take on the Sabbath, viz., about 2,000 yards or cubits (estimates vary). The regulation was not a Mosaic enactment, but a rabbinical tradition, based upon an exposition of Exod. 16:29, and a comparison of the width of the suburb of a Levitical city as enjoined in Num. 35:4, 5, and the distance between the ark and the people at the crossing of the Jordan, Josh. 3:4. In regard to Acts 1:12, there is no discrepancy between this and Luke 24:50, where the RV rightly translates by "over against Beth any," which does not fix the exact spot of the Ascension.

2. ***hodoiporia*** (*3597*), "a wayfaring, journeying" (No. 1, and ***poros***, "a way, a passage"), is used of the Lord's journey to Samaria, John 4:6, and of Paul's "journeyings," 2 Cor. 11:26. Cf. B, No. 1.

### B. Verbs.

1. ***hodoiporeo*** (*3596*), "to travel, journey" (akin to A, No. 2), is found in Acts 10:9.

2. ***hodeuo*** (*3593*), "to be on the way, journey" (from ***hodos***, "a way"), the simplest form of the verbs denoting "to journey," is used in the parable of the good Samaritan, Luke 10:33.

3. ***sunodeuo*** (*4922*), ***sun***, "with," and No. 2, "to journey with," occurs in Acts 9:7.

4. ***euodoo*** (*2137*), "to help on one's way" (***eu***, "well," and ***hodos***), is used in the passive voice with the meaning "to have a prosperous journey"; so the KJV of Rom. 1:10; the RV. "I may be prospered" rightly expresses the metaphorical use which the verb acquired, without reference to a "journey"; see 1 Cor. 16:2; 3 John 2.

## JOY (Noun and Verb), JOYFULNESS, JOYFULLY, JOYOUS

### A. Nouns.

1. ***chara*** (*5479*), "joy, delight" (akin to ***chairo***, "to rejoice"), is found frequently in Matthew and Luke, and especially in John, once in Mark (4:16, KJV, "gladness"); it is absent from 1 Cor. (though the verb is used three times), but is frequent in 2 Cor., where the noun is used five times, and the verb eight times, suggestive of the apostle's relief in comparison with the circumstances of the First Epistle; in Col. 1:11, KJV, "joyfulness." The word is sometimes used, by metonymy, of the occasion or cause of "joy," Luke 2:10; in 2 Cor. 1:15, in some mss., for ***charis***, "benefit"; Phil. 4:1, where the readers are called the apostle's "joy"; so 1 Thess. 2:19, 20; Heb. 12:2, of the object of Christ's "joy"; Jas. 1:2, where it is connected with falling into trials; perhaps also in Matt. 25:21, 23, where some regard it as signifying, concretely, the circumstances attending cooperation in the authority of the Lord.

2. ***agalliasis*** (*20*), "exultation, exuberant joy." Cf. B, No. 3, below.

3. ***euphrosune*** (*2167*) is rendered "joy" in the KJV of Acts 2:28, RV, "gladness," as in 14:17.

### B. Verbs.

1. ***chairo*** (*5463*), "to rejoice, be glad," is translated "joyfully" in Luke 19:6, lit., "rejoicing"; "we joyed," 2 Cor. 7:13; "I joy," Phil. 2:17; "do ye joy," 2:18; "joying," Col. 2:5; "we joy," 1 Thess. 3:9. It is contrasted with weeping and sorrow, e.g., in John 16:20, 22; Rom. 12:15; 1 Cor. 7:30 (cf. Ps. 30:5).

2. ***kauchaomai*** (*2744*), "to boast, glory, exult," is rendered "we joy," in Rom. 5:11, KJV. It would have been an advantage to translate this word distinctively by the verbs "to glory" or "to exult."

3. ***agalliao*** (*21*), "to exult, rejoice greatly," is translated "with exceeding joy" in 1 Pet. 4:13 (middle voice), lit., "(ye rejoice, ***chairo***) exulting." Cf. A, No. 2.

## JUDGE (Noun and Verb)

***Old Testament***

### A. Verb.

***shapat*** (8199), "to judge, deliver, rule." In many contexts this root has a judicial sense. ***shapat*** refers to the activity of a third party who sits over two parties at odds with one another. This third party hears their cases against one another and decides where the right is and what to do about it (he functions as both judge and jury), Gen. 16:5, 6, Here, Abram acts according to Nuzu law.

***shapat*** also speaks of the accomplishing of a sentence. Both this concept and those of hearing the case and rendering a decision are seen in Gen. 18:25; 1 Sam. 3:13. In some cases "judging" really means delivering from injustice or oppression, 1 Sam. 24:15, or the process of maintaining order and law within a group, Judg. 4:4. The military deliverer was the head over a volunteer army summoned when danger threatened (militia), so Saul became a judge and king, 1 Sam. 8:6–18.

***mishpat*** (4941), "judgment; rights." This word has two main senses; 1) the act of sitting as a judge, hearing a case, and rendering a proper verdict, Eccl. 12:14; 2) ***mishpat*** can also refer to the "rights" belonging to someone, Exod. 23:6. The noun ***shepatim*** refers to "acts of judgment," Num. 33:4.

### *New Testament*

**A. Nouns.**

1. ***krites*** (*2923*), "a judge," is used (a) of God, Heb. 12:23, where the order in the original is "to a Judge who is God of all"; this is really the significance; it suggests that He who is the Judge of His people is at the same time their God; that is the order in 10:30; the word is also used of God in Jas. 4:12, RV; (b) of Christ, Acts 10:42; 2 Tim. 4:8; Jas. 5:9; (c) of a ruler in Israel in the times of the Judges, Acts 13:20; (d) of a Roman procurator, Acts 24:10; (e) of those whose conduct provides a standard of "judging," Matt. 12:27; Luke 11:19; (f) in the forensic sense, of one who tries and decides a case, Matt. 5:25 (twice); Luke 12:14 (some mss. have No. 2 here); 12:58 (twice); 18:2; 18:6 (lit., "the judge of unrighteousness," expressing subjectively his character); Acts 18:15; (g) of one who passes, or arrogates to himself, judgment on anything, Jas. 2:4.

2. ***dikastes*** (*1348*) denotes "a judge," Acts 7:27, 35.

**B. Verbs.**

1. ***krino*** (*2919*) primarily denotes "to separate, select, choose"; hence, "to determine," and so "to judge, pronounce judgment." The uses of this verb in the NT may be analyzed as follows: (a) to assume the office of a judge, Matt. 7:1; John 3:17; (b) to undergo process of trial, John 3:18; 16:11; 18:31; Jas. 2:12; (c) to give sentence, Acts 15:19; 16:4; 21:25; (d) to condemn, John 12:48; Acts 13:27; Rom. 2:27; (e) to execute judgment upon, 2 Thess. 2:12; Acts 7:7; (f) to be involved in a lawsuit, whether as plaintiff, Matt. 5:40; 1 Cor. 6:1; or as defendant, Acts 23:6; (g) to administer affairs, to govern, Matt. 19:28; cf. Judg. 3:10; (h) to form an opinion, Luke 7:43; John 7:24; Acts 4:19; Rom. 14:5; (i) to make a resolve, Acts 3:13; 20:16 1 Cor. 2:2.

2. ***anakrino*** (*350*), "to examine, investigate, question," is rendered "judged" in 1 Cor. 2:14 (KJV, "are . . . discerned"), said of the things of the Spirit of God; in v. 15, "judgeth," said of the exercise of a discerning "judgment" of all things as to their true value, by one who is spiritual; in the same verse, "is judged (of no man)," i.e., the merely natural mind cannot estimate the motives of the spiritual; in 4:3, "I should be judged," i.e., as to examining and passing sentence on the fulfillment or nonfulfillment of the apostle's stewardship; so in the same verse, "I judge (not mine own self)," and in v. 4 "(he that) judgeth (me is the Lord)"; in 14:24, "he is judged (of all)," i.e., the light of the heart-searching testimony of the assembly probes the conscience of the unregenerate, sifting him judicially.

3. ***diakrino*** (*1252*) denotes "to separate throughout" (***dia***, and No. 1), "discriminate, discern," and hence "to decide, to judge" (also "to contend, to hesitate, to doubt"); it is rendered "to judge" in 1 Cor. 6:5, in the sense of arbitrating; in 11:31 (1st part), the RV has "(if we) discerned (ourselves)," KJV "(if we would) judge" (***krino***, No. 1, is used in the 2nd part); so in 14:29, RV, "discern" (KJV, "judge").

## JUDGMENT

1. ***krisis*** (*2920*) primarily denotes "a separating," then, "a decision, judgment," most frequently in a forensic sense, and especially of divine "judgment."

J

2. ***krima*** (*2917*) denotes the result of the action signified by the verb ***krino***, "to judge"; it is used (a) of a decision passed on the faults of others, Matt. 7:2; (b) of "judgment" by man upon Christ, Luke 24:20; (c) of God's "judgment" upon men, e.g., Rom. 2:2, 3; 3:8; 5:16; 11:33; 13:2; 1 Cor. 11:29; Gal. 5:10; Heb. 6:2; Jas. 3:1; through Christ, e.g., John 9:39; (d) of the right of "judgment," Rev. 20:4; (e) of a lawsuit, 1 Cor. 6:7.

3. ***hemera*** (*2250*), "a day," is translated "judgment" in 1 Cor. 4:3, where "man's judgment" (lit., "man's day," marg.) is used of the present period in which man's mere "judgment" is exercised, a period of human rebellion against God, cf. Rev. 1:10, "The Lord's Day," a period of divine judgments.

4. ***gnome*** (*1106*), primarily "a means of knowing" (akin to ***ginosko***, "to know"), came to denote "a mind, understanding"; hence (a) "a purpose," Acts 20:3; (b) "a royal purpose, a decree," Rev. 17:17 (KJV, "will"); (c) "judgment, opinion," 1 Cor. 1:10, "(in the same) judgment"; Rev. 17:13, "mind"; (d) "counsel, advice," 1 Cor. 7:25, "(I give my) judgment"; 7:40, "(after my) judgment"; Philem. 14, "mind."

**B. Adjective.**

***hupodikos*** (*5267*), "brought to trial, answerable to" (***hupo***, "under," ***dike***, "justice"), Rom. 3:19, is translated "under the judgment," RV (KJV, "guilty").

## JUDGMENT SEAT

1. ***bema*** (*968*), primarily, "a step, a pace" (akin to ***baino***, "to go"), as in Acts 7:5, trans-

lated "to set (his foot) on," lit., "footroom," was used to denote a raised place or platform, where was the place of assembly; from the platform orations were made. The word became used for a tribune, two of which were provided in the law courts of Greece, one for the accuser and one for the defendant; it was applied to the tribunal of a Roman magistrate or ruler, Matt. 27:19; John 19:13; Acts 12:21, translated "throne"; 18:12, 16, 17; 25:6, 10, 17.

In two passages the word is used of the divine tribunal before which all believers are hereafter to stand. In Rom. 14:10 it is called "The judgment seat of God," RV (KJV, "of Christ"), according to the most authentic mss. The same tribunal is called "the judgment seat of Christ," 2 Cor. 5:10, to whom the Father has given all judgment, John 5:22, 27; this is different than the "Great White Throne," Rev. 20:11, at which only "the dead" will appear.

2. ***kriterion*** (*2922*) primarily "a means of judging" (akin to ***krino***, "to judge": Eng., "criterion"), then, a tribunal, law court, or "lawsuit," 1 Cor. 6:2.

## JURISDICTION

***exousia*** (*1849*), "power, authority," is used, by metonymy, to denote "jurisdiction," in Luke 23:7.

## JUST, JUSTLY

### A. Adjectives.

1. ***dikaios*** (*1342*) was first used of persons observant of ***dike***, "custom, rule, right," especially in the fulfillment of duties towards gods and men, and of things that were in accordance with right. The Eng. word "righteous" was formerly spelled "rightwise," i.e., (in a) straight way. In the NT it denotes "righteous," a state of being right, or right conduct, judged whether by the divine standard, or according to human standards, of what is right. Said of God, it designates the perfect agreement between His nature and His acts (in which He is the standard for all men). It is used (1) in the broad sense, of persons: (a) of God, e.g., John 17:25; Rom. 3:26; 1 John 1:9; 2:29; 3:7; (b) of Christ, e.g., Acts 3:14; 7:52; 22:14; 2 Tim. 4:8; 1 Pet. 3:18; 1 John 2:1; (c) of men, Matt. 1:19; Luke 1:6; Rom. 1:17; 2:13; 5:7. (2) of things; blood (metaphorical), Matt. 23:35; Christ's judgment, John 5:30; any circumstance, fact or deed, Matt. 20:4 (v. 7, in some mss.); Luke 12:57; Acts 4:19; Eph. 6:1; Phil. 1:7; 4:8; Col. 4:1; 2 Thess. 1:6; "the commandment" (the Law), Rom. 7:12; works, 1 John 3:12, the ways of God, Rev. 15:3.

2. ***endikos*** (*1738*), "just, righteous" (***en***, "in," ***dike***, "right"), is said of the condemnation of those who say "Let us do evil, that good may come," Rom. 3:8; of the recompense of reward of transgressions under the Law, Heb. 2:2.

### B. Adverb.

***dikaios*** (*1346*), "justly, righteously, in accordance with what is right," is said (a) of God's judgment, 1 Pet. 2:23; (b) of men, Luke 23:41, "justly"; 1 Cor. 15:34, RV, "righteously" (KJV, "to righteousness"); 1 Thess. 2:10, RV, "righteously"; Titus 2:12.

## JUSTICE

***dike*** (*1349*), primarily "custom, usage," came to denote "what is right"; then, "a judicial hearing"; hence, "the execution of a sentence," "punishment," 2 Thess. 1:9, RV; Jude 7, (KJV, "vengeance").

## JUSTIFICATION, JUSTIFIER, JUSTIFY

### A. Nouns.

1. ***dikaiosis*** (*1347*) denotes the act of pronouncing righteous, justification, acquittal"; its precise meaning is determined by that of the verb ***dikaioo***, "to justify" (see B); it is used twice in the Epistle to the Romans, and there alone in the NT, signifying the establishment of a person as just by acquittal from guilt. In Rom. 4:25 the phrase "for our justification," is, lit., "because of our justification," because all that was necessary on God's part for our "justification" had been effected in the death of Christ. On this account He was raised from the dead. In 5:18, "justification of life" means "justification which results in life" (cf. v. 21). That God "justifies" the believing sinner on the ground of Christ's death, involves His free gift of life.

2. ***dikaioma*** (*1345*) has three distinct meanings, and seems best described comprehensively as "a concrete expression of righteousness"; it is a declaration that a person or thing is righteous, and hence it represents the expression and effect of ***dikaiosis*** (No. 1). It signifies (a) "an ordinance," Luke 1:6; Rom. 1:32, i.e., what God has declared to be right; Rom. 2:26, righteous requirements enjoined by the Law; so 8:4, "ordinance of the Law," i.e., collectively, the precepts of the Law, all that it demands as right; in Heb. 9:1, 10, ordinances connected with the tabernacle ritual; (b) "a sentence of acquittal," by which God acquits men of their guilt, on the conditions (1) of His grace in Christ, through His expiatory sacrifice, (2) the acceptance of Christ by faith, Rom.

5:16; (c) "a righteous act," Rom. 5:18, "(through one) act of righteousness," RV.

**B. Verb.**

***dikaioo*** (*1344*) primarily "to deem to be right," signifies, in the NT, (a) "to show to be right or righteous"; in the passive voice, to be justified, Matt. 11:19; Luke 7:35; Rom. 3:4; 1 Tim. 3:16; (b) "to declare to be righteous, to pronounce righteous," (1) by man, concerning God, Luke 7:29 (see Rom. 3:4, above); concerning himself, Luke 10:29; 16:15; (2) by God concerning men, who are declared to be righteous before Him on certain conditions laid down by Him.

Ideally the complete fulfillment of the law of God would provide a basis of "justification" in His sight, Rom. 2:13. But no such case has occurred in mere human experience, and therefore no one can be "justified" on this ground, Rom. 3:9–20; Gal. 2:16; 3:10, 11; 5:4. From this negative presentation in Rom. 3, the apostle proceeds to show that He is, through Christ, as "a propitiation . . . by (***en***, "instrumental") His blood," 3:25, RV, "the Justifier of him that hath faith in Jesus" (v. 26), "justification" being the legal and formal acquittal from guilt by God as Judge, the pronouncement of the sinner as righteous, who believes on the Lord Jesus Christ. In v. 24, "being justified" is in the present continuous tense, indicating the constant process of "justification" in the succession of those who believe and are "justified." In 5:1, "being justified" is in the aorist, or point, tense, indicating the definite time at which each person, upon the exercise of faith, was justified. In 8:1, "justification" is presented as "no condemnation." That "justification" is in view here is confirmed by the preceding chapters and by verse 34.

"Justification" is primarily and gratuitously by faith, subsequently and evidentially by works. In regard to "justification" by works, the so-called contradiction between James and the apostle Paul is only apparent. Paul has in mind Abraham's attitude toward God, his acceptance of God's word, not upon Abraham's character or actions, but upon the contrast between faith and the lack of it, namely, unbelief, cf. Rom. 11:20. James (2:21–26) is occupied with the contrast between faith that is real and faith that is false, a faith barren and dead, which is not faith at all. So with righteousness, or "justification": Paul is occupied with a right relationship with God, James, with right conduct. Paul testifies that the ungodly can be "justified" by faith, James that only the right-doer is "justified."

# K

## KEEP, KEEPING

### *Old Testament*

**A. Verb.**

***natsach*** (5329), "to keep, oversee, have charge over." The word appears as "to set forward" in the sense of "to oversee or to lead" in 1 Chron. 23:4, 2 Chron. 34:12, Ezra 3:8, and Ezra 3:9.

**B. Participle.**

***natseach*** (5329), "overseer; director." ***natseach*** is found in the Book of Psalms a total of 55 times in the titles of various psalms, Ps. 5, 6, 9, et al. with the meaning, "To the choirmaster" (JB, RSV). Other versions render it "choir director" (NASB); "chief musician" (KJV); and "leader" (NAB). The significance of this title is not clear. Cf. also that the word refers to "overseers" in 2 Chron. 2:18.

**C. Adjective.**

***natsach*** is used only in Jer. 8:5 in the sense of "enduring."

### *New Testament*

**A. Verbs.**

1. ***tereo*** (*5083*) denotes (a) "to watch over, preserve, keep, watch," e.g., Acts 12:5, 6; 16:23; in 25:21, RV (1st part), "kept" (KJV, "reserved"); the present participle is translated "keepers" in Matt. 28:4, lit. "the keeping (ones)"; it is used of the "keeping" power of God the Father and Christ, exercised over His people, John 17:11, 12, 15; 1 Thess. 5:23, "preserved"; 1 John 5:18, where "He that was begotten of God," RV, is said of Christ as the Keeper ("keepeth him," RV, for KJV, "keepeth himself"); Jude 1, RV, "kept for Jesus Christ" (KJV, "preserved in Jesus Christ"), Rev. 3:10; of their inheritance, 1 Pet. 1:4 ("reserved"); of judicial reservation by God in view of future doom, 2 Pet. 2:4, 9, 17; 3:7; Jude 6, 13; of "keeping" the faith, 2 Tim. 4:7; the unity of the Spirit, Eph. 4:3; oneself, 2 Cor. 11:9; 1 Tim. 5:22; Jas. 1:27; figuratively, one's garments, Rev. 16:15; (b) "to observe, to give heed to," as of keeping commandments, etc., e.g., Matt. 19:17; John 14:15; 15:10; 17:6; Jas. 2:10; 1 John 2:3, 4, 5; 3:22, 24; 5:2 (in some mss.), 3; Rev. 1:3; 2:26; 3:8, 10; 12:17; 14:12; 22:7, 9.

2. ***diatereo*** (*1301*), "to keep carefully" (***dia***, intensive, and No. 1), is said of "the mother of Jesus," in keeping His sayings in her heart, Luke 2:51, and of the command of the apostles and elders in Jerusalem to gentile converts in the churches to "keep" themselves from the evils mentioned in Acts 15:29.

3. ***suntereo*** (*4933*) denotes "to preserve, keep safe, keep close" (***sun***, "together with," used intensively, and No. 1), in Luke 2:19, as in v. 51 (see No. 2, above), of the mother of Jesus in regard to the words of the shepherds; in Mark 6:20 it is used of Herod's preservation of John the Baptist from Herodias, RV, "kept (him) safe," KJV, "observed (him)" (marg., "kept"); in Matt. 9:17 (in some mss., Luke 5:38), of the preservation of wineskins.

4. ***phulasso*** (*5442*) denotes (a) "to guard, watch, keep watch," e.g., Luke 2:8; in the passive voice, 8:29; (b) "to keep by way of protection," e.g., Luke 11:21; John 12:25; 17:12 (2nd part; No. 1 in 1st part and in v. 11); (c) metaphorically, "to keep a law precept," etc., e.g., Matt. 19:20 and Luke 18:21, "have observed"; Luke 11:28; John 12:47 (in the best mss.); Acts 7:53; 16:4; 21:24; Rom. 2:26; Gal. 6:13; 1 Tim. 5:21 ("observe"); in the middle voice, Mark 10:20 ("have observed"); (d) in the middle voice, "to keep oneself from," Acts 21:25; elsewhere translated by the verb "to beware."

5. ***diaphulasso*** (*1314*), an intensive form of No. 4, "to guard thoroughly."

6. ***phroureo*** (*5432*), "to keep with a military guard," e.g., Gal. 3:23, RV, "kept in ward."

7. ***krateo*** (*2902*), "to be strong, get possession of, hold fast," is used in Mark 9:10, "(and) they kept (the saying)," i.e., they held fast to the Lord's command to refrain from telling what they had seen in the mount of Transfiguration.

**B. Noun.**

***teresis*** (*5084*), akin to A, No. 1, denotes (a) "a watching," and hence, "imprisonment, prison," Acts 4:3 and 5:18, "ward," RV (KJV, "hold" and "prison"); (b) "keeping," 1 Cor. 7:19.

## TO KEEP, WATCH, GUARD

**A. Verb.**

***natsar*** (5341), "to watch, to guard, to keep." ***natsar*** is frequently used to express the idea of "guarding" something, such as a vineyard, Isa. 27:3, or a fortification, Nah. 2:1. "To watch" one's speech is a frequent concern, so advice is given "to watch" one's mouth, Prov. 13:3, the tongue, Ps. 34:13, and the lips, Ps. 141:3. Many references are made to God as the one who "preserves" His people from dangers of all kinds, Deut. 32:10; Ps. 31:23.

***shamar*** (8104), "to keep, tend, watch over, retain." ***shamar*** means "to keep" in the sense of "tending" and taking care of. So God put Adam "into the garden of Eden to dress it and to keep it," in the sense of taking care of it, as with God and his people, Gen. 2:15; 2 Kings 22:14; Job 2:6; Ps. 121:4.

The word also means "to keep" in the sense of "watching over" or giving attention to, 1 Sam. 26:15; "to watch, observe," 1 Sam. 1:12; "to watch over" in the sense of seeing that one observes the covenant, keeping one to a covenant, Gen. 18:19. ***shamar*** also signifies fulfilling a responsibility, Judg. 1:24. In a third group of passages this verb means "to keep" in the sense of saving or "retaining," Gen. 41:35.

**B. Nouns.**

***mishmar*** (4929), "guard; guardpost," a group of soldiers, Gen. 40:3; a place, "guardpost," Neh. 7:3.

***mishmeret*** (4931), "those who guard; obligation," a guard-man, 2 Kings 11:5; a charge or obligation, Gen. 26:5.

## KEY

***kleis*** (*2807*), "a key," is used metaphorically (a) of "the keys of the kingdom of heaven," which the Lord committed to Peter, Matt. 16:19, by which he would open the door of faith, as he did to Jews at Pentecost, and to Gentiles in the person of Cornelius, acting as one commissioned by Christ, through the power of the Holy Spirit; he had precedence over his fellow disciples, not in authority, but in the matter of time, on the ground of his confession of Christ (v. 16); equal authority was committed to them (18:18); (b) of "the key of knowledge," Luke 11:52, i.e., knowledge of the revealed will of God, by which men entered into the life that pleases God; this the religious leaders of the Jews had presumptuously "taken away," so that they neither entered in themselves, nor permitted their hearers to do so; (c) of "the keys of death and of Hades," Rev. 1:18,, indicative of the authority of the Lord over the bodies and souls of men; (d) of "the key of David," Rev. 3:7, a reference to Isa. 22:22, speaking of the deposition of Shebna and the investiture of Eliakim, in terms evidently messianic, the metaphor being that of the right of entrance upon administrative authority; the mention of David is symbolic of complete sovereignty; (e) of "the key of the pit of the abyss," Rev. 9:1; here the symbolism is that of competent authority; the pit represents a shaft or deep entrance into the region, from whence issued smoke, symbolic of blinding delusion; (f) of "the key of the abyss," Rev. 20:1; this is to be distinguished from (e): the symbolism is that of the complete supremacy of God over the region of the lost, in which, by angelic agency, Satan is destined to be confined for a thousand years.

## KILL

### *Old Testament*

***shachat*** (7819), "to slaughter, kill," i.e., take the life of an animal or human, Gen. 22:10; of animals for food, 1 Sam. 14:32, 34; Isa. 22:13; of killing people, Judg. 12:6; 1 Kings 18:40; 2 Kings 10:7, 14. Another word with the same above usage, is ***harag***, "kill, slay," especially animals, though also great numbers of people Gen. 4:8; also vv. 14–15; Num. 31:7–8.

***rashach***, "to murder," occurs primarily in the legal material of the Old Testament. This is not a surprise, as God's law included regulations on life and provisions for dealing with the murderer. The Decalogue gives the general principle in a simple statement, which contains the first occurrence of the verb: "Thou shalt not kill [murder]," Exod. 20:13.

The Old Testament recognizes the distinction between premeditated murder and unintentional killing. In order to assure the rights of the manslayer, who unintentionally killed someone, the law provided for three cities of refuge, Num. 35; Deut. 19; Josh. 20; 21. Accidental killing has different, less severe penalties.

The prophets use ***rashach*** to describe the effect of injustice and lawlessness in Israel, Hos. 4:1–2; cf. Isa. 1:21; Jer. 7:9. The psalmist, too, metaphorically expresses the deprivation of the rights of helpless murder victims, Ps. 94:6.

### *New Testament*

1. ***apokteino*** (*615*), "to kill," is used (a) physically, e.g., Matt. 10:28; 14:5, "put . . . to death," similarly rendered in John 18:31; often of Christ's death; in Rev. 2:13, RV "was killed" (KJV, "was slain"); 9:15, RV, "kill" (KJV, "slay"); 11:13, RV, "were killed" (KJV, "were slain"); so in 19:21; (b) metaphorically, Rom. 7:11, of the power of sin, which is personified, as "finding occasion, through the commandment," and inflicting deception and spiritual death, i.e., separation from God, realized through the presentation of the commandment to conscience, breaking in upon the fancied state of freedom; the argument shows the power of the

Law, not to deliver from sin, but to enhance its sinfulness; in 2 Cor. 3:6, "the letter killeth," signifies not the literal meaning of Scripture as contrasted with the spiritual, but the power of the Law to bring home the knowledge of guilt and its punishment; in Eph. 2:16 "having slain the enmity" describes the work of Christ through His death in annulling the enmity, "the Law" (v. 15), between Jew and Gentile, reconciling regenerate Jew and Gentile to God in spiritual unity "in one body."

2. ***anaireo*** (*337*) denotes (a) "to take up" (***ana***, "up," ***haireo***, "to take"), said of Pharaoh's daughter, in "taking up" Moses, Acts 7:21; (b) "to take away" in the sense of removing, Heb. 10:9, of the legal appointment of sacrifices, to bring in the will of God in the sacrificial offering of the death of Christ; (c) "to kill," used physically only (not metaphorically as in No. 1), e.g., Luke 22:2; in 2 Thess. 2:8, instead of the future tense of this verb, some texts (followed by RV marg.) read the future of ***analisko***, "to consume."

3. ***thuo*** (*2380*) primarily denotes "to offer firstfruits to a god"; then (a) "to sacrifice by slaying a victim," Acts 14:13, 18, to do sacrifice; 1 Cor. 10:20, to sacrifice; 1 Cor. 5:7, "hath been sacrificed," of the death of Christ as our Passover; (b) "to slay, kill," Matt. 22:4; Mark 14:12; Luke 15:23, 27, 30; 22:7; John 10:10; Acts 10:13; 11:7.

## KIN, KINSFOLK, KINSMAN, KINSWOMAN

### A. Adjective.

***sungenes*** (*4773*), primarily denoting "congenital, natural, innate" (***sun***, "with," ***genos***, "a family, race, offspring"), then, "akin to," is used as a noun, denoting (a) of "family relationship, kin, a kinsman, kinsfolk(s)," Luke 1:58, RV, "kinsfolk" (KJV, "cousins"); 14:12; 21:16; John 18:26; Acts 10:24; (b) of "tribal or racial kinship, fellow nationals," Rom. 9:3; 16:7, 11, 21.

### B. Nouns.

1. ***sungenis*** (*4773v*), a late feminine form of A (some mss. have ***sungenes***), denotes "a kinswoman," Luke 1:36, RV, "kinswoman" (KJV, "cousin").

2. ***sungeneus*** (*4773***), an alternative form of A, is used in Mark 6:4, "kin," and Luke 2:44, "kinsfolk."

## KIND (Noun)

1. ***genos*** (*1085*), akin to ***ginomai***, "to become," denotes (a) "a family," Acts 4:6; 7:13 (KJV, "kindred"); 13:26, "stock"; (b) "an offspring," Acts 17:28; Rev. 22:16; (c) "a nation, a race," Mark 7:26; Acts 4:36, KJV, "of the country (of Cyprus)"; ***genos*** does not mean "a country"; the word here signifies "parentage"; 7:19, (KJV, "kindred"); 18:2, 24, (KJV, "born"); 2 Cor. 11:26, "countrymen"; Gal. 1:14 (KJV, "nation"); Phil. 3:5, "stock"; 1 Pet. 2:9 (KJV, "generation"); (d) "a kind, sort, class," Matt. 13:47, "kind"; in some mss. in 17:21, KJV, "kind"; Mark 9:29, "kind"; 1 Cor. 12:10, 28, "kinds" (KJV, "diversities"); 14:10 (ditto).

2. ***phusis*** (*5449*) among its various meanings denotes "the nature, the natural constitution or power of a person or thing," and is translated "kind" in Jas. 3:7 (twice), "kind" (of beasts, etc.), and "(man)kind," lit., "human kind."

## KIND (Adjective), KIND (be), KINDLY, KINDNESS

### A. Adjective.

***chrestos*** (*5543*), "serviceable, good, pleasant" (of things), "good, gracious, kind" (of persons), is translated "kind" in Luke 6:35, of God; in Eph. 4:32, enjoined upon believers.

### B. Verb.

***chresteuomai*** (*5541*), akin to A, "to be kind," is said of love, 1 Cor. 13:4.

### C. Nouns.

1. ***chrestotes*** (*5544*), akin to A, and B, used of "goodness of heart, kindness," is translated "kindness" in 2 Cor. 6:6; Gal. 5:22, RV (KJV, "gentleness"); Eph. 2:7; Col. 3:12; Titus 3:4.

2. ***philanthropia*** (*5363*), (Eng., "philanthropy"), denotes "kindness," and is so translated in Acts 28:2 and in Titus 3:4, the latter of the "kindness" of God.

### D. Adverb.

***philanthropos*** (*5364*), akin to C, No. 2, "humanely, kindly," is translated "kindly" in Acts 27:3 (KJV, "courteously").

## KINDLE

1. ***hapto*** (*681*), properly, "to fasten to," is used in Acts 28:2 (in the most authentic mss., some mss. have No. 3), of "kindling a fire."

2. ***periapto*** (*4012* and *681*), properly, "to tie about, attach" (***peri***, "around," and No. 1), is used of "lighting" a fire in the midst of a court in Luke 22:55 (some mss. have No. 1).

3. ***anapto*** (*381*), "to light up" (***ana***, "up," and No. 1), is used (a) literally, in Jas. 3:5, "kindleth"; (b) metaphorically, in the passive voice, in Luke 12:49, of the "kindling" of the fire of hostility.

## KING

### A. Noun.

***basileus*** (*935*), "a king" (cf. Eng., "Basil"), e.g., Matt. 1:6, is used of the Roman emperor in 1 Pet. 2:13, 17 (a command of general application); of Herod the Tetrarch (used by courtesy), Matt. 14:9; of Christ, as the "King" of the Jews, e.g., Matt, 2:2; 27:11, 29, 37; as the "King" of Israel, Mark 15:32; John 1:49; 12:13; as "King of kings," Rev. 17:14; 19:16; as "the King" in judging nations and men at the establishment of the millennial kingdom, Matt. 25:34, 40; of God, "the great King," Matt. 5:35; "the King eternal, incorruptible, invisible," 1 Tim. 1:17; "King of kings," 1 Tim. 6:15; "King of the ages," Rev. 15:3, RV (KJV, "saints"). Christ's "kingship" was predicted in the OT, e.g., Ps. 2:6, and in the NT, e.g., Luke 1:32, 33; He came as such e.g., Matt. 2:2; John 18:37; was rejected and died as such, Luke 19:14; Matt. 27:37; is now a "King" Priest, after the order of Melchizedek, Heb. 5:6; 7:1, 17; and will reign for ever and ever, Rev. 11:15.

### B. Adjectives.

1. ***basileios*** (*934*), denoting "royal," as in 1 Pet. 2:9, is used in the plural, of the courts or palaces of kings, Luke 7:25, "kings' courts"; a possible meaning is "among royal courtiers or persons."

2. ***basilikos*** (*937*), "royal, belonging to a king," is used in Acts 12:20 with "country" understood, "their country was fed from the king's," lit., "the royal (country)."

## KINGDOM

### *Old Testament*

***malkut*** (4438), "kingdom; reign; rule." The word ***malkut*** denotes: (1) the territory of the kingdom, Esth. 1:4; (2) the accession to the throne, Esth. 4:14; (3) the year of rule, Esth. 2:16; and (4) anything "royal" or "kingly," Esth. 1:2; royal wine, Esth. 1:7; royal crown, Esth. 1:11; royal word, Esth. 1:19; royal garment, Esth. 6:8, royal palace, Esth. 1:9, royal scepter, Ps. 45:6, and finally, "glory," Ps. 145:11–12.

***mamlakah*** (4467), "kingdom; sovereignty; dominion; reign," is the area and people that constitute a "kingdom." The word refers to non-Israelite nations who are ruled by a ***melek***, "king," Isa. 23:17. ***mamlikah*** is a synonym for ***'am***, "people," and ***goy***, "nation," Ps. 105:13. The word also denotes Israel as God's "kingdom," Exod. 19:6. The Davidic king was the theocratic agent by whom God ruled over and blessed His people, 2 Sam. 7:16. Nevertheless, the one ***mamlakah*** after Solomon was divided into two kingdoms which Ezekiel predicted would be reunited, Ezek. 37:22.

Close to the basic meaning is the usage of ***mamlakah*** to denote "king," i.e., one who heads the kingdom, 1 Sam. 10:18. The word further has the meaning of the royal "rule," the royal "sovereignty," and the "dominion." The royal "sovereignty" was taken from Saul because of his disobedience, 1 Sam. 28:17. "Royal sovereignty" is also the sense in Jer. 27:1. The Old Testament further defines as expressions of the royal "rule" all things associated with the king: (1) the throne: "And it shall be, when he sitteth upon the throne of his kingdom, that he shall write him a copy of this law in a book out of that which is before the priests the Levites," Deut. 17:18; (2) the pagan sanctuary supported by the throne: "But prophesy not again any more at Beth-el: for it is the king's chapel, and it is the king's court," Amos 7:13; and (3) a royal city, 1 Sam. 27:5.

All human rule is under God's control. Consequently the Old Testament fully recognizes the kingship of God. The Lord ruled as king over His people Israel, 1 Chron. 29:11. He graciously ruled over His people through David and his followers until the Exile, 2 Chron. 13:5.

***melek*** (4428), "king." This word occurs about 2,513 times in the Old Testament. It is found several times in Gen. 14:1: "And it came to pass in the days of Amraphel king of Shinar, Arioch king of Ellasar, Chedorlaomer king of Elam, and Tidal king of nations."

### *New Testament*

***basileia*** (*932*) is primarily an abstract noun, denoting "sovereignty, royal power, dominion," e.g., Rev. 17:18, translated "(which) reigneth," lit., "hath a kingdom" (RV marg.); then, by metonymy, a concrete noun, denoting the territory or people over whom a king rules, e.g., Matt. 4:8; Mark 3:24. It is used especially of the "kingdom" of God and of Christ.

The Kingdom of God is (a) the sphere of God's rule, Ps. 22:28; 145:13; Dan. 4:25; Luke 1:52; Rom. 13:1, 2. Since, however, this earth is the scene of universal rebellion against God, e.g., Luke 4:5, 6; 1 John 5:19; Rev. 11:15–18, the "kingdom" of God is (b) the sphere in which, at any given time, His rule is acknowledged. God has not relinquished His sovereignty in the face of rebellion, demoniac and human, but has declared His purpose to establish it, Dan. 2:44; 7:14; 1 Cor. 15:24, 25. Meantime, seeking willing obedience, He gave His law to a nation and appointed kings to administer His "kingdom" over it, 1 Chron. 28:5. Israel, however, though declaring still a nominal allegiance shared in the common rebellion, Isa. 1:2–4, and, after they had rejected the Son of God, John 1:11 (cf. Matt. 21:33–43), were "cast away," Rom. 11:15, 20, 25. Henceforth God calls upon men everywhere, without distinction of race or nationality, to submit voluntarily to His rule. Thus the "kingdom" is said to be "in mystery" now, Mark 4:11, that is, it does not come within the range of the natural powers of observation, Luke 17:20, but is spiritually discerned, John 3:3 (cf. 1 Cor. 2:14). When, hereafter, God asserts His rule universally, then the "kingdom" will be in glory, that is, it will be manifest to all; cf. Matt. 25:31–.34; Phil. 2:9–11; 2 Tim. 4:1, 18.

The fundamental principle of the Kingdom is declared in the words of the Lord spoken in the midst of a company of Pharisees, "the Kingdom of God is in the midst of you," Luke 17:21 (marg.), where the King is, there is the Kingdom. Thus at the present time and on earth, where the King is and where His rule is acknowledged, is, first, in the heart of the individual believer, Acts 4:19; Eph. 3:17; 1 Pet. 3:15; and then in the churches of God, 1 Cor. 12:3, 5, 11; 14:37; cf. Col. 1:27, where for "in" read "among."

Entrance into the Kingdom of God is by the new birth, Matt. 18:3; John 3:5, for nothing that a man may be by nature, or can attain to by any form of self-culture, avails in the spiritual realm. And as the new nature, received in the new birth, is made evident by obedience, it is further said that only such as do the will of God shall enter into His Kingdom, Matt. 7:21, where, however, the context shows that the reference is to the future, as in 2 Pet. 1:10, 11. Cf. also 1 Cor. 6:9, 10; Gal. 5:21; Eph. 5:5.

The expression "Kingdom of God" occurs four times in Matthew, "Kingdom of the Heavens" usually taking its place. The latter (cf. Dan. 4:26) does not occur elsewhere in NT, but see 2 Tim. 4:18, "His heavenly Kingdom.". . . This Kingdom is identical with the Kingdom of the Father (cf. Matt. 26:29 with Mark 14:25), and with the Kingdom of the Son (cf. Luke 22:30). Thus there is but one Kingdom, variously described: of the Son of Man, Matt. 13:41; of Jesus, Rev. 1:9; of Christ Jesus, 2 Tim. 4:1; "of Christ and God," Eph. 5:5; "of our Lord, and of His Christ," Rev. 11:15; "of our God, and the authority of His Christ," 12:10; "of the Son of His love," Col. 1:13.

The Apostle Paul often speaks of the Kingdom of God, not dispensationally but morally, e.g., in Rom. 14:17; 1 Cor. 4:20, but never so of the Kingdom of Heaven. "God" is not the equivalent of "the heavens." He is everywhere and above all dispensations, whereas "the heavens" are distinguished from the earth, until the Kingdom comes in judgment and power and glory (Rev. 11:15, RV) when rule in heaven and on earth will be one.

While, then, the sphere of the Kingdom of God and the Kingdom of Heaven are at times identical, yet the one term cannot be used indiscriminately for the other. In the "Kingdom of Heaven" (32 times in Matt.), heaven is in antithesis to earth, and the phrase is limited to the Kingdom in its earthly aspect for the time being, and is used only dispensationally and in connection with Israel. In the "Kingdom of God," in its broader aspect, God is in antithesis to "man" or "the world," and the term signifies the entire sphere of God's rule and action in relation to the world. It has a moral and spiritual force and is a general term for the Kingdom at any time. The Kingdom of Heaven is always the Kingdom of God, but the Kingdom of God is not limited to the Kingdom of Heaven, until in their final form, they become identical, e.g., Rev. 11:15, RV; John 3:5; Rev. 12:10.

## KNEEL

***gonupeteo*** (*1120*) denotes "to bow the knees, kneel," the act of one imploring aid, Matt. 17:14; Mark 1:40; of one expressing reverence and honor, Mark 10:17; in mockery, Matt. 27:29.

## KNIT TOGETHER

***sumbibazo*** (*4822*) signifies "to cause to coalesce, to join or knit together," Eph. 4:16, RV, "knit together" (KJV, "compacted)"; Col. 2:2, where some would assign the alternative meaning, "to instruct," as, e.g., in 1 Cor. 2:16; in Col. 2:19, "knit together," it is said of the church, as the body of which Christ is the Head.

## KNOW, KNOWN, KNOWLEDGE, UNKNOWN

### *Old Testament*

### A. Verbs.

***nakar*** (5234), "to know, regard, recognize, pay attention to, be acquainted with." The basic meaning of the term is a physical apprehension, whether through sight, touch, or hearing. Darkness sometimes makes recognition impossible, Ruth 3:14. People are often "recognized" by their voices, Judg. 18:3. ***nakar*** sometimes has the meaning "pay attention to," a special kind of recognition. Ruth 2:19. This verb can mean "to be acquainted with," a kind of intellectual awareness, " Job 7:10; cf. Ps. 103:16. The sense of "to distinguish" is seen in Ezra 3:13,

***yada'*** (3045), "to know." Essentially ***yada'*** means: (1) to know by observing and reflecting (thinking), and (2) to know by experiencing. The first sense appears in Gen. 8:11, where Noah "knew" the waters had abated as a result of seeing the freshly picked olive leaf in the dove's mouth; he "knew" it after observing and thinking about what he had seen. He did not actually see or experience the abatement himself.

In contrast to this knowing through reflection is the knowing which comes through experience with the senses, by investigation and proving, by reflection and consideration (firsthand knowing). Consequently ***yada'*** is used in synonymous parallelism with "hear," Exod. 3:7, "see," Gen. 18:21, and "perceive, see," Job 28:7.

Thirdly, this verb can represent that kind of knowing which one learns and can give back, Gen. 4:9; 12:11. One can also "know" by being told by a witness, Lev. 5:1. In addition to the essentially cognitive knowing already presented, this verb has a purely experiential side. The "knower" has actual involvement with or in the object of the knowing. So Potiphar was unconcerned about (literally, "did not know about") what was in his house, Gen. 39:6—he had no actual contact with it. In Gen. 4:1 Adam's knowing Eve also refers to direct contact with her—in a sexual relationship. In Gen. 18:19 God says He "knows" Abraham; He cared for him in the sense that He chose him from among other men and saw to it that certain things happened to him. The emphasis is on the fact that God "knew" him intimately and personally.

***yada'*** in the intensive and causative stems is used to express a particular concept of revelation. God did not make Himself known by His name Jehovah to Abraham, Isaac, and Jacob. He did reveal that name to them, that He was the God of the covenant. Nevertheless, the covenant was not fulfilled (they did not possess the Promised Land) until the time of Moses. The statement in Exod. 6:3 implies that now God was going to make Himself known "by His name"; He was going to lead them to possess the land. God makes Himself known through revelatory acts such as bringing judgment on the wicked, Ps. 9:16, and deliverance to His people, Isa. 66:14. He also reveals Himself through the spoken word—for example, by the commands given through Moses, Ezek. 20:11, by promises like those given to David, 2 Sam. 7:21.

**B. Noun.**

***da'at*** (1847), "knowledge," Gen. 2:9; Exod. 31:3.

***New Testament***

**A. Verbs.**

1. ***ginosko*** (*1097*) signifies "to be taking in knowledge, to come to know, recognize, understand," or "to understand completely," e.g., Mark 13:28, 29; John 13:12; 15:18; 21:17; 2 Cor. 8:9; Heb. 10:34; 1 John 2:5; 4:2, 6 (twice), 7, 13; 5:2, 20; in its past tenses it frequently means "to know in the sense of realizing," the aorist or point tense usually indicating definiteness, Matt. 13:11; Mark 7:24; John 7:26; in 10:38 "that ye may know (aorist tense) and understand, (present tense)"; 19:4; Acts 1:7; 17:19; Rom. 1:21; 1 Cor. 2:11 (2nd part), 14; 2 Cor. 2:4; Eph. 3:19; 6:22; Phil. 2:19; 3:10; 1 Thess. 3:5; 2 Tim. 2:19; Jas. 2:20; 1 John 2:13 (twice), 14; 3:6; 4:8; 2 John 1; Rev. 2:24; 3:3, 9. In the passive voice, it often signifies "to become known," e.g., Matt. 10:26; Phil. 4:5. In the sense of complete and absolute understanding on God's part, it is used, e.g., in Luke 16:15; John 10:15 (of the Son as well as the Father); 1 Cor. 3:20. In Luke 12:46, KJV, it is rendered "he is . . . aware."

In the NT ***ginosko*** frequently indicates a relation between the person "knowing" and the object known; in this respect, what is "known" is of value or importance to the one who knows, and hence the establishment of the relationship, e.g., especially of God's "knowledge," 1 Cor. 8:3, "if any man love God, the same is known of Him"; Gal. 4:9, "to be known of God"; here the "knowing" suggests approval and bears the meaning "to be approved"; so in 2 Tim. 2:19; cf. John 10:14, 27; Gen. 18:19; Nah. 1:7; the relationship implied may involve remedial chastisement, Amos 3:2. The same idea of appreciation as well as "knowledge" underlies several statements concerning the "knowledge" of God and His truth on the part of believers, e.g., John 8:32; 14:20, 31; 17:3; Gal. 4:9 (1st part); 1 John 2:3–13, 14; 4:6, 8, 16; 5:20; such "knowledge" is obtained, not by mere intellectual activity, but by operation of the Holy Spirit consequent upon acceptance of Christ. Nor is such "knowledge" marked by finality; see e.g., 2 Pet. 3:18; Hos. 6:3, RV.

The verb is also used to convey the thought of connection or union, as between man and woman, Matt. 1:25; Luke 1:34.

2. ***oida*** (Perf. of *1492*), from the same root as ***eidon***, "to see," is a perfect tense with a

present meaning, signifying, primarily, "to have seen or perceived"; hence, "to know, to have knowledge of," whether absolutely, as in divine knowledge, e.g., Matt. 6:8, 32; John 6:6, 64; 8:14; 11:42; 13:11; 18:4; 2 Cor. 11:31; 2 Pet. 2:9; Rev. 2:2, 9, 13, 19; 3:1, 8, 15; or in the case of human "knowledge," to know from observation, e.g., 1 Thess. 1:4, 5; 2:1; 2 Thess. 3:7.

The differences between ***ginosko*** (No. 1) and ***oida*** demand consideration: (a) ***ginosko***, frequently suggests inception or progress in "knowledge," while ***oida*** suggests fullness of "knowledge," e.g., John 8:55; (b) while ***ginosko*** frequently implies an active relation between the one who "knows" and the person or thing "known" (see No. 1, above), ***oida*** expresses the fact that the object has simply come within the scope of the "knower's" perception; thus in Matt. 7:23 "I never knew you" (***ginosko***) suggests "I have never been in approving connection with you," whereas in 25:12, "I know you not" (***oida***) suggests "you stand in no relation to Me."

3. ***epiginosko*** (*1921*) denotes (a) "to observe, fully perceive, notice attentively, discern, recognize" (***epi***, "upon," and No. 1); it suggests generally a directive, a more special, recognition of the object "known" than does No. 1; it also may suggest advanced "knowledge" or special appreciation; thus, in Rom. 1:32, "knowing the ordinance of God" (***epiginosko***) means "knowing full well," whereas in verse 21 "knowing God" (***ginosko***) simply suggests that they could not avoid the perception.

4. ***proginosko*** (*4267*), "to know beforehand," is used (a) of the divine "foreknowledge" concerning believers, Rom. 8:29; Israel, 11:2; Christ as the Lamb of God, 1 Pet. 1:20, RV, "foreknown" (KJV, "foreordained"); (b) of human previous "knowledge," of a person, Acts 26:5, RV, "having knowledge of" (KJV, "which knew"); of facts, 2 Pet. 3:17.

5. ***sunoida*** (*4923*), ***sun***, "with," and No. 2, a perfect tense with a present meaning, denotes (a) "to share the knowledge of, be privy to," Acts 5:2; (b) "to be conscious of," especially of guilty consciousness, 1 Cor. 4:4, "I know nothing against (KJV, by) myself." The verb is connected with ***suneidon***, found in Acts 12:12; 14:6 (in the best texts).

6. ***gnorizo*** (*1107*) signifies (a) "to come to know, discover, know," Phil. 1:22, "I wot (not)," i.e., "I know not," "I have not come to know" (the RV, marg. renders it, as under (b), "I do not make known"); (b) "to make known," whether (I) communicating things before "unknown," Luke 2:15, 17; in the latter some mss. have the verb ***diagnorizo*** (hence the KJV, "made known abroad)"; John 15:15, "I have made known"; 17:26; Acts 2:28; 7:13 (1st part); Rom. 9:22, 23; 16:26 (passive voice); 2 Cor. 8:1, "we make known (to you)," RV, KJV, "we do (you) to wit"; Eph. 1:9; 3:3, 5, 10 (all three in the passive voice); 6:19, 21; Col. 1:27; 4:7, 9, "shall make known" (KJV, "shall declare"); 2 Pet. 1:16; or (II), reasserting things already "known," 1 Cor. 12:3, "I give (you) to understand" (the apostle reaffirms what they knew); 15:1, of the gospel; Gal. 1:11 (he reminds them of what they well knew, the ground of his claim to apostleship); Phil. 4:6 (passive voice), of requests to God.

## B. Adjectives.

1. ***gnostos*** (*1110*), a later form of ***gnotos*** (from No. 1), most frequently denotes "known"; it is used ten times in the Acts, always with that meaning (save in 4:16, where it means "notable"); twice in the Gospel of John, 18:15, 16; in Luke 2:44 and 23:49 it denotes "acquaintance"; elsewhere only in Rom. 1:19, "(that which) may be known (of God)," lit., "the knowable of God," referring to the physical universe, in the creation of which God has made Himself "knowable," that is, by the exercise of man's natural faculties, without such supernatural revelations as those given to Israel.

2. ***phaneros*** (*5318*), "visible, manifest," is translated "known" in Matt. 12:16 and Mark 3:12.

## C. Nouns.

1. ***gnosis*** (*1108*), primarily "a seeking to know, an enquiry, investigation" (akin to A, No. 1), denotes, in the NT, "knowledge," especially of spiritual truth; it is used (a) absolutely, in Luke 11:52; Rom. 2:20; 15:14; 1 Cor. 1:5; 8:1 (twice), 7, 10, 11; 13:2, 8; 14:6; 2 Cor. 6:6; 8:7; 11:6; Eph. 3:19; Col. 2:3; 1 Pet. 3:7; 2 Pet. 1:5, 6; (b) with an object: in respect of (1) God, 2 Cor. 2:14; 10:5; (2) the glory of God, 2 Cor. 4:6; (3) Christ Jesus, Phil. 3:8; 2 Pet. 3:18; (4) salvation, Luke 1:77; (c) subjectively, of God's "knowledge," Rom. 11:33; the word of "knowledge," 1 Cor. 12:8; "knowledge" falsely so called, 1 Tim. 6:20.

2. ***epignosis*** (*1922*), akin to A, No. 3, denotes "exact or full knowledge, discernment, recognition," and is a strengthened form of No. 1, expressing a fuller or a full "knowledge," a greater participation by the "knower" in the object "known," thus more powerfully influencing him. It is not found in the Gospels and Acts. Paul uses it 15 times (16 if Heb. 10:26 is included) out of the 20 occurrences; Peter 4 times, all in his 2nd Epistle. Contrast Rom. 1:28 (***epignosis***) with the simple verb in v. 21. "In all the four Epistles of the first Roman cap-

tivity it is an element in the Apostle's opening prayer for his correspondents' well-being, Phil. 1:9; Eph. 1:17; Col. 1:9; Philem. 6" (Lightfoot).

It is used with reference to God in Rom. 1:28; 10:2; Eph. 1:17; Col. 1:10; 2 Pet. 1:3; God and Christ, 2 Pet. 1:2; Christ, Eph. 4:13; 2 Pet. 1:8; 2:20; the will of the Lord, Col. 1:9; every good thing, Philem. 6, RV (KJV, "acknowledging"); the truth, 1 Tim. 2:4; 2 Tim. 2:25, RV; 3:7; Titus 1:1, RV; the mystery of God. Col. 2:2, RV, "(that they) may know" (KJV, "to the acknowledgment of"), lit., "into a full knowledge." It is used without the mention of an object in Phil. 1:9; Col. 3:10, RV, "(renewed) unto knowledge."

# L

## LABORER, FELLOW LABORER

***ergates*** (*2040*), akin to ***ergazomai***, "to work," and ***ergon***, "work," denotes (a) "a field laborer, a husbandman," Matt. 9:37, 38; 20:1, 2, 8; Luke 10:2 (twice); Jas. 5:4; (b) "a workman, laborer," in a general sense, Matt. 10:10; Luke 10:7; Acts 19:25; 1 Tim. 5:18; it is used (c) of false apostles and evil teachers, 2 Cor. 11:13; Phil. 3:2, (d) of a servant of Christ, 2 Tim. 2:15; (e) of evildoers, Luke 13:27.

## LACK, LACKING

**A. Noun.**

***husterema*** (*5303*) denotes (a) "that which is lacking, deficiency, shortcoming" (akin to ***hustereo***, "to be behind, in want"), 1 Cor. 16:17; Phil. 2:30; Col. 1:24.

**B. Verb.**

***hustereo*** (*5302*), akin to A, "to come or be behind," is used in the sense of "lacking" certain things, Matt. 19:20; Mark 10:21; Luke 22:35; in the sense of being inferior, 1 Cor. 12:24 (middle voice).

## LADY

***kuria*** (*2959*) is the person addressed in 2 John 1 and 5. Not improbably it is a proper name, but one who had a special relation with the local church.

## LAMB

1. ***aren*** (*704*), a noun the nominative case of which is found only in early times occurs in Luke 10:3. In normal usage it was replaced by ***arnion*** (No. 2), of which it is the equivalent.

2. ***arnion*** (*721*) is a diminutive in form, but the diminutive force is not to be pressed. The general tendency in the vernacular was to use nouns in ***-ion*** freely, apart from their diminutive significance. It is used only by the apostle John, (a) in the plural, in the Lord's command to Peter, John 21:15, with symbolic reference to young converts; (b) elsewhere, in the singular, in the Apocalypse, some 28 times, of Christ as the "Lamb" of God, the symbolism having reference to His character and His vicarious Sacrifice, as the basis both of redemption and of divine vengeance. He is seen in the position of sovereign glory and honor, e.g., 7:17, which He shares equally with the Father, 22:1, 3, the center of angelic beings and of the redeemed and the object of their veneration, e.g. 5:6, 8, 12, 13; 15:3, the Leader and Shepherd of His saints, e.g., 7:17; 14:4, the Head of his spiritual bride, e.g., 21:9, the luminary of the heavenly and eternal city, 21:23, the One to whom all judgment is committed, e.g., 6:1, 16; 13:8, the Conqueror of the foes of God and His people, 17:14; the song that celebrates the triumph of those who "gain the victory over the Beast," is the song of Moses . . . and the song of the Lamb 15:3. His sacrifice, the efficacy of which avails for those who accept the salvation thereby provided, forms the ground of the execution of divine wrath for the rejector, and the defier of God, 14:10; (c) in the description of the second "Beast," Rev. 13:11, seen in the vision "like a lamb," suggestive of his acting in the capacity of a false messiah, a travesty of the true.

3. ***amnos*** (*286*), "a lamb," is used figuratively of Christ, in John 1:29, 36, with the article, pointing Him out as the expected One, the One to be well known as the personal fulfillment and embodiment of all that had been indicated in the OT, the One by whose sacrifice deliverance from divine judgment was to be obtained; in Acts 8:32 and 1 Pet. 1:19, the absence of the article stresses the nature and character of His sacrifice as set forth in the symbolism. The reference in each case is to the lamb of God's providing, Gen. 22:8, and the Paschal lamb of God's appointment for sacrifice in Israel, e.g., Ex. 12:5, 14, 27 (cf. 1 Cor. 5:7).

## LAMP

1. ***lampas*** (*2985*) denotes "a torch" (akin to ***lampo***, "to shine"), frequently fed, like a "lamp," with oil from a little vessel used for the purpose (the ***angeion*** of Matt. 25:4); they held little oil and would frequently need replenishing, as in the parable of the ten virgins, Matt. 25:1, 3, 4, 7, 8; John 18:3, "torches"; Acts 20:8, "lights"; Rev. 4:5; 8:10.

2. ***luchnos*** (*3088*) frequently mistranslated "candle," is a portable "lamp" usually set on a stand; the word is used literally, Matt. 5:15; Mark 4:21; Luke 8:16; 11:33, 36; 15:8; Rev. 18:23; 22:5; (b) metaphorically, of Christ as the Lamb, Rev. 21:23, RV, "lamp" (KJV, "light"); of John the Baptist, John 5:35, RV, "the lamp" (KJV, "a . . . light"); of the eye, Matt. 6:22, and Luke

11:34, RV, "lamp"; of spiritual readiness, Luke 12:35, RV, "lamps"; of "the word of prophecy," 2 Pet. 1:19, RV, "lamp."

## LANGUAGE

***dialektos*** (*1258*), primarily "a conversation, discourse" (akin to ***dialegomai***, "to discourse or discuss"), came to denote "the language or dialect of a country or district," in the KJV and RV of Acts 2:6 it is translated "language"; in the following the RV retains "language," for KJV, "tongue," Acts 1:19; 2:8; 21:40; 22:2; 26:14.

## LASCIVIOUS, LASCIVIOUSNESS

***aselgeia*** (*766*) denotes "excess, licentiousness, absence of restraint, indecency, wantonness"; "lasciviousness" in Mark 7:22, one of the evils that proceed from the heart; in 2 Cor. 12:21, one of the evils of which some in the church at Corinth had been guilty; in Gal. 5:19, classed among the works of the flesh; in Eph. 4:19, among the sins of the unregenerate who are "past feeling"; so in 1 Pet. 4:3; in Jude 4, of that into which the grace of God had been turned by ungodly men; it is translated "wantonness" in Rom. 13:13.

## LAUGH, LAUGH TO SCORN

1. ***gelao*** (*1070*), "to laugh," is found in Luke 6:21, 25. This signifies loud laughter in contrast to demonstrative weeping.

2. ***katagelao*** (*2606*) denotes "to laugh scornfully at," more emphatic than No. 1 (***kata***, "down," used intensively, and No. 1), and signifies derisive laughter, Matt. 9:24; Mark 5:40; Luke 8:53.

## LAUGHTER

***gelos*** (*1071*), corresponding to LAUGH, 1, denotes "laughter," Jas. 4:9.

## LAW

### *Old Testament*

**A. Noun.**

***torah*** (8451), "law; direction; instruction," Prov. 13:14; Job 22:22. The "instruction" of the sages of Israel, who were charged with the education of the young, was intended to cultivate in the young a fear of the Lord so that they might live in accordance with God's expectations, Prov. 28:7; cf. 3:1; 4:2; 7:2; also a parent, Prov. 31:26.

The "instruction" given by God to Moses and the Israelites became known as "the law" or "the direction" (***ha-torah***), and quite frequently as "the Law of the Lord," Ps. 119:1; or "the Law of God," Neh. 8:18; or "Law of Moses," Mal. 4:4. The word can refer to the whole of the "law," Ps. 78:5; or to particulars, Deut. 4:44.

God had communicated the "law" that Israel might observe and live, Deut. 4:8. The king was instructed to have a copy of the "law" prepared for him at his coronation, Deut. 17:18. The priests were charged with the study and teaching of, as well as the jurisprudence based upon, the "law," Jer. 18:18. The "law" was retaught in Josiah's day, 2 Chron. 34:15. Jeremiah prophesied concerning God's new dealing with His people in terms of the New Covenant, in which God's law is to be internalized, God's people would willingly obey Him, Jer. 31:33. The last prophet of the Old Testament reminded and challenged God's people to remember the "law," Mal. 4:4.

**B. Verb.**

***yarah*** (3384), "to throw, cast, direct, teach, instruct." The noun ***torah*** is derived from this root. The meaning "to cast" appears in Gen. 31:51; "to teach" in 1 Sam. 12:23.

### *New Testament*

**A. Noun.**

***nomos*** (*3551*), akin to ***nemo***, "to divide out, distribute," primarily meant "that which is assigned"; hence, "usage, custom," and then, "law, law as prescribed by custom, or by statute"; the word ***ethos***, "custom," was retained for unwritten "law," while ***nomos*** became the established name for "law" as decreed by a state and set up as the standard for the administration of justice.

In the NT it is used

(a) of "law" in general, e.g., Rom. 2:12, 13, "a law" (RV), expressing a general principle relating to "law"; v. 14, last part; 3:27, "By what manner of law?" i.e., "by what sort of principle (has the glorying been excluded)?"; 4:15 (last part); 5:13, referring to the period between Adam's trespass and the giving of the Law; 7:1 (1st part, RV marg., "law"); against those graces which constitute the fruit of the Spirit "there is no law," Gal. 5:23.

(b) of a force or influence impelling to action, Rom. 7:21, 23 (1st part), "a different law," RV.

(c) of the Mosaic Law, the "law" of Sinai, (1) with the definite article, e.g., Matt. 5:18; John 1:17; Rom. 2:15, 18, 20, 26, 27; 3:19; 4:15; 7:4, 7, 14, 16, 22; 8:3, 4, 7; Gal. 3:10, 12, 19, 21, 24; 5:3; Eph. 2:15; Phil. 3:6; 1 Tim. 1:8; Heb. 7:19; Jas. 2:9; (2) without the article, thus stressing the Mosaic Law in its quality as "law," e.g.,

Rom. 2:14 (1st part); 5:20; 7:9, where the stress in the quality lies in this, that "the commandment which was unto (i.e., which he thought would be a means of) life," he found to be "unto (i.e., to have the effect of revealing his actual state of) death"; 10:4; 1 Cor. 9:20; Gal. 2:16, 19, 21; 3:2, 5, 10 (1st part), 11, 18, 23; 4:4, 5, 21 (1st part); 5:4, 18; 6:13; Phil. 3:5, 9; Heb. 7:16; 9:19; Jas. 2:11; 4:11; (in regard to the statement in Gal. 2:16, that "a man is not justified by the works of the Law."

The following phrases specify "laws" of various kinds; (a) "the law of Christ," Gal. 6:2, i.e., either given by Him (as in the Sermon on the Mount and in John 13:14, 15; 15:4), or the "law" or principle by which Christ Himself lived (Matt. 20:28; John 13:1); these are not actual alternatives, for the "law" imposed by Christ was always that by which He Himself lived in the "days of His flesh." He confirmed the "Law" as being of divine authority (cf. Matt. 5:18); yet He presented a higher standard of life than perfunctory obedience to the current legal rendering of the "Law," a standard which, without annulling the "Law," He embodied in His own character and life (see, e.g., Matt. 5:21–48; this breach with legalism is especially seen in regard to the ritual or ceremonial part of the "Law" in its wide scope); He showed Himself superior to all human interpretations of it; (b) "a law of faith," Rom. 3:27, i.e., a principle which demands only faith on man's part; (c) "the law of my mind," Rom. 7:23, that principle which governs the new nature in virtue of the new birth; (d) "the law of sin," Rom. 7:23, the principle by which sin exerts its influence and power despite the desire to do what is right; "of sin and death," 8:2, death being the effect; (e) "the law of liberty," Jas. 1:25; 2:12, a term comprehensive of all the Scriptures, not a "law" of compulsion enforced from without, but meeting with ready obedience through the desire and delight of the renewed being who is subject to it; into it he looks, and in its teaching he delights; he is "under law (*ennomos*, 'in law,' implying union and subjection) to Christ," 1 Cor. 9:21; cf., e.g., Ps. 119:32, 45, 97; 2 Cor. 3:17; (f) "the royal law," Jas. 2:8, i.e., the "law" of love, royal in the majesty of its power, the "law" upon which all others hang, Matt. 22:34–40; Rom. 13:8; Gal. 5:14; (g) "the law of the Spirit of life," Rom. 8:2, i.e., the animating principle by which the Holy Spirit acts as the imparter of life (cf. John 6:63); (h) "a law of righteousness," Rom. 9:31, i.e., a general principle presenting righteousness as the object and outcome of keeping a "law," particularly the "Law" of Moses (cf. Gal. 3:21); (i) "the law of a carnal commandment," Heb. 7:16, i.e., the "law" respecting the Aaronic priesthood, which appointed men conditioned by the circumstances and limitations of the flesh. In the Epistle to the Hebrews the "Law" is treated of especially in regard to the contrast between the Priesthood of Christ and that established under the "law" of Moses, and in regard to access to God and to worship. In these respects the "Law" "made nothing perfect," 7:19. There was "a disannulling of a foregoing commandment . . . and a bringing in of a better hope." This is established under the "new Covenant," a covenant instituted on the basis of "better promises," 8:6.

### B. Verbs.

1. ***nomotheteo*** (*3549*), (a) used intransitively, signifies "to make laws"; in the passive voice, "to be furnished with laws," Heb. 7:11, "received the law," lit., "was furnished with (the) law"; (b) used transitively, it signifies "to ordain by law, to enact"; in the passive voice, Heb. 8:6.

2. ***paranomeo*** (*3891*), "to transgress law" (***para***, "contrary to," and ***nomos***), is used in the present participle in Acts 23:3, and translated "contrary to the law," lit., "transgressing the law."

### C. Adjectives.

1. ***nomikos*** (*3544*) denotes "relating to law"; Titus 3:9.

2. ***ennomos*** (*1772*), (a) "lawful, legal," lit., "in law" (***en***, "in," and ***nomos***), or strictly, "what is within the range of law," is translated "lawful" in Acts 19:39, KJV (RV, "regular"), of the legal tribunals in Ephesus; (b) "under law" (RV), in relation to Christ, 1 Cor. 9:21; the word as used by the apostle suggests not merely the condition of being under "law," but the intimacy of a relation established in the loyalty of a will devoted to his Master.

## LAWFUL, LAWFULLY

### A. Verb.

***exesti*** (*1832*), an impersonal verb, signifying "it is permitted, it is lawful" (or interrogatively, "is it lawful?"), occurs most frequently in the synoptic Gospels and the Acts; elsewhere in John 5:10; 18:31; 1 Cor. 6:12; 10:23; 2 Cor. 12:4; in Acts 2:29, it is rendered "let me (speak)," lit., "it being permitted"; in the KJV of 8:37, "thou mayest," lit., "it is permitted"; 16:21; in 21:37, "may I," lit., "is it permitted?"

### B. Adverb.

***nomimos*** (*3545*), "lawfully," is used in 1 Tim. 1:8, "the Law is good, if a man use it lawfully," i.e., agreeably to its design; the meaning here is that, while no one can be justified or obtain eternal life through its instrumentality, the believer is to have it in his heart and to fulfill its requirements; walking "not after the flesh but after the spirit," Rom. 8:4, he will "use it lawfully." In 2 Tim. 2:5 it is used of contending in the games and adhering to the rules.

## LAWGIVER

***nomothetes*** (*3550*), "a lawgiver," occurs in Jas. 4:12, as one who gives law.

## LAWLESS, LAWLESSNESS

**A. Adjective.**

***anomos*** (*459*), "without law," also denotes "lawless," and is so rendered in the RV of Acts 2:23, "lawless (men)," marg., "(men) without the law," KJV, "wicked (hands)"; 2 Thess. 2:8, "the lawless one" (KJV, "that wicked"), of the man of sin (v. 4); in 2 Pet. 2:8, of deeds (KJV, "unlawful"), where the thought is not simply that of doing what is unlawful, but of flagrant defiance of the known will of God.

**B. Noun.**

***anomia*** (*458*), "lawlessness," akin to A, is most frequently translated "iniquity"; in 2 Thess. 2:7, RV, "lawlessness" (KJV, "iniquity"); "the mystery of lawlessness" is not recognized by the world, for it does not consist merely in confusion and disorder (see A); the display of "lawlessness" by the "lawless" one (v. 8) will be the effect of the attempt by the powers of darkness to overthrow the divine government. In 1 John 3:4, the RV adheres to the real meaning of the word, "every one that doeth sin (a practice, not the committal of an act) doeth also lawlessness: and sin is lawlessness." This definition of sin sets forth its essential character as the rejection of the law, or will, of God and the substitution of the will of self.

## LAWYER

***nomikos*** (*3544*), an adjective, "learned in the law" (see Titus 3:9), is used as a noun, "a lawyer," Matt. 22:35; Luke 7:30; 10:25; 11:45, 46, 52 (v. 53 in some mss.); 14:3; Titus 3:13, where Zenas is so named. As there is no evidence that he was one skilled in Roman jurisprudence, the term may be regarded in the usual NT sense as applying to one skilled in the Mosaic Law.

## LAYING ON

***epithesis*** (*1936*), "a laying on" (***epi***, "on," ***tithemi***, "to put"), is used in the NT (a) of the "laying" on of hands by the apostles accompanied by the impartation of the Holy Spirit in outward demonstration, in the cases of those in Samaria who had believed, Acts 8:18; such supernatural manifestations were signs especially intended to give witness to Jews as to the facts of Christ and the faith, they were thus temporary; there is no record of their continuance after the time and circumstances narrated in Acts 19 (in v. 6 of which the corresponding verb ***epitithemi*** is used), nor was the gift delegated by the apostles to others; (b) of the similar act by the elders of a church on occasions when a member of a church was set apart for a particular work, having given evidence of qualifications necessary for it, as in the case of Timothy, 1 Tim. 4:14; of the impartation of a spiritual gift through the laying on of the hands of the apostle Paul, 2 Tim. 1:6, RV, "laying"; KJV, "putting."

The principle underlying the act was that of identification on the part of him who did it with the animal or person upon whom the hands were laid.

## LEAN

1. ***anakeimai*** (*345*), "to be laid up, to lie," is used of reclining at table, John 13:23, 25, 28.

2. ***anapipto*** (*377*), lit., "to fall back," is used of reclining at a repast and translated "leaning back," in John 13:25, RV (the KJV follows the mss. which have ***epipipto***, and renders it "lying"); in 21:20, "leaned back."

## LEARN, LEARNED (be)

1. ***manthano*** (*3129*) denotes (a) "to learn" (akin to ***mathetes***, "a disciple"), "to increase one's knowledge," or "be increased in knowledge," frequently "to learn by inquiry, or observation," e.g., Matt. 9:13; 11:29; 24:32; Mark 13:28; John 7:15; Rom. 16:17; 1 Cor. 4:6; 14:35; Phil. 4:9; 2 Tim. 3:14; Rev. 14:3; said of "learning" Christ, Eph. 4:20, not simply the doctrine of Christ, but Christ Himself, a process not merely of getting to know the person but of so applying the knowledge as to walk differently from the rest of the Gentiles; (b) "to ascertain," Acts 23:27, RV, "learned" (KJV, "understood"); Gal. 3:2, "This only would I learn from you," perhaps with a tinge of irony in the enquiry, the answer to which would settle the question of the validity of the new Judaistic gospel they were receiving; (c) "to learn by use and practice, to acquire the habit of, be accustomed to," e.g., Phil. 4:11; 1 Tim. 5:4, 13; Titus 3:14; Heb. 5:8.

2. ***ginosko*** (*1097*), "to know by observation and experience," is translated "to learn," in the RV of Mark 15:45; John 12:9.

3. ***akriboo*** (*198*), "to learn carefully," is so translated in Matt. 2:7, 16, RV (KJV, "diligently enquired").

4. ***mueo*** (*3453*), "to initiate into mysteries," is translated "I have learned the secret" (passive voice, perfect tense) in Phil. 4:12, RV (KJV, "I am instructed").

## LEARNING (Noun)

1. ***gramma*** (*1121*), "a letter," is used in the plural in Acts 26:24, with the meaning "learning": "(thy much) learning (doth turn thee to madness)," RV, possibly an allusion to the Jewish Scriptures.

2. ***didaskalia*** (*1319*), "teaching, instruction" (akin to ***didasko***, "to teach"), is translated "learning" in Rom. 15:4.

## LEAST

1. ***elachistos*** (*1646*), "least," is a superlative degree formed from the word ***elachus***, "little," the place of which was taken by ***mikros*** (the comparative degree being ***elasson***, "less"); it is used of (a) size, Jas. 3:4; (b) amount; of the management of affairs, Luke 16:10 (twice), 19:17, "very little"; (c) importance, 1 Cor. 6:2, "smallest (matters)"; (d) authority: of commandments, Matt. 5:19; (e) estimation, as to persons, Matt. 5:19 (2nd part); 25:40, 45; 1 Cor. 15:9; as to a town, Matt. 2:6; as to activities or operations, Luke 12:26; 1 Cor. 4:3, "a very small thing."

2. ***elachistoteros*** (*1647*), a comparative degree formed from No. 1, is used in Eph. 3:8, "less than the least."

3. ***mikroteros*** (*3398*), is used of (a) size, Matt. 13:32, KJV, "the least," RV, "less"; Mark 4:31 [cf. No. 1 (a)]; (b) estimation, Matt. 11:11 and Luke 7:28, KJV, "least," RV, "but little," marg., "lesser" (in the kingdom of heaven), those in the kingdom itself being less than John the Baptist [cf. No. 1 (e)]; Luke 9:48.

## LEAVEN (Noun and Verb)

### A. Noun.

***zume*** (*2219*), "leaven, sour dough, in a high state of fermentation," was used in general in making bread. It required time to fulfill the process. Hence, when food was required at short notice, unleavened cakes were used, e.g., Gen. 18:6; 19:3; Exod. 12:8. The Israelites were forbidden to use "leaven" for seven days at the time of Passover, that they might be reminded that the Lord brought them out of Egypt "in haste," Deut. 16:3, with Exod. 12:11; the unleavened bread, insipid in taste, reminding them, too, of their afflictions, and of the need of self-judgment, is called "the bread of affliction." "Leaven" was forbidden in all offerings to the Lord by fire, Lev. 2:11; 6:17. Being bred of corruption and spreading through the mass of that in which it is mixed, and therefore symbolizing the pervasive character of evil, "leaven" was utterly inconsistent in offerings which typified the propitiatory sacrifice of Christ.

In the OT "leaven" is not used in a metaphorical sense. In the NT it is used (a) metaphorically (1) of corrupt doctrine, Matt. 13:33 and Luke 13:21, of error as mixed with the truth (there is no valid reason for regarding the symbol here differently from its application elsewhere in the NT); Matt. 16:6, 11; Mark 8:15 (1st part); Luke 12:1; that the kingdom of heaven is likened to "leaven," does not mean that the kingdom is "leaven." The same statement, as made in other parables, shows that it is the whole parable which constitutes the similitude of the kingdom; the history of Christendom confirms the fact that the pure meal of the doctrine of Christ has been adulterated with error; (2) of corrupt practices, Mark 8:15 (2nd part), the reference to the Herodians being especially applied to their irreligion; 1 Cor. 5:7, 8; (b) literally in Matt. 16:12, and in the general statements in 1 Cor. 5:6 and Gal. 5:9, where the implied applications are to corrupt practice and corrupt doctrine respectively.

### B. Verb.

***zumoo*** (*2220*) signifies "to leaven, to act as leaven," passive voice in Matt. 13:33 and Luke 13:21; active voice in 1 Cor. 5:6 and Gal. 5:9.

## LEFT (Adjective)

1. ***aristeros*** (*710*), is used (a) of the "left" hand, in Matt. 6:3; in connection with the armor of righteousness, in 2 Cor. 6:7; (b) in the phrase "on the left," Mark 10:37; Luke 23:33.

2. ***euonumos*** (*2176*), lit., "of good name," or "omen," a word adopted to avoid the ill-omen attaching to the "left" (omens from the "left" being unlucky), is used euphemistically for No. 1, either (a) simply as an adjective in Rev. 10:2, of the "left" foot; in Acts 21:3, "on the left"; or (b) with the preposition ***ex*** (for ***ek***), signifying "on the left hand," Matt. 20:21, 23; 25:33, 41; 27:38; Mark 10:40; 15:27.

## LEGION

***legion*** (*3003*), otherwise spelled ***legeon***, "a legion," occurs in Matt. 26:53, of angels; in Mark 5:9, 15, and Luke 8:30, of demons. Among the Romans a "legion" was primarily a chosen (***lego***, "to choose") body of soldiers divided into ten cohorts, and numbering from 4,200 to 6,000 men.

## LEND, LENDER

**A. Verb.**

***daneizo*** (*1115v*) is translated "to lend" in Luke 6:34, 35.

**B. Noun.**

***danistes*** or ***daneistes*** (*1157*) denotes a moneylender (akin to A), translated "lender" in Luke 7:41, RV (KJV, "creditor").

## LEPER

***lepros*** (*3015*), an adjective, primarily used of "psoriasis," characterized by an eruption of rough scaly patches; later, "leprous," but chiefly used as a noun, "a leper," Matt. 8:2; 10:8; 11:5; Mark 1:40; Luke 4:27; 7:22; 17:12; especially of Simon. mentioned in Matt. 26:6: Mark 14:3.

## LEPROSY

***lepra*** (*3014*), akin to ***lepros***, is mentioned in Matt. 8:3; Mark 1:42; Luke 5:12, 13. In the removal of other maladies the verb "to heal" (***iaomai***) is used, but in the removal of "leprosy," the verb "to cleanse" (***katharizo***), except in the statement concerning the Samaritan, Luke 17:15, "when he saw that he was healed." Matt. 10:8 and Luke 4:27 indicate that the disease was common in the nation.

## LETTER

***gramma*** (*1121*) primarily denotes "that which is traced or drawn, a picture"; then, "that which is written," (a) "a character, letter of the alphabet," 2 Cor. 3:7; "written," lit., "(in) letters," Gal. 6:11; here the reference is not to the length of the epistle (Paul never uses ***gramma***, either in the singular or the plural of his epistles; of these he uses ***epistole***, No. 2), but to the size of the characters written by his own hand (probably from this verse to the end, as the use of the past tense, "I have written," is, according to Greek idiom, the equivalent of our "I am writing"). Moreover, the word for "letters" is here in the dative case, ***grammasin***, "with (how large) letters"; (b) "a writing, a written document, a bond" (KJV, "bill") Luke 16:6, 7; (c) "a letter, by way of correspondence," Acts 28:21; (d) the Scriptures of the OT, 2 Tim. 3:15; (e) "learning," John 7:15, "letters"; Acts 26:24, "(much) learning" (lit., "many letters"); in the papyri an illiterate person is often spoken of as one who does not know "letters," "which never means anything else than inability to write" (Moulton and Milligan); (f) "the letter," the written commandments of the Word of God, in contrast to the inward operation of the Holy Spirit under the New Covenant, Rom. 2:27, 29; 7:6; 2 Cor. 3:6; (g) "the books of Moses," John 5:47.

## LIAR

**A. Noun.**

***pseustes*** (*5583*), "a liar," occurs in John 8:44, 55; Rom. 3:4; 1 Tim. 1:10; Titus 1:12; 1 John 1:10; 2:4, 22; 4:20; 5:10.

**B. Adjective.**

***pseudes*** (*5571*), "lying, false" (Eng. "pseudo-"), rendered "false" in Acts 6:13 and in the RV of Rev. 2:2 (KJV, "liars"), is used as a noun, "liars," in Rev. 21:8.

## LIBERAL, LIBERALITY, LIBERALLY

**A. Noun.**

1. ***haplotes*** (*572*) denotes (a) "simplicity, sincerity, unaffectedness" (from ***haplous***, "single, simple," in contrast to ***diplous***, "double"), Rom. 12:8, "simplicity"; 2 Cor. 11:3 (in some mss. in 1:12); Eph. 6:5 and Col. 3:22, "singleness"; (b) "simplicity as manifested in generous giving," "liberality," 2 Cor. 8:2; 9:11 (KJV, "bountifulness," RV marg., "singleness"); 9:13 (KJV, "liberal").

**B. Adverb.**

***haplos*** (*574*), "liberally, with singleness of heart," is used in Jas. 1:5 of God as the gracious and "liberal" Giver.

## LIBERTY

**A. Noun.**

***aphesis*** (*859*), "dismissal, release, forgiveness," is rendered "liberty" in the KJV of Luke 4:18, RV, "release."

**B. Adjective.**

***eleutheros*** (*1658*) is rendered "at liberty" in 1 Cor. 7:39, KJV (RV "free").

## LIE (falsehood: Noun and Verb)

**A. Nouns.**

1. ***pseudos*** (*5579*), "a falsehood, lie." is translated "lie" in John 8:44 (lit., "the lie"); Rom. 1:25, where it stands by metonymy for an idol, as, e.g., in Isa. 44:20; Jer. 10:14; 13:25; Amos 2:4 (plural); 2 Thess. 2:11, with special reference to the lie of v. 4, that man is God (cf. Gen. 3:5); 1 John 2:21, 27; Rev. 21:27; 22:15; in Eph. 4:25, KJV "lying," RV, "falsehood," the practice; in Rev. 14:5, RV, "lie." (some mss. have ***dolos***, "guile," KJV); 2 Thess. 2:9, where "lying wonders" is, lit., "wonders of falsehood," i.e., wonders calculated to deceive (cf. Rev. 13:13–15), the purpose being to deceive people into the

acknowledgement of the spurious claim to deity on the part of the Man of Sin.

2. ***pseusma*** (*5582*), "a falsehood," or "an acted lie," Rom. 3:7, where "my lie" is not idolatry, but either the universal false attitude of man toward God or that with which his detractors charged the apostle; the former seems to be the meaning.

**B. Adjectives.**

1. ***pseudologos*** (*5573*) denotes "speaking falsely" (***pseudes***, "false," ***logos***, "a word") in 1 Tim. 4:2, where the adjective is translated "that speak lies," RV (KJV, "speaking lies") and is applied to "demons," the actual utterances being by their human agents.

2. ***apseudes*** (*893*) denotes "free from falsehood" (***a***, negative, ***pseudes***, "false"), truthful, Titus 1:2, of God, "who cannot lie."

**C. Verb.**

***pseudo*** (*5574*), "to deceive by lies" (always in the middle voice in the NT), is used (a) absolutely, in Matt. 5:11, "falsely," lit., "lying" (v, marg.); Rom. 9:1; 2 Cor. 11:31; Gal. 1:20; Col. 3:9 (where the verb is followed by the preposition ***eis***, "to"); 1 Tim. 2:7; Heb. 6:18; Jas. 3:14 (where it is followed by the preposition ***kata***, "against"); 1 John 1:6; Rev. 3:9; (b) transitively, with a direct object (without a preposition following), Acts 5:3 (with the accusative case) "to lie to (the Holy Ghost)," RV marg., "deceive"; v. 4 (with the dative case) "thou hast (not) lied (unto men, but unto God)."

## LIFE, LIVING, LIFETIME, LIFE-GIVING

**A. Nouns.**

1. ***zoe*** (*2222*) (Eng., "zoo," "zoology") is used in the NT "of life as a principle, life in the absolute sense, life as God has it, that which the Father has in Himself, and which He gave to the Incarnate Son to have in Himself, John 5:26, and which the Son manifested in the world, 1 John 1:2. From this life man has become alienated in consequence of the Fall, Eph. 4:18, and of this life men become partakers through faith in the Lord Jesus Christ, John 3:15, who becomes its Author to all such as trust in Him, Acts 3:15, and who is therefore said to be 'the life' of the believer, Col. 3:4, for the life that He gives He maintains, John 6:35, 63. Eternal life is the present actual possession of the believer because of his relationship with Christ, John 5:24; 1 John 3:14, and that it will one day extend its domain to the sphere of the body is assured by the Resurrection of Christ, 2 Cor. 5:4; 2 Tim. 1:10. This life is not merely a principle of power and mobility, however, for it has moral associations which are inseparable from it, as of holiness and righteousness. Death and sin, life and holiness, are frequently contrasted in the Scriptures.

Death came through sin, Rom. 5:12, which is rebellion against God. Sin thus involved the forfeiting of the "life." "The life of the flesh is in the blood," Lev. 17:11. Therefore the impartation of "life" to the sinner must be by a death caused by the shedding of that element which is the life of the flesh. "It is the blood that maketh atonement by reason of the life" (*id.* RV). The separation from God caused by the forfeiting of the "life" could be removed only by a sacrifice in which the victim and the offerer became identified. This which was appointed in the typical offerings in Israel received its full accomplishment in the voluntary sacrifice of Christ. The shedding of the blood in the language of Scripture involves the taking or the giving of the "life." Since Christ had no sins of his own to die for, His death was voluntary and vicarious, John 10:15 with Isa. 53:5, 10, 12; 2 Cor. 5:21. In His sacrifice He endured the divine judgment due to man's sin. By this means the believer becomes identified with Him in His deathless "life," through His resurrection, and enjoys conscious and eternal fellowship with God.

2. ***bios*** (*979*) (cf. Eng. words beginning with *bio-*), is used in three respects (a) of "the period or duration of life," e.g., in the KJV of 1 Pet. 4:3, "the time past of our life" (the RV follows the mss. which omit "of our life"); Luke 8:14; 2 Tim. 2:4; (b) of "the manner of life, life in regard to its moral conduct," 1 Tim. 2:2; 1 John 2:16; (c) of "the means of life, livelihood, maintenance, living," Mark 12:44; Luke 8:43; 15:12, 30; 21:4; 1 John 3:17, "goods," RV (KJV, "good").

3. ***psuche*** (*5590*), besides its meanings, "heart, mind, soul," denotes "life" in two chief respects, (a) "breath of life, the natural life," e.g., Matt. 2:20; 6:25; Mark 10:45; Luke 12:22; Acts 20:10; Rev. 8:9; 12:11 (cf. Lev. 17:11; Esth. 8:11); (b) "the seat of personality," e.g., Luke 9:24, explained in v. 25 as "own self."

4. ***biosis*** (*981*), from ***bioo***, "to spend one's life, to live," denotes "a manner of life," Acts 26:4.

**B. Adjective.**

***biotikos*** (*982*), "pertaining to life" (***bios***), is translated "of this life," in Luke 21:34, with reference to cares; in 1 Cor. 6:3 "(things) that pertain to this life," and v. 4, "(things) pertaining to this life," i.e., matters of this world, concerning which Christians at Corinth were engaged in public lawsuits one with another; such matters were to be regarded as relatively unimportant in view of the great tribunals to come under the jurisdiction of saints hereafter.

### C. Verb.

***zoopoieo*** (2227), "to make alive, cause to live, quicken" (from ***zoe***, "life," and ***poieo***, "to make"), is used as follows:

(a) of God as the bestower of every kind of life in the universe, 1 Tim. 6:13, and, particularly, of resurrection life, John 5:21; Rom. 4:17; (b) of Christ, who also is the bestower of resurrection life, John 5:21 (2nd part); 1 Cor. 15:45; cf. v. 22; (c) of the resurrection of Christ in "the body of His glory," 1 Pet. 3:18; (d) of the power of reproduction inherent in seed, which presents a certain analogy with resurrection, 1 Cor. 15:36; (e) of the 'changing,' or 'fashioning anew,' of the bodies of the living, which corresponds with, and takes place at the same time as, the resurrection of the dead in Christ, Rom. 8:11; (f) of the impartation of spiritual life, and the communication of spiritual sustenance generally, John 6:63; 2 Cor. 3:6; Gal. 3:2.

## LIGHT, Noun, and Verb (bring to, give), LIGHTEN

*Old Testament*

### A. Verb.

***'or*** (216), "to become light, become lighted up (of daybreak), give light, cause light to shine." ***'or*** means "to become light" in Gen. 44:3; "to give light" in Num. 8:2.

### B. Nouns.

***'or*** (216), "light." "Light" is the opposite of "darkness"; or figurative, Isa. 5:20, 30. In Hebrew various antonyms of ***'or*** are used in parallel constructions, Isa. 9:2. The basic meaning of ***'or*** is "daylight," cf. Gen. 1:3. In the Hebrew mind the "day" began at the rising of the sun," 2 Sam. 23:4; of light from heavenly bodies, Isa. 30:26.

In the metaphorical use ***'or*** signifies life over against death, Ps. 56:13. To walk in the "light" of the face of a superior, Prov. 16:15, or of God, Ps. 89:15, is an expression of a joyful, blessed life in which the quality of life is enhanced.

The noun ***'ur*** means "shine; light-giving," Isa. 50:11. ***'orah*** refers to "light," Ps. 139:12. ***ma'or*** also means "light," Gen. 1:16.

*New Testament*

### A. Noun.

***phos*** (*5457*), akin to ***phao***, "to give light" (from roots ***pha***– and ***phan***–, expressing "light as seen by the eye," and, metaphorically, as "reaching the mind," whence ***phaino***, "to make to appear," ***phaneros***, "evident," etc.); cf. Eng., "phosphorus" (lit., "light-bearing"). "Primarily light is a luminous emanation, probably of force, from certain bodies, which enables the eye to discern form and color. Light requires an organ adapted for its reception (Matt. 6:22). Where the eye is absent, or where it has become impaired from any cause, light is useless. Man, naturally, is incapable of receiving spiritual light inasmuch as he lacks the capacity for spiritual things, 1 Cor. 2:14. Hence believers are called 'sons of light,' Luke 16:8, not merely because they have received a revelation from God, but because in the New Birth they have received the spiritual capacity for it.

Apart from natural phenomena, light is used in Scripture of (a) the glory of God's dwelling-place, 1 Tim. 6:16; (b) the nature of God, 1 John 1:5; (c) the impartiality of God, Jas. 1:17; (d) the favor of God, Ps. 4:6; of the King, Prov. 16:15; of an influential man, Job 29:24; (e) God, as the illuminator of His people, Isa. 60:19, 20; (f) the Lord Jesus as the illuminator of men, John 1:4, 5, 9; 3:19; 8:12; 9:5; 12:35, 36, 46; Acts 13:47; (g) the illuminating power of the Scriptures, Ps. 119:105; and of the judgments and commandments of God, Isa. 51:4; Prov. 6:23, cf. Ps. 43:3; (h) the guidance of God, Job 29:3; Ps. 112:4; Isa. 58:10; and, ironically, of the guidance of man, Rom. 2:19; (i) salvation, 1 Pet. 2:9; (j) righteousness, Rom. 13:12; 2 Cor. 11:14, 15; 1 John 2:9, 10; (k) witness for God, Matt. 5:14, 16; John 5:35; (1) prosperity and general well-being, Esth. 8:16; Job 18:18; Isa. 58:8–10.

### B. Verb.

***photizo*** (*5461*), used (a) intransitively, signifies "to shine, give light," Rev. 22:5; (b) transitively, (1) "to illumine, to light, enlighten, to be lightened," Luke 11:36; Rev. 21:23; in the passive voice, Rev. 18:1; metaphorically, of spiritual enlightenment, John 1:9; Eph. 1:18; 3:9, "to make . . . see"; Heb. 6:4; 10:32, "ye were enlightened," RV (KJV, "illuminated"); (2) "to bring to light," 1 Cor. 4:5 (of God's act in the future); 2 Tim. 1:10 (of God's act in the past).

### C. Adjective.

***photeinos*** (*5460*), from ***phos*** (see A), "bright," is rendered "full of light" in Matt. 6:22; Luke 11:34, 36 (twice), figuratively, of the single-mindedness of the eye, which acts as the lamp of the body; in Matt. 17:5, "bright," of a cloud.

## LIKE, LIKE (as to, unto), (be) LIKE, (make) LIKE, LIKE (things), LIKEN

### A. Adjectives.

1. ***homoios*** (*3664*), "like, resembling, such as, the same as," is used (a) of appearance or

form John 9:9; Rev. 1:13, 15; 2:18; 4:3 (twice), 6, 7; 9:7 (twice), 10, 19; 11:1; 13:2, 11; 14:14; (b) of ability, condition, nature, Matt. 22:39; Acts 17:29; Gal. 5:21, "such like," lit., "and the (things) similar to these"; 1 John 3:2; Rev. 13:4; 18:18; 21:11, 18; (c) of comparison in parables, Matt. 13:31, 33, 44, 45, 47; 20:1; Luke 13:18, 19, 21; (d) of action, thought, etc. Matt. 11:16; 13:52; Luke 6:47, 48, 49; 7:31, 32; 12:36; John 8:55; Jude 7.

2. ***paromoios*** (*3946*), "much like" (***para***, "beside," and No. 1), is used in Mark 7:13, in the neuter plural, "(many such) like things."

**B. Verbs.**

1. ***homoioo*** (*3666*), "to make like" (akin to A, No. 1), is used (a) especially in the parables, with the significance of comparing, "likening," or, in the passive voice, "being likened," Matt. 7:24, 26; 11:16; 13:24; 18:23; 22:2 (RV, "likened"); 25:1; Mark 4:30; Luke 7:31; 13:18, RV, "liken" (KJV, "resemble"); v. 20; in several of these instances the point of resemblance is not a specific detail, but the whole circumstances of the parable; (b) of making "like," or, in the passive voice, of being made or becoming "like," Matt. 6:8; Acts 14:11, "in the likeness of (men)," lit., "being made like" (aorist participle, passive); Rom. 9:29; Heb. 2:17, of Christ in being "made like" unto His brethren, i.e., in partaking of human nature, apart from sin (cf. v. 14).

2. ***paromoiazo*** (*3945*), "to be like" (from ***para***, "by," and a verbal form from ***homoios***, A, No. 1), is used in Matt. 23:27 (perhaps with intensive force), in the Lord's comparison of the scribes and Pharisees to whitened sepulchres.

3. ***aphomoioo*** (*871*), "to make like" (***apo***, "from," and No. 1), is used in Heb. 7:3, of Melchizedek as "made like" the Son of God, i.e., in the facts related and withheld in the Genesis record.

## LIKEMINDED

1. ***isopsuchos*** (*2473*), lit., "of equal soul" (***isos***, "equal," ***psuche***, "the soul"), is rendered "likeminded" in Phil. 2:20.

2. ***homophron*** (*3675*), (***homos***, "the same," ***phren***, "the mind"), occurs in 1 Pet. 3:8, RV, "likeminded" (KJV, "of one mind").

## LIKENESS, LIKENESS OF (in the)

### *Old Testament*

**A. Verb.**

***damah*** (1819), "to be like, resemble" and so make a comparison of similar things, Ps. 102:6.

**B. Noun.**

***demut*** (1823), "likeness; shape; figure; form; pattern." First, the word means "pattern," in the sense of the specifications from which an actual item is made, 2 Kings 16:10. Second, ***demut*** means "shape" or "form," the thing(s) made after a given pattern, in general, 2 Chron. 4:3; or a particular shape, Ezek. 1:10, 26. Third, ***demut*** signifies the original after which a thing is patterned, Gen. 1:26.

### *New Testament*

1. ***homoioma*** (*3667*) denotes "that which is made like something, a resemblance," (a) in the concrete sense, Rev. 9:7, "shapes" (RV, marg., "likenesses"); (b) in the abstract sense, Rom. 1:23, RV, "(for) the likeness (of an image)"; the KJV translates it as a verb, "(into an image) made like to"; the association here of the two words ***homoioma*** and ***eikon*** serves to enhance the contrast between the idol and "the glory of the incorruptible God," and is expressive of contempt; in 5:14, "(the) likeness of Adam's transgression" (KJV, "similitude"); in 6:5, "(the) likeness (of His death); in 8:3, "(the) likeness (of sinful flesh); in Phil. 2:7, "the likeness of men." The expression 'likeness of men' does not of itself imply, still less does it exclude or diminish, the reality of the nature which Christ assumed.

2. ***homoiosis*** (*3669*), "a making like," is translated "likeness" in Jas. 3:9, RV (KJV, "similitude").

3. ***homoiotes*** (*3665*) is translated "likeness" in Heb. 7:15, RV (KJV, "similitude").

## LIVE

### *Old Testament*

**A. Verb.**

***chayah*** (2421), "to live," in the intensive form, ***chayah*** means "to preserve alive," Gen. 6:19; or, "to bring to life," Isa. 57:15. "To live" is more than physical existence, Deut. 8:3; 30:16.

**B. Noun.**

***chay*** (2416), "living thing; life." The use of this word occurs only in the oath formula "as *X* lives," literally, "by the life of *X*," Judg. 8:19. This formula summons the power of a superior to sanction the statement asserted, Gen. 42:15; 1 Sam. 1:26. The feminine form of the word, ***chayyah***, means "living being," especially animals, Gen. 8:1; even preying, usually wild, animals, Job 37:8. In another nuance the word describes land animals as distinct from birds and fish, Gen. 1:28. Also creatures in a vision are "living animals," Ezek. 1:5. The plural, ***chayyim***, is a general word for the state of living as opposed to that of death, Gen. 3:14; 6:17; 27:46; Deut. 30:15.

The "tree of life" is the tree which gives one eternal, everlasting "life," Gen. 2:9. In another nuance this word suggests a special quality of "life," life as a special gift from God (a gift of salvation), Deut. 30:19; or, persons living, Num. 16:48.

### C. Adjective.

***chay*** (2416), "alive; living." The word ***chay*** is used both as an adjective and as a noun. Used adjectivally it modifies men, animals, and God, but never plants, Gen. 2:7. ***chay*** describes flesh (animal meat or human flesh) under the skin, or "raw flesh," Lev. 13:10; 1 Sam. 2:15.

Applied to liquids, ***chay*** means "running"; it is used metaphorically describing something that moves, Gen. 26:19. In Jer. 2:13 the NASB translates "living" waters, or waters that give life, cf. Jer. 17:13; Zech. 14:8. The Song of Solomon uses the word in a figure of speech describing one's wife; she is "a well of living waters," 4:15. The emphasis is not on the fact that the water flows but on its freshness; it is not stagnant, and therefore is refreshing and pleasant when consumed.

#### *New Testament*

1. ***zao*** (*2198*), "to live, be alive," is used in the NT of "(a) God, Matt. 16:16; John 6:57; Rom. 14:11; (b) the Son in Incarnation, John 6:57; (c) the Son in Resurrection, John 14:19; Acts 1:3; Rom. 6:10; 2 Cor. 13:4; Heb. 7:8; (d) spiritual life, John 6:57; Rom. 1:17; 8:13b; Gal. 2:19, 20; Heb. 12:9; (e) the present state of departed saints, Luke 20:38; 1 Pet. 4:6; (f) the hope of resurrection, 1 Pet. 1:3; (g) the resurrection of believers, 1 Thess. 5:10; John 5:25; Rev. 20:4, and of unbelievers, v. 5, cf. v. 13; (h) the way of access to God through the Lord Jesus Christ, Heb. 10:20; (i) the manifestation of divine power in support of divine authority, 2 Cor. 13:4b; cf. 12:10, and 1 Cor. 5:5; (j) bread, figurative of the Lord Jesus, John 6:51; (k) a stone, figurative of the Lord Jesus, 1 Pet. 2:4; (1) water, figurative of the Holy Spirit, John 4:10; 7:38; (m) a sacrifice, figurative of the believer, Rom. 12:1; (n) stones, figurative of the believer, 1 Pet. 2:5; (o) the oracles, ***logion***, Acts 7:38, and word, ***logos***, Heb. 4:12; 1 Pet. 1:23, of God; (p) the physical life of men, 1 Thess. 4:15; Matt. 27:63; Acts 25:24; Rom. 14:9; Phil. 1:21 (in the infinitive mood used as a noun with the article, 'living'), 22; 1 Pet. 4:5; (q) the maintenance of physical life, Matt. 4:4; 1 Cor. 9:14; (r) the duration of physical life, Heb. 2:15; (s) the enjoyment of physical life, 1 Thess. 3:8; (t) the recovery of physical life from the power of disease, Mark 5:23; John 4:50; (u) the recovery of physical life from the power of death, Matt. 9:18; Acts 9:41; Rev. 20:5; (v) the course, conduct, and character of men, (1) good, Acts 26:5; 2 Tim. 3:12; Titus 2:12; (2) evil, Luke 15:13; Rom. 6:2; 8:13a; 2 Cor. 5:15b; Col. 3:7; (3) undefined, Rom. 7:9; 14:7; Gal. 2:14; (w) restoration after alienation, Luke 15:32.

2. ***sunzao*** (*4800*), "to live together with" (***sun***, "with," and ***zao***, "to live"), may be included with ***zao*** in the above analysis as follows: (g) Rom. 6:8; 2 Tim. 2:11; (s), 2 Cor. 7:3.

3. ***anazao*** (*326*) ***ana***, "again," and ***zao***, denotes "to live again," "to revive," Luke 15:24.

4. ***zoogoneo*** (*2225*) denotes "to preserve alive" (from ***zoos***, "alive," and ***ginomai***, "to come to be, become, be made"); in Luke 17:33, "shall preserve (it)," i.e., his life, RV marg., "save (it) alive"; cf. the parallels ***sozo***, "to save," in Matt. 16:25, and ***phulaso***, "to keep," in John 12:25; in Acts 7:19, "live," negatively of the efforts of Pharaoh to destroy the babes in Israel; in 1 Tim. 6:13, according to the best mss. (some have ***zoopoieo***, "to cause to live"), "quickeneth" (RV, marg., "preserveth . . . alive," the preferable rendering).

## LIVE LONG

***makrochronios*** (*3118*), an adjective denoting "of long duration, long-lived" (***makros***, "long," ***chronos***, "time"), is used in Eph. 6:3, "(that thou mayest) live long," lit., "(that thou mayest be) long-lived."

## LOCUST

***akris*** (*200*) occurs in Matt. 3:4 and Mark 1:6, of the animals themselves, as forming part of the diet of John the Baptist; they are used as food; the Arabs stew them with butter, after removing the head, legs and wings; as part of a plague, see Rev. 9:3, 7.

## LODGE, LODGING

### A. Verb.

***xenizo*** (*3579*), "to receive as a guest" (***xenos***, "a guest, stranger"), "to entertain, lodge," is used in the active voice in Acts 10:23; 28:7, RV, "entertained" (KJV, "lodged"); Heb. 13:2, "have entertained"; in the passive voice, Acts 10:6 (lit., "he is entertained"), 18, 32; 21:16. Its other meaning, "to think strange," is found in 1 Pet. 4:4, 12.

### B. Noun.

***xenia*** (*3578*), akin to A, denotes (a) "hospitality, entertainment," Philem. 22; (b) by metonymy, "a place of entertainment, a lodging-place," Acts 28:23 (some put Philem. 22 under this section).

## LOINS

***osphus*** (*3751*) is used (a) in the natural sense in Matt. 3:4; Mark 1:6; (b) as "the seat of generative power," Heb. 7:5, 10; metaphorically in Acts 2:30; (c) metaphorically, (1) of girding the "loins" in readiness for active service for the Lord, Luke 12:35; (2) the same, with truth, Eph. 6:14, i.e., bracing up oneself so as to maintain perfect sincerity and reality as the counteractive in Christian character against hypocrisy and falsehood; (3) of girding the "loins" of the mind, 1 Pet. 1:13, RV, "girding," suggestive of the alertness necessary for sobriety and for setting one's hope perfectly on "the grace to be brought . . . at the revelation of Jesus Christ" (the present participle, "girding," is introductory to the rest of the verse).

## LONG (Verb), LONG (after, for), LONGING

### A. Verb.

***epipotheo*** (*1971*), "to long for greatly" (a strengthened form of ***potheo***, "to long for," not found in the NT), is translated "I long," in Rom. 1:11; in 2 Cor. 5:2, RV, "longing" (KJV, "earnestly desiring"); in 1 Thess. 3:6 and 2 Tim. 1:4, RV, "longing" (KJV, "desiring greatly"); to long after, in 2 Cor. 9:14; Phil. 1:8; 2:26; to long for, in 1 Pet. 2:2, RV (KJV, "desire"); Jas. 4:5, RV, "long."

### B. Adjective.

***epipothetos*** (*1973*), akin to A, and an intensive form of ***pothetos***, "desired, greatly desired," "longed for," is used in Phil. 4:1.

### C. Nouns.

1. ***epipothia*** (*1974*), "a longing" (akin to A and B), is found in Rom. 15:23, RV "longing" (KJV, "great desire").

2. ***epipothesis*** (*1972*), "a longing" (perhaps stressing the process more than No. 1), is found in 2 Cor. 7:7, RV, "longing" (KJV, "earnest desire"); 7:11, RV, "longing" (KJV, "vehement desire").

## LONGSUFFERING (Noun and Verb)

### A. Noun.

***makrothumia*** (*3115*), "forbearance, patience, longsuffering" (***makros***, "long," ***thumos***, "temper"), is usually rendered "longsuffering," Rom. 2:4; 9:22; 2 Cor. 6:6; Gal. 5:22; Eph. 4:2; Col. 1:11; 3:12; 1 Tim. 1:16; 2 Tim. 3:10; 4:2; 1 Pet. 3:20; 2 Pet. 3:15; "patience" in Heb. 6:12 and Jas. 5:10.

### B. Verb.

***makrothumeo*** (*3114*), akin to A, "to be patient, longsuffering, to bear with," lit., "to be long-tempered," is rendered by the verb "to be longsuffering" in Luke 18:7, RV (KJV, "bear long"); in 1 Thess. 5:14, RV (KJV, "be patient"); so in Jas. 5:7, 8; in 2 Pet. 3:9, KJV and RV, "is longsuffering."

## LOOK

### *Old Testament*

***nabat*** (5027), "to look, regard, behold," commonly used of physical "looking," Exod. 3:6; also in a figurative sense to mean a spiritual and inner apprehension, 1 Sam. 16:7. The sense of "consider" (with insight) is expressed in Isa. 51:1–2,12.

### *New Testament*

### A. Verbs.

1. ***blepo*** (*991*), primarily, "to have sight, to see," then, "observe, discern, perceive," frequently implying special contemplation, is rendered by the verb "to look" in Luke 9:62, "looking (back)"; John 13:22 "(the disciples) looked (one on another)"; Acts 1:9, RV, "were looking" (KJV, "beheld"); 3:4, "look (on us)"; 27:12, RV, "looking," KJV, "that lieth (towards)," of the haven Phoenix; Eph. 5:15, RV, "look (therefore carefully how ye walk)," KJV, "see (that ye walk circumspectly)"; Rev. 11:9 and 18:9, RV, "look upon" (KJV, "shall see"). There are many cognate words related to this root, which can give different ways, positions, and intensities to the way one "looks."

2. ***eidon*** (*3708*), used as the aorist tense of ***horao***, "to see," in various senses, is translated "to look," in the KJV of John 7:52, RV, "see"; Rev. 4:1 (RV, "I saw"); so in 6:8; 14:1, 14 (as in KJV of v. 6), and 15:5.

3. ***epeidon*** (*1896*) denotes "to look upon" (***epi***, "upon"), (a) favorably, Luke 1:25 (b) unfavorably, in Acts 4:29.

4. ***skopeo*** (*4648*), "to look at, consider" (Eng., "scope"), implying mental consideration, is rendered "while we look . . . at" in 2 Cor. 4:18; "looking to" (KJV, "on") in Phil. 2:4.

5. ***episkopeo*** (*1983*), lit., "to look upon" (***epi***, and No. 4), is rendered "looking carefully" in Heb. 12:15, RV (KJV, "looking diligently"), ***epi*** being probably intensive here; in 1 Pet. 5:2, "to exercise the oversight, to visit, care for."

6. ***episkeptomai*** (*1980*), a later form of No. 5, "to visit," has the meaning of "seeking out," and is rendered "look ye out" in Acts 6:3.

## LOOK (for), LOOKING (after, for)

### A. Verbs.

1. ***prosdokao*** (*4328*), "to await, expect" (***pros***, "to" or "towards," ***dokeo***, "to think, be of opinion"), is translated "to look for," e.g., in Matt. 11:3; 2 Pet. 3:12, 13, 14; the RV renders it by the verb "to expect, to be in expectation," in some instances, as does the KJV in Luke 3:15; Acts 3:5.

2. ***prosdechomai*** (*4327*), "to receive favorably," also means "to expect," and is rendered "to look for," e.g., in Luke 2:38; 23:51; Acts 24:15, RV (KJV, "allow"); Titus 2:13; Jude 21.

3. ***ekdechomai*** (*1551*), primarily "to receive from another," hence, "to expect, to await," is translated "he looked for" in Heb. 11:10; in 1 Cor. 16:11, KJV, "I look for" (RV, "I expect").

### B. Nouns.

1. ***prosdokia*** (*4329*); akin to A, No. 1, is translated "a looking after" in Luke 21:26, KJV ("expectation," as in Acts 12:11, KJV and RV).

2. ***ekdoche*** (*1561*), akin to A, No. 3, is translated "looking for" in Heb. 10:27, KJV.

## LORD, LORDSHIP

### *Old Testament*

***'adon*** (113), or ***'adonay*** (113), "lord; master; Lord," ***'adon*** basically describes the one who occupies the position of a "master" or "lord" over a slave or servant, Gen. 24:9. It is used of kings, rulers, and officials, Gen. 45:8; cf. 42:30. ***'adon*** is often used as a term of polite address, much like "sir," or "madame," Gen. 18:12; 32:18.

When applied to God, ***'adon*** is used in several senses. It signifies His position as the one who has authority (like a master) over His people to reward the obedient and punish the disobedient, Hos. 12:14. In such contexts God is conceived as a Being who is sovereign ruler and almighty master; or title of respect, Ps. 8:1. In the form ***'adonay*** the word means "Lord" par excellence or "Lord over all," Josh. 3:11, where He is called the "Lord of all the earth".

***Yahweh*** (3068), "Lord." The four letters of this word (***YHWH***) appear without their own vowels, and the exact pronunciation is uncertain (although Yahweh is most probable). The Hebrew text does insert the vowels for ***'adonay***. The meaning of the divine personal name, ***YHWH***, relates to the verb "to be." It translates "I am who I am," Exod. 3:14. The meaning of this is debated: one focus is that this God was an eternal, self-existent One with unique being; another focus is that He "will be" present to the people of his covenant promise to Abraham. ***YHWH*** often has the personal focus of relationship, Gen. 4:26; 12:8; Exod. 3:14–17; 6:2–8.

### *New Testament*

### A. Nouns.

1. ***kurios*** (*2962*), properly an adjective, signifying "having power" (***kuros***) or "authority," is used as a noun, variously translated in the NT, "'Lord,' 'master,' 'Master,' 'owner,' 'Sir,' a title of wide significance, occurring in each book of the NT except Titus and the Epistles of John. It is used (a) of an owner, as in Luke 19:33, cf. Matt. 20:8; Acts 16:16; Gal. 4:1; or of one who has the disposal of anything, as the Sabbath, Matt. 12:8; (b) of a master, i.e., one to whom service is due on any ground, Matt. 6:24; 24:50; Eph. 6:5; (c) of an Emperor or King, Acts 25:26; Rev. 17:14; (d) of idols, ironically, 1 Cor. 8:5, cf. Isa. 26:13; (e) as a title of respect addressed to a father, Matt. 21:30, a husband, 1 Pet. 3:6, a master, Matt. 13:27; Luke 13:8, a ruler, Matt. 27:63, an angel, Acts 10:4; Rev. 7:14; (f) as a title of courtesy addressed to a stranger, John 12:21; 20:15; Acts 16:30; from the outset of His ministry this was a common form of address to the Lord Jesus, alike, by the people, Matt. 8:2; John 4:11, and by His disciples, Matt. 8:25; Luke 5:8; John 6:68; (g) ***kurios*** is the Sept. and NT representative of Heb. Jehovah ('LORD' in Eng. versions), see Matt. 4:7; Jas. 5:11, e.g., of ***'adon***, Lord, Matt. 22:44, and of ***'adonay***, Lord, 1:22; it also occurs for ***'elohim***, God, 1 Pet. 1:25.

His purpose did not become clear to the disciples until after His resurrection, and the revelation of His Deity consequent thereon. Thomas, when he realized the significance of the presence of a mortal wound in the body of a living man, immediately joined with it the absolute title of Deity, saying, "My Lord and my God," John 20:28. Thereafter, except in Acts 10:4 and Rev. 7:14, there is no record that ***kurios*** was ever again used by believers in addressing any except God and the Lord Jesus; cf. Acts 2:47 with 4:29, 30.

How soon and how completely the lower meaning had been superseded is seen in Peter's declaration in his first sermon after the resurrection, "God hath made Him—Lord," Acts 2:36, and that in the house of Cornelius, "He is Lord of all," 10:36, cf. Deut. 10:14; Matt. 11:25; Acts 17:24. In his writings the implications of his early teaching are confirmed and developed. Thus Ps. 34:8, "O taste and see that Jehovah is good," is applied to the Lord Jesus, 1 Pet. 2:3, and "Jehovah of Hosts, Him shall ye sanctify," Isa. 8:13, becomes "sanctify in your hearts Christ as Lord," 3:15.

So also James who uses ***kurios*** alike of God, 1:7 (cf. v. 5); 3:9; 4:15; 5:4, 10, 11, and of the Lord Jesus, 1:1 (where the possibility that ***kai*** is intended epexegetically, i.e. = even, cf. 1 Thess. 3:11, should not be overlooked); 2:1 (lit., "our Lord Jesus Christ of glory," cf. Ps. 24:7; 29:3; Acts 7:2; 1 Cor. 2:8; 5:7, 8, while the language of 4:10; 5:15, is equally applicable to either.

Jude, v. 4, speaks of "our only—Lord, Jesus Christ," and immediately, v. 5, uses "Lord" of God, as he does later, vv. 9, 14.

Paul ordinarily uses ***kurios*** of the Lord Jesus, 1 Cor. 1:3, e.g., but also on occasion, of God, in quotations from the OT, 1 Cor. 3:20, e.g., and in his own words, 1 Cor. 3:5, cf. v. 10. It is equally appropriate to either in 1 Cor. 7:25; 2 Cor. 3:16; 8:21; 1 Thess. 4:6, and if 1 Cor. 11:32 is to be interpreted by 10:21, 22, the Lord Jesus is intended, but if by Heb. 12:5–9, then ***kurios*** here also = God. 1 Tim. 6:15, 16 is probably to be understood of the Lord Jesus, cf. Rev. 17:14.

Though John does not use "Lord" in his Epistles, and though, like the other Evangelists, he ordinarily uses the personal Name in his narrative, yet he occasionally speaks of Him as "the Lord," John 4:1; 6:23; 11:2; 20:20; 21:12.

The full significance of this association of Jesus with God under the one appellation, "Lord," is seen when it is remembered that these men belonged to the only monotheistic race in the world. To associate with the Creator one known to be a creature, however exalted, though possible to Pagan philosophers, was quite impossible to a Jew.

It is not recorded that in the days of His flesh any of His disciples either addressed the Lord, or spoke of Him, by His personal Name. Where Paul has occasion to refer to the facts of the gospel history he speaks of what the Lord Jesus said, Acts 20:35, and did, 1 Cor. 11:23, and suffered, 1 Thess. 2:15; 5:9, 10. It is our Lord Jesus who is coming, 1 Thess. 2:19, etc. In prayer also the title is given, 3:11; Eph. 1:3; the sinner is invited to believe on the Lord Jesus, Acts 16:31; 20:21, and the saint to look to the Lord Jesus for deliverance, Rom. 7:24, 25, and in the few exceptional cases in which the personal Name stands alone a reason is always discernible in the immediate context.

2. ***despotes*** (*1203*), "a master, lord, one who possesses supreme authority," is used in personal address to God in Luke 2:29; Acts 4:24; Rev. 6:10; with reference to Christ, 2 Pet. 2:1; Jude 4; elsewhere it is translated "master," "masters," 1 Tim. 6:1, 2; 2 Tim. 2:21 (of Christ); Titus 2:9; 1 Pet. 2:18.

## B. Verbs.

1. ***kurieuo*** (*2961*) denotes "to be lord of, to exercise lordship over," Luke 22:25; Rom. 6:9, 14; 7:1; 14:9; 2 Cor. 1:24; 1 Tim. 6:15.

2. ***katakurieuo*** (*2634*), a strengthened form of No. 1, is rendered "lording it" in 1 Pet. 5:3.

## C. Adjective.

***kuriakos*** (*2960*), from ***kurios*** (A, No. 1), signifies "pertaining to a lord or master"; "lordly" is not a legitimate rendering for its use in the NT, where it is used only of Christ; in 1 Cor. 11:20, of the Lord's Supper, or the Supper of the Lord; in Rev. 1:10, of the Day of the Lord.

# LOSE, (suffer) LOSS, LOST

1. ***apollumi*** (*622*) signifies (I) In the active voice, (a) "to destroy, destroy utterly, kill," e.g., Matt. 10:28; Mark 1:24; 9:22; (b) "to lose utterly," e.g., Matt. 10:42, of "losing" a reward; Luke 15:4 (1st part), of "losing" a sheep; Luke 9:25, of "losing" oneself (of the "loss" of well-being hereafter); metaphorically, John 6:39, of failing to save; 18:9, of Christ's not "losing" His own; (II), in the middle voice (a) "to perish," of things, e.g., John 6:12 "(that nothing) be lost"; of persons, e.g., Matt. 8:25, "we perish"; of the "loss" of eternal life, usually (always in the RV) translated to perish, John 3:16; 17:12, KJV, "is lost," RV, "perished"; 2 Cor. 4:3, "are perishing," KJV, "are lost"; (b) "to be lost," e.g., Luke 15:4 (2nd part), "which is lost"; metaphorically, from the relation between shepherd and flock, of spiritual destitution and alienation from God, Matt. 10:6, "(the) lost (sheep)" of the house of Israel; Luke 19:10 (the perfect tense translated "lost" is here intransitive).

2. ***zemioo*** (*2210*), "to damage" (akin to ***zemia***, "damage," e.g., Acts 27:10, 21), is used in the NT, in the passive voice, signifying "to suffer loss, forfeit, lose," Matt. 16:26; Mark 8:36, of losing one's soul or life; Luke 9:25, RV, "forfeit (his own self)," KJV, "be cast away" (for the preceding verb see No. 1); 1 Cor. 3:15, "he shall suffer loss," i.e., at the Judgment-Seat of Christ (see v. 13 with 2 Cor. 5:10); 2 Cor. 7:9, "(that) ye might suffer loss," RV (KJV, "might receive damage"); though the apostle did regret the necessity of making them sorry by his letter, he rejoiced that they were made sorry after a godly sort, and that they thus suffered no spiritual loss, which they would have done had their sorrow been otherwise than after a godly manner; in Phil. 3:8, "I suffered the loss (of all things)," RV, i.e., of all things which he formerly counted gain (especially those in verses 5 and 6, to which the article before "all things" points).

## LOSS

***zemia*** (*2209*), akin to No. 2, above, is used in Acts 27:10, RV, "loss" (KJV, "damage"); v. 21, KJV and RV, "loss," of ship and cargo; in Phil. 3:7, 8 of the apostle's estimate of the things which he formerly valued, and of all things on account of "the excellency of the knowledge of Christ Jesus."

## LOT, LOTS

### *Old Testament*

***goral*** (1486), "lot," i.e., a pebble, stick, or stone, with special markings, which was thrown to discover God's decisions, Lev. 16:8, usually with a "yes," or "no," Josh. 15:1. In an extended use the word ***goral*** represents the idea "fate" or "destiny," Isa. 17:14. Since God is viewed as controlling all things absolutely, the result of the casting of the "lot" is divinely controlled, Prov. 16:33. Thus, providence (divine control of history) is frequently figured as one's "lot."

### *New Testament*

**A. Noun.**

***kleros*** (*2819*) denotes (a) an object used in casting or drawing lots, which consisted of bits, or small tablets, of wood or stone (the probable derivation is from ***klao***, "to break"); these were sometimes inscribed with the names of persons, and were put into a receptacle or a garment ("a lap," Prov. 16:33), from which they were cast, after being shaken together; he whose "lot" first fell out was the one chosen. The method was employed in a variety of circumstances, e.g., of dividing or assigning property, Matt. 27:35; Mark 15:24; Luke 23:34; John 19:24 (cf., e.g., Num. 26:55); of appointing to office, Acts 1:26 (cf., e.g., 1 Sam. 10:20); for other occurrences in the OT, see, e.g., Josh. 7:14 (the earliest instance in Scripture), Lev. 16:7–10; Esth. 3:7; 9:24; (b) "what is obtained by lot, an allotted portion," e.g., of the ministry allotted to the apostles, Acts 1:17; of those the spiritual care of, and charge over, whom is assigned to elders, 1 Pet. 5:3.

**B. Verb.**

***lanchano*** (*2975*) denotes (a) "to draw lots," John 19:24; (b) "to obtain by lot, to obtain," Luke 1:9, "his lot was," lit., "he received by lot," i.e., by divine appointment; Acts 1:17, of the portion "allotted" by the Lord to His apostles in their ministry (cf. A, above); 2 Pet. 1:1, "that have obtained (a like precious faith)," i.e., by its being "allotted" to them, not by acquiring it for themselves, but by divine grace (an act independent of human control, as in the casting of "lots").

## LOVE (Noun and Verb)

### *Old Testament*

**A. Verb.**

***'ahab*** (157), or ***'aheb*** (157), "to love; like," i.e., a strong emotional attachment to and desire either to possess or to be in the presence of the object; familial, romantic, or friendship, Gen. 22:2; 24:67; Gen. 34:3; Ruth 4:15. In a very few instances ***'ahab*** (or ***'aheb***) may signify sexual lust, cf. 2 Sam. 13:1. Making love usually is represented by ***yada'***, "to know," or by ***shakab***, "to lie with." Though ***'ahab*** can also mean this, 1 Kings 11:1; cf. Jer. 2:25; Zech. 13:6.

***'ahab*** (or ***'aheb***) sometimes depicts a special strong attachment a servant may have toward a master under whose dominance he wishes to remain, Exod. 21:5. Perhaps there is an overtone here of family love; he "loves" his master as a son "loves" his father, cf. Deut. 15:16; 1 Sam. 16:21; 18:16.

**B. Noun.**

***'ahabah*** (160), "love," (see Verb. above) has the same range of meanings as the verb. It can refer to family, friend, romantic, or sexual "love," as a state of being, or actions of strong affection and commitment, Gen. 29:20; Deut. 7:8; 1 Sam. 18:3; In Hos. 3:1.

**C. Participle.**

***'ahab*** (157), "friend," Prov. 14:20.

### *New Testament*

**A. Verbs.**

1. ***agapao*** (*25*) and the corresponding noun ***agape*** are used in the NT (a) to describe the attitude of God toward His Son, John 17:26; the human race, generally, John 3:16; Rom. 5:8, and to such as believe on the Lord Jesus Christ particularly John 14:21; (b) to convey His will to His children concerning their attitude one toward another, John 13:34, and toward all men, 1 Thess. 3:12; 1 Cor. 16:14; 2 Pet. 1:7; (c) to express the essential nature of God, 1 John 4:8.

Love can be known only from the actions it prompts. God's love is seen in the gift of His Son, 1 John 4:9, 10. But obviously this is not the love of complacency, or affection, that is, it was not drawn out by any excellency in its objects, Rom. 5:8. It was an exercise of the divine will in deliberate choice, made without assignable cause save that which lies in the nature of God Himself, cf. Deut. 7:7, 8.

Love had its perfect expression among men in the Lord Jesus Christ, 2 Cor. 5:14; Eph. 2:4;

L

3:19; 5:2; Christian love is the fruit of His Spirit in the Christian, Gal. 5:22. Christian love has God for its primary object, and expresses itself first of all in implicit obedience to His commandments, John 14:15, 21, 23; 15:10; 1 John 2:5; 5:3; 2 John 6. Self-will, that is, self-pleasing, is the negation of love to God.

Christian love, whether exercised toward the brethren, or toward men generally, is not an impulse from the feelings, it does not always run with the natural inclinations, nor does it spend itself only upon those for whom some affinity is discovered. Love seeks the welfare of all, Rom. 15:2, and works no ill to any, 13:8–10; love seeks opportunity to do good to "all men, and especially toward them that are of the household of the faith," Gal. 6:10. See further 1 Cor. 13 and Col. 3:12–14.

2. ***phileo*** (*5368*) is to be distinguished from ***agapao*** in this, that ***phileo*** more nearly represents "tender affection." The two words are used for the "love" of the Father for the Son, John 3:35 (No. 1), and 5:20 (No. 2); for the believer, 14:21 (No. 1) and 16:27 (No. 2); both, of Christ's "love" for a certain disciple, 13:23 (No. 1), and 20:2 (No. 2). Yet the distinction between the two verbs remains, and they are never used indiscriminately in the same passage; if each is used with reference to the same objects, as just mentioned, each word retains its distinctive and essential character.

***phileo*** is never used in a command to men to "love" God; it is, however, used as a warning in 1 Cor. 16:22; ***agapao*** is used instead, e.g., Matt. 22:37; Luke 10:27; Rom. 8:28; 1 Cor. 8:3; 1 Pet. 1:8; 1 John 4:21. The distinction between the two verbs finds a conspicuous instance in the narrative of John 21:15–17.

### B. Nouns.

1. ***agape*** (*26*), the significance of which has been pointed out in connection with A, No. 1, is always rendered "love" in the RV where the KJV has "charity," a rendering nowhere used in the RV; in Rom. 14:15, where the KJV has "charitably," the RV, adhering to the translation of the noun, has "in love."

2. ***philanthropia*** (*5363*) denotes, lit., "love for man" (***phileo*** and ***anthropos***, "man"); hence, "kindness," Acts 28:2, in Titus 3:4, "(His) love toward man."

## LOVE FEASTS

***agape*** (*26*) is used in the plural in Jude 12, 2 Pet. 2:13; this refers to the common meals of the early churches (cf. 1 Cor. 11:21).

## LOVER

This is combined with other words, forming compound adjectives as follows:

1. ***philotheos*** (*5377*), "a lover of God," 2 Tim. 3:4.

2. ***philoxenos*** (*5382*), "loving strangers" (***xenia***, "hospitality"), translated "a lover of hospitality" in Titus 1:8, KJV (RV, "given to h."); elsewhere, in 1 Tim. 3:2; 1 Pet. 4:9.

3. ***philagathos*** (*5358*), "loving that which is good" (***agathos***), Titus 1:8, "a lover of good," RV.

4. ***philarguros*** (*5366*), "loving money" (***arguros***, "silver"), translated "lovers of money" in Luke 16:14; 2 Tim. 3:2, RV (KJV, "covetous").

5. ***philautos*** (*5367*), "loving oneself," 2 Tim. 3:2, RV.

6. ***philedonos*** (*5369*), "loving pleasure" (***hedone***, "pleasure"), 2 Tim. 3:4, "lovers of pleasure."

## LOVING-KINDNESS

### A. Noun.

***chesed*** (2617), "loving-kindness; steadfast love; grace; mercy; faithfulness; goodness; devotion." The word refers primarily to mutual and reciprocal rights (always grounded in truth) and obligations between the parties of a relationship (especially Yahweh and Israel), 1 Kings 8:23. But ***chesed*** is not only a matter of obligation; it is also of generosity. It is not only a matter of loyalty, but also of mercy. The weaker party seeks the protection and blessing of the patron and protector, but he may not lay absolute claim to it. The stronger party remains committed to his promise, but retains his freedom, especially with regard to the manner in which he will implement those promises. ***chesed*** implies personal involvement and commitment in a relationship beyond the rule of law.

Marital love is often related to ***chesed***. Marriage certainly is a legal matter, and there are legal sanctions for infractions. Yet the relationship, if sound, far transcends mere legalities. The prophet Hosea applies the analogy to Yahweh's ***chesed*** to Israel within the covenant (e.g., 2:21). Hence, "devotion" is sometimes the single English word best capable of capturing the nuance of the original. The RSV attempts to bring this out by its translation, "steadfast love." Hebrew writers often underscored the element of steadfastness (or strength) by pairing ***chesed*** with ***'emet*** ("truth, reliability") and ***'emunah*** ("faithfulness").

Man exercises ***chesed*** toward various units within the community—toward family and relatives, but also to friends, guests, masters, and servants. ***chesed*** toward the lowly and needy is often specified. The Bible prominently uses the term ***chesed*** to summarize and characterize a life of sanctification within, and in response to, the covenant. Thus, Hos. 6:6 states that God desires "mercy [RSV, "steadfast love"] and not sacrifice" (i.e., faithful living in addition to worship). Similarly, Mic. 6:8 features ***chesed*** in the prophets' summary of biblical ethics.

Behind all these uses with man as subject, however, stand the repeated references to God's ***chesed***. It is one of His most central characteristics. God's loving-kindness is offered to His people, who need redemption from sin, enemies, and troubles. A recurrent refrain describing God's nature is "abounding/plenteous in ***chesed***," Exod. 34:6; Neh. 9:17; Ps. 103:8; Jonah 4:2. The entire history of Yahweh's covenantal relationship with Israel can be summarized in terms of ***chesed***. It is the one permanent element in the flux of covenantal history. Even the Creation is the result of God's ***chesed***, Ps. 136:5–9. His love lasts for a "thousand generations," Deut. 7:9; cf. Deut. 5:10 and Exod. 20:6, indeed "forever" (especially in the refrains of certain psalms, such as Ps. 136).

The association of ***chesed*** with "covenant" keeps it from being misunderstood as mere providence or love for all creatures; it applies primarily to God's particular love for His chosen and covenanted people. "Covenant" also stresses the reciprocity of the relationship; but since God's ***chesed*** is ultimately beyond the covenant, it will not ultimately be abandoned, even when the human partner is unfaithful and must be disciplined, Isa. 54:8, 10. Since its final triumph and implementation is eschatological, ***chesed*** can imply the goal and end of all salvation-history, Ps. 85:7, 10; 130:7; Mic. 7:20.

### B. Adjective.

***chasid*** (2623), "pious; devout; faithful; godly." The adjective ***chasid***, derived from ***chesed***, is often used to describe the faithful Israelite. God's ***chesed*** provides the pattern, model, and strength by which the life of the ***chasid*** is to be directed. One reference to the "godly" man appears in Ps. 12:1.

## LOW (to bring, to make), LOW (estate, degree)

### A. Verb.

***tapeinoo*** (*5013*), "to bring low, to humble," is translated "shall be brought low" in Luke 3:5.

### B. Adjective.

***tapeinos*** (*5011*) denotes "of low degree or estate," Rom. 12:16, "things that are lowly," RV (KJV, "men of low estate").

### C. Noun.

***tapeinosis*** (*5014*), "abasement, humiliation, low estate," is translated "low estate" in Luke 1:48; in Jas. 1:10, "that he is made low," lit., "in his abasement."

## LOWER (Adjective, and Verb, to make), LOWEST

### A. Adjectives.

1. ***katoteros*** (*2737*), the comparative degree of ***kato***, "beneath," is used in Eph. 4:9, of Christ's descent into "the lower parts of the earth"; two of the various interpretations of this phrase are (1) that the earth is in view in contrast to heaven, (2) that the region is that of hades, the Sheol of the OT. Inasmuch as the passage is describing the effects not merely of the Incarnation but of the death and resurrection of Christ, the second interpretation is to be accepted.

2. ***eschatos*** (*2078*), "last, utmost, lowest," is rendered "lowest" in Luke 14:9, 10, of the "lowest" place at a meal.

### B. Verb.

***elattoo*** (*1642*) denotes "to make less" (***elatton***, "less"), and is used in the active voice in Heb. 2:7, and in the passive in v. 9, "was made . . . lower," and John 3:30, lit., "be made less."

## LOWLINESS, LOWLY

***tapeinophrosune*** (*5012*), "lowliness of mind, humbleness," is translated "lowliness" or "lowliness of mind" in Acts 20:19, RV; Eph. 4:2; Phil. 2:3.

## LUCRE (filthy)

### A. Noun.

***kerdos*** (*2771*), "gain," Phil. 1:21 and 3:7; "lucre" in Titus 1:11 (preceded by ***aischros***, "filthy").

### B. Adjectives.

1. ***aischrokerdes*** (*146*) denotes "greedy of base gains" (***aischros***, and A, as above), 1 Tim. 3:8, "greedy of filthy lucre"; so the RV in Titus 1:7, KJV, "given to filthy lucre." In some mss. 1 Tim. 3:3.

2. ***aischrokerdos*** (*147*) denotes "from eagerness for base gain," 1 Pet. 5:2, "for filthy lucre."

## LUKEWARM

***chliaros*** *(5513)*, "tepid, warm" (akin to ***chlio***, "to become warm," not found in the NT or Sept.), is used metaphorically in Rev. 3:16, of the state of the Laodicean church, which afforded no refreshment to the Lord.

## LUST (Noun and Verb)

### A. Noun.

***epithumia*** *(1939)* denotes "strong desire" of any kind, the various kinds being frequently specified by some adjective. The word is used of a good desire in Luke 22:15; Phil. 1:23, and 1 Thess. 2:17 only. Everywhere else it has a bad sense. In Rom. 6:12 the injunction against letting sin reign in our mortal body to obey the "lust" thereof, refers to those evil desires which are ready to express themselves in bodily activity. They are equally the "lusts" of the flesh, Rom. 13:14; Gal. 5:16, 24; Eph. 2:3; 2 Pet. 2:18; 1 John 2:16, a phrase which describes the emotions of the soul, the natural tendency towards things evil. Such "lusts" are not necessarily base and immoral, they may be refined in character, but are evil if inconsistent with the will of God.

Other descriptions besides those already mentioned are:—"of the mind," Eph. 2:3; "evil (desire)," Col. 3:5; "the passion of," 1 Thess. 4:5, RV; "foolish and hurtful," 1 Tim. 6:9; "youthful," 2 Tim. 2:22; "divers," 2 Tim. 3:6 and Titus 3:3; "their own," 2 Tim. 4:3; 2 Pet. 3:3; Jude 16; "worldly," Titus 2:12; "his own," Jas. 1:14; "your former," 1 Pet. 1:14, RV; "fleshly," 2:11; "of men," 4:2; "of defilement," 2 Pet. 2:10; "of the eyes," 1 John 2:16; of the world ("thereof"), v. 17; "their own ungodly," Jude 18. In Rev. 18:14 "(the fruits) which thy soul lusted after" is, lit., "of thy soul's lust."

### B. Verb.

***epithumeo*** *(1937)*, akin to A, has the same twofold meaning as the noun, namely (a) "to desire," used of the Holy Spirit against the flesh, Gal. 5:17; of the Lord Jesus, Luke 22:15, "I have desired"; of the holy angels, 1 Pet. 1:12; of good men, for good things, Matt. 13:17; 1 Tim. 3:1; Heb. 6:11; of men, for things without moral quality, Luke 15:16; 16:21; 17:22; Rev. 9:6; (b) of "evil desires," in respect of which it is translated "to lust" in Matt. 5:28; 1 Cor. 10:6; Gal. 5:17; Jas. 4:2; to covet, Acts 20:23; Rom. 7:7; 13:9.

# M

## MAD, MADNESS

**A. Verbs.**

1. ***mainomai*** (*3105*), "to rage, be mad," is translated by the verb "to be mad" in John 10:20; Acts 12:15; 26:24, 25; 1 Cor. 14:23.

2. ***emmainomai*** (*1693*), an intensive form of No. 1, prefixed by ***en***, "in," implying "fierce rage, to be furious against"; it is rendered "being exceedingly mad" in Acts 26:11 (cf. 9:1).

**B. Nouns.**

1. ***mania*** (*3130*), akin to A, and transliterated into English, denotes "frenzy, madness," Acts 26:24 "(thy much learning doth turn thee to) madness," RV; KJV, "(doth make thee) mad."

2. ***anoia*** (*454*), lit., "without understanding" (***a***, negative, ***nous***, "mind, understanding"), denotes "folly," 2 Tim. 3:9, and this finding its expression in violent rage, Luke 6:11.

3. ***paraphronia*** (*3913*), "madness" (from ***para***, "contrary to," and ***phren***, "the mind"), is used in 2 Pet. 2:16.

## MAGISTRATE

1. ***strategos*** (*4755*), besides its application to "the captain of the Temple," denotes "a magistrate or governor," Acts 16:20, 22, 35, 36, 38. These were, in Latin terminology, the *duumviri* or *praetores*, so called in towns which were Roman colonies. They were attended by lictors or "sergeants," who executed their orders. In the circumstances of Acts 16 they exceeded their powers, in giving orders for Roman citizens to be scourged; hence they became suppliants.

## MAGNIFICENCE

***megaleiotes*** (*3168*) denotes "splendor, magnificence" (from ***megaleios***, "magnificent," mighty," Acts 2:11, ***megas***, "great"), translated "magnificence" in Acts 19:27, of the splendor of the goddess Diana. In Luke 9:43, RV (KJV, "mighty power"); in 2 Pet. 1:16, "majesty."

## MAGNIFY

### *Old Testament*

**A. Verb.**

***gadal*** (1431), "to become strong, grow up, be great or wealthy, evidence oneself as great (magnified), be powerful, significant, or valuable." This verb can signify the increasing of size and age as with the maturing process of human life, Gen. 21:8; or animals, 2 Sam. 12:3; and plants, Isa. 44:14; anything that can grow, Dan. 8:9. ***gadal*** can represent the status of "being great or wealthy," Gen. 24:35. In the intensive stem the verb sets forth a fact, "I will make great," Gen. 12:2.

This word is sometimes used with the meaning "to be great, to evidence oneself as great," Num. 14:17. This meaning of "great," is to have high status and honor in the esteem of others, 2 Sam. 7:22. Another emphasis of ***gadal*** is "to be great, powerful, important, or valuable." This nuance arises when the word is applied to kings, as when Pharaoh said to Joseph, Gen. 41:40. The nuance "to be valuable" appears in 1 Sam. 26:24. In the reflexive stem ***gadal*** may signify "to magnify oneself." When God is the subject this is proper, Ezek. 38:23. When spoken of a proud person though it is improper pride and boasting, Isa. 10:15; Job 19:5.



**B. Nouns.**

***gedullah*** (1420), "greatness; great things." It means "greatness," as a state or condition, Ps. 71:21; or an object or event, 2 Sam. 7:21.

***godel*** (1433), "greatness." ***godel*** means "greatness" in terms of spatial size, Ezek. 31:7; of divine power, Ps. 79:11; of divine dignity, Deut. 32:3; of divine majesty, Deut. 3:24; of divine mercy, Num. 14:19; or insolence, Isa. 9:9.

***migdal*** (4026), "strong place," Gen. 11:4–5; "wooden podium," Neh. 8:4.

**C. Adjective.**

***gadol*** (1419), "great." ***gadol*** is used of extended dimension, Gen. 1:21, of number, Gen. 12:2, of power, Deut. 4:37, of punishment, Gen. 4:13, and of value or importance, Gen. 39:9. "Great," is used in such a variety of ways, that it is best to summarize that it is used with quantities, states of being, numbers of collections or masses, or spatial sizes, even to denote intensity.

### *New Testament*

***megaluno*** (*3170*), "to make great" (***megas***), is translated "to magnify" in Luke 1:46; in v. 58, RV, "had magnified (His mercy)," KJV, "had shewed great (mercy)"; Acts 5:13; 10:46;

19:17; 2 Cor. 10:15, RV (KJV, "we shall be enlarged"), i.e., by their faith in its practical effect he will be so assisted as to enlarge the scope of his gospel ministry and carry its message to regions beyond them.

## MAID, MAIDEN, MAIDSERVANT

### *Old Testament*

***betulah*** (1330), "maiden, virgin." This word can mean "virgin," as a female who has not yet had sexual intercourse, Deut. 22:17, 19, 21. In several passages this word merely means a grown-up girl or a "maiden," who may or may not have known a man, Jer. 31:4, 21. The other nations are also called ***betuloth:*** Isa. 23:12—Sidon; Isa. 47:1—Babylon; Jer. 46:11—Egypt. These nations are hardly being commended for their purity!

### *New Testament*

***paidiske*** (*3814*), translated "maid," "maids," in the KJV and RV in Mark 14:66, 69; Luke 22:56, in the RV (KJV, "damsel"), in Matt. 26:69; John 18:17; Acts 12:13; 16:16; in Luke 12:45, "maidservants" (KJV "maidens"); in Gal. 4:22, 23, 30, 31, RV, "handmaid" (KJV, "bondmaid" or "bondwoman").

## MAJESTY

***megalosune*** (*3172*), from ***megas***, "great," denotes "greatness, majesty"; it is used of God the Father, signifying His greatness and dignity, in Heb. 1:3, "the Majesty (on high)," and 8:1, "the Majesty (in the Heavens)"; and in an ascription of praise acknowledging the attributes of God in Jude 25.

## TO MAKE (CUT) A COVENANT

### A. Verb.

***karat*** (3772), "to cut off, cut down, fell, cut or make (a covenant or agreement)." Basically ***karat*** means "to sever" something from something else by cutting it with a blade. The nuance depends upon the thing being cut off. In the case of a branch, one "cuts it down," Num. 13:23, and one "[swings] the axe to cut down the tree," Deut. 19:5. The word is also used of "chopping down" wooden idols, Exod. 34:13. ***karat*** can signify "chopping off" a man's head and feet, 1 Sam. 5:4.

"To cut off" can mean "to exterminate or destroy," Gen. 9:11. ***karat*** can be used of spiritual and social extermination. A person "cut off" in this manner is not necessarily killed but may be driven out of the family and removed from the blessings of the covenant, Gen. 17:14.

One of the best known uses of this verb is "to make" a covenant. The process by which God made a covenant with Abraham is called "cutting," Gen. 15:18. Animals were literally severed into two parts. Later, "cutting" a covenant did not necessarily include this act of literal "cutting," but seems to be an allusion to the Abrahamic covenantal process, cf. Jer. 34:18. In such a covenant the one passing through the pieces pledged his faithfulness to the covenant, Neh. 9:38.

### B. Noun.

***keritut*** (3748), refers to a "bill of divorcement." This word implies the cutting off of a marriage by means of a "bill of divorcement," Deut. 24:1.

## MAKER

***demiourgos*** (*1217*), lit., "one who works for the people" (from ***demos***, "people," ***ergon***, "work"; an ancient inscription speaks of the magistrates of Tarsus as ***demiourgoi:*** the word was formerly used thus regarding several towns in Greece; it is also found used of an artist), came to denote, in general usage, a builder or "maker," and is used of God as the "Maker" of the heavenly city, Heb. 11:10.

## MALEFACTOR

1. ***kakourgos*** (*2557*), an adjective, lit., "evil-working" (***kakos***, "evil," ***ergon***, "work"), is used as a noun, translated "malefactor(-s)" in Luke 23:32, 33, 39, and in the RV in 2 Tim. 2:9 (KJV, "evil doer").

2. ***kakopoios*** (*2555*), an adjective, lit., "doing evil," is used in 1 Pet. 2:12, 14; 3:16 (in some mss.); 4:15.

## MALICE, MALICIOUSNESS, MALICIOUS

***kakia*** (*2549*), "badness in quality" (the opposite of ***arete***, "excellence"), "the vicious character generally" (Lightfoot), is translated "malice" in 1 Cor. 5:8; 14:20; Eph. 4:31; Col. 3:8; Titus 3:3; 1 Pet. 2:1.

## MAMMON

***mamonas*** (*3126*), a common Aramaic word for "riches," akin to a Hebrew word signifying "to be firm, steadfast" (whence "Amen"), hence, "that which is to be trusted"; Gesenius regards it as derived from a Heb. word signifying "treasure," Gen. 43:23; it is personified in Matt. 6:24; Luke 16:9, 11, 13.

## MAN (See also MEN)

### *Old Testament*

### Nouns.

***'adam*** (120) is translated "person, human," which means a single human being of either sex, Psa. 49:20.

***'adam*** is translated "humankind, mankind," meaning a class of beings created by God without regard to sex, with a focus as a class of creature, distinct from animals, plants, or even spiritual beings, Gen. 1:26. Similarly, ***'adam*** also refers to the first human who was directly created by God, in his image, from the (red?) dust of the ground, Gen. 2:20. Note that one has to carefully distinguish each of the above meanings to ***'adam***, according to context, especially in the first chapters of Genesis.

***ben 'adam*** are two Hebrew words, translated "son of man" and means low class person, i.e., a person of low social status, implying poverty, Prov. 49:2

***ben 'adam*** is also translated "son of man" and has the far more common meaning in the Bible of a person who is in the class of humanity, as contrasted to other classes of supernatural beings, Ezek 2:1.

The Fall greatly affected the nature of "man," but he did not cease to be in God's image, Gen. 9:6. Fallen "man" occupies a new and lower position before God, Gen. 6:5; cf. 8:21. No longer does "man" have perfect communion with the Creator; he is now under the curse of sin and death.

***geber*** (1397), "man." The root meaning "to be strong" is no longer obvious in the usage of ***geber***, since it is often indistinguishable from ***'ish***, Jer. 22:30. Other synonyms to ***geber*** are ***zakar***, "male," Jer. 30:6; ***'enosh***, "man," Job 4:17; and ***'adam***, "man," Job 14:10. A ***geber*** denotes a "male," as an antonym of a "woman," Deut. 22:5.

***'ish*** (376) can be translated "man," with the meaning of a male or female human as a class or kind in contrast to other classes of created beings, Exod. 19:13. More specifically, ***'ish*** can be translated "man," with the meaning of a mature, adult male of a created species (usually a human), Gen. 2:24; 7:2. Even more particularly, ***'ish*** can be translated "husband," with the meaning of a male spouse in a marriage, Gen. 16:3.

***'ish*** can be translated "each, every," with the meaning of one or every one of a totality, with a focus on the individual parts of a whole group, collections of things, of a mass of things, Gen. 40:5. ***'ish*** also can be translated "anyone, whoever, someone, a certain one," with a reference to whom or what is spoken about which is not explicit, Lev. 15:5. With the Hebrew word ***lo*** (not) translates as "none, not anyone," with the meaning of a negative reference to an entity, event, or state, a kind of opposite to the first pronouns, Gen. 23:6.

***'ish*** can also be a kind of helper word to change a Hebrew noun of an idea or concept into a noun about an individual person related to that abstract idea. For example, ***'ish mashchit***, "destroyer," is translated in form as "man of destruction," Prov. 28:24. Or another example is ***'ish matsut***, "enemy," but is in form translated "man of strife," Isa. 41:12. Space would not allow all the samples, for they are many.

Another meaning of ***'ish*** in combination with other words is ***zera 'ish***, translated " offspring," formally translated "seed of man," with the meaning of a child of a parent, 1 Sam. 1:11.

Yet another meaning of ***'ish*** in combination with other words is ***'ish shem***, translated "well-known person," with the meaning of a person known in the community, with a generally favorable view, and so has high status and community standing, Num. 16:2.

So also another meaning of ***'ish*** in combination with other words is ***'ish el 'ach***, translated, "to each other, to one another, among yourselves," with a formal translation, "each (or *man*) to his brother," and so this phrase has the meaning of a reciprocal reference of two or more associating with one another in some way, Gen. 37:19; 42:21,28; Exod. 16:15; 25:20; 37:9; Num. 14:4; 2 Kin. 7:6; Jer. 13:14; 23:35; 25:26; Ezek. 24:23

Lastly a meaning of ***'ish*** in combination with other words is ***'ish 'elohim***, translated "prophet," with a formal translation of "man of God," with the meaning of one who speaks words that a deity gives by vision, words, or other forms of revelation, Deut. 33:1; 1 Sam. 9:6; 1 Kin. 13:1–31.

***'enosh*** (582), "man." ***'enosh*** has the meaning of man as a class of being, with a focus on the frailty and mortality of mankind, Ps. 103:15.

### *New Testament*

1. ***anthropos*** (*444*) is used (a) generally, of "a human being, male or female," without reference to sex or nationality, e.g., Matt. 4:4; 12:35; John 2:25; (b) in distinction from God, e.g., Matt. 19:6; John 10:33; Gal. 1:11; Col. 3:23; (c) in distinction from animals, etc., e.g., Luke 5:10; (d) sometimes, in the plural, of "men and women," people, e.g., Matt. 5:13, 16; in Mark 11:2 and 1 Tim. 6:16, lit., "no one of men"; (e) in some instances with a suggestion of human frailty and imperfection e.g., 1 Cor. 2:5; Acts 14:15 (2nd part); (f) in the phrase translated "after man," "after the manner of men," "as a man" (KJV), lit. "according to (***kata***) man," is used only by the apostle Paul, of (1) the practices of fallen humanity 1 Cor. 3:3; (2) anything

of human origin, Gal. 1:11; (3) the laws that govern the administration of justice among men, Rom. 3:5; (4) the standard generally accepted among men, Gal. 3:15; (5) an illustration not drawn from Scripture, 1 Cor. 9:8; (6) probably equals "to use a figurative expression,," i.e., to speak evil of men with whom he had contended at Ephesus as "beasts" (cf. 1 Cor. 4:6), 1 Cor. 15:32.

(g) in the phrase "the inward man," the regenerate person's spiritual nature personified, the inner self of the believer, Rom. 7:22, as approving of the law of God; in Eph. 3:16, as the sphere of the renewing power of the Holy Spirit; in 2 Cor. 4:16 (where ***anthropos*** is not repeated), in contrast to "the outward man," the physical frame, the "man" as cognizable by the senses; the "inward" man is identical with "the hidden man of the heart," 1 Pet. 3:4.

(h) in the expressions "the old man," "the new man," which are confined to Paul's epistles, the former standing for the unregenerate nature personified as the former self of a believer, which, having been crucified with Christ, Rom. 6:6, is to be apprehended practically as such, and to be "put off," Eph. 4:22; Col. 3:9, being the source and seat of sin; the latter, "the new man," standing for the new nature personified as the believer's regenerate self, a nature "created in righteousness and holiness of truth," Eph. 4:24, and having been "put on" at regeneration, Col. 3:10; being "renewed after the image of Him that created him," it is to be "put on" in practical apprehension of these facts.

2. ***aner*** (*435*) is never used of the female sex; it stands (a) in distinction from a woman, Acts 8:12; 1 Tim. 2:12; as a husband, Matt. 1:16; John 4:16; Rom. 7:2; Titus 1:6; (b) as distinct from a boy or infant, 1 Cor. 13:11; metaphorically in Eph. 4:13; (c) in conjunction with an adjective or noun, e.g., Luke 5:8, lit., "a man, a sinner"; 24:19, lit., "a man, a prophet."

## MAN'S, OF MAN, MANKIND (see also MEN)

***anthropinos*** (*442*), "human, belonging to man," is used (a) of man's wisdom, in 1 Cor. 2:13 (some mss. have it in v. 4, where indeed it is implied; see, however, the RV); (b) of "man's judgment," 1 Cor. 4:3; (c) of "mankind," Jas. 3:7, lit., "the human nature," RV marg. (KJV marg., "nature of man"); (d) of human ordinance, 1 Pet. 2:13.

## MANGER

***phatne*** (*5336*), "a manger," Luke 2:7, 12, 16, also denotes "a stall," 13:15.

## MANIFEST (Adjective and Verb)

### A. Adjectives.

1. ***emphanes*** (*1717*), manifest (akin to ***emphaino***, "to show in, to exhibit"; ***en***, "in," ***phaino***, "to cause to shine"), is used (a) literally in Acts 10:40, RV "(gave Him to be made) manifest"; (b) metaphorically in Rom. 10:20, "(I was made) manifest."

2. ***phaneros*** (*5318*), "open to sight, visible, manifest" (the root ***phan***—, signifying "shining," exists also in No. 1), is translated "manifest" in Luke 8:17; Acts 4:16; 7:13, RV (KJV, "known"); Rom. 1:19; 1 Cor. 3:13; 11:19; 14:25; Gal. 5:19; Phil. 1:13; 1 Tim. 4:15 (KJV "appear"); 1 John 3:10.

3. ***aphanes*** (*852*) denotes "unseen, hidden," Heb. 4:13, "not manifest" (***a***, negative and ***phaino***).

### B. Verbs.

1. ***phaneroo*** (*5319*), "to make visible, clear, manifest, known" (akin to A, No. 2), is used especially in the writings of the apostles John and Paul, occurring 9 times in the Gospel, 9 times in 1 John, 2 in Rev.; in the Pauline Epistles (including Heb.) 24 times; in the other Gospels, only in Mark, 3 times; elsewhere in 1 Pet. 1:20; 5:4.

The true meaning is "to uncover, lay bare, reveal." The following are variations in the rendering, which should be noted: Mark 16:12, 14 (RV, "was manifested," KJV, "appeared"); John 21:1 (RV, "manifested," KJV, "shewed"; cf. v. 14); Rom. 1:19 (RV, "manifested," KJV, "hath shewed"); 2 Cor. 3:3 (RV, "being made manifest," KJV, "are manifestly declared"); 2 Cor. 5:10; 7:12 and Rev. 3:18 (RV, "be made manifest," KJV, "appear"); 2 Cor. 11:6 (RV, "we have made it manifest," KJV, "we have been thoroughly made manifest"); Col. 1:26 (RV "hath it been manifested," KJV, "is made manifest"); 3:4 (RV, "be manifested," KJV, "appear"; so 1 Pet. 5:4); 1 Tim. 3:16 (RV, "was manifested," KJV, "was manifest"); 2 Tim. 1:10 (RV, "hath . . . been manifested," KJV, "is . . . made manifest"; cf. Rom. 16:26, 2 Cor. 4:10, 11; 1 Pet. 1:20); Heb. 9:26 (RV, "hath He been manifested," KJV, "hath He appeared"); 1 John 2:28; 3:2 (RV, "is . . . made manifest," KJV, "doth appear").

2. ***emphanizo*** (*1718*), akin to A, No. 1, is translated "to manifest, make manifest," in John 14:21, 22; Heb. 11:14.

## MANIFESTATION

***phanerosis*** (*5321*), "a manifestation," occurs in 1 Cor. 12:7 and 2 Cor. 4:2.

## MANNA

***manna*** (*3131*), the supernaturally provided food for Israel during their wilderness journey, for details see Exod. 16 and Num. 11; cf. John 6:31–35. The "hidden manna" is promised as one of the rewards of the overcomer, Rev. 2:17. None of the natural substances called "manna" is to be identified with that which God provided for Israel.

## MANNER

### A. Nouns.

1. ***ethos*** (*1485*), "a habit, custom" (akin to the verb ***etho***, "to be accustomed"), is always translated "custom" in the RV ("manner" in the KJV of John 19:40; Acts 15:1; 25:16; Heb. 10:25).

2. ***ethos*** (*2239*), primarily "a haunt, abode," then, "a custom, manner," occurs in the plural in 1 Cor. 15:33, i.e., ethical conduct, morals.

3. ***tropos*** (*5158*), "a turning, fashion, manner, character, way of life," is translated "manner" in Acts 1:11, with reference to the Lord's ascension and return, in Jude 7, of the similarity of the evil of those mentioned in vv. 6 and 7.

### B. Adverb.

***homoios*** (*3668*), akin to the adjective ***homoios***, "like," signifies in "like manner, equally"; in the following the RV has "in like manner" for KJV, "likewise"; Matt. 27:41; Mark 4:16; Luke 10:32; 13:3; 16:25; John 5:19; (Heb. 9:21); Jas. 2:25; 1 Pet. 3:1, 7; Rev. 8:12; in Rev. 2:15 the KJV "which thing I hate" translates a variant reading (***ho miso***).

### C. Verb.

***tropophoreo*** (*5159*), "to bear another's manners," is translated "suffered He (their) manners" in Acts 13:18.

## MANSERVANT

***pais*** (*3816*), "a child, boy, youth," also means "a servant, attendant," Luke 12:45.

## MANSIONS

***mone*** (*3438*), primarily "a staying abiding" (akin to ***meno***, "to abide"), denotes an "abode" (Eng., "manor," "manse," etc.), translated "mansions" in John 14:2; "abode" in v. 23. There is nothing in the word to indicate separate compartments in heaven; neither does it suggest temporary resting places on the road.

## MANSLAYERS

***androphonos*** (*409*), from ***aner***, "a man," and ***phoneus***, "a murderer," occurs in the plural in 1 Tim. 5:9.

## MARAN-ATHA

***maran-atha*** (*3134*), an expression used in 1 Cor. 16:22, is the Greek spelling for two Aramaic words, likely meaning the "Our Lord, come," or "O Lord, come." The character of the context, however, indicates that the apostle is making a statement rather than expressing a desire or uttering a prayer. As to the reason why it was used, most probably it was a current phrase of joy among early Christians, as embodying the consummation of their desires.

## MARK (Noun)

1. ***charagma*** (*5480*) denotes "a stamp, impress," translated "mark" in Rev. 13:16, 17; etc.

2. ***stigma*** (*4742*) denotes "a tattooed mark" or "a mark burnt in, a brand" (akin to ***stizo***, "to prick"), translated "marks" in Gal. 6:17. It is probable that the apostle refers to the physical sufferings he had endured since he began to proclaim Jesus as Messiah and Lord [e.g., at Lystra and Philippi. It is probable, too, that this reference to his scars was intended to set off the insistence of the Judaizers upon a body-mark which cost them nothing. Over against the circumcision they demanded as a proof of obedience to the law he set the indelible tokens, sustained in his own body, of his loyalty to the Lord Jesus. As to the origin of the figure, it was indeed customary for a master to brand his slaves, but this language does not suggest that the apostle had been branded by His Master.

M

## MARKET, MARKETPLACE

***agora*** (*58*), primarily "an assembly," or, in general, "an open space in a town." In the NT it denotes "a place of assembly, a public place or forum, a marketplace." A variety of circumstances, connected with it as a public gathering place, is mentioned, e.g., business dealings such as the hiring of laborers, Matt. 20:3; the buying and selling of goods, Mark 7:4 (involving risk of pollution); the games of children, Matt. 11:16; Luke 7:32; exchange of greetings, Matt. 23:7; Mark 12:38; Luke 11:43; 20:46; the holding of trials, Acts 16:19; public discussions, Acts 17:17. Mark 6:56 records the bringing of the sick there. The word always carries with it the idea of publicity, in contrast to private circumstances.

## MARRIAGE (give in), MARRY

### A. Noun.

***gamos*** (*1062*), "a marriage, wedding," or "wedding feast," is used to denote (a) the ceremony and its proceedings, including the "marriage feast," John 2:1, 2; of the "marriage ceremony" only, figuratively, Rev. 19:7, as distinct from the "marriage feast" (v. 9); (b) "the marriage feast," RV in Matt. 22:2–4, 9; in v. 8, 10, "wedding"; in 25:10, RV "marriage feast"; so Luke 12:36; 14:8; in Matt. 22:11, 12, the "wedding garment" is, lit., "a garment of a wedding." In Rev. 19, where, under the figure of a "marriage," the union of Christ, as the Lamb of God, with His heavenly bride is so described, the marriage itself takes place in heaven during the Parousia, v. 7 (the aorist or point tense indicating an accomplished fact; the bride is called "His wife"); the "marriage feast" or supper is to take place on earth, after the Second Advent, v. 9. That Christ is spoken of as the Lamb points to His atoning sacrifice as the ground upon which the spiritual union takes place. The background of the phraseology lies in the OT description of the relation of God to Israel, e.g., Isa. 54:4,ff.; Ezek. 16:7,ff.; Hos. 2:19; (c) "marriage" in general, including the "married" state, which is to be "had in honor," Heb. 13:4, RV.

**B. Verbs.**

1. ***gameo*** (*1060*), "to marry" (akin to A), is used (a) of "the man," Matt. 5:32; 19:9, 10; 22:25 (RV; KJV, "married a wife"); v. 30; 24:38; Mark 6:17; 10:11; 12:25; Luke 14:20; 16:18; 17:27, RV, "married" (AV, "married wives"); 20:34, 35; 1 Cor. 7:28 (1st part); v. 33; (b) of "the woman," in the active voice, Mark 10:12; 1 Cor. 7:28 (last part); ver. 34; 1 Tim. 5:11, 14; in the passive voice, 1 Cor. 7:39; (c) of "both sexes," 1 Cor. 7:9, 10, 36; 1 Tim. 4:3.

2. ***gamizo*** (*1061v*), "to give in marriage," is used in the passive voice in Matt. 22:30 (2nd clause); Mark 12:25; Luke 17:27; 20:35 (last word), passive; in the active voice, Matt. 24:38; further, of giving a daughter in "marriage," 1 Cor. 7:38 (twice), which, on the whole, may be taken as the meaning. In this part of the Epistle, the apostle was answering a number of questions on matters about which the church at Corinth had written to him, and in this particular matter the formal transition from "marriage" in general to the subject of giving a daughter in "marriage," is simple. Eastern customs naturally would involve the inclusion of the latter in the inquiry and the reply.

## MARVEL (Noun and Verb), MARVELLOUS

### *Old Testament*

**A. Verb.**

***pala'*** (6381), "to be marvelous, be extraordinary, be beyond one's power to do, do wonderful acts." ***pala'*** is used primarily with God as its subject, expressing actions that are beyond the bounds of human powers or expectations, Ps. 118:23. Deliverance from Egypt was the result of God's wondrous acts, Exod. 3:20. Praise is constantly due God for all His wonderful deeds, Ps. 9:1. At the same time, God does not require anything of His people that is too hard for them, Deut. 30:11.

**B. Noun.**

***pele'*** (6382), "wonder; marvel." This noun frequently expresses the "wonder," the extraordinary aspects, of God's dealings with His people, Exod. 15:11; Ps. 77:11; Isa. 9:6; 29:14.

### *New Testament*

**A. Noun.**

***thauma*** (*2295*), "a wonder" (akin to ***theaomai***, "to gaze in wonder"), is found in the most authentic mss. in 2 Cor. 11:14 (some mss. have the adjective ***thaumastos:*** see C, below), "(no) marvel"; in Rev. 17:6, RV, "wonder" (KJV, "admiration"), said of John's astonishment at the vision of the woman described as Babylon the Great.

**B. Verbs.**

1. ***thaumazo*** (*2296*) signifies "to wonder at, marvel" (akin to A); the following are RV differences from the KJV: Luke 2:33, "were marveling" for "marveled"; Luke 8:25 and 11:14, "marveled" for "wondered"; 9:43, "were marveling" for "wondered"; 2 Thess. 1:10, "marveled at" for "admired" (of the person of Christ at the time of the shining forth of His Parousia, at the Second Advent).

2. ***ekthaumazo*** (*1537*) and (*2296*), a strengthened form of No. 1 (***ek***, intensive), is found in the best mss. in Mark 12:17, RV, "wondered greatly" (some mss. have No. 1).

**C. Adjective.**

***thaumastos*** (*2298*), "marvellous" (akin to A and B), is said (a) of the Lord's doing in making the rejected Stone the Head of the corner, Matt. 21:42; Mark 12:11; (b) of the erstwhile blind man's astonishment that the Pharisees knew not from whence Christ had come, and yet He had given him sight, John 9:30, RV, "the marvel," KJV, "a marvellous thing"; (c) of the spiritual light into which believers are brought, 1 Pet. 2:9; (d) of the vision of the seven angels having the seven last plagues, Rev. 15:1; (e) of the works of God, 15:3.

## MASTER (Noun and Verb)

**A. Nouns.**

1. ***didaskalos*** (*1320*), "a teacher" (from ***didasko***, "to teach"), is frequently rendered

"Master" in the four Gospels, as a title of address to Christ, e.g., Matt. 8:19; Mark 4:38 (there are more instances in Luke than in the other Gospels); John 1:38, where it interprets "Rabbi"; 20:16, where it interprets "Rabboni." It is used by Christ of Himself in Matt. 23:8 and John 13:13–14; by others concerning Him, Matt. 17:24; 26:18; Mark 5:35; 14:14; Luke 8:49; 22:11; John 11:28. In John 3:10, the Lord uses it in addressing Nicodemus, RV, "the teacher" (KJV, "a master"), where the article does not specify a particular "teacher," but designates the member of a class; for the class see Luke 2:46, "the doctors" (RV, marg., "teachers"). It is used of the relation of a disciple to his "master," in Matt. 10:24, 25; Luke 6:40. It is not translated "masters" in the rest of the NT, save in the KJV of Jas. 3:1 "(be not many) masters," where obviously the RV "teachers" is the meaning.

2. ***kurios*** (*2962*), "a lord, one who exercises power," is translated "masters" in Matt. 6:24; 15:27; Mark 13:35; Luke 16:13; Acts 16:16, 19; Rom. 14:4, KJV (RV, "lord"); Eph. 6:5, 9 (twice), the 2nd time of Christ; so in Col. 3:22; 4:1.

3. ***despotes*** (*1203*), one who has "absolute ownership and uncontrolled power," is translated "masters" in 1 Tim. 6:1, 2; Titus 2:9; 1 Pet. 2:18; of Christ, 2 Tim. 2:21; 2 Pet. 2:1, RV (for KJV, Lord); in Jude 4, RV, it is applied to Christ "(our only) Master (and Lord, Jesus Christ)," KJV "(the only) Lord (God)"; in Rev. 6:10, RV, in an address to God, "O Master" (KJV, "O Lord"). It is rendered "Lord" in Luke 2:29 and Acts 4:24.

4. ***rabbei*** (*4461*) was an Aramaic word signifying "my master," a title of respectful address to Jewish teachers, Matt. 26:25. In the following the RV has "Rabbi" for KJV "Master"; Matt. 26:25, 49; Mark 9:5; 11:21; 14:45; John 4:31; 9:2; 11:8. In other passages the KJV has "Rabbi," Matt 23:7–8; John 1:38, 49; 3:2, 26; 6:25.

5. ***epistates*** (*1988*) denotes "a chief, a commander, overseer master." It is used by the disciples in addressing the Lord, in recognition of His authority rather than His instruction; it occurs only in Luke 5:5; 8:24, 45; 9:33, 49; 17:13.

### B. Verb.

***katakurieuo*** (*2634*), "to exercise lordship" (***kata***, "down upon," ***kurios***, "a lord"), is translated "mastered" in Acts 19:16, RV, of the action of the evil spirit on the sons of Sceva (KJV, "overcame").

## MASTERBUILDER

***architekton*** (*753*), from ***arche***, "rule, beginning," and ***tekton***, "an artificer" (whence Eng., "architect"), "a principal artificer," is used figuratively by the apostle in 1 Cor. 3:10, of his work in laying the foundation of the local church in Corinth, inasmuch as the inception of the spiritual work there devolved upon him.

## MEASURE (Noun and Verb)

### *Old Testament*

### A. Verb.

***madad*** (4058), "to measure, measure off, extend." The basic meaning of the verb is to measure a volume, or length against a normal standard, the way we use feet and pounds to "measure things, Exod. 16:18; Deut. 21:2; Num. 35:5. ***madad*** can express the idea of extending, stretching, 1 Kings 17:21.

### B. Noun.

***middah*** (4060), "measure; measurement; extent; size; stature; section; area." This noun refers to the act of "measurement," Lev. 19:35; Ezek. 41:17. Second, ***middah*** means the thing measured, or the "size." Exod. 26:2; Ps. 39:4; 1 Chron. 11:23. Third, ***middah*** sometimes represents a "measured portion" of a thing, Neh. 3:11.

### *New Testament*

### A. Nouns.

***metron*** (*3358*) denotes (I) "that which is used for measuring, a measure," (a) of "a vessel," figuratively, Matt. 23:32; Luke 6:38 (twice); in John 3:34, with the preposition ***ek***, "(He giveth not the Spirit) by measure," RV (which is a necessary correction; the italicized words "*unto him*," KJV, detract from the meaning). Not only had Christ the Holy Spirit without "measure," but God so gives the Spirit through Him to others. It is the ascended Christ who gives the Spirit to those who receive His testimony and set their seal to this, that God is true. The Holy Spirit is imparted neither by degrees, nor in portions, as if He were merely an influence; He is bestowed personally upon each believer, at the time of the New Birth; (b) of "a graduated rod or rule for measuring," figuratively, Matt. 7:2; Mark 4:24; literally, Rev. 21:15 (in the best mss.; see the RV); v. 17; (II) "that which is measured, a determined extent, a portion measured off," Rom. 12:3; 2 Cor. 10:13 (twice); Eph. 4:7, "(according to the) measure (of the gift of Christ)"; the gift of grace is "measured" and given according to the will of Christ; whatever the endowment, His is the bestowment and the adjustment; v. 13, "the measure (of the stature of the fullness of Christ)," the standard of spiritual stature being the fullness which is essentially Christ's; v. 16, "(according to the working in due) measure (of each several part)," i.e., according to the effectual working of the ministration rendered in due "measure" by every part.

**B. Adjective.**

***ametros*** (*280*), "without measure" (***a***, negative, and A), is used in the neuter plural in an adverbial phrase in 2 Cor. 10:13, 15, ***eis ta ametra***, lit., "unto the (things) without measure," RV, "(we will not glory) beyond our measure," KJV, "(we will not boast) of things without measure," referring to the sphere divinely appointed for the apostle as to his gospel ministry; this had reached to Corinth, and by the increase of the faith of the church there, would extend to regions beyond. His opponents had no scruples about intruding into the spheres of other men's work.

**C. Verbs.**

1. ***metreo*** (*3354*), "to measure" (akin to A), is used (a) of space, number, value, etc., Rev. 11:1, 2; 21:15, 16, 17; metaphorically, 2 Cor. 10:12; (b) in the sense of "measuring" out, giving by "measure," Matt. 7:2, "ye mete" (some mss. have No. 2); Mark 4:24; in some mss. in Luke 6:38.

2. ***antimetreo*** (*488*), "to measure in return" (***anti***, "back, in return" and No. 1), is used in the passive voice, and found in some mss. in Matt. 7:2 (the most authentic have No. 1); in Luke 6:38 the most authentic have this verb.

## MEDIATOR

***mesites*** (*3316*), lit., "a go-between" (from ***mesos***, "middle," and ***eimi***, "to go"), is used in two ways in the NT, (a) "one who mediates" between two parties with a view to producing peace, as in 1 Tim. 2:5, though more than mere "mediatorship" is in view, for the salvation of men necessitated that the Mediator should Himself possess the nature and attributes of Him towards whom He acts, and should likewise participate in the nature of those for whom He acts (sin apart); only by being possessed both of deity and humanity could He comprehend the claims of the one and the needs of the other; further, the claims and the needs could be met only by One who, Himself being proved sinless, would offer Himself an expiatory sacrifice on behalf of men; (b) "one who acts as a guarantee" so as to secure something which otherwise would not be obtained. Thus in Heb. 8:6; 9:15; 12:24 Christ is the Surety of "the better covenant," "the new covenant," guaranteeing its terms for His people.

In Gal. 3:19 Moses is spoken of as a "mediator," and the statement is made that "a mediator is not a mediator of one," v. 20, that is, of one party. Here the contrast is between the promise given to Abraham and the giving of the Law. The Law was a covenant enacted between God and the Jewish people, requiring fulfillment by both parties. But with the promise to Abraham, all the obligations were assumed by God, which is implied in the statement, "but God is one."

## MEDITATE

### *Old Testament*

***hagah*** (1897), "to meditate, moan, growl, utter, speak." This word means to think about something in earnest, often with the focus on thinking about future plans and contingencies, possibly speaking to God or oneself in low tones. It seems to be an onomatopoetic term, reflecting the sighing and low sounds one may make while musing, at least as the ancients practiced it, Josh. 1:8; Ps. 1:2. ***hagah*** also expresses the "growl" of lions, Isa. 31:4; "coo" of doves, Isa. 38:14.

### *New Testament*

1. ***meletao*** (3191), primarily, "to care for" (akin to ***melete***, "care"; cf. ***melei***, "it is a care"), denotes (a) "to attend to, practice," 1 Tim. 4:15, RV, "be diligent in" (KJV, "meditate upon"); to practice is the prevalent sense of the word, and the context is not against this significance in the RV rendering; some mss. have it in Mark 13:11; (b) "to ponder, imagine," Acts 4:25.

2. ***promeletao*** (4304), "to premeditate," is used in Luke 21:14.

## MEEK, MEEKNESS

**A. Adjective.**

***praus*** or ***praos*** (*4239*) denotes "gentle, mild, meek"; for its significance see the corresponding noun, below, B. Christ uses it of His own disposition, Matt. 11:29; He gives it in the third of His Beatitudes, 5:5; it is said of Him as the King Messiah, 21:5, from Zech. 9:9; it is an adornment of the Christian profession, 1 Pet. 3:4.

**B. Nouns.**

1. ***prautes***, or ***praotes***, an earlier form, (*4240*) denotes "meekness." In its use in Scripture, in which it has a fuller, deeper significance than in non-scriptural Greek writings, it consists not in a person's outward behavior only; nor yet in his relations to his fellow-men; as little in his mere natural disposition. Rather it is an inwrought grace of the soul; and the exercises

of it are first and chiefly towards God. It is that temper of spirit in which we accept His dealings with us as good, and therefore without disputing or resisting; it is closely linked with the word ***tapeinophrosune*** [humility], and follows directly upon it, Eph. 4:2; Col. 3:12; cf. the adjectives in the Sept. of Zeph. 3:12, "meek and lowly."

The meaning of ***prautes*** is not readily expressed in English, for the terms meekness, mildness, commonly used, suggest weakness and pusillanimity to a greater or less extent, whereas ***prautes*** does nothing of the kind. Nevertheless, it is difficult to find a rendering less open to objection than "meekness"; "gentleness" has been suggested, but as ***prautes*** describes a condition of mind and heart, and as "gentleness" is appropriate rather to actions, this word is no better than that used in both English Versions. It must be clearly understood, therefore, that the meekness manifested by the Lord and commended to the believer is the fruit of power. The common assumption is that when a man is meek it is because he cannot help himself; but the Lord was "meek" because he had the infinite resources of God at His command. Described negatively, meekness is the opposite to self-assertiveness and self-interest; it is equanimity of spirit that is neither elated nor cast down, simply because it is not occupied with self at all.

2. ***praupathia***, "a meek disposition, meekness" (***praus***, "meek," ***pascho***, "to suffer"), is found in the best texts in 1 Tim. 6:11.

## MEMBER

***melos*** (*3196*), "a limb of the body," is used (a) literally, Matt. 5:29–30; Rom. 6:13 (twice), 19 (twice); 7:5, 23 (twice); 12:4 (twice); 1 Cor. 12:12 (twice), 14, 18–20, 22, 25–26 (twice); Jas. 3:5, 6; 4:1; in Col. 3:5, "mortify therefore your members which are upon the earth"; since our bodies and their "members" belong to the earth, and are the instruments of sin, they are referred to as such (cf. Matt. 5:29–30; Rom. 7:5, 23, mentioned above); the putting to death is not physical, but ethical; as the physical "members" have distinct individualities, so those evils, of which the physical "members" are agents, are by analogy regarded as examples of the way in which the "members" work if not put to death; this is not precisely the same as "the old man," v. 9, i.e., the old nature, though there is a connection; (b) metaphorically, "of believers as members of Christ," 1 Cor. 6:15 (1st part); of one another, Rom. 12:5 (as with the natural illustration, so with the spiritual analogy, there is not only vital unity, and harmony in operation, but diversity, all being essential to effectivity; the unity is not due to external organization but to common and vital union in Christ); there is stress in v. 5 upon "many" and "in Christ" and "members"; 1 Cor. 12:27 (of the "members" of a local church as a body); Eph. 4:25 (of the "members" of the whole Church as the mystical body of Christ); in 1 Cor. 6:15 (2nd part), of one who practices fornication.

## MEMORIAL

***mnemosunon*** (*3422*) denotes "a memorial," that which keeps alive the memory of someone or something (from ***mnemon***, "mindful"), Matt. 26:13; Mark 14:9; Acts 10:4.

## MEN-PLEASERS

***anthropareskos*** (*441*), an adjective signifying "studying to please men" (***anthropos***, "man," ***aresko***, "to please"), designates, "not simply one who is pleasing to men . . . , but one who endeavors to please men and not God" (Cremer). It is used in Eph. 6:6 and Col. 3:22.

## MEN-STEALERS

***andrapodistes*** (*405*), "a slave dealer, kidnapper," from ***andrapodon***. The verb ***andrapodizo*** supplied the noun "with the like odious meaning," which appears in 1 Tim. 1:10.

## MEND

***katartizo*** (*2675*), from ***kata***, "down," intensive and ***artios***, "fit," has three meanings, (a) "to mend, repair," Matt. 4:21; Mark 1:19, of nets; (b) "to complete, furnish completely, equip, prepare," Luke 6:40; Rom. 9:22; Heb, 11:3 and in the middle voice, Matt. 21:16; Heb. 10:5; (c) "ethically, to prepare, perfect," Gal. 6:1; 1 Thess. 3:10; 1 Pet. 5:10; Heb. 13:21; and in the passive voice, 1 Cor. 1:10; 2 Cor. 13:11.

## MENTION (Noun and Verb)

### A. Noun.

***mneia*** (*3417*), "remembrance, mention" (akin to ***mimnesko***, "to remind, remember"), is always used in connection with prayer, and translated "mention" in Rom. 1:9; Eph. 1:16; 1 Thess. 1:2; Philem. 4, in each of which it is preceded by the verb to make; "remembrance" in Phil. 1:3; 1 Thess. 3:6; 2 Tim. 1:3. Some mss. have it in Rom. 12:13, instead of ***chreiais***, necessities.

### B. Verb.

***mnemoneuo*** (*3421*), which most usually means "to call to mind, remember," signifies "to make mention of," in Heb. 11:22.

## MERCHANDISE (Noun, and Verb, to make)

### A. Nouns.

1. ***emporia*** (*1711*) denotes "commerce, business, trade" [akin to No. 2, and to ***emporos***, "one on a journey," "a merchant"], occurs in Matt. 22:5.

2. ***emporion*** (*1712*) denotes "a trading place, exchange" (Eng., "emporium"), John 2:16, "(a house) of merchandise."

### B. Verb.

***emporeuomai*** (*1710*) primarily signifies "to travel," especially for business; then, "to traffic, trade," Jas. 4:13; then, "to make a gain of, make merchandise of," 2 Pet. 2:3.

## MERCIFUL (Adjective, and Verb, to be), MERCY (Noun, and Verb, to have, etc.)

### A. Nouns.

1. ***eleos*** (*1656*) "is the outward manifestation of pity; it assumes need on the part of him who receives it, and resources adequate to meet the need on the part of him who shows it. It is used (a) of God, who is rich in mercy, Eph. 2:4, and who has provided salvation for all men, Titus 3:5, for Jews, Luke 1:72, and Gentiles, Rom. 15:9. He is merciful to those who fear him, Luke 1:50, for they also are compassed with infirmity, and He alone can succor them. Hence they are to pray boldly for mercy, Heb. 4:16, and if for themselves, it is seemly that they should ask for mercy for one another, Gal. 6:16; 1 Tim. 1:2. When God brings His salvation to its issue at the Coming of Christ, His people will obtain His mercy, 2 Tim. 1:16; Jude 21; (b) of men; for since God is merciful to them, He would have them show mercy to one another, Matt. 9:13; 12:7; 23:23; Luke 10:37; Jas. 2:13.

2. ***oiktirmos*** (*3628*), "pity, compassion for the ills of others," is used (a) of God, Who is "the Father of mercies," 2 Cor. 1:3; His "mercies" are the ground upon which believers are to present their bodies a living sacrifice, holy, acceptable to God, as their reasonable service, Rom. 12:1; under the Law he who set it at nought died without compassion, Heb. 10:28; (b) of men; believers are to feel and exhibit compassions one toward another, Phil. 2:1, RV "compassions," and Col. 3:12, RV "(a heart) of compassion"; in these two places the word is preceded by No. 3, rendered "tender mercies" in the former, and "a heart" in the latter, RV.

3. ***splanchnon*** (*4698*), "affections, the heart," always in the plural in the NT, has reference to "feelings of kindness, goodwill, pity," Phil. 2:1, RV, "tender mercies."

### B. Verbs.

1. ***eleeo*** (*1653*), akin to A, No. 1, signifies, in general, "to feel sympathy with the misery of another," and especially sympathy manifested in act, (a) in the active voice, "to have pity or mercy on, to show mercy" to, e.g., Matt. 9:27; 15:22; 17:15; 18:33; 20:30, 31 (three times in Mark, four in Luke); Rom. 9:15, 16, 18; 11:32; 12:8; Phil. 2:27; Jude 22, 23; (b) in the passive voice, "to have pity or mercy shown one, to obtain mercy," Matt. 5:7; Rom. 11:30, 31; 1 Cor. 7:25; 2 Cor. 4:1; 1 Tim. 1:13, 16; 1 Pet. 2:10.

2. ***oikteiro*** (*3627*), akin to A, No. 2, "to have pity on" (from ***oiktos***, "pity": ***oi***, an exclamation, = oh!), occurs in Rom. 9:15 (twice), where it follows No. 1 (twice); the point established there and in Exod. 33:19, from the Sept. of which it is quoted, is that the "mercy" and compassion shown by God are determined by nothing external to His attributes. Speaking generally ***oikteiro*** is a stronger term than ***eleeo***.

3. ***hilaskomai*** (*2433*) in profane Greek meant "to conciliate, appease, propitiate, cause the gods to be reconciled"; their goodwill was not regarded as their natural condition, but as something to be earned. The heathen believed their gods to be naturally alienated in feeling from man. In the NT the word never means to conciliate God; it signifies (a) "to be propitious, merciful," Luke 18:13, in the prayer of the publican; (b) "to expiate, make propitiation for," Heb. 2:17, "make propitiation."

That God is not of Himself already alienated from man, see John 3:16. His attitude toward the sinner does not need to be changed by his efforts. With regard to his sin, an expiation is necessary, consistently with God's holiness and for His righteousness' sake, and that expiation His grace and love have provided in the atoning sacrifice of His Son; man, himself a sinner, justly exposed to God's wrath (John 3:36), could never find an expiation. As Lightfoot says, "when the NT writers speak at length on the subject of Divine wrath, the hostility is represented, not as on the part of God, but of men." Through that which God has accomplished in Christ, by His death, man, on becoming regenerate, escapes the merited wrath of God. The making of this expiation [(b) above], with its effect in the mercy of God (a) is what is expressed in ***hilaskomai***.

### C. Adjectives.

1. ***eleemon*** (*1655*), "merciful," akin to A, No. 1, not simply possessed of pity but actively compassionate, is used of Christ as a High Priest, Heb. 2:17, and of those who are like God, Matt. 5:7 (cf. Luke 6:35, 36, where the RV, "sons" is to be read, as representing characteristics resembling those of their Father).

2. ***oiktirmon*** (*3629*) pitiful, compassionate for the ills of others," a stronger term than No. 1 (akin to A, No. 2), is used twice in Luke 6:36, "merciful" (of the character of God, to be expressed in His people); Jas. 5:11, RV, "merciful," KJV, "of tender mercy."

3. ***hileos*** (*2436*), "propitious, merciful" (akin to B, No. 3), was used in profane Greek just as in the case of the verb (which see). There is nothing of this in the use of the word in Scripture. The quality expressed by it there essentially appertains to God, though man is undeserving of it. It is used only of God, Heb. 8:12; in Matt. 16:22, "Be it far from Thee" (Peter's word to Christ) may have the meaning given in the RV marg., "(God) have mercy on Thee," lit., "propitious to Thee" (KJV marg., "Pity Thyself").

4. ***aneleos*** or ***anileos*** (*448*), "unmerciful, merciless," occurs in Jas. 2:13, said of judgment on him who shows no mercy.

## MERCY SEAT

***hilasterion*** (*2435*), "the lid or cover of the ark of the covenant," signifies the Propitiatory, so called on account of the expiation made once a year on the great Day of Atonement, Heb. 9:5. For the formation see Exod. 25:17–21.

## MERRY (to be, to make)

***euphraino*** (*2165*), in the active voice, "to cheer, make glad," 2 Cor. 2:2, is used everywhere else in the passive voice, signifying, "to be happy, rejoice, make merry," and translated "to be merry" in Luke 12:19; 15:23, 24, 29, 32; in 16:19, "fared (sumptuously)"; in Rev. 11:10, make merry.

## MESSAGE

1. ***angelia*** (*31*), akin to ***angello***, "to bring a message, proclaim," denotes a "message, proclamation, news," 1 John 1:5 [some mss. have ***epangelia***]; 1 John 3:11, where the word is more precisely defined (by being followed by the conjunction "that," expressing the purpose that we should love one another) as being virtually equivalent to an order.

2. ***kerugma*** (*2782*), "that which is proclaimed by a herald, a proclamation, preaching," is translated "the message" in Titus 1:3, RV (KJV, preaching).

## MESSENGER

1. ***angelos*** (*32*), "a messenger, an angel, one sent," is translated "messenger," of John the Baptist, Matt. 11:10; Mark 1:2; Luke 7:27; in the plural, of John's "messengers," 7:24; of those whom Christ sent before Him when on His journey to Jerusalem, 9:52; of Paul's "thorn in the flesh," "a messenger of Satan," 2 Cor. 12:7; of the spies as received by Rahab, Jas. 2:25.

2. ***apostolos*** (*652*), "an apostle," is translated "messengers" in 2 Cor. 8:23 regarding Titus and "the other brethren," whom Paul describes to the church at Corinth as "messengers of the churches," in respect of offerings from those in Macedonia for the needy in Judea; in Phil. 2:25, of Epaphroditus as the "messenger" of the church at Philippi to the apostle in ministering to his need; RV marg. in each case, "apostle."

## MESSIAH (See also CHRIST)

### A. Nouns.

***mashiach*** (4899), "anointed one; Messiah." First, ***mashiach*** refers to one who is anointed with oil, symbolizing the reception of the Holy Spirit, enabling him to do an assigned task. Kings, 1 Sam. 24:6, high priests, and some prophets, 1 Kings 19:16, were so anointed, Lev. 4:3. In the case of Cyrus, he was anointed with God's Spirit only and commissioned an "anointed deliverer" of Israel, Isa. 45:1. The patriarchs, too, are called "anointed ones," Ps. 105:15. Second, the word is sometimes transliterated "Messiah." After the promise to David, 2 Sam. 7:13, ***mashiach*** refers immediately to the Davidic dynasty, but ultimately it points to the "Messiah," Jesus the Christ, Ps. 2:2; Dan. 9:25; cf. John 1:41.

M

### B. Verb.

***mashach*** (*4886*), "to smear with oil or paint, anoint." The objects of this verb are people, sacrificial victims, and objects of worship. Aaron and his sons are the objects of this verb in Exod. 30:30.

## MIGHT (Noun), MIGHTY, MIGHTILY, MIGHTIER

### *Old Testament*

***geburah*** (1369), "might." The primary meaning of ***geburah*** is "power" or "physical strength." Certain animals are known for their "strength," such as horses, Ps. 147:10, and crocodiles, Job 41:4. Man also demonstrates "might" in heroic acts, Judg. 8:21, and in war, Isa. 3:25. David's powerful regime is expressed as a "kingship of ***geburah***," 1 Chron. 29:30. Since both physical strength and wisdom were necessary for leadership, these two qualities are joined together, Prov. 8:14. God is of course the ultimate example of combining might and wisdom, Ps. 54:1; 65:6

*New Testament*

### A. Nouns.

1. ***dunamis*** (*1411*), "power," (a) used relatively, denotes "inherent ability, capability, ability to perform anything," e.g., Matt. 25:15, "ability"; Acts 3:12, "power"; 2 Thess. 1:7, RV, "(angels) of His power" (KJV, "mighty"); Heb. 11:11, RV, "power" (KJV, "strength"); (b) used absolutely, denotes (1) "power to work, to carry something into effect," e.g., Luke 24:49; (2) "power in action," e.g., Rom. 1:16; 1 Cor. 1:18; it is translated "might" in the KJV of Eph. 1:21 (RV, "power"); so 3:16; Col. 1:11 (1st clause); 2 Pet. 2:11; in Rom. 15:19, KJV, this noun is rendered "mighty"; RV, "(in the) power of signs."

2. ***ischus*** (*2479*) denotes "might, strength, power," (a) inherent and in action as used of God, Eph. 1:19, RV, "(the strength, ***kratos***, of His) might," KJV, "(His mighty) power," i.e., power (over external things) exercised by strength; Eph. 6:10, "of His might"; 2 Thess. 1:9, RV, "(from the glory) of His might" (KJV "power"); Rev. 5:12, RV, "might" (KJV, "strength"); 7:12, "might"; (b) as an endowment, said (1) of angels, 2 Pet. 2:11; here the order is No. 2 and No. 1, RV, "might and power," which better expresses the distinction than the KJV, "power and might"; in some mss. in Rev. 18:2 it is said of the voice of an angel; the most authentic mss. have the adjective ***ischuros***, "mighty"; (2) of men, Mark 12:30, 33; Luke 10:27.

### B. Adjectives.

1. ***dunatos*** (*1415*), "powerful, mighty" (akin to A, No. 1), is used, with that significance, (1) of God, Luke 1:49, "mighty"; Rom. 9:22, "power" (here the neuter of the adjective is used with the article, as a noun, equivalent to ***dunamis***); frequently with the meaning "able"; (2) of Christ, regarded as a prophet, Luke 24:19 ("in deed and word"); (3) of men: Moses, Acts 7:22 ("in his words and works"); Apollos, 18:24, "in the Scriptures"; of those possessed of natural power, 1 Cor. 1:26; of those possessed of spiritual power, 2 Cor. 10:4. For the shades of meaning in the translation "strong," see Rom. 15:1; 2 Cor. 12:10; 13:9.

2. ***ischuros*** (*2478*), "strong, mighty" (akin to A, No. 2, and with corresponding adjectival significance), is usually translated "strong"; "mighty" in Luke 15:14 (of a famine); Rev. 19:6 (of thunders); 19:18 (of men): in the following, where the KJV has "mighty," the RV substitutes "strong," 1 Cor. 1:27; Rev. 6:15 (KJV, "mighty men"); 18:10, 21; Heb. 11:34, RV, "(waxed) mighty" (KJV, "valiant").

3. ***ischuroteros*** (*2478**), "stronger, mightier," the comparative degree of No. 2, is translated "mightier" in Matt. 3:11; Mark 1:7; Luke 3:16; "stronger" in Luke 11:22; 1 Cor. 1:25; 10:22.

4. ***biaios*** (*972*), "violent" (from ***bia***, "force, violence, strength," found in Acts 5:26; 21:35; 24:7; 27:41), occurs in Acts 2:2, of wind.

### C. Verb.

***dunateo*** (*1414*), "to be powerful" (akin to A, No. 1 and B, No. 1), is found in the most authentic mss. in Rom. 14:4 (some have ***dunatos***, B, No. 1), RV "(the Lord) hath power," KJV, "(God) is able"; similarly, as regard mss., in 2 Cor. 9:8, where the RV and KJV have "(God) is able"; in 2 Cor. 13:3, KJV, "is mighty," RV, "is powerful" (according to the general significance of ***dunamis***).

## MILLSTONE

### A. Noun.

***mulos*** (*3458*) denotes "a handmill," consisting of two circular stones, one above the other, the lower being fixed. From the center of the lower a wooden pin passes through a hole in the upper, into which the grain is thrown, escaping as flour between the stones and falling on a prepared material below them. The handle is inserted into the upper stone near the circumference. Small stones could be turned by one woman (millgrinding was a work deemed fit only for women and slaves; cf. Judg. 16:21); larger ones were turned by two or more.

Still larger ones were turned by an ass (***onikos***), Matt. 18:6, RV, "a great millstone" (marg., "a millstone turned by an ass"), indicating the immediate and overwhelming drowning of one who causes one young believer to stumble; Mark 9:42 (where some mss. have ***lithos mulikos***, "a stone of a mill," as in Luke 17:2).

### B. Adjectives.

1. ***mulikos*** (*3457*), "of a mill," occurs in Luke 17:2.

2. ***mulinos*** (*3458(v)*), "made of millstone," is used with ***lithos***, "a stone"; and with the adjective ***megas***, "great," in the best mss. in Rev. 18:21 (some have the word ***mulos***.

## MIND (Noun and Verb)

### A. Nouns.

1. ***nous*** (*3563*), "mind," denotes, speaking generally, the seat of reflective consciousness, comprising the faculties of perception and un-

derstanding, and those of feeling, judging and determining.

Its use in the NT may be analyzed as follows: it denotes (a) the faculty of knowing, the seat of the understanding, Luke 24:45; Rom. 1:28; 14:5; 1 Cor. 14:15, 19; Eph. 4:17; Phil. 4:7; Col. 2:18; 1 Tim. 6:5; 2 Tim. 3:8; Titus 1:15; Rev. 13:18; 17:9; (b) counsels, purpose, Rom. 11:34 (of the "mind" of God); 12:2; 1 Cor. 1:10; 2:16, twice (1) of the thoughts and counsels of God, (2) of Christ, a testimony to His Godhood; Eph. 4:23; (c) the new nature, which belongs to the believer by reason of the new birth, Rom. 7:23, 25, where it is contrasted with "the flesh," the principle of evil which dominates fallen man. Under (b) may come 2 Thess. 2:2, where it stands for the determination to be steadfast amidst afflictions, through the confident expectation of the day of rest and recompense mentioned in the first chapter.

2. ***dianoia*** (*1271*), lit. "a thinking through, or over, a meditation, reflecting," signifies (a) like No. 1, "the faculty of knowing, understanding, or moral reflection," (1) with an evil significance, a consciousness characterized by a perverted moral impulse, Eph. 2:3 (plural); 4:18; (2) with a good significance, the faculty renewed by the Holy Spirit, Matt. 22:37; Mark 12:30; Luke 10:27; Heb. 8:10; 10:16; 1 Pet. 1:13; 1 John 5:20; (b) "sentiment, disposition" (not as a function but as a product); (1) in an evil sense, Luke 1:51, "imagination"; Col. 1:21; (2) in a good sense, 2 Pet. 3:1.

3. ***ennoia*** (*1771*), "an idea, notion, intent," is rendered "mind" in 1 Pet. 4:1.

4. ***noema*** (*3540*), "thought, design," is rendered "minds" in 2 Cor. 3:14; 4:4; 11:3; Phil. 4:7.

5. ***phronema*** (*5427*) denotes "what one has in the mind, the thought" (the content of the process expressed in ***phroneo***, "to have in mind, to think"); or "an object of thought"; in Rom. 8:6 (KJV, "to be carnally minded" and "to be spiritually minded"), the RV, adhering to the use of the noun, renders by "the mind of the flesh," in vv. 6 and 7, and "the mind of the spirit," in v. 6. In v. 27 the word is used of the "mind" of the Holy Spirit.

## B. Verbs.

1. ***phroneo*** (*5426*) signifies (a) "to think, to be minded in a certain way"; (b) "to think of, be mindful of." It implies moral interest or reflection, not mere unreasoning opinion. Under (a) it is rendered by the verb "to mind" in the following: Rom. 8:5, "(they that are after the flesh) do mind (the things of the flesh)"; 12:16, "be of (the same) mind," lit., "minding the same," and "set (not) your mind on," RV, KJV, "mind (not)"; 15:5, "to be of (the same) mind," RV, (KJV, "to be like-minded"); so the RV in 2 Cor. 13:11, KJV, "be of (one) mind"; Gal. 5:10, "ye will be (none otherwise) minded"; Phil. 1:7, RV, "to be (thus) minded," KJV, "to think (this)"; 2:2, RV, "be of (the same) mind," KJV, "be likeminded," and "being . . . of (one) mind," lit., "minding (the one thing)"; 2:5, RV, "have (this) mind," KJV, "let (this) mind be," lit., "mind this"; 3:15, "let us . . . be (thus) minded," and "(if) . . . ye are (otherwise) minded" (some mss. have the verb in v. 16); 3:19, "(who) mind (earthly things)"; 4:2, "be of (the same) mind"; Col. 3:2, RV and KJV marg., "set your mind," lit., "mind (the things above)," KJV, "set your affection."

2. ***sophroneo*** (*4993*) signifies (a) "to be of sound mind," or "in one's right mind, sober-minded" (***sozo***, "to save," ***phren***, "the mind"), Mark 5:15 and Luke 8:35, "in his right mind"; 2 Cor. 5:13, RV, "we are of sober mind" (KJV, "we be sober"); (b) "to be temperate, self-controlled," Titus 2:6, "to be sober-minded"; 1 Pet. 4:7, RV, "be ye . . . of sound mind" (KJV, "be ye sober").

## C. Adjective.

***homophron*** (*3675*), "agreeing, of one mind" (***homos***, "same," ***phren***, "the mind"), is used in 1 Pet. 3:8.

M

# MINDED

1. ***boulomai*** (*1014*), "to wish, will, desire, purpose" (akin to ***boule***, "counsel, purpose"), is translated "was minded" in Matt. 1:19; Acts 15:37, RV (KJV, "determined"); 18:27, RV (KJV, "was disposed"); 19:30, RV (KJV, "would have"); 5:33, RV, "were minded" (KJV, "took counsel"); 18:15, RV, "I am (not) minded (to be)," KJV, "I will (be no)"; Heb. 6:17, "being minded," RV (KJV, "willing"), said of God.

2. ***bouleuo*** (*1011*), "to take counsel," is translated "to be minded" in Acts 27:39; 2 Cor. 1:17, middle voice in each case.

# MINDFUL OF (to be)

1. ***mimnesko*** (*5403*), the tenses of which are from the older verb ***mnaomai***, signifies "to remind"; but in the middle voice, "to remember, to be mindful of," in the sense of caring for, e.g., Heb. 2:6, "Thou art mindful"; in 13:3, "remember"; in 2 Tim. 1:4, RV, "remembering" (KJV, "being mindful of"); so in 2 Pet. 3:2.

2. ***mnemoneuo*** (*3421*), "to call to mind, remember," is rendered "they had been mindful" in Heb. 11:15.

# MINGLE

***kerannumi*** (*2767*), "to mix, to mingle," chiefly of the diluting of wine, implies "a mixing of two things, so that they are blended and form a compound, as in wine and water. It is used in Rev. 18:6.

## MINISTER (Noun and Verb)

### *Old Testament*

**A. Verb.**

***sharat*** (8334), "to minister, serve, officiate." As a term for serving or ministering, ***sharat*** is to be distinguished from the term for more menial serving, ***'abad***, from which the word meaning "slave" or "servant" is derived. ***sharat*** is characteristically used of "serving" done by royal household workers, 2 Sam. 13:17; 1 Kings 10:5. In the manner of the modern "public servant" idea, the word is used in reference to court officials and royal servants, 1 Chron. 27:1; 28:1; Esth. 1:10. This term is used most frequently as the special term for service in worship to the Lord, Deut. 10:8; Num. 16:9; Ezek. 44:11–14.

**B. Noun.**

***sharat*** (8334), "minister; servant." The noun form of the verb appears several times meaning "minister" or "servant." As humans, Exod. 24:13; or angels, Ps. 103:21; cf. Ps. 104:4.

### *New Testament*

**A. Nouns.**

1. ***diakonos*** (*1249*), "a servant, attendant, minister, deacon," is translated "minister" in Mark 10:43; Rom. 13:4 (twice); 15:8; 1 Cor. 3:5; 2 Cor. 3:6; 6:4; 11:15 (twice); Gal. 2:17; Eph. 6:21; Col. 1:7, 23, 25; 4:7; 1 Thess. 3:2; 1 Tim. 4:6.

2. ***leitourgos*** (*3011*) denoted among the Greeks, firstly, "one who discharged a public office at his own expense," then, in general, "a public servant, minister." In the NT it is used (a) of Christ, as a "Minister of the sanctuary" (in the Heavens), Heb. 8:2; (b) of angels, Heb. 1:7 (Ps. 104:4); (c) of the apostle Paul, in his evangelical ministry, fulfilling it as a serving priest, Rom. 15:16; that he used it figuratively and not in an ecclesiastical sense, is obvious from the context; (d) of Epaphroditus, as ministering to Paul's needs on behalf of the church at Philippi, Phil. 2:25; here, representative service is in view; (e) of earthly rulers, who though they do not all act consciously as servants of God, yet discharge functions which are the ordinance of God, Rom. 13:6.

**B. Verbs.**

1. ***diakoneo*** (*1247*), akin to A, No. 1, signifies "to be a servant, attendant, to serve, wait upon, minister." In the following it is translated "to minister," except where "to serve" is mentioned: it is used (a) with a general significance, e.g., Matt. 4:11; 20:28; Mark 1:13; 10:45; John 12:26 ("serve," twice); Acts 19:22; Philem. 13; (b) of waiting at table, "ministering" to the guests, Matt. 8:15; Luke 4:39; 8:3; 12:37; 17:8, "serve"; 22:26, "serve," v. 27, "serveth," twice; the 2nd instance, concerning the Lord, may come under (a); so of women preparing food, etc., Mark 1:31; Luke 10:40, "serve"; John 12:2, "served"; (c) of relieving one's necessities, supplying the necessaries of life, Matt. 25:44; 27:55; Mark 15:41; Acts 6:2, "serve"; Rom. 15:25; Heb. 6:10; more definitely in connection with such service in a local church, 1 Tim. 3:10, 13 [there is nothing in the original representing the word "office"; RV, "let them serve as deacons," "they that have served (well) as deacons"]; (d) of attending, in a more general way, to anything that may serve another's interests, as of the work of an amanuensis, 2 Cor. 3:3 (metaphorical): of the conveyance of material gifts for assisting the needy, 2 Cor. 8:19, 20, RV, "is ministered" (KJV, "is administered"); of a variety of forms of service, 2 Tim. 1:18; of the testimony of the OT prophets, 1 Pet. 1:12; of the ministry of believers one to another in various ways, 1 Pet. 4:10, 11 (not here of discharging ecclesiastical functions).

2. ***leitourgeo*** (*3008*), (akin to A, No. 2), in classical Greek, signified at Athens "to supply public offices at one's own cost, to render public service to the State"; hence, generally, "to do service," said, e.g., of service to the gods. In the NT it is used (a) of the prophets and teachers in the church at Antioch, who "ministered to the Lord," Acts 13:2; (b) of the duty of churches of the Gentiles to "minister" in "carnal things" to the poor Jewish saints at Jerusalem, in view of the fact that the former had "been made partakers" of the "spiritual things" of the latter, Rom. 15:27; (c) of the official service of priests and Levites under the Law, Heb. 10:11.

## MINISTERING, MINISTRATION, MINISTRY

**A. Nouns.**

1. ***diakonia*** (*1248*), "the office and work of a ***diakonos***," "service, ministry," is used (a) of domestic duties, Luke 10:40; (b) of religious and spiritual "ministration," (1) of apostolic "ministry," e.g., Acts 1:17, 25; 6:4; 12:25; 21:19; Rom. 11:13, RV (KJV, "office"); (2) of the service of believers, e.g., Acts 6:1; Rom. 12:7; 1 Cor. 12:5, RV, "ministrations" (KJV, "administrations"); 1 Cor. 16:15; 2 Cor. 8:4; 9:1, 12, RV, "ministration"; v. 13; Eph. 4:12, RV, "ministering" (KJV,

"the ministry," not in the sense of an ecclesiastical function); 2 Tim. 4:11, RV, "(for) ministering"; collectively of a local church, Acts 11:29, "relief" (RV marg. "for ministry"); Rev. 2:19, RV, "ministry" (KJV, "service"); of Paul's service on behalf of poor saints, Rom. 15:31; (3) of the "ministry" of the Holy Spirit in the gospel, 2 Cor. 3:8; (4) of the "ministry" of angels, Heb. 1:14, RV, "to do service" (KJV, "to minister"); (5) of the work of the gospel, in general, e.g., 2 Cor. 3:9, "of righteousness"; 5:18, "of reconciliation"; (6) of the general "ministry" of a servant of the Lord in preaching and teaching, Acts 20:24; 2 Cor. 4:1; 6:3; 11:8; 1 Tim. 1:12, RV, "(to His) service"; 2 Tim. 4:5; undefined in Col. 4:17; (7) of the Law, as a "ministration" of death, 2 Cor. 3:7; of condemnation, 3:9.

2. ***leitourgia*** (*3009*), akin to ***leitourgos***, to which the meanings of ***leitourgia*** correspond, is used in the NT of "sacred ministrations," (a) priestly, Luke 1:23; Heb. 8:6; 9:21; (b) figuratively, of the practical faith of the members of the church at Philippi regarded as priestly sacrifice, upon which the apostle's lifeblood might be poured out as a libation, Phil. 2:17; (c) of the "ministration" of believers one to another, regarded as priestly service, 2 Cor. 9:12; Phil. 2:30.

### B. Adjective.

***leitourgikos*** (*3010*), "of or pertaining to service, ministering," is used in Heb. 1:14, of angels as "ministering spirits."

## MIRACLE

1. ***dunamis*** (*1411*), "power, inherent ability," is used of works of a supernatural origin and character, such as could not be produced by natural agents and means. It is translated "miracles" in the RV and KJV in Acts 8:13 (where variant readings give the words in different order); 19:11; 1 Cor. 12:10, 28, 29; Gal. 3:5; KJV only, in Acts 2:22 (RV, "mighty works"); Heb. 2:4 (RV, "powers"). In Gal. 3:5, the word may be taken in its widest sense, to include "miracles" both physical and moral.

2. ***semeion*** (*4592*), "a sign, mark, token" (akin to ***semaino***, "to give a sign"; ***sema***, "a sign"), is used of "miracles" and wonders as signs of divine authority; it is translated "miracles" in the RV and KJV of Luke 23:8; Acts 4:16, 22; most usually it is given its more appropriate meaning "sign," "signs," e.g., Matt. 12:38, 39, and in every occurrence in the Synoptists, except Luke 23:8; in the following passages in John's Gospel the RV substitutes "sign" or "signs" for the KJV "miracle or miracles"; 2:11, 23; 3:2; 4:54; 6:2, 14, 26; 7:31; 9:16; 10:41; 11:47; 12:18, 37; the KJV also has "signs" elsewhere in this Gospel; in Acts, RV, "signs," KJV, "miracles," in 6:8; 8:6; 15:12; elsewhere only in Rev. 13:14; 16:14; 19:20.

## MISERABLE, MISERABLY, MISERY

### A. Adjectives.

1. ***eleeinos*** (*1652*), "pitiable, miserable" (from ***eleos***, "mercy, pity"), is used in Rev. 3:17, in the Lord's description of the church at Laodicea; here the idea is probably that of a combination of "misery" and pitiableness.

2. ***kakos*** (*2556*), "bad, evil," is translated "miserable" in Matt. 21:41, RV (KJV, "wicked").

### B. Adverb.

***kakos*** (*2560*), "badly, ill," is translated "miserably" in Matt. 21:41 (see A, No. 2). Adhering to the meaning "evil," and giving the designed stress, the sentence may be rendered, "evil (as they are) he will evilly destroy them."

### C. Noun.

***talaiporia*** (*5004*), "hardship, suffering, distress" (akin to ***talaiporos***, "wretched," Rom. 7:24; Rev. 3:17, and to ***talaiporeo***, in the middle voice, "to afflict oneself," in Jas. 4:9, "be afflicted"), is used as an abstract noun, "misery," in Rom. 3:16; as a concrete noun, "miseries," in Jas. 5:1.

M

## MIST

1. ***achlus*** (*887*), "a mist," especially a dimness of the eyes, is used in Acts 13:11.

2. ***homichle*** (*3658a*), "a mist" (not so thick as ***nephos*** and ***nephele***, "a cloud"), occurs in 2 Pet. 2:17 (1st part), RV, "mists"; some mss. have ***nephelai***, "clouds" (KJV)."

3. ***zophos*** (*2217*) is rendered "mist" in the KJV of 2 Pet. 2:17 (2nd part), RV, "blackness"; "murkiness" would be a suitable rendering.

## MOCK, MOCKER, MOCKING

### A. Verbs.

1. ***empaizo*** (*1702*), a compound of ***paizo***, "to play like a child" (***pais***), "to sport, jest," prefixed by ***en***, "in" or "at," is used only in the Synoptics, and, in every instance, of the "mockery" of Christ, except in Matt. 2:16 (there in the sense of deluding, or deceiving, of Herod by the wise men) and in Luke 14:29, of ridicule cast upon the one who after laying a foundation of a tower is unable to finish it. The word is used (a) prophetically by the Lord, of His impending sufferings, Matt. 20:19; Mark 10:34; Luke 18:32; (b) of the actual insults inflicted upon Him by the men who had taken Him from Gethsemane, Luke 22:63; by Herod and

his soldiers, Luke 23:11; by the soldiers of the governor, Matt. 27:29, 31; Mark 15:20; Luke 23:36; by the chief priests, Matt. 27:41; Mark 15:31.

2. ***mukterizo*** (*3456*), from ***mukter***, "the nose," hence, "to turn up the nose at, sneer at, treat with contempt," is used in the passive voice in Gal. 6:7, where the statement "God is not mocked" does not mean that men do not mock Him; the apostle vividly contrasts the essential difference between God and man. It is impossible to impose upon Him who discerns the thoughts and intents of the heart.

3. ***chleuazo*** (*5512*), "to jest, mock, jeer at" (from ***chleue***, "a jest"), is said of the ridicule of some of the Athenian philosophers at the apostle's testimony concerning the resurrection of the dead, Acts 17:32.

4. ***diachleuazo***, an intensive form of No. 3, "to scoff at," whether by gesture or word, is said of those who jeered at the testimony given on the Day of Pentecost, Acts 2:13 (some mss. have No. 3).

**B. Nouns.**

1. ***empaiktes*** (*1703*), "a mocker" (akin to A, No. 1), is used in 2 Pet. 3:3, RV, "mockers," (KJV, "scoffers"); Jude 18, RV and KJV, "mockers."

2. ***empaigmos*** (*1701*), the act of the ***empaiktes***, "a mocking," is used in Heb. 11:36, "mockings."

3. ***empaigmone*** (*1702d*), an abstract noun, "mockery," is used in 2 Pet. 3:3 (some mss. omit it, as in KJV): (see also No. 1, above).

## MODEST

***kosmios*** (*2887*), "orderly, well-arranged, decent, modest" (akin to ***kosmos***, in its primary sense as "harmonious arrangement adornment"; cf. ***kosmikos***, of the world, which is related to ***kosmos*** in its secondary sense as the world), is used in 1 Tim. 2:9 of the apparel with which Christian women are to adorn themselves; in 3:2 (RV, "orderly"; KJV, "of good behavior"), of one of the qualifications essential for a bishop or overseer.

## MOMENT

1. ***atomos*** (*823*) lit. means "indivisible" (from ***a***, negative, and ***temno***, "to cut"; Eng., "atom"); hence it denotes "a moment," 1 Cor. 15:52.

2. ***stigme*** (*4743*), "a prick, a point" (akin to ***stizo***, "to prick"), is used metaphorically in Luke 4:5, of a "moment," with ***chronos***, "a moment (of time)."

## MONEY

1. ***argurion*** (*694*), properly, "a piece of silver," denotes (a) "silver," e.g., Acts 3:6; (b) a "silver coin," often in the plural, "pieces of silver," e.g., Matt. 26:15; so 28:12, where the meaning is "many, (***hikanos***) pieces of silver"; (c) "money"; it has this meaning in Matt. 25:18, 27; 28:15; Mark 14:11; Luke 9:3; 19:15, 23; 22:5; Acts 8:20 (here the RV has "silver").

2. ***chrema*** (*5536*), lit., "a thing that one uses" (akin to ***chraomai*** "to use"), hence, (a) "wealth, riches," Mark 10:23, 24; Luke 18:24; (b) "money," Acts 4:37, singular number, "a sum of money"; plural in 8:18, 20; 24:26.

3. ***chalkos*** (*5475*), "copper," is used, by metonymy, of "copper coin," translated "money," in Mark 6:8; 12:41.

4. ***kerma*** (*2772*), primarily "a slice" (akin to ***keiro***, "to cut short"), hence, "a small coin, change," is used in the plural in John 2:15, "the changers' money," probably considerable heaps of small coins.

5. ***nomisma*** (*3546*), primarily "that which is established by custom" (***nomos***, "a custom, law"), hence, "the current coin of a state, currency," is found in Matt. 22:19, "(tribute) money."

## MONEY (love of)

***philarguria*** (*5365*), from ***phileo***, "to love," and ***arguros***, "silver," occurs in 1 Tim. 6:10 (cf. ***philarguros***, "covetous, avaricious"). Trench contrasts this with ***pleonexia***, "covetousness."

## MONTH, MONTHS

1. ***men*** (*3376*), connected with ***mene***, "the moon," akin to a Sanskrit root *ma*—, "to measure" (the Sanskrit *masa* denotes both moon and month, cf., e.g., Lat. *mensis*, Eng., "moon" and "month," the moon being in early times the measure of the "month"). The interval between the 17th day of the second "month" (Gen. 7:11) and the 17th day of the seventh "month," is said to be 150 days (8:3, 4), i.e., five months of 30 days each; hence the year would be 360 days (cf. Dan. 7:25; 9:27; 12:7 with Rev. 11:2–3; 12:6, 14; 13:5; whence we conclude that 3 1/2 years or 42 months = 1260 days, i.e., one year = 60 days); this was the length of the old Egyptian year; later, five days were added to correspond to the solar year. The Hebrew year was as nearly solar as was compatible with its commencement, coinciding with the new moon, or first day of the "month." This was a regular feast day, Num. 10:10; 28:11–14; the Passover coincided with the full moon (the 14th of the month Abib).

Except in Gal. 4:10; Jas. 5:17; Rev. 9:5, 10, 15; 11:2; 13:5; 22:2, the word is found only in Luke's writings, Luke 1:24, 26, 36, 56; 4:25; Acts 7:20; 18:11; 19:8; 20:3; 28:11, examples of Luke's care as to accuracy of detail.

## MOON

1. ***selene*** (*4582*), from ***selas***, "brightness" (the Heb. words are ***yareach***, "wandering," and ***lebanah***, "white"), occurs in Matt. 24:29; Mark 13:24; Luke 21:25; Acts 2:20; 1 Cor. 15:41; Rev. 6:12; 8:12; 12:1; 21:23. In Rev. 12:1, "the moon under her feet" is suggestive of derived authority, just as her being clothed with the sun is suggestive of supreme authority; everything in the symbolism of the passage centers in Israel. In 6:12 the similar symbolism of the sun and "moon" is suggestive of the supreme authority over the world, and of derived authority, at the time of the execution of divine judgments upon nations at the close of the present age.

2. ***neomenia*** (*3561*), or ***noumeniua***, denoting "a new moon" (***neos***, "new," ***men***, "a month,") is used in Col. 2:16, of a Jewish festival. Judaistic tradition added special features in the liturgy of the synagogue in connection with the observance of the first day of the month, the new "moon" time.

## MORTAL, MORTALITY

***thnetos*** (*2349*), "subject or liable to death, mortal" (akin to ***thnesko***, "to die"), occurs in Rom. 6:12, of the body, where it is called "mortal," not simply because it is liable to death, but because it is the organ in and through which death carries on its death-producing activities; in 8:11, the stress is on the liability to death, and the quickening is not reinvigoration but the impartation of life at the time of the Rapture, as in 1 Cor. 15:53, 54 and 2 Cor. 5:4 (RV, "what is mortal"; KJV, "mortality"); in 2 Cor. 4:11, it is applied to the flesh, which stands, not simply for the body, but the body as that which consists of the element of decay, and is thereby death-doomed. Christ's followers are in this life delivered unto death, that His life may be manifested in that which naturally is the seat of decay and death. That which is subject to suffering is that in which the power of Him who suffered here is most manifested.

## MORTIFY

1. ***thanatoo*** (*2289*), "to put to death" (from ***thanatos***, "death," akin to ***thnetos***, "mortal," see above), is translated "mortify" in Rom. 8:13 (Amer. RV, "put to death"); in 7:4, "ye were made dead" (passive voice), betokens the act of God on the believer, through the death of Christ; here in 8:13 it is the act of the believer himself, as being responsible to answer to God's act, and to put to death "the deeds of the body."

2. ***nekroo*** (*3499*), "to make dead" (from ***nekros***), is used figuratively in Col. 3:5 and translated "mortify" (Amer. RV, "put to death").

## MOTE

***karphos*** (*2595*), "a small, dry stalk, a twig, a bit of dried stick," is used metaphorically of a minor fault, Matt. 7:3, 4, 5; Luke 6:41, 42.

## MOTH

***ses*** (*4597*) denotes "a clothes moth," Matt. 6:19, 20; Luke 12:33.

## MOTHER

### *Old Testament*

***'em*** (517), "mother, grandmother, caregiver, source." ***'em*** is translated "mother," with the meaning of biological or adoptive female parent of any creature, Gen. 2:24; Exod. 22:30. ***'em*** is also translated "grandmother," with the meaning of the mother of one's parents, 1 Kin. 15:10,13; 2 Chron. 15:16. ***'em*** is translated "care giver, provider," (lit. "mother") with the meaning of one who cares, helps, and protects an object as a figurative extension of a biological mother who cares for a child, Judg. 5:7; 2 Sam. 20:19. ***'em*** is translated "fork of the road," with the meaning of an intersecting point in two different paths, as a particular place on a path or road, Ezek. 21:21.

***'em*** is also used in combination with other Hebrew words, ***min beten 'em***, translated "birth," with a literal translation of "from womb of mother," with the meaning of the time of one's coming into the world from the womb, Judg. 16:17; Job 31:18; cf. also "loins of the mother," Isa. 49:1.

### *New Testament*

1. ***meter*** (*3384*) is used (a) of the natural relationship, e.g., Matt. 1:18; 2 Tim. 1:5; (b) figuratively, (1) of "one who takes the place of a mother," Matt. 12:49, 50; Mark 3:34, 35; John 19:27; Rom. 16:13; 1 Tim. 5:2; (2) of "the heavenly and spiritual Jerusalem," Gal. 4:26. (3) symbolically, of "Babylon," Rev. 17:5, as the source from which has proceeded the religious harlotry.

2. ***ametor*** (*282*), "without a mother" (***a***, negative, and No. 1), is used in Heb. 7:3, of the Genesis record of Melchizedek, certain details concerning him being purposely omitted, in order to conform the description to facts about Christ as the Son of God. The word has been found in this sense in the writings of Euripides the dramatist and Herodotus the historian.

## MOUNT, MOUNTAIN

### *Old Testament*

***har*** (2022), "mountain range; mountainous region; mount." ***har*** has the normal meaning of an elevated geographical area, translated "hill," or "mountain," either general or named specifically; this can also refer to a series of mountains, as a mountain-range, Gen. 8:4; Gen. 31:21; Josh. 21:11.

In the poetical literature of the Old Testament, the view of the world held by men of that era finds its reflection. One can speak of the foundations of the mountains as rooted in the underworld, Deut. 32:22, serving to support the earth as the "bars" of the earth, Jonah 2:6. Mountain peaks may be said to reach into the heavens where God dwells, Isa. 24:21; in Gen. 11:4, the men who built the tower at Babel erroneously thought they were going to reach God's dwelling place. "Mountains" often serve as a symbol of strength, Zech. 4:7, inasmuch as they carried mythological significance since many people thought of them as sacred areas, Jer. 3:22–23, and they were the locations of strong fortresses, Josh. 10:6. Even the "mountains" tremble before the Lord; He is mightier than they are, Job 14:18.

### *New Testament*

***oros*** (*3735*) is used (a) without specification, e.g., Luke 3:5 (distinct from ***bounos***, "a hill"); John 4:20; (b) of "the Mount of Transfiguration," Matt. 17:1, 9; Mark 9:2, 9; Luke 9:28, 37 (KJV, "hill"); 2 Pet. 1:18; (c) of "Zion," Heb. 12:22; Rev. 14:1; (d) of "Sinai," Acts 7:30, 38; Gal. 4:24, 25; Heb. 8:5; 12:20; (e) of "the Mount of Olives," Matt. 21:1; 24:3; Mark 11:1; 13:3; Luke 19:29, 37; 22:39; John 8:1; Acts 1:12; (f) of "the hill districts as distinct from the lowlands," especially of the hills above the Sea of Galilee, e.g., Matt. 5:1; 8:1; 18:12; Mark 5:5; (g) of "the mountains on the east of Jordan" and "those in the land of Ammon" and "the region of Petra," etc., Matt. 24:16; Mark 13:14; Luke 21:21; (h) proverbially, "of overcoming difficulties, or accomplishing great things," 1 Cor. 13:2; cf. Matt. 17:20; 21:21; Mark 11:23; (i) symbolically, of "a series of the imperial potentates of the Roman dominion, past and future," Rev. 17:9.

## MOURN, MOURNING

### *Old Testament*

***'abal*** (56), "to mourn, lament." When ***'abal*** is used of mourning for the dead in a literal sense, the word is found in prose sections and in the reflexive form, indicating action back on the subject, Gen. 37:34. When used in the figurative sense, ***'abal*** expresses "mourning" by gates, Isa. 3:26, by the land, Isa. 24:4, and by pastures, Amos 1:2. In addition to mourning for the dead, "mourning" may be over Jerusalem, Isa. 66:10, over sin, Ezra 10:6, or over God's judgment, Exod. 33:4. One may pretend to be a mourner, 2 Sam. 14:2, simply by putting on mourning clothes.

### *New Testament*

**A. Verbs.**

1. ***kopto*** (*2875*), to cut or beat, used in the middle voice of "beating the breast or head in mourning" (cf. Luke 23:27), is translated "shall mourn" in Matt. 24:30.

2. ***pentheo*** (*3996*), "to mourn for, lament," is used (a) of mourning in general, Matt. 5:4; 9:15; Luke 6:25; (b) of sorrow for the death of a loved one, Mark 16:10; (c) of "mourning" for the overthrow of Babylon and the Babylonish system, Rev. 18:11, 15, RV, "mourning" (KJV, "wailing"); v. 19 (ditto); (d) of sorrow for sin or for condoning it, Jas. 4:9; 1 Cor. 5:2; (e) of grief for those in a local church who show no repentance for evil committed, 2 Cor. 12:21, RV, "mourn" (KJV, "bewail").

3. ***threneo*** (*2354*), "to lament, wail" (akin to ***threnos***, "a lamentation, a dirge"), is used (a) in a general sense, of the disciples during the absence of the Lord, John 16:20, "lament"; (b) of those who sorrowed for the sufferings and the impending crucifixion of the Lord, Luke 23:27, "lamented"; the preceding word is ***kopto*** (No. 1); (c) of "mourning" as for the dead, Matt. 11:17, RV, "wailed" (KJV, "have mourned"); Luke 7:32 (ditto).

**B. Nouns.**

1. ***odurmos*** (*3602*), "lamentation, mourning," is translated "mourning" in Matt. 2:18 and 2 Cor. 7:7.

2. ***penthos*** (*3997*), akin to A, No. 2, "mourning," is used in Jas. 4:9; Rev. 18:7 (twice), RV, "mourning" (KJV, "sorrow"); v. 8, "mourning"; 21:4, RV, "mourning" (KJV, "sorrow").

## MOUTH

### *Old Testament*

***peh*** (6310) "mouth; edge; opening; entrance; collar; utterance; order; command; evidence." ***peh*** can be translated "mouth," meaning of the entrance orifice of the body on the face, for ingestion, breathing, and communication, Gen. 8:11; Num. 22:28; 1 Sam. 14:27. It should be noted that the mouth may include the area of the mouth, including lips and tongue. Other renderings related to the mouth include "taste," meaning of a desire for tasting a certain food, Gen. 25:28, and the related state of "hunger," with the meaning of the physical desire for food, Prov. 16:26; and "communication, speech," meaning the speaking function of the mouth that gives information, exhortation, or commands, Gen. 41:40.

***peh*** can be translated more generally, "opening," meaning the entrance area to a space, making that space accessible, like a door or gate "opening," or more limited space as a "collar," on a piece of clothing, Gen. 29:2; Exod. 28:32; Psa. 133:2. ***peh*** can be translated "edge," the sharp, thin shape of a sword or knife, Gen. 34:26. This can also mean "double-edged," as the shape of a sword or knife, Judg. 3:16. So also ***peh*** can be translated "part, number, portion," a single unit of something which can be numbered, Gen. 47:12; Deut. 21:17; 2 Kin. 2:9. Then ***peh*** can be translated "end, border, extremity," the outer geographical limits of the boundaries of a space, 2 Kin. 10:21; 21:16.

Finally, ***peh*** can also be used in a combination of Hebrew words. One of the more common phrases is ***peh el peh***, translated "face to face," (lit. "mouth to mouth") with the meaning of a position of persons across from each other, Num. 12:8, and in some contexts it has a focus on personal relationship, Jer. 32:4; 34:3. The phrase ***pi shenayim*** (literally, "two mouths") has two different meanings. In Deut. 21:17 it means "double portion" (two parts). This same phrase, however, also means "two thirds," Zech. 13:8.

### *New Testament*

***stoma*** (*4750*), akin to ***stomachos*** (which originally meant "a throat, gullet"), is used (a) of "the mouth" of man, e.g., Matt. 15:11; of animals, e.g., Matt. 17:27; 2 Tim. 4:17 (figurative); Heb. 11:33; Jas. 3:3; Rev. 13:2 (2nd occurrence); (b) figuratively of "inanimate things," of the "edge" of a sword, Luke 21:24; Heb. 11:34; of the earth, Rev. 12:16; (c) figuratively, of the "mouth," as the organ of speech, (1) of Christ's words, e.g., Matt. 13:35; Luke 11:54; Acts 8:32; 22:14; 1 Pet. 2:22; (2) of human, e.g., Matt. 18:16; 21:16; Luke 1:64; Rev. 14:5; as emanating from the heart, Matt. 12:34; Rom. 10:8, 9; of prophetic ministry through the Holy Spirit, Luke 1:70; Acts 1:16; 3:18; 4:25; of the destructive policy of two world potentates at the end of this age, Rev. 13:2, 5, 6; 16:13 (twice); of shameful speaking, Eph. 4:29 and Col. 3:8; (3) of the Devil speaking as a dragon or serpent, Rev. 12:15, 16; 16:13; (d) figuratively, in the phrase "face to face" (lit., "mouth to mouth"), 2 John 12; 3 John 14; (e) metaphorically, of "the utterances of the Lord, in judgment," 2 Thess. 2:8; Rev. 1:16; 2:16; 19:15, 21; of His judgment upon a local church for its lukewarmness, Rev. 3:16; (f) by metonymy, for "speech," Matt. 18:16; Luke 19:22; 21:15; 2 Cor. 13:1.

## MULTIPLY

### *Old Testament*

**A. Verb.**

***rabah*** (7235), "to multiply, become numerous, become great." Basically this word connotes numerical increase, either of things or of a length of time, Gen. 1:22; cf. Job 29:18. ***rabah*** sometimes refers to increasing in wealth, although in such cases the material is clearly specified, cf. Deut. 8:13. In a special nuance this verb signifies the process of growing up, Job 39:4. ***rabah*** can also be used of the end product, Ezek. 16:7. A somewhat different nuance occurs in Ezek. 19:2, where the verb speaks of a parent's care for an offspring.

**B. Nouns.**

***marbeh***, which appears once means "abundance," Isa. 33:23. ***marbit***, which is found 5 times, refers to a "greater number," 1 Sam. 2:33, or the "greater half," 2 Chron. 9:6. ***tarbut*** has a single appearance to mean " increase," Num. 32:14. ***tarbit***, which occurs 6 times, can mean "interest, increment, usury," Lev. 25:36.

### *New Testament*

1. ***plethuno*** (*4129*), used (a) transitively, denotes "to cause to increase, to multiply," 2 Cor. 9:10; Heb. 6:14 (twice); in the passive voice, "to be multiplied," Matt. 24:12, RV, "(iniquity) shall be multiplied" (KJV, "shall abound"); Acts 6:7; 7:17; 9:31; 12:24; 1 Pet. 1:2; 2 Pet. 1:2; Jude 2; (b) intransitively it denotes "to be multiplying," Acts 6:1, RV, "was multiplying" (KJV, "was multiplied").

2. ***pleonazo*** (*4121*), used intransitively, "to abound," is translated "being multiplied" in the RV of 2 Cor. 4:15 (KJV, "abundant"); the active voice, aorist tense, here would be more accurately rendered "having superabounded" or "superabounding" or "multiplying.

## MULTITUDE

### *Old Testament*

**A. Noun.**

***hamon*** (1995), "multitude; lively commotion; agitation; tumult; uproar; commotion; turmoil; noise; crowd; abundance." The word represents a "lively commotion or agitation," Isa. 63:15; the stirring or agitation of a crowd of people, 2 Sam. 18:29. In Isa. 17:12 the word is synonymously parallel to ***sha'on***, "rumbling."

***hamon*** sometimes means a "multitude or crowd" from which a tumult may arise. Frequently the word represents a large army, Judg. 4:7; cf. 1 Sam. 14:16. Elsewhere ***hamon*** represents a whole people, 2 Sam. 6:19. Finally, any great throng, or a great number of people, Gen. 17:4; or of things, 1 Chron. 29:16; Ps. 37:16; cf. Eccl. 5:10. Finally, ***hamon*** refers to a group of people organized around a king, specifically, his courtiers, Ezek. 31:2.

**B. Verb.**

***hamah*** (1993), "to make a noise, be tumultuous, roar, groan, bark, sound, moan," Psalm 83:2.

***New Testament***

***ochlos*** (*3793*) is used frequently in the four Gospels and the Acts; elsewhere only in Rev. 7:9; 17:15; 19:1, 6; it denotes (a) "a crowd or multitude of persons, a throng," e.g., Matt. 14:14, 15; 15:33; often in the plural, e.g., Matt. 4:25; 5:1; with ***polus***, "much" or "great," it signifies "a great multitude," e.g., Matt. 20:29, or "the common people," Mark 12:37, perhaps preferably "the mass of the people." Field supports the meaning in the text, but either rendering is suitable. The mass of the people was attracted to Him (for the statement "heard Him gladly" cf. what is said in Mark 6:20 of Herod Antipas concerning John the Baptist); in John 12:9, "the common people," RV, stands in contrast with their leaders (v. 10); Acts 24:12, RV, "crowd"; (b) "the populace, an unorganized multitude," in contrast to ***demos***, "the people as a body politic," e.g., Matt. 14:5; 21:26; John 7:12 (2nd part); (c) in a more general sense, "a multitude or company," e.g., Luke 6:17, RV, "a (great) multitude (of His disciples)," KJV, "the company"; Acts 1:15, "a multitude (of persons)," RV, KJV, "the number (of names)"; Acts 24:18, RV, "crowd" (KJV, "multitude").

## MURDER

***phonos*** (*5408*) is used (a) of a special act, Mark 15:7; Luke 23:19, 25; (b) in the plural, of "murders" in general, Matt. 15:19; Mark 7:21 (Gal. 5:21, in some inferior mss.); Rev. 9:21; in the singular, Rom. 1:29; (c) in the sense of "slaughter," Heb. 11:37, "they were slain with the sword," lit., "(they died by) slaughter (of the sword)"; in Acts 9:1, "slaughter."

## MURDERER

1. ***phoneus*** (*5406*), akin to ***phoneuo*** and ***phonos***, is used (a) in a general sense, in the singular, 1 Pet. 4:15; in the plural, Rev. 21:8; 22:15; (b) of those guilty of particular acts, Matt. 22:7; Acts 3:14, lit. "a man (***aner***), a murderer"; 7:52; 28:4.

2. ***anthropoktonos*** (*443*), an adjective, lit., "manslaying," used as a noun, "a manslayer, murderer" (***anthropos***, "a man," ***kteino***, "to slay"), is used of Satan, John 8:44; of one who hates his brother, and who, being a "murderer," has not eternal life, 1 John 3:15 (twice).

3. ***patroloas*** (or ***patral—***) (*3964*) "a murderer of one's father," occurs in 1 Tim. 1:9.

## MURMUR, MURMURING

**A. Verbs.**

1. ***gonguzo*** (*1111*), "to mutter, murmur, grumble, say anything in a low tone" (Eng., "gong"), an onomatopoeic word, representing the significance by the sound of the word, as in the word "murmur" itself, is used of the laborers in the parable of the householder, Matt. 20:11; of the scribes and Pharisees, against Christ, Luke 5:30; of the Jews, John 6:41, 43, of the disciples, 6:61; of the people, 7:32 (of debating secretly); of the Israelites, 1 Cor. 10:10 (twice).

2. ***diagonguzo*** (*1234*), lit., "to murmur through" (***dia***, i.e., "through a whole crowd," or "among themselves"), is always used of indignant complaining, Luke 15:2; 19:7.

**B. Noun.**

***gongusmos*** (*1112*), "a murmuring, muttering" (akin to A, No. 1), is used (a) in the sense of secret debate among people, John 7:12 (as with the verb in v. 32); (b) of displeasure or complaining (more privately than in public), said of Grecian Jewish converts against Hebrews, Acts 6:1; in general admonitions, Phil. 2:14; 1 Pet. 4:9, RV, "murmuring" (KJV "grudging").

## MURMURER

***gongustes*** (*1113*), "a murmurer" (akin to A, No. 1, and B, above), "one who complains," is used in Jude 16, especially perhaps of utterances against God (see v. 15).

## MYRRH

**A. Noun.**

***smurna*** (*4666*), whence the name "Smyrna," a word of Semitic origin, Heb., ***mor***, from a root meaning "bitter," is a gum resin from a shrubby tree, which grows in Yemen and neighboring regions of Africa; the fruit is smooth and somewhat larger than a pea. The color of myrrh varies from pale reddish-yellow to reddish-brown or red. The taste is bitter, and the substance astringent, acting as an antiseptic and a stimulant. It was used as a perfume, Ps. 45:8, where the language is symbolic of the graces of the Messiah; Prov. 7:17; Song of Sol. 1:13; 5:5; it was one of the ingredients of the "holy anointing oil" for the priests, Ex. 30:23 (RV, "flowing myrrh"); it was used also for the purification of women, Esth. 2:12; for embalming, John 19:39; as an anodyne see B), it was one of the gifts of the Magi, Matt. 2:11.

### B. Verb.

***smurnizo*** *(4669)* is used transitively in the NT, with the meaning "to mingle or drug with myrrh," Mark 15:23; the mixture was doubtless offered to deaden the pain (Matthew's word "gall" suggests that "myrrh" was not the only ingredient). Christ refused to partake of any such means of alleviation; He would retain all His mental power for the complete fulfillment of the Father's will.

## MYSTERY

***musterion*** *(3466)*, primarily that which is known to the ***mustes***, "the initiated" (from ***mueo***, "to initiate into the mysteries"; cf. Phil. 4:12, ***mueomai***, "I have learned the secret," RV). In the NT it denotes, not the mysterious (as with the Eng. word), but that which, being outside the range of unassisted natural apprehension, can be made known only by divine revelation, and is made known in a manner and at a time appointed by God, and to those only who are illumined by His Spirit. In the ordinary sense a "mystery" implies knowledge withheld; its Scriptural significance is truth revealed. Hence the terms especially associated with the subject are "made known," "manifested," "revealed," "preached," "understand," "dispensation." The definition given above may be best illustrated by the following passage: "the mystery which hath been hid from all ages and generations: but now hath it been manifested to His saints" (Col. 1:26, RV). It is used of:

(a) spiritual truth generally, as revealed in the gospel, 1 Cor. 13:2; 14:2 [cf. 1 Tim. 3:9]. Among the ancient Greeks "the mysteries" were religious rites and ceremonies practiced by secret societies into which any one who so desired might be received. Those who were initiated into these "mysteries" became possessors of certain knowledge, which was not imparted to the uninitiated, and were called "the perfected," cf. 1 Cor. 2:6–16 where the Apostle has these "mysteries" in mind and presents the gospel in contrast thereto; here "the perfected" are, of course the believers, who alone can perceive the things revealed; (b) Christ, who is God Himself revealed under the conditions of human life, Col. 2:2; 4:3, and submitting even to death, 1 Cor. 2:1 [in some mss., for ***marturion***, testimony], 7, but raised from among the dead, 1 Tim. 3:16, that the will of God to coordinate the universe in Him, and subject it to Him, might in due time be accomplished, Eph. 1:9 (cf. Rev. 10:7), as is declared in the gospel Rom. 16:25; Eph. 6:19; (c) the Church, which is Christ's Body, i.e., the union of redeemed men with God in Christ, Eph. 5:32 [cf. Col. 1:27]; (d) the rapture into the presence of Christ of those members of the Church which is His Body who shall be alive on the earth at His Parousia, 1 Cor. 15:51; (e) the operation of those hidden forces that either retard or accelerate the Kingdom of Heaven (i.e., of God), Matt. 13:11; Mark 4:11; (f) the cause of the present condition of Israel, Rom. 11:25; (g) the spirit of disobedience to God, 2 Thess. 2:7; Rev. 17:5, 7, cf. Eph. 2:2.

To these may be added (h) the seven local churches, and their angels, seen in symbolism, Rev. 1:20; (i) the ways of God in grace, Eph. 3:9. The word is used in a comprehensive way in 1 Cor. 4:1.

# N

## NAIL (Noun and Verb)

### A. Noun.

***helos*** (2247) A device to fasten an object to another object, made of tempered metal such as iron, and pounded into a sharpened point on one end, and a blunt end on the other, Used in the Crucifixion by nailing through the hole in the wrist bones (so, considered the upper part of the hand), and just above the ankle bones, John 20:25.

### B. Verb.

***proseloo*** (4338), "to nail to" (***pros***, "to," and a verbal form of A), is used in Col. 2:14, in which the figure of a bond (ordinances of the Law) is first described as cancelled, and then removed; the idea in the verb itself is not that of the cancellation, to which the taking out of the way was subsequent, but of nailing up the removed thing in triumph to the cross. The death of Christ not only rendered the Law useless as a means of salvation, but gave public demonstration that it was so.

## NAKED (Adjective and Verb), NAKEDNESS

### *Old Testament*

### A. Nouns.

***'erwah*** (6172), "nakedness; indecent thing." This word represents male or female sexual organs. In its first biblical appearance ***'erwah*** implies shameful exposure, Gen. 9:22–23; symbolical of shame, Lam. 1:8; euphemism for cohabitation, Lev. 18:6. The phrase "indecent thing" represents any uncleanness. In Deut. 24:1 ***'erwah*** appears to bear this emphasis on any violation of the laws of purity—if a groom is dissatisfied with his bride, Deut. 22:13ff. The "undefended parts" or "nakedness" of a land is represented by ***'erwah*** in Gen. 42:9.

***ma'ar***, which refers to "sexual nakedness," appears in a figurative sense in Nah. 3:5. ***'Erom*** appears as a noun abstract in several instances, Ezek. 16:7, 39.

Two nouns, ***ta'ar*** and ***morah***, have a different significance. ***ta'ar***, which occurs 13 times, means "razor," Num. 6:5, or a "knife" to sharpen scribal pens, Jer. 36:23. The word's meaning of a "sword sheath," 1 Sam. 17:51, has a cognate in Ugaritic. ***morah*** also means "razor,"1 Sam. 1:11.

### B. Adjectives.

***'arom*** (6174), "naked," Gen. 2:25. Another adjective, is ***'eryah***, with the same meaning is found in Ezek. 16:22.

### C. Verb.

***'arah*** (6168), "to pour out," Isa. 32:15; "make bare," Lev. 20:19; "destroy," Isa. 3:17; "spread oneself out," Ps. 37:35.

### *New Testament*

### A. Adjective.

***gumnos*** (1131) signifies (a) "unclothed," Mark 14:52; in v. 51 it is used as a noun ("*his*" and "*body*" being italicized); (b) "scantily or poorly clad," Matt. 25:36, 38, 43, 44; Acts 19:16 (with torn garments); Jas. 2:15; (c) "clad in the undergarment only" (the outer being laid aside), John 21:7; (d) metaphorically, (1) of "a bare seed," 1 Cor. 15:37; (2) of "the soul without the body," 2 Cor. 5:3; (3) of "things exposed to the all-seeing eye of God," Heb. 4:13; (4) of "the carnal condition of a local church," Rev. 3:17; (5) of "the similar state of an individual," 16:15; (6) of "the desolation of religious Babylon," 17:16.

### B. Verb.

***gumniteuo*** (1130), "to be naked or scantily clad" (akin to A), is used in 1 Cor. 4:11. In the *Koine* writings it is used of being light-armed.

### C. Noun.

***gumnotes*** (1132), "nakedness" (akin to A), is used (a) of "want of sufficient clothing," Rom. 8:35; 2 Cor. 11:27; (b) metaphorically, of "the nakedness of the body," said of the condition of a local church, Rev. 3:18.

## NAME

### *Old Testament*

***shem*** (8034), "name; reputation; memory; renown." Sometimes this word is used in the sense of a name as an identification appears in Gen. 2:19, though not always. ***shem*** can be a synonym for "reputation" or "fame," Gen. 11:4. To "give a name for one" is to make him famous, 2 Sam. 7:23. If a name goes forth for one, his "reputation" of fame is made known, Ezek. 16:14. Fame may include power, 2 Sam. 23:18.

This word is sometimes a synonym for "memory," 2 Sam. 14:7. In this respect "name" may include property, or an inheritance, Num. 27:4. ***shem*** can connote "renown" and "continuance" (in those remaining after one), Num. 16:2. This significance is in the phrase "to raise up his name after him," cf. Deut. 9:14; 25:6; Ruth 4:5.

### *New Testament*

#### A. Noun.

***onoma*** (*3686*) is used (I) in general of the "name" by which a person or thing is called, e.g., Mark 3:16, 17, "(He) surnamed," lit., "(He added) the name"; 14:32, lit., "(of which) the name (was)"; Luke 1:63; John 18:10, sometimes translated "named," e.g., Luke 8:5, "named (Zacharias)," lit., "by name"; in the same verse, "named (Elizabeth)," lit., "the name of her," an elliptical phrase, with "was" understood; Acts 8:9, RV, "by name," 10:1; the "name" is put for the reality in Rev. 3:1; in Phil. 2:9, the "Name" represents "the title and dignity" of the Lord, as in Eph. 1:21 and Heb. 1:4;

(II) for all that a "name" implies, of authority, character, rank, majesty, power, excellence, etc., of everything that the "name" covers: (a) of the "Name" of God as expressing His attributes, etc., e.g., Matt. 6:9; Luke 1:49; John 12:28; 17:6, 26; Rom. 15:9; 1 Tim. 6:1; Heb. 13:15; Rev. 13:6; (b) of the "Name" of Christ, e.g., Matt. 10:22; 19:29; John 1:12; 2:23; 3:18; Acts 26:9; Rom. 1:5; Jas. 2:7; 1 John 3:23; 3 John 7; Rev. 2:13; 3:8; also the phrases rendered "in the name"; these may be analyzed as follows: (1) representing the authority of Christ, e.g., Matt. 18:5 (with ***epi***, "on the ground of My authority"); so Matt. 24:5 (falsely) and parallel passages; as substantiated by the Father, John 14:26; 16:23 (last clause), RV; (2) in the power of (with ***en***, "in"), e.g., Mark 16:17; Luke 10:17; Acts 3:6; 4:10; 16:18; Jas. 5:14; (3) in acknowledgement or confession of, e.g., Acts 4:12; 8:16; 9:27, 28; (4) in recognition of the authority of (sometimes combined with the thought of relying or resting on), Matt. 18:20; cf. 28:19; Acts 8:16; 9:2 (***eis***, "into"); John 14:13; 15:16; Eph. 5:20; Col. 3:17; (5) owing to the fact that one is called by Christ's "Name" or is identified with Him, e.g. 1 Pet. 4:14 (with ***en***, "in"); with ***heneken***, "for the sake of," e.g., Matt. 19:29; with ***dia***, "on account of," Matt. 10:22; 24:9; Mark 13:13; Luke 21:17; John 15:21; 1 John 2:12; Rev. 2:3.

(III) as standing, by metonymy, for "persons," Acts 1:15; Rev. 3:4; 11:13 (RV, "persons").

#### B. Verbs.

1. ***onomazo*** (*3687*) denotes (a) "to name," "mention," or "address by name," Acts 19:13, RV, "to name" (KJV, "to call"); in the passive voice, Rom. 15:20; Eph. 1:21; 5:3; to make mention of the "Name" of the Lord in praise and worship, 2 Tim. 2:19; (b) "to name, call, give a name to," Luke 6:13, 14; passive voice, 1 Cor. 5:11, RV, "is named" (KJV, "is called"); Eph. 3:15 (some mss. have the verb in this sense in Mark 3:14 and 1 Cor. 5:1).

2. ***eponomazo*** (*2028*), "to call by a name, surname" (***epi***, "on," and No. 1), is used in Rom. 2:17, passive voice, RV, "bearest the name of" (KJV, "art called").

3. ***prosagoreuo*** (*4316*) primarily denotes "to address, greet, salute"; hence, "to call by name," Heb. 5:10, RV, "named (of God, a High Priest)" (KJV, "called"), expressing the formal ascription of the title to Him whose it is; "called" does not adequately express the significance.

4. ***kaleo*** (*2564*), "to call," is translated "named" in Acts 7:58, RV (KJV, "whose name was").

## NARRATIVE

***diegesis*** (*1335*), translated "a declaration" in the KJV of Luke 1:1, denotes a "narrative," RV (akin to ***diegeomai***, "to set out in detail, recount, describe").

## NARROW

#### A. Adjective.

***stenos*** (*4728*), from a root ***sten-***, seen in ***stenazo***, "to groan," ***stenagmos***, "groaning" (Eng., "stenography," lit., "narrow writing"), is used figuratively in Matt. 7:13, 14, of the gate which provides the entrance to eternal life; "narrow" because it runs counter to natural inclinations, and "the way" is similarly characterized; so in Luke 13:24 (where the more intensive word ***agonizomai***, "strive," is used); RV, "narrow" (KJV, "strait") in each place.

#### B. Verb.

***thlibo*** (*2346*), "to press," is translated "narrow" in Matt. 7:14, KJV, lit., "narrowed" (RV, "straitened"; the verb is in the perfect participle, passive voice), i.e., hemmed in, like a mountain gorge; the way is rendered "narrow" by the divine conditions, which make it impossible for any to enter who think the entrance depends upon self-merit, or who still incline towards sin, or desire to continue in evil.

## NATION

### *Old Testament*

***goy*** (1471), "nation; people; heathen." ***goy*** refers to a "people or nation," usually with overtones of territorial or governmental unity/

identity, Gen. 12:2; cf. Num. 14:12. So ***goy*** represents a group of individuals who are considered as a unit with respect to origin, language, land, jurisprudence, and government, Gen. 10:5; Deut. 4:32ff. The word ***'am***, "people, nation," suggests subjective personal interrelationships based on common familial ancestry and/or a covenantal union, while ***goy*** suggests a political entity with a land of its own, Exod. 33:13. ***goy*** may be used of a people, however, apart from its territorial identity, Exod. 19:6.

***goy*** is sometimes almost a derogatory name for non-Israelite groups, or the "heathen," Lev. 26:33. This negative connotation is not always present, however, when the word is used of the heathen, Num. 23:9.

### *New Testament*

1. ***ethnos*** (*1484*), originally "a multitude," denotes (a) "a nation" or "people," e.g., Matt. 24:7; Acts 10:35; the Jewish people, e.g., Luke 7:5; 23:2; John 11:48, 50–52; Acts 10:22; 24:2, 10, 17; in Matt. 21:43, the reference is to Israel in its restored condition, (b) in the plural "the nations" as distinct from Israel.

2. ***genos*** (*1085*), "a race," Philip. 3:5.

3. ***allophulos*** (*246*), "foreign, of another race" (***allos***, "another," ***phulon***, "a tribe"), is used in Acts 10:28, "one of another nation."

## NATURAL, NATURALLY

### A. Adjectives.

1. ***phusikos*** (*5446*) originally signifying "produced by nature, inborn," from ***phusis***, "nature," cf. Eng., "physical," "physics," etc., denotes (a) "according to nature," Rom. 1:26, 27; (b) "governed by mere natural instincts," 2 Pet. 2:12, RV, "(born) mere animals," KJV and RV marg., "natural (brute beasts)."

2. ***psuchikos*** (*5591*), "belonging to the ***psuche***, soul" (as the lower part of the immaterial in man), "natural, physical," describes the man in Adam and what pertains to him (set in contrast to ***pneumatikos*** "spiritual"), 1 Cor. 2:14; 15:44 (twice), 46 (in the latter used as a noun); Jas. 3:15, "sensual" (RV marg., "natural" or "animal"), here relating perhaps more especially to the mind, a wisdom in accordance with, or springing from, the corrupt desires and affections; so in Jude 19.

### B. Noun.

***genesis*** (*1078*), "birth," is used in Jas. 1:23, of the "natural face," lit., "the face of his birth," "what God made him to be" (Hort).

### C. Adverb.

***phusikos*** (*5447*), "naturally, by nature" (akin to A, No. 1), is used in Jude 10.

## NATURE

1. ***phusis*** (*5449*), from ***phuo***, "to bring forth, produce," signifies (a) "the nature" (i.e., the natural powers or constitution) of a person or thing, Eph. 2:3; Jas. 3:7 ("kind"); 2 Pet. 1:4; (b) "origin, birth," Rom. 2:27, one who by birth is a Gentile, uncircumcised, in contrast to one who, though circumcised, has become spiritually uncircumcised by his iniquity; Gal. 2:15; (c) "the regular law or order of nature," Rom. 1:26, against "nature" (***para***, "against"); 2:14, adverbially, "by nature"; 1 Cor. 11:14; Gal. 4:8, "by nature (are no gods)," here "nature" is the emphatic word, and the phrase includes demons, men regarded as deified, and idols; these are gods only in name (the negative, ***me***, denies not simply that they were gods, but the possibility that they could be).

2. ***genesis*** (*1078*) is used in the phrase in Jas. 3:6, "the wheel of nature," or "course of life," with a focus on the constant changes in life.

## NEED, NEEDS, NEEDFUL

### *Old Testament*

### A. Noun.

***'ebyon*** (34), "needy (person)." This noun refers, first, to someone who is poor in a material sense. Such a one may have lost the land of his inheritance, Exod. 23:11. He has come into difficult financial straits, Job 30:25, and perhaps lacks clothing, Job 31:19, or food, Ps. 132:15. Secondly, ***'ebyon*** may refer to the lack of social standing which causes a need for protection, Exod. 23:6; Job 29:16; cf. Prov. 31:9; Rom. 3:14–15. Divine provisions are encased in the Mosaic stipulations such as the seventh-year reversion of ancestral hereditary lands, Exod. 23:11, cancellation of loans, Deut. 15:4, and special extension of loans, Deut. 15:7, 9, 11. Thirdly, this noun sometimes describes one's spiritual condition before God, Amos 2:6. In this verse ***'ebyon*** is in synonymous parallelism to "righteous," which means that it describes a moral quality.

### B. Verb.

***'abah*** (14), "to accede, accept, consent." This verb means "to consent to" in Deut. 13:8.

### *New Testament*

### A. Nouns.

1. ***chreia*** (*5532*) denotes "a need," in such expressions as "there is a need"; or "to have need of" something, e.g., Matt. 3:14; 6:8; 9:12.

In Luke 10:42 it is translated "needful," where the "one thing" is surely not one dish, or one person, but is to be explained according to Matt. 6:33 and 16:26. In Eph. 4:29, for the KJV, "(to) the use (of edifying)," the RV more accurately has "(for edifying) as the need may be," marg., "the building up of the need," i.e., "to supply that which [is] needed in each case"; so Westcott, who adds "The need represents a gap in the life which the wise word 'builds up,' fills up solidly and surely." In Phil. 4:19 the RV has "every need of yours" (KJV, "all your need"); in 1 Thess. 4:12, RV, "need" (KJV, "lack"); in Acts 28:10, RV, "(such things) as we needed" (KJV, "as were necessary"), lit., "the things for the needs (plural)."

2. ***ananke*** (*318*), "a necessity, need," is translated "it must needs be" in Matt. 18:7, with the verb "to be" understood (according to the best mss.); in Luke 14:18, "I must needs" translates the verb ***echo***, "to have," with this noun as the object, lit., "I have need"; in Rom. 13:5 "(ye) must needs," lit., "(it is) necessary (to be subject)."

**B. Verbs.**

1. ***chrezo*** (*5535*), "to need, to have need of" (akin to ***chre***, "it is necessary, fitting"), is used in Matt. 6:32; Luke 11:8; 12:30; Rom. 16:2, RV, "may have need" (KJV, "hath need"); 2 Cor. 3:1.

2. ***dei*** (*1163*), an impersonal verb, signifying "it is necessary," is rendered "must needs" in Mark 13:7; John 4:4; Acts 1:16, KJV (RV, "it was needful"); 17:3, KJV (RV, "it behooved"); (in some mss. in Acts 21:22); 2 Cor. 11:30; 12:1; in Acts 15:5, "it was needful."

3. ***deon*** (*1163***), the neuter of the present participle of No. 2, is used as a noun, signifying "that which is needful, due, proper," in 1 Pet. 1:6, with the meaning "need," "(if) need (be)," with the verb to be understood.

4. ***prosdeomai*** (*4326*), "to want besides, to need in addition" (***pros***, "besides," ***deomai***, "to want"), is used in Acts 17:25, "(as though) He needed (anything)"; the literal sense of ***pros*** is not to be stressed.

5. ***opheilo*** (*3784*), "to owe, be bound, obliged to do something," is translated "must ye needs," in 1 Cor. 5:10; in 7:36 it is used impersonally, signifying "it is due," and followed by the infinitive mood of ***ginomai***, "to become, to occur, come about," lit. "it is due to become," translated "(if) need (so) require."

**C. Adjectives.**

1. ***anankaioteros*** (*316**), the comparative degree of ***anankaios***, "necessary," is translated "more needful" in Phil. 1:24.

2. ***epitedeios*** (*2006*), primarily, "suitable, convenient," then, "useful, necessary," is translated "needful" in Jas. 2:16, neuter plural, "necessaries."

## NEEDLE

1. ***rhaphis*** (*4476*), from ***rhapto***, "to sew," occurs in Matt. 19:24; Mark 10:25.

2. ***belone*** (*956*), akin to ***belos***, "a dart," denotes a sharp point, hence, "a needle," Luke 18:25 (some mss. have No. 1).

***Note:*** The idea of applying "the needle's eye" to small gates seems to be a modern one; there is no ancient trace of it. The Lord's object in the statement is to express human impossibility and there is no need to endeavor to soften the difficulty by taking the needle to mean anything more than the ordinary instrument. An attempt is sometimes made to explain the words as a reference to the small door, a little over 2 feet square, in the large heavy gate of a walled city. This mars the figure and receives no justification from the language and traditions of Palestine.

## NEGLECT, NEGLIGENT

1. ***ameleo*** (*272*) denotes (a) "to be careless, not to care" (***a***, negative, ***melei***, "it is a care"; from ***melo***, "to care, to be a care"), Matt. 22:5, "made light of"; (b) "to be careless of, neglect," 1 Tim. 4:14; Heb. 2:3; 8:9, "I regarded (them) not."

2. ***paratheoreo*** (*3865*), primarily, "to examine side by side, compare" (***para***, "beside," ***theoreo***, "to look at"), hence, "to overlook, to neglect," is used in Acts 6:1, of the "neglect" of widows in the daily ministration in Jerusalem.

## NEIGHBOR

1. ***geiton*** (*1069*), lit., "one living in the same land," denotes "a neighbor," always plural in the NT, Luke 14:12; 15:6, 9; John 9:5.

2. ***perioikos*** (*4040*), an adjective, lit., "dwelling around" (***peri***, "around," ***oikos***, "a dwelling"), is used as a noun in Luke 1:58, "neighbors".

3. ***plesion*** (*4139*), the neuter of the adjective ***plesios*** (from ***pelas***, "near"), is used as an adverb accompanied by the article, lit., "the (one) near"; hence, one's "neighbor."

This and Nos. 1 and 2 have a wider range of meaning than that of the Eng. word "neighbor." There were no farmhouses scattered over the agricultural areas of Palestine; the populations, gathered in villages, went to and fro to their toil. Hence domestic life was touched at every point by a wide circle of neighborhood. The terms for neighbor were therefore of a very comprehensive scope. This may be seen from the chief characteristics of the privileges and duties of neighborhood as set forth in

Scripture, (a) its helpfulness, e.g., Prov. 27:10; Luke 10:36; (b) its intimacy, e.g., Luke 15:6, 9; Heb. 8:11; (c) its sincerity and sanctity, e.g., Ex. 22:7, 10; Prov. 3:29; 14:21; Rom. 13:10; 15:2; Eph. 4:25; Jas. 4:12. The NT quotes and expands the command in Lev. 19:18, "to love one's neighbor as oneself"; see, e.g., Matt. 5:43; 19:19; 22:39; Mark 12:31, 33; Luke 10:27; Gal. 5:14; Jas. 2:8.

## NEW; NEW MOON

### *Old Testament*

**A. Verb.**

***chadash*** (2318), "to renew," i.e., to reaffirm a relationship and have a prior state or condition exist once again, 1 Sam. 11:14.

**B.enlNoun.**

***chodesh*** (2320), "new moon; month." The word refers to the day on which the crescent of the moon reappears, 1 Sam. 20:24; so a feast day occurs at this time, Isa. 1:14.

***chodesh*** can refer to a "month," or the period from one new moon to another, Gen. 38:24; Exod. 13:4.

**C. Adjective.**

***chadash*** (2319), "new; renewed." ***chadash*** means "new" both in the sense of recent or fresh (as the opposite of old) and in the sense of something not previously existing, a king, Exod. 1:8; new song (not existing before), Isa. 42:10; new contrasted to the former, Isa. 42:9; Jer. 31:31–34; cf. Ezek. 11:19; 18:31.

### *New Testament*

1. ***kainos*** *(2537)* denotes "new," of that which is unaccustomed or unused, not "new" in time, recent, but "new" as to form or quality, of different nature from what is contrasted as old. "The new tongues," ***kainos***, of Mark 16:17 are the "other tongues," ***heteros***, of Acts 2:4. These languages, however, were "new" and "different," not in the sense that they had never been heard before, or that they were new to the hearers, for it is plain from v. 8 that this is not the case; they were new languages to the speakers, different from those in which they were accustomed to speak.

The new things that the Gospel brings for present obedience and realization are: a new covenant, Matt. 26:28 in some texts; a new commandment, John 13:34; a new creative act, Gal. 6:15; a new creation, 2 Cor. 5:17; a new man, i.e., a new character of manhood, spiritual and moral, after the pattern of Christ, Eph. 4:24; a new man, i.e., "the Church which is His (Christ's) body," Eph. 2:15.

The new things that are to be received and enjoyed hereafter are: a new name, the believer's, Rev. 2:17; a new name, the Lord's, Rev. 3:12; a new song, Rev. 5:9; a new Heaven and a new Earth, Rev. 21:1; the new Jerusalem, Rev. 3:12; 21:2; "And He that sitteth on the Throne said, Behold, I make all things new," Rev. 21:5.

***kainos*** is translated "fresh" in the RV of Matt. 9:17; Mark 2:22 (in the best texts) and Luke 5:38, of wineskins.

2. ***neos*** *(3501)* signifies "new" in respect of time, that which is recent; it is used of the young, and so translated, especially the comparative degree "younger"; accordingly what is ***neos*** may be a reproduction of the old in quality or character. ***neos*** and ***kainos*** are sometimes used of the same thing, but there is a difference, as already indicated. Thus the "new man" in Eph. 2:15 (***kainos***) is "new" in differing in character; so in 4:24; but the "new man" in Col. 3:10 (***neos***) stresses the fact of the believer's "new" experience, recently begun, and still proceeding. "The old man in him . . . dates as far back as Adam; a new man has been born, who therefore is fitly so called" [i.e., ***neos***], Trench, *Syn.* Sec. lx. The "New" Covenant in Heb. 12:24 is "new" (***neos***) compared with the Mosaic, nearly fifteen hundred years before; it is "new" (***kainos***) compared with the Mosaic, which is old in character, ineffective, 8:8, 13; 9:15.

3. ***prosphatos*** *(4732)*, originally signifying "freshly slain," acquired the general sense of "new," as applied to flowers, oil, misfortune, etc. It is used in Heb. 10:20 of the "living way" which Christ "dedicated for us . . . through the veil . . . His flesh" (which stands for His expiatory death by the offering of His body, v. 10).

## NEWNESS

***kainotes*** *(2538)*, akin to ***kainos***, is used in the phrases (a) "newness of life," Rom. 6:4, i.e., life of a new quality; the believer, being a new creation (2 Cor. 5:17), is to behave himself consistently with this in contrast to his former manner of life; (b) "newness of the spirit," RV, Rom. 7:6, said of the believer's manner of serving the Lord. While the phrase stands for the new life of the quickened spirit of the believer, it is impossible to dissociate this (in an objective sense) from the operation of the Holy Spirit, by whose power the service is rendered.

## NOBLE

### *Old Testament*

**A. Nouns.**

***'addir*** (117), "noble; principal; stately one." As a noun, ***'addir*** is paralleled to "mighty" in

Judg. 5:13. The word also occurs in Jer. 14:3 and Jer. 30:21. In 2 Chron. 23:20 ***'addir*** is paralleled to "captains and governors." The word is applied to the Messiah; the Messiah is none other than God Himself, Isa. 33:21.

Two less frequently occurring nouns are ***'adderet*** and ***'eder***. ***'adderet*** may mean "luxurious outer garment, mantle, cloak," Gen. 25:25; ***'eder*** may refer to a "luxurious outer garment," Mic. 2:8.

**B. Adjectives.**

***'addir*** (117), "mighty; majestic." In its first appearance the adjective ***'addir*** describes God's superior (majestic) holiness which was demonstrated by His delivering Israel from Egyptian bondage, Exod. 15:11. The idea of superior power is also suggested here, cf. Exod. 15:6; 1 Sam. 4:8. It is God's eternal and sovereign might which overcame His enemies, Ps. 136:18—He was/is mightier than mighty kings. Hence, His name (His person) is lauded as sovereign in power and majesty, Ps. 8:1; Ps. 93:4.

Two other adjectives are related to this word. ***'adderet*** used as an adjective and a noun appears 12 times. In Ezek. 17:8 the word implies "noble or majestic": "It was planted in a good soil by great waters . . . that it might be a goodly [***'adderet***] vine." ***'eder*** occurs once as an adjective, Zech. 11:13; there it modifies the value of an amount of money.

**C. Verb.**

***'adar*** (142), "to be majestic," Isa. 42:21.

***New Testament***

1. ***eugenes*** (*2104*), an adjective, lit., "well born" (***eu***, "well," and ***genos***, "a family, race"), (a) signifies "noble," 1 Cor. 1:26; (b) is used with ***anthropos***, "a man," i.e., "a nobleman," in Luke 19:12.

2. ***eugenesteros*** (*2104**), the comparative degree of No. 1, occurs in Acts 17:11, "more noble," i.e., "more noble-minded."

3. ***kratistos*** (*2903*) is translated "most noble" in the KJV of Acts 24:3 and 26:25 (RV, most excellent).

## NOBLEMAN

***basilikos*** (*937*), an adjective, "royal, belonging to a king" (***basileus***), is used of the command, "thou shalt love thy neighbor as thyself," "the royal law," Jas. 2:8; this may mean a law which covers or governs other laws and therefore has a specially regal character (as Hort suggests), or because it is made by a King (a meaning which Deissmann assigns) with whom there is no respect of persons; it is used with the pronoun ***tis***, "a certain one," in John 4:46, 49, of a courtier, one in the service of a king, "a nobleman" (some mss. have the noun ***basiliskos***, "a petty king," in these two verses). It is used of a country in Acts 12:20, "the king's (country)," and of royal apparel in v. 21.

## NOISE

**A. Adverb.**

***rhoizedon*** (*4500*), from ***rhoizos***, "the whistling of an arrow," signifies "with rushing sound," as of roaring flames, and is used in 2 Pet. 3:10, of the future passing away of the heavens.

**B. Verbs.**

1. ***akouo*** (*191*), "to hear," is translated "it was noised" in Mark 2:1 (passive voice), of the rapid spread of the information that Christ was "in the house" in Capernaum.

2. ***dialaleo*** (*1255*), lit., "to speak through," is rendered "were noised abroad" in Luke 1:65.

## NOSE

**A. Noun.**

***'ap*** (639) is translated by many different words, with their corresponding meanings:

***'ap*** usually means parts of the body; and can be translated "nostril," meaning the breathing passage of the nose, as a particular part of the nose, Gen. 2:7; or "nose," meaning any part of the nose, internal cartilage or external protuberance of any creature, Gen. 3:19; 24:47; Pr 11:22; "face," meaning the entire front of the head, including eyes, nose, mouth, chin, etc., Gen. 19:1; or translated "breath," meaning the vapor and air which comes out of the lungs through the mouth, Song. 7:8.

***'ap*** is also used figuratively, translated "anger, wrath, resentment," and so meaning to have a strong feeling of displeasure over a person or a situation, as a figurative extension of the nose as an area that can change color when blood rushes to it when one is angry, Gen. 27:45; and in phrases Gen. 30:2, it can mean "quick-tempered, hot-tempered," so pertaining to being angry with relatively little provocation, Prov. 14:17. "Long of nose" is "patient, slow to anger, tolerant, enduring," meaning not being easily angered in a potentially hostile situation, as a figurative extension of a nose not changing color (getting "hot") when one is angry, Prov. 16:32.

***'ap*** can also be translated "before," lit., "face," meaning a spatial position in front of another object, 1 Sam. 25:23. ***'ap*** is also translated "double portion," meaning an amount which is a multiple of twice as much, as a figurative extension of a pair of nostrils, 1 Sam. 1:5. ***'ap*** lastly, is translated "pride, arrogance," meaning an improper haughtiness and self-confidence, as a moral failure, as a figurative extension of having one's nose high in the air, Psa. 10:4.

**B. Verb.**

***'anap*** (*599*), "to be angry," Isa. 12:1.

## NOTABLE, OF NOTE

1. ***gnostos*** (*1110*), an adjective, signifying "known" (from ***ginosko***, "to know"), is used (a) as an adjective, most usually translated "known," whether of facts, e.g., Acts 1:19; 2:14; 4:10; or persons, John 18:15–16; it denotes "notable" in Acts 4:16, of a miracle; (b) as a noun, "acquaintance," Luke 2:44 and 23:49.

2. ***episemos*** (*1978*), primarily meant "bearing a mark," e.g., of money "stamped, coined," (from ***epi***, "upon," and ***sema***, "a mark, a sign"; cf. ***semaino***, "to give a sign, signify, indicate," and ***semeioo***, "to note"); it is used in the NT, metaphorically, (a) in a good sense, Rom. 16:7, "of note, illustrious," said of Andronicus and Junias; (b) in a bad sense, Matt. 27:16, "notable," of the prisoner Barabbas.

3. ***epiphanes*** (*2016*), "illustrious, renowned, notable" (akin to ***epiphaino***, "to show forth, appear"; Eng., "epiphany"), is translated "notable" in Acts 2:20, of the great Day of the Lord. The appropriateness of this word (compared with Nos. 1 and 2) to that future occasion is obvious.

## NOTE (Verb)

***semeioo*** (*4593*), from ***semeion***, "a sign, token," signifies "to mark, to note," in the middle voice, "to note for oneself," and is so used in 2 Thess. 3:14, in an injunction to take cautionary note of one who refuses obedience to the apostle's word by the Epistle.

## NOUGHT (for, bring to, come to, set at)

**A. Pronoun.**

***ouden*** (*3762*), "nothing" (the neuter of ***oudeis***, no one), is translated "nought" in Acts 5:36.

**B. Adverb.**

***dorean*** (*1432*), "freely, as a gift," is translated "for nought" in Gal. 2:21, RV (KJV, "in vain"); in 2 Thess. 3:8, in a denial by the apostle that he lived on the hospitality of others at Thessalonica.

**C. Verbs.**

1. ***katargeo*** (*2673*) is used in 1 Cor. 1:28, "(that) He might bring to nought"; 1 Cor. 2:6 (passive voice in the original); 1 Cor. 6:13, RV, "will bring to nought" (KJV "will destroy"); so 2 Thess. 2:8 and Heb. 2:14.

2. ***exoutheneo*** (*1848*), "to set at nought, treat with utter contempt, despise," is translated "set at nought" in Luke 18:9, RV (KJV, "despised"); in 23:11, "set (Him) at nought"; "was set at nought" in Acts 4:11; in Rom. 14:3, RV, "set at nought" (KJV, "despise"); v. 10, "set at nought."

3. ***exoudeneo*** or ***exoudenoo*** (*1847*) has the same meaning as No. 2, and is virtually the same word (***outhen*** being another form of ***ouden***, "nothing"), i.e., "to treat as nothing" (***ex***, intensive), and is translated "be set at nought" in Mark 9:12.

4. ***ekpipto*** (*1601*), "to fall out," is used in Rom. 9:6 in the sense of falling from its place, failing, of the word of God, RV, "hath come to nought" (KJV, "hath taken none effect").

5. ***atheteo*** (*114*), "to set aside, reject," is translated "set at nought" in Heb. 10:28, RV (KJV, "despised"); so Jude 8.

## NOURISH, NOURISHMENT

1. ***trepho*** (*5142*), "to rear, feed, nourish," is translated by the verb "to nourish" in Jas. 5:5 (of luxurious living); Rev. 12:14 (of God's care for Israel against its enemies); so v. 6, RV (KJV, feed); in Acts 12:20, RV, "was fed" (KJV, "was nourished").

2. ***anatrepho*** (*397*), "to nurse, bring up" (***ana***, "up," and No. 1), is translated "nourished" in Acts 7:20 (KJV, "nourished up"); in 21, "nourished," KJV and RV.

3. ***ektrepho*** (*1625*), ***ek***, "from, out of," and No. 1, primarily used of children, "to nurture, rear," is translated "nurture" of the care of one's own flesh, Eph. 5:29, and in Eph. 6:4, RV (KJV, "bring . . . up").

4. ***entrepho*** (*1789*), "to train up, nurture," is used metaphorically, in the passive voice, in 1 Tim. 4:6, of being "nourished" in the faith.

## NOVICE

***neophutos*** (*3504*), an adjective, lit., "newly-planted" (from ***neos***, "new," and ***phuo***, "to bring forth, produce"), denotes "a new convert, neophyte, novice," 1 Tim. 3:6, of one who by inexperience is unfit to act as a bishop or overseer in a church.

## TO NUMBER, VISIT, PUNISH

**A. Verb.**

***paqad*** (6485), "to number, visit, be concerned with, look after, make a search for, punish." The verb is used in an expression which is unique to Hebrew and which shows great intensity of meaning. Such an occurrence appears in Exod. 3:16ff., in which it is used twice in two different grammatical forms to portray the intensity of the action; the text reads (literally): "Looking after, I have looked after" (KJV, "I have surely visited"). The usage refers to God's intervention in His saving the children of Israel from their bondage in Egypt. The same verb in a similar expression can also be used for divine intervention for punishment: "Shall I not *visit* them for these things?," Jer. 9:9, which means literally: "Shall I not *punish* them for these things?"

However, the most common usage of the verb in the whole of the Old Testament is in the sense of "drawing up, mustering, or numbering," i.e., count and add up collections of objects or persons; as of troops for marching or battle, Exod. 30:12; or take a census, Num. 14:29.

**B. Noun.**

***paqid*** (6496), "one who looks after." This noun, possibly means "one who draws up troops," hence "officer," 2 Chron. 24:11; Jer. 20:1.

## NURSE

***trophos*** (*5162*), translated "nurse" in 1 Thess. 2:7, there denotes a "nursing" mother, as is clear from the statement "cherisheth her own children"; this is also confirmed by the word ***epios***, "gentle" (in the same verse), which was commonly used of the kindness of parents towards children.

N

# O

## OATH

1. ***horkos*** (*3727*) is primarily equivalent to ***herkos***, "a fence, an enclosure, that which restrains a person"; hence, "an oath." The Lord's command in Matt. 5:33 was a condemnation of the minute and arbitrary restrictions imposed by the scribes and Pharisees in the matter of adjurations, by which God's Name was profaned. The injunction is repeated in Jas. 5:12. The language of the apostle Paul, e.g., in Gal. 1:20 and 1 Thess. 5:27 was not inconsistent with Christ's prohibition, read in the light of its context. Contrast the "oaths" mentioned in Matt. 14:7, 9; 26:72; Mark 6:26.

Heb. 6:16 refers to the confirmation of a compact among men, guaranteeing the discharge of liabilities; in their disputes "the oath is final for confirmation." This is referred to in order to illustrate the greater subject of God's "oath" to Abraham, confirming His promise; cf. Luke 1:73; Acts 2:30.

2. ***horkomosia*** (*3728*) denotes "an affirmation on oath" (from No. 1 and ***omnumi***, "to swear"). This is used in Heb. 7:20–21 (twice), 28, of the establishment of the Priesthood of Christ, the Son of God, appointed a Priest after the order of Melchizedek, and "perfected for evermore."

## OBEDIENCE, OBEDIENT, OBEY

### A. Nouns.

1. ***hupakoe*** (*5218*), "obedience" (***hupo***, "under," ***akouo***, "to hear"), is used (a) in general, Rom. 6:16 (1st part), RV, "(unto) obedience," KJV, "(to) obey"; here "obedience" is not personified, as in the next part of the verse, "servants . . . of obedience" [see (c)], but is simply shown to be the effect of the presentation mentioned; (b) of the fulfillment of apostolic counsels, 2 Cor. 7:15; 10:6; Philem. 21; (c) of the fulfillment of God's claims or commands, Rom. 1:5 and 16:26, "obedience of faith," which grammatically might be objective, to the faith (marg.), or subjective, as in the text. Since faith is one of the main subjects of the Epistle, and is the initial act of obedience in the new life, as well as an essential characteristic thereof, the text rendering is to be preferred; Rom. 6:16 (2nd part); 15:18, RV "(for) the obedience," KJV, "(to make) obedient"; 16:19; 1 Pet. 1:2, 14, RV, "(children of) obedience," i.e., characterized by "obedience," KJV, "obedient (children)"; v. 22, RV, "obedience (to the truth)," KJV, "obeying (the truth)"; (d) of "obedience" to Christ (objective), 2 Cor. 10:5; (e) of Christ's "obedience," Rom. 5:19 (referring to His death; cf. Phil. 2:8); Heb. 5:8, which refers to His delighted experience in constant "obedience" to the Father's will (not to be understood in the sense that He learned to obey).

2. ***hupotage*** (*5292*), subjection (***hupo***, "under," ***tasso***, "to order"), is translated "obedience" in 2 Cor. 9:13, RV (KJV, "subjection").

### B. Verbs.

1. ***hupakouo*** (*5219*), "to listen, attend" (as in Acts 12:13), and so, "to submit, to obey," is used of "obedience" (a) to God, Heb. 5:9; 11:8; (b) to Christ, by natural elements, Matt. 8:27; Mark 1:27; 4:41; Luke 8:25; (c) to disciples of Christ, Luke 17:6; (d) to the faith, Acts 6:7; the gospel, Rom. 10:16; 2 Thess. 1:8; Christian doctrine, Rom. 6:17 (as to a form or mold of teaching); (e) to apostolic injunctions, Phil. 2:12; 2 Thess. 3:14; (f) to Abraham by Sarah, 1 Pet. 3:6; (g) to parents by children, Eph. 6:1; Col. 3:20; (h) to masters by servants, Eph. 6:5; Col. 3:22; (i) to sin, Rom. 6:12; (j) in general, Rom. 6:16.

2. ***peitho*** (*3982*), "to persuade, to win over," in the passive and middle voices, "to be persuaded, to listen to, to obey," is so used with this meaning, in the middle voice, e.g., in Acts 5:36–37 (in v. 40, passive voice, "they agreed"); Rom. 2:8; Gal. 5:7; Heb. 13:17; Jas. 3:3. The "obedience" suggested is not by submission to authority, but resulting from persuasion.

***peitho*** and ***pisteuo***, "to trust," are closely related etymologically; the difference in meaning is that the former implies the obedience that is produced by the latter, cf. Heb. 3:18–19, where the disobedience of the Israelites is said to be the evidence of their unbelief. Faith is of the heart, invisible to men; obedience is of the conduct and may be observed. When a man obeys God he gives the only possible evidence that in his heart he believes God. Of course it is persuasion of the truth that results in faith (we believe because we are persuaded that the thing is true, a thing does not become true because it is believed), but ***peitho***, in NT suggests an actual and outward result of the inward persuasion and consequent faith.

3. ***peitharcheo*** (*3980*), "to obey one in authority" (No. 2, and ***arche***, "rule"), is translated "obey" in Acts 5:29, 32; "to be obedient," Titus

3:1, RV (KJV, "to obey magistrates"); in Acts 27:21, "hearkened."

4. ***apeitheo*** (*544*), "to disobey, be disobedient" (***a***, negative, and No. 2), is translated "obey not" in Rom. 2:8; 1 Pet. 3:1; 4:17.

**C. Adjective.**

***hupekoos*** (*5255*), "obedient" (akin to A, No. 1), "giving ear, subject," occurs in Acts 7:39, RV, "(would not be) obedient," KJV, "(would not) obey"; 2 Cor. 2:9; Phil. 2:8, where the RV "***even***" is useful as making clear that the "obedience" was not to death but to the Father.

## OBSERVATION, OBSERVE

**A. Noun.**

***parateresis*** (*3907*), "attentive watching" (akin to ***paratereo***, "to observe"), is used in Luke 17:20, of the manner in which the kingdom of God (i.e., the operation of the spiritual kingdom in the hearts of men) does not come, "in such a manner that it can be watched with the eyes" (Grimm-Thayer), or, as KJV marg., "with outward show."

**B. Verb.**

***paratereo*** (*3906*), "to watch closely, observe narrowly," is translated "ye observe" in Gal. 4:10, where the middle voice suggests that their religious observance of days, etc. was not from disinterested motives, but with a view to their own advantage.

## ODOR

***osme*** (*3744*), "a smell, an odor" (akin to ***ozo***, "to smell"), is translated "odor" in John 12:3; it is used metaphorically in Eph. 5:2, RV, "an odor (of a sweet smell)," KJV, "(a sweet smelling) savor," of the effects Godward of the sacrifice of Christ; in Phil. 4:18 of the effect of sacrifice, on the part of those in the church at Philippi, who sent material assistance to the apostle in his imprisonment. The word is translated "savor" in 2 Cor. 2:14, 16 (twice).

## OFFENCE (OFFENSE)

**A. Nouns.**

1. ***skandalon*** (*4625*) originally was "the name of the part of a trap to which the bait is attached, hence, the trap or snare itself, as in Rom. 11:9, RV, "stumblingblock," quoted from Psa. 69:22, and in Rev. 2:14, for Balaam's device was rather a trap for Israel than a stumblingblock to them, and in Matt. 16:23, for in Peter's words the Lord perceived a snare laid for Him by Satan.

In NT ***skandalon*** is always used metaphorically, and ordinarily of anything that arouses prejudice, or becomes a hindrance to others, or causes them to fall by the way. Sometimes the hindrance is in itself good, and those stumbled by it are the wicked.

Thus it is used (a) of Christ in Rom. 9:33, "(a rock) of offense"; so 1 Pet. 2:8; 1 Cor. 1:23 (KJV and RV, "stumblingblock"), and of His cross, Gal. 5:11 (RV, ditto); of the "table" provided by God for Israel, Rom. 11:9; (b) of that which is evil, e.g., Matt. 13:41, RV, "things that cause stumbling" (KJV, "things that offend"), lit., "all stumblingblocks"; 18:7, RV, "occasions of stumbling" and "occasion"; Luke 17:1 (ditto); Rom. 14:13, RV, "an occasion of falling" (KJV, "an occasion to fall"), said of such a use of Christian liberty as proves a hindrance to another; 16:17, RV, "occasions of stumbling," said of the teaching of things contrary to sound doctrine; 1 John 2:10, "occasion of stumbling," of the absence of this in the case of one who loves his brother and thereby abides in the light. Love, then, is the best safeguard against the woes pronounced by the Lord upon those who cause others to stumble.

2. ***proskomma*** (*4348*), "an obstacle against which one may dash his foot" (akin to ***proskopto***, "to stumble" or "cause to stumble"; ***pros***, "to or against," ***kopto***, "to strike"), is translated "offense" in Rom. 14:20, in v. 13, "a stumblingblock," of the spiritual hindrance to another by a selfish use of liberty (cf. No. 1 in the same verse); so in 1 Cor. 8:9. It is used of Christ, in Rom. 9:32–33, RV, "(a stone) of stumbling," and 1 Pet. 2:8, where the KJV also has this rendering.

3. ***proskope*** (*4349*), like No. 2, and formed from the same combination, occurs in 2 Cor. 6:3, RV, "occasion of stumbling" (KJV, "offense"), something which leads others into error or sin.

**B. Adjective.**

***aproskopos*** (*677*), akin to A, No. 3, with ***a***, negative, prefixed, is used (a) in the active sense, "not causing to stumble," in 1 Cor. 10:32, metaphorically of "refraining from doing anything to lead astray" either Jews or Greeks or the church of God (i.e., the local church), RV, "no occasion of stumbling" (KJV, "none offense"); (b) in the passive sense, "blameless, without stumbling," Acts 24:16, "(a conscience) void of offense"; Phil. 1:10, "void of (KJV, without) offense." The adjective is found occasionally in the papyri writings.

## OFFEND

***skandalizo*** (*4624*), signifies "to put a snare or stumblingblock in the way," always metaphorically in the NT, in the same ways as the noun, which see. It is used 14 times in Matthew, 8 in Mark, twice in Luke, twice in John; elsewhere in 1 Cor. 8:13 (twice) and 2 Cor. 11:29. It is absent in the most authentic mss. in Rom. 14:21. The RV renders it by the verb "to stumble," or "cause to stumble," in every place save the following, where it uses the verb "to offend," Matt. 13:57; 15:12; 26:31, 33; Mark 6:3; 14:27, 29.

## OFFENDER

***opheiletes*** (*3781*), "a debtor," is translated "offenders" in Luke 13:4, RV (RV and KJV marg., "debtors"; KJV, "sinners").

## OFFER, OFFERING

### *Old Testament*

### A. Verb.

***qarab*** (7126), "to offer, come near, approach"; i.e., to approach spatially, apart from any sense of intimacy, Gen. 12:11; Exod. 32:19; Num. 9:6. This verb also is used of temporal "nearness," in the sense that something is about to occur, like a special occasion, or any occasion, even presenting sacrifice or meeting God, Deut. 15:9; Exod. 16:9. The word is also used of the imminence of foreboding events, Gen. 27:41. ***qarab*** is used also in the sense of relationship which is not spatial, Ps. 27:2, 3; in sexual relations, Gen. 20:4; cf. Deut. 22:14; Isa. 8:3.

### B. Nouns.

***qorban*** (7133), "offering; oblation," i.e., valuable products of the land and flock presented to the Lord, Lev. 1:2. Some other related nouns appear less frequently: ***qarob***, "neighbor," Exod. 32:27; ***qirbah*** occurs twice with the meaning of drawing near to worship God and offer sacrifice, Ps. 73:28; Isa. 58:2.

***minchah*** (4503), "grain offering; offering; tribute; present; gift; sacrifice; oblation." ***minchah*** is used many times in the Old Testament to designate a "gift" or "present" which is given by one person to another, Gen. 32:13–15; 43:11; 1 Kings 10:25. Frequently ***minchah*** is used in the sense of "tribute" paid to a king or overlord, so a gift which is more or less required, Judg. 3:15–23; 2 Sam. 8:2; Ps. 72:10. ***minchah*** is often used to refer to any "offering" or "gift" made to God, the produce of flock or the ground, Gen. 4:3–5; or later sacrifices in the Torah, Lev. 2:14; 14:10, 21; 23:13; Num. 7:13. Note that the KJV translators regularly use "meat" instead of "grain" to translate this word.

***minchah*** provides an interesting symbolism for the prophet when he refers to the restoration of the Jews, Isa. 66:20. In his vision of the universal worship of God, even in Gentile lands, Malachi saw the ***minchah*** given as "a pure offering" to God by believers everywhere, Mal. 1:11.

***terumah*** (8641), "heave offering; offering; oblation." In more than a third of its occurrences in the text, the KJV translates ***terumah*** as "heave offering," all of these instances being found in Exodus, Leviticus, Numbers (where the majority are found), and Deuteronomy. This translation apparently is derived from the fact that the word is based on the common Semitic root, "to be high, exalted." The inference seems to be that such "offerings" were raised high by the priest in some sort of motion as it was placed on the altar. This is clearly illustrated in Num. 15:20. ***terumah*** often is used to designate those gifts or contributions to God, but which were set apart specifically for the priests, Num. 5:9. Such "offerings" were to go to the priests because of a special covenant God had made, Num. 18:19, RSV. Such offerings, or contributions, sometimes were of grain or grain products, Lev. 7:13–14. Part of the animal sacrifices was also designated as a ***terumah*** for the priests, Lev. 7:32; cf. Lev. 10:14–15; Num. 6:20. This portion was for the sustenance of the priest, Deut. 14:28–29.

In order to provide for the materials necessary for the construction of the wilderness tabernacle, Moses was instructed to receive a voluntary "offering" or ***terumah***, Exod. 25:3–9; 35:5, 6–8. The ***terumah*** sometimes was an "offering" which had the meaning of a tax, an obligatory assessment which was made against every Israelite male who was twenty years old or older, to be paid for the support of the tabernacle and later, the temple, Exod. 30:11–16; or as a ransom to God, 2 Sam. 24:1; or for a king's taxes, 1 Kings 12.

A very different use of ***terumah*** is found in Ezek. 45:1; 48:9, 20–21, where it refers to an "oblation" which was that portion of land on which the post-exilic temple was to be built, as well as accommodations for the priests and Levites. This tract of land is referred to as "the holy oblation," Ezek. 48:20; RSV, "holy portion," since it belongs to God just as much as the ***terumah*** which was given to Him as a sacrifice.

***qorban*** (7133), "offering; oblation; sacrifice." ***qorban*** may be translated as "that which one brings near to God or the altar." It is not surprising, then, that the word is used as a general term for all sacrifices, whether animal or vegetable. The very first reference to "sacrifice" in Leviticus is to the ***qorban*** as a burnt "offering," Lev. 1:2–3; cf. Lev. 1:10; 3:2, 6; 4:23; or any offering of precious metals or other valuable materials, Num. 7:1–89.

***qurban*** (7133), "wood offering." ***qurban*** is closely related to ***qarban***, and it is found in Neh. 10:34; 13:31. Here it refers to the "wood offering" which was to be provided for the burning of the sacrifices in the Second Temple. Lots were to be cast among the people, priests, and Levites to determine who would bring in the "wood offering" or fuel at the scheduled times throughout the year.

***'olah*** (5930), "whole burnt offering," ***'olah***, is similar in meaning to the above words of sacrifice and offering to God. The special feature of this word is that it is an animal given as a sin offering and presented whole (and skinned) to God. The offering was then wholly consumed by fire on the altar, Gen. 8:20; Lev. 1:3–15. The animal skin was given to the priest as his portion, Lev. 7:8. The ***'olah*** was the most common sacrifice, given daily and also at special times, Exod. 29:38–42; Num. 28:11–29. The central significance of ***'olah*** as the "whole burnt offering" was the total surrender of the heart and life of the offerer to God. Sin offerings could accompany them when the offerer was especially concerned with a covering or expiation for sin, 2 Chron. 29:27. When peace offerings accompanied "burnt offerings," the offerer's concern focused on fellowship with God, 2 Chron. 29:31–35. Before the Mosaic legislation, it appears, the "whole burnt offering" served the full range of meanings expressed in all the various Mosaic sacrifices.

***'ishsheh*** (801), "fire offering." All legitimate sacrifices had to be presented before God at His altar, and all of them involved burning to some degree. Thus they may all be called fire offerings. The word ***'ishsheh*** first occurs in Exod. 29:18: "And thou shalt burn the whole ram upon the altar: it is a burnt offering unto the Lord: it is a sweet savor, an offering made by fire unto the Lord."

***'asham*** (817), "guilt offering; offense; guilt; gift of restitution; gift of atonement." The most frequent meaning of the word is "guilt offering," Lev. 5:6. This specialized kind of sin offering, Lev. 5:7, was to be offered when someone had been denied what was due to him. The valued amount defrauded was to be repaid plus 20 percent, Lev. 5:16; 6:5. Ritual infractions and periods of leprosy and defilement took from God a commodity or service rightfully belonging to Him and required repayment plus restitution. Every violation of property rights required paying full reparation and the restitution *price* (*20* percent) to the one violated as well as presenting the guilt offering to God as the Lord of all (i.e., as a feudal lord over all). If the offended party was dead, reparation and restitution were made to God (i.e., given to the priests; Num. 5:5–10), usually a ram was offered, Lev. 14:14. In some passages, ***'asham*** is used of an offense against God and the guilt incurred by it, Gen. 26:10. In two verses, Num. 5:7–8, ***'asham*** represents the repayment made to one who has been wronged. This basic idea is extended so that the word comes to mean a gift made to God to remove guilt, 1 Sam. 6:3, or atone for sin, Isa. 53:10, other than the specified offerings to be presented at the altar.

## C. Adjectives.

***qarob*** (7138), "near," can represent nearness in space, Gen. 19:20; Ezek. 6:12; and an epistemological nearness, Deut. 30:14.

The adjective ***qareb*** parallels ***qarob*** in meaning. It represents intimate proximity (usually in a cultic context referring to cultic activity), Ezek. 45:4.

### *New Testament*

## A. Verbs.

1. ***prosphero*** (*4374*), primarily, "to bring to" (***pros***, "to," ***phero***, "to bring"), also denotes "to offer," (a) of the sacrifice of Christ Himself, Heb. 8:3; of Christ in virtue of his High Priesthood (RV, "this *high priest*"; KJV, "this man"); 9:14, 25 (negative), 28; 10:12; (b) of offerings under, or according to, the Law, e.g., Matt. 8:4; Mark 1:44; Acts 7:42; 21:26; Heb. 5:1, 3; 8:3; 9:7, 9; 10:1–2, 8, 11; (c) of "offerings" previous to the Law, Heb. 11:4, 17 (of Isaac by Abraham); (d) of gifts "offered" to Christ, Matt. 2:11, RV, "offered" (KJV, "presented unto"); (e) of prayers "offered" by Christ, Heb. 5:7; (f) of the vinegar "offered" to Him in mockery by the soldiers at the cross, Luke 23:36; (g) of the slaughter of disciples by persecutors, who think they are "offering" service to God, John 16:2, RV (KJV, "doeth"); (h) of money "offered" by Simon the sorcerer, Acts 8:18.

2. ***anaphero*** (*399*), primarily, "to lead" or "carry up" (***ana***), also denotes "to offer," (a) of Christ's sacrifice, Heb. 7:27; (b) of sacrifices under the Law, Heb. 7:27; (c) of such previous to the Law, Jas. 2:21 (of Isaac by Abraham); (d) of praise, Heb. 13:15; (e) of spiritual sacrifices in general, 1 Pet. 2:5.

3. ***spendo*** (*4689*), "to pour out as a drink offering, make a libation," is used figuratively in the passive voice in Phil. 2:17, "offered" (RV marg., "poured out as a drink offering"; KJV marg., "poured forth"). In 2 Tim. 4:6, "I am already being offered," RV (marg., "poured out as a drink-offering"), the apostle is referring

to his approaching death, upon the sacrifice of his ministry. This use of the word is exemplified in the papyri writings.

**B. Nouns.**

1. ***prosphora*** (*4376*), lit., "a bringing to" (akin to A, No. 1), hence an "offering," in the NT a sacrificial "offering," (a) of Christ's sacrifice, Eph. 5:2; Heb. 10:10 (of His body); 10:14; negatively, of there being no repetition, 10:18; (b) of "offerings" under, or according to, the Law, Acts 21:26; Heb. 10:5, 8; (c) of gifts in kind conveyed to needy Jews, Acts 24:17; (d) of the presentation of believers themselves (saved from among the Gentiles) to God, Rom. 15:16.

2. ***holokautoma*** (*3646*), "a burnt offering," see ***'olah*** in Old Testament section

3. ***anathema*** (*334*) denotes "a gift set up in a temple, a votive offering" (***ana***, "up," ***tithemi***, "to place"), Luke 21:5, RV "offerings" (KJV, "gifts").

## OFFICE

**A. Nouns.**

1. ***praxis*** (*4234*), "a doing, deed" (akin to ***prasso***, "to do or practice"), also denotes "an acting" or "function," translated "office" in Rom. 12:4.

2. ***hieroteia*** (*2405*), or ***hieratia***, denotes "a priest's office," Luke 1:9; Heb. 7:5, RV, "priest's office" (KJV "office of the priesthood").

**B. Verb.**

***hierateuo*** (*2407*), "to officiate as a priest" (akin to A, No. 2), is translated "he executed the priest's office" in Luke 1:8. The word is frequent in inscriptions.

## OFFICER

1. ***huperetes*** (*5257*), is translated "officer," with the following applications, (a) to a magistrate's attendant, Matt. 5:25; (b) to officers of the synagogue, or officers or bailiffs of the Sanhedrin, Matt. 26:58; Mark 14:54, 65; John 7:32, 45–46; 18:3, 12, 18, 22; 19:6; Acts 5:22, 26.

2. ***praktor*** (*4233*), lit., "one who does," or "accomplishes" (akin to ***prasso***, "to do"), was used in Athens of one who exacts payment, a collector (the word is frequently used in the papyri of a public accountant); hence, in general, a court "officer," an attendant in a court of justice (so Deissmann); the word is used in Luke 12:58 (twice).

## OFFSCOURING

***peripsema*** (*4067*), "that which is wiped off"; in NT it means, "refuse, rubbish," i.e., "scum."

## OFFSPRING

1. ***gennema*** (*1081*), akin to ***gennao***, "to beget," denotes "the offspring of men and animals," Matt. 3:7; 12:34; 23:33; Luke 3:7, RV, "offspring" (KJV, "generation").

2. ***genos*** (*1085*), "a race, family," denotes "an offspring," Acts 17:28, 29; Rev. 22:16.

## OIL

### *Old Testament*

**A. Noun.**

***shemen*** (8081), "(olive) oil; olive; perfume; olivewood." ***shemen*** means olive "oil," i.e., the viscous plant-oil that is derived by crushing and draining the liquid out of the olive fruit, Gen. 28:18; Exod. 25:6; 2 Kings 9:6. Olive oil was used in a wide variety of ceremonies, 2 Sam. 14:2; Ps. 23:5; cf. Lev. 14:17. ***shemen*** is used as a preservative on shield-leather, 2 Sam. 1:21, and in baking, Exod. 29:2, and as a medication, Ezek. 16:9, or lamp oil, Exod. 25:6. Its many uses made olive oil a valuable trade item, Ezek. 27:17, and of course food, Isa. 25:6. ***shemen*** is "a kind of perfume," or olive oil mixed with certain sweet-smelling herbs and ground-up barks as a perfume, Song of Sol. 1:3.

**B. Verb.**

The verb ***saman***, means "to grow or be fat," Neh. 9:25; Jer. 5:28.

**C. Adjective.**

The adjective ***shaman***, translated "fat," Ezek. 34:16; "rich" in the sense of fattening, Gen. 49:20; "fertile," Num. 13:20; "robust or muscular," Judg. 3:29; and "large," Hab. 1:16.

### *New Testament*

***elaion*** (*1637*), "olive oil"; in the NT the uses mentioned were (a) for lamps, in which the "oil" is a symbol of the Holy Spirit, Matt. 25:3–4, 8; (b) as a medicinal agent, for healing, Luke 10:34; (c) for anointing at feasts, Luke 7:46; (d) on festive occasions, Heb. 1:9, where the reference is probably to the consecration of kings; (e) as an accompaniment of miraculous power, Mark 6:13, or of the prayer of faith, Jas. 5:14. For its general use in commerce, see Luke 16:6; Rev. 6:6; 18:13.

## OINTMENT

***muron*** (*3464*), a word derived by the ancients from ***muro***, "to flow," or from ***murra***, "myrrh-oil" (it is probably of foreign origin). The "ointment" is mentioned in the NT in connection with the anointing of the Lord on the occasions recorded in Matt. 26:7, 9, 12; Mark 14:3–4; Luke 7:37–38, 46; John 11:2; 12:3 (twice), 5. The alabaster cruse mentioned in the passages in Matthew, Mark and Luke was the best of its kind, and the spikenard was one of the costliest of perfumes. "Ointments" were used in preparing a body for burial, Luke 23:56 ("ointments"). Of the act of the woman mentioned in Matt. 26:6–13, the Lord said, "she did it to prepare Me for burial"; her devotion led her to antedate the customary ritual after death, by showing both her affection and her understanding of what was impending. For the use of the various kinds of "ointments" as articles of commerce, see Rev. 18:13.

## OLD

### A. Adjectives.

1. ***archaios*** (*744*), "original, ancient" (from ***arche***, "a beginning": Eng., "archaic," "archaeology," etc.), is used (a) of persons belonging to a former age," (to) them of old time," Matt. 5:21, 33, RV; in some mss. v. 27; the RV rendering is right; not ancient teachers are in view; what was said to them of old time was "to be both recognized in its significance and estimated in its temporary limitations, Christ intending His words to be regarded not as an abrogation, but a deepening and fulfilling" (Cremer); of prophets, Luke 9:8, 19; (b) of time long gone by, Acts 15:21; (c) of days gone by in a person's experience, Acts 15:7, "a good while ago," lit., "from old (days)," i.e., from the first days onward in the sense of originality, not age; (d) of Mnason, "an early disciple," Acts 21:16, RV, not referring to age, but to his being one of the first who had accepted the gospel from the beginning of its proclamation; (e) of things which are "old" in relation to the new, earlier things in contrast to things present, 2 Cor. 5:17, i.e., of what characterized and conditioned the time previous to conversion in a believer's experience, RV, "they are become new," i.e., they have taken on a new complexion and are viewed in an entirely different way; (f) of the world (i.e., the inhabitants of the world) just previous to the Flood, 2 Pet. 2:5; (g) of the Devil, as "that old serpent," Rev. 12:9; 20:2, "old," not in age, but as characterized for a long period by the evils indicated.

2. ***palaios*** (*3820*), akin to Eng., "paleontology," etc., "of what is of long duration, old in years," etc., a garment, wine (in contrast to new), Matt. 9:16–17; Mark 2:21–22 (twice); Luke 5:36–37, 39 (twice); of the treasures of divine truth, Matt. 13:52 (compared with new); of what belongs to the past, e.g., the believer's former self before his conversion, his "old man"; "old" because it has been superseded by that which is new, Rom. 6:6; Eph. 4:22 (in contrast to ***kainos***); Col. 3:9 (in contrast to ***neos***); of the covenant in connection with the Law, 2 Cor. 3:14; of leaven, metaphorical of moral evil, 1 Cor. 5:7, 8 (in contrast to ***neos***); of that which was given long ago and remains in force, an "old" commandment, 1 John 2:7 (twice), that which was familiar and well known in contrast to that which is fresh (***kainos***).

3. ***presbuteros*** (*4245*), "older, elder," is used in the plural, as a noun, in Acts 2:17, "old men."

### B. Nouns.

1. ***geron*** (*1088*) denotes "an old man" (from the same root comes Eng., "gray"), John 3:4.

2. ***presbutes*** (*4246*), "an old man," Luke 1:18, is translated "aged" in Titus 2:2; Philem. 9.

3. ***geras*** (*1094*), "old age," occurs in Luke 1:36.

### C. Adverbs.

1. ***palai*** (*3819*) denotes "long ago, of old," Heb. 1:1, RV, "of old time" (KJV, "in time past"); in Jude 4, "of old"; it is used as an adjective in 2 Pet. 1:9, "(his) old (sins)," lit., "his sins of old."

2. ***ekpalai*** (*1597*), "from of old, for a long time" (***ek***, "from," and No. 1), occurs in 2 Pet. 2:3, RV, "from of old" (KJV, "of a long time"); 3:5.

***Note:*** In 1 Pet. 3:5, KJV, the particle ***pote***, "once, formerly, ever, sometime," is translated "in the old time" (RV, "aforetime"); in 2 Pet. 1:21, "in old time" (RV, "ever"), KJV marg., "at any time."

O

### D. Verbs.

1. ***palaioo*** (*3822*), akin to A, No. 2, denotes, in the active voice, "to make or declare old," Heb. 8:13 (1st part); in the passive voice, "to become old," of things worn out by time and use, Luke 12:33; Heb. 1:11, "shall wax old," lit., "shall be made old," i.e., worn out; in 8:13 (2nd part), RV, "is becoming old" (KJV "decayeth"); here and in the 1st part of the verse, the verb may have the meaning "to abrogate."

2. ***gerasko*** (*1095*), from ***geras***, "old age" (akin to B, No. 1), "to grow old," is translated "thou shalt be old," in John 21:18; "waxeth aged," Heb. 8:13, RV (KJV, "waxeth old").

## OLDNESS

***palaiotes*** (*3821*), from ***palaios***, occurs in Rom. 7:6, of "the letter," i.e., "the law," with its rules of conduct, mere outward conformity to which has yielded place in the believer's service to a response to the inward operation of the Holy Spirit. The word is contrasted with ***kainotes***, "newness."

## OLD WIVES'

***graodes*** *(1126)*, an adjective, signifying "old-womanish" (from ***graus***, "an old woman"), is said of fables, in 1 Tim. 4:7.

## ONCE (at; for all)

1. ***hapax*** *(530)* denotes (a) "once, one time," 2 Cor. 11:25; Heb. 9:7, 26–27; 12:26–27; in the phrase "once and again," lit., "once and twice," Phil. 4:16; 1 Thess. 2:18; (b) "once for all," of what is of perpetual validity, not requiring repetition, Heb. 6:4; 9:28; 10:2; 1 Pet. 3:18; Jude 3, RV, "once for all" (KJV, "once"); v. 5 (ditto); in some mss. 1 Pet. 3:20 (so the KJV).

2. ***ephapax*** *(2178)*, a strengthened form of No. 1 (***epi***, "upon"), signifies (a) "once for all," Rom. 6:10; Heb. 7:27, RV (KJV, "once"); 9:12 (ditto); 10:10; (b) "at once," 1 Cor. 15:6.

3. ***pote*** *(4218)* denotes "once upon a time, formerly, sometime," e.g., Rom. 7:9; Gal. 1:23, 1st part, RV, "once" (KJV, "in times past"); 2nd part, KJV and RV, "once"; Gal. 2:6, RV marg., "what they once were" (to be preferred to the text, "whatsoever they were"), the reference probably being to the association of the twelve apostles with the Lord during His ministry on earth; upon this their partisans based their claim for the exclusive authority of these apostles, which Paul vigorously repudiated; in Eph. 5:8, RV, "once" (KJV, "sometimes").

## ONE ANOTHER or ONE . . . ANOTHER, ONE . . . THE OTHER

This translates a number of words and phrases in Greek, and one of the meanings of "one another" in English has the basic idea of reciprocity, i.e., the state or condition in which one has a relationship with another person, and in which one person does similar acts and words. The word in itself can have a negative or positive associative meaning. Here is an edited list of the "one-anothers" in the New Testament representing the Greek word ***allelon*** or ***allelous***, which has the idea of mutuality and reciprocity. It is a beautiful and edifying concept pertaining to Christian interpersonal relationships. Jesus commands that Christians are to love one another, John 13:34–35; 15:12, 17. The NT writers give the Church varied exhortations to promote a rich church life, see Rom. 12:10, 16; 13:8; 14:13, 19; 15:5,7, 14; 16:16; 1 Cor.11:33; 12:25; Gal. 5:13, 15, 26; 6:2; Eph. 4:2,25, 32; 5:21; Phil. 2:3; Col. 3:9, 13; 1 Thess. 3:12; 4:9, 18; 5:11,15; Heb. 10:24; James 4:11; 5:9, 16; 1 Pet. 1:22; 4:9; 5:5; 1 John.3:11.

## ONLY

1. ***monos*** *(3441)*, "alone, solitary," is translated "only," e.g., in Matt. 4:10; 12:4; 17:8; 1 Cor. 9:6; 14:36; Phil. 4:15; Col. 4:11; 2 John 1; it is used as an attribute of God in John 5:44; 17:3; Rom. 16:27; 1 Tim. 1:17; 1 Tim. 6:15–16; Jude 4, 25; Rev. 15:4.

2. ***monogenes*** *(3439)*, "only begotten" (No. 1 and ***genos***, "offspring"), has the meaning "only," of human offspring, in Luke 7:12; 8:42; 9:38; the term is one of endearment, or status, as well as of singleness in some contexts.

## ONLY BEGOTTEN

***monogenes*** *(3439)* is used five times, all in the writings of the apostle John, of Christ as the Son of God; it is translated "only begotten" in Heb. 11:17 of the relationship of Isaac to Abraham.

With reference to Christ, the phrase "the only begotten from the Father," John 1:14 indicates that as the Son of God He was the sole representative of the Being and character of the One who sent Him. In the original the definite article is omitted both before "only begotten" and before "Father," and its absence in each case serves to lay stress upon the characteristics referred to in the terms used. The apostle's object is to demonstrate what sort of glory it was that he and his fellow apostles had seen. That he is not merely making a comparison with earthly relationships is indicated by ***para***, "from." The glory was that of a unique relationship and the word "begotten" does not imply a beginning of His Sonship. It suggests relationship indeed, but must be distinguished from generation as applied to man.

We can only rightly understand the term "the only begotten" when used of the Son, in the sense of unoriginated relationship. "The begetting is not an event of time, however remote, but a fact irrespective of time. The Christ did not *become*, but necessarily and eternally *is* the Son. He, a Person, possesses every attribute of pure Godhood. This necessitates eternity, absolute being; in this respect He is not 'after' the Father" (Moule). The expression also suggests the thought of the deepest affection, as in the case of the OT word ***yachid***, variously rendered, "only one," Gen. 22:2, 12; "only son," Jer. 6:26; Amos 8:10; Zech. 12:10; "only beloved," Prov. 4:3, and "darling," Ps. 22:20; 35:17.

In John 1:18 the clause "the only begotten son, which is in the bosom of the Father," expresses both His eternal union with the Father in the Godhead and the ineffable intimacy and love between them, the Son sharing all the Father's counsels and enjoying all His affections. Another reading is ***monogenes theos***, "God only-begotten." In John 3:16 the statement, "God so loved the world that He gave His only begotten son," must not be taken to mean that Christ became the only begotten son by incarnation. The value and the greatness of the gift lay in the Sonship of Him who was given. His Sonship was not the effect of His being given. In John 3:18 the phrase "the name of the only begotten son of God" lays stress upon the full revelation of God's character and will, His love and grace, as conveyed in the name of One who, being in a unique relationship to Him, was provided by Him as the object of faith. In 1 John 4:9 the statement "God hath sent His only begotten son into the world" does not mean that God sent out into the world one who at His birth in Bethlehem had become His Son.

## OPEN, OPENING

### A. Verbs.

1. ***anoigo*** (*455*) is used (1) transitively, (a) literally, of "a door or gate," e.g., Acts 5:19; graves, Matt. 27:52; a sepulchre, Rom. 3:13; a book, e.g., Luke 4:17; Rev. 5:2–5; 10:8; the seals of a roll, e.g., Rev. 5:9; 6:1; the eyes, Acts 9:40; the mouth of a fish, Matt. 17:27; "the pit of the abyss," Rev. 9:2, RV; heaven and the heavens, Matt. 3:16; Luke 3:21; Acts 10:11; Rev. 19:11; "the temple of the tabernacle of the testimony in heaven," Rev. 15:5; by metonymy, for that which contained treasures, Matt. 2:11; (b) metaphorically, e.g., Matt. 7:7–8; 25:11; Rev. 3:7; Hebraistically, "to open the mouth," of beginning to speak, e.g., Matt. 5:2; 13:35; Acts 8:32, 35; 10:34; 18:14; Rev. 13:6 (cf., e.g., Num. 22:28; Job. 3:1; Isa. 50:5); and of recovering speech, Luke 1:64; of the earth "opening," Rev. 12:16; of the "opening" of the eyes, Acts 26:18; the ears, Mark 7:35 (in the best mss.; some have No. 2); (2) intransitively (perfect tense, active, in the Greek), (a) literally, of "the heaven," John 1:51, RV, "opened"; (b) metaphorically, of "speaking freely," 2 Cor. 6:11.

2. ***dianoigo*** (*1272*), "to open up completely" (***dia***, "through," intensive, and No. 1), is used (a) literally, Luke 2:23; Acts 7:56, in the best mss.; (b) metaphorically, of the eyes, Mark 7:34; Luke 24:31; of the Scriptures, v. 32 and Acts 17:3; of the mind, Luke 24:45, RV (KJV, "understanding"); of the heart, Acts 16:14.

### B. Nouns.

1. ***anoixis*** (*457*), "an opening" (akin to A, No. 1), is used in Eph. 6:19, metaphorically of the "opening" of the mouth as in A, No. 1 (2), (b).

2. ***ope*** (*3692*), "an opening, a hole," is used in Jas. 3:11, of the opening of a fountain.

## OPENLY

***parrhesia*** (*3954*), "freedom of speech, boldness," is used adverbially in the dative case and translated "openly" in Mark 8:32, of a saying of Christ; in John 7:13, of a public statement; in 11:54, of Christ's public appearance; in 7:26 and 18:20, of His public testimony; preceded by the preposition ***en***, "in," John 7:4, lit., "in boldness" (cf. v. 10, RV, "publicly).

## OPPORTUNITY

### A. Nouns.

1. ***kairos*** (*2540*), primarily, "a due measure," is used of "a fixed and definite period, a time, season," and is translated "opportunity" in Gal. 6:10 and Heb. 11:15.

2. ***eukairia*** (*2120*), "a fitting time, opportunity" (***eu***, "well," and No. 1), occurs in Matt. 26:16 and Luke 22:6.

### B. Verb.

***eukaireo*** (*2119*), "to have time or leisure" (akin to A, No. 2), is translated "he shall have opportunity" in 1 Cor. 16:12, RV (KJV, "convenient time").

## OPPOSE

1. ***antitasso*** (*498*) is used in the middle voice in the sense of setting oneself against (***anti***, "against," ***tasso***, "to order, set"), "opposing oneself to," Acts 18:6; elsewhere rendered by the verb "to resist," Rom. 13:2; Jas. 4:6; 5:6; 1 Pet. 5:5.

2. ***antidiatithemi*** (*475*) signifies "to place oneself in opposition, oppose" (***anti***, "against," ***dia***, "through," intensive, ***tithemi***, "to place"), 2 Tim. 2:25.

## OPPOSITIONS

***antithesis*** (*477*), "a contrary position" (***anti***, "against," ***tithemi***, "to place"; Eng., "antithesis"), occurs in 1 Tim. 6:20.

## OPPRESS

***katadunasteuo*** (*2616*), "to exercise power over" (***kata***, "down," ***dunastes***, "a potentate": ***dunamai*** "to have power"), "to oppress," is used, in the passive voice, in Acts 10:38; in the active, in Jas. 2:6.

## ORACLE

***logion*** (*3051*), a diminutive of ***logos***, "a word, narrative, statement," denotes "a divine response or utterance, an oracle"; it is used of

(a) the contents of the Mosaic Law, Acts 7:38; (b) all the written utterances of God through OT writers, Rom. 3:2; (c) the substance of Christian doctrine, Heb. 5:12; (d) the utterances of God through Christian teachers, 1 Pet. 4:11.

## ORATION

***demegoreo*** (*1215*), from ***demos***, "the people" and ***agoreuo***, "to speak in the public assembly, to deliver an oration," occurs in Acts 12:21.

## ORATOR

***rhetor*** (*4489*), from an obsolete present tense, ***rheo***, "to say" (cf. Eng., "rhetoric"), denotes "a public speaker, an orator," Acts 24:1, of Tertullus. Such a person, distinct from the professional lawyer, was hired, as a professional speaker, to make a skillful presentation of a case in court. His training was not legal but rhetorical.

## ORDAIN

1. ***kathistemi*** (*2525*), from ***kata***, "down," or "over against," and ***histemi***, "to cause to stand, to set," is translated "to ordain" in the KJV of Titus 1:5; Heb. 5:1; 8:3.

2. ***tasso*** (*5021*) is translated "to ordain," in Acts 13:48 and Rom. 13:1.

3. ***diatasso*** (*1299*) is translated "to ordain" in 1 Cor. 7:17; 9:14; Gal. 3:19, the last in the sense of "administered."

4. ***horizo*** (*3724*) is twice used of Christ as divinely "ordained" to be the Judge of men, Acts 10:42; 17:31.

5. ***krino*** (*2919*), "to divide, separate, decide, judge," is translated "ordained" in Acts 16:4, of the decrees by the apostles and elders in Jerusalem.

## ORDER (Noun and Verb)

### A. Nouns.

1. ***taxis*** (*5010*), "an arranging, arrangement, order" (akin to ***tasso***, "to arrange, draw up in order"), is used in Luke 1:8 of the fixed succession of the course of the priests; of due "order," in contrast to confusion, in the gatherings of a local church, 1 Cor. 14:40; of the general condition of such, Col. 2:5 (some give it a military significance here); of the divinely appointed character or nature of a priesthood, of Melchizedek, as foreshadowing that of Christ, Heb. 5:6, 10; 6:20; 7:11 (where also the character of the Aaronic priesthood is set in contrast); 7:17 (in some mss, v. 21).

2. ***tagma*** (*5001*), a more concrete form of No. 1, signifying "that which has been arranged in order," was especially a military term, denoting "a company"; it is used metaphorically in 1 Cor. 15:23 of the various classes of those who have part in the first resurrection.

### B. Verbs.

1. ***anatassomai*** (*392*), "to arrange in order" (***ana***, "up," and the middle voice of ***tasso***, "to arrange"), is used in Luke 1:1, KJV, "to set forth in order" (RV, "to draw up"); the probable meaning is to bring together and so arrange details in "order."

2. ***diatasso*** (*1299*), "to appoint, arrange, charge, give orders to," is used, in the middle voice, in Acts 24:23, "gave order" (RV); 1 Cor. 11:34, "will I set in order"; in the active voice, in 1 Cor. 16:1, "I gave order" (RV).

3. ***epidiorthoo*** (*1930*), "to set in order" (***epi*** "upon," ***dia***, "through, intensive," and ***orthos***, "straight"), is used in Titus 1:5, in the sense of setting right again what was defective, a commission to Titus, not to add to what the apostle himself had done, but to restore what had fallen into disorder since the apostle had labored in Crete; this is suggested by the ***epi***.

### C. Adverb.

***kathexes*** (*2517*) is translated "in order" in Luke 1:3; Acts 11:4, RV (KJV, "by order); Acts 18:23.

## ORDERLY

***kosmios*** (*2887*), an adjective signifying "decent, modest, orderly" (akin to ***kosmos***, "order, adornment"), is translated "modest" in 1 Tim. 2:9; "orderly" in 3:2, RV (KJV, "of good behavior").

## ORDINANCE

### A. Nouns.

1. ***diatage*** (*1296*) is translated "ordinances," in Rom. 13:2.

2. ***dogma*** (*1378*) is translated "ordinances" in Eph. 2:15 and Col. 2:14.

3. ***ktisis*** (*2937*), "a creation, creature," is translated "ordinance" in 1 Pet. 2:13.

### B. Verb.

***dogmatizo*** (*1379*), akin to A, No. 2, "to decree," signifies, in the middle voice, "to subject oneself to an ordinance," Col. 2:20.

## OVERCOME

1. ***nikao*** (*3528*), is used (a) of God, Rom. 3:4 (a law term), RV, "mightest prevail"; (b) of Christ, John 16:33; Rev. 3:21; 5:5; 17:14; (c) of His followers, Rom. 12:21 (2nd part); 1 John 2:13–14; 4:4; 5:4–5; Rev. 2:7, 11, 17, 26; 3:5, 12, 21; 12:11; 15:2; 21:7; (d) of faith, 1 John 5:4; (e) of evil (passive voice), Rom. 12:21; (f) of predicted human potentates, Rev. 6:2; 11:7; 13:7.

2. ***hettaomai*** (*2274*), "to be made inferior, be enslaved," is rendered "is (are) overcome," in 2 Pet. 2:19–20.

3. ***katakurieuo*** (*2634*) is translated "overcome" in Acts 19:16.

## OVERFLOW, OVERFLOWING

### A. Verbs.

1. ***huperperisseuo*** (*5248*), "to abound more exceedingly," Rom. 5:20, is used in the middle voice in 2 Cor. 7:4, RV, "I overflow (with joy)," KJV, "I am exceeding (joyful)."

2. ***katakluzo*** (*2626*), "to inundate, deluge," is used in the passive voice in 2 Pet. 3:6, of the Flood.

### B. Noun.

***perisseia*** (*4050*) is translated "overflowing" in Jas. 1:21, RV.

## OVERLOOK

***hupereidon*** (*5237*), "to overlook" (an aorist form), is used in Acts 17:30, RV (KJV, "winked at"), i.e., God bore with them without interposing by way of punishment, though the debasing tendencies of idolatry necessarily developed themselves.

## OVERSHADOW

1. ***episkiazo*** (*1982*), "to throw a shadow upon" (***epi***, "over," ***skia***, "a shadow"), "to overshadow," is used (a) of the bright cloud at the Transfiguration, Matt. 17:5; Mark 9:7; Luke 9:34; (b) metaphorically of the power of "the Most High" upon the Virgin Mary, Luke 1:35; (c) of the apostle Peter's shadow upon the sick, Acts 5:15.

2. ***kataskiazo*** (*2683*), lit., "to shadow down," is used of the "overshadowing" (RV) of the cherubim of glory above the mercy seat, Heb. 9:5 (KJV, "shadowing").

## OVERSIGHT (exercise, take)

***episkopeo*** (*1983*), lit., "to look upon" (***epi***, "upon," ***skopeo***, "to look at, contemplate"), is found in 1 Pet. 5:2 (some ancient authorities omit it), "exercising the oversight," RV (KJV, "taking . . ."); "exercising" is the right rendering; the word does not imply the entrance upon such responsibility, but the fulfillment of it. It is not a matter of assuming a position, but of the discharge of the duties. The word is found elsewhere in Heb. 12:15, "looking carefully," RV.

## OVERTAKE

1. ***katalambano*** (*2638*), "to lay hold of," has the significance of "overtaking," metaphorically, in John 12:35 (RV, "overtake," KJV, "come upon") and 1 Thess. 5:4.

2. ***prolambano*** (*4301*), "to anticipate" (***pro***, "before," ***lambano***, "to take"), is used of the act of Mary, in Mark 14:8; of forestalling the less favored at a social meal, 1 Cor. 11:21; of being "overtaken" in any trespass, Gal. 6:1, where the meaning is not that of detecting a person in the act, but of his being caught by the trespass, through his being off his guard (see 5:21 and contrast the premeditated practice of evil in 5:26). The modern Greek version is "even if a man, through lack of circumspection, should fall into any sin."

## OWE

### A. Verbs.

1. ***opheilo*** (*3784*), "to owe, to be a debtor" (in the passive voice, "to be owed, to be due"), is translated by the verb "to owe" in Matt. 18:28 (twice); Luke 7:41; 16:5, 7; Rom. 13:8; in 15:27, RV, "they (gentile converts) owe it" (KJV, "it is their duty"); Philem. 18.

2. ***prosopheilo*** (*4359*), "to owe besides" (***pros***, "in addition," and No. 1), is used in Philem. 19, "thou owest (to me even thine own self) besides," i.e., "thou owest me already as much as Onesimus," debt, and in addition "even thyself" (not "thou owest me much more").

### B. Noun.

***opheiletes*** (*3781*), "a debtor" (akin to A, No. 1), is translated "which owed" in Matt. 18:24, lit., "a debtor (of ten thousand talents)."



## OWN (Adjective)

1. ***gnesios***, primarily, "lawfully begotten," and hence "true, genuine," is translated "own" in the KJV of 1 Tim. 1:2 and Titus 1:4 (RV, "true").

2. In Acts 5:4, "was it not thine own?" is, lit., "did it not remain (***meno***) to thee?"

3. In Jude 6 (1st part), KJV, ***heauton***, "of themselves," "their own" (RV), is rendered "their"; in the 2nd part, RV, ***idios***, one's own, is translated "their proper" (KJV, "their own").

4. In Gal. 1:14, RV, ***sunelikiotes***, is rendered "of mine own age" (KJV, "my equals"; marg., "equals in years").

## OWNER

1. ***kurios*** (*2962*), "one having power" (***kuros***) or "authority, a lord, master," signifies "an owner" in Luke 19:33.

2. ***naukleros*** (*3490*), "a ship owner" (***naus***, "a ship," ***kleros***, "a lot"), "a shipmaster," occurs in Acts 27:11, "(the) owner of the ship."

# P

## PAIN (Noun and Verb)

### A. Nouns.

1. ***ponos*** (*4192*) is translated "pain" in Rev. 16:10; 21:4; "pains" in 16:11.

2. ***odin*** (*5604*), "a birth pang, travail pain," is rendered "travail," metaphorically, in Matt. 24:8 and Mark 13:8, RV (KJV, "sorrows"); by way of comparison, in 1 Thess. 5:3; translated "pains (of death)," Acts 2:24 (RV, "pangs").

### B. Verb.

***bosanizo*** (*928*) primarily signifies "to rub on the touchstone, to put to the test" (from ***basanos***, "a touchstone," a dark stone used in testing metals); hence, "to examine by torture," and, in general, "to distress"; in Rev. 12:2, "in pain," RV (KJV, "pained"), in connection with parturition.

## PALACE

***praitorion*** (*4232*) signified originally "a general's (praetor's) tent." Then it was applied to "the council of army officers"; then to "the official residence of the governor of a province"; finally, to "the imperial bodyguard." In the KJV the word appears only once, Mark 15:16, "the hall, called Praetorium" (RV, "within the court which is the Praetorium," marg., "palace"); in the Greek of the NT it also occurs in Matt. 27:27, KJV, "the common hall," marg., "the governor's house"; RV, "palace," see marg.; John 18:28 (twice), KJV, "the hall of judgment"; and "judgment hall," marg., "Pilate's house," RV, "palace"; 18:33 and 19:9, KJV, "judgment hall," RV, "palace," see marg.; so in Acts 23:35; in Phil. 1:13, KJV, "in all the palace," marg., "Caesar's court," RV, "throughout the whole praetorian guard," marg., "in the whole Praetorium."

In the Gospels the term denotes the official residence in Jerusalem of the Roman governor, and the various translations of it in our versions arose from a desire either to indicate the special purpose for which that residence was used on the occasion in question, or to explain what particular building was intended. But whatever building the governor occupied was the Praetorium. It is most probable that in Jerusalem he resided in the well-known palace of Herod. Pilate's residence has been identified with the castle of Antonia, which was occupied by the regular garrison. The probability is that it was the same as Herod's palace. Herod's palace in Caesarea was used as the Praetorium there, and the expression in Acts 23:35, marg., "Herod's praetorium," is abbreviated from "the praetorium of Herod's palace."

In Phil. 1:13, marg., "the whole Praetorium" has been variously explained. It has been spoken of as "the palace," in connection with 4:22, where allusion is made to believers who belong to Caesar's household. Others have understood it of the barracks of the "praetorian" guard, but Lightfoot shows that this use of the word cannot be established, neither can it be regarded as referring to the barracks of the "palace" guard. The phrase "and to all the rest" in 1:13 indicates that persons are meant. Mommsen, followed by Ramsay (*St. Paul the Traveller*, p. 357) regards it as improbable that the apostle was committed to the "praetorian" guard and holds the view that Julius the centurion, who brought Paul to Rome, belonged to a corps drafted from legions in the provinces, whose duty it was to supervise the corn supply and perform police service, and that Julius probably delivered his prisoners to the commander of his corps. Eventually Paul's case came before the praetorian council, which is the "praetorium" alluded to by the apostle, and the phrase "to all the rest" refers to the audience of the trial.

## PALM (of the hand)

### *Old Testament*

***kap*** (3709), "palm (of hand)." ***kap*** is often translated "hand," with the meaning of a body part on the end of arms (including the fingers), very important for manipulation and ability to do things, 2 Sam. 18:14. Also it is translated "palm of the hand," meaning the padded part of the hand, when face up can make a shallow pool to hold liquid in the hand, Lev. 14:15. Sometimes translated "sole of the foot, paw" meaning the padded, very bottom part of the foot, that makes contact with the ground (of any footed creature), Deut. 58:56; Lev. 11:27. ***kap*** can also be translated "control," meaning to be under the power of another, Judg. 6:13.

***kap*** can also be different useful objects. It can be translated "handle," meaning a part of a door lock and bolt assembly that you grab to lock, close, or open, Song. Sol. 5:5. Also it can be translated "pocket of a sling," meaning the part of a sling that holds the stone before release, 1 Sam. 25:29. Another translation is "socket, joint" meaning the opening or hollow place of a joint to connect the parts, Gen. 32:33. Lastly for objects, it can be translated "dish, shallow pan," meaning a metal container, shallow (as an extension of the shallow part of the hand), Num. 7:14–80. Note: in context this pan refers to an incense burning container.

***kap*** can also be used in combination with other Hebrew words; ***kap*** is translated "handful," meaning an amount that can be held in the hand, as a general measure of volume Lev. 9:17; 1 Kin. 17:12. Note: it is not clear if the hand is clenched or open in the measure. ***sim nephesh be kap***, can be translated "live in danger," (lit. take life in palm), meaning to take a great risk, that might even endanger one's life, 1 Sam. 19:5.

## PAPER

***chartes*** (*5489*), "a sheet of paper made of strips of papyrus," 2 John 12. The pith of the stem of the plant was cut into thin strips, placed side by side to form a sheet. Another layer was laid upon this at right angles to it. The two layers were united by moisture and pressure with the natural sap of the plant. The sheets, after being dried and polished, were ready for use. Normally, the writing is on that side of the papyrus on which the fibers lie horizontally, parallel to the length of the roll, but where the material was scarce the writer used the other side also (cf. Rev. 5:1).

## PARABLE

1. ***parabole*** (*3850*) lit. denotes "a placing beside" (akin to ***paraballo***, "to throw" or "lay beside, to compare"). It signifies "a placing of one thing beside another" with a view to comparison (some consider that the thought of comparison is not necessarily contained in the word). In the NT it is found outside the gospels, only in Heb. 9:9 and 11:19. It is generally used of a somewhat lengthy utterance or narrative drawn from nature or human circumstances, the object of which is to set forth a spiritual lesson, e.g., those in Matt. 13 and Synoptic parallels; sometimes it is used of a short saying or proverb, e.g., Matt. 15:15; Mark 3:23; 7:17; Luke 4:23; 5:36; 6:39. It is the lesson that is of value; the hearer must catch the analogy if he is to be instructed (this is true also of a proverb). Such a narrative or saying, dealing with earthly things with a spiritual meaning, is distinct from a fable, which attributes to things what does not belong to them in nature.

2. ***paroimia*** (*3942*) denotes "a wayside saying" (from ***paroimos***, "by the way"), "a byword," "maxim," or "problem," 2 Pet. 2:22. The word is sometimes spoken of as a "parable," John 10:6, i.e., a figurative discourse (RV marg., "proverb"); see also 16:25, 29, where the word is rendered "proverbs" (marg. "parables") and "proverb."

## PARADISE

***paradeisos*** (*3857*) is an Oriental word, first used by the historian Xenophon, denoting "the parks of Persian kings and nobles." It is of Persian origin (Old Pers. ***pairidaeza***, akin to Gk. ***peri***, "around," and ***teichos***, "a wall") whence it passed into Greek.

In Luke 23:43, the promise of the Lord to the repentant robber was fulfilled the same day; Christ, at His death, having committed His spirit to the Father, went in spirit immediately into Heaven itself, the dwelling place of God (the Lord's mention of the place as "paradise" must have been a great comfort to the malefactor; to the oriental mind it expressed the sum total of blessedness). Thither the apostle Paul was caught up, 2 Cor. 12:4, spoken of as "the third heaven" (v. 3 does not introduce a different vision), beyond the heavens of the natural creation (see Heb. 4:14, RV, with reference to the Ascension). The same region is mentioned in Rev. 2:7, where the "tree of life," the figurative antitype of that in Eden, held out to the overcomer, is spoken of as being in "the Paradise of God" (RV), marg., "garden," as in Gen. 2:8.

## PARCHMENT

***membrana*** (*3200*) is a Latin word, properly an adjective, from ***membrum***, "a limb," but denoting "skin, parchment." The word ***membrana*** is found in 2 Tim. 4:13, where Timothy is asked to bring to the apostle "the books, especially the parchments." The writing material was prepared from the skin of the sheep or goat. The skins were first soaked in lime for the purpose of removing the hair, and then shaved, washed, dried, stretched and ground or smoothed with fine chalk or lime and pumice stone. The finest kind is called "vellum," and is made from the skins of calves or kids.

## PARENTS

***goneus*** (*1118*), "a begetter, a father" (akin to ***ginomai***, "to come into being, become"), is used in the plural in the NT, Matt. 10:21; Mark 13:12; six times in Luke (in Luke 2:43, RV, "His parents," KJV, "Joseph and His mother"); six in

John; elsewhere, Rom. 1:30; 2 Cor. 12:14 (twice); Eph. 6:1; Col. 3:20; 2 Tim. 3:2.

## PARTAKE, PARTAKER

### A. Nouns.

1. ***koinonos*** (*2844*), an adjective, signifying "having in common" (***koinos***, "common"), is used as a noun, denoting "a companion, partner, partaker," translated "partakers" in Matt. 23:30; 1 Cor. 10:18, KJV; 2 Cor. 1:7; Heb. 10:33, RV; 2 Pet. 1:4; "partaker" in 1 Pet. 5:1.

2. ***sunkoinonos*** (*4791*) denotes "partaking jointly with" (***sun***, and No. 1), Rom. 11:17, RV, "(didst become) partaker with them" (KJV, "partakest"); 1 Cor. 9:23, RV, "a joint partaker," i.e., with the gospel, as cooperating in its activity; the KJV misplaces the "with" by attaching it to the superfluous italicized pronoun "*you*"; Phil. 1:7, "partakers with (me of grace)," RV, and KJV marg.; not as KJV text, "partakers (of my grace)"; Rev. 1:9, "partaker with (you in the tribulation, etc.)," KJV, "companion."

### B. Verbs.

1. ***koinoneo*** (*2841*), "to have a share of, to share with, take part in" (akin to A, No. 1), is translated "to be partaker of" in 1 Tim. 5:22; Heb. 2:14 (1st part), KJV, "are partakers of," RV, "are sharers in"; 1 Pet. 4:13; 2 John 11, RV, "partaketh in" (KJV, "is partaker of"); in the passive voice in Rom. 15:27.

2. ***metecho*** (*3348*), "to partake of, share in" (***meta***, "with," ***echo***, "to have"), is translated "of partaking" in 1 Cor. 9:10, RV (KJV, "be partaker of"); "partake of" in 9:12, RV (KJV, "be partakers of"); so in 10:17, 21: in v. 30 "partake"; in Heb. 2:14, the KJV "took part of" is awkward; Christ "partook of" flesh and blood, RV; cf. No. 1 in this verse; in Heb. 5:13, metaphorically, of receiving elementary spiritual teaching, RV, "partaketh of (milk)," KJV, "useth"; in Heb. 7:13, it is said of Christ (the antitype of Melchizedek) as "belonging to" (so RV) or "partaking of" (RV marg.) another tribe than that of Levi (KJV, "pertaineth to").

3. ***antilambano*** (*482*), "to take hold of, to lay hold of" something before one, has the meaning "to partake of" in 1 Tim. 6:2, RV, "partake of," marg., "lay hold of," KJV, "are . . . partakers of" (***anti***, "in return for," ***lambano***, "to take or receive"); the benefit mentioned as "partaken" of by the masters would seem to be the improved quality of the service rendered; the benefit of redemption is not in view here.

4. ***metalambano*** (*3335*), "to have, or get, a share of," is translated "to be partaker (or partakers) of" in 2 Tim. 2:6 and Heb. 12:10.

5. ***summerizo*** (*4829*), primarily, "to distribute in shares" (***sun***, "with," ***meros***, "a part"), in the middle voice, "to have a share in," is used in 1 Cor. 9:13, KJV, "are partakers with (the altar)," RV, "have their portion with," i.e., they feed with others on that which, having been sacrificed, has been placed upon an altar; so the believer feeds upon Christ (who is the altar in Heb. 13:10).

## PARTIAL, PARTIALITY

### A. Verb.

***diakrino*** (*1252*), "to separate, distinguish, discern, judge, decide," Jas. 2:4.

### B. Noun.

***prosklisis*** (*4346*) denotes "inclination" (***pros***, "towards," ***klino***, "to lean"); it is used with ***kata*** in 1 Tim. 5:21, lit., "according to partiality."

### C. Adjective.

***adiakritos*** (*87*) primarily signifies "not to be parted," hence, "without uncertainty," or "indecision," Jas. 3:17, KJV, "without partiality" (marg. "wrangling"), RV, "without variance" (marg., "Or, doubtfulness Or, partiality"). In the Sept., Prov. 25:1.

## PARTITION

***phragmos*** (*5418*), primarily "a fencing" in (akin to ***phrasso***, "to fence in, stop, close"), is used metaphorically in Eph. 2:14, of "the middle wall of partition"; "the partition" is epexegetic of "the middle wall," namely, the "partition" between Jew and Gentile. J. A. Robinson suggests that Paul had in mind the barrier between the outer and inner courts of the Temple, notices fixed to which warned Gentiles not to proceed further on pain of death.

## PARTNER

1. ***koinonos*** (*2844*), an adjective, signifying "having in common" (***koinos***), is used as a noun, "partners" in Luke 5:10, "partner" in 2 Cor. 8:23; Philem. 17 (in spiritual life and business).

2. ***metochos*** (*3353*), an adjective, signifying "having with, sharing," is used as a noun, "partners" in Luke 5:7.

## PASS, PASS BY, COME TO PASS

1. ***parerchomai*** (*3928*), from ***para***, "by," ***erchomai***, "to come" or "go," denotes (I), literally, "to pass, pass by," (a) of persons, Matt. 8:28; Mark 6:48; Luke 18:37; Acts 16:8; (b) of things, Matt. 26:39, 42; of time, Matt. 14:15; Mark 14:35; Acts 27:9, KJV, "past" (RV, "gone by"); 1 Pet. 4:3; (II), metaphorically, (a) "to pass away, to perish," Matt. 5:18; 24:34, 35; Mark 13:30, 31;

Luke 16:17; 21:32, 33; 2 Cor. 5:17; Jas. 1:10; 2 Pet. 3:10; (b) "to pass by, disregard, neglect, pass over," Luke 11:42; 15:29, "transgressed."

2. ***dierchomai*** (*1330*) denotes "to pass through or over," (a) of persons, e.g., Matt. 12:43, RV, "passeth (KJV, walketh) through"; Mark 4:35, KJV, "pass (RV, go) over"; Luke 19:1, 4; Heb. 4:14, RV, "passed through" (KJV "into"); Christ "passed through" the created heavens to the throne of God; (b) of things, e.g., Matt. 19:24, "to go through"; Luke 2:35, "shall pierce through" (metaphorically of a sword).

3. ***aperchomai*** (*565*), "to go away," is rendered "to pass" in Rev. 9:12; 11:14; "passed away" in Rev. 21:4.

## PASSION

### A. Noun.

***pathema*** (*3804*), "a suffering" or "a passive emotion," is translated "passions" in Rom. 7:5, RV, "(sinful) passions," KJV, "motions," and Gal. 5:24, RV.

### B. Verb.

***pascho*** (*3958*), "to suffer," is used as a noun, in the aorist infinitive with the article, and translated "passion" in Acts 1:3, of the suffering of Christ at Calvary.

### C. Adjective.

***homoiopathes*** (*3663*), "of like feelings or affections," is rendered "of like passions" in Acts 14:15 (RV marg., "nature"); in Jas. 5:17, RV, ditto (KJV, "subject to like passions").

## PASSOVER

***pascha*** (*3957*), the Greek spelling of the Aramaic word for the Passover, from the Hebrew ***pasach***, "to pass over, to spare," a feast instituted by God in commemoration of the deliverance of Israel from Egypt, and anticipatory of the expiatory sacrifice of Christ. The word signifies (I) "the Passover Feast," e.g., Matt. 26:2; John 2:13, 23; 6:4; 11:55; 12:1; 13:1; 18:39; 19:14; Acts 12:4; Heb. 11:28; (II), by metonymy, (a) "the Paschal Supper," Matt. 26:18, 19; Mark 14:16; Luke 22:8, 13; (b) "the Paschal lamb," e.g., Mark 14:12, cf. Exod. 12:21; Luke 22:7; (c) "Christ Himself," 1 Cor. 5:7.

## PASTURE

***nome*** (*3542*) denotes (a) "pasture, pasturage," figuratively in John 10:9; (b) "grazing, feeding," figuratively in 2 Tim. 2:17, of the doctrines of false teachers, lit., "their word will have feeding as a gangrene."

## PATIENCE, PATIENT, PATIENTLY

### A. Nouns.

1. ***hupomone*** (*5281*), lit., "an abiding under" (***hupo***, "under," ***meno***, "to abide"), is almost invariably rendered "patience." "Patience, which grows only in trial"; Jas. 1:3 may be passive, i.e., "endurance," as, (a) in trials, generally, Luke 21:19 (which is to be understood by Matt. 24:13), cf. Rom. 12:12; Jas. 1:12; (b) in trials incident to service in the gospel, 2 Cor. 6:4; 12:12; 2 Tim. 3:10; (c) under chastisement, which is trial viewed as coming from the hand of God our Father, Heb. 12:7; (d) under undeserved affliction, 1 Pet. 2:20; or active, i.e. "persistence, perseverance," as (e) in well doing, Rom. 2:7 (KJV, "patient continuance"); (f) in fruit bearing, Luke 8:15; (g) in running the appointed race, Heb. 12:1.

2. ***makrothumia*** (*3115*), "longsuffering," is rendered "patience" in Heb. 6:12; Jas. 5:10.

### B. Verbs.

1. ***hupomeno*** (*5278*), akin to A, No. 1, (a) used intransitively, means "to tarry behind, still abide," Luke 2:43; Acts 17:14; (b) transitively, "to wait for," Rom. 8:24 (in some mss.), "to bear patiently, endure," translated "patient" (present participle) in Rom. 12:12; "ye take it patiently," 1 Pet. 2:20 (twice).

2. ***makrothumeo*** (*3114*), akin to A, No. 2, "to be long-tempered," is translated "to have patience," or "to be patient," in Matt. 18:26, 29; 1 Thess. 5:14, KJV (RV, "be longsuffering"); Jas. 5:7 (1st part, "be patient"; 2nd part, RV, "being patient," KJV, "hath long patience"); in Heb. 6:15, RV, "having (KJV, after he had) patiently endured."

P

## PATRIARCH

***patriarches*** (*3966*), from ***patria***, "a family," and ***archo***, "to rule," is found in Acts 2:29; 7:8, 9; Heb. 7:4.

## PATTERN

### A. Nouns.

1. ***tupos*** (*5179*) is translated "pattern" in Titus 2:7, KJV; Heb. 8:5 (KJV and RV).

2. ***hupotuposis*** (*5296*) is translated "pattern" in 1 Tim. 1:16, KJV; 2 Tim. 1:13, RV.

### B. Adjective.

***antitupos*** (*499*) is translated "like in pattern" in Heb. 9:24, RV.

## PAVEMENT

***lithostrotos*** (*3038*), an adjective, denoting "paved with stones" (***lithos***, "a stone," and ***stronnuo***, "to spread"), especially of tesselated work, is used as a noun in John 19:13, of a place near the Praetorium in Jerusalem, called Gabbatha, a Greek transliteration of an Aramaic word.

## PAY (Verb), PAYMENT

1. ***apodidomi*** (*591*), "to give back, to render what is due, to pay," used of various obligations in this respect, is translated "to pay, to make payment," in Matt. 5:26; 18:25 (twice), 26, 28, 29, 30, 34; 20:8, RV (KJV, "give").

2. ***teleo*** (*5055*), "to bring to an end, complete, fulfill," has the meaning "to pay" in Matt. 17:24 and Rom. 13:6.

## PEACE, PEACEABLE, PEACEABLY

### *Old Testament*

**A. Nouns.**

***shalom*** (7965), "peace; completeness; welfare; health." The use of ***shalom*** is frequent (237 times) and varied in its semantic range. The first two occurrences in Genesis already indicate the changes in meaning, "at ease," Gen. 15:15; and "unharmed," Gen. 26:29. Yet, both uses are essentially the same, as they express the root meaning of "to be whole," Ps. 41:9; cf. Jer. 20:10. The relationship is one of harmony and wholeness, which is the opposite of the state of strife and war, Ps. 120:7. ***shalom*** as a harmonious state of the soul and mind encourages the development of the faculties and powers. The state of being at ease is experienced both externally and internally. In Hebrew it finds expression in the phrase ***beshalom*** ("in peace"): "I will both lay me down in peace [***beshalom***], and sleep: for thou, Lord, only makest me dwell in safety," Ps. 4:8.

Closely associated to the above is the meaning "welfare," specifically personal "welfare" or "health," 2 Sam. 20:9. ***shalom*** also signifies "peace," indicative of a prosperous relationship between two or more parties. ***shalom*** in this sense finds expression in speech, Jer. 9:8; in diplomacy, Judg. 4:17; in warfare, Deut. 20:11.

Isaiah prophesied concerning the "prince of peace," Isa. 9:6, whose kingdom was to introduce a government of "peace," Isa. 9:7. Ezekiel spoke about the new covenant as one of "peace," Ezek. 37:26. Psalm 122 is one of those great psalms in celebration of and in prayer for the "peace of Jerusalem."

Another related noun is ***shelem***, "peace offering," Exod. 24:5.

**B. Verbs.**

***shalem*** (7999), "to be complete, be sound," 1 Kings 9:25. Another verb, ***shalam***, means "to make peace," Prov. 16:7.

**C. Adjective.**

***shalem*** (8003), "complete; perfect," Gen. 15:16; the word means "perfect" in Deut. 25:15.

### *New Testament*

**A. Noun.**

***eirene*** (*1515*) occurs in each of the books of the NT, save 1 John and except in Acts 7:26 ['(at) one again'] it is translated "peace" in the RV. It describes (a) harmonious relationships between men, Matt. 10:34; Rom. 14:19; (b) between nations, Luke 14:32; Acts 12:20; Rev. 6:4; (c) friendliness, Acts 15:33; 1 Cor. 16:11; Heb. 11:31; (d) freedom from molestation, Luke 11:21; 19:42; Acts 9:31 (RV, 'peace,' KJV, 'rest'); 16:36; (e) order, in the State, Acts 24:2 (RV, 'peace,' KJV, 'quietness'); in the churches, 1 Cor. 14:33; (f) the harmonized relationships between God and man, accomplished through the gospel, Acts 10:36; Eph. 2:17; (g) the sense of rest and contentment consequent thereon, Matt. 10:13; Mark 5:34; Luke 1:79; 2:29; John 14:27; Rom. 1:7; 3:17; 8:6; in certain passages this idea is not distinguishable from the last, Rom. 5:1.

"The God of peace" is a title used in Rom. 15:33; 16:20; Phil. 4:9; 1 Thess. 5:23; Heb. 13:20; cf. 1 Cor. 14:33; 2 Cor. 13:11. The corresponding Heb. word ***shalom*** primarily signifies "wholeness": see its use in Josh. 8:31, "unhewn"; Ruth 2:12, "full"; Neh. 6:15, "finished"; Isa. 42:19, marg., "made perfect." Hence there is a close connection between the title in 1 Thess. 5:23 and the word ***holokleros***, "entire," in that verse.

**B. Verb.**

***eireneuo*** (*1514*), primarily, "to bring to peace, reconcile," denotes in the NT, "to keep peace or to be at peace": in Mark 9:50, RV, the Lord bids the disciples "be at peace" with one another, gently rebuking their ambitious desires; in Rom. 12:18 (RV, "be at peace," KJV, "live peaceably") the limitation "if it be possible, as much as in you liveth," seems due to the phrase "with all men," but is not intended to excuse any evasion of the obligation imposed by the command; in 2 Cor. 13:11 it is rendered "live in peace," a general exhortation to believers; in 1 Thess. 5:13, "be at peace (among yourselves)."

**C. Adjective.**

***eirenikos*** (*1516*), akin to A, denotes "peaceful." It is used (a) of the fruit of righteousness, Heb. 12:11, "peaceable" (or "peaceful") because it is produced in communion with God the Father, through His chastening; (b) of "the wisdom that is from above," Jas. 3:17.

## PEACE (hold one's)

***sigao*** *(4601)* signifies (a), used intransitively, "to be silent" (from ***sige***, "silence"), translated "to hold one's peace," in Luke 9:36; 18:39; 20:26; Acts 12:17; 15:13 (in v. 12, "kept silence"; similarly rendered in 1 Cor. 14:28, 30, KJV, "hold his peace," 34); (b) used transitively, "to keep secret"; in the passive voice, "to be kept secret," Rom. 16:25, RV, "hath been kept in silence."

## PEACEMAKER

***eirenopoios*** *(1518)*, an adjective signifying peace making (***eirene***, and ***poieo***, "to make"), is used in Matt. 5:9, "peacemakers."

## PENTECOST

***pentekostos*** *(4005)*, an adjective denoting "fiftieth," is used as a noun, with "day" understood, i.e., the "fiftieth" day after the Passover, counting from the second day of the Feast, Acts 2:1; 20:16; 1 Cor. 16:8. For the divine instructions to Israel see Exod. 23:16; 34:22; Lev. 23:15–21; Num. 28:26–31; Deut. 16:9–11.

## PEOPLE

### *Old Testament*

***'am*** (5971), "people; relative." The word bears subjective and personal overtones. First, ***'am*** represents a familial relationship. In Ruth 3:11 the word means "male kinsmen." In the plural the word refers to all the individuals who are related to a person through his father, Lev. 21:4. Second, ***'am*** may signify those relatives (including women and children) who are grouped together locally whether or not they permanently inhabit a given location, Gen. 32:7. Third, this word may refer to the whole of a nation formed and united primarily by their descent from a common ancestor, Gen. 11:6. ***'am*** may also include those who enter by religious adoption and marriage, Exod. 1:9. Later the basic unity in a common covenant relationship with God becomes the unifying factor underlying ***'am***. When they left Egypt, the people of Israel were joined by many others, Exod. 12:38.

***'am*** can mean all those physical ancestors who lived previously and are now dead, Gen. 25:8. There might be covenantal overtones here in the sense that Abraham was gathered to all those who were true believers. Jesus argued that such texts taught the reality of life after death, Matt. 22:32.

***'am*** can represent the individuals who together form a familial (and covenantal) group within a larger group, Judg. 5:18 There is no distinction between the concepts "militia" and "kinsmen," Josh. 8:1, 5. ***'am*** may signify the inhabitants of a city regardless of their familial or covenantal relationship; it is a territorial or political term, Ruth 4:9.

Finally, sometimes ***'am*** used of an entire nation has political and territorial overtones. As such it may be paralleled to the Hebrew word with such overtones (***goy***), Deut. 14:2; cf. Exod. 19:5–6.

### *New Testament*

1. ***laos*** (2992) is used of (a) "the people at large," especially of people assembled, e.g., Matt. 27:25; Luke 1:21; 3:15; Acts 4:27; (b) "a people of the same race and language," e.g., Rev. 5:9; in the plural, e.g., Luke 2:31; Rom. 15:11; Rev. 7:9; 11:9; especially of Israel, e.g., Matt. 2:6; 4:23; John 11:50; Acts 4:8; Heb. 2:17; in distinction from their rulers and priests, e.g., Matt. 26:5; Luke 20:19; Heb. 5:3; in distinction from Gentiles, e.g., Acts 26:17, 23; Rom. 15:10; (c) of Christians as the people of God, e.g., Acts 15:14; Titus 2:14; Heb. 4:9; 1 Pet. 2:9.

2. ***demos*** *(1218)*, "the common people, the people generally" (Eng., "demagogue," "democracy," etc.), especially the mass of the "people" assembled in a public place, Acts 12:22; 17:5; 19:30, 33.

3. ***ethnos*** *(1484)* denotes (a) "a nation," e.g., Matt. 24:7; Acts 10:35; "the Jewish people," e.g., Luke 7:5; Acts 10:22; 28:19; (b) in the plural, "the rest of mankind" in distinction from Israel or the Jews, e.g., Matt. 4:15; Acts 28:28; (c) "the people of a city," Acts 8:9; (d) gentile Christians, e.g., Rom. 10:19; 11:13; 15:27; Gal. 2:14.



## PERCEIVE

1. ***ginosko*** *(1097)*, "to know by experience and observation," is translated "to perceive" in Matt. 12:15, RV (KJV, "knew"); 16:8; 21:45; 22:18; 26:10, RV, (KJV, "understood"); Mark 8:17; 12:12 and 15:10, RV (KJV, "knew"); so Luke 9:11; 18:34; in Luke 7:39, RV (KJV, "known"); 20:19; John 6:15; 8:27, RV (KJV, "understood"); 16:19, RV (KJV, "knew"); Acts 23:6; Gal. 2:9; in 1 John 3:16, KJV, "perceive" (RV, "know," perfect tense, lit., "we have perceived," and therefore "know").

2. ***epiginosko*** *(1921)*, a strengthened form of No. 1, "to gain a full knowledge of, to become fully acquainted with," is translated "to perceive" in Mark 5:30, RV (KJV, "knowing"); Luke 1:22; 5:22; Acts 19:34, RV (KJV, knew).

## PERFECT (Adjective and Verb), PERFECTLY

### *Old Testament*

### A. Adjective.

***tamim*** (8549), "perfect; blameless; sincerity; entire; whole; complete; full." ***tamim*** means "complete," in the sense of the entire or whole thing, Lev. 3:9; a "whole" time period, Josh. 10:13; Lev. 23:15; a "full" year, Lev. 25:30. This word may also mean "intact," or not cut up into pieces, Ezek. 15:5. ***tamim*** may mean incontestable or free from objection, so "perfect," Deut. 18:13; 32:4; meets all the requirements of God's law, cf. Ps. 18:23.

In several contexts the word has a wider background. When one is described by it, there is nothing in his outward activities or internal disposition that is odious to God, Gen. 6:9. This word describes his entire relationship to God. In Judg. 9:16, where ***tamim*** describes a relationship between men it is clear that more than mere external activity is meant, Gen. 17:1; with Rom. 4 where Paul argues that Abraham fulfilled God's condition but that he did so only through faith.

### B. Noun.

***tom*** (8537), "completeness," Job 21:23; innocency or simplicity, 2 Sam. 15:11; integrity, Gen. 20:5.

### C. Verb.

***tamam*** (8552), "to be complete, be finished, be consumed, be without blame," Gen. 47:18.

### *New Testament*

### A. Adjectives.

1. ***teleios*** (*5049*) signifies "having reached its end" (***telos***), "finished, complete perfect." It is used (I) of persons, (a) primarily of physical development, then, with ethical import, "fully grown, mature," 1 Cor. 2:6; 14:20 ("men"; marg., "of full age"); Eph. 4:13; Phil. 3:15; Col. 1:28; 4:12; in Heb. 5:14, RV, "fullgrown" (marg., "perfect"), KJV, "of full age" (marg., "perfect"); (b) "complete," conveying the idea of goodness without necessary reference to maturity or what is expressed under (a) Matt. 5:48; 19:21; Jas. 1:4 (2nd part); 3:2. It is used thus of God in Matt. 5:48; (II), of "things, complete, perfect," Rom. 12:2; 1 Cor. 13:10 (referring to the complete revelation of God's will and ways, whether in the completed Scriptures or in the hereafter); Jas. 1:4 (of the work of patience); v. 25; 1 John 4:18.

2. ***teleioteros*** (*5046**), the comparative degree of No. 1, is used in Heb. 9:11, of the very presence of God.

### B. Verbs.

1. ***teleioo*** (*5048*), "to bring to an end by completing or perfecting," is used (I) of "accomplishing"; (II), of "bringing to completeness," (a) of persons: of Christ's assured completion of His earthly course, in the accomplishment of the Father's will, the successive stages culminating in His death, Luke 13:32; Heb. 2:10, to make Him "perfect," legally and officially, for all that He would be to His people on the ground of His sacrifice; cf. 5:9; 7:28, RV, "perfected" (KJV, "consecrated"); of His saints, John 17:23, RV, "perfected" (KJV, "made perfect"); Phil. 3:12; Heb. 10:14; 11:40 (of resurrection glory); 12:23 (of the departed saints); 1 John 4:18, of former priests (negatively), Heb. 9:9; similarly of Israelites under the Aaronic priesthood, 10:1; (b) of things, Heb. 7:19 (of the ineffectiveness of the Law); Jas. 2:22 (of faith made "perfect" by works); 1 John 2:5, of the love of God operating through him who keeps His word; 4:12, of the love of God in the case of those who love one another; 4:17, of the love of God as "made perfect with" (RV) those who abide in God, giving them to be possessed of the very character of God, by reason of which "as He is, even so are they in this world."

2. ***epiteleo*** (*2005*), "to bring through to the end" (***epi***, intensive, in the sense of "fully," and ***teleo***, "to complete"), is used in the middle voice in Gal. 3:3, "are ye (now) perfected," continuous present tense, indicating a process, lit., "are ye now perfecting yourselves"; in 2 Cor. 7:1, "perfecting (holiness)"; in Phil. 1:6, RV, "will perfect (it)," KJV, "will perform."

3. ***katartizo*** (*2675*), "to render fit, complete," is used of mending nets, Matt. 4:21; Mark 1:19, and is translated "restore" in Gal. 6:1. It does not necessarily imply, however, that that to which it is applied has been damaged, though it may do so, as in these passages; it signifies, rather, right ordering and arrangement, Heb. 11:3, "framed"; it points out the path of progress, as in Matt. 21:16; Luke 6:40; cf. 2 Cor. 13:9; Eph. 4:12, where corresponding nouns occur. It indicates the close relationship between character and destiny, Rom. 9:22, "fitted." It expresses the pastor's desire for the flock, in prayer, Heb. 13:21, and in exhortation, 1 Cor. 1:10, RV, "perfected" (KJV, "perfectly joined"); 2 Cor. 13:11, as well as his conviction of God's purpose for them, 1 Pet. 5:10. It is used of the Incarnation of the Word in Heb. 10:5, "prepare," quoted from Ps. 40:6 (Sept.), where it is apparently intended to describe the unique creative act involved in the Virgin Birth,

Luke 1:35. In 1 Thess. 3:10 it means to supply what is necessary, as the succeeding words show."*

### C. Adverbs.

1. ***akribos*** (*199*), accurately, is translated "perfectly" in 1 Thess. 5:2, where it suggests that Paul and his companions were careful ministers of the Word.

2. ***akribesteron*** (*197*), the comparative degree of No. 1, Acts 18:26; 23:15.

3. ***teleios*** (*5049*), "perfectly," is so translated in 1 Pet. 1:13, RV (KJV, "to the end"), of setting one's hope on coming grace.

## PERFECTION, PERFECTING (noun), PERFECTNESS

### A. Nouns.

1. ***katartisis*** (*2676*), "a making fit," is used figuratively in an ethical sense in 2 Cor. 13:9, RV, "perfecting" (KJV, "perfection"), implying a process leading to consummation (akin to ***katartizo***).

2. ***katartismos*** (*2677*) denotes, in much the same way as No. 1, "a fitting or preparing fully," Eph. 4:12.

3. ***teleiosis*** (*5050*) denotes "a fulfillment, completion, perfection, an end accomplished as the effect of a process," Heb. 7:11; in Luke 1:45, RV, "fulfillment" (KJV, "performance").

4. ***teleiotes*** (*5047*) denotes much the same as No. 3, but stressing perhaps the actual accomplishment of the end in view, Col. 3:14, "perfectness"; Heb. 6:1, "perfection."

### B. Verb.

***telesphoreo*** (*5052*), "to bring to a completion" or "an end in view" (***telos***, "an end," ***phero***, "to bear"), is said of plants, Luke 8:14.

## PERFORM, PERFORMANCE

1. ***teleo*** (*5055*), "to finish," is translated "performed" in Luke 2:39, KJV.

2. ***apoteleo*** (*658*), "to bring to an end, accomplish," is translated "I perform" in Luke 13:32, RV (KJV, "I do"); some mss. have No. 3; in Jas. 1:15, it is used of sin, "fullgrown" RV (KJV, "finished").

3. ***epiteleo*** (*2005*), Rom. 15:28, KJV, "performed" (RV, "accomplished"); 2 Cor. 8:11, KJV, "perform" (RV, "complete"); Phil. 1:6, KJV, "perform" (RV, "perfect").

4. ***poieo*** (*4160*), "to do," is translated "to perform" in Rom. 4:21; in Luke 1:72, KJV (RV, "to show").

5. ***apodidomi*** (*591*), "to give back, or in full," is translated "thou . . . shalt perform" in Matt. 5:33.

## PERISH

#### *Old Testament*

### A. Verb.

***'abad*** (6), "to perish, die, be lost, go astray, go to ruin, succumb, be carried off, fail." Basically ***'abad*** represents the disappearance of someone or something. In its strongest sense the word means "to die or to cease to exist," Lev. 26:38; or "utterly destroy," Num. 33:52. A somewhat different emphasis of ***'abad*** is "to go to ruin" or "to be ruined," Exod. 10:7; Num. 21:29–30. Closely related to the immediately preceding emphasis is that of "to succumb." This use of ***'abad*** focuses on the process rather than the conclusion, Num. 17:12–13; 18:5.

***'abad*** can also speak of being carried off to death or destruction by some means, Num. 16:33. This same nuance appears when God says the people will "perish" from off the land if they do not keep the covenant, Deut. 4:26. The verb may mean to disappear but not be destroyed, in other words "to be lost," Deut. 22:3; so, "lost sheep," Jer. 50:6. Another nuance of the verb is "to go astray" in the sense of wandering, Deut. 26:5.

Finally, ***'abad*** can be applied to human qualities which are lessening or have lessened, Deut. 32:28. The word can also be used of the failure of human wisdom as in Ps. 146:4: as for men "his breath goeth forth, he returneth to his earth; in that very day his thoughts perish."

P

### B. Nouns.

There are three nouns related to the verb. ***'abedah***, which is found 4 times, refers to a "thing which has been lost," Exod. 22:9. The noun ***'abaddon*** occurs 6 times and means "the place of destruction," Job 26:6. ***'abdan*** occurs once with the meaning "destruction," Esth. 9:5.

#### *New Testament*

1. ***apollumi*** (*622*), "to destroy," signifies, in the middle voice, "to perish," and is thus used (a) of things, e.g., Matt. 5:29, 30; Luke 5:37; Acts 27:34, RV, "perish" (in some texts ***pipto***, "to fall," as KJV); Heb. 1:11; 2 Pet. 3:6; Rev. 18:14 (2nd part), RV, "perished" (in some texts ***aperchomai***, "to depart," as KJV); (b) of persons, e.g., Matt. 8:25; John 3:(15), 16; 10:28; 17:12, RV, "perished" (KJV, "is lost"); Rom. 2:12; 1 Cor. 1:18, lit., "the perishing," where the perfective force of the verb implies the completion of the process of destruction; 8:11; 15:18; 2 Pet. 3:9; Jude 11.

2. ***sunapollumi*** *(4881)*, in the middle voice, denotes "to perish together" (***sun***, "with," and No. 1), Heb. 11:31.

3. ***aphanizo*** *(853)*, "to make unseen" (***a***, negative, ***phaino***, "to cause to appear"), in the passive voice, is translated "perish" in Acts 13:41 (RV, marg., "vanish away").

4. ***diaphtheiro*** *(1311)*, "to corrupt," is rendered "perish" in 2 Cor. 4:16, KJV (RV, "is decaying").

## PERMISSION

***sungnome*** *(4774)*, lit., "a joint opinion, mind or understanding," "a fellow feeling," hence, "a concession, allowance," is translated "permission," in contrast to "commandment," in 1 Cor. 7:6.

## PERMIT

***epitrepo*** *(2010)*, lit., "to turn to," "to entrust," signifies "to permit," Acts 26:1; 1 Cor. 14:34; 1 Cor. 16:7; 1 Tim. 2:12, RV "permit" (KJV,"suffer"); Heb. 6:3.

## PERPLEX, PERPLEXITY

### A. Verbs

1. ***aporeo*** *(639)* is rendered "perplexed" in 2 Cor. 4:8, and in the most authentic mss. in Luke 24:4.

2. ***diaporeo*** *(1280)*, "was much perplexed" in Luke 9:7.

### B. Noun.

***aporia*** *(640)*, akin to A, No. 1, is translated "perplexity" in Luke 21:25 (lit., "at a loss for a way," ***a***, negative, ***poros***, "a way, resource"), of the distress of nations, finding no solution to their embarrassments; papyri illustrations are in the sense of being at one's wit's end, at a loss how to proceed, without resources.

## PERSECUTE, PERSECUTION

### A. Verbs.

1. ***dioko*** *(1377)* has the meanings (a) "to put to flight, drive away," (b) "to pursue," whence the meaning "to persecute," Matt. 5:10–12, 44; 10:23; 23:34; Luke 11:49 (No. 2 in some mss.); 21:12; John 5:16; 15:20 (twice); Acts 7:52; 9:4, 5, and similar passages; Rom. 12:14; 1 Cor. 4:12; 15:9; 2 Cor. 4:9, KJV (RV, "pursued"); Gal. 1:13, 23; 4:29; Gal. 5:11, RV, "am . . . persecuted" (KJV, "suffer persecution"); so 6:12; Phil. 3:6; 2 Tim. 3:12, "shall suffer persecution"; Rev. 12:13.

2. ***ekdioko*** *(1559)*, ***ek***, "out," and No. 1, is used in 1 Thess. 2:15, KJV, "persecuted" (RV, "drove out").

### B. Noun.

***diogmos*** *(1375)*, akin to A, No. 1 occurs in Matt. 13:21; Mark 4:17; 10:30; Acts 8:1; 13:50; Rom. 8:35; 2 Cor. 12:10; 2 Thess. 1:4; 2 Tim. 3:11, twice.

## PERSECUTOR

***dioktes*** *(1376)*, akin to ***dioko***, 1 Tim. 1:13.

## PERSEVERANCE

***proskarteresis*** *(4343)* occurs in Eph. 6:18.

## PERSON

1. ***prosopon*** *(4383)*, is translated "person" or "persons" in Matt. 22:16; Mark 12:14; Luke 20:21; 2 Cor. 1:11; 2 Cor. 2:10; Gal. 2:6; Jude 16, lit., "(admiring, or showing respect of, RV) persons."

2. ***anthropos*** *(444)*, a generic name for man, is translated "persons" in Rev. 11:13, RV (KJV, "men").

## PERSONS (respect of)

### A. Nouns.

1. ***prosopolemptes*** *(4381)* denotes "a respecter of persons" (***prosopon***, "a face" or "person," ***lambano***, "to lay hold of"), Acts 10:34.

2. ***prosopolempsia*** (in inferior texts without the letter m) *(4382)* denotes "respect of persons, partiality" (akin to No. 1), the fault of one who, when responsible to give judgment, has respect to the position, rank, popularity, or circumstances of men, instead of their intrinsic conditions, preferring the rich and powerful to those who are not so, Rom. 2:11; Eph. 6:9; Col. 3:25; Jas. 2:1.

### B. Verb.

***prosopolempteo*** *(4380)*, "to have respect of persons," Jas. 2:9.

### C. Adverb.

***aprosopolemptos*** *(678)*, "without respect of persons, impartially" (***a***, negative), occurs in 1 Pet. 1:17.

## PERSUADE

1. ***peitho*** *(3982)* in the active voice, signifies "to apply persuasion, to prevail upon or win over, to persuade," bringing about a change of mind by the influence of reason or moral considerations, e.g., in Matt. 27:20; 28:14; Acts 13:43; 19:8; in the passive voice, "to be persuaded, believe," e.g., Luke 16:31; 20:6; Acts 17:4, RV (KJV, "believed"); 21:14; 26:26; Rom. 8:38; 14:14; 15:14; 2 Tim. 1:5, 12; Heb. 6:9; 11:13, in some mss.; 13:18, RV (KJV, "trust").

2. ***anapeitho*** (*374*), "to persuade, induce," in an evil sense (***ana***, "back," and No. 1), is used in Acts 18:13.

## PERSUASIVE, PERSUASIVENESS

### A. Adjective.

***peithos*** (*3981*), an adjective (akin to ***peitho***), not found elsewhere, is translated "persuasive" in 1 Cor. 2:4, RV (KJV, "enticing").

### B. Noun.

***pithanologia*** (*4086*), "persuasiveness of speech," is used in Col. 2:4, RV.

## PERSUASION

***peismone*** (*3988*), akin to ***peitho***, is used in Gal. 5:8, where the meaning is "this influence that has won you over, or that seems likely to do so"; the use of ***peitho***, in the sense of "to obey," in v. 7, suggests a play upon words here.

## PERTAIN TO

***metecho*** (*3348*), in Heb. 7:13, means "belong to."

## PERVERSE, PERVERT

1. ***apostrepho*** (*654*), "to turn away" (***apo***, "from," ***strepho***, "to turn"), is used metaphorically in the sense of "perverting" in Luke 23:14 (cf. No. 2 in v. 2).

2. ***diastrepho*** (*1294*), "to distort, twist" (***dia***, "through," and ***strepho***), is translated "to pervert" in Luke 23:2 (cf. No. 1 in v. 14); Acts 13:10 [in v. 8, "to turn aside" (KJV, "away")]; in the perfect participle, passive voice, it is translated "perverse," lit., "turned aside, corrupted," in Matt. 17:17; Luke 9:41; Acts 20:30; Phil. 2:15.

3. ***metastrepho*** (*3344*), "to transform into something of an opposite character" (***meta***, signifying "a change," and ***strepho***,) as the Judaizers sought to "pervert the gospel of Christ," Gal. 1:7; cf. "the sun shall be turned into darkness," Acts 2:20; laughter into mourning and joy to heaviness, Jas. 4:9.

4. ***ekstrepho*** (*1612*), "to turn inside out" (***ek***, "out"), "to change entirely," is used metaphorically in Titus 3:11, RV, "is perverted" (KJV, "is subverted").

## PESTILENCE, PESTILENT FELLOW

### *Old Testament*

***deber*** (1698), "pestilence." The meaning of ***deber*** is best denoted by the English word "pestilence" or "plague," cf. 2 Sam. 24:13ff. The nature of the "plague" (bubonic or other) is often difficult to determine from the contexts, as the details of medical interest are not given or are scanty. In the prophetical writings, the "plague" occurs with other disasters: famine, flood, and the sword, Jer. 14:12.

### *New Testament*

***loimos*** (*3061*), "a pestilence, any deadly infectious malady," is used in the plural in Luke 21:11 (in some mss., Matt. 24:7); in Acts 24:5, metaphorically, "a pestilent fellow."

## PETITION

***aitema*** (*155*), from ***aiteo***, "to ask" is rendered "petitions" in 1 John 5:15.

## PHARISEES

***pharisaios*** (*5330*), from an Aramaic word ***peras*** (found in Dan. 5:28), signifying "to separate," owing to a different manner of life from that of the general public. The "Pharisees" and Sadducees appear as distinct parties in the latter half of the 2nd cent. B.C., though they represent tendencies traceable much earlier in Jewish history, tendencies which became pronounced after the return from Babylon (537 B.C.). The immediate progenitors of the two parties were, respectively, the Hasidaeans and the Hellenizers; the latter, the antecedents of the Sadducees, aimed at removing Judaism from its narrowness and sharing in the advantages of Greek life and culture. The Hasidaeans, a transcription of the Hebrew ***chasidim***, i.e., "pious ones," were a society of men zealous for religion, who acted under the guidance of the scribes, in opposition to the godless Hellenizing party; they scrupled to oppose the legitimate high priest even when he was on the Greek side. Thus the Hellenizers were a political sect, while the Hasidaeans, whose fundamental principle was complete separation from non-Jewish elements, were the strictly legal party among the Jews, and were ultimately the more popular and influential party. In their zeal for the Law they almost deified it and their attitude became merely external, formal, and mechanical. They laid stress, not upon the righteousness of an action, but upon its formal correctness. Consequently their opposition to Christ was inevitable; His manner of life and teaching was essentially a condemnation of theirs; hence His denunciation of them, e.g., Matt. 6:2, 5, 16; 15:7 and chapter 23.

While the Jews continued to be divided into these two parties, the spread of the testimony of the gospel must have produced what in the public eye seemed to be a new sect, and in the extensive development which took place at Antioch, Acts 11:19–26, the name "Christians" seems to have become a popular term applied to the disciples as a sect, the primary cause, however, being their witness to Christ. The opposition of both "Pharisees" and Sadducees (still mutually antagonistic, Acts 23:6–10) against the new "sect" continued unabated during apostolic times.

## PHILOSOPHER

***philosophos*** (*5386*), lit., "loving wisdom" (***philos***, "loving," ***sophia***, "wisdom"), occurs in Acts 17:18.

## PHILOSOPHY

***philosophia*** (*5385*) denotes "the love and pursuit of wisdom," hence, "philosophy," the investigation of truth and nature; in Col. 2:8, the so-called "philosophy" of false teachers.

## PHYLACTERY

***phulakterion*** (*5440*), primarily "an outpost," or "fortification" (***phulax***, "a guard"), then, "any kind of safeguard," became used especially to denote "an amulet." In the NT it denotes a prayer fillet, "a phylactery," a small strip of parchment, with portions of the Law written on it; it was fastened by a leather strap either to the forehead or to the left arm over against the heart, to remind the wearer of the duty of keeping the commandments of God in the head and in the heart; cf. Ex. 13:16; Deut. 6:8; 11:18. It was supposed to have potency as a charm against evils and demons. The Pharisees broadened their "phylacteries" to render conspicuous their superior eagerness to be mindful of God's Law, Matt. 23:5.

## PIERCE

1. ***diikneomai*** (*1338*), "to go through, penetrate" (***dia***, "through," ***ikneomai***, "to go"), is used of the power of the Word of God, in Heb. 4:12, "piercing."

2. ***dierchomai*** (*1330*), "to go through," is translated "shall pierce through" in Luke 2:35.

3. ***ekkenteo*** (*1574*), primarily, "to prick out" (***ek***, "out," ***kenteo***, "to prick"), signifies "to pierce," John 19:37; Rev. 1:7.

4. ***nusso*** (*3572*), "to pierce" or "pierce through," often of inflicting severe or deadly wounds, is used of the piercing of the side of Christ, John 19:34 (in some mss., Matt. 27:49).

5. ***peripeiro*** (*4044*), "to put on a spit," hence, "to pierce," is used metaphorically in 1 Tim. 6:10, of torturing one's soul with many sorrows, "have pierced (themselves) through."

## PIETY (to shew)

***eusebeo*** (*2151*), "to reverence, to show piety" towards any to whom dutiful regard is due (akin to ***eusebes***, "pious, godly, devout"), is used in 1 Tim. 5:4 of the obligation on the part of children and grandchildren (RV) to express in a practical way their dutifulness "towards their own family"; in Acts 17:23 of worshiping God.

## PILGRIM

***parepidemos*** (*3927*), an adjective signifying "sojourning in a strange place, away from one's own people" (***para***, "from," expressing a contrary condition, and ***epidemeo***, "to sojourn"; ***demos***, "a people"), is used of OT saints, Heb. 11:13, "pilgrims" (coupled with ***xenos***, "a foreigner"); of Christians, 1 Pet. 1:1, "sojourners (of the Dispersion)," RV; 2:11, "pilgrims" (coupled with ***paroikos***, "an alien, sojourner"); the word is thus used metaphorically of those to whom Heaven is their own country, and who are sojourners on earth.

## PILLAR

### Old Testament

***'ayil*** (352), "pillar, post," meaning a vertical piece of finished wood used in construction, 1 Kings 6:31.

***mashshebah*** (4676), "pillar; monument; sacred stone," This word refers to a "pillar" as a personal memorial in 2 Sam. 18:18. In Gen. 28:18 the "monument" is a memorial of the Lord's appearance. ***mashshebah*** is used in connection with the altar built by Moses in Exod. 24:4, and it refers to "sacred stones or pillars."

### New Testament

***stulos*** (*4769*), "a column supporting the weight of a building," is used (a) metaphorically, of those who bear responsibility in the churches, as of the elders in the church at Jerusalem, Gal. 2:9; of a local church as to its responsibility, in a collective capacity, to maintain the doctrines of the faith by teaching and practice, 1 Tim. 3:15; some would attach this and the next words to the statement in v. 16; the connection in the Eng. versions seems preferable; (b) figuratively in Rev. 3:12, indicating a firm and permanent position in the spiritual, heavenly and eternal Temple of God; (c) illustratively, of the feet of the angel in the vision in Rev. 10:1, seen as flames rising like columns of fire indicative of holiness and consuming power, and thus reflecting the glory of Christ as depicted in 1:15; cf. Ezek. 1:7.

## PINNACLE

***pterugion*** (*4419*) denotes (a) "a little wing" (diminutive of ***pterux***, "a wing"); (b) "anything like a wing, a turret, battlement," of the temple in Jerusalem, Matt. 4:5 and Luke 4:9 (of the

***hieron***, "the entire precincts," or parts of the main building, as distinct from the ***naos***, "the sanctuary"). This "wing" has been regarded (1) as the apex of the sanctuary, (2) the top of Solomon's porch, (3) the top of the Royal Portico, which Josephus describes as of tremendous height.

## PIOUS

***chacid*** (2623), "one who is pious, godly." Basically, ***chasid*** means one who practices "loving-kindness," so translated the "pious" or "godly one."

## PIPE (Noun and Verb)

### A. Noun.

***aulos*** (*836*), "a wind instrument," e.g., "a flute" (connected with ***aemi***, "to blow"), occurs in 1 Cor. 14:7.

### B. Verb.

***auleo*** (*832*), "to play on an ***aulos***," is used in Matt. 11:17; Luke 7:32; 1 Cor. 14:7 (2nd part).

## PIT

### *Old Testament*

***be'er*** (875), "pit; well." ***be'er*** means a "well" in which there may be water. Such a "well" may have a narrow enough mouth that it can be blocked with a stone which a single, strong man could move, Gen. 29:2, 10. In the desert country of the ancient Near East a "well" was an important place and its water the source of deep satisfaction for the thirsty. This concept pictures the role of a wife for a faithful husband, Prov. 5:15.

A "pit" may contain something other than water, like slimepits, Gen. 14:10. A "pit" may contain nothing as does the "pit" which becomes one's grave, Ps. 55:23. In some passages the word was to represent more than a depository for the body but a place where one exists after death, Ps. 69:15.

### *New Testament*

1. ***phrear*** (*5421*), "a well, dug for water" (distinct from ***pege***, "a fountain"), denotes "a pit" in Rev. 9:1, 2, RV, "the pit (of the abyss)," "the pit," i.e., the shaft leading down to the abyss, KJV, "(bottomless) pit"; in Luke 14:5, RV, well (KJV, "pit"); in John 4:11, 12, "well."

2. ***bothunos*** (*999*) is rendered "pit" in Matt. 12:11.

## PITIABLE (most)

***eleeinoeros*** (*1652**), the comparative degree of ***eleeinos***, "miserable, pitiable" (***eleos***, "pity"), is used in 1 Cor. 15:19, "most pitiable" (RV), lit., "more pitiable than all men."

## PITIFUL, PITY

1. ***polusplanchnos*** (*4184*) denotes "very pitiful" or "full of pity" (***polus***, "much," ***splanchnon***, "the heart"; in the plural, "the affections"), occurs in Jas. 5:11, RV, "full of pity."

2. ***eusplanchnos*** (*2155*), "compassionate, tenderhearted," lit., "of good heartedness" (***eu***, "well," and ***splanchnon***), is translated "pitiful" in 1 Pet. 3:8, KJV, RV, "tenderhearted," as in Eph. 4:32.

## PLAGUE

1. ***mastix*** (*3148*), "a whip, scourge," Acts 22:24, "by scourging"; Heb. 11:36, "scourgings," is used metaphorically of "disease" or "suffering," Mark 3:10; 5:29, 34; Luke 7:21.

2. ***plege*** (*4127*), "a stripe, wound" (akin to ***plesso***, "to smite"), is used metaphorically of a calamity, "a plague," Rev. 9:20; 11:6; 15:1, 6, 8; 16:9, 21 (twice); 18:4, 8; 21:9; 22:18.

## PLAY

***paizo*** (*3815*), properly, "to play as a child" (***pais***), hence denotes "to play" as in dancing and making merry, 1 Cor. 10:7.

## PLEAD

### *Old Testament*

### A. Verb.

***rib*** (7378), "to plead, strive, conduct a legal case, make a charge." The prophets use ***rib*** frequently to indicate that God has an indictment, a legal case, against Israel, Amos 7:4. Micah 6 is a classic example of such a legal case against Judah, calling on the people "to plead" their case (6:1) and progressively showing how only God has a valid case (6:8).

P

### B. Noun.

***rib*** (7379), "strife; dispute," Mic. 6:2.

### *New Testament*

***entunchano*** (*1793*), "to make petition," is used of the "pleading" of Elijah against Israel, Rom. 11:2, RV, "pleadeth with" (KJV, "maketh intercession to").

## PLEASE, PLEASING (Noun), WELL-PLEASING, PLEASURE

### A. Verbs.

1. ***aresko*** (*700*) signifies (a) "to be pleasing to, be acceptable to," Matt. 14:6; Mark 6:22; Acts 6:5; Rom. 8:8; 15:2; 1 Cor. 7:32–34; Gal. 1:10; 1 Thess. 2:15; 4:1 (where the preceding ***kai***, "and," is epexegetical, "even," explaining the "walking," i.e., Christian manner of life as "pleasing" God; in Gen. 5:22, where the He-

brew has "Enoch walked with God," the Sept. has "Enoch pleased God"; cf. Mic. 6:8; Heb. 11:5); 2 Tim. 2:4; (b) "to endeavor to please," and so, "to render service," doing so evilly in one's own interests, Rom. 15:1, which Christ did not, v. 3; or unselfishly, 1 Cor. 10:33; 1 Thess. 2:4.

2. ***euaresteo*** (*2100*) signifies "to be well-pleasing" (***eu***, "well," and a form akin to No. 1); in the active voice, Heb. 11:5, RV, "he had been "well-pleasing" (unto God)," KJV, "he pleased"; so v. 6; in the passive voice, Heb. 13:16.

3. ***eudokeo*** (*2106*) signifies (a) "to be well pleased, to think it good" [***eu***, "well," and ***dokeo***], not merely an understanding of what is right and good as in ***dokeo***, but stressing the willingness and freedom of an intention or resolve regarding what is good, e.g., Luke 12:32, "it is (your Father's) good pleasure"; so Rom. 15:26, 27, RV; 1 Cor. 1:21; Gal. 1:15; Col. 1:19; 1 Thess. 2:8, RV, "we were well pleased" (KJV, "we were willing"); this meaning is frequently found in the papyri in legal documents; (b) "to be well pleased with," or "take pleasure in," e.g., Matt. 3:17; 12:18; 17:5; 1 Cor. 10:5; 2 Cor. 12:10; 2 Thess. 2:12; Heb. 10:6, 8, 38; 2 Pet. 1:17.

4. ***thelo*** (*2309*), "to will, wish, desire," is translated "it pleased (Him)" in 1 Cor. 12:18; 15:38, RV.

5. ***spatalao*** (*4684*), "to live riotously," is translated "giveth herself to pleasure" in 1 Tim. 5:6, RV (KJV, "liveth in pleasure"); "taken your pleasure" in Jas. 5:5, KJV, "been wanton."

### B. Adjectives.

1. ***arestos*** (*701*) denotes "pleasing, agreeable," John 8:29, RV, "(the things that are) pleasing," KJV, "(those things that) please," KJV and RV in 1 John 3:22; in Acts 6:2, "fit" (RV marg., "pleasing"); 12:3, "it pleased," lit., "it was pleasing."

### C. Noun.

***areskeia*** (or -***ia***) (*699*), a "pleasing," a giving pleasure, Col. 1:10, of the purpose Godward of a walk worthy of the Lord (cf. 1 Thess. 4:1).

## PLEASURE

#### *Old Testament*

### A. Noun.

***chepets*** (2656), "pleasure; delight; desire; request; affair; thing." This word often means "pleasure" or "delight," 1 Sam. 15:22; acceptable words, Eccl. 12:10, i.e., words that were both true and aesthetically pleasing; "willingly" [in delight], Prov. 31:13. ***chepets*** can mean not simply what one takes pleasure in or what gives someone delight but one's wish or desire, 2 Sam. 23:5; "to grant a request," 1 Kings 5:8; precious stones, Isa. 54:12. Third, ***chepets*** sometimes represents *one's affairs* as that *in which one takes delight*, Eccl. 3:1. In Isa. 58:13 the first occurrence of this word means "pleasure" or "delight." Finally, in one passage this word means "affair" in the sense of a "thing" or "situation," Eccl. 5:8.

### B. Verb.

***chapets*** (2654), "to take pleasure in, take care of, desire, delight in, have delight in," 2 Sam. 15:26.

### C. Adjective.

***chapets*** (2655), "delighting in, having pleasure in," Ps. 35:27.

#### *New Testament*

### A. Nouns.

1. ***hedone*** (*2237*), "pleasure," is used of the gratification of the natural desire or sinful desires (akin to ***hedormai***, "to be glad," and ***hedeos***, "gladly"), Luke 8:14; Titus 3:3; Jas. 4:1, 3, RV, "pleasures" (KJV, "lusts"); in the singular, 2 Pet. 2:13.

2. ***eudokia*** (*2107*), "good pleasure," Eph. 1:5, 9; Phil. 2:13; 2 Thess. 1:11.

3. ***apolausis*** (*619*), "enjoyment," is used with ***echo***, "to have," and rendered "enjoy the pleasures" (lit., "pleasure") in Heb. 11:25.

### B. Adjective.

***philedonos*** (*5369*), "loving pleasure" (***philos***, "loving," and A, No. 1), occurs in 2 Tim. 3:4, RV, "lovers of pleasure" (KJV, ". . . pleasures").

## PLENTEOUS

***polus*** (*4183*), "much," is rendered "plenteous" in Matt. 9:37, of a harvest of souls, and Luke 10:2, RV (KJV, "great").

## PLOT

***epiboule*** (*1917*), lit., "a plan against" (***epi***, "against," ***boule***, "a counsel, plan"), is translated "plot" in the RV (KJV, "laying await" and "lying in wait") in Acts 9:24; 20:3, 19; 23:30.

## PLUCK (out)

1. ***tillo*** (*5089*) is used of "plucking off ears of corn," Matt. 12:1; Mark 2:23; Luke 6:1.

2. ***harpazo*** (*726*), "to seize, snatch," is rendered "pluck" in John 10:28, 29, KJV, RV, "snatch."

3. ***exaireo*** (*1807*), "to take out" (***ex*** for ***ek***, "out," haireo, "to take"), is translated "pluck out," of the eye as the occasion of sin, in Matt. 5:29; 18:9, indicating that, with determination and promptitude, we are to strike at the root of unholy inclinations, ridding ourselves of whatever would stimulate them.

4. ***exorusso*** (*846*), "to dig out or up," is rendered "ye would have plucked out (your eyes)" in Gal. 4:15, an indication of their feelings of gratitude to, and love for, the apostle. The metaphor affords no real ground for the supposition of a reference to some weakness of his sight, and certainly not to the result of his temporary blindness at his conversion, the recovery from which must have been as complete as the infliction. There would be some reason for such an inference had the pronoun "ye" been stressed; but the stress is on the word "eyes"; their devotion prompted a readiness to part with their most treasured possession on his behalf.

5. ***ekrizoo*** (*1610*), "to pluck up by the roots" (***ek***, "out," ***rhiza***, "a root"), is so translated in Jude 12 (figuratively), and in the KJV in Luke 17:6, RV, "rooted up"; "root up," Matt. 13:29; "shall be rooted up," 15:13.

## POINT, POINTS

### A. Noun.

***kephalaion*** (*2774*), the neuter of the adjective ***kephalaios***, "of the head," is used as a noun, signifying (a) "a sum, amount, of money," Acts 22:28; (b) "a chief point," Heb. 8:1, not the summing up of the subject, as the KJV suggests, for the subject was far from being finished in the Epistle; on the contrary, in all that was being set forth by the writer "the chief point" consisted in the fact that believers have "a High Priest" of the character already described.

### B. Verb.

***deloo*** (*1213*), "to make plain" (***delos***, "evident"), is translated "did point unto" in 1 Pet. 1:11, RV (KJV, "did signify"), of the operation of "the Spirit of Christ" in the prophets of the Old Testament in "pointing" on to the time and its characteristics, of the sufferings of Christ and subsequent glories.

## POLLUTE, POLLUTION

### *Old Testament*

***chalal*** (2490), "to pollute, defile, profane, begin." The most frequent use of this Hebrew root is in the sense of "to pollute, defile." This may be a ritual defilement, such as that resulting from contact with a dead body, Lev. 21:4; ceremonial profaning of the sacred altar by the use of tools in order to shape the stones, Exod. 20:25. In more than 50 instances, this root is used in the sense of "to begin," Gen. 4:26.

### *New Testament*

***alisgema*** (*234*), akin to a late verb ***alisgeo***, "to pollute," denotes "a pollution, contamination," Acts 15:20; "pollutions of idols," i.e., all the contaminating associations connected with idolatry including meats from sacrifices offered to idols.

## POMP

***phantasia*** (*5325*), as a philosophic term, denoted "an imagination"; then, "an appearance," like ***phantasma***, "an apparition"; later, "a show, display, pomp" (Eng., "phantasy"), Acts 25:23. In the Sept., Hab. 2:18; 3:10; Zech. 10:1.

## PONDER

***sumballo*** (*4820*), "to throw together, confer," etc., has the meaning "to ponder," i.e., "to put one thing with another in considering circumstances," in Luke 2:19.

## POOR

### *Old Testament*

### A. Nouns.

***'ani*** (6041), "poor; weak; afflicted; humble." This noun is frequently used in synonymous parallelism with ***'ebyon*** ("needy") and/or ***dal*** ("poor"). It differs from both in emphasizing some kind of disability or distress. A hired servant as one who is in a lower (oppressive) social and material condition is described both as an ***'ebyon*** and ***'ani***, Deut. 24:14–15. An ***'ani*** can call on God for defense. Financially, the ***'ani*** lives from day to day and is socially defenseless, being subject to oppression, Exod. 22:25. The godly protect and deliver the "afflicted," Isa. 10:2; Ezek. 18:17, while the ungodly take advantage of them, increasing their oppressed condition, Isa. 58:7. The king is especially charged to protect the ***'ani***: "Open thy mouth, judge righteously, and plead the cause of the poor and needy," Prov. 31:9.

***'ani*** can refer to one who is physically oppressed, Isa. 51:21. Physical oppression is sometimes related to spiritual oppression as in Ps. 22:24; 25:16; 68:10. In such cases spiritual poverty and want are clearly in view. Sometimes the word means "humble" or "lowly," as it does in Zech. 9:9; cf. Ps. 18:27; Prov. 3:34; Isa. 66:2.

***dal*** (1800), "one who is low, poor, reduced, helpless, weak." ***dal*** is related to, but differs from, ***'ani*** (which suggests affliction of some kind), ***'ebyon*** (which emphasizes need), and ***rash*** (which suggests destitution). The ***dallim*** constituted the middle class of Israel—those who were physically deprived (in the ancient world the majority of people were poor). For example, the ***dallim*** may be viewed as the opposite of the rich, Exod. 30:15; cf. Ruth 3:10; Prov. 10:15.

In addition, the word may connote social poverty or lowliness. As such, ***dal*** describes those who are the counterparts of the great, Lev. 19:15; cf. Amos 2:7; of low status, or weak, Judg. 6:15; cf. 2 Sam. 3:1. God commands that society protect the poor, the lowly, and the weak, Exod. 23:2–3; cf. Lev. 14:21; Isa. 10:2. He also warns that if men fail to provide justice, He will do so, Isa. 11:4. A fourth emphasis appears in Gen. 41:19 (the first biblical appearance of the word), where ***dal*** is contrasted to "healthy" or "fat," 2 Sam. 13:4.

**B. Verbs.**

***dalal*** (1809), "to be low, hang down," Ps. 79:8.

***'anah*** (6031), "to afflict, oppress, humble," Gen. 15:13.

**C. Adjective.**

***'anaw*** (6035), "humble; poor; meek." ***'anaw*** depicts the objective condition as well as the subjective stance of Moses. He was entirely dependent on God and saw that he was, Num. 12:3.

***New Testament***

**A. Adjectives.**

1. ***ptochos*** (*4434*), has the broad sense of "poor," (a) literally, e.g., Matt. 11:5; 26:9, 11; Luke 21:3 (with stress on the word, "a conspicuously poor widow"); John 12:5, 6, 8; 13:29; Jas. 2:2, 3, 6; the "poor" are constantly the subjects of injunctions to assist them, Matt. 19:21; Mark 10:21; Luke 14:13, 21; 18:22; Rom. 15:26; Gal. 2:10; (b) metaphorically, Matt. 5:3; Luke 6:20; Rev. 3:17.

2. ***penichros*** (*3998*), akin to B, "needy, poor," is used of the widow in Luke 21:2 (cf. No. 1, of the same woman, in v. 3); it is used frequently in the papyri.

**B. Noun.**

***penes*** (*3993*), "a laborer" (akin to ***penomai***, "to work for one's daily bread"), is translated "poor" in 2 Cor. 9:9.

## PORCH

1. ***stoa*** (*4745*), "a portico," is used (a) of the "porches" at the pool of Bethesda, John 5:2; (b) of the covered colonnade in the Temple, called Solomon's "porch," John 10:23; Acts 3:11; 5:12 a portico on the eastern side of the temple; this and the other "porches" existent in the time of Christ were almost certainly due to Herod's restoration.

2. ***pulon*** (*440*), akin to ***pule***, "a gate" (Eng., "pylon"), is used of "a doorway, porch or vestibule" of a house or palace, Matt. 26:71. In the parallel passage Mark 14:68, No. 3 is used, and ***pulon*** doubtless stands in Matt. 26 for ***proaulion***.

3. ***proaulion*** (*4259*), "the exterior court" or "vestibule," between the door and the street, in the houses of well-to-do folk, Mark 14:68, "porch" (RV marg., "forecourt").

## PORTION

**A. Nouns.**

1. ***meros*** (*3313*), "a part," is translated "portion" in Matt. 24:51; Luke 12:46; 15:12.

2. ***kleros*** (*2819*), "a lot," is translated "portion" in Acts 1:17, RV.

3. ***meris*** (*3310*), "a part," is translated "portion" in 2 Cor. 6:15, RV.

**B. Verb.**

***summerizo*** (*4829*), "to have a part with" (akin to A, No. 3), is translated "have their portion with" in 1 Cor. 9:13. RV.

**C. Adverb**

***polumeros*** (*4181*) signifies "in many parts" or "portions" (***polus***, "many," and A, No. 1), Heb. 1:1, RV (KJV, "at sundry times").

## POSSIBLE

**A. Adjective.**

***dunatos*** (*1415*), "strong, mighty, powerful, able (to do)," in its neuter form signifies "possible," Matt. 19:26; 24:24; 26:39; Mark 9:23; 10:27; 13:22; 14:35, 36; Luke 18:27; Acts 2:24; 20:16 (27:39, in some mss; ***dunamai***, "to be able," in the most authentic, RV, "they could"); Rom. 12:18; Gal. 4:15.

**B. Verb.**

***eimi*** (*1510*), "to be," is used in the third person singular, impersonally, with the meaning "it is possible," negatively in 1 Cor. 11:20, RV, (KJV, "it is not"), and Heb. 9:5, "we cannot," lit., "it is not possible."

## POVERTY

***ptocheia*** (*4432*), "destitution," is used of the "poverty" which Christ voluntarily experienced on our behalf, 2 Cor. 8:9; of the destitute condition of saints in Judea, v. 2; of the condition of the church in Smyrna, Rev. 2:9, where the word is used in a general sense.

## POWER (Noun, and Verb, to have, bring under)

***Old Testament***

***koach*** (3581), "strength; power; force; ability." The basic meaning of ***koach*** is an ability to do something. Samson's "strength" lay in his hair, Judg. 16:5, and we must keep in mind that his "strength" had been demonstrated against the Philistines. Nations and kings exert their "powers," Josh. 17:17; Dan. 8:24. In the Old Testament it is recognized that by eating one gains "strength," 1 Sam. 28:22, whereas one loses one's "abilities" in fasting, 1 Sam. 28:20. A special sense of ***koach*** is the meaning "property," Ezra 2:69. A proverb warns against adultery, because one's "strength," or one's wealth, may be taken by others, Prov. 5:10.

In the Old Testament, God had demonstrated His "strength" to Israel. The language of God's "strength" is highly metaphorical. God's right hand gloriously manifests His "power," Exod. 15:6; loud, Ps. 29:4; power, Exod. 32:11.

### *New Testament*

**A. Nouns.**

1. ***dunamis*** (*1411*), is sometimes used, by metonymy, of persons and things, e.g., (a) of God, Matt. 26:64; Mark 14:62; (b) of angels, e.g., perhaps in Eph. 1:21, RV, "power," KJV, "might" (cf. Rom. 8:38; 1 Pet. 3:22); (c) of that which manifests God's "power": Christ, 1 Cor. 1:24; the gospel, Rom. 1:16; (d) of mighty works (RV, marg., "power" or "powers"), e.g., Mark 6:5, "mighty work"; so 9:39, RV (KJV, "miracle"); Acts 2:22 (ditto); 8:13, "miracles"; 2 Cor. 12:12, RV, "mighty works" (KJV, "mighty deeds").

2. ***exousia*** (*1849*) denotes "freedom of action, right to act"; used of God, it is absolute, unrestricted, e.g., Luke 12:5 (RV marg., "authority"); in Acts 1:7 "right of disposal" is what is indicated; used of men, authority is delegated. Angelic beings are called "powers" in Eph. 3:10 (cf. 1:21); 6:12; Col. 1:16; 2:15 (cf. 2:10).

3. ***ischus*** (*2479*), "ability, force, strength," is nowhere translated "power" in the RV (KJV in 2 Thess. 1:9).

4. ***kratos*** (*2904*) is translated "power" in the RV and KJV in 1 Tim. 6:16; Heb. 2:14; in Eph. 1:19 (last part); 6:10, KJV, "power" (RV, "strength").

**B. Verb.**

***exousiazo*** (*1850*), "to exercise authority" (akin to A, No. 2), is used (a) in the active voice, Luke 22:25, RV, "have authority" (KJV, "exercise authority"), of the "power" of rulers; 1 Cor. 7:4 (twice), of marital relations and conditions; (b) in the passive voice, 1 Cor. 6:12, to be brought under the "power" of a thing; here, this verb and the preceding one connected with it, ***exesti***, present a ***paronomasia***, which Lightfoot brings out as follows: "All are within my power; but I will not put myself under the power of any one of all things."

## POWERFUL, POWERFULLY

**Adjective.**

***ischuros*** (*2478*), "strong, mighty," akin to ***ischus***, is translated "powerful" in 2 Cor. 10:10, KJV (RV, "strong).

**B. Adverb.**

***eutonos*** (*2159*) signifies "vigorously, vehemently" (***eu***, "well," ***teino***, "to stretch"), Luke 23:10, "vehemently," of the accusation of the chief priests and scribes against Christ; Acts 18:28, RV, "powerfully" (KJV, "mightily"), of Apollos in confuting Jews. In the Sept., Josh. 6:8.

## PRAISE

### *Old Testament*

**A. Verbs.**

***halal*** (1984), "to praise, celebrate, glory, sing (praise), boast." While ***halal*** is often used simply to indicate "praise" of people, including the king, 2 Chron. 23:12, or the beauty of Absalom, 2 Sam. 14:25, the word is usually used in reference to the "praise" of God. Indeed, not only all living things but all created things, including the sun and moon, are called upon "to praise" God, Ps. 148:2–5, 13; 150:1. Typically, such "praise" is called for and expressed in the sanctuary, especially in times of special festivals, Isa. 62:9. The Book of Psalms contains more than half the occurrences of ***halal*** in its various forms.

The word ***halal*** is the source of "Hallelujah," a Hebrew expression of "praise" to God which has been taken over into virtually every language of mankind. The Hebrew "Hallelujah" is generally translated "*Praise the Lord!*" The Hebrew term is more technically translated "*Let us praise Yah*," the term "Yah" being a shortened form of "Yahweh," Ps. 68:4; cf. Rev. 19:1, 3–4, 6.

***yadah*** (3034), "to give thanks, laud, praise." As is to be expected, this word is found most frequently in the Book of Psalms (some 70 times). As an expression of thanks or praise, it is a natural part of ritual or public worship as well as personal praise to God, Ps. 30:9, 12; 35:18.

**B. Nouns.**

***tehillah*** (8416), "glory; praise; song of praise; praiseworthy deeds." ***tehillah*** denotes a quality or attribute of some person or thing, "glory or praiseworthiness," Deut. 10:21. Israel is God's "glory" when she exists in a divinely exalted and blessed state, Isa. 62:7; cf. Jer.

P

13:11. Second, in some cases ***tehillah*** represents the words or song by which God is publicly lauded, or by which His "glory" is publicly declared, Ps. 22:22, 25. In a third nuance ***tehillah*** is a technical-musical term for a song (***shir***) which exalts or praises God: "David's psalm of praise" (heading for Ps. 145; v. 1 in the Hebrew. Finally, ***tehillah*** may represent deeds which are worthy of "praise," or deeds for which the doer deserves "praise and glory," Exod. 15:11.

***todah*** (8426), "thanksgiving." ***todah*** is used to indicate "thanksgiving" in songs of worship, Ps. 26:7; 42:4. Sometimes the word is used to refer to the thanksgiving choir or procession, Neh. 12:31, 38. One of the peace offerings was designated the thanksgiving offering, Lev. 7:12.

### *New Testament*

#### A. Nouns.

1. ***ainos*** (*136*), primarily "a tale, narration," came to denote "praise"; in the NT only of praise to God, Matt. 21:16; Luke 18:43.

2. ***epainos*** (*1868*), a strengthened form of No. 1 (***epi*** upon), denotes "approbation, commendation, praise"; it is used (a) of those on account of, and by reason of, whom as God's heritage, "praise" is to be ascribed to God, in respect of His glory (the exhibition of His character and operations), Eph. 1:12 in v. 14, of the whole company, the church, viewed as "*God's* own possession" (RV); in v. 6, with particular reference to the glory of His grace towards them; in Phil. 1:11, as the result of "the fruits of righteousness" manifested in them through the power of Christ; (b) of "praise" bestowed by God, upon the Jew spiritually (Judah  "praise"), Rom. 2:29; bestowed upon believers hereafter at the judgment seat of Christ, 1 Cor. 4:5 (where the definite article indicates that the "praise" will be exactly in accordance with each person's actions); as the issue of present trials, "at the revelation of Jesus Christ," 1 Pet. 1:7; (c) of whatsoever is "praiseworthy," Phil. 4:8; (d) of the approbation by churches of those who labor faithfully in the ministry of the gospel, 2 Cor. 8:18; (e) of the approbation of well-doers by human rulers, Rom. 13:3; 1 Pet. 2:14.

3. ***ainesis*** (*133*), "praise" (akin to No. 1), is found in Heb. 13:15, where it is metaphorically represented as a sacrificial offering.

#### B. Verbs

1. ***aineo*** (*134*), "to speak in praise of, to praise" (akin to A, No. 1), is always used of "praise" to God, (a) by angels, Luke 2:13; (b) by men, Luke 2:13; 19:37; 24:53; Acts 2:20, 47; 3:8, 9; Rom. 15:11 (No. 2 in some texts); Rev. 19:5.

2. ***epaineo*** (*1867*), akin to A, No. 2, is rendered "praise," 1 Cor. 11:2, 17, 22.

3. ***humneo*** (*5214*) denotes (a) transitively, "to sing, to laud, sing to the praise of" (Eng., "hymn"), Acts 16:25, KJV, "sang praises" (RV, "singing hymns"); Heb. 2:12, RV, "will I sing (Thy) praise," KJV, "will I sing praise (unto Thee)," lit., "I will hymn Thee"; (b) intransitively, "to sing," Matt. 26:30; Mark 14:26, in both places of the singing of the paschal hymns (Ps. 113–118, and 136), called by Jews the Great Hallel.

4. ***psallo*** (*5567*), primarily, "to twitch" or "twang" (as a bowstring, etc.), then, "to play" (a stringed instrument with the fingers), in the NT, to sing a hymn, sing "praise"; in Jas. 5:13, RV, "sing praise" (KJV, "sing psalms").

## PRATE

***phluareo*** (*5396*) signifies "to talk nonsense" (from ***phluo***, "to babble"; cf. the adjective ***phluaros***, "babbling, garrulous, tattlers," 1 Tim. 5:13), "to raise false accusations," 3 John 10.

## PRAY, PRAYER

### *Old Testament*

#### A. Verb.

***palal*** (6419), "to pray, intervene, mediate, judge." In the intensive form ***palal*** expresses the idea of "to mediate, to come between two parties," always between human beings, 1 Sam. 2:25; "to mediate" requires "making a judgment," as in Ezek. 16:52.

The first occurrence of ***palal*** in the Old Testament is in Gen. 20:7, where the reflexive or reciprocal form of the verb expresses the idea of "interceding for, prayer in behalf of." Samuel "intercedes" continually for Israel, 1 Sam. 12:23. Prayer is directed not only toward Yahweh but toward pagan idols as well, Isa. 44:17. Sometimes prayer is made to Yahweh that He would act against an enemy, 2 Kings 19:20.

#### B. Noun.

***tepillah*** (8605), "prayer." This word means to "make a request," which when referring to asking God is translated "prayer," 1 Kings 8:28; or as a title in scripture, psalm title in 5 psalms; Hab. 3:1, related to music in some way.

### *New Testament*

#### A. Verbs.

1. ***euchomai*** (*2172*), "to pray (to God)," is used with this meaning in 2 Cor. 13:7; v. 9, RV, "pray" (KJV, "wish"); Jas. 5:16; 3 John 2, RV,

"pray" (KJV, wish). Even when the RV and KJV translate by "I would," Acts 26:29, or "wished for," Acts 27:29 (RV, marg., "prayed"), or "could wish," Rom. 9:3 (RV, marg., "could pray"), the indication is that "prayer" is involved.

2. ***proseuchomai*** (*4336*), "to pray," is always used of "prayer" to God, and is the most frequent word in this respect, especially in the Synoptists and Acts, once in Romans, 8:26; in Ephesians, 6:18; in Philippians, 1:9; in 1 Timothy, 2:8; in Hebrews, 13:18; in Jude, v. 20. For the injunction in 1 Thess. 5:17.

### B. Nouns.

1. ***euche*** (*2171*), akin to A, No. 1, denotes "a prayer," Jas. 5:15; "a vow," Acts 18:18 and 21:23.

2. ***proseuche*** (*4335*), akin to A, No. 2, denotes (a) "prayer" (to God), the most frequent term, e.g., Matt. 21:22; Luke 6:12, where the phrase is not to be taken literally as if it meant, "the prayer of God" (subjective genitive), but objectively, "prayer to God." In Jas. 5:17, "He prayed fervently," RV, is, lit., "he prayed with prayer" (a Hebraistic form): Eph. 6:18; Phil. 4:6; 1 Tim. 2:1; 5:5; (b) "a place of prayer," Acts 16:13, 16, a place outside the city wall, RV.

3. ***deesis*** (*1162*), primarily "a wanting, a need," then, "an asking, entreaty, supplication," in the NT is always addressed to God and always rendered "supplication" or "supplications" in the RV; in the KJV "prayer," or "prayers," in Luke 1:13; 2:37; 5:33; Rom. 10:1; 2 Cor. 1:11; 9:14; Phil. 1:4 (in the 2nd part, "request"); 1:19; 2 Tim. 1:3; Heb. 5:7; Jas. 5:16; 1 Pet. 3:12.

## PREACH, PREACHING

### A. Verbs.

1. ***euangelizo*** (*2097*) is almost always used of "the good news" concerning the Son of God as proclaimed in the gospel [exceptions are e.g., Luke 1:19; 1 Thess. 3:6, in which the phrase "to bring (or show) good (or glad) tidings" does not refer to the gospel]; Gal. 1:8 (2nd part). With reference to the gospel the phrase "to bring, or declare, good, or glad, tidings" is used in Acts 13:32; Rom. 10:15; Heb. 4:2.

In Luke 4:18 the RV "to preach good tidings" gives the correct quotation from Isaiah, rather than the KJV "to preach the Gospel."

2. ***kerusso*** (*2784*) signifies (a) "to be a herald," or, in general, "to proclaim," e.g., Matt. 3:1; Mark 1:45, "publish"; in Luke 4:18, RV, "to proclaim," KJV, "to preach"; so verse 19; Luke 12:3; Acts 10:37; Rom. 2:21; Rev. 5:2. In 1 Pet. 3:19 the probable reference is, not to glad tidings (which there is no real evidence that Noah preached, nor is there evidence that the spirits of antediluvian people are actually "in prison"), but to the act of Christ after His resurrection in proclaiming His victory to fallen angelic spirits; (b) "to preach the gospel as a herald," e.g., Matt. 24:14; Mark 13:10, RV, "be preached" (KJV, "be published"); 14:9; 16:15, 20; Luke 8:1; 9:2; 24:47; Acts 8:5; 19:13; 28:31; Rom. 10:14, present participle, lit., "(one) preaching," "a preacher"; 10:15 (1st part); 1 Cor. 1:23; 15:11, 12; 2 Cor. 1:19; 4:5; 11:4; Gal. 2:2; Phil. 1:15; Col. 1:23; 1 Thess. 2:9; 1 Tim. 3:16; (c) "to preach the word," 2 Tim. 4:2 (of the ministry of the Scriptures, with special reference to the gospel).

3. ***prokerusso*** (*4296*), lit., "to proclaim as a herald" (***pro***, before, and No. 2), is used in Acts 13:24, "had first preached." Some mss. have the verb in Acts 3:20.

### B. Nouns.

***kerugma*** (*2782*), "a proclamation by a herald" (akin to A, No. 2), denotes "a message, a preaching" (the substance of what is "preached" as distinct from the act of "preaching"), Matt. 12:41; Luke 11:32; Rom. 16:25; 1 Cor. 1:21; 2:4; 15:14; in 2 Tim. 4:17 and Titus 1:3, RV, "message," marg., "proclamation," KJV, "preaching."

## PREACHER

***kerux*** (*2783*), "a herald" (akin to A, No. 2 and B, above), is used (a) of the "preacher" of the gospel, 1 Tim. 2:7; 2 Tim. 1:11; (b) of Noah, as a "preacher" of righteousness, 2 Pet. 2:5.

## PRECEDE

***phthano*** (*5348*), "to anticipate, to come sooner," is translated "shall (in no wise) precede" in 1 Thess. 4:15, RV (KJV, "prevent"), i.e., "shall in no wise obtain any advantage over" (the verb does not convey the thought of a mere succession of one event after another); the apostle, in reassuring the bereaved concerning their departed fellow believers, declares that, as to any advantage, the dead in Christ will "rise first."

## PRECEPT

1. ***entole*** (*1785*), "a commandment," is translated "precept" in Mark 10:5 (RV, "commandment"); so Heb. 9:19.

2. ***entalma*** (*1778*) is always translated "precepts" in the RV, Matt. 15:9.

## PRECIOUS, PRECIOUSNESS

### *Old Testament*

### A. Adjective.

***yaqar*** (3368), "precious; rare; excellent; weighty; noble." First, ***yaqar*** means "precious"

P

in the sense of being rare and valuable, 2 Sam. 12:30; or, "rare," 1 Sam. 3:1. Second, the word can focus on the value of a thing, Ps. 36:7. Third, this word means "weighty," Eccl. 10:1; or "noble," Lam. 4:2.

**B. Verb.**

***yaqar*** (3365), "to be difficult, be valued from, be valued or honored, be precious," 1 Sam. 26:21.

**C. Noun.**

***yeqar*** (3366), "precious thing; value; price; splendor; honor." The word signifies "value or price," Zech. 11:13; "splendor," Esth. 1:4; "honor," Esth. 8:16.

***New Testament***

1. ***timios*** (*5093*), translated "precious," e.g., in Jas. 5:7; 1 Pet. 1:19; 2 Pet. 1:4; in 1 Cor. 3:12, KJV (RV, "costly").

2. ***entimos*** (1784),"precious," 1 Pet. 2:4, 6.

3. ***poluteles*** (*4185*), "very expensive," translated "very precious" in Mark 14:3, KJV (RV, "very costly).

4. ***polutimos*** (*4186*), "of great value"; comparative degree in 1 Pet. 1:7.

5. ***barutimos*** (*927*), "of great value, exceeding precious" (***barus***, "weighty," ***time***, value), is used in Matt. 26:7.

## PREDESTINATE

***proorizo*** (*4309*): "to make a choice," the full theological implications are much debated, Acts 4:28; Rom. 8:29, 30; 1 Cor. 2:7; Eph 1:5, 11.

## PREEMINENCE (to have the)

1. ***proteuo*** (*4409*), "to be first" (***protos***), "to be preeminent," is used of Christ in relation to the Church, Col. 1:18.

2. ***philoproteuo*** (*5383*), lit., "to love to be preeminent" (***philos***, "loving"), "to strive to be first," is said of Diotrephes, 3 John 9.

## PREFER, PREFERRING

***proegeomai*** (*4285*), "to go before and lead," is used in Rom. 12:10, in the sense of taking the lead in showing deference one to another, "(in honor) preferring one another."

## PREJUDICE

***prokrima*** (*4299*) denotes "prejudging" (akin to ***prokrino***, "to judge beforehand"), 1 Tim. 5:21, RV, "prejudice" (marg., "preference"), preferring one person, another being put aside, by unfavorable judgment due to partiality.

## PRESENCE

**Noun.**

***parousia*** (*3952*): lit. "coming," so meaning the being present in a place, with a focus on the return of the person, Matt. 24:37. This can refer to the presence of any person, but Christians look forward to the return of Christ.

## PRESENT (to be)

**A. Verbs.**

1. ***pareimi*** (*3918*) signifies (a) "to be by, at hand or present," of persons, e.g., Luke 13:1; Acts 10:33; 24:19; 1 Cor. 5:3; 2 Cor. 10:2, 11; Gal. 4:18, 20; of things, John 7:6, of a particular season in the Lord's life on earth, "is (not yet) come," or "is not yet at hand"; Heb. 12:11, of chastening "(for the) present" (the neuter of the present participle, used as a noun); in 13:5 "such things as ye have" is, lit., "the things that are present"; 2 Pet. 1:12, of the truth "(which) is with (you)" (not as KJV, "the present truth," as if of special doctrines applicable to a particular time); in v. 9 "he that lacketh" is lit., "to whom are not present"; (b) "to have arrived or come," Matt. 26:50, "thou art come," RV; John 11:28; Acts 10:21; Col. 1:6.

2. ***enistemi*** (*1764*), "to set in," or, in the middle voice and perfect tense of the active voice, "to stand in, be present," is used of the present in contrast with the past, Heb. 9:9, where the RV correctly has "(for the time) ***now*** present" (for the incorrect KJV, "then present"); in contrast to the future, Rom. 8:38; 1 Cor. 3:22; Gal. 1:4, "present"; 1 Cor. 7:26, where "the present distress" is set in contrast to both the past and the future; 2 Thess. 2:2, where the RV, "is ***now*** present" gives the correct meaning (KJV, incorrectly, "is at hand"); the saints at Thessalonica, owing to their heavy afflictions were possessed of the idea that "the day of the Lord," RV (not as KJV, "the day of Christ"), had begun; this mistake the apostle corrects; 2 Tim. 3:1, "shall come."

**B. Adverb.**

***nun*** (*3568*), "now," is translated "present," with reference to this age or period ("world"), in Rom. 8:18; 11:5; 2 Tim. 4:10; Titus 2:12.

## PRESENT (Verb)

***paristemi*** (*3936*) denotes, when used transitively, "to place beside" (***para***, "by," ***histemi***, "to set"), "to present," e.g., Luke 2:22; Acts 1:3, "He shewed (Himself)"; 9:41; 23:33; Rom. 6:13 (2nd part), RV, "present," KJV "yield"; so 6:19 (twice); 12:1; 2 Cor. 4:14; 11:2; Eph. 5:27; Col. 1:22, 28; 2 Tim. 2:15, RV (KJV, "shew").

## PRESERVE

1. ***tereo*** (*5083*) is translated "to preserve" in 1 Thess. 5:23, where the verb is in the singular number, as the threefold subject, "spirit and soul and body," is regarded as the unit, consti-

tuting the person. The aorist or "point" tense regards the continuous "preservation" of the believer as a single, complete act, without reference to the time occupied in its accomplishment; in Jude 1, KJV (RV, "kept").

2. ***phulasso*** (*5442*), "to guard, protect, preserve," is translated "preserved" in 2 Pet. 2:5, RV (KJV, "saved").

## PREVAIL

1. ***ischuo*** (*2480*), "to be strong, powerful," is translated "to prevail" in Acts 19:16, 20; Rev. 12:8.

2. ***katischuo*** (*2729*), "to be strong against" (***kata***, "against," and No. 1), is used in Matt. 16:18, negatively of the gates of Hades; positively in Luke 21:36.

3. ***nikao*** (*3528*), "to conquer, prevail," is used as a law term in Rom. 3:4, "(that) Thou . . . mightest prevail [KJV, 'overcome'] (when Thou comest into judgment)"; that the righteousness of the judge's verdict compels an acknowledgement on the part of the accused, is inevitable where God is the judge. God's promises to Israel provided no guarantee that an unrepentant Jew would escape doom. In Rev. 5:5, KJV, "hath prevailed" (RV, "hath overcome").

## PRICE

### A. Noun.

***time*** (*5092*) denotes "a valuing," hence, objectively, (a) "price paid or received," Matt. 27:6, 9; Acts 4:34 (plural); 5:2, 3; 7:16, RV, "price (in silver)," KJV, "sum (of money)"; 19:19 (plural); 1 Cor. 6:20; 7:23; (b) "value, honor, preciousness."

### B. Verb.

***timao*** (*5091*), "to fix the value, to price," is translated "was priced" and "did price" in the RV of Matt. 27:9 (KJV, "was valued" and "did value").

### C. Adjectives

1. ***poluteles*** (*4185*), "of great price," 1 Pet. 3:4.

2. ***polutimos*** (*4186*), "of great price," Matt. 13:46.

## PRIDE

### A. Nouns.

1. ***alazonia*** (or ***—eia***) (*212*) is translated "pride" in 1 John 2:16, KJV.

2. ***huperephania*** (*5243*), "pride," Mark 7:22.

### B. Verb.

***tuphoo*** (*5187*), "lifted up with pride," 1 Tim. 3:6, KJV (RV, "puffed up").

## PRIEST

### *Old Testament*

### A. Noun.

***kohen*** (3548), "priest." This word means a person specially authorized by position or heritage, who is a worker or servant of a deity, with a special focus on worship and liturgical duties, and must be "clean" ceremonially in the god's eyes: Egyptian "priests," Gen. 41:50; 46:20; 47:26; Philistine, 1 Sam. 6:2; of Dagon, 1 Sam. 5:5; of Baal, 2 Kings 10:19; of Chemosh, Jer. 48:7; and (the most common use), of the Lord, the true God, Num. 16:5–7.

The Priesthood of Aaron is the most common in the OT, Exod. 28:1, 41; 29:9, 29–30. However, not all individuals born in the family of Aaron could serve as "priest." Certain physical deformities excluded a man from that perfection of holiness which a "priest" should manifest before Yahweh, Lev. 21:17–23.

A priest of Yahweh must go through rigorous ceremonies to keep "clean" and so presentable to work in a consecrated area, and wear special clothing, Exod. 29:1–37 and Lev. 8. The duties of the priesthood were very clearly defined by the Mosaic law. These duties were assumed on the eighth day of the service of consecration, Lev. 9:1. Another function of the priests was to act as teachers of the Law, Lev. 10:10–11; Deut. 33:10; 2 Chron. 5:3; 17:7–9; Ezek. 44:23; Mal. 2:6–9; medical diagnosis, Lev. 13–14; be sentencing judges, and other civil matters, Deut. 21:5; 2 Chron. 19:8–11.

### B. Verb.

***kahan*** (3547), "to act as a priest." This verb, which appears 23 times in biblical Hebrew, is derived from the noun ***kohen.*** The verb appears only in the intensive stem, Exod. 28:1.

### *New Testament*

1. ***hiereus*** (*2409*), "one who offers sacrifice and has the charge of things pertaining thereto," is used (a) of a "priest" of the pagan god Zeus, Acts 14:13; (b) of Jewish "priests," e.g., Matt. 8:4; 12:4, 5; Luke 1:5, where allusion is made to the 24 courses of "priests" appointed for service in the Temple, cf. 1 Chron. 24:4ff.; John 1:19; Heb. 8:4; (c) of believers, Rev. 1:6; 5:10; 20:6. Israel was primarily designed as a nation to be a kingdom of "priests," offering service to God, e.g., Ex. 19:6, the Israelites having renounced their obligations, Ex. 20:19, the Aaronic priesthood was selected for the purpose, till Christ came to fulfill His ministry in offering up Himself; since then the Jewish priesthood has been abrogated, to be resumed nationally, on behalf of Gentiles, in

the millennial kingdom, Is. 61:6; 66:21. Meanwhile all believers, from Jews and Gentiles, are constituted "a kingdom of priests," Rev. 1:6, "a holy priesthood," 1 Pet. 2:5, and "royal," v. 9. The NT knows nothing of a sacerdotal class in contrast to the laity; all believers are commanded to offer the sacrifices mentioned in Rom. 12:1; Phil. 2:17; 4:18; Heb. 13:15, 16; 1 Pet. 2:5; (d) of Christ, Heb. 5:6; 7:11, 15, 17, 21; 8:4 (negatively); (e) of Melchizedek, as the foreshadower of Christ, Heb. 7:1, 3.

2. ***archiereus*** (*749*) designates (a) "the high priests" of the Levitical order, frequently called "chief priests" in the NT, including "ex-high priests" and members of "high priestly" families, e.g., Matt. 2:4; 16:21; 20:18; 21:15; in the singular, a "high priest," e.g., Abiathar, Mark 2:26; Annas and Caiaphas, Luke 3:2, where the RV rightly has "in the high priesthood of A. and C." (cf. Acts 4:6). As to the combination of the two in this respect, Annas was the "high priest" from A.D. 7–14, and, by the time referred to, had been deposed for some years; his son-in-law, Caiaphas, the fourth "high priest" since his deposition, was appointed about A.D. 24. That Annas was still called the "high priest" is explained by the facts (1) that by the Mosaic law the high priesthood was held for life, Num. 35:25; his deposition was the capricious act of the Roman procurator, but he would still be regarded legally and religiously as "high priest" by the Jews; (2) that he probably still held the office of deputy-president of the Sanhedrin, cf. 2 Kings 25:18; (3) that he was a man whose age, wealth and family connections gave him a preponderant influence, by which he held the real sacerdotal power; indeed at this time the high priesthood was in the hands of a clique of some half dozen families; the language of the writers of the gospels is in accordance with this, in attributing the high priesthood rather to a caste than a person; (4) the "high priests" were at that period mere puppets of Roman authorities who deposed them at will, with the result that the title was used more loosely than in former days.

The divine institution of the priesthood culminated in the "high priest," it being his duty to represent the whole people, e.g., Lev. 4:15, 16; ch. 16. The characteristics of the Aaronic "high priests" are enumerated in Heb. 5:1–4; 8:3; 9:7, 25; in some mss., 10:11 (RV, marg.); 13:11.

(b) Christ is set forth in this respect in the Ep. to the Hebrews, where He is spoken of as "a high priest," 4:15; 5:5, 10; 6:20; 7:26; 8:1, 3 (RV); 9:11; "a great high priest," 4:14; "a great priest," 10:21; "a merciful and faithful high priest," 2:17; "the Apostle and high priest of our confession," 3:1, RV; "a high priest after the order of Melchizedek," 5:10. One of the great objects of this Epistle is to set forth the superiority of Christ's High Priesthood as being of an order different from and higher than the Aaronic, in that He is the Son of God (see especially 7:28), with a priesthood of the Melchizedek order. Seven outstanding features of His priesthood are stressed, (1) its character, 5:6, 10; (2) His commission, 5:4, 5; (3) His preparation, 2:17; 10:5; (4) His sacrifice, 8:3; 9:12, 14, 27, 28; 10:4–12; (5) His sanctuary, 4:14; 8:2; 9:11, 12, 24; 10:12, 19; (6) His ministry, 2:18; 4:15; 7:25; 8:6; 9:15, 24; (7) its effects, 2:15; 4:16; 6:19, 20; 7:16, 25; 9:14, 28; 10:14–17, 22, 39; 12:1; 13:13–17.

## PRIESTHOOD, PRIEST'S OFFICE

**Nouns.**

1. ***hierateuma*** (*2406*) denotes "a priesthood" (akin to ***hierateuo***), "a body of priests," consisting of all believers, the whole church (not a special order from among them), called "a holy priesthood," 1 Pet. 2:5; "a royal priesthood," v. 9; the former term is associated with offering spiritual sacrifices, the latter with the royal dignity of showing forth the Lord's excellencies (RV).

2. ***hierosune*** (*2420*), "a priesthood," signifies the office, quality, rank and ministry of "a priest," Heb. 7:11, 12, 24, where the contrasts between the Levitical "priesthood" and that of Christ are set forth.

3. ***hierateia*** (*2405*), "a priesthood," denotes the priest's office, Luke 1:9; Heb. 7:5, RV, "priest's office."

## PRINCE

### *Old Testament*

***nashi'*** (5387), "prince; chief; leader." This noun is clearly associated with leadership, both Israelite and non-Israelite, sometimes called a "prince," and so be a leader by one's heritage or position in the clan, Gen. 17:20; cf. 25:16; or "ruler," Exod. 16:22; or "leader," Exod. 34:31; cf. Josh. 22:30.

### *New Testament*

1. ***archegos*** (*747*), primarily an adjective signifying "originating, beginning," is used as a noun, denoting "a founder, author, prince or leader," Acts 3:15, "Prince" (marg., "Author"); 5:31.

2. ***archon*** (*758*), aside from human rulers, (a) of Christ, as "the Ruler (KJV, Prince) of the kings of the earth," Rev. 1:5; (b) of the Devil, as "prince" of this world, John 12:31; 14:30; 16:11; of the power of the air, Eph. 2:2, "the air" being that sphere in which the inhabitants of the

world live and which, through the rebellious and godless condition of humanity, constitutes the seat of his authority; (c) of Beelzebub, the "prince" of the demons, Matt. 9:24; 12:24; Mark 3:22; Luke 11:15.

## PRINCIPAL

***protos*** (*4413*), "first," is translated "principal men" in the RV of Luke 19:47 and Acts 25:2.

## PRINCIPALITY

***arche*** (*746*), "beginning, government, rule," is used of supra-mundane beings who exercise rule, called "principalities"; (a) of holy angels, Eph. 3:10, the church in its formation being to them the great expression of "the manifold (or "much-varied") wisdom of God"; Col. 1:16; (b) of evil angels, Rom. 8:38; Col. 2:15.

## PRINCIPLES

1. ***arche*** (*746*), "beginning," is used in Heb. 6:1, in its relative significance, of the beginning of the thing spoken of; here "the first principles of Christ," lit., "the account (or word) of the beginning of Christ," denotes the teaching relating to the elementary facts concerning Christ.

2. ***stoicheion*** (*4747*) is translated "principles" in Heb. 5:12.

## PRISON, PRISON-HOUSE

***phulake*** (*5438*), denotes a "prison," e.g., Matt. 14:10; Mark 6:17; Acts 5:19; 2 Cor. 11:23; in 2 Cor. 6:5 and Heb. 11:36 it stands for the condition of imprisonment; in Rev. 2:10; 18:2, "hold" (twice, RV, marg., "prison"; in the 2nd case, KJV, "cage"); 20:7.

## PRISONER

1. ***desmios*** (*1198*), an adjective, primarily denotes "binding, bound," then, as a noun, "the person bound, a captive, prisoner" (akin to ***deo***, "to bind"), Matt. 27:15, 16; Mark 15:6; Acts 16:25, 27; 23:18; 25:14, RV (KJV, "in bonds"), 27; 28:16, 17; Eph. 3:1; 4:1; 2 Tim. 1:8; Philem. 1, 9; in Heb. 10:34 and 13:3, "in bonds."

2. ***desmotes*** (*1202*), akin to No. 1, occurs in Acts 27:1, 42.

3. ***sunaichmalotos*** (*4869*), "a fellow prisoner," primarily "one of fellow captives in war" (from ***aichme***, "a spear," and ***haliskomai***, "to be taken"), is used by Paul of Andronicus and Junias, Rom. 16:7; of Epaphras, Philem. 23; of Aristarchus, Col. 4:10.

## PRIVATE, PRIVATELY

### A. Adjective.

***idios*** (*2398*), one's own, is translated "private" in 2 Pet. 1:20.

### B. Adverbial Phrase.

***kat 'idian*** is translated "privately" in Matt. 24:3; Mark 4:34, RV (KJV, "when they were alone"); 6:32 (KJV only); 7:33, RV; 9:28; 13:3; Luke 10:23; Acts 23:19; Gal. 2:2. Contrast 2:14.

## PRIZE

1. ***brabeion*** (*1017*), "a prize bestowed in connection with the games" (akin to ***brabeus***, "an umpire," and ***brabeuo***, "to decide, arbitrate," "rule," Col. 3:15), 1 Cor. 9:24, is used metaphorically of "the reward" to be obtained hereafter by the faithful believer, Phil. 3:14; the preposition ***eis***, "unto," indicates the position of the goal. The "prize" is not "the high calling," but will be bestowed in virtue of, and relation to, it, the heavenly calling, Heb. 3:1, which belongs to all believers and directs their minds and aspirations heavenward; for the "prize" see especially 2 Tim. 4:7, 8.

2. ***harpagmos*** (*725*), akin to ***harpazo***, "to seize, carry off by force," is found in Phil. 2:6, "(counted it not) a prize," RV (marg., "a thing to be grasped"), KJV, "(thought it not) robbery"; it may have two meanings, (a) in the active sense, "the act of seizing, robbery," a meaning in accordance with a rule connected with its formation, (b) in the passive sense, "a thing held as a prize."

## PROCLAIM

1. ***kerusso*** (*2784*) is translated "to proclaim" in the RV, for KJV, "to preach," in Matt. 10:27; Luke 4:19; Acts 8:5; 9:20.

2. ***katangello*** (*2605*), "to declare, proclaim," is translated "to proclaim" in the RV, for KJV, to "show," in Acts 16:17; 26:23; 1 Cor. 11:26, where the verb makes clear that the partaking of the elements at the Lord's Supper is a "proclamation" (an evangel) of the Lord's death; in Rom. 1:8, for KJV, "spoken of"; in 1 Cor. 2:1, for KJV, "declaring."

## PROCONSUL

***anthupatos*** (*446*), from ***anti***, "instead of," and ***hupatos***, "supreme," denotes "a consul, one acting in place of a consul, a proconsul, the governor of a senatorial province" (i.e., one which had no standing army). The "proconsuls" were of two classes, (a) exconsuls, the rulers of the provinces of Asia and Africa, who were therefore "proconsuls" (b) those who were ex-praetors or "proconsuls" of other senatorial provinces (a praetor being virtually the same as a consul). To the former belonged the "proconsuls" at Ephesus, Acts 19:38 (KJV, "deputies"); to the latter, Sergius Paulus in Cyprus, Acts 13:7, 8, 12, and Gallio at Corinth, 18:12. In the NT times Egypt was governed by a prefect.

Provinces in which a standing army was kept were governed by an imperial legate (e.g., Quirinius in Syria, Luke 2:2).

## PROFANE (Adjective and Verb)

### A. Adjective.

***bebelos*** (*952*), primarily, "permitted to be trodden, accessible" (from ***baino***, "to go," whence ***belos***, "a threshold"), hence, "unhallowed, profane" (opposite to ***hieros***, "sacred"), is used of (a) persons, 1 Tim. 1:9; Heb. 12:16; (b) things, 1 Tim. 4:7; 6:20; 2 Tim. 2:16.

### B. Verb.

***bebeloo*** (*953*), primarily, "to cross the threshold," hence, "to profane, pollute," occurs in Matt. 12:5 and Acts 24:6 (the latter as in 21:28, 29.

## PROFESS, PROFESSION

### A. Verbs.

1. ***epangello*** (*1861*), "to announce, proclaim, profess," is rendered "to profess" in 1 Tim. 2:10, of godliness, and 6:21, of "the knowledge . . . falsely so called."

2. ***homologeo*** (*3670*) is translated "to profess" in Matt. 7:23 and Titus 1:16; in 1 Tim. 6:12, KJV (RV, "confess").

3. ***phasko*** (*5335*), "to affirm, assert."

### B. Noun.

***homologia*** (*3671*), akin to A, No. 2, "confession," is translated "profession" and "professed" in the KJV only.

## PROFIT (Noun and Verb), PROFITABLE, PROFITING

### A. Nouns.

1. ***opheleia*** (*5622*) primarily denotes "assistance"; then, "advantage, benefit, profit," in Rom. 3:1.

2. ***ophelos*** (*3786*), "profit" in Jas. 2:14, 16.

3. ***sumpheron*** (*4851d*), the neuter form of the present participle of ***sumphero***, is used as a noun with the article in Heb. 12:10, "(for our) profit"; in some mss. in 1 Cor. 7:35 and 10:33; in 1 Cor. 12:7, preceded by ***pros***, "with a view to, towards," translated "to profit withal," lit., "towards the profiting."

4. ***sumphoros*** (*4851d*), akin to No. 3, an adjective, signifying "profitable, useful, expedient," is used as a noun, and found in the best texts, with the article, in 1 Cor. 7:35 and 10:33 (1st part), the word being understood in the 2nd part.

### B. Verbs.

1. ***sumphero*** (*4851*), "to be profitable," Matt. 5:29, 30; Acts 20:20.

2. ***opheleo*** (*5623*), akin to A, No. 1, is translated "to profit" in Matt. 15:5; 16:26; Mark 7:11; 8:36; Luke 9:25, RV; John 6:63; Rom. 2:25; 1 Cor. 13:3; 14:6; Gal. 5:2; Heb. 4:2; 13:9.

### C. Adjectives.

1. ***chresimos*** (*5539*), "useful" (akin to ***chraomai***, "to use"), is translated as a noun in 2 Tim. 2:14, "to (no) profit," lit., "to (nothing) profitable.

2. ***euchrestos*** (*2173*), "useful, serviceable" (***eu***, "well," ***chrestos***, "serviceable," akin to ***chraomai***, see No. 1), is used in Philem. 11, "profitable," in contrast to ***achrestos***, "unprofitable" (***a***, negative), with a delightful play upon the name "Onesimus," signifying "profitable" (from ***onesis***, "profit"), a common name among slaves. Perhaps the prefix ***eu*** should have been brought out by some rendering like "very profitable," "very serviceable," the suggestion being that whereas the runaway slave had done great disservice to Philemon, now after his conversion, in devotedly serving the apostle in his confinement, he had thereby already become particularly serviceable to Philemon himself, considering that the latter would have most willingly rendered service to Paul, had it been possible.

3. ***ophelimos*** (*5624*), "useful, profitable" (akin to B, No. 2), is translated "profitable" in 1 Tim. 4:8, both times in the RV (KJV, "profiteth" in the 1st part), of physical exercise, and of godliness; in 2 Tim. 3:16 of the God-breathed Scriptures; in Titus 3:8, of maintaining good works.

## PROLONG

***parateino*** (*3905*), "to stretch out along" (***para***, "along," ***teino***, "to stretch"), is translated "prolonged" in Acts 20:7.

## PROMISE (Noun and Verb)

### A. Noun.

1. ***epangelia*** (*1860*), primarily a law term, denoting "a summons" (***epi***, "upon," ***angello***, "to proclaim, announce"), also meant "an undertaking to do or give something, a promise." Except in Acts 23:21 it is used only of the "promises" of God. It frequently stands for the thing "promised," and so signifies a gift graciously bestowed, not a pledge secured by negotiation; thus, in Gal. 3:14, "the promise of the Spirit" denotes "the promised Spirit": cf. Luke 24:49; Acts 2:33 and Eph. 1:13; so in Heb. 9:15, "the promise of the eternal inheritance" is "the promised eternal inheritance." On the other hand, in Acts 1:4, "the promise of the Father," is the "promise" made by the Father.

In Gal. 3:16, the plural "promises" is used because the one "promise" to Abraham was variously repeated, Gen. 12:1–3; 13:14–17; 15:18; 17:1–14; 22:15–18, and because it contained the germ of all subsequent "promises"; cf. Rom. 9:4; Heb. 6:12; 7:6; 8:6; 11:17; Gal. 3 is occupied with showing that the "promise" was conditional upon faith and not upon the fulfillment of the Law. The Law was later than, and inferior to, the "promise," and did not annul it, v. 21; cf. 4:23, 28. Again, in Eph. 2:12, "the covenants of the promise" does not indicate different covenants, but a covenant often renewed, all centering in Christ as the "promised" Messiah-Redeemer, and comprising the blessings to be bestowed through Him.

In 2 Cor. 1:20 the plural is used of every "promise" made by God: cf. Heb. 11:33; in 7:6, of special "promises" mentioned. For other applications of the word, see, e.g., Eph. 6:2; 1 Tim. 4:8; 2 Tim. 1:1; Heb. 4:1; 2 Pet. 3:4, 9; in 1 John 1:5 some mss. have this word, instead of ***angelia***, "message."

The occurrences of the word in relation to Christ and what centers in Him, may be arranged under the headings (1) the contents of the "promise," e.g., Acts 26:6; Rom. 4:20; 1 John 2:25; (2) the heirs, e.g., Rom. 9:8; 15:8; Gal. 3:29; Heb. 11:9; (3) the conditions, e.g., Rom. 4:13, 14; Gal. 3:14–22; Heb. 10:36.

### B. Verbs.

1. ***epangello*** (*1861*), "to announce, proclaim," has in the NT the two meanings "to profess" and "to promise," each used in the middle voice; "to promise" (a) of "promises" of God, Acts 7:5; Rom. 4:21; in Gal. 3:19, passive voice; Titus 1:2; Heb. 6:13; 10:23; 11:11; 12:26; Jas. 1:12; 2:5; 1 John 2:25; (b) made by men, Mark 14:11; 2 Pet. 2:19.

2. ***proepangello*** (*4279*), in the middle voice, "to promise before" ***pro***, and No. 1), occurs in Rom. 1:2; 2 Cor. 9:5.

## PRONOUNCE

***lego*** (*3004*), "to say, declare," is rendered "pronounceth (blessing)" in Rom. 4:6, RV, which necessarily repeats the verb in v. 9 (it is absent from the original), for KJV, "*cometh*" (italicized).

## PROOF

***dokimion*** (*1383*), "a test, a proof," is rendered "proof" in Jas. 1:3, RV (KJV, "trying"); it is regarded by some as equivalent to ***dokimeion***, "a crucible, a test"; it is the neuter form of the adjective ***dokimios***, used as a noun, which has been taken to denote the means by which a man is tested and "proved" (Mayor), in the same sense as ***dokime*** in 2 Cor. 8:2; the same phrase is used in 1 Pet. 1:7.

## PROPER

***asteios*** (*791*) is translated "proper" in Heb. 11:23, RV, "goodly."

## PROPHECY, PROPHESY, PROPHESYING

### *Old Testament*

### A. Verb.

***naba'*** (5012), "to prophesy." This word means to speak God's message to the people, under the influence of the divine spirit, 1 Kings 22:8; Jer. 29:27; Ezek. 37:10; by compulsion, Amos 3:8; cf. Jer. 20:7; possibly in an ecstatic experience, 1 Sam. 10:6, 11; 19:20. Music is sometimes spoken of as a means of prophesying, as in 1 Chron. 25:1–3. The false prophets, although not empowered by the divine spirit, are spoken of as prophesying, Jer. 23:21. The false prophet is roundly condemned because he speaks a non-authentic word, Ezek. 13:2–3.

"To prophesy" is much more than the prediction of future events. Indeed, the first concern of the prophet is to speak God's word to the people of his own time, calling them to covenant faithfulness. The prophet's message is conditional, dependent upon the response of the people. Thus, by their response to this word, the people determine in large part what the future holds, as is well illustrated by the response of the Ninevites to Jonah's preaching. Of course, prediction does enter the picture at times, such as in Nahum's prediction of the fall of Nineveh, Nah. 2:13, and in the various messianic passages, Isa. 9:1–6; 11:1–9; 52:13–53:12)

### B. Noun.

***nabi'*** (5030), "prophet." ***nabi'*** represents "prophet," whether a true or false prophet, male or female, cf. Deut. 13:1–5; Isa. 8:3. True prophets were mouthpieces of the true God, Exod. 7:1; 1 Chron. 29:29. This basic meaning of ***nabi'*** is supported by other passages, Deut. 18:14–22. A prophet was held to a very high standard, Deut. 18:19, 20.

In the plural ***nabi'*** is used of some who do not function as God's mouthpieces. In the time of Samuel there were men who followed him. They went about praising God (frequently with song) and trying to stir the people to return to God, 1 Sam. 10:5, 10; 19:20. The word is also used of "heathen prophets," 1 Kings 18:19.

*New Testament*

**A. Noun.**

***propheteia*** (*4394*) signifies "the speaking forth of the mind and counsel of God" (***pro***, "forth," ***phemi***, "to speak"; in the NT it is used (a) of the gift, e.g., Rom. 12:6; 1 Cor. 12:10; 13:2; (b) either of the exercise of the gift or of that which is "prophesied," e.g., Matt. 13:14; 1 Cor. 13:8; 14:6, 22 and 1 Thess. 5:20, "prophesying (s)"; 1 Tim. 1:18; 4:14; 2 Pet. 1:20, 21; Rev. 1:3; 11:6; 19:10; 22:7, 10, 18, 19.

In such passages as 1 Cor. 12:28; Eph. 2:20, the "prophets" are placed after the "Apostles," since not the prophets of Israel are intended, but the "gifts" of the ascended Lord, Eph. 4:8, 11; cf. Acts 13:1; the purpose of their ministry was to edify, to comfort, and to encourage the believers, 1 Cor. 14:3, while its effect upon unbelievers was to show that the secrets of a man's heart are known to God, to convict of sin, and to constrain to worship, vv. 24, 25.

**B. Adjective.**

***prophetikos*** (*4397*), "of or relating to prophecy," or "proceeding from a prophet, prophetic," is used of the OT Scriptures, Rom. 16:26, "of the prophets," lit., "(by) prophetic (Scriptures)"; 2 Pet. 1:19, "the word of prophecy (*made* more sure)," i.e., confirmed by the person and work of Christ (KJV, "a more sure, etc."), lit., "the prophetic word."

**C. Verb.**

***propheteuo*** (*4395*), "to be a prophet, to prophesy," is used (a) with the primary meaning of telling forth the divine counsels, e.g., Matt. 7:22; 26:68; 1 Cor. 11:4, 5; 13:9; 14:1, 3–5, 24, 31, 39; Rev. 11:3; (b) of foretelling the future, e.g., Matt. 15:7; John 11:51; 1 Pet. 1:10; Jude 14.

## PROPHET

1. ***prophetes*** (*4396*), "one who speaks forth or openly," "a proclaimer of a divine message," denoted among the Greeks an interpreter of the oracles of the gods.

In the NT the word is used (a) of "the OT prophets," e.g., Matt. 5:12; Mark 6:15; Luke 4:27; John 8:52; Rom. 11:3; (b) of "prophets in general," e.g., Matt. 10:41; 21:46; Mark 6:4; (c) of "John the Baptist," Matt. 21:26; Luke 1:76; (d) of "prophets in the churches," e.g., Acts 13:1; 15:32; 21:10; 1 Cor. 12:28, 29; 14:29, 32, 37; Eph. 2:20; 3:5; 4:11; (e) of "Christ, as the aforepromised Prophet," e.g., John 1:21; 6:14; 7:40; Acts 3:22; 7:37, or, without the article, and, without reference to the Old Testament, Mark 6:15; Luke 7:16; in Luke 24:19 it is used with ***aner***, "a man"; John 4:19; 9:17; (f) of "two witnesses" yet to be raised up for special purposes, Rev. 11:10, 18; (g) of "the Cretan poet Epimenides," Titus 1:12; (h) by metonymy, of "the writings of prophets," e.g., Luke 24:27; Acts 8:28.

2. ***pseudoprophetes*** (*5578*), "a false prophet," is used of such (a) in OT times, Luke 6:26; 2 Pet. 2:1; (b) in the present period since Pentecost, Matt. 7:15; 24:11, 24; Mark 13:22; Acts 13:6; 1 John 4:1; (c) with reference to a false "prophet" destined to arise as the supporter of the "Beast" at the close of this age, Rev. 16:13; 19:20; 20:10 (himself described as "another beast," 13:11).

## PROPHETESS

***prophetis*** (*4398*), the feminine of ***prophetes*** (see above), is used of Anna, Luke 2:36; of the self-assumed title of "the woman Jezebel" in Rev. 2:20.

## PROPITIATION

**A. Verb.**

***hilaskomai*** (*2433*) was used amongst the Greeks with the significance "to make the gods propitious, to appease, propitiate," inasmuch as their good will was not conceived as their natural attitude, but something to be earned first. This use of the word is foreign to the Greek Bible, with respect to God whether in the Sept. or in the NT. It is never used of any act whereby man brings God into a favorable attitude or gracious disposition. It is God who is "propitiated" by the vindication of His holy and righteous character, whereby through the provision He has made in the vicarious and expiatory sacrifice of Christ, He has so dealt with sin that He can show mercy to the believing sinner in the removal of his guilt and the remission of his sins.

Thus in Luke 18:13 it signifies "to be propitious" or "merciful to" (with the person as the object of the verb), and in Heb. 2:17 "to expiate, to make propitiation for" (the object of the verb being sins); here the RV, "to make propitiation" is an important correction of the KJV "to make reconciliation." Through the "propitiatory" sacrifice of Christ, he who believes upon Him is by God's own act delivered from justly deserved wrath, and comes under the covenant of grace. Never is God said to be reconciled, a fact itself indicative that the enmity exists on man's part alone, and that it is man who needs to be reconciled to God, and not God to man. God is always the same and, since He is Himself immutable, His relative attitude does change towards those who change. He can act differently towards those who come to Him by faith, and solely on the ground of the "propitiatory" sacrifice of Christ, not because He has changed, but because He ever acts according to His unchanging righteousness.

The expiatory work of the Cross is therefore the means whereby the barrier which sin interposes between God and man is broken down. By the giving up of His sinless life sacrificially, Christ annuls the power of sin to separate between God and the believer.

In the OT the Hebrew verb ***kaphar*** is connected with ***kopher***, "a covering," and is used in connection with the burnt offering, e.g., Lev. 1:4; 14:20; 16:24, the guilt offering, e.g., Lev. 5:16, 18, the sin offering, e.g., Lev. 4:20, 26, 31, 35, the sin offering and burnt offering together, e.g., Lev. 5:10; 9:7, the meal offering and peace offering, e.g., Ezek. 45:15, 17, as well as in other respects. It is used of the ram offered at the consecration of the high priest, Ex. 29:33, and of the blood which God gave upon the altar to make "propitiation" for the souls of the people, and that because "the life of the flesh is in the blood," Lev. 17:11, and "it is the blood that maketh atonement by reason of the life" (RV). Man has forfeited his life on account of sin and God has provided the one and only way whereby eternal life could be bestowed, namely, by the voluntary laying down of His life by His Son, under divine retribution. Of this the former sacrifices appointed by God were foreshadowings.

**B. Nouns.**

1. ***hilasterion*** (*2435*), akin to A, is regarded as the neuter of an adjective signifying "propitiatory." In the Sept. it is used adjectivally in connection with ***epithema***, "a cover," in Exod. 25:17 and 37:6, of the lid of the ark, but it is used as a noun (without ***epithema***), of locality, in Exod. 25:18, 19, 20, 21, 22; 31:7; 35:12; 37:7, 8, 9; Lev. 16:2, 13, 14, 15; Num. 7:89, and this is its use in Heb. 9:5.

Elsewhere in the NT it occurs in Rom. 3:25, where it is used of Christ Himself; the RV text and punctuation in this verse are important: "whom God set forth to be a propitiation, through faith, by His blood." The phrase "by His blood" is to be taken in immediate connection with "propitiation." Christ, through His expiatory death, is the personal means by whom God shows the mercy of His justifying grace to the sinner who believes. His "blood" stands for the voluntary giving up of His life, by the shedding of His blood in expiatory sacrifice under divine judgment righteously due to us as sinners, faith being the sole condition on man's part.

2. ***hilasmos*** (*2434*), akin to ***hileos*** ("merciful, propitious"), signifies "an expiation, a means whereby sin is covered and remitted." It is used in the NT of Christ Himself as "the propitiation," in 1 John 2:2 and 4:10, signifying that He Himself, through the expiatory sacrifice of His death, is the personal means by whom God shows mercy to the sinner who believes on Christ as the One thus provided. In the former passage He is described as "the propitiation for our sins; and not for ours only, but also for the whole world." The italicized addition in the KJV, "the sins of," gives a wrong interpretation. What is indicated is that provision is made for the whole world, so that no one is, by divine predetermination, excluded from the scope of God's mercy; the efficacy of the "propitiation," however, is made actual for those who believe. In 4:10, the fact that God "sent His Son to be the propitiation for our sins," is shown to be the great expression of God's love toward man, and the reason why Christians should love one another.

## PROPORTION

***analogia*** (*356*), Cf. Eng., "analogy," signified in classical Greek "the right relation, the coincidence or agreement existing or demanded according to the standard of the several relations, not agreement as equality" (Cremer). It is used in Rom. 12:6, where "let us prophesy according to the proportion of our faith," RV, recalls v. 3. It is a warning against going beyond what God has given and faith receives.



## PROSELYTE

***proselutos*** (*4339*), akin to ***proserchomai***, "to come to," primarily signifies "one who has arrived, a stranger"; in the NT it is used of converts to Judaism, or foreign converts to the Jewish religion, Matt. 23:15; Acts 2:10; 6:5; 13:43. There seems to be no connection necessarily with Palestine, for in Acts 2:10 and 13:43 it is used of those who lived abroad.

## PROSPER

### *Old Testament*

***tsaleach*** (6743), "to succeed, prosper." This word generally expresses the idea of a successful venture, as contrasted with failure. The source of such success is God, 2 Chron. 26:5

### *New Testament*

***euodoo*** (*2137*), "to help on one's way" (***eu***, "well," ***hodos***, "a way or journey"), is used in the passive voice signifying "to have a prosperous journey," Rom. 1:10; metaphorically, "to prosper, be prospered," 1 Cor. 16:2, RV, "(as) he may prosper," KJV, "(as God) hath prospered (him)," lit., "in whatever he may be prospered," i.e., in material things; the continuous tense suggests the successive circumstances of varying prosperity as week follows week; in 3 John 2, of the "prosperity" of physical and spiritual health.

## PROUD

***huperephanos*** (*5244*) signifies "showing oneself above others, preeminent" (***huper***, "above," ***phainomai***, "to appear, be manifest"); it is always used in Scripture in the bad sense of "arrogant, disdainful, proud," Luke 1:51; Rom. 1:30; 2 Tim. 3:2; Jas. 4:6; 1 Pet. 5:5.

## PROVE

### A. Verbs.

1. ***dokimazo*** (*1381*), "to test, prove," with the expectation of approving, is translated "to prove" in Luke 14:19; Rom. 12:2; 1 Cor. 3:13, RV (KJV, "shall try"); 11:28, RV (KJV, "examine"); 2 Cor. 8:8, 22; 13:5; Gal. 6:4; Eph. 5:10; 1 Thess. 2:4 (2nd part), RV (KJV, "trieth"); 5:21; 1 Tim. 3:10; in some mss., Heb. 3:9 (the most authentic have the noun ***dokimasia***, "a proving"); 1 Pet. 1:7, RV (KJV, "tried"); 1 John 4:1, RV (KJV, "try").

2. ***peirazo*** (*3985*), "to try," either in the sense of attempting, e.g., Acts 16:7, or of testing, is rendered "to prove" in John 6:6.

### B. Noun.

***peirasmos*** (*3986*), (a) "a trying, testing," (b) "a temptation," is used in sense (a) in 1 Pet. 4:12, with the preposition ***pros***, "towards" or "with a view to," RV, "to prove" (KJV, "to try"), lit., "for a testing."

## PROVIDE, PROVIDENCE, PROVISION

### A. Verbs.

1. ***hetoimazo*** (*2090*), "to prepare," is translated "hast provided" in Luke 12:20, KJV.

2. ***ktaomai*** (*2932*), "to get, to gain," is rendered "provide" in Matt. 10:9.

3. ***paristemi*** (*3936*), "to present," signifies "to provide" in Acts 23:24.

4. ***problepo*** (*4265*), "to foresee," is translated "having provided" in Heb. 11:40.

5. ***pronoeo*** (*4306*), "to take thought for, provide," is translated "provide . . . for" in 1 Tim. 5:8; in Rom. 12:17 and 2 Cor. 8:21, RV, to take thought for (KJV, "to provide").

### B. Noun.

***pronoia*** (*4307*), "forethought" (***pro***, "before," ***noeo***, "to think"), is translated "providence" in Acts 24:2; "provision" in Rom. 13:14.

## PROVINCE

1. ***eparcheia***, or ***—ia*** (*1885*) was a technical term for the administrative divisions of the Roman Empire. The original meaning was the district within which a magistrate, whether consul or praetor, exercised supreme authority. The word *provincia* acquired its later meaning when Sardinia and Sicily were added to the Roman territories, 227 B.C. On the establishment of the empire the proconsular power over all "provinces" was vested in the emperor. Two "provinces," Asia and Africa, were consular, i.e., held by ex-consuls; the rest were praetorian. Certain small "provinces," e.g. Judea and Cappadocia, were governed by procurators. They were usually districts recently added to the empire and not thoroughly Romanized. Judea was so governed in the intervals between the rule of native kings; ultimately it was incorporated in the "province" of Syria. The "province" mentioned in Acts 23:34 and 25:1 was assigned to the jurisdiction of an ***eparchos***, "a prefect or governor."

2. ***kanon*** (*2583*) originally denoted "a straight rod," used as a ruler or measuring instrument, or, in rare instances, "the beam of a balance," the secondary notion being either (a) of keeping anything straight, as of a rod used in weaving, or (b) of testing straightness, as a carpenter's rule; hence its metaphorical use to express what serves "to measure or determine" anything. By a common transition in the meaning of words, "that which measures," was used for "what was measured." In general the word thus came to serve for anything regulating the actions of men, as a standard or principle. In Gal. 6:16, those who "walk by this rule (***kanon***)" are those who make what is stated in vv. 14 and 15 their guiding line in the matter of salvation through faith in Christ alone, apart from works, whether following the principle themselves or teaching it to others. In 2 Cor. 10:13, 15, 16, it is translated "province," RV (KJV, "rule" and "line of things"; marg., "line"; RV marg., "limit" or "measuring rod.") Here it signifies the limits of the responsibility in gospel service as measured and appointed by God.

## PROVOCATION, PROVOKE

### *Old Testament*

***ka'as*** (3707), "to provoke, vex, make angry." This word means to be intensely displeased with another, often implying that an action venting the anger will occur, Deut. 4:25; 2 Kings 23:19.

*New Testament*

**A. Nouns.**

1. ***parapikrasmos*** (*3894*), from ***para***, "amiss" or "from," used intensively, and ***pikraino***, "to make bitter" (***pikros***, "sharp, bitter"), "provocation," occurs in Heb. 3:8, 15.

2. ***paroxusmos*** (*3948*) denotes "a stimulation" (Eng., "paroxysm"), (cf. B, No. 2): in Heb. 10:24, "to provoke," lit., "unto a stimulation (of love)."

**B. Verbs.**

1. ***parapikraino*** (*3893*), "to embitter, provoke" (akin to A, No. 1), occurs in Heb. 3:16.

2. ***paroxuno*** (*3947*), primarily, "to sharpen" (akin to A, No. 2), is used metaphorically, signifying "to rouse to anger, to provoke," in the passive voice, in Acts 17:16, RV, "was provoked" (KJV, "was stirred"); in 1 Cor. 13:5, RV, "is not provoked" (the word "easily" in KJV, represents no word in the original).

3. ***parorgizo*** (*3949*), "to provoke to wrath."

4. ***parazeloo*** (*3863*), "to provoke to jealousy."

## PRUDENCE, PRUDENT

**A. Nouns.**

1. ***phronesis*** (*5428*), akin to ***phroneo***, "to have understanding" (***phren***, "the mind"), denotes "practical wisdom, prudence in the management of affairs." It is translated "wisdom" in Luke 1:17; "prudence" in Eph. 1:8.

2. ***sunesis*** (*4907*), "understanding," is rendered "prudence" in 1 Cor. 1:19, RV (KJV, "understanding"); it suggests quickness of apprehension, the penetrating consideration which precedes action.

**B. Adjective.**

***sunetos*** (*4908*) signifies "intelligent, sagacious, understanding" (akin to ***suniemi***, "to perceive"), translated "prudent" in Matt. 11:25, KJV (RV, "understanding"); Luke 10:21 (ditto); Acts 13:7, RV, "(a man) of understanding"; in 1 Cor. 1:19, "prudent," RV and KJV.

## PSALM

***psalmos*** (*5568*) primarily denoted "a striking or twitching with the fingers (on musical strings)"; then, "a sacred song, sung to musical accompaniment, a psalm." It is used (a) of the OT book of "Psalms," Luke 20:42; 24:44; Acts 1:20; (b) of a particular "psalm," Acts 13:33 (cf. v. 35); (c) of "psalms" in general, 1 Cor. 14:26; Eph. 5:19; Col. 3:16.

## PUBLIC

***demosios*** (*1219*), "belonging to the people" (***demos***, "the people"), is translated "public" in Acts 5:18, RV, "public (ward)," KJV, "common (prison)."

## PUBLICAN

***telones*** (*5057*) primarily denoted "a farmer of the tax" (from ***telos***, "toll, custom, tax"), then, as in the NT, a subsequent subordinate of such, who collected taxes in some district, "a tax gatherer"; such were naturally hated intensely by the people; they are classed with "sinners," Matt. 9:10, 11; 11:9; Mark 2:15, 16; Luke 5:30; 7:34; 15:1; with harlots, Matt. 21:31, 32; with "the Gentile," Matt. 18:17; some mss. have it in Matt. 5:47, the best have ***ethnikoi***, "Gentiles." See also Matt. 5:46; 10:3; Luke 3:12; 5:27, 29; 7:29; 18:10, 11, 13.

## PUBLISH

1. ***kerusso*** (*2784*), "to be a herald, to proclaim, preach," is translated "to publish" in Mark 1:45; 5:20; 7:36; 13:10, KJV (RV, "preached"); Luke 8:39.

2. ***diaphero*** (*1308*), "to bear through," is translated "was published" in Acts 13:49, KJV (RV, "was spread abroad").

3. ***ginomai*** (*1096*), "to become, come to be," is translated "was published" in Acts 10:37, lit., "came to be."

4. ***diangello*** (*1229*), "to publish abroad," is so translated in Luke 9:60, RV (KJV, "preach"), and Rom. 9:17.

## PUFF (up)

1. ***phusioo*** (*5448*), "to puff up, blow up, inflate" (from ***phusa***, "bellows"), is used metaphorically in the NT, in the sense of being "puffed" up with pride, 1 Cor. 4:6, 18, 19; 5:2; 8:1; 13:4; Col. 2:18.

2. ***tuphoo*** (*5187*) is always rendered "to puff up" in the RV.

## PUNISH

1. ***kolazo*** (*2849*) primarily denotes "to curtail, prune, dock" (from ***kolos***, "docked"); then, "to check, restrain, punish"; it is used in the middle voice in Acts 4:21; passive voice in 2 Pet. 2:9, KJV, "to be punished" (RV, "under punishment," lit., "being punished"), a futurative present tense.

2. ***timoreo*** (*5097*), primarily, "to help," then, "to avenge" (from ***time***, "value, honor," and ***ouros***, "a guardian"), i.e., "to help" by redressing injuries, is used in the active voice in Acts 26:11, RV, "punishing" (KJV, "I punished"); passive voice in 22:5, lit., "(that) they may be punished."

## PUNISHMENT

1. ***ekdikesis*** (*1557*): for 1 Pet. 2:14, KJV, "punishment" (RV, "vengeance").

2. ***epitimia*** (*2009*) in the NT denotes "penalty, punishment," 2 Cor. 2:6. Originally it signified the enjoyment of the rights and privileges of citizenship; then it became used of the estimate (***time***) fixed by a judge on the infringement of such rights, and hence, in general, a "penalty."

3. ***kolasis*** (*2851*), akin to ***kolazo***, "punishment," is used in Matt. 25:46, "(eternal) punishment," and 1 John 4:18, "(fear hath) punishment," RV (KJV, "torment"), which there describes a process, not merely an effect; this kind of fear is expelled by perfect love; where God's love is being perfected in us, it gives no room for the fear of meeting with His reprobation; the "punishment" referred to is the immediate consequence of the sense of sin, not a holy awe but a slavish fear, the negation of the enjoyment of love.

4. ***dike*** (*1349*), "justice," or "the execution of a sentence," is translated "punishment" in Jude 7, RV (KJV, "vengeance").

## PURCHASE

1. ***peripoieo*** (*4046*) signifies "to gain" or "get for oneself, purchase"; middle voice in Acts 20:28 and 1 Tim. 3:13 (RV "gain"); see GAIN.

2. ***agorazo*** (*59*) is rendered "to purchase" in the RV of Rev. 5:9; 14:3, 4.

## PURE, PURENESS, PURITY

### A. Adjectives.

1. ***hagnos*** (*53*), "pure from defilement, not contaminated" (from the same root as ***hagios***, "holy"), is rendered "pure" in Phil. 4:8; 1 Tim. 5:22; Jas. 3:17; 1 John 3:3.

2. ***katharos*** (*2513*), "pure," as being cleansed, e.g., Matt. 5:8; 1 Tim. 1:5; 3:9; 2 Tim. 1:3; 2:22; Titus 1:15; Heb. 10:22; Jas. 1:27; 1 Pet. 1:22; Rev. 15:6; 21:18; 22:1 (in some mss.).

3. ***eilikrines*** (*1506*) signifies "unalloyed, pure"; (a) it was used of unmixed substances; (b) in the NT it is used of moral and ethical "purity," Phil. 1:10, "sincere"; so the RV in 2 Pet. 3:1 (KJV, "pure"). Some regard the etymological meaning as "tested by the sunlight" (Cremer).

### B. Nouns.

1. ***hagnotes*** (*54*), the state of being ***hagnos*** (A, No. 1), occurs in 2 Cor. 6:6, "pureness"; 11:3, in the best mss., "(and the) purity," RV.

2. ***hagneia*** (*47*), synonymous with No. 1, "purity," occurs in 1 Tim. 4:12; 5:2, where it denotes the chastity which excludes all impurity of spirit, manner, or act.

## PURGE (to cleanse)

1. ***kathairo*** (*2508*), akin to ***katharos***, "to cleanse," is used of pruning, John 15:2, KJV, "purgeth" (RV, "cleanseth").

2. ***ekkathairo*** (*1571*), "to cleanse out, cleanse thoroughly," is said of "purging" out leaven, 1 Cor. 5:7; in 2 Tim. 2:21, of "purging" oneself from those who utter "profane babblings," vv. 16–18.

3. ***diakathairo*** (*1223* and *2508*), "to cleanse thoroughly," is translated "will thoroughly purge" in Luke 3:17.

4. ***kathakizo*** (*2511*), "to cleanse, make clean," is translated "purging (all meats)," in Mark 7:19, KJV, RV, "making (all meats) clean"; Heb. 9:14, KJV, "purge" (RV, "cleanse"); so 9:22 (for v. 23, see PURIFY) and 10:2.

5. ***diakatharizo*** (*1245*), "to cleanse thoroughly," is translated "will thoroughly purge" in Matt. 3:12, KJV.

## PURIFICATION, PURIFY, PURIFYING

### A. Nouns.

1. ***katharismos*** (*2512*) is rendered "a cleansing," Mark 1:44; Luke 5:14; in Heb. 1:3, RV, "purification."

2. ***katharotes*** (*2514*), "cleansing," Heb. 9:13.

3. ***hagnismos*** (*49*) denotes "a ceremonial purification," Acts 21:26, for the circumstances of which with reference to the vow of a Nazirite (RV), see Num. 6:9–13.

### B. Verbs.

1. ***hagnizo*** (*48*), akin to ***hagnos***, "pure," "to purify, cleanse from defilement," is used of "purifying" (a) ceremonially, John 11:55; Acts 21:24, 26 (cf. No. 3 above); 24:18; (b) morally, the heart, Jas. 4:8; the soul, 1 Pet. 1:22; oneself, 1 John 3:3.

2. ***katharizo*** (*2511*), "to cleanse, make free from admixture," is translated "to purify" in Acts 15:9, KJV (RV, "cleansing"); Titus 2:14; Heb. 9:23, KJV (RV, "cleansed").

## PURPLE

### A. Noun.

***porphura*** (*4209*) originally denoted the "purple-fish," then, "purple dye" (extracted from certain shell fish): hence, "a purple garment," Mark 15:17, 20; Luke 16:19; Rev. 18:12.

### B. Adjective.

***porphureos*** (*4210*), "purple, a reddish purple," a color extracted from certain shell fish, is used of the robe put in mockery on Christ, John 19:2, 5; Rev. 18:16, as a noun (with ***himation***, "a garment," understood).

## PURPOSE (Noun and Verb)

### A. Nouns.

1. ***boulema*** (*1013*), "a purpose or will" (akin to ***boulomai***, "to will, wish, purpose"), "a deliberate intention," occurs in Acts 27:43, "purpose"; Rom. 9:19, "will"; 1 Pet. 4:3, in the best mss. (some have ***thelema***), KJV, "will," RV, "desire."

2. ***prothesis*** (*4286*), "a setting forth" (used of the "showbread"), "a purpose" (akin to B, No. 2), is used (a) of the "purposes of God," Rom. 8:28; 9:11; Eph. 1:11; 3:11; 2 Tim. 1:9; (b) of "human purposes," as to things material, Acts 27:13; spiritual, Acts 11:23; 2 Tim. 3:10.

3. ***gnome*** (*1106*), "an opinion, purpose, judgment," is used in the genitive case with ***ginomai***, "to come to be," in Acts 20:3, "he purposed," KJV (RV, "he determined"), lit., "he came to be of purpose."

### B. Verbs.

1. ***bouleuo*** (*1011*), "to take counsel, resolve," always in the middle voice in the NT, "to take counsel with oneself," to determine with oneself, is translated "I purpose" in 2 Cor. 1:17 (twice).

2. ***protithemi*** (*4388*), "to set before, set forth" (***pro***, "before," and No. 2, akin to A, No. 2), is used in Rom. 3:25, "set forth," RV marg., "purposed," KJV marg., "foreordained," middle voice, which lays stress upon the personal interest which God had in so doing; either meaning, "to set forth" or "to purpose," would convey a scriptural view, but the context bears out the former as being intended here; in Rom. 1:13, "I purposed"; Eph. 1:9, "He purposed (in Him)," RV.

# Q

## QUATERNION

***tetradion*** (*5069*), "a group of four" (***tetra***—,"four"), occurs in Acts 12:4. A "quaternion" was a set of four men occupied in the work of a guard, two soldiers being chained to the prisoner and two keeping watch; alternatively one of the four watched while the other three slept. The night was divided into four watches of three hours each; there would be one "quaternion" for each watch by day and by night.

## QUENCH, UNQUENCHABLE

**A. Verb.**

***sbennumi*** (*4570*) is used (a) of "quenching" fire or things on fire, Matt. 12:20, quoted from Isa. 42:3, figurative of the condition of the feeble; Heb. 11:34; in the passive voice, Matt. 25:8, of torches, RV, "are going out," lit., "are being quenched"; of the retributive doom hereafter of sin unrepented of and unremitted in this life, Mark 9:48 (in some mss. in vv. 44, 46); (b) metaphorically, of "quenching" the fire-tipped darts of the evil one, Eph. 6:16; of "quenching" the Spirit, by hindering His operations in oral testimony in the church gatherings of believers, 1 Thess. 5:19. The peace, order, and edification of the saints were evidence of the ministry of the Spirit among them, 1 Cor. 14:26, 32, 33, 40, but if, through ignorance of His ways, or through failure to recognize, or refusal to submit to, them, or through impatience with the ignorance or self-will of others, the Spirit was quenched, these happy results would be absent.

**B. Adjective.**

***asbestos*** (*762*), "not quenched" (***a***, negative, and A), is used of the doom of persons described figuratively as "chaff," Matt. 3:12 and Luke 3:17, "unquenchable"; of the fire of Gehenna, Mark 9:43, RV, "unquenchable fire" (in some mss. v. 45).

## QUESTION (Noun and Verb), QUESTIONING

**A. Nouns.**

1. ***zetesis*** (*2214*), primarily "a seeking, search" (***zeteo***, "to seek"), is used in John 3:25; Acts 25:20, RV, "(being perplexed) how to inquire (concerning these things)," KJV "(because I doubted of such manner) of questions," lit., "being perplexed as to the inquiry (or discussion) concerning these things"; in 1 Tim. 1:4 (in some mss.); 6:4; 2 Tim. 2:23; Titus 3:9.

2. ***zetema*** (*2213*), synonymous with No. 1, but, generally speaking, suggesting in a more concrete form the subject of an inquiry, occurs in Acts 15:2; 18:15; 23:29; 25:19; 26:3.

**B. Verbs.**

1. ***suzeteo*** (*4802*) or ***sunzeteo***, "to search together," "to discuss, dispute," is translated "to question" (or "question with or together") in Mark 1:27; 8:11; 9:10, 14, 16; 12:28, RV (KJV, "reasoning together"); Luke 22:23, RV (KJV, "inquire"); 24:15, RV (KJV, "reasoned").

2. ***eperotao*** (*1905*), "to ask," is translated "asked . . . a question," in Matt. 22:35, 41; in Luke 2:46, "asking . . . questions"; "questioned" in Luke 23:9.

## QUICKEN

***suzoopoieo*** (*4806*) or ***sunzoopoieo***, "to quicken together with, make alive with," is used in Eph. 2:5; Col. 2:13, of the spiritual life with Christ, imparted to believers at their conversion.

## QUIET, QUIETNESS

**A. Adjectives.**

1. ***eremos*** (*2263*), "quiet, tranquil," occurs in 1 Tim. 2:2, RV, "tranquil" (KJV, "quiet"); it indicates tranquillity arising from without.

2. ***hesuchios*** (*2272*) has much the same meaning as No. 1, but indicates "tranquillity arising from within," causing no disturbance to others. It is translated "quiet" in 1 Tim. 2:2, RV (KJV, "peaceable"); "quiet" in 1 Pet. 3:4, where it is associated with "meek," and is to characterize the spirit or disposition.

**B. Verbs**

***hesuchazo*** (*2270*), akin to A, No. 2, "to be still, to live quietly."

**C. Nouns.**

1. ***eirene*** (*1515*), "peace," is translated "quietness" in Acts 24:2, KJV (RV, "peace").

2. ***hesuchia*** (*2271*), akin to A, No. 2, and B. No. 1, denotes "quietness," 2 Thess. 3:12; it is so translated in the RV of 1 Tim. 2:11, 12

(KJV, "silence"); in Acts 22:2, RV, "(they were the more) quiet," KJV, "(they kept the more) silence," lit., "they kept quietness the more."

## QUIT

1. ***apallasso*** (525), "to free from," is used in the passive voice in Luke 12:58, RV, "to be quit" (KJV, "to be delivered").

2. ***andrizo*** (*407*) signifies "to make a man of" (***aner***, "a man"); in the middle voice, in 1 Cor. 16:13, "to play the man," "quit you like men."

# R

## RABBI

***rabbei*** or ***rabbi*** (*4461*), from a word ***rab***, primarily denoting "master" in contrast to a slave; this with the added pronominal suffix signified "my master" and was a title of respect by which teachers were addressed. The suffix soon lost its specific force, and in the NT the word is used as courteous title of address. It is applied to Christ in Matt. 26:25, 49; Mark 9:5; 11:21; 14:45; John 1:38 (where it is interpreted as ***didaskalos***, "master," marg., "teacher"; v. 49; 3:2; 4:31; 6:25; 9:2; 11:8; to John the Baptist in John 3:26. In Matt. 23:7, 8 Christ forbids his disciples to covet or use it. In the latter verse it is again explained as ***didaskalos***, "master."

## RABBONI

***rabbounei*** or ***rabboni*** (*4462*), formed in a similar way to the above, was an Aramaic form of a title even more respectful than Rabbi, and signified "My great master"; in its use in the NT the pronominal force of the suffix is apparently retained (contrast Rabbi above); it is found in Mark 10:51 in the best texts, RV, "Rabboni" (KJV, "Lord"), addressed to Christ by blind Bartimaeus, and in John 20:16 by Mary Magdalene.

## RACA

***raka*** (*4469*) is an Aramaic word akin to the Heb. ***req***, "empty," the first ***a*** being due to a Galilean change. In the KJV of 1611 it was spelled ***racha***; in the edition of 1638, ***raca***. It was a word of utter contempt, signifying "empty," intellectually rather than morally, "empty-headed," like Abimelech's hirelings, Judg. 9:4, and the "vain" man of Jas. 2:20; condemned by Christ, Matt. 5:22.

## RACE (contest)

***agon*** (*73*) is translated "race" in Heb. 12:1, one of the modes of athletic contest, this being the secondary meaning of the word.

## RAGE, RAGING

***phruasso*** (*5433*) was primarily used of "the snorting, neighing and prancing of horses"; hence, metaphorically, of "the haughtiness and insolence of men," Acts 4:25.

## RAIL

***blasphemeo*** (*987*), a verb, "to blaspheme, rail, revile," is translated "to rail at, or on," in Matt. 27:39, RV (KJV, "reviled"); Mark 15:29; Luke 23:39; 2 Pet. 2:10, RV (KJV, "to speak evil of"); 2:12, RV (KJV, "speak evil of").

## RAINBOW

***iris*** (*2463*), whence Eng., "iris," the flower, describes the "rainbow" seen in the heavenly vision, "round about the throne, like an emerald to look upon," Rev. 4:3; emblematic of the fact that, in the exercise of God's absolute sovereignty and perfect counsels, He will remember His covenant concerning the earth, Gen. 9:9–17.

## RAISE (up)

1. ***egeiro*** (*1453*), for the various meanings of which, is used (a) of "raising" the dead, active and passive voices, e.g. of the resurrection of Christ, Matt. 16:21; 17:23; 20:19, RV; 26:32, RV, "(after) I am raised up" (KJV, "... risen again"); Luke 9:22; 20:37; John 2:19; Acts 3:15; 4:10 [not 5:30, see (c) below]; 10:40 [not 13:23 in the best texts, see (c) below]; 13:30, 37; Rom. 4:24, 25; 6:4, 9; 7:4; 8:11 (twice); 8:34, RV; 10:9; 1 Cor. 6:14 (1st part); 15:13, 14, RV; 15:15 (twice), 16, 17; 15:20, RV; 2 Cor. 4:14; Gal. 1:1; Eph. 1:20; Col. 2:12; 1 Thess. 1:10; 1 Pet. 1:21; in 2 Tim. 2:8, RV, "risen"; (b) of the resurrection of human beings, Matt. 10:8; 11:5; Matt. 27:52. RV (KJV, "arose"); Mark 12:26, RV; Luke 7:22; John 5:21; 12:1, 9, 17; Acts 26:8; 1 Cor. 15:29 and 32, RV; 15:35, 42, 43 (twice), 44, 52; 2 Cor. 1:9; 4:14; Heb. 11:19; (c) of "raising" up a person to occupy a place in the midst of a people, said of Christ, Acts 5:30; in 13:23, KJV only (the best texts have ***ago***, to bring, RV, "hath . . . brought"); of David, Acts 13:22 (for v. 33 see No. 2); (d) metaphorically, of a horn of salvation, Luke 1:69; (e) of children, from stones, by creative power, Luke 3:8; (f) of the Temple, as the Jews thought, John 2:20, RV, "wilt Thou raise (it) Up" (KJV, "rear"); (g) of "lifting" up a person, from physical infirmity, Mark 1:31, RV, "raised . . . up" (KJV, "lifted"); so 9:27; Acts 3:7; 10:26, RV (KJV, "took"); Jas. 5:15, "shall raise . . . up"; (h) metaphorically, of "raising" up affliction, Phil. 1:17, RV (in the best texts; the KJV, v. 16, following those which have ***epiphero***, has "to add").

2. ***anistemi*** (*450*), translated "to raise or raise up," (a) of the resurrection of the dead by Christ, John 6:39, 40, 44, 54; (b) of the resurrection of Christ from the dead, Acts 2:24 (for v. 30 see RV, ***kathizo***, "to set," as in the best texts); 2:32; 13:34, see (c) below; Acts 17:31; (c) of "raising" up a person to occupy a place in the midst of a nation, said of Christ, Acts 3:26; 7:37; 13:33, RV, "raised up Jesus," not here by resurrection from the dead, as the superfluous "again" of the KJV would suggest; this is confirmed by the latter part of the verse, which explains the "raising" up as being by way of His incarnation, and by the contrast in v. 34, where stress is laid upon His being "raised" from the dead, the same verb being used: (d) of "raising" up seed, Matt. 22:24; (e) of being "raised" from natural sleep, Matt. 1:24, KJV.

## RANSOM

***lutron*** (*3383*), lit., "a means of loosing" (from ***luo***, "to loose"), occurs frequently in the Sept., where it is always used to signify "equivalence." Thus it is used of the "ransom" for a life, e.g., Exod. 21:30, of the redemption price of a slave, e.g., Lev. 19:20, of land, 25:24, of the price of a captive, Isa. 45:13. In the NT it occurs in Matt. 20:28 and Mark 10:45, where it is used of Christ's gift of Himself as "a ransom for many."

## RAVENING

***harpax*** (*727*), an adjective signifying "rapacious," is translated "ravening" (of wolves) in Matt. 7:15.

## READ, READING

***anaginosko*** (*314*), primarily, "to know certainly, to know again, recognize" (***ana***, "again," ***ginosko***, "to know"), is used of "reading" written characters, e.g., Matt. 12:3, 5; 21:16; 24:15; of the private "reading" of Scripture, Acts 8:28, 30, 32; of the public "reading" of Scripture, Luke 4:16; Acts 13:27; 15:21; 2 Cor. 3:15; Col. 4:16 (thrice); 1 Thess. 5:27; Rev. 1:3.

## READINESS

1. ***prothumia*** (*4288*), "eagerness, willingness, readiness" (***pro***, "forward," ***thumos***, "mind, disposition"), akin to ***prothumos***, is translated "readiness of mind" in Acts 17:11, "readiness" in 2 Cor. 8:11; in v. 12, RV (KJV, "a willing mind"); in v. 19, RV "(our) readiness," KJV, "(your) ready mind"; in 9:2, RV, "readiness."

2. ***hetoimos*** (*2092*), an adjective, is used with ***echo***, "to have," and ***en***, "in," idiomatically, as a noun in 2 Cor. 10:6, RV, "being in readiness" (KJV, "having in readiness"), of the apostle's aim for the church to be obedient to Christ.

## READY

***hetoimos*** (*2092*), "prepared, ready" (akin to ***hetoimasia***, "preparation"), is used (a) of persons, Matt. 24:44; 25:10; Luke 12:40; 22:33; Acts 23:15, 21 (for 2 Cor. 10:6, see above); Titus 3:1; 1 Pet. 3:15; (b) of things, Matt. 22:4 (2nd part), 8; Mark 14:15, RV, "ready" (KJV, "prepared"); Luke 14:17; John 7:6; 2 Cor. 9:5; 10:16, RV, "things ready" (KJV, "things made ready"); 1 Pet. 1:5.

## REAP

***therizo*** (*2325*), "to reap" (akin to ***theros***, "summer, harvest"), is used (a) literally, Matt. 6:26; 25:24, 26; Luke 12:24; 19:21, 22; Jas. 5:4 (2nd part), KJV, "have reaped"; (b) figuratively or in proverbial expressions, John 4:36 (twice), 37, 38, with immediate reference to bringing Samaritans into the kingdom of God, in regard to which the disciples would enjoy the fruits of what Christ Himself had been doing in Samaria; the Lord's words are, however, of a general application in respect of such service; in 1 Cor. 9:11, with reference to the right of the apostle and his fellow missionaries to receive material assistance from the church, a right which he forbore to exercise; in 2 Cor. 9:6 (twice), with reference to rendering material help to the needy, either "sparingly" or "bountifully," the "reaping" being proportionate to the sowing; in Gal. 6:7, 8 (twice), of "reaping" corruption, with special reference, according to the context, to that which is naturally shortlived transient (though the statement applies to every form of sowing to the flesh), and of "reaping" eternal life (characteristics and moral qualities being in view), as a result of sowing "to the Spirit," the reference probably being to the new nature of the believer, which is, however, under the controlling power of the Holy Spirit, v. 9, the "reaping" (the effect of well doing) being accomplished, to a limited extent, in this life, but in complete fulfillment at and beyond the judgment seat of Christ; diligence or laxity here will then produce proportionate results; in Rev. 14:15 (twice), 16, figurative of the discriminating judgment divinely to be fulfilled at the close of this age, when the wheat will be separated from the tares (see Matt. 13:30).



## REASON (Noun)

***logos*** (*3056*), "a word," etc., has also the significance of "the inward thought itself, a reckoning, a regard, a reason," translated "reason" in Acts 18:14, in the phrase "reason would," ***kata logon***, lit., "according to reason (I would bear with you)"; in 1 Pet. 3:15, "a reason (concerning the hope that is in you)."

## REASON (Verb)

1. ***dialogizomai*** (*1260*), "to bring together different reasons and reckon them up, to reason," is used in the NT (a) chiefly of thoughts and considerations which are more or less objectionable, e.g., of the disciples who "reasoned" together, through a mistaken view of Christ's teaching regarding leaven, Matt. 16:7, 8 and Mark 8:16, 17; of their "reasoning" as to who was the greatest among them, Mark 9:33, RV, "were ye reasoning," KJV, "ye disputed"; of the scribes and Pharisees in criticizing Christ's claim to forgive sins, Mark 2:6, 8 (twice) and Luke 5:21, 22; of the chief priests and elders in considering how to answer Christ's question regarding John's baptism, Matt. 21:25; Mark 11:31.

2. ***sullogizomai*** (*4817*), "to compute" (***sun***, "with," and ***logizomai***, cf. Eng., "syllogism"), also denotes "to reason," and is so rendered in Luke 20:5.

## REASONABLE

***logikos*** (*3050*), pertaining to "the reasoning faculty, reasonable, rational," is used in Rom. 12:1, of the service (***latreia***) to be rendered by believers in presenting their bodies "a living sacrifice, holy, acceptable to God." The sacrifice is to be intelligent, in contrast to those offered by ritual and compulsion; the presentation is to be in accordance with the spiritual intelligence of those who are new creatures in Christ and are mindful of "the mercies of God."

## TO REBEL

### A. Verb.

***marah*** (4784), "to rebel, be contentious." ***marah*** signifies an opposition to someone motivated by pride, Deut. 21:18; cf. Isa. 3:8 (NASB). More particularly, the word generally connotes a rebellious attitude against God, Deut. 9:7; Jer. 4:17. The primary meaning of ***marah*** is "to disobey," 1 Kings 13:21; cf. 13:26. The Old Testament sometimes specifically states that someone "rebelled" against the Lord; at other times it may refer to a rebelling against the word of the Lord, Ps. 105:28; 107:11, or against the mouth of God, Num. 20:24; Deut. 1:26, 43; 9:23; 1 Sam. 12:14–15. The intent of the Hebrew is to signify the act of defying the command of God, Lam. 1:18. An individual, Deut. 21:18, 20, a nation, Num. 20:24, and a city, Zeph. 3:1, may be described as "being rebellious." Zephaniah gave a vivid image of the nature of the rebellious spirit, Zeph. 3:1–2, RSV.

### B. Nouns.

***meri*** (4805), "rebellion," Deut. 31:27; cf. Prov. 17:11. The noun ***meratayim*** means "double rebellion." This reference to Babylon, Jer. 50:21, is generally made a proper name, "Merathaim."

### C. Adjective.

***meri*** (4805), "rebellious," Ezek. 2:8.

## REBUKE (Verb and Noun)

### A. Verbs.

1. ***epitimao*** (*2008*), primarily, "to put honor upon," then, "to adjudge," hence signifies "to rebuke." Except for 2 Tim. 4:2 and Jude 9, it is confined in the NT to the Synoptic Gospels, where it is frequently used of the Lord's rebukes to (a) evil spirits, e.g., Matt. 17:18; Mark 1:25; 9:25; Luke 4:35, 41; 9:42; (b) winds, Matt. 8:26; Mark 4:39; Luke 8:24; (c) fever, Luke 4:39; (d) disciples, Mark 8:33; Luke 9:55; contrast Luke 19:39. For rebukes by others see Matt. 16:22; 19:13; 20:31; Mark 8:32; 10:13; 10:48, RV, "rebuked" (KJV, "charged"); Luke 17:3; 18:15, 39; 23:40.

2. ***elencho*** (*1651*), "to convict, refute, reprove," is translated "to rebuke" in the KJV of the following (the RV always has the verb "to reprove"): 1 Tim. 5:20; Titus 1:13; 2:15; Heb. 12:5; Rev. 3:19.

3. ***epiplesso*** (*1969*), "to strike at" (***epi***, "upon" or "at," ***plesso***, "to strike, smite"), hence, "to rebuke," is used in the injunction against "rebuking" an elder, 1 Tim. 5:1.

### B. Noun.

***elenxis*** (*1649*), akin to A, No. 2, denotes "rebuke"; in 2 Pet. 2:16, it is used with ***echo***, "to have," and translated "he was rebuked," lit., "he had rebuke."

## RECKON, RECKONING

#### *Old Testament*

### A. Verb.

***yachas*** (3187), "to reckon (according to race or family)," 1 Chron. 5:17; cf. 1 Chron. 7:5 and Ezra 2:62.

### B. Noun.

***yachas*** (3188), "genealogy." This word appears in the infinitive form as a noun to indicate a register or table of genealogy, 1 Chron. 7:40; cf. 2 Chron. 31:18.

#### *New Testament*

***logizomai*** (*3049*) is properly used (a) of "numerical calculation," e.g., Luke 22:37; (b) metaphorically, "by a reckoning of characteristics or reasons, to take into account," Rom. 2:26, "shall . . . be reckoned," RV (KJV, "counted"), of "reckoning" uncircumcision for circumcision by God's estimate in contrast to that of the Jew regarding his own condition (v. 3); in 4:3, 5, 6, 9, 11, 22, 23, 24, of "reckoning" faith for righteousness, or "reckoning" righteousness to persons, in all of which the RV uses the verb "to reckon" instead of the KJV "to count or to impute"; in v. 4 the subject is treated by way of contrast between grace and debt, which latter involves the "reckoning" of a reward for works; what is owed as a debt cannot be "reckoned" as a favor, but the faith of Abraham and his spiritual children sets them outside the category of those who seek to be justified by self-effort, and, *vice versa*, the latter are excluded from the grace of righteousness bestowed on the sole condition of faith; so in Gal. 3:6 (RV, "was reckoned," KJV, "was accounted"); since Abraham, like all the natural descendants of Adam, was a sinner, he was destitute of righteousness in the sight of God; if, then, his relationship with God was to be rectified (i.e., if he was to be justified before God), the rectification could not be brought about by works of merit on his part; in Jas. 2:23, RV, "reckoned," the subject is viewed from a different standpoint.

## RECOMPENCE, RECOMPENSE

### *Old Testament*

***shalam*** (7999), "to recompense, reward, be whole, be complete, sound." In its first occurrence in the Old Testament, the word has the sense of "repaying" or "restoring": "Why have you returned evil for good?" Gen. 44:4, RSV. Sometimes it means "to complete or finish," 1 Kings 9:25. In Lev. 24:18, ***shalam*** describes compensation for injury.

### *New Testament*

**A. Nouns.**

1. ***antapodoma*** (*468*), akin to ***antapodidomi***, "to recompense" (see below), lit., "a giving back in return" (***anti***, "in return," ***apo***, back, ***didomi***, "to give"), a requital, recompence, is used (a) in a favorable sense, Luke 14:12; (b) in an unfavorable sense, Rom. 11:9, indicating that the present condition of the Jewish nation is the retributive effect of their transgressions, on account of which that which was designed as a blessing ("their table") has become a means of judgment.

2. ***antapodosis*** (*469*), derived, like No. 1, from ***antapodidomi***, is rendered "recompense" in Col. 3:24, RV (KJV, "reward").

**B. Verb.**

***antapodidomi*** (*467*), akin to A, No. 1 and No. 2, "to give back as an equivalent, to requite, recompense" (the ***anti*** expressing the idea of a complete return), is translated "render" in 1 Thess. 3:9, here only in the NT of thanksgiving to God; elsewhere it is used of "recompense," whether between men (but in that case only of good, not of evil, see No. 2 in 1 Thess. 5:15), Luke 14:14 *a*, cf. the corresponding noun in v. 12; or between God and evil-doers, Rom. 12:19, RV (KJV, "repay"); Heb. 10:30, cf. the noun in Rom. 11:9; or between God and those who do well, Luke 14:14 *b*; Rom. 11:35, cf. the noun in Col. 3:24; in 2 Thess. 1:6 both reward and retribution are in view.

## RECONCILE

***katallasso*** (*2644*) properly denotes "to change, exchange" (especially of money); hence, of persons, "to change from enmity to friendship, to reconcile." With regard to the relationship between God and man, the use of this and connected words shows that primarily "reconciliation" is what God accomplishes, exercising His grace towards sinful man on the ground of the death of Christ in propitiatory sacrifice under the judgment due to sin, 2 Cor. 5:19, where both the verb and the noun are used. By reason of this men in their sinful condition and alienation from God are invited to be "reconciled" to Him; that is to say, to change their attitude, and accept the provision God has made, whereby their sins can be remitted and they themselves be justified in His sight in Christ.

The removal of God's wrath does not contravene His immutability. He always acts according to His unchanging righteousness and lovingkindness, and it is because He changes not that His relative attitude does change towards those who change. All His acts show that He is Light and Love. Anger, where there is no personal element, is a sign of moral health if, and if only, it is accompanied by grief. There can be truest love along with righteous indignation, Mark 3:5, but love and enmity cannot exist together. It is important to distinguish "wrath" and "hostility." The change in God's relative attitude toward those who receive the "reconciliation" only proves His real unchangeableness. Not once is God said to be "reconciled." The enmity is alone on our part. It was we who needed to be "reconciled" to God, not God to us, and it is propitiation, which His righteousness and mercy have provided, that makes the "reconciliation" possible to those who receive it.

The subject finds its great unfolding in 2 Cor. 5:18–20, which states that God "reconciled us (believers) to Himself through Christ," and that "the ministry of reconciliation" consists in this, "that God was in Christ reconciling the world unto Himself." The insertion of a comma in the KJV after the word "Christ" is misleading; the doctrine stated here is not that God was in Christ (the unity of the Godhead is not here in view), but that what God has done in the matter of reconciliation He has done in Christ, and this is based upon the fact that "Him who knew no sin He made to be sin on our behalf; that we might become the righteousness of God in Him." On this ground the command to men is "be ye reconciled to God."

## RECOVER

***sozo*** (*4982*), "to save," is sometimes used of "healing" or "restoration to health," the latter in John 11:12, RV, "he will recover," marg., "be saved" (KJV, "he shall do well").

## REDEEM, REDEMPTION

### *Old Testament*

**A. Verbs.**

***ga'al*** (1350), "to redeem, deliver, avenge, act as a kinsman." This word's basic use had to do with the deliverance of persons or property that had been sold for debt, as in Lev. 25:25–47. A poor man may sell himself to a fellow Israelite, Lev. 25:39, or to an alien living in Israel, Lev. 25:47. The responsibility "to redeem" belonged to the nearest relative—brother, uncle, uncle's son, or a blood relative from his family, Lev. 25:25, 48–49. The person (kinsman) who "redeemed" the one in financial difficulties was known as a kinsman-redeemer, as the NIV translates the word in Ruth 2:20. In Deut. 19:6 the redeemer is called the "avenger of blood" whose duty it was to execute the murderer of his relative. The verb occurs in this sense 12 times and is translated "revenger" in KJV, Num. 35:19, 21, 24, 27, or "avenger," Num. 35:12; always so in NASB and NIV. The Book of Ruth is a beautiful account of the kinsman-redeemer. The greater usage of this word group is of God who promised to redeem, Exod. 6:6; cf. Ps. 77:15; Exod. 15:13; Ps. 78:35.

The Book of Isaiah evidences the word "Redeemer" used of God 13 times, all in chapters 41—63, and ***ga'al*** is used 9 times of God, first in 43:1. Israel's "Redeemer" is "the Holy One of Israel," 41:14, "the creator of Israel, your King," 43:14–15.

***padah*** (6299), "to redeem, ransom." ***padah*** indicates that some intervening or substitutionary action effects a release from an undesirable condition; save from death, 1 Sam. 14:45; from slavery, Exod. 21:8; Lev. 19:20. The word is connected with the laws of the firstborn, Exod. 13:15. God accepted the separation of the tribe of Levi for liturgical service in lieu of all Israelite firstborn, Num. 3:40ff. However, the Israelite males still had to be "redeemed" (***padah***) from this service by payment of specified "redemption money," Num. 3:44–51.

When God is the subject of ***padah***, the word emphasizes His complete, sovereign freedom to liberate human beings. Sometimes God is said to "redeem" individuals, Abraham, Isa. 29:22; David, 1 Kings 1:29; and often in the Psalter, e.g., 26:11; 21:5; 71:23; but usually Israel, the elect people, is the beneficiary.

***kapar*** (3722), "to ransom, atone, expiate, propitiate." On its most basic level of meaning, ***kapar*** denotes a material transaction or "ransom." Sometimes man is the subject of ***kapar***, 2 Sam. 21:3. Moses ascends the mountain yet a third time in an effort to "make an atonement" for the people's sin (apparently merely by intercession, although this is not explicitly stated). God is often the subject of ***kapar*** in this general sense, too. In 2 Chron. 30:18, Hezekiah prays for God to "pardon" those who were not ritually prepared for the Passover. At the conclusion of the Song of Moses, Yahweh is praised because He "will atone for His land and His people," Deut. 32:43, NASB. Similar general uses of the word appear in Ps. 65:3; 78:38; and Dan. 9:24. Jeremiah once uses ***kapar*** to pray bitterly that Yahweh not "forgive" the iniquity of those plotting to slay him, Jer. 18:23, and in Ps. 79:9 the word means "to purge" sin. Most often ***kapar*** is used in connection with specific rites, and the immediate subject is a priest. All types of ritual sacrifice are explained in terms of ***kapar***. We find the priests' smearing of blood on the altar during the "sin offering" (***chatta't***) described as "atonement," Exod. 29: 36–37; Lev. 4:20, 31; 10:17; Num. 28:22; 29:5; Neh. 10:33.

Most English versions prefer to render ***kapar*** with the more neutral term "atone" or even "ransom." But various translations often have "expiate" or "propitiate" as well. The terms are partly synonymous. In any sacrifice, the action is directed both toward God (*propitiation*) and toward the offense (*expiation*).

**B. Noun.**

***ge'ullah*** (1353), "(right of) redemption." This word is used in regard to deliverance of persons or property that had been sold for debt. The law required that the "right of redemption" of land and of persons be protected, Lev. 25:24, 48. The redemption price was determined by the number of years remaining until the release of debts in the year of jubilee, Lev. 25:27–28.

***pedut***: "ransom or redemption," Ps. 111:9.

*New Testament*

**A. Verbs.**

1. ***exagorazo*** (*1805*), a strengthened form of ***agorazo***, "to buy," denotes "to buy out" (***ex*** for ***ek***), especially of purchasing a slave with a view to his freedom. It is used metaphorically in Gal. 3:13 and 4:5, of the deliverance by Christ of Christian Jews from the Law and its curse.

2. ***lutroo*** (*3084*), "to release on receipt of ransom" (akin to ***lutron***, "a ransom"), is used in the middle voice, signifying "to release by paying a ransom price, to redeem" (a) in the natural sense of delivering, Luke 24:21, of setting Israel free from the Roman yoke; (b) in a spiritual sense, Titus 2:14, of the work of Christ in "redeeming" men "from all iniquity" (***anomia***, "lawlessness," the bondage of self-will which rejects the will of God); 1 Pet. 1:18 (passive voice), "ye were redeemed," from a vain manner of life, i.e., from bondage to tradition. In both instances the death of Christ is stated as the means of "redemption."

**B. Noun.**

***apolutrosis*** (*629*), a strengthened form of No. 1, lit., "a releasing, for (i.e., on payment of) a ransom." It is used of (a) "deliverance" from physical torture, Heb. 11:35; (b) the deliverance of the people of God at the coming of Christ with His glorified saints, "in a cloud with power and great glory," Luke 21:28, a "redemption" to be accomplished at the "outshining of His Parousia," 2 Thess. 2:8, i.e., at His second advent; (c) forgiveness and justification, "redemption" as the result of expiation, deliverance from the guilt of sins, Rom. 3:24, "through the redemption that is in Christ Jesus"; Eph. 1:7, defined as "the forgiveness of our trespasses," RV; so Col. 1:14, "the forgiveness of our sins," indicating both the liberation from the guilt and doom of sin and the introduction into a life of liberty, "newness of life" (Rom. 6:4,; Heb. 9:15), "for the redemption of the transgressions that were under the first covenant," RV, here "redemption of" is equivalent to "redemption from," the genitive case being used of the object from which the "redemption" is effected, not from the consequence of the transgressions, but from the transgressions themselves; (d) the deliverance of the believer from the presence and power of sin, and of his body from bondage to corruption, at the coming (the Parousia in its inception) of the Lord Jesus, Rom. 8:23; 1 Cor. 1:30; Eph. 1:4; 4:30.

## REFRAIN

***pauo*** (*3973*), "to stop," is used in the active voice in the sense of "making to cease, restraining" in 1 Pet. 3:10, of causing the tongue to refrain from evil; elsewhere in the middle voice.

## REFRESH, REFRESHING

**A. Verbs.**

1. ***anapauo*** (*373*), "to give intermission from labor, to give rest, refresh" (***ana***, "back," ***pauo***, "to cause to cease"), is translated "to refresh" in 1 Cor. 16:18; 2 Cor. 7:13; Philem. 7, 20.

2. ***sunanapauomai*** (*4875*), "to lie down, to rest with" (***sun***, "with," and No. 1 in the middle voice), is used metaphorically of being "refreshed" in spirit with others, in Rom. 15:32, KJV, "may with (you) be refreshed" (RV, ". . . find rest").

**B. Noun.**

***anapsuxis*** (*403*), "a refreshing," occurs in Acts 3:19.

## REFUSE (Verb)

1. ***arneomai*** (*720*), "to deny, renounce, reject," in late Greek came to signify "to refuse to acknowledge, to disown," and is translated "to refuse" in Acts 7:35; Heb. 11:24.

2. ***paraiteomai*** (*3868*), denotes "to refuse" in Acts 25:11; 1 Tim. 4:7; 5:11; 2 Tim. 2:23, RV (KJV, "avoid"); Titus 3:10, RV (marg., "avoid"; KJV, "reject"); Heb. 12:25 (twice), perhaps in the sense of "begging off."

R

## REGARD

1. ***phroneo*** (*5426*), "to think, set the mind on," implying moral interest and reflection, is translated "to regard" in Rom. 14:6 (twice); the second part in the KJV represents an interpolation and is not part of the original.

2. ***oligoreo*** (*3643*) denotes "to think little of" (***oligos***, "little," ***ora***, "care"), "to regard lightly," Heb. 12:5, RV (KJV, "despise").

3. ***prosecho*** (*4337*), "to take or give heed," is translated "they had regard" in Acts 8:11, KJV (RV, "they gave heed).

## REGENERATION

***palingenesia*** (*3824*), "new birth" (***palin***, "again," ***genesis***, "birth"), is used of "spiritual regeneration," Titus 3:5, involving the communication of a new life, the two operating powers to produce which are "the word of truth," Jas. 1:18; 1 Pet. 1:23, and the Holy Spirit, John 3:5, 6; the ***loutron***, "the laver, the washing," is explained in Eph. 5:26, "having cleansed it by the washing (***loutron***) of water with the word."

The new birth and "regeneration" do not represent successive stages in spiritual experience, they refer to the same event but view it in different aspects. The new birth stresses the communication of spiritual life in contrast to antecedent spiritual death; "regeneration" stresses the inception of a new state of things in contrast with the old; hence the connection of the use of the word with its application to Israel, in Matt. 19:28. Some regard the ***kai*** in Titus 3:5 as epexegetic, "even"; but, as Scripture marks two distinct yet associated operating powers, there is not sufficient ground for this interpretation.

## REGRET

***metamelomai*** (*3338*), a verb, "to regret, to repent one," is translated "to regret" in 2 Cor. 7:8, RV (twice), KJV, "repent."

## REIGN (Verb and Noun)

### *Old Testament*

***malak*** (4427), "to reign, be king (or queen)." Basically the word means to fill the functions of ruler over someone. To hold such a position was to function as the commander-in-chief of the army, the chief executive of the group, and to be an important, if not central, religious figure. The king was the head of his people and, therefore, in battle was the king to be killed, his army would disperse until a new king could be chosen, Gen. 36:31; Ps. 2:6; cf. 2 Kings 11:3.

### *New Testament*

1. ***basileuo*** (*936*), "to reign," is used (I) literally, (a) of God, Rev. 11:17; 19:6, in each of which the aorist tense (in the latter, translated "reigneth") is "ingressive," stressing the point of entrance; (b) of Christ, Luke 1:33; 1 Cor. 15:25; Rev. 11:15; as rejected by the Jews, Luke 19:14, 27; (c) of the saints, hereafter, 1 Cor. 4:8 (2nd part), where the apostle, casting a reflection upon the untimely exercise of authority on the part of the church at Corinth, anticipates the due time for it in the future (see No. 2); Rev. 5:10; 20:4, where the aorist tense is not simply of a "point" character, but "constative," that is, regarding a whole action as having occurred, without distinguishing any steps in its progress (in this instance the aspect is future); v. 6; 22:5; (d) of earthly potentates, Matt. 2:22; 1 Tim. 6:15, where "kings" is, lit., "them that reign"; (II), metaphorically, (a) of believers, Rom. 5:17, where "shall reign in life" indicates the activity of life in fellowship with Christ in His sovereign power, reaching its fullness hereafter; 1 Cor. 4:8 (1st part), of the carnal pride that laid claim to a power not to be exercised until hereafter; (b) of divine grace, Rom. 5:21; (c) of sin, Rom. 5:21; 6:12; (d) of death, Rom. 5:14, 17.

2. ***sunbasileuo*** (*4821*), "to reign together with" (***sun***, "with," and No. 1), is used of the future "reign" of believers together and with Christ in the kingdom of God in manifestation, 1 Cor. 4:8 (3rd part); of those who endure, 2 Tim. 2:12. cf. Rev. 20:6.

## REINS

***nephros*** (*3510*), "a kidney" (Eng., "nephritis," etc.), usually in the plural, is used metaphorically of "the will and the affections," Rev. 2:23, "reins" (cf. Ps. 7:9; Jer. 11:20; 17:10; 20:12). The feelings and emotions were regarded as having their seat in the "kidneys."

## REJECT

**A. Verbs.**

1. ***apodokimazo*** (*593*), "to reject" as the result of examination and disapproval (***apo***, "away from," ***dokimazo***, "to approve"), is used (a) of the "rejection" of Christ by the elders and chief priests of the Jews, Matt. 21:42; Mark 8:31; 12:10; Luke 9:22; 20:17; 1 Pet. 2:4, 7 (KJV, "disallowed"); by the Jewish people, Luke 17:25; (b) of the "rejection" of Esau from inheriting "the blessing," Heb. 12:17.

2. ***atheteo*** (*114*), properly, "to do away" with what has been laid down, to make ***atheton*** (i.e., "without place," ***a***, negative, ***tithemi***, "to place"), hence, besides its meanings "to set aside, make void, nullify, disannul," signifies "to reject"; in Mark 6:26, regarding Herod's pledge to Salome, it almost certainly has the meaning "to break faith with." In Mark 7:9 "ye reject (the commandment)" means "ye set aside"; in Luke 7:30, "ye reject" may have the meaning of "nullifying or making void the counsel of God"; in Luke 10:16 (four times), "rejecteth," RV (KJV, "despiseth"); "rejecteth" in John 12:48; "reject" in 1 Cor. 1:19 (KJV, "bring to nothing"); 1 Thess. 4:8, "to despise," where the reference is to the charges in v. 2; in 1 Tim. 5:12 RV, "have rejected" (KJV, "have cast off").

3. ***ekptuo*** (*1609*), "to spit out" (***ek***, "out," and ***ptuo***, "to spit"), i.e., "to abominate, loathe," is used in Gal. 4:14, "rejected" (marg., "spat out"), where the sentence is elliptical: "although my disease repelled you, you did not refuse to hear my message."

**B. Adjective.**

1. ***adokimos*** (*96*), "not standing the test," is translated "rejected" in 1 Cor. 9:27, RV; Heb. 6:8, KJV and RV.

## REJOICE

### *Old Testament*

**A. Verb.**

***samach*** (8055), "to rejoice, be joyful." ***samach*** usually refers to a spontaneous emotion or extreme happiness which is expressed in some visible and/or external manner. It does not normally represent an abiding state of well-being or feeling. This emotion arises at festivals, circumcision feasts, wedding feasts, harvest feasts, the overthrow of one's enemies, and other such events. The men of Jabesh broke out joyously when they were told that they would be delivered from the Philistines, 1 Sam. 11:9. The verb ***samach*** suggests three elements: (1) a spontaneous, unsustained feeling of jubilance, 1 Sam. 18:6; (2) a feeling so strong that it finds expression in some external act, Exod. 4:27; (3) a feeling prompted by some external and unsustained stimulus, Exod. 4:14.

**B. Noun.**

***simchah*** (8057), "joy." ***simchah*** is both a technical term for the external expression of "joy," Gen. 31:27; and (usually) a representation of the abstract feeling or concept "joy," Deut. 28:47.

**C. Adjective.**

***sameach*** (8056), "joyful; glad," Deut. 16:15.

### *New Testament*

1. ***chairo*** (*5463*), "to rejoice," is most frequently so translated. As to this verb, the following are grounds and occasions for "rejoicing," on the part of believers: in the Lord, Phil. 3:1; 4:4; His incarnation, Luke 1:14; His power, Luke 13:17; His presence with the Father, John 14:28; His presence with them, John 16:22; 20:20; His ultimate triumph, 8:56; hearing the gospel, Acts 13:48; their salvation, Acts 8:39; receiving the Lord, Luke 19:6; their enrollment in Heaven, Luke 10:20; their liberty in Christ, Acts 15:31; their hope, Rom. 12:12 (cf. Rom. 5:2; Rev. 19:7); their prospect of reward, Matt. 5:12; the obedience and godly conduct of fellow believers, Rom. 16:19, RV, "I rejoice" (KJV, "I am glad"); 2 Cor. 7:7, 9; 13:9; Col. 2:5; 1 Thess. 3:9; 2 John 4; 3 John 3; the proclamation of Christ, Phil. 1:18; the gospel harvest, John 4:36; suffering with Christ, Acts 5:41; 1 Pet. 4:13; suffering in the cause of the gospel, 2 Cor. 13:9 (1st part); Phil. 2:17 (1st part); Col. 1:24; in persecutions, trials and afflictions, Matt. 5:12; Luke 6:23; 2 Cor. 6:10; the manifestation of grace, Acts 11:23; meeting with fellow believers, 1 Cor. 16:17, RV, "I rejoice"; Phil. 2:28; receiving tokens of love and fellowship, Phil. 4:10; the "rejoicing" of others, Rom. 12:15; 2 Cor. 7:13; learning of the well-being of others, 2 Cor. 7:16.

2. ***agalliao*** (*21*), "to rejoice greatly, to exult," is used, (I) in the active voice, of "rejoicing" in God, Luke 1:47; in faith in Christ, 1 Pet. 1:8, RV (middle voice in some mss.), "ye rejoice greatly"; in the event of the marriage of the Lamb, Rev. 19:7, "be exceeding glad," RV; (II), in the middle voice, (a) of "rejoicing" in persecutions, Matt. 5:12 (2nd part); in the light of testimony for God, John 5:35; in salvation received through the gospel, Acts 16:34, "he rejoiced greatly," RV; in salvation ready to be revealed, 1 Pet. 1:6; at the revelation of His glory, 1 Pet. 4:13, "with exceeding joy," lit., "ye may rejoice, exulting"; (b) of Christ's "rejoicing" (greatly) "in the Holy Spirit," Luke 10:21, RV; said of His praise, as foretold in Ps. 16:9, quoted in Acts 2:26; (c) of Abraham's "rejoicing," by faith, to see Christ's day, John 8:56.

4. ***euphraino*** (*2165*), in the active voice, "to cheer, gladden" (***eu***, "well," ***phren***, "the mind"), signifies in the passive voice "to rejoice, make merry"; it is translated "to rejoice" in Acts 2:26, RV, "was glad," KJV, "did . . . rejoice," of the heart of Christ as foretold in Ps. 16:9 [cf. No. 3, 11 (b)]; in Acts 7:41, of Israel's idolatry; in Rom. 15:10 with the Jews in their future deliverance by Christ from all their foes, at the establishment of the messianic kingdom) the apostle applies it to the effects of the gospel.

## RELEASE

***apoluo*** (*630*), "to loose from," is translated "to release" in Matt. 18:27, RV (KJV, "loosed"); 27:15, 17, 21, 26; Mark 15:6, 9, 11, 15; Luke 6:37 (twice), RV (KJV, "forgive" and "ye shall be forgiven"); 23:16 (v. 17, in some mss.), 18, 20, 25; 23:22, RV (KJV, "let . . . go"); John 18:39 (twice); 19:10; in 19:12, in the 1st part, KJV and RV; in the 2nd part, RV, "release" (KJV, "let . . . go"); so in Acts 3:13.

## RELIEF

***anesis*** (*425*), "a loosening, relaxation" (akin to ***aniemi***, "to send away, let go, loosen"), is translated "relief" in 2 Cor. 2:13 and 7:5 (KJV, "rest").

## RELIEVE

***eparkeo*** (*1884*) signifies "to be strong enough for," and so either "to ward off," or "to aid, to relieve" (a strengthened form of ***arkeo***, which has the same three meanings, ***epi*** being intensive); it is used in 1 Tim. 5:10, 16 (twice).

## RELIGION

***threskeia*** (*2356*) signifies "religion" in its external aspect (akin to ***threskos***, see below), "religious worship," especially the ceremonial service of "religion"; it is used of the "religion" of the Jews, Acts 26:5; of the "worshiping" of angels, Col. 2:18, which they themselves repudiate (Rev. 22:8, 9); "there was an officious parade of humility in selecting these lower beings as intercessors rather than appealing directly to the Throne of Grace" (Lightfoot); in Jas. 1:26, 27 the writer purposely uses the word to set in contrast that which is unreal and deceptive, and the "pure religion" which consists in visiting "the fatherless and widows in their affliction," and in keeping oneself "unspotted from the world." He is "not herein affirming . . . these offices to be the sum total, nor yet the great essentials, of true religion, but declares them to be the body, the ***threskeia***, of which godliness, or the love of God, is the informing soul" (Trench). Cf. also ***threskos*** (*2357*), "religious, careful of the externals of divine service," Jas. 1:26.

## REMAINDER; REMNANT

### A. Nouns.

***yether*** (3499), "remainder; remnant." The more general meaning of ***yether*** is "whatever remains" from the whole of a single unit of something: prey, Num. 31:32; or a collection: giants, Deut. 3:11; the kingdom, Josh. 13:27; and the people, Judg. 7:6. The prophets used ***she'erit*** as a technical term for "the remnant of Israel," Hag. 2:2–3; cf. Mic. 5:3.

### B. Verb.

***yathar*** (3498), "to be superfluous," Dan. 10:13.

## REMEMBER, REMEMBRANCE, REMINDED

*Old Testament*

### A. Verb.

***zakar*** (2142), "to remember, think of, mention." This word basically means to "recall information," but usually has the added focus that a response to a need or situation will also occur, implying that there is a relationship, or a renewal of an old relationship, Gen. 8:1; 18:17–33; 19:29; Exod. 6:5–6; Lev. 26:40–45; Psa. 98:3; 105:8, 42; 106:45; Jer. 31:34. Men also "remember." Joseph said to Pharaoh's butler: "But think on me . . . , and make mention of me unto Pharaoh . . ." Gen. 40:14.; cf. Ps. 20:7. The covenant commanded Israel to "remember this day, in which ye came out from Egypt . . ." Exod. 13:3; to "remember the sabbath day . . ." Exod. 20:8.

### B. Nouns.

***zeker*** (2143), "remembrance; memorial," Exod. 3:15; cf. Ps. 30:4; 135:13. Moses was told to write an account of the war with Amalek, Exod. 17:14.

The noun ***zikkaron*** has similar meanings. God gave the bronze plates covering the altar, Num. 16:40, and the heap of stones at the Jordan, Josh. 4:7, 20–24, as perpetual "memorials" for the sons of Israel. The names of the twelve tribes of Israel were engraved on two stones that were attached to the ephod as "stones of memorial unto the children of Israel: and Aaron shall bear their names before the Lord," Exod. 28:12; cf. v. 29.

*New Testament*

### A. Verbs.

1. ***mimnesko*** (*3403*), from the older form ***mnaomai***, in the active voice signifies "to remind"; in the middle voice, "to remind oneself of," hence, "to remember, to be mindful of"; the later form is found only in the present tense, in Heb. 2:6, "are mindful of," and 13:3, "remember"; the perfect tense in 1 Cor. 11:2 and in 2 Tim. 1:4 (RV, "remembering," KJV, "being mindful of"), is used with a present meaning. RV variations from the KJV are, in Luke 1:54, RV, "that He might remember" (KJV, "in remembrance of"); 2 Pet. 3:2, "remember" (KJV, "be mindful of"); Rev. 16:19 (passive voice), "was remembered" (KJV, "came in remembrance"). The passive voice is used also in Acts 10:31, KJV and RV, "are had in remembrance."

2. ***mnemoneuo*** (*3421*) signifies "to call to mind, remember"; it is used absolutely in Mark 8:18; everywhere else it has an object, (a) persons, Luke 17:32; Gal. 2:10; 2 Tim. 2:8, where the RV rightly has "remember Jesus Christ, risen from the dead"; Paul was not reminding Timothy (nor did he need to) that Christ was raised from the dead (KJV), what was needful for him was to "remember" (to keep in mind) the One who rose, the Source and Supplier of all his requirements; (b) things, e.g., Matt. 16:9; John 15:20; 16:21; Acts 20:35; Col. 4:18; 1 Thess. 1:3; 2:9; Heb. 11:15, "had been mindful of"; 13:7; Rev. 18:5; (c) a clause, representing a circumstance, etc., John 16:4; Acts 20:31; Eph. 2:11; 2 Thess. 2:5; Rev. 2:5; 3:3; in Heb. 11:22 it signifies "to make mention of."

3. ***anamimnesko*** (*363*), ***ana***, "back," and No. 1, signifies in the active voice "to remind, call to one's mind," 1 Cor. 4:17, "put (KJV, bring) . . . into remembrance"; so 2 Tim. 1:6; in the passive voice, "to remember, call to (one's own) mind," Mark 11:21, "calling to remembrance"; 14:72, "called to mind"; 2 Cor. 7:15, "remembereth"; Heb. 10:32, "call to remembrance."

4. ***hupomimnesko*** (*5279*) signifies "to cause one to remember, put one in mind of" (***hupo***, "under," often implying suggestion, and No. 1), John 14:26, "shall . . . bring . . . to (your) remembrance"; 2 Tim. 2:14, "put . . . in remembrance"; Titus 3:1, "put . . . in mind"; 3 John 10, RV, "I will bring to remembrance" (KJV, "I will remember"); Jude 5, "to put . . . in remembrance." In Luke 22:61 it is used in the passive voice, "(Peter) remembered," lit., "was put in mind."

**B. Nouns.**

1. ***anamnesis*** (*364*), "a remembrance" (***ana***, "up," or "again," and A, No. 1), is used (a) in Christ's command in the institution of the Lord's Supper, Luke 22:19; 1 Cor. 11:24, 25, not "in memory of" but in an affectionate calling of the Person Himself to mind; (b) of the "remembrance" of sins, Heb. 10:3, RV, "a remembrance" (KJV, "a remembrance again"; but the prefix ***ana*** does not here signify "again"); what is indicated, in regard to the sacrifices under the Law, is not simply an external bringing to "remembrance," but an awakening of mind.

2. ***hupomnesis*** (*5280*) denotes "a reminding, a reminder"; in 2 Tim. 1:5 it is used with ***lambano***, "to receive," lit., "having received a reminder," RV, "having been reminded" (KJV, "when I call to remembrance"); in 2 Pet. 1:13 and 3:1, "remembrance."

3. ***mneia*** (*3417*) denotes "a remembrance," or "a mention."

4. ***mneme*** (*3420*) denotes "a memory" (akin to ***mnaomai***, A, No. 1), "remembrance, mention," 2 Pet. 1:15, "remembrance."

## REMISSION, REMIT

**A. Nouns.**

1. ***aphesis*** (*859*), "a dismissal, release" (from ***aphiemi***, B), is used of the forgiveness of sins and translated "remission" in Matt. 26:28; Mark 1:4; Luke 1:77; 3:3; 24:47; Acts 2:38; 5:31 (KJV, "forgiveness"); 10:43; 13:38, RV (KJV, "forgiveness"); 26:18 (ditto); Heb. 9:22; 10:18.

2. ***paresis*** (*3929*), "a passing by of debt or sin," Rom. 3:25, KJV, "remission" (RV and KJV marg., "passing over").

**B. Verb.**

***aphiemi*** (*863*), "to send away" (akin to A, No. 1), is translated "to remit" in John 20:23 (twice), KJV (RV, "to forgive"). Scripture makes clear that the Lord's words could not have been intended to bestow the exercise of absolution, which Scripture declares is the prerogative of God alone.

## REMNANT

### *Old Testament*

**A. Nouns.**

***she'erit*** (7611), "rest; remnant; residue." The idea of the "remnant" plays a prominent part in the divine economy of salvation throughout the Old Testament. The "remnant" concept is applied especially to the Israelites who survived such calamities as war, pestilence, and famine—people whom the Lord in His mercy spared to be His chosen people, 2 Kings 19:31; cf. Ezra 9:14. The Israelites repeatedly suffered major catastrophes that brought them to the brink of extinction. So they often prayed as in Jer. 42:2. Isaiah used the word ***she'erit*** 5 times to denote those who would be left after the Assyrian invasions, Isa. 37:32. Micah also announced the regathering of the Jewish people after the Exile, Mic. 2:12; 4:7; 5:7–8; 7:18. Jeremiah discussed the plight of the Jews who fled to Egypt after Jerusalem's capture by Nebuchadnezzar, Jer. 40:11, 15. Zephaniah, a seventh-century prophet, identified the "remnant" with the poor and humble, 2:3, 7; 3:12–13. Zechariah announced that a "remnant" would be present at the time of the coming of the Messiah's kingdom, 12:10–13:1; 13:8–9.

***she'ar*** (7605), "rest; remnant; residue," Isa. 10:20.

**B. Verb.**

***sha'ar*** (7604), "to remain, be left over." In the pre-exilic period, this remnant idea is stressed by Isaiah. Isaiah tells of the judgment on the earth from which a remnant will "remain," Isa. 24:6. In the writing prophets, the idea of the "remnant" acquired a growing significance. Yet the idea may be found as early as the Pentateuch. The idea of "those being left" or "having escaped," especially a portion of the Israelite people, may be traced back to Deut. 4:27: "And the Lord shall scatter you among the nations, and ye shall be left few in number among the heathen, whither the Lord shall lead you," cf. Deut. 28:62. In these passages, Moses warns that if Israel failed to live up to the stipulations of the Mosaic covenant, the Lord would scatter them among the nations, and then He would regather a "remnant."

### *New Testament*

1. ***loipos*** (*3062*), an adjective (akin to ***leipo***, "to leave") signifying "remaining," is used as a noun and translated "the rest" in the RV, where the KJV has "the remnant," Matt. 22:6; Rev. 11:13; 12:17; 19:21.

2. ***leimma*** (*3005*), "that which is left" (akin to ***leipo***, "to leave"), "a remnant," is used in Rom. 11:5, "there is a remnant," more lit., "there has come to be a remnant," i.e., there is a spiritual "remnant" saved by the gospel from the midst of apostate Israel. While in one sense there has been and is a considerable number, yet, compared with the whole nation, past and present, the "remnant" is small, and as such is an evidence of God's electing grace (see v. 4).

3. ***hupoleimma*** (*5259*, and *3005*), ***hupo***, "under," signifying "diminution," and No. 2, is used in Rom. 9:27; cf. Isa. 10:22, 23 and Hosea 1:10.

## RENDER

1. ***apodidomi*** (*591*), "to give up or back," is translated "to render," (a) of righteous acts, (1) human, Matt. 21:41; 22:21; Mark 12:17; Luke 16:2, RV (KJV, "give"); Luke 20:25; Rom. 13:7, 1 Cor. 7:3; (2) divine, Matt. 16:27, RV, "shall render" (KJV, "shall reward"), an important RV change; Rom. 2:6; 2 Tim. 4:14, RV (KJV, "reward"); Rev. 18:6 (ditto); 22:12, RV (KJV, "give"); (b) of unrighteous acts, Rom. 12:17, RV (KJV, "recompense"); 1 Thess. 5:15; 1 Pet. 3:9.

2. ***antapodidomi*** (*467*), to give in return for," is translated "render" in 1 Thess. 3:9.

## RENEW, RENEWING (Verb and Noun)

### A. Verbs.

1. ***anakainoo*** (*341*), "to make new" (***ana***, "back" or "again," ***kainos***, "new," not recent but different), "to renew," is used in the passive voice in 2 Cor. 4:16, of the daily renewal of "the inward man" (in contrast to the physical frame), i.e., of the "renewal" of spiritual power; in Col. 3:10, of "the new man" (in contrast to the old unregenerate nature), which "is being renewed unto knowledge," RV (cf. No. 3 in Eph. 4:23), i.e., the true knowledge in Christ, as opposed to heretical teachings.

2. ***anakainizo*** (*340*) is a variant form of No. 1, used in Heb. 6:6, of the impossibility of "renewing" to repentance those Jews who professedly adhered to the Christian faith, if, after their experiences of it (not actual possession of its regenerating effects), they apostatized into their former Judaism.

3. ***ananeoo*** (*365*), "to renew, make young" (***ana***, as in No. 1, and ***neos***, "recent," not different), is used in Eph. 4:23, "be renewed (in the spirit of your mind)." The "renewal" here mentioned is not that of the mind itself in its natural powers of memory, judgment and perception, but "the spirit of the mind," which, under the controlling power of the indwelling Holy Spirit, directs its bent and energies Godward in the enjoyment of "fellowship with the Father and with His Son, Jesus Christ," and of the fulfillment of the will of God. The word is frequent in inscriptions and in the papyri.

### B. Noun.

***anakainosis*** (*342*), akin to A, No. 1, "a renewal," is used in Rom. 12:2, "the renewing (of your mind)," i.e., the adjustment of the moral and spiritual vision and thinking to the mind of God, which is designed to have a transforming effect upon the life; in Titus 3:5, where "the renewing of the Holy Spirit" is not a fresh bestowment of the Spirit, but a revival of His power, developing the Christian life; this passage stresses the continual operation of the indwelling Spirit of God; the Romans passage stresses the willing response on the part of the believer.

## RENOUNCE

1. ***apeipon*** (*550*), lit., "to tell from" (***apo***, "from," ***eipon***, an aorist form used to supply parts of ***lego***, "to say"), signifies "to renounce," 2 Cor. 4:2 (middle voice), of disowning "the hidden things of shame."

2. ***apotasso*** (*657*), "to set apart, to appoint," in NT meaning "taking leave of," Acts 18:18; Luke 14:33.

## REPAY

1. ***antapodidomi*** (*467*), "to give in return for," is translated "I will repay" in Rom. 12:19, KJV (RV, "I will recompense").

2. ***apotino*** or ***apotio*** (*661*), signifying "to pay off" (***apo***, "off," ***tino***, "to pay a fine"), is used in Philem. 19, of Paul's promise to "repay."

## REPENT, REPENTANCE

### *Old Testament*

***nacham*** (5162), "to repent, comfort." ***nacham*** apparently translates "to repent" about 40 times and "to comfort" about 65 times in the Old Testament. Most uses of the term in the Old Testament are connected with God's repentance, which means choose a particular course of action (often as a response to a change in a person's attitude or change in a situation), as a figurative way of saying to "change his mind," Jer. 18:8, 10; Joel 2:13 God usually changed His mind and "repented" of His actions because of man's intercession and repentance of his evil deeds. Moses pleaded with God as the intercessor for Israel, Exod. 32:12, 14; Jonah 3:10. In such instances, God "repented," or changed His mind, to bring about a change of plan. Again, however, God remained faithful to His absolutes of righteousness in His relation to and with man.

When referring to a human, it means to turn away from wickedness, and so have change from an apostate state to a state of belief and acceptance in a relationship, Jer. 8:6; 31:19, 20.

***nacham*** may also mean "to comfort," i.e., bring acts of kindness and favor, and encouraging words to another, Ezek. 14:23; the connection between "comfort" and "repent" here resulted from the calamity God brought upon Jerusalem as a testimony to the truth of His Word. David "comforted" Bathsheba after the death of her child born in sin, 2 Sam. 12:24; this probably indicates his repentance of what had happened in their indiscretion.

***New Testament***

### A. Verbs.

1. ***metanoeo*** (*3340*), lit., "to perceive afterwards" (***meta***, "after," implying "change," ***noeo***, "to perceive"; ***nous***, "the mind, the seat of moral reflection"), in contrast to ***pronoeo***, "to perceive beforehand," hence signifies "to change one's mind or purpose," always, in the NT, involving a change for the better, an amendment, and always, except in Luke 17:3, 4, of "repentance" from sin. The word is found in the Synoptic Gospels (in Luke, nine times), in Acts five times, in the Apocalypse twelve times, eight in the messages to the churches, 2:5 (twice), 16, 21 (twice), RV, "she willeth not to repent" (2nd part); 3:3, 19 (the only churches in those chapters which contain no exhortation in this respect are those at Smyrna and Philadelphia); elsewhere only in 2 Cor. 12:21.

2. ***metamelomai*** (*3338*), ***meta***, as in No. 1, and ***melo***, "to care for," is used in the passive voice with middle voice sense, signifying "to regret, to repent oneself," Matt. 21:29, RV, "repented himself"; v. 32, RV, "ye did (not) repent yourselves" (KJV, "ye repented not"); 27:3, "repented himself"; 2 Cor. 7:8 (twice), RV, "regret" in each case; Heb. 7:21, where alone in the NT it is said (negatively) of God.

### B. Adjective.

***ametameletos*** (*278*), "not repented of, unregretted" (***a***, negative, and a verbal adjective of A, No. 2), signifies "without change of purpose"; it is said (a) of God in regard to his "gifts and calling," Rom. 11:29; (b) of man, 2 Cor. 7:10.

### C. Noun.

***metanoia*** (*3341*), "afterthought, change of mind, repentance," corresponds in meaning to A, No. 1, and is used of "repentance" from sin or evil, except in Heb. 12:17, where the word "repentance" seems to mean, not simply a change of Isaac's mind, but such a change as would reverse the effects of his own previous state of mind. Esau's birthright-bargain could not be recalled; it involved an irretrievable loss.

As regards "repentance" from sin, (a) the requirement by God on man's part is set forth, e.g., in Matt. 3:8; Luke 3:8; Acts 20:21; 26:20; (b) the mercy of God in giving "repentance" or leading men to it is set forth, e.g., in Acts 5:31; 11:18; Rom. 2:4; 2 Tim. 2:25. The most authentic mss. omit the word in Matt. 9:13 and Mark 2:17, as in the RV.

In the NT the subject chiefly has reference to "repentance" from sin, and this change of mind involves both a turning from sin and a turning to God. The parable of the Prodigal Son is an outstanding illustration of this. Christ began His ministry with a call to "repentance," Matt. 4:17, but the call is addressed, not as in the OT to the nation, but to the individual. In the Gospel of John, as distinct from the Synoptic Gospels, referred to above, "repentance" is not mentioned, even in connection with John the Baptist's preaching; in John's gospel and 1st epistle the effects are stressed, e.g., in the new birth, and, generally, in the active turning from sin to God by the exercise of faith (John 3:3; 9:38; 1 John 1:9), as in the NT in general.



## REPETITIONS (use vain)

***battalogeo*** or ***battologeo*** (*945*), "to repeat idly," is used in Matt. 6:7, "use (not) vain repetitions"; the meaning "to stammer" is scarcely to be associated with this word. The word is probably from an Aramaic phrase and onomatopoeic in character, "repetitive babbling."

## REPORT (Noun and Verb)

### A. Nouns.

1. ***euphemia*** (*2162*), "a good report, good reputation" (***eu***, "well," ***pheme*** "a saying or report"), is used in 2 Cor. 6:8.

2. ***dusphemia*** (*1426*), "evil-speaking, defamation" (***dus***-, an inseparable prefix, the opposite to ***eu***, "well"), is used in 2 Cor. 6:8.

**B. Adjective.**

***euphemos*** *(2613)*, akin to A, No. 1, primarily, "uttering words or sounds of good omen," then, "avoiding ill-omened words," and hence "fair-sounding," "of good report," is so rendered in Phil. 4:8.

**C. Verbs.**

1. ***apangello*** *(518)*, "to report" (***apo***, "from," ***angello***, "to give a message"), "announce, declare" (by a messenger, speaker, or writer), is translated "reported" in Acts 4:23; 16:36, RV (KJV, "told"); v. 38 (some mss. have No. 2; KJV, "told"); "report" in 1 Cor. 14:25, KJV (RV, "declaring"); 1 Thess. 1:9, RV, "report" (KJV, "shew"); so Acts 28:21.

2. ***anangello*** *(312)*, "to bring back word," in later Greek came to have the same meaning as No. 1, "to announce, declare"; it is translated "are reported" in 1 Pet. 1:12, KJV (RV, "have been announced").

## REPROACH (Noun and Verb), REPROACHFULLY

### *Old Testament*

**A. Noun.**

***cherpah*** (2781), "reproach." "Reproach" has a twofold usage. On the one hand, the word denotes the state in which one finds himself. The unmarried woman, Isa. 4:1, or the woman without children, Gen. 30:23, carried a sense of disgrace in a society where marriage and fertility were highly spoken of. The destruction of Jerusalem and the Exile brought Judah to the state of "reproach," Dan. 9:16.

Whatever the occasion of the disgrace was, whether defeat in battle, exile, or enmity, the psalmist prayed for deliverance from the "reproach," Ps. 119:22—see context; cf. Ps. 109:25; cf. also the prophets use, Jer. 29:18; cf. Ezek. 5:14. However, the Lord graciously promised to remove the "reproach" at the accomplishment of His purpose, Isa. 25:8.

**B. Verb.**

***charap*** (2778), "to say sharp things, reproach," Ps. 42:10.

### *New Testament*

**A. Nouns.**

1. ***oneidismos*** *(3680)*, "a reproach, defamation," is used in Rom. 15:3; 1 Tim. 3:7; Heb. 10:33; 11:26; 13:13.

2. ***oneidos*** *(3681)*, akin to No. 1, is used in Luke 1:25 in the concrete sense of "a matter of reproach, a disgrace." To have no children was, in the Jewish mind, more than a misfortune, it might carry the implication that this was a divine punishment for some secret sin.

3. ***atimia*** *(819)*, "dishonor," is translated "reproach" in 2 Cor. 11:21, KJV (RV, "disparagement).

**B. Verbs.**

1. ***oneidizo*** *(3679)*, akin to A, Nos. 1 and 2, signifies (a), in the active voice, "to reproach, upbraid," Matt. 5:11, RV, "shall reproach" (KJV, "shall revile"); 11:20, "to upbraid"; 27:44, RV, "cast . . . reproach" [KJV, "cast . . . in (His) teeth"]; Mark 15:32 RV, "reproached" (KJV, "reviled"); 16:14 "upbraided"; Luke 6:22 "shall reproach," Rom. 15:3; Jas. 1:5, "upbraideth"; (b) in the passive voice, "to suffer reproach, be reproached," 1 Tim. 4:10 (in some mss. in the 2nd part); 1 Pet. 4:14.

2. ***hubrizo*** *(5195)*, akin to ***hubris***, used transitively, denotes "to outrage, insult, treat insolently"; it is translated "Thou reproachest" in Luke 11:45. The word is much stronger than "to reproach"; the significance is "Thou insultest (even us)," i.e., who are superior to ordinary Pharisees.

## REPROBATE

***adokimos*** *(96)*, signifying "not standing the test, rejected" (***a***, negative, ***dokimos***, "approved"), was primarily applied to metals, cf. Isa. 1:22; it is used always in the NT in a passive sense, (a) of things, Heb. 6:8, "rejected," of land that bears thorns and thistles; (b) of persons, Rom. 1:28, of a "reprobate mind," a mind of which God cannot approve, and which must be rejected by Him, the effect of refusing "to have God in their knowledge"; in 1 Cor. 9:27; 2 Cor. 13:5, 6, 7, where the RV rightly translates the adjective "reprobate" (KJV, "reprobates"), here the reference is to the great test as to whether Christ is in a person; in 2 Tim. 3:8 of those "reprobate concerning the faith," i.e., men whose moral sense is perverted and whose minds are beclouded with their own speculations; in Titus 1:16, of the defiled, who are "unto every good work reprobate," i.e., if they are put to the test in regard to any good work (in contrast to their profession), they can only be rejected.

## REPROOF, REPROVE

### *Old Testament*

***yakach*** (3198), "to decide, prove, convince, judge." It is evident in most of the uses of ***yakach*** that there is a value judgment involved, as in Job 5:17; Ps. 50:21; Prov. 3:12, RSV.

*New Testament*

**A. Noun.**

***elegmos*** (*1650*), "a reproof" (akin to B), is found in the best texts in 2 Tim. 3:16 (some mss. have ***elenchos***, which denotes "a proof, proving, test," as in Heb. 11:1, "proving," RV marg., "test").

**B. Verb.**

***elencho*** (*1651*), "to convict, rebuke, reprove," is translated "to reprove" in Luke 3:19; John 3:20, RV marg., "convicted"; the real meaning here is "exposed" (KJV marg., "discovered"); Eph. 5:11, 13, where "to expose" is again the significance; in John 16:8, KJV, "will reprove" (RV, "will convict"); in 1 Cor. 14:24, RV, "reproved" (KJV, "convinced"); in the following the RV has "to reprove," for KJV, "to rebuke," 1 Tim. 5:20; Titus 2:15; Heb. 12:5; Rev. 3:19.

## REPUTATION, REPUTE

***dokeo*** (*1380*) signifies (a) "to be of opinion" (akin to ***doxa***, "an opinion"), "to suppose," e.g., Luke 12:51; 13:2; (b) "to seem, to be reputed"; in Gal. 2:2, RV, "who were of repute" (KJV, "which were of reputation"); in 2:6 (twice), and 9, RV, "were reputed" and "were of repute" (KJV, "seemed"); in each case the present participle of the verb with the article is used, lit., "(well) thought of" by them, persons held in consideration; in v. 6, RV, "(those) who were reputed to be somewhat" (KJV "who seemed to be somewhat"): so v. 9. where there is no irony [cf. the rendering "are accounted" in Mark 10:42 (i.e., not rulers nominally)], Paul recognized that James, Cephas, and John were, as they were "reputed" by the church at Jerusalem, its responsible guides; (c) impersonally, "to think, to seem good."

## REQUEST (Noun and Verb)

**A. Nouns.**

1. ***aitema*** (*155*) denotes "that which has been asked for" (akin to ***aiteo***, "to ask"); in Luke 23:24, RV, "what they asked for" (KJV, "as they required"), lit., "their request (should be done, ***ginomai***)"; in Phil. 4:6, "requests"; in 1 John 5:15, "petitions."

2. ***deesis*** (*1162*), "an asking, entreaty, supplication," is translated "request" in Phil. 1:4, KJV (RV, supplication).

**B. Verbs.**

1. ***deomai*** (*1189*), akin to A, No. 2, "to beseech, pray, request," in Rom. 1:10.

2. ***aiteo*** (*154*), "to ask," is translated "to make request" in Col. 1:9, RV (KJV, "to desire").

3. ***erotao*** (*2065*), "to ask," is translated "to make request" in 1 John 5:16.

## REQUIRE

1. ***zeteo*** (*2212*), "to seek, seek after," also signifies "to require, demand," "shall be required," Luke 12:48; in 1 Cor. 4:2, "it is required (in stewards)."

2. ***ekzeteo*** (*1567*), "to seek out" (***ek***, "out," and No. 1), also denotes "to demand, require," Luke 11:50, 51, of executing vengeance for the slaughter of the prophets, cf. 2 Sam. 4:11; Ezek. 3:18.

3. ***apaiteo*** (*523*), "to ask back, demand back" (***apo***, "from," or "back," ***aiteo***, "to ask"), is translated "shall be required" in Luke 12:20, lit. "do they require," in the impersonal sense; elsewhere, Luke 6:30, "to ask again." It is used in the papyri frequently in the sense of "demanding, making demands."

## RESCUE

***exaireo*** (*1807*), "to take out" (***ek***, "from," ***haireo***, "to take"), is used of "delivering" from persons and circumstances, and translated "rescued" in Acts 23:27.

## RESERVE

***tereo*** (*5083*), "to guard, keep, preserve, give heed to," is translated "to reserve," (a) with a happy issue, 1 Pet. 1:4; (b) with a retributive issue, 2 Pet. 2:4; v. 9, KJV (RV, "keep"); 2:17; 3:7; Jude 6, KJV (RV, "hath kept"); v. 13; (c) with the possibility either of deliverance or execution, Acts 25:21, KJV (RV, kept).

## RESIST

1. ***anthistemi*** (*436*), "to set against" (***anti***, "against," ***histemi***, "to cause to stand"), used in the middle (or passive) voice and in the intransitive 2nd aorist and perfect active, signifying "to withstand, oppose, resist," is translated "to resist" in Matt. 5:39; Acts 6:10, KJV (RV, withstand); Rom. 9:19, KJV (RV, "withstandeth"); 13:2 (2nd and 3rd parts; for 1st part, see No. 3), KJV (RV, "withstandeth" and "withstand"); Gal. 2:11, RV (KJV, "withstood"); 2 Tim. 3:8 (2nd part), KJV (RV, "withstand"); Jas. 4:7; 1 Pet. 5:9, KJV (RV, "withstand"); "to withstand" in Acts 13:8; Eph. 6:13; 2 Tim. 3:8 (1st part); 4:15.

2. ***antikathistemi*** (*478*), "to stand firm against" (***anti***, "against," ***kathistemi***, "to set down," ***kata***), is translated "ye have (not) resisted" in Heb. 12:4.

3. ***antitasso*** (*498*), ***anti***, "against," ***tasso***, "to arrange," originally a military term, "to range in battle against," and frequently so found in the papyri, is used in the middle voice signify-

ing "to set oneself against, resist," (a) of men, Acts 18:6, "opposed themselves"; elsewhere "to resist," of resisting human potentates, Rom. 13:2; (b) of God, Jas. 4:6; 5:6, negatively, of leaving persistent evildoers to pursue their self-determined course, with eventual retribution, 1 Pet. 5:5.

4. ***antipipto*** (*496*), lit., and primarily, "to fall against or upon" (***anti***, "against," ***pipto***, "to fall"), then, "to strive against, resist," is used in Acts 7:51 of "resisting" the Holy Spirit.

## RESPECT (Noun and Verb)

### A. Noun.

***meros*** (*3313*), "a part," has occasionally the meaning of "a class" or "category," and, used in the dative case with ***en***, "in," signifies "in respect of," 2 Cor. 3:10, "in (this) respect"; 9:3, RV, KJV, "in (this) behalf"; Col. 2:16, "in respect of (a feast day)."

### B. Verbs.

1. ***apoblepo*** (*578*), "to look away from all else at one object" (***apo***, "from"), hence, "to look steadfastly," is translated "he had respect" in Heb. 11:26, KJV (RV, "looked").

2. ***epiblepo*** (*1914*), "to look upon" (***epi***), is translated "have respect" in Jas. 2:3 (RV "regard").

## REST (Noun and Verb)

*Old Testament*

***nuach*** (5117), "to rest, remain, be quiet." ***nuach*** sometimes indicates a complete envelopment and thus permeation, as in the spirit of Elijah "resting" on Elisha, 2 Kings 2:15, the hand of God "resting" on the mountain, Isa. 25:10, and when Wisdom "resteth in the heart of him that hath understanding," Prov. 14:33. Frequently ***nuach*** means "to be quiet" or "to rest" after hard work, Exod. 20:11, from onslaught of one's enemies, Esth. 9:16, from trouble, Job 3:26, and in death, Job 3:17.

It should be noted that while ***nuach*** is used sometimes as a synonym for ***shabat***, "to cease, to rest," Exod. 20:11, ***shabat*** really is basically "to cease" from work which may imply rest, but not necessarily so. The writer of Gen. 2:3 is not stressing rest from work but rather God ceasing from His creative work since it was complete.

*New Testament*

### A. Nouns.

1. ***anapausis*** (*372*), "cessation, refreshment, rest" (***ana***, "up," ***pauo***, "to make to cease"), the constant word in the Sept. for the Sabbath "rest," is used in Matt. 11:29; here the contrast seems to be to the burdens imposed by the Pharisees. Christ's "rest" is not a "rest" from work, but in work, "not the rest of inactivity but of the harmonious working of all the faculties and affections—of will, heart, imagination, conscience—because each has found in God the ideal sphere for its satisfaction and development" (J. Patrick, in *Hastings' Bib. Dic.*); it occurs also in Matt. 12:43; Luke 11:24; Rev. 4:8, RV, "(they have no) rest" [KJV, "(they) rest (not)"], where the noun is the object of the verb ***echo***, "to have"; so in 14:11.

2. ***katapausis*** (*2663*), in classical Greek, denotes "a causing to cease" or "putting to rest"; in the NT, "rest, repose"; it is used (a) of God's "rest," Acts 7:49; Heb. 3:11, 18; 4:1, 3 (twice), RV (1st part), "that rest" (the KJV, "rest," is ambiguous), 5, 11; (b) in a general statement, applicable to God and man, 4:10.

3. ***anesis*** (*425*), translated "rest" in 2 Cor. 2:13, KJV (RV, "relief"); 7:5 (ditto); in 2 Thess. 1:7, the subject is not the "rest" to be granted to the saints, but the divine retribution on their persecutors; hence the phrase "and to you that are afflicted rest with us," is an incidental extension of the idea of recompense, and is to be read parenthetically. The time is not that at which the saints will be relieved of persecution, as in 1 Thess. 4:15–17, when the Parousia of Christ begins, but that at which the persecutors will be punished, namely, at the epiphany (or out-shining) of His Parousia (2 Thess. 2:8). For similar parentheses characteristic of epistolary writings see v. 10; 1 Thess. 1:6, 2:15, 16.

4. ***sabbatismos*** (*4520*), "a Sabbath-keeping," is used in Heb. 4:9, RV, "a sabbath rest," KJV marg., "a keeping of a sabbath" (akin to ***sabbatizo***, "to keep the Sabbath," used, e.g., in Exod. 16:30, not in the NT); here the sabbath-keeping is the perpetual sabbath "rest" to be enjoyed uninterruptedly by believers in their fellowship with the Father and the Son, in contrast to the weekly Sabbath under the Law. Because this sabbath "rest" is the "rest" of God Himself, 4:10, its full fruition is yet future, though believers now enter into it. In whatever way they enter into divine "rest," that which they enjoy is involved in an indissoluble relation with God.

5. ***koimesis*** (*2838*), "a resting, reclining" (akin to ***keimai***, "to lie"), is used in John 11:13, of natural sleep, translated "taking rest," RV.

### B. Verbs.

1. ***anapauo*** (*373*), akin to A, No. 1, in the active voice, signifies "to give intermission from labor, to give rest, to refresh," Matt. 11:28; 1 Cor. 16:18, "have refreshed"; Philem. 20, "refresh"; passive voice, "to be rested, refreshed,"

2 Cor. 7:13, "was refreshed"; Philem. 7, "are refreshed"; in the middle voice, "to take or enjoy rest," Matt. 26:45; Mark 6:31; 14:41; Luke 12:19, "take thine ease"; 1 Pet. 4:14; Rev. 6:11; 14:13. In the papyri it is found as an agricultural term, e.g., of giving land "rest" by sowing light crops upon it. In inscriptions it is found on gravestones of Christians, followed by the date of death (Moulton and Milligan).

2. ***katapauo*** (*2664*), akin to A, No. 2, used transitively, signifies "to cause to cease, restrain," Acts 14:18; "to cause to rest," Heb. 4:8; intransitively, "to rest," Heb. 4:4, 10.

3. ***episkenoo*** (*1981*), "to spread a tabernacle over" (***epi***, "upon," ***skene***, "a tent"), is used metaphorically in 2 Cor. 12:9, "may rest upon (me)," RV, marg., "cover," "spread a tabernacle over."

4. ***kataskenoo*** (*2681*), "to pitch one's tent, lodge," is translated "shall rest," in Acts 2:26, KJV (RV, "shall dwell").

5. ***hesuchazo*** (*2270*), "to be still, to rest from labor," is translated "they rested" in Luke 23:56.

6. ***epanapauo*** (*1879*), "to cause to rest," is used in the middle voice, metaphorically, signifying "to rest upon" (***epi***, "upon," and No. 1), in Luke 10:6 and Rom. 2:17.

## REST (the)

1. ***loipos*** (*3062*), "remaining," is frequently used to mean "the rest," and is generally so translated in the RV (KJV, "others" in Luke 8:10; Acts 28:9; Eph. 2:3; 1 Thess. 4:13; 5:6; 1 Tim. 5:20; KJV, "other" in Luke 18:11; Acts 17:9; Rom. 1:13; 2 Cor. 12:13; 13:2; Gal. 2:13; Phil. 1:13; 4:3); the neut. plur., lit., "remaining things," is used in Luke 12:26; 1 Cor. 11:34.

2. ***epiloipos*** (*1954*), signifying "still left, left over" (***epi***, "over," and No. 1), is used in the neuter with the article in 1 Pet. 4:2, "the rest (of your time)."

## RESTLESS

***akatastatos*** (*182*), "unsettled, unstable, disorderly" (***a***, negative, ***kathistemi***, "to set in order"), is translated "unstable" in Jas. 1:8; "restless" in 3:8, RV [in the latter, the KJV "unruly" represents the word ***akataschetos***, signifying "that cannot be restrained" (***a***, negative, ***katecho***, "to hold down, restrain").

## RESTORATION

***apokatastasis*** (*605*), from ***apo***, "back, again," ***kathistemi***, "to set in order," is used in Acts 3:21, RV, "restoration" (KJV, "restitution"). In the papyri it is used of a temple cell of a goddess, a "repair" of a public way, the "restoration" of estates to rightful owners, a "balancing" of accounts. Apart from papyri illustrations the word is found in an Egyptian reference to a consummating agreement of the world's cyclical periods, an idea somewhat similar to that in the Acts passage (Moulton and Milligan).

## RESTORE

1. ***apodidomi*** (*591*), "to give back," is translated "I restore" in Luke 19:8.

2. ***apokathistemi*** or the alternative form ***apokathistano*** (*600*) is used (a) of "restoration" to a former condition of health, Matt. 12:13; Mark 3:5; 8:25; Luke 6:10; (b) of the divine "restoration" of Israel and conditions affected by it, including the renewal of the covenant broken by them, Matt. 17:11; Mark 9:12; Acts 1:6; (c) of "giving" or "bringing" a person back, Heb. 13:19. In the papyri it is used of financial restitution, of making good the breaking of a stone by a workman by his substituting another, of the reclamation of land, etc. (Moulton and Milligan).

3. ***katartizo*** (*2675*), "to mend, to furnish completely," is translated "restore" in Gal. 6:1, metaphorically, of the "restoration," by those who are spiritual, of one overtaken in a trespass, such a one being as a dislocated member of the spiritual body.

## RESTRAIN

***katecho*** (*2722*), "to hold fast or down," is translated "restraineth" in 2 Thess. 2:6 and 7. In v. 6 lawlessness is spoken of as being "restrained" in its development: in v. 7 "one that restraineth" is, lit., "the restrainer" (the article with the present participle, "the restraining one"); this may refer to an individual, as in the similar construction in 1 Thess. 3:5, "the tempter" (cf. 1:10, lit., "the Deliverer"); or to a number of persons presenting the same characteristics, just as "the believer" stands for all believers, e.g., Rom. 9:33; 1 John 5:10. V. 6 speaks of a principle, v. 7 of the principle as embodied in a person or series of persons; cf. what is said of "the power" in Rom. 13:3, 4, a phrase representing all such rulers. Probably such powers, i.e., "constituted governments," are the "restraining" influence here intimated (specifications being designedly withheld).

## RESURRECTION

1. ***anastasis*** (*386*) denotes (I) "a raising up," or "rising" (***ana***, "up," and ***histemi***, "to cause to stand"), Luke 2:34, "the rising up"; the KJV "again" obscures the meaning; the Child would be like a stone against which many in Israel would stumble while many others would find in its strength and firmness a means of

their salvation and spiritual life; (II), of "resurrection" from the dead, (a) of Christ, Acts 1:22; 2:31; 4:33; Rom. 1:4; 6:5; Phil. 3:10; 1 Pet. 1:3; 3:21; by metonymy, of Christ as the Author of "resurrection," John 11:25; (b) of those who are Christ's at His Parousia, Luke 14:14, "the resurrection of the just"; Luke 20:33, 35, 36; John 5:29 (1st part), "the resurrection of life"; 11:24; Acts 23:6; 24:15 (1st part); 1 Cor. 15:21, 42; 2 Tim. 2:18; Heb. 11:35 (2nd part); Rev. 20:5, "the first resurrection"; hence the insertion of "is" stands for the completion of this "resurrection," of which Christ was "the firstfruits"; 20:6; (c) of "the rest of the dead," after the Millennium (cf. Rev. 20:5); John 5:29 (2nd part), "the resurrection of judgment"; Acts 24:15 (2nd part), "of the unjust"; (d) of those who were raised in more immediate connection with Christ's "resurrection," and thus had part already in the first "resurrection," Acts 26:23 and Rom. 1:4 (in each of which "dead" is plural; see Matt. 27:52); (e) of the "resurrection" spoken of in general terms, Matt. 22:23; Mark 12:18; Luke 20:27; Acts 4:2; 17:18; 23:8; 24:21; 1 Cor. 15:12, 13; Heb. 6:2; (f) of those who were raised in OT times, to die again, Heb. 11:35 (1st part), lit., "out of resurrection."

2. ***exanastasis*** (*1815*), ***ek***, "from" or "out of," and No. 1, Phil. 3:11, followed by ***ek***, lit., "the out-resurrection from among the dead."

3. ***egersis*** (*1454*), "a rousing" (akin to ***egeiro***, "to arouse, to raise"), is used of the "resurrection" of Christ, in Matt. 27:53.

## REVEAL

1. ***apokalupto*** (*601*) signifies "to uncover, unveil" (***apo***, "from," ***kalupto***, "to cover"); both verbs are used in Matt. 10:26; in Luke 12:2, ***apokalupto*** is set in contrast to ***sunkalupto***, "to cover up, cover completely." "The NT occurrences of this word fall under two heads, subjective and objective. The subjective use is that in which something is presented to the mind directly, as, (a) the meaning of the acts of God, Matt. 11:25; Luke 10:21; (b) the secret of the Person of the Lord Jesus, Matt. 16:17; John 12:38; (c) the character of God as Father, Matt. 11:27; Luke 10:22; (d) the will of God for the conduct of His children, Phil. 3:15; (e) the mind of God to the prophets of Israel, 1 Pet. 1:12, and of the Church, 1 Cor. 14:30; Eph. 3:5.

The objective use is that in which something is presented to the senses, sight or hearing, as, referring to the past, (f) the truth declared to men in the gospel, Rom. 1:17; 1 Cor. 2:10; Gal. 3:23; (g) the Person of Christ to Paul on the way to Damascus, Gal. 1:16; (h) thoughts before hidden in the heart, Luke 2:35; referring to the future, (i) the coming in glory of the Lord Jesus, Luke 17:30; (j) the salvation and glory that await the believer, Rom. 8:18; 1 Pet. 1:5; 5:1; (k) the true value of service, 1 Cor. 3:13; (l) the wrath of God (at the Cross, against sin, and, at the revelation of the Lord Jesus, against the sinner), Rom. 1:18; (m) the Lawless One, 2 Thess. 2:3, 6, 8.

2. ***chrematizo*** (*5537*), "to give divine admonition, instruction, revelation," is translated "it had been revealed," in Luke 2:26.

## REVELATION

***apokalupsis*** (*602*), "an uncovering" (akin to ***apokalupto***; see above), is used in the NT of (a) the drawing away by Christ of the veil of darkness covering the Gentiles, Luke 2:32; cf. Isa. 25:7; (b) 'the mystery,' the purpose of God in this age, Rom. 16:25; Eph. 3:3; (c) the communication of the knowledge of God to the soul, Eph. 1:17; (d) an expression of the mind of God for the instruction of the church, 1 Cor. 14:6, 26, for the instruction of the Apostle Paul, 2 Cor. 12:1, 7; Gal. 1:12, and for his guidance, Gal. 2:2; (e) the Lord Jesus Christ, to the saints at His Parousia, 1 Cor. 1:7, RV (KJV, 'coming'); 1 Pet. 1:7, RV (KJV, 'appearing'), 13; 4:13; (f) the Lord Jesus Christ when He comes to dispense the judgments of God, 2 Thess. 1:7; cf. Rom. 2:5; (g) the saints, to the creation, in association with Christ in His glorious reign, Rom. 8:19, RV, 'revealing' (KJV, 'manifestation'); (h) the symbolic forecast of the final judgments of God, Rev. 1:1 (hence the Greek title of the book, transliterated 'Apocalypse' and translated 'Revelation').

## REVEL, REVELING

1. ***truphe*** (*5172*), "luxuriousness, daintiness, reveling," is translated freely by the verb "to revel" in 2 Pet. 2:13, RV (KJV, "to riot"), lit., "counting reveling in the daytime a pleasure." In Luke 7:25 it is used with ***en***, "in," and translated "delicately."

2. ***komos*** (*2970*), "a revel, carousal," the concomitant and consequence of drunkenness, is used in the plural, Rom. 13:13, translated by the singular, RV, "reveling" (KJV, "rioting"); Gal. 5:21 and 1 Pet. 4:3, "revelings."

## REVERENCE (Noun and Verb)

### A. Verbs.

1. ***entrepo*** (*1788*), lit., "to turn in" (i.e., upon oneself), "to put to shame," denotes, when used in the passive voice, "to feel respect for, to show deference to, to reverence," Matt. 21:37; Mark 12:6; Luke 20:13; Heb. 12:9.

2. ***phobeo*** (*5399*), "to fear," is used in the passive voice in the NT; in Eph. 5:33 of reverential

fear on the part of a wife for a husband, KJV, "reverence" (RV, "fear").

**B. Noun**

***eulabeia*** (*2124*), "caution, reverence," is translated "reverence" in Heb. 12:28 (1st part in the best mss; some have ***aidos***).

## REVERENT

***hieroprepes*** (*2412*), "suited to a sacred character, reverend" (***hieros***, "sacred," ***prepo***, "to be fitting"), is translated "reverent" in Titus 2:3, RV (KJV, "as becometh holiness").

## REVILE, REVILING, REVILER

**A. Verbs.**

1. ***loidoreo*** (*3058*) denotes "to abuse, revile," John 9:28; Acts 23:4; 1 Cor. 4:12; 1 Pet. 2:23 (1st clause).

2. ***oneidizo*** (*3679*), "to reproach, upbraid," is translated "to revile" in Matt. 5:11, KJV, and Mark 15:32 (RV, "reproach").

3. ***blasphemeo*** (*987*), "to speak profanely, rail at," is translated "reviled" in Matt. 27:39, KJV (RV, "railed on"); Luke 22:65, RV, "reviling" (KJV, "blasphemously").

4. ***antiloidoreo*** (*486*), "to revile back or again" (***anti***, and No. 1), is found in 1 Pet. 2:23 (2nd clause).

**B. Adjective.**

***loidoros*** (*3060*), akin to A, No. 1, "abusive, railing, reviling," is used as a noun, 1 Cor. 5:11, RV, "a reviler" (KJV "a railer"); 6:10, "revilers."

**C. Noun.**

***loidoria*** (*3059*), akin to A, No. 1, and B, "abuse, railing," is used in 1 Tim. 5:14, RV, "for (***charin***, 'for the sake of') reviling" (KJV, "to speak reproachfully"—a paraphrase); 1 Pet. 3:9 (twice), RV, "reviling" (KJV, "railing").

## REVIVE

1. ***anathallo*** (*330*), "to flourish anew" (***ana***, "again, anew," ***thallo***, "to flourish or blossom"), hence, "to revive," is used metaphorically in Phil. 4:10, RV, "ye have revived (your thought for me)," KJV, "(your care of me) hath flourished again."

2. ***anazao*** (*326*), "to live again" (***ana***, "and" ***zao***, "to live"), "to regain life," is used of moral "revival," Luke 15:24, "is alive again"; (b) of sin, Rom. 7:9, "revived," lit., "lived again" i.e., it sprang into activity, manifesting the evil inherent in it; here sin is personified, by way of contrast to the man himself. Some mss. have it in Rom. 14:9, for ***zao***, as in the RV, which italicizes "***again***."

## REWARD (Noun and Verb)

**A. Noun.**

***misthos*** (*3408*), primarily "wages, hire," and then, generally, "reward," (a) received in this life, Matt. 5:46; 6:2, 5, 16; Rom. 4:4; 1 Cor. 9:17, 18; of evil "rewards," Acts 1:18; (b) to be received hereafter, Matt. 5:12; 10:41 (twice), 42; Mark 9:41; Luke 6:23, 35; 1 Cor. 3:8, 14; 2 John 8; Rev. 11:18; 22:12.

**B. Verb.**

***apodidomi*** (*591*), "to give back," is nowhere translated "to reward" in the RV; KJV, Matt. 6:4, 6, 18; Matt. 16:27; 2 Tim. 4:14; Rev. 18:6.

## REWARDER

***misthapodotes*** (*3406*), "one who pays wages" (***misthos***, "wages," ***apo***, "back," ***didomi***, "to give"), is used by metonymy in Heb. 11:6, of God, as the "Rewarder" of those who "seek after Him" (RV).

## RICH, RICHES, RICHLY, RICH MAN

**A. Adjective.**

***plousios*** (*4145*), akin to B, C, No. 1, "rich, wealthy," is used (I) literally, (a) adjectivally (with a noun expressed separately) in Matt. 27:57; Luke 12:16; 14:12; 16:1, 19; (without a noun), 18:23; 19:2; (b) as a noun, singular, a "rich" man (the noun not being expressed), Matt. 19:23, 24; Mark 10:25; 12:41; Luke 16:21, 22; 18:25; Jas. 1:10, 11, "the rich," "the rich (man)"; plural, Mark 12:41, lit., "rich (ones)"; Luke 6:24 (ditto); 21:1; 1 Tim. 6:17, "(them that are) rich," lit., "(the) rich"; Jas. 2:6, RV, "the rich"; 5:1, RV, "ye rich"; Rev. 6:15 and 13:16, RV, "the rich"; (II), metaphorically, of God, Eph. 2:4 ("in mercy"); of Christ, 2 Cor. 8:9; of believers, Jas. 2:5, RV, "(***to be***) rich (in faith)"; Rev. 2:9, of spiritual "enrichment" generally; 3:17, of a false sense of "enrichment."

**B. Verbs.**

1. ***plouteo*** (*4147*), "to be rich," in the aorist or point tense, "to become rich," is used (a) literally, Luke 1:53, "the rich," present participle, lit., "(ones or those) being rich"; 1 Tim. 6:9, 18; Rev. 18:3, 15, 19 (all three in the aorist tense); (b) metaphorically, of Christ, Rom. 10:12 (the passage stresses the fact that Christ is Lord; see v. 9, and the RV); of the "enrichment" of believers through His poverty, 2 Cor. 8:9 (the aorist tense expressing completeness, with permanent results); so in Rev. 3:18, where the spiritual "enrichment" is conditional upon righteousness of life and conduct; of a false sense of "enrichment," 1 Cor. 4:8 (aorist), RV, "ye are become rich" (KJV, "ye are rich"); Rev. 3:17 (perfect tense, RV, "I . . . have gotten

riches," KJV, "I am . . . increased with goods"); of not being "rich" toward God, Luke 12:21.

2. ***ploutizo*** (*4148*), "to make rich, enrich," is rendered "making (many) rich" in 2 Cor. 6:10 (metaphorical of "enriching" spiritually).

### C. Nouns

1. ***ploutos*** (*4149*) is used in the singular (I) of material "riches," used evilly, Matt. 13:22: Mark 4:19; Luke 8:14; 1 Tim. 6:17; Jas. 5:2; Rev. 18:17; (II) of spiritual and moral "riches," (a) possessed by God and exercised towards men, Rom. 2:4, "of His goodness and forbearance and longsuffering"; 9:23 and Eph. 3:16, "of His glory" (i.e., of its manifestation in grace towards believers); Rom. 11:33, of His wisdom and knowledge; Eph. 1:7 and 2:7, "of His grace"; 1:18, "of the glory of His inheritance in the saints"; 3:8, "of Christ"; Phil. 4:19, "in glory in Christ Jesus," RV; Col. 1:27, "of the glory of this mystery . . . Christ in you, the hope of glory"; (b) to be ascribed to Christ, Rev. 5:12; (c) of the effects of the gospel upon the Gentiles, Rom. 11:12 (twice); (d) of the full assurance of understanding in regard to the mystery of God, even Christ, Col. 2:2, RV; (e) of the liberality of the churches of Macedonia, 2 Cor. 8:2 (where "the riches" stands for the spiritual and moral value of their liberality); (f) of "the reproach of Christ" in contrast to this world's treasures, Heb. 11:26.

2. ***chrema*** (*5536*), "what one uses or needs" (***chraomai***, "to use"), "a matter, business," hence denotes "riches," Mark 10:23, 24; Luke 18:24.

### D. Adverb.

***plousios*** (*4146*), "richly, abundantly," akin to A, is used in Col. 3:16; 1 Tim. 6:17; Titus 3:6, RV, "richly" (KJV, "abundantly"); 2 Pet. 1:11 (ditto).

## RIGHT (opp. to left), RIGHT HAND, RIGHT SIDE

#### *Old Testament*

***yamin*** (3225), "right hand." This word has cognates attested in Ugaritic, Arabic, Syriac, Aramaic, and Ethiopic. It appears about 137 times and in all periods of biblical Hebrew.

First, the word represents the bodily part called the "right hand," simply as opposed to the left hand, Gen. 48:13; with the associative meaning of strength and authority or high status, Exod. 15:6; 20:4; Deut. 4:15–19; Ps. 77:10. Second, ***yamin*** represents the direction, to the "right," which means "south," in our language, since the orientation is to stand in the direction of the sunrise, Gen. 13:9; or in some contexts, "the right side," with no reference to a compass direction, Exod. 14:29. Third, ***yamin*** can be used of bodily parts other than the right hand, Judg. 3:16.

#### *New Testament*

***dexios*** (*1188*), an adjective, used (a) of "the right" as opposite to the left, e.g., Matt. 5:29, 30; Rev. 10:5, RV, "right hand"; in connection with armor (figuratively), 2 Cor. 6:7; with ***en***, followed by the dative plural, Mark 16:5; with ***ek***, and the genitive plural, e.g., Matt. 25:33, 34; Luke 1:11; (b) of giving the "right hand" of fellowship, Gal. 2:9, betokening the public expression of approval by leaders at Jerusalem of the course pursued by Paul and Barnabas among the Gentiles; the act was often the sign of a pledge, e.g., 2 Kings 10:15; 1 Chron. 29:24, marg.; Ezra 10:19; Ezek. 17:18; figuratively, Lam. 5:6; it is often so used in the papyri; (c) metaphorically of "power" or "authority," Acts 2:33; with ***ek***, signifying "on," followed by the genitive plural, Matt. 26:64; Mark 14:62; Heb. 1:13; (d) similarly of "a place of honor in the messianic kingdom," Matt. 20:21; Mark 10:37.

## RIGHT (not wrong—Noun and Adjective), RIGHTLY

### A. Noun.

***exousia*** (*1849*), "authority, power," is translated "right" in the RV, for KJV, "power," in John 1:12; Rom. 9:21; 1 Cor. 9:4, 5, 6, 12 (twice), 18; 2 Thess. 3:9, where the "right" is that of being maintained by those among whom the ministers of the gospel had labored, a "right" possessed in virtue of the "authority" given them by Christ, Heb. 13:10; Rev. 22:14.

***exousia*** first denotes "freedom to act" and then "authority for the action." This is first true of God, Acts 1:7. It was exercised by the Son of God, as from, and in conjunction with, the Father when the Lord was upon earth, in the days of His flesh, Matt. 9:6; John 10:18, as well as in resurrection, Matt. 28:18; John 17:2. All others hold their freedom to act from God (though some of them have abused it), whether angels, Eph. 1:21, or human potentates, Rom. 13:1. Satan offered to delegate his authority over earthly kingdoms to Christ, Luke 4:6, who, though conscious of His "right" to it, refused, awaiting the divinely appointed time.

### B. Adjectives.

1. ***dikaios*** (*1342*), "just, righteous, that which is in accordance with" ***dike***, "rule, right, justice," is translated "right" in Matt. 20:4; v. 7, KJV only (RV omits, according to the most authentic mss., the clause having been inserted from v. 4, to the detriment of the narrative);

Luke 12:57; Acts 4:19; Eph. 6:1; Phil. 1:7, RV (KJV, "meet"); 2 Pet. 1:13 (KJV, "meet").

2. ***euthus*** (*2117*), "straight," hence, metaphorically, "right," is so rendered in Acts 8:21, of the heart; 13:10, of the ways of the Lord; 2 Pet. 2:15.

## RIGHTEOUS, RIGHTEOUSLY

### *Old Testament*

**A. Verb.**

***tsadaq*** (6663), "to be righteous, be in the right, be justified, be just." The basic meaning of ***tsadaq*** is "to be righteous." It is a legal term which involves the whole process of justice. God "is righteous" in all of His relations, and in comparison with Him man is not righteous: "Shall mortal man be more just [righteous] than God?" Job 4:17. In a derived sense, the case presented may be characterized as a just cause in that all facts indicate that the person is to be cleared of all charges. Isaiah called upon the nations to produce witnesses who might testify that their case was right, 43:9. Job was concerned about his case and defended it before his friends, 9:15. ***tsadaq*** may also be used to signify the outcome of the verdict, when a man is pronounced "just" and is judicially cleared of all charges. Job believed that the Lord would ultimately vindicate him against his opponents, Job 13:18.

In its causative pattern, the meaning of the verb brings out more clearly the sense of a judicial pronouncement of innocence: "If there be a controversy between men, and they come unto judgment, that the judges may judge them; then they shall justify [***tsadaq***] the righteous [***tsaddiq***], and condemn the wicked," Deut. 25:1. The Israelites were charged with upholding righteousness in all areas of life. When the court system failed became of corruption, the wicked were falsely "justified" and the poor were robbed of justice because of trumped-up charges. Absalom, thus, gained a large following by promising justice to the landowner, 2 Sam. 15:4. God, however, assured Israel that justice would be done in the end: "Thou shalt not wrest the judgment of thy poor in his cause. Keep thee far from a false matter; and the innocent and righteous slay thou not: for I will not justify the wicked," Exod. 23:6–7. The righteous person followed God's example. The psalmist exhorts his people to change their judicial system, Ps. 82:3.

**B. Nouns.**

***tsedeq*** (6664); ***tsedaqah*** (6666), "righteousness." Exegetes have spilled much ink in an attempt to understand contextually the words ***tsedeq*** and ***tsedaqah.*** The conclusions of the researchers indicate a twofold significance. On the one hand, the relationships among people and of a man to his God can be described as ***tsedeq***, supposing the parties are faithful to each other's expectations. It is a relational word. In Jacob's proposal to Laban, Jacob used the word ***tsedaqah*** to indicate the relationship. The KJV gives the following translation of ***tsedaqah:*** "So shall my righteousness answer for me in time to come, when it shall come for my hire before thy face . . ." Gen. 30:33. The NASB gives the word "righteousness" in a marginal note, but prefers the word "honesty" in the text itself. The NEB reads "fair offer" instead. Finally, the NIV has: "And my honesty [***tsedaqah***] will testify for me in the future, whenever you check on the wages you have paid me." On the other hand, "righteousness" as an abstract or as the legal status of a relationship is also present in the Old Testament. The *locus classicus* is Gen. 15:6: ". . . And he [the Lord] counted it to him [Abraham] for righteousness."

***tsedeq*** and ***tsedaqah*** are legal terms signifying justice in conformity with the Law, Deut. 16:20; the judicial process, Jer. 22:3, the justice of the king as judge, 1 Kings 10:9; Ps. 119:121; Prov. 8:15, and also the source of justice, God Himself: "Judge me, O Lord my God, according to thy righteousness; and let them not rejoice over me. . . . And my tongue shall speak of thy righteousness and of thy praise all the day long," Ps. 35:24, 28.

The word "righteousness" also embodies all that God expects of His people. The verbs associated with "righteousness" indicate the practicality of this concept. One judges, deals, sacrifices, and speaks righteously; and one learns, teaches, and pursues after righteousness. Based upon a special relationship with God, the Old Testament saint asked God to deal righteously with him: "Give the king thy judgments, O God, and thy righteousness unto the king's son," Ps. 72:1.

**C. Adjective.**

***tsaddiq*** (6662), "righteous; just," of God, Exod. 9:27; of a nation, Gen. 20:4.

### *New Testament*

**A. Adjective.**

***dikaios*** (*1342*) signifies "just," without prejudice or partiality, e.g., of the judgment of God, 2 Thess. 1:5, 6; of His judgments, Rev. 16:7; 19:2; of His character as Judge, 2 Tim. 4:8; Rev. 16:5; of His ways and doings, Rev. 15:3.

In the following the RV substitutes "righteous" for the KJV "just"; Matt. 1:19; 13:49;

27:19, 24; Mark 6:20; Luke 2:25; 15:7; 20:20; 23:50; John 5:30; Acts 3:14; 7:52; 10:22; 22:14; Rom. 1:17; 7:12; Gal. 3:11; Heb. 10:38; Jas. 5:6; 1 Pet. 3:18; 2 Pet. 2:7; 1 John 1:9; Rev. 15:3.

**B. Adverb.**

***dikaios*** *(1346)* is translated "righteously" in 1 Cor. 15:34, RV "(awake up) righteously," KJV, "(awake to) righteousness"; 1 Thess. 2:10, RV (KJV, "justly"); Titus 2:12; 1 Pet. 2:23.

## RIGHTEOUSNESS

***dikaiosune*** *(1343)* is "the character or quality of being right or just"; it was formerly spelled "rightwiseness," which clearly expresses the meaning. It is used to denote an attribute of God, e.g., Rom. 3:5, the context of which shows that "the righteousness of God" means essentially the same as His faithfulness, or truthfulness, that which is consistent with His own nature and promises; Rom. 3:25, 26 speaks of His "righteousness" as exhibited in the death of Christ, which is sufficient to show men that God is neither indifferent to sin nor regards it lightly. On the contrary, it demonstrates that quality of holiness in Him which must find expression in His condemnation of sin.

***dikaiosune*** is found in the sayings of the Lord Jesus, (a) of whatever is right or just in itself, whatever conforms to the revealed will of God, Matt. 5:6, 10, 20; John 16:8, 10; (b) whatever has been appointed by God to be acknowledged and obeyed by man, Matt. 3:15; 21:32; (c) the sum total of the requirements of God, Matt. 6:33; (d) religious duties, Matt. 6:1 (distinguished as almsgiving, man's duty to his neighbor, vv. 2–4, prayer, his duty to God, vv. 5–15, fasting, the duty of self-control, vv. 16–18).

In the preaching of the apostles recorded in Acts the word has the same general meaning. So also in Jas. 1:20, 3:18, in both Epp. of Peter, 1st John and the Revelation. In 2 Pet. 1:1, "the righteousness of our God and Savior Jesus Christ," is the righteous dealing of God with sin and with sinners on the ground of the death of Christ. "Word of righteousness," Heb. 5:13, is probably the gospel, and the Scriptures as containing the gospel, wherein is declared the righteousness of God in all its aspects.

This meaning of ***dikaiosune***, right action, is frequent also in Paul's writings, as in all five of its occurrences in Rom. 6; Eph. 6:14, etc. But for the most part he uses it of that gracious gift of God to men whereby all who believe on the Lord Jesus Christ are brought into right relationship with God. This righteousness is unattainable by obedience to any law, or by any merit of man's own, or any other condition than that of faith in Christ . . . . The man who trusts in Christ becomes "the righteousness of God in Him," 2 Cor. 5:21, i.e., becomes in Christ all that God requires a man to be, all that he could never be in himself. Because Abraham accepted the Word of God, making it his own by that act of the mind and spirit which is called faith, and, as the sequel showed, submitting himself to its control, therefore God accepted him as one who fulfilled the whole of His requirements, Rom. 4:3.

Righteousness is not said to be imputed to the believer save in the sense that faith is imputed ("reckoned" is the better word) for righteousness. It is clear that in Rom. 4:6, 11, "righteousness reckoned" must be understood in the light of the context, "faith reckoned for righteousness," vv. 3, 5, 9, 22. "For" in these places is ***eis***, which does not mean "instead of," but "with a view to." The faith thus exercised brings the soul into vital union with God in Christ, and inevitably produces righteousness of life, that is, conformity to the will of God.

## RIOT, RIOTING, RIOTOUS, RIOTOUSLY

**A. Noun.**

***asotia*** *(810)*, "prodigality, a wastefulness, profligacy" (***a***, negative, ***sozo***, "to save"), is rendered "riot" in Eph. 5:18, RV (KJV, "excess"); Titus 1:6 and 1 Pet. 4:4 (KJV and RV, "riot"). The corresponding verb is found in a papyrus writing, telling of "riotous living."

**B. Adverb.**

***asotos*** *(811)*, "wastefully" (akin to A), is translated "with riotous living" in Luke 15:13; though the word does not necessarily signify "dissolutely," the parable narrative makes clear that this is the meaning here.

## ROAR, ROARING

**A. Verbs.**

1. ***mukaomai*** *(3455)*, properly of oxen, "to low, bellow," is used of a lion, Rev. 10:3.

2. ***oruomai*** *(5612)*, "to howl" or "roar," is used of a lion, 1 Pet. 5:8, as a simile of Satan.

**B. Noun.**

***echos*** *(2279)*, "a noise" or "sound" (Eng., "echo"), is used of the "roaring" of the sea in Luke 21:25, in the best mss., "for the roaring (of the sea and the billows)," RV; some mss. have the present participle of ***echeo***, "to sound," KJV "(the sea and the waves) roaring."

## ROB

1. ***sulao*** (*4813*), "to plunder, spoil," is translated "I robbed" in 2 Cor. 11:8.

2. ***katabrabeuo*** (*2603*), "to give judgment against, to condemn" (***kata***, "against," and ***brabeus***, "an umpire"; cf. ***brabeion***, "a prize in the games," 1 Cor. 9:24; Phil. 3:14, and ***brabeuo***, "to act as an umpire, arbitrate," Col. 3:15), occurs in Col. 2:18, RV, "let (no man) rob (you) of your prize" (KJV, ". . . beguile . . . of your reward"), said of false teachers who would frustrate the faithful adherence of the believers to the truth, causing them to lose their reward. Another rendering closer to the proper meaning of the word, as given above, is "let no man decide for or against you" (i.e., without any notion of a prize); this suitably follows the word "judge" in v. 16, i.e., "do not give yourselves up to the judgment and decision of any man" (KJV, marg., "judge against").

## ROBBER

1. ***lestes*** (*3027*), "a robber, brigand" (akin to ***leia***, "booty"), "one who plunders openly and by violence" (in contrast to ***kleptes***, "a thief," see below), is always translated "robber" or "robbers" in the RV, as the KJV in John 10:1, 8, 18:40; 2 Cor. 11:26; the KJV has "thief" or "thieves" in Matt. 21:13, and parallel passages; 26:55, and parallel passages; 27:38, 44 and Mark 15:27; Luke 10:30, 36; but "thief" is the meaning of ***kleptes***.

2. ***hierosulos*** (*2417*), an adjective signifying "robbing temples" (***hieron***, "a temple," and ***sulao***, "to rob"), is found in Acts 19:37.

## ROCK

### *Old Testament*

***tsur*** (6697), "rock; rocky wall; cliff; rocky hill; mountain; rocky surface; boulder." This can mean the material that the earth (hard and often very heavy) is made up of, from the size of a huge rock wall or cliff (which is often high up and so hard to get to, making a natural "fortress"), Exod. 17:6; of mountains, Isa. 2:10, 19; or boulders, Num. 23:9; or a flat rock, 2 Sam. 21:10; cf. Prov. 30:19.

"Rock" is frequently used to picture God's support and defense of His people, Deut. 32:15. In some cases this noun is an epithet, or meaningful name, of God, Deut. 32:4, or of heathen gods: "For their rock [god] is not as our Rock [God] . . ." Deut. 32:31.

### *New Testament*

1. ***petra*** (*4073*) denotes "a mass of rock," as distinct from ***petros***, "a detached stone or boulder," or a stone that might be thrown or easily moved. For the nature of ***petra***, see Matt. 7:24, 25; 27:51, 60; Mark 15:46; Luke 6:48 (twice), a type of a sure foundation (here the true reading is as in the RV, "because it had been well builded"); Rev. 6:15, 16, cf. Isa. 2:19ff.; Hos. 10:8; Luke 8:6, 13, used illustratively; 1 Cor. 10:4 (twice), figuratively, of Christ; in Rom. 9:33 and 1 Pet. 2:8, metaphorically, of Christ; in Matt. 16:18, metaphorically, of Christ and the testimony concerning Him; here the distinction between ***petra***, concerning the Lord Himself, and ***petros***, the apostle, is clear.

2. ***spilas*** (*4694*), "a rock or reef," over which the sea dashes, is used in Jude 12, "hidden rocks," RV, metaphorical of men whose conduct is a danger to others. A late meaning ascribed to it is that of "spots," (KJV), but that rendering seems to have been influenced by the parallel passage in 2 Pet. 2:13, where ***spiloi***, "spots," occurs.

## ROCKY

***petrodes*** (*4075*), "rock-like" (***petra***, "a rock," ***eidos***, "a form, appearance"), is used of "rock" underlying shallow soil, Matt. 13:5, 20, RV, "the rocky places" (KJV, "stony places"); Mark 4:5, RV, "the rocky ground" (KJV, "stony ground"); v. 16, RV, "rocky places" (KJV, "stony ground").

## ROD

**A. Noun.**

***rhabdos*** (*4464*), "a staff, rod, scepter," is used (a) of Aaron's "rod," Heb. 9:4; (b) a staff used on a journey, Matt. 10:10, RV, "staff" (KJV, "staves"); so Luke 9:3; Mark 6:8, "staff"; Heb. 11:21, "staff"; (c) a ruler's staff, a "scepter," Heb. 1:8 (twice); elsewhere a "rod," Rev. 2:27; 12:5; 19:15; (d) a "rod" for chastisement (figuratively), 1 Cor. 4:21; (e) a measuring rod, Rev. 11:1.

**B. Verb.**

***rhabdizo*** (*4463*), "to beat with a rod," is used in Acts 16:22, RV, "to beat . . . with rods"; 2 Cor. 11:25. The "rods" were those of the Roman lictors or "sergeants" (***rhabdouchoi***, lit., "rod-bearers"); the Roman beating with "rods" is distinct from the Jewish infliction of stripes.

## ROLL (Noun and Verb)

**A. Verb.**

***heilisso***, or ***helisso*** (*1507*), "to roll," or "roll up," is used (a) of the "rolling" up of a mantle, illustratively of the heavens, Heb. 1:12, RV; (b) of the "rolling" up of a scroll, Rev. 6:14, illustratively of the removing of the heaven.

**B. Noun.**

***kephalis*** (*2777*), lit., "a little head" (a diminutive of ***kephale***, "a head"; Lat., ***capitulum***, a diminutive of ***caput***), hence, "a capital of a column," then, "a roll" (of a book), occurs in Heb. 10:7, RV, "in the roll" (KJV, "in the volume"), lit., "in the heading of the scroll" (from Ps. 40:7).

## ROUSE

***exupnos*** (*1853*), "roused out of sleep" (***ek***, "out of," ***hupnos***, "sleep"), occurs in Acts 16:27.

## ROYAL

1. ***basileios*** (*934*), from ***basileus***, "a king," is used in 1 Pet. 2:9 of the priesthood consisting of all believers.

2. ***basilikos*** (*937*), "belonging to a king," is translated "royal" in Acts 12:21; Jas. 2:8.

## RUDIMENTS

***stoicheion*** (*4747*), "one of a row or series," is translated "rudiments" in the RV of Gal. 4:3, 9; Heb. 5:12, and the KJV and RV of Col. 2:8, 20.

## RUIN

1. ***rhegma*** (*4485*), akin to ***rhegnumi***, "to break," denotes "a cleavage, fracture," in NT by metonymy, that which is broken, "a ruin," Luke 6:49.

2. ***katestrammena*** (*2690***), the neuter plural, perfect participle, passive, of ***katastrepho***, "to overturn," is translated "ruins" in Acts 15:16.

## RULE (Noun and Verb)

### *Old Testament*

***mashal*** (4910), "to rule, reign, have dominion." ***mashal*** is used most frequently in the text to express the "ruling or dominion" of one person over another, Gen. 3:16; 24:2. Cain is advised "to rule over" or "master" sin, Gen. 4:7. Joseph's brothers respond to his dreams with the angry question: "Shalt thou indeed reign over us?" Gen. 37:8.

As Creator and Sovereign over His world, God "ruleth by his power for ever," Ps. 66:7. When God allowed Israel to have a king, it was with the condition that God was still the ultimate King and that first loyalty belonged to Him, Deut. 17:14–20. This theocratic ideal is perhaps best expressed by Gideon: "I will not rule over you, neither shall my son rule over you: the Lord shall rule over you," Judg. 8:23.

### *New Testament*

**A. Nouns.**

1. ***arche*** (*746*), "a beginning," etc., denotes "rule," Luke 20:20, RV, "rule" (KJV, "power"); 1 Cor. 15:24; Eph. 1:21, RV, "rule" (KJV, "principality").

2. ***kanon*** (*2583*) is translated "rule" in the KJV of 2 Cor. 10:13, 15; in Gal. 6:16, KJV and RV; in Phil. 3:16, KJV (RV, in italics).

**B. Verbs.**

1. ***oikodespoteo*** (*3616*), from ***oikos***, "a house," and ***despotes***, "a master," signifies "to rule the household"; so the RV in 1 Tim. 5:14 (KJV, "guide the house").

2. ***hegeomai*** (*2233*), "to lead," is translated "to rule" in Heb. 13:7, 17, 24 (KJV marg., in the first two, "are the guides" and "guide."

3. ***poimaino*** (*4165*), "to act as a shepherd, tend flocks," is translated "to rule" in Rev. 2:27; 12:5; 19:15, all indicating that the governing power exercised by the Shepherd is to be of a firm character; in Matt. 2:6, KJV, "shall rule" (RV, "shall be shepherd of").

## RULER

1. ***archon*** (*758*), "a ruler, chief, prince," is translated "rulers," e.g., in 1 Cor. 2:6, 8, RV (KJV, "princes"); "ruler," Rev. 1:5 (KJV, prince).

2. ***kosmokrator*** (*2888*) denotes "a ruler of this world" (contrast ***pantokrator***, "almighty"). In Greek literature, in Orphic hymns, etc., and in rabbinic writings, it signifies a "ruler" of the whole world, a world lord. In the NT it is used in Eph. 6:12, "the world rulers (of this darkness)," RV, KJV, "the rulers (of the darkness) of this world."

## RUMOR

1. ***akoe*** (*189*), "a hearing," is translated "rumor" in Matt. 24:6; Mark 13:7.

2. ***echos*** (*2279*), "a noise, sound," is translated "rumor" in Luke 4:37, RV (KJV, "fame").

# S

## SABACHTHANI

***sabachthani*** (*4518*), an Aramaic word signifying "Thou hast forsaken Me," is recorded as part of the utterance of Christ on the cross, Matt. 27:46; Mark 15:34, a quotation from Ps. 22:1. Recently proposed renderings which differ from those of the KJV and RV have not been sufficiently established to require acceptance.

## SABAOTH

***sabaoth*** (*4519*) is the transliteration of a Hebrew word which denotes "hosts" or "armies," Rom. 9:29; Jas. 5:4. While the word "hosts" probably had special reference to angels, the title "the LORD of hosts" became used to designate Him as the One who is supreme over all the innumerable hosts of spiritual agencies, or of what are described as "the armies of heaven." Eventually it was used as equivalent to "the LORD all-sovereign."

## SABBATH

***sabbaton*** (*4521*) The observation of the seventh day of the week, enjoined upon Israel, was a sign between God and His earthly people, based upon the fact that after the six days of creative operations He rested, Exod. 31:16, 17, with 20:8–11. The OT regulations were developed and systematized to such an extent that they became a burden upon the people (who otherwise rejoiced in the rest provided) and a byword for absurd extravagance. Two treatises of the Mishna (the *Shabbath* and *Erubin*) are entirely occupied with regulations for the observance; so with the discussions in the Gemara, on rabbinical opinions. The effect upon current opinion explains the antagonism roused by the Lord's cures wrought on the "Sabbath," e.g., Matt. 12:9–13; John 5:5–16, and explains the fact that on a "Sabbath" the sick were brought to be healed after sunset, e.g., Mark 1:32. According to rabbinical ideas, the disciples, by plucking ears of corn (Matt. 12:1; Mark 2:23), and rubbing them (Luke 6:1), broke the "sabbath" in two respects; for to pluck was to reap, and to rub was to thresh. The Lord's attitude towards the "sabbath" was by way of freeing it from these vexatious traditional accretions by which it was made an end in itself, instead of a means to an end (Mark 2:27).

In the Epistles the only direct mentions are in Col. 2:16, "a sabbath day," RV (which rightly has the singular, see 1st parag., above), where it is listed among things that were "a shadow of the things to come" (i.e., of the age introduced at Pentecost), and in Heb. 4:4–11, where the perpetual ***sabbatismos*** is appointed for believers; inferential references are in Rom. 14:5 and Gal. 4:9–11. For the first three centuries of the Christian era the first day of the week was never confounded with the "sabbath"; the confusion of the Jewish and Christian institutions was due to declension from apostolic teaching.

## SACRED

***hieros*** (*2413*) denotes "consecrated to God," e.g., the Scriptures, 2 Tim. 3:15, RV, "sacred" (KJV "holy"); it is used as a noun in the neuter plural in 1 Cor. 9:13, RV, "sacred things" (KJV, "holy things"). The neuter singular, ***hieron***, denotes "a temple."

## SACRIFICE (Noun and Verb)

### *Old Testament*

***zebach*** (2077), "sacrifice." The basic meaning of ***zebach*** is "sacrifice." When a "sacrifice" had been slaughtered by the priest, he then offered it to God. The purpose was not just to create communion between God and man; rather, the "sacrifice" represented the principle that, without the shedding of blood, there is no forgiveness of sins, Lev. 17:11; cf. Heb. 9:22. In the act of "sacrifice" the faithful Israelite submitted himself to the priest, who, in keeping with the various detailed regulations (see Leviticus), offered the "sacrifice" in accordance with God's expectations. The "sacrifices" are the Passover "sacrifice," Exod. 12:27, "sacrifice" of the peace offering, Lev. 3:1ff., "sacrifice" of thanksgiving, Lev. 7:12, and "sacrifice" of the priest's offering, ***qarban***; Lev. 7:16. The ***zebach*** was not like the burnt offering (***'olah***), which was completely burnt on the altar; and it was unlike the sin offering (***chatta't***), where the meat was given to the priest, for most of the meat of the ***zebach*** was returned to the person who made the "sacrifice." The fat was burned on the altar, Lev. 3:4–5, and the blood was poured out around the altar, 3:2. The person who made the ***zeb-***

***ach*** had to share the meat with the officiating priest, Exod. 29:28; Lev. 7:31–35; Deut. 18:3.

The prophets looked with condemnation on apostate Israel's "sacrifices": "To what purpose is the multitude of your sacrifices unto me? saith the Lord: I am full of the burnt offerings of rams, and the fat of fed beasts; and I delight not in the blood of bullocks, or of lambs, or of he goats," Isa. 1:11. Hosea spoke about the necessity of Israel's love for God, Hos. 6:6. Samuel the prophet rebuked Saul with familiar words, 1 Sam. 15:22. David knew the proper response to God when he had sinned, Ps. 51:16–17.

### *New Testament*

**A. Noun.**

***thusia*** (*2378*) primarily denotes "the act of offering"; then, objectively, "that which is offered" (a) of idolatrous "sacrifice," Acts 7:41; (b) of animal or other "sacrifices," as offered under the Law, Matt. 9:13; 12:7; Mark 9:49; 12:33; Luke 2:24; 13:1; Acts 7:42; 1 Cor. 10:18; Heb. 5:1; 7:27 (RV, plural); 8:3; 9:9; 10:1, 5, 8 (RV, plural), 11; 11:4; (c) of Christ, in His "sacrifice" on the cross, Eph. 5:2; Heb. 9:23, where the plural antitypically comprehends the various forms of Levitical "sacrifices" in their typical character; 9:26; 10:12, 26; (d) metaphorically, (1) of the body of the believer, presented to God as a living "sacrifice," Rom. 12:1; (2) of faith, Phil. 2:17; (3) of material assistance rendered to servants of God, Phil. 4:18; (4) of praise, Heb. 13:15; (5) of doing good to others and communicating with their needs, Heb. 13:16; (6) of spiritual "sacrifices" in general, offered by believers as a holy priesthood, 1 Pet. 2:5.

**B. Verb.**

***thuo*** (*2380*) is used of "sacrificing by slaying a victim," (a) of the "sacrifice" of Christ, 1 Cor. 5:7, RV, "hath been sacrificed" (KJV, "is sacrificed"); (b) of the Passover "sacrifice," Mark 14:12, RV, "they sacrificed" (KJV, "they killed"); Luke 22:7, RV, "(must) be sacrificed," KJV, "(must) be killed"; (c) of idolatrous "sacrifices," Acts 14:13, 18; 1 Cor. 10:20 (twice).

## SAFE, SAFELY, SAFETY

**A. Nouns.**

1. ***asphaleia*** (*803*), "certainty, safety," is translated "safety" in Acts 5:23; 1 Thess. 5:3.

2. ***soteria*** (*4991*), "salvation," is translated "safety" in Acts 27:34, RV (KJV, "health").

**B. Verbs.**

1. ***diasozo*** (*1295*), "to bring safely through danger," and, in the passive voice, "to come safe through" (***dia***, "through," ***sozo***, "to save"), is translated "bring safe" in Acts 23:24; "escaped safe" in 27:44.

2. ***hugiaino*** (*5198*), "to be sound, healthy" (Eng., "hygiene," etc.), is translated "safe and sound" in Luke 15:27, lit., "being healthy."

## SAINT(S)

***hagios*** (*40*), used as a noun in the singular in Phil. 4:21, where ***pas***, "every," is used with it. In the plural, as used of believers, it designates all such and is not applied merely to persons of exceptional holiness, or to those who, having died, were characterized by exceptional acts of "saintliness." See especially 2 Thess. 1:10, where "His saints" are also described as "them that believed," i.e., the whole number of the redeemed.

## SALT (Noun, Adjective and Verb), SALTNESS

**A. Noun.**

***halas*** (*251*), a late form of ***hals*** (found in some mss. in Mark 9:49), is used (a) literally in Matt. 5:13 (2nd part); Mark 9:50 (1st part, twice); Luke 14:34 (twice); (b) metaphorically, of "believers," Matt. 5:13 (1st part); of their "character and condition," Mark 9:50 (2nd part); of "wisdom" exhibited in their speech, Col. 4:6.

Being possessed of purifying, perpetuating and antiseptic qualities, "salt" became emblematic of fidelity and friendship among eastern nations. To eat of a person's "salt" and so to share his hospitality is still regarded thus among the Arabs. So in Scripture, it is an emblem of the covenant between God and His people, Num. 18:19; 2 Chron. 13:5; so again when the Lord says "Have salt in yourselves, and be at peace one with another" (Mark 9:50). In the Lord's teaching it is also symbolic of that spiritual health and vigor essential to Christian virtue and counteractive of the corruption that is in the world, e.g., Matt. 5:13, see (b) above. Food is seasoned with "salt" (see B); every meal offering was to contain it, and it was to be offered with all offerings presented by Israelites, as emblematic of the holiness of Christ, and as betokening the reconciliation provided for man by God on the ground of the death of Christ, Lev. 2:13. To refuse God's provision in Christ and the efficacy of His expiatory sacrifice is to expose oneself to the doom of being "salted with fire," Mark 9:49.

**B. Verb.**

***halizo*** (*233*), akin to A, signifies "to sprinkle" or "to season with salt," Matt. 5:13; Mark 9:49.

**C. Adjectives.**

1. ***halukos*** (*252*) occurs in Jas. 3:12, "salt (water)."

2. ***analos*** (*358*) denotes "saltless" (***a***, negative, ***n***, euphonic, and A), insipid, Mark 9:50, "have lost its saltness," lit., "have become (***ginomai***) saltless (***analos***)."

## SALVATION

**A. Nouns.**

1. ***soteria*** (*4991*) denotes "deliverance, preservation, salvation." "Salvation" is used in the NT (a) of material and temporal deliverance from danger and apprehension, (1) national, Luke 1:69, 71; Acts 7:25, RV marg., "salvation" (text, "deliverance"); (2) personal, as from the sea, Acts 27:34; RV, "safety" (KJV, "health"); prison, Phil. 1:19; the flood, Heb. 11:7; (b) of the spiritual and eternal deliverance granted immediately by God to those who accept His conditions of repentance and faith in the Lord Jesus, in whom alone it is to be obtained, Acts 4:12, and upon confession of Him as Lord, Rom. 10:10; for this purpose the gospel is the saving instrument, Rom. 1:16; Eph. 1:13; (c) of the present experience of God's power to deliver from the bondage of sin, e.g., Phil. 2:12, where the special, though not the entire, reference is to the maintenance of peace and harmony; 1 Pet. 1:9; this present experience on the part of believers is virtually equivalent to sanctification; for this purpose, God is able to make them wise, 2 Tim. 3:15; they are not to neglect it, Heb. 2:3; (d) of the future deliverance of believers at the Parousia of Christ for His saints, a salvation which is the object of their confident hope, e.g., Rom. 13:11; 1 Thess. 5:8, and v. 9, where "salvation" is assured to them, as being deliverance from the wrath of God destined to be executed upon the ungodly at the end of this age (see 1 Thess. 1:10); 2 Thess. 2:13; Heb. 1:14; 9:28; 1 Pet. 1:5; 2 Pet. 3:15; (e) of the deliverance of the nation of Israel at the second advent of Christ at the time of "the epiphany (or shining forth) of His Parousia" (2 Thess. 2:8); Luke 1:71; Rev. 12:10; (f) inclusively, to sum up all the blessings bestowed by God on men in Christ through the Holy Spirit, e.g., 2 Cor. 6:2; Heb. 5:9; 1 Pet. 1:9, 10; Jude 3; (g) occasionally, as standing virtually for the Savior, e.g., Luke 19:9; cf. John 4:22; (h) in ascriptions of praise to God, Rev. 7:10, and as that which it is His prerogative to bestow, 19:1 (RV).

2. ***soterion*** (*4992*), the neuter of the adjective, is used as a noun in Luke 2:30; 3:6, in each of which it virtually stands for the Savior, as in No. 1 (g); in Acts 28:28, as in No. 1 (b); in Eph. 6:17, where the hope of "salvation" [see No. 1 (d)] is metaphorically described as "a helmet."

**B. Adjective.**

***soterios*** (*4992***), "saving, bringing salvation," describes the grace of God, in Titus 2:11.

## SANCTIFICATION, SANCTIFY

### *Old Testament*

**A. Verb.**

***qadash*** (6942), "to sanctify, be holy." In the primary stem the verb signifies an act whereby, or a state wherein, people or things are set aside for worship of God: they are consecrated or "made sacred." By this act and in this state the thing or person consecrated is to be withheld from workaday use (or profane use) and to be treated with special care as a possession of God, Exod. 29:21. There are also overtones of ethical-moral (spiritual) holiness here since the atoning blood was applied to the people involved. The state appears to be emphasized when the word is used in Exod. 29:37. In some cases "set aside for God," means destruction, 2 Sam. 6:6ff., while in others it means such things are to be used only by those who are ritualistically pure, Num. 4:15; 1 Sam. 21:6.

In the passive stem the verb means "to prove oneself holy," Num. 20:13. This proving refers not to an act of judgment against sin (an ethical-moral holiness) but a miraculous act of deliverance. Another emphasis is "to be treated as holy, Isa. 5:16; Deut. 6:3, 5ff.

***qadash*** can mean "to declare something holy" or to declare it to be said exclusively for celebrating God's glory, Exod. 20:8; or a pagan god, 2 Kings 10:20. The word comes to mean "to declare" and "to make proper preparations for war, Jer. 6:4; cf. Mic. 3:5; Jer. 51:27. This stem may also be used of putting something or someone into a state reserved exclusively for God's use, Exod. 13:2, 12–13; 1 Sam. 1:24.

***qadash*** may also be used in the sense of making something or someone cultically pure and meeting all God's requirements for purity in persons or things used in the formal worship of Him. This act appears in Exod. 19:10. Although the primary emphasis here is ritualistic, there are ethical-moral overtones. Thus, God directed Moses to have the artisans make special clothing for Aaron, Exod. 28:4.

***qadash*** is also applied to the consecration of things by placing them into a state of ritualistic or cultic purity and dedicating them solely to God's use, cultic use; cf. Exod. 29:36; Lev. 16:19. In some cases consecrating something to God requires no act upon the object, but leaving it entirely alone. Moses acknowledges to God that "the people cannot come up to mount Sinai: for thou chargedst us, saying, Set bounds about the mount, and sanctify it," Exod. 19:23. In the causative stem the word means "to give for God's use," Exod. 28:38. The act whereby someone gives things to God is also described by the word ***qadash***. The priests performed the actual consecration ceremony while an individual decided that something he owned was to be given to God, 2 Sam. 8:11.

God's consecrating something or someone may also mean that He accepts that person or thing as in His service, 1 Kings 9:3; Jer. 1:5; cf. 12:3. This verb also means "to prepare to approach God," Zeph. 1:7.

**B. Nouns.**

***qodesh*** (6944), "holy thing." First, ***qodesh*** is used of things or people belonging to God. All Israel is holy, Exod. 30:31, separated to God's service, and therefore should keep itself separated to that service by observing the distinction between things holy (allowed by God) and things unclean, Lev. 10:10.

***qodesh*** can also be used of what God makes a person, place, or thing to be. He designates a place to be His (Exod. 3:5—the first biblical appearance of the word), that is, separate and unique. Even more, God designates His sanctuary a holy place, Exod. 36:1. The outer part of the sanctuary is *the* holy place, the inner part the holy of holies, Exod. 26:33, and the altar a most holy place. This means that to varying degrees these places are identified with the holy God, 2 Sam. 6:10–11, the God who is separate from and hates all that is death and/or associated with death and idolatry, Ezek. 39:25.

The noun ***miqdash***, represents a "sacred place" or "sanctuary," a place set aside by men upon God's direction and acceptance as the place where He meets them and they worship Him, Exod. 15:17.

**C. Adjective.**

***qadosh*** (6918), "holy." The adjective ***qados*** occurs about 116 times in biblical Hebrew and in all periods. This adjective is more focused in emphasis than the noun ***qodesh***. ***qadosh*** can refer (infrequently) to cultic holiness, or ritualistic ceremonial holiness, Num. 5:17. Its most frequent use, however, represents God's majestic, 1 Sam. 2:2, moral, Lev. 11:44, and dynamistic holiness; holiness as power; 1 Sam. 6:20.

***New Testament***

**A. Noun.**

***hagiasmos*** (*38*), "sanctification," is used of (a) separation to God, 1 Cor. 1:30; 2 Thess. 2:13; 1 Pet. 1:2; (b) the course of life befitting those so separated, 1 Thess. 4:3, 4, 7; Rom. 6:19, 22; 1 Tim. 2:15; Heb. 12:14. Sanctification is that relationship with God into which men enter by faith in Christ, Acts 26:18; 1 Cor. 6:11, and to which their sole title is the death of Christ, Eph. 5:25, 26; Col. 1:22; Heb. 10:10, 29; 13:12.

Sanctification is also used in NT of the separation of the believer from evil things and ways. This sanctification is God's will for the believer, 1 Thess. 4:3, and His purpose in calling him by the gospel, v. 7; it must be learned from God, v. 4, as He teaches it by His Word, John 17:17, 19, cf. Ps. 17:4; 119:9, and it must be pursued by the believer, earnestly and undeviatingly, 1 Tim. 2:15; Heb. 12:14. For the holy character, ***hagiosune***, 1 Thess. 3:13, is not vicarious, i.e., it cannot be transferred or imputed, it is an individual possession, built up, little by little, as the result of obedience to the Word of God, and of following the example of Christ, Matt. 11:29; John 13:15; Eph. 4:20; Phil. 2:5, in the power of the Holy Spirit, Rom. 8:13; Eph. 3:16.

**B. Verb.**

***hagiazo*** (*37*), "to sanctify," "is used of (a) the gold adorning the Temple and of the gift laid on the altar, Matt. 23:17, 19; (b) food, 1 Tim. 4:5; (c) the unbelieving spouse of a believer, 1 Cor. 7:14; (d) the ceremonial cleansing of the Israelites, Heb. 9:13; (e) the Father's Name, Luke 11:2; (f) the consecration of the Son by the Father, John 10:36; (g) the Lord Jesus devoting Himself to the redemption of His people, John 17:19; (h) the setting apart of the believer for God, Acts 20:32; cf. Rom. 15:16; (i) the effect on the believer of the Death of Christ, Heb. 10:10, said of God, and 2:11; 13:12, said of the Lord Jesus; (j) the separation of the believer from the world in his behavior—by the Father through the Word, John 17:17, 19; (k) the believer who turns away from such things as dishonor God and His gospel, 2 Tim. 2:21; (l) the acknowledgment of the Lordship of Christ, 1 Pet. 3:15.

## SANCTUARY

1. ***hagion*** (*39*), the neuter of the adjective ***hagios***, "holy," is used of those structures which are set apart to God, (a) of "the tabernacle" in the wilderness, Heb. 9:1, RV, "its sanctuary, a *sanctuary* of this world" (KJV, "a worldly sanctuary"); in v. 2 the outer part is called "the

Holy place," RV (KJV, "the sanctuary"); here the neuter plural ***hagia*** is used, as in v. 3.

2. ***naos*** (*3485*) is used of the inner part of the Temple in Jerusalem, in Matt. 23:35, RV, "sanctuary."

## SAPPHIRE

***sappheiros*** (*4552*) is mentioned in Rev. 21:19 (RV, marg., "***lapis lazuli***") as the second of the foundations of the wall of the heavenly Jerusalem (cf. Isa. 54:11). It was one of the stones in the high priest's breastplate, Exod. 28:18; 39:11; as an intimation of its value see Job 28:16; Ezek. 28:13. See also Exod. 24:10; Ezek. 1:26; 10:1. The sapphire has various shades of blue and ranks next in hardness to the diamond.

## SATAN

### *Old Testament*

***satan*** (7854), "adversary; Satan." This word has two clear references: (a) an evil being who is the opponent of the true God, Job 1:6–12; 2:1–7; (b) a human being who is an opponent to God or another human. Ps. 38:20; 71:13; Ps. 109:4; cf. also 2 Sam. 16:5ff. God can also be the "adversary." When Balaam went to curse the sons of Israel, God warned him not to do so. When the prophet persisted, God disciplined him, Num. 22:22; with Solomon, 1 Kings 11:14. One must carefully read in some contexts to decide who the "satan," or "Satan" is. But in the New Testament, it nearly always refers to the person of Satan.

### *New Testament*

***satanas*** (*4567*), a Greek form derived from the Aramaic (Heb., ***satan***), "an adversary," is used (a) of an angel of Jehovah in Num. 22:22 (the first occurrence of the Word in the OT); (b) of men, e.g., 1 Sam. 29:4; Ps. 38:20; 71:13; four in Ps. 109; (c) of "Satan," the Devil, some seventeen or eighteen times in the OT; in Zech. 3:1, where the name receives its interpretation, "to be (his) adversary," RV (see marg.; KJV, "to resist him").

In the NT the word is always used of "Satan," the adversary (a) of God and Christ, e.g., Matt. 4:10; 12:26; Mark 1:13; 3:23, 26; 4:15; Luke 4:8 (in some mss.); 11:18; 22:3; John 13:27; (b) of His people, e.g., Luke 22:31; Acts 5:3; Rom. 16:20; 1 Cor. 5:5; 7:5; 2 Cor. 2:11; 11:14; 12:7; 1 Thess. 2:18; 1 Tim. 1:20; 5:15; Rev. 2:9, 13 (twice), 24; 3:9; (c) of mankind, Luke 13:16; Acts 26:18; 2 Thess. 2:9; Rev. 12:9; 20:7.

His doom, sealed at the Cross, is foretold in its stages in Luke 10:18; Rev. 20:2, 10. Believers are assured of victory over him, Rom. 16:20.

The appellation was given by the Lord to Peter, as a "Satan-like" man, on the occasion when he endeavored to dissuade Him from death, Matt. 16:23; Mark 8:33.

"Satan" is not simply the personification of evil influences in the heart, for he tempted Christ, in whose heart no evil thought could ever have arisen (John 14:30; 2 Cor. 5:21; Heb. 4:15); moreover his personality is asserted in both the OT and the NT, and especially in the latter, whereas if the OT language was intended to be figurative, the NT would have made this evident.

## SATISFY

### *Old Testament*

***saba'*** (7646), "to be satisfied, sated, surfeited." ***saba'*** expresses the idea of "being filled, sated," Exod. 16:8; often in reference to eating, Jer. 50:19. ***saba'*** sometimes expresses "being surfeited with," as in Prov. 25:16; Isa. 1:11. ***saba'*** often indicates God "satisfying, supplying," man with his material needs, Ps. 103:5. But even when God "fed them to the full," Israel was not satisfied and went after strange gods, Jer. 5:7.

### *New Testament*

1. ***chortazo*** (*5526*), "to fill or satisfy with food," is translated "satisfy" in Mark 8:4, KJV (RV, "to fill").

2. ***empiplemi*** or ***empletho*** (*1705*), "to fill up, fill full, satisfy" (***en***, "in," ***pimplemi*** or ***pletho***, "to fill"), is used metaphorically in Rom. 15:24, of taking one's fill of the company of others, RV, "I shall have been satisfied" (KJV, "I be . . . filled").

## SAVE, SAVING

### *Old Testament*

**A. Verb.**

***yasha'*** (3467), "to help, deliver, save." ***yasha'*** signifies to remove someone from a burden or job, Josh. 10:6. ***yasha'*** is used in other situations as when Jephthah tells the Ephraimites that they had been summoned to the war at a crucial time but did not respond, Judg. 12:2. Militarily the word can also be used of "helping," emphasizing the union of forces so as to forge a single and stronger fighting unit. This is no last-ditch stand for the unit being helped, 2 Sam. 10:11–19.

In the realm of justice and civil law ***yasha'*** represents an obligation on the part of anyone who hears an outcry of one being mistreated, Deut. 22:27; cf. 28:29. Therefore, one may appeal especially to the king as the one obligated to help maintain one's rights, 2 Sam.

14:4; cf. 2 Kings 6:26. The king also "delivered" his people from subjection to their enemies, 1 Sam. 10:27; Hos. 13:10. The word appears in many prayer petitions: "Arise, O Lord; save me, O my God . . ." Ps. 3:7; 20:9; 72:4.

**B. Nouns.**

***yesu'ah*** (3444), "salvation." This word refers primarily to God's acts of help which have already occurred and been experienced. In Gen. 49:18 (the first biblical occurrence), the word includes the idea of "salvation" through divinely appointed means and from inequity. In 1 Sam. 14:45 ***yeshu'ah*** is used of a human act, Isa. 12:3. The noun ***teshu'ah*** also means "salvation," 1 Sam. 11:13; rendered "deliverance," Judg. 15:18; or "victory," 2 Sam. 19:2.

The noun ***yesha'*** signifies that which God will do in man's behalf, 2 Sam. 22:3, or that which has been done by Him for man, 2 Sam. 22:36.

***New Testament***

1. ***sozo*** (*4982*), a verb, "to save," is used (as with the noun ***soteria***, "salvation") (a) of material and temporal deliverance from danger, suffering, etc., e.g., Matt. 8:25; Mark 13:20; Luke 23:35; John 12:27; 1 Tim. 2:15; 2 Tim. 4:18 (KJV, "preserve"); Jude 5; from sickness, Matt. 9:22, "made . . . whole" (RV, marg., "saved"); so Mark 5:34; Luke 8:48; Jas. 5:15; (b) of the spiritual and eternal salvation granted immediately by God to those who believe on the Lord Jesus Christ, e.g., Acts 2:47, RV "(those that) were being saved"; 16:31; Rom. 8:24, RV, "were we saved"; Eph. 2:5, 8; 1 Tim. 2:4; 2 Tim. 1:9; Titus 3:5; of human agency in this, Rom. 11:14; 1 Cor. 7:16; 9:22; (c) of the present experiences of God's power to deliver from the bondage of sin, e.g., Matt. 1:21; Rom. 5:10; 1 Cor. 15:2; Heb. 7:25; Jas. 1:21; 1 Pet. 3:21; of human agency in this, 1 Tim. 4:16; (d) of the future deliverance of believers at the second coming of Christ for His saints, being deliverance from the wrath of God to be executed upon the ungodly at the close of this age and from eternal doom, e.g., Rom. 5:9; (e) of the deliverance of the nation of Israel at the second advent of Christ, e.g., Rom. 11:26; (f) inclusively for all the blessings bestowed by God on men in Christ, e.g., Luke 19:10; John 10:9; 1 Cor. 10:33; 1 Tim. 1:15; (g) of those who endure to the end of the time of the Great Tribulation, Matt. 10:22; Mark 13:13; (h) of the individual believer, who, though losing his regard at the judgment seat of Christ hereafter, will not lose his salvation, 1 Cor. 3:15; 5:5; (i) of the deliverance of the nations at the Millennium, Rev. 21:24 (in some mss.).

2. ***diasozo*** (*1295*), "to bring safely through" (***dia***, "through," and No. 1), is used (a) of the healing of the sick by the Lord, Matt. 14:36, RV, "were made whole" (KJV adds "perfectly"); Luke 7:3; (b) of bringing "safe" to a destination, Acts 23:24; (c) of keeping a person "safe," 27:43; (d) of escaping through the perils of shipwreck, 27:44; 28:1, 4, passive voice; (e) through the Flood, 1 Pet. 3:20.

## SAVIOR

***soter*** (*4990*), "a savior, deliverer, preserver," is used (a) of God, Luke 1:47; 1 Tim. 1:1; 2:3; 4:10 (in the sense of "preserver," since He gives "to all life and breath and all things"); Titus 1:3; 2:10; 3:4; Jude 25; (b) of Christ, Luke 2:11; John 4:42; Acts 5:31; 13:23 (of Israel); Eph. 5:23 (the sustainer and preserver of the church, His "body"); Phil. 3:20 (at His return to receive the Church to Himself); 2 Tim. 1:10 (with reference to His incarnation, "the days of His flesh"); Titus 1:4 (a title shared, in the context, with God the Father); 2:13, RV, "our great God and Savior Jesus Christ," the pronoun "our," at the beginning of the whole clause, includes all the titles; Titus 3:6; 2 Pet. 1:1, "our God and Savior Jesus Christ; RV, where the pronoun "our," coming immediately in connection with "God," involves the inclusion of both titles as referring to Christ, just as in the parallel in v. 11, "our Lord and Savior Jesus Christ" (KJV and RV); these passages are therefore a testimony to His deity; 2 Pet. 2:20; 3:2, 18; 1 John 4:14.

## SAY

1. ***lego*** (*3004*), primarily to pick out, gather," chiefly denotes "to say, speak, affirm," whether of actual speech, e.g., Matt. 11:17, or of unspoken thought, e.g., Matt. 3:9, or of a message in writing, e.g., 2 Cor. 8:8. The 2nd aorist form ***eipon*** is used to supply that tense, which is lacking in ***lego***.

2. ***phemi*** (*5346*), "to declare, say," (a) is frequently used in quoting the words of another, e.g., Matt. 13:29; 26:61; (b) is interjected into the recorded words, e.g., Acts 23:35; (c) is used impersonally, 2 Cor. 10:10.

## SCATTER

***Old Testament***

***puts*** (6327), "to scatter, disperse, be scattered." ***puts***, in the sense of "scattering," often has an almost violent connotation to it, 1 Sam. 11:11. Such "scattering" of forces seems to have been a common thing after defeats in battle, 1 Kings 22:17; 2 Kings 25:5. Many references are made to Israel as a people and nation "being scattered" among the nations, especially in the imagery of a scattered flock of sheep, Ezek. 34:5–6; Zech. 13:7.

In a figurative sense, this word is used to refer to lightning as arrows which God "scatters," 2 Sam. 22:15. According to Job, "the clouds scatter his lightning," Job 37:11, RSV. No harvest is possible unless first the seeds "are scattered" in rows, Isa. 28:25.

*New Testament*

**A. Verbs.**

1. ***skorpizo*** (*4650*) is used in Matt. 12:30; Luke 11:23; John 10:12; 16:32; 2 Cor. 9:9, RV.

2. ***diaskorpizo*** (*1287*), "to scatter abroad," is rendered "to scatter" in Matt. 25:24, 26, RV (KJV, "strawed"); 26:31; Mark 14:27; Luke 1:51; John 11:52; Acts 5:37, RV.

3. ***diaspeiro*** (*1289*), "to scatter abroad" (***dia***, "throughout," ***speiro***, "to sow seed"), is used in Acts 8:1, 4; 11:19, all of the church in Jerusalem "scattered" through persecution; the word in general is suggestive of the effects of the "scattering" in the sowing of the spiritual seed of the Word of life.

**B. Noun.**

***diaspora*** (*1290*), "a dispersion," is rendered "scattered abroad" in Jas. 1:1, KJV; "scattered" in 1 Pet. 1:1, KJV.

## SCHISM

***schisma*** (*4978*), "a rent, division," is translated "schism" in 1 Cor. 12:25, metaphorically of the contrary condition to that which God has designed for a local church in "tempering the body together" (v. 24), the members having "the same care one for another" ("the same" being emphatic).

## SCHOOL

***schole*** (*4981*) (whence Eng., "school") primarily denotes "leisure," then, "that for which leisure was employed, a disputation, lecture"; hence, by metonymy, "the place where lectures are delivered, a school," Acts 19:9.

## SCIENCE

***gnosis*** (*1108*) is translated "science" in the KJV of 1 Tim. 6:20; the word simply means "knowledge" (RV), where the reference is to the teaching of the Gnostics (lit., "the knowers") "falsely called knowledge." Science in the modern sense of the word, viz., the investigation, discovery, and classification of secondary laws, is unknown in Scripture.

## SCOFF

***ekmukterizo*** (*1592*), "to hold up the nose in derision at" (***ek***, "from," used intensively, ***mukterizo***, "to mock"; from ***mukter***, "the nose"), is translated "scoffed at" in Luke 16:14, RV (KJV, "derided"), of the Pharisees in their derision of Christ on account of His teaching; in 23:35 (ditto), of the mockery of Christ on the cross by the rulers of the people.

## SCOURGE (Noun and Verb)

**A. Noun.**

***phragellion*** (*5416*), "a whip" (from Latin, ***flagellum***), is used of the "scourge" of small cords which the Lord made and employed before cleansing the Temple, John 2:15. However He actually used it, the whip was in itself a sign of authority and judgment.

**B. Verbs.**

1. ***phragelloo*** (*5417*) (akin to A: Latin, ***flagello***; Eng., "flagellate"), is the word used in Matt. 27:26, and Mark 15:15, of the "scourging" endured by Christ and administered by the order of Pilate. Under the Roman method of "scourging," the person was stripped and tied in a bending posture to a pillar, or stretched on a frame. The "scourge" was made of leather thongs, weighted with sharp pieces of bone or lead, which tore the flesh of both the back and the breast (cf. Ps. 22:17). Eusebius (*Chron.*) records his having witnessed the suffering of martyrs who died under this treatment.

2. ***mastigoo*** (*3146*), akin to ***mastix*** (see below), is used (a) as mentioned under No. 1; (b) of Jewish "scourgings," Matt. 10:17 and 23:34; (c) metaphorically, in Heb. 12:6, of the "chastening" by the Lord administered in love to His spiritual sons.

3. ***mastizo*** (*3147*), akin to No. 2, occurs in Acts 22:25 (see No. 1, above).

## SCOURGING (-S)

***mastix*** (*3148*), "a whip, scourge," is used (a) with the meaning "scourging," in Acts 22:24, of the Roman method, (b) in Heb. 11:36, of the "sufferings" of saints in the OT times. Among the Hebrews the usual mode, legal and domestic, was that of beating with a rod (see 2 Cor. 11:25); (c) metaphorically, of "disease" or "suffering."

S

## SCRIBE (-S)

***grammateus*** (*1122*), from ***gramma***, "a writing," denotes "a scribe, a man of letters, a teacher of the law"; the "scribes" are mentioned frequently in the Synoptists, especially in connection with the Pharisees, with whom they virtually formed one party (see Luke 5:21), sometimes with the chief priests, e.g., Matt. 2:4; Mark 8:31; 10:33; 11:18, 27; Luke 9:22. They are mentioned only once in John's gospel, 8:3, three times in the Acts, 4:5; 6:12; 23:9; elsewhere only in 1 Cor. 1:20, in the singular. They were considered naturally qualified to teach in the synagogues, Mark 1:22. They were ambitious of honor, e.g., Matt. 23:5–11, which they demanded especially from their pupils, and which was readily granted them, as well as by the people generally. Like Ezra, Ezra 7:12, the "scribes" were found originally among the priests and Levites. The priests being the official interpreters of the Law, the "scribes" ere long became an independent company; though they never held political power, they became leaders of the people.

## SCRIPTURE

***graphe*** (*1124*), akin to ***grapho***, "to write" (Eng., "graph," "graphic," etc.), primarily denotes "a drawing, painting"; then "a writing," (a) of the OT Scriptures, (1) in the plural, the whole, e.g., Matt. 21:42; 22:29; John 5:39; Acts 17:11; 18:24; Rom. 1:2, where "the prophets" comprises the OT writers in general; 15:4; 16:26, lit., "prophetic writings," expressing the character of all the Scriptures; (2) in the singular in reference to a particular passage, e.g., Mark 12:10; Luke 4:21; John 2:22; 10:35 (though applicable to all); 19:24, 28, 36, 37; 20:9; Acts 1:16; 8:32, 35; Rom. 4:3; 9:17; 10:11; 11:2; Gal. 3:8, 22; 4:30; 1 Tim. 5:18, where the 2nd quotation is from Luke 10:7, from which it may be inferred that the apostle included Luke's gospel as "Scripture" alike with Deuteronomy, from which the first quotation is taken; in reference to the whole, e.g. Jas. 4:5 (see RV, a separate rhetorical question from the one which follows); in 2 Pet. 1:20, "no prophecy of Scripture," a description of all, with special application to the OT in the next verse; (b) of the OT Scriptures (those accepted by the Jews as canonical) and all those of the NT which were to be accepted by Christians as authoritative, 2 Tim. 3:16; these latter were to be discriminated from the many forged epistles and other religious "writings" already produced and circulated in Timothy's time. Such discrimination would be directed by the fact that "every Scripture," characterized by inspiration of God, would be profitable for the purposes mentioned; so the RV. The KJV states truth concerning the completed canon of Scripture, but that was not complete when the apostle wrote to Timothy.

The Scriptures are frequently personified by the NT writers (as by the Jews, John 7:42), (a) as speaking with divine authority, e.g., John 19:37; Rom. 4:3; 9:17, where the Scripture is said to speak to Pharaoh, giving the message actually sent previously by God to him through Moses; Jas. 4:5 (see above); (b) as possessed of the sentient quality of foresight, and the active power of preaching, Gal. 3:8, where the Scripture mentioned was written more than four centuries after the words were spoken. The Scripture, in such a case, stands for its divine Author with an intimation that it remains perpetually characterized as the living voice of God. This divine agency is again illustrated in Gal. 3:22 (cf. v. 10 and Matt. 11:13).

## SEA

### *Old Testament*

***yam*** (3220), "sea; ocean." This word refers to the body of water as distinct from the land bodies (continents and islands) and the sky (heavens), Exod. 20:11. Used in this sense ***yam*** means "ocean," Gen. 1:10; or fresh water body, Num. 34:11. ***yam*** is used of the "great basin" or "bath," as a small body of water, 1 Kings 7:23; Jer. 27:19. ***yam*** is also used of mighty rivers such as the Nile, Isa. 19:5; Ezek. 32:2. The word is sometimes used of the direction "west" or "westward," Gen. 13:14; Ezek. 42:19. Exod. 10:19 uses ***yam*** as an adjective modifying "wind."

In some instances the word ***yam*** may represent the Canaanite god *Yamm*, Job 9:8. If understood as a statement about Yamm, this passage would read: "and tramples upon the back of Yamm."

### *New Testament*

1. ***thalassa*** (*2281*) is used (a) chiefly literally, e.g., "the Red Sea," Acts 7:36; 1 Cor. 10:1; Heb. 11:29; the "sea" of Galilee or Tiberias, Matt. 4:18; 15:29; Mark 6:48, 49, where the acts of Christ testified to His deity; John 6:1; 21:1; in general, e.g., Luke 17:2; Acts 4:24; Rom. 9:27; Rev. 16:3; 18:17; 20:8, 13; 21:1; in combination with No. 2, Matt. 18:6; (b) metaphorically, of "the ungodly men" described in Jude 13 (cf. Isa. 57:20); (c) symbolically, in the apocalyptic vision of "a glassy sea like unto crystal," Rev. 4:6, emblematic of the fixed purity and holiness of all that appertains to the authority and judicial dealings of God; in 15:2, the same, "mingled with fire," and, standing by it (RV) or on it (KJV and RV marg.), those who had "come victorious from the beast" (ch. 13); of the wild and restless condition of nations, Rev. 13:1 (see 17:1, 15), where "he stood" (RV) refers to the dragon, not John (KJV); from the midst of this state arises the beast, symbolic of the final gentile power dominating the federated nations of the Roman world (see Dan., chs. 2, 7, etc.).

2. ***pelagos*** *(989)*, "the deep sea, the deep," is translated "the depth" in Matt. 18:6, and is used of the "Sea of Cilicia" in Acts 27:5. ***pelagos*** signifies "the vast expanse of open water"; ***thalassa***, "the sea as contrasted with the land."

## SEAL (Noun and Verb)

### A. Noun.

***sphragis*** *(4973)* denotes (a) "a seal" or "signet," Rev. 7:2, "the seal of the living God," an emblem of ownership and security, here combined with that of destination (as in Ezek. 9:4), the persons to be "sealed" being secured from destruction and marked for reward; (b) "the impression" of a "seal" or signet, (1) literal, a "seal" on a book or roll, combining with the ideas of security and destination those of secrecy and postponement of disclosures, Rev. 5:1, 2, 5, 9; 6:1, 3, 5, 7, 9, 12; 8:1; (2) metaphorical, Rom. 4:11, said of "circumcision," as an authentication of the righteousness of Abraham's faith, and an external attestation of the covenant made with him by God; the rabbis called circumcision "the seal of Abraham"; in 1 Cor. 9:2, of converts as a "seal" or authentication of Paul's apostleship; in 2 Tim. 2:19, "the firm foundation of God standeth, having this seal, The Lord knoweth them that are His," RV, indicating ownership, authentication, security and destination, "and, Let every one that nameth the Name of the Lord depart from unrighteousness," indicating a ratification on the part of the believer of the determining counsel of God concerning him; Rev. 9:4 distinguishes those who will be found without the "seal" of God on their foreheads [see (a) above and B].

### B. Verb.

***sphragizo*** *(4972)*, "to seal" (akin to A), is used to indicate (a) security and permanency (attempted but impossible), Matt. 27:66; on the contrary, of the doom of Satan, fixed and certain, Rev. 20:3, RV, "sealed it over"; (b) in Rom. 15:28, "when . . . I have . . . sealed to them this fruit," the formal ratification of the ministry of the churches of the Gentiles in Greece and Galatia to needy saints in Judea, by Paul's faithful delivery of the gifts to them; this material help was the fruit of his spiritual ministry to the Gentiles, who on their part were bringing forth the fruit of their having shared with them in spiritual things; the metaphor stresses the sacred formalities of the transaction (Deissmann illustrates this from the papyri of Fayyum, in which the "sealing" of sacks guarantees the full complement of the contents); (c) secrecy and security and the postponement of disclosure, Rev. 10:4; in a negative command 22:10; (d) ownership and security, together with destination, Rev. 7:3, 4, 5 (as with the noun in v. 2; see A); the same three indications are conveyed in Eph. 1:13, in the metaphor of the "sealing" of believers by the gift of the Holy Spirit, upon believing (i.e., at the time of their regeneration, not after a lapse of time in their spiritual life, "having also believed"—not as KJV, "after that ye believed"; the aorist participle marks the definiteness and completeness of the act of faith); the idea of destination is stressed by the phrase "the Holy Spirit of promise" (see also v. 14); so 4:30, "ye were sealed unto the day of redemption"; so in 2 Cor. 1:22, where the middle voice intimates the special interest of the Sealer in His act; (e) authentication by the believer (by receiving the witness of the Son) of the fact that "God is true," John 3:33; authentication by God in sealing the Son as the Giver of eternal life (with perhaps a figurative allusion to the impress of a mark upon loaves), 6:27.

## SEARCH

1. ***eraunao*** or ***ereunao***, an earlier form, *(2045)*, "to search, examine," is used (a) of God, as "searching" the heart, Rom. 8:27; (b) of Christ, similarly, Rev. 2:23; (c) of the Holy Spirit, as "searching" all things, 1 Cor. 2:10, acting in the spirit of the believer; (d) of the OT prophets, as "searching" their own writings concerning matters foretold of Christ, testified by the Spirit of Christ in them, 1 Pet. 1:11 (cf. No. 2); (e) of the Jews, as commanded by the Lord to "search" the Scriptures, John 5:39, KJV, and RV marg., "search," RV text, "ye search," either is possible grammatically; (f) of Nicodemus as commanded similarly by the chief priests and Pharisees, John 7:52.

2. ***exeraunao*** *(1830)*, a strengthened form of No. 1 (***ek***, or ***ex***, "out"), "to search out," is used in 1 Pet. 1:10, "searched diligently"; cf. No. 1 (d).

3. ***exetazo*** *(1833)*, "to examine closely, inquire carefully" (from ***etazo***, "to examine"), occurs in Matt. 2:8, RV, "search out."

## SEASON (Noun)

### A. Nouns.

1. ***kairos*** *(2540)*, primarily, "due measure, fitness, proportion," is used in the NT to signify "a season, a time, a period" possessed of certain characteristics, frequently rendered "time" or "times"; in the following the RV substitutes "season" for the KJV "time," thus distinguishing the meaning from ***chronos*** (see No. 2): Matt. 11:25; 12:1; 14:1; 21:34; Mark 11:13; Acts 3:19; 7:20; 17:26; Rom. 3:26; 5:6; 9:9; 13:11;

1 Cor. 7:5; Gal. 4:10; 1 Thess. 2:17, lit., "for a season (of an hour)," 2 Thess. 2:6; in Eph. 6:18, "at all seasons" (KJV, "always"); in Titus 1:3, "His own seasons" (marg., "its"; KJV, "in due times"); in the preceding clause ***chronos*** is used.

2. ***chronos*** (*5550*), whence Eng. words beginning with "chron"—, denotes "a space of time," whether long or short: (a) it implies duration, whether longer, e.g., Acts 1:21, "(all the) time"; Acts 13:18; 20:18, RV, "(all the) time" (KJV, "at all seasons"); or shorter, e.g., Luke 4:5; (b) it sometimes refers to the date of an occurrence, whether past, e.g., Matt. 2:7, or future, e.g., Acts 3:21; 7:17.

***chronos*** marks quantity, ***kairos***, quality. Sometimes the distinction between the two words is not sharply defined as, e.g., in 2 Tim. 4:6, though even here the apostle's "departure" signalizes the time (***kairos***). In Rev. 10:6 ***chronos*** has the meaning "delay" (RV, marg.), an important rendering for the understanding of the passage (the word being akin to ***chronizo***, "to take time, to linger, delay," Matt. 24:48; Luke 12:45).

3. ***hora*** (*5610*), "an hour," is translated "season" in John 5:35; 2 Cor. 7:8; Philem. 15.

### B. Adverbs.

1. ***akairos*** (*171*) denotes "out of season, unseasonably" (akin to ***akairos***, "unseasonable," ***a***, negative, and A, No. 1), 2 Tim. 4:2.

2. ***eukairos*** (*2122*), "in season" (***eu***, "well"), 2 Tim. 4:2; it occurs also in Mark 14:11, "conveniently."

## SEASON (Verb)

***artuo*** (*741*), "to arrange, make ready" (cf. ***artios***, "fitted"), is used of "seasoning," Mark 9:50; Luke 14:34; Col. 4:6.

## SECRET, SECRETLY

#### *Old Testament*

***sod*** (5475), "secret or confidential plan(s); secret or confidential talk; secret; council; gathering; circle." ***sod*** means, first, "confidential talk," Ps. 64:2. In Prov. 15:22 the word refers to plans which one makes on one's own and before they are shared by others, Prov. 25:9. Second, the word represents a group of intimates with whom one shares confidential matters, Gen. 49:6; Jer. 6:11; Ps. 55:14.

#### *New Testament*

1. ***kruptos*** (*2927*), adj., "secret, hidden" (akin to ***krupto***, "to hide"), Eng., "crypt," "cryptic," etc., is used as an adjective and rendered "secret" in Luke 8:17, KJV (RV, "hid"); in the neuter, with ***en***, "in," as an adverbial phrase, "in secret," with the article, Matt. 6:4, 6 (twice in each v.), without the article, John 7:4, 10; 18:20; in the neuter plural, with the article, "the secrets (of men)," Rom. 2:16; of the heart, 1 Cor. 14:25; in Luke 11:33, KJV, "a secret place" (RV, "cellar").

2. ***apokruphos*** (*614*) (whence "Apocrypha"), "hidden," is translated "kept secret" in Mark 4:22, KJV (RV, "made secret"); "secret" in Luke 8:17, RV (KJV, "hid").

3. ***kruphaios*** (*2928d*) occurs in the best mss. in Matt. 6:18 (twice; some have No. 1).

### B. Verb.

***krupto*** (*2928*), "to hide," is translated "secretly" in John 19:38 [perfect participle, passive voice, lit., "(but) having been hidden"], referring to Nicodemus as having been a "secret" disciple of Christ; in Matt. 13:35, KJV, it is translated "kept secret" (RV, "hidden").

## SECURE (Verb)

***perikrates*** (*4031*), an adjective, signifies "having full command of" (***peri***, "around, about," ***krateo***, "to be strong, to rule"); it is used with ***ginomai***, "to become," in Acts 27:16, RV, "to secure (the boat)," KJV, "to come by."

## SECURITY

#### *Old Testament*

### A. Nouns.

***mibtach*** (4009), "the act of confiding; the object of confidence; the state of confidence or security." The word refers to "the act of confiding" in Prov. 21:22, ***mibtach*** means the "object of confidence" in Job 8:14 and the "state of confidence or security" in Prov. 14:26.

***betach*** is a noun meaning "security, trust." One occurrence is in Isa. 32:17.

### B. Verb.

***batach*** (982), "to be reliant, trust, be unsuspecting," Deut. 28:52.

### C. Adjective.

***betach*** (983), "secure," Judg. 8:11; cf. Isa. 32:17.

### D. Adverb.

***betach*** (983), "securely." In its first occurrence ***betach*** emphasizes the status of a city which was certain of not being attacked, Gen. 34:25. Thus the city was unsuspecting regarding the impending attack.

#### *New Testament*

***hikanos*** (*2425*), "sufficient," is used in its neuter form with the article, as a noun, in Acts 17:9, "(when they had taken) security," i.e., satisfaction, lit., "the sufficient," 1 Thess. 2:18.

## SEDITION

### A. Nouns.

1. ***stasis*** *(4714)*, "a dissension, an insurrection," is translated "sedition" in Acts 24:5, KJV.

2. ***dichostasia*** *(1370)*, lit., "a standing apart" (***dicha***, "asunder, apart," ***stasis***, "a standing"), hence "a dissension, division," is translated "seditions" in Gal. 5:20, KJV.

### B. Verb.

***anastatoo*** *(387)*, "to excite, unsettle," or "to stir up to sedition," is so translated in Acts 21:38, RV (KJV, "madest an uproar"); in 17:6, "have turned (the world) upside down," i.e., "causing tumults"; in Gal. 5:12, RV, "unsettle" (KJV, "trouble"), i.e., by false teaching (here in the continuous present tense, lit., "those who are unsettling you"). The word was supposed not to have been used in profane authors. It has been found, however, in several of the papyri writings.

## SEDUCE, SEDUCING

### A. Verbs.

1. ***planao*** *(4105)*, "to cause to wander, lead astray," is translated "to seduce" in 1 John 2:26, KJV (RV, "lead . . . astray"); in Rev. 2:20, "to seduce."

2. ***apoplanao*** *(635)* is translated "seduce" in Mark 13:22 (RV, "lead astray").

### B. Adjective.

***planos*** *(4108)*, akin to A, lit., "wandering," then, "deceiving," is translated "seducing in 1 Tim. 4:1.

## SEE, SEEING

### *Old Testament*

### A. Verb.

***ra'ah*** (7200), "to see, observe, perceive, get acquainted with, gain understanding, examine, look after (see to), choose, discover." Basically ***ra'ah*** connotes seeing with one's eyes, Gen. 27:1. The second primary meaning is "to perceive," or to be consciously aware of—so idols "neither see, nor hear," Deut. 4:28. Third, ***ra'ah*** can represent perception in the sense of hearing something, Gen. 2:19. In Isa. 44:16 the verb means "to enjoy."

This verb has several further extended meanings. For example, ***ra'ah*** can refer to "perceiving or ascertaining" something apart from seeing it with one's eyes, as when Hagar saw that she had conceived, Gen. 16:4. It can represent mentally recognizing that something is true, Gen. 26:28. Seeing and hearing together can mean "to gain understanding," Isa. 52:15; "to distinguish," Mal. 3:18.

In addition to these uses of ***ra'ah*** referring to intellectual seeing, there is seeing used in the sense of living. "To see the light" is to live life, Job 3:16; cf. 33:28. It can mean "experience" in the sense of what one is aware of as he lives, Job 4:8.

A fourth idea of seeing is "to examine," Gen. 39:23. Used in this sense ***ra'ah*** can imply looking upon with joy or pain. Hagar asked that she not be allowed to look on the death of Ishmael, Gen. 21:16. This verb may be used of attending to or visiting, 2 Sam. 13:5.

### B. Nouns.

***ro'eh*** (7203), "seer; vision." ***ro'eh***, which occurs 11 times, refers to a "prophet," emphasizing the means by which revelation was received; 1 Sam. 9:9; and to "vision," Isa. 28:7.

***mar'ah*** means "visionary appearance" or "(prophetic) vision," Gen. 46:2 and "looking glasses," Exod. 38:8.

### *New Testament*

1. ***blepo*** *(991)*, "to have sight," is used of bodily vision, e.g., Matt. 11:4; and mental, e.g. Matt. 13:13, 14; it is said of God the Father in Matt. 6:4, 6, 18; of Christ as "seeing" what the Father doeth, John 5:19. It especially stresses the thought of the person who "sees."

2. ***horao*** *(3708)*, with the form ***eidon***, serving for its aorist tense, and ***opsomai***, for its future tense (middle voice), denotes "to see," of bodily vision, e.g., John 6:36; and mental, e.g., Matt. 8:4; it is said of Christ as "seeing" the Father, John 6:46, and of what He had "seen" with the Father, 8:38. It especially indicates the direction of the thought to the object "seen."

3. ***aphorao*** *(872)*, with ***apeidon*** serving as the aorist tense, "to look away from one thing so as to see another" (***apo***, "from," and No. 2), as in Heb. 12:2, simply means "to see" in Phil. 2:23.

4. ***kathorao*** *(2529)*, lit., "to look down" (***kata***, and No. 2), denotes "to discern clearly," Rom. 1:20, "are clearly seen."

5. ***diablepo*** *(1227)*, "to see clearly" (***dia***, "through," and No. 1), is used in Matt. 7:5; Luke 6:42; in Mark 8:25, RV, "he looked steadfastly" (No. 6 is used in the next clause; No. 1 in v. 24, and No. 2 in the last part).

6. ***emblepo*** *(1689)*, "to look at" (***en***, "in," and No. 1), used of earnestly looking, is translated "saw" in Mark 8:25 (last part); "could (not) see" in Acts 22:11.

7. ***anablepo*** *(308)*, "to look up," is translated "see," of the blind, in Luke 7:22, KJV (RV, "receive their sight").

## SEED

1. ***sperma*** (*4690*), akin to ***speiro***, "to sow" (Eng., "sperm," "spermatic," etc.), has the following usages, (a) agricultural and botanical, e.g., Matt. 13:24, 27, 32 (for the KJV of vv. 19, 20, 22, 23, as in the RV); 1 Cor. 15:38; 2 Cor. 9:10; (b) physiological, Heb. 11:11; (c) metaphorical and by metonymy for "offspring, posterity," (1) of natural offspring, e.g., Matt. 22:24, 25, RV, "seed" (KJV, "issue"); John 7:42; 8:33, 37; Acts 3:25; Rom. 1:3; 4:13, 16, 18; 9:7 (twice), 8, 29; 11:1; 2 Cor. 11:22; Heb. 2:16; 11:18; Rev. 12:17; Gal. 3:16, 19, 29; in the 16th v., "He saith not, And to seeds, as of many; but as of one, And to thy seed, which is Christ," quoted from the Sept. of Gen. 13:15 and 17:7, 8, there is especial stress on the word "seed," as referring to an individual (here, Christ) in fulfillment of the promises to Abraham—a unique use of the singular. While the plural form "seeds," neither in Hebrew nor in Greek, would have been natural any more than in English (it is not so used in Scripture of human offspring; its plural occurrence is in 1 Sam, 8:15, of crops), yet if the divine intention had been to refer to Abraham's natural descendants, another word could have been chosen in the plural, such as "children"; all such words were, however, set aside, "seed" being selected as one that could be used in the singular, with the purpose of showing that the "seed" was Messiah. Some of the rabbis had even regarded "seed," e.g., in Gen. 4:25 and Isa. 53:10, as referring to the Coming One. Descendants were given to Abraham by other than natural means, so that through him Messiah might come, and the point of the apostle's argument is that since the fulfillment of the promises of God is secured alone by Christ, they only who are "in Christ" can receive them; (2) of spiritual offspring, Rom. 4:16, 18; 9:8; here "the children of the promise are reckoned for a seed" points, firstly, to Isaac's birth as being not according to the ordinary course of nature but by divine promise, and, secondly, by analogy, to the fact that all believers are children of God by spiritual birth, Gal. 3:29.

As to 1 John 3:9, "his seed abideth in him," it is possible to understand this as meaning that children of God (His "seed") abide in Him, and do not go on doing (practicing) sin (the verb "to commit" does not represent the original in this passage). Alternatively, the "seed" signifies the principle of spiritual life as imparted to the believer, which abides in him without possibility of removal or extinction; the child of God remains eternally related to Christ, he who lives in sin has never become so related, he has not the principle of life in him. This meaning suits the context and the general tenor of the Epistle.

2. ***sporos*** (*4703*), akin to No. 1, properly "a sowing," denotes "seed sown," (a) natural, Mark 4:26, 27; Luke 8:5, 11 (the natural being figuratively applied to the Word of God); 2 Cor. 9:10 (1st part); (b) metaphorically of material help to the needy, 2 Cor. 9:10 (2nd part), RV, "(your) seed for sowing" (KJV, "seed sown").

3. ***spora*** (*4701*), akin to No. 1, and like No. 2, "a sowing, seedtime," denotes "seed sown," 1 Pet. 1:23, of human offspring.

## SEEK

### *Old Testament*

### A. Verbs.

***baqash*** (1245), "to seek, search, consult." ***baqash*** means "to seek" to find something that is lost or missing, or, at least, whose location is unknown, Gen. 37:15; 1 Sam. 13:14; 1 Kings 10:24. The sense "seek to secure" emphasizes the pursuit of a wish or the accomplishing of a plan. Moses asked the Levites who rebelled against the unique position of Aaron and his sons, Num. 16:10. This word may have an emotional coloring, such as, "to aim at, devote oneself to, and be concerned about," Ps. 4:2. Cultically one may "seek" to secure God's favor or help, 2 Chron. 20:4.

This sense of "seeking to secure" may also be used of seeking one's life (***nepesh***). God told Moses to "go, return into Egypt: for all the men are dead which sought thy life," Exod. 2:15; 4:19.

Theologically, this verb can be used not only "to seek" a location before the Lord (to stand before Him in the temple and seek to secure His blessing), but it may also be used of a state of mind, Deut. 4:29. In instances such as this where the verb is used in synonymous parallelism with ***darash***, the two verbs have the same meaning.

***darash*** (1875), "to seek, inquire, consult, ask, require, frequent." One of the most frequent uses of this word is in the expression "to inquire of God," which sometimes indicates a private seeking of God in prayer for direction, Gen. 25:22, and often it refers to the contacting of a prophet who would be the instrument of God's revelation, 1 Sam. 9:9; 1 Kings 22:8; or seek pagan gods or demons, Deut. 18:10–11; cf. 1 Sam. 28:3ff. This word is often used to describe the "seeking of" the Lord in the sense of entering into covenantal relationship with Him. The prophets often used ***darash*** as they called on the people to make an about-face in living and instead "seek ye the Lord while he may be found . . ." Isa. 55:6.

**B. Noun.**

***midrash*** can mean "study; commentary; story," 2 Chron. 13:22; 2 Chron. 24:27.

*New Testament*

1. ***zeteo*** (*2212*) signifies (a) "to seek, to seek for," e.g., Matt. 7:7, 8; 13:45; Luke 24:5; John 6:24; of plotting against a person's life, Matt. 2:20; Acts 21:31; Rom. 11:3; metaphorically, to "seek" by thinking, to "seek" how to do something, or what to obtain, e.g., Mark 11:18; Luke 12:29; to "seek" to ascertain a meaning, John 16:19, "do ye inquire"; to "seek" God, Acts 17:27, RV; Rom. 10:20; (b) "to seek or strive after, endeavor, to desire," e.g., Matt. 12:46, 47, RV, "seeking" (KJV, "desiring"); Luke 9:9, RV, "sought" (KJV, "desired"); John 7:19, RV, "seek ye" (KJV, "go ye about"); so v. 20; Rom. 10:3, RV, "seeking" (AV, "going about"); of "seeking" the kingdom of God and His righteousness, in the sense of coveting earnestly, striving after, Matt. 6:33; "the things that are above," Col. 3:1; peace, 1 Pet. 3:11; (c) "to require or demand," e.g., Mark 8:12; Luke 11:29 (some mss. have No. 4); 1 Cor. 4:2, "it is required"; 2 Cor. 13:3, "ye seek."

2. ***anazeteo*** (*327*), "to seek carefully" (***ana***, "up," used intensively, and No. 1), is used of searching for human beings, difficulty in the effort being implied, Luke 2:44, 45 (some mss. have No. 1 in the latter v.), Acts 11:25; numerous illustrations of this particular meaning in the papyri are given by Moulton and Milligan.

3. ***ekzeteo*** (*1567*) signifies (a) "to seek out (***ek***) or after, to search for"; e.g., God, Rom. 3:11; the Lord, Acts 15:17; in Heb. 11:6, RV, "seek after" (KJV, "diligently seek"); 12:17, RV, "sought diligently" (KJV, "sought carefully"); 1 Pet. 1:10, RV, "sought" (KJV, "have inquired"), followed by ***exeraunao***, "to search diligently," (b) "to require or demand," Luke 11:50, 51.

4. ***epizeteo*** (*1934*), "to seek after" (directive, ***epi***, "towards") is always rendered in the RV, by some form of the verb "to seek," Acts 13:7, "sought" (KJV, "desired"); 19:39, "seek" (KJV, "inquire"); Phil. 4:17, "seek for" (KJV, "desire"), twice; elsewhere, Matt. 6:32; 12:39; 16:4; Mark 8:12 (in some texts); Luke 12:30; Acts 12:19; Rom. 11:7; Heb. 11:14; 13:14.

## SEEM

***dokeo*** (*1380*) denotes (a) "to be of opinion" (akin to ***doxa***, "opinion"), e.g., Luke 8:18, RV, "thinketh" (KJV, "seemeth"); so 1 Cor. 3:18; to think, suppose, Jas. 1:26, RV, "thinketh himself (KJV, "seem"); (b) "to seem, to be reputed," e.g., Acts 17:18; 1 Cor. 11:16; 12:22; 2 Cor. 10:9; Heb. 4:1; 12:11; for Gal. 2:2, 6, 9; (c) impersonally (1) to think, (2) to "seem" good, Luke 1:3; Acts 15:22, RV, "it seemed good" (KJV, "it pleased"); 15:25, 28 (v. 34 in some mss.); in Heb. 12:10, the neuter of the present participle is used with the article, lit., "the (thing) seeming good," RV, "(as) seemed good," KJV, "after (their own) pleasure."

## SELF-WILLED

***authades*** (*829*), "self-pleasing" (***autos***, "self," ***hedomai***, "to please"), denotes one who, dominated by self-interest, and inconsiderate of others, arrogantly asserts his own will, "self-willed," Titus 1:7; 2 Pet. 2:10 (the opposite of ***epieikes***, "gentle," e.g., 1 Tim. 3:3), "one so far overvaluing any determination at which he has himself once arrived that he will not be removed from it."

## SELL

*Old Testament*

***makar*** (4376), "to sell," i.e., an exchange of money, services, or other bartered good, as a way to do business, Gen. 25:31. Anything tangible may be "sold": land, Gen. 47:20; houses, Lev. 25:29; Exod. 21:35; Gen. 37:27–28.

***makar*** is often used in the figurative sense to express various actions. Nineveh is accused of "selling" or "betraying" other nations, Nah. 3:4. Frequently it is said that God "sold" Israel into the power of her enemies, meaning that He gave them over entirely into their hands, Judg. 2:14. Similarly, it was said that "the Lord shall sell Sisera into the hand of a woman," Judg. 4:9. "To be sold" sometimes means to be given over to death, Esth. 7:4.

*New Testament*

1. ***poleo*** (*4453*), "to exchange or barter, to sell," is used in the latter sense in the NT, six times in Matthew, three in Mark, six in Luke; in John only in connection with the cleansing of the Temple by the Lord, 2:14, 16; in Acts only in connection with the disposing of property for distribution among the community of believers, 4:34, 37; 5:1; elsewhere, 1 Cor. 10:25; Rev. 13:17.

2. ***piprasko*** (*4097*), from an earlier form, ***perao***, "to carry across the sea for the purpose of selling or to export," is used (a) literally, Matt. 13:46; 18:25; 26:9; Mark 14:5; John 12:5; Acts 2:45; 4:34; 5:4; (b) metaphorically, Rom. 7:14, "sold under sin," i.e., as fully under the domination of sin as a slave is under his master.

S

## SENSES

***aistheterion*** *(145)*, "sense, the faculty of perception, the organ of sense" (akin to ***aisthanomai***, "to perceive"), is used in Heb. 5:14, "senses," the capacities for spiritual apprehension.

## SENTENCE

### A. Nouns.

1. ***krima*** *(2917)*, "a judgment," a decision passed on the faults of others, is used especially of God's judgment upon men, and translated "sentence" in 2 Pet. 2:3, RV (KJV, judgment).

2. ***katadike*** *(2613)*, "a judicial sentence, condemnation," is translated "sentence" in Acts 25:15, RV (KJV, "judgment"); some mss. have ***dike***.

### B. Verbs.

1. ***krino*** *(2919)*, "to judge, to adjudge," is translated "(my) sentence is" in Acts 15:19, KJV, RV, "(my) judgment is," lit., "I (***ego***, emphatic) judge," introducing the substance or draft of a resolution.

2. ***epikrino*** *(1948)*, "to give sentence," is used in Luke 23:24.

## SEPARATE

*Old Testament*

### A. Verbs.

***parad*** (6504), "to divide, separate." This word often expresses separation of people from each other, sometimes with hostility, Gen. 13:9. A reciprocal separation seems to be implied in the birth of Jacob and Esau, Gen. 25:23. Sometimes economic status brings about separation, Prov. 19:4.

***nazar*** (5144), "to separate, be separated." "To separate" and "to consecrate" are not distinguished from one another in the early Old Testament books. For example, the earliest use of ***nazar*** in the Pentateuch is in Lev. 15:31.

In prophetic literature, the verb ***nazar*** indicates Israel's deliberate separation from Jehovah to dedication of foreign gods or idols. In Hos. 9:10, the various versions differ in their rendering of ***nazar***. The prophet Ezekiel employed ***nazar***, Ezek. 14:7.

### B. Noun.

***nazir*** (5139), "one who is separated; Nazirite." There are 16 occurrences of the word in the Old Testament. The earliest use of ***nazir*** is found in Gen. 49:26; cf. Deut. 33:16. Most frequently in Old Testament usage, ***nazir*** is an appellation for one who vowed to refrain from certain things for a period of time, Num. 6:13. According to Num. 6, a lay person of either sex could take a special vow of consecration to God's service for a certain period of time. A "Nazirite" usually made a vow voluntarily; however, in the case of Samson, Judg. 13:5, 7, his parents dedicated him for life. Whether or not this idea of separation to God was distinctive alone to Israel has been debated. Num. 6:1–23 laid down regulatory laws pertaining to Naziritism. There were two kinds of "Nazirites": the temporary and the perpetual. The first class was much more common than the latter kind. From the Bible we have knowledge only of Samson, Samuel, and John the Baptist as persons who were lifelong "Nazirites." During the time of his vow, a "Nazirite" was required to abstain from wine and every kind of intoxicating drink. He was also forbidden to cut the hair of his head or to approach a dead body, even that of his nearest relative. If a "Nazirite" accidentally defiled himself, he had to undergo certain rites of purification and then had to begin the full period of consecration over again. The "Nazirite" was "holy unto the Lord," and he wore upon his head a diadem of his consecration.

*New Testament*

### A. Verbs.

1. ***aphorizo*** *(873)*, "to mark off by bounds" (***apo***, "from," ***horizo***, "to determine"; ***horos***, "a limit"), "to separate," is used of (a) the Divine action in setting men apart for the work of the gospel, Rom. 1:1; Gal. 1:15; (b) the Divine judgment upon men, Matt. 13:49; 25:32; (c) the separation of Christians from unbelievers, Acts 19:9; 2 Cor. 6:17; (d) the separation of believers by unbelievers, Luke 6:22; (e) the withdrawal of Christians from their brethren, Gal. 2:12. In (c) is described what the Christian must do, in (d) what he must be prepared to suffer, and in (e) what he must avoid.

2. ***chorizo*** *(5563)*, "to put asunder, separate," is translated "to separate" in Rom. 8:35, 39; in the middle voice, "to separate oneself, depart"; in the passive voice in Heb. 7:26, RV, "separated" (KJV, "separate"), the verb here relates to the resurrection of Christ, not, as KJV indicates, to the fact of His holiness in the days of His flesh; the list is progressive in this respect that the first three qualities apply to His sinlessness, the next to His resurrection, the last to His ascension.

3. ***apodiorizo*** *(592)*, "to mark off" (***apo***, "from," ***dia***, "asunder," ***horizo***, "to limit"), hence denotes metaphorically to make "separations," Jude 19, RV (KJV, "separate themselves"), of persons who make divisions (in

contrast with v. 20); there is no pronoun in the original representing "themselves."

**B. Preposition.**

***choris*** (*5565*), "apart from, without" (cf. ***aneu***, "without," a rarer word than this), is translated "separate from" in Eph. 2:12 (KJV, without).

## SERGEANT (-S)

***rhabdouchos*** (*4465*), "a rod bearer," one who carries a staff of office, was, firstly, an umpire or judge, later, a Roman lictor, Acts 16:35, 38. The duty of these officials was to attend Roman magistrates to execute their orders, especially administering punishment by scourging or beheading.

## SERPENT

***ophis*** (*3789*): the characteristics of the "serpent" as alluded to in Scripture are mostly evil (though Matt. 10:16 refers to its caution in avoiding danger); its treachery, Gen. 49:17; 2 Cor. 11:3; its venom, Ps. 58:4; 1 Cor. 10:9; Rev. 9:19; its skulking, Job 26:13; its murderous proclivities, e.g., Ps. 58:4; Prov. 23:32; Eccl. 10:8, 11; Amos 5:19; Mark 16:18; Luke 10:19; the Lord used the word metaphorically of the scribes and Pharisees, Matt. 23:33 (cf. Matt. 3:7; 12:34). The general aspects of its evil character are intimated in the Lord's rhetorical question in Matt. 7:10 and Luke 11:11. Its characteristics are concentrated in the arch-adversary of God and man, the Devil, metaphorically described as the serpent, 2 Cor. 11:3; Rev. 12:9, 14, 15; 20:2.

## SERVANT

**A. Nouns.**

1. ***doulos*** (*1401*), an adjective, signifying "in bondage," Rom. 6:19 (neuter plural, agreeing with ***mele***, "members"), is used as a noun, and as the most common and general word for "servant," frequently indicating subjection without the idea of bondage; it is used (a) of natural conditions, e.g., Matt. 8:9; 1 Cor. 7:21, 22 (1st part); Eph. 6:5; Col. 4:1; 1 Tim. 6:1; frequently in the four Gospels; (b) metaphorically of spiritual, moral and ethical conditions: "servants" (1) of God, e.g., Acts 16:17; Titus 1:1; 1 Pet. 2:16; Rev. 7:3; 15:3; the perfect example being Christ Himself, Phil. 2:7; (2) of Christ, e.g., Rom. 1:1; 1 Cor. 7:22 (2nd part); Gal. 1:10; Eph. 6:6; Phil. 1:1; Col. 4:12; Jas. 1:1; 2 Pet. 1:1; Jude 1; (3) of sin, John 8:34 (RV, "bondservants"); Rom. 6:17, 20; (4) of corruption, 2 Pet. 2:19 (RV, "bondservants"); cf. the verb ***douloo*** (see B).

2. ***diakonos*** (*1249*), translated "servant" or "servants" in Matt. 22:13 (RV marg., "ministers"); 23:11 (RV marg., ditto); Mark 9:35, KJV (RV, "minister"); John 2:5, 9; 12:26; Rom. 16:1.

3. ***pais*** (*3816*), denotes "an attendant"; it is translated "servant" (a) of natural conditions, in Matt. 8:6, 8, 13; 14:2; Luke 7:7 ("menservants" in 12:45); 15:26; (b) of spiritual relation to God, (1) of Israel, Luke 1:54; (2) of David, Luke 1:69; Acts 4:25; (3) of Christ, so declared by God the Father, Matt. 12:18; spoken of in prayer, Acts 4:27, 30, RV (KJV, "child"); Acts 4; Matt. 12.

4. ***oiketes*** (*3610*), "a house servant" (***oikeo***, "to dwell," ***oikos***, "a house"), is translated "servant" in Luke 16:13 (RV marg., "household servant"); so Rom. 14:4 and 1 Pet. 2:18; in Acts 10:7, KJV and RV, "household servants."

**B. Verb.**

***douloo*** (*1402*), "to enslave, to bring into bondage" (akin to A, No. 1), e.g., 1 Cor. 9:19, RV, "I brought (myself) under bondage (to all)," KJV, "I made myself servant," denotes in the passive voice, "to be brought into bondage, to become a slave or servant," rendered "ye became servants (of righteousness)" in Rom. 6:18; "being . . . become servants (to God)," v. 22.

## SERVE

### *Old Testament*

**A. Verbs.**

***sharat*** (8334), "to serve, minister." ***sharat*** often denotes "service" rendered in connection with Israel's worship, 1 Sam. 2:11; 3:1. This kind of "service" was to honor only the Lord, for Israel was not to be "as the heathen, as the families of the countries; to serve wood and stone," Ezek. 20:32.

In a number of situations, the word is used to denote "service" rendered to a fellow human being. Though the person "served" usually is of a higher rank or station in life, this word never describes a slave's servitude to his master, Num. 3:6; cf. 8:26. Elisha "ministered" to Elijah, 1 Kings 19:21. Abishag is said to have "ministered" unto David, 1 Kings 1:15. Various kinds of officials "ministered" to David, 1 Chron. 28:1. David's son, Amnon had a "servant that ministered unto him," 2 Sam. 13:17.

***'abad*** (5647), "to serve, cultivate, enslave, work." ***'abad*** is often used toward God: ". . . Ye shall serve God upon this mountain," Exod. 3:12, meaning "to worship," Deut. 6:13, or ". . . hearken diligently unto my commandments which I command you this day, to love the Lord your God, and to serve him . . ." Deut. 11:13; Ps. 100:2.

S

**B. Nouns.**

***'abodah*** (5656), "work; labors; service." The more general meaning of ***'abodah*** is close to our English word for "work," field work, 1 Chron. 27:26; daily "work," Ps. 104:23; linen industry, 1 Chron. 4:21. The more limited meaning of the word is "service." Israel was in the "service" of the Lord, Josh. 22:27. Whenever God's people were not fully dependent on Him, they had to choose to serve the Lord God or human kings with their requirements of forced "labor" and tribute, 2 Chron. 12:8. Further specialization of the usage is in association with the tabernacle and the temple. The priests were chosen for the "service" of the Lord, Num. 3:7. The Levites also had many important functions in and around the temple; they sang, played musical instruments, and were secretaries, scribes, and doorkeepers, 2 Chron. 34:13; cf. 8:14. Thus anything, people and objects, 1 Chron. 28:13, associated with the temple was considered to be in the "service" of the Lord.

***'ebed*** (5650), "servant." This words represents a person usually an indentured servant, possibly to pay off a debt, Exod. 21:2; hired, 1 Kings 5:6; yet they can also be slaves bought and sold, Lev 25:44. ***'ebed*** was used as a mark of humility and courtesy, as in Gen. 18:3. The "servant" was not a free man. He was subject to the will and command of his master. But one might willingly and lovingly submit to his master, Exod. 21:5, remaining in his service when he was not obliged to do so. Hence it is a very fitting description of the relationship of man to God.

Of prime significance is the use of "my servant" for the Messiah in Isaiah, 42:1–7; 49:1–7; 50:4–10; 52:13–53:12. Israel was a blind and deaf "servant," Isa. 42:18–22. So the Lord called "my righteous servant," Isa. 53:11; cf. 42:6 "[to bear] the sin of many," Isa. 53:12, "that thou mayest be my salvation unto the end of the earth," Isa. 49:6.

***sharat*** (8334), "servant; minister." This word is most regularly translated "minister," Josh. 1:1; Ezek. 46:24. The privilege of serving the Lord is not restricted to human beings, Ps. 103:21. Fire and wind, conceived poetically as persons, are also God's "ministers," Ps. 104:3–4.

***New Testament***

1. ***diakoneo*** (*1247*), "to minister" (akin to ***diakonos***, "to render any kind of service"), is translated "to serve," e.g., in Luke 10:40; 12:37; 17:8; 22:26, 27 (twice).

2. ***douleuo*** (*1398*), "to serve as a ***doulos***" (No. 1, above), is used (a) of serving God (and the impossibility of serving mammon also), Matt. 6:24 and Luke 16:13; Rom. 7:6; in the gospel, Phil. 2:22; (b) Christ, Acts 20:19; Rom. 12:11; 14:18; 16:18; Eph. 6:7; Col. 3:24; (c) the law of God, Rom. 7:25; (d) one another, Gal. 5:13, RV, "be servants to" (KJV, "serve"); (e) a father, Luke 15:29 (with a suggestion of acting as a slave); (f) earthly masters, Matt. 6:24; Luke 16:13; 1 Tim. 6:2, RV, "serve"; (g) the younger by the elder, Rom. 9:12; (h) of being in bondage to a nation, Acts 7:7; Gal. 4:25, to the Romans, actually, though also spiritually to Judaizers; (i) to idols, Gal. 4:8, RV, "were in bondage" (KJV, "did service"); (j) to "the weak and beggarly rudiments," v. 9 (RV), "to be in bondage" (aorist tense in the best texts, suggesting "to enter into bondage"), i.e., to the religion of the Gentiles ("rudiments" being used in v. 3 of the religion of the Jews); (k) sin, Rom. 6:6, RV, "be in bondage" (KJV, "serve"); (l) "divers lusts and pleasures," Titus 3:3; (m) negatively, to any man—a proud and thoughtless denial by the Jews, John 8:33.

3. ***latreuo*** (*3000*), primarily "to work for hire" (akin to ***latris***, "a hired servant"), signifies (1) to worship, (2) to "serve"; in the latter sense it is used of service (a) to God, Matt. 4:10; Luke 1:74 ("without fear"); 4:8; Acts 7:7; 24:14, RV, "serve" (KJV, "worship"); 26:7; 27:23; Rom. 1:9 ("with my spirit"); 2 Tim. 1:3; Heb. 9:14; 12:28, KJV, "we may serve," RV, "we may offer service"; Rev. 7:15; (b) to God and Christ ("the Lamb"), Rev. 22:3; (c) in the tabernacle, Heb. 8:5, RV; 13:10; (d) to "the host of heaven," Acts 7:42, RV, "to serve" (KJV, "to worship"); (e) to "the creature," instead of the Creator, Rom. 1:25.

4. ***hupereteo*** (*5256*), translated "to serve" in Acts 13:36; there is a contrast intimated between the service of David, lasting for only a generation, and the eternal character of Christ's ministry as the One who not having seen corruption was raised from the dead.

## SERVICE, SERVING

1. ***diakonia*** (*1248*) is rendered "service" in Rom. 15:31, KJV; "serving" in Luke 10:40.

2. ***leitourgia*** (*3009*) is rendered "service" in 2 Cor. 9:12; Phil. 2:17, 30.

3. ***latreia*** (*2999*), akin to ***latreuo*** (see No. 3, above), primarily "hired service," is used (a) of the "service" of God in connection with the tabernacle, Rom. 9:4; Heb. 9:1, "divine service"; v. 6, plural, RV, "services" (KJV, "service," and, in italics, "of God"); (b) of the intelligent "service" of believers in presenting their bodies to God, a living sacrifice, Rom. 12:1, RV marg., "worship"; (c) of imagined "ser-

vice" to God by persecutors of Christ's followers, John 16:2.

## SEVEN

***hepta*** (*2033*), whence Eng. words beginning with "hept"–,corresponds to the Heb. ***sheba'*** (which is akin to ***saba'***, signifying "to be full, abundant"), sometimes used as an expression of fullness, e.g., Ruth 4:15: it generally expresses completeness, and is used most frequently in the Apocalypse; it is not found in the Gospel of John, nor between the Acts and the Apocalypse, except in Heb. 11:30 (in Rom. 11:4 the numeral is ***heptakischilioi***, "seven thousand"); in Matt. 22:26 it is translated "seventh" (marg., "seven").

## SEVEN TIMES

***heptakis*** (*2034*) occurs in Matt. 18:21, 22; Luke 17:4 (twice).

## SEVENTY

***hebdomekonta*** (*1440*) occurs in Luke 10:1, 17; in Acts 7:14 it precedes ***pente***, "five," lit., "seventy-five," rendered "threescore and fifteen."

## SEVENTY TIMES

***hebdomekontakis*** (*1441*) occurs in Matt. 18:22, where it is followed by ***hepta***, "seven," "seventy times seven"; RV marg. has "seventy times and seven," which many have regarded as the meaning; cf. Gen. 4:24; whether this is literal or figurative or a greater number is debated among the sources,

The Lord's reply "until seventy times seven" was indicative of completeness, the absence of any limit, and was designed to turn away Peter's mind from a merely numerical standard. God's forgiveness is limitless; so should man's be.

## SEVERITY

1. ***apotomia*** (*663*), "steepness, sharpness" (***apo***, "off," ***temno***, "to cut"; ***tome***, "a cutting"), is used metaphorically in Rom. 11:22 (twice) of "the severity of God," which lies in His temporary retributive dealings with Israel. In the papyri it is used of exacting to the full the provisions of a statute.

2. ***apheidia*** (*857*), primarily "extravagance" (***a***, negative, ***pheidomai***, "to spare"), hence, "unsparing treatment, severity," is used in Col. 2:23, RV, "severity (to the body)," KJV, "neglecting of" (marg., "punishing, not sparing"); here it refers to ascetic discipline; it was often used among the Greeks of courageous exposure to hardship and danger.

## SHADOW (Noun)

1. ***skia*** (*4639*) is used (a) of "a shadow," caused by the interception of light, Mark 4:32; Acts 5:15; metaphorically of the darkness and spiritual death of ignorance, Matt. 4:16; Luke 1:79; (b) of "the image" or "outline" cast by an object, Col. 2:17, of ceremonies under the Law; of the tabernacle and its appurtenances and offerings, Heb. 8:5; of these as appointed under the Law, Heb. 10:1.

2. ***aposkiasma*** (*644*), "a shadow," is rendered "shadow that is cast" in Jas. 1:17, RV; the KJV makes no distinction between this and No. 1. The probable significance of this word is "overshadowing" or "shadowing-over" (which ***apo*** may indicate), and this with the genitive case of ***trope***, "turning," yields the meaning "shadowing-over of mutability" implying an alternation of "shadow" and light; of this there are two alternative explanations, namely, "overshadowing" (1) not caused by mutability in God, or (2) caused by change in others, i.e., "no changes in this lower world can cast a shadow on the unchanging Fount of light."

## SHAMBLES

***makellon*** (*3111*), a term of late Greek borrowed from the Latin ***macellum***, denotes a "meat market," translated "shambles" in 1 Cor. 10:25.

## SHAME (Noun, and Verb)

### *Old Testament*

**A. Verb.**

***bosh*** (954), "to be ashamed, feel ashamed." The word has overtones of being or feeling worthless. ***bosh*** means "to be ashamed" in Isa. 1:29.

**B. Noun.**

***boshet*** (1322), "shame; shameful thing." This word means a "shameful thing" as a reference to Baal, Jer. 3:24; cf. Jer. 11:13; Hos. 9:10. This substitution also occurs in proper names: Ish-bosheth, 2 Sam. 2:8, the "man of shame," was originally Esh-baal, cf. 1 Chron. 8:33.

This word means both "shame and worthlessness, 1 Sam. 20:30; 2 Chron. 32:21.

### *New Testament*

**A. Nouns.**

1. ***atimia*** (*819*) signifies (a) "shame, disgrace," Rom. 1:26, "vile (passions)," RV, lit., "(passions) of shame"; 1 Cor. 11:14; (b) "dishonor," e.g., 2 Tim. 2:20, where the idea of disgrace or "shame" does not attach to the use of the word; the meaning is that while in a

great house some vessels are designed for purposes of honor, others have no particular honor (***time***) attached to their use (the prefix ***a*** simply negatives the idea of honor).

2. ***entrope*** (*1791*), 1 Cor. 6:5 and 15:34.

3. ***aschemosune*** (*808*) denotes (a) "unseemliness," Rom. 1:27, RV (AV, "that which is unseemly"); (b) "shame, nakedness," Rev. 16:15.

**B. Adjective.**

***aischros*** (*150*), "base, shameful" (akin to ***aischos***, "shame"), of that which is opposed to modesty or purity, is translated as a noun in 1 Cor. 11:6; 14:35, KJV (RV, "shameful"); Eph. 5:12; in Titus 1:11, "filthy (lucre)," lit., "shameful (gain)."

**C. Verbs.**

1. ***atimazo*** (*818*), "to dishonor, put to shame (akin to A, No. 1).

2. ***entrepo*** (*1788*), lit., "to turn in upon, to put to shame" (akin to A, No. 2), is translated "to shame (you)" in 1 Cor. 4:14.

3. ***kataischuno*** (*2617*), "to put to shame" (***kata***, perhaps signifying "utterly"), is translated "ye . . . shame (them)" in 1 Cor. 11:22, KJV, RV, "ye . . . put (them) to shame."

## SHAMEFASTNESS (KJV, SHAMEFACEDNESS)

***aidos*** (*127*), "a sense of shame, modesty," is used regarding the demeanor of women in the church, 1 Tim. 2:9 (some mss. have it in Heb. 12:28 for ***deos***, "awe": here only in NT). Shamefastness is that modesty which is "fast" or rooted in the character . . . The change to "shamefacedness" is the more to be regretted because shamefacedness . . . has come rather to describe an awkward diffidence, such as we sometimes call sheepishness.

## SHAPE

1. ***eidos*** (*1491*), rendered "shape" in the KJV of Luke 3:22 and John 5:37.

2. ***homoioma*** (*3667*), rendered "shapes" in Rev. 9:7.

## SHARP, SHARPER, SHARPLY, SHARPNESS

**A. Adjectives.**

1. ***oxus*** (*3691*) denotes (a) of a sword, Rev. 1:16 (b) of motion, "swift," Rom. 3:15.

2. ***tomos*** (*5114**), akin to ***temno***, "to cut" [Eng., "(ana)tomy," etc.], is used metaphorically in the comparative degree, ***tomoteros***, in Heb. 4:12, of the Word of God.

**B. Adverb.**

***apotomos*** (*664*) signifies "abruptly, curtly," lit., "in a manner that cuts" (***apo***, "from," ***temno***, "to cut"), hence "sharply, severely," 2 Cor. 13:10, RV, "(that I may not . . . deal) sharply," KJV, "(use) sharpness"; the pronoun "you" is to be understood, i.e., "that I may not use (or deal with) . . . sharply"; Titus 1:13, of rebuking.

## SHEAR, SHEARER, SHORN

***keiro*** (*2751*) is used (a) of "shearing sheep," Acts 8:32, "shearer," lit., "the (one) shearing": (b) in the middle voice, "to have one's hair cut off, be shorn," Acts 18:18; 1 Cor. 11:6 (twice; cf. ***xurao***, "to shave").

## SHED

1. ***ekcheo*** (*1632*), "to pour out," is translated "to shed" or "to shed forth" in Acts 2:33; Titus 3:6, KJV; of "shedding" blood in murder, Rom. 3:15.

2. ***ekchuno***, or ***ekchunno*** (*1632*), a later form of No. 1, is used of the voluntary giving up of His life by Christ through the "shedding" of His blood in crucifixion as an atoning sacrifice, Matt. 26:28; Mark 14:24; Luke 22:20, KJV, "is shed," RV, "is poured out"; these passages do not refer to the effect of the piercing of His side (which took place after His death); of the murder of servants of God, Matt. 23:35; Luke 11:50; Acts 22:20 (in the best texts; others have No. 1); of the love of God in the hearts of believers through the Holy Spirit, Rom. 5:5. For the "pouring out" of the Holy Spirit, Acts 10:45. (The form in the last two passages might equally well come from No. 1, above.)

## SHEEP

1. ***probaton*** (*4263*), from ***probaino***, "to go forward," i.e., of the movement of quadrupeds, was used among the Greeks of small cattle, sheep and goats; in the NT, of "sheep" only (a) naturally, e.g., Matt. 12:11, 12; (b) metaphorically, of those who belong to the Lord, the lost ones of the house of Israel, Matt. 10:6; of those who are under the care of the Good Shepherd, e.g., Matt. 26:31; John 10:1, lit., "the fold of the sheep," and vv. 2–27; 21:16, 17 in some texts; Heb. 13:20; of those who in a future day, at the introduction of the millennial kingdom, have shown kindness to His persecuted earthly people in their great tribulation, Matt. 25:33; of the clothing of false shepherds, Matt. 7:15; (c) figuratively, by way of simile, of Christ, Acts 8:32; of the disciples, e.g., Matt. 10:16; of true followers of Christ in general, Rom. 8:36; of the former wayward condition of those who had come under His Shepherd care, 1 Pet. 2:25; of the multitudes who sought the help of Christ in the days of His flesh, Matt. 9:36; Mark 6:34.

2. ***probation*** (*4263**), a diminutive of No. 1, "a little sheep," is found in the best texts in John 21:16, 17 (some have No. 1); distinct from ***arnia***, "lambs" (v. 15), but used as a term of endearment.

## SHEET

***othone*** (*3607*) primarily denoted "fine linen," later, "a sheet," Acts 10:11; 11:5.

## SHEOL

***she'ol*** (7585), "Sheol." First, the word means the state of death," Ps. 6:5; cf. 18:5. It is the final resting place of all men, Job 21:13. "Sheol" is parallel to Hebrew words for "pit" or "hell," Job 26:6, "corruption" or "decay," Ps. 16:10, and "destruction," Prov. 15:11. Second, "Sheol" is used of a place of conscious existence after death, Gen. 37:35. All men go to "Sheol," Ps. 16:10. The wicked receive punishment there, Num. 16:30; Deut. 32:22; Ps. 9:17. They are put to shame and silenced in "Sheol," Ps. 31:17. Jesus alluded to Isaiah's use of ***she'ol***, 14:13–15, in pronouncing judgment on Capernaum, Matt. 11:23, translating "Sheol" as "Hades" or "Hell," meaning the place of conscious existence and judgment.

## SHEPHERD

### *Old Testament*

**A. Verb.**

***ra'ah*** (7462), "to pasture, shepherd." ***ra'ah*** represents what a shepherd allows domestic animals to do when they feed on grasses in the fields, Gen. 29:7. ***ra'ah*** can also represent the entire job of a shepherd, Gen. 37:2. Used metaphorically this verb represents a leader's or a ruler's relationship to his people, 2 Sam. 5:2; fig. to provide nourishment or "to enliven," Prov. 10:21.

***ra'ah*** is used intransitively describing what cattle do when they feed on the grass of the field, Gen. 41:2. This usage is applied metaphorically to men in Isa. 14:30.

**B. Nouns.**

***ro'eh*** (7462), "shepherd." This noun occurs about 62 times in the Old Testament. It is applied to God, the Great Shepherd, who pastures or feeds His sheep, Ps. 23:1–4; cf. John 10:11. This concept of God, the Great Shepherd, is very old, having first appeared in the Bible on Jacob's lips in Gen. 49:24: "From thence is the shepherd, the stone of Israel."

### *New Testament*

***poimen*** (*4166*) is used (a) in its natural significance, Matt. 9:36; 25:32; Mark 6:34; Luke 2:8, 15, 18, 20; John 10:2, 12; (b) metaphorically of Christ, Matt. 26:31; Mark 14:27; John 10:11, 14, 16; Heb. 13:20; 1 Pet. 2:25; (c) metaphorically of those who act as pastors in the churches, Eph. 4:11.

## SHEW (SHOW)

1. ***deiknumi***, or ***deiknuo***, (*1166*) denotes (a) "to show, exhibit," e.g., Matt. 4:8; 8:4; John 5:20; 20:20; 1 Tim. 6:15; (b) "to show by making known," Matt. 16:21; Luke 24:40; John 14:8, 9; Acts 10:28; 1 Cor. 12:31; Rev. 1:1; 4:1; 22:6; (c) "to show by way of proving," Jas. 2:18; 3:13.

2. ***anadeiknumi*** (*322*) signifies (a) "to lift up and show, show forth, declare" (***ana***, "up," and No. 1), Acts 1:24; (b) to "appoint," Luke 10:1.

3. ***endeiknumi*** (*1731*) signifies (1) "to show forth, prove" (middle voice), said (a) of God as to His power, Rom. 9:17; His wrath, 9:22; the exceeding riches of His grace, Eph. 2:7; (b) of Christ, as to His longsuffering, 1 Tim. 1:16; (c) of Gentiles, as to "the work of the Law written in their hearts," Rom. 2:15; (d) of believers, as to the proof of their love, 2 Cor. 8:24; all good fidelity, Titus 2:10; meekness, 3:2; love toward God's Name, Heb. 6:10; diligence in ministering to the saints, v. 11; (2) "to manifest by evil acts," 2 Tim. 4:14, "did (me much evil)," marg., "showed."

4. ***epideiknumi*** (*1925*), ***epi***, "upon," intensive, and No. 1, signifies (a) "to exhibit, display," Matt. 16:1; 22:19; 24:1; Luke 17:14 (in some mss. 24:40; No. 1 in the best texts); in the middle voice, "to display," with a special interest in one's own action, Acts 9:39; (b) "to point out, prove, demonstrate," Acts 18:28; Heb. 6:17.

5. ***hupodeiknumi*** (*5263*), primarily, "to show secretly (***hupo***, 'under'), or by tracing out," hence, "to make known, warn," is translated "to show" in Luke 6:47; Acts 9:16; in 20:35, KJV (RV, "I gave . . . an example").

## SHEWBREAD

The phrase rendered "the shewbread" is formed by the combination of the nouns ***prothesis***, "a setting forth" (***pro***, "before," ***tithemi***, "to place") and ***artos***, "a loaf" (in the plural), each with the article, Matt. 12:4; Mark 2:26 and Luke 6:4, lit., "the loaves of the setting forth"; in Heb. 9:2, lit., "the setting forth of the loaves." The corresponding OT phrases are lit., "bread of the face," Exod. 25:30, i.e., the presence, referring to the Presence of God (cf. Isa. 63:9 with Exod. 33:14, 15); "the bread of ordering," 1 Chron. 9:32, marg. In Num. 4:7 it is called "the continual bread"; in 1 Sam. 21:4, 6, "holy bread" (KJV, "hallowed"). In the Sept. of 1 Kings 7:48, it is called "the bread of the offering" (***prosphora***, "a bearing towards").

The twelve loaves, representing the tribes of Israel, were set in order every Sabbath day before the Lord, "on the behalf of the children," Lev. 24:8, RV (marg., and KJV, "from"), "an everlasting covenant." The loaves symbolized the fact that on the basis of the sacrificial atonement of the Cross, believers are accepted before God, and nourished by Him in the person of Christ. The showbread was partaken of by the priests, as representatives of the nation. Priesthood now being coextensive with all who belong to Christ, 1 Pet. 2:5, 9, He, the Living Bread, is the nourishment of all, and where He is, there, representatively, they are.

## SHEWING

***anadeixis*** (*323*), "a shewing forth" (***ana***, "up or forth," and ***deiknumi***, "to show"), is translated "showing" in Luke 1:80.

## SHINE, SHINING

### A. Verbs.

1. ***phaino*** (*5316*), "to cause to appear," denotes, in the active voice, "to give light, shine," John 1:5; 5:35; in Matt. 24:27, passive voice; so Phil. 2:15, RV, "ye are seen" (for KJV, "ye shine"); 2 Pet. 1:19 (active); so 1 John 2:8, Rev. 1:16; in 8:12 and 18:23 (passive); 21:23 (active).

2. ***epiphaino*** (*2014*), "to shine upon" (***epi***, "upon," and No. 1), is so translated in Luke 1:79, RV (KJV, "to give light").

3. ***lampo*** (*2989*), "to shine as a torch," occurs in Matt. 5:15, 16, 17:2; Luke 17:24; Acts 12:7; 2 Cor. 4:6 (twice).

4. ***eklampo*** (*1584*), "to shine forth" (***ek***, "out" and No. 3), is used in Matt. 13:43, of the future shining "forth" of the righteous "in the Kingdom of their Father."

5. ***perilampo*** (*4034*), "to shine around" (***peri***, "around," and No. 3), is used in Luke 2:9, "shone round about," of the glory of the Lord; so in Acts 26:13, of the light from Heaven upon Saul of Tarsus.

### B. Noun.

***astrape*** (*796*), denotes (a) "lightning," (b) "bright shining," of a lamp, Luke 11:36.

## SHOUT (Noun and Verb)

### A. Noun.

***keleusma*** (*2752*), "a call, summons, shout of command," John 5:28.

### B. Verb.

***epiphoneo*** (*2019*), "to call out" (***epi***, "upon," ***phoneo***, "to utter a sound"), is translated "shouted" in Acts 12:22, RV (KJV, "gave a shout").

## SHOW (make a)

***deigmatizo*** (*1165*), "to make a show of, expose," is used in Col. 2:15 of Christ's act regarding the principalities and powers, displaying them "as a victor displays his captives or trophies in a triumphal procession" (Lightfoot). Some regard the meaning as being that He showed the angelic beings in their true inferiority. For its other occurrence, Matt. 1:19.

## SHRINE

***naos*** (*3485*), "the inmost part of a temple, a shrine," is used in the plural in Acts 19:24, of the silver models of the pagan "shrine" in which the image of Diana (Greek Artemis) was preserved. The models were large or small, and were signs of wealth and devotion on the part of purchasers. The variety of forms connected with the embellishment of the image provided "no little business" for the silversmiths.

## SHUT, SHUT UP

### *Old Testament*

***cagar*** (5462), "to shut, close, shut up or imprison." The obvious use of this verb is to express the "shutting" of doors and gates, and it is used in this way many times in the text, Gen. 19:10; Josh. 2:7. More specialized uses are: fat closing over the blade of a sword, Judg. 3:22, and closing up a breach in city walls, 1 Kings 11:27. Figuratively, men may "close their hearts to pity," Ps. 17:10. In the books of Samuel, ***cagar*** is used in the special sense of "to deliver up," implying that all avenues of escape "are closed," 1 Sam. 17:46; cf. 1 Sam. 24:18; 26:8; 2 Sam. 18:28. In Lev. 13–14, in which the priest functions as a medical inspector of contagious diseases, ***cagar*** is used a number of times in the sense of "to isolate," Lev. 13:5, 11, 21, 26.

### *New Testament*

1. ***kleio*** (*2808*) is used (a) of things material, Matt. 6:6; 25:10; Luke 11:7; John 20:19, 26; Acts 5:23; 21:30; Rev. 20:3; figuratively, 21:25; (b) metaphorically, of the kingdom of heaven, Matt. 23:13; of heaven, with consequences of famine, Luke 4:25; Rev. 11:6; of compassion, 1 John 3:17.

2. ***apokleio*** (*608*), to shut fast (***apo***, away from, and No. 1), is used in Luke 13:25, expressing the impossibility of entrance after the closing.

3. ***katakleio*** (*2623*), lit., to shut down" (the ***kata*** has, however, an intensive use), signifies "to shut up in confinement," Luke 3:20; Acts 26:10.

## SICK, SICKLY, SICKNESS

### *Old Testament*

**A. Verb.**

***chalah*** (2470), "to be sick, weak." A meaning of ***chalah*** is physical weakness, Judg. 16:7; or being in a wounded state, 2 Kings 8:29; or not top-quality livestock, Mal. 1:8. This word is sometimes used in the figurative sense of over-exerting oneself, thus becoming "weak," Jer. 12:13; or even "love-sick," Song of Sol. 2:5.

**B. Noun.**

***choli*** (2483), "sickness." The use of this word in the description of the Suffering Servant in Isa. 53:3–4 has resulted in various translations. The RSV, KJV, and NASB render it "grief." It is "sufferings" in the NEB, JB, TEV and "infirmity" in the NAB. The meaning of "sickness" occurs in Deut. 7:15.

### *New Testament*

**A. Verb.**

***astheneo*** (*770*), lit., "to be weak, feeble" (***a***, negative, ***sthenos***, "strength"), is translated "to be sick," e.g., in Matt. 10:8, "(the) sick"; 25:36; v. 39 in the best texts (some have B); Mark 6:56; Luke 4:40; 7:10 (RV omits the word); 9:2; John 4:46; 5:3, RV (KJV, "impotent folk"); v. 7; 6:2, RV (KJV, "were diseased"); 11:1–3, 6; Acts 9:37; 19:12; Phil. 2:26, 27; 2 Tim. 4:20; Jas. 5:14.

**B. Adjective.**

***asthenes*** (*772*), lit., "without strength," hence, "feeble, weak," is used of "bodily debility," Matt. 25:43 (for v. 39, see A, No. 1), 44; some texts have it in Luke 9:2 (the best omit it, the meaning being "to heal" in general); 10:9; Acts 5:15, 16; in 4:9 it is rendered "impotent."

**C. Noun.**

***astheneia*** (*769*), "weakness, sickness" (akin to A and B), is translated "sickness" in John 11:4.

## SIGH

1. ***stenazo*** (*4727*), "to groan," is translated "He sighed" in Mark 7:34.

2. ***anastenazo*** (*389*), "to sigh deeply" (***ana***, "up," suggesting "deep drawn," and No. 1), occurs in Mark 8:12.

## SIGHT (verb)

***anablepo*** (*308*), "to look up," also denotes "to receive or recover sight" (akin to A, No. 5), e.g., Matt. 11:5; 20:34; Mark 10:51, 52; Luke 18:41–43; John 9:11, 15, 18 (twice); Acts 9:12, 17, 18; 22:13.

## SIGN

### *Old Testament*

***'ot*** (226), "sign; mark." This word represents something by which a person or group is characteristically marked, i.e., a symbol or signal that has meaning, without necessarily using verbal words, Gen. 4:15; Exod. 8:23; Num. 2:2; Josh. 2:12, 18. The word also means "sign" as a reminder of one's duty, Gen. 9:12. In passages such as Exod. 4:8 ***'ot*** represents a miraculous "sign," as an act of power signaling God's deliverance, cf. Deut. 13:1–5. Several passages use ***'ot*** of omens and/or indications of future events, 1 Sam. 14:10; or "warning sign," Num. 16:38.

### *New Testament*

***semeion*** (*4592*), "a sign, mark, indication, token," is used (a) of that which distinguished a person or thing from others, e.g., Matt. 26:48; Luke 2:12; Rom. 4:11; 2 Cor. 12:12 (1st part); 2 Thess. 3:17, "token," i.e., his autograph attesting the authenticity of his letters; (b) of a "sign" as a warning or admonition, e.g., Matt. 12:39, "the sign of (i.e., consisting of) the prophet Jonas"; 16:4; Luke 2:34; 11:29, 30; (c) of miraculous acts (1) as tokens of divine authority and power, e.g., Matt. 12:38, 39 (1st part); John 2:11, RV, "signs"; 3:2 (ditto); 4:54, "(the second) sign," RV; 10:41 (ditto); 20:30; in 1 Cor. 1:22, "the Jews ask for signs," RV, indicates that the Apostles were met with the same demand from Jews as Christ had been: "signs were vouchsafed in plenty, signs of God's power and love, but these were not the signs which they sought. . . . They wanted signs of an outward Messianic Kingdom, of temporal triumph, of material greatness for the chosen people. . . . With such cravings the Gospel of a 'crucified Messiah' was to them a stumblingblock indeed" (Lightfoot); 1 Cor. 14:22; (2) by demons, Rev. 16:14; (3) by false teachers or prophets, indications of assumed authority, e.g., Matt. 24:24; Mark 13:22; (4) by Satan through his special agents, 2 Thess. 2:9; Rev. 13:13, 14; 19:20; (d) of tokens portending future events, e. g., Matt. 24:3, where "the sign of the Son of Man" signifies, subjectively, that the Son of Man is Himself the "sign" of what He is about to do; Mark 13:4; Luke 21:7, 11, 25; Acts 2:19; Rev. 12:1, RV; 12:3, RV; 15:1.

## SIGNS (to make)

***enneuo*** (*1770*), "to nod to" (***en***, "in," ***neuo***, "to nod"), denotes "to make a sign to" in Luke 1:62.

## SIGNIFY

***semaino*** (*4591*), "to give a sign, indicate," "to signify," is so translated in John 12:33; 18:32;

21:19; Acts 11:28; 25:27; Rev. 1:1, where perhaps the suggestion is that of expressing by signs.

## SILENCE

### A. Noun.

***sige*** *(4602)* occurs in Acts 21:40; Rev. 8:1, where the "silence" is introductory to the judgments following the opening of the seventh seal.

### B. Verb.

***phimoo*** *(5392)*, "to muzzle," is rendered "to put to silence" in Matt. 22:34; 1 Pet. 2:15.

## SILVER

### A. Noun.

***keseph*** (3701), "silver; money; price; property." This refers to the precious metal which comes from the earth. It can mean unprocessed "metal ore silver," Prov. 25:4; cf. Job 28:1; or refined silver from ore, in jewelry, bars, lumps, etc., as a form of wealth and exchange, Gen. 24:53; 1 Kings 10:21; Lev. 25:50. ***keseph*** sometimes represents the color "silver," Ps. 68:13.

## SIN (Noun and Verb)

### *Old Testament*

### A. Nouns.

***'awen*** (205), "iniquity; vanity; sorrow." ***'awen*** may be a general term for a crime or offense, Micah 2:1. In some passages, the word refers to falsehood or deception, Ps. 36:3; Zech. 10:2.

***'asham*** (817), "sin; guilt; guilt offering; trespass; trespass offering." ***'asham*** implies the condition of "guilt" incurred through some wrongdoing, Gen. 26:10. The word may also refer to the offense itself which entails the guilt, Jer. 51:5; Ps. 68:21.

Most occurrences of ***'asham*** refer to the compensation given to satisfy someone who has been injured, or to the "trespass offering" or "guilt offering" presented on the altar by the repentant offender after paying a compensation of six-fifths of the damage inflicted, Num. 5:7–8. The "trespass offering" was the blood sacrifice of a ram, Lev. 5:18; cf. Lev. 7:5, 7; 14:12–13.

***'amal*** (5999), "evil; trouble; misfortune; mischief; grievance; wickedness; labor." In general, ***'amal*** refers either to the trouble and suffering which sin causes the sinner or to the trouble that he inflicts upon others. Jer. 20:18 depicts self-inflicted sorrow, cf. also Deut. 26:7.

***'awon*** (5771), "iniquity." ***'awon*** portrays sin as a perversion of life (a twisting out of the right way), a perversion of truth (a twisting into error), or a perversion of intent (a bending of rectitude into willful disobedience). The word "iniquity" is the best single-word equivalent, although the Latin root ***iniquitas*** really means "injustice; unfairness; hostile; adverse." ***'awon*** occurs frequently throughout the Old Testament in parallelism with other words related to sin, such as ***chatta't*** ("sin") and ***pesha'*** ("transgression"). Some examples are 1 Sam. 20:1: "And David . . . said before Jonathan, what have I done? what is mine iniquity [***'awon***]? and what is my sin [***chatta't***] before thy father, that he seeketh my life?" cf. Isa. 43:24; Jer. 5:25. Also note Job 14:17: "My transgression [***pesha'***] is sealed up in a bag, and thou sewest up mine iniquity [***'awon***]," cf. Ps. 107:17; Isa. 50:1.

The penitent wrongdoer recognized his "iniquity," Isa. 59:12; cf. 1 Sam. 3:13. "Iniquity" is something to be confessed, Lev. 16:21; Neh. 9:2; cf. Ps. 38:18. The grace of God may remove or forgive "iniquity": "And unto him he said, Behold, I have caused thine iniquity to pass from thee . . ." Zech. 3:4; cf. 2 Sam. 24:10. His atonement may cover over "iniquity": "By mercy and truth iniquity is purged; and by the fear of the Lord men depart from evil," Prov. 16:6; cf. Ps. 78:38.

***rasha'*** (7563), "wicked; criminal; guilty." ***rasha'*** generally connotes a turbulence and restlessness, cf. Isa. 57:21, or something disjointed or ill-regulated. In some instances, ***rasha'*** carries the sense of being "guilty of crime": "Thou shalt not raise a false report: put not thine hand with the wicked to be an unrighteous witness," Exod. 23:1; "Take away the wicked from before the king, and his throne shall be established in righteousness," Prov. 25:5. "An ungodly witness scorneth judgment: and the mouth of the *wicked* [plural form] devoureth iniquity," Prov. 19:28; cf. Prov. 20:26 The ***rasha'*** is guilty of hostility to God and His people, Ps. 7:9; 17:13; Isa. 13:11; Hab. 1:13.

***chatta't*** (2403), "sin; sin-guilt; sin-purification; sin offering." The basic nuance of this word is "sin" conceived as missing the road or mark (155 times). ***chatta't*** can refer to an offense against a man, Gen. 31:36. It is such passages which prove that ***chatta't*** is not simply a general word for "sin"; since Jacob used two different words, he probably intended two different nuances. In addition, a full word study shows basic differences between ***chatta't*** and other words rendered "sin." For the most part this word represents a sin against God, Lev. 4:14. Men are to return from "sin," which is a path, a life-style, or act deviating from that which God has marked out, 1 Kings 8:35. They should depart from "sin," 2 Kings

10:31, be concerned about it, Ps. 38:18, and confess it, Num. 5:7. The noun first appears in Gen. 4:7, where Cain is warned that "sin lieth at the door."

***chatta't*** means "sin offering.". The law of the "sin offering" is recorded in Lev. 4–5:13; 6:24–30. This was an offering for some specific "sin" committed unwittingly, without intending to do it and perhaps even without knowing it at the time (Lev. 4:2; 5:15).

***chet'***, means "sin" in the sense of missing the mark or the path. This may be sin against either a man, Gen. 41:9; or God, Deut. 9:18. Second, it connotes the "guilt" of such an act, Num. 27:3.

**B. Adjectives.**

***rasha'*** (7563), "wicked; guilty," Deut. 25:2, this word refers to a person "guilty of a crime," Jer. 5:26. ***rasha'*** is used specifically of murderers in 2 Sam. 4:11.

***ra'*** (7451), "bad; evil; wicked; sore." ***ra'*** refers to that which is "bad" or "evil," in a wide variety of applications. A greater number of the word's occurrences signify something morally evil or hurtful, often referring to man or men: "Then answered all the wicked men and men of Belial, of those that went with David . . ." 1 Sam. 30:22; Esth. 7:6; Job 35:12; cf. Ps. 10:15. ***ra'*** is also used to denote evil words, Prov. 15:26, evil thoughts, Gen. 6:5, or evil actions, Deut. 17:5, Neh. 13:17. Ezek. 6:11 depicts grim consequences for Israel as a result of its actions.

In less frequent uses, ***ra'*** implies severity, Ezek. 14:21; cf. Deut. 6:22; unpleasantness, Deut. 7:15; cf. Deut. 28:59; deadliness, Ezek. 5:16; cf. "hurtful sword," Ps. 144:10; or sadness, Neh. 2:2. The word may also refer to something of poor or inferior quality, such as "bad" land, Num. 13:19, "naughty" figs, Jer. 24:2, "ill-favored" cattle, Gen. 41:3, 19, or a "bad" sacrificial animal, Lev. 27:10, 12, 14.

**C. Verbs.**

***'abar*** (5674), "to transgress, cross over, pass over." This word occurs as a verb only when it refers to sin. ***'abar*** often carries the sense of "transgressing" a covenant or commandment—i.e., the offender "passes beyond" the limits set by God's law and falls into transgression and guilt. This meaning appears in Num. 14:41: "And Moses said, wherefore now do ye transgress the commandment of the Lord? but it shall not prosper." Another example is in Judg. 2:20: "And the anger of the Lord was hot against Israel; and he said, Because that this people hath transgressed my covenant which I commanded their fathers, and have not hearkened unto my voice," cf. 1 Sam. 15:24; Hos. 8:1.

Most frequently, ***'abar*** illustrates the motion of "crossing over" or "passing over." (The Latin ***transgredior***, from which we get our English word *transgress*, has the similar meaning of "go beyond" or "cross over.") This word refers to crossing a stream or boundage, "pass through," Num. 21:22, invading a country, "passed over," Judg. 11:32, crossing a boundary against a hostile army, "go over," 1 Sam. 14:4, marching over, "go over," Isa. 51:23, overflowing the banks of a river or other natural barriers, "pass through," Isa. 23:10, passing a razor over one's head, "come upon," Num. 6:5, and the passing of time "went over," 1 Chron. 29:30.

***chata'*** (2398), "to miss, sin, be guilty, forfeit, purify." The basic meaning of this verb "to miss aim," is illustrated in Judg. 20:16.

From this basic meaning comes the word's chief usage to indicate moral failure toward both God and men, and certain results of such wrongs. The first occurrence of the verb is in Gen. 20:6, God's word to Abimelech after he had taken Sarah: "Yes, I know that in the integrity of your heart you have done this, and also I have kept you from sinning against Me," NASB; cf. Gen. 39:9.

Sin against God is defined in Josh. 7:11: "Israel hath sinned, and they have also transgressed my covenant which I commanded them. . . ." Also note Lev. 4:27: "And if any one of the common people sin through ignorance, while he doeth somewhat against any of the commandments of the Lord concerning things which ought not to be done, and be guilty." The verb may also refer to the result of wrongdoing, as in Gen. 43:9: "then let me bear the blame for ever." Deut. 24:1–4, after forbidding adulterous marriage practices, concludes: "for that is abomination before the Lord: and thou shalt not cause the land to sin . . ." (KJV); the RSV renders this passage: "You shall not bring guilt upon the land." Similarly, those who pervert justice are described as "those who by a word make a man out to be guilty," Isa. 29:21, NIV. This leads to the meaning in Lev. 9:15: "And he . . . took the goat . . . and slew it, and offered it for sin." The effect of the offerings for sin is described in Ps. 51:7: "Purge me with hyssop, and I shall be clean"; cf. Num. 19:1–13.

### *New Testament*

**A. Noun.**

***hamartia*** (266) is, lit., "a missing of the mark," but this etymological meaning is largely lost sight of in the NT. It is the most comprehensive term for moral obliquity. It is used of "sin" as (a) a principle or source of action, or an inward element producing acts, e.g., Rom. 3:9; 5:12, 13, 20; 6:1, 2; 7:7 (abstract for concrete); 7:8 (twice), 9, 11, 13, "sin, that it might be shown to be sin," i.e., "sin became death to me, that it might be exposed in its heinous character": in the last clause, "sin might become exceeding sinful," i.e., through the holiness of the Law, the true nature of sin was designed to be manifested to the conscience;

(b) a governing principle or power, e.g., Rom. 6:6, "(the body) of sin," here "sin" is spoken of as an organized power, acting through the members of the body, though the seat of "sin" is in the will (the body is the organic instrument); in the next clause, and in other passages, as follows, this governing principle is personified, e.g., Rom. 5:21; 6:12, 14, 17; 7:11, 14, 17, 20, 23, 25; 8:2; 1 Cor. 15:56; Heb. 3:13; 11:25; 12:4; Jas. 1:15 (2nd part);

(c) a generic term (distinct from specific terms such as No. 2 yet sometimes inclusive of concrete wrong doing, e.g., John 8:21, 34, 46; 9:41; 15:22, 24; 19:11); in Rom. 8:3, "God, sending His own Son in the likeness of sinful flesh," lit., "flesh of sin," the flesh stands for the body, the instrument of indwelling "sin" [Christ, preexistently the Son of God, assumed human flesh, "of the substance of the Virgin Mary"; the reality of incarnation was His, without taint of sin, and *as an offering* for sin," i.e., "a sin offering," "condemned sin in the flesh," i.e., Christ, having taken human nature, "sin" apart (Heb. 4:15), and having lived a sinless life, died under the condemnation and judgment due to our "sin"; for the generic sense see further, e.g., Heb. 9:26; 10:6, 8, 18; 13:11; 1 John 1:7, 8; 3:4 (1st part; in the 2nd part, "sin" is defined as "lawlessness," RV), 8, 9; in these verses the KJV use of the verb to commit is misleading; not the committal of an act is in view, but a continuous course of "sin," as indicated by the RV, "doeth." The apostle's use of the present tense of ***poieo***, "to do," virtually expresses the meaning of ***prasso***, "to practice," which John does not use (it is not infrequent in this sense in Paul's Epp., e.g., Rom. 1:32, RV; 2:1; Gal. 5:21; Phil. 4:9); 1 Pet. 4:1 (singular in the best texts), lit., "has been made to cease from sin," i.e., as a result of suffering in the flesh, the mortifying of our members, and of obedience to a Savior who suffered in flesh. Such no longer lives in the flesh, "to the lusts of men, but to the will of God"; sometimes the word is used as virtually equivalent to a condition of "sin," e.g., John 1:29, "the sin (not sins) of the world"; 1 Cor. 15:17; or a course of "sin," characterized by continuous acts, e.g., 1 Thess. 2:16; in 1 John 5:16 (2nd part) the RV marg., is probably to be preferred, "there is sin unto death," not a special act of "sin," but the state or condition producing acts; in v. 17, "all unrighteousness is sin" is not a definition of "sin" (as in 3:4), it gives a specification of the term in its generic sense;

(d) a sinful deed, an act of "sin," e.g., Matt. 12:31; Acts 7:60; Jas. 1:15 (1st part); 2:9; 4:17; 5:15, 20; 1 John 5:16 (1st part).

### B. Verb.

***hamartano*** (*264*), lit., "to miss the mark," is used in the NT (a) of "sinning" against God, (1) by angels, 2 Pet. 2:4; (2) by man, Matt. 27:4; Luke 15:18, 21 (heaven standing, by metonymy, for God); John 5:14; 8:11; 9:2, 3; Rom. 2:12 (twice); 3:23; 5:12, 14, 16; 6:15; 1 Cor. 7:28 (twice), 36; 15:34; Eph. 4:26; 1 Tim. 5:20; Titus 3:11; Heb. 3:17; 10:26; 1 John 1:10; in 2:1 (twice), the aorist tense in each place, referring to an act of "sin"; on the contrary, in 3:6 (twice), 8, 9, the present tense indicates, not the committal of an act, but the continuous practice of "sin"; in 5:16 (twice) the present tense indicates the condition resulting from an act, "unto death" signifying "tending towards death"; (b) against Christ, 1 Cor. 8:12; (c) against man, (1) a brother, Matt. 18:15, RV, "sin" (KJV, "trespass"); v. 21; Luke 17:3, 4, RV, "sin" (KJV, "trespass"); 1 Cor. 8:12; (2) in Luke 15:18, 21, against the father by the Prodigal Son, "in thy sight" being suggestive of befitting reverence; (d) against Jewish law, the Temple, and Caesar, Acts 25:8, RV, "sinned" (KJV, "offended"); (e) against one's own body, by fornication, 1 Cor. 6:18; (f) against earthly masters by servants, 1 Pet. 2:20, RV, "(when) ye sin (and are buffeted for it)," KJV, "(when ye be buffeted) for your faults," lit., "having sinned."

## SINCERE, SINCERELY, SINCERITY

### A. Adjectives.

1. ***adolos*** (*97*), "guileless, pure," is translated "sincere" in 1 Pet. 2:2, KJV, "without guile," RV.

2. ***gnesios*** (*1103*), "true, genuine, sincere," is used in the neuter, as a noun, with the article, signifying "sincerity," 2 Cor. 8:8 (of love).

### B. Adverb.

***hagnos*** (*55*) denotes "with pure motives," is rendered "sincerely" in Phil. 1:17, RV (v. 16, KJV).

### C. Noun.

***eilikrinia*** (or ***—eia***) (*1505*), denotes "sincerity, purity"; it is described metaphorically in 1 Cor. 5:8 as "unleavened (bread)"; in 2 Cor.

1:12, "sincerity (of God)," RV, KJV, "(godly) sincerity," it describes a quality possessed by God, as that which is to characterize the conduct of believers; in 2 Cor. 2:17 it is used of the rightful ministry of the Scriptures.

## SINFUL

***hamartolos*** *(268)*, an adjective, akin to ***hamartano***, "to sin," is used as an adjective, "sinful" in Mark 8:38; Luke 5:8; 19:7; 24:7; John 9:16, 24; Rom. 7:13.

## SING, SINGING

### *Old Testament*

**A. Verbs.**

***ranan*** (7442), "to sing, shout, cry out." ***ranan*** is often used to express joy, exultation, which seems to demand loud singing, especially when it is praise to God, Isa. 12:6); cries aloud, Prov. 8:3; shout for joy, Ps. 32:11.

***shir*** (7891), "to sing." Over one quarter of the instances of ***shir*** are found in the Book of Psalms, often in the imperative form, calling the people to express their praise to God in singing, Ps. 96:1. Frequently ***shir*** is found in parallelism with ***zamar***, "to sing," Ps. 68:4, 32.

**B. Participle.**

***shir*** (7891), "singers"; Levitical "singers," 1 Chron. 15:16; female singers, 2 Sam. 19:35; 2 Chron. 35:25; Eccl. 2:8.

**C. Noun.**

***shir*** (7892), "song." ***shir*** is used of a joyous, triumphal, religious, "song" in Gen. 31:27; Judg. 5:12; Neh. 12:46. The book that is commonly designated "The Song of Solomon" actually has the title "The Song of Songs" in Hebrew.

### *New Testament*

***ado*** *(103)* is used always of "praise to God," (a) intransitively, Eph. 5:19; Col. 3:16; (b) transitively, Rev. 5:9; 14:3; 15:3.

## SINGLE

***haplous*** *(573)*, "simple, single," is used in a moral sense in Matt. 6:22 and Luke 11:34, said of the eye; "singleness" of purpose keeps us from the snare of having a double treasure and consequently a divided heart.

## SINGLENESS

***aphelotes*** *(858)* denotes "simplicity," Acts 2:46; the idea here is that of an unalloyed benevolence expressed in act.

## SINNER

***hamartolos*** *(268)*, lit., "one who misses the mark" (a meaning not to be pressed), is an adjective, most frequently used as a noun; it is the most usual term to describe the fallen condition of men; it is applicable to all men, Rom. 5:8, 19. In the Synoptic Gospels the word is used not infrequently, by the Pharisees, of publicans (tax collectors) and women of ill repute, e.g., "a woman which was in the city, a sinner," Luke 7:37; "a man that is a sinner," 19:7. In Gal. 2:15, in the clause "not sinners of the Gentiles," the apostle is taking the Judaizers on their own ground, ironically reminding them of their claim to moral superiority over Gentiles; he proceeds to show that the Jews are equally sinners with Gentiles.

## SISTER

### *Old Testament*

***'achot*** (269), "sister." ***'achot*** can mean a female sibling, Gen. 4:22; or one's half-sister, Gen. 20:12; or aunt on the father's side, Lev. 18:12; 20:19; or on the mother's side, Lev. 18:13; 20:19. The use of ***'achot*** more generally denotes female relatives, Gen. 24:60. This meaning lies behind the metaphorical use, where two divisions of a nation, i.e., Judah and Israel; Jer. 3:7, and two cities, i.e., Sodom and Samaria; Ezek. 16:46, are portrayed as sisters—Hebrew names of geographical entities are feminine. The more specialized meaning "beloved" is found only in Song of Sol. 4:9.

### *New Testament*

***adelphe*** *(79)* is used (a) of natural relationship, e.g., Matt. 19:29; of the "sisters" of Christ, the children of Joseph and Mary after the virgin birth of Christ, e.g., Matt. 13:56; (b) of "spiritual kinship" with Christ, an affinity marked by the fulfillment of the will of the Father, Matt. 12:50; Mark 3:35; of spiritual relationship based upon faith in Christ, Rom. 16:1; 1 Cor. 7:15; 9:5, KJV and RV marg.; Jas. 2:15; Philem. 2, RV.



## SLACK (Verb), SLACKNESS

**A. Verb.**

***braduno*** *(1019)*, used intransitively signifies "to be slow, to tarry" (***bradus***, "slow"), said negatively of God, 2 Pet. 3:9, "is (not) slack"; in 1 Tim. 3:15, translated "(if) I tarry."

**B. Noun.**

***bradutes*** *(1022)*, "slowness" (akin to A), is rendered "slackness" in 2 Pet. 3:9.

## SLANDERER

***diabolos*** *(1228)*, an adjective, "slanderous, accusing falsely," 1 Tim. 3:11; 2 Tim. 3:3; Titus 2:3.

## SLAUGHTER

*Old Testament*

### A. Verb.

***zabach*** (2076), "to slaughter, sacrifice." This word often means to kill an animal, for the use of making a sacrifice to God, Exod. 20:24. While there were grain and incense offerings prescribed as part of the Mosaic laws dealing with sacrifice, see Lev. 2, the primary kind of sacrifice was the blood offering which required the slaughter of an animal, cf. Deut. 17:1; 1 Chron. 15:26. ***zabach*** is also used as a term for "slaughter for eating," 1 Kings 19:21.

### B. Nouns.

***zebach*** (2077), "sacrifice." This noun occurs more than 160 times in biblical Hebrew. The "sacrifice" which was part of a covenant ritual involved the sprinkling of the blood on the people and upon the altar, which presumably symbolized God as the covenant partner, see Exod. 24:6–8. Another special "sacrifice" was "the sacrifice of the feast of the Passover," Exod. 34:25. In this case the sacrificial lamb provided the main food for the Passover meal, and its blood was sprinkled on the doorposts of the Israelite homes as a sign to the death angel.

The "sacrifice" of animals was in no way unique to Israelite religion, for sacrificial rituals generally are part of all ancient religious cults. Indeed, the mechanics of the ritual were quite similar, especially between Israelite and Canaanite religions. However, the differences are very clear in the meanings which the rituals had as they were performed either to capricious Canaanite gods or for the one true God who kept His covenant with Israel. The noun ***zebach*** is used of "sacrifices" to the one true God in Gen. 46:1, cf. Exod. 10:25; Neh. 12:43. The noun refers to "sacrifices" to other deities in Exod. 34:15. cf. Num. 25:2; 2 Kings 10:19. The idea of "sacrifice" certainly is taken over into the New Testament, for Christ became "the Lamb of God, who takes away the sin of the world," John 1:29, RSV. The writer of Hebrews makes much of the fact that with the "sacrifice" of Christ, no more sacrifices are necessary, Heb. 9.

***mizbeach*** (4196), "altar." Frequent use is obviously another direct evidence of the centrality of the sacrificial system in Israel. The first appearance of ***mizbeach*** is in Gen. 8:20, where Noah built an "altar" after the Flood. Countless "altars" are referred to as the story of Israel progresses on the pages of the Old Testament: that of Noah, Gen. 8:20; of Abram at Sichem, Gen. 12:7, at Beth-el, Gen. 12:8, and at Moriah, Gen. 22:9; of Isaac at Beersheba, Gen. 26:25; of Jacob at Shechem, Gen. 33:20; of Moses at Horeb, Exod. 24:4, of Samuel at Ramah, 1 Sam. 7:17; of the temple in Jerusalem, 1 Kings 6:20; 8:64; and of the two "altars" planned by Ezekiel for the restored temple, Ezek. 41:22; 43:13–17.

*New Testament*

***sphage*** (*4967*) is used in two quotations from the Sept., Acts 8:32 from Isa. 53:7, and Rom. 8:36 from Ps. 44:22; in the latter the quotation is set in a strain of triumph, the passage quoted being an utterance of sorrow. In Jas. 5:5 there is an allusion to Jer. 12:3, the luxurious rich, getting wealth by injustice, spending it on their pleasures, are "fattening themselves like sheep unconscious of their doom."

## SLAVE

***soma*** (*4983*), "a body," is translated "slaves" in Rev. 18:13 (RV and KJV marg., "bodies"), an intimation of the unrighteous control over the bodily activities of "slaves"; the next word "souls" stands for the whole being.

## SLAY, SLAIN, SLEW

1. ***apokteino*** (*615*), the usual word for "to kill," is so translated in the RV wherever possible (e.g., for KJV, "to slay," in Luke 11:49; Acts 7:52; Rev. 2:13; 9:15; 11:13; 19:21); in the following the verb "to kill" would not be appropriate, Rom. 7:11, "slew," metaphorically of sin, as using the commandment; Eph. 2:16, "having slain," said metaphorically of the enmity between Jew and Gentile.

2. ***anaireo*** (*337*), "to take away, destroy, kill," is rendered "to slay" in Matt. 2:16; Acts 2:23; 5:33, 36; 9:29, KJV (RV, "to kill"); 10:39; 13:28; 22:20; 23:15, RV; in 2 Thess. 2:8 the best texts have this verb (for ***analisko***, "to consume," KJV and RV marg.); hence the RV, "shall slay," of the destruction of the man of sin.

3. ***sphazo*** or ***sphatto*** (*4969*), "to slay," especially of victims for sacrifice, is used (a) of taking human life, 1 John 3:12 (twice); Rev. 6:4, RV, "slay" (KJV, "kill"); in 13:3, probably of assassination, RV, "smitten (unto death)," KJV, "wounded (to death)," RV marg., "slain"; 18:24; (b) of Christ, as the Lamb of sacrifice, Rev. 5:6, 9, 12; 6:9; 13:8.

4. ***katasphazo*** (*2695v*), "to kill off" (***kata***, used intensively, and No. 3), is used in Luke 19:27.

## SLEIGHT

***kubia*** (or ***—eia***) (*2940*) denotes "dice playing"; hence, metaphorically, "trickery, sleight,"

Eph. 4:14. The Eng. word is connected with "sly" ("not with slight").

## SLOTHFUL

1. ***nothros*** *(3576)*, "indolent, sluggish," is rendered "slothful" in Heb. 6:12, KJV.

2. ***okneros*** *(3636)*, "shrinking, irksome," is translated "slothful" in Matt. 25:26, and Rom. 12:11, where "in diligence not slothful," RV, might be rendered "not flagging in zeal."

## SLOW

***bradus*** *(1021)* is used twice in Jas. 1:19, in an exhortation to "be slow to speak" and "slow to wrath"; in Luke 24:25, metaphorically of the understanding.

## SLUGGISH

***nothros*** *(3576)*, translated "sluggish" in Heb. 6:12, RV; here it is set in contrast to confident and constant hope; in 5:11 ("dull") to vigorous growth in knowledge.

## SLUMBER (Verb)

***nustazo*** *(3573)* denotes "to nod in sleep" (akin to ***neuo***, "to nod"), "fall asleep," and is used (a) of natural slumber, Matt. 25:5; (b) metaphorically in 2 Pet. 2:3, negatively, of the destruction awaiting false teachers.

## SMITE

1. ***patasso*** *(3960)*, "to strike, smite," is used (I) literally, of giving a blow with the hand, or fist or a weapon, Matt. 26:51, RV, "smote" (KJV, "struck"); Luke 22:49, 50; Acts 7:24; 12:7; (II) metaphorically, (a) of judgment meted out to Christ, Matt. 26:31; Mark 14:27; (b) of the infliction of disease, by an angel, Acts 12:23; of plagues to be inflicted upon men by two divinely appointed witnesses, Rev. 11:6; (c) of judgment to be executed by Christ upon the nations, Rev. 19:15, the instrument being His Word, described as a sword.

2. ***tupto*** *(5180)*, "to strike, smite, beat," is rendered "to smite" in Matt. 24:49, KJV (RV, "beat"); 27:30; Mark 15:19; Luke 6:29; 18:13; in some texts in 22:64 (1st part: RV omits; for the 2nd part see No. 3); 23:48; Acts 23:2, 3 (twice).

3. ***paio*** *(3817)* signifies "to strike or smite" (a) with the hand or fist, Matt. 26:68; Luke 22:64 (see No. 2); (b) with a sword, Mark 14:47; John 18:10, KJV (RV, "struck"); (c) with a sting, Rev. 9:5, "striketh."

4. ***dero*** *(1194)*, "to flay, to beat," akin to ***derma***, "skin," is translated "to smite" in Luke 22:63, KJV (RV, "beat"); John 18:23; 2 Cor. 11:20.

6. ***rhapizo*** *(4474)*, primarily "to strike with a rod" (***rhapis***, "a rod"), then, "to strike the face with the palm of the hand or the clenched fist," is used in Matt. 5:39; 26:67, where the marg. of KJV and RV has "with rods."

7. ***sphazo*** *(4969)*, "to slay," is translated "smitten unto death" in Rev. 13:3.

## SMOOTH

***leois*** *(3006)*, "smooth," occurs in Luke 3:5, figurative of the change in Israel from self-righteousness, pride and other forms of evil, to repentance, humility and submission.

## SNARE

1. ***pagis*** *(3803)*, "a trap, a snare" (akin to ***pegnumi***, "to fix," and ***pagideuo***, "to ensnare," which see), is used metaphorically of (a) the allurements to evil by which the Devil "ensnares" one, 1 Tim. 3:7; 2 Tim. 2:26; (b) seductions to evil, which "ensnare" those who "desire to be rich," 1 Tim. 6:9; (c) the evil brought by Israel upon themselves by which the special privileges divinely granted them and centering in Christ, became a "snare" to them, their rejection of Christ and the Gospel being the retributive effect of their apostasy, Rom. 11:9; (d) of the sudden judgments of God to come upon those whose hearts are "overcharged with surfeiting, and drunkenness, and cares of this life," Luke 21:34 (v. 35 in KJV).

2. ***brochos*** *(1029)*, "a noose, slipknot, halter," is used metaphorically in 1 Cor. 7:35, "a snare" (RV, marg., "constraint," "noose").

## SOBER, SOBERLY, SOBERMINDED

### A. Adjective.

***sophron*** *(4998)* denotes "of sound mind" (***sozo***, "to save," ***phren***, "the mind"); hence, "self-controlled, soberminded," always rendered "sober-minded" in the RV; in 1 Tim. 3:2 and Titus 1:8, KJV, "sober"; in Titus 2:2, KJV, "temperate"; in 2:5, KJV, "discreet."

### B. Verbs.

1. ***nepho*** *(3525)* signifies "to be free from the influence of intoxicants"; in the NT, metaphorically, it does not in itself imply watchfulness, but is used in association with it, 1 Thess. 5:6, 8; 2 Tim. 4:5; 1 Pet. 1:13; 4:7, RV (KJV, "watch"); 5:8.

2. ***sophroneo*** *(4993)*, akin to A, is rendered "to think soberly," Rom. 12:3; "to be sober," 2 Cor. 5:13; "to be soberminded," Titus 2:6; in 1 Pet. 4:7, KJV "be ye sober" (RV, "of sound mind").

3. ***sophronizo*** *(4994)* denotes "to cause to be of sound mind, to recall to one's senses"; in Titus 2:4, RV, it is rendered "they may train" (KJV, "they may teach . . . to be sober," marg., "wise"); "train" expresses the meaning more

adequately; the training would involve the cultivation of sound judgment and prudence.

## SOBERNESS, SOBRIETY

***sophrosune*** (*4997*) denotes "soundness of mind," Acts 26:25, "soberness"; 1 Tim. 2:9, 15, "sobriety."

## SOJOURN, SOJOURNER, SOJOURNING

### *Old Testament*

**A. Verb.**

***gur*** (1481), "to dwell as a client, sojourn." This verb means "to dwell in a land as a client." The first occurrence of the word is in Gen. 12:10, where it is reported that Abram journeyed to Egypt and dwelt there as a client, Gen. 21:23.

**B. Nouns.**

***ger*** (1616), "client; stranger." A "client" was not simply a foreigner (***nakri***) or a stranger (***zar***). He was a permanent resident, once a citizen of another land, who had moved into his new residence. Frequently he left his homeland under some distress, as when Moses fled to Midian, Exod. 2:22. Whether the reason for his journey was to escape some difficulty or merely to seek a new place to dwell, he was one who sought acceptance and refuge. Consequently he might also call himself a ***toshab***, a settler. Neither the settler nor the "client" could possess land. In the land of Canaan the possession of land was limited to members or descendants of the original tribal members. Only they were full citizens who enjoyed all the rights of citizenry, which meant sharing fully in the inheritance of the gods and forefathers—the feudal privileges and responsibilities, cf. Ezek. 47:22.

In Israel a ***ger***, like a priest, could possess no land and enjoyed the special privileges of the third tithe. Every third year the tithe of the harvest was to be deposited at the city gate with the elders and distributed among those in need, Deut. 14:29. In the eschaton such "clients" were to be treated as full citizens. Ezek. 47:22. Under the Mosaic law aliens were not slaves but were usually in the service of some Israelite whose protection they enjoyed, Deut. 24:14. This, however, was not always the case. Sometimes a "client" was rich and an Israelite would be in his service, Lev. 25:47.

The ***ger*** was to be treated (except for feudal privileges and responsibilities) as an Israelite, being responsible to and protected by the law, Deut. 1:16; Lev. 18:26; Lev. 24:22. The ***ger*** also enjoyed the Sabbath rest, Lev. 25:6, and divine protection, Deut. 10:18. God commanded Israel to love the "client" as himself, Lev. 19:34.

### *New Testament*

**A. Verb.**

***paroikeo*** (*3939*) denotes "to dwell beside, among or by" (***para***, "beside," ***oikeo***, "to dwell"); then, "to dwell in a place as a ***paroikos***, a stranger," Luke 24:18, RV, "Dost thou (alone) sojourn . . .?" [marg., "Dost thou sojourn (alone)" is preferable], KJV, "art thou (only) a stranger?" (***monos***, "alone," is an adjective, not an adverb); in Heb. 11:9, RV, "he became a sojourner" (KJV, "he sojourned"), the RV gives the force of the aorist tense.

**B. Adjective.**

***paroikos*** (*3941*), an adjective, akin to A, No. 1, lit., "dwelling near" (see above), then, "foreign, alien" (found with this meaning in inscriptions), hence, as a noun, "a sojourner," is used with ***eimi***, "to be," in Acts 7:6, "should sojourn," lit., "should be a sojourner"; in 7:29, RV, "sojourner" (KJV, "stranger"); in Eph. 2:19, RV, "sojourners" (KJV, "foreigners"), the preceding word rendered "strangers" is ***xenos***; in 1 Pet. 2:11, RV, ditto (KJV, "strangers").

**C. Noun.**

***paroikia*** (*3940*), "a sojourning" (akin to A and B), occurs in Acts 13:17, rendered "they sojourned," RV, KJV, "dwelt as strangers," lit., "in the sojourning"; in 1 Pet. 1:17, "sojourning."

## SOLID

***stereos*** (*4731*), meaning "solid" in Heb. 5:12, 14, of food.

## SON

***huios*** (*5207*) primarily signifies the relation of offspring to parent (see John 9:18–20; Gal. 4:30). It is often used metaphorically of prominent moral characteristics (see below). "It is used in the NT of (a) male offspring, Gal. 4:30; (b) legitimate, as opposed to illegitimate offspring, Heb. 12:8; (c) descendants, without reference to sex, Rom. 9:27; (d) friends attending a wedding, Matt. 9:15; (e) those who enjoy certain privileges, Acts 3:25; (f) those who act in a certain way, whether evil, Matt. 23:31, or good, Gal. 3:7; (g) those who manifest a certain character, whether evil, Acts 13:10; Eph. 2:2, or good, Luke 6:35; Acts 4:36; Rom. 8:14; (h) the destiny that corresponds with the character, whether evil, Matt. 23:15; John 17:12; 2 Thess. 2:3, or good, Luke 20:36; (i) the dignity of the relationship with God whereunto men are brought by the Holy Spirit when they believe on the Lord Jesus Christ, Rom. 8:19; Gal. 3:26. . . .

The Apostle John does not use ***huios***, "son," of the believer, he reserves that title for the Lord; but he does use ***teknon***, "child," as in his Gospel, 1:12; 1 John 3:1, 2; Rev. 21:7 (***huios***) is a quotation from 2 Sam. 7:14. The Lord Jesus used ***huios*** in a very significant way, as in Matt. 5:9, "Blessed are the peacemakers, for they shall be called the sons of God," and vv. 44, 45, "Love your enemies, and pray for them that persecute you; that ye may be (become) sons of your Father which is in heaven." The disciples were to do these things, not in order that they might become children of God, but that, being children (note "your Father" throughout), they might make the fact manifest in their character, might "become sons." See also 2 Cor. 6:17, 18.

As to moral characteristics, the following phrases are used: (a) sons of God, Matt. 5:9, 45; Luke 6:35; (b) sons of the light, Luke 16:8; John 12:36; (c) sons of the day, 1 Thess. 5:5; (d) sons of peace, Luke 10:6; (e) sons of this world, Luke 16:8; (f) sons of disobedience, Eph. 2:2; (g) sons of the evil one, Matt. 13:38, cf. "of the Devil," Acts 13:10; (h) son of perdition, John 17:12; 2 Thess. 2:3. It is also used to describe characteristics other than moral, as: (i) sons of the resurrection, Luke 20:36; (j) sons of the Kingdom, Matt. 8:12; 13:38; (k) sons of the bridechamber, Mark 2:19; (1) sons of exhortation, Acts 4:36; (m) sons of thunder, Boanerges, Mark 3:17.

### *The Son of God*

In this title the word "Son" is used sometimes (a) of relationship, sometimes (b) of the expression of character. Thus, e.g., when the disciples so addressed Him, Matt. 14:33; 16:16; John 1:49, when the centurion so spoke of Him, Matt. 27:54, they probably meant that (b) He was a manifestation of God in human form. But in such passages as Luke 1:32, 35; Acts 13:33, which refer to the humanity of the Lord Jesus, . . . the word is used in sense (a).

The Lord Jesus Himself used the full title on occasion, John 5:25; 9:35 [some mss. have "the Son of Man"; see RV marg.]; 11:4, and on the more frequent occasions on which He spoke of Himself as "the Son," the words are to be understood as an abbreviation of "the Son of God," not of "The Son of Man"; this latter He always expressed in full; see Luke 10:22; John 5:19, etc.

John uses both the longer and shorter forms of the title in his Gospel, see 3:16–18; 20:31, e.g., and in his Epistles; cf. Rev. 2:18. So does the writer of Hebrews, 1:2; 4:14; 6:6, etc. An eternal relation subsisting between the Son and the Father in the Godhead is to be understood. That is to say, the Son of God, in His eternal relationship with the Father, is not so entitled because He at any time began to derive His being from the Father (in which case He could not be co-eternal with the Father), but because He is and ever has been the expression of what the Father is; cf. John 14:9, "he that hath seen Me hath seen the Father." The words of Heb. 1:3, "Who being the effulgence of His (God's) glory, and the very image of His (God's) substance" are a definition of what is meant by "Son of God." Thus absolute Godhead, not Godhead in a secondary or derived sense, is intended in the title.

Other titles of Christ as the "Son of God" are: "His Son," 1 Thess. 1:10 (in Acts 13:13, 26, RV, ***pais*** is rendered "servant"); "His own Son," Rom. 8:32; "My beloved Son," Matt. 3:17; "His Only Begotten Son," John 3:16; "the Son of His love," Col. 1:13.

In addressing the Father in His prayer in John 17 He says, "Thou lovedst Me before the foundation of the world." Accordingly in the timeless past the Father and the "Son" existed in that relationship, a relationship of love, as well as of absolute Deity. In this passage the "Son" gives evidence that there was no more powerful plea in the Father's estimation than that co-eternal love existing between the Father and Himself.

The declaration "Thou art My Son, this day have I begotten Thee," Ps. 2:7, quoted in Acts 13:33; Heb. 1:5; 5:5, refers to the birth of Christ, not to His resurrection. In Acts 13:33 the verb "raise up" is used of the raising up of a person to occupy a special position in the nation, as of David in verse 22 (so of Christ as a Prophet in 3:22 and 7:37). The word "again" in the KJV in v. 33 represents nothing in the original. The RV rightly omits it. In v. 34 the statement as to the resurrection of Christ receives the greater stress in this respect through the emphatic contrast to that in v. 33 as to His being raised up in the nation, a stress imparted by the added words "from the dead." Accordingly v. 33 speaks of His incarnation, v. 34 of His resurrection.

S

### *Son of Man*

In the NT this is a designation of Christ, almost entirely confined to the Gospels. Elsewhere it is found in Acts 7:56, the only occasion where a disciple applied it to the Lord and in Rev. 1:13; 14:14 (see below).

"Son of Man" is the title Christ used of Himself; John 12:34 is not an exception, for the quotation by the multitude was from His own statement. The title is found especially in the Synoptic Gospels. The occurrences in John's gospel, 1:51; 3:13, 14; 5:27; 6:27, 53, 62; 8:28 (9:35 in some texts); 12:23, 34 (twice); 13:31, are not parallel to those in the Synoptic Gospels. In the latter the use of the title falls into two groups, (a) those in which it refers to Christ's humanity, His earthly work, sufferings and death, e.g., Matt. 8:20; 11:19; 12:40; 26:2, 24; (b) those which refer to His glory in resurrection and to that of His future advent, e.g., Matt. 10:23; 13:41; 16:27, 28; 17:9; 24:27, 30 (twice), 37, 39, 44.

While it is a messianic title it is evident that the Lord applied it to Himself in a distinctive way, for it indicates more than Messiahship, even universal headship on the part of One who is Man. It therefore stresses His manhood, manhood of a unique order in comparison with all other men, for He is declared to be of heaven, 1 Cor. 15:47, and even while here below, was "the Son of Man, which is in Heaven," John 3:13. As the "Son of Man" He must be appropriated spiritually as a condition of possessing eternal life, John 6:53. In His death, as in His life, the glory of His Manhood was displayed in the absolute obedience and submission to the will of the Father (12:23; 13:31), and, in view of this, all judgment has been committed to Him, who will judge in full understanding experimentally of human conditions, sin apart, and will exercise the judgment as sharing the nature of those judged, John 5:22, 27. Not only is He man, but He is "Son of Man," not by human generation but, according to the Semitic usage of the expression, partaking of the characteristics (sin apart) of manhood belonging to the category of mankind. Twice in the Apocalypse, 1:13 and 14:14, He is described as "One like unto a Son of man," RV (KJV, ". . . the Son of Man"), cf. Dan. 7:13. He who was thus seen was indeed the "Son of Man," but the absence of the article in the original serves to stress what morally characterizes Him as such. Accordingly in these passages He is revealed, not as the Person known by the title, but as the One who is qualified to act as the Judge of all men. He is the same Person as in the days of His flesh, still continuing His humanity with His Deity. The phrase "like unto" serves to distinguish Him as there seen in His glory and majesty in contrast to the days of His humiliation.

## SOOTHSAYING

***manteuomai*** (*3132*), "to divine, practice divination" (from ***mantis***, "a seer, diviner"), occurs in Acts 16:16. The word is allied to ***mainomai***, "to rave," and ***mania***, "fury" displayed by those who were possessed by the evil spirit (represented by the pagan god or goddess) while delivering their oracular messages. Trench draws a distinction between this verb and ***propheteuo***, not only as to their meanings, but as to the fact of the single occurrence of ***manteuomai*** in the NT, contrasted with the frequency of ***propheteuo***, exemplifying the avoidance by NT writers of words the employment of which "would tend to break down the distinction between heathenism and revealed religion."

## SOP

***psomion*** (*5596*), a diminutive of ***psomos***, "a morsel," denotes "a fragment, a sop," John 13:26 (twice), 27, 30. It had no connection with the modern meaning of "sop," something given to pacify (as in the classical expression "a sop to Cerberus").

## SORCERER

1. ***magos*** (*3097*), (a) "one of a Median caste, a magician"; (b) "a wizard, sorcerer, a pretender to magic powers, a professor of the arts of witchcraft," Acts 13:6, 8, where Bar-Jesus was the Jewish name, Elymas, an Arabic word meaning "wise." Hence the name Magus, "the magician," originally applied to Persian priests.

2. ***pharmakos*** (*5333*), an adjective signifying "devoted to magical arts," is used as a noun, "a sorcerer," especially one who uses drugs, potions, spells, enchantments, Rev. 21:8, in the best texts (some have ***pharmakeus***), and 22:15.

## SORCERY

### A. Nouns.

1. ***pharmakia*** (or ***—eia***) (*5331*) (Eng., "pharmacy," etc.) primarily signified "the use of medicine, drugs, spells"; then, "poisoning"; then, "sorcery," Gal. 5:20, RV, "sorcery" (KJV, "witchcraft"), mentioned as one of "the works of the flesh." See also Rev. 9:21; 18:23.

2. ***magia*** (or ***—eia***) (*3095*), "the magic art," is used in the plural in Acts 8:11.

### B. Verb.

***mageuo*** (*3096*), akin to A, No. 2, "to practice magic," Acts 8:9, "used sorcery," is used as in A, No. 2, of Simon Magnus.

## SORE (Noun, Verb)

### A. Noun.

***helkos*** (*1668*), "a sore" or "ulcer" (primarily a wound), occurs in Luke 16:21; Rev. 16:2, 11.

**B. Verb.**

***helkoo*** (*1669*), "to wound, to ulcerate," is used in the passive voice, signifying "to suffer from sores," to be "full of sores," Luke 16:20 (perfect participle).

## SORROW (Noun and Verb), SORROWFUL

**A. Nouns.**

1. ***lupe*** (*3077*), "grief, sorrow," is translated "sorrow" in Luke 22:45; John 16:6, 20–22; Rom. 9:2, RV (KJV, "heaviness"); 2 Cor. 2:1, RV; 2:3, 7; 7:10 (twice); Phil. 2:27 (twice).

2. ***odune*** (*3601*), "pain, consuming grief, distress," whether of body or mind, is used of the latter, Rom. 9:2, RV, "pain"; 1 Tim. 6:10.

3. ***odin*** (*5604*), "a birth-pang, travail, pain," "sorrows," Matt. 24:8; Mark 13:8.

4. ***penthos*** (*3997*), "mourning," "sorrow," Rev. 18:7 (twice); 21:4.

**B. Verb.**

***odunao*** (*3600*), "to cause pain" (akin to A, No. 2), is used in the middle voice in Luke 2:48; Acts 20:38.

**C. Adjective.**

***perilupos*** (*4036*), "very sad, deeply grieved" (***peri***, intensive), is used in Matt. 26:38 and Mark 14:34, "exceeding sorrowful"; Mark 6:26; Luke 18:23 (v. 24 in some mss.).

## SORRY

**A. Verb.**

***lupeo*** (*3076*) is rendered "to be sorry" (passive voice) in Matt. 14:9, KJV (RV, "grieved"); 17:23; 18:31; 2 Cor. 2:2 [1st part, active voice, "make sorry" (as in 7:8, twice); 2nd part, passive]; 2:4, RV, "made sorry"; 9:9 and 11, RV, "ye were made sorry."

**B. Adjective.**

***perilupos*** (*4036*) is translated "exceeding sorry" in Mark 6:26.

## SOUL

### *Old Testament*

**A. Noun.**

***nephesh*** (5315), "soul; self; life; person; heart." The Hebrew contrasts two other concepts which are not found in the Greek and Latin tradition: "the inner self" and "the outer appearance" or, as viewed in a different context, "what one is to oneself" as opposed to "what one appears to be to one's observers." The inner person is ***nephesh***, while the outer person, or reputation, is ***shem***, most commonly translated "name." In narrative or historical passages of the Old Testament, ***nephesh*** can be translated as "life" or "self," as in Lev. 17:11. It is often translated as the common pronoun "I" or "me, my," Ps 16:10, often with a focus on the animate life of the person. The soul can have physical cravings and desires, Psa 109:7; seat of emotions, Psa. 10:3. See the New Testament section for the unique perspectives of the eternal aspects of the soul.

**B. Verb.**

***naphash*** means "to breathe; respire; be refreshed," Exod. 23:12; 31:17; 2 Sam. 16:14.

### *New Testament*

***psuche*** (*5590*) denotes "the breath, the breath of life," then "the soul," in its various meanings. The NT uses may be analyzed approximately as follows:

(a) the natural life of the body, Matt. 2:20; Luke 12:22; Acts 20:10; Rev. 8:9; 12:11; cf. Lev. 17:11; 2 Sam. 14:7; Esth. 8:11; (b) the immaterial, invisible part of man, Matt. 10:28; Acts 2:27; cf. 1 Kings 17:21; (c) the disembodied (or "unclothed" or "naked," 2 Cor. 5:3, 4) man, Rev. 6:9; (d) the seat of personality, Luke 9:24, explained as = "own self," v. 25; Heb. 6:19; 10:39; cf. Isa. 53:10 with 1 Tim. 2:6; (e) the seat of the sentient element in man, that by which he perceives, reflects, feels, desires, Matt. 11:29; Luke 1:46; 2:35; Acts 14:2, 22; cf. Ps. 84:2; 139:14; Isa. 26:9; (f) the seat of will and purpose, Matt. 22:37; Acts 4:32; Eph. 6:6; Phil. 1:27; Heb. 12:3; cf. Num. 21:4; Deut. 11:13; (g) the seat of appetite, Rev. 18:14; cf. Ps. 107:9; Prov. 6:30; Isa. 5:14 ("desire"); 29:8; (h) persons, individuals, Acts 2:41, 43; Rom. 2:9; Jas. 5:20; 1 Pet. 3:20; 2 Pet. 2:14; cf. Gen. 12:5; 14:21 ("persons"); Lev. 4:2 ('any one'); Ezek. 27:13; of dead bodies, Num. 6:6, lit., "dead soul"; and of animals, Lev. 24:18, lit., "soul for soul"; (i) the equivalent of the personal pronoun, used for emphasis and effect:—1st person, John 10:24 ("us"); Heb. 10:38; cf. Gen. 12:13; Num. 23:10; Judg. 16:30; Ps. 120:2 ("me"); 2nd person, 2 Cor. 12:15; Heb. 13:17; Jas. 1:21; 1 Pet. 1:9; 2:25; cf. Lev. 17:11; 26:15; 1 Sam. 1:26; 3rd person, 1 Pet. 4:19; 2 Pet. 2:8; (j) an animate creature, human or other, 1 Cor. 15:45; Rev. 16:3; cf. Gen. 1:24; 2:7, 19; (k) "the inward man," the seat of the new life, Luke 21:19 (cf. Matt. 10:39); 1 Pet. 2:11; 3 John 2.

Body and soul are the constituents of the man according to Matt. 6:25; 10:28; Luke 12:20; Acts 20:10; body and spirit according to Luke 8:55; 1 Cor. 5:3; 7:34; Jas. 2:26. In Matt. 26:38 the emotions are associated with the soul, in John 13:21 with the spirit; cf. also Ps. 42:11 with 1 Kings 21:5. In Ps. 35:9 the soul rejoices in God, in Luke 1:47 the spirit. Apparently, then, the relationships may be thus summed up; ***soma***, body, and ***pneuma***, spirit, may be separated, ***pneuma*** and ***psuche***, soul, can only be distinguished.

## SOUND (Noun and Verb)

**A. Noun.**

***phone*** (*5456*), most frequently "a voice," is translated "sound" in Matt. 24:31 (KJV marg., "voice"); John 3:8, KJV (RV, "voice"); so 1 Cor. 14:7 (1st part), 8; Rev. 1:15; 18:22 (2nd part, RV, "voice"); KJV and RV in 9:9 (twice); in Acts 2:6, RV, "(this) sound (was heard)," KJV, "(this) was noised abroad."

**B. Verbs.**

1. ***echeo*** (*2278*), akin to A, No. 2, occurs in 1 Cor. 13:1, "sounding (brass)"; in some mss., Luke 21:25.

2. ***execheo*** (*1837*), "to sound forth as a trumpet" or "thunder" (***ex***, "out," and No. 1), is used in 1 Thess. 1:8, "sounded forth," passive voice, lit., "has been sounded out." In the Sept., Joel 3:14.

## SOUND (Health), BE SOUND

**A. Adjective.**

***hugies*** (*199*), "whole, healthy," is used metaphorically of "sound speech," Titus 2:8.

**B. Verb.**

***hugiaino*** (*5198*), "to be healthy, sound in health" (Eng., "hygiene," etc.), translated "safe and sound" in Luke 15:27, is used metaphorically of doctrine, 1 Tim. 1:10; 2 Tim. 4:3; Titus 1:9; 2:1; of words, 1 Tim. 6:3, RV (KJV, "wholesome," RV marg., "healthful"); 2 Tim. 1:13; "in the faith," Titus 1:13 (RV marg., "healthy"); "in faith," Titus 2:2 (RV marg., ditto).

## SOUNDNESS

***holokleria*** (*3647*), "completeness, soundness," Acts 3:16.

## SOW (Verb), SOWER

*Old Testament*

**A. Verb.**

***zara'*** (2232), "to sow, scatter seed, make pregnant." In an agricultural society such as ancient Israel, ***zara'*** would be most important and very commonly used, especially to describe the annual sowing of crops, Judg. 6:3; Gen. 26:12. Used in the figurative sense, it is said that Yahweh "will sow" Israel in the land, Hos. 2:23; Jer. 31:27; Ps. 126:5. "Sow seed" means "conceive [***zara***] seed [***zera'***]," Num. 5:28.

**B. Noun.**

***zera'*** (2233), "seed; sowing; seedtime; harvest; offspring; descendant(s); posterity." ***zera'*** frequently means "seed," i.e., that which propagates a new generation of plants, shrubs, or trees, Gen. 47:19; some seed may be eaten, cf. Lev. 27:30.

***zera'*** sometimes means "semen," or a man's "seed," Lev. 15:16. ***zera'*** often means "offspring." Only rarely is this nuance applied to animals, Gen. 3:15. This verse uses the word in several senses. The first appearance means both the descendants of the snake and those of the spiritual being who used the snake (evil men). The second appearance of the word refers to all the descendants of the woman and ultimately to a particular descendant (Christ). In Gen. 4:25 ***zera'*** appears not as a collective noun but refers to a particular and immediate "offspring"; upon the birth of Seth, Eve said: "God . . . hath appointed me another seed [offspring]. . . ." Gen. 46:6 uses the word (in the singular) of one's entire family including children and grandchildren, cf. Gen. 17:12. One's larger family, including all immediate relatives, is included in the word in passages such as 1 Kings 11:14. The word is used of an entire nation of people in Esth. 10:3.

*New Testament*

***speiro*** (*4687*), "to sow seed," is used (1) literally, especially in the Synoptic Gospels; elsewhere, 1 Cor. 15:36, 37; 2 Cor. 9:10, "the sower," (2) metaphorically, (a) in proverbial sayings, e.g., Matt. 13:3, 4; Luke 19:21, 22; John 4:37; 2 Cor. 9:6; (b) in the interpretation of parables, e.g., Matt. 13:19–23 (in these vv., RV, "was sown," for KJV, "received seed"); (c) otherwise as follows: of "sowing" spiritual things in preaching and teaching, 1 Cor. 9:11; of the interment of the bodies of deceased believers, 1 Cor. 15:42–44; of ministering to the necessities of others in things temporal (the harvest being proportionate to the "sowing"), 2 Cor. 9:6, 10 (see above); of "sowing" to the flesh, Gal. 6:7, 8 ("that" in v. 7 is emphatic, "that and that only," what was actually "sown"); in v. 8, ***eis***, "unto," signifies "in the interests of"; of the "fruit of righteousness" by peacemakers, Jas. 3:18.

## SPARE, SPARINGLY

**A. Verb.**

***pheidomai*** (*5339*), "to spare," i.e., "to forego" the infliction of that evil or retribution which was designed, is used with a negative in Acts 20:29; Rom. 8:32; 11:21 (twice); 2 Cor. 13:2; 2 Pet. 2:4, 5; positively, in 1 Cor. 7:28; 2 Cor. 1:3; rendered "forbear" in 2 Cor. 12:6.

**B. Adverb.**

***pheidomenos*** (*5340*), akin to A, "sparingly," occurs in 2 Cor. 9:6 (twice), of sowing and reaping.

## SPARROW

***strouthion*** (*4765*), a diminutive of ***strouthos***, "a sparrow," occurs in Matt. 10:29, 31; Luke 12:6, 7.

## SPEAK

### *Old Testament*

**A. Verb.**

***dabar*** (1696), "to speak, say." This verb focuses not only on the content of spoken verbal communication but also and especially on the time and circumstances of what is said. Unlike ***'amar***, "to say," ***dabar*** often appears without any specification of what was communicated. Those who "speak" are primarily persons (God or men) or organs of speech. In Gen. 8:15 (the first occurrence of this verb) God "spoke" to Noah, while in Gen. 18:5 one of the three men "spoke" to Abraham.

**B. Nouns.**

***dabar*** (1697), "word, matter; something." The noun ***dabar*** refers, first, to what is said, to the actual "word" itself, Gen. 11:1. This noun can also be used of the content of speaking. When God "did according to the word of Moses," Exod. 8:13, He granted his request. The noun can connote "matter" or "affair," as in Gen. 12:17, where it is reported that God struck Pharaoh's household with plagues because of the "matter of Sarah" (KJV, "because of Sarai"). ***dabar*** can be used as a more general term in the sense of "something"—so in Gen. 24:66 the "everything" (KJV, "all things") is literally "all of something(s)"; it is an indefinite generalized concept rather than a reference to everything in particular.

As a biblical phrase "the word of the Lord" is quite important; it occurs about 242 times. Against the background just presented it is important to note that "word" here may focus on the content (meaning) of what was said, but it also carries overtones of the actual "words" themselves. It was the "word of the Lord" that came to Abram in a vision after his victory over the kings who had captured Lot, Gen. 15:1.

The "word" of God indicates God's thoughts and will. This should be contrasted with His name, which indicates His person and presence. Therefore, God's "word" is called "holy" only once, cf. Ps. 105:42, while His name is frequently called "holy."

There is much discussion regarding the "word" as a hypostatization of divine reality and attributes as seen, for example, in John 1:1: "In the beginning was the Word." This theme is rooted in such Old Testament passages as Isa. 9:8: "The Lord sent a word into Jacob . . ." cf. 55:10–11; Ps. 107:20; 147:15. Some scholars argue that this is no more than the poetical device of personification and does not foreshadow John's usage. Their evidence is that human attributes are frequently separated from a man and objectivized as if they had a separate existence, cf. Ps. 85:11–12.

### *New Testament*

1. ***laleo*** (*2980*), is used several times in 1 Cor. 14; the command prohibiting women from speaking in a church gathering, vv. 34, 35, is regarded by some as an injunction against chattering, a meaning which is absent from the use of the verb everywhere else in the NT; it is to be understood in the same sense as in vv. 2, 3–6, 9, 11, 13, 18, 19, 21, 23, 27–29, 39.

2. ***proslaleo*** (*4354*), "to speak to or with" (***pros***, "to," and No. 2), is used in Acts 13:43 and 28:20.

3. ***phthengomai*** (*5350*), "to utter a sound or voice," is translated "to speak" in Acts 4:18; 2 Pet. 2:16; in 2:18, KJV, "speak" (RV, "utter").

4. ***apophthengomai*** (*669*), "to speak forth" (***apo***, "forth," and No. 4), is so rendered in Acts 2:14, RV (KJV, "said"), and 26:25; in 2:2 it denotes to give utterance.

5. ***sullaleo*** (*4814*), "to speak together" (***sun***, "with," and No. 2), is rendered "spake together" in Luke 4:36, RV.

## SPEAKER (chief)

In Acts 14:12 the verb ***hegeomai***, "to lead the way, be the chief," is used in the present participle with the article (together equivalent to a noun), followed by the genitive case of ***logos***, "speech," with the article, the phrase being rendered "the chief speaker," lit., "the leader of the discourse."

## SPEAKING (evil, much)

***polulogia*** (*4180*), "loquacity," "much speaking" (***polus***, "much," ***logos***, "speech"), is used in Matt. 6:7. In the Sept., Prov. 10:19.

## SPECIAL

***tuchon***, the 2nd aorist participle of ***tunchano***, "to happen, meet with, chance," is used with a negative signifying "not common or ordinary, special," Acts 19:11; so in 28:2.

## SPECTACLE

***theatron*** (*2302*), akin to ***theaomai***, "to behold," denotes (a) "a theater" (used also as a place of assembly), Acts 19:29, 31; (b) "a spectacle, a show," metaphorically in 1 Cor. 4:9.

## SPEECH

1. ***logos*** (*3056*), rendered "word," signifies "speech," as follows: (a) "discourse," e.g., Luke 20:20, RV, "speech" (KJV, "words"); Acts 14:12; 20:7; 1 Cor. 2:1, 4; 4:19, KJV (RV, "word"); 2 Cor. 10:10; (b) "the faculty of speech," e.g., 2 Cor. 11:6; (c) "the manner of speech," e.g., Matt. 5:37, RV, "speech" (KJV, "communication"); Col. 4:6; (d) "manner of instruction," Titus 2:8; 1 Cor. 14:9, RV (KJV, "words"); Eph. 4:29, RV (KJV, "communication").

2. ***lalia*** (*2981*), akin to ***laleo***, denotes "talk, speech," (a) of "a dialect," Matt. 26:73; Mark 14:70; (b) "utterances," John 4:42, RV, "speaking" (KJV, "saying"); 8:43.

3. ***eulogia*** (*2129*) has the meaning "fair speaking, flattering speech" in Rom. 16:18, RV, "fair speech" (KJV, "fair speeches"); cf. also Rom. 16:18.

## SPEECHLESS

1. ***eneos*** (or ***enneos***) (*1769*), "dumb, speechless," occurs in Acts 9:7.

2. ***kophos***, which means either "deaf" or "dumb," is translated "speechless" in Luke 1:22.

## SPEND, SPENT

1. ***dapanao*** (*1159*) denotes (a) "to expend, spend," Mark 5:26: 2 Cor. 12:15 (1st part: for "be spent," see No. 2); (b) "to consume, squander," Luke 15:14; Jas. 4:3.

2. ***ekdapanao*** (*1550*), lit., "to spend out" (***ek***), an intensive form of No. 1, "to spend entirely," is used in 2 Cor. 12:15, in the passive voice, with reflexive significance, "to spend oneself out (for others)," "will . . . be spent," RV marg., "spent out" (see No. 1).

3. ***prosdapanao*** (*4325*), "to spend besides" (***pros***, and No. 1), is used in Luke 10:35, "thou spendest more."

4. ***prosanalisko*** (*4321*), "to spend besides," a strengthened form of ***analisko***, "to expend, consume," occurs in most texts in Luke 8:43.

## SPEW (KJV, SPUE)

***emeo*** (*1692*), "to vomit" (cf. Eng., "emetic"), is used in Rev. 3:16, figuratively of the Lord's utter abhorrence of the condition of the church at Laodicea.

## SPIKENARD

***nardos*** (*3487*), is derived, through the Semitic languages (Heb. ***nerd***, Syriac ***nardin***), from the Sanskrit ***nalada***, "a fragrant oil," procured from the stem of an Indian plant. The Arabs call it the "Indian spike." The adjective ***pistikos*** is attached to it in the NT, Mark 14:3; John 12:3; ***pistikos***, if taken as an ordinary Greek word, would signify "genuine." There is evidence, however, that it was regarded as a technical term. It has been suggested that the original reading was ***pistakes***, i.e., the *Pistacia Terebinthus*, which grows in Cyprus, Syria, Palestine, etc., and yields a resin of very fragrant odor, and in such inconsiderable quantities as to be very costly. Nard was frequently mixed with aromatic ingredients . . . so when scented with the fragrant resin of the ***pistake*** it would quite well be called ***nardos pistakes***.

## SPIRIT

### *Old Testament*

***ruach*** (7307), "breath; air; strength; wind; breeze; spirit; courage; temper; Spirit." First, this word means "breath," air for breathing, air that is being breathed, Jer. 14:6; catching the breath is to revive, Judg. 15:19; overwhelmed is breathless, 1 Kings 10:4–5; one must pass air over the vocal cords to speak, Ps. 33:6; cf. Exod. 15:8; Job 4:9; 19:17. Second, this word can be used with emphasis on the invisible, intangible, fleeting quality of "air": "O remember that my life is wind: mine eyes shall no more see good," Job 7:7. There may be a suggestion of purposelessness, uselessness, or even vanity (emptiness), Jer. 5:13; "empty knowledge," Job 15:2; cf. Eccl. 1:14, 17; "nothing," Prov. 11:29. Third, ***ruach*** can mean "wind," Gen. 3:8; Exod. 10:13, 19; Jer. 4:11; Amos 4:13. Fourth, the wind represents direction, as a compass direction, Jer. 49:36.

Fifth, ***ruach*** frequently represents the element of life in a man, his natural "spirit," Gen. 7:21–22; of animals, cf. Ps. 104:29. On the other hand, in Prov. 16:2 the word appears to mean more than just the element of life; it seems to mean "soul." Sixth, ***ruach*** is often used of a man's mind-set, disposition, or "temper," Ps. 32:2; Ezek. 13:3. ***ruach*** can represent particular dispositions, Josh. 2:11; cf. Josh. 5:1; Job 15:13. Another disposition represented by this word is "temper," Eccl. 10:4. David prayed that God would "restore unto me the joy of thy salvation; and uphold me with thy free Spirit," Ps. 51:12.

Seventh, the Bible often speaks of God's "Spirit," the third person of the Trinity. This is the use of the word in its first biblical occurrence: "And the earth was without form, and void; and darkness was upon the face of the deep. And the Spirit of God moved upon the face of the waters," Gen. 1:2. Isa. 63:10–11 and

Ps. 51:12 specifically speak of the "holy or free Spirit." Eighth, the non-material beings (angels) in heaven are sometimes called "spirits": "And there came forth a spirit, and stood before the Lord, and said, I will persuade him," 1 Kings 22:21; cf. 1 Sam. 16:14.

### *New Testament*

***pneuma*** (*4151*) primarily denotes "the wind" (akin to ***pneo***, "to breathe, blow"); also "breath"; then, especially "the spirit," which, like the wind, is invisible, immaterial and powerful. The NT uses of the word may be analyzed approximately as follows:

(a) the wind, John 3:8 (where marg. is, perhaps, to be preferred); Heb. 1:7; (b) the breath, 2 Thess. 2:8; Rev. 11:11; 13:15; (c) the immaterial, invisible part of man, Luke 8:55; Acts 7:59; 1 Cor. 5:5; Jas. 2:26; (d) the disembodied (or 'unclothed,' or 'naked,' 2 Cor. 5:3, 4) man, Luke 24:37, 39; Heb. 12:23; 1 Pet. 4:6; (e) the resurrection body, 1 Cor. 15:45; 1 Tim. 3:16; 1 Pet. 3:18; (f) the sentient element in man, that by which he perceives, reflects, feels, desires, Matt. 5:3; 26:41; Mark 2:8; Luke 1:47, 80; Acts 17:16; 20:22; 1 Cor. 2:11; 5:3, 4; 14:4, 15; 2 Cor. 7:1; cf. Gen. 26:35; Isa. 26:9; Ezek. 13:3; Dan. 7:15; (g) purpose, aim, 2 Cor. 12:18; Phil. 1:27; Eph. 4:23; Rev. 19:10; cf. Ezra 1:5; Ps. 78:8; Dan. 5:12; (h) the equivalent of the personal pronoun, used for emphasis and effect: 1st person, 1 Cor. 16:18; cf. Gen. 6:3; 2nd person, 2 Tim. 4:22; Philem. 25; cf. Ps. 139:7; 3rd person, 2 Cor. 7:13; cf. Isa. 40:13; (i) character, Luke 1:17; Rom. 1:4; cf. Num. 14:24; (j) moral qualities and activities: bad, as of bondage, as of a slave, Rom. 8:15; cf. Isa. 61:3; stupor, Rom. 11:8; cf. Isa. 29:10; timidity, 2 Tim. 1:7; cf. Josh. 5:1; good, as of adoption, i.e., liberty as of a son, Rom. 8:15; cf. Ps. 51:12; meekness, 1 Cor. 4:21; cf. Prov. 16:19; faith, 2 Cor. 4:13; quietness, 1 Pet. 3:4; cf. Prov. 14:29; (k) the Holy Spirit, e.g., Matt. 4:1 (see below); Luke 4:18; (l) 'the inward man' (an expression used only of the believer, Rom. 7:22; 2 Cor. 4:16; Eph. 3:16); the new life, Rom. 8:4–6, 10, 16; Heb. 12:9; cf. Ps. 51:10; (m) unclean spirits, demons, Matt. 8:16; Luke 4:33; 1 Pet. 3:19; cf. 1 Sam. 18:10; (n) angels, Heb. 1:14; cf. Acts 12:15; (o) divine gift for service, 1 Cor. 14:12, 32; (p) by metonymy, those who claim to be depositories of these gifts, 2 Thess. 2:2; 1 John 4:1–3; (q) the significance, as contrasted with the form, of words, or of a rite, John 6:63; Rom. 2:29; 7:6; 2 Cor. 3:6; (r) a vision, Rev. 1:10; 4:2; 17:3; 21:10.

### *The Holy Spirit*

The "Holy Spirit" is spoken of under various titles in the NT ("Spirit" and "Ghost" are renderings of the same word, ***pneuma***; the advantage of the rendering "Spirit" is that it can always be used, whereas "Ghost" always requires the word "Holy" prefixed.) In the following list the omission of the definite article marks its omission in the original (concerning this see below): "Spirit, Matt. 22:43; Eternal Spirit, Heb. 9:14; the Spirit, Matt. 4:1; Holy Spirit, Matt. 1:18; the Holy Spirit, Matt. 28:19; the Spirit, the Holy, Matt. 12:32; the Spirit of promise, the Holy, Eph. 1:13; Spirit of God, Rom. 8:9; Spirit of (the) living God, 2 Cor. 3:3; the Spirit of God, 1 Cor. 2:11; the Spirit of our God, 1 Cor. 6:11; the Spirit of God, the Holy, Eph. 4:30; the Spirit of glory and of God, 1 Pet. 4:14; the Spirit of Him that raised up Jesus from the dead (i.e., God), Rom. 8:11; the Spirit of your Father, Matt. 10:20; the Spirit of His Son, Gal. 4:6; Spirit of (the) Lord, Acts 8:39; the Spirit of (the) Lord, Acts 5:9; (the) Lord, (the) Spirit, 2 Cor. 3:18; the Spirit of Jesus, Acts 16:7; Spirit of Christ, Rom. 8:9; the Spirit of Jesus Christ, Phil. 1:19; Spirit of adoption, Rom. 8:15; the Spirit of truth, John 14:17; the Spirit of life, Rom. 8:2; the Spirit of grace, Heb. 10:29.

The use or absence of the article in the original where the "Holy Spirit" is spoken of cannot always be decided by grammatical rules, nor can the presence or absence of the article alone determine whether the reference is to the "Holy Spirit." Examples where the Person is meant when the article is absent are Matt. 22:43 (the article is used in Mark 12:36); Acts 4:25, RV (absent in some texts); 19:2, 6; Rom. 14:17; 1 Cor. 2:4; Gal. 5:25 (twice); 1 Pet. 1:2. Sometimes the absence is to be accounted for by the fact that ***pneuma*** (like ***theos***) is substantially a proper name, e.g., in John 7:39. As a general rule the article is present where the subject of the teaching is the Personality of the Holy Spirit, e.g., John 14:26, where He is spoken of in distinction from the Father and the Son. See also 15:26 and cf. Luke 3:22.

In Gal. 3:3, in the phrase "having begun in the Spirit," it is difficult to say whether the reference is to the "Holy Spirit" or to the quickened spirit of the believer; that it possibly refers to the latter is not to be determined by the absence of the article, but by the contrast with "the flesh"; on the other hand, the contrast may be between the "Holy Spirit" who in the believer sets His seal on the perfect work of Christ, and the flesh which seeks to better itself by works of its own. There is no preposition before either noun, and if the reference is to the quickened spirit it cannot be dissociated from the operation of the "Holy Spirit." In Gal. 4:29 the phrase "after the Spirit" signifies "by supernatural power," in contrast to "after the flesh," i.e., "by natural power," and the reference must be to the "Holy Spirit"; so in 5:17.

The full title with the article before both ***pneuma*** and ***hagios*** (the "resumptive" use of the article), lit., "the Spirit the Holy," stresses the character of the Person, e.g., Matt. 12:32; Mark 3:29; 12:36; 13:11; Luke 2:26; 10:21 (RV); John 14:26; Acts 1:16; 5:3; 7:51; 10:44, 47; 13:2; 15:28; 19:6; 20:23, 28; 21:11; 28:25; Eph. 4:30; Heb. 3:7; 9:8; 10:15.

The Personality of the Spirit is emphasized at the expense of strict grammatical procedure in John 14:26; 15:26; 16:8, 13, 14, where the emphatic pronoun ***ekeinos***, "He," is used of Him in the masculine, whereas the noun ***pneuma*** is neuter in Greek, while the corresponding word in Aramaic, the language in which our Lord probably spoke, is feminine (***rucha***, cf. Heb. ***ruach***). The rendering "itself" in Rom. 8:16, 26, due to the Greek gender, is corrected to "Himself" in the RV.

## SPIRIT (OF THE DEAD), NECROMANCER

***'ob*** (178), "spirit (of the dead); necromancer; pit." The word usually represents the troubled spirit (or spirits) of the dead, Isa. 29:4. Its second meaning, "necromancer," refers to a professional who claims to summon forth such spirits when requested (or hired) to do so, Lev. 19:31—first occurrence; 1 Sam. 28:8.

God forbade Israel to seek information by this means, which was so common among the pagans, Lev. 19:31; Deut. 18:11. Perhaps the pagan belief in manipulating one's basic relationship to a god (or gods) explains the relative silence of the Old Testament regarding life after death. Yet God's people believed in life after death, from early times, e.g., Gen. 37:35; Isa. 14:15ff. Necromancy was so contrary to God's commands that its practitioners were under the death penalty, Deut. 13. Necromancers' unusual experiences do not prove that they truly had power to summon the dead. For example, the medium of Endor could not snatch Samuel out of God's hands against His wishes. But in this particular incident, it seems that God rebuked Saul's apostasy, either through a revived Samuel or through a vision of Samuel. Mediums do not have power to summon the spirits of the dead, since this is reprehensible to God and contrary to His will.

## SPIRITUAL

### A. Adjective.

***pneumatikos*** (*4152*) always connotes the ideas of invisibility and of power; it is in fact an after-Pentecost word. In the NT it is used as follows: (a) the angelic hosts, lower than God but higher in the scale of being than man in his natural state, are "spiritual hosts," Eph. 6:12; (b) things that have their origin with God, and which, therefore, are in harmony with His character, as His law is, are "spiritual," Rom. 7:14; (c) "spiritual" is prefixed to the material type in order to indicate that what the type sets forth, not the type itself, is intended, 1 Cor. 10:3, 4; (d) the purposes of God revealed in the gospel by the Holy Spirit, 1 Cor. 2:13a, and the words in which that revelation is expressed, are "spiritual," 13b, matching, or combining, spiritual things with spiritual words [or, alternatively, "interpreting spiritual things to spiritual men," see (e) below]; "spiritual songs" are songs of which the burden is the things revealed by the Spirit, Eph. 5:19; Col. 3:16; "spiritual wisdom and understanding" is wisdom in, and understanding of, those things, Col. 1:9; (e) men in Christ who walk so as to please God are "spiritual," Gal. 6:1; 1 Cor. 2:13b, 15; 3:1; 14:37; (f) the whole company of those who believe in Christ is a "spiritual house," 1 Pet. 2:5a; (g) the blessings that accrue to regenerate men at this present time are called "spiritualities," Rom. 15:27; 1 Cor. 9:11; "spiritual blessings," Eph. 1:3; "spiritual gifts," Rom. 1:11; (h) the activities Godward of regenerate men are "spiritual sacrifices," 1 Pet. 2:5b; their appointed activities in the churches are also called "spiritual gifts," lit., "spiritualities," 1 Cor. 12:1; 14:1; (i) the resurrection body of the dead in Christ is "spiritual," i.e., such as is suited to the heavenly environment, 1 Cor. 15:44; (j) all that is produced and maintained among men by the operations of the Spirit of God is "spiritual," 1 Cor. 15:46.

### B. Adverb.

***pneumatikos*** (*4153*), "spiritually," occurs in 1 Cor. 2:14, with the meaning as (j) above, and Rev. 11:8, with the meaning as in (c). Some mss. have it in 1 Cor. 2:13.

## SPITEFULLY (ENTREAT)

***hubrizo*** (*5195*), used transitively, denotes "to outrage, treat insolently"; "to entreat shamefully" in Matt. 22:6, RV (KJV, "spitefully"); so in Luke 18:32, RV; in Acts 14:5 (KJV, "use despitefully"); in 1 Thess. 2:2, KJV and RV; in Luke 11:45, "reproachest."

## SPLENDOR

***hod*** (1935), "splendor; majesty; authority." The basic significance of "splendor and majesty" with overtones of superior power and position is attested in the application of this word to kings, Jer. 22:18; of weather, Job 37:22. In many cases ***hod*** focuses on "dignity and splendor" with overtones of superior power and position but not to the degree seen in oriental kings: "And thou shalt put some of thine honor upon him, that all the congregation of the children of Israel may be obedient," Num. 27:20—the first occurrence of the word. When used of the olive tree, Hos. 14:6, ***hod*** focuses on its "splendor and dignity" as the most desired and desirable of the trees, cf. Judg. 9:9–15.

## SPOIL (Noun and Verb), SPOILING

### A. Nouns.

1. ***skulon*** (*4661*), used in the plural, denotes "arms stripped from a foe"; "spoils" in Luke 11:22.

2. ***akrothinion*** (*205*), primarily "the top of a heap" (***akros***, "highest, top," and ***this***, "a heap"), hence "firstfruit offerings," and in war "the choicest spoils, Heb. 7:4.

3. ***harpage*** (*724*), "pillage," is rendered "spoiling" in Heb. 10:34.

### B. Verbs.

1. ***diarpazo*** (*1283*), "to plunder," is found in Matt. 12:29, 2nd part (the 1st has ***harpazo***, in the best texts), lit., "(then) he will completely (***dia***, intensive) spoil (his house)"; Mark 3:27 (twice).

2. ***harpazo*** (*726*), "to seize, snatch away," is rendered "spoil" in Matt. 12:29a (see No. 1).

3. ***sulagogeo*** (*4812*), "to carry off as spoil, lead captive" (***sule***, "spoil," ***ago***, "to lead"), is rendered "maketh spoil of" in Col. 2:8, RV (KJV, "spoil"), rather "carry you off as spoil." The false teacher, through his "philosophy and vain deceit," would carry them off as so much booty.

4. ***apekduo*** (*554*), in the middle voice is translated "having spoiled" in Col. 2:15, KJV, RV, "having put off from Himself (the principalities and the powers)." These are regarded by some as the unsinning angels, because they are mentioned twice before in the Epistle (1:16; 2:10).

## SPOT (Noun and Verb)

### A. Nouns.

1. ***spilos*** (*4696*), "a spot or stain," is used metaphorically (a) of moral blemish, Eph. 5:27; (b) of lascivious and riotous persons, 2 Pet. 2:13.

2. ***spilas*** (*4694*) is rendered "spots" in Jude 12, KJV.

### B. Verb.

***spiloo*** (*4695*), akin to A, No. 1, is used in Jude 23, in the clause "hating even the garment spotted by the flesh," the garment representing that which, being brought into contact with the polluting element of the flesh, becomes defiled.

### C. Adjective.

***aspilos*** (*784*), "unspotted, unstained" (***a***, negative, and A), is used of a lamb, 1 Pet. 1:19; metaphorically, of keeping a commandment without alteration and in the fulfillment of it, 1 Tim. 6:14; of the believer in regard to the world, Jas. 1:27, and free from all defilement in the sight of God, 2 Pet. 3:14.

## SPRINKLE, SPRINKLING

### *Old Testament*

***zaraq*** (2236), "to throw; sprinkle; strew; toss; scatter abundantly." This word expresses the "throwing" or "sprinkling" of blood against the sacrificial altar or on the people. Thus, it appears very often in Leviticus, 1:5, 11; 3:2, 8, 13 et al. Ezekiel's version of "the New Covenant" includes the "sprinkling" of the water of purification, Ezek. 36:25. In the first use of ***zaraq*** in the Old Testament, it describes the "throwing" a handful of dust into the air which would settle down on the Egyptians and cause boils, Exod. 9:8, 10.

### *New Testament*

### A. Verb.

***rhantizo*** (*4472*), "to sprinkle" (a later form of ***rhaino***), is used in the active voice in Heb. 9:13, of "sprinkling" with blood the unclean, a token of the efficacy of the expiatory sacrifice of Christ, His blood signifying the giving up of His life in the shedding of His blood (cf. 9:22) under divine judgment upon sin (the voluntary act to be distinguished from that which took place after His death in the piercing of His side); so again in vv. 19, 21 (see B); in Heb. 10:22, passive voice, of the purging (on the ground of the same efficacy) of the hearts of believers from an evil conscience.

### B. Nouns.

1. ***rhantismos*** (*4473*), "sprinkling," akin to A, is used of the "sprinkling" of the blood of Christ, in Heb. 12:24 and 1 Pet. 1:2, an allusion to the use of the blood of sacrifices, appointed for Israel, typical of the sacrifice of Christ (see under A).

2. ***proschusis*** (*4378*), "a pouring or sprinkling upon," occurs in Heb. 11:28, of the "sprinkling" of the blood of the Passover lamb.

## SPY (Noun and Verb)

**A. Nouns.**

1. ***enkathetos*** (*1455*), an adjective denoting "suborned to lie in wait" (***en***, "in," ***kathiemi***, "to send down"), is used as a noun in Luke 20:20, "spies."

2. ***kataskopos*** (*2685*) denotes "a spy" (***kata***, "down," signifying "closely," and ***skopeo***, "to view"), Heb. 11:31.

**B. Verb.**

***kataskopeo*** (*2684*), "to view closely" (akin to A, No. 2), "spy out, search out" with a view to overthrowing, is used in Gal. 2:4.

## STAR

1. ***aster*** (*792*), "a star," Matt. 2:2–10; 24:29; Mark 13:25; 1 Cor. 15:41; Rev. 6:13; 8:10–12; 9:1; 12:1, 4, is used metaphorically, (a) of Christ, as "the morning star," figurative of the approach of the day when He will appear as the "sun of righteousness," to govern the earth in peace, an event to be preceded by the rapture of the Church, Rev. 2:28; 22:16, the promise of the former to the overcomer being suggestive of some special personal interest in Himself and His authority; (b) of the angels of the seven churches, Rev. 1:16, 20; 2:1; 3:1; (c) of certain false teachers, described as "wandering stars," Jude 13, as if the "stars," intended for light and guidance, became the means of deceit by irregular movements.

2. ***astron*** (*798*), practically the same as No. 1, is used (a) in the sing. in Acts 7:43, "the star of the god Rephan," RV, the symbol or "figure," probably of Saturn, worshiped as a god, apparently the same as Chiun in Amos 5:26 (Rephan being the Egyptian deity corresponding to Saturn, Chiun the Assyrian); (b) in the plur., Luke 21:25; Acts 27:20; Heb. 11:12.

## STATUE

***tselem*** (6754), "statue; image; copy." This word signifies an "image or copy" of something in the sense of a replica, 1 Sam. 6:5; Ezek. 23:14. The word also means "image" in the sense of essential nature, Gen. 5:3. Human nature in its internal and external characteristics is what is meant here rather than an exact duplicate. So, too, God made man in His own "image," reflecting some of His own perfections: perfect in knowledge, righteousness, and holiness, and with dominion over the creatures, Gen. 1:26. Being created in God's "image" meant being created male and female, in a loving unity of more than one person, Gen. 1:27. It is noteworthy that in Gen. 1:26 (the first occurrence of the word) the "image" of God is represented by two Hebrew words (***tselem*** and ***demut***); by ***tselem*** alone in Gen. 1:27 and 9:6; and by ***demut*** alone in Gen. 5:1. This plus the fact that in other contexts the words are used exactly the same leads to the conclusion that the use of both in passages such as Gen. 1:26 is for literary effect.

## STATUTE, ORDINANCE

**A. Nouns.**

***choq*** (2706), "statute; prescription; rule; law; regulation." The word ***choq*** also signifies "law," or "statute." In a general sense it refers to the "laws" of nature like rain, Job 28:26; cf. Jer. 5:22; and the celestial bodies, Ps. 148:6; Jer. 31:35–36. Moreover, the word ***choq*** denotes a "law" promulgated in a country, Gen. 47:26.

Finally, and most important, the "law" given by God is also referred to as a ***choq***: "When they have a matter, they come unto me; and I judge between one and another, and I do make them know the statutes [***choq***] of God, and his laws [***torah***]," Exod. 18:16. The word's synonyms are ***mitswah***, "commandment"; ***mishpat***, "judgment"; ***berit***, "covenant"; ***torah***, "law"; and ***'edut***, "testimony." It is not easy to distinguish between these synonyms, as they are often found in conjunction with each other: "Ye shall diligently keep the commandments [***mitswah***] of the Lord your God, and his testimonies [***'edah***], and his statutes [***choq***], which he hath commanded thee," Deut. 6:17.

***chuqqah*** (2708), "statute; regulation; prescription; term," is found for the first time in God's words of commendation about Abraham to Isaac: "Because that Abraham obeyed my voice, and kept my charge, my commandments [***mitswah***], my statutes [***chuqqah***], and my laws [***torah***]" (Gen. 26:5), together with its synonyms ***mishmeret***, ***mitswah***, and ***torah***. In non-religious usage, the word ***chuqqah*** refers to the customs of the nations, Lev. 18:3; cf. 20:23. The reason for the requirement to abstain from the pagan practices is that they were considered to be degenerate, Lev. 18:30.

The most significant usage of ***chuqqah*** is God's "law." It is more specific in meaning than ***choq***. Whereas ***choq*** is a general word for "law," ***chuqqah*** denotes the "law" of a particular festival or ritual. There is the "law" of the Passover, Exod. 12:14, Unleavened Bread, Exod. 12:17, Feast of Tabernacles, Lev. 23:41, the Day of Atonement, Lev. 16:29ff., the priesthood, Exod. 29:9, and the blood and fat, Lev. 3:17.

The word ***chuqqah*** has many synonyms. At times it forms a part of a series of three: "Beware that thou forget not the Lord thy God, in not keeping his commandments [***mitswah***], and his judgments [***mishpat***], and his statutes [***chuqqah***], which I command thee this day" (Deut. 8:11), and at other times of a series of four: "Therefore thou shalt love the Lord thy God, and keep his charge [***mishmeret***], and his statutes [***chuqqah***] and his judgments [***mishpat***], and his commandments [***mitswah***], always," Deut. 11:1; cf. Gen. 26:5 with ***torah*** instead of ***mishpat***.

The "statutes" of people are to be understood as the practices contrary to God's expectations, Mic. 6:16; Ezek. 5:6; 33:15.

**B. Verb.**

***chaqaq*** (2710), "to cut in, determine, decree." ***chaqaq*** is used in Isa. 22:16 with the meaning "to cut in."

## STEAL

***klepto*** (*2813*), "to steal," akin to ***kleptes***, "a thief" (cf. Eng., "kleptomania"), occurs in Matt. 6:19, 20; 19:18; 27:64; 28:13; Mark 10:19; Luke 18:20; John 10:10; Rom. 2:21 (twice); 13:9; Eph. 4:28 (twice).

## STEDFAST, STEDFASTNESS

**A. Adjectives.**

1. ***bebaios*** (*949*), "firm, secure" (akin to ***baino***, "to go"), is translated "steadfast" in 2 Cor. 1:7; Heb. 2:2; 3:14, KJV (RV, "firm"); 6:19.
2. ***hedraios*** (*1476*) primarily denotes "seated" (***hedra***, "a seat"); hence, "steadfast," metaphorical of moral fixity, 1 Cor. 7:37; 15:58; Col. 1:23, RV (KJV, "settled").
3. ***stereos*** (*4731*), firm, is rendered "steadfast" in 1 Pet. 5:9.

**B. Nouns.**

1. ***stereoma*** (*4733*), primarily "a support, foundation," denotes "strength, steadfastness," Col. 2:5.
2. ***sterigmos*** (*4740*), "a setting firmly, supporting," then "fixedness, steadfastness" (akin to ***sterizo***, "to establish"), is used in 2 Pet. 3:17.

## STEEP

***kremnos*** (*2911*), "a steep bank," occurs in Matt. 8:32; Mark 5:13; Luke 8:33, RV, "the steep" (KJV, "a steep place").

## STEWARD, STEWARDSHIP

**A. Nouns.**

1. ***oikonomos*** (*3623*) primarily denoted "the manager of a household or estate" (***oikos***, "a house," ***nemo***, "to arrange"), "a steward" (such were usually slaves or freedmen), Luke 12:42; 16:1, 3, 8; 1 Cor. 4:2; Gal. 4:2, RV (KJV, "governors"); in Rom. 16:23, the "treasurer (RV) of a city; it is used metaphorically, in the wider sense, of a "steward" in general, (a) of preachers of the gospel and teachers of the Word of God, 1 Cor. 4:1; (b) of elders or bishops in churches, Titus 1:7; (c) of believers generally, 1 Pet. 4:10.
2. ***oikonomia*** (*3622*) is rendered "stewardship" in Luke 16:2, 3, 4, and in the RV in 1 Cor. 9:17.

**B. Verb.**

***oikonomeo*** (*3621*), akin to A, signifies "to be a house steward," Luke 16:2.

## STIFF-NECKED

***sklerotrachelos*** (*4644*), from ***skleros***, "harsh, hard," ***trachelos***, "a neck," is used metaphorically in Acts 7:51.

## STIR, STIR UP (Noun and Verb)

**A. Noun.**

***tarachos*** (*5017*), akin to ***tarache***, "trouble," and ***tarasso***, "to trouble," is rendered "stir" in Acts 12:18; 19:23.

**B. Verbs.**

1. ***anazopureo*** (*329*) denotes "to kindle afresh," or "keep in full flame" (***ana***, "up," or "again," ***zoos***, "alive," ***pur***, "fire"), and is used metaphorically in 2 Tim. 1:6, where "the gift of God" is regarded as a fire capable of dying out through neglect. The verb was in common use in the vernacular of the time.
2. ***seio*** (*4579*), "to move to and fro," is rendered "was stirred" in Matt. 21:10, RV (KJV, "was moved).
3. ***anaseio*** (*383*) primarily denotes "to shake back or out, move to and fro"; then, "to stir up," used metaphorically in Mark 15:11, RV, "stirred . . . up" (KJV, "moved"), and Luke 3:14; 23:5.
4. ***saleuo*** (*4531*), "stirred up" in Acts 17:13.
5. ***erethizo*** (*2042*), "hath stirred" in 2 Cor. 9:2, RV.
6. ***anastatoo*** (*387*), "to excite, unsettle" (akin to ***anistemi***, "to raise up," and ***anastasis***, "a raising"), is used (a) of "stirring up" to sedition, and tumult, Acts 17:6, "turned . . . upside down"; 21:38, RV, "stirred up to sedition," KJV, "madest an uproar"; (b) "to upset" by false teaching, Gal. 5:12, RV, "unsettle" (KJV, "trouble").

## STONE (Noun, Verb, and Adjective)

### *Old Testament*

***'eben*** (68), "stone." Beyond their use as a construction material, stones served as covers for wells, Gen. 29:3ff., storage containers, Exod. 7:19, weights, Deut. 25:13; Prov. 11:1, and slingstones, 1 Sam. 17:49. Plumblines were suspended stones, Isa. 34:11; pavement was sometimes made of "stone," 2 Kings 16:17; and the Bible speaks of hailstones, Josh. 10:11; Ezek. 13:11ff. The Israelite custom of cave burials presumes stone tombs, Isa. 14:19; on 3 occasions when bodies were not interred, they were heaped with "stones," Josh. 7:26; 8:29; 2 Sam. 18:17; an instrument for capital punishment, Lev. 24:23; Num. 15:35–36; Deut. 22:21, 24; carving into idols, Lev. 26:1.

Precious "stones" such as onyx, Gen. 2:12, and sapphire, Ezek. 1:26, are mentioned frequently in the Bible, especially with regard to the high priest's ephod and breastplate, Exod. 39:6ff. The expensiveness of the high priest's garments corresponded to the special workmanship of the most holy place where Aaron served.

In certain texts, ***'eben*** has been given theological interpretations. God is called the "stone of Israel" in Gen. 49:24. And several occurrences of ***'eben*** in the Old Testament have been viewed as messianic, as evidenced by the Greek Old Testament, rabbinic writings, and the New Testament, among them: Gen. 28:18; Ps. 118:22; Isa. 8:14; 28:16; Dan. 2:34; Zech. 4:7.

***New Testament***

**A. Nouns.**

1. ***lithos*** (*3037*) is used (1) literally, of (a) the "stones" of the ground, e.g., Matt. 4:3, 6; 7:9; (b) "tombstones," e.g., Matt. 27:60, 66; (c) "building stones," e.g., Matt. 21:42; (d) "a millstone," Luke 17:2; cf. Rev. 18:21; (e) the "tables (or tablets)" of the Law, 2 Cor. 3:7; (f) "idol images," Acts 17:29; (g) the "treasures" of commercial Babylon, Rev. 18:12, 16; (II), metaphorically, of (a) Christ, Rom. 9:33; 1 Pet. 2:4, 6, 8; (b) believers, 1 Pet. 2:5; (c) spiritual edification by scriptural teaching, 1 Cor. 3:12; (d) the adornment of the foundations of the wall of the spiritual and heavenly Jerusalem, Rev. 21:19; (e) the adornment of the seven angels in Rev. 15:6, RV (so the best texts; some have ***linon***, "linen," KJV); (f) the adornment of religious Babylon, Rev. 17:4; (III) figuratively, of Christ, Rev. 4:3; 21:11, where "light" stands for "Light-giver" (***phoster***).

2. ***psephos*** (*5586*), "a smooth stone, a pebble," worn smooth as by water, or polished (akin to ***psao***, "to rub"), denotes (a) by metonymy, a vote (from the use of "pebbles" for this purpose; cf. ***psephizo***, "to count"), Acts 26:10, RV (KJV, "voice"); (b) a (white) "stone" to be given to the overcomer in the church at Pergamum, Rev. 2:17 (twice); a white "stone" was often used in the social life and judicial customs of the ancients; festal days were noted by a white "stone," days of calamity by a black; in the courts a white "stone" indicated acquittal, a black condemnation. A host's appreciation of a special guest was indicated by a white "stone" with the name or a message written on it; this is probably the allusion here.

**B. Verbs.**

1. ***lithoboleo*** (*3036*), "to pelt with stones" (A, No. 1, and ***ballo***, "to throw"), "to stone to death," occurs in Matt. 21:35; 23:37; Luke 13:34 (John 8:5 in some mss.: see No. 2); Acts 7:58, 59; 14:5; Heb. 12:20.

2. ***lithazo*** (*3034*), "to stone," virtually equivalent to No. 1, but not stressing the casting, occurs in John 8:5 (in the most authentic mss.); 10:31–33; 11:8; Acts 5:26; 14:19; 2 Cor. 11:25; Heb. 11:37.

## STOP

***phrasso*** (*5420*), "to fence in" (akin to ***phragmos***, "a fence"), "close, stop," is used (a) metaphorically, in Rom. 3:19, of "preventing" all excuse from Jew and Gentile, as sinners; in 2 Cor. 11:10, lit., "this boasting shall not be stopped to me"; passive voice in both; (b) physically, of the mouths of lions, Heb. 11:33 (active voice).

## STORE (Verb)

1. ***thesaurizo*** (*2343*), "to lay up, store up," is rendered "in store" (lit., "storing"), with a view to help a special case of need, 1 Cor. 16:2; said of the heavens and earth in 2 Pet. 3:7, RV, "have been stored up (for fire)," marg., "stored (with fire)," KJV, "kept in store (reserved unto fire)."

2. ***apothesaurizo*** (*597*), "to treasure up, store away" (***apo***), is used in 1 Tim. 6:19, of "laying up in store" a good foundation for the hereafter by being rich in good works.

## STORY

***tristegos*** (*5152*), an adjective denoting "of three stories," occurs in Acts 20:9 (with ***oikema***, "a dwelling," understood), RV, "the third story" (KJV, "the third loft").

## STRAIN OUT

***diulizo*** (*1368*), primarily denotes "to strain thoroughly" (***dia***, "through," intensive, ***hulizo***, "to strain"), then, "to strain out," as through a sieve or strainer, as in the case of wine, so as to remove the unclean midge, Matt. 23:24, RV (KJV, "strain at").

## STRANGE

**A. Adjectives.**

1. ***xenos*** (*3581*) denotes (a) "foreign, alien," Acts 17:18, of gods; Heb. 13:9, of doctrines;

(b) "unusual," 1 Pet. 4:12, 2nd part, of the fiery trial of persecution (for 1st part, see B).

2. ***allotrios*** (*245*) denotes (a) "belonging to another" (***allos***); (b) "alien, foreign, strange," Acts 7:6; Heb. 11:9, KJV, RV, "(a land) not his own."

3. ***paradoxos*** (*3861*), "contrary to received opinion" (***para***, "beside," ***doxa***, "opinion"; Eng. "paradoxical"), is rendered "strange things" in Luke 5:26.

4. ***exo*** (*1845*), outside, is rendered "strange" in Acts 26:11, KJV.

**B. Verb.**

***xenizo*** (*3579*) denotes "to think something strange," 1 Pet. 4:4, 12, passive voice, i.e., "they are surprised," and "be (not) surprised"; in Acts 17:20, the present participle, active, is rendered "strange," i.e., "surprising."

## STRANGER

**A. Adjectives (used as nouns).**

1. ***xenos*** (*3581*), "strange" (see No. 1 above), denotes "a stranger, foreigner," Matt. 25:35, 38, 43, 44; 27:7; Acts 17:21; Eph. 2:12, 19; Heb. 11:13; 3 John 5.

2. ***allotrios*** (*245*), "strangers," Matt. 17:25, 26; John 10:5 (twice): see No. 2, above.

3. ***allogenes*** (*241*) (***allos***, "another," ***genos***, "a race") occurs in Luke 17:18.

**B. Verb.**

***xenodocheo*** (*3580*), "to receive strangers" (***xenos***, No. 1, above, and ***dechomai***, "to receive"), occurs in 1 Tim. 5:10, RV, "(if) she hath used hospitality to strangers," KJV, "(if) she have lodged strangers."

**C. Noun.**

***philoxenia*** (*5381*), "love of strangers," occurs in Rom. 12:13, "hospitality," and Heb. 13:2, RV, "to show love unto strangers," KJV, "to entertain strangers."

## STRANGLED

***pniktos*** (*4156*), from ***pnigo***, "to choke," i.e., kill but not let the blood, Acts 15:20, 29; 21:25; cf. Lev. 17:13, 14.

## STRENGTH, STRENGTHEN

### *Old Testament*

***chayil*** (2458), "strength; power; wealth; property; capable; valiant; army; troops; influential; upper-class people (courtiers)." First, this word signifies a faculty or "power," the ability to effect or produce something. The word is used of physical "strength" in the sense of power that can be exerted, Eccl. 10:10. Quite often this word appears in a military context. Here it is the physical strength, power, and ability to perform in battle that is in view, 1 Sam. 2:4; cf. Ps. 18:32, 39. Ps. 33:17 applies the word to a war horse. An interesting use of ***chayil*** appears in Num. 24:17–18, where Balaam prophesied the destruction of Moab and Edom at the hands of Israel. Second, ***chayil*** means "wealth, property," Gen. 34:29; cf. Deut. 8:18; Ruth 4:11. Third, several passages use the word in the sense of "able," i.e., have the capacity or potency to actualize an event, Gen. 47:6; Ruth 3:11; Prov. 12:4. When used in some contexts, the word may be translated "valiant," 1 Sam. 14:52; cf. Num. 24:18; 1 Sam. 14:48. Fourth, this word sometimes means "army," Exod. 14:4. The word can also refer to the army as troops in the sense of a combination of a lot of individuals. Under such an idea the word can represent the members of an army distributed to perform certain functions, 2 Chron. 17:2. Fifth, ***chayil*** sometimes represents the "upper class," who, as in all feudal systems, were at once soldiers, wealthy, and influential; Sanballat "spake before his brethren and the army of Samaria," i.e., in the royal court, Neh. 4:2. The Queen of Sheba was accompanied by a large escort of upper-class people from her homeland: "And she came to Jerusalem with a very great train," 1 Kings 10:2.

### *New Testament*

**A. Nouns.**

1. ***dunamis*** (*1411*) is rendered "strength" in the RV and KJV of Rev. 1:16; elsewhere the RV gives the word its more appropriate meaning "power," for KJV, "strength," 1 Cor. 15:56; 2 Cor. 1:8; 12:9; Heb. 11:11; Rev. 3:8; 12:10.

2. ***ischus*** (*2479*), "ability, strength," is rendered "strength" in Mark 12:30, 33; Luke 10:27; in Rev. 5:12, KJV (RV, "might").

3. ***kratos*** (*2904*), "force, might," is rendered "strength" in Luke 1:51, RV and KJV; RV, "strength" (KJV, "power") in Eph. 1:19 and 6:10.

**B. Verbs.**

1. ***dunamoo*** (*1412*), "to strengthen," occurs in Col. 1:11, and in the best texts in Heb. 11:34, "were made strong" (some have No. 2); some have it in Eph. 6:10 (the best have No. 2).

2. ***endunamoo*** (*1743*), "to make strong," is rendered "increased . . . in strength" in Acts 9:22; "to strengthen" in Phil. 4:13; 2 Tim. 2:1, RV, "be strengthened"; 4:17.

3. ***ischuo*** (*2480*), akin to A, No. 2, "to have strength," is so rendered in Mark 5:4, RV (KJV, "could"); in Luke 16:3, RV, "I have not strength to" (KJV, "I cannot").

4. ***enischuo*** (*1765*), akin to A, No. 2, a strengthened form of No. 3, is used in Luke 22:43 and Acts 9:19.

5. ***krataioo*** (*2901*), "to strengthen," is rendered "to be strengthened" in Eph. 3:16.

6. ***sthenoo*** (*4599*), from ***sthenos***, "strength," occurs in 1 Pet. 5:10, in a series of future tenses, according to the best texts, thus constituting divine promises.

## STRICKEN (in years)

***probaino*** (*4260*), "to go forward," is used metaphorically of age, in Luke 1:7, 18, with the phrases "in their (her) days," translated "well stricken in years" (see marg.); in 2:36, "of a great age" (marg., "advanced in many days").

## STRIFE

### *Old Testament*

**A. Verb.**

***rib*** (7378), "to strive, contend," i.e., struggle or strife: physical, Exod. 21:18; verbal, Judg. 6:32.

**B. Nouns.**

***rib*** (7379), "strife; quarrel; dispute; case; contentions; cause." The noun ***rib*** is used of conflicts outside the realm of law cases and courts, Gen. 13:7–8. ***rib*** sometimes represents a "dispute" between two parties. This "dispute" is set in the context of a mutual law structure binding both parties and a court which is empowered to decide and execute justice. This may involve "contention" between two unequal parties (an individual and a group), as when all Israel quarreled with Moses, asserting that he had not kept his end of the bargain by adequately providing for them. Moses appealed to the Judge, who vindicated him by sending water from a rock (cliff?) smitten by Moses: "And he called the name of the place Massah, and Meribah, because of the chiding [quarrel] of the children of Israel . . ." Exod. 17:7. God decided who was the guilty party, Moses or Israel. The "contention" may be between two individuals as in Deut. 25:1, where the two disputants go to court (having a "case or dispute" does not mean one is a wrongdoer): "If there be a controversy between men, and they come unto judgment, that the judges may judge them; then they shall justify the righteous, and condemn the wicked." So in Isa. 1:23 the unjust judge accepts a bribe and does not allow the widow's just "cause" (NASB, "widow's plea") to come before him. Prov. 25:8–9 admonishes the wise to "debate thy cause with thy neighbor" when that neighbor has "put thee to shame."

### *New Testament*

1. ***eris*** (*2054*), "strife, contention," is the expression of "enmity," Rom. 1:29, RV, "strife" (KJV, "debate"); 13:13; 1 Cor. 1:11, "contentions" (RV and KJV); 3:3; 2 Cor. 12:20, RV, "strife" (KJV, "debates"); Gal. 5:20, RV, "strife" (KJV, "variance"); Phil. 1:15; 1 Tim. 6:4; Titus 3:9, RV, "strifes" (KJV, "contentions").

2. ***erithia*** (or ***—eia***) (*2052*), 2 Cor. 12:20.

## STRIKER

***plektes*** (*4131*), "a striker, a brawler" (akin to ***plesso***, "to strike," smite), occurs in 1 Tim. 3:3; Titus 1:7.

## STRIVE

1. ***agonizomai*** (*75*), "to contend" (Eng., "agonize"), is rendered "to strive" in Luke 13:24; 1 Cor. 9:25; Col. 1:29; 4:12, RV (KJV, "laboring fervently").

2. ***machomai*** (*3164*), "to fight, to quarrel, dispute," is rendered "to strive" in John 6:52; Acts 7:26; 2 Tim. 2:24.

3. ***diamachomai*** (*1264*), "to struggle against" (***dia***, intensive, and No. 2), is used of "contending" in an argument, Acts 23:9, "strove."

4. ***erizo*** (*2051*), "to wrangle, strive" (***eris***, "strife"), is used in Matt. 12:19.

5. ***logomacheo*** (*3054*), "to strive about words" (***logos***, "a word," and No. 2), is used in 2 Tim. 2:14.

6. ***antagonizomai*** (*464*), "to struggle against" (***anti***), is used in Heb. 12:4, "striving against."

7. ***sunagonizomai*** (*4865*), "to strive together with" (***sun***), is used in Rom. 15:30.

8. ***sunathleo*** (*4866*), "to strive together," Phil. 1:27.

## STRONG, STRONGER

### *Old Testament*

**A. Verb.**

***chazaq*** (2388), "to be strong, strengthen, harden, take hold of." In the sense of personal strength ***chazaq*** is first used in Deut. 11:8 in the context of the covenant, Deut. 3:28. The covenant promise accompanies the injunction to "be strong and of a good courage," Deut. 31:6. The same encouragement was given to the returned captives as they renewed the work of rebuilding the temple, Zech. 8:9, 13; cf. Hag. 2:4.

***chazaq***, can mean pure physical strength: as in a building up, of a city, Judg. 1:28; 2 Kings 12:6; 2 Chron. 26:9. In battle ***chazaq*** means: "So David prevailed over the Philistine . . ." 1 Sam. 17:50.

In summary, this word group describes the physical and moral strength of man and society. God communicates strength to men, even to the enemies of His people as chastisement for His own. Men may turn their strength into stubbornness against God.

**B. Adjective.**

***chazaq*** (2389), "strong; mighty; heavy; severe; firm; hard." First, the word means "firm" or "hard" in the sense that something is impenetrable, like rock, Ezek. 3:8–9; or metals, Job 37:18. Second, this word means "strong." In its basic meaning it refers to physical strength, cf. Deut. 4:15, 19; able to effect, Num. 13:18; have healthy animals, Ezekiel 34:16. Third, ***chazaq*** means "heavy." When applied to a battle or war, it describes the event(s) as severe, 1 Sam. 14:52. The word is also used to indicate a severe sickness, 1 Kings 17:17, and famine, 1 Kings 18:2.

***New Testament***

**A. Adjectives.**

1. ***dunatos*** (*1415*), "powerful, mighty," is translated "strong," in Rom. 15:1, where the "strong" are those referred to in ch. 14, in contrast to "the weak in faith," those who have scruples in regard to eating meat and the observance of days; 2 Cor. 12:10, where the strength lies in bearing sufferings in the realization that the endurance is for Christ's sake; 2 Cor. 13:9, where "ye are strong" implies the good spiritual condition which the apostle desires for the church at Corinth in having nothing requiring his exercise of discipline (contrast No. 2 in 1 Cor. 4:10).

2. ***ischuros*** (*2478*), "strong, mighty," is used of (a) persons: (1) God, Rev. 18:8; (2) angels, Rev. 5:2; 10:1; 18:21; (3) men, Matt. 12:29 (twice) and parallel passages; Heb. 11:34, KJV, "valiant" (RV, "mighty"); Rev. 6:15 (in the best texts; some have No. 1); 19:18, "mighty"; metaphorically, (4) the church at Corinth, 1 Cor. 4:10, where the apostle reproaches them ironically with their unspiritual and self-complacent condition; (5) of young men in Christ spiritually strong, through the Word of God, to overcome the evil one, 1 John 2:14; of (b) things: (1) wind, Matt. 14:30 (in some mss.), "boisterous"; (2) famine, Luke 15:14; (3) things in the mere human estimate, 1 Cor. 1:27; (4) Paul's letters, 2 Cor. 10:10; (5) the Lord's crying and tears, Heb. 5:7; (6) consolation, 6:18; (7) the voice of an angel, Rev. 18:2 (in the best texts; some have ***megas***, "great"); (8) Babylon, Rev. 18:10; (9) thunderings, Rev. 19:6.

**B. Verbs.**

1. ***endunamoo*** (*1743*), "to make strong" (***en***, "in," ***dunamis***, "power"), "to strengthen," is rendered "waxed strong" in Rom. 4:20, RV (KJV, "was strong"); "be strong," Eph. 6:10; "were made strong," Heb. 11:34.

2. ***krataioo*** (*2901*), "to strengthen" (akin to ***kratos***, "strength"), is rendered (a) "to wax strong," Luke 1:80; 2:40; "be strong," 1 Cor. 16:13, lit., "be strengthened"; "to be strengthened," Eph. 3:16 (passive voice in each place).

## STRONGHOLDS

***ochuroma*** (*3794*), "a stronghold, fortress" (akin to ***ochuroo***, "to make firm"), is used metaphorically in 2 Cor. 10:4, of those things in which mere human confidence is imposed.

## STUMBLE

***Old Testament***

***kashal*** (3782), "to stumble, stagger, totter, be thrown down." Other than literal stumbling, Lev. 26:37, this word is often used figuratively to describe the consequences of divine judgment on sin, Jer. 6:21; cf. also Jer. 50:32.

***New Testament***

1. ***proskopto*** (*4350*), "to strike against," is used of "stumbling," (a) physically, John 11:9, 10; (b) metaphorically, (1) of Israel in regard to Christ, whose Person, teaching, and atoning death, and the gospel relating thereto, were contrary to all their ideas as to the means of righteousness before God, Rom. 9:32; 1 Pet. 2:8; (2) of a brother in the Lord in acting against the dictates of his conscience, Rom. 14:21.

2. ptaio (*4417*), "to cause to stumble," signifies, intransitively, "to stumble," used metaphorically in Rom. 11:11, in the sense (b) (1) in No. 1; with moral significance in Jas. 2:10 and 3:2 (twice), RV, "stumble" (KJV, "offend"); in 2 Pet. 1:10, RV, "stumble" (KJV, "fall").

## STUPID FELLOW

***kesil*** (3684), "stupid fellow; dull person; fool." The ***kesil*** is "insolent" in religion and "stupid or dull" in wise living Ps. 92:6, 7; Prov. Prov. 1:22.

## STUPOR

***katanuxis*** (*2659*), "a pricking" (akin to ***katanusso***, "to strike" or "prick violently," Acts 2:37), is used in Rom. 11:8, RV, "stupor" (KJV, "slumber").

## SUBDUE

***katagonizomai*** (*2610*), primarily, "to struggle against" (***kata***, "against," ***agon***, "a contest"), came to signify "to conquer," Heb. 11:33, "subdued."

## SUBJECT (Verb)

***hupotasso*** (*5293*), primarily a military term, "to rank under" (***hupo***, "under," ***tasso***, "to arrange"), denotes (a) "to put in subjection, to subject," Rom. 8:20 (twice); in the following, the RV, has to subject for KJV, "to put under," 1 Cor. 15:27 (thrice), 28 (3rd clause); Eph. 1:22; Heb. 2:8 (4th clause); in 1 Cor. 15:28 (1st clause), for KJV "be subdued"; in Phil. 3:21, for KJV, "subdue"; in Heb. 2:5, KJV, "hath . . . put in subjection"; (b) in the middle or passive voice, to subject oneself, to obey, be subject to, Luke 2:51; 10:17, 20; Rom. 8:7; 10:3, RV, "did (not) subject themselves" [KJV, "have (not) submitted themselves"]; 13:1, 5; 1 Cor. 14:34, RV, "be in subjection" (KJV, "be under obedience"); 15:28 (2nd clause); 16:16 RV, "be in subjection" (KJV, "submit, etc."); so Col. 3:18; Eph. 5:21, RV, "subjecting yourselves" (KJV, "submitting, etc."); v. 22, RV in italics, according to the best texts; v. 24, "is subject"; Titus 2:5, 9, RV, "be in subjection" (KJV, "be obedient"); 3:1, RV, "to be in subjection" (KJV, "to be subject"); Heb. 12:9, "be in subjection"; Jas. 4:7, RV, "be subject" (KJV, "submit yourselves"); so 1 Pet. 2:13; v. 18, RV, "be in subjection"; so 3:1, KJV and RV; v. 5, similarly; 3:22, "being made subject"; 5:5, RV, "be subject" (KJV, "submit yourselves"); in some texts in the 2nd part, as KJV.

## SUBMIT

***hupeiko*** (*5226*), "to retire, withdraw" (***hupo***, under, ***eiko***, "to yield"), hence, "to yield, submit," is used metaphorically in Heb. 13:17, of "submitting" to spiritual guides in the churches.

## SUBORN

***hupoballo*** (*5260*), "to throw or put under, to subject," denoted "to suggest, whisper, prompt"; hence, "to instigate," translated "suborned" in Acts 6:11. To "suborn" in the legal sense is to procure a person who will take a false oath. The idea of making suggestions is probably present in this use of the word.

## SUBSTANCE

1. ***ouisia*** (*3776*), derived from a present participial form of ***eimi***, "to be," denotes "substance, property," Luke 15:12, 13, RV, "substance," KJV, "goods" and "substance."

2. ***huparchonta*** (*5224*), the neuter plural of the present participle of ***huparcho***, "to be in existence," is used as a noun with the article, signifying one's "goods," and translated "substance" in Luke 8:3.

3. ***huparxis*** (*5223*), existence (akin to No. 2), possession.

4. ***hupostasis*** (*5287*), is translated "substance" (a) in Heb. 1:3, of Christ as "the very image" of God's "substance"; here the word has the meaning of the real nature of that to which reference is made in contrast to the outward manifestation (see the preceding clause); it speaks of the divine essence of God existent and expressed in the revelation of His Son. The KJV, "person" is an anachronism; the word was not so rendered till the 4th cent. Most of the earlier Eng. versions have "substance"; (b) in Heb. 11:1 it has the meaning of "confidence, assurance" (RV), marg., "the giving substance to," KJV, "substance," something that could not equally be expressed by ***elpis***, "hope."

## SUBTLY

***katasophizomai*** (*2686*), "to deal subtly," Acts 7:19.

## SUBVERT, SUBVERTING

### A. Verb.

***anaskeuazo*** (*384*), primarily, "to pack up baggage" (***ana***, "up," ***skeuos***, "a vessel"), hence, from a military point of view, "to dismantle a town, to plunder," is used metaphorically in Acts 15:24, of unsettling or "subverting" the souls of believers. In the papyri it is used of going bankrupt.

### B. Noun.

***katastrophe*** (*2692*), "an overthrow," 2 Pet. 2:6 (Eng. "catastrophe"), is rendered "subverting" in 2 Tim. 2:14.

## SUCCORER

***prostatis*** (*4368*), a feminine form of ***prostates***, denotes "a protectress, patroness"; it is used metaphorically of Phoebe in Rom. 16:2.

## SUCK (GIVE SUCK), SUCKLING

***thelazo*** (*2337*), from ***thele***, "a breast," is used (a) of the mother, "to suckle," Matt. 24:19; Mark 13:17; Luke 21:23; in some texts in 23:29 (the best have ***trepho***); (b) of the young, "to suck," Matt. 21:16, "sucklings"; Luke 11:27.

## SUFFER

(a) *to permit*

1. ***eao*** (*1439*), "to let, permit," is translated "to suffer" in Matt. 24:43; Luke 4:41; 22:51; Acts 14:16; 16:7; 19:30; 28:4; 1 Cor. 10:13.

2. ***proseao*** (*4330*), "to permit further" (***pros***, and No. 1), occurs in Acts 27:7.

3. ***epitrepo*** (*2010*), rendered "to suffer" in KJV and RV in Matt. 8:21; Mark 10:4; Luke

9:59; Acts 28:16; RV only, Luke 9:61 (KJV, "let"); KJV only, Acts 21:39; in some texts, Matt. 8:31, KJV only.

4. ***aphiemi*** (*863*), "to send away," signifies "to permit, suffer," in Matt. 3:15 (twice); Matt. 19:14; 23:13; Mark 1:34; 5:19, 37; 10:14; 11:16; Luke 8:51; 12:39, KJV (RV, "left"); 18:16; John 12:7, RV, KJV and RV marg., "let (her) alone"; Rev. 11:9.

(b) *to endure suffering*

1. ***anecho*** (*430*), in the middle voice, "to bear with," is rendered "to suffer" in Matt. 17:17 and parallel passages; KJV only, 1 Cor. 4:12 (RV, "endure"); 2 Cor. 11:19, 20 and Heb. 13:22 (RV, bear with).

2. ***pascho*** (*3958*), "to suffer," is used (I) of the "sufferings" of Christ (a) at the hands of men, e.g., Matt. 16:21; 17:12; 1 Pet. 2:23; (b) in His expiatory and vicarious sacrifice for sin, Heb. 9:26; 13:12; 1 Pet. 2:21; 3:18; 4:1; (c) including both (a) and (b), Luke 22:15; 24:26, 46; Acts 1:3, "passion"; 3:18; 17:3; Heb. 5:8; (d) by the antagonism of the evil one, Heb. 2:18; (II), of human "suffering" (a) of followers of Christ, Acts 9:16; 2 Cor. 1:6; Gal. 3:4; Phil. 1:29; 1 Thess. 2:14; 2 Thess. 1:5; 2 Tim. 1:12; 1 Pet. 3:14, 17; 5:10; Rev. 2:10; in identification with Christ in His crucifixion, as the spiritual ideal to be realized, 1 Pet. 4:1; in a wrong way, 4:15; (b) of others, physically, as the result of demoniacal power, Matt. 17:15, RV, "suffereth (grievously)," KJV, "is (sore) vexed"; cf. Mark 5:26; in a dream, Matt. 27:19; through maltreatment, Luke 13:2; 1 Pet. 2:19, 20; by a serpent (negatively), Acts 28:5, RV, "took"; (c) of the effect upon the whole body through the "suffering" of one member, 1 Cor. 12:26, with application to a church.

3. ***propascho*** (*4310*), "to suffer before" (***pro***, and No. 2), occurs in 1 Thess. 2:2.

4. ***sumpascho*** (*4841*), "to suffer with" (***sun***, and No. 2), is used in Rom. 8:17 of "suffering" with Christ; in 1 Cor. 12:26 of joint "suffering" in the members of the body.

5. ***hupecho*** (*5254*), "to hold under" (***hupo***, "under," ***echo***, "to have or hold"), is used metaphorically in Jude 7 of "suffering" punishment.

6. ***kakoucheo*** (*2558*), "to ill-treat" (***kakos***, "evil," and ***echo***, "to have"), is used in the passive voice in Heb. 11:37, RV, "evil entreated" (KJV, "tormented"); in 13:3, RV, "are evil entreated" (KJV, "suffer adversity").

7. ***sunkakoucheomai*** (*4778*), "to endure adversity with," is used in Heb. 11:25 (***sun***, "with," and No. 6), RV, "to be evil entreated with," KJV, "to suffer affliction with."

8. ***makrothumeo*** (*3114*) is rendered "suffereth long" in 1 Cor. 13:4.

9. ***adikeo*** (*91*), "to do wrong, injustice" (***a***, negative, ***dike***, "right"), is used in the passive voice in 2 Pet. 2:13, RV, "suffering wrong" (some texts have ***komizo***, "to receive," KJV); there is a play upon words here which may be brought out thus, "being defrauded (of the wages of fraud)," a use of the verb illustrated in the papyri.

## SUFFERING

***pathema*** (*3804*) is rendered "sufferings" in the RV (KJV, "afflictions") in 2 Tim. 3:11; Heb. 10:32; 1 Pet. 5:9; in Gal. 5:24, "passions (KJV, "affections").

## SUFFICE, SUFFICIENT

### A. Verbs.

1. ***arkeo*** (*714*), "to suffice," is rendered "is sufficient" in John 6:7; 2. Cor. 12:9; "it sufficeth" in John 14:8.

2. ***hikanoo*** (*2427*), "to make sufficient, render fit," is translated "made (us) sufficient" in 2 Cor. 3:6, RV (KJV, "hath made . . . able").

### B. Adjectives.

1. ***hikanos*** (*2425*), akin to A, No. 2, "enough, sufficient, fit," etc. is translated "sufficient" in 2 Cor. 2:6, 16; 3:5.

2. ***arketos*** (*713*), akin to A, No. 1, used with ***eimi***, "to be," is translated "may suffice" in 1 Pet. 4:3.

## SUFFICIENCY

### *Old Testament*

***day*** (1767), "sufficiency; the required; enough." Often used with the meaning of that which is enough or an amount which is sufficient for a need or standard, Exod. 36:7; Jer. 49:9. There are many special uses of ***day*** where the basic meaning is in the background and the context dictates a different nuance. In Job 39:25 the word preceded by the preposition ***be*** may be rendered "as often as": "As often as the trumpet sounds he says, Aha!" (NASB). When preceded by the preposition ***ke***, "as," the word usually means "according to": ". . . The judge shall cause him to lie down, and to be beaten before his face, according to his fault, by a certain number," Deut. 25:2. Preceded by ***min***, "from," the word sometimes means "regarding the need," 1 Sam. 7:16.

### *New Testament*

1. ***autarkeia*** (*841*) (***autos***, "self," ***arkeo***, see A, above; Eng., "autarchy"), "contentment," 1 Tim. 6:6, is rendered "sufficiency" in 2 Cor. 9:5.

2. ***hikanotes*** (*2426*) is rendered "sufficiency" in 2 Cor. 3:5.

S

## SUM (Noun), SUM UP

***anakephalaioo*** (*346*), "to sum up, gather up" (***ana***, "up," ***kephale***, "a head"), "to present as a whole," is used in the passive voice in Rom. 13:9, RV, "summed up" (KJV, "briefly comprehended"), i.e., the one commandment expresses all that the Law enjoins, and to obey this one is to fulfill the Law (cf. Gal. 5:14); middle voice in Eph. 1:10, RV, "sum up" (KJV, "gather together"), of God's purpose to "sum up" all things in the heavens and on the earth in Christ, a consummation extending beyond the limits of the church, though the latter is to be a factor in its realization.

## SUMPTUOUS, SUMPTUOUSLY

### A. Adjective.

***lampros*** (*2986*), "bright," is rendered "sumptuous" in Rev. 18:14, RV.

### B. Adverb.

***lampros*** (*2988*), the corresponding adverb, is used in Luke 16:19, "sumptuously."

## SUPERFLUOUS

***perissos*** (*4053*), "abundant, more than sufficient," is translated "superfluous" in 2 Cor. 9:1.

## SUPERSCRIPTION

***epigraphe*** (*1923*), lit., "an overwriting" (***epi***, "over," ***grapho***, "to write") (the meaning of the anglicized Latin word "superscription"), denotes "an inscription, a title." On Roman coins the emperor's name was inscribed, Matt. 22:20; Mark 12:16; Luke 20:24. In the Roman Empire, in the case of a criminal on his way to execution, a board on which was inscribed the cause of his condemnation, was carried before him or hung round his neck; the inscription was termed a "title" (***titlos***). The four Evangelists state that at the crucifixion of Christ the title was affixed to the cross, Mark (15:26), and Luke (23:38), call it a "superscription"; Mark says it was "written over" (***epigrapho***, the corresponding verb). Matthew calls it "His accusation"; John calls it "a title" (a technical term). The wording varies: the essential words are the same, and the variation serves to authenticate the narratives, showing that there was no consultation leading to an agreement as to the details.

## SUPERSTITIOUS

***deisidaimon*** (*1175*), "reverent to the deity" (***deido***, "to fear"; ***daimon***, "a demon," or "pagan god"), occurs in Acts 17:22 in the comparative degree, rendered "somewhat superstitious," RV (KJV, "too superstitious"), a meaning which the word sometimes has; others, according to its comparative form, advocate the meaning "more religious (than others)," "quite religious" (cf. the noun in 25:19).

## SUPPLICATION

1. ***deesis*** (*1162*) is always translated "supplication," or the plural, in the RV.

2. ***hiketeria*** (*2428*) is the feminine form of the adjective ***hiketerios***, denoting "of a suppliant," and used as a noun, formerly "an olive branch" carried by a suppliant (***hiketes***), then later, "a supplication," used with No. 1 in Heb. 5:7.

## SUPPLY (Noun and Verb)

### A. Verbs.

1. ***choregeo*** (*5524*) primarily, among the Greeks, signified "to lead a stage chorus or dance" (***choros***, and ***hegeomai***, "to lead"), then, "to defray the expenses of a chorus"; hence, later, metaphorically, "to supply," 2 Cor. 9:10 (2nd part; see also No. 2), RV, "supply" (KJV "minister"); 1 Pet. 4:11, RV, "supplieth" (KJV, "giveth").

2. ***epichoregeo*** (*2023*), "to supply fully, abundantly" (a strengthened form of No. 1), is rendered "to supply" in the RV of 2 Cor. 9:10 (1st part) and Gal. 3:5 (for KJV, "to minister"), where the present continuous tense speaks of the work of the Holy Spirit in all His ministrations to believers individually and collectively; in Col. 2:19, RV, "being supplied" (KJV, "having nourishment ministered"), of the work of Christ as the Head of the church His body, in 2 Pet. 1:5, "supply" (KJV, "add"); in v. 11, "shall be . . . supplied" (KJV, "shall be ministered"), of the reward hereafter which those are to receive, in regard to positions in the kingdom of God, for their fulfillment here of the conditions mentioned.

3. ***anapleroo*** (*378*), "to fill up, fulfill," is rendered "to supply" in 1 Cor. 16:17 and Phil. 2:30.

4. ***prosanapleroo*** (*4322*), "to fill up by adding to, to supply fully" (***pros***, "to," and No. 3), is translated "supplieth" in 2 Cor. 9:12, KJV (RV, "filleth up the measure of"); in 11:9, RV and KJV, "supplied."

### B. Noun.

***epichoregia*** (*2024*), "a full supply," occurs in Eph. 4:16, "supplieth," lit., "by the supply of every joint," metaphorically of the members of the church, the body of which Christ is the Head, and Phil. 1:19, "the supply (of the Spirit of Jesus Christ)," i.e., "the bountiful supply"; here "of the Spirit" may be taken either in the subjective sense, the Giver, or the objective, the Gift.

## SUPPOSE

1. ***nomizo*** (*3543*), "to consider, suppose, think," is rendered "to suppose" in Matt. 20:10; Luke 2:34; 3:23; Acts 7:25; 14:19; 16:27; 21:29; 1 Tim. 6:5; in 1 Cor. 7:26, KJV (RV, "I think"); in Acts 16:13, the RV adheres to the meaning "to suppose," "(where) we supposed (there was a place of prayer)"; this word also signifies "to practice a custom" (***nomos***) and is commonly so used by Greek writers. Hence the KJV, "was wont (to be made)"; it is rendered "to think" in Matt. 5:17; 10:34; Acts 8:20; 17:29; 1 Cor. 7:36.

2. ***dokeo*** (*1380*), "to be of opinion," is translated "to suppose" in Mark 6:49; Luke 24:37; John 20:15; Acts 27:13; in the following, KJV "suppose," RV, "think," Luke 12:51; 13:2; Heb. 10:29. It is most frequently rendered "to think," always in Matthew; always in John, except 11:31, "supposing," RV [where the best texts have this verb (for ***lego***, KJV, "saying")], and 20:15 (see above).

3. ***hupolambano*** (*5274*), when used of mental action, signifies "to suppose," Luke 7:43, and Acts 2:15.

4. ***huponoeo*** (*5282*), "to suspect, to conjecture," is translated "suppose ye" in Acts 13:25, RV (KJV, "think ye"); "I supposed" in 25:18.

## SUPREME

***huperecho*** (*5242*), "to be superior, to excel," is translated "supreme" in 1 Pet. 2:13.

## SURE

### A. Adjectives.

1. ***asphales*** (*804*), "safe," is translated "sure" in Heb. 6:19.

2. ***bebaios*** (*949*), "firm, steadfast," is used of (a) God's promise to Abraham, Rom. 4:16; (b) the believer's hope, Heb. 6:19, "steadfast"; (c) the hope of spiritual leaders regarding the welfare of converts, 2 Cor. 1:7, "steadfast"; (d) the glorying of the hope, Heb. 3:6, "firm"; (e) the beginning of our confidence, 3:14, RV, "firm" (KJV, "steadfast"); (f) the Law given at Sinai, Heb. 2:2, "steadfast"; (g) the testament (or covenant) fulfilled after a death, 9:17, "of force"; (h) the calling and election of believers, 2 Pet. 1:10, to be made "sure" by the fulfillment of the injunctions in vv. 5–7; (i) the word of prophecy, "*made* more sure," 2 Pet. 1:19, RV, KJV, "a more sure (word of prophecy)"; what is meant is not a comparison between the prophecies of the OT and NT, but that the former have been confirmed in the person of Christ (vv. 16–18).

### B. Verb.

***asphalizo*** (*805*), "to make safe or sure" (akin to A, No. 1), is rendered "to make sure" in Matt. 27:64, 65, 66, of the sepulchre of Christ; elsewhere, Acts 16:24, of making feet fast in the stocks.

## SURETY (Noun)

***enguos*** (*1450*) primarily signifies "bail," the bail who personally answers for anyone, whether with his life or his property (to be distinguished from ***mesites***, "a mediator"); it is used in Heb. 7:22, "(by so much also hath Jesus become) the Surety (of a better covenant)," referring to the abiding and unchanging character of His Melchizedek priesthood, by reason of which His suretyship is established by God's oath (vv. 20, 21). As the Surety, He is the personal guarantee of the terms of the new and better covenant, secured on the ground of His perfect sacrifice (v. 27).

## SURFEITING

***kraipale*** (*2897*) signifies "the giddiness and headache resulting from excessive wine-bibbing, a drunken nausea," "surfeiting," Luke 21:34. Trench distinguishes this and the synonymous words, ***methe***, "drunkenness," ***oinophlugia***, "wine-bibbing" (KJV, "excess of wine," 1 Pet. 4:3), ***komos***, "revelling."

## SURNAME

***epikaleo*** (*1941*), "to put a name upon" (***epi***, "upon," ***kaleo***, "to call"), "to surname," is used in this sense in the passive voice, in some texts in Matt. 10:3 (it is absent in the best); in Luke 22:3, in some texts (the best have ***kaleo***, "to call"); Acts 1:23; 4:36; 10:5, 18, 32; 11:13; 12:12, 25; in some texts, 15:22 (the best have ***kaleo***).

## SWADDLING CLOTHES

***sparganoo*** (*4683*), "to swathe" (from ***sparganon***, "a swathing band"), signifies "to wrap in swaddling clothes" in Luke 2:7, 12. The idea that the word means "rags" is without foundation.

S

## SWEAR, SWORN

### *Old Testament*

***shaba'*** (7650), "to swear; take an oath." Often "to swear or to take an oath" is to strongly affirm a promise, with sanctions for not following through, often divine sanctions, Josh. 6:22. David and Jonathan strongly affirmed their love for each other with an oath, 1 Sam. 20:17. Allegiance to God is pledged by an oath, Isa. 19:18. Zephaniah condemns the idolatrous priests "that worship and that swear by the Lord, and that swear by Malcham [the Ammonite god]," Zeph. 1:5.

*New Testament*

***omnumi*** or ***omnuo*** (*3660*) is used of "affirming or denying by an oath," e.g., Matt. 26:74; Mark 6:23; Luke 1:73; Heb. 3:11, 18; 4:3; 7:21; accompanied by that by which one swears, e.g., Matt. 5:34, 36; 23:16; Heb. 6:13, 16; Jas. 5:12; Rev. 10:6.

## SWEET

***glukus*** (*1099*) (cf. Eng., "glycerin," "glucose"), occurs in Jas. 3:11, 12 (KJV, "fresh" in this verse); Rev. 10:9, 10.

## SWERVE

***astocheo*** (*795*), "to miss the mark," is translated "having swerved" in 1 Tim. 1:6. Moulton and Milligan illustrate the use of the verb from the papyri, e.g., of a man in extravagant terms bewailing the loss of a pet fighting cock, "(I am distraught, for my cock) has failed (me)."

## SWORD

*Old Testament*

**A. Noun.**

***chereb*** (2719), "sword; dagger; flint knife; chisel." Usually ***chereb*** represents an implement that can be or is being used in war, such as a "sword," Gen. 34:26. It can also refer to a shorter sword, a "dagger," Judg. 3:16; or any knife, Josh. 5:2; or hewing instrument, Exod. 20:25.

This two-edged "sword" can be compared to a tongue; words can be sharp and cut, and wound and kill, Ps. 57:4. This usage tells us not only about the shape of the "sword" but that such a tongue is a violent, merciless, attacking weapon. In Gen. 27:40 "sword" is symbolic of violence: "And by thy sword shalt thou live. . . ." Prov. 5:4 uses ***chereb*** (of a long two-edged "sword") to depict the grievous result of dealing with an adulteress; it is certain death: "But her end is bitter as wormwood, sharp as a two-edged sword."

The "sword" is frequently depicted as an agent of God. It is not only used to safeguard the garden of Eden, but figures the judgment of God executed upon His enemies: "For my sword shall be bathed in heaven: behold, it shall come down upon Idumea . . ." (Isa. 34:5; cf. Deut. 28:22).

**B. Verb.**

***charab*** means "to smite down, slaughter." This verb, which appears 3 times in biblical Hebrew, has cognates in Arabic. The word appears in 2 Kings 3:23: "This is blood: the kings are surely slain."

*New Testament*

1. ***machaira*** (*3162*), "a short sword or dagger" (distinct from No. 2), e.g., Matt. 26:47, 51, 52 and parallel passages; Luke 21:24; 22:38, possibly "a knife"; Heb. 4:12; metaphorically and by metonymy, (a) for ordinary violence, or dissensions, that destroy peace, Matt. 10:34; (b) as the instrument of a magistrate or judge, e.g., Rom. 13:4; (c) of the Word of God, "the sword of the Spirit," probing the conscience, subduing the impulses to sin, Eph. 6:17.

2. ***rhomphaia*** (*4501*), a word of somewhat doubtful origin, denoted "a Thracian weapon of large size," whether a sword or spear is not certain, but usually longer than No. 1; it occurs (a) literally in Rev. 6:8; (b) metaphorically, as the instrument of anguish, Luke 2:35; of judgment, Rev. 1:16; 2:12, 16; 19:15, 21, probably figurative of the Lord's judicial utterances.

## SYNAGOGUE

***sunagoge*** (*4864*), properly "a bringing together" (***sun***, "together," ***ago***, "to bring"), denoted (a) "a gathering of things, a collection," then, of "persons, an assembling, of Jewish religious gatherings," e.g., Acts 9:2; an assembly of Christian Jews, Jas. 2:2, RV, "synagogue" (KJV, marg.; text, "assembly"); a company dominated by the power and activity of Satan, Rev. 29; 39; (b) by metonymy, "the building" in which the gathering is held, e.g. Matt. 6:2; Mark 1:21. The origin of the Jewish "synagogue" is probably to be assigned to the time of the Babylonian exile. Having no temple, the Jews assembled on the Sabbath to hear the Law read, and the practice continued in various buildings after the return.

## SYNAGOGUE (put out of the)

***aposunagogos*** (*656*), an adjective denoting "expelled from the congregation, excommunicated," is used (a) with ***ginomai***, "to become, be made," John 9:22; 12:42; (b) with ***poieo***, "to make," John 16:2. This excommunication involved prohibition not only from attendance at the "synagogue," but from all fellowship with Israelites.

## SYNAGOGUE (ruler of the)

***archisunagogos*** (*752*) denotes "the administrative official," with the duty of preserving order and inviting persons to read or speak in the assembly, Mark 5:22, 35, 36, 38; Luke 8:49; 13:14; Acts 13:15; "chief ruler" (KJV) in Acts 18:8, 17.

# T

## TABERNACLE

### *Old Testament*

**A. Noun.**

***mishkan*** (4908), "dwelling place; tabernacle; shrine." This was a construction made of leather and goat hair, which was moveable. This construction was used as a holy place to worship the Lord, Exod. 25:9; Lev. 15:31; cf. Num. 19:13. The Tabernacle was built in the time of Moses and remained the holy place of Israel until the Temple was built, 2 Sam. 7:6; Ps. 132:4–5. The meaning of ***mishkan*** was also extended to include the whole area surrounding the temple, including as much as the city Jerusalem, Ps. 46:4; 87:2.

The defilement of the city and the temple area was sufficient reason for God to leave the temple, Ezek. 10, and to permit the destruction of His "dwelling place" by the brutish Babylonians, Ps. 74:7. In the Lord's providence He had planned to restore His people and the temple so as to assure them of His continued presence, Ezek. 37:27–28. John comments that Jesus Christ was God's "tabernacle": "And the Word was made flesh, and dwelt among us, (and we beheld his glory, the glory as of the only begotten of the Father,) full of grace and truth," John 1:14, and Jesus later referred to Himself as the temple: "But He spake of the temple of his body," John 2:21.

**B. Verb.**

***shakan*** (7934), "to dwell, inhabit," Ps. 37:27.

### *New Testament*

1. ***skene*** (*4633*), "a tent, booth, tabernacle," is used of (a) tents as dwellings, Matt. 17:4; Mark 9:5; Luke 9:33; Heb. 11:9, KJV, "tabernacles" (RV, "tents"); (b) the Mosaic tabernacle, Acts 7:44; Heb. 8:5; 9:1 (in some mss.); 9:8, 21, termed "the tent of meeting," RV (i.e., where the people were called to meet God), a preferable description to "the tabernacle of the congregation," as in the KJV in the OT; the outer part 9:2, 6; the inner sanctuary, 9:3; (c) the heavenly prototype, Heb. 8:2; 9:11; Rev. 13:6; 15:5; 21:3 (of its future descent); (d) the eternal abodes of the saints, Luke 16:9, RV, "tabernacles" (KJV, "habitations"); (e) the Temple in Jerusalem, as continuing the service of the tabernacle, Heb. 13:10; (f) the house of David, i.e., metaphorically of his people, Acts 15:16; (g) the portable shrine of the god Moloch, Acts 7:43.

2. ***skenos*** (*4636*), the equivalent of No. 1, is used metaphorically of the body as the "tabernacle" of the soul, 2 Cor. 5:1, 4.

3. ***skenoma*** (*4638*) occurs in Acts 7:46; 2 Pet. 1:13, 14.

4. ***skenopegia*** (*4634*), properly "the setting up of tents or dwellings" (No. 1, and ***pegnumi***, "to fix"), represents the word "tabernacles" in "the feast of tabernacles," John 7:2. This feast, one of the three Pilgrimage Feasts in Israel, is called "the feast of ingathering" in Exod. 23:16; 34:22; it took place at the end of the year, and all males were to attend at the "tabernacle" with their offerings. In Lev. 23:34; Deut. 16:13, 16; 31:10; 2 Chron. 8:13; Ezra 3:4 (cf. Neh. 8:14–18), it is called "the feast of tabernacles" (or "booths," ***sukkoth***), and was appointed for seven days at Jerusalem from the 15th to the 22nd Tishri (approximately October), to remind the people that their fathers dwelt in these in the wilderness journeys. Cf. Num. 29:15–38, especially v. 35–38, for the regulations of the eighth or "last day, the great day of the feast" (John 7:37).

## TABLE

1. ***trapeza*** (*5132*) is used of (a) "a dining table," Matt. 15:27; Mark 7:28; Luke 16:21; 22:21, 30; (b) "the table of shewbread," Heb. 9:2; (c) by metonymy, of "what is provided on the table" (the word being used of that with which it is associated), Acts 16:34; Rom. 11:9 (figurative of the special privileges granted to Israel and centering in Christ); 1 Cor. 10:21 (twice), "the Lord's table," denoting all that is provided for believers in Christ on the ground of His death (and thus expressing something more comprehensive than the Lord's Supper); "the table of demons," denoting all that is partaken of by idolaters as the result of the influence of demons in connection with their sacrifices; (d) "a moneychanger's table," Matt. 21:12; Mark 11:15; John 2:15; (e) "a bank," Luke 19:23; (f) by metonymy for "the distribution of money," Acts 6:2.

2. ***plax*** (*4109*) primarily denotes "anything flat and broad," hence, "a flat stone, a tablet," 2 Cor. 3:3 (twice); Heb. 9:4.

## TALK (Noun and Verb)

**A. Noun.**

***leros*** (*3026*) denotes "foolish talk, nonsense," Luke 24:11, RV, "idle talk" (KJV, "idle tales").

**B. Verbs.**

1. ***laleo*** (*2980*), "to speak, say," is always translated "to speak" in the RV, where the KJV renders it by "to talk," Matt. 12:46; Mark 6:50; Luke 24:32; John 4:27 (twice); 9:37; 14:30; Acts 26:31; Rev. 4:1; 17:1; 21:9, 15. The RV rendering is preferable; the idea of "chat" or "chatter" is entirely foreign to the NT, and should never be regarded as the meaning in 1 Cor. 14:34, 35.

2. ***sullaleo*** (*4814*), "to speak with" (***sun***), is translated "to talk with," Matt. 17:3; Mark 9:4; Luke 9:30.

3. ***homileo*** (*3656*), "to be in company with, consort with" (***homilos***, "a throng"; ***homilia***, "company"), hence, "to converse with," is rendered "to talk with," Acts 20:11.

4. ***sunomileo*** (*4926*), "to converse, talk with," occurs in Acts 10:27.

## TALKERS (vain)

***mataiologos*** (*3151*), an adjective denoting "talking idly" (***mataios***, "vain, idle," ***lego***, "to speak"), is used as a noun (plural) in Titus 1:10.

## TALKING (vain, foolish)

1. ***mataiologia*** (*3150*), a noun corresponding to the above, is used in 1 Tim. 1:6, RV, "vain talking" (KJV, "vain jangling").

2. ***morologia*** (*3473*), from ***moros***, "foolish, dull, stupid," and ***lego***, is used in Eph. 5:4; it denotes more than mere idle "talk." Trench describes it as "that 'talk of fools' which is foolishness and sin together."

## TAME

***damazo*** (*1150*), "to subdue, tame," is used (a) naturally in Mark 5:4 and Jas. 3:7 (twice); (b) metaphorically, of the tongue, in Jas. 3:8.

## TANNER

***burseus*** (*1038*), "a tanner" (from ***bursa***, "a hide"), occurs in Acts 9:43; 10:6, 32.

## TARES

***zizanion*** (*2215*) is a kind of darnel, the commonest of the four species, being the bearded, growing in the grain fields, as tall as wheat and barley, and resembling wheat in appearance. It was credited among the Jews with being degenerate wheat. The rabbis called it "bastard." The seeds are poisonous to man and herbivorous animals, producing sleepiness, nausea, convulsions and even death (they are harmless to poultry). The plants can be separated out, but the custom, as in the parable, is to leave the cleaning out till near the time of harvest, Matt. 13:25–27, 29, 30, 36, 38, 40. The Lord describes the tares as "the sons of the evil *one*"; false teachings are not distinguishable from their propagandists.

## TARRY

1. ***meno*** (*3306*), "to abide," is translated by the verb "to abide," in the RV, for KJV, "to tarry," in Matt. 26:38; Mark 14:34; Luke 24:29; John 4:40; Acts 9:43; 18:20; the RV retains the verb "to tarry" in John 21:22, 23; in Acts 20:5, KJV, "tarried" (RV, "were waiting"). Some mss. have it in Acts 20:15 (KJV, "tarried").

2. ***epimeno*** (*1961*), to abide, continue, a strengthened form of No. 1, is translated "to tarry" in Acts 10:48; 21:4, 10; 28:12, 14; 1 Cor. 16:7, 8; Gal. 1:18, RV (KJV, "abode").

3. ***hupomeno*** (*5278*), "to endure," is rendered "tarried behind" in Luke 2:43.

4. ***prosmeno*** (*4357*), "to abide still, continue," is translated "tarried" in Acts 18:18, suggesting patience and steadfastness in remaining after the circumstances which preceded; in 1 Tim. 1:3, RV, "to tarry" (KJV, "to abide still").

5. ***diatribo*** (*1304*), is invariably rendered "to tarry," in the RV; KJV, twice, John 3:22; Acts 25:6; "continued" in John 11:54; Acts 15:35; "abode," Acts 12:19; 14:3, 28; 20:6; "abiding," 16:12, "had been," 25:14.

6. ***chronizo*** (*5549*), "to spend or while away time"; "to tarry," Matt. 25:5; Luke 1:21; Heb. 10:37.

7. ***braduno*** (*1019*), "to be slow," is rendered "I tarry long," 1 Tim. 3:15; "is . . . slack," 2 Pet. 3:9.

8. ***kathizo*** (*2523*), "to make to sit down," or, intransitively, "to sit down," is translated "tarry ye" in Luke 24:49.

9. ***mello*** (*3195*), "to be about to," is rendered "(why) tarriest thou?" in Acts 22:16.

10. ***ekdechomai*** (*1551*), "to expect, await" (***ek***, "from," ***dechomai***, "to receive"), is translated "tarry" in 1 Cor. 11:33, KJV (RV, "wait).

## TASTE

***geuo*** (*1089*), "to make to taste," is used in the middle voice, signifying "to taste" (a) naturally, Matt. 27:34; Luke 14:24; John 2:9; Col. 2:21; (b) metaphorically, of Christ's "tasting" death, implying His personal experience in voluntarily undergoing death, Heb. 2:9; of believers (negatively) as to "tasting" of death,

Matt. 16:28; Mark 9:1; Luke 9:27; John 8:52; of "tasting" the heavenly gift (different from receiving it), Heb. 6:4; "the good word of God, and the powers of the age to come," 6:5; "that the Lord is gracious," 1 Pet. 2:3.

## TATTLER

***phluaros*** (*5397*), "babbling, garrulous" (from ***phluo***, "to babble": cf. ***phluareo***, "to prate against"), is translated "tattlers" in 1 Tim. 5:13.

## TAUGHT (Adjective)

1. ***didaktos*** (*1318*), primarily "what can be taught," then, "taught," is used (a) of persons, John 6:45; (b) of things, 1 Cor. 2:13 (twice), "(not in words which man's wisdom) teacheth, (but which the Spirit) teacheth," lit., "(not in words) taught (of man's wisdom, but) taught (of the Spirit)."

2. ***theodidaktos*** (*2312*), "God-taught" (***theos***, "God," and No. 1), occurs in 1 Thess. 4:9, lit., "God-taught (persons)"; while the missionaries had "taught" the converts to love one another, God had Himself been their Teacher. Cf. John 6:45 (see No. 1).

## TEACH

### *Old Testament*

**A. Verbs.**

***lamad*** (3925), "to teach, learn, cause to learn." In its simple, active form, this verb has the meaning "to learn," but it is also found in a form giving the causative sense, "to teach," Deut. 4:1. In Deut. 5:1 ***lamad*** is used of learning God's laws, cf. Ps. 119:7.

***yarah*** (3384), "throw, teach, shoot, point out." The basic idea of "to throw" is easily extended to mean the shooting of arrows, 1 Sam. 20:36–37. "To throw" seems to be further extended to mean "to point," by which fingers are thrown in a certain direction, Gen. 46:28; Prov. 6:13. From this meaning it is only a short step to the concept of teaching as the "pointing out" of fact and truth. Thus, Bezalel was inspired by God "to teach" others his craftsmanship, Exod. 35:34; the false prophets "teach" lies, Isa. 9:15; and the father "taught" his son, Prov. 4:4.

**B. Noun.**

***torah*** (8451), "direction; instruction; guideline." ***torah*** is much more than law or a set of rules. ***torah*** is not restriction or hindrance, but instead the means whereby one can reach a goal or ideal. In the truest sense, ***torah*** was given to Israel to enable her to truly become and remain God's special people. One might say that in keeping ***torah***, Israel was kept. Unfortunately, Israel fell into the trap of keeping ***torah*** as something imposed, and for itself, rather than as a means of becoming what God intended for her. The means became the end. Instead of seeing ***torah*** as a guideline, it became an external body of rules, and thus a weight rather than a freeing and guiding power. This burden, plus the legalism of Roman law, forms the background of the New Testament tradition of law, especially as Paul struggles with it in his Letter to the church at Rome.

**C. Adjective.**

***limmud*** means "taught." This adjective forms an exact equivalent to the New Testament idea of "disciple, one who is taught," Isa. 8:16: 54:13.

### *New Testament*

**A. Verbs.**

1. ***didasko*** (*1321*) is used (a) absolutely, "to give instruction," e.g., Matt. 4:23; 9:35; Rom. 12:7; 1 Cor. 4:17; 1 Tim. 2:12; 4:11; (b) transitively, with an object, whether persons, e.g., Matt. 5:2; 7:29, and frequently in the Gospels and Acts, or things "taught," e.g., Matt. 15:9; 22:16; Acts 15:35; 18:11; both persons and things, e.g., John 14:26; Rev. 2:14, 20.

2. ***katecheo*** (*2727*), rendered "to teach" in 1 Cor. 14:19, KJV (RV, "instruct"); Gal. 6:6 (twice).

3. ***heterodidaskaleo*** (*2085*), "to teach a different doctrine" (***heteros***, "different," to be distinguished from ***allos***, "another of the same kind," is used in 1 Tim. 1:3; 6:3, RV, KJV, "teach (no) other doctrine" and "teach otherwise," of what is contrary to the faith.

**B. Adjective.**

***didaktikos*** (*1317*), "skilled in teaching" (akin to No. 1 above: Eng., "didactic"), is translated "apt to teach" in 1 Tim. 3:2; 2 Tim. 2:24.

## TEACHER, FALSE TEACHERS

1. ***didaskalos*** (*1320*) is rendered "teacher" or "teachers" in Matt. 23:8, by Christ, of Himself; in John 3:2 of Christ; of Nicodemus in Israel, 3:10, RV; of "teachers" of the truth in the churches, Acts 13:1; 1 Cor. 12:28, 29; Eph. 4:11; Heb. 5:12; Jas. 3:1, RV; by Paul of his work among the churches, 1 Tim. 2:7; 2 Tim. 1:11; of "teachers," wrongfully chosen by those who have "itching ears," 2 Tim. 4:3.

2. ***kalodidaskalos*** (*2567*) denotes "a teacher of what is good" (***kalos***), Titus 2:3.

3. ***pseudodidaskalos*** (*5572*), "a false teacher," occurs in the plural in 2 Pet. 2:1.

## TEARS

***dakruon*** or ***dakru*** (*1144*), akin to ***dakruo***, "to weep," is used in the plural, Mark 9:24; Luke 7:38, 44 (with the sense of washing therewith the Lord's feet); Acts 20:19, 31; 2 Cor. 2:4; 2 Tim. 1:4; Heb. 5:7; 12:17; Rev. 7:17; 21:4.

## TEDIOUS (to be)

***enkopto*** (*1465*), "to hinder," is rendered "to be tedious" in Acts 24:4, of detaining a person unnecessarily.

## TELL

### *Old Testament*

**A. Verb.**

***nagad*** (5046), "to tell, explain, inform." The first emphasis of the word is "to tell," i.e., speak verbal information to another, often reporting an event, Gen. 9:22; or giving an important message, Gen. 14:13; finally, ***nagad*** means "to explain or reveal" something one does not otherwise know, Gen. 3:11. 1 Sam. 27:11; Isa. 58:1.

**B. Noun.**

***nagid*** (5057), "chief leader." In 1 Sam. 9:16 the word is used as a "chief leader" that is equivalent to a king, 1 Chron. 9:11, 20.

**C. Preposition.**

***neged*** (5048), "before; in the presence of; in the sight of; in front of; in one's estimation; straight ahead." Basically the word indicates that its object is immediately "before" something or someone. It is used in Gen. 2:18, where God said He would make Adam "a help meet for him," or someone to correspond to him, just as the males and females of the animals corresponded to (matched) one another. To be immediately "before" the sun is to be fully in the sunlight, Num. 25:4. In Exod. 10:10 Pharaoh told Moses that evil was immediately "before" his face, or was in his mind. ***neged*** signifies "in front of," Exod. 19:2, "before" in the sense of "in one's estimation," Isa. 40:17, and "straight ahead (before)," Josh. 6:5.

**D. Adverb.**

***neged*** (5048), "opposite; over against," Gen. 21:16.

### *New Testament*

1. ***lego*** (*3004*) and the 2nd aorist form ***eipon***, used to supply this tense in ***lego***, are frequently translated "to tell," e.g., Matt. 2:13, RV, "I tell," KJV, "I bring (thee) word"; 10:27.

2. ***laleo*** (*2980*), rendered "to speak," in the RV (for KJV, "to tell"), e.g., Matt. 26:13; Luke 1:45; 2:17, 18, 20; Acts 11:14; 27:25; but RV and KJV, "to tell" in John 8:40; Acts 9:6; 22:10.

3. ***apangello*** (*518*), "to announce, declare, report" (usually as a messenger), is frequently rendered "to tell," e.g., Matt. 8:33; 14:12.

4. ***anangello*** (*312*), "to bring back word, announce," is sometimes rendered "to tell," e.g., John 5:15; 2 Cor. 7:7.

## TEMPERANCE, TEMPERATE

**A. Noun.**

***enkrateia*** (*1466*), from ***kratos***, "strength," occurs in Acts 24:25; Gal. 5:23; 2 Pet. 1:6 (twice), in all of which it is rendered "temperance"; the RV marg., "self-control" is the preferable rendering, as "temperance" is now limited to one form of self-control; the various powers bestowed by God upon man are capable of abuse; the right use demands the controlling power of the will under the operation of the Spirit of God; in Acts 24:25 the word follows "righteousness," which represents God's claims, self-control being man's response thereto; in 2 Pet. 1:6, it follows "knowledge," suggesting that what is learned requires to be put into practice.

**B. Adjectives.**

1. ***enkrates*** (*1468*), akin to A, denotes "exercising self-control," rendered "temperate" in Titus 1:8.

2. ***nephalios*** (*3524*), translated "temperate" in 1 Tim. 3:2, RV (KJV, "vigilant"); in 3:11 and Titus 2:2, RV (KJV, "sober").

**C. Verb.**

***enkrateuomai*** (*1467*), akin to A and B, No. 1, rendered "is temperate" in 1 Cor. 9:25, is used figuratively of the rigid self-control practiced by athletes with a view to gaining the prize.

## TEMPEST

1. ***thuella*** (*2366*), "a hurricane, cyclone, whirlwind" (akin to ***thuo***, "to slay," and ***thumos***, "wrath"), is used in Heb. 12:18.

2. ***seismos*** (*4578*), "a shaking" (Eng., "seismic," etc.), is used of a "tempest" in Matt. 8:24.

3. ***cheimon*** (*5494*), "winter, a winter storm," hence, in general, "a tempest," is so rendered in Acts 27:20.

4. ***lailaps*** (*2978*), "a tempest," 2 Pet. 2:17, KJV.

## TEMPESTUOUS

***tuphonikos*** (*5189*), from ***tuphon***, "a hurricane, typhoon," is translated "tempestuous" in Acts 27:14.

## TEMPLE

### *Old Testament*

***hekal*** (1964), "palace; temple." This is a construction, often very beautiful and ornate, as the dwelling place of a king or a god (or the true God), 1 Sam. 1:9. The word "palace" in English versions is a residence for a king, 1 Kings 21:1; of the king of Babylon, 2 Kings 20:18; of Nineveh, Nah. 2:6. ***hekal*** with the meaning "temple" is generally clarified in the context by two markers that follow. The first marker is the addition "of the Lord," Ezra 3:10; it was a holy place, Ps. 79:1. Sometimes the definite article suffices to identify the "temple in Jerusalem," Isa. 6:1; Ezekiel's temple, Ezek. 41.

The Old Testament also speaks about the heavenly ***hekal***, the ***hekal*** of God. It is difficult to decide on a translation, whether "palace" or "temple." Most versions opt in favor of the "temple" idea: "Hear, all ye people; hearken, O earth, and all that therein is: and let the Lord God be witness against you, the Lord from his holy temple," Mic. 1:2; cf. Ps. 5:7; 11:4; Hab. 2:20.

### *New Testament*

1. ***hieron*** (*2411*), the neuter of the adjective ***hieros***, "sacred," is used as a noun denoting "a sacred place, a temple," that of Artemis (Diana), Acts 19:27; that in Jerusalem, Mark 11:11, signifying the entire building with its precincts, or some part thereof, as distinct from the ***naos***, "the inner sanctuary" (see No. 2); apart from the Gospels and Acts, it is mentioned only in 1 Cor. 9:13. Christ taught in one of the courts, to which all the people had access. ***hieron*** is never used figuratively. The Temple mentioned in the Gospels and Acts was begun by Herod in 20 B.C., and destroyed by the Romans in A.D. 70.

2. ***naos*** (*3485*), "a shrine or sanctuary," was used (a) among the heathen, to denote the shrine containing the idol, Acts 17:24; 19:24 (in the latter, miniatures); (b) among the Jews, the sanctuary in the "Temple," into which only the priests could lawfully enter, e.g., Luke 1:9, 21, 22; Christ, as being of the tribe of Judah, and thus not being a priest while upon the earth (Heb. 7:13, 14; 8:4), did not enter the ***naos***; for 2 Thess. 2:4; (c) by Christ metaphorically, of His own physical body, John 2:19, 21; (d) in apostolic teaching, metaphorically, (1) of the church, the mystical body of Christ, Eph. 2:21; (2) of a local church, 1 Cor. 3:16, 17; 2 Cor. 6:16; (3) of the present body of the individual believer, 1 Cor. 6:19; (4) of the "Temple" seen in visions in the Apocalypse, 3:12; 7:15; 11:19; 14:15, 17; 15:5, 6, 8; 16:1, 17; (5) of the Lord God Almighty and the Lamb, as the "Temple" of the new and heavenly Jerusalem, Rev. 21:22.

## TEMPORAL

***proskairos*** (*4340*), "for a season" (***pros***, "for," ***kairos***, "a season"), is rendered "temporal" in 2 Cor. 4:18.

## TEMPT

### A. Verbs.

1. ***peirazo*** (*3985*) signifies (1) "to try, attempt, assay"; (2) "to test, try, prove," in a good sense, said of Christ and of believers, Heb. 2:18, where the context shows that the temptation was the cause of suffering to Him, and only suffering, not a drawing away to sin, so that believers have the sympathy of Christ as their High Priest in the suffering which sin occasions to those who are in the enjoyment of communion with God; so in the similar passage in 4:15; in all the temptations which Christ endured, there was nothing within Him that answered to sin. There was no sinful infirmity in Him. While He was truly man, and His divine nature was not in any way inconsistent with His Manhood, there was nothing in Him such as is produced in us by the sinful nature which belongs to us; in Heb. 11:37, of the testing of OT saints; in 1 Cor. 10:13, where the meaning has a wide scope, the verb is used of "testing" as permitted by God, and of the believer as one who should be in the realization of his own helplessness and his dependence upon God; in a bad sense, "to tempt" (a) of attempts to ensnare Christ in His speech, e.g., Matt. 16:1; 19:3; 22:18, 35, and parallel passages; John 8:6; (b) of temptations to sin, e.g., Gal. 6:1, where one who would restore an erring brother is not to act as his judge, but as being one with him in liability to sin, with the possibility of finding himself in similar circumstances, Jas. 1:13, 14; of temptations mentioned as coming from the Devil, Matt. 4:1; and parallel passages; 1 Cor. 7:5; 1 Thess. 3:5; (c) of trying or challenging God, Acts 15:10; 1 Cor. 10:9 (2nd part); Heb. 3:9; the Holy Spirit, Acts 5:9: cf. No. 2.

2. ***ekpeirazo*** (*1598*), an intensive form of the foregoing, is used in much the same way as No. 1 (2) (c), in Christ's quotation from Deut. 6:16, in reply to the Devil, Matt. 4:7; Luke 4:12; so in 1 Cor. 10:9, RV, "the Lord" (KJV, "Christ"); of the lawyer who "tempted" Christ, Luke 10:25.

### B. Adjective.

***apeirastos*** (*551*), "untempted, untried" (***a***, negative, and A, No. 1), occurs in Jas. 1:13, with ***eimi***, "to be," "cannot be tempted," "untemptable" (Mayor).

## TEMPTATION

***peirasmos*** (*3986*), akin to A, above, is used of (1) "trials" with a beneficial purpose and effect, (a) of "trials" or "temptations," divinely permitted or sent, Luke 22:28; Acts 20:19; Jas. 1:2; 1 Pet. 1:6; 4:12, RV, "to prove," KJV, "to try"; 2 Pet. 2:9 (singular); Rev. 3:10, RV, "trial" (KJV, "temptation"); in Jas. 1:12, "temptation" apparently has meanings (1) and (2) combined, and is used in the widest sense; (b) with a good or neutral significance, Gal. 4:14, of Paul's physical infirmity, "a temptation" to the Galatian converts, of such a kind as to arouse feelings of natural repugnance; (c) of "trials" of a varied character, Matt. 6:13 and Luke 11:4, where believers are commanded to pray not to be led into such by forces beyond their own control; Matt. 26:41; Mark 14:38; Luke 22:40, 46, where they are commanded to watch and pray against entering into "temptations" by their own carelessness or disobedience; in all such cases God provides "the way of escape," 1 Cor. 10:13 (where ***peirasmos*** occurs twice). (2) Of "trial" definitely designed to lead to wrong doing, "temptation," Luke 4:13; 8:13; 1 Tim. 6:9; (3) of "trying" or challenging God, by men, Heb. 3:8.

## TEMPTER

The present participle of ***peirazo***, "to tempt," preceded by the article, lit., "the (one) tempting," is used as a noun, describing the Devil in this character, Matt. 4:3; 1 Thess. 3:5. See TEMPT 1, above.

## TENDER

***hapalos*** (527), "soft, tender," is used of the branch of a tree, Matt. 24:32; Mark 13:28.

## TENTMAKERS

***skenopoios*** (*4635*), an adjective, "tentmaking," is used as a noun in Acts 18:3.

## TERM (appointed)

***prothesmios*** (*4287*), an adjective denoting "appointed beforehand," is used as a noun, ***prothesmia*** (grammatically feminine, with ***hemera***, "a day," understood), as in Greek law, "a day appointed before," Gal. 4:2, RV, "the term appointed," i.e., "a stipulated date" (KJV, "the time appointed").

## TERRESTRIAL

***epigeios*** (*1919*), "on earth, earthly" (***epi***, "on," ***ge***, "the earth"), is rendered "terrestrial" in 1 Cor. 15:40 (twice), in contrast to ***epouranios***, "heavenly."

## TERRIFY

**A. Verbs.**

1. ***ptoeo*** (*4422*), "to terrify," is used in the passive voice, Luke 21:9; 24:37.

2. ***ekphobeo*** (*1629*), "to frighten away" (***ek***, "out," ***phobos***, "fear"), occurs in 2 Cor. 10:9.

3. ***pturo*** (*4426*), "to scare," Phil. 1:28.

**B. Adjective.**

***emphobos*** (*1719*), "terrified," is so rendered in the RV of Acts 24:25.

## TERROR

1. ***phobos*** (*5401*), "fear," is rendered "terror" in Rom. 13:3; in 2 Cor. 5:11 and 1 Pet. 3:14, KJV (RV, "fear").

2. ***phobetron*** (*5400*), "that which causes fright, a terror," is translated "terrors" in Luke 21:11, RV (KJV, "fearful sights").

## TO TEST

**A. Verb.**

***tsarap*** (6884), "to refine, try, smelt, test." ***tsarap*** has the meaning "to refine" in rabbinic and modern Hebrew, but lost the primary significance of "to smelt," and then also a meaning, "test, try." Jeremiah describes the process of smelting and refining, Jer. 6:30; Isa. 40:19; 41:7. ***tsarap*** is also used metaphorically with the sense "to refine by means of suffering," Ps. 66:10–12; Isa. 1:25. Those who were thus purified are those who call on the name of the Lord and receive the gracious benefits of the covenant, Zech. 13:9. The coming of the messenger of the covenant (Jesus Christ) is compared to the work of a smith, Mal. 3:2–3. The believer can take comfort in the Word of God which alone on earth is tried and purified and by which we can be purified: "Thy promise is well tried, and thy servant loves it," Ps. 119:140, RSV; cf. Ps. 18:30; Prov. 30:5.

**B. Nouns.**

Two nouns derived from the verb ***tsarap*** occur rarely. ***tsorpi*** occurs once to mean "goldsmith," Neh. 3:31. ***matsrep*** occurs twice and refers to a "crucible," Prov. 17:3; cf. Prov. 27:21.

## TESTATOR

***diatithemi*** (*1303*), "to arrange, dispose," is used only in the middle voice in the NT; in Heb. 9:16, 17. "There can be little doubt that the word (***diatheke***) must be invariably taken in this sense of 'covenant' in the NT, and especially in a book . . . so impregnated with the language of the Sept. as the Epistle to the Hebrews" (Hatch). We may render somewhat literally thus: For where a covenant (is), a death (is) necessary to be brought in of the one covenanting; for a covenant over dead ones (victims) is sure, since never has it force when the one covenanting lives [Christ being especially in view]. The writer is speaking from a Jewish point of view, not from that of the Greeks. "To adduce the fact that in the case of wills the death of the testator is the condition of validity, is, of course, no proof at all that a death is necessary to make a covenant valid . . . To support his argument, proving the necessity of Christ's death, the writer adduces the general law that he who makes a covenant does so at the expense of life" (Marcus Dods). This refers not to the making of a will (a testator), but the making of a covenant.

## TESTIFY

1. ***martureo*** (*3140*), rendered "to bear witness, to witness," in the RV, where KJV renders it "to testify," John 2:25; 3:11, 32; 5:39; 15:26; 21:24; 1 Cor. 15:15; Heb. 7:17; 11:4; 1 John 4:14; 5:9; 3 John 3. In the following, however, the RV, like the KJV, has the rendering "to testify," John 4:39, 44; 7:7; 13:21; Acts 26:5; Rev. 22:16, 18, 20.

2. ***epimartureo*** (*1957*), "to bear witness to" (a strengthened form of No. 1), is rendered "testifying" in 1 Pet. 5:12.

3. ***marturomai*** (*3143*), primarily, "to summon as witness," then, "to bear witness" (sometimes with the suggestion of solemn protestation), is rendered "to testify" in Acts 20:26, RV (KJV, "I take . . . to record"); 26:22, in the best texts (some have No. 1), RV; Gal. 5:3; Eph. 4:17; 1 Thess. 2:11, in the best texts (some have No. 1), RV, "testifying" (KJV, "charged").

4. ***diamarturomai*** (*1263*), "to testify or protest solemnly," an intensive form of No. 3, is translated "to testify" in Luke 16:28; Acts 2:40; 8:25; 10:42; 18:5; 20:21, 23, 24; 23:11; 28:23; 1 Thess. 4:6; Heb. 2:6; "to charge" in 1 Tim. 5:21; 2 Tim. 2:14; 4:8.

5. ***promarturomai*** (*4303*), "to testify beforehand," occurs in 1 Pet. 1:11, where the pronoun "it" should be "He" (the "it" being due to the grammatically neuter form of ***pneuma***; the personality of the Holy Spirit requires the masculine pronoun).

## TESTIMONY

### *Old Testament*

***'edut*** (5715), "testimony; ordinance." This word refers to the Ten Commandments as a solemn divine charge or duty. In particular, it represents those commandments as written on the tablets and existing as a reminder and "testimony" of Israel's relationship and responsibility to God, Exod. 31:18. Elsewhere these tablets are called simply "the testimony," Exod. 25:16. Since they were kept in the ark, it became known as the "ark of the testimony," Exod. 25:22, or simply "the testimony": "As the Lord commanded Moses, so Aaron laid it up before the Testimony, to be kept," Exod. 16:34. The word sometimes refers to the entire law of God, Ps. 19:7. Here ***'edut*** is synonymously parallel to "law," making it a synonym to that larger concept. Special or particular laws are sometimes called "testimonies," 1 Kings 2:3.

### *New Testament*

1. ***marturion*** (*3142*), "a testimony, witness," is almost entirely translated "testimony" in both KJV and RV. The only place where both have "witness" is Acts 4:33. In Acts 7:44 and Jas. 5:3, the RV has "testimony" (KJV, "witness").

In 2 Thess. 1:10, "our testimony unto you," RV, refers to the fact that the missionaries, besides proclaiming the truths of the gospel, had borne witness to the power of these truths. ***kerugma***, "the thing preached, the message," is objective, having especially to do with the effect on the hearers; ***marturion*** is mainly subjective, having to do especially with the preacher's personal experience.

2. ***marturia*** (*3141*), "witness, evidence, testimony," is almost always rendered "witness" in the RV (for KJV, "testimony" in John 3:32, 33; 5:34; 8:17; 21:24, and always for KJV, "record," e.g., 1 John 5:10, 11), except in Acts 22:18 and in the Apocalypse, where both, with one exception, have "testimony," 1:2, 9; 6:9; 11:7; 12:11, 17; 19:10 (twice); 20:4 (KJV, "witness"). In 19:10, "the testimony of Jesus" is objective, the "testimony" or witness given to Him (cf. 1:2, 9; as to those who will bear it, see Rev. 12:17, RV). The statement "the testimony of Jesus is the spirit of prophecy," is to be understood in the light, e.g., of the "testimony" concerning Christ and Israel in the Psalms, which will be used by the godly Jewish remnant in the coming time of "Jacob's Trouble." All such "testimony" centers in and points to Christ.

## TETRARCH

### A. Noun.

***tetraarches*** or ***tetrarches*** (*5076*) denotes "one of four rulers" (***tetra***, "four," ***arche***, "rule"), properly, "the governor of the fourth part of a region"; hence, "a dependent princeling," or "any petty ruler" subordinate to kings or ethnarchs; in the NT, Herod Antipas, Matt. 14:1; Luke 3:19; 9:7; Acts 13:1.

**B. Verb.**

***tetraarcheo*** or ***tetrarcheo*** (*5075*), "to be a tetrarch," occurs in Luke 3:1 (thrice), of Herod Antipas, his brother Philip and Lysanias. Antipas and Philip each inherited a fourth part of his father's dominions. Inscriptions bear witness to the accuracy of Luke's details.

## THANK, THANKS (Noun and Verb), THANKFUL, THANKFULNESS, THANKSGIVING, THANKWORTHY

**A. Nouns.**

1. ***charis*** (*5485*), rendered "thank" in Luke 6:32, 33, 34; in 17:9, "doth he thank" is lit., "hath he thanks to"; it is rendered "thanks (be to God)" in Rom. 6:17, RV (KJV, "God be thanked"); "thanks" in 1 Cor. 15:57; in 1 Tim. 1:12 and 2 Tim. 1:3, "I thank" is, lit., "I have thanks"; "thankworthy," 1 Pet. 2:19, KJV (RV, "acceptable").

2. ***eucharistia*** (*2169*), ***eu***, "well," ***charizomai***, "to give freely" (Eng., "eucharist"), denotes (a) "gratitude," "thankfulness," Acts 24:3; (b) "giving of thanks, thanksgiving," 1 Cor. 14:16; 2 Cor. 4:15; 9:11, 12 (plur.); Eph. 5:4; Phil. 4:6; Col. 2:7; 4:2; 1 Thess. 3:9 ("thanks"); 1 Tim. 2:1 (plur.); 4:3, 4; Rev. 4:9, "thanks"; 7:12.

**B. Verbs.**

1. ***eucharisteo*** (*2168*), akin to A, No. 2, "to give thanks," (a) is said of Christ, Matt. 15:36; 26:27; Mark 8:6; 14:23; Luke 22:17, 19; John 6:11, 23; 11:41; 1 Cor. 11:24; (b) of the Pharisee in Luke 18:11 in his self-complacent prayer; (c) is used by Paul at the beginning of all his epistles, except 2 Cor. (see, however, ***eulogetos*** in 1:3), Gal., 1 Tim., 2 Tim. (see, however, ***charin echo***, 1:3), and Titus, (1) for his readers, Rom. 1:8; Eph. 1:16; Col. 1:3; 1 Thess. 1:2; 2 Thess. 1:3 (cf. 2:13); virtually so in Philem. 4; (2) for fellowship shown, Phil. 1:3; (3) for God's gifts to them, 1 Cor. 1:4; (d) is recorded (1) of Paul elsewhere, Acts 27:35; 28:15; Rom. 7:25; 1 Cor. 1:14; 14:18; (2) of Paul and others, Rom. 16:4; 1 Thess. 2:13; of himself, representatively, as a practice, 1 Cor. 10:30; (3) of others, Luke 17:16; Rom. 14:6 (twice); 1 Cor. 14:17; Rev. 11:17; (e) is used in admonitions to the saints, the Name of the Lord Jesus suggesting His character and example, Eph. 5:20; Col. 1:12; 3:17; 1 Thess. 5:18; (f) as the expression of a purpose, 2 Cor. 1:11, RV; (g) negatively of the ungodly, Rom. 1:21. "Thanksgiving" is the expression of joy Godward, and is therefore the fruit of the Spirit (Gal. 5:22); believers are encouraged to abound in it (e.g., Col. 2:7, and see C, below).

2. ***exomologeo*** (*1843*), in the middle voice, signifies "to make acknowledgment," whether of sins (to confess), or in the honor of a person, as in Rom. 14:11; 15:9 (in some mss. in Rev. 3:5); this is the significance in the Lord's address to the Father, "I thank (Thee)," in Matt. 11:25 and Luke 10:21, the meaning being "I make thankful confession" or "I make acknowledgment with praise."

3. ***anthomologeomai*** (*437*), "to acknowledge fully, to celebrate fully (***anti***) in praise with thanksgiving," is used of Anna in Luke 2:35.

**C. Adjective.**

***eucharistos*** (*2170*), primarily, "gracious, agreeable" (as in the Sept., Prov. 11:16, of a wife, who brings glory to her husband), then "grateful, thankful," is so used in Col. 3:15.

## THEATER

***theatron*** (*2302*), "a theater," was used also as "a place of assembly," Acts 19:29, 31; in 1 Cor. 4:9 it is used of "a show" or "spectacle."

## THEFT

1. ***klope*** (*2829*), akin to ***klepto***, "to steal," is used in the plural in Matt. 15:19; Mark 7:22.

2. ***klemma*** (*2809*), "a thing stolen," and so, "a theft," is used in the plural in Rev. 9:21.

## THIEF, THIEVES

1. ***kleptes*** (*2812*) is used (a) literally, Matt. 6:19, 20; 24:43; Luke 12:33, 39; John 10:1, 10; 12:6; 1 Cor. 6:10; 1 Pet. 4:15; (b) metaphorically of "false teachers," John 10:8; (c) figuratively, (1) of the personal coming of Christ, in a warning to a local church, with most of its members possessed of mere outward profession and defiled by the world, Rev. 3:3; in retributive intervention to overthrow the foes of God, 16:15; (2) of the Day of the Lord, in divine judgment upon the world, 2 Pet. 3:10 and 1 Thess. 5:2, 4.

2. ***lestes*** (*3027*) is frequently rendered "thieves" in the KJV, e.g., Matt. 21:13.

## THINK

### *Old Testament*

**A. Verb.**

***chashab*** (2803), "to think, devise, purpose, esteem, count, imagine, impute." ***chashab*** can be translated as "devise" in association with the sense of "to think and reckon." A gifted person of God "devises" excellent works in gold and other choice objects, Exod. 35:35. The word may deal with evil, as when Haman "devised" an evil plot against the Jewish people, Esth. 8:3. The word may mean "think." Some "thought" to do away with David by sending him against the Philistines, 1 Sam. 18:25; Judah "thought" Tamar to be a harlot, Gen. 38:15; and Eli "thought" Hannah was drunk, 1 Sam. 1:13. God repented of the evil concerning the judgment he "thought" to bring upon Israel, Jer. 18:8. Those who fear the Lord may also "think" upon His name, Mal. 3:16. ***chashab*** may be rendered "to purpose" or "esteem," Job 41:27. A classic usage of "esteem" appears in Isa. 53:3–4.

Translated as "count," the word is used in a number of ways. It had a commercial connotation, as when land was being redeemed and the price was established, based on the value of crops until the next year of Jubilee, Lev. 25:27; Num. 18:30.

Other unique translations of ***chashab*** occur. In order to approach God, Asaph had to remember and "consider" the days of old, Ps. 77:5. God had a controversy with Nebuchadnezzar, king of Babylon, because he "conceived" a plan against Him and His people, Jer. 49:30. The prophet Amos cites people who "invent" instruments of music and enjoy it, Amos 6:5. Huram of Tyre sent a man to help Solomon in the building of the temple, who knew how to "find out" all the works of art—i.e., he could work in various metals and fabrics to design a work of beauty, 2 Chron. 2:14. Joseph had to remind his brethren that he did not seek to do them harm because they had sold him into slavery, since God "meant" it for the good of the preservation of Jacob's sons, Gen. 50:20.

### B. Adjective.

***chashab*** (2803), "cunning," Exod. 38:23. This meaning of ***chashab*** as "cunning" appears 11 times in Exodus. But this skill was more than human invention—it indicated how the Spirit of God imparts wisdom, understanding, and knowledge, cf. Exod. 36:8; 39:3.

#### *New Testament*

1. ***dokeo*** (*1380*), "to suppose, to think, to form an opinion," which may be either right or wrong, is sometimes rendered "to think," e.g., Matt. 3:9; 6:7.

2. ***hegeomai*** (*2233*), rendered "to think" in Acts 26:2; 2 Cor. 9:5, "I thought"; Phil. 2:6, KJV (RV, "counted"); 2 Pet. 1:13.

3. ***noeo*** (*3539*), "to perceive, understand, apprehend," is rendered "think" in Eph. 3:20.

4. ***huponoeo*** (*5282*), "to suppose, surmise" (***hupo***, "under," and No. 3), is rendered "to think" in Acts 13:25, KJV (RV, "suppose).

5. ***logizomai*** (*3049*), "to reckon," is rendered "to think," in Rom. 2:3, KJV (RV, "reckonest"); 1 Cor. 13:5, KJV, RV, "taketh (not) account of," i.e., love does not reckon up or calculatingly consider the evil done to it (something more than refraining from imputing motives); 13:11, "I thought"; in the following, for the KJV, "to think," in 2 Cor. 3:5, RV, "to account"; 10:2 (twice), "count"; 10:7, "consider"; 10:11, "reckon"; 12:6, "account." In Phil. 4:8, "think on (these things)," it signifies "make those things the subjects of your thoughtful consideration," or "carefully reflect on them" (RV marg., "take account of").

6. ***phroneo*** (*5426*), "to be minded in a certain way" (***phren***, "the mind"), is rendered "to think," in Rom. 12:3 (2nd and 3rd occurrences).

7. ***axioo*** (*515*), "to regard as worthy" (***axios***), "to deem it suitable," is rendered "thought (not) good" in Acts 15:38.

8. ***enthumeomai*** (*1760*), "to reflect on, ponder," is used in Matt. 1:20; 9:4.

9. ***huperphroneo*** (*5252*), "to be overproud, high-minded," occurs in Rom. 12:3, rendered "to think of himself more highly."

10. ***dienthumeomai*** (*1223*) and *1760*), "to consider deeply" (***dia***, intensive), is used of Peter in Acts 10:19, in the best texts.

## THIRST (Noun and Verb), THIRSTY (to be), ATHIRST

### A. Noun.

***dipsos*** (*1373*), "thirst" (cf. Eng., "dipsomania"), occurs in 2 Cor. 11:27.

### B. Verb.

***dipsao*** (*1372*) is used (a) in the natural sense, e.g., Matt. 25:35, 37, 42; in v. 44, "athirst" (lit., "thirsting"); John 4:13, 15; 19:28; Rom. 12:20; 1 Cor. 4:11; Rev. 7:16; (b) figuratively, of spiritual "thirst," Matt. 5:6; John 4:14; 6:35; 7:37; in Rev. 21:6 and 22:17, "that is athirst."

## THOUGHT (Noun)

1. ***epinoia*** (*1963*), "a thought by way of a design" (akin to ***epinoeo***, "to contrive," ***epi***, intensive, ***noeo***, "to consider"), is used in Acts 8:22.

2. ***noema*** (*3540*), "a purpose, device of the mind," is rendered "thought" in 2 Cor. 10:5, "thoughts" in Phil. 4:7.

3. ***dianoema*** (*1270*), "a thought," occurs in Luke 11:17, where the sense is that of "machinations."

4. ***enthumesis*** (*1761*), is translated "thoughts" in Matt. 9:4; 12:25; Heb. 4:12.

## THOUGHT (to take)

1. ***merimnao*** (*3309*) denotes "to be anxious, careful." For the KJV, "to take thought," the RV substitutes "to be anxious" in Matt. 6:25, 27, 28, 31, 34; 10:19; Luke 12:11, 22, 25, 26.

2. ***promerimnao*** (*4305*), "to be anxious beforehand," occurs in Mark 13:11.

3. ***phroneo*** (*5426*): for Phil. 4:10, RV, "ye did take thought."

4. ***pronoeo*** (*4306*), "to provide," is rendered "to take thought" in Rom. 12:17 and 2 Cor. 8:21.

## THREATEN

1. ***apeileo*** (*546*) is used of Christ, negatively, in 1 Pet. 2:23; in the middle voice, Acts 4:17, where some texts have the noun ***apeile*** in addition, hence the KJV, "let us straitly threaten," lit., "let us threaten . . . with threatening."

2. ***prosapeileo*** (*4324*), "to threaten further" (***pros***, and No. 1), occurs in the middle voice in Acts 4:21.

## THREATENING

***apeile*** (*547*), akin to ***apeileo*** (see above), occurs in Acts 4:29 (in some mss. v. 17); 9:1; Eph. 6:9.

## THRONE

### *Old Testament*

***kisse'*** (3678), "throne; seat." In the Old Testament the basic meaning of ***kisse'*** is "seat" or "chair." Visitors were seated on a chair, 1 Kings 2:19, as well as guests, 2 Kings 4:10, and older men, 1 Sam. 1:9. When the king or elders assembled to administer justice, they sat on the throne of justice, Prov. 20:8; cf. Ps. 9:4. In these contexts ***kisse'*** is associated with honor. However, in the case of the prostitute, Prov. 9:14, and soldiers who set up their chairs, Jer. 1:15—***kisse'*** may mean "throne" here; cf. KJV, NASB, NIV), ***kisse'*** signifies a place and nothing more. The more frequent sense of ***kisse'*** is "throne" or "seat of honor," also known as the "royal seat": "And it shall be, when he sitteth upon the throne of his kingdom, that he shall write him a copy of this law in a book out of that which is before the priests the Levites," Deut. 17:18; cf. 1 Kings 1:46. Since the Davidic dynasty received the blessing of God, the Old Testament has a number of references to "the throne of David," 2 Sam. 3:10; Jer. 22:2, 30; 36:30; Isa. 9:7.

The word ***kisse'*** was also used to represent "kingship" and the succession to the throne. David had sworn that Solomon would sit on his "throne," 1 Kings 1:13; cf. 2 Kings 10:3. Above all human kingship and "thrones" was the God of Israel, Ps. 47:8; Isa. 6:1; Jer. 3:17.

### *New Testament*

1. ***thronos*** (*2362*), "a throne, a seat of authority," is used of the "throne" (a) of God, e.g., Heb. 4:16, "the throne of grace," i.e., from which grace proceeds; 8:1; 12:2; Rev. 1:4; 3:21 (2nd part); 4:2 (twice); 5:1; frequently in Rev.; in 20:12, in the best texts, "the throne" (some have ***theos***, "God," KJV); cf. 21:3; Matt. 5:34; 23:22; Acts 7:49; (b) of Christ, e.g. Heb. 1:8; Rev. 3:21 (1st part); 22:3; His seat of authority in the Millennium, Matt. 19:28 (1st part); (c) by metonymy for angelic powers, Col. 1:16; (d) of the Apostles in millennial authority, Matt. 19:28 (2nd part); Luke 22:30; (e) of the elders in the heavenly vision, Rev. 4:4 (2nd and 3rd parts), RV, "thrones" (KJV, "seats"); so 11:16; (f) of David, Luke 1:32; Acts 2:30; (g) of Satan, Rev. 2:13, RV, "throne" (KJV, "seat"); (h) of "the beast," the final and federal head of the revived Roman Empire, Rev. 13:2; 16:10.

2. ***bema*** (*968*), used of the throne or tribunal of Herod, Acts 12:21.

## THUNDER, THUNDERING

***bronte*** (*1027*): aside from the lit. meaning, used fig. in Mark 3:17 "sons of thunder" is the interpretation of Boanerges, the name applied by the Lord to James and John; their fiery disposition is seen in 9:38 and Luke 9:54.

## TIDINGS (give)

### A. Noun.

***phasis*** (*5334*), akin to ***phemi***, "to speak," denotes "information," especially against fraud or other delinquency, and is rendered "tidings" in Acts 21:31.

### B. Verbs.

1. ***euangelizo*** (*2097*) is used of any message designed to cheer those who receive it; it is rendered "to bring, declare, preach," or "show good or glad tidings," e.g., Luke 1:19; 2:10; 3:18, RV; 4:43, RV; 7:22, RV; 8:1; Acts 8:12 and 10:36, RV; 14:15, RV; in 1 Thess. 3:6, "brought us glad (KJV, good) tidings"; in Heb. 4:2, RV, "we have had good tidings preached."

## TIE

1. ***deo*** (*1210*), "to bind," is rendered "to tie" in Matt. 21:2; Mark 11:2, 4; Luke 19:30.

2. ***proteino*** (*4385*), "to stretch out or forth," is used of preparations for scourging, Acts 22:25, RV, "had tied (him) up" (KJV, "bound").

## TIME

### *Old Testament*

### A. Noun.

***'et*** (6256), "time; period of time; appointed time; proper time; season." Basically this noun connotes "time" conceived as an opportunity or season. First, the word signifies an appointed, fixed, and set time or period, Esth.

1:13. God alone, however, knows and reveals such "appointed times," Jer. 8:12. This noun also is used of the concept "proper or appropriate time," Eccl. 7:17. It is used of the "appropriate or suitable time" for a given activity in life, Eccl. 3:11; cf. Ps. 104:27. Finally, the "appropriate time" for divine judgment is represented by *'et*, Ps. 119:126. A third use connotes "season," or a regular fixed period of time such as springtime, Gen. 18:10; or rainy season, Ezra 10:13. This noun also is applied to differing "extensions of time," as when the sun is setting, Gen. 8:11; or a special occasion, Mic. 5:3; or other periods of time, Exod. 18:22; Dan. 12:11.

### B. Verb.

***'anah*** means "to be exercised." The noun ***'et*** may be derived from this verb which occurs only 3 times in Hebrew poetry (cf. Eccl. 1:13). In later Hebrew this root means "to worry."

#### *New Testament*

1. ***chronos*** (*5550*), a noun, denotes "a space of time," whether short, e.g., Matt. 2:7; Luke 4:5, or long, e.g., Luke 8:27; 20:9; or a succession of "times," shorter, e.g., Acts 20:18, or longer, e.g., Rom. 16:25, RV, "times eternal"; or duration of "time," e.g., Mark 2:19, 2nd part, RV, "while" (KJV, "as long as"), lit., "for whatever time."

2. ***kairos*** (*2540*), primarily "due measure, due proportion," when used of "time," signified "a fixed or definite period, a season," sometimes an opportune or seasonable "time," e.g., Rom. 5:6, RV, "season"; Gal. 6:10, "opportunity." In Mark 10:30 and Luke 18:30, "this time" (***kairos***), i.e., "in this lifetime," is contrasted with "the coming age." In 1 Thess. 5:1, "the times and the seasons," "times" (***chronos***) refers to the duration of the interval previous to the Parousia of Christ and the length of "time" it will occupy, as well as other periods; "seasons" refers to the characteristics of these periods.

3. ***hora*** (*5610*), primarily, "any time or period fixed by nature," is translated "time" in Matt. 14:15; Luke 14:17; Rom. 13:11, "high time"; in the following the RV renders it "hour," for KJV, "time," Matt. 18:1; Luke 1:10; John 16:2, 4, 25; 1 John 2:18 (twice); Rev. 14:15; in Mark 6:35, RV, "day"; in 1 Thess. 2:17, RV, "a short (season)," lit., "(the season, KJV, 'time') of an hour."

## TITHE (Verb)

1. ***dekatoo*** (*1183*), from ***dekatos***, "tenth," in the active voice denotes "to take tithes of," Heb. 7:6, RV, "hath taken (KJV, received) tithes"; in the passive, "to pay tithes," 7:9, RV, "hath paid (KJV, 'payed') tithes."

2. ***apodekatoo*** (*586*) denotes (a) "to tithe" (***apo***, "from," ***dekatos***, "tenth"), Matt. 23:23 (KJV, "pay tithe of"); Luke 11:42; in Luke 18:12 (where the best texts have the alternative form ***apodekateuo***), "I give tithes"; (b) "to exact tithes" from Heb. 7:5.

3. ***apodekateuo*** (*586v*), "to give tithes," in Luke 18:12 (some texts have No. 2).

## TITLE

***titlos*** (*5102*), from Latin ***titulus***, is used of the inscription above the cross of Christ, John 19:19, 20.

## TITTLE

***keraia*** or ***kerea*** (*2762*), "a little horn" (***keras***, "a horn"), was used to denote the small stroke distinguishing one Hebrew letter from another. The rabbis attached great importance to these; hence the significance of the Lord's statements in Matt. 5:18 and Luke 16:17, charging the Pharisees with hypocrisy, because, while professing the most scrupulous reverence to the Law, they violated its spirit.

## TOIL (Verb and Noun)

### A. Verbs.

1. ***kopiao*** (*2872*), "to be weary, to labor," is rendered "to toil" in Matt. 6:28; Luke 5:5 (12:27 in some mss.); in 1 Cor. 4:12, RV (KJV, "we labor").

2. ***basanizo*** (*928*), primarily, "to rub on the touchstone, to put to the test," then, "to examine by torture" (***basanos***, "touchstone, torment"), hence denotes "to torture, torment, distress"; in the passive voice it is rendered "toiling" in Mark 6:48, KJV (RV, "distressed").

### B. Noun.

***kopos*** (*2873*), "labor, trouble," is rendered "toil" in Rev. 2:2, RV (KJV, "labor").

## TOKEN



1. ***semeion*** (*4592*), "a sign, token or indication," is translated "token" in 2 Thess. 3:17, of writing of the closing salutations, the apostle using the pen himself instead of his amanuensis, his autograph attesting the authenticity of his Epistles.

2. ***sussemon*** (*4953*), "a fixed sign or signal, agreed upon with others" (***sun***, "with"), is used in Mark 14:44, "a token."

3. ***endeigma*** (*1730*), "a plain token, a proof" (akin to ***endeiknumi***, "to point out, prove"), is used in 2 Thess. 1:5 "a manifest token," said of the patient endurance and faith of the persecuted saints at Thessalonica, affording proof

to themselves of their new life, and a guarantee of the vindication by God of both Himself and them.

4. ***endeixis*** (*1732*), "a pointing out, showing forth," is rendered "evident token" in Phil. 1:28.

## TOLERABLE

***anektos*** (*414*) (akin to ***anecho***, in the middle voice, "to endure"), is used in its comparative form, ***anektoteros***, in Matt. 10:15; 11:22, 24; Luke 10:12, 14; some texts have it in Mark 6:11.

## TOMB

1. ***mnemeion*** (*3419*) is almost invariably rendered "tomb" or "tombs" in the RV, never "grave," sometimes "sepulchre"; in the KJV, "tomb" in Matt. 8:28; 27:60; Mark 5:2; 6:29.

2. ***mnema*** (*3418*), rendered "tombs" in Mark 5:3, 5; Luke 8:27.

3. ***taphos*** (*5028*), akin to ***thapto***, "to bury," is translated "tombs" in Matt. 23:29; elsewhere "sepulchre."

## TOMORROW

### *Old Testament*

**A. Noun.**

***machar*** (4279), "tomorrow," i.e., "the day following the present day," Exod. 16:23; as noun, Prov. 27:1.

**B. Adverbs.**

***machar*** (4279), "tomorrow," i.e., pertaining to a time of the next day, Exod. 19:10; meaning "later," in some passages, Gen. 30:33.

***machorat*** (4283), "the next day," related to the noun ***machar***, ***machorat*** is joined to the preposition ***min*** to mean "on the next day," Gen. 19:34; cf. also 1 Sam. 30:17.

**C. Verb.**

***'achar*** means "to be behind, tarry, defer," i.e., to extend a period of time, Judg. 5:28.

### *New Testament*

***aurion*** (*839*) is used either without the article, e.g., Matt. 6:30; 1 Cor. 15:32; Jas. 4:13; or with the article in the feminine form, to agree with ***hemera***, "day," e.g., Matt. 6:34; Acts 4:3, RV, "the morrow" (KJV, "next day"); Jas. 4:14; preceded by ***epi***, "on," e.g., Luke 10:35; Acts 4:5.

## TONGUE (-S)

### *Old Testament*

***lashon*** (3956), "tongue; language; speech." The basic meaning of ***lashon*** is "tongue," which as an organ of the body refers to humans, Lam. 4:4, and animals, Exod. 11:7; Job 41:1. The extended meaning of the word as an organ of speech occurs more frequently. A person may be "heavy" or "slow" of tongue or have a stammering "tongue," Exod. 4:10; or he may be fluent and clear, Isa. 32:4. "Tongue" with the meaning "speech" has as a synonym ***peh***, "mouth," Ps. 66:17, and more rarely ***sapah***, "lip," Job 27:4.

A further extension of meaning is "language." In Hebrew both ***sapah*** and ***lashon*** denote a foreign "language": "For with stammering lips and another tongue will he speak to this people," Isa. 28:11. The foreigners to the "language" are well described in these words, Isa. 33:19.

***lashon*** also refers to objects that are shaped in the form of a tongue. Most important is the "tongue of fire," which even takes the character of "eating" or "devouring," Isa. 5:24. The association in Isaiah of God's appearance in judgment with smoke and fire gave rise to a fine literary description of the Lord's anger: "Behold, the name of the Lord cometh from far, burning with his anger, and the burden thereof is heavy: his lips are full of indignation, and his tongue as a devouring fire," Isa. 30:27. Notice the words "lips" and "tongue" here with the meaning of "flames of fire," even though the language evokes the representation of a tongue (as an organ of the body) together with a tongue (of fire). Also a bar of gold, Josh. 7:21, and a bay of the sea, Isa. 11:15, shaped in the form of a tongue were called ***lashon***.

### *New Testament*

**A. Nouns.**

1. ***glossa*** (*1100*) is used of (1) the "tongues . . . like as of fire" which appeared at Pentecost; (2) "the tongue," as an organ of speech, e.g., Mark 7:33; Rom. 3:13; 14:11; 1 Cor. 14:9; Phil. 2:11; Jas. 1:26; 3:5, 6, 8; 1 Pet. 3:10; 1 John 3:18; Rev. 16:10; (3) (a) "a language," coupled with ***phule***, "a tribe," ***laos***, "a people," ***ethnos***, "a nation," seven times in the Apocalypse, 5:9; 7:9; 10:11; 11:9; 13:7; 14:6; 17:15; (b) "the supernatural gift of speaking in another language without its having been learnt"; in Acts 2:4–13 the circumstances are recorded from the viewpoint of the hearers; to those in whose language the utterances were made it appeared as a supernatural phenomenon; to others, the stammering of drunkards; what was uttered was not addressed primarily to the audience but consisted in recounting "the mighty works of God"; cf. 2:46; in 1 Cor., chapters 12 and 14, the use of the gift of "tongues" is mentioned as exercised in the gatherings of local churches; 12:10 speaks of the gift in general terms, and couples with it that of "the

interpretation of tongues"; chapt. 14 gives instruction concerning the use of the gift, the paramount object being the edification of the church; unless the "tongue" was interpreted the speaker would speak "not unto men, but unto God," v. 2; he would edify himself alone, v. 4, unless he interpreted, v. 5, in which case his interpretation would be of the same value as the superior gift of prophesying, as he would edify the church, vv. 4–6; he must pray that he may interpret, v. 13; if there were no interpreter, he must keep silence, v. 28, for all things were to be done "unto edifying," v. 26. "If I come . . . speaking with tongues, what shall I profit you," says the apostle (expressing the great object in all oral ministry), "unless I speak to you either by way of revelation, or of knowledge, or of prophesying, or of teaching?" (v. 6). "Tongues" were for a sign, not to believers, but to unbelievers, v. 22, and especially to unbelieving Jews (see v. 21): cf. the passages in the Acts.

There is no evidence of the continuance of this gift after apostolic times nor indeed in the later times of the apostles themselves; this provides confirmation of the fulfillment in this way of 1 Cor. 13:8, that this gift would cease in the churches, just as would "prophecies" and "knowledge" in the sense of knowledge received by immediate supernatural power (cf. 14:6). The completion of the Holy Scriptures has provided the churches with all that is necessary for individual and collective guidance, instruction, and edification.

2. ***dialektos*** (*1258*), "language" (Eng., "dialect"), is rendered "tongue" in the KJV of Acts 1:19; 2:6, 8; 21:40; 22:2; 26:14.

### B. Adjective.

***heteroglossos*** (*2804*) is rendered "strange tongues" in 1 Cor. 14:21, RV (***heteros***, "another of a different sort").

### C. Adverb.

***hebraisti*** (or ***ebraisti***, Westcott and Hort) (*1447*) denotes (a) "in Hebrew," Rev. 9:11, RV (AV, "in the Hebrew tongue"); so 16:16; (b) in the Aramaic vernacular of Palestine, John 5:2, KJV, "in the Hebrew tongue" (RV, "in Hebrew"); in 19:13, 17, KJV, "in the Hebrew" (RV, "in Hebrew"); in v. 20, KJV and RV, "in Hebrew"; in 20:16, RV only, "in Hebrew (Rabboni)."

## TORMENT (Noun and Verb)

### A. Nouns.

1. ***basanismos*** (*929*), akin to ***basanizo***, used of divine judgments in Rev. 9:5; 14:11; 18:7, 10, 15.

2. ***basanos*** (*931*), primarily "a touchstone," employed in testing metals, hence, "torment," is used (a) of physical diseases, Matt. 4:24: (b) of a condition of retribution in Hades, Luke 16:23, 28.

### B. Verbs.

1. ***basanizo*** (*928*), translated "to torment," (a) of sickness, Matt. 8:6; (b) of the doom of evil spirits, Mark 5:7; Luke 8:28; (c) of retributive judgments upon impenitent mankind at the close of this age, Rev. 9:5; 11:10; (d) upon those who worship the Beast and his image and receive the mark of his name, 14:10; (e) of the doom of Satan and his agents, 20:10.

2. ***kakoucheo*** (*2558*), "to treat evilly," in the passive voice is translated "tormented" in Heb. 11:37, KJV (RV, "evil entreated").

3. ***odunao*** (*3600*), rendered, "I am (thou art) tormented" in Luke 16:24, 25, KJV.

## TORMENTOR

***basanistes*** (*930*), properly, "a torturer," "one who elicits information by torture," is used of jailers, Matt. 18:34.

## TORTURE (Verb)

***tumpanizo*** (*5178*) primarily denotes "to beat a drum" (***tumpanon***, "a kettledrum," Eng., "tympanal," "tympanitis," "tympanum"), hence, "to torture by beating, to beat to death," Heb. 11:35.

## TOUCH (Verb)

*Old Testament*

### A. Verb.

***naga'*** (5060), "to touch, strike, reach, smite." Meaning physical touch, this word is used involving various kinds of objects, Gen. 32:25, 32; Exod. 19:12; Lev. 5:2–3. Sometimes ***naga'*** is used figuratively in the sense of emotional involvement, 1 Sam. 10:26; NEB; or sexual contact, Gen. 20:6; or divine chastisement, Job 19:21.

### B. Noun.

***nega'*** (5061), "plague: stroke; wound." This noun formed from ***naga'*** occurs about 76 times in the Old Testament. The word refers to a "plague" most frequently, Gen. 12:17; Exod. 11:1. ***nega'*** can also mean "stroke," Deut. 17:8; 21:5, or "wound," Prov. 6:33. Each meaning carries with it the sense of a person "being stricken or smitten in some way."

*New Testament*

1. ***hapto*** (*681*), primarily, "to fasten to," hence, of fire, "to kindle," denotes, in the mid-

dle voice (a) "to touch," e.g., Matt. 8:3, 15; 9:20, 21, 29; (b) "to cling to, lay hold of," John 20:17; here the Lord's prohibition as to clinging to Him was indicative of the fact that communion with Him would, after His ascension, be by faith, through the Spirit; (c) "to have carnal intercourse with a woman," 1 Cor. 7:1; (d) "to have fellowship and association with unbelievers," 2 Cor. 6:17; (e) (negatively) "to adhere to certain Levitical and ceremonial ordinances," in order to avoid contracting external defilement, or to practice rigorous asceticism, all such abstentions being of "no value against the indulgence of the flesh," Col. 2:21, KJV (RV, "handle"); (f) "to assault," in order to sever the vital union between Christ and the believer, said of the attack of the Evil One, 1 John 5:18.

2. ***thingano*** (*2345*), "to touch," a lighter term than No. 1, though Heb. 11:28 approximates to it, in expressing the action of the Destroyer of the Egyptian firstborn; in Heb. 12:20 it signifies "to touch," and is not to be interpreted by Ps. 104:32, "He toucheth the hills and they smoke"; in Col. 2:21, RV (KJV, handle).

3. ***prospsauo*** (*4379*), "to touch upon, to touch slightly," occurs in Luke 11:46.

4. ***pselaphao*** (*5584*), "to feel, to handle," is rendered "that might be touched" in Heb. 12:18.

5. ***katago*** (*2609*), to bring down, is used of bringing a ship to land in Acts 27:3.

6. ***sumpatheo*** (*4834*), rendered "be touched with" in Heb. 4:15.

7. ***paraballo*** (*3846*), rendered "touched at" in Acts 20:15, RV.

## TOWN

1. ***komopolis*** (*2969*), denotes a country town," Mark 1:38, "a large village" usually without walls.

2. ***kome*** (*2968*), "a village," or "country town without walls." The RV always renders this "village" or "villages," KJV, "town" or "towns," Matt. 10:11; Mark 8:23, 26 (twice), 27; Luke 5:17; 9:6, 12; John 7:42; 11:1, 30.

## TOWN CLERK

***grammateus*** (*1122*), "a writer, scribe," is used in Acts 19:35 of a state "clerk," an important official, variously designated, according to inscriptions found in Graeco-Asiatic cities. He was responsible for the form of decrees first approved by the Senate, then sent for approval in the popular assembly, in which he often presided. The decrees having been passed, he sealed them with the public seal in the presence of witnesses. Such an assembly frequently met in the theater. The Roman administration viewed any irregular or unruly assembly as a grave and even capital offense, as tending to strengthen among the people the consciousness of their power and the desire to exercise it. In the circumstances at Ephesus the town clerk feared that he might himself be held responsible for the irregular gathering.

## TRACE

### A. Verb.

***parakoloutheo*** (*3877*), "to follow up," is used of investigating or "tracing" a course of events, Luke 1:3, where the writer, humbly differentiating himself from those who possessed an essential apostolic qualification, declares that he "traced the course of all things" (RV) about which he was writing (KJV, "having had . . . understanding, etc.").

### B. Adjective.

***anexichniastos*** (*421*) signifies "that cannot be traced out" (***a***, negative, ***ex***, for ***ek***, "out," ***ichnos***, "a track"), is rendered "past tracing out" in Rom. 11:33, RV (KJV, "past finding out"); in Eph. 3:8, "unsearchable."

## TRADE (Noun and Verb)

### A. Verbs.

1. ***ergazomai*** (*2038*), "to work," is rendered "traded" in Matt. 25:16; in Rev. 18:17, KJV, "trade," RV, "gain their living."

2. ***pragmateuomai*** (*4231*) is rendered "trade ye" in Luke 19:13.

3. ***diapragmateuomai*** (*1281*), "to accomplish by traffic, to gain by trading," occurs in Luke 19:15.

4. ***emporeuomai*** (*1710*) is rendered "trade" in Jas. 4:13.

### B. Nouns.

1. ***techne*** (*5078*), "an art" (Eng., "technique," "technical"), is used in Acts 18:3 (2nd part) of a "trade," RV (KJV, "occupation").

2. ***meros*** (*3313*), "a portion," is used of "a trade" in Acts 19:27.

## TRADITION

***paradosis*** (*3862*), "a handing down or on" (akin to ***paradidomi***, "to hand over, deliver"), denotes "a tradition," and hence, by metonymy, (a) "the teachings of the rabbis," interpretations of the Law, which was thereby made void in practice, Matt. 15:2, 3, 6; Mark 7:3, 5, 8, 9, 13; Gal. 1:14; Col. 2:8; (b) of "apostolic teaching," 1 Cor. 11:2, RV, "traditions" (KJV, "ordinances"), of instructions concerning the gatherings of believers (instructions of wider scope than ordinances in the limited sense); in 2 Thess. 2:15, of Christian doctrine in general, where the apostle's use of the word constitutes a denial that what he preached originated with himself, and a claim for its divine authority (cf. ***paralambano***, "to receive," 1 Cor. 11:23; 15:3); in 2 Thess. 3:6, it is used of instructions concerning everyday conduct.

## TRAITOR

***prodotes*** (*4273*) denotes "a betrayer, traitor"; the latter term is assigned to Judas, virtually as a title, in Luke 6:16; in 2 Tim. 3:4 it occurs in a list of evil characters, foretold as abounding in the last days.

## TRAMPLE

***katapateo*** (*2662*), "to tread down, trample under foot," is rendered "trample in Matt. 7:6.

## TRANCE

***ekstasis*** (*1611*), denotes "a trance" in Acts 10:10; 11:5; 22:17, a condition in which ordinary consciousness and the perception of natural circumstances were withheld, and the soul was susceptible only to the vision imparted by God.

## TRANSFIGURE

***metamorphoo*** (*3339*), "to change into another form" (***meta***, implying change, and ***morphe***, "form:" is used in the passive voice (a) of Christ's "transfiguration," Matt. 17:2; Mark 9:2; Luke (in 9:29) avoids this term, which might have suggested to gentile readers the metamorphoses of heathen gods, and uses the phrase ***egeneto heteron***, "was altered," lit., "became (***ginomai***) different (***heteros***)"; (b) of believers, Rom. 12:2, "be ye transformed," the obligation being to undergo a complete change which, under the power of God, will find expression in character and conduct; ***morphe*** lays stress on the inward change, ***schema*** lays stress on the outward; the present continuous tenses indicate a process; 2 Cor. 3:18 describes believers as being "transformed (RV) into the same image" (i.e., of Christ in all His moral excellencies), the change being effected by the Holy Spirit.

## TRANSFORM

1. ***metamorphoo*** (*3339*) is rendered "transformed" in Rom. 12:2.

2. ***metaschematizo*** (*3345*) in the passive voice is rendered "to be transformed" in the KJV of 2 Cor. 11:13, 14, 15.

## TRANSGRESS, TRANSGRESSION

### *Old Testament*

**A. Verb.**

***pasha'*** (6586), "to transgress, rebel." The basic sense of ***pasha'*** is "to rebel." There are two stages of rebellion. First, the whole process of rebellion has independence in view, 2 Kings 1:1. Second, the final result of the rebellion is the state of independence, 2 Kings 8:20, NASB. A more radical meaning is the state of rebellion in which there is no end of the rebellion in view, 1 Kings 12:19. Thus far, the usage has a king or a nation as the object of the revolt. Translations generally give the rendering "transgress" for ***pasha'*** when the act is committed against the Lord, Hos. 7:13. This meaning also appears in Isa. 66:24.

**B. Noun.**

***pesha'*** (6588), "transgression; guilt; punishment; offering." A cognate of this word appears in Ugaritic. ***pesha'*** appears 93 times and in all periods of biblical Hebrew.

Basically, this noun signifies willful deviation from, and therefore rebellion against, the path of godly living. This emphasis is especially prominent in Amos 2:4: "For three transgressions of Judah, and for four, I will not turn away the punishment thereof; because they have despised the law of the Lord, and have not kept his commandments, and their lies caused them to err, after the which their fathers have walked." Such a willful rebellion from a prescribed or agreed-upon path may be perpetrated against another man, "Jacob answered and said to Laban, What is my trespass? What is my sin, that thou hast so hotly pursued after me?"; Gen. 31:36—the first occurrence of the word. Jacob is asking what he has done by way of violating or not keeping his responsibility (contract) with Laban. A nation can sin in this sense against another nation: "For three transgressions of Damascus, and for four . . . because they have threshed Gilead with threshing instruments of iron," Amos 1:3.

This word sometimes represents the guilt of such a transgression: "I am clean, without [guilt of] transgression, I am innocent; neither is there iniquity in me," Job 33:9.

***pesha'*** can signify the punishment for transgression: "And a host was given him against the daily sacrifice by reason of transgression," Dan. 8:12; "How long shall be the vision concerning the daily sacrifice, and [punishment for] the transgression of desolation, to give both the sanctuary and the host to be trodden under foot?"; Dan. 8:13.

Finally, in Mic. 6:7 ***pesha'*** signifies an offering for "transgression": "Shall I give my firstborn for my transgression [NASB, "for my rebellious acts"]?"

*New Testament*

**A. Verbs.**

1. ***parabaino*** (*3845*), lit., "to go aside" (***para***), hence "to go beyond," is chiefly used metaphorically of "transgressing" the tradition of the elders, Matt. 15:2; the commandment of God, 15:3; in Acts 1:25, of Judas, KJV, "by transgression fell" (RV, "fell away"); in 2 John 9 some texts have this verb (KJV, "transgresseth"), the best have ***proago***.

2. ***huperbaino*** (*5233*), lit., "to go over" (***huper***), used metaphorically and rendered "transgress" in 1 Thess. 4:6 (KJV, "go beyond"), i.e., of "overstepping" the limits separating chastity from licentiousness, sanctification from sin.

3. ***parerchomai*** (*3928*), "to come by" (***para***, "by," ***erchomai***, "to come"), "pass over," and hence, metaphorically, "to transgress," is so used in Luke 15:29.

**B. Nouns.**

1. ***parabasis*** (*3847*), akin to A, No. 1, primarily "a going aside," then, "an overstepping," is used metaphorically to denote "transgression" (always of a breach of law): (a) of Adam, Rom. 5:14; (b) of Eve, 1 Tim. 2:14; (c) negatively, where there is no law, since "transgression" implies the violation of law, none having been enacted between Adam's "transgression" and those under the Law, Rom. 4:15; (d) of "transgressions" of the Law, Gal. 3:19, where the statement "it was added because of transgressions" is best understood according to Rom. 4:15; 5:13 and 5:20; the Law does not make men sinners, but makes them "transgressors"; hence sin becomes "exceeding sinful," Rom. 7:7, 13. Conscience thus had a standard external to itself; by the Law men are taught their inability to yield complete obedience to God, that thereby they may become convinced of their need of a Savior; in Rom. 2:23, RV, "transgression (of the Law)," KJV, "breaking (the Law)"; Heb. 2:2; 9:15.

2. ***paranomia*** (*3892*), "law-breaking" (***para***, "contrary to," ***nomos***, "law"), is rendered "transgression" in 2 Pet. 2:16, RV (KJV, "iniquity").

## TRANSGRESSOR

1. ***parabates*** (*3848*), lit. and primarily, "one who stands beside," then, "one who oversteps the prescribed limit, a transgressor"; so Rom. 2:25, RV (KJV, "a breaker"); v. 27, RV, "a transgressor" (KJV, "dost transgress"); Gal. 2:18; Jas. 2:9, 11.

2. ***anomos*** (*459*), "without law" (***a***-, negative), is translated "transgressors" in Luke 22:37 (in some texts, Mark 15:28), in a quotation from Isa. 53:12.

## TRANSLATE, TRANSLATION

**A. Verbs.**

1. ***methistemi*** or ***methistano*** (*3179*), "to change, remove" (***meta***, implying "change," ***histemi***, "to cause to stand"), is rendered "hath translated" in Col. 1:13.

2. ***metatithemi*** (*3346*), "to transfer to another place" (***meta***, "change," ***tithemi***, "to put"), is rendered "to translate" in Heb. 11:5 (twice).

**B. Noun.**

***metathesis*** (*3331*), "a change of position" (akin to A, No. 2), is rendered "translation" in Heb. 11:5.

## TRAVAIL (Noun and Verb)

**A. Nouns.**

1. ***mochthos*** (*3449*), "labor, involving painful effort," is rendered "travail" in 2 Cor. 11:27, RV (KJV, "painfulness"); in 1 Thess. 2:9 and 2 Thess. 3:8 it stresses the toil involved in the work.

2. ***odin*** (*5604*), a birth pang, "travail pain," is used illustratively in 1 Thess. 5:3 of the calamities which are to come upon men at the beginning of the Day of the Lord; the figure used suggests the inevitableness of the catastrophe.

**B. Verbs.**

1. ***odino*** (*5605*), akin to A, No. 2, is used negatively in Gal. 4:27, "(thou) that travailest (not)," quoted from Isa. 54:1; the apostle applies the circumstances of Sarah and Hagar (which doubtless Isaiah was recalling) to show that, whereas the promise by grace had temporarily been replaced by the works of the Law (see Gal. 3:17), this was now reversed, and, in the fulfillment of the promise to Abraham, the number of those saved by the gospel would far exceed those who owned allegiance to the Law. Isa. 54 has primary reference to the future prosperity of Israel restored to God's favor, but frequently the principles underlying events recorded in the OT extend beyond their immediate application.

In 4:19 the apostle uses it metaphorically of a second travailing on his part regarding the churches of Galatia; his first was for their deliverance from idolatry (v. 8), now it was for their deliverance from bondage to Judaism.

There is no suggestion here of a second regeneration necessitated by defection. There is a hint of reproach, as if he was enquiring whether they had ever heard of a mother experiencing second birth pangs for her children.

In Rev. 12:2 the woman is figurative of Israel; the circumstances of her birth pangs are mentioned in Isa. 66:7 (see also Micah 5:2, 3). Historically the natural order is reversed. The Manchild, Christ, was brought forth at His first advent; the travail is destined to take place in "the time of Jacob's trouble," the "great tribulation," Matt. 24:21; Rev. 7:14. The object in 12:2 in referring to the birth of Christ is to connect Him with His earthly people Israel in their future time of trouble, from which the godly remnant, the nucleus of the restored nation, is to be delivered, Jer. 30:7.

2. ***sunodino*** (*4944*), "to be in travail together," is used metaphorically in Rom. 8:22, of the whole creation.

3. ***tikto*** (*5088*), "to beget," is rendered "travail" in John 16:21.

## TREASURE (Noun and Verb)

### A. Nouns.

1. ***thesauros*** (*2344*) denotes (1) "a place of safe keeping" (possibly akin to ***tithemi***, "to put"), (a) "a casket," Matt. 2:11; (b) "a storehouse," Matt. 13:52; used metaphorically of the heart, Matt. 12:35, twice (RV, "out of his treasure"); Luke 6:45; (2) "a treasure," Matt. 6:19, 20, 21; 13:44; Luke 12:33, 34; Heb. 11:26; "treasure" (in heaven or the heavens), Matt. 19:21; Mark 10:21; Luke 18:22; in these expressions (which are virtually equivalent to that in Matt. 6:1, "with your Father which is in Heaven") the promise does not simply refer to the present life, but looks likewise to the hereafter; in 2 Cor. 4:7 it is used of "the light of the knowledge of the glory of God in the face of Jesus Christ," descriptive of the gospel, as deposited in the earthen vessels of the persons who proclaim it (cf. v. 4); in Col. 2:3, of the wisdom and knowledge hidden in Christ.

2. ***gaza*** (*1047*), a Persian word, signifying "royal treasure," occurs in Acts 8:27.

### B. Verb.

***thesaurizo*** (*2343*), akin to A, No. 1, is used metaphorically in Rom. 2:5 of "treasuring up wrath."

## TREASURY

1. ***gazophulakion*** (*1049*), from ***gaza***, "a treasure," ***phulake***, "a guard," is used by Josephus for a special room in the women's court in the Temple in which gold and silver bullion was kept. This seems to be referred to in John 8:20; in Mark 12:41 (twice), 43 and Luke 21:1 it is used of the trumpet-shaped or ram's-horn-shaped chests, into which the temple offerings of the people were cast. There were 13 chests, six for such gifts in general, seven for distinct purposes.

2. ***korbanas*** (*2878*), signifying "the place of gifts," denoted the Temple "treasury," Matt. 27:6.

## TREATISE

***logos*** (*3056*), "a word," denotes "a treatise or written narrative" in Acts 1:1.

## TREE

### *Old Testament*

***'ets*** (6086), "tree; wood; timber; stick; stalk." This word may signify a single "tree," as it does in Gen. 2:9; or genus of tree, Isa. 41:19. ***'ets*** can mean "wood as a material from which things are constructed, as a raw material to be carved, Exod. 31:5. Large unprocessed pieces of "wood or timber" are also signified by ***'ets***, Hag. 1:8. The end product of wood already processed and fashioned into something may be indicated by ***'ets***, Lev. 11:32. This word means "stick" or "piece of wood" in Ezek. 37:16. This may also refer to a "pole" or "gallows," Gen. 40:19. ***'ets*** one time means "stalk," Josh. 2:6.

***'ayil*** (352), "large, mighty tree." This does not mean a particular genus or species of tree but merely a large, mighty tree, Isa. 1:29.

***'elon*** (436), "large tree." This noun is probably related to ***'ayil***, "large tree," Judg. 9:37.

### *New Testament*

1. ***dendron*** (*1186*), "a living, growing tree" (cf. Eng., "rhododendron," lit., "rose tree"), known by the fruit it produces, Matt. 12:33; Luke 6:44; certain qualities are mentioned in the NT; "a good tree," Matt. 7:17, 18; 12:33; Luke 6:43; "a corrupt tree" (ditto); in Jude 12, metaphorically, of evil teachers, "autumn trees (KJV, 'trees whose fruit withereth') without fruit, twice dead, plucked up by the roots," RV; in Luke 13:19 in some texts, "a great tree," KJV (RV, "a tree"); for this and Matt. 13:32; in Luke 21:29 "the fig tree" is illustrative of Israel, "all the trees" indicating gentile nations.

2. ***xulon*** (*3586*), "wood, a piece of wood, anything made of wood," is used, with the rendering "tree," (a) in Luke 23:31, where "the green tree" refers either to Christ, figuratively of all His living power and excellencies, or to the life of the Jewish people while still inhabiting their land, in contrast to "the dry," a figure fulfilled in the horrors of the Roman massacre and devastation in A.D. 70 (cf. the Lord's parable in

Luke 13:6–9; see Ezek. 20:47, and cf. 21:3); (b) of "the cross," the tree being the ***stauros***, the upright pale or stake to which Romans nailed those who were thus to be executed, Acts 5:30; 10:39; 13:29; Gal. 3:13; 1 Pet. 2:24; (c) of "the tree of life," Rev. 2:7; 22:2 (twice), 14, 19, RV, KJV, "book."

## TREMBLE, TREMBLING

### A. Verbs.

1. ***tremo*** (*5141*), "to tremble, especially with fear," is used in Mark 5:33; Luke 8:47 (Acts 9:6, in some mss.); 2 Pet. 2:10, RV, "they tremble (not)," KJV, "they are (not) afraid."

2. ***seio*** (*4579*), "to move to and fro, shake," is rendered "will I make to tremble" in Heb. 12:26, RV (KJV, "I shake").

### B. Noun.

***tromos*** (*5156*), "a trembling" (akin to A, No. 1), occurs in Mark 16:8, RV, "trembling (... had come upon them)"; 1 Cor. 2:3; 2 Cor. 7:15; Eph. 6:5; Phil. 2:12.

## TRESPASS (Noun and Verb)

***Old Testament***

### A. Verb.

***ma'al*** (4603), "to trespass, act unfaithfully." ***ma'al*** has basically the meaning "to sin," Lev. 5:15. Second, the meaning of ***ma'al*** is further expressed by a verb indicating the intent of being unfaithful to one's neighbor for personal profit, Lev 6:2. The offense is against God, even when one acts unfaithfully against one's neighbor, 2 Chron. 29:6. Dan. 9:7. In view of the additional significance of "treachery," many versions translate the verb "to act unfaithfully" or "to act treacherously" instead of "to transgress" or "to commit a trespass." Both the verb and the noun have strongly negative overtones, which the translator must convey in English, Ezek. 14:13.

***ma'al*** generally expresses man's unfaithfulness to God, Lev. 26:40; Deut. 32:51; 2 Chron. 12:2; Ezra 10:2; Ezek. 14:13. The word further signifies man's unfaithfulness to his fellow man; particularly it is illustrative of unfaithfulness in marriage, Num. 5:12–13; Lev. 6:2.

### B. Noun.

***ma'al*** (4604), "trespass; unfaithful, treacherous act." In addition to the primary sense of "trespass," given in KJV, there may be an indication of the motivation through which the sin was committed. Most of the usages support the idea of "faithlessness, treachery," Josh. 7:1. Joshua challenged Israel not to follow the example of Achan, and so be faithless, Josh. 22:20. In 2 Chron. 29:19 the "faithlessness" was committed against God.

***New Testament***

### A. Noun.

***paraptoma*** (*3900*), primarily "a false step, a blunder" (akin to ***parapipto***, "to fall away," Heb. 6:6), lit., "a fall beside," used ethically, denotes "a trespass," a deviation, from uprightness and truth, Matt. 6:14, 15 (twice); 18:35, in some mss.; Mark 11:25, 26; in Romans the RV substitutes "trespass" and "trespasses" for KJV, "offense" and "offenses," 4:25, "for (i.e., because of) our trespasses"; 5:15 (twice), where the trespass is that of Adam (in contrast to the free gift of righteousness, v. 17, a contrast in the nature and the effects); 5:16, where "of many trespasses" expresses a contrast of quantity; the condemnation resulted from one "trespass," the free gift is "of (***ek***, expressing the origin, and throwing stress upon God's justifying grace in Christ) many trespasses"; v. 17, introducing a contrast between legal effects and those of divine grace; v. 18, where the RV, "through one trespass," is contrasted with "one act of righteousness"; this is important, the difference is not between one man's "trespass" and Christ's righteousness (as KJV), but between two acts, that of Adam's "trespass" and the vicarious death of Christ; v. 20; in 2 Cor. 5:19, KJV and RV, "trespasses"; in Eph. 1:7, RV, "trespasses" (KJV, "sins"); in 2:1, RV, "(dead through your) trespasses," KJV, "(dead in) trespasses"; 2:5, RV, "(dead through our) trespasses," KJV, "(dead in) sins"; so Col. 2:13 (1st part); in the 2nd part, KJV and RV, "trespasses."

In Gal. 6:1, RV, "(in any) trespass" (KJV, "fault"), the reference is to "the works of the flesh" (5:19), and the thought is that of the believer's being found off his guard, the "trespass" taking advantage of him; in Jas. 5:16, KJV, "faults" (RV, "sins" translates the word ***hamartias***, which is found in the best texts), auricular confession to a priest is not in view here or anywhere else in Scripture; the command is comprehensive, and speaks either of the acknowledgment of sin where one has wronged another, or of the unburdening of a troubled conscience to a godly brother whose prayers will be efficacious, or of open confession before the church.

In Rom. 11:11, 12, the word is used of Israel's "fall," i.e., their deviation from obedience to God and from the fulfillment of His will (to be distinguished from the verb ***ptaio***, "fall," in the 1st part of v. 11, which indicates the impossibility of recovery).

**B. Verb.**

***hamartano*** (*264*), "to sin," is translated "to trespass," in the KJV of Matt. 18:15, and Luke 17:3, 4 (RV, "to sin").

## TRIAL

1. ***dokime*** (*1382*), rendered "trial" in 2 Cor. 8:2, KJV (RV, "proof").

2. ***peira*** (*3984*), "a making trial, an experiment," is used with ***lambano***, "to receive or take," in Heb. 11:29, rendered "assaying," and v. 36, in the sense of "having experience of" (akin to ***peirao***, "to assay, to try"), "had trial."

3. ***peirasmos*** (*3986*), akin to No. 2, is rendered "trials" in Acts 20:19, RV.

4. ***purosis*** (*4451*), akin to ***puroo***, "to set on fire," signifies (a) "a burning"; (b) "a refining," metaphorically in 1 Pet. 4:12, "fiery trial," or rather "trial by fire," referring to the refining of gold (1:7).

## TRIBE (-S)

### *Old Testament*

**A. Nouns.**

***matteh*** (4294), "staff; rod; shaft; branch; tribe." The basic meaning of ***matteh*** is "staff." The use of the "staff" was in shepherding. Judah was a shepherd and gave his "staff" to his daughter-in-law, Tamar, as a pledge of sending her a kid of the flock, Gen. 38:17–18; cf. also Exod. 4:2ff.; Exod. 17:9. The "staff" was also a token of authority. The Egyptian magicians had "staffs" as symbols of their authority over the magical realm by which they duplicated several miracles, Exod. 7:12; even the authority of a nation, Isa. 9:4; 10:5–6; or authority of God, Ps. 110:2. A derived sense of ***matteh*** is "tribe," which means one of the major subdivisions of a national unit, comprising thousands of persons, Josh. 14:1.

***shebet*** (7626), "tribe; rod." The "rod" as a tool is used by the shepherd, Lev. 27:32, and the teacher, 2 Sam. 7:14. It is a symbol of authority in the hands of a ruler, whether it is the scepter, Amos 1:5, 8, or an instrument of warfare and oppression, Ps. 2:9; cf. Zech. 10:11. The symbolic element comes to expression in a description of the messianic rule, Isa. 11:4. The word ***shebet*** is most frequently used to denote a "tribe," a division in a nation, Gen. 49:16; Exod. 28:21. Jeremiah referred to all of Israel as the "tribe," 51:19.

**B. Verb.**

***natah*** (5186), "to stretch out, spread out, extend," Exod. 9:22.

### *New Testament*

1. ***phule*** (*5443*), "a company of people united by kinship or habitation, a clan, tribe," is used (a) of the peoples of the earth, Matt. 24:30; in the following the RV has "tribe(-s)" for KJV, "kindred(-s)," Rev. 1:7; 5:9; 7:9; 11:9; 13:7; 14:6; (b) of the "tribes" of Israel, Matt. 19:28; Luke 2:36; 22:30; Acts 13:21; Rom. 11:1; Phil. 3:5; Heb. 7:13, 14; Jas. 1:1; Rev. 5:5; 7:4–8; 21:12.

2. ***dodekaphulos*** (*1429*), an adjective signifying "of twelve tribes" (***dodeka***, "twelve," and No. 1), used as a noun in the neuter, occurs in Acts 26:7.

## TRIBULATION

***thlipsis*** (*2347*), is translated "tribulation" in the RV (for KJV, "affliction") in Mark 4:17; 13:19; plural in 2 Thess. 1:4, KJV, "tribulations," RV, "afflictions"; in Acts 14:22 "many tribulations" (KJV, "much tribulation"); in Matt. 24:9, "unto tribulation" (KJV, "to be afflicted"); in 2 Cor. 1:4; 7:4; 2 Thess. 1:6, KJV, "tribulation" for RV, "affliction"; RV and KJV, "tribulation(-s)," e.g., in Rom. 2:9; 5:3 (twice); 8:35; 12:12; Eph. 3:13; Rev. 1:9; 2:9, 10, 22.

In Rev. 7:14, "the great tribulation," RV, lit., "the tribulation, the great one" (not as KJV, without the article), is not that in which all saints share; it indicates a definite period spoken of by the Lord in Matt. 24:21, 29; Mark 13:19, 24, where the time is mentioned as preceding His second advent, and as a period in which the Jewish nation, restored to Palestine in unbelief by gentile instrumentality, will suffer an unprecedented outburst of fury on the part of the antichristian powers confederate under the Man of Sin (2 Thess. 2:10–12; cf. Rev. 12:13–17); in this tribulation gentile witnesses for God will share (Rev. 7:9), but it will be distinctly "the time of Jacob's trouble," Jer. 30:7; its beginning is signalized by the setting up of the "abomination of desolation" (Matt. 24:15; Mark 13:14, with Dan. 11:31; 12:11).

## TRIBUTE

1. ***phoros*** (*5411*), akin to ***phero***, "to bring," denotes "tribute" paid by a subjugated nation, Luke 20:22; 23:2; Rom. 13:6, 7.

2. ***kensos*** (*2778*), Lat. and Eng., "census," denotes "a poll tax," Matt. 17:25; 22:17, 19; Mark 12:14.

3. ***didrachmon*** (*1323*), "the half-shekel," is rendered "tribute" in Matt. 17:24 (twice).

## TRIUMPH

***thriambeuo*** (*2358*) denotes (a) "to lead in triumph," used of a conqueror with reference to the vanquished, 2 Cor. 2:14. Theodoret paraphrases it, "He leads us about here and there and displays us to all the world." This is in agreement with evidences from various sources. Those who are led are not captives exposed to humiliation, but are displayed as the glory and devoted subjects of Him who leads (see the context). This is so even if there is a reference to a Roman "triumph." On such occasions the general's sons, with various officers, rode behind his chariot (Livy, xlv. 40). But there is no necessary reference here to a Roman "triumph."

In Col. 2:15 the circumstances and subjects are quite different, and relate to Christ's victory over spiritual foes at the time of His death; accordingly the reference may be to the triumphant display of the defeated.

## TROUBLE (Noun and Verb)

### A. Noun.

***thlipsis*** (*2347*), rendered "trouble" in the KJV of 1 Cor. 7:28 (RV, "tribulation"); 2 Cor. 1:4 (2nd clause), 8 (RV, "affliction").

### B. Verbs.

1. ***tarasso*** (*5015*), akin to ***tarache***, is used (1) in a physical sense, John 5:7 (in some mss. v. 4), (2) metaphorically, (a) of the soul and spirit of the Lord, John 11:33, where the true rendering is "He troubled Himself"; (b) of the hearts of disciples, 14:1, 27; (c) of the minds of those in fear or perplexity, Matt. 2:3; 14:26; Mark 6:50; Luke 1:12; 24:38; 1 Pet. 3:14; (d) of subverting the souls of believers, by evil doctrine, Acts 15:24; Gal. 1:7; 5:10; (e) of stirring up a crowd, Acts 17:8; v. 13 in the best texts, "troubling (the multitudes)," RV.

2. ***diatarasso*** (*1298*), "to agitate greatly" (***dia***, "throughout," and No. 1), is used of the Virgin Mary, Luke 1:29.

3. ***ektarasso*** (*1613*), "to throw into great trouble, agitate," is used in Acts 16:20, "do exceedingly trouble (our city)."

4. ***thlibo*** (*2346*), "to afflict," is rendered "to trouble" in the KJV, e.g., 2 Cor. 4:8 (RV, "pressed"); 7:5.

5. ***enochleo*** (*1776*), from ***en***, "in," ***ochlos***, "a throng, crowd," is used in Heb. 12:15 of a root of bitterness; in Luke 6:18 (in the best texts; some have ***ochleo***), RV, "were troubled" (KJV, "were vexed").

6. ***parenochleo*** (*3926*), "to annoy concerning anything" (***para***, and No. 5), occurs in Acts 15:19, "we trouble (not them)."

7. ***skullo*** (*4660*), primarily "to flay," hence, "to vex, annoy" ("there was a time when the Greek, in thus speaking, compared his trouble to the pains of flaying alive," Moulton, *Proleg.*, p. 89), is used in the active voice in Mark 5:35; Luke 8:49; in the passive voice, Matt. 9:36, in the best texts, RV, "they were distressed" (some have ***ekluo***, KJV, "they fainted"); in the middle voice, Luke 7:6, "trouble (not thyself)." The word is frequent in the papyri.

8. ***anastatoo*** (*387*) is rendered "trouble" in Gal. 5:12, KJV.

9. ***thorubeo*** (*2350*), akin to ***thorubos***, "a tumult," in the middle voice, "to make an uproar," is rendered "trouble not yourselves" in Acts 20:10, KJV.

10. ***throeo*** (*2360*), "to make an outcry" (***throos***, "a tumult"), is used in the passive voice, Matt. 24:6; Mark 13:7; Luke 24:37; 2 Thess. 2:2.

11. ***thorubazo*** (*2351*), "to disturb, to trouble" (akin to No. 9), is used in Luke 10:41, in the best texts (in some, ***turbazo***, with the same meaning).

12. ***ademoneo*** (*85*), "to be much troubled, distressed" (perhaps from ***a***, negative, and ***demon***, "knowing," the compound therefore originally suggesting bewilderment), is translated "sore troubled" in Matt. 26:37 and Mark 14:33, RV (KJV, "very heavy"); so the RV in Phil. 2:26 (KJV, "full of heaviness"); Lightfoot renders it "distressed," a meaning borne out in the papyri.

13. ***diaponeo*** (*1278*) denotes "to work out with toil," hence, "to be sore troubled"; so the RV in Acts 4:2 and 16:18 (KJV, "grieved"); Mark 14:4 in some texts.

## TRUE, TRULY, TRUTH

### A. Adjectives.

1. ***alethes*** (*227*), primarily, "unconcealed, manifest" (***a***, negative, ***letho***, "to forget," = ***lanthano***, "to escape notice"), hence, actual, "true to fact," is used (a) of persons, "truthful," Matt. 22:16; Mark 12:14; John 3:33; 7:18; 8:26; Rom. 3:4; 2 Cor. 6:8; (b) of things, "true," conforming to reality, John 4:18, "truly," lit., "true"; 5:31, 32; in the best texts, 6:55 (twice), "indeed"; 8:13, 14 (v. 16 in some texts: see No. 2), 17; 10:41; 19:35; 21:24; Acts 12:9; Phil. 4:8; Titus 1:13; 1 Pet. 5:12; 2 Pet. 2:22; 1 John 2:8, 27; 3 John 1:2.

2. ***alethinos*** (*228*), akin to No. 1, denotes "true" in the sense of real, ideal, genuine; it is used (a) of God, John 7:28 (cf. No. 1 in 7:18, above); 17:3; 1 Thess. 1:9; Rev. 6:10; these declare that God fulfills the meaning of His Name; He is "very God," in distinction from all other gods, false gods (***alethes***, see John 3:33 in No. 1, signifies that He is veracious, "true" to His utterances, He cannot lie); (b) of Christ, John 1:9; 6:32; 15:1; 1 John 2:8; 5:20 (thrice); Rev. 3:7, 14; 19:11; His judgment, John 8:16 (in the best texts, instead of No. 1); (c) God's words, John 4:37; Rev. 19:9, 21:5; 22:6; the last three

are equivalent to No. 1; (d) His ways, Rev. 15:3; (e) His judgments, Rev. 16:7; 19:2; (f) His riches, Luke 16:11; (g) His worshipers, John 4:23; (h) their hearts, Heb. 10:22; (i) the witness of the apostle John, John 19:35; (j) the spiritual, antitypical tabernacle, Heb. 8:2; 9:24, not that the wilderness tabernacle was false, but that it was a weak and earthly copy of the heavenly.

3. ***gnesios*** (*1103*), primarily "lawfully begotten" (akin to ***ginomai***, "to become"), hence, "true, genuine, sincere," is used in the apostle's exhortation to his "true yoke-fellow" in Phil. 4:3.

### B. Verb.

***aletheuo*** (*226*) signifies "to deal faithfully or truly with anyone" (cf. Gen. 42:16, Sept., "whether ye deal truly or no"), Eph. 4:15, "speaking the truth"; Gal. 3:16, "I tell (you) the truth," where probably the apostle is referring to the contents of his epistle.

### C. Noun.

***aletheia*** (*225*), "truth," is used (a) objectively, signifying "the reality lying at the basis of an appearance; the manifested, veritable essence of a matter" (Cremer), e.g., Rom. 9:1; 2 Cor. 11:10; especially of Christian doctrine, e.g., Gal. 2:5, where "the truth of the Gospel" denotes the "true" teaching of the Gospel, in contrast to perversions of it; Rom. 1:25, where "the truth of God" may be "the truth concerning God" or "God whose existence is a verity"; but in Rom. 15:8 "the truth of God" is indicative of His faithfulness in the fulfillment of His promises as exhibited in Christ; the word has an absolute force in John 14:6; 17:17; 18:37, 38; in Eph. 4:21, where the RV, "even as truth is in Jesus," gives the correct rendering, the meaning is not merely ethical "truth," but "truth" in all its fullness and scope, as embodied in Him; He was the perfect expression of the truth; this is virtually equivalent to His statement in John 14:6; (b) subjectively, "truthfulness," "truth," not merely verbal, but sincerity and integrity of character, John 8:44; 3 John 3, RV; (C) in phrases, e.g., "in truth" (***epi***, "on the basis of"), Mark 12:14; Luke 20:21; with ***en***, "in," 2 Cor. 6:7; Col. 1:6; 1 Tim. 2:7, RV (KJV, "in . . . verity"), 1 John 3:18; 2 John 1, 3, 4.

### D. Adverbs.

1. ***alethos*** (*230*), "truly, surely," is rendered "of a truth" in Matt. 14:33; 26:73 and Mark 14:70, RV, (KJV, "surely"); Luke 9:27; 12:44; 21:3; John 6:14; 7:40; 17:8, RV, "of a truth (KJV, surely); Acts 12:11, RV (KJV, "of a surety"); "in truth," 1 Thess. 2:13; "truly," Matt. 27:54; Mark 15:39.

2. ***gnesios*** (*1104*), "sincerely, honorably" (akin to A, No. 3), is rendered "truly" (marg., "genuinely") in Phil. 2:20 (KJV, "naturally").

## TRUMP, TRUMPET

### A. Noun.

***salpinx*** (*4536*) is used (1) of the natural instrument, 1 Cor. 14:8; (2) of the supernatural accompaniment of divine interpositions, (a) at Sinai, Heb. 12:19; (b) of the acts of angels at the second advent of Christ, Matt. 24:31; (c) of their acts in the period of divine judgments preceding this, Rev. 8:2, 6, 13; 9:14; (d) of a summons to John to the presence of God, Rev. 1:10; 4:1; (e) of the act of the Lord in raising from the dead the saints who have fallen asleep and changing the bodies of those who are living, at the Rapture of all to meet Him in the air, 1 Cor. 15:52, where "the last trump" is a military allusion, familiar to Greek readers, and has no connection with the series in Rev. 8:6 to 11:15; there is a possible allusion to Num. 10:2–6, with reference to the same event, 1 Thess. 4:16, "the (lit., a) trump of God" (the absence of the article suggests the meaning "a trumpet such as is used in God's service").

### B. Verb.

***salpizo*** (*4537*), "to sound a trumpet," Matt. 6:2; as in (2) (c) above, Rev. 8:6, 7 8, 10, 12, 13; 9:1, 13; 10:7; 11:15; as in (2) (e) 1 Cor. 15:52.

## TRUMPETER

***salpistes*** (*4538*) occurs in Rev. 18:22.

## TRUST (Noun and Verb)

### A. Noun.

***pepoithesis*** (*4006*) is rendered "trust" in 2 Cor. 3:4, KJV.

### B. Verbs.

1. ***peitho*** (*3982*), intransitively, in the perfect and pluperfect active, "to have confidence, trust," is rendered "to trust" in Matt. 27:43; Mark 10:24; Luke 11:22; 18:9; 2 Cor. 1:9; 10:7; Phil, 2:24; 3:4, KJV (RV, "to have confidence"); Heb. 2:13; in the present middle, Heb. 13:18, KJV (RV, "are persuaded").

2. ***pisteuo*** (*4100*), "to entrust," or, in the passive voice, "to be entrusted with," is rendered "to commit to one's trust," in Luke 16:11; 1 Tim. 1:11; "to be put in trust with," 1 Thess. 2:4, KJV (RV, "to be intrusted").

## TRY, TRIED

1. ***dokimazo*** (*1381*) is rendered "to try" in the KJV in 1 Cor. 3:13; 1 Thess. 2:4; 1 Pet. 1:7; 1 John 4:1.

2. ***peirazo*** (*3985*) is rendered "to try" in Heb. 11:17; Rev. 2:2, 10; 3:10. In Acts 16:7 it is rendered "assayed"; in 24:6, RV, "assayed" (KJV, "hath gone about").

## TUMULT

1. ***akatastasia*** (*181*) is rendered "tumults" in Luke 21:9, RV; 2 Cor. 6:5; 12:20.

2. ***thorubos*** (*2351*), "a noise, uproar, tumult," is rendered "tumult" in Matt. 27:24 and Mark 5:38; in Matt. 26:5, RV (KJV, "uproar"), so in Mark 14:2; in Acts 20:1, "uproar," KJV and RV; in 24:18, "tumult"; in 21:34, KJV, "tumult" (RV, "uproar").

## TWINKLING

***rhipe*** (*4493*), akin to ***rhipto***, "to hurl," was used of any rapid movement, e.g., the throw of a javelin, the rush of wind or flame; in 1 Cor. 15:52 of the "twinkling" of an eye.

# U

## UNBELIEF

1. ***apistia*** *(570)*, "unbelief," Matt. 13:58; Mark 9:24; Rom. 3:3.

2. ***apeitheta*** *(543)* is always rendered "disobedience" in the RV; Rom. 11:30, 32; Heb. 4:6, 11.

## UNBELIEVER

***apistos*** *(571)*, an adjective, is used as a noun, rendered "unbeliever" in 2 Cor. 6:15 and 1 Tim. 5:8, RV; plural in 1 Cor. 6:6 and 2 Cor. 6:14; KJV only, Luke 12:46 (RV, "unfaithful").

## UNBELIEVING

**A. Adjective.**

***apistos*** *(571)*, "unbelieving," Matt. 17:17.

**B. Verb.**

***apeitheo*** *(544)*, "refuse to believe," John 3:36.

## UNBLAMEABLE, UNBLAMEABLY

**A. Adjective.**

***amemptos*** *(273)*, "unblameable" (from ***a***, negative, and ***memphomai***, "to find fault"), is so rendered in 1 Thess. 3:13, i.e., "free from all valid charge."

**B. Adverb.**

***amemptos*** *(274)* is used in 1 Thess. 2:10, "unblameably," signifying that no charge could be maintained, whatever charges might be made.

## UNCERTAIN, UNCERTAINLY, UNCERTAINTY

**A. Adjective.**

***adelos*** *(82)* denotes (a) "unseen"; with the article, translated "which appear not" (***a***, negative, ***delos***, "evident"), Luke 11:44; (b) "uncertain, indistinct," 1 Cor. 14:8.

**B. Adverb.**

***adelos*** *(84)*, "uncertainly" (akin to A), occurs in 1 Cor. 9:26.

**C. Noun.**

***adelotes*** *(83)*, "uncertainty" (akin to A and B), occurs in 1 Tim. 6:17, "(the) uncertainty (of riches)," RV (the KJV translates it as an adjective, "uncertain"), i.e., riches the special character of which is their "uncertainty"; the Greek phrase is a rhetorical way of stressing the noun "riches"; when a genitive (here "of riches") precedes the governing noun (here "uncertainty") the genitive receives emphasis.

## UNCHANGEABLE

***aparabatos*** *(531)* is used of the priesthood of Christ, in Heb. 7:24.

## UNCLEAN

### *Old Testament*

**A. Verb.**

***tame'*** (2930), "to be unclean," usually with the meaning of ceremonial uncleanness, Lev. 11:26. ***tame'*** is the opposite of ***taher***, "to be pure."

**B. Noun.**

***tum'ah*** (2932), "uncleanness." This noun is means ceremonial uncleanness, Num. 5:19; ethical and religious uncleanness, Lev 16:16.

**C. Adjective.**

***tame'*** (2931), "unclean." This adjective occurs usually in Leviticus, with the meaning of ceremonial or ritual cleanness, so as to be pure to the Lord, Lev. 5:2. The usage of ***tame'*** in the Old Testament resembles that of ***tahor***, "pure." First, uncleanness is a state of being. The leper was compelled to announce his uncleanness wherever he went, Lev. 13:45; however, even here there is a religious overtone, in that his uncleanness was ritual. Hence, it is more appropriate to recognize that the second usage is most basic. ***tame'*** in the religio-cultic sense is a technical term denoting a state of being ceremonially unfit, Num. 19:22; even from genital issues, Lev. 15:2, 25.

### *New Testament*

**A. Adjectives.**

1. ***akathartos*** *(169)*, "unclean, impure" (***a***, negative, ***kathairo***, "to purify"), is used (a) of "unclean" spirits, frequently in the Synoptists, not in John's gospel; in Acts 5:16; 8:7; Rev. 16:13; 18:2a (in the 2nd clause the birds are apparently figurative of destructive satanic agencies); (b) ceremonially, Acts 10:14, 28; 11:8; 1 Cor. 7:14; (c) morally, 2 Cor. 6:17, including (b), RV; "no unclean thing"; Eph. 5:5; Rev. 17:4, RV, "the unclean things" (KJV follows the text which have the noun ***akathartes***, "the filthiness").

2. ***koinos*** *(2839)*, "common," is translated "unclean" in Rom. 14:14 (thrice).

### B. Verb.

***koinoo*** *(2840)*, to make ***koinos***, "to defile," is translated "unclean" in Heb. 9:13, KJV, where the perfect participle, passive, is used with the article, hence the RV, "them that have been defiled."

### C. Noun.

***akatharsia*** *(167)*, akin to A, No. 1, denotes "uncleanness," (a) physical, Matt. 23:27 (instances in the papyri speak of tenants keeping houses in good condition); (b) moral, Rom. 1:24; 6:19; 2 Cor. 12:21; Gal. 5:19; Eph. 4:19; 5:3; Col. 3:5; 1 Thess. 2:3 (suggestive of the fact that sensuality and evil doctrine are frequently associated); 4:7.

## UNCONDEMNED

***akatakritos*** *(178)*, rendered "uncondemned" in Acts 16:37; 22:25, properly means "without trial, not yet tried."

## UNCOVER

***apostegazo*** *(648)* signifies "to unroof" (***apo***, from, ***stege***, "a roof"), Mark 2:4.

## UNDEFILED

***amiantos*** *(283)*, "undefiled, free from contamination" (***a***, negative, ***miaino***, "to defile"), is used (a) of Christ, Heb. 7:26; (b) of pure religion, Jas. 1:27; (c) of the eternal inheritance of believers, 1 Pet. 1:4; (d) of the marriage bed as requiring to be free from unlawful sexual intercourse, Heb. 13:4.

## UNDERSTAND, UNDERSTOOD

*Old Testament*

### A. Verbs.

***sakal*** (7919), "to be prudent, act wisely, give attention to, ponder, prosper." The basic meaning of ***sakal*** seems to be "to look at, to give attention to," as illustrated in this parallelism: "That they may see, and know, and consider, and understand . . ." Isa. 41:20. From this develops the connotation of insight, intellectual comprehension, Jer. 9:23–24. As here, it is frequently used along with and in parallelism to the Hebrew ***yada'***, "to know" (primarily experientially). As is true of ***chakam***, "to be wise," ***sakal*** never concerns abstract prudence, but acting prudently, Amos 5:13; Ps. 36:3.

***bin*** (995), "to understand, be able, deal wisely, consider, pay attention to, regard, notice, discern, perceive, inquire." ***bin*** appears in Jer. 9:12 with the meaning "to understand"; Job 6:30, "to discern"; and in Deut. 32:7 it means "to consider."

### B. Nouns.

***binah*** (998), "understanding." This noun represents the "act of understanding," Dan. 1:20. Elsewhere ***binah*** signifies the faculty "understanding," Job 20:3. In other passages the object of knowledge, in the sense of what one desires to know, is indicated by ***binah***, Deut. 4:6; cf. 1 Chron. 22:12.

***tebunah*** (8394), "understanding." This word, which occurs 42 times, is also a wisdom term. Like ***binah***, it represents the act, Job 26:12, faculty, Exod. 31:3, object, Prov. 2:3.

***maskil*** (4905), "didactic psalm(?)." This noun form, derived from ***sakal***, is found in the title of 13 psalms and also in Ps. 47:7. Scholars are not agreed on the significance of this term, but on the basis of the general meaning of ***sakal***, such psalms must have been considered didactic or teaching psalms.

*New Testament*

### A. Verbs.

1. ***suniemi*** *(4920)*, primarily, "to bring or set together," is used metaphorically of "perceiving, understanding, uniting" (***sun***), so to speak, the perception with what is perceived, e.g., Matt. 13:13–15, 19, 23, 51; 15:10; 16:12; 17:13, and similar passages in Mark and Luke; Acts 7:25 (twice); 28:26, 27; in Rom. 3:11, the present participle, with the article, is used as a noun, lit., "there is not the understanding (one)," in a moral and spiritual sense; Rom. 15:21; 2 Cor. 10:12, RV, "are (without) understanding," KJV, "are (not) wise"; Eph. 5:17, RV, "understand."

2. ***noeo*** *(3539)*, "to perceive with the mind," as distinct from perception by feeling, is so used in Matt. 15:17, KJV, "understand," RV, "perceive"; 16:9, 11; 24:15 (here rather perhaps in the sense of considering) and parallels in Mark (not in Luke); John 12:40; Rom. 1:20; 1 Tim. 1:7; Heb. 11:3; in Eph. 3:4, KJV, "may understand" (RV, "can perceive"); 3:20, "think"; 2 Tim. 2:7, "consider."

3. ***ginosko*** *(1097)*, "to know, to come to know," is translated "to understand" in the KJV in Matt. 26:10 and John 8:27 (RV, "to perceive"); KJV and RV in John 8:43; 10:6; in 10:38, RV (in some texts ***pisteuo***, KJV, "believe"); KJV and RV in 12:16; 13:7 RV, KJV, "know"; Acts 8:30; in Phil. 1:12, KJV, RV, "know" (in some texts, Acts 24:11, KJV).

### B. Adjectives.

1. ***eusemos*** *(2154)*, primarily denotes "conspicuous" or "glorious" (as in Ps. 81:3, Sept.; RV, "solemn"), then, "distinct, clear to understanding," 1 Cor. 14:9, "easy to be understood" (KJV, marg., "significant").

2. ***dusnoetos*** (*1425*), "hard to be understood," occurs in 2 Pet. 3:16.

## UNDERSTANDING

### A. Nouns.

1. ***nous*** (*3563*), translated "understanding" in Luke 24:45, KJV (RV, "mind"); 1 Cor. 14:14, 15 (twice), 19; Phil. 4:7; Rev. 13:18.

2. ***sunesis*** (*4907*), akin to ***suniemi***, "to set together, to understand," denotes (a) "the understanding, the mind or intelligence," Mark 12:33; (b) "understanding, reflective thought," Luke 2:47; 1 Cor. 1:19, RV, "prudence," Eph. 3:4, RV (AV, "knowledge"); Col. 1:9; 2:2; 2 Tim. 2:7.

3. ***dianoia*** (*1271*), rendered "understanding" in Eph. 4:18; 1 John 5:20.

### B. Adjective.

***asunetos*** (*801*), "without understanding or discernment" (***a***, negative, ***sunetos***, "intelligent, understanding"), is translated "without understanding" in Matt. 15:16; Mark 7:18; Rom. 1:31; 10:19, RV, "void of understanding" (KJV, "foolish"); in Rom. 1:21, RV, "senseless" (KJV, "foolish").

## UNFAITHFUL

***apistos*** (*571*), "unbelieving, faithless," is translated "unfaithful" in Luke 12:46, RV (KJV, "unbelievers").

## UNGODLINESS, UNGODLY

### A. Noun.

***asebeia*** (*763*), "impiety, ungodliness," is used of (a) general impiety, Rom. 1:18; 11:26; 2 Tim. 2:16; Titus 2:12; (b) "ungodly" deeds, Jude 15, RV, "works of ungodliness"; (c) of lusts or desires after evil things, Jude 18. It is the opposite of ***eusebeia***, "godliness."

### B. Adjective.

***asebes*** (*765*), "impious, ungodly" (akin to A), "without reverence for God," not merely irreligious, but acting in contravention of God's demands, Rom. 4:5; 5:6; 1 Tim. 1:9; 1 Pet. 4:18; 2 Pet. 2:5 (v. 6 in some mss.); 3:7; Jude 4, 15 (twice).

### C. Verb.

***asebeo*** (*764*), akin to A and B, signifies (a) "to be or live ungodly," 2 Pet. 2:6; (b) "to commit ungodly deeds," Jude 15.

## UNHOLY

1. ***anosios*** (*462*), "unholy, profane," occurs in 1 Tim. 1:9; 2 Tim. 3:2.

2. ***koinon*** (*2839*), the neut. of ***koinos***, "common," is translated "an unholy thing" in Heb. 10:29.

## UNITY

***henotes*** (*1775*), from ***hen***, the neuter of ***heis***, "one." is used in Eph. 4:3, 13.

## UNJUST

***adikos*** (*94*), "not in conformity with ***dike***, "right," is rendered "unjust" in the KJV and RV in Matt. 5:45; Luke 18:11; Acts 24:15; elsewhere for the KJV "unjust" the RV has "unrighteous.

## UNLAWFUL

***athemitos*** (*111*), a late form for ***athemistos*** (***themis***, "custom, right"; in classical Greek "divine law"), "contrary to what is right," is rendered "an unlawful thing" (neuter) in Acts 10:28; in 1 Pet. 4:3, "abominable."

## UNLEARNED

1. ***agrammatos*** (*62*), lit., "unlettered" (***grammata***, "letters": ***grapho***, "to write") Acts 4:13, means either; "unversed in the learning of the Jewish schools"; or "one who cannot write."

2. ***amathes*** (*261*), "unlearned" (***manthano***, "to learn"), is translated "unlearned" in 2 Pet. 3:16, KJV (RV, "ignorant").

3. ***apaideutos*** (*521*), "uninstructed" (***paideuo***, "to train, teach"), is translated "unlearned" in 2 Tim. 2:23, KJV (RV, "ignorant").

## UNLOOSE

***luo*** (*3089*), "to loose," is rendered "to unloose" in Mark 1:7; Luke 3:16; John 1:27; in Acts 13:25, RV.

## UNMARRIED

***agamos*** (*22*), ***a***, negative, ***gameo***, "to marry," occurs in 1 Cor. 7:8, 11, 32, 34.

## UNMERCIFUL

***aneleemon*** (*415*), "without mercy" (***a***, negative, ***n***, euphonic, ***eleemon***, "merciful"), occurs in Rom. 1:31.

## UNPREPARED

***aparaskeuastos*** (*532*), "unprepared," occurs in 2 Cor. 9:4.



## UNPROFITABLE, UNPROFITABLENESS

### A. Adjectives.

1. ***achreios*** (*888*), "useless" (***chreia***, "use"), "unprofitable," occurs in Matt. 25:30 and Luke 17:10.

2. ***achrestos*** (*890*), "unprofitable, unserviceable" (***chrestos***, "serviceable"), is said of Onesimus, Philem. 11, antithetically to ***euchrestos***, "profitable," with a play on the name of the converted slave (from ***onesis***, "profit").

3. ***alusiteles*** (*255*), "not advantageous, not making good the expense involved" (***lusiteles***, "useful") occurs in Heb. 13:17.

4. ***anopheles*** (*512*), "not beneficial or serviceable" (***a***, negative, ***n***, euphonic, ***opheleo***, "to do good, to benefit"), is rendered "unprofitable" in Titus 3:9; in the neuter, used as a noun, "unprofitableness," Heb. 7:18, said of the Law as not accomplishing that which the "better hope" could alone bring.

**B. Verb.**

***achreoo***, or ***achreioo*** (*889*), akin to A, No. 1, "to make useless," occurs in Rom. 3:12, in the passive voice, rendered "they have . . . become unprofitable."

## UNREASONABLE

***alogos*** (*249*), "without reason, irrational," is rendered "unreasonable" in Acts 25:27.

## UNRIGHTEOUS

***adikos*** (*94*), not conforming to ***dike***, "right," is translated "unrighteous" in Luke 16:10 (twice), RV, 11; Rom. 3:5; 1 Cor. 6:1, RV; 6:9; Heb. 6:10; 1 Pet. 3:18, RV; 2 Pet. 2:9, RV.

## UNRIGHTEOUSNESS

**A. Noun.**

***adikia*** (*93*) denotes (a) "injustice," Luke 18:6, lit., "the judge of injustice"; Rom. 9:14; (b) "unrighteousness, iniquity," e.g., Luke 16:8, lit., "the steward of unrighteousness," RV marg., i.e., characterized by "unrighteousness"; Rom. 1:18, 29; 2:8; 3:5; 6:13; 1 Cor. 13:6, RV, "unrighteousness"; 2 Thess. 2:10, "[with all (lit., 'in every) deceit'] of unrighteousness," i.e., deceit such as "unrighteousness" uses, and that in every variety; Antichrist and his ministers will not be restrained by any scruple from words or deeds calculated to deceive; 2 Thess. 2:12, of those who have pleasure in it, not an intellectual but a moral evil; distaste for truth is the precursor of the rejection of it; 2 Tim. 2:19, RV; 1 John 1:9, which includes (c); (c) "a deed or deeds violating law and justice" (virtually the same as ***adikema***, "an unrighteous act"), e.g., Luke 13:27, "iniquity"; 2 Cor. 12:13, "wrong," the wrong of depriving another of what is his own, here ironically of a favor; Heb. 8:12, 1st clause, "iniquities," lit., "unrighteousnesses" (plural, not as KJV); 2 Pet. 2:13, 15, RV, "wrongdoing," KJV, "unrighteousness"; 1 John 5:17.

**B. Verb.**

***adikeo*** (*91*), "to do wrong," is rendered in Rev. 22:11, RV, firstly, "he that is unrighteous," lit., "the doer of unrighteousness" (present participle of the verb, with the article), secondly, "let him do unrighteousness (still)," the retributive and permanent effect of a persistent course of unrighteous-doing (KJV, "he that is unjust, let him be unjust").

## UNRULY

1. ***anupotaktos*** (*506*), "not subject to rule" (***a***, negative, ***n***, euphonic, ***hupotasso***, "to put in subjection"), is used (a) of things, Heb. 2:8, RV, "not subject" (KJV, "not put under"); (b) of persons, "unruly," 1 Tim. 1:9, RV (KJV, "disobedient"); Titus 1:6, 10.

2. ***ataktos*** (*814*) is rendered "unruly" in 1 Thess. 5:14, KJV (marg. and RV, "disorderly).

## UNSEARCHABLE

1. ***anexeraunetos***, or ***anexereunetos*** (*419*), (***a***, negative, ***n***, euphonic, ***ex*** [***ek***], "out," ***eraunao***, "to search, examine"), is used in Rom. 11:33, of the judgments of God.

2. ***anexichniastos*** (*421*), with the same prefixes as in No. 1 and an adjectival form akin to ***ichneuo***, "to trace out" (***ichnos***, "a footprint, a track"), is translated "unsearchable" in Eph. 3:8, of the riches of Christ; in Rom. 11:33, "past tracing out," of the ways of the Lord (cf. No. 1, in the same verse). The ways of God are the outworkings of His judgment. Of the two questions in v. 34, the first seems to have reference to No. 1, the second to No. 2.

## UNSEEMLINESS, UNSEEMLY

***aschemosune*** (*808*), from ***aschemon***, "unseemly," is rendered "unseemliness" in Rom. 1:27, RV.

## UNSPEAKABLE

1. ***anekdiegetos*** (*411*) denotes "inexpressible" (***a***, negative, ***n***, euphonic, ***ekdiegeomai***, "to declare, relate"), 2 Cor. 9:15, "unspeakable" (of the gift of God); regarding the various explanations of the gift, it seems most suitable to view it as the gift of His Son.

2. ***aneklaletos*** (*412*) denotes "unable to be told out" (***eklaleo***, "to speak out"), 1 Pet. 1:8, of the believer joy.

3. ***arrhetos*** (*731*), primarily, "unspoken" (***a***, negative, ***rhetos***, "spoken"), denotes "unspeakable," 2 Cor. 12:4, of the words heard by Paul when caught up into paradise. The word is common in sacred inscriptions especially in connection with the Greek Mysteries; hence Moulton and Milligan suggest the meaning "words too sacred to be uttered."

## UNSTABLE, UNSTEADFAST

1. ***asteriktos*** (*793*), (***a***, negative, ***sterizo***, "to fix"), is used in 2 Pet. 2:14; 3:16, KJV, "unstable," RV, "unsteadfast."

2. ***akatastatos*** (*182*), from ***kathistemi***, "to set in order," is rendered "unstable" in Jas. 1:8.

## UNTHANKFUL

***acharistos*** (*884*) denotes "ungrateful, thankless" (***charis***, "thanks"), Luke 6:35; 2 Tim. 3:2.

## UNVEILED

***akatakaluptos*** (*177*), "uncovered" (***a***, negative, ***katakalupto***, "to cover"), is used in 1 Cor. 11:5, 13, RV, "unveiled," with reference to the injunction forbidding women to be "unveiled" in a church gathering. Whatever the character of the covering, it is to be on her head as "a sign of authority" (v. 10), RV, the meaning of which is indicated in v. 3 in the matter of headships, and the reasons for which are given in vv. 7–9, and in the phrase "because of the angels," intimating their witness of, and interest in, that which betokens the headship of Christ.

## UNWASHED

***aniptos*** (*449*), "unwashed" (***a***, negative, ***nipto***, "to wash"), occurs in Matt. 15:20; Mark 7:2 (v. 5 in some mss.).

## UNWISE

1. ***anoetos*** (*453*) is translated "unwise" in Rom. 1:14, KJV.

2. ***aphron*** (*878*) is translated "unwise" in Eph. 5:17, KJV.

3. ***asophos*** (*781*), rendered "unwise" in Eph. 5:15, RV (KJV, "fools.)"

## UNWORTHILY, UNWORTHY

### A. Adverb.

***anaxios*** (*371*) is used in 1 Cor. 11:27, of partaking of the Lord's Supper "unworthily," i.e., treating it as a common meal, the bread and cup as common things, not apprehending their solemn symbolic import.

### B. Adjective.

***anaxios*** (*370*) is used in 1 Cor. 6:2. In modern Greek it signifies "incapable."

## UPRIGHT, UPRIGHTNESS

*Old Testament*

### A. Adjective.

***yashar*** (3477), "upright; right; righteous; just." The basic meaning is the root meaning "to be straight" in the sense of "to be level." The legs of the creatures in Ezekiel's vision were straight, Ezek. 1:7. The Israelites designated an easy road for traveling as a "level road." It had few inclines and declines compared to the mountain roads, cf. Jer. 31:9.

***yashar*** with the meaning "right" pertains to things and to abstracts. Samuel promised himself to instruct God's people in "the good and the right way," 1 Sam. 12:23. Nehemiah thanked God for having given just ordinances, Neh. 9:13. Based on His revelation God expected His people to please Him in being obedient to Him, Deut. 6:18.

When ***yashar*** pertains to people, it is best translated "just" or "upright." God is the standard of uprightness for His people, Ps. 25:8. His word, Ps. 33:4, judgments, Ps. 19:9, and ways, Hos. 14:9, reveal His uprightness and are a blessing to His people. The believer follows Him in being "upright" in heart, Ps. 32:11; cf. 7:10; 11:2.

### B. Verb.

***yashar*** (3474), "to be straight, be smooth, be right." One occurrence of the verb is in 1 Chron. 13:4: "And all the congregation said that they would do so: for the thing was right in the eyes of all the people." In this usage ***yashar*** has the sense of being pleasing or agreeable. In Hab. 2:4 the word implies an ethical uprightness.

### C. Nouns.

***yosher*** (3476), "straightness," Prov. 2:13.

Other nouns occur less frequently. ***yishrah*** means "uprightness" and occurs once, 1 Kings 3:6. The noun ***yeshurun*** is an honorific title for Israel, Deut. 32:15; 33:5. ***mishor*** means "level place, uprightness." In 1 Kings 20:23 ***mishor*** refers to "level country"; in Isa. 11:4 the word refers to "uprightness."

*New Testament*

***euthutes*** (*2118*), from ***euthus***, "straight," is rendered "uprightness" in Heb. 1:8, RV, KJV, "righteousness," marg., "rightness," or, "straightness."

## UPROAR (Verbs)

***thorubeo*** (*2350*), used in the middle voice, denotes "to make a noise or uproar," or, transitively, in the active voice, "to trouble, throw into confusion," Acts 17:5.



## URGE

(1) In Acts 13:50, KJV, ***parotruno***, "to urge on" (RV), is rendered "stirred up." (2) In Acts 13:43, ***peitho***, "to persuade," is rendered "urged," RV (KJV, "persuaded"). (3) ***enecho*** is rendered "to urge" in Luke 11:53.

## USURY

***Note:*** The RV, "interest," Matt. 25:27; Luke 19:23, is the preferable rendering of ***tokos*** here.

## UTTER

1. ***laleo*** (*2980*), "to speak," is rendered "to utter" in 2 Cor. 12:4 and Rev. 10:3, 4 (twice).

2. ***ereugomai*** (*2044*), primarily, "to spit or spue out," or, of oxen, "to bellow, roar," hence, "to speak aloud, utter," occurs in Matt. 13:35.

3. ***aphiemi*** (*863*), "to send forth," is used of "uttering" a cry, Mark 15:37, of Christ's final "utterance" on the cross, RV, "uttered" (KJV, "cried").

## UTTERANCE

***logos*** (*3056*), "a word," is translated "utterance" in 1 Cor. 1:5; 2 Cor. 8:7; Eph. 6:19.

# V

## VAIN, IN VAIN, VAINLY

**A. Adjectives.**

1. ***kenos*** (*2756*), "empty," with special reference to quality, is translated "vain" (as an adjective) in Acts 4:25; 1 Cor. 15:10, 14 (twice); Eph. 5:6; Col. 2:8; Jas. 2:20.

2. ***mataios*** (*3152*), "void of result," is used of (a) idolatrous practices, Acts 14:15, RV, "vain things" (KJV, "vanities"); (b) the thoughts of the wise, 1 Cor. 3:20; (c) faith, if Christ is not risen, 1 Cor. 15:17; (d) questionings, strifes, etc., Titus 3:9; (e) religion, with an unbridled tongue, Jas. 1:26; (f) manner of life, 1 Pet. 1:18.

**B. Verbs.**

1. ***mataioo*** (*3154*), "to make vain, or foolish," corresponding in meaning to A, No. 2, occurs in Rom. 1:21, "became vain."

2. ***kenoo*** (*2758*), "to empty," corresponding to A, No. 1, is translated "should be in vain" in 2 Cor. 9:3, KJV.

**C. Adverbs.**

1. ***maten*** (*3155*), properly the accusative case of ***mate***, "a fault, a folly," signifies "in vain, to no purpose," Matt. 15:9; Mark 7:7.

2. ***dorean*** (*1432*), the accusative of ***dorea***, "a gift," is used adverbially, denoting (a) "freely" (see FREE, D); (b) "uselessly," "in vain," Gal. 2:21, KJV (RV, "for nought").

3. ***eike*** (*1500*) denotes (a) "without cause," "vainly," Col. 2:18; (b) "to no purpose," "in vain," Rom. 13:4; Gal. 3:4 (twice); 4:11.

## VAINGLORY, VAINGLORIOUS

**A. Nouns.**

1. ***kenodoxia*** (*2754*), from ***kenos***, "vain, empty," ***doxa***, "glory," is used in Phil. 2:3.

2. ***alazoneia***, or ***-ia*** (*212*) denotes "boastfulness, vaunting," translated "vainglory" in 1 John 2:16, RV (KJV, "pride"); in Jas. 4:16, RV, "vauntings" (KJV, "boastings").

**B. Adjective.**

***kenodoxos*** (*2755*), akin to A, No. 1, is rendered "vainglorious" in Gal. 5:26, RV (KJV, "desirous of vain glory").

## VALUE

**A. Verb.**

***diaphero*** (*1308*), used intransitively, means "to differ, to excel," hence "to be of more value," Matt. 6:26, RV, "are (not) ye of (much) more value" (KJV, "better"); 12:12 and Luke 12:24, ditto; Matt. 10:31; Luke 12:7.

**B. Noun.**

***time*** (*5092*) denotes "a valuing, a price, honor"; in Col. 2:23, RV, "(not of any) value (against the indulgence of the flesh)" [KJV, "(not in any) honor . . ."], i.e., the ordinances enjoined by human tradition are not of any value to prevent (***pros***, "against"; cf. Acts 26:14) indulgence of the flesh.

## VANISH, VANISHING

**A. Verb.**

***aphanizo*** (*853*), "to render unseen," is translated "vanisheth away" in Jas. 4:14 (passive voice, lit., "is made to disappear").

**B. Noun.**

***aphanismos*** (*854*), (***a***, negative, ***phaino***, "to cause to appear" akin to A), occurs in Heb. 8:13, RV, "(nigh unto) vanishing away"; the word is suggestive of abolition.

## VANITY

***mataiotes*** (*3153*), "emptiness as to results," akin to ***mataios***, is used (a) of the creation, Rom. 8:20, as failing of the results designed, owing to sin; (b) of the mind which governs the manner of life of the Gentiles, Eph. 4:17; (c) of the "great swelling *words*" of false teachers, 2 Pet. 2:18.

## VAPOR

***atmis*** (*822*) is used of "smoke," Acts 2:19; figuratively of human life, Jas. 4:14.

## VARIABLENESS, VARIATION

***parallage*** (*3883*) denotes, in general, "a change" (Eng., "parallax," the difference between the directions of a body as seen from two different points), "a transmission" from one condition to another; it occurs in Jas. 1:17, RV, "variation" (KJV, "variableness"); the reference may be to the sun, which "varies" its position in the sky.

## VARIANCE

***dichazo*** (*1369*), "to cut apart, divide in two," is used metaphorically in Matt. 10:35, "to set at variance."

## VAUNT (ONESELF)

***perpereuomai*** (*4068*), "to boast or vaunt oneself" (from ***perperos***, "vainglorious, braggart," not in the NT), is used in 1 Cor. 13:4, negatively of love.

## VEHEMENTLY

1. ***deinos*** (*1171*), is rendered "vehemently" in Luke 11:53.

2. ***eutonos*** (*2159*), vigorously, is translated "vehemently" in Luke 23:10, of accusations against Christ.

3. ***ekperissos*** (*1537* and *4053*), formed from ***ek***, "out of," and the adverb ***perissos***, "exceedingly, the more," is found in Mark 14:31, in the best texts (some have ***ek perissou***, the genitive case of the adjective ***perissos***, "more"), RV, "exceeding vehemently" (KJV, "the more vehemently"), of Peter's protestation of loyalty; the RV gives the better rendering.

## VEIL

1. ***katapetasma*** (*2665*), lit., "that which is spread out" (***petannumi***) "before" (***kata***), hence, "a veil," is used (a) of the inner "veil" of the tabernacle, Heb. 6:19; 9:3; (b) of the corresponding "veil" in the Temple, Matt. 27:51; Mark 15:38; Luke 23:45; (c) metaphorically of the "flesh" of Christ, Heb. 10:20, i.e., His body which He gave up to be crucified, thus by His expiatory death providing a means of the spiritual access of believers, the "new and living way," into the presence of God.

2. ***kalumma*** (*2571*), "a covering," is used (a) of the "veil" which Moses put over his face when descending Mount Sinai, thus preventing Israel from beholding the glory, 2 Cor. 3:13; (b) metaphorically of the spiritually darkened vision suffered retributively by Israel, until the conversion of the nation to their Messiah takes place, vv. 14, 15, 16.

3. ***peribolaion*** (*4018*), rendered "a veil" in the KJV marg. of 1 Cor. 11:15.

## VENGEANCE

***ekdikesis*** (*1557*), lit., ("that which proceeds) out of justice," not, as often with human "vengeance," out of a sense of injury or merely out of a feeling of indignation. The word is most frequently used of divine "vengeance," e.g., Rom. 12:19; Heb. 10:30. The judgments of God are holy and right (Rev. 16:7), and free from any element of self-gratification or vindictiveness.

## VERILY

1. ***alethos*** (*230*), "truly" (akin to ***aletheia***, "truth"), is translated "verily" in 1 John 2:5.

2. ***amen*** (*281*), the transliteration of a Heb. word = "truth," is usually translated "verily" in the four Gospels; in John's gospel the Lord introduces a solemn pronouncement by the repeated word "verily, verily" twenty-five times.

## VESSEL

### *Old Testament*

***keli*** (3627), "vessel," can mean an utensil or container of many different kinds and made of many different materials. It is similar to the way we use "thing," as a descriptor, as in "hand me that *thing*." Context will best demand what the meaning of the *thing* is: receptacle; stuff; clothing; utensil; tool; instrument; ornament or jewelry; armor or weapon, Gen. 31:37; Lev. 6:28; 1 Sam. 17:22 the word is used of baggage; or cargo, Jon. 1:5. Ships are called "receptacles," presumably because they can hold people, Isa. 18:2.

This word may be used of various "implements or tools": "Simeon and Levi are brethren instruments of cruelty are in their habitations," Gen. 49:5. In Jer. 22:7 the word represents "tools" with which trees may be cut down: "And I will prepare destroyers against thee, every one with his weapons: and they shall cut down thy choice cedars, and cast them into the fire." Isaac told Esau to take his gear, his quiver, and his bow, "and go out to the field, and take me some venison," Gen. 27:3.

Weapons for war are called "implements": "And they [the Israelites] went after them unto Jordan: and, lo, all the way was full of garments and vessels, which the Syrians had cast away in their haste," 2 Kings 7:15. A bearer of implements is an armor-bearer, Judg. 9:54. A house of arms or an armory is referred to in 2 Kings 20:13.

In Amos 6:5 and such passages, 2 Chron. 5:13; 7:6; 23:13; cf. Ps. 71:22, "musical instruments" are called ***kelim:*** "That chant to the sound of the viol, and invent to themselves instruments of music. . . ."

### *New Testament*

***skeuos*** (*4632*) is used (a) of "a vessel or implement" of various kinds, Mark 11:16; Luke 8:16; John 19:29; Acts 10:11, 16; 11:5; 27:17 (a sail); Rom. 9:21; 2 Tim. 2:20; Heb. 9:21; Rev. 2:27; 18:12; (b) of "goods or household stuff," Matt. 12:29 and Mark 3:27, "goods"; Luke 17:31, RV, "goods" (KJV, "stuff"); (c) of "persons," (1) for the service of God, Acts 9:15, "a (chosen) vessel"; 2 Tim. 2:21, "a vessel (unto honor)"; (2) the "subjects" of divine wrath, Rom. 9:22; (3) the "subjects" of divine mercy, Rom. 9:23; (4) the human frame, 2 Cor. 4:7; perhaps 1 Thess. 4:4; (5) a husband and wife, 1 Pet. 3:7;

of the wife, probably, 1 Thess. 4:4; while the exhortation to each one "to possess himself of his own vessel in sanctification and honor" is regarded by some as referring to the believer's body, the view that the "vessel" signifies the wife, and that the reference is to the sanctified maintenance of the married state, is supported by the facts that in 1 Pet. 3:7 the same word ***time***, "honor," is used with regard to the wife, again in Heb. 13:4, ***timios***, "honorable" (RV, "in honor") is used in regard to marriage; further, the preceding command in 1 Thess. 4 is against fornication, and the succeeding one (v. 6) is against adultery.

## VEX

1. ***ochleo*** (*3791*), "to disturb, trouble," is used in the passive voice, of being "troubled" by evil spirits, Acts 5:16.

2. ***basanizo*** (*928*), "to torment," is translated "vexed" in 2 Pet. 2:8.

## VICTORY, VICTORIOUS

**A. Nouns.**

1. ***nike*** (*3529*), "victory," is used in 1 John 5:4.

2. ***nikos*** (*3534*), a later form of No. 1, is used in Matt. 12:20; 1 Cor. 15:54, 55, 57.

**B. Verb.**

***nikao*** (*3528*), "to conquer, overcome," is translated "(them) that come victorious (from)" in Rev. 15:2, RV (KJV, "that had gotten the victory").

## VILE

**A. Noun.**

***atimia*** (*819*), "dishonor," is translated "vile" in Rom. 1:26, RV, marg., "(passions) of dishonor."

**B. Adjectives.**

1. ***rhuparos*** (*4508*), "filthy dirty," is used (a) literally, of old shabby clothing, Jas. 2:2, "vile"; (b) metaphorically, of moral defilement, Rev. 22:11 (in the best texts).

2. ***poneros*** (*4190*), "evil," is translated "vile" in Acts 17:5, RV (KJV, "lewd").

## VILLAGE

***kome*** (*2968*), "a village," or "country town," primarily as distinct from a walled town, occurs in the Gospels; elsewhere only in Acts 8:25. The difference between ***polis***, "a city," and ***kome***, is maintained in the NT, as in Josephus. Among the Greeks the point of the distinction was not that of size or fortification, but of constitution and land. In the OT the city and the village are regularly distinguished. The Mishna makes the three distinctions, a large city, a city, and a village.

The RV always substitutes "village(-s)" for KJV, "town(-s)," Matt. 10:11; Mark 8:23, 26, 27; Luke 5:17; 9:6, 12; John 7:42; 11:1, 30.

## VILLANY

1. ***rhadiourgia*** (*4468*) lit. and primarily denotes "ease in working" (***rhadios***, "easy," ***ergon***, "work"), "easiness, laziness"; hence "recklessness, wickedness," Acts 13:10, RV, "villany," KJV, "mischief." In the papyri it is used of "theft."

2. ***rhadiourgema*** (*4467*), "a reckless act" (akin to No. 1), occurs in Acts 18:14, RV, "villany" (KJV, "lewdness").

## VINEGAR

***oxos*** (*3690*), akin to ***oxus***, "sharp," denotes "sour wine," the ordinary drink of laborers and common soldiers; it is used in the four Gospels of the "vinegar" offered to the Lord at His crucifixion. In Matt. 27:34 the best texts have ***oinos***, "wine" (RV). Some have ***oxos*** (KJV, "vinegar"), but Mark 15:23 (KJV and RV) confirms the RV in the passage in Matthew. This, which the soldiers offered before crucifying, was refused by Him, as it was designed to alleviate His sufferings; the "vinegar" is mentioned in Mark 15:36; so Luke 23:36, and John 19:29, 30.

## VINEYARD

***kerem*** (3754), "vineyard." Isaiah gives a vivid description of the work involved in the preparation, planting, and cultivation of a "vineyard," Isa. 5:1–7. The "vineyard" was located on the slopes of a hill, Isa. 5:1. The soil was cleared of stones before the tender vines were planted, Isa. 5:2. A watchtower provided visibility over the "vineyard," Isa. 5:2; and a winevat and place for crushing the grapes were hewn out of the rock, Isa. 5:2. When all the preparations were finished, the "vineyard" was ready and in a few years it was expected to produce crops. In the meantime the ***kerem*** required regular pruning, Lev. 25:3–4. The time between planting and the first crop was of sufficient import as to free the owner from military duty, Deut. 20:6.

The words "vineyard" and "olive grove," (***zayit***) are often found together in the biblical text. These furnished the two major permanent agricultural activities in ancient Israel, as both required much work and time before the crops came in. God promised that the ownership of the "vineyards" and orchards of the Canaanites was to go to His people as a blessing from Him, Deut. 6:11–12. The "vineyards" were located mainly in the hill country and in the low-lying hill country. The Bible mentions the "vineyard" at Timnath, Judg. 14:5, Jezreel, 1 Kings 21:1, the hill country of Samaria, Jer. 31:5, and even at En-gedi, Song of Sol. 1:14.

The metaphorical use of ***kerem*** allows the prophet Isaiah to draw an analogy between the "vineyard" and Israel, Isa. 5:7. It has also been suggested that the "vineyard" in the Song of Solomon is better understood metaphorically as "person," cf. Song of Sol. 1:6.

## VIOLENCE, VIOLENT, VIOLENTLY

### *Old Testament*

**A. Noun.**

***chamas*** (2555), "violence; wrong; maliciousness." Basically ***chamas*** connotes the disruption of the divinely established order of things. It has a wide range of nuances within this legal sphere. The expression "a witness in the case of violent wrongdoing" means someone who bears witness in a case having to do with such an offense, cf. Deut. 19:16. In this context the truthfulness of the witness is not established except upon further investigation, Deut. 19:18. Once he was established as a false witness, the penalty for the crime concerning which he bore false witness was to be executed against the liar, cf. Deut. 19:19.

***chamas*** perhaps connotes a "violent wrongdoing" which has not been righted, the guilt of which lies on an entire area (its inhabitants) disrupting their relationship with God and thereby interfering with His blessings, Gen. 6:11; 16:5.

**B. Verb.**

***chamas*** (2554) means "to treat violently," Jer. 22:3.

### *New Testament*

**A. Nouns.**

1. ***bia*** (*970*) denotes "force, violence," said of men, Acts 5:26; 21:35; 24:7; of waves, 27:41.

2. ***biastes*** (*973*), "a forceful or violent man," is used in Matt. 11:12.

**B. Verbs.**

1. ***diaseio*** (*1286*), "to shake violently," is used in Luke 3:14, "do violence," including intimidation.

2. ***biazo*** (*971*), in the passive voice, is rendered "suffereth violence" in Matt. 11:12;

## VIPER

***echidna*** (*2191*) is probably a generic term for "poisonous snakes." It is rendered "viper" in the NT, (a) of the actual creature, Acts 28:3; (b) metaphorically in Matt. 3:7; 12:34; 23:33; Luke 3:7.

## VIRGIN

### *Old Testament*

***'almah*** (5959), "virgin; maiden." That ***'almah*** can mean "virgin" is quite clear in Song of Sol. 6:8. The word ***'almah*** represents those who are eligible for marriage but are neither wives (queens) nor concubines. These "maidens" all loved the king and longed to be chosen to be with him (to be his bride), even as did the Shulamite who became his bride, 1:3–4. In Gen. 24:43 the word describes Rebekah, of whom it is said in Gen. 24:16 that she was a "maiden" with whom no man had had relations. Thus ***'almah*** appears to be used more of the concept "virgin" than that of "maiden," yet always of a woman who had not borne a child. This makes it the ideal word to be used in Isa. 7:14, since the word ***betulah*** emphasizes virility more than virginity. The reader of Isa. 7:14 in the days preceding the birth of Jesus would read that a "virgin who is a maiden" would conceive a child. This was a possible, but irregular, use of the word since the word can refer merely to the unmarried status of the one so described. The child immediately in view was the son of the prophet and his wife (cf. Isa. 8:3) who served as a sign to Ahaz that his enemies would be defeated by God. On the other hand, the reader of that day must have been extremely uncomfortable with this use of the word, since its primary connotation is "virgin" rather than "maiden." Thus the clear translation of the Greek in Matt. 1:23 whereby this word is rendered "virgin" satisfies its fullest implication. Therefore, there was no embarrassment to Isaiah when his wife conceived a son by him, since the word ***'almah*** allowed for this. Neither is there any embarrassment in Matthew's understanding of the word.

### *New Testament*

***parthenos*** (*3933*) is used (a) of "the Virgin Mary," Matt. 1:23; Luke 1:27 [cf. "virginity," Luke 2:36]; (b) of the ten "virgins" in the parable, Matt. 25:1, 7, 11; (c) of the "daughters" of Philip the evangelist, Acts 21:9; (d) those concerning whom the apostle Paul gives instructions regarding marriage, 1 Cor. 7:25, 28, 34; in vv. 36, 37, 38, the subject passes to that of "virgin *daughters*" (RV), which almost certainly formed one of the subjects upon which the church at Corinth sent for instructions from the apostle; one difficulty was relative to the discredit which might be brought upon a father (or guardian), if he allowed his daughter or ward to grow old unmarried. The interpretation that this passage refers to a man and woman already in some kind of relation by way of a spiritual marriage and living together in a vow of virginity and celibacy, is untenable if only in view of the phraseology of the passage; (e) figuratively, of "a local church" in its relation to Christ, 2 Cor. 11:2; (f) metaphorically of "chaste persons," Rev. 14:4.

## VIRGINITY

***parthenia*** *(3932)*, akin to the above, occurs in Luke 2:36.

## VIRTUE

***arete*** *(703)* properly denotes whatever procures preeminent estimation for a person or thing; hence, "intrinsic eminence, moral goodness, virtue," (a) of God, 1 Pet. 2:9, "excellencies" (KJV, "praises"); here the original and general sense seems to be blended with the impression made on others, i.e., renown, excellence or praise (Hort); in 2 Pet. 1:3, "(by His own glory and) virtue," RV (instrumental dative), i.e., the manifestation of His divine power; this significance is frequently illustrated in the papyri and was evidently common in current Greek speech; (b) of any particular moral excellence, Phil. 4:8; 2 Pet. 1:5 (twice), where virtue is enjoined as an essential quality in the exercise of faith, RV, "(in your faith supply) virtue."

## VISION

### *Old Testament*

### A. Nouns.

***chazon*** (2377), "vision," i.e., a means of divine revelation. First, it refers to the means itself, to a prophetic "vision" by which divine messages are communicated, Ezek. 12:22. Second, this word represents the message received by prophetic "vision," Prov. 29:18. Finally, ***chazon*** can represent the entirety of a prophetic or prophet's message as it is written down, Isa. 1:1. Thus the word inseparably related to the content of a divine communication focuses on the means by which that message is received, Isa. 29:7.

***chizzayon*** (2384), "vision." This noun, which occurs 9 times, refers to a prophetic "vision" in Joel 2:28: "And it shall come to pass afterward, that I will pour out my spirit upon all flesh; and your sons and your daughters shall prophesy, your old men shall dream dreams, your young men shall see visions." ***chizzayon*** refers to divine communication in 2 Sam. 7:17 (the first biblical occurrence) and to an ordinary dream in Job 4:13.

### B. Verb.

***chazah*** (2372), "to see, behold, select for oneself." It means "to see or behold" in general, Prov. 22:29, "to see" in a prophetic vision, Num. 24:4, and "to select for oneself," Exod. 18:21. In Lam. 2:14 the word means "to see" in relation to prophets' vision.

### *New Testament*

1. ***horama*** *(3705)*, "that which is seen" (***horao***), denotes (a) "a spectacle, sight," Matt. 17:9; Acts 7:31 ("sight"); (b) "an appearance, vision," Acts 9:10 (v. 12 in some mss.): 10:3, 17, 19; 11:5; 12:9; 16:9, 10; 18:9.

2. ***horasis*** *(3706)*, "sense of sight," is rendered "visions" in Acts 2:17; Rev. 9:17.

3. ***optasia*** *(3701)* (a late form of ***opsis***, "the act of seeing"), from ***optano***, "to see, a coming into view," denotes a "vision" in Luke 1:22; 24:23; Acts 26:19; 2 Cor. 12:1.

## VISIT

***episkeptomai*** *(1980)*, primarily, "to inspect" (a late form of ***episkopeo***, "to look upon, care for, exercise oversight"), signifies (a) "to visit" with help, of the act of God, Luke 1:68, 78; 7:16; Acts 15:14; Heb. 2:6; (b) "to visit" the sick and afflicted, Matt. 25:36, 43; Jas. 1:27; (c) "to go and see," "pay a visit to," Acts 7:23; 15:36; (d) "to look out" certain men for a purpose, Acts 6:3.

2. ***historeo*** *(2477)*, from ***histor***, "one learned in anything," denotes "to visit" in order to become acquainted with, Gal. 1:18, RV, "visit" (KJV, "see"), RV marg., "become acquainted with."

3. ***epiphero*** *(2018)*, for which see BRING, No. 6, is rendered "visiteth (with wrath)" in Rom. 3:5, RV, KJV, "taketh (vengeance)."

## VISITATION

***episkope*** *(1984)*, denotes "a visitation," whether in mercy, Luke 19:44, or in judgment, 1 Pet. 2:12.



## VOID

1. ***kenoo*** *(2758)*, "to empty, make of no effect," is rendered "to make void," in Rom. 4:14; 1 Cor. 1:17, RV; 9:15; 2 Cor. 9:3, RV.

2. ***atheteo*** *(114)*, rendered "to make void" in Gal. 2:21, RV (KJV, "frustrate"); 3:15, RV.

3. ***akuroo*** *(208)*, "to make void" in Matt. 15:6; Mark 7:13, RV.

## VOLUNTARY

In Col. 2:18, ***thelo*** is rendered "(in a) voluntary (humility)," present participle, i.e., "being a voluntary (in humility)," KJV marg., RV marg., "of his own mere will (by humility)," ***en***, "in," being rendered as instrumental; what was of one's own mere will, with the speciousness of humility, would mean his being robbed of his prize.

## VOW

### *Old Testament*

**A. Verb.**

***nadar*** (5087), "to vow," i.e., to make a promise to another, with sanctions for not completing the promise. Numbers 30 deals with the law concerning vows.

**B. Noun.**

***neder*** (5088), "vow; votive offering." The vow has two basic forms, the unconditional and the conditional. The unconditional is an "oath" where someone binds himself without expecting anything in return, Ps. 116:14. The conditional "vow" generally had a preceding clause before the oath giving the conditions which had to come to pass before the "vow" became valid, Gen. 28:20–22.

"Vows" usually occurred in serious situations. Jacob needed the assurance of God's presence before setting out for Padan-aram, Gen. 28:20–22; Jephthah made a rash "vow" before battle, Judg. 11:30; cf. Num. 21:1–3; Hannah greatly desired a child, 1 Sam. 1:11, when she made a "vow." Once a vow was made, it must be kept. One cannot annul the "vow." However, the Old Testament allows for "redeeming" the "vow"; by payment of an equal amount in silver, a person, a field, or a house dedicated by "vow" to the Lord could be redeemed, Lev. 27:1–25. This practice, however, declined in Jesus' time, and therefore the Talmud frowns upon the practice of "vowing" and refers to those who vow as "sinners."

***neder*** signifies a kind of offering, Deut. 12:6. In particular the word represents a kind of peace or "votive offering," Ezra 7:16. It also is a kind of thank offering, Nah. 1:15. Here even Gentiles expressed their thanks to God presumably with a gift promised upon condition of deliverance, cf. Num. 21:1–3.

### *New Testament*

***euche*** (*2171*) denotes also "a vow," Acts 18:18; 21:23; Jas. 5:15, "prayer."

# W

## WAGES

1. ***opsonion*** (*3800*), denotes (a) "soldier's pay," Luke 3:14; 1 Cor. 9:7 ("charges"); (b) in general, "hire, wages of any sort," used metaphorically, Rom. 6:23, of sin; 2 Cor. 11:8, of material support which Paul received from some of the churches which he had established and to which he ministered in spiritual things; their support partly maintained him at Corinth, where he forebore to receive such assistance (vv. 9, 10).

2. ***misthos*** (*3408*), "hire," is rendered "wages" in John 4:36; in 2 Pet. 2:15, KJV (RV, hire).

## WAIL, WAILING

(1) ***alalazo*** is rendered "to wail" in Mark 5:38. (2) ***kopto*** is rendered "to wail" in Rev. 1:7, KJV (RV, "shall mourn") and 18:9, RV, "wail" (KJV, "lament"). (3) ***pentheo*** is rendered "to wail" in Rev. 18:15, 19, KJV. (4) ***klauthmos*** is rendered "wailing" in Matt. 13:42, 50, KJV. (5) In Matt. 11:17 and Luke 7:32, KJV, ***threneo***, "to wail" (RV), is rendered to mourn.

## WAIT

1. ***ekdechomai*** (*1551*), rendered "to wait" in John 5:3, KJV; Acts 17:16; 1 Cor. 11:33, RV.

2. ***apekdechomai*** (*553*), "to await or expect eagerly," is rendered "to wait for" in Rom. 8:19, 23, 25; 1 Cor. 1:7; Gal. 5:5; Phil. 3:20, RV (KJV, "look for"); Heb. 9:28, RV (KJV, "look for"), here "them that wait" represents believers in general, not a section of them; 1 Pet. 3:20 (in the best texts; some have No. 1).

3. ***prosdechomai*** (*4327*), "to look for" with a view to favorable reception, is rendered "to wait for" in Mark 15:43; Luke 2:25; 12:36; 23:51.

4. ***prosdokao*** (*4328*), "to await," is rendered "to wait for" in Luke 1:21; 8:40; Acts 10:24; in 27:33, RV "ye wait" (KJV, "have tarried").

5. ***anameno*** (*362*), "to wait for," is used in 1 Thess. 1:10, of "waiting" for the Son of God from heaven; the word carries with it the suggestion of "waiting" with patience and confident expectancy.

6. ***perimeno*** (*4037*), "to await an event," is used in Acts 1:4, of "waiting" for the Holy Spirit, "the promise of the Father."

7. ***proskartereo*** (*4342*), to continue steadfastly, is rendered "to wait on," in Mark 3:9 and Acts 10:7.

## WAKE

***gregoreo*** (*1127*), translated "wake" in 1 Thess. 5:10, is rendered "watch" in the RV marg., as in the text in v. 6, and the RV in the twenty-one other places in which it occurs in the NT (save 1 Pet. 5:8, "be watchful"). It is not used in the metaphorical sense of "to be alive"; here it is set in contrast with ***katheudo***, "to sleep," which is never used by the apostle with the meaning "to be dead" (it has this meaning only in the case of Jairus' daughter). Accordingly the meaning here is that of vigilance and expectancy as contrasted with laxity and indifference. All believers will live together with Christ from the time of the Rapture described in ch. 4; for all have spiritual life now, though their spiritual condition and attainment vary considerably. Those who are lax and fail to be watchful will suffer loss (1 Cor. 3:15; 9:27; 2 Cor. 5:10, e.g.), but the apostle is not here dealing with that aspect of the subject. What he does make clear is that the Rapture of believers at the second coming of Christ will depend solely on the death of Christ for them, and not upon their spiritual condition. The Rapture is not a matter of reward, but of salvation.

## WALK

### *Old Testament*

**A. Verb.**

***halak*** (1980), "to go, walk, behave." Essentially, this root refers to linear movement without any suggestion of direction, or elevation change: of man, Gen. 9:23; of beasts, Gen. 3:14; or inanimate objects Gen. 2:14. This root is used in various other special ways. It may be used to emphasize that a certain thing occurred; Jacob "went" and got the kid his mother requested, in other words, he actually did the action, Gen. 27:14. In Gen. 8:3 the waters of the flood steadily receded from the surface of the earth. Sometimes this verb implies movement away from, as in Gen. 18:33, when the Lord "departed" from Abraham.

God is said to "walk" or "go" in three senses. First, there are certain cases where He assumed some kind of physical form. For example, Adam and Eve heard the sound of God "walking" to and fro in the garden of

Eden, Gen. 3:8. He "walks" on the clouds, Ps. 104:3, or in the heavens, Job 22:14; these are probably anthropomorphisms (God is spoken of as if He had bodily parts). Even more often God is said to accompany His people, Exod. 33:14, to go to redeem (deliver) them from Egypt, 2 Sam. 7:23, and to come to save them, Ps. 80:2. Men may also "walk . . . after the imagination of their evil heart," or act stubbornly, Jer. 3:17. The pious followed or practiced God's commands; they "walked" in righteousness, Isa. 33:15, in humility, Mic. 6:8, and in integrity, Ps. 15:2.

**B. Nouns.**

***halikah*** (1979), "course; doings; traveling company; caravan; procession." This noun occurs 6 times in the Old Testament.

This word conveys several nuances. In Nah. 2:5 ***halikah*** refers to a "course," Prov. 31:27; "traveling-company" or "caravan," Job 6:19; "procession," Ps. 68:24.

Several other related nouns occur infrequently. ***mahalak***, which appears 5 times, means "passage," Ezek. 42:4; "journey," Neh. 2:6. ***helek*** occurs twice and means a "visitor," 2 Sam. 12:4.

***New Testament***

1. ***peripateo*** (*4043*) is used (a) physically, in the Synoptic Gospels (except Mark 7:5); always in the Acts except in 21:21; never in the Pauline Epistles, nor in those of John; (b) figuratively, signifying the whole round of the activities of the individual life, whether of the unregenerate, Eph. 4:17, or of the believer, 1 Cor. 7:17; Col. 2:6. It is applied to the observance of religious ordinances, Acts 21:21; Heb. 13:9, marg., as well as to moral conduct. The Christian is to walk in newness of life, Rom. 6:4, after the spirit, 8:4, in honesty, 13:13, by faith, 2 Cor. 5:7, in good works, Eph. 2:10, in love, 5:2, in wisdom, Col. 4:5, in truth, 2 John 4, after the commandments of the Lord, v. 6. And, negatively, not after the flesh, Rom. 8:4; not after the manner of men, 1 Cor. 3:3; not in craftiness, 2 Cor. 4:2; not by sight, 5:7; not in the vanity of the mind, Eph. 4:17; not disorderly, 2 Thess. 3:6.

2. ***poreuo*** (*4198*), used in the middle voice and rendered "to walk" in Luke 1:6, of the general activities of life; so in Luke 13:33, KJV, "walk" (RV, "go on My way"); Acts 9:31; 14:16; 1 Pet. 4:3; 2 Pet. 2:10; Jude 16, 18.

3. ***stoicheo*** (*4748*), from ***stoichos***, "a row," signifies "to walk in line," and is used metaphorically of "walking" in relation to others (No. 1 is used more especially of the individual walk); in Acts 21:24, it is translated "walkest orderly"; in Rom. 4:12, "walk (in . . . steps)"; in Gal. 5:25 it is used of walking "by the Spirit," RV, in an exhortation to keep step with one another in submission of heart to the Holy Spirit, and therefore of keeping step with Christ, the great means of unity and harmony in a church (contrast No. 1 in v. 16; v. 25 begins a new section which extends to 6:10); in 6:16 it is used of walking by the rule expressed in vv. 14, 15; in Phil. 3:16 the reference is to the course pursued by the believer who makes "the prize of the high calling" the object of his ambition.

4. ***orthopodeo*** (*3716*), "to walk in a straight path" (***orthos***, "straight," ***pous***, "a foot"), is used metaphorically in Gal. 2:14, signifying a "course of conduct" by which one leaves a straight track for others to follow ("walked . . . uprightly").

## WALLET

***pera*** (*4082*), "a traveler's leather bag or pouch for holding provisions," is translated "wallet" in the RV (KJV, "scrip"), Matt. 10:10; Mark 6:8; Luke 9:3; 10:4; 22:35, 36.

## WALLOW (Verb and Noun)

**A. Verb.**

***kulio*** (*2947*) in the active voice denotes "to roll, roll along"; in the middle voice in Mark 9:20, rendered "wallowed."

**B. Noun.**

***kulismos*** (*2946***), "a rolling, wallowing," akin to A (some texts have ***kulisma***), is used in 2 Pet. 2:22, of the proverbial sow that had been washed.

## WANT (Noun and Verb)

**A. Nouns.**

1. ***husteresis*** (*5304*), akin to B, No. 1 (below), occurs in Mark 12:14 and Phil. 4:11.

2. ***husterema*** (*5305*) denotes (more concretely than No. 1) (a) "that which is lacking"; (b) "need, poverty, want," rendered "want" in Luke 21:4 (KJV, "penury"); 2 Cor. 8:14 (twice); 9:12; 11:9 (2nd occurrence), RV, "want" (KJV, "that which was lacking").

3. ***chreia*** (*5532*) is rendered "want" in Phil. 2:25, KJV (RV, need).

**B. Verbs.**

1. ***hustereo*** (*5302*) signifies "to be in want," Luke 15:14; 2 Cor. 11:9 (1st occurrence); Phil. 4:12, RV (KJV "to suffer need"); in John 2:3, KJV, "wanted" (RV, "failed").

2. ***leipo*** (*3007*), "to leave," is rendered "to be wanting" in Titus 1:5 and 3:13, and in the KJV in Jas. 1:4.

## WANTONNESS, WANTON, WANTONLY

### A. Nouns.

1. ***aselgeia*** *(766)*, "lasciviousness, licentiousness," is rendered "wantonness" in 2 Pet. 2:18, KJV.

2. ***strenos*** *(4764)*, "insolent luxury," is rendered "wantonness" in Rev. 18:3, RV (marg., "luxury"; KJV, "delicacies," not a sufficiently strong rendering).

### B. Verbs.

1. ***streniao*** *(4763)*, akin to A, No. 2, "to run riot," is rendered "waxed wanton" in Rev. 18:7, RV, and "lived wantonly" in v. 8. The root of the verb is seen in the Latin *strenuus*.

2. ***katastreniao*** *(2691)*, an intensive form of No. 1, "to wax wanton against," occurs in 1 Tim. 5:11.

## WAR (Verb and Noun)

*Old Testament*

### A. Noun.

***milchamah*** (4421), "war; battle; skirmish; combat." This word means "war," the over-all confrontation of two forces, Gen. 14:2. It can refer to the engagement in hostilities considered as a whole, the "battle," Gen. 14:8. ***milchamah*** sometimes represents the art of soldiering, or "combat," Exod. 15:3.

There are several principles which were supposed to govern "war" in the Old Testament. Unjust violence was prohibited, but "war" as a part of ancient life was led, Judg. 4:13, and used by God, Num. 21:14. If it was preceded by sacrifices recognizing His leadership and sovereignty, 1 Sam. 7:9, and if He was consulted and obeyed, Judg. 20:23, Israel was promised divine protection, Deut. 20:1–4. Not one life would be lost, Josh. 10:11. At the beginning Israel's army consisted of every man over twenty and under fifty, Num. 1:2–3. Sometimes only certain segments of this potential citizens' army were summoned, Num. 31:3–6. There were several circumstances which could exempt one from "war," Num. 1:48–49; Deut. 20:5–8. Under David and Solomon there grew a professional army. It was especially prominent under Solomon, whose army was renowned for its chariotry. Cities outside Palestine were to be offered terms of surrender before being attacked. Compliance meant subjugation to slavery, Deut. 20:10–11. Cities and peoples within the Promised Land were to be utterly wiped out. They were under the ban, Deut. 2:34; 3:6; 20:16–18.

### B. Verb.

***lacham*** (3898), "to engage in battle, fight, wage war," Exod. 1:10.

*New Testament*

### A. Verbs.

1. ***polemeo*** *(4170)* (Eng., "polemics"), "to fight, to make war," is used (a) literally, Rev. 12:7 (twice), RV; 13:4; 17:14; 19:11; (b) metaphorically, Rev. 2:16, RV; (C) hyperbolically, Jas. 4:2.

2. ***strateuo*** *(4754)*, used in the middle voice, "to make war" (from ***stratos***, "an encamped army"), is translated "to war" in 2 Cor. 10:3; metaphorically, of spiritual "conflict," 1 Tim. 1:18; 2 Tim. 2:3, KJV; Jas. 4:1; 1 Pet. 2:11.

3. ***antistrateuomai*** *(497)*, "to make war against," (***anti***), Rom. 7:23.

### B. Noun.

***polemos*** *(4171)*, "war" (akin to A, No. 1), is so translated in the RV, for KJV, "battle," 1 Cor. 14:8; Rev. 9:7, 9; 16:14; 20:8; for KJV, "fight," Heb. 11:34; KJV and RV in Jas. 4:1, hyperbolically of private "quarrels"; elsewhere, literally, e.g., Matt. 24:6; Rev. 11:7.

## WARD

1. ***phulake*** *(5438)*, "a guard," is used of the place where persons are kept under guard (akin to ***phulax***, "a keeper"), and translated "ward" in Acts 12:10.

2. ***teresis*** *(5084)* primarily denotes "a watching" (***tereo***, "to watch"); hence "imprisonment, ward," Acts 4:3 (KJV, "hold"); 5:18, RV, "(public) ward" [KJV, "(common) prison"].

## WARE OF

***phulasso*** *(5442)* denotes "to guard, watch"; in 2 Tim. 4:15.

## WARFARE

***strateia***, or ***-tia*** *(4756)*, primarily "a host or army," came to denote "a warfare," and is used of spiritual "conflict" in 2 Cor. 10:4; 1 Tim. 1:15.

## WARN

1. ***noutheteo*** *(3560)*, "to put in mind, warn," is translated "to warn" in the KJV; the RV always translates this word by the verb "to admonish."

2. ***hupodeiknumi*** *(5263)*, primarily, "to show secretly" (***hupo***, "under," ***deiknumi***, "to show"), hence, generally, "to teach, make known," is translated "to warn" in Matt. 3:7; Luke 3:7; 12:5, RV (KJV, "forewarn").

3. ***chrematizo*** *(5537)*, translated "to warn" in Matt. 2:12, 22; Acts 10:22; Heb. 8:5, RV (KJV, "admonished"); 11:7; 12:25, RV (KJV, "spake").

## WASH

### *Old Testament*

***rachas*** (7364), "to wash, bathe." When the word is used figuratively to express vengeance, the imagery is a bit more gruesome, Ps. 58:10. Pilate's action in Matt. 27:24 is reminiscent of the psalmist's statement, "I will wash mine hands in innocency," Ps. 26:6. Literally, used to describe cleansing meat, Exod. 29:17. ***rachas*** is frequently used in the sense of "bathing," Exod. 2:5; 2 Sam. 11:2.

***kabas*** (3526), "to wash." The word is used in the Old Testament primarily in the sense of "washing" clothes, both for ordinary cleansing, 2 Sam. 19:24, and for ritual cleansing, Exod. 19:10, 14; Lev. 11:25.

### *New Testament*

1. ***nipto*** (*3538*) is chiefly used of "washing part of the body," John 13:5–6, 8 (twice, figuratively in 2nd clause), 12, 14 (twice); in 1 Tim. 5:10, including the figurative sense; in the middle voice, to wash oneself, Matt. 6:17; 15:2; Mark 7:3; John 9:7, 11, 15; 13:10.

2. ***louo*** (*3068*) signifies "to bathe, to wash the body," (a) active voice, Acts 9:37; 16:33; (b) passive voice, John 13:10, RV, "bathed" (KJV, "washed"); Heb. 10:22, lit., "having been washed as to the body," metaphorical of the effect of the Word of God upon the activities of the believer; (c) middle voice, 2 Pet. 2:22. Some inferior mss. have it instead of ***luo***, "to loose," in Rev. 1:5 (see RV).

3. ***apolouo*** (*628*), "to wash off or away," is used in the middle voice, metaphorically, "to wash oneself," in Acts 22:16, where the command to Saul of Tarsus to "wash away" his sins indicates that by his public confession, he would testify to the removal of his sins, and to the complete change from his past life; this "washing away" was not in itself the actual remission of his sins, which had taken place at his conversion; the middle voice implies his own particular interest in the act (as with the preceding verb "baptize," lit., "baptize thyself," i.e., "get thyself baptized"); the aorist tenses mark the decisiveness of the acts; in 1 Cor. 6:11, lit., "ye washed yourselves clean"; here the middle voice (rendered in the passive in KJV and RV, which do not distinguish between this and the next two passives; see RV marg.) again indicates that the converts at Corinth, by their obedience to the faith, voluntarily gave testimony to the complete spiritual change divinely wrought in them.

4. ***baptizo*** (*907*) is rendered "washed" in Luke 11:38.

## WASHING

1. ***baptismos*** (*909*) denotes "the act of washing, ablution," with special reference to purification, Mark 7:4 (in some texts, v. 8); Heb. 6:2, "baptisms"; 9:10, "washings."

2. ***loutron*** (*3067*), "a bath, a laver" (akin to ***louo***, see above), is used metaphorically of the Word of God, as the instrument of spiritual cleansing, Eph. 5:26; in Titus 3:5.

## WASTE (Noun and Verb)

### A. Noun.

***apoleia*** (*684*), "destruction," is translated "waste" in Matt. 26:8; Mark 14:4.

### B. Verbs.

1. ***diaskorpizo*** (*1287*), "to scatter abroad," is used metaphorically of "squandering property," Luke 15:13; 16:1.

2. ***portheo*** (*4199*), "to ravage," is rendered "wasted" in Gal. 1:13, KJV.

3. ***lumaino*** (*3075*), "to outrage, maltreat," is used in the middle voice in Acts 8:3, of Saul's treatment of the church, RV, "laid waste" (KJV, "made havoc of").

## WATCH (Noun and Verb), WATCHERS, WATCHFUL, WATCHINGS

### *Old Testament*

### A. Nouns.

***mishmeret*** (4931); ***mishmar*** (4929), "watch; guard; post; confinement; prison; custody; division." The noun ***mishmar*** means a "military watch over a city," Neh. 4:9. ***mishmar*** can also represent a "place of confinement," such as a jail, Gen. 40:3; 42:17. ***mishmar*** sometimes represents a group of attendants, especially in the temple. In this nuance the word may represent the temple guard-units, 1 Chron. 26:16. However, in Neh. 12:24 the service rendered is the Levitical service in general, therefore, "division corresponding to division." All these Levitical "divisions" constituted the full services of the temple, Neh. 13:14.

***mishmeret*** often is used to represent a more abstract idea than ***mishmar***, whereas ***mishmar*** means the units of Levites who served the Lord (perhaps with the exception of Neh. 13:30, where ***mishmeret*** may mean "service-unit"). ***mishmeret*** refers to the priestly or Levitical service itself, Lev. 8:35; Num. 3:25 .This word often refers to divine obligation or service in general, a non-cultic obligation, Gen. 26:5; cf. Deut. 11:1.

**B. Verb.**

***shamar*** (8104), "to keep, watch," Job 14:16.

***New Testament***

**A. Nouns.**

1. ***phulake*** (*5438*) is used (a) with the meaning "a watch," actively, "a guarding," Luke 2:8, lit., "(keeping, ***phulasso***) watches"; (b) of "the time during which guard was kept by night, a watch of the night," Matt. 14:25; 24:43; Mark 6:48; Luke 12:38.

2. ***koustodia*** (*2892*), from Lat., ***custodia*** (cf. Eng., "custody"), is rendered "watch" in Matt. 27:65, 66 and 28:11, KJV.

3. ***agrupnia*** (*70*), "sleeplessness" (akin to B, No. 3), is rendered "watchings" in 2 Cor. 6:5; 11:27.

**B. Verbs.**

1. ***gregoreo*** (*1127*), "to watch," is used (a) of "keeping awake," e.g., Matt. 24:43; 26:38, 40, 41; (b) of "spiritual alertness," e.g., Acts 20:31; 1 Cor. 16:13; Col. 4:2; 1 Thess. 5:6, 10; 1 Pet. 5:8, RV, "be watchful" (KJV, "be vigilant"); Rev. 3:2, 3; 16:15.

2. ***paratereo*** (*3906*), "to observe," especially with sinister intent, is rendered "to watch" in Mark 3:2; Luke 6:7; 14:1; 20:20; Acts 9:24.

3. ***agrupneo*** (*69*), "to be sleepless" (from ***agreuo***, "to chase," and ***hupnos***, "sleep"), is used metaphorically, "to be watchful," in Mark 13:33; Luke 21:36; Eph. 6:18; Heb. 13:17. The word expresses not mere wakefulness, but the "watchfulness" of those who are intent upon a thing.

## WATER (Noun and Verb), WATERING, WATERLESS

***Old Testament***

***mayim*** (4325), "water; flood." First, "water" is one of the original basic substances, which in moderation and proper amounts gives and sustains life, This is water of any kind, fresh, stale, salt, sweet, from a well or cistern, or from a river or spring, Gen. 1:2; 26:19; Jer. 8:14. The phrase, ***me raglayim*** ("water of one's feet") is urine, 2 Kings 18:27; cf. Isa. 25:10.

This word is used figuratively in many senses. ***mayim*** symbolizes danger or distress: "He sent from above, he took me; he drew me out of many waters," 2 Sam. 22:17. Outbursting force is represented by ***mayim*** in 2 Sam. 5:20. Thus the word is used to picture something impetuous, violent, and overwhelming, Job 27:20. In other passages "water" is used to represent timidity, Josh. 7:5. Related to this nuance is the connotation "transitory," Job 11:16. In Isa. 32:2 "water" represents that which is refreshing. Outpoured "water" represents bloodshed, Deut. 12:16, wrath, Hos. 5:10, justice, Amos 5:24; KJV, "judgment," and strong feelings, Job 3:24.

***tehom*** (8415), "deep water; ocean; water table; waters; flood of waters." The word represents the "deep water" whose surface freezes when cold, Job 38:30. In Ps. 135:6 ***tehom*** is used of the "ocean" in contrast to the seas. The word has special reference to the deep floods or sources of water. Sailors in the midst of a violent storm "mount up to the heaven, they go down again to the depths," Ps. 107:26. ***tehom*** can represent an inexhaustible source of water or, by way of poetic comparison, of blessing: "with blessings of heaven above, blessings of the deep that lieth under," Gen. 49:25. In such contexts the word represents the "water table" always available below the surface of the earth—what was tapped by digging wells, out of which flowed springs, and what was one with the waters beneath the surface of oceans, lakes, seas, and rivers.

***New Testament***

**A. Noun.**

***hudor*** (*5204*), whence Eng. prefix, "hydro-," is used (a) of the natural element, Jas. 3:12 (b) The word "water" is used symbolically in John 3:5, either (1) of the Word of God, as in 1 Pet. 1:23 (cf. the symbolic use in Eph. 5:26), or, in view of the preposition ***ek***, "out of," (2) of the truth conveyed by baptism, this being the expression, not the medium, the symbol, not the cause, of the believer's identification with Christ in His death, burial and resurrection. So the New Birth is, in one sense, the setting aside of all that the believer was according to the flesh, for it is evident that there must be an entirely new beginning. Some regard the ***kai***, "and," in John 3:5, as epexegetic, = "even," in which case the "water" would be emblematic of the Spirit, as in John 7:38 (cf. 4:10, 14), but not in 1 John 5:8. where the Spirit and the "water" are distinguished. "The water of life," Rev. 21:6 and 22:1, 17, is emblematic of the maintenance of spiritual life in perpetuity. In Rev. 17:1 "the waters" are symbolic of nations, peoples, etc.

**B. Verb.**

***potizo*** (*4222*), "to give to drink," is used (a) naturally in Luke 13:15, "watering," with reference to animals; (b) figuratively, with reference to spiritual ministry to converts, 1 Cor. 3:6–8.

## WAY

### *Old Testament*

**A. Nouns.**

***derek*** (1870), "way (path, road, highway); distance; journey; manner, conduct; condition; destiny." This word refers to a path, a road, or a highway, Gen. 3:24; or a distance between two points, Gen. 30:36. In other passages ***derek*** refers to the action or process of "taking a journey," Gen. 45:23. In an extended nuance ***derek*** means "undertaking," Isa. 58:13; cf. Gen. 24:21; Deut. 28:29. In another emphasis this word connotes how and what one does, a "manner, custom, behavior, mode of life," Gen. 19:31. In 1 Kings 2:4 ***derek*** is applied to an activity that controls one, one's life-style. In 1 Kings 16:26 ***derek*** is used of Jeroboam's attitude. ***derek*** also refers to a "condition" in the sense of what has happened to someone. This is clear by the parallelism of Isa. 40:27. In one passage ***derek*** signifies the overall course and fixed path of one's life, or his "destiny," Jer. 10:23.

***'orach*** (734), "way; path; course; conduct; manner." In meaning this word parallels Hebrew ***derek***, Gen. 49:17; Judg. 5:6; Ps. 19:5; Prov. 9:15. ***'orach*** signifies the ground itself as the path upon which one treads, Isa. 41:3. In Job 30:12 the word seems to represent an obstruction or dam. The word can refer to a recurring life event typical of an individual or a group. In its first biblical occurrence, Gen. 18:11, it is used of "the manner of women" (menstruation). Job 16:22 mentions the "way whence I shall not return," or death, while other passages speak of life actions, Job 34:11; literally, "conduct," or life-style, Prov. 15:10.

**B. Verb.**

***'arach*** means "to go, wander," Job 34:7–8.

### *New Testament*

***hodos*** (*3598*) denotes (a) "a natural path, road, way," frequent in the Synoptic Gospels; elsewhere, e.g., Acts 8:26; 1 Thess. 3:11; Jas. 2:25; Rev. 16:12; (b) "a traveler's way"; (C) metaphorically, of "a course of conduct," or "way of thinking," e.g., of righteousness, Matt. 21:32; 2 Pet. 2:21; of God, Matt. 22:16, and parallels, i.e., the "way" instructed and approved by God; so Acts 18:26 and Heb. 3:10, "My ways" (cf. Rev. 15:3); of the Lord, Acts 18:25; "that leadeth to destruction," Matt. 7:13; ". . . unto life," 7:14; of peace, Luke 1:79; Rom. 3:17; of Paul's "ways" in Christ, 1 Cor. 4:17 (plural); "more excellent" (of love), 1 Cor. 12:31; of truth, 2 Pet. 2:2; of the right "way," 2:15; of Balaam (*ibid.*), of Cain, Jude 11; of a "way" consisting in what is from God, e.g., of life, Acts 2:28 (plural); of salvation, Acts 16:17; personified, of Christ as the means of access to the Father, John 14:6; of the course followed and characterized by the followers of Christ, Acts 9:2; 19:9, 23; 24:22.

2. ***parodos*** (*938*), "a passing or passage," is used with ***en***, "in," 1 Cor. 16:7, "by the way" (lit, "in passing").

3. ***tropos*** (*5158*), "a turning, a manner," is translated "way" in Rom. 3:2, "(every) way"; Phil. 1:18, "(in every) way."

## WEAK, WEAKENED, WEAKER, WEAKNESS

**A. Adjectives.**

1. ***asthenes*** (*772*), lit., "strengthless," is translated "weak," (a) of physical "weakness," Matt. 26:41; Mark 14:38; 1 Cor. 1:27; 4:10; 11:30 (a judgment upon spiritual laxity in a church); 2 Cor. 10:10; 1 Pet. 3:7 (comparative degree); (b) in the spiritual sense, said of the rudiments of Jewish religion, in their inability to justify anyone, Gal. 4:9; of the Law, Heb. 7:18; in Rom. 5:6, RV, "weak" (KJV, "without strength"), of the inability of man to accomplish his salvation; (c) morally or ethically, 1 Cor. 8:7, 10; 9:22; (d) rhetorically, of God's actions according to the human estimate, 1 Cor. 1:25, "weakness," lit., "the weak things of God."

2. ***adunatos*** (*102*), lit., "not powerful," is translated "weak" in Rom. 15:1, of the infirmities of those whose scruples arise through lack of faith (see 14:22, 23), in the same sense as No. 1 (c); the change in the adjective (cf. 14:1) is due to the contrast with ***dunatoi***, the "strong," who have not been specifically mentioned as such in ch. 14.

**B. Verb.**

***astheneo*** (*770*), "to lack strength," is used in much the same way as A, No. 1, and translated "being . . . weak" in Rom. 4:19, KJV (RV, "being weakened"); 8:3; 14:1, 2 (in some texts, 1 Cor. 8:9); 2 Cor. 11:21, 29 (twice); 12:10; 13:3, 4, 9.

**C. Noun.**

***astheneia*** (*769*), rendered "weakness," of the body, 1 Cor. 2:3; 15:43; 2 Cor. 11:30, RV; 12:5 (plural, RV), 9, 10, RV; Heb. 11:34; in 2 Cor. 13:4, "He was crucified through weakness" is said in respect of the physical sufferings to which Christ voluntarily submitted in giving Himself up to the death of the cross.

## WEAKER ONE, LITTLE ONE

***tap*** (2945), "weaker one; child; little one." Basically this word signifies those members of a nomadic tribe who are not able to march or who can only march to a limited extent. The word implies the "weaker ones." Thus we read of the men and the ***tapim***, or the men and those who were unable to move quickly over long stretches, Gen. 43:8; 50:7–8. In several passages ***tap*** represents only the children and old ones, Gen. 34:26, 29.

## WEALTH

### *Old Testament*

***hon*** (1952), "wealth; substance; riches; possessions; enough." ***hon*** usually refers to movable goods considered as "wealth," Prov. 6:31; cf. Ezek. 27:12. "Wealth" can be good and a sign of blessing, Ps. 112:3. The creation is God's wealth, Ps. 119:14. In the Proverbs "wealth" is usually an indication of ungodliness, Prov. 10:15. Finally, ***hon*** means "enough," only in Prov. 30:15–16.

### *New Testament*

***euporia*** (*2142*), primarily "facility" (***eu***, "well," ***poros***, "a passage"), hence "plenty, wealth," occurs in Acts 19:25.

## WEAR, WEARING

**A. Verbs.**

1. ***phoreo*** (*5409*), a frequentative form of ***phero***, "to bear," and denoting "repeated or habitual action," is chiefly used of clothing, weapons, etc., of soft raiment, Matt. 11:8; fine clothing, Jas. 2:3; the crown of thorns, John 19:5.

2. ***endidusko*** (*1737*), "to put on," is used in the active voice in Mark 15:17 (in good mss.; some have No. 3); in Luke 8:27 (middle voice), in some texts; the best have No. 3.

3. ***enduo*** (*1746*) is rendered "to wear" in Luke 8:27 (middle voice; see No. 2).

4. ***klino*** (*2827*), "to bend, decline," is used of a day, "wearing" away, Luke 9:12 (in 24:29, is far spent).

5. ***hupopiazo*** (*5299*) is translated "wear (me) out" in Luke 18:5, RV (KJV, "weary").

**B. Noun.**

***perithesis*** (*4025*), "a putting around or on" (***peri***, "around," ***tithemi***, "to put"), is used in 1 Pet. 3:3 of "wearing" jewels of gold (RV).

## WEARY

1. ***kopiao*** (*2872*), "to grow weary, be beaten out" (***kopos***, "a beating, toil"), is used of the Lord in John 4:6 (used in His own word "labor" in Matt. 11:28), in Rev. 2:3, RV.

2. ***kamno*** (*2577*), "to be weary," is rendered "to wax weary" in Heb. 12:3, RV.

3. ***ekkakeo*** or ***enkakeo*** (*1573*), rendered "to be weary" in Gal. 6:9; 2 Thess. 3:13.

## WEEP, WEEPING

**A. Verbs.**

1. ***klaio*** (*2799*) is used of "any loud expression of grief," especially in mourning for the dead, Matt. 2:18; Mark 5:38, 39; 16:10; Luke 7:13; 8:52 (twice); John 11:31, 33 (twice); 20:11 (twice), 13, 15; Acts 9:39; otherwise, e.g., in exhortations, Luke 23:28; Rom. 12:15; Jas. 4:9; 5:1; negatively, "weep not," Luke 7:13; 8:52; 23:28; Rev. 5:5 (cf. Acts 21:13); in 18:9, RV, "shall weep" (KJV, "bewail").

2. ***dakruo*** (*1145*), "to shed tears" (***dakruon***, "a tear"), is used only of the Lord Jesus, John 18:35.

**B. Noun.**

***klauthmos*** (*2805*), akin to A, No. 1, denotes "weeping, crying," Matt. 2:18; 8:12; 13:42, 50, RV (KJV, "wailing"); 22:13; 24:51; 25:30; Luke 13:28; Acts 20:37.

## WELCOME

1. ***apodechomai*** (*588*), "to receive gladly," is rendered "to welcome" in the RV of Luke 8:40; 9:11.

2. ***hupolambano*** (*5274*), "to take up, to entertain," is rendered "to welcome" in 3 John 8, RV, of a hearty "welcome" to servants of God.

## WELL PLEASED

**A. Noun.**

***eudokia*** (*2107*), "good pleasure," occurs in the genitive case in Luke 2:14, lit., "(men) of good pleasure" (so RV marg.), RV, "(men) in whom He is well pleased" (the genitive is objective); the KJV, "good will (toward men)," follows the inferior texts which have the nominative.

**B. Verb.**

***eudokeo*** (*2106*), "to be well pleased."

## WELL-PLEASING

**A. Adjective.**

***euarestos*** (*2101*) is used in Rom. 12:1, 2, translated "acceptable (RV marg., "well-pleasing"); in the following the RV has "well-pleasing," Rom. 14:18; 2 Cor. 5:9; Eph. 5:10; in Phil. 4:18 and Col. 3:20 (RV and KJV); in Titus 2:9, RV, "well-pleasing" (KJV, "please . . . well"); in Heb. 13:21, RV and KJV.

**B. Verb.**

***euaresteo*** (*2100*), akin to A, is rendered "to be well-pleasing" in Heb. 11:5, 6, RV (KJV, "please"); in Heb. 13:16, "is well pleased."

**C. Noun.**

***eudokia*** (*2107*), lit., "good pleasure," is rendered "well-pleasing" in Matt. 11:26 and Luke 10:21.

## WHALE

***ketos*** (*2785*) means "a huge fish, a sea monster," Matt. 12:40.

## WHISPERER, WHISPERING

1. ***psithuristes*** (*5588*), "a whisperer," occurs in an evil sense in Rom. 1:29.
2. ***psithurismos*** (*5587*), "a whispering," is used of "secret slander" in 2 Cor. 12:20.

## WICKED

### *Old Testament*

**A. Nouns.**

***rasha'*** (7563), "wicked; ungodly; guilty." The narrow meaning of ***rasha'*** lies in the concept of "wrongdoing" or "being in the wrong." It is a legal term. The person who has sinned against the law is guilty, " Prov. 28:4. ***rasha'*** also denotes the category of people who have done wrong, are still living in sin, and are intent on continuing with wrongdoing, the "wicked," Ps. 10:4; he challenges God, Ps. 10:13. In his way of life the "wicked" loves violence, Ps. 11:5, oppresses the righteous, Ps. 17:9, does not repay his debts, Ps. 37:21, and lays a snare to trap the righteous, Ps. 119:110.

Two other related nouns occur in the Old Testament. ***resha'***, means "wickedness," Deut. 9:27. ***rish'ah***, refers to "wickedness" or "guilt," Deut. 9:4.

**B. Adjective.**

***rasha'*** (7563), "wicked; guilty," Deut. 25:2. The characteristics of a "wicked" person qualify him as a godless, impious man, 2 Sam. 4:11; cf. Ezek. 3:18–19.

**C. Verb.**

***rasha'*** (7561), "to be wicked, act wickedly," 2 Chron. 6:37.

### *New Testament*

***poneros*** (*4190*), translated "wicked" in the KJV and RV in Matt. 13:49; 18:32; 25:26; Luke 19:22; Acts 18:14; 1 Cor. 5:13; in the following the RV substitutes "evil" for KJV, "wicked": Matt. 12:45 (twice); 13:19; 16:4; Luke 11:26; Col. 1:21; 2 Thess. 3:2; and in the following, where Satan is mentioned as "the (or that) evil one": Matt. 13:38; Eph. 6:16; 1 John 2:13, 14; 3:12 (1st part); 5:18; in v. 19 for AV, "wickedness"; he is so called also in KJV and RV in John 17:15; 2 Thess. 3:3; KJV only in Luke 11:4; in 3 John 10, KJV, the word is translated "malicious," RV, "wicked."

## WICKEDNESS

### *Old Testament*

***beliya'al*** (1100), "wickedness; wicked; destruction." The basic meaning of this word appears in a passage such as Judg. 20:13, where the sons of ***beliya'al*** are perpetrators of wickedness (they raped and murdered a man's concubine). The psalmist uses ***beliya'al*** as a synonym of death, Ps. 18:4, NASB.

### *New Testament*

1. ***poneria*** (*4189*), akin to ***poneros***, is always rendered "wickedness" save in Acts 3:26.
2. ***kakia*** (*2549*), "evil," is rendered "wickedness" in Acts 8:22; RV in Jas. 1:21, KJV, "naughtiness."

## WIDOW

### *Old Testament*

***'almanah*** (490), "widow." The word represents a woman who, because of the death of her husband, has lost her social and economic position. The gravity of her situation was increased if she had no children. In such a circumstance she returned to her father's home and was subjected to the Levirate rule whereby a close male relative surviving her husband was to produce a child through her in her husband's behalf, Gen. 38:11. Even if children had been born before her husband's death, a widow's lot was not a happy one, 2 Sam. 14:5. Israel was admonished to treat "widows" and other socially disadvantaged people with justice, God Himself standing as their protector, Exod. 22:21–24.

Wives whose husbands shut them away from themselves are sometimes called "widows," 2 Sam. 20:3. Destroyed, plundered Jerusalem is called a "widow," Lam. 1:1.

### *New Testament*

***chera*** (*5503*), Matt. 28:13 (in some texts); Mark 12:40, 42, 43; Luke 2:37; 4:25, 26, lit., "a woman a widow"; 7:12; 18:3, 5; 20:47; 21:2, 3; Acts 6:1; 9:39, 41; 1 Tim. 5:3 (twice), 4, 5, 11, 16 (twice); Jas. 1:27; 1 Tim. 5:9 refers to elderly "widows" (not an ecclesiastical "order"), recognized, for relief or maintenance by the church (cf. vv. 3, 16), as those who had fulfilled the conditions mentioned; where relief could be ministered by those who had relatives that were "widows" (a likely circumstance in large families), the church was not to be responsible; there is an intimation of the tendency to shelve individual responsibility at the expense of church funds. In Rev. 18:7, it is used figuratively of a city forsaken.

## WIFE, WIVES

1. ***gune*** (*1135*) denotes (1) "a woman, married or unmarried"; (2) "a wife," e.g., Matt. 1:20; 1 Cor. 7:3, 4; in 1 Tim. 3:11, RV, "women," the reference may be to the "wives" of deacons, as the KJV takes it.

2. ***gunaikeios*** (*1134*), an adjective denoting "womanly, female," is used as a noun in 1 Pet. 3:7, KJV, "wife," RV, "woman."

## WIFE'S MOTHER

***penthera*** (*3994*) denotes "a mother-in-law," Matt. 8:14; 10:35; Mark 1:30; Luke 4:38; 12:53 (twice).

## WILDERNESS

1. ***eremia*** (*2047*), "an uninhabited place," is translated "wilderness" in the KJV of Matt. 15:33 and Mark 8:4 (RV, "a desert place"); RV and KJV, "wilderness" in 2 Cor. 11:26.

2. ***eremos*** (*2048*), an adjective signifying "desolate, deserted, lonely," is used as a noun, and rendered "wilderness" 32 times in the KJV; in Matt. 24:26 and John 6:31, RV, "wilderness" (KJV, "desert"). For the RV, "deserts" in Luke 5:16 and 8:29.

## WILES

***methodia***, or ***—eia*** (*3180*) denotes "craft, deceit" (***meta***, "after," ***hodos***, "a way"), "a cunning device, a wile," and is translated "wiles (of error)" in Eph. 4:14, RV [AV paraphrases it, "they lie in wait (to deceive)"], lit., "(with a view to) the craft (singular) of deceit"; in 6:11, "the wiles (plural) (of the Devil.)"

## WILL, WOULD

### *Old Testament*

***'abah*** (14), "to will, be willing, consent," Gen. 24:5. It is to be noted that in all but 2 instances of its use in the Old Testament (Job 39:9; Isa. 1:19), the word is used with a negation, to indicate lack of willingness or consent. Even in these two positive uses, there seems to be a negative aspect or expectation implied.

### *New Testament*

### A. Nouns.

1. ***thelema*** (*2307*) signifies (a) objectively, "that which is willed, of the will of God," e.g., Matt. 18:14; Mark 3:35, the fulfilling being a sign of spiritual relationship to the Lord, John 4:34; 5:30; 6:39, 40; Acts 13:22, plural, "my desires"; Rom. 2:18; 12:2, lit., "the will of God, the good and perfect and acceptable"; here the repeated article is probably resumptive, the adjectives describing the will, as in the Eng. versions; Gal. 1:4; Eph. 1:9; 5:17, "of the Lord"; Col. 1:9; 4:12; 1 Thess. 4:3; 5:18, where it means "the gracious design," rather than "the determined resolve"; 2 Tim. 2:26, which should read "which have been taken captive by him" [(***autou***), i.e., by the Devil; the RV, "by the Lord's servant" is an interpretation; it does not correspond to the Greek] unto His (***ekeinou***) will" (i.e., "God's will"; the different pronoun refers back to the subject of the sentence, viz., God); Heb. 10:10; Rev. 4:11, RV, "because of Thy will"; of human will, e.g., 1 Cor. 7:37; (b) subjectively, the "will" being spoken of as the emotion of being desirous, rather than as the thing "willed"; of the "will" of God, e.g., Rom. 1:10; 1 Cor. 1:1; 2 Cor. 1:1; 8:5; Eph. 1:1, 5, 11; Col. 1:1; 2 Tim. 1:1; Heb. 10:7, 9, 36; 1 John 2:17; 5:14; of human "will," e.g., John 1:13; Eph. 2:3, "the desires of the flesh"; 1 Pet. 4:3 (in some texts); 2 Pet. 1:21.

2. ***thelesis*** (*2308*) denotes "a willing, a wishing" [similar to No. 1 (b)], Heb. 2:4.

3. ***boulema*** (*1013*), "a deliberate design, that which is purposed," Rom. 9:19; 1 Pet. 4:3 (in the best texts).

4. ***eudokia*** (*2107*) (***eu***, "well," ***dokeo***, "to think") is rendered "good will" in Luke 2:14; Phil. 1:15.

### B. Adjective.

***hekon*** (*1635*), "of free will, willingly," occurs in Rom. 8:20, RV, "of its own will" (KJV, "willingly"); 1 Cor. 9:17, RV, "of my own will" (KJV, "willingly").

### C. Verbs.

When "will" is not part of the translation of the future tense of verbs, it represents one of the following:

1. ***thelo*** (*2309*), expresses "desire" or "design"; it is most frequently translated by "will" or "would"; see especially Rom. 7:15, 16, 18–21. In 1 Tim. 2:4, RV, "willeth" signifies the gracious "desire" of God for all men to be saved; not all are "willing" to accept His condition, depriving themselves either by the self-established criterion of their perverted reason, or because of their self-indulgent preference for sin. In John 6:21, the KJV renders the verb "willingly" (RV, "they were willing"); in 2 Pet. 3:5, KJV, the present participle is translated "willingly" (RV, "wilfully").

The following are RV renderings for the KJV, "will": Matt. 16:24, 25, "would"; "wouldest," 19:21 and 20:21; "would," 20:26, 27; Mark 8:34, 35; 10:43, 44; "would fain," Luke 13:31; "would," John 6:67; "willeth," 7:17; in 8:44, "it is your will (to do)"; "wouldest," Rom. 13:3; "would," 1 Cor. 14:35 and 1 Pet. 3:10.

2. ***boulomai*** (*1014*), expresses the deliberate exercise of volition more strongly than No. 1, and is rendered as follows in the RV, where the KJV has "will": Matt. 11:27 and Luke 10:22, "willeth"; Jas. 4:4, "would"; in Jas. 3:4, RV, "willeth" (KJV, "listeth"). In Jas. 1:18 the perfect participle is translated "of His own will," lit. "having willed."

## WINE

### *Old Testament*

***yayin*** (3196), "wine." This is the usual Hebrew word for naturally fermented grape, capable of intoxicating if overused. It is usually rendered "wine," Gen. 14:18; cf. 27:25. Passages such as Ezek. 27:18 inform us that "wine" was an article of commerce. Proverbs recommends that kings avoid "wine" and beer but that it be given to those troubled with problems that they might drink and forget their problems, Prov. 31:4–7. "Wine" was used to make merry, to make one feel good without being intoxicated, 2 Sam. 13:28. Second, "wine" was used in rejoicing before the Lord. Once a year all Israel is to gather in Jerusalem. The money realized from the sale of a tithe of all their harvest was to be spent, Deut. 14:26. "Wine" was offered to God at His command as part of the prescribed ritual, Exod. 29:40. In Gen. 9:24 ***yayin*** means drunkenness.

***tirosh*** is distinguished from ***yayin*** by referring only to new wine not fully fermented; ***yayin*** includes "wine" at any stage. In Gen. 27:28 (the first biblical occurrence of the word) Jacob's blessing includes the divine bestowal of an abundance of new wine. In 1 Sam. 1:15 ***yayin*** parallels ***shekar***, "grain or fruit drink." ***shekar*** in early times included wine, Num. 28:7, but meant strong drink made from any fruit or grain, Num. 6:3. People in special states of holiness were forbidden to drink "wine," such as the Nazirites, Num. 6:3, Samson's mother, Judg. 13:4, and priests approaching God, Lev. 10:9.

### *New Testament*

1. ***oinos*** (*3631*) is the general word for "wine." The mention of the bursting of the wineskins, Matt. 9:17; Mark 2:22; Luke 5:37, implies fermentation.

The drinking of "wine" could be a stumbling block and the apostle enjoins abstinence in this respect, as in others, so as to avoid giving an occasion of stumbling to a brother, Rom. 14:21. Contrast 1 Tim. 5:23, which has an entirely different connection. The word is used metaphorically (a) of the evils ministered to the nations by religious Babylon, 14:8; 17:2; 18:3; (b) of the contents of the cup of divine wrath upon the nations and Babylon, Rev. 14:10; 16:19; 19:15.

2. ***gleukos*** (*1098*) denotes sweet "new wine," or "must," Acts 2:13, where the accusation shows that it was intoxicant and must have been undergoing fermentation some time.

## WINEBIBBER

***oinopotes*** (*3630*), "a wine drinker" (***oinos***, and ***potes***, "a drinker"), is used in Matt. 11:19; Luke 7:34.

## WINEPRESS, WINE-VAT

***lenos*** (*3025*) denotes "a trough or vat," used especially for the treading of grapes, Matt. 21:33. Not infrequently they were dug out in the soil or excavated in a rock, as in the rock vats in Palestine today. In Rev. 14:19, 20 (twice) and 19:15 (where ***oinos*** is added, lit.. "the winepress of the wine") the word is used metaphorically with reference to the execution of divine judgment upon the gathered foes of the Jews at the close of this age preliminary to the establishment of the millennial kingdom.

## WISDOM

1. ***sophia*** (*4678*) is used with reference to (a) God, Rom. 11:33; 1 Cor. 1:21, 24; 2:7; Eph. 3:10; Rev. 7:12; (b) Christ, Matt. 13:54; Mark 6:2; Luke 2:40, 52; 1 Cor. 1:30; Col. 2:3; Rev. 5:12; (c) "wisdom" personified, Matt. 11:19; Luke 7:35; 11:49; (d) human "wisdom" (1) in spiritual things, Luke 21:15; Acts 6:3, 10; 7:10; 1 Cor. 2:6 (1st part); 12:8; Eph. 1:8, 17; Col. 1:9, RV, "(spiritual) wisdom," 28; 3:16; 4:5; Jas. 1:5; 3:13, 17; 2 Pet. 3:15; Rev. 13:18; 17:9; (2) in the natural sphere, Matt. 12:42; Luke 11:31; Acts 7:22; 1 Cor. 1:17, 19, 20, 21 (twice), 22; 2:1, 4, 5, 6 (2nd part), 13; 3:19; 2 Cor. 1:12; Col. 2:23; (3) in its most debased form, Jas. 3:15, "earthly, sensual, devilish" (marg., "demoniacal").

2. ***phronesis*** (*5428*), "understanding, prudence," i.e., a right use of ***phren***, "the mind," is translated "wisdom" in Luke 1:17.

## WISE, WISER, WISELY

### *Old Testament*

**A. Adjective.**

***chakam*** (2450), "wise; skillful; practical." The ***chakam*** in secular usage signified a man who was a "skillful" craftsman. The manufacturers of the objects belonging to the tabernacle were known to be wise, or experienced in their crafts, Exod. 36:4. Even the man who was skillful in making idols was recognized as a craftsman, Isa. 40:20; cf. Jer. 10:9.

Based on the characterization of wisdom as a skill, a class of counselors known as "wise men" arose. They were to be found in Egypt, Gen. 41:8, in Babylon, Jer. 50:35, in Tyre, Ezek. 27:9, in Edom, Obad. 8, and in Israel. In pagan cultures the "wise" man practiced magic and divination, Exod. 7:11; Isa. 44:25.

The religious sense of ***chakam*** excludes delusion, craftiness, shrewdness, and magic. God is the source of wisdom, as He is "wise," Isa. 31:2. The man or woman who, fearing God, lives in accordance with what God expects and what is expected of him in a God-fearing society is viewed as an integrated person. He is "wise" in that his manner of life projects the fear of God and the blessing of God rests upon him. Even as the craftsman is said to be skillful in his trade, the Old Testament ***chakam*** was learning and applying wisdom to every situation in life, and the degree in which he succeeded was a barometer of his progress on the road of wisdom.

### B. Nouns.

***chokmah*** (2451), "wisdom; experience; shrewdness." ***chokmah*** is the knowledge and the ability to make the right choices at the opportune time. The consistency of making the right choice is an indication of maturity and development. The prerequisite for "wisdom" is the fear of the Lord: "The fear of the Lord is the beginning of knowledge: but fools despise wisdom and instruction," Prov. 1:7. "Wisdom" is viewed as crying out for disciples who will do everything to pursue her, Prov. 1:20. The person who seeks ***chokmah*** diligently will receive understanding, Prov. 2:6; he will benefit in his life by walking with God, Prov. 2:20. The advantages of "wisdom" are many, Prov. 3:2–4. The prerequisite is a desire to follow and imitate God as He has revealed Himself in Jesus Christ, without self-reliance and especially *not* in a spirit of pride, Prov. 1:5–7. The fruits of ***chokmah*** are many, and the Book of Proverbs describes the characters of the ***chakam*** and ***chokmah***.

The importance of "wisdom" explains why books were written about it. Songs were composed in celebration of "wisdom," Job 28. Even "wisdom" is personified in Proverbs. ***chokmah*** as a person stands for that divine perfection of "wisdom" which is manifest in God's creative acts. As a divine perfection it is visible in God's creative acts, Prov. 8:1, 12, 22, 30, 32.

### C. Verb.

***chakam*** (2449), "to be wise, act wisely, make wise, show oneself wise," Prov. 23:15; cf. Ps. 119:98 where ***chakam*** means "to make wise."

*New Testament*

### A. Adjectives.

1. ***sophos*** (*4680*) is used of (a) God, Rom. 16:27; in 1 Tim. 1:17 and Jude 25 ***sophos*** is absent, in the best mss. (see the RV), the comparative degree, ***sophoteros***, occurs in 1 Cor. 1:25, where "foolishness" is simply in the human estimate; (b) spiritual teachers in Israel, Matt. 23:34; (c) believers endowed with spiritual and practical wisdom, Rom. 16:19; 1 Cor. 3:10; 6:5; Eph. 5:15; Jas. 3:13; (d) Jewish teachers in the time of Christ, Matt. 11:25; Luke 10:21; (e) the naturally learned, Rom. 1:14, 22; 1 Cor. 1:19, 20, 26, 27; 3:15–20.

2. ***phronimos*** (*5429*), "prudent, sensible, practically wise," Matt. 7:24; 10:16; 24:45; 25:2, 4, 8, 9; Luke 12:42; 16:8 (comparative degree, ***phronimoteros***); 1 Cor. 10:15; in an evil sense, "wise (in your own conceits)," lit., "wise (in yourselves)," i.e., "judged by the standard of your self-complacency," Rom. 11:25; 12:16; ironically, 1 Cor. 4:10; 2 Cor. 11:19.

### B. Noun.

***magos*** (*3097*) denotes "a Magian," one of a sacred caste, originally Median, Matt. 2:1, 7, 16.

### C. Verbs.

1. ***sophizo*** (*4679*) is rendered "to make wise" in 2 Tim. 3:15.

2. ***suniemi*** or ***sunio*** (*4920*), "to perceive, understand," is used negatively in 2 Cor. 10:12, KJV, "are not wise" (RV, "are without understanding").

### D. Adverb.

***phronimos*** (*5430*), "wisely" (akin to A, No. 2), occurs in Luke 16:8.

## WISH

1. ***euchomai*** (*2172*) is rendered "to wish" in Acts 27:29 (RV marg., "prayed"); so Rom. 9:3; in 2 Cor. 13:9 and 3 John 2, RV, "pray."

2. ***boulomai*** (*1014*), in Mark 15:15, RV, is translated "wishing" (KJV, "willing"); so 2 Pet. 3:9; in Acts 25:22, RV, "could wish" (KJV, "would).

3. ***thelo*** (*2309*), in 1 Cor. 16:7, RV, is translated "wish" (KJV, "will"); Gal. 4:20, "I could wish" (KJV, "I desire").

## WITNESS (Noun and Verb)

### *Old Testament*

### A. Noun.

***'ed*** (5707), "witness." This word has to do with the legal or judicial sphere. First, in the area of civil affairs the word can mean someone who is present at a legal transaction and can confirm it if necessary. Such people worked as notaries, e.g., for an oral transfer of property, Ruth 4:7, 9. At a later time the "witnesses" not only acted to attest the transaction and to confirm it orally, but they signed a document or deed of purchase. Thus "witness" takes on the new nuance of those able and willing to affirm the truth of a transaction by affixing their signatures, Jer. 32:12. An object or animal(s) can signify the truthfulness of an act or agreement. Its very existence or the acceptance of it by both parties (in the case of the animals given to Abimelech in Gen. 21:30) bears witness, Gen. 31:44; or stone pillar or heap as a further "witness," Gen. 31:48.

In Mosaic criminal law the accused has the right to be faced by his/her accuser and to give evidence of his/her innocence. In the case of a newly married woman charged by her own husband, his testimony is sufficient to prove her guilty of adultery unless her parents have clear evidence proving her virginity before her marriage, Deut. 22:14ff. Usually the accused is faced with someone who either saw or heard of his guilt, Lev. 5:1. Heavy penalties fell on anyone who lied to a court. The ninth commandment may well have immediate reference to such a concrete court situation, Exod. 20:16. If so, it serves to sanction proper judicial procedure, to safeguard individuals from secret accusation and condemnation and giving them the right and privilege of self-defense. In the exchange between Jacob and Laban mentioned above, Jacob also cites God as a "witness," Gen. 31:50, between them, the one who will see violations; God, however, is also the Judge. Although human courts are (as a rule) to keep judge and "witness" separate, the "witnesses" do participate in executing the penalty upon the guilty party, Deut. 17:7, even as God does.

### B. Verb.

***'ud*** (5749), "to take as witness, bear witness, repeat, admonish, warn, assure protection, relieve." In 1 Kings 21:10 ***'ud*** means "to bear witness"; "to warn" in Jer. 6:10.

### *New Testament*

### A. Nouns.

1. ***martus*** or ***martur*** (*3144*) (whence Eng., "martyr," one who bears "witness" by his death) denotes "one who can or does aver what he has seen or heard or knows"; it is used (a) of God, Rom. 1:9; 2 Cor. 1:23; Phil. 1:8; 1 Thess. 2:5, 10 (2nd part); (b) of Christ, Rev. 1:5; 3:14; (c) of those who "witness" for Christ by their death, Acts 22:20; Rev. 2:13; Rev. 17:6; (d) of the interpreters of God's counsels, yet to "witness" in Jerusalem in the times of the Antichrist, Rev. 11:3; (e) in a forensic sense, Matt. 18:16; 26:65; Mark 14:63; Acts 6:13; 7:58; 2 Cor. 13:1; 1 Tim. 5:19; Heb. 10:28; (f) in a historical sense, Luke 11:48; 24:48; Acts 1:8, 22; 2:32; 3:15; 5:32; 10:39, 41; 13:31; 22:15; 26:16; 1 Thess. 2:10 (1st part); 1 Tim. 6:12; 2 Tim. 2:2; Heb. 12:1, "(a cloud) of witnesses," here of those mentioned in ch. 11, those whose lives and actions testified to the worth and effect of faith, and whose faith received "witness" in Scripture, 1 Pet. 5:1.

2. ***marturia*** (*3141*), "testimony, a bearing witness," is translated "witness" in Mark 14:55, 56, 59; Luke 22:71; John 1:7, 19 (RV); 3:11, 32 and 33 (RV); 5:31, 32, 34 (RV), 36; RV in 8:13, 14, 17; 19:35; 21:24; KJV in Titus 1:13; KJV and RV in 1 John 5:9 (thrice), 10a; RV in 10b, 11; 3 John 12.

3. ***marturion*** (*3142*), "testimony or witness as borne, a declaration of facts," is translated "witness" in Matt. 24:14, KJV; Acts 4:33; 7:44 (KJV); Jas. 5:3 (KJV).

4. ***pseudomartus*** or ***-tur*** (*5571* and *3144*) denotes "a false witness," Matt. 26:60; 1 Cor. 15:15.

5. ***pseudomarturia*** (*5577*), "false witness," occurs in Matt. 15:19; 26:59.

### B. Verbs.

1. ***martureo*** (*3140*) denotes (I) "to be a ***martus***" (see A, No. 1), or "to bear witness to," sometimes rendered "to testify"; it is used of the witness (a) of God the Father to Christ, John 5:32, 37; 8:18 (2nd part); 1 John 5:9, 10; to others, Acts 13:22; 15:8; Heb. 11:2, 4 (twice), 5, 39; (b) of Christ, John 3:11, 32; 4:44; 5:31; 7:7; 8:13, 14, 18 (1st part); 13:21; 18:37; Acts 14:3; 1 Tim. 6:13; Rev. 22:18, 20; of the Holy Spirit, to Christ, John 15:26; Heb. 10:15; 1 John 5:7, 8, RV, which rightly omits the latter part of v. 7; it finds no support in Scripture; (c) of the Scriptures, to Christ, John 5:39; Heb. 7:8, 17; (d) of the works of Christ, to Himself, and of the circumstances connected with His death, John 5:36; 10:25; 1 John 5:8; (e) of prophets and apostles, to the righteousness of God, Rom. 3:21; to

Christ, John 1:7, 8, 15, 32, 34; 3:26; 5:33, RV; 15:27; 19:35; 21:24; Acts 10:43; 23:11; 1 Cor. 15:15; 1 John 1:2; 4:14; Rev. 1:2; to doctrine, Acts 26:22 (in some texts, so KJV; see No. 2); to the Word of God, Rev. 1:2; (f) of others, concerning Christ, Luke 4:22; John 4:39; 12:17; (g) of believers to one another, John 3:28; 2 Cor. 8:3; Gal. 4:15; Col. 4:13; 1 Thess. 2:11 (in some texts: see No. 2); 3 John 3, 6, 12 (2nd part); (h) of the apostle Paul concerning Israel, Rom. 10:2; (i) of an angel, to the churches, Rev. 22:16; (j) of unbelievers, concerning themselves, Matt. 23:31; concerning Christ, John 18:23; concerning others, John 2:25; Acts 22:5; 26:5; (II), "to give a good report, to approve of," Acts 6:3; 10:22; 16:2; 22:12; 1 Tim. 5:10; 3 John 12 (1st part); some would put Luke 4:22 here.

2. ***marturomai*** (*3143*), strictly meaning "to summon as a witness," signifies "to affirm solemnly, adjure," and is used in the middle voice only, rendered "to testify" in Acts 20:26, RV (KJV, "I take . . . to record"); 26:22, RV, in the best texts [see No. 1 (e)]; Gal. 5:3; Eph. 4:17; 1 Thess. 2:11, in the best texts [see No. 1 (g)].

3. ***summartureo*** (*4828*) denotes "to bear witness with" (***sun***), Rom. 2:15; 8:16; 9:1.

4. ***sunepimartureo*** (*4901*) denotes "to join in bearing witness with others," Heb. 2:4.

5. ***katamartureo*** (*2649*) denotes "to witness against" (***kata***), Matt. 26:62; 27:13; Mark 14:60 (in some mss., 15:4, for ***kategoreo***, "to accuse," RV).

6. ***pseudomartureo*** (*5576*), "to bear false witness" (***pseudes***, "false"), occurs in Matt. 19:18; Mark 10:19; 14:56, 57; Luke 18:20; in some texts, Rom. 13:9.

### C. Adjective.

***amarturos*** (*267*) denotes "without witness" (***a***, negative, and ***martus***), Acts 14:17.

## WOE

***ouai*** (*3759*), an interjection, is used (a) in denunciation, Matt. 11:21; 18:7 (twice); eight times in ch. 23; 24:19; 26:24; Mark 13:17; 14:21; Luke 6:24, 25 (twice), 26; 10:13; six times in ch. 11; 17:1; 21:23; 22:22; 1 Cor. 9:16; Jude 11; Rev. 8:13 (thrice); 12:12; as a noun, Rev. 9:12 (twice); 11:14 (twice); (b) in grief, "alas," Rev. 18:10, 16, 19 (twice in each).

## WOMAN

### *Old Testament*

***'ishshah*** (802), "woman; wife; betrothed one; bride; each." This noun connotes one who is a female human being regardless of her age or virginity. Therefore, it appears in correlation to "man" (***ish***), Gen. 2:22, 23. The stress on the family role of a "wife" appears in passages such as Gen. 8:16. In Lam. 2:20 ***'ishshah*** is a synonym for "mother," Gen. 29:21 (cf. Deut. 22:24. This word can also be used figuratively describing foreign warriors and/or heroes as "women," in other words as weak, unmanly, and cowardly," Isa. 19:16. In a few passages ***'ishshah*** means "each" or "every," Exod. 3:22; cf. Amos 4:3.

### *New Testament*

1. ***gune*** (*1135*), "woman" unmarried or married, e.g., Matt. 11:11; 14:21; Luke 4:26, of a "widow"; Rom. 7:2; in the vocative case, used in addressing a "woman," it is a term not of reproof or severity, but of endearment or respect, Matt. 15:28; John 2:4, where the Lord's words to His mother at the wedding in Cana, are neither rebuff nor rebuke. The question is, lit., "What to Me and to thee?" and the word "woman," the term of endearment, follows this. The meaning is "There is no obligation on Me or you, but love will supply the need." She confides in Him, He responds to her faith. There was lovingkindness in both hearts. His next words about "His hour" suit this; they were not unfamiliar to her. Cana is in the path to Calvary; Calvary was not yet, but it made the beginning of signs possible. See also 4:21; 19:26.

2. ***gunaikarion*** (*1133*), a diminutive of No. 1, a "little woman," is used contemptuously in 2 Tim. 3:6, "a silly woman."

3. ***presbuteros*** (*4245*), "elder, older," in the feminine plural, denotes "elder women" in 1 Tim. 5:2.

4. ***presbutis*** (*4247*), the feminine of ***presbutes***, "aged," is used in the plural and translated "aged women" in Titus 2:3.

5. ***theleia*** (*2338***), the feminine of the adjective ***thelus***, denotes "female," and is used as a noun, Rom. 1:26, 27.

## WOMB

1. ***koilia*** (*2836*) denotes "the womb," Matt. 19:12; Luke 1:15, 41, 42, 44; 2:21; 11:27; 23:29; John 3:4; Acts 3:2; 14:8; Gal. 1:15.

2. ***gaster*** (*1064*), is rendered "womb" in Luke 1:31.

3. ***metra*** (*3388*), the matrix (akin to meter "a mother"), occurs in Luke 2:23; Rom. 4:19.

## WONDER (Noun and Verb)

### *Old Testament*

***mopet*** (4159), "wonder; sign; portent." First, this word signifies a divine act or a special display of divine power, Exod. 4:21. Second, the word can represent a "sign" from God or a token of a future event, 1 Kings 13:3; Zech. 3:8.

*New Testament*

1. ***teras*** (*5059*), a noun, "something strange," causing the beholder to marvel, is always used in the plural, always rendered "wonders," and generally follows ***semeia***, "signs"; the opposite order occurs in Acts 2:22, 43; 6:8, RV; 7:36; in Acts 2:19 "wonders" occurs alone. A sign is intended to appeal to the understanding, a "wonder" appeals to the imagination, a power (***dunamis***) indicates its source as supernatural. "Wonders" are manifested as divine operations in thirteen occurrences (9 times in Acts); three times they are ascribed to the work of Satan through human agents, Matt. 24:24; Mark 13:22 and 2 Thess. 2:9.

2. ***thambos*** (*2285*), "amazement," is rendered "wonder" in Acts 3:10.

## WONDERFUL (THING, WORK)

(1) In Matt. 7:22, KJV, ***dunamis*** (in the plural) is rendered "wonderful works" (RV, "mighty works," marg., "powers"). (2) In Acts 2:11, KJV, the adjective ***megaleios***, "magnificent," in the neuter plural with the article, is rendered "the wonderful works" (RV, "the mighty works"). (3) In Matt. 21:15, the neuter plural of the adjective ***thaumasios***, "wonderful," is used as a noun, "wonderful things," lit., "wonders."

## WONT

***etho*** (*1486*), "to be accustomed," is used in the pluperfect tense (with imperfect meaning), ***eiotha***, rendered "was wont" in Matt. 27:15; Mark 10:1.

## WORD

1. ***logos*** (*3056*) denotes (I) "the expression of thought"—not the mere name of an object—(a) as embodying a conception or idea, e.g., Luke 7:7; 1 Cor. 14:9, 19; (b) a saying or statement, (1) by God, e.g., John 15:25; Rom. 9:9; 9:28, RV, "word" (KJV, "work"); Gal. 5:14; Heb. 4:12; (2) by Christ, e.g., Matt. 24:35 (plur.); John 2:22; 4:41; 14:23 (plur.); 15:20. In connection with (1) and (2) the phrase "the word of the Lord," i.e., the revealed will of God (very frequent in the OT), is used of a direct revelation given by Christ, 1 Thess. 4:15; of the gospel, Acts 8:25; 13:49; 15:35, 36; 16:32; 19:10; 1 Thess. 1:8; 2 Thess. 3:1; in this respect it is the message from the Lord, delivered with His authority and made effective by His power (cf. Acts 10:36); for other instances relating to the gospel see Acts 13:26; 14:3; 15:7; 1 Cor. 1:18, RV; 2 Cor. 2:17; 4:2; 5:19; 6:7; Gal. 6:6; Eph. 1:13; Phil. 2:16; Col. 1:5; Heb. 5:13; sometimes it is used as the sum of God's utterances, e.g., Mark 7:13; John 10:35; Rev. 1:2, 9; (c) discourse, speech, of instruction, etc., e.g., Acts 2:40; 1 Cor. 2:13; 12:8; 2 Cor. 1:18; 1 Thess. 1:5; 2 Thess. 2:15; Heb. 6:1, RV, marg.; doctrine, e.g., Matt. 13:20; Col. 3:16; 1 Tim. 4:6; 2 Tim. 1:13; Titus 1:9; 1 John 2:7;

(II) "The Personal Word," a title of the Son of God; this identification is substantiated by the statements of doctrine in John 1:1–18, declaring in verses 1 and 2 (1) His distinct and superfinite Personality, (2) His relation in the Godhead (***pros***, "with," not mere company, but the most intimate communion), (3) His deity; in v. 3 His creative power; in v. 14 His incarnation ("became flesh," expressing His voluntary act; not as KJV, "was made"), the reality and totality of His human nature, and His glory "as of the only begotten from the Father," RV (marg., "an only begotten from a father"), the absence of the article in each place lending stress to the nature and character of the relationship; His was the ***shekinah*** glory in open manifestation; v. 18 consummates the identification: "the only-begotten Son (RV marg., many ancient authorities read "God only begotten,"), which is in the bosom of the Father, He hath declared Him," thus fulfilling the significance of the title "***Logos***," the "Word," the personal manifestation, not of a part of the divine nature, but of the whole deity.

The title is used also in 1 John 1, "the Word of life" combining the two declarations in John 1:1 and 4 and Rev. 19:13.

2. ***rhema*** (*4487*) denotes "that which is spoken, what is uttered in speech or writing"; in the singular, "a word," e.g., Matt. 12:36; 27:14; 2 Cor. 12:4; 13:1; Heb. 12:19; in the plural, speech, discourse, e.g., John 3:34; 8:20; Acts 2:14; 6:11, 13; 11:14; 13:42; 26:25; Rom. 10:18; 2 Pet. 3:2; Jude 17; it is used of the gospel in Rom. 10:8 (twice), 17, RV, "the word of Christ" (i.e., the "word" which preaches Christ); 10:18; 1 Pet. 1:25 (twice); of a statement, command, instruction, e.g., Matt. 26:75; Luke 1:37, RV, "(no) word (from God shall be void of power)," v. 38; Acts 11:16; Heb. 11:3.

## WORK (Noun and Verb), WROUGHT

*Old Testament*

### A. Verbs.

***pa'al*** (6466), "to do, work." It is used primarily as a poetic synonym for the much more common verb ***'ashah***, "to do, to make, Exod. 15:17; Ps. 15:2.

***'ashah*** (6213), "to make, do, create." In its primary sense this verb represents the production of various objects. This includes making images and idols, Exod. 20:4; Isa. 44:17. In Gen. 12:5 ***'ashah*** means "to acquire." Used in association with "Sabbath" or the name of other holy days, this word signifies "keeping" or "celebrating": "All the congregation of Israel shall keep it [the Passover]," Exod. 12:47. In a related sense the word means "to spend" a day, Eccl. 6:12.

***'ashah*** may represent the relationship of an individual to another in his action or behavior, in the sense of what one does, Gen. 12:18. With the particle ***le*** the verb signifies inflicting upon another some act or behavior, Gen. 20:9. With the particle ***'im*** the word may mean "to show," or "to practice" something toward someone, Gen. 24:12. In Gen. 26:29 ***'ashah*** appears twice in the sense "to practice toward." Used of plants this verb signifies "bringing forth." In Gen. 1:11 it means "to bear fruit," Hos. 8:7; or branches, Ezek. 17:8.

This verb is also applied specifically to all aspects of divine acts and actions. In the general sense of His actions toward His people Israel, the word first occurs in Gen. 12:2, where God promises "to make" Abram a great nation. ***'ashah*** is also the most general Old Testament expression for divine creating. Every aspect of this activity is described by this word, Exod. 20:11. This word is used of God's acts effecting the entire created world and individual men, Exod. 20:6. God's acts and words perfectly correspond, so that what He says He does, and what He does is what He has said, Gen. 21:1; Ps. 115:3.

## B. Noun.

***ma'aseh*** (4639), "work; deed; labor; behavior." The basic meaning of ***ma'aseh*** is "work." Lamech used the word to signify agricultural labor, Gen. 5:29. The Israelites were commanded to celebrate the Festival of the Firstfruits, as it signified the blessing of God upon their "labors," Exod. 23:16. It is not to be limited to this. As the word is the most general word for "work," it may be used to refer to the "work" of a skillful craftsman, Exod. 26:1, a weaver, 26:36, a jeweler, 28:11, and a perfumer, 30:25.

The phrase "work of one's hands" signifies the worthlessness of the idols fashioned by human hands, Hos. 14:3. However, the prayer of the psalmist includes the request that the "works" of God's people might be established, Ps. 90:17. Since the righteous work out God's work and are a cause of God's rejoicing, Ps. 104:31. In addition to "work," ***ma'aseh*** also denotes "deed," "practice," or "behavior," Gen. 44:15. The Israelites were strongly commanded not to imitate the grossly immoral behavior of the Canaanites and the surrounding nations, Lev. 18:3; cf. Exod. 23:24.

Thus far, we have dealt with ***ma'aseh*** from man's perspective. The word may have a positive connotation ("work, deed") as well as a negative ("corrupt practice"). The Old Testament also calls us to celebrate the "work" of God. The psalmist was overwhelmed with the majesty of the Lord, as he looked at God's "work" of creation, Ps. 8:3; cf. 19:1; 102:25. The God of Israel demonstrated His love by His mighty acts of deliverance on behalf of Israel, Josh. 24:31; cf. versions. All of God's "works" are characterized by faithfulness to His promises and covenant, Ps. 33:4.

### *New Testament*

## A. Nouns.

1. ***ergon*** (*2041*) denotes (I) "work, employment, task," e.g., Mark 13:34; John 4:34; 17:4; Acts 13:2; Phil. 2:30; 1 Thess. 5:13; in Acts 5:38 with the idea of enterprise; (II), "a deed, act," (a) of God, e.g., John 6:28, 29; 9:3; 10:37; 14:10; Acts 13:41; Rom. 14:20; Heb. 1:10; 2:7; 3:9; 4:3, 4, 10; Rev. 15:3; (b) of Christ, e.g., Matt. 11:2; especially in John, 5:36; 7:3, 21; 10:25, 32, 33, 38; 14:11, 12; 15:24; Rev. 2:26; (c) of believers, e.g., Matt. 5:16; Mark 14:6; Acts 9:36; Rom. 13:3; Col. 1:10; 1 Thess. 1:3, "work of faith," here the initial act of faith at conversion (turning to God, v. 9); in 2 Thess. 1:11, "*every* work of faith," RV, denotes every activity undertaken for Christ's sake; 2:17; 1 Tim. 2:10; 5:10; 6:18; 2 Tim. 2:21; 3:17; Titus 2:7, 14; 3:1, 8, 14; Heb. 10:24; 13:21; frequent in James, as the effect of faith [in 1:25, KJV, "(a doer) of the work," RV, "(a doer) that worketh"]; 1 Pet. 2:12; Rev. 2:2 and in several other places in chs. 2 and 3; 14:13; (d) of unbelievers, e.g., Matt. 23:3, 5; John 7:7; Acts 7:41 (for idols); Rom. 13:12; Eph. 5:11; Col. 1:21; Titus 1:16 (1st part); 1 John 3:12; Jude 15, RV; Rev. 2:6, RV; of those who seek justification by works, e.g., Rom. 9:32; Gal. 3:10; Eph. 2:9; described as the works of the law, e.g., Gal. 2:16; 3:2, 5; dead works, Heb. 6:1; 9:14; (e) of Babylon, Rev. 18:6; (f) of the Devil, John 8:41; 1 John 3:8.

2. ***ergasia*** (*2039*) denotes "a work" or "business," also "a working, performance," Eph. 4:19, where preceded by ***eis***, "to," it is rendered "to work" (marg., "to make a trade of").

## B. Verbs.

1. ***ergazomai*** (*2038*) is used (I) intransitively, e.g., Matt. 21:28; John 5:17; 9:4 (2nd part); Rom. 4:4, 5; 1 Cor. 4:12; 9:6; 1 Thess. 2:9; 4:11; 2 Thess. 3:8, 10–12; (II) transitively, (a) "to work something, produce, perform," e.g., Matt. 26:10, "she hath wrought"; John 6:28, 30; 9:4 (1st part); Acts 10:35; 13:41; Rom. 2:10; 13:10; 1 Cor. 16:10;

2 Cor. 7:10a, in the best texts, some have No. 2; Gal. 6:10, RV, "let us work"; Eph. 4:28; Heb. 11:33; 2 John 8; (b) "to earn by working, work for," John 6:27, RV, "work" (KJV, "labor").

2. ***katergazomai*** (*2716*), an emphatic form of No. 1, signifies "to work out, achieve, effect by toil," rendered "to work" (past tense, "wrought") in Rom. 1:27; 2:9, RV; 4:15 (the Law brings men under condemnation and so renders them subject to divine wrath); 5:3; 7:8, 13; 15:18; 2 Cor. 4:17; 5:5; 7:10 (see No. 1), 11; 12:12; Phil. 2:12, where "your own salvation" refers especially to freedom from strife and vainglory; Jas. 1:3, 20; 1 Pet. 4:3.

3. ***energeo*** (*1754*), lit., "to work in" (***en***, and A, No. 1), "to be active, operative," is used of (a) God, 1 Cor. 12:6; Gal. 2:8; 3:5; Eph. 1:11, 20; 3:20; Phil. 2:13a; Col. 1:29; (b) the Holy Spirit, 1 Cor, 12:11; (c) the Word of God, 1 Thess. 2:13 (middle voice; KJV, 'effectually worketh'); (d) supernatural power, undefined, Matt. 14:2; Mark 6:14; (e) faith, as the energizer of love, Gal. 5:6; (f) the example of patience in suffering, 2 Cor. 1:6; (g) death (physical) and life (spiritual), 2 Cor. 4:12; (h) sinful passions, Rom. 7:5; (i) the spirit of the Evil One, Eph. 2:2; (j) the mystery of iniquity, 2 Thess. 2:7. (k) the active response of believers to the inworking of God, Phil. 2:13b, RV, "to work (for)," KJV, "to do (of)"; (l) the supplication of the righteous, Jas. 5:16, RV, "in its working" (KJV, "effectual fervent").

4. ***poieo*** (*4160*), "to do," is rendered "to work" in Matt. 20:12, KJV (RV, "spent"); Acts 15:12, "had wrought"; 19:11; 21:19; Heb. 13:21; Rev. 16:14; 19:20; 21:27, KJV (RV, "maketh"; marg., "doeth").

5. ***sunergeo*** (*4903*), "to work with or together" (***sun***), occurs in Mark 16:20; Rom. 8:28, "work together"; 1 Cor. 16:16, "helpeth with"; 2 Cor. 6:1, "workers together," present participle, "working together"; the "*with Him*" represents nothing in the Greek; Jas. 2:22, "wrought with."

6. ***ginomai*** (*1096*), "to become, take place," is rendered "wrought" in Mark 6:2; Acts 5:12, "were . . . wrought."

## WORKER, WORKFELLOW, FELLOW WORKERS, WORKMAN

1. ***ergates*** (*2040*) is translated "workers" in Luke 13:27 ("of iniquity"); 2 Cor. 11:13 ("deceitful"); Phil. 3:2 ("evil"); "workman," Matt. 10:10, KJV (RV, "laborer"); "workman," 2 Tim. 2:15; "workmen," Acts 19:25.

2. ***sunergos*** (*4904*) denotes "a worker with," and is rendered "workfellow" in Rom. 16:21, KJV, RV, "fellow worker"; in Col. 4:11, "fellow workers" (see RV). See the RV, "God's fellow workers," in 1 Cor. 3:9.

## WORKING

1. ***energeia*** (*1753*) (Eng., "energy") is used (1) of the "power" of God, (a) in the resurrection of Christ, Eph. 1:19; Col. 2:12, RV, "working" (KJV, "operation"); (b) in the call and enduement of Paul, Eph. 3:7; Col. 1:29; (c) in His retributive dealings in sending "a working of error" (KJV, "strong delusion") upon those under the rule of the Man of Sin who receive not the love of the truth, but have pleasure in unrighteousness, 2 Thess. 2:11; (2) of the "power" of Christ (a) generally, Phil. 3:21; (b) in the church, individually, Eph. 4:16; (3) of the power of Satan in energizing the Man of Sin in his "parousia," 2 Thess. 2:9, "coming."

2. ***energema*** (*1755*), "what is wrought," the effect produced by No. 1, occurs in 1 Cor. 12:6, RV, "workings" (KJV, "operations"); v. 10.

## WORLD

1. ***kosmos*** (*2889*), primarily "order, arrangement, ornament, adornment" (1 Pet. 3:3), is used to denote (a) the "earth," e.g., Matt. 13:35; John 21:25; Acts 17:24; Rom. 1:20 (probably here the universe: it had this meaning among the Greeks, owing to the order observable in it); 1 Tim. 6:7; Heb. 4:3; 9:26; (b) the "earth" in contrast with Heaven, 1 John 3:17 (perhaps also Rom. 4:13); (c) by metonymy, the "human race, mankind," e.g., Matt. 5:14; John 1:9 [here "that cometh (RV, 'coming') into the world" is said of Christ, not of "every man"; by His coming into the world He was the light for all men]; v. 10; 3:16, 17 (thrice), 19; 4:42, and frequently in Rom., 1 Cor. and 1 John; (d) "Gentiles" as distinguished from Jews, e.g., Rom. 11:12, 15, where the meaning is that all who will may be reconciled (cf. 2 Cor. 5:19); (e) the "present condition of human affairs," in alienation from and opposition to God, e.g., John 7:7; 8:23; 14:30; 1 Cor. 2:12; Gal. 4:3; 6:14; Col. 2:8; Jas. 1:27; 1 John 4:5 (thrice); 5:19; (f) the "sum of temporal possessions," Matt. 16:26; 1 Cor. 7:31 (1st part); (g) metaphorically, of the "tongue" as "a world (of iniquity)," Jas. 3:6, expressive of magnitude and variety.

2. ***aion*** (*165*), "an age, a period of time," marked in the NT usage by spiritual or moral characteristics, is sometimes translated "world"; the RV marg. always has "age." The following are details concerning the world in this respect; its cares, Matt. 13:22; its sons, Luke 16:8; 20:34; its rulers, 1 Cor. 2:6, 8; its wisdom, 1 Cor. 1:20; 2:6; 3:18; its fashion, Rom. 12:2; its character, Gal. 1:4; its god, 2 Cor. 4:4. The phrase "the end of the world" should be rendered "the end of the age," in most places; in 1 Cor. 10:11, KJV, "the ends (***tele***) of the world,"

RV, "the ends of the ages," probably signifies the fulfillment of the divine purposes concerning the ages in regard to the church. In Heb. 11:3 [lit., "the ages (have been prepared)"] the word indicates all that the successive periods contain; cf. 1:2.

3. ***oikoumene*** (*3625*), "the inhabited earth," is used (a) of the whole inhabited world, Matt. 24:14; Luke 4:5; 21:26; Rom. 10:18; Heb. 1:6; Rev. 3:10; 16:14; by metonymy, of its inhabitants, Acts 17:31; Rev. 12:9; (b) of the Roman Empire, the world as viewed by the writer or speaker, Luke 2:1; Acts 11:28; 24:5; by metonymy, of its inhabitants, Acts 17:6; 19:27; (c) the inhabited world in a coming age, Heb. 2:5.

## WORLDLY

***kosmikos*** (*2886*), "pertaining to this world," is used (a) in Heb. 9:1, of the tabernacle, KJV, "worldly," RV, "of this world" (i.e., made of mundane materials, adapted to this visible world, local and transitory); (b) in Titus 2:12, ethically, of "worldly lusts," or desires.

## WORMWOOD

***apsinthos*** (*894*) (Eng., "absinthe"), a plant both bitter and deleterious, and growing in desolate places, figuratively suggestive of "calamity" (Lam. 3:15) and injustice (Amos 5:7), is used in Rev. 8:11 (twice; in the 1st part as a proper name).

## WORSE

### A. Adjectives.

1. ***cheiron*** (*5501*), used as the comparative degree of ***kakos***, "evil," describes (a) the condition of certain men, Matt. 12:45; Luke 11:26; 2 Pet. 2:20; (b) evil men themselves and seducers, 2 Tim. 3:13; (c) indolent men who refuse to provide for their own households, and are worse than unbelievers, 1 Tim. 5:8, RV; (d) a rent in a garment, Matt. 9:16; Mark 2:21; (e) an error, Matt. 27:64; (f) a person suffering from a malady, Mark 5:26; (g) a possible physical affliction, John 5:14; (h) a punishment, Heb. 10:29, "sorer."

2. ***elasson*** or ***elatton*** (*1640*) is said of wine in John 2:10.

3. ***hesson*** or ***hetton*** (*2276*), "less, inferior," used in the neuter, after ***epi***, "for," is translated "worse" in 1 Cor. 11:17; in 2 Cor. 12:15 the neuter, used adverbially, is translated "the less."

### B. Verbs.

1. ***hustereo*** (*5302*) is rendered "are we the worse" in 1 Cor. 8:8.

2. ***proecho*** (*4281*), "to hold before, promote," is rendered "are we better" in Rom. 3:9, KJV (passive voice); RV, "are we in worse case."

## WORSHIP (Verb and Noun), WORSHIPING

### *Old Testament*

***shachah*** (7812), "to worship, prostrate oneself, bow down." The act of bowing down in homage is generally done before a superior or a ruler. Thus, David "bowed" himself before Saul, 1 Sam. 24:8. Sometimes it is a social or economic superior to whom one bows, as when Ruth "bowed" to the ground before Boaz, Ruth 2:10. In a dream, Joseph saw the sheaves of his brothers "bowing down" before his sheaf, Gen. 37:5, 9–10. ***shachah*** is used as the common term for coming before God in worship, as in 1 Sam. 15:25 and Jer. 7:2.

### *New Testament*

### A. Verbs.

1. ***proskuneo*** (*4352*), "to make obeisance, do reverence to" (from ***pros***, "towards," and ***kuneo***, "to kiss"), is the most frequent word rendered "to worship." It is used of an act of homage or reverence (a) to God, e.g., Matt. 4:10; John 4:21–24; 1 Cor. 14:25; Rev. 4:10; 5:14; 7:11; 11:16; 19:10 (2nd part) and 22:9; (b) to Christ, e.g., Matt. 2:2, 8, 11; 8:2; 9:18; 14:33; 15:25; 20:20; 28:9, 17; John 9:38; Heb. 1:6, in a quotation from the Sept. of Deut. 32:43, referring to Christ's second advent; (c) to a man, Matt. 18:26; (d) to the Dragon, by men, Rev. 13:4; (e) to the Beast, his human instrument, Rev. 13:4, 8, 12; 14:9, 11; (f) the image of the Beast, 13:15; 14:11; 16:2; (g) to demons, Rev. 9:20; (h) to idols, Acts 7:43.

2. ***sebomai*** (*4576*), "to revere," stressing the feeling of awe or devotion, is used of "worship" (a) to God, Matt. 15:9; Mark 7:7; Acts 16:14; 18:7, 13; (b) to a goddess, Acts 19:27.

3. ***sebazomai*** (*4573*), akin to No. 2, "to honor religiously," is used in Rom. 1:25.

4. ***latreuo*** (*3000*), "to serve, to render religious service or homage," is translated "to worship" in Phil. 3:3, "(who) worship (by the Spirit of God)," RV, KJV, "(which) worship (God in the spirit)"; the RV renders it "to serve" (for KJV, "to worship") in Acts 7:42; 24:14; KJV and RV, "(the) worshipers" in Heb. 10:2, present participle, lit., "(the ones) worshiping."

5. ***eusebeo*** (*2151*), "to act piously towards," is translated "ye worship" in Acts 17:23.



### B. Nouns.

1. ***sebasma*** (*4574*) denotes "an object of worship" (akin to A, No. 3); Acts 17:23; in 2 Thess. 2:4, "that is worshiped"; every object of "worship," whether the true God or pagan idols, will come under the ban of the Man of Sin.

2. ***ethelothreskeia*** (or ***-ia***) (*1479*), "will-worship" (***ethelo***, "to will," ***threskeia***, "worship"), occurs in Col. 2:23, voluntarily adopted "worship," whether unbidden or forbidden, not that which is imposed by others, but which one affects.

3. ***threskeia*** (*2356*), translated "worshiping" in Col. 2:18.

## WORSHIPER

1. ***proskunetes*** (*4353*), akin to ***proskuneo***, occurs in John 4:23.

2. ***neokoros*** (*3511*) is translated "worshiper" in Acts 19:35 KJV.

3. ***theosebes*** (*2318*) denotes "reverencing God" (***theos***, "God," ***sebomai***, "to revere"), and is rendered "a worshiper of God" in John 9:35.

## WORTHY, WORTHILY

### A. Adjectives.

1. ***axios*** (*514*), "of weight, worth, worthy," is said of persons and their deeds: (a) in a good sense, e.g., Matt. 10:10, 11, 13 (twice), 37 (twice), 38; 22:8; Luke 7:4; 10:7; 15:19, 21; John 1:27; Acts 13:25; 1 Tim. 5:18; 6:1; Heb. 11:38; Rev. 3:4; 4:11; 5:2, 4, 9, 12; (b) in a bad sense, Luke 12:48; 23:15; Acts 23:29; 25:11, 25; 26:31; Rom. 1:32; Rev. 16:6.

2. ***hikanos*** (*2425*), "sufficient," is translated "worthy" in this sense in Matt. 3:11 (marg., "sufficient"); so 8:8; Mark 1:7; Luke 3:16; 7:6.

3. ***enochos*** (*1777*), "held in, bound by," is translated "worthy (of death)" in Matt. 26:66 and Mark 14:64, RV (marg., "liable to"; KJV, "guilty").

### B. Verbs.

1. ***axioo*** (*515*), "to think or count worthy," is used (1) of the estimation formed by God (a) favorably, 2 Thess. 1:11, "may count (you) worthy (of your calling)," suggestive of grace (it does not say "may make you worthy"); Heb. 3:3, "of more glory," of Christ in comparison with Moses; (b) unfavorably, 10:29, "of how much sorer punishment"; (2) by a centurion (negatively) concerning himself, Luke 7:7; (3) by a church, regarding its elders, 1 Tim. 5:17, where "honor" stands probably for "honorarium," i.e., "material support."

2. ***kataxioo*** (*2661*), a strengthened form of No. 1, occurs in Luke 20:35; 21:36, in some texts; Acts 5:41; 2 Thess. 1:5.

### C. Adverb.

***axios*** (*516*), "worthily," so translated in the RV [with one exception, see (c)], for KJV, "worthy" and other renderings, (a) "worthily of God," 1 Thess. 2:12, of the Christian walk as it should be; 3 John 6, RV, of assisting servants of God in a way which reflects God's character and thoughts; (b) "worthily of the Lord," Col. 1:10; of the calling of believers, Eph. 4:1, in regard to their "walk" or manner of life; (c) "worthy of the gospel of Christ," Phil. 1:27, of a manner of life in accordance with what the gospel declares; (d) "worthily of the saints," RV, of receiving a fellow believer, Rom. 16:2, in such a manner as befits those who bear the name of "saints."

## WOT

1. ***oida***, "to know," in Acts 3:17; 7:40; Rom. 11:2.

2. ***gnorizo***, "to come to know," in Phil. 1:22.

## WOUND (Noun and Verb)

### A. Noun.

***trauma*** (*5134*), "a wound," occurs in Luke 10:34.

### B. Verb.

***traumaizo*** (*5135*), "to wound" (from A), occurs in Luke 20:12 and Acts 19:16.

## WRANGLINGS

***diaparatribe*** (*3859v*), found in 1 Tim. 6:5, denotes "constant strife," "obstinate contests" (Ellicott), "mutual irritations" (Field), KJV, "perverse disputings" (marg., "gallings one of another"), RV "wranglings." Some texts have ***paradiatribe***. The preposition ***dia-*** is used intensively, indicating thoroughness, completeness. The simple word ***paratribe*** (not found in the NT), denotes "hostility, enmity."

## WRATH

### *Old Testament*

### A. Noun.

***chemah*** (2534), "wrath; heat; rage; anger." The word indicates a state of anger. Most of the usage involves God's "anger." His "wrath" is expressed against Israel's sin in the wilderness, Deut. 9:19. The psalmist prayed for God's mercy in the hour of God's "anger," Ps. 6:1.

***chemah*** also denotes man's reaction to everyday circumstances. Man's "rage" is a dangerous expression of his emotional state, as it inflames everybody who comes close to the person in rage. "Wrath" may arise for many reasons. Proverbs speaks strongly against ***chemah***, as jealousy, 6:34; cf. "Wrath is cruel, and anger is outrageous; but who is able to stand before envy?" Prov. 27:4; cf. Ezek. 16:38. The man in rage may be culpable of crime and be condemned, Job 19:29. The wise response to "rage" is a soft answer, Prov. 15:1.

***chemah*** is associated with ***qin'ah***, "jealousy," and also with ***naqam***, "vengeance," as the angered person intends to save his name or avenge himself on the person who provoked him. In God's dealing with Israel He was jealous of His Holy name, for which reason He had to deal justly with idolatrous Israel by avenging Himself, Ezek. 24:8; but He also avenges His people against their enemies, Nah. 1:2.

There are two special meanings of ***chemah***. One is "heat," Ezek. 3:14; the other is "poison," or "venom," Deut. 32:33.

**B. Verb.**

***yacham*** (3179), "to be fiery, be hot." This verb, which occurs only 10 times in biblical Hebrew, is the root of the noun ***chemah***.

In Deut. 19:6 ***yacham*** means "to be hot": "Lest the avenger of the blood pursue the slayer, while his heart is hot, and overtake him. . . ."

***New Testament***

1. ***thumos*** (*2372*), "hot anger, passion," translated "wrath" in Luke 4:28; Acts 19:28; Rom. 2:8, RV; Gal. 5:20; Eph. 4:31; Col. 3:8; Heb. 11:27; Rev. 12:12; 14:8, 10, 19; 15:1, 7; 16:1; 18:3; "wraths" in 2 Cor. 12:20; "fierceness" in Rev. 16:19; 19:15 (followed by No. 1).

2. ***parorgismos*** (*3950*) occurs in Eph. 4:26.

## WRESTLE, WRESTLING

***pale*** (*3823*), "a wrestling" (akin to ***pallo***, "to sway, vibrate"), is used figuratively in Eph. 6:12, of the spiritual conflict engaged in by believers, RV, "(our) wrestling," KJV, "(we) wrestle."

## WRETCHED

***talaiporos*** (*5005*), "distressed, miserable, wretched," is used in Rom. 7:24 and Rev. 3:17.

## WRITE, WROTE, WRITTEN

***Old Testament***

**A. Verb.**

***katab*** (3789), "to write, inscribe, describe, take dictation, engrave." Basically, this verb represents writing down a message. The judgment (ban) of God against the Amalekites was to be recorded in the book, Exod. 17:14. One may "write" upon a stone or "write" a message upon it, Deut. 27:2–3. This use of the word implies something more than keeping a record of something so that it will be remembered. This is obvious in the first passage because the memory of Amalek is "to be recorded" and also blotted out. In such passages "to be recorded," therefore, refers to the unchangeableness and binding nature of the Word of God. God has said it, it is fixed, and it will occur. An extended implication in the case of divine commands is that man must obey what God "has recorded," Deut. 27:2–3.

Sometimes ***katab*** appears to mean "to inscribe" and "to cover with inscription," Exod. 31:18. The verb means not only to write in a book but "to write a book," not just to record something in a few lines on a scroll but to complete the writing, Exod. 32:32. Here "book" probably refers to a scroll rather than a codex-book in the present-day sense.

Among the special uses of ***katab*** is the meaning "to record a survey," Josh. 18:4. A second extended nuance of ***katab*** is "to receive dictation," Jer. 36:4. The word can also be used of signing one's signature, Neh. 9:38.

**B. Nouns.**

***ketab*** (3791), "something written; register; scripture." In 1 Chron. 28:19 ***ketab*** is used to mean "something written," such as an "edict." The word also refers to a "register," Ezra 2:62, and to "scripture," Dan. 10:21.

Two other related nouns are ***ketobet*** and ***miktab***. ***ketobet*** occurs once to mean something inscribed, specifically a "tatooing" (Lev. 19:28). ***miktab*** appears about 9 times and means "something written, a writing" (Exod. 32:16; Isa. 38:9).

***New Testament***

**A. Verbs.**

1. ***grapho*** (*1125*) is used (a) of "forming letters" on a surface or writing material, John 8:6; Gal. 6:11, where the apostle speaks of his having "written" with large letters in his own hand, which not improbably means that at this point he took the pen from his amanuensis and finished the epistle himself; this is not negatived by the fact that the verb is in the aorist or past definite tense, lit., "I wrote," for in Greek idiom the writer of a letter put himself beside the reader and spoke of it as having been "written" in the past; in Eng. we should say "I am writing," taking our point of view from the time at which we are doing it; cf. Philem. 19 (this Ep. is undoubtedly a holograph), where again the equivalent English translation is in the present tense (see also Acts 15:23; Rom. 15:15); possibly the apostle, in Galatians, was referring to his having "written" the body of the epistle but the former alternative seems the more likely; in 2 Thess. 3:17 he says that the closing salutation is written by his own hand and speaks of it as "the token in every epistle" which some understand as a purpose for the future rather than a custom; see, however, 1 Cor. 16:21 and Col. 4:18. The absence of the token from the other epistles of Paul can

be explained differently, their authenticity not being dependent upon this; (b) "to commit to writing, to record," e.g., Luke 1:63; John 19:21, 22; it is used of Scripture as a standing authority, "it is written," e.g., Mark 1:2; Rom. 1:17 (cf. 2 Cor. 4:13); (c) of "writing directions or giving information," e.g., Rom. 10:5, "(Moses) writeth," RV (KJV, "describeth"); 15:15; 2 Cor. 7:12; (d) of "that which contained a record or message," e.g., Mark 10:4, 5; John 19:19; 21:25; Acts 23:25.

2. ***epistello*** (*1989*) denotes "to send a message by letter, to write word" (***stello***, "to send"; Eng., "epistle"), Acts 15:20; 21:25 (some mss. have ***apostello***, "to send"); Heb. 13:22.

3. ***prographo*** (*4270*) denotes "to write before," Rom. 15:4 (in the best texts; some have ***grapho***); Eph. 3:3.

4. ***engrapho*** (*1449*) denotes "to write in," Luke 10:20; 2 Cor. 3:2, 3.

5. ***epigrapho*** (*1924*) is rendered "to write over or upon" (***epi***) in Mark 15:26; figuratively, on the heart, Heb. 8:10; 10:16; on the gates of the heavenly Jerusalem, Rev. 21:12.

**B. Adjective.**

***graptos*** (*1123*), from A, No. 1, "written," occurs in Rom. 2:15.

## WRONG (Noun and Verb), WRONGDOER, WRONGDOING

**A. Nouns.**

1. ***adikia*** (*93*), ***a***, negative, ***dike***, "right," is translated "wrong" in 2 Pet. 2:13 (2nd part), 15, RV, "wrongdoing" (KJV, unrighteousness); in 2 Cor. 12:13, it is used ironically.

2. ***adikema*** (*92*) denotes "a misdeed, injury," in the concrete sense (in contrast to No. 1), Acts 18:14, "a matter of wrong"; 24:20, RV, "wrongdoing" (KJV, "evil doing").

**B. Verb.**

***adikeo*** (*91*), "to do wrong," is used (a) intransitively, to act unrighteously, Acts 25:11, RV, "I am a wrongdoer" (KJV, ". . . an offender"); 1 Cor. 6:8; 2 Cor. 7:12 (1st part); Col. 3:25 (1st part); cf. Rev. 22:11; (b) transitively, "to wrong," Matt. 20:13; Acts 7:24 (passive voice), 26, 27; 25:10; 2 Cor. 7:2, v. 12 (2nd part; passive voice); Gal. 4:12, "ye did (me no) wrong," anticipating a possible suggestion that his vigorous language was due to some personal grievance; the occasion referred to was that of his first visit; Col. 3:25 (2nd part), lit., "what he did wrong," which brings consequences both in this life and at the judgment seat of Christ; Philem. 18; 2 Pet. 2:13 (1st part); in the middle or passive voice, "to take or suffer wrong, to suffer (oneself) to be wronged," 1 Cor. 6:7.

## WRONGFULLY

***adikos*** (*95*), akin to the above, occurs in 1 Pet. 2:19.

## WROTH (be)

### *Old Testament*

**A. Verb.**

***qatsap*** (7107), "to be wroth, angry." The general meaning of ***qatsap*** is a strong emotional outburst of anger, especially when man is the subject of the reaction, Gen. 40:2–3; cf. 41:10; Exod. 16:20. In these examples an exalted person demonstrated his anger in radical measures against his people, Esth. 2:21.

The noun derived from ***qatsap*** particularly refers to God's anger. The object of the anger is often indicated by the preposition ***'al*** ("against"), Deut. 9:19. The Lord's anger expresses itself against disobedience, Lev. 10:6, and sin, Eccl. 5:5ff. However, people themselves can be the cause for God's anger, Ps. 106:32.

**B. Noun.**

***qetsep*** (7110), "wrath." One occurrence of God's "wrath" is in 2 Chron. 29:8; man's wrath, Esth. 1:18.

### *New Testament*

1. ***orgizo*** (*3710*), always in the middle or passive voice in the NT, is rendered "was (were) wroth" in Matt. 18:34; 22:7; Rev. 11:18, RV, (KJV, were angry); 12:17, RV, "waxed wroth."

2. ***thumoo*** (*2373*) signifies "to be very angry" (from ***thumos***, "wrath, hot anger"), "to be stirred into passion," Matt. 2:16, of Herod (passive voice).

3. ***cholao*** (*5520*), primarily, "to be melancholy" (***chole***, "gall"), signifies "to be angry," John 7:23, RV, "are ye wroth" (KJV, ". . . angry").

# Y

## YEAR

### Old Testament

***shanah*** *(8141), "year." There are several ways of determining what a "year" is. First, the "year" may be based on the relationship between the seasons and the sun, the solar year or agricultural year. Second, it can be based on a correlation of the seasons and the moon (lunar year). Third, the "year" may be decided on the basis of the correlation between the movement of the earth and the stars (stellar year). At many points the people of the Old Testament period set the seasons according to climatic or agricultural events, such as harvest, Exod. 23:16.*

*The Gezer calendar shows that by the time it was written (about the tenth century* B.C.*) some in Palestine were using the lunar calendar, since it exhibits an attempt to correlate the agricultural and lunar systems. The lunar calendar began in the spring (the month Nisan, March-April) and had twelve lunations, or periods between new moons. It was necessary periodically to add a thirteenth month in order to synchronize the lunar calendar and the number of days in a solar year. The lunar calendar also seems to have underlain Israel's religious system with a special rite to celebrate the first day of each lunar month, Num. 28:11–15. The major feasts, however, seem to be based on the agricultural cycle, and the date on which they were celebrated varied from year to year according to work in the fields, e.g., Deut. 16:9–12. This solar-agricultural year beginning in the spring is similar to (if not derived from) the Babylonian calendar.*

### New Testament

**A. Nouns.**

1. ***etos*** (*2094*) is used (a) to mark a point of time at or from which events take place, e.g., Luke 3:1 (dates were frequently reckoned from the time when a monarch began to reign); in Gal. 3:17 the time of the giving of the Law is stated as 430 "years" after the covenant of promise given to Abraham; there is no real discrepancy between this and Ex. 12:40; the apostle is not concerned with the exact duration of the interval, it certainly was not less than 430 "years"; the point of the argument is that the period was very considerable; Gal. 1:18 and 2:1 mark events in Paul's life; as to the former the point is that three "years" elapsed before he saw any of the apostles; in 2:1 the 14 "years" may date either from his conversion or from his visit to Peter mentioned in 1:18; the latter seems the more natural. (b) to mark a space of time, e.g., Matt. 9:20; Luke 12:19; 13:11; John 2:20; Acts 7:6, where the 400 "years" mark not merely the time that Israel was in bondage in Egypt, but the time that they sojourned or were strangers there, Heb. 3:17; Rev. 20:2–7; (c) to date an event from one's birth, e.g., Mark 5:42; Luke 2:42; 3:23; John 8:57; Acts 4:22; 1 Tim. 5:9; (d) to mark recurring events, Luke 2:41 (with ***kata***, used distributively); 13:7; (e) of an unlimited number, Heb. 1:12.

2. ***eniautos*** (*1763*), originally "a cycle of time," is used (a) of a particular time marked by an event, e.g., Luke 4:19; John 11:49, 51; 18:13; Gal. 4:10; Rev. 9:15; (b) to mark a space of time, Acts 11:26; 18:11; Jas. 4:13; 5:17; (c) of that which takes place every year, Heb. 9:7.

3. ***dietia*** (*1333*) denotes "a space of two years" (***dis***, "twice," and No. 1), Acts 24:27; 25:30.

4. ***trietia*** (*5148*) denotes "a space of three years" (***treis***, "three," and No. 1) Acts 20:31.

**B. Adjectives.**

1. ***dietes*** (*1332*), akin to A, No. 3, denotes "lasting two years, two years old," Matt. 2:16.

2. ***hekatontaetes*** (*1541*) denotes "a hundred years old," Rom. 4:19.

**C. Adverb.**

***perusi*** (*4070*), "last year, a year ago" (from ***pera***, "beyond"), is used with ***apo***, "from" 2 Cor. 8:10; 9:2.

## YOKE, YOKED

**A. Nouns.**

1. ***zugos*** (*2218*), "a yoke," serving to couple two things together, is used (1) metaphorically, (a) of submission to authority, Matt. 11:29, 30, of Christ's "yoke," not simply imparted by Him but shared with Him; (b) of bondage, Acts 15:10 and Gal. 5:1, of bondage to the Law as a supposed means of salvation; (c) of bond service to masters, 1 Tim. 6:1; (2) to denote "a balance," Rev. 6:5.

2. ***zeugos*** (*2201*), "a pair of animals," Luke 14:19.

2. ***elasson*** (*1640*) is rendered "younger" in Rom. 9:12.

**B. Verb.**

***heterozugeo*** (*2086*), "to be unequally yoked," is used metaphorically in 2 Cor. 6:14.

## YOKEFELLOW

***sunzugos*** or ***suzugos*** (*4805*), Phil. 4:3, "a yokefellow, fellow laborer"; probably here it is a proper name, "Synzygus."

## YOUNG, YOUNG (children, daughter, man, men, woman, women)

1. ***neoteros*** (*3501*), the comparative degree of ***neos***, "new, youthful," is translated "young" in John 21:18; in the plural, Acts 5:6, "young men" (marg., "younger"); Titus 2:6, KJV, RV, "younger men."

2. ***neos*** (*3501*), in the feminine plural, denotes "young women," Titus 2:4.

3. ***neanias*** (*3494*), "a young man," occurs in Acts 7:58; 20:9; 23:17, 18 (in some texts).

4. ***neaniskos*** (*3495*), a diminutive of No. 3, "a youth, a young man," occurs in Matt. 19:20, 22; Mark 14:51 (1st part; RV omits in 2nd part); 16:5; Luke 7:14; Acts 2:17; 5:10 (i.e., attendants); 23:18 (in the best texts), 22; 1 John 2:13, 14, of the second branch of the spiritual family.

5. ***nossos*** or ***neossos*** (*3502*), "a young bird" (akin to No. 2), is translated "young" in Luke 2:24; cf. also 13:34, and Matt. 23:37.

## YOUNGER

1. ***neoteros*** (*3501*), occurs in Luke 15:12, 13; 22:26; 1 Tim. 5:1 ("younger men"); 5:2, feminine; v. 11, "younger (widows)"; v. 14, "younger (widows), 1 Pet. 5:5.

## YOUTH

### *Old Testament*

***na'ar*** (5288), "youth; lad; young man." The basic meaning of ***na'ar*** is "youth," over against an older man. At times it may signify a very young child, Isa. 7:16. Generally ***na'ar*** denotes a "young man" who is of marriageable age but is still a bachelor. We must keep in mind the opposition of youth and old age, so that we can better understand that Jeremiah, while claiming to be only a "youth," was not necessarily a youngster, Jer. 1:6; cf. also Absalom, 2 Sam. 18:5.

Another meaning of ***na'ar*** is "servant," usually with a focus on the servant as a youth, 1 Sam. 14:1. The ***na'ar*** ("servant") addressed his employer as "master," Judg. 19:11. Kings and officials had "attendants" who were referred to by the title ***na'ar***, Esth. 2:2. When a ***na'ar*** is commissioned to carry messages, he is a "messenger." Thus, we see that the meaning of the word ***na'ar*** as "servant" does not denote a "slave" or a performer of low duties. He carried important documents, was trained in the art of warfare, and even gave counsel to the king.

### *New Testament*

***neotes*** (*3503*), from ***neos***, "new," occurs in Mark 10:20; Luke 18:21; Acts 26:4; 1 Tim. 4:12.

## YOUTHFUL

***neoterikos*** (*3512*), from ***neoteros***, "new," is used especially of qualities, of lusts, 2 Tim. 2:22.

# Z

## ZEAL

***zelos*** (*2205*) denotes "zeal" in the following passages: John 2:17, with objective genitive, i.e., "zeal for Thine house"; so in Rom. 10:2, "a zeal for God"; in 2 Cor. 7:7, RV, "(your) zeal (for me)," KJV, "(your) fervent mind (toward me)"; used absolutely in 7:11; 9:2; Phil. 3:6 (in Col. 4:13 in some texts; the best have ***ponos***, labor, RV).

## ZEALOUS

### A. Noun.

***zelotes*** (*2207*) is used adjectivally, of "being zealous" (a) "of the Law," Acts 21:20; (b) "toward God," lit., "of God," 22:3, RV, "for God"; (c) "of spiritual gifts," 1 Cor. 14:12, i.e., for exercise of spiritual gifts (lit., "of spirits," but not to be interpreted literally); (d) "for (KJV, 'of') the traditions of my fathers," Gal. 1:14, of Paul's loyalty to Judaism before his conversion; (e) "of good works," Titus 2:14.

The word is, lit., "a zealot," i.e., "an uncompromising partisan." The "Zealots" was a name applied to an extreme section of the Pharisees, bitterly antagonistic to the Romans. Josephus (*Antiq*. xviii. 1. 1, 6; *B.J.* ii. 8. 1) refers to them as the "fourth sect of Jewish philosophy" (i.e., in addition to the Pharisees, Sadducees, and Essenes), founded by Judas of Galilee (cf. Acts 5:37). After his rebellion in A.D. 6, the Zealots nursed the fires of revolt, which, bursting out afresh in A.D. 66, led to the destruction of Jerusalem in 70. To this sect Simon, one of the apostles, had belonged, Luke 6:15; Acts 1:13. The equivalent Hebrew and Aramaic term was "Cananaean" (Matt. 10:4); this is not connected with Canaan, as the KJV "Canaanite" would suggest, but is derived from Heb. ***qanna***, "jealous."

### B. Verbs.

1. ***zeloo*** (*2206*), "to be jealous," also signifies "to seek or desire eagerly"; in Gal. 4:17, RV, "they zealously seek (you)," in the sense of taking a very warm interest in, so in v. 18, passive voice, "to be zealously sought" (KJV, "to be zealously affected"), i.e., to be the object of warm interest on the part of others; some texts have this verb in Rev. 3:19 (see No. 2).

2. ***zeleuo***, a late and rare form of No. 1, is found in the best texts in Rev. 3:19, "be zealous."